THE OPEN BIBLE®

To

From

Date

Occasion

THE OPEN BIBLE®

NEW KING JAMES VERSION®

RED LETTER EDITION

with Read-Along References® and Read-Along Translations®
Biblical Cyclopedic Index
The Christian's Guide to the New Life
Book Introductions and Outlines
Visual Survey of the Bible
Special Study Aids

THOMAS NELSON
Since 1798

NASHVILLE DALLAS MEXICO CITY RIO DE JANEIRO

The text of the New King James Version (NKJV) may be quoted or reprinted without prior written permission with the following qualifications:

(1) up to and including 1,000 verses may be quoted in printed form as long as the verses quoted amount to less than 50% of a complete book of the Bible and make up less than 50% of the total work in which they are quoted;
(2) all NKJV quotations must conform accurately to the NKJV text.

Any use of the NKJV text must include a proper acknowledgment as follows:

Scripture taken from the New King James Version. Copyright © 1979, 1980, 1982 by Thomas Nelson, Inc. Used by permission. All rights reserved.

However, when quotations from the NKJV text are used in church bulletins, orders of service, Sunday School lessons, church newsletters and similar works in the course of religious instruction or services at a place of worship or other religious assembly, the following notice may be used at the end of each quotation: "NKJV."

For quotation requests not covered by the above guidelines, write to Thomas Nelson Publishers, Attn: Bible Rights and Permissions, P.O. Box 141000, Nashville, Tennessee 37214-1000.

Printed in Colombia

1 2 3 4 5 6 7 - QG - 17 16 15 14 13 12

Welcome to . . .

THE OPEN BIBLE®

The intent of this study Bible is to make the Scriptures an open and rewarding book for personal Bible study and to give an overview of the whole Bible message. In combining scholarly commentary with the latest revision of the trusted King James Version, the publisher is pleased to present the labors of learned and reverent men and women who have sought to clarify the meaning of the Scriptures and bring the treasures of God's Holy Word into the possession of the reader. To that end, the following special features are provided.

The text is that of the New King James Version. It has been produced with the conviction that the words of Scripture as originally penned in the Hebrew and Greek were inspired by God. Since they are the eternal Word of God, the Holy Scriptures speak with fresh power to each generation, to give wisdom that leads to salvation, that men and women may serve Christ to the glory of God.

The following paragraphs describe *The Open Bible*®'s many special features, which have been prepared by eminent scholars under the supervision of Thomas Nelson Publishers:

Notes that serve to clarify the text are Read-Along References® and Read-Along Translations®. The symbol "R" beside a word denotes a Read-Along Reference®, which lists at the end of the verse other passages that have similar meanings or further bearing on the word or phrase indicated. This exciting cross-reference method of Bible study ties together the magnificent truths of Scripture. The symbol "T" beside a word or phrase indicates a Read-Along Translation®, an easy-to-understand equivalent, alternate, or literal translation at the end of the verse. When the symbol "*" is used, a textual note is given at the end of the page. When more than one reference or translation follows a verse, a center point "•" is used for division. When space does not allow the letter (R or T) to precede the word or phrase referenced, then it follows immediately at the end of the word or first word of the phrase referenced. The asterisk (*) always follows the word or phrase.

Before each book of the Bible there is an introduction and outline of the book. These introductions are extensive and scholarly, and the outlines are designed to give an overview of the book. Related charts provide an at-a-glance summary of the book's content.

The *Biblical Cyclopedic Index* is one of the major study aids in *The Open Bible*®. A marvel in itself, this distinctive section combines the most useful features of a concordance, reference system, and index. With the *BCI,* the serious Bible student will find the riches of the Word unfolding in logical fashion. For the busy pastor or speaker, searching the Scriptures for a message, the *Biblical Cyclopedic Index* provides one of the most helpful tools to the explication of the Scriptures in published form today.

Another very noteworthy study feature is "The Christian's Guide to the New Life," whose thirty-two outlines cover the major teachings of the Bible. Its study notes are placed at the foot of the page near related passages, and they are chained by book-chapter-verse and page number of the next related outline point so that you can easily follow the development of each doctrine. With the "Christian's Guide" you can actually cover the material of an advanced course in systematic theology, but in a much easier and clearer manner.

For convenience in Bible study, on the Contents page you'll find a listing of *Bible Study Helps* included in *The Open Bible*®. These helps provide a wealth of information normally found only in a complete library of books.

Among the articles in the *Bible Study Helps* section are "How to Study the Bible," "Harmony of the Gospels," and "Teachings and Illustrations of Christ by Subject." "The Visual Survey of the Bible," which begins immediately following the Old Testament, gives you a visual overview of the whole of Scripture.

The *Biblical Information* section features many items not commonly understood in the Scriptures, plus countless bits of practical information in concise form. Of special interest is the article "The Greatest Archaeological Discoveries," which includes photographs and scholarly discussion of many significant archaeological finds.

Messianic prophecies are indicated in *The Open Bible*® by stars placed with the references in the appropriate passages. An outline star (☆) is used to indicate a prophecy later fulfilled in Jesus Christ. A solid star (★) is used to indicate a prophecy that has been fulfilled in Jesus Christ.

This study edition of the Holy Bible is intended to make it an Open Book for the reverent reader. It is hoped that this unique edition will truly make the Scripture plain enough so all can have an Open Bible.

The Publisher

CONTRIBUTORS
to the Study Aids

JEAN M. ALLEY, B.A., M.A.
Biblical Cyclopedic Index (Old Testament Word Studies), Contributing Editor
Nashville, Tennessee

KENNETH D. BOA, Ph.D., D.Phil.
Visual Survey of the Bible, Author; Introductions to the Books of the Bible, Co-Author
Director of Publications, Search Ministries
Atlanta, Georgia

†WICK BROOMALL, A.M., Th.M.
Biblical Cyclopedic Index
Minister, Presbyterian Church
Augusta, Georgia

W. A. CRISWELL, D.D., Ph.D.
The Scarlet Thread of Redemption
Pastor, First Baptist Church
Dallas, Texas

ARTHUR L. FARSTAD, Th.D.
Consulting Editor
Bible Editor
Dallas, Texas

PAUL R. FINK, Ed.S., Th.D.
The Christian's Guide to the New Life, Contributing Editor
Professor of Pastoral Ministries, Liberty Baptist College
Lynchburg, Virginia

DONALD E. HOKE, D.D.
How to Study the Bible
Pastor, Cedar Springs Presbyterian Church
Knoxville, Tennessee

GEORGE KNIGHT, B.A., B.D., Th.M.
Visual Bible Study Aids, Editor
Nashville, Tennessee

†R. G. LEE, LL.D., Ph.D.
A Guide to Christian Workers
Pastor-Evangelist
Nashville, Tennessee

MYLES LORENZEN, Th.M.
Visual Survey of the Bible, Contributor
Co-Pastor, Fellowship Bible Church
Roswell, Georgia

† Deceased

JIM BILL McINTEER, B.A.
Harmony of the Gospels
Minister, West End Church of Christ
Nashville, Tennessee

JOSEPH B. SNIDER, B.A., Th.M.
The Christian's Guide to the New Life, Contributing Editor
Indianapolis, Indiana

JEFFREY T. TUCKER, B.A., M.Div., M.A., Ph.D.
Biblical Cyclopedic Index (New Testament Word Studies), Contributing Editor
Nashville, Tennessee

†MERRILL F. UNGER, Th.D., Ph.D.
The Greatest Archaeological Discoveries
Professor Emeritus, Dallas Theological Seminary
Dallas, Texas

C. M. WARD, D.D.
A Guide to Christian Workers
Assemblies of God Radio Evangelist
Santa Cruz, California

WILLIAM WHITE, Ph.D.
The Greatest Archaeological Discoveries
Consulting Editor
Warrington, Pennsylvania

BRUCE H. WILKINSON, Th.M.
Outlines to the Books of the Bible, Author; Introductions to the Books of the Bible, Co-Author and Executive Editor
Founder and President, Walk Thru the Bible Ministries
Atlanta, Georgia

NEAL D. WILLIAMS, Th.D.
The Christian's Guide to the New Life, Contributing Editor
Assistant Professor of Biblical Studies, Liberty Baptist College
Lynchburg, Virginia

HAROLD L. WILLMINGTON, D.Min.
The Christian's Guide to the New Life, Executive Editor
Vice President, Liberty Baptist College
Lynchburg, Virginia
Books of the Old and New Testaments and Their Abbreviations

Books of the Old and New Testaments

Alphabetically

In Sequence

CONTENTS
of The Open Bible®

I. Text

II. Bible Study Helps

III. Biblical Information

FOREWORD

For the past several centuries English-speaking peoples have cherished the King James Version of the Bible. This love does not come from a desire to preserve a tradition for tradition's sake. Rather, the opposite is true: the King James Version has become a tradition because it is loved for its scholarship, literary form, and devotional quality.

During its long history the translation has been revised in accordance with changes in English speech and our growing knowledge of the original text of the Scriptures. Previous major revisions were prepared in 1629, 1638, 1762, and 1769. It is our hope that the present volume, the fifth major revision of the King James Version, will preserve for our own period of history the most revered Bible of the English-speaking world.

The King James Version

In the summer of 1603, when King James was on his way to London to receive the English crown, he was presented with a petition of grievances by clergy holding Puritan convictions, which led the king to call a conference "for hearing and for the determining of things pretended to be amiss in the church." This conference was convened for three days, January 14–16, 1604, and was known as the Hampton Court Conference. During his conference Dr. John Rainolds, the leader of the Puritan party and the president of Corpus Christi College, Oxford, made the motion that a new translation of the Bible be undertaken. Though the majority present were against the motion, it appealed to the king, and he ordered that such a translation be undertaken. Fifty-four of the best biblical scholars in Great Britain were brought together for this great task, divided into six groups—three to work on a translation of the Old Testament and three on the New Testament. Two groups for the Old and New Testaments were to meet at Oxford, two at Cambridge, and two at Westminster.

The result of this action was an English translation which bore the following title: *The Holy Bible, Conteyning the Old Testament, and the New, Newly Translated out of the Original tongues: & with the former Translations diligently compared and revised: by his Majesties special Comandement. Appointed to be read in Churches. Imprinted at London by Robert Barker, Printer to the Kings most excellent Majestie. Anno Dom. 1611.* While this version is called "the Authorized Version," no act of Parliament was ever passed approving it. King James vigorously promoted such an undertaking, but there was no subsequent official act. Nevertheless, the work soon made its own way to a position of leading acceptance among clergy and laity. It was to hold that position for over three centuries.

A New King James Version

In the latter part of the nineteenth century, F. H. A. Scrivener observed that the King James Bible, ". . . so laborious, so generally accurate, so close, so abhorrent of paraphrase, so grave and weighty in word and rhythm, so intimately bound up with the religious convictions of the English people, will never yield its hard earned supremacy, save to some reverential and well-considered revision of which it has been adapted as the basis, that shall be happy enough to retain its characteristic excellence, while amending its venial [trifling] errors and supplying its unavoidable defect."

The versions of 1881, 1901, and 1952 had used a New Testament Greek text that differed considerably from the traditional text and from the great majority of biblical manuscripts. There was growing concern among large segments of the Christian community that there was insufficient reason for many of these differences.

In 1975 Thomas Nelson Publishers, successor to the British firm that had first published the English Revised Version (1885), the American Standard Version (1901), and the Revised Standard Version (1952), determined to evaluate interest in a possible new revision. Such a revision would retain the traditional text while taking account of variant readings in footnotes.

Because any revision of the Scriptures must meet the needs of public worship, Christian education and personal reading and study, leading clergymen and lay Christians were invited to meetings in Chicago, Illinois, and Nashville, Tennessee, in 1975, and in London, England, in 1976, to discuss the need for revision. Almost one hundred church leaders from a broad spectrum of Christian churches gave strong endorsement to a new revision.

Biblical scholars representing a broad cross section of evangelical Christendom were selected to work on this major project. They came from Canada, England, Scotland, New Zealand, Australia, the Netherlands, and Taiwan, as well as from the United States, so that the New King James Version would reflect internationally accepted English usage.

Each translator worked privately and recommended changes in the King James text. In the translator's work he used the *Biblia Hebraica*

Stuttgartensia (for the Old Testament) or the Scrivener Greek Text (for the New Testament) and a copy of the 1611 King James Version as revise3d in 1769 (the edition in general use today). His work was then submitted to the executive editor for the Old or New Testament. An elaborate concordance and word studies of the English, Greek, and Hebrew were prepared especially for this revision by the executive editors and their associates. In addition, using the original texts, the King James Bible, and the guidelines, the executive editor for the Old or New Testament carefully reviewed each scholar's work. Where necessary, they made recommendations for further changes or, in some cases, for restoration of the King James reading.

Each book was then submitted to the English editor to be checked for grammatical accuracy, literary beauty, and the effective communication of the content.

Throughout the entire editing process, the work was regularly reviewed by the clergy and lay advisors who served on the British and North American Overview Committees.

The final exhaustive review process was carried out by a separate Executive Review Committee for each Testament over a period of four years.

All suggested changes were collated by the executive editors. Copies of each book showing all suggested changes were then reviewed in extensive study sessions by the entire Executive Review Committee for each Testament.

The review process was completed in July 1981, at St. Andrews University in northeast Scotland, not far from King James's residence, historic Stirling Castle. During part of this time the North American Committee was joined in its activity by the distinguished members of the British Overview Committee. AS in the older version of the King James Bible words added to the English text for purposes of clarity, which were not in the original Hebrew or Greek, were indicated to be shown in italics. This work was carried out by the Old and New Testament executive editors. Subject headings were developed jointly by the executive editors and the English editor.

The New King James Version was thus prepared with profound reverence for the Word of God and with deep appreciation of the wise traditions established by the translators of 1611. It was the prayer of the current revisers that the work in which they labored indeed be, as Dr. Scrivener had said years before, a "reverential and well-considered revision . . . retaining the characteristic excellencies" of the King James Bible.'

PREFACE

Purpose

In the preface to the 1611 edition, the translators of the Authorized Version, known popularly as the King James Bible, state that it was not their purpose "to make a new translation . . . but to make a good one better." Indebted to the earlier work of William Tyndale and others, they saw their best contribution to consist in revising and enhancing the excellence of the English versions which had sprung from the Reformation of the sixteenth century. In harmony with the purpose of the King James scholars, the translators and editors of the present work have not pursued a goal of innovation. They have perceived the Holy Bible, New King James Version, as a continuation of the labors of the earlier translators, thus unlocking for today's readers the spiritual treasures found especially in the Authorized Version of the Holy Scriptures.

A Living Legacy

For nearly four hundred years, and throughout several revisions of its English form, the King James Bible has been deeply revered among the English-speaking peoples of the world. The precision of translation for which it is historically renowned, and its majesty of style, have enabled that monumental version of the Word of God to become the mainspring of the religion, language, and legal foundations of our civilization.

Although the Elizabethan period and our own era share in zeal for technical advance, the former period was more aggressively devoted to classical learning. Along with this awakened concern for the classics came a flourishing companion interest in the Scriptures, an interest that was enlivened by the conviction that the manuscripts were providentially handed down and were a trustworthy record of the inspired Word of God. The King James translators were committed to producing an English Bible that would be a precise translation, and by no means a paraphrase or a broadly approximate rendering. On the one hand, the scholars were almost as familiar with the original languages of the Bible as with their native English. On the other hand, their reverence for the divine Author and His Word assured a translation of the Scriptures in which only a principle of utmost accuracy could be accepted.

In 1786 Catholic scholar Alexander Geddes said of the King James Bible, "If accuracy and strictest attention to the letter of the text be supposed to constitute an excellent version, this is of all versions the most excellent." George Bernard Shaw became a literary legend in our century because of his severe and often humorous criticisms of our most cherished values. Surprisingly, however, Shaw pays the following tribute to the scholars commissioned by King James: "The translation was extraordinarily well done because to the translators what they were translating was not merely a curious collection of ancient books written by different authors in different stages of culture, but the Word of God divinely revealed through His chosen and expressly inspired scribes. In this conviction they carried out their work with boundless reverence and care and achieved a beautifully artistic result." History agrees with these estimates. Therefore, while seeking to unveil the excellent *form* of the traditional English Bible, special care has also been taken in the present edition to preserve the work of *precision* which is the legacy of the 1611 translators.

Complete Equivalence in Translation

Where new translation has been necessary in the New King James Version, the most complete representation of the original has been rendered by considering the history of usage and etymology of words in their contexts. This principle of complete equivalence seeks to preserve all of the information in the text, while presenting it in good literary form. Dynamic equivalence, a recent procedure in Bible translation, commonly results in paraphrasing where a more literal rendering is needed to reflect a specific and vital sense. For example, complete equivalence truly renders the original text in expressions such as "lifted her voice and wept" (Gen. 21:16); "I gave you cleanness of teeth" (Amos 4:6); "Jesus met them, saying, 'Rejoice!'" (Matt. 28:9); and "Woman, what does your concern have to do with Me?" (John 2:4). Complete equivalence translates fully, in order to provide an English text that is both accurate and readable.

In keeping with the principle of complete equivalence, it is the policy to translate interjections which are commonly omitted in modern language renderings of the Bible. As an example, the interjection *behold,* in the older King James editions, continues to have a place in English usage, especially in dramatically calling attention to a spectacular scene, or an event of profound importance such as the Immanuel prophecy of Isaiah 7:14. Consequently, *behold* is retained for these occasions in the present edition. However, the Hebrew and Greek originals for this word can be translated variously, depending on the circumstances in the passage. Therefore, in addition to *behold,* words such as *indeed, look, see,* and *surely* are also rendered to convey the appropriate sense suggested by the context in each case.

In faithfulness to God and to our readers, it was deemed appropriate that all participating scholars sign a statement affirming their belief in the verbal and plenary inspiration of Scripture, and in the inerrancy of the original autographs.

Devotional Quality

The King James scholars readily appreciated the intrinsic beauty of divine revelation. They accordingly disciplined their talents to render well-chosen English words of their time, as well as a graceful, often musical arrangement of language, which has stirred the hearts of Bible readers through the years. The translators, the committees, and the editors of the present edition, while sensitive to the late-twentieth-century English idiom, and while adhering faithfully to the Hebrew, Aramaic, and Greek texts, have sought to maintain those lyrical and devotional qualities that are so highly regarded in the Authorized Version. This devotional quality is especially apparent in the poetic and prophetic books, although even the relatively plain style of the Gospels and Epistles cannot strictly be likened, as sometimes suggested, to modern newspaper style. The Koine Greek of the New Testament is influenced by the Hebrew background of the writers, for whom even the gospel narratives were not merely flat utterance, but often song in various degrees of rhythm.

The Style

Students of the Bible applaud the timeless devotional character of our historic Bible. Yet it is also universally understood that our language, like all living languages, has undergone profound change since 1611. Subsequent revisions of the King James Bible have sought to keep abreast of changes in English speech. The present work is a further step toward this objective. Where obsolescence and other reading difficulties exist, present-day vocabulary, punctuation, and grammar have been carefully integrated. Words representing ancient objects, such as *chariot* and *phylactery,* have no modern substitutes and are therefore retained.

A special feature of the New King James Version is its conformity to the thought flow of the 1611 Bible. The reader discovers that the sequence and selection of words, phrases, and clauses of the new edition, while much clearer, are so close to the traditional that there is remarkable ease in listening to the reading of either edition while following with the other.

In the discipline of translating biblical and other ancient languages, a standard method of transliteration, that is, the English spelling of untranslated words, such as names of persons and places, has never been commonly adopted. In keeping with the design of the present work, the King James spelling of untranslated words is retained, although made uniform throughout. For example, instead of the spellings *Isaiah* and *Elijah* in the Old Testament, and *Esaias* and *Elias* in the New Testament, *Isaiah* and *Elijah* now appear in both Testaments.

King James doctrinal and theological terms, for example, *propitiation, justification,* and *sanctification,* are generally familiar to English-speaking peoples. Such terms have been retained except where the original language indicates need for a more precise translation.

Readers of the Authorized Version will immediately be struck by the absence of several pronouns: *thee, thou,* and *ye* are replaced by the simple *you,* while *your* and *yours* are substituted for *thy* and *thine* as applicable. *Thee, thou, thy,* and *thine* were once forms of address to express a special relationship to human as well as divine persons. These pronouns are no longer part of our language. However, reverence for God in the present work is preserved by capitalizing pronouns, including *You, Your,* and *Yours,* which refer to Him. Additionally, capitalization of these pronouns benefits the reader by clearly distinguishing divine and human persons referred to in a passage. Without such capitalization the distinction is often obscure, because the antecedent of a pronoun is not always clear in the English translation.

In addition to the pronoun usages of the seventeenth century, the *-eth* and *-est* verb endings, so familiar in the earlier King James editions, are now obsolete. Unless a speaker is schooled in these verb endings, there is common difficulty in selecting the correct form to be used with a given subject of the verb in vocal prayer. That is, should we use *love, loveth,* or *lovest*? *do, doeth, doest,* or *dost*? *have, hath,* or *hast*? Because these forms are obsolete, contemporary English usage has been substituted for the previous verb endings.

In older editions of the King James Version, the frequency of the connective *and* far exceeded the limits of present English usage. Also, biblical linguists agree that the Hebrew and Greek original words for this conjunction may commonly be translated otherwise, depending on the immediate context. Therefore, instead of *and,* alternatives such as *also, but, however, now, so, then,* and *thus* are accordingly rendered in the present edition, when the original language permits.

The real character of the Authorized Version does not reside in its archaic pronouns or verbs or other grammatical forms of the seventeenth century, but rather in the care taken by its scholars to impart the letter and spirit of the original text in a majestic and reverent style.

The Old Testament Text

The Hebrew Bible has come down to us through the scrupulous care of ancient scribes who copied the original text in successive generations. By the sixth century A.D. the scribes were succeeded by a group known as the Masoretes, who continued to preserve the sacred Scriptures for another five hundred years in a form known as the Masoretic Text. Babylonia, Palestine, and Tiberias were the main centers of Masoretic activity; but by the tenth century A.D. the Masoretes of Tiberias, led by the family of ben Asher, gained the ascendancy. Through subsequent editions, the ben Asher text became in the twelfth century the only recognized form of the Hebrew Scriptures.

Daniel Bomberg printed the first Rabbinic Bible in 1516–17; that work was followed in 1524–25 by a second edition prepared by Jacob ben Chayyim and also published by Bomberg. The text of ben Chayyim was adopted in most subsequent Hebrew Bibles, including those used by the King James translators. The ben Chayyim text was also used for the first two editions of Rudolph Kittel's *Biblia Hebraica* of 1906 and 1912. In 1937 Paul Kahle published a third edition of *Biblia Hebraica*. This edition was based on the oldest dated manuscript of the ben Asher text, the Leningrad Manuscript B19a (A.D. 1008), which Kahle regarded as superior to that used by ben Chayyim.

For the New King James Version the text used was the 1967/1977 Stuttgart edition of the *Biblia Hebraica,* with frequent comparisons being made with the Bomberg edition of 1524–25. The Septuagint (Greek) Version of the Old Testament and the Latin Vulgate also were consulted. In addition to referring to a variety of ancient versions of the Hebrew Scriptures, the New King James Version draws on the resources of relevant manuscripts from the Dead Sea caves. In the few places where the Hebrew was so obscure that the 1611 King James was compelled to follow one of the versions, but where information is now available to resolve the problems, the New King James Version follows the Hebrew text. Significant variations are recorded in the textual footnotes at the end of text pages.

The New Testament Text

There is more manuscript support for the New Testament than for any other body of ancient literature. Over five thousand Greek, eight thousand Latin, and many more manuscripts in other languages attest the integrity of the New Testament. There is only one basic New Testament used by Protestants, Roman Catholics, and Orthodox, by conservatives and liberals. Minor variations in hand copying have appeared through the centuries, before mechanical printing began about A.D. 1450.

Some variations exist in the spelling of Greek words, in word order, and in similar details. These ordinarily do not show up in translation and do not affect the sense of the text in any way.

Other manuscript differences such as omission or inclusion of a word or a clause, and two paragraphs in the Gospels, should not overshadow the overwhelming degree of *agreement* which exists among the ancient records. Bible readers may be assured that the most important differences in English New Testaments of today are due, not to manuscript divergence, but to the way in which translators view the task of translation: How literally should the text be rendered? How does the translator view the matter of biblical inspiration? Does the translator adopt a paraphrase when a literal rendering would be quite clear and more to the point? The New King James Version follows the historic precedent of the Authorized Version in maintaining a literal approach to translation, except where the idiom of the original language cannot be translated directly into our tongue.

The King James New Testament was based on the traditional text of the Greek-speaking churches, first published in 1516, and later called the Textus Receptus or Received Text. Although based on the relatively few available manuscripts, these were representative of many more which existed at the time but only became known later. In the late nineteenth century, B. Westcott and F. Hort taught that this text had been officially edited by the fourth-century church, but a total lack of historical evidence for this event has forced a revision of the theory. It is now widely held that the Byzantine Text that largely supports the Textus Receptus has as much right as the Alexandrian or any other tradition to be weighed in determining the text of the New Testament.

Since the 1880s most contemporary translations of the New Testament have relied upon a relatively few manuscripts discovered chiefly in the late nineteenth and early twentieth centuries. Such translations depend primarily on two manuscripts, Codex Vaticanus and Codex Sinaiticus, because of their greater age. The Greek text obtained by using these sources and the related papyri (our most ancient manuscripts) is known as the Alexandrian Text. However, some scholars have grounds for doubting the faithfulness of Vaticanus and Sinaiticus, since they often disagree with one another, and Sinaiticus exhibits excessive omission.

A third viewpoint of New Testament scholarship holds that the best text is based on the consensus of the majority of existing Greek manuscripts. This text is called the Majority

Text. Most of these manuscripts are in substantial agreement. Even though many are late, and none is earlier than the fifth century, usually their readings are verified by papyri, ancient versions, quotations from the early church fathers, or a combination of these. The Majority Text is similar to the Textus Receptus, but it corrects those readings which have little or no support in the Greek manuscript tradition.

Today, scholars agree that the science of New Testament textual criticism is in a state of flux. Very few scholars still favor the Textus Receptus as such, and then often for its historical prestige as the text of Luther, Calvin, Tyndale, and the King James Version. For about a century most have followed a Critical Text (so called because it is edited according to specific principles of textual criticism) which depends heavily upon the Alexandrian type of text. More recently many have abandoned this Critical Text (which is quite similar to the one edited by Westcott and Hort) for one that is more eclectic. Finally, a small but growing number of scholars prefer the Majority Text, which is close to the traditional text except in the Revelation.

In light of these facts, and also because the New King James Version is the fifth revision of a historic document translated from specific Greek texts, the editors decided to retain the traditional text in the body of the New Testament and to indicate major Critical and Majority Text variant readings in the textual footnotes. Although these variations are duly indicated in the textual footnotes of the present edition, it is most important to emphasize that fully eighty-five percent of the New Testament text is the same in the Textus Receptus, the Alexandrian Text, and the Majority Text.

Special Abbreviations

Arab.	Arabic
Aram.	Aramaic
Bg.	the 1524–25 edition of the Hebrew Old Testament published by Daniel Bomberg (see Preface, “The Old Testament Text”)
cf.	compare
ch., chs.	chapter, chapters
DSS	Dead Sea Scrolls
e.g.	for example
et al.	and others
etc.	and so forth
fem.	feminine
f., ff.	following verse, following verses
Gr.	Greek
Heb.	Hebrew
i.e.	that is
Kt.	Kethib (literally, in Aramaic, “written”)—the written words of the Hebrew Old Testament preserved by the Masoretes (see “Qr.”)
Lat.	Latin
lit.	literally
LXX	Septuagint—an ancient translation of the Old Testament into Greek
M	Majority Text (see Preface, “The New Testament Text”)
ms., mss.	manuscript, manuscripts
masc.	masculine
MT	Masoretic Text—the traditional Hebrew Old Testament (see Preface, “The Old Testament Text”)
NU	the most prominent modern Critical Text of the Greek New Testament, published in the twenty-sixth edition of the *N*estle-Aland Greek New Testament and in the third edition of the *U*nited Bible Societies’ Greek New Testament (see Preface, “The New Testament Text”)
pl.	plural
Qr.	Qere (literally, in Aramaic, “read”)—certain words read aloud, differing from the written words, in the Masoretic tradition of the Hebrew Old Testament (see “Kt.”)
Sam.	Samaritan Pentateuch—a variant Hebrew edition of the books of Moses, used by the Samaritan community
sing.	singular
Syr.	Syriac
Tg.	Targum—an Aramaic paraphrase of the Old Testament
TR	Textus Receptus or Received Text (see Preface, “The New Testament Text”)
v., vv.	verse, verses
vss.	versions—ancient translations of the Bible
Vg.	Vulgate—an ancient translation of the Bible into Latin, translated and edited by Jerome

HOW TO US

ALTERNATE TRANSLATIONS are set in italic type and preceded by the word "Or"; these words are different from those in the text, but they are justified by the original languages.

ITALIC TYPE in the Bible text indicates wo that are not in the original languages of brew, Aramaic, or Greek, but have been s plied by the translators for clarity in Englisl

The swift of foot shall not [*] escape,
Nor shall he who rides a horse deliver
himself. *Or save*
16 The most courageous men of might
Shall flee naked in that day,"
Says the LORD.

CHAPTER 3

Israel's Judgment Is Deserved (Present)

HEAR this word that the LORD has spoken against you, O children of Israel, against the whole family which I brought up from the land of Egypt, saying:

2 "You[R] only have I known of all the families of the earth; [Deut. 7:6]
[R]Therefore I will punish you for all your iniquities." [Rom. 2:9]

3 Can two walk together, unless they are agreed?
4 Will a lion roar in the forest, when he has no prey?
Will a young lion cry out of his den, if he has caught nothing?
5 Will a bird fall into a snare on the earth, where there is no trap for it?
Will a snare spring up from the earth, if it has caught nothing at all?
6 If a trumpet is blown in a city, will not the people be afraid? *ram's horn*
[R]If there is calamity in a city, will not the LORD have done *it?* Is. 45:7

7 Surely the Lord GOD does nothing,
Unless He reveals His secret to His servants the prophets. [John 15:15]
8 A lion has roared!
Who will not fear?
The Lord GOD has spoken!
[R]Who can but prophesy? Acts 4:20

9 "Proclaim in the palaces at Ashdod,*
And in the palaces in the land of Egypt, and say:
'Assemble on the mountains of Samaria;
See great tumults in her midst,
And the oppressed within her.
10 For they [R]do not know to do right,'
Says the LORD, Jer. 4:22

'Who store up violence and [T]
their palaces.' "

Israel's Judgment Is Describe

11 Therefore thus says the Lor

"An adversary *shall be* all aro
land;
He shall sap your strength f
And your palaces shall be pl
12 Thus says the LORD:

"As a shepherd [T]takes from t
a lion
Two legs or a piece of an ear
So shall the children of Israe
out
Who dwell in Samaria—
In the corner of a bed and o
of a couch!
13 Hear and testify against the
Jacob,"
Says the Lord GOD, the God
14 "That in the day I punish Isra
transgressions,
I will also visit *destruction* o
of [R]Bethel;
And the horns of the altar sh
off
And fall to the ground.
15 I will destroy the winter ho
with the summer house;
The [T]houses of ivory shall pe
And the great houses shall h
end,"
Says the LORD.

CHAPTER 4

Israel's Judgment Is Deserve

HEAR this word, you cows of
who *are* on the mountain o
Who oppress the [R]poor,
Who crush the needy,
Who say to your husbands,*
let us [R]drink!"

3:9 So with MT; LXX Assyria 3:12 [...] possibly *on the cover* 4:1 Lit. *their* [...] *lords*

3:2 Selection of Israel—The selection of Israel as a special nation to God was part of Go[...] 1158—Rom. 11:2). Historically, the selection of Israel began with the Lord's promise to A[...] make you a great nation" (Page 14—Gen. 12:2). The name *Israel* actually is from the new na[...] gave to Abraham's grandson, Jacob. It was occasioned by Jacob's spiritual victory at the [...] (Page 35—Gen. 32:28). This fact explains why his descendants are often called the childre[...]
The motivation for the Lord's choice of Israel as His select nation did not lie in any spec[...] possessed. Its people were, in fact, the least in number among all the nations (Page 182–[...] Rather, the Lord chose them because of His love for them and because of His covenant [...] This fact does not mean that God did not love other nations, because it was through Israel th[...] to bring forth the Savior and to bless the entire world (Page 14—Gen. 12:3).
Now turn to Page 587—Ps. 78:4. History of Israel.

The superior "T" and italic type in its related reference indicate an EQUIVALENT TRANSLATION, which is similar in meaning; translating the text word helps clarify the meaning.

CAPS and SMALL CAPS are used to identify places where the covenant name of God, *YHWH,* appears in the text (translated as "LORD" or "GOD").

CONCEPTUAL REFERENCES are marked with a superior "R" to point out the referenced word or phrase in the text. The cross-reference in square brackets refers to a passage similar in concept.

ASTERISKS indicate important textual information. Corresponding notes are found at the foot of the right-hand text column on the same page with the related asterisk.

LITERAL TRANSLATION for a particular wo or phrase in the text is denoted with a super letter "T" and the abbreviation "Lit." in the no

THE OPEN BIBLE®

ROSS-REFERENCES, marked with a superior letter "R," point out verses that will explain the referenced word or phrase.

An OUTLINE STAR and a SOLID STAR indicate messianic references. The outline star indicates a prophecy that at the time of the writing had yet to be fulfilled. The solid star identifies the fulfillment of a prophecy.

urns to Nazareth—Luke 2:39

en Herod was dead, behold, an Lord appeared in a dream to Jo- t,
"Arise, take the young Child and and go to the land of Israel, for sought the young Child's life are
Luke 2:39 • Matt. 2:16
arose, took the young Child and and came into the land of Israel.
n he heard that Archelaus was r Judea instead of his father as afraid to go there. And being od in a Rdream, he turned aside on of Galilee. Matt. 2:12, 13, 19
came and dwelt in a city called hat it might be fulfilled Rwhich by the prophets, "He shall be arene." John 1:45, 46 • Judg. 13:5★

CHAPTER 3

Person of John the Baptist
Mark 1:2–6; Luke 3:3–6

days John the Baptist came ; in the wilderness of Judea, ng, "Repent, for Rthe kingdom of hand!" Dan. 2:44; Mal. 4:5, 6★
is he who was spoken of by the h, saying:

e of one crying in the
ness:
the way of the LORD; Luke 1:76
s paths straight.' "*

ohn himself was clothed in with a leather belt around his is food was Rlocusts and Rwild
Mark 1:6 • Lev. 11:22 • 1 Sam. 14:25, 26
usalem, all Judea, and all the re- the Jordan went out to him e baptized by him in the Jordan, eir sins. Acts 19:4, 18

eaching of John the Baptist
: 1:7, 8; Luke 3:7–9, 16, 17

n he saw many of the Pharisees es coming to his baptism, he said ood of vipers! Who warned you to wrath to come?

8 "Therefore bear fruits worthy of repentance,
9 "and do not think to say to yourselves, R'We have Abraham as *our* father.' For I say to you that God is able to raise up children to Abraham from these stones. John 8:33
10 "And even now the ax is laid to the root of the trees. RTherefore every tree which does not bear good fruit is cut down and thrown into the fire. Matt. 7:19
11 R"I indeed baptize you with water unto repentance, but He who is coming after me is mightier than I, whose sandals I am not worthy to carry. He will baptize you with the Holy Spirit and fire.* Acts 2:4, 33
12 R"His winnowing fan *is* in His hand, and He will thoroughly clean out His threshing floor, and gather His wheat into the barn; but He will Rburn up the chaff with unquenchable fire." Mal. 3:3 • Matt. 13:30

Baptism of Jesus—Mark 1:9–11; Luke 3:21–23

13 Then Jesus came from Galilee to John at the Jordan to be baptized by him.
14 And John *tried to* prevent Him, saying, "I need to be baptized by You, and are You coming to me?"
15 But Jesus answered and said to him, "Permit *it to be so* now, for thus it is fitting for us to fulfill all righteousness." Then he allowed Him.
16 When He had been baptized, Jesus came up immediately from the water; and behold, the heavens were opened to Him, and He* saw Rthe Spirit of God descending like a dove and alighting upon Him. Is. 11:2; 42:1★
17 RAnd suddenly a voice *came* from heaven, saying, R"This is My beloved Son, in whom I am well pleased." John 12:28 • Ps. 2:7

CHAPTER 4

First Temptation—Mark 1:12, 13; Luke 4:1–4

THEN RJesus was led up by Rthe Spirit into the wilderness to be tempted by the devil. Mark 1:12 • Ezek. 3:14
2 And when He had fasted forty days and forty nights, afterward He was hungry.

3:3 Is. 40:3★ 3:11 M omits *and fire* 3:16 Or *he*

e Father of Christ—Every new Christian eventually wonders in what sense God may be er of Christ and Christ the Son of God. The answer to this question is not a simple one. First, gnize that the title "Son of God" does not speak of physical nature, for God is spirit (Page 24), and Christ was the Son of God before He assumed a human body in Bethlehem (Page 16; Page 1198—Gal. 4:4). Passages which use terms implying physical origin must be taken sense (Page 1258—Heb. 1:5). title expresses a unique relationship. Christ distinguished His sonship from that of His dis- 105—John 20:17). He is begotten of God in a sense that no one else is (Page 1081—John ome call it "eternal generation," signifying the timelessness of this "God from God" relation-

(continued on next page)

SUBJECT HEADS and PARALLEL PASSAGES have been added to assist in identifying main subjects of the text that follows and in locating other passages in Scripture that speak to the same subjects.

RED LETTER type is used in the New Testament to signify words of Jesus Christ.

POETRY and OBLIQUE TYPE set apart certain portions of Bible text. Poetry is structured as contemporary verse to reflect the poetic form and beauty of the original Hebrew, Aramaic, or Greek language. Oblique type in the New Testament text indicates quotations from the Old Testament.

IE CHRISTIAN'S GUIDE TO THE NEW LIFE is a point-by-point study of basic Bible ctrines that covers the material of an advanced course in systematic theology. The in- oduction leads you to the page of the first underlined verse. Detailed notes at the bottom the page discuss the passage. Then they refer you to the next verses for study.

EXPLANATION OF FORMAT

The format of this volume is designed to enhance the vividness and devotional quality of the Holy Scriptures and to assist the reader in personal study. To this end, special features have been incorporated in the text of the Bible and in special study aids on each page.

Read-Along® Study Aids

Superior R's and T's usually precede the referenced word or phrase in the text whereas *asterisks* always follow the referenced word or phrase (examples: [R]glory, [T]minister, king of Israel*). When space does not allow the superior letter to precede the referenced word or phrase, the superior immediately follows the referenced word or the first word of the phrase (example: [R]king[T]).

Superior R's indicate cross-references. These cross-references point out verses that will enhance the reader's understanding of the referenced word or phrase in the text; they also identify Old Testament sources of New Testament quotations. A cross-reference in *square brackets* (example: [Deut. 12:5]) is a *conceptual cross-reference;* that is, it refers to a passage similar in concept to the referenced passage in the text.

A superior R can also indicate a prophecy of the Messiah. The reference at the end of the verse will be followed by an outline or solid star. The outline star indicates a prophecy that at the time of the writing had yet to be fulfilled. The solid star indicates the fulfillment of a prophecy.

Superior T's indicate translation notes. There are four kinds of these notes:

— equivalent translations (in italic type with no introductory words; example, *mercy*), which are roughly similar in meaning to the translations in the text and help to clarify them;

— alternate translations (in italic type, preceded by "Or"; example: Or *mercy*), which are different from those in the text but are justified by the original languages;

— literal translations (in italic type, preceded by "Lit."; example: Lit. *mercy*); and

— notes that explain words or phrases in the text (in roman type; example: Mercy).

Words set in in roman type in translation notes are explanatory only and are not translated from the original languages.

Asterisks are used to indicate important textual information. The corresponding note is found at the foot of the right-hand column of Bible text on the same page on which the asterisk appears. *Textual notes* point out significant textual variants in both the Old and New Testaments. The sources of these variant readings are identified by abbreviations listed under "Special Abbreviations" on page 13.

The notes in the present edition of the New Testament make no evaluation of readings (and so terms such as "better manuscripts" are avoided), but they do clearly indicate the sources of readings that diverge from the traditional text, whether they be from the modern eclectic or "critical" text (NU), which depends heavily upon the Alexandrian type of text, or from the Majority Text (M). (See the Preface, "The New Testament Text," for an explanation of these terms.) Thus, a clearly defined statement of the variants, representing all textual persuasions, is provided for the benefit of interested readers.

Subject headings indicate the main subjects of the sections of text that follow them. These headings are not found in the original Hebrew, Aramaic, or Greek, but have been added to assist the reader in identifying topics and transitions in the biblical content. Whenever a parallel passage in Scripture exists, reference to that parallel is made with the subject heading.

The Text

Italic type in the text (example: God saw that *it was* good) indicates words that are not found in the original languages but that are needed for clarity in English.

Oblique type in the New Testament text (example: *Behold, a virgin shall be with child*) indicates quotations from the Old Testament.

Paragraph breaks are indicated by verse numbers in bold type (example: **Genesis 1:6**) or, when a paragraph begins within a verse, by indentation (example: **Genesis 35:22**).

Quotation marks in the text follow modern English usage. For easier reading, only the marks denoting the most recently opened quotations are repeated in a new verse.

Personal pronouns and certain nouns are capitalized when they refer to Deity.

Poetry is structured as contemporary verse to reflect the poetic form and beauty of the original language.

The covenant name of God in the Old Testament, represented by the Hebrew consonants *YHWH,* is translated "LORD" or "GOD" (using capital letters as shown), as it has been throughout the history of the King James Bible. In this edition the capitalized form is also used whenever the covenant name is quoted in the New Testament from a passage in the Old Testament.

HOW TO STUDY THE BIBLE

The Bible is the greatest book ever written. In it God Himself speaks to humankind. It is a book of divine instruction. It offers comfort in sorrow, guidance in perplexity, advice for our problems, rebuke for our sins, and daily inspiration for our every need.

The Bible is not simply one book. It is an entire library of books covering the whole range of literature. It includes history, poetry, drama, biography, prophecy, philosophy, science, and inspirational reading. Little wonder, then, that all or part of the Bible has been translated into more than 1,200 languages, and every year more copies of the Bible are sold than of any other single book.

The Bible alone truly answers the greatest questions that people of all ages have asked: **"Where have I come from?" "Where am I going?" "Why am I here?" "How can I know the truth?"** For the Bible reveals the truth about God, explains the origin of human beings, points out the only way to salvation and eternal life, and explains the age-old problem of sin and suffering.

The great theme of the Bible is the Lord Jesus Christ and His work of redemption for humankind. The Person and work of Jesus Christ are promised, prophesied, and pictured in the types and symbols of the Old Testament. In all of His truth and beauty, the Lord Jesus Christ is revealed in the Gospels; and the full meanings of His life, His death, and His resurrection are explained in the Epistles. His glorious coming again to earth in the future is unmistakably foretold in the Book of Revelation. The great purpose of the written Word of God, the Bible, is to reveal the living Word of God, the Lord Jesus Christ (read John 1:1–18).

Dr. Wilbur M. Smith relates seven great things that the study of the Bible will do for us:

1. The Bible discovers sin and convicts us of it.

2. The Bible helps cleanse us from the pollutions of sin.

3. The Bible imparts strength.

4. The Bible instructs us in what we are to do.

5. The Bible provides us with a sword for victory over sin.

6. The Bible makes our lives fruitful.

7. The Bible gives us power to pray.

You do not need a whole library of books to study the Bible. The Bible is its own best commentator and interpreter. With all of the instructive helps that you have in this new Bible, you have a whole lifetime of Bible study.

I. Personal Bible Study

A. Devotional Bible Study

The Bible is not an end in itself, but is a means to the end of knowing God and doing His will. The apostle Paul said, "Be diligent to present yourself approved to God, a worker who does not need to be ashamed, rightly dividing the word of truth" (**2 Tim. 2:15**). God has given us the Bible in order that we might know Him and that we might do His will here on earth.

Therefore, devotional Bible study is the most important kind of Bible study. Devotional Bible study means reading and studying the Word of God in order that we may hear God's voice and that we may know how to do His will and to live a better Christian life.

A great scientist and medical doctor, Howard A. Kelly (Professor of Gynecology at Johns Hopkins University from 1889 through 1940), was also an avid student of the Bible. He once said: "The very best way to study the Bible is simply to read it daily with close attention and with prayer to see the light that shines from its pages, to meditate upon it, and to continue to read it until somehow it works itself, its words, its expressions, its teachings, its habits of thought, and its presentation of God and His Christ into the very warp and woof of one's being."

For your devotional reading and study of the Bible, here are several important, practical suggestions:

1. Begin your Bible reading with prayer (**Ps. 119:18; John 16:13, 14, 15**).

2. Take brief notes on what you read. Keep a small notebook for your Bible study (see number 4 below).

3. Read slowly through one chapter, or perhaps two or three chapters, or perhaps just one paragraph at a time. After reading, ask yourself what this passage means. Then reread it.

4. It is often very helpful in finding out the true meaning of a chapter or passage to ask yourself the following questions, then write the answers in your notebook:

a. What is the main subject of this passage?

b. Who are the persons revealed in this passage: Who is speaking? About whom is he speaking? Who is acting?

c. What is the key verse of this passage?

d. What does this passage teach me about the Lord Jesus Christ?

e. Does this passage portray any sin for me to confess and forsake?

f. Does this passage contain any command for me to obey?

g. Is there any promise for me to claim?

h. Is there any instruction for me to follow?

Not all of these questions may be answered in every passage.

5. Keep a spiritual diary. Either in your Bible study notebook mentioned above (number 2), or in a separate notebook entitled, "My Spiritual Diary," write down daily what God says to you through the Bible. Write down the sins that you confess or the commands you should obey.

6. Memorize passages of the Word of God. No one is ever too old to memorize the Word of God. Write verses on cards with the reference on one side and the verse on the other. Carry these cards with you and review them while you're waiting on a train, standing in lunch line, and so on.

Other persons prefer to memorize whole passages or chapters of the Bible. A small pocket Bible will help you to review these passages when you have spare moments. One of the best ways is to spend a few minutes every night before going to sleep, in order that your subconscious mind may help you fix these passages of God's Word in your mind while you're asleep (**Ps. 119:11**).

To meditate means "to reflect, to ponder, to consider, to dwell in thought." Through meditation the Word of God will become meaningful and real to you, and the Holy Spirit will use this time to apply the Word of God to your own life and its problems.

7. Obey the Word of God. As Paul said to Timothy in 2 Timothy 3:16: "All Scripture *is* given by inspiration of God, and *is* profitable for doctrine, for reproof, for correction, for instruction in righteousness." The Bible has been given to us that we may live a holy life, well-pleasing to God. Therefore God says, "But be doers of the word, and not hearers only" (**James 1:22**).

8. The Navigators, a group of men banded together just before World War II to encourage Bible study among Christian servicemen, developed a splendid plan for a personal, devotional study.

a. After prayer, first read the Bible passage slowly and silently; then read it again aloud.

b. In a large notebook divide the paper into columns and head each column as follows: Chapter title, Key verse, Significant truth, Cross-references, Difficulties in this passage (personal or possible), Application to me, and Summary or outline of the passage. In each of these columns, write the information desired.

Do not try to adopt all of these methods at once, but start out slowly, selecting those methods and suggestions that appeal to you. You will find, as millions of others have before you, that the more you read and study the Word of God, the more you'll want to read it. Therefore, the following suggestions of Bible study are made for those who wish to make a more intensive study of the Bible truths.

B. Study for Bible Knowledge

There are many valuable methods of Bible study. One may study the Bible, as if with a telescope, to see the great truths that stand out in every book. Or one may study the Bible as if with a microscope to find all of the marvelous details that are in this mine of spiritual riches. In this section there are several proven methods with which a person may conduct more intensive Bible study. The most important thing is to follow faithfully some systematic method of Bible study.

Bible Study by Chapters. In the Bible there are 1,189 chapters in the Old and New Testaments. In a little over three years, a person could make an intensive study of the whole Bible, taking a chapter a day. It is usually a good practice to start your Bible study in the New Testament.

1. Read through the chapter carefully, seeking to find its main subject or subjects.

2. As you read each chapter, give it a title that suggests its main content. If you are reading the Gospel of John, for example, you might give each chapter titles like this:

ch. 1 "Jesus Christ, the Word of God"
ch. 2 "The Wedding at Cana"
ch. 3 "The New Birth"
ch. 4 "The Woman at the Well"
ch. 5 "The Healing of the Man at the Pool of Bethesda"
ch. 6 "The Feeding of the 5,000"

3. Reread the chapter and make a simple outline, including its main thoughts. For example, for **John 1,** you might make an outline like this:

"Jesus Christ, the Word of God":

a. Jesus Christ was the eternal Word of God, **1–9**.

b. Jesus Christ came into the world, **10–18**.

c. John witnesses that Christ is to come, **19–28**.

d. John says that Jesus is the Lamb of God, **29–37**.

e. Jesus Christ calls His first disciples, **38–51**.

4. Concerning each chapter, ask and answer the questions suggested in item number 4 of devotional Bible study hints above. Especially take note of any practical or theological problems in this chapter. Then, using your concordance, look up the key words in those verses and find out what other portions of the Bible say about this question or problem. Compare Scripture with Scripture to find its true meaning. Usually, to understand a Bible chapter, you must study it together with the preceding or following chapters.

Bible Study by Paragraphs. A paragraph is several sentences of thought in writing. When an author changes the subject of emphasis in writing, he usually begins a new paragraph. The beginning of a paragraph in this Bible is indicated by a boldface verse number. Studying the Bible by paragraphs like this is often called analytic Bible study.

1. Read the paragraph carefully for its main thought or subject.

2. In order to find the relation of the important words and sentences in this paragraph, it is often helpful to rewrite the text. For example, if you were going to study the paragraph on prayer in the Sermon on the Mount found in **Matthew 6:5–8**, you could rewrite this text:

"And when you pray, you shall not be like the hypocrites. For they love to pray standing in the synagogues and on the corners of the streets, that they may be seen by men. Assuredly, I say to you, they have their reward.

"But you, when you pray, go into your room, and when you have shut your door, pray to your Father who *is* in the secret *place;* and your Father who sees in secret will reward you openly.

"And when you pray, do not use vain repetitions as the heathen *do.* For they think that they will be heard for their many words.

"Therefore do not be like them. For your Father knows the things you have need of before you ask Him."

3. From the text you've now rewritten so that you can see the relationship of the various parts of the paragraph, it is easy to make a simple outline. For example, using **Matthew 6:5–15,** your outline of this passage would be something like this:

"Jesus Teaches Us How to Pray"—**Matthew 6:5–15**.

a. How not to pray **Matthew 6:5, 7, 8**.
  (1) Hypocritically in public, **6:5**.
  (2) With useless repetition, **6:7, 8**.

b. How to pray: **Matthew 6:6, 9–13**.
  (1) In private to your heavenly Father, **6:6**.
  (2) Following the pattern of Jesus' model prayer, **6:9–13**.

4. It is helpful also to look up in the concordance important words *that occur* in this paragraph, for example, the words "hypocrites" and "heathen." By comparing other passages of the Bible that teach about prayer, you'll be kept from making any mistakes concerning the true nature, conditions, and results of prayer according to the will of God.

Bible Study by Verses. In studying the historical passages of the Bible, such as most of the Old Testament or parts of the Gospels, each verse may have only one simple meaning.

But many verses in both the Old and New Testaments are rich with many great Bible truths that will demand more detailed study. There are many ways for you to study a single Bible verse.

1. Study it by the verbs in the verse. For example, if you were studying **John 3:16** you would find the following verbs: "loved . . . gave . . . should not perish . . . have . . ."

You could make a comparative list like this:

God loved	Humankind believes
God gave	Humankind shall not perish
	Humankind has everlasting life.

Or simply take the nouns in this wonderful verse: "God . . . world . . . only begotten Son . . . whoever . . . everlasting life."

2. Study a verse through the personalities revealed. For example, once again taking **John 3:16,** these very simple but significant points are brought to light: "God . . . only begotten Son . . . whoever . . . Him.

3. Study a verse by looking for the great ideas revealed in it. Let us look again at **John 3:16** as our example. We might title this verse, "The greatest verse in the Bible." The following ideas are found in it:

"God"—the greatest Person
"so loved"—the greatest devotion
"the world"—the greatest number
"He gave"—the greatest act
"His only begotten Son"—the greatest gift
"that whoever believes"—the greatest condition
"should not perish"—the greatest mercy
"have everlasting life"—the greatest result

4. Sometimes a combination of these various ideas applied to a verse will bring the richest results. For example, take **Romans 5:1:**

"Therefore"—This verse depends on **4:25**. Our justification is based on and is guaranteed by Jesus' resurrection.
"justified"—made righteous.
"by faith"—method of our justification (see also **3:24; 4:9**).
"have"—not future, but present tense—we have this *now*.
"peace with God"—We were enemies, but now there is peace between us and God because of what Christ has done.
"through our Lord Jesus Christ"—the way to peace with God is only through Jesus Christ.

Bible Study by Books. After you have begun to study the Bible by chapters or paragraphs or verses, you will be ready to study the Bible by books.

1. There are several methods of Bible book study.

a. One is called the inductive method. This is

a method of studying in detail the contents of a Bible book and then drawing from these details general conclusions or principles concerning the contents and purpose of the book.

b. Another method of book study is called the synthetic method. By this method, one reads the Bible book several times to receive the general impressions of the main ideas and purpose of the book without attention to the details. (It is sometimes hard to distinguish these two methods.)

c. In some cases the study of a Bible book becomes a historical study, if that book relates the history of a nation or an individual in a particular period of time. For example, the Book of Exodus tells the history of the children of Israel from the death of Joseph in Egypt until the erecting of the tabernacle in the wilderness in the time of Moses. This covers approximately 400 years.

The principles of Bible book study, whether inductive or synthetic, are very similar. Such study will require more time than the previous methods mentioned, but it will be amply rewarding.

2. Here are some methods for Bible study by books:

a. Read the book through to get the perspective and the general emphasis of the book.

b. Reread the book many times, each time asking yourself a relevant question and jotting down the answers you find as you read. Here are the most important questions to ask:

First reading: What is the central theme or emphasis of this book? What is the key verse?

Second reading: Remembering the theme of the book, see how it is emphasized and developed. Look for any special problems or applications.

Third reading: What does it tell me about the author and his circumstances when he wrote this book?

Fourth reading: What does the book tell me about the people to whom the book was written and their circumstances, needs, or problems?

Fifth reading: What are the main divisions of the book? Is there any outline apparent in the logical organization and development of the book? During this reading, divide the text into the paragraphs as you see them and then give a title to each paragraph. Draw a line down the right side *of the outline and on the other side write* any problems, questions, words, or ideas that require further study by comparison with other passages in the Bible.

Sixth and successive readings: Look for other facts and/or information that your earlier readings have suggested. By now certain words will stand out in the book. See how often they recur. (For example, as you read Philippians, you will soon find that the word "joy" occurs many times. This is one of the key words of the book, so note its occurrences and the circumstances surrounding it.)

As you read and reread a book, you'll find that you begin to see its structure and its outline very clearly. It is true, however, that there are other outlines for any given book. It depends on the principle of division that you select. For example, as you study Paul's letter to the Romans, you might adopt the outline that Dr. G. Allen Fleece, president of Columbia Bible College, has written:

The Book of Romans

Subject: "The Gospel," 1:16

I. The Gospel for the lost sinner, 1—5
II. The Gospel for the Christian, 6—8
III. The Gospel for the whole world, 9—11
IV. The Gospel applied to daily living, 12—16

Of course, each of these great sections of this remarkable book can be divided into smaller subjects with great profit.

This method, applied to a book that is mainly historical, will also enable you to find a clear outline. In the case of a historical book, the outline will be largely chronological. The Book of Acts lends itself to this kind of study and outline.

The Book of Acts

Subject: "The Gospel Witness in the First Century"

Key verse: 1:8

Outline:

I. Introduction: The apostles receive power, 1:1—2:4
II. The witness in Jerusalem, 2:5—7:60
III. The witness in Judea and Samaria, 8:1—11:18
IV. The beginning of the witness to the end of the earth, 11:19—28:31

Once again, more careful study will give the details and further subdivisions of each of these great units of gospel history in this inspired record of the origin of the Christian church.

Bible Study by Words. There are two profitable and helpful ways of studying great words or subjects in the Word of God.

1. Word study by Bible books. Certain words have special significance in certain Bible books. For example, after studying the Gospel of John as a book and by chapters, you'll find it instructive and inspiring to trace the words "believe" and "belief." They occur almost 100 times. By reading the book hurriedly and underlining each passage where the words "believe" and "belief" occur, you'll understand why Bible scholars contend that the purpose of the Gospel of John is expressed by the author in **John 20:31.**

2. General word study. The fine index and concordance in this Bible will be a great help. Through the study of great Bible words, you can soon become familiar with the great doctrines of the Bible and understand the great theological principles which the Bible reveals.

With the concordance you might begin with the study of the word "grace." By tracing the occurrences of this word through the Old Testament and then into the New Testament, you will come to see that God has always dealt with His people in grace, and you will find in a concrete way the great truth of **Ephesians 2:8.**

Bible Study by Topics. Closely related to the method of study by words is the study according to great topics or subjects: Bible prayers, Bible promises, Bible sermons, Bible songs, Bible poems, and so on.

Or one might study Bible geography by reading rapidly through and looking for rivers, seas, and mountains highlighted in Scripture. For example, the mountaintop experiences in the life of Abraham are a thrilling study.

Another challenging study is to read rapidly through the Gospels and Epistles looking for the Lord's commands to us. The list of Bible topics is unlimited.

First, for a topical study on prayer, look up the word "prayer" or "pray" in your concordance. Look up every form of these words and such related words as "ask" and "intercession." After you have looked up these verses, study them and bring together all the teaching on prayer that you find. You will find conditions of prayer, words to be used in prayer, results to expect from prayer, when to pray, and where to pray.

Bible Study Through Biography. The Bible is a record of God's revealing Himself to people and through people. The Old Testament as well as the New is rich in such biographical studies. Here are a few:

The life of Noah: Genesis 5:32—10:32
The life of Abraham: Genesis 12—25
The life of Joseph: Genesis 37—50
The life of Deborah: Judges 4; 5

Let us summarize various methods for studying the great Bible biographies:

1. Read the Bible book or passages in which this person's life is prominent, for example, Abraham in **Genesis 12—25,** plus references to Abraham in **Hebrews 11** and **Romans 4.**

2. Trace character with your concordance.

3. Be careful to note indirect references to the person in other portions of Scripture.

Conclusion. There are many other methods of studying the Bible, for example, the psychological method, the sociological method, the cultural method, and the philosophical method. Use all the Bible study methods suggested above. From time to time, change your method so that you'll not become too accustomed to any one method or tired from delving too deeply into one type of study.

The great thrill of Bible study is discovering these eternal truths of God's Word for yourself and embarking on the adventure of obeying them and experiencing the blessing in your personal life.

II. Family Bible Study

Nothing is more important in a Christian home than the family altar. At a convenient time, when all members of the family are home, father or mother should lead them in worship of God and in reading His Word. A simple program for family worship includes singing a hymn, an opening prayer by a family member, a brief Bible study, and a concluding period of prayer in which all members take part.

The family altar and Bible study will bind the family together, eliminate juvenile delinquency, foster deeper love, and enable each member to become a stronger, better Christian. Since family Bible study usually includes small children, it is wise to avoid deep, difficult topics and study something of interest and help to all. Such subjects might be Bible biographies as outlined above, stories of miracles and deeds of Jesus as revealed in the Gospels, miracles in the Old Testament, and other narrative portions of the Bible. It is wise to keep the study brief and to concentrate on a short passage of Scripture. For example, a study of the life of Moses could be divided into units like this:

First day: The birth of Moses: Exodus 2:1–10

Second day: Moses' great choice and great mistake: Hebrews 11:24–27; Exodus 2:11–15

Third day: Moses' wilderness training: Exodus 2:16–25

Fourth day: Moses' call to serve God: Exodus 3:1–22

Fifth day: Moses' argument with God: Exodus 4:1–17

Sixth day: Moses' return to Egypt: Exodus 4:18–31

Here are several practical hints on how to make your family Bible study interesting and profitable to all:

1. Keep your family Bible study reasonably short: one brief chapter or several paragraphs a day.

2. Have each member read a verse.

3. Appoint one family member to lead in worship each day and select the passage to read. This one may appoint others to help in the family worship.

4. Read through a Bible book, a chapter, or several paragraphs each day. As you read, together decide on a name or a title for each chapter and memorize this.

5. After reading the passage, have each member in the family explain one verse or one paragraph.

6. Let the leader prepare five or ten questions on the Bible passage and ask various members of the family to answer these questions after the passage has been read.

7. Study the beautiful maps in your Bible together, and trace Paul's journeys or the wandering of the children of Israel in Egypt.

8. Study Bible topics together. Assign verses concerning a topic or great word to each member of the family. Let each read a verse and tell what the verse teaches about the topic or word.

9. After the Bible reading, have each member tell what this verse means or how it can be applied to personal life.

10. Make up Bible games by having each member make up questions to try to stump the others.

11. Study a Bible book together, using the hints given above. There are many wonderful ways to make the Bible the heart of your home.

III. Principles of Bible Interpretation

Since the Bible was written by many men over a period covering 1,500 years, and since the last author of the Bible has been dead 1,900 years, there are definite problems in understanding the exact meaning of certain passages of the Bible.

There is a need to interpret clearly certain passages of the Bible because there is a gap between the way we think and the words we use today and the way of thinking and the words that these Bible writers used thousands of years ago. Bible scholars have pointed out that there are language gaps—differences in words that we use; there are cultural gaps—different customs were in vogue then. There are geographical gaps—certain rivers that are spoken of in the Bible have long since dried up. Some places that are spoken of frequently in the Bible are not on our modern maps. And then there are historical gaps—the Bible speaks of kings and empires that existed years ago.

Therefore, there is a need for Bible interpretation. This is a fascinating study in itself, but I want to give you just a few principles of interpretation of the Bible that will keep you from error and help you understand the difficult passages of the Word of God.

1. Always remember that the Bible is God's infallible, inerrantly inspired Word. There are no mistakes in the Bible. God has included everything in the Bible that He wants you to know and that is necessary for you to know concerning salvation and your Christian life.

2. The second principle of interpretation is to interpret the Bible in the light of its historical background. There are three aspects of this:

a. Study the personal circumstances of the writer. In studying The Revelation, it is important to understand where John was and what he was doing when God gave him this marvelous revelation. See **Revelation 1:1–10**.

b. The second aspect of this principle is to study the culture and customs of the country at the time that the writing or story was taking place. For example, to understand the Book of Ruth, it is important to study the customs concerning widows, redemptions of property, and so on, as they are explained in **Leviticus 25** and **Deuteronomy 25**.

c. A third aspect of this principle is to study and interpret the Bible in the light of the actual historical situation and events that were taking place at the time of the story. For example, in studying the Gospels it is important to realize that the entire land of Palestine and all of the Jews were being governed and oppressed by the Roman Empire at that time.

3. Interpret the Bible according to the purpose and plan of each book.

Every Bible book has its specific purpose intended by the Holy Spirit to bring some special message to humankind. For example, it is important to remember that **1 John** (see **1 John 5:13**) was written to Christians. Therefore the promise in **1 John 1:9** is specifically applied to Christians.

4. One of the most important principles of interpretation is always to interpret according to the context of a verse.

The "context" includes the verses immediately preceding and immediately following the verse you are studying. If you do not take care to interpret the verse according to the context, you could make the Bible teach atheism. For the Bible itself says, "*There is* no God" (**Ps. 14:1**). But the context makes very clear what this verse means: The whole sentence says, "The fool has said in his heart, '*There is* no God.' "

Always study the passage immediately preceding and immediately following any verse, word, or topic to make sure that you see this truth in the setting that God intended.

5. Always interpret according to the correct meaning of words. You can find the correct meaning of a word in several ways. First of all, look up the usage of the word in other parts of the Bible to find how it was used in that generation. Another way is to look up its background or its root. You could do this with the use of a dictionary. Still another way is to look up the synonyms—words that are similar in meaning but slightly different: for example, "prayer," "intercession," "supplication."

6. Also interpret the Bible according to all of the parallel passages that deal with the subject and according to the message of the entire Bible.

The more you read the Bible, the more you will understand that in it God is revealing His way of salvation to humankind from beginning to end. And when you come to a difficult passage, think of it in the light of the overall purpose of the Bible. For example, the animal sacrifices of the Old Testament are meant to be a picture of the perfect sacrifice of Jesus Christ on the cross.

If you will follow these simple guidelines, you will be kept from error and extremes, and you will be helped to understand correctly the teachings of even the more difficult passages in God's Word.

THE CHRISTIAN'S GUIDE TO THE NEW LIFE

The Christian's Guide to the New Life offers a complete doctrinal overview of the Scripture to assist you in a practical, simplified method of studying your Bible. The study breaks into seven main areas that tell us how to become contented and mature Christians. The seven main subjects branch out so they cover all the important areas of biblical theology. This unique study feature places before the Bible student an explanation of God's Word with hundreds of scriptural references.

For the student just beginning Bible study, *The Christian's Guide to the New Life* covers in a fundamental way how to become a Christian and then walks the believer through the Christian life. The easy-to-use references lead the reader toward a comprehensive, practical knowledge of God's Word.

The general organization of *The Christian's Guide to the New Life* includes seven main areas of study:

Knowing God's Word
Understanding God's Being
Understanding Other Spirit Beings
Beginning the New Life
Growing in the New Life
Facing Problems in the New Life
Recognizing God's Institutions

These areas of study are subdivided into thirty-two individual "Christian's Guides" with appropriate Bible references. All the material is organized in a simple format to assist you in more easily understanding the Bible, the inspired Word of God. Each numbered "Christian's Guide" has several discussions of Bible texts appearing on the page where the text occurs. For example, within the main area of study "Knowing God's Word" is "Christian's Guide" (1) "How God's Word Came to Us." There are three discussions concerning how God's Word came to us: on page 203 is "Revelation of God's Word"; on page 737 is "Inspiration of God's Word"; and on page 633 is "Illumination of God's Word."

This article, *The Christian's Guide to the New Life,* will serve as a general introduction, index, and guide to the various "Christian's Guides." Each time you study one of the discussions in the Bible the last line will tell you where to turn for the next discussion. When you finish a main area of study, such as "Knowing God's Word," the last line in the last discussion will tell you to turn to this article, *The Christian's Guide to the New Life.* Then, after reading the synopsis of the next main area of study, you will be ready to turn to the first discussion and follow the development of that area of study throughout the Bible text.

The Christian's Guide to the New Life can be used in three easy ways: monthly study, daily study, and topical study.

- Monthly study—For thirty-two days study one of the numbered "Christian's Guides." Read all of the discussions and look up the listed references.
- Daily study—Once a day for 123 days study a single discussion in the Bible text. Read the complete discussion and look up the listed references.
- Topical study—Using this article, *The Christian's Guide to the New Life,* as an index, study individual "Christian's Guides" and discussions that interest you or meet needs in your life.

You are now ready to begin using *The Christian's Guide to the New Life.* For each of the seven main areas of study a synopsis and an organization are provided. For each of the "Christian's Guides" page numbers and Scripture references are given to help you find the various discussions in the Bible, Also look for this symbol (Q) on the opening verse connected with each "Christian's Guide" in the text and for a crown symbol superimposed over the text of the "Christian's Guide" itself.

Knowing God's Word

Synopsis

Christians should know the Bible for many reasons, but the primary one is because God is its Author. All Bible students know that God is Creator (Gen. 1:1), Redeemer (Is. 60:16), and Judge (Gen. 18:25), but do we think of Him as the Author of the Bible? Human writers feel it vital that we read their books; it is much more important that we read God's Book, the Bible.

About fourteen centuries before Christ, our Bible had its beginnings in the Sinai desert. In this arid place, God spoke to Moses, who had once been a prince in Egypt and was nearly 120 years old at the time. At the Lord's command, Moses picked up his pen and began writing Scripture's first five books, Genesis through Deuteronomy. More than 1,500 years later, the divine manuscript was completed on a lonely, windswept island in the Mediterranean Sea by a former fisherman, John the apostle. From Genesis through Revelation there are sixty-six divinely inspired books. Over the centuries, approximately forty authors—representing varied backgrounds and writing styles—served as channels for God's Word. Yet, in spite of these variations in time and talent, the completed work displays a marvelous historical, theological, geographical, topical, and biographical unity.

The Bible's practical benefits for us may well be summarized under two headings: knowing and growing. The Bible proclaims the good news of the gospel that we might know God; it explains the will of God that all of us may grow spiritually before Him.

Scripture also reveals our place within God's program and answers crucial questions pertaining to our origin, purpose, and destiny. Because God has revealed His unchanging truths, the Christian faith provides real answers and guidance to every generation. Although we cannot grasp how individual events fit into God's program (Eccl. 11:5), we can understand God's basic plan in order to come to know and serve Him. Few joys can compare with realizing our places in God's program and working to fulfill our destinies.

Organization

Understanding God's Being

Synopsis

The Bible reveals the nature of God as spirit, unity, and trinity. He is a spirit—a personal, infinite being (John 4:24); He is one—one in substance or nature and incapable of being divided into separate parts (Deut. 6:4); and He is three—eternally existing in three coequal Persons (Matt. 28:19). While great mystery surrounds God's nature, it is reassuring to know that our God is above us.

God's attributes are merely words we use to describe how God is and how He acts toward us. Among these attributes are love, holiness, constancy, justice, truth, eternalness, omniscience (all-knowledge), omnipresence (all-presence), and omnipotence (all-powerfulness). The fact that we can grasp and understand this much about God is evidence of God's desire that all peoples may know Him.

The word "Father" is variously applied in the Bible. When God is spoken of as the Father of all humankind, it is as Creator; as the Father of Christ, it expresses an eternal, unique relationship; as the Father of believers, it denotes a relationship established by grace; and as Father of Israel, it indicates a bond established by covenant. However "Father" is used, it is a deliberately chosen word to communicate one of the primary ways God wants us to conceive of Him.

The title "Son of God" is one that Jesus never directly applied to Himself; but when others applied it to Him, Jesus willingly accepted it as a claim to His own deity (John 10:24–38). Jesus often referred to Himself as "the Son," which was certainly an abbreviation for "the Son of God." Because Jesus was the Son of God, we have confidence that He spoke with the authoritative words of God. The Son of God also accepted the role of Lamb of God in order to die in the place of sinners and provide forgiveness of sins for all who believe. It can be said that as our relationship with the Son of God determines whether we will become Christians, our relationship with the Spirit of God determines what kind of believers we will be.

Organization

6. God the Father
God the Father of All
Page 968—Mal. 2:10
God the Father of Christ
Page 979—Matt. 3:17
God the Father of Believers
Page 1154—Rom. 8:15

7. The Son of God
The Person of the Son of God
Page 691—Is. 9:6
The Earthly Life of the Son of God
Page 1094—John 10:10
The Ministry of the Son of God
Page 1028—Mark 10:45
The Lamb of God
Page 731—Is. 53:7

8. The Holy Spirit
The Person of the Holy Spirit
Page 1206—Eph. 4:3
The Work of the Holy Spirit in Salvation
Page 1250—Titus 3:5
The Work of the Holy Spirit in Christian Living
Page 1171—1 Cor. 6:19

9. The Trinity
Unity of the Trinity
Page 5—Gen. 1:26
Persons of the Trinity
Page 1192—2 Cor. 13:14
Interaction Within the Trinity
Page 1204—Eph. 1:4, 7, 13

Understanding Other Spirit Beings

Synopsis

At some point before God created the heavens and the earth He created a class of spirit beings known in the Bible as angels. A large number of these beings were created, and their primary purposes were to worship and serve God. There seems to be some organization among angels with seraphim, cherubim, and archangels having status above the others.

Apparently still before the creation of the universe, perhaps a third of the angels rebelled against God in support of a chief angel named Lucifer who desired to usurp God's power and glory. These fallen angels lost their heavenly position. They continue to oppose God's purposes however they can.

Good angels serve as messengers from God to humankind and minister to Christians as God directs them. They may protect or guide us. They may be agents of punishment for unbelievers. Since angels are spirit beings, most of their activity escapes notice, but biblical stories show they are capable of being visible and audible.

The fallen angels serve Satan as they attempt to frustrate the plans of God. There is an unseen spiritual struggle between good and fallen angels. Christians also engage in spiritual warfare against them by resisting temptation and obeying God's Word. After the Last Judgment, Satan and his angels will be consigned forever to the lake of fire.

Organization

10. Angels
Angels: Spirit Beings
Page 601—Ps. 104:4
Angels: Messengers and Servants
Page 1258—Heb. 1:14
Angels: Interaction with Humans
Page 879—Dan. 6:22

11. Demons
Demons: Fallen Angels
Page 1320—Rev. 12:9
Demons: Relation to Satan
Page 989—Matt. 12:24
Demons: Interaction with Humans
Page 1057—Luke 11:24–26

12. Satan
Satan: Fall of Satan
Page 696—Is. 14:12–15
Satan: Role in Fall of Humans
Page 1092—John 8:44
Satan: Strategies of Satan
Page 1185—2 Cor. 2:11
Satan: Destiny of Satan
Page 1006—Matt. 25:41

Beginning the New Life

Synopsis

Human beings are by nature sinful and need the righteousness of God. We must be separated from sin and set apart to righteousness. If we are to approach God, we must do so on God's terms—we must have new lives in which our sins have been forgiven and obliterated.

It is one thing to be convinced of the need for the new life, but it is an entirely differen t thing to acquire the new life. When we are "saved," we are said to be new creatures (2 Cor. 5:17); to have passed from death to life (John 5:24); to have been transferred from the rule of darkness to the kingdom of God's Son (Col. 1:13); to have been born again (John 3:3); and to have been adopted by God (Gal. 4:4, 5). These wonderful results of having new life in Christ are offered freely to all who trust in Christ for salvation.

One of the most thrilling benefits of finding new life in Christ is "everlasting [eternal] life." We enter a new, personal relationship with God that gives us a fullness of spiritual vitality, and this new life is a gift that will never die. God can accomplish a life-changing transformation for all who truly believe in Christ. Once we are reconciled to God through Christ, we discover a basis for reconciliation to people around us who formerly seemed our bitter enemies.

Organization

13. Need for the New Life
Holiness of God
Page 687—Is. 6:3
Adam's Sin
Page 6—Gen. 3:6, 7
Individual Sin
Page 667—Eccl. 7:20

14. Way to the New Life
New Life: A Free Gift
Page 1153—Rom. 6:23
New Life: Based on Christ's Death
Page 1220—Col. 1:22
New Life: Received by Faith
Page 1131—Acts 16:31

15. Results of the New Life
Everlasting Life
Page 1086—John 5:24
New Nature
Page 1187—2 Cor. 5:17
Christ's Righteousness
Page 738—Is. 61:10
Placed into God's Family
Page 1295—1 John 3:2
Reconciliation Between Enemies
Page 1123—Acts 10:14, 15
Empowered by God
Page 1112—Acts 1:8

16. Assurance of the New Life
Promise of God
Page 1249—Titus 1:2
Witness of the Spirit
Page 1296—1 John 3:24
Changed Life
Page 1170—1 Cor. 6:11

Growing in the New Life

Synopsis

Bible reading, memorization, meditation, study, and obedience form the foundation for Christian growth. The adage is ever true: "Sin will keep you from God's Word, or God's Word will keep you from sin."

Prayer may be the most neglected element of growth. Prayer is talking with and listening to God. We talk to Him with our lips and heart, and He tells us His will through His Word. Prayer is a two-way conversation. Spiritual maturity depends on systematic prayer.

Worship is a third essential to spiritual growth. Worship involves honoring God, engaging in private and public devotion, and joyfully witnessing for the Lord. Christians who submit to the lordship of Christ in reverence and service will grow in their spiritual lives.

The Bible describes the Christian life as a "walk in the Spirit" (Gal. 5:16). Walking pictures the step-by-step character of the spiritual life. Living by the Spirit's power is a moment-by-moment yielding to His will that results in a display of the fruit of the Spirit (Gal. 5:22, 23). Walking in the Spirit involves confession of sin, yielding to God, and being controlled by the Spirit.

Organization

17. Bible Study
Reading God's Word
Page 491—Neh. 8:3
Memorizing God's Word
Page 527—Job 22:22
Meditating upon God's Word
Page 214—Josh. 1:8
Obedience to God's Word
Page 205—Deut. 31:12

18. Prayer
Praise
Page 625—Ps. 150:1
Confession
Page 1293—1 John 1:9
Petition
Page 273—1 Sam. 1:17
Thanksgiving
Page 1215—Phil. 4:6
Commitment
Page 642—Prov. 16:3

19. Stewardship
Using Spiritual Gifts
Page 1175—1 Cor. 12:1–10
Serving
Page 1199—Gal. 5:13
Giving
Page 1189—2 Cor. 9:6–8

20. Worship
The Meaning of Worship
Page 416—1 Chr. 16:29
The Expressions of Worship
Page 1268—Heb. 13:15
The Reasons for Worship
Page 439—2 Chr. 7:3

21. Participation in the Local Church
Definition of the Local Church
Page 1162—Rom. 16:5
The Reason for Participation in the Local Church
Page 1265—Heb. 10:25
Benefits of Participation in the Local Church
Page 1114—Acts 2:42–47

22. Sharing Our Faith
Sharing Our Faith: Why?
Page 1011—Matt. 28:19
Sharing Our Faith: What?
Page 1178—1 Cor. 15:3, 4
Sharing Our Faith: How to Prepare
Page 476—Ezra 7:10
Sharing Our Faith: How to Do It
Page 1226—1 Thess. 1:5
Sharing Our Faith: When?
Page 1245—2 Tim. 4:2

23. Walking in the Spirit
Walking in the Spirit: Confession
Page 584—Ps. 73:1
Walking in the Spirit: Yielding
Page 1158—Rom. 12:1, 2
Walking in the Spirit: Filling
Page 1208—Eph. 5:18

Facing Problems in the New Life

Synopsis

Just as we have problems in our physical lives, we also experience problems in our spiritual or new lives. Facing and conquering difficulties cause us to grow and be strengthened, whether our problems are physical or spiritual. As we grow in our new strength, we bring glory to God as He demonstrates His faithfulness and that His grace is sufficient for every need (2 Cor. 12:9). Some of the problems that are common in the new life are sin, temptation, doubt, suffering, and knowing the will of God.

Organization

24. Sin
What Sin Is
Page 572—Ps. 51:2
What Sin Does
Page 736—Is. 59:2
What Should Be Done About Sin
Page 561—Ps. 32:5

25. Temptation
Temptation by the World
Page 1294—1 John 2:15
Temptation by the Flesh
Page 1033—Mark 14:38
Temptation by Satan
Page 420—1 Chr. 21:1

26. Doubt
Occasions of Doubt
Page 815—Lam. 5:20
Sources of Doubt
Page 940—Hab. 1:2
Cure for Doubt
Page 357—1 Kin. 18:21

27. Suffering
Kinds of Suffering
Page 1282—1 Pet. 3:17
Purposes of Suffering
Page 513—Job 2:7
Responses to Suffering
Page 513—Job 1:21
Examples of Suffering
Page 788—Jer. 37:15

28. Knowing the Will of God
Knowing the Will of God Through the Scriptures
Page 393—2 Kin. 23:3
Knowing the Will of God Through Prayer and Fasting
Page 882—Dan. 9:3, 4
Knowing the Will of God Through Submission to the Spirit
Page 688—Is. 6:8
Knowing the Will of God Through Circumstances and Counsel
Page 650—Prov. 24:6

Recognizing God's Institutions

Synopsis

God gave humanity four basic institutions: the family, human government, Israel, and the church. It may be observed that each of these institutions demonstrates a characteristic or attribute of God.

- The family illustrates the unity of God (Gen. 2:24; Deut. 6:4).
- Human government illustrates the judgment of God (Rom. 13:1, 2).
- Israel illustrates the election of God (Rom. 9:1–18; 11:1–5).
- The church illustrates the love of God (Eph. 5:22–27).

The family was the first institution God created. Through the family God illustrates the complex relationships that exist in the Trinity and the loving relationship between Christ and His church. He created all the heavens and the earth and the things in them that they might prepare the way for and sustain the crown of His creation—humanity.

God's purpose in human government is that it serve as both a custodian and an enforcer of His eternal law. It has been correctly noted that all the thousands of good and practical laws passed by hundreds of legislative bodies and rulers throughout history are in reality only amplifications of the Ten Commandments.

God's selection of Israel as a special nation may puzzle the Bible student, but His choice becomes obvious through study. When God promised Abraham that he would become the father of a great nation, He also promised that He would bless all peoples through that nation (Gen. 12:1–3). Israel was to be a channel of blessing as well as a recipient.

The church, illustrating God's love for us, is the fourth institution through which God works. The universal church—the Body of Christ (Col. 1:18)—comprises all believers since the institution of the church.

Organization

MONIES, WEIGHTS, AND MEASURES

The Hebrews probably first used coins in the Persian period (500–350 B.C.). However, minting began around 700 B.C. in other nations. Prior to this, precious metals were weighed, not counted as money.

Some units appear as both measures of money and measures of weights. This comes from naming the coins after their weight. For example, the shekel was a weight long before it became the name of a coin.

It is helpful to relate biblical monies to current values. But we cannot make exact equivalents. The fluctuating value of money's purchasing power is difficult to determine in our own day. It is even harder to evaluate currencies used two- to three-thousand years ago.

Therefore, it is best to choose a value meaningful over time, such as a common laborer's daily wage. One day's wage corresponds to the ancient Jewish system (a silver shekel is four days' wages) as well as to the Greek and Roman systems (the drachma and the denarius were each coins representing a day's wage).

The monies chart below takes a current day's wage as thirty-two dollars. Though there are differences of economies and standards of living, this measure will help us apply meaningful values to the monetary units in the chart and in the biblical text.

Monies

Unit	*Monetary Value*	*Equivalents*	*Translations*
Jewish Weights			
Talent	gold—$5,760,000[1] silver—$384,000	3,000 shekels; 6,000 bekas	talent
Shekel	gold—$1,920 silver—$128	4 days' wages; 2 bekas; 20 gerahs	shekel
Beka	gold—$960 silver—$64	½ shekel; 10 gerahs	bekah
Gerah	gold—$96 silver—$6.40	1/20 shekel	gerah
Persian Coins			
Daric	gold—$1,280[2] silver—$64	2 days' wages; ½ Jewish silver shekel	dram
Greek Coins			
Tetradrachma (Stater)	$128	4 drachmas	piece of money
Didrachma	$64	2 drachmas	tribute
Drachma	$32	1 day's wage	piece of silver
Lepton	$.25	½ of a Roman kodrantes	mite
Roman Coins			
Aureus	$800	25 denarii	
Denarius	$32	1 day's wage	pence, penny
Assarius	$2	1/16 of a denarius	farthing
Kodrantes	$.50	¼ of an assarius	farthing

[1]Value of gold is fifteen times the value of silver.
[2]Value of gold is twenty times the value of silver.

Weights

Unit	*Weight*	*Equivalents*	*Translations*
Jewish Weights			
Talent	c. 75 pounds for common talent, c. 150 pounds for royal talent	60 minas; 3,000 shekels	talent
Mina	1.25 pounds	50 shekels	mina
Shekel	c. .4 ounce (11.4 grams) for common shekel c. .8 ounce for royal shekel	2 bekas; 20 gerahs	shekel
Beka	c. .2 ounce (5.7 grams)	½ shekel; 10 gerahs	half a shekel
Gerah	c. .02 ounce (.57 grams)	1/20 shekel	gerah
Roman Weight			
Litra	12 ounces		pound

Measures of Length

Unit	*Length*	*Equivalents*	*Translations*
Day's journey	c. 20 miles		day's journey
Roman mile	4,854 feet	8 stadia	mile
Sabbath day's journey	3,637 feet	6 stadia	Sabbath day's journey
Stadion	606 feet	⅛ Roman mile	furlong
Rod	9 feet (10.5 feet in Ezekiel)	3 paces; 6 cubits	measuring reed, reed
Fathom	6 feet	4 cubits	fathom
Pace	3 feet	⅓ rod; 2 cubits	pace
Cubit	18 inches	½ pace; 2 spans	cubit
Span	9 inches	½ cubit; 3 handbreadths	span
Handbreadth	3 inches	⅓ span; 4 fingers	handbreadth
Finger	.75 inches	¼ handbreadth	finger

Dry Measures

Unit	*Measure*	*Equivalents*	*Translations*
Homer	6.52 bushels	10 ephahs	homer
Kor	6.52 bushels	1 homer; 10 ephahs	cor, measure
Lethech	3.26 bushels	½ kor	half homer
Ephah	.65 bushel, 20.8 quarts	1/10 homer	ephah

Dry Measures—Continued

Unit	*Measure*	*Equivalents*	*Translations*
Modius	7.68 quarts		bushel
Seah	7 quarts	⅓ ephah	measure
Omer	2.08 quarts	$\frac{1}{10}$ ephah; 1⅘ kab	omer
Kab	1.16 quarts	4 logs	cab
Choenix	1 quart		measure
Xestes	1$\frac{1}{16}$ pints		pot
Log	.58 pint	¼ kab	log

Liquid Measures

Unit	*Measure*	*Equivalents*	*Translations*
Kor	60 gallons	10 baths	kor
Metretes	10.2 gallons		gallon
Bath	6 gallons	6 hins	measure, bath
Hin	1 gallon	2 kabs	hin
Kab	2 quarts	4 logs	kab
Log	1 pint	¼ kab	log

Biblical Cyclopedic Index

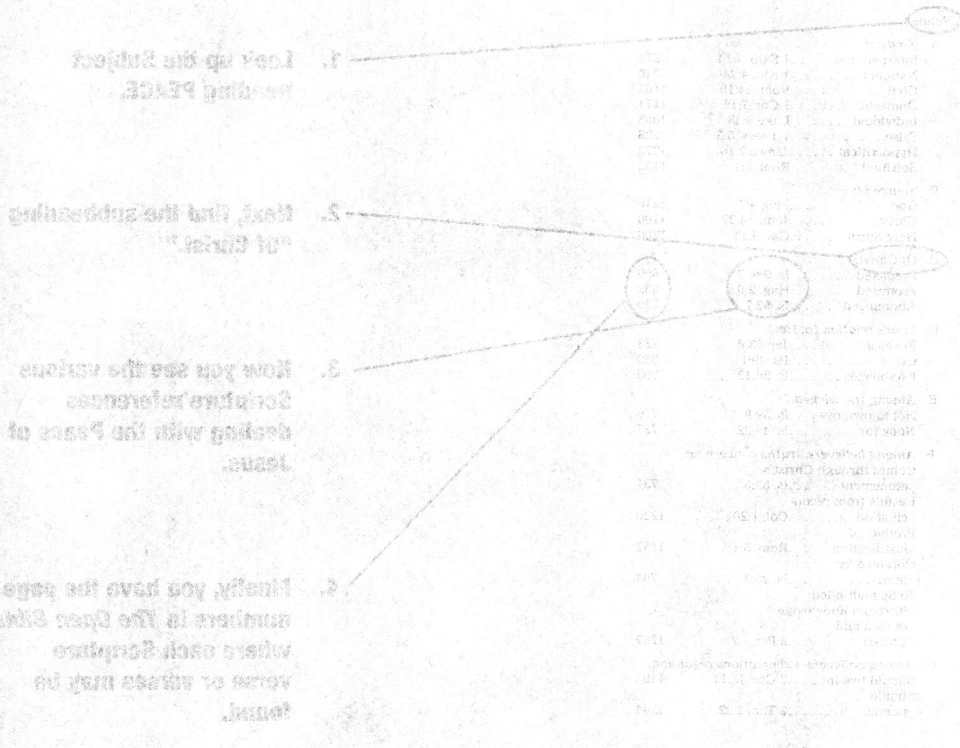

How to Use
The Biblical Cyclopedic Index

The Biblical Cyclopedic Index is a special kind of subject index that combines the best features of a concordance, a topical index, the usable features of a syllabus and other related study aids in one unique, quick, easy-to-use form. The Index offers advantages for personal Bible study that not even a combination of the above study helps would provide.

With over 8,000 subjects, names, places, things, concepts, events, and doctrines of the Bible, the BCI truly "opens" the Bible. It not only includes the Scripture references for the individual subjects (by appropriate subheadings), it goes one convenient step further: it gives the actual page numbers in *The Open Bible*® where each Scripture verse or verses may be found.

An example will illustrate. Suppose you need to prepare a study lesson on "The Peace of Jesus." Follow four easy steps:

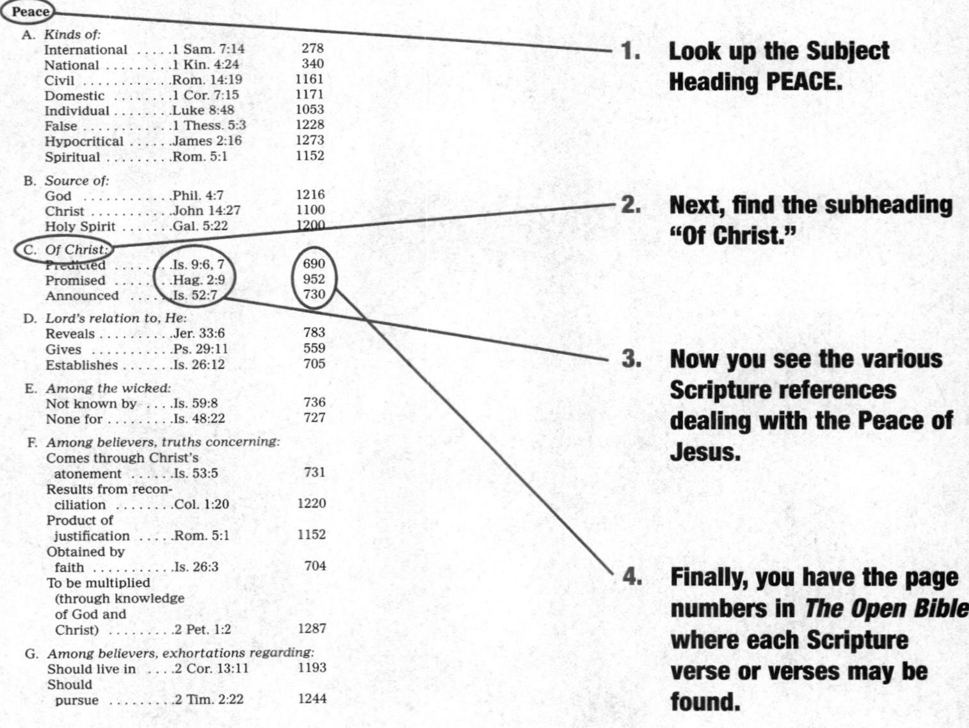

Peace

A. *Kinds of:*
International . . . . .1 Sam. 7:14 278
National . . . . .1 Kin. 4:24 340
Civil . . . . .Rom. 14:19 1161
Domestic . . . . .1 Cor. 7:15 1171
Individual . . . . .Luke 8:48 1053
False . . . . .1 Thess. 5:3 1228
Hypocritical . . . . . .James 2:16 1273
Spiritual . . . . .Rom. 5:1 1152

B. *Source of:*
God . . . . .Phil. 4:7 1216
Christ . . . . .John 14:27 1100
Holy Spirit . . . . . . .Gal. 5:22 1200

C. *Of Christ:*
Predicted . . . . . . .Is. 9:6, 7 690
Promised . . . . . . .Hag. 2:9 952
Announced . . . . . .Is. 52:7 730

D. *Lord's relation to, He:*
Reveals . . . . .Jer. 33:6 783
Gives . . . . .Ps. 29:11 559
Establishes . . . . . . .Is. 26:12 705

E. *Among the wicked:*
Not known by . . . .Is. 59:8 736
None for . . . . .Is. 48:22 727

F. *Among believers, truths concerning:*
Comes through Christ's atonement . . . . . .Is. 53:5 731
Results from reconciliation . . . . .Col. 1:20 1220
Product of justification . . . . .Rom. 5:1 1152
Obtained by faith . . . . .Is. 26:3 704
To be multiplied (through knowledge of God and Christ) . . . . .2 Pet. 1:2 1287

G. *Among believers, exhortations regarding:*
Should live in . . . .2 Cor. 13:11 1193
Should pursue . . . . .2 Tim. 2:22 1244

The Biblical Cyclopedic Index has provided two important sources of information for you. First, you have the scriptural material needed to prepare or study your lesson. Second, you have this material in order as it appears in the Bible, so you have a ready-made outline for your personal use.

Biblical Cyclopedic Index

FROM GENESIS TO REVELATION

ARRANGED ALPHABETICALLY GIVING THE BOOK, CHAPTER, VERSE AND PAGE
WHERE EVERY REFERENCE IN THIS INDEX IS FOUND

SUBJECT	REFERENCE	PAGE

A

Aaron—*bright*

A. *Ancestry and family of:*
- Descendant of Levi ... Ex. 6:16-20 ... 60
- Son of Amram and Jochebed ... Ex. 6:20 ... 61
- Moses' older brother ... Ex. 7:1, 7 ... 61
- Brother of Miriam ... Ex. 15:20 ... 70
- Husband of Elisheba ... Ex. 6:23 ... 61
- Father of Nadab, Abihu, Eleazar, and Ithamar ... Ex. 6:23 ... 61

B. *Position of:*
- Moses' helper ... Ex. 4:13-31 ... 59
- Becomes "prophet" to Moses ... Ex. 7:1, 2 ... 61
- God inspired ... Ex. 12:1 ... 65
- Commissioned, with Moses to deliver Israelites from Egypt ... Ex. 6:13, 26 ... 60; Josh. 24:5 ... 236
- Inferior to that of Melchizedek ... Heb. 7:11-19 ... 1262

C. *Special privileges of:*
- Appears before Pharaoh ... Ex. 5:1-4 ... 59
- Performs miracles ... Ex. 7:9, 10, 19, 20 ... 61
- Supports Moses' hands ... Ex. 17:10-12 ... 71
- Ascends Mt. Sinai ... Ex. 19:24 ... 74; Ex. 24:1, 9 ... 77
- Sees God's glory ... Ex. 24:9, 10 ... 78
- Judges Israel in Moses' absence ... Ex. 24:14 ... 78
- Allowed inside the veil ... Lev. 16:15 ... 114
- Blesses the people ... Lev. 9:22 ... 106
- Intercedes for Miriam ... Num. 12:10-12 ... 145

D. *Sins of:*
- Tolerates idolatry ... Ex. 32:1-4 ... 85
- Permits evil ... Ex. 32:21-25 ... 86
- Conspires against Moses ... Num. 12:1-16 ... 145
- With Moses, fails at Meribah ... Num. 20:1-13, 24 ... 153

E. *Character of:*
- A good speaker ... Ex. 4:14 ... 59
- Weak in crises ... Ex. 32:1-24 ... 85
- Subject to jealousy ... Num. 12:1, 2 ... 145
- Conscious of guilt ... Num. 12:11 ... 145
- Submissive ... Lev. 10:1-7 ... 106
- A saint ... Ps. 106:16 ... 603

F. *Priesthood of:*
- Chosen by God ... Ex. 28:1 ... 81
- Sons, in office ... Lev. 8:1-36 ... 104
- Anointed with oil ... Ex. 30:25, 30 ... 85
- Duties given ... Ex. 30:7-10 ... 84
- Garments prescribed ... Ex. 39:1-31 ... 93
- Ordained to teach ... Lev. 10:8, 11 ... 107
- Set apart to offer sacrifices ... Lev. 9:1-24 ... 106; Heb. 5:1-4 ... 1261
- Alone enters within the holy place ... Ex. 30:10 ... 84; Heb. 9:7, 25 ... 1263
- Intercedes for others ... Num. 16:46-48 ... 151
- Confirmed by God ... Num. 17:8-10 ... 151; Heb. 9:4 ... 1263
- Hereditary ... Num. 20:23-28 ... 154
- For lifetime ... Heb. 7:23 ... 1262
- Inferior to Melchizedek's ... Heb. 7:11-19 ... 1262

G. *Death and successor of:*
- Lives 123 years ... Num. 33:39 ... 168
- Death ... Num. 20:23-29 ... 154
- Eleazar, son of, successor ... Num. 20:25-28 ... 154; Deut. 10:6 ... 185

Aaronites—*descendants of Aaron*
- Fight with David ... 1 Chr. 12:27 ... 413
- Under Zadok ... 1 Chr. 27:17 ... 426

Ab—*fifth month of the Jewish year*
- Aaron died in ... Num. 33:38 ... 168
- See Jewish calendar

Ab—*father*
- A part of many Hebrew names (e.g., Abinadab, Abner, Abijah) ... 1 Sam. 7:1 ... 278

Abaddon—*a Hebrew word translated "destruction"*
- Designates ruin in ... Job 31:12 ... 532
- Parallel with Sheol in ... Job 26:6 ... 529
- Refers to death ... Job 28:22 ... 530
- Personified ... Rev. 9:11 ... 1318

Abagtha
- A eunuch under King Ahasuerus ... Esth. 1:10 ... 502

Abanah—*a river flowing through Damascus*
- Spoken of highly by Naaman ... 2 Kin. 5:12 ... 373

Abandon—*desert*

A. *Required for:*
- Safety ... Gen. 19:12-26 ... 20; Acts 27:41-44 ... 1143
- Salvation ... Phil. 3:7-10 ... 1215
- Service ... Matt. 10:37-39 ... 987
- Sanctification ... 2 Cor. 6:14-18 ... 1187
- Spiritual success ... Heb. 11:24-27 ... 1266

B. *Aspects of:*
- Land, commanded ... Gen. 12:1-5 ... 14
- Idolatry, admonished ... Ex. 32:1-10 ... 85
- One's ministry, rebuked ... 1 Kin. 19:3-18 ... 359
- Family, regretted ... 1 Sam. 30:1-6 ... 301
- The tabernacle, remembered ... Jer. 7:12 ... 756
- Jerusalem, lamented ... Matt. 23:37, 38 ... 1003

C. *Of people to judgment because of:*
- Sin ... Gen. 6:5-7 ... 9
- Rebellion ... 1 Sam. 15:16-26 ... 286
- Unbelief ... Matt. 23:37-39 ... 1003
- Rejecting God ... Rom. 1:21-32 ... 1149
- Sexual immorality ... 1 Cor. 5:1-5 ... 1169
- Apostasy ... Heb. 10:26-29 ... 1265

Abarim—*regions beyond*
- Moses sees the Promised Land from ... Num. 27:12 ... 162

Abasement—*degradation; humiliation*

A. *As a judgment for:*
- Stubbornness ... 2 Kin. 14:8-14 ... 382
- Defaming God ... 2 Chr. 32:1-22 ... 460
- Pride ... Is. 14:12-17 ... 695
- Haman's prejudice ... Esth. 7:4-10 ... 506
- Arrogance ... Dan. 4:33, 37 ... 876; Acts 12:20-23 ... 1126

B. *As a virtue, seen in:*
- Nineveh's repentance ... Jon. 3:1-10 ... 923; Matt. 12:41 ... 990
- A tax collector's unworthiness ... Luke 18:13, 14 ... 1066
- Paul's life ... 1 Cor. 9:19-23 ... 1173
- Christ's humiliation ... Phil. 2:5-8 ... 1214

C. *Rewards of, seen in:*
- Healing ... 2 Kin. 5:11-14 ... 373
- Elevation ... Matt. 23:12 ... 1002
- Restoration ... Luke 15:11-24 ... 1063
- Renewed service ... 1 Cor. 15:9, 10 ... 1178

Abate—*diminish, desist*
- Floodwaters ... Gen. 8:8, 11 ... 11
- Moses' natural force not ... Deut. 34:7 ... 209
- Anger of Ephraim ... Judg. 8:3 ... 248

Abba—*an Aramaic word meaning "father"*
- Used by Christ ... Mark 14:36 ... 1033
- Expressive of sonship ... Rom. 8:15 ... 1154

Abda—*servant* (of God)
1. The father of Adoniram ... 1 Kin. 4:6 ... 339

SUBJECT	REFERENCE	PAGE
Buys burial place for Sarah	Gen. 23:1-20	23
Obtains wife for Isaac	Gen. 24:1-67	24
Marries Keturah; fathers other children; dies	Gen. 25:1-10	26
D. *Characteristics of:*		
Friend of God	2 Chr. 20:7	448
Obedient	Gen. 22:1-18	22
Giving	Gen. 14:20 Heb. 7:1, 2, 4	16 1262
Generous	Gen. 13:8, 9	15
Courageous	Gen. 14:13-16	16
Independent	Gen. 14:21-23	16
Man of prayer	Gen. 18:23-33	19
Man of faith	Gen. 15:6	17
Rich man	Gen. 13:2	15
Mighty prince	Gen. 23:5, 6	23
Good provider	Gen. 25:5, 6	26
E. *References to, in the New Testament:*		
Ancestor of Jesus	Matt. 1:1	977
In the line of faith	Heb. 11:8-10	1265
Christ the true Seed of	Gal. 3:16	1198
Foresees Christ's day	John 8:56	1092
Hears the gospel preached	Gal. 3:8	1198
Justified by faith	Rom. 4:1-12	1151
Faith of, seen in works	James 2:21-23	1273
Father of true believers	Matt. 8:11 Rom. 4:11-25 Gal. 3:7, 29	1381 984 1198
Sees the eternal city	Heb. 11:8-10, 13-16	1265
Covenant with, still valid	Luke 1:73 Acts 3:25	1043 1115
Sons of, illustrate covenants	Gal. 4:22-31	1199
Tithing of, has deeper meaning	Heb. 7:9, 10	1262
Headship of, in marriage	1 Pet. 3:5-7	1281
Eternal home of, in heaven	Luke 16:19-25	1064

Abraham's bosom

SUBJECT	REFERENCE	PAGE
Expressive of heavenly status	Luke 16:22, 23	1064

Abram (see Abraham)

Abronah—*passage*

SUBJECT	REFERENCE	PAGE
Israelite encampment	Num. 33:34	168

Absalom—*the father of peace*

SUBJECT	REFERENCE	PAGE
Son of David	2 Sam. 3:3	308
A handsome man	2 Sam. 14:25	319
Receives Tamar after her rape by Amnon	2 Sam. 13:20	317
Slays Amnon for raping Tamar	2 Sam. 13:22-33	317
Flees from David	2 Sam. 13:34-39	318
Returns through Joab's intrigue	2 Sam. 14:1-24	318
Fathers children	2 Sam. 14:27	319
Reconciled to David	2 Sam. 14:28-33	319
Alienates the people from David	2 Sam. 15:1-6	319
Conspires against David	2 Sam. 15:7-12	319
Forces David from Jerusalem	2 Sam. 15:13-29	319
Receives Hushai	2 Sam. 15:31-37	320
Hears Ahithophel's counsel	2 Sam. 16:20-23	321
Prefers Hushai's counsel	2 Sam. 17:5-14	321
Strategy of, revealed to David	2 Sam. 17:15-22	322
Masses his army against David	2 Sam. 17:24-26	322
Caught and slain by Joab	2 Sam. 18:9-18	323
Death of, brings sorrow to David	2 Sam. 18:19-33	323
Joab rebukes David for mourning over	2 Sam. 19:1-8	324
Death of, unites Israel again to David	2 Sam. 19:9-15	324

Absence

SUBJECT	REFERENCE	PAGE
A. *Of physical relations:*		
A child from its father	Gen. 37:32-35	39
Israel's ark	1 Sam. 4:21, 22	277
Israel from her land	2 Chr. 36:17-21	465
Believers from one another	Phil. 1:25-27	1213
Believers from Christ	2 Cor. 5:6-9	1186
B. *Of God's Spirit as:*		
Judgment on the world	Gen. 6:3	9
Judgment on an individual	1 Sam. 16:14	287
Unable to flee	Ps. 139:7-12	619
C. *Of graces:*		
Holy Spirit	Jude 19	1307
Faith	2 Thess. 3:2	1233
Love	2 Tim. 3:2	1244
Holiness	Rev. 22:11	1328
Righteousness	Rev. 22:11	1328

Absenteeism—*habitual absence from*

SUBJECT	REFERENCE	PAGE
Work, condemned	2 Thess. 3:6-14	1233
Church, rebuked	Heb. 10:25	1265

Abstain—*to refrain from*

SUBJECT	REFERENCE	PAGE
A. *From moral evil:*		
Vindictiveness	2 Sam. 16:5-14	321
Idolatry	Acts 15:20, 29	1129
Sexual immorality	Acts 15:20	1129
Sexual sins	1 Thess. 4:3	1228
Fleshly lusts	1 Pet. 2:11	1280
Every form of evil	1 Thess. 5:22	1229
B. *From things:*		
Food	2 Sam. 12:16, 23	316
Married relations	Ex. 19:15 1 Cor. 7:5	73 1171
Meats	Rom. 14:1-23 1 Cor. 8:1-13	1160 1172
C. *From unauthorized commands:*		
Forbidding to marry	1 Tim. 4:3	1239
Requiring man-made ceremonies	Col. 2:20-23	1221
Abstaining from foods	1 Tim. 4:3	1239

Abstinence—*to refrain from*

SUBJECT	REFERENCE	PAGE
Blood	Acts 15:20	1129
Evil	1 Thess. 5:22	1229
Eating	Acts 27:21	1143
Sexual immorality	Acts 15:20 1 Thess. 4:3	1129 1228
Idolatry	Acts 15:20	1129
Intoxicants	Prov. 23:31	650
Lust	1 Pet. 2:11	1280
Things offered to idols	Acts 15:29	1130
Meats contaminated	Acts 15:20	1129

Abstinence—*to refrain from strong drink*

SUBJECT	REFERENCE	PAGE
A. *Required of:*		
Priests	Lev. 10:9	107
Kings	Prov. 31:4	657
Nazirites	Num. 6:1-4	138
B. *Failure of, a cause of:*		
Sudden death	1 Sam. 25:36-38	297
Delirium tremens	Prov. 23:31-35	650
Insensibility to justice	Is. 5:11, 12, 22, 23	686
Error in judgment	Is. 28:7	706
Moral callousness	Is. 56:12	734
Revelry	Dan. 5:2-4	877
Debauchery	Hab. 2:15, 16	941
A weaker brother's stumble	Rom. 14:20, 21	1161
Excess	Eph. 5:18	1208
C. *Examples of:*		
Manoah's wife	Judg. 13:3, 4, 7	254
Samson	Judg. 16:17	257
Hannah	1 Sam. 1:15	273
Rechabites	Jer. 35:1-19	785
Daniel	Dan. 1:8	871
John the Baptist	Luke 1:13-15	1041

Abundance—*plentiful supply*

SUBJECT	REFERENCE	PAGE
A. *Of material things:*		
Spices	1 Kin. 10:10	348
Rain	1 Kin. 18:41	358
Metals	1 Chr. 22:3, 14	421
Trees	1 Chr. 22:4 Neh. 9:25	421 493
Sacrifices	1 Chr. 29:21	429
Camels	2 Chr. 14:15	445
Great numbers	2 Chr. 15:9	445
Flocks and herds	2 Chr. 18:2 2 Chr. 32:29	447 461
Money	2 Chr. 24:11	452
Weapons	2 Chr. 32:5	460
Riches	Ps. 52:7	573
Milk	Is. 7:22	689
Wine	Is. 56:12	734
Horses	Ezek. 26:10	844
Labors	2 Cor. 11:23	1191
B. *Of God's spiritual blessings:*		
Goodness	Ex. 34:6	88
Pardon	Is. 55:7	733
Peace and truth	Jer. 33:6	783
Answers to our prayers	Eph. 3:20	1206
Grace	1 Tim. 1:14	1237
Mercy	1 Pet. 1:3	1279
C. *Of spiritual things:*		
Predicted for gospel times	Is. 35:2	713
Realized in the Messiah	Ps. 72:7	583
Given to the gentle	Ps. 37:11	564
Through Christ	Rom. 5:17, 18, 20	1152
By grace	Eph. 1:3-6	1204
D. *Of good things for Christians:*		
Greater usefulness	Matt. 13:11-13	990
Greater reward	Matt. 25:29	1005
Spiritual life	John 10:10	1094
Grace	Rom. 5:17	1152
Christian service	1 Cor. 15:10	1178
Joy	2 Cor. 8:2	1188

SUBJECT REFERENCE PAGE

Abundance—continued
Thanksgiving ... 2 Cor. 4:15 1186; 2 Cor. 9:12 1190
Rejoicing ... Phil. 1:26 1214
Holy Spirit ... Titus 3:5, 6 1250
Entrance in God's kingdom ... 2 Pet. 1:11 1287
E. *Of undesirable things:*
Witchcraft ... Is. 47:9 725
Idleness ... Ezek. 16:49 832
F. *Characteristics of:*
Given to the obedient ... Lev. 26:3-13 124
Useful in God's work ... 2 Chr. 24:11 452
Cannot satisfy fully ... Eccl. 5:10-12 665
Not to be trusted ... Ps. 52:7 573
Subject to conditions ... Mal. 3:10-12 969; Matt. 6:32, 33 983
Can be taken away ... Luke 12:13-21 1059
Not a sign of real worth ... Luke 12:15 1059
G. *Obtained by:*
Putting away sin ... 2 Chr. 15:8, 9 445
Following God's commands ... 2 Chr. 17:3-5 446
Given by God ... Job 36:31 537
Through Christ ... John 10:10 1094

Abuse—*application to a wrong purpose*
A. *Of physical things:*
Sexual perversions ... Gen. 19:5-9, 31-38 20
Torture ... Judg. 16:21 257
B. *Of spiritual things:*
Misuse of authority ... Num. 20:10-13 154; 1 Cor. 9:18 1173
Using the world wrongly ... 1 Cor. 7:31 1172
Perverting the truth ... 2 Pet. 2:10-22 1288
Corrupting God's ordinances ... 1 Sam. 2:12-17 274; 1 Cor. 11:17-22 1175
C. *Manifested by:*
Unbelieving ... Mark 15:29-32 1035

Abyss
Translated:
"Bottomless pit" ... Rev. 9:1, 2, 11 1318; Rev. 17:8 1324

Acacia Grove
1. Israel's last camp before crossing the Jordan ... Josh. 3:1 216
Scene of Baalam's attempted curse ... Num. 22–24 156
Sin of Baal of Peor here ... Num. 25:1-18 159
Site of Joshua's commission ... Num. 27:12-23 162
War with Midianites here ... Num. 31:1-54 165
Reuben and Gad receive inheritance here ... Num. 32:1-42 166
Scene of Moses' final address ... Deut. 1–34 175
Spies sent from ... Josh. 2:1 215
2. Valley blessed by the Lord ... Joel 3:18 905

Acacia wood
Used in:
Making the ark ... Ex. 25:10, 13 78
Table of showbread ... Ex. 37:10 91
Altar of incense ... Ex. 30:1 84
Altar of burnt offering ... Ex. 38:1, 6 92
Tabernacle boards ... Ex. 26:15-37 80

Accad—*a city in the land of Shinar*
One of the towns in Nimrod's kingdom ... Gen. 10:10 13

Acceptance—*the reception of one's person or service*
A. *Objects of, before God:*
Righteousness and justice ... Prov. 21:3 647
Our words and meditations ... Ps. 19:14 555
Our dedication ... Rom. 12:1, 2 1158
Service ... Rom. 14:18 1161
Giving ... Rom. 15:16, 27 1161
Offerings ... Phil. 4:18 1216
Intercession ... 1 Tim. 2:1-3 1237
Helping parents ... 1 Tim. 5:4 1239
Spiritual sacrifices ... 1 Pet. 2:5 1280
B. *Qualifications of, seen in:*
Coming at God's time ... Is. 49:8 727; 2 Cor. 6:2 1187
Meeting God's requirements ... Job 42:8, 9 541
Receiving divine sign ... Judg. 6:9-21 246
Noting God's response ... 1 Sam. 7:8-10 278; John 12:28-30 1097
Responding to God's renewal ... Ezek. 20:40-44 837
Manifesting spiritual rectitude ... Mic. 6:6-8 931
C. *Persons disqualified for, such as:*
Blemished sacrifices ... Mal. 1:8, 10, 13 967
Those who swear deceitfully ... Ps. 24:3-6 557

Access to God
A. *By means of:*
Christ ... John 14:6 1099
Christ's blood ... Eph. 2:13 1205
Holy Spirit ... Eph. 2:18 1205
Faith ... Rom. 5:2 1152
Clean hands ... Ps. 24:3-5 557
God's grace ... Eph. 1:6 1204
Prayer ... Matt. 6:6 982
B. *Characteristics of:*
On God's choosing ... Ps. 65:4 578
Sinners commanded to seek ... Is. 55:6, 7 733; James 4:8 1274
With confidence ... Heb. 4:16 1261
Boldness ... Eph. 3:12 1206
Results from reconciliation ... Col. 1:21, 22 1220
Open to Gentiles ... Acts 14:27 1129
Experienced in Christ's priesthood ... Heb. 7:19-25 1262
Sought by God's people ... Ps. 27:4 558
Bold in prayer ... Heb. 4:16 1261
A blessing to be chosen ... Ps. 65:4 578

Accident—*event not foreseen*
A. *Caused by:*
An animal ... Num. 22:25 156
A fall ... 2 Sam. 4:4 309
B. *Explanation of:*
Known to God ... Deut. 29:29 203; Prov. 16:9, 33 642
Misunderstood by people ... Luke 13:4, 5 1061
Subject to God's providence ... Rom. 8:28 1155

Acco—*a seaport 8 miles north of Mt. Carmel (modern Acre)*
Assigned to Asher ... Judg. 1:31 241
Called Ptolemais in the New Testament ... Acts 21:7 1136

Accommodation—*adaptation caused by human limitations*
A. *Physically, caused by:*
Age ... Gen. 33:13-15 35
Strength and size ... 1 Sam. 17:38-40 289
Inability to repay ... Luke 7:41, 42 1051
B. *Spiritually, caused by:*
Humankind's blindness ... Matt. 13:10-14 990
Absence of the Spirit ... John 16:12, 13 1101
Carnality ... 1 Cor. 3:1, 2 1168
Spiritual immaturity ... Rom. 14:1-23 1160
Humankind's present limitations ... 1 Cor. 2:7-16 1168
Degrees of light ... Heb. 9:7-15 1263

Accomplish—*to fulfill*
A. *Of God's Word concerning:*
Judah's captivity ... Dan. 9:2 882
Judah's return ... 2 Chr. 36:22, 23 466
God's sovereign plan ... Is. 55:11 733
Christ's suffering ... Luke 18:31 1066
Christ's death ... John 19:28-30 1104
B. *Of human things:*
Food ... 1 Kin. 5:9 341

Accord—*united agreement*
A. *Descriptive of:*
A spontaneous response ... Acts 12:10 1126
United in spirit ... Acts 12:20 1126
Voluntary action ... 2 Cor. 8:17 1189
Single-mindedness ... Josh. 9:2 221
Spiritual unity ... Acts 1:14 1112
B. *Manifested in:*
Fellowship ... Acts 2:46 1114
Prayer ... Acts 4:24 1116
Opposition ... Acts 7:57 1120
Response ... Acts 8:6 1120
Decisions ... Acts 15:25 1130
Mind ... Phil. 2:2 1214

Accountability—*responsibility for own acts*
A. *Kinds of:*
Universal ... Rom. 14:12 1160
Personal ... 2 Sam. 12:1-15 315
Personal and family ... Josh. 7:1-26 219
Personal and national ... 2 Sam. 24:1-17 330
Delayed but exacted ... 2 Sam. 21:1-14 326
Final ... Rom. 2:1-12 1149
B. *Determined by:*
Federal headship ... Gen. 3:1-24 9; Rom. 5:12-21 1152
Personal responsibility ... Ezek. 18:1-32 834
Faithfulness ... Matt. 25:14-30 1004
Knowledge ... Luke 12:47, 48 1060
Conscience ... Rom. 2:12-16 1149
Greater light ... Rom. 2:17-29 1150

SUBJECT REFERENCE PAGE

SUBJECT — REFERENCE — PAGE

Joins other cities against Chedorlaomer ... Gen. 14:1-4, 8 ... 16
Destroyed with Sodom and Gomorrah ... Gen. 19:24-28 ... 20

Admatha—*God-given*

One of Ahasuerus's chamberlains ... Esth. 1:13-15 ... 502

Administer—*serve; execute; manage*

Applied to:
Judgment ... 1 Kin. 3:28 ... 339
Vengeance ... Jer. 21:12 ... 770
Justice ... 2 Sam. 8:15 ... 313

Administration—*the management or disposition of affairs*

Of gifts to Jerusalem saints ... 2 Cor. 8:19, 20 ... 1189
Of spiritual gifts ... {1 Cor. 12:5 / 2 Cor. 9:12} ... 1175 / 1190

Admiration—*exceptional esteem*

Reserved for saints ... 2 Thess. 1:10 ... 1232
Flattering, shown by false teachers ... Jude 16 ... 1307

Admonition—*wise words spoken against evil acts; warning*

A. *Performed by:*
God ... Heb. 8:5 ... 1263
Earthly fathers ... Eph. 6:4 ... 1209
Leaders ... 1 Thess. 5:12 ... 1228
Christians ... Rom. 15:14 ... 1161

B. *Directed against:*
A remnant ... Jer. 42:19 ... 792
Elders ... Acts 20:28-35 ... 1136
Those who will not work ... {2 Thess. 3:10, 15} ... 1233
Divisive individual ... Titus 3:10 ... 1250

C. *Sources of in:*
Scriptures ... 1 Cor. 10:11 ... 1174
Wise words ... Eccl. 12:11, 12 ... 670
Spiritual knowledge ... Col. 3:16 ... 1221

Adna—*pleasure*

1. One who divorced his foreign wife ... Ezra 10:18, 30 ... 479
2. Postexilic priest ... Neh. 12:12, 15 ... 496

Adnah—*pleasure*

1. Captain of Saul ... 1 Chr. 12:20 ... 413
2. Chief captain of Jehoshaphat ... 2 Chr. 17:14 ... 446

Adonai—*Lord*

The Hebrew title for God (translated "Lord") expressing lordship (found in the following five compound words)

Adoni-Bezek—*lord of Bezek*

A king of Bezek ... Judg. 1:3-7 ... 240

Adonijah—*my Lord is Yahweh*

1. David's fourth son ... 2 Sam. 3:2, 4 ... 308
   Attempts to usurp throne ... 1 Kin. 1:5-53 ... 335
   Desires Abishag as wife ... 1 Kin. 2:13-18 ... 337
   Executed by Solomon ... 1 Kin. 2:19-25 ... 337
2. A teacher ... 2 Chr. 17:8, 9 ... 446
3. A Jew who signed the document ... {Neh. 9:38; 10:16} ... 494

Probably the same as Adonikam in ... Ezra 2:13 ... 470

Adonikam—*my Lord has risen*

Descendants of, return from exile ... Ezra 2:13 ... 470

Adoniram, Adoram—*my Lord is exalted*

A son of Abda ... 1 Kin. 4:6 ... 339
Official under David, Solomon, and Rehoboam ... {2 Sam. 20:24 / 1 Kin. 5:14 / 1 Kin. 12:18} ... 326 / 341 / 350
Stoned by angry Israelites ... 1 Kin. 12:18 ... 350
Called Hadoram ... 2 Chr. 10:18 ... 442

Adoni-Zedek—*my Lord is righteous*

An Amorite king of Jerusalem ... Josh. 10:1-5 ... 222
Defeated and slain by Joshua ... Josh. 10:6-27 ... 222

Adoption—*the legal act of investing with sonship*

A. *Used naturally of:*
Eliezer under Abraham ... Gen. 15:2-4 ... 17
Joseph's sons under Jacob ... {Gen. 48:5, 14, 16} ... 50
Moses under Pharaoh's daughter ... {Ex. 2:10 / Acts 7:21} ... 57 / 1119
Esther under Mordecai ... Esth. 2:7 ... 503

B. *Used spiritually of Israel as:*
Elected by God ... {Deut. 14:1, 2 / Rom. 11:1-32} ... 189 / 1157
Blessed by God ... Rom. 9:4 ... 1155
Realized in history ... Ex. 4:22, 23 ... 59

C. *Used spiritually of the Gentiles as:*
Predicted in the prophets ... Is. 65:1 ... 741
Confirmed by faith ... Rom. 10:20 ... 1157
Realized in the new covenant ... {Eph. 2:12 / Eph. 3:1-6} ... 1205 / 1205

D. *The time of:*
Past, predestined to ... Rom. 8:29 ... 1155
Present, regarded as sons ... {John 1:12, 13 / John 3:1-11} ... 1081 / 1083
Future, glorified as sons ... {Rom. 8:19, 23 / 1 John 3:2} ... 1155 / 1295

E. *The source of:*
By God's grace ... Rom. 4:16, 17 ... 1151
By faith ... Gal. 3:7, 26 ... 1198
Through Christ ... Gal. 4:4, 5 ... 1198

F. *Assurances of, by:*
Spirit's witness ... Rom. 8:16 ... 1154
Spirit's leading ... Rom. 8:14 ... 1154
"Abba, Father" ... Rom. 8:15 ... 1154
Changed life ... 1 John 3:9-17 ... 1295
Father's chastening ... {Prov. 3:11, 12 / Heb. 12:5-11} ... 631 / 1267

G. *The blessings of:*
A new nature ... 2 Cor. 5:17 ... 1187
A new name ... {Is. 62:2, 12 / Rev. 3:12} ... 739 / 1314
Access to God ... Eph. 2:18 ... 1205
Fatherly love ... 1 John 3:1 ... 1295
Help in prayer ... Matt. 6:5-15 ... 982

Spiritual unity ... {John 17:11, 21 / Eph. 2:18-22} ... 1102 / 1205
A glorious inheritance ... {John 14:1-3 / Rom. 8:17, 18} ... 1099 / 1155

Adoraim—*double honor*

A city fortified by Rehoboam ... 2 Chr. 11:5, 9 ... 442

Adoram (see Adoniram)

Adoration—*reverential praise*

A. *Rendered falsely to:*
Idols ... {Is. 44:15, 17, 19} ... 722
An image ... Dan. 3:5-7 ... 874
Heavenly hosts ... 2 Kin. 17:16 ... 386
Satan ... Luke 4:6-8 ... 1046
People ... Acts 10:25, 26 ... 1124
Angels ... Col. 2:18, 23 ... 1221

B. *Rendered properly to God:*
Illustrated ... Is. 6:1-5 ... 687
Taught ... Ps. 95–100 ... 599
Proclaimed ... Rev. 4:8-11 ... 1315

C. *Rendered properly to Christ as God by:*
Wise men ... Matt. 2:1, 11 ... 978
Leper ... Matt. 8:2 ... 984
Ruler ... Matt. 9:18 ... 985
Disciples ... Matt. 14:22, 33 ... 992
Woman ... Matt. 15:25 ... 993
Mother ... Matt. 20:20 ... 998
Blind man ... John 9:1, 38 ... 1092
Every creature ... Phil. 2:10, 11 ... 1214

See Worship

Adornment

A. *Used literally of:*
A harlot ... Rev. 17:3, 4 ... 1323
A woman ... {Is. 3:16-24 / 1 Tim. 2:9} ... 685 / 1238
A building ... Luke 21:5 ... 1070
A bride ... Rev. 21:2 ... 1326

B. *Used spiritually of:*
Believer as justified ... Is. 61:10 ... 738
Believer as sanctified ... Titus 2:10 ... 1250
Israel restored ... Jer. 31:4 ... 780
Saintly woman ... 1 Tim. 2:9 ... 1238

C. *Guidelines for:*
In modesty ... 1 Tim. 2:9 ... 1238
Not external ... 1 Pet. 3:3-5 ... 1281

Adrammelech—*Adar is king*

1. A god worshiped by the Samaritans ... 2 Kin. 17:31 ... 386
2. Killed Sennacherib ... {2 Kin. 19:36, 37 / Is. 37:38} ... 390 / 716

Adramyttium—*a seaport of Mysia in Asia Minor*

Travels of Paul ... Acts 27:2-6 ... 1142

Adriatic Sea

A part or the whole of the Adriatic Sea named after Adria, a city of Italy ... Acts 27:27 ... 1143

Adriel—*my help is God*

Marries Saul's eldest daughter ... 1 Sam. 18:19 ... 290
Sons of, slain to atone Saul's crime ... 2 Sam. 21:8, 9 ... 326

Adullam—*refuge*

A town of Canaan ... {Gen. 38:1, 12, 20} ... 40
Conquered by Joshua ... Josh. 12:7, 15 ... 225

SUBJECT — REFERENCE — PAGE

Afflictions—continued
- Part of gospel ... 1 Thess. 1:6 ... 1226
- Must not be shaken by ... 1 Thess. 3:3 ... 1227
- Commendable examples of ... 2 Tim. 3:11 ... 1245
- Momentary ... 2 Cor. 4:17 ... 1186
- Cannot separate from God ... Rom. 8:35-39 ... 1155
- Deliverance from, promised ... Ps. 34:19 ... 562
- Terminated at Christ's return ... 2 Thess. 1:4-7 ... 1232

See Trials

Afraid—*overcome with fear*

A. *Caused by:*
- Nakedness ... Gen. 3:10 ... 7
- Unusual dream ... Gen. 28:16, 17 ... 30
- God's presence ... Ex. 3:6 ... 57
- Moses' approach ... Ex. 34:30 ... 89
- A burning mountain ... Deut. 5:5 ... 180
- Giant's raging ... 1 Sam. 17:11, 24 ... 288
- A prophet's words ... 1 Sam. 28:20 ... 300
- Angel's sword ... 1 Chr. 21:30 ... 421
- God's deeds ... Ps. 65:8 ... 578
- Gabriel's presence ... Dan. 8:17 ... 881
- A terrifying storm ... Jon. 1:5, 10 ... 922
- Peter's sinking ... Matt. 14:30 ... 992
- Changed person ... Mark 5:15 ... 1020
- Heavenly hosts ... Luke 2:9 ... 1043

B. *Overcome by:*
- The Lord's presence ... Ps. 3:5, 6 ... 547
- Trusting God ... Ps. 27:1-3 ... 558
- God's protection ... Ps. 91:4, 5 ... 595
- Stability of heart ... Ps. 112:7, 8 ... 607
- God's coming judgment ... Is. 10:24-26 ... 693
- The Messiah's advent ... Is. 40:9-11 ... 717
- God's sovereign power ... Is. 51:12, 13 ... 729
- Christ's comforting words ... Matt. 14:27 ... 992

Afternoon—*part of the day following noon*
- Called cool of the day ... Gen. 3:8 ... 7

Afterthought—*a later reflection*
- Of Esau ... Heb. 12:16, 17 ... 1267
- Of the Israelites ... Num. 14:40-45 ... 148
- Of one of two sons ... Matt. 21:28-30 ... 1000
- Of the lost son ... Luke 15:17 ... 1063
- Of the unjust steward ... Luke 16:1-8 ... 1064
- Of the rich man in hell ... Luke 16:23-31 ... 1064
- Of Judas ... Matt. 27:3-5 ... 1008

Afterward(s)
- Your hands shall be ... Judg. 7:11 ... 248
- Those who are invited ... 1 Sam. 9:13 ... 280
- David's conscience bothered him ... 1 Sam. 24:5 ... 295
- His mouth will ... Prov. 20:17 ... 646
- Jesus finds him ... John 5:14 ... 1086

Agabus—*he loved*
- A Christian prophet who foretells a famine and warns Paul ... Acts 11:27, 28 ... 1125; Acts 21:10, 11 ... 1136

Agag—*flaming or violent*
1. A king of Amalek in Balaam's prophecy ... Num. 24:7 ... 158
2. Amalekite king spared by Saul, but slain by Samuel ... 1 Sam. 15:8, 9, 20-24, 32, 33 ... 286

Agagite—*descendant of Agag*
- A title applied to the father of Haman, enemy of the Jews ... Esth. 3:1, 10 ... 503

Agape—*Greek word rendered "love"*
- Descriptive of God ... 1 John 4:8 ... 1296
- Demanded toward God ... Matt. 22:37 ... 1001
- Demanded toward neighbors ... Matt. 22:39 ... 1001
- Fulfills Law ... Matt. 22:40 ... 1001
- Activity of described ... 1 Cor. 13:1-13 ... 1176

Agate—*a stone of translucent quartz*
- Worn by the high priest ... Ex. 28:19 ... 81; Ex. 39:12 ... 93
- Sold by Syrians ... Ezek. 27:16 ... 845

Age—*time counted by years*

A. *Handicaps of, seen in:*
- Physical infirmities ... Gen. 48:10 ... 50
- Unwillingness to adventure ... 2 Sam. 19:31-39 ... 325
- Declining strength ... Ps. 71:9 ... 582
- Deterioration of body ... Eccl. 12:1-7 ... 670

B. *Glories of, manifested in:*
- Wisdom ... Job 12:12 ... 520
- Maturity ... Job 5:26 ... 516
- Spiritual beauty ... Prov. 16:31 ... 643
- Fruitfulness ... Ps. 92:12-15 ... 596
- Judgment ... 1 Kin. 12:6-8 ... 350
- Strong faith ... Josh. 24:15, 29 ... 236

C. *Attitude of others toward:*
- Respect ... Lev. 19:32 ... 117
- Disrespect ... 2 Chr. 36:17 ... 465
- Insolence ... Is. 3:5 ... 685

D. *Unusual things connected with:*
- Retaining physical vigor ... Deut. 34:7 ... 209
- Becoming a father ... Gen. 18:9-15 ... 19; Luke 1:18, 36 ... 1041
- Living to see Christ ... Luke 2:25-32 ... 1044
- Knowing kind of death in ... John 21:18, 19 ... 1107

E. *Attaining unto, by:*
- Honoring parents ... Ex. 20:12 ... 74; Eph. 6:2, 3 ... 1209
- Keeping God's law ... Prov. 3:1, 2 ... 630
- Following wisdom ... Prov. 3:13, 16 ... 631
- The fear of the Lord ... Ps. 128:1, 6 ... 616
- Keeping from evil ... Ps. 34:11-14 ... 562
- God's promise ... Gen. 15:15 ... 17

F. *Those of Bible times who lived beyond age of 100:*
- Methuselah ... Gen. 5:27 ... 9
- Jared ... Gen. 5:20 ... 9
- Noah ... Gen. 9:29 ... 13
- Adam ... Gen. 5:5 ... 9
- Seth ... Gen. 5:8 ... 9
- Cainan ... Gen. 5:14 ... 9
- Enosh ... Gen. 5:11 ... 9
- Mahalalel ... Gen. 5:17 ... 9
- Lamech ... Gen. 5:31 ... 9
- Enoch ... Gen. 5:23 ... 9
- Terah ... Gen. 11:32 ... 14
- Isaac ... Gen. 35:28 ... 37
- Abraham ... Gen. 25:7 ... 26
- Jacob ... Gen. 47:28 ... 49
- Ishmael ... Gen. 25:17 ... 26
- Jehoiada ... 2 Chr. 24:15 ... 453
- Sarah ... Gen. 23:1 ... 23
- Aaron ... Num. 33:39 ... 168
- Moses ... Deut. 34:7 ... 209
- Joseph ... Gen. 50:26 ... 52
- Joshua ... Josh. 24:29 ... 237

Agee—*fugitive*
- Shammah's father ... 2 Sam. 23:11 ... 329

Ages—*extended periods of time*
- Descriptive of the times before Christ ... Eph. 3:5 ... 1205
- Descriptive of eternity ... Eph. 2:7 ... 1205

Agitation—*a disturbance*

A. *Physically of:*
- Mountain ... Ex. 19:16-18 ... 73
- The earth ... Matt. 27:51-53 ... 1010
- The world ... Ps. 46:2-6 ... 570
- End-time events ... Luke 21:25-27 ... 1070
- World's end ... 2 Pet. 3:7-12 ... 1288

B. *Emotionally of:*
- Extreme grief ... 2 Sam. 19:1-4 ... 324
- Remorse ... Matt. 27:3, 4 ... 1008
- Fear ... Matt. 28:1-4 ... 1010

C. *Figuratively of:*
- Messiah's advent ... Hag. 2:6, 7 ... 952
- Enraged people ... Acts 4:25-28 ... 1116
- The wicked ... Is. 57:20 ... 735
- The drunkard ... Prov. 23:29-35 ... 65

Agony—*extreme suffering*

Descriptive of:
- Christ in Gethsemane ... Luke 22:44 ... 1072
- Christ on the cross ... Mark 15:34-37 ... 1035
- Paul's sufferings ... 2 Cor. 1:8, 9 ... 1184
- The Christians' race ... 1 Cor. 9:24, 25 ... 1173

Agree, agreement

A. *Forbidden between:*
- Israel and pagans ... Ex. 34:12-16 ... 88
- God and Baal ... 1 Kin. 18:21-40 ... 357
- Believers, demons ... 1 Cor. 10:21 ... 1174
- Truth, error ... 1 John 4:1-6 ... 1296

B. *Necessary between:*
- Prophecy, fulfillment ... Acts 15:15 ... 1129
- Doctrine, life ... James 2:14-21 ... 1273
- Words, performance ... 2 Cor. 10:9-11 ... 1190
- Believers in prayer ... Matt. 18:19 ... 996
- Adversaries ... Matt. 5:24, 25 ... 981
- Christian workers ... Gal. 2:7-9 ... 1197

C. *Examples of:*
- Laban and Jacob ... Gen. 31:43-53 ... 33

SUBJECT — REFERENCE — PAGE

Anchor—continued

- Figuratively of the believer's hope . . . Heb. 6:19 — 1262

Ancient—*that which is old*

- Applied to the beginning (eternity) . . . Is. 45:21 — 724
- Applied to something very old . . . Prov. 22:28 — 649
- Applied to old men (elders) . . . Ps. 119:100 — 612; 1 Sam. 24:13 — 296

Ancient of Days

- Title applied to God . . . Dan. 7:9, 13, 22 — 880

Andrew—*manly*

- A fisherman . . . Matt. 4:18 — 980
- A disciple of John the Baptist . . . John 1:40 — 1082
- Brought Peter to Christ . . . John 1:40-42 — 1082
- Called to Christ's discipleship . . . Matt. 4:18, 19 — 980
- Enrolled among the Twelve . . . Matt. 10:2 — 986
- Told Jesus about a lad's lunch . . . John 6:8, 9 — 1087
- Carried a request to Jesus . . . John 12:20-22 — 1097
- Sought further light on Jesus' words . . . Mark 13:3, 4 — 1031
- Met in the Upper Room . . . Acts 1:13 — 1112

Andronicus—*conqueror of men*

- A notable Christian at Rome . . . Rom. 16:7 — 1162

Anem—*double fountain*

- Levitical city . . . 1 Chr. 6:73 — 407

Aner—*waterfall*

1. Amorite chief . . . Gen. 14:13, 24 — 16
2. A Levitical city . . . 1 Chr. 6:70 — 407

Angels—*heavenly beings created by God*

A. *Described as:*
- Spiritual beings . . . Heb. 1:13, 14 — 1258
- Created . . . Ps. 148:2, 5 — 624; Col. 1:16 — 1220
- Immortal . . . Luke 20:36 — 1069
- Holy . . . Matt. 25:31 — 1005
- Innumerable . . . Heb. 12:22 — 1267
- Wise . . . 2 Sam. 14:17, 20 — 318
- Powerful . . . Ps. 103:20 — 600
- Elect . . . 1 Tim. 5:21 — 1240
- Respectful of authority . . . Jude 9 — 1306
- Sexless . . . Matt. 22:30 — 1001
- Invisible . . . Num. 22:22-31 — 156
- Obedient . . . Ps. 103:20 — 600
- Possessing emotions . . . Luke 15:10 — 1063
- Judged in future by Christians . . . 1 Cor. 6:3 — 1170
- Concerned in human things . . . 1 Pet. 1:12 — 1279
- Incarnate in human form at times . . . Gen. 18:2-8 — 19
- Not perfect . . . Job 4:18 — 515
- Organized in ranks or orders . . . Is. 6:1-3 — 687; 1 Thess. 4:16 — 1228

B. *Ministry of, toward believers:*
- Guide . . . Gen. 24:7, 40 — 24
- Provide for . . . 1 Kin. 19:5-8 — 359
- Protect . . . Ps. 34:7 — 562; Ps. 91:11 — 595; Dan. 6:22 — 879
- Deliver . . . Acts 12:7-11 — 1125
- Gather . . . Matt. 24:31 — 1004
- Direct activities . . . Acts 8:26 — 1121
- Comfort . . . Acts 27:23, 24 — 1143
- Minister to . . . Heb. 1:14 — 1258

C. *Ministry of, toward unbelievers:*
- A destruction . . . Gen. 19:1, 13 — 20
- A curse . . . Judg. 5:23 — 245
- A pestilence . . . 2 Sam. 24:15-17 — 330
- Sudden death . . . Acts 12:23 — 1126
- Persecution . . . Ps. 35:5, 6 — 563

D. *Ministry of, in Christ's life, to:*
- Announce His conception . . . Matt. 1:20, 21 — 978
- Herald His birth . . . Luke 2:10-12 — 1043
- Sustain Him . . . Matt. 4:11 — 980
- Witness His resurrection . . . 1 Tim. 3:16 — 1238
- Proclaim His resurrection . . . Matt. 28:5-7 — 1010
- Accompany Him to heaven . . . Acts 1:9-11 — 1112

E. *Ministry of, on special occasions, at:*
- The world's creation . . . Job 38:7 — 538
- Sinai . . . Acts 7:38, 53 — 1119
- Satan's binding . . . Rev. 20:1-3 — 1326
- Christ's return . . . Matt. 13:41, 49 — 991; 1 Thess. 4:16 — 1228

F. *Appearance of, during the Old Testament, to:*
- Abraham . . . Gen. 18:2-15 — 19
- Hagar . . . Gen. 16:7-14 — 17
- Lot . . . Gen. 19:1-22 — 20
- Jacob . . . Gen. 28:10-12 — 30
- Moses . . . Ex. 3:1, 2 — 57
- Balaam . . . Num. 22:31-35 — 156
- Joshua . . . Josh. 5:13-15 — 218
- All Israel . . . Judg. 2:1-4 — 242
- Gideon . . . Judg. 6:11-24 — 246
- Manoah . . . Judg. 13:6-21 — 254
- David . . . 2 Sam. 24:16, 17 — 330
- Elijah . . . 1 Kin. 19:2-8 — 359
- Daniel . . . Dan. 6:21, 22 — 879
- Zechariah . . . Zech. 2:3 — 956

G. *Appearances of, during the New Testament, to:*
- Zacharias . . . Luke 1:11-20 — 1041
- The virgin Mary . . . Luke 1:26-38 — 1041
- Joseph . . . Matt. 1:20-25 — 978
- Shepherds . . . Luke 2:8-15 — 1043
- Certain women . . . Matt. 28:1-7 — 1010
- Mary Magdalene . . . John 20:11-13 — 1105
- The apostles . . . Acts 1:10, 11 — 1112
- Peter . . . Acts 5:19, 20 — 1117
- Philip . . . Acts 8:26 — 1121
- Cornelius . . . Acts 10:3-32 — 1123
- Paul . . . Acts 27:23, 24 — 1143
- John . . . Rev. 1:1 — 1312
- Seven churches . . . Rev. 1:20 — 1313

Angels, fallen

- Fall of, by pride . . . Is. 14:12-15 — 695; Jude 6 — 1306
- Seen by Christ . . . Luke 10:18 — 1056
- Make war on saints . . . Rev. 12:7-17 — 1320
- Imprisoned . . . 2 Pet. 2:4 — 1287
- Everlasting fire prepared for . . . Matt. 25:41 — 1005

Angel of God, the—*distinct manifestation of God*

A. *Names of:*
- Angel of God . . . Gen. 21:17 — 22
- Angel of the Lord . . . Gen. 22:11 — 23
- Captain of the army of the Lord . . . Josh. 5:14 — 218

B. *Appearances of, to:*
- Hagar . . . Gen. 16:7, 8 — 17; Gen. 21:17 — 22
- Abraham . . . Gen. 18:1-33 — 19; Gen. 22:11, 15 — 23
- Jacob . . . Gen. 31:11-13 — 33; Gen. 32:24-30 — 35
- Moses . . . Ex. 3:1, 2 — 57
- Children of Israel . . . Ex. 13:21, 22 — 68; Ex. 14:19 — 68
- Balaam . . . Num. 22:22-35 — 156
- Joshua . . . Judg. 2:1 — 242
- Donkey and Manoah and wife . . . Judg. 13:1-21 — 254
- David . . . 1 Chr. 21:16-18 — 420
- Zechariah, in vision, concerning Joshua . . . Zech. 3:1-10 — 956

C. *Divine characteristics:*
- Deliver Israel . . . 2 Kin. 19:14-20, 35, 36 — 389
- Extend blessings . . . Gen. 16:7-12 — 17
- Pardon sin . . . Ex. 23:20-22 — 77

Angels' food

- Eaten by humans . . . Ps. 78:25 — 587
- Eaten by Elijah . . . 1 Kin. 19:5-8 — 359

Anger of God

A. *Caused by humankind's:*
- Sin . . . Num. 32:10-15 — 166
- Unbelief . . . Ps. 78:21, 22 — 587
- Error . . . 2 Sam. 6:7 — 310
- Disobedience . . . Josh. 7:1, 11, 12 — 219
- Idolatry . . . Judg. 2:11-14 — 242

B. *Described as:*
- Sometimes delayed . . . 2 Kin. 23:25-27 — 394
- Slow . . . Neh. 9:17 — 493
- Brief . . . Ps. 30:5 — 559
- Restrained . . . Ps. 78:38 — 588
- Fierceness . . . Ps. 78:49, 50 — 588
- Consuming . . . Ps. 90:7 — 595
- Powerful . . . Ps. 90:11 — 595
- Not forever . . . Mic. 7:18 — 932
- To be feared . . . Ps. 76:7 — 586

C. *Visitation of, upon:*
- Miriam and Aaron . . . Num. 12:9-15 — 145
- Israelites . . . Num. 11:4-10 — 144
- Balaam . . . Num. 22:21, 22 — 156
- Moses . . . Deut. 4:21, 22 — 179
- Israel . . . Deut. 9:8 — 184
- Aaron . . . Deut. 9:20 — 185
- Wicked cities . . . Deut. 29:23 — 203
- A land . . . Deut. 29:24-28 — 203
- A king . . . 2 Chr. 25:15, 16 — 454

D. *Deliverance from, by:*
- Intercessory prayer . . . Num. 11:1, 2 — 144; Deut. 9:19, 20 — 185
- Decisive action . . . Num. 25:3-12 — 159
- Obedience . . . Deut. 13:16-18 — 188
- Executing the guilty . . . Josh. 7:1, 10-26 — 219

See Wrath of God

Anger of Jesus

- Provoked by unbelievers . . . Mark 3:1-6 — 1017
- In the temple . . . Matt. 21:12 — 999; Mark 11:15 — 1029

Anger, human

A. *Caused by:*
- A brother's deception . . . Gen. 27:42-45 — 29
- A wife's complaint . . . Gen. 30:1, 2 — 31
- Rape . . . Gen. 34:1-7 — 35

SUBJECT REFERENCE PAGE

Anub—*strong*

A man of Judah ...... 1 Chr. 4:8 403

Anvil—*a block for forging hot metals*

Used figuratively in .... Is. 41:7 719

Anxiety—*a disturbed state of mind produced by real or imaginary fears*

A. *Caused by:*
- Brother's hatred .... Gen. 32:6-12 34
- Son's rebellion .... 2 Sam. 18:24-33 323
- King's decree .... Esth. 4:1-17 504
- Child's absence .... Luke 2:48 1044
- Son's sickness .... John 4:46-49 1085
- Friend's delay .... 2 Cor. 2:12, 13 1185

B. *Overcome by:*
- Trust .... Ps. 37:1-5 564
- Reliance upon the Holy Spirit .... Mark 13:11 1031
- God's provision .... Luke 12:22-30 1059
- Upward look ..... Luke 21:25-28 1070
- Assurance of God's sovereignty ..... Rom. 8:28 1155
- Angel's word .... Acts 27:21-25 1143
- Prayer .... Phil. 4:6 1215
- God's care .... 1 Pet. 5:6, 7 1283

See Cares, worldly

Ape—*a monkey*

Article of trade ...... 1 Kin. 10:22 348

Apelles

A Christian in Rome .... Rom. 16:10 1162

Apharsathchites

Assyrian colonists in Samaria opposing Zerubbabel's work .... Ezra 4:9 473

Aphek—*strength, fortress*

1. A town in Plain of Sharon .... Josh. 12:18 225
   - Site of Philistine camp ...... 1 Sam. 4:1 276; 1 Sam. 29:1 300
2. A city assigned to Asher .... Josh. 19:30 231
3. Border city .... Josh. 13:4 225
4. A city in Jezreel ...... 1 Kin. 20:26-30 360
   - Syria's defeat prophesied here .... 2 Kin. 13:14-19 382

Aphekah—*fortress*

A city of Judah ..... Josh. 15:53 228

Aphiah—*striving*

An ancestor of King Saul .... 1 Sam. 9:1 279

Aphik—*strength, fortress*

Spared by Asher ..... Judg. 1:31 241

See Aphek 2

Apocalypse—*an unveiling of something unknown*

The Greek word usually translated "revelation" .... Rom. 16:25 1163; Gal. 1:12 1196

Apocrypha—*hidden things*

Writings in Greek written during the period between the Testaments; rejected by Protestants as uninspired

Apollonia—*pertaining to Apollo*

A town between Amphipolis and Thessalonica .... Acts 17:1 1132

Apollos—*a short or pet name for Apollonios*

- An Alexandrian Jew mighty in the Scriptures .... Acts 18:24, 25 1134
- Receives further instruction .... Acts 18:26 1134
- Sent to preach in Achaia .... Acts 18:27, 28 1134
- A minister in Corinth .... 1 Cor. 1:12 1167; 1 Cor. 3:4, 22 1168
- Cited by Paul .... 1 Cor. 4:6 1169
- Urged to revisit Corinth .... 1 Cor. 16:12 1180
- Journey of, noted by Paul .... Titus 3:13 1250

Apollyon—*the destroyer*

Angel of the bottomless pit .... Rev. 9:11 1318

Apostasy—*a falling away from God's truth*

A. *Kinds of:*
- National .... 1 Kin. 12:26-33 351; 2 Kin. 21:1-9 391
- Individual ...... Heb. 3:12 1260
- Satanic .... Rev. 12:7-9 1320
- Angelic .... 2 Pet. 2:4 1287
- General .... 2 Tim. 3:1-5 1244
- Imputed .... Acts 21:21 1137
- Final .... 2 Thess. 2:3 1232
- Irremedial .... Heb. 6:1-8 1261

B. *Caused by:*
- Satan .... Luke 22:31 1071
- False teachers .... Acts 20:29, 30 1136
- Perversion of Scripture .... 2 Tim. 4:3, 4 1245
- Persecution ...... Matt. 13:21 990
- Unbelief .... Heb. 4:9-11 1260
- Love of world .... 2 Tim. 4:10 1245
- Hardened heart .... Acts 7:54, 57 1120
- Spiritual blindness .... Acts 28:25-27 1144

C. *Manifested in:*
- Resisting truth .... 2 Tim. 3:7, 8 1245
- Resorting to deception ..... 2 Cor. 11:13-15 1191
- Reverting to immorality ..... 2 Pet. 2:14, 19-22 1288

D. *Safeguards against, found in:*
- God's Word .... Ps. 119:11 610; 2 Tim. 3:13-17 1245
- Spiritual growth .... 2 Pet. 1:5-11 1287
- Indoctrination .... Acts 20:29-31 1136
- Faithfulness ..... Matt. 24:42-51 1004
- Spiritual perception .... 1 John 4:1-6 1296
- Being grounded in the truth .... Eph. 4:13-16 1207
- Using God's armor .... Eph. 6:10-20 1209
- Preaching the Word .... 2 Tim. 4:2, 5 1245

E. *Examples of, seen in:*
- Israelites .... Ex. 32:1-35 85
- Saul .... 1 Sam. 15:11 286
- Solomon .... 1 Kin. 11:1-10 348
- Amaziah .... 2 Chr. 25:14-16 454
- Judas .... Matt. 26:14-16 1006
- Hymenaeus and Philetus .... 2 Tim. 2:17, 18 1244
- Demas .... 2 Tim. 4:10 1245
- Certain men .... Jude 4 1306

Apostles—*men divinely commissioned to represent Christ*

A. *Descriptive of:*
- Christ .... Heb. 3:1 1259
- The twelve .... Matt. 10:2 986
- Others (Barnabas, James, etc.) .... Acts 14:14 1128; Gal. 1:19 1197
- Simon Peter ...... Matt. 10:2 986
- Andrew .... Matt. 10:2 986
- James, son of Zebedee .... Matt. 10:2 986
- John .... Matt. 10:2 986
- Philip .... Matt. 10:3 986
- Bartholomew (Nathanael) .... Matt. 10:3 986; John 1:45 1082
- Thomas .... Matt. 10:3 986
- Matthew (Levi) .... Matt. 10:3 986; Luke 5:27 1048
- James, son of Alphaeus .... Matt. 10:3 986
- Thaddaeus (Judas) .... Matt. 10:3 986; John 14:22 1099
- Simon the Zealot .... Luke 6:15 1049
- Judas Iscariot .... Matt. 10:4 986
- Matthias .... Acts 1:26 1113
- Paul .... 2 Cor. 1:1 1184
- Barnabas .... Acts 14:14 1128
- James, the Lord's brother .... Gal. 1:19 1197
- Silvanus and Timothy .... 1 Thess. 1:1 1226; 1 Thess. 2:9 1227
- Andronicus and Junia .... Rom. 16:7 1162

B. *Mission of, to:*
- Perform miracles .... Matt. 10:1, 8 986
- Preach gospel ... Matt. 28:19, 20 1011
- Witness Christ's resurrection ...... Acts 1:22 1113; Acts 10:40-42 1124
- Write Scripture .... Eph. 3:5 1205
- Establish the church .... Eph. 2:20 1205

C. *Limitations of, before Pentecost:*
- Lowly in position .... Matt. 4:18 980
- Unlearned .... Acts 4:13 1116
- Subject to disputes .... Matt. 20:20-28 998
- Faith often obscure .... Matt. 16:21-23 995
- Need of instruction ..... Matt. 17:4, 9-13 995

D. *Position of, after Pentecost:*
- Interpreted prophecy .... Acts 2:14-36 1113
- Defended truth .... Phil. 1:7, 17 1213
- Exposed heretics .... Gal. 1:6-9 1196
- Upheld discipline .... 2 Cor. 13:1-6 1192
- Established churches .... Rom. 15:17-20 1161

Appaim—*nostrils*

A man of Judah ...... 1 Chr. 2:30, 31 402

Apparel—*clothing*

A. *Kinds of:*
- Harlot's .... Gen. 38:14, 15 40
- Virgin's .... 2 Sam. 13:18 317
- Mourner's .... 2 Sam. 12:19, 20 316
- Gorgeous .... Luke 7:25 1051
- Rich .... Ezek. 27:24 845
- Worldly .... 1 Pet. 3:3 1281
- Showy .... Luke 16:19 1064
- Official .... 1 Kin. 10:5 347
- Royal .... Esth. 6:8 506
- Priestly .... Ezra 3:10 472
- Angelic .... Acts 1:10 1112
- Heavenly .... Rev. 19:8 1325

SUBJECT REFERENCE PAGE

Asking in prayer—continued

Unselfishness ... James 4:2, 3 — 1274
In Christ's name ... John 14:13, 14 — 1099; John 15:16 — 1100

Asnah—*thornbush*

The head of a family of Nethinims ... Ezra 2:50 — 471

Asp—*a deadly snake*

Figurative of man's evil nature ... Ps. 140:3 — 620; Rom. 3:13 — 1150

Aspatha—*horse-given*

A son of Haman ... Esth. 9:7 — 507

Asphalt

In Babel's tower ... Gen. 11:3 — 13
In Moses' ark ... Ex. 2:3 — 57
Kings fall in ... Gen. 14:10 — 16

Aspiration—*exalted desire combined with holy zeal*

A. *Centered in:*
God Himself ... Ps. 42:1, 2 — 568
God's kingdom ... Matt. 6:33 — 983
The high calling ... Phil. 3:8-14 — 1215
Heaven ... Col. 3:1, 2 — 1221
Acceptableness with Christ ... 2 Tim. 2:4 — 1244

B. *Inspired by:*
Christ's love ... 2 Cor. 5:14-16 — 1187
Work yet to be done ... Rom. 15:18-20 — 1161; 2 Cor. 10:13-18 — 1190
Christ's grace ... 2 Cor. 12:9-15 — 1192
The reward ... 2 Tim. 4:7, 8 — 1245
The Lord's return ... Matt. 24:42-47 — 1004; 1 John 3:1-3 — 1295
World's end ... 2 Pet. 3:11-14 — 1288

Asriel—*God has filled with joy*

A descendant of Manasseh and progenitor of the Asrielites ... Num. 26:31 — 160; Josh. 17:2 — 229; 1 Chr. 7:14 — 407

Assassination—*killing by secret and sudden assault*

A. *Actual cases of:*
Eglon by Ehud ... Judg. 3:17, 20, 21 — 243
Sisera by Jael ... Judg. 4:17-21 — 244
Abner by Joab ... 2 Sam. 3:27 — 308
Ishbosheth by sons of Rimmon ... 2 Sam. 4:5-8 — 309
Amnon by Absalom ... 2 Sam. 13:28, 29 — 317
Absalom by Joab ... 2 Sam. 18:14 — 323
Amasa by Joab ... 2 Sam. 20:10 — 325
Elah by Zimri ... 1 Kin. 16:8-10 — 355
Ben-Hadad by Hazael ... 2 Kin. 8:7, 8, 15 — 376
Jehoram by Jehu ... 2 Kin. 9:24 — 377
Ahaziah by Jehu ... 2 Kin. 9:27 — 378
Jezebel by Jehu ... 2 Kin. 9:30-37 — 378
Joash by servants ... 2 Kin. 12:20, 21 — 381
Zechariah by Shallum ... 2 Kin. 15:8-10 — 383
Shallum by Menahem ... 2 Kin. 15:14 — 384
Pekahiah by Pekah ... 2 Kin. 15:25 — 384
Pekah by Hoshea ... 2 Kin. 15:30 — 384
Amon by servants ... 2 Kin. 21:23 — 391
Gedaliah by Ishmael ... 2 Kin. 25:25 — 396
Sennacherib by his sons ... 2 Kin. 19:36, 37 — 390

B. *Attempted cases of:*
Jacob by Esau ... Gen. 27:41-45 — 29
Joseph by his brothers ... Gen. 37:18-22 — 39
David by Saul ... 1 Sam. 19:10-18 — 291
David by Absalom ... 2 Sam. 15:10-14 — 319
Joash by Athaliah ... 2 Kin. 11:1-3 — 379
Ahasuerus by servants ... Esth. 2:21-23 — 503
Jesus by the Jews ... Luke 4:14, 28-30 — 1046; John 7:1 — 1089
Paul by the Jews ... Acts 9:23-25 — 1122; Acts 23:12-31 — 1139

C. *Crime of:*
Against God's image in man ... Gen. 9:6 — 12
Punishable by death ... Ex. 21:12-15 — 75; Num. 35:33 — 170
Not to be condoned ... Deut. 19:11-13 — 193
Puts the guilty under a curse ... Deut. 27:24 — 200
Abhorred by the righteous ... 2 Sam. 4:4-12 — 309

Assembly—*a large gathering for official business*

A. *Descriptive of:*
Israel as a people ... Num. 10:2-8 — 143
Israel as a nation ... Judg. 20:1, 2 — 261; 2 Chr. 30:23 — 459
God's elect people ... Ps. 111:1 — 607
A civil court ... Acts 19:32-41 — 1135
A church gathering ... James 2:2-4 — 1273

B. *Purposes of:*
Proclaim war ... Judg. 10:17, 18 — 252; 1 Sam. 14:20 — 284
Establish the ark in Zion ... 1 Kin. 8:1-6 — 344
Institute reforms ... Ezra 9:4-15 — 478; Neh. 9:1, 2 — 492
Celebrate victory ... Esth. 9:17, 18 — 508
Condemn Christ ... Matt. 26:3, 4, 57 — 1006
Worship God ... Acts 4:31 — 1116; Heb. 10:25 — 1265

C. *Significant ones, at:*
Sinai ... Ex. 19:1-19 — 73
Joshua's farewell ... Josh. 23:1-16 — 235; Josh. 24:1-28 — 236
David's coronation ... 2 Sam. 5:1-3 — 309
The temple's dedication ... 2 Chr. 5:1-14 — 436
Josiah's reformation ... 2 Kin. 23:1-3, 21-23 — 392
Ezra's reading the Law ... Neh. 8:1-18 — 490
Jesus' trial ... Matt. 27:11-26 — 1008
Pentecost ... Acts 2:1-21 — 1113
The Jerusalem Council ... Acts 15:5-21 — 1129

Assent—*agreeing to the truth of a statement or fact*

A. *Concerning good things:*
Accepting God's covenant ... Ex. 19:7, 8 — 73
Agreeing to reforms ... 1 Sam. 7:3, 4 — 278; Ezra 10:1-12, 19 — 479
Accepting a scriptural decision ... Acts 15:13-22 — 1129
Receiving Christ as Savior ... Rom. 10:9, 10 — 1157

B. *Concerning evil things:*
Tolerating idolatry ... Jer. 44:15-19 — 793
Condemning Christ to death ... Matt. 27:17-25 — 1009
Putting Stephen to death ... Acts 7:51-60 — 1120
Refusing to hear the gospel ... Acts 13:44-51 — 1128

Asshur—*level plain*

1. One of the sons of Shem; progenitor of the Assyrians ... Gen. 10:22 — 13; 1 Chr. 1:17 — 400
2. The chief god of the Assyrians; seen in names like Ashurbanipal (Osnapper) ... Ezra 4:10 — 473
3. A city in Assyria or the nation of Assyria ... Num. 24:22, 24 — 159

Asshurim—*mighty ones*

Descendants of Abraham by Keturah ... Gen. 25:3 — 26

Assir—*prisoner*

1. A son of Korah ... Ex. 6:24 — 61; 1 Chr. 6:22 — 406
2. A son of Ebiasaph ... 1 Chr. 6:23, 37 — 406
3. A son of King Jeconiah ... 1 Chr. 3:17 — 403

Assistance, divine

A. *Offered, in:*
Battle ... 2 Chr. 20:5-17 — 448
Trouble ... Ps. 50:15 — 572
Crises ... Luke 21:14, 15 — 1070
Prayer ... Rom. 8:16-27 — 1154
Testimony ... 2 Tim. 4:17 — 1245
Wisdom ... James 1:5-8 — 1272

B. *Given:*
Internally ... Phil. 2:13 — 1214; Heb. 13:21 — 1268
By God ... 2 Cor. 8:9 — 1188; 1 John 4:9, 10 — 1296
By Christ ... Phil. 4:13 — 1216
By the Spirit ... Zech. 4:6 — 957
By God's Word ... 1 Thess. 2:13 — 1227
By grace ... 1 Cor. 15:10 — 1178
By prayer ... James 5:15-18 — 1275
By trusting God ... Ps. 37:3-7 — 564
By God's providence ... Rom. 8:28 — 1155

Association—*joining together for mutually beneficial purposes*

A. *Among believers, hindered by:*
Sin ... Acts 5:1-11 — 1116
Friction ... Acts 6:1-6 — 1118
Inconsistency ... Gal. 2:11-14 — 1197
Disagreement ... Acts 15:36-40 — 1130
Selfishness ... 3 John 9-11 — 1303
Ambition ... Matt. 20:20-24 — 998
Error ... 2 John 7-11 — 1300
Partiality ... James 2:1-5 — 1273

B. *Among believers, helped by:*
Common faith ... Acts 2:42-47 — 1114
Mutual helpfulness ... Gal. 6:1-5 — 1200
United prayer ... Matt. 18:19, 20 — 996
Impending dangers ... Neh. 4:1-23 — 486
Grateful praise ... Acts 4:23-33 — 1116

See Alliance with evil; Fellowship

SUBJECT	REFERENCE	PAGE
Backsliding—continued		
E. *Examples of, among believers:*		
Lot	Gen. 19:1-22	20
David	2 Sam. 11:1-5 Ps. 51:1-19	314 572
Peter	Matt. 26:69-75 Luke 22:31, 32	1008 1071
Galatians	Gal. 1:6 Gal. 4:9-11	1196 1198
Corinthians	1 Cor. 5:1-13	1169
Churches of Asia	2 Tim. 1:15 Rev. 2: 3	1243 1313
See Apostasy		
Badger		
1. *Probably a specie of dolphin or porpoise*		
Skins of, used in tabernacle coverings	Ex. 26:14 Ex. 35:7	80 89
Used for sandals	Ezek. 16:10	831
2. *The Syrian rock hyrax*		
Called "rock hyrax"	Lev. 11:5 Deut. 14:7	107 189
Lives among rocks	Ps. 104:18	601
Likened to people	Prov. 30:26	657
Bag—*a purse or pouch*		
A. *Used for:*		
Money	2 Kin. 12:10	381
Stones	1 Sam. 17:40, 49	289
Food ("vessels")	1 Sam. 9:7	280
Weights	Deut. 25:13 Prov. 16:11	198 642
B. *Figurative of:*		
Forgiveness	Job 14:17	521
True righteousness	Prov. 16:11	642
True riches	Luke 12:33	1060
Insecure riches	Hag. 1:6	951
Bahurim—*young men*		
A village near Jerusalem	2 Sam. 3:16	308
Where Shimei cursed David	2 Sam. 16:5	321
Where two men hid in a well	2 Sam. 17:17, 18	322
Bakbakkar—*investigator*		
A Levite	1 Chr. 9:15	409
Bakbuk—*a flask*		
Head of post-exilic family	Ezra 2:51 Neh. 7:53	471 490
Bakbukiah—*Yahweh has poured out*		
1. A Levite of high position	Neh. 11:17	495
2. Levite porter	Neh. 12:25	496
Baker—*one who cooks food* (bread)		
A. *Kinds of:*		
Household	Gen. 18:6	19
Public	Jer. 37:21	788
Royal	Gen. 40:1, 2	41
B. *Features of:*		
Usually a woman's job	Lev. 26:26	125
Considered menial	1 Sam. 8:13	279
Balaam—*destroyer of the people*		
A. *Information concerning:*		
A son of Beor	Num. 22:5	156
From Mesopotamia	Deut. 23:4	196
A soothsayer	Josh. 13:22	226
A prophet	2 Pet. 2:15	1288
Killed because of his sin	Num. 31:1-8	165
B. *Mission of:*		
Balak sent to curse Israel	Num. 22:5-7 Josh. 24:9	156 236
Hindered by speaking donkey	Num. 22:22-35 2 Pet. 2:16	156 1288
Curse becomes a blessing	Deut. 23:4, 5 Josh. 24:10	196 236
C. *Prophecies of:*		
Under divine control	Num. 22:18, 38 Num. 23:16, 20, 26	156 157
By the Spirit's prompting	Num. 24:2	158
Blessed Israel three times	Num. 24:10	158
Spoke of the Messiah in final message	Num. 24:14-19	158
D. *Nature of:*		
"Unrighteousness"—greed	2 Pet. 2:14, 15	1288
"Error"—rebellion	Jude 11	1306
Baladan—(Marduk) *has given a son*		
Father of Merodach-Baladan (*also spelled* Berodach-Baladan)	2 Kin. 20:12	390
Balak, Balac—*empty*		
A Moabite king	Num. 22:4	156
Hired Balaam to curse Israel	Num. 22–24	156
Balances—*an instrument for weighing; scales*		
A. *Used for weighing:*		
Things	Lev. 19:36	117
Money	Jer. 32:10	782
B. *Laws concerning:*		
Must be just	Lev. 19:36	117
False, an abomination	Prov. 11:1	637
Deceit, condemned	Amos 8:5	914
C. *Figurative of:*		
God's justice	Job 31:6	532
Human smallness	Ps. 62:9 Is. 40:12, 15	577 717
God's judgment	Dan. 5:27	878
Human tribulation	Rev. 6:5	1316
Baldness—*a head without hair*		
A. *Natural:*		
Not a sign of leprosy	Lev. 13:40, 41	110
Elisha mocked for	2 Kin. 2:23, 24	370
B. *Artificial:*		
A sign of mourning	Is. 22:12	701
An idolatrous practice	Lev. 21:5 Deut. 14:1	119 189
Inflicted upon captives	Deut. 21:12	194
Forbidden to priests	Ezek. 44:20	863
A part of Nazirite vow	Num. 6:2, 9, 18	138
C. *Figurative of judgment, upon:*		
Israel	Is. 3:24 Amos 8:10	685 914
Moab	Is. 15:2	697
Philistia	Jer. 47:5	796
Tyre	Ezek. 27:2, 31	844
Ball—*spherical object*		
Prophetic	Is. 22:18	702
Ballad singers		
Rendered "those who speak in proverbs"	Num. 21:27	155
Balm—*an aromatic resin or gum*		
A product of Gilead	Jer. 8:22	757
Sent to Joseph	Gen. 43:11	45
Exported to Tyre	Ezek. 27:17	845
Healing qualities of	Jer. 46:11 Jer. 51:8	795 802
Bamah—*high place*		
A place of idolatry	Ezek. 20:29	837
Bamoth—*high places*		
Encampment site	Num. 21:19, 20	155
Also called Bamoth Baal	Josh. 13:17	226
Bamoth Baal—*high places of Baal*		
Assigned to Reuben	Josh. 13:17	226
Ban (see Excommunication)		
Bandage		
Used as disguise	1 Kin. 20:37-41	361
In prophecy against Egypt	Ezek. 30:20-22	848
Bani—*built*		
1. Gadite warrior	2 Sam. 23:36	330
2. A Judahite	1 Chr. 9:4	409
3. A postexilic family	Ezra 2:10 Neh. 10:14	470 494
4. A Merarite Levite	1 Chr. 6:46	406
5. A Levite; father of Rehum	Neh. 3:17	486
6. Signed document	Neh. 10:13	494
7. Head of Levitical family	Ezra 10:34	480
8. A postexilic Levite	Ezra 10:38	480
9. A descendant of Asaph	Neh. 11:22	496
Banishment—*forceful expulsion from one's place*		
A. *Political, of:*		
Absalom by David	2 Sam. 14:13, 14	318
The Jews into exile	2 Chr. 36:20, 21	465
The Jews from Rome	Acts 18:2	1133
B. *Moral and spiritual, of:*		
Adam and Eve from Eden	Gen. 3:22-24	7
Cain from others	Gen. 4:12, 14	8
Lawbreaker	Ezra 7:26	477
John to Patmos	Rev. 1:9	1312
Satan from heaven	Rev. 12:7-9	1320
The wicked to lake of fire	Rev. 20:15 Rev. 21:8	1326 1327
Bank—*A place for money*		
Exchange charges	John 2:15	1083
Interest paid on deposits	Matt. 25:27 Luke 19:23	1005 1067
Bankruptcy—*inability to pay one's debts*		
A. *Literal:*		
Condition of David's men	1 Sam. 22:1, 2	293

SUBJECT REFERENCE PAGE

Belteshazzar—*Bel protect his life*

Daniel's Babylonian name ... Dan. 1:7 ... 871

Ben—*son*

Levite porter ... 1 Chr. 15:18 ... 415

Benaiah—*Yahweh has built*

1. Jehoiada's son ... 2 Sam. 23:20 ... 329
   A mighty man ... 2 Sam. 23:20, 21 ... 329
   David's bodyguard ... 2 Sam. 8:18 ... 313
   Faithful to David ... 2 Sam. 15:18 ... 320; 2 Sam. 20:23 ... 326
   Escorts Solomon to the throne ... 1 Kin. 1:38-40 ... 336
   Executes Adonijah, Joab, and Shimei ... 1 Kin. 2:25, 29-34 ... 337; 1 Kin. 2:46 ... 338
   Commander-in-chief ... 1 Kin. 2:28-35 ... 338
2. One of David's mighty men ... 2 Sam. 23:30 ... 330
   Divisional commander ... 1 Chr. 27:14 ... 426
3. Levite musician ... 1 Chr. 15:18-20 ... 415
4. Priestly trumpeter ... 1 Chr. 15:24 ... 415; 1 Chr. 16:6 ... 415
5. Levite of Asaph's family ... 2 Chr. 20:14 ... 449
6. Simeonite ... 1 Chr. 4:36 ... 404
7. Levite overseer ... 2 Chr. 31:13 ... 460
8. Father of leader Pelatiah ... Ezek. 11:1, 13 ... 827

9-12. Four postexilic Jews who divorced their foreign wives ... Ezra 10:25-43 ... 480

Ben-Ammi—*son of my kinsman*

Son of Lot; father of the Ammonites ... Gen. 19:38 ... 21

Ben-Deker—*piercing; mattock*

One of Solomon's officers ... 1 Kin. 4:9 ... 339

Bene Berak—*sons of berak* (lightning)

A town of Dan ... Josh. 19:45 ... 231

Benediction—*an act of blessing*

A. *Characteristics of:*
   Instituted by God ... Gen. 1:22, 28 ... 4
   Divinely approved ... Deut. 10:8 ... 185
   Aaronic form ... Num. 6:23-26 ... 139
   Apostolic form ... 2 Cor. 13:14 ... 1193
   Jesus' last words ... Luke 24:50, 51 ... 1076

B. *Pronounced upon:*
   Creation ... Gen. 1:22, 28 ... 4
   New world ... Gen. 9:1, 2 ... 11
   Abraham ... Gen. 14:19, 20 ... 16
   Marriage ... Gen. 24:60 ... 25
   Son (Jacob) ... Gen. 27:27-29 ... 28
   Monarch (Pharaoh) ... Gen. 47:7, 10 ... 49
   Sons (Joseph's) ... Gen. 48:15, 16, 20 ... 50
   Tribes (Israel's) ... Deut. 33:1-29 ... 208
   Foreigner ... Ruth 1:8, 9 ... 266
   People ... 2 Sam. 6:18 ... 311
   Jesus ... Luke 2:34 ... 1044
   Song of Zacharias ... Luke 1:68-79 ... 1042
   Children's blessing ... Mark 10:16 ... 1027

Benefactor—*one who bestows benefits*

A. *Materially, God as:*
   Israel's ... Deut. 7:6-26 ... 182
   Unbeliever's ... Acts 14:15-18 ... 1128
   Christian's ... Phil. 4:19 ... 1216

B. *Spiritually:*
   By God ... Eph. 1:3-6 ... 1204
   Through Christ ... Eph. 2:13-22 ... 1205
   For enrichment ... Eph. 1:16-19 ... 1204

C. *Attitudes toward:*
   Murmuring ... Num. 11:1-10 ... 144
   Forgetfulness ... Ps. 106:7-14 ... 603
   Rejection ... Acts 13:44-47 ... 1128
   Remembrance ... Luke 7:1-5 ... 1050
   Gratefulness ... Acts 13:48 ... 1128

Benefice—*an enriching act or gift*

Manifested by a church ... Phil. 4:15-17 ... 1216
Encouraged in a friend ... Philem. 17-22 ... 1253
Justified in works ... James 2:14-17 ... 1273
Remembered in heaven ... 1 Tim. 6:17-19 ... 1240

Bene Jaakan—*sons of Jaakan*

A wilderness station ... Num. 33:31 ... 168

Benevolence—*generosity toward others*

A. *Exercised toward:*
   The poor ... Gal. 2:10 ... 1197
   The needy ... Eph. 4:28 ... 1207
   Enemies ... Prov. 25:21 ... 652
   God's servant ... Phil. 4:14-17 ... 1216

B. *Measured by:*
   Ability ... Acts 11:29 ... 1125
   Love ... 1 Cor. 13:3 ... 1176
   Sacrifice ... Mark 12:41-44 ... 1031
   Bountifulness ... 2 Cor. 9:6-15 ... 1189

C. *Blessings of:*
   Fulfills a grace ... Rom. 12:6, 13 ... 1159
   Performs a spiritual sacrifice ... Heb. 13:16 ... 1268
   Makes us "more blessed" ... Acts 20:35 ... 1136
   Enriches the giver ... Prov. 11:25 ... 637; Is. 58:10, 11 ... 735
   Reward ... 1 Tim. 6:17-19 ... 1240

Ben-Hadad—*son of the god Hadad*

1. Ben-Hadad I, king of Damascus. Hired by Asa, king of Judah, to attack Baasha, king of Israel ... 1 Kin. 15:18-21 ... 354
2. Ben-Hadad II, king of Damascus. Makes war on Ahab, king of Israel ... 1 Kin. 20:1-21 ... 359
   Defeated by Israel ... 1 Kin. 20:26-34 ... 360
   Fails in siege against Samaria ... 2 Kin. 6:24-33 ... 374; 2 Kin. 7:6-20 ... 375
   Killed by Hazael ... 2 Kin. 8:7-15 ... 376
3. Ben-Hadad III, king of Damascus. Loses all Israelite conquests made by Hazael, his father ... 2 Kin. 13:3-25 ... 381

Ben-Hail—*son of strength*

A teacher ... 2 Chr. 17:7 ... 446

Ben-Hanan—*son of the gracious one*

A son of Shimon ... 1 Chr. 4:20 ... 404

Ben Hesed—*son of mercy*

Father of one of Solomon's officers ... 1 Kin. 4:7, 10 ... 339

Beninu—*our son*

A Levite document signer ... Neh. 10:13 ... 494

Benjamin—*son of the right hand*

Jacob's youngest son ... Gen. 35:16-20 ... 37
Jacob's favorite son ... Gen. 42:4 ... 44; Gen. 43:1-14 ... 45
Loved by Joseph ... Gen. 43:29-34 ... 45
Judah intercedes for ... Gen. 44:18-34 ... 46
Joseph's gifts to ... Gen. 45:22 ... 47
Father of five sons ... 1 Chr. 8:1, 2 ... 408
Head of a tribe ... Num. 26:38-41 ... 160
Jacob's prophecy concerning ... Gen. 49:27 ... 51

Benjamin (others bearing this name)

1. A son of Bilhan ... 1 Chr. 7:10 ... 407
2. Son of Harim ... Ezra 10:18, 31, 32 ... 479
   Same as in ... Neh. 3:23 ... 486

Benjamin, tribe of

A. *Background features of:*
   Descendants of Jacob's youngest son ... Gen. 35:17, 18, 24 ... 37
   Family divisions of ... Num. 26:38-41 ... 160
   Strength of ... Num. 1:36, 37 ... 132
   Bounds of ... Josh. 18:11-28 ... 230
   Prophecies respecting ... Gen. 49:27 ... 51; Deut. 33:12 ... 208

B. *Memorable events of:*
   Almost destroyed for protecting men of Gibeah ... Judg. 20:12-48 ... 261
   Wives provided for, to preserve the tribe ... Judg. 21:1-23 ... 262
   Furnished Israel her first king ... 1 Sam. 9:1-17 ... 279
   Hailed David's return ... 2 Sam. 19:16, 17 ... 324
   12,000 sealed ... Rev. 7:8 ... 1317

C. *Celebrities belonging to:*
   Ehud, a judge ... Judg. 3:15 ... 243
   Saul, Israel's first king ... 1 Sam. 9:1 ... 279
   Abner, David's general ... 1 Sam. 17:55 ... 289
   Mordecai ... Esth. 2:5 ... 503
   The apostle Paul ... Phil. 3:5 ... 1215

Beno—*his son*

A Merarite Levite ... 1 Chr. 24:26, 27 ... 423

Ben-Oni—*son of my sorrow*

Rachel's name for Benjamin ... Gen. 35:16-18 ... 37

Ben-Zoheth—*son of Zoheth*

A man of Judah ... 1 Chr. 4:20 ... 404

Beon—*house of On*

A locality east of Jordan ... Num. 32:3 ... 166
Same as Baal Meon ... Num. 32:37, 38 ... 167

Beor—*a burning*

1. Father of Bela ... Gen. 36:32 ... 38

SUBJECT	REFERENCE	PAGE
Beor—continued		
2. Father of Balaam	Num. 22:5 2 Pet. 2:15	156 1288
Bera—*excellent*		
A king of Sodom	Gen. 14:2	16
Berachah—*blessing*		
1. David's warrior	1 Chr. 12:3	412
2. A valley in Judah near Tekoa	2 Chr. 20:26	449
Berachiah, Berechiah—*blessed by Yahweh*		
1. Asaph's father	1 Chr. 6:39	406
2. Levite door-keepers	1 Chr. 15:23, 24	415
3. Head man of Ephraim	2 Chr. 28:12	456
4. Son of Zerubbabel	1 Chr. 3:20	403
5. Levite	1 Chr. 9:16	409
6. Postexilic workman	Neh. 3:4, 30	485
7. Father of Zechariah	Zech. 1:1, 7 Matt. 23:35	955 1003
Beraiah—*Yahweh has created*		
A Benjamite chief	1 Chr. 8:21	408
Berea—*watered*		
A city of Macedonia visited by Paul	Acts 17:10-15	1132
Bereavement—*the emotional state after a loved one's death*		
A. *General attitudes in:*		
Horror	Ex. 12:29, 30	66
Great emotion	2 Sam. 18:33	323
Complaint	Ruth 1:20, 21	266
Genuine sorrow	Gen. 37:33-35	39
Submission	Job 1:18-21	513
B. *Christian attitudes in:*		
Unlike world's	1 Thess. 4:13-18	1228
Yet sorrow allowed	John 11:32-35 Acts 9:39	1096 1123
With hope of reunion	John 11:20-27	1095
C. *Unusual circumstances of, mourning:*		
Forbidden	Lev. 10:6	107
Of great length	Gen. 50:1-11	51
Turned to joy	Matt. 28:8 John 11:41-44	1010 1096
Bered—*hail*		
1. A place in the wilderness of Shur	Gen. 16:7, 14	17
2. An Ephraimite	1 Chr. 7:20	408
Beri—*belonging to a well*		
An Asherite	1 Chr. 7:36	408
Beriah—*evil*		
1. Son of Asher	Gen. 46:17	48
2. Ephraim's son	1 Chr. 7:22, 23	408
3. Chief of Benjamin	1 Chr. 8:13, 16	408
4. Levite	1 Chr. 23:10, 11	422
Beriites		
Descendants of Beriah	Num. 26:44	161
Berites		
A people in north Palestine	2 Sam. 20:14, 15	326
Berith—*covenant*		
Shechem idol	Judg. 9:46	251
Same as Baal-Berith	Judg. 8:33 Judg. 9:4	249 250
Bernice—*victorious*		
Sister of Herod Agrippa II	Acts 25:13, 23	1141
Hears Paul's defense	Acts 26:1-30	1141
Berodach-Baladan		
A king of Babylon	2 Kin. 20:12-19	390
Also called Merodach-Baladan	Is. 39:1	717
Berothah, Berothai—*wells*		
City of Syria taken by David	2 Sam. 8:8	313
Boundary in the ideal kingdom	Ezek. 47:16	866
Beryl—*a precious stone*		
In breastplate of high priest	Ex. 28:15-21 Ex. 39:8-14	81 93
Ornament of a king	Ezek. 28:12, 13	846
Describes a lover	Song 5:14	677
Applied to an angel	Dan. 10:5, 6	884
Wheels like color of	Ezek. 1:16	820
In New Jerusalem	Rev. 21:20	1327
Besai		
A family head	Ezra 2:49	471
Besodeiah—*in the counsel of Yahweh*		
Father of Meshullam	Neh. 3:6	485
Besor—*cold*		
A brook south of Ziklag	1 Sam. 30:9, 10, 21	301
Bestial—*beastlike*		
Condemned	Ex. 22:19	76
Punishment of	Lev. 20:13	118
Best seats—*seats or places of honor*		
Sought by scribes and Pharisees	Matt. 23:1, 6 Mark 12:38, 39	1002 1031
Not to be sought	Luke 14:7-11	1062
Betah—*trust, confidence*		
Cities of Hadadezer	2 Sam. 8:8	313
Called Tibhath	1 Chr. 18:8	418
Beten—*valley*		
City of Asher	Josh. 19:25	231
Beth—*house*		
Second letter of the Hebrew alphabet	Ps. 119:9-16	610
Bethabara—*house of passage*		
A place beyond Jordan where John baptized	John 1:28	1082
Beth Acacia		
A town of Judah	Judg. 7:22	248
Beth Anath—*house of Anath* (the goddess)		
A town of Naphtali	Josh. 19:38, 39	231
Canaanites remain in	Judg. 1:33	242
Beth Anoth—*house of Anoth* (the goddess)		
A town of Judah	Josh. 15:59	228
Bethany—*house of poverty*		
A town on Mt. of Olives	Luke 19:29	1067
Home of Lazarus	John 11:1	1095
Home of Simon, the leper	Matt. 26:6	1006
Jesus visits there	Mark 11:1, 11, 12	1028
Scene, Ascension	Luke 24:50, 51	1076
Beth Aphrah—*house of dust*		
A Philistine city; symbolic of doom	Mic. 1:10	927
Beth Arabah—*house of desert*		
A village of Judah	Josh. 15:6, 61	227
Assigned to Benjamin	Josh. 18:21, 22	230
Beth Arbel—*house of God's ambush*		
A town destroyed by Shalman	Hos. 10:14	897
Beth Aven—*house of nothingness* (vanity)		
A town of Benjamin	Josh. 7:2	219
Israel defeated Philistines there	1 Sam. 13:5	283
Beth Baal Meon		
City of Reuben	Josh. 13:17	226
Beth Barah—*house of the ford*		
A passage over Jordan	Judg. 7:24	248
Beth Biri—*house of my creation*		
A town of Simeon	1 Chr. 4:31	404
Probably same as Beth Lebaoth	Josh. 19:6	230
Beth Car—*house of a lamb*		
Site of Philistines' retreat	1 Sam. 7:11	278
Beth Dagon—*house of Dagon*		
1. Village of Judah	Josh. 15:41	228
2. Town of Asher	Josh. 19:27	231
Beth Diblathaim—*house of fig cakes*		
A Moabite town	Jer. 48:21, 22	797
Bethel—*house of God*		
1. A town of Benjamin	Judg. 21:19	263
Abraham settles near	Gen. 12:7, 8	15
Site of Abraham's altar	Gen. 13:3, 4	15
Scene of Jacob's ladder	Gen. 28:10-19	30
Luz becomes Bethel	Gen. 28:19	30
Jacob returns to	Gen. 35:1-15	36

SUBJECT REFERENCE PAGE

SUBJECT | REFERENCE | PAGE

Chesil—*a fool*
- A village of Judah ... Josh. 15:30 ... 228
- Probably same as Bethul and Bethuel ... Josh. 19:4 ... 230; 1 Chr. 4:30 ... 404

Chest—*case or box*
- For offering ... 2 Kin. 12:9, 10 ... 381
- For levy fixed by Moses ... 2 Chr. 24:8, 9 ... 452
- Used to safeguard valuables ... 1 Sam. 6:8-15 ... 277

Chestnut tree—*plane tree*
- Used by Jacob ... Gen. 30:37 ... 32
- In Eden, God's garden ... Ezek. 31:8, 9 ... 849

Chesulloth—*loins or slopes*
- A border town of Issachar ... Josh. 19:18 ... 231

Chezib—*deceitful*
- Birthplace of Shelah ... Gen. 38:5 ... 40
- Same as Azib ... Josh. 15:44 ... 228

Chicken—*domestic fowl*
- Hen and brood ... Luke 13:34 ... 1062
- Rooster ... Luke 22:34 ... 1071

Chicks—*the young of a hen*
- Figurative of Israel ... Matt. 23:37 ... 1003

Chiding—*to reprove or rebuke*

A. *Between men:*
- Jacob with Laban ... Gen. 31:36 ... 33
- Israelites with Moses ... Ex. 17:2 ... 71
- Ephraimites with Gideon ... Judg. 7:24, 25 ... 248; Judg. 8:1 ... 248
- Paul with Peter ... Gal. 2:11, 14 ... 1197

B. *By Christ, because of:*
- Unbelief ... Matt. 11:20-24 ... 988
- Spiritual dullness ... Matt. 16:8-12 ... 994
- Censoriousness ... Mark 10:13-16 ... 1027
- Sluggishness ... Matt. 26:40 ... 1007

Chidon—*a javelin*
- Where Uzza was struck dead ... 1 Chr. 13:9, 10 ... 414
- Called Nachon ... 2 Sam. 6:6 ... 310

Childbearing
- Agreeable to God's command ... Gen. 1:28 ... 6
- Result of marriage ... 1 Tim. 5:14 ... 1239
- Attended with pain ... Gen. 3:16 ... 7
- Productive of joy ... John 16:21 ... 1101
- Productive of the Messiah ... Luke 2:7 ... 1043
- Means of salvation ... 1 Tim. 2:15 ... 1238
- Expressed in symbols ... Rev. 12:2, 5 ... 1320

Childhood, characteristics of
- Dependence ... 1 Thess. 2:7 ... 1227
- Immaturity ... 1 Cor. 13:11 ... 1176
- Foolishness ... Prov. 22:15 ... 649
- Unstableness ... Eph. 4:14 ... 1207
- Humility ... Matt. 18:1-5 ... 996
- Need for instruction ... Prov. 22:6 ... 648
- Influence on adults ... Is. 49:15 ... 728

Childishness—*an immature spirit*
- Manifested by Saul ... 1 Sam. 18:8, 9 ... 290
- Seen in Haman ... Esth. 6:6-9 ... 506

Childlikeness
- Requirement of God's kingdom ... Mark 10:15 ... 1027
- An element in spiritual growth ... 1 Pet. 2:2 ... 1280
- A model to be followed ... 1 Cor. 14:20 ... 1177

Children, figurative
- Disciples of a teacher ... Mark 10:24 ... 1027
- God's own ... Rom. 8:16, 17 ... 1154
- Christians ... Eph. 5:8 ... 1208
- Devil's own ... 1 John 3:10 ... 1295
- Those who show such trait ... Matt. 11:16-19 ... 988

See Sonship of believers

Children, illegitimate

A. *Characteristics of:*
- No inheritance ... Gal. 4:30 ... 1199
- Not in congregation ... Deut. 23:2 ... 196
- Despised ... Judg. 11:2 ... 252

B. *Examples of:*
- Moab and Ammon ... Gen. 19:36-38 ... 21
- Sons of Tamar by Judah ... Gen. 38:12-30 ... 40
- Jephthah ... Judg. 11:1 ... 252

C. *Figurative of:*
- A mixed race ... Zech. 9:6 ... 960
- The unregenerate state ... Heb. 12:8 ... 1267

Children, natural

A. *Right estimate of:*
- God's gifts ... Gen. 33:5 ... 35
- God's heritage ... Ps. 127:3-5 ... 616
- Crown of old men ... Prov. 17:6 ... 643

B. *Characteristics of:*
- Imitate parents ... 1 Kin. 15:11, 26 ... 354
- Diverse in nature ... Gen. 25:27 ... 26
- Playful ... Matt. 11:16-19 ... 988

C. *Capacities of:*
- Glorify God ... Matt. 21:15, 16 ... 999
- Come to Christ ... Mark 10:13-16 ... 1027
- Understand Scripture ... 2 Tim. 3:15 ... 1245
- Receive the promises ... Acts 2:39 ... 1114
- Believe ... Matt. 18:6 ... 996
- Receive training ... Eph. 6:4 ... 1209
- Worship in God's house ... 1 Sam. 1:24, 28 ... 273

D. *Parental obligations toward:*
- Nourishment ... 1 Sam. 1:22 ... 273
- Discipline ... Eph. 6:4 ... 1209
- Instruction ... Gal. 4:1, 2 ... 1198
- Employment ... 1 Sam. 17:15 ... 288
- Inheritance ... Luke 12:13, 14 ... 1059

E. *Duties of:*
- Obedience ... Eph. 6:1-3 ... 1209
- Honor to parents ... Heb. 12:9 ... 1267
- Respect for age ... 1 Pet. 5:5 ... 1283
- Care for parents ... 1 Tim. 5:4 ... 1239
- Obedience to God ... Deut. 30:2 ... 203
- Remembering God ... Eccl. 12:1 ... 670

F. *Description of ungrateful:*
- Stubborn ... Deut. 21:18-21 ... 195
- Scorners ... Prov. 30:17 ... 657
- Robbers ... Prov. 28:24 ... 655
- Strikers ... Ex. 21:15 ... 75
- Cursers ... Lev. 20:9 ... 118

G. *Examples of good:*
- Isaac ... Gen. 22:6-10 ... 23
- Joseph ... Gen. 45:9, 10 ... 47
- Jephthah's daughter ... Judg. 11:34-36 ... 253
- Samuel ... 1 Sam. 2:26 ... 275
- David ... 1 Sam. 17:20 ... 288
- Josiah ... 2 Chr. 34:1-3 ... 462
- Esther ... Esth. 2:20 ... 503
- Daniel ... Dan. 1:1-6 ... 871
- John the Baptist ... Luke 1:80 ... 1043
- Jesus ... Luke 2:51 ... 1044
- In the temple ... Matt. 21:15, 16 ... 999
- Timothy ... 2 Tim. 3:15 ... 1245

H. *Examples of bad:*
- Esau ... Gen. 26:34, 35 ... 28
- Job's haters ... Job 19:18 ... 525
- Sons of Eli ... 1 Sam. 2:12, 17 ... 274
- Sons of Samuel ... 1 Sam. 8:1-3 ... 279
- Absalom ... 2 Sam. 15:10 ... 319
- Adonijah ... 1 Kin. 1:5, 6 ... 335
- Elisha's mockers ... 2 Kin. 2:22, 23 ... 370
- Adram-melech ... 2 Kin. 19:37 ... 390

I. *Acts performed upon:*
- Naming ... Ruth 4:17 ... 269
- Blessing ... Luke 1:67, 76-79 ... 1042
- Circumcision ... Luke 2:21 ... 1043

J. *Murder of:*
- By Pharaoh ... Ex. 1:15, 16 ... 56
- By Herod the Great ... Matt. 2:16-18 ... 978
- In war ... Num. 31:12-17 ... 165

K. *Jesus' relationship with:*
- Blessed them ... Matt. 19:13-15 ... 997
- Healed them ... Matt. 15:22-28 ... 993
- Raised girl from dead ... Matt. 9:18, 19, 23-25 ... 1025; Luke 8:49-56 ... 1053

Chileab—*restraint of father*
- A son of David ... 2 Sam. 3:3 ... 308
- Also called Daniel ... 1 Chr. 3:1 ... 403

Chilion—*wasting away*
- Elimelech's son ... Ruth 1:2 ... 266
- Orpah's deceased husband ... Ruth 1:4, 5 ... 266
- Boaz redeems his estate ... Ruth 4:9 ... 268

Chilmad
- A town or country trading with Tyre ... Ezek. 27:23 ... 845

Chimham—*pining*
- A son of Barzillai ... 2 Sam. 19:37-40 ... 325
- Inn bearing his name ... Jer. 41:17 ... 791

Chinnereth, Chinneroth—*lyre*
1. A city of Naphtali ... Deut. 3:17 ... 178
2. The region of Chinneroth ... 1 Kin. 15:20 ... 354
   Same as plain of Gennesaret ... Matt. 14:34 ... 993
3. The Old Testament name for Sea of Galilee ... Num. 34:11 ... 169
   Also called Lake of Gennesaret and Sea of Galilee ... Matt. 4:18 ... 1374; Luke 5:1 ... 980

SUBJECT REFERENCE PAGE

Commission—*special assignment*

A. *Kinds of:*
Christ's—to humankind ....John 3:16-18 1083
Israel's—to the Gentiles ....Acts 13:45-47 1128
The church's—to the world ....Matt. 28:19, 20 1011

B. *Requirements of:*
Faithfulness ......2 Tim. 4:1-8 1245
Diligence ....Rom. 15:15-32 1161
Willingness ......1 Sam. 3:9, 10 275

Common—*public; general*

Normal, natural ......1 Cor. 10:13 1174
Ceremonially unclean ....Acts 10:14 1123
Ordinary people ......Jer. 26:23 776
Shared togetherness ....Acts 2:44 1114
Things believed alike ....Titus 1:4 1249

Common people

Burial place of ....Jer. 26:23 776

Commonwealth—*a nation*

Descriptive of Israel ....Eph. 2:12 1205

Communion of the Lord's Supper (see Lord's Supper)

Communion of the saints (see Fellowship)

Communion with Christ

A. *Based on:*
Redemption ......Heb. 2:10-13 1259
Regeneration ....1 Cor. 6:14-17 1171
Resurrection (spiritual) ....Col. 3:1-3 1221

B. *Identifies Christians, in:*
Name ....1 Pet. 4:12-16 1283
Character ....John 14:23 1100
Hope ....1 John 3:1-3 1295

Communion with God

A. *Prerequisites of:*
Reconciliation ....2 Cor. 5:18, 19 1187
Acceptance of Christ ....John 14:6 1099
Obedience ....John 14:23 1100
Holiness ....2 Cor. 6:14-18 1187

B. *Saints:*
Desire such ......Heb. 11:10 1266
Seek it through prayer ....Matt. 6:6-15 982
Realized fully in eternity ....Rev. 7:13-17 1317

Communism, Christian

A. *Supposedly found in:*
Early church .....Acts 2:44, 45 1114

B. *Differs from modern Communism:*
In being voluntary ....Acts 5:4 1116
Confined to Christians ......Acts 4:32 1116
Not under government control ....Acts 4:34-37 1116

Companion—*a fellow worker*

Wife ....Mal. 2:14 969
Companion in tribulation ....Rev. 1:9 1312
Coworker ....Ezra 4:7, 9, 11 473
Fellow fool ....Prov. 13:20 639
Fellow believer ......Ps. 119:63 611
Fellow worker ......Phil. 2:23, 25 1214

Companions, evil

A. *Cause:*
Rebellion ....Num. 16:1-50 149
Idolatry ....Ex. 32:1-8 85
Violence, death ...Acts 23:12-22 1139
Persecution ......Acts 17:5-9 1132

B. *Warnings against:*
Do not consent with them ....Prov. 1:10-19 629
Avoid them ......1 Cor. 5:9-11 1170
Remember their end ....{Rev. 22:11, 14, 15} 1328

Comparison—*likeness; similarity*

A. *Worthy comparisons, between:*
God's holiness and human sinfulness ......{Is. 46:12, 13 725; Is. 55:6-9 733}
Christ's glory and humiliation ....Phil. 2:5-11 1214
Israel's call and responsibility ....Rom. 2:17-29 1150
Faith and unbelief ....Matt. 12:41, 42 990
Former and present unbelief ....Matt. 11:20-24 988
Old and new covenants ....2 Cor. 3:6-18 1185
The believer's status now and hereafter ....1 John 3:1-3 1295

B. *Unworthy comparisons, based on:*
Position ....Num. 16:3 149
Privileges ....1 Cor. 3:1-9 1168
Wealth ....James 2:1-9 1273

Compassion—*suffering with another, mercy*

A. *God's, described as:*
Overabundant ....Ps. 86:13, 15 592
New every morning ....Lam. 3:22, 23 812
Great ....Is. 54:7 732
Kindled ....Hos. 11:8 897

B. *God's, expressed:*
Fully ....Ps. 78:38 588
Sovereignly ....Rom. 9:15 1156
Unfailingly ....Lam. 3:22 812
Willingly ....Luke 15:18-20 1063

C. *Christ's, expressed toward the:*
Weary ....Matt. 11:28-30 988
Tempted ....Heb. 2:17, 18 1259
Helpless ....Mark 9:20-22 1025
Sorrowful ....Luke 7:13, 14 1050
Multitude ....Matt. 15:32 994
Sick ....{Matt. 20:34 999; Mark 1:41 1016}

D. *Examples of:*
David in sorrow ....Ps. 51:1-12 572
God to Israel ......Hos. 11:8 897
Christ to sinners ....Matt. 9:12, 13 985

E. *Christian's:*
Commanded ....{Zech. 7:9 958; Col. 3:12 1221; Jude 22 1307}
Expressed ....{1 Pet. 3:8 1282; Heb. 10:34 1265}
Illustrated ....Luke 10:30, 33 1056
Unified ....Phil. 2:1, 2 1214

Complete—*to finish*

Used of:
Purification rites .....Esth. 2:12 503
Priestly ministry ......Luke 1:23 1041
Time of pregnancy ....Luke 2:6 1043

Complicity—*partnership in wrongdoing*

In Adam's sin ....Rom. 5:12 1152
In the sins of others ....Ps. 50:18 572
In national guilt ......Matt. 27:24-26 1009

Composure—*calmness; tranquility; self-possession*

Before enemies ......Neh. 4:1-23 486
Under great strain ....Acts 27:21-26 1143
Facing death ....Acts 7:59, 60 1120
Lack of ....Dan. 6:18-20 879

Compromise—*agreement by concession*

A. *Forbidden with:*
Ungodly ....Ps. 1:1 546
Evil ....Rom. 12:9 1159
Unbelievers ......2 Cor. 6:14-18 1187
False teachers ....{Gal. 1:8-10 1196; 2 John 7-11 1300}
Spiritual darkness ....Eph. 5:11 1208

B. *Examples:*
Lot ....{Gen. 13:12, 13 16; Gen. 19:1-29 20}
Samson ....Judg. 16:1-21 256
Solomon ....1 Kin. 11:1-14 348
Asa ....2 Chr. 16:1-9 446
Jehoshaphat ......{2 Chr. 18:1-3 447; 2 Chr. 19:1, 2 448; 2 Chr. 20:35-37 450}

Concealment—*keeping something secret*

Of sin, impossible ....Is. 29:15 708
Of intrigue, exposed ....Esth. 2:21-23 503
Of intentions, revealed ....Acts 23:12-22 1139

Conceit—*self-flattery*

A. *Of persons:*
Goliath ....{1 Sam. 17:42-44} 289
Haman ....Esth. 6:6-9 506
The wicked ....Prov. 6:12-17 633
Christians, deplored ....Rom. 12:16 1159

B. *Characteristic of:*
False teachers ....1 Tim. 6:3, 4 1240
New convert ....1 Tim. 3:6 1238

Conceited—*a self-righteous spirit; haughty*

Christians warned against ....Rom. 11:20 1158
Rich tempted to ......1 Tim. 6:17 1240
To prevail in last days ....2 Tim. 3:1-5 1244

Conception of children

In marriage ....Gen. 21:1-3 21
In adultery ....2 Sam. 11:2-5 314
In virginity ....Matt. 1:18-21 978

Conclude—*to finish*

The main issue ......Eccl. 12:13 670

Concubine—*a "wife" who is not legally a wife*

A. *Features regarding:*
Could be divorced ....Gen. 21:10-14 22
Has certain rights ....Deut. 21:10-14 194
Children of, legitimate ......Gen. 22:24 23
Unfaithfulness of ....Judg. 19:1, 2 259
Source of trouble ....Gen. 21:9-14 22
Incompatible with Christianity .....Matt. 19:5 997

B. *Men who had:*
Abraham ....Gen. 25:6 2
Nahor ....Gen. 22:23, 24 23
Jacob ....Gen. 30:1, 4 31
Eliphaz ....Gen. 36:12 3
Gideon ....Judg. 8:30, 31 249
The Levite ....Judg. 19:1 25
Saul ....2 Sam. 3:7 308

SUBJECT REFERENCE PAGE

SUBJECT REFERENCE PAGE

SUBJECT — REFERENCE — PAGE

SUBJECT | REFERENCE | PAGE

SUBJECT REFERENCE PAGE

SUBJECT REFERENCE PAGE

Fearlessness—*without fear*

A. *Source of:*
- Believing God's promises .... Num. 13:30 ... 146
- Challenge of duty .... Ex. 32:26-29 ... 86
- Regard for God's holiness .... Num. 25:1-9 ... 159
- Believing God .... Acts 27:22-26 ... 1143

B. *Exemplified by:*
- Abram .... Gen. 14:14-16 ... 16
- Jonathan .... 1 Sam. 14:6-14 ... 284
- David .... 1 Sam. 17:34-37 ... 289
- Nehemiah .... Neh. 4:1-23 ... 486
- Hebrew men .... Dan. 3:16-30 ... 874
- Peter and John .... Acts 4:13 ... 1116
- Paul .... Acts 21:10-14 ... 1136

Feasts, Hebrew

A. *Annual:*
- Passover .... Ex. 12:1-14 ... 65; Lev. 23:5-8 ... 120
- Unleavened Bread .... Ex. 12:15-20 ... 66
- Harvest (Weeks or Pentecost) .... Ex. 23:16 ... 77
- Firstfruits .... Lev. 23:9-14 ... 120
- Tabernacles .... Lev. 23:34-44 ... 121

B. *Other, celebrated:*
- Sabbath .... Ex. 20:8-11 ... 74; Lev. 23:2, 3 ... 120
- Sabbath year .... Lev. 25:1-7 ... 122
- Year of Jubilee .... Lev. 25:8-17 ... 123
- The New Moon .... Num. 28:11-15 ... 162; Ps. 81:3 ... 590
- Dedication .... John 10:22 ... 1094
- Purim .... Esth. 9:18-32 ... 508

C. *Purposes of:*
- Unify the nation .... Deut. 12:5-14 ... 187
- Worship God .... Ex. 5:1 ... 59
- Illustrate spiritual truths .... John 7:37-39 ... 1090
- Foretell the Messiah .... 1 Cor. 11:23-26 ... 1175

D. *Brief history of:*
- Pre-Sinaitic observance .... Ex. 12:1-27 ... 65
- Three instituted at Sinai .... Ex. 23:14-17 ... 77
- Celebrated in the wilderness .... Num. 9:3-5 ... 142
- Again at beginning of conquest .... Josh. 5:10, 11 ... 217
- At dedication of temple .... 1 Kin. 8:2, 65 ... 344
- "Dedication" introduced by Solomon .... 2 Chr. 7:9-11 ... 439
- Idolatrous counterfeits introduced by Jeroboam .... 1 Kin. 12:27-33 ... 351
- Observed in Hezekiah's reign .... 2 Chr. 30:1 ... 458
- Perversion of, by Jews .... Is. 1:13, 14 ... 683
- Restored in Josiah's reformation .... 2 Kin. 23:22, 23 ... 394
- Failure in, cause of exile .... 2 Chr. 36:20, 21 ... 465
- Restored after the Exile .... Ezra 3:4 ... 472
- Purim instituted by Mordecai .... Esth. 9:17-32 ... 508
- Christ attends .... John 2:23 ... 1083; John 13:1 ... 1098
- Christ fulfills the Passover .... 1 Cor. 5:7, 8 ... 1170
- Christianity begins with Pentecost .... Acts 2:1-41 ... 1113
- All fulfilled in Christ .... 2 Cor. 3:3-18 ... 1185

Feasts, social

A. *Worldly, occasions of:*
- Idolatry .... Ex. 32:6 ... 86
- Drunkenness .... 1 Sam. 25:36 ... 297
- Proud display .... Esth. 1:1-8 ... 502
- Profane carousals .... Dan. 5:1-16 ... 877
- Licentiousness .... Mark 6:21, 22 ... 1021

B. *Proper, occasions of:*
- Refreshment .... Gen. 19:1-3 ... 20
- Reconciliation .... Gen. 31:54, 55 ... 34
- Reunion .... Gen. 43:16-34 ... 45
- Restoration .... Luke 15:22-24 ... 1063

See Entertainment

Feeble—*powerless*
- Moab .... Is. 16:14 ... 698

Feed—*to supply food to*

A. *Used naturally of:*
- Food for men .... 2 Sam. 19:33 ... 325
- Food for animals .... Gen. 30:36 ... 32
- God's provision .... Matt. 6:26 ... 983

B. *Used figuratively of:*
- Messiah .... Ezek. 34:23 ... 853
- Good deeds .... Matt. 25:37 ... 1005
- Supernatural supply .... Rev. 12:6 ... 1320
- Elemental teaching .... 1 Cor. 3:2 ... 1168
- Change of nature .... Is. 11:7 ... 693
- Corruption .... Ps. 49:14 ... 571
- Vanity .... Hos. 12:1 ... 897

C. *Miracles:*

Feeding children of Israel:
- Manna .... Ex. 16:4 ... 70
- Quail .... Ex. 16:13 ... 70

Feeding Elijah:
- By ravens .... 1 Kin. 17:4-6 ... 356
- Widow's oil and meal .... 1 Kin. 17:8-16 ... 356

By Elisha feeds:
- 100 prophets with 20 loaves .... 2 Kin. 4:42-44 ... 372
- Sons of the prophets .... 2 Kin. 4:38-41 ... 372

By Jesus feeds:
- 4,000 .... Matt. 15:32-38 ... 994
- 5,000 .... John 6:1-13 ... 1087

Feet—*the lower parts of the body*

A. *Acts performed by or on, indicating:*
- Subjection .... Josh. 10:24 ... 223
- Conquest .... 2 Sam. 22:39 ... 328
- Humiliation .... Judg. 5:27 ... 246
- Submission and entreaty .... 1 Sam. 25:24, 41 ... 297
- Great love .... Luke 7:38, 44-46 ... 1051
- Worship .... Rev. 19:10 ... 1325
- Learner's position .... Luke 10:39 ... 1057
- Humility .... John 13:5-14 ... 1098
- Changed nature .... Luke 8:35 ... 1053
- Rejection .... Matt. 10:14 ... 986

B. *Figurative of:*
- God's holiness .... Ex. 3:5 ... 57
- God's nature .... Ex. 24:10 ... 78
- Clouds .... Nah. 1:3 ... 935
- God's messengers .... Is. 52:7 ... 730; Rom. 10:15 ... 1157
- Final conquest .... Rom. 16:20 ... 1162

C. *Unusual features concerning:*
- No swelling .... Neh. 9:21 ... 493
- Lameness .... 2 Sam. 9:3, 13 ... 313
- Neglected .... 2 Sam. 19:24 ... 324
- Impotent .... Acts 14:8-10 ... 1128
- Binding .... Acts 21:11 ... 1136

See Foot

Feet washing
- Performed on guests .... Gen. 18:4 ... 19
- Proffered by Abigail .... 1 Sam. 25:40, 41 ... 297
- On Jesus, with tears .... Luke 7:44 ... 1051
- Performed by Jesus .... John 13:5 ... 1098
- Duty of saints .... 1 Tim. 5:10 ... 1239

Felix—*happy*
- Governor of Judea .... Acts 23:24, 26 ... 1139
- Letter addressed to .... Acts 23:25-30 ... 1139
- Paul's defense before .... Acts 24:1-21 ... 1140
- Convicted, but unchanged .... Acts 24:22-25 ... 1140
- Subject to bribery .... Acts 24:26, 27 ... 1140

Fellow citizens
- With the saints .... Eph. 2:19 ... 1205

Fellow countryman
- Shall not hate .... Lev. 19:17 ... 117
- Becomes poor .... Lev. 25:25 ... 123
- Judge righteously .... Deut. 1:16 ... 175
- Lord gives rest .... Deut. 3:20 ... 178
- Save some .... Rom. 11:14 ... 1158

Fellow servant
- Who owed a hundred denarii .... Matt. 18:28-33 ... 997
- Evil slave beats .... Matt. 24:48, 49 ... 1004
- Were to be killed .... Rev. 6:11 ... 1316
- Who hold fast the testimony of Jesus .... Rev. 19:10 ... 1325
- Who heed the words .... Rev. 22:9 ... 1327

Fellowship—*sharing together*

A. *Based upon common:*
- Purpose .... Ps. 133:1-3 ... 617
- Belief .... Acts 2:42 ... 1114
- Conviction .... 1 Pet. 3:8 ... 1282
- Work .... Neh. 4:1-23 ... 486
- Hope .... Heb. 11:39, 40 ... 1266
- Faith .... 1 Sam. 20:30-42 ... 292
- Suffering .... Dan. 3:16-30 ... 874
- Need .... 2 Cor. 8:1-15 ... 1188

B. *Persons sharing together:*
- Father, the Son, and Christians .... 1 John 1:3 ... 1293
- Christ and Christians .... 1 Cor. 1:9 ... 1167
- Holy Spirit and Christians .... Phil. 2:1 ... 1214
- Apostles .... Acts 2:42 ... 1114
- Believers .... 1 John 1:7 ... 1293

C. *Things shared together:*
- Material things .... 2 Cor. 8:4 ... 1188
- Suffering .... Phil. 3:10 ... 1215
- The gospel ministry .... Gal. 2:9 ... 1197
- Gospel privileges .... Phil. 1:5 ... 1213
- Gospel mystery .... Eph. 3:9 ... 1206
- Lord's Supper .... Mark 14:22-25 ... 1033; 1 Cor. 10:16, 17 ... 1174

SUBJECT REFERENCE PAGE

SUBJECT REFERENCE PAGE

SUBJECT	REFERENCE	PAGE
Omnipotence (All-powerful)	Jer. 32:17, 27	782
Omnipresence (Ever-present)	Ps. 139:7-12	619
Omniscience (All-knowing)	1 John 3:20	1295
Foreknowledge	Is. 48:3, 5	726
Wise	Acts 15:18	1129
E. *Moral attributes of:*		
Goodness (see Goodness of God)		
Hatred	Ps. 5:5, 6	547
Holiness	Rev. 4:8	1315
Impartiality	1 Pet. 1:17	1280
Justice	Ps. 89:14	594
Long-suffering	Ex. 34:6, 7	88
Love	1 John 4:8, 16	1296
Mercy	Lam. 3:22, 23	812
Peace	Gal. 3:15	1198
Truth	Ps. 117:2	609
Vengeance	Deut. 32:34-41	207
Wrath	Deut. 32:22	207
F. *Human expressions applied to:*		
Fear	Deut. 32:26, 27	207
Grief	Gen. 6:6	9
Repentance	Gen. 6:7	9
Jealousy	Ex. 34:14	88
Swearing	Jer. 44:26	794
Laughing	Ps. 2:4	546
Sleeping	Ps. 78:65	588
Human parts:		
Face	Num. 6:25, 26	139
Eyes	2 Chr. 16:9	446
Ears	Neh. 1:6	484
Nose	Ex. 15:8	69
Mouth	Deut. 8:3	183
Voice	Gen. 3:9, 10 Ex. 15:26	7 70
Hand	Ezra 7:9	476
Fingers	Ps. 8:3	549
Arms	Deut. 33:27	209
Back	Ex. 33:21-23	88
Feet	Ps. 18:9	553
G. *Titles given to:*		
Creator	Is. 40:12, 22, 26	717
Judge	Ps. 96:10, 13	597
King	Ps. 47:2, 7, 8	570
Defender	Ps. 59:1	576
Preserver	Ps. 121:3-8	614
Shepherd	Gen. 49:24	51
Healer	Ex. 15:26	70
H. *Works of, described as:*		
Awesome	Ps. 66:3	579
Incomparable	Ps. 86:8	592
Great	Ps. 92:5	596
Manifold	Ps. 104:24	601
Marvelous	Ps. 139:14	620
Wondrous	1 Chr. 16:9	415
I. *Ways of, described as:*		
Perfect	Ps. 18:30	553
Knowledgeable	Ps. 86:11	592
Made known	Ps. 103:7	600
Righteous	Ps. 145:17	623
Not like human	Is. 55:8, 9	733
Everlasting	Hab. 3:6	942
Inscrutable	Rom. 11:33	1158
Just and true	Rev. 15:3	1322

See Goodness of God; Love of God; Power of God

Godhead—*the Deity*

SUBJECT	REFERENCE	PAGE
Revealed to humankind	Rom. 1:20	1149
Corrupted by humankind	Acts 17:29	1133
Incarnated in Jesus Christ	Col. 2:9	1221

Godliness—*holy living*

SUBJECT	REFERENCE	PAGE
Profitable	1 Tim. 4:7, 8	1239
Perverted	1 Tim. 6:5	1240
Pursue	1 Tim. 6:11	1240
Duty	Titus 2:12	1250

See Holiness of Christians

Gods, false

SUBJECT	REFERENCE	PAGE
A. *Names of:*		
Adrammelech (Syria)	2 Kin. 17:31	386
Anammelech (Babylon)	2 Kin. 17:31	386
Ashtoreth (Canaan)	1 Kin. 11:5, 33	348
Baal (Canaan)	1 Kin. 18:19	357
Baal of Peor (Moab)	Num. 25:1-9	159
Beelzebub (Philistine)	Luke 11:19-23	1057
Bel (Babylon)	Jer. 51:44	804
Calf worship (Egypt)	Ex. 32:1-6	85
Chemosh (Moab)	1 Kin. 11:7	348
Dagon (Philistine)	1 Sam. 5:1-7	277
Diana (Ephesian)	Acts 19:34	1135
Hermes (Greek)	Acts 14:12, 13	1128
Milcom (Ammon)	1 Kin. 11:5	348
Molech (Ammon)	1 Kin. 11:7	348
Nebo (Babylon)	Is. 46:1	724
Nisroch (Assyria)	2 Kin. 19:37	390
Rimmon (Syria)	2 Kin. 5:18	373
Tammuz (Babylon)	Ezek. 8:14	825
Zeus (Greek)	Acts 14:12, 13	1128
B. *Evils connected with:*		
Immorality	Num. 25:1-9	159
Prostitution	2 Kin. 23:7	393
Divination	Lev. 20:1-6	117
Sacrilege	Dan. 5:4	877
Pride	2 Kin. 18:28-35	388
Persecution	1 Kin. 19:1-3	359
Child sacrifice	Jer. 7:29-34	756

Gog—*mountain*

SUBJECT	REFERENCE	PAGE
1. Reubenite	1 Chr. 5:4	404
2. Prince of Rosh, Meshech, and Tubal	Ezek. 38:2, 3	856
3. Leader of the final battle	Rev. 20:8-15	1326

Golan—*circuit*

SUBJECT	REFERENCE	PAGE
City of Bashan	Deut. 4:43	180
Assigned to Levites	Josh. 21:27	233
City of refuge	Josh. 20:8	232

Gold

SUBJECT	REFERENCE	PAGE
A. *Found in:*		
Havilah	Gen. 2:11, 12	8
Ophir	1 Kin. 9:28	347
Sheba	1 Kin. 10:2, 10	347
Arabia	2 Chr. 9:14	441
B. *Used for:*		
Money	Matt. 10:9	986
Offerings	Ex. 35:22 1 Sam. 6:4	89 277
Gift	Matt. 2:11	978
Tabernacle:		
Frame	Ex. 26:29, 32	80
Furnishings	Ex. 25:10-40 Ex. 30:3-5	78 84
Priest's garment	Ex. 39:2-30	93
Temple:		
Building	1 Kin. 6:20-35	342
Furnishings	1 Kin. 7:48-51	344
Shields	1 Kin. 10:16, 17	348
Holy adornment	Ex. 28:4-6	81
Jewelry	Gen. 24:22	24
Physical adornment	Ex. 36:34, 38	91
Idols	Ex. 32:31	87
C. *Figurative of:*		
Saints refined	Job 23:10	528
Babylonian Empire	Dan. 2:38	873
Redeemed	2 Tim. 2:20	1244
Faith purified	1 Pet. 1:7	1279
Christ's doctrine	Rev. 3:18	1315

Golden apples

SUBJECT	REFERENCE	PAGE
Appropriate word	Prov. 25:11	652

Golden city

SUBJECT	REFERENCE	PAGE
Babylon called	Is. 14:4	695

Golden rule

SUBJECT	REFERENCE	PAGE
For Christian conduct	Matt. 7:12 Luke 6:31	983 1049

Golden wedge

SUBJECT	REFERENCE	PAGE
Figurative term	Is. 13:12	695

Goldsmiths

SUBJECT	REFERENCE	PAGE
In building the tabernacle	Ex. 31:1-4	85
Refiners	Mal. 3:3	969
Shapers of objects	Ex. 25:11, 18	78
Makers of idols	Num. 33:52	168
Guilds	Neh. 3:8, 32	485

Golgotha—*place of a skull*

SUBJECT	REFERENCE	PAGE
Where Jesus died	Matt. 27:33-35	1009

Goliath—*exile*

SUBJECT	REFERENCE	PAGE
1. Giant of Gath	1 Sam. 17:4	288
Challenged Israel	1 Sam. 17:8-11	288
Killed by David	1 Sam. 17:50	289
2. Brother of above; killed by Elhanan	2 Sam. 21:19	327

See Giants

Gomer—*completion*

SUBJECT	REFERENCE	PAGE
1. Son of Japheth	Gen. 10:2, 3 1 Chr. 1:5, 6	13 400
Northern nation	Ezek. 38:6	856
2. Wife of Hosea	Hos. 1:2, 3	890

Gomorrah—*submersion*

SUBJECT	REFERENCE	PAGE
In a fruitful valley	Gen. 13:10	16
Defeated by Chedorlaomer	Gen. 14:8-11	16
Destroyed by God	Gen. 19:23-29	20
Symbol of evil	Is. 1:10	683
Symbol of destruction	Amos 4:11	911
Punishment of	Matt. 10:15	986

Good for evil

SUBJECT	REFERENCE	PAGE
Illustrated by Joseph	Gen. 45:5-15	47
Christian duty	Luke 6:27, 35 Rom. 12:14, 20	1049 1159

SUBJECT REFERENCE PAGE

SUBJECT REFERENCE PAGE

Harlot—continued
- Connected with idolatry . . . Ex. 34:15, 16 . . . 88
- Brings spiritual error . . . Hos. 4:10-19 . . . 892
- Cause of divorce . . . Jer. 3:8, 14 . . . 750

C. *Prohibitions concerning:*
- Forbidden in Israel . . . Lev. 19:29 . . . 117
- Priests not to marry . . . Lev. 21:1, 7, 14 . . . 118
- To be shamed . . . Prov. 5:3-20 . . . 632
- Punishment . . . Lev. 21:9 . . . 119

D. *Examples of:*
- Tamar . . . Gen. 38:13-20 . . . 40
- Rahab . . . Josh. 2:1-21 . . . 215
- Jephthah's mother . . . Judg. 11:1 . . . 252
- Samson's . . . Judg. 16:1 . . . 256
- Hosea's wife . . . Hos. 1:2 . . . 890
- The great . . . Rev. 17:1-18 . . . 1323

E. *Figurative of:*
- Tyre . . . Is. 23:15, 17 . . . 702
- Israel . . . Is. 1:21 . . . 683
- Spiritual adultery . . . Is. 57:7-9 . . . 734; Rev. 17:1-18 . . . 1323

See Adultery

Harmony—*agreement, cooperation*
- Husband and wife . . . 1 Cor. 7:3-6 . . . 1171; Eph. 5:22, 23 . . . 1208; Col. 3:18, 19 . . . 1222
- Christians . . . John 13:34, 35 . . . 1099; Rom. 15:5-7 . . . 1161
- Christians and unbelievers . . . Rom. 12:16-18 . . . 1159; Heb. 12:14 . . . 1267

Harnepher
- Asherite . . . 1 Chr. 7:36 . . . 408

Harness—*to equip*
- Horses . . . Jer. 46:4 . . . 794

Harod—*fountain of trembling*
- Well near Gideon's camp . . . Judg. 7:1 . . . 247

Harodite
- Inhabitant of Harod . . . 2 Sam. 23:25 . . . 329
- Same as Harorite . . . 1 Chr. 11:27 . . . 412

Haroeh—*the seer*
- Judahite . . . 1 Chr. 2:50, 52 . . . 402
- Called Reaiah . . . 1 Chr. 4:2 . . . 403

Harosheth Hagoyim—*carving of the nations*
- Residence of Sisera . . . Judg. 4:2, 13, 16 . . . 244

Harp—*a stringed musical instrument*

Used by:
- The wicked . . . Is. 5:11, 12 . . . 686
- David . . . 1 Sam. 16:16, 23 . . . 287
- Prophets . . . 1 Sam. 10:5 . . . 281
- Temple orchestra . . . 1 Chr. 16:5 . . . 415
- Temple worshipers . . . Ps. 33:2 . . . 561
- Celebrators . . . 2 Chr. 20:27, 28 . . . 449
- Jewish captives . . . Ps. 137:2 . . . 619
- Worshipers in heaven . . . Rev. 5:8 . . . 1316

Harpoon—*a barbed spear for hunting large fish*
- Used against Leviathan . . . Job 41:7 . . . 540

Harsha—*enchanter*
- Head of temple servants . . . Ezra 2:43, 52 . . . 471; Neh. 7:46, 54 . . . 489

Harum—*exalted*
- Judahite . . . 1 Chr. 4:8 . . . 403

Harumaph—*flat-nosed*
- Father of Jedaiah . . . Neh. 3:10 . . . 485

Haruphite
- Designation of Shephatiah . . . 1 Chr. 12:5 . . . 412
- Member of Hariph's family . . . Neh. 7:24 . . . 489

Haruz—*active*
- Father-in-law of King Manasseh . . . 2 Kin. 21:19 . . . 391

Harvest—*the time when the crops are ripe*

A. *Occasion of:*
- Great joy . . . Is. 9:3 . . . 690
- Bringing the first-fruits . . . Lev. 23:10 . . . 120
- Remembering the poor . . . Lev. 19:9, 10 . . . 117

B. *Figuratively of:*
- Seasons of grace . . . Jer. 8:20 . . . 757
- Judgment . . . Jer. 51:33 . . . 804
- God's wrath . . . Rev. 14:15 . . . 1322
- Gospel opportunities . . . Matt. 9:37, 38 . . . 986
- World's end . . . Matt. 13:30, 39 . . . 991
- Measure of fruitfulness . . . 2 Cor. 9:6 . . . 1189

C. *Promises concerning:*
- To continue . . . Gen. 8:22 . . . 11
- Rain . . . Jer. 5:24 . . . 754
- Patience . . . James 5:7 . . . 1274

D. *Failure caused by:*
- Drought . . . Amos 4:7 . . . 911
- Locusts . . . Joel 1:4 . . . 902
- Sin . . . Is. 17:4-12 . . . 698

Hasadiah—*Yahweh has been gracious*
- Son of Zerubbabel . . . 1 Chr. 3:20 . . . 403

Hashabiah—*Yahweh has imputed*
1. Merarite Levite . . . 1 Chr. 6:44, 45 . . . 406
   Perhaps the same as in . . . 1 Chr. 9:14 . . . 409
2. Levite musician . . . 1 Chr. 25:3, 19 . . . 424
3. Kohathite Levite . . . 1 Chr. 26:30 . . . 425
4. Levite ruler . . . 1 Chr. 27:17 . . . 426
5. Chief Levite during Josiah's reign . . . 2 Chr. 35:9 . . . 464
6. Postexilic Levite . . . Ezra 8:19, 24 . . . 477
   Probably the same as in . . . Neh. 10:11 . . . 494
7. Postexilic ruler . . . Neh. 3:17 . . . 486
8. Descendant of Asaph . . . Neh. 11:22 . . . 496
9. Priest in the time of Joiakim . . . Neh. 12:21 . . . 496

Hashabnah—*covenant sealer*
- Signed covenant . . . Neh. 10:25 . . . 494

Hashabniah—*Yahweh has regarded me*
1. Father of Hattush . . . Neh. 3:10 . . . 485
2. Postexilic Levite . . . Neh. 9:5 . . . 492

Probably the same as Hashabiah 6

Hashbadana—*thoughtful judge*
- Assistant to Ezra . . . Neh. 8:4 . . . 490

Hashem—*shining*
- Father of David's warriors . . . 1 Chr. 11:34 . . . 412
- Also called Jashen . . . 2 Sam. 23:32 . . . 330

Hashmonah—*fertility*
- Israelite encampment . . . Num. 33:29 . . . 168

Hashub, Hasshub—*thoughtful*
1. Postexilic workman . . . Neh. 3:11 . . . 485
2. Signer of the covenant . . . Neh. 10:23 . . . 494
3. Levite chief . . . Neh. 11:15 . . . 495

Hashubah—*esteemed*
- Son of Zerubbabel . . . 1 Chr. 3:19, 20 . . . 403

Hashum—*opulent*
- Founder of postexilic family . . . Ezra 2:19 . . . 471
- Assists Ezra and signs document . . . Neh. 8:4 . . . 490; Neh. 10:18 . . . 494

Hasrah—*want*
- Grandfather of Shallum . . . 2 Chr. 34:22 . . . 463
- Called Harhas . . . 2 Kin. 22:14 . . . 392

Hassenaah—*thorny*
- Father of postexilic workmen . . . Neh. 3:3 . . . 485
- Same as Senaah . . . Ezra 2:35 . . . 471; Neh. 7:38 . . . 489

Hassenuah—*thorny*
- Benjamite family . . . 1 Chr. 9:7 . . . 409
- Called Senuah . . . Neh. 11:7-9 . . . 495

Haste—*to do something quickly*
- Prompted by good . . . 2 Chr. 35:21 . . . 464; Luke 19:5, 6 . . . 1067
- Prompted by evil . . . Prov. 14:29 . . . 640; Prov. 28:20 . . . 655

Hasupha—*naked*
- Head of temple servants . . . Ezra 2:43 . . . 471; Neh. 7:46 . . . 489

Hate—*to dislike something with strong feeling*

A. *Meanings of:*
- React as God does . . . Rev. 2:6 . . . 1313
- Twist moral judgments . . . Prov. 8:36 . . . 635
- Esteem of less value . . . John 12:25 . . . 1097
- Make a vital distinction . . . Luke 14:26 . . . 1062
- Despise . . . Is. 1:14 . . . 683

B. *Causes of:*
- Parental favoritism . . . Gen. 37:4, 5 . . . 39
- Rape . . . 2 Sam. 13:14, 15, 22 . . . 317
- Failure to please . . . 1 Kin. 22:8 . . . 362
- God's purpose . . . Ps. 105:25 . . . 602
- Six things God hates . . . Prov. 6:16-19 . . . 633
- Belonging to Christ . . . Matt. 24:9, 10 . . . 1003
- Evil nature . . . John 3:20 . . . 1083

SUBJECT REFERENCE PAGE

I

SUBJECT — REFERENCE — PAGE

- Light of the world — John 8:12 — 1091; John 9:5 — 1093
- Door of the sheep — John 10:7, 9 — 1094
- Good shepherd — John 10:11, 14 — 1094
- Resurrection and the life — John 11:25 — 1095
- Way, truth, and life — John 14:6 — 1099
- True vine — John 15:1, 5 — 1100

Ibleam—*he destroys the people*

- City assigned to Manasseh — Josh. 17:11, 12 — 229
- Canaanites remain in — Judg. 1:27 — 241
- Called Bileam — 1 Chr. 6:70 — 407
- Ahaziah slain near — 2 Kin. 9:27 — 378

Ibneiah—*Yahweh builds up*

- Head of a Benjamite family — 1 Chr. 9:8 — 409

Ibnijah—*Yahweh builds up*

- Father of Reuel — 1 Chr. 9:8 — 409

Ibri—*a Hebrew*

- Son of Jaaziah — 1 Chr. 24:27 — 423

Ibzan—*active*

- Judge of Israel — Judg. 12:8 — 254
- Father of 60 children — Judg. 12:8, 9 — 254

Ice

Figurative of:

- By reason of — Job 6:16 — 516

Ichabod—*inglorious*

- Son of Phinehas — 1 Sam. 4:19-22 — 276

Iconium—*imagelike*

- City of Asia Minor; visited by Paul — Acts 13:51 — 1128
- Many converts in — Acts 14:1-6 — 1128
- Paul visits again — Acts 14:21 — 1128
- Timothy's ministry — Acts 16:1, 2 — 1130
- Paul persecuted — 2 Tim. 3:11 — 1245

Iconoclast—*a breaker of images*

- Moses, an angry — Ex. 32:19, 20 — 86
- Gideon, an inspired — Judg. 6:25-32 — 247
- Jehu, a subtle — 2 Kin. 10:18-31 — 379
- Josiah, a reforming — 2 Kin. 23:12-25 — 393

Idalah—*memorial of God*

- Border town of Zebulun — Josh. 19:15 — 231

Idbash—*honey-sweet*

- Man of Judah — 1 Chr. 4:3 — 403

Iddo—*festal*

1. Chief officer under David — 1 Chr. 27:21 — 426
2. Father of Ahinadab — 1 Kin. 4:14 — 340
3. Leader of Jews at Casiphia — Ezra 8:17-20 — 477
4. Gershonite Levite — 1 Chr. 6:20, 21 — 405; Called Adaiah — 1 Chr. 6:41 — 406
5. Seer whose writings are cited — 2 Chr. 9:29 — 441
6. Grandfather of Zechariah the prophet — Zech. 1:1, 7 — 955
7. Postexilic priest — Neh. 12:4, 16 — 496

Identification—*proving something or somebody to be what it or he really is*

A. *Among men:*

- At birth — Gen. 25:22-26 — 26
- By the life — Luke 6:43-45 — 1050
- By speech — Judg. 12:6 — 254
- By a search — 2 Kin. 10:23 — 379
- By a kiss — Matt. 26:48, 49 — 1007

B. *Of Christ the Messiah, by:*

- A divine sign — John 1:31-34 — 1082
- A divine voice — Matt. 17:5 — 995
- Divine works — Matt. 11:2-6 — 987
- Human testimony — John 3:26-36 — 1084
- Scriptures — John 5:39-47 — 1087

C. *Of spiritual things:*

- New birth — 2 Cor. 5:17 — 1187
- Apostates — Matt. 7:22, 23 — 984
- Antichrist — 2 Thess. 2:1-12 — 1232
- Believers and unbelievers — Matt. 25:31-46 — 1005

Identifying with Christ

A. *Proper time, when tempted:*

- To harm — Prov. 1:10-19 — 629
- To violate convictions — Dan. 1:8 — 871
- To conform to world — Rom. 12:2 — 1159
- To rebellion — Rom. 13:1-5 — 1159
- With improper associations — 2 Cor. 6:14-17 — 1187
- To learn evil — Rom. 16:19 — 1162; Prov. 19:27 — 646

B. *Results:*

- Hatred — John 17:14 — 1102
- Separation — Luke 6:22, 23 — 1049
- Suffering — 1 Pet. 2:20, 21 — 1281
- Witness — 1 Pet. 3:15 — 1282
- Good conscience — 1 Pet. 3:16 — 1282

C. *Basis:*

- Future glory — Rom. 8:18 — 1155
- Life of Christ — Gal. 2:20 — 1197
- Reward — 2 Tim. 2:12 — 1244

Idleness—*inactivity; slothfulness*

A. *Consequences of:*

- Poverty — Prov. 20:13 — 646
- Begging — Prov. 20:4 — 646
- Hunger — Prov. 19:15 — 645
- Bondage — Prov. 12:24 — 638
- Ruin — Prov. 24:30-34 — 651

B. *Admonitions against, consider:*

- Ant — Prov. 6:6-11 — 633
- Ideal woman — Prov. 31:10-31 — 657
- Lord — John 9:4 — 1093
- Apostles — 2 Thess. 3:7-9 — 1233
- Judgment — 1 Cor. 3:8-15 — 1168

See Laziness; Slothfulness

Idol makers

- Maachah — 1 Kin. 15:13 — 354
- Foreign peoples — Is. 45:16 — 724
- Men of Judah — Is. 2:1, 20 — 684
- People of Jerusalem — Ezek. 22:3 — 839

Idol making

- Described by Isaiah — Is. 44:9-18 — 722

Idols, idolatry—*worship of idols*

A. *Described as:*

- Irrational — Acts 17:29 — 1133
- Degrading — Rom. 1:22, 23 — 1149
- Demonical — 1 Cor. 10:20, 21 — 1174
- Defiling — 2 Cor. 6:15-18 — 1187
- Enslaving — Gal. 4:8, 9 — 1198
- Abominable — 1 Pet. 4:3 — 1282

B. *Brief history of:*

- Begins in humankind's apostasy — Rom. 1:21-25 — 1149
- Prevails in Ur — Josh. 24:2, 14 — 236
- In Laban's household — Gen. 31:19-35 — 33
- Judgments on Egyptian — Num. 33:4 — 167
- Brought from Egypt by Israel — Josh. 24:14 — 236
- Forbidden in Law at Sinai — Ex. 20:1-5 — 74
- Warnings against, at Sinai — Ex. 34:13-16 — 88
- Israel yields to, at Sinai — Ex. 32:1-8 — 85
- Moabites entice Israel to — Num. 25:1-18 — 159
- Early zeal against — Josh. 22:10-34 — 234
- Gideon destroys — Judg. 6:25-32 — 247
- Gideon becomes an occasion of — Judg. 8:24-27 — 249
- Enticements to Baalism — Judg. 10:6-16 — 252
- Levite corrupted by — Judg. 17:1-13 — 258
- Danites establish, at Shiloh — Judg. 18:30, 31 — 259
- Overthrow of Philistines' — 1 Sam. 5:1-12 — 277
- Revival against, under Samuel — 1 Sam. 7:3-6 — 278
- Solomon yields to — 1 Kin. 11:1-8 — 348
- Jeroboam establishes in Jerusalem — 1 Kin. 12:26-33 — 351; 2 Chr. 11:14, 15 — 443
- Rehoboam tolerates in Judah — 1 Kin. 14:22-24 — 353
- Conflict—Elijah and Ahab — 1 Kin. 18:1-46 — 357
- Wicked kings of Israel — 1 Kin. 21:25, 26 — 362; 2 Kin. 16:2, 3 — 384
- Prophet denounces in Israel — Hos. 4:12-19 — 893
- Cause of Israel's exile — 2 Kin. 17:5-23 — 385
- Judah follows Israel's example — 2 Chr. 28:1-4 — 455
- Manasseh climaxes Judah's apostasy in — 2 Kin. 21:1-18 — 391; 2 Chr. 33:1-11 — 461
- Reformation against, under Asa — 2 Chr. 14:3-5 — 444
- Under Hezekiah — 2 Chr. 29:15-19 — 457
- Under Josiah — 2 Kin. 23:1-20 — 392
- Prophets denounce in Judah — Jer. 16:11-21 — 765
- Cause of Judah's exile — 2 Kin. 23:26, 27 — 394

C. *Christians warned against:*

- No company with — 1 Cor. 5:11 — 1170
- Flee from — 1 Cor. 10:14 — 1174
- No fellowship with — 1 Cor. 10:19, 20 — 1174
- Keep from — 1 John 5:21 — 1297
- Testify against — Acts 14:15 — 1128
- Turn from — 1 Thess. 1:9 — 1226

D. *Enticements to, due to:*

- Heathen background — Josh. 24:2 — 236; Ezek. 16:44, 45 — 832
- Contact with idolaters — Num. 25:1-6 — 159
- Intermarriage — 1 Kin. 11:1-13 — 348
- Imagined good — Jer. 44:15-19 — 793

SUBJECT REFERENCE PAGE

SUBJECT REFERENCE PAGE

K

SUBJECT REFERENCE PAGE

SUBJECT	REFERENCE	PAGE
Miracles of the Bible—continued		
Uzziah afflicted with leprosy	2 Chr. 26:16-21	455
Three men protected from the fiery furnace	Dan. 3:19-27	874
Daniel delivered from the lion's den	Dan. 6:16-23	879
Preservation of Jonah in stomach of fish three days	Jon. 2:1-10	923
Miracles of the Bible—*New Testament*		
Of Christ (listed chronologically):		
Water made wine (Cana)	John 2:1-11	1082
Son of nobleman healed (Cana)	John 4:46-54	1085
Passed unseen through crowd (Nazareth)	Luke 4:28-30	1046
Man with unclean spirit in synagogue cured (Capernaum)	Mark 1:23-26	1016
	Luke 4:33-35	1047
Peter's mother-in-law healed (Capernaum)	Matt. 8:14-17	984
	Mark 1:29-31	1016
	Luke 4:38, 39	1047
Net full of fishes (Lower Galilee)	Luke 5:1-11	1047
Leper cleansed (Capernaum)	Matt. 8:1-4	984
	Mark 1:40-45	1016
	Luke 5:12-15	1047
Paralytic cured (Capernaum)	Matt. 9:1-8	985
	Mark 2:3-12	1017
	Luke 5:18-26	1048
Man healed (Jerusalem)	John 5:1-9	1085
Withered hand restored (Galilee)	Matt. 12:10-13	988
	Mark 3:1-5	1017
	Luke 6:6-11	1049
Centurion's servant cured of paralysis (Capernaum)	Matt. 8:5-13	984
	Luke 7:1-10	1050
Widow's son raised from dead (Nain)	Luke 7:11-17	1050
Demon-possessed man healed (Galilee)	Matt. 12:22, 23	989
	Luke 11:14	1057
Windstorm stilled (Lower Galilee)	Matt. 8:23-27	985
	Mark 4:37-41	1019
	Luke 8:22-25	1052
Two demon-possessed men cured (Gadara)	Matt. 8:28-34	985
	Mark 5:1-20	1020
	Luke 8:26-39	1052
Raised Jairus's daughter (Capernaum)	Matt. 9:24-26	986
	Mark 5:23	1020
	Luke 8:41	1053
Woman with flow of blood healed (Capernaum)	Matt. 9:20-22	986
	Mark 5:25-34	1020
	Luke 8:43-48	1053
Blind men cured (Capernaum)	Matt. 9:27-31	986
Mute spirit cast out (Capernaum)	Matt. 9:32, 33	986
Five thousand fed (Lower Galilee)	Matt. 14:15-21	992
	Mark 6:35-44	1022
	Luke 9:10-17	1054
	John 6:1-14	1087
Walking on the sea (Lower Galilee)	Matt. 14:25-33	992
	Mark 6:48-52	1022
	John 6:15-21	1087
Canaanite's or Syro-Phoenician's daughter healed (District of Tyre)	Matt. 15:21-28	993
	Mark 7:24-30	1023
Four thousand fed (Lower Galilee)	Matt. 15:32-39	994
	Mark 8:1-9	1024
Deaf and dumb man cured (Lower Galilee)	Mark 7:31-37	1023
Blind man healed (Bethsaida)	Mark 8:22-26	1024
Demon cast out of boy (near Caesarea)	Matt. 17:14-18	995
	Mark 9:14-29	1025
	Luke 9:37-43	1055
Tribute money provided (Capernaum)	Matt. 17:24-27	996
Passed unseen through crowd (in temple)	John 8:59	1092
Ten lepers cleansed (Samaria)	Luke 17:11-19	1065
Man born blind, healed (Jerusalem)	John 9:1-7	1092
Lazarus raised from dead (Bethany)	John 11:38-44	1096
Woman with sickness cured (Perea)	Luke 13:11-17	1061
Man with dropsy cured (Perea)	Luke 14:1-6	1062
Two blind men cured (Jericho)	Matt. 20:29-34	999
	Mark 10:46-52	1028
	Luke 18:35-43	1066
Fig tree withered (Mt. Olivet)	Matt. 21:18-22	1000
	Mark 11:12-14	1028
Malchus's ear healed (Gethsemane)	Luke 22:50, 51	1072
Second net full of fishes (Lower Galilee)	John 21:1-14	1106
Resurrection of Christ	Luke 24:6	1074
	John 10:18	1094
Appearances of Christ after His resurrection, to:		
Mary Magdalene (Jerusalem)	Mark 16:9	1036
Other women (Jerusalem)	Matt. 28:9	1010
Two disciples (Emmaus)	Luke 24:15-31	1075
Peter (Jerusalem)	1 Cor. 15:5	1178
Ten apostles, Thomas absent (Jerusalem)	John 20:19, 24	1105
Eleven apostles, Thomas present (Jerusalem)	John 20:26-28	1106
Seven disciples fishing (Lower Galilee)	John 21:1-24	1106
Eleven disciples (Galilee)	Matt. 28:16, 17	1010
Five hundred brethren	1 Cor. 15:6	1178
James	1 Cor. 15:7	1178
Eleven apostles on day of His ascension (Bethany)	Acts 1:2-9	1112
Paul at his conversion	Acts 9:1-5	1121
	1 Cor. 15:8	1178
Those associated with Peter:		
Lame man cured	Acts 3:6	1115
Death of Ananias and Sapphira	Acts 5:5, 10	1117
Sick healed	Acts 5:15	1117
Aeneas healed of paralysis	Acts 9:34	1122
Dorcas restored to life	Acts 9:40	1123
His release from prison	Acts 12:7-11	1125
Those associated with Paul:		
His sight restored	Acts 9:17, 18	1122
	Acts 22:12, 13	1138
Elymas blinded	Acts 13:11	1126
Lame man cured	Acts 14:10	1128
Girl freed of evil spirits	Acts 16:18	1131
	Acts 19:11, 12	1134
Earthquake at Philippi	Acts 16:25, 26	1131
Evil spirits overcame Sceva's seven sons	Acts 19:13-16	1134
Eutychus restored to life	Acts 20:10	1135
Unharmed by viper's bite	Acts 28:5	1144
Publius's father healed	Acts 28:8	1144
Other miracles of the New Testament:		
Outpouring of the Holy Spirit	Acts 2:1-21	1113
Gift of tongues	Acts 2:3, 4, 11	1113
	Acts 10:46	1124
	Acts 19:6	1134
Apostles freed from prison	Acts 5:19	1117
	Acts 12:7-11	1125
Agabus's prophecies	Acts 11:28	1125
	Acts 21:11	1136
Visions:		
Three apostles'	Matt. 17:1, 2	995
	Luke 9:32	1054
Of Christ, by dying:		
Stephen	Acts 7:55, 56	1120
Ananias's	Acts 9:10	1122
Peter's	Acts 10:1-48	1123
	Acts 11:1-30	1124
Cornelius's	Acts 10:3, 4, 30-32	1123
Paul's	Acts 16:9	1130
	2 Cor. 12:1-5	1191
John's on Patmos	Rev. 1–10	1312
	Rev. 4–22	1315
Miracles by the seventy	Luke 10:17	1056
Stephen performed great miracles	Acts 6:8	1118
Philip cast out unclean spirits	Acts 8:6-13	1120
Miracles pretended, or false		
Egyptian magicians	Ex. 7:11-22	61
	Ex. 8:18, 19	62
In support of false religions	Deut. 13:1-3	188
Witch of En Dor	1 Sam. 28:9-12	299
False prophets	Matt. 7:22, 23	984
	Matt. 24:24	1003
False christs	Matt. 24:24	1003
Deceive the ungodly	Rev. 13:13	1321
	Rev. 19:20	1326
Sign of apostasy	2 Thess. 2:3, 9	1232
	Rev. 13:13	1321
Mire—*deep mud*		
A. *Places of:*		
Dungeon	Jer. 38:22	789
Streets	Is. 10:6	692
B. *Figurative of:*		
Affliction	Job 30:19	532
Insecurity	Is. 57:20	735
Plentifulness	Zech. 9:3	960
Miriam—*obstinacy* (stubbornness)		
1. Sister of Aaron and Moses	Num. 26:59	161
Watches over Moses in river	Ex. 2:4-6	57
Calls Moses' mother as nurse to help with Moses for Pharaoh's daughter	Ex. 2:7, 8	57
Chosen by God; called a prophetess	Ex. 15:20	70
Leads in victory song	Ex. 15:20, 21	70
Opposes Moses	Num. 12:1, 2	145
Punished for rebellion	Num. 12:3-16	145
Buried at Kadesh	Num. 20:1	153
2. Judahite	1 Chr. 4:17	404
Mirmah—*deceit*		
Benjamite	1 Chr. 8:10	408
Mirror		
In the tabernacle	Ex. 38:8	92
Of cast metal	Job 37:18	537
Used figuratively	1 Cor. 13:12	1176
	2 Cor. 3:18	1186
	James 1:23, 25	1272
Mirth—*a spirit of gaiety*		
Occasions of	Gen. 31:27	33
	Neh. 8:10-12	491
	Jer. 25:10, 11	774
Absence of	Hos. 2:11	891
	Prov. 14:13	640
Inadequacy of	Eccl. 2:1, 2	662
Miscarriage—*premature ejection of a fetus from the mother's womb, resulting in the death of the fetus*		
Against the wicked	Ps. 58:8	576

SUBJECT REFERENCE PAGE

SUBJECT REFERENCE PAGE

SUBJECT REFERENCE PAGE

SUBJECT REFERENCE PAGE

SUBJECT REFERENCE PAGE

SUBJECT REFERENCE PAGE

SUBJECT REFERENCE PAGE

Q

R

SUBJECT REFERENCE PAGE

SUBJECT REFERENCE PAGE

SUBJECT	REFERENCE	PAGE
Salvation—continued		
Deliverance from enemies	2 Chr. 20:17	449
Messiah	Matt. 1:21	978
B. *Source of, in:*		
God's grace	Eph. 2:5, 8	1205
God's love	Rom. 5:8	1152
God's mercy	Titus 3:5	1250
Christ alone	Acts 4:12	1116
Cross	1 Cor. 1:18	1167
C. *History of:*		
Promised to Adam	Gen. 3:15	7
Announced to Abram	Gen. 12:1-3	14
Revealed to the prophets	1 Pet. 1:10-12	1279
Longed for by the saints	Ps. 119:81, 174	612
Promised to Gentiles	Is. 45:21, 22	724
To be realized in the Messiah	Is. 59:16, 17	736
Seen in Christ's birth	Luke 1:69, 77	1042
Christ, the author	Heb. 5:9	1261
Appeared to all people	Titus 2:11	1250
Proclaimed to Israel	Zech. 9:9	960
Accomplished on the cross	John 3:14, 15	1083
Preached through the gospel	Eph. 1:13	1204
Rejected by Israel	Acts 13:26-46	1127
Extended to Gentiles	Acts 28:28	1144
This age, day of	2 Cor. 6:2	1187
God's longsuffering in	2 Pet. 3:9	1288
Final, nearer each day	Rom. 13:11	1160
Consummated in the Second Advent	Heb. 9:28	1264
Praise for, in heaven	Rev. 7:10	1317
D. *Requirements of:*		
Confession	Acts 2:21 Rom. 10:10	1113 1157
Repentance	Mark 1:15	1016
Faith	John 3:14-18	1083
Regeneration	John 3:3-8	1083
Holy Scripture	2 Tim. 3:15	1245
Believe	Rom. 10:9	1157
E. *Negative blessings of, deliverance from:*		
Sin	Matt. 1:21	978
Satan's power	Heb. 2:14, 15	1259
Wrath	Rom. 5:9	1152
Eternal death	John 3:16, 17	1083
F. *Positive blessings of:*		
Chosen to	2 Thess. 2:13	1232
Appointed to	1 Thess. 5:9	1228
Kept unto	1 Pet. 1:5	1279
Rejoiced in	1 Pet. 4:13	1283
To be worked out	Phil. 2:12	1214
G. *Temporal aspects of:*		
Past	Eph. 2:8	1205
Present	1 Cor. 1:18	1167
Future	Heb. 9:28	1264
Samaria—*watchtower*		
1. Capital of Israel	1 Kin. 16:24-29	355
Built by Omri	1 Kin. 16:23, 24	355
Israel's "crown of pride"	Is. 28:1	706
Besieged twice by Ben-Hadad	1 Kin. 20:1-22	359
Miraculously saved	2 Kin. 6:8-23	374
Worshipers of Baal destroyed	2 Kin. 10:1-28	378
Taken captive; people of, exiled	2 Kin. 17:6	385
Threatened with divine judgment	Is. 28:1-4 Amos 3:11, 12	706 910
Repopulated with foreigners	2 Kin. 17:24-41	386
2. Name of northern kingdom	1 Kin. 21:1	361
3. District of Palestine in Christ's time	Luke 17:11-19	1065
Preaching in, forbidden by Christ	Matt. 10:5	986
Preaching of gospel in, commanded	Acts 1:8	1112
Churches established there	Acts 9:31	1122
Paul preached there	Acts 15:3	1129
Samaritans—*inhabitants of Samaria*		
Of mixed blood and defiled religion	2 Kin. 17:24-41	386
Seek alliance with Jews	Ezra 4:1-4	472
Jews did not associate with	John 4:9	1084
Christ and the Samaritan woman	John 4:5-42	1084
Story of "the Good Samaritan"	Luke 10:30-37	1056
Jesus heals a Samaritan leper	Luke 17:11-19	1065
A town of, rejects Jesus	Luke 9:52-55	1055
Beliefs of	John 4:25	1085
Converts among	Acts 8:5-25	1120
Samek		
Fifteenth letter of the Hebrew alphabet	Ps. 119:113-120	613
Samgar-Nebo—*be gracious, Nebo*		
Prince of Nebuchadnezzar	Jer. 39:3	789
Samlah—*a garment*		
Edomite king	Gen. 36:36, 37	38
Samos—*an island off the coast of Lydia*		
Visited by Paul	Acts 20:15	1135
Samothrace—*an island in the Aegean Sea*		
Visited by Paul	Acts 16:11	1130
Samson—*sunlike*		
A. *Life of:*		
Judge from tribe of Dan	Judg. 13:2, 5	254
Birth of, predicted	Judg. 13:3-7	254
God's Spirit moves him	Judg. 13:24, 25	255
Desired a Philistine wife	Judg. 14:1-9	255
Posed a riddle	Judg. 14:10-14	255
Betrayed, kills 30 men	Judg. 14:15-20	255
Enticed by Delilah, loses strength	Judg. 16:4-20	257
Blinded and bound	Judg. 16:21	257
Destroyed over 3,000 in his death	Judg. 16:22-31 Heb. 11:32	257 1266
Listed as a man of faith	Heb. 11:32	1266
B. *Character of:*		
Weaknesses:		
Attracted to foreign women	Judg. 14:1-4 Judg. 16:1 Judg. 16:4	255 256 257
Takes revenge	Judg. 15:1-8	256
Disregard for his Nazirite vow	Judg. 13:4, 5 Judg. 14:8, 9 Judg. 16:19	254 255 257
Strengths:		
Dependence on God	Judg. 15:18, 19	256
Repentance that restored	Judg. 16:28-31	258
Samuel—*name of God* (a godly name)		
A. *Life of:*		
Born in answer to Hannah's prayer	1 Sam. 1:5-21	273
Before birth, dedicated to God as a Nazirite	1 Sam. 1:11, 22	273
Brought to Shiloh; reared by Eli	1 Sam. 1:24-28	273
His mother praised God for	1 Sam. 2:1-10	274
The child Samuel called by God	1 Sam. 3:2-10	275
Delivered God's rebuke to Eli	1 Sam. 3:11-18	275
Recognized as a prophet	1 Sam. 3:20, 21	276
Became a circuit judge	1 Sam. 7:15-17	279
Called Israel to repentance	1 Sam. 7:3-6	278
Samuel's sons rejected by Israel; they ask for a king	1 Sam. 8:1-6	279
Anointed Saul as king	1 Sam. 10:1	280
Advised Saul God had rejected him as king	1 Sam. 13:13, 14 1 Sam. 15:28	283 287
Anointed David as king	1 Sam. 16:13	287
Woman of En Dor calls up spirit of; he foretells Saul's defeat and death	1 Sam. 28:11-20	299
Lamented in death	1 Sam. 25:1	296
B. *Ministry of:*		
Served as priest	1 Sam. 2:11, 18 1 Chr. 6:1, 28	274 405
Served as prophet, seer	1 Sam. 3:19-21	276
Served as judge	1 Sam. 7:15-17	279
Organized gatekeepers	1 Chr. 9:22 1 Chr. 26:28	410 425
Inspired as a writer	1 Chr. 29:29	429
Inspired as a prophet	Acts 3:24	1115
Faithful to God	Heb. 11:32-34	1266
Industrious in service	1 Chr. 9:22	410
Devout in life	Jer. 15:1	764
Powerful in prayer	Ps. 99:6	598
Samuel, Books of—*two books of the Old Testament*		
A. *1 Samuel:*		
Birth of Samuel	1 Sam. 1:19-28	273
Hannah's song	1 Sam. 2:1-10	274
The ark captured	1 Sam. 4:1-11	276
The ark returned	1 Sam. 6:1-21	277
Saul chosen as king	1 Sam. 9:1-27	279
Saul anointed	1 Sam. 10:1-27	280

SUBJECT — REFERENCE — PAGE

Sedition—*attack upon an established government*

Miriam and Aaron, against Moses ... Num. 12:1-13 ... 145
Paul accused of, by Jews and Tertullus ... Acts 24:1-9 ... 1140

Seducers—*those who lead others astray*

A. *Agents of:*
Evil leaders ... 2 Kin. 21:9 ... 391

B. *Characteristics of:*
Lead to evil ... Rev. 2:20 ... 1314
Preach false message ... Ezek. 13:9, 10 ... 829

Seed—*the essential element of transmitting life*

A. *Descriptive of:*
One's ancestry ... Gen. 12:7 ... 15
Messianic line ... Gen. 21:12 ... 22
Christ ... Gal. 3:16, 19 ... 1198

B. *Figurative of true believers:*
Born of God ... 1 Pet. 1:23 ... 1280
Abraham's true children ... Gal. 3:29 ... 1198
Children of promise ... Rom. 9:7, 8 ... 1156
Including Israel's faithful ... Rom. 9:29 ... 1156

C. *Sowing of, figurative of:*
God's Word ... Matt. 13:3, 32 ... 990
Spiritual blessings ... 1 Cor. 9:11 ... 1173
Christ's death ... John 12:24 ... 1097
Christian's body ... 1 Cor. 15:36-49 ... 1179

Seeking—*trying to obtain*

A. *Things of the world:*
Material things ... Matt. 6:32 ... 983
One's life ... Luke 17:33 ... 1065
One's selfish interest ... Phil. 2:21 ... 1214
Pleasing others ... Gal. 1:10 ... 1196
One's own glory ... John 7:18 ... 1089

B. *Things of the Spirit:*
True wisdom ... Prov. 2:4 ... 630
God's kingdom ... Matt. 6:33 ... 983
Another's benefit ... 2 Cor. 12:14 ... 1192
Peace ... 1 Pet. 3:11 ... 1282
Heavenly country ... Heb. 11:14 ... 1266

Seers—*prophets*

Amos ... Amos 7:12 ... 913
Asaph ... 2 Chr. 29:30 ... 458
Gad ... 2 Sam. 24:11 ... 330
Heman ... 1 Chr. 25:5 ... 424
Samuel ... 1 Sam. 9:19 ... 280
Zadok ... 2 Sam. 15:27 ... 320
Iddo ... 2 Chr. 9:29 ... 441
Hanani ... 2 Chr. 16:7 ... 446
Jeduthun ... 2 Chr. 35:15 ... 464

Segub—*exalted*

1. Son of Hiel ... 1 Kin. 16:34 ... 356
2. Son of Hezron ... 1 Chr. 2:21, 22 ... 402

Seir—*hairy; shaggy*

1. Mt. Seir ... Gen. 14:6 ... 16
Home of Esau ... Gen. 32:3 ... 34
Mountain range of Edom ... Gen. 36:21 ... 38
Horites dispossessed by Esau's descendants ... Deut. 2:12 ... 176
Refuge of Amalekite remnant ... 1 Chr. 4:42, 43 ... 404
Desolation of ... Ezek. 35:15 ... 854
2. Landmark on Judah's boundary ... Josh. 15:10 ... 227

Seirah—*rough*

Ehud's refuge ... Judg. 3:26 ... 243

Seize—*to take or keep fast, hold*

Used of:
Darkness ... Job 3:6 ... 514
Inheritance being taken ... Matt. 21:38 ... 1000

Sela

Place in Edom ... 2 Kin. 14:7 ... 382

Selah

Musical term found in Psalms ... Ps. 3:2 ... 547
Found in ... Hab. 3:3, 9, 13 ... 942

Seled—*exultation*

Judahite ... 1 Chr. 2:30 ... 402

Seleucia—*a city on the seacoast of Syria*

Paul and Barnabas embark from ... Acts 13:4 ... 1126

Self-abasement

Jacob, before Esau ... Gen. 33:3-10 ... 35
Moses, before God ... Ex. 3:11 ... 58
Roman, before Christ ... Luke 7:7-9 ... 1050
Christ, true example of ... Phil. 2:5-8 ... 1214

Self-acceptance—*having the proper attitude toward oneself*

A. *By Christians, based on:*
Planned before birth by God ... Ps. 139:13-16 ... 620
Workmanship of God ... Ps. 138:8 ... 619; Eph. 2:10 ... 1205
Christ has provided life ... John 10:10 ... 1094
God's desire for human fellowship ... John 17:3 ... 1102
God's love ... Rom. 5:8 ... 1152
Living epistle of God ... 2 Cor. 3:2 ... 1185
Complete in Christ ... Col. 2:10 ... 1221
Chosen by God ... 1 Pet. 2:9 ... 1280

B. *Hindered by false attitudes:*
Looking on outward appearance ... 1 Sam. 16:7 ... 287
Questioning God's direction ... Is. 45:9 ... 723
Doubting God's grace ... 2 Cor. 12:9, 10 ... 1192

Self-condemnation

Caused by one's:
Heart ... 1 John 3:20 ... 1295
Conscience ... John 8:7-9 ... 1090
Sins ... 2 Sam. 24:17 ... 330
Mouth ... Job 9:20 ... 518
Evil works ... Matt. 23:31 ... 1002

Self-control

A. *Origin of:*
Brought about by Christ ... Luke 8:35 ... 1053
Christian grace ... 2 Pet. 1:6 ... 1287

B. *Elements involved in:*
Ruling one's spirit ... Prov. 16:32 ... 643; Col. 3:14-17 ... 1221
Soberness ... Rom. 12:3 ... 1159
Control of the body ... 1 Cor. 9:27 ... 1173

C. *Hindered by:*
Fleshly lusts ... 1 Pet. 2:11 ... 1280
Tongue ... Ps. 39:1, 2 ... 566
Drink ... Prov. 23:29-35 ... 650
Sexual sins ... 1 Thess. 4:3, 4 ... 1228
Unclean spirit ... Mark 5:2-16 ... 1020
Self-expressionism ... Prov. 25:28 ... 653

Self-control, lack of—*uncontrolled indulgence of the passions*

A. *Expressed in:*
Unbridled sexual morals ... Ex. 32:6, 18, 25 ... 86
Abnormal sexual desires ... 2 Sam. 13:1-15 ... 317
Unnatural sexual appetites ... Gen. 19:5-9 ... 20; Rom. 1:26, 27 ... 1149

B. *Sources of:*
Lust ... 1 Pet. 4:2, 3 ... 1282
Satan ... 1 Cor. 7:5 ... 1171
Apostasy ... 2 Tim. 3:3 ... 1244

Self-deception

A. *Factors contributing to:*
Scoffers ... 2 Pet. 3:3, 4 ... 1288
Worldliness ... Matt. 24:48-51 ... 1004
False teaching ... 1 Thess. 5:3 ... 1228

B. *Examples of:*
Babylon ... Is. 47:7-11 ... 725
Jewish women ... Jer. 44:16-19 ... 793
Jewish leaders ... John 8:33, 41 ... 1091

Self-denial

A. *Expressed by:*
"Denying" ... Titus 2:12 ... 1250
"No longer should live" ... 1 Pet. 4:2 ... 1282
"Does not forsake" ... Luke 14:33 ... 1063
"Take his cross" ... Matt. 10:38 ... 987
"Crucified the flesh" ... Gal. 5:24 ... 1200
"Put off" ... Eph. 4:22 ... 1207
"Put to death" ... Col. 3:5 ... 1221

B. *Objects for:*
Appetite ... Prov. 23:2 ... 649
Sinful pleasures ... Heb. 11:25, 26 ... 1266
Worldly ambitions ... Matt. 16:24-26 ... 995

C. *Willingness to, manifested by:*
Judah ... Gen. 44:33 ... 47
Moses ... Ex. 32:32 ... 87
Paul ... Acts 20:22-24 ... 1136

D. *Commended as:*
Christian duty ... Rom. 12:1, 2 ... 1158
Rewardable ... Luke 18:28-30 ... 1066

Self-exaltation

A. *Manifested by:*
Satan ... Is. 14:12-15 ... 695
Antichrist ... 2 Thess. 2:4 ... 1232
Wicked ... Ps. 73:9 ... 584

B. *Evils of, seen in:*
Self-abasement ... Matt. 23:12 ... 1002
Pride ... Prov. 16:18 ... 642

C. *Antidotes for:*
Humility ... Prov. 15:33 ... 642
Christ's example ... Phil. 2:5-8 ... 1214

See Pride

Self-examination

A. *Purposes of, to:*
Test one's faith ... 2 Cor. 13:5 ... 1192

SUBJECT REFERENCE PAGE

SUBJECT REFERENCE PAGE

Shaalbonite—*an inhabitant of Shaalbim*

Eliahba called ... 2 Sam. 23:32 ... 330

Shaalim—*district of foxes*

Mentioned in Saul's pursuit ... 1 Sam. 9:4 ... 279

Shaaph—*friendship*

1. Descendant of Caleb ... 1 Chr. 2:47 ... 402
2. Son of Caleb ... 1 Chr. 2:49 ... 402

Shaaraim, Sharaim—*double gate*

1. Village in Judah ... Josh. 15:36 ... 228
2. City of Simeon ... 1 Chr. 4:31 ... 404

Shaashgaz

Persian eunuch ... Esth. 2:14 ... 503

Shabbethai—*Sabbath-born*

Postexilic Levite ... Ezra 10:15 ... 479
Interprets the Law ... Neh. 8:7, 8 ... 491

Shadow

A. *Used literally of:*
- Peter's ... Acts 5:15 ... 1117
- Mountain ... Judg. 9:36 ... 251
- Sundial ... 2 Kin. 20:9-11 ... 390

B. *Used figuratively of:*
- Protection ... Ps. 91:1 ... 595
- Brevity ... Ps. 102:11 ... 599
- Change ... James 1:17 ... 1272
- Death ... Matt. 4:16 ... 980
- Types ... Col. 2:17 ... 1221
- Old Testament period ... Heb. 10:1 ... 1264

Shadrach

Hananiah's Babylonian name ... Dan. 1:3, 7 ... 871
Deported by Nebuchadnezzar ... Dan. 1:6, 7 ... 871
Refused defiling food ... Dan. 1:8-20 ... 871
Refused to bow to image ... Dan. 3:8-18 ... 874
Cast into the fiery furnace ... Dan. 3:19-23 ... 874
Delivered by God ... Dan. 3:24-28 ... 875
Promoted by Nebuchadnezzar ... Dan. 3:29, 30 ... 875

Shageh—*wandering*

Father of one of David's mighty men ... 1 Chr. 11:34 ... 412

Shaharaim—*double dawn*

Benjamite ... 1 Chr. 8:8-11 ... 408

Shahazimah—*heights*

Town of Issachar ... Josh. 19:17, 22 ... 231

Shake—*to move violently*

A. *Descriptive of:*
- Thunder ... Ps. 77:18 ... 586
- Earthquakes ... Acts 4:31 ... 1116
- Fear ... Matt. 28:4 ... 1010

B. *Used figuratively of:*
- Fear ... Is. 14:16 ... 696
- Second Advent ... Heb. 12:26, 27 ... 1267
- Rejection ... Luke 9:5 ... 1054; Acts 18:6 ... 1133

Shalisha—*a third part*

Shallecheth—*a casting out*

Gate of Solomon's temple ... 1 Chr. 26:16 ... 425

Shallum—*recompense*

1. King of Israel ... 2 Kin. 15:10-15 ... 383
2. Husband of Huldah ... 2 Kin. 22:14 ... 392
3. Judahite ... 1 Chr. 2:40, 41 ... 402
4. Simeonite ... 1 Chr. 4:25 ... 404
5. Father of Hilkiah ... 1 Chr. 6:12, 13 ... 405
6. Naphtali's son ... 1 Chr. 7:13 ... 407
7. Family of gatekeepers ... Ezra 2:42 ... 471
8. Father of Jehizkiah ... 2 Chr. 28:12 ... 456
9. One who divorced his foreign wife ... Ezra 10:24 ... 480
10. Another who divorced his foreign wife ... Ezra 10:42 ... 480
11. Son of Hallohesh ... Neh. 3:12 ... 485
12. Jeremiah's uncle ... Jer. 32:7 ... 782
13. Father of Maaseiah ... Jer. 35:4 ... 785

Shalmai—*Yahweh is recompenser*

Head of a family of Nethinim ... Ezra 2:46 ... 471

Shalman

Contraction of Shalmaneser ... Hos. 10:14 ... 897

Shalmaneser—*Shulmanu* (a god) *is chief*

Assyrian king ... 2 Kin. 17:3 ... 385

Shama—*He* (God) *has heard*

Son of Hotham ... 1 Chr. 11:44 ... 412

Shamariah—*Yahweh has kept*

Son of Rehoboam ... 2 Chr. 11:18, 19 ... 443

Shame—*a feeling of guilt*

A. *Caused by:*
- Rape ... 2 Sam. 13:13 ... 317
- Defeat ... 2 Chr. 32:21 ... 461
- Folly ... Prov. 3:35 ... 631
- Idleness ... Prov. 10:5 ... 636
- Pride ... Prov. 11:2 ... 637
- A wicked wife ... Prov. 12:4 ... 638
- Lying ... Prov. 13:5 ... 639
- Stubbornness ... Prov. 13:18 ... 639
- Haste in speech ... Prov. 18:13 ... 644
- Mistreatment of parents ... Prov. 19:26 ... 645
- Evil companions ... Prov. 28:7 ... 654
- Juvenile delinquency ... Prov. 29:15 ... 656
- Nakedness ... Is. 47:3 ... 725
- Idolatry ... Jer. 2:26, 27 ... 749
- Impropriety ... 1 Cor. 11:6 ... 1174
- Lust ... Phil. 3:19 ... 1215

B. *Of the unregenerate:*
- Hardened in ... Jer. 8:12 ... 757
- Pleasure in ... Rom. 1:26, 27, 32 ... 1149
- Vessels of ... Rom. 9:21 ... 1156
- Glory in ... Phil. 3:19 ... 1215

C. *In the Christian life, of:*
- Former life ... Rom. 6:21 ... 1153
- Sinful things ... Eph. 5:12 ... 1208
- Improper behavior ... 1 Cor. 11:14, 22 ... 1175
- In gospel of Christ no ... Rom. 1:16 ... 1149

Shamer (see Shemer)

Shamgar—*cupbearer*

Judge of Israel; struck down 600 Philistines ... Judg. 3:31 ... 244

Shamhuth—*desolation*

Commander in David's army ... 1 Chr. 27:8 ... 425

Shamir—*a sharp point*

1. Town in Judah ... Josh. 15:1, 48 ... 227
2. Town in Ephraim ... Judg. 10:1 ... 251
3. Levite ... 1 Chr. 24:24 ... 423

Shamma—*astonishment*

Asherite ... 1 Chr. 7:36, 37 ... 408

Shammah—*waste*

1. Son of Reuel ... Gen. 36:13, 17 ... 38
2. Son of Jesse ... 1 Sam. 16:9 ... 287
   Called Shimea ... 1 Chr. 2:13 ... 402
3. One of David's mighty men ... 2 Sam. 23:11 ... 329
   Also called Shammoth the Harorite ... 1 Chr. 11:27 ... 412

Shammai—*celebrated*

1. Grandson of Jerahmeel ... 1 Chr. 2:26, 28 ... 402
2. Descendant of Caleb ... 1 Chr. 2:44, 45 ... 402
3. Descendant of Judah ... 1 Chr. 4:17 ... 404

Shammoth—*waste*

One of David's mighty men ... 1 Chr. 11:27 ... 412

Shammua—*renowned*

1. Reubenite spy ... Num. 13:2-4 ... 146
2. Son of David ... 2 Sam. 5:13, 14 ... 310
3. Levite ... Neh. 11:17 ... 495
4. Postexilic priest ... Neh. 12:1, 18 ... 496

Shamsherai—*sunlike*

Son of Jeroham ... 1 Chr. 8:26, 27 ... 409

Shapham—*youthful*

Gadite ... 1 Chr. 5:12 ... 405

Shaphan—*prudent, shy*

Scribe under Josiah ... 2 Kin. 22:3 ... 392
Takes Book of the Law to Josiah ... 2 Kin. 22:8-10 ... 392
Is sent to Huldah for interpretation ... 2 Kin. 22:14 ... 392
Assists in repairs of temple ... 2 Chr. 34:8 ... 462
Father of notable son ... Jer. 36:10-12, 25 ... 786

Shaphat—*he has judged*

1. Simeonite spy ... Num. 13:2-5 ... 146
2. Son of Shemaiah ... 1 Chr. 3:22 ... 403
3. Gadite chief ... 1 Chr. 5:11, 12 ... 405
4. One of David's herdsmen ... 1 Chr. 27:29 ... 426
5. Father of the prophet Elisha ... 1 Kin. 19:16, 19 ... 359

Shaphir—*glittering*

Town of Judah ... Mic. 1:11 ... 927

Sharai—*Yahweh is deliverer*

Divorced his foreign wife ... Ezra 10:34, 40 ... 480

Sharar—*firm*

Father of Ahiam ... 2 Sam. 23:33 ... 330

SUBJECT REFERENCE PAGE

Sharezer, Sherezer—*protect the king*

1. Son of Sennacherib ... Is. 37:37, 38 ... 716
2. Sent to Zechariah concerning fasting ... Zech. 7:1-3 ... 958

Sharon—*plain*

1. Coastal plain between Joppa and Mt. Carmel ... 1 Chr. 27:29 ... 426
   Famed for roses ... Song 2:1 ... 674
   Inhabitants turn to the Lord ... Acts 9:35 ... 1122
2. Pasture east of the Jordan ... 1 Chr. 5:16 ... 405

Sharonite—*an inhabitant of Sharon*

Shitrai called ... 1 Chr. 27:29 ... 426

Sharp—*having a keen edge; biting*

A. *Descriptive of:*
   Stone ... Ex. 4:25 ... 59
   Knives ... Josh. 5:2, 3 ... 217
   Plowshare ... 1 Sam. 13:20, 21 ... 284
   Rocks ... 1 Sam. 14:4 ... 284
   Arrows ... Is. 5:28 ... 687
   Razor ... Ps. 52:2 ... 573

B. *Used to compare a sword with:*
   Tongue ... Ps. 57:4 ... 575
   Adulteress ... Prov. 5:4 ... 632
   Mouth ... Is. 49:2 ... 727
   God's Word ... Heb. 4:12 ... 1260

C. *Figurative of:*
   Deceitfulness ... Ps. 52:2 ... 573
   Falsehood ... Prov. 25:18 ... 652
   Contention ... Acts 15:39 ... 1130
   Severe rebuke ... 2 Cor. 13:10 ... 1193
   Christ's conquest ... Rev. 14:14-18 ... 1322

Sharuhen—*abode of pleasure*

Town of Judah assigned to Simeon ... Josh. 19:1, 6 ... 230
Called Sharaim ... Josh. 15:36 ... 228
Called Shaaraim ... 1 Chr. 4:31 ... 404

Shashai—*whitish*

Divorced his foreign wife ... Ezra 10:34, 40 ... 480

Shashak—*assaulter*

Benjamite ... 1 Chr. 8:14, 25 ... 408

Shaul—*asked* (of God)

1. Son of Simeon ... Gen. 46:10 ... 48
   Founder of a tribal family ... Num. 26:13 ... 160
2. Kohathite Levite ... 1 Chr. 6:24 ... 406

Shave—*to cut off the hair*

A. *Used worthily to express:*
   Accommodation ... Gen. 41:14 ... 42
   Cleansing ... Lev. 14:8, 9 ... 111
   Commitment ... Deut. 21:10-13 ... 194
   Mourning ... Job 1:18-20 ... 513
   Sorrow ... Jer. 41:5 ... 791

B. *Used unworthily to express:*
   Defeat of a Nazirite ... Judg. 16:19 ... 257
   Contempt ... 2 Sam. 10:4 ... 314
   Unnaturalness ... 1 Cor. 11:5, 6 ... 1174

Shaveh—*plain*

Valley near Salem; Abram meets king of Sodom here ... Gen. 14:17, 18 ... 16

Shaveh Kiriathaim—*plain of Kiriathaim*

Plain near Kiriathaim inhabited by the Emim ... Gen. 14:5 ... 16

Shavsha, Shisha—*nobility*

David's secretary ... 1 Chr. 18:14, 16 ... 418
Serves under Solomon also ... 1 Kin. 4:3 ... 339

Sheal—*asking*

Divorced his foreign wife ... Ezra 10:29 ... 480

Shealtiel—*I have asked God*

Son of King Jeconiah and father of Zerubbabel ... 1 Chr. 3:17 ... 403; Ezra 5:2 ... 474

Sheariah—*Yahweh has esteemed*

Descendant of Saul ... 1 Chr. 9:44 ... 410

Shear-Jashub—*a remnant shall return*

Symbolic name given to Isaiah's son ... Is. 7:3 ... 688

Sheba—*seven; an oath*

1. City in territory assigned to Simeon ... Josh. 19:1, 2 ... 230
2. Benjamite insurrectionist ... 2 Sam. 20:1-22 ... 325
3. Descendant of Cush through Raamah ... Gen. 10:7 ... 13
4. Descendant of Shem ... Gen. 10:28 ... 13
5. Grandson of Abraham and Keturah ... Gen. 25:3 ... 26
6. Gadite chief ... 1 Chr. 5:13 ... 405
7. Land of, occupied by Sabeans, famous traders ... Job 1:15 ... 512; Ps. 72:10 ... 583
   Queen of, visits Solomon; marvels at his wisdom ... 1 Kin. 10:1-13 ... 347
   Mentioned by Christ ... Matt. 12:42 ... 990

Shebah—*seven; an oath*

Name given to a well and town (Beersheba) ... Gen. 26:31-33 ... 28

Shebaniah—*Yahweh has returned me*

1. Levite trumpeter ... 1 Chr. 15:24 ... 415
2. Levite; offers prayer and signs covenant ... Neh. 9:4, 5 ... 492
3. Levite who signs covenant ... Neh. 10:12 ... 494
4. Priest who signs covenant ... Neh. 10:4 ... 494

Shebarim—*breakings*

Place near Ai ... Josh. 7:5 ... 219

Shebat

Eleventh month of the Hebrew year ... Zech. 1:7 ... 955

Sheber—*breaking*

Son of Caleb ... 1 Chr. 2:48 ... 402

Shebna—*perhaps an abbreviation of Shebaniah*

Treasurer under Hezekiah ... Is. 22:15 ... 701
Demoted to position of scribe ... 2 Kin. 19:2 ... 388
Man of pride and luxury; replaced by Eliakim ... Is. 22:19-21 ... 702

Shebuel—*God is renown*

1. Son of Gershon ... 1 Chr. 23:16 ... 422
2. Son of Heman ... 1 Chr. 25:4 ... 424

Shecaniah, Shechaniah—*Yahweh has dwelt*

1. Descendant of Zerubbabel ... 1 Chr. 3:21, 22 ... 403
2. Postexilic returnee ... Ezra 8:5 ... 477
3. Descendant of Aaron ... 1 Chr. 24:11 ... 423
4. Priest ... 2 Chr. 31:15 ... 460
5. Divorced his foreign wife ... Ezra 10:2, 3 ... 479
6. Father of Shemaiah ... Neh. 3:29 ... 486
   Probably same as number 1
7. Postexilic priest ... Neh. 12:3, 7 ... 496
8. Father-in-law of Tobiah ... Neh. 6:18 ... 488

Shechem—*shoulder*

1. Son of Hamor; seduces Dinah, Jacob's daughter ... Gen. 34:1-26 ... 35
   Deceived and killed by Levi and Simeon ... Gen. 34:13-18, 25, 26 ... 36
2. Son of Gilead; founder of a tribal family ... Num. 26:31 ... 160
3. Son of Shemida ... 1 Chr. 7:19 ... 408
4. Ancient city of Ephraim ... Gen. 33:18 ... 35
   Abram camps near ... Gen. 12:6 ... 15
   Jacob buys ground here ... Gen. 33:18, 19 ... 35
   Inhabitants of, slaughtered by Simeon and Levi ... Gen. 34:25-29 ... 36
   Becomes city of refuge ... Josh. 20:7 ... 232
   Joseph buried here ... Josh. 24:32 ... 237
   Joshua's farewell address here ... Josh. 24:1, 25 ... 236
   Center of idol worship ... Judg. 9:1, 4-7 ... 249
   Town destroyed ... Judg. 9:23, 45 ... 250
   Jeroboam made king here ... 1 Kin. 12:1-19 ... 350
   Name of, used poetically ... Ps. 108:7 ... 605

Shed—*to pour out*

A. *Descriptive of:*
   Blood ... Gen. 9:6 ... 12
   Holy Spirit ... Titus 3:6 ... 1250

B. *As applied to blood, indicative of:*
   Justifiable execution ... Gen. 9:6 ... 12
   Unjustifiable murder ... Gen. 37:22 ... 39
   Unacceptable sacrifice ... Lev. 17:1-5 ... 115
   Attempted vengeance ... 1 Sam. 25:31, 34 ... 297
   Unpardonable ... 2 Kin. 24:4 ... 395
   Abomination ... Prov. 6:16, 17 ... 633
   Heinous crime ... Is. 59:7 ... 736
   New covenant ... Matt. 26:28 ... 1007
   Martyrdom ... Acts 27:20 ... 1143

Shedeur—*shedder of light*

Reubenite leader ... Num. 1:5 ... 131

Sheep—*a domesticated animal*

A. *Characteristics of:*
   Domesticated ... 2 Sam. 12:3 ... 315

SUBJECT — REFERENCE — PAGE

18. Leading man under Ezra .... Ezra 8:16 — 477
19. Priest who divorced his foreign wife .... Ezra 10:21 — 480
20. Man who divorced his foreign wife .... Ezra 10:31 — 480
21. Prophet hired by Sanballat .... Neh. 6:10-14 — 488
22. Priest who signs covenant .... Neh. 10:1, 8 — 494
23. Participant in dedication service .... Neh. 12:34 — 497
24. Postexilic priest .... Neh. 12:35 — 497
25. Levite musician .... Neh. 12:36 — 497

Shemariah—*Yahweh keeps*

1. Mighty man of Benjamin .... 1 Chr. 12:5 — 412
2. Son of Rehoboam ..... 2 Chr. 11:18, 19 — 443
3. Divorced his foreign wife .... Ezra 10:31, 32 — 480

Shemeber—*splendor of heroism*

King of Zeboiim ..... Gen. 14:2 — 16

Shemed—*destruction*

Son of Elpaal .... 1 Chr. 8:12 — 408

Shemer, Shamer—*guard*

1. Sells Omri hill on which Samaria is built .... 1 Kin. 16:23, 24 — 355
2. Levite .... 1 Chr. 6:46 — 406
3. Asherite .... 1 Chr. 7:30, 34 — 408

Shemida—*fame of knowing*

Descendant of Manasseh; founder of the Shemidaites .... Num. 26:29, 32 — 160

Sheminith—*eighth*

Musical term .... 1 Chr. 15:21 — 415

Shemiramoth—*fame of the highest*

1. Levite musician in David's time .... 1 Chr. 15:18, 20 — 415
2. Levite teacher under Jehoshaphat ...... 2 Chr. 17:8 — 446

Shemuel—*name of God*

1. Grandson of Issachar .... 1 Chr. 7:1, 2 — 407
2. Representative of Simeon .... Num. 34:20 — 169

Shen—*tooth; a pointed rock*

Rock west of Jerusalem .... 1 Sam. 7:12 — 278

Shenazzar

Son of Jeconiah ...... 1 Chr. 3:18 — 403

Shepham—*nakedness*

Place near the Sea of Galilee .... Num. 34:11 — 169

Shephatiah—*Yahweh judges*

1. Benjamite warrior .... 1 Chr. 12:5 — 412
2. Son of David ..... 2 Sam. 3:4 — 308
3. Simeonite chief .... 1 Chr. 27:16 — 426
4. Son of King Jehoshaphat ...... 2 Chr. 21:2 — 450
5. Opponent of Jeremiah .... Jer. 38:1 — 788
6. Descendant of Judah .... Neh. 11:4 — 495
7. Servant of Solomon whose descendants return from exile .... Ezra 2:57 — 471

Shepher—*beauty*

Israelite encampment .... Num. 33:23 — 168

Shepherd—*one who cares for the sheep*

A. *Duties of, toward his flock:*
- Defend .... 1 Sam. 17:34-36 — 289
- Water .... Gen. 29:2-10 — 30
- Give rest to ...... Jer. 33:12 — 784
- Know .... John 10:3-5 — 1094
- Number .... Jer. 33:13 — 784
- Secure pasture for .... 1 Chr. 4:39-41 — 404
- Search for the lost .... Ezek. 34:12-16 — 853; Luke 15:4, 5 — 1063

B. *Good, described as:*
- Faithful .... Gen. 31:38-40 — 33
- Fearless .... 1 Sam. 17:34-36 — 289
- Unselfish .... Luke 15:3-6 — 1063
- Considerate ...... Gen. 33:13, 14 — 35
- Believing .... Luke 2:8-20 — 1043

C. *Bad, described as:*
- Unfaithful .... Ezek. 34:1-10 — 852
- Cowardly .... John 10:12, 13 — 1094
- Selfish .... Is. 56:11, 12 — 734
- Ruthless .... Ex. 2:17, 19 — 57
- Unbelieving ...... Jer. 50:6 — 800

D. *Descriptive of:*
- God .... Ps. 78:52, 53 — 588
- Christ .... John 10:11 — 1094; Heb. 13:20 — 1268
- Joshua .... Num. 27:16-23 — 162
- David .... 2 Sam. 5:2 — 309
- Judges .... 1 Chr. 17:6 — 417
- National leaders .... Jer. 49:19 — 799
- Cyrus .... Is. 44:28 — 723
- Church elders ..... 1 Pet. 5:2 — 1283

Shepherd, Jesus the Good

A. *Described prophetically in His:*
- Prophetic position (teaching) ...... Is. 40:10, 11 — 717
- Priestly position (sacrifice) .... Zech. 13:7 — 963; Matt. 26:31 — 1007
- Kingly position (ruling) .... Ezek. 37:24 — 856; Matt. 2:6 — 978

B. *Described typically as:*
- Good .... John 10:11, 14 — 1094
- Chief .... 1 Pet. 5:4 — 1283
- Great .... Heb. 13:20 — 1268
- Gentle .... Is. 40:11 — 717
- One who separates .... Matt. 25:31-46 — 1005

Shepho—*unconcern*

Son of Shobal .... Gen. 36:23 — 38

Sherebiah—*Yahweh has sent burning heat*

1. Levite family returning with Ezra .... Ezra 8:18 — 477
2. Levite who assists Ezra .... Neh. 8:7 — 491

Sheresh—*root*

Grandson of Manasseh .... 1 Chr. 7:16 — 408

Sheshach—(probably a cryptogram)

Symbolic of Babylon .... Jer. 25:26 — 774

Sheshai—*whitish*

Descendant of Anak .... Num. 13:22 — 146
Driven out by Caleb .... Josh. 15:14 — 227
Destroyed by Judah .... Judg. 1:10 — 241

Sheshan—*whitish*

Jerahmeelite .... 1 Chr. 2:31-35 — 402

Sheshbazzar—*sin (the moon-god) protect the father*

Prince of Judah ...... Ezra 1:8, 11 — 470

Shethar—*star*

Persian prince .... Esth. 1:14 — 502

Shethar-Boznai—*starry splendor*

Official of Persia .... Ezra 5:3, 6 — 474

Sheva—*self-satisfying*

1. Son of Caleb ..... 1 Chr. 2:43, 49 — 402
2. David's scribe .... 2 Sam. 20:25 — 326

Shibboleth—*stream, or ear of corn*

Password .... Judg. 12:5, 6 — 254

Shicron—*drunkenness*

Town of Judah .... Josh. 15:11 — 227

Shield—*a protective armor*

A. *Uses of:*
- Protection .... 2 Chr. 14:8 — 445
- Treasures in war .... 1 Kin. 14:25, 26 — 353
- Riches .... 2 Chr. 32:27 — 461
- Ornamenting public buildings .... 1 Kin. 10:17 — 348

B. *Figurative of:*
God's:
- Protection ...... Ps. 33:20 — 562
- Favor .... Ps. 5:12 — 547
- Salvation ...... Ps. 18:35 — 554
- Truth .... Ps. 91:4 — 595
- Faith .... Eph. 6:16 — 1209
- Rulers .... Ps. 47:9 — 570

Shiggaion—*a musical term*

Plural form:
Shigionoth .... Hab. 3:1 — 942

Shihor—*black; turbid*

Name given to the Nile .... Is. 23:3 — 702
Israel's southwestern border .... Josh. 13:3 — 225

Shihor Libnath—*turbid stream of Libnath*

Small river in Asher's territory .... Josh. 19:26 — 231

Shilhi—*Yahweh has sent*

Father of Azubah .... 1 Kin. 22:42 — 363

Shilhim—*missiles*

Town in south Judah .... Josh. 15:1, 32 — 227

Shillem—*compensation*

Son of Naphtali ...... Gen. 46:24 — 48

Shiloah—*sent*

A pool of Jerusalem, figurative of God's protection .... Is. 8:6 — 689
See Siloam

Shiloh

1. Town of Ephraim .... Judg. 21:19 — 263
   - Center of religious worship .... Judg. 18:31 — 259
   - Canaan divided here .... Josh. 18:1, 10 — 229
   - Benjamites seize women here .... Judg. 21:19-23 — 263

SUBJECT REFERENCE PAGE

SUBJECT REFERENCE PAGE

SUBJECT	REFERENCE	PAGE
Womb—continued		
Helpless	Ps. 22:9, 10	556
Sustained	Ps. 71:6	582
Estranged	Ps. 58:3	575
Women of the Bible, named		
Abi, wife of Ahaz	2 Kin. 18:1, 2	387
Abigail		
(1) wife of Nabal	1 Sam. 25:3	296
(2) sister of David	1 Chr. 2:15, 16	402
Abihail, wife of Abishur	1 Chr. 2:29	402
Abijah, wife of Hezron	1 Chr. 2:24	402
Abishag, nurse of David	1 Kin. 1:1-3	335
Abital, David's wife	2 Sam. 3:2, 4	308
Achsah, daughter of Caleb	Josh. 15:16	227
Adah		
(1) a wife of Lamech	Gen. 4:19	8
(2) Canaanite wife of Esau	Gen. 36:2	37
Ahinoam		
(1) wife of Saul	1 Sam. 14:50	286
(2) a Jezreelitess, wife of David	1 Sam. 25:43	298
Anah, daughter of Zibeon	Gen. 36:2	37
Anna, an aged widow	Luke 2:36, 37	1044
Apphia, a Christian of Colosse	Philem. 2	1253
Asenath, wife of Joseph	Gen. 41:45	43
Atarah, wife of Jerahmeel	1 Chr. 2:26	402
Athaliah, mother of Ahaziah	2 Kin. 8:26	376
Azubah		
(1) first wife of Caleb	1 Chr. 2:18	402
(2) daughter of Shilhi	1 Kin. 22:42	363
Baara, wife of Shaharaim	1 Chr. 8:8	408
Basemath		
(1) daughter of Elon	Gen. 26:34	28
(2) third wife of Esau	Gen. 36:2, 3	37
Bathsheba, wife of David	2 Sam. 11:3, 27	314
Bernice, sister of Agrippa	Acts 25:13	1141
Bilhah, Rachel's handmaid	Gen. 29:29	31
Bithiah, daughter of a pharaoh	1 Chr. 4:18	404
Candace, a queen	Acts 8:27	1121
Chloe, woman of Corinth	1 Cor. 1:11	1167
Claudia, Christian of Rome	2 Tim. 4:21	1246
Cozbi, Midianite slain	Num. 25:15-18	159
Damaris, woman of Athens	Acts 17:34	1133
Deborah		
(1) Rebekah's nurse	Gen. 35:8	37
(2) judge	Judg. 4:4	244
Delilah, Philistine woman	Judg. 16:4, 5	257
Dinah, daughter of Jacob	Gen. 30:19, 21	31
Dorcas, called Tabitha	Acts 9:36	1122
Drusilla, wife of Felix	Acts 24:24	1140
Eglah, one of David's wives	2 Sam. 3:5	308
Elizabeth, mother of John the Baptist	Luke 1:5, 13	1041
Elisheba, wife of Aaron	Ex. 6:23	61
Ephah, concubine of Caleb	1 Chr. 2:46	402
Ephrath, mother of Hur	1 Chr. 2:19	402
Esther, a Jewess who became queen of Persia	Esth. 2:16, 17	503
Eunice, mother of Timothy	2 Tim. 1:5	1243
Euodia, a laborer with Paul	Phil. 4:2	1215
Eve, first woman	Gen. 3:20	7
Gomer, wife of Hosea	Hos. 1:2, 3	890
Hagar, Sarai's maid	Gen. 16:1	17
Haggith, wife of David	2 Sam. 3:2, 4	308
Hammoleketh, mother of Ishhod	1 Chr. 7:18	408
Hamutal, daughter of Jeremiah	2 Kin. 23:31	394
Hannah, mother of Samuel	1 Sam. 1:20	273
Hazelelponi, in genealogies of Judah	1 Chr. 4:1-3	403
Helah, one of the wives of Ashhur	1 Chr. 4:5	403
Hephzibah, mother of Manasseh	2 Kin. 21:1	391
Herodias, sister-in-law of Herod	Matt. 14:3-6	992
Hodesh, wife of Shaharaim	1 Chr. 8:8, 9	408
Hoglah, a daughter of Zelophehad	Num. 26:33	160
Huldah, a prophetess	2 Kin. 22:14	392
Hushim, a Moabitess	1 Chr. 8:8-11	408
Iscah, daughter of Haran	Gen. 11:29	14
Jael, wife of Heber	Judg. 4:17	244
Jecholiah, wife of Amaziah	2 Kin. 15:1, 2	383
Jedidah, mother of Josiah	2 Kin. 22:1	392
Jehoaddan, wife of Joash	2 Kin. 14:1, 2	382
Jehosheba, daughter of Joram	2 Kin. 11:2	379
Jemimah, Job's daughter	Job 42:12, 14	541
Jerioth, wife of Caleb	1 Chr. 2:18	402
Jerusha, daughter of Zadok	2 Kin. 15:33	384
Jezebel, wife of Ahab	1 Kin. 16:30, 31	356
Joanna, wife of Chuza	Luke 8:3	1052
Jochebed, mother of Moses	Ex. 6:20	61
Judith, daughter of Beeri	Gen. 26:34	28
Julia, Christian woman of Rome	Rom. 16:15	1162
Keren-Happuch, Job's daughter	Job 42:14	541
Keturah, second wife of Abraham	Gen. 25:1	26
Keziah, daughter of Job	Job 42:14	541
Leah, wife of Jacob	Gen. 29:21-25	31
Lois, grandmother of Timothy	2 Tim. 1:5	1243
Lo-Ruhamah, daughter of Gomer	Hos. 1:3-6	890
Lydia, first Christian convert in Europe	Acts 16:14	1131
Maacah, Maachah		
(1) daughter of Nahor	Gen. 22:23, 24	23
(2) daughter of Talmai	2 Sam. 3:3	308
(3) granddaughter of Abishalom	1 Kin. 15:2	354
(4) grandmother of Asa	1 Kin. 15:9, 10	354
(5) concubine of Caleb	1 Chr. 2:48	402
(6) wife of Machir	1 Chr. 7:16	408
(7) wife of Jeiel	1 Chr. 8:29 1 Chr. 9:35	409 410
Mahalath		
(1) wife of Esau	Gen. 28:9	29
(2) granddaughter of David	2 Chr. 11:18	443
Mahlah, daughter of Zelophehad	Num. 26:33	160
Mara, another name for Naomi	Ruth 1:20	266
Martha, friend of Christ	Luke 10:38-41	1056
Mary		
(1) mother of Jesus	Matt. 1:16	977
(2) Mary Magdalene	Matt. 27:56-61	1010
(3) Mary, sister of Martha	Luke 10:38, 39	1056
(4) Mary, wife of Clopas	John 19:25	1104
(5) Mary, mother of Mark	Acts 12:12	1126
(6) a Christian at Rome	Rom. 16:6	1162
Matred, mother-in-law of Hadar	Gen. 36:39	38
Mehetabel, daughter of Matred	Gen. 36:39	38
Merab, King Saul's eldest daughter	1 Sam. 14:49	285
Meshullemeth, wife of Manasseh	2 Kin. 21:18, 19	391
Michal, daughter of King Saul	1 Sam. 14:49	285
Milcah		
(1) daughter of Haran	Gen. 11:29	14
(2) daughter of Zelophehad	Num. 26:33	160
Miriam		
(1) sister of Moses	Ex. 15:20	70
(2) disputed daughter of Ezrah	1 Chr. 4:17	404
Naamah		
(1) daughter of Lamech	Gen. 4:19-22	8
(2) wife of Solomon	1 Kin. 14:21	353
Naarah, one of the wives of Ashhur	1 Chr. 4:5	403
Naomi, wife of Elimelech	Ruth 1:2	266
Nehushta, daughter of Elnathan	2 Kin. 24:8	395
Noadiah, a false prophetess	Neh. 6:14	488
Noah, daughter of Zelophehad	Num. 26:33	160
Oholah	Ezek. 23:4	840
Oholibah	Ezek. 23:4	840
Orpah, sister-in-law of Ruth	Ruth 1:4	266
Peninnah, one of the wives of Elkanah	1 Sam. 1:1, 2	272
Persis, convert of early church	Rom. 16:12	1162
Phoebe, a deaconess	Rom. 16:1, 2	1162
Priscilla, wife of Aquila	Acts 18:2	1133
Puah, a midwife	Ex. 1:15	56
Rachel, wife of Jacob	Gen. 29:28	31
Rahab, aid to Israel's spies	Josh. 2:1-3	215
Reumah, mother of Tebah	Gen. 22:24	23
Rhoda, a girl	Acts 12:13	1126
Rizpah, concubine of Saul	2 Sam. 3:7	308
Ruth, daughter-in-law of Naomi	Ruth 1:3, 4	266
Salome, wife of Zebedee	Matt. 27:56 Mark 15:40	1010 1035

SUBJECT REFERENCE PAGE

Zephaniah, Book of—*a book of the Old Testament*
Coming judgment .... Zeph. 1:2-18 945
Call to repentance .... Zeph. 2:1-3 946
The nations judged .... Zeph. 2:4-15 946
Jerusalem is blessed .... Zeph. 3:9-20 947

Zephath—*watchtower*
Canaanite town destroyed by Simeon and Judah .... Judg. 1:17 241
See Hormah

Zephathah
Valley near Mareshah .... 2 Chr. 14:10 445

Zepho, Zephi—*watch*
Grandson of Esau and a chief of Edom .... Gen. 36:15, 19 38; 1 Chr. 1:36 401

Zephon—*watching*
Son of Gad and tribal head .... Num. 26:15 160
Called Ziphion .... Gen. 46:16 48

Zer—*rock*
City assigned to Naphtali .... Josh. 19:32, 35 231

Zerah—*dawning*
1. Son of Reuel and chief of Edom .... Gen. 36:17, 19 38; 1 Chr. 1:44 401
2. Son of Judah .... Num. 26:20 160
Ancestor of Achan .... Josh. 7:1-18 219
3. Son of Simeon and tribal head .... Num. 26:12, 13 160
Called Zohar .... Gen. 46:10 48
4. Gershomite Levite .... 1 Chr. 6:20, 21, 41 405
5. Ethiopian general defeated by King Asa .... 2 Chr. 14:8-15 445

Zerahiah—*Yahweh is appearing*
1. Ancestor of Ezra .... Ezra 7:1, 4, 5 475
2. Son of Pahath-Moab .... Ezra 8:4 477

Zered—*willow bush*
Brook and valley crossed by Israel .... Num. 21:12 155

Zereda, Zeredah—*the fortress*
1. City of Ephraim; birthplace of Jeroboam .... 1 Kin. 11:26 349
2. City in the Jordan Valley .... 2 Chr. 4:17 436
Same as Zaretan in .... 1 Kin. 7:46 344

Zererah
Town in the Jordan Valley .... Judg. 7:22 248
Same as Zaretan .... 1 Kin. 7:46 344

Zeresh—*golden*
Wife of Haman .... Esth. 5:10, 14 505

Zereth—*splendor*
Judahite .... 1 Chr. 4:5-7 403

Zereth Shahar—*the splendor of dawn*
City of Reuben .... Josh. 13:19 226

Zeror—*bundle*
Benjamite .... 1 Sam. 9:1 279

Zeruah—*smitten; leprous*
Mother of King Jeroboam I .... 1 Kin. 11:26 349

Zerubbabel—*seed of Babel*
Descendant of David .... 1 Chr. 3:19 403
Leader of Jewish exiles .... Neh. 7:6, 7 489
Restores worship in Jerusalem .... Ezra 3:1-8 472
Rebuilds the temple .... Zech. 4:1-14 957
Prophecy concerning .... Hag. 2:23 952
Ancestor of Christ .... Matt. 1:12, 13 977; Luke 3:27 1045

Zeruiah—*balm*
Half sister of David .... 1 Chr. 2:16 402
Mother of Joab, Abishai, and Asahel .... 2 Sam. 2:18 307

Zetham—*olive tree*
Gershonite Levite .... 1 Chr. 23:7, 8 422

Zethan—*olive tree*
Benjamite .... 1 Chr. 7:6, 10 407

Zethar—*sacrifice*
One of the seven eunuchs of King Ahasuerus .... Esth. 1:10 502

Zia—*the trembler*
Gadite .... 1 Chr. 5:11, 13 405

Ziba—*plant*
Saul's servant .... 2 Sam. 9:9 313
Befriends David .... 2 Sam. 16:1-4 320
Accused of deception by Mephibosheth .... 2 Sam. 19:17-30 324

Zibeon—*hyena*
Son of Seir and a clan chief .... Gen. 36:20, 21 38

Zibia—*gazelle*
Benjamite and household head .... 1 Chr. 8:8, 9 408

Zibiah—*gazelle*
Mother of King Jehoash .... 2 Kin. 12:1 380

Zichri—*famous*
1. Kohathite Levite .... Ex. 6:21 61
2, 3, 4. Three Benjamites .... 1 Chr. 8:19, 23, 27 408
5. Son of Asaph .... 1 Chr. 9:15 409
6. Descendant of Moses .... 1 Chr. 26:25 425
7. Reubenite .... 1 Chr. 27:16 426
8. Judahite .... 2 Chr. 17:16 447
9. Mighty man in Pekah's army .... 2 Chr. 28:7 456
10. Benjamite .... Neh. 11:9 495
11. Postexilic priest .... Neh. 12:17 496

Ziddim—*sides*
City of Naphtali .... Josh. 19:35 231

Ziha
Head of a Nethinim family .... Ezra 2:43 471

Ziklag—*winding*
City on the border of Judah .... Josh. 15:1, 31 227
Assigned to Simeon .... Josh. 19:1, 5 230
Held by David .... 1 Sam. 27:6 299
Overthrown by Amalekites .... 1 Sam. 30:1-31 301
Occupied by returnees .... Neh. 11:28 496

Zillah—*shadow*
One of Lamech's wives .... Gen. 4:19-23 8

Zillethai—*shadow of Yahweh*
1. Benjamite .... 1 Chr. 8:20 408
2. Manassite captain .... 1 Chr. 12:20 413

Zilpah—*a drop*
Leah's maid .... Gen. 29:24 31
Mother of Gad and Asher .... Gen. 30:9-13 31

Zimmah—*counsel*
Gershonite Levite .... 1 Chr. 6:20, 42, 43 405

Zimran—*antelope*
Son of Abraham and Keturah .... Gen. 25:1, 2 26

Zimri—*pertaining to an antelope*
1. Grandson of Judah .... 1 Chr. 2:3-6 401
Called Zabdi .... Josh. 7:1-18 219
2. Simeonite prince slain by Phinehas .... Num. 25:6-14 159
3. Benjamite .... 1 Chr. 8:1, 36 408
4. King of Israel for seven days .... 1 Kin. 16:8-20 355
5. Place or people otherwise unknown .... Jer. 25:25 774

Zin—*lowland*
Wilderness through which the Israelites passed .... Num. 20:1 153
Border of Judah and Edom .... Josh. 15:1-3 227

Zina—*abundance*
Son of Shimei .... 1 Chr. 23:10 422

Zion—*fortress*
A. *Used literally of:*
Jebusite fortress captured by David .... 2 Sam. 5:6-9 310
Place from which Solomon brings the ark .... 2 Chr. 5:2 436
Area occupied by the temple .... Is. 8:18 690
B. *Used figuratively of:*
Israel as a people of God .... 2 Kin. 19:21 389
God's spiritual kingdom .... Ps. 125:1 615
Eternal city .... Heb. 12:22, 28 1267
Heaven .... Rev. 14:1 1321

Zior—*smallness*
Town of Judah .... Josh. 15:54 228

Ziph—*refining place*
1. Town in south Judah .... Josh. 15:24 228
2. City in the hill country of Judah .... Josh. 15:55 228
David hides from Saul in wilderness here .... 1 Sam. 23:14, 15 295
3. Son of Jehallelel .... 1 Chr. 4:16 404

Read Your Bible Through In a Year

A systematic division of the books of the Bible, primarily for reading.

JANUARY

Date	MORNING	EVENING
	MATT.	**GEN.**
1	1	1, 2, 3
2	2	4, 5, 6
3	3	7, 8, 9
4	4	10, 11, 12
5	5: 1–26	13, 14, 15
6	5:27–48	16, 17
7	6: 1–18	18, 19
8	6:19–34	20, 21, 22
9	7	23, 24
10	8: 1–17	25, 26
11	8:18–34	27, 28
12	9: 1–17	29, 30
13	9:18–38	31, 32
14	10: 1–20	33, 34, 35
15	10:21–42	36, 37, 38
16	11	39, 40
17	12: 1–23	41, 42
18	12:24–50	43, 44, 45
19	13: 1–30	46, 47, 48
20	13:31–58	49, 50
		EX.
21	14: 1–21	1, 2, 3
22	14:22–36	4, 5, 6
23	15: 1–20	7, 8
24	15:21–39	9, 10, 11
25	16	12, 13
26	17	14, 15
27	18: 1–20	16, 17, 18
28	18:21–35	19, 20
29	19	21, 22
30	20: 1–16	23, 24
31	20:17–34	25, 26

FEBRUARY

Date	MORNING	EVENING
	MATT.	**EX.**
1	21: 1–22	27, 28
2	21:23–46	29, 30
3	22: 1–22	31, 32, 33
4	22:23–46	34, 35
5	23: 1–22	36, 37, 38
6	23:23–39	39, 40
		LEV.
7	24: 1–28	1, 2, 3
8	24:29–51	4, 5
9	25: 1–30	6, 7
10	25:31–46	8, 9, 10
11	26: 1–25	11, 12
12	26:26–50	13
13	26:51–75	14
14	27: 1–26	15, 16
15	27:27–50	17, 18
16	27:51–66	19, 20
17	28	21, 22
	MARK	
18	1: 1–22	23, 24
19	1:23–45	25
20	2	26, 27
		NUM.
21	3: 1–19	1, 2
22	3:20–35	3, 4
23	4: 1–20	5, 6
24	4:21–41	7, 8
25	5: 1–20	9, 10, 11
26	5:21–43	12, 13, 14
27	6: 1–29	15, 16
28	6:30–56	17, 18, 19
29	7: 1–13	20, 21, 22

MARCH

Date	MORNING	EVENING
	MARK	**NUM.**
1	7:14–37	23, 24, 25
2	8: 1–21	26, 27
3	8:22–38	28, 29, 30
4	9: 1–29	31, 32, 33
5	9:30–50	34, 35, 36
		DEUT.
6	10: 1–31	1, 2
7	10:32–52	3, 4
8	11: 1–18	5, 6, 7
9	11:19–33	8, 9, 10
10	12: 1–27	11, 12, 13
11	12:28–44	14, 15, 16
12	13: 1–20	17, 18, 19
13	13:21–37	20, 21, 22
14	14: 1–26	23, 24, 25
15	14:27–53	26, 27
16	14:54–72	28, 29
17	15: 1–25	30, 31
18	15:26–47	32, 33, 34
		JOSH.
19	16	1, 2, 3
	LUKE	
20	1: 1–20	4, 5, 6
21	1:21–38	7, 8, 9
22	1:39–56	10, 11, 12
23	1:57–80	13, 14, 15
24	2: 1–24	16, 17, 18
25	2:25–52	19, 20, 21
26	3	22, 23, 24
		JUDG.
27	4: 1–30	1, 2, 3
28	4:31–44	4, 5, 6
29	5: 1–16	7, 8
30	5:17–39	9, 10
31	6: 1–26	11, 12

APRIL

Date	MORNING	EVENING
	LUKE	**JUDG.**
1	6:27–49	13, 14, 15
2	7: 1–30	16, 17, 18
3	7:31–50	19, 20, 21
		RUTH
4	8: 1–25	1, 2, 3, 4
		1 SAM.
5	8:26–56	1, 2, 3
6	9: 1–17	4, 5, 6
7	9:18–36	7, 8, 9
8	9:37–62	10, 11, 12
9	10: 1–24	13, 14
10	10:25–42	15, 16
11	11: 1–28	17, 18
12	11:29–54	19, 20, 21
13	12: 1–31	22, 23, 24
14	12:32–59	25, 26
15	13: 1–22	27, 28, 29
16	13:23–35	30, 31
		2 SAM.
17	14: 1–24	1, 2
18	14:25–35	3, 4, 5
19	15: 1–10	6, 7, 8
20	15:11–32	9, 10, 11
21	16	12, 13
22	17: 1–19	14, 15
23	17:20–37	16, 17, 18
24	18: 1–23	19, 20
25	18:24–43	21, 22
26	19: 1–27	23, 24
		1 KIN.
27	19:28–48	1, 2
28	20: 1–26	3, 4, 5
29	20:27–47	6, 7
30	21: 1–19	8, 9

MAY

Date	MORNING	EVENING
	LUKE	**1 KIN.**
1	21:20–38	10, 11
2	22: 1–20	12, 13
3	22:21–46	14, 15
4	22:47–71	16, 17, 18
5	23: 1–25	19, 20
6	23:26–56	21, 22
		2 KIN.
7	24: 1–35	1, 2, 3
8	24:36–53	4, 5, 6
	JOHN	
9	1: 1–28	7, 8, 9
10	1:29–51	10, 11, 12
11	2	13, 14
12	3: 1–18	15, 16
13	3:19–38	17, 18
14	4: 1–30	19, 20, 21
15	4:31–54	22, 23
16	5: 1–24	24, 25
		1 CHR.
17	5:25–47	1, 2, 3
18	6: 1–21	4, 5, 6
19	6:22–44	7, 8, 9
20	6:45–71	10, 11, 12
21	7: 1–27	13, 14, 15
22	7:28–53	16, 17, 18
23	8: 1–27	19, 20, 21
24	8:28–59	22, 23, 24
25	9: 1–23	25, 26, 27
26	9:24–41	28, 29
		2 CHR.
27	10: 1–23	1, 2, 3
28	10:24–42	4, 5, 6
29	11: 1–29	7, 8, 9
30	11:30–57	10, 11, 12
31	12: 1–26	13, 14

JUNE

Date	MORNING	EVENING
	JOHN	**2 CHR.**
1	12:27–50	15, 16
2	13: 1–20	17, 18
3	13:21–38	19, 20
4	14	21, 22
5	15	23, 24
6	16	25, 26, 27
7	17	28, 29
8	18: 1–18	30, 31
9	18:19–40	32, 33
10	19: 1–22	34, 35, 36
		EZRA
11	19:23–42	1, 2
12	20	3, 4, 5
13	21	6, 7, 8
	ACTS	
14	1	9, 10
		NEH.
15	2: 1–21	1, 2, 3
16	2:22–47	4, 5, 6
17	3	7, 8, 9
18	4: 1–22	10, 11
19	4:23–37	12, 13
		ESTH.
20	5: 1–21	1, 2
21	5:22–42	3, 4, 5
22	6	6, 7, 8
23	7: 1–21	9, 10
		JOB
24	7:22–43	1, 2
25	7:44–60	3, 4
26	8: 1–25	5, 6, 7
27	8:26–40	8, 9, 10
28	9: 1–21	11, 12, 13
29	9:22–43	14, 15, 16
30	10: 1–23	17, 18, 19

JULY

Date	MORNING ACTS	EVENING JOB
1	10:24–48	20, 21
2	11	22, 23, 24
3	12	25, 26, 27
4	13: 1–25	28, 29
5	13:26–52	30, 31
6	14	32, 33
7	15: 1–21	34, 35
8	15:22–41	36, 37
9	16: 1–21	38, 39, 40
10	16:22–40	41, 42
		PS.
11	17: 1–15	1, 2, 3
12	17:16–34	4, 5, 6
13	18	7, 8, 9
14	19: 1–20	10, 11, 12
15	19:21–41	13, 14, 15
16	20: 1–16	16, 17
17	20:17–38	18, 19
18	21: 1–17	20, 21, 22
19	21:18–40	23, 24, 25
20	22	26, 27, 28
21	23: 1–15	29, 30
22	23:16–35	31, 32
23	24	33, 34
24	25	35, 36
25	26	37, 38, 39
26	27: 1–26	40, 41, 42
27	27:27–44	43, 44, 45
28	28	46, 47, 48
	ROM.	
29	1	49, 50
30	2	51, 52, 53
31	3	54, 55, 56

AUGUST

Date	MORNING ROM.	EVENING PS.
1	4	57, 58, 59
2	5	60, 61, 62
3	6	63, 64, 65
4	7	66, 67
5	8: 1–21	68, 69
6	8:22–39	70, 71
7	9: 1–15	72, 73
8	9:16–33	74, 75, 76
9	10	77, 78
10	11: 1–18	79, 80
11	11:19–36	81, 82, 83
12	12	84, 85, 86
13	13	87, 88
14	14	89, 90
15	15: 1–13	91, 92, 93
16	15:14–33	94, 95, 96
17	16	97, 98, 99
	1 COR.	
18	1	100, 101, 102
19	2	103, 104
20	3	105, 106
21	4	107, 108, 109
22	5	110, 111, 112
23	6	113, 114, 115
24	7: 1–19	116, 117, 118
25	7:20–40	119: 1– 88
26	8	119: 89–176
27	9	120, 121, 122
28	10: 1–18	123, 124, 125
29	10:19–33	126, 127, 128
30	11: 1–16	129, 130, 131
31	11:17–34	132, 133, 134

SEPTEMBER

Date	MORNING 1 COR.	EVENING PS.
1	12	135, 136
2	13	137, 138, 139
3	14: 1–20	140, 141, 142
4	14:21–40	143, 144, 145
5	15: 1–28	146, 147
6	15:29–58	148, 149, 150
		PROV.
7	16	1, 2
	2 COR.	
8	1	3, 4, 5
9	2	6, 7
10	3	8, 9
11	4	10, 11, 12
12	5	13, 14, 15
13	6	16, 17, 18
14	7	19, 20, 21
15	8	22, 23, 24
16	9	25, 26
17	10	27, 28, 29
18	11: 1–15	30, 31
		ECCL.
19	11:16–33	1, 2, 3
20	12	4, 5, 6
21	13	7, 8, 9
	GAL.	
22	1	10, 11, 12
		SONG
23	2	1, 2, 3
24	3	4, 5
25	4	6, 7, 8
		IS.
26	5	1, 2
27	6	3, 4
	EPH.	
28	1	5, 6
29	2	7, 8
30	3	9, 10

OCTOBER

Date	MORNING EPH.	EVENING IS.
1	4	11, 12, 13
2	5: 1–16	14, 15, 16
3	5:17–33	17, 18, 19
4	6	20, 21, 22
	PHIL.	
5	1	23, 24, 25
6	2	26, 27
7	3	28, 29
8	4	30, 31
	COL.	
9	1	32, 33
10	2	34, 35, 36
11	3	37, 38
12	4	39, 40
	1 THESS.	
13	1	41, 42
14	2	43, 44
15	3	45, 46
16	4	47, 48, 49
17	5	50, 51, 52
	2 THESS.	
18	1	53, 54, 55
19	2	56, 57, 58
20	3	59, 60, 61
	1 TIM.	
21	1	62, 63, 64
22	2	65, 66
		JER.
23	3	1, 2
24	4	3, 4, 5
25	5	6, 7, 8
26	6	9, 10, 11
	2 TIM.	
27	1	12, 13, 14
28	2	15, 16, 17
29	3	18, 19
30	4	20, 21
	TITUS	
31	1	22, 23

NOVEMBER

Date	MORNING TITUS	EVENING JER.
1	2	24, 25, 26
2	3	27, 28, 29
3	**PHILEM.**	30, 31
	HEB.	
4	1	32, 33
5	2	34, 35, 36
6	3	37, 38, 39
7	4	40, 41, 42
8	5	43, 44, 45
9	6	46, 47
10	7	48, 49
11	8	50
12	9	51, 52
		LAM.
13	10: 1–18	1, 2
14	10:19–39	3, 4, 5
		EZEK.
15	11: 1–19	1, 2
16	11:20–40	3, 4
17	12	5, 6, 7
18	13	8, 9, 10
	JAMES	
19	1	11, 12, 13
20	2	14, 15
21	3	16, 17
22	4	18, 19
23	5	20, 21
	1 PET.	
24	1	22, 23
25	2	24, 25, 26
26	3	27, 28, 29
27	4	30, 31, 32
28	5	33, 34
	2 PET.	
29	1	35, 36
30	2	37, 38, 39

DECEMBER

Date	MORNING 2 PET.	EVENING EZEK.
1	3	40, 41
	1 JOHN	
2	1	42, 43, 44
3	2	45, 46
4	3	47, 48
		DAN.
5	4	1, 2
6	5	3, 4
7	**2 JOHN**	5, 6, 7
8	**3 JOHN**	8, 9, 10
9	**JUDE**	11, 12
	REV.	**HOS.**
10	1	1, 2, 3, 4
11	2	5, 6, 7, 8
12	3	9, 10, 11
13	4	12, 13, 14
14	5	**JOEL**
		AMOS
15	6	1, 2, 3
16	7	4, 5, 6
17	8	7, 8, 9
18	9	**OBAD.**
19	10	**JON.**
		MIC.
20	11	1, 2, 3
21	12	4, 5
22	13	6, 7
23	14	**NAH.**
24	15	**HAB.**
25	16	**ZEPH.**
26	17	**HAG.**
		ZECH.
27	18	1, 2, 3, 4
28	19	5, 6, 7, 8
29	20	9, 10, 11, 12
30	21	13, 14
31	22	**MAL.**

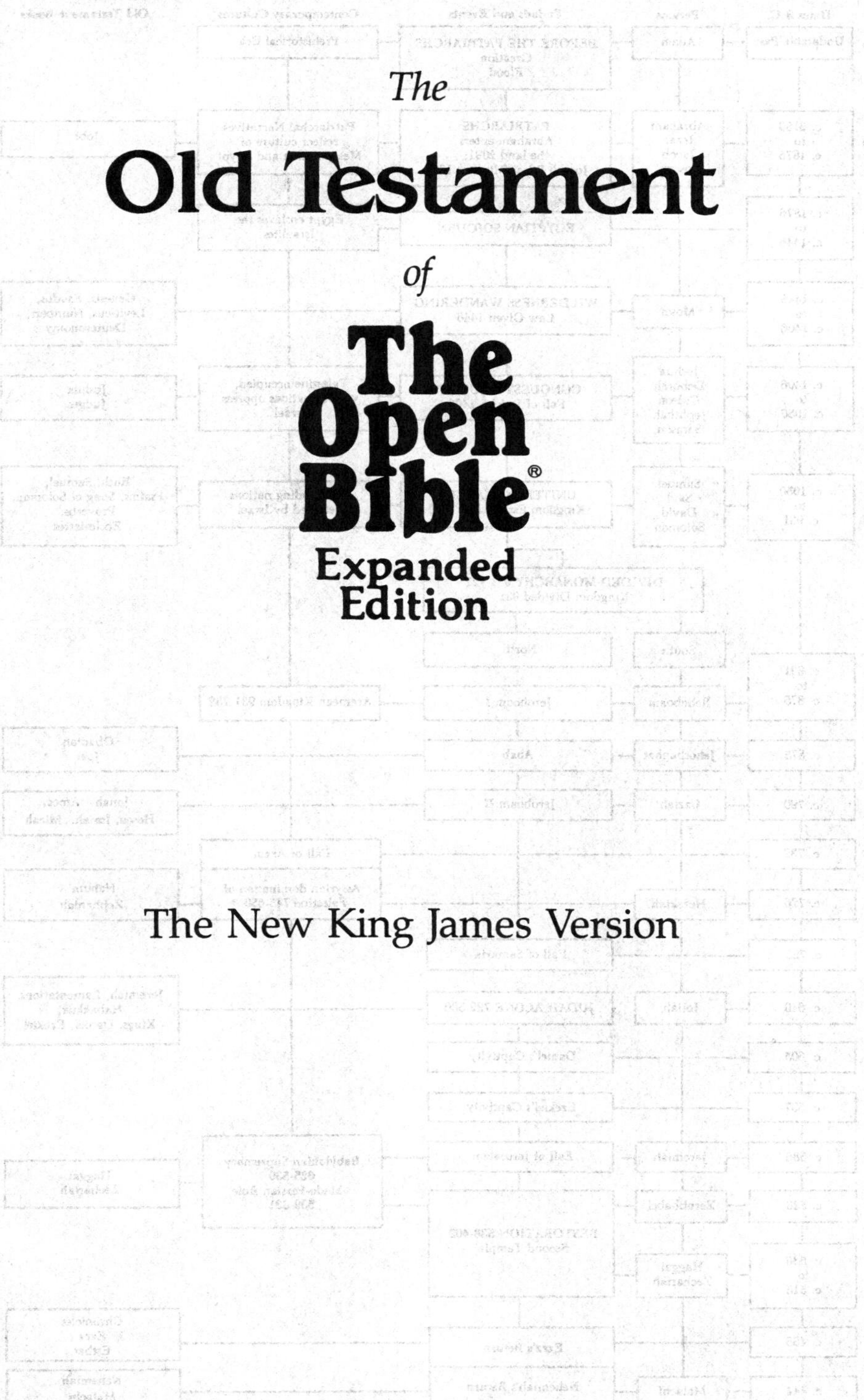

The

Old Testament

of

The Open Bible®

Expanded Edition

The New King James Version

Old Testament Chronology

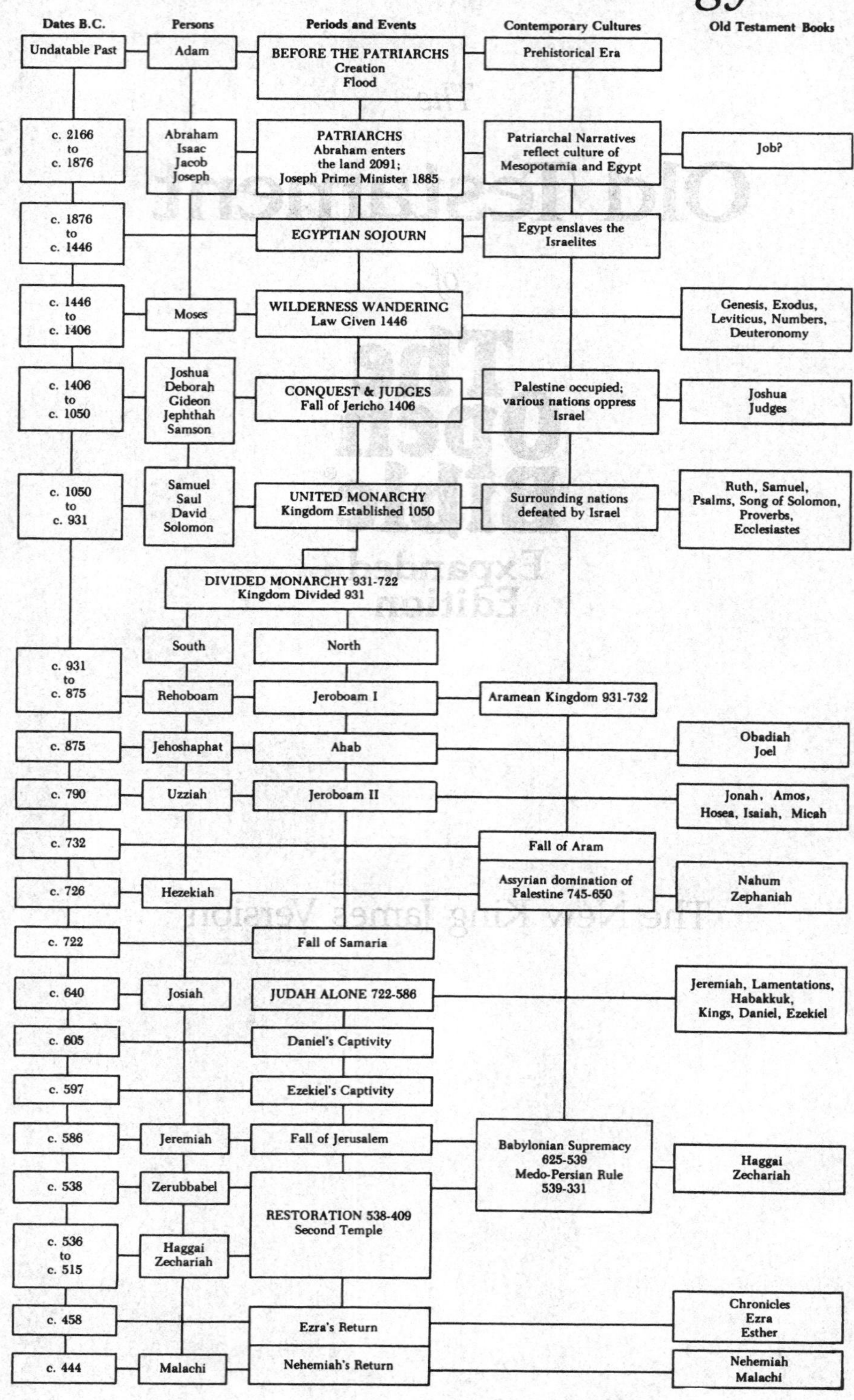

THE FIRST BOOK OF MOSES CALLED

GENESIS

THE BOOK OF GENESIS

The first part of Genesis focuses on the beginning and spread of sin in the world and culminates in the devastating flood in the days of Noah. The second part of the book focuses on God's dealings with one man, Abraham, through whom God promises to bring salvation and blessing to the world. Abraham and his descendants learn firsthand that it is always safe to trust the Lord in times of famine and feasting, blessing and bondage. From Abraham . . . to Isaac . . . to Jacob . . . to Joseph . . . God's promises begin to come to fruition in a great nation possessing a great land.

Genesis is a Greek word meaning "origin," "source," "generation," or "beginning." The original Hebrew title *Bereshith* means "In the Beginning."

The literary structure of Genesis is clear and is built around eleven separate units, each headed with the word *generations* in the phrase "These are the generations" or "The book of the generations": (1) Introduction to the Generations (1:1—2:3); (2) Heaven and Earth (2:4—4:26); (3) Adam (5:1—6:8); (4) Noah (6:9—9:29); (5) Sons of Noah (10:1—11:9); (6) Shem (11:10–26); (7) Terah (11:27—25:11); (8) Ishmael (25:12–18); (9) Isaac (25:19—35:29); (10) Esau (36:1—37:1); (11) Jacob (37:2—50:26).

THE AUTHOR OF GENESIS

Although Genesis does not directly name its author, and although Genesis ends some three centuries before Moses was born, the whole of Scripture and church history are unified in their adherence to the Mosaic authorship of Genesis.

The Old Testament is replete with both direct and indirect testimonies to the Mosaic authorship of the entire Pentateuch (Ex. 17:14; Lev. 1:1, 2; Num. 33:2; Deut. 1:1; Josh. 1:7; 1 Kin. 2:3; 2 Kin. 14:6; Ezra 6:18; Neh. 13:1; Dan. 9:11–13; Mal. 4:4). The New Testament also contains numerous testimonies (Matt. 8:4; Mark 12:26; Luke 16:29; John 7:19; Acts 26:22; Rom. 10:19; 1 Cor. 9:9; 2 Cor. 3:15).

The early church openly held to the Mosaic authorship, as does the first-century Jewish historian Josephus. As would be expected, the Jerusalem Talmud supports Moses as author.

It would be difficult to find a man in all the range of Israel's life who was better prepared or qualified to write this history. Trained in the "wisdom of the Egyptians" (Acts 7:22), Moses had been providentially prepared to understand and integrate, under the inspiration of God, all the available records, manuscripts, and oral narratives.

THE TIME OF GENESIS

Genesis divides neatly into three geographical settings: (1) the Fertile Crescent (1—11); (2) Israel (12—36); (3) Egypt (37—50).

The setting of the first eleven chapters changes rapidly as it spans more than two thousand years and fifteen hundred miles, and paints the majestic acts of the Creation, the Garden of Eden, the Noahic Flood, and the towering citadel of Babel.

The middle section of Genesis rapidly funnels down from the broad brim of the two millennia spent in the Fertile Crescent to less than two hundred years in the little country of Canaan. Surrounded by the rampant immorality and idolatry of the Canaanites, the godliness of Abraham rapidly degenerates into gross immorality in some of his descendants.

In the last fourteen chapters, God dramatically saves the small Israelite nation from extinction by transferring the seventy persons to Egypt so that they may grow and multiply. Egypt is an unexpected womb for the growth of God's chosen nation Israel, to be sure, but one in which they are isolated from the maiming influence of Canaan.

Genesis spans more time than any other book in the Bible; in fact, it covers more than all sixty-five other books of the Bible put together.

Utilizing the same threefold division noted above, the following dates can be assigned:

A. 2,000 or more years, 4000–2090 B.C. (Gen. 1—11)
   1. Creation, 4000 B.C. or earlier (Gen. 1:1)
   2. Death of Terah, 2090 B.C. (Gen. 11:32)

B. 193 years, 2090–1897 B.C. (Gen. 12—36)
   1. Death of Terah, 2090 B.C. (Gen. 11:32)
   2. Joseph to Egypt, c. 1897 B.C. (Gen. 37:2)

C. 93 years, 1897–1804 B.C. (Gen. 37—50)
   1. Joseph to Egypt, c. 1897 B.C. (Gen. 37:2)
   2. Death of Joseph, 1804 B.C. (Gen. 50:26)

THE CHRIST OF GENESIS

Genesis moves from the general to the specific in its messianic predictions: Christ is the Seed of the woman (3:15), from the line of Seth (4:25), the son of Shem (9:27), the descendant of Abraham (12:3), of Isaac (21:12), of Jacob (25:23), and of the tribe of Judah (49:10).

Christ is also seen in people and events that serve as types. (A "type" is a historical fact that illustrates a spiritual truth.) Adam is "a type of Him who was to come" (Rom. 5:14). Both entered the world through a special act of God as sinless men. Adam is the head of the old creation; Christ is the Head of the new creation. Abel's acceptable offering of a blood sacrifice points to Christ, and there is a parallel in his murder by Cain. Melchizedek ("Righteous King") is "made like the Son of God" (Heb. 7:3). He is the king of Salem ("Peace") who brings forth bread and wine and is the priest of the Most High God. Joseph is also a type of Christ. Joseph and Christ are both objects of special love by their fathers, both are hated by their brothers, both are rejected as rulers over their brothers, both are conspired against and sold for silver, both are condemned though innocent, and both are raised from humiliation to glory by the power of God.

KEYS TO GENESIS

Key Word: Beginnings—Genesis gives the beginning of almost everything, including the beginning of the universe, life, man, sabbath, death, marriage, sin, redemption, family, literature, cities, art, language, and sacrifice.

Key Verses: Genesis 3:15; 12:3—"And I will put enmity between you and the woman, and between your seed and her Seed; He shall bruise your head, and you shall bruise His heel" (3:15).

"I will bless those who bless you, and I will curse him who curses you; and in you all the families of the earth shall be blessed" (12:3).

Key Chapter: Genesis 15—Central to all of Scripture is the Abrahamic covenant, which is given in 12:1–3 and ratified in 15:1–21. Israel receives three specific promises: (1) the promise of a great land—"from the river of Egypt to the great river, the River Euphrates" (15:18); (2) the promise of a great nation—"and I will make your descendants as the dust of the earth" (13:16); and (3) the promise of a great blessing—"I will bless you and make your name great; and you shall be a blessing" (12:2).

SURVEY OF GENESIS

Genesis is not so much a history of man as it is the first chapter in the history of the *redemption* of man. As such, Genesis is a highly selective spiritual interpretation of history. Genesis is divided into four great events (1—11) and four great people (12—50).

The Four Great Events: Chapters 1—11 lay the foundation upon which the whole Bible is built and center on four key events. (1) *Creation:* God is the sovereign Creator of matter, energy, space, and time. Man is the pinnacle of the Creation. (2) *Fall:* Creation is followed by corruption. In the first sin man is separated from God (Adam from God), and in the second sin, man is separated from man (Cain from Abel). In spite of the devastating curse of the Fall, God promises hope of redemption through the Seed of the woman (3:15). (3) *Flood:* As man multiplies, sin also multiplies until God is compelled to destroy humanity with the exception of Noah and his family. (4) *Nations:* Genesis teaches the unity of the human race: we are all children of Adam through Noah, but because of rebellion at the Tower of Babel, God fragments the single culture and language of the post-flood world and scatters people over the face of the earth.

The Four Great People: Once the nations are scattered, God focuses on one man and his descendants through whom He will bless all nations (12—50). (1) *Abraham:* The calling of Abraham (12) is the pivotal point of the book. The three covenant promises God makes to Abraham (land, descendants, and blessing) are foundational to His program of bringing salvation upon the earth. (2) *Isaac:* God establishes

FOCUS	FOUR EVENTS				FOUR PEOPLE			
REFERENCE	1:1——3:1——6:1——10:1——12:1——25:19——27:1——37:1—50:26							
DIVISION	CREATION	FALL	FLOOD	NATIONS	ABRAHAM	ISAAC	JACOB	JOSEPH
TOPIC	HUMAN RACE				HEBREW RACE			
	HISTORICAL				BIOGRAPHICAL			
LOCATION	FERTILE CRESCENT (Eden-Haran)				CANAAN (Haran-Canaan)			EGYPT (Canaan-Egypt)
TIME	c. 2000 YEARS (c. 4004–2090 B.C)				193 YEARS (2090–1897 B.C.)			93 YEARS (1897–1804 B.C.)

His covenant with Isaac as the spiritual link with Abraham. (3) *Jacob:* God transforms this man from selfishness to servanthood and changes his name to Israel, the father of the twelve tribes. (4) *Joseph:* Jacob's favorite son suffers at the hands of his brothers and becomes a slave in Egypt. After his dramatic rise to the rulership of Egypt, Joseph delivers his family from famine and brings them out of Canaan to Goshen.

Genesis ends on a note of impending bondage with the death of Joseph. There is great need for the redemption that is to follow in the Book of Exodus.

OUTLINE OF GENESIS

Part One: Primeval History (1:1—11:9)

I. The Creation ....1:1—2:25

A. Creation of the World....................1:1—2:3
B. Creation of Human Beings 2:4–25

II. The Fall ....3:1—5:32

A. The Fall of Man and Woman....................3:1–24
1. The Temptation 3:1–5
2. The Fall....................3:6, 7
3. Judgment on Man and Woman 3:8–24
B. After the Fall: Conflicting Family Lines ....4:1—5:32
1. The Initial Conflict 4:1–15
2. The Ungodly Line of Cain 4:16–24
3. The Godly Line of Seth ....4:25—5:32

III. The Judgment of the Flood ....6:1—9:29

A. Causes of the Flood 6:1–5
1. The Ungodly Multiply 6:1–4
2. The Ungodly Sin Continually 6:5
B. Judgment of the Flood....................6:6–22
1. The Ungodly to Be Destroyed 6:6, 7
2. The Godly to Be Saved 6:8–22
C. The Flood....................7:1—8:19
1. The Ark Is Entered 7:1–10
2. The Earth Is Flooded....................7:11–24
3. The Flood Recedes 8:1–19
D. Results of the Flood ....8:20—9:17
1. Noah Worships God 8:20–22
2. God's Covenant with Noah....................9:1–17
E. After the Flood: The Sin of the Godly Line....................9:18–29
1. The Sons of Noah 9:18, 19
2. Ham's Sin 9:20–24
3. The Curse on Canaan 9:25–27
4. Noah's Death....................9:28, 29

IV. The Judgment on the Tower of Babel....................10:1—11:9

A. Family Lines After the Flood....................10:1–32
1. The Family of Japheth....................10:1–5
2. The Family of Ham 10:6–14
3. The Family of Canaan 10:15–20
4. The Family of Shem....................10:21–32
B. Judgment on All the Family Lines....................11:1–9
1. Construction of the Tower 11:1–3
2. Rebellion at the Tower....................11:4
3. Judgment on All the Family Lines ..11:5–9

Part Two: Patriarchal History (11:10—50:26)

I. The Life of Abraham ....11:10—25:18

A. Introduction of Abram....................11:10–32
1. Abram's Family Line 11:10–26
2. Abram's Past 11:27–32
B. The Covenant of God with Abram ....12:1—25:18
1. Initiation of the Covenant 12:1–20
2. Separation to the Covenant.....13:1—14:24
3. Ratification of the Covenant.....15:1—16:16
4. Institution of the Covenant: Circumcision....................17:1–27
5. Testing of the Covenant....................18:1—20:18
6. Consummation of the Covenant....................21:1—25:18

II. The Life of Isaac....................25:19—26:35

A. The Family of Isaac 25:19–34
B. The Failure of Isaac....................26:1–33
C. The Failure of Esau....................26:34, 35

III. The Life of Jacob....................27:1—36:43

A. Jacob Gains Esau's Blessing....................27:1—28:9
B. Jacob's Life at Haran....................28:10—31:55
1. Jacob's Dream 28:10–22
2. Jacob's Labors....................29:1—30:43
3. Jacob's Flight....................31:1–55
C. Jacob's Return ....32:1—33:20
1. Jacob Fights with the Angel....................32:1–32
2. Jacob Makes Peace with Esau 33:1–20
D. Jacob's Residence in Canaan....................34:1—35:29
1. The Defilement of Dinah 34:1–31
2. The Devotion at Bethel....................35:1–15
3. The Deaths of Rachel and Isaac....................35:16–29
E. The History of Esau 36:1–43

IV. The Life of Joseph ....37:1—50:26

A. The Corruption of Joseph's Family....................37:1—38:30

1. Joseph's Family Sins Against Him 37:1–36
2. Joseph's Family Sins with the Canaanites 38:1–30

B. The Exaltation of Joseph....................39:1—41:57
1. Joseph's Test with the Egyptian Woman....................39:1–23
2. Joseph's Test with the Egyptian Society....................40:1–23
3. Joseph's Test with Pharaoh's Dreams 41:1–36
4. Joseph's Exaltation over Egypt....41:37–57

C. The Salvation of Jacob's Family....................42:1—50:26
1. Joseph's Brothers Visit Egypt 42:1–38
2. Joseph's Brothers' Second Journey to Egypt....................43:1—45:28
3. Jacob's Family Safe in Egypt...46:1—47:26
4. Jacob Blesses the Family in Egypt....................47:27—49:32
5. Jacob Dies in Egypt....................49:33—50:14
6. Joseph Dies in Egypt....................50:15–26

CHAPTER 1

Creation of the World

IN the [R]beginning [R]God created the heavens
and the earth. [John 1:1–3] • Acts 17:24
2 The earth was [R]without form, and void;
and darkness *was** on the face of the deep.
[R]And the Spirit of God was hovering over the
face of the waters. Jer. 4:23 • Is. 40:13, 14
3 Then God said, [R]"Let there be [R]light"; and
there was light. 2 Cor. 4:6 • [Heb. 11:3]
4 And God saw the light, that *it was* good;
and God divided the light from the darkness.
5 God called the light Day, and the [R]dark-
ness He called Night. So the evening and the
morning were the first day. Ps. 19:2; 33:6
6 Then God said, "Let there be a [T]firma-
ment in the midst of the waters, and let it di-
vide the waters from the waters." *expanse*
7 Thus God made the firmament, and di-
vided the waters which *were* under the firma-
ment from the waters which *were* [R]above the
firmament; and it was so. Ps. 148:4
8 And God called the firmament Heaven.
So the evening and the morning were the sec-
ond day.
9 Then God said, [R]"Let the waters under
the heavens be gathered together into one
place, and [R]let the dry *land* appear"; and it
was so. Job 26:10 • Ps. 24:1, 2; 33:7; 95:5
10 And God called the dry *land* Earth, and
the gathering together of the waters He called
Seas. And God saw that *it was* good.
11 Then God said, "Let the earth [R]bring forth
grass, the herb *that* yields seed, *and* the [R]fruit
tree *that* yields fruit according to its kind,
whose seed *is* in itself, on the earth"; and it
was so. Heb. 6:7 • 2 Sam. 16:1
12 And the earth brought forth grass, the
herb *that* yields seed according to its kind,
and the tree *that* yields fruit, whose seed *is* in
itself according to its kind. And God saw that
it was good.
13 So the evening and the morning were the
third day.
14 Then God said, "Let there be lights in the
firmament of the heavens to divide the day
from the night; and let them be for signs and
seasons, and for days and years;
15 "and let them be for lights in the firma-
ment of the heavens to give light on the
earth"; and it was so.
16 Then God made two great [T]lights: the
[R]greater light to rule the day, and the [R]lesser
light to rule the night. *He made* [R]the stars
also. *luminaries* • Ps. 136:8 • Ps. 8:3 • Job 38:7
17 God set them in the firmament of the
[R]heavens to give light on the earth, Gen. 15:5
18 and to rule over the day and over the
night, and to divide the light from the dark-
ness. And God saw that *it was* good.
19 So the evening and the morning were the
fourth day.
20 Then God said, "Let the waters abound
with an abundance of living creatures, and let
birds fly above the earth across the face of the
[T]firmament of the heavens." *expanse*
21 So [R]God created great sea creatures and
every living thing that moves, with which the
waters abounded, according to their kind, and
every winged bird according to its kind. And
God saw that *it was* good. Ps. 104:25–28
22 And God blessed them, saying, [R]"Be
fruitful and multiply, and fill the waters in
the seas, and let birds multiply on the
earth." Gen. 8:17
23 So the evening and the morning were the
fifth day.
24 Then God said, "Let the earth bring forth
the living creature according to its kind: cattle
and creeping thing and beast of the earth,
each according to its kind"; and it was so.
25 And God made the beast of the earth ac-
cording to its kind, cattle according to its
kind, and everything that creeps on the earth
according to its kind. And God saw that *it was*
good.
26 Then God said, "Let Us make man in Our
image, according to Our likeness; [R]let them
have dominion over the fish of the sea, over
the birds of the air, and over the cattle, over
all* the earth and over every creeping thing
that creeps on the earth." Gen. 9:2
27 So God created man in His *own* image; in

1:2 Words in italic type have been added for clarity. They are not found in the original Hebrew or Aramaic. **1:26** Syr. *all the wild animals of*

the image of God He created him; [R]male and
female He created them. Matt. 19:4
28 Then God blessed them, and God said to
them, [R]"Be fruitful and multiply; fill the
earth and [R]subdue it; have dominion over
the fish of the sea, over the birds of the air,
and over every living thing that moves on
the earth." Gen. 9:1, 7 • 1 Cor. 9:27
29 And God said, "See, I have given you
every herb *that* yields seed which *is* on the
face of all the earth, and every tree whose
fruit yields seed; to you it shall be for food.
30 "Also, to [R]every beast of the earth, to
every [R]bird of the air, and to everything that
creeps on the earth, in which *there is* [T]life, *I*
have given every green herb for food"; and it
was so. Ps. 145:15 • Job 38:41 • *a living soul*
31 Then God saw everything that He had
made, and indeed *it was* very good. So the
evening and the morning were the sixth day.

CHAPTER 2

THUS the heavens and the earth, and [R]all
the host of them, were finished. Ps. 33:6
2 [R]And on the seventh day God ended His
work which He had done, and He rested on
the seventh day from all His work which He
had done. Ex. 20:9–11; 31:17
3 Then God blessed the seventh day and
sanctified it, because in it He rested from all
His work which God had created and made.

Creation of Man

4 [R]This *is* the history* of the heavens and
the earth when they were created, in the day
that the LORD God made the earth and the
heavens, Gen. 1:1
5 before any [R]plant of the field was in the
earth and before any herb of the field had
grown. For the LORD God had not [R]caused it to
rain on the earth, and *there was* no man to till
the ground; Gen. 1:11, 12 • Gen. 7:4
6 but a mist went up from the earth and wa-
tered the whole face of the ground.
7 And the LORD God formed man *of* the
dust of the ground, and [R]breathed into his
[R]nostrils the breath of life; and [R]man became
a living being. Job 33:4 • Gen. 7:22 • 1 Cor. 15:45
8 The LORD God planted a garden [R]east-
ward in [R]Eden, and there He put the man
whom He had formed. Gen. 3:23, 24 • Gen. 4:16
9 And out of the ground the LORD God
made every tree grow that is pleasant to the
sight and good for food. The tree of life *was*
also in the midst of the garden, and the tree of
the knowledge of good and evil.
10 Now a river went out of Eden to water the
garden, and from there it parted and became
four riverheads.
11 The name of the first *is* Pishon; it *is* the
one which skirts [R]the whole land of Havilah,
where *there is* gold. Gen. 25:18
12 And the gold of that land *is* good. [R]Bdel-
lium and the onyx stone *are* there. Num. 11:7
13 The name of the second river *is* Gihon; it
is the one which goes around the whole land
of Cush.
14 The name of the third river *is* Hiddekel;* it
is the one which goes toward the east of As-
syria. The fourth river *is* the Euphrates.

15 Then the LORD God took [T]the man and put
him in the garden of Eden to [T]tend and keep
it. Or *Adam* • *cultivate*
16 And the LORD God commanded the man,
saying, "Of every tree of the garden you may
freely eat;
17 "but of the tree of the knowledge of good

2:4 Heb. *toledoth*, lit. *generations* **2:14** Or *Tigris*

1:26 Unity of the Trinity—Historically other monotheistic religions have accused Christians of worshiping three Gods: the Father, the Son, and the Holy Spirit. Early and medieval Judaism, for instance, just could not conceive of any theological explanation that vindicated Christianity of the charge of polytheism.

Christians always have affirmed the great monotheistic statements of the OT (Deut. 4:35; 6:4; Is. 44:6–20; Zech. 14:9). Christian theologians also have wrestled through the centuries with how to express the unity of God's Being while recognizing distinctions among the three Persons interacting and fellowshiping within Him. The early church fathers spoke of one divine essence or substance that could not be divided. Within that one essence are three personal distinctions: the Father, Son, and Holy Spirit. No one has improved on that description.

The NT, which teaches the deity of Father (John 6:27), Son (John 1:1; 20:28), and Holy Spirit (Acts 5:3, 4), also stresses the unity of God (Mark 12:29–32; John 17:3; 1 Cor. 8:4–6; 1 Tim. 2:5). The mystery of the Trinity should remind us that when we contemplate the nature of God we reach the limits of finite human understanding. At the same time, the complexity of human personality, which somehow reflects the divine personality, should cause us not to be surprised by how multifaceted He is.

Now turn to Page 1192—2 Cor. 13:14: Persons of the Trinity.

2:15–17 The Edenic Covenant—The covenant in Eden is the first of the general or universal covenants. In it, Adam is charged to: (1) populate the earth (Gen. 1:28); (2) subdue the earth (Gen. 1:28); (3) exercise dominion over the animal creation (Gen. 1:28); (4) care for the Garden of Eden and enjoy its fruit (Gen. 1:29; 2:15); and (5) refrain from eating the fruit of the tree of the knowledge of good and evil, under penalty of death (Gen. 2:16, 17). The Edenic covenant was terminated by man's disobedience, when Adam and Eve ate of the fruit of the tree of the knowledge of good and evil, resulting in their spiritual and physical deaths. This failure necessitated the establishment of the covenant with Adam (Page 7—Gen. 3:14–21).

Now turn to page 7—Gen. 3:14–21: The Adamic Covenant.

and evil you shall not eat, for in the day that you eat of it you shall surely die."

18 And the LORD God said, "*It is* not good that man should be alone; [R]I will make him a helper comparable to him." 1 Cor. 11:8, 9

19 [R]Out of the ground the LORD God formed every beast of the field and every bird of the air, and [R]brought *them* to [T]Adam to see what he would call them. And whatever Adam called each living creature, that *was* its name. Gen. 1:20, 24 • Ps. 8:6 • Or *the man*

20 So Adam gave names to all cattle, to the birds of the air, and to every beast of the field. But for Adam there was not found a helper comparable to him.

21 And the LORD God caused a [R]deep sleep to fall on Adam, and he slept; and He took one of his ribs, and closed up the flesh in its place. 1 Sam. 26:12

22 Then the rib which the LORD God had taken from man He made into a woman, [R]and He brought her to the man. 1 Tim. 2:13

23 And Adam said:

"This *is* now [R]bone of my bones
And flesh of my flesh; Gen. 29:14
She shall be called Woman,
Because she was taken out of Man."

24 [R]Therefore a man shall leave his father and mother and be joined to his wife, and they shall become one flesh. Matt. 19:5

25 And they were both naked, the man and his wife, and were not ashamed.

CHAPTER 3

Temptation

NOW the serpent was [R]more cunning than any beast of the field which the LORD God had made. And he said to the woman, "Has God indeed said, 'You shall not eat of every tree of the garden'?" 2 Cor. 11:3

2 And the woman said to the serpent, "We may eat the fruit of the trees of the garden;

3 "but of the fruit of the tree which *is* in the midst of the garden, God has said, 'You shall not eat it, nor shall you [R]touch it, lest you die.'" Ex. 19:12, 13

4 [R]Then the serpent said to the woman, "You will not surely die. [2 Cor. 11:3]

5 "For God knows that in the day you eat of it your eyes will be opened, and you will be like God, knowing good and evil."

The Fall

6 So when the woman saw that the tree *was* good for food, that it *was* pleasant to the eyes, and a tree desirable to make *one* wise, she took of its fruit and ate. She also gave to her husband with her, and he ate.

7 Then the eyes of both of them were opened, [R]and they knew that they *were* naked; and they sewed fig leaves together and made themselves coverings. Gen. 2:25

2:18–25 How the Family Began—Gen. 2:18–25 fills in the details of the simple statement in Gen. 1:27: "Male and female He created them." This account particularly amplifies the "and female" part of the statement and shows how woman was created. Three observations can be made on the passage that will help us to understand how the family began:

a. The need for woman (vv. 18–20). Woman is absolutely essential in God's plan. It was God who observed, "*It is* not good that man should be alone" (v. 18) and determined to make a "helper" for Adam. Woman's role in the will of God was to be a "helper" who was suitable to man in every particular mental, spiritual, emotional, social, and physical need. God undertook an orientation program to show man the need that He alone had observed. He brought to man the birds and beasts He had created, so that man should exercise his dominion over them (v. 28) and name them (v. 19). However, in v. 20 it is noted that for Adam there was no "helper" similar to himself.

b. The provision of woman for man (vv. 21–24). God caused Adam to go to sleep, and God removed one of his "ribs." Exactly what God removed is not known, but it was adequate for His purpose. He "made" (lit., *built*) a woman (v. 22) whom Adam recognized as being his equal, "bone of my bones and flesh of my flesh." This resulted in what has become known as the universal law of marriage (v. 24), in which it can be seen that: (1) the responsibility for marriage is on the man's shoulders—he is to "leave his father and mother"; (2) the responsibility for keeping the union together is on the man's shoulders—he is to "be joined to" his wife; and (3) the union is indissoluble—"they shall become one flesh."

c. The state of the first man and woman (v. 25). From the beginning the man and woman were "naked" in each other's presence and "were not ashamed." There is no shame in nudity when it occurs within the right context—the marital union. This passage clearly teaches that (1) sex was God's idea and is not sinful; (2) sex came before the Fall, and if the Fall had never taken place there still would be sexual relations between a husband and his wife; and (3) propagation of the species is one, but not the exclusive, purpose for sex. The Bible gives two other reasons for sex: (1) to promote love between the husband and wife (Page 1268—Heb. 13:4), and (2) to prevent fornication—the unlawful satisfaction of the God-given sexual desire (Page 1171—1 Cor. 7:2).

Now turn to Page 181—Deut. 6:4–9: Three Essentials for a Christian Home.

3:6, 7 Adam's Sin—Adam's sin does not seem to be a very great sin from the human perspective. All he did was take a bite of some fruit. Adam's sin is serious in that the fruit was of "the tree of the knowledge of good and evil," of which God said that he was not to eat under penalty of death (Page 5—Gen. 2:17). Up to this time Adam was morally innocent. When he sinned, he by nature became a sinner. As such he

Judgment on Man and Woman

8 And they heard [R]the sound of the LORD
God walking in the garden in the cool of the
day, and Adam and his wife [R]hid themselves
from the presence of the LORD God among the
trees of the garden. Job 38:1 • Job 31:33
9 Then the LORD God called to Adam and
said to him, "Where *are* you?"
10 So he said, "I heard Your voice in the gar-
den, [R]and I was afraid because I was naked;
and I hid myself." Gen. 2:25
11 And He said, "Who told you that you *were*
naked? Have you eaten from the tree of which
I commanded you that you should not eat?"
12 Then the man said, [R]"The woman whom
You gave *to be* with me, she gave me of the
tree, and I ate." [Prov. 28:13]
13 And the LORD God said to the woman,
"What *is* this you have done?" The woman
said, "The serpent deceived me, and I ate."
14 So the LORD God said to the serpent:

"Because you have done this,
You *are* cursed more than all cattle,
And more than every beast of the field;
On your belly you shall go,
And [R]you shall eat dust
All the days of your life. Deut. 28:15–20
15 And I will put enmity
Between you and the woman,
And between your seed and her Seed;
[R]He shall bruise your head,
And you shall bruise His heel." Rom. 16:20☆

16 To the woman He said:

"I will greatly multiply your sorrow and
your conception;
[R]In pain you shall bring forth children;
Your desire *shall be* for your husband,
And he shall rule over you." John 16:21

17 Then to Adam He said, "Because you have
heeded the voice of your wife, and have eaten
from the tree of which I commanded you, say-
ing, 'You shall not eat of it':

[R]"Cursed *is* the ground for your sake;
In toil you shall eat *of* it
All the days of your life. Rom. 8:20–22
18 Both thorns and thistles it shall [T]bring
forth for you, *cause to grow*
And you shall eat the herb of the field.
19 [R]In the sweat of your face you shall eat
bread 2 Thess. 3:10
Till you return to the ground,
For out of it you were taken;
[R]For dust you *are*, Gen. 2:7; 5:5
And to dust you shall return."

20 And Adam called his wife's name Eve,
because she was the mother of all living.
21 Also for Adam and his wife the LORD God
made tunics of skin, and clothed them.

22 Then the LORD God said, "Behold, the
man has become like one of Us, to know good
and evil. And now, lest he put out his hand
and take also of the tree of life, and eat, and
live forever"—
23 therefore the LORD God sent him out of

---

died. He died spiritually immediately, and he began to die physically. Adam was the first man ever to live upon the face of the earth. From Adam and Eve come every other human being who ever has lived upon the face of the earth. Thus Adam is the "federal head" from whom every other man came. Like begets like. Apples beget apples. Dogs beget dogs. Human beings beget human beings. Since Adam became a sinner before Eve conceived a child, every human being descended from him is a sinner just like him except Christ. Because of Adam's sin, death entered into the human race (Page 1152—Rom. 5:12–14); every human being needs to have the new life.

Now turn to Page 667—Eccl. 7:20: Individual Sin.

3:14–21 The Adamic Covenant—The covenant with Adam is the second general or universal covenant. It could be called the covenant with humankind, for it sets forth the conditions that will hold sway until the curse of sin is lifted (cf. Page 693—Is. 11:6–10; Page 1155—Rom. 8:18–23). According to the covenant, the conditions that will prevail are:

a. The serpent, the tool used by Satan to effect the fall of Adam and Eve, is cursed. The curse affects not only the instrument, the serpent, but also the indwelling energizer, Satan. Great physical changes took place in the serpent. Apparently it was upright; now it will go on its belly (v. 14). It was the most desirable animal of the animal creation; now it is the most loathsome. The sight or thought of a snake should be an effective reminder of the devastating effects of sin.
b. Satan is judged—he will enjoy limited success ("you shall bruise His heel," v. 15), but ultimately he will be judged ("He shall bruise your head," v. 15).
c. The first prophecy of the coming of the Messiah is given (v. 15).
d. There will be a multiplication of conception, necessitated by the introduction of death into the human race (v. 16).
e. There will be pain in childbirth (v. 16).
f. The woman's relationship with her husband is distorted (v. 16).
g. The ground is cursed and will bring forth weeds among the food that man must eat for his existence (vv. 17–19).
h. The creation resists man's efforts to order it. He toils in frustration all his life long (v. 19).
i. In sinning, man dies spiritually, and ultimately will die physically. His flesh will decay until it returns to dust from which it was originally taken (v. 19).

Now turn to Page 11—Gen. 9:1–19: The Noahic Covenant.

the garden of Eden [R]to till the ground from which he was taken. Gen. 4:2; 9:20

24 So [R]He drove out the man; and He placed [R]cherubim [R]at the east of the garden of Eden, and a flaming sword which turned every way, to guard the way to the tree of [R]life. Ezek. 31:3, 11 • Ps. 104:4 • Gen. 2:8 • Gen. 2:9

CHAPTER 4

The Initial Conflict

NOW Adam knew Eve his wife, and she conceived and bore Cain, and said, "I have acquired a man from the LORD."

2 Then she bore again, this time his brother Abel. Now Abel was a keeper of sheep, but Cain was a tiller of the ground.

3 And in the process of time it came to pass that Cain brought an offering of the fruit [R]of the ground to the LORD. Num. 18:12

4 Abel also brought of the firstborn of his flock and of their fat. And the LORD [R]respected Abel and his offering, Heb. 11:4

5 but He did not respect Cain and his offering. And Cain was very angry, and his countenance fell.

6 So the LORD said to Cain, "Why are you angry? And why has your countenance fallen?

7 "If you do well, will you not be accepted? And if you do not do well, sin lies at the door. And its desire *is* [T]for you, but you should rule over it." Lit. *toward*

8 Now Cain talked with Abel his brother;* and it came to pass, when they were in the field, that Cain rose up against Abel his brother and [R]killed him. [1 John 3:12–15]

9 Then the LORD said to Cain, "Where *is* Abel your brother?" He said, [R]"I do not know. *Am* I my brother's keeper?" John 8:44

10 And He said, "What have you done? The voice of your brother's blood [R]cries out to Me from the ground. Heb. 12:24

11 "So now [R]you *are* cursed from the earth, which has opened its mouth to receive your brother's blood from your hand. Gen. 3:14

12 "When you till the ground, it shall no longer yield its strength to you. A fugitive and a vagabond you shall be on the earth."

13 And Cain said to the LORD, "My [T]punishment *is* greater than I can bear! *iniquity*

14 "Surely You have driven me out this day from the face of the ground; I shall be hidden from Your face; I shall be a fugitive and a vagabond on the earth, and it will happen *that* anyone who finds me will kill me."

15 And the LORD said to him, "Therefore,* whoever kills Cain, vengeance shall be taken on him [R]sevenfold." And the LORD set a [R]mark on Cain, lest anyone finding him should kill him. Gen. 4:24 • Ezek. 9:4, 6

The Ungodly Line of Cain

16 Then Cain [R]went out from the [R]presence of the LORD and dwelt in the land of Nod on the east of Eden. 2 Kin. 13:23; 24:20 • Jon. 1:3

17 And Cain knew his wife, and she conceived and bore Enoch. And he built a city, [R]and called the name of the city after the name of his son—Enoch. Ps. 49:11

18 To Enoch was born Irad; and Irad begot Mehujael, and Mehujael begot Methushael, and Methushael begot Lamech.

19 Then Lamech took for himself [R]two wives: the name of one *was* Adah, and the name of the second *was* Zillah. Gen. 2:24

20 And Adah bore Jabal. He was the father of those who dwell in tents and have livestock.

21 His brother's name *was* Jubal. He was the father of all those who play the harp and [T]flute. *pipe*

22 And as for Zillah, she also bore Tubal-Cain, an instructor of every craftsman in bronze and iron. And the sister of Tubal-Cain *was* Naamah.

23 Then Lamech said to his wives:

"Adah and Zillah, hear my voice;
Wives of Lamech, listen to my speech!
For I have [T]killed a man for wounding
me, *slain a man for my wound*
Even a young man for hurting me.
24 If Cain shall be avenged sevenfold,
Then Lamech seventy-sevenfold."

The Godly Line of Seth
1 Chr. 1:1–4; Luke 3:36–38

25 And Adam knew his wife again, and she bore a son and [R]named him Seth, "For God has appointed another seed for me instead of Abel, whom Cain killed." Gen. 5:3

26 And as for Seth, to him also a son was born; and he named him Enosh.* Then *men* began to call on the name of the LORD.

CHAPTER 5

THIS is the book of the genealogy of Adam. In the day that God created man, He made him in the likeness of God.

2 He created them [R]male and female, and blessed them and called them Mankind in the day they were created. Mark 10:6

3 And Adam lived one hundred and thirty years, and begot *a son* in his own likeness, after his image, and named him Seth.

4 After he begot Seth, [R]the days of Adam were eight hundred years; [R]and he had sons and daughters. Luke 3:36–38 • Gen. 1:28; 4:25

4:8 Sam., LXX, Syr., Vg. add *"Let us go out to the field."* **4:15** So with MT, Tg.; LXX, Syr., Vg. *Not so;* **4:26** Gr. *Enos,* Luke 3:38

5 So all the days that Adam lived were nine
hundred and thirty years; and he died.
6 Seth lived one hundred and five years,
and begot [R]Enosh. Gen. 4:26
7 After he begot Enosh, Seth lived eight
hundred and seven years, and had sons and
daughters.
8 So all the days of Seth were nine hundred
and twelve years; and he died.
9 Enosh lived ninety years, and begot
Cainan.*
10 After he begot Cainan, Enosh lived eight
hundred and fifteen years, and had sons and
daughters.
11 So all the days of Enosh were nine hun-
dred and five years; and he died.
12 Cainan lived seventy years, and begot
Mahalalel.
13 After he begot Mahalalel, Cainan lived
eight hundred and forty years, and had sons
and daughters.
14 So all the days of Cainan were nine hun-
dred and ten years; and he died.
15 Mahalalel lived sixty-five years, and
begot Jared.
16 After he begot Jared, Mahalalel lived
eight hundred and thirty years, and had sons
and daughters.
17 So all the days of Mahalalel were
eight hundred and ninety-five years; and he
died.
18 Jared lived one hundred and sixty-two
years, and begot [R]Enoch. Jude 14, 15
19 After he begot Enoch, Jared lived eight
hundred years, and had sons and daugh-
ters.
20 So all the days of Jared were nine hun-
dred and sixty-two years; and he died.
21 Enoch lived sixty-five years, and begot
Methuselah.
22 After he begot Methuselah, Enoch
[R]walked with God three hundred years, and
had sons and daughters. Gen. 6:9; 17:1; 24:40
23 So all the days of Enoch were three hun-
dred and sixty-five years.
24 And Enoch walked with God; and he *was*
not, for God [R]took him. Heb. 11:5
25 Methuselah lived one hundred and
eighty-seven years, and begot Lamech.
26 After he begot Lamech, Methuselah lived
seven hundred and eighty-two years, and had
sons and daughters.
27 So all the days of Methuselah were nine
hundred and sixty-nine years; and he died.
28 Lamech lived one hundred and eighty-
two years, and had a son.
29 And he called his name Noah, saying,
"This *one* will comfort us concerning our
work and the toil of our hands, because of the
ground which the LORD has cursed."
30 After he begot Noah, Lamech lived five
hundred and ninety-five years, and had sons
and daughters.
31 So all the days of Lamech were seven
hundred and seventy-seven years; and he
died.
32 And Noah was five hundred years old,
and Noah begot Shem, Ham, and Japheth.

CHAPTER 6

The Ungodly Multiply

NOW it came to pass, [R]when men began to
multiply on the face of the earth, and
daughters were born to them, Gen. 1:28
2 that the sons of God saw the daughters
of men, that they *were* beautiful; and they
[R]took wives for themselves of all whom they
chose. Deut. 7:3, 4
3 And the LORD said, [R]"My Spirit shall not
[R]strive* with man forever, for he *is* indeed
flesh; yet his days shall be one hundred and
twenty years." [Gal. 5:16, 17] • 2 Thess. 2:7
4 There were giants on the earth in those
days, and also afterward, when the sons of
God came in to the daughters of men and they
bore *children* to them. Those *were* the mighty
men who *were* of old, men of renown.

The Ungodly Sin Continually

5 Then the LORD* saw that the wickedness
of man *was* great in the earth, and *that* every
[R]intent[T] of the thoughts of his heart *was* only
evil continually. Gen. 8:21 • *thought*

The Ungodly to Be Destroyed

6 And [R]the LORD was sorry that He had
made man on the earth, and [R]He was grieved
in His [R]heart. 1 Sam. 15:11, 29 • Is. 63:10 • Mark 3:5
7 So the LORD said, "I will [R]destroy man
whom I have created from the face of the
earth, both man and beast, creeping thing and
birds of the air, for I am sorry that I have
made them." Gen. 7:4, 23

The Godly to Be Saved

8 But Noah [R]found grace in the eyes of the
LORD. Gen. 19:19
9 This is the genealogy of Noah. [R]Noah was
a just man, perfect in his generations. Noah
[R]walked with God. 2 Pet. 2:5 • Gen. 5:22, 24
10 And Noah begot three sons: [R]Shem, Ham,
and Japheth. Gen. 5:32; 7:13
11 The earth also was corrupt before God,
and the earth was filled with violence.
12 So God [R]looked upon the earth, and in-
deed it was corrupt; for all flesh had cor-
rupted their way on the earth. Ps. 14:2; 53:2, 3
13 And God said to Noah, "The end of all
flesh has come before Me, for the earth is
filled with violence through them; and behold,
I will destroy them with the earth.
14 "Make yourself an ark of gopherwood;

5:9 Heb. *Qenan* **6:3** LXX, Syr., Tg., Vg. *abide*
6:5 So with MT, Tg.; Vg. *God;* LXX LORD *God*

make [T]rooms in the ark, and cover it inside and outside with pitch. Lit. *compartments* or *nests*

15 "And this is how you shall make it: The length of the ark *shall be* three hundred [T]cubits, its width fifty cubits, and its height thirty cubits. A cubit is about 18 inches.

16 "You shall make a window for the ark, and you shall finish it to a cubit from above; and set the door of the ark in its side. You shall make it *with* lower, second, and third *decks.*

17 [R]"And behold, I Myself am bringing [R]floodwaters on the earth, to destroy from under heaven all flesh in which *is* the breath of life; everything that *is* on the earth shall [R]die. 2 Pet. 2:5 • 2 Pet. 3:6 • Luke 16:22

18 "But I will establish My [R]covenant with you; and [R]you shall go into the ark—you, your sons, your wife, and your sons' wives with you. Gen. 8:20—9:17; 17:7 • Gen. 7:1, 7, 13

19 "And of every living thing of all flesh you shall bring [R]two of every *sort* into the ark, to keep *them* alive with you; they shall be male and female. Gen. 7:2, 8, 9, 14–16

20 "Of the birds after their kind, of animals after their kind, and of every creeping thing of the earth after its kind, two of every *kind* will come to you to keep *them* alive.

21 "And you shall take for yourself of all food that is eaten, and you shall gather *it* to yourself; and it shall be food for you and for them."

22 [R]Thus Noah did; according to all that God commanded him, so he did. Gen. 7:5

CHAPTER 7

The Ark Is Entered

THEN the [R]LORD said to Noah, "Come into the ark, you and all your household, because I have seen *that* you *are* righteous before Me in this generation. Matt. 11:28

2 "You shall take with you seven each of every [R]clean animal, a male and his female; [R]two each of animals that *are* unclean, a male and his female; Lev. 11 • Lev. 10:10

3 "also seven each of birds of the air, male and female, to keep [T]the species alive on the face of all the earth. Lit. *seed*

4 "For after seven more days I will cause it to rain on the earth forty days and forty nights, and I will destroy from the face of the earth all living things that I have made."

5 [R]And Noah did according to all that the LORD commanded him. Gen. 6:22

6 Noah *was* [R]six hundred years old when the floodwaters were on the earth. Gen. 5:4

7 [R]So Noah, with his sons, his wife, and his sons' wives, went into the ark because of the waters of the flood. Matt. 24:38

8 Of clean animals, of animals that *are* unclean, of birds, and of everything that creeps on the earth,

9 two by two they went into the ark to Noah, male and female, as God had commanded Noah.

10 And it came to pass after seven days that the waters of the flood were on the earth.

The Earth Is Flooded

11 In the six hundredth year of Noah's life, in the second month, the seventeenth day of the month, on [R]that day all the fountains of the great deep were broken up, and the windows of heaven were opened. Matt. 24:39

12 [R]And the rain was on the earth forty days and forty nights. Gen. 7:4, 17

13 On the very same day Noah and Noah's sons, Shem, Ham, and Japheth, and Noah's wife and the three wives of his sons with them, entered the ark—

14 [R]they and every beast after its kind, all cattle after their kind, every creeping thing that creeps on the earth after its kind, and every bird after its kind, every bird of every [R]sort. Gen. 6:19 • Gen. 1:21

15 And they [R]went into the ark to Noah, two by two, of all flesh in which *is* the breath of life. Gen. 6:19, 20; 7:9

16 So those that entered, male and female of all flesh, went in [R]as God had commanded him; and the LORD shut him in. Gen. 7:2, 3

17 Now the flood was on the earth forty days. The waters increased and lifted up the ark, and it rose high above the earth.

18 The waters prevailed and greatly increased on the earth, and the ark moved about on the surface of the waters.

19 And the waters prevailed exceedingly on the earth, and all the high hills under the whole heaven were covered.

20 The waters prevailed fifteen cubits upward, and the mountains were covered.

21 [R]And all flesh died that moved on [T]the earth: birds and cattle and beasts and every creeping thing that creeps on the earth, and every man. Gen. 6:7, 13, 17; 7:4 • *the land*

22 All in [R]whose nostrils *was* the breath of the spirit* of life, all that *was* on the dry *land,* died. Gen. 2:7

23 So He destroyed all living things which were on the face of the ground: both man and cattle, creeping thing and bird of the air. They were destroyed from the earth. Only [R]Noah and those who *were* with him in the ark remained *alive.* 2 Pet. 2:5

24 [R]And the waters prevailed on the earth one hundred and fifty days. Gen. 8:3, 4

CHAPTER 8

The Flood Recedes

THEN God [R]remembered Noah, and every living thing, and all the animals that *were* with him in the ark. [R]And God made a wind

7:22 LXX, Vg. omit *of the spirit*

to pass over the earth, and the waters sub-
sided. Gen. 19:29 • Ex. 14:21; 15:10
2 [R]The fountains of the deep and the win-
dows of heaven were also stopped, and the
rain from heaven was restrained. Gen. 7:11
3 And the waters receded continually from
the earth. At the end [R]of the hundred and fifty
days the waters decreased. Gen. 7:24
4 Then the ark rested in the seventh month,
the seventeenth day of the month, on the
mountains of Ararat.
5 And the waters decreased continually
until the tenth month. In the tenth *month*, on
the first *day* of the month, the tops of the
mountains were seen.
6 So it came to pass, at the end of forty
days, that Noah opened [R]the window of the
ark which he had made. Gen. 6:16
7 Then he sent out a raven, which kept
going to and fro until the waters had dried up
from the earth.
8 He also sent out from himself a dove, to
see if the waters had receded from the face of
the ground.
9 But the dove found no resting place for
the sole of her foot, and she returned into the
ark to him, for the waters *were* on the face of
the whole earth. So he put out his hand and
took her, and drew her into the ark to himself.
10 And he waited yet another seven days,
and again he sent the dove out from the
ark.
11 Then the dove came to him in the
evening, and behold, a freshly plucked olive
leaf *was* in her mouth; and Noah knew that
the waters had receded from the earth.
12 So he waited yet another seven days and
sent out the dove, which did not return again
to him anymore.
13 And it came to pass in the six hundred
and first year, in the first *month*, the first *day*
of the month, that the waters were dried up
from the earth; and Noah removed the cover-
ing of the ark and looked, and indeed the sur-
face of the ground was dry.
14 And in the second month, on the twenty-
seventh day of the month, the earth was dried.
15 Then God spoke to Noah, saying,
16 "Go out of the ark, [R]you and your wife,
and your sons and your sons' wives with
you. Gen. 7:13
17 "Bring out with you every living thing
of all flesh that *is* with you: birds and cat-
tle and every creeping thing that creeps on the
earth, so that they may abound on the
earth, and [R]be fruitful and multiply on the
earth." Gen. 1:22, 28; 9:1, 7
18 So Noah went out, and his sons and his
wife and his sons' wives with him.
19 Every animal, every creeping thing, every
bird, *and* whatever creeps on the earth, ac-
cording to their families, went out of the ark.

Noah Worships God

20 Then Noah built an [R]altar to the LORD,
and took of [R]every clean animal and of every
clean bird, and offered [R]burnt offerings on the
altar. Gen. 12:7 • Lev. 11 • Ex. 10:25
21 And the LORD smelled a soothing aroma.
Then the LORD said in His heart, "I will never
again curse the ground for man's sake, al-
though the imagination of man's heart *is* evil
from his youth; nor will I again destroy every
living thing as I have done.

22 "While the earth [R]remains,
Seedtime and harvest,
Cold and heat,
Winter and summer,
And [R]day and night
Shall not cease." Is. 54:9 • Jer. 33:20, 25

CHAPTER 9

God's Covenant with Noah

SO God blessed Noah and his sons, and
said to them: [R]"Be fruitful and multiply,
and fill the earth.* Gen. 1:28, 29; 8:17; 9:7, 19
2 [R]"And the fear of you and the dread of you
shall be on every beast of the earth, on every
bird of the air, on all that move *on* the earth,
and on all the fish of the sea. They are given
into your hand. Ps. 8:6
3 "Every moving thing that lives shall be
food for you. I have given you [R]all things, even
as the green herbs. Rom. 14:14, 20
4 [R]"But you shall not eat flesh with its life,
that is, its blood. 1 Sam. 14:33, 34
5 "Surely for your lifeblood I will demand *a
reckoning;* [R]from the hand of every beast I
will require it, and from the hand of man.

9:1 Cf. Gen. 1:28

9:1–19 The Noahic Covenant—The covenant with Noah is the third general or universal covenant. Noah has just passed through the universal flood in which all the world's population had been wiped out. Only Noah, his wife, his three sons, and their wives—eight people—constitute the world's population. Noah might have thought that the things provided by the covenant with Adam had now been changed. However, God gives the Noahic covenant so that Noah and all the human race to follow might know that the provisions made in the Adamic covenant remain in effect with one notable addition: the principle of human government, which includes the responsibility of suppressing the outbreak of sin and violence, so that it will not be necessary to destroy the earth again by a flood. The provisions of the covenant are:
a. The responsibility to populate the earth is reaffirmed (v. 1).
b. The subjection of the animal kingdom to humankind is reaffirmed (v. 2).

(continued on next page)

From the hand of every [R]man's brother I will
require the life of man. Ex. 21:28 • Acts 17:26

6 "Whoever [R]sheds man's blood,
By man his blood shall be shed;
[R]For in the image of God
He made man. Lev. 24:17 • Gen. 1:26, 27
7 And as for you, [R]be fruitful and multiply;
Bring forth abundantly in the earth
And multiply in it." Gen. 9:1, 19

8 Then God spoke to Noah and to his sons
with him, saying:
9 "And as for Me, [R]behold, I establish [R]My
covenant with you and with your descen-
dants* after you, Gen. 6:18 • Is. 54:9
10 [R]"and with every living creature that *is*
with you: the birds, the cattle, and every beast
of the earth with you, of all that go out of the
ark, every beast of the earth. Ps. 145:9
11 "Thus I establish My covenant with you:
Never again shall all flesh be cut off by the
waters of the flood; never again shall there be
a flood to destroy the earth."
12 And God said: [R]"This *is* the sign of the
covenant which I make between Me and you,
and every living creature that *is* with you, for
perpetual generations: Gen. 9:13, 17; 17:11
13 "I set [R]My rainbow in the cloud, and it
shall be for the sign of the covenant between
Me and the earth. Ezek. 1:28
14 "It shall be, when I bring a cloud over the
earth, that the rainbow shall be seen in the
cloud;
15 "and [R]I will remember My covenant
which *is* between Me and you and every liv-
ing creature of all flesh; the waters shall
never again become a flood to destroy all
flesh. Lev. 26:42, 45
16 "The rainbow shall be in the cloud, and I
will look on it to remember the everlasting
covenant between God and every living crea-
ture of all flesh that *is* on the earth."
17 And God said to Noah, "This *is* the sign of
the covenant which I have established be-
tween Me and all flesh that *is* on the earth."

The Sons of Noah

18 Now the sons of Noah who went out of
the ark were Shem, Ham, and Japheth. [R]And
Ham *was* the father of Canaan. Gen. 9:25–27
19 [R]These three *were* the sons of Noah,
[R]and from these the whole earth was popu-
lated. Gen. 5:32 • 1 Chr. 1:4

Ham's Sin

20 And Noah began *to be* a [R]farmer, and he
planted a vineyard. Gen. 3:19, 23; 4:2
21 Then he drank of the wine and was
drunk, and became uncovered in his tent.
22 And Ham, the father of Canaan, saw the
nakedness of his father, and told his two
brothers outside.
23 [R]But Shem and Japheth took a garment,
laid *it* on both their shoulders, and went
backward and covered the nakedness of
their father. Their faces *were* [T]turned away,
and they did not see their father's naked-
ness. Ex. 20:12 • Lit. *backwards*
24 So Noah awoke from his wine, and knew
what his younger son had done to him.

9:9 Lit. *seed*

(continued from previous page)

c. People are permitted to eat the flesh of animals. However, they are to refrain from eating blood (vv. 3, 4).
d. The sacredness of human life is established. Whatever sheds human blood, whether human or beast, must be put to death (vv. 5, 6).
e. This covenant is confirmed to Noah, all humankind, and every living creature on the face of the earth (vv. 9, 10).
f. The promise is given never to destroy the earth again by a universal flood (v. 11). The next time God destroys the earth, the means will be fire (Page 1288—2 Pet. 3:10).
g. The rainbow is designated as a testimony of the existence of this covenant and the promise never to destroy the earth by flood. As long as we can see the rainbow, we will know that the Noahic covenant is in existence (vv. 12–17).

Now turn to Page 15—Gen. 12:1–3: The Abrahamic Covenant.

9:5 The Origin of Human Government—It has been assumed that human government was officially instituted after the Great Flood in Gen. 9. However, some form of law and order undoubtedly existed prior to this period. This is strongly suggested by both Jesus and Jude. Jesus in Luke 17:26, 27 says that prior to the Flood in Noah's day people conducted their affairs in much the same manner as we do today. Jude gives us the text of a message Enoch preached to sinners prior to the Flood (Page 1306—Jude 14, 15). We learn that one of the main factors that brought about the Flood was human disobedience to the revealed law of God.

At any rate, there is certainly no doubt concerning the source of human government. God Himself is its divine author. Two individuals give testimony to this fact. Daniel reminds King Nebuchadnezzar that "the Most High rules in the kingdom of men, and gives it to whomever He chooses" (Page 876—Dan. 4:25). The apostle Paul exhorts Christians to be subject to the laws of human government because all earthly powers exist through God's divine permission (Page 1159—Rom. 13).

If one rightly understands the origin of human government, then the conclusion is reached that lawless anarchy is not only rebellion against human authority, but actual blasphemy against the divine Creator Himself.

Now turn to Page 1159—Rom. 13:1–4: The Function of Human Government.

The Curse on Canaan

25 Then he said:

[R]"Cursed *be* Canaan; Deut. 27:16
A [R]servant of servants
He shall be to his brethren." Josh. 9:23

26 And he said:

[R]"Blessed *be* the LORD,
The God of Shem, Gen. 14:20; 24:27
And may Canaan be his servant.
27 May God [R]enlarge Japheth, Gen. 10:2–5
And may he dwell in the tents of Shem;
And may Canaan be his servant."

Noah's Death

28 And Noah lived after the flood three hun-
dred and fifty years.
29 So all the days of Noah were nine hun-
dred and fifty years; and he died.

CHAPTER 10

The Family of Japheth—1 Chr. 1:5–7

NOW this *is* the genealogy of the sons of
Noah: Shem, Ham, and Japheth. And
sons were born to them after the flood.
2 [R]The sons of Japheth *were* Gomer,
Magog, Madai, Javan, Tubal, Meshech, and
Tiras. 1 Chr. 1:5–7
3 The sons of Gomer *were* Ashkenaz,
Riphath,* and Togarmah.
4 The sons of Javan *were* Elishah, Tarshish,
Kittim, and Dodanim.*
5 From these the coastland *peoples* of the
Gentiles were separated into their lands,
everyone according to his language, accord-
ing to their families, into their nations.

The Family of Ham—1 Chr. 1:8–12

6 [R]The sons of Ham *were* Cush, Mizraim,
Put,* and Canaan. 1 Chr. 1:8–16
7 The sons of Cush *were* Seba, Havilah,
Sabtah, Raamah, and Sabtechah; and the
sons of Raamah *were* Sheba and Dedan.
8 Cush begot [R]Nimrod; he began to be a
mighty one on the earth. Mic. 5:6
9 He was a mighty [R]hunter before the LORD;
therefore it is said, "Like Nimrod the mighty
hunter before the LORD." Jer. 16:16
10 [R]And the beginning of his kingdom was
[R]Babel, Erech, Accad, and Calneh, in the land
of Shinar. Mic. 5:6 • Gen. 11:9
11 From that land he went [R]to Assyria and
built Nineveh, Rehoboth Ir, Calah, Mic. 5:6
12 and Resen between Nineveh and Calah
(that *is* the principal city).
13 Mizraim begot Ludim, Anamim, Le-
habim, Naphtuhim,
14 Pathrusim, and Casluhim (from whom
came the Philistines and Caphtorim).

The Family of Canaan—1 Chr. 1:13–16

15 Canaan begot Sidon his firstborn, and
[R]Heth; Gen. 23:3
16 [R]the Jebusite, the Amorite, and the Gir-
gashite; Gen. 14:7; 15:19–21
17 the Hivite, the Arkite, and the Sinite;
18 the Arvadite, the Zemarite, and the
Hamathite. Afterward the families of the
Canaanites were dispersed.
19 And the border of the Canaanites was
from Sidon as you go toward Gerar, as far as
Gaza; then as you go toward Sodom, Gomor-
rah, Admah, and Zeboiim, as far as Lasha.
20 These *were* the sons of Ham, according to
their families, according to their languages, in
their lands *and* in their nations.

The Family of Shem—1 Chr. 1:17–23

21 And *children* were born also to Shem, the
father of all the children of Eber, the brother
of Japheth the elder.
22 The sons of Shem *were* Elam, Asshur,
[R]Arphaxad, Lud, and Aram. Luke 3:36
23 The sons of Aram *were* Uz, Hul, Gether,
and Mash.*
24 Arphaxad begot [R]Salah,* and Salah begot
Eber. Gen. 11:12
25 [R]To Eber were born two sons: the name
of one *was* [T]Peleg, for in his days the earth
was divided; and his brother's name *was* Jok-
tan. 1 Chr. 1:19 • Lit. *Division*
26 Joktan begot Almodad, Sheleph, Ha-
zarmaveth, Jerah,
27 Hadoram, Uzal, Diklah,
28 Obal,* Abimael, Sheba,
29 Ophir, Havilah, and Jobab. All these *were*
the sons of Joktan.
30 And their dwelling place was from Mesha
as you go toward Sephar, the mountain of the
east.
31 These *were* the sons of Shem, according
to their families, according to their languages,
in their lands, according to their nations.
32 [R]These *were* the families of the sons of
Noah, according to their generations, in their
nations; and from these the nations were di-
vided on the earth after the flood. Gen. 10:1

CHAPTER 11

Construction of the Tower

NOW the whole earth had one language
and one [T]speech. Lit. *lip*
2 And it came to pass, as they journeyed
from the east, that they found a plain in the
land of Shinar, and they dwelt there.
3 Then they said to one another, "Come, let

10:3 *Diphath*, 1 Chr. 1:6 **10:4** Sam. *Rodanim* and 1 Chr. 1:7 **10:6** Or *Phut* **10:23** LXX *Meshech* and 1 Chr. 1:17 **10:24** So with MT, Vg., Tg.; LXX *Arphaxad begot Cainan, and Cainan begot Salah* (cf. Luke 3:35, 36) **10:28** *Ebal*, 1 Chr. 1:22

us make bricks and [T]bake *them* thoroughly." They had brick for stone, and they had asphalt for mortar. Lit. *burn*

Rebellion at the Tower

4 And they said, "Come, let us build ourselves a city, and a tower [R]whose top *is* in the heavens; let us make a name for ourselves, lest we be scattered abroad over the face of the whole earth." Deut. 1:28; 9:1

Judgment on All the Family Lines

5 [R]But the LORD came down to see the city and the tower which the sons of men had built. Gen. 18:21

6 And the LORD said, "Indeed [R]the people *are* one and they all have [R]one language, and this is what they begin to do; now nothing that they [R]propose to do will be withheld from them. Gen. 9:19 • Gen. 11:1 • Ps. 2:1

7 "Come, [R]let Us go down and there confuse their language, that they may not understand one another's speech." Gen. 1:26

8 So [R]the LORD scattered them abroad from there over the face of all the earth, and they ceased building the city. [Luke 1:51]

9 Therefore its name is called [T]Babel, [R]because there the LORD confused the language of all the earth; and from there the LORD scattered them abroad over the face of all the earth. Lit. *Confusion,* Babylon • 1 Cor. 14:23

Abram's Family Line
1 Chr. 1:24–27; Luke 3:34–36

10 This *is* the genealogy of Shem: Shem *was* one hundred years old, and begot Arphaxad two years after the flood.

11 After he begot Arphaxad, Shem lived five hundred years, and begot sons and daughters.

12 Arphaxad lived thirty-five years, [R]and begot Salah. Luke 3:35

13 After he begot Salah, Arphaxad lived four hundred and three years, and begot sons and daughters.

14 Salah lived thirty years, and begot Eber.

15 After he begot Eber, Salah lived four hundred and three years, and begot sons and daughters.

16 [R]Eber lived thirty-four years, and begot [R]Peleg. 1 Chr. 1:19 • Luke 3:35

17 After he begot Peleg, Eber lived four hundred and thirty years, and begot sons and daughters.

18 Peleg lived thirty years, and begot Reu.

19 After he begot Reu, Peleg lived two hundred and nine years, and begot sons and daughters.

20 Reu lived thirty-two years, and begot [R]Serug. Luke 3:35

21 After he begot Serug, Reu lived two hundred and seven years, and begot sons and daughters.

22 Serug lived thirty years, and begot Nahor.

23 After he begot Nahor, Serug lived two hundred years, and begot sons and daughters.

24 Nahor lived twenty-nine years, and begot [R]Terah. Josh. 24:2

25 After he begot Terah, Nahor lived one hundred and nineteen years, and begot sons and daughters.

26 Now Terah lived seventy years, and [R]begot Abram, Nahor, and Haran. 1 Chr. 1:26

Abram's Past

27 This *is* the genealogy of Terah: Terah begot [R]Abram, Nahor, and Haran. Haran begot Lot. Gen. 11:31; 17:5

28 And Haran died before his father Terah in his native land, in Ur of the Chaldeans.

29 Then Abram and Nahor took wives: the name of Abram's wife *was* [R]Sarai, and the name of Nahor's wife, [R]Milcah, the daughter of Haran the father of Milcah and the father of Iscah. Gen. 17:15; 20:12 • Gen. 22:20, 23; 24:15

30 But [R]Sarai was barren; she had no child. Gen. 16:1, 2

31 And Terah took his son Abram and his grandson Lot, the son of Haran, and his daughter-in-law Sarai, his son Abram's wife, and they went out with them from Ur of the Chaldeans to go to the land of Canaan; and they came to Haran and dwelt there.

32 So the days of Terah were two hundred and five years, and Terah died in Haran.

CHAPTER 12

Initiation of the Covenant

NOW the [R]LORD had said to Abram:

"Get out of your country,
From your family Acts 7:2, 3
And from your father's house,
To a land that I will show you.
2 [R]I will make you a great nation;
I will bless you Deut. 26:5
And make your name great;
[R]And you shall be a blessing. Gen. 28:4
3 [R]I will bless those who bless you,
And I will curse him who curses you;
And in [R]you all the families of the earth
shall be blessed." Num. 24:9 • Acts 3:25☆

12:1–3 The Abrahamic Covenant—The covenant with Abraham is the first of the theocratic covenants (pertaining to the rule of God). It is unconditional, depending solely upon God who obligates Himself in grace, indicated by the unconditional declaration, "I will," to bring to pass the promised blessings. The Abrahamic covenant is the basis of all the other theocratic covenants and provides for blessings in three areas:

4 So Abram departed as the LORD had spoken to him, and Lot went with him. And Abram *was* seventy-five years old when he departed from Haran.

5 Then Abram took Sarai his wife and Lot his brother's son, and all their possessions that they had gathered, and the people whom they had acquired in Haran, and they departed to go to the land of Canaan. So they came to the land of Canaan.

6 Abram [R]passed through the land to the place of Shechem, [R]as far as the terebinth tree of Moreh.* And the Canaanites *were* then in the land. Heb. 11:9 • Deut. 11:30

7 [R]Then the LORD appeared to Abram and said, "To your descendants I will give this land." And there he built an altar to the LORD, who had appeared to him. Gen. 17:1

8 And he moved from there to the mountain east of Bethel, and he pitched his tent *with* Bethel on the west and Ai on the east; there he built an altar to the LORD and [R]called on the name of the LORD. Gen. 4:26

9 So Abram journeyed, [R]going on still toward the South.* Gen. 13:1, 3; 20:1; 24:62

10 Now there was [R]a famine in the land, and Abram [R]went down to Egypt to dwell there, for the famine *was* [R]severe in the land. Gen. 26:1 • Ps. 105:13 • Gen. 43:1

11 And it came to pass, when he was close to entering Egypt, that he said to Sarai his wife, "Indeed I know that you *are* [R]a woman of beautiful countenance. Gen. 12:14; 26:7

12 "Therefore it will happen, when the Egyptians see you, that they will say, 'This *is* his wife'; and they [R]will kill me, but they will let you live. Gen. 20:11; 26:7

13 [R]"Please say you *are* my sister, that it may be well with me for your sake, and that I* may live because of you." Gen. 20:1–18

14 So it was, when Abram came into Egypt, that the Egyptians saw the woman, that she *was* very beautiful.

15 The princes of Pharaoh also saw her and commended her to Pharaoh. And the woman was taken to Pharaoh's house.

16 He [R]treated Abram well for her sake. He [R]had sheep, oxen, male donkeys, male and female servants, female donkeys, and camels. Gen. 20:14 • Gen. 13:2

17 But the LORD [R]plagued Pharaoh and his house with great plagues because of Sarai, Abram's wife. 1 Chr. 16:21

18 And Pharaoh called Abram and said, "What *is* this you have done to me? Why did you not tell me that she *was* your wife?

19 "Why did you say, 'She *is* my sister'? I might have taken her as my wife. Now therefore, here is your wife; take *her* and go your way."

20 [R]So Pharaoh commanded *his* men concerning him; and they sent him away, with his wife and all that he had. [Prov. 21:1]

CHAPTER 13

Abram's Separation from Lot

THEN Abram went up from Egypt, he and his wife and all that he had, and [R]Lot with him, to the South.* Gen. 12:4; 14:12, 16

2 [R]Abram *was* very rich in livestock, in silver, and in gold. Gen. 24:35; 26:14

3 And he went on his journey [R]from the South as far as Bethel, to the place where his tent had been at the beginning, between Bethel and Ai, Gen. 12:8, 9

4 to the [R]place of the altar which he had made there at first. And there Abram called on the name of the LORD. Gen. 12:7, 8; 21:33

5 Lot also, who went with Abram, had flocks and herds and tents.

6 Now [R]the land was not able to [T]support them, that they might dwell together, for their possessions were so great that they could not dwell together. Gen. 36:7 • Lit. *bear*

7 And there was [R]strife between the herdsmen of Abram's livestock and the herdsmen of Lot's livestock. The Canaanites and the Perizzites then dwelt in the land. Gen. 26:20

8 So Abram said to Lot, [R]"Please let there be no strife between you and me, and between my herdsmen and your herdsmen; for we *are* brethren. 1 Cor. 6:7

9 "*Is* not the whole land before you? Please separate from me. If *you take* the left, then I will go to the right; or, if *you go* to the right, then I will go to the left."

12:6 Heb. *Alon Moreh* **12:9** Heb. *Negev* **12:13** Lit. *my soul* **13:1** Heb. *Negev*

---

(1) national—"I will make you a great nation," (2) personal—"I will bless you and make your name great; and you shall be a blessing," and (3) universal—"in you all families of the earth shall be blessed." This covenant was first given in broad outline and was later confirmed to Abraham in greater detail (cf. Page 16—Gen. 13:14–17; 15:1–7, 18–21; 17:1–8). The Abrahamic covenant constitutes an important link in all that God began to do, has done throughout history, and will continue to do until the consummation of history. It is the one purpose of God for humans into which all of God's programs and works fit. The personal aspects of the Abrahamic covenant are fourfold: (1) to be the father of a great nation, (2) to receive personal blessing, (3) to receive personal honor and reputation, and (4) to be the source of blessing to others. The universal aspects of the covenant are threefold: (1) blessings for those people and nations that bless Abraham and the nation that comes from him; (2) cursings upon those people and nations that curse Abraham and Israel; and (3) blessings upon all the families of the earth through the Messiah, who, according to the flesh, is Abraham's son and provides salvation for the entire world.

Now turn to Page 73—Ex. 19:5–8: The Mosaic Covenant.

10 And Lot lifted his eyes and saw all [R]the plain of Jordan, that it *was* well watered everywhere (before the LORD [R]destroyed Sodom and Gomorrah) [R]like the garden of the LORD, like the land of Egypt as you go toward Zoar. Gen. 19:17–29 • Gen. 19:24 • Gen. 2:8, 10

11 Then Lot chose for himself all the plain of Jordan, and Lot journeyed east. And they separated from each other.

12 Abram dwelt in the land of Canaan, and Lot dwelt in the cities of the plain and pitched *his* tent even as far as Sodom.

13 But the men of Sodom *were* exceedingly wicked and sinful against the LORD.

God's Promise to Abram

14 And the LORD said to Abram, after Lot [R]had separated from him: "Lift your eyes now and look from the place where you are—[R]northward, southward, eastward, and westward; Gen. 13:11 • Gen. 28:14

15 "for all the land which you see [R]I give to you and your descendants* forever. Acts 7:5

16 "And I will make your descendants as the dust of the earth; so that if a man could number the dust of the earth, *then* your descendants also could be numbered.

17 "Arise, walk in the land through its length and its width, for I give it to you."

18 [R]Then Abram moved *his* tent, and went and [R]dwelt by the terebinth trees of Mamre,* which *are* in Hebron, and built an altar there to the LORD. Gen. 26:17 • Gen. 14:13

CHAPTER 14

Abram Rescues Lot

AND it came to pass in the days of Amraphel king [R]of Shinar, Arioch king of Ellasar, Chedorlaomer king of Elam, and Tidal king of nations,* Gen. 10:10; 11:2

2 *that* they made war with Bera king of Sodom, Birsha king of Gomorrah, Shinab king of Admah, Shemeber king of Zeboiim, and the king of Bela (that is, Zoar).

3 All these joined together in the Valley of Siddim [R](that is, the Salt Sea). Num. 34:12

4 Twelve years [R]they served Chedorlaomer, and in the thirteenth year they rebelled. Gen. 9:26

5 In the fourteenth year Chedorlaomer and the kings that *were* with him came and attacked [R]the Rephaim in Ashteroth Karnaim, [R]the Zuzim in Ham, the Emim in Shaveh Kiriathaim, Gen. 15:20 • Deut. 2:20

6 [R]and the Horites in their mountain of Seir, as far as El Paran, which *is* by the wilderness. Deut. 2:12, 22

7 Then they turned back and came to En Mishpat (that *is*, Kadesh), and attacked all the country of the Amalekites, and also the Amorites who dwelt in Hazezon Tamar.

8 And the king of Sodom, the king of Gomorrah, the king of Admah, the king of Zeboiim, and the king of Bela (that *is*, Zoar) went out and joined together in battle in the Valley of Siddim

9 against Chedorlaomer king of Elam, Tidal king of nations,* Amraphel king of Shinar, and Arioch king of Ellasar—four kings against five.

10 Now the Valley of Siddim *was full of* [R]asphalt pits; and the kings of Sodom and Gomorrah fled; *some* fell there, and the remainder fled to the mountains. Gen. 11:3

11 Then they took [R]all the goods of Sodom and Gomorrah, and all their provisions, and went their way. Gen. 14:16, 21

12 They also took Lot, Abram's [R]brother's son [R]who dwelt in Sodom, and his goods, and departed. Gen. 11:27; 12:5 • Gen. 13:12

13 Then one who had escaped came and told Abram the [R]Hebrew, for he dwelt by the terebinth trees of Mamre* the Amorite, brother of Eshcol and brother of Aner; and they *were* allies with Abram. Gen. 39:14; 40:15

14 Now [R]when Abram heard that his brother was taken captive, he armed his three hundred and eighteen trained *servants* who were born in his own house, and went in pursuit as far as Dan. Gen. 19:29

15 He divided his forces against them by night, and he and his servants [R]attacked them and pursued them as far as Hobah, which *is* north of Damascus. Is. 41:2, 3

16 So he brought back all the goods, and also brought back his brother Lot and his goods, as well as the women and the people.

Abram Refuses Reward

17 And the king of Sodom [R]went out to meet him at the Valley of Shaveh (that *is*, the King's Valley), [R]after his return from the defeat of Chedorlaomer and the kings who *were* with him. 1 Sam. 18:6 • Heb. 7:1

18 Then [R]Melchizedek king of Salem brought out bread and wine; he *was* the priest of God Most High. Heb. 7:1–10

19 And he blessed him and said:

"Blessed be Abram of God Most High,
Possessor of heaven and earth;
20 And [R]blessed be God Most High,
Who has delivered your enemies into
your hand." Gen. 24:27

And he [R]gave him a tithe of all. Heb. 7:4

21 Now the king of Sodom said to Abram, "Give me the [T]persons, and take the goods for yourself." Lit. *souls*

22 But Abram [R]said to the king of Sodom, "I [R]have raised my hand to the LORD, God

13:15 Lit. *seed* **13:18** Heb. *Alon Mamre* **14:1** Heb. *goyim* **14:9** Heb. *goyim* **14:13** Heb. *Alon Mamre*

Most High, [R]the Possessor of heaven and
earth, Gen. 14:2, 8, 10 • Dan. 12:7 • Gen. 14:19
23 "that [R]I *will take* nothing, from a thread to
a sandal strap, and that I will not take any-
thing that *is* yours, lest you should say, 'I have
made Abram rich'— 2 Kin. 5:16
24 "except only what the young men have
eaten, and the portion of the men who went
with me: Aner, Eshcol, and Mamre; let them
take their portion."

CHAPTER 15

God's Promise of Children

AFTER these things the word of the LORD
came to Abram [R]in a vision, saying, "Do
not be afraid, Abram. I *am* your shield, your
exceedingly great reward." Dan. 10:1
2 But Abram said, "Lord GOD, what will You
give me, seeing I go childless, and the heir of
my house *is* Eliezer of Damascus?"
3 Then Abram said, "Look, You have given
me no offspring; indeed [R]one[T] born in my
house is my heir!" Gen. 14:14 • *a servant*
4 And behold, the word of the LORD *came* to
him, saying, "This one shall not be your heir,
but one who [R]will come from your own body
shall be your heir." 2 Sam. 7:12
5 Then He brought him outside and said,
"Look now toward heaven, and [R]count the
[R]stars if you are able to number them." And
He said to him, [R]"So shall your [R]descendants
be." Ps. 147:4 • Jer. 33:22 • Ex. 32:13 • Gen. 17:19
6 And he believed in the LORD, and He ac-
counted it to him for righteousness.
7 Then He said to him, "I *am* the LORD,
who [R]brought you out of [R]Ur of the
Chaldeans, [R]to give you this land to inherit
it." Gen. 12:1 • Gen. 11:28, 31 • Ps. 105:42, 44
8 And he said, "Lord GOD, [R]how shall I
know that I will inherit it?" Luke 1:18
9 So He said to him, "Bring Me a three-
year-old heifer, a three-year-old female goat, a
three-year-old ram, a turtledove, and a young
pigeon."
10 Then he brought all these to Him and [R]cut
them in two, down the middle, and placed
each piece opposite the other; but he did not
cut the birds in two. Jer. 34:18
11 And when the vultures came down on the
carcasses, Abram drove them away.
12 Now when the sun was going down, a
deep sleep fell upon Abram; and behold, hor-
ror *and* great darkness fell upon him.
13 Then He said to Abram: "Know certainly
[R]that your descendants will be strangers in a
land *that is* not theirs, and will serve them,
and [R]they will afflict them four hundred
years. Ex. 1:11 • Ex. 12:40
14 "And also the nation whom they serve [R]I
will judge; afterward [R]they shall come out
with great possessions. Ex. 6:6 • Ex. 12:36
15 "Now as for you, [R]you shall go [R]to your fa-
thers in peace; [R]you shall be buried at a good
old age. Job 5:26 • Gen. 25:8; 47:30 • Gen. 25:8
16 "But [R]in the fourth generation they shall
return here, for the iniquity of the Amorites
[R]*is* not yet complete." Ex. 12:41 • Matt. 23:32
17 And it came to pass, when the sun went
down and it was dark, that behold, there ap-
peared a smoking oven and a burning torch
that passed between those pieces.
18 On the same day the LORD [R]made a
covenant with Abram, saying: Gen. 24:7
[R]"To your descendants I have given this
land, from the river of Egypt to the great river,
the River Euphrates— Gen. 12:7; 17:8
19 "the Kenites, the Kenezzites, the Kad-
monites,
20 "the Hittites, the Perizzites, the Rephaim,
21 "the Amorites, the Canaanites, the Gir-
gashites, and the Jebusites."

CHAPTER 16

A Carnal Plan for Children

NOW Sarai, Abram's wife, had borne him
no *children.* And she had an Egyptian
maidservant whose name was Hagar.
2 [R]So Sarai said to Abram, "See now, the
LORD has restrained me from bearing *chil-
dren.* Please, go in to my maid; perhaps I shall
obtain children by her." And Abram heeded
the voice of Sarai. Gen. 30:3
3 Then Sarai, Abram's wife, took Hagar her
maid, the Egyptian, and gave her to her hus-
band Abram to be his wife, after Abram had
dwelt ten years in the land of Canaan.
4 So he went in to Hagar, and she con-
ceived. And when she saw that she had con-
ceived, her mistress became [R]despised in her
[T]eyes. [Prov. 30:21, 23] • *sight*
5 Then Sarai said to Abram, "My wrong *be*
upon you! I gave my maid into your embrace;
and when she saw that she had conceived, I
became despised in her eyes. [R]The LORD judge
between you and me." Gen. 31:53
6 [R]So Abram said to Sarai, "Indeed your
maid *is* in your hand; do to her as you please."
And when Sarai dealt harshly with her, she
fled from her presence. 1 Pet. 3:7
7 Now the [R]Angel of the LORD found her by
a spring of water in the wilderness, by the
spring on the way to Shur. Gen. 21:17, 18
8 And He said, "Hagar, Sarai's maid, where
have you come from, and where are you
going?" She said, "I am fleeing from the pres-
ence of my mistress Sarai."
9 The Angel of the LORD said to her, "Re-
turn to your mistress, and [R]submit yourself
under her hand." [Titus 2:9]
10 Then the Angel of the LORD said to her, [R]"I
will multiply your descendants exceedingly,
so that they shall not be counted for multi-
tude." Gen. 17:20
11 And the Angel of the LORD said to her:

"Behold, you *are* with child,
[R]And you shall bear a son.
You shall call his name [T]Ishmael,
Because the LORD has heard your
affliction. Luke 1:13, 31 • Lit. *God Hears*

12 [R]He shall be a wild man;
His hand *shall be* against every man,
And every man's hand against him.
[R]And he shall dwell in the presence of all
his brethren." Gen. 21:20 • Gen. 25:18

13 Then she called the name of the LORD who spoke to her, You-Are-[T]the-God-Who-Sees; for she said, "Have I also here seen Him [R]who sees me?" Heb. *El Roi* • Gen. 31:42

14 Therefore the well was called [R]Beer Lahai Roi;* observe, *it is* [R]between Kadesh and Bered. Gen. 24:62 • Num. 13:26

15 So [R]Hagar bore Abram a son; and Abram named his son, whom Hagar bore, Ishmael. Gal. 4:22

16 Abram *was* eighty-six years old when Hagar bore Ishmael to Abram.

CHAPTER 17

Institution of the Covenant: Circumcision

WHEN Abram was ninety-nine years old, the LORD [R]appeared to Abram and said to him, "I *am* Almighty God; walk before Me and be blameless. Gen. 12:7; 18:1

2 "And I will make My [R]covenant between Me and you, and [R]will multiply you exceedingly." Gen. 15:18 • Gen. 12:2; 13:16; 15:5; 18:18

3 Then Abram fell on his face, and God talked with him, saying:

4 "As for Me, behold, My covenant is with you, and you shall be [R]a father of [T]many nations. [Rom. 4:11, 12, 16] • Lit. *multitude of nations*

5 "No longer shall [R]your name be called [T]Abram, but your name shall be Abraham; [R]for I have made you a father of many nations. Neh. 9:7 • Lit. *Exalted Father* • Rom. 4:17

6 "I will make you exceedingly fruitful; and I will make [R]nations of you, and [R]kings shall come from you. Gen. 17:16; 35:11 • Matt. 1:6

7 "And I will [R]establish My covenant between Me and you and your descendants after you in their generations, for an everlasting covenant, to be God to you and [R]your descendants after you. [Gal. 3:17]☆ • Rom. 9:8

8 "Also I give to you and your descendants after you the land in which you are a stranger, all the land of Canaan, as an everlasting possession; and I will be their God."

9 And God said to Abraham: "As for you, [R]you shall keep My covenant, you and your descendants after you throughout their generations. Ex. 19:5

10 "This *is* My covenant which you shall keep, between Me and you and your descendants after you: [R]Every male child among you shall be circumcised; Acts 7:8

11 "and you shall be circumcised in the flesh of your foreskins, and it shall be a sign of the covenant between Me and you.

12 "He who is eight days old among you [R]shall be circumcised, every male child in your generations, he who is born in your house or bought with money from any foreigner who is not your descendant. Lev. 12:3

13 "He who is born in your house and he who is bought with your money must be circumcised, and My covenant shall be in your flesh for an everlasting covenant.

14 "And the uncircumcised male child, who is not circumcised in the flesh of his foreskin, that person shall be cut off from his people; he has broken My covenant."

15 Then God said to Abraham, "As for Sarai your wife, you shall not call her name Sarai, but Sarah *shall be* her name.

16 "And I will bless her [R]and also give you a son by her; then I will bless her, and she shall be *a mother* [R]*of* nations; kings of peoples shall be from her." Gen. 18:10 • Gen. 35:11

17 Then Abraham fell on his face [R]and laughed, and said in his heart, "Shall *a child* be born to a man who is one hundred years old? And shall Sarah, who is ninety years old, bear *a child?*" Gen. 17:3; 18:12; 21:6

18 And Abraham [R]said to God, "Oh, that Ishmael might live before You!" Gen. 18:23

19 Then God said: "No, [R]Sarah your wife shall bear you a son, and you shall call his name Isaac; I will establish My covenant with him for an everlasting covenant, *and* with his descendants after him. [Gal. 4:28]☆

20 "And as for Ishmael, I have heard you. Behold, I have blessed him, and will make him fruitful, and [R]will multiply him exceedingly. He shall beget twelve princes, and I will make him a great nation. Gen. 16:10

21 "But My [R]covenant I will establish with Isaac, [R]whom Sarah shall bear to you at this set time next year." Gen. 26:2–5 • Gen. 21:2

22 Then He finished talking with him, and God went up from Abraham.

23 So Abraham took Ishmael his son, all who were born in his house and all who were bought with his money, every male among the men of Abraham's house, and circumcised the flesh of their foreskins that very same day, as God had said to him.

24 Abraham *was* ninety-nine years old when he was circumcised in the flesh of his foreskin.

25 And Ishmael his son *was* thirteen years old when he was circumcised in the flesh of his foreskin.

26 That very same day Abraham was circumcised, and his son Ishmael;

27 and all the men of his house, born in the house or bought with money from a foreigner, were circumcised with him.

16:14 Lit. *Well of the One Who Lives and Sees Me*

CHAPTER 18

Sarah's Faith Is Tested

THEN the LORD appeared to him by the terebinth trees of Mamre,* as he was sitting in the tent door in the heat of the day.

2 [R]So he lifted his eyes and looked, and behold, three men were standing by him; [R]and when he saw *them,* he ran from the tent door to meet them, and bowed himself to the ground, Heb. 13:2 • Gen. 19:1

3 and said, "My Lord, if I have now found favor in Your sight, do not pass on by Your servant.

4 "Please let [R]a little water be brought, and wash your feet, and rest yourselves under the tree. Gen. 19:2; 24:32; 43:24

5 "And [R]I will bring a morsel of bread, that [R]you may refresh your hearts. After that you may pass by, inasmuch as you have come to your servant." They said, "Do as you have said." Judg. 6:18, 19; 13:15, 16 • Judg. 19:5

6 So Abraham hurried into the tent to Sarah and said, "Quickly, make ready three measures of fine meal; knead *it* and make cakes."

7 And Abraham ran to the herd, took a tender and good calf, gave *it* to a young man, and he hastened to prepare it.

8 So [R]he took butter and milk and the calf which he had prepared, and set *it* before them; and he stood by them under the tree as they ate. Gen. 19:3

9 Then they said to him, "Where *is* Sarah your wife?" So he said, "Here, in the tent."

10 And He said, "I will certainly return to you [R]according to the time of life, and behold, [R]Sarah your wife shall have a son." (Sarah was listening in the tent door which *was* behind him.) 2 Kin. 4:16 • Rom. 9:9

11 Now [R]Abraham and Sarah were old, well advanced in age; *and* Sarah [R]had passed the age of childbearing.* Gen. 17:17 • Gen. 31:35

12 Therefore Sarah laughed within herself, saying, "After I have grown old, shall I have pleasure, my lord being old also?"

13 And the LORD said to Abraham, "Why did Sarah laugh, saying, 'Shall I surely bear *a child,* since I am old?'

14 [R]"Is anything too hard for the LORD? [R]At the appointed time I will return to you, according to the time of life, and Sarah shall have a son." Jer. 32:17 • Gen. 17:21; 18:10

15 But Sarah denied *it,* saying, "I did not laugh," for she was afraid. And He said, "No, but you did laugh!"

Abraham's Faith Is Tested

16 Then the men rose from there and looked toward Sodom, and Abraham went with them to send them on the way.

17 And the LORD said, [R]"Shall I hide from Abraham what I am doing, Ps. 25:14

18 "since Abraham shall surely become a great and mighty nation, and all the nations of the earth shall be blessed in him?

19 "For I have known him, in order [R]that he may command his children and his household after him, that they keep the way of the LORD, to do righteousness and justice, that the LORD may bring to Abraham what He has spoken to him." [Deut. 4:9, 10; 6:6, 7]

20 And the LORD said, "Because [R]the outcry against Sodom and Gomorrah is great, and because their sin is very grave, Gen. 4:10

21 [R]"I will go down now and see whether they have done altogether according to the outcry against it that has come to Me; and if not, [R]I will know." Gen. 11:5 • Deut. 8:2; 13:3

22 Then the men turned away from there [R]and went toward Sodom, but Abraham still stood before the LORD. Gen. 18:16; 19:1

23 And Abraham [R]came near and said, [R]"Would You also destroy the righteous with the wicked? [Heb. 10:22] • Num. 16:22

24 "Suppose there were fifty righteous within the city; would You also destroy the place and not spare *it* for the fifty righteous that were in it?

25 "Far be it from You to do such a thing as this, to slay the righteous with the wicked, so [R]that the righteous should be as the wicked; far be it from You! Shall not the Judge of all the earth do right?" Is. 3:10, 11

26 So the LORD said, [R]"If I find in Sodom fifty righteous within the city, then I will spare all the place for their sakes." Jer. 5:1

27 Then Abraham answered and said, "Indeed now, I who *am* [R]*but* dust and ashes have taken it upon myself to speak to the Lord: [Gen. 3:19]

28 "Suppose there were five less than the fifty righteous; would You destroy all of the city for *lack of* five?" So He said, "If I find there forty-five, I will not destroy *it.*"

29 And he spoke to Him yet again and said, "Suppose there should be forty found there?" So He said, "I will not do *it* for the sake of forty."

30 Then he said, "Let not the Lord be angry, and I will speak: Suppose thirty should be found there?" So He said, "I will not do *it* if I find thirty there."

31 And he said, "Indeed now, I have taken it upon myself to speak to the Lord: Suppose twenty should be found there?" So He said, "I will not destroy *it* for the sake of twenty."

32 Then he said, "Let not the Lord be angry, and I will speak but once more: Suppose ten should be found there?" And He said, "I will not destroy *it* for the sake of ten."

33 So the LORD went His way as soon as He had finished speaking with Abraham; and Abraham returned to his place.

18:1 Heb. *Alon Mamre* **18:11** Lit. *the manner of women had ceased to be with Sarah*

CHAPTER 19

Destruction of Sodom and Gomorrah

NOW [R]the two angels came to Sodom in the evening, and Lot was sitting in the gate of Sodom. When Lot saw *them,* he rose to meet them, and he bowed himself with his face toward the ground. Gen. 18:2, 16, 22

2 And he said, "Here now, my lords, please [R]turn in to your servant's house and spend the night, and wash your feet; then you may rise early and go on your way." And they said, [R]"No, but we will spend the night in the open square." [Heb. 13:2] • Luke 24:28

3 But he insisted strongly; so they turned in to him and entered his house. [R]Then he made them a feast, and baked [R]unleavened bread, and they ate. Gen. 18:6–8 • Ex. 12:8

4 Now before they lay down, the men of the city, the men of Sodom, both old and young, all the people from every quarter, surrounded the house.

5 [R]And they called to Lot and said to him, "Where are the men who came to you tonight? [R]Bring them out to us that we may know them *carnally.*" Is. 3:9 • Judg. 19:22

6 So Lot went out to them through the doorway, shut the door behind him,

7 and said, "Please, my brethren, do not do so wickedly!

8 [R]"See now, I have two daughters who have not known a man; please, let me bring them out to you, and you may do to them as you wish; only do nothing to these men, since this is the reason they have come under the shadow of my roof." Judg. 19:24

9 And they said, "Stand back!" Then they said, "This one [R]came in to stay *here,* and he keeps acting as a judge; now we will deal worse with you than with them." So they pressed hard against the man Lot, and came near to break down the door. 2 Pet. 2:7, 8

10 But the men reached out their hands and pulled Lot into the house with them, and shut the door.

11 And they [R]struck the men who *were* at the doorway of the house with blindness, both small and great, so that they became weary *trying* to find the door. Gen. 20:17, 18

12 Then the men said to Lot, "Have you anyone else here? Son-in-law, your sons, your daughters, and whomever you have in the city—take *them* out of this place!

13 "For we will destroy this place, because the [R]outcry against them has grown great before the face of the LORD, and the LORD has sent us to destroy it." Gen. 18:20

14 So Lot went out and spoke to his sons-in-law, [R]who had married his daughters, and said, "Get up, get out of this place; for the LORD will destroy this city!" But to his sons-in-law he seemed to be joking. Matt. 1:18

15 When the morning dawned, the angels urged Lot to hurry, saying, [R]"Arise, take your wife and your two daughters who are here, lest you be consumed in the punishment of the city." Rev. 18:4

16 And while he lingered, the men [R]took hold of his hand, his wife's hand, and the hands of his two daughters, the LORD being merciful to him, and they brought him out and set him outside the city. 2 Pet. 2:7

17 So it came to pass, when they had brought them outside, that he* said, "Escape for your life! Do not look behind you nor stay anywhere in the plain. Escape to the mountains, lest you be destroyed."

18 Then Lot said to them, "Please, [R]no, my lords! Acts 10:14

19 "Indeed now, your servant has found favor in your sight, and you have increased your mercy which you have shown me by saving my life; but I cannot escape to the mountains, lest some evil overtake me and I die.

20 "See now, this city *is* near *enough* to flee to, and it *is* a little one; please let me escape there (*is* it not a little one?) and my soul shall live."

21 And he said to him, "See, [R]I have favored you concerning this thing also, in that I will not overthrow this city for which you have spoken. Job 42:8, 9

22 "Hurry, escape there. For I cannot do anything until you arrive there." Therefore the name of the city was called Zoar.

23 The sun had risen upon the earth when Lot entered Zoar.

24 Then the LORD rained [R]brimstone and [R]fire on Sodom and Gomorrah, from the LORD out of the heavens. Deut. 29:23 • Lev. 10:2

25 So He overthrew those cities, all the plain, all the inhabitants of the cities, and [R]what grew on the ground. Ps. 107:34

26 But his wife looked back behind him, and she became [R]a pillar of salt. Luke 17:32

27 And Abraham went early in the morning to the place where [R]he had stood before the LORD. Gen. 18:22

28 Then he looked toward Sodom and Gomorrah, and toward all the land of the plain; and he saw, and behold, [R]the smoke of the land which went up like the smoke of a furnace. Rev. 9:2; 18:9

29 And it came to pass, when God destroyed the cities of the plain, that God [R]remembered Abraham, and sent Lot out of the midst of the overthrow, when He overthrew the cities in which Lot had dwelt. Gen. 8:1

The Sin of Lot

30 Then Lot went up out of Zoar and [R]dwelt in the mountains, and his two daughters were with him; for he was afraid to dwell in Zoar.

19:17 LXX, Syr., Vg. *they*

And he and his two daughters dwelt in a cave. Gen. 19:17, 19

31 Now the firstborn said to the younger, "Our father *is* old, and *there is* no man on the earth [R]to come in to us as is the custom of all the earth. Gen. 16:2, 4; 38:8, 9

32 "Come, let us make our father drink wine, and we will lie with him, that we may preserve the lineage of our father."

33 So they made their father drink wine that night. And the firstborn went in and lay with her father, and he did not know when she lay down or when she arose.

34 It happened on the next day that the firstborn said to the younger, "Indeed I lay with my father last night; let us make him drink wine tonight also, and you go in *and* lie with him, that we may preserve the [T]lineage of our father." Lit. *seed*

35 Then they made their father drink wine that night also. And the younger arose and lay with him, and he did not know when she lay down or when she arose.

36 Thus both the daughters of Lot were with child by their father.

37 The firstborn bore a son and called his name Moab; [R]he *is* the father of the Moabites to this day. Deut. 2:9

38 And the younger, she also bore a son and called his name Ben-Ammi; he *is* the father of the people of Ammon to this day.

CHAPTER 20

The Test of Abimelech

AND Abraham journeyed from [R]there to the South, and dwelt between Kadesh and Shur, and stayed in Gerar. Gen. 18:1

2 Now Abraham said of Sarah his wife, [R]"She *is* my sister." And Abimelech king of Gerar sent and took Sarah. Gen. 12:11–13

3 But [R]God came to Abimelech [R]in a dream by night, and said to him, [R]"Indeed you *are* a dead man because of the woman whom you have taken, for she *is* a man's wife." Ps. 105:14 • Job 33:15 • Gen. 20:7

4 But Abimelech had not come near her; and he said, "Lord, [R]will You slay a righteous nation also? Gen. 18:23–25

5 "Did he not say to me, 'She *is* my sister'? And she, even she herself said, 'He *is* my brother.' [R]In the [T]integrity of my heart and innocence of my hands I have done this." 2 Kin. 20:3 • *innocence*

6 And God said to him in a dream, "Yes, I know that you did this in the integrity of your heart. For [R]I also withheld you from sinning [R]against Me; therefore I did not let you touch her. 1 Sam. 25:26, 34 • Gen. 39:9

7 "Now therefore, restore the man's wife; [R]for he *is* a prophet, and he will pray for you and you shall live. But if you do not restore *her,* [R]know that you shall surely die, you and all who *are* yours." 1 Sam. 7:5 • Gen. 2:17

8 So Abimelech rose early in the morning, called all his servants, and told all these things in their hearing; and the men were very much afraid.

9 And Abimelech called Abraham and said to him, "What have you done to us? How have I [T]offended you, [R]that you have brought on me and on my kingdom a great sin? You have done deeds to me [R]that ought not to be done." *sinned against* • Gen. 26:10; 39:9 • Gen. 34:7

10 Then Abimelech said to Abraham, "What did you have in view, that you have done this thing?"

11 And Abraham said, "Because I thought, surely the fear of God *is* not in this place; and they will kill me on account of my wife.

12 "But indeed [R]*she is* truly my sister. She *is* the daughter of my father, but not the daughter of my mother; and she became my wife. Gen. 11:29

13 "And it came to pass, when God caused me to wander from my father's house, that I said to her, 'This *is* your kindness that you should do for me: in every place, wherever we go, say of me, "He *is* my brother."' "

14 Then Abimelech [R]took sheep, oxen, and male and female servants, and gave *them* to Abraham; and he restored Sarah his wife to him. Gen. 12:16

15 And Abimelech said, "See, my land *is* before you; dwell where it pleases you."

16 Then to Sarah he said, "Behold, I have given your brother a thousand *pieces* of silver; [R]indeed this vindicates you* [R]before all who *are* with you and before everybody." Thus she was rebuked. Gen. 26:11 • Mal. 2:9

17 So Abraham [R]prayed to God; and God healed Abimelech, his wife, and his female servants. Then they bore *children;* Job 42:9

18 for the LORD [R]had closed up all the wombs of the house of Abimelech because of Sarah, Abraham's wife. Gen. 12:17

CHAPTER 21

Birth of Isaac

AND the LORD [R]visited Sarah as He had said, and the LORD did for Sarah [R]as He had spoken. 1 Sam. 2:21 • [Gal. 4:23, 28]

2 For Sarah [R]conceived and bore Abraham a son in his old age, at the set time of which God had spoken to him. Heb. 11:11, 12

3 And Abraham called the name of his son who was born to him—whom Sarah bore to him—[R]Isaac.[T] Gen. 17:19, 21 • Lit. *Laughter*

4 Then Abraham [R]circumcised his son Isaac when he was eight days old, [R]as God had commanded him. Acts 7:8 • Gen. 17:10, 12

20:16 Lit. *is a covering of the eyes for you to all*

5 Now Abraham was one hundred years old when his son Isaac was born to him.

6 And Sarah said, "God has made me laugh, *and* all who hear will laugh with me."

7 She also said, "Who would have said to Abraham that Sarah would nurse children? For I have borne *him* a son in his old age."

8 So the child grew and was weaned. And Abraham made a great feast on the same day that Isaac was weaned.

9 And Sarah saw the son of Hagar [R]the Egyptian, whom she had borne to Abraham, [R]scoffing.[T] Gen. 16:1, 4, 15 • [Gal. 4:29] • Lit. *laughing*

10 Therefore she said to Abraham, [R]"Cast out this bondwoman and her son; for the son of this bondwoman shall not be heir with my son, *namely* with Isaac." Gal. 3:18

11 And the matter was very displeasing in Abraham's sight because of his son.

12 But God said to Abraham, "Do not let it be displeasing in your sight because of the lad or because of your bondwoman. Whatever Sarah has said to you, listen to her voice; for [R]in Isaac your seed shall be called. [Rom. 9:7, 8]☆

13 "Yet I will also make [R]a nation of the son of the bondwoman, because he *is* your seed." Gen. 16:10; 17:20; 21:18; 25:12–18

14 So Abraham rose early in the morning, and took bread and [T]a skin of water; and putting *it* on her shoulder, he gave *it* and the boy to Hagar, and [R]sent her away. Then she departed and wandered in the Wilderness of Beersheba. A water bottle made of skins • John 8:35

15 And the water in the skin was used up, and she placed the boy under one of the shrubs.

16 Then she went and sat down across from *him* at a distance of about a bowshot; for she said to herself, "Let me not see the death of the boy." So she sat opposite *him,* and lifted her voice and wept.

17 And [R]God heard the voice of the lad. Then the [R]angel of God called to Hagar out of heaven, and said to her, "What ails you, Hagar? Fear not, for God has heard the voice of the lad where he *is.* Ex. 3:7 • Gen. 22:11

18 "Arise, lift up the lad and hold him with your hand, for [R]I will make him a great nation." Gen. 16:10; 21:13; 25:12–16

19 Then [R]God opened her eyes, and she saw a well of water. And she went and filled the skin with water, and gave the lad a drink. Num. 22:31

20 So God [R]was with the lad; and he grew and dwelt in the wilderness, [R]and became an archer. Gen. 28:15; 39:2, 3, 21 • Gen. 16:12

21 He dwelt in the Wilderness of Paran; and his mother [R]took a wife for him from the land of Egypt. Gen. 24:4

22 And *it* came to pass at that time that [R]Abimelech and Phichol, the commander of his army, spoke to Abraham, saying, "God *is* with you in all that you do. Gen. 20:2, 14

23 "Now therefore, [R]swear[T] to me by God that you will not deal falsely with me, with my offspring, or with my posterity; but that according to the kindness that I have done to you, you will do to me and to the land in which you have dwelt." Josh. 2:12 • *take an oath*

24 And Abraham said, "I will swear."

25 Then Abraham rebuked Abimelech because of a well of water which Abimelech's servants [R]had seized. Gen. 26:15, 18, 20–22

26 And Abimelech said, "I do not know who has done this thing; you did not tell me, nor had I heard *of it* until today."

27 So Abraham took sheep and oxen and gave them to Abimelech, and the two of them [R]made a covenant. Gen. 26:31; 31:44

28 And Abraham set seven ewe lambs of the flock by themselves.

29 Then Abimelech asked Abraham, "What *is the meaning of* these seven ewe lambs which you have set by themselves?"

30 And he said, "You will take *these* seven ewe lambs from my hand, that they may be my witness that I have dug this well."

31 Therefore he [R]called that place Beersheba,* because the two of them swore an oath there. Gen. 21:14; 26:33

32 Thus they made a covenant at Beersheba. So Abimelech rose with Phichol, the commander of his army, and they returned to the land of the Philistines.

33 Then *Abraham* planted a tamarisk tree in Beersheba, and [R]there called on the name of the LORD, the Everlasting God. Gen. 4:26

34 And Abraham stayed in the land of the Philistines many days.

CHAPTER 22

Offering of Isaac

NOW it came to pass after these things that God tested Abraham, and said to him, "Abraham!" And he said, "Here I am."

2 Then He said, "Take now your son, your only *son* Isaac, whom you love, and go to the land of Moriah, and offer him there as a burnt offering on one of the mountains of which I shall tell you."

3 So Abraham rose early in the morning and saddled his donkey, and took two of his young men with him, and Isaac his son; and he split the wood for the burnt offering, and arose and went to the place of which God had told him.

4 Then on the third day Abraham lifted his eyes and saw the place afar off.

5 And Abraham said to his young men, "Stay here with the donkey; the lad* and I will

21:31 Lit. *Well of the Oath* or *Well of the Seven*
22:5 Or *young man*

go yonder and worship, and we will [R]come back to you." [Heb. 11:19]

6 So Abraham took the wood of the burnt offering and [R]laid *it* on Isaac his son; and he took the fire in his hand, and a knife, and the two of them went together. John 19:17

7 But Isaac spoke to Abraham his father and said, "My father!" And he said, "Here I am, my son." Then he said, "Look, the fire and the wood, but where *is* the [T]lamb for a burnt offering?" *Or goat*

8 And Abraham said, "My son, God will provide for Himself the lamb for a burnt offering." So the two of them went together.

9 Then they came to the place of which God had told him. And Abraham built an altar there and placed the wood in order; and he bound Isaac his son and [R]laid him on the altar, upon the wood. [Heb. 11:17–19]

10 And Abraham stretched out his hand and took the knife to slay his son.

11 But the [R]Angel of the LORD called to him from heaven and said, "Abraham, Abraham!" So he said, "Here I am." Gen. 16:7–11; 21:17, 18

12 And He said, "Do not lay your hand on the lad, or do anything to him; for now I know that you fear God, since you have not withheld your son, your only *son*, from Me."

13 Then Abraham lifted his eyes and looked, and there behind *him was* a ram caught in a thicket by its horns. So Abraham went and took the ram, and offered it up for a burnt offering instead of his son.

14 And Abraham called the name of the place, The-LORD-Will-Provide;* as it is said *to* this day, "In the Mount of the LORD it shall be provided."

15 Then the Angel of the LORD called to Abraham a second time out of heaven,

16 and said: [R]"By Myself I have sworn, says the LORD, because you have done this thing, and have not withheld your son, your only *son*— Ps. 105:9

17 "blessing I will bless you, and multiplying I will multiply your descendants as the stars of the heaven and as the sand which *is* on the seashore; and your descendants shall possess the gate of their enemies.

18 [R]"In your seed all the nations of the earth shall be blessed, because you have obeyed My voice." Gal. 3:16☆

19 So Abraham returned to his young men, and they rose and went together to Beersheba; and Abraham dwelt at Beersheba.

20 Now it came to pass after these things that it was told Abraham, saying, "Indeed [R]Milcah also has borne children to your brother Nahor: Gen. 11:29; 24:15

21 [R]"Huz his firstborn, Buz his brother, Kemuel the father [R]of Aram, Job 1:1 • Job 32:2

22 "Chesed, Hazo, Pildash, Jidlaph, and Bethuel."

23 And [R]Bethuel begot Rebekah.* These eight Milcah bore to Nahor, Abraham's brother. Gen. 24:15

24 His concubine, whose name was Reumah, also bore Tebah, Gaham, Thahash, and Maachah.

CHAPTER 23

Death of Sarah

SARAH lived one hundred and twenty-seven years; *these were* the years of the life of Sarah.

2 So Sarah died in [R]Kirjath Arba (that *is,* [R]Hebron) in the land of Canaan, and Abraham came to mourn for Sarah and to weep for her. Josh. 14:15; 15:13; 21:11 • Gen. 13:18; 23:19

3 Then Abraham stood up from before his dead, and spoke to the sons of [R]Heth, saying, Gen. 10:15; 15:20

4 [R]"I *am* a foreigner and a visitor among you. [R]Give me property for a burial place among you, that I may bury my dead out of my sight." [Gen. 17:8] • Acts 7:5, 16

5 And the sons of Heth answered Abraham, saying to him,

6 "Hear us, my lord: You *are* [R]a mighty prince among us; bury your dead in the choicest of our burial places. None of us will withhold from you his burial place, that you may bury your dead." Gen. 13:2; 14:14; 24:35

7 Then Abraham stood up and bowed himself to the people of the land, the sons of Heth.

8 And he spoke with them, saying, "If it is your wish that I bury my dead out of my sight, hear me, and [T]meet with Ephron the son of Zohar for me, *entreat*

9 "that he may give me the cave of [R]Machpelah which he has, which *is* at the end of his field. Let him give it to me at the full price, as property for a burial place among you." Gen. 25:9

10 Now Ephron dwelt among the sons of Heth; and Ephron the Hittite answered Abraham in the presence of the sons of Heth, all who [R]entered at the gate of his city, saying, Gen. 23:18; 34:20, 24

11 "No, my lord, hear me: I give you the field and the cave that *is* in it; I give it to you in the presence of the sons of my people. I give it to you. Bury your dead!"

12 Then Abraham bowed himself down before the people of the land;

13 and he spoke to Ephron in the hearing of the people of the land, saying, "If you *will give it,* please hear me. I will give you money for the field; take *it* from me and I will bury my dead there."

14 And Ephron answered Abraham, saying to him,

22:14 Heb. *YHWH Yireh* **22:23** *Rebecca,* Rom. 9:10

15 "My lord, listen to me; the land *is worth*
four hundred shekels of silver. What *is* that
between you and me? So bury your dead."
16 And Abraham listened to Ephron; and
Abraham [R]weighed out the silver for Ephron
which he had named in the hearing of the
sons of Heth, four hundred shekels of silver,
currency of the merchants. Jer. 32:9, 10
17 So [R]the field of Ephron which *was* in
Machpelah, which *was* before Mamre, the
field and the cave which *was* in it, and all the
trees that *were* in the field, which *were*
within all the surrounding borders, were
deeded Gen. 25:9; 49:29–32; 50:13
18 to Abraham as a possession in the pres-
ence of the sons of Heth, before all who went
in at the gate of his city.
19 And after this, Abraham buried Sarah his
wife in the cave of the field of Machpelah, be-
fore Mamre (that *is*, Hebron) in the land of
Canaan.
20 So the field and the cave that *is* in it were
deeded to Abraham by the sons of Heth as
property for a burial place.

CHAPTER 24

Isaac's Marriage

NOW Abraham [R]was old, well advanced in
age; and the LORD [R]had blessed Abra-
ham in all things. Gen. 18:11; 21:5 • Gen. 12:2
2 So Abraham said to the oldest servant of
his house, who ruled over all that he had,
"Please, put your hand under my thigh,
3 "and I will make you [R]swear by the LORD,
the God of heaven and the God of the earth,
that [R]you will not take a wife for my son from
the daughters of the Canaanites, among
whom I dwell; Gen. 14:19, 22 • Deut. 7:3
4 "but you shall go to my country and to my
family, and take a wife for my son Isaac."
5 And the servant said to him, "Perhaps the
woman will not be willing to follow me to this
land. Must I take your son back to the land
from which you came?"
6 But Abraham said to him, "Beware that
you do not take my son back there.
7 "The LORD God of heaven, who [R]took me
from my father's house and from the land of
my family, and who spoke to me and swore
to me, saying, [R]'To your descendants* I give
this land,' He will send His angel before you,
and you shall take a wife for my son from
there. Gen. 12:1; 24:3 • Gen. 12:7; 13:15; 15:18
8 "And if the woman is not willing to follow
you, then you will be released from this oath;
only do not take my son back there."
9 So the servant put his hand under the
thigh of Abraham his master, and swore to
him concerning this matter.
10 Then the servant took ten of his mas-
ter's camels and departed, [R]for all his mas-
ter's goods *were in* his hand. And he arose
and went to Mesopotamia, to [R]the city of
Nahor. Gen. 24:2, 22 • Gen. 11:31, 32; 22:20; 27:43; 29:5
11 And he made his camels kneel down out-
side the city by a well of water at evening
time, the time [R]when women go out to draw
water. Ex. 2:16
12 Then he [R]said, "O LORD God of my mas-
ter Abraham, please [R]give me success this
day, and show kindness to my master Abra-
ham. Ex. 3:6, 15 • Neh. 1:11
13 "Behold, *here* [R]I stand by the well of
water, and the daughters of the men of the
city are coming out to draw water. Gen. 24:43
14 "Now let it be that the young woman to
whom I say, 'Please let down your pitcher that
I may drink,' and she says, 'Drink, and I will
also give your camels a drink'—*let* her *be the
one* You have appointed for Your servant
Isaac. And by this I will know that You have
shown kindness to my master."
15 And it happened, [R]before he had finished
speaking, that behold, Rebekah, who was
born to Bethuel, son of Milcah, the wife of
Nahor, Abraham's brother, came out with her
pitcher on her shoulder. Is. 65:24
16 Now the young woman [R]*was* very beauti-
ful to behold, a virgin; no man had known her.
And she went down to the well, filled her
pitcher, and came up. Gen. 12:11; 26:7
17 And the servant ran to meet her and said,
"Please let me drink a little water from your
pitcher."
18 [R]So she said, "Drink, my lord." Then she
quickly let her pitcher down to her hand, and
gave him a drink. [1 Pet. 3:8, 9]
19 And when she had finished giving him a
drink, she said, "I will draw *water* for your
camels also, until they have finished drinking."
20 Then she quickly emptied her pitcher into
the trough, ran back to the well to draw *water*,
and drew for all his camels.
21 And the man, wondering at her, re-
mained silent so as to know whether [R]the
LORD had made his journey prosperous or
not. Gen. 24:12–14, 27, 52
22 So it was, when the camels had finished
drinking, that the man took a golden [R]nose
ring weighing half a shekel, and two
bracelets for her wrists weighing ten *shekels*
of gold, Ex. 32:2, 3
23 and said, "Whose daughter *are* you? Tell
me, please, is there room *in* your father's
house for us [T]to lodge?" *to spend the night*
24 So she said to him, [R]"I *am* the daughter of
Bethuel, Milcah's son, whom she bore to
Nahor." Gen. 22:23; 24:15
25 Moreover she said to him, "We have both
straw and feed enough, and room to lodge."
26 Then the man [R]bowed down his head and
worshiped the LORD. Ex. 4:31
27 And he said, [R]"Blessed *be* the LORD God

24:7 Lit. *seed*

of my master Abraham, who has not for-
saken [R]His mercy and His truth toward my
master. As for me, being on the way, the
LORD [R]led me to the house of my master's
brethren." Ex. 18:10 • Gen. 32:10 • Gen. 24:21, 48
28 So the young woman ran and told her
mother's household these things.
29 Now Rebekah had a brother whose name
was [R]Laban, and Laban ran out to the man by
the well. Gen. 29:5, 13
30 So it came to pass, when he saw the nose
ring, and the bracelets on his sister's wrists,
and when he heard the words of his sister Re-
bekah, saying, "Thus the man spoke to me,"
that he went to the man. And there he stood
by the camels at the well.
31 And he said, "Come in, [R]O blessed of the
LORD! Why do you stand outside? For I have
prepared the house, and a place for the
camels." Judg. 17:2
32 Then the man came to the house. And he
unloaded the camels, and [R]provided straw
and feed for the camels, and water to [R]wash
his feet and the feet of the men who *were* with
him. Gen. 43:24 • Gen. 19:2
33 *Food* was set before him to eat, but he
said, "I will not eat until I have told about my
errand." And he said, "Speak on."
34 So he said, "I *am* Abraham's servant.
35 "The LORD [R]has blessed my master
greatly, and he has become great; and He has
given him flocks and herds, silver and gold,
male and female servants, and camels and
donkeys. Gen. 13:2; 24:1
36 "And Sarah my master's wife [R]bore a son
to my master when she was old; and to him he
has given all that he has. Gen. 21:1–7
37 "Now my master [R]made me swear, saying,
'You shall not take a wife for my son from the
daughters of the Canaanites, in whose land I
dwell; Gen. 24:2–4
38 [R]'but you shall go to my father's house
and to my family, and take a wife for my
son.' Gen. 24:4
39 [R]"And I said to my master, 'Perhaps the
woman will not follow me.' Gen. 24:5
40 [R]"But he said to me, 'The LORD, [R]before
whom I walk, will send His angel with you
and prosper your way; and you shall take a
wife for my son from my family and from my
father's house. Gen. 24:7 • Gen. 5:22, 24; 17:1
41 [R]'You will be clear from this oath when
you arrive among my family; for if they will
not give *her* to you, then you will be released
from my oath.' Gen. 24:8
42 "And this day I came to the well and said,
'O LORD God of my master Abraham, if You
will now prosper the way in which I go,
43 [R]'behold, I stand by the well of water; and
it shall come to pass that when the virgin
comes out to draw *water,* and I say to her,
"Please give me a little water from your
pitcher to drink," Gen. 24:13
44 'and she says to me, "Drink, and I will
draw for your camels also,"—*let* her *be* the
woman whom the LORD has appointed for my
master's son.'
45 [R]"But before I had finished speaking in
my heart, there was Rebekah, coming out
with her pitcher on her shoulder; and she
went down to the well and drew *water.* And I
said to her, 'Please let me drink.' Gen. 24:15
46 "And she made haste and let her pitcher
down from her *shoulder,* and said, 'Drink, and
I will give your camels a drink also.' So I
drank, and she gave the camels a drink also.
47 "Then I asked her, and said, 'Whose
daughter *are* you?' And she said, 'The daugh-
ter of Bethuel, Nahor's son, whom Milcah
bore to him.' So I put the nose ring on her
nose and the bracelets on her wrists.
48 [R]"And I bowed my head and worshiped
the LORD, and blessed the LORD God of my
master Abraham, who had led me in the way
of truth to [R]take the daughter of my master's
brother for his son. Gen. 24:26, 52 • Gen. 22:23
49 "Now if you will [R]deal kindly and truly
with my master, tell me. And if not, tell me,
that I may turn to the right hand or to the
left." Josh. 2:14
50 Then Laban and Bethuel answered and
said, "The thing comes from the LORD; we
cannot speak to you either bad or good.
51 [R]"Here *is* Rebekah before you; take *her*
and go, and let her be your master's son's
wife, as the LORD has spoken." Gen. 20:15
52 And it came to pass, when Abraham's ser-
vant heard their words, that he worshiped the
LORD, *bowing himself* to the earth.
53 Then the servant brought out jewelry of
silver, jewelry of gold, and clothing, and gave
them to Rebekah. He also gave precious
things to her brother and to her mother.
54 And he and the men who *were* with him
ate and drank and stayed all night. Then they
arose in the morning, and he said, [R]"Send me
away to my master." Gen. 30:25
55 But her brother and her mother said, "Let
the young woman stay with us *a few* days, at
least ten; after that she may go."
56 And he said to them, "Do not [T]hinder me,
since the LORD has prospered my way; send
me away so that I may go to my master." *delay*
57 So they said, "We will call the young
woman and ask her personally."
58 Then they called Rebekah and said to her,
"Will you go with this man?" And she said, "I
will go."
59 So they sent away Rebekah their sister
[R]and her nurse, and Abraham's servant and
his men. Gen. 35:8
60 And they blessed Rebekah and said to her:

"Our sister, *may* you *become*
[R] *The mother of* thousands of ten
thousands; Gen. 17:16

And may your descendants possess
The gates of those who hate them."

61 Then Rebekah and her maids arose, and
they rode on the camels and followed the
man. So the servant took Rebekah and de-
parted.
62 Now Isaac came from the way of Beer
Lahai Roi, for he dwelt in the South.
63 And Isaac went out [R]to meditate in the
field in the evening; and he lifted his eyes
and looked, and there, the camels *were* com-
ing. Josh. 1:8
64 Then Rebekah lifted her eyes, and when
she saw Isaac [R]she dismounted from her
camel; Josh. 15:18
65 for she had said to the servant, "Who *is*
this man walking in the field to meet us?" The
servant said, "It *is* my master." So she took a
veil and covered herself.
66 And the servant told Isaac all the things
that he had done.
67 Then Isaac brought her into his mother
Sarah's tent; and he took Rebekah and she
became his wife, and he loved her. So Isaac
was comforted after his mother's *death*.

CHAPTER 25

Abraham Dies—1 Chr. 1:28–33

ABRAHAM again took a wife, and her
name *was* [R]Keturah. 1 Chr. 1:32, 33
2 And she bore him Zimran, Jokshan,
Medan, Midian, Ishbak, and Shuah.
3 Jokshan begot Sheba and Dedan. And the
sons of Dedan were Asshurim, Letushim, and
Leummim.
4 And the sons of Midian *were* Ephah,
Epher, Hanoch, Abidah, and Eldaah. All these
were the children of Keturah.
5 And [R]Abraham gave all that he had to
Isaac. Gen. 24:35, 36
6 But Abraham gave gifts to the sons of the
concubines which Abraham had; and while
he was still living he [R]sent them eastward,
away from Isaac his son, to [R]the country of the
east. Gen. 21:14 • Judg. 6:3
7 This *is* the sum of the years of Abraham's
life which he lived: one hundred and seventy-
five years.
8 Then Abraham breathed his last and died
in a good old age, an old man and full *of
years*, and was gathered to his people.
9 And [R]his sons Isaac and Ishmael buried
him in the cave of [R]Machpelah, which *is* be-
fore Mamre, in the field of Ephron the son of
Zohar the Hittite, Gen. 35:29; 50:13 • Gen. 23:9, 17
10 [R]the field which Abraham purchased
from the sons of Heth. There Abraham was
buried, and Sarah his wife. Gen. 23:3–16
11 And it came to pass, after the death of
Abraham, that God blessed his son Isaac. And
Isaac dwelt at Beer Lahai Roi.
12 Now this *is* the genealogy of Ishmael,
Abraham's son, whom Hagar the Egyptian,
Sarah's maidservant, bore to Abraham.
13 And these *were* the names of the sons of
Ishmael, by their names, according to their
generations: The firstborn of Ishmael, Neba-
joth; then Kedar, Adbeel, Mibsam,
14 Mishma, Dumah, Massa,
15 Hadar,* Tema, Jetur, Naphish, and Ked-
emah.
16 These *were* the sons of Ishmael and these
were their names, by their towns and their
[T]settlements, [R]twelve princes according to
their nations. *camps* • Gen. 17:20
17 These *were* the years of the life of Ish-
mael: one hundred and thirty-seven years;
and [R]he breathed his last and died, and was
gathered to his people. Gen. 25:8; 49:33
18 [R](They dwelt from Havilah as far as Shur,
which *is* east of Egypt as you go toward As-
syria.) He [T]died [R]in the presence of all his
brethren. 1 Sam. 15:7 • *fell* • Gen. 16:12
19 This *is* the genealogy of Isaac, Abraham's
son. [R]Abraham begot Isaac. Matt. 1:2
20 Isaac was forty years old when he took
Rebekah as wife, [R]the daughter of Bethuel the
Syrian of Padan Aram, the sister of Laban the
Syrian. Gen. 22:23; 24:15, 29, 67
21 Now Isaac pleaded with the LORD for his
wife, because she *was* barren; [R]and the LORD
granted his plea, [R]and Rebekah his wife con-
ceived. 1 Chr. 5:20 • Rom. 9:10–13
22 But the children struggled together
within her; and she said, "If *all is* well, why *am
I like* this?" [R]So she went to inquire of the
LORD. 1 Sam. 1:15; 9:9; 10:22
23 And the LORD said to her:

[R]"Two nations *are* in your womb,
Two peoples shall be separated from
your body; Gen. 17:4–6, 16; 24:60
One people shall be stronger than [R]the
other, 2 Sam. 8:14
And the older shall serve the younger."

24 So when her days were fulfilled *for her* to
give birth, indeed *there were* twins in her
womb.
25 And the first came out red. *He was* [R]like a
hairy garment all over; so they called his
name Esau.* Gen. 27:11, 16, 23
26 Afterward his brother came out, and [R]his
hand took hold of Esau's heel; so his name
was called Jacob.* Isaac *was* sixty years old
when she bore them. Hos. 12:3
27 So the boys grew. And Esau was a skillful
hunter, a man of the field; but Jacob was a
mild man, dwelling in tents.
28 And Isaac loved Esau because he ate *of
his* game, but Rebekah loved Jacob.

25:15 MT *Hadad* **25:25** Lit. *Hairy* **25:26** *Supplanter* or *Deceitful*, lit. *One Who Takes the Heel*

29 Now Jacob cooked a stew; and Esau came
in from the field, and he *was* weary.
30 And Esau said to Jacob, "Please feed me
with that same red *stew,* for I *am* weary."
Therefore his name was called Edom.*
31 But Jacob said, "Sell me your birthright
as of this day."
32 And Esau said, "Look, I *am* about to die;
so what *is* this birthright to me?"
33 Then Jacob said, [T]"Swear to me as of this
day." So he swore to him, and [R]sold his
birthright to Jacob. *Take an oath* • Heb. 12:16
34 And Jacob gave Esau bread and stew of
lentils; then [R]he ate and drank, arose, and
went his way. Thus Esau [R]despised *his*
birthright. Eccl. 8:15 • Heb. 12:16, 17

CHAPTER 26

The Failure of Isaac

THERE was a famine in the land, besides
[R]the first famine that was in the days of
Abraham. And Isaac went to Abimelech king
of the Philistines, in Gerar. Gen. 12:10
2 Then the LORD appeared to him and said:
[R]"Do not go down to Egypt; live in the land of
which I shall tell you. Gen. 12:7; 17:1
3 [R]"Dwell in this land, and [R]I will be with
you and [R]bless you; for to you and your de-
scendants I give all these lands, and I will per-
form the oath which I swore to Abraham your
father. Heb. 11:9 • Gen. 28:13, 15 • Gen. 12:2
4 "And I will make your descendants multi-
ply as the stars of heaven; I will give to your
descendants all these lands; [R]and in your
seed all the nations of the earth shall be
blessed; Gen. 12:3; 22:18; Gal. 3:8☆
5 [R]"because Abraham obeyed My voice and
kept My charge, My commandments, My
statutes, and My laws." Gen. 22:16, 18
6 So Isaac dwelt in Gerar.
7 And the men of the place asked about his
wife. And [R]he said, "She *is* my sister"; for [R]he
was afraid to say, "*She is* my wife," *because
he thought,* "lest the men of the place kill me
for Rebekah, because she *is* beautiful to be-
hold." Gen. 12:13; 20:2, 12, 13 • Prov. 29:25
8 Now it came to pass, when he had been
there a long time, that Abimelech king of the
Philistines looked through a window, and saw,
and there was Isaac, [T]showing endearment to
Rebekah his wife. *caressing*
9 Then Abimelech called Isaac and said,
"Quite obviously she *is* your wife; so how
could you say, 'She *is* my sister'?" Isaac said to
him, "Because I said, 'Lest I die on account of
her.' "
10 And Abimelech said, "What *is* this you
have done to us? One of the people might
soon have lain with your wife, and [R]you would
have brought guilt on us." Gen. 20:9
11 So Abimelech charged all *his* people, say-
ing, "He who [R]touches this man or his wife
shall surely be put to death." Ps. 105:15
12 Then Isaac sowed in that land, and
reaped in the same year [R]a hundredfold; and
the LORD [R]blessed him. Matt. 13:8, 23 • Gen. 24:1
13 The man [R]began to prosper, and contin-
ued prospering until he became very prosper-
ous; [Prov. 10:22]
14 for he had possessions of flocks and pos-
sessions of herds and a great number of ser-
vants. So the Philistines envied him.
15 Now the Philistines had stopped up all
the wells [R]which his father's servants had dug
in the days of Abraham his father, and they
had filled them with earth. Gen. 21:25, 30
16 And Abimelech said to Isaac, "Go away
from us, for [R]you are much mightier than
we." Ex. 1:9
17 Then Isaac departed from there and
[T]pitched his tent in the Valley of Gerar, and
dwelt there. *camped*
18 And Isaac dug again the wells of water
which they had dug in the days of Abraham
his father, for the Philistines had stopped
them up after the death of Abraham. [R]He
called them by the names which his father
had called them. Gen. 21:31
19 Also Isaac's servants dug in the valley,
and found a well of running water there.
20 But the herdsmen of Gerar quarreled with
Isaac's herdsmen, saying, "The water *is* ours."
So he called the name of the well Esek,* be-
cause they quarreled with him.
21 Then they dug another well, and they
quarreled over that *one* also. So he called its
name Sitnah.*
22 And he moved from there and dug an-
other well, and they did not quarrel over it. So
he called its name Rehoboth,* because he
said, "For now the LORD has made room for
us, and we shall be fruitful in the land."
23 Then he went up from there to Beersheba.
24 And the LORD appeared to him the same
night and said, "I *am* the God of your father
Abraham; do not fear, for I *am* with you. I will
bless you and multiply your descendants for
My servant Abraham's sake."
25 So he [R]built an altar there and [R]called on
the name of the LORD, and he pitched his
tent there; and there Isaac's servants dug a
well. Gen. 12:7, 8; 13:4, 18; 22:9; 33:20 • Ps. 116:17
26 Then Abimelech came to him from Gerar
with Ahuzzath, one of his friends, and Phichol
the commander of his army.
27 And Isaac said to them, "Why have you
come to me, [R]since you hate me and have sent
me away from you?" Judg. 11:7
28 But they said, "We have certainly seen
that the LORD [R]is with you. So we said, 'Let
there now be an oath between us, between

25:30 Lit. *Red* **26:20** Lit. *Quarrel* **26:21** Lit. *Enmity*
26:22 Lit. *Spaciousness*

you and us; and let us make a [T]covenant with you, Gen. 21:22, 23 • *treaty*

29 'that you will do us no harm, since we have not touched you, and since we have done nothing to you but good and have sent you away in peace. [R]You *are* now the blessed of the LORD.' " Gen. 24:31

30 [R]So he made them a feast, and they ate and drank. Gen. 19:3

31 Then they arose early in the morning and [R]swore an oath with one another; and Isaac sent them away, and they departed from him in peace. Gen. 21:31

32 It came to pass the same day that Isaac's servants came and told him about the well which they had dug, and said to him, "We have found water."

33 So he called it Shebah.* Therefore the name of the city *is* Beersheba* to this day.

The Failure of Esau

34 [R]When Esau was forty years old, he took as wives Judith the daughter of Beeri the Hittite, and Basemath the daughter of Elon the Hittite. Gen. 28:8; 36:2

35 And [R]they were a grief of mind to Isaac and Rebekah. Gen. 27:46; 28:1, 8

CHAPTER 27

Jacob Gains Esau's Blessing

NOW it came to pass, when Isaac was [R]old and [R]his eyes were so dim that he could not see, that he called Esau his older son and said to him, "My son." And he answered him, "Here I am." Gen. 35:28 • Gen. 48:10

2 Then he said, "Behold now, I am old. I do not know the day of my death.

3 "Now therefore, please take your weapons, your quiver and your bow, and go out to the field and hunt game for me.

4 "And make me [T]savory food, such as I love, and bring *it* to me that I may eat, that my soul may bless you before I die." *tasty*

5 Now Rebekah was listening when Isaac spoke to Esau his son. And Esau went to the field to hunt game and to bring *it*.

6 So Rebekah spoke to Jacob her son, saying, "Indeed I heard your father speak to Esau your brother, saying,

7 'Bring me game and make [T]savory food for me, that I may eat it and bless you in the presence of the LORD before my death.' *tasty*

8 "Now therefore, my son, obey my voice according to what I command you.

9 "Go now to the flock and bring me from there two choice kids of the goats, and I will make [R]savory food from them for your father, such as he loves. Gen. 27:4

10 "Then you shall take *it* to your father, that he may eat *it*, and that he [R]may bless you before his death." Gen. 27:4; 48:16

11 And Jacob said to Rebekah his mother, "Look, [R]Esau my brother *is* a hairy man, and I *am* a smooth-*skinned* man. Gen. 25:25

12 "Perhaps my father will [R]feel me, and I shall seem to be a deceiver to him; and I shall bring [R]a curse on myself and not a blessing." Gen. 27:21, 22 • Deut. 27:18

13 But his mother said to him, [R]"*Let* your curse *be* on me, my son; only obey my voice, and go, get *them* for me." Gen. 43:9

14 And he went and got *them* and brought *them* to his mother, and his mother made savory food, such as his father loved.

15 Then Rebekah took [R]the choice clothes of her elder son Esau, which *were* with her in the house, and put them on Jacob her younger son. Gen. 27:27

16 And she put the skins of the kids of the goats on his hands and on the smooth part of his neck.

17 Then she gave the savory food and the bread, which she had prepared, into the hand of her son Jacob.

18 So he went to his father and said, "My father." And he said, "Here I am. Who *are* you, my son?"

19 Jacob said to his father, "I *am* Esau your firstborn; I have done just as you told me; please arise, sit and eat of my game, [R]that your soul may bless me." Gen. 27:4

20 But Isaac said to his son, "How *is it* that you have found *it* so quickly, my son?" And he said, "Because the LORD your God brought *it* to me."

21 Then Isaac said to Jacob, "Please come near, that I may feel you, my son, whether you *are* really my son Esau or not."

22 So Jacob went near to Isaac his father, and he felt him and said, "The voice *is* Jacob's voice, but the hands *are* the hands of Esau."

23 And he did not recognize him, because [R]his hands were hairy like his brother Esau's hands; so he blessed him. Gen. 27:16

24 Then he said, "*Are* you really my son Esau?" He said, "I *am*."

25 He said, "Bring *it* near to me, and I will eat of my son's game, so [R]that my soul may bless you." So he brought *it* near to him, and he ate; and he brought him wine, and he drank. Gen. 27:4, 10, 19, 31

26 Then his father Isaac said to him, "Come near now and kiss me, my son."

27 And he came near and [R]kissed him; and he smelled the smell of his clothing, and blessed him and said: Gen. 29:13

"Surely, [R]the smell of my son
Is like the smell of a field
Which the LORD has blessed. Song 4:11

26:33 Lit. *Oath* or *Seven* • Lit. *Well of the Oath* or *Well of the Seven*

28 Therefore may [R]God give you Heb. 11:20
Of [R]the dew of heaven, Deut. 33:13, 28
Of [R]the fatness of the earth, Gen. 45:18
And [R]plenty of grain and wine. Deut. 7:13
29[R] Let peoples serve you, Gen. 9:25; 25:23
And nations bow down to you.
Be master over your brethren,
And [R]let your mother's sons bow down
to you. Gen. 37:7, 10; 49:8
Cursed *be* everyone who curses you,
And blessed *be* those who bless you!"

30 Now it happened, as soon as Isaac had
finished blessing Jacob, and Jacob had
scarcely gone out from the presence of Isaac
his father, that Esau his brother came in from
his hunting.
31 He also had made savory food, and
brought it to his father, and said to his father,
"Let my father arise and eat of his son's game,
that your soul may bless me."
32 And his father Isaac said to him, "Who
are you?" So he said, "I *am* your son, your
firstborn, Esau."
33 Then Isaac trembled exceedingly, and
said, "Who? Where *is* the one who hunted
game and brought *it* to me? I ate all *of it* be-
fore you came, and I have blessed him—[R]*and*
indeed he shall be blessed." Gen. 25:23; 28:3, 4
34 When Esau heard the words of his father,
[R]he cried with an exceedingly great and bitter
cry, and said to his father, "Bless me—me also,
O my father!" [Heb. 12:17]
35 But he said, "Your brother came with de-
ceit and has taken away your blessing."
36 And *Esau* said, [R]"Is he not rightly named
Jacob? For he has supplanted me these two
times. He took away my birthright, and now
look, he has taken away my blessing!" And he
said, "Have you not reserved a blessing for
me?" Gen. 25:26, 32–34
37 Then Isaac answered and said to Esau,
[R]"Indeed I have made him your master, and
all his brethren I have given to him as ser-
vants; with [R]grain and wine I have sus-
tained him. What shall I do now for you, my
son?" 2 Sam. 8:14 • Gen. 27:28, 29
38 And Esau said to his father, "Have you
only one blessing, my father? Bless me—me
also, O my father!" And Esau lifted up his
voice [R]and wept. Heb. 12:17
39 Then Isaac his father answered and said
to him:

"Behold, [R]your dwelling shall be of the
fatness of the earth, Heb. 11:20
And of the dew of heaven from above.
40 By your sword you shall live,
And you shall serve your brother;
And [R]it shall come to pass, when you
become restless,
That you shall break his yoke from your
neck." 2 Kin. 8:20–22

41 So Esau [R]hated Jacob because of the
blessing with which his father blessed him,
and Esau said in his heart, "The days of
mourning for my father are at hand; then I
will kill my brother Jacob." Gen. 26:27; 32:3–11
42 And the words of Esau her older son were
told to Rebekah. So she sent and called Jacob
her younger son, and said to him, "Surely
your brother Esau comforts himself concern-
ing you *by intending* to kill you.
43 "Now therefore, my son, obey my voice:
arise, flee to my brother Laban in Haran.
44 "And stay with him a [R]few days, until your
brother's fury turns away, Gen. 31:41
45 "until your brother's anger turns away
from you, and he forgets what you have done
to him; then I will send and bring you from
there. Why should I be bereaved also of you
both in one day?"
46 And Rebekah said to Isaac, "I am weary
of my life because of the daughters of
Heth; if Jacob takes a wife of the daughters
of Heth, like these *who are* the daughters
of the land, what good will my life be to
me?"

CHAPTER 28

THEN Isaac called Jacob and [R]blessed
him, and [T]charged him, and said to him:
[R]"You shall not take a wife from the daughters
of Canaan. Gen. 27:33 • *commanded* • Gen. 24:3
2 [R]"Arise, go to Padan Aram, to the house of
Bethuel your mother's father; and take your-
self a wife from there of the daughters of
Laban your mother's brother. Hos. 12:12

3 "May [R]God Almighty bless you,
And make you fruitful and multiply you,
That you may be an assembly of
peoples; Gen. 17:16; 35:11; 48:3
4 And give you the blessing of Abraham,
To you and your descendants with you,
That you may inherit the land
[R]In which you are a stranger,
Which God gave to Abraham." Gen. 17:8

5 So Isaac sent Jacob away, and he went to
Padan Aram, to Laban the son of Bethuel the
Syrian, the brother of Rebekah, the mother of
Jacob and Esau.
6 Esau saw that Isaac had blessed Jacob
and sent him away to Padan Aram to take
himself a wife from there, *and that* as he
blessed him he gave him a charge, saying,
"You shall not take a wife from the daughters
of Canaan,"
7 and that Jacob had obeyed his father and
his mother and had gone to Padan Aram.
8 Also Esau saw that the daughters of
Canaan did not please his father Isaac.
9 So Esau went to Ishmael and [R]took Ma-
halath the daughter of Ishmael, Abraham's

son, the sister of Nebajoth, to be his wife in
addition to the wives he had. Gen. 26:34, 35

Jacob's Dream

10 Now Jacob [R]went out from Beersheba
and went toward [R]Haran. Hos. 12:12 • Gen. 12:4
11 So he came to a certain place and stayed
there all night, because the sun had set. And
he took one of the stones of that place and put
it at his head, and he lay down in that place to
sleep.
12 Then he dreamed, and behold, a ladder
was set up on the earth, and its top reached to
heaven; and there [R]the angels of God were as-
cending and descending on it. John 1:51
13 [R]And behold, the LORD stood above it and
said: [R]"I *am* the LORD God of Abraham your
father and the God of Isaac; the land on which
you lie I will give to you and your descen-
dants. Gen. 35:1; 48:3 • Gen. 26:24
14 "Also your descendants shall be as the
dust of the earth; you shall spread abroad to
the west and the east, to the north and the
south; and in you and in your seed all the fam-
ilies of the earth shall be blessed.
15 "Behold, [R]I *am* with you and will [R]keep
you wherever you go, and will [R]bring you
back to this land; for I will not leave you
until I have done what I have spoken to
you." Gen. 26:3, 24; 31:3 • Gen. 48:16 • Gen. 35:6
16 Then Jacob awoke from his sleep and
said, "Surely the LORD is in [R]this place, and I
did not know *it*." Ex. 3:5
17 And he was afraid and said, "How awe-
some *is* this place! This *is* none other than the
house of God, and this *is* the gate of heaven!"
18 Then Jacob rose early in the morning,
and took the stone that he had put at his
head, [R]set it up as a pillar, [R]and poured oil on
top of it. Gen. 31:13, 45 • Lev. 8:10–12
19 And he called the name of [R]that place
Bethel;* but the name of that city had been
Luz previously. Judg. 1:23, 26
20 Then Jacob made a vow, saying, "If God
will be with me, and keep me in this way that
I am going, and give me [R]bread to eat and
clothing to put on, 1 Tim. 6:8
21 "so that [R]I come back to my father's
house in peace, [R]then the LORD shall be my
God. Judg. 11:31 • Deut. 26:17
22 "And this stone which I have set as a pil-
lar [R]shall be God's house, [R]and of all that
You give me I will surely give a [T]tenth to
You." Gen. 35:7, 14 • Gen. 14:20 • *tithe*

CHAPTER 29

Jacob's Labors

SO Jacob went on his journey and came
to the land of the people of the East.
2 And he looked, and saw a [R]well in the
field; and behold, there *were* three flocks of
sheep lying by it; for out of that well they wa-
tered the flocks. A large stone *was* on the
well's mouth. Gen. 24:10, 11
3 Now all the flocks would be gathered
there; and they would roll the stone from the
well's mouth, water the sheep, and put the
stone back in its place on the well's mouth.
4 And Jacob said to them, "My brethren,
where *are* you from?" And they said, "We *are*
from [R]Haran." Gen. 11:31; 28:10
5 Then he said to them, "Do you know [R]La-
ban the son of Nahor?" And they said, "We
know him." Gen. 24:24, 29; 28:2
6 So he said to them, "Is he well?" And they
said, "*He is* well. And look, his daughter Ra-
chel is coming with the sheep."
7 Then he said, "Look, *it is* still [T]high day; *it
is* not time for the cattle to be gathered to-
gether. Water the sheep, and go and feed
them." *early in the day*
8 But they said, "We cannot until all the
flocks are gathered together, and they have
rolled the stone from the well's mouth; then
we water the sheep."
9 Now while he was still speaking with
them, [R]Rachel came with her father's sheep,
for she was a shepherdess. Ex. 2:16
10 And it came to pass, when Jacob saw Ra-
chel the daughter of Laban his mother's
brother, and the sheep of Laban his mother's
brother, that Jacob went near and [R]rolled the
stone from the well's mouth, and watered the
flock of Laban his mother's brother. Ex. 2:17
11 Then Jacob [R]kissed Rachel, and lifted up
his voice and wept. Gen. 33:4; 45:14, 15
12 And Jacob told Rachel that he *was* her fa-
ther's relative and that he *was* Rebekah's son.
So she ran and told her father.
13 Then it came to pass, when Laban heard
the report about Jacob his sister's son, that he
ran to meet him, and embraced him and
kissed him, and brought him to his house. So
he told Laban all these things.
14 And Laban said to him, [R]"Surely you *are*
my bone and my flesh." And he stayed with
him for a month. Gen. 2:23; 37:27
15 Then Laban said to Jacob, "Because you
are my relative, should you therefore serve
me for nothing? Tell me, [R]what *should* your
wages *be*?" Gen. 30:28; 31:41
16 Now Laban had two daughters: the name
of the elder *was* Leah, and the name of the
younger *was* Rachel.
17 Leah's eyes *were* delicate, but Rachel was
beautiful of form and appearance.
18 Now Jacob loved Rachel; so he said, [R]"I
will serve you seven years for Rachel your
younger daughter." Gen. 31:41
19 And Laban said, "*It is* better that I give
her to you than that I should give her to an-
other man. Stay with me."
20 So Jacob [R]served seven years for Rachel,

28:19 Lit. *House of God*

and they seemed *only* a few days to him because of the love he had for her. Gen. 30:26

21 Then Jacob said to Laban, "Give *me* my wife, for my days are fulfilled, that I may [R]go in to her." Judg. 15:1

22 And Laban gathered together all the men of the place and made a feast.

23 Now it came to pass in the evening, that he took Leah his daughter and brought her to Jacob; and he went in to her.

24 And Laban gave his maid [R]Zilpah to his daughter Leah *as* a maid. Gen. 30:9, 10

25 So it came to pass in the morning, that behold, it *was* Leah. And he said to Laban, "What is this you have done to me? Was it not for Rachel that I served you? Why then have you [R]deceived me?" 1 Sam. 28:12

26 And Laban said, "It must not be done so in our [T]country, to give the younger before the firstborn. Lit. *place*

27 "Fulfill her week, and we will give you this one also for the service which you will serve with me still another seven years."

28 Then Jacob did so and fulfilled her week. So he gave him his daughter Rachel as wife also.

29 And Laban gave his maid [R]Bilhah to his daughter Rachel as a maid. Gen. 30:3–5

30 Then *Jacob* also went in to Rachel, and he also [R]loved Rachel more than Leah. And he served with Laban [R]still another seven years. Deut. 21:15–17 • Gen. 30:26; 31:41

31 When the LORD [R]saw that Leah *was* [T]unloved, He [R]opened her womb; but Rachel *was* barren. Ps. 127:3 • Lit. *hated* • Gen. 30:1

32 So Leah conceived and bore a son, and she called his name Reuben;* for she said, "The LORD has surely [R]looked on my affliction. Now therefore, my husband will love me." Deut. 26:7

33 Then she conceived again and bore a son, and said, "Because the LORD has heard that I *am* [T]unloved, He has therefore given me this *son* also." And she called his name Simeon.* Lit. *hated*

34 She conceived again and bore a son, and said, "Now this time my husband will become attached to me, because I have borne him three sons." Therefore his name was called Levi.*

35 And she conceived again and bore a son, and said, "Now I will praise the LORD." Therefore she called his name [R]Judah.* Then she stopped bearing. Matt. 1:2

CHAPTER 30

NOW when Rachel saw that [R]she bore Jacob no children, Rachel [R]envied her sister, and said to Jacob, "Give me children, or else I die!" Gen. 16:1, 2; 29:31 • Gen. 37:11

2 And Jacob's anger was aroused against Rachel, and he said, [R]"*Am* I in the place of God, who has withheld from you the fruit of the womb?" 1 Sam. 1:5

3 So she said, "Here is [R]my maid Bilhah; go in to her, [R]and she will bear *a child* on my knees, [R]that I also may have children by her." Gen. 16:2 • Gen. 50:23 • Gen. 16:2, 3

4 Then she gave him Bilhah her maid [R]as wife, and Jacob went in to her. Gen. 16:3, 4

5 And Bilhah conceived and bore Jacob a son.

6 Then Rachel said, "God has [R]judged my case; and He has also heard my voice and given me a son." Therefore she called his name Dan.* Lam. 3:59

7 And Rachel's maid Bilhah conceived again and bore Jacob a second son.

8 Then Rachel said, "With great wrestlings I have wrestled with my sister, *and* indeed I have prevailed." So she called his name Naphtali.*

9 When Leah saw that she had stopped bearing, she took Zilpah her maid and [R]gave her to Jacob as wife. Gen. 30:4

10 And Leah's maid Zilpah bore Jacob a son.

11 Then Leah said, "A troop comes!"* So she called his name Gad.*

12 And Leah's maid Zilpah bore Jacob a second son.

13 Then Leah said, "I am happy, for the daughters [R]will call me blessed." So she called his name Asher.* Luke 1:48

14 Now Reuben went in the days of wheat harvest and found mandrakes in the field, and brought them to his mother Leah. Then Rachel said to Leah, [R]"Please give me *some* of your son's mandrakes." Gen. 25:30

15 But she said to her, "*Is it* a small matter that you have taken away my husband? Would you take away my son's mandrakes also?" And Rachel said, "Therefore he will lie with you tonight for your son's mandrakes."

16 When Jacob came out of the field in the evening, Leah went out to meet him and said, "You must come in to me, for I have surely hired you with my son's mandrakes." And he lay with her that night.

17 And God listened to Leah, and she conceived and bore Jacob a fifth son.

18 Leah said, "God has given me my wages, because I have given my maid to my husband." So she called his name Issachar.*

19 Then Leah conceived again and bore Jacob a sixth son.

20 And Leah said, "God has endowed me *with* a good endowment; now my husband

29:32 Lit. *See, a Son* **29:33** Lit. *Heard* **29:34** Lit. *Attached* **29:35** Lit. *Praise* **30:6** Lit. *Judge* **30:8** Lit. *My Wrestling* **30:11** So with Qr., Syr., Tg.; Kt., LXX, Vg. *in fortune* • Lit. *Troop* or *Fortune* **30:13** Lit. *Happy* **30:18** Lit. *Wages*

will dwell with me, because I have borne him six sons." So she called his name Zebulun.*

21 Afterward she bore a [R]daughter, and called her name Dinah. Gen. 34:1

22 Then God remembered Rachel, and God listened to her and opened her womb.

23 And she conceived and bore a son, and said, "God has taken away my reproach."

24 So she called his name Joseph,* and said, [R]"The LORD shall add to me another son." Gen. 35:16–18

25 And it came to pass, when Rachel had borne Joseph, that Jacob said to Laban, [R]"Send me away, that I may go to my own place and to my country. Gen. 24:54, 56

26 "Give *me* my wives and my children [R]for whom I have served you, and let me go; for you know my service which I have done for you." Gen. 29:18–20, 27, 30

27 And Laban said to him, "Please *stay*, if I have found favor in your eyes, *for* [R]I have learned by experience that the LORD has blessed me for your sake." Gen. 26:24; 39:3

28 Then he said, [R]"Name me your wages, and I will give *it*." Gen. 29:15; 31:7, 41

29 So *Jacob* said to him, [R]"You know how I have served you and how your livestock has been with me. Gen. 31:6, 38–40

30 "For what you had before I *came was* little, and it has increased to a great amount; the LORD has blessed you [T]since my coming. And now, when shall I also [R]provide for my own house?" Lit. *at my foot* • [1 Tim. 5:8]

31 So he said, "What shall I give you?" And Jacob said, "You shall not give me anything. If you will do this thing for me, I will again feed and keep your flocks:

32 "Let me pass through all your flock today, removing from there all the speckled and spotted sheep, and all the brown ones among the lambs, and the spotted and speckled among the goats; and [R]*these* shall be my wages. Gen. 31:8

33 "So my [R]righteousness will answer for me in time to come, when the subject of my wages comes before you: every one that *is* not speckled and spotted among the goats, and brown among the lambs, will be considered stolen, if *it is* with me." Ps. 37:6

34 And Laban said, "Oh, that it were according to your word!"

35 So he removed that day the male goats that were [R]speckled and spotted, all the female goats that were speckled and spotted, every one that had *some* white in it, and all the brown ones among the lambs, and gave *them* into the hand of his sons. Gen. 31:9–12

36 Then he put three days' journey between himself and Jacob, and Jacob fed the rest of Laban's flocks.

37 Now Jacob took for himself rods of green poplar and of the almond and chestnut trees, peeled white strips in them, and exposed the white which *was* in the rods.

38 And the rods which he had peeled, he set before the flocks in the gutters, in the watering troughs where the flocks came to drink, so that they should conceive when they came to drink.

39 So the flocks conceived before the rods, and the flocks brought forth streaked, speckled, and spotted.

40 Then Jacob separated the lambs, and made the flocks face toward the streaked and all the brown in the flock of Laban; but he put his own flocks by themselves and did not put them with Laban's flock.

41 And it came to pass, whenever the stronger livestock conceived, that Jacob placed the rods before the eyes of the livestock in the gutters, that they might conceive among the rods.

42 But when the flocks were feeble, he did not put *them* in; so the feebler were Laban's and the stronger Jacob's.

43 Thus the man became exceedingly prosperous, and had large flocks, female and male servants, and camels and donkeys.

CHAPTER 31

Jacob's Flight

NOW *Jacob* heard the words of Laban's sons, saying, "Jacob has taken away all that was our father's, and from what was our father's he has acquired all this [R]wealth." Ps. 49:16

2 And Jacob saw the [R]countenance of Laban, and indeed it *was* not [R]*favorable* toward him as before. Gen. 4:5 • Deut. 28:54

3 Then the LORD said to Jacob, [R]"Return to the land of your fathers and to your family, and I will be with you." Gen. 28:15, 20, 21

4 So Jacob sent and called Rachel and Leah to the field, to his flock,

5 and said to them, [R]"I see your father's [T]countenance, that it *is* not *favorable* toward me as before; but the God of my father [R]has been with me. Gen. 31:2, 3 • Lit. *face* • Is. 41:10

6 "And [R]you know that with all my might I have served your father. Gen. 30:29; 31:38–41

7 "Yet your father has deceived me and [R]changed my wages ten times, but God did not allow him to hurt me. Gen. 29:25; 31:41

8 "If he said thus: [R]'The speckled shall be your wages,' then all the flocks bore speckled. And if he said thus: 'The streaked shall be your wages,' then all the flocks bore streaked. Gen. 30:32

9 "So God has taken away the livestock of your father and given *them* to me.

10 "And it happened, at the time when the flocks conceived, that I lifted my eyes and saw

30:20 Lit. *Dwelling* **30:24** Lit. *He Will Add*

in a dream, and behold, the rams which leaped upon the flocks *were* streaked, speckled, and gray-spotted.

11 "Then [R]the Angel of God spoke to me in a dream, saying, 'Jacob.' And I said, 'Here I am.' Gen. 16:7–11; 22:11, 15; 31:13; 48:16

12 "And He said, 'Lift your eyes now and see, all the rams which leap on the flocks *are* streaked, speckled, and gray-spotted; for I have seen all that Laban is doing to you.

13 'I *am* the God of Bethel, where you anointed the pillar *and* where you made a vow to Me. Now arise, get out of this land, and return to the land of your family.' "

14 Then Rachel and Leah answered and said to him, "Is there still any portion or inheritance for us in our father's house?

15 "Are we not considered strangers by him? For he has sold us, and also completely consumed our money.

16 "For all these riches which God has taken from our father are *really* ours and our children's; now then, whatever God has said to you, do it."

17 Then Jacob rose and set his sons and his wives on camels.

18 And he carried away all his livestock and all his possessions which he had gained, his acquired livestock which he had gained in Padan Aram, to go to his father Isaac in the land of [R]Canaan. Gen. 17:8; 33:18

19 Now Laban had gone to shear his sheep, and Rachel had stolen the [R]household[T] idols that were her father's. Judg. 17:5 • Heb. *teraphim*

20 And Jacob stole away, unknown to Laban the Syrian, in that he did not tell him that he intended to flee.

21 So he fled with all that he had. He arose and crossed the river, and [R]headed toward the mountains of Gilead. 2 Kin. 12:17

22 And Laban was told on the third day that Jacob had fled.

23 Then he took [R]his brethren with him and pursued him for seven days' journey, and he overtook him in the mountains of Gilead. Gen. 13:8

24 But God [R]had come to Laban the Syrian in a dream by night, and said to him, "Be careful that you speak to Jacob neither good nor bad." Gen. 20:3; 31:29; 46:2–4

25 So Laban overtook Jacob. Now Jacob had pitched his tent in the mountains, and Laban with his brethren pitched in the mountains of Gilead.

26 And Laban said to Jacob: "What have you done, that you have stolen away unknown to me, and carried away my daughters like captives *taken* with the sword?

27 "Why did you flee away secretly, and steal away from me, and not tell me; for I might have sent you away with joy and songs, with timbrel and harp?

28 "And you did not allow me [R]to kiss my sons and my daughters. Now [R]you have done foolishly in so doing. Gen. 31:55 • 1 Sam. 13:13

29 "It is in my power to do you harm, but the [R]God of your father spoke to me last night, saying, 'Be careful that you speak to Jacob neither good nor bad.' Gen. 28:13; 31:5

30 "And now you have surely gone because you greatly long for your father's house, *but* why did you [R]steal my gods?" Judg. 17:5; 18:24

31 Then Jacob answered and said to Laban, "Because I was [R]afraid, for I said, 'Perhaps you would take your daughters from me by force.' Gen. 26:7; 32:7, 11

32 "With whomever you find your gods, [R]do not let him live. In the presence of our brethren, identify what I have of yours and take *it* with you." For Jacob did not know that Rachel had stolen them. Gen. 44:9

33 And Laban went into Jacob's tent, into Leah's tent, and into the two maids' tents, but he did not find *them*. Then he went out of Leah's tent and entered Rachel's tent.

34 Now Rachel had taken the household idols, put them in the camel's saddle, and sat on them. And Laban [T]searched all about the tent but did not find *them*. Lit. *felt*

35 And she said to her father, "Let it not displease my lord that I cannot [R]rise before you, for the manner of women *is* with me." And he searched but did not find the [T]household idols. Lev. 19:32 • Heb. *teraphim*

36 Then Jacob was angry and rebuked Laban, and Jacob answered and said to Laban: "What *is* my [T]trespass? What *is* my sin, that you have so hotly pursued me? *transgression*

37 "Although you have searched all my things, what part of your household things have you found? Set *it* here before my brethren and your brethren, that they may judge between us both!

38 "These twenty years I *have been* with you; your ewes and your female goats have not miscarried their young, and I have not eaten the rams of your flock.

39 [R]"That which was torn *by beasts* I did not bring to you; I bore the loss of it. [R]You required it from my hand, *whether* stolen by day or stolen by night. Ex. 22:10 • Ex. 22:10–13

40 "*There* I was! In the day the drought consumed me, and the frost by night, and my sleep departed from my eyes.

41 "Thus I have been in your house twenty years; I served you fourteen years for your two daughters, and six years for your flock, and you have changed my wages ten times.

42 [R]"Unless the God of my father, the God of Abraham and [R]the Fear of Isaac, had been with me, surely now you would have sent me away empty-handed. God has seen my affliction and the labor of my hands, and rebuked *you* last night." Ps. 124:1, 2 • Is. 8:13

43 And Laban answered and said to Jacob,

"*These* daughters *are* my daughters, and
these children *are* my children, and *this* flock
is my flock; all that you see *is* mine. But what
can I do this day to these my daughters or to
their children whom they have borne?
44 "Now therefore, come, [R]let us make a
covenant, you and I, and let it be a witness be-
tween you and me." Gen. 21:27, 32; 26:28
45 So Jacob [R]took a stone and set it up *as* a
pillar. Gen. 28:18; 35:14
46 Then Jacob said to his brethren, "Gather
stones." And they took stones and made a
heap, and they ate there on the heap.
47 Laban called it Jegar Sahadutha,* but Ja-
cob called it Galeed.*
48 And Laban said, [R]"This heap *is* a witness
between you and me this day." Therefore its
name was called Galeed, Josh. 24:27
49 also [R]Mizpah,* because he said, "May the
LORD watch between you and me when we are
absent one from another. Judg. 10:17
50 "If you afflict my daughters, or if you take
other wives besides my daughters, *although*
no man *is* with us—see, God *is* witness be-
tween you and me!"
51 Then Laban said to Jacob, "Here is this
heap and here is *this* pillar, which I have
placed between you and me.
52 "This heap *is* a witness, and *this* pillar
is a witness, that I will not pass beyond
this heap to you, and you will not pass beyond
this heap and this pillar to me, for harm.
53 "The God of Abraham, the God of Nahor,
and the God of their father [R]judge between
us." And Jacob [R]swore by [R]the Fear of his
father Isaac. Gen. 16:5 • Gen. 21:23 • Gen. 31:42
54 Then Jacob offered a sacrifice on the
mountain, and called his brethren to eat
bread. And they ate bread and stayed all night
on the mountain.
55 And early in the morning Laban arose,
and [R]kissed his sons and daughters and
blessed them. Then Laban departed and re-
turned to his place. Gen. 29:11, 13; 31:28, 43

CHAPTER 32

Jacob Fights with the Angel

SO Jacob went on his way, and [R]the
angels of God met him. Num. 22:31
2 When Jacob saw them, he said, "This *is*
God's [R]camp." And he called the name of that
place Mahanaim.* Josh. 5:14
3 Then Jacob sent messengers before him
to Esau his brother [R]in the land of Seir, the
country of Edom. Gen. 14:6; 33:14, 16
4 And he commanded them, saying,
[R]"Speak thus to my lord Esau, 'Thus your ser-
vant Jacob says: "I have dwelt with Laban and
stayed there until now. Prov. 15:1
5 [R]"I have oxen, donkeys, flocks, and male
and female servants; and I have sent to tell
my lord, that [R]I may find favor in your
sight." ' " Gen. 30:43 • Gen. 33:8, 15
6 Then the messengers returned to Jacob,
saying, "We came to your brother Esau, and
[R]he also is coming to meet you, and four hun-
dred men *are* with him." Gen. 33:1
7 So Jacob was greatly afraid and [R]dis-
tressed; and he divided the people that *were*
with him, and the flocks and herds and
camels, into two companies. Gen. 32:11; 35:3
8 And he said, "If Esau comes to the one
company and [T]attacks it, then the other com-
pany which is left will escape." Lit. *strikes*
9 [R]Then Jacob said, [R]"O God of my father
Abraham and God of my father Isaac, the
LORD [R]who said to me, 'Return to your coun-
try and to your family, and I will deal well
with you': [Ps. 50:15] • Gen. 28:13; 31:42 • Gen. 31:3
10 "I am not worthy of the least of all the
[R]mercies and of all the truth which You have
shown Your servant; for I crossed over this
Jordan with [R]my staff, and now I have become
two companies. Gen. 24:27 • Job 8:7
11 [R]"Deliver me, I pray, from the hand of my
brother, from the hand of Esau; for I fear him,
lest he come and attack me *and* the mother
with the children. Ps. 59:1, 2
12 "For [R]You said, 'I will surely treat you
well, and make your descendants as the [R]sand
of the sea, which cannot be numbered for
multitude.' " Gen. 28:13–15 • Gen. 22:17
13 So he lodged there that same night, and
took what [T]came to his hand as [R]a present for
Esau his brother: *he had received* • Gen. 43:11
14 two hundred female goats and twenty
male goats, two hundred ewes and twenty
rams,
15 thirty milk camels with their colts, forty
cows and ten bulls, twenty female donkeys
and ten foals.
16 Then he delivered *them* to the hand of his
servants, every drove by itself, and said to his
servants, "Pass over before me, and put some
distance between successive droves."
17 And he commanded the first one, saying,
"When Esau my brother meets you and asks
you, saying, 'To whom do you belong, and
where are you going? Whose *are* these in
front of you?'
18 "then you shall say, 'They *are* your
servant Jacob's. It *is* a present sent to my lord
Esau; and behold, he also *is* behind us.' "
19 So he commanded the second, the third,
and all who followed the droves, saying, "In
this manner you shall speak to Esau when
you find him;
20 "and also say, 'Behold, your servant Jacob
is behind us.' " For he said, "I will [R]appease
him with the present that goes before me, and

31:47 Lit., in Aram., *Heap of Witness* • Lit., in Heb., *Heap of Witness* **31:49** Lit. *Watch* **32:2** Lit. *Double Camp*

afterward I will see his face; perhaps he will
accept me." [Prov. 21:14]
21 So the present went on over before him,
but he himself lodged that night in the camp.
22 And he arose that night and took his two
wives, his two female servants, and his
eleven sons, [R]and crossed over the ford of
Jabbok. Deut. 3:16
23 He took them, sent them [T]over the brook,
and sent over what he had. *across*
24 Then Jacob was left alone; and a Man
wrestled with him until the breaking of day.
25 Now when He saw that He did not prevail
against him, He [T]touched the socket of his hip;
and the socket of Jacob's hip was out of joint
as He wrestled with him. *struck*
26 And [R]He said, "Let Me go, for the day
breaks." But he said, [R]"I will not let You go un-
less You bless me!" Luke 24:28 • Hos. 12:4
27 So He said to him, "What *is* your name?"
He said, "Jacob."
28 And He said, [R]"Your name shall no longer
be called Jacob, but Israel;* for you have
[R]struggled with God and with men, and have
prevailed." Gen. 35:10 • Hos. 12:3, 4
29 Then Jacob asked, saying, "Tell *me* Your
name, I pray." And He said, [R]"Why *is* it *that*
you ask about My name?" And He [R]blessed
him there. Judg. 13:17, 18 • Gen. 35:9
30 So Jacob called the name of the place Pe-
niel:* "For [R]I have seen God face to face, and
my life is preserved." Gen. 16:13
31 Just as he crossed over Penuel* the sun
rose on him, and he limped on his hip.
32 Therefore to this day the children of Is-
rael do not eat the muscle that shrank, which
is on the hip socket, because He [T]touched the
socket of Jacob's hip in the muscle that
shrank. *struck*

CHAPTER 33

Jacob Makes Peace with Esau

NOW Jacob lifted his eyes and looked, and
there, [R]Esau was coming, and with him
were four hundred men. So he divided the
children among Leah, Rachel, and the two
maidservants. Gen. 32:6
2 And he put the maidservants and their
children in front, Leah and her children be-
hind, and Rachel and Joseph last.
3 Then he crossed over before them and
[R]bowed himself to the ground seven times,
until he came near to his brother. Gen. 18:2
4 [R]But Esau ran to meet him, and embraced
him, [R]and fell on his neck and kissed him, and
they wept. Gen. 32:28 • Gen. 45:14, 15
5 And he lifted his eyes and saw the women
and children, and said, "Who *are* these with
you?" So he said, "The children [R]whom God
has graciously given your servant." Gen. 48:9
6 Then the maidservants came near, they
and their children, and bowed down.
7 And Leah also came near with her chil-
dren, and they bowed down. Afterward Jo-
seph and Rachel came near, and they bowed
down.
8 Then Esau said, "What *do* you *mean by*
[R]all this company which I met?" And he said,
"*These are* [R]to find favor in the sight of my
lord." Gen. 32:13–16 • Gen. 32:5
9 But Esau said, "I have enough, my
brother; keep what you have for yourself."
10 And Jacob said, "No, please, if I have now
found favor in your sight, then receive my
present from my hand, inasmuch as I [R]have
seen your face as though I had seen the face of
God, and you were pleased with me. Gen. 43:3
11 "Please, take my blessing that is brought
to you, because God has dealt graciously with
me, and because I have enough." So he urged
him, and he took *it*.
12 Then Esau said, "Let us take our journey;
let us go, and I will go before you."
13 But Jacob said to him, "My lord knows
that the children *are* weak, and the flocks and
herds which are nursing *are* with me. And if
the men should drive them hard one day, all
the flock will die.
14 "Please let my lord go on ahead before his
servant. I will lead on slowly at a pace which
the livestock that go before me, and the chil-
dren, are able to endure, until I come to my
lord [R]in Seir." Gen. 32:3; 36:8
15 And Esau said, "Now let me leave with
you *some* of the people who *are* with me." But
he said, "What need is there? [R]Let me find
favor in the sight of my lord." Ruth 2:13
16 So Esau returned that day on his way to
Seir.
17 And Jacob journeyed to [R]Succoth, built
himself a house, and made [T]booths for his
livestock. Therefore the name of the place is
called Succoth.* Josh. 13:27 • *shelters*
18 Then Jacob came safely to [R]the city of
Shechem, which *is* in the land of Canaan,
when he came from Padan Aram; and he
pitched his tent before the city. John 3:23
19 And [R]he bought the parcel of [T]land, where
he had pitched his tent, from the children of
Hamor, Shechem's father, for one hundred
pieces of money. John 4:5 • Lit. *the field*
20 Then he erected an altar there and called
it [R]El Elohe Israel.* Gen. 35:7

CHAPTER 34

The Defilement of Dinah

NOW [R]Dinah the daughter of Leah, whom
she had borne to Jacob, went out to see
the daughters of the land. Gen. 30:21

32:28 Lit. *Prince with God* **32:30** Lit. *Face of God*
32:31 Lit. *Face of God; same as Peniel*, v. 30
33:17 Lit. *Booths* **33:20** Lit. *God, the God of Israel*

2 And when Shechem the son of Hamor the
Hivite, prince of the country, saw her, he took
her and lay with her, and violated her.

3 His soul [T]was strongly attracted to Dinah
the daughter of Jacob, and he loved the young
woman and spoke [T]kindly to the young
woman. Lit. *clung to* • *tenderly*

4 So Shechem [R]spoke to his father Hamor,
saying, "Get me this young woman as a
wife." Judg. 14:2

5 And Jacob heard that he had defiled
Dinah his daughter. Now his sons were with
his livestock in the field; so Jacob [R]held[T] his
peace until they came. 2 Sam. 13:22 • *kept silent*

6 Then Hamor the father of Shechem went
out to Jacob to speak with him.

7 And the sons of Jacob came in from the
field when they heard *it;* and the men were
grieved and very angry, because he [R]had done
a disgraceful thing in Israel by lying with Ja-
cob's daughter, [R]a thing which ought not to be
done. Judg. 20:6 • 2 Sam. 13:12

8 But Hamor spoke with them, saying, "The
soul of my son Shechem longs for your
daughter. Please give her to him as a wife.

9 "And make marriages with us; give your
daughters to us, and take our daughters to
yourselves.

10 "So you shall dwell with us, and the land
shall be before you. Dwell and trade in it, and
acquire possessions for yourselves in it."

11 Then Shechem said to her father and her
brothers, "Let me find favor in your eyes, and
whatever you say to me I will give.

12 "Ask me ever so much [R]dowry[T] and gift,
and I will give according to what you say to
me; but give me the young woman as a
wife." Ex. 22:16, 17 • *bride-price*

13 But the sons of Jacob answered
Shechem and Hamor his father, and spoke
[R]deceitfully, because he had defiled Dinah
their sister. Gen. 31:7

14 And they said to them, "We cannot do
this thing, to give our sister to one who is
[R]uncircumcised, for [R]that *would be* a re-
proach to us. Ex. 12:48 • Josh. 5:2–9

15 "But on this *condition* we will consent to
you: If you will become as we *are,* if every
male of you is circumcised,

16 "then we will give our daughters to you,
and we will take your daughters to us; and we
will dwell with you, and we will become one
people.

17 "But if you will not heed us and be cir-
cumcised, then we will take our daughter and
be gone."

18 And their words pleased Hamor and
Shechem, Hamor's son.

19 So the young man did not delay to do the
thing, because he delighted in Jacob's daugh-
ter. He *was* [R]more honorable than all the
household of his father. 1 Chr. 4:9

20 And Hamor and Shechem his son came to
the [R]gate of their city, and spoke with the men
of their city, saying: Ruth 4:1, 11

21 "These men *are* at peace with us. There-
fore let them dwell in the land and trade in it.
For indeed the land *is* large enough for them.
Let us take their daughters to us as wives, and
let us give them our daughters.

22 "Only on this *condition* will the men con-
sent to dwell with us, to be one people: if
every male among us is circumcised as they
are circumcised.

23 "*Will* not their livestock, their property,
and every animal of theirs *be* ours? Only let
us consent to them, and they will dwell with
us."

24 And all who went out of the gate of his
city heeded Hamor and Shechem his son;
every male was circumcised, all who [R]went
out of the gate of his city. Gen. 23:10, 18

25 Now it came to pass on the third day,
when they were in pain, that two of the
sons of Jacob, Simeon and Levi, Dinah's
brothers, each took his sword and came
boldly upon the city and killed all the males.

26 And they killed Hamor and Shechem his
son with the edge of the sword, and took
Dinah from Shechem's house, and went out.

27 The sons of Jacob came upon the slain,
and plundered the city, because their sister
had been defiled.

28 They took their sheep, their oxen, and
their donkeys, what *was* in the city and what
was in the field,

29 and all their wealth. All their little ones
and their wives they took captive; and they
plundered even all that *was* in the houses.

30 Then Jacob said to Simeon and Levi,
[R]"You have [R]troubled me [R]by making me ob-
noxious among the inhabitants of the land,
among the Canaanites and the Perizzites;
[R]and since I *am* few in number, they will
gather themselves together against me and
kill me. I shall be destroyed, my household
and I." Gen. 49:6 • Josh. 7:25 • Ex. 5:21 • Deut. 4:27

31 But they said, "Should he treat our sister
like a harlot?"

CHAPTER 35

The Devotion at Bethel

THEN God said to Jacob, "Arise, go up to
[R]Bethel and dwell there; and make an
altar there to God, [R]who appeared to you
[R]when you fled from the face of Esau your
brother." Gen. 28:19; 31:13 • Gen. 28:13 • Gen. 27:43

2 And Jacob said to his household and to
all who *were* with him, "Put away the foreign
gods that *are* among you, purify yourselves,
and change your garments.

3 "Then let us arise and go up to Bethel;
and I will make an altar there to God, [R]who

answered me in the day of my distress [R]and has been with me in the way which I have gone." Gen. 32:7, 24 • Gen. 28:15, 20; 31:3, 42

4 So they gave Jacob all the foreign [T]gods which *were* in their hands, and the [R]earrings which *were* in their ears; and Jacob hid them under [R]the terebinth tree which *was* by Shechem. *idols* • Hos. 2:13 • Josh. 24:26

5 And they journeyed, and [R]the terror of God was upon the cities that *were* all around them, and they did not pursue the sons of Jacob. Ex. 15:16; 23:27

6 So Jacob came to [R]Luz (that *is,* Bethel), which *is* in the land of Canaan, he and all the people who *were* with him. Gen. 28:19, 22

7 And he [R]built an altar there and called the place El Bethel,* because [R]there God appeared to him when he fled from the face of his brother. Eccl. 5:4 • Gen. 28:13

8 Now [R]Deborah, Rebekah's nurse, died, and she was buried below Bethel under the terebinth tree. So the name of it was called Allon Bachuth.* Gen. 24:59

9 Then [R]God appeared to Jacob again, when he came from Padan Aram, and [R]blessed him. Josh. 5:13 • Gen. 32:29

10 And God said to him, "Your name *is* Jacob; [R]your name shall not be called Jacob anymore, but Israel shall be your name." So He called his name Israel. Gen. 17:5

11 Also God said to him: [R]"I *am* God Almighty. [R]Be fruitful and multiply; [R]a nation and a company of nations shall proceed from you, and kings shall come from your body. Ex. 6:3 • Gen. 9:1, 7 • Gen. 17:5, 6, 16; 28:3; 48:4

12 "The [R]land which I gave Abraham and Isaac I give to you; and to your descendants after you I give this land." Gen. 12:7; 13:15

13 Then God [R]went up from him in the place where He talked with him. Gen. 17:22

14 So Jacob [R]set up a pillar in the place where He talked with him, a pillar of stone; and he poured a drink offering on it, and he poured oil on it. Gen. 28:18, 19; 31:45

15 And Jacob called the name of the place where God spoke with him, Bethel.

The Deaths of Rachel and Isaac

16 Then they journeyed from Bethel. And when there was but a little distance to go to Ephrath, Rachel labored *in childbirth,* and she had hard labor.

17 Now it came to pass, when she was in hard labor, that the midwife said to her, "Do not fear; you will have this son also."

18 And so it was, as her soul was departing (for she died), that she called his name Ben-Oni;* but his father called him Benjamin.*

19 So Rachel died and was buried on the way to Ephrath (that *is,* Bethlehem).

20 And Jacob set a pillar on her grave, which *is* the pillar of Rachel's grave [R]to this day. 1 Sam. 10:2

21 Then Israel journeyed and pitched his tent beyond [R]the tower of Eder. Mic. 4:8

22 And it happened, when Israel dwelt in that land, that Reuben went and [R]lay with Bilhah his father's concubine; and Israel heard *about it.* Gen. 49:4

Now the sons of Jacob were twelve:

23 the sons of Leah *were* [R]Reuben, Jacob's firstborn, and Simeon, Levi, Judah, Issachar, and Zebulun; Ex. 1:1–4

24 the sons of Rachel *were* Joseph and Benjamin;

25 the sons of Bilhah, Rachel's maidservant, *were* Dan and Naphtali;

26 and the sons of Zilpah, Leah's maidservant, *were* Gad and Asher. These *were* the sons of Jacob who were born to him in Padan Aram.

27 Then Jacob came to his father Isaac at Mamre, or Kirjath Arba* (that *is,* Hebron), where Abraham and Isaac had dwelt.

28 Now the days of Isaac were one hundred and eighty years.

29 So Isaac breathed his last and died, and [R]was gathered to his people, *being* old and full of days. And [R]his sons Esau and Jacob buried him. Gen. 15:15; 25:8; 49:33 • Gen. 25:9

CHAPTER 36

The History of Esau—1 Chr. 1:35–42

NOW this *is* the genealogy of Esau, [R]who is Edom. Gen. 25:30

2 [R]Esau took his wives from the daughters of Canaan: Adah the daughter of Elon the Hittite; Aholibamah the daughter of Anah, the daughter of Zibeon the Hivite; Gen. 26:34

3 and [R]Basemath, Ishmael's daughter, sister of Nebajoth. Gen. 28:9

4 Now [R]Adah bore Eliphaz to Esau, and Basemath bore Reuel. 1 Chr. 1:35

5 And Aholibamah bore Jeush, Jaalam, and Korah. These *were* the sons of Esau who were born to him in the land of Canaan.

6 Then Esau took his wives, his sons, his daughters, and all the persons of his household, his cattle and all his animals, and all his goods which he had gained in the land of Canaan, and went to a country away from the presence of his brother Jacob.

7 [R]For their possessions were too great for them to dwell together, and the land where they were strangers could not support them because of their livestock. Gen. 13:6, 11

8 So Esau dwelt in [R]Mount Seir. [R]Esau *is* Edom. Gen. 32:3 • Gen. 36:1, 19

9 And this *is* the genealogy of Esau the father of the Edomites in Mount Seir.

35:7 Lit. *God of the House of God* **35:8** Lit. *Terebinth of Weeping* **35:18** Lit. *Son of My Sorrow* • Lit. *Son of the Right Hand* **35:27** Lit. *Town* or *City of Arba*

10 These *were* the names of Esau's sons:
[R]Eliphaz the son of Adah the wife of Esau,
and Reuel the son of Basemath the wife of
Esau. 1 Chr. 1:35
11 And the sons of Eliphaz were Teman,
Omar, Zepho,* Gatam, and Kenaz.
12 Now Timna was the concubine of Eli-
phaz, Esau's son, and she bore [R]Amalek to
Eliphaz. These *were* the sons of Adah, Esau's
wife. Num. 24:20
13 These *were* the sons of Reuel: Nahath,
Zerah, Shammah, and Mizzah. These were
the sons of Basemath, Esau's wife.
14 These were the sons of [T]Aholibamah,
Esau's wife, the daughter of Anah, the daugh-
ter of Zibeon. And she bore to Esau: Jeush,
Jaalam, and Korah. Or *Oholibamah*
15 These *were* the chiefs of the sons of Esau.
The sons of Eliphaz, the firstborn *son* of Esau,
were Chief Teman, Chief Omar, Chief Zepho,
Chief Kenaz,
16 Chief Korah,* Chief Gatam, *and* Chief
Amalek. These *were* the chiefs of Eliphaz in
the land of Edom. They *were* the sons of
Adah.
17 These *were* the sons of Reuel, Esau's son:
Chief Nahath, Chief Zerah, Chief Shammah,
and Chief Mizzah. These *were* the chiefs of
Reuel in the land of Edom. These *were* the
sons of Basemath, Esau's wife.
18 And these *were* the sons of Aholibamah,
Esau's wife: Chief Jeush, Chief Jaalam, and
Chief Korah. These *were* the chiefs *who de-
scended* from Aholibamah, Esau's wife, the
daughter of Anah.
19 These *were* the sons of Esau, who is
Edom, and these *were* their chiefs.
20 [R]These *were* the sons of Seir [R]the Horite
who inhabited the land: Lotan, Shobal,
Zibeon, Anah, 1 Chr. 1:38–42 • Gen. 14:6
21 Dishon, Ezer, and Dishan. These *were* the
chiefs of the Horites, the sons of Seir, in the
land of Edom.
22 And the sons of Lotan were Hori and
Hemam.* Lotan's sister *was* Timna.
23 These *were* the sons of Shobal: Alvan,*
Manahath, Ebal, Shepho,* and Onam.
24 These *were* the sons of Zibeon: both Ajah
and Anah. This *was the* Anah who found the
water* in the wilderness as he pastured the
donkeys of his father Zibeon.
25 These *were* the children of Anah: Di-
shon and [T]Aholibamah the daughter of
Anah. Or *Oholibamah*
26 These *were* the sons of Dishon:* Hem-
dan,* Eshban, Ithran, and Cheran.
27 These *were* the sons of Ezer: Bilhan, Zaa-
van, and Akan.*
28 These *were* the sons of Dishan: [R]Uz and
Aran. Job 1:1
29 These *were* the chiefs of the Horites:
Chief Lotan, Chief Shobal, Chief Zibeon,
Chief Anah,
30 Chief Dishon, Chief Ezer, and Chief Di-
shan. These *were* the chiefs of the Horites, ac-
cording to their chiefs in the land of Seir.
31 [R]Now these *were* the kings who reigned
in the land of Edom before any king reigned
over the children of Israel: 1 Chr. 1:43
32 Bela the son of Beor reigned in Edom,
and the name of his city *was* Dinhabah.
33 And when Bela died, Jobab the son of
Zerah of Bozrah reigned in his place.
34 When Jobab died, Husham of the land of
the Temanites reigned in his place.
35 And when Husham died, Hadad the son
of Bedad, who attacked Midian in the field of
Moab, reigned in his place. And the name of
his city *was* Avith.
36 When Hadad died, Samlah of Masrekah
reigned in his place.
37 And when Samlah died, Saul of
Rehoboth-*by*-the-River reigned in his place.
38 When Saul died, Baal-Hanan the son of
Achbor reigned in his place.
39 And when Baal-Hanan the son of Achbor
died, Hadar* reigned in his place; and the
name of his city *was* Pau.* His wife's name
was Mehetabel, the daughter of Matred, the
daughter of Mezahab.
40 And these *were* the names of the chiefs of
Esau, according to their families and their
places, by their names: Chief Timnah, Chief
Alvah,* Chief Jetheth,
41 Chief [T]Aholibamah, Chief Elah, Chief
Pinon, Or *Oholibamah*
42 Chief Kenaz, Chief Teman, Chief Mibzar,
43 Chief Magdiel, and Chief Iram. These
were the chiefs of Edom, according to their
dwelling places in the land of their posses-
sion. Esau *was* the father of the Edomites.

CHAPTER 37

Joseph's Family Sins Against Him

NOW Jacob dwelt in the land [R]where his
father was a stranger, in the land of
Canaan. Gen. 17:8; 23:4; 28:4; 36:7
2 This *is* the history of Jacob. Joseph, *being*
seventeen years old, was feeding the flock
with his brothers. And the lad *was* with the
sons of Bilhah and the sons of Zilpah, his fa-
ther's wives; and Joseph brought a bad report
of them to his father.
3 Now Israel loved Joseph more than all his
children, because he *was* [R]the son of his old
age. Also he [R]made him a tunic of *many* col-
ors. Gen. 44:20 • Gen. 37:23, 32

36:11 *Zephi*, 1 Chr. 1:36 **36:16** Sam. omits *Chief Korah* **36:22** *Homam*, 1 Chr. 1:39 **36:23** *Alian*, 1 Chr. 1:40 • *Shephi*, 1 Chr. 1:40 **36:24** So with MT, Vg. (*hot springs*); LXX *Jamin*; Tg. *mighty men;* Talmud *mules* **36:26** Heb. *Dishan* • *Hamran*, 1 Chr. 1:41 **36:27** *Jaakan*, 1 Chr. 1:42 **36:39** Sam., Syr. *Hadad* and 1 Chr. 1:50 • *Pai*, 1 Chr. 1:50 **36:40** *Aliah*, 1 Chr. 1:51

4 But when his brothers saw that their father loved him more than all his brothers, they [R]hated him and could not speak peaceably to him. Gen. 27:41; 49:23

5 Now Joseph had a dream, and he told *it* to his brothers; and they hated him even more.

6 So he said to them, "Please hear this dream which I have dreamed:

7 [R]"There we were, binding sheaves in the field. Then behold, my sheaf arose and also stood upright; and indeed your sheaves stood all around and bowed down to my sheaf." Gen. 42:6, 9; 43:26; 44:14

8 And his brothers said to him, "Shall you indeed reign over us? Or shall you indeed have dominion over us?" So they hated him even more for his dreams and for his words.

9 Then he dreamed still another dream and told it to his brothers, and said, "Look, I have dreamed another dream. And this time, [R]the sun, the moon, and the eleven stars bowed down to me." Gen. 46:29; 47:25

10 So he told *it* to his father and his brothers; and his father rebuked him and said to him, "What *is* this dream that you have dreamed? Shall your mother and I and [R]your brothers indeed come to bow down to the earth before you?" Gen. 27:29

11 And [R]his brothers envied him, but his father kept the matter *in mind.* Acts 7:9

12 Then his brothers went to feed their father's flock in [R]Shechem. Gen. 33:18–20

13 And Israel said to Joseph, "Are not your brothers feeding *the flock* in Shechem? Come, I will send you to them." So he said to him, "Here I am."

14 Then he said to him, "Please go and see if it is well with your brothers and well with the flocks, and bring back word to me." So he sent him out of the Valley of [R]Hebron, and he went to Shechem. Gen. 13:18; 23:2, 19; 35:27

15 Now a certain man found him, and there he was, wandering in the field. And the man asked him, saying, "What are you seeking?"

16 So he said, "I am seeking my brothers. [R]Please tell me where they are feeding *their flocks.*" Song 1:7

17 And the man said, "They have departed from here, for I heard them say, 'Let us go to Dothan.' " So Joseph went after his brothers and found them in [R]Dothan. 2 Kin. 6:13

18 Now when they saw him afar off, even before he came near them, [R]they conspired against him to kill him. Mark 14:1

19 Then they said to one another, "Look, this [T]dreamer is coming! Lit. *master of dreams*

20 "Come therefore, let us now kill him and cast him into some pit; and we shall say, 'Some wild beast has devoured him.' We shall see what will become of his dreams!"

21 But [R]Reuben heard *it,* and he delivered him out of their hands, and said, "Let us not kill him." Gen. 42:22

22 And Reuben said to them, "Shed no blood, *but* cast him into this pit which *is* in the wilderness, and do not lay a hand on him"—that he might deliver him out of their hands, and bring him back to his father.

23 So it came to pass, when Joseph had come to his brothers, that they [R]stripped Joseph *of* his tunic, the tunic of *many* colors that *was* on him. Matt. 27:28

24 Then they took him and cast him into a pit. And the pit *was* empty; *there was* no water in it.

25 [R]And they sat down to eat a meal. Then they lifted their eyes and looked, and there was a company of [R]Ishmaelites, coming from Gilead with their camels, bearing spices, balm, and myrrh, on their way to carry *them* down to Egypt. Prov. 30:20 • Gen. 16:11, 12

26 So Judah said to his brothers, "What profit *is there* if we kill our brother and [R]conceal his blood? Gen. 37:20

27 "Come and let us sell him to the Ishmaelites, and [R]let not our hand be upon him, for he *is* our brother *and* our flesh." And his brothers listened. 1 Sam. 18:17

28 Then Midianite traders passed by; so *the brothers* pulled Joseph up and lifted him out of the pit, and sold him to the Ishmaelites for [R]twenty *shekels* of silver. And they took Joseph to Egypt. Matt. 27:9

29 Then Reuben returned to the pit, and indeed Joseph *was* not in the pit; and he [R]tore his clothes. Job 1:20

30 And he returned to his brothers and said, "The lad [R]*is* no *more;* and I, where shall I go?" Gen. 42:13, 36

31 So they took [R]Joseph's tunic, killed a kid of the goats, and dipped the tunic in the blood. Gen. 37:3, 23

32 Then they sent the tunic of *many* colors, and they brought *it* to their father and said, "We have found this. Do you know whether it *is* your son's tunic or not?"

33 And he recognized it and said, "*It is* my son's tunic. A wild beast has devoured him. Without doubt Joseph is torn to pieces."

34 Then Jacob [R]tore his clothes, put sackcloth on his waist, and [R]mourned for his son many days. 2 Sam. 3:31 • Gen. 50:10

35 And all his sons and all his daughters [R]arose to comfort him; but he refused to be comforted, and he said, "For [R]I shall go down into the grave to my son in mourning." Thus his father wept for him. 2 Sam. 12:17 • Gen. 25:8

36 Now [R]the Midianites* had sold him in Egypt to Potiphar, an officer of Pharaoh *and* captain of the guard. Gen. 39:1

37:36 MT *Medanites*

CHAPTER 38

Joseph's Family Sins with the Canaanites

IT came to pass at that time that Judah
departed from his brothers, and visited a
certain Adullamite whose name *was* Hirah.
2 And Judah saw there a daughter of a cer-
tain Canaanite whose name *was* Shua, and he
married her and went in to her.
3 So she conceived and bore a son, and he
called his name [R]Er. Gen. 46:12
4 She conceived again and bore a son, and
she called his name [R]Onan. Num. 26:19
5 And she conceived yet again and bore a
son, and called his name [R]Shelah. He was at
Chezib when she bore him. Num. 26:20
6 Then Judah [R]took a wife for Er his first-
born, and her name *was* Tamar. Gen. 21:21
7 But [R]Er, Judah's firstborn, was wicked in
the sight of the LORD, [R]and the LORD killed
him. Gen. 46:12 • 1 Chr. 2:3
8 And Judah said to Onan, "Go in to
[R]your brother's wife and marry her, and raise
up an heir to your brother." Deut. 25:5, 6
9 But Onan knew that the heir would not be
[R]his; and it came to pass, when he went in to
his brother's wife, that he emitted on the
ground, lest he should give an heir to his
brother. Deut. 25:6
10 And the thing which he did displeased the
LORD; therefore He killed him also.
11 Then Judah said to Tamar his daughter-
in-law, [R]"Remain a widow in your father's
house till my son Shelah is grown." For he
said, "Lest he also die like his brothers." And
Tamar went and dwelt [R]in her father's
house. Ruth 1:12, 13 • Lev. 22:13
12 Now in the process of time the daughter
of Shua, Judah's wife, died; and Judah [R]was
comforted, and went up to his sheepshearers
at Timnah, he and his friend Hirah the Adul-
lamite. 2 Sam. 13:39
13 And it was told Tamar, saying, "Look,
your father-in-law is going up [R]to Timnah to
shear his sheep." Josh. 15:10, 57
14 So she took off her widow's garments,
covered *herself* with a veil and wrapped her-
self, and [R]sat in an open place which *was* on
the way to Timnah; for she saw [R]that Shelah
was grown, and she was not given to him as a
wife. Prov. 7:12 • Gen. 38:11, 26
15 When Judah saw her, he thought she *was*
a harlot, because she had covered her face.
16 Then he turned to her by the way, and
said, "Please let me come in to you"; for he did
not know that she *was* his daughter-in-law. So
she said, "What will you give me, that you
may come in to me?"
17 And he said, [R]"I will send a young goat
from the flock." So she said, "Will you give *me*
a pledge till you send *it?*" Ezek. 16:33
18 Then he said, "What pledge shall I give
you?" So she said, [R]"Your signet and cord, and
your staff that *is* in your hand." Then he gave
them to her, and went in to her, and she con-
ceived by him. Gen. 38:25; 41:42
19 So she arose and went away, and [R]laid
aside her veil and put on the garments of her
widowhood. Gen. 38:14
20 And Judah sent the young goat by the
hand of his friend the Adullamite, to receive
his pledge from the woman's hand, but he did
not find her.
21 Then he asked the men of that place, say-
ing, "Where is the harlot who *was* openly by
the roadside?" And they said, "There was no
harlot in this *place*."
22 So he returned to Judah and said, "I can-
not find her. Also, the men of the place said
there was no harlot in this *place*."
23 Then Judah said, "Let her take *them* for
herself, lest we be shamed; for I sent this
young goat and you have not found her."
24 And it came to pass, about three months
after, that Judah was told, saying, "Tamar
your daughter-in-law has [R]played the harlot;
furthermore she *is* with child by harlotry." So
Judah said, "Bring her out [R]and let her be
burned!" Judg. 19:2 • Lev. 20:14
25 When she *was* brought out, she sent
to her father-in-law, saying, "By the man to
whom these belong, I *am* with child." And she
said, "Please determine whose these *are*—the
signet and cord, and staff."
26 So Judah [R]acknowledged *them* and said,
"She has been more righteous than I, because
I did not give her to Shelah my son." And he
never knew her again. Gen. 37:33
27 Now it came to pass, at the time for giving
birth, that behold, twins *were* in her womb.
28 And so it was, when she was giving birth,
that *the one* put out *his* hand; and the midwife
took a scarlet *thread* and bound it on his
hand, saying, "This one came out first."
29 Then it happened, as he drew back his
hand, that his brother came out unexpectedly;
and she said, "How did you break through?
This breach *be* upon you!" Therefore his
name was called [R]Perez.* Gen. 46:12
30 Afterward his brother came out who had
the scarlet *thread* on his hand. And his name
was called [R]Zerah. 1 Chr. 2:4

CHAPTER 39

Joseph's Test with the Egyptian Woman

NOW Joseph had been taken [R]down to
Egypt. And Potiphar, an officer of
Pharaoh, captain of the guard, an Egyptian,
bought him from the Ishmaelites who had
taken him down there. Gen. 12:10; 43:15
2 [R]The LORD was with Joseph, and he was a

38:29 Lit. *Breach* or *Breakthrough*

successful man; and he was in the house of his master the Egyptian. Acts 7:9

3 And his master saw that the LORD *was* with him and that the LORD [R]made all he did [T]to prosper in his hand. Ps. 1:3 • *to be a success*

4 So Joseph [R]found favor in his sight, and served him. Then he made him [R]overseer of his house, and all *that* he had he put under his authority. Gen. 18:3; 19:19; 39:21 • Gen. 24:2

5 So it was, from the time *that* he had made him overseer of his house and all that he had, that [R]the LORD blessed the Egyptian's house for Joseph's sake; and the blessing of the LORD was on all that he had in the house and in the field. Gen. 18:26; 30:27

6 Thus he left all that he had in Joseph's hand, and he did not know what he had except for the bread which he ate. Now Joseph was handsome in form and appearance.

7 And it came to pass after these things that his master's wife cast longing eyes on Joseph, and she said, "Lie with me."

8 But he refused and said to his master's wife, "Look, my master does not know what *is* with me in the house, and he has committed all that he has to my hand.

9 "*There is* no one greater in this house than I, nor has he kept back anything from me but you, because you *are* his wife. [R]How then can I do this great wickedness, and [R]sin against God?" Prov. 6:29, 32 • Ps. 51:4

10 So it was, as she spoke to Joseph day by day, that he [R]did not heed her, to lie with her *or* to be with her. Prov. 1:10

11 But it happened about this time, when Joseph went into the house to do his work, and none of the men of the house *was* inside,

12 that she caught him by his garment, saying, "Lie with me." But he left his garment in her hand, and fled and ran outside.

13 And so it was, when she saw that he had left his garment in her hand and fled outside,

14 that she called to the men of her house and spoke to them, saying, "See, he has brought in to us a [R]Hebrew to [T]mock us. He came in to me to lie with me, and I cried out with a loud voice. Gen. 14:13; 41:12 • *laugh at*

15 "And it happened, when he heard that I lifted my voice and cried out, that he left his garment with me, and fled and went outside."

16 So she kept his garment with her until his master came home.

17 Then she [R]spoke to him with words like these, saying, "The Hebrew servant whom you brought to us came in to me to mock me; Ex. 23:1

18 "so it happened, as I lifted my voice and cried out, that he left his garment with me and fled outside."

19 So it was, when his master heard the words which his wife spoke to him, saying, "Your servant did to me after this manner," that his [R]anger was aroused. Prov. 6:34, 35

20 Then Joseph's master took him and [R]put him into the [R]prison, a place where the king's prisoners *were* confined. And he was there in the prison. Ps. 105:18 • Gen. 40:3, 15

21 But the LORD was with Joseph and showed him mercy, and He gave him favor in the sight of the keeper of the prison.

22 And the keeper of the prison [R]committed to Joseph's hand all the prisoners who *were* in the prison; whatever they did there, it was his doing. Gen. 39:4; 40:3, 4

23 The keeper of the prison did not look into anything *that was* under *Joseph's** authority, because [R]the LORD was with him; and whatever he did, the LORD made *it* prosper. Gen. 39:2, 3

CHAPTER 40

Joseph's Test with the Egyptian Society

IT came to pass after these things *that* the butler and the baker of the king of Egypt offended their lord, the king of Egypt.

2 And Pharaoh was angry with his two officers, the chief butler and the chief baker.

3 So he put them in custody in the house of the captain of the guard, in the prison, the place where Joseph *was* confined.

4 And the captain of the guard charged Joseph with them, and he served them; so they were in custody for a while.

5 Then the butler and the baker of the king of Egypt, who *were* confined in the prison, had a dream, both of them, each man's dream in one night *and* each man's dream with its *own* interpretation.

6 And Joseph came in to them in the morning and looked at them, and saw that they *were* [T]sad. *dejected*

7 So he asked Pharaoh's officers who *were* with him in the custody of his lord's house, saying, [R]"Why do you look *so* sad today?" Neh. 2:2

8 And they said to him, [R]"We each have had a dream, and *there is* no interpreter of it." So Joseph said to them, [R]"Do not interpretations belong to God? Tell *them* to me, please." Gen. 41:15 • [Dan. 2:11, 20–22, 27, 28, 47]

9 Then the chief butler told his dream to Joseph, and said to him, "Behold, in my dream a vine *was* before me,

10 "and in the vine *were* three branches; it *was* as though it budded, its blossoms shot forth, and its clusters brought forth ripe grapes.

11 "Then Pharaoh's cup *was* in my hand; and I took the grapes and pressed them into Pharaoh's cup, and placed the cup in Pharaoh's hand."

12 And Joseph said to him, [R]"This *is* the interpretation of it: The three branches [R]*are* three days. Dan. 2:36; 4:18, 19 • Gen. 40:18; 42:17

13 "Now within three days Pharaoh will [R]lift

39:23 Lit. *his hand*

up your head and restore you to your [T]place,
and you will put Pharaoh's cup in his hand ac-
cording to the former manner, when you were
his butler. 2 Kin. 25:27 • *position*
14 "But [R]remember me when it is well with
you, and [R]please show kindness to me; make
mention of me to Pharaoh, and get me out of
this house. Luke 23:42 • Josh. 2:12
15 "For indeed I was [R]stolen away from the
land of the Hebrews; [R]and also I have done
nothing here that they should put me into the
dungeon." Gen. 37:26–28 • Gen. 39:20
16 When the chief baker saw that the inter-
pretation was good, he said to Joseph, "I also
was in my dream, and there *were* three white
baskets on my head.
17 "In the uppermost basket *were* all
kinds of baked goods for Pharaoh, and the
birds ate them out of the basket on my head."
18 So Joseph answered and said, [R]"This *is*
the interpretation of it: The three baskets *are*
three days. Gen. 40:12
19 "Within three days Pharaoh will lift off
your head from you and hang you on a
tree; and the birds will eat your flesh from
you."
20 Now it came to pass on the third day,
which was Pharaoh's birthday, that he made a
feast for all his servants; and he lifted up the
head of the chief butler and of the chief baker
among his servants.
21 Then he [R]restored the chief butler to his
butlership again, and [R]he placed the cup in
Pharaoh's hand. Gen. 40:13 • Neh. 2:1
22 But he [R]hanged the chief baker, as Joseph
had interpreted to them. Gen. 40:19
23 Yet the chief butler did not remember Jo-
seph, but [R]forgot him. Eccl. 9:15, 16

CHAPTER 41

Joseph's Test with Pharaoh's Dreams

THEN it came to pass, at the end of two
full years, that [R]Pharaoh had a dream; and
behold, he stood by the river. Gen. 40:5
2 Suddenly there came up out of the river
seven cows, fine looking and fat; and they fed
in the meadow.
3 Then behold, seven other cows came up
after them out of the river, ugly and gaunt,
and stood by the *other* cows on the bank of
the river.
4 And the ugly and gaunt cows ate up the
seven fine looking and fat cows. So Pharaoh
awoke.
5 He slept and dreamed a second time; and
suddenly seven heads of grain came up on
one stalk, plump and good.
6 Then behold, seven thin heads, blighted
by the east wind, sprang up after them.
7 And the seven thin heads devoured the
seven plump and full heads. So Pharaoh
awoke, and indeed, *it was* a dream.
8 Now it came to pass in the morning that
his spirit was troubled, and he sent and called
for all the magicians of Egypt and all its [R]wise
men. And Pharaoh told them his dreams, but
there was no one who could interpret them
for Pharaoh. Matt. 2:1
9 Then the chief butler spoke to Pharaoh,
saying: "I remember my faults this day.
10 "When Pharaoh was [R]angry with his ser-
vants, [R]and put me in custody in the house of
the captain of the guard, *both* me and the
chief baker, Gen. 40:2, 3 • Gen. 39:20
11 [R]"we each had a dream in one night, he
and I. Each of us dreamed according to the in-
terpretation of his *own* dream. Gen. 40:5
12 "Now there *was* a young Hebrew man
with us there, a servant of the captain of the
guard. And we told him, and he interpreted
our dreams for us; to each man he interpreted
according to his *own* dream.
13 "And it came to pass, just as he inter-
preted for us, so it happened. He restored me
to my office, and he hanged him."
14 [R]Then Pharaoh sent and called Joseph,
and they brought him quickly out of the dun-
geon; and he shaved, changed his clothing,
and came to Pharaoh. Ps. 105:20
15 And Pharaoh said to Joseph, "I have had a
dream, and *there is* no one who can interpret
it. [R]But I have heard it said of you *that* you can
understand a dream, to interpret it." Dan. 5:16
16 So Joseph answered Pharaoh, saying, [R]"*It*
is not in me; [R]God will give Pharaoh an an-
swer of peace." Dan. 2:30 • Dan. 2:22, 28, 47
17 Then Pharaoh said to Joseph: "Behold,
[R]in my dream I stood on the bank of the
river. Gen. 41:1
18 "Suddenly seven cows came up out of the
river, fine looking and fat; and they fed in the
meadow.
19 "Then behold, seven other cows came up
after them, poor and very ugly and gaunt,
such ugliness as I have never seen in all the
land of Egypt.
20 "And the gaunt and ugly cows ate up the
first seven, the fat cows.
21 "When they had eaten them up, no one
would have known that they had eaten them,
for they *were* just as ugly as at the beginning.
So I awoke.
22 "Also I saw in my dream, and suddenly
seven [T]heads came up on one stalk, full and
good. Heads of grain
23 "Then behold, seven heads, withered,
thin, *and* blighted by the east wind, sprang up
after them.
24 "And the thin heads devoured the seven
good heads. So [R]I told *this* to the magicians,
but *there was* no one who could explain *it* to
me." Is. 8:19
25 Then Joseph said to Pharaoh, "The
dreams of Pharaoh *are* one; God has shown
Pharaoh what He *is* about to do:

26 “The seven good cows *are* seven years,
and the seven good [T]heads *are* seven years;
the dreams *are* one. Heads of grain
27 “And the seven thin and ugly cows which
came up after them *are* seven years, and the
seven empty heads blighted by the east wind
are seven years of famine.
28 [R]“This *is* the thing which I have spoken to
Pharaoh. God has shown Pharaoh what He *is*
about to do. [Gen. 41:25, 32]
29 “Indeed seven years of great plenty will
come throughout all the land of Egypt;
30 “but after them seven years of famine will
[R]arise, and all the plenty will be forgotten in
the land of Egypt; and the famine [R]will de-
plete the land. Gen. 41:54, 56 • Gen. 47:13
31 “So the plenty will not be known in the
land because of the famine following, for it
will be very severe.
32 “And the dream was repeated to
Pharaoh twice because the [R]thing *is* estab-
lished by God, and God will shortly bring it
to pass. Num. 23:19
33 “Now therefore, let Pharaoh select a dis-
cerning and wise man, and set him over the
land of Egypt.
34 “Let Pharaoh do *this*, and let him appoint
[T]officers over the land, [R]to collect one-fifth *of
the produce* of the land of Egypt in the seven
plentiful years. *overseers* • [Prov. 6:6–8]
35 “And let them gather all the food of those
good years that are coming, and store up
grain under the authority of Pharaoh, and let
them keep food in the cities.
36 “Then that food shall be as a reserve for
the land for the seven years of famine which
shall be in the land of Egypt, that the land
may not perish during the famine.”

Joseph’s Exaltation over Egypt

37 So the advice was good in the eyes of
Pharaoh and in the eyes of all his servants.
38 And Pharaoh said to his servants, “Can
we find *such a one* as this, a man [R]in whom *is*
the Spirit of God?” Num. 27:18
39 Then Pharaoh said to Joseph, “Inasmuch
as God has shown you all this, *there is* no one
as discerning and wise as you.
40 [R]“You shall be [T]over my house, and all my
people shall be ruled according to your word;
only in regard to the throne will I be greater
than you.” Ps. 105:21 • In charge of
41 And Pharaoh said to Joseph, “See, I have
set you over all the land of Egypt.”
42 Then Pharaoh took his signet ring off his
hand and put it on Joseph’s hand; and he
clothed him in garments of fine linen and put
a gold chain around his neck.
43 And he had him ride in the second [R]char-
iot which he had; and they cried out before
him, “Bow the knee!” So he set him over all
the land of Egypt. Gen. 46:29
44 Pharaoh also said to Joseph, “I *am*
Pharaoh, and without your consent no man
may lift his hand or foot in all the land of
Egypt.”
45 And Pharaoh called Joseph’s name
Zaphnath-Paaneah. And he gave him as a
wife [R]Asenath, the daughter of Poti-Pherah
priest of On. So Joseph went out over *all* the
land of Egypt. Gen. 46:20
46 Joseph was thirty years old when he
stood before Pharaoh king of Egypt. And Jo-
seph went out from the presence of Pharaoh,
and went throughout all the land of Egypt.
47 Now in the seven plentiful years the
ground brought forth abundantly.
48 So he gathered up all the food of the
seven years which were in the land of Egypt,
and laid up the food in the cities; he laid up in
every city the food of the fields which sur-
rounded them.
49 Joseph gathered very much grain, [R]as the
sand of the sea, until he stopped counting, for
it was immeasurable. Gen. 22:17
50 [R]And to Joseph were born two sons be-
fore the years of famine came, whom Ase-
nath, the daughter of Poti-Pherah priest of
On, bore to him. Gen. 46:20; 48:5
51 Joseph called the name of the firstborn
Manasseh:* “For God has made me forget all
my toil and all my [R]father’s house.” Ps. 45:10
52 And the name of the second he called
Ephraim:* “For God has caused me to be fruit-
ful in the land of my affliction.”
53 Then the seven years of plenty which
were in the land of Egypt ended,
54 [R]and the seven years of famine began to
come, [R]as Joseph had said. The famine was in
all lands, but in all the land of Egypt there was
bread. Acts 7:11 • Gen. 41:30
55 So when all the land of Egypt was fam-
ished, the people cried to Pharaoh for bread.
Then Pharaoh said to all the Egyptians, “Go to
Joseph; whatever he says to you, do.”
56 The famine was over all the face of the
earth, and Joseph opened all the storehouses*
and sold to the Egyptians. And the famine be-
came severe in the land of Egypt.
57 [R]So all countries came to Joseph in Egypt
to [R]buy *grain*, because the famine was severe
in all lands. Ezek. 29:12 • Gen. 27:28, 37

CHAPTER 42

Joseph’s Brothers Visit Egypt

WHEN [R]Jacob saw that there was grain in
Egypt, Jacob said to his sons, “Why do
you look at one another?” Acts 7:12
2 And he said, “Indeed I have heard that
there is grain in Egypt; go down to that place
and buy for us there, that we may [R]live and
not die.” Gen. 43:8

41:51 Lit. *Making Forgetful* **41:52** Lit. *Fruitfulness*
41:56 Lit. *all that was in them*

3 So Joseph's ten brothers went down to
buy grain in Egypt.
4 But Jacob did not send Joseph's brother
Benjamin with his brothers, for he said, "Lest
some calamity befall him."
5 And the sons of Israel went to buy *grain*
among those who journeyed, for the famine
was [R]in the land of Canaan. Acts 7:11
6 Now Joseph *was* governor [R]over the land;
and it was he who sold to all the people of the
land. And Joseph's brothers came and
[R]bowed down before him with *their* faces to
the earth. Gen. 41:41, 55 • Gen. 37:7–10; 41:43
7 Joseph saw his brothers and recognized
them, but he acted as a stranger to them and
spoke roughly to them. Then he said to them,
"Where do you come from?" And they said,
"From the land of Canaan to buy food."
8 So Joseph recognized his brothers, but
they did not recognize him.
9 Then Joseph [R]remembered the dreams
which he had dreamed about them, and said
to them, "You *are* spies! You have come to see
the nakedness of the land!" Gen. 37:5–9
10 And they said to him, "No, my lord, but
your servants have come to buy food.
11 "We *are* all one man's sons; we *are* honest
men; your servants are not spies."
12 But he said to them, "No, but you have
come to see the nakedness of the land."
13 And they said, "Your servants *are* twelve
brothers, the sons of one man in the land of
Canaan; and in fact, the youngest *is* with our
father today, and one *is* no more."
14 But Joseph said to them, "It *is* as I spoke
to you, saying, 'You *are* spies!'
15 "In this *manner* you shall be tested: [R]By
the life of Pharaoh, you shall not leave this
place unless your youngest brother comes
here. 1 Sam. 1:26; 17:55
16 "Send one of you, and let him bring your
brother; and you shall be kept in prison, that
your words may be tested to see whether
there is any truth in you; or else, by the life of
Pharaoh, surely you *are* spies!"
17 So he [T]put them all together in prison
[R]three days. Lit. *gathered* • Gen. 40:4, 7, 12
18 Then Joseph said to them the third day,
"Do this and live, [R]*for* I fear God: Lev. 25:43
19 "If you *are* honest *men,* let one of your
brothers be confined to your prison house; but
you, go and carry grain for the famine of your
houses.
20 "And [R]bring your youngest brother to me;
so your words will be verified, and you shall
not die." And they did so. Gen. 42:34
21 Then they said to one another, [R]"We *are*
truly guilty concerning our brother, for we
saw the anguish of his soul when he pleaded
with us, and we would not hear; therefore this
distress has come upon us." Hos. 5:15
22 And Reuben answered them, saying,
[R]"Did I not speak to you, saying, 'Do not sin
against the boy'; and you would not listen?
Therefore behold, his blood is now [R]required
of us." Gen. 37:21, 22, 29 • Gen. 9:5, 6
23 But they did not know that Joseph under-
stood *them,* for he spoke to them through an
interpreter.
24 And he turned himself away from them
and wept. Then he returned to them again,
and talked with them. And he took Simeon
from them and bound him before their eyes.
25 Then Joseph [R]gave a command to fill
their sacks with grain, to [R]restore every
man's money to his sack, and to give them
provisions for the journey. [R]Thus he did for
them. Gen. 44:1 • Gen. 43:12 • [Rom. 12:17, 20, 21]
26 So they loaded their donkeys with the
grain and departed from there.
27 But as [R]one *of them* opened his sack to
give his donkey feed at the encampment, he
saw his money; and there it was, in the mouth
of his sack. Gen. 43:21, 22
28 So he said to his brothers, "My money has
been restored, and there it is, in my sack!"
Then their hearts failed *them* and they were
afraid, saying to one another, "What *is* this
that God has done to us?"
29 Then they went to Jacob their father in
the land of Canaan and told him all that had
happened to them, saying:
30 "The man *who is* lord of the land [R]spoke
[T]roughly to us, and took us for spies of the
country. Gen. 42:7 • *harshly*
31 "But we said to him, 'We *are* honest *men;*
we are not spies.
32 'We *are* twelve brothers, sons of our
father; one *is* no *more,* and the youngest *is*
with our father this day in the land of
Canaan.'
33 "Then the man, the lord of the country,
said to us, [R]'By this I will know that you *are*
honest *men:* Leave one of your brothers *here*
with me, take *food for* the famine of your
households, and be gone. Gen. 42:15, 19, 20
34 'And bring your [R]youngest brother to me;
so I shall know that you *are* not spies, but
that you *are* honest *men.* I will grant your
brother to you, and you may [R]trade in the
land.' " Gen. 42:20; 43:3, 5 • Gen. 34:10
35 Then it happened as they emptied their
sacks, that surprisingly [R]each man's bundle of
money *was* in his sack; and when they and
their father saw the bundles of money, they
were afraid. Gen. 43:12, 15, 21
36 And Jacob their father said to them, "You
have bereaved me: Joseph is no *more,* Simeon
is no *more,* and you want to take Benjamin.
All these things are against me."
37 Then Reuben spoke to his father, saying,
"Kill my two sons if I do not bring him *back* to
you; put him in my hands, and I will bring him
back to you."
38 But he said, "My son shall not go down
with you, for [R]his brother is dead, and he is

left alone. If any calamity should befall him
along the way in which you go, then you
would bring down my gray hair with sorrow
to the grave." Gen. 37:22; 42:13; 44:20, 28

CHAPTER 43

Joseph's Brothers' Second Journey to Egypt

NOW the famine *was* severe in the land.
2 And it came to pass, when they had
eaten up the grain which they had brought
from Egypt, that their father said to them, "Go
[R]back, buy us a little food." Gen. 42:2
3 But Judah spoke to him, saying, "The
man solemnly warned us, saying, 'You shall
not see my face unless your [R]brother *is* with
you.' Gen. 42:20; 43:5; 44:23
4 "If you send our brother with us, we will
go down and buy you food.
5 "But if you will not send *him*, we will not
go down; for the man said to us, 'You shall not
see my face unless your brother *is* with you.' "
6 And Israel said, "Why did you deal *so*
wrongfully with me *as* to tell the man whether
you had still *another* brother?"
7 But they said, "The man asked us point-
edly about ourselves and our family, saying,
'*Is* your father still alive? Have you *another*
brother?' And we told him according to these
words. Could we possibly have known that he
would say, 'Bring your brother down'?"
8 Then Judah said to Israel his father,
"Send the lad with me, and we will arise and
go, that we may [R]live and not die, both we and
you *and* also our little ones. Gen. 42:2
9 "I myself will be surety for him; from my
hand you shall require him. If I do not bring
him *back* to you and set him before you, then
let me bear the blame forever.
10 "For if we had not lingered, surely by now
we would have returned this second time."
11 And their father Israel said to them, "If *it*
must be so, then do this: Take some of the best
fruits of the land in your vessels and [R]carry
down a present for the man—a little balm and
a little honey, spices and myrrh, pistachio nuts
and almonds. Gen. 32:20; 33:10
12 "Take double money in your hand, and
take back in your hand the money [R]that was
returned in the mouth of your sacks; perhaps
it was an oversight. Gen. 42:25, 35; 43:21
13 "Take your brother also, and arise, go
back to the man.
14 "And may God [R]Almighty give you mercy
before the man, that he may release your
other brother and Benjamin. If I am bereaved,
I am bereaved!" Gen. 17:1; 28:3
15 So the men took that present and Benja-
min, and they took double money in their
hand, and arose and went [R]down to Egypt;
and they stood before Joseph. Gen. 39:1
16 When Joseph saw Benjamin with them,
he said to the [R]steward of his house, "Take
these men to my home, and slaughter an ani-
mal and make ready; for *these* men will dine
with me at noon." Gen. 24:2; 39:4; 44:1
17 Then the man did as Joseph ordered, and
the man brought the men into Joseph's house.
18 Now the men were [R]afraid because they
were brought into Joseph's house; and they
said, "*It is* because of the money, which was
returned in our sacks the first time, that we
are brought in, so that he may make a case
against us and seize us, to take us as slaves
with our donkeys." Gen. 42:28
19 When they drew near to the steward of
Joseph's house, they talked with him at the
door of the house,
20 and said, "O sir, [R]we indeed came down
the first time to buy food; Gen. 42:3, 10
21 "but [R]it happened, when we came to the
encampment, that we opened our sacks, and
there, *each* man's money *was* in the mouth of
his sack, our money in full weight; so we have
brought it back in our hand. Gen. 42:27
22 "And we have brought down other money
in our hands to buy food. We do not know who
put our money in our sacks."
23 But he said, "Peace *be* with you, do not be
afraid. Your God and the God of your father
has given you treasure in your sacks; I had
your money." Then he brought [R]Simeon out to
them. Gen. 42:24
24 So the man brought the men into Jo-
seph's house and [R]gave *them* water, and they
washed their feet; and he gave their donkeys
feed. Gen. 18:4; 19:2; 24:32
25 Then they made the present ready for Jo-
seph's coming at noon, for they heard that
they would eat bread there.
26 And when Joseph came home, they
brought him the present which *was* in their
hand into the house, and [R]bowed down before
him to the earth. Gen. 37:7, 10; 42:6; 44:14
27 Then he asked them about *their* well-
being, and said, "*Is* your father well, the old
man of whom you spoke? *Is* he still alive?"
28 And they answered, "Your servant our fa-
ther *is* in good health; he *is* still alive." [R]And
they bowed their heads down and prostrated
themselves. Gen. 37:7, 10
29 Then he lifted his eyes and saw his
brother Benjamin, [R]his mother's son, and
said, "*Is* this your younger brother of whom
you spoke to me?" And he said, "God be gra-
cious to you, my son." Gen. 35:17, 18
30 Now [R]his heart yearned for his brother;
so Joseph made haste and sought *somewhere*
to weep. And he went into *his* chamber and
[R]wept there. 1 Kin. 3:26 • Gen. 42:24
31 Then he washed his face and came out;
and he restrained himself, and said, "Serve
the [R]bread." Gen. 43:25
32 So they set him a place by himself, and
them by themselves, and the Egyptians who
ate with him by themselves; because the

Egyptians could not eat food with the [R]He-
brews, for that *is* [R]an abomination to the
Egyptians. Gen. 41:12 • Gen. 46:34
33 And they sat before him, the firstborn ac-
cording to his [R]birthright and the youngest ac-
cording to his youth; and the men looked in
astonishment at one another. Gen. 27:36
34 Then he took servings to them from be-
fore him, but Benjamin's serving was [R]five
times as much as any of theirs. So they drank
and were merry with him. Gen. 35:24

CHAPTER 44

AND he commanded [T]the [R]steward of his
house, saying, [R]"Fill the men's sacks
with food, as much as they can carry, and
put each man's money in the mouth of his
sack. Lit. *the one overseer* • Gen. 43:16 • Gen. 42:25
2 "Also put my cup, the silver cup, in the
mouth of the sack of the youngest, and his
grain money." So he did according to the word
that Joseph had spoken.
3 As soon as the morning dawned, the men
were sent away, they and their donkeys.
4 When they had gone out of the city, *and*
were not *yet* far off, Joseph said to his stew-
ard, "Get up, follow the men; and when you
overtake them, say to them, 'Why have you
[R]repaid evil for good? 1 Sam. 25:21
5 '*Is* not this *the one* from which my lord
drinks, and with which he indeed practices
divination? You have done evil in so doing.' "
6 So he overtook them, and he spoke to
them these same words.
7 And they said to him, "Why does my lord
say these words? Far be it from us that your
servants should do such a thing.
8 "Look, we brought back to you from the
land of Canaan [R]the money which we found
in the mouth of our sacks. How then could
we steal silver or gold from your lord's
house? Gen. 43:21
9 "With whomever of your servants it is
found, [R]let him die, and we also will be my
lord's slaves." Gen. 31:32
10 And he said, "Now also *let* it *be* according
to your words; he with whom it is found shall
be my slave, and you shall be blameless."
11 Then each man speedily let down his sack
to the ground, and each opened his sack.
12 So he searched. He began with the oldest
and left off with the youngest; and the cup
was found in Benjamin's sack.
13 Then they [R]tore their clothes, and each
man loaded his donkey and returned to the
city. 2 Sam. 1:11
14 So Judah and his brothers came to Jo-
seph's house, and he *was* still there; and they
fell before him on the ground.
15 And Joseph said to them, "What deed *is*
this you have done? Did you not know that
such a man as I can certainly practice divina-
tion?"
16 Then Judah said, "What shall we say to
my lord? What shall we speak? Or how shall
we clear ourselves? God has [R]found out the
iniquity of your servants; here we are, my
lord's slaves, both we and *he* also with whom
the cup was found." [Num. 32:23]
17 But he said, "Far be it from me that I
should do so; the man in whose hand the cup
was found, he shall be my slave. And as for
you, go up in peace to your father."
18 Then Judah came near to him and said:
"O my lord, please let your servant speak a
word in my lord's hearing, and [R]do not let
your anger burn against your servant; for you
are even like Pharaoh. Ex. 32:22
19 "My lord asked his servants, saying,
'Have you a father or a brother?'
20 "And we said to my lord, 'We have a
father, an old man, and [R]a child of *his* old age,
who is young; his brother is dead, and he
alone is left of his mother's children, and his
father loves him.' Gen. 37:3; 43:8; 44:30
21 "Then you said to your servants, [R]'Bring
him down to me, that I may set my eyes on
him.' Gen. 42:15, 20
22 "And we said to my lord, 'The lad cannot
leave his father, for *if* he should leave his
father, *his father* would die.'
23 "But you said to your servants, 'Unless
your youngest brother comes down with you,
you shall see my face no more.'
24 "So it was, when we went up to your ser-
vant my father, that we told him the words of
my lord.
25 "And [R]our father said, 'Go back *and* buy
us a little food.' Gen. 43:2
26 "But we said, 'We cannot go down;
if our youngest brother is with us, then we
will go down; for we may not see the
man's face unless our youngest brother *is*
with us.'
27 "Then your servant my father said to us,
'You know that my wife bore me two sons;
28 'and the one went out from me, and I said,
[R]"Surely he is torn to pieces"; and I have not
seen him since. Gen. 37:31–35
29 'But if you take this one also from
me, and calamity befalls him, you shall bring
down my gray hair with sorrow to the grave.'
30 "Now therefore, when I come to your
servant my father, and the lad *is* not with
us, since [R]his life is bound up in the lad's
life, [1 Sam. 18:1; 25:29]
31 "it will happen, when he sees that the lad
is not *with us,* that he will die. So your ser-
vants will bring down the gray hair of your
servant our father with sorrow to the grave.
32 "For your servant became surety for the
lad to my father, saying, [R]'If I do not bring him
back to you, then I shall bear the blame before
my father forever.' Gen. 43:9

33 "Now therefore, please let your servant remain instead of the lad as a slave to my lord, and let the lad go up with his brothers.

34 "For how shall I go up to my father if the lad *is* not with me, lest perhaps I see the evil that would [T]come upon my father?" Lit. *find*

CHAPTER 45

THEN Joseph could not restrain himself before all those who stood by him, and he cried out, "Make everyone go out from me!" So no one stood with him while Joseph made himself known to his brothers.

2 And he wept aloud, and the Egyptians and the house of Pharaoh heard *it.*

3 Then Joseph said to his brothers, [R]"I *am* Joseph; does my father still live?" But his brothers could not answer him, for they were dismayed in his presence. Acts 7:13

4 And Joseph said to his brothers, "Please come near to me." So they came near. Then he said: "I *am* Joseph your brother, [R]whom you sold into Egypt. Gen. 37:28; 39:1

5 "But now, do not therefore be grieved or angry with yourselves because you sold me here; [R]for God sent me before you to preserve life. Gen. 45:7, 8; 50:20

6 "For these two years the [R]famine *has been* in the land, and *there are* still five years in which *there will be* neither plowing nor harvesting. Gen. 43:1; 47:4, 13

7 "And God sent me before you to preserve a posterity for you in the earth, and to save your lives by a great deliverance.

8 "So now *it was* not you *who* sent me here, but [R]God; and He has made me [R]a father to Pharaoh, and lord of all his house, and a [R]ruler throughout all the land of Egypt. [Rom. 8:28] • Is. 22:21 • Gen. 41:43; 42:6

9 "Hurry and go up to my father, and say to him, 'Thus says your son Joseph: "God has made me lord of all Egypt; come down to me, do not [T]tarry. *delay*

10 "You shall dwell in the land of Goshen, and you shall be near to me, you and your children, your children's children, your flocks and your herds, and all that you have.

11 "There I will [R]provide for you, lest you and your household, and all that you have, come to poverty; for *there are* still five years of famine." ' Gen. 47:12

12 "And behold, your eyes and the eyes of my brother Benjamin see that *it is* [R]my mouth that speaks to you. Gen. 42:23

13 "So you shall tell my father of all my glory in Egypt, and of all that you have seen; and you shall hurry and [R]bring my father down here." Acts 7:14

14 Then he fell on his brother Benjamin's neck and wept, and Benjamin wept on his neck.

15 Moreover he [R]kissed all his brothers and wept over them, and after that his brothers talked with him. Gen. 48:10

16 Now the report of it was heard in Pharaoh's house, saying, "Joseph's brothers have come." So it pleased Pharaoh and his servants well.

17 And Pharaoh said to Joseph, "Say to your brothers, 'Do this: Load your animals and depart; go to the land of Canaan.

18 'Bring your father and your households and come to me; I will give you the best of the land of Egypt, and you will eat [R]the [T]fat of the land. Gen. 27:28; 47:6 • The choicest produce

19 'Now you are commanded—do this: Take carts out of the land of Egypt for your little ones and your wives; bring your father and come.

20 'Also do not be concerned about your goods, for the best of all the land of Egypt *is* yours.' "

21 Then the sons of Israel did so; and Joseph gave them [R]carts, according to the command of Pharaoh, and he gave them provisions for the journey. Gen. 45:19; 46:5

22 He gave to all of them, to each man, [R]changes of garments; but to Benjamin he gave three hundred *pieces* of silver and [R]five changes of garments. 2 Kin. 5:5 • Gen. 43:34

23 And he sent to his father these *things:* ten donkeys loaded with the good things of Egypt, and ten female donkeys loaded with grain, bread, and food for his father for the journey.

24 So he sent his brothers away, and they departed; and he said to them, "See that you do not become troubled along the way."

25 Then they went up out of Egypt, and came to the land of Canaan to Jacob their father.

26 And they told him, saying, "Joseph *is* still alive, and he *is* governor over all the land of Egypt." And Jacob's heart stood still, because he did not believe them.

27 But when they told him all the words which Joseph had said to them, and when he saw the carts which Joseph had sent to carry him, the spirit [R]of Jacob their father revived. Judg. 15:19

28 Then Israel said, "*It is* enough. Joseph my son *is* still alive. I will go and see him before I die."

CHAPTER 46

Jacob's Family Safe in Egypt

SO Israel took his journey with all that he had, and came to [R]Beersheba, and offered sacrifices [R]to the God of his father Isaac. Gen. 21:31, 33; 26:32, 33; 28:10 • Gen. 28:13

2 Then God spoke to Israel [R]in the visions of the night, and said, "Jacob, Jacob!" And he said, "Here I am." Gen. 15:1; 22:11; 31:11

3 So He said, "I *am* God, the God of your father; do not fear to go down to Egypt, for I will make of you a great nation there.

4 "I will go down with you to Egypt, and I
will also surely bring you up *again;* and Jo-
seph will put his hand on your eyes."
5 Then Jacob arose from Beersheba; and
the sons of Israel carried their father Jacob,
their little ones, and their wives, in the carts
which Pharaoh had sent to carry him.
6 So they took their livestock and their
goods, which they had acquired in the land of
Canaan, and went to Egypt, [R]Jacob and all his
descendants with him. Deut. 26:5
7 His sons and his sons' sons, his daughters
and his sons' daughters, and all his descen-
dants he brought with him to Egypt.
8 Now these *were* the names of the children
of Israel, Jacob and his sons, who went to
Egypt: Reuben *was* Jacob's firstborn.
9 The [R]sons of Reuben *were* Hanoch, Pallu,
Hezron, and Carmi. Ex. 6:14
10 [R]The sons of Simeon *were* Jemuel,*
Jamin, Ohad, Jachin,* Zohar,* and Shaul, the
son of a Canaanite woman. Ex. 6:15
11 The sons of [R]Levi *were* Gershon, Kohath,
and Merari. 1 Chr. 6:1, 16
12 The sons of [R]Judah *were* Er, Onan, She-
lah, Perez, and Zerah (but Er and Onan died
in the land of Canaan). The sons of Perez
were Hezron and Hamul. 1 Chr. 2:3; 4:21
13 The sons of Issachar *were* Tola, Puvah,*
Job,* and Shimron.
14 The [R]sons of Zebulun *were* Sered, Elon,
and Jahleel. Num. 26:26
15 These *were* the sons of Leah, whom she
bore to Jacob in Padan Aram, with his daugh-
ter Dinah. All the persons, his sons and his
daughters, *were* thirty-three.
16 The sons of Gad *were* Ziphion,* Haggi,
Shuni, Ezbon,* Eri, Arodi,* and Areli.
17 [R]The sons of Asher *were* Jimnah,
Ishuah, Isui, Beriah, and Serah, their sister.
And the sons of Beriah *were* Heber and
Malchiel. 1 Chr. 7:30
18 These *were* the sons of Zilpah, whom
Laban gave to Leah his daughter; and these
she bore to Jacob: sixteen persons.
19 The [R]sons of Rachel, [R]Jacob's wife, *were*
Joseph and Benjamin. Gen. 35:24 • Gen. 44:27
20 [R]And to Joseph in the land of Egypt were
born Manasseh and Ephraim, whom Asenath,
the daughter of Poti-Pherah priest of On, bore
to him. Gen. 41:45, 50–52; 48:1
21 [R]The sons of Benjamin *were* Belah,
Becher, Ashbel, Gera, Naaman, Ehi, Rosh,
Muppim, Huppim,* and Ard. 1 Chr. 7:6; 8:1
22 These *were* the sons of Rachel, who were
born to Jacob: fourteen persons in all.
23 The son of Dan *was* Hushim.*
24 [R]The sons of Naphtali *were* Jahzeel,*
Guni, Jezer, and Shillem.* Num. 26:48
25 These *were* the sons of Bilhah, whom
Laban gave to Rachel his daughter, and she
bore these to Jacob: seven persons in all.
26 [R]All the persons who went with Jacob to
Egypt, who came from his body, [R]besides Ja-
cob's sons' wives, *were* sixty-six persons in
all. Ex. 1:5 • Gen. 35:11
27 And the sons of Joseph who were born to
him in Egypt *were* two persons. [R]All the per-
sons of the house of Jacob who went to Egypt
were seventy. Deut. 10:22
28 Then he sent Judah before him to Jo-
seph, [R]to point out before him *the way* to
Goshen. And they came [R]to the land of
Goshen. Gen. 31:21 • Gen. 47:1
29 So Joseph made ready his chariot and
went up to Goshen to meet his father Israel;
and he presented himself to him, and fell on
his neck and wept on his neck a good while.
30 And Israel said to Joseph, [R]"Now let me
die, since I have seen your face, because you
are still alive." Luke 2:29, 30
31 Then Joseph said to his brothers and to
his father's household, [R]"I will go up and tell
Pharaoh, and say to him, 'My brothers and
those of my father's house, who *were* in the
land of Canaan, have come to me. Gen. 47:1
32 'And the men *are* [R]shepherds, for their oc-
cupation has been to feed livestock; and they
have brought their flocks, their herds, and all
that they have.' Gen. 47:3
33 "So it shall be, when Pharaoh calls you
and says, 'What is your occupation?'
34 "that you shall say, 'Your servants' [R]occu-
pation has been with livestock [R]from our
youth even till now, both we *and* also our
fathers,' that you may dwell in the land of
Goshen; for every shepherd *is* an abomination
to the Egyptians." Gen. 47:3 • Gen. 30:35

CHAPTER 47

THEN Joseph [R]went and told Pharaoh,
and said, "My father and my brothers,
their flocks and their herds and all that they
possess, have come from the land of
Canaan; and indeed they *are* in [R]the land of
Goshen." Gen. 46:31 • Gen. 45:10; 46:28; 50:8
2 And he took five men from among his
brothers and presented them to Pharaoh.
3 Then Pharaoh said to his brothers,
[R]"What *is* your occupation?" And they said to
Pharaoh, "Your servants *are* shepherds, both
we *and* also our fathers." Gen. 46:33
4 And they said to Pharaoh, [R]"We have
come to dwell in the land, because your ser-
vants have no pasture for their flocks, for the
famine *is* severe in the land of Canaan. Now
therefore, please let your servants dwell in the
land of Goshen." Deut. 26:5

46:10 *Nemuel,* 1 Chr. 4:24 • *Jarib,* 1 Chr. 4:24 • *Zerah,* 1 Chr. 4:24 **46:13** *Puah,* Num. 26:23; 1 Chr. 7:1 • *Jashub,* Num. 26:24; 1 Chr. 7:1 **46:16** Sam., LXX *Zephon* and Num. 26:15 • *Ozni,* Num. 26:16 • *Arod,* Num. 26:17 **46:21** *Hupham,* Num. 26:39 **46:23** *Shuham,* Num. 26:42 **46:24** *Jahziel,* 1 Chr. 7:13 • *Shallum,* 1 Chr. 7:13

5 Then Pharaoh spoke to Joseph, saying,
"Your father and your brothers have come to
you.
6 [R]"The land of Egypt *is* before you. Have
your father and brothers dwell in the best of
the land; let them dwell in the land of Goshen.
And if you know *any* competent men among
them, then make them chief herdsmen over
my livestock." Gen. 20:15
7 Then Joseph brought in his father Jacob
and set him before Pharaoh; and Jacob
[R]blessed Pharaoh. Gen. 47:10; 48:15, 20
8 Pharaoh said to Jacob, "How old *are*
you?"
9 And Jacob said to Pharaoh, [R]"The days of
the years of my pilgrimage *are* [R]one hundred
and thirty years; few and evil have been the
days of the years of my life, and they have
not attained to the days of the years of the
life of my fathers in the days of their pilgrim-
age." [Heb. 11:9, 13] • Gen. 47:28
10 So Jacob [R]blessed Pharaoh, and went out
from before Pharaoh. Gen. 47:7
11 And Joseph situated his father and his
brothers, and gave them a possession in the
land of Egypt, in the best of the land, in the
land of [R]Rameses, [R]as Pharaoh had com-
manded. Ex. 1:11; 12:37 • Gen. 47:6, 27
12 Then Joseph provided [R]his father, his
brothers, and all his father's household with
bread, according to the number in *their* fami-
lies. Gen. 45:11; 50:21
13 Now *there was* no bread in all the land;
for the famine *was* very severe, [R]so that the
land of Egypt and the land of Canaan lan-
guished because of the famine. Gen. 41:30
14 [R]And Joseph gathered up all the money
that was found in the land of Egypt and in the
land of Canaan, for the grain which they
bought; and Joseph brought the money into
Pharaoh's house. Gen. 41:56; 42:6
15 So when the money failed in the land of
Egypt and in the land of Canaan, all the Egyp-
tians came to Joseph and said, "Give us bread,
for [R]why should we die in your presence? For
the money has failed." Gen. 47:19
16 Then Joseph said, "Give your livestock,
and I will give you *bread* for your livestock, if
the money is gone."
17 So they brought their livestock to Joseph,
and Joseph gave them bread *in exchange* for
the horses, the flocks, the cattle of the herds,
and for the donkeys. Thus he [T]fed them with
bread *in exchange* for all their livestock that
year. *supplied*
18 When that year had ended, they came to
him the next year and said to him, "We will
not hide from my lord that our money is gone;
my lord also has our herds of livestock. There
is nothing left in the sight of my lord but our
bodies and our lands.
19 "Why should we die before your eyes,
both we and our land? Buy us and our land
for bread, and we and our land will be ser-
vants of Pharaoh; give *us* seed, that we may
[R]live and not die, that the land may not be
desolate." Gen. 43:8
20 Then Joseph [R]bought all the land of
Egypt for Pharaoh; for every man of the
Egyptians sold his field, because the famine
was severe upon them. So the land became
Pharaoh's. Jer. 32:43
21 And as for the people, he moved them
into the cities,* from *one* end of the borders of
Egypt to the *other* end.
22 [R]Only the land of the [R]priests he did not
buy; for the priests had rations *allotted to
them* by Pharaoh, and they ate their rations
which Pharaoh gave them; therefore they did
not sell their lands. Ezra 7:24 • Gen. 41:45
23 Then Joseph said to the people, "Indeed I
have bought you and your land this day for
Pharaoh. Look, *here is* seed for you, and you
shall sow the land.
24 "And it shall come to pass in the harvest
that you shall give one-fifth to Pharaoh. Four-
fifths shall be your own, as seed for the field
and for your food, for those of your house-
holds and as food for your little ones."
25 So they said, "You have saved [R]our lives;
let us find favor in the sight of my lord, and we
will be Pharaoh's servants." Gen. 33:15
26 And Joseph made it a law over the land
of Egypt to this day, *that* Pharaoh should
have one-fifth, [R]except for the land of the
priests only, *which* did not become Pha-
raoh's. Gen. 47:22

Jacob Blesses the Family in Egypt

27 So Israel [R]dwelt in the land of Egypt, in
the country of Goshen; and they had posses-
sions there and [R]grew and multiplied exceed-
ingly. Gen. 47:11 • Gen. 17:6; 26:4; 35:11; 46:3
28 And Jacob lived in the land of Egypt sev-
enteen years. So the length of Jacob's life was
one hundred and forty-seven years.
29 When the time [R]drew near that Israel
must die, he called his son Joseph and said to
him, "Now if I have found favor in your sight,
please put your hand under my thigh, and
deal kindly and truly with me. Please do not
bury me in Egypt, Deut. 31:14
30 "but [R]let me lie with my fathers; you shall
carry me out of Egypt and [R]bury me in their
burial place." And he said, "I will do as you
have said." 2 Sam. 19:37 • Gen. 49:29; 50:5–13
31 Then he said, "Swear to me." And he
swore to him. So [R]Israel bowed himself on the
head of the bed. 1 Kin. 1:47

CHAPTER 48

NOW it came to pass after these things
that Joseph was told, "Indeed your

47:21 So with MT, Tg.; Sam., LXX, Vg. *made the people virtual slaves*

father *is* sick"; and he took with him his two
sons, [R]Manasseh and Ephraim. Gen. 46:20
2 And Jacob was told, "Look, your son Jo-
seph is coming to you"; and Israel strength-
ened himself and sat up on the bed.
3 Then Jacob said to Joseph: "God [R]Al-
mighty appeared to me at Luz in the land of
Canaan and blessed me, Gen. 43:14; 49:25
4 "and said to me, 'Behold, I will [R]make you
fruitful and multiply you, and I will make of
you a multitude of people, and [R]give this land
to your descendants after you *as* an everlast-
ing possession.' Gen. 46:3 • Ex. 6:8
5 "And now your [R]two sons, Ephraim and
Manasseh, who were born to you in the land
of Egypt before I came to you in Egypt, *are*
mine; as Reuben and Simeon, they shall be
mine. Josh. 13:7; 14:4
6 "Your [T]offspring [T]whom you beget after
them shall be yours; they will be called by
the name of their brothers in their inheri-
tance. *children* • Who are born to you
7 "But as for me, when I came from Padan,
[R]Rachel died beside me in the land of Ca-
naan on the way, when *there was* but a little
distance to go to Ephrath; and I buried her
there on the way to Ephrath (that is, Bethle-
hem)." Gen. 35:9, 16, 19, 20
8 Then Israel saw Joseph's sons, and said,
"Who *are* these?"
9 And Joseph said to his father, "They *are*
my sons, whom God has given me in this
place." And he said, "Please bring them to me,
and [R]I will bless them." Gen. 27:4; 47:15
10 Now [R]the eyes of Israel were dim with
age, *so that* he could not see. Then Joseph
brought them near him, and he kissed them
and embraced them. Gen. 27:1
11 And Israel said to Joseph, "I had not
thought to see your face; but in fact, God has
also shown me your offspring!"
12 So Joseph brought them from beside his
knees, and he bowed down with his face to
the earth.
13 And Joseph took them both, Ephraim
with his right hand toward Israel's left hand,
and Manasseh with his left hand toward Is-
rael's right hand, and brought *them* near him.
14 Then Israel stretched out his right hand
and [R]laid *it* on Ephraim's head, who *was* the
younger, and his left hand on Manasseh's
head, guiding his hands knowingly, for Ma-
nasseh *was* the firstborn. Matt. 19:15
15 And [R]he blessed Joseph, and said:

"God, [R]before whom my fathers Abraham
and Isaac walked,
The God who has fed me all my life long
to this day, [Heb. 11:21] • Gen. 17:1; 24:40
16 The Angel [R]who has redeemed me from
all evil, Gen. 22:11, 15–18; 28:13–15; 31:11
Bless the lads;
Let [R]my name be named upon them,
And the name of my fathers Abraham
and Isaac; Amos 9:12
And let them [R]grow into a multitude in
the midst of the earth." Num. 26:34, 37

17 Now when Joseph saw that his father
[R]laid his right hand on the head of Ephraim, it
displeased him; so he took hold of his father's
hand to remove it from Ephraim's head to
Manasseh's head. Gen. 48:14
18 And Joseph said to his father, "Not so, my
father, for this *one is* the firstborn; put your
right hand on his head."
19 But his father refused and said, [R]"I know,
my son, I know. He also shall become a peo-
ple, and he also shall be great; but truly his
younger brother shall be greater than he, and
his descendants shall become a multitude of
nations." Gen. 48:14
20 So he blessed them that day, saying, "By
you Israel will bless, saying, 'May God make
you as Ephraim and as Manasseh!' " And thus
he set Ephraim before Manasseh.
21 Then Israel said to Joseph, "Behold, I am
dying, but God will be with you and bring you
back to the land of your fathers.
22 "Moreover [R]I have given to you one [T]por-
tion above your brothers, which I took from
the hand [R]of the Amorite with my sword and
my bow." Josh. 24:32 • Gen. 34:28 • Lit. *shoulder*

CHAPTER 49

AND Jacob called his sons and said,
"Gather together, that I may tell you
what shall befall you in the last days:

2 "Gather together and hear, you sons of
Jacob,
And listen to Israel your father.

3 "Reuben, you are [R]my firstborn,
My might and the beginning of my
strength,
The excellency of dignity and the
excellency of power. Gen. 29:32
4 Unstable as water, you shall not excel,
Because you [R]went up to your father's
bed;
Then you defiled *it*—
He went up to my couch. Gen. 35:22

5 "Simeon and Levi *are* brothers;
Instruments of [T]cruelty *are in* their
dwelling place. *violence*
6 [R]Let not my soul enter their council;
Let not my honor be united [R]to their
assembly; Prov. 1:15, 16 • Ps. 26:9
[R]For in their anger they slew a man,
And in their self-will they [T]hamstrung an
ox. Gen. 34:26 • *lamed*
7 Cursed *be* their anger, for *it is* fierce;
And their wrath, for it is cruel!

[R]I will divide them in Jacob
And scatter them in Israel. Josh. 19:1, 9

8"Judah,[R] you *are he* whom your brothers
shall praise; Deut. 33:7
[R]Your hand *shall be* on the neck of your
enemies; Ps. 18:40
[R]Your father's children shall bow down
before you. 1 Chr. 5:2
9 Judah *is* [R]a lion's whelp; [Rev. 5:5]
From the prey, my son, you have gone
up.
He bows down, he lies down as a lion;
And as a lion, who shall rouse him?
10[R]The scepter shall not depart from
Judah, Rev. 5:5☆
Nor [R]a lawgiver from between his feet,
[R]Until Shiloh comes; Ps. 60:7 • Is. 11:1
[R]And to Him *shall be* the obedience of the
people. Ps. 2:6–9; 72:8–11
11 Binding his donkey to the vine,
And his donkey's colt to the choice vine,
He washed his garments in wine,
And his clothes in the blood of grapes.
12 His eyes *are* darker than wine,
And his teeth whiter than milk.

13"Zebulun[R] shall dwell by the haven of the
sea; Deut. 33:18, 19
He *shall become* a haven for ships,
And his border shall adjoin Sidon.

14"Issachar is a strong donkey,
Lying down between two burdens;
15 He saw that rest *was* good,
And that the land *was* pleasant;
He bowed [R]his shoulder to bear *a
burden*, 1 Sam. 10:9
And became a band of slaves.

16"Dan[R] shall judge his people
As one of the tribes of Israel. Deut. 33:22
17[R]Dan shall be a serpent by the way,
A viper by the path, Judg. 18:27
That bites the horse's heels
So that its rider shall fall backward.
18 I have waited for your salvation, O
LORD!

19"Gad,[R] a troop shall tramp upon him,
But he shall triumph at last. Deut. 33:20

20"Bread from Asher *shall be* rich,
And he shall yield royal dainties.

21"Naphtali[R] *is* a deer let loose;
He uses beautiful words. Deut. 33:23

22"Joseph *is* a fruitful bough,
A fruitful bough by a well;
His branches run over the wall.
23 The archers have [R]bitterly grieved him,
Shot *at him* and hated him. Gen. 37:4, 24
24 But his [R]bow remained in strength,
And the arms of his hands were [T]made
strong Job 29:20 • Or *supple*
By the hands of [R]the Mighty *God* of
Jacob Ps. 132:2, 5
(From there [R]*is* the Shepherd, [R]the Stone
of Israel), [Ps. 23:1; 80:1] • Is. 28:16
25[R]By the God of your father who will help
you, Gen. 28:13; 32:9; 35:3; 43:23; 50:17
[R]And by the Almighty [R]who will bless you
With blessings of heaven above,
Blessings of the deep that lies beneath,
Blessings of the breasts and of the
womb. Gen. 17:1; 35:11 • Deut. 33:13
26 The blessings of your father
Have excelled the blessings of my
ancestors,
[R]Up to the utmost bound of the
everlasting hills. Deut. 33:15
They shall be on the head of Joseph,
And on the crown of the head of him
who was separate from his brothers.

27"Benjamin is a ravenous wolf;
In the morning he shall devour the prey,
And at night he shall divide the spoil."

28 All these *are* the twelve tribes of Israel,
and this *is* what their father spoke to them.
And he blessed them; he blessed each one according to his own blessing.
29 Then he charged them and said to them:
"I [R]am to be gathered to my people; bury me
with my fathers in the cave that *is* in the field
of Ephron the Hittite, Gen. 15:15
30 "in the cave that *is* in the field of Mach-
pelah, which *is* before Mamre in the land of
Canaan, [R]which Abraham bought with the
field of Ephron the Hittite as a possession for
a burial place. Gen. 23:3–20
31 "There they buried Abraham and Sarah
his wife, there they buried Isaac and Rebekah
his wife, and there I buried Leah.
32 "The field and the cave that *is* there *were*
purchased from the sons of Heth."

Jacob Dies in Egypt

33 And when Jacob had finished command-
ing his sons, he drew his feet up into the bed
and breathed his last, and was gathered to his
people.

CHAPTER 50

THEN Joseph fell on his father's face, and
wept over him, and kissed him.
2 And Joseph commanded his servants the
physicians to [R]embalm his father. So the
physicians embalmed Israel. Gen. 50:26
3 Forty days were required for him, for
such are the days required for those who are
embalmed; and the Egyptians [R]mourned[T] for
him seventy days. Deut. 34:8 • Lit. *wept*

4 Now when the days of his mourning were past, Joseph spoke to [R]the household of Pharaoh, saying, "If now I have found favor in your eyes, please speak in the hearing of Pharaoh, saying, Esth. 4:2

5 [R]'My father made me swear, saying, "Behold, I am dying; in my grave [R]which I dug for myself in the land of Canaan, there you shall bury me." Now therefore, please let me go up and bury my father, and I will come back.' " Gen. 47:29–31 • Is. 22:16

6 And Pharaoh said, "Go up and bury your father, as he made you swear."

7 So Joseph went up to bury his father; and with him went up all the servants of Pharaoh, the elders of his house, and all the elders of the land of Egypt,

8 as well as all the house of Joseph, his brothers, and his father's house. Only their little ones, their flocks, and their herds they left in the land of Goshen.

9 And there went up with him both chariots and horsemen, and it was a very great gathering.

10 Then they came to the threshing floor of Atad, which *is* beyond the Jordan, and they [R]mourned there with a great and very solemn lamentation. He observed seven days of mourning for his father. Acts 8:2

11 And when the inhabitants of the land, the Canaanites, saw the mourning at the threshing floor of Atad, they said, "This *is* a deep mourning of the Egyptians." Therefore its name was called Abel Mizraim,* which *is* beyond the Jordan.

12 So his sons did for him just as he had commanded them.

13 For his sons carried him to the land of Canaan, and buried him in the cave of the field of Machpelah, before Mamre, which Abraham bought with the field from Ephron the Hittite as property for a burial place.

14 And after he had buried his father, Joseph returned to Egypt, he and his brothers and all who went up with him to bury his father.

Joseph Dies in Egypt

15 When Joseph's brothers saw that their father was dead, [R]they said, "Perhaps Joseph will hate us, and may actually repay us for all the evil which we did to him." [Job 15:21]

16 So they sent *messengers* to Joseph, saying, "Before your father died he commanded, saying,

17 'Thus you shall say to Joseph: "I beg you, please forgive the trespass of your brothers and their sin; for they did evil to you." ' Now, please, forgive the trespass of the servants of the God of your father." And Joseph wept when they spoke to him.

18 Then his brothers also went and [R]fell down before his face, and they said, "Behold, we *are* your servants." Gen. 37:7–10; 41:43; 44:14

19 Joseph said to them, [R]"Do not be afraid, for *am* I in the place of God? Gen. 45:5

20 [R]"But as for you, you meant evil against me; *but* [R]God meant it for good, in order to bring it about as *it is* this day, to save many people alive. Ps. 56:5 • [Acts 3:13–15]

21 "Now therefore, do not be afraid; I will provide for you and your little ones." And he comforted them and spoke kindly to them.

22 So Joseph dwelt in Egypt, he and his father's household. And Joseph lived one hundred and ten years.

23 Joseph saw Ephraim's children [R]to the third *generation.* [R]The children of Machir, the son of Manasseh, were also brought up on Joseph's knees. Job 42:16 • Num. 26:29; 32:39

24 And Joseph said to his brethren, "I am dying; but [R]God will surely visit you, and bring you out of this land to the land [R]of which He swore to Abraham, to Isaac, and to Jacob." Ex. 3:16, 17 • Gen. 26:3; 35:12; 46:4

25 Then [R]Joseph took an oath from the children of Israel, saying, "God will surely visit you, and [R]you shall carry up my [R]bones from here." Ex. 13:19 • Deut. 1:8; 30:1–8 • Ex. 13:19

26 So Joseph died, *being* one hundred and ten years old; and they embalmed him, and he was put in a coffin in Egypt.

50:11 Lit. *Mourning of Egypt*

THE SECOND BOOK OF MOSES CALLED

EXODUS

THE BOOK OF EXODUS

Exodus is the record of Israel's birth as a nation. Within the protective "womb" of Egypt, Jacob's (Israel's) family of seventy rapidly multiplies. At the right time, accompanied with severe "birth pains," an infant nation, numbering between two and three million people, is brought into the world where it is divinely protected, fed, and nurtured.

The Hebrew title, *We'elleh Shemoth,* "Now These *Are* the Names," comes from the first phrase in 1:1. Exodus begins with "Now" to show it as a continuation of Genesis. The Greek title is *Exodus,* a word meaning "exit," "departure," or "going out." The Septuagint uses this word to describe the book by its key event (see 19:1, "gone out"). In Luke 9:31 and in 2 Peter 1:15, the word *exodus* speaks of physical death (Jesus and Peter). This embodies Exodus's theme of redemption, because redemption is accomplished only through death. The Latin title is *Liber Exodus,* "Book of Departure," taken from the Greek title.

THE AUTHOR OF EXODUS

Critics have challenged the Mosaic authorship of Exodus in favor of a series of oral and written documents that were woven together by editors late in Israel's history. Their arguments are generally weak and far from conclusive, especially in view of the strong external and internal evidence that points to Moses as the author.

External Evidence: Exodus has been attributed to Moses since the time of Joshua (cf. Ex. 20:25 with Josh. 8:30–32). Other biblical writers attribute Exodus to Moses: Malachi (Mal. 4:4), the disciples (John 1:45), and Paul (Rom. 10:5). This is also the testimony of Jesus (Mark 7:10; 12:26; Luke 20:37; John 5:46, 47; 7:19, 22, 23). Jewish and Samaritan traditions consistently hold to the Mosaic authorship of Exodus.

Internal Evidence: Portions of Exodus are directly attributed to Moses (Ex. 15; 17:8–14; 20:1–17; 24:4, 7, 12; 31:18; 34:1–27). Moses' usual procedure was to record events soon after they occurred in the form of historical annals. It is clear from Exodus that the author must have been an eyewitness of the Exodus and an educated man. He was acquainted with details about the customs and climate of Egypt and the plants, animals, and terrain of the wilderness. A consistency of style and development also points to a single author. Its antiquity is supported by the frequent use of ancient literary constructions, words, and expressions.

THE TIME OF EXODUS

If the early date for the Exodus (c. 1445 B.C.) is assumed, this book was composed during the forty-year wilderness journey, between 1445 B.C. and 1405 B.C. Moses probably kept an account of God's work, which he then edited in the plains of Moab shortly before his death. Exodus covers the period from the arrival of Jacob in Egypt (c. 1875 B.C.) to the erection of the tabernacle 431 years later in the wilderness (c. 1445 B.C.).

THE CHRIST OF EXODUS

Exodus contains no direct messianic prophecies, but it is full of types and portraits of Christ. Here are seven: (1) *Moses:* In dozens of ways Moses is a type of Christ (Deut. 18:15). Both Moses and Christ are prophets, priests, and kings (although Moses was never made king, he functioned as the ruler of Israel); both are kinsman-redeemers; both are endangered in infancy; both voluntarily renounce power and wealth; both are deliverers, lawgivers, and mediators. (2) *The Passover:* John 1:29, 36 and 1 Corinthians 5:7 make it clear that Christ is our slain God and the Passover Lamb. (3) *The seven feasts:* Each of these feasts portrays some aspect of the ministry of Christ. (4) *The Exodus:* Paul relates baptism to the exodus event because baptism symbolizes death to the old and identification with the new (Rom. 6:2, 3; 1 Cor. 10:1, 2). (5) *The manna and water:* The New Testament applies both to Christ (John 6:31–35, 48–63; 1 Cor. 10:3, 4). (6) *The tabernacle:* In its materials, colors, furniture, and arrangement, the tabernacle clearly speaks of the Person of Christ and the way of redemption. The development is progressive from suffering, blood, and death, to beauty, holiness, and the glory of God. The tabernacle is theology in a physical form. (7) *The High Priest:* In several ways the high priest foreshadows the ministry of Christ, our great High Priest (Heb. 4:14–16; 9:11, 12, 24–28).

KEYS TO EXODUS

Key Word: Redemption—Central to the Book of Exodus is the concept of redemption. Israel was redeemed *from* bondage in Egypt and *into* a covenant relationship with God. From the redemption of Moses in the Nile to the redeeming presence of God in the tabernacle, Exodus records God's overwhelming acts of deliverance, by which He demonstrates His right to be Israel's King.

Key Verses: Exodus 6:6; 19:5, 6—"Therefore say to the children of Israel: 'I *am* the LORD; I will bring you out from under the burdens of the Egyptians, I will rescue you from their bondage, and I will redeem you with an outstretched arm and with great judgments' " (6:6).

" 'Now therefore, if you will indeed obey My voice and keep My covenant, then you shall be a special treasure to Me above all people; for all the earth *is* Mine. And you shall be to Me a kingdom of priests and a holy nation' " (19:5, 6).

Key Chapters: Exodus 12—14—The climax of the entire Old Testament is recorded in chapters 12—14: the salvation of Israel through blood (the Passover) and through power (the Red Sea). The Exodus is the central event of the Old Testament as the Cross is of the New Testament.

SURVEY OF EXODUS

Exodus abounds with God's powerful redemptive acts on behalf of His oppressed people. It begins in pain and ends in liberation; it moves from the groaning of the people to the glory of God. It is the continuation of the story that begins in Genesis with the seventy descendants of Jacob who move from Canaan to Egypt. They have multiplied under adverse conditions to a multitude of over two million people. When the Israelites finally turn to God for deliverance from their bondage, God quickly responds by redeeming them "with an outstretched arm and with great judgments" (6:6). God faithfully fulfills His promise made to Abraham centuries before (Gen. 15:13, 14).

The book falls into two parts: (1) redemption from Egypt (1—18) and (2) revelation from God (19—40).

Redemption from Egypt (1—18): After four centuries of slavery, the people of Israel cry to the God of Abraham, Isaac, and Jacob for deliverance. God has already prepared Moses for this purpose and has commissioned him at the burning bush to stand before Pharaoh as the advocate for Israel. However, Pharaoh hardens his heart: "Who *is* the LORD, that I should obey His voice to let Israel go?" (5:2).

God soon reveals Himself to Pharaoh through a series of object lessons, the ten plagues. These plagues grow in severity until the tenth brings death to the firstborn of every household of Egypt. Israel is redeemed through this plague by means of the Passover lamb. The Israelites' faith in God at this point becomes the basis for their national redemption. As they leave Egypt, God guides them by a pillar of fire and smoke and saves them from Egypt's pursuing army through the miraculous crossing of the sea. In the wilderness He protects and sustains them throughout their journeys.

Revelation from God (19—40): Now that the people have experienced God's deliverance, guidance, and protection, they are ready to be taught what God expects of them. The redeemed people must now be set apart to walk with God. This is why the emphasis moves from narration in chapters 1—18 to legislation in chapters 19—40. On Mount Sinai, Moses receives God's moral, civil, and ceremonial laws, as well as the pattern for the tabernacle to be built in the wilderness. After God judges the people for their worship of the golden calf, the tabernacle is constructed and consecrated. It is a building of beauty in a barren land and reveals much about the Person of God and the way of redemption.

FOCUS	REDEMPTION FROM EGYPT				REVELATION FROM GOD	
REFERENCE	1:1—	2:1—	5:1—	15:22—	19:1—	32:1—40:38
DIVISION	THE NEED FOR REDEMPTION	THE PREPARATION FOR REDEMPTION	THE REDEMPTION OF ISRAEL	THE PRESERVATION OF ISRAEL	THE REVELATION OF THE COVENANT	THE RESPONSE OF ISRAEL TO THE COVENANT
TOPIC	NARRATION				LEGISLATION	
	SUBJECTION		REDEMPTION		INSTRUCTION	
LOCATION	EGYPT			WILDERNESS	MOUNT SINAI	
TIME	430 YEARS			2 MONTHS	10 MONTHS	

OUTLINE OF EXODUS

Part One: Redemption from Egypt (1:1—18:27)

Part Two: Revelation from God (19:1—40:38)

3. Sign of the Covenant: The Sabbath 31:12–17
4. Two Tablets Are Presented 31:18

II. The Response of Israel to the Covenant ....32:1—40:38

A. Israel Willfully Breaks the Covenant....32:1–6
B. Moses Intercedes for Israel's Salvation 32:7–33
1. God to Destroy Israel.......................32:7–10
2. Moses Intercedes for Israel 32:11–14
3. Moses Disciplines Israel..............32:15–29
4. Moses Atones for Israel 32:30–33
C. Moses Convinces God Not to Abandon Israel............................32:34—33:23
1. God Sends His Angel 32:34, 35
2. God Will Not Come into Their Midst...33:1–11
3. God Will Not Abandon Israel 33:12–23
D. God Renews the Covenant with Israel 34:1–35
1. Hewing of the Two Tablets..............34:1–4
2. The Nature of God Is Revealed........34:5–9
3. Renewal of the Covenant................34:10–28
4. Moses Returns from God 34:29–35
E. Israel Willingly Obeys the Covenant..35:1—40:33
1. Israel Brings Offerings in Abundance ....35:1—36:7
2. Israel Builds the Tabernacle....36:8—40:33
F. God Fills the Tabernacle with His Glory..40:34–38

CHAPTER 1

Israel's Rapid Multiplication

NOW these *are* the names of the children
of Israel who came to Egypt; each man
and his household came with Jacob:
2 Reuben, Simeon, Levi, and Judah;
3 Issachar, Zebulun, and Benjamin;
4 Dan, Naphtali, Gad, and Asher.
5 All those who were descendants* of Ja-
cob were [R]seventy* persons (for Joseph was in
Egypt *already*). Gen. 46:26, 27
6 And [R]Joseph died, all his brothers, and all
that generation. Gen. 50:26
7 [R]But the children of Israel were fruitful
and increased abundantly, multiplied and
grew exceedingly mighty; and the land was
filled with them. Acts 7:17

Israel's Severe Affliction

8 Now there arose a new king over Egypt,
[R]who did not know Joseph. Acts 7:18, 19
9 And he said to his people, "Look, the peo-
ple of the children of Israel *are* more and
[R]mightier than we; Gen. 26:16
10 [R]"come, let us [R]deal shrewdly with them,
lest they multiply, and it happen, in the event
of war, that they also join our enemies and
fight against us, and *so* go up out of the
land." Ps. 83:3, 4 • Acts 7:19
11 Therefore they set taskmasters over them
[R]to afflict them with their [R]burdens. And they
built for Pharaoh supply cities, Pithom and
Raamses. Ex. 3:7; 5:6 • Ex. 1:14
12 But the more they afflicted them, the
more they multiplied and grew. And they were
in dread of the children of Israel.
13 So the Egyptians made the children of Is-
rael [R]serve with [T]rigor. Gen. 15:13 • *harshness*
14 And they [R]made their lives bitter with
hard bondage—[R]in mortar, in brick, and in all
manner of service in the field. All their service
in which they made them serve *was* with
rigor. Num. 20:15 • Ps. 81:6

Israel's Planned Extinction

15 Then the king of Egypt spoke to the [R]He-
brew midwives, of whom the name of one
was Shiphrah and the name of the other
Puah; Ex. 2:6
16 and he said, "When you do the duties of a
midwife for the Hebrew women, and see *them*
on the birthstools, if it *is* a [R]son, then you shall
kill him; but if it *is* a daughter, then she shall
live." Acts 7:19
17 But the midwives feared God, and did not
do as the king of Egypt commanded them, but
saved the male children alive.
18 So the king of Egypt called for the mid-
wives and said to them, "Why have you done
this thing, and saved the male children alive?"
19 And the midwives said to Pharaoh, "Be-
cause the Hebrew women *are* not like the
Egyptian women; for they *are* lively and give
birth before the midwives come to them."
20 [R]Therefore God dealt well with the mid-
wives, and the people multiplied and [T]grew
very mighty. [Prov. 11:18] • *became very numerous*
21 And so it was, because the midwives
feared God, [R]that He [T]provided households
for them. 1 Sam. 2:35 • *gave them families*
22 So Pharaoh commanded all his people,
saying, [R]"Every son who is born* you shall
cast into the river, and every daughter you
shall save alive." Acts 7:19

CHAPTER 2

Moses Is Redeemed from Murder

AND a man of the house of Levi went and
took *as wife* a daughter of Levi.
2 So the woman conceived and bore a son.
And when she saw that he *was* a beautiful
child, she hid him three months.

1:5 Lit. *who came from the loins of* • DSS, LXX *seventy-five;* cf. Acts 7:14 **1:22** Sam., LXX, Tg. add *to the Hebrews*

3 But when she could no longer hide him, she took an ark of [R]bulrushes for him, daubed it with [R]asphalt and [R]pitch, put the child in it, and laid *it* in the reeds by the river's bank. Is. 18:2 • Gen. 14:10 • Gen. 6:14

4 [R]And his sister stood afar off, to know what would be done to him. Num. 26:59

5 Then the [R]daughter of Pharaoh came down to bathe at the river. And her maidens walked along the riverside; and when she saw the ark among the reeds, she sent her maid to get it. Acts 7:21

6 And when she opened *it*, she saw the child, and behold, the baby wept. So she had compassion on him, and said, "This is one of the Hebrews' children."

7 Then his sister said to Pharaoh's daughter, "Shall I go and call a nurse for you from the Hebrew women, that she may nurse the child for you?"

8 And Pharaoh's daughter said to her, "Go." So the maiden went and called the child's mother.

9 Then Pharaoh's daughter said to her, "Take this child away and nurse him for me, and I will give *you* your wages." So the woman took the child and nursed him.

10 And the child grew, and she brought him to Pharaoh's daughter, and he became [R]her son. So she called his name Moses,* saying, "Because I drew him out of the water." Acts 7:21

Moses Tries to Redeem by Murder

11 Now it came to pass in those days, [R]when Moses was grown, that he went out to his brethren and looked at their burdens. And he saw an Egyptian beating a Hebrew, one of his brethren. Heb. 11:24–26

12 So he looked this way and that way, and when he saw no one, he [R]killed the Egyptian and hid him in the sand. Acts 7:24, 25

13 And when he went out the second day, behold, two Hebrew men were fighting, and he said to the one who did the wrong, "Why are you striking your companion?"

14 Then he said, [R]"Who made you a prince and a judge over us? Do you intend to kill me as you killed the Egyptian?" So Moses [R]feared and said, "Surely this thing is known!" Acts 7:27, 28 • Judg. 6:27

15 When Pharaoh heard of this matter, he sought to kill Moses. But Moses fled from the face of Pharaoh and dwelt in the land of Midian; and he sat down by a well.

16 [R]Now the priest of Midian had seven daughters. And they came and drew water, and they filled the [R]troughs to water their father's flock. Ex. 3:1; 4:18; 18:12 • Gen. 30:38

17 Then the [R]shepherds came and drove them away; but Moses stood up and helped them, and watered their flock. Gen. 47:3

18 When they came to [R]Reuel[T] their father, he said, "How *is it that* you have come so soon today?" Num. 10:29 • *Jethro*, Ex. 3:1

19 And they said, "An Egyptian delivered us from the hand of the shepherds, and he also drew enough water for us and watered the flock."

20 So he said to his daughters, "And where *is* he? Why *is* it *that* you have left the man? Call him, that he may eat bread."

21 Then Moses was content to live with the man, and he gave [R]Zipporah his daughter to Moses. Ex. 4:25; 18:2

22 And she bore *him* a son. He called his name Gershom,* for he said, "I have been [R]a stranger in a foreign land." Acts 7:29

Israel Calls upon God

23 Now it happened in the process of time that the king of Egypt died. Then the children of Israel groaned because of the bondage, and they cried out; and their cry came up to God because of the bondage.

24 So God [R]heard their groaning, and God remembered His covenant with Abraham, with Isaac, and with Jacob. Ex. 6:5

25 And God looked upon the children of Israel, and God acknowledged *them*.

CHAPTER 3

God Miraculously Appears

NOW Moses was tending the flock of [R]Jethro his father-in-law, [R]the priest of Midian. And he led the flock to the back of the desert, and came to [R]Horeb, [R]the mountain of God. Ex. 4:18 • Ex. 2:16 • Ex. 17:6 • Ex. 18:5

2 And [R]the Angel of the LORD appeared to him in a flame of fire from the midst of a bush. So he looked, and behold, the bush was burning with fire, but the bush *was* not consumed. Deut. 33:16

3 Then Moses said, "I will now turn aside and see this [R]great sight, why the bush does not burn." Acts 7:31

4 So when the LORD saw that he turned aside to look, God called [R]to him from the midst of the bush and said, "Moses, Moses!" And he said, "Here I am." Deut. 33:16

5 Then He said, "Do not draw near this place. Take your sandals off your feet, for the place where you stand *is* holy ground."

6 Moreover He said, "I *am* the God of your father—the God of Abraham, the God of Isaac, and the God of Jacob." And Moses hid his face, for he was afraid to look upon God.

God Calls Moses to Leadership

7 And the LORD said: "I have surely seen the oppression of My people who *are* in Egypt,

2:10 Heb. *Mosheh*, lit. *Drawn Out* **2:22** Lit. *Stranger There*

and have heard their cry because of their
taskmasters, for I know their sorrows.
8 "So I have come down to deliver them out
of the hand of the Egyptians, and to bring
them up from that land to a good and large
land, to a land flowing with milk and honey, to
the place of the Canaanites and the Hittites
and the Amorites and the Perizzites and the
Hivites and the Jebusites.
9 "Now therefore, behold, [R]the cry of the
children of Israel has come to Me, and I have
also seen the oppression with which the
Egyptians oppress them. Ex. 2:23
10 "Come now, therefore, and I will send you
to Pharaoh that you may bring My people, the
children of Israel, out of Egypt."

"Who Am I?"

11 But Moses said to God, "Who *am* I that I
should go to Pharaoh, and that I should bring
the children of Israel out of Egypt?"
12 So He said, [R]"I will certainly be with you.
And this *shall be* a [R]sign to you that I have
sent you: When you have brought the people
out of Egypt, you shall serve God on this
mountain." Gen. 31:3 • Ex. 4:8; 19:3

"What Is His Name?"

13 Then Moses said to God, "Indeed, *when* I
come to the children of Israel and say to them,
'The God of your fathers has sent me to you,'
and they say to me, 'What *is* His name?' what
shall I say to them?"
14 And God said to Moses, "I AM WHO I
AM." And He said, "Thus you shall say to the
children of Israel, [R]'I AM has sent me to
you.' " [John 8:24, 28, 58]
15 Moreover God said to Moses, "Thus you
shall say to the children of Israel: 'The LORD
God of your fathers, the God of Abraham, the
God of Isaac, and the God of Jacob, has sent
me to you. This *is* My name forever, and this
is My memorial to all generations.'
16 "Go and [R]gather the elders of Israel to-
gether, and say to them, 'The LORD God of
your fathers, the God of Abraham, of Isaac,
and of Jacob, appeared to me, saying, [R]"I have
surely visited you and *seen* what is done to
you in Egypt; Ex. 4:29 • Ex. 2:25; 4:31
17 "and I have said [R]I will bring you up out of
the affliction of Egypt to the land of the
Canaanites and the Hittites and the Amorites
and the Perizzites and the Hivites and the
Jebusites, to a land flowing with milk and
honey." ' Gen. 15:13–21; 46:4; 50:24, 25
18 "Then they will heed your voice; and you
shall come, you and the elders of Israel, to the
king of Egypt; and you shall say to him, 'The
LORD God of the Hebrews has met with us;
and now, please, let us go three days' journey
into the wilderness, that we may sacrifice to
the LORD our God.'
19 "But I am sure that the king of Egypt
[R]will not let you go, no, not even by a mighty
hand. Ex. 5:2
20 "So I will [R]stretch out My hand and
strike Egypt with [R]all My wonders which I
will do in its midst; and [R]after that he will let
you go. Ex. 6:6; 9:15 • Deut. 6:22 • Ex. 11:1
21 "And I will give this people favor in the
sight of the Egyptians; and it shall be, when
you go, that you shall not go empty-handed.
22 [R]"But every woman shall ask of her
neighbor, namely, of her who dwells near her
house, [R]articles of silver, articles of gold, and
clothing; and you shall put *them* on your sons
and on your daughters. So you shall plunder
the Egyptians." Ex. 11:2 • Ex. 33:6

CHAPTER 4

"They Will Not Believe Me"

THEN Moses answered and said, "But sup-
pose they will not believe me or listen to
my voice; suppose they say, 'The LORD has not
appeared to you.' "
2 So the LORD said to him, "What *is* that in
your hand?" He said, "A rod."
3 And He said, "Cast it on the ground." So
he cast it on the ground, and it became a ser-
pent; and Moses fled from it.
4 Then the LORD said to Moses, "Reach out
your hand and take *it* by the tail" (and he
reached out his hand and caught it, and it be-
came a rod in his hand),
5 "that they may [R]believe that the [R]LORD
God of their fathers, the God of Abraham, the
God of Isaac, and the God of Jacob, has ap-
peared to you." Ex. 4:31; 19:9 • Ex. 3:6, 15
6 Furthermore the LORD said to him, "Now
put your hand in your bosom." And he put
his hand in his bosom, and when he took it
out, behold, his hand *was* leprous, [R]like
snow. Num. 12:10
7 And He said, "Put your hand in your
bosom again." So he put his hand in his
bosom again, and drew it out of his bosom,
and behold, it was restored like his *other*
flesh.
8 "Then it will be, if they do not believe you,
nor heed the message of the [R]first sign, that
they may believe the message of the latter
sign. Ex. 7:6–13
9 "And it shall be, if they do not believe
even these two signs, or listen to your voice,
that you shall take water from the river* and
pour *it* on the dry *land.* [R]The water which you
take from the river will become blood on the
dry *land.*" Ex. 7:19, 20

"I Am Slow of Speech"

10 Then Moses said to the LORD, "O my Lord,
I *am* not eloquent, neither before nor since

4:9 The Nile

You have spoken to Your servant; but I *am*
slow of speech and slow of tongue."
11 So the LORD said to him, [R]"Who has made
man's mouth? Or who makes the mute, the
deaf, the seeing, or the blind? *Have* not I, the
LORD? Ps. 94:9; 146:8
12 "Now therefore, go, and I will be [R]with
your mouth and teach you what you shall
say." Is. 50:4
13 But he said, "O my Lord, [R]please send
by the hand of whomever *else* You may
send." Jon. 1:3
14 So [R]the anger of the LORD was kindled
against Moses, and He said: "Is not Aaron the
Levite your [R]brother? I know that he can
speak well. And look, he is also coming out to
meet you. When he sees you, he will be glad in
his heart. Num. 11:1, 33 • Num. 26:59
15 "Now [R]you shall speak to him and put the
words in his mouth. And I will be with your
mouth and with his mouth, and I will teach
you what you shall do. Ex. 4:12, 30
16 "So he shall be your spokesman to the
people. And he himself shall be as a mouth for
you, and you shall be to him as God.
17 "And you shall take this rod in your hand,
with which you shall do the signs."

Moses Returns to Egypt

18 So Moses went and returned to [R]Jethro
his father-in-law, and said to him, "Please let
me go and return to my brethren who *are*
in Egypt, and see whether they are still
alive." And Jethro said to Moses, [R]"Go in
peace." Ex. 2:21; 3:1; 4:18 • Judg. 18:6
19 Now the LORD said to Moses in [R]Midian,
"Go, return to Egypt; for all the men who
sought your life are dead." Ex. 3:1; 18:1
20 Then Moses [R]took his wife and his sons
and set them on a donkey, and he returned to
the land of Egypt. And Moses took the rod of
God in his hand. Ex. 18:2–5
21 And the LORD said to Moses, "When you
go back to Egypt, see that you do all those
wonders before Pharaoh which I have put in
your hand. But [R]I will harden his heart, so that
he will not let the people go. John 12:40
22 "Then you shall [R]say to Pharaoh, 'Thus
says the LORD: [R]"Israel *is* My son, [R]My first-
born. Ex. 5:1 • Hos. 11:1 • Jer. 31:9
23 "So I say to you, let My son go that he
may serve Me. But if you refuse to let him
go, indeed [R]I will kill your son, your first-
born." ' " Ex. 11:5; 12:29

Moses Reinstitutes Circumcision

24 And it came to pass on the way, at the [R]en-
campment, that the LORD [R]met him and
sought to kill him. Gen. 42:27 • Num. 22:22
25 Then [R]Zipporah took a sharp stone and
cut off the foreskin of her son and cast *it* at
*Moses'** feet, and said, "Surely you *are* a hus-
band of blood to me!" Ex. 2:21; 18:2
26 So He let him go. Then she said, "You are
a [T]husband of blood!"—because of the cir-
cumcision. *bridegroom*

Israel Accepts the Call of Moses as Deliverer

27 And the LORD said to Aaron, "Go into the
wilderness [R]to meet Moses." So he went and
met him on [R]the mountain of God, and kissed
him. Ex. 4:14 • Ex. 3:1; 18:5; 24:13
28 So Moses told Aaron all the words of the
LORD who had sent him, and all the signs
which He had commanded him.
29 Then Moses and Aaron [R]went and gath-
ered together all the elders of the children of
Israel. Ex. 3:16; 12:21
30 And Aaron spoke all the words which the
LORD had spoken to Moses. Then he did the
signs in the sight of the people.
31 So the people believed; and when they
heard that the LORD had [R]visited the children
of Israel and that He [R]had looked on their af-
fliction, then [R]they bowed their heads and
worshiped. Gen. 50:24 • Ex. 2:25; 3:7 • Gen. 24:26

CHAPTER 5

Pharaoh Rejects Moses

AFTERWARD Moses and Aaron went in
and told Pharaoh, "Thus says the LORD
God of Israel: 'Let My people go, that they
may hold a feast to Me in the wilderness.' "
2 And Pharaoh said, [R]"Who *is* the LORD,
that I should obey His voice to let Israel go? I
do not know the LORD, [R]nor will I let Israel
go." 2 Kin. 18:35 • Ex. 3:19; 7:14
3 So they said, [R]"The God of the Hebrews
has met with us. Please, let us go three days'
journey into the desert and sacrifice to the
LORD our God, lest He fall upon us with pesti-
lence or with the sword." Ex. 3:18; 7:16
4 Then the king of Egypt said to them,
"Moses and Aaron, why do you take the peo-
ple from their work? Get *back* to your [R]la-
bor." Ex. 1:11; 2:11; 6:6
5 And Pharaoh said, "Look, the people of
the land *are* [R]many now, and you make them
rest from their labor!" Ex. 1:7, 9
6 So the same day Pharaoh commanded the
[R]taskmasters of the people and their officers,
saying, Ex. 1:11; 3:7; 5:10, 13, 14
7 "You shall no longer give the people straw
to make [R]brick as before. Let them go and
gather straw for themselves. Ex. 1:14
8 "And you shall lay on them the quota of
bricks which they made before. You shall not
reduce it. For they are idle; therefore they cry
out, saying, 'Let us go *and* sacrifice to our
God.'
9 "Let more work be laid on the men, that
they may labor in it, and let them not regard
false words."

4:25 Lit. *his*

10 And the taskmasters of the people and their officers went out and spoke to the people, saying, "Thus says Pharaoh: 'I will not give you straw.

11 'Go, get yourselves straw where you can find it; yet none of your work will be reduced.' "

12 So the people were scattered abroad throughout all the land of Egypt to gather stubble instead of straw.

13 And the taskmasters forced *them* to hurry, saying, "Fulfill your work, *your* daily quota, as when there was straw."

14 Also the [R]officers of the children of Israel, whom Pharaoh's taskmasters had set over them, were [R]beaten *and* were asked, "Why have you not fulfilled your task in making brick both yesterday and today, as before?" Ex. 5:6 • Is. 10:24

Israel Rejects Moses

15 Then the officers of the children of Israel came and cried out to Pharaoh, saying, "Why are you dealing thus with your servants?

16 "There is no straw given to your servants, and they say to us, 'Make brick!' And indeed your servants *are* beaten, but the fault *is* in your *own* people."

17 But he said, "You *are* idle! Idle! Therefore you say, 'Let us go *and* sacrifice to the LORD.'

18 "Therefore go now *and* work; for no straw shall be given you, yet you shall deliver the quota of bricks."

19 And the officers of the children of Israel saw *that* they *were* in trouble after it was said, "You shall not reduce *any* bricks from your daily quota."

20 Then, as they came out from Pharaoh, they met Moses and Aaron who stood there to meet them.

21 [R]And they said to them, "Let the LORD look on you and judge, because you have made us abhorrent in the sight of Pharaoh and in the sight of his servants, to put a sword in their hand to kill us." Ex. 6:9

Moses Questions God's Plan

22 So Moses returned to the LORD and said, "Lord, why have You brought trouble on this people? Why *is* it You have sent me?

23 "For since I came to Pharaoh to speak in Your name, he has done evil to this people; neither have You delivered Your people at all."

CHAPTER 6

God Reassures Moses

THEN the LORD said to Moses, "Now you shall see what I will do to Pharaoh. For [R]with a strong hand he will let them go, and with a strong hand [R]he will drive them out of his land." Ex. 3:19 • Ex. 12:31, 33, 39

2 And God spoke to Moses and said to him: "I *am* [T]the LORD. Heb. *YHWH*

3 [R]"I appeared to Abraham, to Isaac, and to Jacob, as God Almighty, but *by* My name LORD* I was not known to them. Gen. 17:1

4 "I have also established My covenant with them, [R]to give them the land of Canaan, the land of their pilgrimage, [R]in which they were strangers. Lev. 25:23 • Gen. 28:4

5 "And [R]I have also heard the groaning of the children of Israel whom the Egyptians keep in bondage, and I have remembered My covenant. Ex. 2:24

6 "Therefore say to the children of Israel: [R]'*I am* the LORD; [R]I will bring you out from under the burdens of the Egyptians, I will rescue you from their bondage, and I will redeem you with an outstretched arm and with great judgments. Deut. 6:12 • Deut. 26:8

7 'I will take you as My people, and I will be your God. Then you shall know that I *am* the LORD your God who brings you out from under the burdens of the Egyptians.

8 'And I will bring you into the land which I [R]swore to give to Abraham, Isaac, and Jacob; and I will give it to you *as* a heritage: I *am* the LORD.' " Gen. 15:18; 26:3

Moses Reassures Israel

9 So Moses spoke thus to the children of Israel; [R]but they did not heed Moses, because of [R]anguish[T] of spirit and cruel bondage. Ex. 5:21 • Ex. 2:23 • Lit. *shortness*

God Recommissions Moses

10 And the LORD spoke to Moses, saying,

11 "Go in, tell Pharaoh king of Egypt to let the children of Israel go out of his land."

12 And Moses spoke before the LORD, saying, "The children of Israel have not heeded me. How then shall Pharaoh heed me, for [R]I *am* of uncircumcised lips?" Jer. 1:6

13 Then the LORD spoke to Moses and Aaron, and gave them a [R]command[T] for the children of Israel and for Pharaoh king of Egypt, to bring the children of Israel out of the land of Egypt. Deut. 31:14 • *charge*

14 These *are* the heads of their fathers' houses: The sons of Reuben, the firstborn of Israel, *were* Hanoch, Pallu, Hezron, and Carmi. These are the families of Reuben.

15 [R]And the sons of Simeon *were* Jemuel,* Jamin, Ohad, Jachin, Zohar, and Shaul the son of a Canaanite woman. These *are* the families of Simeon. Gen. 46:10

16 These *are* the names of the sons of Levi according to their generations: Gershon, Kohath, and Merari. And the years of the life of Levi *were* one hundred and thirty-seven.

17 The sons of Gershon *were* Libni and Shimi according to their families.

18 And [R]the sons of Kohath *were* Amram,

6:3 Heb. *YHWH*, traditionally *Jehovah* **6:15** *Nemuel*, Num. 26:12

Izhar, Hebron, and Uzziel. And the years of
the life of Kohath *were* one hundred and
thirty-three. 1 Chr. 6:2, 18
19 [R]The sons of Merari *were* Mahli and
Mushi. These *are* the families of Levi accord-
ing to their generations. 1 Chr. 6:19; 23:21
20 Now [R]Amram took for himself [R]Jochebed,
his father's sister, as wife; and she bore him
Aaron and Moses. And the years of the life
of Amram *were* one hundred and thirty-
seven. Ex. 2:1, 2 • Num. 26:59
21 [R]The sons of Izhar *were* Korah, Nepheg,
and Zichri. 1 Chr. 6:37, 38
22 And [R]the sons of Uzziel *were* Mishael,
Elzaphan, and Zithri. Lev. 10:4
23 Aaron took to himself Elisheba, daughter
of [R]Amminadab, sister of Nahshon, as wife;
and she bore him [R]Nadab, Abihu, Eleazar, and
Ithamar. Ruth 4:19, 20 • Lev. 10:1
24 And [R]the sons of Korah *were* Assir, Elka-
nah, and Abiasaph. These are the families of
the Korahites. Num. 26:11
25 Eleazar, Aaron's son, took for himself one
of the daughters of Putiel as wife; and [R]she
bore him Phinehas. These *are* the heads of the
fathers' houses of the Levites according to
their families. Num. 25:7, 11
26 These *are the same* Aaron and Moses to
whom the LORD said, "Bring out the children
of Israel from the land of Egypt according to
their [R]armies."[T] Ex. 7:4; 12:17, 51 • *hosts*
27 These *are* the ones who spoke to Pharaoh
king of Egypt, [R]to bring out the children of Is-
rael from Egypt. These *are the same* Moses
and Aaron. Ps. 77:20

Moses Objects

28 And it came to pass, on the day the LORD
spoke to Moses in the land of Egypt,
29 that the LORD spoke to Moses, saying, "I
am the LORD. [R]Speak to Pharaoh king of
Egypt all that I say to you." Ex. 6:11; 7:2
30 But Moses said before the LORD, "Behold,
[R]I *am* of uncircumcised lips, and how shall
Pharaoh heed me?" Ex. 4:10; 6:12

CHAPTER 7

God Reassures Moses

SO the LORD said to Moses: "See, I have
made you *as* God to Pharaoh, and Aaron
your brother shall be your prophet.
2 "You [R]shall speak all that I command
you. And Aaron your brother shall tell
Pharaoh to send the children of Israel out of
his land. Ex. 4:15
3 "And [R]I will harden Pharaoh's heart, and
[R]multiply My signs and My wonders in the
land of Egypt. Ex. 4:21; 9:12 • Ex. 11:9
4 "But [R]Pharaoh will not heed you, so
[R]that I may lay My hand on Egypt and bring
My armies *and* My people, the children of Is-
rael, out of the land of Egypt by great judg-
ments. Ex. 3:19, 20; 10:1; 11:9 • Ex. 9:14
5 "And the Egyptians [R]shall know that I *am*
the LORD, when I [R]stretch out My hand on
Egypt and bring out the children of Israel
from among them." Ps. 9:16 • Ex. 9:15
6 Then Moses and Aaron did *so;* just as the
LORD commanded them, so they did.
7 And Moses *was* [R]eighty years old and
Aaron eighty-three years old when they
spoke to Pharaoh. Deut. 29:5; 31:2; 34:7

Aaron's Rod Swallows Pharaoh's Rods

8 Then the LORD spoke to Moses and
Aaron, saying,
9 "When Pharaoh speaks to you, saying,
[R]'Show a miracle for yourselves,' then you
shall say to Aaron, [R]'Take your rod and cast *it*
before Pharaoh, *and* let it become a ser-
pent.' " Is. 7:11 • Ex. 4:2, 3, 17
10 So Moses and Aaron went in to Pharaoh,
and they did so, just [R]as the LORD com-
manded. And Aaron cast down his rod before
Pharaoh and before his servants, and it [R]be-
came a serpent. Ex. 7:9 • Ex. 4:3
11 But Pharaoh also [R]called the wise men
and [R]the sorcerers; so the magicians of Egypt,
they also did in like manner with their en-
chantments. Gen. 41:8 • 2 Tim. 3:8
12 For every man threw down his rod, and
they became serpents. But Aaron's rod swal-
lowed up their rods.
13 And Pharaoh's heart grew hard, and he
did not heed them, as the LORD had said.

First Plague: Blood

14 So the LORD said to Moses: "Pharaoh's
heart *is* hard; he refuses to let the people go.
15 "Go to Pharaoh in the morning, when he
goes out to the [R]water, and you shall stand by
the river's bank to meet him; and [R]the rod
which was turned to a serpent you shall take
in your hand. Ex. 2:5; 8:20 • Ex. 4:2, 3; 7:10
16 "And you shall say to him, [R]'The LORD
God of the Hebrews has sent me to you, say-
ing, "Let My people go, that they may serve
Me in the wilderness"; but indeed, until now
you would not hear! Ex. 3:13, 18; 4:22
17 'Thus says the LORD: "By this you shall
know that I *am* the LORD. Behold, I will strike
the waters which *are* in the river with the rod
that *is* in my hand, and they shall be turned
[R]to blood. Rev. 11:6; 16:4, 6
18 "And the fish that *are* in the river shall
die, the river shall stink, and the Egyptians
will [R]loathe[T] to drink the water of the
river." ' " Ex. 7:24 • *be weary of drinking*
19 Then the LORD spoke to Moses, "Say to
Aaron, 'Take your rod and stretch out your
hand over the waters of Egypt, over their
streams, over their rivers, over their ponds,
and over all their pools of water, that they
may become blood. And there shall be blood

throughout all the land of Egypt, both in *buckets of* wood and *pitchers of* stone.' "

20 And Moses and Aaron did so, just as the LORD commanded. So he [R]lifted up the rod and struck the waters that *were* in the river, in the sight of Pharaoh and in the sight of his servants. And all the waters that *were* in the river were turned to blood. Ex. 17:5

21 The fish that *were* in the river died, the river stank, and the Egyptians could not drink the water of the river. So there was blood throughout all the land of Egypt

22 [R]Then the magicians of Egypt did so with their enchantments; and Pharaoh's heart grew hard, and he did not heed them, [R]as the LORD had said. Ex. 7:11 • Ex. 3:19; 7:3

23 And Pharaoh turned and went into his house. Neither was his heart moved by this.

24 So all the Egyptians dug all around the river for water to drink, because they could not drink the water of the river.

25 And seven days passed after the LORD had struck the river.

CHAPTER 8

Second Plague: Frogs

AND the LORD spoke to Moses, "Go to Pharaoh and say to him, 'Thus says the LORD: "Let My people go, [R]that they may serve Me. Ex. 3:12, 18; 4:23; 5:1, 3

2 "But if you [R]refuse to let *them* go, behold, I will smite all your territory with [R]frogs. Ex. 7:14; 9:2 • Rev. 16:13

3 "So the river shall bring forth frogs abundantly, which shall go up and come into your house, into your [R]bedroom, on your bed, into the houses of your servants, on your people, into your ovens, and into your kneading bowls. Ps. 105:30

4 "And the frogs shall come up on you, on your people, and on all your servants." ' "

5 Then the LORD spoke to Moses, "Say to Aaron, [R]'Stretch out your hand with your rod over the streams, over the rivers, and over the ponds, and cause frogs to come up on the land of Egypt.' " Ex. 7:19

6 So Aaron stretched out his hand over the waters of Egypt, and [R]the frogs came up and covered the land of Egypt. Ps. 78:45

7 [R]And the magicians did so with their [T]enchantments, and brought up frogs on the land of Egypt. Ex. 7:11, 22 • *secret arts*

8 Then Pharaoh called for Moses and Aaron, and said, [R]"Entreat the LORD that He may take away the frogs from me and from my people; and I will let the people go, that they may sacrifice to the LORD." Ex. 10:17

9 And Moses said to Pharaoh, "Accept the honor of saying when I shall intercede for you, for your servants, and for your people, to destroy the frogs from you and your houses, *that* they may remain in the river only."

10 So he said, "Tomorrow." And he said, "*Let it be* according to your word, that you may know that [R]*there is* no one like the LORD our God. Ex. 9:14; 15:11

11 "And the frogs shall depart from you, from your houses, from your servants, and from your people. They shall remain in the river only."

12 Then Moses and Aaron went out from Pharaoh. And Moses [R]cried out to the LORD concerning the frogs which He had brought against Pharaoh. Ex. 8:30; 9:33; 10:18; 32:11

13 So the LORD did according to the word of Moses. And the frogs died out of the houses, out of the courtyards, and out of the fields.

14 They gathered them together in heaps, and the land stank.

15 But when Pharaoh saw that there was [R]relief, he hardened his heart and did not heed them, as the LORD had said. Eccl. 8:11

Third Plague: Lice

16 So the LORD said to Moses, "Say to Aaron, 'Stretch out your rod, and strike the dust of the land, so that it may become [T]lice throughout all the land of Egypt.' " *gnats*

17 And they did so. For Aaron stretched out his hand with his rod and struck the dust of the earth, and it became lice on man and beast. All the dust of the land became lice throughout all the land of Egypt.

18 Now [R]the magicians so worked with their [T]enchantments to bring forth lice, but they [R]could not. So there were lice on man and beast. Ex. 7:11, 12; 8:7 • *secret arts* • Dan. 5:8

19 Then the magicians said to Pharaoh, "This *is* [R]the finger of God." But Pharaoh's heart grew hard, and he did not heed them, just as the LORD had said. Ex. 7:5; 10:7

Fourth Plague: Flies

20 And the LORD said to Moses, [R]"Rise early in the morning and stand before Pharaoh as he comes out to the water. Then say to him, 'Thus says the LORD: "Let My people go, that they may serve Me. Ex. 7:15; 9:13

21 "Or else, if you will not let My people go, behold, I will send swarms *of flies* on you and your servants, on your people and into your houses. The houses of the Egyptians shall be full of swarms *of flies*, and also the ground on which they *stand*.

22 "And in that day I will set apart the land of [R]Goshen, in which My people dwell, that no swarms *of flies* shall be there, in order that you may know that I *am* the LORD in the midst of the [R]land. Gen. 50:8 • Ex. 9:29

23 "I will make a difference* between My people and your people. Tomorrow this [R]sign shall be." ' " Ex. 4:8

24 And the LORD did so. [R]Thick swarms *of*

8:23 Lit. *set a ransom*, Ex. 9:4; 11:7

flies came into the house of Pharaoh, *into* his servants' houses, and into all the land of Egypt. The land was corrupted because of the swarms *of flies.* Ps. 78:45; 105:31

25 Then Pharaoh called for Moses and Aaron, and said, "Go, sacrifice to your God in the land."

26 And Moses said, "It is not right to do so, for we would be sacrificing [R]the abomination of the Egyptians to the LORD our God. If we sacrifice the abomination of the Egyptians before their eyes, then will they not [T]stone us? Gen. 43:32; 46:34 • Put us to death by stoning

27 "We will go three days' journey into the wilderness and sacrifice to the LORD our God as [R]He will command us." Ex. 3:12

28 So Pharaoh said, "I will let you go, that you may sacrifice to the LORD your God in the wilderness; only you shall not go very far away. Intercede for me."

29 Then Moses said, "Indeed I am going out from you, and I will entreat the LORD, that the swarms *of flies* may depart tomorrow from Pharaoh, from his servants, and from his people. But let Pharaoh not [R]deal deceitfully anymore in not letting the people go to sacrifice to the LORD." Ex. 8:8, 15

30 So Moses went out from Pharaoh and [R]entreated the LORD. Ex. 8:12

31 And the LORD did according to the word of Moses; He removed the swarms *of flies* from Pharaoh, from his servants, and from his people. Not one remained.

32 But Pharaoh hardened his heart at this time also; neither would he let the people go.

CHAPTER 9

Fifth Plague: Disease on Beasts

THEN the LORD said to Moses, [R]"Go in to Pharaoh and tell him, 'Thus says the LORD God of the Hebrews: "Let My people go, that they may serve Me. Ex. 4:23; 8:1

2 "For if you [R]refuse to let *them* go, and still hold them, Ex. 8:2

3 "behold, the hand of the LORD will be on your cattle in the field, on the horses, on the donkeys, on the camels, on the oxen, and on the sheep—a very severe pestilence.

4 "And the LORD will make a difference between the livestock of Israel and the livestock of Egypt. So nothing shall die of all *that* belongs to the children of Israel." ' "

5 Then the LORD appointed a set time, saying, "Tomorrow the LORD will do this thing in the land."

6 So the LORD did this thing on the next day, and [R]all the livestock of Egypt died; but of the livestock of the children of Israel, not one died. Ps. 78:48, 50

7 Then Pharaoh sent, and indeed, not even one of the livestock of the Israelites was dead. But the heart of Pharaoh became hard, and he did not let the people go.

Sixth Plague: Boils on Man and Beast

8 So the LORD said to Moses and Aaron, "Take for yourselves handfuls of ashes from a furnace, and let Moses scatter it toward the heavens in the sight of Pharaoh.

9 "And it will become fine dust in all the land of Egypt, and it will cause [R]boils that break out in sores on man and beast throughout all the land of Egypt." Rev. 16:2

10 Then they took ashes from the furnace and stood before Pharaoh, and Moses scattered *them* toward heaven. And *they* caused [R]boils that break out in sores on man and beast. Deut. 28:27

11 And the [R]magicians could not stand before Moses because of the [R]boils, for the boils were on the magicians and on all the Egyptians. [Ex. 8:18, 19] • Job 2:7

12 But the LORD hardened the heart of Pharaoh; and he [R]did not heed them, just as the LORD had spoken to Moses. Ex. 7:13

Seventh Plague: Hail

13 Then the LORD said to Moses, [R]"Rise early in the morning and stand before Pharaoh, and say to him, 'Thus says the LORD God of the Hebrews: "Let My people go, that they may [R]serve Me, Ex. 8:20 • Ex. 9:1

14 "for at this time I will send all My plagues to your very heart, and on your servants and on your people, [R]that you may know that *there is* none like Me in all the earth. Ex. 8:10

15 "Now if I had [R]stretched out My hand and struck you and your people with [R]pestilence, then you would have been cut off from the earth. Ex. 3:20; 7:5 • Ex. 5:3

16 "But indeed for [R]this *purpose* I have raised you up, that I may show My power *in* you, and that My [R]name may be declared in all the earth. [Rom. 9:17, 18] • 1 Kin. 8:43

17 "As yet you exalt yourself against My people in that you will not let them go.

18 "Behold, tomorrow about this time I will cause very heavy hail to rain down, such as has not been in Egypt since its founding until now.

19 "Therefore send now *and* gather your livestock and all that you have in the field, for the hail shall come down on every man and every animal which is found in the field and is not brought home; and they shall die." ' "

20 He who feared the word of the LORD among the servants of Pharaoh made his servants and his livestock flee to the houses.

21 But he who did not regard the word of the LORD left his servants and his livestock in the field.

22 Then the LORD said to Moses, "Stretch out your hand toward heaven, that there may be hail in all the land of Egypt—on man, on

beast, and on every herb of the field, through-
out the land of Egypt."
23 And Moses stretched out his rod toward
heaven; and the LORD sent thunder and hail,
and fire darted to the ground. And the LORD
rained hail on the land of Egypt.
24 So there was hail, and fire mingled with
the hail, so very heavy that there was none
like it in all the land of Egypt since it became
a nation.
25 And the [R]hail struck throughout the
whole land of Egypt, all that *was* in the field,
both man and beast; and the hail struck every
herb of the field and broke every tree of the
field. Ps. 78:47, 48; 105:32, 33
26 Only in the land of Goshen, where the
children of Israel *were*, there was no hail.
27 And Pharaoh sent and [R]called for Moses
and Aaron, and said to them, "I have sinned
this time. [R]The LORD *is* righteous, and my peo-
ple and I *are* wicked. Ex. 8:8 • 2 Chr. 12:6
28 [R]"Entreat the LORD, that there may be no
more mighty thundering and hail, for *it is*
enough. I will let you go, and you shall stay no
longer." Ex. 8:8, 28; 10:17
29 So Moses said to him, "As soon as I have
gone out of the city, I will spread out my
hands to the LORD; the thunder will cease, and
there will be no more hail, that you may know
that the earth *is* the LORD's.
30 "But as for you and your servants, [R]I
know that you will not yet fear the LORD
God." [Is. 26:10]
31 Now the flax and the barley were struck,
[R]for the barley *was* in the head and the flax
was in bud. Ruth 1:22; 2:23
32 But the wheat and the spelt were not
struck, for they *are* [T]late crops. Lit. *darkened*
33 So Moses went out of the city from
Pharaoh and spread out his hands to the
LORD; then the thunder and the hail ceased,
and the rain was not poured on the earth.
34 And when Pharaoh saw that the rain, the
hail, and the thunder had ceased, he sinned
yet more; and he hardened his heart, he and
his servants.
35 So [R]the heart of Pharaoh was hard; nei-
ther would he let the children of Israel go, as
the LORD had spoken by Moses. Ex. 4:21

CHAPTER 10

Eighth Plague: Locusts

NOW the LORD said to Moses, "Go in to
Pharaoh; for I have hardened his heart
and the hearts of his servants, that I may
show these signs of Mine before him,
2 "and that [R]you may tell in the hearing of
your son and your son's son the mighty things
I have done in Egypt, and My signs which I
have done among them, that you may know
that I *am* the LORD." Joel 1:3
3 So Moses and Aaron came in to Pharaoh
and said to him, "Thus says the LORD God of
the Hebrews: 'How long will you refuse to
[R]humble yourself before Me? Let My people
go, that they may serve Me. [1 Kin. 21:29]
4 'Or else, if you refuse to let My people go,
behold, tomorrow I will bring [R]locusts into
your territory. Rev. 9:3
5 'And they shall cover the face of the earth,
so that no one will be able to see the earth;
and [R]they shall eat the residue of what is left,
which remains to you from the hail, and they
shall eat every tree which grows up for you
out of the field. Ex. 9:32
6 'They shall [R]fill your houses, the houses
of all your servants, and the houses of all
the Egyptians—which neither your fathers
nor your fathers' fathers have seen, since
the day that they were on the earth to this
day.'" And he turned and went out from
Pharaoh. Ex. 8:3, 21
7 Then Pharaoh's servants said to him,
"How long shall this man be [R]a snare to us?
Let the men go, that they may serve the LORD
their God. Do you not yet know that Egypt is
destroyed?" Ex. 23:33
8 So Moses and Aaron were brought again
to Pharaoh, and he said to them, "Go, serve
the LORD your God. Who *are* the ones that are
going?"
9 And Moses said, "We will go with our
young and our old; with our sons and our
daughters, with our flocks and our herds we
will go, for [R]we must hold a feast to the
LORD." Ex. 5:1; 7:16
10 Then he said to them, "The LORD had bet-
ter be with you when I let you and your little
ones go! Beware, for evil is ahead of you.
11 "Not so! Go now, you *who are* men, and
serve the LORD, for that is what you desired."
And they were driven [R]out from Pharaoh's
presence. Ex. 10:28
12 Then the LORD said to Moses, [R]"Stretch
out your hand over the land of Egypt for the
locusts, that they may come upon the land of
Egypt, and [R]eat every herb of the land—all
that the hail has left." Ex. 7:19 • Ex. 10:5, 15
13 So Moses stretched out his rod over the
land of Egypt, and the LORD brought an east
wind on the land all that day and all *that*
night. When it was morning, the east wind
brought the locusts.
14 And [R]the locusts went up over all the land
of Egypt and rested on all the territory of
Egypt. *They were* very severe; previously
there had been no such locusts as they, nor
shall there be such after them. Ps. 78:46
15 For they [R]covered the face of the whole
earth, so that the land was darkened; and they
[R]ate every herb of the land and all the fruit of
the trees which the hail had left. So there re-
mained nothing green on the trees or on the
plants of the field throughout all the land of
Egypt. Ex. 10:5 • Ps. 105:35

16 Then Pharaoh called for Moses and Aaron in haste, and said, "I have sinned against the LORD your God and against you.

17 "Now therefore, please forgive my sin only this once, and [R]entreat[T] the LORD your God, that He may take away from me this death only." 1 Kin. 13:6 • *make supplication to*

18 So he [R]went out from Pharaoh and entreated the LORD. Ex. 8:30

19 And the LORD turned a very strong west wind, which took the locusts away and blew them into the Red Sea. There remained not one locust in all the territory of Egypt.

20 But the LORD [R]hardened Pharaoh's heart, and he did not let the children of Israel go. Ex. 4:21; 10:1; 11:10

Ninth Plague: Darkness

21 Then the LORD said to Moses, [R]"Stretch out your hand toward heaven, that there may be darkness over the land of Egypt, darkness *which* may even be felt." Ex. 9:22

22 So Moses stretched out his hand toward heaven, and there was [R]thick darkness in all the land of Egypt three days. Ps. 105:28

23 They did not see one another; nor did anyone rise from his place for three days. [R]But all the children of Israel had light in their dwellings. Ex. 8:22, 23

24 Then Pharaoh called to Moses and [R]said, "Go, serve the LORD; only let your flocks and your herds be kept back. Let your [R]little ones also go with you." Ex. 8:8, 25; 10:8 • Ex. 10:10

25 But Moses said, "You must also give us sacrifices and burnt offerings, that we may sacrifice to the LORD our God.

26 "Our livestock also shall go with us; not a hoof shall be left behind. For we must take some of them to serve the LORD our God, and even we do not know with what we must serve the LORD until we arrive there."

27 But the LORD hardened Pharaoh's heart, and he would not let them go.

28 Then Pharaoh said to him, [R]"Get away from me! Take heed to yourself and see my face no more! For in the day you see my face you shall die!" Ex. 10:11

29 So Moses said, "You have spoken well. [R]I will never see your face again." Heb. 11:27

CHAPTER 11

Tenth Plague: Death Announced

AND the LORD said to Moses, "I will bring one more plague on Pharaoh and on Egypt. Afterward he will let you go from here. When he lets *you* go, he will surely drive you out of here altogether.

2 "Speak now in the hearing of the people, and let every man ask from his neighbor and every woman from her neighbor, [R]articles of silver and articles of gold." Ex. 3:22; 12:35, 36

3 And the LORD gave the people favor in the sight of the Egyptians. Moreover the man [R]Moses *was* very great in the land of Egypt, in the sight of Pharaoh's servants and in the sight of the people. Deut. 34:10–12

4 Then Moses said, "Thus says the LORD: [R]'About midnight I will go out into the midst of Egypt; Ex. 12:12, 23, 29

5 'and [R]all the firstborn in the land of Egypt shall die, from the firstborn of Pharaoh who sits on his throne, even to the firstborn of the female servant who *is* behind the handmill, and all the firstborn of the animals. Ex. 4:23; 12:12, 29

6 [R]'Then there shall be a great cry throughout all the land of Egypt, [R]such as was not like it *before,* nor shall be like it again. Ex. 12:30 • Ex. 10:14

7 [R]'But against none of the children of Israel [R]shall a dog move its tongue, against man or beast, that you may know that the LORD does make a difference between the Egyptians and Israel.' Ex. 8:22 • Josh. 10:21

8 "And all these your servants shall come down to me and bow down to me, saying, 'Get out, and all the people who follow you!' After that I will go out." [R]Then he went out from Pharaoh in great anger. Heb. 11:27

9 But the LORD said to Moses, "Pharaoh will not heed you, so that My wonders may be multiplied in the land of Egypt."

10 So Moses and Aaron did all these wonders before Pharaoh; and the LORD hardened Pharaoh's heart, and he did not let the children of Israel go out of his land.

CHAPTER 12

Instructions for the Passover

NOW the LORD spoke to Moses and Aaron in the land of Egypt, saying,

2 [R]"This month *shall be* your beginning of months; it *shall be* the first month of the year to you. Deut. 16:1

3 "Speak to all the congregation of Israel, saying: 'On the [R]tenth of this month every man shall take for himself a lamb, according to the house of *his* father, a lamb for a household. Josh. 4:19

4 'And if the household is too small for the lamb, let him and his neighbor next to his house take *it* according to the number of the persons; according to each man's need you shall make your count for the lamb.

5 'Your lamb shall be [R]without blemish, a male of the first year. You may take *it* from the sheep or from the goats. [1 Pet. 1:19]

6 'Now you shall keep it until the [R]fourteenth day of the same month. Then the whole assembly of the congregation of Israel shall kill it at twilight. Lev. 23:5

7 'And they shall take *some* of the blood and put *it* on the two doorposts and on the lintel of the houses where they eat it.

8 'Then they shall eat the flesh on that
night; roasted in fire, with unleavened bread
and with bitter *herbs* they shall eat it.
9 'Do not eat it raw, nor boiled at all with
water, but [R]roasted in fire—its head with its
legs and its entrails. Deut. 16:7
10 [R]'You shall let none of it remain until
morning, and what remains of it until morn-
ing you shall burn with fire. Ex. 16:19; 23:18
11 'And thus you shall eat it: *with* a belt on
your waist, your sandals on your feet, and
your staff in your hand. So you shall eat it in
haste. It *is* the LORD's Passover.
12 'For I will pass through the land of Egypt
on that night, and will strike all the firstborn
in the land of Egypt, both man and beast; and
against all the gods of Egypt I will execute
judgment: I *am* the LORD.
13 'Now the blood shall be a sign for you on
the houses where you *are*. And when I see the
blood, I will pass over you; and the plague
shall not be on you to destroy *you* when I
strike the land of Egypt.
14 'So this day shall be to you a memorial;
and you shall keep it as a feast to the LORD
throughout your generations. You shall keep it
as a feast by an everlasting ordinance.
15 [R]'Seven days you shall eat unleavened
bread. On the first day you shall remove
leaven from your houses. For whoever eats
leavened bread from the first day until the
seventh day, [R]that [T]person shall be cut off
from Israel. Lev. 23:6 • Gen. 17:14 • *soul*
16 'On the first day *there shall be* [R]a holy
convocation, and on the seventh day there
shall be a holy convocation for you. No man-
ner of work shall be done on them; but *that*
which everyone must eat—that only may be
prepared by you. Lev. 23:2, 7, 8
17 'So you shall observe *the Feast of* Un-
leavened Bread, for [R]on this same day I will
have brought your [T]armies out of the land of
Egypt. Therefore you shall observe this day
throughout your generations as an everlast-
ing ordinance. Ex. 12:14; 13:3, 10 • *hosts*
18 [R]'In the first *month*, on the fourteenth day
of the month at evening, you shall eat unleav-
ened bread, until the twenty-first day of the
month at evening. Lev. 23:5–8
19 'For [R]seven days no leaven shall be
found in your houses, since whoever eats
what is leavened, that same person shall be
cut off from the congregation of Israel,
whether *he is* a stranger or a native of the
land. Ex. 12:15; 23:15; 34:18
20 'You shall eat nothing leavened; in all your
dwellings you shall eat unleavened bread.' "

Participation in the Passover

21 Then [R]Moses called for all the elders of Is-
rael and said to them, "Pick out and take
lambs for yourselves according to your fami-
lies, and kill the Passover *lamb*. [Heb. 11:28]
22 [R]"And you shall take a bunch of hyssop,
dip *it* in the blood that *is* in the basin, and
[R]strike the lintel and the two doorposts with
the blood that *is* in the basin. And none of you
shall go out of the door of his house until
morning. Heb. 11:28 • Ex. 12:7
23 "For the LORD will pass through to strike
the Egyptians; and when He sees the blood on
the lintel and on the two doorposts, the LORD
will pass over the door and [R]not allow [R]the de-
stroyer to come into your houses to strike
you. Rev. 7:3; 9:4 • Heb. 11:28
24 "And you shall observe this thing as an
ordinance for you and your sons forever.
25 "It will come to pass when you come to
the land which the LORD will give you, [R]just
as He promised, that you shall keep this ser-
vice. Ex. 3:8, 17
26 [R]"And it shall be, when your children
say to you, 'What do you mean by this ser-
vice?' Ex. 10:2; 13:8, 14, 15
27 "that you shall say, [R]'It *is* the Passover
sacrifice of the LORD, who passed over the
houses of the children of Israel in Egypt when
He struck the Egyptians and delivered our
households.' " So the people bowed their
heads and worshiped. Ex. 12:11
28 Then the children of Israel went away and
did *so*; just as the LORD had commanded Mo-
ses and Aaron, so they did.

Redemption Through the Passover

29 And it came to pass at midnight that [R]the
LORD struck all the firstborn in the land of
Egypt, from the firstborn of Pharaoh who sat
on his throne to the firstborn of the captive
who *was* in the dungeon, and all the firstborn
of livestock. Num. 8:17; 33:4
30 So Pharaoh rose in the night, he, all his
servants, and all the Egyptians; and there was
a great cry in Egypt, for *there was* not a house
where *there was* not one dead.
31 Then he [R]called for Moses and Aaron by
night, and said, "Rise, go out from among
my people, [R]both you and the children of Is-
rael. And go, serve the LORD as you have
[R]said. Ex. 10:28, 29 • Ex. 8:25; 11:1 • Ex. 10:9
32 [R]"Also take your flocks and your herds, as
you have said, and be gone; and bless me
also." Ex. 10:9, 26
33 And the Egyptians urged the people, that
they might send them out of the land in haste.
For they said, "We *shall* all *be* dead."
34 So the people took their dough before it
was leavened, having their kneading bowls
bound up in their clothes on their shoulders.
35 Now the children of Israel had done ac-
cording to the word of Moses, and they had
asked from the Egyptians [R]articles of silver,
articles of gold, and clothing. Ex. 3:21, 22
36 And the LORD had given the people favor
in the sight of the Egyptians, so that they

granted them *what they requested.* Thus they plundered the Egyptians.

Freedom Because of the Passover

37 Then [R]the children of Israel journeyed from [R]Rameses to Succoth, about [R]six hundred thousand men on foot, besides children. Num. 33:3, 5 • Gen. 47:11 • Ex. 38:26

38 A [R]mixed multitude went up with them also, and flocks and herds—a great deal of [R]livestock. Num. 11:4 • Deut. 3:19

39 And they baked unleavened cakes of the dough which they had brought out of Egypt; for it was not leavened, because they were driven out of Egypt and could not wait, nor had they prepared provisions for themselves.

40 Now the [T]sojourn of the children of Israel who lived in Egypt* *was* [R]four hundred and thirty years. Length of the stay • Acts 7:6

41 And it came to pass at the end of the four hundred and thirty years—on that very same day—it came to pass that [R]all the armies of the LORD went out from the land of Egypt. Ex. 3:8, 10; 6:6; 7:4

42 It *is* a night of solemn observance to the LORD for bringing them out of the land of Egypt. This *is* that night of the LORD, a solemn observance for all the children of Israel throughout their generations.

43 And the LORD said to Moses and Aaron, "This *is* [R]the ordinance of the Passover: No foreigner shall eat it. Num. 9:14

44 "But every man's servant who is bought for money, when you have [R]circumcised him, then he may eat it. Gen. 17:12, 13

45 [R]"A sojourner and a hired servant shall not eat it. Lev. 22:10

46 "In one house it shall be eaten; you shall not carry any of the flesh outside the house, nor shall you break one of its bones.

47 [R]"All the congregation of Israel shall keep it. Ex. 12:6

48 "And [R]when a stranger dwells with you *and wants* to keep the Passover to the LORD, let all his males be circumcised, and then let him come near and keep it; and he shall be as a native of the land. For no uncircumcised person shall eat it. Num. 9:14

49 "One law shall be for the native-born and for the stranger who dwells among you."

50 Thus all the children of Israel did; as the LORD commanded Moses and Aaron, so they did.

51 [R]And it came to pass, on that very same day, that the LORD brought the children of Israel out of the land of Egypt [R]according to their armies. Ex. 12:41; 20:2 • Ex. 6:26

CHAPTER 13

Sanctification as a Result of the Passover

THEN the LORD spoke to Moses, saying,

2 [R]"Consecrate[T] to Me all the firstborn, whatever opens the womb among the children of Israel, *both* of man and beast; it is Mine." Luke 2:23☆ • *Set apart*

3 And Moses said to the people: [R]"Remember this day in which you went out of Egypt, out of the house of [T]bondage; for [R]by strength of hand the LORD brought you out of this *place.* No leavened bread shall be eaten. Deut. 16:3 • Lit. *slaves* • Ex. 3:20; 6:1

4 [R]"On this day you are going out, in the month Abib. Ex. 12:2; 23:15; 34:18

5 "And it shall be, when the LORD [R]brings you into the [R]land of the Canaanites and the Hittites and the Amorites and the Hivites and the Jebusites, which He [R]swore to your fathers to give you, a land flowing with milk and honey, that you shall keep this service in this month. Ex. 3:8, 17 • Gen. 17:8 • Ex. 6:8

6 [R]"Seven days you shall eat unleavened bread, and on the seventh day *there shall be* a feast to the LORD. Ex. 12:15–20

7 "Unleavened bread shall be eaten seven days. And [R]no leavened bread shall be seen among you, nor shall leaven be seen among you in all your quarters. Ex. 12:19

8 "And you shall [R]tell your son in that day, saying, '*This is done* because of what the LORD did for me when I came up from Egypt.' Ex. 10:2; 12:26; 13:14

9 "It shall be as [R]a sign to you on your hand and as a memorial between your eyes, that the LORD's law may be in your mouth; for with a strong hand the LORD has brought you out of Egypt. Deut. 6:8; 11:18

10 "You shall therefore keep this ordinance in its season from year to year.

11 "And it shall be, when the LORD [R]brings you into the land of the [R]Canaanites, as He swore to you and your fathers, and gives it to you, Ex. 13:5 • Num. 21:3

12 [R]"that you shall set apart to the LORD all that open the womb, that is, every firstborn that comes from an animal which you have; the males *shall be* the LORD's. Lev. 27:26

13 "But [R]every firstborn of a donkey you shall redeem with a lamb; and if you will not redeem *it,* then you shall break its neck. And all the firstborn of man among your sons [R]you shall redeem. Ex. 34:20 • Num. 3:46, 47

14 [R]"So it shall be, when your son asks you in time to come, saying, 'What *is* this?' that you shall say to him, [R]'By strength of hand the LORD brought us out of Egypt, out of the house of bondage. Deut. 6:20 • Ex. 13:3, 9

15 'And it came to pass, when Pharaoh was stubborn about letting us go, that [R]the LORD killed all the firstborn in the land of Egypt, both the firstborn of man and the firstborn of beast. Therefore I sacrifice to the LORD all males that open the womb, but all the firstborn of my sons I redeem.' Ex. 12:29

12:40 Sam., LXX *Egypt and Canaan*

16 "It shall be as [R]a sign on your hand and
as frontlets between your eyes, for by
strength of hand the LORD brought us out of
Egypt." Ex. 13:9

God Leads Israel

17 Then it came to pass, when Pharaoh had
let the people go, that God did not lead them
by way of the land of the Philistines, although
that *was* near; for God said, "Lest perhaps the
people change their minds when they see war,
and return to Egypt."
18 So God [R]led the people around *by* way of
the wilderness of the Red Sea. And the chil-
dren of Israel went up in orderly ranks out of
the land of Egypt. Num. 33:6
19 And Moses took the bones* of Joseph
with him, for he had placed the children of Is-
rael under solemn oath, saying, [R]"God will
surely visit you, and you shall carry up my
bones from here with you." Ex. 4:31
20 So [R]they took their journey from [R]Suc-
coth and camped in Etham at the edge of the
wilderness. Num. 33:6–8 • Ex. 12:37
21 And [R]the LORD went before them by day
in a pillar of cloud to lead the way, and by
night in a pillar of fire to give them light, so as
to go by day and night. Deut. 1:33
22 He did not take away the pillar of cloud
by day or the pillar of fire by night *from* be-
fore the people.

CHAPTER 14

NOW the LORD spoke to Moses, saying:
2 "Speak to the children of Israel, that
they turn and camp before Pi Hahiroth, be-
tween Migdol and the sea, opposite Baal
Zephon; you shall camp before it by the sea.

Pharaoh Follows Israel

3 "For Pharaoh will say of the children of
Israel, [R]'They *are* bewildered by the land; the
wilderness has closed them in.' Ps. 71:11
4 "Then [R]I will harden Pharaoh's heart, so
that he will pursue them; and I will gain honor
over Pharaoh and over all his army, that the
Egyptians may know that I *am* the LORD." And
they did so. Ex. 4:21; 7:3; 14:17
5 Now it was told the king of Egypt that the
people had fled, and [R]the heart of Pharaoh and
his servants was turned against the people;
and they said, "Why have we done this, that we
have let Israel go from serving us?" Ps. 105:25
6 So he [T]made ready his chariot and took
his people with him. *harnessed*
7 Also, he took [R]six hundred choice chari-
ots, and all the chariots of Egypt with cap-
tains over every one of them. Ex. 15:4
8 And the LORD [R]hardened the heart of
Pharaoh king of Egypt, and he pursued the
children of Israel; and [R]the children of Israel
went out with boldness. Ex. 14:4 • Num. 33:3
9 So the [R]Egyptians pursued them, all the
horses *and* chariots of Pharaoh, his horsemen
and his army, and overtook them camping
by the sea beside Pi Hahiroth, before Baal
Zephon. Josh. 24:6

Israel Rebels Against God

10 And when Pharaoh drew near, the chil-
dren of Israel lifted their eyes, and behold, the
Egyptians marched after them. So they were
very afraid, and the children of Israel [R]cried
out to the LORD. Neh. 9:9
11 [R]Then they said to Moses, "Because
there were no graves in Egypt, have you
taken us away to die in the wilderness? Why
have you so dealt with us, to bring us up out
of Egypt? Ps. 106:7, 8
12 "*Is* this not the word that we told you in
Egypt, saying, 'Let us alone that we may serve
the Egyptians'? For *it would have been* better
for us to serve the Egyptians than that we
should die in the wilderness."

God Opens the Red Sea

13 And Moses said to the people, "Do not be
afraid. Stand still, and see the salvation of the
LORD, which He will accomplish for you
today. For the Egyptians whom you see today,
you shall see again no more forever.
14 [R]"The LORD will fight for you, and you
shall hold your peace." Deut. 1:30; 3:22
15 And the LORD said to Moses, "Why do you
cry to Me? Tell the children of Israel to go for-
ward.
16 "But lift up your rod, and stretch out your
hand over the sea and divide it. And the chil-
dren of Israel shall go on dry *ground* through
the midst of the sea.
17 "And I indeed will harden the hearts of
the Egyptians, and they shall follow them. So
I will gain honor over Pharaoh and over all
his army, his chariots, and his horsemen.
18 "Then the Egyptians shall know that I *am*
the LORD, when I have gained honor for My-
self over Pharaoh, his chariots, and his horse-
men."
19 And the Angel of God, [R]who went before
the camp of Israel, moved and went behind
them; and the pillar of cloud went from before
them and stood behind them. [Is. 63:9]
20 So it came between the camp of the Egyp-
tians and the camp of Israel. Thus it was a
cloud and darkness *to the one*, and it gave
light by night *to the other*, so that the one did
not come near the other all that night.
21 Then Moses stretched out his hand over
the sea; and the LORD caused the sea to go
back by a strong east wind all that night, and
made the sea into dry *land*, and the waters
were [R]divided. Is. 63:12, 13

13:19 Gen. 50:25

22 So [R]the children of Israel went into the midst of the sea on the dry *ground,* and the waters *were* [R]a wall to them on their right hand and on their left. Ex. 15:19 • Ex. 14:29

23 And the Egyptians pursued and went after them into the midst of the sea, all Pharaoh's horses, his chariots, and his horsemen.

24 Now it came to pass, in the morning [R]watch, that [R]the LORD looked down upon the army of the Egyptians through the pillar of fire and cloud, and He [T]troubled the army of the Egyptians. Judg. 7:19 • Ex. 13:21 • *confused*

25 And He took off* their chariot wheels, so that they drove them with difficulty; and the Egyptians said, "Let us flee from the face of Israel, for the LORD [R]fights for them against the Egyptians." Ex. 7:5; 14:4, 14, 18

26 Then the LORD said to Moses, "Stretch out your hand over the sea, that the waters may come back upon the Egyptians, on their chariots, and on their horsemen."

27 And Moses stretched out his hand over the sea; and when the morning appeared, the sea [R]returned to its full depth, while the Egyptians were fleeing into it. So the LORD [R]overthrew[T] the Egyptians in the midst of the sea. Josh. 4:18 • Ex. 15:1, 7 • Lit. *shook off*

28 Then [R]the waters returned and covered the chariots, the horsemen, *and* all the army of Pharaoh that came into the sea after them. Not so much as one of them remained. Ps. 78:53; 106:11

29 But [R]the children of Israel had walked on dry *land* in the midst of the sea, and the waters *were* a wall to them on their right hand and on their left. Ps. 66:6; 78:52, 53

30 So the LORD saved Israel that day out of the hand of the Egyptians, and Israel saw the Egyptians dead on the seashore.

31 Thus Israel saw the great work which the LORD had done in Egypt; so the people feared the LORD, and [R]believed the LORD and His servant Moses. John 2:11; 11:45

CHAPTER 15

Israel Praises God

THEN [R]Moses and the children of Israel sang this song to the LORD, and spoke, saying: Ps. 106:12

"I will [R]sing to the LORD, Is. 12:1–6
For He has triumphed gloriously!
The horse and its rider
He has thrown into the sea!

2 The LORD *is* my strength and song,
And He has become my salvation;
He *is* my God, and I will praise Him;
My father's God, and I will exalt Him.

3 The LORD *is* a man of [R]war; Rev. 19:11
The LORD *is* His [R]name. Ps. 24:8; 83:18

4 [R]Pharaoh's chariots and his army He has cast into the sea; Ex. 14:28
[R]His chosen captains also are drowned in the Red Sea. Ex. 14:7

5 The depths have covered them;
They sank to the bottom like a stone.

6 "Your [R]right hand, O LORD, has become glorious in power; Ps. 17:7; 118:15
Your right hand, O LORD, has dashed the enemy in pieces.

7 And in the greatness of Your [R]excellence
You have overthrown those who rose against You; Deut. 33:26
You sent forth [R]Your wrath; Ps. 78:49, 50
It consumed them like stubble.

8 And [R]with the blast of Your nostrils
The waters were gathered together;
[R]The floods stood upright like a heap;
The depths congealed in the heart of the sea. Ex. 14:21, 22, 29 • Ps. 78:13

9 [R]The enemy said, 'I will pursue,
I will overtake, Judg. 5:30
I will [R]divide the spoil; Is. 53:12
My desire shall be satisfied on them.
I will draw my sword,
My hand shall destroy them.'

10 You blew with Your wind,
The sea covered them;
They sank like lead in the mighty waters.

11 "Who[R] *is* like You, O LORD, among the [T]gods? 1 Kin. 8:23 • *mighty ones*
Who *is* like You, glorious in holiness,
Fearful in praises, doing wonders?

12 You stretched out Your right hand;
The earth swallowed them.

13 You in Your mercy have led forth
The people whom You have redeemed;
You have guided *them* in Your strength
To [R]Your holy habitation. Ps. 78:54

14 "The [R]people will hear *and* be afraid;
[R]Sorrow[T] will take hold of the inhabitants of Philistia. Josh. 2:9 • Ps. 48:6 • *Anguish*

15 [R]Then [R]the chiefs of Edom will be dismayed; Gen. 36:15, 40 • Deut. 2:4
[R]The mighty men of Moab, Num. 22:3, 4
Trembling will take hold of them;
[R]All the inhabitants of Canaan will [R]melt away. Josh. 5:1 • Josh. 2:9–11, 24

16 Fear and dread will fall on them;
By the greatness of Your arm
They will be *as* still as a stone,
Till Your people pass over, O LORD,
Till the people pass over
[R]Whom You have purchased. Jer. 31:11

17 You will bring them in and [R]plant them
In the [R]mountain of Your inheritance,
In the place, O LORD, *which* You have made Ps. 44:2; 80:8, 15 • Ps. 2:6; 78:54, 68

14:25 Sam., LXX, Syr. *bound*

For Your own dwelling,
The sanctuary, O LORD, *which* Your
hands have established.

18 "The LORD shall reign forever and ever."

19 For the horses of Pharaoh went with his chariots and his horsemen into the sea, and the LORD brought back the waters of the sea upon them. But the children of Israel went on dry *land* in the midst of the sea.

20 Then Miriam [R]the prophetess, [R]the sister of Aaron, took the timbrel in her hand; and all the women went out after her with timbrels and with dances. Judg. 4:4 • Num. 26:59

21 And Miriam [R]answered them:

[R]"Sing to the LORD, 1 Sam. 18:7 • Ex. 15:1
For He has triumphed gloriously!
The horse and its rider
He has thrown into the sea!"

Preserved from Thirst

22 So Moses brought Israel from the Red Sea; then they went out into the Wilderness of Shur. And they went three days in the wilderness and found no [R]water. Num. 20:2

23 Now when they came to [R]Marah, they could not drink the waters of Marah, for they *were* bitter. Therefore the name of it was called Marah.* Num. 33:8

24 And the people complained against Moses, saying, "What shall we drink?"

25 So he cried out to the LORD, and the LORD showed him a tree. When he cast *it* into the waters, the waters were made sweet. There He made a statute and an ordinance for them, and there He tested them,

26 and said, [R]"If you diligently heed the voice of the LORD your God and do what is right in His sight, give ear to His commandments and keep all His statutes, I will put none of the diseases on you which I have brought on the Egyptians. For I *am* the LORD [R]who heals you." Deut. 7:12, 15 • Ex. 23:25

27 Then they came to Elim, where there *were* twelve wells of water and seventy palm trees; so they camped there by the waters.

CHAPTER 16

Preserved from Hunger

AND they [R]journeyed from Elim, and all the congregation of the children of Israel came to the Wilderness of Sin, which is between Elim and Sinai, on the fifteenth day of the second month after they departed from the land of Egypt. Num. 33:10, 11

2 Then the whole congregation of the children of Israel [R]complained against Moses and Aaron in the wilderness. 1 Cor. 10:10

3 And the children of Israel said to them, [R]"Oh, that we had died by the hand of the LORD in the land of Egypt, [R]when we sat by the pots of meat *and* when we ate bread to the full! For you have brought us out into this wilderness to kill this whole assembly with hunger." Lam. 4:9 • Num. 11:4, 5

4 Then the LORD said to Moses, "Behold, I will rain bread from heaven for you. And the people shall go out and gather a certain quota every day, that I may test them, whether they will walk in My law or not.

5 "And it shall be on the sixth day that they shall prepare what they bring in, and it shall be twice as much as they gather daily."

6 Then Moses and Aaron said to all the children of Israel, [R]"At evening you shall know that the LORD has brought you out of the land of Egypt. Ex. 6:7

7 "And in the morning you shall see [R]the glory of the LORD; for He hears your complaints against the LORD. But what *are* we, that you complain against us?" John 11:4, 40

8 Also Moses said, "*This shall be seen* when the LORD gives you meat to eat in the evening, and in the morning bread to the full; for the LORD hears your complaints which you make against Him. And what *are* we? Your complaints *are* not against us but [R]against the LORD." 1 Sam. 8:7

9 Then Moses spoke to Aaron, "Say to all the congregation of the children of Israel, [R]'Come near before the LORD, for He has heard your complaints.'" Num. 16:16

10 Now it came to pass, as Aaron spoke to the whole congregation of the children of Israel, that they looked toward the wilderness, and behold, the glory of the LORD [R]appeared in the cloud. Num. 16:19

11 And the LORD spoke to Moses, saying,

12 [R]"I have heard the complaints of the children of Israel. Speak to them, saying, [R]'At twilight you shall eat meat, and [R]in the morning you shall be filled with bread. And you shall know that I *am* the LORD your God.'" Ex. 16:8 • Ex. 16:6 • Ex. 16:7

13 So it was that quails came up at evening and covered the camp, and in the morning the dew lay all around the camp.

14 And when the layer of dew lifted, there, on the surface of the wilderness, was [R]a small round [R]substance, *as* fine as frost on the ground. Num. 11:7, 8 • Ps. 147:16

15 So when the children of Israel saw *it,* they said to one another, "What is it?" For they did not know what it *was.* And Moses said to them, [R]"This *is* the bread which the LORD has given you to eat. 1 Cor. 10:3

16 "This is the thing which the LORD has commanded: 'Let every man gather it [R]according to each one's need, one [R]omer for each person, *according to the* number of per-

15:23 Lit. *Bitter*

sons; let every man take for *those* who *are* in his tent.' " Ex. 12:4 • Ex. 16:32, 36

17 Then the children of Israel did so and gathered, some more, some less.

18 So when they measured *it* by omers, [R]he who gathered much had nothing left over, and he who gathered little had no lack. Every man had gathered according to each one's need. 2 Cor. 8:15

19 And Moses said, "Let no one [R]leave any of it till morning." Ex. 12:10; 16:23; 23:18

20 Notwithstanding they did not [T]heed Moses. But some of them left part of it until morning, and it bred worms and stank. And Moses was angry with them. *listen to*

21 So they gathered it every morning, every man according to his need. And when the sun became hot, it melted.

22 And so it was, on the sixth day, *that* they gathered twice as much bread, two omers for each one. And all the rulers of the congregation came and told Moses.

23 Then he said to them, "This *is what* the LORD has said: 'Tomorrow *is* [R]a Sabbath rest, a holy Sabbath to the LORD. Bake what you will bake *today*, and boil what you will boil; and lay up for yourselves all that remains, to be kept until morning.' " Gen. 2:3

24 So they laid it up till morning, as Moses commanded; and it did not [R]stink, nor were there any worms in it. Ex. 16:20

25 Then Moses said, "Eat that today, for today *is* a Sabbath to the LORD; today you will not find it in the field.

26 [R]"Six days you shall gather it, but on the seventh day, the Sabbath, there will be none." Ex. 20:9, 10

27 Now it happened *that some* of the people went out on the seventh day to gather, but they found none.

28 And the LORD said to Moses, "How long [R]do you refuse to keep My commandments and My laws? 2 Kin. 17:14

29 "See! For the LORD has given you the Sabbath; therefore He gives you on the sixth day bread for two days. Let every man remain in his place; let no man go out of his place on the seventh day."

30 So the people rested on the seventh day.

31 And the house of Israel called its name Manna.* And [R]it *was* like white coriander seed, and the taste of it *was* like wafers *made* with honey. Num. 11:7–9

32 Then Moses said, "This *is* the thing which the LORD has commanded: 'Fill an omer with it, to be kept for your generations, that they may see the bread with which I fed you in the wilderness, when I brought you out of the land of Egypt.' "

33 And Moses said to Aaron, [R]"Take a pot and put an omer of manna in it, and lay it up before the LORD, to be kept for your generations." Heb. 9:4

34 As the LORD commanded Moses, so Aaron laid it up [R]before the Testimony, to be kept. Num. 17:10

35 And the children of Israel [R]ate manna forty years, until they came to an inhabited land; they ate manna until they came to the border of the land of Canaan. Deut. 8:3, 16

36 Now an omer *is* one-tenth of an ephah.

CHAPTER 17

Preserved from Thirst Again

THEN [R]all the congregation of the children of Israel set out on their journey from the Wilderness of [R]Sin, according to the commandment of the LORD, and camped in Rephidim; but *there was* no water for the people to drink. Ex. 16:1 • Num. 33:11–15

2 [R]Therefore the people contended with Moses, and said, "Give us water, that we may drink." So Moses said to them, "Why do you contend with me? Why do you [R]tempt the LORD?" Num. 20:2, 3, 13 • [Deut. 6:16]

3 And the people thirsted there for water, and the people [R]complained against Moses, and said, "Why *is* it you have brought us up out of Egypt, to kill us and our children and our livestock with thirst?" Ex. 16:2, 3

4 So Moses [R]cried out to the LORD, saying, "What shall I do with this people? They are almost ready to stone me!" Ex. 14:15

5 And the LORD said to Moses, [R]"Go on before the people, and take with you some of the elders of Israel. Also take in your hand your rod with which [R]you struck the river, and go. Ezek. 2:6 • Num. 20:8

6 "Behold, I will stand before you there on the rock in Horeb; and you shall strike the rock, and water will come out of it, that the people may drink." And Moses did so in the sight of the elders of Israel.

7 So he called the name of the place [R]Massah* and Meribah,* because of the contention of the children of Israel, and because they tempted the LORD, saying, "Is the LORD among us or not?" Num. 20:13, 24; 27:14

Preserved from Defeat

8 [R]Now Amalek came and fought with Israel in Rephidim. Gen. 36:12

9 And Moses said to Joshua, "Choose us some men and go out, fight with Amalek. Tomorrow I will stand on the top of the hill with [R]the rod of God in my hand." Ex. 4:20

10 So Joshua did as Moses said to him, and fought with Amalek. And Moses, Aaron, and Hur went up to the top of the hill.

11 And so it was, when Moses held up his hand, that Israel prevailed; and when he let down his hand, Amalek prevailed.

16:31 Lit. *What?* Ex. 16:15 **17:7** Lit. *Tempted* • Lit. *Contention*

12 But Moses' hands *became* heavy; so they took a stone and put *it* under him, and he sat on it. And Aaron and Hur supported his hands, one on one side, and the other on the other side; and his hands were steady until the going down of the sun.

13 So Joshua defeated Amalek and his people with the edge of the sword.

14 Then the LORD said to Moses, "Write this *for* a memorial in the book and recount *it* in the hearing of Joshua, that [R]I will utterly blot out the remembrance of Amalek from under heaven." 1 Sam. 15:3

15 And Moses built an altar and called its name, The-LORD-Is-My-Banner;*

16 for he said, "Because the LORD has sworn: the LORD *will have* war with Amalek from generation to generation."

CHAPTER 18

Preserved from Chaos—Deut. 1:12–17

AND [R]Jethro, the priest of Midian, Moses' father-in-law, heard of all that [R]God had done for Moses and for Israel His people—that the LORD had brought Israel out of Egypt. Ex. 2:16, 18; 3:1 • [Ps. 106:2, 8]

2 Then Jethro, Moses' father-in-law, took [R]Zipporah, Moses' wife, after he had sent her back, Ex. 2:21; 4:20–26

3 with her two sons, of whom the name of one *was* Gershom (for he said, "I have been a stranger in a foreign land")*

4 and the name of the other *was* Eliezer* (for *he said,* "The God of my father *was* my [R]help, and delivered me from the sword of Pharaoh"); Gen. 49:25

5 and Jethro, Moses' father-in-law, came with his sons and his wife to Moses in the wilderness, where he was encamped at [R]the mountain of God. Ex. 3:1, 12; 4:27; 24:13

6 Now he had said to Moses, "I, your father-in-law Jethro, am coming to you with your wife and her two sons with her."

7 So Moses [R]went out to meet his father-in-law, bowed down, and kissed him. And they asked each other about *their* well-being, and they went into the tent. Gen. 18:2

8 And Moses told his father-in-law all that the LORD had done to Pharaoh and to the Egyptians for Israel's sake, all the hardship that had come upon them on the way, and *how* the LORD had delivered them.

9 Then Jethro rejoiced for all the [R]good which the LORD had done for Israel, whom He had delivered out of the hand of the Egyptians. [Is. 63:7–14]

10 And Jethro said, [R]"Blessed *be* the LORD, who has delivered you out of the hand of the Egyptians and out of the hand of Pharaoh, *and* who has delivered the people from under the hand of the Egyptians. Gen. 14:20

11 "Now I know that the LORD *is* [R]greater than all the gods; for in the very thing in which they behaved [R]proudly, *He was* above them." 2 Chr. 2:5 • Luke 1:51

12 Then Jethro, Moses' father-in-law, took* a burnt [R]offering and *other* sacrifices *to offer* to God. And Aaron came with all the elders of Israel [R]to eat bread with Moses' father-in-law before God. Ex. 24:5 • Deut. 12:7

13 And so it was, on the next day, that Moses [R]sat to judge the people; and the people stood before Moses from morning until evening. Matt. 23:2

14 So when Moses' father-in-law saw all that he did for the people, he said, "What *is* this thing that you are doing for the people? Why do you alone [T]sit, and all the people stand before you from morning until evening?" Sit as judge

15 And Moses said to his father-in-law, "Because [R]the people come to me to inquire of God. Lev. 24:12

16 "When they have [R]a [T]difficulty, they come to me, and I judge between one and another; and I make known the statutes of God and His laws." Ex. 24:14 • *dispute*

17 So Moses' father-in-law said to him, "The thing that you do *is* not good.

18 "Both you and these people who *are* with you will surely wear yourselves out. For this thing *is* too much for you; [R]you are not able to perform it by yourself. Num. 11:14, 17

19 "Listen now to my voice; I will give you counsel, and God will be with you: Stand before God for the people, so that you may [R]bring the difficulties to God. Num. 9:8; 27:5

20 "And you shall [R]teach them the statutes and the laws, and show them the way in which they must walk and [R]the work they must do. Deut. 5:1 • Deut. 1:18

21 "Moreover you shall select from all the people [R]able men, such as [R]fear God, [R]men of truth, [R]hating covetousness; and place *such* over them *to be* rulers of thousands, rulers of hundreds, rulers of fifties, and rulers of tens. Acts 6:3 • 2 Sam. 23:3 • Ezek. 18:8 • Deut. 16:19

22 "And let them judge the people at all times. [R]Then it will be *that* every great matter they shall bring to you, but every small matter they themselves shall judge. So it will be easier for you, for [R]they will bear *the burden* with you. Deut. 1:17 • Num. 11:17

23 "If you do this thing, and God *so* commands you, then you will be able to endure, and all this people will also go to their [R]place in peace." Ex. 16:29

24 So Moses heeded the voice of his father-in-law and did all that he had said.

25 And Moses chose able men out of all Israel, and made them heads over the people:

17:15 Heb. *YHWH Nissi* **18:3** Cf. Ex. 2:22 **18:4** Lit. *My God Is Help* **18:12** So with MT, LXX; Syr., Tg., Vg. *offered*

rulers of thousands, rulers of hundreds, rulers
of fifties, and rulers of tens.
26 So they judged the people at all times; the
hard cases they brought to Moses, but they
judged every small case themselves.
27 Then Moses let his father-in-law depart,
and he went his way to his own land.

CHAPTER 19

Location of the Giving of the Covenant

IN the third month after the children of Is-
rael had gone out of the land of Egypt, on
the same day, [R]they came *to* the Wilderness of
Sinai. Num. 33:15
2 For they had departed from [R]Rephidim,
had come *to* the Wilderness of Sinai, and
camped in the wilderness. So Israel camped
there before [R]the mountain. Ex. 17:1 • Ex. 3:1

Purpose of the Covenant

3 And Moses went up to God, and the LORD
[R]called to him from the mountain, saying,
"Thus you shall say to the house of Jacob, and
tell the children of Israel: Ex. 3:4
4 'You have seen what I did to the Egyp-
tians, and *how* [R]I bore you on eagles' wings
and brought you to Myself. Is. 63:9
5 'Now therefore, if you will indeed obey
My voice and keep My covenant, then [R]you
shall be a special treasure to Me above all
people; for all the earth *is* Mine. Ps. 135:4
6 'And you shall be to Me a [R]kingdom of
priests and a [R]holy nation.' These *are* the
words which you shall speak to the children
of Israel." [1 Pet. 2:5, 9] • Deut. 7:6; 14:21; 26:19

Israel Accepts the Covenant

7 So Moses came and called for the [R]el-
ders of the people, and [T]laid before them all
these words which the LORD commanded
him. Ex. 4:29, 30 • *set*
8 Then [R]all the people answered together
and said, "All that the LORD has spoken we
will do." So Moses brought back the words of
the people to the LORD. Deut. 5:27; 26:17

Israelites Sanctify Themselves

9 And the LORD said to Moses, "Behold, I
come to you in the thick cloud, [R]that the peo-
ple may hear when I speak with you, and be-
lieve you forever." So Moses told the words of
the people to the LORD. Deut. 4:12, 36
10 Then the LORD said to Moses, "Go to the
people and consecrate them today and tomor-
row, and let them wash their clothes.
11 "And let them be ready for the third day.
For on the third day the LORD will come down
upon Mount Sinai in the sight of all the peo-
ple.
12 "You shall set bounds for the people all
around, saying, 'Take heed to yourselves *that*
you do *not* go up to the mountain or touch its
base. [R]Whoever touches the mountain shall
surely be put to death. Heb. 12:20
13 'Not a hand shall touch him, but he shall
surely be stoned or shot *with an arrow;*
whether man or beast, he shall not live.' When
the trumpet sounds long, they shall come near
the mountain."
14 So Moses went down from the mountain
to the people and sanctified the people, and
they washed their clothes.
15 And he said to the people, "Be ready for
the third day; do not come near *your* wives."
16 Then it came to pass on the third day, in
the morning, that there were [R]thunderings
and lightnings, and a thick cloud on the
mountain; and the sound of the trumpet was
very loud, so that all the people who *were* in
the camp trembled. Heb. 12:18, 19
17 And [R]Moses brought the people out of the
camp to meet with God, and they stood at the
foot of the mountain. Deut. 4:10
18 Now [R]Mount Sinai *was* completely in
smoke, because the LORD descended upon it
in fire. Its smoke ascended like the smoke of a

19:5–8 The Mosaic Covenant—The covenant with Moses is the second of the theocratic covenants (pertaining to the rule of God) and is conditional. It is introduced by the conditional formula, "if you will indeed obey My voice . . . then you shall be a special treasure." This covenant was given to the nation Israel so that those who believed God's promise given to Abraham in the Abrahamic covenant (Page 14—Gen. 12:1–3) would know how they should conduct themselves. The Mosaic covenant in its entirety governs three areas of their lives: (1) the commandments governed their personal lives particularly as they related to God (Page 74—Ex. 20:1–26); (2) the judgments governed their social lives particularly as they related to one another (Page 75—Ex. 21:1—24:11); and (3) the ordinances governed their religious lives so that the people would know how to approach God on the terms that He dictates (Page 78—Ex. 24:12—31:18). The Mosaic covenant in no way replaced or set aside the Abrahamic covenant. Its function is clearly set forth by Paul (Page 1198—Gal. 3:17–19), who points out that the law, the Mosaic covenant, came 430 years after the Abrahamic covenant. The Mosaic covenant was added alongside the Abrahamic covenant so that the people of Israel would know how to conduct their lives until "the seed," the Christ, comes and makes the complete and perfect sacrifice, toward which the sacrifices of the Mosaic covenant only point. The Mosaic covenant was never given so that by keeping it people could be saved, but so that they might realize that they cannot do what God wants them to do even when God writes it down on tablets of stone. The law was given that people might realize their helplessness and hopelessness when left to themselves and that their only hope is to receive the righteousness of God by faith in Jesus (Page 1198—Gal. 3:22–24).

Now turn to Page 202—Deut. 29:10–15; 30:11–20: The Palestinian Covenant.

furnace, and the [R]whole mountain* quaked greatly. Deut. 4:11 • Ps. 68:8

19 And when the blast of the trumpet sounded long and became louder and louder, [R]Moses spoke, and [R]God answered him by voice. Heb. 12:21 • Ps. 81:7

20 Then the LORD came down upon Mount Sinai, on the top of the mountain. And the LORD called Moses to the top of the mountain, and Moses went up.

21 And the LORD said to Moses, "Go down and warn the people, lest they break through [R]to gaze at the LORD, and many of them perish. 1 Sam. 6:19

22 "Also let the priests who come near the LORD consecrate themselves, lest the LORD [R]break out against them." 2 Sam. 6:7, 8

23 But Moses said to the LORD, "The people cannot come up to Mount Sinai; for You warned us, saying, [R]'Set bounds around the mountain and consecrate it.' " Ex. 19:12

24 Then the LORD said to him, "Away! Get down and then come up, you and Aaron with you. But do not let the priests and the people break through to come up to the LORD, lest He break out against them."

25 So Moses went down to the people and spoke to them.

CHAPTER 20

Commandments Relating to God

AND God spoke all these words, saying:

2 [R]"I *am* the LORD your God, who brought you out of the land of Egypt, out of the house of bondage. Hos. 13:4

3 [R]"You shall have no other gods before Me. Jer. 25:6; 35:15

4 "You shall not make for yourself a carved image—any likeness *of anything* that *is* in heaven above, or that *is* in the earth beneath, or that *is* in the water under the earth;

5 you shall not bow down to them nor serve them. For I, the LORD your God, *am* a jealous God, visiting the iniquity of the fathers upon the children to the third and fourth *generations* of those who hate Me,

6 but [R]showing mercy to thousands, to those who love Me and keep My commandments. Deut. 7:9

7 [R]"You shall not take the name of the LORD your God in vain, for the LORD will not hold *him* guiltless who takes His name in vain. Lev. 19:12

8 [R]"Remember the Sabbath day, to keep it holy. Lev. 26:2

9 [R]Six days you shall labor and do all your work, Luke 13:14

10 but the [R]seventh day *is* the Sabbath of the LORD your God. *In it* you shall do no work: you, nor your son, nor your daughter, nor your male servant, nor your female servant, nor your cattle, nor your stranger who *is* within your gates. Gen. 2:2, 3

11 For [R]in six days the LORD made the heavens and the earth, the sea, and all that *is* in them, and rested the seventh day. Therefore the LORD blessed the Sabbath day and hallowed it. Ex. 31:17

Commandments Relating to Humans

12 [R]"Honor your father and your mother, that your days may be [R]long upon the land which the LORD your God is giving you. Lev. 19:3; Deut. 5:16

13 [R]"You shall not murder. Rom. 13:9

14 "You shall not commit adultery.

15 [R]"You shall not steal. Lev. 19:11, 13

16 [R]"You shall not bear false witness against your neighbor. Deut. 5:20

17 "You shall not covet your neighbor's house; you shall not covet your neighbor's wife, nor his male servant, nor his female servant, nor his ox, nor his donkey, nor anything that *is* your neighbor's."

The Response of Israel

18 Now [R]all the people [R]witnessed the thunderings, the lightning flashes, the sound of the trumpet, and the mountain smoking; and when the people saw *it,* they trembled and stood afar off. Heb. 12:18, 19 • Rev. 1:10, 12

19 Then they said to Moses, [R]"You speak with us, and we will hear; but let not God speak with us, lest we die." Heb. 12:19

20 And Moses said to the people, [R]"Do not fear; [R]for God has come to test you, and [R]that His fear may be before you, so that you may not sin." [Is. 41:10, 13] • [Deut. 13:3] • Is. 8:13

21 So the people stood afar off, but Moses drew near [R]the thick darkness where God *was.* Ex. 19:16

Provision for Approaching God

22 Then the LORD said to Moses, "Thus you shall say to the children of Israel: 'You have seen that I have talked with you [R]from heaven. Deut. 4:36; 5:24, 26

23 'You shall not make *anything to be* [R]with Me—gods of silver or gods of gold you shall not make for yourselves. Ex. 32:1, 2, 4

24 'An altar of earth you shall make for Me, and you shall sacrifice on it your burnt offerings and your peace offerings, [R]your sheep and your oxen. In every [R]place where I record My name I will come to you, and I will [R]bless you. Ex. 24:5 • 2 Chr. 6:6 • Gen. 12:2

25 'And [R]if you make Me an altar of stone, you shall not build it of hewn stone; for if

19:18 LXX *all the people*

you [R]use your tool on it, you have profaned it. Deut. 27:5 • Josh. 8:30, 31

26 'Nor shall you go up by steps to My altar, that your [R]nakedness may not be exposed on it.' Ex. 28:42, 43

CHAPTER 21

Rights of Persons

"NOW these *are* the judgments which you shall [R]set before them: Deut. 4:14; 6:1

2 [R]"If you buy a Hebrew servant, he shall serve six years; and in the seventh he shall go out free and pay nothing. Jer. 34:14

3 "If he comes in by himself, he shall go out by himself; if he *comes in* married, then his wife shall go out with him.

4 "If his master has given him a wife, and she has borne him sons or daughters, the wife and her children shall be her master's, and he shall go out by himself.

5 [R]"But if the servant plainly says, 'I love my master, my wife, and my children; I will not go out free,' Deut. 15:16, 17

6 "then his master shall bring him to the [R]judges. He shall also bring him to the door, or to the doorpost, and his master shall pierce his ear with an awl; and he shall serve him forever. Ex. 12:12; 22:8, 9

7 "And if a man [R]sells his daughter to be a female slave, she shall not go out as the male slaves do. Neh. 5:5

8 "If she does not please her master, who has betrothed her to himself, then he shall let her be redeemed. He shall have no right to sell her to a foreign people, since he has dealt deceitfully with her.

9 "And if he has betrothed her to his son, he shall deal with her according to the custom of daughters.

10 "If he takes another *wife*, he shall not diminish her food, her clothing, [R]and her marriage rights. [1 Cor. 7:3, 5]

11 "And if he does not do these three for her, then she shall go out free, without *paying* money.

12 [R]"He who strikes a man so that he dies shall surely be put to death. [Matt. 26:52]

13 "However, if he did not lie in wait, but God delivered *him* into his hand, then I will appoint for you a place where he may flee.

14 "But if a man acts with [R]premeditation against his neighbor, to kill him by treachery, [R]you shall take him from My altar, that he may die. Deut. 19:11, 12 • 1 Kin. 2:28–34

15 "And he who strikes his father or his mother shall surely be put to death.

16 [R]"He who kidnaps a man and [R]sells him, or if he is [R]found in his hand, shall surely be put to death. Deut. 24:7 • Gen. 37:28 • Ex. 22:4

17 "And he who curses his father or his mother shall surely be put to death.

18 "If men contend with each other, and one strikes the other with a stone or with *his* fist, and he does not die but is confined to *his* bed,

19 "if he rises again and walks about outside [R]with his staff, then he who struck *him* shall be acquitted. He shall only pay *for* the loss of his time, and shall provide *for him* to be thoroughly healed. 2 Sam. 3:29

20 "And if a man beats his male or female servant with a rod, so that he dies under his hand, he shall surely be punished.

21 "Notwithstanding, if he remains alive a day or two, he shall not be punished; for he *is* his [R]property. Lev. 25:44–46

22 "If men [T]fight, and hurt a woman with child, so that she gives birth prematurely, yet no harm follows, he shall surely be punished accordingly as the woman's husband imposes on him; and he shall [R]pay as the judges *determine*. *struggle* • Ex. 18:21, 22; 21:30

23 "But if *any* harm follows, then you shall give life for life,

24 [R]"eye for eye, tooth for tooth, hand for hand, foot for foot, Lev. 24:20

25 "burn for burn, wound for wound, stripe for stripe.

26 "If a man strikes the eye of his male or female servant, and destroys it, he shall let him go free for the sake of his eye.

27 "And if he knocks out the tooth of his male or female servant, he shall let him go free for the sake of his tooth.

28 "If an ox gores a man or a woman to death, then the ox shall surely be stoned, and its flesh shall not be eaten; but the owner of the ox *shall be* acquitted.

29 "But if the ox [T]tended to thrust with its horn in times past, and it has been made known to his owner, and he has not kept it confined, so that it has killed a man or a woman, the ox shall be stoned and its owner also shall be put to death. *was inclined*

30 "If there is imposed on him a sum of money, then he shall pay [R]to redeem his life, whatever is imposed on him. Num. 35:31

31 "Whether it has gored a son or gored a daughter, according to this judgment it shall be done to him.

32 "If the ox gores a male or female servant, he shall give to their master thirty shekels of silver, and the ox shall be stoned.

Rights of Property

33 "And if a man opens a pit, or if a man digs a pit and does not cover it, and an ox or a donkey falls in it,

34 "the owner of the pit shall make *it* good; he shall give money to their owner, but the dead *animal* shall be his.

35 "If one man's ox hurts another's, so that it dies, then they shall sell the live ox and divide the money from it; and the dead *ox* they shall also divide.

36 "Or if it was known that the ox tended to

thrust in time past, and its owner has not kept it confined, he shall surely pay ox for ox, and the dead animal shall be his own.

CHAPTER 22

"IF a man steals an ox or a sheep, and slaughters it or sells it, he shall [R]restore five oxen for an ox and four sheep for a sheep. 2 Sam. 12:6

2 "If the thief is found [R]breaking in, and he is struck so that he dies, *there shall be* no guilt for his bloodshed. Matt. 6:19; 24:43

3 "If the sun has risen on him, *there shall be* guilt for his bloodshed. He should make full restitution; if he has nothing, then he shall be [R]sold for his theft. Ex. 21:2

4 "If the theft is certainly found alive in his hand, whether it is an ox or donkey or sheep, he shall [R]restore double. Prov. 6:31

5 "If a man causes a field or vineyard to be grazed, and lets loose his animal, and it feeds in another man's field, he shall make restitution from the best of his own field and the best of his own vineyard.

6 "If fire breaks out and catches in thorns, so that stacked grain, standing grain, or the field is consumed, he who kindled the fire shall surely make restitution.

7 "If a man [R]delivers to his neighbor money or articles to keep, and it is stolen out of the man's house, [R]if the thief is found, he shall pay double. Lev. 6:1–7 • Ex. 22:4

8 "If the thief is not found, then the master of the house shall be brought to the [R]judges *to see* whether he has put his hand into his neighbor's goods. Ex. 21:6, 22; 22:28

9 "For any kind of trespass, *whether it concerns* an ox, a donkey, a sheep, or clothing, *or* for any kind of lost thing which *another* claims to be his, the [R]cause of both parties shall come before the judges; *and* whomever the judges condemn shall pay double to his neighbor. Deut. 25:1

10 "If a man delivers to his neighbor a donkey, an ox, a sheep, or any animal to keep, and it dies, is hurt, or driven away, no one seeing *it,*

11 "*then* an [R]oath of the LORD shall be between them both, that he has not put his hand into his neighbor's goods; and the owner of it shall accept *that,* and he shall not make *it* good. Heb. 6:16

12 "But if, in fact, it is stolen from him, he shall make restitution to the owner of it.

13 "If it is [R]torn to pieces *by a beast, then* he shall bring it as evidence, *and* he shall not make good what was torn. Gen. 31:39

14 "And if a man borrows *anything* from his neighbor, and it becomes injured or dies, the owner of it not *being* with it, he shall surely make *it* good.

15 "If its owner *was* with it, he shall not make *it* good; if it *was* hired, it came for its hire.

Proper Conduct

16 "If a man entices a virgin who is not betrothed, and lies with her, he shall surely pay the bride-price for her *to be* his wife.

17 "If her father utterly refuses to give her to him, he shall pay money according to the [R]bride-price of virgins. Gen. 34:12

18 [R]"You shall not permit a sorceress to live. 1 Sam. 28:3–10

19 [R]"Whoever lies with an animal shall surely be put to death. Lev. 18:23; 20:15, 16

20 "He who sacrifices to *any* god, except to the LORD only, he shall be utterly destroyed.

21 [R]"You shall neither mistreat a [T]stranger nor oppress him, for you were strangers in the land of Egypt. Deut. 10:19 • *sojourner*

22 [R]"You shall not afflict any widow or fatherless child. [James 1:27]

23 "If you afflict them in any way, *and* they cry at all to Me, I will surely hear their cry;

24 "and My [R]wrath will become hot, and I will kill you with the sword; [R]your wives shall be widows, and your children fatherless. Ps. 69:24 • Ps. 109:9

25 [R]"If you lend money to *any of* My people *who are* poor among you, you shall not be like a moneylender to him; you shall not charge him [R]interest. Lev. 25:35–37 • Ps. 15:5

26 [R]"If you ever take your neighbor's garment as a pledge, you shall return it to him before the sun goes down. Deut. 24:6, 10–13

27 "For that *is* his only covering, it *is* his garment for his skin. What will he sleep in? And it will be that when he cries to Me, I will hear, for I *am* [R]gracious. Ex. 34:6, 7

28 [R]"You shall not revile God, nor curse a [R]ruler of your people. Eccl. 10:20 • Acts 23:5

29 "You shall not delay *to offer* the first of your ripe produce and your juices. The firstborn of your sons you shall give to Me.

30 [R]"Likewise you shall do with your oxen *and* your sheep. It shall be with its mother [R]seven days; on the eighth day you shall give it to Me. Deut. 15:19 • Lev. 22:27

31 "And you shall be holy men to Me: you shall not eat meat torn *by beasts* in the field; you shall throw it to the dogs.

CHAPTER 23

Proper Justice

"YOU [R]shall not circulate a false report. Do not put your hand with the wicked to be an unrighteous witness. Ps. 101:5

2 "You shall not follow a crowd to do evil; nor shall you testify in a dispute so as to turn aside after many to pervert *justice.*

3 "You shall not show partiality to a [R]poor man in his dispute. Deut. 1:17; 16:19

4 [R]"If you meet your enemy's ox or his don-

key going astray, you shall surely bring it
back to him again. [Rom. 12:20]
5 [R]"If you see the donkey of one who hates
you lying under its burden, and you would re-
frain from helping it, you shall surely help
him with it. Deut. 22:4
6 [R]"You shall not pervert the judgment of
your poor in his dispute. Eccl. 5:8
7 [R]"Keep yourself far from a false matter;
do not kill the innocent and righteous. For I
will not justify the wicked. Eph. 4:25
8 "And [R]you shall take no bribe, for a bribe
blinds the discerning and perverts the words
of the righteous. Prov. 15:27; 17:8, 23
9 "Also [R]you shall not oppress a [T]stranger,
for you know the heart of a stranger, be-
cause you were strangers in the land of
Egypt. Ex. 22:21 • *sojourner*

Sabbatical Year

10 [R]"Six years you shall sow your land and
gather in its produce, Lev. 25:1–7
11 "but the seventh *year* you shall let it rest
and lie fallow, that the poor of your people
may eat; and what they leave, the beasts of the
field may eat. In like manner you shall do with
your vineyard *and* your olive grove.
12 [R]"Six days you shall do your work, and on
the seventh day you shall rest, that your ox
and your donkey may rest, and the son of
your female servant and the stranger may be
refreshed. Luke 13:14
13 "And in all that I have said to you, [R]be cir-
cumspect and [R]make no mention of the name
of other gods, nor let it be heard from your
mouth. 1 Tim. 4:16 • Josh. 23:7

Three National Feasts

14 [R]"Three times you shall keep a feast to Me
in the year: Ex. 23:17; 34:22–24
15 [R]"You shall keep the Feast of Unleavened
Bread (you shall eat unleavened bread seven
days, as I commanded you, at the time ap-
pointed in the month of Abib, for in it you
came out of Egypt; [R]none shall appear before
Me empty); Ex. 12:14–20 • Ex. 22:29; 34:20
16 "and the Feast of Harvest, the firstfruits of
your labors which you have sown in the field;
and the Feast of Ingathering at the end of the
year, when you have gathered in *the fruit of*
your labors from the field.
17 "Three times in the year all your males
shall appear before the Lord GOD.*
18 "You shall not offer the blood of My sac-
rifice with leavened bread; nor shall the fat of
My sacrifice remain until morning.
19 [R]"The first of the firstfruits of your land
you shall bring into the house of the LORD
your God. [R]You shall not boil a young goat in
its mother's milk. Deut. 26:2, 10 • Deut. 14:21

Conquest Regulations

20 [R]"Behold, I send an Angel before you to
keep you in the way and to bring you into the
place which I have prepared. Ex. 3:2
21 "Beware of Him and obey His voice; do
not provoke Him, for He will not pardon your
transgressions; for My name *is* in Him.
22 "But if you indeed obey His voice and do
all that I speak, then [R]I will be an enemy to
your enemies and an adversary to your adver-
saries. Deut. 30:7
23 [R]"For My Angel will go before you and
[R]bring you in to the Amorites and the Hittites
and the Perizzites and the Canaanites and the
Hivites and the Jebusites; and I will cut them
off. Ex. 23:20 • Josh. 24:8, 11
24 "You shall not bow down to their gods,
nor serve them, [R]nor do according to their
works; [R]but you shall utterly overthrow them
and completely break down their *sacred* pil-
lars. Deut. 12:30, 31 • Num. 33:52
25 "So you shall [R]serve the LORD your God,
and [R]He will bless your bread and your water.
And [R]I will take sickness away from the midst
of you. Deut. 6:13 • Deut. 28:5 • Ex. 15:26
26 [R]"No one shall suffer miscarriage or be
barren in your land; I will [R]fulfill the number
of your days. Deut. 7:14; 28:4 • 1 Chr. 23:1
27 "I will send My fear before you, I will
[R]cause confusion among all the people to
whom you come, and will make all your ene-
mies turn *their* backs to you. Deut. 7:23
28 "And I will send hornets before you,
which shall drive out the Hivite, the Canaan-
ite, and the Hittite from before you.
29 [R]"I will not drive them out from before
you in one year, lest the land become desolate
and the beasts of the field become too numer-
ous for you. Deut. 7:22
30 "Little by little I will drive them out from
before you, until you have increased, and you
inherit the land.
31 "And I will set your bounds from the Red
Sea to the sea, Philistia, and from the desert to
the River.* For I will deliver the inhabitants of
the land into your hand, and you shall drive
them out before you.
32 [R]"You shall make no covenant with them,
nor with their gods. Ex. 34:12, 15
33 "They shall not dwell in your land, lest
they make you sin against Me. For *if* you
serve their gods, [R]it will surely be a snare to
you." Ps. 106:36

CHAPTER 24

The Covenant Is Ratified Through Blood

NOW He said to Moses, "Come up to
the LORD, you and Aaron, [R]Nadab and
Abihu, [R]and seventy of the elders of Israel,
and worship from afar. Lev. 10:1, 2 • Num. 11:16
2 "And Moses alone shall come near the

23:17 Heb. *YHWH*, usually translated LORD
23:31 Heb. *Nahar*, the Euphrates

LORD, but they shall not come near; nor shall
the people go up with him."
3 So Moses came and told the people all the
words of the LORD and all the judgments. And
all the people answered with one voice and
said, [R]"All the words which the LORD has said
we will do." Ex. 19:8; 24:7
4 And Moses [R]wrote all the words of the
LORD. And he rose early in the morning, and
built an altar at the foot of the mountain, and
twelve [R]pillars according to the twelve tribes
of Israel. Deut. 31:9 • Gen. 28:18
5 Then he sent young men of the children
of Israel, who offered [R]burnt offerings and
sacrificed peace offerings of oxen to the
LORD. Ex. 18:12; 20:24
6 And Moses [R]took half the blood and put *it*
in basins, and half the blood he sprinkled on
the altar. Heb. 9:18
7 Then he [R]took the Book of the Covenant
and read in the hearing of the people. And
they said, "All that the LORD has said we will
do, and be obedient." Heb. 9:19
8 And Moses took the blood, sprinkled *it* on
the people, and said, "This is the blood of the
covenant which the LORD has made with you
according to all these words."

The God of the Covenant Is Revealed

9 Then Moses went up, also Aaron, Nadab,
and Abihu, and seventy of the elders of Israel,
10 and they saw the God of Israel. And *there*
was under His feet as it were a paved work of
sapphire stone, and it was like the [R]very heav-
ens in *its* clarity. Matt. 17:2
11 But on the nobles of the children of Israel
He did not lay His hand. So they saw God, and
they [R]ate and drank. 1 Cor. 10:18

The Revelation Is Given on Mount Sinai

12 Then the LORD said to Moses, [R]"Come up
to Me on the mountain and be there; and I will
give you tablets of stone, and the law and
commandments which I have written, that
you may teach them." Ex. 24:2, 15
13 So Moses arose with [R]his assistant
Joshua, and Moses went up to the mountain
of God. Ex. 32:17
14 And he said to the elders, "Wait here for
us until we come back to you. Indeed, Aaron
and [R]Hur *are* with you. If any man has a diffi-
culty, let him go to them." Ex. 17:10, 12
15 Then Moses went up into the mountain,
and a cloud covered the mountain.
16 Now the glory of the LORD rested on
Mount Sinai, and the cloud covered it six
days. And on the seventh day He called to Mo-
ses out of the midst of the cloud.
17 The sight of the glory of the LORD *was*
like [R]a consuming fire on the top of the
mountain in the eyes of the children of Is-
rael. Deut. 4:26, 36; 9:3
18 So Moses went into the midst of the cloud
and went up into the mountain. And [R]Moses
was on the mountain forty days and forty
nights. Ex. 34:28

CHAPTER 25

The Offering for the Tabernacle

THEN the LORD spoke to Moses, saying:
2 "Speak to the children of Israel, that
they bring Me an [T]offering. [R]From everyone
who gives it willingly with his heart you shall
take My offering. *heave offering* • Ex. 35:4–9, 21
3 "And this *is* the offering which you shall
take from them: gold, silver, and bronze;
4 "blue, purple, and scarlet *thread,* fine
linen, and goats' *hair;*
5 "ram skins dyed red, [T]badger skins, and
acacia wood; Or *dolphin*
6 "oil for the light, and spices for the
anointing oil and for the sweet incense;
7 "onyx stones, and stones to be set in the
[R]ephod and in the breastplate. Ex. 28:4, 6–14

The Purpose of the Tabernacle

8 "And let them make Me a [R]sanctuary, that
I may dwell among them. Heb. 9:1, 2
9 "According to all that I show you, *that is,*
the pattern of the tabernacle and the pattern
of all its furnishings, just so you shall make *it.*

The Ark of the Covenant

10 [R]"And they shall make an ark of acacia
wood; two and a half cubits *shall be* its length,
a cubit and a half its width, and a cubit and a
half its height. Ex. 37:1–9
11 "And you shall overlay it with pure gold,
inside and out you shall overlay it, and shall
make on it a molding of gold all around.
12 "You shall cast four rings of gold for it,
and put *them* in its four corners; two rings
shall be on one side, and two rings on the
other side.
13 "And you shall make poles *of* acacia
wood, and overlay them with gold.
14 "You shall put the poles into the rings on
the sides of the ark, that the ark may be car-
ried by them.
15 "The poles shall be in the rings of the ark;
they shall not be taken from it.
16 "And you shall put into the ark [R]the Testi-
mony which I will give you. Heb. 9:4
17 [R]"You shall make a mercy seat of pure
gold; two and a half cubits *shall be* its length
and a cubit and a half its width. Ex. 37:6
18 "And you shall make two cherubim of
gold; of hammered work you shall make them
at the two ends of the mercy seat.
19 "Make one cherub at one end, and the
other cherub at the other end; you shall make
the cherubim at the two ends of it *of one piece*
with the mercy seat.
20 "And [R]the cherubim shall stretch out *their*
wings above, covering the mercy seat with

their wings, and they shall face one another; the faces of the cherubim *shall be* toward the mercy seat. 1 Kin. 8:7

21 "You shall put the mercy seat on top of the ark, and [R]in the ark you shall put the Testimony that I will give you. Ex. 25:16

22 "And there I will meet with you, and I will speak with you from above the mercy seat, from between the two cherubim which *are* on the ark of the Testimony, about everything which I will give you in commandment to the children of Israel.

The Table of Showbread

23 "You shall also make a table of acacia wood; two cubits *shall be* its length, a cubit its width, and a cubit and a half its height.

24 "And you shall overlay it with pure gold, and make a molding of gold all around.

25 "You shall make for it a frame of a handbreadth all around, and you shall make a gold molding for the frame all around.

26 "And you shall make for it four rings of gold, and put the rings on the four corners that *are* at its four legs.

27 "The rings shall be close to the frame, as holders for the poles to bear the table.

28 "And you shall make the poles of acacia wood, and overlay them with gold, that the table may be carried with them.

29 "You shall make [R]its dishes, its pans, its pitchers, and its bowls for pouring. You shall make them of pure gold. Ex. 37:16

30 "And you shall set the [R]showbread on the table before Me always. Lev. 24:5–9

The Golden Lampstand

31 [R]"You shall also make a lampstand of pure gold; the lampstand shall be of hammered work. Its shaft, its branches, its bowls, its *ornamental* knobs, and flowers shall be *of one piece.* Zech. 4:2

32 "And six branches shall come out of its sides: three branches of the lampstand out of one side, and three branches of the lampstand out of the other side.

33 [R]"Three bowls *shall be* made like almond *blossoms* on one branch, *with* an *ornamental* knob and a flower, and three bowls made like almond *blossoms* on the other branch, *with* an *ornamental* knob and a flower—and so for the six branches that come out of the lampstand. Ex. 37:19

34 "On the lampstand itself four bowls *shall be* made like almond *blossoms, each with* its *ornamental* knob and flower.

35 "And *there shall be* a knob under the *first* two branches of the same, a knob under the *second* two branches of the same, and a knob under the *third* two branches of the same, according to the six branches that extend from the lampstand.

36 "Their knobs and their branches *shall be of one piece;* all of it *shall be* one hammered piece of pure gold.

37 "You shall make seven lamps for it, and [R]they shall arrange its lamps so that they [R]give light in front of it. Lev. 24:3, 4 • Num. 8:2

38 "And its wick-trimmers and their trays *shall be* of pure gold.

39 "It shall be made of a talent of pure gold, with all these utensils.

40 "And [R]see to it that you make *them* according to the pattern which was shown you on the mountain. [Heb. 8:5]

CHAPTER 26

The Curtains of Linen

"MOREOVER [R]you shall make the tabernacle *with* ten curtains *of* fine woven linen, and blue, purple, and scarlet *thread;* with artistic designs of cherubim you shall weave them. Ex. 36:8–19

2 "The length of each curtain *shall be* twenty-eight cubits, and the width of each curtain four cubits. And every one of the curtains shall have [T]the same measurements. Lit. *one measure*

3 "Five curtains shall be coupled to one another, and *the other* five curtains *shall be* coupled to one another.

4 "And you shall make loops of blue *yarn* on the edge of the curtain on the selvedge of *one* set, and likewise you shall do on the outer edge of *the other* curtain of the second set.

5 "Fifty loops you shall make in the one curtain, and fifty loops you shall make on the edge of the curtain that *is* on the end of the second set, that the loops may be clasped to one another.

6 "And you shall make fifty clasps of gold, and couple the curtains together with the clasps, so that it may be one tabernacle.

7 [R]"You shall also make curtains of goats' *hair,* to be a tent over the tabernacle. You shall make eleven curtains. Ex. 36:14

8 "The length of each curtain *shall be* thirty cubits, and the width of each curtain four cubits; and the eleven curtains shall all have the same measurements.

9 "And you shall couple five curtains by themselves and six curtains by themselves, and you shall double over the sixth curtain at the forefront of the tent.

10 "You shall make fifty loops on the edge of the curtain that is outermost in *one* set, and fifty loops on the edge of the curtain of the second set.

11 "And you shall make fifty bronze clasps, put the clasps into the loops, and couple the tent together, that it may be one.

12 "The remnant that remains of the curtains of the tent, the half curtain that remains, shall hang over the back of the tabernacle.

13 "And a cubit on one side and a cubit on

the other side, of what remains of the length
of the curtains of the tent, shall hang over the
sides of the tabernacle, on this side and on
that side, to cover it.
14 R"You shall also make a covering of ram
skins dyed red for the tent, and a covering of
badger skins above that. Ex. 35:7, 23; 36:19

The Boards and Sockets

15 "And for the tabernacle you shall make
the boards of acacia wood, standing upright.
16 "Ten cubits *shall be* the length of a board,
and a cubit and a half *shall be* the width of
each board.
17 "Two tenons *shall be* in each board for
binding one to another. Thus you shall make
for all the boards of the tabernacle.
18 "And you shall make the boards for the
tabernacle, twenty boards for the south side.
19 "You shall make forty sockets of silver
under the twenty boards: two sockets under
each of the boards for its two tenons.
20 "And for the second side of the taberna-
cle, the north side, *there shall be* twenty
boards
21 "and their forty sockets of silver: two
sockets under each of the boards.
22 "For the far side of the tabernacle, west-
ward, you shall make six boards.
23 "And you shall also make two boards for
the two back corners of the tabernacle.
24 "They shall be coupled together at the
bottom and they shall be coupled together at
the top by one ring. Thus it shall be for both of
them. They shall be for the two corners.
25 "So there shall be eight boards with their
sockets of silver—sixteen sockets—two sock-
ets under each of the boards.
26 "And you shall make bars of acacia wood:
five for the boards on one side of the taberna-
cle,
27 "five bars for the boards on the other side
of the tabernacle, and five bars for the boards
of the side of the tabernacle, for the far side
westward.
28 "The middle bar shall pass through the
midst of the boards from end to end.
29 "You shall overlay the boards with gold,
make their rings of gold *as* holders for the
bars, and overlay the bars with gold.
30 "And you shall raise up the tabernacle
Raccording to its pattern which you were
shown on the mountain. Acts 7:44

The Inner Veil

31 R"You shall make a veil woven of blue,
purple, and scarlet *thread,* and fine woven
linen. It shall be woven with an artistic design
of cherubim. Matt. 27:51
32 "You shall hang it upon the four pillars of
acacia *wood* overlaid with gold. Their hooks
shall be gold, upon four sockets of silver.
33 "And you shall hang the veil from the
clasps. Then you shall bring the ark of the
Testimony in there, behind the veil. The veil
shall be a divider for you between Rthe holy
place and the Most Holy. Heb. 9:2, 3
34 "You shall put the mercy seat upon the
ark of the Testimony in the Most Holy.
35 R"You shall set the table outside the veil,
and Rthe lampstand across from the table on
the side of the tabernacle toward the south;
and you shall put the table on the north
side. Ex. 40:22 • Ex. 40:24

The Outer Veil

36 R"You shall make a screen for the door of
the tabernacle, *woven of* blue, purple, and
scarlet *thread,* and fine woven linen, made by
a weaver. Ex. 36:37
37 "And you shall make for the screen five
pillars of acacia *wood,* and overlay them with
gold; their hooks *shall be* gold, and you shall
cast five sockets of bronze for them.

CHAPTER 27

The Bronze Altar

"YOU shall make Ran altar of acacia
wood, five cubits long and five cubits
wide—the altar shall be square—and its
height *shall be* three cubits. Ex. 38:1
2 "You shall make its horns on its four cor-
ners; its horns shall be of one piece with it.
And you shall overlay it with bronze.
3 "Also you shall make its pans to receive
its ashes, and its shovels and its basins and its
forks and its firepans; you shall make all its
utensils of bronze.
4 "You shall make a grate for it, a network
of bronze; and on the network you shall make
four bronze rings at its four corners.
5 "You shall put it under the rim of the altar
beneath, that the network may be midway up
the altar.
6 "And you shall make poles for the altar,
poles of acacia wood, and overlay them with
bronze.
7 "The poles shall be put in the rings, and
the poles shall be on the two sides of the altar
to bear it.
8 "You shall make it hollow with boards;
Ras it was shown you on the mountain, so
shall they make *it.* Ex. 25:40; 26:30

The Court of the Tabernacle

9 "You shall also make the court of the tab-
ernacle. For the south side *there shall be*
hangings for the court *made of* fine woven
linen, one hundred cubits long for one side.
10 "And its twenty pillars and their twenty
sockets *shall be* bronze. The hooks of the pil-
lars and their bands *shall be* silver.
11 "Likewise along the length of the north
side *there shall be* hangings one hundred *cu-
bits* long, with its twenty pillars and their

twenty sockets of bronze, and the hooks of
the pillars and their bands of silver.
12 "And along the width of the court on the
west side *shall be* hangings of fifty cubits,
with their ten pillars and their ten sockets.
13 "The width of the court on the east side
shall be fifty cubits.
14 "The hangings on *one* side *of the gate*
shall be fifteen cubits, *with* their three pillars
and their three sockets.
15 "And on the other side *shall be* hangings
of fifteen *cubits, with* their three pillars and
their three sockets.
16 "For the gate of the court *there shall be* a
screen twenty cubits long, *woven of* blue, pur-
ple, and scarlet *thread*, and fine woven linen,
made by a weaver. It *shall have* four pillars
and four sockets.
17 "All the pillars around the court shall
have bands of silver; their [R]hooks *shall be* of
silver and their sockets of bronze. Ex. 38:19
18 "The length of the court *shall be* one hun-
dred cubits, the width fifty throughout, and
the height five cubits, *made of* fine woven
linen, and its sockets of bronze.
19 "All the utensils of the tabernacle for all
its service, all its pegs, and all the pegs of the
court, *shall be* of bronze.

The Oil for the Lamp

20 "And [R]you shall command the children of
Israel that they bring you pure oil of pressed
olives for the light, to cause the lamp to burn
continually. Lev. 24:1–4
21 "In the tabernacle of meeting, outside the
veil which *is* before the Testimony, [R]Aaron
and his sons shall tend it from evening until
morning before the LORD. *It shall be* a statute
forever to their generations on behalf of the
children of Israel. Ex. 30:8

CHAPTER 28

The Command to Make the Priests' Clothes

"NOW take Aaron your brother, and his
sons with him, from among the chil-
dren of Israel, that he may minister to Me as
[R]priest, Aaron *and* Aaron's sons: [R]Nadab,
Abihu, Eleazar, and Ithamar. Heb. 5:4 • Lev. 10:1
2 "And you shall make holy garments for
Aaron your brother, for glory and for beauty.
3 "So [R]you shall speak to all *who are* gifted
artisans, whom I have filled with the spirit of
wisdom, that they may make Aaron's gar-
ments, to consecrate him, that he may minis-
ter to Me as priest. Ex. 31:6; 36:1
4 "And these *are* the garments which they
shall make: a breastplate, an ephod,* a robe, a
skillfully woven tunic, a turban, and [R]a sash.
So they shall make holy garments for Aaron
your brother and his sons, that he may minis-
ter to Me as priest. Lev. 8:7
5 "They shall take the gold, blue, purple,
and scarlet *thread*, and the fine linen,

The Ephod

6 [R]"and they shall make the ephod of gold,
blue, purple, *and* scarlet *thread*, and fine
woven linen, artistically worked. Ex. 39:2–7
7 "It shall have two shoulder straps joined
at its two edges, and *so* it shall be joined to-
gether.
8 "And the intricately woven band of the
ephod, which *is* on it, shall be of the same
workmanship, *made of* gold, blue, purple, and
scarlet *thread*, and fine woven linen.
9 "Then you shall take two onyx [R]stones
and engrave on them the names of the sons of
Israel: Ex. 35:27
10 "six of their names on one stone and six
names on the other stone, in order of their
[R]birth. Gen. 29:31—30:24; 35:16–18
11 "With the work of an [R]engraver in stone,
like the engravings of a signet, you shall en-
grave the two stones with the names of the
sons of Israel. You shall set them in settings of
gold. Ex. 35:35
12 "And you shall put the two stones on the
shoulders of the ephod *as* memorial stones for
the sons of Israel. So Aaron shall bear their
names before the LORD on his two shoulders
[R]as a memorial. Josh. 4:7
13 "You shall also make settings of gold,
14 "and you shall make two chains of pure
gold like braided cords, and fasten the
braided chains to the settings.

The Breastplate

15 [R]"You shall make the breastplate of judg-
ment. Artistically woven according to the
workmanship of the ephod you shall make it:
of gold, blue, purple, and scarlet *thread*, and
fine woven linen, you shall make it. Ex. 39:8–21
16 "It shall be doubled into a square: a span
shall be its length, and a span *shall be* its
width.
17 [R]"And you shall put settings of stones in
it, four rows of stones: *The first* row *shall be* a
[T]sardius, a topaz, and an emerald; *this shall be*
the first row; Ex. 39:10 • Or *ruby*
18 "the second row *shall be* a turquoise, a
sapphire, and a diamond;
19 "the third row, a [T]jacinth, an agate, and an
amethyst; Or *amber*
20 "and the fourth row, a [T]beryl, an [T]onyx,
and a jasper. They shall be set in gold set-
tings. Or *yellow jasper* • Or *carnelian*
21 "And the stones shall have the names of
the sons of Israel, twelve according to their
names, *like* the engravings of a signet, each
one with its own name; they shall be accord-
ing to the twelve tribes.

28:4 Ornamented vest

22 "You shall make chains for the breastplate at the end, like braided cords of pure gold.

23 "And you shall make two rings of gold for the breastplate, and put the two rings on the two ends of the breastplate.

24 "Then you shall put the two braided *chains* of gold in the two rings which are on the ends of the breastplate;

25 "and the *other* two ends of the two braided *chains* you shall fasten to the two settings, and put them on the shoulder straps of the ephod in the front.

26 "You shall make two rings of gold, and put them on the two ends of the breastplate, on the edge of it, which is on the inner side of the ephod.

27 "And two *other* rings of gold you shall make, and put them on the two shoulder straps, underneath the ephod toward its front, right at the seam above the [T]intricately woven band of the ephod. *ingenious work of*

28 "They shall bind the breastplate by means of its rings to the rings of the ephod, using a blue cord, so that it is above the intricately woven band of the ephod, and so that the breastplate does not come loose from the ephod.

29 "So Aaron shall [R]bear the names of the sons of Israel on the breastplate of judgment over his heart, when he goes into the holy *place,* as a memorial before the LORD continually. Ex. 28:12

The Urim and Thummim

30 "And you shall put in the breastplate of judgment the Urim and the Thummim,* and they shall be over Aaron's heart when he goes in before the LORD. So Aaron shall bear the judgment of the children of Israel over his heart before the LORD continually.

The Robe of the Ephod

31 [R]"You shall make the robe of the ephod all of blue. Ex. 39:22–26

32 "There shall be an opening for his head in the middle of it; it shall have a woven binding all around its opening, like the opening in a coat of mail, so that it does not tear.

33 "And upon its hem you shall make pomegranates of blue, purple, and scarlet, all around its hem, and bells of gold between them all around:

34 "a golden bell and a pomegranate, a golden bell and a pomegranate, upon the hem of the robe all around.

35 "And it shall be upon Aaron when he ministers, and its sound will be heard when he goes into the holy *place* before the LORD and when he comes out, that he may not die.

The Holy Crown

36 [R]"You shall also make a plate of pure gold and engrave on it, *like* the engraving of a signet: Ex. 39:30, 31

HOLINESS TO THE LORD.

37 "And you shall put it on a blue cord, that it may be on the turban; it shall be on the front of the turban.

38 "So it shall be on Aaron's forehead, that Aaron may [R]bear the iniquity of the holy things which the children of Israel hallow in all their holy gifts; and it shall always be on his forehead, that they may be [R]accepted before the LORD. [1 Pet. 2:24] • Lev. 1:4; 22:27; 23:11

The Priest's Coat

39 "You shall [R]skillfully weave the tunic of fine linen *thread,* you shall make the turban of fine linen, and you shall make the sash of woven work. Ex. 35:35; 39:27–29

40 [R]"For Aaron's sons you shall make tunics, and you shall make sashes for them. And you shall make hats for them, for glory and [R]beauty. Ezek. 44:17, 18 • Ex. 28:2

41 "So you shall put them on Aaron your brother and on his sons with him. You shall [R]anoint them, [R]consecrate them, and [T]sanctify them, that they may minister to Me as priests. Lev. 10:7 • Lev. 8 • *set them apart*

42 "And you shall make for them linen trousers to cover their nakedness; they shall reach from the waist to the thighs.

43 "They shall be on Aaron and on his sons when they come into the tabernacle of meeting, or when they come near [R]the altar to minister in the holy *place,* that they [R]do not incur [T]iniquity and die. [R]*It shall be* a statute forever to him and his descendants after him. Ex. 20:26 • Num. 9:13; 18:22 • *guilt* • Ex. 27:21

CHAPTER 29

The Consecration of the Priests

"AND this is what you shall do to them to hallow them for ministering to Me as priests: [R]Take one young bull and two rams without blemish, [Heb. 7:26–28]

2 "and [R]unleavened bread, unleavened cakes mixed with oil, and unleavened wafers anointed with oil (you shall make them of wheat flour). Lev. 2:4; 6:19–23

3 "You shall put them in one basket and bring them in the basket, with the bull and the two rams.

4 "And Aaron and his sons you shall bring to the door of the tabernacle of meeting, and you shall wash them with water.

5 [R]"Then you shall take the garments, put the tunic on Aaron, and the robe of the ephod, the ephod, and the breastplate, and gird him with [R]the intricately woven band of the ephod. Ex. 28:2 • Ex. 28:8

6 "You shall put the turban on his head, and put the holy crown on the turban.

28:30 Lit. *Lights and the Perfections*

7 "And you shall take the anointing oil, pour *it* on his head, and anoint him.

8 "Then [R]you shall bring his sons and put tunics on them. Ex. 28:39, 40

9 "And you shall gird them with sashes, Aaron and his sons, and put the hats on them. [R]The priesthood shall be theirs for a perpetual statute. So you shall [R]consecrate Aaron and his sons. Num. 3:10 • Ex. 28:41

10 "You shall also have the bull brought before the tabernacle of meeting, and [R]Aaron and his sons shall put their hands on the head of the bull. Lev. 1:4; 8:14

11 "Then you shall kill the bull before the LORD, *by* the door of the tabernacle of meeting.

12 "You shall take *some* of the blood of the bull and put *it* on [R]the horns of the altar with your finger, and [R]pour all the blood beside the base of the altar. Lev. 8:15 • Ex. 27:2

13 "And you shall take all the fat that covers the entrails, the fatty lobe *attached* to the liver, and the two kidneys and the fat that *is* on them, and burn *them* on the altar.

14 "But [R]the flesh of the bull, with its skin and its offal, you shall burn with fire outside the camp. It *is* a sin offering. Lev. 4:11, 12

15 [R]"You shall also take one ram, and Aaron and his sons shall [R]put their hands on the head of the ram; Lev. 8:18 • Lev. 1:4–9

16 "and you shall kill the ram, and you shall take its blood and [R]sprinkle *it* all around on the altar. Ex. 24:6

17 "Then you shall cut the ram in pieces, wash its entrails and its legs, and put *them* with its pieces and with its head.

18 "And you shall burn the whole ram on the altar. It *is* a [R]burnt offering to the LORD; it *is* a sweet aroma, an offering made by fire to the LORD. Ex. 20:24

19 [R]"You shall also take the other ram, and Aaron and his sons shall put their hands on the head of the ram. Lev. 8:22

20 "Then you shall kill the ram, and take some of its blood and put *it* on the tip of the right ear of Aaron and on the tip of the right ear of his sons, on the thumb of their right hand and on the big toe of their right foot, and sprinkle the blood all around on the altar.

21 "And you shall take some of the blood that is on the altar, and some of the anointing oil, and sprinkle *it* on Aaron and on his garments, on his sons and on the garments of his sons with him; and [R]he and his garments shall be hallowed, and his sons and his sons' garments with him. [Heb. 9:22]

22 "Also you shall take the fat of the ram, the fat tail, the fat that covers the entrails, the fatty lobe *attached to* the liver, the two kidneys and the fat on them, the right thigh (for it *is* a ram of consecration),

23 "one loaf of bread, one cake *made with* oil, and one wafer from the basket of the unleavened bread that *is* before the LORD;

24 "and you shall put all these in the hands of Aaron and in the hands of his sons, and you shall [R]wave them *as* a wave offering before the LORD. Lev. 7:30; 10:14

25 [R]"You shall receive them back from their hands and burn *them* on the altar as a burnt offering, as a sweet aroma before the LORD. It *is* an offering made by fire to the LORD. Lev. 8:28

26 "Then you shall take [R]the breast of the ram of Aaron's consecration and wave it *as* a wave offering before the LORD; and it shall be your portion. Lev. 7:31, 34; 8:29

27 "And from the ram of the consecration you shall consecrate the breast of the wave offering which is waved, and the thigh of the heave offering which is raised, of *that* which *is* for Aaron and of *that* which is for his sons.

28 "It shall be from the children of Israel *for* Aaron and his sons [R]by a statute forever. For it is a heave offering; it shall be a heave offering from the children of Israel from the sacrifices of their peace offerings, *that is*, their heave offering to the LORD. Lev. 10:15

29 "And the holy garments of Aaron shall be his sons' after him, to be anointed in them and to be consecrated in them.

30 [R]"That son who becomes priest in his place shall put them on for seven days, when he enters the tabernacle of meeting to minister in the holy *place*. Num. 20:28

31 "And you shall take the ram of the consecration and boil its flesh in the holy place.

32 "Then Aaron and his sons shall eat the flesh of the ram, and the [R]bread that *is* in the basket, *by* the door of the tabernacle of meeting. Matt. 12:4

33 "They shall eat those things with which the atonement was made, to consecrate *and* to sanctify them; [R]but an outsider shall not eat *them*, because they *are* holy. Lev. 22:10

34 "And if any of the flesh of the consecration offerings, or of the bread, remains until the morning, then [R]you shall burn the remainder with fire. It shall not be eaten, because it *is* holy. Lev. 7:18; 8:32

35 "Thus you shall do to Aaron and his sons, according to all that I have commanded you. [R]Seven days you shall consecrate them. Lev. 8:33–35

36 "And you shall offer a bull every day *as* a sin offering for atonement. You shall cleanse the altar when you make atonement for it, and you shall anoint it to sanctify it.

37 "Seven days you shall make atonement for the altar and sanctify it. And the altar shall be most holy. [R]Whatever touches the altar must be holy.* Matt. 23:19

The Continual Offerings of the Priests

38 "Now this *is* what you shall offer on the altar: two lambs of the first year, [R]day by day continually. Dan. 12:11

29:37 Cf. Num. 4:15 and Hag. 2:11–13

39 "One lamb you shall offer [R]in the morning, and the other lamb you shall offer at twilight. Ezek. 46:13–15

40 "With the one lamb shall be one-tenth *of an ephah* of flour mixed with one-fourth of a hin of pressed oil, and one-fourth of a hin of wine *as* a drink offering.

41 "And the other lamb you shall [R]offer at twilight; and you shall offer with it the grain offering and the drink offering, as in the morning, for a sweet aroma, an offering made by fire to the LORD. 2 Kin. 16:15

42 "*This shall be* a continual burnt offering throughout your generations *at* the door of the tabernacle of meeting before the LORD, where I will meet you to speak with you.

43 "And there I will meet with the children of Israel, and *the tabernacle* [R]shall be sanctified by My glory. 1 Kin. 8:11

44 "So I will consecrate the tabernacle of meeting and the altar. I will also [R]consecrate both Aaron and his sons to minister to Me as priests. Lev. 21:15

45 [R]"I will dwell among the children of Israel and will be their God. [Rev. 21:3]

46 "And they shall know that I *am* the LORD their God, who [R]brought them up out of the land of Egypt, that I may dwell among them. I *am* the LORD their God. Lev. 11:45

CHAPTER 30

The Altar of Incense

"YOU shall make an altar to burn incense on; you shall make it of acacia wood.

2 "A cubit *shall be* its length and a cubit its width—it shall be square—and two cubits *shall be* its height. Its horns *shall be* of one piece with it.

3 "And you shall overlay its top, its sides all around, and its horns with pure gold; and you shall make for it a [T]molding of gold all around. *border*

4 "Two gold rings you shall make for it, under the molding on both its sides. You shall place *them* on its two sides, and they will be holders for the poles with which to bear it.

5 "You shall make the poles of acacia wood, and overlay them with gold.

6 "And you shall put it before the veil that *is* before the ark of the Testimony, before the mercy seat that *is* over the Testimony, where I will meet with you.

7 "Aaron shall burn on it [R]sweet incense every morning; when he tends the lamps, he shall burn incense on it. 1 Sam. 2:28

8 "And when Aaron lights the lamps [T]at twilight, he shall burn incense on it, a perpetual incense before the LORD throughout your generations. Lit. *between the two evenings*

9 "You shall not offer strange incense on it, or a burnt offering, or a grain offering; nor shall you pour a drink offering on it.

10 "And [R]Aaron shall make atonement upon its horns once a year with the blood of the sin offering of atonement; once a year he shall make atonement upon it throughout your generations. It *is* most holy to the LORD." Lev. 16:3–34

The Ransom Money

11 Then the LORD spoke to Moses, saying:

12 [R]"When you take the census of the children of Israel for their number, then every man shall give [R]a ransom for himself to the LORD, when you number them, that there may be no plague among them when *you* number them. Num. 1:2; 26:2 • [1 Pet. 1:18, 19]

13 [R]"This is what everyone among those who are numbered shall give: half a shekel according to the shekel of the sanctuary (a shekel *is* twenty gerahs). The half-shekel *shall be* an offering to the LORD. Matt. 17:24

14 "Everyone included among those who are numbered, from twenty years old and above, shall give an offering to the LORD.

15 "The [R]rich shall not give more and the poor shall not give less than half a shekel, when *you* give an offering to the LORD, to make atonement for yourselves. [Eph. 6:9]

16 "And you shall take the atonement money of the children of Israel, and [R]shall [T]appoint it for the service of the tabernacle of meeting, that it may be a memorial for the children of Israel before the LORD, to make atonement for yourselves." Ex. 38:25–31 • *give*

The Laver of Bronze

17 Then the LORD spoke to Moses, saying:

18 [R]"You shall also make a [T]laver of bronze, with its base also of bronze, for washing. You shall [R]put it between the tabernacle of meeting and the altar. And you shall put water in it, Ex. 38:8 • *basin* • Ex. 40:30

19 "for Aaron and his sons [R]shall wash their hands and their feet in water from it. Ex. 40:31, 32

20 "When they go into the tabernacle of meeting, or when they come near the altar to minister, to burn an offering made by fire to the LORD, they shall wash with water, lest they die.

21 "So they shall wash their hands and their feet, lest they die. And it shall be a statute forever to them—to him and his descendants throughout their generations."

The Anointing Oil

22 Moreover the LORD spoke to Moses, saying:

23 "Also take for yourself quality spices—five hundred *shekels* of liquid myrrh, half as much sweet-smelling cinnamon (two hundred and fifty *shekels*), two hundred and fifty *shekels* of sweet-smelling cane,

24 "five hundred *shekels* of [R]cassia, accord-

ing to the shekel of the sanctuary, and a [R]hin of olive oil. Ps. 45:8 • Ex. 29:40

25 "And you shall make from these a holy anointing oil, an ointment compounded according to the art of the perfumer. It shall be [R]a holy anointing oil. Ex. 37:29; 40:9

26 "With it you shall anoint the tabernacle of meeting and the ark of the Testimony;

27 "the table and all its utensils, the lampstand and its utensils, and the altar of incense;

28 "the altar of burnt offering with all its utensils, and the laver and its base.

29 "You shall consecrate them, that they may be most holy; [R]whatever touches them must be holy.* Ex. 29:37

30 [R]"And you shall anoint Aaron and his sons, and consecrate them, that *they* may minister to Me as priests. Lev. 8:12

31 "And you shall speak to the children of Israel, saying: 'This shall be a holy anointing oil to Me throughout your generations.

32 'It shall not be poured on man's flesh; nor shall you make *any other* like it, according to its composition. [R]It *is* holy, *and* it shall be holy to you. Ex. 30:25, 37

33 'Whoever compounds *any* like it, or whoever puts *any* of it on an outsider, [R]shall be cut off from his people.' " Gen. 17:14

The Incense

34 And the LORD said to Moses: [R]"Take sweet spices, stacte and onycha and galbanum, and pure frankincense with *these* sweet spices; there shall be equal amounts of each. Ex. 25:6; 37:29

35 "You shall make of these an incense, a compound [R]according to the art of the perfumer, salted, pure, *and* holy. Ex. 30:25

36 "And you shall beat *some* of it very fine, and put some of it before the Testimony in the tabernacle of meeting where I will meet with you. It shall be most holy to you.

37 "But *as for* the incense which you shall make, [R]you shall not make any for yourselves, according to its composition. It shall be to you holy for the LORD. Ex. 30:32

38 "Whoever makes *any* like it, to smell it, he shall be cut off from his people."

CHAPTER 31

Instructions for Building the Tabernacle

THEN the LORD spoke to Moses, saying:

2 [R]"See, I have called by name Bezalel the [R]son of Uri, the son of Hur, of the tribe of Judah. Ex. 35:30—36:1 • 1 Chr. 2:20

3 "And I have filled him with the Spirit of God, in wisdom, in understanding, in knowledge, and in all *manner of* workmanship,

4 "to design artistic works, to work in gold, in silver, in bronze,

5 "in cutting jewels for setting, in carving wood, and to work in all *manner of* workmanship.

6 "And I, indeed I, have appointed with him Aholiab the son of Ahisamach, of the tribe of Dan; and I have put wisdom in the hearts of all the gifted artisans, that they may make all that I have commanded you:

7 "the tabernacle of meeting, the ark of the Testimony and the mercy seat that *is* on it, and all the furniture of the tabernacle—

8 [R]"the table and its utensils, [R]the pure *gold* lampstand with all its utensils, the altar of incense, Ex. 37:10–16 • Ex. 37:17–24

9 "the altar of burnt offering with all its utensils, and the laver and its base—

10 "the garments of ministry,* the holy garments for Aaron the priest and the garments of his sons, to minister as priests,

11 "and the anointing oil and sweet incense for the holy *place*. According to all that I have commanded you they shall do."

Sign of the Covenant: The Sabbath

12 And the LORD spoke to Moses, saying,

13 "Speak also to the children of Israel, saying: 'Surely My Sabbaths you shall keep, for it *is* a sign between Me and you throughout your generations, that *you* may know that I *am* the LORD who sanctifies you.

14 [R]'You shall keep the Sabbath, therefore, for *it is* holy to you. Everyone who [T]profanes it shall surely be put to death; for whoever does *any* work on it, that person shall be cut off from among his people. Ex. 20:8 • *defiles*

15 'Work shall be done for [R]six days, but the [R]seventh *is* the Sabbath of rest, holy to the LORD. Whoever does *any* work on the Sabbath day, he shall surely be put to death. Ex. 20:9–11 • Gen. 2:2

16 'Therefore the children of Israel shall keep the Sabbath, to observe the Sabbath throughout their generations *as* a perpetual covenant.

17 'It *is* [R]a sign between Me and the children of Israel forever; for [R]*in* six days the LORD made the heavens and the earth, and on the seventh day He rested and was refreshed.' " Ex. 31:13 • Gen. 1:31; 2:2, 3

Two Tablets Are Presented

18 And when He had made an end of speaking with him on Mount Sinai, He gave Moses two tablets of the Testimony, tablets of stone, written with the finger of God.

CHAPTER 32

Israel Willfully Breaks the Covenant

NOW when the people saw that Moses delayed coming down from the mountain,

30:29 Cf. Num. 4:15 and Hag. 2:11–13 **31:10** Or *woven garments*

the people [R]gathered together to Aaron, and said to him, [R]"Come, make us gods that shall [R]go before us; for *as for* this Moses, the man who [R]brought us up out of the land of Egypt, we do not know what has become of him." Ex. 17:1–3 • Acts 7:40 • Ex. 13:21 • Ex. 32:8

2 And Aaron said to them, "Break off the [R]golden earrings which *are* in the ears of your wives, your sons, and your daughters, and bring *them* to me." Ex. 11:2; 35:22

3 So all the people broke off the golden earrings which *were* in their ears, and brought *them* to Aaron.

4 And he received *the gold* from their hand, and he fashioned it with an engraving tool, and made a molded calf. Then they said, "This *is* your god, O Israel, that brought you out of the land of Egypt!"

5 So when Aaron saw *it*, he built an altar before it. And Aaron made a proclamation and said, "Tomorrow *is* a feast to the LORD."

6 Then they rose early on the next day, offered burnt offerings, and brought peace offerings; and the people [R]sat down to eat and drink, and rose up to play. Num. 25:2

God to Destroy Israel

7 And the LORD said to Moses, [R]"Go, get down! For your people whom you brought out of the land of Egypt [R]have corrupted *themselves.* Deut. 9:8–21 • Gen. 6:11, 12

8 "They have turned aside quickly out of the way which I commanded them. They have made themselves a molded calf, and worshiped it and sacrificed to it, and said, [R]'This *is* your god, O Israel, that brought you out of the land of Egypt!' " 1 Kin. 12:28

9 And the LORD said to Moses, [R]"I have seen this people, and indeed it *is* a [T]stiff-necked people! [Acts 7:51] • *stubborn*

10 "Now therefore, [R]let Me alone, that [R]My wrath may burn hot against them and I may [T]consume them. And I will make of you a great nation." Deut. 9:14, 19 • Ex. 22:24 • *destroy*

Moses Intercedes for Israel

11 Then Moses pleaded with the LORD his God, and said: "LORD, why does Your wrath burn hot against Your people whom You have brought out of the land of Egypt with great power and with a mighty hand?

12 [R]"Why should the Egyptians speak, and say, 'He brought them out to harm them, to kill them in the mountains, and to consume them from the face of the earth'? Turn from Your fierce wrath, and [R]relent from this harm to Your people. Num. 14:13–19 • Ex. 32:14

13 "Remember Abraham, Isaac, and Israel, Your servants, to whom You [R]swore by Your own self, and said to them, 'I will multiply your descendants as the stars of heaven; and all this land that I have spoken of I give to your descendants, and they shall inherit *it* forever.' "* [Heb. 6:13]

14 So the LORD relented from the harm which He said He would do to His people.

Moses Disciplines Israel

15 And Moses turned and went down from the mountain, and the two tablets of the Testimony *were* in his hand. The tablets *were* written on both sides; on the one *side* and on the other they were written.

16 Now the [R]tablets *were* the work of God, and the writing *was* the writing of God engraved on the tablets. Ex. 31:18

17 And when Joshua heard the noise of the people as they shouted, he said to Moses, "*There is* a noise of war in the camp."

18 But he said:

"*It is* not the noise of the shout of victory,
Nor the noise of the cry of defeat,
But the sound of singing I hear."

19 So it was, as soon as he came near the camp, that [R]he saw the calf *and* the dancing. So Moses' anger became hot, and he cast the tablets out of his hands and broke them at the foot of the mountain. Deut. 9:16, 17

20 Then he took the calf which they had made, burned *it* in the fire, and ground *it* to powder; and he scattered *it* on the water and made the children of Israel drink *it.*

21 And Moses said to Aaron, [R]"What did this people do to you that you have brought *so* great a sin upon them?" Gen. 26:10

22 So Aaron said, "Do not let the anger of my lord become hot. [R]You know the people, that they *are set* on evil. Deut. 9:24

23 "For they said to me, 'Make us gods that shall go before us; *as for* this Moses, the man who brought us out of the land of Egypt, we do not know what has become of him.'

24 "And I said to them, 'Whoever has any gold, let them break *it* off.' So they gave *it* to me, and I cast it into the fire, and this calf came out."

25 Now when Moses saw that the people *were* [R]unrestrained (for Aaron [R]had not restrained them, to *their* shame among their enemies), Ex. 33:4, 5 • 2 Chr. 28:19

26 then Moses stood in the entrance of the camp, and said, "Whoever *is* on the LORD's side—*come* to me!" And all the sons of Levi gathered themselves together to him.

27 And he said to them, "Thus says the LORD God of Israel: 'Let every man put his sword on his side, and go in and out from entrance to entrance throughout the camp, and [R]let every man kill his brother, every man his companion, and every man his neighbor.' " Num. 25:5–13

28 So the sons of Levi did according to the

32:13 Gen. 13:15 and 22:17

word of Moses. And about three thousand men of
the people fell that day.
29 Then Moses said, "Consecrate yourselves
today to the LORD, that He may bestow on you a
blessing this day, for every man has opposed his
son and his brother."

Moses Atones for Israel

30 Now it came to pass on the next day that
Moses said to the people, [R]"You have commit-
ted a great sin. So now I will go up to the
LORD; [R]perhaps I can make atonement for
your sin." 1 Sam. 12:20, 23 • 2 Sam. 16:12
31 Then Moses [R]returned to the LORD and
said, "Oh, these people have committed a
great sin, and have [R]made for themselves a
god of gold! Deut. 9:18 • Ex. 20:23
32 "Yet now, if You will forgive their sin—but
if not, I pray, [R]blot me [R]out of Your book which
You have written." Ps. 69:28 • Dan. 12:1
33 And the LORD said to Moses, [R]"Whoever
has sinned against Me, I will [R]blot him out of
My book. [Ezek. 18:4; 33:2, 14, 15] • Ex. 17:14

God Sends His Angel

34 "Now therefore, go, lead the people to *the
place* of which I have [R]spoken to you. Behold,
My Angel shall go before you. Nevertheless,
[R]in the day when I [R]visit for punishment, I
will visit punishment upon them for their
sin." Ex. 3:17 • Deut. 32:35 • Ps. 89:32
35 So the LORD plagued the people because
of [R]what they did with the calf which Aaron
made. Neh. 9:18

CHAPTER 33

The Tabernacle Is Moved Outside the Camp

THEN the LORD said to Moses, "Depart *and*
go up from here, you and the people
whom you have brought out of the land of
Egypt, to the land of which I swore to Abra-
ham, Isaac, and Jacob, saying, [R]'To your de-
scendants I will give it.' Gen. 12:7
2 "And I will send *My* Angel before you,
[R]and I will drive out the Canaanite and the
Amorite and the Hittite and the Perizzite and
the Hivite and the Jebusite. Josh. 24:11
3 "*Go up* [R]to a land flowing with milk and
honey; for I will not go up in your midst, lest
[R]I consume you on the way, for you *are* a stiff-
necked people." Ex. 3:8 • Num. 16:21, 45
4 And when the people heard this bad
news, [R]they mourned, [R]and no one put on his
ornaments. Num. 14:1, 39 • Ezra 9:3
5 For the LORD had said to Moses, "Say to
the children of Israel, 'You *are* a stiff-necked
people. I could come up into your midst in one
moment and consume you. Now therefore,
take off your ornaments, that I may [R]know
what to do to you.' " [Ps. 139:23]
6 So the children of Israel stripped them-
selves of their ornaments by Mount Horeb.
7 Moses took his tent and pitched it outside
the camp, far from the camp, and called it the
tabernacle of meeting. And it came to pass
that everyone who [R]sought the LORD went out
to the tabernacle of meeting which *was* out-
side the camp. Deut. 4:29

Moses Talks to God

8 So it was, whenever Moses went out to
the tabernacle, *that* all the people rose, and
each man stood [R]*at* his tent door and
watched Moses until he had gone into the
tabernacle. Num. 16:27
9 And it came to pass, when Moses entered
the tabernacle, that the pillar of cloud de-
scended and stood *at* the door of the taberna-
cle, and *the LORD* talked with Moses.
10 All the people saw the pillar of cloud
standing *at* the tabernacle door, and all the
people rose and [R]worshiped, each man *in* his
tent door. Ex. 4:31
11 So [R]the LORD spoke to Moses face to face,
as a man speaks to his friend. And he would
return to the camp, but his servant Joshua the
son of Nun, a young man, did not depart from
the tabernacle. Num. 12:8

God Will Show Moses the Way

12 Then Moses said to the LORD, "See, [R]You
say to me, 'Bring up this people.' But You
have not let me know whom You will send
with me. Yet You have said, [R]'I know you by
name, and you have also found grace in My
sight.' Ex. 3:10; 32:34 • Ex. 33:17
13 "Now therefore, I pray, [R]if I have found
grace in Your sight, [R]show me now Your way,
that I may know You and that I may find grace
in Your sight. And consider that this nation *is*
Your people." Ex. 34:9 • Ps. 25:4
14 And He said, [R]"My Presence will go *with
you*, and I will give you rest." Is. 63:9
15 Then he said to Him, [R]"If Your Presence
does not go *with us*, do not bring us up from
here. Ex. 33:3
16 "For how then will it be known that Your
people and I have found grace in Your sight,
except You go with us? So we shall be sepa-
rate, Your people and I, from all the people
who *are* upon the face of the earth."
17 So the LORD said to Moses, [R]"I will also do
this thing that you have spoken; for you have
found grace in My sight, and I know you by
name." [James 5:16]

God Shows Moses His Glory

18 And he said, "Please, show me [R]Your
glory." [1 Tim. 6:16]
19 Then He said, "I will make all My good-
ness pass before you, and I will proclaim the
name of the LORD before you. [R]I will be gra-
cious to whom I will be [R]gracious, and I will
have compassion on whom I will have com-
passion." [Rom. 9:15, 16, 18] • [Rom. 4:4, 16]

20 But He said, "You cannot see My face; for
no man shall see Me, and live."
21 And the LORD said, "Here is a place by
Me, and you shall stand on the rock.
22 "So it shall be, while My glory passes by,
that I will put you [R]in the cleft of the rock,
and will [R]cover you with My hand while I
pass by. Is. 2:21 • Ps. 91:1, 4
23 "Then I will take away My hand, and you
shall see My back; but My face shall [R]not be
seen." [John 1:18]

CHAPTER 34

Hewing of the Two Tablets

AND the LORD said to Moses, "Cut two
tablets of stone like the first *ones*, and I
will write on *these* tablets the words that were
on the first tablets which you broke.
2 "So be ready in the morning, and come up
in the morning to Mount Sinai, and present
yourself to Me there [R]on the top of the moun-
tain. Ex. 19:11, 18, 20
3 "And no man shall [R]come up with you,
and let no man be seen throughout all the
mountain; let neither flocks nor herds feed be-
fore that mountain." Ex. 19:12, 13; 24:9–11
4 So he cut two tablets of stone like the first
ones. Then Moses rose early in the morning
and went up Mount Sinai, as the LORD had
commanded him; and he took in his hand the
two tablets of stone.

The Nature of God Is Revealed

5 Now the LORD descended in the [R]cloud
and stood with him there, and [R]proclaimed
the name of the LORD. Ex. 19:9 • Ex. 33:19
6 And the LORD passed before him and pro-
claimed, "The LORD, the LORD God, merciful
and gracious, longsuffering, and abounding in
goodness and truth,
7 "keeping mercy for thousands, [R]forgiving
iniquity and transgression and sin, [R]by no
means clearing *the guilty*, visiting the iniquity
of the fathers upon the children and the chil-
dren's children to the third and the fourth
generation." Ps. 103:3, 4 • Job 10:14
8 So Moses made haste and bowed his head
toward the earth, and worshiped.
9 Then he said, "If now I have found grace
in Your sight, O Lord, let my Lord, I pray, go
among us, even though we *are* a stiff-necked
people; and pardon our iniquity and our sin,
and take us as Your inheritance."

Renewal of the Covenant

10 And He said: "Behold, [R]I make a
covenant. Before all your people I will [R]do
marvels such as have not been done in all the
earth, nor in any nation; and all the people
among whom you *are* shall see the work of
the LORD. For it *is* an awesome thing that I will
do with you. Deut. 5:2 • Ps. 77:14
11 [R]"Observe what I command you this day.
Behold, [R]I am driving out from before you the
Amorite and the Canaanite and the Hittite
and the Perizzite and the Hivite and the Jeb-
usite. Deut. 6:25 • Ex. 23:20–33; 33:2
12 [R]"Take heed to yourself, lest you make a
covenant with the inhabitants of the land
where you are going, lest it be a snare in your
midst. Ex. 23:32, 33
13 "But you shall [R]destroy their altars, break
their *sacred* pillars, and [R]cut down their
wooden images Deut. 12:3 • 2 Kin. 18:4
14 "(for you shall worship [R]no other god, for
the LORD, whose [R]name *is* Jealous, *is* a [R]jeal-
ous God), [Ex. 20:3–5] • [Is. 9:6; 57:15] • [Deut. 4:24]
15 "lest you make a covenant with the in-
habitants of the land, and they play the harlot
with their gods and make sacrifice to their
gods, and *one of them* invites you and you
[R]eat of his sacrifice, 1 Cor. 8:4, 7, 10
16 "and you take of [R]his daughters for your
sons, and his daughters [R]play the harlot with
their gods and make your sons play the harlot
with their gods. Gen. 28:1 • Num. 25:1, 2
17 [R]"You shall make no molded gods for
yourselves. Ex. 20:4, 23; 32:8
18 "The Feast of Unleavened Bread you shall
keep. Seven days you shall eat unleavened
bread, as I commanded you, in the appointed
time of the month of Abib; for in the month of
Abib you came out from Egypt.
19 [R]"All that open the womb *are* Mine, and
every male firstborn among your livestock,
whether ox or sheep. Ex. 13:2; 22:29
20 "But [R]the firstborn of a donkey you shall
redeem with a lamb. And if you will not re-
deem *him*, then you shall break his neck. All
the firstborn of your sons you shall redeem.
And none shall appear before Me [R]empty-
handed. Ex. 13:13 • Ex. 22:29; 23:15
21 [R]"Six days you shall work, but on the sev-
enth day you shall rest; in plowing time and in
harvest you shall rest. Ex. 20:9
22 "And you shall observe the Feast of
Weeks, of the firstfruits of wheat harvest, and
the Feast of Ingathering at the year's end.
23 [R]"Three times in the year all your men
shall appear before the Lord, the LORD God of
Israel. Ex. 23:14–17
24 "For I will [R]cast out the nations before you
and enlarge your borders; neither will any
man covet your land when you go up to ap-
pear before the LORD your God three times in
the year. [Ex. 33:2]
25 "You shall not offer the blood of My sac-
rifice with leaven, [R]nor shall the sacrifice of
the Feast of the Passover be left until morn-
ing. Ex. 12:10
26 [R]"The first of the firstfruits of your land
you shall bring to the house of the LORD your
God. You shall not boil a young goat in its
mother's milk." Ex. 23:19
27 Then the LORD said to Moses, "Write

[R]these words, for according to the tenor of
these words I have made a covenant with you
and with Israel." Deut. 31:9
28 [R]So he was there with the LORD forty days
and forty nights; he neither ate bread nor
drank water. And [R]He wrote on the tablets the
words of the covenant, the Ten Command-
ments.* Ex. 24:18 • Ex. 34:1, 4

Moses Returns from God

29 Now it was so, when Moses came down
from Mount Sinai (and the two tablets of the
Testimony *were* in Moses' hand when he
came down from the mountain), that Moses
did not know that [R]the skin of his face shone
while he talked with Him. 2 Cor. 3:7
30 So when Aaron and all the children of Is-
rael saw Moses, behold, the skin of his face
shone, and they were afraid to come near him.
31 Then Moses called to them, and Aaron
and all the rulers of the congregation re-
turned to him; and Moses talked with them.
32 Afterward all the children of Israel came
near, [R]and he gave them as commandments
all that the LORD had spoken with him on
Mount Sinai. Ex. 24:3
33 And when Moses had finished speaking
with them, he put a veil on his face.
34 But whenever Moses went in before the
LORD to speak with Him, he would take the
veil off until he came out; and he would come
out and speak to the children of Israel what-
ever he had been commanded.
35 And whenever the children of Israel saw
the face of Moses, that the skin of Moses' face
shone, then Moses would put the veil on his
face again, until he went in to speak with
Him.

CHAPTER 35

Israel Brings Offerings in Abundance

THEN Moses gathered all the congregation
of the children of Israel together, and said
to them, "These *are* the words which the LORD
has commanded *you* to do:
2 "Work shall be done for six days, but the
seventh day shall be a holy day for you, a Sab-
bath of rest to the LORD. Whoever does any
work on it shall be put to death.
3 "You shall kindle no fire throughout your
dwellings on the Sabbath day."
4 And Moses spoke to all the congregation
of the children of Israel, saying, "This *is* the
thing which the LORD commanded, saying:
5 'Take from among you an offering to the
LORD. [R]Whoever *is* of a willing heart, let him
bring it as an offering to the LORD: [R]gold, sil-
ver, and bronze; Ex. 25:2 • Ex. 38:24
6 [R]'blue, purple, and scarlet *thread,* fine
linen, and [R]goats' *hair;* Ex. 36:8 • Ex. 36:14
7 'ram skins dyed red, badger skins, and
acacia wood;
8 'oil for the light, and spices for the anoint-
ing oil and for the sweet incense;
9 'onyx stones, and stones to be set in the
ephod and in the breastplate.
10 [R]'All *who are* gifted artisans among you
shall come and make all that the LORD has
commanded: Ex. 31:2–6; 36:1, 2
11 [R]'the tabernacle, its tent, its covering, its
clasps, its boards, its bars, its pillars, and its
sockets; Ex. 26:1, 2; 36:14
12 'the ark and its poles, *with* the mercy seat,
and the veil of the covering;
13 'the [R]table and its poles, all its utensils,
[R]and the showbread; Ex. 25:23 • Ex. 25:30
14 'also the lampstand for the light, its uten-
sils, its lamps, and the oil for the light;
15 [R]'the incense altar, its poles, [R]the anoint-
ing oil, [R]the sweet incense, and the screen
for the door at the entrance of the taberna-
cle; Ex. 30:1 • Ex. 30:25 • Ex. 30:34–38
16 [R]'the altar of burnt offering with its
bronze grating, its poles, all its utensils, *and*
the laver and its base; Ex. 27:1–8
17 [R]'the hangings of the court, its pillars,
their sockets, and the screen for the gate of
the court; Ex. 27:9–18
18 'the pegs of the tabernacle, the pegs of the
court, and their cords;
19 [R]'the garments of ministry,* for minister-
ing in the holy *place*—the holy garments for
Aaron the priest and the garments of his sons,
to minister as priests.' " Ex. 31:10
20 And all the congregation of the children
of Israel departed from the presence of Moses.
21 Then everyone came whose heart was
stirred, and everyone whose spirit was will-
ing, *and* they brought the LORD's offering for
the work of the tabernacle of meeting, for all
its service, and for the holy garments.
22 They came, both men and women, as
many as had a willing heart, *and* brought ear-
rings and nose rings, rings and necklaces, all
jewelry of gold, that is, every man who *made*
an offering of gold to the LORD.
23 And [R]every man, with whom was found
blue, purple, and scarlet *thread,* fine linen,
and goats' *hair,* red skins of rams, and badger
skins, brought *them.* 1 Chr. 29:8
24 Everyone who offered an offering of sil-
ver or bronze brought the LORD's offering.
And everyone with whom was found acacia
wood for any work of the service, brought *it.*
25 All the women *who were* [R]gifted artisans
spun yarn with their hands, and brought what
they had spun, of blue, purple, *and* scarlet,
and fine linen. Ex. 28:3; 31:6; 36:1
26 And all the women whose hearts stirred
with wisdom spun yarn of goats' *hair.*
27 [R]The rulers brought onyx stones, and the
stones to be set in the ephod and in the breast-
plate, Ezra 2:68

34:28 Lit. *Ten Words* **35:19** Or *woven garments*

28 and spices and oil for the light, for the anointing oil, and for the sweet incense.

29 The children of Israel brought a freewill offering to the LORD, all the men and women whose hearts were willing to bring *material* for all kinds of work which the LORD, by the hand of Moses, had commanded to be done.

30 And Moses said to the children of Israel, "See, [R]the LORD has called by name Bezalel the son of Uri, the son of Hur, of the tribe of Judah; Ex. 31:1–6

31 "and He has filled him with the Spirit of God, in wisdom and understanding, in knowledge and all manner of workmanship,

32 "to design artistic works, to work in gold and silver and bronze,

33 "in cutting jewels for setting, in carving wood, and to work in all manner of artistic workmanship.

34 "And He has put in his heart the ability to teach, *in* him and [R]Aholiab the son of Ahisamach, of the tribe of Dan. Ex. 31:6

35 "He has [R]filled them with skill to do all manner of work of the engraver and the designer and the tapestry maker, in blue, purple, and scarlet *thread,* and fine linen, and of the weaver—those who do every work and those who design artistic works. 1 Kin. 7:14

CHAPTER 36

"AND Bezalel and Aholiab, and every gifted artisan in whom the LORD has put wisdom and understanding, to know how to do all manner of work for the service of the [R]sanctuary,[T] shall do according to all that the LORD has commanded." Ex. 25:8 • *holy place*

2 Then Moses called Bezalel and Aholiab, and every gifted artisan in whose heart the LORD had put wisdom, everyone whose heart was stirred, to come and do the work.

3 And they received from Moses all the offering which the children of Israel had brought for the work of the service of making the sanctuary. So they continued bringing to him freewill offerings every morning.

4 Then all the craftsmen who were doing all the work of the sanctuary came, each from the work he was doing,

5 and they spoke to Moses, saying, [R]"The people bring much more than enough for the service of the work which the LORD commanded *us* to do." [2 Cor. 8:2, 3]

6 So Moses gave a commandment, and they caused it to be proclaimed throughout the camp, saying, "Let neither man nor woman do any more work for the offering of the sanctuary." And the people were restrained from bringing,

7 for the material they had was sufficient for all the work to be done—indeed too [R]much. 1 Kin. 8:64

The Curtains

8 Then all the gifted artisans among them who worked on the tabernacle made ten curtains woven of fine linen, and of blue, purple, and scarlet *thread; with* artistic designs of cherubim they made them.

9 The length of each curtain *was* twenty-eight cubits, and the width of each curtain four cubits; the curtains *were* all the same size.

10 And he coupled five curtains to one another, and *the other* five curtains he coupled to one another.

11 He made loops of blue *yarn* on the edge of the curtain on the selvedge of one set; likewise he did on the outer edge of *the other* curtain of the second set.

12 [R]Fifty loops he made on one curtain, and fifty loops he made on the edge of the curtain on the end of the second set; the loops held one *curtain* to another. Ex. 26:5

13 And he made fifty clasps of gold, and coupled the curtains to one another with the clasps, that it might be one tabernacle.

14 [R]He made curtains of goats' *hair* for the tent over the tabernacle; he made eleven curtains. Ex. 26:7

15 The length of each curtain *was* thirty cubits, and the width of each curtain four cubits; the eleven curtains *were* the same size.

16 He coupled five curtains by themselves and six curtains by themselves.

17 And he made fifty loops on the edge of the curtain that is outermost in one set, and fifty loops he made on the edge of the curtain of the second set.

18 He also made fifty bronze clasps to couple the tent together, that it might be one.

19 [R]Then he made a covering for the tent of ram skins dyed red, and a covering of [T]badger skins above *that.* Ex. 26:14 • Or *dolphin*

The Boards

20 For the tabernacle [R]he made boards of acacia wood, standing upright. Ex. 26:15–29

21 The length of each board *was* ten cubits, and the width of each board a cubit and a half.

22 Each board had two tenons [R]for binding one to another. Thus he made for all the boards of the tabernacle. Ex. 26:17

23 And he made boards for the tabernacle, twenty boards for the south side.

24 Forty sockets of silver he made to go under the twenty boards: two sockets under each of the boards for its two tenons.

25 And for the other side of the tabernacle, the north side, he made twenty boards

26 and their forty sockets of silver: two sockets under each of the boards.

27 For the west side of the tabernacle he made six boards.

28 He also made two boards for the two back corners of the tabernacle.

29 And they were coupled at the bottom and
[T]coupled together at the top by one ring.
Thus he made both of them for the two cor-
ners. Lit. *doubled*
30 So there were eight boards and their
sockets—sixteen sockets of silver—two sock-
ets under each of the boards.
31 And he made bars of acacia wood: five for
the boards on one side of the tabernacle,
32 five bars for the boards on the other side
of the tabernacle, and five bars for the boards
of the tabernacle on the far side westward.
33 And he made the middle bar to pass
through the boards from one end to the other.
34 He overlaid the boards with gold, made
their rings of gold *to be* holders for the bars,
and overlaid the bars with gold.

The Veils

35 And he made a veil of blue, purple, and
scarlet *thread,* and fine woven linen; it was
worked *with* an artistic design of cherubim.
36 He made for it four pillars of acacia *wood,*
and overlaid them with gold, with their hooks
of gold; and he cast four sockets of silver for
them.
37 He also made a screen for the tabernacle
door, of blue, purple, and scarlet *thread,* and
fine woven linen, made by a weaver,
38 and its five pillars with their hooks. And
he overlaid their capitals and their rings with
gold, but their five sockets *were* bronze.

CHAPTER 37

The Ark of the Covenant

THEN [R]Bezalel made the ark of acacia
wood; two and a half cubits *was* its length,
a cubit and a half its width, and a cubit and a
half its height. Ex. 35:30; 36:1
2 He overlaid it with pure gold inside and
outside, and made a molding of gold all
around it.
3 And he cast for it four rings of gold *to be
set* in its four corners: two rings on one side,
and two rings on the other side of it.
4 He made poles of acacia wood, and over-
laid them with gold.
5 And he put the poles into the rings at the
sides of the ark, to bear the ark.
6 He also made the [R]mercy seat of pure
gold; two and a half cubits *was* its length and
a cubit and a half its width. Ex. 25:17
7 He made two cherubim of beaten gold; he
made them of one piece at the two ends of the
mercy seat:
8 one cherub at one end on this side, and
the other cherub at the *other* end on that side.
He made the cherubim at the two ends *of one
piece* with the mercy seat.
9 The cherubim spread out *their* wings
above, *and* covered the [R]mercy seat with
their wings. They faced one another; the
faces of the cherubim were toward the mercy
seat. Ex. 25:20

The Table of Showbread

10 He made [R]the table of acacia wood; two
cubits *was* its length, a cubit its width, and a
cubit and a half its height. Ex. 25:23–29
11 And he overlaid it with pure gold, and
made a molding of gold all around it.
12 Also he made a frame of a handbreadth
all around it, and made a molding of gold for
the frame all around it.
13 And he cast for it four rings of gold, and
put the rings on the four corners that *were* at
its four legs.
14 The rings were close to the frame, as
holders for the poles to bear the table.
15 And he made the poles of acacia wood to
bear the table, and overlaid them with gold.
16 He made of pure gold the utensils which
were on the table: its dishes, its cups, its
bowls, and its pitchers for pouring.

The Gold Lampstand

17 He also made the [R]lampstand of pure
gold; of hammered work he made the lamp-
stand. Its shaft, its branches, its bowls, its *or-
namental* knobs, and its flowers were of the
same piece. Ex. 25:31–39
18 And six branches came out of its sides:
three branches of the lampstand out of one
side, and three branches of the lampstand out
of the other side.
19 There were three bowls made like almond
blossoms on one branch, with an *ornamental*
knob and a flower, and three bowls made like
almond *blossoms* on the other branch, with
an *ornamental* knob and a flower—and so for
the six branches coming out of the lampstand.
20 And on the lampstand itself *were* four
bowls made like almond *blossoms, each with*
its *ornamental* knob and flower.
21 *There was* a knob under the *first* two
branches of the same, a knob under the *sec-
ond* two branches of the same, and a knob
under the *third* two branches of the same, ac-
cording to the six branches extending from it.
22 Their knobs and their branches were of
one piece; all of it *was* one hammered piece of
pure gold.
23 And he made its seven lamps, its wick-
trimmers, and its trays of pure gold.
24 Of a talent of pure gold he made it, with
all its utensils.

The Altar of Incense

25 He made the incense altar of acacia
wood. Its length *was* a cubit and its width a
cubit—*it was* square—and two cubits *was* its
height. Its horns were *of one piece* with it.
26 And he overlaid it with pure gold: its top,
its sides all around, and its horns. He also
made for it a molding of gold all around it.

27 He made two rings of gold for it under its molding, by its two corners on both sides, as holders for the poles with which to bear it.

28 And he [R]made the poles of acacia wood, and overlaid them with gold. Ex. 30:5

29 He also made [R]the holy anointing oil and the pure incense of sweet spices, according to the work of the perfumer. Ex. 30:23–25

CHAPTER 38

The Altar of Burnt Offerings

HE made [R]the altar of burnt offering of acacia wood; five cubits *was* its length and five cubits its width—*it was* square—and its height *was* three cubits. Ex. 27:1–8

2 He made its horns on its four corners; the horns were *of one piece* with it. And he overlaid it with bronze.

3 He made all the utensils for the altar: the pans, the shovels, the basins, the forks, and the firepans; all its utensils he made of bronze.

4 And he made a grate of bronze network for the altar, under its rim, midway from the bottom.

5 He cast four rings for the four corners of the bronze grating, *as* holders for the poles.

6 And he made the poles of acacia wood, and overlaid them with bronze.

7 Then he put the poles into the rings on the sides of the altar, with which to bear it. He made the altar hollow with boards.

The Bronze Laver

8 He made [R]the laver of bronze and its base of bronze, from the bronze mirrors of the serving women who assembled at the door of the tabernacle of meeting. Ex. 30:18

The Court

9 Then he made the court on the south side; the hangings of the court *were of* fine woven linen, one hundred cubits long.

10 There *were* twenty pillars for them, with twenty bronze sockets. The hooks of the pillars and their bands *were* silver.

11 On the north side *the hangings were* one hundred cubits *long*, with twenty pillars and their twenty bronze sockets. The hooks of the pillars and their bands *were* silver.

12 And on the west side *there were* hangings of fifty cubits, with ten pillars and their ten sockets. The hooks of the pillars and their bands *were* silver.

13 For the east side *the hangings were* fifty cubits.

14 The hangings of one side *of the gate were* fifteen cubits *long*, *with* their three pillars and their three sockets,

15 and the same for the other side of the court gate; on this side and that *were* hangings of fifteen cubits, *with* their three pillars and their three sockets.

16 All the hangings of the court all around *were of* fine woven linen.

17 The sockets for the pillars *were* bronze, the hooks of the pillars and their bands *were* silver, and the overlay of their capitals *was* silver; and all the pillars of the court had bands of silver.

18 The screen for the gate of the court *was* woven of blue, purple, and scarlet *thread*, and of fine woven linen. The length *was* twenty cubits, and the height along its width *was* five cubits, corresponding to the hangings of the court.

19 And *there were* four pillars *with* their four sockets of bronze; their hooks *were* silver, and the overlay of their capitals and their bands *was* silver.

20 All the pegs of the tabernacle, and of the court all around, *were* bronze.

The Sum of Materials

21 This is the inventory of the tabernacle, the tabernacle of the Testimony, which was counted according to the commandment of Moses, for the service of the Levites, by the hand of Ithamar, son of Aaron the priest.

22 [R]Bezalel the son of Uri, the son of Hur, of the tribe of Judah, made all that the LORD had commanded Moses. Ex. 31:2, 6

23 And with him *was* [R]Aholiab the son of Ahisamach, of the tribe of Dan, an engraver and designer, a weaver of blue, purple, and scarlet *thread*, and of fine linen. Ex. 31:6

24 All the gold that was used in all the work of the holy *place*, that is, the gold of the [R]offering, was twenty-nine talents and seven hundred and thirty shekels, according to the shekel of the sanctuary. Ex. 35:5, 22

25 And the silver from those who were [R]numbered of the congregation *was* one hundred talents and one thousand seven hundred and seventy-five shekels, according to the shekel of the sanctuary: Ex. 30:11–16

26 [R]a bekah for each man (*that is*, half a shekel, according to the shekel of the sanctuary), for everyone included in the numbering from twenty years old and above, for [R]six hundred and three thousand, five hundred and fifty *men*. Ex. 30:13, 15 • Num. 1:46; 26:51

27 And from the hundred talents of silver were cast [R]the sockets of the sanctuary and the bases of the veil: one hundred sockets from the hundred talents, one talent for each socket. Ex. 26:19, 21, 25, 32

28 Then from the one thousand seven hundred and seventy-five *shekels* he made hooks for the pillars, overlaid their capitals, and [R]made bands for them. Ex. 27:17

29 The offering of bronze *was* seventy talents and two thousand four hundred shekels.

30 And with it he made the sockets for the

door of the tabernacle of meeting, the bronze
altar, the bronze grating for it, and all the
utensils for the altar,
31 the sockets for the court all around, the
bases for the court gate, all the pegs for the
tabernacle, and all the pegs for the court all
around.

CHAPTER 39

The Clothes for the Priest

OF the [R]blue, purple, and scarlet *thread*
they made garments of ministry,* for
ministering in the holy *place,* and made the
holy garments for Aaron, [R]as the LORD had
commanded Moses. Ex. 25:4; 35:23 • Ex. 28:4
2 [R]He made the [R]ephod of gold, blue, pur-
ple, and scarlet *thread,* and of fine woven
linen. Ex. 28:6–14 • Lev. 8:7
3 And they beat the gold into thin sheets
and cut *it into* threads, to work *it* in *with* the
blue, purple, and scarlet *thread,* and the fine
linen, *into* artistic designs.
4 They made shoulder straps for it to cou-
ple *it* together; it was coupled together at its
two edges.
5 And the intricately woven band of his
ephod that *was* on it *was* of the same work-
manship, *woven of* gold, blue, purple, and
scarlet *thread,* and *of* fine woven linen, as the
LORD had commanded Moses.
6 [R]And they set onyx stones, enclosed in
[T]settings of gold; they were engraved, as
signets are engraved, with the names of the
sons of Israel. Ex. 28:9–11 • *plaited work*
7 He put them on the shoulders of the
ephod *as* memorial stones for the sons of Is-
rael, as the LORD had commanded Moses.
8 And he made the breastplate, artistically
woven like the workmanship of the ephod, of
gold, blue, purple, and scarlet *thread,* and of
fine woven linen.
9 They made the breastplate square by
doubling it; a span *was* its length and a span
its width when doubled.
10 [R]And they set in it four rows of stones: a
row with a sardius, a topaz, and an emerald
was the first row; Ex. 28:17
11 the second row, a turquoise, a sapphire,
and a diamond;
12 the third row, a jacinth, an agate, and an
amethyst;
13 the fourth row, a beryl, an onyx, and a
jasper. *They were* enclosed in settings of gold
in their mountings.
14 *There were* [R]twelve stones according to
the names of the sons of Israel: according to
their names, *engraved like* a signet, each one
with its own name according to the twelve
tribes. Rev. 21:12
15 And they made chains for the breastplate
at the ends, like braided cords of pure gold.
16 They also made two settings of gold and
two gold rings, and put the two rings on the
two ends of the breastplate.
17 And they put the two braided *chains* of
gold in the two rings on the ends of the breast-
plate.
18 The two ends of the two braided *chains*
they fastened in the two settings, and put
them on the shoulder straps of the ephod in
the front.
19 And they made two rings of gold and put
them on the two ends of the breastplate, on
the edge of it, which *was* on the inward side of
the ephod.
20 They made two *other* gold rings and put
them on the two shoulder straps, underneath
the ephod toward its front, right at the seam
above the intricately woven band of the ephod.
21 And they bound the breastplate by means
of its rings to the rings of the ephod with a
blue cord, so that it would be above the intri-
cately woven band of the ephod, and that the
breastplate would not come loose from the
ephod, as the LORD had commanded Moses.
22 [R]He made the [R]robe of the ephod of
woven work, all of blue. Ex. 28:31–35 • Ex. 29:5
23 And *there was* an opening in the middle
of the robe, like the opening in a coat of mail,
with a woven binding all around the opening,
so that it would not tear.
24 They made on the hem of the robe pome-
granates of blue, purple, and scarlet, and of
fine woven *linen.*
25 And they made [R]bells of pure gold, and
put the bells between the pomegranates on
the hem of the robe all around between the
pomegranates: Ex. 28:33
26 a bell and a pomegranate, a bell and a
pomegranate, all around the hem of the robe
to [T]minister in, as the LORD had commanded
Moses. *serve*
27 They made tunics, artistically woven of
fine linen, for Aaron and his sons,
28 [R]a turban of fine linen, exquisite hats of
fine linen, [R]short trousers of fine woven
linen, Ex. 28:4, 39 • Ex. 28:42
29 and a sash of fine woven linen with blue,
purple, and scarlet *thread,* made by a weaver,
as the LORD had commanded Moses.
30 Then they made the plate of the holy
crown of pure gold, and wrote on it an in-
scription *like* the engraving of a signet:

HOLINESS TO THE LORD.

31 And they tied to it a blue cord, to fasten *it*
above on the turban, as the LORD had com-
manded Moses.

The Tabernacle Is Inspected by Moses

32 Thus all the work of the tabernacle of
the tent of meeting was [R]finished. And the

39:1 Or *woven garments*

children of Israel did [R]according to all that
the LORD had commanded Moses; so they
did. Ex. 40:17 • Ex. 25:40; 39:42, 43
33 And they brought the tabernacle to Mo-
ses, the tent and all its furnishings: its clasps,
its boards, its bars, its pillars, and its sockets;
34 the covering of ram skins dyed red, the
covering of badger skins, and the veil of the
covering;
35 the ark of the Testimony with its poles,
and the mercy seat;
36 the table, all its utensils, and the [R]show-
bread; Ex. 25:23–30
37 the pure *gold* lampstand with its lamps
(the lamps set in order), all its utensils, and
the oil for light;
38 the gold altar, the anointing oil, and the
sweet incense; the screen for the tabernacle
door;
39 the bronze altar, its grate of bronze, its
poles, and all its utensils; the laver with its
base;
40 the hangings of the court, its pillars and
its sockets, the screen for the court gate, its
cords, and its pegs; all the utensils for the
service of the tabernacle, for the tent of meet-
ing;
41 and the garments of ministry,* to [T]minis-
ter in the holy *place:* the holy garments for
Aaron the priest, and his sons' garments, to
minister as priests. *serve*
42 According to all that the LORD had com-
manded Moses, so the children of Israel [R]did
all the work. Ex. 35:10
43 Then Moses looked over all the work, and
indeed they had done it; as the LORD had com-
manded, just so they had done it. And Moses
[R]blessed them. Lev. 9:22, 23

CHAPTER 40

The Tabernacle Is Erected

THEN the LORD spoke to Moses, saying:
2 "On the first day of the [R]first month you
shall set up [R]the tabernacle of the tent of
meeting. Ex. 12:2; 13:4 • Ex. 26:1, 30; 40:17
3 [R]"You shall put in it the ark of the Testi-
mony, and [T]partition off the ark with the
veil. Num. 4:5 • *screen*
4 [R]"You shall bring in the table and arrange
the things that are to be set in order on it; and
you shall bring in the lampstand and [T]light its
lamps. Ex. 26:35; 40:22 • *set up*
5 [R]"You shall also set the altar of gold for
the incense before the ark of the Testimony,
and put up the screen for the door of the tab-
ernacle. Ex. 40:26
6 "Then you shall set the [R]altar of the burnt
offering before the door of the tabernacle of
the tent of meeting. Ex. 39:39
7 "And [R]you shall set the laver between the
tabernacle of meeting and the altar, and put
water in it. Ex. 30:18; 40:30
8 "You shall set up the court all around, and
hang up the screen at the court gate.
9 "And you shall take the anointing oil, and
[R]anoint the tabernacle and all that *is* in it; and
you shall hallow it and all its utensils, and it
shall be holy. Ex. 30:26
10 "You shall anoint the altar of the burnt of-
fering and all its utensils, and consecrate the
altar. The altar shall be most holy.
11 "And you shall anoint the laver and its
base, and consecrate it.
12 [R]"Then you shall bring Aaron and his
sons to the door of the tabernacle of meeting
and wash them with water. Lev. 8:1–13
13 "You shall put the holy garments on
Aaron, and anoint him and consecrate him,
that he may minister to Me as priest.
14 "And you shall bring his sons and clothe
them with tunics.
15 "You shall anoint them, as you anointed
their father, that they may minister to Me as
priests; for their anointing shall surely be [R]an
everlasting priesthood throughout their gen-
erations." Num. 25:13
16 Thus Moses did; according to all that the
LORD had commanded him, so he did.
17 And it came to pass in the first month of
the second year, on the first *day* of the month,
that the tabernacle was raised up.
18 So Moses raised up the tabernacle, fas-
tened its sockets, set up its boards, put in its
bars, and raised up its pillars.
19 And he spread out the tent over the tab-
ernacle and put the covering of the tent on top
of it, as the LORD had commanded Moses.
20 He took [R]the Testimony and put *it* into the
ark, inserted the poles through the rings of
the ark, and put the mercy seat on top of the
ark. Ex. 25:16
21 And he brought the ark into the taberna-
cle, [R]hung up the veil of the covering, and par-
titioned off the ark of the Testimony, as the
LORD had commanded Moses. Ex. 26:33
22 [R]He put the table in the tabernacle of
meeting, on the north side of the tabernacle,
outside the veil; Ex. 26:35
23 [R]and he set the bread in order upon it be-
fore the LORD, as the LORD had commanded
Moses. Ex. 40:4
24 [R]He put the lampstand in the tabernacle
of meeting, across from the table, on the south
side of the tabernacle; Ex. 26:35
25 and [R]he lit the lamps before the LORD, as
the LORD had commanded Moses. Ex. 25:37
26 [R]He put the gold altar in the tabernacle of
meeting in front of the veil; Ex. 30:1, 6
27 [R]and he burned sweet incense on it, as the
LORD had commanded Moses. Ex. 30:7
28 [R]He hung up the screen *at* the door of the
tabernacle. Ex. 26:36; 40:5
29 [R]And he put the altar of burnt offering *be-*

39:41 Or *woven garments*

fore the door of the tabernacle of the tent of
meeting, and offered upon it the burnt offer-
ing and the grain offering, as the LORD had
commanded Moses. Ex. 40:6
30 [R]He set the laver between the tabernacle
of meeting and the altar, and put water there
for washing; Ex. 30:18; 40:7
31 and Moses, Aaron, and his sons would
[R]wash their hands and their feet *with water*
from it. Ex. 30:19, 20
32 Whenever they went into the tabernacle
of meeting, and when they came near the
altar, they washed, [R]as the LORD had com-
manded Moses. Ex. 30:19
33 [R]And he raised up the court all around the
tabernacle and the altar, and hung up the
screen of the court gate. So Moses [R]finished
the work. Ex. 27:9–18; 40:8 • [Heb. 3:2–5]

God Fills the Tabernacle with His Glory

34 Then the [R]cloud covered the tabernacle of
meeting, and the [R]glory of the LORD filled the
tabernacle. 1 Kin. 8:10, 11 • Lev. 9:6, 23
35 And Moses [R]was not able to enter the tab-
ernacle of meeting, because the cloud rested
above it, and the glory of the LORD filled the
tabernacle. 1 Kin. 8:11
36 Whenever the cloud was taken up from
above the tabernacle, the children of Israel
would go onward in all their journeys.
37 But [R]if the cloud was not taken up, then
they did not journey till the day that it was
taken up. Num. 9:19–22
38 For [R]the cloud of the LORD *was* above the
tabernacle by day, and fire was over it by
night, in the sight of all the house of Israel,
throughout all their journeys. Ex. 13:21

Weights

Unit	*Weight*	*Equivalents*	*Translations*
Jewish Weights			
Talent	c. 75 pounds for common talent, c. 150 pounds for royal talent	60 minas; 3,000 shekels	talent
Mina	1.25 pounds	50 shekels	mina
Shekel	c. .4 ounce (11.4 grams) for common shekel; c. .8 ounce for royal shekel	2 bekas; 20 gerahs	shekel
Beka	c. .2 ounce (5.7 grams)	½ shekel; 10 gerahs	half a shekel
Gerah	c. .02 ounce (.57 grams)	1/20 shekel	gerah
Roman Weight			
Litra	12 ounces		pound

THE THIRD BOOK OF MOSES CALLED

LEVITICUS

THE BOOK OF LEVITICUS

Leviticus is God's guidebook for His newly redeemed people, showing them how to worship, serve, and obey a holy God. Fellowship with God through sacrifice and obedience shows the awesome holiness of the God of Israel. Indeed, " 'you shall be holy, for I the LORD your God *am* holy' " (19:2).

Leviticus focuses on the worship and walk of the nation of God. In Exodus, Israel was redeemed and established as a kingdom of priests and a holy nation. Leviticus shows how God's people are to fulfill their priestly calling.

The Hebrew title is *Wayyiqra,* "And He Called." The Talmud refers to Leviticus as the "Law of the Priests," and the "Law of the Offerings." The Greek title appearing in the Septuagint is *Leuitikon,* "That Which Pertains to the Levites." From this word, the Latin Vulgate derived its name *Leviticus,* which was adopted as the English title. This title is slightly misleading because the book does not deal with the Levites as a whole but more with the priests, a segment of the Levites.

THE AUTHOR OF LEVITICUS

The kind of arguments used to confirm the Mosaic authorship of Genesis and Exodus also apply to Leviticus because the Pentateuch is a literary unit. In addition to these arguments, others include the following:

External Evidence: (1) A uniform ancient testimony supports the Mosaic authorship of Leviticus. (2) Ancient parallels to the Levitical system of trespass offerings have been found in the Ras Shamra Tablets dating from about 1400 B.C. and discovered on the coast of northern Syria. (3) Christ ascribes the Pentateuch (which includes Leviticus) to Moses (cf. Matt. 8:2–4 and Lev. 14:1–4; Matt. 12:4 and Lev. 24:9; see also Luke 2:22).

Internal Evidence: (1) Fifty-six times in the twenty-seven chapters of Leviticus it is stated that God imparted these laws to Moses (see 1:1; 4:1; 6:1, 24; 8:1). (2) The Levitical Code fits the time of Moses. Economic, civil, moral, and religious considerations show it to be ancient. Many of the laws are also related to a migratory lifestyle.

THE TIME OF LEVITICUS

No geographical movement takes place in Leviticus: the children of Israel remain camped at the foot of Mount Sinai (25:1, 2; 26:46; 27:34). The new calendar of Israel begins with the first Passover (Ex. 12:2): and, according to Exodus 40:17, the tabernacle is completed exactly one year later.

Leviticus picks up the story at this point, and its events occur in the first month of the second year. Numbers 1:1 opens at the beginning of the second month. Moses probably wrote much of Leviticus during that first month and may have put it in its final form shortly before his death in Moab, about 1405 B.C.

THE CHRIST OF LEVITICUS

The Book of Leviticus is replete with types and allusions to the Person and work of Jesus Christ. Some of the more important include: (1) *The five offerings:* The burnt offering typifies Christ's total offering in submission to His Father's will. The meal offering typifies Christ's sinless service. The peace offering is a type of the fellowship believers have with God through the work of the Cross. The sin offering typifies Christ as our guilt-bearer. The trespass offering typifies Christ's payment for the damage of sin. (2) *The high priest:* There are several comparisons and contrasts between Aaron, the first high priest, and Christ, our eternal High Priest. (3) *The seven feasts:* Passover speaks of the substitutionary death of the Lamb of God. Christ died on the day of Passover. Unleavened Bread speaks of the holy walk of the believer (1 Cor. 5:6–8). Firstfruits speaks of Christ's resurrection as the firstfruits of the resurrection of all believers (1 Cor. 15:20–23). Christ rose on the Day of the Firstfruits. Pentecost speaks of the descent of the Holy Spirit after Christ's ascension. Trumpets, the Day of Atonement, and Tabernacles speak of events associated with the second advent of Christ. This may be why these three are separated by a long gap from the first four in Israel's annual cycle.

KEYS TO LEVITICUS

Key Word: Holiness—Leviticus centers on the concept of the holiness of God and how an unholy people can acceptably approach Him and then remain in continued fellowship. The way to God is only through blood sacrifice, and the walk with God is only through obedience to His laws.

Key Verses: Leviticus 17:11; 20:7, 8—" 'For the life of the flesh *is* in the blood, and I have given it to you upon the altar to make atonement for your souls; for it *is* the blood *that* makes atonement for the soul' " (17:11).

"Consecrate yourselves therefore, and be holy,

for I *am* the LORD your God. And you shall keep My statutes, and perform them: I *am* the LORD who sanctifies you" (20:7, 8).

Key Chapter: Leviticus 16—The Day of Atonement (*"Yom Kippur"*) was the most important single day in the Hebrew calendar as it was the only day the high priest entered into the Most Holy Place to "make atonement for you, to cleanse you, *that* you may be clean from all your sins before the LORD" (16:30).

SURVEY OF LEVITICUS

It has been said that it took God only one night to get Israel out of Egypt, but it took forty years to get Egypt out of Israel. In Exodus, Israel is redeemed and established as a kingdom of priests and a holy nation; and in Leviticus, Israel is taught how to fulfill their priestly call. They have been led out from the land of bondage in Exodus and into the sanctuary of God in Leviticus. They move from redemption to service, from deliverance to dedication. This book serves as a handbook for the Levitical priesthood, giving instructions and regulations for worship. Used to guide a newly redeemed people into worship, service, and obedience to God, Leviticus falls into two major sections: (1) sacrifice (1—17) and (2) sanctification (18—27).

Sacrifice (1—17): This section teaches that God must be approached by the sacrificial offerings (1—7), by the mediation of the priesthood (8—10), by the purification of the nation from uncleanness (11—15), and by the provision for national cleansing and fellowship (16 and 17). The blood sacrifices remind the worshipers that because of sin the holy God requires the costly gift of life (17:11). The blood of the innocent sacrificial animal becomes the substitute for the life of the guilty offerer: "without shedding of blood there is no remission" (Heb. 9:22).

Sanctification (18—27): The Israelites serve a holy God who requires them to be holy as well. To be holy means to be "set apart" or "separated." They are to be separated *from* other nations *unto* God. In Leviticus the idea of holiness appears eighty-seven times, sometimes indicating ceremonial holiness (ritual requirements) and at other times moral holiness (purity of life). This sanctification extends to the people of Israel (18—20), the priesthood (21 and 22), their worship (23 and 24), their life in Canaan (25 and 26), and their special vows (27). It is necessary to remove the defilement that separates the people from God so that they can have a walk of fellowship with their Redeemer.

FOCUS	SACRIFICE				SANCTIFICATION				
REFERENCE	1:1——8:1——11:1——16:1——18:1——21:1——23:1——25:1——27:1——27:34								
DIVISION	THE LAWS OF				THE LAWS OF SANCTIFICATION				
	THE OFFERINGS	CONSECRATION OF THE PRIESTS	CONSECRATION OF THE PEOPLE	NATIONAL ATONEMENT	FOR THE PEOPLE	FOR THE PRIESTS	IN WORSHIP	IN THE LAND OF CANAAN	THROUGH VOWS
TOPIC	THE WAY TO GOD				THE WALK WITH GOD				
	THE LAWS OF ACCEPTABLE APPROACH TO GOD				THE LAWS OF CONTINUED FELLOWSHIP WITH GOD				
LOCATION	MOUNT SINAI								
TIME	c. 1 MONTH								

OUTLINE OF LEVITICUS

Part One: The Laws of Acceptable Approach to God: Sacrifice (1:1—17:16)

I. The Laws of Acceptable Approach to God .... 1:1—7:38

A. Laws of Approach to God When in Fellowship .... 1:1—3:17
1. The Burnt Offering 1:1–17
2. The Grain Offering 2:1–16
3. The Peace Offering 3:1–17

B. Laws of Approach to God When Out of Fellowship .... 4:1—6:7
1. The Sin Offering .... 4:1—5:13
2. The Trespass Offering .... 5:14—6:7

C. Laws for Administering Offering .... 6:8—7:38
1. The Burnt Offering 6:8–13
2. The Grain Offering 6:14–23
3. The Sin Offering 6:24–30

Part Two: The Laws of Acceptable Walk with God: Sanctification (18:1—27:34)

CHAPTER 1

The Burnt Offering

NOW the LORD [R]called to Moses, and spoke
to him [R]from the tabernacle of meeting,
saying, Ex. 19:3; 25:22 • Ex. 40:34
2 "Speak to the children of Israel, and say
to them: [R]'When any one of you brings an of-
fering to the LORD, you shall bring your offer-
ing of the livestock—of the herd and of the
flock. Lev. 22:18, 19
3 'If his offering *is* a burnt sacrifice of the
herd, let him offer a male [R]without blemish;
he shall offer it of his own free will at the
door of the tabernacle of meeting before the
LORD. Eph. 5:27
4 [R]'Then he shall put his hand on the head
of the burnt offering, and it will be [R]ac-
cepted on his behalf to make atonement for
him. Lev. 3:2, 8, 13; 4:15 • [Rom. 12:1]
5 'He shall kill the [R]bull before the LORD;
and the priests, Aaron's sons, shall bring the
blood [R]and sprinkle the blood all around on
the altar that *is by* the door of the tabernacle
of meeting. Mic. 6:6 • [Heb. 12:24]
6 'And he shall [R]skin the burnt offering and
cut it into its pieces. Lev. 7:8
7 'The sons of Aaron the priest shall put
[R]fire on the altar, and [R]lay the wood in order
on the fire. Mal. 1:10 • Gen. 22:9
8 'Then the priests, Aaron's sons, shall lay
the parts, the head, and the fat in order on the
wood that *is* on the fire upon the altar;
9 'but he shall wash its entrails and its legs
with water. And the priest shall burn all on the
altar as a burnt sacrifice, an offering made by
fire, a sweet aroma to the LORD.
10 'If his offering *is* of the flocks—of the
sheep or of the goats—as a burnt sacrifice, he
shall bring a male without blemish.
11 [R]'He shall kill it on the north side of
the altar before the LORD; and the priests, Aar-
on's sons, shall sprinkle its blood all around
on the altar. Lev. 1:5
12 'And he shall cut it into its pieces, with its
head and its fat; and the priest shall lay them
in order on the wood that *is* on the fire upon
the altar;
13 'but he shall wash the entrails and the
legs with water. Then the priest shall bring *it*
all and burn *it* on the altar; it *is* a burnt sacri-
fice, an [R]offering made by fire, a sweet aroma
to the LORD. Num. 15:4–7; 28:12–14
14 'And if the burnt sacrifice of his offering
to the LORD *is* of birds, then he shall bring his
offering of turtledoves or young pigeons.
15 'The priest shall bring it to the altar,
[T]wring off its head, and burn *it* on the altar; its
blood shall be drained out at the side of the
altar. Lit. *nip* or *chop off*
16 'And he shall remove its crop with its
feathers and cast it [R]beside the altar on the
east side, into the place for ashes. Lev. 6:10
17 'Then he shall split it at its wings, *but*
[R]shall not divide *it* completely; and the
priest shall burn it on the altar, on the wood
that *is* on the fire. [R]It *is* a burnt sacrifice, an
offering made by fire, a sweet aroma to the
LORD. Gen. 15:10 • Lev. 1:9, 13

CHAPTER 2

The Grain Offering

'WHEN anyone offers [R]a grain offering
to the LORD, his offering shall be *of*
fine flour. And he shall pour oil on it, and put
[R]frankincense on it. Num. 15:4 • Lev. 5:11
2 'He shall bring it to Aaron's sons, the
priests, one of whom shall take from it his
handful of fine flour and oil with all the frank-
incense. And the priest shall burn [R]*it as* a me-
morial on the altar, an offering made by fire, a
sweet aroma to the LORD. Lev. 2:9
3 [R]'The rest of the grain offering *shall be*
Aaron's and his sons'. *It is* most holy of the of-
ferings to the LORD made by fire. Lev. 7:9
4 'And if you bring as an offering a
grain offering baked in the oven, *it shall be*
unleavened cakes of fine flour mixed with oil,
or unleavened wafers anointed with oil.
5 'But if your offering *is* a grain offering
baked in a [T]pan, *it shall be of* fine flour, un-
leavened, mixed with oil. *flat plate* or *griddle*
6 'You shall break it in pieces and pour oil
on it; it *is* a grain offering.
7 'If your offering *is* a grain offering *baked*
in a [R]covered pan, it shall be made *of* fine
flour with oil. Lev. 7:9
8 'You shall bring the grain offering that is
made of these things to the LORD. And when it
is presented to the priest, he shall bring it to
the altar.
9 'Then the priest shall take from the grain
offering a memorial portion, and burn *it* on
the altar. *It is* an [R]offering made by fire, a
sweet aroma to the LORD. Ex. 29:18

10 ‘And [R]what is left of the grain offering *shall be* Aaron’s and his sons’. *It is* most holy of the offerings to the LORD made by fire. Lev. 2:3; 6:16

11 ‘No grain offering which you bring to the LORD shall be made with leaven, for you shall burn no leaven nor any honey in any offering to the LORD made by fire.

12 [R]‘As for the offering of the firstfruits, you shall offer them to the LORD, but they shall not be burned on the altar for a sweet aroma. Lev. 23:10, 11, 17, 18

13 ‘And every offering of your grain offering [R]you shall season with salt; you shall not allow the salt of the covenant of your God to be lacking from your grain offering. With all your offerings you shall offer salt. [Col. 4:6]

14 ‘If you offer a grain offering of your firstfruits to the LORD, [R]you shall offer for the grain offering of your firstfruits green heads of grain roasted on the fire, grain beaten from [R]full heads. Lev. 23:10, 14 • 2 Kin. 4:42

15 ‘And you shall put oil on it, and lay frankincense on it. It *is* a grain offering.

16 ‘Then the priest shall burn [R]the memorial portion: *part* of its beaten grain and *part* of its oil, with all the frankincense, as an offering made by fire to the LORD. Lev. 2:2

CHAPTER 3

The Peace Offering

‘WHEN his offering *is* a [R]sacrifice of a peace offering, if he offers *it* of the herd, whether male or female, he shall offer it without blemish before the LORD. Lev. 7:11

2 ‘And [R]he shall lay his hand on the head of his offering, and kill it *at* the door of the tabernacle of meeting; and Aaron’s sons, the priests, shall [R]sprinkle the blood all around on the altar. Lev. 1:4, 5; 16:21 • Lev. 1:5

3 ‘Then he shall offer from the sacrifice of the peace offering an offering made by fire to the LORD. The fat that covers the entrails and all the fat that *is* on the entrails,

4 ‘the two kidneys and the fat that *is* on them by the flanks, and the fatty lobe *attached* to the liver above the kidneys, he shall remove;

5 ‘and Aaron’s sons shall burn it on the altar upon the burnt sacrifice, which *is* on the wood that *is* on the fire, *as* an offering made by fire, a sweet aroma to the LORD.

6 ‘If his offering as a sacrifice of a peace offering to the LORD *is* of the flock, *whether* male or female, [R]he shall offer it without blemish. Lev. 3:1; 22:20–24

7 ‘If he offers a lamb as his offering, then he shall [R]offer it before the LORD. 1 Kin. 8:62

8 ‘And he shall lay his hand on the head of his offering, and kill it before the tabernacle of meeting; and Aaron’s sons shall sprinkle its blood all around on the altar.

9 ‘Then he shall offer from the sacrifice of the peace offering, as an offering made by fire to the LORD, its fat *and* the whole fat tail which he shall remove close to the backbone. And the fat that covers the entrails and all the fat that *is* on the entrails,

10 ‘the two kidneys and the fat that *is* on them by the flanks, and the fatty lobe *attached* to the liver above the kidneys, he shall remove;

11 ‘and the priest shall burn *them* on the altar *as* [R]food, an offering made by fire to the LORD. Num. 28:2

12 ‘And if his [R]offering *is* a goat, then he shall offer it before the LORD. Num. 15:6–11

13 ‘He shall lay his hand on its head and kill it before the tabernacle of meeting; and the sons of Aaron shall sprinkle its blood all around on the altar.

14 ‘Then he shall offer from it his offering, as an offering made by fire to the LORD. The fat that covers the entrails and all the fat that *is* on the entrails,

15 ‘the two kidneys and the fat that *is* on them by the flanks, and the fatty lobe *attached* to the liver above the kidneys, he shall remove;

16 ‘and the priest shall burn them on the altar *as* food, an offering made by fire for a sweet aroma; all the fat *is* the LORD’s.

17 ‘*This shall be* a [R]perpetual statute throughout your generations in all your dwellings: you shall eat neither fat nor blood.’ ” Lev. 6:18; 7:36; 17:7; 23:14

CHAPTER 4

The Sin Offering

NOW the LORD spoke to Moses, saying,

2 “Speak to the children of Israel, saying: [R]‘If a person sins [T]unintentionally against any of the commandments of the LORD *in anything* which ought not to be done, and does any of them, Lev. 5:15–18 • *through error*

3 [R]‘if the anointed priest sins, bringing guilt on the people, then let him offer to the LORD for his sin which he has sinned [R]a young bull without blemish as a [R]sin offering. Lev. 8:12 • Lev. 3:1; 9:2 • Lev. 9:7

4 ‘He shall bring the bull [R]to the door of the tabernacle of meeting before the LORD, lay his hand on the bull’s head, and kill the bull before the LORD. Lev. 1:3, 4; 4:15

5 ‘Then the anointed priest [R]shall take some of the bull’s blood and bring it to the tabernacle of meeting. Lev. 16:14

6 ‘The priest shall dip his finger in the blood and sprinkle some of the blood seven times before the LORD, in front of the [R]veil of the sanctuary. Ex. 40:21, 26

7 ‘And the priest shall put some of the blood on the horns of the altar of sweet incense before the LORD, which is in the tabernacle of

meeting; and he shall pour the remaining blood of the bull at the base of the altar of the burnt offering, which is at the door of the tabernacle of meeting.

8 'He shall take from it all the fat of the bull as the sin offering. The fat that covers the entrails and all the fat which *is* on the entrails,

9 'the two kidneys and the fat that *is* on them by the flanks, and the fatty lobe *attached* to the liver above the kidneys, he shall remove,

10 [R]'as it was taken from the bull of the sacrifice of the peace offering; and the priest shall burn them on the altar of the burnt offering. Lev. 3:3–5

11 [R]'But the bull's hide and all its flesh, with its head and legs, its entrails and offal— Ex. 29:14

12 'the whole bull he shall carry outside the camp to a clean place, where the ashes are poured out, and [R]burn it on wood with fire; where the ashes are poured out it shall be burned. [Heb. 13:11, 12]

13 'Now if the whole congregation of Israel sins unintentionally, and the thing is hidden from the eyes of the assembly, and they have done *something against* any of the commandments of the LORD *in anything* which should not be done, and are guilty;

14 'when the sin which they have committed becomes known, then the assembly shall offer a young bull for the sin, and bring it before the tabernacle of meeting.

15 'And the elders of the congregation [R]shall lay their hands on the head of the bull before the LORD. Then the bull shall be killed before the LORD. Lev. 1:3, 4

16 'The anointed priest shall bring some of the bull's blood to the tabernacle of meeting.

17 'Then the priest shall dip his finger in the blood and sprinkle *it* seven times before the LORD, in front of the veil.

18 'And he shall put *some* of the blood on the horns of the altar which *is* before the LORD, which *is* in the tabernacle of meeting; and he shall pour the remaining blood at the base of the altar of burnt offering, which is at the door of the tabernacle of meeting.

19 'He shall take all the fat from it and burn *it* on the altar.

20 'And he shall do with the bull as he did with the bull as a sin offering; thus he shall do with it. So the priest shall make atonement for them, and it shall be forgiven them.

21 'Then he shall carry the bull outside the camp, and burn it as he burned the first bull. It *is* a sin offering for the assembly.

22 'When a [T]ruler has sinned, and [R]done *something* unintentionally *against* any of the commandments of the LORD his God *in anything* which should not be done, and is guilty, *leader* • Lev. 4:2, 13, 27

23 'or [R]if his sin which he has committed [T]comes to his knowledge, he shall bring as his offering a kid of the goats, a male without blemish. Lev. 4:14; 5:4 • *is made known to him*

24 'And [R]he shall lay his hand on the head of the goat, and kill it at the place where they kill the burnt offering before the LORD. It *is* a sin offering. [Is. 53:6]

25 [R]'The priest shall take some of the blood of the sin offering with his finger, put *it* on the horns of the altar of burnt offering, and pour its blood at the base of the altar of burnt offering. Lev. 4:7, 18, 30, 34

26 'And he shall burn all its fat on the altar, like [R]the fat of the sacrifice of the peace offering. [R]So the priest shall make atonement for him concerning his sin, and it shall be forgiven him. Lev. 3:3–5 • Lev. 4:20

27 [R]'If [T]anyone of the common people sins unintentionally by doing *something against* any of the commandments of the LORD *in anything* which ought not to be done, and is guilty, Num. 15:27 • Lit. *any soul*

28 'or [R]if his sin which he has committed comes to his knowledge, then he shall bring as his offering a kid of the goats, a female without blemish, for his sin which he has committed. Lev. 4:23

29 [R]'And he shall lay his hand on the head of the sin offering, and kill the sin offering at the place of the burnt offering. Lev. 1:4

30 'Then the priest shall take *some* of its blood with his finger, put *it* on the horns of the altar of burnt offering, and pour all *the remaining* blood at the base of the altar.

31 [R]'He shall remove all its fat, as fat is removed from the sacrifice of the peace offering; and the priest shall burn it on the altar for a [R]sweet aroma to the LORD. So the priest shall make atonement for him, and it shall be forgiven him. Lev. 3:14 • Ex. 29:18

32 'If he brings a lamb as his sin offering, he shall bring a female without blemish.

33 'Then he shall [R]lay his hand on the head of the sin offering, and kill it as a sin offering at the place where they kill the burnt offering. Num. 8:12

34 'The priest shall take *some* of the blood of the sin offering with his finger, put *it* on the horns of the altar of burnt offering, and pour all *the remaining* blood at the base of the altar.

35 'He shall remove all its fat, as the fat of the lamb is removed from the sacrifice of the peace offering. Then the priest shall burn it on the altar, according to the offerings made by fire to the LORD. So the priest shall make atonement for his sin that he has committed, and it shall be forgiven him.

CHAPTER 5

'IF a person sins in [R]hearing the utterance of an oath, and *is* a witness, whether he has seen or known *of the matter*—if he does not tell *it*, he bears guilt. Prov. 29:24

2 'Or [R]if a person touches any unclean
thing, whether *it is* the carcass of an unclean
beast, or the carcass of unclean livestock, or
the carcass of unclean creeping things, and he
is unaware of it, he also shall be unclean and
guilty. Num. 19:11–16
3 'Or if he touches human uncleanness—
whatever uncleanness with which a man may
be defiled, and he is unaware of it—when he
realizes *it*, then he shall be guilty.
4 'Or if a person swears, speaking thought-
lessly with *his* lips [R]to do evil or [R]to do good,
whatever *it is* that a man may pronounce by
an oath, and he is unaware of it—when he re-
alizes *it*, then he shall be guilty in any of these
matters. Acts 23:12 • [James 5:12]
5 'And it shall be, when he is guilty in any
of these *matters*, that he shall [R]confess that
he has sinned in that *thing*; Prov. 28:13
6 'and he shall bring his trespass offering to
the LORD for his sin which he has committed,
a female from the flock, a lamb or a kid of the
goats as a sin offering. So the priest shall
make atonement for him concerning his sin.
7 'If he is not able to bring a lamb, then he
shall bring to the LORD, for his trespass which
he has committed, two [R]turtledoves or two
young pigeons: one as a sin offering and the
other as a burnt offering. Lev. 1:14
8 'And he shall bring them to the priest,
who shall offer *that* which *is* for the sin offer-
ing first, and wring off its head from its neck,
but shall not divide *it* completely.
9 'Then he shall sprinkle *some* of the blood
of the sin offering on the side of the altar,
and the [R]rest of the blood shall be drained
out at the base of the altar. It *is* a sin offer-
ing. Lev. 4:7, 18, 30, 34
10 'And he shall offer the second *as* a burnt
offering according to the prescribed manner.
So the priest shall make atonement on his be-
half for his sin which he has committed, and
it shall be forgiven him.
11 'But if he is not able to bring two turtle-
doves or two young pigeons, then he who
sinned shall bring for his offering one-tenth
of an ephah of fine flour as a sin offering. He
shall put no oil on it, nor shall he put frankin-
cense on it, for it *is* a sin offering.
12 'Then he shall bring it to the priest, and
the priest shall take his handful of it [R]as a me-
morial portion, and burn *it* on the altar ac-
cording to the offerings made by fire to the
LORD. It *is* a sin offering. Lev. 2:2
13 [R]'The priest shall make atonement for
him, for his sin that he has committed in any
of these matters; and it shall be forgiven him.
[R]*The rest* shall be the priest's as a grain offer-
ing.' " Lev. 4:26 • Lev. 2:3; 6:17, 26

The Trespass Offering

14 Then the LORD spoke to Moses, saying:
15 [R]"If a person commits a trespass, and
sins unintentionally in regard to the holy
things of the LORD, then [R]he shall bring to
the LORD as his trespass offering a ram with-
out blemish from the flocks, with your valua-
tion in shekels of silver according to [R]the
shekel of the sanctuary, as a trespass offer-
ing. Lev. 4:2; 22:14 • Ezra 10:19 • Ex. 30:13
16 "And he shall make restitution for the
harm that he has done in regard to the holy
thing, and shall add one-fifth to it and give it
to the priest. So the priest shall make atone-
ment for him with the ram of the trespass of-
fering, and it shall be forgiven him.
17 "If a person sins, and commits any of
these things which are forbidden to be done
by the commandments of the LORD, [R]though
he does not know *it*, yet he is guilty and shall
bear his iniquity. Lev. 4:2, 13, 22, 27
18 "And he shall bring to the priest a ram
without blemish from the flock, with your val-
uation, as a trespass offering. So the priest
shall make atonement for him regarding his
ignorance in which he erred and did not know
it, and it shall be forgiven him.
19 "It is a trespass offering; he has certainly
trespassed against the LORD."

CHAPTER 6

AND the LORD spoke to Moses, saying:
2 "If a person sins and [R]commits a tres-
pass against the LORD by [R]lying to his neigh-
bor about what was delivered to him for
safekeeping, or about a pledge, or about a
robbery, or if he has [R]extorted from his neigh-
bor, Num. 5:6 • Lev. 19:11 • Prov. 24:28
3 "or if he [R]has found what was lost and lies
concerning it, and [R]swears falsely—in any one
of these things that a man may do in which he
sins: Deut. 22:1–4 • Ex. 22:11
4 "then it shall be, because he has sinned
and is guilty, that he shall [T]restore [R]what he
has stolen, or the thing which he has ex-
torted, or what was delivered to him for
safekeeping, or the lost thing which he
found, *return* • Lev. 24:18, 21
5 "or all that about which he has sworn
falsely. He shall [R]restore its full value, add
one-fifth more to it, *and* give it to whomever
it belongs, on the day of his trespass offer-
ing. Lev. 5:16
6 "And he shall bring his trespass offering
to the LORD, [R]a ram without blemish from the
flock, with your [T]valuation, as a trespass of-
fering, to the priest. Lev. 1:3; 5:15 • *appraisal*
7 "So the priest shall make atonement for
him before the LORD, and he shall be forgiven
for any one of these things that he may have
done in which he trespasses."

The Burnt Offering

8 Then the LORD spoke to Moses, saying,
9 "Command Aaron and his sons, saying,

'This *is* the law of the burnt offering: The burnt offering *shall be* on the hearth upon the altar all night until morning, and the fire of the altar shall be kept burning on it.

10 [R]'And the priest shall put on his linen garment, and his linen trousers he shall put on his body, and take up the ashes of the burnt offering which the fire has consumed on the altar, and he shall put them [R]beside the altar. Ex. 28:39–43 • Lev. 1:16

11 'Then he shall take off his garments, put on other garments, and carry the ashes outside the camp to a clean place.

12 'And the fire on the altar shall be kept burning on it; it shall not be put out. And the priest shall burn wood on it every morning, and lay the burnt offering in order on it; and he shall burn on it [R]the fat of the peace offerings. Lev. 3:3, 5, 9, 14

13 'A fire shall always be burning on the [R]altar; it shall never go out. Lev. 1:7

The Grain Offering

14 'This *is* the law of the grain offering: The sons of Aaron shall offer it on the altar before the LORD.

15 'He shall take from it his handful of the fine flour of the grain offering, with its oil, and all the frankincense which *is* on the grain offering, and shall burn *it* on the altar *for* a sweet aroma, as a memorial to the LORD.

16 'And the remainder of it Aaron and his sons shall eat; with unleavened bread it shall be eaten in a holy place; in the court of the tabernacle of meeting they shall eat it.

17 'It shall not be baked with leaven. I have given it *as* their portion of My offerings made by fire; it *is* most holy, like the sin offering and the [R]trespass offering. Lev. 7:7

18 'All the males among the children of Aaron may eat it. *It shall be* a statute forever in your generations concerning the offerings made by fire to the LORD. Everyone who touches them must be holy.' "*

19 And the LORD spoke to Moses, saying,

20 [R]"This *is* the offering of Aaron and his sons, which they shall offer to the LORD, *beginning* on the day when he is anointed: one-tenth of an [R]ephah of fine flour as a daily grain offering, half of it in the morning and half of it at night. Ex. 29:2 • Ex. 16:36

21 "It shall be made in a pan with oil. *When it is* mixed, you shall bring it in. The baked pieces of the grain offering you shall offer *for* a sweet aroma to the LORD.

22 "The priest from among his sons, [R]who is anointed in his place, shall offer it. *It is* a statute forever to the LORD. [R]It shall be [T]wholly burned. Lev. 4:3 • Ex. 29:25 • *completely*

23 "For every grain offering for the priest shall be wholly burned. It shall not be eaten."

The Sin Offering

24 Also the LORD spoke to Moses, saying,

25 "Speak to Aaron and to his sons, saying, 'This *is* the law of the sin offering: [R]In the place where the burnt offering is killed, the sin offering shall be killed before the LORD. It *is* most holy. Lev. 1:1, 3, 5, 11

26 'The priest who offers it for sin shall eat it. In a holy place it shall be eaten, in the court of the tabernacle of meeting.

27 [R]'Everyone who touches its flesh must be holy.* And when its blood is sprinkled on any garment, you shall wash that on which it was sprinkled, in a holy place. Ex. 29:37

28 'But the earthen vessel in which it is boiled [R]shall be broken. And if it is boiled in a bronze pot, it shall be both scoured and rinsed in water. Lev. 11:33; 15:12

29 'All the males among the priests may eat it. It *is* most holy.

30 'But no sin offering from which *any* of the blood is brought into the tabernacle of meeting, to make atonement in the holy [R]*place,** shall be [R]eaten. It shall be [R]burned in the fire. Ex. 26:33 • Lev. 6:16, 23, 26 • Lev. 16:27

CHAPTER 7

The Trespass Offering

'LIKEWISE [R]this *is* the law of the trespass offering (it *is* most holy): Lev. 5:14—6:7

2 'In the place where they kill the burnt offering they shall kill the trespass offering. And its blood he shall sprinkle all around on the altar.

3 'And he shall offer from it all its fat. The fat tail and the fat that covers the entrails,

4 'the two kidneys and the fat that *is* on them by the flanks, and the fatty lobe *attached* to the liver above the kidneys, he shall remove;

5 'and the priest shall burn them on the altar *as* an offering made by fire to the LORD. It *is* a trespass offering.

6 [R]'Every male among the priests may eat it. It shall be eaten in a holy place. [R]It *is* most holy. Lev. 6:16–18, 29 • Lev. 2:3

7 [R]'The trespass offering *is* like the sin offering; *there is* one law for them both: the priest who makes atonement with it shall have *it*. Lev. 6:24–30; 14:13

8 'And the priest who offers anyone's burnt offering, that priest shall have for himself the skin of the burnt offering which he has offered.

9 'Also [R]every grain offering that is baked in the oven and all that is prepared in the covered pan, or [T]in a pan, shall be the priest's who offers it. Lev. 2:3, 10 • *on a griddle*

6:18 Cf. Num. 4:15 and Hag. 2:11–13 **6:27** Cf. Num. 4:15 and Hag. 2:11–13 **6:30** The Most Holy Place when capitalized

10 'Every grain offering, *whether* mixed with oil or dry, shall belong to all the sons of Aaron, to one *as much* as the other.

The Peace Offering

11 'This *is* the law of the sacrifice of peace offerings which he shall offer to the LORD:

12 'If he offers it for a thanksgiving, then he shall offer, with the sacrifice of thanksgiving, unleavened cakes mixed with oil, unleavened wafers [R]anointed with oil, or cakes of blended flour mixed with oil. Num. 6:15

13 'Besides the cakes, *as* his offering he shall offer leavened bread with the sacrifice of thanksgiving of his peace offering.

14 'And from it he shall offer one cake from each offering *as* a heave offering to the LORD. It shall belong to the priest who sprinkles the blood of the peace offering.

15 [R]'The flesh of the sacrifice of his peace offering for thanksgiving shall be eaten the same day it is offered. He shall not leave any of it until morning. Lev. 22:29, 30

16 'But [R]if the sacrifice of his offering *is* a vow or a voluntary offering, it shall be eaten the same day that he offers his sacrifice; but on the next day the remainder of it also may be eaten; Lev. 19:5–8

17 'the remainder of the flesh of the sacrifice on the third day must be burned with fire.

18 'And if *any* of the flesh of the sacrifice of his peace offering is eaten at all on the third day, it shall not be accepted, nor shall it be [R]imputed to him; it shall be an abomination *to* him who offers it, and the person who eats of it shall bear guilt. Num. 18:27

19 'The flesh that touches any unclean thing shall not be eaten. It shall be burned with fire. And as for the *clean* flesh, all who are [T]clean may eat of it. *pure*

20 'But the person who eats the flesh of the sacrifice of the peace offering that *belongs* to the [R]LORD, while he is unclean, that person shall be cut off from his people. [Heb. 2:17]

21 'Moreover the person who touches any unclean thing, *such as* [R]human uncleanness, *an* unclean animal, or any [R]abominable unclean thing,* and who eats the flesh of the sacrifice of the peace offering that *belongs* to the LORD, that person shall be cut off from his people.' " Lev. 5:2, 3, 5 • Ezek. 4:14

22 And the LORD spoke to Moses, saying,

23 "Speak to the children of Israel, saying: [R]'You shall not eat any fat, of ox or sheep or goat. Lev. 3:17; 17:10–15

24 'And the fat of an animal that dies *naturally*, and the fat of what is torn by wild beasts, may be used in any other way; but you shall by no means eat it.

25 'For whoever eats the fat of the animal of which men offer an offering made by fire to the LORD, the person who eats *it* shall be cut off from his people.

26 [R]'Moreover you shall not eat any blood in any of your dwellings, *whether* of bird or beast. Acts 15:20, 29

27 'Whoever eats any blood, that person shall be cut off from his people.' "

28 Then the LORD spoke to Moses, saying,

29 "Speak to the children of Israel, saying: [R]'He who offers the sacrifice of his peace offering to the LORD shall bring his offering to the LORD from the sacrifice of his peace offering. Lev. 3:1; 22:21

30 'His own hands shall bring the offerings made by fire to the LORD. The fat with the breast he shall bring, that the breast may be waved *as* a wave offering before the LORD.

31 [R]'And the priest shall burn the fat on the altar, but the [R]breast shall be Aaron's and his sons'. Lev. 3:5, 11, 16 • Deut. 18:3

32 [R]'Also the right thigh you shall give to the priest *as* a heave offering from the sacrifices of your peace offerings. Num. 6:20

33 'He among the sons of Aaron, who offers the blood of the peace offering and the fat, shall have the right thigh for *his* part.

34 'For [R]the breast of the wave offering and the thigh of the heave offering I have taken from the children of Israel, from the sacrifices of their peace offerings, and I have given them to Aaron the priest and to his sons from the children of Israel by a statute forever.' " Lev. 10:14, 15

35 This *is* the consecrated portion for Aaron and his sons, from the offerings made by fire to the LORD, on the day when *Moses* presented them to [T]minister to the LORD as priests. *serve*

36 The LORD commanded this to be given to them by the children of Israel, [R]on the day that He anointed them, *by* a statute forever throughout their generations. Lev. 8:12, 30

The Summary of the Offerings

37 This *is* the law [R]of the burnt offering, the grain offering, the sin offering, the trespass offering, the consecrations, and the sacrifice of the peace offering, Lev. 6:9

38 which the LORD commanded Moses on Mount Sinai, on the day when He commanded the children of Israel [R]to offer their offerings to the LORD in the Wilderness of Sinai. Lev. 1:1, 2

CHAPTER 8

Consecration Commanded by God

AND the LORD spoke to Moses, saying:

2 [R]"Take Aaron and his sons with him, and [R]the garments, the anointing oil, a bull as the sin offering, two rams, and a basket of unleavened bread; Ex. 29:1–3 • Ex. 28:2, 4

7:21 So with MT, LXX, Vg.; Sam., Syr., Tg. *swarming thing* (cf. 5:2)

3 "and gather all the congregation together at the door of the tabernacle of meeting."

4 So Moses did as the LORD commanded him. And the congregation was gathered together at the door of the tabernacle of meeting.

5 And Moses said to the congregation, "This *is* what the LORD commanded to be done."

Cleansing the Priests with Water

6 Then Moses brought Aaron and his sons and [R]washed them with water. Heb. 10:22

Special Garments

7 And he [R]put the tunic on him, girded him with the sash, clothed him with the robe, and put the ephod on him; and he girded him with the intricately woven band of the ephod, and with it tied *the ephod* on him. Ex. 39:1–31

8 Then he put the breastplate on him, and he put the Urim and the Thummim* in the breastplate.

9 [R]And he put the turban on his head. Also on the turban, on its front, he put the golden plate, the holy crown, as the LORD had commanded Moses. Ex. 28:36, 37; 29:6

Anointing with Oil

10 [R]Also Moses took the anointing oil, and anointed the tabernacle and all that *was* in it, and consecrated them. Ex. 30:26–29

11 He sprinkled some of it on the altar seven times, anointed the altar and all its utensils, and the laver and its base, to [T]consecrate them. *set them apart* for the LORD

12 And he [R]poured some of the anointing oil on Aaron's head and anointed him, to consecrate him. Ps. 133:2

13 [R]Then Moses brought Aaron's sons and put tunics on them, girded them with sashes, and put hats on them, as the LORD had commanded Moses. Ex. 29:8

Consecrating with Blood

14 [R]And he brought the bull for the sin offering. Then Aaron and his sons [R]laid their hands on the head of the bull for the sin offering, Ezek. 43:19 • Lev. 4:4

15 and Moses killed *it*. [R]Then he took the blood, and put *some* on the horns of the altar all around with his finger, and purified the altar. And he poured the blood at the base of the altar, and consecrated it, to make [T]atonement for it. Lev. 4:7 • Lit. *covering*

16 [R]Then he took all the fat that *was* on the entrails, the fatty lobe *attached to* the liver, and the two kidneys with their fat, and Moses burned *them* on the altar. Ex. 29:13

17 But the bull, its hide, its flesh, and its offal, he burned with fire outside the camp, as the LORD had commanded Moses.

18 [R]Then he brought the ram as the burnt offering. And Aaron and his sons laid their hands on the head of the ram, Ex. 29:15

19 and Moses killed *it*. Then he sprinkled the blood all around on the altar.

20 And he cut the ram into pieces; and Moses [R]burned the head, the pieces, and the fat. Lev. 1:8

21 Then he washed the entrails and the legs in water. And Moses burned the whole ram on the altar. It *was* a burnt sacrifice for a [T]sweet aroma, an offering made by fire to the LORD, [R]as the LORD had commanded Moses. *pleasing* • Ex. 29:18

22 And [R]he brought the second ram, the ram of consecration. Then Aaron and his sons laid their hands on the head of the ram, Ex. 29:19, 31

23 and Moses killed *it*. Also he took *some* of its blood and put it on the tip of Aaron's right ear, on the thumb of his right hand, and on the big toe of his right foot.

24 Then he brought Aaron's sons. And Moses put *some* of the [R]blood on the tips of their right ears, on the thumbs of their right hands, and on the big toes of their right feet. And Moses sprinkled the blood all around on the altar. [Heb. 9:13, 14, 18–23]

25 [R]Then he took the fat and the fat tail, all the fat that *was* on the entrails, the fatty lobe *attached to* the liver, the two kidneys and their fat, and the right thigh; Ex. 29:22

26 [R]and from the basket of unleavened bread that was before the LORD he took one unleavened cake, a cake of bread *anointed with* oil, and one wafer, and put *them* on the fat and on the right thigh; Ex. 29:23

27 and he put all *these* [R]in Aaron's hands and in his sons' hands, and waved them *as* a wave offering before the LORD. Ex. 29:24

28 [R]Then Moses took them from their hands and burned *them* on the altar, on the burnt offering. They *were* consecration offerings for a sweet aroma. That *was* an offering made by fire to the LORD. Ex. 29:25

29 And [R]Moses took the breast and waved it *as* a wave offering before the LORD. It was Moses' part of the ram of consecration, as the LORD had commanded Moses. Ps. 99:6

30 Then [R]Moses took some of the anointing oil and some of the blood which *was* on the altar, and sprinkled *it* on Aaron, on his garments, on his sons, and on the garments of his sons with him; and he consecrated Aaron, his garments, his sons, and the garments of his sons with him. Ex. 29:21; 30:30

The Priests Are to Remain in the Tabernacle

31 And Moses said to Aaron and his sons, [R]"Boil the flesh *at* the door of the tabernacle of meeting, and eat it there with the bread that *is* in the basket of consecration offerings, as I

8:8 Lit. *Lights and the Perfections*, Ex. 28:30

commanded, saying, 'Aaron and his sons shall eat it.' Ex. 29:31, 32

32 [R]"What remains of the flesh and of the bread you shall burn with fire. Ex. 29:34

33 "And you shall not go outside the door of the tabernacle of meeting *for* seven days, until the days of your consecration are ended. For [R]seven days he shall consecrate you. Ex. 29:30, 35

34 [R]"As he has done this day, *so* the LORD has commanded to do, to make atonement for you. [Heb. 7:16]

35 "Therefore you shall stay *at* the door of the tabernacle of meeting day and night for seven days, and [R]keep the [T]charge of the LORD, so that you may not die; for so I have been commanded." Deut. 11:1 • *office*

36 So Aaron and his sons did all the things that the LORD had commanded by the hand of Moses.

CHAPTER 9

Offerings for the Priest

IT came to pass on the [R]eighth day that Moses called Aaron and his sons and the elders of Israel. Ezek. 43:27

2 And he said to Aaron, "Take for yourself a young [R]bull as a sin offering and a ram as a burnt offering, without blemish, and offer *them* before the LORD. Lev. 4:1–12

3 "And to the children of Israel you shall speak, saying, [R]'Take a kid of the goats as a sin offering, and a calf and a lamb, *both* of the first year, without blemish, as a burnt offering, Lev. 4:23, 28

4 'also a bull and a ram as peace offerings, to sacrifice before the LORD, and [R]a grain offering mixed with oil; for [R]today the LORD will appear to you.' " Lev. 2:4 • Ex. 29:43

5 So they brought what Moses commanded before the tabernacle of meeting. And all the congregation drew near and stood [T]before the LORD. *in the presence of*

6 Then Moses said, "This *is* the thing which the LORD commanded you to do, and the glory of the LORD will appear to you."

7 And Moses said to Aaron, "Go to the altar, [R]offer your sin offering and your burnt offering, and make atonement for yourself and for the people. Offer the offering of the people, and make atonement for them, as the LORD commanded." [Heb. 5:3–5; 7:27]

8 Aaron therefore went to the altar and killed the calf of the sin offering, which *was* for himself.

9 Then the sons of Aaron brought the blood to him. And he dipped his finger in the blood, put *it* on the horns of the altar, and poured the blood at the base of the altar.

10 [R]But the fat, the kidneys, and the fatty lobe from the liver of the sin offering he burned on the altar, as the LORD had commanded Moses. Lev. 8:16

11 [R]The flesh and the hide he burned with fire outside the camp. Lev. 4:11, 12; 8:17

12 And he killed the burnt offering; and Aaron's sons presented to him the blood, which he sprinkled all around on the altar.

13 [R]Then they presented the burnt offering to him, with its pieces and head, and he burned *them* on the altar. Lev. 8:20

14 [R]And he washed the entrails and the legs, and burned *them* with the burnt offering on the altar. Lev. 8:21

Offerings for the People

15 [R]Then he brought the people's offering, and took the goat, which *was* the sin offering for the people, and killed it and offered it for sin, like the first one. [Is. 53:10]

16 And he brought the burnt offering and offered it [R]according to the [T]prescribed manner. Lev. 1:1–13 • *ordinance*

17 Then he brought the grain offering, took a handful of it, and burned *it* on the altar, besides the burnt sacrifice of the morning.

18 He also killed the bull and the ram *as* [R]sacrifices of peace offerings, which *were* for the people. And Aaron's sons presented to him the blood, which he sprinkled all around on the altar, Lev. 3:1–11

19 and the fat from the bull and the ram—the fatty tail, what covers *the entrails* and the kidneys, and the fatty lobe *attached to* the liver;

20 and they put the fat on the breasts. Then he burned the fat on the altar;

21 but the breasts and the right thigh Aaron waved *as* a wave offering before the LORD, as Moses had commanded.

The Lord Accepts the Offerings

22 Then Aaron lifted his hand toward the people, [R]blessed them, and came down from offering the sin offering, the burnt offering, and peace offerings. Luke 24:50

23 And Moses and Aaron went into the tabernacle of meeting, and came out and blessed the people. Then the glory of the LORD appeared to all the people,

24 and [R]fire came out from before the LORD and consumed the burnt offering and the fat on the altar. When all the people saw *it*, they shouted and fell on their faces. Judg. 6:21

CHAPTER 10

The Sin of Nadab and Abihu

THEN [R]Nadab and Abihu, the sons of Aaron, [R]each took his censer and put fire in it, put incense on it, and offered [R]profane fire before the LORD, which He had not commanded them. Num. 3:2–4 • Lev. 16:12 • Ex. 30:9

2 So fire went out from the LORD and devoured them, and they died before the LORD.

3 And Moses said to Aaron, "This is what
the LORD spoke, saying:

'By those [R]who come near Me Ex. 19:22
I must be regarded as holy;
And before all the people
I must be glorified.' "

So Aaron held his peace.
4 Then Moses called Mishael and Elza-
phan, the sons of Uzziel the uncle of Aaron,
and said to them, "Come near, [R]carry your
brethren from [T]before the sanctuary out of the
camp." Acts 5:6, 10 • *in front of*
5 So they went near and carried them by
their tunics out of the camp, as Moses had
said.
6 And Moses said to Aaron, and to Eleazar
and Ithamar, his sons, "Do not [T]uncover your
heads nor tear your clothes, lest you die, and
[R]wrath come upon all the people. But let
your brethren, the whole house of Israel, be-
wail the burning which the LORD has kin-
dled. An act of mourning • 2 Sam. 24:1
7 "You shall not go out from the door of the
tabernacle of meeting, lest you die, for the
anointing oil of the LORD *is* upon you." And
they did according to the word of Moses.
8 Then the LORD spoke to Aaron, saying:
9 [R]"Do not drink wine or intoxicating drink,
you, nor your sons with you, when you go into
the tabernacle of meeting, lest you die. *It shall
be* a statute forever throughout your genera-
tions, Ezek. 44:21
10 "that you may distinguish between holy
and unholy, and between unclean and clean,
11 "and that you may teach the children of
Israel all the statutes which the LORD has spo-
ken to them by the hand of Moses."

The Sin of Eleazar and Ithamar

12 And Moses spoke to Aaron, and to
Eleazar and Ithamar, his sons who were left:
[R]"Take the grain offering that remains of the
offerings made by fire to the LORD, and eat it
without leaven beside the altar; [R]for it *is* most
holy. Num. 18:9 • Lev. 21:22
13 "You shall eat it in a [R]holy place, because
it *is* your due and your sons' due, of the sacri-
fices made by fire to the LORD; for so I have
been commanded. Num. 18:10
14 [R]"The breast of the wave offering and the
thigh of the heave offering you shall eat in a
clean place, you, your sons, and your daugh-
ters with you; for *they are* your due and your
sons' [R]due, *which* are given from the sacri-
fices of peace offerings of the children of Is-
rael. Num. 18:11 • Num. 18:10
15 [R]"The thigh of the heave offering and the
breast of the wave offering they shall bring
with the offerings of fat made by fire, to offer
as a wave offering before the LORD. And it
shall be yours and your sons' with you, by a
statute forever, as the LORD has com-
manded." Lev. 7:29, 30, 34
16 Then Moses made careful inquiry about
[R]the goat of the sin offering, and there it
was—burned up. And he was angry with
Eleazar and Ithamar, the sons of Aaron *who
were* left, saying, Lev. 9:3, 15
17 [R]"Why have you not eaten the sin offering
in a holy place, since it *is* most holy, and *God*
has given it to you to bear [R]the guilt of the
congregation, to make atonement for them
before the LORD? Lev. 6:24–30 • Ex. 28:38
18 "See! Its blood was not brought inside the
holy *place;** indeed you should have eaten it
in a holy *place,* as I commanded."
19 And Aaron said to Moses, "Look, this day
they have offered their sin offering and their
burnt offering before the LORD, and such
things have befallen me! *If* I had eaten the sin
offering today, would it have been accepted in
the sight of the LORD?"
20 So when Moses heard *that,* he was con-
tent.

CHAPTER 11

Animals of the Earth

NOW the LORD spoke to Moses and Aaron,
saying to them,
2 "Speak to the children of Israel, saying,
'These *are* the animals which you may eat
among all the animals that *are* on the earth:
3 'Among the animals, whatever divides the
hoof, having cloven hooves *and* chewing the
cud—that you may eat.
4 'Nevertheless these you shall [R]not eat
among those that chew the cud or those that
have cloven hooves: the camel, because it
chews the cud but does not have cloven
hooves, is [T]unclean to you; Acts 10:14 • *impure*
5 'the [T]rock hyrax, because it chews the cud
but does not have cloven hooves, *is* [T]unclean
to you; *rock badger* • *impure*
6 'the hare, because it chews the cud but
does not have cloven hooves, *is* unclean to you;
7 'and the swine, though it divides the hoof,
having cloven hooves, yet does not chew the
cud, [R]*is* unclean to you. Is. 65:4
8 'Their flesh you shall not eat, and their
carcasses you shall not touch. [R]They *are* un-
clean to you. Is. 52:11

Living Things in the Waters

9 [R]'These you may eat of all that *are* in the
water: whatever in the water has fins and
scales, whether in the seas or in the rivers—
that you may eat. Deut. 14:9
10 'But all in the seas or in the rivers that do
not have fins and scales, all that move in the
water or any living thing which *is* in the
water, they *are* an abomination to you.

10:18 The Most Holy Place when capitalized

11 'They shall be an abomination to you; you
shall not eat their flesh, but you shall regard
their carcasses as an abomination.
12 'Whatever in the water does not have fins
or scales—that *shall be* an abomination to
you.

Birds of the Air

13 [R]'And these you shall regard as an
abomination among the birds; they shall not
be eaten, they *are* an abomination: the eagle,
the vulture, the buzzard, Is. 66:17
14 'the kite, and the falcon after its kind;
15 'every raven after its kind,
16 'the ostrich, the short-eared owl, the sea
gull, and the hawk after its kind;
17 'the little owl, the fisher owl, and the
screech owl;
18 'the white owl, the jackdaw, and the car-
rion vulture;
19 'the stork, the heron after its kind, the
hoopoe, and the bat.

Winged Insects

20 'All flying insects that creep on *all* fours
shall be an abomination to you.
21 'Yet these you may eat of every flying in-
sect that creeps on *all* fours: those which have
jointed legs above their feet with which to
leap on the earth.
22 'These you may eat: [R]the locust after its
kind, the destroying locust after its kind, the
cricket after its kind, and the grasshopper
after its kind. Matt. 3:4
23 'But all *other* flying insects which have
four feet *shall be* an abomination to you.

The Carcasses of the Unclean Animals

24 'By these you shall become [T]unclean;
whoever touches the carcass of any of them
shall be unclean until evening; *impure*
25 'whoever carries part of the carcass of
any of them [R]shall wash his clothes and be un-
clean until evening: Num. 19:10, 21, 22
26 '*The carcass* of any animal which divides
the foot, but is not cloven-hoofed or does not
chew the cud, *is* unclean to you. Everyone
who touches it shall be unclean.
27 'And whatever goes on its paws, among
all kinds of animals that go on *all* fours, those
are unclean to you. Whoever touches any such
carcass shall be unclean until evening.
28 'Whoever carries *any such* carcass shall
wash his clothes and be unclean until
evening. It *is* unclean to you.

Creeping Things

29 'These also *shall be* unclean to you
among the creeping things that creep on the
earth: the mole, [R]the mouse, and the large
lizard after its kind; Is. 66:17
30 'the gecko, the monitor lizard, the sand
reptile, the sand lizard, and the chameleon.
31 'These *are* unclean to you among all that
creep. Whoever touches them when they are
dead shall be unclean until evening.
32 'Anything on which *any* of them falls,
when they are dead shall be [T]unclean,
whether *it is* any item of wood or clothing or
skin or sack, whatever item *it is*, in which *any*
work is done, [R]it must be put in water. And it
shall be unclean until evening; then it shall be
clean. *impure* • Lev. 15:12
33 'Any [R]earthen vessel into which *any* of
them falls [R]you shall break; and whatever *is* in
it shall be unclean: Lev. 6:28 • Lev. 15:12
34 'in such a vessel, any edible food upon
which water falls becomes unclean, and any
drink that may be drunk from it becomes un-
clean.
35 'And everything on which *a part* of *any
such* carcass falls shall be unclean; *whether it
is* an oven or cooking stove, it shall be broken
down; *for* they *are* unclean, and shall be un-
clean to you.
36 'Nevertheless a spring or a cistern, *in
which there is* plenty of water, shall be clean,
but whatever touches any such carcass be-
comes unclean.
37 'And if a part of *any such* carcass falls on
any planting seed which is to be sown, it *re-
mains* clean.
38 'But if water is put on the seed, and if *a
part* of *any such* carcass falls on it, it *becomes*
[T]unclean to you. *impure*

The Carcasses of the Clean Animals

39 'And if any animal which you may eat
dies, he who touches its carcass shall be [R]un-
clean until evening. Hag. 2:11–13
40 'He who eats of its carcass shall wash his
clothes and be unclean until evening. He also
who carries its carcass shall wash his clothes
and be unclean until evening.

The Purpose of Dietary Laws

41 'And every creeping thing that creeps on
the earth *shall be* [T]an abomination. It shall not
be eaten. *detestable*
42 'Whatever crawls on its belly, whatever
goes on *all* fours, or whatever has many feet
among all creeping things that creep on the
earth—these you shall not eat, for they *are* an
abomination.
43 'You shall not make yourselves [T]abomina-
ble with any creeping thing that creeps; nor
shall you make yourselves unclean with them,
lest you be defiled by them. *impure*
44 'For I *am* the LORD your God. You shall
therefore consecrate yourselves, and [R]you
shall be holy; for I *am* holy. Neither shall you
defile yourselves with any creeping thing that
creeps on the earth. 1 Pet. 1:15, 16
45 'For I *am* the LORD who brings you up out
of the land of Egypt, to be your God. You shall
therefore be holy, for I *am* holy.

46 'This *is* the law [T]of the animals and the birds and every living creature that moves in the waters, and of every creature that creeps on the earth, *concerning*

47 [R]'to distinguish between the unclean and the clean, and between the animal that may be eaten and the animal that may not be eaten.' " Ezek. 44:23

CHAPTER 12

Laws Concerning Childbirth

THEN the LORD spoke to Moses, saying,

2 "Speak to the children of Israel, saying: 'If a woman has conceived, and borne a male child, then [R]she shall be unclean seven days; as in the days of her customary impurity she shall be unclean. Luke 2:22

3 'And on the [R]eighth day the flesh of his foreskin shall be circumcised. Gen. 17:12

4 'She shall then continue in the blood of *her* purification thirty-three days. She shall not touch any [T]hallowed thing, nor come into the sanctuary until the days of her purification are fulfilled. *consecrated*

5 'But if she bears a female child, then she shall be unclean two weeks, as in her customary impurity, and she shall continue in the blood of *her* purification sixty-six days.

6 'When the days of her purification are fulfilled, whether for a son or a daughter, she shall bring to the priest a lamb of the first year as a burnt offering, and a young pigeon or a turtledove as a sin offering, to the door of the tabernacle of meeting

7 'Then he shall offer it before the LORD, and make [T]atonement for her. And she shall be clean from the flow of her blood. This *is* the law for her who has borne a male or a female. Lit. *covering*

8 [R]'And if she is not able to bring a lamb, then she may bring two turtledoves or two young pigeons—one as a burnt offering and the other as a sin offering. [R]So the priest shall make atonement for her, and she will be [T]clean.' " Lev. 5:7 • Lev. 4:26 • *pure*

CHAPTER 13

Examination of People

AND the LORD spoke to Moses and Aaron, saying:

2 "When a man has on the skin of his body a swelling, [R]a scab, or a bright spot, and it becomes on the skin of his body *like* a leprous* sore, [R]then he shall be brought to Aaron the priest or to one of his sons the priests. Is. 3:17 • Mal. 2:7

3 "The priest shall examine the sore on the skin of the body; and if the hair on the sore has turned white, and the sore appears *to be* deeper than the skin of his body, it *is* a leprous sore. Then the priest shall examine him, and pronounce him [T]unclean. *defiled*

4 "But if the bright spot *is* white on the skin of his body, and does not appear *to be* deeper than the skin, and its hair has not turned white, then the priest shall isolate *the one who has* the sore seven days.

5 "And the priest shall examine him on the seventh day; and indeed *if* the sore appears to be as it was, *and* the sore has not spread on the skin, then the priest shall isolate him another seven days.

6 "Then the priest shall examine him again on the seventh day; and indeed *if* the sore has faded, *and* the sore has not spread on the skin, then the priest shall pronounce him clean; it *is only* a scab, and he shall wash his clothes and be clean.

7 "But if the scab should at all spread over the skin, after he has been seen by the priest for his cleansing, he shall be seen by the priest again.

8 "And *if* the priest sees that the scab has indeed spread on the skin, then the priest shall pronounce him unclean. It *is* leprosy.

9 "When the leprous sore is on a person, then he shall be brought to the priest.

10 "And the priest shall examine *him;* and indeed *if* the swelling on the skin *is* white, and it has turned the hair white, and *there is* a spot of raw flesh in the swelling,

11 "it *is* an old leprosy on the skin of his body. The priest shall pronounce him [T]unclean, and shall not isolate him, for he *is* unclean. *defiled*

12 "And if leprosy breaks out all over the skin, and the leprosy covers all the skin of *the one who has* the sore, from his head to his foot, wherever the priest looks,

13 "then the priest shall consider; and indeed *if* the leprosy has covered all his body, he shall pronounce *him* clean *who has* the sore. It has all turned white. He *is* clean.

14 "But when raw flesh appears on him, he shall be unclean.

15 "And the priest shall examine the raw flesh and pronounce him to be unclean; *for* the raw flesh *is* unclean. It *is* leprosy.

16 "Or if the raw flesh changes and turns white again, he shall come to the priest.

17 "And the priest shall examine him; and indeed *if* the sore has turned white, then the priest shall pronounce *him* clean *who has* the sore. He *is* clean.

18 "If the body develops a [R]boil in the skin, and it is healed, Ex. 9:9; 15:26

19 "and in the place of the boil there comes a white swelling or a bright spot, reddish-white, then it shall be shown to the priest;

20 "and *if,* when the priest sees it, it indeed

13:2 Heb. *saraath,* disfiguring skin diseases, including leprosy, and so in vv. 2–46 and 14:2–32

appears deeper than the skin, and its hair has turned white, the priest shall pronounce him unclean. It *is* a leprous sore which has broken out of the boil.

21 "But if the priest examines it, and indeed *there are* no white hairs in it, and it *is* not deeper than the skin, but has faded, then the priest shall isolate him seven days;

22 "and if it should at all spread over the skin, then the priest shall pronounce him unclean. It *is* a [T]leprous sore. *infection*

23 "But if the bright spot stays in one place, *and* has not spread, it *is* the scar of the boil; and the priest shall pronounce him clean.

24 "Or if the body receives a [R]burn on its skin by fire, and the raw *flesh* of the burn becomes a bright spot, reddish-white or white, Is. 3:24

25 "then the priest shall examine it; and indeed *if* the hair of the bright spot has turned white, and it appears deeper than the skin, it *is* leprosy broken out in the burn. Therefore the priest shall pronounce him unclean. It *is* a leprous sore.

26 "But if the priest examines it, and indeed *there are* no white hairs in the bright spot, and it *is* not deeper than the skin, but has faded, then the priest shall isolate him seven days.

27 "And the priest shall examine him on the seventh day. If it has at all spread over the skin, then the priest shall pronounce him unclean. It *is* a leprous sore.

28 "But if the bright spot stays in one place, *and* has not spread on the skin, but has faded, it *is* a swelling from the burn. The priest shall pronounce him clean, for it *is* the scar from the burn.

29 "If a man or woman has a sore on the head or the beard,

30 "then the priest shall examine the sore; and indeed if it appears deeper than the skin, *and there is* in it thin yellow hair, then the priest shall pronounce him unclean. It *is* a scaly leprosy of the head or beard.

31 "But if the priest examines the scaly sore, and indeed it does not appear deeper than the skin, and *there is* no black hair in it, then the priest shall isolate *the one who has* the scale seven days.

32 "And on the seventh day the priest shall examine the sore; and indeed *if* the scale has not spread, and there is no yellow hair in it, and the scale does not appear deeper than the skin,

33 "he shall shave himself, but the scale he shall not shave. And the priest shall isolate *the one who has* the scale another seven days.

34 "On the seventh day the priest shall examine the scale; and indeed *if* the scale has not spread over the skin, and does not appear deeper than the skin, then the priest shall pronounce him clean. He shall wash his clothes and be clean.

35 "But if the scale should at all spread over the skin after his cleansing,

36 "then the priest shall examine him; and indeed *if* the scale has spread over the skin, the priest need not seek for yellow hair. He *is* unclean.

37 "But if the scale appears to be at a standstill, and there is black hair grown up in it, the scale has healed. He *is* clean, and the priest shall pronounce him clean.

38 "If a man or a woman has bright spots on the skin of the body, *specifically* white bright spots,

39 "then the priest shall look; and indeed *if* the bright spots on the skin of the body *are* dull white, it *is* a white spot *that* grows on the skin. He *is* clean.

40 "As for the man whose hair has fallen from his head, he *is* bald, *but* he *is* clean.

41 "He whose hair has fallen from his forehead, he *is* bald on the forehead, *but* he *is* clean.

42 "And if there is on the bald head or bald [R]forehead a reddish-white sore, it *is* leprosy breaking out on his bald head or his bald forehead. 2 Chr. 26:19

43 "Then the priest shall examine it; and indeed *if* the swelling of the sore *is* reddish-white on his bald head or on his bald forehead, as the appearance of leprosy on the skin of the body,

44 "he is a leprous man. He *is* unclean. The priest shall surely pronounce him unclean; his sore *is* on his [R]head. Is. 1:5

45 "Now the leper on whom the sore *is*, his clothes shall be torn and his head bare; and he shall [R]cover his mustache, and cry, [R]'Unclean! Unclean!' Ezek. 24:17, 22 • Lam. 4:15

46 "He shall be unclean. All the days he has the sore he shall be unclean. He *is* unclean, and he shall dwell alone; his dwelling *shall be* [R]outside the camp. Num. 5:1–4; 12:14

Examination of Garments

47 "Also, if a garment has a leprous plague* in it, *whether it is* a woolen garment or a linen garment,

48 "whether *it is* in the warp or woof of linen or wool, whether in leather or in anything made of leather,

49 "and if the plague is greenish or reddish in the garment or in the leather, whether in the warp or in the woof, or in anything made of leather, it *is* a leprous [T]plague and shall be shown to the priest. *mark*

50 "The priest shall examine the plague and isolate *that which has* the plague seven days.

51 "And he shall examine the plague on the seventh day. If the plague has spread in the garment, either in the warp or in the woof,

13:47 A mold, fungus, or similar infestation, and so in vv. 47–59

in the leather *or* in anything made of leather,
the plague *is* [R]an active leprosy. It *is* un-
clean. Lev. 14:44
52 "He shall therefore burn that garment in
which is the plague, whether warp or woof, in
wool or in linen, or anything of leather, for it
is an active leprosy; *the garment* shall be
burned in the fire.
53 "But if the priest examines *it,* and indeed
the plague has not spread in the garment, ei-
ther in the warp or in the woof, or in anything
made of leather,
54 "then the priest shall command that they
wash *the thing* in which *is* the plague; and he
shall isolate it another seven days.
55 "Then the priest shall examine the plague
after it has been washed; and indeed *if* the
plague has not changed its color, though the
plague has not spread, it *is* unclean, and you
shall burn it in the fire; it continues eating
away, *whether* the damage *is* outside or in-
side.
56 "If the priest examines *it,* and indeed the
plague has faded after washing it, then he
shall tear it out of the garment, whether out of
the warp or out of the woof, or out of the
leather.
57 "But if it appears again in the garment, ei-
ther in the warp or in the woof, or in anything
made of leather, it *is* a spreading *plague;* you
shall burn with fire that in which is the
plague.
58 "And if you wash the garment, either warp
or woof, or whatever is made of leather, if the
plague has disappeared from it, then it shall
be washed a second time, and shall be clean.
59 "This *is* the law of the leprous plague in a
garment of wool or linen, either in the warp or
woof, or in anything made of leather, to pro-
nounce it clean or to pronounce it unclean."

CHAPTER 14

Cleansing of People

THEN the LORD spoke to Moses, saying,
2 "This shall be the law of the leper for the
day of his cleansing: He [R]shall be brought to
the priest. Matt. 8:2, 4
3 "And the priest shall go out of the camp,
and the priest shall examine *him;* and indeed,
if the leprosy is healed in the leper,
4 "then the priest shall command to take
for him who is to be cleansed two living *and*
clean birds, [R]cedar wood, [R]scarlet, and [R]hys-
sop. Num. 19:6 • Ex. 25:4 • Ps. 51:7
5 "And the priest shall command that one of
the birds be killed in an earthen vessel over
running water.
6 "As for the living bird, he shall take it, the
cedar wood and the scarlet and the hyssop,
and dip them and the living bird in the blood
of the bird *that was* killed over the running
water.
7 "And he shall [R]sprinkle it [R]seven times
on him who is to be cleansed from the lep-
rosy, and shall pronounce him clean, and
shall let the living bird loose in the open
field. Num. 19:18, 19 • Ps. 51:2
8 "He who is to be cleansed shall wash his
clothes, shave off all his hair, and [R]wash him-
self in water, that he may be clean. After that
he shall come into the camp, and shall stay
outside his tent seven days. [Heb. 10:22]
9 "But on the [R]seventh day he shall shave
all the hair off his head and his beard and his
eyebrows—all his hair he shall shave off. He
shall wash his clothes and wash his body in
water, and he shall be clean. Num. 19:19
10 "And on the eighth day he shall take two
male lambs without blemish, one ewe lamb of
the first year without blemish, three-tenths *of
an ephah* of fine flour mixed with oil as a
grain offering, and one log of oil.
11 "Then the priest who makes *him* clean
shall present the man who is to be made
clean, and those things, before the LORD, *at*
the door of the tabernacle of meeting.
12 "And the priest shall take one male lamb
and [R]offer it as a trespass offering, and the log
of oil, and wave them *as* a wave offering be-
fore the LORD. Lev. 5:6, 18; 6:6; 14:19
13 "Then he shall kill the lamb [R]in the place
where he kills the sin offering and the burnt
offering, in a holy place; for as the sin offering
is the priest's, so *is* the trespass offering. It *is*
most holy. Ex. 29:11
14 "The priest shall take *some* of the blood of
the trespass offering, and the priest shall put
it on the tip of the right ear of him who is to
be cleansed, on the thumb of his right hand,
and on the big toe of his right foot.
15 "And the priest shall take *some* of the log
of oil, and pour *it* into the palm of his own left
hand.
16 "Then the priest shall dip his right finger
in the oil that *is* in his left hand, and shall
[R]sprinkle some of the oil with his finger seven
times before the LORD. Lev. 4:6
17 "And of the rest of the oil in his hand, the
priest shall put *some* on the tip of the right ear
of him who is to be cleansed, on the thumb of
his right hand, and on the big toe of his right
foot, on the blood of the trespass offering.
18 "The rest of the oil that *is* in the priest's
hand he shall put on the head of him who is to
be cleansed. So the priest shall make atone-
ment for him before the LORD.
19 "Then the priest shall offer the sin offer-
ing, and make atonement for him who is to be
cleansed from his uncleanness. Afterward he
shall kill the burnt offering.
20 "And the priest shall offer the burnt offer-
ing and the grain offering on the altar. So the
priest shall make atonement for him, and he
shall be [R]clean. Lev. 14:8, 9
21 "But [R]if he *is* poor and cannot afford it,

then he shall take one male lamb *as* a trespass offering to be waved, to make atonement for him, one-tenth *of an ephah* of fine flour mixed with oil as a grain offering, a log of oil, Lev. 5:7, 11; 12:8; 27:8

22 [R]"and two turtledoves or two young pigeons, such as he is able to afford: one shall be a sin offering and the other a burnt offering. Lev. 12:8; 15:14, 15

23 [R]"He shall bring them to the priest on the eighth day for his cleansing, to the door of the tabernacle of meeting, before the LORD. Lev. 14:10, 11

24 [R]"And the priest shall take the lamb of the trespass offering and the log of oil, and the priest shall wave them *as* a wave offering before the LORD. Lev. 14:12

25 "Then he shall kill the lamb of the trespass offering, and the priest shall take *some* of the blood of the trespass offering and put *it* on the tip of the right ear of him who is to be cleansed, on the thumb of his right hand, and on the big toe of his right foot.

26 "And the priest shall pour some of the oil into the palm of his own left hand.

27 "Then the priest shall sprinkle with his right finger *some* of the oil that *is* in his left hand seven times before the LORD.

28 "And the priest shall put *some* of the oil that *is* in his hand on the tip of the right ear of him who is to be cleansed, on the thumb of the right hand, and on the big toe of his right foot, on the place of the blood of the trespass offering.

29 "The rest of the oil that *is* in the priest's hand he shall put on the head of him who is to be cleansed, to make atonement for him before the LORD.

30 "And he shall offer one of [R]the turtledoves or young pigeons, such as he can afford— Lev. 14:22; 15:14, 15

31 "such as he is able to afford, the one *as* a sin offering and the other *as* a burnt offering, with the grain offering. So the priest shall make atonement for him who is to be cleansed before the LORD.

32 "This *is* the law *for one* who had a leprous sore, who cannot afford [R]the usual cleansing." Lev. 14:10

Cleansing of Houses

33 And the LORD spoke to Moses and Aaron, saying:

34 [R]"When you have come into the land of Canaan, which I give you as a possession, and I put the leprous plague* in a house in the land of your possession, Deut. 7:1; 32:49

35 "and he who owns the house comes and tells the priest, saying, 'It seems to me that *there is* some plague in the house,'

36 "then the priest shall command that they empty the house, before the priest goes *into it* to examine the plague, that all that *is* in the house may not be made unclean; and afterward the priest shall go in to examine the house.

37 "And he shall examine the plague; and indeed *if* the plague *is* on the walls of the house with ingrained streaks, greenish or reddish, which appear to be [T]deep in the wall, Lit. *lower than the wall*

38 "then the priest shall go out of the house, to the door of the house, and [T]shut up the house seven days. *quarantine*

39 "And the priest shall come again on the seventh day and look; and indeed *if* the plague has spread on the walls of the house,

40 "then the priest shall command that they take away the stones in which *is* the plague, and they shall cast them into an unclean place outside the city.

41 "And he shall cause the house to be scraped inside, all around, and the dust that they scrape off they shall pour out in an unclean place outside the city.

42 "Then they shall take other stones and put *them* in the place of *those* stones, and he shall take other mortar and plaster the house.

43 "Now if the plague comes back and breaks out in the house, after he has taken away the stones, after he has scraped the house, and after it is plastered,

44 "then the priest shall come and look; and indeed *if* the plague has spread in the house, it *is* [R]an active leprosy in the house. It *is* unclean. Lev. 13:51

45 "And he shall break down the house, its stones, its timber, and all the plaster of the house, and he shall carry *them* outside the city to an unclean place.

46 "Moreover he who goes into the house at all while it is shut up shall be [T]unclean [R]until evening. *defiled* • Lev. 11:24; 15:5

47 "And he who lies down in the house shall [R]wash his clothes, and he who eats in the house shall wash his clothes. Lev. 14:8

48 "But if the priest comes in and examines *it*, and indeed the plague has not spread in the house after the house was plastered, then the priest shall pronounce the house clean, because the plague is healed.

49 "And [R]he shall take, to cleanse the house, two birds, cedar wood, scarlet, and hyssop. Lev. 14:4

50 "Then he shall kill one of the birds in an earthen vessel over running water;

51 "and he shall take the cedar wood, the hyssop, the scarlet, and the living bird, and dip them in the blood of the slain bird and in the running water, and sprinkle the house seven times.

52 "And he shall [T]cleanse the house with the blood of the bird and the running water and

14:34 Decomposition by mildew, mold, dry rot, etc., and so in vv. 34–53

the living bird, with the cedar wood, the hyssop, and the scarlet. *ceremonially cleanse*

53 "Then he shall let the living bird loose outside the city in the open field, and [R]make atonement for the house, and it shall be clean. Lev. 14:20

The Purpose of the Laws of Leprosy

54 "This *is* the law for any [R]leprous sore and scale, Lev. 13:30; 26:21

55 "for the [R]leprosy of a garment [R]and of a house, Lev. 13:47–52 • Lev. 14:34

56 [R]"for a swelling and a scab and a bright spot, Lev. 13:2

57 "to teach when *it is* unclean and when *it is* clean. This *is* the law of leprosy."

CHAPTER 15

Discharges of the Man

AND the LORD spoke to Moses and Aaron, saying,

2 "Speak to the children of Israel, and say to them: 'When any man has a discharge from his body, his discharge *is* unclean.

3 'And this shall be his uncleanness in regard to his discharge—whether his body runs with his discharge, or his body is stopped up by his discharge, it *is* his uncleanness.

4 'Every bed is [T]unclean on which he who has the discharge lies, and everything on which he sits shall be unclean. *defiled*

5 'And whoever [R]touches his bed shall wash his clothes and bathe in water, and be unclean until evening. Lev. 5:2; 14:46

6 'He who sits on anything on which he who has the [R]discharge sat shall wash his clothes and bathe in water, and be unclean until evening. Deut. 23:10

7 'And he who touches the body of him who has the discharge shall wash his clothes and bathe in water, and be unclean until evening.

8 'If he who has the discharge [R]spits on him who is clean, then he shall wash his clothes and bathe in water, and be unclean until evening. Num. 12:14

9 'Any saddle on which he who has the discharge rides shall be unclean.

10 'Whoever touches anything that was under him shall be unclean until evening. He who carries *any of* those things shall wash his clothes and bathe in water, and be unclean until evening.

11 'And whomever the one who has the discharge touches, and has not rinsed his hands in water, he shall wash his clothes and bathe in water, and be unclean until evening.

12 'The vessel of earth that he who has the discharge touches shall be broken, and every vessel of wood shall be rinsed in water.

13 'And when he who has a discharge is cleansed of his discharge, then he shall count for himself seven days for his cleansing, wash his clothes, and bathe his body in running water; then he shall be clean.

14 'On the eighth day he shall take for himself [R]two turtledoves or two young pigeons, and come before the LORD, to the door of the tabernacle of meeting, and give them to the priest. Lev. 14:22, 23, 30, 31

15 'Then the priest shall offer them, [R]the one *as* a sin offering and the other *as* a burnt offering. [R]So the priest shall make atonement for him before the LORD because of his discharge. Lev. 14:30, 31 • Lev. 14:19, 31

16 [R]'If any man has an emission of semen, then he shall wash all his body in water, and be unclean until evening. Lev. 22:4

17 'And any garment and any leather on which there is semen, it shall be washed with water, and be unclean until evening.

18 'Also, when a woman lies with a man, and *there* is an emission of semen, they shall bathe in water, and [R]be unclean until evening. [1 Sam. 21:4]

Discharges of the Woman

19 'If a woman has a discharge, *and* the discharge from her body is blood, she shall be set apart seven days; and whoever touches her shall be unclean until evening.

20 'Everything that she lies on during her impurity shall be unclean; also everything that she sits on shall be unclean.

21 'Whoever touches her bed shall wash his clothes and bathe in water, and be unclean until evening.

22 'And whoever touches anything that she sat on shall wash his clothes and bathe in water, and be unclean until evening.

23 'If *anything* is on *her* bed or on anything on which she sits, when he touches it, he shall be unclean until evening.

24 'And [R]if any man lies with her at all, so that her impurity is on him, he shall be [T]unclean seven days; and every bed on which he lies shall be unclean. Lev. 18:19; 20:18 • *defiled*

25 'If [R]a woman has a discharge of blood for many days, other than at the time of her *customary* impurity, or if it runs beyond her *usual time of* impurity, all the days of her unclean discharge shall be as the days of her *customary* impurity. She *shall be* unclean. Matt. 9:20

26 'Every bed on which she lies all the days of her discharge shall be to her as the bed of her impurity; and whatever she sits on shall be unclean, as the uncleanness of her impurity.

27 'Whoever touches those things shall be unclean; he shall wash his clothes and bathe in water, and be unclean until evening.

28 'But if she is cleansed of her discharge, then she shall count for herself seven days, and after that she shall be clean.

29 'And on the eighth day she shall take for

herself two turtledoves or two young pigeons,
and bring them to the priest, to the door of the
tabernacle of meeting.
30 'Then the priest shall offer the one *as* a
sin offering and the other *as* a [R]burnt offering,
and the priest shall make atonement for her
before the LORD for the discharge of her
uncleanness. Lev. 5:7

The Purpose of the Laws of Discharge

31 'Thus you shall [R]separate the children of
Israel from their uncleanness, lest they die in
their uncleanness when they defile My taber-
nacle that *is* among them. Deut. 24:8
32 [R]'This *is* the law for one who has a dis-
charge, [R]and *for him* who emits semen and is
unclean thereby, Lev. 15:2 • Lev. 15:16
33 [R]'and for her who is indisposed because
of her *customary* impurity, and for one who
has a discharge, either man [R]or woman,
[R]and for him who lies with her who is un-
clean.' " Lev. 15:19 • Lev. 15:25 • Lev. 15:24

CHAPTER 16

Preparation of the High Priest

NOW the LORD spoke to Moses after [R]the
death of the two sons of Aaron, when
they offered *profane fire* before the LORD, and
died; Lev. 10:1, 2
2 and the LORD said to Moses: "Tell Aaron
your brother [R]not to come at *just* any time
into the Holy *Place* inside the veil, before the
mercy seat which *is* on the ark, lest he die; for
[R]I will appear in the cloud above the mercy
seat. Ex. 30:10 • Ex. 25:21, 22; 40:34
3 [T]"Thus Aaron shall [R]come into the Holy
Place: [R]with *the blood of* a young bull as a
sin offering, and *of* a ram as a burnt offer-
ing. Lit. *With this* • [Heb. 9:7, 12, 24, 25] • Lev. 4:3
4 "He shall put the [R]holy linen tunic and the
linen trousers on his body; he shall be girded
with a linen sash, and with the linen turban he
shall be attired. These *are* holy garments.
Therefore he shall wash his body in water,
and put them on. Ex. 28:39, 42, 43
5 "And he shall take from [R]the congrega-
tion of the children of Israel two kids of the
goats as a sin offering, and one ram as a burnt
offering. Lev. 4:14

Identification of the Sacrifices

6 "Aaron shall offer the bull as a sin offer-
ing, which *is* for himself, and make atonement
for himself and for his house.
7 "He shall take the two goats and present
them before the LORD *at* the door of the tab-
ernacle of meeting.
8 "Then Aaron shall cast lots for the two
goats: one lot for the LORD and the other lot
for the scapegoat.
9 "And Aaron shall bring the goat on which
the LORD's lot fell, and offer it *as* a sin offer-
ing.
10 "But the goat on which the lot fell to be
the scapegoat shall be presented alive before
the LORD, to make [R]atonement upon it, *and*
to let it go as the scapegoat into the wilder-
ness. [1 John 2:2]

Atonement for the Priest

11 "And Aaron shall bring the bull of the sin
offering, which is for [R]himself, and make
atonement for himself and for his house, and
shall kill the bull as the sin offering which *is*
for himself. [Heb. 7:27; 9:7]
12 "Then he shall take [R]a censer full of
burning coals of fire from the altar before
the LORD, with his hands full of [R]sweet in-
cense beaten fine, and bring *it* inside the
veil. Lev. 10:1 • Ex. 30:34–38
13 [R]"And he shall put the incense on the fire
before the LORD, that the cloud of incense may
cover the mercy seat that *is* on the Testimony,
lest he die. Ex. 30:7, 8
14 "He shall take some of the blood of the
bull and sprinkle *it* with his finger on the
mercy seat on the east *side;* and before
the mercy seat he shall sprinkle some of the
blood with his finger seven times.

Atonement for the Tabernacle

15 [R]"Then he shall kill the goat of the sin of-
fering, which *is* for the people, bring its
blood [R]inside the veil, do with that blood as
he did with the blood of the bull, and sprin-
kle it on the mercy seat and before the mercy
seat. [Heb. 2:17] • [Heb. 6:19; 7:27]
16 "So he shall [R]make atonement for the
Holy *Place,* because of the uncleanness of the
children of Israel, and because of their trans-
gressions, for all their sins; and so he shall do
for the tabernacle of meeting which remains
among them in the midst of their unclean-
ness. Ex. 29:36; 30:10
17 "There shall be [R]no man in the tabernacle
of meeting when he goes in to make atone-
ment in the Holy *Place,* until he comes out,
that he may make atonement for himself, for
his household, and for all the assembly of Is-
rael. Luke 1:10
18 "And he shall go out to the altar that *is* be-
fore the LORD, and make atonement for it, and
shall take some of the blood of the bull and
some of the blood of the goat, and put it on the
horns of the altar all around.
19 "Then he shall sprinkle some of the blood
on it with his finger seven times, cleanse it,
and consecrate it from the uncleanness of the
children of Israel.

Atonement for the People

20 "And when he has made an end of aton-
ing for the Holy *Place,* the tabernacle of meet-
ing, and the altar, he shall bring the live goat.

21 "Aaron shall lay both his hands on the head of the live goat, [R]confess over it all the iniquities of the children of Israel, and all their transgressions, concerning all their sins, putting them on the head of the goat, and shall send *it* away into the wilderness by the hand of a suitable man. Lev. 5:5; 26:40

22 "The goat shall bear on itself all their iniquities to an uninhabited land; and he shall release the goat in the wilderness.

23 "Then Aaron shall come into the tabernacle of meeting, [R]shall take off the linen garments which he put on when he went into the Holy *Place,* and shall leave them there. Ezek. 42:14; 44:19

24 "And he shall wash his body with water in a holy place, put on his garments, come out and offer his burnt offering and the burnt offering of the people, and make atonement for himself and for the people.

25 [R]"The fat of the sin offering he shall burn on the altar. Lev. 1:8; 4:10

26 "And he who released the goat as the scapegoat shall wash his clothes [R]and bathe his body in water, and afterward he may come into the camp. Lev. 15:5

27 [R]"The bull *for* the sin offering and the goat *for* the sin offering, whose blood was brought in to make atonement in the Holy *Place,* shall be carried outside the camp. And they shall burn in the fire their skins, their flesh, and their offal. Heb. 13:11

28 "Then he who burns them shall wash his clothes and bathe his body in water, and afterward he may come into the camp.

Purpose of the Day of Atonement

29 "*This* shall be a statute forever for you: [R]In the seventh month, on the tenth *day* of the month, you shall [T]afflict your souls, and do no work at all, *whether* a native of your own country or a stranger who dwells among you. Lev. 23:27–32 • *humble yourselves*

30 "For on that day *the priest* shall make [T]atonement for you, to [R]cleanse you, *that* you may be clean from all your sins before the LORD. Lit. *covering* • Jer. 33:8

31 [R]"It *is* a sabbath of solemn rest for you, and you shall afflict your souls. *It is* a statute forever. Lev. 23:27, 32

32 "And the priest, who is anointed and consecrated to minister as priest in his father's place, shall make atonement, and put on the linen clothes, the holy garments;

33 "then he shall make [T]atonement for the Holy Sanctuary,* and he shall make atonement for the tabernacle of meeting and for the altar, and he shall make atonement for the priests and for all the people of the assembly. Lit. *covering*

34 "This shall be an everlasting statute for you, to make atonement for the children of Israel, for all their sins, once a year." And he did as the LORD commanded Moses.

CHAPTER 17

Laws Concerning the Location of Sacrifices

AND the LORD spoke to Moses, saying,

2 "Speak to Aaron, to his sons, and to all the children of Israel, and say to them, 'This *is* the thing which the LORD has commanded, saying:

3 "Whatever man of the house of Israel who kills an ox or lamb or goat in the camp, or who kills *it* outside the camp,

4 "and does not bring it to the door of the tabernacle of meeting to offer an offering to the LORD before the tabernacle of the LORD, the guilt of bloodshed shall be imputed to that man. He has shed blood; and that man shall be cut off from among his people,

5 "to the end that the children of Israel may bring their sacrifices [R]which they offer in the open field, that they may bring them to the LORD at the door of the tabernacle of meeting, to the priest, and offer them *as* peace offerings to the LORD. Deut. 12:1–27

6 "And the priest shall sprinkle the blood on the altar of the LORD *at* the door of the tabernacle of meeting, and [R]burn the fat for a sweet aroma to the LORD. Num. 18:17

7 "They shall no more offer their sacrifices to demons, after whom they have played the harlot. This shall be a statute forever for them throughout their generations." '

8 "Also you shall say to them: 'Whatever man of the house of Israel, or of the strangers who dwell among you, [R]who offers a burnt offering or sacrifice, Lev. 1:2, 3; 18:26

9 'and does not [R]bring it to the door of the tabernacle of meeting, to offer it to the LORD, that man shall be [T]cut off from among his people. Lev. 14:23 • *Put to death*

Laws Concerning the Use of Blood

10 'And whatever man of the house of Israel, or of the strangers who dwell among you, who eats any blood, I will set My face against that person who eats blood, and will cut him off from among his people.

11 'For the life of the flesh *is* in the blood, and I have given it to you upon the altar to make atonement for your souls; for it *is* the blood *that* makes atonement for the soul.'

12 "Therefore I said to the children of Israel, 'No one among you shall eat blood, nor shall any stranger who dwells among you eat blood.'

13 "Whatever man of the children of Israel, or of the strangers who dwell among you, who hunts and catches any animal or bird that may be eaten, he shall [R]pour out its blood and cover it with dust; Deut. 12:16, 24

14 [R]"for *it is* the life of all flesh. Its blood sustains its life. Therefore I said to the children of

16:33 The Most Holy Place

Israel, 'You shall not eat the blood of any flesh, for the life of all flesh is its blood. Whoever eats it shall be cut off.' Gen. 9:4

15 "And every person who eats what died *naturally* or what was torn *by beasts, whether he is* a native of your own country or a stranger, he shall both wash his clothes and bathe in water, and be unclean until evening. Then he shall be clean.

16 "But if he does not wash *them* or bathe his body, then he shall bear his guilt."

CHAPTER 18

Laws of Sexual Sins

THEN the LORD spoke to Moses, saying,

2 "Speak to the children of Israel, and say to them: 'I am the LORD your God.

3 [R]'According to the doings of the land of Egypt, where you dwelt, you shall not do; and [R]according to the doings of the land of Canaan, where I am bringing you, you shall not do; nor shall you walk in their ordinances. Ezek. 20:7, 8 • Lev. 18:24–30; 20:23

4 [R]'You shall observe My judgments and keep My ordinances, to walk in them: I *am* the LORD your God. Ezek. 20:19

5 'You shall therefore keep My statutes and My judgments, which if a man does, he shall live by them: I *am* the LORD.

6 'None of you shall approach anyone who is near of kin to him, to uncover his nakedness: I *am* the LORD.

7 'The nakedness of your father or the nakedness of your mother you shall not uncover. She *is* your mother; you shall not uncover her nakedness.

8 'The nakedness of your [R]father's wife you shall not uncover; it *is* your father's nakedness. Gen. 35:22

9 [R]'The nakedness of your sister, the daughter of your father, or the daughter of your mother, *whether* born at home or elsewhere, their nakedness you shall not uncover. Deut. 27:22

10 'The nakedness of your son's daughter or your daughter's daughter, their nakedness you shall not uncover; for theirs *is* your own nakedness.

11 'The nakedness of your father's wife's daughter, begotten by your father—she *is* your sister—you shall not uncover her nakedness.

12 [R]'You shall not uncover the nakedness of your father's sister; she *is* near of kin to your father. Lev. 20:19

13 'You shall not uncover the nakedness of your mother's sister, for she *is* near of kin to your mother.

14 [R]'You shall not uncover the nakedness of your father's brother. You shall not approach his wife; she *is* your aunt. Lev. 20:20

15 'You shall not uncover the nakedness of your daughter-in-law—she *is* your son's wife—you shall not uncover her nakedness.

16 'You shall not uncover the nakedness of your brother's wife; it *is* your brother's nakedness.

17 'You shall not uncover the nakedness of a woman and her daughter, nor shall you take her son's daughter or her daughter's daughter, to uncover her nakedness. They *are* near of kin to her. It *is* wickedness.

18 'Nor shall you take a woman [R]as a rival to her sister, to uncover her nakedness while the other is alive. 1 Sam. 1:6, 8

19 'Also you shall not approach a woman to uncover her nakedness as [R]long as she is in her *customary* impurity. Ezek. 18:6

20 [R]'Moreover you shall not lie carnally with your [R]neighbor's wife, to defile yourself with her. [Prov. 6:25–33] • Lev. 20:10

21 'And you shall not let any of your descendants [R]pass through [R]*the fire* to Molech, nor shall you profane the name of your God: I *am* the LORD. Lev. 20:2–5 • 2 Kin. 16:3

22 'You shall not lie with [R]a male as with a woman. It *is* an abomination. Lev. 20:13

23 'Nor shall you mate with any [R]animal, to defile yourself with it. Nor shall any woman stand before an animal to mate with it. It *is* perversion. Ex. 22:19

24 'Do not defile yourselves with any of these things; for by all these the nations are defiled, which I am casting out before you.

25 'For the land is defiled; therefore I visit the punishment of its iniquity upon it, and the land vomits out its inhabitants.

26 [R]'You shall therefore [T]keep My statutes and My judgments, and shall not commit *any* of these abominations, *either* any of your own nation or any stranger who dwells among you Lev. 18:5, 30 • *obey*

27 '(for all these abominations the men of the land have done, who *were* before you, and thus the land is defiled),

28 'lest [R]the land vomit you out also when you defile it, as it vomited out the nations that *were* before you. Jer. 9:19

29 'For whoever commits any of these abominations, the persons who commit *them* shall be cut off from among their people.

30 'Therefore you shall keep My ordinance, so that *you* do not commit *any* of these abominable customs which were committed before you, and that you do not defile yourselves by them: I *am* the LORD your God.' "

CHAPTER 19

Laws of Social Order

AND the LORD spoke to Moses, saying,

2 "Speak to all the congregation of the children of Israel, and say to them: [R]'You shall be holy, for I the LORD your God *am* holy. Lev. 11:44; 20:7, 26

3 [R]'Every one of you shall revere his mother and his father, and keep My Sabbaths: I *am* the LORD your God. Ex. 20:12

4 [R]'Do not turn to idols, [R]nor make for yourselves [T]molded gods: I *am* the LORD your God. Ex. 20:4 • Ex. 34:17 • *molten*

5 'And [R]if you offer a sacrifice of a peace offering to the LORD, you shall offer it of your own free will. Lev. 7:16

6 'It shall be eaten the same day you offer *it*, and on the next day. And if any remains until the third day, it shall be burned in the fire.

7 'And if it is eaten at all on the third day, it *is* an abomination. It shall not be accepted.

8 'Therefore *everyone* who eats it shall bear his iniquity, because he has profaned the hallowed *offering* of the LORD; and that person shall be cut off from his people.

9 [R]'When you reap the harvest of your land, you shall not wholly reap the corners of your field, nor shall you gather the gleanings of your harvest. Deut. 24:19–22

10 'And you shall not glean your vineyard, nor shall you gather *every* grape of your vineyard; you shall leave them for the poor and the stranger: I *am* the LORD your God.

11 'You shall not steal, nor deal falsely, [R]nor lie to one another. Eph. 4:25

12 'And you shall not [R]swear by My name falsely, nor shall you profane the name of your God: I *am* the LORD. Deut. 5:11

13 [R]'You shall not cheat your neighbor, nor rob *him*. [R]The wages of him who is hired shall not remain with you all night until morning. Ex. 22:7–15, 21–27 • Deut. 24:15

14 'You shall not curse the deaf, [R]nor put a stumbling block before the blind, but shall fear your God: I *am* the LORD. Deut. 27:18

15 'You shall do no injustice in judgment. You shall not be partial to the poor, nor honor the person of the mighty. In righteousness you shall judge your neighbor.

16 'You shall not go about *as* a [R]talebearer among your people; nor shall you [R]take a stand against the life of your neighbor: I *am* the LORD. Prov. 11:13; 18:8; 20:19 • 1 Kin. 21:7–19

17 'You shall not hate your brother in your heart. You shall surely rebuke your neighbor, and not bear sin because of him.

18 'You shall not take vengeance, nor bear any grudge against the children of your people, [R]but you shall love your neighbor as yourself: I *am* the LORD. Mark 12:31

19 'You shall keep My statutes. You shall not let your livestock breed with another kind. You shall not sow your field with mixed seed. Nor shall a garment of mixed linen and wool come upon you.

20 'Whoever lies carnally with a woman who *is* betrothed to a man as a concubine, and who has not at all been redeemed nor given her freedom, for this there shall be scourging; *but* they shall not be put to death, because she was not free.

21 'And he shall bring his trespass offering to the LORD, to the door of the tabernacle of meeting, a ram as a trespass offering.

22 'The priest shall make [T]atonement for him with the ram of the trespass offering before the LORD for his sin which he has committed. And the sin which he has committed shall be forgiven him. Lit. *covering*

23 'When you come into the land, and have planted all kinds of trees for food, then you shall count their fruit as [T]uncircumcised. Three years it shall be as uncircumcised to you. It shall not be eaten. *unclean*

24 'But in the fourth year all its fruit shall be holy, a praise to the LORD.

25 'And in the fifth year you may eat its fruit, that it may yield to you its increase: I *am* the LORD your God.

26 'You shall not eat *anything* with the blood, nor shall you practice divination or soothsaying.

27 'You shall not shave around the sides of your head, nor shall you disfigure the edges of your beard.

28 'You shall not [R]make any cuttings in your flesh for the dead, nor tattoo any marks on you: I *am* the LORD. Jer. 16:6

29 [R]'Do not prostitute your daughter, to cause her to be a harlot, lest the land fall into harlotry, and the land become full of wickedness. Deut. 22:21; 23:17, 18

30 'You shall keep My Sabbaths and reverence My sanctuary: I *am* the LORD.

31 'Give no regard to mediums and familiar spirits; do not seek after them, to be defiled by them: I *am* the LORD your God.

32 [R]'You shall rise before the gray headed and honor the presence of an old man, and fear your God: I *am* the LORD. 1 Tim. 5:1

33 'And if a stranger dwells with you in your land, you shall not mistreat him.

34 [R]'The stranger who dwells among you shall be to you as one born among you, and [R]you shall love him as yourself; for you were strangers in the land of Egypt: I *am* the LORD your God. Ex. 12:48 • Deut. 10:19

35 'You shall do no injustice in judgment, in measurement of length, weight, or volume.

36 'You shall have [R]honest scales, honest weights, an honest ephah, and an honest hin: I *am* the LORD your God, who brought you out of the land of Egypt. Deut. 25:13–15

37 [R]'Therefore you shall observe all My statutes and all My judgments, and perform them: I *am* the LORD.' " Lev. 18:4, 5

CHAPTER 20

The Penalty for Worshiping Molech

THEN the LORD spoke to Moses, saying,
2 "Again, you shall say to the children of

Israel: 'Whoever of the children of Israel, or of the strangers who dwell in Israel, who gives *any* of his descendants to Molech, he shall surely be put to death. The people of the land shall stone him with stones.

3 [R]'I will set My face against that man, and will cut him off from his people, because he has given *some* of his descendants to Molech, to defile My sanctuary and profane My holy name. Lev. 17:10

4 'And if the people of the land should in any way [T]hide their eyes from the man, when he gives *some* of his descendants to Molech, and they do not kill him, *disregard*

5 'then I will set My face against that man and against his family; and I will cut him off from his people, and all who prostitute themselves with him to commit harlotry with Molech.

The Penalty for Consulting Spirits

6 'And the person who turns to mediums and familiar spirits, to prostitute himself with them, I will set My face against that person and cut him off from his people.

7 [R]'Consecrate yourselves therefore, and be holy, for I *am* the LORD your God. Lev. 19:2

8 'And you shall keep [R]My statutes, and perform them: [R]I *am* the LORD who [T]sanctifies you. Lev. 19:19, 37 • Ex. 31:13 • *sets you apart*

The Penalty for Cursing Parents

9 'For [R]everyone who curses his father or his mother shall surely be put to death. He has cursed his father or his mother. His blood *shall be* upon him. Ex. 21:17

The Penalty for Committing Sexual Sins

10 [R]'The man who commits adultery with *another* man's wife, *he* who commits adultery with his neighbor's wife, the adulterer and the adulteress, shall surely be put to death. Ex. 20:14

11 'The man who lies with his [R]father's wife has uncovered his father's nakedness; both of them shall surely be put to death. Their blood *shall be* upon them. Lev. 18:7, 8

12 'If a man lies with his [R]daughter-in-law, both of them shall surely be put to death. They have committed perversion. Their blood *shall be* upon them. Lev. 18:15

13 'If a man lies with a male as he lies with a woman, both of them have committed an abomination. They shall surely be put to death. Their blood *shall be* upon them.

14 'If a man marries a woman and her mother, it *is* wickedness. They shall be burned with fire, both he and they, that there may be no wickedness among you.

15 'If a man mates with an [R]animal, he shall surely be put to death, and you shall kill the animal. Lev. 18:23

16 'If a woman approaches any animal and mates with it, you shall kill the woman and the animal. They shall surely be put to death. Their blood *is* upon them.

17 'If a man takes his [R]sister, his father's daughter or his mother's daughter, and sees her nakedness and she sees his nakedness, it *is* a wicked thing. And they shall be [T]cut off in the sight of their people. He has uncovered his sister's nakedness. He shall bear his [T]guilt. Lev. 18:9 • Put to death • *iniquity*

18 [R]'If a man lies with a woman during her sickness and uncovers her nakedness, he has exposed her flow, and she has uncovered the flow of her blood. Both of them shall be cut off from their people. Lev. 15:24

19 'You shall not uncover the nakedness of your [R]mother's sister nor of your father's sister, for that would uncover his near of kin. They shall bear their guilt. Lev. 18:13

20 'If a man lies with his uncle's wife, he has uncovered his uncle's nakedness. They shall bear their sin; they shall die childless.

21 'If a man takes his brother's wife, it *is* an unclean thing. He has uncovered his brother's nakedness. They shall be childless.

The Purpose of the Laws of Sanctification of the People

22 'You shall therefore keep all My [R]statutes and all My judgments, and perform them, that the land where I am bringing you to dwell may not vomit you out. Lev. 18:26

23 [R]'And you shall not walk in the statutes of the nation which I am casting out before you; for they commit all these things, and therefore I abhor them. Lev. 18:3, 24

24 'But [R]I have said to you, "You shall inherit their land, and I will give it to you to possess, a land flowing with milk and honey." I *am* the LORD your God, who has separated you from the peoples. Ex. 3:17

25 'You shall therefore distinguish between clean animals and unclean, between unclean birds and clean, [R]and you shall not make yourselves abominable by beast or by bird, or by any kind of living thing that creeps on the ground, which I have separated from you as unclean. Lev. 11:43

26 'And you shall be holy to Me, for I the LORD *am* holy, and have separated you from the peoples, that you should be Mine.

27 'A man or a woman who is a medium, or who has familiar spirits, shall surely be put to death; they shall stone them with stones. Their blood *shall be* upon them.' "

CHAPTER 21

Laws Concerning Priests

AND the LORD said to Moses, "Speak to the priests, the sons of Aaron, and say to

them: [R]'None shall defile himself for the dead
among his people, Ezek. 44:25
2 'except for his relatives who are nearest
to him: his mother, his father, his son, his
daughter, and his brother;
3 'also his virgin sister who is near to him,
who has had no husband, for her he may de-
file himself.
4 '*Otherwise* he shall not defile himself, *be-
ing* a [T]chief man among his people, to profane
himself. Lit. *master* or *husband*
5 [R]'They shall not make any bald *place* on
their heads, nor shall they shave the edges of
their beards nor make any cuttings in their
flesh. Deut. 14:1
6 'They shall be [R]holy to their God and not
profane the name of their God, for they offer
the offerings of the LORD made by fire, *and* the
[R]bread of their God; [R]therefore they shall be
holy. Ex. 22:31 • Lev. 3:11 • Is. 52:11
7 [R]'They shall not take a wife *who is* a har-
lot or a defiled woman, nor shall they take a
woman divorced from her husband; for *the
priest** is holy to his God. Ezek. 44:22
8 'Therefore you shall consecrate him, for
he offers the bread of your God. He shall be
holy to you, for [R]I the LORD, who [R]sanctify
you, *am* holy. Lev. 11:44, 45 • Lev. 8:12, 30
9 'The daughter of any priest, if she pro-
fanes herself by playing the harlot, she
profanes her father. She shall be [R]burned with
fire. Deut. 22:21

Laws Concerning the High Priest

10 '*He who is* the high priest among his
brethren, on whose head the anointing oil was
[R]poured and who is consecrated to wear the
garments, shall not [R]uncover his head nor tear
his clothes; Lev. 8:12 • Lev. 10:6, 7
11 'nor shall he go [R]near any dead body,
nor defile himself for his father or his
mother; Num. 19:14
12 'nor shall he go out of the sanctuary, nor
profane the sanctuary of his God; for the
[R]consecration of the anointing oil of his God
is upon him: I *am* the LORD. Ex. 29:6, 7
13 'And he shall take a wife in her virginity.
14 'A widow or a divorced woman or a de-
filed woman *or* a harlot—these he shall not
marry; but he shall take a virgin of his own
people as wife.
15 'Nor shall he profane his posterity among
his people, for I the LORD sanctify him.' "

People Prohibited from the Priesthood

16 And the LORD spoke to Moses, saying,
17 "Speak to Aaron, saying: 'No man of your
descendants in *succeeding* generations, who
has *any* defect, may approach to offer the
bread of his God.
18 'For any man who has a defect shall not
approach: a man blind or lame, who has a
marred *face* or any *limb* too long,
19 'a man who has a broken foot or broken
hand,
20 'or is a hunchback or a dwarf, or *a man*
who has a defect in his eye, or eczema or scab,
or is a eunuch.
21 'No man of the descendants of Aaron the
priest, who has a defect, shall come near to
offer the offerings made by fire to the LORD.
He has a defect; he shall not come near to
offer the bread of his God.
22 'He may eat the bread of his God, *both* the
most holy and the holy;
23 'only he shall not go near the [R]veil or ap-
proach the altar, because he has a defect, lest
[R]he profane My sanctuaries; for I the LORD
sanctify them.' " Lev. 16:2 • Lev. 21:12
24 And Moses told *it* to Aaron and his sons,
and to all the children of Israel.

CHAPTER 22

Things Prohibited of the Priesthood

THEN the LORD spoke to Moses, saying,
2 "Speak to Aaron and his sons, that they
[R]separate themselves from the holy things of
the children of Israel, and that they do not
profane My holy name *by* what they dedicate
to Me: I *am* the LORD. Num. 6:3
3 "Say to them: 'Whoever of all your de-
scendants throughout your generations, who
goes near the holy things which the children
of Israel dedicate to the LORD, while he has
uncleanness upon him, that person shall be
cut off from My presence: I *am* the LORD.
4 'Whatever man of the descendants of
Aaron, who *is* a [R]leper or has [R]a discharge,
shall not eat the holy offerings until he is
clean. And whoever touches anything made
unclean *by* a corpse, or a man who has had an
emission of semen, Num. 5:2 • Lev. 15:2
5 'or whoever touches any creeping thing
by which he would be made unclean, or any
person by whom he would become unclean,
whatever his uncleanness may be—
6 'the person who has touched any such
thing shall be unclean until evening, and shall
not eat the holy *offerings* unless he [R]washes
his body with water. Lev. 15:5
7 'And when the sun goes down he shall be
clean; and afterward he may eat the holy *of-
ferings*, because it *is* his food.
8 [R]'Whatever dies *naturally* or is torn *by
beasts* he shall not eat, to defile himself with
it: I *am* the LORD. Lev. 7:24; 11:39, 40; 17:15
9 'They shall therefore keep [R]My [T]ordi-
nance, [R]lest they bear sin for it and die
thereby, if they profane it: I the LORD sanctify
them. Lev. 18:30 • *charge* • Ex. 28:43
10 'No outsider shall eat the holy *offering;*
one who dwells with the priest, or a hired ser-
vant, shall not eat the holy thing.

21:7 Lit. *he*

11 ‘But if the priest [R]buys a person with his
money, he may eat it; and one who is born in
his house may eat his food. Ex. 12:44
12 ‘If the priest’s daughter is married to an
outsider, she may not eat of the holy offerings.
13 ‘But if the priest’s daughter is a widow or
divorced, and has no child, and has returned to
her father’s house as in her youth, she may eat
her father’s food; but no outsider shall eat it.
14 ‘And if a man eats the holy *offering* unin-
tentionally, then he shall restore a holy *offer-
ing* to the priest, and add one-fifth to it.
15 ‘They shall not profane the [R]holy *offer-
ings* of the children of Israel, which they offer
to the LORD, Num. 18:32
16 ‘or allow them to bear the guilt of tres-
pass when they eat their holy *offerings;* for I
the LORD sanctify them.’ ”

Sacrifices Prohibited of the Priesthood

17 And the LORD spoke to Moses, saying,
18 “Speak to Aaron and his sons, and to all
the children of Israel, and say to them:
[R]‘Whatever man of the house of Israel, or of
the strangers in Israel, who offers his sacrifice
for any of his vows or for any of his freewill
offerings, which they offer to the LORD as a
burnt offering— Lev. 1:2, 3, 10
19 [R]‘*you shall offer* of your own free will a
male without blemish from the cattle, from
the sheep, or from the goats. Lev. 1:3
20 [R]‘Whatever has a defect, you shall not
offer, for it shall not be acceptable on your be-
half. Deut. 15:21; 17:1
21 ‘And [R]whoever offers a sacrifice of a
peace offering to the LORD, to fulfill *his* vow,
or a freewill offering from the cattle or the
sheep, it must be perfect to be accepted; there
shall be no defect in it. Lev. 3:1, 6
22 [R]‘Those *that are* blind or broken or
maimed, or have an ulcer or eczema or scabs,
you shall not offer to the LORD, nor make [R]an
offering by fire of them on the altar to the
LORD. Mal. 1:8 • Lev. 1:9, 13; 3:3, 5
23 ‘Either a bull or a lamb that has any limb
[R]too long or too short you may offer *as* a
freewill offering, but for a vow it shall not be
accepted. Lev. 21:18
24 ‘You shall not offer to the LORD what
is bruised or crushed, or torn or cut; nor
shall you make *any offering of them* in your
land.
25 ‘Nor [R]from a foreigner’s hand shall you
offer any of these as the bread of your God,
because their corruption *is* in them, *and*
defects *are* in them. They shall not be ac-
cepted on your behalf.’ ” Num. 15:15, 16
26 And the LORD spoke to Moses, saying:
27 [R]“When a bull or a sheep or a goat is
born, it shall be seven days with its mother;
and from the eighth day and thereafter it shall
be accepted as an offering made by fire to the
LORD. Ex. 22:30
28 “*Whether it is* a cow or ewe, do not kill
both her and her young on the same day.
29 “And when you [R]offer a sacrifice of
thanksgiving to the LORD, offer *it* of your own
free will. Lev. 7:12
30 “On the same day it shall be eaten; you
shall leave [R]none of it until morning: I *am* the
LORD. Lev. 7:15

The Purpose of the Laws of the Priesthood

31 [R]“Therefore you shall keep My com-
mandments, and perform them: I *am* the
LORD. Deut. 4:40
32 “You shall not profane My holy name, but
I will be hallowed among the children of Is-
rael. I *am* the LORD who sanctifies you,
33 “who brought you out of the land of
Egypt, to be your God: I *am* the LORD.”

CHAPTER 23

The Weekly Sabbath

AND the LORD spoke to Moses, saying,
2 “Speak to the children of Israel, and
say to them: ‘The feasts of the LORD, which
you shall proclaim *to be* [R]holy convocations,
these *are* My feasts. Ex. 12:16
3 [R]‘Six days shall work be done, but the
seventh day *is* a Sabbath of solemn rest, a
holy convocation. You shall do no work *on it;*
it *is* the Sabbath of the LORD in all your
dwellings. Luke 13:14

Passover

4 [R]‘These *are* the feasts of the LORD, holy
convocations which you shall proclaim at
their appointed times. Ex. 23:14–16
5 ‘On the fourteenth *day* of the first month
at twilight *is* the LORD’s Passover.

Unleavened Bread

6 ‘And on the fifteenth day of the same
month *is* the Feast of Unleavened Bread to the
LORD; seven days you must eat unleavened
bread.
7 [R]‘On the first day you shall have a holy
convocation; you shall do no [T]customary
work on it. Ex. 12:16 • *occupational*
8 ‘But you shall offer an offering made by
fire to the LORD for seven days. The seventh
day *shall be* a holy convocation; you shall do
no customary work *on it.*’ ”

Firstfruits

9 And the LORD spoke to Moses, saying,
10 “Speak to the children of Israel, and say
to them: ‘When you come into the land which
I give to you, and reap its harvest, then you
shall bring a sheaf of the firstfruits of your
harvest to the priest.
11 ‘He shall [R]wave the sheaf before the LORD,
to be accepted on your behalf; on the day after
the Sabbath the priest shall wave it. Ex. 29:24

12 'And you shall offer on that day, when you wave the sheaf, a male lamb of the first year, without blemish, as a burnt offering to the LORD.

13 'Its grain offering *shall be* two-tenths *of an ephah* of fine flour mixed with oil, an offering made by fire to the LORD, for a [T]sweet aroma; and its drink offering *shall be* of wine, one-fourth of a hin. *pleasing*

14 'You shall eat neither bread nor parched grain nor fresh grain until the same day that you have brought an offering to your God; *it shall be* a statute forever throughout your generations in all your dwellings.

Pentecost

15 'And you shall count for yourselves from the day after the Sabbath, from the day that you brought the sheaf of the wave offering: seven Sabbaths shall be completed.

16 'Count [R]fifty days to the day after the seventh Sabbath; then you shall offer a new grain offering to the LORD. Acts 2:1

17 'You shall bring from your dwellings two wave *loaves* of two-tenths *of an ephah.* They shall be of fine flour; they shall be baked with leaven. *They are* [R]the firstfruits to the LORD. Num. 15:17–21

18 'And you shall offer with the bread seven lambs of the first year, without blemish, one young bull, and two rams. They shall be *as* a burnt offering to the LORD, with their grain offering and their drink offerings, an offering made by fire for a sweet aroma to the LORD.

19 'Then you shall sacrifice [R]one kid of the goats as a sin offering, and two male lambs of the first year as a sacrifice of a [R]peace offering. Num. 28:30 • Lev. 3:1

20 'The priest shall wave them with the bread of the firstfruits *as* a wave offering before the LORD, with the two lambs. They shall be holy to the LORD for the priest.

21 'And you shall proclaim on the same day *that* it is a holy convocation to you. You shall do no customary work *on it. It shall be* a statute forever in all your dwellings throughout your generations.

22 'When you reap the harvest of your land, you shall not wholly reap the corners of your field when you reap, nor shall you gather any gleaning from your harvest. You shall leave them for the poor and for the stranger: I *am* the LORD your God.' "

Trumpets

23 Then the LORD spoke to Moses, saying,

24 "Speak to the children of Israel, saying: 'In the [R]seventh month, on the first *day* of the month, you shall have a sabbath-*rest,* [R]a memorial of blowing of trumpets, a holy convocation. Num. 29:1 • Lev. 25:9

25 'You shall do no customary work *on it;* and you shall offer an offering made by fire to the LORD.' "

Day of Atonement

26 And the LORD spoke to Moses, saying:

27 [R]"Also the tenth *day* of this seventh month *shall be* the Day of Atonement. It shall be a holy convocation for you; you shall afflict your souls, and offer an offering made by fire to the LORD. Num. 29:7

28 "And you shall do no work on that same day, for it *is* the Day of Atonement, to make atonement for you before the LORD your God.

29 "For any person who is not [R]afflicted *in soul* on that same day [R]shall be cut off from his people. Jer. 31:9 • Num. 5:2

30 "And any person who does any work on that same day, [R]that person I will destroy from among his people. Lev. 20:3–6

31 "You shall do no manner of work; *it shall be* a statute forever throughout your generations in all your dwellings.

32 "It *shall be* to you a sabbath of *solemn* rest, and you shall [T]afflict your souls; on the ninth *day* of the month at evening, from evening to evening, you shall [T]celebrate your sabbath." *humble yourselves • observe your sabbath*

Tabernacles

33 Then the LORD spoke to Moses, saying,

34 "Speak to the children of Israel, saying: [R]'The fifteenth day of this seventh month *shall be* the Feast of Tabernacles *for* seven days to the LORD. Num. 29:12

35 'On the first day *there shall be* a holy convocation. You shall do no customary work *on it.*

36 '*For* seven days you shall offer an offering made by fire to the LORD. On the eighth day you shall have a holy convocation, and you shall offer an offering made by fire to the LORD. It *is* a [T]sacred assembly, *and* you shall do no customary work *on it.* *solemn*

37 [R]'These *are* the feasts of the LORD which you shall proclaim *to be* holy convocations, to offer an offering made by fire to the LORD, a burnt offering and a grain offering, a sacrifice and drink offerings, everything on its day— Lev. 23:2, 4

38 [R]'besides the Sabbaths of the LORD, besides your gifts, besides all your vows, and besides all your freewill offerings which you give to the LORD. Num. 29:39

39 'Also on the fifteenth day of the seventh month, when you have [R]gathered in the fruit of the land, you shall keep the feast of the LORD *for* seven days; on the first day *there shall be* a sabbath-*rest,* and on the eighth day a sabbath-*rest.* Ex. 23:16

40 'And [R]you shall take for yourselves on the first day the fruit of beautiful trees, branches of palm trees, the boughs of leafy trees, and willows of the brook; [R]and you

shall rejoice before the LORD your God for seven days. Neh. 8:15 • Deut. 12:7; 16:14, 15

41 'You shall keep it as a feast to the LORD for seven days in the year. *It shall be* a statute forever in your generations. You shall celebrate it in the seventh month.

42 [R]'You shall dwell in booths for seven days. [R]All who are native Israelites shall dwell in booths, [Is. 4:6] • Neh. 8:14–16

43 'that your generations may [R]know that I made the children of Israel dwell in booths when I brought them out of the land of Egypt: I *am* the LORD your God.' " Ex. 10:2

44 So Moses [R]declared to the children of Israel the feasts of the LORD. Lev. 23:2

CHAPTER 24

Oil for the Lamps

THEN the LORD spoke to Moses, saying:

2 [R]"Command the children of Israel that they bring to you pure oil of pressed olives for the light, to make the lamps burn continually. Ex. 27:20, 21

3 "Outside the veil of the Testimony, in the tabernacle of meeting, Aaron shall be in charge of it from evening until morning before the LORD continually; *it shall be* a statute forever in your generations.

4 "He shall be in charge of the lamps on [R]the pure *gold* lampstand before the LORD continually. Ex. 25:31; 31:8; 37:17

The Showbread

5 "And you shall take fine flour and bake twelve [R]cakes with it. Two-tenths *of an ephah* shall be in each cake. Ex. 25:30

6 "You shall set them in two rows, six in a row, on the pure *gold* table before the LORD.

7 "And you shall put pure frankincense on *each* row, that it may be on the bread for a [R]memorial, an offering made by fire to the LORD. Lev. 2:2, 9, 16

8 [R]"Every Sabbath he shall set it in order before the LORD continually, *being taken* from the children of Israel by an everlasting covenant. 1 Chr. 9:32

9 "And it shall be for Aaron and his sons, and they shall eat it in a holy place; for it *is* most holy to him from the offerings of the LORD made by fire, by a perpetual statute."

Law of the Sanctified Name of God

10 Now the son of an Israelite woman, whose father *was* an Egyptian, went out among the children of Israel; and this Israelite *woman's* son and a man of Israel fought each other in the camp.

11 And the Israelite woman's son [R]blasphemed the name *of the LORD* and cursed; and so they brought him to Moses. (His mother's name *was* Shelomith the daughter of Dibri, of the tribe of Dan.) Ex. 22:28

12 Then they [R]put him [T]in custody, [R]that the mind of the LORD might be shown to them. Num. 15:34 • *under guard* • Num. 27:5

13 And the LORD spoke to Moses, saying,

14 "Take outside the camp him who has cursed; then let all who heard *him* [R]lay their hands on his head, and let all the congregation stone him. Deut. 13:9; 17:7

15 "Then you shall speak to the children of Israel, saying: 'Whoever curses his God [R]shall bear his sin. Lev. 20:17

16 'And whoever blasphemes the name of the LORD shall surely be put to death. All the congregation shall certainly stone him, the stranger as well as him who is born in the land. When he blasphemes the name *of the LORD*, he shall be put to death.

17 [R]'Whoever kills any man shall surely be put to death. Ex. 21:12

18 [R]'Whoever kills an animal shall make it good, animal for animal. Lev. 24:21

19 'If a man causes disfigurement of his neighbor, as [R]he has done, so shall it be done to him— Ex. 21:24

20 'fracture for [R]fracture, eye for eye, tooth for tooth; as he has caused disfigurement of a man, so shall it be done to him. Ex. 21:23

21 'And whoever kills an animal shall restore it; but whoever kills a man shall be put to death.

22 'You shall have [R]the same law for the stranger and for one from your own country; for I *am* the LORD your God.' " Ex. 12:49

23 Then Moses spoke to the children of Israel; and they took outside the camp him who had cursed, and stoned him with stones. So the children of Israel did as the LORD commanded Moses.

CHAPTER 25

Law of the Sabbath Year

AND the LORD spoke to Moses on Mount [R]Sinai, saying, Lev. 26:46

2 "Speak to the children of Israel, and say to them: 'When you come into the land which I give you, then the land shall [R]keep a sabbath to the LORD. Lev. 26:34, 35

3 'Six years you shall sow your field, and six years you shall prune your vineyard, and gather its fruit;

4 'but in the seventh year there shall be a sabbath of solemn [R]rest for the land, a sabbath to the LORD. You shall neither sow your field nor prune your vineyard. [Heb. 4:9]

5 [R]'What grows of its own accord of your harvest you shall not reap, nor gather the grapes of your untended vine, *for* it is a year of rest for the land. 2 Kin. 19:29

6 'And the sabbath *produce* of the land shall be food for you: for you, your male and female servants, your hired man, and the stranger who dwells with you,

7 'for your livestock and the beasts that *are*
in your land—all its produce shall be for food.

Law of the Year of Jubilee

8 'And you shall count seven sabbaths of
years for yourself, seven times seven years;
and the time of the seven sabbaths of years
shall be to you forty-nine years.
9 'Then you shall cause the trumpet of the
Jubilee to sound on the tenth *day* of the sev-
enth month; [R]on the Day of Atonement you
shall make the trumpet to sound throughout
all your land. Lev. 23:24, 27
10 'And you shall consecrate the fiftieth year,
and [R]proclaim liberty throughout *all* the land
to all its inhabitants. It shall be a Jubilee for
you; and each of you shall return to his pos-
session, and each of you shall return to his
family. Jer. 34:8, 15, 17
11 'That fiftieth year shall be a Jubilee to
you; in it [R]you shall neither sow nor reap what
grows of its own accord, nor gather *the*
grapes of your untended vine. Lev. 25:5
12 'For it *is* the Jubilee; it shall be holy to
you; you shall eat its produce from the field.
13 [R]'In this Year of Jubilee, each of you shall
return to his possession. Lev. 25:10
14 'And if you sell anything to your neighbor
or buy from your neighbor's hand, you shall
not [R]oppress one another. Lev. 19:13
15 [R]'According to the number of years after
the Jubilee you shall buy from your neighbor,
and according to the number of years of crops
he shall sell to you. Lev. 27:18, 23
16 'According to the multitude of years you
shall increase its price, and according to the
fewer number of years you shall diminish its
price; for he sells to you *according* to the num-
ber *of the years* of the crops.
17 'Therefore [R]you shall not [T]oppress one
another, but you shall fear your God; for I *am*
the LORD your God. Lev. 25:14 • *mistreat*
18 'So you shall observe My statutes and
keep My judgments, and perform them; and
you will dwell in the land in safety.
19 'Then the land will yield its fruit, and
[R]you will eat your fill, and dwell there in
safety. Lev. 26:5
20 'And if you say, [R]"What shall we eat in the
seventh year, since we shall not sow nor
gather in our produce?" Matt. 6:25, 31
21 'Then I will [R]command My blessing on
you in the sixth year, and it will bring forth
produce enough for three years. Deut. 28:8
22 [R]'And you shall sow in the eighth year,
and eat [R]old produce until the ninth year; until
its produce comes in, you shall eat *of* the old
harvest. 2 Kin. 19:29 • Josh. 5:11
23 'The land shall not be sold permanently,
for [R]the land *is* Mine; for you *are* [R]strangers
and sojourners with Me. Ex. 19:5 • Ps. 39:12
24 'And in all the land of your possession
you shall grant redemption of the land.
25 'If one of your brethren becomes poor,
and has sold *some* of his possession, and if his
redeeming relative comes to redeem it, then
he may redeem what his brother sold.
26 'Or if the man has no one to redeem it, but
he himself becomes able to redeem it,
27 'then [R]let him count the years since its
sale, and restore the remainder to the man to
whom he sold it, that he may return to his
possession. Lev. 25:50–52
28 'But if he is not able to have *it* restored
to himself, then what was sold shall remain
in the hand of him who bought it until the
Year of Jubilee; [R]and in the Jubilee it shall be
released, and he shall return to his posses-
sion. Lev. 25:10, 13
29 'If a man sells a house in a walled city,
then he may redeem it within a whole year
after it is sold; *within* a full year he may re-
deem it.
30 'But if it is not redeemed within the space
of a full year, then the house in the walled city
shall belong permanently to him who bought
it, throughout his generations. It shall not be
released in the Jubilee.
31 'However the houses of villages which
have no wall around them shall be counted as
the fields of the country. They may be re-
deemed, and they shall be released in the Ju-
bilee.
32 'Nevertheless the cities of the Levites, *and*
the houses in the cities of their possession, the
Levites may redeem at any time.
33 'And if a man purchases a house from the
Levites, then the house that was sold in the
city of his possession shall be released in the
Jubilee; for the houses in the cities of the
Levites *are* their possession among the chil-
dren of Israel.
34 'But the field of the common-land of their
cities may not be [R]sold, for it *is* their perpetual
possession. Acts 4:36, 37
35 'If one of your brethren becomes poor,
and falls into poverty among you, then you
shall help him, like a stranger or a sojourner,
that he may live with you.
36 [R]'Take no usury or interest from him; but
[R]fear your God, that your brother may live
with you. Ex. 22:25 • Neh. 5:9
37 'You shall not lend him your money for
usury, nor lend him your food at a profit.
38 'I *am* the LORD your God, who brought
you out of the land of Egypt, to give you the
land of Canaan *and* to be your God.
39 'And if *one of* your brethren *who dwells*
by you becomes poor, and sells himself to
you, you shall not compel him to serve as a
slave.
40 'As a hired servant *and* a sojourner he
shall be with you, *and* shall serve you until the
Year of Jubilee.
41 'And *then* he shall depart from you—he
and his children [R]with him—and shall return

to his own family. He shall return to the possession of his fathers. Ex. 21:3

42 'For they *are* [R]My servants, whom I brought out of the land of Egypt; they shall not be sold as slaves. [Rom. 6:22]

43 [R]'You shall not rule over him with rigor, but you shall fear your God. Eph. 6:9

44 'And as for your male and female slaves whom you may have—from the nations that are around you, from them you may buy male and female slaves.

45 'Moreover you may buy [R]the children of the strangers who dwell among you, and their families who are with you, which they beget in your land; and they shall become your property. [Is. 56:3, 6, 7]

46 'And [R]you may take them as an inheritance for your children after you, to inherit *them as* a possession; they shall be your permanent slaves. But regarding your brethren, the children of Israel, you shall not rule over one another with rigor. Is. 14:2

47 'Now if a sojourner or stranger close to you becomes rich, and *one of* your brethren *who dwells* by him becomes poor, and sells himself to the stranger *or* sojourner close to you, or to a member of the stranger's family,

48 'after he is sold he may be redeemed again. One of his brothers may redeem him;

49 'or his uncle or his uncle's son may redeem him; or *anyone* who is near of kin to him in his family may redeem him; or if he is able he may redeem himself.

50 'Thus he shall reckon with him who bought him: The price of his release shall be according to the number of years, from the year that he was sold to him until the Year of Jubilee; *it shall be* [R]according to the time of a hired servant for him. Job 7:1

51 'If *there are* still many years *remaining*, according to them he shall repay the price of his redemption from the money with which he was bought.

52 'And if there remain but a few years until the Year of Jubilee, then he shall reckon with him, *and* according to his years he shall repay him the price of his redemption.

53 'He shall be with him as a yearly hired servant, and he shall not rule with rigor over him in your sight.

54 'And if he is not redeemed in these *years*, then he shall be released in the Year of Jubilee—he and his children with him.

55 'For the children of Israel *are* servants to Me; they *are* My servants whom I brought out of the land of Egypt: I *am* the LORD your God.

CHAPTER 26

Basic Requirements of Obedience

'YOU shall [R]not make idols for yourselves;
neither a carved image nor a *sacred* pillar
shall you rear up for yourselves;
nor shall you set up an engraved stone in
your land, to bow down to it;
for I *am* the LORD your God. Ex. 20:4, 5
2 [R]You shall [T]keep My Sabbaths and reverence My sanctuary: Lev. 19:30 • *observe*
I *am* the LORD.

Conditions and Results of Obedience

3 [R]'If you walk in My statutes and keep
My commandments, and perform
them, Deut. 28:1–14
4 [R]then I will give you rain in its season,
[R]the land shall yield its produce, and
the trees of the field shall yield their
fruit. Is. 30:23 • Ps. 67:6
5 [R]Your threshing shall last till the time of
vintage, and the vintage shall last till
the time of sowing; Amos 9:13
you shall eat your bread to the full, and
dwell in your land safely.
6 [R]I will give peace in the land, and [R]you
shall lie down, and none will make *you*
afraid; Is. 45:7 • Job 11:19
I will rid the land of [R]evil[T] beasts,
and [R]the sword will not go through your
land. 2 Kin. 17:25 • *wild beasts* • Ezek. 14:17
7 You will chase your enemies, and they
shall fall by the sword before you.
8 [R]Five of you shall chase a hundred, and a
hundred of you shall put ten thousand
to flight; Deut. 32:30
your enemies shall fall by the sword before you.

9 'For I will look on you favorably and
make you fruitful, multiply you and
confirm My covenant with you.
10 You shall eat the old harvest, and clear
out the old because of the new.
11 I will set My tabernacle among you, and
My soul shall not abhor you.
12 I will walk among you and be your God,
and you shall be My people.
13 I *am* the LORD your God, who brought you
out of the land of Egypt, that *you* should
not be their slaves;
I have broken the bands of your yoke and
made you walk [T]upright. *erect*

Conditions and Results of Disobedience

14 'But if you do not obey Me, and do not observe all these commandments,
15 and if you despise My statutes, or if your
soul abhors My judgments, so that you
do not perform all My commandments,
but break My covenant,
16 I also will do this to you:
I will even appoint terror over you, [R]wasting disease and fever which shall [R]consume the eyes and cause sorrow of
heart. Deut. 28:22 • 1 Sam. 2:33

And you shall sow your seed in vain, for
your enemies shall eat it.
17 I will set My face against you, and you
shall be defeated by your enemies.
[R]Those who hate you shall reign over you,
and you shall [R]flee when no one pur-
sues you. Ps. 106:41 • Prov. 28:1

18 'And after all this, if you do not obey Me,
then I will punish you [R]seven times
more for your sins. 1 Sam. 2:5
19 I will break the pride of your power;
I [R]will make your heavens like iron and
your earth like bronze. Deut. 28:23
20 And your [R]strength shall be spent in
vain; Ps. 127:1
for your [R]land shall not yield its produce,
nor shall the trees of the land yield their
fruit. Gen. 4:12

21 'Then, if you walk contrary to Me, and are
not willing to obey Me, I will bring on
you seven times more plagues, accord-
ing to your sins.
22 [R]I will also send wild beasts among you,
which shall rob you of your children,
destroy your livestock, and make you
few in number; Deut. 32:24
and your highways shall be desolate.

23 'And if [R]by these things you are not re-
formed by Me, but walk contrary to
Me, Amos 4:6–12
24 [R]then I also will walk contrary to you, and
I will punish you yet seven times for
your sins. Lev. 26:28, 41
25 And [R]I will bring a sword against you that
will execute the vengeance of the
covenant; Ezek. 5:17
when you are gathered together within
your cities [R]I will send pestilence
among you; Deut. 28:21
and you shall be delivered into the hand
of the enemy.
26 When I have cut off your supply of bread,
ten women shall bake your bread in
one oven, and they shall bring back
your bread by weight, and you shall eat
and not be satisfied.

27 'And after all this, if you do not obey Me,
but walk contrary to Me,
28 then I also will walk contrary to you in
fury;
and I, even I, will chastise you seven times
for your sins.
29 [R]You shall eat the flesh of your sons, and
you shall eat the flesh of your daugh-
ters. 2 Kin. 6:28, 29
30 [R]I will destroy your high places, cut down
your incense altars, and cast your car-
casses on the lifeless forms of your
idols; 2 Chr. 34:3
and My soul shall abhor you.
31 I will lay your [R]cities waste and [R]bring
your sanctuaries to desolation, and I
will not smell the fragrance of your
sweet aromas. 2 Kin. 25:4, 10 • Ps. 74:7
32 [R]I will bring the land to desolation, and
your enemies who dwell in it shall be
astonished at it. Jer. 9:11; 18:16
33 [R]I will scatter you among the nations and
draw out a sword after you;
your land shall be desolate and your cities
waste. Deut. 4:27
34 [R]Then the land shall enjoy its sabbaths as
long as it lies desolate and you *are* in
your enemies' land; 2 Chr. 36:21
then the land shall rest and enjoy its sab-
baths.
35 As long as *it* lies desolate it shall rest—
for the time it did not rest on your [R]sab-
baths when you dwelt in it. Lev. 25:2

36 'And as for those of you who are left, I
will send [R]faintness[T] into their hearts in
the lands of their enemies;
the sound of a shaken leaf shall cause
them to flee;
they shall flee as though fleeing from a
sword, and they shall fall when no one
pursues. Ezek. 21:7, 12, 15 • *fear*
37 [R]They shall stumble over one another, as
it were before a sword, when no one
pursues; 1 Sam. 14:15, 16
and [R]you shall have no *power* to stand be-
fore your enemies. Josh. 7:12, 13
38 You shall [R]perish among the nations, and
the land of your enemies shall eat you
up. Deut. 4:26
39 And those of you who are left [R]shall waste
away in their iniquity in your enemies'
lands; Ezek. 4:17; 33:10
also in their fathers' iniquities, which are
with them, they shall waste away.

The Promise of Restoration

40 '*But* if they confess their iniquity and the
iniquity of their fathers, with their
unfaithfulness in which they were
unfaithful to Me, and that they also
have walked contrary to Me,
41 and *that* I also have walked contrary to
them and have brought them into the
land of their enemies;
if their uncircumcised hearts are hum-
bled, and they accept their guilt—
42 then I will [R]remember My covenant with
Jacob, and My covenant with Isaac and
My covenant with Abraham I will re-
member; Ex. 2:24; 6:5
I will [R]remember the land. Ps. 136:23
43 The land also shall be left empty by them,
and will enjoy its sabbaths while it lies
desolate without them;
they will accept their guilt, because they

despised My judgments and because their soul abhorred My statutes.

44 Yet for all that, when they are in the land of their enemies, [R]I will not cast them away, nor shall I abhor them, to utterly destroy them and break My covenant with them; Deut. 4:31
for I *am* the LORD their God.

45 But [R]for their sake I will remember the covenant of their ancestors, whom I brought out of the land of Egypt [R]in the sight of the nations, that I might be their God: [Rom. 11:28] • Ps. 98:2
I *am* the LORD.' "

46 [R]These *are* the statutes and judgments and laws which the LORD made between Himself and the children of Israel on Mount Sinai by the hand of Moses. [John 1:17]

CHAPTER 27

Consecration of Persons

NOW the LORD spoke to Moses, saying,

2 "Speak to the children of Israel, and say to them: [R]'When a man consecrates by a vow certain persons to the LORD, according to your [T]valuation, Num. 6:2 • *appraisal*

3 'if your valuation is of a male from twenty years old up to sixty years old, then your valuation shall be fifty shekels of silver, according to the shekel of the sanctuary.

4 'If it *is* a female, then your valuation shall be thirty shekels;

5 'and if from five years old up to twenty years old, then your valuation for a male shall be twenty shekels, and for a female ten shekels;

6 'and if from a month old up to five years old, then your valuation for a male shall be five shekels of silver, and for a female your valuation shall be three shekels of silver;

7 'and if from sixty years old and above, if *it is* a male, then your valuation shall be fifteen shekels, and for a female ten shekels.

8 'But if he is too poor to pay your valuation, then he shall present himself before the priest, and the priest shall set a value for [R]him; according to the ability of him who vowed, the priest shall value him. Lev. 5:11

Consecration of Animals

9 'If *it is* an animal that men may bring as an offering to the LORD, all that *anyone* gives to the LORD shall be holy.

10 'He shall not substitute it or exchange it, good for bad or bad for good; and if he at all exchanges animal for animal, then both it and the one exchanged for it shall be holy.

11 'If *it is* an unclean animal which they do not offer as a sacrifice to the LORD, then he shall present the animal before the priest;

12 'and the priest shall set a value for it, whether it is good or bad; as you, the priest, value it, so it shall be.

13 [R]'But if he *wants* at all *to* redeem it, then he must add one-fifth to your valuation. Lev. 6:5; 22:14; 27:15, 19

Consecration of Houses

14 'And when a man dedicates his house *to be* holy to the LORD, then the priest shall set a value for it, whether it is good or bad; as the priest values it, so it shall stand.

15 'If he who dedicated it *wants to* [T]redeem his house, then he must add one-fifth of the money of your valuation to it, and it shall be his. *buy back*

Consecration of Fields

16 'If a man [T]dedicates to the LORD *part* of a field of his possession, then your valuation shall be according to the seed for it. A homer of barley seed *shall be valued* at fifty shekels of silver. *sets apart*

17 'If he dedicates his field from the Year of Jubilee, according to your valuation it shall stand.

18 'But if he dedicates his field after the Jubilee, then the priest shall reckon to him the money due according to the years that remain till the Year of Jubilee, and it shall be deducted from your valuation.

19 'And if he who dedicates the field ever wishes to redeem it, then he must add one-fifth of the money of your valuation to it, and it shall belong to him.

20 'But if he does not want to redeem the field, or if he has sold the field to another man, it shall not be redeemed anymore;

21 'but the field, [R]when it is released in the Jubilee, shall be holy to the LORD, as a [R]devoted field; it shall be [R]the possession of the priest. Lev. 25:10, 28, 31 • Lev. 27:28 • Num. 18:14

22 'And if a man dedicates to the LORD a field which he has bought, which is not the field of [R]his possession, Lev. 25:10, 25

23 'then the priest shall reckon to him the worth of your valuation, up to the Year of Jubilee, and he shall give your valuation on that day *as* a holy *offering* to the LORD.

24 'In the Year of Jubilee the field shall return to him from whom it was bought, to the one who *owned* the land as a possession.

25 'And all your valuations shall be according to the shekel of the sanctuary: [R]twenty gerahs to the shekel. Ex. 30:13

Firstborn Clean Animals

26 'But the [R]firstborn of the animals, which should be the LORD's firstborn, no man shall dedicate; whether *it is* an ox or sheep, it *is* the LORD's. Ex. 13:2, 12; 22:30

27 'And if *it is* an unclean animal, then he shall redeem *it* according to your valuation, and [R]shall add one-fifth to it; or if it is not redeemed, then it shall be sold according to your valuation. Lev. 27:11, 12

Devoted Things

28 'Nevertheless no devoted *offering* that
a man may devote to the LORD of all that
he has, *both* man and beast, or the field of his
possession, shall be sold or redeemed; every
devoted *offering is* most holy to the LORD.
29 [R]'No person under the ban, who may be-
come doomed to destruction among men,
shall be redeemed, *but* shall surely be put to
death. Num. 21:2

Tithes

30 'And all the tithe of the land, *whether* of
the seed of the land *or* of the fruit of the tree,
is the LORD's. It *is* holy to the LORD.
31 'If a man wants at all to redeem *any* of his
tithes, he shall add one-fifth to it.
32 'And concerning the tithe of the herd or
the flock, of whatever passes under the rod,
the tenth one shall be holy to the LORD.
33 'He shall not inquire whether it is good or
bad, [R]nor shall he exchange it; and if he ex-
changes it at all, then both it and the one ex-
changed for it shall be holy; it shall not be
redeemed.' " Lev. 27:10

The Conclusion of Leviticus

34 These *are* the commandments which the
LORD commanded Moses for the children of
Israel on Mount [R]Sinai. [Heb. 12:18–29]

Liquid Measures

Unit	*Measure*	*Equivalents*	*Translations*
Kor	60 gallons	10 baths	kor
Metretes	10.2 gallons		gallon
Bath	6 gallons	6 hins	measure, bath
Hin	1 gallon	2 kabs	hin
Kab	2 quarts	4 logs	kab
Log	1 pint	¼ kab	log

THE FOURTH BOOK OF MOSES CALLED

NUMBERS

THE BOOK OF NUMBERS

Numbers is the book of wanderings. It takes its name from the two numberings of the Israelites—the first at Mount Sinai and the second on the plains of Moab. Most of the book, however, describes Israel's experiences as they wander in the wilderness. The lesson of Numbers is clear. While it may be necessary to pass through wilderness experiences, one does not have to live there. For Israel, an eleven-day journey became a forty-year agony.

The title of Numbers comes from the first word in the Hebrew text, *Wayyedabber,* "And He Said." Jewish writings, however, usually refer to it by the fifth Hebrew word in 1:1, *Bemidbar,* "In the Wilderness," which more nearly indicates the content of the book. The Greek title in the Septuagint is *Arithmoi,* "Numbers." The Latin Vulgate followed this title and translated it *Liber Numeri,* "Book of Numbers." These titles are based on the two numberings: the generation of Exodus (Num. 1) and the generation that grew up in the wilderness and conquered Canaan (Num. 26). Numbers has also been called the "Book of the Journeyings," the "Book of the Murmurings," and the "Fourth Book of Moses."

THE AUTHOR OF NUMBERS

The evidence that points to Moses as the author of Numbers is similar to that for the previous books of the Pentateuch. These five books form such a literary unit that they rise or fall together on the matter of authorship.

External Evidence: The Jews, the Samaritans, and the early church give testimony to the Mosaic authorship of Numbers. Also a number of New Testament passages cite events from Numbers and associate them with Moses. These include John 3:14; Acts 7 and 13; 1 Corinthians 10:1–11; Hebrews 3 and 4; and Jude 11.

Internal Evidence: There are more than eighty claims that "the LORD spoke to Moses" (the first is 1:1). In addition, Numbers 33:2 makes this clear statement: "Now Moses wrote down the starting points of their journeys at the command of the LORD." Moses kept detailed records as an eyewitness of the events in this book. As the central character in Exodus through Deuteronomy, he was better qualified than any other man to write these books.

Some scholars have claimed that the third-person references to Moses point to a different author. However, use of the third person was a common practice in the ancient world. Caesar, for example, did the same in his writings.

THE TIME OF NUMBERS

Leviticus covers only one month, but Numbers stretches over almost thirty-nine years (c. 1444–1405 B.C.). It records Israel's movement from the last twenty days at Mount Sinai (1:1; 10:11), the wandering around Kadesh Barnea, and finally the arrival in the plains of Moab in the fortieth year (22:1; 26:3; 33:50; Deut. 1:3). Their tents occupy several square miles whenever they camp since there are probably over two-and-a-half million people (based on the census figures in Numbers 1 and 26). God miraculously feeds and sustains them in the desert—He preserves their clothing and gives them manna, meat, water, leaders, and a promise (14:34).

THE CHRIST OF NUMBERS

Perhaps the clearest portrait of Christ in Numbers is the bronze serpent on the stake, a picture of the Crucifixion (21:4–9): "And as Moses lifted up the serpent in the wilderness, even so must the Son of Man be lifted up" (John 3:14). The rock that quenches the thirst of the multitudes is also a type of Christ: "they drank of that spiritual Rock that followed them, and that Rock was Christ" (1 Cor. 10:4). The daily manna pictures the Bread of Life who later comes down from heaven (John 6:31–33).

Balaam foresees the rulership of Christ: "I see Him, but not now; I behold Him, but not near; a Star shall come out of Jacob; a Scepter shall rise out of Israel" (24:17). The guidance and presence of Christ is seen in the pillar of cloud and fire, and the sinner's refuge in Christ may be seen in the six cities of refuge. The red heifer sacrifice (Num. 19) is also considered a type of Christ.

KEYS TO NUMBERS

Key Word: Wanderings—Numbers records the failure of Israel to believe in the promise of God and the resulting judgment of wandering in the wilderness for forty years.

Key Verses: Numbers 14:22, 23; 20:12—"Because all these men who have seen My glory and the signs which I did in Egypt and in the wilderness, and have put Me to the test now these ten times, and have not heeded My voice, they certainly shall not see the land of which I swore to their fathers, nor shall any of those who rejected Me see it" (14:22, 23).

"Then the LORD spoke to Moses and Aaron, 'Because you did not believe Me, to hallow Me in the eyes of the children of Israel, therefore you shall not bring this assembly into the land which I have given them' " (20:12).

Key Chapter: Numbers 14—The critical turning point of Numbers may be seen in Numbers 14 when Israel rejects God by refusing to go up and conquer the Promised Land. God judges Israel "according to the number of the days in which you spied out the land, forty days, for each day you shall bear your guilt one year, *namely* forty years, and you shall know My rejection" (14:34).

SURVEY OF NUMBERS

Israel as a nation is in its infancy at the outset of this book, only thirteen months after the exodus from Egypt. In Numbers, the book of divine discipline, it becomes necessary for the nation to go through the painful process of testing and maturation. God must teach His people the consequences of irresponsible decisions. The forty years of wilderness experience transform them from a rabble of ex-slaves into a nation ready to take the Promised Land. Numbers begins with the old generation (1:1—10:10), moves through a tragic transitional period (10:11—25:18), and ends with the new generation (26—36) at the doorway to the land of Canaan.

The Old Generation (1:1—10:10): The generation that witnessed God's miraculous acts of deliverance and preservation receives further direction from God while they are still at the foot of Mount Sinai (1:1—10:10). God's instructions are very explicit, reaching every aspect of their lives. He is the Author of order, not confusion; and this is seen in the way He organizes the people around the tabernacle. Turning from the outward conditions of the camp (1—4) to the inward conditions (5—10), Numbers describes the spiritual preparation of the people.

The Tragic Transition (10:11—25:18): Israel follows God step-by-step until Canaan is in sight. Then in the crucial moment at Kadesh they draw back in unbelief. Their murmurings had already become incessant, "Now *when* the people complained, it displeased the LORD; for the LORD heard *it*" (11:1). But their unbelief after sending out the twelve spies at Kadesh Barnea is something God will not tolerate. Their rebellion at Kadesh marks the pivotal point of the book. The generation of the Exodus will not be the generation of the conquest.

Unbelief brings discipline and hinders God's blessing. The old generation is doomed to literally kill time for forty years of wilderness wanderings—one year for every day spent by the twelve spies in inspecting the land. They are judged by disinheritance and death as their journey changes from one of anticipation to one of aimlessness. Only Joshua and Caleb, the two spies who believed God, enter Canaan. Almost nothing is recorded about these transitional years.

The New Generation (26—36): When the transition to the new generation is complete, the people move to the plains of Moab, directly east of the Promised Land (22:1). Before they can enter the land they must wait until all is ready. Here they receive new instructions, a new census is taken, Joshua is appointed as Moses' successor, and some of the people settle in the Transjordan.

Numbers records two generations (1—14 and 21—36), two numberings (1 and 26), two journeyings (10—14 and 21—27), and two sets of instructions (5—9 and 28—36). It illustrates both the kindness and severity of God (Rom. 11:22) and teaches that God's people can move forward only as they trust and depend on Him.

FOCUS	THE OLD GENERATION		THE TRAGIC TRANSITION				THE NEW GENERATION		
REFERENCE	1:1——5:1——10:11—13:1——15:1——20:1—26:1——28:1——31:1—36:13								
DIVISION	ORGANIZATION OF ISRAEL	SANCTIFICATION OF ISRAEL	TO KADESH	AT KADESH	IN WILDERNESS	TO MOAB	REORGANIZATION OF ISRAEL	REGULATIONS OF OFFERINGS AND VOWS	CONQUEST AND DIVISION OF ISRAEL
TOPIC	ORDER		DISORDER				REORDER		
	PREPARATION		POSTPONEMENT				PREPARATION		
LOCATION	MOUNT SINAI		WILDERNESS				PLAINS OF MOAB		
TIME	20 DAYS		38 YEARS 3 MONTHS AND 10 DAYS				c. 5 MONTHS		

OUTLINE OF NUMBERS

Part One: The Preparation of the Old Generation to Inherit the Promised Land (1:1—10:10)

Part Two: The Failure of the Old Generation to Inherit the Promised Land (10:11—25:18)

Part Three: The Preparation of the New Generation to Inherit the Promised Land (26:1—36:13)

CHAPTER 1

The First Census of Israel

NOW the LORD spoke to Moses in the
Wilderness of Sinai, in the tabernacle of
meeting, on the first *day* of the second month,
in the second year after they had come out of
the land of Egypt, saying:
2 "Take a census of all the congregation of
the children of Israel, by their families, by
their fathers' houses, according to the number
of names, every male individually,
3 "from twenty years old and above—all
who *are able to* go to war in Israel. You and
Aaron shall number them by their armies.
4 "And with you there shall be a man from
every tribe, each one the head of his father's
house.
5 "These are the names of the men who
shall stand with you: from Reuben, Elizur the
son of Shedeur;
6 "from Simeon, Shelumiel the son of Zu-
rishaddai;
7 "from Judah, Nahshon the son of Am-
minadab;
8 "from Issachar, Nethanel the son of Zuar;
9 "from Zebulun, Eliab the son of Helon;
10 "from the sons of Joseph: from Ephraim,
Elishama the son of Ammihud; from Ma-
nasseh, Gamaliel the son of Pedahzur;
11 "from Benjamin, Abidan the son of
Gideoni;
12 "from Dan, Ahiezer the son of Am-
mishaddai;
13 "from Asher, Pagiel the son of Ocran;
14 "from Gad, Eliasaph the son of Deuel;*
15 "from Naphtali, Ahira the son of Enan."
16 [R]These *were* [R]chosen from the congrega-
tion, leaders of their fathers' tribes, heads of
the divisions in Israel. Num. 7:2 • Num. 16:2
17 Then Moses and Aaron took these men
who had been mentioned by name,
18 and they assembled all the congregation
together on the first *day* of the second month;
and they recited their ancestry by families, by
their fathers' houses, according to the number
of names, from twenty years old and above,
each one individually.
19 As the LORD commanded Moses, so he
numbered them in the Wilderness of Sinai.
20 Now the [R]children of Reuben, Israel's old-
est son, their genealogies by their families, by
their fathers' house, according to the number
of names, every male individually, from
twenty years old and above, all who *were able
to* go to war: Num. 2:10, 11; 26:5–11
21 those who were numbered of the tribe of
Reuben *were* forty-six thousand five hundred.
22 From the children of Simeon, their ge-
nealogies by their families, by their fathers'
house, of those who were numbered, accord-
ing to the number of names, every male indi-
vidually, from twenty years old and above, all
who *were able to* go to war:
23 those who were numbered of the tribe of

1:14 *Reuel*, Num. 2:14

Simeon *were* fifty-nine thousand three hundred.

24 From the [R]children of Gad, their genealogies by their families, by their fathers' house, according to the number of names, from twenty years old and above, all who *were able to* go to war: Num. 26:15–18

25 those who were numbered of the tribe of Gad *were* forty-five thousand six hundred and fifty.

26 From the [R]children of Judah, their genealogies by their families, by their fathers' house, according to the number of names, from twenty years old and above, all who *were able to* go to war: 2 Sam. 24:9

27 those who were numbered of the tribe of Judah *were* [R]seventy-four thousand six hundred. 2 Chr. 17:14

28 From the [R]children of Issachar, their genealogies by their families, by their fathers' house, according to the number of names, from twenty years old and above, all who *were able to* go to war: Num. 2:5, 6

29 those who were numbered of the tribe of Issachar *were* fifty-four thousand four hundred.

30 From the [R]children of Zebulun, their genealogies by their families, by their fathers' house, according to the number of names, from twenty years old and above, all who *were able to* go to war: Num. 2:7, 8; 26:26, 27

31 those who were numbered of the tribe of Zebulun *were* fifty-seven thousand four hundred.

32 From the sons of Joseph, the children of Ephraim, their genealogies by their families, by their fathers' house, according to the number of names, from twenty years old and above, all who *were able to* go to war:

33 those who were numbered of the tribe of Ephraim *were* forty thousand five hundred.

34 From the [R]children of Manasseh, their genealogies by their families, by their fathers' house, according to the number of names, from twenty years old and above, all who *were able to* go to war: Num. 2:20, 21

35 those who were numbered of the tribe of Manasseh *were* thirty-two thousand two hundred.

36 From the [R]children of Benjamin, their genealogies by their families, by their fathers' house, according to the number of names, from twenty years old and above, all who *were able to* go to war: Num. 26:38–41

37 those who were numbered of the tribe of Benjamin *were* thirty-five thousand four hundred.

38 From the [R]children of Dan, their genealogies by their families, by their fathers' house, according to the number of names, from twenty years old and above, all who *were able to* go to war: Gen. 30:6; 46:23

39 those who were numbered of the tribe of Dan *were* sixty-two thousand seven hundred.

40 From the [R]children of Asher, their genealogies by their families, by their fathers' house, according to the number of names, from twenty years old and above, all who *were able to* go to war: Num. 2:27, 28; 26:44–47

41 those who were numbered of the tribe of Asher *were* forty-one thousand five hundred.

42 From the children of Naphtali, their genealogies by their families, by their fathers' house, according to the number of names, from twenty years old and above, all who *were able to* go to war:

43 those who were numbered of the tribe of Naphtali *were* fifty-three thousand four hundred.

44 These are the ones who were numbered, whom Moses and Aaron numbered, with the leaders of Israel, twelve men, each one representing his father's house.

45 So all who were numbered of the children of Israel, by their fathers' houses, from twenty years old and above, all who *were able to* go to war in Israel—

46 all who were numbered were [R]six hundred and three thousand five hundred and fifty. Ex. 12:37; 38:26

47 But the Levites were not numbered among them by their fathers' tribe;

48 for the LORD had spoken to Moses, saying:

49 [R]"Only the tribe of Levi you shall not number, nor take a census of them among the children of Israel; Num. 2:33; 26:62

50 [R]"but you shall appoint the Levites over the tabernacle of the Testimony, over all its furnishings, and over all things that belong to it; they shall carry the tabernacle and all its furnishings; they shall attend to it and camp around the tabernacle. Ex. 38:21

51 "And when the tabernacle is to go forward, the Levites shall take it down; and when the tabernacle is to be set up, the Levites shall set it up. The outsider who comes near shall be put to death.

52 "The children of Israel shall pitch their tents, [R]everyone by his own camp, everyone by his own standard, according to their armies; Num. 2:2, 34; 24:2

53 "but the Levites shall camp around the tabernacle of the Testimony, that there may be no wrath on the congregation of the children of Israel; and the Levites shall keep charge of the tabernacle of the Testimony."

54 Thus the children of Israel did; according to all that the LORD commanded Moses, so they did.

CHAPTER 2

On the East

AND the LORD spoke to Moses and Aaron, saying:

2 [R]"Everyone of the children of Israel shall camp by his own [T]standard, beside the em-

blems of his father's house; they shall camp [R]some distance from the tabernacle of meeting. Num. 1:52; 24:2 • *banner* • Josh. 3:4

3 "On the [R]east side, toward the rising of the sun, those of the standard of the forces with Judah shall camp according to their armies; and [R]Nahshon the son of Amminadab *shall be* the leader of the children of Judah." Num. 10:5 • 1 Chr. 2:10

4 And his army was numbered at seventy-four thousand six hundred.

5 "Those who camp next to him *shall be* the tribe of Issachar, and Nethanel the son of Zuar *shall be* the leader of the children of Issachar."

6 And his army was numbered at fifty-four thousand four hundred.

7 "Then *comes* the tribe of Zebulun, and Eliab the son of Helon *shall be* the leader of the children of Zebulun."

8 And his army was numbered at fifty-seven thousand four hundred.

9 "All who were numbered according to their armies of the forces with Judah, one hundred and eighty-six thousand four hundred—these shall break camp first.

On the South

10 "On the [R]south side *shall be* the standard of the forces with Reuben according to their armies, and the leader of the children of Reuben *shall be* Elizur the son of Shedeur." Num. 10:6

11 And his army was numbered at forty-six thousand five hundred.

12 "Those who camp next to him *shall be* the tribe of Simeon, and the leader of the children of Simeon *shall be* Shelumiel the son of Zurishaddai."

13 And his army was numbered at fifty-nine thousand three hundred.

14 "Then *comes* the tribe of Gad, and the leader of the children of Gad *shall be* Eliasaph the son of Reuel."*

15 And his army was numbered at forty-five thousand six hundred and fifty.

16 "All who were numbered according to their armies of the forces with Reuben, one hundred and fifty-one thousand four hundred and fifty—[R]they shall [T]be the second to break camp. Num. 10:18 • Lit. *set forth second*

On the Middle

17 [R]"And the tabernacle of meeting shall move out with the camp of the Levites [R]in the middle of the camps; as they camp, so they shall move out, everyone in his place, by their standards. Num. 10:17, 21 • Num. 1:53

On the West

18 "On the west side *shall be* the standard of the forces with Ephraim according to their armies, and the leader of the children of Ephraim *shall be* Elishama the son of Ammihud."

19 And his army was numbered at forty thousand five hundred.

20 "Next to him *comes* the tribe of Manasseh, and the leader of the children of Manasseh *shall be* Gamaliel the son of Pedahzur."

21 And his army was numbered at thirty-two thousand two hundred.

22 "Then *comes* the tribe of Benjamin, and the leader of the children of Benjamin *shall be* Abidan the son of Gideoni."

23 And his army was numbered at thirty-five thousand four hundred.

24 "All who were numbered according to their armies of the forces with Ephraim, one hundred and eight thousand one hundred—they shall be the third to break camp.

On the North

25 "The standard of the forces with Dan *shall be* on the north side according to their armies, and the leader of the children of Dan *shall be* Ahiezer the son of Ammishaddai."

26 And his army was numbered at sixty-two thousand seven hundred.

27 "Those who camp next to him *shall be* the tribe of Asher, and the leader of the children of Asher *shall be* Pagiel the son of Ocran."

28 And his army was numbered at forty-one thousand five hundred.

29 "Then *comes* the tribe of Naphtali, and the leader of the children of Naphtali *shall be* Ahira the son of Enan."

30 And his army was numbered at fifty-three thousand four hundred.

31 "All who were numbered of the forces with Dan, one hundred and fifty-seven thousand six hundred—[R]they shall break camp last, with their standards." Num. 10:25

The Camp Is Arranged

32 These *are* the ones who were numbered of the children of Israel by their fathers' houses. [R]All who were numbered according to their armies of the forces *were* six hundred and three thousand five hundred and fifty. Ex. 38:26

33 But [R]the Levites were not numbered among the children of Israel, just as the LORD commanded Moses. Num. 1:47; 26:57–62

34 Thus the children of Israel [R]did according to all that the LORD commanded Moses; so they camped by their standards and so they broke camp, each one by his family, according to their fathers' houses. Num. 1:54

2:14 *Deuel,* Num. 1:14; 7:42

CHAPTER 3

The Family of Aaron

NOW these *are* the [R]records[T] of Aaron and Moses when the LORD spoke with Moses on Mount Sinai. Ex. 6:16–27 • Lit. *generations*

2 And these *are* the names of the sons of Aaron: Nadab, the [R]firstborn, and [R]Abihu, Eleazar, and Ithamar. Ex. 6:23 • Num. 26:60, 61

3 These *are* the names of the sons of Aaron, [R]the anointed priests, whom he consecrated to minister as priests. Ex. 28:41

4 [R]Nadab and Abihu had died before the LORD when they offered profane fire before the LORD in the Wilderness of Sinai; and they had no children. So Eleazar and Ithamar ministered as priests in the presence of Aaron their father. 1 Chr. 24:2

5 And the LORD spoke to Moses, saying:

The Ministry of the Levites

6 [R]"Bring the tribe of Levi near, and present them before Aaron the priest, that they may serve him. Num. 8:6–22; 18:1–7

7 "And they shall attend to his needs and the needs of the whole congregation before the tabernacle of meeting, to do [R]the work of the tabernacle. Num. 1:50; 8:11, 15, 24, 26

8 "Also they shall attend to all the furnishings of the tabernacle of meeting, and to the needs of the children of Israel, to do the work of the tabernacle.

9 "And you shall give the Levites to Aaron and his sons; they *are* given entirely to him* from among the children of Israel.

10 "So you shall appoint Aaron and his sons, [R]and they shall attend to their priesthood; [R]but the outsider who comes near shall be put to death." Ex. 29:9 • Num. 1:51

11 Then the LORD spoke to Moses, saying:

12 "Now behold, [R]I Myself have taken the Levites from among the children of Israel instead of every firstborn who opens the womb among the children of Israel. Therefore the Levites shall be Mine, Num. 3:41; 8:16; 18:6

13 "because [R]all the firstborn *are* Mine. On the day that I struck all the firstborn in the land of Egypt, I sanctified to Myself all the firstborn in Israel, both man and beast. They shall be Mine: I *am* the LORD." Ex. 13:2

The Census Is Commanded

14 Then the LORD spoke to Moses in the Wilderness of Sinai, saying:

15 "Number the children of Levi by their fathers' houses, by their families; you shall number [R]every male from a month old and above." Num. 3:39; 26:62

16 So Moses numbered them according to the [T]word of the LORD, as he was commanded. Lit. *mouth*

17 These were the sons of Levi by their names: Gershon, Kohath, and Merari.

18 And these *are* the names of the sons of [R]Gershon by their families: [R]Libni and Shimei. Num. 4:38–41 • Ex. 6:17

19 And the sons of Kohath by their families: Amram, Izehar, Hebron, and Uzziel.

20 And the sons of Merari by their families: Mahli and Mushi. These *are* the families of the Levites by their fathers' houses.

The Census of Gershon

21 From Gershon *came* the family of the Libnites and the family of the Shimites; these *were* the families of the Gershonites.

22 Those who were numbered, according to the number of all the males from a month old and above—of those who were numbered *there were* seven thousand five hundred.

23 The families of the Gershonites were to camp behind the tabernacle westward.

24 And the leader of the father's house of the Gershonites *was* Eliasaph the son of Lael.

25 [R]The duties of the children of Gershon in the tabernacle of meeting *included* [R]the tabernacle, [R]the tent with [R]its covering, the screen for the door of the tabernacle of meeting, Num. 4:24–26 • Ex. 25:9 • Ex. 26:1 • Ex. 26:7, 14

26 [R]the screen for the door of the court, [R]the hangings of the court which *are* around the tabernacle and the altar, and [R]their cords, according to all the work relating to them. Ex. 27:9, 12, 14, 15 • Ex. 27:16 • Ex. 35:18

The Census of Kohath

27 [R]From Kohath *came* the family of the Amramites, the family of the Izharites, the family of the Hebronites, and the family of the Uzzielites; these *were* the families of the Kohathites. 1 Chr. 26:23

28 According to the number of all the males, from a month old and above, *there were* eight thousand six* hundred [T]keeping charge of the sanctuary. *taking care of*

29 [R]The families of the children of Kohath were to camp on the south side of the tabernacle. Num. 1:53

30 And the leader of the fathers' house of the families of the Kohathites *was* Elizaphan the son of [R]Uzziel. Lev. 10:4

31 Their duty *included* [R]the ark, [R]the table, [R]the lampstand, [R]the altars, the utensils of the sanctuary with which they ministered, the screen, and all the work relating to them. Ex. 25:10 • Ex. 25:23 • Ex. 25:31 • Ex. 27:1

32 And Eleazar the son of Aaron the priest *was to be* chief over the leaders of the Levites, *with* oversight of those who kept charge of the sanctuary.

3:9 Sam., LXX *Me* **3:28** Some LXX mss. *three*

The Census of Merari

33 From Merari *came* the family of the
Mahlites and the family of the Mushites; these
were the families of Merari.
34 And those who were numbered, accord-
ing to the number of all the males from a
month old and above, *were* six thousand two
hundred.
35 The leader of the fathers' house of the
families of Merari *was* Zuriel the son of Abi-
hail. [R]These *were* to camp on the north side of
the tabernacle. Num. 1:53; 2:25
36 And the appointed duty of the children of
Merari *included* the boards of the tabernacle,
its bars, its pillars, its sockets, its utensils, all
the work relating to them,
37 and the pillars of the court all around,
with their sockets, their pegs, and their cords.

The Summary of the Census

38 [R]Moreover those who were to camp be-
fore the tabernacle on the east, before the tab-
ernacle of meeting, *were* Moses, Aaron, and
his sons, [R]keeping charge of the sanctuary, to
meet the needs of the children of Israel; but
the outsider who came near was to be put to
death. Num. 1:53 • Num. 18:5
39 [R]All who were numbered of the Levites,
whom Moses and Aaron numbered at the
commandment of the LORD, by their families,
all the males from a month old and above,
were twenty-two thousand. Num. 3:43; 4:48

The Substitution of the Levites for the Firstborn

40 Then the LORD said to Moses: [R]"Number
all the firstborn males of the children of Israel
from a month old and above, and take the
number of their names. Num. 3:15
41 [R]"And you shall take the Levites for Me—
I *am* the LORD—instead of all the firstborn
among the children of Israel, and the live-
stock of the Levites instead of all the first-
born among the livestock of the children of
Israel." Num. 3:12, 45
42 So Moses numbered all the firstborn
among the children of Israel, as the LORD
commanded him.
43 And all the firstborn males, according to
the number of names from a month old and
above, of those who were numbered of them,
were twenty-two thousand two hundred and
seventy-three.
44 Then the LORD spoke to Moses, saying:
45 [R]"Take the Levites instead of all the first-
born among the children of Israel, and the
livestock of the Levites instead of their live-
stock. The Levites shall be Mine: I *am* the
LORD. Num. 3:12, 41
46 "And for [R]the redemption of the two hun-
dred and seventy-three of the firstborn of the
children of Israel, who are more than the
number of the Levites, Ex. 13:13, 15
47 "you shall take [R]five shekels for each one
individually; you shall take *them* in the cur-
rency of the shekel of the sanctuary, [R]the
shekel of twenty gerahs. Lev. 27:6 • Ex. 30:13
48 "And you shall give the money, with
which the excess number of them is re-
deemed, to Aaron and his sons."
49 So Moses took the redemption money
from those who were over and above those
who were redeemed by the Levites.
50 From the firstborn of the children of Is-
rael he took the money, [R]one thousand three
hundred and sixty-five *shekels*, according to
the shekel of the sanctuary. Num. 3:46, 47
51 And Moses [R]gave their redemption
money to Aaron and his sons, according to the
word of the LORD, as the LORD commanded
Moses. Num. 3:48

CHAPTER 4

The Ministry of Kohath

THEN the LORD spoke to Moses and Aaron,
saying:
2 "Take a census of the sons of Kohath from
among the children of Levi, by their families,
by their fathers' house,
3 "from thirty years old and above, even to
fifty years old, all who enter the service to do
the work in the tabernacle of meeting.
4 [R]"This *is* the service of the sons of Kohath
in the tabernacle of meeting, *relating to* [R]the
most holy things: Num. 4:15 • Num. 4:19
5 "When the camp prepares to journey,
Aaron and his sons shall come, and they shall
take down [R]the covering veil and cover the
ark of the Testimony with it. Ex. 26:31
6 "Then they shall put on it a covering of
badger skins, and spread over *that* a cloth
entirely of [R]blue; and they shall insert [R]its
poles. Ex. 39:1 • Ex. 25:13
7 "On the [R]table of showbread they shall
spread a blue cloth, and put on it the
dishes, the pans, the bowls, and the pitchers
for pouring; and the [R]showbread* shall be
on it. Ex. 25:23, 29, 30 • Lev. 24:5–9
8 "They shall spread over them a scarlet
cloth, and cover the same with a covering
of badger skins; and they shall insert its poles.
9 "And they shall take a blue cloth and
cover the lampstand of the light, with its
lamps, its wick-trimmers, its trays, and all its
oil vessels, with which they service it.
10 "Then they shall put it with all its utensils
in a covering of badger skins, and put *it* on a
carrying beam.
11 "Over the golden altar they shall spread a
blue cloth, and cover it with a covering
of badger skins; and they shall insert its poles.

4:7 Lit. *continual bread*

12 "Then they shall take all the [R]utensils of
service with which they minister in the sanc-
tuary, put *them* in a blue cloth, cover them
with a covering of badger skins, and put *them*
on a carrying beam. Ex. 25:9
13 "Also they shall take away the ashes from
the altar, and spread a purple cloth over it.
14 "They shall put on it all its implements
with which they minister there—the firepans,
the forks, the shovels, the [T]basins, and all the
utensils of the altar—and they shall spread on
it a covering of badger skins, and insert its
poles. *bowls*
15 "And when Aaron and his sons have fin-
ished covering the sanctuary and all the fur-
nishings of the sanctuary, when the camp is
set to go, then the sons of Kohath shall come
to carry *them;* but they shall not touch any
holy thing, lest they die. These *are* the things
in the tabernacle of meeting which the sons of
Kohath are to carry.
16 "The appointed duty of Eleazar the son of
Aaron the priest *is* [R]the oil for the light, the
sweet incense, the daily grain offering, the
anointing oil, the oversight of all the taberna-
cle, of all that *is* in it, with the sanctuary and
its furnishings." Lev. 24:2
17 Then the LORD spoke to Moses and
Aaron, saying:
18 "Do not cut off the tribe of the families of
the Kohathites from among the Levites;
19 "but do this in regard to them, that they
may live and not die when they approach [R]the
most holy things: Aaron and his sons shall go
in and [T]appoint each of them to his service
and his task. Num. 4:4 • *assign*
20 [R]"But they shall not go in to watch while
the holy things are being covered, lest they
die." Ex. 19:21

The Ministry of Gershon

21 Then the LORD spoke to Moses, saying:
22 "Also take a census of the sons of [R]Ger-
shon, by their fathers' house, by their fami-
lies. Num. 3:22
23 "From thirty years old and above, even to
fifty years old, you shall number them, all
who enter to perform the service, to do the
work in the tabernacle of meeting.
24 "This *is* the service of the families of the
Gershonites, in serving and carrying:
25 "They shall carry the curtains of the tab-
ernacle and the tabernacle of meeting *with* its
covering, the covering of [R]badger skins that *is*
on it, the screen for the door of the tabernacle
of meeting, Ex. 26:14
26 "the screen for the door of the gate of the
court, the hangings of the court which *are*
around the tabernacle and altar, and their
cords, all the furnishings for their service and
all that is made for these things: so shall they
serve.
27 "Aaron and his sons shall [T]assign all the
service of the sons of the Gershonites, all
their tasks and all their service. And you
shall [T]appoint to them all their tasks as their
duty. *command • assign*
28 "This *is* the service of the families of the
sons of Gershon in the tabernacle of meet-
ing. And their duties *shall be* [R]under the au-
thority* of Ithamar the son of Aaron the
priest. Num. 4:33

The Ministry of Merari

29 "*As for* the sons of [R]Merari, you shall
number them by their families and by their fa-
thers' house. Num. 3:33–37
30 "From thirty years old and above, even to
fifty years old, you shall number them, every-
one who enters the service to do the work of
the tabernacle of meeting.
31 "And [R]this *is* [R]what they must carry as all
their service for the tabernacle of meeting: the
boards of the tabernacle, its bars, its pillars,
its sockets, Num. 3:36, 37 • Num. 7:8
32 "and the pillars around the court with
their sockets, pegs, and cords, with all their
furnishings and all their service; and you
shall [R]assign *to each man* by name the items
he must carry. Ex. 25:9; 38:21
33 "This *is* the service of the families of
the sons of Merari, as all their service
for the tabernacle of meeting, under the au-
thority* of Ithamar the son of Aaron the
priest."

The Census of the Working Levites

34 [R]And Moses, Aaron, and the leaders of
the congregation numbered the sons of the
Kohathites by their families and by their fa-
thers' house, Num. 4:2
35 from thirty years old and above, even to
fifty years old, everyone who entered the ser-
vice for work in the tabernacle of meeting;
36 and those who were numbered by their
families were two thousand seven hundred
and fifty.
37 These *were* the ones who were numbered
of the families of the Kohathites, all who
might serve in the tabernacle of meeting,
whom Moses and Aaron numbered according
to the commandment of the LORD by the hand
of Moses.
38 And those who were numbered of the
sons of Gershon, by their families and by their
fathers' house,
39 from thirty years old and above, even
to fifty years old, everyone who entered the
service for work in the tabernacle of meet-
ing—
40 those who were numbered by their fami-
lies, by their fathers' house, were two thou-
sand six hundred and thirty.

4:28 Lit. *hand* **4:33** Lit. *hand*

41 These *are* the ones who were numbered
of the families of the sons of Gershon, of all
who might serve in the tabernacle of meeting,
whom Moses and Aaron numbered according
to the commandment of the LORD.
42 Those of the families of the sons of Me-
rari who were numbered, by their families, by
their fathers' [T]house, *household*
43 from thirty years old and above, even to
fifty years old, everyone who entered the ser-
vice for work in the tabernacle of meeting—
44 those who were numbered by their fami-
lies were three thousand two hundred.
45 These *are* the ones who were numbered
of the families of the sons of Merari, whom
Moses and Aaron numbered according to the
word of the LORD by the hand of Moses.
46 All who were [R]numbered of the Levites,
whom Moses, Aaron, and the leaders of Israel
numbered, by their families and by their fa-
thers' houses, 1 Chr. 23:3–23
47 from thirty years old and above, even to
fifty years old, everyone who came to do the
work of service and the work of bearing bur-
dens in the tabernacle of meeting—
48 those who were numbered were eight
thousand five hundred and eighty.
49 According to the commandment of the
LORD they were numbered by the hand of
Moses, [R]each according to his service and
according to his task; thus were they num-
bered by him, [R]as the LORD commanded
Moses. Num. 4:15, 24, 31 • Num. 4:1, 21

CHAPTER 5

Separation of Unclean Persons

AND the LORD spoke to Moses, saying:
2 "Command the children of Israel that
they put out of the camp every leper, everyone
who has a [R]discharge, and whoever becomes
defiled by a corpse. Lev. 15:2
3 "You shall put out both male and female;
you shall put them outside the camp, that they
may not defile their camps [R]in the midst of
which I dwell." Lev. 26:11, 12
4 And the children of Israel did so, and put
them outside the camp; as the LORD spoke to
Moses, so the children of Israel did.

Separation in Restitution for Sin

5 Then the LORD spoke to Moses, saying,
6 "Speak to the children of Israel: [R]'When a
man or woman commits any sin that men
commit in unfaithfulness against the LORD,
and that person is guilty, Lev. 5:14—6:7
7 'then he shall confess the sin which he
has committed. He shall make restitution for
his trespass [R]in full, plus one-fifth of it, and
give *it* to the one he has wronged. Lev. 6:4, 5
8 'But if the man has no [T]relative to whom
restitution may be made for the wrong, the
restitution for the wrong *must go* to the LORD
for the priest, in addition to [R]the ram of the
atonement with which atonement is made for
him. *redeemer*, Heb. *goel* • Lev. 5:15; 6:6, 7; 7:7
9 'Every [R]offering of all the holy things of
the children of Israel, which they bring to the
priest, shall be his. Ex. 29:28
10 'And every man's [T]holy things shall be
his; whatever any man gives the priest shall
be [R]his.'" *consecrated* • Lev. 10:13

Separation from Suspected Infidelity

11 And the LORD spoke to Moses, saying,
12 "Speak to the children of Israel, and say
to them: 'If any man's wife goes astray and
behaves unfaithfully toward him,
13 'and a man [R]lies with her carnally, and it
is hidden from the eyes of her husband, and it
is concealed that she has defiled herself, and
there was no witness against her, nor was she
[R]caught— Lev. 18:20 • John 8:4
14 'if the spirit of jealousy comes upon him
and he becomes [R]jealous of his wife, who has
defiled herself; or if the spirit of jealousy
comes upon him and he becomes jealous of
his wife, although she has not defiled her-
self— Prov. 6:34
15 'then the man shall bring his wife to the
priest. He shall bring the offering required for
her, one-tenth of an ephah of barley meal; he
shall pour no oil on it and put no frankincense
on it, because it *is* a grain offering of jealousy,
an offering for remembering, for bringing in-
iquity to remembrance.
16 'And the priest shall bring her near, and
set her before the LORD.
17 'The priest shall take holy water in an
earthen vessel, and take some of the dust that
is on the floor of the tabernacle and put *it* into
the water.
18 'Then the priest shall stand the woman
before the LORD, uncover the woman's head,
and put the offering for remembering in her
hands, which *is* the grain offering of jealousy.
And the priest shall have in his hand the bit-
ter water that brings a curse.
19 'And the priest shall put her under oath,
and say to the woman, "If no man has lain
with you, and if you have not gone astray to
uncleanness *while* under your husband's *au-
thority,* be free from this bitter water that
brings a curse.
20 "But if you have gone astray *while* under
your husband's *authority,* and if you have de-
filed yourself and some man other than your
husband has lain with you"—
21 'then the priest shall [R]put the woman
under the oath of the curse, and he shall say
to the woman—[R]"the LORD make you a curse
and an oath among your people, when the
LORD makes your thigh [T]rot and your belly
swell; Josh. 6:26 • Jer. 29:22 • Lit. *fall away*
22 "and may this water that causes the curse
go into your stomach, and make *your* belly

swell and *your* thigh rot." Then the woman shall say, "Amen, so be it."

23 'Then the priest shall write these curses in a book, and he shall scrape *them* off into the bitter water.

24 'And he shall make the woman drink the bitter water that brings a curse, and the water that brings the curse shall enter her *to become* bitter.

25 [R]'Then the priest shall take the grain offering of jealousy from the woman's hand, shall [R]wave the offering before the LORD, and bring it to the altar; Lev. 8:27 • Lev. 2:2, 9

26 'and the priest shall take a handful of the offering, [R]as its memorial portion, burn *it* on the altar, and afterward make the woman drink the water. Lev. 2:2, 9

27 'When he has made her drink the water, then it shall be, if she has defiled herself and behaved unfaithfully toward her husband, that the water that brings a curse will enter her *and become* bitter, and her belly will swell, her thigh will rot, and the woman will become a curse among her people.

28 'But if the woman has not defiled herself, and is clean, then she shall be free and may conceive children.

29 'This *is* the law of jealousy, when a wife, *while* under her husband's *authority*, [R]goes astray and defiles herself, Num. 5:19

30 'or when the spirit of jealousy comes upon a man, and he becomes jealous of his wife; then he shall stand the woman before the LORD, and the priest shall execute all this law upon her.

31 'Then the man shall be free from iniquity, but that woman shall bear her guilt.' "

CHAPTER 6

Sanctification Through the Nazirite Vow

THEN the LORD spoke to Moses, saying,

2 "Speak to the children of Israel, and say to them: 'When either a man or woman consecrates an offering to take the vow of a Nazirite, to separate himself to the LORD,

3 [R]'he shall separate himself from wine and *similar* drink; he shall drink neither vinegar made from wine nor vinegar made from *similar* drink; neither shall he drink any grape juice, nor eat fresh grapes or raisins. Luke 1:15

4 'All the days of his separation he shall eat nothing that is produced by the grapevine, from seed to skin.

5 'All the days of the vow of his separation no [R]razor shall come upon his head; until the days are fulfilled for which he separated himself to the LORD, he shall be holy. *Then* he shall let the locks of the hair of his head grow. 1 Sam. 1:11

6 'All the days that he separates himself to the LORD [R]he shall not go near a dead body. Num. 19:11–22

7 'He shall not make himself unclean even for his father or his mother, for his brother or his sister, when they die, because his separation to God *is* on his head.

8 [R]'All the days of his separation he shall be holy to the LORD. [2 Cor. 6:17, 18]

9 'And if anyone dies very suddenly beside him, and he defiles his consecrated head, then he shall [R]shave his head on the day of his cleansing; on the seventh day he shall shave it. Lev. 14:8, 9

10 'Then [R]on the eighth day he shall bring two turtledoves or two young pigeons to the priest, to the door of the tabernacle of meeting; Lev. 5:7; 14:22; 15:14, 29

11 'and the priest shall offer one as a sin offering and *the* other as a burnt offering, and make atonement for him, because he sinned in regard to the corpse; and he shall sanctify his head that same day.

12 'He shall consecrate to the LORD the days of his separation, and bring a male lamb in its first year [R]as a trespass offering; but the former days shall be [T]lost, because his separation was defiled. Lev. 5:6 • *void*

13 'Now this *is* the law of the Nazirite: [R]When the days of his separation are fulfilled, he shall be brought to the door of the tabernacle of meeting. Acts 21:26

14 'And he shall present his offering to the LORD: one male lamb in its first year without blemish as a burnt offering, one ewe lamb in its first year without blemish [R]as a sin offering, one ram without blemish [R]as a peace offering, Lev. 4:2, 27, 32 • Lev. 3:6

15 'a basket of unleavened bread, [R]cakes of fine flour mixed with oil, unleavened wafers [R]anointed with oil, and their grain offering with their drink offerings. Lev. 2:4 • Ex. 29:2

16 'Then the priest shall bring *them* before the LORD and offer his sin offering and his burnt offering;

17 'and he shall offer the ram as a sacrifice of a peace offering to the LORD, with the basket of unleavened bread; the priest shall also offer its grain offering and its drink offering.

18 [R]'Then the Nazirite shall shave his consecrated head *at* the door of the tabernacle of meeting, and shall take the hair from his consecrated head and put *it* on the fire which is under the sacrifice of the peace offering. Acts 21:23, 24

19 'And the priest shall take the [R]boiled shoulder of the ram, one [R]unleavened cake from the basket, and one unleavened wafer, and [R]put *them* upon the hands of the Nazirite after he has shaved his consecrated *hair*, 1 Sam. 2:15 • Ex. 29:23, 24 • Lev. 7:30

20 'and the priest shall wave them as a wave offering before the LORD; [R]they *are* holy for the priest, together with the breast of the wave offering and the thigh of the heave of-

fering. After that the Nazirite may drink wine.' Ex. 29:27, 28

21 "This is the law of the Nazirite who vows to the LORD the offering for his separation, and besides that, whatever else his hand is able to provide; according to the vow which he takes, so he must do according to the law of his separation."

22 And the LORD spoke to Moses, saying:

23 "Speak to Aaron and his sons, saying, 'This is the way you shall bless the children of Israel. Say to them:

24 "The LORD bless you and keep you;
25 The LORD [R]make His face shine upon
you, Dan. 9:17
And [R]be gracious to you; Mal. 1:9
26 [R]The LORD lift up His countenance upon
you, Ps. 4:6; 89:15
And [R]give you peace." ' Lev. 26:6

27 "So they shall put My name on the children of Israel, and I will bless them."

CHAPTER 7

Israel Gives Donations

NOW it came to pass, when Moses had finished [R]setting up the tabernacle, that he [R]anointed it and consecrated it and all its furnishings, and the altar and all its utensils; so he anointed them and consecrated them. Ex. 40:17–33 • Lev. 8:10, 11

2 Then [R]the leaders of Israel, the heads of their fathers' houses, who *were* the leaders of the tribes and over those who were numbered, made an offering. Num. 1:4

3 And they brought their offering before the LORD, six covered carts and twelve oxen, a cart for *every* two of the leaders, and for each one an ox; and they presented them before the tabernacle.

4 Then the LORD spoke to Moses, saying,

5 "Accept *these* from them, that they may be used in doing the work of the tabernacle of meeting; and you shall give them to the Levites, *to* every man according to his service."

6 So Moses took the carts and the oxen, and gave them to the Levites.

7 Two carts and four oxen he gave to the sons of Gershon, according to their service;

8 [R]and four carts and eight oxen he gave to the sons of Merari, according to their service, under the authority* of Ithamar the son of Aaron the priest. Num. 4:29–33

9 But to the sons of Kohath he gave none, because theirs *was* [R]the service of the holy things, [R]*which* they carried on their shoulders. Num. 4:15 • Num. 4:6–14

10 Now the leaders offered [R]the dedication *offering* for the altar when it was anointed; so the leaders offered their offering before the altar. 2 Chr. 7:5, 9

11 For the LORD said to Moses, "They shall offer their offering, one leader each day, for the dedication of the altar."

12 And the one who offered his offering on the first day *was* [R]Nahshon the son of Amminadab, from the tribe of Judah. Num. 2:3

13 His offering *was* one silver platter, the weight of which *was* one hundred and thirty *shekels,* and one silver bowl of seventy shekels, according to the shekel of the sanctuary, both of them full of fine flour mixed with oil as a [R]grain offering; Lev. 2:1

14 one gold pan of ten *shekels,* full of [R]incense; Ex. 30:34, 35

15 one young bull, one ram, and one male lamb in its first year, as a burnt offering;

16 one kid of the goats as a sin offering;

17 and for the sacrifice of peace offerings: two oxen, five rams, five male goats, and five male lambs in their first year. This *was* the offering of Nahshon the son of Amminadab.

18 On the second day Nethanel the son of Zuar, leader of Issachar, presented *an offering.*

19 *For* his offering he offered one silver platter, the weight of which *was* one hundred and thirty *shekels,* and one silver bowl of seventy shekels, according to the shekel of the sanctuary, both of them full of fine flour mixed with oil as a grain offering;

20 one gold pan of ten *shekels,* full of incense;

21 one young bull, one ram, and one male lamb in its first year, as a burnt offering;

22 one kid of the goats as a sin offering;

23 and as the sacrifice of peace offerings: two oxen, five rams, five male goats, and five male lambs in their first year. This *was* the offering of Nethanel the son of Zuar.

24 On the third day Eliab the son of Helon, leader of the children of Zebulun, *presented an offering.*

25 His offering *was* one silver platter, the weight of which *was* one hundred and thirty *shekels,* and one silver bowl of seventy shekels, according to the shekel of the sanctuary, both of them full of fine flour mixed with oil as a grain offering;

26 one gold pan of ten *shekels,* full of incense;

27 one young bull, one ram, and one male lamb in its first year, as a burnt offering;

28 one kid of the goats as a sin offering;

29 and for the sacrifice of peace offerings: two oxen, five rams, five male goats, and five male lambs in their first year. This *was* the offering of Eliab the son of Helon.

30 On the fourth day [R]Elizur the son of Shedeur, leader of the children of Reuben, *presented an offering.* Num. 1:5; 2:10

31 His offering *was* one silver platter, the

7:8 Lit. *hand*

weight of which *was* one hundred and thirty
shekels, and one silver bowl of seventy
shekels, according to the shekel of the sanctu-
ary, both of them full of fine flour mixed with
oil as a grain offering;
32 one gold pan of ten *shekels,* full of in-
cense;
33 one young bull, one ram, and one male
lamb in its first year, as a burnt offering;
34 one kid of the goats as a sin offering;
35 and as the sacrifice of peace offerings:
two oxen, five rams, five male goats, and five
male lambs in their first year. This *was* the of-
fering of Elizur the son of Shedeur.
36 On the fifth day [R]Shelumiel the son of
Zurishaddai, leader of the children of Simeon,
presented an offering. Num. 1:6
37 His offering *was* one silver platter, the
weight of which *was* one hundred and thirty
shekels, and one silver bowl of seventy
shekels, according to the shekel of the sanctu-
ary, both of them full of fine flour mixed with
oil as a grain offering;
38 one gold pan of ten *shekels,* full of in-
cense;
39 one young bull, one ram, and one male
lamb in its first year, as a burnt offering;
40 one kid of the goats as a sin offering;
41 and as the sacrifice of peace offerings:
two oxen, five rams, five male goats, and five
male lambs in their first year. This *was* the of-
fering of Shelumiel the son of Zurishaddai.
42 On the sixth day [R]Eliasaph the son of
Deuel,* leader of the children of Gad, *pre-
sented an offering.* Num. 1:14; 2:14; 10:20
43 His offering *was* one silver platter, the
weight of which *was* one hundred and thirty
shekels, and one silver bowl of seventy
shekels, according to the shekel of the sanctu-
ary, both of them full of fine flour mixed with
oil as a grain offering;
44 one gold pan of ten *shekels,* full of in-
cense;
45 one young bull, one ram, and one male
lamb in its first year, as a burnt offering;
46 one kid of the goats as a sin offering;
47 and as the sacrifice of peace offerings:
two oxen, five rams, five male goats, and five
male lambs in their first year. This *was* the of-
fering of Eliasaph the son of Deuel.
48 On the seventh day [R]Elishama the son of
Ammihud, leader of the children of Ephraim,
presented an offering. Num. 1:10
49 His offering *was* one silver platter, the
weight of which *was* one hundred and thirty
shekels, and one silver bowl of seventy
shekels, according to the shekel of the sanctu-
ary, both of them full of fine flour mixed with
oil as a grain offering;
50 one gold pan of ten *shekels,* full of in-
cense;
51 one young bull, one ram, and one male
lamb in its first year, as a burnt offering;
52 one kid of the goats as a sin offering;
53 and as the sacrifice of peace offerings:
two oxen, five rams, five male goats, and five
male lambs in their first year. This *was* the of-
fering of Elishama the son of Ammihud.
54 On the eighth day [R]Gamaliel the son of
Pedahzur, leader of the children of Manasseh,
presented an offering. Num. 1:10; 2:20
55 His offering *was* one silver platter, the
weight of which *was* one hundred and thirty
shekels, and one silver bowl of seventy
shekels, according to the shekel of the sanctu-
ary, both of them full of fine flour mixed with
oil as a grain offering;
56 one gold pan of ten *shekels,* full of in-
cense;
57 one young bull, one ram, and one
male lamb in its first year, as a burnt offering;
58 one kid of the goats as a sin offering;
59 and as the sacrifice of peace offerings:
two oxen, five rams, five male goats, and five
male lambs in their first year. This *was* the of-
fering of Gamaliel the son of Pedahzur.
60 On the ninth day [R]Abidan the son of
Gideoni, leader of the children of Benjamin,
presented an offering. Num. 1:11; 2:22
61 His offering *was* one silver platter, the
weight of which *was* one hundred and thirty
shekels, and one silver bowl of seventy
shekels, according to the shekel of the sanctu-
ary, both of them full of fine flour mixed with
oil as a grain offering;
62 one gold pan of ten *shekels,* full of in-
cense;
63 one young bull, one ram, and one male
lamb in its first year, as a burnt offering;
64 one kid of the goats as a sin offering;
65 and as the sacrifice of peace offerings:
two oxen, five rams, five male goats, and five
male lambs in their first year. This *was* the of-
fering of Abidan the son of Gideoni.
66 On the tenth day [R]Ahiezer the son of Am-
mishaddai, leader of the children of Dan, *pre-
sented an offering.* Num. 1:12; 2:25
67 His offering *was* one silver platter, the
weight of which *was* one hundred and thirty
shekels, and one silver bowl of seventy
shekels, according to the shekel of the sanctu-
ary, both of them full of fine flour mixed with
oil as a grain offering;
68 one gold pan of ten *shekels,* full of in-
cense;
69 one young bull, one ram, and one male
lamb in its first year, as a burnt offering;
70 one kid of the goats as a sin offering;
71 and as the sacrifice of peace offerings:
two oxen, five rams, five male goats, and five
male lambs in their first year. This *was*
the offering of Ahiezer the son of Ammishad-
dai.
72 On the eleventh day [R]Pagiel the son of

7:42 *Reuel,* Num. 2:14

Ocran, leader of the children of Asher, *presented an offering.* Num. 1:13; 2:27

73 His offering *was* one silver platter, the weight of which *was* one hundred and thirty *shekels,* and one silver bowl of seventy shekels, according to the shekel of the sanctuary, both of them full of fine flour mixed with oil as a grain offering;

74 one gold pan of ten *shekels,* full of incense;

75 one young bull, one ram, and one male lamb in its first year, as a burnt offering;

76 one kid of the goats as a sin offering;

77 and as the sacrifice of peace offerings: two oxen, five rams, five male goats, and five male lambs in their first year. This *was* the offering of Pagiel the son of Ocran.

78 On the twelfth day [R]Ahira the son of Enan, leader of the children of Naphtali, *presented an offering.* Num. 1:15; 2:29

79 His offering *was* one silver platter, the weight of which *was* one hundred and thirty *shekels,* and one silver bowl of seventy shekels, according to the shekel of the sanctuary, both of them full of fine flour mixed with oil as a grain offering;

80 one gold pan of ten *shekels,* full of incense;

81 one young bull, one ram, and one male lamb in its first year, as a burnt offering;

82 one kid of the goats as a sin offering;

83 and as the sacrifice of peace offerings: two oxen, five rams, five male goats, and five male lambs in their first year. This *was* the offering of Ahira the son of Enan.

84 This *was* [R]the dedication *offering* for the altar from the leaders of Israel, when it was anointed: twelve silver platters, twelve silver bowls, and twelve gold pans. Num. 7:10

85 Each silver platter *weighed* one hundred and thirty *shekels* and each bowl seventy *shekels.* All the silver of the vessels *weighed* two thousand four hundred *shekels,* according to the shekel of the sanctuary.

86 The twelve gold pans full of incense *weighed* ten *shekels* apiece, according to the shekel of the sanctuary; all the gold of the pans *weighed* one hundred and twenty *shekels.*

87 All the oxen for the burnt offering *were* twelve young bulls, the rams twelve, the male lambs in their first year twelve, with their grain offering, and the kids of the goats as a sin offering twelve.

88 And all the oxen for the sacrifice of peace offerings were twenty-four bulls, the rams sixty, the male goats sixty, and the lambs in their first year sixty. This *was* the dedication *offering* for the altar after it was [R]anointed. Num. 7:1, 10

89 Now when Moses went into the tabernacle of meeting to speak with Him, he heard the voice of One speaking to him from above the mercy seat that *was* on the ark of the Testimony, from [R]between the two cherubim; thus He spoke to him. Ps. 80:1; 99:1

CHAPTER 8

The Levites Are Consecrated

AND the LORD spoke to Moses, saying:

2 "Speak to Aaron, and say to him, 'When you arrange the lamps, the seven lamps shall give light in front of the lampstand.' "

3 And Aaron did so; he arranged the lamps to face toward the front of the lampstand, as the LORD commanded Moses.

4 Now this workmanship of the lampstand *was* hammered gold; from its shaft to its flowers it *was* hammered work. According to the pattern which the LORD had shown Moses, so he made the lampstand.

5 Then the LORD spoke to Moses, saying:

6 "Take the Levites from among the children of Israel and cleanse them *ceremonially.*

7 "Thus you shall do to them to cleanse them: Sprinkle [R]water of purification on them, and let them shave all their body, and let them wash their clothes, and *so* make themselves clean. Num. 19:9, 13, 17, 20

8 "Then let them take a young bull with [R]its grain offering of fine flour mixed with oil, and you shall take another young bull as a sin offering. Lev. 2:1

9 [R]"And you shall bring the Levites before the tabernacle of meeting, [R]and you shall gather together the whole congregation of the children of Israel. Ex. 29:4; 40:12 • Lev. 8:3

10 "So you shall bring the Levites before the LORD, and the children of Israel [R]shall lay their hands on the Levites; Lev. 1:4

11 "and Aaron shall [T]offer the Levites before the LORD, *like* a [R]wave offering from the children of Israel, that they may perform the work of the LORD. *present* • Num. 18:6

12 [R]"Then the Levites shall lay their hands on the heads of the young bulls, and you shall offer one as a sin offering and the other as a burnt offering to the LORD, to make atonement for the Levites. Ex. 29:10

13 "And you shall stand the Levites before Aaron and his sons, and then offer them *like* a wave offering to the LORD.

14 "Thus you shall [R]separate the Levites from among the children of Israel, and the Levites shall be [R]Mine. Num. 16:9 • Num. 16:9

15 "After that the Levites shall go in to service the tabernacle of meeting. So you shall cleanse them and [R]offer them, *like* a wave offering. Num. 8:11, 13

16 "For they *are* [R]wholly given to Me from among the children of Israel; I have taken them for Myself [R]instead of all who open the womb, the firstborn of all the children of Israel. Num. 3:9 • Num. 3:12, 45

17 [R]"For all the firstborn among the chil-

dren of Israel *are* Mine, *both* man and beast; on the day that I struck all the firstborn in the land of Egypt I [T]sanctified them to Myself. Ex. 12:2, 12, 13, 15 • *set them apart*

18 "I have taken the Levites instead of all the firstborn of the children of Israel.

19 "And [R]I have given the Levites as a gift to Aaron and his sons from among the children of Israel, to do the work for the children of Israel in the tabernacle of meeting, and to make atonement for the children of Israel, [R]that there be no plague among the children of Israel when the children of Israel come near the sanctuary." Num. 3:9 • Num. 1:53

20 Thus Moses and Aaron and all the congregation of the children of Israel did to the Levites; according to all that the LORD commanded Moses concerning the Levites, so the children of Israel did to them.

21 [R]And the Levites purified themselves and washed their clothes; then Aaron presented them, *like* a wave offering before the LORD, and Aaron made atonement for them to cleanse them. Num. 8:7

22 [R]After that the Levites went in to do their work in the tabernacle of meeting before Aaron and his sons; [R]as the LORD commanded Moses concerning the Levites, so they did to them. Num. 8:15 • Num. 8:5

23 Then the LORD spoke to Moses, saying,

24 "This *is* what *pertains* to the Levites: [R]From twenty-five years old and above one may enter to perform service in the work of the tabernacle of meeting; Num. 4:3

25 "and at the age of fifty years they must cease performing this work, and shall work no more.

26 "They may minister with their brethren in the tabernacle of meeting, [R]to attend to needs, but they *themselves* shall do no work. Thus you shall do to the Levites regarding their duties." Num. 1:53

CHAPTER 9

The Passover Is Celebrated

NOW the LORD spoke to Moses in the Wilderness of Sinai, in the first month of the second year after they had come out of the land of Egypt, saying:

2 "Let the children of Israel keep [R]the Passover at its appointed time. Lev. 23:5

3 "On the fourteenth day of this month, at twilight, you shall keep it at its appointed time. According to all its [T]rites and ceremonies you shall keep it." *statutes*

4 So Moses told the children of Israel that they should keep the Passover.

5 And [R]they kept the Passover on the fourteenth day of the first month, at twilight, in the Wilderness of Sinai; according to all that the LORD commanded Moses, so the children of Israel did. Josh. 5:10

6 Now there were *certain* men who were [R]defiled by a human corpse, so that they could not keep the Passover on that day; [R]and they came before Moses and Aaron that day . Num. 5:2; 19:11–22 • Num. 27:2

7 And those men said to him, "We *became* defiled by a human corpse. Why are we kept from presenting the offering of the LORD at its appointed time among the children of Israel?"

8 And Moses said to them, "Stand still, that [R]I may hear what the LORD will command concerning you." Num. 27:5

9 Then the LORD spoke to Moses, saying,

10 "Speak to the children of Israel, saying: 'If anyone of you or your [T]posterity is unclean because of a corpse, or *is* far away on a journey, he may still keep the LORD's Passover. *descendants*

11 'On [R]the fourteenth day of the second month, at twilight, they may keep it. They shall [R]eat it with unleavened bread and bitter herbs. 2 Chr. 30:2, 15 • Ex. 12:8

12 [R]'They shall leave none of it until morning, [R]nor break one of its bones. According to all the ordinances of the Passover they shall keep it. Ex. 12:10 • Ex. 12:46; John 19:36☆

13 'But the man who *is* clean and is not on a journey, and ceases to keep the Passover, that same person shall be cut off from among his people, because he did not bring the offering of the LORD at its appointed time; that man shall bear his sin.

14 'And if a stranger dwells among you, and would keep the LORD's Passover, he must do so according to the rite of the Passover and according to its ceremony; you shall have one ordinance, both for the stranger and the native of the land.' "

Guidance of the Cloud

15 Now [R]on the day that the tabernacle was raised up, the cloud [R]covered the tabernacle, the tent of the Testimony; from evening until morning it was above the tabernacle like the appearance of fire. Ex. 40:33, 34 • Is. 4:5

16 So it was always: the cloud covered it *by day*, and the appearance of fire by night.

17 Whenever the cloud [R]was taken up from above the tabernacle, after that the children of Israel would journey; and in the place where the cloud settled, there the children of Israel would pitch their tents. Ex. 40:36–38

18 At the command of the LORD the children of Israel would journey, and at the command of the LORD they would camp; [R]as long as the cloud stayed above the tabernacle they remained encamped. 1 Cor. 10:1

19 Even when the cloud continued long, many days above the tabernacle, the children of Israel [R]kept the charge of the LORD and did not journey. Num. 1:53; 3:8

20 So it was, when the cloud was above the tabernacle a few days: according to the com-

mand of the LORD they would remain encamped, and according to the command of the LORD they would journey.

21 So it was, when the cloud remained only from evening until morning: when the cloud was taken up in the morning, then they would journey; whether by day or by night, whenever the cloud was taken up, they would journey.

22 *Whether it was* two days, a month, or a year that the cloud remained above the tabernacle, the children of Israel would remain encamped and not journey; but when it was taken up, they would journey.

23 At the command of the LORD they remained encamped, and at the command of the LORD they journeyed; they [R]kept the charge of the LORD, at the command of the LORD by the hand of Moses. Num. 9:19

CHAPTER 10

Guidance of the Silver Trumpets

AND the LORD spoke to Moses, saying:

2 "Make two silver trumpets for yourself; you shall make them of hammered work; you shall use them for [R]calling the congregation and for directing the movement of the camps. Is. 1:13

3 "When [R]they blow both of them, all the congregation shall gather before you at the door of the tabernacle of meeting. Jer. 4:5

4 "But if they blow *only* one, then the leaders, the [R]heads of the divisions of Israel, shall gather to you. Ex. 18:21

5 "When you sound the [R]advance, [R]the camps that lie on the east side shall then begin their journey. Joel 2:1 • Num. 2:3

6 "When you sound the advance the second time, then the camps that lie [R]on the south side shall begin their journey; they shall sound the call for them to begin their journeys. Num. 2:10

7 "And when the assembly is to be gathered together, [R]you shall blow, but not [R]sound the advance. Num. 10:3 • Joel 2:1

8 [R]"The sons of Aaron, the priests, shall blow the trumpets; and these shall be to you as an [T]ordinance forever throughout your generations. Num. 31:6 • *statute*

9 [R]"When you go to war in your land against the enemy who [R]oppresses you, then you shall sound an alarm with the trumpets, and you will be [R]remembered before the LORD your God, and you will be saved from your enemies. Josh. 6:5 • Judg. 2:18 • Gen. 8:1

10 "Also [R]in the day of your gladness, in your appointed feasts, and at the beginning of your months, you shall blow the trumpets over your burnt offerings and over the sacrifices of your peace offerings; and they shall be [R]a memorial for you before your God: I *am* the LORD your God." Lev. 23:24 • Num. 10:9

Israel Departs Mount Sinai

11 Now it came to pass on the twentieth *day* of the second month, in the second year, that the cloud [R]was taken up from above the tabernacle of the Testimony. Num. 9:17

12 And the children of Israel set out from the [R]Wilderness of Sinai on [R]their journeys; then the cloud settled down in the [R]Wilderness of Paran. Ex. 19:1 • Ex. 40:36 • Gen. 21:21

13 So they started out for the first time [R]according to the command of the LORD by the hand of Moses. Num. 10:5, 6

14 The [T]standard of the camp of the children of Judah [R]set out first according to their armies; over their army was Nahshon the son of Amminadab. *banner* • Num. 2:3–9

15 Over the army of the tribe of the children of Issachar *was* Nethanel the son of Zuar.

16 And over the army of the tribe of the children of Zebulun *was* Eliab the son of Helon.

17 Then the tabernacle was taken down; and the sons of Gershon and the sons of Merari set out, carrying the tabernacle.

18 And the standard of the camp of Reuben set out according to their armies; over their army *was* Elizur the son of Shedeur.

19 Over the army of the tribe of the children of Simeon *was* Shelumiel the son of Zurishaddai.

20 And over the army of the tribe of the children of Gad *was* Eliasaph the son of Deuel.

21 Then the Kohathites set out, carrying the [R]holy things. (The tabernacle would be prepared for their arrival.) Num. 4:4–20; 7:9

22 And [R]the standard of the camp of the children of Ephraim set out according to their armies; over their army *was* Elishama the son of Ammihud. Num. 2:18–24

23 Over the army of the tribe of the children of Manasseh *was* Gamaliel the son of Pedahzur.

24 And over the army of the tribe of the children of Benjamin *was* Abidan the son of Gideoni.

25 Then [R]the standard of the camp of the children of Dan (the rear guard of all the camps) set out according to their armies; over their army *was* Ahiezer the son of Ammishaddai. Num. 2:25–31

26 Over the army of the tribe of the children of Asher *was* Pagiel the son of Ocran.

27 And over the army of the tribe of the children of Naphtali *was* Ahira the son of Enan.

28 [R]Thus *was* the order of march of the children of Israel, according to their armies, when they began their journey. Num. 2:34

29 Now Moses said to Hobab the son of Reuel* the Midianite, Moses' father-in-law, "We are setting out for the place of which the LORD said, 'I will give it to you.' Come with us,

10:29 *Jethro*, Ex. 3:1; LXX *Raguel*

and we will treat you well; for the LORD has promised good things to Israel."

30 And he said to him, "I will not go, but I will depart to my *own* land and to my relatives."

31 So *Moses* said, "Please do not leave, inasmuch as you know how we are to camp in the wilderness, and you can be our eyes.

32 "And it shall be, if you go with us—indeed it shall be—that [R]whatever good the LORD will do to us, the same we will do to you." Judg. 1:16

33 So they departed from [R]the mountain of the LORD on a journey of three days; and the ark of the covenant of the LORD went before them for the three days' journey, to search out a resting place for them. Ex. 3:1

34 And [R]the cloud of the LORD *was* above them by day when they went out from the camp. Ex. 13:21

35 So it was, whenever the ark set out, that Moses said:

[R]"Rise up, O LORD! Ps. 68:1, 2; 132:8
Let Your enemies be scattered,
And let those who hate You flee before
You."

36 And when it rested, he said:

"Return, O LORD,
To the many thousands of Israel."

CHAPTER 11

Israel Complains About Circumstances

NOW *when* the people complained, it displeased the LORD; for the LORD heard *it*, and His anger was aroused. So the fire of the LORD burned among them, and consumed *some* in the outskirts of the camp.

2 Then the people cried out to Moses, and when Moses [R]prayed to the LORD, the fire was [T]quenched. [James 5:16] • *extinguished*

3 So he called the name of the place Taberah,* because the fire of the LORD had burned among them.

Israel Complains About Food

4 Now the mixed multitude who were among them yielded to intense craving; so the children of Israel also wept again and said: "Who will give us meat to eat?

5 "We remember the fish which we ate freely in Egypt, the cucumbers, the melons, the leeks, the onions, and the garlic;

6 "but now [R]our whole being *is* dried up; *there is* nothing at all except this manna *before* our eyes!" Num. 21:5

7 Now the manna *was* like coriander seed, and its color like the color of bdellium.

8 The people went about and gathered *it*, ground *it* on millstones or beat *it* in the mortar, cooked *it* in pans, and made cakes of it; and [R]its taste was like the taste of pastry prepared with oil. Ex. 16:31

9 And [R]when the dew fell on the camp in the night, the manna fell on it. Ex. 16:13, 14

Moses Complains About the People

10 Then Moses heard the people weeping throughout their families, everyone at the door of his tent; and [R]the anger of the LORD was greatly aroused; Moses also was displeased. Ps. 78:21

11 So Moses said to the LORD, "Why have You afflicted Your servant? And why have I not found favor in Your sight, that You have laid the burden of all these people on me?

12 "Did I conceive all these people? Did I beget them, that You should say to me, [R]'Carry them in your bosom, as a guardian carries a nursing child,' to the land which You swore to their fathers? Is. 40:11

13 "Where am I to get meat to give to all these people? For they weep all over me, saying, 'Give us meat, that we may eat.'

Moses Complains About His Own Life

14 [R]"I am not able to bear all these people alone, because the burden *is* too heavy for me. Ex. 18:18

15 "If You treat me like this, please kill me here and now—if I have found favor in Your sight—and [R]do not let me see my wretchedness!" Rev. 3:17

God Provides for Moses

16 So the LORD said to Moses: "Gather to Me [R]seventy men of the elders of Israel, whom you know to be the elders of the people and officers over them; bring them to the tabernacle of meeting, that they may stand there with you. Ex. 18:25; 24:1, 9

17 "Then I will come down and talk with you there. [R]I will take of the Spirit that *is* upon you and will put *the same* upon them; and they shall bear the burden of the people with you, that you may not bear *it* yourself alone. 1 Sam. 10:6

18 "Then you shall say to the people, 'Consecrate yourselves for tomorrow, and you shall eat meat; for you have wept [R]in the hearing of the LORD, saying, "Who will give us meat to eat? For *it was* well with us in Egypt." Therefore the LORD will give you meat, and you shall eat. Ex. 16:7

19 'You shall eat, not one day, nor two days, nor five days, nor ten days, nor twenty days,

20 [R]'but *for* a whole month, until it comes out of your nostrils and becomes loathsome to you, because you have [R]despised the LORD who is among you, and have wept before Him, saying, "Why did we ever come up out of Egypt?" ' " Ps. 78:29; 106:15 • 1 Sam. 10:19

11:3 Lit. *Burning*

21 And Moses said, "The people whom I *am* among *are* six hundred thousand men on foot; yet You have said, 'I will give them meat, that they may eat *for* a whole month.'

22 [R]"Shall flocks and herds be slaughtered for them, to provide enough for them? Or shall all the fish of the sea be gathered together for them, to provide enough for them?" 2 Kin. 7:2

23 And the LORD said to Moses, [R]"Has the LORD's arm been shortened? Now you shall see whether [R]what I say will happen to you or not." Is. 50:2; 59:1 • Num. 23:19

24 So Moses went out and told the people the words of the LORD, and he gathered the seventy men of the elders of the people and placed them around the tabernacle.

25 Then the LORD came down in the cloud, and spoke to him, and took of the Spirit that *was* upon him, and placed *the same* upon the seventy elders; and it happened, [R]when the Spirit rested upon them, that [R]they prophesied, although they never did so again.* 2 Kin. 2:15 • Joel 2:28

26 But two men had remained in the camp: the name of one *was* Eldad, and the name of the other Medad. And the Spirit rested upon them. Now they *were* among those listed, but who [R]had not gone out to the tabernacle; yet they prophesied in the camp. Jer. 36:5

27 And a young man ran and told Moses, and said, "Eldad and Medad are prophesying in the camp."

28 So Joshua the son of Nun, Moses' assistant, *one* of his choice men, answered and said, "Moses my lord, forbid them!"

29 Then Moses said to him, "Are you [T]zealous for my sake? Oh, that all the LORD's people were prophets *and* that the LORD would put His Spirit upon them!" *jealous*

30 And Moses returned to the camp, *both* he and the elders of Israel.

God Provides Quail

31 Now a [R]wind went out from the LORD, and it brought quail from the sea and left *them* fluttering near the camp, about a day's journey on this side and about a day's journey on the other side, all around the camp, and about two cubits above the surface of the ground. Ex. 16:13

32 And the people stayed up all that day, all night, and all the next day, and gathered the quail (he who gathered least gathered ten homers); and they spread *them* out for themselves all around the camp.

God Sends Plagues

33 But while the [R]meat *was* still between their teeth, before it was chewed, the wrath of the LORD was aroused against the people, and the LORD struck the people with a very great plague. Ps. 78:29–31; 106:15

34 So he called the name of that place Kibroth Hattaavah,* because there they buried the people who had yielded to craving.

35 [R]From Kibroth Hattaavah the people moved to Hazeroth, and camped at Hazeroth. Num. 33:17

CHAPTER 12

Miriam and Aaron Rebel

THEN [R]Miriam and Aaron spoke [R]against Moses because of the Ethiopian woman whom he had married; for he had married an Ethiopian woman. Num. 20:1 • Num. 11:1

2 So they said, "Has the LORD indeed spoken only through [R]Moses? [R]Has He not spoken through us also?" And the LORD [R]heard *it.* Num. 16:3 • Mic. 6:4 • Ezek. 35:12, 13

3 (Now the man Moses *was* very humble, more than all men who *were* on the face of the earth.)

Miriam Is Punished

4 [R]Suddenly the LORD said to Moses, Aaron, and Miriam, "Come out, you three, to the tabernacle of meeting!" So the three came out. [Ps. 76:9]

5 [R]Then the LORD came down in the pillar of cloud and stood *in* the door of the tabernacle, and called Aaron and Miriam. And they both went forward. Ex. 19:9; 34:5

6 Then He said,

"Hear now My words:
If there is a prophet among you,
I, the LORD, make Myself known to him
[R]in a vision; Gen. 46:2
I speak to him [R]in a dream. Gen. 31:10
7 Not so with My servant Moses;
He *is* faithful in all My house.
8 I speak with him face to face,
Even plainly, and not in dark sayings;
And he sees the form of the LORD.
Why then were you not afraid
To speak against My servant Moses?"

9 So the anger of the LORD was aroused against them, and He departed.

10 And when the cloud departed from above the tabernacle, [R]suddenly Miriam *became* [R]leprous, as *white as* snow. Then Aaron turned toward Miriam, and there she was, a leper. Deut. 24:9 • 2 Kin. 5:27; 15:5

Moses Intercedes

11 So Aaron said to Moses, "Oh, my lord! Please [R]do not lay [T]this sin on us, in which we have done foolishly and in which we have sinned. 2 Sam. 19:19; 24:10 • *the penalty for this*

12 "Please [R]do not let her be as one dead,

11:25 Tg., Vg. *and they did not cease* **11:34** Lit. *Graves of Craving*

whose flesh is half consumed when he comes
out of his mother's womb!" Ps. 88:4
13 So Moses cried out to the LORD, saying,
"Please [R]heal her, O God, I pray!" Ps. 103:3

Miriam Is Restored

14 Then the LORD said to Moses, "If her
father had but [R]spit in her face, would she not
be shamed seven days? Let her be [R]shut out of
the camp seven days, and afterward she may
be received *again*." Deut. 25:9 • Lev. 13:46
15 [R]So Miriam was shut out of the camp
seven days, and the people did not journey till
Miriam was brought in *again*. Deut. 24:9
16 And afterward the people moved from
[R]Hazeroth and camped in the Wilderness of
Paran. Num. 11:35; 33:17, 18

CHAPTER 13

Investigation of the Promised Land
Deut. 1:22–40

AND the LORD spoke to Moses, saying,
2 [R]"Send men to spy out the land of
Canaan, which I am giving to the children of
Israel; from each tribe of their fathers you
shall send a man, every one a leader among
them." Deut. 1:22; 9:23
3 So Moses sent them [R]from the Wilderness
of Paran according to the command of the
LORD, all of them men who *were* heads of the
children of Israel. Num. 12:16; 32:8
4 Now these *were* their names: from the
tribe of Reuben, Shammua the son of Zaccur;
5 from the tribe of Simeon, Shaphat the son
of Hori;
6 [R]from the tribe of Judah, [R]Caleb the son of
Jephunneh; Num. 34:19 • Josh. 14:6, 7
7 from the tribe of Issachar, Igal the son of
Joseph;
8 from the tribe of Ephraim, [T]Hoshea* the
son of Nun; LXX, Vg. *Oshea*
9 from the tribe of Benjamin, Palti the son
of Raphu;
10 from the tribe of Zebulun, Gaddiel the son
of Sodi;
11 from the tribe of Joseph, *that is*, from the
tribe of Manasseh, Gaddi the son of Susi;
12 from the tribe of Dan, Ammiel the son of
Gemalli;
13 from the tribe of Asher, Sethur the son of
Michael;
14 from the tribe of Naphtali, Nahbi the son
of Vophsi;
15 from the tribe of Gad, Geuel the son of
Machi.
16 These *are* the names of the men whom
Moses sent to spy out the land. And Moses
called Hoshea* the son of Nun, Joshua.
17 Then Moses sent them to spy out the
land of Canaan, and said to them, "Go up this
way into the South, and go up to [R]the moun-
tains, Judg. 1:9
18 "and see what the land is like: whether
the people who dwell in it *are* strong or weak,
few or many;
19 "whether the land they dwell in *is* good or
bad; whether the cities they inhabit *are* like
camps or strongholds;
20 "whether the land *is* rich or poor; and
whether there are forests there or not. [R]Be of
good courage. And bring some of the fruit
of the land." Now the time *was* the season of
the first ripe grapes. Deut. 31:6, 7, 23
21 So they went up and spied out the land
from the Wilderness of Zin as far as Rehob,
near the entrance of [R]Hamath. Josh. 13:5
22 And they went up through the South and
came to [R]Hebron; Ahiman, Sheshai, and Tal-
mai, the descendants of Anak, *were* there.
(Now Hebron was built seven years before
Zoan in Egypt.) Josh. 15:13, 14
23 [R]Then they came to the Valley of Eshcol,
and there cut down a branch with one cluster
of grapes; they carried it between two of them
on a pole. *They* also *brought* some of the
pomegranates and figs. Deut. 1:24, 25
24 The place was called the Valley of [T]Esh-
col,* because of the cluster which the men of
Israel cut down there. Lit. *Cluster*
25 And they returned from spying out the
land after forty days.
26 Now they departed and came back to Mo-
ses and Aaron and all the congregation of the
children of Israel in the Wilderness of Paran,
at Kadesh; they brought back word to them
and to all the congregation, and showed them
the fruit of the land.
27 Then they told him, and said: "We went to
the land where you sent us. It truly flows with
milk and honey, and this *is* its fruit.
28 "Nevertheless the [R]people who dwell in
the land *are* strong; the cities *are* fortified *and*
very large; moreover we saw the descendants
of Anak there. Deut. 1:28; 9:1, 2
29 [R]"The Amalekites dwell in the land of
the South; the Hittites, the Jebusites, and the
Amorites dwell in the mountains; and the
Canaanites dwell by the sea and along
the banks of the Jordan." Judg. 6:3
30 Then [R]Caleb quieted the people before
Moses, and said, "Let us go up at once and
take possession, for we are well able to over-
come it." Num. 14:6, 24
31 But the men who had gone up with him
said, "We are not able to go up against the
people, for they *are* stronger than we."
32 And they gave the children of Israel a bad
report of the land which they had spied out,
saying, "The land through which we have
gone as spies *is* a land that devours its inhab-
itants, and [R]all the people whom we saw in it
are men of *great* stature. Amos 2:9

13:8 LXX, Vg. *Oshea* **13:16** LXX, Vg. *Oshea*
13:24 Lit. *Cluster*

33 "There we saw the giants* (the descendants of Anak came from the giants); and we were [R]like grasshoppers in our own sight, and so we were in their sight." Is. 40:22

CHAPTER 14

Israel Rebels Against God

SO all the congregation lifted up their voices and cried, and the people [R]wept that night. Deut. 1:45

2 [R]And all the children of Israel complained against Moses and Aaron, and the whole congregation said to them, "If only we had died in the land of Egypt! Or if only we had died in this wilderness! Ex. 16:2; 17:3

3 "Why has the LORD brought us to this land to fall by the sword, that our wives and children should become victims? Would it not be better for us to return to Egypt?"

4 So they said to one another, "Let us select a leader and return to Egypt."

5 Then Moses and Aaron fell on their faces before all the assembly of the congregation of the children of Israel.

6 But Joshua the son of Nun and Caleb the son of Jephunneh, *who were* among those who had spied out the land, tore their clothes;

7 and they spoke to all the congregation of the children of Israel, saying: [R]"The land we passed through to spy out *is* an exceedingly good land. Num. 13:27

8 "If the LORD delights in us, then He will bring us into this land and give it to us, 'a land which flows with milk and honey.'*

9 "Only [R]do not rebel against the LORD, [R]nor fear the people of the land, for they *are* our bread; their protection has departed from them, and the LORD *is* with us. Do not fear them." Deut. 1:26; 9:7, 23, 24 • Deut. 7:18

10 [R]And all the congregation said to stone them with stones. Now [R]the glory of the LORD appeared in the tabernacle of meeting before all the children of Israel. Ex. 17:4 • Ex. 16:10

Moses Intercedes

11 Then the LORD said to Moses: "How long will these people reject Me? And how long will they not believe Me, with all the signs which I have performed among them?

12 "I will strike them with the pestilence and disinherit them, and I will make of you a nation greater and mightier than they."

13 And Moses said to the LORD: "Then the Egyptians will hear *it*, for by Your might You brought these people up from among them,

14 "and they will tell *it* to the inhabitants of this land. They have [R]heard that You, LORD, *are* among these people; that You, LORD, are seen face to face and Your cloud stands above them, and You go before them in a pillar of cloud by day and in a pillar of fire by night. Deut. 2:25

15 "Now *if* You kill these people as one man, then the nations which have heard of Your fame will speak, saying,

16 'Because the LORD was not [R]able to bring this people to the land which He swore to give them, therefore He killed them in the wilderness.' Deut. 9:28

17 "And now, I pray, let the power of my Lord be great, just as You have spoken, saying,

18 'The LORD is longsuffering and abundant in mercy, forgiving iniquity and transgression; but He by no means clears *the guilty*, [R]visiting the iniquity of the fathers on the children to the third and fourth *generation*.'* Ex. 20:5

19 "Pardon the iniquity of this people, I pray, according to the greatness of Your mercy, just [R]as You have forgiven this people, from Egypt even until now." Ps. 78:38

Israel to Wander and Die

20 Then the LORD said: "I have pardoned, [R]according to your word; Mic. 7:18–20

21 "but truly, as I live, all the earth shall be filled with the glory of the LORD—

22 [R]"because all these men who have seen My glory and the signs which I did in Egypt and in the wilderness, and have put Me to the test now [R]these ten times, and have not heeded My voice, Deut. 1:35 • Gen. 31:7

23 "they certainly shall not [R]see the land of which I swore to their fathers, nor shall any of those who rejected Me see it. Num. 26:65

24 "But My servant Caleb, because he has a different spirit in him and has followed Me fully, I will bring into the land where he went, and his descendants shall inherit it.

25 "Now the Amalekites and the Canaanites dwell in the valley; tomorrow turn and [R]move out into the wilderness by the Way of the Red Sea." Deut. 1:40

26 And the LORD spoke to Moses and Aaron, saying,

27 [R]"How long *shall I bear with* this evil congregation who complain against Me? I have heard the complaints which the children of Israel make against Me. Ex. 16:28

28 "Say to them, [R]'As I live,' says the LORD, 'just as you have spoken in My hearing, so I will do to you: Heb. 3:16–19

29 'The carcasses of you who have complained against Me shall fall in this wilderness, [R]all of you who were numbered, according to your entire number, from twenty years old and above. Num. 1:45, 46; 26:64

30 [R]'Except for Caleb the son of Jephunneh and Joshua the son of Nun, you shall by no means enter the land which I swore I would make you dwell in. Deut. 1:36–38

31 [R]'But your little ones, whom you said would be victims, I will bring in, and they

13:33 Heb. *nephilim* **14:8** Ex. 3:8 **14:18** Ex. 34:6, 7

shall [T]know the land which [R]you have despised. Deut. 1:39 • *be acquainted with* • Ps. 106:24

32 'But *as for* you, [R]your carcasses shall fall in this wilderness. Num. 26:64, 65; 32:13

33 'And your sons shall [R]be shepherds in the wilderness forty years, and bear the brunt of your infidelity, until your carcasses are consumed in the wilderness. Ps. 107:40

34 [R]'According to the number of the days in which you spied out the land, [R]forty days, for each day you shall bear your guilt one year, *namely* forty years, [R]and you shall know My rejection. Num. 13:25 • Ezek. 4:6 • [Heb. 4:1]

35 [R]'I the LORD have spoken this. I will surely do so to all [R]this evil congregation who are gathered together against Me. In this wilderness they shall be consumed, and there they shall die.' " Num. 23:19 • 1 Cor. 10:5

Spies Die Immediately

36 Now the men whom Moses sent to spy out the land, who returned and made all the congregation complain against him by bringing a bad report of the land,

37 those very men who brought the evil report about the land, [R]died by the plague before the LORD. [1 Cor. 10:10]

38 But Joshua the son of Nun and Caleb the son of Jephunneh remained alive, of the men who went to spy out the land.

Moses Warns Israel—Deut. 1:4–44

39 Then Moses told these words to all the children of Israel, [R]and the people mourned greatly. Ex. 33:4

40 And they rose early in the morning and went up to the top of the mountain, saying, [R]"Here we are, and we will go up to the place which the LORD has promised, for we have sinned!" Deut. 1:41–44

41 And Moses said, "Now why do you [T]transgress the command of the LORD? For this will not succeed. *overstep*

42 [R]"Do not go up, lest you be defeated by your enemies, for the LORD *is* not among you. Deut. 1:42; 31:17

43 "For the Amalekites and the Canaanites *are* there before you, and you shall fall by the sword; [R]because you have turned away from the LORD, the LORD will not be with you." 2 Chr. 15:2

44 [R]But they presumed to go up to the mountaintop. Nevertheless, neither the ark of the covenant of the LORD nor Moses departed from the camp. Deut. 1:43

Amalekites Defeat Israel

45 Then the Amalekites and the Canaanites who dwelt in that mountain came down and attacked them, and drove them back as far as [R]Hormah. Num. 21:3

CHAPTER 15

Offerings to Thank the Lord

AND the LORD spoke to Moses, saying,

2 [R]"Speak to the children of Israel, and say to them: 'When you have come into the land you are to inhabit, which I am giving to you, Lev. 23:10

3 'and you make an offering by fire to the LORD, a burnt offering or a sacrifice, to fulfill a vow or as a freewill offering or in your appointed feasts, to make a sweet aroma to the LORD, from the herd or the flock,

4 'then [R]he who presents his offering to the LORD shall bring a grain offering of one-tenth *of an ephah* of fine flour mixed with one-fourth of a hin of oil; Lev. 2:1; 6:14

5 [R]'and one-fourth of a hin of wine as a drink offering you shall prepare with the burnt offering or the sacrifice, for each [R]lamb. Num. 28:7, 14 • Lev. 1:10; 3:6

6 'Or for a ram you shall prepare as a grain offering two-tenths *of an ephah* of fine flour mixed with one-third of a hin of oil;

7 'and as a drink offering you shall offer one-third of a hin of wine as a sweet aroma to the LORD.

8 'And when you prepare a young bull as a burnt offering, or as a sacrifice to fulfill a vow, or as a peace offering to the LORD,

9 'then shall be offered [R]with the young bull a grain offering of three-tenths *of an ephah* of fine flour mixed with half a hin of oil; Num. 28:12, 14

10 'and you shall bring as the drink offering half a hin of wine as an offering made by fire, a sweet aroma to the LORD.

11 [R]'Thus it shall be done for each young bull, for each ram, or for each lamb or young goat. Num. 28

12 'According to the number that you prepare, so you shall do with everyone according to their number.

13 'All who are native-born shall do these things in this manner, in presenting an offering made by fire, a sweet aroma to the LORD.

14 'And if a stranger [T]dwells with you, or whoever *is* among you throughout your generations, and would present an offering made by fire, a sweet aroma to the LORD, just as you do, so shall he do. As a resident alien

15 [R]'One ordinance *shall be* for you of the assembly and for the stranger who dwells *with you*, an ordinance forever throughout your generations; as you are, so shall the stranger be before the LORD. Num. 9:14

16 'One law and one custom shall be for you and for the stranger who dwells with you.' "*

17 Again the LORD spoke to Moses, saying,

18 [R]"Speak to the children of Israel, and say

15:16 Cf. Ex. 12:49

to them: 'When you come into the land to which I bring you, Deut. 26:1

19 'then it will be, when you eat of [R]the bread of the land, that you shall offer up a heave offering to the LORD. Josh. 5:11, 12

20 [R]'You shall offer up a cake of the first of your ground meal *as* a heave offering; as [R]a heave offering of the threshing floor, so shall you offer it up. Lev. 23:10, 14, 17 • Lev. 2:14

21 'Of the first of your ground meal you shall give to the LORD a heave offering throughout your generations.

Offerings for Unintentional Sins

22 [R]'If you sin unintentionally, and do not observe all these commandments which the LORD has spoken to Moses— Lev. 4:2

23 'all that the LORD has commanded you by the hand of Moses, from the day the LORD gave commandment and onward throughout your generations—

24 'then it will be, [R]if it is unintentionally committed, without the knowledge of the congregation, that the whole congregation shall offer one young bull as a burnt offering, as a sweet aroma to the LORD, with its grain offering and its drink offering, according to the ordinance, and [R]one kid of the goats as a sin offering. Lev. 4:13 • Lev. 4:23

25 [R]'So the priest shall make atonement for the whole congregation of the children of Israel, and it shall be forgiven them, for it was unintentional; they shall bring their offering, an offering made by fire to the LORD, and their sin offering before the LORD, for their unintended sin. [Heb. 2:17]

26 'It shall be forgiven the whole congregation of the children of Israel and the stranger who dwells among them, because all the people *did it* unintentionally.

27 'And [R]if a person sins unintentionally, then he shall bring a female goat in its first year as a sin offering. Lev. 4:27–31

28 [R]'So the priest shall make atonement for the person who sins unintentionally, when he sins unintentionally before the LORD, to make atonement for him; and it shall be forgiven him. Lev. 4:35

29 'You shall have one law for him who sins unintentionally, *for* him who is native-born among the children of Israel and for the stranger who dwells among them.

No Offering for Intentional Sins

30 [R]'But the person who does *anything* presumptuously, *whether he is* native-born or a stranger, that one brings reproach on the LORD, and he shall be cut off from among his people. Deut. 1:43; 17:12

31 'Because he has despised the word of the LORD, and has broken His commandment, that person shall be completely cut off; his [T]guilt *shall be* upon him.' " *iniquity*

32 Now while the children of Israel were in the wilderness, [R]they found a man gathering sticks on the Sabbath day. Ex. 31:14, 15

33 And those who found him gathering sticks brought him to Moses and Aaron, and to all the congregation.

34 They put him [R]under guard, because it had not been explained what should be done to him. Lev. 24:12

35 Then the LORD said to Moses, [R]"The man must surely be put to death; all the congregation shall [R]stone him with stones outside the camp." Ex. 31:14, 15 • Lev. 24:14

36 So, as the LORD commanded Moses, all the congregation brought him outside the camp and stoned him with stones, and he died.

The Tassel on the Garment

37 Again the LORD spoke to Moses, saying,

38 "Speak to the children of Israel: Tell [R]them to make tassels on the corners of their garments throughout their generations, and to put a blue thread in the tassels of the corners. Matt. 23:5

39 "And you shall have the tassel, that you may look upon it and [R]remember all the commandments of the LORD and do them, and that you [R]*may* not [R]follow the harlotry to which your own heart and your own eyes are inclined, Ps. 103:18 • Deut. 29:19 • James 4:4

40 "and that you may remember and do all My commandments, and be [R]holy for your God. [Lev. 11:44, 45]

41 "I *am* the LORD your God, who brought you out of the land of Egypt, to be your God: I *am* the LORD your God."

CHAPTER 16

Korah Rebels Against Moses and Aaron

NOW Korah the son of Izhar, the son of Kohath, the son of Levi, with Dathan and Abiram the sons of Eliab, and On the son of Peleth, sons of Reuben, took *men;*

2 and they rose up before Moses with some of the children of Israel, two hundred and fifty leaders of the congregation, [R]representatives of the congregation, men of renown. Num. 1:16; 26:9

3 They gathered together against Moses and Aaron, and said to them, "*You take* too much upon yourselves, for all the congregation *is* holy, every one of them, and the LORD *is* among them. Why then do you exalt yourselves above the assembly of the LORD?"

4 So when Moses heard *it*, he [R]fell on his face; Num. 14:5; 20:6

5 and he spoke to Korah and all his company, saying, "Tomorrow morning the LORD will show who *is* [R]His and *who is* [R]holy, and will cause *him* to come near to Him. That one

whom He chooses He will cause to come near to Him. [2 Tim. 2:19] • Lev. 21:6–8, 12

6 "Do this: Take censers, Korah and all your company;

7 "put fire in them and put incense in them before the LORD tomorrow, and it shall be *that* the man whom the LORD chooses *is* the holy one. *You take* too much upon yourselves, you sons of Levi!"

8 Then Moses said to Korah, "Hear now, you sons of Levi:

9 "*Is it* [R]a small thing to you that the God of Israel has [R]separated you from the congregation of Israel, to bring you near to Himself, to do the work of the tabernacle of the LORD, and to stand before the congregation to serve them; Is. 7:13 • Deut. 10:8

10 "and that He has brought you near *to Himself*, you and all your brethren, the sons of Levi, with you? And are you seeking the priesthood also?

11 "Therefore you and all your company *are* gathered together against the LORD. [R]And what *is* Aaron that you complain against him?" Ex. 16:7, 8

12 And Moses sent to call Dathan and Abiram the sons of Eliab, but they said, "We will not come up!

13 "*Is it* a small thing that you have brought us up out of [R]a land flowing with milk and honey, to kill us in the wilderness, that you should [R]keep acting like a prince over us? Num. 11:4–6 • Ex. 2:14

14 "Moreover [R]you have not brought us into [R]a land flowing with milk and honey, nor given us inheritance of fields and vineyards. Will you put out the eyes of these men? We will not come up!" Num. 14:1–4 • Ex. 3:8

God Judges Korah

15 Then Moses was very angry, and said to the LORD, [R]"Do not respect their offering. I have not taken one donkey from them, nor have I hurt one of them." Gen. 4:4, 5

16 And Moses said to Korah, "Tomorrow, you and all your company be present before the LORD—you and they, as well as Aaron.

17 "Let each take his censer and put incense in it, and each of you bring his censer before the LORD, two hundred and fifty censers; both you and Aaron, each *with* his censer."

18 So every man took his censer, put fire in it, laid incense on it, and stood at the door of the tabernacle of meeting with Moses and Aaron.

19 And Korah gathered all the congregation against them at the door of the tabernacle of meeting. Then [R]the glory of the LORD appeared to all the congregation. Num. 14:10

20 And the LORD spoke to Moses and Aaron, saying,

21 [R]"Separate yourselves from among this congregation, that I may [R]consume them in a moment." Gen. 19:17 • Ex. 32:10; 33:5

22 Then they [R]fell on their faces, and said, "O God, [R]the God of the spirits of all flesh, shall one man sin, and You be angry with all the congregation?" Num. 14:5 • Num. 27:16

23 So the LORD spoke to Moses, saying,

24 "Speak to the congregation, saying, 'Get away from the tents of Korah, Dathan, and Abiram.' "

25 Then Moses rose and went to Dathan and Abiram, and the elders of Israel followed him.

26 And he spoke to the congregation, saying, "Depart now from the tents of these wicked men! Touch nothing of theirs, lest you be consumed in all their sins."

27 So they got away from around the tents of Korah, Dathan, and Abiram; and Dathan and Abiram came out and stood at the door of their tents, with their wives, their sons, and their little [R]children. Num. 26:11

28 And Moses said: [R]"By this you shall know that the LORD has sent me to do all these works, for *I have* not *done them* [R]of my own will. John 5:36 • John 5:30

29 "If these men die naturally like all men, or if they are visited by the common fate of all men, *then* the LORD has not sent me.

30 "But if the LORD creates [R]a new thing, and the earth opens its mouth and swallows them up with all that belongs to them, and they [R]go down alive into the pit, then you will understand that these men have rejected the LORD." Job 31:3 • [Ps. 55:15]

31 [R]Now it came to pass, as he finished speaking all these words, that the ground split apart under them, Num. 26:10

32 and the earth opened its mouth and swallowed them up, with their households and [R]all the men with Korah, with all *their* goods. Num. 26:10

33 So they and all those with them went down alive into the pit; the earth closed over them, and they perished from among the assembly.

34 Then all Israel who *were* around them fled at their cry, for they said, "Lest the earth swallow us up *also!*"

35 And [R]a fire came out from the LORD and consumed the two hundred and fifty men who were offering incense. Num. 11:1–3

36 Then the LORD spoke to Moses, saying:

37 "Tell Eleazar, the son of Aaron the priest, to pick up the censers out of the blaze, for [R]they are holy, and scatter the fire some distance away. Lev. 27:28

38 "The censers of these men who sinned against their own souls, let them be made into hammered plates as a covering for the altar. Because they presented them before the LORD, therefore they are holy; and they shall be a sign to the children of Israel."

39 So Eleazar the priest took the bronze censers, which those who were burned up had presented, and they were hammered out as a covering on the altar,

40 *to be* a memorial to the children of Israel that no outsider, who *is* not a descendant of Aaron, should come near to offer incense before the LORD, that he might not become like Korah and his companions, just as the LORD had said to him through Moses.

Israel Rebels Against Moses and Aaron

41 On the next day [R]all the congregation of the children of Israel complained against Moses and Aaron, saying, "You have killed the people of the LORD." Num. 14:2

God Judges Israel

42 Now it happened, when the congregation had gathered against Moses and Aaron, that they turned toward the tabernacle of meeting; and suddenly the cloud covered it, and the glory of the LORD appeared.

43 Then Moses and Aaron came before the tabernacle of meeting.

44 And the LORD spoke to Moses, saying,

45 "Get away from among this congregation, that I may consume them in a moment." And they fell on their faces.

46 So Moses said to Aaron, "Take a censer and put fire in it from the altar, put incense *on it,* and take it quickly to the congregation and make [T]atonement for them; [R]for wrath has gone out from the LORD. The plague has begun." Lit. *covering* • Num. 18:5

47 Then Aaron took *it* as Moses commanded, and ran into the midst of the assembly; and already the plague had begun among the people. So he put in the incense and made atonement for the people.

48 And he stood between the dead and the living; so the plague was stopped.

49 Now those who died in the plague were fourteen thousand seven hundred, besides those who died in the Korah incident.

50 So Aaron returned to Moses at the door of the tabernacle of meeting, for the plague had stopped.

CHAPTER 17

Confirmation of the Divine Call

AND the LORD spoke to Moses, saying:

2 "Speak to the children of Israel, and get from them a rod from each father's house, all their leaders according to their fathers' houses—twelve rods. Write each man's name on his rod.

3 "And you shall write Aaron's name on the rod of Levi. For there shall be one rod for the head of *each* father's house.

4 "Then you shall place them in the tabernacle of meeting before [R]the Testimony, [R]where I meet with you. Ex. 25:16 • Ex. 25:22

5 "And it shall be *that* the rod of the man whom I choose will blossom; thus I will rid Myself of the complaints of the children of Israel, which they make against you."

6 So Moses spoke to the children of Israel, and each of their leaders gave him a rod apiece, for each leader according to their fathers' houses, twelve rods; and the rod of Aaron *was* among their rods.

7 And Moses placed the rods before the LORD in the tabernacle of witness.

8 Now it came to pass on the next day that Moses went into the tabernacle of witness, and behold, the [R]rod of Aaron, of the house of Levi, had sprouted and put forth buds, had produced blossoms and yielded ripe almonds. [Ezek. 17:24]

9 Then Moses brought out all the rods from before the LORD to all the children of Israel; and they looked, and each man took his rod.

10 And the LORD said to Moses, "Bring [R]Aaron's rod back before the Testimony, to be kept [R]as a sign against the rebels, [R]that you may put their complaints away from Me, lest they die." Heb. 9:4 • Deut. 9:7, 24 • Num. 17:5

11 Thus did Moses; just as the LORD had commanded him, so he did.

12 So the children of Israel spoke to Moses, saying, "Surely we die, we perish, we all perish!

13 [R]"Whoever even comes near the tabernacle of the LORD must die. Shall we all utterly die?" Num. 1:51, 53; 18:4, 7

CHAPTER 18

Remuneration of the Priesthood

THEN the LORD said to Aaron: [R]"You and your sons and your father's house with you shall [R]bear the [T]iniquity *related to* the sanctuary, and you and your sons with you shall bear the iniquity *associated with* your priesthood. Num. 17:13 • Ex. 28:38 • *guilt*

2 "Also bring with you your brethren of the [R]tribe of Levi, the tribe of your father, that they may be joined with you and serve you while you and your sons *are* with you before the tabernacle of witness. Num. 1:47

3 "They shall attend to your needs and [R]all the needs of the tabernacle; [R]but they shall not come near the articles of the sanctuary and the altar, [R]lest they die—they and you also. Num. 3:25, 31, 36 • Num. 16:40 • Num. 4:15

4 "They shall be joined with you and attend to the needs of the tabernacle of meeting, for all the work of the tabernacle; but an outsider shall not come near you.

5 "And you shall attend to [R]the duties of the sanctuary and the duties of the altar, [R]that there *may* be no more wrath on the children of Israel. Lev. 24:3 • Num. 8:19; 16:46

6 "Behold, I Myself have [R]taken your brethren the Levites from among the children of Israel; [R]*they are* a gift to you, given by the LORD, to do the work of the tabernacle of meeting. Num. 3:12, 45 • Num. 3:9

7 "Therefore you and your sons with you shall attend to your priesthood for everything at the altar and behind the veil; and you shall serve. I give your priesthood *to you* as a gift for service, but the outsider who comes near shall be put to death."

8 And the LORD spoke to Aaron: "Here, [R]I Myself have also given you charge of My heave offerings, all the holy gifts of the children of Israel; I have given them [R]as a portion to you and your sons, as an ordinance forever. Lev. 6:16, 18; 7:28–34 • Ex. 29:29; 40:13, 15

9 "This shall be yours of the most holy things *reserved* from the fire: every offering of theirs, every [R]grain offering and every sin offering and every [R]trespass offering which they render to Me, *shall be* most holy for you and your sons. Lev. 2:2, 3; 10:12, 13 • Lev. 7:7

10 [R]"In a most holy *place* you shall eat it; every male shall eat it. It shall be holy to you. Lev. 6:16, 26

11 "This also *is* yours: [R]the heave offering of their gift, with all the wave offerings of the children of Israel; I have given them to you, and your sons and daughters with you, as an ordinance forever. Everyone who is clean in your house may eat it. Deut. 18:3–5

12 [R]"All the [T]best of the oil, all the best of the new wine and the grain, [R]their firstfruits which they offer to the LORD, I have given them to you. Ex. 23:19 • Lit. *fat* • Ex. 22:29

13 "Whatever first ripe fruit is in their land, [R]which they bring to the LORD, shall be yours. Everyone who is clean in your house may eat it. Ex. 22:29; 23:19; 34:26

14 [R]"Every [T]devoted thing in Israel shall be yours. Lev. 27:1–33 • *consecrated*

15 "Everything that first opens [R]the womb of all flesh, which they bring to the LORD, whether man or beast, shall be yours; nevertheless the firstborn of man you shall surely redeem, and the firstborn of unclean animals you shall redeem. Ex. 13:2

16 "And those redeemed of the devoted things you shall redeem when one month old, according to your valuation, for five shekels of silver, according to the shekel of the sanctuary, which *is* twenty gerahs.

17 [R]"But the firstborn of a cow, the firstborn of a sheep, or the firstborn of a goat you shall not redeem; they *are* holy. You shall sprinkle their blood on the altar, and burn their fat *as* an offering made by fire for a sweet aroma to the LORD. Deut. 15:19

18 "And their flesh shall be yours, just as the [R]wave[T] breast and the right thigh are yours. Ex. 29:26–28 • *breast of the wave offering*

19 "All the heave offerings of the holy things, which the children of Israel offer to the LORD, I have given to you and your sons and daughters with you as an ordinance forever; [R]it *is* a covenant of salt forever before the LORD with you and your descendants with you." 2 Chr. 13:5

20 Then the LORD said to Aaron: "You shall have [R]no inheritance in their land, nor shall you have any portion among them; I *am* your portion and your inheritance among the children of Israel. Josh. 13:14, 33

21 "Behold, I have given the children of Levi all the tithes in Israel as an inheritance in return for the work which they perform, the work of the tabernacle of meeting.

22 [R]"Hereafter the children of Israel shall not come near the tabernacle of meeting, [R]lest they bear sin and die. Num. 1:51 • Lev. 22:9

23 "But the Levites shall perform the work of the tabernacle of meeting, and they shall bear their iniquity; *it shall be* a statute forever, throughout your generations, that among the children of Israel they shall have no inheritance.

24 "For the tithes of the children of Israel, which they offer up *as* a heave offering to the LORD, I have given to the Levites [T]as an inheritance; therefore I have said to them, 'Among the children of Israel they shall have no inheritance.'" *for a possession*

25 Then the LORD spoke to Moses, saying,

26 "Speak thus to the Levites, and say to them: 'When you take from the children of Israel the tithes which I have given you from them as your inheritance, then you shall offer up a heave offering of it to the LORD, [R]a tenth of the tithe. Neh. 10:38

27 'And your heave offering shall be reckoned to you as though *it were* the grain of the [R]threshing floor and as the fullness of the winepress. Num. 15:20

28 'Thus you shall also offer a heave offering to the LORD from all your tithes which you receive from the children of Israel, and you shall give the LORD's heave offering from it to Aaron the priest.

29 'Of all your gifts you shall offer up every heave offering due to the LORD, from all the best of them, the consecrated part of them.'

30 "Therefore you shall say to them: 'When you have lifted up the best of it, then *the rest* shall be accounted to the Levites as the produce of the threshing floor and as the produce of the winepress.

31 'You may eat it in any place, you and your households, for it *is* your reward for your work in the tabernacle of meeting.

32 'And you shall [R]bear no sin because of it, when you have lifted up the best of it. But you shall not profane the holy gifts of the children of Israel, lest you die.'" Lev. 19:8

CHAPTER 19

Purification of the Red Heifer

NOW the LORD spoke to Moses and Aaron, saying,

2 "This *is* the [T]ordinance of the law which the LORD has commanded, saying: 'Speak to

the children of Israel, that they bring you a red heifer without [T]blemish, in which there *is* no [R]defect [R]*and* on which a yoke has never come. *statute • defect* • Lev. 22:20–25 • Deut. 21:3

3 'You shall give it to Eleazar the priest, that he may take it outside the camp, and it shall be slaughtered before him;

4 'and Eleazar the priest shall take some of its blood with his finger, and [R]sprinkle some of its blood seven times directly in front of the tabernacle of meeting. Lev. 4:6

5 'Then the heifer shall be burned in his sight: [R]its hide, its flesh, its blood, and its offal shall be burned. Ex. 29:14

6 'And the priest shall take cedar wood and hyssop and scarlet, and cast *them* into the midst of the fire burning the heifer.

7 [R]'Then the priest shall wash his clothes, he shall bathe in water, and afterward he shall come into the camp; the priest shall be unclean until evening. Lev. 11:25; 15:5

8 'And the one who burns it shall wash his clothes in water, bathe in water, and shall be unclean until evening.

9 'Then a man *who is* clean shall gather up [R]the ashes of the heifer, and store *them* outside the camp in a clean place; and they shall be kept for the congregation of the children of Israel for the water of purification;* it *is* for purifying from sin. [Heb. 9:13, 14]

10 'And the one who gathers the ashes of the heifer shall wash his clothes, and be unclean until evening. It shall be a statute forever to the children of Israel and to the stranger who dwells among them.

11 [R]'He who touches the dead body of anyone shall be unclean seven days. Lev. 21:1

12 [R]'He shall purify himself with the water on the third day and on the seventh day; *then* he will be clean. But if he does not purify himself on the third day and on the seventh day, he will not be clean. Num. 19:19

13 'Whoever touches the body of anyone who has died, and [R]does not purify himself, [R]defiles the tabernacle of the LORD. That person shall be cut off from Israel. He shall be unclean, because [R]the water of purification was not sprinkled on him; his uncleanness *is* still on him. Lev. 22:3–7 • Lev. 15:31 • Num. 8:7

14 'This *is* the law when a man dies in a tent: All who come into the tent and all who *are* in the tent shall be unclean seven days;

15 'and every [R]open vessel, which has no cover fastened on it, *is* unclean. Num. 31:20

16 [R]'Whoever in the open field touches one who is slain by a sword or who has died, or a bone of a man, or a grave, shall be unclean seven days. Num. 19:11; 31:19

17 'And for an unclean *person* they shall take some of the [R]ashes of the heifer burnt for purification from sin, and running water shall be put on them in a vessel. Num. 19:9

18 'A clean person shall take [R]hyssop and dip *it* in the water, sprinkle *it* on the tent, on all the vessels, on the persons who were there, or on the one who touched a bone, the slain, the dead, or a grave. Ps. 51:7

19 'The clean *person* shall sprinkle the unclean on the third day and on the seventh day; and on the seventh day he shall purify himself, wash his clothes, and bathe in water; and at evening he shall be clean.

20 'But the man who is unclean and does not purify himself, that person shall be cut off from among the assembly, because he has [R]defiled the sanctuary of the LORD. The water of purification has not been sprinkled on him; he *is* unclean. Num. 19:13

21 'It shall be a perpetual statute for them. He who sprinkles the water of purification shall wash his clothes; and he who touches the water of purification shall be unclean until evening.

22 'Whatever the unclean *person* touches shall be unclean; and the person who touches *it* shall be unclean until evening.' "

CHAPTER 20

Miriam Dies

THEN the children of Israel, the whole congregation, came into the Wilderness of Zin in the first month, and the people stayed in [R]Kadesh; and [R]Miriam died there and was buried there. Num. 13:26 • Ex. 15:20

The Sin of Israel

2 [R]Now there was no water for the congregation; [R]so they gathered together against Moses and Aaron. Ex. 17:1 • Num. 16:19, 42

3 And the people contended with Moses and spoke, saying: "If only we had died when our brethren died before the LORD!

4 [R]"Why have you brought up the assembly of the LORD into this wilderness, that we and our animals should die here? Ex. 17:3

5 "And why have you made us come up out of Egypt, to bring us to this evil place? It *is* not a place of grain or figs or vines or pomegranates; nor *is* there any water to drink."

6 So Moses and Aaron went from the presence of the assembly to the door of the tabernacle of meeting, and [R]they fell on their faces. And the glory of the LORD appeared to them. Num. 14:5; 16:4, 22, 45

The Command of God

7 Then the LORD spoke to Moses, saying,

8 "Take the rod; you and your brother Aaron gather the congregation together. Speak to the rock before their eyes, and it will yield its water; thus you shall bring water for them out of the rock, and give drink to the congregation and their animals."

19:9 Lit. *impurity*

The Sin of Moses

9 So Moses took the rod [R]from before the
LORD as He commanded him. Num. 17:10
10 And Moses and Aaron gathered the as-
sembly together before the rock; and he said
to them, "Hear now, you rebels! Must we bring
water for you out of this rock?"
11 Then Moses lifted his hand and struck the
rock twice with his rod; [R]and water came out
abundantly, and the congregation and their
animals drank. [1 Cor. 10:4]
12 Then the LORD spoke to Moses and
Aaron, "Because [R]you did not believe Me, to
[R]hallow Me in the eyes of the children of Is-
rael, therefore you shall not bring this as-
sembly into the land which I have given
them." Deut. 1:37; 3:26, 27; 34:5 • Lev. 10:3
13 This *was* the water of Meribah,* because
the children of Israel contended with the
LORD, and He was hallowed among them.

Edom Refuses Passage

14 [R]Now Moses sent messengers from
Kadesh to the king of Edom. "Thus says your
brother Israel: 'You know all the hardship that
has befallen us, Judg. 11:16, 17
15 'how our fathers went down to Egypt, and
we dwelt in Egypt a long time, and the Egyp-
tians afflicted us and our fathers.
16 'When we cried out to the LORD, He heard
our voice and sent the Angel and brought us
up out of Egypt; now here we are in Kadesh, a
city on the edge of your border.
17 'Please let us pass through your country.
We will not pass through fields or vineyards,
nor will we drink water from wells; we will go
along the King's Highway; we will not turn
aside to the right hand or to the left until we
have passed through your territory.' "
18 Then [R]Edom said to him, "You shall not
pass through my *land,* lest I come out against
you with the sword." Num. 24:18
19 So the children of Israel said to him, "We
will go by the Highway, and if I or my live-
stock drink any of your water, [R]then I will pay
for it; let me only pass through on foot, noth-
ing *more.*" Deut. 2:6, 28
20 Then he said, "You shall not pass
through." So Edom came out against them
with many men and with a strong hand.
21 Thus Edom [R]refused to give Israel pas-
sage through his territory; so Israel [R]turned
away from him. Deut. 2:27, 30 • Judg. 11:18

Aaron Dies

22 Now the children of Israel, the whole con-
gregation, journeyed from [R]Kadesh [R]and
came to Mount Hor. Num. 33:37 • Num. 21:4
23 And the LORD spoke to Moses and Aaron
in Mount Hor by the border of the land of
Edom, saying:
24 "Aaron shall [T]be [R]gathered to his people,
for he shall not enter the land which I have
given to the children of Israel, because you re-
belled against My word at the water of
Meribah. Die and join his ancestors • Gen. 25:8
25 [R]"Take Aaron and Eleazar his son, and
bring them up to Mount Hor; Num. 33:38
26 "and strip Aaron of his garments and put
them on Eleazar his son; for Aaron shall be
gathered *to his people* and die there."
27 So Moses did just as the LORD com-
manded, and they went up to Mount Hor in
the sight of all the congregation.
28 [R]Moses stripped Aaron of his garments
and put them on Eleazar his son; and [R]Aaron
died there on the top of the mountain. Then
Moses and Eleazar came down from the
mountain. Ex. 29:29, 30 • Num. 33:38
29 Now when all the congregation saw that
Aaron was dead, all the house of Israel
mourned for Aaron [R]thirty days. Deut. 34:8

CHAPTER 21

Israel's Victory over the Canaanites

THE [R]king of Arad, the Canaanite, who
dwelt in the South, heard that Israel was
coming on the road to Atharim. Then he
fought against Israel and took *some* of them
prisoners. Judg. 1:16
2 [R]So Israel made a vow to the LORD, and
said, "If You will indeed deliver this people
into my hand, then [R]I will utterly destroy their
cities." Gen. 28:20 • Deut. 2:34
3 And the LORD listened to the voice of Is-
rael and delivered up the Canaanites, and
they utterly destroyed them and their cities.
So the name of that place was called
Hormah.*

Israel Complains—Deut. 2:1

4 Then they journeyed from Mount Hor by
the Way of the Red Sea, to go around the land
of Edom; and the soul of the people became
very discouraged on the way.
5 And the people [R]spoke against God and
against Moses: "Why have you brought us up
out of Egypt to die in the wilderness? For
there is no food and no water, and our soul
loathes this worthless bread." Num. 20:4, 5

God Judges with Serpents

6 So the LORD sent [R]fiery serpents among
the people, and they bit the people; and many
of the people of Israel died. Deut. 8:15

The Bronze Serpent

7 Therefore the people came to Moses, and
said, "We have sinned, for we have spoken
against the LORD and against you; pray to the
LORD that He take away the serpents from us."
So Moses prayed for the people.

20:13 Lit. *Contention* **21:3** Lit. *Utter Destruction*

8 Then the LORD said to Moses, [R]"Make a fiery *serpent,* and set it on a pole; and it shall be that everyone who is bitten, when he looks at it, shall live." [John 3:14, 15]

9 So [R]Moses made a bronze serpent, and put it on a pole; and so it was, if a serpent had bitten anyone, when he looked at the bronze serpent, he lived. John 3:14, 15

Journey to Moab

10 Now the children of Israel moved on and [R]camped in Oboth. Num. 33:43, 44

11 And they journeyed from Oboth and camped at Ije Abarim, in the wilderness which *is* east of Moab, toward the sunrise.

12 [R]From there they moved and camped in the Valley of Zered. Deut. 2:13

13 From there they moved and camped on the other side of the Arnon, which *is* in the wilderness that extends from the border of the Amorites; for the Arnon *is* the border of Moab, between Moab and the Amorites.

14 Therefore it is said in the Book of the Wars of the LORD:

"Waheb in Suphah,*
The brooks of the Arnon,
15 And the slope of the brooks
That reaches to the dwelling of Ar,
And lies on the border of Moab."

16 From there *they went* [R]to Beer, which *is* the well where the LORD said to Moses, "Gather the people together, and I will give them water." Judg. 9:21

17 [R]Then Israel sang this song: Ex. 15:1

"Spring up, O well!
All of you sing to it—
18 The well the leaders sank,
Dug by the nation's nobles,
By the lawgiver, with their staves."

And from the wilderness *they went* to Mattanah,

19 from Mattanah to Nahaliel, from Nahaliel to Bamoth,

20 and from Bamoth, *in* the valley that *is* in the country of Moab, to the top of Pisgah which looks down on the wasteland.*

Israel's Victory over the Amorites —Deut. 2:26–36

21 Then [R]Israel sent messengers to Sihon king of the Amorites, saying, Deut. 2:26–37

22 [R]"Let me pass through your land. We will not turn aside into fields or vineyards; we will not drink water from wells. We will go by the King's Highway until we have passed through your territory." Num. 20:16, 17

23 But Sihon would not allow Israel to pass through his territory. So Sihon gathered all his people together and went out against Israel in the wilderness, and he came to Jahaz and fought against Israel.

24 Then [R]Israel defeated him with the edge of the sword, and took possession of his land from the Arnon to the Jabbok, as far as the people of Ammon; for the border of the people of Ammon *was* fortified. Amos 2:9

25 So Israel took all these cities, and Israel [R]dwelt in all the cities of the Amorites, in Heshbon and in all its villages. Amos 2:10

26 For Heshbon *was* the city of Sihon king of the Amorites, who had fought against the former king of Moab, and had taken all his land from his hand as far as the Arnon.

27 Therefore those who speak in [T]proverbs say: *parables*

"Come to Heshbon, let it be built;
Let the city of Sihon be repaired.

28 "For fire went out from Heshbon,
A flame from the city of Sihon;
It consumed [R]Ar of Moab, Is. 15:1
The lords of the heights of the Arnon.
29 Woe to you, [R]Moab! Jer. 48:46
You have perished, O people of
[R]Chemosh! Judg. 11:24
He has given his sons as fugitives,
And his [R]daughters into captivity,
To Sihon king of the Amorites. Is. 16:2

30 "But we have shot at them;
Heshbon has perished as far as Dibon.
Then we laid waste as far as Nophah,
Which *reaches* to [R]Medeba." Is. 15:2

31 Thus Israel dwelt in the land of the Amorites.

32 Then Moses sent to spy out [R]Jazer; and they took its villages and drove out the Amorites who *were* there. Jer. 48:32

Israel's Victory over Bashan—Deut. 3:1–4

33 [R]And they turned and went up by the way to [R]Bashan. So Og king of Bashan went out against them, he and all his people, to battle at Edrei. Deut. 29:7 • Deut. 3:1

34 Then the LORD said to Moses, [R]"Do not fear him, for I have delivered him into your hand, with all his people and his land; and [R]you shall do to him as you did to Sihon king of the Amorites, who dwelt at Heshbon." Deut. 3:2 • Num. 21:24

35 So they defeated him, his sons, and all his people, until there was no survivor left him; and they took possession of his land.

21:14 Ancient unknown places; Vg. *What He did in the Red Sea* **21:20** Heb. *Jeshimon*

CHAPTER 22

Balaam Is Sought by Balak

THEN the children of Israel moved, and
camped in the plains of Moab on the side
of the Jordan *across from* Jericho.
2 Now Balak the son of Zippor saw all that
Israel had done to the Amorites.
3 And [R]Moab was exceedingly afraid of the
people because they *were* many, and Moab
was sick with dread because of the children of
Israel. Ex. 15:15
4 So Moab said to [R]the elders of Midian,
"Now this company will lick up everything
around us, as an ox licks up the grass of the
field." And Balak the son of Zippor *was* king
of the Moabites at that time. Num. 25:15–18
5 Then he sent messengers to Balaam the
son of Beor at Pethor, which *is* near the River*
in the land of the sons of his people,* to call
him, saying: "Look, a people has come from
Egypt. See, they cover the face of the earth,
and are settling next to me!
6 "Therefore please come at once, curse
this people for me, for they *are* too mighty for
me. Perhaps I shall be able to defeat them and
drive them out of the land, for I know that he
whom you bless *is* blessed, and he whom you
curse is cursed."
7 So the elders of Moab and the elders of
Midian departed with the diviner's fee in their
hand, and they came to Balaam and spoke to
him the words of Balak.
8 And he said to them, [R]"Lodge here
tonight, and I will bring back word to you, as
the LORD speaks to me." So the princes of
Moab stayed with Balaam. Num. 22:19
9 [R]Then God came to Balaam and said,
"Who *are* these men with you?" Gen. 20:3
10 So Balaam said to God, "Balak the son of
Zippor, king of Moab, has sent to me, *saying,*
11 'Look, a people has come out of Egypt,
and they cover the face of the earth. Come
now, curse them for me; perhaps I shall be
able to overpower them and drive them out.' "
12 And God said to Balaam, "You shall not
go with them; you shall not curse the people,
for [R]they *are* blessed." [Rom. 11:28]
13 So Balaam rose in the morning and said
to the princes of Balak, "Go back to your land,
for the LORD has refused to give me permis-
sion to go with you."
14 And the princes of Moab rose and went to
Balak, and said, "Balaam refuses to come with
us."
15 Then Balak again sent princes, more nu-
merous and more honorable than they.
16 And they came to Balaam and said to him,
"Thus says Balak the son of Zippor: 'Please let
nothing hinder you from coming to me;
17 'for I will certainly honor you greatly, and
I will do whatever you say to me. Therefore
please come, curse this people for me.' "
18 Then Balaam answered and said to the
servants of Balak, [R]"Though Balak were to
give me his house full of silver and gold, I
could not go beyond the word of the LORD my
God, to do less or more. Num. 22:38; 24:13
19 "Now therefore, please, you also [R]stay
here tonight, that I may know what more the
LORD will say to me." Num. 22:8
20 And God came to Balaam at night and
said to him, "If the men come to call you, rise
and go with them; but only the word which I
speak to you—that you shall do."
21 So Balaam rose in the morning, saddled
his donkey, and went with the princes of
Moab.
22 Then God's anger was aroused because
he went, [R]and the Angel of the LORD took His
stand in the way as an adversary against him.
And he was riding on his donkey, and his two
servants *were* with him. Ex. 4:24
23 Now [R]the donkey saw the Angel of the
LORD standing in the way with His drawn
sword in His hand, and the donkey turned
aside out of the way and went into the field.
So Balaam struck the donkey to turn her back
onto the road. Josh. 5:13
24 Then the Angel of the LORD stood in a
narrow path between the vineyards, *with* a
wall on this side and a wall on that side.
25 And when the donkey saw the Angel of
the LORD, she pushed herself against the wall
and crushed Balaam's foot against the wall;
so he struck her again.
26 Then the Angel of the LORD went further,
and stood in a narrow place where there *was*
no way to turn either to the right hand or to
the left.
27 And when the donkey saw the Angel of
the LORD, she lay down under Balaam; so Ba-
laam's anger was aroused, and he struck the
donkey with his staff.
28 Then the LORD [R]opened the mouth of the
donkey, and she said to Balaam, "What have I
done to you, that you have struck me these
three times?" 2 Pet. 2:16
29 And Balaam said to the donkey, "Be-
cause you have [T]abused me. I wish there
were a sword in my hand, [R]for now I would
kill you!" *mocked* • [Prov. 12:10]
30 [R]So the donkey said to Balaam, "*Am* I not
your donkey on which you have ridden, ever
since *I became* yours, to this day? Was I ever
[T]disposed to do this to you?" And he said,
"No." 2 Pet. 2:16 • *accustomed*
31 Then the LORD [R]opened Balaam's eyes,
and he saw the Angel of the LORD standing in
the way with His drawn sword in His hand;
and he bowed his head and fell flat on his
face. Gen. 21:19
32 And the Angel of the LORD said to him,
"Why have you struck your donkey these

22:5 The Euphrates • Or *the people of Amau*

three times? Behold, I have come out to stand against you, because *your* way is [R]perverse[T] before Me. [2 Pet. 2:14, 15] • *contrary*

33 "The donkey saw Me and turned aside from Me these three times. If she had not turned aside from Me, surely I would also have killed you by now, and let her live."

34 And Balaam said to the Angel of the LORD, "I have sinned, for I did not know You stood in the way against me. Now therefore, if it displeases You, I will turn back."

35 Then the Angel of the LORD said to Balaam, "Go with the men, but only the word that I speak to you, that you shall speak." So Balaam went with the princes of Balak.

36 Now when Balak heard that Balaam was coming, he went out to meet him at the city of Moab, which *is* on the border at the Arnon, the boundary of the territory.

37 Then Balak said to Balaam, "Did I not earnestly send to you, calling for you? Why did you not come to me? Am I not able [R]to honor you?" Num. 22:17; 24:11

38 And Balaam said to Balak, "Look, I have come to you! Now, have I any power at all to say anything? [R]The word that God puts in my mouth, that I must speak." 1 Kin. 22:14

39 So Balaam went with Balak, and they came to Kirjath Huzoth.

40 Then Balak offered oxen and sheep, and he sent *some* to Balaam and to the princes who *were* with him.

The First Oracle of Balaam

41 So it was, the next day, that Balak took Balaam and brought him up to the [R]high places of Baal, that from there he might observe the extent of the people. Num. 21:28

CHAPTER 23

THEN Balaam said to Balak, "Build seven altars for me here, and prepare for me here seven bulls and seven rams."

2 And Balak did just as Balaam had spoken, and Balak and Balaam [R]offered a bull and a ram on *each* altar. Num. 23:14, 30

3 Then Balaam said to Balak, [R]"Stand by your burnt offering, and I will go; perhaps the LORD will come [R]to meet me, and whatever He shows me I will tell you." So he went to a desolate height. Num. 23:15 • Num. 23:4, 16

4 And God met Balaam, and he said to Him, "I have prepared the seven altars, and I have offered on *each* altar a bull and a ram."

5 Then the LORD [R]put a word in Balaam's mouth, and said, "Return to Balak, and thus you shall speak." Deut. 18:18

6 So he returned to him, and there he was, standing by his burnt offering, he and all the princes of Moab.

7 And he [R]took up his [T]oracle and said:

"Balak the king of Moab has brought me
from Aram, Deut. 23:4 • *prophetic discourse*
From the mountains of the east.
'Come, curse Jacob for me,
And come, denounce Israel!'

8 "How[R] shall I curse whom God has not
cursed? Num. 22:12
And how shall I denounce *whom* the
LORD has not denounced?
9 For from the top of the rocks I see him,
And from the hills I behold him;
There! A people dwelling alone,
Not reckoning itself among the nations.

10 "Who can count the dust* of Jacob,
Or number one-fourth of Israel?
Let me die [R]the death of the righteous,
And let my end be like his!" Ps. 116:15

11 Then Balak said to Balaam, "What have you done to me? [R]I took you to curse my enemies, and look, you have blessed *them* bountifully!" Num. 22:11

12 So he answered and said, [R]"Must I not take heed to speak what the LORD has put in my mouth?" Num. 22:38

The Second Oracle of Balaam

13 Then Balak said to him, "Please come with me to another place from which you may see them; you shall see only the outer part of them, and shall not see them all; curse them for me from there."

14 So he brought him to the field of Zophim, to the top of Pisgah, [R]and built seven altars, and offered a bull and a ram on *each* altar. Num. 23:1, 2

15 And he said to Balak, "Stand here by your burnt offering while I meet* *the* LORD over there."

16 Then the LORD met Balaam, and put a word in his mouth, and said, "Go back to Balak, and thus you shall speak."

17 So he came to him, and there he was, standing by his burnt offering, and the princes of Moab were with him. And Balak said to him, "What has the LORD spoken?"

18 Then he took up his oracle and said:

[R]"Rise up, Balak, and hear! Judg. 3:20
Listen to me, son of Zippor!

19 "God[R] *is* not a man, that He should lie,
Nor a son of man, that He should
repent. Mal. 3:6
Has He [R]said, and will He not do?
Or has He spoken, and will He not make
it good? 1 Kin. 8:56

23:10 Or *dust cloud* **23:15** So with MT, Tg., Vg.; Syr. *call;* LXX *go and ask God*

20 Behold, I have received *a command* to
bless;
He has blessed, and I cannot reverse it.

21 "He has not observed iniquity in Jacob,
Nor has He seen [T]wickedness in Israel.
The LORD his God *is* with him, *trouble*
And the shout of a King *is* among them.
22 God brings them out of Egypt;
He has strength like a wild ox.

23 "For *there is* no sorcery against Jacob,
Nor any divination against Israel.
It now must be said of Jacob
And of Israel, 'Oh, what God has done!'
24 Look, a people rises [R]like a lioness,
And lifts itself up like a lion;
[R]It shall not lie down until it devours the
prey, Gen. 49:9 • Gen. 49:27
And drinks the blood of the slain."

25 Then Balak said to Balaam, "Neither
curse them at all, nor bless them at all!"
26 So Balaam answered and said to Balak,
"Did I not tell you, saying, [R]'All that the LORD
speaks, that I must do'?" Num. 22:38

The Third Oracle of Balaam

27 Then Balak said to Balaam, "Please come,
I will take you to another place; perhaps it
will please God that you may curse them for
me from there."
28 So Balak took Balaam to the top of Peor,
that [R]overlooks the wasteland.* Num. 21:20
29 Then Balaam said to Balak, "Build for me
here seven altars, and prepare for me here
seven bulls and seven rams."
30 And Balak did as Balaam had said, and
offered a bull and a ram on *every* altar.

CHAPTER 24

NOW when Balaam saw that it pleased the
LORD to bless Israel, he did not go as at
other times, to seek to use sorcery, but he set
his face toward the wilderness.
2 And Balaam raised his eyes, and saw Is-
rael encamped according to their tribes; and
the Spirit of God came upon him.
3 [R]Then he took up his oracle and said:

"The utterance of Balaam the son of
Beor, Num. 23:7, 18
The utterance of the man whose eyes are
opened,
4 The utterance of him who hears the
words of God,
Who sees the vision of the Almighty,
Who falls down, with eyes wide open:

5 "How lovely are your tents, O Jacob!
Your dwellings, O Israel!
6 Like valleys that stretch out,
Like gardens by the riverside,
[R]Like aloes planted by the LORD, Jer. 17:8
Like cedars beside the waters.
7 He shall pour water from his buckets,
And his seed *shall be* in many waters.

"His king shall be higher than Agag,
And his kingdom shall be exalted.

8 "God[R] brings him out of Egypt;
He has strength like a wild ox;
He shall [R]consume the nations, his
enemies; Num. 23:22 • Num. 14:9; 23:24
He shall [R]break their bones Ps. 2:9
And pierce *them* with his arrows.
9 'He bows down, he lies down as a lion;
And as a lion, who shall rouse him?'*

"Blessed *is* he who blesses you,
And cursed *is* he who curses you."

10 Then Balak's anger was aroused against
Balaam, and he struck his hands together;
and Balak said to Balaam, "I called you to
curse my enemies, and look, you have bounti-
fully blessed *them* these three times!
11 "Now therefore, flee to your place. I said I
would greatly honor you, but in fact, the LORD
has kept you back from honor."
12 So Balaam said to Balak, "Did I not also
speak to your messengers whom you sent to
me, saying,
13 'If Balak were to give me his house full of
silver and gold, I could not go beyond the
word of the LORD, to do good or bad of my
own will. What the LORD says, that I must
speak'?

The Fourth Oracle of Balaam

14 "And now, indeed, I am going to my peo-
ple. Come, I will advise you what this people
will do to your people in the latter days."
15 So he took up his oracle and said:

"The utterance of Balaam the son of Beor,
And the utterance of the man whose
eyes are opened;
16 The utterance of him who hears the
words of God,
And has the knowledge of the Most
High,
Who sees the vision of the Almighty,
Who falls down, with eyes wide open:

17 "I[R] see Him, but not now; Rev. 1:7
I behold Him, but not near;
[R]A Star shall come out of Jacob; Matt. 1:2☆
A Scepter shall rise out of Israel,
And batter the brow of Moab,
And destroy all the sons of tumult.*

23:28 Heb. *Jeshimon* **24:9** Gen. 49:9 **24:17** Heb. *Sheth*, Jer. 48:45

18 "And [R]Edom shall be a possession;
Seir also, his enemies, shall be a
possession, 2 Sam. 8:14
While Israel does [T]valiantly. *mightily*
19 Out of Jacob One shall have dominion,
And destroy the remains of the city."

20 Then he looked on Amalek, and he took
up his oracle and said:

"Amalek *was* first among the nations,
But *shall be* last until he perishes."

21 Then he looked on the Kenites, and he
took up his oracle and said:

"Firm is your dwelling place,
And your nest is set in the rock;
22 Nevertheless Kain shall be burned.
How long until Asshur carries you away
captive?"

23 Then he took up his oracle and said:

"Alas! Who shall live when God does
this?
24 But ships *shall come* from the coasts of
[R]Cyprus,* Gen. 10:4
And they shall afflict Asshur and afflict
[R]Eber, Gen. 10:21, 25
And so shall *Amalek*,* until he perishes."

25 So Balaam rose and departed and re-
turned to his place; Balak also went his way.

CHAPTER 25

Israel Commits Harlotry

NOW Israel remained in Acacia Grove,*
and the [R]people began to commit har-
lotry with the women of Moab. Rev. 2:14
2 [R]They invited the people to the sacrifices
of their gods, and the people ate and bowed
down to their gods. Hos. 9:10

Phinehas Stays the Plague

3 So Israel was joined to Baal of Peor, and
[R]the anger of the LORD was aroused against
Israel. Ps. 106:28, 29
4 Then the LORD said to Moses, [R]"Take all
the leaders of the people and hang the of-
fenders before the LORD, out in the sun, [R]that
the fierce anger of the LORD may turn away
from Israel." Deut. 4:3 • Num. 25:11
5 So Moses said to [R]the judges of Israel,
[R]"Every one of you kill his men who were
joined to Baal of Peor." Ex. 18:21 • Deut. 13:6, 9
6 And indeed, one of the children of Israel
came and presented to his brethren a Midian-
ite woman in the sight of Moses and in the
sight of all the congregation of the children of
Israel, [R]who *were* weeping at the door of the
tabernacle of meeting. Joel 2:17
7 Now [R]when Phinehas the son of Eleazar,
the son of Aaron the priest, saw *it*, he rose
from among the congregation and took a
javelin in his hand; Ps. 106:30
8 and he went after the man of Israel into
the tent and thrust both of them through, the
man of Israel, and the woman through her
body. So [R]the plague was stopped among the
children of Israel. Ps. 106:30
9 And [R]those who died in the plague were
twenty-four thousand. Deut. 4:3
10 Then the LORD spoke to Moses, say-
ing:
11 [R]"Phinehas the son of Eleazar, the son of
Aaron the priest, has turned back My wrath
from the children of Israel, because he was
zealous with My zeal among them, so that I
did not consume the children of Israel in [R]My
zeal. Ps. 106:30 • [Ex. 20:5]
12 "Therefore say, 'Behold, I give to him My
[R]covenant of peace; Is. 54:10
13 'and it shall be to him and his descen-
dants after him a covenant of [R]an everlasting
priesthood, because he was [R]zealous for his
God, and [R]made atonement for the children of
Israel.'" Ex. 40:15 • Acts 22:3 • [Heb. 2:17]
14 Now the name of the Israelite who was
killed, who was killed with the Midianite
woman, *was* Zimri the son of Salu, a leader of
a father's house among the Simeonites.
15 And the name of the Midianite woman
who was killed *was* Cozbi the daughter of
[R]Zur; he *was* head of the people of a father's
house in Midian. Num. 31:8

Israel to Destroy Moab

16 Then the LORD spoke to Moses, saying:
17 [R]"Harass the Midianites, and [T]attack
them; Num. 31:1–3 • *be hostile toward*
18 "for they harassed you with their
[R]schemes[T] by which they seduced you in the
matter of Peor and in the matter of Cozbi, the
daughter of a leader of Midian, their sister,
who was killed in the day of the plague be-
cause of Peor." Rev. 2:14 • *tricks*

CHAPTER 26

The Second Census

AND it came to pass, after the plague, that
the LORD spoke to Moses and Eleazar the
son of Aaron the priest, saying:
2 "Take a census of all the congregation of
the children of Israel from twenty years old
and above, by their fathers' houses, all who
are able to go to war in Israel."
3 So Moses and Eleazar the priest spoke
with them in the plains of Moab by the Jor-
dan, *across from* Jericho, saying:
4 "*Take a census of the people* from twenty

24:24 Heb. *Kittim* • Lit. *he* or *that one* **25:1** Heb. *Shittim*

years old and above, just as the LORD com-
manded Moses and the children of Israel who
came out of the land of Egypt."
5 [R]Reuben *was* the firstborn of Israel. The
children of Reuben *were: of* Hanoch, the fam-
ily of the Hanochites; *of* Pallu, the family of
the Palluites; Ex. 6:14
6 *of* Hezron, the family of the Hezronites; *of*
Carmi, the family of the Carmites.
7 These *are* the families of the Reubenites:
those who were numbered of them were
forty-three thousand seven hundred and
thirty.
8 And the son of Pallu *was* Eliab.
9 The sons of Eliab *were* Nemuel, Dathan,
and Abiram. These *are* the Dathan and Abi-
ram, [R]representatives of the congregation,
who contended against Moses and Aaron in
the company of Korah, when they contended
against the LORD; Num. 1:16; 16:1, 2
10 [R]and the earth opened its mouth and
swallowed them up together with Korah when
that company died, when the fire devoured
two hundred and fifty men; [R]and they became
a sign. Num. 16:32–35 • Num. 16:38–40
11 Nevertheless [R]the children of Korah did
not die. Ex. 6:24
12 The sons of Simeon according to their
families *were: of* Nemuel,* the family of the
Nemuelites; *of* Jamin, the family of the
Jaminites; *of* Jachin,* the family of the Ja-
chinites;
13 *of* Zerah,* the family of the Zarhites; *of*
Shaul, the family of the Shaulites.
14 These *are* the families of the Simeonites:
twenty-two thousand two hundred.
15 The sons of Gad according to their fami-
lies *were: of* Zephon,* the family of the Zeph-
onites; *of* Haggi, the family of the Haggites; *of*
Shuni, the family of the Shunites;
16 *of* Ozni,* the family of the Oznites; *of* Eri,
the family of the Erites;
17 *of* Arod,* the family of the Arodites; *of*
Areli, the family of the Arelites.
18 These *are* the families of the sons of Gad
according to those who were numbered of
them: forty thousand five hundred.
19 [R]The sons of Judah *were* Er and Onan;
and Er and Onan died in the land of
Canaan. Gen. 38:2; 46:12
20 And the sons of Judah according to their
families were: *of* Shelah, the family of the
Shelanites; *of* Perez, the family of the
Parzites; *of* Zerah, the family of the Zarhites.
21 And the sons of Perez were: *of* Hezron,
the family of the Hezronites; *of* Hamul, the
family of the Hamulites.
22 These *are* the families of Judah according
to those who were numbered of them: sev-
enty-six thousand five hundred.
23 The sons of Issachar according to their
families *were: of* Tola, the family of the To-
laites; of Puah,* the family of the Punites;*
24 of Jashub, the family of the Jashubites; of
Shimron, the family of the Shimronites.
25 These *are* the families of Issachar accord-
ing to those who were numbered of them:
sixty-four thousand three hundred.
26 The sons of Zebulun according to their
families *were:* of Sered, the family of the
Sardites; of Elon, the family of the Elonites; of
Jahleel, the family of the Jahleelites.
27 These *are* the families of the Zebulunites
according to those who were numbered of
them: sixty thousand five hundred.
28 The sons of Joseph according to their
families, by Manasseh and Ephraim, *were:*
29 The sons of [R]Manasseh: of [R]Machir, the
family of the Machirites; and Machir begot
Gilead; of Gilead, the family of the Gil-
eadites. Josh. 17:1 • 1 Chr. 7:14, 15
30 These *are* the sons of Gilead: *of* Jeezer,*
the family of the Jeezerites; of Helek, the fam-
ily of the Helekites;
31 *of* Asriel, the family of the Asrielites; *of*
Shechem, the family of the Shechemites;
32 *of* Shemida, the family of the Shemida-
ites; *of* Hepher, the family of the Hepherites.
33 Now Zelophehad the son of Hepher had
no sons, but daughters; and the names of the
daughters of Zelophehad *were* Mahlah, Noah,
Hoglah, Milcah, and Tirzah.
34 These *are* the families of Manasseh; and
those who were numbered of them *were* fifty-
two thousand seven hundred.
35 These *are* the sons of Ephraim according
to their families: of Shuthelah, the family of
the Shuthalhites; of Becher,* the family of the
Bachrites; of Tahan, the family of the Tahan-
ites.
36 And these *are* the sons of Shuthelah: of
Eran, the family of the Eranites.
37 These *are* the families of the sons of
Ephraim according to those who were num-
bered of them: thirty-two thousand five hun-
dred. These *are* the sons of Joseph according
to their families.
38 [R]The sons of Benjamin according to
their families were: of Bela, the family of the
Belaites; of Ashbel, the family of the Ash-
belites; of [R]Ahiram, the family of the Ahi-
ramites; Gen. 46:21 • 1 Chr. 8:1, 2
39 of [R]Shupham,* the family of the
Shuphamites; of Hupham,* the family of the
Huphamites. 1 Chr. 7:12
40 And the sons of Bela were Ard* and Naa-
man: *of Ard,* the family of the Ardites; of Naa-
man, the family of the Naamites.

26:12 *Jemuel,* Gen. 46:10; Ex. 6:15 • *Jarib,* 1 Chr. 4:24 **26:13** *Zohar,* Gen. 46:10 **26:15** *Ziphion,* Gen. 46:16 **26:16** *Ezbon,* Gen. 46:16 **26:17** Sam., Syr. *Arodi* and Gen. 46:16 **26:23** So with Sam., LXX, Syr., Vg.; Heb. *Puvah,* Gen. 46:13; 1 Chr. 7:1 • Sam., LXX, Syr., Vg. *Puaites* **26:30** *Abiezer,* Josh. 17:2 **26:35** *Bered,* 1 Chr. 7:20 **26:39** MT *Shephupham; Shephuphan,* 1 Chr. 8:5 • *Huppim,* Gen. 46:21 **26:40** *Addar,* 1 Chr. 8:3

41 These *are* the sons of Benjamin according to their families; and those who were numbered of them *were* forty-five thousand six hundred.

42 These *are* the sons of Dan according to their families: of Shuham,* the family of the Shuhamites. These *are* the families of Dan according to their families.

43 All the families of the Shuhamites, according to those who were numbered of them, *were* sixty-four thousand four hundred.

44 The sons of Asher according to their families *were:* of Jimna, the family of the Jimnites; of Jesui, the family of the Jesuites; of Beriah, the family of the Beriites.

45 Of the sons of Beriah: of Heber, the family of the Heberites; of Malchiel, the family of the Malchielites.

46 And the name of the daughter of Asher *was* Serah.

47 These *are* the families of the sons of Asher according to those who were numbered of them: fifty-three thousand four hundred.

48 The sons of Naphtali according to their families *were:* of Jahzeel,* the family of the Jahzeelites; of Guni, the family of the Gunites;

49 of Jezer, the family of the Jezerites; of Shillem, the family of the Shillemites.

50 These *are* the families of Naphtali according to their families; and those who were numbered of them *were* forty-five thousand four hundred.

51 These *are* those who were numbered of the children of Israel: six hundred and one thousand seven hundred and thirty.

Method of Dividing the Land

52 Then the LORD spoke to Moses, saying:

53 [R]"To these the land shall be [R]divided as an inheritance, according to the number of names. Josh. 11:23; 14:1 • Num. 33:54

54 [R]"To a large *tribe* you shall give a larger inheritance, and to a small *tribe* you shall give a smaller inheritance. Each shall be given its inheritance according to those who were numbered of them. Num. 33:54

55 "But the land shall be [R]divided by lot; they shall inherit according to the names of the tribes of their fathers. Num. 33:54; 34:13

56 "According to the lot their inheritance shall be divided between the larger and the smaller."

The Levites Have No Inheritance

57 And these *are* those who were numbered of the Levites according to their families: of Gershon, the family of the Gershonites; of Kohath, the family of the Kohathites; of Merari, the family of the Merarites.

58 These *are* the families of the Levites: the family of the Libnites, the family of the Hebronites, the family of the Mahlites, the family of the Mushites, and the family of the Korathites. And Kohath begot Amram.

59 The name of Amram's wife *was* [R]Jochebed the daughter of Levi, who was born to Levi in Egypt; and to Amram she bore Aaron and Moses and their sister Miriam. Ex. 2:1, 2; 6:20

60 [R]To Aaron were born Nadab and Abihu, Eleazar and Ithamar. Num. 3:2

61 And Nadab and Abihu died when they offered profane fire before the LORD.

62 Now those who were numbered of them were twenty-three thousand, every male from a month old and above; for they were not numbered among the other children of Israel, because there was no inheritance given to them among the children of Israel.

The Old Generation Has No Inheritance

63 These *are* those who were numbered by Moses and Eleazar the priest, who numbered the children of Israel in the plains of Moab by the Jordan, *across from* Jericho.

64 But among these there was not a man of those who were numbered by Moses and Aaron the priest when they numbered the children of Israel in the Wilderness of Sinai.

65 For the LORD had said of them, "They [R]shall surely die in the wilderness." So there was not left a man of them, [R]except Caleb the son of Jephunneh and Joshua the son of Nun. Num. 14:26–35 • Num. 14:30

CHAPTER 27

The Special Laws of Inheritance

THEN came the daughters of Zelophehad the son of Hepher, the son of Gilead, the son of Machir, the son of Manasseh, from the families of Manasseh the son of Joseph; and these *were* the names of his daughters: Mahlah, Noah, Hoglah, Milcah, and Tirzah.

2 And they stood before Moses, before Eleazar the priest, and before the leaders and all the congregation, *by* the doorway of the tabernacle of meeting, saying:

3 "Our father [R]died in the wilderness; but he was not in the company of those who gathered together against the LORD, in company with Korah, but he died in his own sin; and he had no sons. Num. 14:35; 26:64, 65

4 "Why should the name of our father be [R]removed from among his family because he had no son? [R]Give us a possession among our father's brothers." Deut. 25:6 • Josh. 17:4

5 So Moses [R]brought their case before the LORD. Ex. 18:13–26

6 And the LORD spoke to Moses, saying:

7 "The daughters of Zelophehad speak *what is* right; [R]you shall surely give them a possession of inheritance among their fa-

26:42 *Hushim,* Gen. 46:23 **26:48** *Jahziel,* 1 Chr. 7:13

ther's brothers, and cause the inheritance of their father to pass to them. Num. 36:2

8 "And you shall speak to the children of Israel, saying: 'If a man dies and has no son, then you shall cause his inheritance to pass to his daughter.

9 'If he has no daughter, then you shall give his inheritance to his brothers.

10 'If he has no brothers, then you shall give his inheritance to his father's brothers.

11 'And if his father has no brothers, then you shall give his inheritance to the relative closest to him in his family, and he shall possess it.' " And it shall be to the children of Israel [R]a statute of judgment, just as the LORD commanded Moses. Num. 35:29

Moses Is Set Aside

12 Now the LORD said to Moses: "Go up into this Mount Abarim, and see the land which I have given to the children of Israel.

13 "And when you have seen it, you also [R]shall be gathered to your people, as Aaron your brother was gathered. Deut. 10:6; 34:5, 6

14 "For in the Wilderness of Zin, during the strife of the congregation, you [R]rebelled against My command to hallow Me at the waters before their eyes." (These *are* the [R]waters of Meribah, at Kadesh in the Wilderness of Zin.) Ps. 106:32, 33 • Ex. 17:7

Joshua Is Appointed

15 Then Moses spoke to the LORD, saying:

16 "Let the LORD, the God of the spirits of all flesh, set a man over the congregation,

17 [R]"who may go out before them and go in before them, who may lead them out and bring them in, that the congregation of the LORD may not be [R]like sheep which have no shepherd." Deut. 31:2 • Zech. 10:2

18 And the LORD said to Moses: "Take Joshua the son of Nun with you, a man [R]in whom *is* the Spirit, and [R]lay your hand on him; Gen. 41:38 • Deut. 34:9

19 "set him before Eleazar the priest and before all the congregation, and [R]inaugurate him in their sight. Deut. 3:28; 31:3, 7, 8, 23

20 "And you shall give *some* of your authority to him, that all the congregation of the children of Israel may be obedient.

21 "He shall stand before Eleazar the priest, who shall inquire before the LORD for him by the judgment of the Urim. At his word they shall go out, and at his word they shall come in, he and all the children of Israel with him—all the congregation."

22 So Moses did as the LORD commanded him. He took Joshua and set him before Eleazar the priest and before all the congregation.

23 And he laid his hands on him [R]and inaugurated him, just as the LORD commanded by the hand of Moses. Deut. 3:28; 31:7, 8

CHAPTER 28

Daily Offering

NOW the LORD spoke to Moses, saying,

2 "Command the children of Israel, and say to them, 'My offering, [R]My food for My offerings made by fire as a sweet aroma to Me, you shall be careful to offer to Me at their appointed time.' Lev. 3:11; 21:6, 8

3 "And you shall say to them, [R]'This *is* the offering made by fire which you shall offer to the LORD: two male lambs in their first year without blemish, day by day, as a regular burnt offering. Ex. 29:38–42

4 'The one lamb you shall offer in the morning, the other lamb you shall offer in the evening,

5 'and [R]one-tenth of an ephah of fine flour as a [R]grain offering mixed with one-fourth of a hin of pressed oil. Ex. 16:36 • Lev. 2:1

6 '*It is* a regular burnt offering which was ordained at Mount Sinai for a sweet aroma, an offering made by fire to the LORD.

7 'And its drink offering *shall be* one-fourth of a hin for each lamb; [R]in a holy *place* you shall pour out the drink to the LORD as an offering. Ex. 29:42

8 'The other lamb you shall offer in the evening; as the morning grain offering and its drink offering, you shall offer *it* as an offering made by fire, a [T]sweet aroma to the LORD. *pleasing*

Weekly Offering

9 'And on the Sabbath day two lambs in their first year, without blemish, and two-tenths *of an ephah* of fine flour as a grain offering, mixed with oil, with its drink offering—

10 '*this is* [R]the burnt offering for every Sabbath, besides the regular burnt offering with its drink offering. Ezek. 46:4

Monthly Offering

11 'At the beginnings of your months you shall present a burnt offering to the LORD: two young bulls, one ram, and seven lambs in their first year, without blemish;

12 [R]'three-tenths *of an ephah* of fine flour as a grain offering, mixed with oil, for each bull; two-tenths *of an ephah* of fine flour as a grain offering, mixed with oil, for the one ram; Num. 15:4–12

13 'and one-tenth *of an ephah* of fine flour, mixed with oil, as a grain offering for each lamb, as a burnt offering of sweet aroma, an offering made by fire to the LORD.

14 'Their drink offering shall be half a hin of wine for a bull, one-third of a hin for a ram, and one-fourth of a hin for a lamb; this *is* the burnt offering for each month throughout the months of the year.

15 'Also one kid of the goats as a sin offering

to the LORD shall be offered, besides the regu-
lar burnt offering and its drink offering.

Passover

16 'On the fourteenth day of the first month
is the Passover of the LORD.

Unleavened Bread

17 [R]'And on the fifteenth day of this month *is*
the feast; unleavened bread shall be eaten for
seven days. Lev. 23:6
18 'On the [R]first day *you shall have* a holy
[T]convocation. You shall do no [T]customary
work. Lev. 23:7 • *assembly* or *gathering* • *occupational*
19 'And you shall present an offering made
by fire as a burnt offering to the LORD: two
young bulls, one ram, and seven lambs in
their first year. [R]Be sure they are without
blemish. Deut. 15:21
20 'Their grain offering shall be of fine flour
mixed with oil: three-tenths *of an ephah* you
shall offer for a bull, and two-tenths for a ram;
21 'you shall offer one-tenth *of an ephah* for
each of the seven lambs;
22 'also [R]one goat *as* a sin offering, to make
[T]atonement for you. Num. 28:15 • Lit. *covering*
23 'You shall offer these besides the burnt
offering of the morning, which *is* for a regular
burnt offering.
24 'In this manner you shall offer the food of
the offering made by fire daily for seven days,
as a sweet aroma to the LORD; it shall be of-
fered besides the regular burnt offering and
its drink offering.
25 'And [R]on the seventh day you shall have a
holy convocation. You shall do no customary
work. Lev. 23:8

Firstfruits

26 'Also [R]on the day of the firstfruits, when
you bring a new grain offering to the LORD at
your *Feast of* Weeks, you shall have a holy
convocation. You shall do no customary
work. Deut. 16:9–12
27 'You shall present a burnt offering as a
sweet aroma to the LORD: two young bulls,
one ram, and seven lambs in their first year,
28 'with their grain offering of fine flour
mixed with oil: three-tenths *of an ephah* for
each bull, two-tenths for the one ram,
29 'and one-tenth for each of the seven lambs;
30 '*also* one kid of the goats, to make [T]atone-
ment for you. Lit. *covering*
31 [R]'Be sure they are without [T]blemish. You
shall present *them* with their drink offerings,
besides the regular burnt offering with its
grain offering. Num. 28:3, 19 • *defect*

CHAPTER 29

Trumpets

'AND in the seventh month, on the first
day of the month, you shall have a holy
convocation. You shall do no customary work.
For you it is a day of blowing the trumpets.
2 'You shall offer a burnt offering as a
sweet aroma to the LORD: one young bull, one
ram, *and* seven lambs in their first year, with-
out blemish.
3 'Their grain offering *shall be* fine flour
mixed with oil: three-tenths *of an ephah* for
the bull, two-tenths for the ram,
4 'and one-tenth for each of the seven
lambs;
5 'also one kid of the goats *as* a sin offering,
to make atonement for you;
6 'besides [R]the burnt offering with its grain
offering for the New Moon, [R]the regular burnt
offering with its grain offering, and their
drink offerings, according to their ordinance,
as a sweet aroma, an offering made by fire to
the LORD. Num. 28:11–15 • Num. 28:3

Atonement

7 [R]'On the tenth *day* of this seventh month
you shall have a holy convocation. You shall
[R]afflict your souls; you shall not do any
work. Lev. 16:29–34; 23:26–32 • Is. 58:5
8 'You shall present a burnt offering to the
LORD *as* a sweet aroma: one young bull, one
ram, *and* seven lambs in their first year. Be
sure they are without blemish.
9 'Their grain offering *shall be of* fine flour
mixed with oil: three-tenths *of an ephah* for
the bull, two-tenths for the one ram,
10 'and one-tenth for each of the seven
lambs;
11 'also one kid of the goats *as* a sin offering,
besides [R]the sin offering for atonement, the
regular burnt offering with its grain offering,
and their drink offerings. Lev. 16:3, 5

Tabernacle

12 'On the fifteenth day of the seventh
month you shall have a holy convocation. You
shall do no customary work, and you shall
keep a feast to the LORD seven days.
13 [R]'You shall present a burnt offering, an of-
fering made by fire as a sweet aroma to the
LORD: thirteen young bulls, two rams, *and*
fourteen lambs in their first year. They shall
be without blemish. Ezra 3:4
14 'Their grain offering *shall be of* fine flour
mixed with oil: three-tenths *of an ephah* for
each of the thirteen bulls, two-tenths for each
of the two rams,
15 'and one-tenth for each of the fourteen
lambs;
16 'also one kid of the goats *as* a sin offering,
besides the regular burnt offering, its grain of-
fering, and its drink offering.
17 'On the [R]second day *present* twelve young
bulls, two rams, fourteen lambs in their first
year without blemish, Lev. 23:36
18 'and their grain offering and their drink
offerings for the bulls, for the rams, and for

the lambs, by their number, [R]according to the ordinance; Num. 15:12; 28:7, 14

19 'also one kid of the goats *as* a sin offering, besides the regular burnt offering with its grain offering, and their drink offerings.

20 'On the third day *present* eleven bulls, two rams, fourteen lambs in their first year without blemish,

21 'and their grain offering and their drink offerings for the bulls, for the rams, and for the lambs, by their number, [R]according to the ordinance; Num. 29:18

22 'also one goat *as* a sin offering, besides the regular burnt offering, its grain offering, and its drink offering.

23 'On the fourth day *present* ten bulls, two rams, *and* fourteen lambs in their first year, without blemish,

24 'and their grain offering and their drink offerings for the bulls, for the rams, and for the lambs, by their number, according to the ordinance;

25 'also one kid of the goats *as* a sin offering, besides the regular burnt offering, its grain offering, and its drink offering.

26 'On the fifth day *present* nine bulls, two rams, *and* fourteen lambs in their first year without blemish,

27 'and their grain offering and their drink offerings for the bulls, for the rams, and for the lambs, by their number, according to the ordinance;

28 'also one goat *as* a sin offering, besides the regular burnt offering, its grain offering, and its drink offering.

29 'On the sixth day *present* eight bulls, two rams, *and* fourteen lambs in their first year without blemish,

30 'and their grain offering and their drink offerings for the bulls, for the rams, and for the lambs, by their number, according to the ordinance;

31 'also one goat *as* a sin offering, besides the regular burnt offering, its grain offering, and its drink offering.

32 'On the seventh day *present* seven bulls, two rams, *and* fourteen lambs in their first year without blemish,

33 'and their grain offering and their drink offerings for the bulls, for the rams, and for the lambs, by their number, according to the ordinance;

34 'also one goat *as* a sin offering, besides the regular burnt offering, its grain offering, and its drink offering.

35 'On the eighth day you shall have a [R]sacred[T] assembly. You shall do no customary work. Lev. 23:36 • *solemn*

36 'You shall present a burnt offering, an offering made by fire as a sweet aroma to the LORD: one bull, one ram, seven lambs in their first year without blemish,

37 'and their grain offering and their drink offerings for the bull, for the ram, and for the lambs, by their number, according to the ordinance;

38 'also one goat *as* a sin offering, besides the regular burnt offering, its grain offering, and its drink offering.

39 'These you shall present to the LORD at your [R]appointed feasts (besides your [R]vowed offerings and your freewill offerings) as your burnt offerings and your grain offerings, as your drink offerings and your peace offerings.' " Lev. 23:1–44 • Lev. 7:16; 22:18, 21, 23; 23:38

40 So Moses told the children of Israel everything, just as the LORD commanded Moses.

CHAPTER 30

The Regulation of Vows

THEN Moses spoke to [R]the heads of the tribes concerning the children of Israel, saying, "This *is* the thing which the LORD has commanded: Num. 1:4, 16; 7:2

2 [R]"If a man makes a vow to the LORD, or [R]swears an oath to bind himself by some agreement, he shall not break his word; he shall [R]do according to all that proceeds out of his mouth. Lev. 27:2 • Matt. 14:9 • Job 22:27

3 "Or if a woman makes a vow to the LORD, and binds *herself* by some agreement while in her father's house in her youth,

4 "and her father hears her vow and the agreement by which she has bound herself, and her father holds his peace, then all her vows shall stand, and every agreement with which she has bound herself shall stand.

5 "But if her father overrules her on the day that he hears, then none of her vows nor her agreements by which she has bound herself shall stand; and the LORD will release her, because her father overruled her.

6 "If indeed she takes a husband, while bound by her vows or by a rash utterance from her lips by which she bound herself,

7 "and her husband hears *it*, and makes no response to her on the day that he hears, then her vows shall stand, and her agreements by which she bound herself shall stand.

8 "But if her husband overrules her on the day that he hears *it*, he shall make void her vow which she took and what she uttered with her lips, by which she bound herself, and the LORD will release her.

9 "Also any vow of a widow or a divorced woman, by which she has bound herself, shall stand against her.

10 "If she vowed in her husband's house, or bound herself by an agreement with an oath,

11 "and her husband heard *it*, and made no response to her *and* did not overrule her, then all her vows shall stand, and every agreement by which she bound herself shall stand.

12 "But if her husband truly made them
void on the day he heard *them*, then what-
ever proceeded from her lips concerning her
vows or concerning the agreement binding
her, it shall not stand; her husband has
made them [T]void, and the LORD will release
her. *annulled* or *invalidated*
13 "Every vow and every binding oath to af-
flict her soul, her husband may confirm it, or
her husband may make it void.
14 "Now if her husband makes no response
whatever to her from day to day, then he con-
firms all her vows or all the agreements that
bind her; he confirms them, because he made
no response to her on the day that he heard
them.
15 "But if he does make them void after he
has heard *them*, then he shall bear her guilt."
16 These *are* the statutes which the LORD
commanded Moses, between a man and his
wife, and between a father and his daughter
in her youth in her father's house.

CHAPTER 31

Destruction of the Midianites

AND the LORD spoke to Moses, saying:
2 [R]"Take vengeance on the Midianites
for the children of Israel. Afterward you shall
be gathered to your people." Num. 25:17
3 So Moses spoke to the people, saying,
"Arm some of yourselves for war, and let them
go against the Midianites to take vengeance
for the LORD on Midian.
4 "A thousand from each tribe of all the
tribes of Israel you shall send to the war."
5 So there were recruited from the divi-
sions of Israel one thousand from *each* tribe,
twelve thousand armed for war.
6 Then Moses sent them to the war, one
thousand from *each* tribe; he sent them to the
war with Phinehas the son of Eleazar the
priest, with the holy articles and [R]the signal
trumpets in his hand. Num. 10:9
7 And they warred against the Midianites,
just as the LORD commanded Moses, and
[R]they killed all the males. Deut. 20:13
8 They killed the kings of Midian with *the
rest of* those who were killed—[R]Evi, Rekem,
Zur, Hur, and Reba, the five kings of Midian.
[R]Balaam the son of Beor they also killed with
the sword. Josh. 13:21 • Josh. 13:22
9 And the children of Israel took the
women of Midian captive, with their little
ones, and took as spoil all their cattle, all their
flocks, and all their goods.
10 They also burned with fire all the cities
where they dwelt, and all their forts.
11 And [R]they took all the spoil and all the
booty—of man and beast. Deut. 20:14
12 Then they brought the captives, the booty,
and the spoil to Moses, to Eleazar the priest,
and to the congregation of the children of Is-
rael, to the camp in the plains of Moab by the
Jordan, *across from* Jericho.
13 And Moses, Eleazar the priest, and all the
leaders of the congregation, went to meet
them outside the camp.
14 But Moses was angry with the officers of
the army, *with* the captains over thousands
and captains over hundreds, who had come
from the battle.
15 And Moses said to them: "Have you kept
[R]all the women alive? Deut. 20:14
16 "Look, these *women* caused the children
of Israel, through the counsel of Balaam, to
trespass against the LORD in the incident of
Peor, and there was a plague among the con-
gregation of the LORD.
17 "Now therefore, [R]kill every male among
the little ones, and kill every woman who has
known a man intimately. Deut. 7:2
18 "But keep alive [R]for yourselves all the
young girls who have not known a man inti-
mately. Deut. 21:10–14

Purification of Israel

19 "And as for you, [R]remain outside the
camp seven days; whoever has killed any per-
son, and whoever has touched any slain, pu-
rify yourselves and your captives on the third
day and on the seventh day. Num. 5:2
20 "Purify every garment, everything made
of leather, everything woven of goats' *hair*,
and everything made of wood."
21 Then Eleazar the priest said to the men of
war who had gone to the battle, "This *is* the
[T]ordinance of the law which the LORD com-
manded Moses: *statute*
22 "Only the gold, the silver, the bronze, the
iron, the tin, and the lead,
23 "everything that can endure fire, you shall
put through the fire, and it shall be clean; and
it shall be purified with the water of purifica-
tion. But all that cannot endure fire you shall
put through water.
24 [R]"And you shall wash your clothes on the
seventh day and be clean, and afterward you
may come into the camp." Lev. 11:25

Distribution of the Spoils

25 Now the LORD spoke to Moses, saying:
26 "Count up the plunder that was [T]taken—
of man and beast—you and Eleazar the
priest and the chief fathers of the congrega-
tion; *captured*
27 "and divide the plunder into two parts,
between those who took part in the war, who
went out to battle, and all the congregation.
28 "And levy a tribute for the LORD on the
men of war who went out to battle: [R]one of
every five hundred of the persons, the cattle,
the donkeys, and the sheep; Num. 31:30, 47
29 "take *it* from their half, and [R]give *it* to
Eleazar the priest as a heave offering to the
LORD. Deut. 18:1–5

30 "And from the children of Israel's half you shall take [R]one of every fifty, drawn from the persons, the cattle, the donkeys, and the sheep, from all the livestock, and give them to the Levites [R]who keep charge of the tabernacle of the LORD." Num. 31:42–47 • Num. 18:3, 4

31 So Moses and Eleazar the priest did as the LORD commanded Moses.

32 The booty remaining from the plunder, which the men of war had taken, was six hundred and seventy-five thousand sheep,

33 seventy-two thousand cattle,

34 sixty-one thousand donkeys,

35 and thirty-two thousand persons in all, of women who had not known a man intimately.

36 And the half, the portion for those who had gone out to war, was in number three hundred and thirty-seven thousand five hundred sheep;

37 and the LORD's [T]tribute of the sheep was six hundred and seventy-five. *tax*

38 The cattle *were* thirty-six thousand, of which the LORD's tribute *was* seventy-two.

39 The donkeys *were* thirty thousand five hundred, of which the LORD's tribute *was* sixty-one.

40 The persons *were* sixteen thousand, of which the LORD's tribute *was* thirty-two persons.

41 So Moses gave the tribute *which was* the LORD's heave offering to Eleazar the priest, as the LORD commanded Moses.

42 And from the children of Israel's half, which Moses separated from the men who fought—

43 now the half belonging to the congregation was three hundred and thirty-seven thousand five hundred sheep,

44 thirty-six thousand cattle,

45 thirty thousand five hundred donkeys,

46 and sixteen thousand persons—

47 and from the children of Israel's half Moses took one of every fifty, drawn from man and beast, and gave them to the Levites, who kept charge of the tabernacle of the LORD, as the LORD commanded Moses.

48 Then the officers who *were* over thousands of the army, the captains of thousands and captains of hundreds, came near to Moses;

49 and they said to Moses, "Your servants have taken a count of the men of war who *are* under our command, and not a man of us is missing.

50 "Therefore we have brought an offering for the LORD, what every man found of ornaments of gold: armlets and bracelets and signet rings and earrings and necklaces, [R]to make [T]atonement for ourselves before the LORD." Ex. 30:12–16 • Lit. *covering*

51 So Moses and Eleazar the priest received the gold from them, all the fashioned ornaments.

52 And all the gold of the offering that they offered to the LORD, from the captains of thousands and captains of hundreds, was sixteen thousand seven hundred and fifty shekels.

53 [R](The men of war had taken spoil, every man for himself.) Deut. 20:14

54 And Moses and Eleazar the priest received the gold from the captains of thousands and of hundreds, and brought it into the tabernacle of meeting as a memorial for the children of Israel before the LORD.

CHAPTER 32

Division of the Land East of Jordan—Deut. 3:12–19

NOW the children of Reuben and the children of Gad had a very great multitude of livestock; and when they saw the land of Jazer and the land of Gilead, that indeed the region *was* a place for livestock,

2 the children of Gad and the children of Reuben came and spoke to Moses, to Eleazar the priest, and to the leaders of the congregation, saying,

3 "Ataroth, Dibon, Jazer, Nimrah, Heshbon, Elealeh, Shebam, Nebo, and Beon,

4 "the country [R]which the LORD defeated before the congregation of Israel, *is* a land for livestock, and your servants have livestock." Num. 21:24, 34, 35

5 Therefore they said, "If we have found favor in your sight, let this land be given to your servants as a possession. Do not take us over the Jordan."

6 And Moses said to the children of Gad and to the children of Reuben: "Shall your brethren go to war while you sit here?

7 "Now why will you discourage the heart of the children of Israel from going over into the land which the LORD has given them?

8 "Thus your fathers did [R]when I sent them away from Kadesh Barnea [R]to see the land. Num. 13:3, 26 • Deut. 1:19–25

9 "For [R]when they went up to the Valley of Eshcol and saw the land, they discouraged the heart of the children of Israel, so that they did not go into the land which the LORD had given them. Deut. 1:24, 28

10 "So the LORD's anger was aroused on that day, and He swore an oath, saying,

11 'Surely none of the men who came up from Egypt, from twenty years old and above, shall see the land of which I swore to Abraham, Isaac, and Jacob, because [R]they have not wholly followed Me, Num. 14:24, 30

12 'except Caleb the son of Jephunneh, the Kenizzite, and Joshua the son of Nun, for they have wholly followed the LORD.'

13 "So the LORD's anger was aroused against Israel, and He made them [R]wander in the wilderness forty years, until all the generation that had done evil in the sight of the LORD was gone. Num. 14:33–35

14 "And look! You have risen in your fathers' place, a brood of sinful men, to increase still more the [R]fierce anger of the LORD against Israel. Deut. 1:34

15 "For if you [R]turn away from following Him, He will once again leave them in the wilderness, and you will destroy all these people." Deut. 30:17, 18

16 Then they came near to him and said: "We will build sheepfolds here for our livestock, and cities for our little ones,

17 "but we ourselves will be armed, ready *to go* before the children of Israel until we have brought them to their place; and our little ones will dwell in the fortified cities because of the inhabitants of the land.

18 [R]"We will not return to our homes until every one of the children of Israel has [T]received his inheritance. Josh. 22:1–4 • *possessed*

19 "For we will not inherit with them on the other side of the Jordan and beyond, [R]because our inheritance has fallen to us on this eastern side of the Jordan." Josh. 12:1

20 Then [R]Moses said to them: "If you do this thing, if you arm yourselves before the LORD for the war, Deut. 3:18

21 "and all your armed men cross over the Jordan before the LORD until He has driven out His enemies from before Him,

22 "and [R]the land is subdued before the LORD, then afterward [R]you may return and be blameless before the LORD and before Israel; and this land shall be your possession before the LORD. Deut. 3:20 • Josh. 22:4

23 "But if you do not do so, then take note, you have sinned against the LORD; and be sure [R]your sin will find you out. Is. 59:12

24 [R]"Build cities for your little ones and folds for your sheep, and do what has proceeded out of your mouth." Num. 32:16

25 And the children of Gad and the children of Reuben spoke to Moses, saying: "Your servants will do as my lord commands.

26 [R]"Our little ones, our wives, our flocks, and all our livestock will be there in the cities of Gilead; Josh. 1:14

27 [R]"but your servants will cross over, every man armed for war, before the LORD to battle, just as my lord says." Josh. 4:12

28 So Moses gave command [R]concerning them to Eleazar the priest, to Joshua the son of Nun, and to the chief fathers of the tribes of the children of Israel. Josh. 1:13

29 And Moses said to them: "If the children of Gad and the children of Reuben cross over the Jordan with you, every man armed for battle before the LORD, and the land is subdued before you, then you shall give them the land of Gilead as a possession.

30 "But if they do not cross over armed with you, they shall have possessions among you in the land of Canaan."

31 Then the children of Gad and the children of Reuben answered, saying: "As the LORD has said to your servants, so we will do.

32 "We will cross over armed before the LORD into the land of Canaan, but the possession of our inheritance *shall remain* with us on this side of the Jordan."

33 So [R]Moses gave to the children of Gad, to the children of Reuben, and to half the tribe of Manasseh the son of Joseph, the kingdom of Sihon king of the Amorites and the kingdom of Og king of Bashan, the land with its cities within the borders, the cities of the surrounding country. Deut. 3:8–17

34 And the children of Gad built [R]Dibon and Ataroth and Aroer, Num. 33:45, 46

35 Atroth and Shophan and [R]Jazer and Jogbehah, Num. 32:1, 3

36 [R]Beth Nimrah and Beth Haran, fortified cities, and folds for sheep. Num. 32:3

37 And the children of Reuben built Heshbon and Elealeh and Kirjathaim,

38 Nebo and Baal Meon (*their* names being changed) and Shibmah; and they gave *other* names to the cities which they built.

39 And the children of Machir the son of Manasseh went to Gilead and took it, and dispossessed the Amorites who *were* in it.

40 So Moses gave Gilead to Machir the son of Manasseh, and he dwelt in it.

41 Also [R]Jair the son of Manasseh went and took its small towns, and called them [R]Havoth Jair.* Deut. 3:14 • Judg. 10:4

42 Then Nobah went and took Kenath and its villages, and he called it Nobah, after his own name.

CHAPTER 33

From Egypt to Sinai

THESE *are* the journeys of the children of Israel, who went out of the land of Egypt by their armies under the [R]hand of Moses and Aaron. Ps. 77:20

2 Now Moses wrote down the starting points of their journeys at the command of the LORD. And these *are* their journeys according to their starting points:

3 They [R]departed from Rameses in the first month, on the fifteenth day of the first month; on the day after the Passover the children of Israel went out with boldness in the sight of all the Egyptians. Ex. 12:37

4 For the Egyptians were burying all *their* firstborn, [R]whom the LORD had killed among them. Also [R]on their gods the LORD had executed judgments. Ex. 12:29 • Is. 19:1

5 [R]Then the children of Israel moved from Rameses and camped at Succoth. Ex. 12:37

6 They departed from [R]Succoth and camped at Etham, which *is* on the edge of the wilderness. Ex. 13:20

32:41 Lit. *Towns of Jair*

7 They moved from Etham and turned back to Pi Hahiroth, which *is* east of Baal Zephon; and they camped near Migdol.

8 They departed from before Hahiroth* and [R]passed through the midst of the sea into the wilderness, went three days' journey in the Wilderness of Etham, and camped at Marah. Ex. 14:22; 15:22, 23

9 They moved from Marah and [R]came to Elim. At Elim *were* twelve springs of water and seventy palm trees; so they camped there. Ex. 15:27

10 They moved from Elim and camped by the Red Sea.

11 They moved from the Red Sea and camped in the [R]Wilderness of Sin. Ex. 16:1

12 They journeyed from the Wilderness of Sin and camped at Dophkah.

13 They departed from Dophkah and camped at Alush.

14 They moved from Alush and camped at [R]Rephidim, where there was no water for the people to drink. Ex. 17:1; 19:2

15 They departed from Rephidim and camped in the Wilderness of Sinai.

From Sinai to Kadesh

16 They moved from the Wilderness of Sinai and camped at Kibroth Hattaavah.

17 They departed from Kibroth Hattaavah and [R]camped at Hazeroth. Num. 11:35

The Wilderness Wanderings

18 They departed from Hazeroth and camped at [R]Rithmah. Num. 12:16

19 They departed from Rithmah and camped at Rimmon Perez.

20 They departed from Rimmon Perez and camped at Libnah.

21 They moved from Libnah and camped at Rissah.

22 They journeyed from Rissah and camped at Kehelathah.

23 They went from Kehelathah and camped at Mount Shepher.

24 They moved from Mount Shepher and camped at Haradah.

25 They moved from Haradah and camped at Makheloth.

26 They moved from Makheloth and camped at Tahath.

27 They departed from Tahath and camped at Terah.

28 They moved from Terah and camped at Mithkah.

29 They went from Mithkah and camped at Hashmonah.

30 They departed from Hashmonah and [R]camped at Moseroth. Deut. 10:6

31 They departed from Moseroth and camped at Bene Jaakan.

32 They moved from [R]Bene Jaakan and camped at Hor Hagidgad. Deut. 10:6

33 They went from Hor Hagidgad and camped at Jotbathah.

34 They moved from Jotbathah and camped at Abronah.

35 They departed from Abronah [R]and camped at Ezion Geber. Deut. 2:8

36 They moved from Ezion Geber and camped in the [R]Wilderness of Zin, which *is* Kadesh. Num. 20:1; 27:14

From Kadesh to Moab

37 They moved from [R]Kadesh and camped at Mount Hor, on the boundary of the land of Edom. Num. 20:22, 23; 21:4

38 Then Aaron the priest went up to Mount Hor at the command of the LORD, and died there in the fortieth year after the children of Israel had come out of the land of Egypt, on the first *day* of the fifth month.

39 Aaron *was* one hundred and twenty-three years old when he died on Mount Hor.

40 Now [R]the king of Arad, the Canaanite, who dwelt in the South in the land of Canaan, heard of the coming of the children of Israel. Num. 21:1

41 So they departed from Mount Hor and camped at Zalmonah.

42 They departed from Zalmonah and camped at Punon.

43 They departed from Punon and [R]camped at Oboth. Num. 21:10

44 They departed from Oboth and camped at Ije Abarim, at the border of Moab.

45 They departed from Ijim* and camped [R]at Dibon Gad. Num. 32:34

46 They moved from Dibon Gad and camped at [R]Almon Diblathaim. Jer. 48:22

47 They moved from Almon Diblathaim [R]and camped in the mountains of Abarim, before Nebo. Deut. 32:49

48 They departed from the mountains of Abarim and camped in the plains of Moab by the Jordan, *across from* Jericho.

49 They camped by the Jordan, from Beth Jesimoth as far as the [R]Abel Acacia Grove* in the plains of Moab. Num. 25:1

Instructions for Conquering Canaan

50 Now the LORD spoke to Moses in the plains of Moab by the Jordan, *across from* Jericho, saying,

51 "Speak to the children of Israel, and say to them: [R]'When you have crossed the Jordan into the land of Canaan, Josh. 3:17

52 [R]'then you shall drive out all the inhabitants of the land from before you, destroy all their engraved stones, destroy all their molded images, and demolish all their [T]high places; Deut. 7:2, 5; 12:3 • Places for pagan worship

33:8 Many Heb. mss., Sam., Syr., Tg., Vg. *from Pi Hahiroth;* cf. Num. 33:7 **33:45** Same as *Ije Abarim,* v. 44 **33:49** Heb. *Abel Shittim*

53 'you shall dispossess *the inhabitants of*
the land and dwell in it, for I have given you
the land to [R]possess. Deut. 11:31
54 'And [R]you shall divide the land by lot as an
inheritance among your families; to the larger
you shall give a larger inheritance, and to the
smaller you shall give a smaller inheritance;
there everyone's *inheritance* shall be whatever
falls to him by lot. You shall inherit according
to the tribes of your fathers. Num. 26:53–56
55 'But if you do not drive out the inhab-
itants of the land from before you, then it shall
be that those whom you let remain *shall be*
[R]irritants in your eyes and thorns in your
sides, and they shall harass you in the land
where you dwell. Josh. 23:13
56 'Moreover it shall be *that* I will do to you
as I thought to do to them.' "

CHAPTER 34

The South

THEN the LORD spoke to Moses, saying,
2 "Command the children of Israel, and
say to them: 'When you come into [R]the land of
Canaan, this *is* the land that shall fall to you
as an inheritance—the land of Canaan to its
boundaries. Gen. 17:8
3 'Your southern border shall be from the
Wilderness of Zin along the border of Edom;
then your southern border shall extend east-
ward to the end of [R]the Salt Sea; Gen. 14:3
4 'your border shall turn from the southern
side of [R]the Ascent of Akrabbim, continue to
Zin, and be on the south of Kadesh Barnea;
then it shall go on to Hazar Addar, and con-
tinue to Azmon; Josh. 15:3
5 'the border shall turn from Azmon [R]to
the Brook of Egypt, and it shall end at the
Sea. Josh. 15:4, 47

The West

6 'As for the [R]western border, you shall
have the Great Sea for a border; this shall be
your western border. Ezek. 47:20

The North

7 'And this shall be your northern border:
From the Great Sea you shall mark out your
border line to [R]Mount Hor; Num. 33:37
8 'from Mount Hor you shall mark out *your
border* [R]to the entrance of Hamath; then the
direction of the border shall be toward
[R]Zedad; Num. 13:21 • Ezek. 47:15
9 'the border shall proceed to Ziphron, and
it shall end at [R]Hazar Enan. This shall be your
northern border. Ezek. 47:17

The East

10 'You shall mark out your eastern border
from Hazar Enan to Shepham;
11 'the border shall go down from Shepham
to Riblah on the east side of Ain; the border
shall go down and reach to the eastern side of
the Sea of Chinnereth;
12 'the border shall go down along the Jor-
dan, and it shall end at [R]the Salt Sea. This
shall be your land with its surrounding
boundaries.' " Num. 34:3
13 Then Moses commanded the children of
Israel, saying: [R]"This *is* the land which you
shall inherit by lot, which the LORD has com-
manded to give to the nine tribes and to the
half-tribe. Josh. 14:1–5
14 "For the tribe of the children of Reuben
according to the house of their fathers, and
the tribe of the children of Gad according to
the house of their fathers, have received *their
inheritance;* and the half-tribe of Manasseh
has received its inheritance.
15 "The two tribes and the half-tribe have re-
ceived their inheritance on this side of the
Jordan, *across from* Jericho eastward, toward
the sunrise."

Officials for Dividing Canaan

16 And the LORD spoke to Moses, saying,
17 "These *are* the names of the men who
shall divide the land among you as an inheri-
tance: [R]Eleazar the priest and Joshua the son
of Nun. Josh. 14:1, 2; 19:51
18 "And you shall take one leader of every
tribe to divide the land for the inheritance.
19 "These *are* the names of the men: from
the tribe of Judah, Caleb the son of Jephun-
neh;
20 "from the tribe of the children of Simeon,
Shemuel the son of Ammihud;
21 "from the tribe of Benjamin, Elidad the
son of Chislon;
22 "a leader from the tribe of the children of
Dan, Bukki the son of Jogli;
23 "from the sons of Joseph: a leader from
the tribe of the children of Manasseh, Hanniel
the son of Ephod,
24 "and a leader from the tribe of the chil-
dren of Ephraim, Kemuel the son of Shiphtan;
25 "a leader from the tribe of the children of
Zebulun, Elizaphan the son of Parnach;
26 "a leader from the tribe of the children of
Issachar, Paltiel the son of Azzan;
27 "a leader from the tribe of the children of
Asher, Ahihud the son of Shelomi;
28 "and a leader from the tribe of the chil-
dren of Naphtali, Pedahel the son of Ammi-
hud."
29 These *are* the ones the LORD commanded
to divide the inheritance among the children
of Israel in the land of Canaan.

CHAPTER 35

Cities for the Levites

AND the LORD spoke to Moses in [R]the
plains of Moab by the Jordan *across
from* Jericho, saying: Num. 33:50

2 [R]"Command the children of Israel that they give the Levites cities to dwell in from the inheritance of their possession, and you shall *also* give the Levites common-land around the cities. Josh. 14:3, 4; 21:2, 3

3 "They shall have the cities to dwell in; and their common-land shall be for their cattle, for their herds, and for all their animals.

4 "The common-land of the cities which you will give the Levites *shall extend* from the wall of the city outward a thousand cubits all around.

5 "And you shall measure outside the city on the east side two thousand cubits, on the south side two thousand cubits, on the west side two thousand cubits, and on the north side two thousand cubits. The city *shall be* in the middle. This shall belong to them as common-land for the cities.

6 "Now among the cities which you will give to the Levites *you shall appoint* [R]six cities of refuge, to which a manslayer may flee. And to these you shall add forty-two cities. Josh. 20:2, 7, 8; 21:3, 13

7 "So all the cities you will give to the Levites *shall be* [R]forty-eight; these *you shall give* with their common-land. Josh. 21:41

8 "And the cities which you will give *shall be* [R]from the possession of the children of Israel; [R]from the larger *tribe* you shall give many, from the smaller you shall give few. Each shall give some of its cities to the Levites, in proportion to the inheritance that each receives." Josh. 21:3 • Num. 26:54; 33:54

Cities of Refuge

9 Then the LORD spoke to Moses, saying,

10 "Speak to the children of Israel, and say to them: [R]'When you cross the Jordan into the land of Canaan, Josh. 20:1–9

11 'then [R]you shall appoint cities to be cities of refuge for you, that the manslayer who kills any person accidentally may flee there. Ex. 21:13

12 [R]'They shall be cities of refuge for you from the avenger, that the manslayer may not die until he stands before the congregation in judgment. Deut. 19:6

13 'And of the cities which you give, you shall have [R]six cities of refuge. Num. 35:6

14 [R]'You shall appoint three cities on this side of the Jordan, and three cities you shall appoint in the land of Canaan, *which* will be cities of refuge. Deut. 4:41

15 'These six cities shall be for refuge for the children of Israel, [R]for the stranger, and for the sojourner among them, that anyone who kills a person accidentally may flee there. Num. 15:16

16 'But if he strikes him with an iron implement, so that he dies, he *is* a murderer; the murderer shall surely be put to death.

17 'And if he strikes him with a stone in the hand, by which one could die, and he does die, he *is* a murderer; the murderer shall surely be put to death.

18 'Or *if* he strikes him with a wooden hand weapon, by which one could die, and he does die, he *is* a murderer; the murderer shall surely be put to death.

19 [R]'The avenger of blood himself shall put the murderer to death; when he meets him, he shall put him to death. Num. 35:21, 24, 27

20 [R]'If he pushes him out of hatred or, [R]while lying in wait, hurls something at him so that he dies, Gen. 4:8 • Ex. 21:14

21 'or in enmity he strikes him with his hand so that he dies, the one who struck *him* shall surely be put to death. He *is* a murderer. The avenger of blood shall put the murderer to death when he meets him.

22 'However, if he pushes him suddenly [R]without enmity, or throws anything at him without lying in wait, Ex. 21:13

23 'or uses a stone, by which a man could die, throwing *it* at him without seeing *him*, so that he dies, while he was not his enemy or seeking his harm,

24 'then the congregation shall judge between the manslayer and the avenger of blood according to these judgments.

25 'So the congregation shall deliver the manslayer from the hand of the avenger of blood, and the congregation shall return him to the city of refuge where he had fled, and [R]he shall remain there until the death of the high priest [R]who was anointed with the holy oil. Josh. 20:6 • Ex. 29:7

26 'But if the manslayer at any time goes outside the limits of the city of refuge where he fled,

27 'and the avenger of blood finds him outside the limits of his city of refuge, and the avenger of blood kills the manslayer, he shall not be guilty of [T]blood, Murder

28 'because he should have remained in his city of refuge until the death of the high priest. But after the death of the high priest the manslayer may return to the land of his possession.

29 'And these *things* shall be [R]a statute of judgment to you throughout your generations in all your dwellings. Num. 27:11

30 'Whoever kills a person, the murderer shall be put to death on the [R]testimony of witnesses; but one witness is not *sufficient* testimony against a person for the death *penalty*. Deut. 17:6; 19:15

31 'Moreover you shall take no ransom for the life of a murderer who *is* guilty of death, but he shall surely be put to death.

32 'And you shall take no ransom for him who has fled to his city of refuge, that he may return to dwell in the land before the death of the priest.

33 'So you shall not pollute the land where

you *are;* for blood [R]defiles the land, and no
atonement can be made for the land, for the
blood that is shed on it, except [R]by the blood
of him who shed it. Ps. 106:38 • Gen. 9:6
34 'Therefore [R]do not defile the land which
you inhabit, in the midst of which I dwell; for
[R]I the LORD dwell among the children of Is-
rael.'" Lev. 18:24, 25 • Ex. 29:45, 46

CHAPTER 36

Special Problems of Inheritance in Canaan

NOW the chief fathers of the families of
the [R]children of Gilead the son of
Machir, the son of Manasseh, of the families
of the sons of Joseph, came near and spoke
before Moses and before the leaders, the chief
fathers of the children of Israel. Num. 26:29
2 And they said: [R]"The LORD commanded
my lord *Moses* to give the land as an inheri-
tance by lot to the children of Israel, and my
lord was commanded by the LORD to give the
inheritance of our brother Zelophehad to his
daughters. Josh. 17:4
3 "Now if they are married to any of the
sons of the *other* tribes of the children of Is-
rael, then their inheritance will be [R]taken
from the inheritance of our fathers, and it will
be added to the inheritance of the tribe into
which they marry; so it will be taken from the
lot of our inheritance. Num. 27:4
4 "And when [R]the Jubilee of the children of
Israel comes, then their inheritance will be
added to the inheritance of the tribe into
which they marry; so their inheritance will be
taken away from the inheritance of the tribe
of our fathers." Lev. 25:10
5 Then Moses commanded the children of
Israel according to the word of the LORD, say-
ing: [R]"What the tribe of the sons of Joseph
speaks is right. Num. 27:7
6 "This *is* what the LORD commands con-
cerning the daughters of Zelophehad, saying,
'Let them marry whom they think best, [R]but
they may marry only within the family of
their father's tribe.' Num. 36:11, 12
7 "So the inheritance of the children of Is-
rael shall not change hands from tribe to
tribe, for every one of the children of Israel
shall [R]keep the inheritance of the tribe of his
fathers. 1 Kin. 21:3
8 "And [R]every daughter who possesses an
inheritance in any tribe of the children of Is-
rael shall be the wife of one of the family of
her father's tribe, so that the children of Israel
each may possess the inheritance of his fa-
thers. 1 Chr. 23:22
9 "Thus no inheritance shall change hands
from *one* tribe to another, but every tribe of
the children of Israel shall keep its own in-
heritance."
10 Just as the LORD commanded Moses, so
did the daughters of Zelophehad;
11 [R]for Mahlah, Tirzah, Hoglah, Milcah, and
Noah, the daughters of Zelophehad, were
married to the sons of their father's broth-
ers. Num. 26:33; 27:1
12 They were married into the families of the
children of Manasseh the son of Joseph, and
their inheritance remained in the tribe of their
father's family.
13 These *are* the commandments and the
judgments which the LORD commanded the
children of Israel by the hand of Moses [R]in the
plains of Moab by the Jordan, *across from* Jer-
icho. Num. 26:3; 33:50

Weights

Unit	*Weight*	*Equivalents*	*Translations*
Jewish Weights			
Talent	c. 75 pounds for common talent, c. 150 pounds for royal talent	60 minas; 3,000 shekels	talent
Mina	1.25 pounds	50 shekels	mina
Shekel	c. .4 ounce (11.4 grams) for common shekel c. .8 ounce for royal shekel	2 bekas; 20 gerahs	shekel
Beka	c. .2 ounce (5.7 grams)	½ shekel; 10 gerahs	half a shekel
Gerah	c. .02 ounce (.57 grams)	¹⁄₂₀ shekel	gerah
Roman Weight			
Litra	12 ounces		pound

THE FIFTH BOOK OF MOSES CALLED

DEUTERONOMY

THE BOOK OF DEUTERONOMY

Deuteronomy, Moses' "Upper Desert Discourse," consists of a series of farewell messages by Israel's 120-year-old leader. It is addressed to the new generation destined to possess the land of promise—those who survived the forty years of wilderness wandering.

Like Leviticus, Deuteronomy contains a vast amount of legal detail, but its emphasis is on the laymen rather than the priests. Moses reminds the new generation of the importance of obedience if they are to learn from the sad example of their parents.

The Hebrew title of Deuteronomy is *Haddebharim,* "The Words," taken from the opening phrase in 1:1, "These *are* the words." The parting words of Moses to the new generation are given in oral and written form so that they will endure to all generations. Deuteronomy has been called "five-fifths of the Law" since it completes the five books of Moses. The Jewish people have also called it *Mishneh Hattorah,* "repetition of the Law," which is translated in the Septuagint as *To Deuteronomion Touto,* "This Second Law." Deuteronomy, however, is not a second law but an adaptation and expansion of much of the original law given on Mount Sinai. The English title comes from the Greek title *Deuteronomion,* "Second Law." Deuteronomy has also been appropriately called the "Book of Remembrance."

THE AUTHOR OF DEUTERONOMY

The Mosaic authorship of Deuteronomy has been vigorously attacked by critics who claim that Moses is only the originator of the tradition on which these laws are based. Some critics grant that part of Deuteronomy may have come from Mosaic times through oral tradition. The usual argument is that it was anonymously written not long before 621 B.C. and used by King Josiah to bring about his reform in that year (2 Kin. 22 and 23). There are several reasons why these arguments are not valid.

External Evidence: (1) The Old Testament attributes Deuteronomy and the rest of the Pentateuch to Moses (see Josh. 1:7; Judg. 3:4; 1 Kin. 2:3; 2 Kin. 14:6; Ezra 3:2; Neh. 1:7; Ps. 103:7; Dan. 9:11; Mal. 4:4). (2) Evidence from Joshua and 1 Samuel indicates that these laws existed in the form of codified written statutes and exerted an influence on the Israelites in Canaan. (3) Christ quotes it as God's Word in turning back Satan's three temptations (Matt. 4:4, 7, 10) and attributes it directly to Moses (Matt. 19:7–9; Mark 7:10; Luke 20:28; John 5:45–47). (4) Deuteronomy is cited more than eighty times in seventeen of the twenty-seven New Testament books. These citations support the Mosaic authorship (see Acts 3:22; Rom. 10:19). (5) Jewish and Samaritan traditions point to Moses.

Internal Evidence: (1) Deuteronomy includes about forty claims that Moses wrote it. Read Deuteronomy 31:24–26 (see also 1:1–5; 4:44–46; 29:1; 31:9). (2) Deuteronomy fits the time of Moses, not Josiah: Canaan is viewed from the outside; the Canaanite religion is seen as a future menace; it assumes the hearers remember Egypt and the wilderness; Israel is described as living in tents; and there is no evidence of a divided kingdom. (3) A serious problem of misrepresentation and literary forgery would arise if this book were written in the seventh century B.C. (4) Geographical and historical details indicate a firsthand knowledge. (5) Deuteronomy follows the treaty form used in the fifteenth and fourteenth centuries B.C. (6) Moses' obituary in chapter 34 was probably written by Joshua.

THE TIME OF DEUTERONOMY

Like Leviticus, Deuteronomy does not progress historically. It takes place entirely on the plains of Moab due east of Jericho and the Jordan River (1:1; 29:1; Josh. 1:2). It covers about one month: combine Deuteronomy 1:3 and 34:8 with Joshua 5:6–12. The book was written at the end of the forty-year period in the wilderness (c. 1405 B.C.) when the new generation was on the verge of entering Canaan. Moses wrote it to encourage the people to believe and obey God in order to receive God's blessings.

THE CHRIST OF DEUTERONOMY

The most obvious portrait of Christ is found in 18:15: "The LORD your God will raise up for you a Prophet like me from your midst, from your brethren. Him you shall hear" (see also 18:16–19; Acts 7:37). Moses is a type of Christ in many ways as he is the only biblical figure other than Christ to fill the three offices of prophet (34:10–12), priest (Ex. 32:31–35), and king (although Moses was not king, he functioned as ruler of Israel; 33:4, 5). Both are in danger of death during childhood; both are saviors, intercessors, and believers; and both are rejected by their brethren. Moses is one of the greatest men who ever lived, combining not just one or two memorable virtues but many.

KEYS TO DEUTERONOMY

Key Word: Covenant—The primary theme of the entire Book of Deuteronomy is the renewal of the covenant. Originally established at Mount Sinai, the covenant is enlarged and renewed on the plains of Moab.

Key Verses: Deuteronomy 10:12, 13; 30:19, 20—"And now, Israel, what does the LORD your God require of you, but to fear the LORD your God, to walk in all His ways and to love Him, to serve the LORD your God with all your heart and with all your soul, *and* to keep the commandments of the LORD and His statutes which I command you today for your good?" (10:12, 13).

"I call heaven and earth as witnesses today against you, *that* I have set before you life and death, blessing and cursing; therefore choose life, that both you and your descendants may live; that you may love the LORD your God, that you may obey His voice, and that you may cling to Him, for He *is* your life and the length of your days; and that you may dwell in the land which the LORD swore to your fathers, to Abraham, Isaac, and Jacob, to give them" (30:19, 20).

Key Chapter: Deuteronomy 27—The formal ratification of the covenant occurs in Deuteronomy 27 as Moses, the priests, the Levites, and all of Israel "take heed and listen, O Israel: This day you have become the people of the LORD your God" (27:9).

SURVEY OF DEUTERONOMY

Deuteronomy, in its broadest outline, is the record of the renewal of the old covenant given at Mount Sinai. This covenant is reviewed, expanded, enlarged, and finally ratified in the plains of Moab. Moses accomplishes this primarily through three sermons that move from a retrospective, to an introspective, and finally to a prospective look at God's dealings with Israel.

Moses' First Sermon (1:1—4:43): Moses reaches into the past to remind the people of two undeniable facts in their history: (1) the moral judgment of God upon Israel's unbelief, and (2) the deliverance and provision of God during times of obedience. The simple lesson is that obedience brings blessing and disobedience brings punishment.

Moses' Second Sermon (4:44—26:19): This moral and legal section is the longest in the book because Israel's future as a nation in Canaan will depend upon a right relationship with God. These chapters review the three categories of the Law: (1) The testimonies (5—11). These are the moral duties—a restatement and expansion of the Ten Commandments plus an exhortation not to forget God's gracious deliverance. (2) The statutes (12:1—16:17). These are the ceremonial duties—sacrifices, tithes, and feasts. (3) The ordinances (16:18—26:19). These are the civil (16:18—20:20) and social (21—26) duties—the system of justice, criminal laws, laws of warfare, rules of property, personal and family morality, and social justice.

Moses' Third Sermon (27—34): In these chapters Moses writes history in advance. He predicts what will befall Israel in the near future (blessings and cursings) and in the distant future (dispersion among the nations and eventual return). Moses lists the terms of the covenant soon to be ratified by the people. Because Moses will not be allowed to enter the land, he appoints Joshua as his successor and delivers a farewell address to the multitude. God Himself buries Moses in an unknown place, perhaps to prevent idolatry. Moses finally enters the Promised Land when he appears with Christ on the Mount of Transfiguration (Matt. 17:3). The last three verses of the Pentateuch (34:10–12) are an appropriate epitaph for this great man.

FOCUS	FIRST SERMON	SECOND SERMON				THIRD SERMON		
REFERENCE	1:1 — 4:44 — 12:1 — 16:18 — 21:1 — 27:1 — 29:1 — 31:1 — 34:12							
DIVISION	REVIEW OF GOD'S ACTS FOR ISRAEL	EXPOSITION OF THE DECALOGUE	CEREMONIAL LAWS	CIVIL LAWS	SOCIAL LAWS	RATIFICATION OF COVENANT	PALESTINIAN COVENANT	TRANSITION OF COVENANT MEDIATOR
TOPIC	WHAT GOD HAS DONE	WHAT GOD EXPECTED OF ISRAEL				WHAT GOD WILL DO		
	HISTORICAL	LEGAL				PROPHETICAL		
LOCATION	PLAINS OF MOAB							
TIME	c. 1 MONTH							

OUTLINE OF DEUTERONOMY

Part One: Moses' First Sermon: "What God Has Done for Israel" (1:1—4:43)

I. The Preamble of the Covenant 1:1–5

II. The Review of God's Acts for Israel ....1:6—4:43

A. From Mount Sinai to Kadesh 1:6–18
B. At Kadesh 1:19–46
C. From Kadesh to Moab 2:1–23
1. "Do Not Meddle with Edom" 2:1–8
2. "Do Not Harass Moab" 2:9–15
3. "Do Not Harass Ammon" 2:16–23
D. Conquest of East Jordan ....2:24—3:29
1. The Conquest of Sihon 2:24–37
2. The Conquest of Og 3:1–11
3. Land Is Granted to Two-and-a-Half Tribes 3:12–20
E. Transition of Leadership 3:21–29
F. Summary of the Covenant 4:1–43

Part Two: Moses' Second Sermon: "What God Expects of Israel" (4:44—26:19)

I. The Introduction to the Law of God ..4:44–49

II. The Exposition of the Decalogue ...5:1—11:32

A. The Covenant of the Great King 5:1–33
1. Setting of the Covenant 5:1–5
2. Commandments of the Covenant 5:6–21
3. Response of Israel 5:22–27
4. Response of God 5:28–33
B. The Command to Teach the Law 6:1–25
C. The Command to Conquer Canaan 7:1–26
D. The Command to Remember the Lord 8:1–20
E. The Commands About Self-Righteousness ....9:1—10:11
1. Moses Rehearses Israel's Rebellion 9:1–29
2. Moses Rehearses God's Mercy 10:1–11
F. The Commands Regarding Blessings and Cursings ....10:12—11:32
1. Love God 10:12–22
2. Study and Obey the Commands 11:1–21
3. Victory Depends upon Obedience 11:22–32

III. The Exposition of the Additional Laws ....12:1—26:19

A. The Exposition of the Ceremonial Laws ....12:1—16:17
1. Law of the Central Sanctuary 12:1–28
2. Law of Idolatry ....12:29—13:18
3. Law of Food 14:1–21
4. Law of the Tithes 14:22–29
5. Law of the Debts 15:1–11
6. Law of the Slaves 15:12–18
7. Law of the Firstborn 15:19–23
8. Law of the Feasts 16:1–17
B. The Exposition of the Civil Laws ....16:18—20:20
1. Law of the Administration of the Judges ....16:18—17:13
2. Law of the Administration of the King 17:14–20
3. Law of the Administration of the Priest and Prophet 18:1–22
4. Cities of Refuge 19:1–14
5. Law of Witnesses 19:15–21
6. Law of Warfare 20:1–20
C. The Exposition of the Social Laws ....21:1—26:19
1. Law of Unknown Murder 21:1–9
2. Law of the Family ....21:10—22:30
3. Law of Acceptance into the Congregation 23:1–23
4. Laws for Harmony in the Nation ....23:24—25:19
5. Law of the Tithe 26:1–15
6. Vow of Israel and of God 26:16–19

Part Three: Moses' Third Sermon: "What God Will Do for Israel" (27:1—34:12)

I. The Ratification of the Covenant in Canaan ....27:1—28:68

A. Erection of the Altar 27:1–8
B. Admonition to Obey the Law 27:9, 10
C. Proclamation of the Curses 27:11–26
D. Warnings of the Covenant 28:1–68
1. Promised Blessings for Obedience .28:1–14
2. Promised Curses for Disobedience 28:15–68

II. The Institution of the Palestinian Covenant ....29:1—30:20

A. The Covenant Is Based on the Power of God 29:1–9
B. Parties of the Covenant 29:10–15
C. Warnings of the Covenant ....29:16—30:10
1. Scattering of Israel 29:16–29
2. Restoration of Israel 30:1–10
D. Ratification of the Palestinian Covenant 30:11–20

III. The Transition of the Covenant Mediator ....31:1—34:12

A. Moses Charges Joshua and Israel 31:1–13
B. God Charges Israel 31:14–21
C. The Book of the Law Is Deposited 31:22–30
D. The Song of Moses 32:1–47
E. The Death of Moses ....32:48—34:12
1. Moses Is Ordered to Mount Nebo 32:48–52
2. Moses Blesses the Tribes 33:1–29
3. Moses Views the Promised Land 34:1–4
4. Moses Dies and Is Mourned 34:5–8
5. Moses Is Replaced by Joshua 34:9
6. Moses Is Extolled in Israel 34:10–12

CHAPTER 1

The Preamble of the Covenant

THESE *are* the words which Moses spoke
to all Israel [R]on this side of the Jordan in
the wilderness, in the plain* opposite Suph,*
between Paran, Tophel, Laban, Hazeroth, and
Dizahab. Deut. 4:44–46
2 *It is* eleven days' *journey* from Horeb by
way of Mount Seir to Kadesh Barnea.
3 Now it came to pass in the fortieth year, in
the eleventh month, on the first *day* of the
month, *that* Moses spoke to the children of Is-
rael according to all that the LORD had given
him as commandments to them,
4 [R]after he had killed Sihon king of the
Amorites, who dwelt in Heshbon, and Og
king of Bashan, who dwelt at Ashtaroth [R]in*
Edrei. Num. 21:23, 24, 33–35 • Josh. 13:12
5 On this side of the Jordan in the land of
Moab, Moses began to explain this law, saying,

From Mount Sinai to Kadesh—Ex. 18:18–26

6 "The LORD our God spoke to us [R]in Horeb,
saying: 'You have dwelt long [R]enough at this
mountain. Ex. 3:1, 12 • Ex. 19:1, 2
7 'Turn and take your journey, and go to the
mountains of the Amorites, to all the neighbor-
ing *places* in the plain,* in the mountains and in
the lowland, in the South and on the seacoast,
to the land of the Canaanites and to Lebanon,
as far as the great river, the River Euphrates.
8 'See, I have set the land before you; go in
and possess the land which the LORD [T]swore
to your fathers—to [R]Abraham, Isaac, and Ja-
cob—to give to them and their descendants
after them.' *promised* • Gen. 12:7
9 "And I spoke to you at that time, saying: 'I
alone am not able to bear you.
10 'The LORD your God has multiplied you,
[R]and here you *are* today, as the stars of
heaven in multitude. Gen. 15:5; 22:17
11 [R]'May the LORD God of your fathers make
you a thousand times more numerous than
you are, and bless you [R]as He has promised
you! 2 Sam. 24:3 • Gen. 15:5
12 'How can I alone bear your problems and
your burdens and your complaints?
13 'Choose wise, understanding, and knowl-
edgeable men from among your tribes, and I
will make them heads over you.'
14 "And you answered me and said, 'The
thing which you have told *us* to do *is* good.'
15 "So I took [R]the heads of your tribes, wise
and knowledgeable men, and made them
heads over you, leaders of thousands, leaders
of hundreds, leaders of fifties, leaders of tens,
and officers for your tribes. Ex. 18:25
16 "Then I commanded your judges at that
time, saying, 'Hear *the cases* between your
brethren, and [R]judge righteously between a
man and his [R]brother or the stranger who is
with him. Deut. 16:18 • Lev. 24:22
17 [R]'You shall not show partiality in judg-
ment; you shall hear the small as well as the
great; you shall not be afraid in any man's
presence, for [R]the judgment *is* God's. The case
that is too hard for you, bring to me, and I will
hear it.' Prov. 24:23–26 • 2 Chr. 19:6
18 "And I commanded you at that time all the
things which you should do.

At Kadesh—Num. 13:1—14:45

19 "So we departed from Horeb, and went
through all that great and terrible wilderness
which you saw on the way to the mountains
of the Amorites, as the LORD our God had
commanded us. Then [R]we came to Kadesh
Barnea. Num. 13:26
20 "And I said to you, 'You have come to the
mountains of the Amorites, which the LORD
our God is giving us.
21 'Look, the LORD your God has set the land
before you; go up *and* possess *it,* as the LORD
God of your fathers has spoken to you; [R]do
not fear or be discouraged.' Josh. 1:6, 9
22 "And every one of you came near to me
and said, 'Let us send men before us, and let
them search out the land for us, and bring
back word to us of the way by which we
should go up, and of the cities into which we
shall come.'
23 "The plan pleased me well; so [R]I took
twelve of your men, one man from *each*
tribe. Num. 13:2, 3
24 [R]"And they departed and went up into the
mountains, and came to the Valley of Eshcol,
and spied it out. Num. 13:21–25
25 "They also took *some* of the fruit of the
land in their hands and brought *it* down to us;
and they brought back word to us, saying, '*It
is* a [R]good land which the LORD our God is giv-
ing us.' Num. 13:27
26 [R]"Nevertheless you would not go up, but
rebelled against the command of the LORD
your God; Num. 14:1–4
27 "and you [R]complained in your tents, and
said, 'Because the LORD [R]hates us, He has
brought us out of the land of Egypt to deliver
us into the hand of the Amorites, to destroy
us. Ps. 106:25 • Deut. 9:28
28 'Where can we go up? Our brethren have
discouraged our hearts, saying, [R]"The people
are greater and taller than we; the cities *are*
great and fortified up to heaven; moreover
we have seen the sons of the [R]Anakim
there." ' Deut. 9:1, 2 • Num. 13:28
29 "Then I said to you, 'Do not be terrified,
[R]or afraid of them. Num. 14:9
30 'The LORD your God, who goes before
you, He will fight for you, according to all He
did for you in Egypt before your eyes,
31 'and in the wilderness where you saw

1:1 Heb. *arabah* • One LXX ms., Tg., Vg. *Red Sea*
1:4 LXX, Syr., Vg. *and;* cf. Josh. 12:4 **1:7** Heb. *arabah*

how the LORD your God carried you, as a
[R]man carries his son, in all the way that you
went until you came to this place.' Is. 63:9
32 "Yet, for all that, [R]you did not believe the
LORD your God, Jude 5
33 "who went in the way before you to
search out a place for you to pitch your tents,
to show you the way you should go, in the fire
by night and in the cloud by day.
34 "And the LORD heard the sound of your
words, and was angry, [R]and took an oath,
saying, Deut. 2:14, 15
35 'Surely not one of these men of this evil
generation shall see that good land of which I
[T]swore to give to your fathers, *promised*
36 [R]'except Caleb the son of Jephunneh; he
shall see it, and to him and his children I am
giving the land on which he walked, because
he wholly followed the LORD.' [Josh. 14:9]
37 [R]"The LORD was also angry with me for
your sakes, saying, 'Even you shall not go in
there. Deut. 3:26; 4:21; 34:4
38 'Joshua the son of Nun, who stands be-
fore you, he shall go in there. Encourage him,
for he shall cause Israel to inherit it.
39 'Moreover your little ones and your chil-
dren, who you say will be victims, who today
[R]have no knowledge of good and evil, they
shall go in there; to them I will give it, and
they shall possess it. Is. 7:15, 16
40 [R]'But *as for* you, turn and take your jour-
ney into the wilderness by the Way of the Red
Sea.' Num. 14:25
41 "Then you answered and said to me, 'We
have sinned against the LORD; we will go up
and fight, just as the LORD our God com-
manded us.' And when everyone of you had
girded on his weapons of war, you were ready
to go up into the mountain.
42 "And the LORD said to me, 'Tell them,
[R]"Do not go up nor fight, for I *am* not among
you; lest you be defeated before your ene-
mies." ' Num. 14:41–43
43 "So I spoke to you; yet you would not lis-
ten, but [R]rebelled against the command of the
LORD, and [R]presumptuously went up into the
mountain. Num. 14:44 • Deut. 17:12, 13
44 "And the Amorites who dwelt in that
mountain came out against you and chased
you [R]as bees do, and drove you back from Seir
to Hormah. Ps. 118:12
45 "Then you returned and wept before the
LORD, but the LORD would not listen to your
voice nor give ear to you.
46 [R]"So you remained in Kadesh many
days, according to the days that you spent
there. Deut. 2:7, 14

CHAPTER 2

"Do Not Meddle with Edom"—Num. 21:4

"THEN we turned and journeyed into the
wilderness of the Way of the Red Sea,
[R]as the LORD spoke to me, and we skirted
Mount Seir for many days. Num. 14:25
2 "And the LORD spoke to me, saying:
3 'You have skirted this mountain [R]long
enough; turn northward. Deut. 2:7, 14
4 'And command the people, saying, "You
are about to pass through the territory of
your brethren, the descendants of Esau, who
live in Seir; and they will be afraid of you.
Therefore watch yourselves carefully.
5 "Do not meddle with them, for I will not
give you *any* of their land, no, not so much as
one footstep, [R]because I have given Mount
Seir to Esau *as* a possession. Gen. 36:8
6 "You shall buy food from them with
money, that you may eat; and you shall also
buy water from them with money, that you
may drink.
7 "For the LORD your God has blessed you
in all the work of your hand. He knows your
trudging through this great wilderness. These
forty years the LORD your God *has been* with
you; you have lacked nothing." '
8 "And when we passed beyond our
brethren, the descendants of Esau who dwell
in Seir, away from the road of the plain,
away from [R]Elath and Ezion Geber, we
[R]turned and passed by way of the Wilderness
of Moab. Judg. 11:18 • Num. 21:4

"Do Not Harass Moab"

9 "Then the LORD said to me, 'Do not harass
Moab, nor contend with them in battle, for I
will not give you *any* of their land *as* a pos-
session, because I have given Ar to the de-
scendants of Lot *as* a possession.' "
10 [R](The Emim had dwelt there in times past,
a people as great and numerous and tall as
[R]the Anakim. Gen. 14:5 • Deut. 9:2
11 They were also regarded as giants,* like
the Anakim, but the Moabites call them
Emim.
12 [R]The Horites formerly dwelt in Seir, but
the descendants of Esau dispossessed them
and destroyed them from before them, and
dwelt in their [T]place, just as Israel did to the
land of their possession which the LORD gave
them.) Deut. 2:22 • *stead*
13 " 'Now rise and cross over [R]the [T]Valley of
the Zered.' So we crossed over the Valley of
the Zered. Num. 21:12 • *Wadi* or *Brook*
14 "And the time we took to come from
Kadesh Barnea until we crossed over the Val-
ley of the Zered *was* thirty-eight years, until
all the generation of the men of war was con-
sumed from the midst of the camp, just as the
LORD had sworn to them.
15 "For indeed the hand of the LORD was
against them, to destroy them from the
midst of the camp until they [T]were con-
sumed. *perished*

2:11 Heb. *rephaim*

"Do Not Harass Ammon"

16 "So it was, when all the men of war had finally perished from among the people,
17 "that the LORD spoke to me, saying:
18 'This day you are to cross over at Ar, the boundary of Moab.
19 'And *when* you come near the people of Ammon, do not harass them or meddle with them, for I will not give you *any* of the land of the people of Ammon *as* a possession, because I have given it to [R]the descendants of Lot *as* a possession.' " Gen. 19:38
20 (That was also regarded as a land of giants;* giants formerly dwelt there. But the Ammonites call them Zamzummim,
21 [R]a people as great and numerous and tall as the Anakim. But the LORD destroyed them before them, and they dispossessed them and dwelt in their place, Deut. 2:10
22 just as He had done for the descendants of Esau, [R]who dwelt in Seir, when He destroyed [R]the Horites from before them. They dispossessed them and dwelt in their place, even to this day. Gen. 36:8 • Gen. 14:6; 36:20–30
23 And [R]the Avim, who dwelt in villages as far as Gaza—[R]the Caphtorim, who came from Caphtor, destroyed them and dwelt in their place.) Josh. 13:3 • Gen. 10:14

The Conquest of Sihon—Num. 21:21–25

24 " 'Rise, take your journey, and [R]cross over the River Arnon. Look, I have given into your hand [R]Sihon the Amorite, king of Heshbon, and his land. Begin to possess *it*, and engage him in battle. Judg. 11:18 • Deut. 1:4
25 [R]'This day I will begin to put the dread and fear of you upon the nations under the whole heaven, who shall hear the report of you, and shall [R]tremble and be in anguish because of you.' Ex. 23:27 • Ex. 15:14–16
26 "And I sent messengers from the Wilderness of Kedemoth to Sihon king of Heshbon, with words of peace, saying,
27 [R]'Let me pass through your land; I will keep strictly to the road, and I will turn neither to the right nor to the left. Judg. 11:19
28 'You shall sell me food for money, that I may eat, and give me water for money, that I may drink; [R]only let me pass through on foot, Num. 20:19
29 'just as the descendants of Esau who dwell in Seir and the Moabites who dwell in Ar did for me, until I cross the Jordan to the land which the LORD our God is giving us.'
30 "But Sihon king of Heshbon would not let us pass through, for the LORD your God [R]hardened his spirit and made his heart obstinate, that He might deliver him into your hand, as *it is* this day. Ex. 4:21
31 "And the LORD said to me, 'See, I have begun to [R]give Sihon and his land over to you. Begin to possess *it*, that you may inherit his land.' Deut. 1:3, 8
32 [R]"Then Sihon and all his people came out against us to fight at Jahaz. Num. 21:23
33 "And [R]the LORD our God delivered him over to us; so [R]we defeated him, his sons, and all his people. Deut. 7:2 • Num. 21:24
34 "We took all his cities at that time, and we [R]utterly destroyed the men, women, and little ones of every city; we left none remaining. Lev. 27:28
35 "We took only the livestock as plunder for ourselves, with the spoil of the cities which we took.
36 [R]"From Aroer, which *is* on the bank of the River Arnon, and *from* the city that *is* in the ravine, as far as Gilead, there was not one city too strong for us; [R]the LORD our God delivered all to us. Deut. 3:12; 4:48 • Ps. 44:3
37 "Only you did not go near the land of the people of Ammon—anywhere along the River [R]Jabbok, or to the cities of the mountains, or [R]wherever the LORD our God had forbidden us. Gen. 32:22 • Deut. 2:5, 9, 19

CHAPTER 3

The Conquest of Og—Num. 21:33–35

"THEN we turned and went up the road to Bashan; and [R]Og king of Bashan came out against us, he and all his people, to battle [R]at Edrei. Num. 21:33–35 • Deut. 1:4
2 "And the LORD said to me, 'Do not fear him, for I have delivered him and all his people and his land into your hand; you shall do to him as you did to Sihon king of the Amorites, who dwelt at Heshbon.'
3 "So the LORD our God also delivered into our hands Og king of Bashan, with all his people, and we [T]attacked him until he had no survivors remaining. *struck*
4 "And we took all his cities at that time; there was not a city which we did not take from them: sixty cities, all the region of Argob, the kingdom of Og in Bashan.
5 "All these cities *were* fortified with high walls, gates, and bars, besides a great many rural towns.
6 "And we utterly destroyed them, as we did to Sihon king [R]of Heshbon, utterly destroying the men, women, and children of every city. Deut. 2:24, 34, 35
7 "But all the livestock and the spoil of the cities we took as booty for ourselves.
8 "And at that time we took the land from the hand of the two kings of the Amorites who *were* on this side of the Jordan, from the River Arnon to Mount Hermon
9 "(the Sidonians call [R]Hermon Sirion, and the Amorites call it Senir), 1 Chr. 5:23
10 "all the cities of the plain, all Gilead, and

2:20 Heb. *rephaim*

all Bashan, as far as Salcah and Edrei, cities
of the kingdom of Og in Bashan.
11 [R]"For only Og king of Bashan remained of
the remnant of the giants.* Indeed his bed-
stead *was* an iron bedstead. (*Is* it not in Rab-
bah of the people of Ammon?) Nine cubits *is*
its length and four cubits its width, according
to the standard cubit. Amos 2:9

Land Is Granted to Two and a Half Tribes
Num. 32:25–41

12 "And this [R]land, *which* we possessed at
that time, [R]from Aroer, which *is* by the River
Arnon, and half the mountains of Gilead and
[R]its cities, I gave to the Reubenites and the
Gadites. Num. 32:33 • Deut. 2:36 • Num. 34:14
13 "The rest of Gilead, and all Bashan, the
kingdom of Og, I gave to half the tribe of Ma-
nasseh. (All the region of Argob, with all
Bashan, was called the land of the giants.*
14 [R]"Jair the son of Manasseh took all the re-
gion of Argob, [R]as far as the border of the
Geshurites and the Maachathites, and called
Bashan after his own name, Havoth Jair,* to
this day.) 1 Chr. 2:22 • Josh. 13:13
15 "Also I gave Gilead to Machir.
16 "And to the Reubenites [R]and the Gadites I
gave from Gilead as far as the River Arnon,
the middle of the river as *the* border, as far as
the River Jabbok, [R]the border of the people of
Ammon; 2 Sam. 24:5 • Num. 21:24
17 "the plain also, with the Jordan as *the*
border, from Chinnereth [R]as far as the east
side of the Sea of the Arabah (the Salt Sea),
below the slopes of Pisgah. Num. 34:11, 12
18 "Then I commanded you at that time, say-
ing: 'The LORD your God has given you this
land to possess. [R]All you men of valor shall
cross over armed before your brethren, the
children of Israel. Num. 32:20
19 'But your wives, your little ones, and your
livestock (I know that you have much live-
stock) shall stay in your cities which I have
given you,
20 'until the LORD has given [R]rest to your
brethren as to you, and they also possess the
land which the LORD your God is giving them
beyond the Jordan. Then each of you may [R]re-
turn to his possession which I have given
you.' Deut. 12:9, 10 • Josh. 22:4

Transition of Leadership

21 "And I commanded Joshua at that time,
saying, 'Your eyes have seen all that the LORD
your God has done to these two kings; so will
the LORD do to all the kingdoms through
which you pass.
22 'You must not fear them, for [R]the LORD
your God Himself fights for you.' Ex. 14:14
23 "Then [R]I pleaded with the LORD at that
time, saying: [2 Cor. 12:8, 9]
24 'O Lord GOD, You have begun to show
Your servant Your greatness and Your [T]mighty
hand, for what god *is there* in heaven or on
earth who can do *anything* like Your works
and Your mighty *deeds*? *strong*
25 'I pray, let me cross over and see [R]the
good land beyond the Jordan, those pleasant
mountains, and Lebanon.' Deut. 4:22
26 "But the LORD [R]was angry with me on
your account, and would not listen to me. So
the LORD said to me: 'Enough of that! Speak
no more to Me of this matter. Num. 20:12
27 [R]'Go up to the top of Pisgah, and lift your
eyes toward the west, the north, the south, and
the east; behold *it* with your eyes, for you shall
not cross over this Jordan. Num. 23:14; 27:12
28 'But command Joshua, and encourage
him and strengthen him; for he shall go over
before this people, and he shall cause them to
inherit the land which you will see.'
29 "So we stayed in [R]the valley opposite Beth
Peor. Deut. 4:46; 34:6

CHAPTER 4

Summary of the Covenant

"NOW, O Israel, listen to [R]the statutes and
the judgments which I teach you to ob-
serve, that you may live, and go in and pos-
sess the land which the LORD God of your
fathers is giving you. [Rom. 10:5]
2 [R]"You shall not add to the word which I
command you, nor take from it, that you may
keep the commandments of the LORD your
God which I command you. Prov. 30:6
3 "Your eyes have seen what the LORD did
at [R]Baal Peor; for the LORD your God has de-
stroyed from among you all the men who fol-
lowed Baal of Peor. Num. 25:1–9
4 "But you who held fast to the LORD your
God *are* alive today, every one of you.
5 "Surely I have taught you statutes and
judgments, just as the LORD my God com-
manded me, that you should act according *to*
them in the land which you go to possess.
6 "Therefore be careful to observe *them;*
for this *is* [R]your wisdom and your under-
standing in the sight of the peoples who will
hear all these statutes, and say, 'Surely this
great nation *is* a wise and understanding peo-
ple.' [2 Tim. 3:15]
7 "For [R]what great nation *is there* that has
[R]God[T] *so* near to it, as the LORD our God *is* to
us, for whatever *reason* we may call upon
Him? [2 Sam. 7:23] • [Is. 55:6] • Or *a god*
8 "And what great nation *is there* that has
such statutes and righteous judgments as are
in all this law which I set before you this day?
9 "Only take heed to yourself, and dili-
gently [R]keep yourself, lest you [R]forget the
things your eyes have seen, and lest they de-
part from your heart all the days of your life.

3:11 Heb. *rephaim* **3:13** Heb. *rephaim* **3:14** Lit. *Towns of Jair*

And teach them to your children and your
grandchildren, Prov. 4:23 • Deut. 29:2–8
10 “*especially concerning* [R]the day you stood
before the LORD your God in Horeb, when the
LORD said to me, ‘Gather the people to Me,
and I will let them hear My words, that they
may learn to fear Me all the days they live on
the earth, and *that* they may teach their chil-
dren.’ Ex. 19:9, 16, 17
11 “Then you came near and stood at the
foot of the mountain, and the mountain
burned with fire to the midst of heaven, with
darkness, cloud, and thick darkness.
12 [R]“And the LORD spoke to you out of the
midst of the fire. You heard the sound of the
words, but saw no [T]form; [R]*you* only *heard* a
voice. Deut. 5:4, 22 • *similitude* • 1 Kin. 19:11–18
13 “So He declared to you His covenant
which He commanded you to perform, the Ten
Commandments; and [R]He wrote them on two
tablets of stone. Ex. 24:12
14 “And [R]the LORD commanded me at that
time to teach you statutes and judgments, that
you might observe them in the land which you
cross over to possess. Ex. 21:1
15 “Take careful heed to yourselves, for you
saw no form when the LORD spoke to you at
Horeb out of the midst of the fire,
16 “lest you act corruptly and make for your-
selves a carved image in the form of any fig-
ure: the likeness of male or female,
17 “the likeness of any animal that *is* on the
earth or the likeness of any winged bird that
flies in the air,
18 “the likeness of anything that creeps on
the ground or the likeness of any fish that *is* in
the water beneath the earth.
19 “And *take heed,* lest you [R]lift your eyes to
heaven, and *when* you see the sun, the moon,
and the stars, [R]all the host of heaven, you feel
driven to [R]worship them and serve them,
which the LORD your God has given to all the
peoples under the whole heaven as a her-
itage. Deut. 17:3 • 2 Kin. 21:3 • [Rom. 1:25]
20 “But the LORD has taken you and
[R]brought you out of the iron furnace, out of
Egypt, to be [R]His people, an inheritance, as
you are this day. Jer. 11:4 • Deut. 7:6; 27:9
21 “Furthermore the LORD was angry with
me for your sakes, and swore that I would not
cross over the Jordan, and that I would not
enter the good land which the LORD your God
is giving you as an inheritance.
22 “But I must die in this land, I must not
cross over the Jordan; but you shall cross over
and possess that good land.
23 “Take heed to yourselves, lest you forget
the covenant of the LORD your God which He
made with you, and make for yourselves a
carved image in the form of anything which
the LORD your God has forbidden you.
24 “For [R]the LORD your God *is* a consuming
fire, [R]a jealous God. Deut. 9:3 • Ex. 20:5; 34:14

25 “When you beget children and grandchil-
dren and have grown old in the land, and
act corruptly and make a carved image in
the form of anything, and [R]do evil in the
sight of the LORD your God to provoke Him
to anger, 2 Kin. 17:17
26 [R]“I call heaven and earth to witness
against you this day, that you will soon ut-
terly perish from the land which you cross
over the Jordan to possess; you will not [T]pro-
long *your* days in it, but will be utterly de-
stroyed. Deut. 30:18, 19 • *live long on it*
27 “And the LORD [R]will scatter you among
the peoples, and you will be left few in num-
ber among the nations where the LORD will
drive you. Deut. 28:62
28 “And [R]there you will serve gods, the
work of men's hands, wood and stone,
[R]which neither see nor hear nor eat nor
smell. Jer. 16:13 • Ps. 115:4–7; 135:15–17
29 [R]“But from there you will seek the LORD
your God, and you will find *Him* if you seek
Him with all your heart and with all your
soul. [2 Chr. 15:4]
30 “When you are in [T]distress, and all these
things come upon you in the [R]latter days,
when you [R]turn to the LORD your God and
obey His voice *tribulation* • Hos. 3:5 • Joel 2:12
31 “(for the LORD your God *is* a merciful
God), He will not forsake you nor [R]destroy
you, nor forget the covenant of your fathers
which He swore to them. Jer. 30:11
32 “For ask now concerning the days that
are past, which were before you, since the day
that God created man on the earth, and *ask*
from one end of heaven to the other, whether
any great *thing* like this has happened, or
anything like it has been heard.
33 [R]“Did *any* people *ever* hear the voice of
God speaking out of the midst of the fire, as
you have heard, and live? Deut. 5:24–26
34 “Or did God *ever* try to go *and* take for
Himself a nation from the midst of *another*
nation, [R]by trials, [R]by signs, by wonders, by
war, [R]by a mighty hand and an outstretched
arm, and by great terrors, according to all that
the LORD your God did for you in Egypt before
your eyes? Deut. 7:19 • Ex. 7:3 • Ex. 13:3
35 “To you it was shown, that you might
know that the LORD Himself *is* God; [R]*there is*
none other besides Him. Mark 12:32
36 “Out of heaven He let you hear His voice,
that He might instruct you; on earth He
showed you His great fire, and you heard His
words out of the midst of the fire.
37 “And because He loved your fathers,
therefore He chose their descendants after
them; and He brought you out of Egypt with
His Presence, with His mighty power,
38 [R]“driving out from before you nations
greater and mightier than you, to bring you in,
to give you their land *as* an inheritance, as *it*
is this day. Deut. 7:1

39 "Therefore know this day, and consider *it*
in your heart, that [R]the LORD Himself *is* God in
heaven above and on the earth beneath; *there*
is no other. Josh. 2:11
40 "You shall therefore keep His statutes and
His commandments which I command you
today, that it may go well with you and with
your children after you, and that you may pro-
long *your* days in the land which the LORD
your God is giving you for all time."
41 Then Moses [R]set apart three cities on this
side of the Jordan, toward the rising of the
sun, Num. 35:6
42 that the manslayer might flee there, who
kills his neighbor unintentionally, without
having hated him in time past, and that by
fleeing to one of these cities he might live:
43 [R]Bezer in the wilderness on the plateau
for the Reubenites, Ramoth in Gilead for the
Gadites, and Golan in Bashan for the Ma-
nassites. Josh. 20:8

The Introduction to the Law of God

44 Now this *is* the law which Moses set be-
fore the children of Israel.
45 These *are* the testimonies, the statutes,
and the judgments which Moses spoke to the
children of Israel after they came out of
Egypt,
46 on this side of the Jordan, in the valley op-
posite Beth Peor, in the land of Sihon king of
the Amorites, who dwelt at Heshbon, whom
Moses and the children of Israel defeated[T]
after they came out of Egypt. *struck*
47 And they took possession of his land and
the land of Og king of Bashan, two kings of
the Amorites, who *were* on this side of the
Jordan, toward the rising of the sun,
48 [R]from Aroer, which *is* on the bank of the
River Arnon, even to Mount Sion* (that is,
[R]Hermon), Deut. 2:36; 3:12 • Deut. 3:9
49 and all the plain on the east side of the
Jordan as far as the Sea of the Arabah, below
the [R]slopes of Pisgah. Deut. 3:17

CHAPTER 5

Setting of the Covenant

AND Moses called all Israel, and said to
them: "Hear, O Israel, the statutes and
judgments which I speak in your hearing
today, that you may learn them and be careful
to observe them.
2 [R]"The LORD our God made a covenant
with us in Horeb. Ex. 19:5
3 "The LORD [R]did not make this covenant
with our fathers, but with us, those who *are*
here today, all of us who *are* alive. Heb. 8:9
4 "The LORD talked with you face to face on
the mountain from the midst of the fire.
5 [R]"I stood between the LORD and you at
that time, to declare to you the word of the
LORD; for [R]you were afraid because of the
fire, and you did not go up the mountain. *He*
said: Gal. 3:19 • Ex. 19:16

Commandments of the Covenant

6 [R]'I *am* the LORD your God who brought
you out of the land of Egypt, out of
the house of bondage. Ex. 20:2–17
7 [R]'You shall have no other gods [T]before
Me. Hos. 13:4 • *besides*
8 'You shall not make for yourself a carved
image—any likeness *of anything* that
is in heaven above, or that *is* in the
earth beneath, or that *is* in the water
under the earth;
9 you shall not bow down to them nor
serve them. For I, the LORD your God,
am a jealous God, visiting the iniq-
uity of the fathers upon the children
to the third and fourth *generations* of
those who hate Me,
10 [R]but showing mercy to thousands, to
those who love Me and keep My com-
mandments. Dan 9:4
11 [R]'You shall not take the name of the LORD
your God in vain, for the LORD will
not hold *him* guiltless who takes His
name in vain. Ex. 20:7
12 [R]Observe the Sabbath day, to [T]keep it
holy, as the LORD your God com-
manded you. Ex. 20:8 • *sanctify it*
13 [R]Six days you shall labor and do all
your work, Ex. 23:12; 35:2
14 but the seventh day *is* the Sabbath of
the LORD your God. *In it* you shall do
no work: you, nor your son, nor your
daughter, nor your male servant, nor
your female servant, nor your ox, nor
your donkey, nor any of your cattle,
nor your stranger who *is* within your
gates, that your male servant and
your female servant may rest as well
as you.
15 [R]And remember that you were a slave
in the land of Egypt, and the LORD
your God brought you out from there
by a mighty hand and by an out-
stretched arm; therefore the LORD
your God commanded you to keep
the Sabbath day. Deut. 15:15
16 [R]'Honor your father and your mother, as
the LORD your God has commanded
you, [R]that your days may be long, and
that it may be well with you in the
land which the LORD your God is giv-
ing you. Lev. 19:3 • Deut. 6:2
17 [R]'You shall not murder. Matt. 5:21
18 'You shall not commit adultery.
19 [R]'You shall not steal. [Rom. 13:9]
20 [R]'You shall not bear false witness against
your neighbor. Ex. 20:16; 23:1
21 [R]'You shall not covet your neighbor's

4:48 Syr. *Sirion*

wife; and you shall not desire your
neighbor's house, his field, his male
servant, his female servant, his ox,
his donkey, or anything that *is* your
neighbor's.' Ex. 20:17

Response of Israel

22 "These words the LORD spoke to all your
assembly, in the mountain from the midst of
the fire, the cloud, and the thick darkness,
with a loud voice; and He added no more. And
[R]He wrote them on two tablets of stone and
gave them to me. Deut. 4:13
23 [R]"So it was, when you heard the voice
from the midst of the darkness, while the
mountain was burning with fire, that you
came near to me, all the heads of your tribes
and your elders. Ex. 20:18, 19
24 "And you said: 'Surely the LORD our God
has shown us His glory and His greatness,
and we have heard His voice from the midst of
the fire. We have seen this day that God
speaks with man; yet he *still* lives.
25 'Now therefore, why should we die? For
this great fire will consume us; [R]if we hear the
voice of the LORD our God anymore, then we
shall die. Deut. 18:16
26 [R]'For who *is there* of all flesh who has
heard the voice of the living God speaking
from the midst of the fire, as we *have*, and
lived? Deut. 4:33
27 'You go near and hear all that the LORD
our God may say, and [R]tell us all that the
LORD our God says to you, and we will hear
and do *it*.' Ex. 20:19

Response of God

28 "Then the LORD heard the voice of your
words when you spoke to me, and the LORD
said to me: 'I have heard the voice of the
words of this people which they have spoken
to you. [R]They are right *in* all that they have
spoken. Deut. 18:17
29 [R]'Oh, that they had such a heart in them
that they would fear Me and [R]always keep
all My commandments, [R]that it might be
well with them and with their children for-
ever! Ps. 81:13 • Deut. 11:1 • Deut. 4:40
30 'Go and say to them, "Return to your tents."
31 'But as for you, stand here by Me, and I
will speak to you all the commandments, the
statutes, and the judgments which you shall
teach them, that they may observe *them* in the
land which I am giving them to possess.'
32 "Therefore you shall [T]be careful to do as
the LORD your God has commanded you; [R]you
shall not turn aside to the right hand or to the
left. *observe* • Deut. 17:20; 28:14
33 "You shall walk in all the ways which the
LORD your God has commanded you, that you
may live and *that it may be* well with you, and
that you may prolong *your* days in the land
which you shall possess.

CHAPTER 6

The Command to Teach the Law

"NOW this *is* the commandment, *and*
these are the statutes and judgments
which the LORD your God has commanded to
teach you, that you may observe *them* in the
land which you are crossing over to possess,
2 "that you may fear the LORD your God, to
keep all His statutes and His commandments
which I command you, you and your son and
your grandson, all the days of your life, and
that your days may be prolonged.
3 "Therefore hear, O Israel, and be careful
to observe *it*, that it may be well with you, and
that you may multiply greatly as the LORD
God of your fathers has promised you—'a
land flowing with milk and honey.'*
4 [R]"Hear, O Israel: The LORD our God, the
LORD *is* one!* [1 Cor. 8:4, 6]
5 [R]"You shall love the LORD your God with
all your heart, [R]with all your soul, and with all
your strength. Matt. 22:37 • 2 Kin. 23:25
6 "And these words which I command you
today shall be in your heart.
7 "You shall teach them diligently to your
children, and shall talk of them when you sit
in your house, when you walk by the way,
when you lie down, and when you rise up.
8 [R]"You shall bind them as a sign on your
hand, and they shall be as frontlets between
your eyes. Prov. 3:3; 6:21; 7:3

6:3 Ex. 3:8 **6:4** Or *The LORD is our God, the LORD alone,* i.e., the only one

---

6:4–9 Three Essentials for a Christian Home—A new generation of Israel is gathered on the plains of Moab to hear Moses review the law in preparation for their entrance to the Promised Land. The previous generation had died in unbelief in the wilderness. Moses begins his instruction by telling the people of Israel what a home is all about. He sets forth three components that must be true if the home is rightly related to God:

a. There must be a revelation of God (6:4). God revealed three things about Himself: (1) His eternality (Yahweh; Hebrew *YHWH*, The Eternal); (2) His plurality (*Elohim*, Hebrew plural of God, there are three Persons in the Godhead); and (3) His unity—"one LORD"—the three Persons of the Godhead constitute one God; each is essential.
b. There must be a response to God's revelation (6:5). The response is to be a total response of love with all one's being, heart, soul, and mind. This is the only fitting response to the eternal God who has revealed Himself.

(continued on next page)

9 "You shall write them on the doorposts of your house and on your gates.

10 "So it shall be, when the LORD your God brings you into the land of which He swore to your fathers, to Abraham, Isaac, and Jacob, to give you large and beautiful cities [R]which you did not build, Josh. 24:13

11 "houses full of all good things, which you did not fill, hewn-out wells which you did not dig, vineyards and olive trees which you did not plant—[R]when you have eaten and are full— Deut. 8:10; 11:15; 14:29

12 "*then* beware, lest you forget the [R]LORD who brought you out of the land of Egypt, from the house of bondage. Deut. 8:11–18

13 "You shall [R]fear the LORD your God and serve Him, and [R]shall take oaths in His name. Matt. 4:10 • Deut. 5:11

14 "You shall not go after other gods, the gods of the peoples who *are* all around you

15 "(for the LORD your God *is* a jealous God among you), lest the anger of the LORD your God be aroused against you and destroy you from the face of the earth.

16 "You shall not [T]tempt the LORD your God as you tempted *Him* in Massah. *test*

17 "You shall [R]diligently keep the commandments of the LORD your God, His testimonies, and His statutes which He has commanded you. Deut. 11:22

18 "And you [R]shall do *what is* right and good in the sight of the LORD, that it may be well with you, and that you may go in and possess the good land of which the LORD swore to your fathers, Ex. 15:26

19 "to cast out all your enemies from before you, as the LORD has spoken.

20 [R]"When your son asks you in time to come, saying, 'What *is the meaning of* the testimonies, the statutes, and the judgments which the LORD our God has commanded you?' Ex. 13:8, 14

21 "then you shall say to your son: 'We were slaves of Pharaoh in Egypt, and the LORD brought us out of Egypt [R]with a mighty hand; Ex. 13:3

22 'and the LORD showed signs and wonders before our eyes, great and severe, against Egypt, Pharaoh, and all his household.

23 'Then He brought us out from there, that He might bring us in, to give us the land of which He swore to our fathers.

24 'And the LORD commanded us to observe all these statutes, to fear the LORD our God, for our good always, that He might preserve us alive, as *it is* this day.

25 'Then [R]it will be righteousness for us, if we are careful to observe all these commandments before the LORD our God, as He has commanded us.' [Rom. 10:3, 5]

CHAPTER 7

The Command to Conquer Canaan

"WHEN the LORD your God brings you into the land which you go to possess, and has cast out many nations before you, the Hittites and the Girgashites and the Amorites and the Canaanites and the Perizzites and the Hivites and the Jebusites, seven nations greater and mightier than you,

2 "and when the LORD your God delivers [R]them over to you, you shall conquer them *and* utterly destroy them. [R]You shall make no covenant with them nor show mercy to them. Num. 31:17 • Josh. 2:14

3 [R]"Nor shall you make marriages with them. You shall not give your daughter to their son, nor take their daughter for your son. 1 Kin. 11:2

4 "For they will turn your sons away from following Me, to serve other gods; [R]so the anger of the LORD will be aroused against you and destroy you suddenly. Deut. 6:15

5 "But thus you shall deal with them: you shall [R]destroy their altars, and break down their *sacred* pillars, and cut down their wooden images,* and burn their carved images with fire. Ex. 23:24; 34:13

6 "For you *are* a [T]holy people to the LORD your God; [R]the LORD your God has chosen you to be a people for Himself, a special treasure above all the peoples on the face of the earth. *set-apart* • Ex. 19:5, 6

7 "The LORD did not set His [R]love on you nor choose you because you were more in number than any other people, for you were the least of all peoples; Deut. 4:37

8 "but [R]because the LORD loves you, and be-

7:5 Heb. *Asherim,* Canaanite deities

(continued from previous page)

c. There must be a threefold responsibility (6:6–9). This threefold responsibility acts as a check upon the proper response. If the earthly father responds to God with love, he will be fulfilling his threefold responsibility. If he fails in any particular, confession of sin is necessary because he does not love God with all his heart, soul, and mind. The threefold responsibility is: (1) to have God's truth govern his heart (6:6)—there must be heart reality, not mere external conformity or ceremony; (2) to have God's truth govern his home—this is evidenced by the fact that the father teaches the truths of God's revelation to his children by both formal (teach diligently) and informal (talk of them) instruction; and (3) to have God's truth govern his habits and conduct personally, privately, and publicly. In short, the home is to be a divine school in which the father is to be the teacher, under Christ.

Now turn to Page 1281—1 Pet. 3:1–6: The Role of the Wife.

cause He would keep the oath which He swore to your fathers, the LORD has brought you out with a mighty hand, and redeemed you from the house of bondage, from the hand of Pharaoh king of Egypt. Deut. 10:15

9 "Therefore know that the LORD your God, He *is* God, [R]the faithful God [R]who keeps covenant and mercy for a thousand generations with those who love Him and keep His commandments; 1 Cor. 1:9 • Neh. 1:5

10 "and He repays those who hate Him to their face, to destroy them. He will not [T]be [R]slack with him who hates Him; He will repay him to his face. *delay* • [2 Pet. 3:9, 10]

11 "Therefore you shall keep the commandment, the statutes, and the judgments which I command you today, to observe them.

12 "Then it shall come to pass, because you listen to these judgments, and keep and do them, that the LORD your God will keep with you the covenant and the mercy which He swore to your fathers.

13 "And He will love you and bless you and multiply you; He will also bless the fruit of your womb and the fruit of your land, your grain and your new wine and your oil, the increase of your cattle and the offspring of your flock, in the land of which He swore to your fathers to give you.

14 "You shall be blessed above all peoples; there shall not be a male or female barren among you or among your livestock.

15 "And the LORD will take away from you all sickness, and will afflict you with none of the [R]terrible diseases of Egypt which you have known, but will lay *them* on all those who hate you. Ex. 9:14; 15:26

16 "Also you shall [T]destroy all the peoples whom the LORD your God delivers over to you; your eye shall have no pity on them; nor shall you serve their gods, for that *will* be a snare to you. *consume* • Judg. 8:27

17 "If you should say in your heart, 'These nations are greater than I; how can I dispossess them?'—

18 "you shall not be afraid of them, *but* you shall remember well what the LORD your God did to Pharaoh and to all Egypt:

19 [R]"the great trials which your eyes saw, the signs and the wonders, the mighty hand and the outstretched arm, by which the LORD your God brought you out. So shall the LORD your God do to all the peoples of whom you are afraid. Deut. 4:34; 29:3

20 [R]"Moreover the LORD your God will send the hornet among them until those who are left, who hide themselves from you, are destroyed. Josh. 24:12

21 "You shall not be terrified of them; for the LORD your God, the great and awesome God, *is* among you.

22 "And the LORD your God will drive out those nations before you [R]little by little; you will be unable to [T]destroy them at once, lest the beasts of the field become *too* numerous for you. Ex. 23:29, 30 • *consume*

23 "But the LORD your God will deliver them over to you, and will inflict defeat upon them until they are destroyed.

24 "And [R]He will deliver their kings into your hand, and you will destroy their name from under heaven; [R]no one shall be able to stand [T]against you until you have destroyed them. Josh. 10:24, 42; 12:1–24 • Josh. 23:9 • *before*

25 "You shall burn the carved images of their gods with fire; you shall not covet the silver or gold *that is* on them, nor take *it* for yourselves, lest you be snared by it; for it *is* an abomination to the LORD your God.

26 "Nor shall you bring an abomination into your house, lest you be doomed to destruction like it. You shall utterly detest it and utterly abhor it, [R]for it *is* an [T]accursed thing. Deut. 13:17 • *devoted* or *banned*

CHAPTER 8

The Command to Remember the Lord

"EVERY commandment which I command you today [R]you must be careful to observe, that you may live and multiply, and go in and possess the land of which the LORD swore to your fathers. Deut. 4:1; 6:24

2 "And you shall remember that the LORD your God [R]led you all the way these forty years in the wilderness, to humble you *and* [R]test you, [R]to know what *was* in your heart, whether you would keep His commandments or not. Amos 2:10 • Ex. 16:4 • [John 2:25]

3 "So He humbled you, allowed you to hunger, and [R]fed you with manna which you did not know nor did your fathers know, that He might make you know that man shall [R]not live by bread alone; but man lives by every *word* that proceeds from the mouth of the LORD. Ex. 16:12, 14, 35 • Matt. 4:4

4 [R]"Your garments did not wear out on you, nor did your foot swell these forty years. Neh. 9:21

5 [R]"You should [T]know in your heart that as a man chastens his son, *so* the LORD your God chastens you. 2 Sam. 7:14 • *consider*

6 "Therefore you shall keep the commandments of the LORD your God, [R]to walk in His ways and to fear Him. [Deut. 5:33]

7 "For the LORD your God is bringing you into a good land, [R]a land of brooks of water, of fountains and springs, that flow out of valleys and hills; Deut. 11:9–12

8 "a land of wheat and barley, of vines and fig trees and pomegranates, a land of olive oil and honey;

9 "a land in which you will eat bread without scarcity, in which you will lack nothing; a land whose stones *are* iron and out of whose hills you can dig copper.

10 "When you have eaten and are full, then you shall bless the LORD your God for the good land which He has given you.

11 "Beware that you do not forget the LORD your God by not keeping His commandments, His judgments, and His statutes which I command you today,

12 [R]"lest—*when* you have eaten and are [T]full, and have built beautiful houses and dwell *in them;* Hos. 13:6 • *satisfied*

13 "and *when* your herds and your flocks multiply, and your silver and your gold are [T]multiplied, and all that you have is multiplied; *increased*

14 [R]"when your heart [T]is lifted up, and you [R]forget the LORD your God who brought you out of the land of Egypt, from the house of bondage; 1 Cor. 4:7 • *becomes proud* • Ps. 106:21

15 "who [R]led you through that great and terrible wilderness, *in which were* fiery serpents and scorpions and thirsty land where there was no water; who brought water for you out of the flinty rock; Is. 63:12–14

16 "who fed you in the wilderness with manna, which your fathers did not know, that He might humble you and that He might test you, to do you good in the end—

17 "then you say in your heart, 'My power and the might of my hand have gained me this wealth.'

18 "And you shall remember the LORD your God, [R]for *it is* He who gives you power to get wealth, [R]that He may [T]establish His covenant which He swore to your fathers, as *it is* this day. Hos. 2:8 • Deut. 7:8, 12 • *confirm*

19 "Then it shall be, if you by any means forget the LORD your God, and follow other gods, and serve them and worship them, [R]I testify against you this day that you shall surely perish. Deut. 4:26; 30:18

20 "As the nations which the LORD destroys before you, [R]so you shall perish, because you would not be obedient to the voice of the LORD your God. [Dan. 9:11, 12]

CHAPTER 9

Moses Rehearses Israel's Rebellion

"HEAR, O Israel: You *are* to cross over the Jordan today, and go in to dispossess nations greater and mightier than yourself, cities great and fortified up to heaven,

2 "a people great and tall, the descendants of the Anakim, whom you know, and *of whom* you heard *it said,* 'Who can stand before the descendants of Anak?'

3 "Therefore understand today that the LORD your God *is* He who goes over before you *as* a consuming fire. He will destroy them and bring them down before you; so you shall drive them out and destroy them quickly, as the LORD has said to you.

4 [R]"Do not think in your heart, after the LORD your God has cast them out before you, saying, 'Because of my righteousness the LORD has brought me in to possess this land'; but *it is* because of the wickedness of these nations *that* the LORD is driving them out from before you. Deut. 8:17

5 [R]"*It is* not because of your righteousness or the uprightness of your heart *that* you go in to possess their land, but because of the wickedness of these nations *that* the LORD your God drives them out from before you, and that He may fulfill the [R]word which the LORD swore to your fathers, to Abraham, Isaac, and Jacob. [Titus 3:5] • Gen. 50:24

6 "Therefore understand that the LORD your God is not giving you this good land to possess because of your righteousness, for you *are* a [R]stiff-necked people. Deut. 31:27

7 "Remember! Do not forget how you [R]provoked the LORD your God to wrath in the wilderness. [R]From the day that you departed from the land of Egypt until you came to this place, you have been rebellious against the LORD. Num. 14:22 • Ex. 14:11

8 "Also [R]in Horeb you provoked the LORD to wrath, so that the LORD was angry *enough* with you to have destroyed you. Ex. 32:1–8

9 [R]"When I went up into the mountain to receive the tablets of stone, the tablets of the covenant which the LORD made with you, then I stayed on the mountain forty days and [R]forty nights. I neither ate bread nor drank water. Deut. 5:2–22 • Ex. 24:18

10 [R]"Then the LORD delivered to me two tablets of stone written with the finger of God, and on them *were* all the words which the LORD had spoken to you on the mountain from the midst of the fire [R]in the day of the assembly. Deut. 4:13 • Ex. 19:17

11 "And it came to pass, at the end of forty days and forty nights, *that* the LORD gave me the two tablets of stone, the tablets of the covenant.

12 "Then the LORD said to me, 'Arise, go down quickly from here, for your people whom you brought out of Egypt have acted corruptly; they have quickly turned aside from the way which I commanded them; they have made themselves a molded image.'

13 "Furthermore [R]the LORD spoke to me, saying, 'I have seen this people, and indeed they are a stiff-necked people. Ex. 32:9

14 [R]'Let Me alone, that I may destroy them and blot out their name from under heaven; [R]and I will make of you a nation mightier and greater than they.' Ex. 32:10 • Num. 14:12

15 [R]"So I turned and came down from the mountain, and the mountain burned with fire; and the two tablets of the covenant *were* in my two hands. Ex. 32:15–19

16 "And [R]I looked, and behold, you had sinned against the LORD your God—had made for yourselves a molded calf! You had turned

aside quickly from the way which the LORD had commanded you. Ex. 32:19

17 "Then I took the two tablets and threw them out of my two hands and [R]broke them before your eyes. Ex. 32:19

18 "And I [R]fell[T] down before the LORD, as at the first, forty days and forty nights; I neither ate bread nor drank water, because of all your sin which you committed in doing wickedly in the sight of the LORD, to provoke Him to anger. Ex. 34:28 • *prostrated myself*

19 [R]"For I was afraid of the anger and hot displeasure with which the LORD was angry with you, to destroy you. But the LORD listened to me at that time also. Ex. 32:10, 11

20 "And the LORD was very angry with Aaron *and* would have destroyed him; so I prayed for Aaron also at the same time.

21 "Then I took your sin, the calf which you had made, and burned it with fire and crushed it *and* ground *it* very small, until it was as fine as dust; and I [R]threw its dust into the brook that descended from the mountain. Ex. 32:20

22 "Also at [R]Taberah and [R]Massah and [R]Kibroth Hattaavah you provoked the LORD to wrath. Num. 11:1, 3 • Ex. 17:7 • Num. 11:4, 34

23 "Likewise, [R]when the LORD sent you from Kadesh Barnea, saying, 'Go up and possess the land which I have given you,' then you rebelled against the commandment of the LORD your God, and [R]you did not believe Him nor obey His voice. Num. 13:3 • Ps. 106:24, 25

24 "You have been rebellious against the LORD from the day that I knew you.

25 [R]"Thus I [T]prostrated myself before the LORD; forty days and forty nights I kept prostrating myself, because the LORD had said He would destroy you. Deut. 9:18 • *fell down*

26 "Therefore I prayed to the LORD, and said: 'O Lord GOD, do not destroy Your people and [R]Your inheritance whom You have redeemed through Your greatness, whom You have brought out of Egypt with a mighty hand. Deut. 32:9

27 'Remember Your servants, Abraham, Isaac, and Jacob; do not look on the stubbornness of this people, or on their wickedness or their sin,

28 'lest the land from which You brought us should say, "Because the LORD was not able to bring them to the land which He promised them, and because He hated them, He has brought them out to kill them in the wilderness."

29 'Yet they *are* Your people and Your inheritance, whom You brought out by Your mighty power and by Your outstretched arm.'

CHAPTER 10

Moses Rehearses God's Mercy

"AT that time the LORD said to me, 'Hew for yourself two tablets of stone like the first, and come up to Me on the mountain and make yourself an [R]ark of wood. Ex. 25:10

2 'And I will write on the tablets the words that were on the first tablets, which you broke; and you shall put them in the ark.'

3 "So I made an ark of acacia wood, hewed two tablets of stone like the first, and went up the mountain, having the two tablets in my hand.

4 "And He wrote on the tablets according to the first writing, the Ten [T]Commandments, [R]which the LORD had spoken to you in the mountain from the midst of the fire in the day of the assembly; and the LORD gave them to me. Lit. *Words* • Ex. 20:1; 34:28

5 "Then I turned and came down from the mountain, and put the tablets in the ark which I had made; and there they are, just as the LORD commanded me."

6 (Now the children of Israel journeyed from the wells of Bene Jaakan to Moserah, where Aaron [R]died, and where he was buried; and Eleazar his son ministered as priest in his stead. Num. 20:25–28; 33:38

7 [R]From there they journeyed to Gudgodah, and from Gudgodah to Jotbathah, a land of [T]rivers of water. Num. 33:32–34 • *brooks*

8 At that time [R]the LORD separated the tribe of Levi [R]to bear the ark of the covenant of the LORD, to stand before the LORD to minister to Him and to bless in His name, to this day. Num. 3:6 • Num. 4:5, 15; 10:21

9 [R]Therefore Levi has no portion nor inheritance with his brethren; the LORD *is* his inheritance, just as the LORD your God promised him.) Deut. 18:1, 2

10 "As at the first time, I stayed in the mountain forty days and forty nights; [R]the LORD also heard me at that time, *and* the LORD chose not to destroy you. Ex. 32:14

11 "Then the LORD said to me, 'Arise, begin *your* journey before the people, that they may go in and possess the land which I swore to their fathers to give them.'

Love God

12 "And now, Israel, what does the LORD your God require of you, but to fear the LORD your God, to walk in all His ways and to love Him, to serve the LORD your God with all your heart and with all your soul,

13 "*and* to keep the commandments of the LORD and His statutes which I command you today [R]for your good? Deut. 6:24

14 "Indeed heaven and the highest heavens belong to the [R]LORD your God, *also* the earth with all that *is* in it. [Neh. 9:6]

15 "The LORD delighted only in your fathers, to love them; and He chose their [T]descendants after them, you above all peoples, as *it is* this day. Lit. *seed*

16 "Therefore circumcise the foreskin of your heart, and be stiff-necked no longer.

17 "For the LORD your God *is* [R]God of gods
and [R]Lord of lords, the great God, mighty and
awesome, who [R]shows no partiality nor takes
a bribe. Dan. 2:47 • Rev. 19:16 • Acts 10:34
18 [R]"He administers justice for the fatherless
and the widow, and loves the stranger, giving
him food and clothing. Ps. 68:5; 146:9
19 "Therefore love the stranger, for you were
strangers in the land of Egypt.
20 [R]"You shall fear the LORD your God; you
shall serve Him, and to Him you shall hold
fast, and take oaths in His name. Matt. 4:10
21 "He *is* your praise, and He *is* your God,
who has done for you these great and awe-
some things which your eyes have seen.
22 "Your fathers went down to Egypt with
seventy persons, and now the LORD your God
has made you as the stars of heaven in multi-
tude.

CHAPTER 11

Study and Obey the Commands

"THEREFORE you shall love the LORD
your God, and keep His charge, His
statutes, His judgments, and His command-
ments always.
2 "Know today that *I do* not *speak* with
your children, who have not known and who
have not seen the [T]chastening of the LORD
your God, His greatness and His mighty hand
and His outstretched arm— *discipline*
3 "His signs and His acts which He did in
the midst of Egypt, to Pharaoh king of Egypt,
and to all his land;
4 "what He did to the army of Egypt, to
their horses and their chariots: how He made
the waters of the Red Sea overflow them as
they pursued you, and *how* the LORD has de-
stroyed them to this day;
5 "what He did for you in the wilderness
until you came to this place;
6 "and what He did to Dathan and Abiram
the sons of Eliab, the son of Reuben: how the
earth opened its mouth and swallowed them
up, their households, their tents, and all the
substance that *was* in their possession, in the
midst of all Israel—
7 "but your eyes have [R]seen every great act
of the LORD which He did. Deut. 29:2
8 "Therefore you shall keep every com-
mandment which I command you today, that
you may [R]be strong, and go in and possess the
land which you cross over to possess, Josh. 1:6, 7
9 "and that you may prolong *your* days in
the land which the LORD swore to give your
fathers, to them and their descendants, 'a land
flowing with milk and honey.'*
10 "For the land which you go to possess *is*
not like the land of Egypt from which you
have come, where you sowed your seed and
watered *it* by foot, as a vegetable garden;
11 "but the land which you cross over to pos-
sess *is* a land of hills and valleys, which
drinks water from the rain of heaven,
12 "a land for which the LORD your God
cares; [R]the eyes of the LORD your God *are* al-
ways on it, from the beginning of the year to
the very end of the year. 1 Kin. 9:3
13 'And it shall be that if you earnestly [T]obey
My commandments which I command you
today, to love the LORD your God and serve
Him with all your heart and with all your
soul, Lit. *listen to*
14 'then I* will give *you* the rain for your
land in its season, the early rain and the latter
rain, that you may gather in your grain, your
new wine, and your oil.
15 [R]'And I will send grass in your fields for
your livestock, that you may [R]eat and be
[T]filled.' Ps. 104:14 • Deut. 6:11 • *satisfied*
16 "Take heed to yourselves, lest your heart
be deceived, and you turn aside and serve
other gods and worship them,
17 "lest the LORD's anger be aroused against
you, and He shut up the heavens so that there
be no rain, and the land yield no produce, and
you perish quickly from the good land which
the LORD is giving you.
18 "Therefore [R]you shall lay up these
words of mine in your heart and in your
[R]soul, and [R]bind them as a sign on your
hand, and they shall be as frontlets between
your eyes. Deut. 6:6–9 • Ps. 119:2, 34 • Deut. 6:8
19 [R]"You shall teach them to your children,
speaking of them when you sit in your house,
when you walk by the way, when you lie
down, and when you rise up. Deut. 6:7
20 "And you shall write them on the door-
posts of your house and on your gates,
21 "that [R]your days and the days of your
children may be multiplied in the land of
which the LORD swore to your fathers to give
them, like [R]the days of the heavens above the
earth. Deut. 4:40 • Ps. 72:5; 89:29

Victory Depends upon Obedience

22 "For if [R]you carefully keep all these com-
mandments which I command you to do—to
love the LORD your God, to walk in all His
ways, and to hold fast to Him— Deut. 11:1
23 "then the LORD will [R]drive out all these
nations from before you, and you will [R]dispos-
sess greater and mightier nations than your-
selves. Deut. 4:38 • Deut. 9:1
24 [R]"Every place on which the sole of your
foot treads shall be yours: [R]from the wilder-
ness and Lebanon, from the river, the River
Euphrates, even to the Western Sea,* shall be
your territory. Josh. 1:3; 14:9 • Gen. 15:18
25 "No man shall be able to stand against
you; the LORD your God will put the dread of

11:9 Ex. 3:8 **11:14** So with MT, Tg.; Sam., LXX, Vg. *He* **11:24** Mediterranean

you and the fear of you upon all the land
where you tread, just as He has said to you.
26 [R]"Behold, I set before you today a bless-
ing and a curse: Deut. 30:1, 15, 19
27 [R]"the blessing, if you obey the command-
ments of the LORD your God which I com-
mand you today; Deut. 28:1–14
28 "and the [R]curse, if you do not obey the
commandments of the LORD your God, but
turn aside from the way which I command
you today, to go after other gods which you
have not known. Deut. 28:15–68
29 "Now it shall be, when the LORD your God
has brought you into the land which you go to
possess, that you shall put the [R]blessing on
Mount Gerizim and the [R]curse on Mount
Ebal. Josh. 8:33 • Deut. 27:13–26
30 "*Are* they not on the other side of the
Jordan, toward the setting sun, in the land of
the Canaanites who dwell in the plain oppo-
site Gilgal, [R]beside the terebinth trees of
Moreh? Gen. 12:6
31 "For you will cross over the Jordan and go
in to possess the land which the LORD your
God is giving you, and you will possess it and
dwell in it.
32 "And you shall be careful to observe all
the statutes and judgments which I set before
you today.

CHAPTER 12

Law of the Central Sanctuary

"THESE [R]*are* the statutes and judgments
which you shall be careful to observe in
the land which the LORD God of your fathers
is giving you to possess, [R]all the days that you
live on the earth. Deut. 6:1 • Deut. 4:9, 10
2 [R]"You shall utterly destroy all the places
where the nations which you shall dispos-
sess served their gods, [R]on the high moun-
tains and on the hills and under every green
tree. Ex. 34:13 • 2 Kin. 16:4; 17:10, 11
3 "And [R]you shall destroy their altars, break
their *sacred* pillars, and burn their wooden
images with fire; you shall cut down the
carved images of their gods and destroy their
names from that place. Num. 33:52
4 "You shall not [R]worship the LORD your
God *with* such *things.* Deut. 12:31
5 "But you shall seek the [R]place where the
LORD your God chooses, out of all your tribes,
to put His name for His dwelling place; and
there you shall go. Ex. 20:24
6 [R]"There you shall take your burnt offer-
ings, your sacrifices, your tithes, the heave of-
ferings of your hand, your vowed offerings,
your freewill offerings, and the firstborn of
your herds and flocks. Lev. 17:3, 4
7 "And [R]there you shall eat before the LORD
your God, and you shall rejoice in all to which
you have put your hand, you and your house-
holds, in which the LORD your God has
blessed you. Deut. 14:26
8 "You shall not at all do as we are doing
here today—[R]every man doing whatever *is*
right in his own eyes— Judg. 17:6; 21:25
9 "for as yet you have not come to the [R]rest
and the inheritance which the LORD your God
is giving you. Deut. 3:20; 25:19
10 "But *when* you cross over the Jordan and
dwell in the land which the LORD your God is
giving you to inherit, and He gives you [R]rest
from all your enemies round about, so that
you dwell in safety, Josh. 11:23
11 "then there will be the place where the
LORD your God chooses to make His name
abide. There you shall bring all that I com-
mand you: your burnt offerings, your sacri-
fices, your tithes, the heave offerings of your
hand, and all your choice offerings which you
vow to the LORD.
12 "And [R]you shall rejoice before the LORD
your God, you and your sons and your
daughters, your male and female servants,
and the [R]Levite who *is* within your gates,
since he has no portion nor inheritance with
you. Deut. 12:18; 26:11 • Deut. 10:9; 14:29
13 "Take heed to yourself that you do not
offer your burnt offerings in every place that
you see;
14 "but in the place which the LORD chooses,
in one of your tribes, there you shall offer
your burnt offerings, and there you shall do
all that I command you.
15 "However, [R]you may slaughter and eat
meat within all your gates, whatever your
heart desires, according to the blessing of the
LORD your God which He has given you; the un-
clean and the clean may eat of it, of the
gazelle and the deer alike. Deut. 12:21
16 "Only you shall not eat the blood; you
shall pour it on the earth like water.
17 "You may not eat within your gates the
tithe of your grain or your new wine or your
oil, of the firstborn of your herd or your flock,
of any of your offerings which you vow, of
your freewill offerings, or of the [T]heave offer-
ing of your hand. *contribution*
18 "But you must eat them before the LORD
your God in the place which the LORD your
God chooses, you and your son and your
daughter, your male servant and your female
servant, and the Levite who *is* within your
gates; and you shall rejoice before the LORD
your God in [T]all to which you put your
hands. all your undertakings
19 [T]"Take heed to yourself that you do not
forsake the Levite as long as you live in your
land. *Be careful*
20 "When the LORD your God [R]enlarges your
border as He has promised you, and you say,
'Let me eat meat,' because you long to eat
meat, you may eat as much meat as your heart
desires. Ex. 34:24

21 “If the place where the LORD your God
chooses to put His name is too far from [R]you,
then you may slaughter from your herd and
from your flock which the LORD has given
you, just as I have commanded you, and you
may eat within your gates as much as your
heart desires. Deut. 14:24
22 “Just as the gazelle and the deer are
eaten, so you may eat them; the unclean and
the clean alike may eat them.
23 “Only be sure that you do not eat the
blood, [R]for the blood *is* the life; you may not
eat the life with the meat. Gen. 9:4
24 “You shall not eat it; you shall pour it on
the earth like water.
25 “You shall not eat it, that it may go well
with you and your children after you, when
you do *what is* right in the sight of the LORD.
26 “Only the holy things which you have,
and your vowed offerings, you shall take and
go to the place which the LORD chooses.
27 “And [R]you shall offer your burnt offer-
ings, the meat and the blood, on the altar of
the LORD your God; and the blood of your
sacrifices shall be poured out on the altar of
the LORD your God, and you shall eat the
meat. Lev. 1:5, 9, 13, 17
28 “Observe and obey all these words which
I command you, [R]that it may go well with you
and your children after you forever, when you
do *what is* good and right in the sight of the
LORD your God. Deut. 12:25

Law of Idolatry

29 “When [R]the LORD your God cuts off from
before you the nations which you go to
dispossess, and you displace them and dwell
in their land, Ex. 23:23
30 “take heed to yourself that you are not en-
snared to follow them, after they are de-
stroyed from before you, and that you do not
inquire after their gods, saying, ‘How did
these nations serve their gods? I also will do
likewise.’
31 “You shall not worship the LORD your God
in that way; for every abomination to the
LORD which He hates they have done to their
gods; for they burn even their sons and
daughters in the fire to their gods.
32 “Whatever I command you, be careful to
observe it; [R]you shall not add to it nor take
away from it. Rev. 22:18, 19

CHAPTER 13

“IF there arises among you a prophet or a
[R]dreamer of dreams, [R]and he gives you a
sign or a wonder, Zech. 10:2 • Matt. 24:24
2 “and [R]the sign or the wonder comes to
pass, of which he spoke to you, saying, ‘Let us
go after other gods’—which you have not
known—‘and let us serve them,’ Deut. 18:22
3 “you shall not listen to the words of that
prophet or that dreamer of dreams, for the
LORD your God is testing you to know
whether you love the LORD your God with all
your heart and with all your soul.
4 “You shall [R]walk after the LORD your God
and fear Him, and keep His commandments
and obey His voice; you shall serve Him and
hold fast to Him. 2 Kin. 23:3
5 “But [R]that prophet or that dreamer of
dreams shall be put to death, because he has
spoken in order to turn *you* away from the
LORD your God, who brought you out of
the land of Egypt and redeemed you from the
house of bondage, to entice you from the way
in which the LORD your God commanded you
to walk. So you shall put away the evil from
your midst. Jer. 14:15
6 [R]“If your brother, the son of your
mother, your son or your daughter, [R]the wife
of your bosom, or your friend [R]who is as
your own soul, secretly entices you, saying,
‘Let us go and serve other gods,’ which you
have not known, neither you nor your fa-
thers, Deut. 17:2 • Gen. 16:5 • 1 Sam. 18:1, 3
7 “of the gods of the people which *are* all
around you, near to you or far off from you,
from *one* end of the earth to the *other* end of
the earth,
8 “you shall [R]not consent to him or listen to
him, nor shall your eye pity him, nor shall you
spare him or conceal him; Prov. 1:10
9 “but you shall surely kill him; your hand
shall be first against him to put him to
[R]death, and afterward the hand of all the peo-
ple. Deut. 17:7
10 “And you shall stone him with stones
until he dies, because he sought to entice you
away from the LORD your God, who brought
you out of the land of Egypt, from the house
of bondage.
11 “So all Israel shall hear and [R]fear, and
not again do such wickedness as this among
you. Deut. 17:13
12 [R]“If you hear someone in one of your
cities, which the LORD your God gives you to
dwell in, saying, Judg. 20:1–48
13 ‘Corrupt men have gone out from among
you and enticed the inhabitants of their city,
saying, “Let us go and serve other gods” ’—
which you have not known—
14 “then you shall inquire, search out, and
ask diligently. And *if it is* indeed true *and* cer-
tain *that* such an [T]abomination was commit-
ted among you, *detestable action*
15 “you shall surely strike the inhabitants of
that city with the edge of the sword, utterly
destroying it, all that is in it and its livestock—
with the edge of the sword.
16 “And you shall gather all its plunder into
the middle of the street, and completely burn
with fire the city and all its plunder, for the
LORD your God. It shall be a heap forever; it
shall not be built again.

17 [R]"So none of the accursed things shall re-
main in your hand, that the LORD may [R]turn
from the fierceness of His anger and show
you mercy, have compassion on you and
[T]multiply you, just as He swore to your fa-
thers, Josh. 6:18 • Josh. 7:26 • *increase*
18 "because you have listened to the voice of
the LORD your God, [R]to keep all His com-
mandments which I command you today, to
do *what is* right in the eyes of the LORD your
God. Deut. 12:25, 28, 32

CHAPTER 14

Law of Food

"YOU *are* the children of the LORD your
God; you shall not cut yourselves nor
shave the front of your head for the dead.
2 [R]"For you *are* a holy people to the LORD
your God, and the LORD has chosen you to be
a people for Himself, a special treasure above
all the peoples who *are* on the face of the
earth. Lev. 20:26
3 [R]"You shall not eat any [T]detestable
thing. Ezek. 4:14 • *abominable*
4 [R]"These *are* the animals which you may
eat: the ox, the sheep, the goat, Lev. 11:2–45
5 "the deer, the gazelle, the roe deer, the
wild goat, the mountain goat,* the antelope,
and the mountain sheep.
6 "And you may eat every animal with
cloven hooves, having the hoof split into two
parts, *and that* chews the cud, among the an-
imals.
7 "Nevertheless, of those that chew the cud
or have cloven hooves, you shall not eat, *such*
as these: the camel, the hare, and the rock
hyrax; for they chew the cud but do not have
cloven hooves; they *are* unclean for you.
8 "Also the swine is unclean for you, be-
cause it has cloven hooves, yet *does* not *chew*
the cud; you shall not eat their flesh or touch
their dead carcasses.
9 [R]"These you may eat of all that *are* in the
waters: you may eat all that have fins and
scales. Lev. 11:9
10 "And whatever does not have fins and
scales you shall not eat; it *is* unclean for you.
11 "All clean birds you may eat.
12 [R]"But these you shall not eat: the eagle,
the vulture, the buzzard, Lev. 11:13
13 "the red kite, the falcon, and the kite after
their kinds;
14 "every raven after its kind;
15 "the ostrich, the short-eared owl, the sea
gull, and the hawk after their kinds;
16 "the little owl, the screech owl, the white
owl,
17 "the jackdaw, the carrion vulture, the
fisher owl,
18 "the stork, the heron after its kind, and
the hoopoe and the bat.
19 "Also every creeping thing that flies is un-
clean for you; they shall not be eaten.
20 "You may eat all clean birds.
21 "You shall not eat anything that dies *of it-*
self; you may give it to the alien who *is* within
your gates, that he may eat it, or you may sell
it to a foreigner; for you *are* a holy people to
the LORD your God. You shall not boil a young
goat in its mother's milk.

Law of the Tithes

22 [R]"You shall truly tithe all the increase of
your grain that the field produces year by
year. Lev. 27:30
23 "And you shall eat before the LORD your
God, in the place where He chooses to make
His name abide, the tithe of your grain and
your new wine and your oil, of the firstborn of
your herds and your flocks, that you may
learn to fear the LORD your God always.
24 "But if the journey is too long for you, so
that you are not able to carry *the tithe, or* if
the place where the LORD your God chooses to
put His name is too far from you, when the
LORD your God has blessed you,
25 "then you shall exchange *it* for money,
take the money in your hand, and go to the
place which the LORD your God chooses.
26 "And you shall spend that money for
whatever your heart desires: for oxen or

14:5 Or *addax*

14:2 Purpose of Israel—The modern-day student of the Bible may well ask why so much of Scripture is taken up with the history of a single nation. Certainly many Christians wonder why one nation should be called "God's chosen people." The answer to this question is bound up in God's purpose for Israel. When God promised Abraham that he would become the father of a great nation, He also promised that He would bless all peoples through that nation (Page 14—Gen. 12:1–3). Therefore Israel was to be a channel of blessing as well as a recipient. Even their deliverance from Egypt was partially designed to show other nations that Israel's God was the only true God (Page 61—Ex. 7:5; 14:18; Page 215—Josh. 2:9–11). It was further prophesied by Isaiah that the Messiah would bring salvation to the Gentiles (Page 727—Is. 49:6). Also in the Psalms there are many invitations to other nations to come and worship the Lord in Israel (Page 546—Ps. 2:10–12; 117:1). Ruth the Moabitess is an example of a foreigner who believed in Israel's God.

It is clear that God's promise to Abraham to bless the whole world through him is still being fulfilled. The life, ministry, and death of Jesus Christ, and the existence and influence of the church today, all came about through God's choice of Israel. All whom the church wins to Christ, whether Jew or Gentile, enter into those great blessings channeled through Israel.

Now turn to Page 427—1 Chr. 28:4–6: Government of Israel.

sheep, for wine or similar drink, for whatever your heart desires; you shall eat there before the LORD your God, and you shall [R]rejoice, you and your household. Deut. 12:7

27 "You shall not [T]forsake the [R]Levite who *is* within your gates, for he has no part nor inheritance with you. *neglect* • Deut. 12:12

28 "At the end of *every* third year you shall bring out the tithe of your produce of that year and store *it* up within your gates.

29 "And the Levite, because he has no portion nor inheritance with you, and the stranger and the fatherless and the widow who *are* within your gates, may come and eat and be satisfied, that the LORD your God may bless you in all the work of your hand which you do.

CHAPTER 15

Law of the Debts

"AT the end of *every* seven years you shall grant a release *of debts.*

2 "And this *is* the form of the release: Every creditor who has lent *anything* to his neighbor shall release *it;* he shall not require *it* of his neighbor or his brother, because it is called the LORD's release.

3 "Of a foreigner you may require *it;* but you shall give up your claim to what is owed by your brother,

4 "except when there may be no poor among you; for the LORD will greatly bless you in the land which the LORD your God is giving you to possess *as* an inheritance—

5 "only if you carefully obey the voice of the LORD your God, to observe with care all these commandments which I command you today.

6 "For the LORD your God will bless you just as He promised you; [R]you shall lend to many nations, but you shall not borrow; you shall reign over many nations, but they shall not reign over you. Deut. 28:12, 44

7 "If there is among you a poor man of your brethren, within any of the gates in your land which the LORD your God is giving you, you shall not harden your heart nor shut your hand from your poor brother,

8 "but [R]you shall open your hand wide to him and willingly lend him sufficient for his need, whatever he needs. Matt. 5:42

9 "Beware lest there be a wicked thought in your heart, saying, 'The seventh year, the year of release, is at hand,' and your eye be evil against your poor brother and you give him nothing, and he cry out to the LORD against you, and it become sin among you.

10 "You shall surely give to him, and your heart should not be grieved when you give to him, because [R]for this thing the LORD your God will bless you in all your works and in all to which you put your hand. 2 Cor. 9:5, 7

11 "For the poor will never cease from the land; therefore I command you, saying, 'You shall open your hand wide to your brother, to your poor and your needy, in your land.'

Law of the Slaves

12 [R]"If your brother, a Hebrew man, or a Hebrew woman, is sold to you and serves you six years, then in the seventh year you shall let him go free from you. Ex. 21:2–6

13 "And when you [T]send him away free from you, you shall not let him go away empty-handed; *set him free*

14 "you shall supply him liberally from your flock, from your threshing floor, and from your winepress. *From what* the LORD has blessed you with, you shall give to him.

15 [R]"You shall remember that you were a slave in the land of Egypt, and the LORD your God redeemed you; therefore I command you this thing today. Deut. 5:15

16 "And [R]if it happens that he says to you, 'I will not go away from you,' because he loves you and your house, since he prospers with you, Ex. 21:5, 6

17 "then you shall take an awl and thrust *it* through his ear to the door, and he shall be your servant forever. Also to your female servant you shall do likewise.

18 "It shall not seem hard to you when you send him away free from you; for he has been worth [R]a double hired servant in serving you six years. Then the LORD your God will bless you in all that you do. Is. 16:14

Law of the Firstborn

19 [R]"All the firstborn males that come from your herd and your flock you shall sanctify to the LORD your God; you shall do no work with the firstborn of your herd, nor shear the firstborn of your flock. Ex. 13:2, 12

20 [R]"You and your household shall eat *it* before the LORD your God year by year in the place which the LORD chooses. Deut. 12:5

21 "But if there is a defect in it, *if it is* lame or blind *or has* any serious defect, you shall not sacrifice it to the LORD your God.

22 "You may eat it within your gates; the unclean and the clean *person* alike *may eat it,* as *if it were* a gazelle or a deer.

23 "Only you shall not eat its blood; you shall pour it on the ground like water.

CHAPTER 16

Law of the Feasts

"OBSERVE the [R]month of Abib, and keep the Passover to the LORD your God, for in the month of Abib the LORD your God brought you out of Egypt by night. Ex. 12:2

2 "Therefore you shall sacrifice the Passover to the LORD your God, from the flock and [R]the herd, in the place where the LORD chooses to put His name. Num. 28:19

3 "You shall eat no leavened bread with it;
[R]seven days you shall eat unleavened bread
with it, *that is*, the bread of affliction (for you
came out of the land of Egypt in haste), that
you may [R]remember the day in which you
came out of the land of Egypt all the days of
your life. Num. 29:12 • Ex. 13:3
4 [R]"And no leaven shall be seen among you
in all your territory for seven days, nor shall
any of the meat which you sacrifice the first
day at twilight remain overnight until [R]morn-
ing. Ex. 13:7 • Num. 9:12
5 "You may not sacrifice the Passover
within any of your gates which the LORD your
God gives you;
6 "but at the place where the LORD your
God chooses to make His name abide, there
you shall sacrifice the Passover [R]at twilight, at
the going down of the sun, at the time you
came out of Egypt. Ex. 12:7–10
7 "And you shall roast and eat *it* [R]in the
place which the LORD your God chooses, and
in the morning you shall turn and go to your
tents. 2 Kin. 23:23
8 "Six days you shall eat unleavened bread,
and [R]on the seventh day there *shall be* a sa-
cred assembly to the LORD your God. You shall
do no work *on it*. Lev. 23:8, 36
9 "You shall count seven weeks for your-
self; begin to count the seven weeks from *the
time* you begin *to put* the sickle to the grain.
10 "Then you shall keep the [R]Feast of Weeks
to the LORD your God with the tribute of a
freewill offering from your hand, which you
shall give [R]as the LORD your God blesses
you. Ex. 34:22 • 1 Cor. 16:2
11 [R]"You shall rejoice before the LORD your
God, you and your son and your daughter,
your male servant and your female servant,
the Levite who *is* within your gates, the
stranger and the fatherless and the widow
who *are* among you, at the place where the
LORD your God chooses to make His name
abide. Deut. 16:14
12 [R]"And you shall remember that you were
a slave in Egypt, and you shall be careful to
observe these statutes. Deut. 15:15
13 [R]"You shall observe the Feast of Taberna-
cles seven days, when you have gathered from
your threshing floor and from your wine-
press. Ex. 23:16
14 "And you shall rejoice in your feast, you
and your son and your daughter, your male
servant and your female servant and the
Levite, the stranger and the fatherless and the
widow, who *are* within your gates.
15 [R]"Seven days you shall keep a sacred
feast to the LORD your God in the place which
the LORD chooses, because the LORD your God
will bless you in all your produce and in all
the work of your hands, so that you surely re-
joice. Lev. 23:39–41
16 "Three times a year all your males shall
appear before the LORD your God in the place
which He chooses: at the Feast of Unleavened
Bread, at the Feast of Weeks, and at the Feast
of Tabernacles; and they shall not appear be-
fore the LORD empty-handed.
17 "Every man *shall give* as he is able, [R]ac-
cording to the blessing of the LORD your God
which He has given you. Deut. 16:10

Law of the Administration of the Judges

18 "You shall appoint judges and officers in
all your gates, which the LORD your God gives
you, according to your tribes, and they shall
judge the people with just judgment.
19 [R]"You shall not pervert justice; you shall
not show partiality, nor take a bribe, for a
bribe blinds the eyes of the wise and twists
the words of the righteous. Ex. 23:2, 6
20 "You shall follow what is altogether just,
that you may live and inherit the land which
the LORD your God is giving you.
21 [R]"You shall not plant for yourself any
tree, as a [T]wooden image, near the altar
which you build for yourself to the LORD your
God. Ex. 34:13 • Or *Asherah*
22 [R]"You shall not set up a sacred pillar,
which the LORD your God hates. Lev. 26:1

CHAPTER 17

"YOU [R]shall not sacrifice to the LORD
your God a bull or sheep which has any
[T]blemish *or* defect, for that *is* an abomination
to the LORD your God. Deut. 15:21 • Lit. *evil thing*
2 "If there is found among you, within any
of your gates which the LORD your God gives
you, a man or a woman who has been wicked
in the sight of the LORD your God, [R]in trans-
gressing His covenant, Josh. 7:11
3 "who has gone and served other gods and
worshiped them, either [R]the sun or moon or
any of the host of heaven, [R]which I have not
commanded, Deut. 4:19 • Jer. 7:22
4 "and it is told you, and you hear *of it*, then
you shall inquire diligently. And if *it is* indeed
true *and* certain that such an abomination has
been committed in Israel,
5 "then you shall bring out to your gates
that man or woman who has committed that
wicked thing, and [R]shall stone to death that
man or woman with stones. Lev. 24:14–16
6 "Whoever is deserving of death shall be
put to death on the testimony of two or three
[R]witnesses; he shall not be put to death on the
testimony of one witness. Num. 35:30
7 "The hands of the witnesses shall be the
first against him to put him to death, and af-
terward the hands of all the people. So you
shall put away the evil from among you.
8 "If a matter arises which is too hard for
you to judge, between degrees of guilt for
bloodshed, between one judgment or another,

or between one punishment or another, matters of controversy within your gates, then you shall arise and go up to the place which the LORD your God chooses.

9 "And you shall come to the priests, the Levites, and to the judge *there* in those days, and inquire *of them;* they shall pronounce upon you the sentence of judgment.

10 "You shall do according to the sentence which they pronounce upon you in that place which the LORD chooses. And you shall be careful to do according to all that they order you.

11 "According to the sentence of the law in which they instruct you, according to the judgment which they tell you, you shall do; you shall not turn aside *to* the right hand or *to* the left from the sentence which they pronounce upon you.

12 "Now the man who acts presumptuously and will not heed the priest who stands to minister there before the LORD your God, or the judge, that man shall die. So you shall put away the evil from Israel.

13 "And all the people shall hear and fear, and no longer act presumptuously.

Law of the Administration of the King

14 "When you come to the land which the LORD your God is giving you, and possess it and dwell in it, and say, [R]'I will set a king over me like all the nations that *are* around me,' 1 Sam. 8:5, 19, 20; 10:19

15 "you shall surely set a king over you whom the LORD your God chooses; *one* from among your brethren you shall set as king over you; you may not set a foreigner over you, who *is* not your brother.

16 "But he shall not multiply [R]horses for himself, nor cause the people [R]to return to Egypt to multiply horses, for the LORD has said to you, 'You shall not return that way again.' 1 Kin. 4:26; 10:26–29 • Ezek. 17:15

17 "Neither shall he multiply wives for himself, lest his heart turn away; nor shall he greatly multiply silver and gold for himself.

18 "Also it shall be, when he sits on the throne of his kingdom, that he shall write for himself a copy of this law in a book, from *the one* before the priests, the Levites.

19 "And [R]it shall be with him, and he shall read it all the days of his life, that he may learn to fear the LORD his God and be careful to observe all the words of this law and these statutes, Ps. 119:97, 98

20 "that his heart may not [T]be lifted above his brethren, that he [R]may not turn aside from the commandment *to* the right hand or *to* the left, and that he may prolong *his* days in his kingdom, he and his children in the midst of Israel. *become proud* • Deut. 5:32

CHAPTER 18

Law of the Administration of the Priest and Prophet

"THE priests, the Levites—all the tribe of Levi—shall have no part nor inheritance with Israel; they shall eat the offerings of the LORD made by fire, and His portion.

2 "Therefore they shall have no inheritance among their brethren; the LORD is their inheritance, as He said to them.

3 "And this shall be the priest's [R]due[T] from the people, from those who offer a sacrifice, whether *it is* bull or sheep: they shall give to the priest the shoulder, the cheeks, and the stomach. Lev. 7:32–34; 1 Sam. 2:13–16, 29 • *right*

4 "The firstfruits of your grain and your new wine and your oil, and the first of the fleece of your sheep, you shall give him.

5 "For [R]the LORD your God has chosen him out of all your tribes [R]to stand to minister in the name of the LORD, him and his sons forever. Ex. 28:1 • Deut. 10:8

6 "So if a Levite comes from any of your gates, from where he dwells among all Israel, and comes with all the desire of his mind to the place which the LORD chooses,

7 "then he may serve in the name of the LORD his God as all his brethren the Levites *do,* who stand there before the LORD.

8 "They shall have equal [R]portions to eat, besides what comes from the sale of his inheritance. 2 Chr. 31:4

9 "When you come into the land which the LORD your God is giving you, [R]you shall not learn to follow the [T]abominations of those nations. Deut. 12:29, 30; 20:16–18 • *detestable acts*

10 "There shall not be found among you *anyone* who makes his son or his daughter pass through the fire, *or one* who practices witchcraft, *or* a soothsayer, or one who interprets omens, or a sorcerer, Is. 8:19

11 [R]"or one who conjures spells, or a medium, or a spiritist, or [R]one who calls up the dead. Lev. 20:27 • 1 Sam. 28:7

12 "For all who do these things *are* an abomination to the LORD, and [R]because of these abominations the LORD your God drives them out from before you. Lev. 18:24

13 "You shall be [T]blameless before the LORD your God. Lit. *perfect*

14 "For these nations which you will dispossess listened to soothsayers and diviners; but as for you, the LORD your God has not appointed such for you.

15 [R]"The LORD your God will raise up for you a Prophet like me from your midst, from your brethren. Him you shall hear, Acts 3:22☆

16 "according to all you desired of the LORD your God in Horeb in the day of the assembly, saying, [R]'Let me not hear again the voice of the LORD my God, nor let me see this great fire anymore, lest I die.' Ex. 20:18, 19

17 "And the LORD said to me: [R]'What they
have spoken is good. Deut. 5:28
18 'I will raise up for them a Prophet like you
from among their brethren, and will put My
words in His mouth, [R]and He shall speak to
them all that I command Him. [John 4:25☆]
19 [R]'And it shall be *that* whoever will not
hear My words, which He speaks in My name,
I will require *it* of him. Acts 3:23☆
20 'But [R]the prophet who presumes to
speak a word in My name, which I have not
commanded him to speak, or [R]who speaks in
the name of other gods, that prophet shall
die.' Jer. 14:14, 15 • Jer. 2:8
21 "And if you say in your heart, 'How shall
we know the word which the LORD has not
spoken?'—
22 [R]"when a prophet speaks in the name of
the LORD, [R]if the thing does not happen or
come to pass, that *is* the thing which the LORD
has not spoken; the prophet has spoken it
[R]presumptuously; you shall not be afraid of
him. Jer. 28:9 • Deut. 13:2 • Deut. 18:20

CHAPTER 19

Cities of Refuge

"WHEN the LORD your God has cut off
the nations whose land the LORD your
God is giving you, and you dispossess them
and dwell in their cities and in their houses,
2 "you shall separate three cities for your-
self in the midst of your land which the LORD
your God is giving you to possess.
3 "You shall prepare roads for yourself, and
divide into three parts the territory of your
land which the LORD your God is giving you to
inherit, that any manslayer may flee there.
4 "And [R]this *is* the case of the manslayer
who flees there, that he may live: Whoever
kills his neighbor unintentionally, not having
hated him in time past— Num. 35:9–34
5 "as when *a man* goes to the woods with
his neighbor to cut timber, and his hand
swings a stroke with the ax to cut down the
tree, and the head slips from the handle and
strikes his neighbor so that he dies—he shall
flee to one of these cities and live;
6 [R]"lest the avenger of blood, while his
anger is hot, pursue the manslayer and over-
take him, because the way is long, and kill
him, though he *was* not deserving of death,
since he had not hated the victim in time
past. Num. 35:12
7 "Therefore I command you, saying, 'You
shall separate three cities for yourself.'
8 "Now if the LORD your God [R]enlarges
your territory, as He swore to [R]your fathers,
and gives you the land which He promised to
give to your fathers, Deut. 12:20 • Gen. 15:18–21
9 "and if you keep all these commandments
and do them, which I command you today, to
love the LORD your God and to walk always in
His ways, [R]then you shall add three more cities
for yourself besides these three, Josh. 20:7–9
10 [R]"lest innocent blood be shed in the midst
of your land which the LORD your God is giv-
ing you *as* an inheritance, and *thus* guilt of
bloodshed be upon you. Deut. 21:1–9
11 "But [R]if anyone hates his neighbor, lies in
wait for him, rises against him and strikes
him mortally, so that he dies, and he flees to
one of these cities, Num. 35:16, 24
12 "then the elders of his city shall send and
bring him from there, and deliver him over to
the hand of the avenger of blood, that he may
die.
13 "Your eye shall not pity him, but you shall
put away *the guilt of* innocent blood from Is-
rael, that it may go well with you.
14 [R]"You shall not remove your neighbor's
landmark, which the men of old have set, in
your inheritance which you will inherit in the
land that the LORD your God is giving you to
possess. Prov. 22:28

Law of Witnesses

15 "One witness shall not rise against a man
concerning any iniquity or any sin that he
commits; by the mouth of two or three wit-
nesses the matter shall be established.
16 "If a false witness rises against any man
to testify against him of wrongdoing,
17 "then both men in the controversy shall
stand before the LORD, before the priests and
the judges who serve in those days.
18 "And the judges shall make careful in-
quiry, and indeed, *if* the witness *is* a false wit-
ness, who has testified falsely against his
brother,
19 "then you shall do to him as he thought to
have done to his brother; so you shall put
away the evil from among you.
20 [R]"And those who remain shall hear and
fear, and hereafter they shall not again com-
mit such evil among you. Deut. 17:13; 21:21
21 [R]"Your eye shall not pity: [R]life *shall be* for
life, eye for eye, tooth for tooth, hand for
hand, foot for foot. Deut. 19:13 • Ex. 21:23, 24

CHAPTER 20

Law of Warfare

"WHEN you go out to battle against your
enemies, and see [R]horses and chari-
ots *and* people more numerous than you, do
not be [R]afraid of them; for the LORD your God
is [R]with you, who brought you up from the
land of Egypt. Ps. 20:7 • Deut. 7:18 • 2 Chr. 13:12
2 "So it shall be, when you are on the verge
of battle, that the priest shall approach and
speak to the people.
3 "And he shall say to them, 'Hear, O Israel:
Today you are on the verge of battle with your
enemies. Do not let your heart faint, do not be

afraid, and do not tremble or be terrified because of them;

4 'for the LORD your God *is* He who goes with you, [R]to fight for you against your enemies, to save you.' Josh. 23:10

5 "Then the officers shall speak to the people, saying: 'What man *is there* who has built a new house and has not [R]dedicated it? Let him go and return to his house, lest he die in the battle and another man dedicate it. Neh. 12:27

6 'Also what man *is there* who has planted a vineyard and has not eaten of it? Let him go and return to his house, lest he die in the battle and another man eat of it.

7 [R]'And what man *is there* who is betrothed to a woman and has not married her? Let him go and return to his house, lest he die in the battle and another man marry her.' Deut. 24:5

8 "The officers shall speak further to the people, and say, [R]'What man *is there who is* fearful and fainthearted? Let him go and return to his house, lest the heart of his brethren faint* like his heart.' Judg. 7:3

9 "And so it shall be, when the officers have finished speaking to the people, that they shall make captains of the armies to lead the people.

10 "When you go near a city to fight against it, then proclaim an offer of peace to it.

11 "And it shall be that if they accept your offer of peace, and open to you, then all the people *who are* found in it shall be placed under tribute to you, and serve you.

12 "Now if *the city* will not make peace with you, but makes war against you, then you shall besiege it.

13 "And when the LORD your God delivers it into your hands, [R]you shall strike every male in it with the edge of the sword. Num. 31:7

14 "But the women, the little ones, [R]the livestock, and all that is in the city, all its spoil, you shall plunder for yourself; and you shall eat the enemies' plunder which the LORD your God gives you. Josh. 8:2

15 "Thus you shall do to all the cities *which are* very far from you, which *are* not of the cities of these nations.

16 "But [R]of the cities of these peoples which the LORD your God gives you *as* an inheritance, you shall let nothing that breathes remain alive, Deut. 7:1–5

17 "but you shall utterly destroy them: the Hittite and the Amorite and the Canaanite and the Perizzite and the Hivite and the Jebusite, just as the LORD your God has commanded you,

18 "lest [R]they teach you to do according to all their abominations which they have done for their gods, and you [R]sin against the LORD your God. Deut. 7:4; 12:30; 18:9 • Ex. 23:33

19 "When you besiege a city for a long time, while making war against it to take it, you shall not destroy its trees by wielding an ax against them; if you can eat of them, do not cut them down to use in the siege, for the tree of the field *is* man's *food*.

20 "Only the trees which you know *are* not trees for food you may destroy and cut down, to build siegeworks against the city that makes war with you, until it is subdued.

CHAPTER 21

Law of Unknown Murder

"IF *anyone* is found slain, lying in the field in the land which the LORD your God is giving you to possess, *and* it is not known who killed him,

2 "then your elders and your judges shall go out and measure *the distance* from the slain man to the surrounding cities.

3 "And it shall be *that* the elders of the city nearest to the slain man will take a heifer which has not been worked *and* which has not pulled with a [R]yoke. Num. 19:2

4 "The elders of that city shall bring the heifer down to a valley with flowing water, which is neither plowed nor sown, and they shall break the heifer's neck there in the valley.

5 "Then the priests, the sons of Levi, shall come near, for [R]the LORD your God has chosen them to minister to Him and to bless in the name of the LORD; [R]by their word every controversy and every [T]assault shall be *settled*. 1 Chr. 23:13 • Deut. 17:8, 9 • Lit. *stroke*

6 "And all the elders of that city nearest to the slain *man* [R]shall wash their hands over the heifer whose neck was broken in the valley. Matt. 27:24

7 "Then they shall answer and say, 'Our hands have not shed this blood, nor have our eyes seen *it*.

8 'Provide atonement, O LORD, for Your people Israel, whom You have redeemed, and do not lay innocent blood to the charge of Your people Israel.' And atonement shall be provided on their behalf for the blood.

9 "So you shall put away the *guilt of* innocent blood from among you when you do *what is* right in the sight of the LORD.

Law of Marriage

10 "When you go out to war against your enemies, and the LORD your God delivers them into your hand, and you take them captive,

11 "and you see among the captives a beautiful woman, and desire her and would take her for your [R]wife, Num. 31:18

12 "then you shall bring her home to your house, and she shall [R]shave her head and trim her nails. Lev. 14:8, 9

13 "She shall put off the clothes of her cap-

20:8 So with MT, Tg.; Sam., LXX, Syr., Vg. *lest he make his brother's heart faint*

tivity, remain in your house, and [R]mourn her
father and her mother a full month; after that
you may go in to her and be her husband, and
she shall be your wife. Ps. 45:10
14 "And it shall be, if you have no delight in
her, then you shall set her free, but you cer-
tainly shall not sell her for money; you shall
not treat her brutally, because you have [R]hum-
bled her. Judg. 19:24
15 "If a man has two wives, one loved [R]and
the other unloved, and they have borne him
children, *both* the loved and the unloved,
and *if* the firstborn son is of her who is
unloved, Gen. 29:33
16 "then it shall be, [R]on the day he bequeaths
his possessions to his sons, *that* he must not
bestow firstborn status on the son of the loved
wife in preference to the son of the unloved,
the *true* firstborn. 1 Chr. 5:2
17 "But he shall acknowledge the son of the
unloved wife *as* the firstborn [R]by giving him a
double portion of all that he has, for he *is* the
beginning of his strength; the right of the
firstborn *is* his. 2 Kin. 2:9

Law of the Rebellious Son

18 "If a man has a stubborn and rebellious
son who will not obey the voice of his father
or the voice of his mother, and *who,* when
they have chastened him, will not heed them,
19 "then his father and his mother shall take
hold of him and bring him out to the elders of
his city, to the gate of his city.
20 "And they shall say to the elders of his
city, 'This son of ours is stubborn and rebel-
lious; he will not obey our voice; he is a glut-
ton and a drunkard.'
21 "Then all the men of his city shall stone
him to death with stones; so you shall put
away the evil from among you, [R]and all Israel
shall hear and fear. Deut. 13:11
22 "If a man has committed a sin [R]deserving
of death, and he is put to death, and you hang
him on a tree, Acts 23:29
23 [R]"his body shall not remain overnight on
the tree, but you shall surely bury him that
day, so that [R]you do not defile the land which
the LORD your God is giving you *as* an inheri-
tance; for [R]he who is hanged *is* accursed of
God. John 19:31 • Lev. 18:25 • Gal. 3:13

CHAPTER 22

Law of the Brother's Property

"YOU [R]shall not see your brother's ox or
his sheep going astray, and [T]hide your-
self from them; you shall certainly bring them
back to your brother. Ex. 23:4 • *ignore them*
2 "And if your brother *is* not near you, or if
you do not know him, then you shall bring it
to your own house, and it shall remain with
you until your brother seeks it; then you shall
restore it to him.
3 "You shall do the same with his donkey,
and so shall you do with his garment; with
any lost thing of your brother's, which he has
lost and you have found, you shall do like-
wise; you must not hide yourself.
4 [R]"You shall not see your brother's donkey
or his ox fall down along the road, and hide
yourself from them; you shall surely help him
lift *them* up again. Ex. 23:5

Law of Separation

5 "A woman shall not wear anything that
pertains to a man, nor shall a man put on a
woman's garment, for all who do so *are* an
abomination to the LORD your God.
6 "If a bird's nest happens to be before you
along the way, in any tree or on the ground,
with young ones or eggs, with the mother sit-
ting on the young or on the eggs, [R]you shall
not take the mother with the young; Lev. 22:28
7 "you shall surely let the mother go, and
take the young for yourself, [R]that it may be
well with you and *that* you may prolong *your*
days. Deut. 4:40
8 "When you build a new house, then you
shall make a parapet for your roof, that you
may not bring guilt of bloodshed on your
household if anyone falls from it.
9 [R]"You shall not sow your vineyard with
different kinds of seed, lest the yield of the
seed which you have sown and the fruit of
your vineyard be defiled. Lev. 19:19
10 [R]"You shall not plow with an ox and a
donkey together. [2 Cor. 6:14–16]
11 [R]"You shall not wear a garment of differ-
ent sorts, *such as* wool and linen mixed to-
gether. Lev. 19:19
12 "You shall make [R]tassels on the four cor-
ners of the clothing with which you cover
yourself. Num. 15:37–41

Law of Marriage

13 "If any man takes a wife, and goes in to
her, and [R]detests her, Deut. 21:15; 24:3
14 "and charges her with shameful conduct,
and brings a bad name on her, and says, 'I
took this woman, and when I came to her I
found she *was* not a virgin,'
15 "then the father and mother of the young
woman shall take and bring out *the evidence
of* the young woman's virginity to the elders
of the city at the gate.
16 "And the young woman's father shall say
to the elders, 'I gave my daughter to this man
as wife, and he detests her.
17 'Now he has charged her with shameful
conduct, saying, "I found your daughter *was*
not a virgin," and yet these *are the evidences
of* my daughter's virginity.' And they shall
spread the cloth before the elders of the city.
18 "Then the elders of that city shall take
that man and punish him;
19 "and they shall fine him one hundred

shekels of silver and give *them* to the father of
the young woman, because he has brought a
bad name on a virgin of Israel. And she shall
be his wife; he cannot divorce her all his days.
20 "But if the thing is true, *and evidences of*
virginity are not found for the young woman,
21 "then they shall bring out the young
woman to the door of her father's house, and
the men of her city shall stone her to death
with [R]stones, because she has done a dis-
graceful thing in Israel, to play the harlot in
her father's house. So you shall put away the
evil from among you. Deut. 21:21
22 [R]"If a man is found lying with a woman
married to a husband, then both of them shall
die—the man that lay with the woman, and
the woman; so you shall put away the evil
from Israel. Lev. 20:10
23 "If a young woman *who* is a virgin is be-
trothed to a husband, and a man finds her in
the city and lies with her,
24 "then you shall bring them both out to
the gate of that city, and you shall stone them
to death with stones, the young woman be-
cause she did not cry out in the city, and the
man because he [R]humbled his neighbor's
wife; so you shall put away the evil from
among you. Deut. 21:14
25 "But if a man finds a betrothed young
woman in the countryside, and the man forces
her and lies with her, then only the man who
lay with her shall die.
26 "But you shall do nothing to the young
woman; *there is* in the young woman no sin
deserving of death, for just as when a man
rises against his neighbor and kills him, even
so *is* this matter.
27 "For he found her in the countryside, *and*
the betrothed young woman cried out, but
there was no one to save her.
28 [R]"If a man finds a young woman *who is*
a virgin, who is not betrothed, and he seizes
her and lies with her, and they are found
out, Ex. 22:16, 17
29 "then the man who lay with her shall give
to the young woman's father fifty *shekels* of
silver, and she shall be his wife because he
has humbled her; he shall not be permitted to
divorce her all his days.
30 "A man shall not take his father's wife,
nor [R]uncover his father's bed. Ezek. 16:8

CHAPTER 23

Law of Acceptance into the Congregation

"HE who is emasculated by crushing or
mutilation shall [R]not enter the assem-
bly of the LORD. Lev. 21:20; 22:24
2 "One of illegitimate birth shall not enter
the assembly of the LORD; even to the tenth
generation none of his *descendants* shall
enter the assembly of the LORD.
3 "An Ammonite or Moabite shall not enter
the assembly of the LORD; even to the tenth
generation none of his *descendants* shall
enter the assembly of the LORD forever,
4 "because they did not meet you with
bread and water on the road when you came
out of Egypt, and because they hired against
you Balaam the son of Beor from Pethor of
Mesopotamia,* to curse you.
5 "Nevertheless the LORD your God would
not listen to Balaam, but the LORD your God
turned the curse into a blessing for you, be-
cause the LORD your God loves you.
6 "You shall not seek their peace nor their
prosperity all your days forever.
7 "You shall not abhor an Edomite, [R]for he
is your brother. You shall not abhor an
Egyptian, because [R]you were an alien in his
land. Obad. 10, 12 • Deut. 10:19
8 "The children of the third generation born
to them may enter the assembly of the LORD.
9 "When the army goes out against your en-
emies, then keep yourself from every wicked
thing.
10 [R]"If there is any man among you who be-
comes unclean by some occurrence in the
night, then he shall go outside the camp; he
shall not come inside the camp. Lev. 15:16
11 "But it shall be, when evening comes, that
he shall wash with water; and when the sun
sets, he may come into the camp.
12 "Also you shall have a place outside the
camp, where you may go out;
13 "and you shall have an implement among
your equipment, and when you sit down out-
side, you shall dig with it and turn and cover
your refuse.
14 "For the LORD your God [R]walks in the
midst of your camp, to deliver you and give
your enemies over to you; therefore your camp
shall be holy, that He may see no unclean thing
among you, and turn away from you. Lev. 26:12
15 [R]"You shall not give back to his master
the slave who has escaped from his master to
you. 1 Sam. 30:15
16 "He may dwell with you in your midst, in
the place which he chooses within one of your
gates, where it seems best to him; [R]you shall
not oppress him. Ex. 22:21
17 "There shall be no *ritual* harlot* [R]of the
daughters of Israel, or a [R]perverted* one of
the sons of Israel. Lev. 19:29 • 2 Kin. 23:7
18 "You shall not bring the wages of a harlot
or the price of a dog to the house of the LORD
your God for any vowed offering, for both of
these *are* [T]an abomination to the LORD your
God. *detestable*
19 [R]"You shall not charge interest to your
brother—interest on money *or* food *or* any-
thing that is lent out at interest. Ex. 22:25

23:4 Heb. *Aram Naharaim* **23:17** Heb. *qedeshah*, fem. of *qadesh* (see following note) • Heb. *qadesh*, one practicing sodomy and prostitution in religious rituals

20 "To a foreigner you may charge interest, but to your brother you shall not charge interest, that the LORD your God may bless you in all to which you set your hand in the land which you are entering to possess.

21 [R]"When you make a vow to the LORD your God, you shall not delay to pay it; for the LORD your God will surely require it of you, and it would be sin to you. Eccl. 5:4, 5

22 "But if you abstain from vowing, it shall not be sin to you.

23 "That which has gone from your lips you shall keep and perform, for you voluntarily vowed to the LORD your God what you have promised with your mouth.

Laws for Harmony in the Nation

24 "When you come into your neighbor's vineyard, you may eat your fill of grapes at your pleasure, but you shall not put *any* in your container.

25 "When you come into your neighbor's standing grain, you may pluck the heads with your hand, but you shall not use a sickle on your neighbor's standing grain.

CHAPTER 24

"WHEN a [R]man takes a wife and marries her, and it happens that she finds no favor in his eyes because he has found some uncleanness in her, and he writes her a certificate of divorce, puts *it* in her hand, and sends her out of his house, [Matt. 5:31; 19:7]

2 "when she has departed from his house, and goes and becomes another man's *wife,*

3 "*if* the latter husband detests her and writes her a certificate of divorce, puts *it* in her hand, and sends her out of his house, or if the latter husband dies who took her as his wife,

4 "*then* her former husband who divorced her must not take her back to be his wife after she has been defiled; for that *is* an abomination before the LORD, and you shall not bring sin on the land which the LORD your God is giving you *as* an inheritance.

5 [R]"When a man has taken a new wife, he shall not go out to war or be charged with any business; he shall be free at home one year, and [R]bring happiness to his wife whom he has taken. Deut. 20:7 • Prov. 5:18

6 "No man shall take the lower or the upper millstone in pledge, for he takes [R]*one's* living in pledge. *life*

7 "If a man is [R]found kidnapping any of his brethren of the children of Israel, and mistreats him or sells him, then that kidnapper shall die; and you shall put away the evil from among you. Ex. 21:16

8 "Take heed in [R]an outbreak of leprosy, that you carefully observe and do according to all that the priests, the Levites, shall teach you; just as I commanded them, *so* you shall be careful to do. Lev. 13:2; 14:2

9 [R]"Remember what the LORD your God did [R]to Miriam on the way when you came out of Egypt! [1 Cor. 10:6] • Num. 12:10

10 "When you [R]lend your brother anything, you shall not go into his house to get his pledge. Matt. 5:42

11 "You shall stand outside, and the man to whom you lend shall bring the pledge out to you.

12 "And if the man *is* poor, you shall not keep his pledge overnight.

13 "You shall in any case return the pledge to him again when the sun goes down, that he may sleep in his own garment and bless you; and it shall be righteousness to you before the LORD your God.

14 "You shall not [R]oppress a hired servant *who is* poor and needy, *whether* one of your brethren or one of the aliens who *is* in your land within your gates. [Mal. 3:5]

15 "Each day [R]you shall give *him* his wages, and not let the sun go down on it, for he *is* poor and has set his heart on it; [R]lest he cry out against you to the LORD, and it be sin to you. Lev. 19:13 • James 5:4

16 [R]"Fathers shall not be put to death for *their* children, nor shall children be put to death for *their* fathers; a person shall be put to death for his own sin. Ezek. 18:20

17 [R]"You shall not pervert justice due the stranger or the fatherless, nor take a widow's garment as a pledge. Ex. 23:6

18 "But [R]you shall remember that you were a slave in Egypt, and the LORD your God redeemed you from there; therefore I command you to do this thing. Deut. 24:22

19 [R]"When you reap your harvest in your field, and forget a sheaf in the field, you shall not go back to get it; it shall be for the stranger, the fatherless, and the widow, that the LORD your God may [R]bless you in all the work of your hands. Lev. 19:9, 10 • Ps. 41:1

20 "When you beat your olive trees, you shall not go over the boughs again; it shall be for the stranger, the fatherless, and the widow.

21 "When you gather the grapes of your vineyard, you shall not glean *it* afterward; it shall be for the stranger, the fatherless, and the widow.

22 "And you shall remember that you were a slave in the land of Egypt; therefore I command you to do this thing.

CHAPTER 25

"IF there is a dispute between men, and they come to court, that *the judges* may judge them, and they [R]justify the righteous and condemn the wicked, Prov. 17:15

2 "then it shall be, if the wicked man [R]deserves to be beaten, that the judge will cause

him to lie down [R]and be beaten in his pres-
ence, according to his guilt, with a certain
number of blows. Prov. 19:29 • Matt. 10:17
3 "Forty blows he may give him *and* no
more, lest he should exceed this and beat him
with many blows above these, and your
brother be humiliated in your sight.
4 [R]"You shall not muzzle an ox while it
[T]treads out *the grain.* [Prov. 12:10] • *threshes*
5 [R]"If brothers dwell together, and one of
them dies and has no son, the widow of the
dead man shall not be *married* to a stranger
outside *the family;* her husband's brother
shall go in to her, take her as his wife, and
perform the duty of a husband's brother to
her. Matt. 22:24
6 "And it shall be *that* the firstborn son
which she bears [R]will succeed to the name of
his dead brother, that [R]his name may not be
blotted out of Israel. Gen. 38:9 • Ruth 4:5, 10
7 "But if the man does not want to take his
brother's wife, then let his brother's wife go
up to the gate to the elders, and say, 'My hus-
band's brother refuses to raise up a name to
his brother in Israel; he will not perform the
duty of my husband's brother.'
8 "Then the elders of his city shall call him
and speak to him. But *if* he stands firm and
says, 'I do not want to take her,'
9 "then his brother's wife shall come to
him in the presence of the elders, [R]remove
his sandal from his foot, spit in his face, and
answer and say, 'So shall it be done to the
man who will not [R]build up his brother's
house.' Ruth 4:7, 8 • Ruth 4:11
10 "And his name shall be called in Israel,
'The house of him who had his sandal re-
moved.'
11 "If *two* men fight together, and the wife of
one draws near to rescue her husband from
the hand of the one attacking him, and puts
out her hand and seizes him by the genitals,
12 "then you shall cut off her hand; [R]your eye
shall not pity *her.* Deut. 7:2; 19:13
13 [R]"You shall not have in your bag differing
weights, a heavy and a light. Mic. 6:11
14 "You shall not have in your house differ-
ing measures, a large and a small.
15 "You shall have a perfect and just weight,
a perfect and just measure, that your days
may be lengthened in the land which the LORD
your God is giving you.
16 "For [R]all who do such things, all who be-
have unrighteously, *are* [T]an abomination to
the LORD your God. Prov. 11:1 • *detestable*
17 "Remember what Amalek did to you on
the way as you were coming out of Egypt,
18 "how he met you on the way and attacked
your rear ranks, all the stragglers at your rear,
when you *were* tired and weary; and he [R]did
not fear God. Rom. 3:18
19 "Therefore it shall be, [R]when the LORD
your God has given you rest from your ene-
mies all around, in the land which the LORD
your God is giving you to possess *as* an in-
heritance, *that* you will [R]blot out the remem-
brance of Amalek from under heaven. You
shall not forget. 1 Sam. 15:3 • Ex. 17:14

CHAPTER 26

Law of the Tithe

"AND it shall be, when you come into the
land which the LORD your God is giving
you *as* an inheritance, and you possess it and
dwell in it,
2 "that you shall take some of the first of all
the produce of the ground, which you shall
bring from your land that the LORD your God
is giving you, and put *it* in a basket and go to
the place where the LORD your God chooses to
make His name abide.
3 "And you shall go to the one who is priest
in those days, and say to him, 'I declare today
to the LORD your* God that I have come to the
country which the LORD swore to our fathers
to give us.'
4 "Then the priest shall take the basket out
of your hand and set it down before the altar
of the LORD your God.
5 "And you shall answer and say before the
LORD your God: 'My father *was* [R]a Syrian,*
about to perish, and [R]he went down to Egypt
and dwelt there, few in number; and there he
became a nation, great, mighty, and popu-
lous. Hos. 12:12 • Acts 7:15
6 'But the Egyptians mistreated us, afflicted
us, and laid hard bondage on us.
7 [R]'Then we cried out to the LORD God of
our fathers, and the LORD heard our voice and
looked on our affliction and our labor and our
oppression. Ex. 2:23–25; 3:9; 4:31
8 'So the LORD brought us out of Egypt with
a mighty hand and with an outstretched arm,
[R]with great terror and with signs and won-
ders. Deut. 4:34; 34:11, 12
9 'He has brought us to this place and has
given us this land, "a land flowing with milk
and honey";*
10 'and now, behold, I have brought the first-
fruits of the land which you, O LORD, have
given me.' Then you shall set it before the
LORD your God, and worship before the LORD
your God.
11 "So [R]you shall rejoice in every good *thing*
which the LORD your God has given to you
and your house, you and the Levite and the
stranger who *is* among you. Deut. 12:7; 16:11
12 "When you have finished laying aside all
the [R]tithe of your increase in the third year—
[R]the year of tithing—and have given *it* to the
Levite, the stranger, the fatherless, and the
widow, so that they may eat within your gates
and be filled, Lev. 27:30 • Deut. 14:28, 29

26:3 LXX *my* **26:5** Or *Aramean* **26:9** Ex. 3:8

13 "then you shall say before the LORD your
God: 'I have removed the holy *tithe* from *my*
house, and also have given them to the Levite,
the stranger, the fatherless, and the widow, ac-
cording to all Your commandments which You
have commanded me; I have not transgressed
Your commandments, [R]nor have I forgotten
them. Ps. 119:141, 153, 176
14 [R]'I have not eaten any of it when in
mourning, nor have I removed *any* of it for an
unclean *use,* nor given *any* of it for the dead. I
have obeyed the voice of the LORD my God,
and have done according to all that You have
commanded me. Hos. 9:4
15 [R]'Look down from Your holy [T]habitation,
from heaven, and bless Your people Israel and
the land which You have given us, just as You
swore to our fathers, "a land flowing with
milk and honey." '* Is. 63:15 • *home*

Vow of Israel and of God

16 "This day the LORD your God commands
you to observe these statutes and judgments;
therefore you shall be careful to observe them
with all your heart and with all your soul.
17 "Today you have [R]proclaimed the LORD to
be your God, and that you will walk in His
ways and keep His statutes, His command-
ments, and His judgments, and that you will
[R]obey His voice. Ex. 20:19 • Deut. 15:5
18 "Also today [R]the LORD has proclaimed you
to be His special people, just as He promised
you, that *you* should keep all His command-
ments, Ex. 6:7; 19:5
19 "and that He will set you [R]high above all
nations which He has made, in praise, in
name, and in honor, and that you may be [R]a
holy people to the LORD your God, just as He
has spoken." Deut. 4:7, 8; 28:1 • [1 Pet. 2:9]

CHAPTER 27

Erection of the Altar

NOW Moses, with the elders of Israel, com-
manded the people, saying: "Keep all the
commandments which I command you today.
2 "And it shall be, on the day when you
cross over the Jordan to the land which the
LORD your God is giving you, that [R]you shall
set up for yourselves large stones, and white-
wash them with lime. Josh. 8:32
3 "You shall write on them all the words of
this law, when you have crossed over, that you
may enter the land which the LORD your God
is giving you, 'a land flowing with milk and
honey,'* just as the LORD God of your fathers
promised you.
4 "Therefore it shall be, when you have
crossed over the Jordan, *that* [R]on Mount Ebal
you shall set up these stones, which I com-
mand you today, and you shall whitewash
them with lime. Deut. 11:29
5 "And there you shall build an altar to the
LORD your God, an altar of stones; you shall
not use an iron *tool* on them.
6 "You shall build with [T]whole stones the
altar of the LORD your God, and offer burnt of-
ferings on it to the LORD your God. *uncut*
7 "You shall offer peace offerings, and shall
eat there, and [R]rejoice before the LORD your
God. Deut. 26:11
8 "And you shall [R]write very plainly on the
stones all the words of this law." Josh. 8:32

Admonition to Obey the Law

9 Then Moses and the priests, the Levites,
spoke to all Israel, saying, "Take heed and lis-
ten, O Israel: This day you have become the
people of the LORD your God.
10 "Therefore you shall obey the voice of the
LORD your God, and observe His command-
ments and His statutes which I command you
today."

Proclamation of the Curses

11 And Moses commanded the people on the
same day, saying,
12 "These shall stand [R]on Mount Gerizim to
bless the people, when you have crossed over
the Jordan: Simeon, Levi, Judah, Issachar, Jo-
seph, and Benjamin; Josh. 8:33
13 "and [R]these shall stand on Mount Ebal to
curse: Reuben, Gad, Asher, Zebulun, Dan, and
Naphtali. Deut. 11:29
14 "And [R]the Levites shall speak with a
loud voice and say to all the men of Is-
rael: Deut. 33:10
15 'Cursed *is* the one who makes a carved or
molded image, an abomination to the LORD,
the work of the hands of the craftsman, and
sets *it* up in secret.'
[R]"And all the people shall answer and say,
'Amen!' Num. 5:22
16 [R]'Cursed *is* the one who treats his father
or his mother with contempt.' Ezek. 22:7
"And all the people shall say, 'Amen!'
17 [R]'Cursed *is* the one who moves his neigh-
bor's landmark.' Deut. 19:14
"And all the people shall say, 'Amen!'
18 [R]'Cursed *is* the one who makes the blind
to wander off the road.' Lev. 19:14
"And all the people shall say, 'Amen!'
19 [R]'Cursed *is* the one who perverts the jus-
tice due the stranger, the fatherless, and
widow.' Ex. 22:21, 22; 23:9
"And all the people shall say, 'Amen!'
20 [R]'Cursed *is* the one who lies with his fa-
ther's wife, because he has uncovered his fa-
ther's bed.' Deut. 22:30
"And all the people shall say, 'Amen!'
21 [R]'Cursed *is* the one who lies with any kind
of animal.' Lev. 18:23; 20:15, 16
"And all the people shall say, 'Amen!'
22 [R]'Cursed *is* the one who lies with his

26:15 Ex. 3:8 **27:3** Ex. 3:8

sister, the daughter of his father or the daughter of his mother.' Lev. 18:9

"And all the people shall say, 'Amen!'

23 [R]'Cursed *is* the one who lies with his mother-in-law.' Lev. 18:17; 20:14

"And all the people shall say, 'Amen!'

24 [R]'Cursed *is* the one who attacks his neighbor secretly.' Ex. 20:13; 21:12

"And all the people shall say, 'Amen!'

25 [R]'Cursed *is* the one who takes a bribe to slay an innocent person.' Ex. 23:7

"And all the people shall say, 'Amen!'

26 [R]'Cursed *is* the one who does not confirm *all* the words of this law by observing them.'

"And all the people shall say, 'Amen!'

CHAPTER 28

Promised Blessings for Obedience

"NOW it shall come to pass, [R]if you diligently obey the voice of the LORD your God, to observe carefully all His commandments which I command you today, that the LORD your God [R]will set you high above all nations of the earth. Ex. 15:26 • Deut. 26:19

2 "And all these blessings shall come upon you and overtake you, because you obey the voice of the LORD your God:

3 "Blessed *shall* you *be* in the city, and blessed *shall* you *be* in the country.

4 "Blessed *shall be* the fruit of your body, the produce of your ground and the increase of your herds, the increase of your cattle and the offspring of your flocks.

5 "Blessed *shall be* your basket and your kneading bowl.

6 [R]"Blessed *shall* you *be* when you come in, and blessed *shall* you *be* when you go out. Ps. 121:8

7 "The LORD will cause your enemies who rise against you to be defeated before your face; they shall come out against you one way and flee before you seven ways.

8 "The LORD will [R]command the blessing on you in your storehouses and in all to which you [R]set your hand, and He will bless you in the land which the LORD your God is giving you. Lev. 25:21 • Deut. 15:10

9 "The LORD will establish you as a holy people to Himself, just as He has sworn to you, if you keep the commandments of the LORD your God and walk in His ways.

10 "Then all peoples of the earth shall see that you are [R]called by the name of the LORD, and they shall be afraid of you. Num. 6:27

11 "And the LORD will grant you plenty of goods, in the fruit of your body, in the increase of your livestock, and in the produce of your ground, in the land of which the LORD swore to your fathers to give you.

12 "The LORD will open to you His good treasure, the heavens, [R]to give the rain to your land in its season, and to bless all the work of your hand. You shall lend to many nations, but you shall not borrow. Lev. 26:4

13 "And the LORD will make [R]you the head and not the tail; you shall be above only, and not be beneath, if you [T]heed the commandments of the LORD your God, which I command you today, and are careful to observe *them*. [Is. 9:14, 15] • *listen to*

14 [R]"So you shall not turn aside from any of the words which I command you this day, *to* the right or the left, to go after other gods to serve them. Deut. 5:32

Promised Curses for Disobedience

15 "But it shall come to pass, [R]if you do not obey the voice of the LORD your God, to observe carefully all His commandments and His statutes which I command you today, that all these curses will come upon you and overtake you: Lev. 26:14–39

16 "Cursed *shall* you *be* in the city, and cursed *shall* you *be* in the country.

17 "Cursed *shall be* your basket and your kneading bowl.

18 "Cursed *shall be* the fruit of your body and the produce of your land, the increase of your cattle and the offspring of your flocks.

19 "Cursed *shall* you *be* when you come in, and cursed *shall* you *be* when you go out.

20 "The LORD will send on you [R]cursing, [R]confusion, and [R]rebuke in all that you set your hand to do, until you are destroyed and until you perish quickly, because of the wickedness of your doings in which you have forsaken Me. Mal. 2:2 • Is. 65:14 • Is. 30:17

21 "The LORD will make the plague cling to you until He has consumed you from the land which you are going to possess.

22 [R]"The LORD will strike you with consumption, with fever, with inflammation, with severe burning fever, with the sword, with scorching, and with mildew; they shall pursue you until you perish. Lev. 26:16

23 "And [R]your heavens which *are* over your head shall be bronze, and the earth which is under you *shall be* iron. Lev. 26:19

24 "The LORD will change the rain of your land to powder and dust; from the heaven it shall come down on you until you are destroyed.

25 [R]"The LORD will cause you to be defeated before your enemies; you shall go out one way against them and flee seven ways before them; and you shall become troublesome to all the kingdoms of the earth. Deut. 32:30

26 "Your carcasses shall be food for all the birds of the air and the beasts of the earth, and no one shall frighten *them* away.

27 "The LORD will strike you with [R]the boils of Egypt, with [R]tumors, with the scab, and with the itch, from which you cannot be healed. Ex. 15:26 • 1 Sam. 5:6

28 “The LORD will strike you with madness
and blindness and confusion of heart.
29 “And you shall [R]grope at noonday, as a
blind man gropes in darkness; you shall not
prosper in your ways; you shall be only op-
pressed and plundered continually, and no
one shall save *you*. Job 5:14
30 [R]“You shall betroth a wife, but another
man shall lie with her; [R]you shall build a
house, but you shall not dwell in it; [R]you shall
plant a vineyard, but shall not gather its
grapes. Jer. 8:10 • Amos 5:11 • Deut. 20:6
31 “Your ox *shall be* slaughtered before your
eyes, but you shall not eat of it; your donkey
shall be violently taken away from before you,
and shall not be restored to you; your sheep
shall be given to your enemies, and you shall
have no one to rescue *them*.
32 “Your sons and your daughters *shall be*
given to [R]another people, and your eyes shall
look and [R]fail *with longing* for them all day
long; and *there shall be* no strength in your
[R]hand. 2 Chr. 29:9 • Ps. 119:82 • Neh. 5:5
33 “A nation whom you have not known
shall eat the fruit of your land and the pro-
duce of your labor, and you shall be only op-
pressed and crushed continually.
34 “So you shall be driven mad because of
the sight which your eyes see.
35 “The LORD will strike you in the knees
and on the legs with severe boils which can-
not be healed, and from the sole of your foot
to the top of your head.
36 “The LORD will [R]bring you and the king
whom you set over you to a nation which nei-
ther you nor your fathers have known, and
[R]there you shall serve other gods—wood and
stone. Jer. 39:1–9 • Deut. 4:28
37 “And you shall become an astonishment,
a proverb, and a byword among all nations
where the LORD will drive you.
38 [R]“You shall carry much seed out to the
field but gather little in, for [R]the locust shall
[T]consume it. Mic. 6:15 • Joel 1:4 • *devour*
39 “You shall plant vineyards and tend *them*,
but you shall neither drink *of* the [R]wine nor
gather the *grapes;* for the worms shall eat
them. Zeph. 1:13
40 “You shall have olive trees throughout all
your territory, but you shall not anoint *your-
self* with the oil; for your olives shall drop off.
41 “You shall beget sons and daughters, but
they shall not be yours; for [R]they shall go into
captivity. Lam. 1:5
42 “Locusts shall [T]consume all your trees
and the produce of your land. *possess*
43 “The alien who *is* among you shall rise
higher and higher above you, and you shall
come down lower and lower.
44 “He shall lend to you, but you shall not
lend to him; he shall be the head, and you
shall be the tail.
45 “Moreover all these curses shall come
upon you and pursue and overtake you, until
you are destroyed, because you [T]did not obey
the voice of the LORD your God, to keep His
commandments and His statutes which He
commanded you. *did not listen to*
46 “And they shall be upon [R]you for a sign
and a wonder, and on your descendants for-
ever. Is. 8:18
47 [R]“Because you did not serve the LORD
your God with joy and gladness of heart, for
the abundance of everything, Neh. 9:35–37
48 “therefore you shall serve your enemies,
whom the LORD will send against you, in hun-
ger, in thirst, in nakedness, and in need of
everything; and He will put a yoke of iron on
your neck until He has destroyed you.
49 [R]“The LORD will bring a nation against
you from afar, from the end of the earth, *as
swift* as the eagle flies, a nation whose lan-
guage you will not understand, Jer. 5:15
50 “a nation of fierce countenance, [R]which
does not respect the elderly nor show favor to
the young. 2 Chr. 36:17
51 “And they shall eat the increase of your
livestock and the produce of your land, until
you are destroyed; they shall not leave you
grain or new wine or oil, *or* the increase of
your cattle or the offspring of your flocks,
until they have destroyed you.
52 “They shall besiege you at all your gates
until your high and fortified walls, in which
you trust, come down throughout all your
land; and they shall besiege you at all your
gates throughout all your land which the
LORD your God has given you.
53 [R]“You shall eat the fruit of your own body,
the flesh of your sons and your daughters
whom the LORD your God has given you, in
the siege and desperate straits in which your
enemy shall distress you. Lev. 26:29
54 “The [T]sensitive and very refined man
among you [R]will be hostile toward his
brother, toward [R]the wife of his bosom, and
toward the rest of his children whom he
leaves behind, Lit. *tender* • Deut. 15:9 • Deut. 13:6
55 “so that he will not give any of them the
flesh of his children whom he will eat, be-
cause he has nothing left in the siege and des-
perate straits in which your enemy shall
distress you at all your gates.
56 “The [T]tender and [T]delicate woman among
you, who would not venture to set the sole of
her foot on the ground because of her deli-
cateness and sensitivity, will refuse* to the
husband of her bosom, and to her son and her
daughter, *sensitive* • *refined*
57 “her [T]placenta which comes out [R]from be-
tween her feet and her children whom she
bears; for she will eat them secretly for lack of
everything in the siege and desperate straits

28:56 Lit. *her eye shall be evil toward*

in which your enemy shall distress you at all
your gates. *afterbirth* • Gen. 49:10
58 "If you do not carefully observe all the
words of this law that are written in this book,
that you may fear this glorious and awesome
name, THE LORD YOUR GOD,
59 "then the LORD will bring upon you and
your descendants [R]extraordinary plagues—
great and prolonged plagues—and serious
and prolonged sicknesses. Dan. 9:12
60 "Moreover He will bring back on you all
the diseases of Egypt, of which you were
afraid, and they shall cling to you.
61 "Also every sickness and every plague,
which *is* not written in this Book of the Law,
will the LORD bring upon you until you are de-
stroyed.
62 "You shall be left few in number, whereas
you were [R]as the stars of heaven in multitude,
because you would not obey the voice of the
LORD your God. Neh. 9:23
63 "And it shall be, *that* just as the LORD [R]re-
joiced over you to do you good and multiply
you, so the LORD will rejoice over you to de-
stroy you and bring you to nothing; and you
shall be plucked[T] from off the land which you
go to possess. Jer. 32:41 • *torn*
64 "Then the LORD [R]will scatter you among
all peoples, from one end of the earth to the
other, and there you shall serve other gods,
which neither you nor your fathers have
known—wood and stone. Jer. 16:13
65 "And [R]among those nations you shall find
no rest, nor shall the sole of your foot have a
resting place; [R]but there the LORD will give
you a trembling heart, failing eyes, and [R]an-
guish of soul. Amos 9:4 • Lev. 26:36 • Lev. 26:16
66 "Your life shall hang in doubt before you;
you shall fear day and night, and have no as-
surance of life.
67 "In the morning you shall say, 'Oh, that it
were evening!' And at evening you shall say,
'Oh, that it were morning!' because of the fear
which terrifies your heart, and because of the
sight which your eyes see.
68 "And the LORD [R]will take you back to
Egypt in ships, by the way of which I said to
you, [R]'You shall never see it again.' And there
you shall be offered for sale to your enemies
as male and female slaves, but no one will buy
you." Hos. 8:13 • Deut. 17:16

CHAPTER 29

The Covenant Is Based on the Power of God

THESE *are* the words of the covenant
which the LORD commanded Moses to
make with the children of Israel in the land of
Moab, besides the [R]covenant which He made
with them in Horeb. Deut. 5:2, 3
2 Now Moses called all Israel and said to
them: [R]"You have seen all that the LORD did
before your eyes in the land of Egypt, to
Pharaoh and to all his servants and to all his
land— Ex. 19:4
3 "the great trials which your eyes have
seen, the signs, and those great wonders.
4 "Yet [R]the LORD has not given you a heart
to perceive and eyes to see and ears to hear, to
this *very* day. [Acts 28:26, 27]
5 [R]"And I have led you forty years in the
wilderness. [R]Your clothes have not worn out
on you, and your sandals have not worn out
on your feet. Deut. 1:3; 8:2 • Deut. 8:4
6 "You have not eaten bread, nor have you
drunk wine or *similar* drink, that you may
know that I *am* the LORD your God.
7 "And when you came to this place, [R]Sihon
king of Heshbon and Og king of Bashan came
out against us to battle, and we conquered
them. Num. 21:23, 24
8 "We took their land and gave it as an in-
heritance to the Reubenites, to the Gadites,
and to half the tribe of Manasseh.
9 "Therefore [R]keep the words of this
covenant, and do them, that you may [R]prosper
in all that you do. Deut. 4:6 • Josh. 1:7

Parties of the Covenant

10 "All of you stand today before the LORD
your God: your leaders and your tribes and
your elders and your officers, all the men of
Israel,
11 "your little ones and your wives—also the
stranger who *is* in your camp, from [R]the one
who cuts your wood to the one who draws
your water— Josh. 9:21, 23, 27
12 "that you may enter into covenant with
the LORD your God, and [R]into His oath,
which the LORD your God makes with you
today, Neh. 10:29
13 "that He may [R]establish you today as a

29:10–15; 30:11–20 The Palestinian Covenant—The covenant concerning Palestine is the third of the theocratic covenants (pertaining to the rule of God). The Palestinian covenant has two aspects: (1) the legal aspects which are immediate and conditional (Page 199—Deut. 27—29); and (2) the grace aspects which are future and unconditional (Page 203—Deut. 30:1–9). The enjoyment of the immediate blessings are introduced by the conditional formula: "if you diligently obey the voice of the LORD your God . . . the LORD your God will set you high above all nations of the earth" (Page 200—Deut. 28:1). Sadly, Israel did not meet the condition of obedience, and is still experiencing God's curses and punishment for their disobedience (Page 200—Deut. 28:15–68). The unconditional grace aspects of the Palestinian covenant have yet to be realized. God will regather the scattered people of Israel and establish them in the land He has promised unconditionally to give them. Deut. concludes the Palestinian covenant with a final warning and challenge for obedience (Page 203—Deut. 30:1–20).

Now turn to Page 312—2 Sam. 7:4–17: The Davidic Covenant.

people for Himself, and *that* He may be God
to you, just as He has spoken to you, and just
as He has sworn to your fathers, to Abraham,
Isaac, and Jacob. Deut. 28:9
14 "I make this covenant and this oath, [R]not
with you alone, [Jer. 31:31]
15 "but with *him* who stands here with us
today before the LORD our God, as well as
with *him* who *is* not here with us today

Scattering of Israel

16 (for you know that we dwelt in the land of
Egypt and that we came through the nations
which you passed by,
17 and you saw their abominations and their
idols which *were* among them—wood and
stone and silver and gold);
18 "so that there may not be among you man
or woman or family or tribe, whose heart
turns away today from the LORD our God, to
go *and* serve the gods of these nations, and
that there may not be among you a root bear-
ing bitterness or wormwood;
19 "and so it may not happen, when he hears
the words of this curse, that he blesses himself
in his heart, saying, 'I shall have peace, even
though I follow the dictates* of my heart'—as
though the drunkard could be included with
the sober.
20 "The LORD would not spare him; for then
the anger of the LORD and His jealousy would
burn against that man, and every curse that is
written in this book would settle on him, and
the LORD would blot out his name from under
heaven.
21 "And the LORD would separate him from
all the tribes of Israel for adversity, according
to all the curses of the covenant that are writ-
ten in this Book of the Law,
22 "so that the coming generation of your
children who rise up after you, and the for-
eigner who comes from a far land, would
say, when they [R]see the plagues of that land
and the sicknesses which the LORD has laid
on it: Jer. 19:8; 49:17; 50:13
23 'The whole land *is* brimstone, [R]salt, and
burning; it is not sown, nor does it bear, nor
does any grass grow there, like the overthrow
of Sodom and Gomorrah, Admah, and Ze-
boiim, which the LORD overthrew in His anger
and His wrath.' Zeph. 2:9
24 "All nations would say, [R]'Why has the
LORD done so to this land? What does the heat
of this great anger mean?' 1 Kin. 9:8
25 "Then *people* would say: 'Because they
have forsaken the covenant of the LORD God
of their fathers, which He made with them
when He brought them out of the land of
Egypt;
26 'for they went and served other gods and
worshiped them, gods that they did not know
and that He had not given to them.
27 'Then the anger of the LORD was aroused
against this land, [R]to bring on it every curse
that is written in this book. Dan. 9:11
28 'And the LORD [R]uprooted them from their
land in anger, in wrath, and in great indigna-
tion, and cast them into another land, as *it is*
this day.' 1 Kin. 14:15
29 "The secret *things belong* to the LORD our
God, but those *things which are* revealed *be-
long* to us and to our children forever, that *we*
may do all the words of this law.

CHAPTER 30

Restoration of Israel

"NOW it shall come to pass, when all
these things come upon you, the bless-
ing and the curse which I have set before you,
and you call *them* to mind among all the na-
tions where the LORD your God drives you,
2 "and you return to the LORD your God and
obey His voice, according to all that I com-
mand you today, you and your children, with
all your heart and with all your soul,
3 [R]"that the LORD your God will bring you

29:19 *walk in the stubbornness* or *imagination*

29:29 Revelation of God's Word—Revelation may be defined as that process by which God imparted to human beings truths they otherwise could not know. The details of creation in Genesis 1 and 2 are an example of revelation. As the first human was not created until the sixth day, we could not have possibly known the events occurring prior to this until God gave the facts to Moses.

We know God spoke to the human authors of our Bible; but just how did He speak? Was it in Hebrew? Greek? Angelic language? He spoke to them in their own language. God's call to young Samuel in the temple (Page 275—1 Sam. 3:1–10) proves this, for the boy at first mistook God's voice for that of the aged priest Eli. Sometimes God spoke through angels: Gabriel was sent from heaven to tell Mary she would give birth to the Messiah (Page 1041—Luke 1:26–37). On other occasions the Lord spoke directly to individuals, as He did to Noah concerning the Great Flood (Page 9—Gen. 6:13–21).

One of God's methods of communication in Scripture is to reveal His message through dreams and visions: The wise men (Page 978—Matt. 2:12) were warned in a dream not to return to Herod, while Peter was later instructed in a vision to minister to Cornelius (Page 1123—Acts 10:10–16). God has communicated in many different ways. He revealed Himself to Moses from a burning bush (Page 57—Ex. 3:4) and to Moses, Aaron, and Miriam out of a cloud (Page 145—Num. 12:4, 5).

One of the most important ways that divine truths were given in the Old Testament was through the Angel of the Lord. Most Bible students perceive this heavenly messenger to be the preincarnate Christ Himself. For example, it is the Angel of the Lord who reassured Joshua on the eve of a battle (Page 218—Josh. 5:13–15).

Now turn to Page 737—Is. 59:21: Inspiration of God's Word.

back from captivity, and have compassion on
you, and [R]gather you again from all the na-
tions where the LORD your God has scattered
you. Jer. 29:14 • Ezek. 34:13
4 [R]"If *any* of you are driven out to the far-
thest *parts* under heaven, from there the LORD
your God will gather you, and from there He
will bring you. Neh. 1:9
5 "Then the LORD your God will bring you
to the land which your fathers possessed, and
you shall possess it. He will prosper you and
multiply you more than your fathers.
6 "And [R]the LORD your God will circumcise
your heart and the heart of your descen-
dants, to love the LORD your God with all
your heart and with all your soul, that you
may live. Deut. 10:16
7 "Also the LORD your God will put all these
curses on your enemies and on those who
hate you, who persecuted you.
8 "And you will [R]again obey the voice of the
LORD and do all His commandments which I
command you today. Zeph. 3:20
9 [R]"The LORD your God will make you
abound in all the work of your hand, in the
[T]fruit of your body, in the increase of your
livestock, and in the produce of your land for
good. For the LORD will again [R]rejoice over
you for good as He rejoiced over your fa-
thers, Deut. 28:11 • *offspring* • Jer. 32:41
10 "if you obey the voice of the LORD your
God, to keep His commandments and His
statutes which are written in this Book of the
Law, *and* if you turn to the LORD your God
with all your heart and with all your soul.

11 "For this commandment which I com-
mand you today [R]*is* [T]not *too* mysterious for
you, nor *is* it far off. Is. 45:19 • *not hidden from*
12 "It *is* not in heaven, that you should say,
'Who will ascend into heaven for us and bring
it to us, that we may hear it and do it?'
13 "Nor *is* it beyond the sea, that you should
say, 'Who will go over the sea for us and bring
it to us, that we may hear it and do it?'
14 "But the word *is* very near you, [R]in your
mouth and in your heart, that you may do
it. Rom. 10:8
15 "See, [R]I have set before you today life and
good, death and evil, Deut. 30:1, 19
16 "in that I command you today to love the
LORD your God, to walk in His ways, and to
keep His commandments, His statutes, and
His judgments, that you may live and multi-
ply; and the LORD your God will bless you in
the land which you go to possess.
17 "But if your heart turns away so that you
do not hear, and are drawn away, and worship
other gods and serve them,
18 [R]"I announce to you today that you shall
surely perish; you shall not prolong *your* days
in the land which you cross over the Jordan to
go in and possess. Deut. 4:26; 8:19
19 [R]"I call heaven and earth as witnesses
today against you, *that* [R]I have set before you
life and death, blessing and cursing; therefore
choose life, that both you and your descen-
dants may live; Deut. 4:26 • Deut. 30:15
20 "that you may love the LORD your God,
that you may obey His voice, and that you
may cling to Him, for He *is* your [R]life and the
length of your days; and that you may dwell in
the land which the LORD swore to your fa-
thers, to Abraham, Isaac, and Jacob, to give
them." [John 11:25; 14:6]

CHAPTER 31

Moses Charges Joshua and Israel

THEN Moses went and spoke these words
to all Israel.
2 And he said to them: "I [R]*am* one hun-
dred and twenty years old today. I can no
longer [R]go out and come in. Also the LORD
has said to me, [R]'You shall not cross over
this Jordan.' Deut. 34:7 • 1 Kin. 3:7 • Num. 20:12
3 "The LORD your God Himself crosses over
before you; He will destroy these nations from
before you, and you shall dispossess them.
Joshua himself crosses over before you, just
as the LORD has said.
4 [R]"And the LORD will do to them [R]as He
did to Sihon and Og, the kings of the Amo-
rites and their land, when He destroyed
them. Deut. 3:21 • Num. 21:24, 33
5 [R]"The LORD will give them over to you,
that you may do to them according to every
commandment which I have commanded
you. Deut. 7:2; 20:10–20
6 "Be strong and of good courage, do not
fear nor be afraid of them; for the LORD your
God, He *is* the One who goes with you. He will
not leave you nor forsake you."
7 Then Moses called Joshua and said to
him in the sight of all Israel, [R]"Be strong and
of good courage, for you must go with this
people to the land which the LORD has sworn
to their fathers to give them, and you shall
cause them to inherit it. Deut. 31:23
8 "And the LORD, [R]He *is* the One who goes
before you. [R]He will be with you, He will not
leave you nor forsake you; do not fear nor be
dismayed." Ex. 13:21 • Josh. 1:5
9 So Moses wrote this law and delivered it
to the priests, the sons of Levi, [R]who bore the
ark of the covenant of the LORD, and to all the
elders of Israel. Josh. 3:3
10 And Moses commanded them, saying: "At
the end of *every* seven years, at the appointed
time in the [R]year of release, [R]at the Feast of
Tabernacles, Deut. 15:1, 2 • Lev. 23:34
11 "when all Israel comes to [R]appear before
the LORD your God in the place which He
chooses, [R]you shall read this law before all Is-
rael in their hearing. Deut. 16:16 • Josh. 8:34

12 [R]"Gather the people together, men and
women and little ones, and the stranger who
is within your gates, that they may hear and
that they may learn to fear the LORD your God
and carefully observe all the words of this
law, Deut. 4:10
13 "and *that* their children, [R]who have not
known it, [R]may hear and learn to fear the
LORD your God as long as you live in the
land which you cross the Jordan to pos-
sess." Deut. 11:2 • Ps. 78:6, 7

God Charges Israel

14 Then the LORD said to Moses, [R]"Behold,
the days approach when you must die; call
Joshua, and present yourselves in the taber-
nacle of meeting, that [R]I may [T]inaugurate
him." So Moses and Joshua went and pre-
sented themselves in the tabernacle of meet-
ing. Num. 27:13 • Deut. 3:28 • *commission*
15 Now the LORD appeared at the tabernacle
in a pillar of cloud, and the pillar of cloud
stood above the door of the tabernacle.
16 And the LORD said to Moses: "Behold, you
will rest with your fathers; and this people
will rise and [R]play the harlot with the gods of
the foreigners of the land, where they go *to be*
among them, and they will forsake Me and
[R]break My covenant which I have made with
them. Ex. 34:15 • Judg. 2:20
17 "Then My anger shall be aroused
against them in that day, and [R]I will forsake
them, and I will [R]hide My face from them,
and they shall be devoured. And many evils
and troubles shall befall them, so that they
will say in that day, [R]'Have not these evils
come upon us because our God *is* not among
us?' 2 Chr. 15:2 • Deut. 32:20 • Judg. 6:13
18 "And I will surely hide My face in that day
because of all the evil which they have done,
in that they have turned to other gods.
19 "Now therefore, write down this song for
yourselves, and teach it to the children of Is-
rael; put it in their mouths, that this song may
be [R]a witness for Me against the children of
Israel. Deut. 31:22, 26
20 "When I have brought them to the land
flowing with milk and honey, of which I
swore to their fathers, and they have eaten
and filled themselves [R]and grown fat, [R]then
they will turn to other gods and serve them;
and they will provoke Me and break My
covenant. Deut. 32:15–17 • Deut. 31:16
21 "Then it shall be, when many evils and
troubles have come upon them, that this song
will testify against them as a witness; for it
will not be forgotten in the mouths of their
descendants, for [R]I know the inclination [R]of
their behavior today, even before I have
brought them to the land of which I swore *to
give them*." Hos. 5:3 • Amos 5:25, 26

The Book of the Law Is Deposited

22 Therefore Moses wrote this song the
same day, and taught it to the children of Is-
rael.
23 [R]Then He inaugurated Joshua the son of
Nun, and said, [R]"Be strong and of good
courage; for you shall bring the children of Is-
rael into the land of which I swore to them,
and I will be with you." Num. 27:23 • Deut. 31:7
24 So it was, when Moses had completed
writing the words of this law in a book, when
they were finished,
25 that Moses commanded the Levites, who
bore the ark of the covenant of the LORD, say-
ing:
26 "Take this Book of the Law, [R]and put it be-
side the ark of the covenant of the LORD your
God, that it may be there [R]as a witness against
you; 2 Kin. 22:8 • Deut. 31:19
27 "for I know your rebellion and your stiff
neck. *If* today, while I am yet alive with you,
you have been rebellious against the LORD,
then how much more after my death?
28 "Gather to me all the elders of your tribes,
and your officers, that I may speak these
words in their hearing and call heaven and
earth to witness against them.
29 "For I know that after my death you will
[R]become utterly corrupt, and turn aside from
the way which I have commanded you. And
[R]evil will befall you in the latter days, because

31:12 Obedience to God's Word—Reading, memorizing, and meditating upon the Word of God are of no value without obedience to the Word of God. To obey the Word of God, you do what the Word of God indicates should be done in any situation. Obedience to the Word of God is the only way that the child of God can be pleasing to God in the new life. Obedience to God's Word results in: being treasured by God (Page 73—Ex. 19:5); blessedness (happiness) in life (Page 610—Ps. 119:2); not being ashamed (Page 610—Ps. 119:4–6); understanding (Page 612—Ps. 119:100); avoidance of evil (Page 630—Ps. 119:101); guidance for life (Page 612—Ps. 119:105); safety and freedom from anxiety (Page 612—Prov. 1:33); life (Page 645—Prov. 19:16; Page 834—Ezek. 18:19; Page 1090—John 8:51); God's blessing (Page 683—Is. 1:19); greatness in the kingdom of heaven (Page 981—Matt. 5:19); bearing fruit for God (Page 991—Matt. 13:23); manifesting love for God (Page 1100—John 14:23; Page 1293—1 John 2:5); promise of God's presence (Page 1100—John 14:23; Page 1300—2 John 9); abiding in the love of God (Page 1100—John 15:10); evidence of the doctrine that has been taught (Page 1153—Rom. 6:17); assurance of salvation (Page 1293—1 John 2:3); eternal life (Page 1294—1 John 2:17); dwelling in God (Page 1296—1 John 3:24); love of God's children (Page 1296—1 John 5:2); and entrance into heaven (Page 1327—Rev. 22:7).

Now turn to Page 625—Ps. 150:1: Praise.

you will do evil in the sight of the LORD, to
provoke Him to anger through the work of
your hands." Judg. 2:19 • Deut. 28:15
30 Then Moses spoke in the hearing of all
the assembly of Israel the words of this song
until they were ended:

CHAPTER 32

The Song of Moses

"GIVE [R]ear, O heavens, and I will speak;
And hear, O [R]earth, the words of my mouth. Deut. 4:26 • Jer. 6:19
2 Let my [T]teaching drop as the rain,
My speech distill as the dew, *doctrine*
[R]As raindrops on the tender herb,
And as showers on the grass. Ps. 72:6
3 For I proclaim the name of the LORD:
Ascribe greatness to our God.
4 *He is* [R]the Rock, His work *is* perfect;
For all His ways *are* justice, Ps. 18:2
[R]A God of truth and without injustice;
Righteous and upright *is* He. Is. 65:16

5 "They[R] have corrupted themselves;
They are not His children,
Because of their blemish: Deut. 4:25; 31:29
A perverse and crooked generation.
6 Do you thus deal with the LORD
O foolish and unwise people?
Is He not [R]your Father, *who* [R]bought you? Is. 63:16 • Ps. 74:2
Has He not [R]made you and established you? Deut. 32:15

7 "Remember[R] the days of old, Ps. 44:1
Consider the years of many generations.
Ask your father, and he will show you;
Your elders, and they will tell you:
8 When the Most High [R]divided their inheritance to the nations, Acts 17:26
When He [R]separated the sons of Adam,
He set the boundaries of the peoples
According to the number of the children of Israel. Gen. 11:8
9 For the LORD's portion *is* His people;
Jacob *is* the place of His inheritance.

10 "He found him [R]in a desert land Jer. 2:6
And in the wasteland, a howling wilderness;
He encircled him, He instructed him,
He kept him as the apple of His eye.
11 [R]As an eagle stirs up its nest, Is. 31:5
Hovers over its young,
Spreading out its wings, taking them up,
Carrying them on its wings,
12 *So* the LORD alone led him,
And *there was* no foreign god with him.

13 "He[R] made him ride in the heights of the earth, Is. 58:14
That he might eat the produce of the fields;
He made him draw honey from the rock,
And oil from the flinty rock;
14 Curds from the cattle, and milk of the flock,
[R]With fat of lambs; Ps. 81:16
And rams of the breed of Bashan, and goats,
With the choicest wheat;
And you drank wine, the [R]blood of the grapes. Gen. 49:11

15 "But Jeshurun grew fat and kicked;
[R]You grew fat, you grew thick,
You are obese! Deut. 31:20
Then he [R]forsook God *who* [R]made him,
And scornfully esteemed the Rock of his salvation. Is. 1:4 • Is. 51:13
16 [R]They provoked Him to jealousy with foreign *gods;* 1 Cor. 10:22
With [T]abominations they provoked Him to anger. *detestable acts*
17 [R]They sacrificed to demons, not to God,

32:7 God's Work in the Past—The Bible's revelation of God's work in the past provides an informative and exciting panorama of centuries of divine activity toward people.

First, it gives humankind an *education* in truths unknowable apart from divine revelation. For example, the creation of man and woman described in Genesis 1 and 2 answers two most basic questions: "Who am I?" and "Where did I come from?" Only God Himself could disclose these facts.

Second, the Bible sets forth a mass of historical *evidence* for the truthfulness of the Christian faith. The most outstanding of these evidences are fulfilled prophecy, the miracles of Christ, and Christ's death and resurrection. The believer's faith is thus grounded in historical events and is far removed from what some have called "a leap into the dark."

Third, the Bible records *examples* to help present-day Christians. Various failures of Israel and the resulting judgments of God are often cited in the New Testament as things to avoid, for example, their idolatry and grumbling in the wilderness (Page 1174—1 Cor. 10:11), and their unbelief at Kadesh (Page 1260—Heb. 4:11). Paul is said to be a living example for believers to follow (Page 1169—1 Cor. 4:16; 11:1), as is Jesus' humility in the midst of suffering (Page 1281—1 Pet. 2:21).

Fourth, the Bible provides *encouragement* for Christians in their life and witness. If God could use an adulterer and murderer like David, then God can certainly use struggling Christians today if they possess David's devotion to the Lord. Likewise, if God saved Saul of Tarsus, the chief enemy of the early church (Page 1121—Acts 9:1–31), then surely He can save the people with whom Christians daily share their faith.

Now turn to Page 620—Ps. 139:14: God's Work in Our Lives.

To gods they did not know, Rev. 9:20
To new *gods*, new arrivals
That your fathers did not fear.
18[R] Of the Rock *who* begot you, you are
unmindful, Is. 17:10
And have [R]forgotten the God who
fathered you. Jer. 2:32

19 "And[R] when the LORD saw *it*, He spurned
them,
Because of the provocation of His sons
and His daughters. Judg. 2:14
20 And He said: 'I will hide My face from
them,
I will see what their end *will be*,
For they *are* a perverse generation,
Children in whom *is* no faith.
21[R] They have provoked Me to jealousy by
what is not God; Ps. 78:58
They have moved Me to anger [R]by their
foolish idols. Ps. 31:6
But [R]I will provoke them to jealousy by
those who are not a nation;
I will move them to anger by a foolish
nation. Rom. 10:19
22 For [R]a fire is kindled in My anger,
And shall burn to the [T]lowest [T]hell;
It shall consume the earth with her
increase, Lam. 4:11 • *lowest part of*
And set on fire the foundations of the
mountains. Or *Sheol*

23 'I will heap disasters on them;
I will spend My arrows on them.
24 *They shall be* wasted with hunger,
Devoured by pestilence and bitter
destruction;
I will also send against them the [R]teeth
of beasts, Lev. 26:22
With the poison of serpents of the dust.
25 The sword shall destroy outside;
There shall be terror within
For the young man and virgin,
The nursing child with the man of gray
hairs.
26[R] I would have said, "I will dash them in
pieces, Ezek. 20:23
I will make the memory of them to cease
from among men,"
27 Had I not feared the wrath of the enemy,
Lest their adversaries should
misunderstand,
Lest they should say, [R]"Our hand *is*
high; Is. 10:12–15
And it is not the LORD who has done all
this." '

28 "For they *are* a nation void of counsel,
Nor *is there any* understanding in them.
29[R] Oh, that they were wise, *that* they
understood this, [Luke 19:42]
That they would consider their [R]latter
end! Deut. 31:29
30 How could one chase a thousand,
And two put ten thousand to flight,
Unless their Rock had sold them,
And the LORD had surrendered them?
31 For their rock *is* not like our Rock,
[R]Even our enemies themselves *being*
judges. [1 Sam. 4:7, 8]
32 For [R]their vine *is* of the vine of Sodom
And of the fields of Gomorrah;
Their grapes *are* grapes of gall,
Their clusters *are* bitter. Is. 1:8–10
33 Their wine *is* the poison of serpents,
And the cruel venom of cobras.

34 '*Is* this not laid up in store with Me,
Sealed up among My treasures?
35[R] Vengeance is Mine, and recompense;
Their foot shall slip in *due* time;
[R]For the day of their calamity *is* at hand,
And the things to come hasten upon
them.' Heb. 10:30 • 2 Pet. 2:3
36 "For[R] the LORD will judge His people
[R]And have compassion on His servants,
When He sees that *their* power is gone,
And [R]*there is* no one *remaining*, bond or
free. Ps. 135:14 • Jer. 31:20 • 2 Kin. 14:26
37 He will say: 'Where *are* their gods,
The rock in which they sought refuge?
38 Who ate the fat of their sacrifices,
And drank the wine of their drink
offering?
Let them rise and help you,
And be your refuge.

39 'Now see that [R]I, *even* I, *am* He,
And [R]*there is* no God besides Me;
I kill and I make alive;
I wound and I heal;
Nor *is there any* who can deliver from
My hand. Is. 41:4; 43:10 • Is. 45:5
40 For I raise My hand to heaven,
And say, "*As* I live forever,
41 If I [T]whet My glittering sword, *sharpen*
And My hand takes hold on judgment,
I will render vengeance to My enemies,
And repay those who hate Me.
42 I will make My arrows drunk with blood,
And My sword shall devour flesh,
With the blood of the slain and the
captives,
From the heads of the leaders of the
enemy." '

43 "Rejoice,[R] O Gentiles, *with* His people;*
For He will [R]avenge the blood of His
servants, Rom. 15:10 • Rev. 6:10; 19:2
And render vengeance to His adversaries;
He [R]will provide atonement for His land
and His people." Ps. 65:3; 79:9; 85:1

32:43 DSS fragment adds *And let all the gods (angels) worship Him;* cf. LXX and Heb. 1:6

44 So Moses came with Joshua* the son of
Nun and spoke all the words of this song in
the hearing of the people.
45 Moses finished speaking all these words
to all Israel,
46 and he said to them: [R]"Set your hearts on
all the words which I testify among you today,
which you shall command your [R]children to
be careful to observe—all the words of this
law. Ezek. 40:4; 44:5 • Deut. 11:19
47 "For it *is* not a futile thing for you, be-
cause it *is* your life, and by this word you shall
prolong *your* days in the land which you cross
over the Jordan to possess."

Moses Is Ordered to Mount Nebo

48 Then the LORD spoke to Moses that very
same day, saying:
49 [R]"Go up this mountain of the Abarim,
Mount Nebo, which *is* in the land of Moab,
across from Jericho; view the land of Canaan,
which I give to the children of Israel as a pos-
session; Num. 27:12–14
50 "and die on the mountain which you as-
cend, and be gathered to your people, just as
Aaron your brother died on Mount Hor and
was gathered to his people;
51 "because [R]you trespassed against Me
among the children of Israel at the waters of
Meribah Kadesh, in the Wilderness of Zin, be-
cause you did not hallow Me in the midst of
the children of Israel. Num. 20:11–13
52 "Yet you shall see the land before *you,*
though you shall not go there, into the land
which I am giving to the children of Israel."

CHAPTER 33

Moses Blesses the Tribes

NOW this *is* [R]the blessing with which Mo-
ses [R]the man of God blessed the children
of Israel before his death. Gen. 49:28 • Ps. 90
2 And he said:

[R]"The LORD came from Sinai, Ps. 68:8, 17
And dawned on them from [R]Seir;
He shone forth from [R]Mount Paran,
And He came with [R]ten thousands of
saints; Deut. 2:1, 4 • Num. 10:12 • Dan. 7:10
From His right hand
Came a fiery law for them.
3 Yes, [R]He loves the people; Hos. 11:1
All His saints *are* in Your hand;
They [R]sit down at Your feet; [Luke 10:39]
Everyone receives Your words.
4 Moses commanded a law for us,
A heritage of the congregation of
Jacob.
5 And He was [R]King in [R]Jeshurun,
When the leaders of the people were
gathered, Ex. 15:18 • Deut. 32:15
All the tribes of Israel together.

6 "Let [R]Reuben live, and not die,
Nor let his men be few." Gen. 49:3, 4

7 And this he said of Judah:

"Hear, LORD, the voice of Judah,
And bring him to his people;
[R]Let his hands be sufficient for him,
And may You be [R]a help against his
enemies." Gen. 49:8 • Ps. 146:5

8 And of [R]Levi he said: Gen. 49:5
[R]"*Let* Your Thummim and Your Urim *be*
with Your holy one, Ex. 28:30
[R]Whom You tested at Massah,
And with whom You contended at the
waters of Meribah, Ps. 81:7
9 Who says of his father and mother,
'I have not [R]seen them'; [Gen. 29:32]
[R]Nor did he acknowledge his brothers,
Or know his own children; Ex. 32:26–28
For [R]they have observed Your word
And kept Your covenant. Mal. 2:5, 6
10 [R]They shall teach Jacob Your judgments,
And Israel Your law. Lev. 10:11
They shall put incense before You,
[R]And a whole burnt sacrifice on Your
altar. Ps. 51:19
11 Bless his substance, LORD,
And [R]accept the work of his hands;
Strike the loins of those who rise against
him, 2 Sam. 24:23
And of those who hate him, that they
rise not again."

12 Of Benjamin he said:

"The beloved of the LORD shall dwell in
safety by Him,
Who shelters him all the day long;
And he shall dwell between His
shoulders."

13 And of Joseph he said:

[R]"Blessed of the LORD *is* his land,
With the precious things of heaven, with
the [R]dew, Gen. 49:22–26 • Gen. 27:28
And the deep lying beneath,
14 With the precious fruits of the sun,
With the precious produce of the
months,
15 With the best things of [R]the ancient
mountains, Gen. 49:26
With the precious things [R]of the
everlasting hills, Hab. 3:6
16 With the precious things of the earth and
its fullness,
And the favor of [R]Him who dwelt in the
bush. Ex. 3:2–4

32:44 Heb. *Hoshea,* Num. 13:8, 16

Let *the blessing* come 'on the head of
Joseph,
And on the crown of the head of him
who was separate from his brothers.'*
17 His glory *is like* a [R]firstborn bull,
And his horns *like* the [R]horns of the wild
ox; 1 Chr. 5:1 • Num. 23:22
Together with them
[R]He shall push the peoples Ps. 44:5
To the ends of the earth;
[R]They *are* the ten thousands of Ephraim,
And they *are* the thousands of
Manasseh." Gen. 48:19

18 And of Zebulun he said:

"Rejoice, Zebulun, in your going out,
And Issachar in your tents!
19 They shall [R]call the peoples *to* the
mountain; Is. 2:3
There [R]they shall offer sacrifices of
righteousness; Ps. 4:5; 51:19
For they shall partake *of* the abundance
of the seas
And *of* treasures hidden in the sand."

20 And of Gad he said:

"Blessed *is* he who [R]enlarges Gad;
He dwells as a lion, 1 Chr. 12:8
And tears the arm and the crown of his
head.
21 [R]He provided the first *part* for himself,
Because a lawgiver's portion was
reserved there. Num. 32:16, 17
He came *with* the heads of the people;
He administered the justice of the
LORD,
And His judgments with Israel."

22 And of Dan he said:

"Dan *is* a lion's whelp;
[R]He shall leap from Bashan." Josh. 19:47

23 And of Naphtali he said:

"O Naphtali, satisfied with favor,
And full of the blessing of the LORD,
Possess the west and the south."

24 And of Asher he said:

[R]Asher *is* most blessed of sons; Gen. 49:20
Let him be favored by his brothers,
And let him [R]dip his foot in oil. Job 29:6
25 Your sandals *shall be* iron and bronze;
As your days, *so shall* your strength *be*.

26 "*There is* [R]no one like the God of
[R]Jeshurun, Ex. 15:11 • Deut. 32:15
Who rides the heavens to help you,
And in His excellency on the clouds.
27 The eternal God *is your* [R]refuge,
And underneath *are* the everlasting
arms; [Ps. 90:1; 91:2, 9]
[R]He will thrust out the enemy from before
you, Deut. 9:3–5
And will say, 'Destroy!'
28 Then Israel shall dwell in safety,
The fountain of Jacob alone,
In a land of grain and new wine;
His heavens shall also drop dew.
29 [R]Happy *are* you, O Israel! Ps. 144:15
[R]Who *is* like you, a people saved by the
LORD, 2 Sam. 7:23
[R]The shield of your help Ps. 115:9
And the sword of your majesty!
Your enemies shall submit to you,
And [R]you shall tread down their [T]high
places." Num. 33:52 • Places for pagan worship

CHAPTER 34

Moses Views the Promised Land

THEN Moses went up from the plains of
Moab [R]to Mount Nebo, to the top of Pis-
gah, which is across from Jericho. And the
LORD showed him all the land of Gilead as far
as Dan, Deut. 32:49
2 all Naphtali and the land of Ephraim and
Manasseh, all the land of Judah as far as the
Western Sea,*
3 the South, and the plain of the Valley of
Jericho, [R]the city of palm trees, as far as
Zoar. 2 Chr. 28:15
4 Then the LORD said to him, [R]"This *is* the
land of which I swore to give Abraham,
Isaac, and Jacob, saying, 'I will give it to your
descendants.' [R]I have caused you to see *it*
with your eyes, but you shall not cross over
there." Gen. 12:7 • Deut. 3:27

Moses Dies and Is Mourned

5 [R]So Moses the servant of the LORD died
there in the land of Moab, according to the
word of the LORD. Deut. 32:50; Josh. 1:1, 2
6 And He buried him in a valley in the land
of Moab, opposite Beth Peor; but [R]no one
knows his grave to this day. Jude 9
7 Moses *was* one hundred and twenty years
old when he died. His eyes were not dim nor
his natural vigor diminished.
8 And the children of Israel wept for Moses
in the plains of Moab [R]thirty days. So the
days of weeping *and* mourning for Moses
ended. Gen. 50:3, 10

Moses Is Replaced by Joshua

9 Now Joshua the son of Nun was full of the
[R]spirit of wisdom, for [R]Moses had laid his
hands on him; so the children of Israel heeded

33:16 Gen. 49:26 **34:2** Mediterranean

him, and did as the LORD had commanded
Moses. Is. 11:2 • Num. 27:18, 23

Moses Is Extolled in Israel

10 But since then there [R]has not arisen in Is-
rael a prophet like Moses, [R]whom the LORD
knew face to face, Deut. 18:15, 18 • Ex. 33:11
11 in all [R]the signs and wonders which the
LORD sent him to do in the land of Egypt, be-
fore Pharaoh, before all his servants, and in
all his land, Deut. 7:19
12 and by all that mighty power and all the
great terror which Moses performed in the
sight of all Israel.

THE BOOK OF

JOSHUA

THE BOOK OF JOSHUA

Joshua, the first of the twelve historical books (Joshua—Esther), forges a link between the Pentateuch and the remainder of Israel's history. Through three major military campaigns involving more than thirty enemy armies, the people of Israel learn a crucial lesson under Joshua's capable leadership: victory comes through faith in God and obedience to His word, rather than through military might or numerical superiority.

The title of this book is appropriately named after its central figure, Joshua. His original name is *Hoshea,* "Salvation" (Num. 13:8); but Moses evidently changes it to *Yehoshua* (Num. 13:16), "Yahweh Is Salvation." He is also called *Yeshua,* a shortened form of *Yehoshua.* This is the Hebrew equivalent of the Greek name *Iesous* ("Jesus"). Thus, the Greek title given to the book in the Septuagint is *Iesous Naus,* "Joshua the Son of Nun." The Latin title is *Liber Josue,* the "Book of Joshua."

His name is symbolic of the fact that, although he is the leader of the Israelite nation during the conquest, the Lord is the Conqueror.

THE AUTHOR OF JOSHUA

Although it cannot be proven, Jewish tradition seems correct in assigning the authorship of this book to Joshua himself. Joshua 24:26 makes this clear statement: "Then Joshua wrote these words in the Book of the Law of God." This refers at least to Joshua's farewell charge, if not to the book as a whole (see also 18:9). Joshua, as Israel's leader and an eyewitness of most of the events, was the person best qualified to write the book. He even uses the first person in one place (5:6, "us"; "we" appears in some manuscripts of 5:1). The book was written soon after the events occurred: Rahab was still alive (6:25). Other evidences for early authorship are the detailed information about Israel's campaigns and use of the ancient names of Canaanite cities.

The unity of style and organization suggests a single authorship for the majority of the book. Three small portions, however, must have been added after Joshua's death. These are: (1) Othniel's capture of Kirjath Sepher (15:13–19; cf. Judg. 1:9–15), (2) Dan's migration to the north (19:47; cf. Judg. 18:27–29), and (3) Joshua's death and burial (24:29–33). These may have been inserted early in the time of the judges by Eleazer the priest and his son Phinehas (24:33).

Joshua, born a slave in Egypt, becomes a conqueror in Canaan. He serves as personal attendant to Moses, as one of the twelve spies (of whom only he and Caleb believed God), and as Moses' successor. His outstanding qualities are obedient faith, courage, and dedication to God and His word.

THE TIME OF JOSHUA

Joshua divides neatly into three geographical settings: (1) the Jordan River (1—5); (2) Canaan (6—13:7); and (3) the twelve tribes situated on both sides of the Jordan (13:8—24:33).

The setting of the first five chapters begins east of the Jordan as Joshua replaces Moses, crosses the Jordan on dry land, and finally prepares for war west of the Jordan.

Like a wise general, Joshua utilizes the divide-and-conquer strategy; and his campaign leads him to central Canaan (6—8), southern Canaan (9 and 10), and finally to northern Canaan (11 and 12).

After listing those areas yet to be conquered (13:1–7), Joshua undertakes the long task of dividing the Promised Land to all the tribes. First, he settles those two-and-a-half tribes east of the Jordan (13:8–33) and then the nine-and-a-half tribes west of the Jordan (14:1—19:51). Completing this, he is free to assign the six Cities of Refuge and the forty-eight Cities of Levites, which are scattered among all the tribes.

The Book of Joshua cannot be dated precisely, but utilizing the same threefold division noted above, the following dates can be assigned:

A. One month, March–April, 1405 B.C. (Josh. 1—5)
   1. Death of Moses, March 1405 B.C. (Deut. 34:5–9)
   2. Crossing the Jordan, April 10, 1405 B.C. (Josh. 4:19)

B. Seven years, April 1405–1398 B.C. (Josh. 6:1—13:7)
   1. Caleb forty years old at Kadesh (Josh. 14:7)
   2. Caleb eighty-five years old at that time (Josh. 14:10)
      Note: forty-five years less thirty-eight years of wandering leaves seven years.

C. Eight years, 1398/7–1390 B.C. (Josh. 13:8–24)
   1. Division begun, 1398/7 B.C. (Josh. 14:7–10)
   2. Joshua dies at 110, c. 1390 B.C. (Josh. 24:29)

THE CHRIST OF JOSHUA

Although there are no direct messianic prophecies in the book, Joshua is clearly a type of Christ. His name *Yeshua* ("Yahweh Is Salvation") is the Hebrew equivalent of the name "Jesus." In his role of triumphantly leading his people into their possessions, he foreshadows the One who will bring "many sons to glory" (Heb. 2:10). "Now thanks *be* to God who always leads us in triumph in Christ" (2 Cor. 2:14; see Rom. 8:37). Joshua succeeds Moses and wins the victory unreached by Moses. Christ will succeed the Mosaic Law and win the victory unreachable by the Law (John 1:17; Rom. 8:2–4; Gal. 3:23–25; Heb. 7:18, 19).

The "Commander of the army of the LORD" (5:13–15) met by Joshua is evidently a preincarnate appearance of Christ (cf. Josh. 5:15 with Ex. 3:2).

Rahab's scarlet cord portrays safety through the blood (Heb. 9:19–22); and amazingly, this Gentile woman is found in Christ's genealogy (Matt. 1:5).

KEYS TO JOSHUA

Key Word: Conquest—The entire Book of Joshua describes the entering, conquering, and occupying of the land of Canaan. The book begins with a statement of the promise of conquest, "Moses My servant is dead. Now therefore, arise, go over this Jordan . . . Every place that the sole of your foot will tread upon I have given you" (1:2, 3) and ends with the completion of conquest "that not one thing has failed of all the good things which the LORD your God spoke concerning you. All have come to pass for you; not one word of them has failed" (23:14).

Key Verses: Joshua 1:8; 11:23—"This Book of the Law shall not depart from your mouth, but you shall meditate in it day and night, that you may observe to do according to all that is written in it. For then you will make your way prosperous, and then you will have good success" (1:8).

"So Joshua took the whole land, according to all that the LORD had said to Moses; and Joshua gave it as an inheritance to Israel according to their divisions by their tribes. Then the land rested from war" (11:23).

Key Chapter: Joshua 24—Some of the most critical periods in Israel's history are the transitions of leadership: Moses to Joshua; Joshua to the judges; the judges to the kings, and so on. Before his death and in preparation for a major transition of leadership by one man (Joshua) to many (the judges), Joshua reviews for the people God's fulfillment of His promises and then challenges them to review their commitment to the covenant (24:24, 25), which is the foundation for all successful national life.

SURVEY OF JOSHUA

Joshua resumes the narrative where Deuteronomy left off, and takes Israel from the wilderness to the Promised Land. Israel has now reached its climactic point of fulfilling the centuries-old promise in Genesis of a homeland. The first half of Joshua (1:1—13:7) describes the seven-year conquest of the land, and the second half (13:8—24:33) gives the details of the division and settlement of the land.

Conquest (1:1—13:7): The first five chapters record the spiritual, moral, physical, and military preparation of Joshua and the people for the impending conquest of Canaan. Joshua is given a charge by God to complete the task begun by Moses (1:2). After being encouraged by God, Joshua sends out two spies who come back with a favorable report (in contrast to the spies of the previous generation). Obedience and faith are united in the miraculous crossing of the Jordan River (3:1—4:24).

Joshua's campaign in central Canaan (6:1—8:35) places a strategic wedge between the northern and southern cities preventing a mas-

FOCUS	CONQUEST OF CANAAN		SETTLEMENT IN CANAAN			
REFERENCE	1:1	6:1	13:8	14:1	20:1	22:1—24:33
DIVISION	PREPARATION OF ISRAEL	CONQUEST OF CANAAN	SETTLEMENT OF EAST JORDAN	SETTLEMENT OF WEST JORDAN	SETTLEMENT OF RELIGIOUS COMMUNITY	CONDITIONS FOR CONTINUED SETTLEMENT
TOPIC	ENTERING CANAAN	CONQUERING CANAAN	DIVIDING CANAAN			
	PREPARATION	SUBJECTION	POSSESSION			
LOCATION	JORDAN RIVER	CANAAN	TWO AND A HALF TRIBES—EAST JORDAN NINE AND A HALF TRIBES—WEST JORDAN			
TIME	c. 1 MONTH	c. 7 YEARS	c. 8 YEARS			

sive Canaanite alliance against Israel. This divide-and-conquer strategy proves effective, but God's directions for taking the first city (Jericho) sound like foolishness from a military point of view. The Lord uses this to test the people and to teach them that Israel's success in battle will always be by His power and not their own might or cleverness. Sin must be dealt with at once because it brings severe consequences and defeat at Ai (7:1–26).

The southern and northern campaigns (9:1—13:7) are also successful, but an unwise oath made to the deceptive Gibeonites forces Israel to protect them and to disobey God's command to eliminate the Canaanites.

Settlement (13:8—24:33): Joshua is growing old, and God tells him to divide the land among the twelve tribes. Much remains to be won, and the tribes are to continue the conquest by faith after Joshua's death. Joshua 13:8—21:45 describes the allocation of the land to the various tribes as well as the inheritances of Caleb (14 and 15) and the Levites (21).

The last chapters (22:1—24:33) record the conditions for continued successful settlement in Canaan. Access to God, as well as His forgiveness, come only through the divinely established sacrificial system; and civil war almost breaks out when the eastern tribes build an altar that is misinterpreted by the western tribes.

Realizing that blessing comes from God only as Israel obeys His covenant, Joshua preaches a moving sermon, climaxed by Israel's renewal of her allegiance to the covenant.

OUTLINE OF JOSHUA

Part One: The Conquest of Canaan (1:1—13:7)

I. Israel Is Prepared for the Conquest .... 1:1—5:15

- A. Joshua Replaces Moses 1:1–18
  1. Joshua Is Commissioned by God 1:1–9
  2. Joshua Commands Israel 1:10–15
  3. Joshua Is Accepted by Israel 1:16–18
- B. Joshua Prepares Israel Militarily .... 2:1—5:1
  1. Joshua Spies Canaan 2:1–24
  2. Joshua Leads Israel into Canaan .... 3:1—5:1
- C. Joshua Prepares Israel Spiritually 5:2–12
  1. Circumcision Is Practiced 5:2–9
  2. Passover Is Celebrated 5:10, 11
  3. From Manna to Corn 5:12
- D. The Commander of the Lord Appears 5:13–15

II. The Conquest of Canaan by Israel ... 6:1—13:7

- A. Conquest of Central Canaan .... 6:1—8:35
  1. Victory at Jericho 6:1–27
  2. Defeat at Ai 7:1–26
  3. Victory at Ai 8:1–29
  4. Result of the Victories 8:30–35
- B. Conquest of Southern Canaan .... 9:1—10:43
  1. Failure with the Gibeonites 9:1–27
  2. Victory over the Amorites 10:1–43
- C. Conquest of Northern Canaan 11:1–15
- D. Conquest of Canaan Is Summarized .... 11:16—12:24
  1. The Summary of Conquered Territory 11:16–23
  2. The Summary of Conquered Kings 12:1–24
- E. Unconquered Parts of Canaan 13:1–7

Part Two: The Settlement in Canaan (13:8—24:33)

I. The Settlement East of the Jordan 13:8–33

- A. Geographical Boundaries 13:8–13
- B. Tribal Boundaries 13:14–33
  1. Boundaries of Levi 13:14
  2. Boundaries of Reuben 13:15–23
  3. Boundaries of Gad 13:24–28
  4. Boundaries of the Half-Tribe of Manasseh 13:29–33

II. The Settlement West of the Jordan .... 14:1—19:51

- A. The First Settlement Done at Gilgal .... 14:1—17:18
  1. Method of Setting Tribal Boundaries 14:1–5
  2. Boundaries of Judah .... 14:6—15:63
  3. Boundaries of the Tribes of Joseph .... 16:1—17:18
- B. The Second Settlement Done at Shiloh .... 18:1—19:51
  1. The Remaining Tribes Move to Shiloh 18:1
  2. New Method of Setting Tribal Boundaries 18:2–10
  3. Boundaries of Benjamin 18:11–28
  4. Boundaries of Simeon 19:1–9
  5. Boundaries of Zebulun 19:10–16
  6. Boundaries of Issachar 19:17–23
  7. Boundaries of Asher 19:24–31
  8. Boundaries of Naphtali 19:32–39
  9. Boundaries of Dan 19:40–48
  10. Boundaries of Joshua 19:49–51

III. The Settlement of the Religious Community .... 20:1—21:45

- A. Six Cities of Refuge 20:1–9
- B. Selection of the Levitical Cities 21:1–42
  1. The Families to Be Assigned Cities 21:1–7
  2. Cities for the Kohathites 21:8–26

CHAPTER 1

Joshua Is Commissioned by God

AFTER the death of Moses the servant of
the LORD, it came to pass that the LORD
spoke to Joshua the son of Nun, Moses' [R]as-
sistant, saying: Ex. 24:13
2 [R]"Moses My servant is dead. Now there-
fore, arise, go over this Jordan, you and all
this people, to the land which I am giving to
them—the children of Israel. Deut. 34:5
3 [R]"Every place that the sole of your foot
will tread upon I have given you, as I said to
Moses. Deut. 11:24
4 [R]"From the wilderness and this Lebanon
as far as the great river, the River Euphrates,
all the land of the Hittites, and to the Great
Sea toward the going down of the sun, shall
be your territory. Gen. 15:18
5 [R]"No man shall *be able to* stand before
you all the days of your life; [R]as I was with
Moses, *so* I will be with you. I will not leave
you nor forsake you. Deut. 7:24 • Ex. 3:12
6 [R]"Be strong and of good courage, for to
this people you shall [T]divide as an inheritance
the land which I swore to their fathers to give
them. Deut. 31:7, 23 • *give as a possession*
7 "Only be strong and very courageous,
that you may observe to do according to all
the law [R]which Moses My servant com-
manded you; [R]do not turn from it to the right
hand or to the left, that you may prosper
wherever you go. Deut. 31:7 • Deut. 5:32
8 [R]"This Book of the Law shall not depart
from your mouth, but you shall meditate in it
day and night, that you may observe to do ac-
cording to all that is written in it. For then you
will make your way prosperous, and then you
will have good success. Josh. 8:34
9 [R]"Have I not commanded you? Be strong
and of good courage; [R]do not be afraid, nor be
dismayed, for the LORD your God *is* with you
wherever you go." Deut. 31:7 • Ps. 27:1

Joshua Commands the Tribes West of the Jordan

10 Then Joshua commanded the officers of
the people, saying,
11 "Pass through the camp and command
the people, saying, 'Prepare provisions for
yourselves, for [R]within three days you will
cross over this Jordan, to go in to possess the
land which the LORD your God is giving you to
possess.' " Deut. 9:1

Joshua Commands the Tribes East of the Jordan

12 And to the Reubenites, the Gadites, and
half the tribe of Manasseh Joshua spoke, say-
ing,
13 "Remember [R]the word which Moses the
servant of the LORD commanded you, saying,
'The LORD your God is giving you rest and is
giving you this land.' Num. 32:20–28
14 "Your wives, your little ones, and your
livestock shall remain in the land which Mo-
ses gave you on this side of the Jordan. But
you shall pass before your brethren armed, all
your mighty men of valor, and help them,
15 "until the LORD has given your brethren

1:8 Meditating upon God's Word—Joshua had just succeeded Moses in the leadership of the nation Israel. Moses had led the nation for forty years and had the benefit that all the wisdom and culture of Egypt and the king's household could provide. Moses was a seasoned, multitalented man who had walked closely with God. Joshua, by contrast, was relatively untried. He was assuming an awesome responsibility in taking command of two-and-a-half million people. If anyone needed a formula for success, Joshua did. Likely there were many well-meaning people with all kinds of advice and formulas to help Joshua in the seemingly impossible task that lay ahead. What comfort and assurance it must have been as the LORD (Yahweh) spoke directly to Joshua, assuring him of His presence with him as He had been with Moses (Josh. 1:5), and giving him the key to success—meditating upon God's Word.

Joshua is to meditate upon the Word of God day and night (i.e., at all times), and is promised (1) prosperity and (2) good success in the God-given task that lies ahead. Reading and memorizing God's Word provide the basis for meditating upon God's Word. You meditate upon the Word of God by rehearsing its thoughts over and over in order to understand its implications for the situations of life. Meditating upon the Word of God will guarantee prosperity and success in the new life.

Now turn to Page 205—Deut. 31:12: Obedience to God's Word.

rest, as He *gave* you, and they also have
taken possession of the land which the LORD
your God is giving them. [R]Then you shall re-
turn to the land of your possession and enjoy
it, which Moses the LORD's servant gave you
on this side of the Jordan toward the sun-
rise." Josh. 22:1–4

Joshua Is Accepted by Israel

16 So they answered Joshua, saying, "All
that you command us we will do, and wher-
ever you send us we will go.
17 "Just as we heeded Moses in all things, so
we will heed you. Only the LORD your God be
with you, as He was with Moses.
18 "Whoever rebels against your command
and does not heed your words, in all that you
command him, shall be put to death. Only be
strong and of good courage."

CHAPTER 2

The Faith of Rahab

NOW Joshua the son of Nun sent out two
men [R]from Acacia Grove* to spy se-
cretly, saying, "Go, view the land, especially
Jericho." So they went, and [R]came to the
house of a harlot named [R]Rahab, and lodged
there. Num. 25:1 • James 2:25 • Matt. 1:5
2 And [R]it was told the king of Jericho, say-
ing, "Behold, men have come here tonight
from the children of Israel to search out the
country." Josh. 2:22
3 So the king of Jericho sent to Rahab, say-
ing, "Bring out the men who have come to
you, who have entered your house, for they
have come to search out all the country."
4 [R]Then the woman took the two men and
hid them. So she said, "Yes, the men came to
me, but I did not know where they *were*
from. 2 Sam. 17:19, 20
5 "And it happened as the gate was being
shut, when it was dark, that the men went out.
Where the men went I do not know; pursue
them quickly, for you may overtake them."
6 (But she had brought them up to the roof
and hidden them with the stalks of flax, which
she had laid in order on the roof.)
7 Then the men pursued them by the road
to the Jordan, to the fords. And as soon as
those who pursued them had gone out, they
shut the gate.
8 Now before they lay down, she came up
to them on the roof,
9 and said to the men: [R]"I know that the
LORD has given you the land, that [R]the terror
of you has fallen on us, and that all the inhab-
itants of the land are fainthearted because of
you. Deut. 1:8 • Deut. 2:25; 11:25
10 "For we have heard how the LORD [R]dried
up the water of the Red Sea for you when you
came out of Egypt, and what you did to the
two kings of the Amorites who *were* on the
other side of the Jordan, Sihon and Og, whom
you utterly destroyed. Ex. 14:21
11 "And as soon as we [R]heard *these things*,
our hearts melted; neither did there remain
any more courage in anyone because of you,
for the LORD your God, He *is* God in heaven
above and on earth beneath. Ex. 15:14, 15
12 "Now therefore, I beg you, [R]swear to me
by the LORD, since I have shown you kind-
ness, that you also will show kindness to
[R]my father's house, and [R]give me a true
token, 1 Sam. 20:14, 15, 17 • 1 Tim. 5:8 • Josh. 2:18
13 "and spare my father, my mother, my
brothers, my sisters, and all that they have,
and deliver our lives from death."
14 So the men answered her, "Our lives for
yours, if none of you tell this business of ours.
And it shall be, when the LORD has given us
the land, that [R]we will deal kindly and truly
with you." Judg. 1:24
15 Then she let them down by a rope
through the window, for her house *was* on the
city wall; she dwelt on the wall.
16 And she said to them, "Get to the moun-
tain, lest the pursuers meet you. Hide there
three days, until the pursuers have returned.
Afterward you may go your way."
17 So the men said to her: "We *will be*
[R]blameless of this oath of yours which you
have made us swear, Ex. 20:7
18 [R]"unless, *when* we come into the land, you
bind this line of scarlet cord in the window
through which you let us down, [R]and unless
you bring your father, your mother, your
brothers, and all your father's household to
your own home. Josh. 2:12 • Josh. 6:23
19 "So it shall be *that* whoever goes outside
the doors of your house into the street, his
blood *shall be* on his own head, and we *will be*
guiltless. And whoever is with you in the
house, [R]his blood *shall be* on our head if a
hand is laid on him. 1 Kin. 2:32
20 "And if you tell this business of ours, then
we will be [T]free from your oath which you
made us swear." *free from obligation to*
21 Then she said, "According to your words,
so *be* it." And she sent them away, and they
departed. And she bound the scarlet cord in
the window.

The Faith of the Spies

22 They departed and went to the mountain,
and stayed there three days until the pursuers
returned. The pursuers sought *them* all along
the way, but did not find *them*.
23 So the two men returned, descended from
the mountain, and crossed over; and they
came to Joshua the son of Nun, and told him
all that had befallen them.
24 And they said to Joshua, "Truly the LORD
has delivered all the land into our hands, for

2:1 Heb. *Shittim*

indeed all the inhabitants of the country are fainthearted because of us."

CHAPTER 3

The Miraculous Crossing of the Jordan

THEN Joshua rose early in the morning; and they set out [R]from Acacia Grove* and came to the Jordan, he and all the children of Israel, and lodged there before they crossed over. Josh. 2:1

2 So it was, [R]after three days, that the officers went through the camp; Josh. 1:10, 11

3 and they commanded the people, saying, [R]"When you see the ark of the covenant of the LORD your God, and the priests, the Levites, bearing it, then you shall set out from your place and go after it. Num. 10:33

4 [R]"Yet there shall be a space between you and it, about two thousand cubits by measure. Do not come near it, that you may know the way by which you must go, for you have not passed *this* way before." Ex. 19:12

5 And Joshua said to the people, [R]"Sanctify yourselves, for tomorrow the LORD will do wonders among you." Josh. 7:13

6 Then Joshua spoke to the priests, saying, [R]"Take up the ark of the covenant and cross over before the people." So they took up the ark of the covenant and went before the people. Num. 4:15

7 And the LORD said to Joshua, "This day I will begin to [R]exalt you in the sight of all Israel, that they may know that, as I was with Moses, *so* I will be with you. Josh. 4:14

8 "You shall command [R]the priests who bear the ark of the covenant, saying, 'When you have come to the edge of the water of the Jordan, [R]you shall stand in the Jordan.' " Josh. 3:3 • Josh. 3:17

9 So Joshua said to the children of Israel, "Come here, and hear the words of the LORD your God."

10 And Joshua said, "By this you shall know that [R]the living God *is* among you, and *that* He will without fail [R]drive out from before you the [R]Canaanites and the Hittites and the Hivites and the Perizzites and the Girgashites and the Amorites and the Jebusites: 1 Thess. 1:9 • Ex. 33:2 • Acts 13:19

11 "Behold, the ark of the covenant of [R]the Lord of all the earth is crossing over before you into the Jordan. Zech. 4:14; 6:5

12 "Now therefore, [R]take for yourselves twelve men from the tribes of Israel, one man from every tribe. Josh. 4:2, 4

13 "And it shall come to pass, as soon as the soles of the feet of the priests who bear the ark of the LORD, the Lord of all the earth, shall rest in the waters of the Jordan, *that* the waters of the Jordan shall be cut off, the waters that come down from upstream, and they shall stand as a heap."

14 So it was, when the people set out from their camp to cross over the Jordan, with the priests bearing the [R]ark of the covenant before the people, Acts 7:44, 45

15 and as those who bore the ark came to the Jordan, and the feet of the priests who bore the ark dipped in the edge of the water (for the [R]Jordan overflows all its banks during the whole time of harvest), 1 Chr. 12:15

16 that the waters which came down from upstream stood *still, and* rose in a heap very far away at Adam, the city that *is* beside [R]Zaretan. So the waters that went down into the Sea of the Arabah, [R]the Salt Sea, failed, *and* were cut off; and the people crossed over opposite Jericho. Deut. 3:17 • Gen. 14:3

17 Then the priests who bore the ark of the covenant of the LORD stood firm on dry ground in the midst of the Jordan; [R]and all Israel crossed over on dry ground, until all the people had crossed completely over the Jordan. Ex. 3:8; 6:1–8; 14:21, 22, 29; 33:1

CHAPTER 4

The Memorial of the Crossing

AND it came to pass, when all the people had completely crossed over the Jordan, that the LORD spoke to Joshua, saying:

2 "Take for yourselves twelve men from the people, one man from every tribe,

3 "and command them, saying, 'Take for yourselves twelve stones from here, out of the midst of the Jordan, from the place where the priests' feet stood firm. You shall carry them over with you and leave them in the lodging place where you lodge tonight.' "

4 Then Joshua called the twelve men whom he had appointed from the children of Israel, one man from every tribe;

5 and Joshua said to them: "Cross over before the ark of the LORD your God into the midst of the Jordan, and each one of you take up a stone on his shoulder, according to the number of the tribes of the children of Israel,

6 "that this may be a sign among you when your children ask in time to come, saying, 'What do these stones *mean* to you?'

7 "Then you shall answer them that [R]the waters of the Jordan were cut off before the ark of the covenant of the LORD; when it crossed over the Jordan, the waters of the Jordan were cut off. And these stones shall be for [R]a memorial to the children of Israel forever." Josh. 3:13, 16 • Num. 16:40

8 And the children of Israel did so, just as Joshua commanded, and took up twelve stones from the midst of the Jordan, as the LORD had spoken to Joshua, according to the number of the tribes of the children of Israel,

3:1 Heb. *Shittim*

and carried them over with them to the place
where they lodged, and laid them down there.
9 Then Joshua set up twelve stones in the
midst of the Jordan, in the place where the feet
of the priests who bore the ark of the covenant
stood; and they are there to this day.
10 So the priests who bore the ark stood
in the midst of the Jordan until everything
was finished that the LORD had commanded
Joshua to speak to the people, according to all
that Moses had commanded Joshua; and the
people hurried and crossed over.
11 Then it came to pass, when all the people
had completely crossed over, that the [R]ark of
the LORD and the priests crossed over in the
presence of the people. Josh. 3:11
12 And the men of Reuben, the men of Gad,
and half the tribe of Manasseh crossed over
armed before the children of Israel, as Moses
had spoken to them.
13 About forty thousand [T]prepared for war
crossed over before the LORD for battle, to the
plains of Jericho. *equipped*
14 On that day the LORD [R]exalted[T] Joshua in
the sight of all Israel; and they feared him, as
they had feared Moses, all the days of his
life. Josh. 3:7 • *made Joshua great*
15 Then the LORD spoke to Joshua, saying,
16 "Command the priests who bear [R]the ark
of the Testimony to come up from the Jor-
dan." Ex. 25:16, 22
17 Joshua therefore commanded the priests,
saying, "Come up from the Jordan."
18 And it came to pass, when the priests
who bore the ark of the covenant of the LORD
had come from the midst of the Jordan, *and*
the soles of the priests' feet touched the dry
land, that the waters of the Jordan returned to
their place [R]and overflowed all its banks as
before. Josh. 3:15
19 Now the people came up from the Jordan
on the tenth *day* of the first month, and they
camped [R]in Gilgal on the east border of Jeri-
cho. Josh. 5:9
20 And [R]those twelve stones which they
took out of the Jordan, Joshua set up in Gil-
gal. Josh. 4:3; 5:9, 10
21 Then he spoke to the children of Israel,
saying: [R]"When your children ask their fa-
thers in time to come, saying, 'What *are* these
stones?' Josh. 4:6
22 "then you shall let your children know,
saying, [R]'Israel crossed over this Jordan on
[R]dry land'; Deut. 26:5–9 • Josh. 3:17
23 "for the LORD your God dried up the wa-
ters of the Jordan before you until you had
crossed over, as the LORD your God did to the
Red Sea, [R]which He dried up before us until
we had crossed over, Ex. 14:21
24 [R]"that all the peoples of the earth may
know the hand of the LORD, that it *is* [R]mighty,
that you may [R]fear the LORD your God for-
ever." 1 Kin. 8:42 • 1 Chr. 29:12 • Jer. 10:7

CHAPTER 5

The Canaanites Fear Israel

SO it was, when all the kings of the Amo-
rites who *were* on the west side of the Jor-
dan, and all the kings of the Canaanites [R]who
were by the sea, heard that the LORD had
dried up the waters of the Jordan from before
the children of Israel until we* had crossed
over, that their heart melted; and there was no
spirit in them any longer because of the chil-
dren of Israel. Num. 13:29

Circumcision Is Practiced

2 At that time the LORD said to Joshua,
"Make [R]flint knives for yourself, and circum-
cise the sons of Israel again the second
time." Ex. 4:25
3 So Joshua made flint knives for himself,
and circumcised the sons of Israel at the hill
of the foreskins.*
4 And this *is* the reason why Joshua cir-
cumcised them: All the people who came out
of Egypt *who were* males, all the men of war,
had died in the wilderness on the way, after
they had come out of Egypt.
5 For all the people who came out had been
circumcised, but all the people born in the
wilderness, on the way as they came out of
Egypt, had not been circumcised.
6 For the children of Israel walked forty
years in the wilderness, till all the people *who*
were men of war, who came out of Egypt,
were consumed, because they did not obey
the voice of the LORD—to whom the LORD
swore that [R]He would not show them the land
which the LORD had sworn to their fathers
that He would give us, "a land flowing with
milk and honey."* Heb. 3:11
7 Then Joshua circumcised [R]their sons
whom He raised up in their place; for they
were uncircumcised, because they had not
been circumcised on the way. Deut. 1:39
8 So it was, when they had finished cir-
cumcising all the people, that they stayed in
their places in the camp [R]till they were
healed. Gen. 34:25
9 Then the LORD said to Joshua, "This day I
have rolled away [R]the reproach of Egypt from
you." Therefore the name of the place is called
Gilgal* to this day. Gen. 34:14

Passover Is Celebrated

10 Now the children of Israel camped in Gil-
gal, and kept the Passover [R]on the fourteenth
day of the month at twilight on the plains of
Jericho. Ex. 12:6
11 And they ate of the produce of the land
on the day after the Passover, unleavened

5:1 So with Kt.; Qr., some Heb. mss. and editions, LXX, Syr., Tg., Vg. *they* **5:3** Heb. *Gibeath Haaraloth* **5:6** Ex. 3:8 **5:9** Lit. *Rolling*

bread and [T]parched grain, on the very same
day. *roasted*

From Manna to Corn

12 Then [R]the manna ceased on the day after
they had eaten the produce of the land; and
the children of Israel no longer had manna,
but they ate the food of the land of Canaan
that year. Ex. 16:35

The Commander of the Lord Appears

13 And it came to pass, when Joshua was by
Jericho, that he lifted his eyes and looked, and
behold, a Man stood opposite him with His
sword drawn in His hand. And Joshua went to
Him and said to Him, "*Are* You for us or for
our adversaries?"
14 So He said, "No, but *as* Commander of the
army of the LORD I have now come." And
Joshua [R]fell on his face to the earth and [R]wor-
shiped, and said to Him, "What does my Lord
say to His servant?" Gen. 17:3 • Ex. 34:8
15 Then the Commander of the LORD's army
said to Joshua, [R]"Take your sandal off your
foot, for the place where you stand *is* holy."
And Joshua did so. Ex. 3:5

CHAPTER 6

Victory at Jericho

NOW [R]Jericho was securely shut up be-
cause of the children of Israel; none went
out, and none came in. Josh. 2:1
2 And the LORD said to Joshua: "See! I have
given Jericho into your hand, its [R]king, *and*
the mighty men of valor. Deut. 7:24
3 "You shall march around the city, all *you*
men of war; you shall go all around the city
once. This you shall do six days.
4 "And seven priests shall bear seven
[R]trumpets of rams' horns before the ark. But
the seventh day you shall march around the
city [R]seven times, and [R]the priests shall blow
the trumpets. Lev. 25:9 • 1 Kin. 18:43 • Num. 10:8
5 "It shall come to pass, when they make a
long *blast* with the ram's horn, *and* when you
hear the sound of the trumpet, that all the
people shall shout with a great shout; then
the wall of the city will fall down flat. And the
people shall go up every man straight before
him."
6 Then Joshua the son of Nun called the
priests and said to them, "Take up the ark of
the covenant, and let seven priests bear seven
trumpets of rams' horns before the ark of the
LORD."
7 And he said to the people, "Proceed, and
march around the city, and let him who is
armed advance before the ark of the LORD."
8 So it was, when Joshua had spoken to the
people, that the seven priests bearing the
seven trumpets of rams' horns before the LORD
advanced and blew the trumpets, and the
ark of the covenant of the LORD followed
them.
9 The armed men went before the priests
who blew the trumpets, [R]and the rear guard
came after the ark, while *the priests* contin-
ued blowing the trumpets. Num. 10:25
10 Now Joshua had commanded the people,
saying, "You shall not shout or make any
noise with your voice, nor shall a word pro-
ceed out of your mouth, until the day I say to
you, 'Shout!' Then you shall shout."
11 So he had the ark of the LORD circle the
city, going around *it* once. Then they came
into the camp and lodged in the camp.
12 And Joshua rose early in the morning,
and the priests took up the ark of the LORD.
13 Then seven priests bearing seven trum-
pets of rams' horns before the ark of the LORD
went on continually and blew with the trum-
pets. And the armed men went before them.
But the rear guard came after the ark of the
LORD, while *the priests* continued blowing the
trumpets.
14 And the second day they marched around
the city once and returned to the camp. So
they did six days.
15 But it came to pass on the seventh day
that they rose early, about the dawning of the
day, and marched around the city seven times
in the same manner. On that day only they
marched around the city seven times.
16 And the seventh time it happened, when
the priests blew the trumpets, that Joshua
said to the people: "Shout, for the LORD has
given you the city!
17 "Now the city shall be doomed by the
LORD to destruction, it and all who *are* in it.
Only [R]Rahab the harlot shall live, she and all
who *are* with her in the house, because she
hid the messengers that we sent. Matt. 1:5
18 "And you, [R]by all means abstain from the
accursed things, lest you become accursed
when you take of the accursed things, and
make the camp of Israel a curse, [R]and trou-
ble it. Deut. 7:26 • Josh. 7:1, 12, 25
19 "But all the silver and gold, and vessels of
bronze and iron, *are* [T]consecrated to the LORD;
they [T]shall come into the treasury of the
LORD." *set apart* • *shall go*
20 So the people shouted when *the priests*
blew the trumpets. And it happened when the
people heard the sound of the trumpet, and
the people shouted with a great shout, that
[R]the wall fell down flat. Then the people went
up into the city, every man straight before
him, and they took the city. Heb. 11:30
21 And they [R]utterly destroyed all that *was*
in the city, both man and woman, young and
old, ox and sheep and donkey, with the edge
of the sword. Deut. 7:2; 20:16, 17
22 But Joshua had said to the two men who
had spied out the country, "Go into the har-
lot's house, and from there bring out the

woman and all that she has, [R]as you swore to
her." Josh. 2:12–19
23 And the young men who had been spies
went in and brought out Rahab, her father,
her mother, her brothers, and all that she had.
So they brought out all her relatives and left
them outside the camp of Israel.
24 But they burned the city and all that *was*
in it with fire. Only the silver and gold, and
the vessels of bronze and iron, they put into
the treasury of the house of the LORD.
25 And Joshua spared Rahab the harlot, her
father's household, and all that she had. So
[R]she dwells in Israel to this day, because she
hid the messengers whom Joshua sent to spy
out Jericho. [Matt. 1:5]
26 Then Joshua [T]charged *them* at that time,
saying, [R]"Cursed *be* the man before the LORD
who rises up and builds this city Jericho; he
shall lay its foundation with his firstborn,
and with his youngest he shall set up its
gates." *warned* • 1 Kin. 16:34
27 So the LORD was with Joshua, and his
fame spread throughout all the country.

CHAPTER 7

Defeat at Ai

BUT the children of Israel committed a
[R]trespass regarding the [R]accursed things,
for Achan the son of Carmi, the son of
Zabdi,* the son of Zerah, of the tribe of Ju-
dah, took of the accursed things; so the anger
of the LORD burned against the children of Is-
rael. Josh. 7:20, 21 • Josh. 6:17–19
2 Now Joshua sent men from Jericho to Ai,
which *is* beside Beth Aven, on the east side of
Bethel, and spoke to them, saying, "Go up and
spy out the country." So the men went up and
spied out Ai.
3 And they returned to Joshua and said to
him, "Do not let all the people go up, but let
about two or three thousand men go up and
attack Ai. Do not weary all the people there,
for *the people of Ai are* few."
4 So about three thousand men went up
there from the people, [R]but they fled before
the men of Ai. Lev. 26:17
5 And the men of Ai struck down about
thirty-six men, for they chased them *from* be-
fore the gate as far as Shebarim, and struck
them down on the descent; therefore [R]the[T]
hearts of the people melted and became like
water. Lev. 26:36 • *the people's courage failed*
6 Then Joshua tore his clothes, and fell to
the earth on his face before the ark of the
LORD until evening, he and the elders of Israel;
and they put dust on their heads.
7 And Joshua said, "Alas, Lord [T]GOD, [R]why
have You brought this people over the Jordan
at all—to deliver us into the hand of the
Amorites, to destroy us? Oh, that we had been
content, and dwelt on the other side of the
Jordan! Heb. *YHWH,* LORD • Ex. 17:3
8 "O Lord, what shall I say when Israel
turns its [T]back before its enemies? Lit. *neck*
9 "For the Canaanites and all the inhab-
itants of the land will hear *it,* and surround
us, and [R]cut off our name from the earth.
Then [R]what will You do for Your great
name?" Deut. 32:26 • Ex. 32:12
10 So the LORD said to Joshua: "Get up! Why
do you lie thus on your face?
11 "Israel has sinned, and they have also
transgressed My covenant which I com-
manded them. For they have even taken some
of the accursed things, and have both stolen
and [R]deceived; and they have also put *it*
among their own stuff. Acts 5:1, 2
12 "Therefore the children of Israel could
not stand before their enemies, *but* turned
their backs before their enemies, because
they have become doomed to destruction.
Neither will I be with you anymore, unless
you destroy the accursed from among you.
13 "Get up, [R]sanctify[T] the people, and say,
[R]'Sanctify yourselves for tomorrow, because
thus says the LORD God of Israel: "*There is* an
accursed thing in your midst, O Israel; you
cannot stand before your enemies until you
take away the accursed thing from among
you." Ex. 19:10 • *set apart* • Josh. 3:5
14 'In the morning therefore you shall be
brought according to your tribes. And it shall
be *that* the tribe which the LORD takes shall
come according to families; and the family
which the LORD takes shall come by house-
holds; and the household which the LORD
takes shall come man by man.
15 [R]'Then it shall be *that* he who is taken
with the accursed thing shall be burned with
fire, he and all that he has, because he has
[R]transgressed the covenant of the LORD, and
because he [R]has done a disgraceful thing in
Israel.'" 1 Sam. 14:38, 39 • Josh. 7:11 • Gen. 34:7
16 So Joshua rose early in the morning and
brought Israel by their tribes, and the tribe of
Judah was taken.
17 He brought the clan of Judah, and he took
the family of the Zarhites; and he brought the
family of the Zarhites man by man, and Zabdi
was taken.
18 Then he brought his household man by
man, and Achan the son of Carmi, the son of
Zabdi, the son of Zerah, of the tribe of Judah,
[R]was taken. 1 Sam. 14:42
19 Now Joshua said to Achan, "My son, I beg
you, [R]give glory to the LORD God of Israel,
[R]and make confession to Him, and [R]tell me
now what you have done; do not hide *it* from
me." Jer. 13:16 • Num. 5:6, 7 • 1 Sam. 14:43
20 And Achan answered Joshua and said,

7:1 *Zimri,* 1 Chr. 2:6

"Indeed I have sinned against the LORD God of
Israel, and this is what I have done:
21 "When I saw among the spoils a beautiful
Babylonian garment, two hundred shekels of
silver, and a wedge of gold weighing fifty
shekels, I [T]coveted them and took them. And
there they are, hidden in the earth in the midst
of my tent, with the silver under it." *desired*
22 So Joshua sent messengers, and they ran
to the tent; and there it was, hidden in his tent,
with the silver under it.
23 And they took them from the midst of the
tent, brought them to Joshua and to all the
children of Israel, and laid them out before
the LORD.
24 Then Joshua, and all Israel with him, took
Achan the son of Zerah, the silver, the gar-
ment, the wedge of gold, his sons, his daugh-
ters, his oxen, his donkeys, his sheep, his tent,
and all that he had, and they brought them to
the Valley of Achor.
25 And Joshua said, "Why have you troubled
us? The LORD will trouble you this day." [R]So
all Israel stoned him with stones; and they
burned them with fire after they had stoned
them with stones. Deut. 17:5
26 Then they raised over him a great heap of
stones, still there to this day. So the LORD
turned from the fierceness of His anger.
Therefore the name of that place has been
called the Valley of Achor* to this day.

CHAPTER 8

Victory at Ai

NOW the LORD said to Joshua: "Do not be
afraid, nor be dismayed; take all the peo-
ple of war with you, and arise, go up to Ai.
See, I have given into your hand the king of
Ai, his people, his city, and his land.
2 "And you shall do to Ai and its king as
you did to [R]Jericho and its king. Only [R]its spoil
and its cattle you shall take as booty for
yourselves. Lay an ambush for the city be-
hind it." Josh. 6:21 • Deut. 20:14
3 So Joshua arose, and all the people of
war, to go up against Ai; and Joshua chose
thirty thousand mighty men of valor and sent
them away by night.
4 And he commanded them, saying: "Be-
hold, [R]you shall lie in ambush against the city,
behind the city. Do not go very far from the
city, but all of you be ready. Judg. 20:29
5 "Then I and all the people who *are* with
me will approach the city; and it will come
about, when they come out against us as at
the first, that we shall flee before them.
6 "For they will come out after us till we
have drawn them from the city, for they will
say, '*They are* fleeing before us as at the first.'
Therefore we will flee before them.
7 "Then you shall rise from the ambush and
seize the city, for the LORD your God will de-
liver it into your hand.
8 "And it will be, when you have taken the
city, *that* you shall set the city on fire. Ac-
cording to the commandment of the LORD you
shall do. See, I have commanded you."
9 Joshua therefore sent them out; and they
went to lie in ambush, and stayed between
Bethel and Ai, on the west side of Ai; but
Joshua lodged that night among the people.
10 Then Joshua rose up early in the morning
and mustered the people, and went up, he and
the elders of Israel, before the people to Ai.
11 [R]And all the people of war who *were*
with him went up and drew near; and they
came before the city and camped on the
north side of Ai. Now a valley *lay* between
them and Ai. Josh. 8:5
12 So he took about five thousand men and
set them in ambush between Bethel and Ai, on
the west side of [T]the city. Ai
13 And when they had set the people, all the
army that *was* on the north of the city, and its
rear guard on the west of the city, Joshua
went that night into the midst of the valley.
14 Now it happened, when the king of Ai
saw *it*, that the men of the city hurried and
rose early and went out against Israel to bat-
tle, he and all his people, at an appointed
place before the plain. But he [R]did not know
that *there was* an ambush against him behind
the city. Judg. 20:34
15 And Joshua and all Israel [R]made as if they
were beaten before them, and fled by the way
of the wilderness. Judg. 20:36
16 So all the people who *were* in Ai were
called together to pursue them. And they pur-
sued Joshua and were drawn away from the
city.
17 There was not a man left in Ai or Bethel
who did not go out after Israel. So they left the
city open and pursued Israel.
18 Then the LORD said to Joshua, "Stretch
out the spear that *is* in your hand toward Ai,
for I will give it into your hand." And Joshua
stretched out the spear that *was* in his hand
toward the city.
19 So *those in* ambush arose quickly out of
their place; they ran as soon as he had
stretched out his hand, and they entered the city
and took it, and hurried to set the city on fire.
20 And when the men of Ai looked behind
them, they saw, and behold, the smoke of the
city ascended to heaven. So they had no
power to flee this way or that way, and the
people who had fled to the wilderness turned
back on the pursusers.
21 Now when Joshua and all Israel saw that
the ambush had taken the city and that the
smoke of the city ascended, they turned back
and struck down the men of Ai.

7:26 Lit. *Trouble*

22 Then the others came out of the city against them; so they were *caught* in the midst of Israel, some on this side and some on that side. And they struck them down, so that they [R]let none of them remain or escape. Deut. 7:2

23 But the king of Ai they took alive, and brought him to Joshua.

24 And it came to pass when Israel had made an end of slaying all the inhabitants of Ai in the field, in the wilderness where they pursued them, and when they all had fallen by the edge of the sword until they were consumed, that all the Israelites returned to Ai and struck it with the edge of the sword.

25 So it was *that* all who fell that day, both men and women, *were* twelve thousand—all the people of Ai.

26 For Joshua did not draw back his hand, with which he stretched out the spear, until he had [R]utterly destroyed all the inhabitants of Ai. Josh. 6:21

27 [R]Only the livestock and the spoil of that city Israel took as booty for themselves, according to the word of the LORD which He had commanded Joshua. Num. 31:22, 26

28 So Joshua burned Ai and made it a heap forever, a desolation to this day.

29 [R]And the king of Ai he hanged on a tree until evening. [R]And as soon as the sun was down, Joshua commanded that they should take his corpse down from the tree, cast it at the entrance of the gate of the city, and raise over it a great heap of stones *that remains* to this day. Josh. 10:26 • Deut. 21:22, 23

Israel Worships the Lord

30 Now Joshua built an altar to the LORD God of Israel [R]in Mount Ebal, Deut. 27:4–8

31 as Moses the servant of the LORD had commanded the children of Israel, as it is written in the Book of the Law of Moses: [R]"an altar of whole stones over which no man has wielded an iron *tool*."* And [R]they offered on it burnt offerings to the LORD, and sacrificed peace offerings. Ex. 20:25 • Ex. 20:24

Israel Renews the Covenant

32 And there, in the presence of the children of Israel, he wrote on the stones a copy of the law of Moses, which he had written.

33 Then all Israel, with their elders and officers and judges, stood on either side of the ark before the priests, the Levites, [R]who bore the ark of the covenant of the LORD, [R]the stranger as well as he who was born among them. Half of them *were* in front of Mount Gerizim and half of them in front of Mount Ebal, as Moses the servant of the LORD had commanded before, that they should bless the people of Israel. Deut. 31:9, 25 • Deut. 31:12

34 And afterward [R]he read all the words of the law, the blessings and the cursings, according to all that is written in the [R]Book of the Law. Neh. 8:3 • Josh. 1:8

35 There was not a word of all that Moses had commanded which Joshua did not read before all the assembly of Israel, [R]with the women, the little ones, and the strangers who were living among them. Deut. 31:12

CHAPTER 9

Failure with the Gibeonites

AND it came to pass when [R]all the kings who *were* on this side of the Jordan, in the hills and in the lowland and in all the coasts of [R]the Great Sea toward Lebanon—[R]the Hittite, the Amorite, the Canaanite, the Perizzite, the Hivite, and the Jebusite—heard *about it*, Josh. 3:10 • Num. 34:6 • Ex. 3:17; 23:23

2 that they gathered together to fight with Joshua and Israel with one accord.

3 But when the inhabitants of [R]Gibeon [R]heard what Joshua had done to Jericho and Ai, Josh. 9:17, 22; 10:2; 21:17 • Josh. 6:27

4 they worked craftily, and went and [T]pretended to be ambassadors. And they took old sacks on their donkeys, old wineskins torn and [T]mended, *acted as envoys* • Lit. *tied up*

5 old and patched sandals on their feet, and old garments on themselves; and all the bread of their provision was dry *and* moldy.

6 And they went to Joshua, to the camp at Gilgal, and said to him and to the men of Israel, "We have come from a far country; now therefore, make a covenant with us."

7 Then the men of Israel said to the Hivites, "Perhaps you dwell among us; so how can we make a covenant with you?"

8 But they said to Joshua, "We *are* your servants." And Joshua said to them, "Who *are* you, and where do you come from?"

9 So they said to him: [R]"From a very far country your servants have come, because of the name of the LORD your God; for we have [R]heard of His fame, and all that He did in Egypt, Deut. 20:15 • Josh. 2:9, 10; 5:1

10 "and all that He did to the two kings of the Amorites who *were* beyond the Jordan—to Sihon king of Heshbon, and Og king of Bashan, who was at Ashtaroth.

11 "Therefore our elders and all the inhabitants of our country spoke to us, saying, 'Take provisions with you for the journey, and go to meet them, and say to them, "We *are* your servants; now therefore, make a covenant with us." '

12 "This bread of ours we took hot *for* our provision from our houses on the day we departed to come to you. But now look, it is dry and moldy.

8:31 Deut. 27:5, 6

13 "And these wineskins which we filled
were new, and see, they are torn; and these
our garments and our sandals have become
old because of the very long journey."
14 Then the men of Israel took some of their
provisions; [R]but they did not ask counsel of
the LORD. Num. 27:21
15 So Joshua [R]made peace with them, and
made a covenant with them to let them live;
and the rulers of the congregation swore to
them. 2 Sam. 21:2
16 And it happened at the end of three days,
after they had made a covenant with them,
that they heard that they *were* their neighbors
who dwelt near them.
17 Then the children of Israel journeyed and
came to their cities on the third day. Now their
cities *were* [R]Gibeon, Chephirah, Beeroth, and
Kirjath Jearim. Josh. 18:25
18 But the children of Israel did not [T]attack
them, [R]because the rulers of the congregation
had sworn to them by the LORD God of Israel.
And all the congregation complained against
the rulers. *strike* • Ps. 15:4
19 Then all the rulers said to all the congre-
gation, "We have sworn to them by the LORD
God of Israel; now therefore, we may not
touch them.
20 "This we will do to them: We will let them
live, lest wrath be upon us because of the oath
which we swore to them."
21 And the rulers said to them, "Let them
live, but let them be [R]woodcutters and water
carriers for all the congregation, as the rulers
had promised them." Deut. 29:11
22 Then Joshua called for them, and he
spoke to them, saying, "Why have you de-
ceived us, saying, [R]'We *are* very far from you,'
when you dwell near us? Josh. 9:6, 9
23 "Now therefore, you *are* [R]cursed, and
none of you shall be freed from being slaves—
woodcutters and water carriers for the house
of my God." Gen. 9:25
24 So they answered Joshua and said, "Be-
cause your servants were clearly told that the
LORD your God [R]commanded His servant Mo-
ses to give you all the land, and to destroy all
the inhabitants of the land from before you;
therefore [R]we were very much afraid for our
lives because of you, and have done this
thing. Deut. 7:1, 2 • Ex. 15:14
25 "And now, here we are, [R]in your hands; do
with us as it seems good and right to do to
us." Gen. 16:6
26 So he did to them, and delivered them out
of the hand of the children of Israel, so that
they did not kill them.
27 And that day Joshua made them
[R]woodcutters and water carriers for the con-
gregation and for the altar of the LORD, [R]in the
place which He would choose, even to this
day. Josh. 9:21, 23 • Deut. 12:5

CHAPTER 10

Victory over the Amorites

NOW it came to pass when Adoni-
Zedek king of Jerusalem [R]heard how
Joshua had taken Ai and had utterly destroyed
it—as he had done to Jericho and its king, so
he had done to Ai and its king—and how the
inhabitants of Gibeon had made peace with Is-
rael and were among them, Josh. 9:1
2 that they [R]feared greatly, because Gibeon
was a great city, like one of the royal cities,
and because it *was* greater than Ai, and all its
men *were* mighty. Ex. 15:14–16
3 Therefore Adoni-Zedek king of Jerusa-
lem sent to Hoham king of Hebron, Piram
king of Jarmuth, Japhia king of Lachish, and
Debir king of Eglon, saying,
4 "Come up to me and help me, that we may
attack Gibeon, for it has made peace with
Joshua and with the children of Israel."
5 Therefore the five kings of the [R]Amo-
rites, the king of Jerusalem, the king of He-
bron, the king of Jarmuth, the king of
Lachish, *and* the king of Eglon, [R]gathered to-
gether and went up, they and all their armies,
and camped before Gibeon and made war
against it. Num. 13:29 • Josh. 9:2
6 And the men of Gibeon sent to Joshua at
the camp [R]at Gilgal, saying, "Do not forsake
your servants; come up to us quickly, save us
and help us, for all the kings of the Amorites
who dwell in the mountains have gathered to-
gether against us." Josh. 5:10
7 So Joshua ascended from Gilgal, he and
[R]all the people of war with him, and all the
mighty men of valor. Josh. 8:1
8 And the LORD said to Joshua, [R]"Do not
fear them, for I have delivered them into your
hand; [R]not a man of them shall [R]stand before
you." Josh. 11:6 • Josh. 1:5, 9 • Josh. 21:44
9 Joshua therefore came upon them sud-
denly, having marched all night from Gilgal.
10 So the LORD [R]routed them before Israel,
killed them with a great slaughter at Gibeon,
chased them along the road that goes to Beth
Horon, and struck them down as far as
[R]Azekah and Makkedah. Is. 28:21 • Josh. 15:35
11 And it happened, as they fled before Is-
rael *and* were on the descent of Beth Horon,
[R]that the LORD cast down large hailstones
from heaven on them as far as Azekah, and
they died. *There were* more who died from the
hailstones than the children of Israel killed
with the sword. Is. 30:30
12 Then Joshua spoke to the LORD in the day
when the LORD delivered up the Amorites be-
fore the children of Israel, and he said in the
sight of Israel:

[R]"Sun, stand still over Gibeon; Hab. 3:11
And Moon, in the Valley of Aijalon."

13 So the sun stood still,
And the moon stopped,
Till the people had revenge
Upon their enemies.

[R]*Is* this not written in the Book of Jasher? So
the sun stood still in the midst of heaven, and
did not hasten to go *down* for about a whole
day. 2 Sam. 1:18
14 And there has been [R]no day like that, be-
fore it or after it, that the LORD heeded the
voice of a man; for [R]the LORD fought for Is-
rael. Is. 38:7, 8 • Deut. 1:30; 20:4
15 [R]Then Joshua returned, and all Israel with
him, to the camp at Gilgal. Josh. 10:43
16 But these five kings had fled and hidden
themselves in a cave at Makkedah.
17 And it was told Joshua, saying, "The five
kings have been found hidden in the cave at
Makkedah."
18 So Joshua said, "Roll large stones against
the mouth of the cave, and set men by it to
guard them.
19 "And do not stay *there* yourselves, *but*
pursue your enemies, and attack their rear
guard. Do not allow them to enter their cities,
for the LORD your God has delivered them
into your hand."
20 Then it happened, while Joshua and the
children of Israel made an end of slaying
them with a very great slaughter, till they had
finished, that those who escaped entered for-
tified cities.
21 And all the people returned to the camp,
to Joshua at Makkedah, in peace. [R]No one
moved his tongue against any of the children
of Israel. Ex. 11:7
22 Then Joshua said, "Open the mouth of the
cave, and bring out those five kings to me
from the cave."
23 And they did so, and brought out those five
kings to him from the cave: the king of Jerusa-
lem, the king of Hebron, the king of Jarmuth,
the king of Lachish, *and* the king of Eglon.
24 So it was, when they brought out those
kings to Joshua, that Joshua called for all the
men of Israel, and said to the captains of the
men of war who went with him, "Come near,
put your feet on the necks of these kings."
And they drew near and [R]put their feet on
their necks. Mal. 4:3
25 Then Joshua said to them, "Do not be
afraid, nor be dismayed; be strong and of
good courage, for thus the LORD will do to all
your enemies against whom you fight."
26 And afterward Joshua struck [T]them and
killed them, and hanged them on five trees;
and they [R]were hanging on the trees until
evening. The kings • Josh. 8:29
27 So it was at the time of the going down of
the sun *that* Joshua commanded, and they
took them down from the trees, cast them into
the cave where they had been hidden, and laid
large stones against the cave's mouth, *which*
remain until this very day.
28 On that day Joshua took Makkedah, and
struck it and its king with the edge of the
sword. He utterly destroyed them*—all the
people who *were* in it. He let none remain. He
also did to the king of Makkedah as he had
done to the king of Jericho.
29 Then Joshua passed from Makkedah, and
all Israel with him, to [R]Libnah; and they
fought against Libnah. Josh. 15:42; 21:13
30 And the LORD also delivered it and its
king into the hand of Israel; he struck it and
all the people who *were* in it with the edge of
the sword. He let none remain in it, but did to
its king as he had done to the king of Jericho.
31 Then Joshua passed from Libnah, and
all Israel with him, to Lachish; and they en-
camped against it and fought against it.
32 And the LORD delivered Lachish into the
hand of Israel, who took it on the second day,
and struck it and all the people who *were* in it
with the edge of the sword, according to all
that he had done to Libnah.
33 Then Horam king of Gezer came up to
help Lachish; and Joshua struck him and his
people, until he left him none remaining.
34 From Lachish Joshua passed to Eglon,
and all Israel with him; and they encamped
against it and fought against it.
35 They took it on that day and struck it with
the edge of the sword; all the people who *were*
in it he utterly destroyed that day, according
to all that he had done to Lachish.
36 So Joshua went up from Eglon, and all Is-
rael with him, to [R]Hebron; and they fought
against it. Josh. 14:13–15; 15:13
37 And they took it and struck it with the
edge of the sword—its king, all its cities, and
all the people who *were* in it; he left none re-
maining, according to all that he had done to
Eglon, but utterly destroyed it and all the peo-
ple who *were* in it.
38 Then Joshua returned, and all Israel
with him, to [R]Debir; and they fought against
it. Josh. 15:15
39 And he took it and its king and all its
cities; they struck them with the edge of the
sword and utterly destroyed all the people
who *were* in it. He left none remaining; as he
had done to Hebron, so he did to Debir and its
king, as he had done also to Libnah and its
king.
40 So Joshua conquered all the land: the
[R]mountain country and the South* and the
lowland and the wilderness slopes, and all
their kings; he left none remaining, but utterly
destroyed all that breathed, as the LORD God
of Israel had commanded. Deut. 1:7

10:28 So with MT and most authorities; many Heb. mss., some LXX mss., and some Tg. mss. *it*
10:40 Heb. *Negev*, and so throughout the book

41 And Joshua conquered them from Kadesh Barnea as far as Gaza, and all the country of Goshen, even as far as Gibeon.

42 All these kings and their land Joshua took at one time, [R]because the LORD God of Israel fought for Israel. Josh. 10:14

43 Then Joshua returned, and all Israel with him, to the camp at Gilgal.

CHAPTER 11

Conquest of Northern Canaan

AND it came to pass, when Jabin king of Hazor heard *these things,* that he sent to Jobab king of Madon, to the king of Shimron, to the king of Achshaph,

2 and to the kings who *were* from the north, in the mountains, in the plain south of [R]Chinneroth, in the lowland, and in the heights of Dor on the west, Num. 34:11

3 to the Canaanites in the east and in the west, the Amorite, the Hittite, the Perizzite, the Jebusite in the mountains, and the Hivite below Hermon in the land of Mizpah.

4 So they went out, they and all their armies with them, *as* many people *as* the sand that *is* on the seashore in multitude, with very many horses and chariots.

5 And when all these kings had met together, they came and camped together at the waters of Merom to fight against Israel.

6 But the LORD said to Joshua, "Do not be afraid because of them, for tomorrow about this time I will deliver all of them slain before Israel. You shall hamstring their horses and burn their chariots with fire."

7 So Joshua and all the people of war with him came against them suddenly by the waters of Merom, and they attacked them.

8 And the LORD delivered them into the hand of Israel, who defeated them and chased them to Greater Sidon, to the Brook [R]Misrephoth,* and to the Valley of Mizpah eastward; they attacked them until they left none of them remaining. Josh. 13:6

9 So Joshua did to them as the LORD had told him: he hamstrung their horses and burned their chariots with fire.

10 Joshua turned back at that time and took Hazor, and struck its king with the sword; for Hazor was formerly the head of all those kingdoms.

11 And they struck all the people who *were* in it with the edge of the sword, utterly destroying *them.* There was none left breathing. Then he burned Hazor with fire.

12 So all the cities of those kings, and all their kings, Joshua took and struck with the edge of the sword. He utterly destroyed them, [R]as Moses the servant of the LORD had commanded. Num. 33:50–56

13 But *as for* the cities that stood on their mounds,* Israel burned none of them, except Hazor only, *which* Joshua burned.

14 And all the spoil of these cities and the livestock, the children of Israel took as booty for themselves; but they struck every man with the edge of the sword until they had destroyed them, and they left none breathing.

15 As the LORD had commanded Moses his servant, so Moses commanded Joshua, and so Joshua did. He left nothing undone of all that the LORD had commanded Moses.

The Summary of Conquered Territory

16 Thus Joshua took all this land: [R]the mountain country, all the South, [R]all the land of Goshen, the lowland, and the Jordan plain*—the mountains of Israel and its lowlands, Josh. 12:8 • Josh. 10:40, 41

17 [R]from Mount Halak and the ascent to Seir, even as far as Baal Gad in the Valley of Lebanon below Mount Hermon. He captured [R]all their kings, and struck them down and killed them. Josh. 12:7 • Deut. 7:24

18 Joshua made war a long time with all those kings.

19 There was not a city that made peace with the children of Israel, except [R]the Hivites, the inhabitants of Gibeon. All *the others* they took in battle. Josh. 9:3–7

20 For [R]it was of the LORD to harden their hearts, that they should come against Israel in battle, that He might utterly destroy them, *and* that they might receive no mercy, but that He might destroy them, as the LORD had commanded Moses. Deut. 2:30

21 And at that time Joshua came and cut off [R]the Anakim from the mountains: from Hebron, from Debir, from Anab, from all the mountains of Judah, and from all the mountains of Israel; Joshua utterly destroyed them with their cities. Num. 13:22, 33

22 None of the Anakim were left in the land of the children of Israel; they remained only in Gaza, in Gath, and in Ashdod.

23 So Joshua took the whole land, according to all that the LORD had said to Moses; and Joshua gave it as an inheritance to Israel according to their divisions by their tribes. Then the land rested from war.

CHAPTER 12

Kings Are Conquered by Moses

THESE *are* the kings of the land whom the children of Israel defeated, and whose land they possessed on the other side of the Jordan toward the rising of the sun, [R]from the River Arnon to Mount Hermon, and all the eastern Jordan plain: Num. 21:24

11:8 Heb. *Misrephoth Maim,* lit. *Burnings of Water*
11:13 Heb. *tel,* a heap of successive city ruins
11:16 Heb. *arabah*

2 *One king was* Sihon king of the Amorites, who dwelt in Heshbon *and* ruled half of Gilead, from Aroer, which is on the bank of the River Arnon, from the middle of that river, even as far as the River Jabbok, *which is* the border of the Ammonites,

3 and [R]the eastern Jordan plain from the Sea of Chinneroth as far as the Sea of the Arabah (the Salt Sea), [R]the road to Beth Jeshimoth, and southward below the slopes of Pisgah. Deut. 3:17 • Josh. 13:20

4 *The other king was* [R]Og king of Bashan and his territory, *who was* of [R]the remnant of the giants, [R]who dwelt at Ashtaroth and at Edrei, Num. 21:33 • Deut. 3:11 • Deut. 1:4

5 and reigned over [R]Mount Hermon, [R]over Salcah, over all Bashan, as far as the border of the Geshurites and the Maachathites, and over half of Gilead *to* the border of Sihon king of Heshbon. Deut. 3:8 • Deut. 3:10

6 These Moses the servant of the LORD and the children of Israel had conquered; and Moses the servant of the LORD had given it *as* a possession to the Reubenites, the Gadites, and half the tribe of Manasseh.

Kings Are Conquered by Joshua

7 And these *are* the kings of the country [R]which Joshua and the children of Israel conquered on this side of the Jordan, on the west, from Baal Gad in the Valley of Lebanon as far as Mount Halak and the ascent to [R]Seir, which Joshua [R]gave to the tribes of Israel *as* a possession according to their divisions, Josh. 11:17 • Gen. 14:6; 32:3 • Josh. 11:23

8 in the mountain country, in the lowlands, in the *Jordan* plain, in the slopes, in the wilderness, and in the South—the Hittites, the Amorites, the Canaanites, the Perizzites, the Hivites, and the Jebusites:

9 [R]the king of Jericho, one; the king of Ai, which *is* beside Bethel, one; Josh. 6:2

10 [R]the king of Jerusalem, one; the king of Hebron, one; Josh. 10:23

11 the king of Jarmuth, one; the king of Lachish, one;

12 the king of Eglon, one; [R]the king of Gezer, one; Josh. 10:33

13 [R]the king of Debir, one; the king of Geder, one; Josh. 10:38, 39

14 the king of Hormah, one; the king of Arad, one;

15 [R]the king of Libnah, one; the king of Adullam, one; Josh. 10:29, 30

16 [R]the king of Makkedah, one; [R]the king of Bethel, one; Josh. 10:28 • Judg. 1:22

17 the king of Tappuah, one; [R]the king of Hepher, one; 1 Kin. 4:10

18 the king of Aphek, one; the king of [T]Lasharon, one; Or *Sharon*

19 the king of Madon, one; [R]the king of Hazor, one; Josh. 11:10

20 the king of [R]Shimron Meron, one; the king of Achshaph, one; Josh. 11:1; 19:15

21 the king of Taanach, one; the king of Megiddo, one;

22 [R]the king of Kedesh, one; the king of Jokneam in Carmel, one; Josh. 19:37; 20:7

23 the king of Dor in the heights of Dor, one; the king of the people of Gilgal, one;

24 the king of Tirzah, one—[R]all the kings, thirty-one. Deut. 7:24

CHAPTER 13

Unconquered Parts of Canaan

NOW Joshua [R]was old, advanced in years. And the LORD said to him: "You are old, advanced in years, and there remains very much land yet to be possessed. Josh. 14:10

2 [R]"This is the land that yet remains: [R]all the territory of the Philistines and all [R]*that of* the Geshurites, Judg. 3:1–3 • Joel 3:4 • 2 Sam. 3:3

3 [R]"from Sihor, which *is* east of Egypt, as far as the border of Ekron northward (*which* is counted as Canaanite); the [R]five lords of the Philistines—the Gazites, the Ashdodites, the Ashkelonites, the Gittites, and the Ekronites; also the Avites; Jer. 2:18 • Judg. 3:3

4 "from the south, all the land of the Canaanites, and Mearah that belongs to the Sidonians [R]as far as Aphek, to the border of [R]the Amorites; Josh. 12:18; 19:30 • Judg. 1:34

5 "the land of [R]the Gebalites,* and all Lebanon, toward the sunrise, from Baal Gad below Mount Hermon as far as the entrance to Hamath; 1 Kin. 5:18; Ezek. 27:9

6 "all the inhabitants of the mountains from Lebanon as far as the Brook Misrephoth,* *and* all the Sidonians—them I will drive out from before the children of Israel; only [T]divide it by lot to Israel as an inheritance, as I have commanded you. *apportion*

7 "Now therefore, divide this land as an inheritance to the nine tribes and half the tribe of Manasseh."

Geographical Boundaries

8 With the other half-tribe the Reubenites and the Gadites received their inheritance, [R]which Moses had given them, beyond the Jordan eastward, as Moses the servant of the LORD had given them: Num. 32:33

9 from Aroer which *is* on the bank of the River Arnon, and the town that *is* in the midst of the ravine, [R]and all the plain of Medeba as far as Dibon; Num. 21:30

10 all the cities of Sihon king of the Amorites, who reigned in Heshbon, as far as the border of the children of Ammon;

11 [R]Gilead, and the border of the Geshurites

13:5 Or *Giblites* **13:6** Heb. *Misrephoth Maim*, lit. *Burnings of Water*

and Maachathites, all Mount Hermon, and all
Bashan as far as Salcah; Josh. 12:5
12 all the kingdom of Og in Bashan, who
reigned in Ashtaroth and Edrei, who re-
mained of the remnant of the giants; for Mo-
ses had defeated and cast out these.
13 Nevertheless the children of Israel [R]did
not drive out the Geshurites or the Ma-
achathites, but the Geshurites and the Ma-
achathites dwell among the Israelites until
this day. Josh. 13:11

Boundaries of Levi

14 [R]Only to the tribe of Levi he had given no
inheritance; the sacrifices of the LORD God of
Israel made by fire *are* their inheritance, as
He said to them. Josh. 14:3, 4

Boundaries of Reuben

15 [R]And Moses had given to the tribe of the
children of Reuben *an inheritance* according
to their families. Num. 34:14
16 Their territory was from Aroer, which *is*
on the bank of the River Arnon, [R]and the city
that *is* in the midst of the ravine, [R]and all the
plain by Medeba; Num. 21:28 • Num. 21:30
17 [R]Heshbon and all its cities that *are* in
the plain: Dibon, Bamoth Baal, Beth Baal
Meon, Num. 21:28, 30
18 Jahaza, Kedemoth, Mephaath,
19 [R]Kirjathaim, Sibmah, Zereth Shahar on
the mountain of the valley, Num. 32:37
20 Beth Peor, [R]the slopes of Pisgah, and Beth
Jeshimoth— Deut. 3:17
21 all the cities of the plain and all the king-
dom of Sihon king of the Amorites, who
reigned in Heshbon, whom Moses had struck
with the princes of Midian: Evi, Rekem, Zur,
Hur, and Reba, who *were* princes of Sihon
dwelling in the country.
22 The children of Israel also killed with
the sword [R]Balaam the son of Beor, the
[T]soothsayer, among those who were killed by
them. Num. 22:5; 31:8 • *diviner*
23 And the border of the children of Reuben
was the bank of the Jordan. This *was* the in-
heritance of the children of Reuben according
to their families, the cities and their villages.

Boundaries of Gad

24 [R]Moses also had given *an inheritance* to
the tribe of Gad, to the children of Gad ac-
cording to their families. Num. 34:14
25 [R]Their territory was Jazer, and all the
cities of Gilead, [R]and half the land of the Am-
monites as far as Aroer, which *is* before Rab-
bah, Num. 32:1, 35 • Judg. 11:13, 15
26 and from Heshbon to Ramath Mizpah
and Betonim, and from Mahanaim to the bor-
der of Debir,
27 and in the valley [R]Beth Haram, Beth Nim-
rah, Succoth, and Zaphon, the rest of the
kingdom of Sihon king of Heshbon, with the
Jordan as *its* border, as far as the edge of the
Sea of Chinnereth, on the other side of the
Jordan eastward. Num. 32:36
28 This *is* the inheritance of the children of
Gad according to their families, the cities and
their villages.

Boundaries of the Half-Tribe of Manasseh

29 [R]Moses also had given *an inheritance* to
half the tribe of Manasseh; it was for half the
tribe of the children of Manasseh according to
their families: Num. 34:14
30 Their territory was from Mahanaim, all
Bashan, all the kingdom of Og king of
Bashan, and [R]all the towns of Jair which are
in Bashan, sixty cities; Num. 32:41
31 half of Gilead, and Ashtaroth and Edrei,
cities of the kingdom of Og in Bashan, *were*
for the [R]children of Machir the son of Ma-
nasseh, for half of the children of Machir ac-
cording to their families. Num. 32:39, 40
32 These *are the areas* which Moses had
[T]distributed as an inheritance in the plains of
Moab on the other side of the Jordan, by Jeri-
cho eastward. *apportioned*
33 But to the tribe of Levi Moses had given
no inheritance; the LORD God of Israel *was*
their inheritance, as He had said to them.

CHAPTER 14

Method of Setting Tribal Boundaries

THESE *are the areas* which the children of
Israel inherited in the land of Canaan,
[R]which Eleazar the priest, Joshua the son of
Nun, and the heads of the fathers of the tribes
of the children of Israel distributed as an in-
heritance to them. Num. 34:16–29
2 Their inheritance *was* by lot, as the LORD
had commanded by the hand of Moses, for the
nine tribes and the half-tribe.
3 For Moses had given the inheritance of
the two tribes and the half-tribe on the other
side of the Jordan; but to the Levites he had
given no inheritance among them.
4 For the children of Joseph were two
tribes: Manasseh and Ephraim. And they gave
no part to the Levites in the land, except cities
to dwell *in*, with their common-lands for their
livestock and their property.
5 [R]As the LORD had commanded Moses, so
the children of Israel did; and they divided the
land. Josh. 21:2

Boundaries of Caleb

6 Then the children of Judah came to
Joshua in Gilgal. And Caleb the son of Je-
phunneh the Kenizzite said to him: "You
know [R]the word which the LORD said to Moses
the man of God concerning you and me in
Kadesh Barnea. Num. 14:24, 30
7 "I *was* forty years old when Moses the
servant of the LORD sent me from Kadesh

Barnea to spy out the land, and I brought back
word to him as *it was* in my heart.
8 "Nevertheless [R]my brethren who went
up with me made the heart of the people
melt, but I wholly [R]followed the LORD my
God. Num. 13:31, 32 • Num. 14:24
9 "So Moses swore on that day, saying,
[R]'Surely the land where your foot has trodden
shall be your inheritance and your children's
forever, because you have wholly followed the
LORD my God.' Num. 14:23, 24
10 "And now, behold, the LORD has kept me
[R]alive, [R]as He said, these forty-five years,
ever since the LORD spoke this word to Mo-
ses while Israel wandered in the wilderness;
and now, here I am this day, eighty-five years
old. Num. 14:24, 30, 38 • Josh. 5:6
11 "As yet I *am as* strong this day as on the
day that Moses sent me; just as my strength
was then, so now *is* my strength for war, both
for going out and for coming in.
12 "Now therefore, give me this mountain of
which the LORD spoke in that day; for you
heard in that day how [R]the Anakim *were*
there, and *that* the cities *were* great *and* forti-
fied. [R]It may be that the LORD *will be* with me,
and I shall be able to drive them out as the
LORD said." Num. 13:28, 33 • Rom. 8:31
13 And Joshua [R]blessed him, [R]and gave He-
bron to Caleb the son of Jephunneh as an in-
heritance. Josh. 22:6 • Josh. 10:37; 15:13
14 [R]Hebron therefore became the inheri-
tance of Caleb the son of Jephunneh the
Kenizzite to this day, because he wholly fol-
lowed the LORD God of Israel. Josh. 21:12
15 And [R]the name of Hebron formerly was
Kirjath Arba (*Arba was* the greatest man
among the Anakim). [R]Then the land had rest
from war. Gen. 23:2 • Josh. 11:23

CHAPTER 15

Boundaries of the Remainder of Judah

SO *this* was the [T]lot of the tribe of the chil-
dren of Judah according to their families:
[R]The border of Edom at the [R]Wilderness of
Zin southward *was* the extreme southern
boundary. *allotment* • Num. 34:3 • Num. 33:36
2 And their [R]southern border began at the
shore of the Salt Sea, from the bay that faces
southward. Num. 34:3, 4
3 Then it went out to the southern side of
the Ascent of Akrabbim, passed along to Zin,
ascended on the south side of Kadesh Barnea,
passed along to Hezron, went up to Adar, and
went around to Karkaa.
4 *From there* it passed [R]toward Azmon and
went out to the Brook of Egypt; and the bor-
der ended at the sea. This shall be your south-
ern border. Num. 34:5
5 The east border *was* the Salt Sea as far as
the mouth of the Jordan. And the border on
the northern quarter *began* at the bay of the
sea at the mouth of the Jordan.
6 The border went up to [R]Beth Hoglah and
passed north of Beth Arabah; and the border
went up [R]to the stone of Bohan the son of Reu-
ben. Josh. 18:19, 21 • Josh. 18:17
7 Then the border went up toward [R]Debir
from [R]the Valley of Achor, and it turned north-
ward toward Gilgal, which *is* before the As-
cent of Adummim, which *is* on the south side
of the valley. The border continued toward
the waters of En Shemesh and ended at En
Rogel. Josh. 13:26 • Josh. 7:26
8 And the border went up [R]by the Valley of
the Son of Hinnom to the southern slope of
the Jebusite *city* (which *is* Jerusalem). The
border went up to the top of the mountain that
lies before the Valley of Hinnom westward,
which *is* at the end of the Valley of Rephaim*
northward. Josh. 18:16
9 Then the border went around from the
top of the hill to the fountain of the water of
Nephtoah, and extended to the cities of Mount
Ephron. And the border went around to
Baalah (which *is* Kirjath Jearim).
10 Then the border turned westward from
Baalah to Mount Seir, passed along to the side
of Mount Jearim on the north (which *is*
Chesalon), went down to Beth Shemesh, and
passed on to [R]Timnah. Gen. 38:13
11 And the border went out to the side of
[R]Ekron northward. Then the border went
around to Shicron, passed along to Mount
Baalah, and extended to Jabneel; and the bor-
der ended at the sea. Josh. 19:43
12 The west border *was* [R]the coastline of the
Great Sea. This *is* the boundary of the chil-
dren of Judah all around according to their
families. Num. 34:6, 7
13 Now to Caleb the son of Jephunneh he
gave a share among the children of Judah, ac-
cording to the commandment of the LORD to
Joshua, *namely*, Kirjath Arba, which *is* He-
bron (*Arba was* the father of Anak).
14 Caleb drove out [R]the three sons of Anak
from there: Sheshai, Ahiman, and Talmai, the
children of Anak. Judg. 1:10, 20
15 Then [R]he went up from there to the in-
habitants of Debir (formerly the name of
Debir *was* Kirjath Sepher). Judg. 1:11
16 [R]And Caleb said, "He who attacks Kirjath
Sepher and takes it, to him I will give Achsah
my daughter as wife." Judg. 1:12
17 So [R]Othniel the son of Kenaz, the brother
of Caleb, took it; and he gave him Achsah his
daughter as wife. Judg. 1:13; 3:9
18 Now it was so, when she came *to him*,
that she persuaded him to ask her father for a
field. So she dismounted from *her* donkey,
and Caleb said to her, "What do you wish?"
19 She answered, "Give me a blessing; since

15:8 Lit. *Giants*

you have given me land in the South, give me also springs of water." So he gave her the upper springs and the lower springs.

20 This *was* the inheritance of the tribe of the children of Judah according to their families:

21 The cities at the limits of the tribe of the children of Judah, toward the border of Edom in the South, were Kabzeel, [R]Eder, Jagur, Gen. 35:21

22 Kinah, Dimonah, Adadah,

23 Kedesh, Hazor, Ithnan,

24 [R]Ziph, Telem, Bealoth, 1 Sam. 23:14

25 Hazor, Hadattah, Kerioth, Hezron (which *is* Hazor),

26 Amam, Shema, Moladah,

27 Hazar Gaddah, Heshmon, Beth Pelet,

28 Hazar Shual, Beersheba, Bizjothjah,

29 Baalah, Ijim, Ezem,

30 Eltolad, Chesil, [R]Hormah, Josh. 19:4

31 Ziklag, Madmannah, Sansannah,

32 Lebaoth, Shilhim, Ain, and Rimmon: all the cities *are* twenty-nine, with their villages.

33 In the lowland: [R]Eshtaol, Zorah, Ashnah, Judg. 13:25; 16:31

34 Zanoah, En Gannim, Tappuah, Enam,

35 Jarmuth, Adullam, Socoh, Azekah,

36 Sharaim, Adithaim, Gederah, and Gederothaim: fourteen cities with their villages;

37 Zenan, Hadashah, Migdal Gad,

38 Dilean, Mizpah, [R]Joktheel, 2 Kin. 14:7

39 [R]Lachish, Bozkath, Eglon, 2 Kin. 14:19

40 Cabbon, Lahmas,* Kithlish,

41 Gederoth, Beth Dagon, Naamah, and Makkedah: sixteen cities with their villages;

42 [R]Libnah, Ether, Ashan, Josh. 21:13

43 Jiphtah, Ashnah, Nezib,

44 Keilah, Achzib, and Mareshah: nine cities with their villages;

45 Ekron, with its towns and villages;

46 from Ekron to the sea, all that *lay* near [R]Ashdod, with their villages; Josh. 11:22

47 Ashdod with its towns and villages, Gaza with its towns and villages—as far as [R]the Brook of Egypt and [R]the Great Sea with *its* coastline. Josh. 15:4 • Num. 34:6

48 And in the mountain country: Shamir, Jattir, Sochoh,

49 Dannah, Kirjath Sannah (which *is* Debir),

50 Anab, Eshtemoh, Anim,

51 [R]Goshen, Holon, and Giloh: eleven cities with their villages; Josh. 10:41; 11:16

52 Arab, Dumah, Eshean,

53 Janum, Beth Tappuah, Aphekah,

54 Humtah, [R]Kirjath Arba (which *is* Hebron), and Zior: nine cities with their villages; Josh. 14:15

55 Maon, Carmel, Ziph, Juttah,

56 Jezreel, Jokdeam, Zanoah,

57 Kain, Gibeah, and Timnah: ten cities with their villages;

58 Halhul, Beth Zur, Gedor,

59 Maarath, Beth Anoth, and Eltekon: six cities with their villages;

60 Kirjath Baal (which *is* Kirjath Jearim) and Rabbah: two cities with their villages.

61 In the wilderness: Beth Arabah, Middin, Secacah,

62 Nibshan, the City of Salt, and [R]En Gedi: six cities with their villages. 1 Sam. 23:29

63 As for the Jebusites, the inhabitants of Jerusalem, [R]the children of Judah could not drive them out; [R]but the Jebusites dwell with the children of Judah at Jerusalem to this day. 2 Sam. 5:6 • Judg. 1:21

CHAPTER 16

Boundaries of Joseph

THE lot [T]fell to the children of Joseph from the Jordan, by Jericho, to the waters of Jericho on the east, to the [R]wilderness that goes up from Jericho through the mountains to Bethel, Lit. *went out* • Josh. 8:15; 18:12

2 then went out from [R]Bethel to Luz,* passed along to the border of the Archites at Ataroth, Josh. 18:13

3 and went down westward to the boundary of the Japhletites, [R]as far as the boundary of Lower Beth Horon to [R]Gezer; and it ended at the sea. 2 Chr. 8:5 • 1 Kin. 9:15

4 So the children of Joseph, Manasseh and Ephraim, took their inheritance.

Boundaries of Ephraim

5 [R]The border of the children of Ephraim, according to their families, was *thus:* The border of their inheritance on the east side was [R]Ataroth Addar [R]as far as Upper Beth Horon. Judg. 1:29 • Josh. 18:13 • 2 Chr. 8:5

6 And the border went out toward the sea on the north side of [R]Michmethath; then the border went around eastward to Taanath Shiloh, and passed by it on the east of Janohah. Josh. 17:7

7 Then it went down from Janohah to Ataroth and Naarah,* reached to Jericho, and came out at the Jordan.

8 The border went out from [R]Tappuah westward to the [R]Brook Kanah, and it ended at the sea. This *was* the inheritance of the tribe of the children of Ephraim according to their families. Josh. 17:8 • Josh. 17:9

9 [R]The separate cities for the children of Ephraim *were* among the inheritance of the children of Manasseh, all the cities with their villages. Josh. 17:9

10 [R]And they did not drive out the Canaanites who dwelt in Gezer; but the Canaanites dwell among the Ephraimites to this day and have become forced laborers. Judg. 1:29

15:40 Or *Lahmam* **16:2** LXX *to Bethel*
16:7 *Naaran,* 1 Chr. 7:28

CHAPTER 17

Boundaries of the Half-Tribe of Manasseh

THERE was also a lot for the tribe of Ma-
nasseh, for he *was* the firstborn of Joseph:
namely for [R]Machir the firstborn of Ma-
nasseh, the father of Gilead, because he was a
man of war; therefore he was given [R]Gilead
and Bashan. Gen. 50:23 • Deut. 3:15
2 And there was *a lot* for the rest of the
children of Manasseh according to their fam-
ilies: for the children of Abiezer,* the children
of Helek, the children of Asriel, the children
of Shechem, the children of Hepher, and the
children of Shemida; these *were* the male
children of Manasseh the son of Joseph ac-
cording to their families.
3 But Zelophehad the son of Hepher, the
son of Gilead, the son of Machir, the son of
Manasseh, had no sons, but only daughters.
And these *are* the names of his daughters:
Mahlah, Noah, Hoglah, Milcah, and Tirzah.
4 And they came near before [R]Eleazar the
priest, before Joshua the son of Nun, and
before the rulers, saying, [R]"The LORD com-
manded Moses to give us an [T]inheritance
among our brothers." Therefore, according
to the commandment of the LORD, he gave
them an inheritance among their father's
brothers. Josh. 14:1 • Num. 27:2–11 • *possession*
5 Ten shares fell to [R]Manasseh, besides the
land of Gilead and Bashan, which *were* on the
other side of the Jordan, Josh. 22:7
6 because the daughters of Manasseh re-
ceived an inheritance among his sons; and the
rest of Manasseh's sons had the land of
Gilead.
7 And the territory of Manasseh was from
Asher to Michmethath, that *lies* east of She-
chem; and the border went along south to the
inhabitants of En Tappuah.
8 Manasseh had the land of Tappuah, but
Tappuah on the border of Manasseh *belonged*
to the children of Ephraim.
9 And the [T]border descended to the [T]Brook
Kanah, southward to the brook. [R]These cities
of Ephraim *are* among the cities of Ma-
nasseh. The border of Manasseh *was* on the
north side of the brook; and it ended at the
sea. *boundary* • *Wadi* • Josh. 16:9
10 Southward *it was* Ephraim's, northward
it was Manasseh's, and the sea was its border.
Manasseh's territory was adjoining Asher on
the north and Issachar on the east.
11 And in Issachar and in Asher, [R]Manasseh
had Beth Shean and its towns, Ibleam and its
towns, the inhabitants of Dor and its towns,
the inhabitants of En Dor and its towns, the
inhabitants of Taanach and its towns, and the
inhabitants of Megiddo and its towns—three
hilly regions. 1 Chr. 7:29
12 Yet [R]the children of Manasseh could not
drive out *the inhabitants of* those cities, but
the Canaanites were determined to dwell in
that land. Judg. 1:19, 27, 28
13 And it happened, when the children of Is-
rael grew strong, that they put the Canaanites
to [R]forced labor, but did not utterly drive them
out. Josh. 16:10
14 Then the children of Joseph spoke to
Joshua, saying, "Why have you given us *only*
one lot and one share to inherit, since we *are*
[R]a great people, inasmuch as the LORD has
blessed us until now?" Gen. 48:19
15 So Joshua answered them, "If you *are* a
great people, *then* go up to the forest *country*
and clear a place for yourself there in the land
of the Perizzites and the giants, since the
mountains of Ephraim are too confined for
you."
16 But the children of Joseph said, "The
mountain country is not enough for us; and all
the Canaanites who dwell in the land of the
valley have chariots of iron, *both those* who
are of Beth Shean and its towns and *those*
who *are* of the Valley of Jezreel."
17 And Joshua spoke to the house of Jo-
seph—to Ephraim and Manasseh—saying,
"You *are* a great people and have great power;
you shall not have *only* one lot,
18 "but the mountain country shall be
yours. Although it *is* wooded, you shall cut it
down, and its [T]farthest extent shall be yours;
for you shall drive out the Canaanites,
[R]though they have iron chariots *and* are
strong." Lit. *goings out* • Deut. 20:1

CHAPTER 18

The Remaining Tribes Move to Shiloh

NOW the whole congregation of the chil-
dren of Israel assembled together [R]at
Shiloh, and [R]set up the tabernacle of meeting
there. And the land was subdued before
them. Jer. 7:12 • Judg. 18:31

New Method of Setting Tribal Boundaries

2 But there remained among the children of
Israel seven tribes which had not yet received
their inheritance.
3 Then Joshua said to the children of Israel:
[R]"How long will you neglect to go and possess
the land which the LORD God of your fathers
has given you? Judg. 18:9
4 "Pick out from among you three men for
each tribe, and I will send them; they shall
rise and go through the land, survey it ac-
cording to their inheritance, and come *back* to
me.
5 "And they shall divide it into seven parts.
Judah shall remain in their territory on the
south, and the house of Joseph shall remain in
their territory on the north.

17:2 *Jeezer,* Num. 26:30

6 "You shall therefore survey the land in seven parts and bring *the survey* here to me, [R]that I may cast lots for you here before the LORD our God. Josh. 14:2; 18:10

7 "But the Levites have no part among you, for the priesthood of the LORD *is* their inheritance. And Gad, Reuben, and half the tribe of Manasseh have received their inheritance beyond the Jordan on the east, which Moses the servant of the LORD gave them."

8 Then the men arose to go away; and Joshua charged those who went to [T]survey the land, saying, "Go, walk [R]through the land, survey it, and come back to me, that I may cast lots for you here before the LORD in Shiloh." *describe in writing* • Gen. 13:17

9 So the men went, passed through the land, and wrote the survey in a book in seven parts by cities; and they came to Joshua at the camp in Shiloh.

10 Then Joshua cast [R]lots for them in Shiloh before the LORD, and there Joshua divided the land to the children of Israel according to their divisions. Acts 13:19

Boundaries of Benjamin

11 [R]Now the lot of the tribe of the children of Benjamin came up according to their families, and the territory of their lot came out between the children of Judah and the children of Joseph. Judg. 1:21

12 [R]Their border on the north side began at the Jordan, and the border went up to the side of Jericho on the north, and went up through the mountains westward; it ended at the Wilderness of Beth Aven. Josh. 16:1

13 The border went over from there toward Luz, to the side of Luz (which *is* Bethel) southward; and the border descended to Ataroth Addar, near the hill that *lies* on the south side of Lower Beth Horon.

14 Then the border extended around the west side to the south, from the hill that *lies* before Beth Horon southward; and [T]it ended at [R]Kirjath Baal (which *is* Kirjath Jearim), a city of the children of Judah. This *was* the west side. Lit. *its goings out were* • Josh. 15:9

15 The south side *began* at the end of Kirjath Jearim, and the border extended on the west and went out to [R]the spring of the waters of Nephtoah. Josh. 15:9

16 Then the border came down to the end of the mountain that *lies* before [R]the Valley of the Son of Hinnom, which *is* in the Valley of the Rephaim* on the north, descended to the Valley of Hinnom, to the side of the Jebusite *city* on the south, and descended to [R]En Rogel. Josh. 15:8 • Josh. 15:7

17 And it went around from the north, went out to En Shemesh, and extended toward Geliloth, which is before the Ascent of Adummim, and descended to [R]the stone of Bohan the son of Reuben. Josh. 15:6

18 Then it passed along toward the north side of Arabah,* and went down to Arabah.

19 And the border passed along to the north side of Beth Hoglah; then the border ended at the north bay at the [R]Salt Sea, at the south end of the Jordan. This *was* the southern boundary. Josh. 15:2, 5

20 The Jordan was its border on the east side. This *was* the inheritance of the children of Benjamin, according to its boundaries all around, according to their families.

21 Now the cities of the tribe of the children of Benjamin, according to their families, were Jericho, Beth Hoglah, Emek Keziz,

22 Beth Arabah, Zemaraim, Bethel,

23 Avim, Parah, Ophrah,

24 Chephar Haammoni, Ophni, and Gaba: twelve cities with their villages;

25 [R]Gibeon, Ramah, Beeroth, 1 Kin. 3:4, 5

26 Mizpah, Chephirah, Mozah,

27 Rekem, Irpeel, Taralah,

28 Zelah, Eleph, [R]Jebus (which *is* Jerusalem), Gibeath, *and* Kirjath: fourteen cities with their villages. This was the inheritance of the children of Benjamin according to their families. Josh. 15:8, 63

CHAPTER 19

Boundaries of Simeon

THE [R]second lot came out for Simeon, for the tribe of the children of Simeon according to their families. [R]And their inheritance was within the inheritance of the children of Judah. Judg. 1:3 • Josh. 19:9

2 [R]They had in their inheritance Beersheba (Sheba), Moladah, 1 Chr. 4:28

3 Hazar Shual, Balah, Ezem,

4 Eltolad, Bethul, Hormah,

5 Ziklag, Beth Marcaboth, Hazar Susah,

6 Beth Lebaoth, and Sharuhen: thirteen cities and their villages;

7 Ain, Rimmon, Ether, and Ashan: four cities and their villages;

8 and all the villages that *were* all around these cities as far as Baalath Beer, [R]Ramah of the South. This *was* the inheritance of the tribe of the children of Simeon according to their families. 1 Sam. 30:27

9 The inheritance of the children of Simeon *was included* in the share of the children of Judah, for the share of the children of Judah was [T]too much for them. [R]Therefore the children of Simeon had *their* inheritance within the inheritance of [T]that people. *too large* • Josh. 19:1 • Lit. *them*

Boundaries of Zebulun

10 The third lot came out for the children of Zebulun according to their families, and the border of their inheritance was as far as Sarid.

18:16 Lit. *Giants* **18:18** *Beth Arabah,* Josh. 15:6; 18:22

11 [R]Their border went toward the west and
to Maralah, went to Dabbasheth, and ex-
tended along the brook that is [R]east of
Jokneam. Gen. 49:13 • Josh. 12:22
12 Then from Sarid it went eastward toward
the sunrise along the border of Chisloth
Tabor, and went out toward [R]Daberath,
bypassing Japhia. 1 Chr. 6:72
13 And from there it passed along on the
east of [R]Gath Hepher, toward Eth Kazin,
and extended to Rimmon, which borders on
Neah. 2 Kin. 14:25
14 Then the border went around it on the
north side of Hannathon, and it ended in the
Valley of Jiphthah El.
15 Included were Kattath, Nahallal, Shim-
ron, Idalah, and Bethlehem: twelve cities with
their villages.
16 This *was* the inheritance of the children
of Zebulun according to their families, these
cities with their villages.

Boundaries of Issachar

17 The fourth lot came out to Issachar, for
the children of Issachar according to their
families.
18 And their territory went to Jezreel, and
included Chesulloth, Shunem,
19 Haphraim, Shion, Anaharath,
20 Rabbith, Kishion, Abez,
21 Remeth, En Gannim, En Haddah, and
Beth Pazzez.
22 And the border reached to Tabor, Sha-
hazimah, and [R]Beth Shemesh; their border
ended at the Jordan: sixteen cities with their
villages. Josh. 15:10
23 This *was* the inheritance of the tribe of
the children of Issachar according to their
families, the cities and their villages.

Boundaries of Asher

24 [R]The fifth lot came out for the tribe of
the children of Asher according to their fam-
ilies. Judg. 1:31, 32
25 And their territory included Helkath,
Hali, Beten, Achshaph,
26 Alammelech, Amad, and Mishal; it
reached to [R]Mount Carmel westward, along
the Brook Shihor Libnath. Jer. 46:18
27 It turned toward the sunrise to Beth
Dagon; and it reached to Zebulun and to the
Valley of Jiphthah El, then northward beyond
Beth Emek and Neiel, bypassing [R]Cabul
which was on the left, 1 Kin. 9:13
28 including Ebron,* Rehob, Hammon, and
Kanah, as far as Greater Sidon.
29 And the border turned to Ramah and to
the fortified city of Tyre; then the border
turned to Hosah, and ended at the sea by the
region of [R]Achzib. Judg. 1:31
30 Also Ummah, Aphek, and Rehob *were in-
cluded:* twenty-two cities with their villages.
31 This *was* the inheritance of the tribe of
the children of Asher according to their fami-
lies, these cities with their villages.

Boundaries of Naphtali

32 [R]The sixth lot came out to the children of
Naphtali, for the children of Naphtali accord-
ing to their families. Judg. 1:33
33 And their border began at Heleph, en-
closing the territory from the terebinth tree in
Zaanannim, Adami Nekeb, and Jabneel, as far
as Lakkum; it ended at the Jordan.
34 [R]From Heleph the border extended west-
ward to Aznoth Tabor, and went out from
there toward Hukkok; it adjoined Zebulun on
the south side and Asher on the west side, and
ended at Judah by the Jordan toward the sun-
rise. Deut. 33:23
35 And the fortified cities *are* Ziddim, Zer,
Hammath, Rakkath, Chinnereth,
36 Adamah, Ramah, Hazor,
37 [R]Kedesh, Edrei, En Hazor, Josh. 20:7
38 Iron, Migdal El, Horem, Beth Anath, and
Beth Shemesh: nineteen cities with their vil-
lages.
39 This *was* the inheritance of the tribe of
the children of Naphtali according to their
families, the cities and their villages.

Boundaries of Dan

40 [R]The seventh lot came out for the tribe of
the children of Dan according to their fami-
lies. Judg. 1:34–36
41 And the territory of their inheritance was
Zorah, Eshtaol, Ir Shemesh,
42 Shaalabbin, Aijalon, Jethlah,
43 Elon, Timnah, [R]Ekron, Judg. 1:18
44 Eltekeh, Gibbethon, Baalath,
45 Jehud, Bene Berak, Gath Rimmon,
46 Me Jarkon, and Rakkon, with the region
[T]near [T]Joppa. *over against* • Heb. *Japho*
47 And the [R]border of the children of Dan
went beyond these, because the children of
Dan went up to fight against Leshem and took
it; and they struck it with the edge of the
sword, took possession of it, and dwelt in it.
They called Leshem, Dan, after the name of
Dan their father. Judg. 18
48 This *is* the inheritance of the tribe of the
children of Dan according to their families,
these cities with their villages.

Boundaries of Joshua

49 When they had [T]made an end of dividing
the land as an inheritance according to their
borders, the children of Israel gave an inher-
itance among them to Joshua the son of
Nun. *finished*
50 According to the word of the LORD they
gave him the city which he asked for, Timnath

19:28 So with MT, Tg., Vg.; a few Heb. mss. *Abdon* (cf. 21:30 and 1 Chr. 6:74)

Serah in the mountains of Ephraim; and he built the city and dwelt in it.

51 These *were* the inheritances which Eleazar the priest, Joshua the son of Nun, and the heads of the fathers of the tribes of the children of Israel divided as an inheritance by lot in Shiloh before the LORD, at the door of the tabernacle of meeting. So they made an end of dividing the country.

CHAPTER 20

Cities of Refuge

THE LORD also spoke to Joshua, saying,

2 "Speak to the children of Israel, saying: Appoint for yourselves cities of refuge, of which I spoke to you through Moses,

3 'that the slayer who kills a person accidentally *or* unintentionally may flee there; and they shall be your refuge from the avenger of blood.

4 'And when he flees to one of those cities, and stands at the entrance of the gate of the city, and declares his case in the hearing of the elders of that city, they shall take him into the city as one of them, and give him a place, that he may dwell among them.

5 [R]'Then if the avenger of blood pursues him, they shall not deliver the slayer into his hand, because he struck his neighbor unintentionally, but did not hate him beforehand. Num. 35:12

6 'And he shall dwell in that city until he stands before the congregation for judgment, *and* until the death of the one who is high priest in those days. Then the slayer may return and come to his own city and his own house, to the city from which he fled.' "

7 So they appointed [R]Kedesh in Galilee, in the mountains of Naphtali, [R]Shechem in the mountains of Ephraim, and Kirjath Arba (which *is* Hebron) in [R]the mountains of Judah. 1 Chr. 6:76 • Josh. 21:21 • Luke 1:39

8 And on the other side of the Jordan, by Jericho eastward, they assigned [R]Bezer in the wilderness on the plain, from the tribe of Reuben, [R]Ramoth in Gilead, from the tribe of Gad, and [R]Golan in Bashan, from the tribe of Manasseh. Deut. 4:43 • Josh. 21:38 • Josh. 21:27

9 These were the cities appointed for all the children of Israel and for the stranger who dwelt among them, that whoever killed a person accidentally might flee there, and not die by the hand of the avenger of blood until he stood before the congregation.

CHAPTER 21

The Families to Be Assigned Cities— 1 Chr. 6:54–81

THEN the heads of the fathers' *houses* of the [R]Levites came near to [R]Eleazar the priest, to Joshua the son of Nun, and to the heads of the fathers' *houses* of the tribes of the children of Israel. Num. 35:1–8 • Josh. 14:1

2 And they spoke to them at [R]Shiloh in the land of Canaan, saying, [R]"The LORD commanded through Moses to give us cities to dwell in, with their common-lands for our livestock." Josh. 18:1 • Num. 35:2

3 So the children of Israel gave to the Levites from their inheritance, at the commandment of the LORD, these cities and their common-lands:

4 Now the lot came out for the families of the Kohathites. And [R]the children of Aaron the priest, *who were* of the Levites, [R]had thirteen cities by lot from the tribe of Judah, from the tribe of Simeon, and from the tribe of Benjamin. Josh. 21:8, 19 • Josh. 19:51

5 [R]The rest of the children of Kohath had ten cities by lot from the families of the tribe of Ephraim, from the tribe of Dan, and from the half-tribe of Manasseh. Josh. 21:20

6 And [R]the children of Gershon had thirteen cities by lot from the families of the tribe of Issachar, from the tribe of Asher, from the tribe of Naphtali, and from the half-tribe of Manasseh in Bashan. Josh. 21:27

7 [R]The children of Merari according to their families had twelve cities from the tribe of Reuben, from the tribe of Gad, and from the tribe of Zebulun. Josh. 21:34

Cities for the Kohathites

8 [R]And the children of Israel gave these cities with their common-lands by lot to the Levites, [R]as the LORD had commanded by the hand of Moses. Josh. 21:3 • Num. 35:2

9 So they gave from the tribe of the children of Judah and from the tribe of the children of Simeon these cities which are [T]designated by name, Lit. *called*

10 which were for the children of Aaron, one of the families of the Kohathites, *who were* of the children of Levi; for the lot was theirs first.

11 [R]And they gave them Kirjath Arba (*Arba was* the father of Anak), which *is* Hebron, in the mountains of Judah, with the common-land surrounding it. 1 Chr. 6:55

12 But [R]the fields of the city and its villages they gave to Caleb the son of Jephunneh as his possession. Josh. 14:14

13 Thus [R]to the children of Aaron the priest they gave [R]Hebron with its common-land (a city of refuge for the slayer), Libnah with its common-land, 1 Chr. 6:57 • Josh. 15:54; 20:2, 7

14 [R]Jattir with its common-land, Eshtemoa with its common-land, Josh. 15:48

15 [R]Holon with its common-land, Debir with its common-land, 1 Chr. 6:58

16 [R]Ain with its common-land, [R]Juttah with its common-land, and [R]Beth Shemesh with its common-land: nine cities from those two tribes; 1 Chr. 6:59 • Josh. 15:55 • Josh. 15:10

17 and from the tribe of Benjamin, [R]Gibeon with its common-land, [R]Geba with its common-land, Josh. 18:25 • Josh. 18:24

18 Anathoth with its common-land, and Almon with its common-land: four cities.

19 All the cities of the children of Aaron, the priests, *were* thirteen cities with their common-lands.

20 [R]And the families of the children of Kohath, the Levites, the rest of the children of Kohath, even they had the cities of their lot from the tribe of Ephraim. 1 Chr. 6:66

21 For they gave them [R]Shechem with its common-land in the mountains of Ephraim (a city of refuge for the slayer), [R]Gezer with its common-land, Josh. 20:7 • Judg. 1:29

22 Kibzaim with its common-land, and Beth Horon with its common-land: four cities;

23 and from the tribe of Dan, Eltekeh with its common-land, Gibbethon with its common-land,

24 [R]Aijalon with its common-land, *and* Gath Rimmon with its common-land: four cities; Josh. 10:12

25 and from the half-tribe of Manasseh, Tanach with its common-land and Gath Rimmon with its common-land: two cities.

26 All the ten cities with their common-lands were for the rest of the families of the children of Kohath.

Cities for the Gershonites

27 [R]Also to the children of Gershon, of the families of the Levites, from the *other* half-tribe of Manasseh, *they gave* Golan in Bashan with its common-land (a city of refuge for the slayer), and Be Eshterah with its common-land: two cities; 1 Chr. 6:71

28 and from the tribe of Issachar, Kishion with its common-land, Daberath with its common-land,

29 Jarmuth with its common-land, *and* En Gannim with its common-land: four cities;

30 and from the tribe of Asher, Mishal with its common-land, Abdon with its common-land,

31 Helkath with its common-land, and Rehob with its common-land: four cities;

32 and from the tribe of Naphtali, [R]Kedesh in Galilee with its common-land (a city of refuge for the slayer), Hammoth Dor with its common-land, and Kartan with its common-land: three cities. Josh. 20:7

33 All the cities of the Gershonites according to their families *were* thirteen cities with their common-lands.

Cities for the Merarites

34 And to the families of the children of Merari, the rest of the Levites, from the tribe of Zebulun, Jokneam with its common-land, Kartah with its common-land,

35 Dimnah with its common-land, *and* Nahalal with its common-land: four cities;

36 and from the tribe of Reuben, [R]Bezer with its common-land, Jahaz with its common-land, Josh. 20:8

37 Kedemoth with its common-land, and Mephaath with its common-land: four cities;*

38 and from the tribe of Gad, [R]Ramoth in Gilead with its common-land (a city of refuge for the slayer), Mahanaim with its common-land, Josh. 20:8

39 Heshbon with its common-land, *and* Jazer with its common-land: four cities in all.

40 So all the cities for the children of Merari according to their families, the rest of the families of the Levites, were *by* their lot twelve cities.

41 All the cities of the Levites within the possession of the children of Israel *were* forty-eight cities with their common-lands.

42 Every one of these cities had its common-land surrounding it; thus *were* all these cities.

The Settlement of Israel Is Completed

43 So the LORD gave to Israel [R]all the land of which He had sworn to give to their fathers, and they took possession of it and dwelt in it. Gen. 12:7; 26:3, 4; 28:4, 13, 14

44 [R]The LORD gave them rest all around, according to all that He had sworn to their fathers. And not a man of all their enemies stood against them; the LORD delivered all their enemies into their hand. Deut. 7:23, 24

45 [R]Not a word failed of any good thing which the LORD had spoken to the house of Israel. All came to pass. Josh. 23:14

CHAPTER 22

Joshua Challenges the Eastern Tribes

THEN Joshua called the Reubenites, the Gadites, and half the tribe of Manasseh,

2 and said to them: "You have kept [R]all that Moses the servant of the LORD commanded you, and have obeyed my voice in all that I commanded you. Num. 32:20–22

3 "You have not [T]left your brethren these many days, up to this day, but have kept the charge of the commandment of the LORD your God. *forsaken*

4 "And now the LORD your God has given rest to your brethren, as He promised them; now therefore, return and go to your tents *and* to the land of your possession, [R]which Moses the servant of the LORD gave you on the other side of the Jordan. Num. 32:33

5 "But [R]take careful heed to do the commandment and the law which Moses the servant of the LORD commanded you, to love the LORD your God, to walk in all His ways, to keep His commandments, to hold fast to Him,

21:37 So with LXX, Vg. (cf. 1 Chr. 6:78, 79); MT, Bg., Tg. omit vv. 36, 37

and to serve Him with all your heart and with all your soul." Deut. 6:6, 17; 11:22

6 So Joshua blessed them and sent them away, and they went to their tents.

7 Now to half the tribe of Manasseh Moses had given a possession in Bashan, [R]but to the *other* half of it Joshua gave *a possession* among their brethren on this side of the Jordan, westward. And indeed, when Joshua sent them away to their tents, he blessed them, Josh. 17:1–13

8 and spoke to them, saying, "Return with much riches to your tents, with very much livestock, with silver, with gold, with bronze, with iron, and with very much clothing. [R]Divide the [T]spoil of your enemies with your brethren." 1 Sam. 30:24 • *plunder*

9 So the children of Reuben, the children of Gad, and half the tribe of Manasseh returned, and departed from the children of Israel at Shiloh, which *is* in the land of Canaan, to go to [R]the country of Gilead, to the land of their possession, which they had obtained according to the word of the LORD by the hand of Moses. Num. 32:1, 26, 29

Construction of the Altar

10 And when they came to the region of the Jordan which *is* in the land of Canaan, the children of Reuben, the children of Gad, and half the tribe of Manasseh built an altar there by the Jordan—a great, impressive altar.

Misunderstanding of the Altar

11 Now the children of Israel heard *someone* say, "Behold, the children of Reuben, the children of Gad, and half the tribe of Manasseh have built an altar on the frontier of the land of Canaan, in the region of the Jordan—on the children of Israel's side."

12 And when the children of Israel heard *of it*, [R]the whole congregation of the children of Israel gathered together at Shiloh to go to war against them. Josh. 18:1

13 Then the children of Israel [R]sent [R]Phinehas the son of Eleazar the priest to the children of Reuben, to the children of Gad, and to half the tribe of Manasseh, into the land of Gilead, Deut. 13:14 • Ex. 6:25

14 and with him ten rulers, one ruler each from the chief house of every tribe of Israel; and each one *was* the head of the house of his father among the divisions* of Israel.

15 Then they came to the children of Reuben, to the children of Gad, and to half the tribe of Manasseh, to the land of Gilead, and they spoke with them, saying,

16 "Thus says the whole congregation of the LORD: 'What [R]treachery *is* this that you have committed against the God of Israel, to turn away this day from following the LORD, in that you have built for yourselves an altar, [R]that you might rebel this day against the LORD? Deut. 12:5–14 • Lev. 17:8, 9

17 '*Is* the iniquity [R]of Peor not enough for us, from which we are not cleansed till this day, although there was a plague in the congregation of the LORD, Num. 25:1–9

18 'but that you must turn away this day from following the LORD? And it shall be, if you rebel today against the LORD, that tomorrow [R]He will be angry with the whole congregation of Israel. Num. 16:22

19 [T]'Nevertheless, if the land of your possession *is* unclean, *then* cross over to the land of the possession of the LORD, [R]where the LORD's tabernacle stands, and take possession among us; but do not rebel against the LORD, nor rebel against us, by building yourselves an altar besides the altar of the LORD our God. *However* • Josh. 18:1

20 [R]'Did not Achan the son of Zerah [T]commit a trespass in the accursed thing, and wrath fell on all the congregation of Israel? And that man did not perish alone in his iniquity.' " Josh. 7:1–26 • *act unfaithfully*

Explanation of the Altar

21 Then the children of Reuben, the children of Gad, and half the tribe of Manasseh answered and said to the heads of the divisions* of Israel:

22 "The LORD God of gods, the LORD God of gods, He knows, and let Israel itself know—if *it is* in rebellion, or if in treachery against the LORD, do not save us this day.

23 "If we have built ourselves an altar to turn from following the LORD, or if to offer on it burnt offerings or grain offerings, or if to offer peace offerings on it, let the LORD Himself [R]require *an account*. 1 Sam. 20:16

24 "But in fact we have done it [T]for fear, for a reason, saying, 'In time to come your descendants may speak to our descendants, saying, "What have you to do with the LORD God of Israel? Lit. *from fear*

25 "For the LORD has made the Jordan a border between you and us, *you* children of Reuben and children of Gad. You have no part in the LORD." So your descendants would make our descendants cease fearing the LORD.'

26 "Therefore we said, 'Let us now prepare to build ourselves an altar, not for burnt offering nor for sacrifice,

27 'but *that* it *may be* [R]a witness between you and us and our generations after us, that we may [R]perform the service of the LORD before Him with our burnt offerings, with our sacrifices, and with our peace offerings; that your descendants may not say to our descendants in time to come, "You have no part in the LORD." ' Gen. 31:48 • Deut. 12:5, 14

28 "Therefore we said that it will be, when

22:14 Lit. *thousands* **22:21** Lit. *thousands*

they say *this* to us or to our generations in
time to come, that we may say, 'Here is the
replica of the altar of the LORD which our fa-
thers made, though not for burnt offerings
nor for sacrifices; but it *is* a witness between
you and us.'
29 "Far be it from us that we should rebel
against the LORD, and turn from following the
LORD this day, to build an altar for burnt of-
ferings, for grain offerings, or for sacrifices,
besides the altar of the LORD our God which *is*
before His tabernacle."

Celebration by the Western Tribes

30 Now when Phinehas the priest and the
rulers of the congregation, the heads of the di-
visions* of Israel who *were* with him, heard
the words that the children of Reuben, the
children of Gad, and the children of Ma-
nasseh spoke, it pleased them.
31 Then Phinehas the son of Eleazar the
priest said to the children of Reuben, the chil-
dren of Gad, and the children of Manasseh,
"This day we perceive that the LORD *is*
[R]among us, because you have not committed
this treachery against the LORD. Now you
have delivered the children of Israel out of the
hand of the LORD." Lev. 26:11, 12
32 And Phinehas the son of Eleazar the
priest, and the rulers, returned from the chil-
dren of Reuben and the children of Gad, from
the land of Gilead to the land of Canaan, to
the children of Israel, and brought back word
to them.
33 So the thing pleased the children of Is-
rael, and the children of Israel [R]blessed God;
they spoke no more of going against them in
battle, to destroy the land where the children
of Reuben and Gad dwelt. 1 Chr. 29:20
34 The children of Reuben and the chil-
dren of Gad* called the altar, *Witness*, "For
it is a witness between us that the LORD *is*
God."

CHAPTER 23

A Reminder from History

NOW it came to pass, a long time after the
LORD [R]had given rest to Israel from all
their enemies round about, that Joshua was
old, advanced in age. Josh. 21:44; 22:4
2 And Joshua [R]called for all Israel, for their
elders, for their heads, for their judges, and
for their officers, and said to them: "I am old,
advanced in age. Deut. 31:28
3 "You have seen all that the [R]LORD your
God has done to all these nations because of
you, for the [R]LORD your God *is* He who has
fought for you. Ps. 44:3 • Deut. 1:30
4 "See, [R]I have divided to you by lot these
nations that remain, to be an inheritance for
your tribes, from the Jordan, with all the na-
tions that I have cut off, as far as the Great
Sea westward. Josh. 13:2, 6; 18:10
5 "And the LORD your God [R]will expel them
from before you and drive them out of your
sight. So you shall possess their land, as the
LORD your God promised you. Ex. 23:30
6 [R]"Therefore be very courageous to keep
and to do all that is written in the Book of the
Law of Moses, lest you turn aside from it to
the right hand or to the left, Josh. 1:7
7 "*and* lest you go among these nations,
these who remain among you. You shall not
make mention of the name of their gods, nor
cause *anyone* to swear *by them;* you shall not
serve them nor bow down to them,
8 "but you shall hold fast to the LORD your
God, as you have done to this day.
9 [R]"For the LORD has [T]driven out from be-
fore you great and strong nations; but *as for*
you, no one has been able to stand against
you to this day. Deut. 7:24; 11:23 • *dispossessed*
10 "One man of you shall chase a thousand,
for the LORD your God *is* He who fights for
you, [R]as He promised you. Ex. 14:14
11 "Therefore take careful heed to your-
selves, that you love the LORD your God.
12 "Or else, if indeed you do [R]go back, and
cling to the remnant of these nations—these
that remain among you—and [R]make mar-
riages with them, and go in to them and they
to you, [2 Pet. 2:20, 21] • Deut. 7:3, 4
13 "know for certain that [R]the LORD your
God will no longer drive out these nations
from before you. [R]But they shall be snares and
traps to you, and scourges on your sides and
thorns in your eyes, until you perish from this
good land which the LORD your God has given
you. Judg. 2:3 • Ex. 23:33; 34:12
14 "Behold, this day [R]I *am* going the way of
all the earth. And you know in all your hearts
and in all your souls that [R]not one thing has
failed of all the good things which the LORD
your God spoke concerning you. All have
come to pass for you; not one word of them
has failed. 1 Kin. 2:2 • Josh. 21:45
15 [R]"Therefore it shall come to pass, that as
all the good things have come upon you
which the LORD your God promised you, so
the LORD will bring upon you [R]all harmful
things, until He has destroyed you from this
good land which the LORD your God has given
you. Deut. 28:63 • Deut. 28:15–68
16 "When you have transgressed the
covenant of the LORD your God, which He
commanded you, and have gone and served
other gods, and bowed down to them, then the
[R]anger of the LORD will burn against you, and
you shall perish quickly from the good land
which He has given you." Deut. 4:24–28

22:30 Lit. *thousands* **22:34** LXX adds *and half the tribe of Manasseh.*

CHAPTER 24

Renewal of the Covenant

THEN Joshua gathered all the tribes of Israel to [R]Shechem and called for the elders of Israel, for their heads, for their judges, and for their officers; and they presented themselves before God. Gen. 35:4

2 And Joshua said to all the people, "Thus says the LORD God of Israel: [R]'Your fathers, *including* Terah, the father of Abraham and the father of Nahor, dwelt on the other side of the River* in old times; and [R]they served other gods. Gen. 11:7–32 • Josh. 24:14

3 'Then I took your father Abraham from the other side of the River, led him throughout all the land of Canaan, and multiplied his descendants and gave him Isaac.

4 'To Isaac I gave [R]Jacob and Esau. To [R]Esau I gave the mountains of Seir to possess, [R]but Jacob and his children went down to Egypt. Gen. 25:24–26 • Deut. 2:5 • Gen. 46:1, 3, 6

5 'Also I sent Moses and Aaron, and I plagued Egypt, according to what I did among them. Afterward I brought you out.

6 'Then I brought your fathers out of Egypt, and you came to the sea; and the Egyptians pursued your fathers with chariots and horsemen to the Red Sea.

7 'So they cried out to the LORD; and He put [R]darkness between you and the Egyptians, brought the sea upon them, and covered them. And [R]your eyes saw what I did in Egypt. Then you dwelt in the wilderness [R]a long time. Ex. 14:20 • Deut. 4:34 • Josh. 5:6

8 'And I brought you into the land of the Amorites, who dwelt on the other side of the Jordan, [R]and they fought with you. But I gave them into your hand, that you might possess their land, and I destroyed them from before you. Num. 21:21–35

9 'Then [R]Balak the son of Zippor, king of Moab, arose to make war against Israel, and [R]sent and called Balaam the son of Beor to curse you. Judg. 11:25 • Num. 22:2–14

10 [R]'But I would not listen to Balaam; therefore he continued to bless you. So I delivered you out of his hand. Deut. 23:5

11 'Then you went over the Jordan and came to Jericho. And the men of Jericho fought against you—*also* the Amorites, the Perizzites, the Canaanites, the Hittites, the Girgashites, the Hivites, and the Jebusites. But I delivered them into your hand.

12 [R]'I sent the hornet before you which drove them out from before you, *also* the two kings of the Amorites, *but* [R]not with your sword or with your bow. Ex. 23:28 • Ps. 44:3

13 'I have given you a land for which you did not labor, and [R]cities which you did not build, and you dwell in them; you eat of the vineyards and olive groves which you did not plant.' Deut. 6:10, 11

14 [R]"Now therefore, fear the LORD, serve Him in [R]sincerity and in truth, and put away the gods which your fathers served on the other side of the River and in Egypt. Serve the LORD! 1 Sam. 12:24 • 2 Cor. 1:12

15 "And if it seems evil to you to serve the LORD, choose for yourselves this day whom you will serve, whether the gods which your fathers served that *were* on the other side of the River, or the gods of the Amorites, in whose land you dwell. But as for me and my house, we will serve the LORD."

16 So the people answered and said: "Far be it from us that we should forsake the LORD to serve other gods;

17 "for the LORD our God *is* He who brought us and our fathers up out of the land of Egypt, from the house of bondage, who did those great signs in our sight, and preserved us in all the way that we went and among all the people through whom we passed.

18 "And the LORD drove out from before us all the people, including the Amorites who dwelt in the land. [R]We also will serve the LORD, for He *is* our God." Ps. 116:16

19 But Joshua said to the people, "You cannot serve the LORD, for He *is* a holy God. He *is* a jealous God; He will not forgive your transgressions nor your sins.

20 [R]"If you forsake the LORD and serve foreign gods, [R]then He will turn and do you harm and consume you, after He has done you good." Ezra 8:22 • Deut. 4:24–26

21 And the people said to Joshua, "No, but we will serve the LORD!"

22 So Joshua said to the people, "You *are* witnesses against yourselves that you have chosen the LORD for yourselves, to serve Him." And they said, "*We are* witnesses!"

23 "Now therefore," *he said,* "put away the foreign gods which *are* among you, and incline your heart to the LORD God of Israel."

24 And the people [R]said to Joshua, "The LORD our God we will serve, and His voice we will obey!" Deut. 5:24–27

25 So Joshua made a covenant with the people that day, and made for them a statute and an ordinance in Shechem.

26 Then Joshua wrote these words in the Book of the Law of God. And he took a large stone, and set it up there under the oak that *was* by the sanctuary of the LORD.

27 And Joshua said to all the people, "Behold, this stone shall be a witness to us, for it has heard all the words of the LORD which He spoke to us. It shall therefore be a witness to you, lest you deny your God."

28 So [R]Joshua let the people depart, each to his own inheritance. Judg. 2:6, 7

24:2 The Euphrates

Joshua and Eleazar Die

29 [R]Now it came to pass after these things
that Joshua the son of Nun, the servant of the
LORD, died, *being* one hundred and ten years
old. Judg. 2:8
30 And they buried him within the border of
his inheritance at [R]Timnath Serah, which *is* in
the mountains of Ephraim, on the north side
of Mount Gaash. Josh. 19:50
31 [R]Israel served the LORD all the days of
Joshua, and all the days of the elders who
outlived Joshua, who had [R]known all the
works of the LORD which He had done for Is-
rael. Judg. 2:7 • Deut. 11:2
32 [R]The bones of Joseph, which the children of
Israel had brought up out of Egypt, they buried
at Shechem, in the plot of ground [R]which Jacob
had bought from the sons of Hamor the father of
Shechem for one hundred pieces of silver, and
which had become an inheritance of the chil-
dren of Joseph. Gen. 50:25 • Gen. 33:19
33 And [R]Eleazar the son of Aaron died. They
buried him in a hill *belonging to* Phinehas his
son, which was given to him in the mountains
of Ephraim. Ex. 28:1

Jewish Feasts

Feast of	*Month on Jewish Calendar*	*Day*	*Corresponding Month*	*References*
*Passover (Unleavened Bread)	Nisan	14–21	Mar.–Apr.	Ex. 12:43–13:10; Matt. 26:17–20
*Pentecost (Firstfruits or Weeks)	Sivan	6 (50 days after Passover)	May–June	Deut. 16:9–12; Acts 2:1
Trumpets, *Rosh Hashanah*	Tishri	1, 2	Sept.–Oct.	Num. 29:1–6
Day of Atonement, *Yom Kippur*	Tishri	10	Sept.–Oct.	Lev. 23:26–32; Heb. 9:7
*Tabernacles (Booths or Ingathering)	Tishri	15–22	Sept.–Oct.	Neh. 8:13–18; John 7:2
Dedication (Lights), *Hanukkah*	Chislev	25 (8 days)	Nov.–Dec.	John 10:22
Purim (Lots)	Adar	14, 15	Feb.–Mar.	Esth. 9:18–32

*The three major feasts for which all males of Israel were required to travel to the Temple in Jerusalem (Ex. 23:14–19).

THE BOOK OF

JUDGES

THE BOOK OF JUDGES

The Book of Judges stands in stark contrast to Joshua. In Joshua an obedient people conquered the land through trust in the power of God. In Judges, however, a disobedient and idolatrous people are defeated time and time again because of their rebellion against God.

In seven distinct cycles of sin to salvation, Judges shows how Israel had set aside God's law and in its place substituted *"what was* right in his own eyes" (21:25). The recurring result of abandonment from God's law is corruption from within and oppression from without. During the nearly four centuries spanned by this book, God raises up military champions to throw off the yoke of bondage and to restore the nation to pure worship. But all too soon the "sin cycle" begins again as the nation's spiritual temperature grows steadily colder.

The Hebrew title is *Shophetim,* meaning "judges," "rulers," "deliverers," or "saviors." *Shophet* not only carries the idea of maintaining justice and settling disputes, but it is also used to mean "liberating" and "delivering." First the judges deliver the people; then they rule and administer justice. The Septuagint used the Greek equivalent of this word, *Kritai* ("Judges"). The Latin Vulgate called it *Liber Judicum,* the "Book of Judges." This book could also appropriately be titled "The Book of Failure."

THE AUTHOR OF JUDGES

The author of Judges is anonymous, but Samuel or one of his prophetic students may have written it. Jewish tradition contained in the Talmud attributes Judges to Samuel, and certainly he was the crucial link between the period of the judges and the period of the kings.

It is clear from 18:31 and 20:27 that the book was written after the ark was removed from Shiloh (1 Sam. 4:3–11). The repeated phrase "In those days *there was* no king in Israel" (17:6; 18:1; 19:1; 21:25) shows that Judges was also written after the commencement of Saul's reign but before the divided kingdom. The fact that the Jebusites were dwelling in Jerusalem "to this day" (1:21) means that it was written before 1004 B.C. when David dispossessed the Jebusites (2 Sam. 5:5–9). Thus, the book was written during the time of Samuel; and it is likely that Samuel compiled this book from oral and written source material. His prophetic ministry clearly fits the moral commentary of Judges, and the consistent style and orderly scheme of Judges point to a single compiler.

Judges 18:30 contains a phrase that poses a problem to this early date of composition: "until the day of the captivity of the land." If this refers to the 722 B.C. Assyrian captivity of Israel it could have been inserted by a later editor. It is more likely a reference to the Philistine captivity of the land during the time of the judges. This event is described as "captivity" in Psalm 78:61.

THE TIME OF JUDGES

If Judges was not written by Samuel, it was at least written by one of his contemporaries between 1043 B.C. (the beginning of Saul's reign) and 1004 B.C. (David's capture of Jerusalem).

Joshua's seven-year conquest is general in nature; much of the land remains to be possessed (Josh. 13:1). There are still important Canaanite strongholds to be taken by the individual tribes. Some of the nations have been left to "test Israel" (Judg. 3:1, 4). During this time, the Egyptians maintain strong control along the coastal routes, but they are not interested in the hill country where Israel is primarily established.

The events covered in Judges range from about 1380 B.C. to 1045 B.C. (c. 335 years), but the period of the judges extends another thirty years since it includes the life of Samuel (1 Sam. 1:1—25:1). Evidently, the rulerships of some of the judges overlap because not all of them ruled over the entire land. Judges describes the cycles of apostasy, oppression, and deliverance in the southern region (3:7–31), the northern region (4:1—5:31), the central region (6:1—10:5), the eastern region (10:6—12:15), and the western region (13:1—16:31). The spread of apostasy covers the whole land.

THE CHRIST OF JUDGES

Each judge is a savior and a ruler, a spiritual and political deliverer. Thus, the judges portray the role of Christ as the Savior-King of His people. The Book of Judges also illustrates the need for a righteous king.

Including 1 Samuel, seventeen judges are mentioned altogether. Some are warrior-rulers (for example, Othniel and Gideon), one is a priest (Eli), and two are prophets (Samuel and Deborah). This gives a cumulative picture of the three offices of Christ, who excelled all His predecessors in that He was the ultimate Prophet, Priest, and King.

KEYS TO JUDGES

Key Word: Cycles—The Book of Judges is written more on a thematic than a chronological basis (chs. 16—21 actually precede chs. 3—15). The author uses the accounts of the various judges to prove the utter failure of living out the closing verse of Judges: "Everyone did *what was* right in his own eyes." To accomplish this, the author uses a five-point cycle to recount the repeated spiral of disobedience, destruction, and defeat. The five parts are: (1) sin, (2) servitude, (3) supplication, (4) salvation, and (5) silence.

Key Verses: Judges 2:20, 21; 21:25—"Then the anger of the LORD was hot against Israel; and He said, 'Because this nation has transgressed My covenant which I commanded their fathers, and has not heeded My voice, I also will no longer drive out before them any of the nations which Joshua left when he died' " (2:20, 21).

"In those days *there was* no king in Israel; everyone did *what was* right in his own eyes" (21:25).

Key Chapter: Judges 2—The second chapter of Judges is a miniature of the whole book as it records the transition of the godly to the ungodly generation, the format of the cycles, and the purpose of God in not destroying the Canaanites.

SURVEY OF JUDGES

Following the death of Joshua, Israel plunges into a 350-year Dark Age. After Joshua and the generation of the conquest pass on, "another generation arose after them who did not know the LORD nor the work which He had done for Israel" (2:10; see also 2:7–10; Josh. 24:31). Judges opens with a description of Israel's deterioration, continues with seven cycles of oppression and deliverance, and concludes with two illustrations of Israel's depravity.

Deterioration (1:1—3:4): Judges begins with short-lived military successes after Joshua's death, but quickly turns to the repeated failure of all the tribes to drive out their enemies. The people feel the lack of a unified central leader, but the primary reasons for their failure are a lack of faith in God and a lack of obedience to Him (2:1–3). Compromise leads to conflict and chaos. Israel does not drive out the inhabitants (1:21, 27, 29, 30); instead of removing the moral cancer spread by the inhabitants of Canaan, they contract the disease. The Canaanite gods literally become a snare to them (2:3). Judges 2:11–23 is a microcosm of the pattern found in Judges 3—16.

Deliverances (3:5—16:31): This section describes seven apostasies (fallings away from God), seven servitudes, and seven deliverances. Each of the seven cycles has five steps: sin, servitude, supplication, salvation, and silence. These also can be described by the words *rebellion, retribution, repentance, restoration,* and *rest.* The seven cycles connect together as a descending spiral of sin (2:19). Israel vacillates between obedience and apostasy as the people continually fail to learn from their mistakes. Apostasy grows, but the rebellion is not continual. The times of rest and peace are longer than the times of bondage. The monotony of Israel's sins can be contrasted with the creativity of God's methods of deliverance.

The judges are military and civil leaders during this period of loose confederacy. Thirteen are mentioned in this book, and four more are found in 1 Samuel (Eli, Samuel, Joel, and Abijah).

Depravity (17:1—21:25): These chapters illustrate (1) religious apostasy (17 and 18) and (2) social and moral depravity (19—21) during the period of the judges. Chapters 19—21 contain one of the worst tales of degradation in the Bible. Judges closes with a key to understanding the period: "everyone did *what was* right in his own eyes" (21:25). The people are not doing what is wrong in their own eyes, but what is "evil in the sight of the LORD" (2:11).

FOCUS	DETERIORATION		DELIVERANCE						DEPRAVITY		
REFERENCE	1:1——2:1——3:5——4:1——6:1——10:6——12:8——13:1——17:1——19:1——20:1-21:25										
DIVISION	ISRAEL FAILS TO COMPLETE THE CONQUEST	GOD JUDGES ISRAEL	SOUTHERN CAMPAIGN	NORTHERN CAMPAIGN (1st)	CENTRAL CAMPAIGN	EASTERN CAMPAIGN	NORTHERN CAMPAIGN (2nd)	WESTERN CAMPAIGN	SIN OF IDOLATRY	SIN OF IMMORALITY	SIN OF CIVIL WAR
TOPIC	CAUSES OF THE CYCLES		CURSE OF THE CYCLES						CONDITION DURING THE CYCLES		
	LIVING WITH THE CANAANITES		WAR WITH THE CANAANITES						LIVING LIKE THE CANAANITES		
LOCATION	CANAAN										
TIME	c. 350 YEARS										

OUTLINE OF JUDGES

Part One: The Deterioration of Israel and Failure to Complete the Conquest of Canaan (1:1—3:4)

Part Two: The Deliverance of Israel During the Seven Cycles (3:5—16:31)

Part Three: The Depravity of Israel in Sinning Like the Canaanites (17:1—21:25)

CHAPTER 1

Failure of Judah

NOW after the [R]death of Joshua it came to pass that the children of Israel [R]asked the LORD, saying, "Who shall be first to go up for us against the Canaanites to fight against them?" Josh. 24:29 • Num. 27:21

2 And the LORD said, [R]"Judah shall go up. Indeed I have delivered the land into his hand." Gen. 49:8, 9

3 So Judah said to Simeon his brother, "Come up with me to my allotted territory, that we may fight against the Canaanites; and I will likewise go with you to your allotted territory." And Simeon went with him.

4 Then Judah went up, and the LORD delivered the Canaanites and the Perizzites into their hand; and they killed ten thousand men at [R]Bezek. 1 Sam. 11:8

5 And they found Adoni-Bezek in Bezek, and fought against him; and they defeated the Canaanites and the Perizzites.

6 Then Adoni-Bezek fled, and they pursued him and caught him and cut off his thumbs and big toes.

7 And Adoni-Bezek said, "Seventy kings with their thumbs and big toes cut off used to gather *scraps* under my table; [R]as I have done, so God has repaid me." Then they brought him to Jerusalem, and there he died. Lev. 24:19

8 Now [R]the children of Judah fought against Jerusalem and took it; they struck it with the edge of the sword and set the city on fire. Josh. 15:63

9 [R]And afterward the children of Judah went down to fight against the Canaanites who dwelt in the mountains, in the South,* and in the lowland. Josh. 10:36; 11:21; 15:13

10 Then Judah went against the Canaanites who dwelt in Hebron. (Now the name of Hebron *was* formerly Kirjath Arba.) And they killed Sheshai, Ahiman, and Talmai.

11 [R]From there they went against the inhabitants of Debir. (The name of Debir *was* formerly Kirjath Sepher.) Josh. 15:15

12 Then Caleb said, "Whoever attacks Kirjath Sepher and takes it, to him I will give my daughter Achsah as wife."

13 And Othniel the son of Kenaz, [R]Caleb's younger brother, took it; so he gave him his daughter Achsah as wife. Judg. 3:9

14 [R]Now it happened, when she came *to him,* that she urged him* to ask her father for a field. And she dismounted from *her* donkey, and Caleb said to her, "What do you wish?" Josh. 15:18, 19

15 So she said to him, [R]"Give me a blessing; since you have given me land in the South, give me also springs of water." And Caleb gave her the upper springs and the lower springs. Gen. 33:11

16 [R]Now the children of the Kenite, Moses' father-in-law, went up [R]from the City of Palms with the children of Judah into the Wilderness of Judah, which *lies* in the South *near* Arad; and they went and dwelt among the people. Num. 10:29–32 • Deut. 34:3

17 [R]And Judah went with his brother Simeon, and they attacked the Canaanites who inhabited Zephath, and utterly destroyed it. So the name of the city was called [R]Hormah. Judg. 1:3 • Num. 21:3

18 Also Judah took [R]Gaza with its territory, Ashkelon with its territory, and Ekron with its territory. Josh. 11:22

19 So the LORD was with Judah. And they drove out the mountaineers, but they could not drive out the inhabitants of the lowland, because they had chariots of iron.

20 [R]And they gave Hebron to Caleb, as Moses had said. Then he expelled from there the three sons of Anak. Josh. 14:9, 14

Failure of Benjamin

21 But the children of Benjamin did not drive out the Jebusites who inhabited Jerusalem; so the Jebusites dwell with the children of Benjamin in Jerusalem to this day.

Failure of Tribes of Joseph

22 And the [T]house of Joseph also went up against Bethel, [R]and the LORD *was* with them. *family* • Judg. 1:19

23 So the [T]house of Joseph [R]sent men to spy out Bethel. (The name of the city *was* formerly [R]Luz.) *family* • Josh. 2:1; 7:2 • Gen. 28:19

24 And when the spies saw a man coming out of the city, they said to him, "Please show us the entrance to the city, and [R]we will show you mercy." Josh. 2:12, 14

25 So he showed them the entrance to the city, and they struck the city with the edge of the sword; but they let the man and all his family go.

26 And the man went to the land of the Hittites, built a city, and called its name Luz, which *is* its name to this day.

27 [R]However, Manasseh did not drive out *the inhabitants of* Beth Shean and its villages, or [R]Taanach and its villages, or the inhabitants of Dor and its villages, or the inhabitants of Ibleam and its villages, or the inhabitants of Megiddo and its villages; for the Canaanites were determined to dwell in that land. Josh. 17:11–13 • Josh. 21:25

28 And it came to pass, when Israel was strong, that they put the Canaanites [T]under tribute, but did not completely drive them out. *to forced labor*

29 [R]Nor did Ephraim drive out the Canaanites who dwelt in Gezer; so the Canaanites dwelt in Gezer among them. Josh. 16:10

Failure of Zebulun

30 Nor did [R]Zebulun drive out the inhabitants of Kitron or the inhabitants of Nahalol; so the Canaanites dwelt among them, and were put under tribute. Josh. 19:10–16

Failure of Asher

31 Nor did Asher drive out the inhabitants of Acco or the inhabitants of Sidon, or of Ahlab, Achzib, Helbah, Aphik, or Rehob.

32 So the Asherites [R]dwelt among the Canaanites, the inhabitants of the land; for they did not drive them out. Ps. 106:34, 35

1:9 Heb. *Negev,* and so throughout the book
1:14 LXX, Vg. *he urged her*

Failure of Naphtali

33 [R]Nor did Naphtali drive out the inhabitants of Beth Shemesh or the inhabitants of Beth Anath; but they dwelt among the Canaanites, the inhabitants of the land. Nevertheless the inhabitants of Beth Shemesh and Beth Anath were put under tribute to them. Josh. 19:32–39

Failure of Dan

34 And the Amorites forced the children of Dan into the mountains, for they would not allow them to come down to the valley;

35 and the Amorites were determined to dwell in Mount Heres, [R]in Aijalon, and in Shaalbim;* yet when the strength of the house of Joseph became greater, they were put under tribute. Josh. 19:42

36 Now the boundary of the Amorites *was* [R]from the Ascent of Akrabbim, from Sela, and upward. Josh. 15:3

CHAPTER 2

Angel Announces Judgment

THEN the Angel of the LORD came up from Gilgal to Bochim, and said: "I led you up from Egypt and brought you to the land of which I swore to your fathers; and I said, 'I will never break My covenant with you.

2 'And you shall make no [T]covenant with the inhabitants of this land; you shall tear down their altars.' But you have not obeyed My voice. Why have you done this? *treaty*

3 "Therefore I also said, 'I will not drive them out before you; but they shall be *thorns* in your side,* and [R]their gods shall be a [R]snare to you.'" Judg. 3:6 • Ps. 106:36

4 So it was, when the Angel of the LORD spoke these words to all the children of Israel, that the people lifted up their voices and wept.

5 Then they called the name of that place Bochim;* and they sacrificed there to the LORD.

Godly Generation Dies

6 And when Joshua had dismissed the people, the children of Israel went each to his own inheritance to possess the land.

7 [R]So the people served the LORD all the days of Joshua, and all the days of the elders who outlived Joshua, who had seen all the great works of the LORD which He had done for Israel. Josh. 24:31

8 Now [R]Joshua the son of Nun, the servant of the LORD, died *when he was* one hundred and ten years old. Josh. 24:29

9 [R]And they buried him within the border of his inheritance at [R]Timnath Heres, in the mountains of Ephraim, on the north side of Mount Gaash. Josh. 24:30 • Josh. 19:49, 50

10 When all that generation had been gathered to their fathers, another generation arose after them who did not know the LORD nor the work which He had done for Israel.

Judgment of God Is Described

11 Then the children of Israel did evil in the sight of the LORD, and served the Baals;

12 and they forsook the LORD God of their fathers, who had brought them out of the land of Egypt; and they followed other gods from *among* the gods of the people who *were* all around them, and they bowed down to them; and they provoked the LORD to anger.

13 They forsook the LORD [R]and served Baal and the Ashtoreths.* Judg. 10:6

14 And the anger of the LORD was hot against Israel. So He delivered them into the hands of plunderers who despoiled them; and He sold them into the hands of their enemies all around, so that they could no longer stand before their enemies.

15 Wherever they went out, the hand of the LORD was against them for calamity, as the LORD had said, and as the LORD had sworn to them. And they were greatly distressed.

16 Nevertheless, [R]the LORD raised up judges who delivered them out of the hand of those who plundered them. Ps. 106:43–45

17 Yet they would not listen to their judges, but they [R]played the harlot with other gods, and bowed down to them. They turned quickly from the way in which their fathers walked, in obeying the commandments of the LORD; they did not do so. Ex. 34:15

18 And when the LORD raised up judges for them, [R]the LORD was with the judge and delivered them out of the hand of their enemies all the days of the judge; [R]for the LORD was moved to pity by their groaning because of those who oppressed them and harassed them. Josh. 1:5 • Gen. 6:6

19 And it came to pass, when the judge was dead, that they reverted and behaved more corruptly than their fathers, by following other gods, to serve them and bow down to them. They did not cease from their own doings nor from their stubborn way.

Enemy Is Left as a Test

20 Then the anger of the LORD was hot against Israel; and He said, "Because this nation has [R]transgressed My covenant which I commanded their fathers, and has not heeded My voice, [Josh. 23:16]

21 "I also will no longer drive out before them any of the nations which Joshua [R]left when he died, Josh. 23:4, 5, 13

22 "so [R]that through them I may [R]test Israel, whether they will keep the ways of the LORD,

1:35 *Shaalabbin,* Josh. 19:42 **2:3** LXX, Tg., Vg. *enemies to you* **2:5** Lit. *Weeping* **2:13** Canaanite goddesses

to walk in them as their fathers kept *them*, or
not." Judg. 3:1, 4 • Deut. 8:2, 16; 13:3
23 Therefore the LORD left those nations,
without driving them out immediately; nor
did He deliver them into the hand of Joshua.

CHAPTER 3

NOW these *are* [R]the nations which the
LORD left, that He might test Israel by
them, *that is*, all who had not known any of
the wars in Canaan Judg. 1:1; 2:21, 22
2 (*this was* only so that the generations of
the children of Israel might be taught to know
war, at least those who had not formerly
known it),
3 *namely*, [R]five lords of the Philistines, all
the Canaanites, the Sidonians, and the
Hivites who dwelt in Mount Lebanon, from
Mount Baal Hermon to the entrance of
Hamath. Josh. 13:3
4 And they were *left, that He might* test Is-
rael by them, to [T]know whether they would
obey the commandments of the LORD, which
He had commanded their fathers by the hand
of Moses. *find out*

The Judge Othniel

5 Thus the children of Israel dwelt among
the Canaanites, the Hittites, the Amorites, the
Perizzites, the Hivites, and the Jebusites.
6 And they took their daughters to be their
wives, and gave their daughters to their sons;
and they served their gods.
7 So the children of Israel did evil in the
sight of the LORD. They forgot the LORD their
God, and served the Baals and Asherahs.*
8 Therefore the anger of the LORD was hot
against Israel, and He sold them into the hand
of [R]Cushan-Rishathaim king of Mesopotamia;
and the children of Israel served Cushan-
Rishathaim eight years. Hab. 3:7
9 When the children of Israel [R]cried out to
the LORD, the LORD [R]raised up a deliverer for
the children of Israel, who delivered them:
[R]Othniel the son of Kenaz, Caleb's younger
brother. Judg. 3:15 • Judg. 2:16 • Judg. 1:13
10 The Spirit of the LORD came upon him,
and he judged Israel. He went out to war, and
the LORD delivered Cushan-Rishathaim king
of Mesopotamia into his hand; and his hand
prevailed over Cushan-Rishathaim.
11 So the land had rest for forty years. Then
Othniel the son of Kenaz died.

The Judge Ehud

12 [R]And the children of Israel again did evil
in the sight of the LORD. So the LORD strength-
ened [R]Eglon king of Moab against Israel, be-
cause they had done evil in the sight of the
LORD. Judg. 2:19 • 1 Sam. 12:9
13 Then he gathered to himself the people of
Ammon and [R]Amalek, went and [T]defeated Is-
rael, and took possession of [R]the City of
Palms. Judg. 5:14 • *struck* • Judg. 1:16
14 So the children of Israel [R]served Eglon
king of Moab eighteen years. Deut. 28:48
15 But when the children of Israel [R]cried out
to the LORD, the LORD raised up a deliverer
for them: Ehud the son of Gera, the Ben-
jamite, a [R]left-handed man. By him the chil-
dren of Israel sent tribute to Eglon king of
Moab. Ps. 78:34 • Judg. 20:16
16 Now Ehud made himself a dagger (it was
double-edged and a cubit in length) and fas-
tened it under his clothes on his right thigh.
17 So he brought the tribute to Eglon king of
Moab. (Now Eglon *was* a very fat man.)
18 And when he had finished presenting the
tribute, he sent away the people who had car-
ried the tribute.
19 But he himself turned back [R]from the
stone images that *were* at Gilgal, and said, "I
have a secret message for you, O king." He
said, "Keep silence!" And all who attended
him went out from him. Josh. 4:20
20 So Ehud came to him (now he was sitting
upstairs in his cool private chamber). Then
Ehud said, "I have a message from God for
you." So he arose from *his* seat.
21 Then Ehud reached with his left hand,
took the dagger from his right thigh, and
thrust it into his belly.
22 Even the [T]hilt went in after the blade, and
the fat closed over the blade, for he did not
draw the dagger out of his belly; and his en-
trails came out. *handle*
23 Then Ehud went out through the porch
and shut the doors of the upper room behind
him and locked them.
24 When he had gone out, *Eglon's** servants
came to look, and *to their* surprise, the doors
of the upper room were locked. So they said,
"He is probably [R]attending to his needs in the
cool chamber." 1 Sam. 24:3
25 So they waited till they were embar-
rassed, and still he had not opened the doors
of the upper room. Therefore they took the
key and opened *them*. And there was their
master, fallen dead on the floor.
26 But Ehud had escaped while they de-
layed, and passed beyond the [T]stone images
and escaped to Seirah. Tg. *quarries*
27 And it happened, when he arrived, that
[R]he blew the trumpet in the [R]mountains of
Ephraim, and the children of Israel went
down with him from the mountains; and he
led them. 1 Sam. 13:3 • Josh. 17:15
28 Then he said to them, "Follow *me*, for [R]the
LORD has delivered your enemies the Mo-
abites into your hand." So they went down
after him, seized the [R]fords of the Jordan

3:7 Name or symbol for Canaanite goddesses
3:24 Lit. *his*

leading to Moab, and did not allow anyone to
cross over. Judg. 7:9, 15 • Josh. 2:7
29 And at that time they killed about ten
thousand men of Moab, all stout men of valor;
not a man escaped.
30 So Moab was subdued that day under the
hand of Israel. And [R]the land had rest for
eighty years. Judg. 3:11

The Judge Shamgar

31 After him was Shamgar the son of Anath,
who killed six hundred men of the Philistines
[R]with an ox goad; and he also delivered [R]Is-
rael. 1 Sam. 17:47 • 1 Sam. 4:1

CHAPTER 4

Deborah and Barak Are Called

WHEN Ehud was dead, [R]the children of
Israel again did [R]evil in the sight of the
LORD. Judg. 2:19 • Judg. 2:11
2 So the LORD sold them into the hand of
Jabin king of Canaan, who reigned in Hazor.
The commander of his army *was* Sisera, who
dwelt in Harosheth Hagoyim.
3 And the children of Israel cried out to the
LORD; for Jabin had nine hundred chariots of
iron, and for twenty years he had harshly op-
pressed the children of Israel.
4 Now Deborah, a prophetess, the wife of
Lapidoth, was judging Israel at that time.
5 And she would sit under the palm tree of
Deborah between Ramah and Bethel in the
mountains of Ephraim. And the children of Is-
rael came up to her for judgment.
6 Then she sent and called for [R]Barak the
son of Abinoam from [R]Kedesh in Naphtali,
and said to him, "Has not the LORD God of Is-
rael commanded, 'Go and [T]deploy *troops* at
Mount Tabor; take with you ten thousand men
of the sons of Naphtali and of the sons of
Zebulun; Heb. 11:32 • Josh. 19:37; 21:32 • *march*
7 'and against you [R]I will deploy Sisera,
the commander of Jabin's army, with his
chariots and his multitude at the [R]River
Kishon; and I will [T]deliver him into your
hand'?" Ex. 14:4 • Ps. 83:9, 10 • Lit. *draw*
8 And Barak said to her, "If you will go with
me, then I will go; but if you will not go with
me, I will not go!"
9 So she said, "I will surely go with you;
nevertheless there will be no glory for you in
the journey you are taking, for the LORD will
[R]sell Sisera into the hand of a woman." Then
Deborah arose and went with Barak to Ke-
desh. Judg. 2:14
10 And Barak called [R]Zebulun and Naphtali
to Kedesh; he went up with ten thousand men
[R]under his command,* and Deborah went up
with him. Judg. 5:18 • 1 Kin. 20:10
11 Now Heber the Kenite, of the children of
Hobab the father-in-law of Moses, had sepa-
rated himself from the Kenites and pitched his
tent near the terebinth tree at Zaanaim, which
is beside Kedesh.

Canaanites Are Defeated

12 And they reported to Sisera that Barak
the son of Abinoam had gone up to Mount
Tabor.
13 So Sisera gathered together all his chari-
ots, nine hundred chariots of iron, and all the
people who *were* with him, from Harosheth
Hagoyim to the River Kishon.
14 Then Deborah said to Barak, [T]"Up! For
this *is* the day in which the LORD has delivered
Sisera into your hand. [R]Has not the LORD gone
out before you?" So Barak went down from
Mount Tabor with ten thousand men follow-
ing him. *Arise!* • Deut. 9:3; 31:3
15 And the LORD routed Sisera and all *his*
chariots and all *his* army with the edge of the
sword before Barak; and Sisera alighted from
his chariot and fled away on foot.
16 But Barak pursued the chariots and the
army as far as Harosheth Hagoyim, and all
the army of Sisera fell by the edge of the
sword; not a man was [R]left. Ex. 14:28
17 However, Sisera had fled away on foot to
the tent of Jael, the wife of Heber the Kenite;
for *there was* peace between Jabin king of
Hazor and the house of Heber the Kenite.
18 And Jael went out to meet Sisera, and
said to him, "Turn aside, my lord, turn aside to
me; do not fear." And when he had turned
aside with her into the tent, she covered him
with a [T]blanket. *rug*
19 Then he said to her, "Please give me a lit-
tle water to drink, for I am thirsty." So she
opened [R]a jug of milk, gave him a drink, and
covered him. Judg. 5:24–27
20 And he said to her, "Stand at the door of
the tent, and if any man comes and inquires of
you, and says, 'Is there any man here?' you
shall say, 'No.'"
21 Then Jael, Heber's wife, took a tent peg
and took a hammer in her hand, and went
softly to him and drove the peg into his tem-
ple, and it went down into the ground; for he
was fast asleep and weary. So he died.
22 And then, as Barak pursued Sisera, Jael
came out to meet him, and said to him,
"Come, I will show you the man whom you
seek." And when he went into her *tent*, there
lay Sisera, dead with the peg in his temple.
23 So on that day God subdued Jabin king of
Canaan in the presence of the children of Is-
rael.
24 And the hand of the children of Israel
grew stronger and stronger against Jabin
king of Canaan, until they had destroyed
Jabin king of Canaan.

4:10 Lit. *at his feet*

CHAPTER 5

Song of Deborah and Barak

THEN Deborah and Barak the son of Abinoam sang on that day, saying:

2"When leaders lead in Israel,
[R]When the people [T]willingly offer
themselves, 2 Chr. 17:16 • *volunteer*
Bless the LORD!

3"Hear,[R] O kings! Give ear, O princes!
I, *even* [R]I, will sing to the LORD;
I will sing praise to the LORD God of
Israel. Deut. 32:1, 3 • Ps. 27:6

4"LORD, [R]when You went out from Seir,
When You marched from [R]the field of
Edom, Deut. 33:2 • Ps. 68:8
The earth trembled and the heavens
poured,
The clouds also poured water;
5[R]The mountains [T]gushed before the LORD,
[R]This Sinai, before the LORD God of
Israel. Ps. 97:5 • Ex. 19:18 • *flowed*

6"In the days of Shamgar, son of Anath,
In the days of [R]Jael, Judg. 4:17
[R]The highways were deserted,
And the travelers walked along the
byways. Is. 33:8
7 Village life ceased, it ceased in Israel,
Until I, Deborah, arose,
Arose a mother in Israel.
8 They chose [R]new gods; Deut. 32:17
Then *there was* war in the gates;
Not a shield or spear was seen among
forty thousand in Israel.
9 My heart *is* with the rulers of Israel
Who offered themselves willingly with
the people.
Bless the LORD!

10"Speak, you who ride on white [R]donkeys,
Who sit in judges' attire, Judg. 10:4; 12:14
And who walk along the road.
11 Far from the noise of the archers, among
the watering places,
There they shall recount the righteous
acts of the LORD,
The righteous acts *for* His villagers in
Israel;
Then the people of the LORD shall go
down to the gates.

12"Awake,[R] awake, Deborah! Ps. 57:8
Awake, awake, sing a song!
Arise, Barak, and lead your captives
away,
O son of Abinoam!

13"Then the survivors came down, the
people against the nobles;
The LORD came down for me against the
mighty.
14 From Ephraim *were* those whose roots
were in [R]Amalek. Judg. 3:13
After you, Benjamin, with your peoples,
From Machir rulers came down,
And from Zebulun those who bear the
recruiter's staff.
15 And the princes of Issachar* *were* with
Deborah;
As Issachar, so *was* Barak
Sent into the valley under his
command;*
Among the divisions of Reuben
There were great resolves of heart.
16 Why did you sit among the sheepfolds,
To hear the pipings for the flocks?
The divisions of Reuben have great
searchings of heart.
17 Gilead stayed beyond the Jordan,
And why did Dan remain on ships?*
[R]Asher continued at the seashore,
And stayed by his inlets. Josh. 19:29, 31
18[R]Zebulun *is* a people *who* jeopardized
their lives to the point of death,
Naphtali also, on the heights of the
battlefield. Judg. 4:6, 10

19"The kings came *and* fought,
Then the kings of Canaan fought
In [R]Taanach, by the waters of Megiddo;
They took no spoils of silver. Judg. 1:27
20 They fought from the heavens;
The stars from their courses fought
against Sisera.
21[R]The torrent of Kishon swept them away,
That ancient torrent, the torrent of
Kishon. Judg. 4:7
O my soul, march on in strength!
22 Then the horses' hooves pounded,
The galloping, galloping of his steeds.
23'Curse Meroz,' said the angel* of the
LORD,
'Curse its inhabitants bitterly,
Because they did not come to the help of
the LORD,
To the help of the LORD against the
mighty.'

24"Most blessed among women is Jael,
The wife of Heber the Kenite;
Blessed is she among women in tents.
25 He asked for water, she gave milk;
She brought out cream in a lordly bowl.
26 She stretched her hand to the tent peg,
Her right hand to the workmen's
hammer;
She pounded Sisera, she pierced his
head,

5:15 So with LXX, Syr., Tg., Vg.; MT *And my princes in Issachar* • Lit. *at his feet* **5:17** Or *at ease* **5:23** Or *Angel*

She split and struck through his temple.
27 At her feet he sank, he fell, he lay still;
At her feet he sank, he fell;
Where he sank, there he fell dead.

28 "The mother of Sisera looked through the window,
And cried out through the lattice,
'Why is his chariot *so* long in coming?
Why tarries the clatter of his chariots?'
29 Her wisest ladies answered her,
Yes, she answered herself,
30 'Are they not finding and dividing the spoil:
To every man a girl *or* two;
For Sisera, plunder of dyed garments,
Plunder of garments embroidered and dyed,
Two pieces of dyed embroidery for the neck of the looter?'

31 "Thus let all Your enemies [R]perish, O LORD! Ps. 92:9
But *let* those who love Him *be* [R]like the [R]sun 2 Sam. 23:4 • Ps. 37:6; 89:36, 37
When it comes out in full strength."

So the land had rest for forty years.

CHAPTER 6

Israel Sins

THEN the children of Israel did [R]evil in the sight of the LORD. So the LORD delivered them into the hand of [R]Midian for seven years, Judg. 2:11 • Num. 22:4; 31:1–3

2 and the hand of Midian prevailed against Israel. Because of the Midianites, the children of Israel made for themselves the dens, [R]the caves, and the strongholds which *are* in the mountains. 1 Sam. 13:6

3 So it was, whenever Israel had sown, Midianites would come up; also Amalekites and the [R]people of the East would come up against them. Judg. 7:12

4 Then they would encamp against them and destroy the produce of the earth as far as Gaza, and leave no sustenance for Israel, neither sheep nor ox nor donkey.

5 For they would come up with their livestock and their tents, coming in as numerous as locusts; both they and their camels were [T]without number; and they would enter the land to destroy it. *innumerable*

6 So Israel was greatly impoverished because of the Midianites, and the children of Israel [R]cried out to the LORD. Hos. 5:15

7 And it came to pass, when the children of Israel cried out to the LORD because of the Midianites,

8 that the LORD sent a prophet to the children of Israel, who said to them, "Thus says the LORD God of Israel: 'I brought you up from Egypt and brought you out of the [R]house of [T]bondage; Josh. 24:17 • *slavery*

9 'and I delivered you out of the hand of the Egyptians and out of the hand of all who oppressed you, and [R]drove them out before you and gave you their land. Ps. 44:2, 3

10 'Also I said to you, "I *am* the LORD your God; [R]do not fear the gods of the Amorites, in whose land you dwell." But you have not obeyed My voice.' " 2 Kin. 17:35, 37, 38

Gideon Called

11 Now the Angel of the LORD came and sat under the terebinth tree which *was* in Ophrah, which *belonged* to Joash [R]the Abiezrite, while his son [R]Gideon threshed wheat in the winepress, in order to hide *it* from the Midianites. Josh. 17:2 • Heb. 11:32

12 And the Angel of the LORD appeared to him, and said to him, "The LORD *is* [R]with you, you mighty man of valor!" Josh. 1:5

13 Gideon said to Him, "O my lord,* if the LORD is with us, why then has all this happened to us? And where *are* all His miracles which our fathers told us about, saying, 'Did not the LORD bring us up from Egypt?' But now the LORD has forsaken us and delivered us into the hands of the Midianites."

14 Then the LORD turned to him and said, [R]"Go in this might of yours, and you shall save Israel from the hand of the Midianites. [R]Have I not sent you?" 1 Sam. 12:11 • Josh. 1:9

15 So he said to Him, "O my Lord,* how can I save Israel? Indeed [R]my clan *is* the weakest in Manasseh, and I *am* the least in my father's house." 1 Sam. 9:21

16 And the LORD said to him, [R]"Surely I will be with you, and you shall [T]defeat the Midianites as one man." Ex. 3:12 • Lit. *strike*

17 Then he said to Him, "If now I have found favor in Your sight, then show me a sign that it is You who talk with me.

18 [R]"Do not depart from here, I pray, until I come to You and bring out my offering and set *it* before You." And He said, "I will wait until you come back." Gen. 18:3, 5

19 [R]So Gideon went in and prepared a young goat, and unleavened bread from an ephah of flour. The meat he put in a basket, and he put the broth in a pot; and he brought *them* out to Him under the terebinth tree and presented *them*. Gen. 18:6–8

20 The Angel of God said to him, "Take the meat and the unleavened bread and [R]lay *them* on this rock, and [R]pour out the broth." And he did so. Judg. 13:19 • 1 Kin. 18:33, 34

21 Then the Angel of the LORD put out the end of the staff that *was* in His hand, and touched the meat and the unleavened bread; and fire rose out of the rock and consumed

6:13 Heb. *adoni,* used of man **6:15** Heb. *Adonai,* used of God

the meat and the unleavened bread. And the
Angel of the LORD departed out of his sight.
22 Now Gideon [R]perceived that He *was* the
Angel of the LORD. So Gideon said, "Alas, O
Lord GOD! [R]For I have seen the Angel of the
LORD face to face." Judg. 13:21, 22 • Gen. 16:13
23 Then the LORD said to him, "Peace *be* with
you; do not fear, you shall not die."
24 So Gideon built an altar there to the LORD,
and called it The-LORD-*Is*-Peace.* To this day it
is still [R]in Ophrah of the Abiezrites. Judg. 8:32
25 Now it came to pass the same night that
the LORD said to him, "Take your father's
young bull, the second bull of seven years old,
and [R]tear down the altar of [R]Baal that your fa-
ther has, and cut down the wooden image*
that *is* beside it; Judg. 2:2 • Judg. 3:7
26 "and build an altar to the LORD your God
on top of this rock in the proper arrangement,
and take the second bull and offer a burnt
sacrifice with the wood of the image which
you shall cut down."
27 So Gideon took ten men from among his
servants and did as the LORD had said to him.
But because he feared his father's household
and the men of the city too much to do *it* by
day, he did *it* by night.
28 And when the men of the city arose early
in the morning, there was the altar of Baal,
torn down; and the wooden image that *was*
beside it was cut down, and the second bull
was being offered on the altar *which had been*
built.
29 So they said to one another, "Who has
done this thing?" And when they had inquired
and asked, they said, "Gideon the son of Joash
has done this thing."
30 Then the men of the city said to Joash,
"Bring out your son, that he may die, because
he has torn down the altar of Baal, and be-
cause he has cut down the wooden image that
was beside it."
31 But Joash said to all who stood against
him, "Would you [T]plead for Baal? Would you
save him? Let the one who would plead for
him be put to death by morning! If he *is* a god,
let him plead for himself, because his altar
has been torn down!" *contend*
32 Therefore on that day he called him
Jerubbaal,* saying, "Let Baal plead against
him, because he has torn down his altar."
33 Then all [R]the Midianites and Amalekites,
the people of the East, gathered together; and
they crossed over and encamped in [R]the Valley
of Jezreel. Judg. 6:3 • Josh. 17:16
34 But [R]the Spirit of the LORD came upon
Gideon; then he blew the trumpet, and the
Abiezrites gathered behind him. Judg. 3:10
35 And he sent messengers throughout all
Manasseh, who also gathered behind him. He
also sent messengers to [R]Asher, [R]Zebulun,
and Naphtali; and they came up to meet
them. Judg. 5:17; 7:23 • Judg. 4:6, 10; 5:18
36 So Gideon said to God, "If You will save
Israel by my hand as You have said—
37 [R]"look, I shall put a fleece of wool on the
threshing floor; if there is dew on the fleece
only, and *it is* dry on all the ground, then I
shall know that You will save Israel by my
hand, as You have said." [Ex. 4:3–7]
38 And it was so. When he rose early the
next morning and squeezed the fleece to-
gether, he wrung the dew out of the fleece, a
bowlful of water.
39 Then Gideon said to God, [R]"Do not be
angry with me, but let me speak just once
more: Let me test, I pray, just once more with
the fleece; let it now be dry only on the
fleece, but on all the ground let there be
dew." Gen. 18:32
40 And God did so that night. It was dry on
the fleece only, but there was dew on all the
ground.

CHAPTER 7

Midianites Defeated

THEN [R]Jerubbaal (that *is*, Gideon) and all
the people who *were* with him rose early
and encamped beside the well of Harod, so
that the camp of the Midianites was on the
north side of them by the hill of Moreh in the
valley. Judg. 6:32
2 And the LORD said to Gideon, "The people
who *are* with you *are* too many for Me to give
the Midianites into their hands, lest Israel
[R]claim glory for itself against Me, saying, 'My
own hand has saved me.' Deut. 8:17
3 "Now therefore, proclaim in the hearing
of the people, saying, [R]'Whoever *is* fearful and
afraid, let him turn and depart at once from
Mount Gilead.' " And twenty-two thousand of
the people returned, and ten thousand re-
mained. Deut. 20:8
4 But the LORD said to Gideon, "The people
are still *too* many; bring them down to the
water, and I will test them for you there. Then
it will be, *that* of whom I say to you, 'This one
shall go with you,' the same shall go with you;
and of whomever I say to you, 'This one shall
not go with you,' the same shall not go."
5 So he brought the people down to the
water. And the LORD said to Gideon, "Every-
one who laps from the water with his tongue,
as a dog laps, you shall set apart by himself;
likewise everyone who gets down on his
knees to drink."
6 And the number of those who lapped,
putting their hand to their mouth, was three
hundred men; but all the rest of the people got
down on their knees to drink water.
7 Then the LORD said to Gideon, [R]"By the
three hundred men who lapped I will save

6:24 Heb. *YHWH Shalom* **6:25** Heb. *Asherah*, a
Canaanite goddess **6:32** Lit. *Let Baal Plead*

you, and deliver the Midianites into your
hand. Let all the *other* people go, every man
to his [T]place." 1 Sam. 14:6 • *home*
8 So the people took provisions and their
trumpets in their hands. And he sent away all
the rest of Israel, every man to his tent, and
retained those three hundred men. Now the
camp of Midian was below him in the valley.
9 It happened on the same [R]night that the
LORD said to him, "Arise, go down against
the camp, for I have delivered it into your
hand. Judg. 6:25
10 "But if you are afraid to go down, go
down to the camp with Purah your servant,
11 "and you shall hear what they say; and afterward your hands shall be strengthened to
go down against the camp." Then he went
down with Purah his servant to the outpost of
the armed men who *were* in the camp.
12 Now the Midianites and Amalekites, all
the people of the East, were lying in the valley
[R]as numerous as locusts; and their camels
were without number, as the sand by the
seashore in multitude. Judg. 6:5
13 And when Gideon had come, there was a
man telling a dream to his companion. He
said, "I have had a dream: *To my* surprise, a
loaf of barley bread tumbled into the camp of
Midian; it came to a tent and struck it so that
it fell and overturned, and the tent collapsed."
14 Then his companion answered and said,
"This *is* nothing else but the sword of Gideon
the son of Joash, a man of Israel! Into his
hand [R]God has delivered Midian and the
whole camp." Judg. 6:14, 16
15 And so it was, when Gideon heard the
telling of the dream and its interpretation,
that he worshiped. He returned to the camp of
Israel, and said, "Arise, for the LORD has delivered the camp of Midian into your hand."
16 Then he divided the three hundred men
into three companies, and he put a trumpet
into every man's hand, with empty pitchers,
and torches inside the pitchers.
17 And he said to them, "Look at me and do
likewise; watch, and when I come to the edge
of the camp you shall do as I do:
18 "When I blow the trumpet, I and all who
are with me, then you also blow the trumpets
on every side of the whole camp, and say, '*The
sword of* the LORD and of Gideon!' "
19 So Gideon and the hundred men who
were with him came to the outpost of the
camp at the beginning of the middle watch,
just as they had posted the watch; and they
blew the trumpets and broke the pitchers that
were in their hands.
20 Then the three companies blew the trumpets and broke the pitchers—they held the
torches in their left hands and the trumpets in
their right hands for blowing—and they cried,
"The sword of the LORD and of Gideon!"
21 And [R]every man stood in his place all
around the camp; [R]and the whole army ran
and cried out and fled. 2 Chr. 20:17 • 2 Kin. 7:7
22 When the three hundred [R]blew the trumpets, [R]the LORD set every man's sword against
his companion throughout the whole camp;
and the army fled to Beth Acacia,* toward
Zererah, as far as the border of Abel Meholah,
by Tabbath. Josh. 6:4, 16, 20 • Is. 9:4
23 And the men of Israel gathered together
from [R]Naphtali, Asher, and all Manasseh, and
pursued the Midianites. Judg. 6:35
24 Then Gideon sent messengers throughout all the [R]mountains of Ephraim, saying,
"Come down against the Midianites, and
seize from them the watering places as far as
Beth Barah and the Jordan." Then all the men
of Ephraim gathered together and seized the
watering places as far as [R]Beth Barah and the
Jordan. Judg. 3:27 • John 1:28
25 And they captured two princes of the
Midianites, Oreb and Zeeb. They killed Oreb
at the rock of Oreb, and Zeeb they killed at
the winepress of Zeeb. They pursued Midian
and brought the heads of Oreb and Zeeb to
Gideon on the other side of the Jordan.

CHAPTER 8

NOW [R]the men of Ephraim said to him,
"Why have you done this to us by not
calling us when you went to fight with the
Midianites?" And they reprimanded him
sharply. Judg. 12:1
2 So he said to them, "What have I done
now in comparison with you? *Is* not the gleaning *of the grapes* of Ephraim better than the
vintage of [R]Abiezer? Judg. 6:11
3 [R]"God has delivered into your hands the
princes of Midian, Oreb and Zeeb. And what
was I able to do in comparison with you?"
Then their [R]anger toward him subsided when
he said that. Judg. 7:24, 25 • Prov. 15:1
4 When Gideon came [R]to the Jordan, he
and [R]the three hundred men who *were* with
him crossed over, exhausted but still in pursuit. Judg. 7:25 • Judg. 7:6
5 Then he said to the men of [R]Succoth,
"Please give loaves of bread to the people who
follow me, for they are exhausted, and I am
pursuing Zebah and Zalmunna, kings of Midian." Gen. 33:17
6 And the leaders of Succoth said, [R]"*Are* the
hands of Zebah and Zalmunna now in your
hand, that [R]we should give bread to your
army?" Judg. 8:15 • 1 Sam. 25:11
7 So Gideon said, "For this cause, when the
LORD has delivered Zebah and Zalmunna
into my hand, [R]then I will tear your flesh
with the thorns of the wilderness and with
briers!" Judg. 8:16
8 Then he went up from there [R]to Penuel

7:22 Heb. *Beth Shittah*

and spoke to them in the same way. And the
men of Penuel answered him as the men of
Succoth had answered. Gen. 32:30, 31
9 So he also spoke to the men of Penuel,
saying, "When I [R]come back in peace, [R]I will
tear down this tower!" 1 Kin. 22:27 • Judg. 8:17
10 Now Zebah and Zalmunna *were* at
Karkor, and their armies with them, about fif-
teen thousand, all who were left of [R]all the
army of the people of the East; for [R]one hun-
dred and twenty thousand men who drew the
sword had fallen. Judg. 7:12 • Judg. 6:5
11 Then Gideon went up by the road of those
who dwell in tents on the east of Nobah and
Jogbehah; and he [T]attacked the army while
the camp felt secure. Lit. *struck*
12 When Zebah and Zalmunna fled, he pur-
sued them; and he [R]took the two kings of Mid-
ian, Zebah and Zalmunna, and routed the
whole army. Ps. 83:11
13 Then Gideon the son of Joash returned
from battle, from the Ascent of Heres.
14 And he caught a young man of the men of
Succoth and interrogated him; and he wrote
down for him the leaders of Succoth and its
elders, seventy-seven men.
15 Then he came to the men of Succoth and
said, "Here are Zebah and Zalmunna, about
whom you [R]ridiculed me, saying, '*Are* the
hands of Zebah and Zalmunna now in your
hand, that we should give bread to your weary
men?' " Judg. 8:6
16 And he took the elders of the city, and
thorns of the wilderness and briers, and with
them he taught the men of Succoth.
17 Then he tore down the tower of [R]Penuel
and killed the men of the city. 1 Kin. 12:25
18 And he said to Zebah and Zalmunna,
"What kind of men *were they* whom you
killed at [R]Tabor?" So they answered, "As you
are, so *were* they; each one resembled the son
of a king." Judg. 4:6
19 Then he said, "They *were* my brothers,
the sons of my mother. *As* the LORD lives, if
you had let them live, I would not kill you."
20 And he said to Jether his firstborn, "Rise,
kill them!" But the youth would not draw his
sword; for he was afraid, because he *was* still
a youth.
21 So Zebah and Zalmunna said, "Rise your-
self, and kill us; for as a man *is, so is* his
strength." So Gideon arose and killed Zebah
and Zalmunna, and took the crescent orna-
ments that *were* on their camels' necks.

Gideon Judges

22 Then the men of Israel said to Gideon,
[R]"Rule over us, both you and your son, and
your grandson also; for you have delivered us
from the hand of Midian." [Judg. 9:8]
23 But Gideon said to them, "I will not rule
over you, nor shall my son rule over you; [R]the
LORD shall rule over you." 1 Sam. 8:7
24 Then Gideon said to them, "I would like to
make a request of you, that each of you would
give me the earrings from his plunder." For
they had golden earrings, [R]because they *were*
Ishmaelites. Gen. 37:25, 28
25 So they answered, "We will gladly give
them." And they spread out a garment, and
each man threw into it the earrings from his
plunder.
26 Now the weight of the gold earrings that
he requested was one thousand seven hun-
dred *shekels* of gold, besides the crescent or-
naments, pendants, and purple robes which
were on the kings of Midian, and besides the
chains that *were* around their camels' necks.
27 Then Gideon made it into an ephod and
set it up in his city, Ophrah. And all Israel
played the harlot with it there. It became a
snare to Gideon and to his house.
28 Thus Midian was subdued before the chil-
dren of Israel, so that they lifted their heads
no more. And the country was quiet for forty
years in the days of Gideon.
29 Then [R]Jerubbaal the son of Joash went
and dwelt in his own house. Judg. 6:32; 7:1
30 Gideon had seventy sons who were his
own offspring, for he had many wives.
31 [R]And his concubine who *was* in Shechem
also bore him a son, whose name he called
Abimelech. Judg. 9:1
32 Now Gideon the son of Joash died [R]at a
good old age, and was buried in the tomb of
Joash his father, [R]in Ophrah of the Abiez-
rites. Gen. 25:8 • Judg. 6:24; 8:27

Confusion After Gideon Dies

33 So it was, [R]as soon as Gideon was dead,
that the children of Israel again [R]played the
harlot with the Baals, and made Baal-Berith
their god. Judg. 2:19 • Judg. 2:17
34 Thus the children of Israel [R]did not re-
member the LORD their God, who had deliv-
ered them from the hands of all their enemies
on every side; Deut. 4:9
35 nor did they show kindness to the house
of Jerubbaal (Gideon) in accordance with the
good he had done for Israel.

CHAPTER 9

Deception of Abimelech

THEN Abimelech the son of Jerubbaal
went to Shechem, to [R]his mother's broth-
ers, and spoke with them and with all the
family of the house of his mother's father,
saying, Judg. 8:31, 35
2 "Please speak in the hearing of all the
men of Shechem: 'Which is better for you,
that all [R]seventy of the sons of Jerubbaal
reign over you, or that one reign over you?'
Remember that I *am* your own flesh and
[R]bone." Judg. 8:30; 9:5, 18 • Gen. 29:14
3 And his mother's brothers spoke all these

words concerning him in the hearing of all the
men of Shechem; and their heart was inclined
to follow Abimelech, for they said, "He is our
[R]brother." Gen. 29:15
4 So they gave him seventy *shekels* of silver
from the temple of [R]Baal-Berith, with which
Abimelech hired worthless and reckless men;
and they followed him. Judg. 8:33
5 Then he went to his father's house at
Ophrah and [R]killed his brothers, the seventy
sons of Jerubbaal, on one stone. But Jotham
the youngest son of Jerubbaal was left, be-
cause he hid himself. 2 Kin. 11:1, 2
6 And all the men of Shechem gathered to-
gether, all of Beth Millo, and they went and
made Abimelech king beside the terebinth
tree at the pillar that *was* in Shechem.

Revelation of Jotham

7 Now when they told Jotham, he went
and stood on top of [R]Mount Gerizim, and
lifted his voice and cried out. And he said to
them: Deut. 11:29; 27:12

"Listen to me, you men of Shechem,
That God may listen to you!

8 "The[R] trees once went forth to anoint a
king over them. 2 Kin. 14:9
And they said to the olive tree,
[R]'Reign over us!' Judg. 8:22, 23
9 But the olive tree said to them,
'Should I cease giving my oil,
[R]With which they honor God and men,
And go to sway over trees?' [John 5:23]

10 "Then the trees said to the fig tree,
'You come *and* reign over us!'
11 But the fig tree said to them,
'Should I cease my sweetness and my
good fruit,
And go to sway over trees?'
12 "Then the trees said to the vine,
'You come *and* reign over us!'
13 But the vine said to them,
'Should I cease my new wine,
[R]Which cheers *both* God and men,
And go to sway over trees?' Ps. 104:15

14 "Then all the trees said to the bramble,
'You come *and* reign over us!'
15 And the bramble said to the trees,
'If in truth you anoint me as king over
you,
Then come *and* take shelter in my
[R]shade; Is. 30:2
But if not, [R]let fire come out of the
bramble Num. 21:28
And devour the cedars of Lebanon!'

16 "Now therefore, if you have acted in truth
and sincerity in making Abimelech king, and
if you have dealt well with Jerubbaal and his
house, and have done to him [R]as he de-
serves— Judg. 8:35
17 "for my [R]father fought for you, risked his
life, and [R]delivered you out of the hand of
Midian; Judg. 7 • Judg. 8:22
18 "but you have risen up against my father's
house this day, and killed his seventy sons on
one stone, and made Abimelech, the son of his
female servant, king over the men of She-
chem, because he is your brother—
19 "if then you have acted in truth and sin-
cerity with Jerubbaal and with his house this
day, *then* [R]rejoice in Abimelech, and let him
also rejoice in you. Is. 8:6
20 "But if not, [R]let fire come from Abimelech
and devour the men of Shechem and Beth
Millo; and let fire come from the men of
Shechem and from Beth Millo and devour
Abimelech!" Judg. 9:15, 45, 56, 57
21 And Jotham ran away and fled; and he
went to [R]Beer and dwelt there, for fear of
Abimelech his brother. Num. 21:16

Destruction of Shechem

22 After Abimelech had reigned over Israel
three years,
23 [R]God sent a [R]spirit of ill will between
Abimelech and the men of Shechem; and the
men of Shechem dealt treacherously with
Abimelech, Is. 19:14 • 1 Sam. 16:14; 18:9, 10
24 [R]that the crime *done* to the seventy sons
of Jerubbaal might be settled and their
[R]blood be laid on Abimelech their brother,
who killed them, and on the men of She-
chem, who aided him in the killing of his
brothers. 1 Kin. 2:32 • Num. 35:33
25 And the men of Shechem set [T]men in am-
bush against him on the tops of the moun-
tains, and they robbed all who passed by
them along that way; and it was told Abim-
elech. Lit. *liers-in-wait for*
26 Now Gaal the son of Ebed came with his
brothers and went over to Shechem; and the
men of Shechem put their confidence in him.
27 So they went out into the fields, and gath-
ered *grapes* from their vineyards and trod
them, and made merry. And they went into
[R]the house of their god, and ate and drank,
and cursed Abimelech. Judg. 9:4
28 Then Gaal the son of Ebed said, "Who *is*
Abimelech, and who *is* Shechem, that we
should serve him? *Is he* not the son of Jerub-
baal, and *is not* Zebul his officer? Serve the
men of Hamor the father of Shechem; but
why should we serve him?
29 [R]"If only this people were under my au-
thority!* Then I would remove Abimelech." So
he* said to Abimelech, "Increase your army
and come out!" 2 Sam. 15:4
30 When Zebul, the ruler of the city, heard

9:29 Lit. *hand* • So with MT, Tg.; DSS *they;* LXX *I*

the words of Gaal the son of Ebed, his anger was aroused.

31 And he sent messengers to Abimelech secretly, saying, "Take note! Gaal the son of Ebed and his brothers have come to Shechem; and here they are, fortifying the city against you.

32 "Now therefore, get up by night, you and the people who *are* with you, and [T]lie in wait in the field. Set up an ambush

33 "And it shall be, as soon as the sun is up in the morning, *that* you shall rise early and rush upon the city; and *when* he and the people who are with him come out against you, you may then do to them [T]as you find opportunity." Lit. *as your hand can find*

34 So Abimelech and all the people who *were* with him rose by night, and lay in wait against Shechem in four companies.

35 When Gaal the son of Ebed went out and stood in the entrance to the city gate, Abimelech and the people who *were* with him rose from lying in wait.

36 And when Gaal saw the people, he said to Zebul, "Look, people are coming down from the tops of the mountains!" But Zebul said to him, "You see the shadows of the mountains as *if they were* men."

37 So Gaal spoke again and said, "See, people are coming down from the center of the land, and another company is coming from the Diviners'* Terebinth Tree."

38 Then Zebul said to him, "Where indeed *is* your mouth now, with which you [R]said, 'Who is Abimelech, that we should serve him?' *Are* not these the people whom you despised? Go out, if you will, and fight with them now." Judg. 9:28, 29

39 So Gaal went out, leading the men of Shechem, and fought with Abimelech.

40 And Abimelech chased him, and he fled from him; and many fell wounded, to the *very* entrance of the gate.

41 Then Abimelech dwelt at Arumah, and Zebul drove out Gaal and his brothers, so that they would not dwell in Shechem.

42 And it came about on the next day that the people went out into the field, and they told Abimelech.

43 So he took his people, divided them into three companies, and lay in wait in the field. And he looked, and there were the people, coming out of the city; and he rose against them and [T]attacked them. Lit. *struck*

44 Then Abimelech and the company that *was* with him rushed forward and stood at the entrance of the gate of the city; and the *other* two companies rushed upon all who *were* in the fields and killed them.

45 So Abimelech fought against the city all that day; he took the city and killed the people who *were* in it; and he [R]demolished the city and sowed it with salt. 2 Kin. 3:25

46 Now when all the men of the tower of Shechem had heard *that,* they entered the stronghold of the temple of the god Berith.

47 And it was told Abimelech that all the men of the tower of Shechem were gathered together.

48 Then Abimelech went up to Mount [R]Zalmon, he and all the people who *were* with him. And Abimelech took an ax in his hand and cut down a bough from the trees, and took it and laid *it* on his shoulder; then he said to the people who were with him, "What you have seen me do, make haste *and* do as I *have done.*" Ps. 68:14

49 So each of the people likewise cut down his own bough and followed Abimelech, put *them* against the [T]stronghold, and set the stronghold on fire above them, so that all the people of the tower of Shechem died, about a thousand men and women. *fortified room*

Death of Abimelech

50 Then Abimelech went to Thebez, and he encamped against Thebez and took it.

51 But there was a strong tower in the city, and all the men and women—all the people of the city—fled there and shut themselves in; then they went up to the top of the tower.

52 So Abimelech came as far as the tower and fought against it; and he drew near the door of the tower to burn it with fire.

53 But a certain woman [R]dropped an upper millstone on Abimelech's head and crushed his skull. 2 Sam. 11:21

54 Then he called quickly to the young man, his armorbearer, and said to him, "Draw your sword and kill me, lest men say of me, 'A woman killed him.' " So his young man thrust him through, and he died.

55 And when the men of Israel saw that Abimelech was dead, they departed, every man to his [T]place. *home*

56 [R]Thus God repaid the wickedness of Abimelech, which he had done to his father by killing his seventy brothers. Job 31:3

57 And all the evil of the men of Shechem God returned on their own heads, and on them came [R]the curse of Jotham the son of Jerubbaal. Judg. 9:20

CHAPTER 10

The Judge Tola

AFTER Abimelech there arose to save Israel Tola the son of Puah, the son of Dodo, a man of Issachar; and he dwelt in Shamir in the mountains of Ephraim.

2 He judged Israel twenty-three years; and he died and was buried in Shamir.

9:37 Heb. *Meonenim*

The Judge Jair

3 After him arose Jair, a Gileadite; and he
judged Israel twenty-two years.
4 Now he had thirty sons who rode on
thirty donkeys; they also had thirty towns,
[R]which are called "Havoth Jair"* to this day,
which *are* in the land of Gilead. Deut. 3:14
5 And Jair died and was buried in Camon.

Israel Sins

6 Then the children of Israel again did evil
in the sight of the LORD, and [R]served the Baals
and the Ashtoreths, the gods of Syria, the
gods of Sidon, the gods of Moab, the gods of
the people of Ammon, and the gods of the
Philistines; and they forsook the LORD and did
not serve Him. Judg. 2:13
7 So the anger of the LORD was hot against
Israel; and He [R]sold them into the hands of
the Philistines and into the hands of the peo-
ple of Ammon. 1 Sam. 12:9
8 From that year they harassed and op-
pressed the children of Israel for eighteen
years—all the children of Israel who *were* on
the other side of the Jordan in the [R]land of the
Amorites, in Gilead. Num. 32:33
9 Moreover the people of Ammon crossed
over the Jordan to fight against Judah also,
against Benjamin, and against the house of
Ephraim, so that Israel was severely distressed.
10 [R]And the children of Israel cried out to
the LORD, saying, "We have sinned against
You, because we have both forsaken our God
and served the Baals!" 1 Sam. 12:10
11 So the LORD said to the children of Israel,
"*Did I* not *deliver you* from the Egyptians and
from the Amorites and from the people of
Ammon and from the Philistines?
12 "Also [R]the Sidonians [R]and Amalekites
and Maonites* oppressed you; and you cried
out to Me, and I delivered you from their
hand. Judg. 1:31; 5:19 • Judg. 6:3; 7:12
13 [R]"Yet you have forsaken Me and served
other gods. Therefore I will deliver you no
more. [Jer. 2:13]
14 "Go and [R]cry out to the gods which you
have chosen; let them deliver you in your time
of distress." Deut. 32:37, 38
15 And the children of Israel said to the
LORD, "We have sinned! [R]Do to us whatever
seems best to You; only deliver us this day, we
pray." 1 Sam. 3:18
16 [R]So they put away the foreign gods from
among them and served the LORD. And [R]His
soul could no longer endure the misery of Is-
rael. Jer. 18:7, 8 • Is. 63:9
17 Then the people of Ammon gathered to-
gether and encamped in Gilead. And the chil-
dren of Israel assembled together and
encamped in [R]Mizpah. Judg. 11:11, 29
18 And the people, the leaders of Gilead,
said to one another, "Who *is* the man who will
begin the fight against the people of Ammon?
He shall [R]be head over all the inhabitants of
Gilead." Judg. 11:8, 11

CHAPTER 11

Jephthah Is Called

NOW Jephthah the Gileadite was a mighty
man of valor, but he *was* the son of a har-
lot; and Gilead begot Jephthah.
2 Gilead's wife bore sons; and when his
wife's sons grew up, they drove Jephthah out,
and said to him, "You shall have [R]no inheri-
tance in our father's house, for you *are* the
son of another woman." Gen. 21:10
3 Then Jephthah fled from his brothers and
dwelt in the land of Tob; and [R]worthless men
banded together with Jephthah and went out
raiding with him. 1 Sam 22:2
4 It came to pass after a time that the peo-
ple of Ammon made war against Israel.
5 And so it was, when the people of Ammon
made war against Israel, that the elders of
Gilead went to get Jephthah from the land of
Tob.
6 Then they said to Jephthah, "Come and
be our commander, that we may fight against
the people of Ammon."
7 So Jephthah said to the elders of Gilead,
"Did you not hate me, and expel me from my
father's house? Why have you come to me
now when you are in distress?"
8 And the elders of Gilead said to Jephthah,
"That is why we have turned again to you
now, that you may go with us and fight
against the people of Ammon, and be our
head over all the inhabitants of Gilead."
9 So Jephthah said to the elders of Gilead,
"If you take me back home to fight against the
people of Ammon, and the LORD delivers them
to me, shall I be your head?"
10 And the elders of Gilead said to Jephthah,
"The LORD will be a witness between us, if we
do not do according to your words."
11 Then Jephthah went with the elders of
Gilead, and the people made him head and
commander over them; and Jephthah spoke
all his words before the LORD in Mizpah.

Jephthah Judges

12 Now Jephthah sent messengers to the
king of the people of Ammon, saying, "What
do you have against me, that you have come
to fight against me in my land?"
13 And the king of the people of Ammon an-
swered the messengers of Jephthah, "Because
Israel took away my land when they came up
out of Egypt, from the Arnon as far as the Jab-
bok, and to the Jordan. Now therefore, restore
those *lands* peaceably.

10:4 Lit. *Towns of Jair,* Num. 32:41; Deut. 3:14
10:12 LXX mss. *Midianites*

14 So Jephthah again sent messengers to the
king of the people of Ammon,
15 and said to him, "Thus says Jephthah: 'Is-
rael did not take away the land of Moab, nor
the land of the people of Ammon;
16 'for when Israel came up from Egypt, they
walked through the wilderness as far as the
Red Sea and came to Kadesh.
17 'Then Israel sent messengers to the king
of Edom, saying, "Please let me pass through
your land." But the king of Edom would not
heed. And in like manner they sent to the king
of Moab, but he would not *consent*. So Israel
remained in Kadesh.
18 'And they [R]went along through the wilder-
ness and bypassed the land of Edom and the
land of Moab, came to the east side of the land
of Moab, and encamped on the other side of
the Arnon. But they did not enter the border
of Moab, for the Arnon *was* the border of
Moab. Deut. 2:9, 18, 19
19 'Then Israel sent messengers to Sihon
king of the Amorites, king of Heshbon; and Is-
rael said to him, "Please let us pass through
your land into our place."
20 [R]But Sihon did not trust Israel to pass
through his territory. So Sihon gathered all
his people together, encamped in Jahaz, and
fought against Israel. Deut. 2:27
21 'And the LORD God of Israel delivered
Sihon and all his people into the hand of Is-
rael, and they defeated them. Thus Israel
gained possession of all the land of the Amo-
rites, who inhabited that country.
22 'They took possession of [R]all the terri-
tory of the Amorites, from the Arnon to the
Jabbok and from the wilderness to the Jor-
dan. Deut. 2:36, 37
23 'And now the LORD God of Israel has dis-
possessed the Amorites from before His peo-
ple Israel; should you then possess it?
24 'Will you not possess whatever Chemosh
your god gives you to possess? So whatever
the LORD our God takes possession of before
us, we will possess.
25 'And now, *are* you any better than [R]Balak
the son of Zippor, king of Moab? Did he ever
strive against Israel? Did he ever fight against
them? Num. 22:2
26 'While Israel dwelt in [R]Heshbon and its
villages, in Aroer and its villages, and in all
the cities along the banks of the Arnon, for
three hundred years, why did you not recover
them within that time? Num. 21:25, 26
27 'Therefore I have not sinned against you,
but you wronged me by fighting against me.
May the LORD, [R]the Judge, render judgment
this day between the children of Israel and the
people of Ammon.' " Gen. 18:25
28 However, the king of the people of
Ammon did not heed the words which Jeph-
thah sent him.

Jephthah Vows

29 Then the Spirit of the LORD came upon
Jephthah, and he passed through Gilead and
Manasseh, and passed through Mizpah of
Gilead; and from Mizpah of Gilead he ad-
vanced *toward* the people of Ammon.
30 And Jephthah [R]made a vow to the LORD,
and said, "If You will indeed deliver the people
of Ammon into my hands, Gen. 28:20
31 "then it will be that whatever comes out of
the doors of my house to meet me, when I re-
turn in peace from the people of Ammon,
[R]shall surely be the LORD's, and I will offer it
up as a burnt offering." Lev. 27:2, 3, 28
32 So Jephthah advanced toward the people
of Ammon to fight against them, and the LORD
delivered them into his hands.
33 And he [T]defeated them from Aroer as far
as [R]Minnith—twenty cities—and to Abel
Keramim,* with a very great slaughter. Thus
the people of Ammon were subdued before
the children of Israel. Lit. *struck* • Ezek. 27:17
34 When Jephthah came to his house at Miz-
pah, there was [R]his daughter, coming out to
meet him with timbrels and dancing; and she
was his only child. Besides her he had neither
son nor daughter. Ex. 15:20
35 And it came to pass, when he saw her,
that he [R]tore his clothes, and said, "Alas, my
daughter! You have brought me very low! You
are among those who trouble me! For I have
given my word to the LORD, and I cannot go
back on it." Gen. 37:29, 34
36 So she said to him, "My father, *if* you have
given your word to the LORD, do to me ac-
cording to what has gone out of your mouth,
because the LORD has avenged you of your en-
emies, the people of Ammon."
37 Then she said to her father, "Let this
thing be done for me: let me alone for two
months, that I may go and wander on the
mountains and [T]bewail my virginity, my
[T]friends and I." *lament* • *companions*
38 So he said, "Go." And he sent her away *for*
two months; and she went with her friends,
and bewailed her virginity on the mountains.
39 And it was so at the end of two months
that she returned to her father, and he [R]car-
ried out his vow with her which he had
vowed. She [T]knew no man. And it became a
custom in Israel Judg. 11:31 • Remained a virgin
40 *that* the daughters of Israel went four
days each year to [T]lament the daughter of
Jephthah the Gileadite. *commemorate*

CHAPTER 12

Ephraim Is Conquered

THEN [R]the men of Ephraim gathered to-
gether, crossed over toward Zaphon, and

11:33 Lit. *Plain of Vineyards*

said to Jephthah, "Why did you cross over to fight against the people of Ammon, and did not call us to go with you? We will burn your house down on you with fire!" Judg. 8:1

2 And Jephthah said to them, "My people and I were in a great struggle with the people of Ammon; and when I called you, you did not deliver me out of their hands.

3 "So when I saw that you would not deliver *me,* I [R]took my life in my hands and crossed over against the people of Ammon; and the LORD delivered them into my hand. Why then have you come up to me this day to fight against me?" 1 Sam. 19:5; 28:21

4 Now Jephthah gathered together all the men of Gilead and fought against Ephraim. And the men of Gilead defeated Ephraim, because they said, "You Gileadites [R]*are* fugitives of Ephraim among the Ephraimites *and* among the Manassites." 1 Sam. 25:10

5 The Gileadites seized the [R]fords of the Jordan before the Ephraimites *arrived.* And when *any* Ephraimite who escaped said, "Let me cross over," the men of Gilead would say to him, "*Are* you an Ephraimite?" If he said, "No," Josh. 22:11

6 then they would say to him, "Then say, 'Shibboleth'!" And he would say, "Sibboleth," for he could not pronounce *it* right. Then they would take him and kill him at the fords of the Jordan. There fell at that time forty-two thousand Ephraimites.

7 And Jephthah judged Israel six years. Then Jephthah the Gileadite died and was buried in among the cities of Gilead.

The Judge Ibzan

8 After him, Ibzan of Bethlehem judged Israel.

9 He had thirty sons. And he gave away thirty daughters in marriage, and brought in thirty daughters from elsewhere for his sons. He judged Israel seven years.

10 Then Ibzan died and was buried at Bethlehem.

The Judge Elon

11 After him, Elon the Zebulunite judged Israel. He judged Israel ten years.

12 And Elon the Zebulunite died and was buried at Aijalon in the country of Zebulun.

The Judge Abdon

13 After him, Abdon the son of Hillel the Pirathonite judged Israel.

14 He had forty sons and thirty grandsons, who [R]rode on seventy young donkeys. He judged Israel eight years. Judg. 5:10; 10:4

15 Then Abdon the son of Hillel the Pirathonite died and was buried in Pirathon in the land of Ephraim, [R]in the mountains of the Amalekites. Judg. 3:13, 27; 5:14

CHAPTER 13

Miraculous Birth of Samson

AGAIN the children of Israel [R]did evil in the sight of the LORD, and the LORD delivered them [R]into the hand of the Philistines for forty years. Judg. 2:11 • 1 Sam. 12:9

2 Now there was a certain man from [R]Zorah, of the family of the Danites, whose name *was* Manoah; and his wife *was* barren and had no children. Josh. 19:41

3 And the Angel of the LORD appeared to the woman and said to her, "Indeed now, you are barren and have borne no children, but you shall conceive and bear a son.

4 "Now therefore, please be careful [R]not to drink wine or *similar* drink, and not to eat anything unclean. Num. 6:2, 3, 20

5 "For behold, you shall conceive and bear a son. And no [R]razor shall come upon his head, for the child shall be [R]a Nazirite to God from the womb; and he shall [R]begin to deliver Israel out of the hand of the Philistines." Num. 6:5 • Num. 6:2 • 1 Sam. 7:13

6 So the woman came and told her husband, saying, "A Man of God came to me, and His [R]countenance *was* like the countenance of the Angel of God, very awesome; but I did not ask Him where He *was* from, and He did not tell me His name. Matt. 28:3

7 "And He said to me, 'Behold, you shall conceive and bear a son. Now drink no wine or *similar* drink, nor eat anything unclean, for the child shall be a Nazirite to God from the womb to the day of his death.' "

8 Then Manoah prayed to the LORD, and said, "O my Lord, please let the Man of God whom You sent come to us again and teach us what we shall do for the child who will be born."

9 And God listened to the voice of Manoah, and the Angel of God came to the woman again as she was sitting in the field; but Manoah her husband *was* not with her.

10 Then the woman ran in haste and told her husband, and said to him, "Look, the Man who came to me the *other* day has just now appeared to me!"

11 So Manoah arose and followed his wife. When he came to the Man, he said to Him, "Are You the Man who spoke to this woman?" And He said, "I *am.*"

12 Manoah said, "Now let Your words come *to pass!* What will be the boy's rule of life, and his work?"

13 So the Angel of the LORD said to Manoah, "Of all that I said to the woman let her be careful.

14 "She may not eat anything that comes from the vine, nor may she drink wine or *similar* drink, nor eat anything unclean. All that I commanded her let her observe."

15 Then Manoah said to the Angel of the

LORD, "Please [R]let us detain You, and we will
prepare a young goat for You." Gen. 18:5
16 And the Angel of the LORD said to
Manoah, "Though you detain Me, I will not
eat your food. But if you offer a burnt offering,
you must offer it to the LORD." (For Manoah
did not know He *was* the Angel of the LORD.)
17 Then Manoah said to the Angel of the
LORD, "What *is* Your name, that when Your
words come *to pass* we may honor You?"
18 And the Angel of the LORD said to him,
[R]"Why do you ask My name, seeing it *is* won-
derful?" Gen. 32:29
19 So Manoah took the young goat with the
grain offering, and offered it upon the rock to
the LORD. And He did a wondrous thing while
Manoah and his wife looked on—
20 it happened as the flame went up toward
heaven from the altar—the Angel of the LORD
ascended in the flame of the altar! When
Manoah and his wife saw *this*, they [R]fell on
their faces to the ground. Ezek. 1:28
21 When the Angel of the LORD appeared no
more to Manoah and his wife, then Manoah
knew that He *was* the Angel of the LORD.
22 And Manoah said to his wife, "We shall
surely die, because we have seen God!"
23 But his wife said to him, "If the LORD had
desired to kill us, He would not have accepted
a burnt offering and a grain offering from our
hands, nor would He have shown us all these
things, nor would He have told us *such things*
as these at this time."
24 So the woman bore a son and called his
name [R]Samson; and [R]the child grew, and the
LORD blessed him. Heb. 11:32 • 1 Sam. 3:19
25 [R]And the Spirit of the LORD began to
move upon him at Mahaneh Dan* [R]between
Zorah and Eshtaol. Judg. 3:10 • Judg. 18:11

CHAPTER 14

Sinful Marriage of Samson

NOW Samson went down [R]to Timnah, and
saw a woman in Timnah of the daugh-
ters of the Philistines. Josh. 15:10, 57
2 So he went up and told his father and
mother, saying, "I have seen a woman in Tim-
nah of the daughters of the Philistines; now
therefore, get her for me as a wife."
3 Then his father and mother said to him,
"*Is there* no woman among the daughters of
[R]your brethren, or among all my people, that
you must go and get a wife from the [R]uncir-
cumcised Philistines?" And Samson said to
his father, "Get her for me, for she pleases me
well." Gen. 24:3, 4 • Gen. 34:14
4 But his father and mother did not know
that it was [R]of the LORD—that He was seeking
an occasion to move against the Philistines.
For at that time the Philistines had dominion
over Israel. Josh. 11:20
5 So Samson went down to Timnah with his
father and mother, and came to the vineyards
of Timnah.
Now *to his* surprise, a young lion *came*
roaring against him.
6 And [R]the Spirit of the LORD came might-
ily upon him, and he tore the lion apart as
one would have torn apart a young goat,
though *he had* nothing in his hand. But he did
not tell his father or his mother what he had
done. Judg. 3:10
7 Then he went down and talked with the
woman; and she pleased Samson well.
8 After some time, when he returned to get
her, he turned aside to see the carcass of the
lion. And behold, a swarm of bees and honey
were in the carcass of the lion.
9 He took some of it in his hands and went
along, eating. When he came to his father
and mother, he gave *some* to them, and they
also ate. But he did not tell them that he had
taken the honey out of the [R]carcass of the
lion. Lev. 11:27
10 So his father went down to the woman.
And Samson gave a feast there, for young
men used to do so.
11 And it happened, when they saw him, that
they brought thirty companions to be with him.
12 Then Samson said to them, "Let me
[R]pose a riddle to you. If you can correctly
solve and explain it to me [R]within the seven
days of the feast, then I will give you thirty
linen garments and thirty [R]changes of cloth-
ing. Ezek. 17:2 • Gen. 29:27 • 2 Kin. 5:22
13 "But if you cannot explain *it* to me, then
you shall give me thirty linen garments and
thirty changes of clothing." And they said to
him, [R]"Pose your riddle, that we may hear
it." Ezek. 17:2
14 So he said to them:

"Out of the eater came something to eat,
And out of the strong came something
sweet."

Now for three days they could not explain the
riddle.
15 But it came to pass on the seventh* day
that they said to Samson's wife, [R]"Entice
your husband, that he may explain the rid-
dle to us, [R]or else we will burn you and your
father's house with fire. Have you invited us
in order to take what is ours? *Is that* not
so?" Judg. 16:5 • Judg. 15:6
16 Then Samson's wife wept on him, and
said, [R]"You only hate me! You do not love me!
You have posed a riddle to the sons of my peo-
ple, but you have not explained *it* to me." And
he said to her, "Look, I have not explained *it*
to my father or my mother; so should I ex-
plain *it* to you?" Judg. 16:15

13:25 Lit. *Camp of Dan*, Judg. 18:12 **14:15** So with MT, Tg., Vg.; LXX, Syr. *fourth*

17 Now she had wept on him the seven days while their feast lasted. And it happened on the seventh day that he told her, because she pressed him so much. Then she explained the riddle to the sons of her people.

18 So the men of the city said to him on the seventh day before the sun went down:

"What *is* sweeter than honey?
And what *is* stronger than a lion?"

And he said to them:

"If you had not plowed with my heifer,
You would not have solved my riddle!"

19 Then [R]the Spirit of the LORD came upon him mightily, and he went down to Ashkelon and killed thirty of their men, took their apparel, and gave the changes *of clothing* to those who had explained the riddle. So his anger was aroused, and he went back up to his father's house. Judg. 3:10; 13:25

20 And Samson's wife was *given* to his companion, who had been his best man.

CHAPTER 15

Judgeship of Samson

AFTER a while, in the time of wheat harvest, it happened that Samson visited his wife with a young goat. And he said, "Let me go in to my wife, into *her* room." But her father would not permit him to go in.

2 Her father said, "I really thought that you thoroughly [R]hated her; therefore I gave her to your companion. *Is* not her younger sister better than she? Please, take her instead." Judg. 14:20

3 And Samson said to them, "This time I shall be blameless regarding the Philistines if I harm them!"

4 Then Samson went and caught three hundred foxes; and he took torches, turned *the foxes* tail to tail, and put a torch between each pair of tails.

5 When he had set the torches on fire, he let *the foxes* go into the standing grain of the Philistines, and burned up both the shocks and the standing grain, as well as the vineyards *and* olive groves.

6 Then the Philistines said, "Who has done this?" And they answered, "Samson, the son-in-law of the Timnite, because he has taken his wife and given her to his companion." So the Philistines came up and burned her and her father with fire.

7 Samson said to them, "Since you would do a thing like this, I will surely take revenge on you, and after that I will cease."

8 So he attacked them hip and thigh with a great slaughter; then he went down and dwelt in the cleft of the rock of Etam.

9 Now the Philistines went up, encamped in Judah, and deployed themselves [R]against Lehi. Judg. 15:19

10 And the men of Judah said, "Why have you come up against us?" So they answered, "We have come up to [T]arrest Samson, to do to him as he has done to us." Lit. *bind*

11 Then three thousand men of Judah went down to the cleft of the rock of Etam, and said to Samson, "Do you not know that the Philistines rule over us? What *is* this you have done to us?" And he said to them, "As they did to me, so I have done to them."

12 But they said to him, "We have come down to arrest you, that we may deliver you into the hand of the Philistines." Then Samson said to them, "Swear to me that you will not kill me yourselves."

13 So they spoke to him, saying, "No, but we will tie you securely and deliver you into their hand; but we will surely not kill you." And they bound him with two new ropes and brought him up from the rock.

14 When he came to Lehi, the Philistines came shouting against him. Then [R]the Spirit of the LORD came mightily upon him; and the ropes that *were* on his arms became like flax that is burned with fire, and his bonds broke loose from his hands. Judg. 3:10; 14:6

15 He found a fresh jawbone of a donkey, reached out his hand and took it, and [R]killed a thousand men with it. Lev. 26:8

16 Then Samson said:

"With the jawbone of a donkey,
Heaps upon heaps,
With the jawbone of a donkey
I have slain a thousand men!"

17 And so it was, when he had finished speaking, that he threw the jawbone from his hand, and called that place Ramath Lehi.*

18 Then he became very thirsty; so he cried out to the LORD and said, "You have given this great deliverance by the hand of Your servant; and now shall I die of thirst and fall into the hand of the uncircumcised?"

19 So God split the hollow place that *is* in Lehi,* and water came out, and he drank; and [R]his spirit returned, and he revived. Therefore he called its name En Hakkore,* which is in Lehi to this day. Is. 40:29

20 And he judged Israel twenty years [R]in the days of the Philistines. Judg. 13:1

CHAPTER 16

Failure of Samson

NOW Samson went to Gaza and saw a harlot there, and went in to her.

15:17 Lit. *Jawbone Height* **15:19** Lit. *Jawbone*, Judg. 15:14 • Lit. *Spring of the Caller*

2 *When* the Gazites *were told,* "Samson
has come here!" they [R]surrounded *the place*
and lay in wait for him all night at the gate of
the city. They were quiet all night, saying, "In
the morning, when it is daylight, we will kill
him." 1 Sam. 23:26
3 And Samson lay *low* till midnight; then
he arose at midnight, took hold of the doors of
the gate of the city and the two gateposts,
pulled them up, bar and all, put *them* on his
shoulders, and carried them to the top of the
hill that faces Hebron.
4 Afterward it happened that he loved a
woman in the Valley of Sorek, whose name
was Delilah.
5 And the [R]lords of the Philistines came up
to her and said to her, [R]"Entice him, and find
out where his great strength *lies,* and by
what *means* we may overpower him, that we
may bind him to afflict him; and every one of
us will give you eleven hundred *pieces* of sil-
ver." Josh. 13:3 • Judg. 14:15
6 So Delilah said to Samson, "Please tell me
where your great strength *lies,* and with what
you may be bound to afflict you."
7 And Samson said to her, "If they bind me
with seven fresh bowstrings, not yet dried,
then I shall become weak, and be like any
other man."
8 So the lords of the Philistines brought up
to her seven fresh bowstrings, not yet dried,
and she bound him with them.
9 Now *men were* lying in wait, staying with
her in the room. And she said to him, "The
Philistines *are* upon you, Samson!" But he
broke the bowstrings as a strand of yarn
breaks when it touches fire. So the secret of
his strength was not known.
10 Then Delilah said to Samson, "Look, you
have mocked me and told me lies. Now, please
tell me what you may be bound with."
11 So he said to her, "If they bind me se-
curely with [R]new ropes that have never been
used, then I shall become weak, and be like
any *other* man." Judg. 15:13
12 Therefore Delilah took new ropes and
bound him with them, and said to him, "The
Philistines *are* upon you, Samson!" And *men
were* lying in wait, staying in the room. But he
broke them off his arms like a thread.
13 Delilah said to Samson, "Until now you
have mocked me and told me lies. Tell me
what you may be bound with." And he said to
her, "If you weave the seven locks of my head
into the web of the loom"—
14 So she wove *it* tightly with the batten of
the loom, and said to him, "The Philistines *are*
upon you, Samson!" But he awoke from his
sleep, and pulled out the batten and the web
from the loom.
15 Then she said to him, [R]"How can you say,
'I love you,' when your heart *is* not with me?
You have mocked me these three times, and
have not told me where your great strength
lies." Judg. 14:16
16 And it came to pass, when she pestered
him daily with her words and pressed him, *so*
that his soul was vexed to death,
17 that he [R]told her all his heart, and said to
her, "No razor has ever come upon my head,
for I *have been* a Nazirite to God from my
mother's womb. If I am shaven, then my
strength will leave me, and I shall become
weak, and be like any *other* man." [Mic. 7:5]
18 When Delilah saw that he had told her all
his heart, she sent and called for the lords of
the Philistines, saying, "Come up once more,
for he has told me all his heart." So the lords
of the Philistines came up to her and brought
the money in their hand.
19 [R]Then she lulled him to sleep on her
knees, and called for a man and had him
shave off the seven locks of his head. Then
she began to torment him,* and his strength
left him. Prov. 7:26, 27
20 And she said, "The Philistines *are* upon
you, Samson!" So he awoke from his sleep,
and said, "I will go out as before, at other
times, and shake myself free!" But he did
not know that the LORD [R]had departed from
him. [Josh. 7:12]
21 Then the Philistines took him and put out
his eyes, and brought him down to Gaza. They
bound him with bronze fetters, and he be-
came a grinder in the prison.
22 However, the hair of his head began to
grow again after it had been shaven.
23 Now the lords of the Philistines gathered
together to offer a great sacrifice to Dagon
their god, and to rejoice. And they said:

"Our god has delivered into our hands
Samson our enemy!"

24 When the people saw him, they [R]praised
their god; for they said: Dan. 5:4

"Our god has delivered into our hands
our enemy,
The destroyer of our land,
And the one who multiplied our dead."

25 So it happened, when their hearts were
[R]merry, that they said, "Call for Samson, that
he may perform for us." So they called for
Samson from the prison, and he performed
for them. And they stationed him between the
pillars. Judg. 9:27
26 Then Samson said to the lad who held
him by the hand, "Let me feel the pillars
which support the temple, so that I can lean
on them."
27 Now the temple was full of men and
women. All the lords of the Philistines *were*

16:19 So with MT, Tg., Vg.; LXX *he began to be weak,*

there—about three thousand men and women on the [R]roof watching while Samson performed. Deut. 22:8

28 Then Samson called to the LORD, saying, "O Lord GOD, [R]remember me, I pray! Strengthen me, I pray, just this once, O God, that I may with one *blow* take vengeance on the Philistines for my two eyes!" Jer. 15:15

29 And Samson took hold of the two middle pillars which supported the temple, and he braced himself against them, one on his right and the other on his left.

30 Then Samson said, "Let me die with the Philistines!" And he pushed with *all his* might, and the temple fell on the lords and all the people who *were* in it. So the dead that he killed at his death were more than he had killed in his life.

31 And his brothers and all his father's household came down and took him, and brought *him* up and buried him between Zorah and Eshtaol in the tomb of his father Manoah. He had judged Israel twenty years.

CHAPTER 17

Example of Personal Idolatry

NOW there was a man from the mountains of Ephraim, whose name *was* [R]Micah. Judg. 18:2

2 And he said to his mother, "The eleven hundred *shekels* of silver that were taken from you, and on which you put a curse, even saying it in my ears—here *is* the silver with me; I took it." And his mother said, "*May you be* blessed by the LORD, my son!"

3 So when he had returned the eleven hundred *shekels* of silver to his mother, his mother said, "I had wholly dedicated the silver from my hand to the LORD for my son, to make a carved image and a molded image; now therefore, I will return it to you."

4 Thus he returned the silver to his mother. Then his mother [R]took two hundred *shekels* of silver and gave them to the silversmith, and he made it into a carved image and a molded image; and they were in the house of Micah. Is. 46:6

5 The man Micah had a [R]shrine, and made an [R]ephod and household idols;* and he consecrated one of his sons, who became his priest. Judg. 18:24 • Judg. 8:27; 18:14

6 [R]In those days *there was* no king in Israel; [R]everyone did *what was* right in his own eyes. Judg. 18:1; 19:1 • Deut. 12:8

7 Now there was a young man from Bethlehem in Judah, of the family of Judah; he *was* a Levite, and was staying there.

8 The man departed from the city of Bethlehem in Judah to stay wherever he could find *a place*. Then he came to the mountains of Ephraim, to the house of Micah, as he journeyed.

9 And Micah said to him, "Where do you come from?" So he said to him, "I *am* a Levite from Bethlehem in Judah, and I am on my way to find *a place* to stay."

10 Micah said to him, "Dwell with me, [R]and be a [R]father and a priest to me, and I will give you ten *shekels* of silver per year, a suit of clothes, and your sustenance." So the Levite went in. Judg. 18:19 • Gen. 45:8

11 Then the Levite was content to dwell with the man; and the young man became like one of his sons to him.

12 So Micah [R]consecrated the Levite, and the young man [R]became his priest, and lived in the house of Micah. Judg. 17:5 • Judg. 18:30

13 Then Micah said, "Now I know that the LORD will be good to me, since I have a Levite as [R]priest!" Judg. 18:4

CHAPTER 18

Example of Tribal Idolatry

IN those days *there was* no king in Israel. And in those days the tribe of the Danites was seeking an inheritance for itself to dwell in; for until that day *their* inheritance among the tribes of Israel had not fallen to them.

2 So the children of Dan sent five men of their family from their territory, men of valor from [R]Zorah and Eshtaol, [R]to spy out the land and search it. They said to them, "Go, search the land." So they went to the mountains of Ephraim, to the house of Micah, and lodged there. Judg. 13:25 • Num. 13:17

3 While they *were* at the house of Micah, they recognized the voice of the young Levite. They turned aside and said to him, "Who brought you here? What are you doing in this *place*? What do you have here?"

4 He said to them, "Thus and so Micah did for me. He has [R]hired me, and I have become his priest." Judg. 17:10, 12

5 So they said to him, "Please inquire of God, that we may know whether the journey on which we go will be prosperous."

6 And the priest said to them, [R]"Go in peace. The presence of the LORD *be* with you on your way." 1 Kin. 22:6

7 So the five men departed and went to [R]Laish. They saw the people who *were* there, [R]how they dwelt safely, in the manner of the Sidonians, quiet and secure. *There were* no rulers in the land who might put *them* to shame for anything. They *were* far from the [R]Sidonians, and they had no ties with anyone.* Josh. 19:47 • Judg. 18:27–29 • Judg. 10:12

8 Then *the spies* came back to their brethren at Zorah and Eshtaol, and their brethren said to them, "What *is* your *report?*"

17:5 Heb. *teraphim* **18:7** So with MT, Tg., Vg.; LXX *with Syria*

9 So they said, [R]"Arise, let us go up against
them. For we have seen the land, and indeed
it *is* very good. *Would* you [R]*do* nothing? Do
not hesitate to go, *and* enter to possess the
land. Num. 13:30 • 1 Kin. 22:3
10 "When you go, you will come to a [R]se-
cure people and a large land. For God has
given it into your hands, [R]a place where
there is no lack of anything that *is* on the
earth." Judg. 18:7, 27 • Deut. 8:9
11 And six hundred men of the family of the
Danites went from there, from Zorah and
Eshtaol, armed with weapons of war.
12 Then they went up and encamped in Kir-
jath Jearim in Judah. (Therefore they call that
place Mahaneh Dan* to this day. There *it is*,
west of Kirjath Jearim.)
13 And they passed from there to the moun-
tains of Ephraim, and came to [R]the house of
Micah. Judg. 18:2
14 [R]Then the five men who had gone to spy
out the country of Laish answered and said
to their brethren, "Do you know that [R]there
are in these houses an ephod, household
idols, a carved image, and a molded image?
Now therefore, consider what you should
do." 1 Sam. 14:28 • Judg. 17:5
15 So they turned aside there, and came to
the house of the young Levite man—to the
house of Micah—and greeted him.
16 The six hundred men armed with their
weapons of war, who *were* of the children of
Dan, stood by the entrance of the gate.
17 Then [R]the five men who had gone to spy
out the land went up. Entering there, they
took [R]the carved image, the ephod, the house-
hold idols, and the molded image. The priest
stood at the entrance of the gate with the six
hundred men *who were* armed with weapons
of war. Judg. 18:2, 14 • Judg. 17:4, 5
18 When these went into Micah's house and
took the carved image, the ephod, the house-
hold idols, and the molded image, the priest
said to them, "What are you doing?"
19 And they said to him, "Be quiet, [R]put your
hand over your mouth, and come with us; be
a father and a priest to us. *Is it* better for you
to be a priest to the household of one man, or
that you be a priest to a tribe and a family in
Israel?" Job 21:5; 29:9; 40:4
20 So the priest's heart was glad; and he
took the ephod, the household idols, and the
carved image, and took his place among the
people.
21 Then they turned and departed, and put
the little ones, the livestock, and the goods in
front of them.
22 When they were a good way from the
house of Micah, the men who *were* in the
houses near Micah's house gathered together
and overtook the children of Dan.
23 And they called out to the children of
Dan. So they turned around and said to
Micah, [R]"What ails you, that you have gath-
ered such a company?" 2 Kin. 6:28
24 So he said, "You have taken away my
gods which I made, and the priest, and you
have gone away. Now what more do I have?
How can you say to me, 'What ails you?' "
25 And the children of Dan said to him, "Do
not let your voice be heard among us, lest an-
gry men fall upon you, and you lose your life,
with the lives of your household!"
26 Then the children of Dan went their way.
And when Micah saw that they *were* too
strong for him, he turned and went back to his
house.
27 So they took *the things* Micah had made,
and the priest who had belonged to him, and
went to Laish, to a people quiet and secure;
[R]and they struck them with the edge of the
sword and burned the city with fire. Josh. 19:47
28 *There was* no deliverer, because it *was*
[R]far from Sidon, and they had no ties with
anyone. It was in the valley that belongs [R]to
Beth Rehob. So they rebuilt the city and dwelt
there. Judg. 18:7 • 2 Sam. 10:6
29 And [R]they called the name of the city
Dan, after the name of Dan their father, who
was born to Israel. However, the name of the
city formerly *was* Laish. Josh. 19:47
30 Then the children of Dan set up for them-
selves the carved image; and Jonathan the
son of Gershom, the son of Manasseh,* and
his sons were priests to the tribe of Dan until
the day of the captivity of the land.
31 So they set up for themselves Micah's
carved image which he made, all the time that
the house of God was in Shiloh.

CHAPTER 19

Example of Personal Immorality

AND it came to pass in those days, when
there was no king in Israel, that there
was a certain Levite staying in the remote
mountains of Ephraim. He took for himself a
concubine from Bethlehem in Judah.
2 But his concubine played the harlot
against him, and went away from him to her
father's house at Bethlehem in Judah, and
was there four whole months.
3 Then her husband arose and went after
her, to [R]speak [T]kindly to her *and* bring her
back, having his servant and a couple of don-
keys with him. So she brought him into her fa-
ther's house; and when the father of the
young woman saw him, he was glad to meet
him. Gen. 34:3; 50:21 • Lit. *to her heart*
4 Now his father-in-law, the young woman's
father, detained him; and he stayed with him
three days. So they ate and drank and lodged
there.

18:12 Lit. *Camp of Dan* **18:30** LXX, Vg. *Moses*

5 Then it came to pass on the fourth day
that they arose early in the morning, and he
stood to depart; but the young woman's father
said to his son-in-law, [R]"Refresh your heart
with a morsel of bread, and afterward go your
way." Gen. 18:5
6 So they sat down, and the two of them ate
and drank together. Then the young woman's
father said to the man, "Please be content to
stay all night, and let your heart be merry."
7 And when the man stood to depart, his
father-in-law urged him; so he lodged there
again.
8 Then he arose early in the morning on the
fifth day to depart, but the young woman's
father said, "Please refresh your heart." So
they delayed until afternoon; and both of
them ate.
9 And when the man stood to depart—
he and his concubine and his servant—his
father-in-law, the young woman's father, said
to him, "Look, the day is now drawing toward
evening; please spend the night. See, the day
is coming to an end; lodge here, that your
heart may be merry. Tomorrow go your way
early, so that you may get home."
10 However, the man was not willing to
spend that night; so he rose and departed, and
came to opposite Jebus (that *is*, Jerusalem).
With him were the two saddled donkeys; his
concubine *was* also with him.

Example of Tribal Immorality

11 They *were* near Jebus, and the day was
far spent; and the servant said to his master,
"Come, please, and let us turn aside into this
city of the Jebusites and lodge in it."
12 But his master said to him, "We will not
turn aside here into a city of foreigners, who
are not of the children of Israel; we will go on
[R]to Gibeah." Josh. 18:28
13 So he said to his servant, "Come, let us
draw near to one of these places, and spend
the night in Gibeah or in Ramah."
14 And they passed by and went their way;
and the sun went down on them near Gibeah,
which belongs to Benjamin.
15 They turned aside there to go in to lodge
in Gibeah. And when he went in, he sat down
in the open square of the city, for no one
would [R]take them into *his* house to spend the
night. Matt. 25:43
16 Just then an old man came in from [R]his
work in the field at evening, who also *was*
from the mountains of Ephraim; he was stay-
ing in Gibeah, whereas the men of the place
were Benjamites. Ps. 104:23
17 And when he raised his eyes, he saw the
traveler in the open square of the city; and the
old man said, "Where are you going, and
where do you come from?"
18 So he said to him, "We *are* passing from
Bethlehem in Judah toward the remote moun-
tains of Ephraim; I *am* from there. I went to
Bethlehem in Judah; *now* I am going to the
house of the LORD. But there *is* no one who
will take me into his house,
19 "although we have both straw and fodder
for our donkeys, and bread and wine for my-
self, for your female servant, and for the
young man *who is* with your servant; *there is*
no lack of anything."
20 And the old man said, [R]"Peace *be* with
you! However, *let* all your needs *be* my re-
sponsibility; [R]only do not spend the night in
the open square." Gen. 43:23 • Gen. 19:2
21 So he brought him into his house, and
gave fodder to the donkeys. And they washed
their feet, and ate and drank.
22 As they were enjoying themselves, sud-
denly certain men of the city, perverted men,*
surrounded the house *and* beat on the door.
They spoke to the master of the house, the old
man, saying, [R]"Bring out the man who came
to your house, that we may know him *car-*
nally!" [Rom. 1:26, 27]
23 But [R]the man, the master of the house,
went out to them and said to them, "No, my
brethren! I beg you, do not act *so* wickedly!
Seeing this man has come into my house, do
not commit this outrage. Gen. 19:6, 7
24 [R]"Look, *here is* my virgin daughter and
*the man's** concubine; let me bring them out
now. [R]Humble them, and do with them as you
please; but to this man do not do such a vile
thing!" Gen. 19:8 • Gen. 34:2
25 But the men would not heed him. So the
man took his concubine and brought *her* out
to them. And they knew her and abused her
all night until morning; and when the day
began to break, they let her go.
26 Then the woman came as the day was
dawning, and fell down at the door of the man's
house where her master *was*, till it was light.
27 When her master arose in the morning,
and opened the doors of the house and went
out to go his way, there was his concubine,
fallen *at* the door of the house with her hands
on the threshold.
28 And he said to her, "Get up and let us be
going." But [R]there was no answer. So the man
lifted her onto the donkey; and the man got up
and went to his place. Judg. 20:5
29 When he entered his house he took a
knife, laid hold of his concubine, and [R]di-
vided her into twelve pieces, limb by limb,*
and sent her throughout all the territory of Is-
rael. 1 Sam. 11:7
30 And so it was that all who saw it said, "No
such deed has been done or seen from the day
that the children of Israel came up from the
land of Egypt until this day. Consider it, [R]con-
fer, and speak up!" Judg. 20:7

19:22 Lit. *sons of Belial* **19:24** Lit. *his* **19:29** Lit. *with her bones*

CHAPTER 20

War Between Israel and Benjamin

SO [R]all the children of Israel came out, from [R]Dan to Beersheba, as well as from the land of Gilead, and the congregation gathered together as one man before the LORD at Mizpah. Josh. 22:12 • 2 Sam. 3:10; 24:2

2 And the leaders of all the people, all the tribes of Israel, presented themselves in the assembly of the people of God, four hundred thousand foot soldiers who drew the sword.

3 (Now the children of Benjamin heard that the children of Israel had gone up to Mizpah.) Then the children of Israel said, "Tell *us*, how did this wicked deed happen?"

4 So the Levite, the husband of the woman who was murdered, answered and said, "My concubine and [R]I went into Gibeah, which belongs to Benjamin, to spend the night. Judg. 19:15

5 [R]"And the men of Gibeah rose against me, and surrounded the house at night because of me. They intended to kill me, [R]but instead they ravished my concubine so that she died. Judg. 19:22 • Judg. 19:25, 26

6 "So [R]I took hold of my concubine, cut her in pieces, and sent her throughout all the territory of the inheritance of Israel, because they [R]committed lewdness and outrage in Israel. Judg. 19:29 • Josh. 7:15

7 "Look! All of you *are* children of Israel; [R]give your advice and counsel here and now!" Judg. 19:30

8 So all the people arose as one man, saying, "None *of us* will go to his tent, nor will any turn back to his house;

9 "but now this *is* the thing which we will do to Gibeah: *We will go up* against it by lot.

10 "We will take ten men out of *every* hundred throughout all the tribes of Israel, a hundred out of *every* thousand, and a thousand out of *every* ten thousand, to make provisions for the people, that when they come to Gibeah in Benjamin, they may repay all the vileness that they have done in Israel."

11 So all the men of Israel were gathered against the city, united together as one man.

12 [R]Then the tribes of Israel sent men through all the tribe of Benjamin, saying, "What *is* this wickedness that has occurred among you? Deut. 13:14

13 "Now therefore, deliver up the men, [R]the perverted men* who *are* in Gibeah, that we may put them to death and remove the evil from Israel!" But the children of Benjamin would not listen to the voice of their brethren, the children of Israel. Deut. 13:13

14 Instead, the children of Benjamin gathered together from their cities to Gibeah, to go to battle against the children of Israel.

15 And from their cities at that time [R]the children of Benjamin numbered twenty-six thousand men who drew the sword, besides the inhabitants of Gibeah, who numbered seven hundred select men. Num. 1:36, 37

16 Among all this people *were* seven hundred select men *who were* [R]left-handed; every one could sling a stone at a hair's *breadth* and not miss. 1 Chr. 12:2

17 Now besides Benjamin, the men of Israel numbered four hundred thousand men who drew the sword; all of these *were* men of war.

18 Then the children of Israel arose and went up to the house of God* to inquire of God. They said, "Which of us shall go up first to battle against the children of Benjamin?" The LORD said, "Judah first!"

19 So the children of Israel rose in the morning and encamped against Gibeah.

20 And the men of Israel went out to battle against Benjamin, and the men of Israel put themselves in battle array to fight against them at Gibeah.

21 Then [R]the children of Benjamin came out of Gibeah, and on that day cut down to the ground twenty-two thousand men of the Israelites. [Gen. 49:27]

22 And the people, that is, the men of Israel, encouraged themselves and again formed the battle line at the place where they had put themselves in array on the first day.

23 [R]Then the children of Israel went up and wept before the LORD until evening, and asked counsel of the LORD, saying, "Shall I again draw near for battle against the children of my brother Benjamin?" And the LORD said, "Go up against him." Judg. 20:26, 27

24 So the children of Israel approached the children of Benjamin on the second day.

25 And [R]Benjamin went out against them from Gibeah on the second day, and cut down to the ground eighteen thousand more of the children of Israel; all these drew the sword. Judg. 20:21

26 Then all the children of Israel, that is, all the people, went up and came to the house of God* and wept. They sat there before the LORD and fasted that day until evening; and they offered burnt offerings and peace offerings before the LORD

27 So the children of Israel inquired of the LORD ([R]the ark of the covenant of God *was* there in those days, Josh. 18:1

28 [R]and Phinehas the son of Eleazar, the son of Aaron, [R]stood before it in those days), saying, "Shall I yet again go out to battle against the children of my brother Benjamin, or shall I cease?" And the LORD said, "Go up, for tomorrow I will deliver them into your hand." Josh. 24:33 • Deut. 10:8; 18:5

29 Then Israel [R]set men in ambush all around Gibeah. Josh. 8:4

30 And the children of Israel went up against

20:13 Lit. *sons of Belial* **20:18** Or *Bethel* **20:26** Or *Bethel*

the children of Benjamin on the third day, and
put themselves in battle array against Gibeah
as at the other times.
31 So the children of Benjamin went out
against the people, *and* were drawn away
from the city. They began to strike down *and*
kill some of the people, as at the other times,
in the highways [R](one of which goes up to
Bethel and the other to Gibeah) and in the
field, about thirty men of Israel. Judg. 21:19
32 And the children of Benjamin said, "They
are defeated before us, as at first." But the
children of Israel said, "Let us flee and draw
them away from the city to the highways."
33 So all the men of Israel rose from their
place and put themselves in battle array at
Baal Tamar. Then Israel's men in ambush
burst forth from their position in the plain of
Geba.
34 And ten thousand select men from all Is-
rael came against Gibeah, and the battle was
fierce. But *the Benjamites** did not know that
disaster *was* upon them.
35 The LORD defeated Benjamin before Is-
rael. And the children of Israel destroyed that
day twenty-five thousand one hundred Ben-
jamites; all these drew the sword.
36 So the children of Benjamin saw that they
were defeated. [R]The men of Israel had given
ground to the Benjamites, because they relied
on the men in ambush whom they had set
against Gibeah. Josh. 8:15
37 [R]And the men in ambush quickly rushed
upon Gibeah; the men in ambush spread out
and struck the whole city with the edge of the
sword. Josh. 8:19
38 Now the appointed signal between the
men of Israel and the men in ambush was that
they would make a great cloud of [R]smoke rise
up from the city, Josh. 8:20
39 whereupon the men of Israel would turn
in battle. Now Benjamin had begun to strike
and kill about thirty of the men of Israel. For
they said, "Surely they are defeated before us,
as *in* the first battle."
40 But when the cloud began to rise from the
city in a column of smoke, the Benjamites
looked behind them, and there was the whole
city going up *in smoke* to heaven.
41 And when the men of Israel turned back,
the men of Benjamin panicked, for they saw
that disaster had come upon them.
42 Therefore they [T]turned *their backs* before
the men of Israel in the direction of the
wilderness; but the battle overtook them, and
whoever *came* out of the cities they destroyed
in their midst. *fled*
43 They surrounded the Benjamites, chased
them, *and* easily trampled them down as far
as the front of Gibeah toward the east.
44 And eighteen thousand men of Benjamin
fell; all these *were* men of valor.
45 Then they* turned and fled toward the
wilderness to the rock of [R]Rimmon; and they
cut down five thousand of them on the high-
ways. Then they pursued them relentlessly
up to Gidom, and killed two thousand of
them. Josh. 15:32
46 So all who fell of Benjamin that day were
twenty-five thousand men who drew the
sword; all these *were* men of valor.
47 [R]But six hundred men turned and fled to-
ward the wilderness to the rock of Rimmon,
and they stayed at the rock of Rimmon for
four months. Judg. 21:13
48 And the men of Israel turned back
against the children of Benjamin, and struck
them down with the edge of the sword—from
every city, men and beasts, all who were
found. They also set fire to all the cities they
came to.

CHAPTER 21

Israel's Foolish Vow

NOW the men of Israel had sworn an oath
at Mizpah, saying, "None of us shall give
his daughter to Benjamin as a wife."
2 Then the people came [R]to the house of
God,* and remained there before God till
evening. They lifted up their voices and wept
bitterly, Judg. 20:18, 26
3 and said, "O LORD God of Israel, why has
this come to pass in Israel, that today there
should be one tribe *missing* in Israel?"
4 So it was, on the next morning, that the
people rose early and [R]built an altar there,
and offered burnt offerings and peace offer-
ings. 2 Sam. 24:25
5 The children of Israel said, "Who *is there*
among all the tribes of Israel who did not
come up with the assembly to the LORD?"
[R]For they had made a great oath concerning
anyone who had not come up to the LORD at
Mizpah, saying, "He shall surely be put to
death." Judg. 20:1–3
6 And the children of Israel grieved for
Benjamin their brother, and said, "One tribe is
cut off from Israel today.
7 "What shall we do for wives for those
who remain, seeing we have sworn by the
LORD that we will not give them our daughters
as wives?"

Men at Jabesh Gilead Murdered

8 And they said, "What one *is there* from
the tribes of Israel who did not come up to
Mizpah to the LORD?" And, in fact, no one had
come to the camp from [R]Jabesh Gilead to the
assembly. 1 Sam. 11:1; 31:11
9 For when the people were counted, in-
deed, not one of the inhabitants of Jabesh
Gilead *was* there.
10 So the congregation sent out there twelve

20:34 Lit. *they* **20:45** LXX *the rest* **21:2** Or *Bethel*

thousand of their most valiant men, and com-
manded them, saying, [R]"Go and strike the in-
habitants of Jabesh Gilead with the edge of
the sword, including the women and chil-
dren. Num. 31:17
11 "And this *is* the thing that you shall do:
[R]You shall utterly destroy every male, and
every woman who has known a man inti-
mately." Num. 31:17
12 So they found among the inhabitants of
Jabesh Gilead four hundred young virgins
who had not known a man intimately; and
they brought them to the camp at [R]Shiloh,
which is in the land of Canaan. Josh. 18:1
13 Then the whole congregation sent *word*
to the children of Benjamin [R]who *were* at the
rock of Rimmon, and announced peace to
them. Judg. 20:47
14 So Benjamin came back at that time, and
they gave them the women whom they had
saved alive of the women of Jabesh Gilead;
and yet they had not found enough for them.
15 And the people [R]grieved for Benjamin,
because the LORD had made a void in the
tribes of Israel. Judg. 21:6

Women of Shiloh Kidnapped

16 Then the elders of the congregation said,
"What shall we do for wives for those who re-
main, since the women of Benjamin have
been destroyed?"
17 And they said, "*There must be* an inheri-
tance for the survivors of Benjamin, that a
tribe may not be destroyed from Israel.
18 "However, we cannot give them wives
from our daughters, for the children of Israel
have sworn an oath, saying, 'Cursed *be* the
one who gives a wife to Benjamin.' "
19 Then they said, "In fact, *there is* a yearly
[R]feast of the LORD in [R]Shiloh, which *is* north of
Bethel, on the east side of the highway that
goes up from Bethel to Shechem, and south of
Lebonah." Lev. 23:2 • 1 Sam. 1:3
20 Therefore they instructed the children of
Benjamin, saying, "Go, lie in wait in the vine-
yards,
21 "and watch; and just when the daughters
of Shiloh come out [R]to perform their dances,
then come out from the vineyards, and every
man catch a wife for himself from the daugh-
ters of Shiloh; then go to the land of Benja-
min. Judg. 11:34
22 "Then it shall be, when their fathers or
their brothers come to us to complain, that we
will say to them, 'Be kind to them for our
sakes, because we did not take a wife for any
of them in the war; for *it is* not *as though* you
have given the *women* to them at this time,
making yourselves guilty of your oath.' "
23 And the children of Benjamin did so;
they took enough wives for their number
from those who danced, whom they caught.
Then they went and returned to their inheri-
tance, and they [R]rebuilt the cities and dwelt in
them. Judg. 20:48
24 So the children of Israel departed from
there at that time, every man to his tribe and
family; they went out from there, every man
to his inheritance.
25 [R]In those days *there was* no king in Is-
rael; [R]everyone did *what was* right in his own
eyes. Judg. 17:6; 18:1; 19:1 • Judg. 17:6

THE BOOK OF

RUTH

THE BOOK OF RUTH

Ruth is a cameo story of love, devotion, and redemption set in the grim context of the days of the judges. It is the story of a Moabite woman who forsakes her pagan heritage in order to cling to the people of Israel and to the God of Israel. Because of her *faithfulness* in a time of national *faithlessness,* God rewards her by giving her a new husband (Boaz), a son (Obed), and a privileged position in the lineage of David and Christ (she is the great-grandmother of David).

Ruth is the Hebrew title of this book. This name may be a Moabite modification of the Hebrew word *reuit,* meaning "friendship" or "association." The Septuagint entitles the book *Routh,* the Greek equivalent of the Hebrew name. The Latin title is *Ruth,* a transliteration of *Routh.*

THE AUTHOR OF RUTH

The author of Ruth is not given anywhere in the book, nor is he known from any other biblical passage. Talmudic tradition attributes it to Samuel but this is unlikely since David appears in Ruth 4:17, 22, and Samuel died before David's coronation (1 Sam. 25:1). Ruth was probably written during David's reign since Solomon's name is not included in the genealogy. The anonymity of the book, however, should not detract from its spiritual value or literary beauty.

THE TIME OF RUTH

Ruth divides neatly into four distinct settings: (1) the country of Moab (1:1–18); (2) a field in Bethlehem (1:19—2:23); (3) a threshing floor in Bethlehem (3:1–18); and (4) the city of Bethlehem (4:1–22).

The setting of the first eighteen verses is Moab, a region northeast of the Dead Sea. The Moabites, descendants of Lot, worshiped Chemosh and other pagan gods. Scripture records two times when they fight against Israel (Judg. 3:12–30 and 1 Sam. 14:47). Ruth takes place about two centuries after the first war and about eighty years before the second.

Ruth 1:1 gives the setting of the remainder of the book: "Now it came to pass, in the days when the judges ruled." This is a time of apostasy, warfare, decline, violence, moral decay, and anarchy. Ruth provides a cameo of the other side of the story—the godly remnant who remain true to the laws of God.

Because Ruth is written more to tell a beautiful story than to give all the historical facts of that period, the assignment of time is somewhat difficult. Utilizing the same fourfold division noted above, the following can be assigned:

A. Ruth 1:1–18 (see 1:4): The country of Moab (c. ten years)
B. Ruth 1:19—2:23 (see 1:22; 2:23): A field in Bethlehem (months)
C. Ruth 3:1–18 (see 3:2, 8, 14, 18): A threshing floor in Bethlehem (one day)
D. Ruth 4:1–22 (see 4:13–16): The city of Bethlehem (c. one year)

THE CHRIST OF RUTH

The concept of the kinsman-redeemer or *goel* (3:9, "close relative") is an important portrayal of the work of Christ. The *goel* must (1) be related by blood to those he redeems (Deut. 25:5, 7–10; John 1:14; Rom. 1:3; Phil. 2:5–8; Heb. 2:14, 15); (2) be able to pay the price of redemption (2:1; 1 Pet. 1:18, 19); (3) be willing to redeem (3:11; Matt. 20:28; John 10:15, 18; Heb. 10:7); (4) be free himself (Christ was free from the curse of sin). The word *goel,* used thirteen times in this short book, presents a clear picture of the mediating work of Christ.

KEYS TO RUTH

Key Word: Kinsman-Redeemer—The Hebrew word for kinsman (*goel*) appears thirteen times in Ruth and basically means "one who redeems." By buying back the land of Naomi, as well as marrying Ruth and fathering a son to keep the family line alive, Boaz acts as a redeemer.

Key Verses: Ruth 1:16; 3:11—"But Ruth said: 'Entreat me not to leave you, *or to* turn back from following after you; for wherever you go, I will go; and wherever you lodge, I will lodge; your people *shall be* my people, and your God my God' " (1:16).

"And now, my daughter, do not fear. I will do for you all that you request, for all the people of my town know that you *are* a virtuous woman" (3:11).

Key Chapter: Ruth 4—In twenty-two short verses, Ruth moves from widowhood and poverty to marriage and wealth (2:1). In exercising the law regulating the redemption of property (Lev. 25:25–34) and the law concerning a brother's duty to raise up seed (children) in the name of the deceased (Deut. 25:5–10), Boaz brings a Moabite woman into the family line of David and eventually of Jesus Christ.

SURVEY OF RUTH

Ruth is the story of a virtuous woman who lives above the norm of her day. Although it was probably written during the time of David, the events take place during the time of the judges. This period in Israel's history was generally a desert of rebellion and immorality, but the story of Ruth stands in contrast as an oasis of integrity and righteousness.

Ruth is "a virtuous woman" (3:11) who shows loyal love to her mother-in-law Naomi and her near-kinsman Boaz. In both relationships, goodness and love are clearly manifested. Her love is demonstrated in chapters 1 and 2 and rewarded in chapters 3 and 4.

Ruth's Love Is Demonstrated (1 and 2): The story begins with a famine in Israel, a sign of disobedience and apostasy (Deut. 25—30). An Israelite named Elimelech ("My God Is King") in a desperate act moves from Bethlehem ("House of Bread"—note the irony) to Moab. Although he seeks life in that land, he and his two sons, Mahlon ("Sick") and Chilion ("Pining"), find only death. The deceased sons leave two Moabite widows, Orpah ("Stubbornness") and Ruth ("Friendship"). Elimelech's widow, Naomi, hears that the famine in Israel is over and decides to return, no longer as Naomi ("Pleasant") but as Mara ("Bitter"). She tells her daughters-in-law to remain in Moab and remarry since there was no security for an unmarried woman in those days. Orpah chooses to leave Naomi and is never mentioned again. Ruth, on the other hand, resolves to cling to Naomi and follow Yahweh, the God of Israel. She therefore gives up her culture, people, and language because of her love.

Naomi's misfortune leads her to think that God is her enemy, but He has plans she does not yet realize. In her plight, she must let Ruth glean at the edge of a field. This is a humiliating and dangerous task because of the character of many of the reapers. However, God's providential care brings her to the field of Boaz, Naomi's kinsman. Boaz ("In Him Is Strength") begins to love, protect, and provide for her.

Ruth's Love Is Rewarded (3 and 4): Boaz takes no further steps toward marriage, so Naomi follows the accepted customs of the day and requests that Boaz exercise his right as kinsman-redeemer. In 3:10–13, Boaz reveals why he has taken no action: he is older than Ruth (perhaps twenty years her senior), and he is not the nearest kinsman. Nevertheless, God rewards Ruth's devotion by giving her Boaz as a husband and by providing her with a son, Obed, the grandfather of David.

FOCUS	RUTH'S LOVE DEMONSTRATED		RUTH'S LOVE REWARDED	
REFERENCE	1:1——1:19——	——3:1——	——4:1——	——4:22
DIVISION	RUTH'S DECISION TO STAY WITH NAOMI	RUTH'S DEVOTION TO CARE FOR NAOMI	RUTH'S REQUEST FOR REDEMPTION BY BOAZ	RUTH'S REWARD OF REDEMPTION BY BOAZ
TOPIC	RUTH AND NAOMI		RUTH AND BOAZ	
	DEATH OF FAMILY	RUTH CARES FOR NAOMI	BOAZ CARES FOR RUTH	BIRTH OF FAMILY
LOCATION	MOAB	FIELDS OF BETHLEHEM	THRESHING FLOOR OF BETHLEHEM	BETHLEHEM
TIME	c. 12 YEARS			

OUTLINE OF RUTH

Part One: Ruth's Love Is Demonstrated (1:1—2:23)

I. Ruth's Decision to Remain with Naomi 1:1–18

A. Ruth's Need to Remain with Naomi 1:1–5

B. Ruth's Opportunity to Leave Naomi 1:6–15

C. Ruth's Choice to Remain with Naomi 1:16–18

II. Ruth's Devotion to Care for Naomi .... 1:19—2:23

A. Ruth and Naomi Return to Bethlehem 1:19–22

B. Ruth Gleans for Food 2:1–23

1. Boaz Meets Ruth 2:1–7
2. Boaz Protects Ruth 2:8–16
3. Boaz Provides for Ruth 2:17–23

Part Two: Ruth's Love Is Rewarded (3:1—4:22)

I. Ruth's Request for Redemption by Boaz 3:1–18

A. Naomi Seeks Redemption for Ruth 3:1–5
B. Ruth Obeys Naomi 3:6–9
C. Boaz Desires to Redeem Ruth 3:10–18

II. Ruth's Reward of Redemption by Boaz 4:1–22

A. Boaz Marries Ruth 4:1–12
B. Ruth Bears a Son, Obed 4:13–15
C. Naomi Receives a New Family 4:16
D. Ruth Is the Great-Grandmother of David 4:17–22

CHAPTER 1

Ruth's Need to Remain with Naomi

NOW it came to pass, in the days when
[R]the judges ruled, that there was a
famine in the land. And a certain man of
[R]Bethlehem, Judah, went to dwell in the coun-
try of [R]Moab, he and his wife and his two
sons. Judg. 2:16–18 • Judg. 17:8 • Gen. 19:37
2 The name of the man *was* Elimelech, the
name of his wife *was* Naomi, and the names
of his two sons *were* Mahlon and Chilion—
[R]Ephrathites of Bethlehem, Judah. And they
went [R]to the country of Moab and remained
there. Gen. 35:19 • Judg. 3:30
3 Then Elimelech, Naomi's husband, died;
and she was left, and her two sons.
4 Now they took wives of the women of
Moab: the name of the one *was* Orpah, and
the name of the other Ruth. And they [T]dwelt
there about ten years. *lived*
5 Then both Mahlon and Chilion also died;
so the woman survived her two sons and her
husband.

Ruth's Opportunity to Leave Naomi

6 Then she arose with her daughters-in-law
that she might return from the country of
Moab, for she had heard in the country of
Moab that the LORD had [R]visited His people
by [R]giving them bread. Ex. 3:16; 4:31 • Matt. 6:11
7 Therefore she went out from the place
where she was, and her two daughters-in-law
with her; and they went on the way to return
to the land of Judah.
8 And Naomi said to her two daughters-in-
law, "Go, return each to her mother's house.
The LORD deal kindly with you, as you have
dealt with the dead and with me.
9 "The LORD grant that you may find [R]rest,
each in the house of her husband." So she
kissed them, and they lifted up their voices
and wept. Ruth 3:1
10 And they said to her, "Surely we will re-
turn with you to your people."
11 But Naomi said, "Turn back, my daugh-
ters; why will you go with me? *Are* there still
sons in my womb, [R]that they may be your hus-
bands? Deut. 25:5
12 "Turn back, my daughters, go—for I am
too old to have a husband. If I should say I
have hope, *if* I should have a husband tonight
and should also bear sons,
13 "would you wait for them till they were
grown? Would you restrain yourselves from
having husbands? No, my daughters; for it
grieves me very much for your sakes that
[R]the hand of the LORD has gone out against
me!" Judg. 2:15
14 Then they lifted up their voices and wept
again; and Orpah kissed her mother-in-law,
but Ruth [R]clung to her. [Prov. 17:17]
15 And she said, "Look, your sister-in-law
has gone back to her people and to her gods;
return after your sister-in-law."

Ruth's Choice to Remain with Naomi

16 But Ruth said:

[T]"Entreat me not to leave you, *Urge me not*
Or to turn back from following after you;
For wherever you go, I will go;
And wherever you lodge, I will lodge;
[R]Your people *shall be* my people,
And your God, my God. Ruth 2:11, 12
17 Where you die, I will die,
And there will I be buried.
The LORD do so to me, and more also,
If *anything but* death parts you and me."

18 [R]When she saw that she [T]was deter-
mined to go with her, she stopped speaking
to her. Acts 21:14 • Lit. *made herself strong to go*

Ruth and Naomi Return to Bethlehem

19 Now the two of them went until they
came to Bethlehem. And it happened, when
they had come to Bethlehem, that [R]all the city
was excited because of them; and the women
said, "*Is* this Naomi?" Matt. 21:10
20 But she said to them, "Do not call me
Naomi;* call me Mara,* for the Almighty has
dealt very bitterly with me.
21 "I went out full, [R]and the LORD has
brought me home again empty. Why do you
call me Naomi, since the LORD has testified
against me, and [T]the Almighty has afflicted
me?" Job 1:21 • Heb. *Shaddai*

1:20 Lit. *Pleasant* • Lit. *Bitter*

22 So Naomi returned, and Ruth the Moabitess her daughter-in-law with her, who returned from the country of Moab. Now they came to Bethlehem [R]at the beginning of barley harvest. 2 Sam. 21:9

CHAPTER 2

Boaz Meets Ruth

THERE was a relative of Naomi's husband, a man of great wealth, of the family of Elimelech. His name *was* Boaz.

2 So Ruth the Moabitess said to Naomi, "Please let me go to the [R]field, and glean heads of grain after *him* in whose sight I may find favor." And she said to her, "Go, my daughter." Lev. 19:9, 10; 23:22

3 Then she left, and went and gleaned in the field after the reapers. And she happened to come to the part of the field *belonging* to Boaz, who *was* of the family of Elimelech.

4 Now behold, Boaz came from [R]Bethlehem, and said to the reapers, [R]"The LORD *be* with you!" And they answered him, "The LORD bless you!" Ruth 1:1 • Ps. 129:7, 8

5 Then Boaz said to his servant who was in charge of the reapers, "Whose young woman *is* this?"

6 So the servant who was in charge of the reapers answered and said, "It *is* the young Moabite woman [R]who came back with Naomi from the country of Moab. Ruth 1:22

7 "And she said, 'Please let me glean and gather after the reapers among the sheaves.' So she came and has continued from morning until now, though she rested a little in the house."

Boaz Protects Ruth

8 Then Boaz said to Ruth, "You will listen, my daughter, will you not? Do not go to glean in another field, nor go from here, but stay close by my young women.

9 "*Let* your eyes *be* on the field which they reap, and go after them. Have I not commanded the young men not to touch you? And when you are thirsty, go to the vessels and drink from what the young men have drawn."

10 So she fell on her face, bowed down to the ground, and said to him, "Why have I found favor in your eyes, that you should take notice of me, since I *am* a foreigner?"

11 And Boaz answered and said to her, "It has been fully reported to me, all that you have done for your mother-in-law since the death of your husband, and *how* you have left your father and your mother and the land of your birth, and have come to a people whom you did not know before.

12 [R]"The LORD repay your work, and a full reward be given you by the LORD God of Israel, [R]under whose wings you have come for refuge." 1 Sam. 24:19 • Ruth 1:16

13 Then she said, [R]"Let me find favor in your sight, my lord; for you have comforted me, and have spoken kindly to your maidservant, [R]though I am not like one of your maidservants." Gen. 33:15 • 1 Sam. 25:41

14 Now Boaz said to her at mealtime, "Come here, and eat of the bread, and dip your piece of bread in the vinegar." So she sat beside the reapers, and he passed parched *grain* to her; and she ate and [R]was satisfied, and kept some back. Ruth 2:18

15 And when she rose up to [T]glean, Boaz commanded his young men, saying, "Let her glean even among the sheaves, and do not [T]reproach her. Gather after the reapers • *rebuke*

16 "Also let *grain* from the bundles fall purposely for her; leave *it* that she may glean, and do not rebuke her."

Boaz Provides for Ruth

17 So she gleaned in the field until evening, and beat out what she had gleaned, and it was about an ephah of [R]barley. Ruth 1:22

18 Then she took *it* up and went into the city, and her mother-in-law saw what she had gleaned. So she brought out and gave to her [R]what she had kept back after she had been satisfied. Ruth 2:14

19 And her mother-in-law said to her, "Where have you gleaned today? And where did you work? Blessed be the one who [R]took notice of you." So she told her mother-in-law with whom she had worked, and said, "The man's name with whom I worked today *is* Boaz." [Ps. 41:1]

20 Then Naomi said to her daughter-in-law, [R]"Blessed *be* he of the LORD, who [R]has not forsaken His kindness to the living and the dead!" And Naomi said to her, "This man *is* a relation of ours, [R]one of our close relatives." 2 Sam. 2:5 • Prov. 17:17 • Ruth 3:9; 4:4, 6

21 Ruth the Moabitess said, "He also said to me, 'You shall stay close by my young men until they have finished all my harvest.'"

22 And Naomi said to Ruth her daughter-in-law, "*It is* good, my daughter, that you go out with his young women, and that people do not meet you in any other field."

23 So she stayed close by the young women of Boaz, to glean until the end of barley harvest and wheat harvest; and she dwelt with her mother-in-law.

CHAPTER 3

Naomi Seeks Redemption for Ruth

THEN Naomi her mother-in-law said to her, "My daughter, shall I not seek security for you, that it may be well with you?

2 "Now Boaz, [R]whose young women you were with, *is he* not our relative? In fact, he is winnowing barley tonight at the threshing floor. Ruth 2:3, 8

3 "Therefore wash yourself and [R]anoint yourself, put on your *best* garment and go down to the threshing floor; *but* do not make yourself known to the man until he has finished eating and drinking. 2 Sam. 14:2

4 "Then it shall be, when he lies down, that you shall notice the place where he lies; and you shall go in, uncover his feet, and lie down; and he will tell you what you should do."

5 And she said to her, "All that you say to me I will do."

Ruth Obeys Naomi

6 So she went down to the threshing floor and did according to all that her mother-in-law instructed her.

7 And after Boaz had eaten and drunk, and [R]his heart was cheerful, he went to lie down at the end of the heap of grain; and she came softly, uncovered his feet, and lay down. Judg. 19:6, 9, 22

8 Now it happened at midnight that the man was startled, and turned himself; and there, a woman was lying at his feet.

9 And he said, "Who *are* you?" So she answered, "I *am* Ruth, your maidservant. [R]Take your maidservant under your wing,* for you are a close relative." Ezek. 16:8

Boaz Desires to Redeem Ruth

10 Then he said, [R]"Blessed *are* you of the LORD, my daughter! For you have shown more kindness at the end than [R]at the beginning, in that you did not go after young men, whether poor or rich. Ruth 2:20 • Ruth 1:8

11 "And now, my daughter, do not fear. I will do for you all that you request, for all the people of my town know that you *are* [R]a virtuous woman. Prov. 12:4; 31:10–31

12 "Now it is true that I *am* a [R]close relative; however, [R]there is a relative closer than I. Ruth 3:9 • Ruth 4:1

13 "Stay this night, and in the morning it shall be *that* if he will perform the duty of a close relative for you—good; let him do it. But if he does not want to perform the duty for you, then I will perform the duty for you, *as* the LORD lives! Lie down until morning."

14 So she lay at his feet until morning, and she arose before one could recognize another. Then he said, "Do not let it be known that the woman came to the threshing floor."

15 Also he said, "Bring the [T]shawl that *is* on you and hold it." And when she held it, he measured six *ephahs* of barley, and laid *it* on her. Then she* went into the city. *cloak*

16 When she came to her mother-in-law, she said, [T]"*Is* that you, my daughter?" Then she told her all that the man had done for her. Or *How are you,*

17 And she said, "These six *ephahs* of barley he gave me; for he said to me, 'Do not go empty-handed to your mother-in-law.' "

18 Then she said, [R]"Sit still, my daughter, until you know how the matter will turn out; for the man will not rest until he has concluded the matter this day." [Ps. 37:3, 5]

CHAPTER 4

Boaz Marries Ruth

NOW Boaz went up to the gate and sat down there; and behold, the close relative of whom Boaz had spoken came by. So Boaz said, "Come aside, friend,* sit down here." So he came aside and sat down.

2 And he took ten men of [R]the elders of the city, and said, "Sit down here." So they sat down. 1 Kin. 21:8

3 Then he said to the close relative, "Naomi, who has come back from the country of Moab, sold the piece of land [R]which *belonged* to our brother Elimelech. Lev. 25:25

4 "And I thought to inform you, saying, [R]'Buy *it* back [R]in the presence of the inhabitants and the elders of my people. If you will redeem *it*, redeem *it;* but if you* will not redeem *it*, *then* tell me, that I may know; [R]for *there is* no one but you to redeem *it*, and I *am* next after you.' " And he said, "I will redeem *it.*" Jer. 32:7, 8 • Gen. 23:18 • Lev. 25:25

5 Then Boaz said, "On the day you buy the field from the hand of Naomi, you must also buy *it* from Ruth the Moabitess, the wife of the dead, [R]to perpetuate* the name of the dead through his inheritance." Matt. 22:24

6 And the close relative said, "I cannot redeem *it* for myself, lest I ruin my own inheritance. You redeem my right of redemption for yourself, for I cannot redeem *it*."

7 Now this *was the custom* in former times in Israel concerning redeeming and exchanging, to confirm anything: one man took off his sandal and gave *it* to the other, and this *was* a confirmation in Israel.

8 Therefore the close relative said to Boaz, "Buy *it* for yourself." So he took off his sandal.

9 And Boaz said to the elders and all the people, "You *are* witnesses this day that I have bought all that was Elimelech's, and all that *was* Chilion's and Mahlon's, from the hand of Naomi.

10 "Moreover, Ruth the Moabitess, the widow of Mahlon, I have acquired as my wife, to perpetuate the name of the dead through his inheritance, [R]that the name of the dead may not be cut off from among his brethren and from his position at the gate.* You *are* witnesses this day." Deut. 25:6

11 And all the people who *were* at the gate,

3:9 Or *Spread the corner of your garment over your maidservant* **3:15** Many Heb. mss., Syr., Vg. *she;* MT, LXX, Tg. *he* **4:1** Heb. *peloni almoni,* lit. *so and so* **4:4** So with many Heb. mss., LXX, Syr., Tg., Vg.; MT *he* **4:5** Lit. *raise up* **4:10** Probably his civic office

and the elders, said, "*We are* witnesses. The
LORD make the woman who is coming to your
house like Rachel and Leah, the two who
built the house of Israel; and may you pros-
per in [R]Ephrathah and be famous in [R]Bethle-
hem. Gen. 35:16–18 • Mic. 5:2
12 "May your house be like the house of
[R]Perez, whom Tamar bore to Judah, because
of the offspring which the LORD will give you
from this young woman." Matt. 1:3

Ruth Bears a Son, Obed

13 So Boaz took Ruth and she became his
wife; and when he went in to her, the LORD
gave her conception, and she bore a son.
14 Then [R]the women said to Naomi, "Blessed
be the LORD, who has not left you this day
without a close relative; and may his name be
famous in Israel! Luke 1:58
15 "And may he be to you a restorer of life
and a nourisher of your old age; for your
daughter-in-law, who loves you, who is better
to you than seven sons, has borne him."

Naomi Receives a Family

16 Then Naomi took the child and laid him
on her bosom, and became a nurse to him.

Ruth Is the Great-Grandmother of David
Matt. 1:3–6

17 Also the neighbor women gave him a
name, saying, "There is a son born to Naomi."
And they called his name Obed. He *is* the fa-
ther of Jesse, the father of David.
18 [R]Now this *is* the genealogy of Perez: Perez
begot Hezron; 1 Chr. 2:4, 5
19 Hezron begot Ram, and Ram begot Am-
minadab;
20 Amminadab begot Nahshon, and Nah-
shon begot [R]Salmon;* Matt. 1:4
21 Salmon begot Boaz, and Boaz begot
Obed;
22 Obed begot Jesse, and Jesse begot [R]Da-
vid. Matt. 1:6

4:20 Heb. *Salmah*

The Jewish Calendar

The Jews used two kinds of calendars:
Civil Calendar—official calendar of kings, childbirth, and contracts
Sacred Calendar—from which festivals were computed.

NAMES OF MONTHS	CORRESPONDS WITH	NO. OF DAYS	MONTH OF CIVIL YEAR	MONTH OF SACRED YEAR
TISHRI	Sept.–Oct.	30 days	1st	7th
HESHVAN	Oct.–Nov.	29 or 30	2nd	8th
CHISLEV	Nov.–Dec.	29 or 30	3rd	9th
TEBETH	Dec.–Jan.	29	4th	10th
SHEBAT	Jan.–Feb.	30	5th	11th
ADAR	Feb.–Mar.	29 or 30	6th	12th
NISAN	Mar.–Apr.	30	7th	1st
IYAR	Apr.–May	29	8th	2nd
SIVAN	May–June	30	9th	3rd
TAMMUZ	June–July	29	10th	4th
AB	July–Aug.	30	11th	5th
*ELUL	Aug.–Sept.	29	12th	6th

The Jewish day was from sunset to sunset, in 8 equal parts:

FIRST WATCH ....SUNSET TO 9 P.M.
SECOND WATCH ....9 P.M. TO MIDNIGHT
THIRD WATCH ....MIDNIGHT TO 3 A.M.
FOURTH WATCH ....3 A.M. TO SUNRISE

FIRST WATCH ....SUNRISE TO 9 A.M.
SECOND WATCH ....9 A.M. TO NOON
THIRD WATCH ....NOON TO 3 P.M.
FOURTH WATCH ....3 P.M. TO SUNSET

*Hebrew months were alternately 30 and 29 days long. Their year, shorter than ours, had 354 days. Therefore, about every 3 years (7 times in 19 years) an extra 29-day-month, VEADAR, was added between ADAR and NISAN.

THE FIRST BOOK OF

SAMUEL

THE BOOK OF 1 SAMUEL

The Book of 1 Samuel describes the transition of leadership in Israel from judges to kings. Three characters are prominent in the book: Samuel, the last judge and first prophet; Saul, the first king of Israel; and David, the king-elect, anointed but not yet recognized as Saul's successor.

The books of 1 and 2 Samuel were originally one book in the Hebrew Bible, known as the "Book of Samuel" or simply "Samuel." This name has been variously translated "The Name of God," "His Name Is God," "Heard of God," and "Asked of God." The Septuagint divides Samuel into two books even though it is one continuous account. This division artificially breaks up the history of David. The Greek (Septuagint) title is *Bibloi Basileion,* "Books of Kingdoms," referring to the later kingdoms of Israel and Judah. First Samuel is called *Basileion Alpha,* "First Kingdoms." Second Samuel and 1 and 2 Kings are called "Second, Third, and Fourth Kingdoms." The Latin Vulgate originally called the books of Samuel and Kings *Libri Regum,* "Books of the Kings." Later the Latin Bible combined the Hebrew and Greek titles for the first of these books, calling it *Liber I Samuelis,* the "First Book of Samuel," or simply "First Samuel."

THE AUTHOR OF 1 SAMUEL

The author of 1 and 2 Samuel is anonymous, but Jewish talmudic tradition says that it was written by Samuel. Samuel may have written the first portion of the book, but his death recorded in 1 Samuel 25:1 makes it clear that he did not write all of 1 and 2 Samuel. Samuel did write a book (10:25), and written records were available. As the head of a company of prophets (10:5; 19:20), Samuel would be a logical candidate for biblical authorship.

First Chronicles 29:29 refers to "the book of Samuel the Seer," "the book of Nathan the Prophet," and "the book of Gad the seer." All three men evidently contributed to these two books; and it is very possible that a single compiler, perhaps a member of the prophetic school, used these chronicles to put together the Book of Samuel. This is also suggested by the unity of plan and purpose and by the smooth transitions between sections.

THE TIME OF 1 SAMUEL

If Samuel wrote the material in the first twenty-four chapters, he did so soon before his death (c. 1015 B.C.). He was born around 1105 B.C. and ministered as a judge and prophet in Israel between about 1067 and 1015 B.C. The books of Samuel end in the last days of David; so they must have been compiled after 971 B.C. The reference in 1 Samuel 27:6 to the divided monarchy in which Judah is separate from Israel indicates a compilation date after Solomon's death in 931 B.C. However, the silence regarding the Assyrian captivity of Israel in 722 B.C. probably means that 1 Samuel was written before this key event.

First Samuel covers the ninety-four-year period from the birth of Samuel to the death of Saul (c. 1105–1011 B.C.). The Philistines strongly oppress Israel from 1087 B.C. until the battle of Ebenezer in 1047 B.C. (7:10–14). However, even after this time the Philistines exercise military and economic control. They live in the coastal plains; and the hill country in which the Israelites dwell protects them from total conquest by the Philistines.

THE CHRIST OF 1 SAMUEL

Samuel is a type of Christ in that he is a prophet, priest, and judge. Highly revered by the people, he brings in a new age.

David is one of the primary Old Testament portrayals of the Person of Christ. He is born in Bethlehem, works as a shepherd, and rules as king of Israel. He is the anointed king who becomes the forerunner of the messianic King. His typical messianic psalms are born of his years of rejection and danger (see Ps. 22). God enables David, a man "after His own heart" (13:14), to become Israel's greatest king. The New Testament specifically calls Christ the "seed of David according to the flesh" (Rom. 1:3) and "the Root and the Offspring of David" (Rev. 22:16).

KEYS TO 1 SAMUEL

Key Word: Transition—First Samuel records the critical transition in Israel from the rule of God through the judges to His rule through the kings.

This transition goes through three stages: Eli to Samuel, Samuel to Saul, and Saul to David.

Key Verses: 1 Samuel 13:14; 15:22—"But now your kingdom shall not continue. The LORD has sought for Himself a man after His own heart, and the LORD has commanded him *to be* commander over His people, because you have not kept what the LORD commanded you" (13:14).

"So Samuel said, 'Has the LORD *as great* delight in burnt offerings and sacrifices, as in obeying the voice of the LORD? Behold, to obey is better than sacrifice, *and* to heed than the fat of rams' " (15:22).

Key Chapter: 1 Samuel 15—First Samuel 15 records the tragic transition of kingship from Saul to David. As in all three changes recorded in 1 Samuel, God removes His blessing from one and gives it to another because of sin. "Because you have rejected the word of the LORD, He also has rejected you from *being* king" (15:23).

SURVEY OF 1 SAMUEL

First Samuel records the crucial transition from the theocracy under the judges to the monarchy under the kings. The book is built around three key men: Samuel (1—7), Saul (8—31), and David (16—31).

Samuel (1—7): Samuel's story begins late in the turbulent time of the judges when Eli is the judge-priest of Israel. The birth of Samuel and his early call by Yahweh are found in chapters 1—3. Because of his responsiveness to God (3:19), he is confirmed as a prophet (3:20, 21) at a time when the "word of the LORD was rare . . . *there was* no widespread revelation" (3:1).

Corruption at Shiloh by Eli's notoriously wicked sons leads to Israel's defeat in the crucial battle with the Philistines (4:1–11). The ark of the covenant, God's "throne" among the people, is lost to the Philistines; the priesthood is disrupted by the deaths of Eli and his sons; and the glory of God departs from the tabernacle (Ichabod, "No Glory," 4:21). Samuel begins to function as the last of the judges and the first in the order of the prophets (Acts 3:24). His prophetic ministry (7:3–17) leads to a revival in Israel, the return of the ark, and the defeat of the Philistines. When Samuel is old and his sons prove to be unjust judges, the people wrongly cry out for a king. They want a visible military and judicial ruler so they can be "like all the nations" (8:5–20).

Saul (8—15): In their impatient demand for a king, Israel chooses less than God's best. Their motive (8:5) and criteria (9:2) are wrong. Saul begins well (9—11), but his good characteristics soon degenerate. In spite of Samuel's solemn prophetic warning (12), Saul and the people begin to act wickedly. Saul presumptuously assumes the role of a priest (cf. 2 Chr. 26:18) and offers up sacrifices (13). He makes a foolish vow (14) and disobeys God's command to destroy the Amalekites (15). Samuel's powerful words in 15:22, 23 evoke a pathetic response in 15:24–31.

Saul and David (16—31): When God rejects Saul, He commissions Samuel to anoint David as Israel's next king. God's king-elect serves in Saul's court (16:14—23:29) and defeats the Philistine Goliath (17). Jonathan's devotion to David leads him to sacrifice the throne (20:30, 31) in acknowledgment of David's divine right to it (18). David becomes a growing threat to the insanely jealous Saul; but he is protected from Saul's wrath by Jonathan, Michal, and Samuel (19).

Saul's open rebellion against God is manifested in his refusal to give up what God has said cannot be his. David is protected again by Jonathan from Saul's murderous intent (20), but Saul becomes more active in his pursuit of David. The future king flees to a Philistine city where he feigns insanity (21), and flees again to Adullam where a band of men forms around him (22).

David continues to escape from the hand of Saul, and on two occasions spares Saul's life when he has the opportunity to take it (24—26). David again seeks refuge among the Philistines, but is not allowed to fight on their side against Israel. Saul, afraid of impending battle against the Philistines, foolishly consults a medium at En Dor to hear the deceased Samuel's advice (28). The Lord rebukes Saul and pronounces his doom; he and his sons are killed by the Philistines on Mount Gilboa (31).

FOCUS	SAMUEL		SAUL		
REFERENCE	1:1—	4:1—	8:1—	13:1—	15:10—31:13
DIVISION	FIRST TRANSITION OF LEADERSHIP: ELI—SAMUEL	JUDGESHIP OF SAMUEL	SECOND TRANSITION OF LEADERSHIP: SAMUEL—SAUL	REIGN OF SAUL	THIRD TRANSITION OF LEADERSHIP: SAUL—DAVID
TOPIC	DECLINE OF JUDGES		RISE OF KINGS		
	ELI	SAMUEL	SAUL		DAVID
LOCATION	CANAAN				
TIME	c. 94 YEARS				

OUTLINE OF 1 SAMUEL

Part One: Samuel, the Last Judge (1:1—7:17)

I. The First Transition of National Leadership: Eli–Samuel ....1:1—3:21

- A. The Birth of the New Leader ....1:1—2:11
  - 1. Hannah's Barrenness 1:1–18
  - 2. Samuel's Birth...1:19–28
  - 3. Hannah's Prophetic Prayer 2:1–11
- B. The Need of the New Leader 2:12–36
  - 1. Sinfulness of Eli's Sons....................2:12–21
  - 2. Compromise of Eli as Father 2:22–36
- C. The Transition from Eli to Samuel 3:1–18
  - 1. The Word of the Lord Does Not Come to Eli..3:1
  - 2. The Word of the Lord Comes to Samuel...3:2–18
- D. Samuel Is Recognized as the New Leader of Israel 3:19–21

II. The Judgeship of Samuel...................4:1—7:17

- A. The Need for Samuel's Leadership ..4:1—6:21
  - 1. Conquest of Israel by Philistia.........4:1–10
  - 2. Eli and His Sons Die 4:11–22
  - 3. The Sin with the Ark ....5:1—6:21
- B. The Victories Under Samuel's Leadership 7:1–17
  - 1. The Acceptable Return of the Ark..7:1, 2
  - 2. Israel Returns to the Lord 7:3–6
  - 3. Israel's Victory over Philistia...........7:7–17

Part Two: Saul, the First King (8:1—31:13)

I. The Second Transition of National Leadership: Samuel–Saul ....8:1—12:25

- A. The Causes of the Transition................8:1–9
  - 1. Israel Rejects Samuel's Sons as Leaders 8:1–5
  - 2. Israel Rejects God as King 8:6–9
- B. The Transition from Samuel to Saul...................................8:10—12:25
  - 1. Samuel Warns Israel 8:10–22
  - 2. God Chooses Saul.........................9:1—10:16
  - 3. Samuel Anoints Saul 10:17–27
  - 4. Israel Makes Saul King..................11:1–15
  - 5. Samuel Confirms Saul....................12:1–25

II. The Reign of King Saul.....................13:1—15:9

- A. The Early Success of King Saul 13:1–4
- B. The Failures of King Saul ....13:5—15:9
  - 1. Saul's Sinful Sacrifices 13:5–23
  - 2. Saul's Selfish Curse 14:1–52
  - 3. Saul's Incomplete Obedience............15:1–9

III. The Third Transition of National Leadership: Saul–David..............15:10—31:13

- A. The Transition of Kingship from Saul to David.................................15:10—18:9
  - 1. God Rejects Saul as King 15:10–35
  - 2. God Anoints David as King...........16:1–13
  - 3. God Takes His Spirit from Saul...16:14–23
  - 4. God Confirms David over Saul ..17:1—18:9
- B. The Attempts of Saul to Slay David..18:10—20:42
  - 1. By Throwing a Spear at David 18:10–16
  - 2. By Tricking David to Fight the Philistines.......................................18:17–30
  - 3. By Commanding His Servants to Kill David 19:1–7
  - 4. By Throwing a Spear at David Again..19:8–10
  - 5. By Sending His Messengers to Kill David 19:11–17
  - 6. By Coming to Kill David at Samuel's House 19:18–24
  - 7. By Commanding Jonathan to Bring David to Be Killed 20:1–42
- C. The Rise of David in Exile..............21:1—28:2
  - 1. David Is Protected by the Priest......21:1–9
  - 2. David Pretends to Be Mad 21:10–15
  - 3. David Builds an Army in the Wilderness ....22:1—26:25
  - 4. David Joins with the Philistines...............................27:1—28:2
- D. The Final Decline of Saul............28:3—31:13
  - 1. God Does Not Answer Saul 28:3–6
  - 2. Saul Visits the Medium 28:7–25
  - 3. David Is Spared from Fighting Saul 29:1–11
  - 4. God Answers David 30:1–8
  - 5. David Kills the Enemy 30:9–31
  - 6. The Enemy Kills Saul.....................31:1–13

CHAPTER 1

Hannah's Barrenness

NOW there was a certain man of Rama-
thaim Zophim, of the mountains of
Ephraim, and his name *was* Elkanah the son
of Jeroham, the son of Elihu,* the son of
Tohu,* the son of Zuph, an Ephraimite.
2 And he had [R]two wives: the name of one
was Hannah, and the name of the other
Peninnah. Peninnah had children, but Han-
nah had no children. Deut. 21:15–17
3 This man went up from his city [R]yearly
[R]to worship and sacrifice to the LORD of hosts
in [R]Shiloh. Also the two sons of Eli, Hophni
and Phinehas, the priests of the LORD, *were*
there. Luke 2:41 • Deut. 12:5–7; 16:16 • Josh. 18:1
4 And whenever the time came for Elkanah

1:1 *Eliel,* 1 Chr. 6:34 • *Toah,* 1 Chr. 6:34

to make an [R]offering, he would give portions
to Peninnah his wife and to all her sons and
daughters. Deut. 12:17, 18
5 But to Hannah he would give a double
portion, for he loved Hannah, [R]although the
LORD had closed her womb. Gen. 16:1; 30:1, 2
6 And her rival also [R]provoked her se-
verely, to make her miserable, because the
LORD had closed her womb. Job 24:21
7 So it was, year by year, when she went up
to the house of the LORD, that she provoked
her; therefore she wept and did not eat.
8 Then Elkanah her husband said to her,
"Hannah, why do you weep? Why do you not
eat? And why is your heart grieved? *Am* I not
[R]better to you than ten sons?" Ruth 4:15
9 So Hannah arose after they had finished
eating and drinking in Shiloh. Now Eli the
priest was sitting on the seat by the doorpost
of the tabernacle* of the LORD.
10 And she *was* in bitterness of soul, and
prayed to the LORD and wept in anguish.
11 Then she [R]made a vow and said, "O
LORD of hosts, if You will indeed [R]look on the
affliction of Your maidservant and [R]remem-
ber me, and not forget Your maidservant, but
will give Your maidservant a male child, then
I will give him to the LORD all the days of
his life, and no razor shall come upon his
head." Num. 30:6–11 • Ps. 25:18 • Gen. 8:1
12 And it happened, as she continued praying
before the LORD, that Eli watched her mouth.
13 Now Hannah spoke in her heart; only her
lips moved, but her voice was not heard.
Therefore Eli thought she was drunk.
14 So Eli said to her, "How long will you be
drunk? Put your wine away from you!"
15 But Hannah answered and said, "No, my
lord, I *am* a woman of sorrowful spirit. I have
drunk neither wine nor intoxicating drink,
but have [R]poured out my soul before the
LORD. Ps. 42:4; 62:8
16 "Do not consider your maidservant a
[R]wicked woman,* for out of the abundance of
my complaint and grief I have spoken until
now." Deut. 13:13
17 Then Eli answered and said, "Go in peace,
and the God of Israel grant your petition
which you have asked of Him."
18 And she said, [R]"Let your maidservant
find favor in your sight." So the woman [R]went
her way and ate, and her face was no longer
sad. Ruth 2:13 • Rom. 15:13

Samuel's Birth

19 Then they rose early in the morning and
worshiped before the LORD, and returned and
came to their house at Ramah. And Elkanah
[R]knew Hannah his wife, and the LORD [R]re-
membered her. Gen. 4:1 • Gen. 21:1
20 So it came to pass in the process of time
that Hannah conceived and bore a son, and
called his name Samuel,* *saying,* "Because I
have asked for him from the LORD."
21 Now the man Elkanah and all his house
[R]went up to offer to the LORD the yearly sacri-
fice and his vow. 1 Sam. 1:3
22 But Hannah did not go up, for she said
to her husband, "*Not* until the child is
weaned; then I will [R]take him, that he may
appear before the LORD and [R]remain there
[R]forever." Luke 2:22 • 1 Sam. 1:11, 28 • Ex. 21:6
23 So [R]Elkanah her husband said to her,
"Do what seems best to you; wait until you
have weaned him. Only let the LORD [T]estab-
lish His* word." Then the woman stayed
and nursed her son until she had weaned
him. Num. 30:7, 10, 11 • *confirm*
24 Now when she had weaned him, she took
him up with her, with three bulls,* one ephah
of flour, and a skin of wine, and brought him
to the house of the LORD in Shiloh. And the
child *was* young.
25 Then they slaughtered a bull, and
[R]brought the child to Eli. Luke 2:22
26 And she said, "O my lord! [R]As your soul

1:9 *palace* or *temple,* Heb. *heykal* **1:16** Lit. *daughter of Belial* **1:20** Lit. *Heard by God* **1:23** So with MT, Tg., Vg.; DSS, LXX, Syr. *your* **1:24** DSS, LXX, Syr. *a three-year-old bull*

1:17 Petition—One great difference between Christianity and all other religions is that the believer has a prayer-hearing and prayer-answering God. In the OT during a contest with Elijah, the priests of Baal make desperate efforts to speak with their god by crying out and cutting themselves, but to no avail. "But *there was* no voice; no one answered" (Page 358—1 Kin. 18:26). How different from these words are those of the psalmist: "*But* certainly God has heard *me;* He has attended to the voice of my prayer" (Page 579—Ps. 66:19).

a. The nature of our petitions. First of all, God has commanded us to pray (Page 983—Matt. 7:7, 8; Page 1237—1 Tim. 2:8). When we pray, our petitions should be made by faith (Page 1272—James 1:6) in the name of Jesus (Page 1099—John 14:13). If these simple rules are followed, we can rest assured our prayers are being heard (Page 1295—1 John 3:22; 5:14, 15).

b. The objects of our prayers. For whom or what should we pray? First of all, we need to pray for ourselves, because unless we are in God's will, He cannot hear our petitions about other things. Thus we should begin by asking for cleansing (Page 1293—1 John 1:9) and wisdom (Page 1272—James 1:5). Other areas of our petitions concern spiritual leaders (Page 1222—Col. 4:3), sick believers (Page 1275—James 5:14, 15), rulers (Page 1237—1 Tim. 2:1–3), and even for our enemies (Page 982—Matt. 5:44).

Now turn to Page 1215—Phil. 4:6: Thanksgiving.

lives, my lord, I *am* the woman who stood by
you here, praying to the LORD. 2 Kin. 4:30
27 R"For this child I prayed, and the LORD
has granted me my petition which I asked of
Him. [Matt. 7:7]
28 "Therefore I also have lent him to the
LORD; as long as he lives he shall be Tlent
to the LORD." So they Rworshiped the LORD
there. *granted* • Gen. 24:26, 52

CHAPTER 2

Hannah's Prophetic Prayer

AND Hannah Rprayed and said: Phil. 4:6

"My heart rejoices in the LORD;
My horn* is exalted in the LORD.
I smile at my enemies,
Because I rejoice in Your salvation.

2 "NoR one is holy like the LORD, Ex. 15:11
For *there is* none besides You,
Nor *is there* any rock like our God.

3 "Talk no more so very proudly;
RLet no arrogance come from your
mouth, Ps. 94:4
For the LORD *is* the God of knowledge;
And by Him actions are weighed.

4 "TheR bows of the mighty men *are*
broken, Ps. 37:15; 46:9
And those who stumbled are girded with
strength.
5 *Those who were* full have hired
themselves out for bread,
And the hungry have ceased *to hunger.*
Even Rthe barren has borne seven,
And Rshe who has many children has
become feeble. Ps. 113:9 • Is. 54:1

6 "TheR LORD kills and makes alive;
He brings down to the grave and brings
up. Deut. 32:39
7 The LORD makes poor and makes rich;
RHe brings low and lifts up. Ps. 75:7
8 He raises the poor from the dust
And lifts the beggar from the ash heap,
RTo set *them* among princes Job 36:7
And make them inherit the throne of glory.

R"For the pillars of the earth *are* the
LORD's, Job 38:4–6
And He has set the world upon them.
9 RHe will guard the feet of His saints,
But the Rwicked shall be silent in
darkness. [1 Pet. 1:5] • [Rom. 3:19]

"For by strength no man shall prevail.
10 The adversaries of the LORD shall be
Rbroken in pieces; Ps. 2:9
RFrom heaven He will thunder against
them.
RThe LORD will judge the ends of the
earth. Ps. 18:13, 14 • Ps. 96:13; 98:9

"He will give strength to His king,
And exalt the horn of His anointed."

11 Then Elkanah went to his house at
Ramah. But the child Tministered to the LORD
before Eli the priest. *served*

Sinfulness of Eli's Sons

12 Now the sons of Eli *were* Rcorrupt;* they
did not know the LORD. Deut. 13:13
13 And the priests' custom with the people
was that when any man offered a sacrifice,
the priest's servant would come with a three-
pronged fleshhook in his hand while the meat
was boiling.
14 Then he would thrust *it* into the pan, or
kettle, or caldron, or pot; and the priest would
take for himself all that the fleshhook brought
up. So they did in RShiloh to all the Israelites
who came there. 1 Sam. 1:3
15 Also, before they Rburned the fat, the
priest's servant would come and say to the
man who sacrificed, "Give meat for roasting
to the priest, for he will not take boiled meat
from you, but raw." Lev. 3:3–5, 16
16 And *if* the man said to him, "They should
really burn the fat first; *then* you may take *as
much* as your heart desires," he would then
answer him, "*No,* but you must give *it* now;
and if not, I will take *it* by force."
17 Therefore the sin of the young men was
very great Rbefore the LORD, for men abhorred
the offering of the LORD. Gen. 6:11
18 But Samuel ministered before the LORD,
even as a child, wearing a linen ephod.
19 Moreover his mother used to make him a
little robe, and bring *it* to him year by year
when she Rcame up with her husband to offer
the yearly sacrifice. 1 Sam. 1:3, 21
20 And Eli Rwould bless Elkanah and his
wife, and say, "The LORD give you descen-
dants from this woman for the Tloan that was
given to the LORD." Then they would go to
their own home. Gen. 14:19 • *gift*
21 And the LORD RvisitedT Hannah, so that
she conceived and bore three sons and two
daughters. Meanwhile the child Samuel grew
before the LORD. Gen. 21:1 • *attended to*

Compromise of Eli as Father

22 Now Eli was very old; and he heard
everything his sons did to all Israel,* and how
they lay with the women who assembled at
the door of the tabernacle of meeting.
23 So he said to them, "Why do you do such
things? For I hear of your evil dealings from
all the people.

2:1 Strength **2:12** Lit. *sons of Belial* **2:22** So with MT, Tg., Vg.; DSS, LXX omit rest of verse

24 "No, my sons! For *it is* not a good report
that I hear. You make the LORD's people trans-
gress.
25 "If one man sins against another, [R]God
will judge him. But if a man [R]sins against
the LORD, who will intercede for him?" Nev-
ertheless they did not heed the voice of their
father, because the LORD desired to kill
them. Deut. 1:17; 25:1, 2 • Num. 15:30
26 And the child Samuel grew in stature, and
in favor both with the LORD and men.
27 Then a [R]man of God came to Eli and said
to him, "Thus says the LORD: [R]'Did I not
clearly reveal Myself to the house of your fa-
ther when they were in Egypt in Pharaoh's
house? 1 Kin. 13:1 • Ex. 4:14–16; 12:1
28 'Did I not [R]choose him out of all the tribes
of Israel *to be* My priest, to offer upon My
altar, to burn incense, and to wear an ephod
before Me? And did I not give to the house of
your father all the offerings of the children of
Israel made by fire? Ex. 28:1, 4
29 'Why do you kick at My sacrifice and My
offering which I have commanded *in My*
dwelling place, and honor your sons more
than Me, to make yourselves fat with the best
of all the offerings of Israel My people?'
30 "Therefore the LORD God of Israel says:
[R]'I said indeed *that* your house and the house
of your father would walk before Me forever.'
But now the LORD says: [R]'Far be it from Me;
for those who honor Me I will honor, and
those who despise Me shall be lightly es-
teemed. Ex. 29:9 • Jer. 18:9, 10
31 'Behold, [R]the days are coming that I will
cut off your [T]arm and the arm of your father's
house, so that there will not be an old man in
your house. 1 Kin. 2:27, 35 • *strength*
32 'And you will see an enemy *in My*
dwelling place, *despite* all the good which
God does for Israel. And there shall not be an
old man in your house forever.
33 'But any of your men *whom* I do not cut
off from My altar shall consume your eyes
and grieve your heart. And all the descen-
dants of your house shall die in the flower of
their age.
34 'Now this *shall be* [R]a sign to you that will
come upon your two sons, on Hophni and
Phinehas: [R]in one day they shall die, both of
them. 1 Kin. 13:3 • 1 Sam. 4:11, 17
35 'Then [R]I will raise up for Myself a faithful
priest *who* shall do according to what *is* in My
heart and in My mind. I will build him a sure
house, and he shall walk before [R]My anointed
forever. 1 Kin. 2:35 • Ps. 18:50
36 [R]'And it shall come to pass that everyone
who is left in your house will come *and* bow
down to him for a piece of silver and a morsel
of bread, and say, "Please, [T]put me in one of
the priestly positions, that I may eat a piece of
bread." ' " 1 Kin. 2:27 • *assign*

CHAPTER 3

The Word of the Lord Does Not Come to Eli

NOW the boy Samuel ministered to the
LORD before Eli. And [R]the word of the
LORD was rare in those days; *there was* no
widespread revelation. Ps. 74:9

The Word of the Lord Comes to Samuel

2 And it came to pass at that time, while Eli
was lying down in his place, and when his
eyes had begun to grow [R]so dim that he could
not see, 1 Sam. 4:15
3 and before the lamp of God went out in
the tabernacle* of the LORD where the ark of
God *was,* and while Samuel was lying down,
4 that the LORD called Samuel. And he an-
swered, "Here I am!"
5 So he ran to Eli and said, "Here I am, for
you called me." And he said, "I did not call; lie
down again." And he went and lay down.
6 Then the LORD called yet again, "Samuel!"
So Samuel arose and went to Eli, and said,
"Here I am, for you called me." He answered,
"I did not call, my son; lie down again."
7 (Now Samuel [R]did not yet know the LORD,
nor was the word of the LORD yet revealed to
him.) 1 Sam. 2:12
8 And the LORD called Samuel again the
third time. So he arose and went to Eli, and
said, "Here I am, for you did call me." Then Eli
perceived that the LORD had called the boy.
9 Therefore Eli said to Samuel, "Go, lie
down; and it shall be, if He calls you, that you
must say, [R]'Speak, LORD, for Your servant
hears.' " So Samuel went and lay down in his
place. 1 Kin. 2:17
10 Now the LORD came and stood and called
as at other times, "Samuel! Samuel!" And
Samuel answered, "Speak, for Your servant
hears."
11 Then the LORD said to Samuel: "Behold, I
will do something in Israel at which both ears
of everyone who hears it will tingle.
12 "In that day I will perform against Eli [R]all
that I have spoken concerning his house, from
beginning to end. 1 Sam. 2:27–36
13 "For I have told him that I will judge his
house forever for the iniquity which he
knows, because his sons made themselves
vile, and he did not restrain them.
14 "And therefore I have sworn to the house
of Eli that the iniquity of Eli's house [R]shall
not be atoned for by sacrifice or offering for-
ever." Num. 15:30, 31
15 So Samuel lay down until morning,* and
opened the doors of the house of the LORD.
And Samuel was afraid to tell Eli the vision.
16 Then Eli called Samuel and said, "Sam-
uel, my son!" He answered, "Here I am."

3:3 *palace* or *temple* **3:15** So with MT, Tg., Vg.; LXX adds *and he arose in the morning*

17 And he said, "What *is* the word that *the* LORD spoke to you? Please do not hide *it* from me. [R]God do so to you, and more also, if you hide anything from me of all the things that He said to you." Ruth 1:17

18 Then Samuel told him everything, and hid nothing from him. And he said, [R]"It *is* the LORD. Let Him do what seems good to Him." Is. 39:8

Samuel Is Recognized as the New Leader of Israel

19 So Samuel [R]grew, and the LORD was with him [R]and let none of his words [T]fall to the ground. 1 Sam. 2:21 • 1 Sam. 9:6 • *fail*

20 And all Israel [R]from Dan to Beersheba knew that Samuel *had been* [T]established as a prophet of the LORD. Judg. 20:1 • *confirmed*

21 Then the LORD appeared again in Shiloh. For the LORD revealed Himself to Samuel in Shiloh by the word of the LORD.

CHAPTER 4

Conquest of Israel by Philistia

AND the word of Samuel came to all Israel.*

Now Israel went out to battle against the Philistines, and encamped beside Ebenezer; and the Philistines encamped in Aphek.

2 Then the [R]Philistines put themselves in battle array against Israel. And when they joined battle, Israel was defeated by the Philistines, who killed about four thousand men of the army in the field. 1 Sam. 12:9

3 And when the people had come into the camp, the elders of Israel said, "Why has the LORD defeated us today before the Philistines? [R]Let us bring the ark of the covenant of the LORD from Shiloh to us, that when it comes among us it may save us from the hand of our enemies." Josh. 6:6–21

4 So the people sent to Shiloh, that they might bring from there the ark of the covenant of the LORD of hosts, [R]who dwells *between* the cherubim. And the two sons of Eli, Hophni and Phinehas, *were* there with the ark of the covenant of God. 1 Sam. 6:2

5 And when the ark of the covenant of the LORD came into the camp, all Israel shouted so loudly that the earth shook.

6 Now when the Philistines heard the noise of the shout, they said, "What *does* the sound of this great shout in the camp of the Hebrews *mean?*" Then they understood that the ark of the LORD had come into the camp.

7 So the Philistines were afraid, for they said, "God has come into the camp!" And they said, [R]"Woe to us! For such a thing has never happened before. Ex. 15:14

8 "Woe to us! Who will deliver us from the hand of these mighty gods? These *are* the gods who struck the Egyptians with all the plagues in the wilderness.

9 [R]"Be strong and conduct yourselves like men, you Philistines, that you do not become servants of the Hebrews, [R]as they have been to you. [T]Conduct yourselves like men, and fight!" 1 Cor. 16:13 • Judg. 13:1 • Lit. *Be men*

10 So the Philistines fought, and [R]Israel was [T]defeated, and every man fled to his tent. There was a very great slaughter, and there fell of Israel thirty thousand foot soldiers. Deut. 28:15, 25 • Lit. *struck down*

Eli and His Sons Die

11 Also [R]the ark of God was captured; and [R]the two sons of Eli, Hophni and Phinehas, died. Ps. 78:60, 61 • 1 Sam. 2:34

12 Then a man of Benjamin ran from the battle line the same day, and [R]came to Shiloh with his clothes torn and [R]dirt on his head. 2 Sam. 1:2 • Josh. 7:6

13 Now when he came, there was Eli, sitting on [R]a seat by the wayside watching,* for his heart trembled for the ark of God. And when the man came into the city and told *it*, all the city cried out. 1 Sam. 1:9; 4:18

14 When Eli heard the noise of the outcry, he said, "What *does* the sound of this tumult *mean?*" And the man came quickly and told Eli.

15 Eli was ninety-eight years old, and his eyes were so dim that he could not see.

16 Then the man said to Eli, "I *am* he who came from the battle. And I fled today from the battle line." And he said, [R]"What happened, my son?" 2 Sam. 1:4

17 So the messenger answered and said, "Israel has fled before the Philistines, and there has been a great slaughter among the people. Also your two sons, Hophni and Phinehas, are dead; and the ark of God has been captured."

18 Then it happened, when he made mention of the ark of God, that Eli fell off the seat backward by the side of the gate; and his neck was broken and he died, for the man was old and heavy. And he had judged Israel forty years.

19 Now his daughter-in-law, Phinehas' wife, was with child, *due* to be delivered; and when she heard the news that the ark of God was captured, and that her father-in-law and her husband were dead, she bowed herself and gave birth, for her labor pains came upon her.

20 And about the time of her death the women who stood by her said to her, "Do not fear, for you have borne a son." But she did not answer, nor did she regard *it*.

4:1 So with MT, Tg.; LXX, Vg. add *And it came to pass in those days that the Philistines gathered themselves together to fight;* LXX adds further *against Israel* **4:13** So with MT, Vg.; LXX *beside the gate watching the road*

21 Then she named the child [R]Ichabod,* say-
ing, [R]"The glory has departed from Israel!"
because the ark of God had been captured
and because of her father-in-law and her hus-
band. 1 Sam. 14:3 • Ps. 26:8; 78:61
22 And she said, "The glory has departed
from Israel, for the ark of God has been cap-
tured."

CHAPTER 5

The Philistines' Sin with the Ark

THEN the Philistines took the ark of God
and brought it [R]from Ebenezer to Ash-
dod. 1 Sam. 4:1; 7:12
2 When the Philistines took the ark of God,
they brought it into the house of [R]Dagon* and
set it by Dagon. 1 Chr. 10:8–10
3 And when the people of Ashdod arose
early in the morning, there was Dagon, [R]fallen
on its face to the earth before the ark of the
LORD. So they took Dagon and [R]set it in its
place again. Is. 19:1; 46:1, 2 • Is. 46:7
4 And when they arose early the next
morning, there was Dagon, fallen on its face
to the ground before the ark of the LORD. [R]The
head of Dagon and both the palms of its
hands *were* broken off on the threshold; only
Dagon's torso* was left of it. Mic. 1:7
5 Therefore neither the priests of Dagon
nor any who come into Dagon's house [R]tread
on the threshold of Dagon in Ashdod to this
day. Zeph. 1:9
6 But the [R]hand of the LORD was heavy on
the people of Ashdod, and He [R]ravaged them
and struck them with tumors,* *both* Ashdod
and its territory. Ex. 9:3 • 1 Sam. 6:5
7 And when the men of Ashdod saw how *it*
was, they said, "The ark of the God of Israel
must not remain with us, for His hand is harsh
toward us and Dagon our god."
8 Therefore they sent and gathered to
themselves all the [R]lords of the Philistines,
and said, "What shall we do with the ark of
the God of Israel?" And they answered, "Let
the ark of the God of Israel be carried away to
[R]Gath." So they carried the ark of the God of
Israel away. 1 Sam. 6:4 • Josh. 11:22
9 So it was, after they had carried it away,
that the hand of the LORD was against the city
with a very great destruction; and He struck
the men of the city, both small and great, and
tumors broke out on them.
10 Therefore they sent the ark of God to
Ekron. So it was, as the ark of God came to
Ekron, that the Ekronites cried out, saying,
"They have brought the ark of the God of Is-
rael to us, to kill us and our people!"
11 So they sent and gathered together all the
lords of the Philistines, and said, "Send away
the ark of the God of Israel, and let it go back
to its own place, so that it does not kill us and
our people." For there was a deadly destruc-
tion throughout all the city; the hand of God
was very heavy there.
12 And the men who did not die were
stricken with the tumors, and the [R]cry of the
city went up to heaven. Jer. 14:2

CHAPTER 6

NOW the ark of the LORD was in the coun-
try of the Philistines seven months.
2 And the Philistines [R]called for the priests
and the diviners, saying, "What shall we do
with the ark of the LORD? Tell us how we
should send it to its place." Gen. 41:8
3 So they said, "If you send away the ark of
the God of Israel, do not send it [R]empty; but
by all means return *it* to Him *with* a trespass
offering. Then you will be healed, and it will
be known to you why His hand is not removed
from you." Deut. 16:16
4 Then they said, "What *is* the trespass of-
fering which we shall return to Him?" They
answered, "Five golden tumors and five
golden rats, *according to* the number of the
lords of the Philistines. For the same plague
was on all of you and on your lords.
5 "Therefore you shall make images of your
tumors and images of your rats that [R]ravage
the land, and you shall [R]give glory to the God
of Israel; perhaps He will lighten[T] His hand
from you, from your gods, and from your
land. 1 Sam. 5:6 • Josh. 7:19 • *ease*
6 "Why then do you harden your hearts as
the Egyptians and Pharaoh hardened their
hearts? When He did mighty things among
them, [R]did they not let the people go, that they
might depart? Ex. 12:31
7 "Now therefore, make a new cart, take
two milk cows which have never been yoked,
and hitch the cows to the cart; and take their
calves home, away from them.
8 "Then take the ark of the LORD and set it
on the cart; and put [R]the articles of gold which
you are returning to Him *as* a trespass offer-
ing in a chest by its side. Then send it away,
and let it go. 1 Sam. 6:4, 5
9 "And watch: if it goes up the road to its
own territory, to Beth Shemesh, *then* He has
done us this great evil. But if not, then we
shall know that *it is* not His hand *that* struck
us—it happened to us by chance."

The Israelites' Sin with the Ark

10 Then the men did so; they took two milk
cows and hitched them to the cart, and shut
up their calves at home.
11 And they set the ark of the LORD on the

4:21 Lit. *Inglorious* **5:2** A Philistine idol **5:4** So with LXX, Syr., Tg., Vg.; MT *Dagon* **5:6** Probably bubonic plague. LXX, Vg. add *And in the midst of their land rats sprang up, and there was a great death panic in the city.*

cart, and the chest with the gold rats and the
images of their tumors.
12 Then the cows headed straight for the
road to Beth Shemesh, *and* went along the
[R]highway, lowing as they went, and did not
turn aside to the right hand or the left. And
the lords of the Philistines went after them to
the border of Beth Shemesh. Num. 20:19
13 Now *the people of* Beth Shemesh *were*
reaping their [R]wheat harvest in the valley; and
they lifted their eyes and saw the ark, and re-
joiced to see *it*. 1 Sam. 12:17
14 Then the cart came into the field of
Joshua of Beth Shemesh, and stood there; a
large stone *was* there. So they split the wood
of the cart and offered the cows as a burnt of-
fering to the LORD.
15 The Levites took down the ark of the
LORD and the chest that *was* with it, in which
were the articles of gold, and put *them* on the
large stone. Then the men of Beth Shemesh
offered burnt offerings and made sacrifices
the same day to the LORD.
16 So when [R]the five lords of the Philistines
had seen *it*, they returned to Ekron the same
day. Josh. 13:3
17 These *are* the golden tumors which the
Philistines returned *as* a trespass offering to
the LORD: one for Ashdod, one for Gaza, one
for Ashkelon, one for Gath, one for Ekron;
18 and the golden rats, *according to* the
number of all the cities of the Philistines *be-
longing* to the five lords, *both* fortified cities
and country villages, even as far as the large
stone of Abel on which they set the ark of the
LORD, *which stone remains* to this day in the
field of Joshua of Beth Shemesh.
19 Then He struck the men of Beth
Shemesh, because they had looked into the
ark of the LORD. He struck fifty thousand and
seventy men* of the people, and the people
lamented because the LORD had struck the
people with a great slaughter.
20 And the men of Beth Shemesh said, "Who
is able to stand before this holy LORD God?
And to whom shall it go up from us?"
21 So they sent messengers to the inhab-
itants of Kirjath Jearim, saying, "The Phi-
listines have brought back the ark of the
LORD; come down *and* take it up with you."

CHAPTER 7

The Acceptable Return of the Ark

THEN the men of Kirjath Jearim came and
took the ark of the LORD, and brought it
into the house of Abinadab on the hill, and
[R]consecrated Eleazar his son to keep the ark
of the LORD. Lev. 21:8
2 So it was that the ark remained in Kirjath
Jearim a long time; it was there twenty years.
And all the house of Israel lamented after the
LORD.

Israel Returns to the Lord

3 Then Samuel spoke to all the house of Is-
rael, saying, "If you return to the LORD with all
your hearts, *then* put away the foreign gods
and the Ashtoreths* from among you, and
prepare your hearts for the LORD, and [R]serve
Him only; and He will deliver you from the
hand of the Philistines." Luke 4:8
4 So the children of Israel put away the
[R]Baals and the Ashtoreths,* and served the
LORD only. Judg. 2:11; 10:16
5 And Samuel said, "Gather all Israel to
Mizpah, and I will pray to the LORD for you."
6 So they gathered together at Mizpah,
[R]drew water, and poured *it* out before the
LORD. And they [R]fasted that day, and said
there, [R]"We have sinned against the LORD."
And Samuel judged the children of Israel at
Mizpah. 2 Sam. 14:14 • Neh. 9:1, 2 • 1 Sam. 12:10

Israel's Victory over Philistia

7 Now when the Philistines heard that the
children of Israel had gathered together at
Mizpah, the lords of the Philistines went up
against Israel. And when the children of Israel
heard *of it*, they were afraid of the Philistines.
8 So the children of Israel said to Samuel,
[R]"Do not cease to cry out to the LORD our God
for us, that He may save us from the hand of
the Philistines." Is. 37:4
9 And Samuel took a suckling lamb and of-
fered *it as* a whole burnt offering to the LORD.
Then Samuel cried out to the LORD for Israel,
and the LORD answered him.
10 Now as Samuel was offering up the burnt
offering, the Philistines drew near to battle
against Israel. But the LORD thundered with a
loud thunder upon the Philistines that day,
and so confused them that they were over-
come before Israel.
11 And the men of Israel went out of Mizpah
and pursued the Philistines, and drove them
back as far as below Beth Car.
12 Then Samuel [R]took a stone and set *it* up
between Mizpah and Shen, and called its
name Ebenezer,* saying, "Thus far the LORD
has helped us." Josh. 4:9; 24:26
13 [R]So the Philistines were subdued, and
they [R]did not come anymore into the terri-
tory of Israel. And the hand of the LORD was
against the Philistines all the days of Sam-
uel. Judg. 13:1 • 1 Sam. 13:5
14 Then the cities which the Philistines had
taken from Israel were restored to Israel, from
Ekron to Gath; and Israel recovered its terri-
tory from the hands of the Philistines. Also
there was peace between Israel and the Amo-
rites.

6:19 Or *He struck seventy men of the people and fifty oxen of a man* **7:3** Images of Canaanite goddesses **7:4** Images of Canaanite goddesses **7:12** Lit. *Stone of Help*

15 And Samuel [R]judged Israel all the days of
his life. 1 Sam. 12:11
16 He went from year to year on a circuit to
Bethel, Gilgal, and Mizpah, and judged Israel
in all those places.
17 But he always returned to Ramah, for his
home *was* there. There he judged Israel, and
there he built an altar to the LORD.

CHAPTER 8

Israel Rejects Samuel's Sons as Leaders

NOW it came to pass when Samuel was
[R]old that he [R]made his [R]sons judges over
Israel. 1 Sam. 12:2 • Deut. 16:18, 19 • Judg. 10:4
2 The name of his firstborn was Joel, and
the name of his second, Abijah; *they were*
judges in Beersheba.
3 But his sons did not walk in his ways;
they turned aside after dishonest gain, took
bribes, and perverted justice.
4 Then all the elders of Israel gathered to-
gether and came to Samuel at Ramah,
5 and said to him, "Look, you are old, and
your sons do not walk in your ways. Now
[R]make us a king to judge us like all the na-
tions." Deut. 17:14, 15

Israel Rejects God as King

6 But the thing displeased Samuel when
they said, "Give us a king to judge us." So
Samuel [R]prayed to the LORD. 1 Sam. 7:9
7 And the LORD said to Samuel, "Heed the
voice of the people in all that they say to you;
for [R]they have not rejected you, but [R]they
have rejected Me, that I should not reign over
them. Ex. 16:8 • 1 Sam. 10:19
8 "According to all the works which they
have done since the day that I brought them
up out of Egypt, even to this day—with which
they have forsaken Me and served other
gods—so they are doing to you also.
9 "Now therefore, heed their voice. How-
ever, you shall solemnly forewarn them, and
[R]show them the behavior of the king who will
reign over them." 1 Sam. 8:11–18

Samuel Warns Israel

10 So Samuel told all the words of the LORD
to the people who asked him for a king.
11 And he said, "This will be the behavior of
the king who will reign over you: He will take
your sons and appoint *them* for his own char-
iots and *to be* his horsemen, and *some* will
run before his chariots.
12 "He will [R]appoint captains over his thou-
sands and captains over his fifties, *will set
some* to plow his ground and reap his harvest,
and *some* to make his weapons of war and
equipment for his chariots. 1 Sam. 22:7
13 "He will take your daughters *to be* per-
fumers, cooks, and bakers.
14 "And [R]he will take the best of your fields,
your vineyards, and your olive groves, and
give *them* to his servants. 1 Kin. 21:7
15 "He will take a tenth of your grain and
your vintage, and give it to his officers and
servants.
16 "And he will take your male servants,
your female servants, your finest young men,*
and your donkeys, and put *them* to his work.
17 "He will take a tenth of your sheep. And
you will be his servants.
18 "And you will cry out in that day because
of your king whom you have chosen for your-
selves, and the LORD [R]will not hear you in that
day." Is. 1:15
19 Nevertheless the people [R]refused to obey
the voice of Samuel; and they said, "No, but
we will have a king over us, Jer. 44:16
20 "that we also may be like all the nations,
and that our king may judge us and go out be-
fore us and fight our battles."
21 And Samuel heard all the words of the
people, and he repeated them in the hearing
of the LORD.
22 So the LORD said to Samuel, [R]"Heed their
voice, and make them a king." And Samuel
said to the men of Israel, "Every man go to his
city." Hos. 13:11

CHAPTER 9

God Chooses Saul

THERE was a man of Benjamin whose
name *was* [R]Kish the son of Abiel, the son
of Zeror, the son of Bechorath, the son of
Aphiah, a Benjamite, a mighty man of
[T]power. 1 Chr. 8:33; 9:36–39 • *wealth*
2 And he had a choice and handsome son
whose name *was* Saul. *There was* not a more
handsome person than he among the children
of Israel. From his shoulders upward *he was*
taller than any of the people.
3 Now the donkeys of Kish, Saul's father,
were lost. And Kish said to his son Saul,
"Please take one of the servants with you, and
arise, go and look for the donkeys."
4 So he passed through the mountains of
Ephraim and through the land of [R]Shalisha, but
they did not find *them*. Then they passed
through the land of Shaalim, and *they were* not
there. Then he passed through the land of the
Benjamites, but they did not find *them*. 2 Kin. 4:42
5 When they had come to the land of Zuph,
Saul said to his servant who *was* with him,
"Come, let [R]us return, lest my father cease
caring about the donkeys and become wor-
ried about us."
1 Sam. 10:2
6 And he said to him, "Look now, *there is* in
this city a man of God, and *he is* an honorable
man; all that he says surely comes to pass. So
let us go there; perhaps he can show us the
way that we should go."

8:16 LXX *cattle*

7 Then Saul said to his servant, "But look, *if*
we go, [R]what shall we bring the man? For the
bread in our vessels is all gone, and *there is*
no present to bring to the man of God. What
do we have?" Judg. 6:18; 13:17
8 And the servant answered Saul again and
said, "Look, I have here at hand one-fourth of
a shekel of silver. I will give *that* to the man of
God, to tell us our way."
9 (Formerly in Israel, when a man went to
inquire of God, he spoke thus: "Come, let us
go to the seer"; for *he who is* now *called* a
prophet was formerly called a seer.)
10 Then Saul said to his servant, "Well said;
come, let us go." So they went to the city
where the man of God *was.*
11 As they went up the hill to the city, [R]they met
some young women going out to draw water,
and said to them, "Is the seer here?" Ex. 2:16
12 And they answered them and said, "Yes,
there he is, just ahead of you. Hurry now; for
today he came to this city, because [R]there is a
sacrifice of the people today [R]on the high
place. Gen. 31:54 • 1 Kin. 3:2
13 "As soon as you come into the city, you
will surely find him before he goes up to the
high place to eat. For the people will not eat
until he comes, because he must bless the sac-
rifice; afterward those who are invited will
eat. Now therefore, go up, for about this time
you will find him."
14 So they went up to the city. As they were
coming into the city, there was Samuel, com-
ing out toward them on his way up to the high
place.
15 Now the LORD had told Samuel in his ear
the day before Saul came, saying,
16 "Tomorrow about this time [R]I will send
you a man from the land of Benjamin, [R]and
you shall anoint him commander over My
people Israel, that he may save My people
from the hand of the Philistines; for I have
looked upon My people, because their cry has
come to Me." Deut. 17:15 • 1 Sam. 10:1
17 So when Samuel saw Saul, the LORD said
to him, [R]"There he is, the man of whom I
spoke to you. This one shall reign over My
people." 1 Sam. 16:12
18 Then Saul drew near to Samuel in the
gate, and said, "Please tell me, where *is* the
seer's house?"
19 Samuel answered Saul and said, "I *am* the
seer. Go up before me to the high place, for
you shall eat with me today; and tomorrow I
will let you go and will tell you all that *is* in
your heart.
20 "But as for your donkeys that were lost
three days ago, do not be anxious about them,
for they have been found. And on whom *is* all
the desire of Israel? *Is it* not on you and on all
your father's house?"
21 And Saul answered and said, [R]"*Am* I not
a Benjamite, of the smallest of the tribes of Is-
rael, and my family the least of all the families
of the tribe* of Benjamin? Why then do you
speak like this to me?" 1 Sam. 15:17
22 Now Samuel took Saul and his servant
and brought them into the hall, and had them
sit in the place of honor among those who
were invited; there *were* about thirty persons.
23 And Samuel said to the cook, "Bring the
portion which I gave you, of which I said to
you, 'Set it apart.' "
24 So the cook took up [R]the thigh with its
upper part and set *it* before Saul. And *Sam-
uel* said, "Here it is, what was kept back. *It*
was set apart for you. Eat; for until this time
it has been kept for you, since I said I invited
the people." So Saul ate with Samuel that
day. Lev. 7:32, 33
25 When they had come down from the high
place into the city, *Samuel* spoke with Saul on
[R]the top of the house.* Deut. 22:8
26 They arose early; and it was about the
dawning of the day that Samuel called to Saul
on the top of the house, saying, "Get up, that I
may send you on your way." And Saul arose,
and both of them went outside, he and Sam-
uel.
27 As they were going down to the outskirts
of the city, Samuel said to Saul, "Tell the ser-
vant to go on ahead of us." And he went on.
"But you stand here awhile, that I may an-
nounce to you the word of God."

CHAPTER 10

THEN [R]Samuel took a flask of oil and
poured *it* on his head, [R]and kissed him
and said: "*Is it* not because [R]the LORD has
anointed you commander over His inheri-
tance?* 2 Kin. 9:3, 6 • Ps. 2:12 • Acts 13:21
2 "When you have departed from me today,
you will find two men by Rachel's tomb in the
territory of Benjamin at Zelzah; and they will
say to you, 'The donkeys which you went to
look for have been found. And now your fa-
ther has ceased caring about the donkeys and
is worrying about you, saying, "What shall I
do about my son?" '
3 "Then you shall go on forward from there
and come to the terebinth tree of Tabor. There
three men going up to God at Bethel will meet
you, one carrying three young goats, another
carrying three loaves of bread, and another
carrying a skin of wine.
4 "And they will [T]greet you and give you

9:21 Lit. *tribes* **9:25** So with MT, Tg.; LXX omits *He spoke with Saul on the top of the house;* LXX, Vg. afterward add *And he prepared a bed for Saul on the top of the house, and he slept.* **10:1** So with MT, Tg., Vg.; LXX *people Israel; and you shall rule the people of the Lord;* LXX, Vg. add *And you shall deliver His people from the hands of their enemies all around them. And this shall be a sign to you, that God has anointed you to be a prince.*

two *loaves* of bread, which you shall receive
from their hands. *ask you about your welfare*
5 "After that you shall come to the hill of
God [R]where the Philistine garrison *is.* And it
will happen, when you have come there to the
city, that you will meet a group of prophets
coming down [R]from the high place with a
stringed instrument, a tambourine, a flute,
and a harp before them; and they will be
prophesying. 1 Sam. 13:2, 3 • 1 Sam. 19:12, 20
6 "Then the Spirit of the LORD will come
upon you, and you will prophesy with them
and be turned into another man.
7 "And let it be, when these [R]signs come to
you, *that* you do as the occasion demands; for
[R]God *is* with you. Ex. 4:8 • Judg. 6:12
8 "You shall go down before me [R]to Gilgal;
and surely I will come down to you to offer
burnt offerings *and* make sacrifices of peace
offerings. [R]Seven days you shall wait, till I
come to you and show you what you should
do." 1 Sam. 11:14, 15; 13:8 • 1 Sam. 13:8–10
9 So it was, when he had turned his back to
go from Samuel, that God [T]gave him another
heart; and all those signs came to pass that
day. *changed his heart*
10 When they came there to the hill, there
was [R]a group of prophets to meet him; then
the Spirit of God came upon him, and he
prophesied among them. 1 Sam. 19:20
11 And it happened, when all who knew him
formerly saw that he indeed prophesied
among the prophets, that the people said to
one another, "What *is* this *that* has come upon
the son of Kish? [R]*Is* Saul also among the
prophets?" Matt. 13:54–57
12 Then a man from there answered and
said, "But [R]who *is* their father?" Therefore it
became a proverb: "*Is* Saul also among the
prophets?" John 5:30, 36
13 And when he had finished prophesying,
he went to the high place.
14 Then Saul's [R]uncle said to him and his
servant, "Where did you go?" So he said, "To
look for the donkeys. When we saw that *they
were* nowhere *to be found,* we went to Sam-
uel." 1 Sam. 14:50
15 And Saul's uncle said, "Tell me, please,
what Samuel said to you."
16 So Saul said to his uncle, "He told us
plainly that the donkeys had been found." But
about the matter of the kingdom, he did not
tell him what Samuel had said.

Samuel Anoints Saul

17 Then Samuel called the people together
[R]to the LORD at Mizpah, Judg. 20:1
18 and said to the children of Israel, [R]"Thus
says the LORD God of Israel: 'I brought up Is-
rael out of Egypt, and delivered you from the
hand of the Egyptians *and* from the hand of
all kingdoms and from those who oppressed
you.' Judg. 6:8, 9
19 "But you have today rejected your God,
who Himself saved you from all your adversi-
ties and your tribulations; and you have said
to Him, 'No, set a king over us!' Now there-
fore, present yourselves before the LORD by
your tribes and by your clans."*
20 And when Samuel had [R]caused all the
tribes of Israel to come near, the tribe of Ben-
jamin was chosen. Acts 1:24, 26
21 When he had caused the tribe of Benja-
min to come near by their families, the family
of Matri was chosen. And Saul the son of Kish
was chosen. But when they sought him, he
could not be found.
22 Therefore they [R]inquired of the LORD fur-
ther, "Has the man come here yet?" And the
LORD answered, "There he is, hidden among
the equipment." 1 Sam. 23:2, 4, 10, 11
23 So they ran and brought him from there;
and when he stood among the people, [R]he was
taller than any of the people from his shoul-
ders upward. 1 Sam. 9:2
24 And Samuel said to all the people, "Do
you see him [R]whom the LORD has chosen, that
there is no one like him among all the peo-
ple?" So all the people shouted and said,
[R]"Long live the king!" 2 Sam. 21:6 • 1 Kin. 1:25
25 Then Samuel explained to the people [R]the
behavior of royalty, and wrote *it* in a book
and laid *it* up before the LORD. And Samuel
sent all the people away, every man to his
house. 1 Sam. 8:11–18
26 And Saul also went home [R]to Gibeah; and
valiant *men* went with him, whose hearts God
had touched. Judg. 20:14
27 [R]But some [R]rebels said, "How can this
man save us?" So they despised him, [R]and
brought him no presents. But he held his
peace. 1 Sam. 11:12 • Deut. 13:13 • 1 Kin. 4:21

CHAPTER 11

Israel Makes Saul King

THEN [R]Nahash the Ammonite came up
and encamped against [R]Jabesh Gilead;
and all the men of Jabesh said to Nahash,
[R]"Make a covenant with us, and we will serve
you." 1 Sam. 12:12 • Judg. 21:8 • Gen. 26:28
2 And Nahash the Ammonite answered
them, "On this *condition* I will make *a covenant*
with you, that I may put out all your right eyes,
and bring [R]reproach on all Israel." Gen. 34:14
3 Then the elders of Jabesh said to him,
"Hold off for seven days, that we may send
messengers to all the territory of Israel. And
then, if *there is* no one to [T]save us, we will
come out to you." *deliver*
4 So the messengers came [R]to Gibeah of
Saul and told the news in the hearing of the
people. And all the people lifted up their
voices and wept. 1 Sam. 10:26; 15:34

10:19 Lit. *thousands*

5 Now there was Saul, coming behind the herd from the field; and Saul said, "What *troubles* the people, that they weep?" And they told him the words of the men of Jabesh.

6 [R]Then the Spirit of God came upon Saul when he heard this news, and his anger was greatly aroused. Judg. 3:10; 6:34; 11:29; 13:25

7 So he took a yoke of oxen and [R]cut them in pieces, and sent *them* throughout all the territory of Israel by the hands of messengers, saying, [R]"Whoever does not go out with Saul and Samuel to battle, so it shall be done to his oxen." And the fear of the LORD fell on the people, and they came out with one consent. Judg. 19:29 • Judg. 21:5, 8, 10

8 When he numbered them in [R]Bezek, the children [R]of Israel were three hundred thousand, and the men of Judah thirty thousand. Judg. 1:5 • 2 Sam. 24:9

9 And they said to the messengers who came, "Thus you shall say to the men of Jabesh Gilead: 'Tomorrow, by *the time* the sun is hot, you shall have help.'" Then the messengers came and reported *it* to the men of Jabesh, and they were glad.

10 Therefore the men of Jabesh said, "Tomorrow we will come out to you, and you may do with us whatever seems good to you."

11 So it was, on the next day, that Saul put the people in three companies; and they came into the midst of the camp in the morning watch, and killed Ammonites until the heat of the day. And it happened that those who survived were scattered, so that no two of them were left together.

12 Then the people said to Samuel, [R]"Who *is* he who said, 'Shall Saul reign over us?' [R]Bring the men, that we may put them to death." 1 Sam. 10:27 • Luke 19:27

13 But Saul said, "Not a man shall be put to death this day, for today the LORD has accomplished salvation in Israel."

14 Then Samuel said to the people, "Come, let us go [R]to Gilgal and renew the kingdom there." 1 Sam. 7:16; 10:8

15 So all the people went to Gilgal, and there they made Saul king [R]before the LORD in Gilgal. [R]There they made sacrifices of peace offerings before the LORD, and there Saul and all the men of Israel rejoiced greatly. 1 Sam. 10:17 • 1 Sam. 10:8

CHAPTER 12

Samuel Confirms Saul

NOW Samuel said to all Israel: "Indeed I have heeded your voice in all that you said to me, and have made a king over you.

2 "And now here is the king, walking before you; and I am old and grayheaded, and look, my sons *are* with you. I have walked before you from my childhood to this day.

3 "Here I am. Witness against me before the LORD and before His anointed: [R]Whose ox have I taken, or whose donkey have I taken, or whom have I cheated? Whom have I oppressed, or from whose hand have I received *any* bribe with which to blind my eyes? I will restore *it* to you." Num. 16:15

4 And they said, [R]"You have not cheated us or oppressed us, nor have you taken anything from any man's hand." Lev. 19:13

5 Then he said to them, "The LORD *is* witness against you, and His anointed *is* witness this day, [R]that you have not found anything [R]in my hand." And they answered, "*He is* witness." Acts 23:9; 24:20 • Ex. 22:4

6 Then Samuel said to the people, [R]"*It is* the LORD who raised up Moses and Aaron, and who brought your fathers up from the land of Egypt. Mic. 6:4

7 "Now therefore, stand still, that I may [R]reason with you before the LORD concerning all the righteous acts of the LORD which He did to you and your fathers: Is. 1:18

8 [R]"When Jacob had gone into Egypt,* and your fathers cried out to the LORD, then the LORD sent Moses and Aaron, who brought your fathers out of Egypt and made them dwell in this place. Gen. 46:5, 6

9 "And when they [R]forgot the LORD their God, He sold them into the hand of [R]Sisera, commander of the army of Hazor, into the hand of the [R]Philistines, and into the hand of the king of Moab; and they fought against them. Judg. 3:7 • Judg. 4:2 • Judg. 3:31; 10:7; 13:1

10 "Then they cried out to the LORD, and said, 'We have sinned, because we have forsaken the LORD and served the Baals and Ashtoreths;* but now deliver us from the hand of our enemies, and we will serve You.'

11 "And the LORD sent Jerubbaal,* Bedan,* Jephthah, and Samuel,* and delivered you out of the hand of your enemies on every side; and you dwelt in safety.

12 "And when you saw that [R]Nahash king of the Ammonites came against you, [R]you said to me, 'No, but a king shall reign over us,' when [R]the LORD your God *was* your king. 1 Sam. 11:1, 2 • 1 Sam. 8:5, 19, 20 • Judg. 8:23

13 "Now therefore, [R]here is the king whom you have chosen *and* whom you have desired. And take note, [R]the LORD has set a king over you. 1 Sam. 10:24 • Hos. 13:11

14 "If you fear the LORD and serve Him and obey His voice, and do not rebel against the commandment of the LORD, then both you and the king who reigns over you will continue following the LORD your God.

15 "However, if you do [R]not obey the voice of

12:8 So with MT, Tg., Vg.; LXX adds *and the Egyptians afflicted them* **12:10** Images of Canaanite goddesses **12:11** Gideon, cf. Judg. 6:25–32; Syr. *Deborah;* Tg. *Gideon* • LXX, Syr. *Barak;* Tg. *Simson* • Syr. *Simson*

the LORD, but [R]rebel against the commandment of the LORD, then the hand of the LORD will be against you, as *it was* against your fathers. Deut. 28:15 • Is. 1:20

16 "Now therefore, [R]stand and see this great thing which the LORD will do before your eyes: Ex. 14:13, 31

17 "*Is* today not the wheat harvest? [R]I will call to the LORD, and He will send thunder and rain, that you may perceive and see that your wickedness *is* great, which you have done in the sight of the LORD, in asking a king for yourselves." [James 5:16–18]

18 So Samuel called to the LORD, and the LORD sent thunder and rain that day; and [R]all the people greatly feared the LORD and Samuel. Ex. 14:31

19 And all the people said to Samuel, [R]"Pray for your servants to the LORD your God, that we may not die; for we have added to all our sins the evil of asking a king for ourselves." Ex. 9:28

20 Then Samuel said to the people, "Do not fear. You have done all this wickedness; yet do not turn aside from following the LORD, but serve the LORD with all your heart.

21 "And do not turn aside; for *then you would go* after empty things which cannot profit or deliver, for they *are* nothing.

22 "For [R]the LORD will not forsake [R]His people, [R]for His great name's sake, because [R]it has pleased the LORD to make you His people. Deut. 31:6 • Is. 43:21 • Jer. 14:21 • Deut. 7:6–11

23 "Moreover, as for me, far be it from me that I should sin against the LORD [R]in ceasing to pray for you; but [R]I will teach you the good and the right way. Rom. 1:9 • Ps. 34:11

24 "Only fear the LORD, and serve Him in truth with all your heart; for consider what great things He has done for you.

25 "But if you still do wickedly, you shall be swept away, both you and your king."

CHAPTER 13

The Early Success of King Saul

SAUL reigned one year; and when he had reigned two years over Israel,*

2 Saul chose for himself three thousand *men* of Israel. Two thousand were with Saul in Michmash and in the mountains of Bethel, and a thousand were with Jonathan in Gibeah of Benjamin. The rest of the people he sent away, every man to his tent.

3 And Jonathan attacked [R]the garrison of the Philistines that *was* in [R]Geba, and the Philistines heard *of it*. Then Saul blew the trumpet throughout all the land, saying, "Let the Hebrews hear!" 1 Sam. 10:5 • 2 Sam. 5:25

4 Now all Israel heard it said *that* Saul had attacked a garrison of the Philistines, and *that* Israel had also become an abomination to the Philistines. And the people were called together to Saul at Gilgal.

Saul's Sinful Sacrifices

5 Then the Philistines gathered together to fight with Israel, thirty* thousand chariots and six thousand horsemen, and people as the sand which *is* on the seashore in multitude. And they came up and encamped in Michmash, to the east of Beth Aven.

6 When the men of Israel saw that they were in danger (for the people were distressed), then the people hid in caves, in thickets, in rocks, in holes, and in pits.

7 And *some of* the Hebrews crossed over the Jordan to the [R]land of Gad and Gilead. As for Saul, he *was* still in Gilgal, and all the people followed him trembling. Num. 32:1–42

8 [R]Then he waited seven days, according to the time set by Samuel. But Samuel did not come to Gilgal; and the people were scattered from him. 1 Sam. 10:8

9 So Saul said, "Bring a burnt offering and peace offerings here to me." And he offered the burnt offering.

10 Now it happened, as soon as he had finished presenting the burnt offering, that Samuel came; and Saul went out to meet him, that he might [T]greet him. Lit. *bless him*

11 And Samuel said, "What have you done?" Saul said, "When I saw that the people were scattered from me, and *that* you did not come within the days appointed, and *that* the Philistines gathered together at Michmash,

12 "then I said, 'The Philistines will now come down on me at Gilgal, and I have not made supplication to the LORD.' Therefore I felt compelled, and offered a burnt offering."

13 And Samuel said to Saul, [R]"You have done foolishly. [R]You have not kept the commandment of the LORD your God, which He commanded you. For now the LORD would have established your kingdom over Israel forever. 2 Chr. 16:9 • 1 Sam. 15:11, 22, 28

14 [R]"But now your kingdom shall not continue. The LORD has sought for Himself a man after His own heart, and the LORD has commanded him *to be* commander over His people, because you have not kept what the LORD commanded you." 1 Sam. 15:28; 31:6

15 Then Samuel arose and went up from Gilgal to Gibeah of Benjamin.* And Saul numbered the people present with him, [R]about six hundred men. 1 Sam. 13:2, 6, 7

16 Saul, Jonathan his son, and the people

13:1 Heb. is difficult; cf. 2 Sam. 5:4; 2 Kin. 14:2; see also 2 Sam. 2:10; Acts 13:21 **13:5** So with MT, LXX, Tg., Vg.; Syr. and some mss. of LXX *three* **13:15** So with MT, Tg.; LXX, Vg. add *And the rest of the people went up after Saul to meet the people who fought against them, going from Gilgal to Gibeah in the hill of Benjamin.*

present with them remained in [T]Gibeah of Benjamin. But the Philistines encamped in Michmash. Heb. *Geba*

17 Then raiders came out of the camp of the Philistines in three companies. One company turned onto the road to [R]Ophrah, to the land of Shual, Josh. 18:23

18 another company turned to the road *to* Beth Horon, and another company turned *to* the road of the border that overlooks the Valley of Zeboim toward the wilderness.

19 Now [R]there was no blacksmith to be found throughout all the land of Israel, for the Philistines said, "Lest the Hebrews make swords or spears." Judg. 5:8

20 But all the Israelites would go down to the Philistines to sharpen each man's plowshare, his mattock, his ax, and his sickle;

21 and the charge for a sharpening was a pim* for the plowshares, the mattocks, the forks, and the axes, and to set the points of the goads.

22 So it came about, on the day of battle, that there was neither sword nor spear found in the hand of any of the people who *were* with Saul and Jonathan. But they were found with Saul and Jonathan his son.

23 [R]And the garrison of the Philistines went out to the pass of Michmash. 1 Sam. 14:1, 4

CHAPTER 14

Saul's Selfish Curse

NOW it happened one day that Jonathan the son of Saul said to the young man who [T]bore his armor, "Come, let us go over to the Philistines' garrison that *is* on the other side." But he did not tell his father. *carried*

2 And Saul was sitting in the outskirts of Gibeah under a pomegranate tree which *is* in Migron. The people who *were* with him *were* about six hundred men.

3 [R]Ahijah the son of Ahitub, Ichabod's brother, the son of Phinehas, the son of Eli, the LORD's priest in Shiloh, was wearing an ephod. But the people did not know that Jonathan had gone. 1 Sam. 22:9, 11, 20

4 Between the passes, by which Jonathan sought to go over [R]to the Philistines' garrison, *there was* a sharp rock on one side and a sharp rock on the other side. And the name of one *was* Bozez, and the name of the other Seneh. 1 Sam. 13:23

5 The front of one faced northward opposite Michmash, and the other southward opposite Gibeah.

6 Then Jonathan said to the young man who bore his armor, "Come, let us go over to the garrison of these [R]uncircumcised; it may be that the LORD will work for us. For nothing restrains the LORD [R]from saving by many or by few." 1 Sam. 17:26, 36 • Judg. 7:4, 7

7 So his armorbearer said to him, "Do all that is in your heart. Go then; here I am with you, according to your heart."

8 Then Jonathan said, "Very well, let us cross over to *these* men, and we will show ourselves to them.

9 "If they say thus to us, 'Wait until we come to you,' then we will stand still in our place and not go up to them.

10 "But if they say thus, 'Come up to us,' then we will go up. For the LORD has delivered them into our hand, and [R]this *will be* a sign to us." Gen. 24:14

11 So both of them showed themselves to the garrison of the Philistines. And the Philistines said, "Look, the Hebrews are coming out of the holes where they have [R]hidden." 1 Sam. 13:6; 14:22

12 Then the men of the garrison called to Jonathan and his armorbearer, and said, "Come up to us, and we will show you something." Jonathan said to his armorbearer, "Come up after me, for the LORD has delivered them into the hand of Israel."

13 And Jonathan climbed up on his hands and knees with his armorbearer after him; and they fell before Jonathan. And as he came after him, his armorbearer killed them.

14 That first slaughter which Jonathan and his armorbearer made was about twenty men within about half an acre of land.*

15 And [R]there was trembling in the camp, in the field, and among all the people. The garrison and [R]the raiders also trembled; and the earth quaked, so that it was [R]a very great trembling. Job 18:11 • 1 Sam. 13:17 • Gen. 35:5

16 Now the watchmen of Saul in Gibeah of Benjamin looked, and *there* was the multitude, melting away; and they [R]went here and there. 1 Sam. 14:20

17 Then Saul said to the people who *were* with him, "Now call the roll and see who has gone from us." And when they had called the roll, surprisingly, Jonathan and his armorbearer *were* not *there*.

18 And Saul said to Ahijah, "Bring the ark* of God here" (for at that time the ark* of God was with the children of Israel).

19 Now it happened, while Saul [R]talked to the priest, that the noise which *was* in the camp of the Philistines continued to increase; so Saul said to the priest, "Withdraw your hand." Num. 27:21

20 Then Saul and all the people who *were* with him assembled, and they went to the battle; and indeed [R]every man's sword was against his neighbor, *and there was* very great confusion. Judg. 7:22

21 Moreover the Hebrews *who* were with the Philistines before that time, who went up with

13:21 About two-thirds shekel weight **14:14** Lit. *half the area plowed by a yoke* of oxen in a day **14:18** So with MT, Tg., Vg.; LXX *ephod* • See preceding note

them into the camp *from the* surrounding
country, they also joined the Israelites who
were with Saul and Jonathan.
22 Likewise all the men of Israel who had
hidden in the mountains of Ephraim, *when*
they heard that the Philistines fled, they also
followed hard after them in the battle.
23 [R]So the LORD saved Israel that day, and
the battle shifted to Beth Aven. Ex. 14:30
24 And the men of Israel were distressed
that day, for Saul had [R]placed the people
under oath, saying, "Cursed *is* the man who
eats *any* food until evening, before I have
taken vengeance on my enemies." So none of
the people tasted food. Josh. 6:26
25 Now all *the people* of the land came to a
forest; and there was honey on the ground.
26 And when the people had come into the
woods, there was the honey, dripping; but no
one put his hand to his mouth, for the people
feared the oath.
27 But Jonathan had not heard his father
charge the people with the oath; therefore he
stretched out the end of the rod that *was* in his
hand and dipped it in a honeycomb, and put
his hand to his mouth; and his [T]countenance
brightened. Lit. *eyes*
28 Then one of the people said, "Your father
strictly charged the people with an oath, say-
ing, 'Cursed *is* the man who eats food this
day.' " And the people were faint.
29 But Jonathan said, "My father has trou-
bled the land. Look now, how my countenance
has brightened because I tasted a little of this
honey.
30 "How much better if the people had eaten
freely today of the spoil of their enemies
which they found! For now would there not
have been a much greater slaughter among
the Philistines?"
31 Now they had [T]driven back the Philistines
that day from Michmash to Aijalon. So the
people were very faint. Lit. *struck*
32 And the people rushed on the [T]spoil, and
took sheep, oxen, and calves, and slaughtered
them on the ground; and the people ate *them*
with the blood. *plunder*
33 Then they told Saul, saying, "Look, the
people are sinning against the LORD by eating
with the blood!" So he said, "You have dealt
treacherously; roll a large stone to me this day."
34 Then Saul said, "Disperse yourselves
among the people, and say to them, 'Bring me
here every man's ox and every man's sheep,
slaughter *them* here, and eat; and do not sin
against the LORD by eating with the blood.' "
So every one of the people brought his ox
with him that night, and slaughtered *it* there.
35 Then Saul [R]built an altar to the LORD.
This was the first altar that he built to the
LORD. 1 Sam. 7:12, 17
36 Now Saul said, "Let us go down after the
Philistines by night, and plunder them until
the morning light; and let us not leave a man
of them." And they said, "Do whatever seems
good to you." Then the priest said, "Let us
draw near to God here."
37 So Saul [R]asked counsel of God, "Shall I go
down after the Philistines? Will You deliver
them into the hand of Israel?" But He did not
answer him that day. Judg. 20:18
38 And Saul said, [R]"Come over here, all you
chiefs of the people, and know and see what
this sin was today. Josh. 7:14
39 "For [R]*as* the LORD lives, who saves Israel,
though it be in Jonathan my son, he shall
surely die." But not a man among all the peo-
ple answered him. 2 Sam. 12:5
40 Then he said to all Israel, "You be on one
side, and my son Jonathan and I will be on the
other side." And the people said to Saul, "Do
what seems good to you."
41 Therefore Saul said to the LORD God of
Israel, [R]"Give a perfect *lot.*"* [R]So Saul and
Jonathan were taken, but the people es-
caped. Acts 1:24–26 • 1 Sam. 10:20, 21
42 And Saul said, "Cast *lots* between my son
Jonathan and me." So Jonathan was taken.
43 Then Saul said to Jonathan, [R]"Tell me
what you have done." And Jonathan told him,
and said, "I only tasted a little honey with the
end of the rod that *was* in my hand. So now I
must die!" Josh. 7:19
44 Saul answered, "God do so and more also;
for you shall surely die, Jonathan."
45 But the people said to Saul, "Shall Jona-
than die, who has accomplished this great de-
liverance in Israel? Certainly not! [R]*As* the
LORD lives, not one hair of his head shall fall
to the ground, for he has worked [R]with God
this day." So the people rescued Jonathan, and
he did not die. 1 Kin. 1:52 • [2 Cor. 6:1]
46 Then Saul returned from pursuing the
Philistines, and the Philistines went to their
own place.
47 So Saul established his sovereignty over
Israel, and fought against all his enemies on
every side, against Moab, against the people
of Ammon, against Edom, against the kings of
Zobah, and against the Philistines. Wherever
he turned, he harassed *them.**
48 And he gathered an army and attacked
the Amalekites, and delivered Israel from the
hands of those who plundered them.
49 [R]The sons of Saul were Jonathan, Jishui,*
and Malchishua. And the names of his two
daughters *were these:* the name of the first-
born Merab, and the name of the younger
Michal. 1 Sam. 31:2

14:41 So with MT, Tg.; LXX, Vg. *Why do You not answer Your servant today? If the injustice is with me or Jonathan my son, O LORD God of Israel, give proof; and if You say it is with Your people Israel, give holiness.* **14:47** LXX, Vg. *prospered*
14:49 *Abinadab,* 1 Chr. 8:33; 9:39

50 The name of Saul's wife *was* Ahinoam the
daughter of Ahimaaz. And the name of the
commander of his army *was* Abner the son of
Ner, Saul's [R]uncle. 1 Sam. 10:14
51 Kish *was* the father of Saul, and Ner the
father of Abner *was* the son of Abiel.
52 Now there was fierce war with the
Philistines all the days of Saul. And when
Saul saw any strong man or any valiant man,
[R]he took him for himself. 1 Sam. 8:11

CHAPTER 15

Saul's Incomplete Obedience

SAMUEL also said to Saul, "The LORD sent
me to anoint you king over His people,
over Israel. Now therefore, heed the voice of
the words of the LORD.
2 "Thus says the LORD of hosts: 'I will pun-
ish Amalek *for* what he did to Israel, [R]how he
ambushed him on the way when he came up
from Egypt. Deut. 25:17–19
3 'Now go and [R]attack Amalek, and [R]utterly
destroy all that they have, and do not spare
them. But kill both man and woman, infant
and nursing child, ox and sheep, camel and
donkey.' " Deut. 25:19 • Num. 24:20
4 So Saul gathered the people together and
numbered them in Telaim, two hundred thou-
sand foot soldiers and ten thousand men of
Judah.
5 And Saul came to a city of Amalek, and
lay in wait in the valley.
6 Then Saul said to [R]the Kenites, [R]"Go, de-
part, get down from among the Amalekites,
lest I destroy you with them. For you
showed kindness to all the children of Israel
when they came up out of Egypt." So the
Kenites departed from among the Ama-
lekites. Num. 24:21 • Gen. 18:25; 19:12, 14
7 [R]And Saul attacked the Amalekites, from
[R]Havilah all the way to Shur, which is east of
Egypt. 1 Sam. 14:48 • Gen. 2:11; 25:17, 18
8 He also took Agag king of the Amalekites
alive, and utterly destroyed all the people with
the edge of the sword.
9 But Saul and the people [R]spared Agag
and the best of the sheep, the oxen, the
fatlings, the lambs, and all *that was* good, and
were unwilling to utterly destroy them. But
everything despised and worthless, that they
utterly destroyed. 1 Sam. 15:3, 15, 19

God Rejects Saul as King

10 Now the word of the LORD came to Sam-
uel, saying,
11 [R]"I greatly regret that I have set up Saul
as king, for he has turned back from follow-
ing Me, and has not performed My command-
ments." And it grieved Samuel, and he cried
out to the LORD all night. Gen. 6:6, 7
12 So when Samuel rose early in the morn-
ing to meet Saul, it was told Samuel, saying,
"Saul went to [R]Carmel, and indeed, he set up
a monument for himself; and he has gone on
around, passed by, and gone down to Gil-
gal." Josh. 15:55
13 Then Samuel went to Saul, and Saul
said to him, [R]"Blessed *are* you of the LORD! I
have performed the commandment of the
LORD." Judg. 17:2
14 But Samuel said, "What then *is* this bleat-
ing of the sheep in my ears, and the lowing of
the oxen which I hear?"
15 And Saul said, "They have brought them
from the Amalekites; [R]for the people spared
the best of the sheep and the oxen, to sacrifice
to the LORD your God; and the rest we have ut-
terly destroyed." [Gen. 3:12, 13]
16 Then Samuel said to Saul, "Be quiet! And
I will tell you what the LORD said to me last
night." And he said to him, "Speak on."
17 So Samuel said, [R]"When you *were* little in
your own eyes, *were* you not head of the
tribes of Israel? And did not the LORD anoint
you king over Israel? 1 Sam. 9:21; 10:22
18 "Now the LORD sent you on a mission, and
said, 'Go, and utterly destroy the sinners, the
Amalekites, and fight against them until they
are [T]consumed.' *exterminated*
19 "Why then did you not obey the voice of
the LORD? Why did you swoop down on the
spoil, and do evil in the sight of the LORD?"
20 And Saul said to Samuel, "But I have
obeyed the voice of the LORD, and gone on the
mission on which the LORD sent me, and
brought back Agag king of Amalek; I have ut-
terly destroyed the Amalekites.
21 "But the people took of the plunder, sheep
and oxen, the best of the things which should
have been utterly destroyed, to sacrifice to the
LORD your God in Gilgal."
22 So Samuel said:

[R]"Has the LORD *as great* delight in burnt
offerings and sacrifices, [Is. 1:11–17]
As in obeying the voice of the LORD?
Behold, to obey is better than sacrifice,
And to heed than the fat of rams.
23 For rebellion *is as* the sin of [T]witchcraft,
And stubbornness *is* as iniquity and
idolatry. *divination*
Because you have rejected the word of
the LORD,
[R]He also has rejected you from *being*
king." 1 Sam. 13:14; 16:1

24 [R]Then Saul said to Samuel, "I have
sinned, for I have transgressed the com-
mandment of the LORD and your words, be-
cause I [R]feared the people and obeyed their
voice. Josh. 7:20 • [Is. 51:12, 13]
25 "Now therefore, please pardon my sin,
and return with me, that I may worship the
LORD."
26 But Samuel said to Saul, "I will not return

with you, for you have rejected the word of the LORD, and the LORD has rejected you from being king over Israel."

27 And as Samuel turned around to go away, [R]*Saul* seized the edge of his robe, and it tore. 1 Kin. 11:30, 31

28 So Samuel said to him, [R]"The LORD has torn the kingdom of Israel from you today, and has given it to a neighbor of yours, *who is* better than you. 1 Kin. 11:31

29 "And also the Strength of Israel [R]will not lie nor relent. For He *is* not a man, that He should relent." Num. 23:19

30 Then he said, "I have sinned; *yet* honor me now, please, before the elders of my people and before Israel, and return with me, that I may worship the LORD your God."

31 So Samuel turned back after Saul, and Saul worshiped the LORD.

32 Then Samuel said, "Bring Agag king of the Amalekites here to me." So Agag came to him cautiously. And Agag said, "Surely the bitterness of death is past."

33 But Samuel said, [R]"As your sword has made women childless, so shall your mother be childless among women." And Samuel hacked Agag in pieces before the LORD in Gilgal. [Gen. 9:6]

34 Then Samuel went to Ramah, and Saul went up to his house at Gibeah of Saul.

35 And Samuel went no more to see Saul until the day of his death. Nevertheless Samuel mourned for Saul, and the LORD regretted that He had made Saul king over Israel.

CHAPTER 16

God Anoints David as King

NOW the LORD said to Samuel, "How long will you mourn for Saul, seeing I have rejected him from reigning over Israel? Fill your horn with oil, and go; I am sending you to Jesse the Bethlehemite. For I have provided Myself a king among his sons."

2 And Samuel said, "How can I go? If Saul hears *it*, he will kill me." But the LORD said, "Take a heifer with you, and say, [R]'I have come to sacrifice to the LORD.' 1 Sam. 9:12

3 "Then invite Jesse to the sacrifice, and I will show you what you shall do; you shall anoint for Me the one I name to you."

4 So Samuel did what the LORD said, and went to Bethlehem. And the elders of the town [R]trembled at his coming, and said, [R]"Do you come peaceably?" 1 Sam. 21:1 • 1 Kin. 2:13

5 And he said, "Peaceably; I have come to sacrifice to the LORD. [R]Sanctify[T] yourselves, and come with me to the sacrifice." Then he consecrated Jesse and his sons, and invited them to the sacrifice. Ex. 19:10 • *Consecrate*

6 So it was, when they came, that he looked at [R]Eliab and said, "Surely the LORD's anointed *is* before Him!" 1 Sam. 17:13, 28

7 But the LORD said to Samuel, "Do not look at his appearance or at his physical stature, because I have [T]refused him. For *the LORD does* not *see* as man sees;* for man [R]looks at the outward appearance, but the LORD looks at the heart." *rejected* • 2 Cor. 10:7

8 So Jesse called Abinadab, and made him pass before Samuel. And he said, "Neither has the LORD chosen this one."

9 Then Jesse made Shammah pass by. And he said, "Neither has the LORD chosen this one."

10 Thus Jesse made seven of his sons pass before Samuel. And Samuel said to Jesse, "The LORD has not chosen these."

11 And Samuel said to Jesse, "Are all the young men here?" Then he said, "There remains yet the youngest, and there he is, keeping the [R]sheep." And Samuel said to Jesse, "Send and bring him. For we will not sit down* till he comes here." 2 Sam. 7:8

12 So he sent and brought him in. Now he *was* [R]ruddy, with bright eyes, and goodlooking. And the LORD said, "Arise, anoint him; for this *is* the one!" 1 Sam. 17:42

13 Then Samuel took the horn of oil and anointed him in the midst of his brothers; and [R]the Spirit of the LORD came upon David from that day forward. So Samuel arose and went to Ramah. Num. 27:18

God Takes His Spirit from Saul

14 [R]But the Spirit of the LORD departed from Saul, and [R]a distressing spirit from the LORD troubled him. Judg. 16:20 • Judg. 9:23

15 And Saul's servants said to him, "Surely, a distressing spirit from God is troubling you.

16 "Let our master now command your servants, *who are* before you, to seek out a man *who is* a skillful player on the harp. And it shall be that he will play it with his hand when the [T]distressing spirit from God is upon you, and you shall be well." Lit. *evil*

17 So Saul said to his servants, [T]"Provide me now a man who can play well, and bring *him* to me." Lit. *Look now for a man for me*

18 Then one of the servants answered and said, "Look, I have seen a son of Jesse the Bethlehemite, *who is* skillful in playing, a mighty man of valor, a man of war, prudent in speech, and a handsome person; and [R]the LORD *is* with him." 1 Sam. 3:19; 18:12, 14

19 Therefore Saul sent messengers to Jesse, and said, "Send me your son David, who *is* with the sheep."

20 And Jesse took a donkey *loaded with* bread, a skin of wine, and a young goat, and sent *them* by his son David to Saul.

16:7 LXX *For God does not see as man sees;* Tg. *It is not by the appearance of a man;* Vg. *Nor do I judge according to the looks of a man* **16:11** So with LXX, Vg.; MT *turn around;* Tg., Syr. *turn away*

21 So David came to Saul and [R]stood before
him. And he loved him greatly, and he became
his armorbearer. Gen. 41:46
22 Then Saul sent to Jesse, saying, "Please
let David stand before me, for he has found
favor in my sight."
23 And so it was, whenever the spirit from
God was upon Saul, that David would take a
harp and play *it* with his hand. Then Saul
would become refreshed and well, and the
distressing spirit would depart from him.

CHAPTER 17

David Defeats Goliath

NOW the Philistines gathered their armies
together to battle, and were gathered at
[R]Sochoh, which *belongs* to Judah; they en-
camped between Sochoh and Azekah, in
Ephes Dammim. Josh. 15:35
2 And Saul and the men of Israel were
gathered together, and they encamped in the
Valley of Elah, and drew up in battle array
against the Philistines.
3 The Philistines stood on a mountain on
one side, and Israel stood on a mountain on
the other side, with a valley between them.
4 And a champion went out from the camp
of the Philistines, named [R]Goliath, from
[R]Gath, whose height *was* six cubits and a
span. 2 Sam. 21:19 • Josh. 11:21, 22
5 *He had* a bronze helmet on his head, and
he *was* [T]armed with a coat of mail, and the
weight of the coat *was* five thousand shekels
of bronze. *clothed with scaled body armor*
6 And *he had* bronze armor on his legs and
a bronze javelin between his shoulders.
7 Now the staff of his spear *was* like a
weaver's beam, and his iron spearhead
weighed six hundred shekels; and a shield-
bearer went before him.
8 Then he stood and cried out to the armies
of Israel, and said to them, "Why have you
come out to line up for battle? *Am* I not a
Philistine, and you the [R]servants of Saul?
Choose a man for yourselves, and let him
come down to me. 1 Sam. 8:17
9 "If he is able to fight with me and kill me,
then we will be your servants. But if I prevail
against him and kill him, then you shall be
our servants and serve us."
10 And the Philistine said, "I defy the armies
of Israel this day; give me a man, that we may
fight together."
11 When Saul and all Israel heard these
words of the Philistine, they were dismayed
and greatly afraid.
12 Now David *was* [R]the son of that
[R]Ephrathite of Bethlehem Judah, whose name
was Jesse, and who had eight sons. And the
man was old, advanced *in years,* in the days of
Saul. Ruth 4:22 • Gen. 35:19
13 The three oldest sons of Jesse had gone to
follow Saul to the battle. The [R]names of his
three sons who went to the battle *were* Eliab
the firstborn, next to him Abinadab, and the
third Shammah. 1 Sam. 16:6, 8, 9
14 David *was* the youngest. And the three
oldest followed Saul.
15 But David occasionally went and re-
turned from Saul [R]to feed his father's sheep at
Bethlehem. 1 Sam. 16:11, 19
16 And the Philistine drew near and pre-
sented himself forty days, morning and
evening.
17 Then Jesse said to his son David, "Take
now for your brothers an ephah of this dried
grain and these ten loaves, and run to your
brothers at the camp.
18 "And carry these ten cheeses to the cap-
tain of *their* thousand, and see how your
brothers fare, and bring back news of them."
19 Now Saul and they and all the men of Is-
rael *were* in the Valley of Elah, fighting with
the Philistines.
20 So David rose early in the morning, left
the sheep with a keeper, and took *the things*
and went as Jesse had commanded him.
And he came to the camp as the army was
going out to the fight and shouting for the
battle.
21 For Israel and the Philistines had drawn
up in battle array, army against army.
22 And David left his supplies in the hand of
the supply keeper, ran to the army, and came
and greeted his brothers.
23 Then as he talked with them, there was
the champion, the Philistine of Gath, Goliath
by name, coming up from the armies of the
Philistines; and he spoke according to the
same words. So David heard *them.*
24 And all the men of Israel, when they saw
the man, fled from him and were dreadfully
afraid.
25 So the men of Israel said, "Have you seen
this man who has come up? Surely he has
come up to defy Israel; and it shall be *that* the
man who kills him the king will enrich with
great riches, [R]will give him his daughter, and
give his father's house exemption *from taxes*
in Israel." Josh. 15:16
26 Then David spoke to the men who stood
by him, saying, "What shall be done for the
man who kills this Philistine and takes away
the reproach from Israel? For who *is* this
uncircumcised Philistine, that he should defy
the armies of the living God?"
27 And the people answered him in this
manner, saying, [R]"So shall it be done for the
man who kills him." 1 Sam. 17:25
28 Now Eliab his oldest brother heard when
he spoke to the men; and Eliab's [R]anger was
aroused against David, and he said, "Why did
you come down here? And with whom have
you left those few sheep in the wilderness? I

know your pride and the insolence of your
heart, for you have come down to see the bat-
tle." [Matt. 10:36]
29 And David said, "What have I done now?
[R]*Is there* not a cause?" 1 Sam. 17:17
30 Then he turned from him toward another
and said the same thing; and these people an-
swered him as the first ones *did*.
31 Now when the words which David spoke
were heard, they reported *them* to Saul; and
he sent for him.
32 Then David said to Saul, "Let no man's
heart fail because of him; your servant will go
and fight with this Philistine."
33 And Saul said to David, [R]"You are not
able to go against this Philistine to fight with
him; for you *are* a youth, and he a man of war
from his youth." Num. 13:31
34 But David said to Saul, "Your servant
used to keep his father's sheep, and when a
[R]lion or a bear came and took a lamb out of
the flock, Judg. 14:5
35 "I went out after it and struck it, and de-
livered *the lamb* from its mouth; and when it
arose against me, I caught *it* by its beard, and
struck and killed it.
36 "Your servant has killed both lion and
bear; and this uncircumcised Philistine will be
like one of them, seeing he has defied the
armies of the living God."
37 Moreover David said, [R]"The LORD, who
delivered me from the paw of the lion and
from the paw of the bear, He will deliver me
from the hand of this Philistine." And Saul
said to David, [R]"Go, and the LORD be with
you!" [2 Cor. 1:10] • 1 Chr. 22:11, 16
38 So Saul clothed David with his armor,
and he put a bronze helmet on his head; he
also clothed him with a coat of mail.
39 David fastened his sword to his armor
and tried to walk, for he had not tested *them*.
And David said to Saul, "I cannot walk with
these, for I have not tested *them*." So David
took them off.
40 Then he took his staff in his hand; and he
chose for himself five smooth stones from the
brook, and put them in a shepherd's bag, in a
pouch which he had, and his sling was in his
hand. And he drew near to the Philistine.
41 So the Philistine came, and began draw-
ing near to David, and the man who bore the
shield *went* before him.
42 And when the Philistine looked about and
saw David, he disdained him; for he was *only*
a youth, ruddy and good-looking.
43 So the Philistine said to David, "*Am* I a
dog, that you come to me with sticks?" And
the Philistine cursed David by his gods.
44 And the Philistine said to David, "Come
to me, and I will give your flesh to the birds of
the air and the beasts of the field!"
45 Then David said to the Philistine, "You
come to me with a sword, with a spear, and
with a javelin. But I come to you in the name
of the LORD of hosts, the God of the armies of
Israel, whom you have defied.
46 "This day the LORD will deliver you into
my hand, and I will strike you and take your
head from you. And this day I will give [R]the
carcasses of the camp of the Philistines to
the birds of the air and the wild beasts of the
earth, that all the earth may know that there
is a God in Israel. Deut. 28:26
47 "Then all this assembly shall know that
the LORD [R]does not save with sword and
spear; for the battle *is* the LORD's, and He will
give you into our hands." Hos. 1:7
48 So it was, when the Philistine arose and
came and drew near to meet David, that Da-
vid hurried and [R]ran toward the army to meet
the Philistine. Ps. 27:3
49 Then David put his hand in his bag and
took out a stone; and he slung *it* and struck
the Philistine in his forehead, so that the stone
sank into his forehead, and he fell on his face
to the earth.
50 So David prevailed over the Philistine
with a [R]sling and a stone, and struck the
Philistine and killed him. But *there was* no
sword in the hand of David. Judg. 3:31
51 Therefore David ran and stood over the
Philistine, took his sword and drew it out of
its sheath and killed him, and cut off his head
with it. And when the Philistines saw that
their champion was dead, they fled.
52 Now the men of Israel and Judah arose
and shouted, and pursued the Philistines as
far as the entrance of the valley* and to the
gates of Ekron. And the wounded of the
Philistines fell along the road to [R]Shaaraim,
even as far as Gath and Ekron. Josh. 15:36
53 Then the children of Israel returned from
chasing the Philistines, and they plundered
their tents.
54 And David took the head of the Philistine
and brought it to Jerusalem, but he put his
armor in his tent.
55 When Saul saw David going out against
the Philistine, he said to [R]Abner, the com-
mander of the army, "Abner, whose son *is* this
youth?" And Abner said, "As your soul lives, O
king, I do not know." 1 Sam. 14:50
56 So the king said, "Inquire whose son this
young man *is*."
57 Then, as David returned from the slaugh-
ter of the Philistine, Abner took him and
brought him before Saul [R]with the head of the
Philistine in his hand. 1 Sam. 17:54
58 And Saul said to him, "Whose son *are*
you, young man?" So David answered, [R]"*I am*
the son of your servant Jesse the Bethle-
hemite." 1 Sam. 17:12

17:52 So with MT, Syr., Tg., Vg.; LXX *Gath*

CHAPTER 18

Jonathan Loves David

NOW when he had finished speaking to Saul, [R]the soul of Jonathan was knit to the soul of David, [R]and Jonathan loved him as his own soul. Gen. 44:30 • 1 Sam. 20:17

2 Saul took him that day, [R]and would not let him go home to his father's house anymore. 1 Sam. 17:15

3 Then Jonathan and David made a [R]covenant, because he loved him as his own soul. 1 Sam. 20:8–17

4 And Jonathan took off the robe that *was* on him and gave it to David, with his armor, even to his sword and his bow and his belt.

Israel Elevates David over Saul

5 So David went out wherever Saul sent him, *and* [T]behaved wisely. And Saul set him over the men of war, and he was accepted in the sight of all the people and also in the sight of Saul's servants. Or *prospered*

6 Now it had happened as they were coming *home,* when David was returning from the slaughter of the [T]Philistine, that [R]the women had come out of all the cities of Israel, singing and dancing, to meet King Saul, with tambourines, with joy, and with musical instruments. *Philistines* • Ex. 15:20, 21

7 So the women [R]sang as they danced, and said: Ex. 15:21

"Saul has slain his thousands,
And David his ten thousands."

8 Then Saul was very angry, and the saying displeased him; and he said, "They have ascribed to David ten thousands, and to me they have ascribed *only* thousands. Now *what* more can he have but the kingdom?"

9 So Saul [T]eyed David from that day forward. Viewed with suspicion

The Attempts of Saul to Slay David: By Throwing a Spear at David

10 And it happened on the next day that [R]the distressing spirit from God came upon Saul, [R]and he prophesied inside the house. So David [R]played *music* with his hand, as at other times; but *there was* a spear in Saul's hand. 1 Sam. 16:14 • 1 Sam. 19:24 • 1 Sam. 16:23

11 And Saul [R]cast the spear, for he said, "I will pin David to the wall!" But David escaped his presence twice. 1 Sam. 19:10; 20:33

12 Now Saul was [R]afraid of David, because [R]the LORD was with him, but had departed from Saul. 1 Sam. 18:15, 29 • 1 Sam. 16:13, 18

13 Therefore Saul removed him from [T]his presence, and made him his captain over a thousand; and [R]he went out and came in before the people. Lit. *himself* • Num. 27:17

14 And David behaved wisely in all his ways, and the LORD *was* with him.

15 Therefore, when Saul saw that he behaved very wisely, he was afraid of him.

16 But [R]all Israel and Judah loved David, because he went out and came in before them. 1 Sam. 18:5

By Tricking David to Fight the Philistines

17 Then Saul said to David, "Here is my older daughter Merab; I will give her to you as a wife. Only be valiant for me, and fight the LORD's battles." For Saul thought, "Let my hand not be against him, but let the hand of the Philistines be against him."

18 So David said to Saul, "Who *am* I, and what *is* my life *or* my father's family in Israel, that I should be son-in-law to the king?"

19 But it happened at the time when Merab, Saul's daughter, should have been given to David, that she was given to [R]Adriel the Meholathite as a wife. 2 Sam. 21:8

20 [R]Now Michal, Saul's daughter, loved David. And they told Saul, and the thing pleased him. 1 Sam. 18:28

21 So Saul said, "I will give her to him, that she may be a snare to him, and that the hand of the Philistines may be against him." Therefore Saul said to David a second time, "You shall be my son-in-law today."

22 And Saul commanded his servants, "Communicate with David secretly, and say, 'Look, the king has delight in you, and all his servants love you. Now therefore, become the king's son-in-law.' "

23 So Saul's servants spoke those words in the hearing of David. And David said, "Does it seem to you *a* light *thing* to be a king's son-in-law, seeing I *am* a poor and lightly esteemed man?"

24 And the servants of Saul told him, saying, "In this manner David spoke."

25 Then Saul said, "Thus you shall say to David: 'The king does not desire any dowry but one hundred foreskins of the Philistines, to take [R]vengeance on the king's enemies.' " But Saul thought to make David fall by the hand of the Philistines. 1 Sam. 14:24

26 So when his servants told David these words, it pleased David well to become the king's son-in-law. Now [R]the days had not expired; 1 Sam. 18:21

27 therefore David arose and went, he and [R]his men, and killed two hundred men of the Philistines. And [R]David brought their foreskins, and they gave them in full count to the king, that he might become the king's son-in-law. Then Saul gave him Michal his daughter as a wife. 1 Sam. 18:13 • 2 Sam. 3:14

28 Thus Saul saw and knew that the LORD *was* with David, and *that* Michal, Saul's daughter, loved him;

29 and Saul was still more afraid of David.
So Saul became David's enemy continually.
30 Then the princes of the Philistines [R]went
out *to war.* And so it was, whenever they went
out, *that* David behaved more wisely than all
the servants of Saul, so that his name became
highly esteemed. 2 Sam. 11:1

CHAPTER 19

By Commanding His Servants to Kill David

Now Saul spoke to Jonathan his son and to
all his servants, that they should kill [R]Da-
vid; but Jonathan, Saul's son, [R]delighted
greatly in David. 1 Sam. 8:8, 9 • 1 Sam. 18:1
2 So Jonathan told David, saying, "My fa-
ther Saul seeks to kill you. Therefore please
be on your guard until morning, and stay in a
secret *place* and hide.
3 "And I will go out and stand beside my fa-
ther in the field where you *are,* and I will
speak with my father about you. Then what I
observe, I will tell [R]you." 1 Sam. 20:8–13
4 Thus Jonathan [R]spoke well of David to
Saul his father, and said to him, "Let not the
king [R]sin against his servant, against David,
because he has not sinned against you, and
because his works *have been* very good to-
ward you. [Prov. 31:8, 9] • [Prov. 17:13]
5 "For he took his [R]life in his hands and
[R]killed the Philistine, and the LORD brought
about a great deliverance for all Israel. You
saw *it* and rejoiced. Why then will you sin
against innocent blood, to kill David without
a cause?" Judg. 9:17; 12:3 • 1 Sam. 17:49, 50
6 So Saul heeded the voice of Jonathan,
and Saul swore, "*As* the LORD lives, he shall
not be killed."
7 Then Jonathan called David, and Jona-
than told him all these things. So Jonathan
brought David to Saul, and he was in his
presence [R]as in times past. 1 Sam. 16:21

By Throwing a Spear at David Again

8 And there was war again; and David went
out and fought with the Philistines, [R]and
struck them with a mighty blow, and they fled
from him. 1 Sam. 18:27; 23:5
9 Now [R]the distressing spirit from the LORD
came upon Saul as he sat in his house with his
spear in his hand. And David was playing *mu-
sic* with *his* hand. 1 Sam. 16:14
10 Then Saul sought to pin David to the wall
with the spear, but he slipped away from
Saul's presence; and he drove the spear into
the wall. So David fled and escaped that night.

By Sending His Messengers to Kill David

11 [R]Saul also sent messengers to David's
house to watch him and to kill him in the
morning. And Michal, David's wife, told him,
saying, "If you do not save your life tonight,
tomorrow you will be killed." Ps. 59:title
12 So Michal let David down through a win-
dow. And he went and fled and escaped.
13 And Michal took an image and laid *it* in
the bed, put a cover of goats' *hair* for his head,
and covered *it* with clothes.
14 So when Saul sent messengers to take
David, she said, "He *is* sick."
15 Then Saul sent the messengers *back* to
see David, saying, "Bring him up to me in the
bed, that I may kill him."
16 And when the messengers had come in,
there was the image in the bed, with a cover
of goats' *hair* for his head.
17 Then Saul said to Michal, "Why have you
deceived me like this, and sent my enemy
away, so that he has escaped?" And Michal
answered Saul, "He said to me, 'Let me go!
Why should I kill you?' "

By Coming to Kill David at Samuel's House

18 So David fled and escaped, and went to
[R]Samuel at Ramah, and told him all that Saul
had done to him. And he and Samuel went
and stayed in Naioth. 1 Sam. 16:13
19 Now it was told Saul, saying, "Take note,
David *is* at Naioth in Ramah!"
20 Then [R]Saul sent messengers to take Da-
vid. And when they saw the group of prophets
prophesying, and Samuel standing *as* leader
over them, the Spirit of God came upon the
messengers of Saul, and they also [R]prophe-
sied. John 7:32 • Joel 2:28
21 And when Saul was told, he sent other
messengers, and they prophesied likewise.
Then Saul sent messengers again the third
time, and they prophesied also.
22 Then he also went to Ramah, and came to
the great well that *is* at Sechu. So he asked,
and said, "Where *are* Samuel and David?"
And *someone* said, "Indeed *they are* at Naioth
in Ramah."
23 So he went there to Naioth in Ramah.
Then [R]the Spirit of God was upon him also,
and he went on and prophesied until he came
to Naioth in Ramah. 1 Sam. 10:10
24 [R]And he also stripped off his clothes and
prophesied before Samuel in like manner, and
lay down [R]naked all that day and all that
night. Therefore they say, "*Is* Saul also among
the prophets?"* Is. 20:2 • Mic. 1:8

CHAPTER 20

By Commanding Jonathan to Bring David to Be Killed

THEN David fled from Naioth in Ramah,
and went and said to Jonathan, "What
have I done? What *is* my iniquity, and what *is*
my sin before your father, that he seeks my
life?"
2 So Jonathan said to him, "By no means!

19:24 Cf. 1 Sam. 10:12

You shall not die! Indeed, my father will do nothing either great or small without first telling me. And why should my father hide this thing from me? It *is* not *so!*"

3 Then David took an oath again, and said, "Your father certainly knows that I have found favor in your eyes, and he has said, 'Do not let Jonathan know this, lest he be grieved.' But [R]truly, *as* the LORD lives and *as* your soul lives, *there is* but a step between me and death." 1 Sam. 27:1

4 So Jonathan said to David, "Whatever you yourself desire, I will do *it* for you."

5 And David said to Jonathan, "Indeed tomorrow *is* the [R]New Moon, and I should not fail to sit with the king to eat. But let me go, that I may hide in the field until the third *day* at evening. Num. 10:10; 28:11–15

6 "If your father misses me at all, then say, 'David earnestly asked *permission* of me that he might run over [R]to Bethlehem, his city, for *there is* a yearly sacrifice there for all the family.' 1 Sam. 16:4; 17:12

7 [R]"If he says thus: '*It is* well,' your servant will be safe. But if he is very angry, be sure that evil is determined by him. 2 Sam. 17:4

8 "Therefore you shall [R]deal kindly with your servant, for you have brought your servant into a covenant of the LORD with you. Nevertheless, [R]if there is iniquity in me, kill me yourself, for why should you bring me to your father?" Josh. 2:14 • 2 Sam. 14:32

9 But Jonathan said, "Far be it from you! For if I knew certainly that evil was determined by my father to come upon you, then would I not tell you?"

10 Then David said to Jonathan, "Who will tell me, or what *if* your father answers you roughly?"

11 And Jonathan said to David, "Come, let us go out into the field." So both of them went out into the field.

12 Then Jonathan said to David: "The LORD God of Israel *is witness!* When I have [T]sounded out my father sometime tomorrow, *or* the third *day,* and indeed *there is* good toward David, and I do not send to you and tell you, *searched out*

13 "may [R]the LORD do so and much more to Jonathan. But if it pleases my father *to do* you evil, then I will report it to you and send you away, that you may go in safety. And [R]the LORD be with you as He has [R]been with my father. Ruth 1:17 • Josh. 1:5 • 1 Sam. 10:7

14 "And you shall not only show me the kindness of the LORD while I still live, that I may not die;

15 "but you shall not cut off your kindness from my [T]house forever, no, not when the LORD has cut off every one of the enemies of David from the face of the earth." *family*

16 So Jonathan made *a covenant* with the house of David, *saying,* "Let the LORD require *it* at the hand of David's enemies."

17 Now Jonathan again caused David to vow, because he loved him; [R]for he loved him as he loved his own soul. 1 Sam. 18:1

18 Then Jonathan said to David, "Tomorrow *is* the New Moon; and you will be missed, because your seat will be empty.

19 "And *when* you have stayed three days, go down quickly and come to [R]the place where you hid on the day of the deed; and remain by the stone Ezel. 1 Sam. 19:2

20 "Then I will shoot three arrows to the side, as though I shot at a target;

21 "and there I will send a lad, *saying,* 'Go, find the arrows.' If I expressly say to the lad, 'Look, the arrows *are* on this side of you; get them and come'—then, as the LORD lives, *there is* safety for you and no harm.

22 "But if I say thus to the young man, 'Look, the arrows *are* beyond you'—go your way, for the LORD has sent you away.

23 "And as for [R]the matter which you and I have spoken of, indeed the LORD *be* between you and me forever." 1 Sam. 20:14, 15

24 Then David hid in the field. And when the New Moon had come, the king sat down to eat the feast.

25 Now the king sat on his seat, as at other times, on a seat by the wall. And Jonathan arose,* and Abner sat by Saul's side, but David's place was empty.

26 Nevertheless Saul did not say anything that day, for he thought, "Something has happened to him; he *is* unclean, surely he *is* [R]unclean." Lev. 7:20, 21; 15:5

27 And it happened the next day, the second *day* of the month, that David's place was empty. And Saul said to Jonathan his son, "Why has the son of Jesse not come to eat, either yesterday or today?"

28 So Jonathan [R]answered Saul, "David earnestly asked *permission* of me *to go* to Bethlehem. 1 Sam. 20:6

29 "And he said, 'Please let me go, for our family has a sacrifice in the city, and my brother has commanded me *to be there.* And now, if I have found favor in your eyes, please let me get away and see my brothers.' Therefore he has not come to the king's table."

30 Then Saul's anger was aroused against Jonathan, and he said to him, "You son of a perverse, rebellious *woman!* Do I not know that you have chosen the son of Jesse to your own shame and to the shame of your mother's nakedness?

31 "For as long as the son of Jesse lives on the earth, you shall not be established, nor your kingdom. Now therefore, send and bring him to me, for he shall surely die."

32 And Jonathan answered Saul his father,

20:25 So with MT, Syr., Tg., Vg.; LXX *he sat across from Jonathan*

and said to him, [R]"Why should he be killed? What has he done?" Gen. 31:36

33 Then Saul cast a spear at him to kill him, by which Jonathan knew that it was determined by his father to kill David.

34 So Jonathan arose from the table in fierce anger, and ate no food the second day of the month, for he was grieved for David, because his father had treated him shamefully.

35 And so it was, in the morning, that Jonathan went out into the field at the time appointed with David, and a little lad *was* with him.

36 Then he said to his lad, "Now run, find the arrows which I shoot." As the lad ran, he shot an arrow beyond him.

37 When the lad had come to the place where the arrow was which Jonathan had shot, Jonathan cried out after the lad and said, "*Is* not the arrow beyond you?"

38 And Jonathan cried out after the lad, "Make haste, hurry, do not delay!" So Jonathan's lad gathered up the arrows and came back to his master.

39 But the lad did not know anything. Only Jonathan and David knew of the matter.

40 Then Jonathan gave his [T]weapons to his lad, and said to him, "Go, carry *them* to the city." *equipment*

41 As soon as the lad had gone, David arose from *a place* toward the south, fell on his face to the ground, and bowed down three times. And they kissed one another; and they wept together, but David more so.

42 Then Jonathan said to David, [R]"Go in peace, since we have both sworn in the name of the LORD, saying, 'May the LORD be between you and me, and between your descendants and my descendants, forever.' " So he arose and departed, and Jonathan went into the city. 1 Sam. 1:17

CHAPTER 21

David Is Protected by the Priest

NOW David came to Nob, to Ahimelech the priest. And Ahimelech was afraid when he met David, and said to him, "Why *are* you alone, and no one is with you?"

2 So David said to Ahimelech the priest, "The king has ordered me on some business, and said to me, 'Do not let anyone know anything about the business on which I send you, or what I have commanded you.' And I have directed *my* young men to such and such a place.

3 "Now therefore, what have you on hand? Give *me* five *loaves of* bread in my hand, or whatever can be found."

4 And the priest answered David and said, "*There is* no common bread on hand; but there is holy bread, if the young men have at least kept themselves from women."

5 Then David answered the priest, and said to him, "Truly, women *have been* kept from us about three days since I came out. And the [R]vessels of the young men are holy, and *the bread is* in effect common, even though it was consecrated [R]in the vessel this day." 1 Thess. 4:4 • Lev. 8:26

6 So the priest [R]gave him holy *bread;* for there was no bread there but the showbread which had been taken from before the LORD, in order to put hot bread *in its place* on the day when it was taken away. Luke 6:3, 4

7 Now a certain man of the servants of Saul *was* there that day, detained before the LORD. And his name *was* [R]Doeg, an Edomite, the chief of the herdsmen who *belonged* to Saul. 1 Sam. 14:47; 22:9

8 And David said to Ahimelech, "Is there not here on hand a spear or a sword? For I have brought neither my sword nor my weapons with me, because the king's business required haste."

9 So the priest said, "The sword of Goliath the Philistine, whom you killed in [R]the Valley of Elah, [R]there it is, wrapped in a cloth behind the ephod. If you will take that, take *it*. For *there is* no other except that one here." And David said, "*There is* none like it; give it to me." 1 Sam. 17:2, 50 • 1 Sam. 31:10

David Pretends to be Mad

10 Then David arose and fled that day from before Saul, and went to Achish the king of Gath.

11 And [R]the servants of Achish said to him, "*Is* this not David the king of the land? Did they not sing of him to one another in dances, saying: Ps. 56:title

'Saul has slain his thousands,
And David his ten thousands'?"*

12 Now David [R]took these words [T]to heart, and was very much afraid of Achish the king of Gath. Luke 2:19 • Lit. *in his heart*

13 So [R]he changed his behavior before them, pretended madness in their hands, scratched on the doors of the gate, and let his saliva fall down on his beard. Ps. 34:title

14 Then Achish said to his servants, "Look, you see the man is insane. Why have you brought him to me?

15 "Have I need of madmen, that you have brought this *fellow* to play the madman in my presence? Shall this *fellow* come into my house?"

CHAPTER 22

David Flees to Adullam—1 Chr. 12:16–18

DAVID therefore departed from there and escaped to the cave of Adullam. So when

21:11 Cf. 1 Sam. 18:7

his brothers and all his father's house heard *it*, they went down there to him.

2 And everyone *who was* in distress, everyone who *was* in debt, and everyone *who was* discontented gathered to him. So he became captain over them. And there were about four hundred men with him.

3 Then David went from there to Mizpah of [R]Moab; and he said to the king of Moab, "Please let my father and mother come here with you, till I know what God will do for me." 2 Sam. 8:2

4 So he brought them before the king of Moab, and they dwelt with him all the time that David was in the stronghold.

5 Now the prophet Gad said to David, "Do not stay in the stronghold; depart, and go to the land of Judah." So David departed and went into the forest of Hereth.

Saul Slays the Priests of God

6 When Saul heard that David and the men who *were* with him had been discovered—now Saul was staying in [R]Gibeah under a tamarisk tree in Ramah, with his spear in his hand, and all his servants standing about him— 1 Sam. 15:34

7 then Saul said to his servants who stood about him, "Hear now, you Benjamites! Will the son of Jesse [R]give every one of you fields and vineyards, *and* make you all captains of thousands and captains of hundreds? 1 Sam. 8:14

8 "All of you have conspired against me, and *there is* no one who reveals to me that [R]my son has made a covenant with the son of Jesse; and *there is* not one of you who is sorry for me or reveals to me that my son has stirred up my servant against me, to lie in wait, as *it is* this day." 1 Sam. 18:3

9 Then answered Doeg the Edomite, who was set over the servants of Saul, and said, "I saw the son of Jesse going to Nob, to [R]Ahimelech the son of Ahitub. 1 Sam. 21:1

10 [R]"And he inquired of the LORD for him, gave him provisions, and gave him the sword of Goliath the Philistine." Num. 27:21

11 So the king sent to call Ahimelech the priest, the son of Ahitub, and all his father's house, the priests who *were* in Nob. And they all came to the king.

12 And Saul said, "Hear now, son of Ahitub!" He answered, "Here I am, my lord."

13 Then Saul said to him, "Why have you conspired against me, you and the son of Jesse, in that you have given him bread and a sword, and have inquired of God for him, that he should rise against me, to lie in wait, as it is this day?"

14 So Ahimelech answered the king and said, "And who among all your servants *is as* [R]faithful as David, who is the king's son-in-law, who goes at your bidding, and is honorable in your house? 1 Sam. 19:4, 5; 20:32; 24:11

15 "Did I then begin to inquire of God for him? Far be it from me! Let not the king impute anything to his servant, *or* to any in the house of my father. For your servant knew nothing of all this, little or much."

16 And the king said, "You shall surely die, Ahimelech, you and all your father's house!"

17 Then the king said to the guards who stood about him, "Turn and kill the priests of the LORD, because their hand also *is* with David, and because they knew when he fled and did not tell it to me." But the servants of the king [R]would not lift their hands to strike the priests of the LORD. Ex. 1:17

18 And the king said to Doeg, "You turn and kill the priests!" So Doeg the Edomite turned and [T]struck the priests, and [R]killed on that day eighty-five men who wore a linen ephod. *attacked* • 1 Sam. 2:31

19 [R]Also Nob, the city of the priests, he struck with the edge of the sword, both men and women, children and nursing infants, oxen and donkeys and sheep—with the edge of the sword. 1 Sam. 22:9, 11

20 [R]Now one of the sons of Ahimelech the son of Ahitub, named Abiathar, escaped and fled after David. 1 Sam. 23:6, 9; 30:7

21 And Abiathar told David that Saul had killed the LORD's priests.

22 So David said to Abiathar, "I knew that day, when Doeg the Edomite *was* there, that he would surely tell Saul. I have caused *the death* of all the persons of your father's [T]house. *family*

23 "Stay with me; do not fear. [R]For he who seeks my life seeks your life, but with me you *shall be* safe." 1 Kin. 2:26

CHAPTER 23

David Smites the Philistines

THEN they told David, saying, "Look, the Philistines are fighting against Keilah, and they are robbing the threshing floors."

2 Therefore David inquired of the LORD, saying, "Shall I go and attack these Philistines?" And the LORD said to David, "Go and attack the Philistines, and save Keilah."

3 But David's men said to him, "Look, we are afraid here in Judah. How much more then if we go to Keilah against the armies of the Philistines?"

4 Then David inquired of the LORD once again. And the LORD answered him and said, "Arise, go down to Keilah. For I will deliver the Philistines into your hand."

5 And David and his men went to Keilah and [R]fought with the Philistines, struck them with a mighty blow, and took away their livestock. So David saved the inhabitants of Keilah. 1 Sam. 19:8

6 Now it happened, when Abiathar the son of Ahimelech [R]fled to David at Keilah,

that he went down *with* an ephod in his
hand. 1 Sam. 22:20
7 And Saul was told that David had gone to
Keilah. So Saul said, "God has delivered him
into my hand, for he has shut himself in by en-
tering a town that has gates and bars."
8 Then Saul called all the people together
for war, to go down to Keilah to besiege David
and his men.
9 When David knew that Saul plotted evil
against him, [R]he said to Abiathar the priest,
"Bring the ephod here." 1 Sam. 23:6; 30:7
10 Then David said, "O LORD God of Israel,
Your servant has certainly heard that Saul
seeks to come to Keilah [R]to destroy the city
for my sake. 1 Sam. 22:19
11 "Will the men of Keilah deliver me into
his hand? Will Saul come down, as Your ser-
vant has heard? O LORD God of Israel, I pray,
tell Your servant." And the LORD said, "He will
come down."
12 Then David said, "Will the men of Keilah
[T]deliver me and my men into the hand of
Saul?" And the LORD said, "They will deliver
you." Lit. *shut up*

Saul Chases David

13 So David and his men, about six hundred,
arose and departed from Keilah and went
wherever they could go. Then it was told Saul
that David had escaped from Keilah; so he
halted the expedition.
14 And David stayed in strongholds in the
wilderness, and remained in [R]the mountains
in the Wilderness of [R]Ziph. Saul [R]sought him
every day, but God did not deliver him into his
hand. Ps. 11:1 • Josh. 15:55 • Ps. 32:7; 54:3, 4
15 So David saw that Saul had come out to
seek his life. And David *was* in the Wilderness
of Ziph in a forest.*
16 Then Jonathan, Saul's son, arose and
went to David in the woods and [T]strengthened
his hand in God. *encouraged him*
17 And he said to him, [R]"Do not fear, for the
hand of Saul my father shall not find you.
You shall be king over Israel, and I shall be
next to you. [R]Even my father Saul knows
that." [Heb. 13:6] • 1 Sam. 20:31; 24:20
18 So the two of them [R]made a covenant
before the LORD. And David stayed in the
woods, and Jonathan went to his own
house. 2 Sam. 9:1; 21:7
19 Then the Ziphites [R]came up to Saul at
Gibeah, saying, "Is David not hiding with us
in strongholds in the woods, in the hill of
Hachilah, which *is* on the south of Jeshi-
mon? 1 Sam. 26:1
20 "Now therefore, O king, come down ac-
cording to all the desire of your soul to come
down; and [R]our part *shall be* to deliver him
into the king's hand." Ps. 54:3
21 And Saul said, "Blessed *are* you of the
LORD, for you have compassion on me.
22 "Please go and find out for sure, and see
the place where his hideout is, *and* who has
seen him there. For I am told he is very crafty.
23 "See therefore, and take knowledge of all
the lurking places where he hides; and come
back to me with certainty, and I will go with
you. And it shall be, if he is in the land, that I
will search for him throughout all the clans*
of Judah."
24 So they arose and went to Ziph before
Saul. But David and his men *were* in the
Wilderness [R]of Maon, in the plain on the
south of Jeshimon. 1 Sam. 25:2
25 When Saul and his men went to seek *him*,
they told David. Therefore he went down to
the rock, and stayed in the Wilderness of
Maon. And when Saul heard *that*, he pursued
David in the Wilderness of Maon.
26 Then Saul went on one side of the moun-
tain, and David and his men on the other
side of the mountain. [R]So David made haste
to get away from Saul, for Saul and his men
[R]were encircling David and his men to take
them. Ps. 31:22 • Ps. 17:9
27 [R]But a messenger came to Saul, saying,
"Hurry and come, for the Philistines have in-
vaded the land!" 2 Kin. 19:9
28 Therefore Saul returned from pursuing
David, and went against the Philistines; so
they called that place the Rock of Escape.*
29 Then David went up from there and dwelt
in strongholds at En Gedi.

CHAPTER 24

David Spares Saul's Life

NOW it happened, when Saul had returned
from following the Philistines, that it was
told him, saying, "Take note! David *is* in the
Wilderness of En Gedi."
2 Then Saul took three thousand chosen
men from all Israel, and went to seek David
and his men on the Rocks of the Wild Goats.
3 So he came to the sheepfolds by the
road, where there *was* a cave; and [R]Saul
went in to attend to his needs. ([R]David and
his men were staying in the recesses of the
cave.) 1 Sam. 24:10 • Ps. 57:title; 142:title
4 Then the men of David said to him, "This
is the day of which the LORD said to you, 'Be-
hold, I will deliver your enemy into your hand,
that you may do to him as it seems good to
you.' " And David arose and secretly cut off a
corner of Saul's robe.
5 Now it happened afterward that [R]David's
heart troubled him because he had cut Saul's
robe. 2 Sam. 24:10
6 And he said to his men, [R]"The LORD forbid
that I should do this thing to my master, the
LORD's anointed, to stretch out my hand

23:15 Or *in Horesh* **23:23** Lit. *thousands*
23:28 Heb. *Sela Hammahlekoth*

against him, seeing he *is* the anointed of the LORD." 1 Sam. 26:11

7 So David [R]restrained his servants with *these* words, and did not allow them to rise against Saul. And Saul got up from the cave and went on *his* way. [Matt. 5:44]

8 David also arose afterward, went out of the cave, and called out to Saul, saying, "My lord the king!" And when Saul looked behind him, David stooped with his face to the earth, and bowed down.

9 And David said to Saul: [R]"Why do you listen to the words of men who say, 'Indeed David seeks your harm'? Ps. 141:6

10 "Look, this day your eyes have seen that the LORD delivered you today into my hand in the cave, and *someone* urged *me* to kill you. But *my eye* spared you, and I said, 'I will not stretch out my hand against my lord, for he *is* the LORD's anointed.'

11 "Moreover, my father, see! Yes, see the corner of your robe in my hand! For in that I cut off the corner of your robe, and did not kill you, know and see that *there is* [R]neither evil nor rebellion in my hand, and I have not sinned against you. Yet you [R]hunt my life to take it. Ps. 7:3; 35:7 • 1 Sam. 26:20

12 "Let the LORD judge between you and me, and let the LORD avenge me on you. But my hand shall not be against you.

13 "As the proverb of the ancients says, 'Wickedness proceeds from the wicked.' But my hand shall not be against you.

14 "After whom has the king of Israel come out? Whom do you pursue? [R]A dead dog? [R]A flea? 2 Sam. 9:8 • 1 Sam. 26:20

15 [R]"Therefore let the LORD be judge, and judge between you and me, and see and [R]plead my case, and deliver me out of your hand." 1 Sam. 24:12 • Ps. 35:1; 43:1; 119:154

16 So it was, when David had finished speaking these words to Saul, that Saul said, "*Is* this your voice, my son David?" And Saul lifted up his voice and wept.

17 [R]Then he said to David: "You *are* [R]more righteous than I; for [R]you have rewarded me with good, whereas I have rewarded you with evil. 1 Sam. 26:21 • Gen. 38:26 • [Matt. 5:44]

18 "And you have shown this day how you have dealt well with me; for when [R]the LORD delivered me into your hand, you did not kill me. 1 Sam. 26:23

19 "For if a man finds his enemy, will he let him get away safely? Therefore may the LORD reward you with good for what you have done to me this day.

20 "And now I know indeed that you shall surely be king, and that the kingdom of Israel shall be established in your hand

21 "Therefore swear now to me by the LORD that you will not cut off my descendants after me, and that you will not destroy my name from my father's house."

22 So David swore to Saul. And Saul went home, but David and his men went up to [R]the stronghold. 1 Sam. 23:29

CHAPTER 25

Samuel the Judge Dies

THEN [R]Samuel died; and the Israelites gathered together and [R]lamented for him, and buried him at his home in Ramah. And David arose and went down to the Wilderness of Paran.* 1 Sam. 28:3 • Deut. 34:8

David Marries Abigail

2 Now *there was* a man [R]in Maon whose business *was* in [R]Carmel, and the man *was* very rich. He had three thousand sheep and a thousand goats. And he was shearing his sheep in Carmel. 1 Sam. 23:24 • Josh. 15:55

3 The name of the man *was* Nabal, and the name of his wife Abigail. And *she was* a woman of good understanding and beautiful appearance; but the man *was* harsh and evil in *his* doings. He *was of the house of* Caleb.

4 When David heard in the wilderness that Nabal was shearing his sheep,

5 David sent ten young men; and David said to the young men, "Go up to Carmel, go to Nabal, and greet him in my name.

6 "And thus you shall say to him who lives *in prosperity:* 'Peace *be* to you, peace to your house, and peace to all that you have!

7 'Now I have heard that you have shearers. Your shepherds were with us, and we did not hurt them, [R]nor was there anything missing from them all the while they were in Carmel. 1 Sam. 25:15, 21

8 'Ask your young men, and they will tell you. Therefore let *my* young men find favor in your eyes, for we come on a feast day. Please give whatever comes to your hand to your servants and to your son David.' "

9 So when David's young men came, they spoke to Nabal according to all these words in the name of David, and waited.

10 Then Nabal answered David's servants, and said, "Who *is* David, and who *is* the son of Jesse? There are many servants nowadays who break away each one from his master.

11 [R]"Shall I then take my bread and my water and my meat that I have killed for my shearers, and give *it* to men when I do not know where they *are* from?" Judg. 8:6, 15

12 So David's young men turned on their heels and went back; and they came and told him all these words.

13 Then David said to his men, "Every man gird on his sword." So every man girded on his sword, and David also girded on his sword. And about four hundred men went

25:1 So with MT, Syr., Tg., Vg.; LXX *Maon*

with David, and two hundred [R]stayed with the supplies. 1 Sam. 30:24

14 Now one of the young men told Abigail, Nabal's wife, saying, "Look, David sent messengers from the wilderness to greet our master; and he reviled them.

15 "But the men *were* very good to us, and [R]we were not hurt, nor did we miss anything as long as we accompanied them, when we were in the fields. 1 Sam. 25:7, 21

16 "They were [R]a wall to us both by night and day, all the time we were with them keeping the sheep. Ex. 14:22

17 "Now therefore, know and consider what you will do, for [R]harm is determined against our master and against all his household. For he *is such* a [R]scoundrel* that *one* cannot speak to him." 1 Sam. 20:7 • Deut. 13:13

18 Then Abigail made haste and [R]took two hundred *loaves* of bread, two skins of wine, five sheep already dressed, five seahs of roasted *grain,* one hundred clusters of raisins, and two hundred cakes of figs, and loaded *them* on donkeys. Gen. 32:13

19 And she said to her servants, "Go on before me; see, I am coming after you." But she did not tell her husband Nabal.

20 So it was, *as* she rode on the donkey, that she went down under cover of the hill; and there were David and his men, coming down toward her, and she met them.

21 Now David had said, "Surely in vain I have protected all that this *fellow* has in the wilderness, so that nothing was missed of all that *belongs* to him. And he has [R]repaid me evil for good. Ps. 109:5

22 "May God do so, and more also, to the enemies of David, if I leave one male of all who *belong* to him by morning light."

23 Now when Abigail saw David, she [R]dismounted quickly from the donkey, fell on her face before David, and bowed down to the ground. Judg. 1:14

24 So she fell at his feet and said: "On me, my lord, *on* me *let* this iniquity *be!* And please let your maidservant [T]speak in your ears, and hear the words of your maidservant. *speak to you*

25 "Please, let not my lord regard this scoundrel Nabal. For as his name *is,* so *is* he: Nabal* *is* his name, and folly *is* with him! But I, your maidservant, did not see the young men of my lord whom you sent.

26 "Now therefore, my lord, [R]*as* the LORD lives and *as* your soul lives, since the LORD has [R]held you back from coming to bloodshed and from [R]avenging yourself with your own hand, now then, let your enemies and those who seek harm for my lord be as Nabal. 2 Kin. 2:2 • Gen. 20:6 • [Rom. 12:19]

27 "And now this present which your maidservant has brought to my lord, let it be given to the young men who follow my lord.

28 "Please forgive the trespass of your maidservant. For [R]the LORD will certainly make for my lord an enduring house, because my lord [R]fights the battles of the LORD, and evil is not found in you throughout your days. 2 Sam. 7:11–16, 27 • 1 Sam. 18:17

29 "Yet a man has risen to pursue you and seek your life, but the life of my lord shall be [R]bound in the bundle of the living with the LORD your God; and the lives of your enemies He shall [R]sling out, *as from* the pocket of a sling. [Col. 3:3] • Jer. 10:18

30 "And it shall come to pass, when the LORD has done for my lord according to all the good that He has spoken concerning you, and has appointed you [R]ruler over Israel, 1 Sam. 13:14; 15:28

31 "that this will be no grief to you, nor offense of heart to my lord, either that you have shed blood without cause, or that my lord has avenged himself. But when the LORD has dealt well with my lord, then remember your maidservant."

32 Then David said to Abigail: [R]"Blessed *is* the LORD God of Israel, who sent you this day to meet me! Luke 1:68

33 "And blessed *is* your advice and blessed *are* you, because you have [R]kept me this day from coming to bloodshed and from avenging myself with my own hand. 1 Sam. 25:26

34 "For indeed, *as* the LORD God of Israel lives, who has [R]kept me back from hurting you, unless you had hurried and come to meet me, surely by morning light no males would have been left to Nabal!" 1 Sam. 25:26

35 So David received from her hand what she had brought him, and said to her, [R]"Go up in peace to your house. See, I have heeded your voice and [R]respected your person." 2 Kin. 5:19 • Gen. 19:21

36 Now Abigail went to Nabal, and there he was, [R]holding a feast in his house, like the feast of a king. And Nabal's heart *was* merry within him, for he *was* very drunk; therefore she told him nothing, little or much, until morning light. 2 Sam. 13:28

37 So it was, in the morning, when the wine had gone from Nabal, and his wife had told him these things, that his heart died within him, and he became *like* a stone.

38 Then it happened, *after* about ten days, that the LORD struck Nabal, and he died.

39 So when David heard that Nabal was dead, he said, [R]"Blessed *be* the LORD, who has [R]pleaded the cause of my reproach from the hand of Nabal, and has kept His servant from evil! For the LORD has returned the wickedness of Nabal on his own head." And David sent and proposed to Abigail, to take her as his wife. 1 Sam. 25:32 • Prov. 22:23

40 When the servants of David had come to Abigail at Carmel, they spoke to her saying,

25:17 Lit. *son of Belial* **25:25** Lit. *Fool*

"David sent us to you, to ask you to become his wife."

41 Then she arose, bowed her face to the earth, and said, "Here is your maidservant, a servant to [R]wash the feet of the servants of my lord." Luke 7:38, 44

42 So Abigail rose in haste and rode on a donkey, attended by five of her maidens; and she followed the messengers of David, and became his wife.

43 David also took Ahinoam of Jezreel, and so both of them were his wives.

44 But Saul had given [R]Michal his daughter, David's wife, to Palti* the son of Laish, who *was* from [R]Gallim. 2 Sam. 3:14 • Is. 10:30

CHAPTER 26

David Saves Saul's Life Again

NOW the Ziphites came to Saul at Gibeah, saying, "Is David not hiding in the hill of Hachilah, opposite Jeshimon?"

2 Then Saul arose and went down to the Wilderness of Ziph, having [R]three thousand chosen men of Israel with him, to seek David in the Wilderness of Ziph. 1 Sam. 13:2; 24:2

3 And Saul encamped in the hill of Hachilah, which *is* opposite Jeshimon, by the road. But David stayed in the wilderness, and he saw that Saul came after him into the wilderness.

4 David therefore sent out spies, and understood that Saul had indeed come.

5 So David arose and came to the place where Saul had encamped. And David saw the place where Saul lay, and [R]Abner the son of Ner, the commander of his army. Now Saul lay within the camp, with the people encamped all around him. 1 Sam. 14:50, 51

6 Then David answered, and said to Ahimelech the Hittite and to Abishai [R]the son of Zeruiah, brother of [R]Joab, saying, "Who will [R]go down with me to Saul in the camp?" And Abishai said, "I will go down with you." 1 Chr. 2:16 • 2 Sam. 2:13 • Judg. 7:10, 11

7 So David and Abishai came to the people by night; and there Saul lay sleeping within the camp, with his spear stuck in the ground by his head. And Abner and the people lay all around him.

8 Then Abishai said to David, [R]"God has delivered your enemy into your hand this day. Now therefore, please, let me strike him [T]at once with the spear, right to the earth; and I will not *have to strike* him a second time!" 1 Sam. 24:4 • Or *one time*

9 But David said to Abishai, "Do not destroy him; [R]for who can stretch out his hand against the LORD's anointed, and be guiltless?" 1 Sam. 24:6, 7

10 David said furthermore, "*As* the LORD lives, [R]the LORD shall strike him, or [R]his day shall come to die, or he shall go out to battle and perish. 1 Sam. 25:26, 38 • [Job 7:1; 14:5]

11 "The LORD forbid that I should stretch out my hand against the LORD's anointed. But please, take now the spear and the jug of water that *are* by his head, and let us go."

12 So David took the spear and the jug of water *by* Saul's head, and they got away; and no man saw or knew *it* or awoke. For they *were* all asleep, because a deep sleep from the LORD had fallen on them.

13 Now David went over to the other side, and stood on the top of a hill afar off, a great distance *being* between them.

14 And David called out to the people and to Abner the son of Ner, saying, "Do you not answer, Abner?" Then Abner answered and said, "Who *are* you, calling out to the king?"

15 So David said to Abner, "*Are* you not a man? And who *is* like you in Israel? Why then have you not guarded your lord the king? For one of the people came in to destroy your lord the king.

16 "This thing that you have done *is* not good. *As* the LORD lives, you deserve to die, because you have not guarded your master, the LORD's anointed. And now see where the king's spear *is*, and the jug of water that *was* by his head."

17 Then Saul knew David's voice, and said, "*Is* that your voice, my son David?" David said, "*It is* my voice, my lord, O king."

18 And he said, [R]"Why does my lord thus pursue his servant? For what have I done, or what evil *is* in my hand? 1 Sam. 24:9, 11–14

19 "Now therefore, please, let my lord the king hear the words of his servant: If the LORD has [R]stirred you up against me, let Him accept an offering. But if *it is* the children of men, *may* they *be* cursed before the LORD, for they have driven me out this day from sharing in the inheritance of the LORD, saying, 'Go, serve other gods.' 2 Sam. 16:11; 24:1

20 "So now, do not let my blood fall to the earth before the face of the LORD. For the king of Israel has come out to seek [R]a flea, as when one hunts a partridge in the mountains." 1 Sam. 24:14

Saul Admits His Guilt

21 Then Saul said, [R]"I have sinned. Return, my son David. For I will harm you no more, because my life was precious in your eyes this day. Indeed I have played the fool and erred exceedingly." 1 Sam. 15:24, 30; 24:17

22 And David answered and said, "Here is the king's spear. Let one of the young men come over and get it.

23 [R]"May the LORD repay every man *for* his righteousness and his faithfulness; for the LORD delivered you into *my* hand today, but I would not stretch out my hand against the LORD's anointed. Ps. 7:8; 18:20; 62:12

25:44 *Paltiel,* 2 Sam. 3:15

24 "And indeed, as your life was valued much this day in my eyes, so let my life be valued much in the eyes of the LORD, and let Him deliver me out of all tribulation."

25 Then Saul said to David, "*May* you *be* blessed, my son David! You shall both do great things and also still [R]prevail." So David went on his way, and Saul returned to his place. Gen. 32:28

CHAPTER 27

David Joins with the Philistines

AND David said in his heart, "Now I shall perish someday by the hand of Saul. *There is* nothing better for me than that I should speedily escape to the land of the Philistines; and Saul will despair of me, to seek me anymore in any part of Israel. So I shall escape out of his hand."

2 Then David arose and went over with the six hundred men who *were* with him to Achish the son of Maoch, king of Gath.

3 So David dwelt with Achish at Gath, he and his men, each man with his household, *and* David [R]with his two wives, Ahinoam the Jezreelitess, and Abigail the Carmelitess, Nabal's widow. 1 Sam. 25:42, 43

4 And it was told Saul that David had fled to Gath; so he sought him no more.

5 Then David said to Achish, "If I have now found favor in your eyes, let them give me a place in some town in the country, that I may dwell there. For why should your servant dwell in the royal city with you?"

6 So Achish gave him Ziklag that day. Therefore [R]Ziklag has belonged to the kings of Judah to this day. Josh. 15:31; 19:5

7 Now the time that David [R]dwelt in the country of the Philistines was one full year and four months. 1 Sam. 29:3

8 And David and his men went up and raided the Geshurites, the Girzites,* and the Amalekites. For those nations were the inhabitants of the land from of old, as you go to Shur, even as far as the land of Egypt.

9 Whenever David [T]attacked the land, he left neither man nor woman alive, but took away the sheep, the oxen, the donkeys, the camels, and the apparel, and returned and came to Achish. Lit. *struck*

10 Then Achish would say, "Where have you made a raid today?" And David would say, "Against the southern *area* of Judah, or against the southern *area* of [R]the Jerahmeelites, or against the southern *area* of [R]the Kenites." 1 Chr. 2:9, 25 • Judg. 1:16

11 David would save neither man nor woman alive, to bring *news* to Gath, saying, "Lest they should inform on us, saying, 'Thus David did.' " And thus *was* his behavior all the time he dwelt in the country of the Philistines.

12 So Achish believed David, saying, "He has made his people Israel utterly abhor him; therefore he will be my servant forever."

CHAPTER 28

NOW [R]it happened in those days that the Philistines gathered their armies together for war, to fight with Israel. And Achish said to David, "You assuredly know that you will go out with me to battle, you and your men." 1 Sam. 29:1, 2

2 So David said to Achish, "Surely you know what your servant can do." And Achish said to David, "Therefore I will make you one of my chief guardians forever."

God Does Not Answer Saul

3 Now [R]Samuel had died, and all Israel had lamented for him and buried him in [R]Ramah, in his own city. And Saul had put [R]the mediums and the spiritists out of the land. 1 Sam. 25:1 • 1 Sam. 1:19 • Deut. 18:10, 11

4 Then the Philistines gathered together, and came and encamped at [R]Shunem. So Saul gathered all Israel together, and they encamped at [R]Gilboa. Josh. 19:18 • 1 Sam. 31:1

5 When Saul saw the army of the Philistines, he was [R]afraid, and his heart trembled greatly. Job 18:11

6 And when Saul inquired of the LORD, the LORD did not answer him, either by dreams or by Urim or by the prophets.

Saul Visits the Medium

7 Then Saul said to his servants, "Find me a woman who is a medium, [R]that I may go to her and inquire of her." And his servants said to him, "In fact, *there is* a woman who is a medium at En Dor." 1 Chr. 10:13

8 So Saul disguised himself and put on other clothes, and he went, and two men with him; and they came to the woman by night. And [R]he said, "Please conduct a séance for me, and bring up for me the one I shall name to you." Deut. 18:10, 11

9 Then the woman said to him, "Look, you know what Saul has done, how he has [R]cut off the mediums and the spiritists from the land. Why then do you lay a snare for my life, to cause me to die?" 1 Sam. 28:3

10 And Saul swore to her by the LORD, saying, "*As* the LORD lives, no punishment shall come upon you for this thing."

11 Then the woman said, "Whom shall I bring up for you?" And he said, "Bring up Samuel for me."

12 When the woman saw Samuel, she cried out with a loud voice. And the woman spoke to Saul, saying, "Why have you deceived me? For you *are* Saul!"

13 And the king said to her, "Do not be afraid. What did you see?" And the woman

27:8 Or *Gezrites*

said to Saul, "I saw [R]a spirit* ascending out of the earth." Ex. 22:28

14 So he said to her, "What *is* his form?" And she said, "An old man is coming up, and he *is* covered with [R]a mantle." And Saul perceived that it *was* Samuel, and he stooped with *his* face to the ground and bowed down. 1 Sam. 15:27

15 Now Samuel said to Saul, "Why have you disturbed me by bringing me up?" And Saul answered, "I am deeply distressed; for the Philistines make war against me, and God has departed from me and does not answer me anymore, neither by prophets nor by dreams. Therefore I have called you, that you may reveal to me what I should do."

16 Then Samuel said: "So why do you ask me, seeing the LORD has departed from you and has become your enemy?

17 "And the LORD has done for Himself* [R]as He spoke by me. For the LORD has torn the kingdom out of your hand and given it to your neighbor, David. 1 Sam. 15:28

18 [R]"Because you did not obey the voice of the LORD nor execute His fierce wrath upon Amalek, therefore the LORD has done this thing to you this day. 1 Chr. 10:13

19 "Moreover the LORD will also deliver Israel with you into the hand of the Philistines. And tomorrow you and your sons *will be* with [R]me. The LORD will also deliver the army of Israel into the hand of the Philistines." Job 3:17–19

20 Immediately Saul fell full length on the ground, and was dreadfully afraid because of the words of Samuel. And there was no strength in him, for he had eaten no food all day or all night.

21 And the woman came to Saul and saw that he was severely troubled, and said to him, "Look, your maidservant has obeyed your voice, and I have [R]put my life in my hands and heeded the words which you spoke to me. Job 13:14

22 "Now therefore, please, heed also the voice of your maidservant, and let me set a piece of bread before you; and eat, that you may have strength when you go on *your* way."

23 But he refused and said, "I will not eat." So his servants, together with the woman, urged him; and he heeded their voice. Then he arose from the ground and sat on the bed.

24 Now the woman had a fatted calf in the house, and she hastened to kill it. And she took flour and kneaded *it*, and baked unleavened bread from it.

25 So she brought *it* before Saul and his servants, and they ate. Then they rose and went away that night.

CHAPTER 29

David Is Spared from Fighting Saul

THEN the Philistines gathered together all their armies at Aphek, and the Israelites encamped by a fountain which *is* in Jezreel.

2 And the [R]lords of the Philistines passed in review by hundreds and by thousands, but David and his men passed in review at the rear with Achish. 1 Sam. 6:4; 7:7

3 Then the princes of the Philistines said, "What *are* these Hebrews *doing here?*" And Achish said to the princes of the Philistines, "*Is* this not David, the servant of Saul king of Israel, who has been with me these days, or these years? And to this day I have found no fault in him since he defected *to me*."

4 But the princes of the Philistines were angry with him; so the princes of the Philistines said to him, "Make this fellow return, that he may go back to the place which you have appointed for him, and do not let him go down with us to battle, lest in the battle he become our adversary. For with what could he reconcile himself to his master, if not with the heads of these men?

5 "*Is* this not David, of whom they sang to one another in dances, saying:

'Saul has slain his thousands,
And David his ten thousands'?"*

6 Then Achish called David and said to him, "Surely, *as* the LORD lives, you have been upright, and your going out and your coming in with me in the army *is* good in my sight. For to this day I have not found evil in you since the day of your coming to me. Nevertheless the lords do not favor you.

7 "Therefore return now, and go in peace, that you may not displease the lords of the Philistines."

8 So David said to Achish, "But what have I done? And to this day what have you found in your servant as long as I have been with you, that I may not go and fight against the enemies of my lord the king?"

9 Then Achish answered and said to David, "I know that you *are* as good in my sight as an angel of God; nevertheless the princes of the Philistines have said, 'He shall not go up with us to the battle.'

10 "Now therefore, rise early in the morning with your master's servants who have come with you.* And as soon as you are up early in the morning and have light, depart."

11 So David and his men rose early to depart in the morning, to return to the land of the Philistines. [R]And the Philistines went up to Jezreel. 2 Sam. 4:4

28:13 Heb. *elohim* **28:17** Or *him*, David **29:5** Cf. 1 Sam. 18:7 **29:10** So with MT, Tg., Vg.; LXX adds *and go to the place which I have selected for you there; and set no bothersome word in your heart, for you are good before me. And rise on your way*

CHAPTER 30

God Answers David

NOW it happened, when David and his men came to [R]Ziklag, on the third day, that the [R]Amalekites had invaded the South and Ziklag, attacked Ziklag and burned it with fire, 1 Sam. 27:6 • 1 Sam. 15:7; 27:8

2 and had taken captive the [R]women and those who *were* there, from small to great; they did not kill anyone, but carried *them* away and went their way. 1 Sam. 27:2, 3

3 So David and his men came to the city, and there it was, burned with fire; and their wives, their sons, and their daughters had been taken captive.

4 Then David and the people who *were* with him lifted up their voices and wept, until they had no more power to weep.

5 And David's two wives, Ahinoam the Jezreelitess, and Abigail the widow of Nabal the Carmelite, had been taken captive.

6 Now David was greatly distressed, for [R]the people spoke of stoning him, because the soul of all the people was [T]grieved, every man for his sons and his daughters. [R]But David strengthened himself in the LORD his God. Ex. 17:4 • Lit. *bitter* • Hab. 3:17–19

7 [R]Then David said to Abiathar the priest, Ahimelech's son, "Please bring the ephod here to me." And [R]Abiathar brought the ephod to David. 1 Sam. 23:2–9 • 1 Sam. 23:6

8 [R]So David inquired of the LORD, saying, "Shall I pursue this troop? Shall I overtake them?" And He answered him, "Pursue, for you shall surely overtake *them* and without fail recover *all*." 1 Sam. 23:2, 4

David Kills the Enemy

9 So David went, he and the six hundred men who *were* with him, and came to the Brook Besor, where those stayed who were left behind.

10 But David pursued, he and four hundred men; [R]for two hundred stayed *behind*, who were so weary that they could not cross the Brook Besor. 1 Sam. 30:9, 21

11 Then they found an Egyptian in the field, and brought him to David; and they gave him bread and he ate, and they let him drink water.

12 And they gave him a piece of a cake of figs and two clusters of raisins. So when he had eaten, his strength came back to him; for he had eaten no bread nor drunk water for three days and three nights.

13 Then David said to him, "To whom do you *belong*, and where *are* you from?" And he said, "I *am* a young man from Egypt, servant of an Amalekite; and my master left me behind, because three days ago I fell sick.

14 "We made an invasion of the southern *area* of [R]the Cherethites, in the *territory* which *belongs* to Judah, and of the southern *area* [R]of Caleb; and we burned Ziklag with fire." 2 Sam. 8:18 • Josh. 14:13; 15:13

15 And David said to him, "Can you take me down to this troop?" So he said, "Swear to me by God that you will neither kill me nor deliver me into the hands of my master, and I will take you down to this troop."

16 And when he had brought him down, there they were, spread out over all the land, [R]eating and drinking and dancing, because of all the great spoil which they had taken from the land of the Philistines and from the land of Judah. 1 Thess. 5:3

17 Then David attacked them from twilight until the evening of the next day. Not a man of them escaped, except four hundred young men who rode on camels and fled.

18 So David recovered all that the Amalekites had carried away, and David rescued his two wives.

19 And nothing of theirs was lacking, either small or great, sons or daughters, spoil or anything which they had taken from them; [R]David recovered all. 1 Sam. 30:8

20 Then David took all the flocks and herds they had driven before those *other* livestock, and said, "This *is* David's spoil."

21 Now David came to the [R]two hundred men who had been so weary that they could not follow David, whom they also had made to stay at the Brook Besor. So they went out to meet David and to meet the people who *were* with him. And when David came near the people, he greeted them. 1 Sam. 30:10

22 Then all the wicked and [R]worthless men* of those who went with David answered and said, "Because they did not go with us, we will not give them *any* of the spoil that we have recovered, except for every man's wife and children, that they may lead *them* away and depart." Deut. 13:13

23 But David said, "My brethren, you shall not do so with what the LORD has given us, who has preserved us and delivered into our hand the troop that came against us.

24 "For who will heed you in this matter? But [R]as his part *is* who goes down to the battle, so *shall* his part *be* who stays by the supplies; they shall share alike." Josh. 22:8

25 So it was, from that day forward; he made it a statute and an ordinance for Israel to this day.

26 Now when David came to Ziklag, he sent *some* of the spoil to the elders of Judah, to his friends, saying, "Here is a present for you from the spoil of the enemies of the LORD"—

27 to *those* who *were* in Bethel, *those* who *were* in [R]Ramoth of the South, *those* who *were* in [R]Jattir, Josh. 19:8 • Josh. 15:48; 21:14

28 *those* who *were* in [R]Aroer, *those* who

30:22 Lit. *men of Belial*

were in [R]Siphmoth, *those* who *were* in [R]Eshte-
moa, Josh. 13:16 • 1 Chr. 27:27 • Josh. 15:50
29 *those* who *were* in Rachal, *those* who
were in the cities of the Jerahmeelites, *those*
who *were* in the cities of the Kenites,
30 *those* who *were* in [R]Hormah, *those* who
were in Chorashan,* *those* who *were* in
Athach, Judg. 1:17
31 *those* who *were* in [R]Hebron, and to all the
places where David himself and his men were
accustomed to rove. 2 Sam. 2:1

CHAPTER 31

The Enemy Kills Saul—1 Chr. 10:1–14

NOW [R]the Philistines fought against Israel;
and the men of Israel fled from before
the Philistines, and fell slain on Mount
[R]Gilboa. 1 Chr. 10:1–12 • 1 Sam. 28:4
2 Then the Philistines followed hard after
Saul and his sons. And the Philistines killed
[R]Jonathan, Abinadab, and Malchishua, Saul's
sons. 1 Sam. 14:49
3 [R]The battle became fierce against Saul.
The archers hit him, and he was severely
wounded by the archers. 2 Sam. 1:6
4 [R]Then Saul said to his armorbearer,
"Draw your sword, and thrust me through
with it, lest [R]these uncircumcised men come
and thrust me through and abuse me." But his
armorbearer would not, for he was greatly
afraid. Therefore Saul took a sword and fell
on it. Judg. 9:54 • 1 Sam. 14:6; 17:26, 36
5 And when his armorbearer saw that Saul
was dead, he also fell on his sword, and died
with him.
6 So Saul, his three sons, his armorbearer,
and all his men died together that same day.
7 And when the men of Israel who *were* on
the other side of the valley, and *those* who
were on the other side of the Jordan, saw that
the men of Israel had fled and that Saul and
his sons were dead, they forsook the cities
and fled; and the Philistines came and dwelt
in them.
8 So it happened the next day, when the
Philistines came to strip the slain, that they
found Saul and his three sons fallen on Mount
Gilboa.
9 And they cut off his head and stripped off
his armor, and sent *word* throughout the land
of the Philistines, to proclaim *it in* the temple
of their idols and among the people.
10 Then they put his armor in the temple of
the [R]Ashtoreths, and they fastened his body to
the wall of Beth Shan.* Judg. 2:13
11 [R]Now when the inhabitants of Jabesh
Gilead heard what the Philistines had done to
Saul, 1 Sam. 11:1–13
12 [R]all the valiant men arose and traveled all
night, and took the body of Saul and the bod-
ies of his sons from the wall of Beth Shan;
and they came to Jabesh and [R]burned them
there. 2 Sam. 2:4–7 • 2 Chr. 16:14
13 Then they took their bones and buried
them under the tamarisk tree at Jabesh, [R]and
fasted seven days. Gen. 50:10

30:30 Or *Borashan* **31:10** *Beth Shean,* Josh. 17:11

Weights

Unit	*Weight*	*Equivalents*	*Translations*
Jewish Weights			
Talent	c. 75 pounds for common talent, c. 150 pounds for royal talent	60 minas; 3,000 shekels	talent
Mina	1.25 pounds	50 shekels	mina
Shekel	c. .4 ounce (11.4 grams) for common shekel c. .8 ounce for royal shekel	2 bekas; 20 gerahs	shekel
Beka	c. .2 ounce (5.7 grams)	½ shekel; 10 gerahs	half a shekel
Gerah	c. .02 ounce (.57 grams)	¹⁄₂₀ shekel	gerah
Roman Weight			
Litra	12 ounces		pound

THE SECOND BOOK OF

SAMUEL

THE BOOK OF 2 SAMUEL

The Book of 2 Samuel records the highlights of David's reign, first over the territory of Judah, and finally over the entire nation of Israel. It traces the ascension of David to the throne, his climactic sins of adultery and murder, and the shattering consequences of those sins upon his family and the nation.

See 1 Samuel for details on the titles of the books of Samuel. The Hebrew title for both books (originally one) is "Samuel." The Greek title for 2 Samuel is *Basileion Beta,* "Second Kingdoms." The Latin title is *Liber Samuelis,* the "Second Book of Samuel," or simply "Second Samuel."

THE AUTHOR OF 2 SAMUEL

Second Samuel was probably compiled by one man who combined the written chronicles of Nathan the prophet and Gad the seer (1 Chr. 29:29). In addition to these written sources, the compiler evidently used another source called "the Book of Jasher" (1:18). See comments under 1 Samuel.

THE TIME OF 2 SAMUEL

The date of the composition for 1 and 2 Samuel was sometime after the death of Solomon (931 B.C.) but before the Assyrian captivity of the northern kingdom (722 B.C.). It is likely that Samuel was composed early in the divided kingdom, perhaps around 900 B.C.

The story of David begins in 1 Samuel 16 and ends in 1 Kings 2. Second Samuel records the major events of David's forty-year rule. His reign in Hebron begins in 1011 B.C. and ends in 1004 B.C. (5:5). His thirty-three-year reign over the united Judah and Israel lasts from 1004 B.C. to 971 B.C.

THE CHRIST OF 2 SAMUEL

As seen in the introduction to 1 Samuel, David is one of the most important types of Christ in the Old Testament. In spite of his sins, he remains a man after God's own heart because of his responsive and faithful attitude toward God. He sometimes fails in his personal life, but he never flags in his relationship to the Lord. Unlike most of the kings who succeed him, he never allows idolatry to become a problem during his reign. He is a true servant of Yahweh, obedient to His law, and an ideal king. His rule is usually characterized by justice, wisdom, integrity, courage, and compassion. Having conquered Jerusalem, he sits upon the throne of Melchizedek, ("Righteous King"; see Gen. 14:18). David is the standard by which all subsequent kings are measured.

Of course, David's life as recorded in chapters 1—10 is a far better portrayal of the future Messiah than is his life as it is seen in 11—24. Sin mars potential. The closest way in which he foreshadows the coming King can be seen in the important covenant God makes with him (7:4–17). David wants to build a house for God; but instead, God makes a house for David. The same three promises of an eternal kingdom, throne, and seed are later given to Christ (Luke 1:32, 33). There are nine different dynasties in the northern kingdom of Israel, but there is only one dynasty in Judah. The promise of a permanent dynasty is fulfilled in Christ, the "Son of David" (Matt. 21:9; 22:42), who will sit upon the throne of David (Is. 9:7; Luke 1:32).

KEYS TO 2 SAMUEL

Key Word: David—The central character of 2 Samuel is David, around whom the entire book is written. The key truth illustrated is the same as the theme of Deuteronomy: obedience brings blessing and disobedience brings judgment.

Key Verses: 2 Samuel 7:12, 13; 22:21—"When your days are fulfilled and you rest with your fathers, I will set up your seed after you, who will come from your body, and I will establish his kingdom. He shall build a house for My name, and I will establish the throne of his kingdom forever" (7:12, 13).

"The LORD rewarded me according to my righteousness; according to the cleanness of my hands He has recompensed me" (22:21).

Key Chapter: 2 Samuel 11—The eleventh chapter of Second Samuel is pivotal for the entire book. This chapter records the tragic sins of David regarding Bathsheba and her husband Uriah. All of the widespread blessings on David's family and his kingdom are quickly removed as God chastises His anointed one.

SURVEY OF 2 SAMUEL

Second Samuel continues the account of the life of David at the point where 1 Samuel concludes. Soon after the death of Saul, the king-elect becomes the king enthroned, first over Judah when he reigns in Hebron for seven-and-a-half years and finally over all Israel when he reigns in Jerusalem for thirty-three years. This book reviews the key events in the forty-year reign of the man who is the halfway point between Abraham and Christ. It can be surveyed in the three divisions: the triumphs of David (1—10), the transgressions of David (11), and the troubles of David (12—24).

The Triumphs of David (1—10): Chapters 1—4 record the seven-year reign of David over the territory of Judah. Even though Saul is David's murderous pursuer, David does not rejoice in his death because he recognizes that Saul has been divinely anointed as king. Saul's son Ishbosheth is installed by Abner as a puppet king over the northern tribes of Israel. David's allies led by Joab defeat Abner and Israel (2:17; 3:1). Abner defects and arranges to unite Israel and Judah under David, but Joab kills Abner in revenge. The powerless Ishbosheth is murdered by his own men, and David is made king of Israel (5:3). David soon captures and fortifies Jerusalem and makes it the civil and religious center of the now united kingdom. Under David's rule the nation prospers politically, spiritually, and militarily. David brings the ark to Jerusalem and seeks to build a house for God (7). His obedience in placing the Lord at the center of his rule leads to great national blessing (8—10). "And the LORD preserved David wherever he went" (8:14).

The Transgressions of David (11): David's crimes of adultery and murder mark the pivotal point of the book. Because of these transgressions, David's victories and successes are changed to the personal, family, and national troubles that are recorded throughout the rest of 2 Samuel.

The Troubles of David (12—24): The disobedience of the king produces chastisement and confusion at every level. David's glory and fame fade, never to be the same again. Nevertheless, David confesses his guilt when confronted by Nathan the prophet and is restored by God. A sword remains in David's house as a consequence of the sin: the baby born to David and Bathsheba dies, his son Amnon commits incest, and his son Absalom murders Amnon.

The consequences continue with Absalom's rebellion against his father. He shrewdly "stole the hearts of the men of Israel" (15:6). David is forced to flee from Jerusalem, and Absalom sets himself up as king. David would have been ruined, but God keeps Absalom from pursuing him until David has time to regroup his forces. Absalom's army is defeated by David's, and Joab kills Absalom in disobedience of David's orders to have him spared.

David seeks to amalgamate the kingdom, but conflict breaks out between the ten northern tribes of Israel and the two southern tribes of Judah and Benjamin. Israel decides to follow a man named Sheba in a revolt against David, but Judah remains faithful to him. This leads to war, and Joab defeats the rebels.

The closing chapters are actually an appendix to the book because they summarize David's words and deeds. They show how intimately the affairs of the people as a whole are tied to the spiritual and moral condition of the king. The nation enjoys God's blessing when David is obedient to the Lord, and it suffers hardship when David disobeys God.

FOCUS	DAVID'S TRIUMPHS			DAVID'S TRANSGRESSIONS	DAVID'S TROUBLES	
REFERENCE	1:1——6:1——8:1——11:1——12:1——13:37——24:25					
DIVISION	POLITICAL TRIUMPHS	SPIRITUAL TRIUMPHS	MILITARY TRIUMPHS	SINS OF ADULTERY AND MURDER	TROUBLES IN DAVID'S HOUSE	TROUBLES IN THE KINGDOM
TOPIC	SUCCESS OBEDIENCE			SIN DISOBEDIENCE	FAILURE JUDGMENT	
LOCATION	DAVID IN HEBRON	DAVID IN JERUSALEM				
TIME	7½ YEARS	33 YEARS				

OUTLINE OF 2 SAMUEL

Part One: The Triumphs of David (1:1—10:19)

I. The Political Triumphs of David......1:1—5:25

A. The Reign of David in Hebron over Judah ......1:1—4:12
1. King Saul Dies 1:1–27
2. David Is Anointed as King over Judah 2:1–7
3. Ishbosheth Is Made King over Israel 2:8–11
4. David and Ishbosheth Fight......2:12—4:12

B. The Reign of David in Jerusalem 5:1–25
1. David Is Anointed to Reign over Israel 5:1–5
2. Conquest of Jerusalem 5:6–10
3. Alliance with Tyre 5:11, 12
4. David's Family 5:13–16
5. Conquest of Philistia 5:17–25

II. The Spiritual Triumphs of David.....6:1—7:29

A. The Transportation of the Ark......6:1–23
1. Incorrect Transportation of the Ark 6:1–11
2. Correct Transportation of the Ark 6:12
3. David Rejoices over the Ark......6:13–15
4. Michal Despises David 6:16–23

B. The Institution of the Davidic Covenant 7:1–29
1. David Is Forbidden to Build God a House 7:1–3
2. God Promises David an Eternal House 7:4–17
3. David Praises God 7:18–29

III. The Military Triumphs of David ......8:1—10:19

A. The Triumphs of David over His Enemies......8:1–12
1. David Defeats Philistia 8:1
2. David Defeats Moab 8:2
3. David Defeats Zobah and Syria......8:3–8
4. David Receives Spoil from His Enemies......8:9–12

B. The Righteous Rule of David ......8:13—9:13
1. David's Righteous Rule over Israel......8:13–18
2. David's Righteous Rule over Mephibosheth......9:1–13

C. The Triumphs of David over Ammon and Syria......10:1–19
1. Insult of Ammon 10:1–5
2. Ammon Is Defeated 10:6–14
3. Syria Is Defeated 10:15–19

Part Two: The Transgressions of David (11:1–27)

I. The Sin of Adultery 11:1–5

II. The Sin of Murder......11:6–27

A. Uriah Does Not Sleep with Bathsheba 11:6–13
B. David Commands Uriah's Murder 11:14–25
C. David and Bathsheba Marry 11:26, 27

Part Three: The Troubles of David (12:1—24:25)

I. The Troubles in David's House.....12:1—13:36

A. Prophecy by Nathan......12:1–14
1. Prophecy of the Sword......12:1–12
2. David Repents for His Sin......12:13, 14

B. David's Son Dies......12:15–25
1. God Takes Away the Son of Adultery......12:15–23
2. God Gives Another Son 12:24, 25

C. Joab's Loyalty to David 12:26–31
D. Incest in David's House......13:1–20
E. Amnon Is Murdered 13:21–36

II. The Troubles in David's Kingdom ......13:37—24:25

A. Rebellion of Absalom ......13:37—17:29
1. Flight of Absalom 13:37–39
2. Return of Absalom 14:1–24
3. Deceit of Absalom......14:25—15:6
4. Rebellion of Absalom 15:7–12
5. Flight of David......15:13—16:14
6. Reign of Absalom......16:15—17:29

B. Absalom's Murder......18:1–33

C. David Is Restored as King......19:1—20:26
1. Reproof of Joab......19:1–7
2. Restoration of David ......19:8—20:26

D. The Commentary on the Reign of David......21:1—24:25
1. Famine 21:1–14
2. War with Philistia......21:15–22
3. Psalms of Thanksgiving......22:1—23:7
4. Deeds of David's Mighty Men 23:8–39
5. The Census and the Plague 24:1–25

CHAPTER 1

King Saul Dies

NOW it came to pass after the [R]death of
Saul, when David had returned from the
slaughter of the Amalekites, and David had
stayed two days in Ziklag, 1 Sam. 31:6
2 on the third day, behold, it happened that
a man came from Saul's camp with his
clothes torn and dust on his head. So it was,
when he came to David, that he fell to the
ground and prostrated himself.
3 And David said to him, "Where have you
come from?" So he said to him, "I have es-
caped from the camp of Israel."
4 Then David said to him, "How did the
matter go? Please tell me." And he answered,
"The people have fled from the battle, many of
the people are fallen and dead, and Saul and
Jonathan his son are dead also."
5 So David said to the young man who told
him, "How do you know that Saul and Jona-
than his son are dead?"
6 Then the young man who told him said,
"As I happened by chance *to be* on [R]Mount
Gilboa, there was Saul, leaning on his spear;
and indeed the chariots and horsemen fol-
lowed hard after him. 1 Sam. 31:1
7 "Now when he looked behind him, he saw
me and called to me. And I answered, 'Here I
am.'
8 "And he said to me, 'Who *are* you?' So I
answered him, 'I *am* an Amalekite.'
9 "He said to me again, 'Please stand over
me and kill me, for [T]anguish has come upon
me, but my life still *remains* in me.' *agony*
10 "So I stood over him and [R]killed him, be-
cause I was sure that he could not live after he
had fallen. And I took the crown that *was* on his
head and the bracelet that *was* on his arm, and
have brought them here to my lord." Judg. 9:54
11 Therefore David took hold of his own
clothes and [R]tore them, and *so did* all the men
who *were* with him. 2 Sam. 3:31; 13:31
12 And they [R]mourned and wept and [R]fasted
until evening for Saul and for Jonathan his
son, for the people of the LORD and for the
house of Israel, because they had fallen by the
sword. 2 Sam. 3:31 • 1 Sam. 31:13
13 Then David said to the young man who
told him, "Where *are* you from?" And he an-
swered, "I *am* the son of an alien, an Ama-
lekite."
14 So David said to him, "How [R]was it you
were not afraid to put forth your hand to de-
stroy the LORD's anointed?" Num. 12:8
15 Then David called one of the young men
and said, "Go near, *and* execute him!" And he
struck him so that he died.
16 So David said to him, "Your blood *is* on
your own head, for [R]your own mouth has tes-
tified against you, saying, 'I have killed the
LORD's anointed.' " Luke 19:22
17 Then David lamented with this lamenta-
tion over Saul and over Jonathan his son,
18 [R]and he told *them* to teach the children of
Judah *the Song of* the Bow; indeed *it is* writ-
ten in the Book of Jasher: 1 Sam. 31:3

19 "The beauty of Israel is slain on your high
places!
[R]How the mighty have fallen! 2 Sam. 1:27
20 [R]Tell *it* not in Gath, Mic. 1:10
Proclaim *it* not in the streets of
[R]Ashkelon— Jer. 25:20
Lest [R]the daughters of the Philistines
rejoice, Ex. 15:20
Lest the daughters of [R]the uncircumcised
triumph. 1 Sam. 31:4

21 "O [R]mountains of Gilboa, 1 Sam. 31:1
[R]*Let there be* no dew nor rain upon you,
Nor fields of offerings. Ezek. 31:15
For the shield of the mighty is [T]cast
away there! Lit. *defiled*
The shield of Saul, not [R]anointed with
oil. 1 Sam. 10:1
22 From the blood of the slain,
From the fat of the mighty,
[R]The bow of Jonathan did not turn back,
And the sword of Saul did not return
empty. 1 Sam. 18:4

23 "Saul and Jonathan *were* beloved and
pleasant in their lives,
And in their [R]death they were not
divided; 1 Sam. 31:2–4
They were swifter than eagles,
They were stronger than lions.

24 "O daughters of Israel, weep over Saul,
Who clothed you in scarlet, with luxury;
Who put ornaments of gold on your
apparel.

25 "How the mighty have fallen in the midst
of the battle!
Jonathan *was* slain in your high places.
26 I am distressed for you, my brother
Jonathan;
You have been very pleasant to me;
Your love to me was wonderful,
Surpassing the love of women.

27 "How the mighty have fallen,
And the weapons of war perished!"

CHAPTER 2

David Is Anointed King over Judah

IT happened after this that David [R]inquired
of the LORD, saying, "Shall I go up to any of
the cities of Judah?" And the LORD said to
him, "Go up." David said, "Where shall I go
up?" And He said, "To Hebron." Judg. 1:1
2 So David went up there, and his two

wives also, Ahinoam the Jezreelitess, and Abigail the widow of Nabal the Carmelite.
3 And David brought up the men who *were*
with him, every man with his household. So they dwelt in the cities of Hebron.
4 [R]Then the men of Judah came, and there they [R]anointed David king over the house of Judah. And they told David, saying, "The men of Jabesh Gilead *were the ones* who buried Saul." 1 Sam. 30:26 • 1 Sam. 16:13
5 So David sent messengers to the men of Jabesh Gilead, and said to them, [R]"You *are* blessed of the LORD, for you have shown this kindness to your lord, to Saul, and have buried him. Ruth 2:20; 3:10
6 "And now may the LORD show kindness and truth to you. I also will repay you this kindness, because you have done this thing.
7 "Now therefore, let your hands be strengthened, and be valiant; for your master Saul is dead, and also the house of Judah has anointed me king over them."

Ishbosheth Is Made King over Israel

8 But Abner the son of Ner, commander of Saul's army, took Ishbosheth* the son of Saul and brought him over to Mahanaim;
9 and he made him king over Gilead, over the Ashurites, over Jezreel, over Ephraim, over Benjamin, and over all Israel.
10 Ishbosheth, Saul's son, *was* forty years old when he began to reign over Israel, and he reigned two years. Only the house of Judah followed David.
11 And [R]the time that David was king in Hebron over the house of Judah was seven years and six months. 2 Sam. 5:5

David's Victory over Ishbosheth

12 Now Abner the son of Ner, and the servants of Ishbosheth the son of Saul, went out from Mahanaim to Gibeon.
13 And [R]Joab the son of Zeruiah, and the servants of David, went out and met them by the pool of Gibeon. So they sat down, one on one side of the pool and the other on the other side of the pool. 1 Chr. 2:16; 11:6
14 Then Abner said to Joab, "Let the young men now arise and compete before us." And Joab said, "Let them arise."
15 So they arose and went over by number, twelve from Benjamin, *followers* of Ishbosheth the son of Saul, and twelve from the servants of David.
16 And each one grasped his opponent by the head and *thrust* his sword in his opponent's side; so they fell down together. Therefore that place was called the Field of Sharp Swords,* which *is* in Gibeon.
17 So there was a very fierce battle that day, and Abner and the men of Israel were beaten before the servants of David.
18 Now the [R]three sons of Zeruiah were there: Joab and Abishai and Asahel. And Asahel *was* [R]*as* fleet of foot [R]as a wild gazelle. 1 Chr. 2:16 • 1 Chr. 12:8 • Ps. 18:33
19 So Asahel pursued Abner, and in going he did not turn to the right hand or to the left from following Abner.
20 Then Abner looked behind him and said, "*Are* you Asahel?" He answered, "I *am*."
21 And Abner said to him, "Turn aside to your right hand or to your left, and lay hold on one of the young men and take his armor for yourself." But Asahel would not turn aside from following him.
22 So Abner said again to Asahel, "Turn aside from following me. Why should I strike you to the ground? How then could I face your brother Joab?"
23 However, he refused to turn aside. Therefore Abner struck him in the stomach with the blunt end of the spear, so that the spear came out of his back; and he fell down there and died on the spot. So it was *that* as many as came to the place where Asahel fell down and died, stood [R]still. 2 Sam. 20:12
24 Joab and Abishai also pursued Abner. And the sun was going down when they came to the hill of Ammah, which *is* before Giah by the road to the Wilderness of Gibeon.
25 Now the children of Benjamin gathered together behind Abner and became a unit, and took their stand on top of a hill.
26 Then Abner called to Joab and said, "Shall the sword devour forever? Do you not know that it will be bitter in the latter end? How long will it be then until you tell the people to return from pursuing their brethren?"
27 And Joab said, "*As* God lives, unless [R]you had spoken, surely then by morning all the people would have given up pursuing their brethren." 2 Sam. 2:14
28 So Joab blew a trumpet; and all the people stood still and did not pursue Israel anymore, nor did they fight anymore.
29 Then Abner and his men went on all that night through the plain, crossed over the Jordan, and went through all Bithron; and they came to Mahanaim.
30 So Joab returned from pursuing Abner. And when he had gathered all the people together, there were missing of David's servants nineteen men and Asahel.
31 But the servants of David had struck down, of Benjamin and Abner's men, three hundred and sixty men who died.
32 Then they took up Asahel and buried him in his father's tomb, which *was in* Bethlehem. And Joab and his men went all night, and they came to Hebron at daybreak.

2:8 *Esh-Baal,* 1 Chr. 8:33; 9:39 **2:16** Heb. *Helkath Hazzurim*

CHAPTER 3

David's Growth over Ishbosheth

NOW there was a long war between the house of Saul and the house of David. But David grew stronger and stronger, and the house of Saul grew weaker and weaker.

2 Sons were born [R]to David in Hebron: His firstborn was Amnon [R]by Ahinoam the Jezreelitess; 1 Chr. 3:1–4 • 1 Sam. 25:42, 43

3 his second, [T]Chileab, by Abigail the widow of Nabal the Carmelite; the third, Absalom the son of Maacah, the daughter of Talmai, king of Geshur; *Daniel*, 1 Chr. 3:1

4 the fourth, Adonijah the son of Haggith; the fifth, Shephatiah the son of Abital;

5 and the sixth, Ithream, by David's wife Eglah. These were born to David in Hebron.

Abner's Murder

6 Now it was so, while there was war between the house of Saul and the house of David, that Abner was strengthening *his hold* on the house of Saul.

7 And Saul had a concubine, whose name *was* [R]Rizpah, the daughter of Aiah. So *Ishbosheth* said to Abner, "Why have you gone in to my father's concubine?" 2 Sam. 21:8–11

8 Then Abner became very angry at the words of Ishbosheth, and said, "*Am* I [R]a dog's head that belongs to Judah? Today I show loyalty to the house of Saul your father, to his brothers, and to his friends, and have not delivered you into the hand of David; and you charge me today with a fault concerning this woman? 1 Sam. 24:14

9 [R]"May God do so to Abner, and more also, if I do not do for David [R]as the LORD has sworn to him— 1 Kin. 19:2 • 1 Chr. 12:23

10 "to transfer the kingdom from the [T]house of Saul, and set up the throne of David over Israel and over Judah, [R]from Dan to Beersheba." *family* • 1 Sam. 3:20

11 And he could not answer Abner another word, because he feared him.

12 Then Abner sent messengers on his behalf to David, saying, "Whose *is* the land?" saying *also*, "Make your covenant with me, and indeed my hand *shall be* with you to bring all Israel to you."

13 And *David* said, "Good, I will make a covenant with you. But one thing I require of you: [R]you shall not see my face unless you first bring Michal, Saul's daughter, when you come to see my face." Gen. 43:3

14 So David sent messengers to Ishbosheth, Saul's son, saying, "Give *me* my wife Michal, whom I betrothed to myself for a hundred foreskins of the Philistines."

15 And Ishbosheth sent and took her from *her* husband, from Paltiel* the son of Laish.

16 Then her husband went along with her to Bahurim, weeping behind her. So Abner said to him, "Go, return!" And he returned.

17 Now Abner had communicated with the elders of Israel, saying, "In time past you were seeking for David *to be* king over you.

18 "Now then, do *it!* [R]For the LORD has spoken of David, saying, 'By the hand of My servant David, I* will save My people Israel from the hand of the Philistines and the hand of all their enemies.' " 2 Sam. 3:9

19 And Abner also spoke in the hearing of [R]Benjamin. Then Abner also went to speak in the hearing of David in Hebron all that seemed good to Israel and the whole house of Benjamin. 1 Chr. 12:29

20 So Abner and twenty men with him came to David at Hebron. And David made a feast for Abner and the men who *were* with him.

21 Then Abner said to David, "I will arise and go, and [R]gather all Israel to my lord the king, that they may make a covenant with you, and that you may reign over all that your heart desires." So David sent Abner away, and he went in peace. 2 Sam. 3:10, 12

22 At that moment the servants of David and Joab came from a raid and brought much [T]spoil with them. But Abner *was* not with David in Hebron, for he had sent him away, and he had gone in peace. *booty*

23 When Joab and all the troops that *were* with him had come, they told Joab, saying, "Abner the son of Ner came to the king, and he sent him away, and he has gone in peace."

24 Then Joab came to the king and said, "What have you done? Look, Abner came to you; why *is* it *that* you sent him away, and he has already gone?

25 "Surely you realize that Abner the son of Ner came to deceive you, to know [R]your going out and your coming in, and to know all that you are doing." 1 Sam. 29:6

26 And when Joab had gone from David's presence, he sent messengers after Abner, who brought him back from the well of Sirah. But David did not know *it*.

27 Now when Abner had returned to Hebron, Joab [R]took him aside in the gate to speak with him privately, and there stabbed him in the stomach, so that he died for the blood of Asahel his brother. 1 Kin. 2:5

28 Afterward, when David heard *it*, he said, "My kingdom and I *are* [T]guiltless before the LORD forever of the blood of Abner the son of Ner. *innocent*

29 "Let it rest on the head of Joab and on all his father's house; and let there never fail to be in the house of Joab one who has a discharge or is a leper, who leans on a staff or falls by the sword, or who lacks bread."

30 So Joab and Abishai his brother killed

3:15 *Palti*, 1 Sam. 25:44 **3:18** So with many Heb. mss., LXX, Syr., Tg.; MT *he*

Abner, because he had killed their brother [R]Asahel at Gibeon in the battle. 2 Sam. 2:23

31 Then David said to Joab and to all the people who were with him, [R]"Tear your clothes, [R]gird yourselves with sackcloth, and mourn for Abner." And King David followed the coffin. Josh. 7:6 • Gen. 37:34

32 So they buried Abner in Hebron; and the king lifted up his voice and wept at the grave of Abner, and all the people wept.

33 And the king sang *a lament* over Abner and said:

"Should Abner die as a fool dies?
34 Your hands were not bound
Nor your feet put into fetters;
As a man falls before wicked men, so
you fell."

Then all the people wept over him again.

35 And when all the people came to persuade David to eat food while it was still day, David took an oath, saying, "God do so to me, and more also, if I taste bread or anything else till the sun goes down!"

36 Now all the people took note *of it,* and it pleased them, since whatever the king did pleased all the people.

37 For all the people and all Israel understood that day that it had not been the king's *intent* to kill Abner the son of Ner.

38 Then the king said to his servants, "Do you not know that a prince and a great man has fallen this day in Israel?

39 "And I *am* weak today, though anointed king; and these men, the sons of Zeruiah, *are* too harsh for me. The LORD shall repay the evildoer according to his wickedness."

CHAPTER 4

Ishbosheth's Murder

WHEN Saul's son* heard that Abner had died in Hebron, [R]he lost heart, and all Israel was [R]troubled. Ezra 4:4 • Matt. 2:3

2 Now Saul's son *had* two men *who were* captains of troops. The name of one *was* Baanah and the name of the other Rechab, the sons of Rimmon the Beerothite, of the children of Benjamin. (For [R]Beeroth also was *part* of Benjamin, Josh. 18:25

3 because the Beerothites fled to [R]Gittaim and have been sojourners there until this day.) Neh. 11:33

4 [R]Jonathan, Saul's son, had a son *who was* lame in *his* feet. He was five years old when the news about Saul and Jonathan came from Jezreel; and his nurse took him up and fled. And it happened, as she made haste to flee, that he fell and became lame. His name *was* Mephibosheth.* 2 Sam. 9:3

5 Then the sons of Rimmon the Beerothite, Rechab and Baanah, set out and came at about the heat of the day to the [R]house of Ishbosheth, who was lying on his bed at noon. 2 Sam. 2:8, 9

6 And they came there, all the way into the house, *as though* to get wheat, and they [T]stabbed him in the stomach. Then Rechab and Baanah his brother escaped. Lit. *struck*

7 For when they came into the house, he was lying on his bed in his bedroom; then they struck him and killed him, beheaded him and took his head, and were all night escaping through the plain.

8 And they brought the head of Ishbosheth to David at Hebron, and said to the king, "Here is the head of Ishbosheth, the son of Saul your enemy, who sought your life; and the LORD has avenged my lord the king this day of Saul and his descendants."

Judgment on the Murder of Ishbosheth

9 But David answered Rechab and Baanah his brother, the sons of Rimmon the Beerothite, and said to them, "*As* the LORD lives, [R]who has redeemed my life from all adversity, Gen. 48:16

10 "when [R]someone told me, saying, 'Look, Saul is dead,' thinking to have brought good news, I arrested him and had him executed in Ziklag—the one who *thought* I would give him a reward for *his* news. 2 Sam. 1:2–16

11 "How much more, when wicked men have killed a righteous person in his own house on his bed? Therefore, shall I not now [R]require his [T]blood at your hand and remove you from the earth?" [Gen. 9:5, 6] • Or *bloodshed*

12 So David [R]commanded his young men, and they executed them, cut off their hands and feet, and hanged *them* by the pool in Hebron. But they took the head of Ishbosheth and buried *it* in the [R]tomb of Abner in Hebron. 2 Sam. 1:15 • 2 Sam. 3:32

CHAPTER 5

David Is Anointed to Reign over Israel
1 Chr. 11:1–3

THEN all the tribes of Israel came to David at Hebron and spoke, saying, "Indeed we *are* your bone and your flesh.

2 "Also, in time past, when Saul was king over us, [R]you were the one who led Israel out and brought them in; and the LORD said to you, 'You shall shepherd My people Israel, and be ruler over Israel.' " 1 Sam. 18:5, 13, 16

3 [R]Therefore all the elders of Israel came to the king at Hebron, [R]and King David made a covenant with them at Hebron [R]before the LORD. And they anointed David king over Israel. 2 Sam. 3:17 • 2 Kin. 11:17 • 1 Sam. 23:18

4 David *was* thirty years old when he began to reign, *and* he reigned forty years.

4:1 Ishbosheth **4:4** *Merib-Baal,* 1 Chr. 8:34; 9:40

5 In Hebron he reigned over Judah [R]seven
years and six months, and in Jerusalem he
reigned thirty-three years over all Israel and
Judah. 2 Sam. 2:11

Conquest of Jerusalem—1 Chr. 11:4–9

6 [R]And the king and his men went to Jeru-
salem against the Jebusites, the inhabitants of
the land, who spoke to David, saying, "You
shall not come in here; but the blind and the
lame will repel you," thinking, "David cannot
come in here." Judg. 1:21
7 Nevertheless David took the stronghold
of Zion (that *is,* the City of David).
8 Now David said on that day, "Whoever
climbs up by way of the water shaft and de-
feats the Jebusites (the lame and the blind,
who are hated by David's soul), *he shall be
chief and captain."** Therefore they say, "The
blind and the lame shall not come into the
house."
9 Then David dwelt in the stronghold, and
called it the City of David. And David built all
around from the Millo* and inward.
10 So David went on and became great, and
the LORD God of hosts *was* with him.

Alliance with Tyre—1 Chr. 14:1, 2

11 Then [R]Hiram [R]king of Tyre sent messen-
gers to David, and cedar trees, and carpen-
ters and masons. And they built David a
house. 1 Kin. 5:1–18 • 1 Chr. 14:1
12 So David knew that the LORD had estab-
lished him as king over Israel, and that He
had [R]exalted His kingdom [R]for the sake of His
people Israel. Num. 24:7 • Is. 45:4

David's Family

13 And [R]David took more concubines and
wives from Jerusalem, after he had come
from Hebron. Also more sons and daughters
were born to David. [Deut. 17:17]
14 Now [R]these *are* the names of those who
were born to him in Jerusalem: Shammua,*
Shobab, Nathan, Solomon, 1 Chr. 3:5–8
15 Ibhar, Elishua,* Nepheg, Japhia,
16 Elishama, Eliada, and Eliphelet.

Conquest of Philistia—1 Chr. 14:9–17

17 [R]Now when the Philistines heard that
they had anointed David king over Israel, all
the Philistines went up to search for David.
And David heard *of it* [R]and went down to the
stronghold. 1 Chr. 11:16 • 2 Sam. 23:14
18 The Philistines also went and deployed
themselves in the Valley of Rephaim.
19 So David inquired of the LORD, saying,
"Shall I go up against the Philistines? Will You
deliver them into my hand?" And the LORD
said to David, "Go up, for I will doubtless de-
liver the Philistines into your hand."
20 So David went to [R]Baal Perazim, and Da-
vid defeated them there; and he said, "The
LORD has broken through my enemies before
me, like a breakthrough of water." Therefore
he called the name of that place Baal Per-
azim.* Is. 28:21
21 And they left their images there, and Da-
vid and his men carried them away.
22 [R]Then the Philistines went up once again
and deployed themselves in the Valley of
Rephaim. 1 Chr. 14:13
23 Therefore [R]David inquired of the LORD,
and He said, "You shall not go up; circle
around behind them, and come upon them in
front of the mulberry trees. 2 Sam. 5:19
24 "And it shall be, when you hear the sound
of marching in the tops of the mulberry trees,
then you shall advance quickly. For then the
LORD will go out before you to strike the camp
of the Philistines."
25 And David did so, as the LORD com-
manded him; and he drove back the
Philistines from Geba* as far as Gezer.

CHAPTER 6

Incorrect Transportation of the Ark
1 Chr. 13:1–14

AGAIN David gathered all *the* choice *men*
of Israel, thirty thousand.
2 And [R]David arose and went with all the
people who *were* with him from Baale Judah
to bring up from there the ark of God,
whose name is called by the Name,* the
LORD of Hosts, [R]who dwells *between* the
cherubim. 1 Chr. 13:5, 6 • Ps. 80:1
3 So they set the ark of God on a new
cart, and brought it out of the house of Abin-
adab, which *was* on [R]the hill; and Uzzah and
Ahio, the sons of Abinadab, drove the new
cart.* 1 Sam. 26:1
4 And they brought it out of [R]the house of
Abinadab, which *was* on the hill, accom-
panying the ark of God; and Ahio went before
the ark. 1 Sam. 7:1
5 Then David and all the house of Israel
[R]played *music* before the LORD on all kinds of
instruments of fir wood, on harps, on stringed
instruments, on tambourines, on sistrums,
and on cymbals. 1 Sam. 18:6, 7
6 And when they came to [R]Nachon's
threshing floor, Uzzah put out *his* [R]*hand* to the
ark of God and took hold of it, for the oxen
stumbled. 1 Chr. 13:9 • Num. 4:15, 19, 20
7 Then the anger of the LORD was aroused
against Uzzah, and God struck him there for
his [T]error; and he died there by the ark of
God. Or *irreverence*

5:8 Cf. 1 Chr. 11:6 **5:9** Lit. *The Landfill*
5:14 *Shimea,* 1 Chr. 3:5 **5:15** *Elishama,* 1 Chr. 3:6
5:20 Lit. *Master of Breakthroughs* **5:25** So with MT, Tg., Vg.; LXX *Gibeon* **6:2** LXX, Tg., Vg. omit *by the Name;* many Heb. mss., Syr. *there* **6:3** LXX adds *with the ark*

8 And David became angry because of the LORD's outbreak against Uzzah; and he called the name of the place Perez Uzzah* to this day.

9 [R]David was afraid of the LORD that day; and he said, "How can the ark of the LORD come to me?" Ps. 119:120

10 So David would not move the ark of the LORD with him into the [R]City of David; but David took it aside into the house of Obed-Edom the [R]Gittite. 2 Sam. 5:7 • 1 Chr. 13:13

11 [R]The ark of the LORD remained in the house of Obed-Edom the Gittite three months. And the LORD blessed Obed-Edom and all his household. 1 Chr. 13:14

Correct Transportation of the Ark
1 Chr. 15:25

12 Now it was told King David, saying, "The LORD has blessed the house of Obed-Edom and all that *belongs* to him, because of the ark of God." So David went and brought up the ark of God from the house of Obed-Edom to the City of David with gladness.

David Rejoices over the Ark
1 Chr. 15:26–28

13 And so it was, when [R]those bearing the ark of the LORD had gone six paces, that he sacrificed oxen and fatted sheep. Josh. 3:3

14 Then David [R]danced before the LORD with all *his* might; and David *was* wearing [R]a linen ephod. Ps. 30:11; 149:3 • 1 Sam. 2:18, 28

15 So David and all the house of Israel brought up the ark of the LORD with shouting and with the sound of the trumpet.

Michal Despises David—1 Chr. 15:29—16:3

16 Now as the ark of the LORD came into the City of David, Michal, Saul's daughter, looked through a window and saw King David leaping and whirling before the LORD; and she despised him in her heart.

17 So [R]they brought the ark of the LORD, and set it in its place in the midst of the tabernacle that David had erected for it. Then David offered burnt offerings and peace offerings before the LORD. 1 Chr. 16:1

18 And when David had finished offering burnt offerings and peace offerings, [R]he blessed the people in the name of the LORD of hosts. 1 Kin. 8:14, 15, 55

19 [R]Then he distributed among all the people, among the whole multitude of Israel, both the women and the men, to everyone a loaf of bread, a piece *of meat,* and a cake of raisins. So all the people departed, everyone to his house. 1 Chr. 16:3

20 [R]Then David returned to bless his household. And Michal the daughter of Saul came out to meet David, and said, "How glorious was the king of Israel today, uncovering himself today in the eyes of the maids of his servants, as one of the base fellows shamelessly uncovers himself!" Ps. 30:title

21 So David said to Michal, "*It was* before the LORD, who chose me instead of your father and all his house, to appoint me ruler over the people of the LORD, over Israel. Therefore I will play *music* before the LORD.

22 "And I will be even more undignified than this, and will be humble in my own sight. But as for the maidservants of whom you have spoken, by them I will be held in honor."

23 Therefore Michal the daughter of Saul had no children to the day of her death.

CHAPTER 7

David Is Forbidden to Build God a House
1 Chr. 17:1, 2

NOW it came to pass [R]when the king was dwelling in his house, and the LORD had given him rest from all his enemies all around, 1 Chr. 17:1–27

2 that the king said to Nathan the prophet, "See now, I dwell in [R]a house of cedar, [R]but the ark of God dwells inside tent [R]curtains." 2 Sam. 5:11 • Acts 7:46 • Ex. 26:1

3 Then Nathan said to the king, "Go, do all that *is* in your [R]heart, for the LORD *is* with you." 1 Kin. 8:17, 18

God Promises David an Eternal House
1 Chr. 17:3–15

4 But it happened that night that the word of the LORD came to Nathan, saying,

5 "Go and tell My servant David, 'Thus says the LORD: [R]"Would you build a house for Me to dwell in? 1 Kin. 5:3, 4; 8:19

6 "For I have not dwelt in a house since the time that I brought the children of Israel up from Egypt, even to this day, but have moved about in a tent and in a tabernacle.

7 "Wherever I have [R]moved about with all the children of Israel, have I ever spoken a word to anyone from the tribes of Israel, whom I commanded [R]to shepherd My people Israel, saying, 'Why have you not built Me a house of cedar?' " ' Lev. 26:11, 12 • 2 Sam. 5:2

8 "Now therefore, thus shall you say to My servant David, 'Thus says the LORD of hosts: [R]"I took you from the sheepfold, from following the sheep, to be ruler over My people, over Israel. 1 Sam. 16:11, 12

9 "And [R]I have been with you wherever you have gone, and have cut off all your enemies from before you, and have made you a great name, like the name of the great men who *are* on the earth. 2 Sam. 5:10

10 "Moreover I will appoint a place for My people Israel, and will plant them, that they may dwell in a place of their own and move

6:8 Lit. *Outburst Against Uzzah*

no more; nor shall the sons of wickedness op-
press them anymore, as previously,
11 [R]"since the time that I commanded judges
to be over My people Israel, and have caused
you to rest from all your enemies. Also the
LORD tells you [R]that He will make you a
house.* Judg. 2:14–16 • 2 Sam. 7:27
12 "When your days are fulfilled and you
rest with your fathers, I will set up your seed
after you, who will come from your body, and
I will establish his kingdom.
13 [R]"He shall build a house for My name,
and I will [R]establish the throne of his kingdom
forever. 1 Kin. 5:5; 8:19 • [Is. 9:7; 49:8]
14 [R]"I will be his Father, and he shall be My
son. If he commits iniquity, I will chasten him
with the rod of men and with the blows of the
sons of men. [Heb. 1:5]
15 "But My mercy shall not depart from him,
[R]as I took *it* from Saul, whom I removed from
before you. 1 Sam. 15:23, 28; 16:14
16 "And your house and your kingdom shall
be established forever before you.* Your
throne shall be established forever." ' "
17 According to all these words and according to all this vision, so Nathan spoke to David.

David Praises God—1 Chr. 17:16–27

18 Then King David went in and sat before
the LORD; and he said: [R]"Who *am* I, O Lord
GOD? And what is my house, that You have
brought me this far? Ex. 3:11
19 "And yet this was a small thing in Your
sight, O Lord GOD; and You have also spoken
of Your servant's house for a great while to
come. [R]*Is* this the manner of man, O Lord
GOD? [Is. 55:8, 9]
20 "Now what more can David say to You?
For You, Lord GOD, know Your servant.
21 "For Your word's sake, and according to
Your own heart, You have done all these great
things, to make Your servant know *them*.
22 "Therefore [R]You are great, O Lord GOD.*
For *there is* none like You, nor *is there any*
God besides You, according to all that we have
heard with our ears. Deut. 10:17
23 "And who *is* like Your people, like Israel,
[R]the one nation on the earth whom God went
to redeem for Himself as a people, to make
for Himself a name—and to do for Yourself
great and awesome deeds for Your land—before [R]Your people whom You redeemed for
Yourself from Egypt, the nations, and their
gods? Ps. 147:20 • Deut. 9:26; 33:29
24 "For [R]You have made Your people Israel
Your very own people forever; and You, LORD,
have become their God. [Deut. 26:18]
25 [R]"Now, O LORD God, the word which You
have spoken concerning Your servant and
concerning his house, establish *it* forever and
do as You have said. Matt. 19:28☆
26 [R]"So let Your name be magnified forever,
saying, 'The LORD of hosts *is* the God over Israel.' And let the house of Your servant David
be established before You. Luke 1:32, 33☆
27 "For You, O LORD of hosts, God of Israel,
have revealed *this* to Your servant, saying, 'I
will build you a house.' Therefore Your servant has found it in his heart to pray this
prayer to You.
28 "And now, O Lord GOD, You are God, and
Your words are true, and You have promised
this goodness to Your servant.
29 "Now therefore, let it please You to bless
the house of Your servant, that it may continue
before You forever; for You, O Lord GOD, have
spoken *it*, and with Your blessing let the house
of Your servant be blessed [R]forever." 2 Sam. 22:51

CHAPTER 8

David Defeats Philistia—1 Chr. 18:1

AFTER this it came to pass that David [T]attacked the Philistines and subdued them.
And David took Metheg Ammah from the
hand of the Philistines. Lit. *struck*

David Defeats Moab—1 Chr. 18:2

2 Then [R]he defeated Moab. Forcing them
down to the ground, he measured them off
with a line. With two lines he measured off

7:11 Royal dynasty **7:16** LXX *Me* **7:22** Tg., Syr. *O LORD God*

7:4–17 The Davidic Covenant—The covenant with David is the fourth of the theocratic covenants (pertaining to the rule of God). In this covenant David is promised three things: (1) a land forever (v. 10); (2) an unending dynasty (vv. 11, 16); and (3) an everlasting kingdom (vv. 13, 16). The birth of Solomon, David's son who is to succeed him, is predicted (v. 12). His particular role is to establish the throne of the Davidic kingdom forever (v. 13). His throne continues, though his seed is cursed in the person of Jeconiah (Coniah), who was the king under whom the nation was carried captive to Babylon. Jeremiah prophesies that no one whose genealogical descent could be traced back to David through Jeconiah and Solomon would ever sit on David's throne (Page 771—Jer. 22:24–30). Joseph, the legal, but not physical, father of Jesus traces his lineage to David through Jeconiah (Page 977—Matt. 1:1–17). David, however, had another son, Nathan. His line was not cursed. Mary, the physical mother of Jesus, traces her lineage back to David through Nathan (Page 1045—Luke 3:23–38). Notice the care and the extent to which God goes to keep His word and to preserve its truthfulness. The virgin birth was absolutely essential not only to assure the sinless character of Jesus but also to fulfill the Davidic covenant. Jesus receives His "blood right" to David's throne through His earthly mother, Mary, and His "legal right" to David's throne through His adoptive earthly father, Joseph. The virgin birth guarantees that one of David's line will sit on David's throne and rule forever, while at the same time preserving intact the curse and restriction on the line of descent through Jeconiah.

Now turn to Page 781—Jer. 31:31–34: The New Covenant.

those to be put to death, and with one full
line those to be kept alive. So the Moabites
became David's [R]servants, *and* [R]brought trib-
ute. Num. 24:17 • 2 Sam. 12:31 • 1 Kin. 4:21

David Defeats Zobah and Syria
1 Chr. 18:3–8

3 David also defeated Hadadezer the son of
Rehob, king of Zobah, as he went to recover
his territory at the River Euphrates.
4 David took from him one thousand *char-
iots,* seven hundred* horsemen, and twenty
thousand foot soldiers. Also David [R]ham-
strung all the chariot horses, except that he
spared *enough* of them for one hundred char-
iots. Josh. 11:6, 9
5 When the Syrians of Damascus came to
help Hadadezer king of Zobah, David killed
twenty-two thousand of the Syrians.
6 Then David put garrisons in Syria of Da-
mascus; and the Syrians became David's ser-
vants, *and* brought tribute. So the LORD
preserved David wherever he went.
7 And David took the shields of gold that
had belonged to the servants of Hadadezer,
and brought them to Jerusalem.
8 Also from Betah* and from [R]Berothai,
cities of Hadadezer, King David took a large
amount of bronze. Ezek. 47:16

David Receives Spoil from His Enemies
1 Chr. 18:9–12

9 When Toi* king of [R]Hamath heard that
David had defeated all the army of Had-
adezer, 1 Kin. 8:65
10 then Toi sent Joram* his son to King
David, to [T]greet him and bless him, because
he had fought against Hadadezer and de-
feated him (for Hadadezer had been at war
with Toi); and *Joram* brought with him arti-
cles of silver, articles of gold, and articles of
bronze. Lit. *ask him of his welfare*
11 King David also [R]dedicated these to the
LORD, along with the silver and gold that he
had dedicated from all the nations which he
had subdued— 1 Kin. 7:51
12 from Syria,* from Moab, from the people
of Ammon, from the [R]Philistines, from
Amalek, and from the spoil of Hadadezer the
son of Rehob, king of Zobah. 2 Sam. 5:17–25

David's Righteous Rule over Israel
1 Chr. 18:13–17

13 And David made *himself* a [R]name when
he returned from killing eighteen thousand
Syrians* in the Valley of Salt. 2 Sam. 7:9
14 He also put garrisons in Edom;
throughout all Edom he put garrisons, and
[R]all the Edomites became David's servants.
And the LORD preserved David wherever he
went. Gen. 27:29, 37–40
15 So David reigned over all Israel; and Da-
vid administered judgment and justice to all
his people.
16 [R]Joab the son of Zeruiah *was* over the
army; [R]Jehoshaphat the son of Ahilud *was*
recorder; 2 Sam. 19:13; 20:23 • 1 Kin. 4:3
17 [R]Zadok the son of Ahitub and Ahimelech
the son of Abiathar *were* the priests; Seraiah*
was the scribe; 1 Chr. 6:4–8; 24:3
18 Benaiah the son of Jehoiada *was over*
both the Cherethites and the Pelethites; and
David's sons were chief ministers.

CHAPTER 9

David's Righteous Rule over Mephibosheth

NOW David said, "Is there still anyone
who is left of the house of Saul, that I
may [R]show him [T]kindness for Jonathan's
sake?" 1 Sam. 18:3; 20:14–16 • *covenant faithfulness*
2 And *there was* a servant of the house of
Saul whose name *was* [R]Ziba. So when they
had called him to David, the king said to
him, "*Are* you Ziba?" He said, "At your ser-
vice!" 2 Sam. 16:1–4; 19:17, 29
3 Then the king said, "*Is* there not still
someone of the house of Saul, to whom I may
show [R]the kindness of God?" And Ziba said to
the king, "There is still a son of Jonathan *who*
is lame in *his* feet." 1 Sam. 20:14
4 So the king said to him, "Where *is* he?"
And Ziba said to the king, "Indeed he *is* in the
house of [R]Machir the son of Ammiel, in Lo
Debar." 2 Sam. 17:27–29
5 Then King David sent and brought him
out of the house of Machir the son of Ammiel,
from Lo Debar.
6 Now when Mephibosheth the son of Jon-
athan, the son of Saul, had come to David, he
fell on his face and prostrated himself. Then
David said, "Mephibosheth?" And he an-
swered, "Here is your servant!"
7 So David said to him, "Do not fear, for I
will surely show you kindness for Jonathan
your father's sake, and will restore to you all
the land of Saul your grandfather; and you
shall eat bread at my table continually."
8 Then he bowed himself, and said, "What
is your servant, that you should look upon
such [R]a dead dog as I?" 2 Sam. 16:9
9 And the king called to Ziba, Saul's ser-
vant, and said to him, [R]"I have given to your
master's son all that belonged to Saul and to
all his house. 2 Sam. 16:4; 19:29
10 "You therefore, and your sons and your
servants, shall work the land for him, and you
shall bring in *the harvest,* that your master's
son may have food to eat. But Mephibosheth

8:4 *seven thousand,* 1 Chr. 18:4 **8:8** *Tibhath,* 1 Chr. 18:8 **8:9** *Tou,* 1 Chr. 18:9 **8:10** *Hadoram,* 1 Chr. 18:10 **8:12** LXX, Syr., Heb. mss. *Edom* **8:13** LXX, Syr., Heb. mss. *Edomites* and 1 Chr. 18:12 **8:17** *Shavsha,* 1 Chr. 18:16

your master's son shall eat bread at my table always." Now Ziba had [R]fifteen sons and twenty servants. 2 Sam. 19:17

11 Then Ziba said to the king, "According to all that my lord the king has commanded his servant, so will your servant do." "As for Mephibosheth," *said the king,* "he shall eat at my table* like one of the king's sons."

12 Mephibosheth had a young son [R]whose name *was* Micha. And all who dwelt in the house of Ziba *were* servants of Mephibosheth. 1 Chr. 8:34

13 So Mephibosheth dwelt in Jerusalem, for he ate continually at the king's table. And he was lame in both his feet.

CHAPTER 10

Insult of Ammon—1 Chr. 19:1–5

IT happened after this that the [R]king of the people of Ammon died, and Hanun his son reigned in his place. 1 Chr. 19:1

2 Then David said, "I will show kindness to Hanun the son of Nahash, as his father showed kindness to me." So David sent by the hand of his servants to comfort him concerning his father. And David's servants came into the land of the people of Ammon.

3 And the princes of the people of Ammon said to Hanun their lord, "Do you think that David really honors your father because he has sent comforters to you? Has David not *rather* sent his servants to you to search the city, to spy it out, and to overthrow it?"

4 Therefore Hanun took David's servants, shaved off half of their beards, cut off their garments in the middle, [R]at their buttocks, and sent them away. Is. 20:4; 47:2

5 When they told David, he sent to meet them, because the men were greatly [T]ashamed. And the king said, "Wait at Jericho until your beards have grown, and *then* return." *humiliated*

Ammon Is Defeated—1 Chr. 19:6–15

6 When the people of Ammon saw that they [R]had made themselves repulsive to David, the people of Ammon sent and hired [R]the Syrians of [R]Beth Rehob and the Syrians of Zoba, twenty thousand foot soldiers; and from the king of Maacah one thousand men, and from Ish-Tob twelve thousand men. Gen. 34:30 • 2 Sam. 8:3, 5 • Judg. 18:28

7 Now when David heard *of it,* he sent Joab and all the army of the mighty men.

8 Then the people of Ammon came out and put themselves in battle array at the entrance of the gate. And [R]the Syrians of Zoba, Beth Rehob, Ish-Tob, and Maacah *were* by themselves in the field. 2 Sam. 10:6

9 When Joab saw that the battle line was against him before and behind, he chose some of Israel's best and put *them* in battle array against the Syrians.

10 And the rest of the people he put under the command of [R]Abishai his brother, that he might set *them* in battle array against the people of Ammon. 2 Sam. 3:30

11 Then he said, "If the Syrians are too strong for me, then you shall help me; but if the people of Ammon are too strong for you, then I will come and help you.

12 [R]"Be of good courage, and let us [R]be strong for our people and for the cities of our God. And may [R]the LORD do *what is* good in His sight." Deut. 31:6 • 1 Cor. 16:13 • 1 Sam. 3:18

13 So Joab and the people who *were* with him drew near for the battle against the Syrians, and they fled before him.

14 When the people of Ammon saw that the Syrians were fleeing, they also fled before Abishai, and entered the city. So Joab returned from the people of Ammon and went to [R]Jerusalem. 2 Sam. 11:1

Syria Is Defeated—1 Chr. 19:16–19

15 When the Syrians saw that they had been defeated by Israel, they gathered together.

16 Then Hadadezer* sent and brought out the Syrians who *were* beyond the River,* and they came to Helam. And [T]Shobach the commander of Hadadezer's army *went* before them. *Shophach,* 1 Chr. 19:16

17 When it was told David, he gathered all Israel, crossed over the Jordan, and came to Helam. And the Syrians set themselves in battle array against David and fought with him.

18 Then the Syrians fled before Israel; and David killed seven hundred charioteers and forty thousand [R]horsemen of the Syrians, and struck Shobach the commander of their army, who died there. 1 Chr. 19:18

19 And when all the kings *who were* servants to Hadadezer* saw that they were defeated by Israel, they made peace with Israel and served them. So the Syrians were afraid to help the people of Ammon anymore.

CHAPTER 11

The Sin of Adultery

IT happened in the spring of the year, at the [R]time when kings go out *to battle,* that David sent Joab and his servants with him, and all Israel; and they destroyed the people of Ammon and besieged Rabbah. But David remained at Jerusalem. 1 Kin. 20:22–26

2 Then it happened one evening that David arose from his bed [R]and walked on the roof of the king's house. And from the roof he saw a woman bathing, and the woman *was* very beautiful to behold. Deut. 22:8

3 So David sent and inquired about the woman. And *someone* said, "Is this not

9:11 LXX *David's table* **10:16** Heb. *Hadarezer* • The Euphrates **10:19** Heb. *Hadarezer*

Bathsheba, the daughter of Eliam, the wife of
Uriah the [R]Hittite?" 1 Sam. 26:6
4 Then David sent messengers, and took
her; and she came to him, and he lay with her,
for she was cleansed from her impurity; and
she returned to her house.
5 And the woman conceived; so she sent
and told David, and said, "I *am* with child."

Uriah Does Not Sleep with Bathsheba

6 Then David sent to Joab, *saying*, "Send
me Uriah the Hittite." And Joab sent Uriah to
David.
7 When Uriah had come to him, David
asked how Joab was doing, and how the peo-
ple were doing, and how the war prospered.
8 And David said to Uriah, "Go down to
your house and [R]wash your feet." So Uriah de-
parted from the king's house, and a gift *of*
food from the king followed him. Gen. 18:4
9 But Uriah slept at the door of the king's
house with all the servants of his lord, and did
not go down to his house.
10 So when they told David, saying, "Uriah
did not go down to his house," David said to
Uriah, "Did you not come from a journey?
Why did you not go down to your house?"
11 And Uriah said to David, [R]"The ark and
Israel and Judah are dwelling in tents, and my
lord Joab and the servants of my lord are en-
camped in the open fields. Shall I then go to
my house to eat and drink, and to lie with my
wife? *As* you live, and *as* your soul lives, I will
not do this thing." 2 Sam. 7:2, 6
12 Then David said to Uriah, "Wait here
today also, and tomorrow I will let you de-
part." So Uriah remained in Jerusalem that
day and the next.
13 Now when David called him, he ate and
drank before him; and he made him [R]drunk.
And at evening he went out to lie on his bed
with the servants of his lord, but he did not go
down to his house. Gen. 19:33, 35

David Commands Uriah's Murder

14 In the morning it happened that David
[R]wrote a letter to Joab and sent *it* by the hand
of Uriah. 1 Kin. 21:8, 9
15 And he wrote in the letter, saying, "Set
Uriah in the forefront of the [T]hottest battle,
and retreat from him, that he may [R]be struck
down and die." *fiercest* • 2 Sam. 12:9
16 So it was, while Joab besieged the city,
that he assigned Uriah to a place where he
knew there *were* valiant men.
17 Then the men of the city came out and
fought with Joab. And *some* of the people of
the servants of David fell; and Uriah the Hit-
tite died also.
18 Then Joab sent and told David all the
things concerning the war,
19 and charged the messenger, saying,
"When you have finished telling the matters
of the war to the king,
20 "if it happens that the king's wrath rises,
and he says to you: 'Why did you approach so
near to the city when you fought? Did you not
know that they would shoot from the wall?
21 'Who struck Abimelech the son of
Jerubbesheth?* Was it not a woman who cast
a piece of a millstone on him from the wall, so
that he died in Thebez? Why did you go near
the wall?'—then you shall say, 'Your servant
Uriah the Hittite is dead also.' "
22 So the messenger went, and came and
told David all that Joab had sent by him.
23 And the messenger said to David, "Surely
the men prevailed against us and came out to
us in the field; then we drove them back as far
as the entrance of the gate.
24 "The archers shot from the wall at your
servants; and *some* of the king's servants are
dead, and your servant Uriah the Hittite is
dead also."
25 Then David said to the messenger, "Thus
you shall say to Joab: 'Do not let this thing
[T]displease you, for the sword devours one as
well as another. Strengthen your attack
against the city, and overthrow it.' So encour-
age him." Lit. *be evil in your sight*

David and Bathsheba Marry

26 When the wife of Uriah heard that Uriah
her husband was dead, she mourned for her
husband.
27 And when her mourning was over, David
sent and brought her to his house, and she
[R]became his wife and bore him a son. But the
thing that David had done [R]displeased the
LORD. 2 Sam. 12:9 • 1 Chr. 21:7

CHAPTER 12

Prophecy of the Sword

THEN the LORD sent Nathan to David. And
[R]he came to him, and [R]said to him: "There
were two men in one city, one rich and the
other poor. Ps. 51:title • 1 Kin. 20:35–41
2 "The rich *man* had exceedingly many
flocks and herds.
3 "But the poor *man* had nothing, except
one little ewe lamb which he had bought and
nourished; and it grew up together with him
and with his children. It ate of his own food
and drank from his own cup and lay in his
bosom; and it was like a daughter to him.
4 "And a traveler came to the rich man, who
refused to take from his own flock and from
his own herd to prepare one for the wayfaring
man who had come to him; but he took the
poor man's lamb and prepared it for the man
who had come to him."
5 So David's anger was greatly aroused

11:21 Gideon; *Jerubbaal*, Judg. 6:32ff

against the man, and he said to Nathan, "*As*
the LORD lives, the man who has done this
shall surely die!
6 "And he shall restore [R]fourfold for the
lamb, because he did this thing and because
he had no pity." [Ex. 22:1]
7 Then Nathan said to David, "You *are* the
man! Thus says the LORD God of Israel: 'I
[R]anointed you king over Israel, and I delivered
you from the hand of Saul. 1 Sam. 16:13
8 'I gave you your master's house and your
master's wives into your keeping, and gave
you the house of Israel and Judah. And if *that*
had been too little, I also would have given
you much more!
9 [R]'Why have you despised the command-
ment of the LORD, to do evil in His sight? You
have killed Uriah the Hittite with the sword;
you have taken his wife *to be* your wife, and
have killed him with the sword of the people
of Ammon. 1 Sam. 15:19
10 'Now therefore, [R]the sword shall never
depart from your house, because you have de-
spised Me, and have taken the wife of Uriah
the Hittite to be your wife.' [Amos 7:9]
11 "Thus says the LORD: 'Behold, I will raise
up adversity against you from your own
house; and I will [R]take your wives before your
eyes and give *them* to your neighbor, and he
shall lie with your wives in the sight of this
sun. 2 Sam. 16:21, 22
12 'For you did *it* secretly, but I will do this
thing before all Israel, before the sun.' "

David Repents for His Sin

13 [R]So David said to Nathan, "I have sinned
against the LORD." And Nathan said to David,
"The LORD also has [R]put away your sin; you
shall not die. 1 Sam. 15:24 • [Mic. 7:18]
14 "However, because by this deed you have
given great occasion to the enemies of the
LORD [R]to blaspheme, the child also *who is*
born to you shall surely die." Is. 52:5

God Takes Away the Son of Adultery

15 Then Nathan departed to his house.
And the LORD struck the child that
Uriah's wife bore to David, and it became ill.
16 David therefore pleaded with God for the
child, and David fasted and went in and [R]lay
all night on the ground. 2 Sam. 13:31
17 So the elders of his house arose *and went*
to him, to raise him up from the ground. But
he would not, nor did he eat food with them.
18 Then on the seventh day it came to pass
that the child died. And the servants of David
were afraid to tell him that the child was dead.
For they said, "Indeed, while the child was
alive, we spoke to him, and he would not heed
our voice. How can we tell him that the child
is dead? He may do some harm!"
19 When David saw that his servants were
whispering, David perceived that the child
was dead. Therefore David said to his ser-
vants, "Is the child dead?" And they said, "He
is dead."
20 So David arose from the ground, washed
and [R]anointed himself, and changed his
clothes; and he went into the house of the
LORD and worshiped. Then he went to his own
house; and when he requested, they set food
before him, and he ate. Ruth 3:3
21 Then his servants said to him, "What *is*
this that you have done? You fasted and wept
for the child *while he was* alive, but when the
child died, you arose and ate food."
22 And he said, "While the child was alive, I
fasted and wept; [R]for I said, 'Who can tell
whether the LORD* will be gracious to me, that
the child may live?' Jon. 3:9
23 "But now he is dead; why should I fast?
Can I bring him back again? I shall go to him,
but he shall not return to me."

God Gives Another Son

24 Then David comforted Bathsheba his
wife, and went in to her and lay with her. So
she bore a son, and he* called his name Sol-
omon. Now the LORD loved him,
25 and He sent *word* by the hand of Nathan
the prophet: So he* called his name Jedidiah,*
because of the LORD.

Joab's Loyalty to David—1 Chr. 20:1–3

26 Now [R]Joab fought against [R]Rabbah of
the people of Ammon, and took the royal
city. 1 Chr. 20:1 • Deut. 3:11
27 And Joab sent messengers to David, and
said, "I have fought against Rabbah, and I
have taken the city's water *supply.*
28 "Now therefore, gather the rest of the
people together and encamp against the city
and take it, lest I take the city and it be called
after my name."
29 So David gathered all the people together
and went to Rabbah, fought against it, and
took it.
30 [R]Then he took their king's crown from his
head. Its weight *was* a talent of gold, with pre-
cious stones. And it was *set* on David's head.
Also he brought out the spoil of the city in
great abundance. 1 Chr. 20:2
31 And he brought out the people who *were*
in it, and put *them to work* with saws and iron
picks and iron axes, and made them cross
over to the brick works. So he did to all the
cities of the people of Ammon. Then David
and all the people returned to Jerusalem.

12:22 Heb. mss., Syr. *God* **12:24** So with Kt., LXX, Vg.; Qr., a few Heb. mss., Syr., Tg. *she* **12:25** Qr., some Heb. mss., Syr., Tg. *she* • Lit. *Beloved of the LORD*

CHAPTER 13

Incest in David's House

AFTER this [R]Absalom the son of David
had a lovely sister, whose name *was* [R]Ta-
mar; and [R]Amnon the son of David loved
her. 2 Sam. 3:2, 3 • 1 Chr. 3:9 • 2 Sam. 3:2
2 Amnon was so distressed over his sister
Tamar that he became sick; for she *was* a vir-
gin. And it was improper for Amnon to do
anything to her.
3 But Amnon had a friend whose name
was Jonadab [R]the son of Shimeah, David's
brother. Now Jonadab *was* a very crafty
man. 1 Sam. 16:9
4 And he said to him, "Why *are* you, the
king's son, becoming thinner day after day?
Will you not tell me?" Amnon said to him, "I
love Tamar, my brother Absalom's sister."
5 So Jonadab said to him, "Lie down on
your bed and pretend to be ill. And when your
father comes to see you, say to him, 'Please let
my sister Tamar come and give me food, and
prepare the food in my sight, that I may see *it*
and eat it from her hand.' "
6 Then Amnon lay down and pretended to
be ill; and when the king came to see him,
Amnon said to the king, "Please let Tamar my
sister come and [R]make a couple of cakes for
me in my sight, that I may eat from her
hand." Gen. 18:6
7 And David sent home to Tamar, saying,
"Now go to your brother Amnon's house, and
prepare food for him."
8 So Tamar went to her brother Amnon's
house; and he was lying down. Then she took
flour and kneaded *it*, made cakes in his sight,
and baked the cakes.
9 And she took the pan and placed *them*
out before him, but he refused to eat. Then
Amnon said, "Have everyone go out from me."
And they all went out from him.
10 Then Amnon said to Tamar, "Bring the
food into the bedroom, that I may eat from
your hand." And Tamar took the cakes which
she had made, and brought *them* to Amnon
her brother in the bedroom.
11 Now when she had brought *them* to him
to eat, [R]he took hold of her and said to her,
"Come, lie with me, my sister." Gen. 39:12
12 But she answered him, "No, my brother,
do not [T]force me, for [R]no such thing should be
done in Israel. Do not do this disgraceful
thing! Lit. *humble me* • [Lev. 18:9–11; 20:17]
13 "And I, where could I take my shame?
And as for you, you would be like one of the
fools in Israel. Now therefore, please speak to
the king; [R]for he will not withhold me from
you." Gen. 20:12
14 However, he would not heed her voice;
and being stronger than she, he [R]forced her
and lay with her. 2 Sam. 12:11
15 Then Amnon hated her [T]exceedingly, so
that the hatred with which he hated her was
greater than the love with which he had
loved her. And Amnon said to her, "Arise, be
gone!" *with a very great hatred*
16 So she said to him, "No, indeed! This evil of
sending me away *is* worse than the other that
you did to me." But he would not listen to her.
17 Then he called his servant who attended
him, and said, "Here! Put this *woman* out,
away from me, and bolt the door behind her."
18 Now she had on [R]a robe of many colors,
for the king's virgin daughters wore such ap-
parel. And his servant put her out and bolted
the door behind her. Gen. 37:3
19 Then Tamar put [R]ashes on her head, and
tore her robe of many colors that *was* on her,
and [R]laid her hand on her head and went
away crying bitterly. Josh. 7:6 • Jer. 2:37
20 And Absalom her brother said to her,
"Has Amnon your brother been with you? But
now hold your peace, my sister. He *is* your
brother; do not take this thing to heart." So
Tamar remained desolate in her brother Ab-
salom's house.

Amnon Is Murdered

21 But when King David heard of all these
things, he was very angry.
22 And Absalom spoke to his brother
Amnon [R]neither good nor bad. For Absalom
[R]hated Amnon, because he had forced his sis-
ter Tamar. Gen. 24:50; 31:24 • [Lev. 19:17, 18]
23 And it came to pass, after two full years,
that Absalom [R]had sheepshearers in Baal
Hazor, which *is* near Ephraim; so Absalom in-
vited all the king's sons. 1 Sam. 25:4
24 Then Absalom came to the king and said,
"Kindly note, your servant has sheepshearers;
please, let the king and his servants go with
your servant."
25 But the king said to Absalom, "No, my
son, let us not all go now, lest we be a burden
to you." Then he urged him, but he would not
go; and he blessed him.
26 Then Absalom said, "If not, please let my
brother Amnon go with us." And the king said
to him, "Why should he go with you?"
27 But Absalom urged him; so he let Amnon
and all the king's sons go with him.
28 Now Absalom had commanded his ser-
vants, saying, "Watch now, when Amnon's
[R]heart is merry with wine, and when I say to
you, 'Strike Amnon!' then kill him. Do not be
afraid. Have I not commanded you? Be coura-
geous and valiant." 1 Sam. 25:36
29 So the servants of Absalom [R]did to
Amnon as Absalom had commanded. Then all
the king's sons arose, and each one got on
[R]his mule and fled. 2 Sam. 12:10 • 2 Sam. 18:9
30 And it came to pass, while they were on
the way, that news came to David, saying,
"Absalom has killed all the king's sons, and
not one of them is left!"

31 So the king arose and tore his garments
and lay on the ground, and all his servants
stood by with their clothes torn.
32 Then [R]Jonadab the son of Shimeah, Da-
vid's brother, answered and said, "Let not my
lord suppose they have killed all the young
men, the king's sons, for only Amnon is dead.
For by the command of Absalom this has been
determined from the day that he forced his
sister Tamar. 2 Sam. 13:3–5
33 "Now therefore, [R]let not my lord the king
take the thing to his heart, to think that all
the king's sons are dead. For only Amnon is
dead." 2 Sam. 19:19
34 Then Absalom fled. And the young man
who was keeping watch lifted his eyes and
looked, and there, many people were coming
from the road on the hillside behind him.*
35 And Jonadab said to the king, "Look, the
king's sons are coming; as your servant said,
so it is."
36 So it was, as soon as he had finished
speaking, that the king's sons indeed came,
and they lifted up their voice and wept. Also
the king and all his servants wept very bitterly.

Flight of Absalom

37 But Absalom fled and went to Talmai the
son of Ammihud, king of Geshur. And *David*
mourned for his son every day.
38 So Absalom fled and went to [R]Geshur,
and was there three years. 2 Sam. 14:23, 32
39 And King David* longed to go to* Absa-
lom. For he had been comforted concerning
Amnon, because he was dead.

CHAPTER 14

Return of Absalom

SO Joab the son of Zeruiah perceived that
the king's heart *was* concerned [R]about
Absalom. 2 Sam. 13:39
2 And Joab sent to Tekoa and brought from
there a wise woman, and said to her, "Please
pretend to be a mourner, and put on mourning
apparel; do not anoint yourself with oil, but
act like a woman who has been mourning a
long time for the dead.
3 "Go to the king and speak to him in this
manner." So Joab [R]put the words in her
mouth. 2 Sam. 14:19
4 And when the woman of Tekoa spoke* to
the king, she fell on her face to the ground
and prostrated herself, and said, [R]"Help, O
king!" 2 Kin. 6:26, 28
5 Then the king said to her, "What troubles
you?" And she answered, [R]"Indeed I *am* a
widow, my husband is dead. [Zech. 7:10]
6 "Now your maidservant had two sons;
and the two fought with each other in the
field, and *there was* no one to part them, but
the one struck the other and killed him.
7 "And now the whole family has risen up
against your maidservant, and they said, 'De-
liver him who struck his brother, that we may
execute him for the life of his brother whom
he killed; and we will destroy the heir also.' So
they would extinguish my ember that is left,
and leave to my husband *neither* name nor
remnant on the earth."
8 Then the king said to the woman, "Go to
your house, and I will give orders concerning
you."
9 And the woman of Tekoa said to the king,
"My lord, O king, *let* the [T]iniquity *be* on me
and on my father's house, and the king and
his throne *be* guiltless." *guilt*
10 So the king said, "Whoever says *anything*
to you, bring him to me, and he shall not touch
you anymore."
11 Then she said, "Please let the king re-
member the LORD your God, and do not per-
mit [R]the avenger of blood to destroy anymore,
lest they destroy my son." And he said, "*As* the
LORD lives, not one hair of your son shall fall
to the ground." Num. 35:19, 21
12 Therefore the woman said, "Please, let
your maidservant speak *another* word to my
lord the king." And he said, "Say on."
13 So the woman said: "Why then have you
schemed such a thing against [R]the people of
God? For the king speaks this thing as one
who is guilty, *in that* the king does not bring
his banished one home again. Judg. 20:2
14 "For we [R]will surely die and *become* like
water spilled on the ground, which cannot be
gathered up again. Yet God does not [R]take
away a life; but He [R]devises means, so that
His banished ones are not [T]expelled from
Him. [Heb. 9:27] • Job 34:19 • Num. 35:15 • *cast out*
15 "Now therefore, I have come to speak of
this thing to my lord the king because the peo-
ple have made me afraid. And your maid-
servant said, 'I will now speak to the king; it
may be that the king will perform the request
of his maidservant.
16 'For the king will hear and deliver his
maidservant from the hand of the man *who
would* destroy me and my son together from
the [R]inheritance of God.' Deut. 32:9
17 "Your maidservant said, 'The word of my
lord the king will now be comforting; for [R]as
the angel of God, so *is* my lord the king in dis-
cerning good and evil. And may the LORD
your God be with you.' " 2 Sam. 19:27
18 Then the king answered and said to the
woman, "Please do not hide from me anything
that I ask you." And the woman said, "Please,
let my lord the king speak."

13:34 LXX adds *And the watchman went and told the king, and said, "I see men from the way of Horonaim, from the regions of the mountains."* **13:39** So with MT, Syr., Vg.; LXX *the spirit of the king;* Tg. *the soul of King David* • So with MT, Tg.; LXX, Vg. *ceased to pursue after* **14:4** Many Heb. mss., LXX, Syr., Vg. *came*

19 So the king said, "*Is* the hand of Joab with
you in all this?" And the woman answered
and said, "*As* you live, my lord the king, no
one can turn to the right hand or to the left
from anything that my lord the king has spo-
ken. For your servant Joab commanded me,
and [R]he put all these words in the mouth of
your maidservant. 2 Sam. 14:3
20 "To bring about this change of affairs
your servant Joab has done this thing; but my
lord *is* wise, [R]according to the wisdom of the
angel of God, to know everything that *is* in the
earth." 2 Sam. 14:17; 19:27
21 And the king said to Joab, "All right, I
have granted this thing. Go therefore, bring
back the young man Absalom."
22 Then Joab fell to the ground on his face
and bowed himself, and [T]thanked the king.
And Joab said, "Today your servant knows
that I have found favor in your sight, my lord,
O king, in that the king has fulfilled the re-
quest of his servant." Lit. *blessed*
23 So Joab arose and went to Geshur, and
brought Absalom to Jerusalem.
24 And the king said, "Let him return to his
own house, but do not let him see my face." So
Absalom returned to his own house, but did
not see the king's face.

Deceit of Absalom

25 Now in all Israel there was no one who
was praised as much as Absalom for his good
looks. [R]From the sole of his foot to the crown
of his head there was no blemish in him. Is. 1:6
26 And when he cut the hair of his head—at
the end of every year he cut *it* because it was
heavy on him—when he cut it, he weighed the
hair of his head at two hundred shekels ac-
cording to the king's standard.
27 To Absalom were born three sons, and
one daughter whose name *was* Tamar. She
was a woman of beautiful appearance.
28 And Absalom dwelt two full years in Jeru-
salem, but did not see the king's face.
29 Therefore Absalom sent for Joab, to send
him to the king, but he would not come to
him. And when he sent again the second time,
he would not come.
30 So he said to his servants, "See, Joab's
field is near mine, and he has barley there; go
and set it on fire." And Absalom's servants set
the field on fire.
31 Then Joab arose and came to Absalom's
house, and said to him, "Why have your ser-
vants set my field on fire?"
32 And Absalom answered Joab, "Look, I
sent to you, saying, 'Come here, so that I may
send you to the king, to say, "Why have I come
from Geshur? *It would be* better for me *to be*
there still." ' Now therefore, let me see the
king's face; but [R]if there is iniquity in me, let
him execute me." 1 Sam. 20:8
33 So Joab went to the king and told him.
And when he had called for Absalom, he
came to the king and bowed himself on his
face to the ground before the king. Then the
king [R]kissed Absalom. Luke 15:20

CHAPTER 15

AFTER this it happened that Absalom pro-
vided himself with chariots and horses,
and fifty men to run before him.
2 Now Absalom would rise early and stand
beside the way to the gate. *So* it was, when-
ever anyone who had a lawsuit came to the
king for a decision, that Absalom would call
to him and say, "What city *are* you from?" And
he would say, "Your servant *is* from such and
such a tribe of Israel."
3 Then Absalom would say to him, "Look,
your [T]case *is* good and right; but *there is* no
deputy of the king to hear you." Lit. *words*
4 Moreover Absalom would say, "Oh, that I
were made judge in the land, and everyone
who has any suit or cause would come to me;
then I would give him justice."
5 And *so* it was, whenever anyone came
near to bow down to him, that he would put
out his hand and take him and kiss him.
6 In this manner Absalom acted toward all
Israel who came to the king for judgment.
[R]So Absalom stole the hearts of the men of Is-
rael. [Rom. 16:18]

Rebellion of Absalom

7 Now it came to pass [R]after forty* years
that Absalom said to the king, "Please, let me
go to [R]Hebron and pay the vow which I made
to the LORD. Deut. 23:21 • 2 Sam. 3:2, 3
8 [R]"For your servant took a vow [R]while I
dwelt at Geshur in Syria, saying, 'If the LORD
indeed brings me back to Jerusalem, then I
will serve the LORD.' " 1 Sam. 16:2 • 2 Sam. 13:38
9 And the king said to him, "Go in peace."
So he arose and went to Hebron.
10 Then Absalom sent spies throughout all
the tribes of Israel, saying, "As soon as you
hear the sound of the trumpet, then you shall
say, 'Absalom reigns in Hebron!' "
11 And with Absalom went two hundred
men [R]invited from Jerusalem, and they
[R]went along innocently and did not know
anything. 1 Sam. 16:3, 5 • Gen. 20:5
12 Then Absalom sent for Ahithophel the
Gilonite, [R]David's counselor, from his city—
from [R]Giloh—while he offered sacrifices. And
the conspiracy grew strong, for the people
with Absalom [R]continually increased in num-
ber. 1 Chr. 27:33 • Josh. 15:51 • Ps. 3:1

Flight of David

13 Now a messenger came to David, saying,
[R]"The hearts of the men of Israel are [T]with Ab-
salom." Judg. 9:3 • Lit. *after*

15:7 LXX mss., Syr., Josephus *four*

14 So David said to all his servants who
were with him at Jerusalem, "Arise, and let us
[R]flee, or we shall not escape from Absalom.
Make haste to depart, lest he overtake us sud-
denly and bring disaster upon us, and strike
the city with the edge of the sword." Ps. 3:title
15 And the king's servants said to the king,
"We *are* your servants, *ready to do* whatever
my lord the king commands."
16 Then the king went out with all his house-
hold after him. But the king left ten women,
concubines, to keep the house.
17 And the king went out with all the people
after him, and stopped at the outskirts.
18 Then all his servants passed before him;
[R]and all the Cherethites, all the Pelethites,
and all the Gittites, six hundred men who had
followed him from Gath, passed before the
king. 2 Sam. 8:18
19 Then the king said to [R]Ittai the Gittite,
"Why are you also going with us? Return
and remain with the king. For you *are* a for-
eigner and also an exile from your own
place. 2 Sam. 18:2
20 "In fact, you came *only* yesterday. Should
I make you wander up and down with us
today, since I go [R]I know not where? Return,
and take your brethren back. Mercy and truth
be with you." 1 Sam. 23:13
21 But Ittai answered the king and said, "*As*
the LORD lives, and *as* my lord the king lives,
surely in whatever place my lord the king
shall be, whether in death or life, even there
also your servant will be."
22 So David said to Ittai, "Go, and cross
over." Then Ittai the Gittite and all his men
and all the little ones who *were* with him
crossed over.
23 And all the country wept with a loud
voice, and all the people crossed over. The
king himself also crossed over the Brook
Kidron, and all the people crossed over to-
ward the way of the wilderness.
24 There was [R]Zadok also, and all the
Levites with him, bearing the [R]ark of the
covenant of God. And they set down the ark
of God, and [R]Abiathar went up until all the
people had finished crossing over from the
city. 2 Sam. 8:17 • Num. 4:15 • 1 Sam. 22:20
25 Then the king said to Zadok, "Carry the
ark of God back into the city. If I find favor
in the eyes of the LORD, He [R]will bring me
back and show me *both* it and [R]His dwelling
place. [Ps. 43:3] • Ex. 15:13
26 "But if He says thus: 'I have no [R]delight in
you,' here I am, [R]let Him do to me as seems
good to Him." Num. 14:8 • 1 Sam. 3:18
27 The king also said to Zadok the priest,
"*Are* you *not* a [R]seer?[T] Return to the city in
peace, and [R]your two sons with you, Ahim-
aaz your son, and Jonathan the son of Abi-
athar. 1 Sam. 9:6–9 • *prophet* • 2 Sam. 17:17–20
28 "See, [R]I will wait in the plains of the
wilderness until word comes from you to in-
form me." 2 Sam. 17:16
29 Therefore Zadok and Abiathar carried
the ark of God back to Jerusalem. And they
remained there.
30 So David went up by the Ascent of the
Mount of Olives, and wept as he went up; and
he [R]had his head covered and went barefoot.
And all the people who *were* with him cov-
ered their heads and went up, weeping as they
went up. Esth. 6:12
31 Then *someone* told David, saying,
[R]"Ahithophel *is* among the conspirators with
Absalom." And David said, "O LORD, I pray,
[R]turn the counsel of Ahithophel into foolish-
ness!" Ps. 3:1, 2; 55:12 • 2 Sam. 16:23; 17:14, 23
32 Now it happened when David had come
to the top *of the mountain,* where he wor-
shiped God—there was Hushai the [R]Archite
coming to meet him [R]with his robe torn and
dust on his head. Josh. 16:2 • 2 Sam. 1:2
33 David said to him, "If you go on with me,
then you will become a burden to me.
34 "But if you return to the city, and say to
Absalom, 'I will be your servant, O king; *as* I
was your father's servant previously, so I *will*
now also *be* your servant,' then you may de-
feat the counsel of Ahithophel for me.
35 "And *do* you not *have* Zadok and Abi-
athar the priests with you there? Therefore it
will be *that* whatever you hear from the
king's house, you shall tell to [R]Zadok and Abi-
athar the priests. 2 Sam. 17:15, 16
36 "Indeed *they have* there [R]with them their
two sons, Ahimaaz, Zadok's *son,* and Jona-
than, Abiathar's *son;* and by them you shall
send me everything you hear." 2 Sam. 15:27
37 So Hushai, David's friend, went into the
city. And Absalom came into Jerusalem.

CHAPTER 16

WHEN[R] David was a little past the top *of
the mountain,* there was Ziba the ser-
vant of Mephibosheth, who met him with a
couple of saddled donkeys, and on them two
hundred *loaves* of bread, one hundred clus-
ters of raisins, one hundred summer fruits,
and a skin of wine. 2 Sam. 15:30, 32
2 And the king said to Ziba, "What do you
mean to do with these?" So Ziba said, "The
donkeys *are* for the king's household to ride
on, the bread and summer fruit for the young
men to eat, and the wine for those who are
faint in the wilderness to drink."
3 Then the king said, "And where *is* your
master's son?" And Ziba said to the king, "In-
deed he is staying in Jerusalem, for he said,
'Today the house of Israel will restore the
kingdom of my father to me.' "
4 So the king said to Ziba, "Here, all that
belongs to Mephibosheth *is* yours." And Ziba

said, "I humbly bow before you, *that* I may find favor in your sight, my lord, O king!"

5 Now when King David came to [R]Bahurim, there was a man from the family of the house of Saul, whose name *was* [R]Shimei the son of Gera, coming from there. He came out, cursing continuously as he came. 2 Sam. 3:16 • 2 Sam. 19:21

6 And he threw stones at David and at all the servants of King David. And all the people and all the mighty men *were* on his right hand and on his left.

7 Also Shimei said thus when he cursed: "Come out! Come out! You bloodthirsty man, [R]you [T]rogue! Deut. 13:13 • *worthless man*

8 "The LORD has [R]brought upon you all [R]the blood of the house of Saul, in whose place you have reigned; and the LORD has delivered the kingdom into the hand of Absalom your son. So now you *are caught* in your own evil, because you are a bloodthirsty man!" Judg. 9:24, 56, 57 • 2 Sam. 1:16

9 Then Abishai the son of Zeruiah said to the king, "Why should this [R]dead dog [R]curse my lord the king? Please, let me go over and take off his head!" 2 Sam. 9:8 • Ex. 22:28

10 But the king said, "What have I to do with you, you sons of Zeruiah? So let him curse, because [R]the LORD has said to him, 'Curse David.' [R]Who then shall say, 'Why have you done so?' " [Lam. 3:38] • [Rom. 9:20]

11 And David said to Abishai and all his servants, "See how [R]my son who [R]came from my own body seeks my life. How much more now *may this* Benjamite? Let him alone, and let him curse; for so the LORD has ordered him. 2 Sam. 12:11 • Gen. 15:4

12 "It may be that the LORD will look on my affliction,* and that the LORD will repay me with good for his cursing this day."

13 And as David and his men went along the road, Shimei went along the hillside opposite him and cursed as he went, threw stones at him and kicked up dust.

14 Now the king and all the people who *were* with him became weary; so they refreshed themselves there.

Reign of Absalom

15 Meanwhile [R]Absalom and all the people, the men of Israel, came to Jerusalem; and Ahithophel *was* with him. 2 Sam. 15:12, 37

16 And so it was, when Hushai the Archite, [R]David's friend, came to Absalom, that [R]Hushai said to Absalom, "*Long* live the king! *Long* live the king!" 2 Sam. 15:37 • 2 Sam. 15:34

17 So Absalom said to Hushai, "*Is* this your loyalty to your friend? [R]Why did you not go with your friend?" 2 Sam. 19:25

18 And Hushai said to Absalom, "No, but whom the LORD and this people and all the men of Israel choose, his I will be, and with him I will remain.

19 "Furthermore, whom should I serve? *Should I* not *serve* in the presence of his son? As I have served in your father's presence, so will I be in your presence."

20 Then Absalom said to Ahithophel, "Give advice as to what we should do."

21 And Ahithophel said to Absalom, "Go in to your father's [R]concubines, whom he has left to keep the house; and all Israel will hear that you [R]are abhorred by your father. Then the hands of all who are with you will be strong." 2 Sam. 15:16; 20:3 • Gen. 34:30

22 So they pitched a tent for Absalom on the top of the house, and Absalom went in to his father's concubines [R]in the sight of all Israel. 2 Sam. 12:11, 12

23 Now the advice of Ahithophel, which he gave in those days, *was* as if one had inquired at the oracle of God. So *was* all the advice of Ahithophel [R]both with David and with Absalom. 2 Sam. 15:12

CHAPTER 17

MOREOVER Ahithophel said to Absalom, "Now let me choose twelve thousand men, and I will arise and pursue David tonight.

2 "I will come upon him while he *is* [R]weary and weak, and make him afraid. And all the people who *are* with him will flee, and I will [R]strike only the king. 2 Sam. 16:14 • Zech. 13:7

3 "Then I will bring back all the people to you. When all return except the man whom you seek, all the people will be at peace."

4 And the saying pleased Absalom and all the [R]elders of Israel. 2 Sam. 5:3; 19:11

5 Then Absalom said, "Now call Hushai the Archite also, and let us hear what he [R]says too." 2 Sam. 15:32–34

6 And when Hushai came to Absalom, Absalom spoke to him, saying, "Ahithophel has spoken in this manner. Shall we do as he says? If not, speak up."

7 So Hushai said to Absalom: "The advice that Ahithophel has given *is* not good at this time.

8 "For," said Hushai, "you know your father and his men, that they *are* mighty men, and they *are* enraged in their minds, like [R]a bear robbed of her cubs in the field; and your father *is* a man of war, and will not camp with the people. Hos. 13:8

9 "Surely by now he is hidden in some pit, or in some *other* place. And it will be, when some of them are overthrown at the first, that whoever hears *it* will say, 'There is a slaughter among the people who follow Absalom.'

10 "And even he *who is* valiant, whose heart *is* like the heart of a lion, will [R]melt

16:12 So with Kt., LXX, Syr., Vg.; Qr. *my eyes;* Tg. *tears of my eyes*

completely. For all Israel knows that your fa-
ther *is* a mighty man, and *those* who *are* with
him *are* valiant men. Josh. 2:11
11 "Therefore I advise that all Israel be fully
gathered to you, from Dan to Beersheba, like
the sand that *is* by the sea for multitude, and
that you go to battle in person.
12 "So we will come upon him in some place
where he may be found, and we will fall on
him as the dew falls on the ground. And of
him and all the men who *are* with him there
shall not be left so much as one.
13 "Moreover, if he has withdrawn into a
city, then all Israel shall bring ropes to that
city; and we will pull it into the river, until
there is not one small stone found there."
14 So Absalom and all the men of Israel said,
"The advice of Hushai the Archite *is* better
than the advice of Ahithophel." For the LORD
had purposed to defeat the good advice of
Ahithophel, to the intent that the LORD might
bring disaster on Absalom.
15 Then Hushai said to Zadok and Abiathar
the priests, "Thus and so Ahithophel advised
Absalom and the elders of Israel, and thus
and so I have advised.
16 "Now therefore, send quickly and tell Da-
vid, saying, 'Do not spend this night in the
plains of the wilderness, but speedily cross
over, lest the king and all the people who *are*
with him be swallowed up.' "
17 [R]Now Jonathan and Ahimaaz [R]stayed at
En Rogel, for they dared not be seen coming
into the city; so a female servant would come
and tell them, and they would go and tell King
David. 2 Sam. 15:27, 36 • Josh. 2:4–6
18 Nevertheless a lad saw them, and told Ab-
salom. But both of them went away quickly
and came to a man's house [R]in Bahurim, who
had a well in his court; and they went down
into it. 2 Sam. 3:16; 16:5
19 [R]Then the woman took and spread a cov-
ering over the well's mouth, and spread
ground grain on it; and the thing was not
known. Josh. 2:4–6
20 And when Absalom's servants came to
the woman at the house, they said, "Where
are Ahimaaz and Jonathan?" So [R]the woman
said to them, "They have gone over the water
brook." And when they had searched and
could not find *them*, they returned to Jerusa-
lem. Josh. 2:3–5
21 Now it came to pass, after they had de-
parted, that they came up out of the well and
went and told King David, and said to Da-
vid, [R]"Arise and cross over the water quickly.
For thus has Ahithophel advised against
you." 2 Sam. 17:15, 16
22 So David and all the people who *were*
with him arose and crossed over the Jordan.
By morning light not one of them was left
who had not gone over the Jordan.
23 Now when Ahithophel saw that his ad-
vice was not followed, he saddled a donkey,
and arose and went home to his house, to his
city. Then he put his household in order, and
[R]hanged himself, and died; and he was buried
in his father's tomb. Matt. 27:5
24 Then David went to [R]Mahanaim. And Ab-
salom crossed over the Jordan, he and all the
men of Israel with him. 2 Sam. 2:8; 19:32
25 And Absalom made [R]Amasa captain of
the army instead of Joab. This Amasa *was* the
son of a man whose name *was* Jithra,* an Is-
raelite,* who had gone in to [R]Abigail the
daughter of Nahash, sister of Zeruiah, Joab's
mother. 1 Kin. 2:5, 32 • 1 Chr. 2:16
26 So Israel and Absalom encamped in the
land of Gilead.
27 Now it happened, when David had come
to Mahanaim, that Shobi the son of Nahash
from Rabbah of the people of Ammon, Machir
the son of Ammiel from Lo Debar, and Barzil-
lai the Gileadite from Rogelim,
28 brought beds and basins, earthen vessels
and wheat, barley and flour, parched *grain*
and beans, lentils and parched *seeds*,
29 honey and curds, sheep and cheese of the
herd, for David and the people who *were* with
him to eat. For they said, "The people are
hungry and weary and thirsty [R]in the wilder-
ness." 2 Sam. 16:2, 14

CHAPTER 18

Absalom's Murder

AND David [T]numbered the people who
were with him, and [R]set captains of
thousands and captains of hundreds over
them. Lit. *attended to* • Ex. 18:25
2 Then David sent out one third of the peo-
ple under the hand of Joab, [R]one third under
the hand of Abishai the son of Zeruiah,
Joab's brother, and one third under the hand
of [R]Ittai the Gittite. And the king said to the
people, "I also will surely go out with you my-
self." Judg. 7:16 • 2 Sam. 15:19–22
3 [R]But the people answered, "You shall not
go out! For if we flee away, they will not care
about us; nor if half of us die, will they care
about us. But *you are* worth ten thousand of
us now. For you are now more help to us in the
city." 2 Sam. 21:17
4 Then the king said to them, "Whatever
seems best to you I will do." So the king stood
beside the gate, and all the people went out by
hundreds and by thousands.
5 Now the king had commanded Joab,
Abishai, and Ittai, saying, "*Deal* gently for
my sake with the young man Absalom."
[R]And all the people heard when the king

17:25 *Jether*, 1 Chr. 2:17 • So with MT, some LXX mss., Tg.; some LXX mss. *Ishmaelite* (cf. 1 Chr. 2:17); Vg. *of Jezrael*

gave all the captains orders concerning Ab-
salom. 2 Sam. 18:12
6 So the people went out into the field of
battle against Israel. And the battle was in the
[R]woods of Ephraim. Josh. 17:15, 18
7 The people of Israel were overthrown
there before the servants of David, and a
great slaughter of twenty thousand took place
there that day.
8 For the battle there was scattered over the
face of the whole countryside, and the woods
devoured more people that day than the
sword devoured.
9 Then Absalom met the servants of David.
Absalom rode on a mule. The mule went
under the thick boughs of a great terebinth
tree, and [R]his head caught in the terebinth; so
he was left hanging between heaven and
earth. And the mule which *was* under him
went on. 2 Sam. 14:26
10 Now a certain man saw *it* and told Joab,
and said, "I just saw Absalom hanging in a
terebinth tree!"
11 So Joab said to the man who told him,
"You just saw *him!* And why did you not strike
him there to the ground? I would have given
you ten *shekels* of silver and a belt."
12 But the man said to Joab, "Though I were
to receive a thousand *shekels* of silver in my
hand, I would not raise my hand against the
king's son. [R]For in our hearing the king com-
manded you and Abishai and Ittai, saying,
'Beware lest anyone *touch* the young man Ab-
salom!'* 2 Sam. 18:5
13 "Otherwise I would have dealt falsely
against my own life. For there is nothing hid-
den from the king, and you yourself would
have set yourself against *me.*"
14 Then Joab said, "I cannot linger with
you." And he took three spears in his hand
and thrust them through Absalom's heart,
while he was *still* alive in the midst of the tere-
binth tree.
15 And ten young men who bore Joab's
armor surrounded Absalom, and struck and
killed him.
16 So Joab blew the trumpet, and the people
returned from pursuing Israel. For Joab held
back the people.
17 And they took Absalom and cast him into
a large pit in the woods, and [R]laid a very large
heap of stones over him. Then all Israel fled,
everyone to his tent. Josh. 7:26; 8:29
18 Now Absalom in his lifetime had taken
and set up a pillar for himself, which *is* in the
King's Valley. For he said, "I have no son to
keep my name in remembrance." He called
the pillar after his own name. And to this day
it is called Absalom's Monument.
19 Then [R]Ahimaaz the son of Zadok said,
"Let me run now and take the news to the
king, how the LORD has [T]avenged him of his
enemies." 2 Sam. 15:36; 17:17 • *vindicated*
20 And Joab said to him, "You shall not take
the news this day, for you shall take the news
another day. But today you shall take no
news, because the king's son is dead."
21 Then Joab said to the Cushite, "Go, tell
the king what you have seen." So the Cushite
bowed himself to Joab and ran.
22 And Ahimaaz the son of Zadok said
again to Joab, "But [T]whatever happens, please
let me also run after the Cushite." So Joab
said, "Why will you run, my son, since you
have no news ready?" Lit. *be what may*
23 "But whatever happens," *he said,* "let me
run." So he said to him, "Run." Then Ahimaaz
ran by way of the plain, and outran the
Cushite.
24 Now David was sitting between the [R]two
gates. And the watchman went up to the
roof over the gate, to the wall, lifted his eyes
and looked, and there was a man, running
alone. 2 Kin. 9:17
25 Then the watchman cried out and told the
king. And the king said, "If he *is* alone, *there
is* news in his mouth." And he came rapidly
and drew near.
26 Then the watchman saw *another* man
running, and the watchman called to the gate-
keeper and said, "There is *another* man, run-
ning alone!" And the king said, "He also
brings news."
27 So the watchman said, [T]"I think the run-
ning of the first is like the running of Ahim-
aaz the son of Zadok." And the king said,
"He *is* a good man, and comes with [R]good
news." Lit. *I see the running* • 1 Kin. 1:42
28 So Ahimaaz called out and said to the
king, "All is well!" Then he bowed down with
his face to the earth before the king, and said,
"Blessed *be* the LORD your God, who has de-
livered up the men who raised their hand
against my lord the king!"
29 The king said, "Is the young man Absa-
lom safe?" Ahimaaz answered, "When Joab
sent the king's servant and *me* your servant, I
saw a great tumult, but I did not know what *it
was about.*"
30 And the king said, "Turn aside *and* stand
here." So he turned aside and stood still.
31 Just then the Cushite came, and the
Cushite said, "There is good news, my lord the
king! For the LORD has avenged you this day
of all those who rose against you."
32 And the king said to the Cushite, "Is the
young man Absalom safe?" So the Cushite
answered, "May the enemies of my lord the
king, and all who rise against you to do harm,
be like *that* young man!"
33 Then the king was deeply moved, and
went up to the chamber over the gate, and
wept. And as he went, he said thus: [R]"O my
son Absalom—my son, my son Absalom—if

18:12 Vss. *'Protect the young man Absalom for me!'*

only I had died in your place! O Absalom my
son, [R]my son!" 2 Sam. 12:10 • 2 Sam. 19:4

CHAPTER 19

Reproof of Joab

AND Joab was told, "Behold, the king is
weeping and mourning for Absalom."
2 So the victory that day was *turned* into
[R]mourning for all the people. For the people
heard it said that day, "The king is grieved for
his son." Esth. 4:3
3 And the people [T]stole back into the city
that day, as people who are ashamed steal
away when they flee in battle. *went by stealth*
4 But the king covered his face, and the
king cried out with a loud voice, "O my son
Absalom! O Absalom, my son, my son!"
5 Then [R]Joab came into the house to the
king, and said, "Today you have disgraced all
your servants who today have saved your life,
the lives of your sons and daughters, the lives
of your wives and the lives of your concu-
bines, 2 Sam. 18:14
6 "in that you love your enemies and hate
your friends. For you have declared today that
you regard neither princes nor servants; for
today I perceive that if Absalom had lived and
all of us had died today, then it would have
pleased you well.
7 "Now therefore, arise, go out and speak
[T]comfort to your servants. For I swear by the
LORD, if you do not go out, not one will stay
with you this night. And that will be worse for
you than all the evil that has befallen you
from your youth until now." Lit. *to the heart of*

Restoration of David

8 Then the king arose and sat in the gate.
And they told all the people, saying, "There is
the king, sitting in the gate." So all the people
came before the king. For everyone of Israel
had fled to his tent.
9 Now all the people were in a dispute
throughout all the tribes of Israel, saying,
"The king saved us from the hand of our [R]en-
emies, he delivered us from the hand of the
Philistines, and now he has fled from the land
because of Absalom. 2 Sam. 8:1–14
10 "But Absalom, whom we anointed over
us, has died in battle. Now therefore, why do
you say nothing about bringing back the
king?"
11 So King David sent to [R]Zadok and Abi-
athar the priests, saying, "Speak to the elders
of Judah, saying, 'Why are you the last to
bring the king back to his house, since the
words of all Israel have come to the king, to
his *very* house? 2 Sam. 15:24
12 'You *are* my brethren, you *are* [R]my bone
and my flesh. Why then are you the last to
bring back the king?' 2 Sam. 5:1
13 [R]"And say to Amasa, '*Are* you not my
bone and my flesh? [R]God do so to me, and
more also, if you are not commander of the
army before me [T]continually in place of
Joab.' " 2 Sam. 17:25 • Ruth 1:17 • *permanently*
14 So he swayed the hearts of all the men of
Judah, [R]just as *the heart of* one man, so that
they sent *this word* to the king: "Return, you
and all your servants!" Judg. 20:1
15 Then the king returned and came to the
Jordan. And Judah came to [R]Gilgal, to go to
meet the king, to escort the king [R]across the
Jordan. Josh. 5:9 • 2 Sam. 17:22
16 And [R]Shimei the son of Gera, a Ben-
jamite, who *was* from Bahurim, hurried and
came down with the men of Judah to meet
King David. 2 Sam. 16:5
17 *There were* a thousand men of Benjamin
with him, and Ziba the servant of the house of
Saul, and his fifteen sons and his twenty ser-
vants with him; and they went over the Jordan
before the king.
18 Then a ferryboat went across to carry
over the king's household, and to do what he
thought good.
Now Shimei the son of Gera fell down be-
fore the king when he had crossed the Jordan.
19 Then he said to the king, "Do not let my
lord impute iniquity to me, or remember what
wrong your servant did on the day that my
lord the king left Jerusalem, that the king
should take *it* to heart.
20 "For I, your servant, know that I have
sinned. Therefore here I am, the first to come
today of all [R]the house of Joseph to go down
to meet my lord the king." Judg. 1:22
21 But Abishai the son of Zeruiah answered
and said, "Shall not Shimei be put to death
for this, [R]because he [R]cursed the LORD's
anointed?" [Ex. 22:28] • [1 Sam. 26:9]
22 And David said, [R]"What have I to do
with you, you sons of Zeruiah, that you
should be adversaries to me today? [R]Shall
any man be put to death today in Israel? For
do I not know that today I *am* king over Is-
rael?" 2 Sam. 3:39; 16:10 • 1 Sam. 11:13
23 Therefore the king said to Shimei, "You
shall not die." And the king swore to him.
24 Now [R]Mephibosheth the son of Saul
came down to meet the king. And he had not
cared for his feet, nor trimmed his mustache,
nor washed his clothes, from the day the
king departed until the day he returned in
peace. 2 Sam. 9:6; 21:7
25 So it was, when he had come to Jerusalem
to meet the king, that the king said to him
[R]"Why did you not go with me, Mephibo-
sheth? 2 Sam. 16:17
26 And he answered, "My lord, O king, my
servant deceived me. For your servant said, 'I
will saddle a donkey for myself, that I may
ride on it and go to the king,' because your
servant *is* lame.
27 "And [R]he has slandered your servant to

my lord the king, but my lord the king *is* like the angel of God. Therefore do *what is* good in your eyes. 2 Sam. 16:3, 4

28 "For all my father's house were but dead men before my lord the king. Yet you set your servant among those who eat at your own table. Therefore what right have I still to [T]cry out anymore to the king?" *complain*

29 So the king said to him, "Why do you speak anymore of your matters? I have said, 'You and Ziba divide the land.'"

30 Then Mephibosheth said to the king, "Rather, let him take it all, inasmuch as my lord the king has come back in peace to his own house."

31 And [R]Barzillai the Gileadite came down from Rogelim and went across the Jordan with the king, to escort him across the Jordan. 1 Kin. 2:7

32 Now Barzillai was a very aged man, eighty years old. And he had provided the king with supplies while he stayed at Mahanaim, for he *was* a very rich man.

33 And the king said to Barzillai, "Come across with me, and I will provide for you while you are with me in Jerusalem."

34 But Barzillai said to the king, "How long have I to live, that I should go up with the king to Jerusalem?

35 "I *am* today [R]eighty years old. Can I discern between the good and bad? Can your servant taste what I eat or what I drink? Can I hear any longer the voice of singing men and singing women? Why then should your servant be a further burden to my lord the king? Ps. 90:10

36 "Your servant will go a little way across the Jordan with the king. And why should the king repay me *with* such a reward?

37 "Please let your servant turn back again, that I may die in my own city, near the grave of my father and mother. But here is your servant [R]Chimham; let him cross over with my lord the king, and do for him what seems good to you." Jer. 41:17

38 And the king answered, "Chimham shall cross over with me, and I will do for him what seems good to you. Now whatever you request of me, I will do for you."

39 Then all the people went over the Jordan. And when the king had crossed over, the king kissed Barzillai and blessed him, and he returned to his own place.

40 Now the king went on to Gilgal, and Chimham* went on with him. And all the people of Judah escorted the king, and also half the people of Israel.

41 Just then all the men of Israel came to the king, and said to the king, "Why have our brethren, the men of Judah, stolen you away and [R]brought the king, his household, and all David's men with him across the Jordan?" 2 Sam. 19:15

42 So all the men of Judah answered the men of Israel, "Because the king *is* a close relative of ours. Why then are you angry over this matter? Have we ever eaten at the king's *expense*? Or has he given us any gift?"

43 And the men of Israel answered the men of Judah, and said, "We have [R]ten shares in the king; therefore we also have more *right* to David than you. Why then do you despise us—were we not the first to advise bringing back our king?" Yet [R]the words of the men of Judah were fiercer than the words of the men of Israel. 1 Kin. 11:30, 31 • Judg. 8:1; 12:1

CHAPTER 20

AND there happened to be there a rebel,* whose name *was* Sheba the son of Bichri, a Benjamite. And he blew a trumpet, and said:

[R]"We have no share in David, 1 Kin. 12:16
Nor do we have inheritance in the son of Jesse;
Every man to his tents, O Israel!"

2 So every man of Israel deserted David, *and* followed Sheba the son of Bichri. But the men of Judah, from the Jordan as far as Jerusalem, remained loyal to their king.

3 Now David came to his house at Jerusalem. And the king took the ten women, [R]his concubines whom he had left to keep the house, and put them in seclusion and supported them, but did not go in to them. So they were shut up to the day of their death, living in widowhood. 2 Sam. 15:16; 16:21, 22

4 And the king said to Amasa, [R]"Assemble the men of Judah for me within three days, and be present here yourself." 2 Sam. 17:25

5 So Amasa went to assemble *the men of* Judah. But he delayed longer than the set time which David had appointed him.

6 And David said to [R]Abishai, "Now Sheba the son of Bichri will do us more harm than Absalom. Take your lord's servants and pursue him, lest he find for himself fortified cities, and escape us." 2 Sam. 21:17

7 So Joab's men, with the Cherethites, the Pelethites, and all the mighty men, went out after him. And they went out of Jerusalem to pursue Sheba the son of Bichri.

8 When they *were* at the large stone which *is* in Gibeon, Amasa came before them. Now Joab was dressed in battle armor; on it was a belt *with* a sword fastened in its sheath at his hips; and as he was going forward, it fell out.

9 Then Joab said to Amasa, "*Are* you in health, my brother?" And Joab took Amasa by the beard with his right hand to kiss him.

10 But Amasa did not notice the sword that *was* in Joab's hand. And [R]he struck him with it [R]in the stomach, and his entrails poured out on the ground; and he did not

19:40 MT *Chimhan* **20:1** Lit. *man of Belial*

strike him again. Thus he died. Then Joab and Abishai his brother pursued Sheba the son of Bichri. 1 Kin. 2:5 • 2 Sam. 2:23

11 Meanwhile one of Joab's men stood near Amasa, and said, "Whoever favors Joab and whoever *is* for David—follow Joab!"

12 But Amasa wallowed in *his* blood in the middle of the highway. And when the man saw that all the people stood still, he moved Amasa from the highway to the field and threw a garment over him, when he saw that everyone who came upon him halted.

13 When he was removed from the highway, all the people went on after Joab to pursue Sheba the son of Bichri.

14 And he went through all the tribes of Israel to [R]Abel and Beth Maachah and all the Berites. So they were gathered together and also went after *Sheba.** 2 Kin. 15:29

15 Then they came and besieged him in Abel of Beth Maachah; and they cast up a siege mound against the city, and it stood by the rampart. And all the people who *were* with Joab battered the wall to throw it down.

16 Then a wise woman cried out from the city, "Hear, hear! Please say to Joab, 'Come nearby, that I may speak with you.' "

17 When he had come near to her, the woman said, "*Are* you Joab?" He answered, "I *am.*" Then she said to him, "Hear the words of your maidservant." And he answered, "I am listening."

18 So she spoke, saying, "They used to talk in former times, saying, 'They shall surely seek *guidance* at Abel,' and so they would end *disputes.*

19 "I *am among the* peaceable *and* faithful in Israel. You seek to destroy a city and a mother in Israel. Why would you swallow up [R]the inheritance of the LORD?" 1 Sam. 26:19

20 And Joab answered and said, "Far be it, far be it from me, that I should swallow up or destroy!

21 "That *is* not so. But a man from the mountains of Ephraim, Sheba the son of Bichri by name, has raised his hand against the king, against David. Deliver him only, and I will depart from the city." So the woman said to Joab, "Watch, his head will be thrown to you over the wall."

22 Then the woman [R]in her wisdom went to all the people. And they cut off the head of Sheba the son of Bichri, and threw *it* out to Joab. Then he blew a trumpet, and they withdrew from the city, every man to his tent. So Joab returned to the king at Jerusalem. [Eccl. 9:13–16]

23 And Joab *was* over all the army of Israel; Benaiah the son of Jehoiada *was* over the Cherethites and the Pelethites;

24 Adoram *was* in charge of revenue; Jehoshaphat the son of Ahilud *was* recorder;

25 Sheva *was* scribe; [R]Zadok and Abiathar *were* the priests; 1 Kin. 4:4

26 [R]and Ira the Jairite was [T]a chief minister under David. 2 Sam. 8:18 • Or *David's priest*

CHAPTER 21

Famine

NOW there was a famine in the days of David for three years, year after year; and David [R]inquired of the LORD. And the LORD answered, "*It is* because of Saul and *his* bloodthirsty house, because he killed the Gibeonites." Num. 27:21

2 So the king called the Gibeonites and spoke to them. Now the Gibeonites *were* not of the children of Israel, but [R]of the remnant of the Amorites; the children of Israel had sworn protection to them, but Saul had sought to kill them in his zeal for the children of Israel and Judah. Josh. 9:3, 15–20

3 Therefore David said to the Gibeonites, "What shall I do for you? And with what shall I make atonement, that you may bless [R]the inheritance of the LORD?" 2 Sam. 20:19

4 And the Gibeonites said to him, "We will have no silver or gold from Saul or from his house, nor shall you kill any man in Israel for us." So he said, "Whatever you say, I will do for you."

5 Then they answered the king, "As for the man who consumed us and plotted against us, *that* we should be destroyed from remaining in any of the territories of Israel,

6 "let seven men of his descendants be delivered to us, and we will hang them before the LORD in Gibeah of Saul, *whom* the LORD chose." And the king said, "I will give *them.*"

7 But the king spared Mephibosheth the son of Jonathan, the son of Saul, because of the LORD's oath that *was* between them, between David and Jonathan the son of Saul.

8 So the king took Armoni and Mephibosheth, the two sons of [R]Rizpah the daughter of Aiah, whom she bore to Saul, and the five sons of Michal* the daughter of Saul, whom she brought up for Adriel the son of Barzillai the Meholathite; 2 Sam. 3:7

9 and he delivered them into the hands of the Gibeonites, and they hanged them on the hill [R]before the LORD. So they fell, *all* seven together, and were put to death in the days of harvest, in the first *days,* in the beginning of barley harvest. 2 Sam. 6:17

10 Now [R]Rizpah the daughter of Aiah took sackcloth and spread it for herself on the rock, [R]from the beginning of harvest until the late rains poured on them from heaven. And she did not allow the birds of the air to rest on them by day nor the beasts of the field by night. 2 Sam. 3:7; 21:8 • Deut. 21:23

11 And David was told what Rizpah the

20:14 Lit. *him* **21:8** *Merab,* 1 Sam. 18:19; 25:44; 2 Sam. 3:14; 6:23

daughter of Aiah, the concubine of Saul, had
done.
12 Then David went and took the bones of
Saul, and the bones of Jonathan his son,
from the men of [R]Jabesh Gilead who had
stolen them from the street of Beth Shan,*
where the [R]Philistines had hung them up,
after the Philistines had struck down Saul in
Gilboa. 1 Sam. 31:11–13 • 1 Sam. 31:8
13 So he brought up the bones of Saul and
the bones of Jonathan his son from there; and
they gathered the bones of those who had
been hanged.
14 They buried the bones of Saul and Jona-
than his son in the country of Benjamin in
[R]Zelah, in the tomb of Kish his father. So they
performed all that the king commanded. And
after that [R]God heeded the prayer for the
land. Josh. 18:28 • 2 Sam. 24:25

War with Philistia—1 Chr. 20:4–8

15 When the Philistines were at war again
with Israel, David and his servants with him
went down and fought against the Philistines;
and David grew faint.
16 Then Ishbi-Benob, who *was* one of the
sons of [T]the [R]giant, the weight of whose
bronze spear *was* three hundred *shekels,* who
was bearing a new *sword,* thought he could
kill David. Or *Rapha* • 2 Sam. 21:18–22
17 But Abishai the son of Zeruiah came to
his aid, and struck the Philistine and killed
him. Then the men of David swore to him,
saying, "You shall go out no more with us to
battle, lest you quench the lamp of Israel."
18 [R]Now it happened afterward that there
was again a battle with the Philistines at
Gob. Then [R]Sibbechai the Hushathite killed
Saph,* who *was* one of the sons of the
giant. 1 Chr. 20:4–8 • 1 Chr. 11:29; 27:11
19 Again there was war at Gob with the
Philistines, where Elhanan the son of Jaare-
Oregim* the Bethlehemite killed *the brother
of* Goliath the Gittite, the shaft of whose spear
was like a weaver's beam.
20 Yet again [R]there was war at Gath, where
there was a man of *great* stature, who had six
fingers on each hand and six toes on each
foot, twenty-four in number; and he also was
born to [T]the giant. 1 Chr. 20:6 • Or *Rapha*
21 So when he defied Israel, Jonathan the
son of Shimea,* David's brother, killed him.
22 [R]These four were born to the giant in
Gath, and fell by the hand of David and by the
hand of his servants. 1 Chr. 20:8

CHAPTER 22

Psalms of Thanksgiving

THEN David spoke to the LORD the words
of this song, on the day when the LORD
had delivered him from the hand of all his en-
emies, and from the hand of Saul.
2 And he said:*

[R]"The LORD *is* my rock and my [R]fortress
and my deliverer; Deut. 32:4 • Ps. 91:2
3 The God of my strength, [R]in whom I will
trust; Heb. 2:13
My [R]shield and the [R]horn of my
salvation, Gen. 15:1 • Luke 1:69
My stronghold and my refuge;
My Savior, You save me from violence.
4 I will call upon the LORD, *who is worthy*
to be praised;
So shall I be saved from my enemies.

5 "When the waves of death surrounded
me,
The floods of ungodliness [T]made me
afraid. Or *overwhelmed*
6 The sorrows of Sheol surrounded me;
The snares of death confronted me.
7 In my distress [R]I called upon the LORD,
And cried out to my God; Ps. 116:4; 120:1
He [R]heard my voice from His temple,
And my cry *entered* His ears. Ex. 3:7

8 "Then [R]the earth shook and trembled;
[R]The foundations of heaven* quaked and
were shaken, Judg. 5:4 • Job 26:11
Because He was angry.
9 Smoke went up from His nostrils,
And devouring [R]fire from His mouth;
Coals were kindled by it. Heb. 12:29
10 He [R]bowed the heavens also, and came
down Is. 64:1
With darkness under His feet.
11 He rode upon a cherub, and flew;
And He was seen* [R]upon the wings of
the wind. Ps. 104:3
12 He made [R]darkness canopies around
Him, Job 36:29
Dark waters *and* thick clouds of the
skies.
13 From the brightness before Him
Coals of fire were kindled.

14 "The LORD thundered from heaven,
And the Most High uttered His voice.
15 He sent out arrows and scattered them;
Lightning bolts, and He vanquished
them.
16 Then the channels of the sea [R]were
seen, Nah. 1:4
The foundations of the world were
uncovered,
At the [R]rebuke of the LORD, Ex. 15:8
At the blast of the breath of His nostrils.

21:12 *Beth Shean,* Josh. 17:11 **21:18** *Sippai,* 1 Chr. 20:4 **21:19** *Jair,* 1 Chr. 20:5 **21:21** *Shammah,* 1 Sam. 16:9 and elsewhere **22:2** Cf. Ps. 18 **22:8** So with MT, LXX, Tg.; Syr., Vg. *hills* (cf. Ps. 18:7) **22:11** So with MT, LXX; many Heb. mss., Syr., Vg. *flew* (cf. Ps. 18:10); Tg. *spoke with power*

17 "He sent from above, He took me,
He drew me out of many waters.
18 He delivered me from my strong enemy,
From those who hated me;
For they were too strong for me.
19 They confronted me in the day of my calamity,
But the LORD was my [R]support. Is. 10:20
20 [R]He also brought me out into a broad place; Ps. 31:8; 118:5
He delivered me because He [R]delighted in me. 2 Sam. 15:26

21 "The[R] LORD rewarded me according to my righteousness; 1 Sam. 26:23
According to the [R]cleanness of my hands
He has recompensed me. Ps. 24:4
22 For I have [R]kept the ways of the LORD,
And have not wickedly departed from my God. Ps. 119:3
23 For all His [R]judgments *were* before me;
And *as for* His statutes, I did not depart from them. [Deut. 6:6–9; 7:12]
24 I was also blameless before Him,
And I kept myself from my iniquity.
25 Therefore the LORD has recompensed me according to my righteousness,
According to my cleanness in His eyes.*

26 "With [R]the merciful You will show Yourself merciful; [Matt. 5:7]
With a blameless man You will show Yourself blameless;
27 With the pure You will show Yourself pure;
And [R]with the devious You will show Yourself shrewd. [Lev. 26:23, 24]
28 You will save the humble people;
But Your eyes *are* on [R]the haughty, *that* You may bring *them* down. Job 40:11

29 "For You *are* my lamp, O LORD;
The LORD shall enlighten my darkness.
30 For by You I can run against a troop;
By my God I can leap over a wall.
31 *As for* God, His way *is* perfect;
The word of the LORD *is* proven;
He *is* a shield to all who trust in Him.

32 "For who *is* God, except the LORD?
And who *is* a rock, except our God?
33 God *is* my strength *and* power,*
And He makes my* way perfect.
34 He makes my* feet like the *feet* of deer,
And sets me on my high places.
35 He teaches my hands [T]to make war,
So that my arms can bend a bow of bronze. Lit. *for the war*

36 "You have also given me the shield of Your salvation;
Your gentleness has made me great.
37 You [R]enlarged my path under me;
So my feet did not slip. Prov. 4:12

38 "I have pursued my enemies and destroyed them;
Neither did I turn back again till they were destroyed.
39 And I have destroyed them and wounded them,
So that they could not rise;
They have fallen [R]under my feet. Mal. 4:3
40 For You have [R]armed me with strength for the battle; [Ps. 18:32]
You have subdued under me [R]those who rose against me. [Ps. 44:5]
41 You have also given me the [R]necks of my enemies, Gen. 49:8
So that I destroyed those who hated me.
42 They looked, but *there was* none to save;
Even [R]to the LORD, but He did not answer them. 1 Sam. 28:6
43 Then I beat them as fine [R]as the dust of the earth; Ps. 18:42
I trod them [R]like dirt in the streets,
And I [T]spread them out. Is. 10:6 • *scattered*

44 "You[R] have also delivered me from the [T]strivings of my people; 2 Sam. 3:1
You have kept me as the [R]head of the nations. *contentions* • Deut. 28:13
[R]A people I have not known shall serve me. [Is. 55:5]
45 The foreigners submit to me;
As soon as they hear, they obey me.
46 The foreigners fade away,
And come frightened* [R]from their hideouts. [Mic. 7:17]

47 "The LORD lives!
Blessed *be* my Rock!
Let God be exalted,
The [R]Rock of my salvation! Ps. 89:26
48 *It is* God who avenges me,
And subdues the peoples under me;
49 He delivers me from my enemies.
You also lift me up above those who rise against me;
You have delivered me from the [R]violent man. Ps. 140:1, 4, 11
50 Therefore I will give thanks to You,
O LORD, among the Gentiles,
And sing praises to Your name.

51 "*He* is the tower of salvation to His king,
And shows mercy to His [R]anointed,

22:25 LXX, Syr., Vg. *the cleanness of my hands in His sight* (cf. Ps. 18:24); Tg. *my cleanness before His word* **22:33** DSS, LXX, Syr., Vg. *It is God who arms me with strength* (cf. Ps. 18:32); Tg. *It is God who sustains me with strength* • So with Qr., LXX, Syr., Tg., Vg. (cf. Ps. 18:32); Kt. *His* **22:34** So with Qr., LXX, Syr., Tg., Vg. (cf. Ps. 18:33); Kt. *His* **22:46** So with LXX, Tg., Vg. (cf. Ps. 18:45); MT *gird themselves*

To David and [R]his descendants
forevermore." Ps. 89:20 • 2 Sam. 7:12–16

CHAPTER 23

NOW these *are* the last words of David.

Thus says David the son of Jesse;
Thus says the man raised up on high,
The anointed of the God of Jacob,
And the sweet psalmist of Israel:

2 "The Spirit of the LORD spoke by me,
And His word *was* on my tongue.
3 The God of Israel said,
The Rock of Israel spoke to me:
'He who rules over men *must be* just,
Ruling [R]in the fear of God. Ex. 18:21
4 And [R]*he shall be* like the light of the
morning *when* the sun rises,
A morning without clouds, Ps. 89:36
Like the tender grass *springing* out of
the earth,
By clear shining after rain.'

5 "Although my house *is* not so with God,
[R]Yet He has made with me an everlasting
covenant, Ps. 89:29
Ordered in all *things* and secure.
For *this is* all my salvation and all *my*
desire;
Will He not make *it* increase?
6 But *the sons* of rebellion *shall* all *be* as
thorns thrust away,
Because they cannot be taken with hands.
7 But the man *who* touches them
Must be [T]armed with iron and the shaft
of a spear, Lit. *filled*
And they shall be utterly burned with
fire in *their* place."

Deeds of David's Mighty Men
1 Chr. 11:10–41

8 These *are* the names of the mighty men
whom David had: Josheb-Basshebeth* the
Tachmonite, chief among the captains.* He
was called Adino the Eznite, because he had
killed eight hundred men at one time.
9 And after him *was* Eleazar the son of
Dodo,* the Ahohite, *one* of the three mighty
men with David when they defied the Phi-
listines *who* were gathered there for battle,
and the men of Israel had retreated.
10 He arose and attacked the Philistines
until his hand was [R]weary, and his hand stuck
to the sword. The LORD brought about a great
victory that day; and the people returned after
him only to plunder. Judg. 8:4
11 And after him *was* [R]Shammah the son of
Agee the Hararite. The Philistines had gath-
ered together into a troop where there was a
piece of ground full of lentils. So the people
fled from the Philistines. 1 Chr. 11:27
12 But he stationed himself in the middle of
the field, defended it, and killed the Philis-
tines. So the LORD brought about a great vic-
tory.
13 Then [R]three of the thirty chief men went
down at harvest time and came to David at
[R]the cave of Adullam. And the troop of
Philistines encamped in [R]the Valley of
Rephaim. 1 Chr. 11:15 • 1 Sam. 22:1 • 2 Sam. 5:18
14 David *was* then in [R]the stronghold, and
the garrison of the Philistines *was* then *in*
Bethlehem. 1 Sam. 22:4, 5
15 And David said with longing, "Oh, that
someone would give me a drink of the water
from the well of Bethlehem, which *is* by the
gate!"
16 So the three mighty men broke through
the camp of the Philistines, drew water from
the well of Bethlehem that *was* by the gate,
and took it and brought *it* to David. Neverthe-
less he would not drink it, but poured it out to
the LORD.
17 And he said, "Far be it from me, O LORD,
that I should do this! Is *this not* the blood of
the men who went in *jeopardy of* their lives?"
Therefore he would not drink it. These things
were done by the three mighty men.
18 Now [R]Abishai the brother of Joab, the son
of Zeruiah, was chief of *another* three.* He
lifted his spear against three hundred *men,*
killed *them,* and won a name among *these*
three. 1 Chr. 11:20
19 Was he not the most honored of three?
Therefore he became their captain. However,
he did not attain to the *first* three.
20 Benaiah *was* the son of Jehoiada, the son
of a valiant man from [R]Kabzeel, who had
done many deeds. [R]He had killed two lion-like
heroes of Moab. He also had gone down and
killed a lion in the midst of a pit on a snowy
day. Josh. 15:21 • Ex. 15:15
21 And he killed an Egyptian, a spectacular
man. The Egyptian *had* a spear in his hand; so
he went down to him with a staff, wrested the
spear out of the Egyptian's hand, and killed
him with his own spear.
22 These *things* Benaiah the son of Jehoiada
did, and won a name among three mighty
men.
23 He was more honored than the thirty, but
he did not attain to the *first* three. And David
appointed him over his guard.
24 [R]Asahel the brother of Joab *was* one of
the thirty; Elhanan the son of Dodo of Bethle-
hem, 2 Sam. 2:18
25 [R]Shammah the Harodite, Elika the Ha-
rodite, 1 Chr. 11:27

23:8 Lit. *One Who Sits in the Seat* (1 Chr. 11:11) • So with MT, Tg.; LXX, Vg. *the three* **23:9** *Dodai,* 1 Chr. 27:4 **23:18** So with MT, LXX, Vg.; some Heb. mss., Syr. *thirty;* Tg. *the mighty men*

26 Helez the Paltite, Ira the son of Ikkesh the
Tekoite,
27 Abiezer the Anathothite, Mebunnai the
Hushathite,
28 Zalmon the Ahohite, Maharai the Ne-
tophathite,
29 Heleb the son of Baanah (the Netoph-
athite), Ittai the son of Ribai from Gibeah of
the children of Benjamin,
30 Benaiah a Pirathonite, Hiddai from the
brooks of [R]Gaash, Judg. 2:9
31 Abi-Albon the Arbathite, Azmaveth the
Barhumite,
32 Eliahba the Shaalbonite (of the sons of
Jashen), Jonathan,
33 [R]Shammah the Hararite, Ahiam the son
of Sharar the Hararite, 2 Sam. 23:11
34 Eliphelet the son of Ahasbai, the son of
the Maachathite, Eliam the son of [R]Ahithophel
the Gilonite, 2 Sam. 15:12
35 Hezrai* the Carmelite, Paarai the Ar-
bite,
36 Igal the son of Nathan of [R]Zobah, Bani
the Gadite, 2 Sam. 8:3
37 Zelek the Ammonite, Naharai the Be-
erothite (armorbearer of Joab the son of
Zeruiah),
38 Ira the Ithrite, Gareb the Ithrite,
39 *and* [R]Uriah the Hittite: thirty-seven in
all. 2 Sam. 11:3, 6

CHAPTER 24

The Census and the Plague—1 Chr. 21:1–17

AGAIN [R]the anger of the LORD was
aroused against Israel, and He moved
David against them to say, [R]"Go, number Is-
rael and Judah." 2 Sam. 21:1, 2 • 1 Chr. 27:23, 24
2 So the king said to Joab the commander
of the army who *was* with him, "Now go
throughout all the tribes of Israel, from Dan to
Beersheba, and count the people, that I may
know the number of the people."
3 And Joab said to the king, "Now may the
LORD your God add to the people a hundred
times more than there are, and may the eyes
of my lord the king see *it*. But why does my
lord the king desire this thing?"
4 Nevertheless the king's word [T]prevailed
against Joab and against the captains of the
army. Therefore Joab and the captains of the
army went out from the presence of the king
to count the people of Israel. *overruled*
5 And they crossed over the Jordan and
camped in [R]Aroer, on the right side of the
town which *is* in the midst of the ravine of
Gad, and toward Jazer. Deut. 2:36
6 Then they came to Gilead and to the land
of Tahtim Hodshi; they came to [R]Dan Jaan
and around to Sidon; Judg. 18:29
7 and they came to the stronghold of [R]Tyre
and to all the cities of the Hivites and the
Canaanites. Then they went out to South Ju-
dah *as far as* Beersheba. Josh. 19:29
8 So when they had gone through all the
land, they came to Jerusalem at the end of
nine months and twenty days.
9 Then Joab gave the sum of the number of
the people to the king. And there were in Is-
rael eight hundred thousand valiant men who
drew the sword, and the men of Judah were
five hundred thousand men.
10 And [R]David's heart condemned him after
he had numbered the people. So [R]David said
to the LORD, "I have sinned greatly in what I
have done; but now, I pray, O LORD, take away
the iniquity of Your servant, for I have done
very foolishly." 1 Sam. 24:5 • 2 Sam. 23:1
11 Now when David arose in the morning,
the word of the LORD came to the prophet
[R]Gad, David's seer, saying, 1 Sam. 22:5
12 "Go and tell David, 'Thus says the LORD:
"I offer you three *things;* choose one of them
for yourself, that I may do *it* to you." ' "
13 So Gad came to David and told him; and
he said to him, "Shall [R]seven* years of famine
come to you in your land? Or shall you flee
three months before your enemies, while they
pursue you? Or shall there be three days'
plague in your land? Now consider and see
what answer I should take back to Him who
sent me." Ezek. 14:21
14 And David said to Gad, "I am in great dis-
tress. Please let us fall into the hand of the
LORD, for His mercies *are* great; but do not let
me fall into the hand of man."
15 So [R]the LORD sent a plague upon Israel
from the morning till the appointed time.
From Dan to Beersheba seventy thousand
men of the people died. 1 Chr. 21:14
16 [R]And when the angel* stretched out His
hand over Jerusalem to destroy it, the LORD
relented from the destruction, and said to the
angel who was destroying the people, "It is
enough; now restrain your hand." And the an-
gel of the LORD was by the threshing floor of
Araunah* the Jebusite. Ex. 12:23
17 Then David spoke to the LORD when he
saw the angel who was striking the people,
and said, "Surely I have sinned, and I have
done wickedly; but these sheep, what have
they done? Let Your hand, I pray, be against
me and against my father's house."
18 And Gad came that day to David and
said to him, [R]"Go up, erect an altar to the
LORD on the threshing floor of Araunah the
Jebusite." 1 Chr. 21:18
19 So David, according to the word of Gad,
went up as the LORD commanded.
20 Now Araunah looked, and saw the king
and his servants coming toward him. So Arau-

23:35 *Hezro,* 1 Chr. 11:37 **24:13** So with MT, Syr., Tg., Vg.; LXX *three* (cf. 1 Chr. 21:12) **24:16** Or *Angel* • *Ornan,* 1 Chr. 21:15

nah went out and bowed before the king with
his face to the ground.
21 Then Araunah said, "Why has my lord the
king come to his servant?" And David said,
"To buy the threshing floor from you, to build
an altar to the LORD, that the plague may be
withdrawn from the people."
22 Now Araunah said to David, "Let my lord
the king take and offer up whatever *seems*
good to him. Look, *here are* oxen for burnt
sacrifice, and threshing implements and the
yokes of the oxen for wood.
23 "All these, O king, Araunah has given to
the king." And Araunah said to the king, "May
the LORD your God accept you."
24 Then the king said to Araunah, "No, but I
will surely buy *it* from you for a price; nor will
I offer burnt offerings to the LORD my God
with that which costs me nothing." So David
bought the threshing floor and the oxen for
fifty shekels of silver.
25 And David built there an altar to the
LORD, and offered burnt offerings and peace
offerings. [R]So the LORD heeded the prayers for
the land, and [R]the plague was withdrawn from
Israel.

2 Sam. 21:14 • 2 Sam. 24:21

Liquid Measures

Unit	*Measure*	*Equivalents*	*Translations*
Kor	60 gallons	10 baths	kor
Metretes	10.2 gallons		gallon
Bath	6 gallons	6 hins	measure, bath
Hin	1 gallon	2 kabs	hin
Kab	2 quarts	4 logs	kab
Log	1 pint	¼ kab	log

THE FIRST BOOK OF THE

KINGS

THE BOOK OF 1 KINGS

The first half of 1 Kings traces the life of Solomon. Under his leadership Israel rises to the peak of her size and glory. Solomon's great accomplishments, including the unsurpassed splendor of the temple he constructs in Jerusalem, bring him worldwide fame and respect. However, Solomon's zeal for God diminishes in his later years, as pagan wives turn his heart away from worship in the temple of God. As a result, the king with the divided heart leaves behind a divided kingdom. For the next century, the Book of 1 Kings traces the twin histories of two sets of kings and two nations of disobedient people who are growing indifferent to God's prophets and precepts.

Like the two books of Samuel, the two books of Kings were originally one in the Hebrew Bible. The original title was *Melechim,* "Kings," taken from the first word in 1:1, *Vehamelech,* "Now King." The Septuagint artificially divided the book of Kings in the middle of the story of Ahaziah into two books. It called the books of Samuel "First and Second Kingdoms" and the books of Kings "Third and Fourth Kingdoms." The Septuagint may have divided Samuel, Kings, and Chronicles into two books each because the Greek required a greater amount of scroll space than did the Hebrew. The Latin title for these books is *Liber Regum Tertius et Quartus,* "Third and Fourth Book of Kings."

THE AUTHOR OF 1 KINGS

The author of 1 and 2 Kings is unknown, but evidence supports the talmudic tradition that Kings was written by the prophet Jeremiah. The author was clearly a prophet/historian as seen in the prophetic exposé of apostasy. Both 1 and 2 Kings emphasize God's righteous judgment on idolatry and immorality. The style of these books is also similar to that found in Jeremiah. The phrase "to this day" in 1 Kings 8:8 and 12:19 indicates a time of authorship prior to the Babylonian captivity (586 B.C.). However, the last two chapters of 2 Kings were written after the captivity, probably by a Jewish captive in Babylon.

Evidently, the majority of 1 and 2 Kings was written before 586 B.C. by a compiler who had access to several historical documents. Some of these are mentioned: "the book of the acts of Solomon" (11:41), "the book of the chronicles of the kings of Israel" (14:19), and "the book of the chronicles of the kings of Judah" (14:29; 15:7). These books may have been a part of the official court records (see 2 Kin. 18:18). In addition, Isaiah 36—39 was probably used as a source (cf. 2 Kin. 18—20).

THE TIME OF 1 KINGS

The Book of Kings was written to the remaining kingdom of Judah before and after its Babylonian exile. The majority was compiled by a contemporary of Jeremiah, if not by Jeremiah himself (c. 646–570 B.C.). It is a record of disobedience, idolatry, and ungodliness, which serves as an explanation for the Assyrian captivity of Israel (722 B.C.) and the Babylonian captivity of Judah (586 B.C.). First Kings covers the 120 years from the beginning of Solomon's reign in 971 B.C. through Ahaziah's reign ending in 851 B.C. The key date is 931 B.C., the year the kingdom was divided into the northern nation of Israel and the southern nation of Judah.

THE CHRIST OF 1 KINGS

Solomon typifies Christ in a number of ways. His fabled wisdom points ahead to "Christ Jesus, who became for us wisdom from God" (1 Cor. 1:30). Solomon's fame, glory, wealth, and honor foreshadow Christ in His kingdom. Solomon's rulership brings knowledge, peace, and worship. However, despite Solomon's splendor, the Son of Man later says of His coming, "indeed a greater than Solomon *is* here" (Matt. 12:42).

The prophet Elijah is more typical of John the Baptist than of Christ, but his prophetic ministry and miraculous works illustrate aspects of the life of Christ.

KEYS TO 1 KINGS

Key Word: Division of the Kingdom—The theme of 1 Kings centers on the fact that the welfare of Israel and Judah depends upon the faithfulness of the people and their king to the covenant. Historically, it was written to give an account of the reigns of the kings from Solomon to Jehoshaphat (Judah) and Ahaziah (Israel). The two books of Kings as a whole trace the monarchy from the point of its greatest prosperity under Solomon to its demise and destruction in the Assyrian and Babylonian captivities.

Theologically, 1 Kings provides a prophetically oriented evaluation of the spiritual and moral causes that led to the political and economic demise of the two kingdoms. The material is too selective to be considered a biography of the kings. For example, Omri was one of Israel's most important rulers from a political point of view, but because of his moral corruption, his achievements are dismissed in a mere eight verses. The lives of these kings are used to teach that observance of God's law produces blessing, but apostasy is rewarded by judgment.

Key Verses: 1 Kings 9:4, 5; 11:11—"Now if you walk before Me as your father David walked, in integrity of heart and in uprightness, to do according to all that I have commanded you, *and* if you keep My statutes and My judgments, then I will establish the throne of your kingdom over Israel forever, as I promised David your father, saying, 'You shall not fail to have a man on the throne of Israel' " (9:4, 5).

"Therefore the LORD said to Solomon, 'Because you have done this, and have not kept My covenant and My statutes, which I have commanded you, I will surely tear the kingdom away from you and give it to your servant' " (11:11).

Key Chapter: 1 Kings 12—The critical turning point in 1 Kings occurs in chapter 12 when the united kingdom becomes the divided kingdom. Solomon dies, and his son Rehoboam becomes king and unwisely leads the nation into a civil war, which tragically rips the nation into two separate, and at times conflicting, nations. Instead of unity, 1 Kings records the history of the two kings, two capitals, and two religions.

SURVEY OF 1 KINGS

The first half of 1 Kings concerns the life of one of the most amazing men who ever lived. More than any man before or since, he knew how to amass and creatively use great wealth. With the sole exception of Jesus Christ, Solomon is the wisest man in human history. He brings Israel to the peak of its size and glory; and yet, the kingdom is disrupted soon after his death, torn in two by civil strife. This book divides clearly into two sections: the united kingdom (1—11) and the divided kingdom (12—22).

United Kingdom (1—11): These chapters give an account of Solomon's attainment of the throne, wisdom, architectural achievements, fame, wealth, and tragic unfaithfulness. Solomon's half-brother Adonijah attempts to take the throne as David's death is nearing, but Nathan the prophet alerts David who quickly directs the coronation of Solomon as coregent (ch. 1). Solomon still has to consolidate his power and deal with those who oppose his rule. Only when this is done is the kingdom "established in the hand of Solomon" (2:46). Solomon's ungodly marriages (cf. 3:1) eventually turn his heart from the Lord, but he begins well with a genuine love for Yahweh and a desire for wisdom. This wisdom leads to the expansion of Israel to the zenith of her power. Solomon's empire stretches from the border of Egypt to the border of Babylonia, and peace prevails.

From a theocratic perspective, Solomon's greatest achievement is the building of the temple. The ark is placed in this exquisite building, which is filled with the glory of God. Solomon offers a magnificent prayer of dedication and binds the people with an oath to remain faithful to Yahweh.

Because the Lord is with him Solomon continues to grow in fame, power, and wealth. However, his wealth later becomes a source of trouble when he begins to purchase forbidden items. He acquires many foreign wives who lead him into idolatry. It is an irony of history that this wisest of men acts as a fool in his old age. God pronounces judgment and foretells that Solomon's son will rule only a fraction of the kingdom (Judah).

Divided Kingdom (12—22): Upon Solomon's death, God's words come to pass. Solomon's son Rehoboam chooses the foolish course of promising more severe taxation. Jeroboam, an officer in Solomon's army, leads the ten northern tribes in revolt. They make him their king,

FOCUS	UNITED KINGDOM			DIVIDED KINGDOM		
REFERENCE	1:1——3:1	——9:1	——12:1	——15:1	——16:29	——22:53
DIVISION	ESTABLISHMENT OF SOLOMON	RISE OF SOLOMON	DECLINE OF SOLOMON	DIVISION OF THE KINGDOM	REIGNS OF VARIOUS KINGS	REIGN OF AHAB WITH ELIJAH
TOPIC	SOLOMON			MANY KINGS		
	KINGDOM IN TRANQUILLITY			KINGDOMS IN TURMOIL		
LOCATION	JERUSALEM: CAPITAL OF UNITED KINGDOM			SAMARIA: CAPITAL OF ISRAEL JERUSALEM: CAPITAL OF JUDAH		
TIME	c. 40 YEARS			c. 90 YEARS		

leaving only Judah and Benjamin in the south under Rehoboam. This is the beginning of a chaotic period with two nations and two sets of kings. Continual enmity and strife exist between the northern and southern kingdoms. The north is plagued by apostasy (Jeroboam sets up a false system of worship) and the south by idolatry. Of all the northern and southern kings listed in this book, only Asa (15:9–24) and Jehoshaphat (22:41–50) do *"what was* right in the eyes of the LORD" (15:11; 22:43). All the others are idolaters, usurpers, and murderers.

Ahab brings a measure of cooperation between the northern and southern kingdoms, but he reaches new depths of wickedness as a king. He is the man who introduces Jezebel's Baal worship to Israel. The prophet Elijah ministers during this low period in Israel's history, providing a ray of light and witness of the word and power of God. But Ahab's encounter with Elijah never brings him to turn from his false gods to God. Ahab's treachery in the matter of Naboth's vineyard causes a prophetic rebuke from Elijah (21). Ahab repents (21:27–29) but later dies in battle because of his refusal to heed the words of Micaiah, another prophet of God.

OUTLINE OF 1 KINGS

Part One: The United Kingdom (1:1—11:43)

Part Two: The Divided Kingdom (12:1—22:53)

1. Miracle of the Drought 17:1–16
2. Miracle of the Resurrection of the Gentile Son 17:17–24
3. Miracle of Fire on Mount Carmel 18:1–40
4. Miracle of the Rain 18:41–46
5. Failings of Elijah...............................19:1–18
6. Call of Elisha.......................................19:19–21

C. Wars with Syria 20:1–43
1. First Victory over Syria 20:1–21
2. Second Victory over Syria..............20:22–43

D. Murder of Naboth 21:1–16
E. Death of Ahab ....21:17—22:40
1. Prediction of Ahab's Death............21:17–29
2. Defeat by Syria 22:1–36
3. Death of Ahab 22:37–40

V. The Reign of Jehoshaphat in Judah 22:41–50

VI. The Reign of Ahaziah in Israel..........22:51–53

CHAPTER 1

Decline of David

NOW King David was [R]old, advanced in
years; and they put covers on him, but he
could not get warm. 1 Chr. 23:1
2 Therefore his servants said to him, "Let a
young woman, a virgin, be sought for our lord
the king, and let her [T]stand before the king,
and let her care for him; and let her lie in
your bosom, that our lord the king may be
warm." Or *serve*
3 So they sought for a lovely young woman
throughout all the territory of Israel, and
found Abishag the [R]Shunammite, and brought
her to the king. Josh. 19:18
4 The young woman *was* very lovely; and
she cared for the king, and served him; but
the king did not know her.

Plot of Adonijah to Be King

5 Then Adonijah the son of Haggith exalted
himself, saying, "I will be king"; and he pre-
pared for himself chariots and horsemen, and
fifty men to run before him.
6 (And his father had not rebuked him at
any time by saying, "Why have you done so?"
He *was* also very good-looking. *His mother*
had borne him after Absalom.)
7 Then he conferred with Joab the son of
Zeruiah and with Abiathar the priest, and
they followed and helped Adonijah.
8 But Zadok the priest, Benaiah the son of
Jehoiada, Nathan the prophet, Shimei, Rei,
and [R]the mighty men who *belonged* to David
were not with Adonijah. 2 Sam. 23:8
9 And Adonijah sacrificed sheep and oxen
and fattened cattle by the stone of Zoheleth,
which *is* by [R]En Rogel; he also invited all his
brothers, the king's sons, and all the men of
Judah, the king's servants. Josh. 15:7; 18:16

Anointing of Solomon

10 But he did not invite Nathan the prophet,
Benaiah, the mighty men, or [R]Solomon his
brother. 2 Sam. 12:24
11 So Nathan spoke to Bathsheba the
mother of Solomon, saying, "Have you not
heard that Adonijah the son of [R]Haggith has
become king, and David our lord does not
know *it?* 2 Sam. 3:4
12 "Come, please, let me now give you ad-
vice, that you may save your own life and the
life of your son Solomon.
13 "Go immediately to King David and say
to him, 'Did you not, my lord, O king, swear to
your maidservant, saying, [R]"Assuredly your
son Solomon shall reign after me, and he
shall sit on my throne"? Why then has Adoni-
jah become king?' 1 Chr. 22:9–13
14 "Then, while you are still talking there
with the king, I also will come in after you and
confirm your words."
15 So Bathsheba went into the chamber to
the king. (Now the king was very old, and
Abishag the Shunammite was serving the
king.)
16 And Bathsheba bowed and did homage to
the king. Then the king said, "What is your
wish?"
17 Then she said to him, "My lord, [R]you
swore by the LORD your God to your maid-
servant, *saying,* 'Assuredly Solomon your son
shall reign after me, and he shall sit on my
throne.' 1 Kin. 1:13, 30
18 "So now, look! Adonijah has become
king; and now, my lord the king, you do not
know about *it.*
19 [R]"He has sacrificed oxen and fattened
cattle and sheep in abundance, and has in-
vited all the sons of the king, Abiathar the
priest, and Joab the commander of the army;
but Solomon your servant he has not in-
vited. 1 Kin. 1:7–9, 25
20 "And as for you, my lord, O king, the eyes
of all Israel *are* on you, that you should tell
them who will sit on the throne of my lord the
king after him.
21 "Otherwise it will happen, when my lord
the king [R]rests with his fathers, that I and
my son Solomon will be counted as offend-
ers." Deut. 31:16
22 And just then, while she was still talking
with the king, Nathan the prophet also came
in.
23 So they told the king, saying, "Here is Na-
than the prophet." And when he came in

before the king, he bowed down before the
king with his face to the ground.
24 And Nathan said, "My lord, O king, have
you said, 'Adonijah shall reign after me, and
he shall sit on my throne'?
25 "For he has gone down today, and has
sacrificed oxen and fattened cattle and sheep
in abundance, and has invited all the king's
sons, and the commanders of the army, and
Abiathar the priest; and look! They are eating
and drinking before him; and they say, '*Long*
live King Adonijah!'
26 "But he has not invited me—me your ser-
vant—nor Zadok the priest, nor Benaiah the
son of Jehoiada, nor your servant Solomon.
27 "Has this thing been done by my lord the
king, and you have not told your servant who
should sit on the throne of my lord the king
after him?"
28 Then King David answered and said,
"Call Bathsheba to me." So she came into the
king's presence and stood before the king.
29 And the king took an oath and said, [R]"*As*
the LORD lives, who has redeemed my life
from every distress, 2 Sam. 4:9; 12:5
30 [R]"just as I swore to you by the LORD God
of Israel, saying, 'Assuredly Solomon your son
shall be king after me, and he shall sit on my
throne in my place,' so I certainly will do this
day." 1 Kin. 1:13, 17
31 Then Bathsheba bowed with *her* face to
the earth, and paid homage to the king, and
said, "Let my lord King David live forever!"
32 And King David said, "Call to me Zadok
the priest, Nathan the prophet, and Benaiah
the son of Jehoiada." So they came before the
king.
33 The king also said to them, [R]"Take with
you the servants of your lord, and have Sol-
omon my son ride on my own mule, and take
him down to Gihon. 2 Sam. 20:6
34 "There let Zadok the priest and Nathan
the prophet [R]anoint him king over Israel; and
[R]blow the horn, and say, '*Long* live King Sol-
omon!' 1 Sam. 10:1; 16:3, 12 • 2 Sam. 15:10
35 "Then you shall come up after him, and
he shall come and sit on my throne, and he
shall be king in my place. For I have ap-
pointed him to be ruler over Israel and Ju-
dah."
36 Benaiah the son of Jehoiada answered
the king and said, "Amen! May the LORD God
of my lord the king say so *too*.
37 [R]"As the LORD has been with my lord the
king, even so may He be with Solomon, and
[R]make his throne greater than the throne of
my lord King David." 1 Sam. 20:13 • 1 Kin. 1:47
38 So Zadok the priest, Nathan the prophet,
[R]Benaiah the son of Jehoiada, the Cherethites,
and the Pelethites went down and had Sol-
omon ride on King David's mule, and took
him to Gihon. 2 Sam. 8:18; 23:20–23
39 Then Zadok the priest took a horn of [R]oil
from the tabernacle and anointed Solomon.
And they blew the horn, and all the people
said, "*Long* live King Solomon!" Ps. 89:20
40 And all the people went up after him; and
the people played the flutes and rejoiced with
great joy, so that the earth *seemed to* split
with their sound.

Submission of Adonijah

41 Now Adonijah and all the guests who
were with him heard *it* as they finished eat-
ing. And when Joab heard the sound of the
horn, he said, "Why *is* the city in such a noisy
uproar?"
42 While he was still speaking, there came
Jonathan, the son of Abiathar the priest. And
Adonijah said to him, "Come in, for you *are* a
prominent man, and bring good news."
43 Then Jonathan answered and said to
Adonijah, "No! Our lord King David has made
Solomon king.
44 "The king has sent with him Zadok the
priest, Nathan the prophet, Benaiah the son of
Jehoiada, the Cherethites, and the Pelethites;
and they have made him ride on the king's
mule.
45 "So Zadok the priest and Nathan the
prophet have anointed him king at Gihon; and
they have gone up from there rejoicing, so
that the city is in an uproar. This *is* the noise
that you have heard.
46 "Also Solomon [R]sits on the throne of the
kingdom. 1 Chr. 29:23
47 "And moreover the king's servants have
gone to bless our lord King David, saying,
'May God make the name of Solomon better
than your name, and may He make his throne
greater than your throne.' [R]Then the king
bowed himself on the bed. Gen. 47:31
48 "Also the king said thus, 'Blessed *be* the
LORD God of Israel, who has [R]given *one* to sit
on my throne this day, while my eyes see
[R]*it!*' " 1 Kin. 3:6 • 2 Sam. 7:12
49 So all the guests who were with Adonijah
were afraid, and arose, and each one went his
way.
50 Now Adonijah was afraid of Solomon; so
he arose, and went and [R]took hold of the
horns of the altar. 1 Kin. 2:28
51 And it was told Solomon, saying, "Indeed
Adonijah is afraid of King Solomon; for look,
he has taken hold of the horns of the altar,
saying, 'Let King Solomon swear to me today
that he will not put his servant to death with
the sword.' "
52 Then Solomon said, "If he proves himself
a worthy man, [R]not one hair of him shall fall
to the earth; but if wickedness is found in him,
he shall die." 1 Sam. 14:45
53 So King Solomon sent them to bring him
down from the altar. And he came and fell
down before King Solomon; and Solomon
said to him, "Go to your house."

CHAPTER 2

David's Charge to Solomon

NOW [R]the days of David drew near that he should die, and he [T]charged Solomon his son, saying: Gen. 47:29 • *commanded*

2 "I go the way of all the earth; be strong, therefore, and prove yourself a man.

3 "And keep the charge of the LORD your God: to walk in His ways, to keep His statutes, His commandments, His judgments, and His testimonies, as it is written in the Law of Moses, that you may prosper in all that you do and wherever you turn;

4 "that the LORD may fulfill His word which He spoke concerning me, saying, 'If your sons take heed to their way, to walk before Me in truth with all their heart and with all their soul,' He said, 'you shall not lack a man on the throne of Israel.'

5 "Moreover you know also what Joab the son of Zeruiah [R]did to me, *and* what he did to the two commanders of the armies of Israel, to [R]Abner the son of Ner and Amasa the son of Jether, whom he killed. And he shed the blood of war in peacetime, and put the blood of war on his belt that *was* around his waist, and on his sandals that *were* on his feet. 2 Sam. 3:39; 18:5, 12, 14 • 2 Sam. 3:27

6 "Therefore do [R]according to your wisdom, and do not let his gray hair go down to the grave in peace. 1 Kin. 2:9

7 "But show kindness to the sons of [R]Barzillai the Gileadite, and let them be among those who eat at your table, for so [R]they came to me when I fled from Absalom your brother. 2 Sam. 19:31–39 • 2 Sam. 17:17–29

8 "And see, *you have* with you [R]Shimei the son of Gera, a Benjamite from Bahurim, who cursed me with a malicious curse in the day when I went to Mahanaim. But he came down to meet me at the Jordan, and I swore to him by the LORD, saying, 'I will not put you to death with the sword.' 2 Sam. 16:5–13

9 "Now therefore, do not hold him guiltless, for you *are* a wise man and know what you ought to do to him; but bring his gray hair down to the grave with blood."

David Dies—1 Chr. 3:4; 29:26–28

10 So [R]David rested with his fathers, and was buried in the City of David. Acts 2:29

11 The period that David [R]reigned over Israel *was* forty years; seven years he reigned in Hebron, and in Jerusalem he reigned thirty-three years. 2 Sam. 5:4, 5

Solomon Is Established as King *1 Chr. 29:23*

12 [R]Then Solomon sat on the throne of his father David; and his kingdom was [R]firmly established. 1 Chr. 29:23 • 2 Chr. 1:1

Adonijah Is Executed

13 Now Adonijah the son of Haggith came to Bathsheba the mother of Solomon. So she said, [R]"Do you come peaceably?" And he said, "Peaceably." 1 Sam. 16:4, 5

14 Moreover he said, "I have something *to say* to you." And she said, "Say it."

15 Then he said, "You know that the kingdom was [R]mine, and all Israel had set their expectations on me, that I should reign. However, the kingdom has been turned over, and has become my brother's; for [R]it was his from the LORD. 1 Kin. 1:11, 18 • [Dan. 2:21]

16 "Now I ask one petition of you; do not deny me." And she said to him, "Say it."

17 Then he said, "Please speak to King Solomon, for he will not refuse you, that he may give me Abishag the Shunammite as wife."

18 So Bathsheba said, "Very well, I will speak for you to the king."

19 Bathsheba therefore went to King Solomon, to speak to him for Adonijah. And the king rose up to meet her and [R]bowed down to her, and sat down on his throne and had a throne set for the king's mother; [R]so she sat at his right hand. [Ex. 20:12] • Ps. 45:9

20 Then she said, "I desire one small petition of you; do not [T]refuse me." And the king said to her, "Ask it, my mother, for I will not refuse you." Lit. *turn away the face*

21 So she said, "Let Abishag the Shunammite be given to Adonijah your brother as wife."

22 And King Solomon answered and said to his mother, "Now why do you ask Abishag the Shunammite for Adonijah? Ask for him the kingdom also—for he *is* my older brother—for him, and for Abiathar the priest, and for Joab the son of Zeruiah."

23 Then King Solomon swore by the LORD, saying, [R]"May God do so to me, and more also, if Adonijah has not spoken this word against his own life! Ruth 1:17

24 "Now therefore, *as* the LORD lives, who has confirmed me and set me on the throne of David my father, and who has established a house* for me, as He [R]promised, Adonijah shall be put to death today!" 2 Sam. 7:11, 13

25 So King Solomon sent by the hand of [R]Benaiah the son of Jehoiada; and he struck him down, and he died. 2 Sam. 8:18

Abiathar Is Removed

26 And to Abiathar the priest the king said, "Go to [R]Anathoth, to your own fields, for you *are* deserving of death; but I will not put you to death at this time, because you carried the ark of the Lord GOD before my father David, and because you were afflicted every time my father was afflicted." Josh. 21:18

2:24 Royal dynasty

27 So Solomon removed Abiathar from being priest to the LORD, that he might fulfill the word of the LORD which He spoke concerning the house of Eli at Shiloh.

Joab Is Executed

28 Then news came to Joab, for Joab [R]had defected to Adonijah, though he had not defected to Absalom. So Joab fled to the tabernacle of the LORD, and [R]took hold of the horns of the altar. 1 Kin. 1:7 • 1 Kin. 1:50

29 And King Solomon was told, "Joab has fled to the tabernacle of the LORD; there *he is,* by the altar." Then Solomon sent Benaiah the son of Jehoiada, saying, "Go, [R]strike him down." 1 Kin. 2:5, 6

30 So Benaiah went to the tabernacle of the LORD, and said to him, "Thus says the king, [R]'Come out!' " And he said, "No, but I will die here." And Benaiah brought back word to the king, saying, "Thus said Joab, and thus he answered me." [Ex. 21:14]

31 Then the king said to him, [R]"Do as he has said, and strike him down and bury him, that you may take away from me and from the house of my father the innocent blood which Joab shed. [Ex. 21:14]

32 "So the LORD [R]will return his blood on his head, because he struck down two men more righteous and better than he, and killed them with the sword—Abner the son of Ner, the commander of the army of Israel, and Amasa the son of Jether, the commander of the army of Judah—though my father David did not know *it.* Judg. 9:24, 57

33 "Their blood shall therefore return upon the head of Joab and [R]upon the head of his descendants forever. [R]But upon David and his descendants, upon his house and his throne, there shall be peace forever from the LORD." 2 Sam. 3:29 • [Prov. 25:5]

34 So Benaiah the son of Jehoiada went up and struck and killed him; and he was buried in his own house in the wilderness.

35 The king put Benaiah the son of Jehoiada in his place over the army, and the king put [R]Zadok the priest in the place of [R]Abiathar. 1 Sam. 2:35 • 1 Kin. 2:27

Shimei Is Executed

36 Then the king sent and called for [R]Shimei, and said to him, "Build yourself a house in Jerusalem and dwell there, and do not go out from there anywhere. 1 Kin. 2:8

37 "For it shall be, on the day you go out and cross [R]the Brook Kidron, know for certain you shall surely die; your blood shall be on your own head." 2 Sam. 15:23

38 And Shimei said to the king, "The saying *is* good. As my lord the king has said, so your servant will do." So Shimei dwelt in Jerusalem many days.

39 Now it happened at the end of three years, that two slaves of Shimei ran away to [R]Achish the son of Maachah, king of Gath. And they told Shimei, saying, "Look, your slaves *are* in Gath!" 1 Sam. 27:2

40 So Shimei arose, saddled his donkey, and went to Achish at Gath to seek his slaves. And Shimei went and brought his slaves from Gath.

41 And Solomon was told that Shimei had gone from Jerusalem to Gath and had come back.

42 Then the king sent and called for Shimei, and said to him, "Did I not make you swear by the LORD, and warn you, saying, 'Know for certain that on the day you go out and travel anywhere, you shall surely die'? And you said to me, 'The word I have heard *is* good.'

43 "Why then have you not kept the oath of the LORD and the commandment that I gave you?"

44 The king said moreover to Shimei, "You know, as your heart acknowledges, [R]all the wickedness that you did to my father David; therefore the LORD will return your wickedness on your own head. 2 Sam. 16:5–13

45 "But King Solomon *shall be* blessed, and [R]the throne of David shall be established before the LORD forever." [Prov. 25:5]

46 So the king commanded Benaiah the son of Jehoiada; and he went out and struck him down, and he died. Thus the kingdom was established in the hand of Solomon.

CHAPTER 3

Unwise Marriage of Solomon

NOW Solomon made a treaty with Pharaoh king of Egypt, and married Pharaoh's daughter; then he brought her to the City of David until he had finished building his own house, and the house of the LORD, and the wall all around Jerusalem.

2 [R]Meanwhile the people sacrificed at the high places, because there was no house built for the name of the LORD until those days. [Deut. 12:2–5, 13, 14]

Request for Wisdom—2 Chr. 1:2–13

3 And Solomon [R]loved the LORD, [R]walking in the statutes of his father David, except that he sacrificed and burned incense at the high places. [Rom. 8:28] • [1 Kin. 3:6, 14]

4 Now [R]the king went to Gibeon to sacrifice there, [R]for that *was* the great high place: Solomon offered a thousand burnt offerings on that altar. 2 Chr. 1:3 • 1 Chr. 16:39; 21:29

5 [R]At Gibeon the LORD appeared to Solomon in a dream by night; and God said, "Ask! What shall I give you?" 1 Kin. 9:2; 11:9

6 And Solomon said: "You have shown great mercy to Your servant David my father, because he walked before You in truth, in righteousness, and in uprightness of heart

with You; You have continued this great kindness for him, and You have given him a son to sit on his throne, as *it is* this day.

7 "Now, O LORD my God, You have made Your servant king instead of my father David, but I *am* a [R]little child; I do not know *how* to go out or come in. Jer. 1:6, 7

8 "And Your servant *is* in the midst of Your people whom You [R]have chosen, a great people, [R]too numerous to be numbered or counted. [Deut. 7:6] • Gen. 13:6; 15:5; 22:17

9 [R]"Therefore give to Your servant an understanding heart [R]to judge Your people, that I may [R]discern between good and evil. For who is able to judge this great people of Yours?" 2 Chr. 1:10 • Ps. 72:1, 2 • [Heb. 5:14]

10 The speech pleased the LORD, that Solomon had asked this thing.

11 Then God said to him: "Because you have asked this thing, and have [R]not asked long life for yourself, nor have asked riches for yourself, nor have asked the life of your enemies, but have asked for yourself understanding to discern justice, [James 4:3]

12 [R]"behold, I have done according to your words; see, I have given you a wise and understanding heart, so that there has not been anyone like you before you, nor shall any like you arise after you. [1 John 5:14, 15]

13 "And I have also [R]given you what you have not asked: both riches and honor, so that there shall not be anyone like you among the kings all your days. [Matt. 6:33]

14 "So [R]if you walk in My ways, to keep My statutes and My commandments, [R]as your father David walked, then I will [R]lengthen your days." [1 Kin. 6:12] • 1 Kin. 15:5 • Ps. 91:16

15 Then Solomon [R]awoke; and indeed it had been a dream. And he came to Jerusalem and stood before the ark of the covenant of the LORD, offered up burnt offerings, offered peace offerings, and [R]made a feast for all his servants. Gen. 41:7 • 1 Kin. 8:65

Display of Solomon's Wisdom

16 Now two women *who were* harlots came to the king, and stood before him.

17 And one woman said, "O my lord, this woman and I dwell in the same house; and I gave birth while she *was* in the house.

18 "Then it happened, the third day after I had given birth, that this woman also gave birth. And we *were* together; [T]no one *was* with us in the house, except the two of us in the house. Lit. *no stranger*

19 "And this woman's son died in the night, because she lay on him.

20 "So she arose in the middle of the night and took my son from my side, while your maidservant slept, and laid him in her bosom, and laid her dead child in my bosom.

21 "And when I rose in the morning to nurse my son, there he was, dead. But when I had examined him in the morning, indeed, he was not my son whom I had borne."

22 Then the other woman said, "No! But the living one *is* my son, and the dead one *is* your son." And the first woman said, "No! But the dead one *is* your son, and the living one *is* my son." Thus they spoke before the king.

23 And the king said, "The one says, 'This *is* my son, who lives, and your son *is* the dead one'; and the other says, 'No! But your son *is* the dead one, and my son *is* the living one.' "

24 Then the king said, "Bring me a sword." So they brought a sword before the king.

25 And the king said, "Divide the living child in two, and give half to one, and half to the other."

26 Then the woman whose son *was* living spoke to the king, for she yearned with compassion for her son; and she said, "O my lord, give her the living child, and by no means kill him!" But the other said, "Let him be neither mine nor yours, *but* divide *him*."

27 So the king answered and said, "Give the first woman the living child, and by no means kill him; she *is* his mother."

National Recognition of Solomon's Wisdom

28 And all Israel heard of the judgment which the king had rendered; and they feared the king, for they saw that the [R]wisdom of God *was* in him to administer justice. 1 Kin. 3:9, 11, 12

CHAPTER 4

Eleven Princes

SO King Solomon was king over all Israel.
2 And these *were* his officials: Azariah the son of Zadok, the priest;

3 Elihoreph and Ahijah, the sons of Shisha, scribes; [R]Jehoshaphat the son of Ahilud, the recorder; 2 Sam. 8:16; 20:24

4 Benaiah the son of Jehoiada, over the army; Zadok and Abiathar, the priests;

5 Azariah the son of Nathan, over the officers; Zabud the son of Nathan, a priest *and* [R]the king's friend; 2 Sam. 15:37; 16:16

6 Ahishar, over the household; and [R]Adoniram the son of Abda, over the labor force. 1 Kin. 5:14

Twelve Governors

7 And Solomon had twelve governors over all Israel, who provided food for the king and his household; each one made provision for one month of the year.

8 These *are* their names: Ben-Hur,* in the mountains of Ephraim;

9 Ben-Deker,* in Makaz, Shaalbim, Beth Shemesh, and Elon Beth Hanan;

4:8 Lit. *Son of Hur* **4:9** Lit. *Son of Deker*

10 Ben-Hesed,* in Arubboth; to him *be-*
longed Sochoh and all the land of Hepher;
11 Ben-Abinadab,* *in* all the regions of Dor;
he had Taphath the daughter of Solomon as
wife;
12 Baana the son of Ahilud, *in* Taanach,
Megiddo, and all Beth Shean, which *is* beside
Zaretan below Jezreel, from Beth Shean to
Abel Meholah, as far as the other side of
Jokneam;
13 Ben-Geber,* in Ramoth Gilead; to him *be-*
longed [R]the towns of Jair the son of Ma-
nasseh, in Gilead; to him *also belonged* the
region of Argob in Bashan—sixty large cities
with walls and bronze gate-bars; Num. 32:41
14 Ahinadab the son of Iddo, *in* Mahanaim;
15 Ahimaaz, in Naphtali; he also took Bas-
emath the daughter of Solomon as wife;
16 Baanah the son of [R]Hushai, in Asher and
Aloth; 1 Chr. 27:33
17 Jehoshaphat the son of Paruah, in Issa-
char;
18 Shimei the son of Elah, in Benjamin;
19 Geber the son of Uri, in the land of
Gilead, *in* the country of Sihon king of the
Amorites, and of Og king of Bashan. *He was*
the only governor who *was* in the land.

Solomon Reigns in Wisdom

20 Judah and Israel *were* as numerous [R]as
the sand by the sea in multitude, eating and
drinking and rejoicing. Gen. 22:17; 32:12
21 So [R]Solomon reigned over all kingdoms
from the River* *to* the land of the Philistines,
as far as the border of Egypt. [R]*They* brought
tribute and served Solomon all the days of
his life. Ps. 72:8 • Ps. 68:29
22 [R]Now Solomon's [T]provision for one day
was thirty [T]kors of fine flour, sixty kors of
meal, Neh. 5:18 • Lit. *bread* • Each about 5 bushels
23 ten fatted oxen, twenty oxen from the
pastures, and one hundred sheep, besides
deer, gazelles, roebucks, and fatted fowl.
24 For he had dominion over all *the region*
on this side of the River* from Tiphsah even to
Gaza, namely over [R]all the kings on this side
of the River; and [R]he had peace on every side
all around him. Ps. 72:11 • 1 Chr. 22:9
25 And Judah and Israel [R]dwelt safely, [R]each
man under his vine and his fig tree, [R]from
Dan as far as Beersheba, all the days of Sol-
omon. [Jer. 23:6] • [Mic. 4:4] • Judg. 20:1
26 [R]Solomon had forty* thousand stalls of
[R]horses for his chariots, and twelve thousand
horsemen. 1 Kin. 10:26 • [Deut. 17:16]
27 And these governors, each man in his
month, provided food for King Solomon and
for all who came to King Solomon's table.
There was no lack in their supply.
28 They also brought barley and straw to the
proper place, for the horses and steeds, each
man according to his charge.
29 And God gave Solomon wisdom and ex-
ceedingly great understanding, and largeness
of heart like the sand on the seashore.
30 Thus Solomon's wisdom excelled the wis-
dom of all the men [R]of the East and all [R]the
wisdom of Egypt. Gen. 25:6 • Is. 19:11, 12
31 For he was wiser than all men—than
Ethan the Ezrahite, and Heman, Chalcol, and
Darda, the sons of Mahol; and his fame was in
all the surrounding nations.
32 He spoke three thousand proverbs, and
his songs were one thousand and five.
33 Also he spoke of trees, from the cedar
tree of Lebanon even to the hyssop that
springs out of the wall; he spoke also of ani-
mals, of birds, of creeping things, and of fish.
34 And men of all nations, from all the kings
of the earth who had heard of his wisdom,
came to hear the wisdom of Solomon.

CHAPTER 5

Temple Materials—2 Chr. 2:3–12

NOW Hiram king of Tyre sent his servants
to Solomon, because he heard that they
had anointed him king in place of his father,
for Hiram had always loved David.
2 Then Solomon sent to Hiram, saying:
3 [R]You know how my father David could
not build a house for the name of the
LORD his God because of the wars which
were fought against him on every side,
until the LORD put *his foes** under the
soles of his feet. 1 Chr. 28:2, 3
4 But now the LORD my God has given me
[R]rest on every side; *there is* neither
adversary nor evil occurrence. 1 Kin. 4:24
5 And behold, I propose to build a house
for the name of the LORD my God, [R]as
the LORD spoke to my father David,
saying, "Your son, whom I will set on
your throne in your place, he shall build
the house for My name." 2 Sam. 7:12, 13
6 Now therefore, command that they cut
down [R]cedars for me from Lebanon; and
my servants will be with your servants,
and I will pay you wages for your
servants according to whatever you say.
For you know *there is* none among us
who has skill to cut timber like the
Sidonians. 2 Chr. 2:8, 10
7 So it was, when Hiram heard the words of
Solomon, that he rejoiced greatly and said,

4:10 Lit. *Son of Hesed* **4:11** Lit. *Son of Abinadab*
4:13 Lit. *Son of Geber* **4:21** The Euphrates
4:24 The Euphrates **4:26** So with MT, most other
authorities; some LXX mss. *four thousand;* cf. 2 Chr.
9:25 **5:3** Lit. *them*

Blessed *be* the LORD this day, for He has
given David a wise son over this great
people!

8 Then Hiram sent to Solomon, saying:

I have considered *the message* which
you sent me, *and* I will do all you desire
concerning the cedar and cypress logs.
9 My servants shall bring *them* down from
Lebanon to the sea; I will float them in
rafts by sea to the place you indicate to
me, and will have them broken apart
there; then you can take *them* away. And
you shall fulfill my desire by giving food
for my household.

10 Then Hiram gave Solomon cedar and cy-
press logs *according to* all his desire.
11 And Solomon gave Hiram twenty thou-
sand kors of wheat *as* food for his household,
and twenty* kors of pressed oil. Thus Sol-
omon gave to Hiram year by year.
12 So the LORD gave Solomon wisdom, [R]as
He had promised him; and there was peace
between Hiram and Solomon, and the two of
them made a treaty together. 1 Kin. 3:12

Temple Laborers

13 Then King Solomon raised up a labor
force out of all Israel; and the labor force was
thirty thousand men.
14 And he sent them to Lebanon, ten thou-
sand a month in shifts: they were one month
in Lebanon *and* two months at home;
Adoniram *was* in charge of the labor force.
15 Solomon had seventy thousand who car-
ried burdens, and eighty thousand who quar-
ried *stone* in the mountains,
16 besides three thousand three hundred*
from the [R]chiefs of Solomon's deputies, who
supervised the people who labored in the
work. 1 Kin. 9:23
17 And the king commanded them to quarry
large stones, costly stones, *and* [R]hewn stones,
to lay the foundation of the temple.* 1 Kin. 6:7
18 So Solomon's builders, Hiram's builders,
and the Gebalites quarried *them;* and they
prepared timber and stones to build the [T]tem-
ple. Lit. *house*

CHAPTER 6

The Temple Is Completed—2 Chr. 3:1–14

AND [R]it came to pass in the four hundred
and eightieth* year after the children of
Israel had come out of the land of Egypt, in
the fourth year of Solomon's reign over Israel,
in the month of Ziv, which *is* the second
month, [R]that he began to build the house of
the LORD. 2 Chr. 3:1, 2 • Acts 7:47
2 Now [R]the house which King Solomon
built for the LORD, its length *was* sixty cu-
bits, its width twenty, and its height thirty
cubits. Ezek. 41:1
3 The vestibule in front of the sanctuary* of
the house *was* [T]twenty cubits long across the
width of the house, *and* the width of *the
vestibule* extended* [T]ten cubits from the front
of the house. About 30 feet • About 15 feet
4 And he made for the house [R]windows
with beveled frames. Ezek. 40:16; 41:16
5 Against the wall of the [T]temple he built
[R]chambers all around, *against* the walls of the
temple, all around the sanctuary and the inner
sanctuary.* Thus he made side chambers all
around it. Lit. *house* • Ezek. 41:6
6 The lowest chamber *was* five cubits wide,
the middle *was* six cubits wide, and the third
was seven cubits wide; for he made narrow
ledges around the outside of the temple, so
that *the support beams* would not be fastened
into the walls of the temple.
7 And [R]the temple, when it was being built,
was built with stone finished at the quarry, so
that no hammer or chisel *or* any iron tool
was heard in the temple while it was being
built. Deut. 27:5, 6
8 The doorway for the middle story* *was* on
the right side of the temple. They went up by
stairs to the middle *story,* and from the middle
to the third.
9 [R]So he built the [T]temple and finished it,
and he paneled the temple with beams and
boards of cedar. 1 Kin. 6:14, 38 • Lit. *house*
10 And he built side chambers against the
entire temple, each five cubits high; they were
attached to the temple with cedar beams.
11 Then the word of the LORD came to Sol-
omon, saying:
12 "*Concerning* this temple which you are
building, [R]if you walk in My statutes, execute
My judgments, keep all My commandments,
and walk in them, then I will perform My
[T]word with you, [R]which I spoke to your father
David. 1 Kin. 2:4; 9:4 • *promise* • [2 Sam. 7:13]
13 "And [R]I will dwell among the children of
Israel, and will not [R]forsake My people Is-
rael." Ex. 25:8 • [Deut. 31:6]
14 So Solomon built the temple and finished
it.
15 And he built the inside walls of the temple
with cedar boards; from the floor of the tem-
ple to the ceiling he paneled the inside with
wood; and he covered the floor of the temple
with planks of cypress.
16 Then he built the twenty-cubit room at

5:11 So with MT, Tg., Vg.; LXX, Syr. *twenty thousand kors* **5:16** So with MT, Tg., Vg.; LXX *six hundred* **5:17** Lit. *house* **6:1** So with MT, Tg., Vg.; LXX *fortieth* **6:3** Heb. *heykal;* here the main room of the temple; elsewhere called the holy place, Ex. 26:33; Ezek. 41:1 • Lit. *it* **6:5** Heb. *debir;* here the inner room of the temple; elsewhere called the Most Holy Place, v. 16 **6:8** So with MT, Vg.; LXX *upper story;* Tg. *ground story*

the rear of the temple, from floor to ceiling, with cedar boards; he built *it* inside as the inner sanctuary, as the Most Holy *Place*.

17 And in front of it the temple sanctuary was forty cubits *long*.

18 The inside of the temple was cedar, carved with ornamental buds and open flowers. All *was* cedar; there was no stone *to be* seen.

19 And he prepared the inner sanctuary inside the temple, to set the ark of the covenant of the LORD there.

20 The inner sanctuary *was* twenty cubits long, twenty cubits wide, and twenty cubits high. He overlaid it with pure gold, and overlaid the altar of cedar.

21 So Solomon overlaid the inside of the temple with pure gold. He stretched gold chains across the front of the inner sanctuary, and overlaid it with gold.

22 The whole temple he overlaid with gold, until he had finished all the temple; also he overlaid with gold [R]the entire altar that *was* by the inner sanctuary. Ex. 30:1, 3, 6

23 Inside the inner sanctuary [R]he made two cherubim *of* olive wood, *each* ten cubits high. 2 Chr. 3:10–12

24 One wing of the cherub *was* five cubits, and the other wing of the cherub five cubits: ten cubits from the tip of one wing to the tip of the other.

25 And the other cherub *was* ten cubits; both cherubim *were* of the same size and shape.

26 The height of one cherub *was* ten cubits, and so *was* the other cherub.

27 Then he set the cherubim inside the inner room;* and [R]they stretched out the wings of the cherubim so that the wing of the one touched *one* wall, and the wing of the other cherub touched the other wall. And their wings touched each other in the middle of the room. 2 Chr. 5:8

28 Also he overlaid the cherubim with gold.

29 Then he carved all the walls of the temple all around, both the inner and outer *sanctuaries,* with carved figures of cherubim, palm trees, and open flowers.

30 And the floor of the temple he overlaid with gold, both the inner and outer *sanctuaries.*

31 For the entrance of the inner sanctuary he made doors *of* olive wood; the lintel *and* doorposts *were* one-fifth *of the wall.*

32 The two doors *were of* olive wood; and he carved on them figures of cherubim, palm trees, and open flowers, and overlaid *them* with gold; and he spread gold on the cherubim and on the palm trees.

33 So for the door of the [T]sanctuary he also made doorposts *of* olive wood, [T]one-fourth *of the wall.* temple • Or *four-sided*

34 And the two doors *were of* cypress wood; [R]two panels *comprised* one folding door, and two panels *comprised* the other folding door. Ezek. 41:23–25

35 Then he carved cherubim, palm trees, and open flowers *on them,* and overlaid *them* with gold applied evenly on the carved work.

36 And he built the [R]inner court with three rows of hewn stone and a row of cedar beams. 1 Kin. 7:12

37 [R]In the fourth year the foundation of the house of the LORD was laid, in the month of [T]Ziv. 1 Kin. 6:1 • Or *Ayyar,* April or May

38 And in the eleventh year, in the month of Bul, which is the eighth month, the house was finished in all its details and according to all its plans. So he was [R]seven years in building it. 1 Kin. 5:5; 6:1; 8:19

CHAPTER 7

Construction of Solomon's House

BUT Solomon took [R]thirteen years to build his own house; so he finished all his house. 2 Chr. 8:1

2 He also built the [R]House of the Forest of Lebanon; its length *was* one hundred cubits, its width fifty cubits, and its height thirty cubits, with four rows of cedar pillars, and cedar beams on the pillars. 2 Chr. 9:16

3 And *it was* paneled with cedar above the beams that *were* on forty-five pillars, fifteen *to* a row.

4 *There were* windows *with beveled frames in* three rows, and window *was* opposite window *in* three tiers.

5 And all the doorways and doorposts *had* rectangular frames; and window *was* opposite window *in* three tiers.

6 He also made the Hall of Pillars: its length *was* fifty cubits, and its width thirty cubits; and in front of them *was* a portico with pillars, and a canopy *was* in front of them.

7 Then he made a hall for the throne, the Hall of Judgment, where he might judge; and *it was* paneled with cedar from floor to ceiling.*

8 And the house where he dwelt *had* another court inside the hall, of like workmanship. Solomon also made a house like this hall for Pharaoh's daughter, [R]whom he had taken *as wife.* 2 Chr. 8:11

9 All these *were of* costly stones cut to size, trimmed with saws, inside and out, from the foundation to the eaves, and also on the outside to the great court.

10 The foundation *was of* costly stones, large stones, some ten cubits and some eight cubits.

11 And above *were* costly stones, hewn to size, and cedar wood.

12 The great court *was* enclosed with three rows of hewn stones and a row of cedar beams. So were the inner court of the house of the LORD and the vestibule of the temple.

6:27 Lit. *house* **7:7** Lit. *floor* of the upper level

Furnishings of the Temple—2 Chr. 3:15—5:1

13 Now King Solomon sent and brought
Huram* from Tyre.
14 He *was* the son of a widow from the tribe
of Naphtali, and his father *was* a man of Tyre,
a bronze worker; he was filled with wisdom
and understanding and skill in working with
all kinds of bronze work. So he came to King
Solomon and did all his work.
15 And he cast two pillars of bronze, each
one eighteen cubits high, and a line of twelve
cubits measured the circumference of each.
16 Then he made two capitals *of* cast bronze,
to set on the tops of the pillars. The height of
one capital *was* five cubits, and the height of
the other capital *was* five cubits.
17 *He made* a lattice network, with wreaths
of chainwork, for the capitals which *were* on
top of the pillars: seven chains for one capital
and seven for the other capital.
18 So he made the pillars, and two rows of
pomegranates above the network all around
to cover the capitals that *were* on top; and
thus he did for the other capital.
19 The capitals which *were* on top of the pil-
lars in the hall *were* in the shape of lilies, four
cubits.
20 The capitals on the two pillars also *had*
pomegranates above, by the convex surface
which *was* next to the network; and there
were two hundred such pomegranates in rows
on each of the capitals all around.
21 [R]Then he set up the pillars by the ves-
tibule of the temple; he set up the pillar on the
right and called its name Jachin, and he set
up the pillar on the left and called its name
Boaz. 2 Chr. 3:17
22 The tops of the pillars were in the shape
of lilies. So the work of the pillars was fin-
ished.
23 And he made [R]the Sea of cast bronze, ten
cubits from one brim to the other; *it was* com-
pletely round. Its height *was* five cubits, and a
line of thirty cubits measured its circumfer-
ence. 2 Chr. 4:2
24 Below its brim *were* ornamental buds en-
circling it all around, ten to a cubit, [R]all the way
around the Sea. The ornamental buds *were*
cast in two rows when it was cast. 2 Chr. 4:3
25 It stood on [R]twelve oxen: three looking to-
ward the north, three looking toward the
west, three looking toward the south, and
three looking toward the east; the Sea *was set*
upon them, and all their back parts *pointed*
inward. Jer. 52:20
26 It *was* a handbreadth thick; and its brim
was shaped like the brim of a cup, *like* a lily
blossom. It contained two thousand* baths.
27 He also made ten carts of bronze; four cu-
bits *was* the length of each cart, four cubits its
width, and three cubits its height.
28 And this *was* the design of the carts: They
had panels, and the panels *were* between
frames;
29 on the panels that *were* between the
frames *were* lions, oxen, and cherubim. And
on the frames *was* a pedestal on top. Below the
lions and oxen *were* wreaths of plaited work.
30 Every cart had four bronze wheels and
axles of bronze, and its four feet had supports.
Under the laver *were* supports of cast *bronze*
beside each wreath.
31 Its opening inside the crown at the top
was one cubit in diameter; and the opening
was round, shaped *like* a pedestal, one and a
half cubits in outside diameter; and also on
the opening *were* engravings, but the panels
were square, not round.
32 Under the panels *were* the four wheels,
and the axles of the wheels *were joined* to the
cart. The height of a wheel *was* one and a half
cubits.
33 The workmanship of the wheels *was* like
the workmanship of a chariot wheel; their
axle pins, their rims, their spokes, and their
hubs *were* all of cast *bronze*.
34 And *there were* four supports at the four
corners of each cart; its supports *were* part of
the cart itself.
35 On the top of the cart, at the height of half
a cubit, *it was* perfectly round. And on the top
of the cart, its flanges and its panels *were* of
the same casting.
36 On the plates of its flanges and on its pan-
els he engraved cherubim, lions, and palm
trees, wherever there was a clear space on
each, with wreaths all around.
37 Thus he made the ten carts. All of them
were of [T]the same mold, one measure, *and* one
shape. *one*
38 Then [R]he made ten lavers of bronze; each
laver contained [T]forty baths, *and* each laver
was four cubits. On each of the ten carts *was*
a laver. 2 Chr. 4:6 • About 240 gallons
39 And he put five carts on the right side of
the house, and five on the left side of the
house. He set the Sea on the right side of the
house, toward the southeast.
40 Huram* made the lavers and the shovels
and the bowls. So Huram finished doing all
the work that he was to do for King Solomon
for the house of the LORD:
41 the two pillars, the *two* bowl-shaped
capitals that *were* on top of the two pillars;
the two [R]networks covering the two bowl-
shaped capitals which *were* on top of the pil-
lars; 1 Kin. 7:17, 18
42 four hundred pomegranates for the two
networks (two rows of pomegranates for each
network, to cover the two bowl-shaped capi-
tals that *were* on top of the pillars);

7:13 Heb. *Hiram;* cf. 2 Chr. 2:13, 14 **7:26** About 12,000 gallons; *three thousand;* cf. 2 Chr. 4:5
7:40 Heb. *Hiram;* cf. 2 Chr. 2:13, 14

43 the ten carts, and ten lavers on the carts;
44 one Sea, and twelve oxen under the Sea;
45 [R]the pots, the shovels, and the bowls. All
these articles which Huram* made for King
Solomon *for* the house of the LORD *were of*
burnished bronze. Ex. 27:3
46 [R]In the plain of Jordan the king had them
cast in clay molds, between [R]Succoth and
[R]Zaretan. 2 Chr. 4:17 • Gen. 33:17 • Josh. 3:16
47 And Solomon did not weigh all the arti-
cles, because *there were* so many; the weight
of the bronze was not determined.
48 Thus Solomon had all the furnishings
made for the house of the LORD: [R]the altar of
gold, and the table of gold on which *was* the
showbread; Ex. 37:25, 26; 2 Chr. 4:8
49 the lampstands of pure gold, five on the
right *side* and five on the left in front of the
inner sanctuary, with the flowers and the lamps
and the wick-trimmers of gold;
50 the basins, the trimmers, the bowls, the
ladles, and the censers of pure gold; and the
hinges of gold, *both* for the doors of the inner
room (the Most Holy *Place*) *and* for the doors
of the main hall of the temple.
51 So all the work that King Solomon had
done for the house of the LORD was finished;
and Solomon brought in the things [R]which his
father David had dedicated: the silver and the
gold and the furnishings. He put them in the
treasuries of the house of the LORD. 2 Sam. 8:11

CHAPTER 8

The Ark Returns—2 Chr. 5:2–12

NOW Solomon assembled the elders of Is-
rael and all the heads of the tribes, the
chief fathers of the children of Israel, to King
Solomon in Jerusalem, that they might bring
up the ark of the covenant of the LORD from
the City of David, which *is* Zion.
2 Therefore all the men of Israel assem-
bled with King Solomon at the [R]feast in the
month of [T]Ethanim, which *is* the seventh
month. Lev. 23:34 • Or *Tishri,* September or October
3 So all the elders of Israel came, [R]and the
priests took up the ark. Num. 4:15; 7:9
4 Then they brought up the ark of the
LORD, [R]the [T]tabernacle of meeting, and all
the holy furnishings that *were* in the taber-
nacle. The priests and the Levites brought
them up. 2 Chr. 1:3 • *tent*
5 Also King Solomon, and all the congrega-
tion of Israel who were assembled with him,
were with him before the ark, sacrificing
sheep and oxen that could not be counted or
numbered for multitude.
6 Then the priests [R]brought in the ark of
the covenant of the LORD to [R]its place, into the
inner sanctuary of the temple, to the Most
Holy *Place,* [R]under the wings of the cheru-
bim. 2 Sam. 6:17 • 1 Kin. 6:19 • 1 Kin. 6:27
7 For the cherubim spread *their* two wings
over the place of the ark, and the cherubim
overshadowed the ark and its poles.
8 The poles [R]extended so that the [T]ends of
the poles could be seen from the holy *place,* in
front of the inner sanctuary; but they could
not be seen from outside. And they are there
to this day. Ex. 25:13–15; 37:4, 5 • *heads*
9 [R]Nothing *was* in the ark [R]except the two
tablets of stone which Moses put there at
Horeb, when the LORD made *a covenant* with
the children of Israel, when they came out of
the land of Egypt. Ex. 25:21 • Deut. 10:5

The Shekinah Returns—2 Chr. 5:13, 14

10 And it came to pass, when the priests
came out of the holy *place,* that the cloud
[R]filled the house of the LORD, Ex. 40:34, 35
11 so that the priests could not continue
ministering because of the cloud; for the
[R]glory of the LORD filled the house of the
LORD. 2 Chr. 7:1, 2

Solomon's Sermon—2 Chr. 6:1–11

12 [R]Then Solomon spoke: 2 Chr. 6:1

"The LORD said He would dwell [R]in the
dark cloud. Ps. 18:11; 97:2
13 [R]I have surely built You an exalted
house, 2 Sam. 7:13
And a place for You to dwell in forever."

14 Then the king turned around and blessed
the whole assembly of Israel, while all the as-
sembly of Israel was standing.
15 And he said: [R]"Blessed *be* the LORD God
of Israel, who [R]spoke with His mouth to my
father David, and with His hand has fulfilled
it, saying, Luke 1:68 • 2 Sam. 7:2, 12, 13, 25
16 'Since the day that I brought My people
Israel out of Egypt, I have chosen no city from
any tribe of Israel *in which* to build a house,
that My name might be there; but I chose Da-
vid to be over My people Israel.'
17 "Now [R]it was in the heart of my father Da-
vid to build a temple* for the name of the
LORD God of Israel. 2 Sam. 7:2, 3
18 [R]"But the LORD said to my father David,
'Whereas it was in your heart to build a tem-
ple for My name, you did well that it was in
your heart. 2 Chr. 6:8, 9
19 'Nevertheless [R]you shall not build the
temple, but your son who will come from
your body, he shall build the temple for My
name.' 2 Sam. 7:5, 12, 13
20 "So the LORD has fulfilled His word
which He spoke; and I have filled the position
of my father David, and sit on the throne of
Israel, [R]as the LORD promised; and I have
built a temple for the name of the LORD God
of Israel. 1 Chr. 28:5, 6

7:45 Heb. *Hiram;* cf. 2 Chr. 2:13, 14 **8:17** Lit. *house,*
and so in vv. 18–20

21 "And there I have made a place for the ark, in which *is* the covenant of the LORD which He made with our fathers, when He brought them out of the land of Egypt."

Solomon's Prayer—2 Chr. 6:12–39

22 Then Solomon stood before [R]the altar of the LORD in the presence of all the assembly of Israel, and [R]spread out his hands toward heaven; 2 Chr. 6:12 • Ezra 9:5

23 and he said: "LORD God of Israel, [R]*there is* no God in heaven above or on earth below like You, [R]who keep *Your* covenant and mercy with Your servants who walk before You with all their hearts. Ex. 15:11 • [Neh. 1:5]

24 "You have kept what You promised Your servant David my father; You have both spoken with Your mouth and fulfilled *it* with Your hand, as *it is* this day.

25 "Therefore, LORD God of Israel, now keep what You promised Your servant David my father, saying, [R]'You shall not fail to have a man sit before Me on the throne of Israel, only if your sons take heed to their way, that they walk before Me as you have walked before Me.' 1 Kin. 2:4; 9:5

26 "And now I pray, O God of Israel, let Your word come true, which You have spoken to Your servant David my father.

27 "But will God indeed dwell on the earth? Behold, heaven and the [R]heaven of heavens cannot contain You. How much less this temple which I have built! 2 Cor. 12:2

28 "Yet regard the prayer of Your servant and his supplication, O LORD my God, and listen to the cry and the prayer which Your servant is praying before You today:

29 "that Your eyes may be open toward this temple night and day, toward the place of which You said, 'My name shall be there,' that You may hear the prayer which Your servant makes [R]toward this place. Dan. 6:10

30 [R]"And may You hear the supplication of Your servant and of Your people Israel, when they pray toward this place. Hear in heaven Your dwelling place; and when You hear, forgive. Neh. 1:6

31 "When anyone sins against his neighbor, and is forced to take [R]an oath, and comes *and* takes an oath before Your altar in this temple, Ex. 22:8–11

32 "then hear in heaven, and act, and judge Your servants, [R]condemning the wicked, bringing his way on his head, and justifying the righteous by giving him according to his righteousness. Deut. 25:1

33 "When Your people Israel are defeated before an enemy because they have sinned against You, and when they turn back to You and confess Your name, and pray and make supplication to You in this temple,

34 "then hear in heaven, and forgive the sin of Your people Israel, and bring them back to the land which You gave to their [R]fathers. [Lev. 26:40–42]

35 "When the heavens are shut up and there is no rain because they have sinned against You, when they pray toward this place and confess Your name, and turn from their sin because You afflict them,

36 "then hear in heaven, and forgive the sin of Your servants, Your people Israel, that You may [R]teach them the good way in which they should walk; and send rain on Your land which You have given to Your people as an inheritance. Ps. 25:4; 27:11; 94:12

37 "When there is famine in the land, pestilence *or* blight *or* mildew, locusts *or* grasshoppers; when their enemy besieges them in the land of their cities; whatever plague or whatever sickness *there is;*

38 "whatever prayer, whatever supplication is made by anyone, *or* by all Your people Israel, when each one knows the plague of his own heart, and spreads out his hands toward this temple:

39 "then hear in heaven Your dwelling place, and forgive, and act, and give to everyone according to all his ways, whose heart You know (for You alone [R]know the hearts of all the sons of men), [1 Sam. 16:7]

40 [R]"that they may fear You all the days that they live in the land which You gave to our fathers. [Ps. 130:4]

41 "Moreover, concerning a foreigner, who *is* not of Your people Israel, but has come from a far country for Your name's sake

42 "(for they will hear of Your great name and Your [R]strong hand and Your outstretched arm), when he comes and prays toward this temple, Deut. 3:24

43 "hear in heaven Your dwelling place, and do according to all for which the foreigner calls to You, [R]that all peoples of the earth may know Your name and [R]fear You, as *do* Your people Israel, and that they may know that this temple which I have built is called by Your name. [1 Sam. 17:46] • Ps. 102:15

44 "When Your people go out to battle against their enemy, wherever You send them, and when they pray to the LORD toward the city which You have chosen and the temple which I have built for Your name,

45 "then hear in heaven their prayer and their supplication, and maintain their [T]cause. *justice*

46 "When they sin against You [R](for *there is* no one who does not sin), and You become angry with them and deliver them to the enemy, and they take them captive to the land of the enemy, far or near; Ps. 130:3

47 "*yet* when they come to themselves in the land where they were carried captive, and repent, and make supplication to You in the land of those who took them captive, [R]saying, 'We have sinned and done wrong, we have committed wickedness'; Dan. 9:5

48 "and *when* they [R]return to You with all
their heart and with all their soul in the land
of their enemies who led them away captive,
and [R]pray to You toward their land which You
gave to their fathers, the city which You have
chosen and the temple which I have built for
Your name: Jer. 29:12–14 • Dan. 6:10
49 "then hear in heaven Your dwelling place
their prayer and their supplication, and main-
tain their [T]cause, *justice*
50 "and forgive Your people who have sinned
against You, and all their transgressions
which they have transgressed against You;
and [R]grant them compassion before those
who took them captive, that they may have
compassion on them Ps. 106:46
51 "(for [R]they *are* Your people and Your in-
heritance, whom You brought out of Egypt,
out of the iron furnace), Deut. 9:26–29
52 [R]"that Your eyes may be open to the sup-
plication of Your servant and the supplication
of Your people Israel, to listen to them when-
ever they call to You. 1 Kin. 8:29
53 "For You separated them from among all
the peoples of the earth *to be* Your inheri-
tance, [R]as You spoke by Your servant Moses,
when You brought our fathers out of Egypt, O
Lord God." Ex. 19:5, 6
54 And so it was, when Solomon had fin-
ished praying all this prayer and supplication
to the LORD, that he arose from before the
altar of the LORD, from kneeling on his knees
with his hands spread up to heaven.
55 Then he stood and blessed all the assem-
bly of Israel with a loud voice, saying:
56 "Blessed *be* the LORD, who has given rest
to His people Israel, according to all that He
promised. There has not failed one word of
all His good promise, which He promised
through His servant Moses.
57 "May the LORD our God be with us, as He
was with our fathers. [R]May He not leave us
nor forsake us, Deut. 31:6
58 "that He may [R]incline our hearts to Him-
self, to walk in all His ways, and to keep His
commandments and His statutes and His
judgments, which He commanded our fa-
thers. Ps. 119:36
59 "And may these words of mine, with
which I have made supplication before the
LORD, be near the LORD our God day and
night, that He may maintain the cause of His
servant and the cause of His people Israel, as
each day may require,
60 [R]"that all the peoples of the earth may
know that [R]the LORD *is* God; *there is* no
other. 1 Sam. 17:46 • Deut. 4:35, 39
61 "Let your [R]heart therefore be [T]loyal to
the LORD our God, to walk in His statutes
and keep His commandments, as at this
day." Deut. 18:13 • Lit. *at peace with*

Israel Rejoices—2 Chr. 7:4–10

62 Then the king and all Israel with him of-
fered sacrifices before the LORD.
63 And Solomon offered a sacrifice of peace
offerings, which he offered to the LORD,
twenty-two thousand bulls and one hundred
and twenty thousand sheep. So the king and
all the children of Israel dedicated the house
of the LORD.
64 On the same day the king consecrated the
middle of the court that *was* in front of the
house of the LORD; for there he offered burnt
offerings, grain offerings, and the fat of the
peace offerings, because the bronze altar that
was before the LORD *was* too small to receive
the burnt offerings, the grain offerings, and
the fat of the peace offerings.
65 At that time Solomon held a feast, and all
Israel with him, a great assembly from the en-
trance of Hamath to the Brook of Egypt, be-
fore the LORD our God, seven days and seven
more days—fourteen days.
66 On the eighth day he sent the people
away; and they blessed the king, and went to
their tents joyful and glad of heart for all the
good that the LORD had done for His servant
David, and for Israel His people.

CHAPTER 9

Reiteration of the Davidic Covenant
2 Chr. 7:11–22

AND [R]it came to pass, when Solomon had
finished building the house of the LORD
and the king's house, and all Solomon's de-
sire which he wanted to do, 2 Chr. 7:11
2 that the LORD appeared to Solomon the
second time, [R]as He had appeared to him at
Gibeon. 1 Kin. 3:5; 11:9
3 And the LORD said to him: [R]"I have heard
your prayer and your supplication that you
have made before Me; I have consecrated this
house which you have built to put My name
there forever, and My eyes and My heart will
be there perpetually. Ps. 10:17
4 "Now if you [R]walk before Me as your fa-
ther David walked, in integrity of heart and in
uprightness, to do according to all that I have
commanded you, *and* if you keep My statutes
and My judgments, Gen. 17:1
5 "then I will establish the throne of your
kingdom over Israel forever, as I promised
David your father, saying, 'You shall not fail to
have a man on the throne of Israel.'
6 [R]"*But* if you or your sons at all [T]turn from
following Me, and do not keep My command-
ments *and* My statutes which I have set before
you, but go and serve other gods and worship
them, 2 Sam. 7:14–16 • *turn back*
7 "then I will cut off Israel from the land
which I have given them; and this house
which I have consecrated for My name I will

cast out of My sight. [R]Israel will be a proverb and a byword among all peoples. Ps. 44:14

8 "And *as for* [R]this house, *which* is exalted, everyone who passes by it will be astonished and will hiss, and say, [R]'Why has the LORD done thus to this land and to this house?' 2 Chr. 7:21 • [Deut. 29:24–26]

9 "Then they will answer, 'Because they forsook the LORD their God, who brought their fathers out of the land of Egypt, and have embraced other gods, and worshiped them and served them; therefore the LORD has brought all this calamity on them.' "

Sale of Cities in Israel—2 Chr. 8:1, 2

10 Now [R]it happened at the end of twenty years, when Solomon had built the two houses, the house of the LORD and the king's house 2 Chr. 8:1

11 [R](Hiram the king of Tyre had supplied Solomon with cedar and cypress and gold, as much as he desired), *that* King Solomon then gave Hiram twenty cities in the land of Galilee. 1 Kin. 5:1

12 Then Hiram went from Tyre to see the cities which Solomon had given him, but they did not please him.

13 So he said, "What *kind of* cities *are* these which you have given me, my brother?" [R]And he called them the land of Cabul,* as they are to this day. Josh. 19:27

14 Then Hiram sent the king one hundred and twenty talents of gold.

Enslavement of the Canaanites—2 Chr. 8:4–18

15 And this *is* the reason for [R]the labor force which King Solomon raised: to build the house of the LORD, his own house, the Millo,* the wall of Jerusalem, Hazor, Megiddo, and Gezer. 1 Kin. 5:13

16 (Pharaoh king of Egypt had gone up and taken Gezer and burned it with fire, [R]had killed the Canaanites who dwelt in the city, and had given it *as* a dowry to his daughter, Solomon's wife.) Josh. 16:10

17 And Solomon built Gezer, Lower [R]Beth Horon, 2 Chr. 8:5

18 [R]Baalath, and Tadmor in the wilderness, in the land *of Judah,* Josh. 19:44

19 all the storage cities that Solomon had, cities for [R]his chariots and cities for his [R]cavalry, and whatever Solomon desired to build in Jerusalem, in Lebanon, and in all the land of his dominion. 1 Kin. 10:26 • 1 Kin. 4:26

20 [R]All the people *who were* left of the Amorites, Hittites, Perizzites, Hivites, and Jebusites, who *were* not of the children of Israel— 2 Chr. 8:7

21 that is, their descendants [R]who were left in the land after them, whom the children of Israel had not been able to destroy completely—from these Solomon raised forced labor, as it is to this day. Judg. 1:21–36; 3:1

22 But of the children of Israel Solomon [R]made no forced laborers, because they *were* men of war and his servants: his officers, his captains, commanders of his chariots, and his cavalry. [Lev. 25:39]

23 Others *were* chiefs of the officials who *were* over Solomon's work: [R]five hundred and fifty, who ruled over the people who did the work. 2 Chr. 8:10

24 But [R]Pharaoh's daughter came up from the City of David to [R]her house which *Solomon** had built for her. [R]Then he built the Millo. 1 Kin. 3:1 • 1 Kin. 7:8 • 2 Sam. 5:9

25 [R]Now three times a year Solomon offered burnt offerings and peace offerings on the altar which he had built for the LORD, and he burned incense with them *on the altar* that *was* before the LORD. So he finished the temple. Ex. 23:14–17

26 King Solomon also built a fleet of ships at Ezion Geber, which *is* near Elath* on the shore of the Red Sea, in the land of Edom.

27 [R]Then Hiram sent his servants with the fleet, seamen who knew the sea, to work with the servants of Solomon. 1 Kin. 5:6, 9

28 And they went to Ophir, and acquired four hundred and twenty talents of gold from there, and brought *it* to King Solomon.

CHAPTER 10

Multiplication of Wealth—2 Chr. 9:1–24

NOW when the [R]queen of Sheba heard of the fame of Solomon concerning the name of the LORD, she came [R]to test him with hard questions. Matt. 12:42 • Judg. 14:12

2 She came to Jerusalem with a very great [T]retinue, with camels that bore spices, very much gold, and precious stones; and when she came to Solomon, she spoke with him about all that was in her heart. *company*

3 So Solomon answered all her questions; there was nothing [T]so difficult for the king that he could not explain *it* to her. *too*

4 And when the queen of Sheba had seen all the wisdom of Solomon, the house that he had built,

5 the food on his table, the seating of his servants, the service of his waiters and their apparel, his cupbearers, and his entryway by which he went up to the house of the LORD, there was no more spirit in her.

6 Then she said to the king: "It was a true report which I heard in my own land about your words and your wisdom.

7 "However I did not believe the words until I came and saw with my own eyes; and indeed the half was not told me. Your wisdom and prosperity exceed the fame of which I heard.

8 "Happy *are* your men and happy *are*

9:13 Lit. *Good for Nothing* **9:15** Lit. *The Landfill*
9:24 Lit. *he;* cf. 2 Chr. 8:11 **9:26** Heb. *Eloth*

these your servants, who stand continually
before you *and* hear your wisdom!
9 "Blessed be the LORD your God, who de-
lighted in you, setting you on the throne of Is-
rael! Because the LORD has loved Israel
forever, therefore He made you king, [R]to do
justice and righteousness." Ps. 72:2
10 Then she gave the king one hundred and
twenty talents of gold, spices in great quan-
tity, and precious stones. There never again
came such abundance of spices as the queen
of Sheba gave to King Solomon.
11 [R]Also, the ships of Hiram, which brought
gold from Ophir, brought great *quantities* of
almug* wood and precious stones from
Ophir. 1 Kin. 9:27, 28
12 [R]And the king made steps of the almug
wood for the house of the LORD and for the
king's house, also harps and stringed instru-
ments for singers. There never again came
such [R]almug wood, nor has the like been seen
to this day. 2 Chr. 9:11 • 2 Chr. 9:10
13 Now King Solomon gave the queen of
Sheba all she desired, whatever she asked, be-
sides what Solomon had given her according
to the royal generosity. So she turned and
went to her own country, she and her ser-
vants.
14 The weight of gold that came to Solomon
yearly was six hundred and sixty-six talents
of gold,
15 besides *that* from the [R]traveling mer-
chants, from the income of traders, [R]from all
the kings of Arabia, and from the governors of
the country. 2 Chr. 1:16 • Ps. 72:10
16 And King Solomon made two hundred
large shields *of* hammered gold; six hundred
shekels of gold went into each shield.
17 He also *made* three hundred shields *of*
hammered gold; three minas of gold went into
each shield. The king put them in the House
of the Forest of Lebanon.
18 Moreover the king made a great throne of
ivory, and overlaid it with pure gold.
19 The throne had six steps, and the top of
the throne *was* round at the back; *there were*
armrests on either side of the place of the
seat, and two lions stood beside the armrests.
20 Twelve lions stood there, one on each side
of the six steps; nothing like *this* had been
made for any *other* kingdom.
21 [R]All King Solomon's drinking vessels
were gold, and all the vessels of the House of
the Forest of Lebanon *were* pure gold. Not
one was silver, for this was accounted as noth-
ing in the days of Solomon. 2 Chr. 9:20
22 For the king had merchant ships* at sea
with the fleet of Hiram. Once every three
years the merchant ships came bringing gold,
silver, ivory, apes, and monkeys.*
23 So King Solomon surpassed all the kings
of the earth in riches and wisdom.
24 Now all the earth sought the presence of
Solomon to hear his wisdom, which God had
put in his heart.
25 Each man brought his present: articles of
silver and gold, garments, armor, spices,
horses, and mules, at a set rate year by year.

Multiplication of Horses
2 Chr. 1:14–17; 9:25–28

26 And Solomon gathered chariots and
horsemen; he had one thousand four hundred
chariots and twelve thousand horsemen,
whom he stationed* in the chariot cities and
with the king at Jerusalem.
27 [R]The king made silver *as common* in Je-
rusalem as stones, and he made cedar trees as
abundant as the sycamores which *are* in the
lowland. 2 Chr. 1:15–17
28 Also Solomon had horses imported from
Egypt and Keveh; the king's merchants
bought them in Keveh at the *current* price.
29 Now a chariot that was imported from
Egypt cost six hundred *shekels* of silver, and a
horse one hundred and fifty; [R]and thus,
through their agents,* they exported *them* to
all the kings of the Hittites and the kings of
Syria. 2 Kin. 7:6, 7

CHAPTER 11

Intermarriage with Foreign Women

BUT King Solomon loved many foreign
women, as well as the daughter of Pha-
raoh: women of the Moabites, Ammonites,
Edomites, Sidonians, *and* Hittites—
2 from the nations of whom the LORD had
said to the children of Israel, "You shall not in-
termarry with them, nor they with you. Surely
they will turn away your hearts after their
gods." Solomon clung to these in love.
3 And he had seven hundred wives,
princesses, and three hundred concubines;
and his wives turned away his heart.

Worship of Idols

4 For it was so, when Solomon was old,
[R]that his wives turned his heart after other
gods; and his [R]heart was not loyal to the LORD
his God, [R]as *was* the heart of his father Da-
vid. [Deut. 17:17] • 1 Kin. 8:61 • 1 Kin. 9:4
5 For Solomon went after Ashtoreth the
goddess of the Sidonians, and after Milcom
the abomination of the Ammonites.
6 Solomon did evil in the sight of the LORD,
and did not fully follow the LORD, as *did* his
father David.
7 Then Solomon built a high place for
Chemosh the abomination of Moab, on the

10:11 *algum*, 2 Chr. 9:10, 11 **10:22** Lit. *ships of Tarshish*, deep-sea vessels • Or *peacocks* **10:26** So with LXX, Syr., Tg., Vg. (cf. 2 Chr. 9:25); MT *led*
10:29 Lit. *by their hands*

hill that *is* east of Jerusalem, and for Molech
the abomination of the people of Ammon.
8 And he did likewise for all his foreign
wives, who burned incense and sacrificed to
their gods.

The Rebuke of God

9 So the LORD became angry with Solomon,
because his heart had turned from the LORD
God of Israel, [R]who had appeared to him
twice, 1 Kin. 3:5; 9:2
10 and [R]had commanded him concerning
this thing, that he should not go after other
gods; but he did not keep what the LORD had
commanded. 1 Kin. 6:12; 9:6, 7
11 Therefore the LORD said to Solomon, "Be-
cause you have done this, and have not kept
My covenant and My statutes, which I have
commanded you, [R]I will surely tear the king-
dom away from you and give it to your [R]ser-
vant. 1 Kin. 11:31; 12:15, 16 • 1 Kin. 11:31, 37
12 "Nevertheless I will not do it in your days,
for the sake of your father David; I will tear it
out of the hand of your son.
13 [R]"However I will not tear away the
whole kingdom; I will give [R]one tribe to your
son [R]for the sake of My servant David, and
for the sake of Jerusalem which I have cho-
sen." 2 Sam. 7:15 • 1 Kin. 12:20 • 2 Sam. 7:15, 16

The Chastisement of God

14 Now the LORD raised up an adversary
against Solomon, Hadad the Edomite; he *was*
a descendant of the king in Edom.
15 [R]For it happened, when David was in
Edom, and Joab the commander of the army
had gone up to bury the slain, after he had
killed every male in Edom 2 Sam. 8:14
16 (because for six months Joab remained
there with all Israel, until he had cut down
every male in Edom),
17 that Hadad fled to go to Egypt, he and
certain Edomites of his father's servants with
him. Hadad *was* still a little child.
18 Then they arose from Midian and came to
Paran; and they took men with them from
Paran and came to Egypt, to Pharaoh king of
Egypt, who gave him a house, apportioned
food for him, and gave him land.
19 And Hadad found great favor in the sight
of Pharaoh, so that he gave him as wife the
sister of his own wife, that is, the sister of
Queen Tahpenes.
20 Then the sister of Tahpenes bore him
Genubath his son, whom Tahpenes weaned
in Pharaoh's house. And Genubath was in
Pharaoh's household among the sons of
Pharaoh.
21 [R]So when Hadad heard in Egypt that Da-
vid rested with his fathers, and that Joab the
commander of the army was dead, Hadad
said to Pharaoh, "Let me depart, that I may go
to my own country." 1 Kin. 2:10, 34
22 Then Pharaoh said to him, "But what
have you lacked with me, that suddenly you
seek to go to your own country?" So he an-
swered, "Nothing, but do let me go anyway."
23 And God raised up *another* adversary
against him, Rezon the son of Eliadah, who
had fled from his lord, [R]Hadadezer king of
Zobah. 2 Sam. 8:3; 10:16
24 So he gathered men to him and became
captain over a band *of raiders*, [R]when David
killed those *of Zobah*. And they went to Da-
mascus and dwelt there, and reigned in Da-
mascus. 2 Sam. 8:3; 10:8, 18
25 He was an adversary of Israel all the days
of Solomon (besides the trouble that Hadad
caused); and he abhorred Israel, and reigned
over Syria.
26 Then Solomon's servant, [R]Jeroboam the
son of Nebat, an Ephraimite from Zereda,
whose mother's name *was* Zeruah, a widow,
also rebelled against the king. 1 Kin. 12:2
27 And this *is* what caused him to rebel
against the king: [R]Solomon had built the Millo
and repaired the damages to the City of David
his father. 1 Kin. 9:15, 24
28 The man Jeroboam *was* a mighty man of
valor; and Solomon, seeing that the young
man was [R]industrious, made him the officer
over all the labor force of the house of Jo-
seph. [Prov. 22:29]
29 Now it happened at that time, when Jer-
oboam went out of Jerusalem, that the
prophet Ahijah the Shilonite met him on the
way; and he had clothed himself with a new
garment, and the two *were* alone in the field.
30 Then Ahijah took hold of the new gar-
ment that *was* on him, and [R]tore it *into* twelve
pieces. 1 Sam. 15:27, 28; 24:5
31 And he said to Jeroboam, "Take for your-
self ten pieces, for [R]thus says the LORD, the
God of Israel: 'Behold, I will tear the kingdom
out of the hand of Solomon and will give ten
tribes to you 1 Kin. 11:11, 13
32 '(but he shall have one tribe for the sake
of My servant David, and for the sake of Jeru-
salem, the city which I have chosen out of all
the tribes of Israel),
33 [R]'because they have* forsaken Me, and
worshiped Ashtoreth the goddess of the Sido-
nians, Chemosh the god of the Moabites, and
Milcom the god of the people of Ammon, and
have not walked in My ways to do *what is*
right in My eyes and *keep* My statutes and My
judgments, as *did* his father David. 1 Kin. 11:5–8
34 'However I will not take the whole king-
dom out of his hand, because I have made him
ruler all the days of his life for the sake of My
servant David, whom I chose because he kept
My commandments and My statutes.
35 'But I will take the kingdom out of his
son's hand and give it to you—ten tribes.

11:33 So with MT, Tg.; LXX, Syr., Vg. *he has*

36 'And to his son I will give one tribe, that
[R]My servant David may always have a lamp
before Me in Jerusalem, the city which I
have chosen for Myself, to put My name
there. [1 Kin. 15:4]
37 'So I will take you, and you shall reign
over all your heart desires, and you shall be
king over Israel.
38 'Then it shall be, if you heed all that I
command you, walk in My ways, and do *what
is* right in My sight, to keep My statutes and
My commandments, as My servant David did,
then I will be with you and build for you an
enduring house, as I built for David, and will
give Israel to you.
39 'And I will afflict the descendants of Da-
vid because of this, but not forever.' "
40 Solomon therefore sought to kill Jer-
oboam. But Jeroboam arose and fled to Egypt,
to Shishak king of Egypt, and was in Egypt
until the death of Solomon.

Death of Solomon—2 Chr. 9:29–31

41 Now the rest of the acts of Solomon, all
that he did, and his wisdom, *are* they not writ-
ten in the book of the acts of Solomon?
42 And the period that Solomon reigned in
Jerusalem over all Israel *was* forty years.
43 [R]Then Solomon rested with his fathers,
and was buried in the City of David his fa-
ther. And Rehoboam his son reigned in his
[R]place. 2 Chr. 9:31 • 2 Chr. 10:1

CHAPTER 12

Request of Israel to Rehoboam
2 Chr. 10:1–5

AND [R]Rehoboam went to [R]Shechem, for all
Israel had gone to Shechem to make him
king. 2 Chr. 10:1 • Judg. 9:6
2 So it happened, when Jeroboam the son
of Nebat heard *it* (he was still in Egypt, for he
had fled from the presence of King Solomon
and had been dwelling in Egypt),
3 that they sent and called him. Then Jer-
oboam and the whole assembly of Israel came
and spoke to Rehoboam, saying,
4 "Your father made our yoke heavy; now
therefore, lighten the burdensome service of
your father, and his heavy yoke which he put
on us, and we will serve you."
5 So he said to them, "Depart *for* three
days, then come back to me." And the people
departed.

Foolish Response of Rehoboam
2 Chr. 10:6–15

6 Then King Rehoboam consulted the el-
ders who stood before his father Solomon
while he still lived, and he said, "How do you
advise *me* to answer these people?"
7 And they spoke to him, saying, [R]"If you
will be a servant to these people today, and
serve them, and answer them, and speak good
words to them, then they will be your servants
forever." 2 Chr. 10:7
8 But he rejected the advice which the el-
ders had given him, and consulted the young
men who had grown up with him, who stood
before him.
9 And he said to them, "What advice do you
give? How should we answer this people who
have spoken to me, saying, 'Lighten the yoke
which your father put on us'?"
10 Then the young men who had grown up
with him spoke to him, saying, "Thus you
should speak to this people who have spoken
to you, saying, 'Your father made our yoke
heavy, but you make *it* lighter on us'—thus
you shall say to them: 'My little *finger* shall be
thicker than my father's waist!
11 'And now, whereas my father put a heavy
yoke on you, I will add to your yoke; my fa-
ther chastised you with whips, but I will chas-
tise you with scourges!' "*
12 So Jeroboam and all the people came to
Rehoboam the third day, as the king had di-
rected, saying, "Come back to me the third
day."
13 Then the king answered the people
[T]roughly, and rejected the advice which the
elders had given him; *harshly*
14 and he spoke to them according to the
advice of the young men, saying, "My father
made your yoke heavy, but I will add to your
yoke; my father chastised you with whips, but
I will chastise you with scourges!"*
15 So the king did not listen to the people;
for [R]the turn *of events* was from the LORD, that
He might fulfill His word, which the LORD had
spoken by Ahijah the Shilonite to Jeroboam
the son of Nebat. Judg. 14:4

Revolt of the Northern Tribes
2 Chr. 10:16–19; 11:1–4

16 Now when all Israel saw that the king did
not listen to them, the people answered the
king, saying:

[R]"What share have we in David?
We have no inheritance in the son of
Jesse. 2 Sam. 20:1
To your tents, O Israel!
Now, see to your own house, O David!"

So Israel departed to their tents.
17 But Rehoboam reigned over [R]the chil-
dren of Israel who dwelt in the cities of Ju-
dah. 1 Kin. 11:13, 36
18 Then King Rehoboam [R]sent Adoram, who
was in charge of the revenue; but all Israel
stoned him with stones, and he died. There-
fore King Rehoboam mounted his chariot in
haste to flee to Jerusalem. 1 Kin. 4:6

12:11 Scourges with points or barbs, lit. *scorpions*
12:14 Lit. *scorpions*

19 So [R]Israel has been in rebellion against
the house of David to this day. 2 Kin. 17:21
20 Now it came to pass when all Israel heard
that Jeroboam had come back, they sent for
him and called him to the congregation, and
made him king over all Israel. There was none
who followed the house of David, but the tribe
of Judah only.
21 And when Rehoboam came to Jerusalem,
he assembled all the house of Judah with the
tribe of [R]Benjamin, one hundred and eighty
thousand chosen *men* who were warriors, to
fight against the house of Israel, that he might
restore the kingdom to Rehoboam the son of
Solomon. 2 Sam. 19:17
22 But [R]the word of God came to Shemaiah
the man of God, saying, 2 Chr. 11:2; 12:5–7
23 "Speak to Rehoboam the son of Solomon,
king of Judah, to all the house of Judah and
Benjamin, and to the rest of the people, say-
ing,
24 'Thus says the LORD: "You shall not go up
nor fight against your brethren the children
of Israel. Let every man return to his house,
[R]for this thing is from Me." ' " Therefore they
obeyed the word of the LORD, and turned back,
according to the word of the LORD. 1 Kin. 12:15

Sin of Jeroboam

25 Then Jeroboam built Shechem in the
mountains of Ephraim, and dwelt there. Also
he went out from there and built Penuel.
26 And Jeroboam said in his heart, "Now the
kingdom may return to the house of David:
27 "If these people [R]go up to offer sacrifices
in the house of the LORD at Jerusalem, then
the heart of this people will turn back to their
lord, Rehoboam king of Judah, and they will
kill me and go back to Rehoboam king of Ju-
dah." [Deut. 12:5–7, 14]
28 Therefore the king asked advice, made
two calves of gold, and said to the people, "It
is too much for you to go up to Jerusalem.
[R]Here are your gods, O Israel, which brought
you up from the land of Egypt!" Ex. 32:4, 8
29 And he set up one in [R]Bethel, and the
other he put in Dan. Gen. 28:19
30 Now this thing became [R]a sin, for the peo-
ple went *to worship* before the one as far as
Dan. 1 Kin. 13:34
31 He made shrines* on the high places,
[R]and made priests from every class of people,
who were not of the sons of Levi. 2 Kin. 17:32
32 Jeroboam ordained a feast on the fif-
teenth day of the eighth month, like the feast
that *was* in Judah, and offered sacrifices on
the altar. So he did at Bethel, sacrificing to the
calves that he had made. [R]And at Bethel he in-
stalled the priests of the high places which he
had made. Amos 7:10–13
33 So he made offerings on the altar which
he had made at Bethel on the fifteenth day
of the eighth month, in the month which he
had [R]devised in his own heart. And he [T]or-
dained a feast for the children of Israel, and
offered sacrifices on the altar and [R]burned
incense. Num. 15:39 • *instituted* • 1 Kin. 13:1

CHAPTER 13

Warning of the Prophet

AND behold, [R]a man of God went from Ju-
dah to Bethel by the word of the LORD,
[R]and Jeroboam stood by the altar to burn in-
cense. 2 Kin. 23:17 • 1 Kin. 12:32, 33
2 Then he cried out against the altar by
the word of the LORD, and said, "O altar,
altar! Thus says the LORD: 'Behold, a child,
[R]Josiah by name, shall be born to the house
of David; and on you he shall sacrifice the
priests of the high places who burn incense
on you, and men's bones shall be [R]burned on
you.' " 2 Kin. 23:15, 16 • [Lev. 26:30]
3 And he gave a sign the same day, saying,
"This *is* the sign which the LORD has spoken:
Surely the altar shall split apart, and the
ashes on it shall be poured out."
4 So it came to pass when King Jeroboam
heard the saying of the man of God, who cried
out against the altar in Bethel, that he
stretched out his hand from the altar, say-
ing, "Arrest him!" Then his hand, which he
stretched out toward him, withered, so that he
could not pull it back to himself.
5 The altar also was split apart, and the
ashes poured out from the altar, according to
the sign which the man of God had given by
the word of the LORD.
6 Then the king answered and said to the
man of God, "Please entreat the favor of the
LORD your God, and pray for me, that my
hand may be restored to me." So the man of
God entreated the LORD, and the king's hand
was restored to him, and became as before.

Sin of the Prophet

7 Then the king said to the man of God,
"Come home with me and refresh yourself,
and [R]I will give you a reward." 1 Sam. 9:7
8 But the man of God said to the king, [R]"If
you were to give me half your house, I would
not go in with you; nor would I eat bread nor
drink water in this place. Num. 22:18; 24:13
9 "For so it was commanded me by the
word of the LORD, saying, [R]'You shall not eat
bread, nor drink water, nor return by the same
way you came.' " [1 Cor. 5:11]
10 So he went another way and did not re-
turn by the way he came to Bethel.
11 Now an old prophet dwelt in Bethel, and
his sons came and told him all the works that
the man of God had done that day in Bethel;
they also told their father the words which he
had spoken to the king.

12:31 Lit. *a house;* cf. 1 Kin. 13:32, lit. houses

12 And their father said to them, "Which way did he go?" For his sons had seen* which way the man of God went who came from Judah.

13 Then he said to his sons, "Saddle the donkey for me." So they saddled the donkey for him; and he rode on it,

14 and went after the man of God, and found him sitting under an oak. Then he said to him, "*Are* you the man of God who came from Judah?" And he said, "I *am.*"

15 Then he said to him, "Come home with me and eat bread."

16 And he said, "I cannot return with you nor go in with you; neither can I eat bread nor drink water with you in this place.

17 "For [T]I have been told [R]by the word of the LORD, 'You shall not eat bread nor drink water there, nor return by going the way you came.' " Lit. *a command came to me by* • 1 Kin. 20:35

18 He said to him, "I too *am* a prophet as you *are,* and an angel spoke to me by the word of the LORD, saying, 'Bring him back with you to your house, that he may eat bread and drink water.' " (He was lying to him.)

19 So he went back with him, and ate bread in his house, and drank water.

Judgment on the Prophet

20 Now it happened, as they sat at the table, that the word of the LORD came to the prophet who had brought him back;

21 and he cried out to the man of God who came from Judah, saying, "Thus says the LORD: 'Because you have disobeyed the word of the LORD, and have not kept the commandment which the LORD your God commanded you,

22 'but you came back, ate bread, and drank water in the [R]place of which *the LORD* said to you, "Eat no bread and drink no water," your corpse shall not come to the tomb of your fathers.' " 1 Kin. 13:9

23 So it was, after he had eaten bread and after he had drunk, that he saddled the donkey for him, the prophet whom he had brought back.

24 When he was gone, a lion met him on the road and killed him. And his corpse was thrown on the road, and the donkey stood by it. The lion also stood by the corpse.

25 And there, men passed by and saw the corpse thrown on the road, and the lion standing by the corpse. Then they went and told *it* in the city where the old prophet dwelt.

26 Now when the prophet who had brought him back from the way heard *it,* he said, "It *is* the man of God who was disobedient to the word of the LORD. Therefore the LORD has delivered him to the lion, which has torn him and killed him, according to the word of the LORD which He spoke to him."

27 And he spoke to his sons, saying, "Saddle the donkey for me." So they saddled *it.*

28 Then he went and found his corpse thrown on the road, and the donkey and the lion standing by the corpse. The lion had not eaten the corpse nor torn the donkey.

29 And the prophet took up the corpse of the man of God, laid it on the donkey, and brought it back. So the old prophet came to the city to mourn, and to bury him.

30 Then he laid the corpse in his own tomb; and they mourned over him, *saying,* [R]"Alas, my brother!" Jer. 22:18

31 So it was, after he had buried him, that he spoke to his sons, saying, "When I am dead, then bury me in the tomb where the man of God *is* buried; [R]lay my bones beside his bones. 2 Kin. 23:17, 18

32 "For the [T]saying which he cried out by the word of the LORD against the altar in Bethel, and against all the shrines* on the high places which *are* in the cities of Samaria, will surely come to pass." Lit. *word*

Continued Sin of Jeroboam

33 [R]After this event Jeroboam did not turn from his evil way, but again he made priests from every class of people for the high places; whoever wished, he consecrated him, and he became *one* of the priests of the high places. 1 Kin. 12:31, 32

34 And this thing was the sin of the house of Jeroboam, so as to exterminate and destroy *it* from the face of the earth.

CHAPTER 14

Judgment on Jeroboam

AT that time Abijah the son of Jeroboam became sick.

2 And Jeroboam said to his wife, "Please arise, and disguise yourself, that they may not recognize you as the wife of Jeroboam, and go to Shiloh. Indeed, Ahijah the prophet *is* there, who told me that [R]*I would be* king over this people. 1 Kin. 11:29–31

3 "Also take with you ten loaves, *some* cakes, and a jar of honey, and go to him; he will tell you what will become of the child."

4 And Jeroboam's wife did so; she arose and went to Shiloh, and came to the house of Ahijah. But Ahijah could not see, for his eyes were glazed by reason of his age.

5 Now the LORD had said to Ahijah, "Here is the wife of Jeroboam, coming to ask you something about her son, for he *is* sick. Thus and thus you shall say to her; for it will be, when she comes in, that she will pretend *to be* another *woman.*"

6 And so it was, when Ahijah heard the sound of her footsteps as she came through the door, he said, "Come in, wife of Jeroboam. Why do you pretend *to be* another *person?* For I *have been* sent to you *with* bad *news.*

13:12 LXX, Syr., Tg., Vg. *showed him* **13:32** Lit. houses

7 "Go, tell Jeroboam, 'Thus says the LORD God of Israel: [R]"Because I exalted you from among the people, and made you ruler over My people Israel, 1 Kin. 16:2

8 "and [R]tore the kingdom away from the house of David, and gave it to you; and *yet* you have not been as My servant David, who kept My commandments and who followed Me with all his heart, to do only *what was* right in My eyes; 1 Kin. 11:31

9 "but you have done more evil than all who were before you, [R]for you have gone and made for yourself other gods and molded images to provoke Me to anger, and [R]have cast Me behind your back— 1 Kin. 12:28 • Ps. 50:17

10 "therefore behold! I will bring disaster on the house of Jeroboam, and will cut off from Jeroboam every male in Israel, [R]bond and free; I will take away the remnant of the house of Jeroboam, as one takes away refuse until it is all gone. Deut. 32:36

11 "The dogs shall eat [R]whoever belongs to Jeroboam and dies in the city, and the birds of the air shall eat whoever dies in the field; for the LORD has spoken!" ' 1 Kin. 16:4; 21:24

12 "Arise therefore, go to your own house. [R]When your feet enter the city, the child shall die. 1 Kin. 14:17

13 "And all Israel shall mourn for him and bury him, for he is the only one of Jeroboam who shall come to the grave, because in him there is found something good toward the LORD God of Israel in the house of Jeroboam.

14 [R]"Moreover the LORD will raise up for Himself a king over Israel who shall cut off the house of Jeroboam; this is the day. What? Even now! 1 Kin. 15:27–29

15 "For the LORD will strike Israel, as a reed is shaken in the water. He will [R]uproot Israel from this [R]good land which He gave to their fathers, and will scatter them [R]beyond the River,* because they have made their wooden images,* provoking the LORD to anger. 2 Kin. 17:6 • [Josh. 23:15, 16] • 2 Kin. 15:29

16 "And He will give Israel up because of the sins of Jeroboam, [R]who sinned and who made Israel sin." 1 Kin. 12:30; 13:34; 15:30, 34

17 Then Jeroboam's wife arose and departed, and came to [R]Tirzah. [R]When she came to the threshold of the house, the child died. Song 6:4 • 1 Kin. 14:12

18 And they buried him; and all Israel mourned for him, [R]according to the word of the LORD which He spoke through His servant Ahijah the prophet. 1 Kin. 14:13

19 Now the rest of the acts of Jeroboam, how he made war and how he reigned, indeed they *are* written in the book of the chronicles of the kings of Israel.

20 The period that Jeroboam reigned *was* twenty-two years. So he rested with his fathers. Then [R]Nadab his son reigned in his place. 1 Kin. 15:25

Sin of Rehoboam

21 And Rehoboam the son of Solomon reigned in Judah. [R]Rehoboam *was* forty-one years old when he became king. He reigned seventeen years in Jerusalem, the city [R]which the LORD had chosen out of all the tribes of Israel, to put His name there. His mother's name *was* Naamah, an Ammonitess. 2 Chr. 12:13 • 1 Kin. 11:32, 36

22 Now Judah did evil in the sight of the LORD, and they provoked Him to jealousy with their sins which they committed, more than all that their fathers had done.

23 For they also built for themselves [R]high places, [R]*sacred* pillars, and wooden images on every high hill and [R]under every green tree. Deut. 12:2 • [Deut. 16:22] • Is. 57:5

24 [R]And there were also perverted persons* in the land. They did according to all the [R]abominations of the nations which the LORD had cast out before the children of Israel. Deut. 23:17 • Deut. 20:18

Judgment on Rehoboam—2 Chr. 12:2–16

25 [R]It happened in the fifth year of King Rehoboam *that* Shishak king of Egypt came up against Jerusalem. 1 Kin. 11:40

26 [R]And he took away the treasures of the house of the LORD and the treasures of the king's house; he took away everything. He also took away all the gold shields which Solomon had made. 2 Chr. 12:9–11

27 Then King Rehoboam made bronze shields in their place, and [T]committed *them* to the hands of the captains of the [T]guard, who guarded the doorway of the king's house. *entrusted* • Lit. *runners*

28 And whenever the king entered the house of the LORD, the guards carried them, then brought them back into the guardroom.

29 [R]Now the rest of the acts of Rehoboam, and all that he did, *are* they not written in the book of the chronicles of the kings of Judah? 2 Chr. 12:15, 16

30 And there was [R]war between Rehoboam and Jeroboam all *their* days. 1 Kin. 12:21–24

31 [R]So Rehoboam rested with his fathers, and was buried with his fathers in the City of David. [R]His mother's name *was* Naamah, an Ammonitess. Then Abijam* his son reigned in his place. 2 Chr. 12:16 • 1 Kin. 14:21

CHAPTER 15

Reign of Abijam in Judah
2 Chr. 13:1, 2; 14:1

IN[R] the eighteenth year of King Jeroboam the son of Nebat, Abijam became king over Judah. 2 Chr. 13:1

14:15 The Euphrates • Heb. *Asherim*, Canaanite deities **14:24** Heb. *qadesh*, one practicing sodomy and prostitution in religious rituals **14:31** *Abijah*, 2 Chr. 12:16

2 He reigned three years in Jerusalem. His
mother's name *was* Maachah the grand-
daughter of [R]Abishalom. 2 Chr. 11:21
3 And he walked in all the sins of his father,
which he had done before him; his heart was
not loyal to the LORD his God, as was the heart
of his father David.
4 Nevertheless [R]for David's sake the LORD
his God gave him a lamp in Jerusalem, by set-
ting up his son after him and by establishing
Jerusalem; 2 Sam. 21:17
5 because David [R]did *what was* right in the
eyes of the LORD, and had not turned aside
from anything that He commanded him all
the days of his life, except in the matter of
Uriah the Hittite. 1 Kin. 9:4; 14:8
6 [R]And there was war between Rehoboam*
and Jeroboam all the days of his life. 1 Kin. 14:30
7 [R]Now the rest of the acts of Abijam, and
all that he did, *are* they not written in the book
of the chronicles of the kings of Judah? And
there was war between Abijam and Jero-
boam. 2 Chr. 13:2–22
8 [R]So Abijam rested with his fathers, and
they buried him in the City of David. Then
Asa his son reigned in his place. 2 Chr. 14:1

Obedience of Asa—2 Chr. 14:2; 15:16–18

9 In the twentieth year of Jeroboam king of
Israel, Asa became king over Judah.
10 And he reigned forty-one years in Jerusa-
lem. His grandmother's name *was* Maachah
the granddaughter of Abishalom.
11 Asa did *what was* right in the eyes of the
LORD, as *did* his father David.
12 And he banished the perverted persons*
from the land, and removed all the idols that
his fathers had made.
13 Also he removed Maachah his grand-
mother from *being* queen mother, because she
had made an obscene image of Asherah.* And
Asa cut down her obscene image and burned
it by the Brook Kidron.
14 [R]But the high places were not removed.
Nevertheless Asa's heart was loyal to the
LORD all his days. 1 Kin. 3:2; 22:43
15 He also brought into the house of the
LORD the things which his father had dedi-
cated, and the things which he himself had
dedicated: silver and gold and utensils.

Disobedience of Asa—2 Chr. 16:1–6

16 Now there was war between Asa and
Baasha king of Israel all their days.
17 And [R]Baasha king of Israel came up
against Judah, and built [R]Ramah, that he
might let none go out or come in to Asa king
of Judah. 2 Chr. 16:1–6 • Josh. 18:25
18 Then Asa took all the silver and gold *that*
was left in the treasuries of the house of the
LORD and the treasuries of the king's house,
and delivered them into the hand of his ser-
vants. And King Asa sent them to [R]Ben-
Hadad the son of Tabrimmon, the son of
Hezion, king of Syria, who dwelt in [R]Damas-
cus, saying, 2 Chr. 16:2 • 1 Kin. 11:23, 24
19 "*Let there be* a treaty between you and
me, as there was between my father and your
father. See, I have sent you a present of silver
and gold. Come and break your treaty with
Baasha king of Israel, so that he will with-
draw from me."
20 So Ben-Hadad heeded King Asa, and
[R]sent the captains of his armies against the
cities of Israel. He attacked [R]Ijon, Dan, Abel
Beth Maachah, and all Chinneroth, with all
the land of Naphtali. 1 Kin. 20:1 • 2 Kin. 15:29
21 Now it happened, when Baasha heard *it*,
that he stopped building Ramah, and re-
mained in [R]Tirzah. 1 Kin. 14:17; 16:15–18
22 [R]Then King Asa made a proclamation
throughout all Judah; none *was* exempted.
And they took away the stones and timber of
Ramah, which Baasha had used for building;
and with them King Asa built Geba of Benja-
min, and Mizpah. 2 Chr. 16:6

Death of Asa—2 Chr. 16:12—17:1

23 The rest of all the acts of Asa, all his
might, all that he did, and the cities which he
built, *are* they not written in the book of the
chronicles of the kings of Judah? But [R]in the
time of his old age he was diseased in his
feet. 2 Chr. 16:11–14
24 So Asa rested with his fathers, and was
buried with his fathers in the City of David his
father. [R]Then [R]Jehoshaphat his son reigned in
his place. 2 Chr. 17:1 • Matt. 1:8

Reign of Nadab in Israel

25 Now [R]Nadab the son of Jeroboam became
king over Israel in the second year of Asa
king of Judah, and he reigned over Israel two
years. 1 Kin. 14:20
26 And he did evil in the sight of the LORD,
and walked in the way of his father, and in his
sin by which he had made Israel sin.
27 Then Baasha the son of Ahijah, of the
house of Issachar, conspired against him. And
Baasha killed him at Gibbethon, which *be-*
longed to the Philistines, while Nadab and all
Israel laid siege to Gibbethon.
28 Baasha killed him in the third year of Asa
king of Judah, and reigned in his place.
29 And it was so, when he became king, *that*
he killed all the house of Jeroboam. He did
not leave to Jeroboam anyone that breathed,
until he had destroyed him, according to [R]the
word of the LORD which He had spoken by His
servant Ahijah the Shilonite, 1 Kin. 14:10–14
30 [R]because of the sins of Jeroboam, which

15:6 So with MT, LXX, Tg., Vg.; some Heb. mss., Syr. *Abijam* **15:12** Heb. *qedeshim*, those practicing sodomy and prostitution in religious rituals **15:13** A Canaanite goddess

he had sinned and by which he had made Is-
rael sin, because of his provocation with
which he had provoked the LORD God of Is-
rael to anger. 1 Kin. 14:9, 16
31 Now the rest of the acts of Nadab, and all
that he did, *are* they not written in the book of
the chronicles of the kings of Israel?

Reign of Baasha in Israel

32 And there was war between Asa and
Baasha king of Israel all their days.
33 In the third year of Asa king of Judah,
Baasha the son of Ahijah became king over
all Israel in Tirzah, and *reigned* twenty-four
years.
34 He did evil in the sight of the LORD, and
walked in the way of Jeroboam, and in his sin
by which he had made Israel sin.

CHAPTER 16

THEN the word of the LORD came to [R]Jehu
the son of [R]Hanani, against [R]Baasha, say-
ing: 2 Chr. 19:2; 20:34 • 2 Chr. 16:7–10 • 1 Kin. 15:27
2 "Inasmuch as I lifted you out of the dust
and made you ruler over My people Israel,
and you have walked in the way of Jeroboam,
and have made My people Israel sin, to pro-
voke Me to anger with their sins,
3 "surely I will [R]take away the posterity of
Baasha and the posterity of his house, and I
will make your house like the house of Jer-
oboam the son of Nebat. 1 Kin. 16:11; 21:21
4 "The dogs shall eat whoever belongs to
Baasha and dies in the city, and the birds of
the air shall eat whoever dies in the fields."
5 Now the rest of the acts of Baasha, what
he did, and his might, [R]*are* they not written in
the book of the chronicles of the kings of Is-
rael? 2 Chr. 16:11
6 So Baasha rested with his fathers and
was buried in [R]Tirzah. Then Elah his son
reigned in his place. 1 Kin. 14:17; 15:21
7 And also the word of the LORD came by
the prophet [R]Jehu the son of Hanani against
Baasha and his house, because of all the evil
that he did in the sight of the LORD in provok-
ing Him to anger with the work of his hands,
in being like the house of Jeroboam, and be-
cause he killed them. 1 Kin. 16:1

Reign of Elah in Israel

8 In the twenty-sixth year of Asa king of Ju-
dah, Elah the son of Baasha became king over
Israel, *and reigned* two years in Tirzah.
9 [R]Now his servant Zimri, commander of
half *his* chariots, conspired against him as he
was in Tirzah drinking himself drunk in the
house of Arza, [R]steward of *his* house in
Tirzah. 2 Kin. 9:30–33 • 1 Kin. 18:3
10 And Zimri went in and struck him and
killed him in the twenty-seventh year of Asa
king of Judah, and reigned in his place.
11 Then it came to pass, when he began to
reign, as soon as he was seated on his throne,
that he killed all the household of Baasha; he
did not leave him one male, neither of his rel-
atives nor of his friends.
12 Thus Zimri destroyed all the household of
Baasha, [R]according to the word of the LORD,
which He spoke against Baasha by Jehu the
prophet, 1 Kin. 16:3
13 for all the sins of Baasha and the sins of
Elah his son, by which they had sinned and by
which they had made Israel sin, in provoking
the LORD God of Israel to anger [R]with their
[T]idols. Deut. 32:21 • Lit. *vanities*
14 Now the rest of the acts of Elah, and all
that he did, *are* they not written in the book of
the chronicles of the kings of Israel?

Reign of Zimri in Israel

15 In the twenty-seventh year of Asa king of
Judah, Zimri had reigned in Tirzah seven
days. And the people *were* encamped
[R]against Gibbethon, which *belonged* to the
Philistines. 1 Kin. 15:27
16 Now the people *who were* encamped
heard it said, "Zimri has conspired and also
has killed the king." So all Israel made Omri,
the commander of the army, king over Israel
that day in the camp.
17 Then Omri and all Israel with him went
up from Gibbethon, and they besieged Tirzah.
18 And it happened, when Zimri saw that
the city was [T]taken, that he went into the
citadel of the king's house and burned the
king's house [T]down upon himself with fire,
and died, *captured* • Lit. *over him*
19 because of the sins which he had com-
mitted in doing evil in the sight of the LORD,
[R]in walking in the [R]way of Jeroboam, and in
his sin which he had committed to make Is-
rael sin. 1 Kin. 15:26, 34 • 1 Kin. 12:25–33
20 Now the rest of the acts of Zimri, and the
treason he committed, *are* they not written in
the book of the chronicles of the kings of Is-
rael?

Reign of Omri in Israel

21 Then the people of Israel were divided
into two parts: half of the people followed
Tibni the son of Ginath, to make him king,
and half followed Omri.
22 But the people who followed Omri pre-
vailed over the people who followed Tibni the
son of Ginath. So Tibni died and Omri reigned.
23 In the thirty-first year of Asa king of Ju-
dah, Omri became king over Israel, *and
reigned* twelve years. Six years he reigned in
[R]Tirzah. 1 Kin. 15:21
24 And he bought the hill of Samaria from
Shemer for two talents of silver; then he built
on the hill, and called the name of the city
which he built, Samaria, after the name of
Shemer, owner of the hill.

25 Omri did evil in the eyes of the LORD, and did worse than all who *were* before him.

26 For he walked in all the ways of Jeroboam the son of Nebat, and in his sin by which he had made Israel sin, provoking the LORD God of Israel to anger with their idols.

27 Now the rest of the acts of Omri which he did, and the might that he showed, *are* they not written in the book of the chronicles of the kings of Israel?

28 So Omri rested with his fathers and was buried in Samaria. Then Ahab his son reigned in his place.

Sin of Ahab

29 In the thirty-eighth year of Asa king of Judah, Ahab the son of Omri became king over Israel; and Ahab the son of Omri reigned over Israel in Samaria twenty-two years.

30 Now Ahab the son of Omri did evil in the sight of the LORD, more than all who *were* before him.

31 And it came to pass, as though it had been a trivial thing for him to walk in the sins of Jeroboam the son of Nebat, [R]that he took as wife Jezebel the daughter of Ethbaal, king of the Sidonians; and he went and served Baal and worshiped him. Deut. 7:3

32 Then he set up an altar for Baal in [R]the temple of Baal, which he had built in Samaria. 2 Kin. 10:21, 26, 27

33 [R]And Ahab made a wooden image.* Ahab did more to provoke the LORD God of Israel to anger than all the kings of Israel who were before him. 2 Kin. 13:6

34 In his days Hiel of Bethel built Jericho. He laid its foundation with Abiram his firstborn, and with his youngest *son* Segub he set up its gates, according to the word of the LORD, which He had spoken through Joshua the son of Nun.*

CHAPTER 17

Prophecy of the Drought

AND Elijah the Tishbite, of the inhabitants of Gilead, said to Ahab, "*As* the LORD God of Israel lives, before whom I stand, there shall not be dew nor rain these years, except at my word."

Miracle of Food

2 Then the word of the LORD came to him, saying,

3 "Get away from here and turn eastward, and hide by the Brook Cherith, which flows into the Jordan.

4 "And it will be *that* you shall drink from the brook, and I have commanded the [R]ravens to feed you there." Job 38:41

5 So he went and did according to the word of the LORD, for he went and stayed by the Brook Cherith, which flows into the Jordan.

6 The ravens brought him bread and meat in the morning, and bread and meat in the evening; and he drank from the brook.

7 And it happened after a while that the brook dried up, because there had been no rain in the land.

8 Then the word of the LORD came to him, saying,

9 "Arise, go to Zarephath, which *belongs* to Sidon, and dwell there. See, I have commanded a widow there to provide for you."

10 So he arose and went to Zarephath. And when he came to the gate of the city, indeed a widow *was* there gathering sticks. And he called to her and said, "Please bring me a little water in a cup, that I may drink."

11 And as she was going to get *it*, he called to her and said, "Please bring me a morsel of bread in your hand."

12 So she said, "As the LORD your God lives, I do not have bread, only a handful of flour in a bin, and a little oil in a jar; and see, I *am* gathering a couple of sticks that I may go in and prepare it for myself and my son, that we may eat it, and die."

13 And Elijah said to her, "Do not fear; go *and* do as you have said, but make me a small cake from it first, and bring *it* to me; and afterward make *some* for yourself and your son.

14 "For thus says the LORD God of Israel: 'The bin of flour shall not be used up, nor shall the jar of oil run dry, until the day the LORD sends rain on the earth.' "

15 So she went away and did according to the word of Elijah; and she and he and her household ate for *many* days.

16 The bin of flour was not used up, nor did the jar of oil run dry, according to the word of the LORD which He spoke by Elijah.

Miracle of the Resurrection of the Gentile Son

17 Now it happened after these things *that* the son of the woman who owned the house became sick. And his sickness was so serious that there was no breath left in him.

18 So she said to Elijah, [R]"What have I to do with you, O man of God? Have you come to me to bring my sin to remembrance, and to kill my son?" Luke 5:8

19 And he said to her, "Give me your son." So he took him out of her arms and carried him to the upper room where he was staying, and laid him on his own bed.

20 Then he cried out to the LORD and said, "O LORD my God, have You also brought tragedy on the widow with whom I lodge, by killing her son?"

21 And he stretched himself out on the child three times, and cried out to the LORD and said, "O LORD my God, I pray, let this child's soul come back to him."

16:33 Heb. *Asherah*, a Canaanite goddess **16:34** Cf. Josh. 6:26

22 Then the LORD heard the voice of Elijah; and the soul of the child came back to him, and he [R]revived. Heb. 11:35

23 And Elijah took the child and brought him down from the upper room into the house, and gave him to his mother. And Elijah said, "See, your son lives!"

24 Then the woman said to Elijah, "Now by this [R]I know that you *are* a man of God, *and* that the word of the LORD in your mouth *is* the truth." John 2:11; 3:2; 16:30

CHAPTER 18

Challenge to Ahab

AND it came to pass *after* many days that the word of the LORD came to Elijah, in the third year, saying, "Go, present yourself to Ahab, and I will send rain on the earth."

2 So Elijah went to present himself to Ahab; and *there was* a severe famine in Samaria.

3 And Ahab had called Obadiah, who *was* [T]in charge of *his* house. (Now Obadiah feared the LORD greatly. Lit. *over the house*

4 For so it was, while Jezebel [T]massacred the prophets of the LORD, that Obadiah had taken one hundred prophets and hidden them, fifty to a cave, and had fed them with bread and water.) Lit. *cut off*

5 And Ahab had said to Obadiah, "Go into the land to all the springs of water and to all the brooks; perhaps we may find grass to keep the horses and mules alive, so that we will not have to kill any livestock."

6 So they divided the land between them to explore it; Ahab went one way by himself, and Obadiah went another way by himself.

7 Now as Obadiah was on his way, suddenly Elijah met him; and he [R]recognized him, and fell on his face, and said, "*Is* that you, my lord Elijah?" 2 Kin. 1:6–8

8 And he answered him, "*It is* I. Go, tell your master, 'Elijah *is here.*' "

9 So he said, "How have I sinned, that you are delivering your servant into the hand of Ahab, to kill me?

10 "*As* the LORD your God lives, there is no nation or kingdom where my master has not sent someone to hunt for you; and when they said, '*He is* not *here,*' he took an oath from the kingdom or nation that they could not find you.

11 "And now you say, 'Go, tell your master, "Elijah *is here*" '!

12 "And it shall come to pass, *as soon as* I am gone from you, that the Spirit of the LORD will carry you to a place I do not know; so when I go and tell Ahab, and he cannot find you, he will kill me. But I your servant have feared the LORD from my youth.

13 "Was it not reported to my lord what I did when Jezebel killed the prophets of the LORD, how I hid one hundred men of the LORD's prophets, fifty to a cave, and fed them with bread and water?

14 "And now you say, 'Go, tell your master, "Elijah *is here.*" ' He will kill me!"

15 Then Elijah said, "*As* the LORD of hosts lives, before whom I stand, I will surely present myself to him today."

16 So Obadiah went to meet Ahab, and told him; and Ahab went to meet Elijah.

17 Then it happened, when Ahab saw Elijah, that Ahab said to him, [R]"*Is that* you, O [R]troubler of Israel?" 1 Kin. 21:20 • Josh. 7:25

18 And he answered, "I have not troubled Israel, but you and your father's house *have,* [R]in that you have forsaken the commandments of the LORD and have followed the Baals. [2 Chr. 15:2]

19 "Now therefore, send *and* gather all Israel to me on [R]Mount Carmel, the four hundred and fifty prophets of Baal, [R]and the four hundred prophets of Asherah,* who eat at Jezebel's table." Josh. 19:26 • 1 Kin. 16:33

Victory on Mount Carmel

20 So Ahab sent for all the children of Israel, and [R]gathered the prophets together on Mount Carmel. 1 Kin. 22:6

21 And Elijah came to all the people, and said, [R]"How long will you falter between two opinions? If the LORD *is* God, follow Him; but if Baal, follow him." But the people answered him not a word. [Matt. 6:24]

18:19 A Canaanite goddess

18:21 Cure for Doubt—The cure for doubt depends to some extent on the thing doubted. However, the real problem is not in the object doubted but in the subject who doubts. Therefore, the following steps should be taken by the doubting Christian:

a. Confess the doubt to God as sin. Doubt is basically unbelief in God and His Word and is therefore sin (Page 1161—Rom. 14:23; Page 1265—Heb. 11:6). God has promised to hear our confession of even the darkest unbelief.

b. Study the evidence for the Christian faith. Christians have nothing to fear by looking into the facts from any source of knowledge. The greatest evidence for the validity of Christianity, the resurrection of Christ, is attested by many proofs. Among these are the empty tomb, post-Resurrection appearances, and transformed disciples. Since the Resurrection is true, it verifies everything the Bible says.

c. Make certain of your salvation. Paul exhorts Christians to examine themselves to make sure they are Christians (Page 1192—2 Cor. 13:5). So did the author of Heb. (Page 1261—Heb. 6:1–9). Salvation from sin is by simple trust in Jesus Christ. Until you are assured of your salvation you will be troubled by enormous doubts.

(continued on next page)

22 Then Elijah said to the people, "I alone am left a prophet of the LORD; but Baal's prophets *are* four hundred and fifty men.

23 "Therefore let them give us two bulls; and let them choose one bull for themselves, cut it in pieces, and lay *it* on the wood, but put no fire *under it;* and I will prepare the other bull, and lay *it* on the wood, but put no fire *under it.*

24 "Then you call on the name of your gods, and I will call on the name of the LORD; and the God who [R]answers by fire, He is God." So all the people answered and said, "It is well spoken." 1 Chr. 21:26

25 Now Elijah said to the prophets of Baal, "Choose one bull for yourselves and prepare *it* first, for you *are* many; and call on the name of your god, but put no fire *under it.*"

26 So they took the bull which was given them, and they prepared *it,* and called on the name of Baal from morning even till noon, saying, "O Baal, [T]hear us!" But *there was* [R]no voice; no one answered. Then they leaped about the altar which they had made. *answer* • Jer. 10:5

27 And so it was, at noon, that Elijah mocked them and said, "Cry [T]aloud, for he *is* a god; either he is meditating, or he is busy, or he is on a journey, *or* perhaps he is sleeping and must be awakened." *with a loud voice*

28 So they cried aloud, and [R]cut themselves, as was their custom, with [T]knives and lances, until the blood gushed out on them. [Deut. 14:1] • *swords*

29 And when midday was past, [R]they prophesied until the *time* of the offering of the *evening* sacrifice. But *there was* [R]no voice; no one answered, no one paid attention. Ex. 29:39, 41 • 1 Kin. 18:26

30 Then Elijah said to all the people, "Come near to me." So all the people came near to him. [R]And he repaired the altar of the LORD *that was* broken down. 2 Chr. 33:16

31 And Elijah took twelve stones, according to the number of the tribes of the sons of Jacob, to whom the word of the LORD had come, saying, "Israel shall be your name."*

32 Then with the stones he built an altar [R]in the name of the LORD; and he made a trench around the altar large enough to hold two seahs of seed. [Col. 3:17]

33 And he [R]put the wood in order, cut the bull in pieces, and laid *it* on the wood, and said, "Fill four waterpots with water, and [R]pour *it* on the burnt sacrifice and on the wood." Lev. 1:6–8 • Judg. 6:20

34 Then he said, "Do *it* a second time," and they did *it* a second time; and he said, "Do *it* a third time," and they did *it* a third time.

35 So the water ran all around the altar; and he also filled the trench with water.

36 And it came to pass, at *the time of* the offering of the *evening* sacrifice, that Elijah the prophet came near and said, "LORD [R]God of Abraham, Isaac, and Israel, let it be known this day that You *are* God in Israel and I *am* Your servant, and *that* I have done all these things at Your word. Ex. 3:6; 4:5

37 "Hear me, O LORD, hear me, that this people may know that You *are* the LORD God, and *that* You have turned their hearts back *to You* again."

38 Then [R]the fire of the LORD fell and consumed the burnt sacrifice, and the wood and the stones and the dust, and it licked up the water that *was* in the trench. 1 Chr. 21:26

39 Now when all the people saw *it,* they fell on their faces; and they said, "The LORD, He *is* God! The LORD, He *is* God!"

40 And Elijah said to them, "Seize the prophets of Baal! Do not let one of them escape!" So they seized them; and Elijah brought them down to the Brook [R]Kishon and executed them there. Judg. 4:7; 5:21

Miracle of the Rain

41 Then Elijah said to Ahab, "Go up, eat and drink; for *there is* the sound of abundance of rain."

42 So Ahab went up to eat and drink. And Elijah went up to the top of Carmel; [R]then he bowed down on the ground, and put his face between his knees, James 5:17, 18

43 and said to his servant, "Go up now, look toward the sea." So he went up and looked, and said, "*There is* nothing." And seven times he said, "Go again."

44 Then it came to pass the seventh *time,* that he said, "There is a cloud, as small as a man's hand, rising out of the sea!" So he said, "Go up, say to Ahab, [T]'Prepare *your chariot,* and go down before the rain stops you.' " Lit. *Bind* or *Harness*

45 Now it happened in the meantime that the

18:31 Gen. 32:28

(continued from previous page)

d. Faithfully study the Word of God. "Faith *comes* by hearing, and hearing by the word of God" (Page 1157—Rom. 10:17).Through study and application of the Bible, our faith is strengthened and matured. Most especially, we must master the doctrines or basic teachings of the Bible if we are to be stable, mature Christians (Page 1239—1 Tim. 4:13, 16; Page 1245—2 Tim. 3:16; Page 1250—Titus 2:1, 10).

e. Pray. The surest way to face doubts when they come is to have an extensive past history of answered prayer. The more a Christian prays with faith, the more that Christian sees God answer prayer; the more a person sees God answer prayer, the stronger that person's faith becomes while the doubt becomes less.

Now turn to Page 1282—1 Pet. 3:17: Kinds of Suffering.

sky became black with clouds and wind, and there was a heavy rain. So Ahab rode away and went to Jezreel.

46 Then the hand of the LORD came upon Elijah; and he girded up his loins and ran ahead of Ahab to the entrance of Jezreel.

CHAPTER 19

Elijah Flees from Jezebel

AND Ahab told Jezebel all that Elijah had done, also how he had [R]executed all the prophets with the sword. 1 Kin. 18:40

2 Then Jezebel sent a messenger to Elijah, saying, [R]"So let the gods do *to me,* and more also, if I do not make your life as the life of one of them by tomorrow about this time." Ruth 1:17

3 And when he saw *that,* he arose and ran for his life, and went to Beersheba, which *belongs* to Judah, and left his servant there.

Elijah Desires to Die

4 But he himself went a day's journey into the wilderness, and came and sat down under a [T]broom tree. And he [R]prayed that he might die, and said, "It is enough! Now, LORD, take my life, for I *am* no better than my fathers!" *juniper* • Num. 11:15

5 Then as he lay and slept under a broom tree, suddenly an angel* touched him, and said to him, "Arise *and* eat."

6 Then he looked, and there by his head *was* a cake baked on [T]coals, and a jar of water. So he ate and drank, and lay down again. *hot stones*

7 And the angel* of the LORD came back the second time, and touched him, and said, "Arise *and* eat, because the journey *is* too great for you."

8 So he arose, and ate and drank; and he went in the strength of that food forty days and [R]forty nights as far as [R]Horeb, the mountain of God. Matt. 4:2 • Ex. 3:1; 4:27

Elijah Has Self-Pity

9 And there he went into a cave, and spent the night in that place; and behold, the word of the LORD *came* to him, and He said to him, "What are you doing here, Elijah?"

10 So he said, [R]"I have been very [R]zealous for the LORD God of hosts; for the children of Israel have forsaken Your covenant, torn down Your altars, and killed Your prophets with the sword. I alone am left; and they seek to take my life." Rom. 11:3 • Ps. 69:9

11 Then He said, "Go out, and stand [R]on the mountain before the LORD." And behold, the LORD [R]passed by, and a great and strong wind tore into the mountains and broke the rocks in pieces before the LORD, *but* the LORD *was* not in the wind; and after the wind an earthquake, *but* the LORD *was* not in the earthquake; Ex. 19:20; 24:12, 18 • Ex. 33:21, 22

12 and after the earthquake a fire, *but* the LORD *was* not in the fire; and after the fire [T]a still small voice. *a delicate whispering voice*

13 So it was, when Elijah heard *it,* that [R]he wrapped his face in his mantle and went out and stood in the entrance of the cave. Suddenly a voice *came* to him, and said, "What are you doing here, Elijah?" Ex. 3:6

14 [R]And he said, "I have been very zealous for the LORD God of hosts; because the children of Israel have forsaken Your covenant, torn down Your altars, and killed Your prophets with the sword. I alone am left; and they seek to take my life." 1 Kin. 19:10

15 Then the LORD said to him: "Go, return on your way to the Wilderness of Damascus; [R]and when you arrive, anoint Hazael *as* king over Syria. 2 Kin. 8:8–15

16 "Also you shall anoint Jehu the son of Nimshi *as* king over Israel. And Elisha the son of Shaphat of Abel Meholah you shall anoint *as* prophet in your place.

17 "It shall be *that* whoever escapes the sword of Hazael, Jehu will kill; and whoever escapes the sword of Jehu, Elisha will kill.

18 [R]"Yet I have reserved seven thousand in Israel, all whose knees have not bowed to Baal, [R]and every mouth that has not kissed him." Rom. 11:4 • Hos. 13:2

Call of Elisha

19 So he departed from there, and found Elisha the son of Shaphat, who *was* plowing *with* twelve yoke *of oxen* before him, and he was with the twelfth. Then Elijah passed by him and threw his mantle on him.

20 And he left the oxen and ran after Elijah, and said, [R]"Please let me kiss my father and my mother, and *then* I will follow you." And he said to him, "Go back again, for what have I done to you?" [Matt. 8:21, 22]

21 So *Elisha* turned back from him, and took a yoke of oxen and slaughtered them and [R]boiled their flesh, using the oxen's equipment, and gave it to the people, and they ate. Then he arose and followed Elijah, and became his servant. 2 Sam. 24:22

CHAPTER 20

First Victory over Syria

NOW [R]Ben-Hadad the king of Syria gathered all his forces together; thirty-two kings *were* with him, with horses and chariots. And he went up and besieged Samaria, and made war against it. 2 Kin. 6:24

2 Then he sent messengers into the city to Ahab king of Israel, and said to him, "Thus says Ben-Hadad:

19:5 Or *Angel* **19:7** Or *Angel*

3 'Your silver and your gold *are* mine; your loveliest wives and children are mine.' "

4 And the king of Israel answered and said, "My lord, O king, just as you say, I and all that I have *are* yours."

5 Then the messengers came back and said, "Thus speaks Ben-Hadad, saying, 'Indeed I have sent to you, saying, "You shall deliver to me your silver and your gold, your wives and your children";

6 'but I will send my servants to you tomorrow about this time, and they shall search your house and the houses of your servants. And it shall be, *that* whatever is [T]pleasant in your eyes, they will put in their hands and take *it*.' " *pleasing*

7 So the king of Israel called all the elders of the land, and said, "Notice, please, and see how this *man* seeks trouble, for he sent to me for my wives, my children, my silver, and my gold; and I did not deny him."

8 And all the elders and all the people said to him, "Do not listen or consent."

9 Therefore he said to the messengers of Ben-Hadad, "Tell my lord the king, 'All that you sent for to your servant the first time I will do, but this thing I cannot do.' " And the messengers departed and brought back word to him.

10 Then Ben-Hadad sent to him and said, "The gods do so to me, and more also, if enough dust is left of Samaria for a handful for each of the people who follow me."

11 So the king of Israel answered and said, "Tell *him*, 'Let not the one who puts on *his armor* boast like the one who takes *it off*.' "

12 And it happened when *Ben-Hadad* heard this message, as he and the kings *were* drinking at the command post, that he said to his servants, "Get ready." And they got ready to attack the city.

13 Suddenly a prophet approached Ahab king of Israel, saying, "Thus says the LORD: 'Have you seen all this great multitude? Behold, I will deliver it into your hand today, and you shall know that I *am* the LORD.' "

14 So Ahab said, "By whom?" And he said, "Thus says the LORD: 'By the young leaders of the provinces.' " Then he said, "Who will set the battle in order?" And he answered, "You."

15 Then he mustered the young leaders of the provinces, and there were two hundred and thirty-two; and after them he mustered all the people, all the children of Israel—seven thousand.

16 So they went out at noon. Meanwhile Ben-Hadad and the thirty-two kings helping him were [R]getting drunk at the command post. 1 Kin. 16:9; 20:12

17 The young leaders of the provinces went out first. And Ben-Hadad sent out *a patrol*, and they told him, saying, "Men are coming out of Samaria!"

18 So he said, "If they have come out for peace, take them alive; and if they have come out for war, take them alive."

19 Then these young leaders of the provinces went out of the city with the army which followed them.

20 And each one killed his man; so the Syrians fled, and Israel pursued them; and Ben-Hadad the king of Syria escaped on a horse with the cavalry.

21 Then the king of Israel went out and attacked the horses and chariots, and killed the Syrians with a great slaughter.

Second Victory over Syria

22 And the prophet came to the king of Israel and said to him, "Go, strengthen yourself; take note, and see what you should do, for in the spring of the year the king of Syria will come up against you."

23 Then the servants of the king of Syria said to him, "Their gods *are* gods of the hills. Therefore they were stronger than we; but if we fight against them in the plain, surely we will be stronger than they.

24 "So do this thing: Dismiss the kings, each from his position, and put captains in their [T]places; *positions*

25 "and you shall muster an army like the army [T]that you have lost, horse for horse and chariot for chariot. Then we will fight against them in the plain; surely we will be stronger than they." And he listened to their voice and did so. Lit. *that fell from you*

26 So it was, in the spring of the year, that Ben-Hadad mustered the Syrians and went up to Aphek to fight against Israel.

27 And the children of Israel were mustered and given provisions, and they went against them. Now the children of Israel encamped before them like two little flocks of goats, while the Syrians filled the [R]countryside. Judg. 6:3–5

28 Then a man of God came and spoke to the king of Israel, and said, "Thus says the LORD: 'Because the Syrians have said, "The LORD *is* God of the hills, but He *is* not God of the valleys," therefore I will deliver all this great multitude into your hand, and you shall know that I *am* the LORD.' "

29 And they encamped opposite each other for seven days. So it was that on the seventh day the battle was joined; and the children of Israel killed one hundred thousand foot soldiers *of* the Syrians in one day.

30 But the rest fled to Aphek, into the city; then a wall fell on twenty-seven thousand of the men *who were* left. And Ben-Hadad fled and went into the city, into an inner chamber.

31 Then his servants said to him, "Look now, we have heard that the kings of the house of Israel *are* merciful kings. Please, let us [R]put sackcloth around our waists and ropes around our heads, and go out to the king of Israel; perhaps he will spare your life." Gen. 37:34

32 So they wore sackcloth around their waists and *put* ropes around their heads, and came to the king of Israel and said, "Your servant Ben-Hadad says, 'Please let me live.' " And he said, "*Is* he still alive? He *is* my brother."

33 Now the men were watching closely to see whether *any sign of mercy would come* from him; and they quickly grasped *at this word* and said, "Your brother Ben-Hadad." So he said, "Go, bring him." Then Ben-Hadad came out to him; and he had him come up into the chariot.

34 So *Ben-Hadad* said to him, "The cities which my father took from your father I will restore; and you may set up marketplaces for yourself in Damascus, as my father did in Samaria." Then *Ahab said,* "I will send you away with this treaty." So he made a treaty with him and sent him away.

35 Now a certain man of [R]the sons of the prophets said to his neighbor by the word of the LORD, "Strike me, please." And the man refused to strike him. 2 Kin. 2:3, 5, 7, 15

36 Then he said to him, "Because you have not obeyed the voice of the LORD, surely, as soon as you depart from me, a lion shall kill you." And as soon as he left him, [R]a lion found him and killed him. 1 Kin. 13:24

37 And he found another man, and said, "Strike me, please." So the man struck him, inflicting a wound.

38 Then the prophet departed and waited for the king by the road, and disguised himself with a bandage over his eyes.

39 Now as the king passed by, he cried out to the king and said, "Your servant went out into the midst of the battle; and there, a man came over and brought a man to me, and said, 'Guard this man; if by any means he is missing, your life shall be for his life, or else you shall pay a talent of silver.'

40 "While your servant was busy here and there, he was gone." Then the king of Israel said to him, "So *shall* your judgment *be;* you yourself have decided *it.*"

41 And he hastened to take the bandage away from his eyes; and the king of Israel recognized him as one of the prophets.

42 Then he said to him, "Thus says the LORD: 'Because you have let slip out of *your* hand a man whom I appointed to utter destruction, therefore your life shall go for his life, and your people for his people.' "

43 So the king of Israel went to his house sullen and displeased, and came to Samaria.

CHAPTER 21

Murder of Naboth

AND it came to pass after these things *that* Naboth the Jezreelite had a vineyard which *was* in [R]Jezreel, next to the palace of Ahab king of Samaria. 1 Kin. 18:45, 46

2 So Ahab spoke to Naboth, saying, "Give me your vineyard, that I may have it for a vegetable garden, because it *is* near, next to my house; and for it I will give you a vineyard better than it. *Or,* if it seems good to you, I will give you its worth in money."

3 But Naboth said to Ahab, "The LORD forbid [R]that I should give the inheritance of my fathers to you!" [Num. 36:7]

4 So Ahab went into his house sullen and displeased because of the word which Naboth the Jezreelite had spoken to him; for he had said, "I will not give you the inheritance of my fathers." And he lay down on his bed, and turned away his face, and would eat no food.

5 But [R]Jezebel his wife came to him, and said to him, "Why is your spirit so sullen that you eat no food?" 1 Kin. 19:1, 2

6 He said to her, "Because I spoke to Naboth the Jezreelite, and said to him, 'Give me your vineyard for money; or else, if it pleases you, I will give you *another* vineyard for it.' And he answered, 'I will not give you my vineyard.' "

7 Then Jezebel his wife said to him, "You now exercise authority over Israel! Arise, eat food, and let your heart be cheerful; I will give you the vineyard of Naboth the Jezreelite."

8 And she wrote letters in Ahab's name, sealed *them* with his seal, and sent the letters to the elders and the nobles who *were* dwelling in the city with Naboth.

9 She wrote in the letters, saying,

Proclaim a fast, and seat Naboth with
high honor among the people;
10 and seat two men, scoundrels, before
him to bear witness against him, saying,
"You have [R]blasphemed God and the
king." *Then* take him out, and stone him,
that he may die. [Ex. 22:28]

11 So the men of his city, the elders and nobles who were inhabitants of his city, did as Jezebel had sent to them, as it *was* written in the letters which she had sent to them.

12 They proclaimed a fast, and seated Naboth with high honor among the people.

13 And two men, scoundrels, came in and sat before him; and the scoundrels witnessed against him, against Naboth, in the presence of the people, saying, "Naboth has blasphemed God and the king!" [R]Then they took him outside the city and stoned him with stones, so that he died. 2 Kin. 9:26

14 Then they sent to Jezebel, saying, "Naboth has been stoned and is dead."

15 And it came to pass, when Jezebel heard that Naboth had been stoned and was dead, that Jezebel said to Ahab, "Arise, take possession of the vineyard of Naboth the Jezreelite, which he refused to give you for money; for Naboth is not alive, but dead."

16 So it was, when Ahab heard that Naboth was dead, that Ahab got up and went down to take possession of the vineyard of Naboth the Jezreelite.

Prediction of Ahab's Death

17 [R]Then the word of the LORD came to [R]Elijah the Tishbite, saying, [Ps. 9:12] • 1 Kin. 19:1

18 "Arise, go down to meet Ahab king of Israel, [R]who *lives* in Samaria. There *he is,* in the vineyard of Naboth, where he has gone down to take possession of it. 2 Chr. 22:9

19 "You shall speak to him, saying, 'Thus says the LORD: "Have you murdered and also taken possession?" ' And you shall speak to him, saying, 'Thus says the LORD: "In the place where dogs licked the blood of Naboth, dogs shall lick your blood, even yours." ' "

20 So Ahab said to Elijah, "Have you found me, O my enemy?" And he answered, "I have found *you,* because you have sold yourself to do evil in the sight of the LORD:

21 'Behold, [R]I will bring calamity on you. I will take away your [R]posterity, and will cut off from Ahab every male in Israel, both bond and free. 1 Kin. 14:10 • 2 Kin. 10:10

22 'I will make your house like the house of Jeroboam the son of Nebat, and like the house of Baasha the son of Ahijah, because of the provocation with which you have provoked *Me* to anger, and made Israel sin.'

23 "And [R]concerning Jezebel the LORD also spoke, saying, 'The dogs shall eat Jezebel by the wall* of Jezreel.' 2 Kin. 9:10, 30–37

24 "The dogs shall eat whoever belongs to Ahab and dies in the city, and the birds of the air shall eat whoever dies in the field."

25 But [R]there was no one like Ahab who sold himself to do wickedness in the sight of the LORD, [R]because Jezebel his wife stirred him up. 1 Kin. 16:30–33; 21:20 • 1 Kin. 16:31

26 And he behaved very abominably in following idols, according to all [R]*that* the Amorites had done, whom the LORD had cast out before the children of Israel. 2 Kin. 21:11

27 So it was, when Ahab heard those words, that he tore his clothes and put sackcloth on his body, and fasted and lay in sackcloth, and went about mourning.

28 And the word of the LORD came to Elijah the Tishbite, saying,

29 "See how Ahab has humbled himself before Me? Because he [R]has humbled himself before Me, I will not bring the calamity in his days. In the days of his son I will bring the calamity on his house." [2 Kin. 22:19]

CHAPTER 22

Promise of Victory by the False Prophets
2 Chr. 18:2–11

NOW three years passed without war between Syria and Israel.

2 Then it came to pass, in the third year, that [R]Jehoshaphat the king of Judah went down to *visit* the king of Israel. 2 Chr. 18:2

3 And the king of Israel said to his servants, "Do you know that [R]Ramoth in Gilead *is* ours, but we hesitate to take it out of the hand of the king of Syria?" Deut. 4:43

4 So he said to Jehoshaphat, "Will you go with me to fight at Ramoth Gilead?" Jehoshaphat said to the king of Israel, [R]"I *am* as you *are,* my people as your people, my horses as your horses." 2 Kin. 3:7

5 Also Jehoshaphat said to the king of Israel, [R]"Please inquire for the word of the LORD today." 2 Kin. 3:11

6 Then the king of Israel [R]gathered the prophets together, about four hundred men, and said to them, "Shall I go against Ramoth Gilead to fight, or shall I refrain?" So they said, "Go up, for the Lord will deliver *it* into the hand of the king." 1 Kin. 18:19

7 And [R]Jehoshaphat said, "*Is there* not still a prophet of the LORD here, that we may inquire of Him?"* 2 Kin. 3:11

8 So the king of Israel said to Jehoshaphat, "*There is* still one man, Micaiah the son of Imlah, by whom we may inquire of the LORD; but I hate him, because he does not prophesy good concerning me, but evil." And Jehoshaphat said, "Let not the king say such things!"

9 Then the king of Israel called an officer and said, "Bring Micaiah the son of Imlah quickly!"

10 The king of Israel and Jehoshaphat the king of Judah, having put on *their* robes, sat each on his throne, at a threshing floor at the entrance of the gate of Samaria; and all the prophets prophesied before them.

11 Now Zedekiah the son of Chenaanah had made [R]horns of iron for himself; and he said, "Thus says the LORD: 'With these you shall [R]gore the Syrians until they are destroyed.' " Zech. 1:18–21 • Deut. 33:17

12 And all the prophets prophesied so, saying, "Go up to Ramoth Gilead and prosper, for the LORD will deliver *it* into the king's hand."

Promise of Defeat by Micaiah
2 Chr. 18:12–27

13 Then the messenger who had gone to call Micaiah spoke to him, saying, "Now listen, the words of the prophets with one accord encourage the king. Please, let your word be like the word of one of them, and speak encouragement."

14 And Micaiah said, "*As* the LORD lives, [R]whatever the LORD says to me, that I will speak." Num. 22:38; 24:13

21:23 So with MT, LXX; some Heb. mss., Syr., Tg., Vg. *plot of ground* instead of *wall* (cf. 2 Kin. 9:36)
22:7 Or *him*

15 Then he came to the king; and the king
said to him, "Micaiah, shall we go to war
against Ramoth Gilead, or shall we refrain?"
And he answered him, "Go and prosper, for
the LORD will deliver *it* into the hand of the
king!"
16 So the king said to him, "How many times
shall I make you swear that you tell me noth-
ing but the truth in the name of the LORD?"
17 Then he said, "I saw all Israel [R]scattered
on the mountains, as sheep that have no
shepherd. And the LORD said, 'These have no
master. Let each return to his house in
peace.'" Matt. 9:36
18 And the king of Israel said to Je-
hoshaphat, "Did I not tell you he would not
prophesy good concerning me, but evil?"
19 Then *Micaiah* said, "Therefore hear the
word of the LORD: [R]I saw the LORD sitting on
His throne, [R]and all the host of heaven
standing by, on His right hand and on His
left. Is. 6:1 • Dan. 7:10
20 "And the LORD said, 'Who will persuade
Ahab to go up, that he may fall at Ramoth
Gilead?' So one spoke in this manner, and an-
other spoke in that manner.
21 "Then a spirit came forward and stood be-
fore the LORD, and said, 'I will persuade him.'
22 "The LORD said to him, 'In what way?' So
he said, 'I will go out and be a lying spirit in
the mouth of all his prophets.' And the LORD
said, [R]'You shall persuade *him*, and also pre-
vail. Go out and do so.' Judg. 9:23
23 [R]"Therefore look! The LORD has put a
lying spirit in the mouth of all these prophets
of yours, and the LORD has declared disaster
against you." [Ezek. 14:9]
24 Now Zedekiah the son of Chenaanah
went near and struck Micaiah on the cheek,
and said, "Which way did the spirit from the
LORD go from me to speak to you?"
25 And Micaiah said, "Indeed, you shall see
on that day when you go into an [R]inner cham-
ber to hide!" 1 Kin. 20:30
26 So the king of Israel said, "Take Micaiah,
and return him to Amon the governor of the
city and to Joash the king's son;
27 "and say, 'Thus says the king: "Put this
fellow in [R]prison, and feed him with bread of
affliction and water of affliction, until I come
in peace."'" 2 Chr. 16:10; 18:25–27
28 But Micaiah said, "If you ever return in
peace, the LORD has not spoken by me." And
he said, "Take heed, all you people!"

Defeat of Israel—2 Chr. 18:28–34

29 So the king of Israel and Jehoshaphat the
king of Judah went up to Ramoth Gilead.
30 And the king of Israel said to Je-
hoshaphat, "I will disguise myself and go into
battle; but you put on your robes." So the king
of Israel [R]disguised himself and went into bat-
tle. 2 Chr. 35:22
31 Now the [R]king of Syria had commanded
the thirty-two captains of his chariots, saying,
"Fight with no one small or great, but only
with the king of Israel." 1 Kin. 20:1
32 So it was, when the captains of the chari-
ots saw Jehoshaphat, that they said, "Surely it
is the king of Israel!" Therefore they turned
aside to fight against him, and Jehoshaphat
[R]cried out. 2 Chr. 18:31
33 And it happened, when the captains of
the chariots saw that it *was* not the king of Is-
rael, that they turned back from pursuing
him.
34 Now a *certain* man drew a bow at ran-
dom, and struck the king of Israel between
the joints of his armor. So he said to the driver
of his chariot, "Turn around and take me out
of the battle, for I am wounded."
35 The battle increased that day; and the
king was propped up in his chariot, facing the
Syrians, and died at evening. The blood ran
out from the wound onto the floor of the
chariot.
36 Then, as the sun was going down, a shout
went throughout the army, saying, "Every
man to his city, and every man to his own
country!"

Death of Ahab

37 So the king died, and was brought to Sa-
maria. And they buried the king in Samaria.
38 Then *someone* washed the chariot at a
pool in Samaria, and the dogs licked up his
blood while the harlots bathed,* according
[R]to the word of the LORD which He had spo-
ken. 1 Kin. 21:19
39 Now the rest of the acts of Ahab, and all
that he did, [R]the ivory house which he built
and all the cities that he built, *are* they not
written in the book of the chronicles of the
kings of Israel? Amos 3:15
40 So Ahab rested with his fathers. Then
Ahaziah his son reigned in his place.

The Reign of Jehoshaphat in Judah
2 Chr. 20:31—21:1

41 [R]Jehoshaphat the son of Asa had become
king over Judah in the fourth year of Ahab
king of Israel. 2 Chr. 20:31
42 Jehoshaphat *was* thirty-five years old
when he became king, and he reigned twenty-
five years in Jerusalem. His mother's name
was Azubah the daughter of Shilhi.
43 And he walked in all the ways of his fa-
ther Asa. He did not turn aside from them,
doing *what was* right in the eyes of the LORD.
Nevertheless the high places were not taken
away, *for* the people offered sacrifices and
burned incense on the high places.
44 Also [R]Jehoshaphat made [R]peace with the
king of Israel. 2 Chr. 19:2 • 2 Chr. 18:1

22:38 Tg., Syr. *they washed his armor*

45 Now the rest of the acts of Jehoshaphat,
the might that he showed, and how he made
war, *are* they not written in the book of the
chronicles of the kings of Judah?
46 [R]And the rest of the perverted persons,*
who remained in the days of his father Asa, he
banished from the land. 1 Kin. 14:24
47 [R]*There was* then no king in Edom, only a
deputy of the king. 2 Sam. 8:14
48 [R]Jehoshaphat [R]made merchant ships*
to go to Ophir for gold; but they never
sailed, for the ships were wrecked at Ezion
Geber. 2 Chr. 20:35–37 • 1 Kin. 10:22
49 Then Ahaziah the son of Ahab said to Je-
hoshaphat, "Let my servants go with your ser-
vants in the ships." But Jehoshaphat would
not.
50 And [R]Jehoshaphat rested with his fathers,
and was buried with his fathers in the City of
David his father. Then Jehoram his son
reigned in his place. 2 Chr. 21:1

The Reign of Ahaziah in Israel

51 [R]Ahaziah the son of Ahab became king
over Israel in Samaria in the seventeenth year
of Jehoshaphat king of Judah, and reigned
two years over Israel. 1 Kin. 22:40
52 He did evil in the sight of the LORD, and
[R]walked in the way of his father and in the
way of his mother and in the way of Jer-
oboam the son of Nebat, who had made Israel
sin; 1 Kin. 15:26; 21:25
53 for [R]he served Baal and worshiped him,
and provoked the LORD God of Israel to
anger, [R]according to all that his father had
done. Judg. 2:11 • 1 Kin. 16:30–32

22:46 Heb. *qadesh*, one practicing sodomy and prostitution in religious rituals **22:48** Or *ships of Tarshish*

THE SECOND BOOK OF THE
KINGS

THE BOOK OF 2 KINGS

The Book of 2 Kings continues the drama begun in 1 Kings—the tragic history of two nations on a collision course with captivity. The author systematically traces the reigning monarchs of Israel and Judah, first by carrying one nation's history forward, then retracing the same period for the other nation.

Nineteen consecutive evil kings rule in Israel, leading to the captivity by Assyria. The picture is somewhat brighter in Judah, where godly kings occasionally emerge to reform the evils of their predecessors. In the end, however, sin outweighs righteousness and Judah is marched off to Babylon. See "The Book of 1 Kings" for more detail concerning the title.

THE AUTHOR OF 2 KINGS

See "The Author of 1 Kings" for a discussion of authorship. If this now divided book was not written by Jeremiah, it probably was written by a prophetic contemporary of his. The majority of 2 Kings was written before the Babylonian captivity (see "to this day" in 17:34, 41).

The literary style of 2 Kings is similar to that of the Book of Jeremiah, and it has been observed that the omission of Jeremiah's ministry in the account of King Josiah and his successors may indicate that Jeremiah himself was the recorder of the events. However, the last two chapters were evidently added to the book after the Babylonian captivity and written by someone other than Jeremiah. The prophet Jeremiah was forced to flee to Egypt (Jer. 43:1–8), not to Babylon. It is interesting that 2 Kings 24:18—25:30 is almost the same as Jeremiah 52.

THE TIME OF 2 KINGS

The last recorded event in 2 Kings is the release of Jehoiachin (25:27–30), which takes place in 560 B.C. Most of 1 and 2 Kings probably was written just prior to 586 B.C., but chapters 24 and 25 were written after Jehoiachin's release, perhaps about 550 B.C.

Chapters 1—17 cover the 131 years from 853 B.C. (King Ahaziah of Israel) to 722 B.C. (the Assyrian captivity of Israel). Chapters 18—25 cover the 155 years from the beginning of Hezekiah's reign in 715 B.C. to the release of Jehoiachin in Babylon in 560 B.C. The united kingdom lasts for 112 years (1043–931 B.C.), the northern kingdom of Israel exists for another 209 years (931–722 B.C.), and the southern kingdom of Judah continues for an additional 136 years (722–586 B.C.). During this 457-year kingdom period, there are great shifts of world power. Egyptian and Assyrian control over Palestine fluctuates; Assyria rises to preeminence, declines, and is finally conquered by Babylon.

The books of Kings show that judgment comes to the kingdoms of Israel and Judah because of their idolatry, immorality, and disunity. Judah lasts 136 years longer than Israel because of the relative goodness of eight of its twenty kings. Israel never breaks away from Jeroboam's idolatrous calf worship, but Judah experiences some periods of revival in the worship of Yahweh. During these years, God sends many of His prophets. Elijah, Elisha, Amos, and Hosea are in the northern kingdom, while in the southern kingdom Obadiah, Joel, Isaiah, Micah, Nahum, Zephaniah, Jeremiah, and Habakkuk are prophesying.

THE CHRIST OF 2 KINGS

Unlike the nine different dynasties in the northern kingdom, the kings of Judah reign as one continuous dynasty. In spite of Queen Athaliah's attempt to destroy the house of David, God remains faithful to His covenant with David (2 Sam. 7) by preserving his lineage. Jesus the Messiah is his direct descendant.

While Elijah is a type of John the Baptist (Matt. 11:14; 17:10–12; Luke 1:17), Elisha reminds us of Christ. Elijah generally lives apart from the people and stresses law, judgment, and repentance. Elisha lives among the people and emphasizes grace, life, and hope.

KEYS TO 2 KINGS

Key Word: Captivities of the Kingdom—Second Kings records both the destruction and captivity of Israel by the Assyrians (2 Kin. 17), as well as the destruction and captivity of Judah by the Babylonians (2 Kin. 25).

The book was written selectively, not exhaustively, from a prophetic viewpoint to teach that the decline and collapse of the two kingdoms occurred because the rulers and people failed to heed the warnings of God's messengers. The spiritual climate of the nation determined its political and economic conditions.

The prophets of Yahweh play a prominent role in 1 and 2 Kings as God uses them to remind the kings of their covenant responsibilities as His theocratic administrators. When the king keeps the covenant, he and the nation are richly blessed. But judgment consistently falls upon those who refuse to obey God's law. God is seen in Kings as the controller of history who reveals His plan and purpose to His people. Unhappily, the people are concerned more with their own plans, and their rejection of God's rule leads to exile at the hands of the Assyrians and Babylonians.

Key Verses: 2 Kings 17:22, 23; 23:27—"For the children of Israel walked in all the sins of Jeroboam which he did; they did not depart from them, until the LORD removed Israel out of His sight, as He had said by all His servants the prophets. So Israel was carried away from their own land to Assyria, *as it is* to this day" (17:22, 23).

"And the LORD said, 'I will also remove Judah from My sight, as I have removed Israel, and will cast off this city Jerusalem which I have chosen, and the house of which I said, "My name shall be there" ' " (23:27).

Key Chapter: 2 Kings 25—The last chapter of 2 Kings records the utter destruction of the City of Jerusalem and its glorious temple. Only the poor of Israel are left, and even some of them flee for their lives to Egypt. Hope is still alive, however, with the remnant in the Babylonian captivity as Evil-Merodach frees Jehoiachin from prison and treats him kindly.

SURVEY OF 2 KINGS

Without interruption 2 Kings continues the narrative of 1 Kings. The twin kingdoms of Israel and Judah pursue a collision course with captivity as the glory of the once united kingdom becomes increasingly diminished. Division has led to decline and now ends in double deportation with Israel captured by Assyria and Judah by Babylon. This book traces the history of the divided kingdom in chapters 1—17 and the history of the surviving kingdom in chapters 18—25.

Divided Kingdom (1—17): These chapters record the story of Israel's corruption in a relentless succession of bad kings from Ahaziah to Hoshea. The situation in Judah during this time (Jehoram to Ahaz) is somewhat better, but far from ideal. This dark period in the northern kingdom of Israel is interrupted only by the ministries of such godly prophets as Elijah and Elisha. At the end of Elijah's miraculous ministry, Elisha is installed and authenticated as his successor. He is a force for righteousness in a nation that never served the true God or worshiped at the temple in Jerusalem. Elisha's ministry is characterized by miraculous provisions of sustenance and life. Through him God demonstrates His gracious care for the nation and His concern for any person who desires to come to Him. However, like his forerunner Elijah, Elisha is basically rejected by Israel's leadership.

Elisha instructs one of his prophetic assistants to anoint Jehu king over Israel. Jehu fulfills the prophecies concerning Ahab's descendants by putting them to death. He kills Ahab's wife Jezebel, his sons, and also the priests of Baal. But he does not depart from the calf worship originally set up by Jeroboam. The loss of the house of Ahab means the alienation of Israel and Judah and the weakening of both. Israel's enemies begin to get the upper hand. Meanwhile, in Judah, Jezebel's daughter Athaliah kills all the descendants of David, except for Joash, and usurps the throne. However, Jehoiada the priest eventually removes her from the throne and places Joash in power. Joash restores the temple and serves God.

Syria gains virtual control over Israel, but there is no response to God's chastisement: the kings and people refuse to repent. Nevertheless, there is a period of restoration under Jeroboam II, but the continuing series of wicked kings in Israel leads to its overthrow by Assyria.

FOCUS	DIVIDED KINGDOM			SURVIVING KINGDOM		
REFERENCE	1:1——9:1	9:1——17:1	17:1——18:1	18:1——22:1	22:1——25:1	25:1——25:30
DIVISION	MINISTRY OF ELISHA UNDER AHAZIAH AND JEHORAM	REIGNS OF TEN KINGS OF ISRAEL AND EIGHT KINGS OF JUDAH	FALL OF ISRAEL	REIGNS OF HEZEKIAH AND TWO EVIL KINGS	REIGNS OF JOSIAH AND FOUR EVIL KINGS	FALL OF JUDAH
TOPIC	ISRAEL AND JUDAH			JUDAH		
	AHAZIAH TO HOSHEA			HEZEKIAH TO ZEDEKIAH		
LOCATION	ISRAEL DEPORTED TO ASSYRIA			JUDAH DEPORTED TO BABYLONIA		
TIME	131 YEARS (853–722 B.C.)			155 YEARS (715–560 B.C.)		

Surviving Kingdom (18—25): Of Israel's nineteen kings, not one is righteous in God's sight. All but one of its nine dynasties are created by murdering the previous king. In Judah, where there is only one dynasty, eight of its twenty rulers do what is right before God. Nevertheless, Judah's collapse finally comes, resulting in the Babylonian exile. Chapters 18—25 read more easily than chapters 1—17 because alternating the histories of the northern and southern kingdoms is no longer necessary. Only Judah remains.

Six years before the overthrow of Israel's capital of Samaria, Hezekiah becomes king of Judah. Because of his exemplary faith and reforms, God spares Jerusalem from Assyria and brings a measure of prosperity to Judah. However, Hezekiah's son Manasseh is so idolatrous that his long reign leads to the downfall of Judah. Even Josiah's later reforms cannot stem the tide of evil, and the four kings who succeed him are exceedingly wicked. Judgment comes with three deportations to Babylon. The third occurs in 586 B.C. when Nebuchadnezzar destroys Jerusalem and the temple. Still, the book ends on a note of hope with God preserving a remnant for Himself.

OUTLINE OF 2 KINGS

Part One: The Divided Kingdom (1:1—17:41)

I. The Reign of Ahaziah in Israel ......1 Kin. 22:51—2 Kin. 1:18

A. Spiritual Evaluation of Ahaziah ......1 Kin. 22:51–53
B. Political Situation Under Ahaziah ......2 Kin. 1:1
C. Death of Ahaziah 1:2–18

II. The Reign of Jehoram in Israel ...2:1—8:15

A. Transition from Elijah to Elisha 2:1–25
1. Chariot of Fire Takes Elijah 2:1–11
2. Authority of Elijah Is Taken by Elisha 2:12–25
B. Spiritual Evaluation of Jehoram 3:1–3
C. Political Situation Under Jehoram ...3:4–27
D. Ministry of Elisha ......4:1—8:15
1. Miracle of the Increase of the Widow's Oil 4:1–7
2. Miracle of the Shunammite's Son 4:8–37
3. Miracle of the Deadly Stew 4:38–41
4. Miracle of the Multiplication of the Loaves 4:42–44
5. Miracle of the Healing of Naaman 5:1–27
6. Miracle of the Floating Ax Head....6:1–7
7. Miracles During the First Syrian Attack 6:8–23
8. Miracles of Elisha During the Second Syrian Attack ......6:24—7:20
9. Elisha's Ministry with the Shunammite Woman 8:1–6
10. Elisha's Ministry with the King of Syria 8:7–15

III. The Reign of Jehoram in Judah 8:16–24

IV. The Reign of Ahaziah in Judah .8:25—9:29

A. Spiritual Evaluation of Ahaziah......8:25–27
B. Political Situation Under Ahaziah ......8:28—9:26
1. Battle Against Syria 8:28, 29
2. Anointing of Jehu King over Israel 9:1–13
3. Execution of Joram 9:14–26
C. Death of Ahaziah 9:27–29

V. The Reign of Jehu in Israel ......9:30—10:36

A. Fulfillment of Elisha's Prophecy ......9:30—10:28
B. Spiritual Evaluation of Jehu 10:29–31
C. Political Situation Under Jehu......10:32, 33
D. Death of Jehu 10:34–36

VI. The Reign of Queen Athaliah in Judah 11:1–16

A. Salvation of Joash 11:1–3
B. Overthrow of Athaliah by Jehoiada 11:4–12
C. Death of Athaliah 11:13–16

VII. The Reign of Joash in Judah..11:17—12:21

A. Renewal of the Covenant 11:17–21
B. Spiritual Evaluation of Joash......12:1–3
C. Spiritual Situation Under Joash 12:4–16
D. Political Situation Under Joash 12:17, 18
E. Death of Joash 12:19–21

VIII. The Reign of Jehoahaz in Israel..........13:1–9

IX. The Reign of Jehoash in Israel 13:10–25

A. Rule of Jehoash 13:10–13
B. Last Prophecies and Death of Elisha 13:14–25
1. Prophecy of Israel's Victory......13:14–19
2. Death of Elisha 13:20
3. Miracle of Resurrection at Elisha's Tomb 13:21
4. Israel's Victory over Syria 13:22–25

X. The Reign of Amaziah in Judah 14:1–22

A. Spiritual Evaluation of Amaziah.......14:1–6
B. Political Situation Under Amaziah .14:7–14
C. Death of Jehoash 14:15, 16
D. Death of Amaziah 14:17–22

XI. The Reign of Jeroboam II in Israel 14:23–29

XII. The Reign of Azariah in Judah 15:1–7

XIII. The Reign of Zechariah in Israel....15:8–12

XIV. The Reign of Shallum in Israel.....15:13–15

XV. The Reign of Menahem in Israel ..15:16–22

CHAPTER 1

Political Situation Under Ahaziah—2 Kin. 3:5

MOAB [R]rebelled against Israel [R]after the death of Ahab. 2 Sam. 8:2 • 2 Kin. 3:5

Death of Ahaziah

2 Now [R]Ahaziah fell through the lattice of his upper room in Samaria, and was injured; so he sent messengers and said to them, "Go, inquire of [R]Baal-Zebub, the god of [R]Ekron, whether I shall recover from this injury." 1 Kin. 22:40 • Matt. 10:25 • 1 Sam. 5:10
3 But the angel* of the LORD said to Elijah the Tishbite, "Arise, go up to meet the messengers of the king of Samaria, and say to them, '*Is it* because *there is* no God in Israel *that* you are going to inquire of Baal-Zebub, the god of Ekron?'
4 "Now therefore, thus says the LORD: 'You shall not come down from the bed to which you have gone up, but you shall surely die.' " So Elijah departed.
5 And when the messengers returned to [T]him, he said to them, "Why have you come back?" Ahaziah
6 So they said to him, "A man came up to meet us, and said to us, 'Go, return to the king who sent you, and say to him, "Thus says the LORD: '*Is it* because *there is* no God in Israel *that* you are sending to inquire of Baal-Zebub, the god of Ekron? Therefore you shall not come down from the bed to which you have gone up, but you shall surely die.' " ' "
7 Then he said to them, "What kind of man

1:3 Or *Angel*

was it who came up to meet you and told you these words?"

8 So they answered him, "A hairy man wearing a leather belt around his waist." And he said, "It *is* Elijah the Tishbite."

9 Then the king sent to him a captain of fifty with his fifty men. So he went up to him; and there he was, sitting on the top of a hill. And he spoke to him: "Man of God, the king has said, 'Come down!' "

10 So Elijah answered and said to the captain of fifty, "If I *am* a man of God, then [R]let fire come down from heaven and consume you and your fifty men." And fire came down from heaven and consumed him and his fifty. Luke 9:54

11 Then he sent to him another captain of fifty with his fifty men. And he answered and said to him: "Man of God, thus has the king said, 'Come down quickly!' "

12 So Elijah answered and said to them, "If I *am* a man of God, let fire come down from heaven and consume you and your fifty men." And the fire of God came down from heaven and consumed him and his fifty.

13 Again, he sent a third captain of fifty with his fifty men. And the third captain of fifty went up, and came and fell on his knees before Elijah, and pleaded with him, and said to him: "Man of God, please let my life and the life of these fifty servants of yours be precious in your sight.

14 "Look, fire has come down from heaven and burned up the first two captains of fifties with their fifties. But let my life now be precious in your sight."

15 And the angel* of the LORD said to Elijah, "Go down with him; do not be afraid of him." So he arose and went down with him to the king.

16 Then he said to him, "Thus says the LORD: 'Because you have sent messengers to inquire of Baal-Zebub, the god of Ekron, *is it* because *there is* no God in Israel to inquire of His word? Therefore you shall not come down from the bed to which you have gone up, but you shall surely die.' "

17 So *Ahaziah* died according to the word of the LORD which Elijah had spoken. Because he had no son, Jehoram* became king in his place, in the second year of Jehoram the son of Jehoshaphat, king of Judah.

18 Now the rest of the acts of Ahaziah which he did, *are* they not written in the book of the chronicles of the kings of Israel?

CHAPTER 2

Chariot of Fire Takes Elijah

AND it came to pass, when the LORD was about to [R]take up Elijah into heaven by a whirlwind, that Elijah went with [R]Elisha from Gilgal. Gen. 5:24 • 1 Kin. 19:16–21

2 Then Elijah said to Elisha, "Stay here, please, for the LORD has sent me on to Bethel." But Elisha said, "*As* the LORD lives, and [R]*as* your soul lives, I will not leave you!" So they went down to Bethel. 1 Sam. 1:26

3 Now the sons of the prophets who *were* at Bethel came out to Elisha, and said to him, "Do you know that the LORD will take away your master from over you today?" And he said, "Yes, I know; keep silent!"

4 Then Elijah said to him, "Elisha, stay here, please, for the LORD has sent me on to Jericho." But he said, "*As* the LORD lives, and *as* your soul lives, I will not leave you!" So they came to Jericho.

5 Now the sons of the prophets who *were* at Jericho came to Elisha and said to him, "Do you know that the LORD will take away your master from over you today?" So he answered, "Yes, I know; keep silent!"

6 Then Elijah said to him, "Stay here, please, for the LORD has sent me on to the Jordan." But he said, "*As* the LORD lives, and *as* your soul lives, I will not leave you!" So the two of them went on.

7 And fifty men of the sons of the prophets went and stood facing *them* at a distance, while the two of them stood by the Jordan.

8 Now Elijah took his mantle, rolled *it* up, and struck the water; and [R]it was divided this way and that, so that the two of them crossed over on dry ground. Ex. 14:21, 22

9 And so it was, when they had crossed over, that Elijah said to Elisha, "Ask! What may I do for you, before I am taken away from you?" Elisha said, "Please let a double portion of your spirit be upon me."

10 So he said, "You have asked a hard thing. *Nevertheless,* if you see me *when I am* taken from you, it shall be so for you; but if not, it shall not be *so*."

11 Then it happened, as they continued on and talked, that suddenly [R]a chariot of fire *appeared* with horses of fire, and separated the two of them; and Elijah [R]went up by a whirlwind into heaven. 2 Kin. 6:17 • Heb. 11:5

Authority of Elijah Is Taken by Elisha

12 And Elisha saw *it,* and he cried out, [R]"My father, my father, the chariot of Israel and its horsemen!" So he saw him no more. And he took hold of his own clothes and tore them into two pieces. 2 Kin. 13:14

13 He also took up the mantle of Elijah that had fallen from him, and went back and stood by the bank of the Jordan.

14 Then he took the mantle of Elijah that had fallen from him, and struck the water, and said, "Where *is* the LORD God of Elijah?" And when he also had struck the water, [R]it was

1:15 Or *Angel* **1:17** The son of Ahab king of Israel, 2 Kin. 3:1

divided this way and that; and Elisha crossed
over. 2 Kin. 2:8
15 Now when the sons of the prophets who
were [R]from Jericho saw him, they said, "The
spirit of Elijah rests on Elisha." And they
came to meet him, and bowed to the ground
before him. 2 Kin. 2:7
16 Then they said to him, "Look now, there
are fifty strong men with your servants.
Please let them go and search for your master,
[R]lest perhaps the Spirit of the LORD has taken
him up and cast him upon some mountain or
into some valley." And he said, "You shall not
send anyone." 1 Kin. 18:12
17 But when they urged him till he was
[R]ashamed, he said, "Send *them!*" Therefore
they sent fifty men, and they searched for
three days but did not find him. 2 Kin. 8:11
18 And when they came back to him, for he
had stayed in Jericho, he said to them, "Did I
not say to you, 'Do not go'?"
19 Then the men of the city said to Elisha,
"Please notice, the situation of this city *is*
pleasant, as my lord sees; but the water *is* bad,
and the ground barren."
20 And he said, "Bring me a new bowl, and
put salt in it." So they brought *it* to him.
21 Then he went out to the source of the
water, and [R]cast in the salt there, and said,
"Thus says the LORD: 'I have [T]healed this
water; from it there shall be no more death or
barrenness.' " Ex. 15:25, 26 • *purified*
22 So the water remains [R]healed to this day,
according to the word of Elisha which he
spoke. Ezek. 47:8, 9
23 Then he went up from there to Bethel;
and as he was going up the road, some youths
came from the city and mocked him, and said
to him, "Go up, you baldhead! Go up, you
baldhead!"
24 So he turned around and looked at them,
and [R]pronounced a curse on them in the name
of the LORD. And two female bears came out
of the woods and mauled forty-two of the
youths. Deut. 27:13–26
25 Then he went from there to [R]Mount
Carmel, and from there he returned to Samaria. 2 Kin. 4:25

CHAPTER 3

Spiritual Evaluation of Jehoram

NOW [R]Jehoram the son of Ahab became
king over Israel at Samaria in the eighteenth year of Jehoshaphat king of Judah, and
reigned twelve years. 2 Kin. 1:17
2 And he did evil in the sight of the LORD,
but not like his father and mother; for he put
away the *sacred* pillar of Baal [R]that his father
had made. 1 Kin. 16:31, 32
3 Nevertheless he persisted in the sins of
Jeroboam the son of Nebat, who had made Israel sin; he did not depart from them.

Political Situation Under Jehoram

4 Now Mesha king of Moab was a sheepbreeder, and he regularly paid the king of Israel one hundred thousand lambs and the
wool of one hundred thousand rams.
5 But it happened, when [R]Ahab died, that
the king of Moab rebelled against the king of
Israel. 2 Kin. 1:1
6 So King Jehoram went out of Samaria at
that time and mustered all Israel.
7 Then he went and sent to Jehoshaphat
king of Judah, saying, "The king of Moab has
rebelled against me. Will you go with me to
fight against Moab?" And he said, "I will go
up; I *am* as you *are*, my people as your people,
my horses as your horses."
8 Then he said, "Which way shall we go
up?" And he answered, "By way of the
Wilderness of Edom."
9 So the king of Israel went with the king of
Judah and the king of Edom, and they
marched on that roundabout route seven
days; and there was no water for the army,
nor for the animals that followed them.
10 And the king of Israel said, "Alas! For the
LORD has called these three kings together to
deliver them into the hand of Moab."
11 But Jehoshaphat said, "*Is there* no
prophet of the LORD here, that we may inquire
of the LORD by him?" So one of the servants of
the king of Israel answered and said, "Elisha
the son of Shaphat *is* here, who poured water
on the hands of Elijah."
12 And Jehoshaphat said, "The word of the
LORD is with him." So the king of Israel and
Jehoshaphat and the king of Edom [R]went
down to him. 2 Kin. 2:25
13 Then Elisha said to the king of Israel,
[R]"What have I to do with you? [R]Go to [R]the
prophets of your father and the prophets of
your mother." But the king of Israel said to
him, "No, for the LORD has called these three
kings *together* to deliver them into the hand
of Moab." [Ezek. 14:3] • Judg. 10:14 • 1 Kin. 22:6–11
14 And Elisha said, [R]"*As* the LORD of hosts
lives, before whom I stand, surely were it not
that I regard the presence of Jehoshaphat
king of Judah, I would not look at you, nor see
you. 1 Kin. 17:1
15 "But now bring me a musician." Then it
happened, when the musician played, that the
hand of the LORD came upon him.
16 And he said, "Thus says the LORD: [R]'Make
this valley full of ditches.' Jer. 14:3
17 "For thus says the LORD: 'You shall not see
wind, nor shall you see rain; yet that valley
shall be filled with water, so that you, your
cattle, and your animals may drink.'
18 "And this is a simple matter in the sight of
the LORD; He will also deliver the Moabites
into your hand.
19 "Also you shall attack every fortified city

and every choice city, and shall cut down
every good tree, and stop up every spring of
water, and ruin every good piece of land with
stones."
20 Now it happened in the morning, when
[R]the grain offering was offered, that suddenly
water came by way of Edom, and the land was
filled with water. Ex. 29:39, 40
21 And when all the Moabites heard that the
kings had come up to fight against them, all
who were able to bear arms and older were
gathered; and they stood at the border.
22 Then they rose up early in the morning,
and the sun was shining on the water; and the
Moabites saw the water on the other side *as*
red as blood.
23 And they said, "This is blood; the kings
have surely struck swords and have killed one
another; now therefore, Moab, to the spoil!"
24 So when they came to the camp of Israel,
Israel rose up and attacked the Moabites, so
that they fled before them; and they entered
their land, killing the Moabites.
25 Then they destroyed the cities, and each
man threw a stone on every good piece of
land and filled it; and they stopped up all the
springs of water and cut down all the good
trees. But they left the stones of [R]Kir Haraseth
intact. However the slingers surrounded and
attacked it. Is. 16:7, 11
26 And when the king of Moab saw that the
battle was too fierce for him, he took with him
seven hundred men who drew swords, to
break through to the king of Edom, but they
could not.
27 Then [R]he took his eldest son who would
have reigned in his place, and offered him *as*
a burnt offering upon the wall; and there was
great [T]indignation against Israel. [R]So they de-
parted from him and returned to *their own*
land. [Amos 2:1] • *wrath* • 2 Kin. 8:20

CHAPTER 4

Miracle of the Increase of the Widow's Oil

A certain woman of the wives of [R]the sons
of the prophets cried out to Elisha, say-
ing, "Your servant my husband is dead, and
you know that your servant feared the LORD.
And the creditor is coming to take my two
sons to be his slaves." 1 Kin. 20:35
2 So Elisha said to her, "What shall I do for
you? Tell me, what do you have in the house?"
And she said, "Your maidservant has nothing
in the house but a jar of oil."
3 Then he said, "Go, borrow vessels from
everywhere, from all your neighbors—empty
vessels; do not gather just a few.
4 "And when you have come in, you shall
shut the door behind you and your sons; then
pour it into all those vessels, and set aside the
full ones."
5 So she went from him and shut the door
behind her and her sons, who brought *the
vessels* to her; and she poured *it* out.
6 Now it came to pass, when the vessels
were full, that she said to her son, "Bring me
another vessel." And he said to her, "*There is*
not another vessel." So the oil ceased.
7 Then she came and told the man of God.
And he said, "Go, sell the oil and pay your
debt; and you *and* your sons live on the rest."

Miracle of the Shunammite's Son

8 Now it happened one day that Elisha
went to Shunem, where there *was* a notable
woman, and she persuaded him to eat some
food. So it was, as often as he passed by, he
would turn in there to eat some food.
9 And she said to her husband, "Look now,
I know that this *is* a holy man of God, who
passes by us regularly.
10 "Please, let us make a small upper room
on the wall; and let us put a bed for him there,
and a table and a chair and a lampstand; so it
will be, whenever he comes to us, he can turn
in there."
11 And it happened one day that he came
there, and he turned in to the upper room and
lay down there.
12 Then he said to Gehazi his servant, "Call
this Shunammite woman." When he had
called her, she stood before him.
13 And he said to him, "Say now to her,
'Look, you have been concerned for us with
all this care. What *can I* do for you? Do you
want me to speak on your behalf to the
king or to the commander of the army?' "
She answered, "I dwell among my own peo-
ple."
14 So he said, "What then *is* to be done for
her?" And Gehazi answered, "Actually, she
has no son, and her husband is old."
15 So he said, "Call her." When he had called
her, she stood in the doorway.
16 Then he said, "About this time next year
you shall embrace a son." And she said, "No,
my lord. Man of God, [R]do not lie to your
maidservant!" 2 Kin. 4:28
17 But the woman conceived, and bore a son
when the appointed time had come, of which
Elisha had told her.
18 And the child grew. Now it happened one
day that he went out to his father, to the
reapers.
19 And he said to his father, "My head, my
head!" So he said to a servant, "Carry him to
his mother."
20 When he had taken him and brought him
to his mother, he sat on her knees till noon,
and *then* died.
21 And she went up and laid him on the bed
of the man of God, shut *the door* upon him,
and went out.
22 Then she called to her husband, and said,
"Please send me one of the young men and

one of the donkeys, that I may run to the man
of God and come back."
23 So he said, "Why are you going to him
today? *It is* neither the New Moon nor the
Sabbath." And she said, "*It is* well."
24 Then she saddled a donkey, and said to
her servant, "Drive, and go forward; do not
slacken the pace for me unless I tell you."
25 And so she departed, and went to the man
of God [R]at Mount Carmel. 2 Kin. 2:25
So it was, when the man of God saw her
afar off, that he said to his servant Gehazi,
"Look, the Shunammite woman!
26 "Please run now to meet her, and say to
her, '*Is it* well with you? *Is it* well with your
husband? *Is it* well with the child?' " And she
answered, "*It is* well."
27 Now when she came to the man of God at
the hill, she caught him by the feet, but Gehazi
came near to push her away. But the man of
God said, "Let her alone; for her soul *is* in
deep distress, and the LORD has hidden *it*
from me, and has not told me."
28 So she said, "Did I ask a son of my lord?
Did I not say, 'Do not deceive me'?"
29 Then he said to Gehazi, [R]"Get yourself
ready, and take my staff in your hand, and be
on your way. If you meet anyone, [R]do not
greet him; and if anyone greets you, do not
answer him; but [R]lay my staff on the face of
the child." 1 Kin. 18:46 • Luke 10:4 • Ex. 7:19
30 And the mother of the child said, [R]"*As*
the LORD lives, and *as* your soul lives, I will
not [R]leave you." So he arose and followed
her. 2 Kin. 2:2 • 2 Kin. 2:4
31 Now Gehazi went on ahead of them, and
laid the staff on the face of the child; but *there
was* neither voice nor hearing. Therefore he
went back to meet him, and told him, saying,
"The child has not awakened."
32 When Elisha came into the house, there
was the child, lying dead on his bed.
33 He [R]went in therefore, shut the door be-
hind the two of them, [R]and prayed to the
LORD. [Matt. 6:6] • 1 Kin. 17:20
34 And he went up and lay on the child, and
put his mouth on his mouth, his eyes on his
eyes, and his hands on his hands; and he
stretched himself out on the child, and the
flesh of the child became warm.
35 He returned and walked back and forth
in the house, and again went up [R]and
stretched himself out on him; then [R]the child
sneezed seven times, and the child opened his
eyes. 1 Kin. 17:21 • 2 Kin. 8:1, 5
36 And he called Gehazi and said, "Call this
Shunammite woman." So he called her. And
when she came in to him, he said, "Pick up
your son."
37 So she went in, fell at his feet, and bowed
to the ground; then she [R]picked up her son
and went out. [Heb. 11:35]

Miracle of the Deadly Stew

38 And Elisha returned to [R]Gilgal, and
there was a [R]famine in the land. Now the
sons of the prophets *were* [R]sitting before
him; and he said to his servant, "Put on the
large pot, and boil stew for the sons of the
prophets." 2 Kin. 2:1 • 2 Kin. 8:1 • Acts 22:3
39 So one went out into the field to gather
herbs, and found a wild vine, and gathered
from it a lapful of wild gourds, and came and
sliced *them* into the pot of stew, though they
did not know *what they were.*
40 Then they served it to the men to eat.
Now it happened, as they were eating the
stew, that they cried out and said, "Man of
God, *there is* [R]death in the pot!" And they
could not eat *it.* Ex. 10:17
41 So he said, "Then bring some flour." And
[R]he put *it* into the pot, and said, "Serve *it* to
the people, that they may eat." And there was
nothing harmful in the pot. Ex. 15:25

Miracle of the Multiplication of the Loaves

42 Then a man came from [R]Baal Shalisha,
[R]and brought the man of God bread of the
firstfruits, twenty loaves of barley bread, and
newly ripened grain in his knapsack. And he
said, "Give *it* to the people, that they may
eat." 1 Sam. 9:4 • [1 Cor. 9:11]
43 But his servant said, [R]"What? Shall I set
this before one hundred men?" He said again,
"Give it to the people, that they may eat; for
thus says the LORD: 'They shall eat and have
some left over.' " John 6:9
44 So he set *it* before them; and they ate
[R]and had *some* left over, according to the
word of the LORD. John 6:13

CHAPTER 5

Miracle of the Healing of Naaman

NOW [R]Naaman, commander of the army of
the king of Syria, was [R]a great and hon-
orable man in the eyes of his master, because
by him the LORD had given victory to Syria.
He was also a mighty man of valor, *but* a
leper. Luke 4:27 • Ex. 11:3
2 And the Syrians had gone out [R]on[T] raids,
and had brought back captive a young girl
from the land of Israel. She waited on Naa-
man's wife. 2 Kin. 6:23; 13:20 • Or *in bands*
3 Then she said to her mistress, "If only my
master *were* with the prophet who *is* in Sa-
maria! For he would heal him of his leprosy."
4 And *Naaman* went in and told his master,
saying, "Thus and thus said the girl who *is*
from the land of Israel."
5 Then the king of Syria said, "Go now, and
I will send a letter to the king of Israel." So he
departed and [R]took with him ten talents of sil-
ver, six thousand *shekels* of gold, and ten
changes of clothing. 1 Sam. 9:8

6 Then he brought the letter to the king of
Israel, which said,

> Now be advised, when this letter comes
> to you, that I have sent Naaman my
> servant to you, that you may heal him of
> his leprosy.

7 And it happened, when the king of Israel
read the letter, that he tore his clothes and
said, "*Am* I God, to kill and make alive, that
this man sends a man to me to heal him of his
leprosy? Therefore please consider, and see
how he seeks a quarrel with me."
8 So it was, when Elisha the man of God
heard that the king of Israel had torn his
clothes, that he sent to the king, saying, "Why
have you torn your clothes? Please let him
come to me, and he shall know that there is a
prophet in Israel."
9 Then Naaman went with his horses and
chariot, and he stood at the door of Elisha's
house.
10 And Elisha sent a messenger to him, say-
ing, "Go and [R]wash in the Jordan seven times,
and your flesh shall be restored to you, and
you shall be clean." John 9:7
11 But Naaman became furious, and went
away and said, "Indeed, I said to myself, 'He
will surely come out *to me,* and stand and call
on the name of the LORD his God, and wave
his hand over the place, and heal the leprosy.'
12 "*Are* not the Abanah* and the Pharpar,
the rivers of Damascus, better than all the wa-
ters of Israel? Could I not wash in them and be
clean?" So he turned and went away in a rage.
13 And his servants came near and spoke to
him, and said, "My father, *if* the prophet had
told you *to do* something great, would you not
have done *it*? How much more then, when he
says to you, 'Wash, and be clean'?"
14 So he went down and dipped seven
times in the Jordan, according to the saying
of the man of God; and his [R]flesh was re-
stored like the flesh of a little child, and [R]he
was clean. Job 33:25 • Luke 4:27; 5:13
15 And he returned to the man of God, he
and all his aides, and came and stood before
him; and he said, "Indeed, now I know that
there is [R]no God in all the earth, except in Is-
rael; now therefore, please take a gift from
your servant." Dan. 2:47; 3:29; 6:26, 27
16 But he said, "*As* the LORD lives, before
whom I stand, I will receive nothing." And he
urged him to take *it,* but he refused.
17 So Naaman said, "Then, if not, please let
your servant be given two mule-loads of
earth; for your servant will no longer offer ei-
ther burnt offering or sacrifice to other gods,
but to the LORD.
18 "Yet in this thing may the LORD pardon
your servant: when my master goes into the
temple of Rimmon to worship there, and he
leans on my hand, and I bow down in the
temple of Rimmon—when I bow down in the
temple of Rimmon, may the LORD please par-
don your servant in this thing."
19 Then he said to him, "Go in peace." So he
departed from him a short distance.
20 But [R]Gehazi, the servant of Elisha the
man of God, said, "Look, my master has
spared Naaman this Syrian, while not receiv-
ing from his hands what he brought; but *as*
the LORD lives, I will run after him and take
something from him." 2 Kin. 4:12; 8:4, 5
21 So Gehazi pursued Naaman. When Naa-
man saw *him* running after him, he got down
from the chariot to meet him, and said, "*Is* all
well?"
22 And he said, "All *is* [R]well. My master has
sent me, saying, 'Indeed, just now two young
men of the sons of the prophets have come to
me from the mountains of Ephraim. Please
give them a talent of silver and two changes
of garments.'" 2 Kin. 4:26
23 So Naaman said, "Please, take two tal-
ents." And he urged him, and bound two tal-
ents of silver in two bags, with two changes of
garments, and handed *them* to two of his ser-
vants; and they carried *them* on ahead of him.
24 When he came to [T]the citadel, he took
them from their hand, and stored *them* away
in the house; then he let the men go, and they
departed. Lit. *the hill*
25 Now he went in and stood before his mas-
ter. Elisha said to him, "Where *did you go,* Ge-
hazi?" And he said, "Your servant did not go
anywhere."
26 Then he said to him, "Did not my heart go
with you when the man turned back from his
chariot to meet you? *Is it* [R]time to receive
money and to receive clothing, olive groves
and vineyards, sheep and oxen, male and fe-
male servants? [Eccl. 3:1, 6]
27 "Therefore the leprosy of Naaman [R]shall
cling to you and your descendants forever."
And he went out from his presence [R]leprous,
as white as snow. [1 Tim. 6:10] • Ex. 4:6

CHAPTER 6

Miracle of the Floating Ax Head

AND [R]the sons of the prophets said to Eli-
sha, "See now, the place where we dwell
with you is too small for us. 2 Kin. 4:38
2 "Please, let us go to the Jordan, and let
every man take a beam from there, and let us
make there a place where we may dwell." So
he answered, "Go."
3 Then one said, [R]"Please consent to go
with your servants." And he answered, "I will
go." 2 Kin. 5:23
4 So he went with them. And when they
came to the Jordan, they cut down trees.

5:12 So with Kt., LXX, Vg.; Qr., Syr., Tg. *Amanah*

5 But as one was cutting down a tree, the iron *ax head* fell into the water; and he cried out and said, "Alas, master! For it was [R]borrowed." [Ex. 22:14]

6 So the man of God said, "Where did it fall?" And he showed him the place. So [R]he cut off a stick, and threw *it* in there; and he made the iron float. 2 Kin. 2:21; 4:41

7 Therefore he said, "Pick *it* up for yourself." So he reached out his hand and took it.

Syria's War Plan

8 Now the [R]king of Syria was making war against Israel; and he consulted with his servants, saying, "My camp *will be* in such and such a place." 2 Kin. 8:28, 29

9 And the man of God sent to the king of Israel, saying, "Beware that you do not pass this place, for the Syrians are coming down there."

10 Then the king of Israel sent *someone* to the place of which the man of God had told him. Thus he warned him, and he was watchful there, not just once or twice.

11 Therefore the heart of the king of Syria was greatly troubled by this thing; and he called his servants and said to them, "Will you not show me which of us *is* for the king of Israel?"

12 And one of his servants said, "None, my lord, O king; but Elisha, the prophet who *is* in Israel, tells the king of Israel the words that you speak in your bedroom."

God's Chariots and Horses

13 So he said, "Go and see where he *is*, that I may send and get him." And it was told him, saying, "Surely *he is* in Dothan."

14 Therefore he sent horses and chariots and a great army there, and they came by night and surrounded the city.

15 And when the servant of the man of God arose early and went out, there was an army, surrounding the city with horses and chariots. And his servant said to him, "Alas, my master! What shall we do?"

16 So he answered, [R]"Do not fear, for [R]those who *are* with us *are* more than those who *are* with them." Ex. 14:13 • [Rom. 8:31]

17 And Elisha prayed, and said, "LORD, I pray, open his eyes that he may see." Then the LORD [R]opened the eyes of the young man, and he saw. And behold, the mountain *was* full of [R]horses and chariots of fire all around Elisha. Num. 22:31 • 2 Kin. 2:11

Syria's Army Is Blinded

18 So when *the Syrians* came down to him, Elisha prayed to the LORD, and said, "Strike this people, I pray, with blindness." And [R]He struck them with blindness according to the word of Elisha. Gen. 19:11

19 Now Elisha said to them, "This *is* not the way, nor *is* this the city. Follow me, and I will bring you to the man whom you seek." But he led them to Samaria.

20 So it was, when they had come to Samaria, that Elisha said, "LORD, open the eyes of these *men*, that they may see." And the LORD opened their eyes, and they saw; and there *they were*, inside Samaria!

21 Now when the king of Israel saw them, he said to Elisha, "My [R]father, shall I kill *them*? Shall I kill *them*?" 2 Kin. 2:12; 5:13; 8:9

22 But he answered, "You shall not kill *them*. Would you kill those whom you have taken captive with your sword and your bow? [R]Set food and water before them, that they may eat and drink and go to their master." [Rom. 12:20]

23 Then he prepared a great feast for them; and after they ate and drank, he sent them away and they went to their master. So [R]the bands of Syrian *raiders* came no more into the land of Israel. 2 Kin. 5:2; 6:8, 9

Siege of Samaria Causes Famine

24 And it happened after this that Ben-Hadad king of Syria gathered all his army, and went up and besieged Samaria.

25 And there was a great [R]famine in Samaria; and indeed they besieged it until a donkey's head was *sold* for eighty *shekels* of silver, and one-fourth of a kab of dove droppings for five *shekels* of silver. 2 Kin. 4:38

26 Then, as the king of Israel was passing by on the wall, a woman cried out to him, saying, "Help, my lord, O king!"

27 And he said, "If the LORD does not help you, where can I find help for you? From the threshing floor or from the winepress?"

28 Then the king said to her, "What is troubling you?" And she answered, "This woman said to me, 'Give your son, that we may eat him today, and we will eat my son tomorrow.'

29 "So [R]we boiled my son, and ate him. And I said to her on the next day, 'Give your son, that we may eat him'; but she has hidden her son." Lev. 26:27–29

Elisha's Prophecies

30 Now it happened, when the king heard the words of the woman, that he [R]tore his clothes; and as he passed by on the wall, the people looked, and there underneath *he had* sackcloth on his body. 1 Kin. 21:27

31 Then he said, [R]"God do so to me and more also, if the head of Elisha the son of Shaphat remains on him today!" Ruth 1:17

32 But Elisha was sitting in his house, and [R]the elders were sitting with him. And *the king* sent a man ahead of him, but before the messenger came to him, he said to the elders, [R]"Do you see how this son of a murderer has sent someone to take away my head? Look, when the messenger comes,

shut the door, and hold him fast at the door.
Is not the sound of his master's feet behind
him?" Ezek. 8:1; 14:1; 20:1 • Luke 13:32
33 And while he was still talking with them,
there was the messenger, coming down to
him; and then *the king* said, "Surely this
calamity *is* from the LORD; [R]why should I wait
for the LORD any longer?" Job 2:9

CHAPTER 7

THEN Elisha said, "Hear the word of the
LORD. Thus says the LORD: 'Tomorrow
about this time a seah of fine flour *shall be*
sold for a shekel, and two seahs of barley for
a shekel, at the gate of Samaria.' "
2 So an officer on whose hand the king
leaned answered the man of God and said,
"Look, [R]*if* the LORD would make windows in
heaven, could this thing be?" And he said, "In
fact, you shall see *it* with your eyes, but you
shall not eat of it." Mal. 3:10
3 Now there were four leprous men [R]at the
entrance of the gate; and they said to one
another, "Why are we sitting here until we
die? [Num. 5:2–4; 12:10–14]
4 "If we say, 'We will enter the city,' the
famine *is* in the city, and we shall die there.
And if we sit here, we die also. Now therefore,
come, let us surrender to the army of the Syr-
ians. If they keep us alive, we shall live; and if
they kill us, we shall only die."
5 And they rose at twilight to go to the
camp of the Syrians; and when they had come
to the outskirts of the Syrian camp, to their
surprise no one *was* there.
6 For the LORD had caused the army of the
Syrians [R]to hear the noise of chariots and the
noise of horses—the noise of a great army; so
they said to one another, "Look, the king of Is-
rael has hired against us [R]the kings of the Hit-
tites and the kings of the Egyptians to attack
us!" 2 Sam. 5:24 • 1 Kin. 10:29
7 Therefore they [R]arose and fled at twilight,
and left the camp intact—their tents, their
horses, and their donkeys—and they fled for
their lives. Ps. 48:4–6
8 And when these lepers came to the out-
skirts of the camp, they went into one tent and
ate and drank, and carried from it silver and
gold and clothing, and went and hid *them;*
then they came back and entered another
tent, and carried *some* from there *also,* and
went and hid *it.*
9 Then they said to one another, "We are
not doing right. This day *is* a day of good
news, and we remain silent. If we wait until
morning light, some [T]punishment will come
upon us. Now therefore, come, let us go and
tell the king's household." Calamity
10 So they went and called to the gatekeep-
ers of the city, and told them, saying, "We
went to the Syrian camp, and surprisingly no
one *was* there, not a human sound—only
horses and donkeys tied, and the tents intact."
11 And the gatekeepers called out, and they
told *it* to the king's household inside.
12 So the king arose in the night and said
to his servants, "Let me now tell you what
the Syrians have done to us. They know that
we *are* [R]hungry; therefore they have gone
out of the camp to [T]hide themselves in the
field, saying, 'When they come out of the
city, we shall catch them alive, and get into
the city.' " 2 Kin. 6:24–29 • Hide themselves in ambush
13 And one of his servants answered and
said, "Please, let several *men* take five of the
remaining horses which are left in the city.
Look, they *may either become* like all the
multitude of Israel that are left in it; or indeed,
I say, they *may become* like all the multitude
of Israel left from those who are consumed; so
let us send them and see."
14 Therefore they took two chariots with
horses; and the king sent them in the direc-
tion of the Syrian army, saying, "Go and see."
15 And they went after them to the Jordan;
and indeed all the road *was* full of garments
and weapons which the Syrians had thrown
away in their haste. So the messengers re-
turned and told the king.
16 Then the people went out and plundered
the tents of the Syrians. So a seah of fine flour
was *sold* for a shekel, and two seahs of barley
for a shekel, [R]according to the word of the
LORD. 2 Kin. 7:1
17 Now the king had appointed the officer
on whose hand he leaned to have charge of
the gate. But the people trampled him in the
gate, and he died, just [R]as the man of God had
said, who spoke when the king came down to
him. 2 Kin. 6:32; 7:2
18 So it happened just as the man of God
had spoken to the king, saying, "Two seahs of
barley for a shekel, and a seah of fine flour for
a shekel, shall be *sold* tomorrow about this
time in the gate of Samaria."
19 Then that officer had answered the man
of God, and said, "Now look, *if* the LORD
would make windows in heaven, could such a
thing be?" And he had said, "In fact, you shall
see *it* with your eyes, but you shall not eat of
it."
20 And so it happened to him, for the people
trampled him in the gate, and he died.

CHAPTER 8

Elisha's Ministry with the Shunammite Woman

THEN Elisha spoke to the woman whose
son he had restored to life, saying, "Arise
and go, you and your household, and stay
wherever you can; for the LORD [R]has called for
a famine, and furthermore, it will come upon
the land for seven years." Hag. 1:11

2 So the woman arose and did according to the saying of the man of God, and she went with her household and dwelt in the land of the Philistines seven years.

3 It came to pass, at the end of seven years, that the woman returned from the land of the Philistines; and she went to make an appeal to the king for her house and for her land.

4 Then the king talked with Gehazi, the servant of the man of God, saying, "Tell me, please, all the great things Elisha has done."

5 Now it happened, as he was telling the king how he had restored the dead to life, that there was the woman whose son he had restored to life, appealing to the king for her house and for her land. And Gehazi said, "My lord, O king, this *is* the woman, and this *is* her son whom Elisha restored to life."

6 And when the king asked the woman, she told him. So the king appointed a certain officer for her, saying, "Restore all that *was* hers, and all the proceeds of the field from the day that she left the land until now."

Elisha's Ministry with the King of Syria

7 Then Elisha went to Damascus, and [R]Ben-Hadad king of Syria was sick; and it was told him, saying, "The man of God has come here." 2 Kin. 6:24

8 And the king said to [R]Hazael, [R]"Take a present in your hand, and go to meet the man of God, and [R]inquire of the LORD by him, saying, 'Shall I recover from this disease?' " 1 Kin. 19:15 • 1 Sam. 9:7 • 2 Kin. 1:2

9 So Hazael went to meet him and took a present with him, of every good thing of Damascus, forty camel-loads; and he came and stood before him, and said, "Your son Ben-Hadad king of Syria has sent me to you, saying, 'Shall I recover from this disease?' "

10 And Elisha said to him, "Go, say to him, 'You shall certainly recover.' However the LORD has shown me that he will really die."

11 Then he [T]set his countenance in a stare until he was ashamed; and the man of God [R]wept. *fixed his gaze* • Luke 19:41

12 And Hazael said, "Why is my lord weeping?" He answered, "Because I know [R]the evil that you will do to the children of Israel: Their strongholds you will set on fire, and their young men you will kill with the sword; and you will dash their children, and rip open their women with child." Amos 1:3, 4

13 So Hazael said, "But what [R]*is* your servant—a dog, that he should do this gross thing?" And Elisha answered, [R]"The LORD has shown me that you *will become* king over Syria." 1 Sam. 17:43 • 1 Kin. 19:15

14 Then he departed from Elisha, and came to his master, who said to him, "What did Elisha say to you?" And he answered, "He told me you would surely recover."

15 But it happened on the next day that he took a thick cloth and dipped *it* in water, and spread *it* over his face so that he died; and Hazael reigned in his place.

The Reign of Jehoram in Judah
2 Chr. 21:5–10, 20

16 Now in the fifth year of Joram the son of Ahab, king of Israel, Jehoshaphat *having been* king of Judah, Jehoram the son of Jehoshaphat began to reign as king of Judah.

17 He was [R]thirty-two years old when he became king, and he reigned eight years in Jerusalem. 2 Chr. 21:5–10

18 And he walked in the way of the kings of Israel, just as the house of Ahab had done, for the daughter of Ahab was his wife; and he did evil in the sight of the LORD.

19 Yet the LORD would not destroy Judah, for the sake of His servant David, [R]as He promised him to give a lamp to him *and* his sons forever. 2 Sam. 7:13

20 In his days [R]Edom revolted against Judah's authority, [R]and made a king over themselves. Gen. 27:40 • 1 Kin. 22:47

21 So Joram* went to Zair, and all his chariots with him. Then he rose by night and attacked the Edomites who had surrounded him and the captains of the chariots; and the troops fled to their tents.

22 Thus Edom has been in revolt against Judah's authority to this day. [R]And Libnah revolted at that time. Josh. 21:13

23 Now the rest of the acts of Joram, and all that he did, *are* they not written in the book of the chronicles of the kings of Judah?

24 So Joram [T]rested with his fathers, and was buried with his fathers in the City of David. Then [R]Ahaziah his son reigned in his place. Died and joined his ancestors • 2 Chr. 22:1, 7

Spiritual Evaluation of Ahaziah
2 Kin. 9:29; 2 Chr. 22:1–4

25 In the twelfth year of Joram the son of Ahab, king of Israel, Ahaziah the son of Jehoram, king of Judah, began to reign.

26 Ahaziah *was* [R]twenty-two years old when he became king, and he reigned one year in Jerusalem. His mother's name *was* Athaliah the granddaughter of Omri, king of Israel. 2 Chr. 22:2

27 [R]And he walked in the way of the house of Ahab, and did evil in the sight of the LORD, like the house of Ahab, for he *was* the son-in-law of the house of Ahab. 2 Chr. 22:3, 4

Battle Against Syria
2 Kin. 9:15, 16; 2 Chr. 22:5, 6

28 Now he went [R]with Joram the son of Ahab to war against Hazael king of Syria at [R]Ramoth Gilead; and the Syrians wounded Joram. 2 Chr. 22:5 • 1 Kin. 22:3, 29

8:21 *Jehoram*, v. 16

29 Then [R]King Joram went back to Jezreel to
recover from the wounds which the Syrians
had inflicted on him at Ramah, when he
fought against Hazael king of Syria. And
Ahaziah the son of Jehoram, king of Judah,
went down to see Joram the son of Ahab in
Jezreel, because he was sick. 2 Kin. 9:15

CHAPTER 9

Anointing of Jehu King over Israel

AND Elisha the prophet called one of the
sons of the prophets, and said to him,
"Get yourself ready, take this flask of oil in
your hand, and go to Ramoth Gilead.
2 "Now when you arrive at that place, look
there for Jehu the son of Jehoshaphat, the son
of Nimshi, and go in and make him rise up
from among [R]his associates, and take him to
an inner room. 2 Kin. 9:5, 11
3 "Then take the flask of oil, and pour *it* on
his head, and say, 'Thus says the LORD: "I have
anointed you king over Israel." ' Then open
the door and flee, and do not delay."
4 So the young man, the servant of the
prophet, went to Ramoth Gilead.
5 And when he arrived, there *were* the cap-
tains of the army sitting; and he said, "I have
a message for you, Commander." Jehu said,
"For which *one* of us?" And he said, "For you,
Commander."
6 Then he arose and went into the house.
And he poured the oil on his head, and said to
him, [R]"Thus says the LORD God of Israel: 'I
have anointed you king over the people of the
LORD, over Israel. 2 Chr. 22:7
7 'You shall strike down the house of Ahab
your master, that I may [R]avenge the blood of
My servants the prophets, and the blood of all
the servants of the LORD, at the hand of
Jezebel. [Deut. 32:35, 41]
8 'For the whole house of Ahab shall perish;
and I will cut off from Ahab all the males in Is-
rael, both bond and free.
9 'So I will make the house of Ahab like
the house of [R]Jeroboam the son of Nebat,
and like the house of [R]Baasha the son of Ahi-
jah. 1 Kin. 14:10; 15:29; 21:22 • 1 Kin. 16:3, 11
10 [R]'The dogs shall eat Jezebel on the plot
of ground at Jezreel, and *there shall be* none
to bury *her.*' " And he opened the door and
fled. 1 Kin. 21:23
11 Then Jehu came out to the servants of
his master, and *one* said to him, "*Is* all well?
Why did [R]this madman come to you?" And he
said to them, "You know the man and his
babble." Jer. 29:26
12 And they said, "A lie! Tell us now." So he
said, "Thus and thus he spoke to me, saying,
'Thus says the LORD: "I have anointed you
king over Israel." ' "
13 Then each man hastened [R]to take his gar-
ment and put *it* [T]under him on the top of the
steps; and they blew trumpets, saying, "Jehu
is king!" Matt. 21:7, 8 • Lit. *under his feet*

Execution of Joram

14 So Jehu the son of Jehoshaphat, the son of
Nimshi, conspired against [R]Joram. (Now Joram
had been defending Ramoth Gilead, he and all
Israel, against Hazael king of Syria. 2 Kin. 8:28
15 But [R]King [T]Joram had returned to
Jezreel to recover from the wounds which
the Syrians had inflicted on him when he
fought with Hazael king of Syria.) And Jehu
said, "If you are so minded, let no one leave
or escape from the city to go and tell *it* in
Jezreel." 2 Kin. 8:29 • *Jehoram*, v. 24
16 So Jehu rode in a chariot and went to
Jezreel, for Joram was laid up there; [R]and
Ahaziah king of Judah had come down to see
Joram. 2 Kin. 8:29
17 Now a watchman stood on the tower in
Jezreel, and he saw the company of Jehu as
he came, and said, "I see a company of men."
And Joram said, "Get a horseman and send
him to meet them, and let him say, [T]'*Is it*
peace?' " Are you peaceful?
18 So the horseman went to meet him, and
said, "Thus says the king: '*Is it* peace?' " And
Jehu said, "What have you to do with peace?
Turn around and follow me." So the watch-
man reported, saying, "The messenger went
to them, but is not coming back."
19 Then he sent out a second horseman who
came to them, and said, "Thus says the king:
'*Is it* peace?' " And Jehu answered, "What
have you to do with peace? Turn around and
follow me."
20 So the watchman reported, saying, "He
went up to them and is not coming back; and
the driving *is* like the driving of Jehu the son
of Nimshi, for he drives furiously!"
21 Then Joram said, "Make ready." And his
chariot was made ready. Then Joram king of
Israel and Ahaziah king of Judah went out,
each in his chariot; and they went out to meet
Jehu, and [T]met him on the property of Naboth
the Jezreelite. Lit. *found*
22 Now it happened, when Joram saw Jehu,
that he said, "*Is it* peace, Jehu?" So he an-
swered, "What peace, as long as the harlotries
of your mother Jezebel and her witchcraft *are*
so many?"
23 Then Joram turned around and fled, and
said to Ahaziah, "Treachery, Ahaziah!"
24 Now Jehu drew his bow with full strength
and shot Jehoram between his arms; and the
arrow came out at his heart, and he sank
down in his chariot.
25 Then *Jehu* said to Bidkar his captain,
"Pick *him* up, *and* throw him into the tract of
the field of Naboth the Jezreelite; for remem-
ber, when you and I were riding together be-
hind Ahab his father, that [R]the LORD laid this
[R]burden upon him: 1 Kin. 21:19, 24–29 • Is. 13:1

26 'Surely I saw yesterday the blood of
Naboth and the blood of his sons,' says the
LORD, [R]'and I will repay you in this plot,' says
the LORD. Now therefore, take *and* throw him
on the plot *of ground,* according to the word
of the LORD." 1 Kin. 21:13, 19

Death of Ahaziah—2 Kin. 8:25; 2 Chr. 22:9

27 But when Ahaziah king of Judah saw
this, he fled by the road to Beth Haggan.* So
Jehu pursued him, and said, [T]"Shoot him also
in the chariot." *And they shot him* at the As-
cent of Gur, which is by Ibleam. Then he fled
to Megiddo, and died there. Lit. *Strike*
28 And his servants carried him in the char-
iot to Jerusalem, and buried him in his tomb
with his fathers in the City of David.
29 In the eleventh year of Joram the son of
Ahab, Ahaziah had become king over Ju-
dah.

Fulfillment of Elijah's Prophecy

30 Now when Jehu had come to Jezreel,
Jezebel heard *of it;* [R]and she put paint on her
eyes and adorned her head, and looked
through a window. Ezek. 23:40
31 Then, as Jehu entered at the gate, she
said, [R]"*Is it* peace, Zimri, murderer of your
master?" 1 Kin. 16:9–20
32 And he looked up at the window, and
said, "Who *is* on my side? Who?" So two *or*
three eunuchs looked out at him.
33 Then he said, "Throw her down." So they
threw her down, and *some* of her blood spat-
tered on the wall and on the horses; and he
trampled her underfoot.
34 And when he had gone in, he ate and
drank. Then he said, "Go now, see to this ac-
cursed *woman,* and bury her, for [R]she was a
king's daughter." 1 Kin. 16:31
35 So they went to bury her, but they found
no more of her than the skull and the feet and
the palms of *her* hands.
36 Therefore they came back and told him.
And he said, "This *is* the word of the LORD,
which He spoke by His servant Elijah the
Tishbite, saying, 'On the plot *of ground* at
Jezreel dogs shall eat the flesh of Jezebel;*
37 'and the corpse of Jezebel shall be [R]as
refuse on the surface of the field, in the plot at
Jezreel, so that they shall not say, "Here *lies*
Jezebel." ' " Ps. 83:10

CHAPTER 10

NOW Ahab had seventy sons in Samaria.
And Jehu wrote and sent letters to Sa-
maria, to the rulers of Jezreel,* to the elders,
and to [T]those who reared Ahab's *sons,* say-
ing: *the guardians of*

2 Now as soon as this letter comes to you,
since your master's sons *are* with you,
and you have chariots and horses, a
fortified city also, and weapons,
3 choose the [T]best qualified of your
master's sons, set *him* on his father's
throne, and fight for your master's
house. most upright

4 But they were exceedingly afraid, and
said, "Look, two kings could not stand up to
him; how then can we stand?"
5 And he who *was* in charge of the house,
and he who *was* in charge of the city, the el-
ders also, and those who reared *the sons,* sent
to Jehu, saying, "We *are* your servants, we will
do all you tell us; but we will not make anyone
king. Do *what is* good in your sight."
6 Then he wrote a second letter to them,
saying:

If you *are* for me and will obey my voice,
take the heads of the men, your master's
sons, and come to me at Jezreel by this
time tomorrow.

Now the king's sons, seventy persons, *were*
with the great men of the city, *who* were rear-
ing them.
7 So it was, when the letter came to them,
that they took the king's sons and slaughtered
seventy persons, put their heads in baskets
and sent *them* to him at Jezreel.
8 Then a messenger came and told him, say-
ing, "They have brought the heads of the king's
sons." And he said, "Lay them in two heaps at
the entrance of the gate until morning."
9 So it was, in the morning, that he went out
and stood, and said to all the people, "You *are*
righteous. Indeed [R]I conspired against my
master and killed him; but who killed all
these? 2 Kin. 9:14–24
10 "Know now that nothing shall [R]fall to the
earth of the word of the LORD which the LORD
spoke concerning the house of Ahab; for the
LORD has done what He spoke [R]by His servant
Elijah." 1 Sam. 3:19 • 1 Kin. 21:17–24, 29
11 So Jehu killed all who remained of the
house of Ahab in Jezreel, and all his great
men and his close acquaintances and his
priests, until he left him none remaining.
12 And he arose and departed and went to
Samaria. On the way, at Beth Eked* of the
Shepherds,
13 [R]Jehu met with the brothers of Ahaziah
king of Judah, and said, "Who *are* you?" So
they answered, "We *are* the brothers of
Ahaziah; we have come down to greet the
sons of the king and the sons of the queen
mother." 2 Chr. 22:8
14 And he said, "Take them alive!" So they

9:27 Lit. *The Garden House* **9:36** 1 Kin. 21:23
10:1 So with MT, Syr., Tg.; LXX *Samaria;* Vg. *city*
10:12 Or *The Shearing House*

took them alive, and [R]killed them at the well
of [T]Beth Eked, forty-two men; and he left none
of them. 2 Chr. 22:8 • Or *The Shearing House*
15 Now when he departed from there, he
met Jehonadab the son of Rechab, *coming to*
meet him; and he greeted him and said to him,
"Is your heart right, as my heart *is* toward
your heart?" And Jehonadab answered, "It is."
Jehu said, "If it is, give *me* your hand." So he
gave *him* his hand, and he took him up to him
into the chariot.
16 Then he said, "Come with me, and see my
[R]zeal for the LORD." So they had him ride in
his chariot. 1 Kin. 19:10
17 And when he came to Samaria, he killed
all who remained to Ahab in Samaria, till he
had destroyed them, according to the word of
the LORD which He spoke to Elijah.
18 Then Jehu gathered all the people to-
gether, and said to them, "Ahab served Baal a
little, Jehu will serve him much.
19 "Now therefore, call to me all the
[R]prophets of Baal, all his servants, and all his
priests. Let no one be missing, for I have a
great sacrifice for Baal. Whoever is missing
shall not live." But Jehu acted deceptively,
with the intent of destroying the worshipers
of Baal. 1 Kin. 18:19; 22:6
20 And Jehu said, "Proclaim a solemn as-
sembly for Baal." So they proclaimed *it.*
21 Then Jehu sent throughout all Israel; and
all the worshipers of Baal came, so that there
was not a man left who did not come. So they
came into the temple* of Baal, and the [R]tem-
ple of Baal was full from one end to the
other. 1 Kin. 16:32
22 And he said to the one in charge of the
wardrobe, "Bring out vestments for all the
worshipers of Baal." So he brought out vest-
ments for them.
23 Then Jehu and Jehonadab the son of
Rechab went into the temple of Baal, and said
to the worshipers of Baal, "Search and see
that no servants of the LORD are here with
you, but only the worshipers of Baal."
24 So they went in to offer sacrifices and
burnt offerings. Now Jehu had appointed for
himself eighty men on the outside, and had
said, "*If* any of the men whom I have brought
into your hands escapes, *whoever lets him es-
cape, it shall be* [R]his life for the life of the
other." 1 Kin. 20:39
25 Now it happened, as soon as he had made
an end of offering the burnt offering, that
Jehu said to the guard and to the captains,
"Go in *and* kill them; let no one come out!"
And they killed them with the edge of the
sword; then the guards and the officers threw
them out, and went into the [T]inner room of the
temple of Baal. Lit. *city*
26 And they brought the *sacred* pillars out of
the temple of Baal and burned them.
27 Then they broke down the *sacred* pillar of
Baal, and tore down the temple of Baal and
made it a refuse dump to this day.
28 Thus Jehu destroyed Baal from Israel.

Spiritual Evaluation of Jehu

29 However Jehu did not turn away from the
sins of Jeroboam the son of Nebat, who had
made Israel sin, *that is,* from the golden
calves that *were* at Bethel and Dan.
30 And the LORD [R]said to Jehu, "Because
you have done well in doing *what is* right in
My sight, *and* have done to the house of Ahab
all that *was* in My heart, your sons shall sit
on the throne of Israel to the fourth *genera-
tion.*" 2 Kin. 9:6, 7
31 But Jehu took no heed to walk in the law
of the LORD God of Israel with all his heart;
for he did not depart from the sins of Jer-
oboam, who had made Israel sin.

Political Situation Under Jehu

32 In those days the LORD began to cut off
parts of Israel; and [R]Hazael conquered them
in all the territory of Israel 2 Kin. 8:12; 13:22
33 from the Jordan eastward: all the land of
Gilead—Gad, Reuben, and Manasseh—from
[R]Aroer, which *is* by the River Arnon, including
Gilead and Bashan. Deut. 2:36

Death of Jehu

34 Now the rest of the acts of Jehu, all that
he did, and all his might, *are* they not written
in the book of the chronicles of the kings of Is-
rael?
35 So Jehu rested with his fathers, and they
buried him in Samaria. Then [R]Jehoahaz his
son reigned in his place. 2 Kin. 13:1
36 And the period that Jehu reigned over Is-
rael in Samaria *was* twenty-eight years.

CHAPTER 11

Salvation of Joash—2 Chr. 22: 10–12

WHEN Athaliah the mother of Ahaziah
saw that her son was dead, she arose
and destroyed all the royal heirs.
2 But Jehosheba, the daughter of King
Joram, sister of [R]Ahaziah, took [T]Joash the son
of Ahaziah, and stole him away from among
the king's sons *who were* being murdered;
and they hid him and his nurse in the bed-
room, from Athaliah, so that he was not
killed. 2 Kin. 8:25 • Or *Jehoash*
3 So he was hidden with her in the house of
the LORD for six years, while Athaliah reigned
over the land.

Overthrow of Athaliah by Jehoiada 2 Chr. 23: 1–11

4 In the seventh year Jehoiada sent and
brought the captains of hundreds—of the

10:21 Lit. *house*

bodyguards and the [T]escorts—and brought them into the house of the LORD to him. And he made a covenant with them and took an oath from them in the house of the LORD, and showed them the king's son. *guards*

5 Then he commanded them, saying, "This *is* what you shall do: One-third of you who come on duty on the Sabbath shall be keeping watch over the king's house,

6 "one-third *shall be* at the gate of Sur, and one-third at the gate behind the escorts. You shall keep the watch of the house, lest it be broken down.

7 "The two contingents of you who go off duty on the Sabbath shall keep the watch of the house of the LORD for the king.

8 "But you shall surround the king on all sides, every man with his weapons in his hand; and whoever comes within range, let him be put to death. You are to be with the king as he goes out and as he comes in."

9 So the captains of the hundreds did according to all that Jehoiada the priest commanded. Each of them took his men who were to be on duty on the Sabbath, with those who were going off duty on the Sabbath, and came to Jehoiada the priest.

10 And the priest gave the captains of hundreds the spears and shields which *had belonged* to King David, [R]that were in the temple of the LORD. 2 Sam. 8:7

11 Then the escorts stood, every man with his weapons in his hand, all around the king, from the right [T]side of the temple to the left side of the temple, by the altar and the house. Lit. *shoulder*

12 And he brought out the king's son, put the crown on him, and *gave him* the [R]Testimony;* they made him king and anointed him, and they clapped their hands and said, "Long live the king!" Ex. 25:16; 31:18

Death of Athaliah—2 Chr. 23:12–15

13 Now when Athaliah heard the noise of the escorts *and* the people, she came to the people *in* the temple of the LORD.

14 When she looked, there was the king standing by [R]a pillar according to custom; and the leaders and the trumpeters were by the king. All the people of the land were rejoicing and blowing trumpets. So Athaliah tore her clothes and cried out, "Treason! Treason!" 2 Chr. 34:31

15 And Jehoiada the priest commanded the captains of the hundreds, the officers of the army, and said to them, "Take her outside [T]under guard, and slay with the sword whoever follows her." For the priest had said, "Do not let her be killed in the house of the LORD." Lit. *between ranks*

16 So they seized her; and she went by way of the horses' entrance *into* the king's house, and there she was killed.

Renewal of the Covenant—2 Chr. 23:16—24:1

17 Then Jehoiada made a covenant between the LORD, the king, and the people, that they should be the LORD's people, and *also* between the king and the people.

18 And all the people of the land went to the temple of Baal, and tore it down. They thoroughly broke in pieces its altars and images, and killed Mattan the priest of Baal before the altars. And the priest appointed officers over the house of the LORD.

19 Then he took the captains of hundreds, the bodyguards, the escorts, and all the people of the land; and they brought the king down from the house of the LORD, and went by way of the gate of the escorts to the king's house. Then he sat on the throne of the kings.

20 So all the people of the land rejoiced; and the city was quiet, for they had slain Athaliah with the sword *in* the king's house.

21 Jehoash *was* [R]seven years old when he became king. 2 Chr. 24:1–14

CHAPTER 12

Spiritual Evaluation of Joash—2 Chr. 24:1, 2

IN the seventh year of Jehu, [R]Jehoash* became king, and he reigned forty years in Jerusalem. His mother's name *was* Zibiah of Beersheba. 2 Chr. 24:1

2 Jehoash did *what was* right in the sight of the LORD all the days in which [R]Jehoiada the priest instructed him. 2 Kin. 11:4

3 But [R]the high places were not taken away; the people still sacrificed and burned incense on the high places. 2 Kin. 14:4; 15:35

Spiritual Situation Under Joash
2 Chr. 24:5–14

4 And Jehoash said to the priests, [R]"All the money of the dedicated gifts that are brought into the house of the LORD—each man's [R]census money, each man's assessment money*—*and* all the money that a man purposes in his heart to bring into the house of the LORD, 2 Kin. 22:4 • Ex. 30:13–16

5 "let the priests take *it* themselves, each from his constituency; and let them repair the [T]damages of the temple, wherever any dilapidation is found." Lit. *breaches*

6 Now it was so, by the twenty-third year of King Jehoash, *that* the priests had not repaired the damages of the temple.

7 [R]So King Jehoash called Jehoiada the priest and the *other* priests, and said to them, "Why have you not repaired the damages of the temple? Now therefore, do not take *more* money from your constituency, but deliver it for repairing the damages of the temple." 2 Chr. 24:6

11:12 Law, Ex. 25:16, 21; Deut. 31:9 **12:1** *Joash,* 2 Kin. 11:2ff. **12:4** Cf. Lev. 27:2ff.

8 And the priests agreed that they would neither receive *more* money from the people, nor repair the damages of the temple.

9 Then Jehoiada the priest took a chest, bored a hole in its lid, and set it beside the altar, on the right side as one comes into the house of the LORD; and the priests who kept the door put [R]there all the money brought into the house of the LORD. Mark 12:41

10 So it was, whenever they saw that *there was* much money in the chest, that the king's scribe and the high priest came up and put it in bags, and counted the money that was found in the house of the LORD.

11 Then they gave the money, which had been apportioned, into the hands of those who did the work, who had the oversight of the house of the LORD; and they [T]paid it out to the carpenters and builders who worked on the house of the LORD, Lit. *weighed*

12 and to masons and stonecutters, and for buying timber and hewn stone, to repair the damage of the house of the LORD, and for all that was paid out to repair the temple.

13 However there were not made for the house of the LORD basins of silver, trimmers, sprinkling-bowls, trumpets, any articles of gold or articles of silver, from the money brought into the house of the LORD.

14 But they gave that to the workmen, and they repaired the house of the LORD with it.

15 Moreover [R]they did not require an account from the men into whose hand they delivered the money to be paid to workmen, for they dealt faithfully. 2 Kin. 22:7

16 [R]The money from the trespass offerings and the money from the sin offerings was not brought into the house of the LORD. It belonged to the priests. [Lev. 5:15, 18]

Political Situation Under Joash

17 Hazael king of Syria went up and fought against Gath, and took it; then Hazael set his face to go up to Jerusalem.

18 And Jehoash king of Judah took all the sacred things that his fathers, Jehoshaphat and Jehoram and Ahaziah, kings of Judah, had dedicated, and his own sacred things, and all the gold found in the treasuries of the house of the LORD and in the king's house, and sent *them* to Hazael king of Syria. Then he went away from Jerusalem.

Death of Joash—2 Chr. 24:25–27

19 Now the rest of the acts of Joash,* and all that he did, *are* they not written in the book of the chronicles of the kings of Judah?

20 And his servants arose and formed a conspiracy, and killed Joash in the house of the Millo,* which goes down to Silla.

21 For Jozachar* the son of Shimeath and Jehozabad the son of Shomer,* his servants, struck him. So he died, and they buried him with his fathers in the City of David. Then [R]Amaziah his son reigned in his place. 2 Chr. 24:27

CHAPTER 13

The Reign of Jehoahaz in Israel

IN the twenty-third year of Joash* the son of Ahaziah, king of Judah, Jehoahaz the son of Jehu became king over Israel in Samaria, *and reigned* seventeen years.

2 And he did evil in the sight of the LORD, and followed the [R]sins of Jeroboam the son of Nebat, who had made Israel sin. He did not depart from them. 1 Kin. 12:26–33

3 Then [R]the anger of the LORD was aroused against Israel, and He delivered them into the hand of [R]Hazael king of Syria, and into the hand of Ben-Hadad the son of Hazael, all *their* days. Judg. 2:14 • 2 Kin. 8:12

4 So Jehoahaz [R]pleaded with the LORD, and the LORD listened to him; for [R]He saw the oppression of Israel, because the king of Syria oppressed them. [Ps. 78:34] • [Ex. 3:7, 9]

5 [R]Then the LORD gave Israel a deliverer, so that they escaped from under the hand of the Syrians; and the children of Israel dwelt in their tents as before. 2 Kin. 13:25; 14:25, 27

6 Nevertheless they did not depart from the sins of the house of Jeroboam, who had made Israel sin, *but* walked in them; [R]and the wooden image* also remained in Samaria. 1 Kin. 16:33

7 For He left of the army of Jehoahaz only fifty horsemen, ten chariots, and ten thousand foot soldiers; for the king of Syria had destroyed them [R]and made them [R]like the dust at threshing. 2 Kin. 10:32 • [Amos 1:3]

8 Now the rest of the acts of Jehoahaz, all that he did, and his might, *are* they not written in the book of the chronicles of the kings of Israel?

9 So Jehoahaz rested with his fathers, and they buried him in Samaria. Then Joash his son reigned in his place.

Rule of Joash—2 Kin. 14:15, 16

10 In the thirty-seventh year of Joash king of Judah, Jehoash* the son of Jehoahaz became king over Israel in Samaria, *and reigned* sixteen years.

11 And he did evil in the sight of the LORD. He did not depart from all the sins of Jeroboam the son of Nebat, who made Israel sin, *but* walked in them.

12 [R]Now the rest of the acts of Joash, all that he did, and his might with which he fought against Amaziah king of Judah, *are* they not written in the book of the chronicles of the kings of Israel? 2 Kin. 14:8–15

12:19 *Jehoash,* vv. 1–18 **12:20** Lit. *The Landfill*
12:21 *Zabad,* 2 Chr. 24:26 • *Shimrith,* 2 Chr. 24:26
13:1 *Jehoash,* 2 Kin. 12:1–18 **13:6** Heb. *Asherah,* a Canaanite goddess **13:10** *Joash,* v. 9

13 So Joash rested with his fathers. Then Jeroboam sat on his throne. And Joash was buried in Samaria with the kings of Israel.

Prophecy of Israel's Victory

14 Elisha had become sick with the illness of which he would die. Then Joash the king of Israel came down to him, and wept over his face, and said, "O my father, my father, the chariots of Israel and their horsemen!"

15 And Elisha said to him, "Take a bow and some arrows." So he took himself a bow and some arrows.

16 Then he said to the king of Israel, "Put your hand on the bow." So he put his hand *on it,* and Elisha put his hands on the king's hands.

17 And he said, "Open the east window"; and he opened *it.* Then Elisha said, "Shoot"; and he shot. And he said, "The arrow of the LORD's deliverance and the arrow of deliverance from Syria; for you must strike the Syrians at Aphek till you have destroyed *them.*"

18 Then he said, "Take the arrows"; so he took *them.* And he said to the king of Israel, "Strike the ground"; so he struck three times, and stopped.

19 And the man of God was angry with him, and said, "You should have struck five or six times; then you would have struck Syria till you had destroyed *it!* But now you will strike Syria *only* three times."

Death of Elisha

20 Then Elisha died, and they buried him. And the *raiding* bands from Moab invaded the land in the spring of the year.

Miracle of Resurrection at Elisha's Tomb

21 So it was, as they were burying a man, that suddenly they spied a band *of raiders;* and they put the man in the tomb of Elisha; and when the man was let down and touched the bones of Elisha, he revived and stood on his feet.

Israel's Victory over Syria

22 And [R]Hazael king of Syria oppressed Israel all the days of Jehoahaz. 2 Kin. 8:12, 13

23 But the LORD was gracious to them, had compassion on them, and regarded them, because of His covenant with Abraham, Isaac, and Jacob, and would not yet destroy them or cast them from His presence.

24 Now Hazael king of Syria died. Then Ben-Hadad his son reigned in his place.

25 And Jehoash* the son of Jehoahaz recaptured from the hand of Ben-Hadad, the son of Hazael, the cities which he had taken out of the hand of Jehoahaz his father by war. Three times Joash defeated him and recaptured the cities of Israel.

CHAPTER 14

Spiritual Evaluation of Amaziah
2 Chr. 25:1–4

IN the second year of Joash the son of Jehoahaz, king of Israel, Amaziah the son of Joash, king of Judah, became king.

2 He was twenty-five years old when he became king, and he reigned twenty-nine years in Jerusalem. His mother's name was Jehoaddan of Jerusalem.

3 And he did *what was* right in the sight of the LORD, yet not like his father David; he did everything [R]as his father Joash had done. 2 Kin. 12:2

4 However the high places were not taken away, and the people still sacrificed and burned incense on the high places.

5 Now it happened, as soon as the kingdom was established in his hand, that he executed his servants [R]who had murdered his father the king. 2 Kin. 12:20

6 But the children of the murderers he did not execute, according to what is written in the Book of the Law of Moses, in which the LORD commanded, saying, [R]"Fathers shall not be put to death for their children, nor shall children be put to death for their fathers; but a person shall be put to death for his own sin."* [Ezek. 18:4, 20]

Political Situation Under Amaziah
2 Chr. 25:11, 17–24

7 He killed ten thousand Edomites in the Valley of Salt, and took Sela by war, and called its name Joktheel to this day.

8 [R]Then Amaziah sent messengers to Jehoash* the son of Jehoahaz, the son of Jehu, king of Israel, saying, "Come, let us face one another *in battle.*" 2 Chr. 25:17, 18

9 And Jehoash king of Israel sent to Amaziah king of Judah, saying, [R]"The thistle that *was* in Lebanon sent to the [R]cedar that *was* in Lebanon, saying, 'Give your daughter to my son as wife'; and a wild beast that *was* in Lebanon passed by and trampled the thistle. Judg. 9:8–15 • 1 Kin. 4:33

10 "You have indeed defeated Edom, and [R]your heart has [T]lifted you up. Glory *in that,* and stay at home; for why should you meddle with trouble so that you fall—you and Judah with you?" Deut. 8:14 • Made you proud

11 But Amaziah would not heed. Therefore Jehoash king of Israel went out; so he and Amaziah king of Judah faced one another at Beth Shemesh, which *belongs* to Judah.

12 And Judah was defeated by Israel, and every man fled to his tent.

13 Then Jehoash king of Israel captured Amaziah king of Judah, the son of Jehoash,

13:25 *Joash,* vv. 12–14, 25 **14:6** Deut. 24:16
14:8 *Joash,* 2 Kin. 13:9, 12–14, 25; 2 Chr. 25:17ff.

the son of Ahaziah, at Beth Shemesh; and he
went to Jerusalem, and broke down the wall
of Jerusalem from the Gate of Ephraim to the
Corner Gate—four hundred cubits.
14 And he took all [R]the gold and silver, all
the articles that were found in the house of
the LORD and in the treasuries of the king's
house, and hostages, and returned to Sa-
maria. 1 Kin. 7:51

Death of Jehoash—2 Kin. 13:12, 13

15 [R]Now the rest of the acts of Jehoash
which he did—his might, and how he fought
with Amaziah king of Judah—*are* they not
written in the book of the chronicles of the
kings of Israel? 2 Kin. 13:12, 13
16 So Jehoash [T]rested with his fathers, and
was buried in Samaria with the kings of Is-
rael. Then Jeroboam his son reigned in his
place. Died and joined his ancestors

Death of Amaziah—2 Chr. 25:25—26:2

17 Amaziah the son of Joash, king of Judah,
lived fifteen years after the death of Jehoash
the son of Jehoahaz, king of Israel.
18 Now the rest of the acts of Amaziah, *are*
they not written in the book of the chronicles
of the kings of Judah?
19 And [R]they formed a conspiracy against
him in Jerusalem, and he fled to [R]Lachish; but
they sent after him to Lachish and killed him
there. 2 Chr. 25:27 • Josh. 10:31
20 Then they brought him on horses, and he
was buried at Jerusalem with his fathers in
the City of David.
21 And all the people of Judah took [R]Aza-
riah,* who *was* sixteen years old, and made him
king instead of his father Amaziah. 2 Kin. 15:13
22 He built Elath and restored it to Judah,
after the king rested with his fathers.

The Reign of Jeroboam II in Israel

23 In the fifteenth year of Amaziah the son
of Joash, king of Judah, Jeroboam the son of
Joash, king of Israel, became king in Samaria,
and reigned forty-one years.
24 And he did evil in the sight of the LORD;
he did not depart from all the [R]sins of Jer-
oboam the son of Nebat, who had made Israel
sin. 1 Kin. 12:26–33
25 He restored the territory of Israel from
the entrance of Hamath to the Sea of the
Arabah, according to the word of the LORD
God of Israel, which He had spoken through
His servant Jonah the son of Amittai, the
prophet who *was* from Gath Hepher.
26 For the LORD saw *that* the affliction of Is-
rael *was* very bitter; and whether bond or
free, there was no helper for Israel.
27 [R]And the LORD did not say that He would
blot out the name of Israel from under
heaven; but He saved them by the hand of Jer-
oboam the son of Joash. [2 Kin. 13:5, 23]
28 Now the rest of the acts of Jeroboam, and
all that he did—his might, how he made war,
and how he recaptured for Israel, from Da-
mascus and Hamath, *what had belonged* to
Judah—*are* they not written in the book of the
chronicles of the kings of Israel?
29 So Jeroboam rested with his fathers, the
kings of Israel. Then [R]Zechariah his son
reigned in his place. 2 Kin. 15:8

CHAPTER 15

The Reign of Azariah in Judah
2 Chr. 26:3–23

IN the twenty-seventh year of Jeroboam
king of Israel, Azariah the son of Amaziah,
king of Judah, [R]became king. 2 Kin. 14:21
2 He was sixteen years old when he became
king, and he reigned fifty-two years in Jerusa-
lem. His mother's name *was* Jecholiah of Je-
rusalem.
3 And he did *what was* right in the sight of
the LORD, according to all that his father
Amaziah had done,
4 except that the high places were not re-
moved; the people still sacrificed and burned
incense on the high places.
5 Then the LORD struck the king, so that
he was a leper until the day of his death; so he
[R]dwelt in an isolated house. And Jotham the
king's son *was* over the *royal* house, judging
the people of the land. [Lev. 13:46]
6 Now the rest of the acts of Azariah, and
all that he did, *are* they not written in the book
of the chronicles of the kings of Judah?
7 So Azariah [T]rested with his fathers, and
[R]they buried him with his fathers in the City
of David. Then Jotham his son reigned in his
place. Died and joined his ancestors • 2 Chr. 26:23

The Reign of Zechariah in Israel

8 In the thirty-eighth year of Azariah king
of Judah, Zechariah the son of Jeroboam
reigned over Israel in Samaria six months.
9 And he did evil in the sight of the LORD,
[R]as his fathers had done; he did not depart
from the sins of Jeroboam the son of Nebat,
who had made Israel sin. 2 Kin. 14:24
10 Then Shallum the son of Jabesh con-
spired against him, and [R]struck and killed him
in front of the people; and he reigned in his
place. Amos 7:9
11 Now the rest of the acts of Zechariah, in-
deed they *are* written in the book of the
chronicles of the kings of Israel.
12 This *was* the word of the LORD which He
spoke to Jehu, saying, "Your sons shall sit on
the throne of Israel to the fourth *generation*."*
And so it was.

14:21 *Uzziah*, 2 Chr. 26:1ff.; Is. 6:1; etc. **15:12** 2 Kin. 10:30

The Reign of Shallum in Israel

13 Shallum the son of Jabesh became king in the thirty-ninth year of Uzziah* king of Judah; and he reigned a full month in Samaria.
14 For Menahem the son of Gadi went up from Tirzah, came to Samaria, and struck Shallum the son of Jabesh in Samaria and killed him; and he reigned in his place.
15 Now the rest of the acts of Shallum, and the conspiracy which he [T]led, indeed they *are* written in the book of the chronicles of the kings of Israel. Lit. *conspired*

The Reign of Menahem in Israel

16 Then from Tirzah, Menahem attacked [R]Tiphsah, all who *were* there, and its territory. Because they did not surrender, therefore he attacked *it*. All the women there who were with child he ripped open. 1 Kin. 4:24
17 In the thirty-ninth year of Azariah king of Judah, Menahem the son of Gadi became king over Israel, *and reigned* ten years in Samaria.
18 And he did evil in the sight of the LORD; he did not depart all his days from the sins of Jeroboam the son of Nebat, who had made Israel sin.
19 [R]Pul* king of Assyria came against the land; and Menahem gave Pul a thousand talents of silver, that his [T]hand might be with him to [R]strengthen the kingdom under his control. Hos. 8:9 • Support • 2 Kin. 14:5
20 And Menahem exacted the money from Israel, from all the very wealthy, from each man fifty shekels of silver, to give to the king of Assyria. So the king of Assyria turned back, and did not stay there in the land.
21 Now the rest of the acts of Menahem, and all that he did, *are* they not written in the book of the chronicles of the kings of Israel?
22 So Menahem rested with his fathers. Then Pekahiah his son reigned in his place.

The Reign of Pekahiah in Israel

23 In the fiftieth year of Azariah king of Judah, Pekahiah the son of Menahem became king over Israel in Samaria, *and reigned* two years.
24 And he did evil in the sight of the LORD; he did not depart from the sins of Jeroboam the son of Nebat, who had made Israel sin.
25 Then Pekah the son of Remaliah, an officer of his, conspired against him and killed him in Samaria, in the citadel of the king's house, along with Argob and Arieh; and with him were fifty men of Gilead. He killed him and reigned in his place.
26 Now the rest of the acts of Pekahiah, and all that he did, indeed they *are* written in the book of the chronicles of the kings of Israel.

The Reign of Pekah in Israel

27 In the fifty-second year of Azariah king of Judah, [R]Pekah the son of Remaliah became king over Israel in Samaria, *and reigned* twenty years. Is. 7:1
28 And he did evil in the sight of the LORD; he did not depart from the sins of Jeroboam the son of Nebat, who had made Israel sin.
29 In the days of Pekah king of Israel, Tiglath-Pileser king of Assyria [R]came and took [R]Ijon, Abel Beth Maachah, Janoah, Kedesh, Hazor, Gilead, and Galilee, all the land of Naphtali; and he carried them captive to Assyria. 1 Chr. 5:26 • 1 Kin. 15:20
30 Then Hoshea the son of Elah led a conspiracy against Pekah the son of Remaliah, and struck and killed him; so he [R]reigned in his place in the twentieth year of Jotham the son of Uzziah. [Hos. 10:3, 7, 15]
31 Now the rest of the acts of Pekah, and all that he did, indeed they *are* written in the book of the chronicles of the kings of Israel.

The Reign of Jotham in Judah—2 Chr. 27:1–9

32 In the second year of Pekah the son of Remaliah, king of Israel, Jotham the son of Uzziah, king of Judah, began to reign.
33 He was twenty-five years old when he became king, and he reigned sixteen years in Jerusalem. His mother's name *was* Jerusha* the daughter of Zadok.
34 And he did *what was* right in the sight of the LORD; he did [R]according to all that his father Uzziah had done. 2 Kin. 15:3, 4
35 However the high places were not removed; the people still sacrificed and burned incense on the high places. He built the Upper Gate of the house of the LORD.
36 Now the rest of the acts of Jotham, and all that he did, *are* they not written in the book of the chronicles of the kings of Judah?
37 In those days the LORD began to send [R]Rezin king of Syria and Pekah the son of Remaliah against Judah. 2 Kin. 16:5–9
38 So Jotham [T]rested with his fathers, and was buried with his fathers in the City of David his father. Then Ahaz his son reigned in his place. Died and joined his ancestors

CHAPTER 16

Spiritual Evaluation of Ahaz—2 Chr. 28:1–4

IN the seventeenth year of Pekah the son of Remaliah, Ahaz the son of Jotham, king of Judah, began to reign.
2 Ahaz *was* twenty years old when he became king, and he reigned sixteen years in Jerusalem; and he did not do *what was* right in

15:13 *Azariah*, 2 Kin. 14:21ff.; 15:1ff. **15:19** Tiglath-Pileser III, v. 29 **15:33** *Jerushah*, 2 Chr. 27:1

the sight of the LORD his God, as his father
David *had done.*
3 But he walked in the way of the kings of
Israel; indeed he made his son pass through
the fire, according to the abominations of the
nations whom the LORD had cast out from be-
fore the children of Israel.
4 And he sacrificed and burned incense on
the [R]high places, [R]on the hills, and under
every green tree. 2 Kin. 15:34, 35 • [Deut. 12:2]

Political Situation Under Ahaz
2 Chr. 28:5, 16, 21; Is. 7:1

5 [R]Then Rezin king of Syria and Pekah the
son of Remaliah, king of Israel, came up to Je-
rusalem to *make* war; and they besieged Ahaz
but could not overcome *him.* Is. 7:1, 4
6 At that time Rezin king of Syria captured
Elath for Syria, and drove the men of Judah
from Elath. Then the Edomites* went to Elath,
and dwell there to this day.
7 So Ahaz sent messengers to [R]Tiglath-
Pileser king of Assyria, saying, "I *am* your ser-
vant and your son. Come up and save me from
the hand of the king of Syria and from the
hand of the king of Israel, who rise up against
me." 1 Chr. 5:26
8 And Ahaz took the silver and gold that
was found in the house of the LORD, and in the
treasuries of the king's house, and sent *it as* a
present to the king of Assyria.
9 So the king of Assyria heeded him; for the
king of Assyria went up against [R]Damascus
and [R]took it, carried *its people* captive to Kir,
and killed Rezin. 2 Kin. 14:28 • Amos 1:5
10 Now King Ahaz went to Damascus to
meet Tiglath-Pileser king of Assyria, and saw
an altar that *was* at Damascus; and King
Ahaz sent to Urijah the priest the design of
the altar and its pattern, according to all its
workmanship.
11 Then Urijah the priest built an altar ac-
cording to all that King Ahaz had sent from
Damascus. So Urijah the priest made *it* before
King Ahaz came back from Damascus.
12 And when the king came back from Da-
mascus, the king saw the altar; and [R]the king
approached the altar and made offerings on
it. 2 Chr. 26:16, 19
13 So he burned his burnt offering and his
grain offering; and he poured his drink offer-
ing and sprinkled the blood of his peace of-
ferings on the altar.
14 He also brought [R]the bronze altar which
was before the LORD, from the front of the
temple—from between the *new* altar and the
house of the LORD—and put it on the north
side of the *new* altar. 2 Chr. 4:1
15 Then King Ahaz commanded Urijah the
priest, saying, "On the great *new* altar burn
the morning burnt offering, the evening grain
offering, the king's burnt sacrifice, and his
grain offering, with the burnt offering of all
the people of the land, their grain offering,
and their drink offerings; and sprinkle on it
all the blood of the burnt offering and all the
blood of the sacrifice. And the bronze altar
shall be for me to inquire *by.*"
16 Thus did Urijah the priest, according to
all that King Ahaz commanded.
17 [R]And King Ahaz cut off the panels of the
carts, and removed the lavers from them; and
he took down the Sea from the bronze oxen
that *were* under it, and put it on a pavement of
stones. 2 Chr. 28:24
18 Also he removed the Sabbath pavilion
which they had built in the temple, and he re-
moved the king's outer entrance from the
house of the LORD, on account of the king of
Assyria.

Death of Ahaz—2 Chr. 28:26, 27

19 Now the rest of the acts of Ahaz which he
did, *are* they not written in the book of the
chronicles of the kings of Judah?
20 So Ahaz rested with his fathers, and
[R]was buried with his fathers in the City of
David. Then Hezekiah his son reigned in his
place. 2 Chr. 28:27

CHAPTER 17

Spiritual Evaluation of Hoshea

IN the twelfth year of Ahaz king of Ju-
dah, Hoshea the son of Elah became king of
Israel in Samaria, *and he reigned* nine years.
2 And he did evil in the sight of the LORD,
but not as the kings of Israel who were before
him.

Imprisonment of Hoshea

3 Shalmaneser king of Assyria came up
against him; and Hoshea became his vassal,
and paid him tribute money.
4 And the king of Assyria uncovered a con-
spiracy by Hoshea; for he had sent messen-
gers to So, king of Egypt, and brought no
tribute to the king of Assyria, as *he had done*
year by year. Therefore the king of Assyria
shut him up, and bound him in prison.

Captivity of Samaria—2 Kin. 18:9–12

5 Now [R]the king of Assyria went through-
out all the land, and went up to Samaria and
besieged it for three years. Hos. 13:16
6 [R]In the ninth year of Hoshea, the king of
Assyria took Samaria and carried Israel away
to Assyria, and placed them in Halah and by
the Habor, the River of Gozan, and in the
cities of the Medes. Hos. 1:4; 13:16

Causes of the Captivity

7 For so it was that the children of Israel
had sinned against the LORD their God, who

16:6 A few ancient mss. *Syrians*

had brought them up out of the land of Egypt,
from under the hand of Pharaoh king of
Egypt; and they had feared other gods,
8 and [R]had walked in the statutes of the na-
tions whom the LORD had cast out from before
the children of Israel, and of the kings of Is-
rael, which they had made. [Lev. 18:3]
9 Also the children of Israel secretly did
against the LORD their God things that *were*
not right, and they built for themselves [T]high
places in all their cities, [R]from watchtower to
fortified city. Places for pagan worship • 2 Kin. 18:8
10 [R]They set up for themselves *sacred* pillars
and wooden images* on every high hill and
under every green tree. Is. 57:5
11 There they burned incense on all the high
places, like the nations whom the LORD had
carried away before them; and they did
wicked things to provoke the LORD to anger,
12 for they served idols, [R]of which the LORD
had said to them, [R]"You shall not do this
thing." [Ex. 20:3–5] • [Deut. 4:19]
13 Yet the LORD testified against Israel and
against Judah, by all of His [R]prophets, every
seer, saying, "Turn from your evil ways, and
keep My commandments *and* My statutes, ac-
cording to all the law which I commanded
your fathers, and which I sent to you by My
servants the prophets." Neh. 9:29, 30
14 Nevertheless they would not hear, but
[R]stiffened their necks, like the necks of their
fathers, who [R]did not believe in the LORD their
God. [Acts 7:51] • Deut. 9:23
15 And they [R]rejected His statutes and His
covenant that He had made with their fathers,
and His testimonies which He had testified
against them; they followed idols, became
idolaters, and *went* after the nations who
were all around them, *concerning* whom the
LORD had charged them that they should not
do like them. Jer. 44:3
16 So they left all the commandments of the
LORD their God, [R]made for themselves a
molded image *and* two calves, made a wooden
image and worshiped all the host of heaven,
and served Baal. 1 Kin. 12:28
17 [R]And they caused their sons and daugh-
ters to pass through the fire, practiced witch-
craft and soothsaying, and sold themselves to
do evil in the sight of the LORD, to provoke
Him to anger. 2 Kin. 16:3
18 Therefore the LORD was very angry with
Israel, and removed them from His sight;
there was none left [R]but the tribe of Judah
alone. 1 Kin. 11:13, 32
19 Also Judah did not keep the command-
ments of the LORD their God, but walked in
the statutes of Israel which they made.
20 And the LORD rejected all the descen-
dants of Israel, afflicted them, and delivered
them into the hand of plunderers, until He
had cast them from His [R]sight. 2 Kin. 24:20
21 For [R]He tore Israel from the house of Da-
vid, and they made Jeroboam the son of
Nebat king. Then Jeroboam drove Israel from
following the LORD, and made them commit a
great sin. 1 Kin. 11:11, 31
22 For the children of Israel walked in all the
sins of Jeroboam which he did; they did not
depart from them,
23 until the LORD removed Israel out of His
sight, as He had said by all His servants the
prophets. So Israel was carried away from
their own land to Assyria, *as it is* to this day.

Sins of the Foreigners

24 [R]Then the king of Assyria brought *people*
from Babylon, Cuthah, Ava, Hamath, and
from Sepharvaim, and placed *them* in the
cities of Samaria instead of the children of Is-
rael; and they took possession of Samaria and
dwelt in its cities. Ezra 4:2, 10
25 And it was so, at the beginning of their
dwelling there, *that* they did not fear the
LORD; therefore the LORD sent lions among
them, which killed *some* of them.
26 So they spoke to the king of Assyria, say-
ing, "The nations whom you have removed
and placed in the cities of Samaria do not
know the rituals of the God of the land; there-
fore He has sent lions among them, and in-
deed, they are killing them because they do
not know the rituals of the God of the land."
27 Then the king of Assyria commanded,
saying, "Send there one of the priests whom
you brought from there; let him go and dwell
there, and let him teach them the rituals of the
God of the land."
28 Then one of the priests whom they had
carried away from Samaria came and dwelt in
Bethel, and taught them how they should fear
the LORD.
29 However every nation continued to make
gods of its own, and put *them* [R]in the shrines
on the high places which the Samaritans had
made, *every* nation in the cities where they
dwelt. 1 Kin. 12:31; 13:32
30 The men of [R]Babylon made Succoth
Benoth, the men of Cuth made Nergal, the
men of Hamath made Ashima, 2 Kin. 17:24
31 [R]and the Avites made Nibhaz and Tartak;
and the Sepharvites burned their children in
fire to Adrammelech and Anammelech, the
gods of Sepharvaim. Ezra 4:9
32 So they feared the LORD, and from every
class they appointed for themselves priests of
the high places, who sacrificed for them in the
shrines of the high places.
33 [R]They feared the LORD, yet served their
own gods—according to the rituals of the na-
tions from among whom they were carried
away. Zeph. 1:5
34 To this day they continue practicing the
former rituals; they do not fear the LORD, nor

17:10 Heb. *Asherim*, Canaanite deities

do they follow their statutes or their ordinances, or the law and commandment which the LORD had commanded the children of Jacob, [R]whom He named Israel, Gen. 32:28

35 with whom the LORD had made a covenant and charged them, saying: "You shall not fear other gods, nor bow down to them nor serve them nor sacrifice to them;

36 "but the LORD, who [R]brought you up from the land of Egypt with great power and [R]an outstretched arm, Him you shall fear, Him you shall worship, and to Him you shall offer sacrifice. Ex. 14:15–30 • Ex. 6:6; 9:15

37 "And the statutes, the ordinances, the law, and the commandment which He wrote for you, you shall be careful to observe forever; you shall not fear other gods.

38 "And the covenant that I have made with you, [R]you shall not forget, nor shall you fear other gods. Deut. 4:23; 6:12

39 "But the LORD your God you shall fear; and He will deliver you from the hand of all your enemies."

40 However they did not obey, but they followed their former rituals.

41 [R]So these nations feared the LORD, yet served their carved images; also their children and their children's children have continued doing as their fathers did, even to this day. 2 Kin. 17:32, 33

CHAPTER 18

Spiritual Evaluation of Hezekiah
2 Chr. 29:1, 2; 31:1

NOW it came to pass in the third year of Hoshea the son of Elah, king of Israel, *that* [R]Hezekiah the son of Ahaz, king of Judah, began to reign. 2 Chr. 28:27; 29:1

2 He was twenty-five years old when he became king, and he reigned twenty-nine years in Jerusalem. His mother's name *was* [R]Abi* the daughter of Zechariah. Is. 38:5

3 And he did *what was* right in the sight of the LORD, according to all that his father David had done.

4 [R]He removed the high places and broke the *sacred* pillars, cut down the wooden image* and broke in pieces the bronze serpent that Moses had made; for until those days the children of Israel burned incense to it, and called it Nehushtan.* 2 Chr. 31:1

5 He [R]trusted in the LORD God of Israel, [R]so that after him was none like him among all the kings of Judah, nor who were before him. 2 Kin. 19:10 • 2 Kin. 23:25

6 For he [R]held fast to the LORD; he did not depart from following Him, but kept His commandments, which the LORD had commanded Moses. Deut. 10:20

7 The LORD was with him; he prospered wherever he went. And he rebelled against the king of Assyria and did not serve him.

8 [R]He [T]subdued the Philistines, as far as Gaza and its territory, [R]from watchtower to fortified city. Is. 14:29 • Lit. *struck* • 2 Kin. 17:9

Invasion of Israel by Assyria—2 Kin. 17:5–7

9 Now it came to pass in the fourth year of King Hezekiah, which *was* the seventh year of Hoshea the son of Elah, king of Israel, *that* Shalmaneser king of Assyria came up against Samaria and besieged it.

10 And at the end of three years they took it. In the sixth year of Hezekiah, that *is,* [R]the ninth year of Hoshea king of Israel, Samaria was taken. 2 Kin. 17:6

11 [R]Then the king of Assyria carried Israel away captive to Assyria, and put them in Halah and by the Habor, the River of Gozan, and in the cities of the Medes, 2 Kin. 17:6

12 because they [R]did not obey the voice of the LORD their God, but transgressed His covenant *and* all that Moses the servant of the LORD had commanded; and they would neither hear nor do *them.* 2 Kin. 17:7–18

First Invasion of Judah by Assyria—Is. 36:1

13 And [R]in the fourteenth year of King Hezekiah, Sennacherib king of Assyria came up against all the fortified cities of Judah and took them. 2 Chr. 32:1

14 Then Hezekiah king of Judah sent to the king of Assyria at Lachish, saying, "I have done wrong; turn away from me; whatever you impose on me I will pay." And the king of Assyria assessed Hezekiah king of Judah three hundred talents of silver and thirty talents of gold.

15 So Hezekiah gave *him* all the silver that was found in the house of the LORD and in the treasuries of the king's house.

16 At that time Hezekiah stripped *the gold from* the doors of the temple of the LORD, and *from* the pillars which Hezekiah king of Judah had overlaid, and gave [T]it to the king of Assyria. Lit. *them*

Second Invasion of Judah by Assyria
2 Chr. 32:9–21; Is. 36:2—37:38

17 Then the king of Assyria sent *the* Tartan,* *the* Rabsaris,* *and the* Rabshakeh* from Lachish, with a great army against Jerusalem, to King Hezekiah. And they went up and came to Jerusalem. When they had come up, they went and stood by the aqueduct from the upper pool, [R]which *was* on the highway to the Fuller's Field. Is. 7:3

18 And when they had called to the king, [R]Eliakim the son of Hilkiah, who *was* over

18:2 *Abijah,* 2 Chr. 29:1ff. **18:4** Heb. *Asherah,* a Canaanite goddess • Lit. *Bronze Thing,* also similar to Heb. *nahash, serpent* **18:17** A title, probably *Commander in Chief* • A title, probably *Chief Officer* • A title, probably *Chief of Staff* or *Governor*

the household, Shebna the [T]scribe, and Joah the son of Asaph, the recorder, came out to them. Is. 22:20 • *secretary*

19 Then *the* Rabshakeh said to them, "Say now to Hezekiah, 'Thus says the great king, the king of Assyria: [R]"What confidence *is* this in which you trust? 2 Chr. 32:10

20 "You speak of *having* plans and power for war; but *they are* [T]mere words. And in whom do you trust, that you rebel against me? Lit. *a word of the lips*

21 [R]"Now look! You are trusting in the staff of this broken reed, Egypt, on which if a man leans, it will go into his hand and pierce it. So *is* Pharaoh king of Egypt to all who trust in him. Ezek. 29:6, 7

22 "But if you say to me, 'We trust in the LORD our God,' *is* it not He [R]whose [T]high places and whose altars Hezekiah has taken away, and said to Judah and Jerusalem, 'You shall worship before this altar in Jerusalem'?" ' 2 Kin. 18:4 • Places for pagan worship

23 "Now therefore, I urge you, give a pledge to my master the king of Assyria, and I will give you two thousand horses—if you are able on your part to put riders on them!

24 "How then will you repel one captain of the least of my master's servants, and put your trust in Egypt for chariots and horsemen?

25 "Have I now come up without the LORD against this place to destroy it? The LORD said to me, 'Go up against this land, and destroy it.' "

26 [R]Then Eliakim the son of Hilkiah, Shebna, and Joah said to *the* Rabshakeh, "Please speak to your servants in [R]Aramaic, for we understand *it;* and do not speak to us in Hebrew* in the hearing of the people who *are* on the wall." Is. 36:11—39:8 • Ezra 4:7

27 But *the* Rabshakeh said to them, "Has my master sent me to your master and to you to speak these words, and not to the men who sit on the wall, who will eat and drink their own waste with you?"

28 Then *the* Rabshakeh stood and called out with a loud voice in [T]Hebrew, and spoke, saying, "Hear the word of the great king, the king of Assyria! Lit. *Judean*

29 "Thus says the king: 'Do not let Hezekiah deceive you, for he shall not be able to deliver you from his hand;

30 'nor let Hezekiah make you trust in the LORD, saying, "The LORD will surely deliver us; this city shall not be given into the hand of the king of Assyria." '

31 "Do not listen to Hezekiah; for thus says the king of Assyria: 'Make *peace* with me by a present and come out to me; and every one of you eat from his own vine and every one from his own fig tree, and every one of you drink the waters of his own cistern;

32 'until I come and take you away to a land like your own land, [R]a land of grain and new wine, a land of bread and vineyards, a land of olive groves and honey, that you may live and not die. But do not listen to Hezekiah, lest he persuade you, saying, "The LORD will deliver us." Deut. 8:7–9; 11:12

33 [R]'Has any of the gods of the nations at all delivered its land from the hand of the king of Assyria? 2 Kin. 19:12

34 'Where *are* the gods of [R]Hamath and Arpad? Where *are* the gods of Sepharvaim and Hena and Ivah? Indeed, have they delivered Samaria from my hand? 2 Kin. 19:13

35 'Who among all the gods of the lands have delivered their countries from my hand, [R]that the LORD should deliver Jerusalem from my hand?' " Dan. 3:15

36 But the people held their peace and answered him not a word; for the king's commandment was, "Do not answer him."

37 Then Eliakim the son of Hilkiah, who *was* over the household, Shebna the scribe, and Joah the son of Asaph, the recorder, came to Hezekiah with *their* clothes torn, and told him the words of *the* Rabshakeh.

CHAPTER 19

AND [R]so it was, when King Hezekiah heard *it,* that he tore his clothes, covered himself with [R]sackcloth, and went into the house of the LORD. Is. 37:1 • Ps. 69:11

2 Then he sent Eliakim, who *was* over the household, Shebna the scribe, and the elders of the priests, covered with sackcloth, to Isaiah the prophet, the son of Amoz.

3 And they said to him, "Thus says Hezekiah: 'This day *is* a day of trouble, and rebuke, and blasphemy; for the children have come to birth, but *there is* no strength to [T]bring them forth. *give birth*

4 [R]'It may be that the LORD your God will hear all the words of *the* Rabshakeh, whom his master the king of Assyria has sent to reproach the living God, and will rebuke the words which the LORD your God has heard. Therefore lift up *your* prayer for the remnant that is left.' " 2 Sam. 16:12

5 So the servants of King Hezekiah came to Isaiah.

6 And Isaiah said to them, "Thus you shall say to your master, 'Thus says the LORD: "Do not be afraid of the words which you have heard, with which the servants of the king of Assyria have blasphemed Me.

7 "Surely I will send [R]a spirit upon him, and he shall hear a rumor and return to his own land; and I will cause him to fall by the sword in his own land." ' " 2 Kin. 19:35–37

8 Then *the* Rabshakeh returned and found the king of Assyria warring against Libnah,

18:26 Lit. *Judean*

for he heard that he had departed [R]from
Lachish. 2 Kin. 18:14, 17
9 And the king heard concerning Tirhakah
king of Ethiopia, "Look, he has come out to
make war with you." So he again sent mes-
sengers to Hezekiah, saying,
10 "Thus you shall speak to Hezekiah king
of Judah, saying: 'Do not let your God [R]in
whom you trust deceive you, saying, "Jerusa-
lem shall not be given into the hand of the
king of Assyria." 2 Kin. 18:5
11 'Look! You have heard what the kings of
Assyria have done to all lands by utterly de-
stroying them; and shall you be delivered?
12 'Have the gods of the nations delivered
those whom my fathers have destroyed,
Gozan and Haran and Rezeph, and the people
of Eden who *were* in Telassar?
13 [R]'Where *is* the king of Hamath, the king
of Arpad, and the king of the city of Sephar-
vaim, Hena, and Ivah?' " 2 Kin. 18:34
14 [R]And Hezekiah received the letter from
the hand of the messengers, and read it; and
Hezekiah went up to the house of the LORD,
and spread it before the LORD. Is. 37:14
15 Then Hezekiah prayed before the LORD,
and said: "O LORD God of Israel, *the One* who
dwells *between* the cherubim, You are God,
You alone, of all the kingdoms of the earth.
You have made heaven and earth.
16 [R]"Incline Your ear, O LORD, and hear; open
Your eyes, O LORD, and see; and hear the
words of Sennacherib, which he has sent to
reproach the living God. Ps. 31:2
17 "Truly, LORD, the kings of Assyria have
laid waste the nations and their lands,
18 "and have cast their gods into the fire; for
they *were* [R]not gods, but [R]the work of men's
hands—wood and stone. Therefore they de-
stroyed them. [Jer. 10:3–5] • [Acts 17:29]
19 "Now therefore, O LORD our God, I pray,
save us from his hand, [R]that all the kingdoms
of the earth may know that You *are* the LORD
God, You alone." Ps. 83:18
20 Then Isaiah the son of Amoz sent to
Hezekiah, saying, "Thus says the LORD God of
Israel: [R]'Because you have prayed to Me
against Sennacherib king of Assyria, [R]I have
heard.' Is. 37:21 • 2 Kin. 20:5
21 "This *is* the word which the LORD has spo-
ken concerning him:

'The virgin, the daughter of Zion,
Has despised you, laughed you to scorn;
The daughter of Jerusalem
Has shaken *her* head behind your back!

22 'Whom have you reproached and
blasphemed?
Against whom have you raised *your*
voice,
And lifted up your eyes on high?
Against the Holy *One* of Israel.
23 [R]By your messengers you have
reproached the Lord, 2 Kin. 18:17
And said: [R]"By the multitude of my
chariots Ps. 20:7
I have come up to the height of the
mountains,
To the limits of Lebanon;
I will cut down its tall cedars
And its choice cypress trees;
I will enter the extremity of its borders,
To its fruitful forest.
24 I have dug and drunk strange water,
And with the soles of my feet I have
[R]dried up Is. 19:6
All the brooks of defense."

25 'Did you not hear long ago
How [R]I made it,
From ancient times that I formed it?
Now I have brought it to pass,
That [R]you should be
For crushing fortified cities *into* heaps
of ruins. [Is. 45:7] • Is. 10:5, 6
26 Therefore their inhabitants had little
power;
They were dismayed and confounded;
They were *as* the grass of the field
And the green herb,
As the grass on the housetops
And *grain* blighted before it is grown.

27 'But [R]I know your dwelling place,
Your going out and your coming in,
And your rage against Me. Ps. 139:1–3
28 Because your rage against Me and your
tumult
Have come up to My ears,
Therefore [R]I will put My hook in your
nose Ezek. 29:4; 38:4
And My bridle in your lips,
And I will turn you back
By the way which you came.

29 'This *shall be* a [R]sign to you: 2 Kin. 20:8, 9

You shall eat this year such as grows [T]of
itself, Without cultivation
And in the second year what springs
from the same;
Also in the third year sow and reap,
Plant vineyards and eat the fruit of them.
30 [R]And the remnant who have escaped of
the house of Judah 2 Chr. 32:22, 23
Shall again take root downward,
And bear fruit upward.
31 For out of Jerusalem shall go a remnant,
And those who escape from Mount Zion.
[R]The zeal of the LORD of hosts* will do
this.' Is. 9:7

19:31 So with many Heb. mss. and ancient vss. (cf. Is. 37:32); MT omits *of hosts*

32 "Therefore thus says the LORD concerning the king of Assyria:

'He shall [R]not come into this city,
Nor shoot an arrow there, Is. 8:7–10
Nor come before it with shield,
Nor build a siege mound against it.
33 By the way that he came,
By the same shall he return;
And he shall not come into this city,'
Says the LORD.
34 'For I will [R]defend this city, to save it
For My own sake and [R]for My servant
David's sake.' " Is. 31:5 • 1 Kin. 11:12, 13

35 And [R]it came to pass on a certain night that the angel* of the LORD went out, and killed in the camp of the Assyrians one hundred and eighty-five thousand; and when *people* arose early in the morning, there were the corpses—all dead. Is. 10:12–19

36 So Sennacherib king of Assyria departed and went away, returned *home*, and remained at [R]Nineveh. Gen. 10:11

37 Now it came to pass, as he was worshiping in the temple of Nisroch his god, that his sons Adrammelech and Sharezer struck him down with the sword; and they escaped into the land of Ararat. Then [R]Esarhaddon his son reigned in his place. Ezra 4:2

CHAPTER 20

Miraculous Recovery of Hezekiah
2 Chr. 32:24; Is. 38:1–8

IN [R]those days Hezekiah was sick and near death. And Isaiah the prophet, the son of Amoz, went to him and said to him, "Thus says the LORD: 'Set your house in order, for you shall die, and not live.' " Is. 38:1–22

2 Then he turned his face toward the wall, and prayed to the LORD, saying,

3 "Remember now, O LORD, I pray, how I have walked before You in truth and with a loyal heart, and have done *what was* good in Your sight." And Hezekiah wept bitterly.

4 And it happened, before Isaiah had gone out into the middle court, that the word of the LORD came to him, saying,

5 "Return and tell Hezekiah the leader of My people, 'Thus says the LORD, the God of David your father: [R]"I have heard your prayer, I have seen [R]your tears; surely I will heal you. On the third day you shall go up to the house of the LORD. Ps. 65:2 • Ps. 39:12; 56:8

6 "And I will add to your days fifteen years. I will deliver you and this city from the hand of the king of Assyria; and [R]I will defend this city for My own sake, and for the sake of My servant David." ' " 2 Kin. 19:34

7 Then [R]Isaiah said, "Take a lump of figs." So they took and laid *it* on the boil, and he recovered. Is. 38:21

8 And Hezekiah said to Isaiah, [R]"What *is* the sign that the LORD will heal me, and that I shall go up to the house of the LORD the third day?" Judg. 6:17, 37, 39

9 Then Isaiah said, [R]"This is the sign to you from the LORD, that the LORD will do the thing which He has spoken: *shall* the shadow go forward ten degrees or go backward ten degrees?" Is. 38:7, 8

10 And Hezekiah answered, "It is an easy thing for the shadow to go down ten [T]degrees; no, but let the shadow go backward ten degrees." Lit. *steps*

11 So Isaiah the prophet cried out to the LORD, and [R]He brought the shadow ten [T]degrees backward, by which it had gone down on the sundial of Ahaz. Is. 38:8 • Lit. *steps*

Judah's Wealth Is Exposed to Babylon
Is. 39:1, 2

12 [R]At that time Berodach-Baladan* the son of Baladan, king of Babylon, sent letters and a present to Hezekiah, for he heard that Hezekiah had been sick. Is. 39:1–8

13 And Hezekiah was attentive to them, and showed them all the house of his treasures—the silver and gold, the spices and precious ointment, and all* his armory—all that was found among his treasures. There was nothing in his house or in all his dominion that Hezekiah did not show them.

Babylonian Exile Is Prophesied—Is. 39:3–8

14 Then Isaiah the prophet went to King Hezekiah, and said to him, "What did these men say, and from where did they come to you?" So Hezekiah said, "They came from a far country, from Babylon."

15 And he said, "What have they seen in your house?" So Hezekiah answered, [R]"They have seen all that *is* in my house; there is nothing among my treasures that I have not shown them." 2 Kin. 20:13

16 Then Isaiah said to Hezekiah, "Hear the word of the LORD:

17 'Behold, the days are coming when all that *is* in your house, and what your fathers have accumulated until this day, [R]shall be carried to Babylon; nothing shall be left,' says the LORD. Jer. 27:21, 22; 52:17

18 'And they shall take away some of your sons who will descend from you, whom you will beget; and they shall be eunuchs in the palace of the king of Babylon.' "

19 So Hezekiah said to Isaiah, [R]"The word of the LORD which you have spoken *is* good!" For he said, "Will there not be peace and truth at least in my days?" 1 Sam. 3:18

19:35 Or *Angel* **20:12** *Merodach-Baladan*, Is. 39:1
20:13 So with many Heb. mss., Syr., Tg.; MT omits *all*

Death of Hezekiah—2 Chr. 32:32, 33

20 Now the rest of the acts of Hezekiah—all his might, and how he made a [R]pool and a tunnel and brought water into the city—*are* they not written in the book of the chronicles of the kings of Judah? Is. 7:3

21 So Hezekiah rested with his fathers. Then Manasseh his son reigned in his place.

CHAPTER 21

Spiritual Evaluation of Manasseh
2 Chr. 33:1–9

MANASSEH [R]*was* twelve years old when he became king, and he reigned fifty-five years in Jerusalem. His mother's name *was* Hephzibah. 2 Chr. 33:1–9

2 And he did evil in the sight of the LORD, [R]according to the abominations of the nations whom the LORD had cast out before the children of Israel. 2 Kin. 16:3

3 For he rebuilt the high places [R]which Hezekiah his father had destroyed; he raised up altars for Baal, and made a wooden image,* [R]as Ahab king of Israel had done; and he worshiped all the host of heaven* and served them. 2 Kin. 18:4, 22 • 1 Kin. 16:31–33

4 [R]He also built altars in the house of the LORD, of which the LORD had said, "In Jerusalem I will put My name." Jer. 7:30; 32:34

5 And he built altars for all the host of heaven in the [R]two courts of the house of the LORD. 1 Kin. 6:36; 7:12

6 [R]Also he made his son pass through the fire, practiced soothsaying, used witchcraft, and consulted spiritists and mediums. He did much evil in the sight of the LORD, to provoke *Him* to anger. [Lev. 18:21; 20:2]

7 He even set a carved image of Asherah* that he had made, in the house of which the LORD had said to David and to Solomon his son, [R]"In this house and in Jerusalem, which I have chosen out of all the tribes of Israel, I will put My name forever; 1 Kin. 8:29; 9:3

8 "and I will not make the feet of Israel wander anymore from the land which I gave their fathers—only if they are careful to do according to all that I have commanded them, and according to all the law that My servant Moses commanded them."

9 But they paid no attention, and Manasseh [R]seduced them to do more evil than the nations whom the LORD had destroyed before the children of Israel. [Prov. 29:12]

10 And the LORD spoke [R]by His servants the prophets, saying, 2 Kin. 17:13

11 "Because Manasseh king of Judah has done these abominations (he has acted more wickedly than all the [R]Amorites who *were* before him, and [R]has also made Judah sin with his idols), Gen. 15:16 • 2 Kin. 21:9

12 "therefore thus says the LORD God of Israel: 'Behold, *I* am bringing *such* calamity upon Jerusalem and Judah, that whoever hears of it, both his ears will tingle.

13 'And I will stretch over Jerusalem [R]the measuring line of Samaria and the plummet of the house of Ahab; [R]I will wipe Jerusalem as *one* wipes a dish, wiping *it* and turning *it* upside down. Amos 7:7, 8 • 2 Kin. 22:16–19

14 'So I will forsake the [R]remnant of My inheritance and deliver them into the hand of their enemies; and they shall become victims of plunder to all their enemies, Jer. 6:9

15 'because they have done evil in My sight, and have provoked Me to anger since the day their fathers came out of Egypt, even to this day.' "

Political Situation Under Manasseh

16 [R]Moreover Manasseh shed very much innocent blood, till he had filled Jerusalem from one end to another, besides his sin by which he made Judah sin, in doing evil in the sight of the LORD. 2 Kin. 24:4

Death of Manasseh

17 Now the rest of the acts of Manasseh—all that he did, and the sin that he committed—*are* they not written in the book of the chronicles of the kings of Judah?

18 So [R]Manasseh rested with his fathers, and was buried in the garden of his own house, in the garden of Uzza. Then his son Amon reigned in his place. 2 Chr. 33:20

The Reign of Amon in Judah
2 Chr. 33:21–25

19 [R]Amon *was* twenty-two years old when he became king, and he reigned two years in Jerusalem. His mother's name *was* Meshullemeth the daughter of Haruz of Jotbah. 2 Chr. 33:21–23

20 And he did evil in the sight of the LORD, as his father Manasseh had done.

21 So he walked in all the ways that his father had walked; and he served the idols that his father had served, and worshiped them.

22 He forsook the LORD God of his fathers, and did not walk in the way of the LORD.

23 [R]Then the servants of Amon [R]conspired against him, and killed the king in his own house. 2 Chr. 33:24, 25 • 2 Kin. 12:20; 14:19

24 But the people of the land [R]executed all those who had conspired against King Amon. Then the people of the land made his son Josiah king in his place. 2 Kin. 14:5

25 Now the rest of the acts of Amon which he did, *are* they not written in the book of the chronicles of the kings of Judah?

26 And he was buried in his tomb in the garden of Uzza. Then Josiah his son reigned in his place.

21:3 Heb. *Asherah*, a Canaanite goddess • The gods of the Assyrians **21:7** A Canaanite goddess

CHAPTER 22

Spiritual Evaluation of Josiah—2 Chr. 34:1, 2

JOSIAH *was* eight years old when he became king, and he reigned thirty-one years in Jerusalem. His mother's name *was* Jedidah the daughter of Adaiah of Bozkath.

2 And he did *what was* right in the sight of the LORD, and walked in all the ways of his father David; he [R]did not turn aside to the right hand or to the left. Deut. 5:32

The Temple Is Repaired—2 Chr. 34:8–13

3 [R]Now it came to pass, in the eighteenth year of King Josiah, *that* the king sent Shaphan the scribe, the son of Azaliah, the son of Meshullam, to the house of the LORD, saying: 2 Chr. 34:8

4 "Go up to Hilkiah the high priest, that he may count the money which has been [R]brought into the house of the LORD, which [R]the doorkeepers have gathered from the people. 2 Kin. 12:4 • 2 Kin. 12:9, 10

5 "And let them [R]deliver it into the hand of those doing the work, who are the overseers in the house of the LORD; let them give it to those who *are* in the house of the LORD doing the work, to repair the damages of the house— 2 Kin. 12:11–14

6 "to carpenters and builders and masons—and to buy timber and hewn stone to repair the house.

7 "However there need be no accounting made with them of the money delivered into their hand, because they deal faithfully."

The Book of the Law Is Discovered 2 Chr. 34:15–18

8 Then Hilkiah the high priest said to Shaphan the scribe, [R]"I have found the Book of the Law in the house of the LORD." And Hilkiah gave the book to Shaphan, and he read it. Deut. 31:24–26

9 So Shaphan the scribe went to the king, bringing the king word, saying, "Your servants have gathered the money that was found in the house, and have delivered it into the hand of those who do the work, who oversee the house of the LORD."

10 Then Shaphan the scribe showed the king, saying, "Hilkiah the priest has given me a book." And Shaphan read it before the king.

Repentance of Josiah—2 Chr. 34:19–22

11 Now it happened, when the king heard the words of the Book of the Law, that he tore his clothes.

12 Then the king commanded Hilkiah the priest, [R]Ahikam the son of Shaphan, Achbor* the son of Michaiah, Shaphan the scribe, and Asaiah a servant of the king, saying, Jer. 26:24

13 "Go, inquire of the LORD for me, for the people and for all Judah, concerning the words of this book that has been found; for great *is* [R]the wrath of the LORD that is aroused against us, because our fathers have not obeyed the words of this book, to do according to all that is written concerning us." [Deut. 29:23–28; 31:17, 18]

14 So Hilkiah the priest, Ahikam, Achbor, Shaphan, and Asaiah went to Huldah the prophetess, the wife of Shallum the son of Tikvah, the son of Harhas, keeper of the wardrobe. (She dwelt in Jerusalem in the Second Quarter.) And they spoke with her.

Prophecy of Blessing—2 Chr. 34:23–28

15 Then she said to them, "Thus says the LORD God of Israel, 'Tell the man who sent you to Me,

16 "Thus says the LORD: 'Behold, [R]I will bring calamity on this place and on its inhabitants—all the words of the book which the king of Judah has read— Deut. 29:27

17 [R]'because they have forsaken Me and burned incense to other gods, that they might provoke Me to anger with all the works of their hands. Therefore My wrath shall be aroused against this place and shall not be quenched.' " ' Deut. 29:25–27

18 "But as for [R]the king of Judah, who sent you to inquire of the LORD, in this manner you shall speak to him, 'Thus says the LORD God of Israel: "*Concerning* the words which you have heard— 2 Chr. 34:26

19 "because your [R]heart was tender, and you humbled yourself before the LORD when you heard what I spoke against this place and against its inhabitants, that they would become a desolation and a curse, and you tore your clothes and wept before Me, I also have heard *you*," says the LORD. [Ps. 51:17]

20 "Surely, therefore, I will gather you to your fathers, and you [R]shall [T]be gathered to your grave in peace; and your eyes shall not see all the calamity which I will bring on this place." ' " So they brought back word to the king. [Is. 57:1, 2] • Die a natural death

CHAPTER 23

Institution of the Covenant—2 Chr. 34:29–32

NOW the king sent them to gather all the elders of Judah and Jerusalem to him.

2 The king went up to the house of the LORD with all the men of Judah, and with him all the inhabitants of Jerusalem—the priests and the prophets and all the people, both small and great. And he [R]read in their hearing all the words of the Book of the Covenant [R]which had been found in the house of the LORD. Deut. 31:10–13 • 2 Kin. 22:8

22:12 *Abdon the son of Micah,* 2 Chr. 34:20

3 Then the king [R]stood by a pillar and made
a [R]covenant before the LORD, to follow the
LORD and to keep His commandments and
His testimonies and His statutes, with all *his*
heart and all *his* soul, to perform the words of
this covenant that were written in this book.
And all the people took a stand for the
covenant. 2 Kin. 11:14 • 2 Kin. 11:17

Reforms Because of the Covenant
2 Chr. 34:33—35:19

4 And the king commanded Hilkiah the
high priest, the [R]priests of the second order,
and the doorkeepers, to bring out of the tem-
ple of the LORD all the articles that were made
for Baal, for Asherah,* and for all the host of
heaven;* and he burned them outside Jerusa-
lem in the fields of Kidron, and carried their
ashes to Bethel. 2 Kin. 25:18
5 Then he removed the idolatrous priests
whom the kings of Judah had ordained to
burn incense on the high places in the cities of
Judah and in the places all around Jerusalem,
and those who burned incense to Baal, to the
sun, to the moon, to the constellations, and to
all the host of heaven.
6 And he brought out the wooden image*
from the house of the LORD, to the Brook
Kidron outside Jerusalem, burned it at the
Brook Kidron and ground *it* to [R]ashes, and
threw its ashes on [R]the graves of the common
people. Ex. 32:20 • 2 Chr. 34:4
7 Then he tore down the *ritual* booths of
the perverted persons* that *were* in the house
of the LORD, [R]where the women wove hang-
ings for the wooden image. Ezek. 16:16
8 And he brought all the priests from the
cities of Judah, and defiled the high places
where the priests had burned incense, from
[R]Geba to Beersheba; also he broke down the
high places at the gates which *were* at the en-
trance of the Gate of Joshua the governor of
the city, which *were* to the left of the city
gate. Josh. 21:17
9 Nevertheless the priests of the high
places did not come up to the altar of the LORD
in Jerusalem, [R]but they ate unleavened bread
among their brethren. 1 Sam. 2:36
10 And he defiled [R]Topheth, which *is* in the
Valley of the Son* of Hinnom, that no man
might make his son or his daughter pass
through the fire to Molech. Is. 30:33
11 Then he removed the horses that the
kings of Judah had [T]dedicated to the sun, at
the entrance to the house of the LORD, by the
chamber of Nathan-Melech, the officer who
was in the court; and he burned the chariots
of the sun with fire. *given*
12 The altars that *were* [R]on the roof, the
upper chamber of Ahaz, which the kings of
Judah had made, and the altars which
[R]Manasseh had made in the two courts of the
house of the LORD, the king broke down and
pulverized there, and threw their dust into the
Brook Kidron. Jer. 19:13 • 2 Kin. 21:5
13 Then the king defiled the high places that
were east of Jerusalem, which *were* on the
south of the Mount of Corruption, which [R]Sol-
omon king of Israel had built for Ashtoreth
the abomination of the Sidonians, for Che-
mosh the abomination of the Moabites, and
for Milcom the abomination of the people of
Ammon. 1 Kin. 11:5–7
14 And he broke in pieces the *sacred* pillars
and cut down the wooden images, and filled
their places with the bones of men.
15 Moreover the altar that *was* at Bethel,
and the high place [R]which Jeroboam the son
of Nebat, who made Israel sin, had made,
both that altar and the high place he broke
down; and he burned the high place *and*
crushed *it* to powder, and burned the wooden
image. 1 Kin. 12:28–33

23:4 A Canaanite goddess • The gods of the Assyrians **23:6** Heb. *Asherah*, a Canaanite goddess **23:7** Heb. *qedeshim*, those practicing sodomy and prostitution in religious rituals **23:10** Kt. *Sons*

23:3 Knowing the Will of God Through the Scriptures—The best way to study a subject often begins with a definition of that subject. What do we mean by the will of God? It is that holy and stated purpose of the Father to make His dear children as much like Christ as possible.

Without doubt the most important factor in finding God's will is the Bible itself. God speaks to us not in some loud voice, but through the Scriptures. *First,* the Scriptures declare He does have a definite will for my life. "The steps of a *good* man are ordered by the LORD" (Page 564—Ps. 37:23). "I will instruct you and teach you in the way you should go" (Page 561—Ps. 32:8). See also Eph. 2:10; Heb. 12:1. *Second,* God desires us to know this will for our lives. "Therefore do not be unwise, but understand what the will of the Lord *is*" (Page 1208—Eph. 5:17). *Third,* this will is continuous. It does not begin when I am thirty years of age. God has a will for children, young people, adults, and senior citizens. See Is. 58:11. *Fourth,* God's will is specific. "Your ears shall hear a word behind you, saying, 'This *is* the way, walk in it' " (Page 709—Is. 30:21). "But the way of the upright *is* a highway" (Page 641—Prov. 15:19). *Fifth,* God's will is profitable (Page 214—Josh. 1:8; Page 546—Ps. 1:1–3).

What is the will of God for us? As we have already noted, it differs from believer to believer. But here are four aspects in the will of God which apply to every Christian:

a. It is His will that we learn more about God (Page 1219—Col. 1:9).
b. It is His will that we grow in grace (Page 1228—1 Thess. 4:3).
c. It is His will that we study His Word (Page 1245—2 Tim. 3:14–17).
d. It is His will that we share our faith (Page 1112—Acts 1:8; Page 1238—1 Tim. 2:4; Page 1288—2 Pet. 3:9).

Now turn to Page 882—Dan. 9:3, 4: Knowing the Will of God Through Prayer and Fasting.

16 As Josiah turned, he saw the tombs that *were* there on the mountain. And he sent and took the bones out of the tombs and burned *them* on the altar, and defiled it according to the [R]word of the LORD which the man of God proclaimed, who proclaimed these words. 1 Kin. 13:2

17 Then he said, "What gravestone *is* this that I see?" So the men of the city told him, "*It is* [R]the tomb of the man of God who came from Judah and proclaimed these things which you have done against the altar of Bethel." 1 Kin. 13:1, 30, 31

18 And he said, "Let him alone; let no one move his bones." So they let his bones alone, with the bones of [R]the prophet who came from Samaria. 1 Kin. 13:11, 31

19 Now Josiah also took away all the shrines of the high places that *were* [R]in the cities of Samaria, which the kings of Israel had made to provoke the LORD* to anger; and he did to them according to all the deeds he had done in Bethel. 2 Chr. 34:6, 7

20 [R]He executed all the priests of the high places who *were* there, on the altars, and [R]burned men's bones on them; and he returned to Jerusalem. 1 Kin. 13:2 • 2 Chr. 34:5

21 Then the king commanded all the people, saying, [R]"Keep the Passover to the LORD your God, [R]as *it is* written in this Book of the Covenant." 2 Chr. 35:1 • Deut. 16:2–8

22 [R]Such a Passover surely had never been held since the days of the judges who judged Israel, nor in all the days of the kings of Israel and the kings of Judah. 2 Chr. 35:18, 19

23 But in the eighteenth year of King Josiah this Passover was held before the LORD in Jerusalem.

24 Moreover Josiah put away those who consulted mediums and spiritists, the household gods and idols, all the abominations that were seen in the land of Judah and in Jerusalem, that he might perform the words of [R]the law which were written in the book that Hilkiah the priest found in the house of the LORD. [Lev. 19:31; 20:27]

25 [R]Now before him there was no king like him, who turned to the LORD with all his heart, with all his soul, and with all his might, according to all the Law of Moses; nor after him did *any* arise like him. 2 Kin. 18:5

26 Nevertheless the LORD did not turn from the fierceness of His great wrath, with which His anger was aroused against Judah, [R]because of all the provocations with which Manasseh had provoked Him. Jer. 15:4

27 And the LORD said, "I will also remove Judah from My sight, as I have removed Israel, and will cast off this city Jerusalem which I have chosen, and the house of which I said, 'My name shall be there.' "*

Political Situation Under Josiah
2 Chr. 35:20–23

28 Now the rest of the acts of Josiah, and all that he did, *are* they not written in the book of the chronicles of the kings of Judah?

29 In his days Pharaoh Necho king of Egypt went to the aid of the king of Assyria, to the River Euphrates; and King Josiah went against him. And *Pharaoh Necho* killed him at Megiddo when he confronted him.

Death of Josiah—2 Chr. 35:24—36:1

30 [R]Then his servants moved his body in a chariot from Megiddo, brought him to Jerusalem, and buried him in his own tomb. And the people of the land took Jehoahaz the son of Josiah, anointed him, and made him king in his father's place. 2 Chr. 35:24

The Reign of Jehoahaz in Judah
2 Chr. 36:2–4

31 [R]Jehoahaz *was* twenty-three years old when he became king, and he reigned three months in Jerusalem. His mother's name *was* [R]Hamutal the daughter of Jeremiah of Libnah. Jer. 22:11 • 2 Kin. 24:18

32 And he did evil in the sight of the LORD, according to all that his fathers had done.

33 Now Pharaoh Necho put him in prison at Riblah in the land of Hamath, that he might not reign in Jerusalem; and he imposed on the land a tribute of one hundred talents of silver and a talent of gold.

34 Then Pharaoh Necho made Eliakim the son of Josiah king in place of his father Josiah, and [R]changed his name to Jehoiakim. And *Pharaoh* took Jehoahaz and went to Egypt, and he* died there. Dan. 1:7

The Reign of Jehoiakim in Judah
2 Chr. 36:5–8

35 So Jehoiakim gave [R]the silver and gold to Pharaoh; but he taxed the land to give money according to the command of Pharaoh; he exacted the silver and gold from the people of the land, from every one according to his assessment, to give *it* to Pharaoh Necho. 2 Kin. 23:33

36 Jehoiakim *was* twenty-five years old when he became king, and he reigned eleven years in Jerusalem. His mother's name *was* Zebudah the daughter of Pedaiah of Rumah.

37 And he did evil in the sight of the LORD, according to all that his fathers had done.

CHAPTER 24

IN [R]his days Nebuchadnezzar king of [R]Babylon came up, and Jehoiakim became his vassal *for* three years. Then he turned and rebelled against him. Dan. 1:1 • 2 Kin. 20:14

23:19 So with LXX, Syr., Vg.; MT, Tg. omit *the LORD*
23:27 1 Kin. 8:29 **23:34** Jehoahaz

2 [R]And the LORD sent against him *raiding*
[T]bands of Chaldeans, bands of Syrians, bands
of Moabites, and bands of the people of
Ammon; He sent them against Judah to de-
stroy it, according to the word of the LORD
which He had spoken by His servants the
prophets. Jer. 25:9; 32:28; 35:11 • *troops*
3 Surely at the commandment of the LORD
this came upon Judah, to remove *them* from
His sight because of the sins of Manasseh, ac-
cording to all that he had done,
4 [R]and also because of the innocent blood
that he had shed; for he had filled Jerusalem
with innocent blood, which the LORD would
not pardon. 2 Kin. 21:16
5 Now the rest of the acts of Jehoiakim, and
all that he did, *are* they not written in the book
of the chronicles of the kings of Judah?
6 [R]So Jehoiakim rested with his fathers.
Then Jehoiachin his son reigned in his
place. Jer. 22:18, 19
7 And [R]the king of Egypt did not come out
of his land anymore, for [R]the king of Babylon
had taken all that belonged to the king of
Egypt from the Brook of Egypt to the River
Euphrates. Jer. 37:5–7 • Jer. 46:2

The Reign of Jehoiachin in Judah
2 Chr. 36:9, 10

8 [R]Jehoiachin *was* eighteen years old when
he became king, and he reigned in Jerusalem
three months. His mother's name *was* Ne-
hushta the daughter of Elnathan of Jerusa-
lem. 2 Chr. 36:9
9 And he did evil in the sight of the LORD,
according to all that his father had done.
10 At that time the servants of Nebuchad-
nezzar king of Babylon came up against Jeru-
salem, and the city was besieged.
11 And Nebuchadnezzar king of Babylon
came against the city, as his servants were be-
sieging it.
12 Then Jehoiachin king of Judah, his
mother, his servants, his princes, and his offi-
cers went out to the king of Babylon; and the
king of Babylon, [R]in the eighth year of his
reign, took him prisoner. 2 Chr. 36:10
13 [R]And he carried out from there all the
treasures of the house of the LORD and the
treasures of the king's house, and he cut in
pieces all the articles of gold which Solomon
king of Israel had made in the temple of the
LORD, as the LORD had said. Is. 39:6
14 Also [R]he carried into captivity all Jeru-
salem: all the captains and all the mighty
men of valor, [R]ten thousand captives, and
[R]all the craftsmen and smiths. None re-
mained except the poorest people of the
land. Jer. 24:1 • 2 Kin. 24:16 • 1 Sam. 13:19
15 And [R]he carried Jehoiachin captive to
Babylon. The king's mother, the king's wives,
his officers, and the mighty of the land he
carried into captivity from Jerusalem to
Babylon. Jer. 22:24–28
16 All the valiant men, seven thousand, and
craftsmen and smiths, one thousand, all *who
were* strong *and* fit for war, these the king of
Babylon brought captive to Babylon.

Spiritual Evaluation of Zedekiah
2 Chr. 36:10–16; Jer. 52:1, 2

17 Then the king of Babylon made Matta-
niah, *Jehoiachin's** uncle, king in his place,
and changed his name to Zedekiah.
18 [R]Zedekiah *was* twenty-one years old
when he became king, and he reigned eleven
years in Jerusalem. His mother's name *was*
[R]Hamutal the daughter of Jeremiah of Lib-
nah. Jer. 52:1 • 2 Kin. 23:31
19 He also did evil in the sight of the LORD,
according to all that Jehoiakim had done.

Political Situation Under Zedekiah
2 Chr. 36:17–20; Jer. 52:3–27

20 For because of the anger of the LORD *this*
happened in Jerusalem and Judah, that He fi-
nally cast them out from His presence. [R]Then
Zedekiah rebelled against the king of Bab-
ylon. Ezek. 17:15

CHAPTER 25

NOW it came to pass [R]in the ninth year of
his reign, in the tenth month, on the
tenth *day* of the month, *that* Nebuchadnezzar
king of Babylon and all his army came
against Jerusalem and encamped against it;
and they built a siege wall against it all
around. Jer. 6:6; 34:2
2 So the city was besieged until the
eleventh year of King Zedekiah.
3 By the ninth *day* of the [R]*fourth* month
the famine had become so severe in the city
that there was no food for the people of the
land. Lam. 4:9, 10
4 Then [R]the city wall was broken through,
and all the men of war *fled* at night by way of
the gate between two walls, which was by the
king's garden, even though the Chaldeans
were still encamped all around against the
city. And [R]*the king** went by way of the
plain.* Jer. 39:2 • Ezek. 12:12
5 But the army of the Chaldeans pursued
the king, and they overtook him in the plains of
Jericho. All his army was scattered from him.
6 So they took the king and brought him up
to the king of Babylon at Riblah, and they
pronounced judgment on him.
7 Then they killed the sons of Zedekiah be-
fore his eyes, [R]put[T] out the eyes of Zedekiah,
bound him with bronze fetters, and took him
to Babylon. Jer. 39:7 • *blinded*

24:17 Lit. *his* **25:4** Lit. *he* • Or *Arabah*, the Jordan Valley

8 And in the fifth month, [R]on the seventh *day* of the month (which *was* the nineteenth year of King Nebuchadnezzar king of Babylon), [R]Nebuzaradan the captain of the guard, a servant of the king of Babylon, came to Jerusalem. Jer. 52:12 • Jer. 39:9

9 He burned the house of the LORD [R]and the king's house; all the houses of Jerusalem, that is, all the houses of the great, [R]he burned with fire. Jer. 39:8 • Jer. 17:27

10 And all the army of the Chaldeans who *were with* the captain of the guard broke down the walls of Jerusalem all around.

11 Then Nebuzaradan the captain of the guard carried away captive the rest of the people *who* remained in the city and the defectors who had deserted to the king of Babylon, with the rest of the multitude.

12 But the captain of the guard [R]left *some* of the poor of the land as vinedressers and farmers. Jer. 39:10; 40:7; 52:16

13 The bronze pillars that *were* in the house of the LORD, and the carts and the bronze Sea that *were* in the house of the LORD, the Chaldeans broke in pieces, and carried their bronze to Babylon.

14 They also took away [R]the pots, the shovels, the trimmers, the spoons, and all the bronze utensils with which the priests ministered. Ex. 27:3

15 The firepans and the basins, the things of solid gold and solid silver, the captain of the guard took away.

16 The two pillars, one Sea, and the carts, which Solomon had made for the house of the LORD, [R]the bronze of all these articles was beyond measure. 1 Kin. 7:47

17 The height of one pillar *was* eighteen cubits, and the capital on it *was* of bronze. The height of the capital was three cubits, and the network and pomegranates all around the capital were all of bronze. The second pillar was the same, with a network.

18 And the captain of the guard took Seraiah the chief priest, Zephaniah the second priest, and the three doorkeepers.

19 He also took out of the city an officer who had charge of the men of war, [R]five men of the king's close associates who were found in the city, the chief recruiting officer of the army, who mustered the people of the land, and sixty men of the people of the land *who were* found in the city. Jer. 52:25

20 So Nebuzaradan, captain of the guard, took these and brought them to the king of Babylon at Riblah.

21 Then the king of Babylon struck them and put them to death at Riblah in the land of Hamath. [R]Thus Judah was carried away captive from its own land. Deut. 28:36, 64

The Governorship of Gedaliah Jer. 40:5—41:18

22 Then he made Gedaliah the son of [R]Ahikam, the son of Shaphan, governor over [R]the people who remained in the land of Judah, whom Nebuchadnezzar king of Babylon had left. 2 Kin. 22:12 • Is. 1:9; Jer. 40:5

23 Now when all the captains of the armies, they and *their* men, heard that the king of Babylon had made Gedaliah governor, they came to Gedaliah at Mizpah—Ishmael the son of Nethaniah, Johanan the son of Careah, Seraiah the son of Tanhumeth the Netophathite, and Jaazaniah* the son of a Maachathite, they and their men.

24 And Gedaliah took an oath before them and their men, and said to them, "Do not be afraid of the servants of the Chaldeans. Dwell in the land and serve the king of Babylon, and it shall be well with you."

25 But [R]it happened in the seventh month that Ishmael the son of Nethaniah, the son of Elishama, of the royal family, came with ten men and struck and killed Gedaliah, the Jews, as well as the Chaldeans who were with him at Mizpah. Jer. 41:1–3

26 And all the people, small and great, and the captains of the armies, arose [R]and went to Egypt; for they were afraid of the Chaldeans. Jer. 43:4–7

The Release of Jehoiachin in Babylon Jer. 52:31–34

27 [R]Now it came to pass in the thirty-seventh year of the captivity of Jehoiachin king of Judah, in the twelfth month, on the twenty-seventh *day* of the month, *that* Evil-Merodach* king of Babylon, in the year that he began to reign, released Jehoiachin king of Judah from prison. Jer. 52:31–34

28 He spoke kindly to him, and gave him a more prominent seat than those of the kings who *were* with him in Babylon.

29 So Jehoiachin changed from his prison garments, and he ate [T]bread regularly before the king all the days of his life. Food

30 And as for his provisions, *there was* a regular ration given him by the king, a portion for each day, all the days of his life.

25:23 *Jezaniah*, Jer. 40:8 **25:27** Lit. *Man of Marduk*

THE FIRST BOOK OF THE

CHRONICLES

THE BOOK OF 1 CHRONICLES

The books of 1 and 2 Chronicles cover the same period of Jewish history described in 2 Samuel through 2 Kings, but the perspective is different. These books are no mere repetition of the same material, but rather form a divine editorial on the history of God's people. While 2 Samuel and 1 and 2 Kings give a political history of Israel and Judah, 1 and 2 Chronicles present a religious history of the Davidic dynasty of Judah. The former are written from a prophetic and moral viewpoint, and the latter from a priestly and spiritual perspective. The Book of 1 Chronicles begins with the royal line of David and then traces the spiritual significance of David's righteous reign.

The books of 1 and 2 Chronicles were originally one continuous work in the Hebrew. The title was *Dibere Hayyamim,* meaning "The Words [accounts, events] of the Days." The equivalent meaning today would be "The Events of the Times." Chronicles was divided into two parts in the third-century B.C. Greek translation of the Hebrew Bible (the Septuagint). At that time it was given the name *Paraleipomenon,* "Of Things Omitted," referring to the things omitted from Samuel and Kings. Some copies add the phrase, *Basileon Iouda,* "Concerning the Kings of Judah." The first book of Chronicles was called *Paraleipomenon Primus,* "The First Book of Things Omitted." The name "Chronicles" comes from Jerome in his Latin Vulgate Bible (A.D. 385–405): *Chronicorum Liber.* He meant his title in the sense of "The Chronicles of the Whole of Sacred History."

THE AUTHOR OF 1 CHRONICLES

Although the text does not identify the author, several facts seem to support the tradition in the Jewish Talmud that Ezra the priest was the author. The content points to a priestly authorship because of the emphasis on the temple, the priesthood, and the theocratic line of David in the southern kingdom of Judah. The narrative also indicates that Chronicles was at least written by a contemporary of Ezra. Chronicles is quite similar in style to the Book of Ezra, and both share a priestly perspective: genealogies, temple worship, ministry of the priesthood, and obedience to the law of God. In addition, the closing verses of 2 Chronicles (36:22, 23) are repeated with minor changes as the opening verses of Ezra (1:1–3). Thus, Chronicles and Ezra may have been one consecutive history as were Luke and Acts.

Ezra was an educated scribe (Ezra 7:6), and according to the apocryphal book of 2 Maccabees 2:13–15, Nehemiah collected an extensive library which was available to Ezra for his use in compiling Chronicles. Many of these documents and sources are listed in the book (see "The Author of 2 Chronicles"). Scholars of Israel accumulated and compared historical material, and the author of Chronicles was actually a compiler who drew from many sources under the guidance and inspiration of the Holy Spirit.

THE TIME OF 1 CHRONICLES

The genealogies in chapters 1—9 cover the time from Adam to David, and chapters 10—29 focus on the thirty-three years of David's rule over the united kingdoms of Israel and Judah (1004–971 B.C.). However, the genealogies extend to about 500 B.C., as seen in the mention of Zerubbabel, grandson of King Jeconiah, who leads the first return of the Jews from exile in 538 B.C., and also Zerubbabel's two grandsons Pelatiah and Jeshaiah (3:21).

Ezra probably completed Chronicles between 450 and 430 B.C. and addressed it to the returned remnant. Ezra leads some of the exiles to Jerusalem in 457 B.C. and ministers to the people as their spiritual leader. During Ezra's time, Nehemiah is the political leader and Malachi is the moral leader. Chronicles spends a disproportionate time on the reigns of David and Solomon because they bring the nation to its pinnacle. The book is written to the people of Israel's "Second Commonwealth" to encourage them and to remind them that they must remain the covenant people of God. This reminds the Jews of their spiritual heritage and identity during the difficult times they are facing.

THE CHRIST OF 1 CHRONICLES

See the introductions to 1 and 2 Samuel for descriptions of David as a type of Christ. The Davidic covenant of 2 Samuel 7 is found again in 1 Chronicles 17:11–14. Solomon fulfilled part, but the promise of the eternality of David's throne can only point to the coming of the Messiah.

The tribe of Judah is placed first in the national genealogy in 1 Chronicles because the monarchy, temple, and Messiah (Gen. 49:10) will come from this tribe. Since the books of Chronicles are the last books of the Hebrew Bible, the genealogies in chapters 1—9 are a preamble to the genealogy of Christ in the first book of the New Testament.

KEYS TO 1 CHRONICLES

Key Verses: 1 Chronicles 17:11–14; 29:11—"And it shall be, when your days are fulfilled, when you must go *to be* with your fathers, that I will set up your seed after you, who will be of your sons; and I will establish his kingdom. He shall build Me a house, and I will establish his throne forever. I will be his Father, and he shall be My son; and I will not take My mercy away from him, as I took *it* from *him* who was before you. And I will establish him in My house and in My kingdom forever; and his throne shall be established forever" (17:11–14).

"Yours, O LORD, *is* the greatness, the power and the glory, the victory and the majesty; for all *that is* in heaven and in earth *is Yours;* Yours is the kingdom, O LORD, and You are exalted as head over all" (29:11).

Key Chapter: 1 Chronicles 17—Pivotal for the Book of 1 Chronicles as well as for the rest of the Scriptures is the Davidic covenant recorded in 2 Samuel 7 and 1 Chronicles 17. God promises David that He will "establish him [David's ultimate offspring, Jesus Christ] in My house and in My kingdom forever; and his throne shall be established forever" (1 Chr. 17:14).

SURVEY OF 1 CHRONICLES

Chronicles retraces the whole story of Israel's history up to the return from captivity in order to give the returned remnant a divine perspective on the developments of their past. The whole Book of 1 Chronicles, like 2 Samuel, is dedicated to the life of David. It begins with the royal line of David (1—9) before surveying key events of the reign of David (10—29).

Royal Line of David (1—9): These nine chapters are the most comprehensive genealogical tables in the Bible. They trace the family tree of David and Israel as a whole, but in a highly selective manner. The genealogies place a disproportionate emphasis on the tribes of Judah and Benjamin because Chronicles is not concerned with the northern kingdom but with the southern kingdom and the Davidic dynasty. They show God at work in selecting and preserving a people for Himself from the beginning of human history to the period after the Babylonian exile. The genealogies move from the patriarchal period (Adam to Jacob; 1:1—2:2) to the national period (Judah, Levi, and the other tribes of Israel; 2:3—9:44). They demonstrate God's keeping of His covenant promises in maintaining the Davidic line through the centuries. The priestly perspective of Chronicles is evident in the special attention given to the tribe of Levi.

Reign of David (10—29): Compared with 2 Samuel, David's life in 1 Chronicles is seen in an entirely different light. This is clear from both the omissions and the additions. Chronicles completely omits David's struggles with Saul, his seven-year reign in Hebron, his various wives, and Absalom's rebellion. It also omits the event in 2 Samuel that hurt the rest of his life—his sin with Bathsheba. Chronicles is written from a more positive perspective, emphasizing God's grace and forgiveness, in order to encourage the Jews who have just returned from captivity. Chronicles adds events not found in 2 Samuel, such as David's preparations for the temple and its worship services.

Only one chapter is given to Saul's reign (10), because his heart was not right with God. David's story begins with his coronation over all Israel after he has already reigned for seven years as king over Judah. Chronicles stresses his deep spiritual commitment, courage, and integrity. It emphasizes his concern for the things of the Lord, including his return of the ark and his desire to build a temple for God. God establishes His crucial covenant with David (17), and

FOCUS	ROYAL LINE OF DAVID	REIGN OF DAVID				
REFERENCE	1:1———	10:1———	13:1———	18:1———	21:1———	28:1———29:30
DIVISION	GENEALOGIES OF DAVID AND ISRAEL	ACCESSION OF DAVID AS KING	ACQUISITION OF THE ARK	VICTORIES OF DAVID	PREPARATION FOR THE TEMPLE	LAST DAYS OF DAVID
TOPIC	GENEALOGY	HISTORY				
	ANCESTRY	ACTIVITY				
LOCATION	ISRAEL					
TIME	THOUSANDS OF YEARS	c. 33 YEARS				

the kingdom is strengthened and expanded under his reign (18—20). His sin in numbering the people is recorded to teach the consequences of disobeying God's law. Most of the rest of the book (22—29) is concerned with David's preparations for the building of the temple and the worship associated with it. The priestly perspective of Chronicles can be seen in the disproportionate space given to the temple and the priests. David is not allowed to build the temple (28:3); but he designs the plans, gathers the materials, prepares the site, and arranges for the Levites, priests, choirs, porters, soldiers, and stewards. The book closes with his beautiful public prayer of praise and the accession of Solomon.

OUTLINE OF 1 CHRONICLES

Part One: The Royal Line of David (1:1—9:44)

Part Two: The Reign of David (10:1—29:30)

1. Desire of David to Build God's House 17:1, 2
2. Covenant of God to Build David's House 17:3–15
3. Praise Prayer of David 17:16–27

III. The Military Victories of King David ....18:1—20:8

A. David's Early Victories Are Summarized 18:1–17
1. Victory over Philistia 18:1
2. Victory over Moab 18:2
3. Victory over Zobah 18:3, 4
4. Victory over Syria 18:5–11
5. Victory over Edom 18:12–17

B. David's Latter Victories Are Summarized ....19:1—20:8
1. Humiliation of David's Servants 19:1–5
2. Victory over the Ammonites 19:6–15
3. Victory over the Syrians 19:16–19
4. Victory over the Ammonites 20:1–3
5. Victory over the Philistine Giants 20:4–8

IV. The Preparation and Organization of Israel for the Temple ....21:1—27:34

A. Sinful Census of David 21:1–30
1. Temptation of David by Satan 21:1–4
2. Enumeration of Israel 21:5, 6
3. Judgment of God 21:7–17
4. Withholding of Judgment by Sacrifices 21:18–30

B. Material Provisions for the Temple's Construction 22:1–5

C. Leaders Are Charged to Construct the Temple 22:6–19
1. David's Charge to Solomon 22:6–16
2. David's Charge to the Leaders 22:17–19

D. Organization of the Temple Leaders ....23:1—26:32
1. Organization of the Levitical Houses 23:1–32
2. Organization of the Courses of the Priests 24:1–31
3. Organization of the Orders of the Musicians 25:1–31
4. Organization of the Gatekeepers 26:1–19
5. Organization of the Treasuries of the Temple 26:20–28
6. Organization of the Officers Outside of the Temple 26:29–32

E. Organization of the Leaders of the Nation of Israel 27:1–34
1. The Twelve Captains of Israel 27:1–15
2. The Leaders of the Twelve Tribes 27:16–24
3. The Royal Officers of David 27:25–31
4. The Counselors of David 27:32–34

V. The Last Days of David ....28:1—29:30

A. Final Exhortations of David 28:1–10
1. Charge to Israel 28:1–8
2. Charge to Solomon 28:9, 10

B. Final Provisions for the Temple ....28:11—29:9
1. Pattern for the Temple 28:11–21
2. Provisions of David for the Temple 29:1–5
3. Provisions of Israel for the Temple 29:6–9

C. David's Final Prayer of Thanksgiving 29:10–19

D. Coronation of Solomon 29:20–25

E. Death of King David 29:26–30

CHAPTER 1

The Genealogy from Adam to Noah
Gen. 5:1–32; Luke 3:36–38

ADAM, [R]Seth, Enosh, Gen. 4:25, 26; 5:3–9
2 Cainan,* Mahalalel, Jared,
3 Enoch, Methuselah, Lamech,
4 Noah,* Shem, Ham, and Japheth.

Sons of Japheth—Gen. 10:2–5

5 [R]The sons of Japheth *were* Gomer,
Magog, Madai, Javan, Tubal, Meshech, and
Tiras. Gen. 10:2–4
6 The sons of Gomer *were* Ashkenaz,
Diphath,* and Togarmah.
7 The sons of Javan *were* Elishah,
Tarshishah,* Kittim, and Rodanim.*

Sons of Ham—Gen. 10:6–18

8 [R]The sons of Ham *were* Cush, Mizraim,
Put, and Canaan. Gen. 10:6
9 The sons of Cush *were* Seba, Havilah,
Sabta,* Raama,* and Sabtecha. The sons of
Raama *were* Sheba and Dedan.
10 Cush [R]begot Nimrod; he began to be a
mighty one on the earth. Gen. 10:8–10, 13
11 Mizraim begot Ludim, Anamim, Le-
habim, Naphtuhim,
12 Pathrusim, Casluhim (from whom came
the Philistines and the Caphtorim).
13 [R]Canaan begot Sidon, his firstborn, and
Heth; Gen. 9:18, 25–27; 10:15
14 the Jebusite, the Amorite, and the Gir-
gashite;
15 the Hivite, the Arkite, and the Sinite;
16 the Arvadite, the Zemarite, and the
Hamathite.

Sons of Shem
Gen. 10:21–29; 11:10–26; Luke 3:34–36

17 The sons of [R]Shem *were* Elam, Asshur,
[R]Arphaxad, Lud, Aram, Uz, Hul, Gether, and
Meshech.* Gen. 10:22–29; 11:10 • Luke 3:36
18 Arphaxad begot Shelah, and Shelah be-
got Eber.
19 To Eber were born two sons: the name of
one *was* Peleg,* for in his days the [T]earth

1:2 Heb. *Qenan* **1:4** So with MT, Vg.; LXX adds *the sons of Noah* **1:6** *Riphath,* Gen. 10:3 **1:7** *Tarshish,* Gen. 10:4 • *Dodanim,* Gen. 10:4 **1:9** *Sabtah,* Gen. 10:7 • *Raamah,* Gen. 10:7 **1:17** *Mash,* Gen. 10:23 **1:19** Lit. *Division,* Gen. 10:25

was divided; and his brother's name *was* Joktan. Or *land*

20 [R]Joktan begot Almodad, Sheleph, Hazarmaveth, Jerah, Gen. 10:26

21 Hadoram, Uzal, Diklah,

22 Ebal,* Abimael, Sheba,

23 Ophir, Havilah, and Jobab. All these *were* the sons of Joktan.

24 [R]Shem, Arphaxad, Shelah, Luke 3:34–36

25 [R]Eber, Peleg, Reu, Gen. 11:15

26 Serug, Nahor, Terah,

27 and Abram, who *is* Abraham.

The Genealogy from Abraham to Isaac Gen. 25:1–4, 12–16

28 [R]The sons of Abraham *were* [R]Isaac and [R]Ishmael. Gen. 21:2, 3 • Gen. 21:2 • Gen. 16:11, 15

29 These *are* their genealogies: The [R]firstborn of Ishmael *was* Nebajoth; then Kedar, Adbeel, Mibsam, Gen. 25:13–16

30 Mishma, Dumah, Massa, Hadad,* Tema,

31 Jetur, Naphish, and Kedemah. These *were* the sons of Ishmael.

32 Now the sons born to Keturah, Abraham's concubine, *were* Zimran, Jokshan, Medan, Midian, Ishbak, and Shuah. The sons of Jokshan *were* Sheba and Dedan.

33 The sons of Midian *were* Ephah, Epher, Hanoch, Abida, and Eldaah. All these were the children of Keturah.

34 And [R]Abraham begot Isaac. The sons of Isaac *were* Esau and Israel. Gen. 21:2

Sons of Esau—Gen. 36:1–30

35 The sons of [R]Esau *were* Eliphaz, Reuel, Jeush, Jaalam, and Korah. Gen. 36:10–19

36 And the sons of Eliphaz *were* Teman, Omar, Zephi,* Gatam, *and* Kenaz; and *by* Timna,* Amalek.

37 The sons of Reuel *were* Nahath, Zerah, Shammah, and Mizzah.

38 The sons of Seir *were* Lotan, Shobal, Zibeon, Anah, Dishon, Ezer, and Dishan.

39 And the sons of Lotan *were* Hori and Homam; Lotan's sister *was* Timna.

40 The sons of Shobal *were* Alian,* Manahath, Ebal, Shephi,* and Onam. The sons of Zibeon *were* Ajah and Anah.

41 The son of Anah *was* [R]Dishon. The sons of Dishon *were* Hamran,* Eshban, Ithran, and Cheran. Gen. 36:25

42 The sons of Ezer *were* Bilhan, Zaavan, *and* Jaakan.* The sons of Dishan *were* Uz and Aran.

Kings of Edom

43 Now these *were* the [R]kings who reigned in the land of Edom before a king reigned over the children of Israel: Bela the son of Beor, and the name of his city was Dinhabah. Gen. 36:31–43

44 And when Bela died, Jobab the son of Zerah of Bozrah reigned in his place.

45 When Jobab died, Husham of the land of the Temanites reigned in his place.

46 And when Husham died, Hadad the son of Bedad, who [T]attacked Midian in the field of Moab, reigned in his place. The name of his city *was* Avith. Lit. *struck*

47 When Hadad died, Samlah of Masrekah reigned in his place.

48 And when Samlah died, Saul of Rehoboth-by-the-River reigned in his place.

49 When Saul died, Baal-Hanan the son of Achbor reigned in his place.

50 And when Baal-Hanan died, Hadad* reigned in his place; and the name of his city was Pai.* His wife's name was Mehetabel the daughter of Matred, the daughter of Mezahab.

Chiefs of Edom

51 Hadad died also. And the chiefs of Edom were Chief Timnah, Chief Aliah,* Chief Jetheth,

52 Chief Aholibamah, Chief Elah, Chief Pinon,

53 Chief Kenaz, Chief Teman, Chief Mibzar,

54 Chief Magdiel, and Chief Iram. These *were* the chiefs of Edom.

CHAPTER 2

The Genealogy of the Sons of Jacob Gen. 29:31—30:24; 35:16–18

THESE *were* the sons of Israel: Reuben, Simeon, Levi, Judah, Issachar, Zebulun,

2 Dan, Joseph, Benjamin, Naphtali, Gad, and Asher.

The Genealogy of the Sons of Judah Gen. 46:12; Ruth 4:18–22; Matt. 1:3–6; Luke 3:31–33

3 The sons of [R]Judah *were* Er, Onan, and Shelah. *These* three were born to him by the daughter of Shua, the Canaanitess. Er, the firstborn of Judah, was wicked in the sight of the LORD; so He killed him. Num. 26:19

4 And [R]Tamar, his daughter-in-law, [R]bore him Perez and Zerah. All the sons of Judah *were* five. Gen. 38:6 • Matt. 1:3

5 The sons of [R]Perez *were* Hezron and Hamul. Ruth 4:18

6 The sons of Zerah *were* [T]Zimri, [R]Ethan, Heman, Calcol, and [T]Dara—five of them in all. *Zabdi,* Josh. 7:1 • 1 Kin. 4:31 • *Darda,* 1 Kin. 4:31

7 The son of [R]Carmi *was* Achar,* the troubler of Israel, who transgressed in the [R]accursed thing. 1 Chr. 4:1 • Josh. 6:18

1:22 *Obal,* Gen. 10:28 **1:30** *Hadar,* Gen. 25:15 **1:36** *Zepho,* Gen. 36:11 • Cf. Gen. 36:12 **1:40** *Alvan,* Gen. 36:23 • *Shepho,* Gen. 36:23 **1:41** *Hemdan,* Gen. 36:26 **1:42** *Akan,* Gen. 36:27 **1:50** *Hadar,* Gen. 36:39 • *Pau,* Gen. 36:39 **1:51** *Alvah,* Gen. 36:40 **2:7** *Achan,* Josh. 7:1

8 The son of Ethan *was* Azariah.
9 Also the sons of Hezron who were born
to him *were* Jerahmeel, [T]Ram, and Che-
lubai.* Aram, Matt. 1:3, 4
10 Ram [R]begot Amminadab, and Ammin-
adab begot Nahshon, [R]leader of the children
of Judah; Matt. 1:4 • Num. 1:7; 2:3
11 Nahshon begot Salma,* and Salma begot
Boaz;
12 Boaz begot Obed, and Obed begot Jesse;
13 Jesse begot Eliab his firstborn, Abinadab
the second, Shimea* the third,
14 Nethanel the fourth, Raddai the fifth,
15 Ozem the sixth, *and* David the seventh.
16 Now their sisters *were* Zeruiah and Abi-
gail. [R]And the sons of Zeruiah *were* Abishai,
Joab, and Asahel—three. 2 Sam. 2:18
17 Abigail bore Amasa; and the father of
Amasa *was* Jether the Ishmaelite.*
18 Caleb the son of Hezron had children by
Azubah, *his* wife, and by Jerioth. Now these
were her sons: Jesher, Shobab, and Ardon.
19 When Azubah died, Caleb took Ephrath*
as his wife, who bore him Hur.
20 And Hur begot Uri, and Uri begot [R]Beza-
lel. Ex. 31:2; 38:22
21 Now afterward Hezron went in to the
daughter of [R]Machir the father of Gilead,
whom he married when he *was* sixty years
old; and she bore him Segub. Num. 27:1
22 Segub begot [R]Jair, who had twenty-three
cities in the land of Gilead. Judg. 10:3
23 [R](Geshur and Syria took from them the
towns of Jair, with Kenath and its towns—
sixty towns.) All these *belonged to* the sons of
Machir the father of Gilead. Deut. 3:14
24 After Hezron died in Caleb Ephrathah,
Hezron's wife Abijah bore him [R]Ashhur the
father of Tekoa. 1 Chr. 4:5
25 The sons of Jerahmeel, the firstborn of
Hezron, *were* Ram, the firstborn, and Bunah,
Oren, Ozem, *and* Ahijah.
26 Jerahmeel had another wife, whose name
was Atarah; she was the mother of Onam.
27 The sons of Ram, the firstborn of Jerah-
meel, were Maaz, Jamin, and Eker.
28 The sons of Onam were Shammai and
Jada. The sons of Shammai *were* Nadab and
Abishur.
29 And the name of the wife of Abishur *was*
Abihail, and she bore him Ahban and Molid.
30 The sons of Nadab *were* Seled and Ap-
paim; Seled died without children.
31 The son of Appaim *was* Ishi, the son of
Ishi *was* Sheshan, and [R]Sheshan's son *was*
Ahlai. 1 Chr. 2:34, 35
32 The sons of Jada, the brother of Sham-
mai, *were* Jether and Jonathan; Jether died
without children.
33 The sons of Jonathan *were* Peleth and
Zaza. These were the sons of Jerahmeel.
34 Now Sheshan had no sons, only daugh-
ters. And Sheshan had an Egyptian servant
whose name *was* Jarha.
35 Sheshan gave his daughter to Jarha his
servant as wife, and she bore him Attai.
36 Attai begot Nathan, and Nathan begot
[R]Zabad; 1 Chr. 11:41
37 Zabad begot Ephlal, and Ephlal begot
[R]Obed; 2 Chr. 23:1
38 Obed begot Jehu, and Jehu begot
Azariah;
39 Azariah begot Helez, and Helez begot
Eleasah;
40 Eleasah begot Sismai, and Sismai begot
Shallum;
41 Shallum begot Jekamiah, and Jekamiah
begot Elishama.
42 The descendants of Caleb the brother of
Jerahmeel *were* Mesha, his firstborn, who
was the father of Ziph, and the sons of Mare-
shah the father of Hebron.
43 The sons of Hebron *were* Korah, Tap-
puah, Rekem, and Shema.
44 Shema begot Raham the father of
Jorkoam, and Rekem begot Shammai.
45 And the son of Shammai *was* Maon, and
Maon *was* the father of Beth Zur.
46 Ephah, Caleb's concubine, bore Haran,
Moza, and Gazez; and Haran begot Gazez.
47 And the sons of Jahdai *were* Regem,
Jotham, Geshan, Pelet, Ephah, and Shaaph.
48 Maachah, Caleb's concubine, bore She-
ber and Tirhanah.
49 She also bore Shaaph the father of Mad-
mannah, Sheva the father of Machbenah and
the father of Gibea. And the daughter of Caleb
was [R]Achsah.[T] Josh. 15:17 • Or *Achsa*
50 These were the descendants of Caleb:
The sons of [R]Hur, the firstborn of Ephra-
thah, *were* Shobal the father of [R]Kirjath
Jearim, 1 Chr. 4:4 • Josh. 9:17; 18:14
51 Salma the father of Bethlehem, *and*
Hareph the father of Beth Gader.
52 And Shobal the father of Kirjath Jearim
had descendants: [T]Haroeh, *and* half of the
families of Manuhoth.* *Reaiah*, 1 Chr. 4:2
53 The families of Kirjath Jearim *were* the
Ithrites, the Puthites, the Shumathites, and the
Mishraites. From these came the Zorathites
and the Eshtaolites.
54 The sons of Salma *were* Bethlehem, the
Netophathites, Atroth Beth Joab, half of the
Manahethites, and the Zorites.
55 And the families of the scribes who dwelt
at Jabez *were* the Tirathites, the Shimeathites,
and the Suchathites. These *were* the Kenites
who came from Hammath, the father of the
house of Rechab.

2:9 *Caleb*, vv. 18, 42 **2:11** *Salmon*, Ruth 4:21; Luke 3:32 **2:13** *Shammah*, 1 Sam. 16:9 **2:17** *Jithra the Israelite*, 2 Sam. 17:25 **2:19** Or *Ephrathah* **2:52** Or *Manuhothites*, same as *Manahethites*, v. 54

CHAPTER 3

The Genealogy of the Sons of David

NOW these were the sons of David who were born to him in Hebron: The firstborn *was* [R]Amnon, by Ahinoam the Jezreelitess; the second, Daniel,* by Abigail the Carmelitess; 2 Sam. 3:2–5

2 the third, Absalom the son of Maacah, the daughter of Talmai, king of Geshur; the fourth, Adonijah the son of Haggith;

3 the fifth, Shephatiah, by Abital; the sixth, Ithream, by his wife Eglah.

4 *These* six were born to him in Hebron. [R]There he reigned seven years and six months, and [R]in Jerusalem he reigned thirty-three years. 2 Sam. 2:11 • 2 Sam. 5:5

5 [R]And these were born to him in Jerusalem: Shimea,* Shobab, Nathan, and [R]Solomon—four by Bathshua* the daughter of Ammiel.* 1 Chr. 14:4–7 • 2 Sam. 12:24, 25

6 Also *there* were Ibhar, Elishama,* Eliphelet,*

7 Nogah, Nepheg, Japhia,

8 Elishama, Eliada,* and Eliphelet—[R]nine *in all.* 2 Sam. 5:14–16

9 *These were* all the sons of David, besides the sons of the concubines, and [R]Tamar their sister. 2 Sam. 13:1

The Genealogy of the Sons of Solomon
Matt. 1:7–12

10 Solomon's son *was* [R]Rehoboam; Abijah* *was* his son, Asa his son, Jehoshaphat his son, 1 Kin. 11:43

11 Joram* his son, [T]Ahaziah his son, Joash* his son, Or *Azariah* or *Jehoahaz*

12 Amaziah his son, Azariah* his son, Jotham his son,

13 Ahaz his son, Hezekiah his son, Manasseh his son,

14 Amon his son, *and* Josiah his son.

15 The sons of Josiah *were* Johanan the firstborn, the second Jehoiakim, the third Zedekiah, and the fourth Shallum.*

16 The sons of [R]Jehoiakim *were* Jeconiah his son *and* Zedekiah* his son. Matt. 1:11

17 And the sons of Jeconiah* *were* Assir,* Shealtiel [R]his son, Matt. 1:12

18 *and* Malchiram, Pedaiah, Shenazzar, Jecamiah, Hoshama, and Nedabiah.

19 The sons of Pedaiah *were* Zerubbabel and Shimei. The sons of Zerubbabel *were* Meshullam, Hananiah, Shelomith their sister,

20 and Hashubah, Ohel, Berechiah, Hasadiah, and Jushab-Hesed—five *in all.*

21 The sons of Hananiah *were* Pelatiah and Jeshaiah, the sons of Rephaiah, the sons of Arnan, the sons of Obadiah, and the sons of Shechaniah.

22 The son of Shechaniah was Shemaiah. The sons of Shemaiah *were* Hattush, Igal, Bariah, Neariah, and Shaphat—six *in all.*

23 The sons of Neariah *were* Elioenai, Hezekiah, and Azrikam—three *in all.*

24 The sons of Elioenai *were* Hodaviah, Eliashib, Pelaiah, Akkub, Johanan, Delaiah, and Anani—seven *in all.*

CHAPTER 4

The Genealogy of Judah

THE sons of Judah *were* [R]Perez, Hezron, Carmi, Hur, and Shobal. Gen. 38:29

2 And Reaiah the son of Shobal begot Jahath, and Jahath begot Ahumai and Lahad. These *were* the families of the Zorathites.

3 These *were* the sons *of the father* of Etam: Jezreel, Ishma, and Idbash; and the name of their sister *was* Hazelelponi;

4 and Penuel *was* the father of Gedor, and Ezer *was the* father of Hushah. These *were* the sons of [R]Hur, the firstborn of Ephrathah the father of Bethlehem. 1 Chr. 2:50

5 And [R]Ashhur the father of Tekoa had two wives, Helah and Naarah. 1 Chr. 2:24

6 Naarah bore him Ahuzzam, Hepher, Temeni, and Haahashtari. These *were* the sons of Naarah.

7 The sons of Helah *were* Zereth, Zohar, and Ethnan;

8 and Koz begot Anub, Zobebah, and the families of Aharhel the son of Harum.

9 Now Jabez was [R]more honorable than his brothers, and his mother called his name Jabez,* saying, "Because I bore *him* in pain." Gen. 34:19

10 And Jabez called on the God of Israel saying, "Oh, that You would bless me indeed, and enlarge my [T]territory, that Your hand would be with me, and that You would keep *me* from evil, that I may not cause pain!" So God granted him what he requested. *border*

11 Chelub the brother of Shuhah begot Mehir, who *was* the father of Eshton.

12 And Eshton begot Beth-Rapha, Paseah, and Tehinnah the father of Ir-Nahash. These *were* the men of Rechah.

13 The sons of Kenaz *were* [R]Othniel and Seraiah. The sons of Othniel *were* Hathath,* Josh. 15:17

14 and Meonothai *who* begot Ophrah. Seraiah begot Joab the father of Ge Harashim,* for they were craftsmen.

15 The sons of [R]Caleb the son of Jephunneh

3:1 *Chileab,* 2 Sam. 3:3 **3:5** *Shammua,* 14:4; 2 Sam. 5:14 • *Bathsheba,* 2 Sam. 11:3 • *Eliam,* 2 Sam. 11:3 **3:6** *Elishua,* 14:5; 2 Sam. 5:15 • *Elpelet,* 14:5 **3:8** *Beeliada,* 14:7 **3:10** *Abijam,* 1 Kin. 15:1 **3:11** *Jehoram,* 2 Kin. 1:17; 8:16 • *Jehoash,* 2 Kin. 12:1 **3:12** *Uzziah,* Is. 6:1 **3:15** *Jehoahaz,* 2 Kin. 23:31 **3:16** *Mattaniah,* 2 Kin. 24:17 **3:17** *Jehoiachin,* 2 Kin. 24:8, or *Coniah,* Jer. 22:24 • Or *Jeconiah the captive were* **4:9** Lit. *He Will Cause Pain* **4:13** LXX, Vg. add *and Meonothai* **4:14** Lit. *Valley of Craftsmen*

were Iru, Elah, and Naam. The son of Elah *was* [T]Kenaz. 1 Chr. 6:56 • Or *Uknaz*
16 The sons of Jehallelel *were* Ziph, Ziphah, Tiria, and Asarel.
17 The sons of Ezrah *were* Jether, Mered, Epher, and Jalon. And *Mered's wife** *bore* Miriam, Shammai, and Ishbah the father of Eshtemoa.
18 (His wife Jehudijah* bore Jered the father of Gedor, Heber the father of Sochoh, and Jekuthiel the father of Zanoah.) And these were the sons of Bithiah the daughter of Pharaoh, whom Mered took.
19 The sons of Hodiah's wife, the sister of Naham, *were* the fathers of Keilah the Garmite and of Eshtemoa the Maachathite.
20 And the sons of Shimon *were* Amnon, Rinnah, Ben-Hanan, and Tilon. And the sons of Ishi *were* Zoheth and Ben-Zoheth.
21 The sons of [R]Shelah [R]the son of Judah *were* Er the father of Lecah, Laadah the father of Mareshah, and the families of the house of the linen workers of the house of Ashbea; Gen. 38:11, 14 • Gen. 38:1–5; 46:12
22 also Jokim, the men of Chozeba, and Joash; Saraph, who ruled in Moab, and Jashubi-Lehem. Now the [T]records are ancient. Lit. *words*
23 These *were* the potters and those who dwell at Netaim* and Gederah;* there they dwelt with the king for his work.

The Genealogy of Simeon—Gen. 46:10

24 The sons of Simeon *were* Nemuel, Jamin, Jarib,* Zerah,* *and* Shaul,
25 Shallum his son, Mibsam his son, and Mishma his son.
26 And the sons of Mishma *were* Hamuel his son, Zacchur his son, and Shimei his son.
27 Shimei had sixteen sons and six daughters; but his brothers did not have many children, nor did any of their families multiply as much as the children of Judah.
28 They dwelt at Beersheba, Moladah, Hazar Shual,
29 [T]Bilhah, Ezem, Tolad, *Balah,* Josh. 19:3
30 Bethuel, Hormah, Ziklag,
31 Beth Marcaboth, Hazar Susim, Beth Biri, and at Shaaraim. These *were* their cities until the reign of David.
32 And their villages *were* Etam, Ain, Rimmon, Tochen, and Ashan—five cities—
33 and all the villages that *were* around these cities as far as Baal.* These *were* their dwelling places, and they maintained their genealogy:
34 Meshobab, Jamlech, and Joshah the son of Amaziah;
35 Joel, and Jehu the son of Joshibiah, the son of Seraiah, the son of Asiel;
36 Elioenai, Jaakobah, Jeshohaiah, Asaiah, Adiel, Jesimiel, and Benaiah;
37 Ziza the son of Shiphi, the son of Allon, the son of Jedaiah, the son of Shimri, the son of Shemaiah—
38 these mentioned by name *were* leaders in their families, and their father's house increased greatly.
39 So they went to the entrance of Gedor, as far as the east side of the valley, to seek pasture for their flocks.
40 And they found rich, good pasture, and the land *was* broad, quiet, and peaceful; for some Hamites formerly lived there.
41 These recorded by name came in the days of Hezekiah king of Judah; and they [R]attacked their tents and the Meunites who were found there, and [R]utterly destroyed them, as it is to this day. So they dwelt in their place, because *there was* pasture for their flocks there. 2 Kin. 18:8 • 2 Kin. 19:11
42 Now *some* of them, five hundred men of the sons of Simeon, went to Mount Seir, having as their captains Pelatiah, Neariah, Rephaiah, and Uzziel, the sons of Ishi.
43 And they defeated [R]the rest of the Amalekites who had escaped. They have dwelt there to this day. 1 Sam. 15:8; 30:17

CHAPTER 5

The Genealogy of Reuben—Gen. 46:8, 9

NOW the sons of Reuben the firstborn of Israel—he *was* indeed the firstborn, but because he defiled his father's bed, his birthright was given to the sons of Joseph, the son of Israel, so that the genealogy is not listed according to the birthright;
2 yet [R]Judah prevailed over his brothers, and from him *came* a ruler, although the birthright was Joseph's— Gen. 49:8, 10
3 the sons of Reuben the firstborn of Israel were Hanoch, Pallu, Hezron, and Carmi.
4 The sons of Joel *were* Shemaiah his son, Gog his son, Shimei his son,
5 Micah his son, Reaiah his son, Baal his son,
6 and Beerah his son, whom Tiglath-Pileser* king of Assyria carried into captivity. He *was* leader of the Reubenites.
7 And his brethren by their families, when the genealogy of their generations was registered: the chief, Jeiel, and Zechariah,
8 and Bela the son of Azaz, the son of Shema, the son of Joel, who dwelt in [R]Aroer, as far as Nebo and Baal Meon. Josh. 12:2
9 Eastward they settled as far as the [T]entrance of the wilderness this side of the River Euphrates, because their cattle had multiplied in the land of Gilead. *beginning*
10 Now in the days of Saul they made war

4:17 Lit. *she* **4:18** Or *His Judean wife* **4:23** Lit. *Plants* • Lit. *Hedges* **4:24** *Jachin,* Gen. 46:10; Num. 26:12 • *Zohar,* Gen. 46:10; Ex. 6:15 **4:33** *Baalath Beer,* Josh. 19:8 **5:6** Heb. *Tilgath-Pilneser*

[R]with the Hagrites, who fell by their hand; and they dwelt in their tents throughout the entire *area* east of Gilead. Gen. 25:12

The Genealogy of Gad

11 And the [R]children of Gad dwelt next to them in the land of [R]Bashan as far as Salcah: Num. 26:15–18 • Josh. 13:11, 24–28
12 Joel *was* the chief, Shapham the next, then Jaanai and Shaphat in Bashan,
13 and their brethren of their father's house: Michael, Meshullam, Sheba, Jorai, Jachan, Zia, and Eber—seven *in all*.
14 These *were* the children of Abihail the son of Huri, the son of Jaroah, the son of Gilead, the son of Michael, the son of Jeshishai, the son of Jahdo, the son of Buz;
15 Ahi the son of Abdiel, the son of Guni, *was* chief of their father's house.
16 And *the Gadites* dwelt in Gilead, in Bashan and in its villages, and in all the [T]common-lands of [R]Sharon within their borders. *open lands* • 1 Chr. 27:29
17 All these were registered by genealogies in the days of Jotham king of Judah, and in the days of Jeroboam king of Israel.
18 The sons of Reuben, the Gadites, and half the tribe of Manasseh *had* forty-four thousand seven hundred and sixty valiant men, men able to bear shield and sword, to shoot with the bow, and skillful in war, who went to war.
19 They made war with the Hagrites, [R]Jetur, Naphish, and Nodab. Gen. 25:15
20 And [R]they were helped against them, and the Hagrites were delivered into their hand, and all who *were* with them, for they [R]cried out to God in the battle. He heeded their prayer, because they [R]put their trust in Him. [1 Chr. 5:22] • 2 Chr. 14:11–13 • Ps. 9:10
21 Then they took away their livestock—fifty thousand of their camels, two hundred and fifty thousand of their sheep, and two thousand of their donkeys—also one hundred thousand of their men;
22 for many fell dead, because the war [R]*was* God's. And they dwelt in their place until [R]the captivity. [Josh. 23:10] • 2 Kin. 15:29

The Genealogy of Manasseh

23 So the children of the half-tribe of Manasseh dwelt in the land. Their *numbers* increased from Bashan to Baal Hermon, that is, to [R]Senir, or Mount Hermon. Deut. 3:9
24 These *were* the heads of their fathers' houses: Epher, Ishi, Eliel, Azriel, Jeremiah, Hodaviah, and Jahdiel. They were mighty men of valor, famous men, *and* heads of their fathers' houses.
25 And they were unfaithful to the God of their fathers, and [R]played the harlot after the gods of the peoples of the land, whom God had destroyed before them. 2 Kin. 17:7
26 So the God of Israel stirred up the spirit of [R]Pul king of Assyria, that is, [R]Tiglath-Pileser* king of Assyria. He carried the Reubenites, the Gadites, and the half-tribe of Manasseh into captivity. He took them to Halah, Habor, Hara, and the river of Gozan to this day. 2 Kin. 15:19 • 2 Kin. 15:29

CHAPTER 6

The High Priestly Line
Gen. 46:11; 1 Chr. 6:50–53

THE sons of Levi *were* [R]Gershon,[T] Kohath, and Merari. Ex. 6:16 • Or *Gershom*, v. 16
2 The sons of Kohath *were* Amram, [R]Izhar, Hebron, and Uzziel. 1 Chr. 6:18, 22
3 The children of Amram *were* Aaron, Moses, and Miriam. And the sons of Aaron *were* Nadab, Abihu, Eleazar, and Ithamar.
4 Eleazar begot Phinehas, *and* Phinehas begot Abishua;
5 Abishua begot Bukki, and Bukki begot Uzzi;
6 Uzzi begot Zerahiah, and Zerahiah begot Meraioth;
7 Meraioth begot Amariah, and Amariah begot Ahitub;
8 [R]Ahitub begot [R]Zadok, and Zadok begot Ahimaaz; 2 Sam. 8:17 • 2 Sam. 15:27
9 Ahimaaz begot Azariah, and Azariah begot Johanan;
10 Johanan begot Azariah (it was he [R]who ministered as priest in the temple that Solomon built in Jerusalem); 2 Chr. 26:17, 18
11 [R]Azariah begot [R]Amariah, and Amariah begot Ahitub; Ezra 7:3 • 2 Chr. 19:11
12 Ahitub begot Zadok, and Zadok begot [T]Shallum; *Meshullam*, 1 Chr. 9:11
13 Shallum begot Hilkiah, and Hilkiah begot Azariah;
14 Azariah begot [R]Seraiah, and Seraiah begot Jehozadak. Neh. 11:11
15 Jehozadak went *into captivity* when the LORD carried Judah and Jerusalem into captivity by the hand of Nebuchadnezzar.

The Levitical Line

16 The sons of Levi *were* [R]Gershon,* Kohath, and Merari. Ex. 6:16
17 These are the names of the sons of Gershon: Libni and Shimei.
18 The sons of Kohath *were* Amram, Izhar, Hebron, and Uzziel.
19 The sons of Merari *were* Mahli and Mushi. Now these *are* the families of the Levites according to their fathers:
20 Of Gershon *were* Libni his son, Jahath his son, [R]Zimmah his son, 1 Chr. 6:42
21 [T]Joah his son, Iddo his son, Zerah his son, *and* Jeatherai his son. *Ethan*, v. 42

5:26 Heb. *Tilgath-Pilneser* **6:16** Heb. *Gershom*, an alternate spelling for *Gershon*, vv. 1, 17, 20, 43, 62, 71

22 The sons of Kohath *were* Amminadab his son, Korah his son, Assir his son,

23 Elkanah his son, Ebiasaph his son, Assir his son,

24 Tahath his son, Uriel his son, Uzziah his son, and Shaul his son.

25 The sons of Elkanah *were* [R]Amasai and Ahimoth. 1 Chr. 6:35, 36

26 *As for* Elkanah,* the sons of Elkanah *were* Zophai* his son, Nahath* his son,

27 Eliab* his son, Jeroham his son, *and* Elkanah his son.

28 The sons of Samuel *were Joel** the firstborn, and Abijah the second.*

29 The sons of Merari *were* Mahli, Libni his son, Shimei his son, Uzzah his son,

30 Shimea his son, Haggiah his son, *and* Asaiah his son.

The Musicians' Guild

31 Now these are [R]the men whom David appointed over the service of song in the house of the LORD, after the [R]ark came to rest. 1 Chr. 15:16–22, 27; 16:4–6 • 1 Chr. 15:25—16:1

32 They were ministering with music before the dwelling place of the tabernacle of meeting, until Solomon had built the house of the LORD in Jerusalem, and they served in their office according to their order.

33 And these *are* the ones who ministered with their sons: Of the sons of the [R]Kohathites *were* Heman the singer, the son of Joel, the son of Samuel, Num. 26:57

34 the son of Elkanah, the son of Jeroham, the son of Eliel,* the son of Toah,*

35 the son of Zuph, the son of Elkanah, the son of Mahath, the son of Amasai,

36 the son of Elkanah, the son of Joel, the son of Azariah, the son of Zephaniah,

37 the son of Tahath, the son of Assir, the son of Ebiasaph, the son of Korah,

38 the son of Izhar, the son of Kohath, the son of Levi, the son of Israel.

39 And his brother [R]Asaph, who stood at his right hand, *was* Asaph the son of Berachiah, the son of Shimea, 2 Chr. 5:12

40 the son of Michael, the son of Baaseiah, the son of Malchijah,

41 the son of [R]Ethni, the son of Zerah, the son of Adaiah, 1 Chr. 6:21

42 the son of Ethan, the son of Zimmah, the son of Shimei,

43 the son of Jahath, the son of Gershon, the son of Levi.

44 Their brethren, the sons of Merari, on the left hand, *were* Ethan the son of Kishi, the son of Abdi, the son of Malluch,

45 the son of Hashabiah, the son of Amaziah, the son of Hilkiah,

46 the son of Amzi, the son of Bani, the son of Shamer,

47 the son of Mahli, the son of Mushi, the son of Merari, the son of Levi.

48 And their brethren, the Levites, *were* appointed to every kind of service of the tabernacle of the house of God.

The Generations of Aaron—1 Chr. 6:3–8

49 [R]But Aaron and his sons offered sacrifices on the altar of burnt offering and on the altar of incense, for all the work of the Most Holy *Place*, and to make atonement for Israel, according to all that Moses the servant of God had commanded. [Num. 18:1–8]

50 Now these *are* the [R]sons of Aaron: Eleazar his son, Phinehas his son, Abishua his son, 1 Chr. 6:4–8

51 Bukki his son, Uzzi his son, Zerahiah his son,

52 Meraioth his son, Amariah his son, Ahitub his son,

53 Zadok his son, *and* Ahimaaz his son.

Cities of the Priests and Levites Josh. 21:1–42

54 Now these *are* their dwelling places throughout their settlements in their territory, for they were *given* by lot to the sons of Aaron, of the family of the Kohathites:

55 [R]They gave them Hebron in the land of Judah, with its surrounding [T]common-lands. Josh. 14:13; 21:11, 12 • *open lands*

56 But the fields of the city and its villages they gave to Caleb the son of Jephunneh.

57 And [R]to the sons of Aaron they gave *one of* the cities of refuge, Hebron; also Libnah with its common-lands, Jattir, Eshtemoa with its common-lands, Josh. 21:13, 19

58 Hilen* with its common-lands, Debir with its common-lands,

59 Ashan* with its common-lands, and Beth Shemesh with its common-lands.

60 And from the tribe of Benjamin: Geba with its common-lands, Alemeth* with its common-lands, and Anathoth with its common-lands. All their cities among their families *were* thirteen.

61 To the rest of the family of the tribe of the Kohathites *they gave* [R]by lot ten cities from half the tribe of Manasseh. Josh. 21:5

62 And to the sons of Gershon, throughout their families, *they gave* thirteen cities from the tribe of Issachar, from the tribe of Asher, from the tribe of Naphtali, and from the tribe of Manasseh in Bashan.

63 To the sons of Merari, throughout their families, *they gave* [R]twelve cities from the tribe of Reuben, from the tribe of Gad, and from the tribe of Zebulun. Josh. 21:7, 34–40

64 So the children of Israel gave *these*

6:26 Cf. v. 35 • *Zuph*, v. 35; 1 Sam. 1:1 • *Toah*, v. 34 **6:27** *Eliel*, v. 34 **6:28** So with LXX, Syr., Arab.; cf. v. 33 and 1 Sam. 8:2 • Heb. *Vasheni* **6:34** *Elihu*, 1 Sam. 1:1 • *Tohu*, 1 Sam. 1:1 **6:58** *Holon*, Josh. 21:15 **6:59** *Ain*, Josh. 21:16 **6:60** *Almon*, Josh. 21:18

cities with their [T]common-lands to the Le-
vites. *open lands*
65 And they gave by lot from the tribe of the
children of Judah, from the tribe of the chil-
dren of Simeon, and from the tribe of the chil-
dren of Benjamin these cities which are called
by *their* names.
66 Now [R]some of the families of the sons of
Kohath *were given* cities as their territory
from the tribe of Ephraim. 1 Chr. 6:61
67 [R]And they gave them *one of* the cities of
refuge, Shechem with its common-lands, in
the mountains of Ephraim, also Gezer with its
common-lands, Josh. 21:21
68 [R]Jokmeam with its common-lands, Beth
Horon with its common-lands, Josh. 21:22
69 Aijalon with its common-lands, and Gath
Rimmon with its common-lands.
70 And from the half-tribe of Manasseh:
Aner with its common-lands and Bileam with
its common-lands, for the rest of the family of
the sons of Kohath.
71 From the family of the half-tribe of Ma-
nasseh the sons of Gershon *were given* Golan
in Bashan with its common-lands and Ash-
taroth with its common-lands.
72 And from the tribe of Issachar: [T]Kedesh
with its common-lands, Daberath with its
common-lands, *Kishon,* Josh. 21:28
73 Ramoth with its common-lands, and
Anem with its common-lands.
74 And from the tribe of Asher: Mashal with
its common-lands, Abdon with its common-
lands,
75 Hukok with its common-lands, and
Rehob with its common-lands.
76 And from the tribe of Naphtali: Kedesh in
Galilee with its common-lands, Hammon with
its common-lands, and Kirjathaim with its
common-lands.
77 From the tribe of Zebulun the rest of
the children of Merari *were given* Rimmon*
with its common-lands and Tabor with its
common-lands.
78 And on the other side of the Jordan,
across from Jericho, on the east side of the
Jordan, *they were given* from the tribe of Reu-
ben: Bezer in the wilderness with its common-
lands, Jahzah with its common-lands,
79 Kedemoth with its common-lands, and
Mephaath with its common-lands.
80 And from the tribe of Gad: Ramoth in
Gilead with its common-lands, Mahanaim
with its common-lands,
81 Heshbon with its common-lands, and
Jazer with its common-lands.

CHAPTER 7

The Genealogy of Issachar—Gen. 46:13

THE sons of Issachar *were* Tola, Puah,*
Jashub, and Shimron—four *in all.*
2 The sons of Tola *were* Uzzi, Rephaiah,
Jeriel, Jahmai, Jibsam, and Shemuel, heads of
their father's house. *The sons* of Tola *were*
mighty men of valor in their generations;
their number in the days of David *was*
twenty-two thousand six hundred.
3 The son of Uzzi *was* Izrahiah, and the
sons of Izrahiah *were* Michael, Obadiah, Joel,
and Ishiah. All five of them *were* chief men.
4 And with them, by their generations, ac-
cording to their fathers' houses, *were* thirty-
six thousand troops ready for war; for they
had many wives and sons.
5 Now their brethren among all the fami-
lies of Issachar *were* mighty men of valor,
listed by their genealogies, eighty-seven thou-
sand in all.

The Genealogy of Benjamin—Gen. 46:21

6 *The sons* of Benjamin *were* Bela, Becher,
and Jediael—three *in all.*
7 The sons of Bela were Ezbon, Uzzi,
Uzziel, Jerimoth, and Iri—five *in all.* They
were heads of *their* fathers' houses, and they
were listed by their genealogies, twenty-two
thousand and thirty-four mighty men of valor.
8 The sons of Becher *were* Zemirah, Joash,
Eliezer, Elioenai, Omri, Jerimoth, Abijah,
Anathoth, and Alemeth. All these *are* the sons
of Becher.
9 And they were recorded by genealogy ac-
cording to their generations, heads of their fa-
thers' houses, twenty thousand two hundred
mighty men of valor.
10 The son of Jediael *was* Bilhan, and the sons
of Bilhan *were* Jeush, Benjamin, Ehud, Che-
naanah, Zethan, Tharshish, and Ahishahar.
11 All these sons of Jediael *were* heads of
their fathers' houses; *there were* seventeen
thousand two hundred mighty men of valor fit
to go out for war *and* battle.
12 Shuppim and Huppim* *were* the sons of
Ir, *and* Hushim *was* the son of Aher.

The Genealogy of Naphtali—Gen. 46:24

13 The [R]sons of Naphtali *were* Jahziel,*
Guni, Jezer, and Shallum,* the sons of Bil-
hah. Num. 26:48–50

The Genealogy of Manasseh

14 The [R]descendants of Manasseh: his Syr-
ian concubine bore him Machir the father of
Gilead, the father of Asriel.* Num. 26:29–34
15 Machir took as his wife *the sister* of Hup-
pim and Shuppim,* whose name *was*
Maachah. The name of *Gilead's* grandson*
was Zelophehad,* but Zelophehad begot only
daughters.

6:77 Heb. *Rimmono,* an alternate spelling of *Rimmon;* 1 Chr. 4:32 **7:1** *Puvah,* Gen. 46:13 **7:12** *Hupham,* Num. 26:39 **7:13** *Jahzeel,* Gen. 46:24 • *Shillem,* Gen. 46:24 **7:14** The son of Gilead (cf. Num. 26:30, 31) **7:15** Cf. v. 12 • Lit. *the second* • cf. Num. 26:30–33

16 (Maachah the wife of Machir bore a son, and she called his name Peresh. The name of his brother *was* Sheresh, and his sons *were* Ulam and Rakem.
17 The son of Ulam *was* [R]Bedan.) These *were* the descendants of Gilead the son of Machir, the son of Manasseh. 1 Sam. 12:11
18 His sister Hammoleketh bore Ishhod, [T]Abiezer, and Mahlah. *Jeezer,* Num. 26:30
19 And the sons of Shemida were Ahian, Shechem, Likhi, and Aniam.

The Genealogy of Ephraim

20 [R]The sons of Ephraim *were* Shuthelah, Bered his son, Tahath his son, Eladah his son, Tahath his son, Num. 26:35–37
21 Zabad his son, Shuthelah his son, and Ezer and Elead. The men of Gath who were born in *that* land killed *them* because they came down to take away their cattle.
22 Then Ephraim their father mourned many days, and his brethren came to comfort him.
23 And when he went in to his wife, she conceived and bore a son; and he called his name Beriah,* because tragedy had come upon his house.
24 Now his daughter *was* Sheerah, who built Lower and Upper [R]Beth Horon and Uzzen Sheerah; Josh. 16:3, 5
25 and Rephah *was* his son, *as well* as Resheph, and Telah his son, Tahan his son,
26 Laadan his son, Ammihud his son, [R]Elishama his son, Num. 10:22
27 Nun* his son, and Joshua his son.
28 Now their [R]possessions and dwelling places *were* Bethel and its towns: to the east Naaran, to the west Gezer and its towns, and Shechem and its towns, as far as Ayyah* and its towns; Josh. 16:1–10
29 and by the borders of the children of Manasseh *were* Beth Shean and its towns, Taanach and its towns, Megiddo and its towns, Dor and its towns. In these dwelt the children of Joseph, the son of Israel.

The Genealogy of Asher—Gen. 46:17

30 The sons of Asher *were* Imnah, Ishvah, Ishvi, Beriah, and their sister Serah.
31 The sons of Beriah *were* Heber and Malchiel, who was the father of Birzaith.*
32 And Heber begot Japhlet, Shomer,* Hotham,* and their sister Shua.
33 The sons of Japhlet *were* Pasach, Bimhal, and Ashvath. These *were* the children of Japhlet.
34 The sons of [R]Shemer *were* Ahi, Rohgah, Jehubbah, and Aram. 1 Chr. 7:32
35 And the sons of his brother Helem *were* Zophah, Imna, Shelesh, and Amal.
36 The sons of Zophah *were* Suah, Harnepher, Shual, Beri, Imrah,
37 Bezer, Hod, Shamma, Shilshah, Jithran,* and Beera.
38 The sons of Jether *were* Jephunneh, Pispah, and Ara.
39 The sons of Ulla *were* Arah, Haniel, and Rizia.
40 All these *were* the children of Asher, heads of *their* fathers' houses, choice men, mighty men of valor, chief leaders. And they were recorded by genealogies among the army fit for battle; their number *was* twenty-six thousand.

CHAPTER 8

The Genealogy of Benjamin—Gen. 46:21

NOW Benjamin begot Bela his firstborn, Ashbel the second, Aharah* the third,
2 Nohah the fourth, and Rapha the fifth.
3 The sons of Bela *were* Addar,* Gera, Abihud,
4 Abishua, Naaman, Ahoah,
5 Gera, Shephuphan, and Huram.
6 These *are* the sons of Ehud, who were the heads of the fathers' *houses* of the inhabitants of [R]Geba, and who forced them to move to [R]Manahath: 1 Chr. 6:60 • 1 Chr. 2:52
7 Naaman, Ahijah, and Gera who forced them to move. He begot Uzza and Ahihud.
8 Also Shaharaim had children in the country of Moab, after he had sent away Hushim and Baara his wives.
9 By Hodesh his wife he begot Jobab, Zibia, Mesha, Malcam,
10 Jeuz, Sachiah, and Mirmah. These *were* his sons, heads of their fathers' *houses.*
11 And by Hushim he begot Abitub and Elpaal.
12 The sons of Elpaal *were* Eber, Misham, and Shemed, who built Ono and Lod with its towns;
13 and Beriah and [R]Shema, who *were* heads of their fathers' *houses* of the inhabitants of Aijalon, who drove out the inhabitants of Gath. 1 Chr. 8:21
14 Ahio, Shashak, Jeremoth,
15 Zebadiah, Arad, Eder,
16 Michael, Ispah, and Joha *were* the sons of Beriah.
17 Zebadiah, Meshullam, Hizki, Heber,
18 Ishmerai, Jizliah, and Jobab *were* the sons of Elpaal.
19 Jakim, Zichri, Zabdi,
20 Elienai, Zillethai, Eliel,
21 Adaiah, Beraiah, and Shimrath *were* the sons of [T]Shimei. *Shema,* 1 Chr. 7:13
22 Ishpan, Eber, Eliel,
23 Abdon, Zichri, Hanan,
24 Hananiah, Elam, Antothijah,

7:23 Lit. *In Tragedy* **7:27** Heb. *Non* **7:28** Many Heb. mss., Bg., LXX, Tg., Vg. *Gazza* **7:31** Or *Birzavith* or *Birzoth* **7:32** *Shemer,* v. 34 • *Helem,* v. 35 **7:37** *Jether,* v. 38 **8:1** *Ahiram,* Num. 26:38 **8:3** *Ard,* Num. 26:40

25 Iphdeiah, and Penuel *were* the sons of Shashak.

26 Shamsherai, Shehariah, Athaliah,

27 Jaareshiah, Elijah, and Zichri *were* the sons of Jeroham.

28 These *were* heads of the fathers' *houses* by their generations, chief men. These dwelt in Jerusalem.

29 Now the father of Gibeon, whose wife's name *was* Maacah, dwelt at Gibeon.

30 And his firstborn son *was* Abdon, then Zur, Kish, Baal, Nadab,

31 Gedor, Ahio, Zecher,

32 and Mikloth, *who* begot Shimeah.* They also dwelt alongside their [T]relatives in Jerusalem, with their brethren. *brethren*

33 [R]Ner* begot Kish, Kish begot Saul, and Saul begot Jonathan, Malchishua, Abinadab,* and Esh-Baal.* 1 Sam. 14:51

34 The son of Jonathan *was* Merib-Baal,* and Merib-Baal begot [R]Micah. 2 Sam. 9:12

35 The sons of Micah *were* Pithon, Melech, [T]Tarea, and Ahaz. *Tahrea,* 1 Chr. 9:41

36 And Ahaz begot Jehoaddah;* Jehoaddah begot Alemeth, Azmaveth, and Zimri; and Zimri begot Moza.

37 Moza begot Binea, Raphah* his son, Eleasah his son, *and* Azel his son.

38 Azel had six sons whose names *were* these: Azrikam, Bocheru, Ishmael, Sheariah, Obadiah, and Hanan. All these *were* the sons of Azel.

39 And the sons of Eshek his brother *were* Ulam his firstborn, Jeush the second, and Eliphelet the third.

40 The sons of Ulam were mighty men of valor—archers. *They* had many sons and grandsons, one hundred and fifty *in all.* These *were* all sons of Benjamin.

CHAPTER 9

The Genealogy of the Twelve Tribes Who Returned

SO [R]all Israel was [T]recorded by genealogies, and indeed, they *were* inscribed in the book of the kings of Israel. But Judah was carried away captive to Babylon because of their unfaithfulness. Ezra 2:59 • *enrolled*

2 And the first inhabitants who *dwelt* in their possessions in their cities *were* Israelites, priests, Levites, and the Nethinim.

3 Now in [R]Jerusalem the children of Judah dwelt, and some of the children of Benjamin, and of the children of Ephraim and Manasseh: Neh. 11:1, 2

4 Uthai the son of Ammihud, the son of Omri, the son of Imri, the son of Bani, of the descendants of Perez, the son of Judah.

5 Of the Shilonites: Asaiah the firstborn and his sons.

6 Of the sons of Zerah: Jeuel, and their brethren—six hundred and ninety.

7 Of the sons of Benjamin: Sallu the son of Meshullam, the son of Hodaviah, the son of Hassenuah;

8 Ibneiah the son of Jeroham; Elah the son of Uzzi, the son of Michri; Meshullam the son of Shephatiah, the son of Reuel, the son of Ibnijah;

9 and their brethren, according to their generations—nine hundred and fifty-six. All these men *were* heads of a father's *house* in their fathers' houses.

The Genealogy of the Priests Who Returned

10 [R]Of the priests: Jedaiah, Jehoiarib, and Jachin; Neh. 11:10–14

11 [T]Azariah the son of Hilkiah, the son of Meshullam, the son of Zadok, the son of Meraioth, the son of Ahitub, the [R]officer over the house of God; *Seraiah,* Neh. 11:11 • Jer. 20:1

12 Adaiah the son of Jeroham, the son of Pashur, the son of Malchijah; Maasai the son of Adiel, the son of Jahzerah, the son of Meshullam, the son of Meshillemith, the son of Immer;

13 and their brethren, heads of their fathers' *houses*—one thousand seven hundred and sixty. *They were* very able men for the work of the service of the house of God.

The Genealogy of the Levites Who Returned

14 Of the Levites: Shemaiah the son of Hasshub, the son of Azrikam, the son of Hashabiah, of the sons of Merari;

15 Bakbakkar, Heresh, Galal, and Mattaniah the son of Micah, the son of [R]Zichri, the son of Asaph; Neh. 11:17

16 [R]Obadiah the son of [R]Shemaiah, the son of Galal, the son of Jeduthun; and Berechiah the son of Asa, the son of Elkanah, who lived in the villages of the Netophathites. Neh. 11:17 • Neh. 11:17

17 And the gatekeepers *were* Shallum, Akkub, Talmon, Ahiman, and their brethren. Shallum *was* the chief.

18 Until then *they had been* gatekeepers for the camps of the children of Levi at the King's Gate on the east.

19 Shallum the son of Kore, the son of Ebiasaph, the son of Korah, and his brethren, from his father's house, the Korahites, *were* in charge of the work of the service, [T]gatekeepers of the tabernacle. Their fathers had been keepers of the entrance to the camp of the LORD. Lit. *thresholds*

20 And [R]Phinehas the son of Eleazar had been the officer over them in time past; the LORD *was* with him. Num. 25:6–13; 31:6

21 [R]Zechariah the son of Meshelemiah *was*

8:32 *Shimeam,* 1 Chr. 9:38 **8:33** Also the son of Gibeon, 1 Chr. 9:36, 39 • *Jishui,* 1 Sam. 14:49 • *Ishbosheth,* 2 Sam. 2:8 **8:34** *Mephibosheth,* 2 Sam. 4:4 **8:36** *Jarah,* 1 Chr. 9:42 **8:37** *Rephaiah,* 1 Chr. 9:43

[T]keeper of the door of the tabernacle of meet-
ing. 1 Chr. 26:2, 14 • *gatekeeper*
22 All those chosen as gatekeepers *were* two
hundred and twelve. [R]They were recorded by
their genealogy, in their villages. David and
Samuel the seer had appointed them to their
trusted office. 1 Chr. 26:1, 2
23 So they and their children *were* in charge
of the gates of the house of the LORD, the
house of the tabernacle, by assignment.
24 The gatekeepers were assigned to the four
directions: the east, west, north, and south.
25 And their brethren in their villages *had* to
come with them from time to time [R]for seven
days. 2 Kin. 11:4–7
26 For in this trusted office *were* four chief
gatekeepers; they were Levites. And they had
charge over the chambers and treasuries of
the house of God.
27 And they lodged *all* around the house of
God because they *had* the [R]responsibility, and
they *were* in charge of opening *it* every morn-
ing. 1 Chr. 23:30–32
28 Now *some* of them were in charge of the
serving vessels, for they brought them in and
took them out by count.
29 *Some* of them *were* appointed over the
furnishings and over all the implements of
the sanctuary, and over the [R]fine flour and the
wine and the oil and the incense and the
spices. 1 Chr. 23:29
30 And *some* of the sons of the priests made
the ointment of the spices.
31 Mattithiah of the Levites, the firstborn of
Shallum the Korahite, had the trusted office
[R]over the things that were baked in the
pans. Lev. 2:5; 6:21
32 And some of their brethren of the sons of
the Kohathites *were* in charge of preparing
the showbread for every Sabbath.
33 These are [R]the singers, heads of the fa-
thers' *houses* of the Levites, *who lodged* in the
chambers, *and were* free *from other duties;*
for they were employed in *that* work day and
night. 1 Chr. 6:31; 25:1
34 These heads of the fathers' *houses* of the
Levites *were* heads throughout their genera-
tions. They dwelt at Jerusalem.

The Genealogy of Saul

35 Jeiel the father of Gibeon, whose wife's
name *was* Maacah, dwelt at Gibeon.
36 His firstborn son *was* Abdon, then Zur,
Kish, Baal, Ner, Nadab,
37 Gedor, Ahio, Zechariah,* and Mikloth.
38 And Mikloth begot Shimeam.* They also
dwelt alongside their relatives in Jerusalem,
with their brethren.
39 [R]Ner begot Kish, Kish begot Saul, and
Saul begot Jonathan, Malchishua, Abinadab,
and Esh-Baal. 1 Chr. 8:33–38
40 The son of Jonathan *was* Merib-Baal, and
Merib-Baal begot Micah.
41 The sons of Micah *were* Pithon, Melech,
Tahrea,* [R]*and Ahaz.** 1 Chr. 8:35
42 And Ahaz begot Jarah;* Jarah begot
Alemeth, Azmaveth, and Zimri; and Zimri
begot Moza;
43 Moza begot Binea, Rephaiah* his son,
Eleasah his son, and Azel his son.
44 And Azel had six sons whose names *were*
these: Azrikam, Bocheru, Ishmael, Sheariah,
Obadiah, and Hanan; these *were* the sons of
Azel.

CHAPTER 10

The House of Saul Dies in Battle
1 Sam. 31:1–7

NOW [R]the Philistines fought against Israel;
and the men of Israel fled from before
the Philistines, and fell slain on Mount
Gilboa. 1 Sam. 31:1, 2
2 Then the Philistines followed hard after
Saul and his sons. And the Philistines killed
Jonathan, [T]Abinadab, and Malchishua, Saul's
sons. *Jishui,* 1 Sam. 14:49
3 The battle became fierce against Saul.
The archers hit him, and he was wounded by
the archers.
4 Then Saul said to his armorbearer, "Draw
your sword, and thrust me through with it, lest
these uncircumcised men come and abuse
me." But his armorbearer would not, for he
was greatly afraid. Therefore Saul took a
sword and fell on it.
5 And when his armorbearer saw that Saul
was dead, he also fell on his sword and died.
6 So Saul and his three sons died, and all
his house died together.
7 And when all the men of Israel who *were*
in the valley saw that they had fled and that
Saul and his sons were dead, they forsook
their cities and fled; then the Philistines came
and dwelt in them.

The Philistines Defile Saul—1 Sam. 31:8–13

8 So it happened the next day, when the
Philistines came to [T]strip the slain, that they
found Saul and his sons fallen on Mount
Gilboa. *plunder*
9 And they stripped him and took his head
and his armor, and sent word *throughout* the
land of the Philistines to proclaim the news *in
the temple* of their idols and among the peo-
ple.
10 [R]Then they put his armor in the [T]temple of
their gods, and fastened his head in the tem-
ple of Dagon. 1 Sam. 31:10 • Lit. *house*
11 And when all Jabesh Gilead heard all that
the Philistines had done to Saul,

9:37 *Zecher,* 1 Chr. 8:31 **9:38** *Shimeah,* 1 Chr. 8:32
9:41 *Tarea,* 1 Chr. 8:35 • So with Arab., Syr., Tg., Vg.
(cf. 8:35); MT, LXX omit *and Ahaz* **9:42** *Jehoaddah,*
1 Chr. 8:36 **9:43** *Raphah,* 1 Chr. 8:37

12 all the valiant men arose and took the
body of Saul and the bodies of his sons; and
they brought them to Jabesh, and buried their
bones under the tamarisk tree at Jabesh, and
fasted seven days.

The Cause of Saul's Death

13 So Saul died for his unfaithfulness which
he had committed against the LORD, because
he did not keep the word of the LORD, and also
because [R]he consulted a medium for guid-
ance. 1 Sam. 28:7
14 But *he* did not inquire of the LORD; there-
fore He killed him, and turned the kingdom
over to David the son of Jesse.

CHAPTER 11

Anointing of David as King—2 Sam. 5:1–3

THEN [R]all Israel came together to David at
Hebron, saying, "Indeed we *are* your bone
and your flesh. 2 Sam. 5:1
2 "Also, in time past, even when Saul was
king, you *were* the one who led Israel out
and brought them in; and the LORD your
[R]God said to you, 'You shall [R]shepherd My
people Israel, and be ruler over My people Is-
rael.'" Ps. 78:70–72 • 2 Sam. 7:7
3 Therefore all the elders of Israel came to
the king at Hebron, and David made a
covenant with them at Hebron before the
LORD. And [R]they anointed David king over Is-
rael, according to the word of the LORD by
[R]Samuel. 2 Sam. 5:3 • 1 Sam. 16:1, 4, 12, 13

Conquest of Jerusalem—2 Sam. 5:6–10

4 And David and all Israel went to Jerusa-
lem, which is Jebus, where the Jebusites *were*,
the inhabitants of the land.
5 But the inhabitants of Jebus said to Da-
vid, "You shall not come in here!" Neverthe-
less David took the stronghold of Zion (that
is, the City of David).
6 Now David said, "Whoever attacks the
Jebusites first shall be [T]chief and captain."
And Joab the son of Zeruiah went up first,
and became chief. Lit. *head*
7 Then David dwelt in the stronghold;
therefore they called it the City of David.
8 And he built the city around it, from the
Millo* to the surrounding area. Joab [T]repaired
the rest of the city. Lit. *revived*
9 So David went on and became great, and
the LORD of hosts *was* with him.

The Chiefs—2 Sam. 23:8–12

10 Now these *were* the heads of the mighty
men whom David had, who strengthened
themselves with him in his kingdom, with all
Israel, to make him king, according to the
word of the LORD concerning Israel.
11 And this *is* the number of the mighty men
whom David had: [R]Jashobeam the son of a
Hachmonite, chief of the captains;* he had
lifted up his spear against three hundred,
killed *by him* at one time. 1 Chr. 27:2
12 After him *was* Eleazar the son of [R]Dodo,
the Ahohite, who *was one* of the three mighty
men. 1 Chr. 27:4
13 He was with David at Pasdammim. Now
there the Philistines were gathered for battle,
and there was a piece of ground full of barley.
So the people fled from the Philistines.
14 But they [T]stationed themselves in the
middle of *that* field, defended it, and killed
the Philistines. So the LORD brought about a
great victory. Lit. *took their stand*

The Thirty Chief Men—2 Sam. 23:13–23

15 Now three of the thirty chief men went
down to the rock to David, into the cave of
Adullam; and the army of the Philistines en-
camped in the Valley of Rephaim.
16 David *was* then in the stronghold, and the
garrison of the Philistines *was* then in Bethle-
hem.
17 And David said with longing, "Oh, that
someone would give me a drink of water from
the well of Bethlehem, which is by the gate!"
18 So the three broke through the camp of
the Philistines, drew water from the well of
Bethlehem that *was* by the gate, and took *it*
and brought *it* to David. Nevertheless David
would not drink it, but poured it out to the
LORD.
19 And he said, "Far be it from me, O my
God, that I should do this! Shall I drink the
blood of these men *who have put* their lives *in
jeopardy*? For at the risk of their lives they
brought it." Therefore he would not drink it.
These things were done by the three mighty
men.
20 Abishai the brother of Joab was chief of
another three.* He had lifted up his spear
against three hundred *men*, killed *them*, and
won a name among *these* three.
21 [R]Of the three he was more honored than
the other two men. Therefore he became their
captain. However he did not attain to the *first*
three. 2 Sam. 23:19
22 Benaiah was the son of Jehoiada, the son
of a valiant man from Kabzeel, who [T]had done
many deeds. [R]He had killed two lion-like he-
roes of Moab. He also had gone down and
killed a lion in the midst of a pit on a snowy
day. *was great in deeds* • 2 Sam. 23:20
23 And he killed an Egyptian, a man of *great*
height, five cubits tall. In the Egyptian's hand
there was a spear like a weaver's beam; and
he went down to him with a staff, wrested the
spear out of the Egyptian's hand, and killed
him with his own spear.

11:8 Lit. *The Landfill* **11:11** So with Qr.; Kt., LXX, Vg. *the thirty* (cf. 2 Sam. 23:8) **11:20** So with MT, LXX, Vg.; Syr. *thirty*

24 These *things* Benaiah the son of Jehoiada
did, and won a name among three mighty
men.
25 Indeed he was more honored than the
thirty, but he did not attain to the *first* three.
And David appointed him over his guard.

The Mighty Warriors—2 Sam. 23:24–39

26 Also the mighty warriors *were* [R]Asahel
the brother of Joab, Elhanan the son of Dodo
of Bethlehem, 2 Sam. 23:24
27 Shammoth the Harorite,* [R]Helez the
Pelonite,* 1 Chr. 27:10
28 [R]Ira the son of Ikkesh the Tekoite, Abiezer
the Anathothite, 1 Chr. 27:9
29 [T]Sibbechai the Hushathite, [T]Ilai the Aho-
hite, *Mebunnai,* 2 Sam. 23:27 • *Zalmon,* 2 Sam. 23:28
30 Maharai the Netophathite, Heled* the son
of Baanah the Netophathite,
31 Ithai* the son of Ribai of Gibeah, of the
sons of Benjamin, Benaiah the Pirathonite,
32 Hurai* of the brooks of Gaash, Abiel* the
Arbathite,
33 Azmaveth the Baharumite,* Eliahba the
Shaalbonite,
34 the sons of Hashem the Gizonite, Jona-
than the son of Shageh the Hararite,
35 Ahiam the son of [T]Sacar the Hararite,
Eliphal the son of Ur, *Sharar,* 2 Sam. 23:33
36 Hepher the Mecherathite, Ahijah the
Pelonite,
37 [T]Hezro the Carmelite, Naarai the son of
Ezbai, *Hezrai,* 2 Sam. 23:38
38 Joel the brother of Nathan, Mibhar the
son of Hagri,
39 Zelek the Ammonite, Naharai the Beroth-
ite* (the armorbearer of Joab the son of
Zeruiah),
40 Ira the Ithrite, Gareb the Ithrite,
41 [R]Uriah the Hittite, Zabad the son of
Ahlai, 2 Sam. 11
42 Adina the son of Shiza the Reubenite (a
chief of the Reubenites) and thirty with him,
43 Hanan the son of Maachah, Joshaphat the
Mithnite,
44 Uzzia the Ashterathite, Shama and Jeiel
the sons of Hotham the Aroerite,
45 Jediael the son of Shimri, and Joha his
brother, the Tizite,
46 Eliel the Mahavite, Jeribai and Joshaviah
the sons of Elnaam, Ithmah the Moabite,
47 Eliel, Obed, and Jaasiel the Mezobaite.

CHAPTER 12

The Mighty Men at Ziklag

NOW [R]these *were* the men who came to
David at [R]Ziklag while he was still a
fugitive from Saul the son of Kish; and they
were among the mighty men, helpers in the
war, 1 Sam. 27:2 • 1 Sam. 27:6
2 armed with bows, using both the right
hand and [R]the left in *hurling* stones and
shooting arrows with the bow. *They were* of
Benjamin, Saul's brethren. Judg. 3:15; 20:16
3 The chief *was* Ahiezer, then Joash, the
sons of [T]Shemaah the Gibeathite; Jeziel and
Pelet the sons of Azmaveth; Berachah, and
Jehu the Anathothite; Or *Hasmaah*
4 Ishmaiah the Gibeonite, a mighty man
among the thirty, and over the thirty; Jere-
miah, Jahaziel, Johanan, and Jozabad the
Gederathite;
5 Eluzai, Jerimoth, Bealiah, Shemariah,
and Shephatiah the Haruphite;
6 Elkanah, Jisshiah, Azarel, Joezer, and
Jashobeam, the Korahites;
7 and Joelah and Zebadiah the sons of
Jeroham of Gedor.
8 *Some* Gadites joined David at the strong-
hold in the wilderness, mighty men of valor,
men trained for battle, who could handle
shield and spear, whose faces *were like* the
faces of lions, and *were* [R]as swift as gazelles
on the mountains: 2 Sam. 2:18
9 Ezer the first, Obadiah the second, Eliab
the third,
10 Mishmannah the fourth, Jeremiah the
fifth,
11 Attai the sixth, Eliel the seventh,
12 Johanan the eighth, Elzabad the ninth,
13 Jeremiah the tenth, and Machbanai the
eleventh.
14 These *were* from the sons of Gad, cap-
tains of the army; the least was over a hun-
dred, and the greatest was over a thousand.
15 These *are* the ones who crossed the Jor-
dan in the first month, when it had over-
flowed all its [R]banks; and they put to flight all
those in the valleys, to the east and to the
west. Josh. 3:15; 4:18, 19
16 Then some of the sons of Benjamin and
Judah came to David at the stronghold.
17 And David went out [T]to meet them, and
answered and said to them, "If you have come
peaceably to me to help me, my heart will be
united with you; but if to betray me to my en-
emies, since *there is* no wrong in my hands,
may the God of our fathers look and bring
judgment." Lit. *before them*
18 Then the Spirit came upon Amasai, chief
of the captains, *and he said:*

" *We are* yours, O David;
We *are* on your side, O son of Jesse!
Peace, peace to you,
And peace to your helpers!
For your God helps you."

So David received them, and made them cap-
tains of the troop.

11:27 *Shammah the Harodite,* 2 Sam. 23:25 • *Paltite,* 2 Sam. 23:26 **11:30** *Heleb,* 2 Sam. 23:29, or *Heldai,* 1 Chr. 27:15 **11:31** *Ittai,* 2 Sam. 23:29 **11:32** *Hiddai,* 2 Sam. 23:30 • *Abi-Albon,* 2 Sam. 23:31
11:33 *Barhumite,* 2 Sam. 23:31 **11:39** *Beerothite,* 2 Sam. 23:37

19 And *some* from Manasseh defected to Da-
vid [R]when he was going with the Philistines to
battle against Saul; but they did not help them,
for the lords of the Philistines sent him away
by agreement, saying, "He may defect to his
master Saul *and endanger* our heads." 1 Sam. 29:2
20 When he went to Ziklag, those of Ma-
nasseh who defected to him were Adnah, Joz-
abad, Jediael, Michael, Jozabad, Elihu, and
Zillethai, captains of the thousands who *were*
from Manasseh.
21 And they helped David against [R]the
bands *of raiders*, for they *were* all mighty
men of valor, and they were captains in the
army. 1 Sam. 30:1, 9, 10
22 For at *that* time they came to David day
by day to help him, until *it was* a great army,
[R]like the army of God. Josh. 5:13–15

The Mighty Men at Hebron

23 Now these *were* the numbers of the divi-
sions *that were* equipped for war, *and* [R]came
to David at [R]Hebron to turn *over* the kingdom
of Saul to him, according to the word of the
LORD: 2 Sam. 2:1–4 • 1 Chr. 11:1
24 of the sons of Judah bearing shield and
spear, six thousand eight hundred [T]armed for
war; *equipped*
25 of the sons of Simeon, mighty men of
valor fit for war, seven thousand one hundred;
26 of the sons of Levi four thousand six hun-
dred;
27 Jehoiada, the leader of the Aaronites, and
with him three thousand seven hundred;
28 [R]Zadok, a young man, a valiant warrior,
and from his father's house twenty-two cap-
tains; 2 Sam. 8:17
29 of the sons of Benjamin, relatives of Saul,
three thousand (until then [R]the greatest part
of them had remained loyal to the house of
Saul); 2 Sam. 2:8, 9
30 of the sons of Ephraim twenty thousand
eight hundred, mighty men of valor, famous
men throughout their father's house;
31 of the half-tribe of Manasseh eighteen
thousand, who were designated by name to
come and make David king;
32 of the sons of Issachar [R]who had under-
standing of the times, to know what Israel
ought to do, their chiefs were two hundred;
and all their brethren were at their com-
mand; Esth. 1:13
33 of Zebulun there were fifty thousand who
went out to battle, expert in war with all
weapons of war, [R]stouthearted men who could
keep ranks; Ps. 12:2
34 of Naphtali one thousand captains, and
with them thirty-seven thousand with shield
and spear;
35 of the Danites who could keep battle for-
mation, twenty-eight thousand six hundred;
36 of Asher, those who could go out to war,
able to keep battle formation, forty thousand;
37 of the Reubenites and the Gadites and the
half-tribe of Manasseh, from the other side of
the Jordan, one hundred and twenty thousand
armed for battle with every *kind* of weapon of
war.
38 All these men of war, who could keep
ranks, came to Hebron with a loyal heart, to
make David king over all Israel; and all the
rest of Israel *were* of [R]one mind to make Da-
vid king. 2 Chr. 30:12
39 And they were there with David three
days, eating and drinking, for their brethren
had prepared for them.
40 Moreover those who were near to them,
from as far away as Issachar and Zebulun and
Naphtali, were bringing food on donkeys and
camels, on mules and oxen—provisions of
flour and cakes of figs and cakes of raisins,
wine and oil and oxen and sheep abundantly,
for *there was* joy in Israel.

CHAPTER 13

Preparation to Move the Ark

THEN David consulted with the [R]captains
of thousands and hundreds, *and* with
every leader. 1 Chr. 11:15; 12:34
2 And David said to all the assembly of Is-
rael, "If *it seems* good to you, and if it is of
the LORD our God, let us send out to our
brethren everywhere *who are* [R]left in all the
land of Israel, and with them to the priests
and Levites *who are* in their cities *and* their
common-lands, that they may gather together
to us; Is. 37:4
3 "and let us bring the ark of our God back
to us, [R]for we have not inquired at it since the
days of Saul." 1 Sam. 7:1, 2
4 Then all the assembly said that they
would do so, for the thing was right in the
eyes of all the people.
5 So [R]David gathered all Israel together,
from [R]Shihor in Egypt to as far as the en-
trance of Hamath, to bring the ark of God
from Kirjath Jearim. 1 Sam. 7:5 • Josh. 13:3

Uzza Dies for Touching the Ark
2 Sam. 6:1–11

6 And David and all Israel went up to
Baalah,* to Kirjath Jearim, which belonged to
Judah, to bring up from there the ark of God
the LORD, who dwells *between* the cherubim,
where *His* name is proclaimed.
7 So they carried the ark of God on a new
cart [R]from the house of Abinadab, and Uzza
and Ahio drove the cart. 1 Sam. 7:1
8 Then [R]David and all Israel played *music*
before God with all *their* might, with [T]sing-
ing, on harps, on stringed instruments, on
tambourines, on cymbals, and with trum-
pets. 2 Sam. 6:5 • *songs*

13:6 *Baale Judah*, 2 Sam. 6:2

9 And when they came to Chidon's* thresh-
ing floor, Uzza put out his hand to hold the
ark, for the oxen stumbled.
10 Then the anger of the LORD was aroused
against Uzza, and He struck him [R]because he
put his hand to the ark; and he [R]died there be-
fore God. [Num. 4:15] • Lev. 10:2
11 And David became angry because of the
LORD's outbreak against Uzza; therefore that
place is called Perez Uzza* to this day.
12 David was afraid of God that day, saying,
"How can I bring the ark of God to me?"
13 So David would not move the ark with
him into the City of David, but took it aside
into the house of Obed-Edom the Gittite.
14 The ark of God remained with the family
of Obed-Edom in his house three months. And
the LORD blessed the house of Obed-Edom
and all that he had.

CHAPTER 14

David's House Is Constructed
2 Sam. 5:11, 12

NOW Hiram king of Tyre sent messengers
to David, and cedar trees, with masons
and carpenters, to build him a house.
2 So David knew that the LORD had estab-
lished him as king over Israel, for his king-
dom was [R]highly exalted for the sake of His
people Israel. Num. 24:7

David's Children in Jerusalem

3 Then David took more wives in Jerusa-
lem, and David begot more sons and daugh-
ters.
4 And these are the names of his children
whom he had in Jerusalem: Shammua,*
Shobab, Nathan, Solomon,
5 Ibhar, Elishua,* Elpelet,*
6 Nogah, Nepheg, Japhia,
7 Elishama, Beeliada,* and Eliphelet.

David's Victory over the Philistines
2 Sam. 5:17–25

8 Now when the Philistines heard that [R]Da-
vid had been anointed king over all Israel, all
the Philistines went up to search for David.
And David heard *of it* and went out against
them. 2 Sam. 5:17–21
9 Then the Philistines went and made a raid
on the Valley of [T]Rephaim. Lit. *Giants*
10 And David [R]inquired of God, saying,
"Shall I go up against the Philistines? Will You
deliver them into my hand?" The LORD said to
him, "Go up, for I will deliver them into your
hand." 1 Sam. 23:2, 4; 30:8
11 So they went up to Baal Perazim, and Da-
vid defeated them there. Then David said,
"God has broken through my enemies by my
hand like a breakthrough of water." Therefore
they called the name of that place Baal Per-
azim.*
12 And when they left their gods there, Da-
vid gave a commandment, and they were
burned with fire.
13 [R]Then the Philistines once again made a
raid on the valley. 2 Sam. 5:22–25
14 Therefore David inquired again of God,
and God said to him, "You shall not go up
after them; circle around them, and come
upon them in front of the mulberry trees.
15 "And it shall be, when you hear a sound of
marching in the tops of the mulberry trees,
then you shall go out to battle, for God has
gone out before you to strike the camp of the
Philistines."
16 So David did as God commanded him,
and they drove back the army of the
Philistines from Gibeon as far as Gezer.
17 Then [R]the fame of David went out into all
lands, and the LORD brought the fear of him
upon all nations. Josh. 6:27

CHAPTER 15

Spiritual Preparation to Move the Ark

DAVID built houses for himself in the City
of David; and he prepared a place for the
ark of God, and pitched a tent for it.
2 Then David said, "No one may carry the
[R]ark of God but the Levites, for the LORD has
chosen them to carry the ark of God and to
minister before Him forever." [Num. 4:15]
3 And David gathered all Israel together at
Jerusalem, to bring up the ark of the LORD to
its place, which he had prepared for it.
4 Then David assembled the children of
Aaron and the Levites:
5 of the sons of Kohath, Uriel the chief,
and one hundred and twenty of his [T]breth-
ren; *kinsmen*
6 of the sons of Merari, Asaiah the chief,
and two hundred and twenty of his brethren;
7 of the sons of Gershom, Joel the chief,
and one hundred and thirty of his brethren;
8 of the sons of Elizaphan, Shemaiah the
chief, and two hundred of his brethren;
9 of the sons of [R]Hebron, Eliel the chief, and
eighty of his brethren; Ex. 6:18
10 of the sons of Uzziel, Amminadab the
chief, and one hundred and twelve of his
brethren.
11 And David called for [R]Zadok and [R]Abi-
athar the priests, and for the Levites: for
Uriel, Asaiah, Joel, Shemaiah, Eliel, and Am-
minadab. 1 Chr. 12:28 • 1 Kin. 2:22, 26, 27
12 He said to them, "You *are* the heads of the
fathers' *houses* of the Levites; sanctify your-
selves, you and your brethren, that you may

13:9 *Nachon*, 2 Sam. 6:6 **13:11** Lit. *Outburst Against Uzza* **14:4** *Shimea*, 1 Chr. 3:5 **14:5** *Elishama*, 1 Chr. 3:6 • *Eliphelet*, 1 Chr. 3:6 **14:7** *Eliada*, 2 Sam. 5:6; 1 Chr. 3:8 **14:11** Lit. *Master of Breakthroughs*

bring up the ark of the LORD God of Israel to *the place* I have prepared for it.
13 "For [R]because you *did* not *do it* the first *time,* [R]the LORD our God broke out against us, because we did not consult Him about the proper order." 2 Sam. 6:3 • 1 Chr. 13:7–11
14 So the priests and the Levites [T]sanctified themselves to bring up the ark of the LORD God of Israel. *consecrated*
15 And the children of the Levites bore the ark of God on their shoulders, by its poles, as [R]Moses had commanded according to the word of the LORD. Ex. 25:14
16 Then David spoke to the leaders of the Levites to appoint their brethren *to be* the singers accompanied by instruments of music, stringed instruments, harps, and cymbals, by raising the voice with resounding joy.
17 So the Levites appointed Heman the son of Joel; and of his brethren, Asaph the son of Berechiah; and of their brethren, the sons of Merari, Ethan the son of Kushaiah;
18 and with them their brethren of the second *rank:* Zechariah, Ben,* Jaaziel, Shemiramoth, Jehiel, Unni, Eliab, Benaiah, Maaseiah, Mattithiah, Elipheleh, Mikneiah, Obed-Edom, and Jeiel, the gatekeepers;
19 the singers, Heman, Asaph, and Ethan, *were* to sound the cymbals of bronze;
20 Zechariah, Aziel, Shemiramoth, Jehiel, Unni, Eliab, Maaseiah, and Benaiah, with strings according to [R]Alamoth; Ps. 46:title
21 Mattithiah, Elipheleh, Mikneiah, Obed-Edom, Jeiel, and Azaziah, to direct with harps on the [R]Sheminith; Ps. 6:title
22 Chenaniah, leader of the Levites, was instructor *in charge of* the music, because he *was* skillful;
23 Berechiah and Elkanah *were* doorkeepers for the ark;
24 Shebaniah, Joshaphat, Nethanel, Amasai, Zechariah, Benaiah, and Eliezer, the priests, [R]were to blow the trumpets before the ark of God; and Obed-Edom and Jehiah, doorkeepers for the ark. [Num. 10:8]

Joyful Transportation of the Ark *2 Sam. 6:12–16*

25 So [R]David, the elders of Israel, and the captains over thousands went to bring up the ark of the covenant of the LORD from the house of Obed-Edom with joy. 1 Kin. 8:1
26 And so it was, when God helped the Levites who bore the ark of the covenant of the LORD, that they offered seven bulls and seven rams.
27 David was clothed with a robe of fine [R]linen, as were all the Levites who bore the ark, the singers, and Chenaniah the music master *with* the singers. David also wore a linen ephod. 1 Sam. 2:18, 28
28 [R]Thus all Israel brought up the ark of the covenant of the LORD with shouting and with the sound of the horn, with trumpets and with cymbals, making music with stringed instruments and harps. 1 Chr. 13:8
29 And it happened, [R]*as* the ark of the covenant of the LORD came to the City of David, that Michal, Saul's daughter, looked through a window and saw King David whirling and playing music; and she despised him in her heart. 2 Sam. 3:13, 14

CHAPTER 16

Offering of Sacrifices—2 Sam. 6:17–19

SO [R]they brought the ark of God, and set it in the midst of the tabernacle that David had erected for it. Then they offered burnt offerings and peace offerings before God. 2 Sam. 6:17
2 And when David had finished offering the burnt offerings and the peace offerings, [R]he blessed the people in the name of the LORD. 1 Kin. 8:14
3 Then he distributed to everyone of Israel, both man and woman, to everyone a loaf of bread, a piece *of meat,* and a cake of raisins.

Appointing Musicians

4 And he appointed some of the Levites to minister before the ark of the LORD, to [R]commemorate, to thank, and to praise the LORD God of Israel: Ps. 38:title; 70:title
5 Asaph the chief, and next to him Zechariah, *then* Jeiel, Shemiramoth, Jehiel, Mattithiah, Eliab, Benaiah, and Obed-Edom: Jeiel with stringed instruments and harps, but Asaph made music with cymbals;
6 Benaiah and Jahaziel the priests regularly *blew* the trumpets before the ark of the covenant of God.

Praise Psalm of David

7 On that day David [R]first delivered *this psalm* into the hand of Asaph and his brethren, to thank the LORD: Ps. 105:1–15

8 [R]Oh, give thanks to the LORD!
Call upon His name; Ps. 105:1–15
Make known His deeds among the
peoples!
9 Sing to Him, sing psalms to Him;
Talk of all His wondrous works!
10 Glory in His holy name;
Let the hearts of those rejoice who seek
the LORD!
11 Seek the LORD and His strength;
Seek His face evermore!
12 Remember His marvelous works which
He has done,
His wonders, and the judgments of His
mouth,

15:18 So with MT, Vg.; LXX omits *Ben*

13 O seed of Israel His servant,
You children of Jacob, His chosen ones!

14 He *is* the LORD our God;
His judgments *are* in all the earth.
15 Remember His covenant forever,
The word which He commanded, for a
thousand generations,
16 *The* [R]*covenant which* He made with
Abraham, Gen. 17:2; 26:3; 28:13; 35:11
And His oath to Isaac,
17 And confirmed it to Jacob for a statute,
To Israel *for* an everlasting covenant,
18 Saying, "To you I will give the land of
Canaan
As the allotment of your inheritance,"
19 When you were few in number,
Indeed very few, and strangers in it.

20 When they went from one nation to
another,
And from *one* kingdom to another
people,
21 He permitted no man to do them wrong;
Yes, He rebuked kings for their sakes,
22 *Saying,* [R]"Do not touch My anointed
ones, Gen. 20:7
And do My prophets no harm."*

23[R] Sing to the LORD, all the earth;
Proclaim the good news of His salvation
from day to day. Ps. 96:1–13
24 Declare His glory among the nations,
His wonders among all peoples.

25 For the LORD *is* great and greatly to be
praised;
He *is* also to be feared above all gods.
26 For all the gods of the peoples *are* idols,
But the LORD made the heavens.

27 Honor and majesty *are* before Him;
Strength and gladness are in His place.

28 Give to the LORD, O families of the
peoples,
Give to the LORD glory and strength.

29 Give to the LORD the glory *due* His name;
Bring an offering, and come before Him.
Oh, worship the LORD in the beauty of
holiness!

30 Tremble before Him, all the earth.
The world also is firmly established,
It shall not be moved.

31 Let the heavens rejoice, and let the earth
be glad;
And let them say among the nations,
"The LORD reigns."
32 Let the sea roar, and all its fullness;
Let the field rejoice, and all that *is* in it.
33 Then the [R]trees of the woods shall
rejoice before the LORD, Is. 55:12, 13
For He is coming to judge the earth.*
34[R] Oh, give thanks to the LORD, for *He is*
good! Ps. 106:1; 107:1; 118:1; 136:1
For His mercy *endures* forever.*
35[R] And say, "Save us, O God of our
salvation; Ps. 106:47, 48
Gather us together, and deliver us from
the Gentiles,
To give thanks to Your holy name,
To triumph in Your praise."

16:22 Cf. vv. 8–22 with Ps. 105:1–15 **16:33** Cf. vv. 23–33 with Ps. 96:1–13 **16:34** Cf. v. 34 with Ps. 106:1

16:29 The Meaning of Worship—Worship refers to the supreme honor or veneration given either in thought or deed to a person or thing. The Bible teaches that God alone is worthy of worship (Page 559—Ps. 29:2), but it also sadly records accounts of those who worshiped other objects. Among those were people (Page 873—Dan. 2:46), false gods (Page 348—2 Kin. 10:19), images and idols (Page 684—Is. 2:8; Page 874—Dan. 3:5), heavenly bodies (Page 391—2 Kin. 21:3), Satan (Page 1321—Rev. 13:4), and demons (Rev. 9:20). It is indeed tragic that many worshiped gods they could carry and not the God who could carry them. God Almighty alone is worthy of worship (Page 1315—Rev. 4:11).

True worship involves at least three important elements:

a. Worship requires reverence. This includes the honor and respect directed toward the Lord in thought and feeling. It is one thing to obey a superior unwillingly; it is quite another to commit one's thoughts and emotions in that obedience. Jesus said that those who worship God must do so "in spirit and truth" (Page 1085—John 4:24). The term "spirit" speaks of the personal nature of worship: It is from my person to God's Person and involves the intellect, emotions, and will. The word "truth" speaks of the content of worship: God is pleased when we worship Him, understanding His true character.
b. Worship includes public expression. This was particularly prevalent in the OT because of the sacrificial system. For example, when a believer received a particular blessing for which he wanted to thank God, it was not sufficient to say it privately; he expressed his thanks publicly with a thank-offering (Page 104—Lev. 7:12).
c. Worship means service. These two concepts are often linked together in Scripture (Page 184—Deut. 8:19). Furthermore, the words for worship in both Testaments originally referred to the labor of slaves for the master. Worship especially includes the joyful service which Christians render to Christ their Master. The concept of worship must not be restricted to church attendance, but should embrace an entire life of obedience to God.

Now turn to Page 1268—Heb. 13:15: The Expressions of Worship.

36 Blessed *be* the LORD God of Israel
From everlasting to everlasting!*

And all [R]the people said, "Amen!" and praised the LORD. Deut. 27:15

Constant Ministry at the Ark

37 So he left [R]Asaph and his brothers there before the ark of the covenant of the LORD to minister before the ark regularly, as every day's work [R]required; 1 Chr. 16:4, 5 • Ezra 3:4

38 and Obed-Edom with his sixty-eight brethren, including Obed-Edom the son of Jeduthun, and Hosah, *to be* gatekeepers;

39 and Zadok the priest and his brethren the priests, before the tabernacle of the LORD at the high place that *was* at Gibeon,

40 to offer burnt offerings to the LORD on the altar of burnt offering regularly [R]morning and evening, and *to do* according to all that is written in the Law of the LORD which He commanded Israel; [Ex. 29:38–42]

41 and with them Heman and Jeduthun and the rest who were chosen, who were designated by name, to give thanks to the LORD, because His mercy *endures* forever;

42 and with them Heman and Jeduthun, to sound aloud with trumpets and cymbals and the musical instruments of God. Now the sons of Jeduthun *were* gatekeepers.

43 [R]Then all the people departed, every man to his house; and David returned to bless his house. 2 Sam. 6:18–20

CHAPTER 17

Desire of David to Build God's House
2 Sam. 7:1–3

NOW it came to pass, when David was dwelling in his house, that David said to Nathan the prophet, "See now, I dwell in a house of cedar, but the ark of the covenant of the LORD *is* under tent curtains."

2 Then Nathan said to David, "Do all that *is* in your heart, for God *is* with you."

Covenant of God to Build David's House
2 Sam. 7:4–17

3 But it happened that night that the word of God came to Nathan, saying,

4 "Go and tell My servant David, 'Thus says the LORD: "You shall [R]not build Me a house to dwell in. [1 Chr. 28:2, 3]

5 "For I have not dwelt in a house since the time that I brought up Israel, even to this day, but have gone from tent to tent, and from *one* tabernacle *to another.*

6 "Wherever I have moved about with all Israel, have I ever spoken a word to any of the judges of Israel, whom I commanded to shepherd My people, saying, 'Why have you not built Me a house of cedar?' " '

7 "Now therefore, thus shall you say to My servant David, 'Thus says the LORD of hosts: "I took you [R]from the sheepfold, from following the sheep, to be [T]ruler over My people Israel. 1 Sam. 16:11–13 • *leader*

8 "And I have been with you wherever you have gone, and have cut off all your enemies from before you, and have [T]made you a name like the name of the great men who *are* on the earth. *given you prestige*

9 "Moreover I will appoint a place for My people Israel, and will plant them, that they may dwell in a place of their own and move no more; nor shall the sons of wickedness oppress them anymore, as previously,

10 "since the time that I commanded judges *to be* over My people Israel. Also I will subdue all your enemies. Furthermore I tell you that the LORD will build you a house.*

11 "And it shall be, when your days are [R]fulfilled, when you must go *to be* with your fathers, that I will [R]set up your seed after you, who will be of your sons; and I will establish his kingdom. 1 Kin. 2:10 • Matt. 1:6☆

12 "He shall build Me a house, and I will establish his throne [R]forever. [Luke 1:33]☆

13 [R]"I will be his Father, and he shall be My son; and I will not take My mercy away from him, [R]as I took *it* from *him* who was before you. Heb. 1:5☆ • [1 Sam. 15:23–28]

14 "And I will establish him in My house and in My kingdom forever; and his [R]throne shall be established forever." ' " Acts 2:30☆

15 According to all these words and according to all this vision, so Nathan spoke to David.

Praise Prayer of David—2 Sam. 7:18–29

16 [R]Then King David went in and sat before the LORD; and he said: "Who *am* I, O LORD God? And what is my house, that You have brought me this far? 2 Sam. 7:18

17 "And *yet* this was a small thing in Your sight, O God; and You have *also* spoken of Your servant's house for a great while to come, and have regarded me according to the rank of a man of high degree, O LORD God.

18 "What more can David *say* to You for the honor of Your servant? For You know Your servant.

19 "O LORD, for Your servant's sake, and according to Your own heart, You have done all this greatness, in making known all these great things.

20 "O LORD, *there is* none like You, nor *is there any* God besides You, according to all that we have heard with our ears.

21 [R]"And who *is* like Your people Israel, the one nation on the earth whom God went to redeem for Himself *as* a people—to make for Yourself a name by great and awesome deeds,

16:36 Cf. vv. 35, 36 with Ps. 106:47, 48 **17:10** Royal dynasty

by driving out nations from before Your peo-
ple whom You redeemed from Egypt? Ps. 147:20
22 "For You have made Your people Israel
Your very own people forever; and You, LORD,
have become their God.
23 "And now, O LORD, the word which You
have spoken concerning Your servant and
concerning his house, *let it* be established for-
ever, and do as You have said.
24 "So let it be established, that Your name
may be magnified forever, saying, 'The LORD
of hosts, the God of Israel, *is* Israel's God.'
And let the house of Your servant David be es-
tablished before You.
25 "For You, O my God, have revealed to Your
servant that You will build him a house. There-
fore Your servant has found it *in his heart* to
pray before You.
26 "And now, LORD, You are God, and have
promised this goodness to Your servant.
27 "Now You have been pleased to bless the
house of Your servant, that it may continue be-
fore You forever; for You have blessed it, O
LORD, and *it shall be* blessed forever."

CHAPTER 18

Victory over Philistia—2 Sam. 8:1

AFTER this [R]it came to pass that David [T]at-
tacked the Philistines, subdued them, and
took Gath and its towns from the hand of the
Philistines. 2 Sam. 8:1–18 • Lit. *struck*

Victory over Moab—2 Sam. 8:2

2 Then he [T]defeated [R]Moab, and the
Moabites became David's [R]servants, *and*
brought tribute. Lit. *struck* • 2 Sam. 8:2 • Ps. 60:8

Victory over Zobah—2 Sam. 8:3, 4

3 And David defeated Hadadezer* king of
Zobah *as far as* Hamath, as he went to estab-
lish his power by the River Euphrates.
4 David took from him one thousand chari-
ots, seven thousand* horsemen, and twenty
thousand foot soldiers. Also David [T]ham-
strung all the chariot *horses*, except that he
spared enough of them for one hundred char-
iots. *crippled*

Victory over Syria—2 Sam. 8:5–13

5 When the Syrians of Damascus came to
help Hadadezer king of Zobah, David killed
twenty-two thousand of the Syrians.
6 Then David put *garrisons* in Syria of Da-
mascus; and the Syrians became David's ser-
vants, *and* brought tribute. So the LORD
preserved David wherever he went.
7 And David took the shields of gold that
were on the servants of Hadadezer, and
brought them to Jerusalem.
8 Also from Tibhath* and from Chun, cities
of Hadadezer, David brought a large amount
of [R]bronze, with which [R]Solomon made the
bronze Sea, the pillars, and the articles of
bronze. 2 Sam. 8:8 • 1 Kin. 7:15, 23
9 Now when Tou* king of Hamath heard
that David had [T]defeated all the army of
Hadadezer king of Zobah, Lit. *struck*
10 he sent Hadoram* his son to King David,
to greet him and bless him, because he had
fought against Hadadezer and defeated him
(for Hadadezer had been at war with Tou);
and *Hadoram brought with him* all kinds of
articles of gold, silver, and bronze.
11 King David also dedicated these to the
LORD, along with the silver and gold that he
had brought from all *these* nations—from
Edom, from Moab, from the [R]people of
Ammon, from the [R]Philistines, and from
[R]Amalek. 2 Sam. 10:14 • 2 Sam. 5:17–25 • 2 Sam. 1:1

Victory over Edom—2 Sam. 8:14–18

12 Moreover [R]Abishai the son of Zeruiah
killed [R]eighteen thousand Edomites* in the
Valley of Salt. 2 Sam. 23:18 • 2 Sam. 8:13
13 He also put garrisons in Edom, and all the
Edomites became David's servants. And the
LORD preserved David wherever he went.
14 So David reigned over all Israel, and
administered judgment and justice to all his
people.
15 Joab the son of Zeruiah *was* over the
army; Jehoshaphat the son of Ahilud *was*
recorder;
16 Zadok the son of Ahitub and Abimelech
the son of Abiathar *were* the priests;
Shavsha* *was* the scribe;
17 [R]Benaiah the son of Jehoiada *was* over
the Cherethites and the Pelethites; and Da-
vid's sons *were* [T]chief ministers at the king's
side. 2 Sam. 8:18 • Lit. *at the hand of the king*

CHAPTER 19

Humiliation of David's Servants 2 Sam. 10:1–5

IT[R] happened after this that Nahash the king
of the people of Ammon died, and his son
reigned in his place. 2 Sam. 10:1–19
2 Then David said, "I will show kindness to
Hanun the son of Nahash, because his father
showed kindness to me." So David sent mes-
sengers to comfort him concerning his father.
And David's servants came to Hanun in the
land of the people of Ammon to comfort him.
3 And the princes of the people of Ammon
said to Hanun, "Do you think that David re-
ally honors your father because he has sent
comforters to you? Did his servants not come
to you to search and to overthrow and to spy
out the land?"

18:3 Heb. *Hadarezer* **18:4** *seven hundred,* 2 Sam. 8:4
18:8 *Betah,* 2 Sam. 8:8 **18:9** *Toi,* 2 Sam. 8:9, 10
18:10 *Joram,* 2 Sam. 8:10 **18:12** *Syrians,* 2 Sam. 8:13
18:16 *Seraiah,* 2 Sam. 8:17, or *Shisha,* 1 Kin. 4:3

4 Therefore Hanun took David's servants, shaved them, and cut off their garments [T]in the middle, at their [R]buttocks, and sent them away. *in half* • Is. 20:4

5 Then *some* went and told David about the men; and he sent to meet them, because the men were greatly ashamed. And the king said, "Wait at Jericho until your beards have grown, and *then* return."

Victory over the Ammonites—2 Sam. 10:6–14

6 When the people of Ammon saw that they had made themselves repulsive to David, Hanun and the people of Ammon sent a thousand talents of silver to hire for themselves chariots and horsemen from Mesopotamia,* from Syrian Maacah, [R]and from Zobah.* 1 Chr. 18:5, 9

7 So they hired for themselves thirty-two thousand chariots, with the king of Maacah and his people, who came and encamped before Medeba. Also the people of Ammon gathered together from their cities, and came to battle.

8 Now when David heard *of it,* he sent Joab and all the army of the mighty men.

9 Then the people of Ammon came out and put themselves in battle array before the gate of the city, and the kings who had come *were* by themselves in the field.

10 When Joab saw that the battle line was against him before and behind, he chose some of Israel's best and put *them* in battle array against the Syrians.

11 And the rest of the people he put under the command of Abishai his brother, and they set *themselves* in battle array against the people of Ammon.

12 Then he said, "If the Syrians are too strong for me, then you shall help me; but if the people of Ammon are too strong for you, then I will help you.

13 "Be of good courage, and let us be strong for our people and for the cities of our God. And may the LORD do *what is* good in His sight."

14 So Joab and the people who *were* with him drew near for the battle against the Syrians, and they fled before him.

15 When the people of Ammon saw that the Syrians were fleeing, they also fled before Abishai his brother, and entered the city. So Joab went to Jerusalem.

Victory over the Syrians—2 Sam. 10:15–19

16 Now when the Syrians saw that they had been defeated by Israel, they sent messengers and brought the Syrians who were beyond the River,* and Shophach* the commander of Hadadezer's army *went* before them.

17 When it was told David, he gathered all Israel, crossed over the Jordan and came upon them, and set up in battle array against them. So when David had set up in *battle* array against the Syrians, they fought with him.

18 Then the Syrians fled before Israel; and David killed seven thousand* charioteers and forty thousand foot soldiers* of the Syrians, and killed Shophach the commander of the army.

19 And when the servants of Hadadezer saw that they were defeated by Israel, they made peace with David and became his servants. So the Syrians were not willing to help the people of Ammon anymore.

CHAPTER 20

Victory over the Ammonites
2 Sam. 11:1; 12:26–31

IT[R] happened in the spring of the year, at the time kings go out *to battle,* that Joab led out the armed forces and ravaged the country of the people of Ammon, and came and besieged Rabbah. But [R]David stayed at Jerusalem. And Joab defeated Rabbah and overthrew it. 2 Sam. 11:1 • 2 Sam. 11:2—12:25

2 Then David [R]took their king's crown from his head, and found it to weigh a talent of gold, and *there were* precious stones in it. And it was set on David's head. Also he brought out the [T]spoil of the city in great abundance. 2 Sam. 12:30, 31 • *plunder*

3 And he brought out the people who *were* in it, and put *them* to work* with saws, with iron picks, and with axes. So David did to all the cities of the people of Ammon. Then David and all the people returned *to* Jerusalem.

Victory over the Philistine Giants
2 Sam. 21:18–22

4 Now it happened afterward [R]that war broke out at Gezer with the Philistines, at which time Sibbechai the Hushathite killed Sippai,* *who was one* of the sons of the giant. And they were subdued. 2 Sam. 21:18

5 Again there was war with the Philistines, and Elhanan the son of Jair* killed Lahmi the brother of Goliath the Gittite, the shaft of whose spear *was* like a weaver's [R]beam. 1 Sam. 17:7

6 Yet again [R]there was war at Gath, where there was a man of *great* stature, with twenty-four fingers and toes, six *on each hand* and six *on each foot;* and he also was born to [T]the giant. 2 Sam. 21:20 • Or *Raphah*

7 So when he defied Israel, Jonathan the son of Shimea,* David's brother, killed him.

19:6 Heb. *Aram Naharaim* • *Zoba,* 2 Sam. 10:6 **19:16** The Euphrates • *Zoba,* 2 Sam. 10:6, or *Shobach,* 2 Sam. 10:16 **19:18** *seven hundred,* 2 Sam. 10:18 • *horsemen,* 2 Sam. 10:18 **20:3** LXX *cut them with* **20:4** *Saph,* 2 Sam. 21:18 **20:5** *Jaare-Oregim,* 2 Sam. 21:19 **20:7** *Shammah,* 1 Sam. 16:9 or *Shimeah,* 2 Sam. 21:21

8 These were born to the giant in Gath, and
they fell by the hand of David and by the hand
of his servants.

CHAPTER 21

Temptation of David by Satan

NOW Satan stood up against Israel, and
moved David to number Israel.
2 So David said to Joab and to the leaders
of the people, "Go, number Israel from Beer-
sheba to Dan, and bring the number of them
to me that I may know *it*."
3 And Joab answered, "May the LORD make
His people a hundred times more than they
are. But, my lord the king, *are* they not all my
lord's servants? Why then does my lord re-
quire this thing? Why should he be a cause of
guilt in Israel?"
4 Nevertheless the king's word prevailed
against Joab. Therefore Joab departed and
went throughout all Israel and came to Jeru-
salem.

Enumeration of Israel

5 Then Joab gave the sum of the number of
the people to David. All Israel *had* one million
one hundred thousand men who drew the
sword, and Judah *had* four hundred and sev-
enty thousand men who drew the sword.
6 [R]But he did not count Levi and Benjamin
among them, for the king's [T]word was abom-
inable to Joab. 1 Chr. 27:24 • *command*

Prayer of David

7 And God was displeased with this thing;
therefore He struck Israel.
8 So David said to God, "I have sinned
greatly, because I have done this thing; but
now, I pray, take away the iniquity of Your ser-
vant, for I have done very foolishly."

Three Choices of David

9 Then the LORD spoke to Gad, David's
[R]seer, saying, 1 Sam. 9:9
10 "Go and tell David, [R]saying, 'Thus says
the LORD: "I offer you three *things;* choose one
of them for yourself, that I may do *it* to
you." ' " 2 Sam. 24:12–14
11 So Gad came to David and said to him,
"Thus says the LORD: 'Choose for yourself,
12 'either three* years of famine, or three
months to be defeated by your foes with the
sword of your enemies overtaking *you,* or else
for three days the sword of the LORD—the
plague in the land, with the angel* of the LORD
destroying throughout all the territory of Is-
rael.' Now consider what answer I should take
back to Him who sent me."
13 And David said to Gad, "I am in great dis-
tress. Please let me fall into the hand of the
LORD, for His mercies *are* very great; but do
not let me fall into the hand of man."

Judgment of Pestilence

14 So the LORD sent a plague upon Israel,
and seventy thousand men of Israel fell.
15 And God sent an angel to Jerusalem to
destroy it. As he* was destroying, the LORD
looked and [R]relented of the disaster, and said
to the angel who was destroying, "It is
enough; now restrain your* hand." And the
angel of the LORD stood by the threshing floor
of Ornan* the Jebusite. Gen. 6:6
16 Then David lifted his eyes and [R]saw the

21:12 *seven,* 2 Sam. 24:13 • Or *Angel,* and so throughout the chapter **21:15** Or *He* • Or *Your* • *Araunah,* 2 Sam. 24:16, 18–24

21:1 Temptation by Satan—The role of Satan against the Christian is well summed up by the meaning of the name Satan—"adversary." He is also called "the devil," meaning "accuser." He can appear as a hideous dragon (Page 1267—Rev. 12:3, 4, 9) or as a beautifully deceptive "angel of light" (Page 1191—2 Cor. 11:14). He stands hatefully opposed to all the work of God and resourcefully promotes defiance among people (Page 1019—Mark 4:15; Page 513—Job 2:4, 5).

When Satan sinned he was expelled from heaven (Page 1056—Luke 10:18), although apparently he still had some access to God (Page 512—Job 1:6). A multitude of angels cast in their lot with him in his fall and subsequently became the demons mentioned often in the Bible (Page 989—Matt. 12:24; Page 1320—Rev. 12:7). Although Satan's doom was secured by Jesus' death on the cross (Page 1101—John 16:11), he will continue to hinder God's program until he and his angels are cast into the lake of fire (Page 1005—Matt. 25:41; Page 1326—Rev. 20:10).

The terrifying work of Satan in the unbeliever is described in Scripture as follows: he blinds their minds (Page 1186—2 Cor. 4:4); he takes the Word of God from their hearts (Page 1052—Luke 8:12); and he controls them (Page 1126—Acts 13:8). In regard to Christians, Satan may accuse them (Page 1320—Rev. 12:10), devour their testimony for Christ (Page 1283—1 Pet. 5:8), deceive them (Page 1191—2 Cor. 11:14), hinder their work (Page 1227—1 Thess. 2:18), tempt them to immorality (Page 1171—1 Cor. 7:5), and even be used by God to discipline Christians (Page 1169—1 Cor. 5:5; Page 1191—2 Cor. 12:7).

The Christian's response to Satan is to recognize his power and deception (Page 1185—2 Cor. 2:11; Page 1209—Eph. 6:11), to adhere steadfastly to the faith (Page 1283—1 Pet. 5:9), to resist him openly (James 4:7), and not to give him opportunities (Page 1207—Eph. 4:27). In practice, the best way to oppose him is to be a growing Christian. Also, in the light of his tremendous power to blind men to the gospel, Christians must always be aggressively and compassionately witnessing to the lost in order to snatch them from Satan's control (Page 1142—Acts 26:18). Believers can respond to temptation by Satan with confidence. We know that nothing can separate us from the love of God (Page 1155—Rom. 8:28–39).

Now turn to Page 1282—1 Pet. 3:17: Kinds of Suffering.

angel of the LORD standing between earth and heaven, having in his hand a drawn sword stretched out over Jerusalem. So David and the elders, clothed in sackcloth, fell on their faces. 2 Chr. 3:1

17 And David said to God, "Was it not I who commanded the people to be numbered? I am the one who has sinned and done evil indeed; but these [R]sheep, what have they done? Let Your hand, I pray, O LORD my God, be against me and my father's house, but not against Your people that they should be plagued." 2 Sam. 7:8

Withholding of Judgment by Sacrifices

18 Therefore, the angel of the LORD commanded Gad to say to David that David should go and erect an altar to the LORD on the threshing floor of Ornan the Jebusite.

19 So David went up at the word of Gad, which he had spoken in the name of the LORD.

20 Now Ornan turned and saw the angel; and his four sons *who were* with him hid themselves, but Ornan continued threshing wheat.

21 So David came to Ornan, and Ornan looked and saw David. And he went out from the threshing floor, and bowed before David with *his* face to the ground.

22 Then David said to Ornan, "Grant me the place of *this* threshing floor, that I may build an altar on it to the LORD. You shall grant it to me at the full price, that the plague may be withdrawn from the people."

23 But Ornan said to David, "Take *it* to yourself, and let my lord the king do *what is* good in his eyes. Look, I *also* give *you* the oxen for burnt offerings, the threshing implements for wood, and the wheat for the grain offering; I give *it* all."

24 Then King David said to Ornan, "No, but I will surely buy *it* for the full price, for I will not take what is yours for the LORD, nor offer burnt offerings with *that which* costs *me* nothing."

25 So David gave Ornan six hundred shekels of gold by weight for the place.

26 And David built there an altar to the LORD, and offered burnt offerings and peace offerings, and called on the LORD; and [R]He answered him from heaven by fire on the altar of burnt offering. Lev. 9:24

27 So the LORD commanded the angel, and he returned his sword to its sheath.

28 At that time, when David saw that the LORD had answered him on the threshing floor of Ornan the Jebusite, he sacrificed there.

29 [R]For the tabernacle of the LORD and the altar of the burnt offering, which Moses had made in the wilderness, *were* at that time at the high place in Gibeon. 1 Kin. 3:4

30 But David could not go before it to inquire of God, for he was afraid of the sword of the angel of the LORD.

CHAPTER 22

Material Provisions for the Temple's Construction

THEN David said, [R]"This *is* the house of the LORD God, and this *is* the altar of burnt offering for Israel." Deut. 12:5

2 So David commanded to gather the [R]aliens who *were* in the land of Israel; and he appointed masons to cut hewn stones to build the house of God. 1 Kin. 9:20, 21

3 And David prepared iron in abundance for the nails of the doors of the gates and for the joints, and bronze in abundance [R]beyond measure, 1 Kin. 7:47

4 and cedar trees in abundance; for the [R]Sidonians and those from Tyre brought much cedar wood to David. 1 Kin. 5:6–10

5 Now David said, [R]"Solomon my son *is* young and inexperienced, and the house to be built for the LORD *must be* exceedingly magnificent, famous and glorious throughout all countries. I will now make preparation for it." So David made abundant preparations before his death. 1 Chr. 29:1, 2

David's Charge to Solomon

6 Then he called for his son Solomon, and [T]charged him to build a house for the LORD God of Israel. *commanded*

7 And David said to Solomon: "My son, as for me, it was in my mind to build a house to the name of the LORD my God;

8 "but the word of the LORD came to me, saying, 'You have shed much blood and have made great wars; you shall not build a house for My name, because you have shed much blood on the earth in My sight.

9 'Behold, a son shall be born to you, who shall be a man of rest; and I will give him rest from all his enemies all around. His name shall be Solomon,* for I will give peace and quietness to Israel in his days.

10 'He shall build a house for My name, and [R]he shall be My son, and I *will be* his Father; and I will establish the throne of his kingdom over Israel forever.' Heb. 1:5☆

11 "Now, my son, may [R]the LORD be with you; and may you prosper, and build the house of the LORD your God, as He has said to you. 1 Chr. 22:16

12 "Only may the LORD [R]give you wisdom and understanding, and give you charge concerning Israel, that you may keep the law of the LORD your God. 1 Kin. 3:9–12

13 [R]"Then you will prosper, if you take care to fulfill the statutes and judgments with which the LORD charged Moses concerning Israel. Be strong and of good courage; do not fear nor be dismayed. 1 Chr. 28:7

14 "Indeed I have taken much trouble to

22:9 Lit. *Peaceful*

prepare for the house of the LORD one hundred thousand talents of gold and one million talents of silver, and bronze and iron [R]beyond measure, for it is so abundant. I have prepared timber and stone also, and you may add to them. 1 Chr. 22:3
15 "Moreover *there are* workmen with you in abundance: woodsmen and stonecutters, and all types of skillful men for every kind of work.
16 "Of gold and silver and bronze and iron *there is* no limit. Arise and begin working, and [R]the LORD be with you." 1 Chr. 22:11

David's Charge to the Leaders

17 David also commanded all the leaders of Israel to help Solomon his son, *saying,*
18 "*Is* not the LORD your God with you? And has He *not* given you rest on every side? For He has given the inhabitants of the land into my hand, and the land is subdued before the LORD and before His people.
19 "Now set your heart and your soul to seek the LORD your God. Therefore arise and build the sanctuary of the LORD God, to bring the ark of the covenant of the LORD and the holy articles of God into the house that is to be built for the name of the LORD."

CHAPTER 23

Enumeration of the Levites

SO when David was old and full of days, he made his son [R]Solomon king over Israel. 1 Kin. 1:33–40
2 And he gathered together all the leaders of Israel, with the priests and the Levites.
3 Now the Levites were numbered from the age of [R]thirty years and above; and the number of individual males was thirty-eight thousand. Num. 4:1–3
4 Of these, twenty-four thousand *were* to look after the work of the house of the LORD, six thousand *were* officers and judges,
5 four thousand *were* gatekeepers, and four thousand [R]praised the LORD with *musical* instruments, "which I made," *said David,* "for giving praise." 1 Chr. 15:16
6 Also [R]David separated them into [T]divisions among the sons of Levi: Gershon, Kohath, and Merari. Ex. 6:16 • *groups*

Organization of the Gershonites

7 Of the [R]Gershonites: Laadan* and Shimei. 1 Chr. 26:21
8 The sons of Laadan: the first Jehiel, then Zetham and Joel—three *in all.*
9 The sons of Shimei: Shelomith, Haziel, and Haran—three *in all.* These were the heads of the fathers' *houses* of Laadan.
10 And the sons of Shimei: Jahath, Zina,* Jeush, and Beriah. These *were* the four sons of Shimei.
11 Jahath was the first and Zizah the second. But Jeush and Beriah did not have many sons; therefore they were assigned as one father's house.

Organization of the Kohathites

12 [R]The sons of Kohath: Amram, Izhar, Hebron, and Uzziel—four *in all.* Ex. 6:18
13 The sons of Amram: Aaron and Moses; and [R]Aaron was set apart, he and his sons forever, that he should sanctify the most holy things, to burn incense before the LORD, to minister to Him, and to give the blessing in His name forever. Heb. 5:4
14 Now the sons of Moses the man of God were reckoned to the tribe of Levi.
15 [R]The sons of Moses *were* Gershon* and Eliezer. Ex. 18:3, 4
16 Of the sons of Gershon, [R]Shebuel* *was* the first. 1 Chr. 26:24
17 Of the descendants of Eliezer, Rehabiah was the first. And Eliezer had no other sons, but the sons of Rehabiah were very many.
18 Of the sons of Izhar, [R]Shelomith *was* the first. 1 Chr. 24:22
19 [R]Of the sons of Hebron, Jeriah *was* the first, Amariah the second, Jahaziel the third, and Jekameam the fourth. 1 Chr. 24:23
20 Of the sons of Uzziel, Michah *was* the first and Jesshiah the second.

Organization of the Merarites

21 [R]The sons of Merari *were* Mahli and Mushi. The sons of Mahli *were* Eleazar and [R]Kish. 1 Chr. 24:26 • 1 Chr. 24:29
22 And Eleazar died, and had no sons, but only daughters; and their [T]brethren, the sons of Kish, took them *as wives.* *kinsmen*
23 [R]The sons of Mushi *were* Mahli, Eder, and Jeremoth—three *in all.* 1 Chr. 24:30

Duties of the Levites

24 These *were* the sons of Levi by their fathers' houses—the heads of the fathers' *houses* as they were counted individually by the number of their names, who did the work for the service of the house of the LORD, from the age of twenty years and above.
25 For David said, "The LORD God of Israel [R]has given rest to His people, that they may dwell in Jerusalem forever"; 1 Chr. 22:18
26 and also to the Levites, "They shall no longer [R]carry the tabernacle, or any of the articles for its service." Num. 4:5, 15; 7:9
27 For by the [R]last words of David the Levites *were* numbered from twenty years old and above; 2 Sam. 23:1
28 because their duty *was* to help the sons of Aaron in the service of the house of the LORD,

23:7 *Libni,* Ex. 6:17 **23:10** LXX, Vg. *Zizah* and v. 11 **23:15** Heb. *Gershom,* 1 Chr. 6:16 **23:16** *Shubael,* 1 Chr. 24:20

in the courts and in the chambers, in the purifying of all holy things and the work of the service of the house of God,
29 both with [R]the showbread and [R]the fine flour for the grain offering, with the unleavened cakes and *what is baked in* the pan, with what is mixed and with all kinds of measures and sizes; Ex. 25:30 • Lev. 6:20
30 to stand every morning to thank and praise the LORD, and likewise at evening;
31 and at every presentation of a burnt offering to the LORD on the Sabbaths and on the New Moons and on the set feasts, by number according to the ordinance governing them, regularly before the LORD;
32 and that they should [R]attend to the needs of the tabernacle of meeting, the needs of the holy *place*, and the needs of the sons of Aaron their brethren in the work of the house of the LORD. 2 Chr. 13:10, 11

CHAPTER 24

Divisions of the Sons of Aaron

NOW *these are* the divisions of the sons of Aaron. [R]The sons of Aaron *were* Nadab, Abihu, Eleazar, and Ithamar. Lev. 10:1–6
2 And Nadab and Abihu died before their father, and had no children; therefore Eleazar and Ithamar ministered as priests.
3 Then David with Zadok of the sons of Eleazar, and [R]Ahimelech of the sons of Ithamar, divided them according to the schedule of their service. 1 Chr. 18:16
4 There were more leaders found of the sons of Eleazar than of the sons of Ithamar, and *thus* they were divided. Among the sons of Eleazar *were* sixteen heads of *their* fathers' houses, and eight heads of their fathers' houses among the sons of Ithamar.
5 Thus they were divided by lot, one group as another, for there were officials of the sanctuary and officials *of the house* of God, from the sons of Eleazar and from the sons of Ithamar.
6 And the scribe, Shemaiah the son of Nethanel, *one of* the Levites, wrote them down before the king, the leaders, Zadok the priest, Ahimelech the son of Abiathar, and the heads of the fathers' *houses* of the priests and Levites, one father's house taken for Eleazar and *one* for Ithamar.
7 Now the first lot fell to Jehoiarib, the second to Jedaiah,
8 the third to Harim, the fourth to Seorim,
9 the fifth to Malchijah, the sixth to Mijamin,
10 the seventh to Hakkoz, the eighth to [R]Abijah, Luke 1:5
11 the ninth to Jeshua, the tenth to Shecaniah,
12 the eleventh to Eliashib, the twelfth to Jakim,
13 the thirteenth to Huppah, the fourteenth to Jeshebeab,
14 the fifteenth to Bilgah, the sixteenth to Immer,
15 the seventeenth to Hezir, the eighteenth to Happizzez,*
16 the nineteenth to Pethahiah, the twentieth to Jehezekel,*
17 the twenty-first to Jachin, the twenty-second to Gamul,
18 the twenty-third to Delaiah, the twenty-fourth to Maaziah.
19 This *was* the schedule of their service [R]for coming into the house of the LORD according to their ordinance by the hand of Aaron their father, as the LORD God of Israel had commanded him. 1 Chr. 9:25

Organization of the Kohathites

20 And the rest of the sons of Levi: of the sons of Amram, Shubael;* of the sons of Shubael, Jehdeiah.
21 Concerning Rehabiah, of the sons of Rehabiah, the first *was* Isshiah.
22 Of the Izharites, Shelomoth;* of the sons of Shelomoth, Jahath.
23 Of the sons *of Hebron,** Jeriah *was the first,** Amariah the second, Jahaziel the third, *and* Jekameam the fourth.
24 *Of* the sons of Uzziel, Michah; of the sons of Michah, Shamir.
25 The brother of Michah, Isshiah; of the sons of Isshiah, Zechariah.

Organization of the Merarites

26 [R]The sons of Merari *were* Mahli and Mushi; the son of Jaaziah, Beno. Ex. 6:19
27 The sons of Merari by Jaaziah *were* Beno, Shoham, Zaccur, and Ibri.
28 Of Mahli: Eleazar, who had no sons.
29 Of Kish: the son of Kish, Jerahmeel.
30 Also [R]the sons of Mushi *were* Mahli, Eder, and Jerimoth. These *were* the sons of the Levites according to their fathers' houses. 1 Chr. 23:23
31 These also cast lots just as their brothers the sons of Aaron did, in the presence of King David, Zadok, Ahimelech, and the heads of the fathers' *houses* of the priests and Levites. The chief fathers *did* just as their younger brethren.

CHAPTER 25

Organization of the Orders of the Musicians

MOREOVER David and the captains of the army separated for the service *some* of the sons of [R]Asaph, of Heman, and of

24:15 LXX, Vg. *Aphses* **24:16** MT *Jehezkel* **24:20** *Shebuel*, 1 Chr. 23:16 **24:22** *Shelomith*, 1 Chr. 23:18 **24:23** Supplied from 23:19 (following some Heb. mss. and LXX mss.)

Jeduthun, who *should* prophesy with harps,
stringed instruments, and cymbals. And the
number of the skilled men performing their
service was: 1 Chr. 6:30, 33, 39, 44
2 Of the sons of Asaph: Zaccur, Joseph,
Nethaniah, and Asharelah;* the sons of
Asaph *were* [T]under the direction of Asaph,
who prophesied according to the order of the
king. Lit. *at the hands of*
3 Of [R]Jeduthun, the sons of Jeduthun:
Gedaliah, Zeri,* Jeshaiah, Shimei, Hasha-
biah, and Mattithiah, six,* under the direction
of their father Jeduthun, who prophesied
with a harp to give thanks and to praise the
LORD. 1 Chr. 16:41, 42
4 Of Heman, the sons of Heman: Bukkiah,
Mattaniah, Uzziel,* Shebuel,* Jerimoth,*
Hananiah, Hanani, Eliathah, Giddalti,
Romamti-Ezer, Joshbekashah, Mallothi,
Hothir, *and* Mahazioth.
5 All these *were* the sons of Heman the
king's seer in the words of God, to exalt his
[R]horn.* For God gave Heman fourteen sons
and three daughters. 1 Chr. 16:42
6 All these *were* under the direction of their
father for the music *in* the house of the LORD,
with cymbals, stringed instruments, and
harps, for the service of the house of God.
Asaph, Jeduthun, and Heman *were* under the
authority of the king.
7 So the [R]number of them, with their
brethren who were instructed in the songs of
the LORD, all who were skillful, *was* two hun-
dred and eighty-eight. 1 Chr. 23:5
8 And they cast lots for their duty, the small
as well as the great, [R]the teacher with the stu-
dent. 2 Chr. 23:13
9 Now the first lot for Asaph came out for
Joseph; the second for Gedaliah, him with his
brethren and sons, twelve;
10 the third for Zaccur, his sons and his
brethren, twelve;
11 the fourth for Jizri,* his sons and his
brethren, twelve;
12 the fifth for Nethaniah, his sons and his
brethren, twelve;
13 the sixth for Bukkiah, his sons and his
brethren, twelve;
14 the seventh for Jesharelah,* his sons and
his brethren, twelve;
15 the eighth for Jeshaiah, his sons and his
brethren, twelve;
16 the ninth for Mattaniah, his sons and his
brethren, twelve;
17 the tenth for Shimei, his sons and his
brethren, twelve;
18 the eleventh for Azarel,* his sons and his
brethren, twelve;
19 the twelfth for Hashabiah, his sons and
his brethren, twelve;
20 the thirteenth for Shubael,* his sons and
his brethren, twelve;
21 the fourteenth for Mattithiah, his sons
and his brethren, twelve;
22 the fifteenth for Jeremoth,* his sons and
his brethren, twelve;
23 the sixteenth for Hananiah, his sons and
his brethren, twelve;
24 the seventeenth for Joshbekashah, his
sons and his brethren, twelve;
25 the eighteenth for Hanani, his sons and
his brethren, twelve;
26 the nineteenth for Mallothi, his sons and
his brethren, twelve;
27 the twentieth for Eliathah, his sons and
his brethren, twelve;
28 the twenty-first for Hothir, his sons and
his brethren, twelve;
29 the twenty-second for Giddalti, his sons
and his brethren, twelve;
30 the twenty-third for Mahazioth, his sons
and his brethren, twelve;
31 the twenty-fourth for Romamti-Ezer, his
sons and his brethren, twelve.

CHAPTER 26

Organization of the Gatekeepers

CONCERNING the divisions of the gate-
keepers: of the Korahites, Meshelemiah
the son of Kore, of the sons of Asaph.
2 And the sons of Meshelemiah *were*
Zechariah the firstborn, Jediael the second,
Zebadiah the third, Jathniel the fourth,
3 Elam the fifth, Jehohanan the sixth,
Eliehoenai the seventh.
4 Moreover the sons of [R]Obed-Edom *were*
Shemaiah the firstborn, Jehozabad the sec-
ond, Joah the third, Sacar the fourth,
Nethanel the fifth, 1 Chr. 15:18, 21
5 Ammiel the sixth, Issachar the seventh,
Peulthai the eighth; for God blessed him.
6 Also to Shemaiah his son were sons born
who governed their fathers' houses, because
they *were* men of great ability.
7 The sons of Shemaiah *were* Othni,
Rephael, Obed, and Elzabad, whose brothers
Elihu and Semachiah *were* able men.
8 All these *were* of the sons of Obed-Edom,
they and their sons and their brethren, able
men with strength for the work: sixty-two of
Obed-Edom.
9 And Meshelemiah had sons and brethren,
eighteen able men.
10 Also [R]Hosah, of the children of Merari,
had sons: Shimri the first (for *though* he was
not the firstborn, his father made him the
first), 1 Chr. 16:38

25:2 *Jesharelah,* v. 14 **25:3** *Jizri,* v. 11 • So with one Heb. ms., LXX mss., *Shimei* completes the total of six sons, v. 17 **25:4** *Azarel,* v. 18 • *Shubael,* v. 20 • *Jeremoth,* v. 22 **25:5** Increase his power or influence **25:11** *Zeri,* v. 3 **25:14** *Asharelah,* v. 2 **25:18** *Uzziel,* v. 4 **25:20** *Shebuel,* v. 4 **25:22** *Jerimoth,* v. 4

11 Hilkiah the second, Tebaliah the third,
Zechariah the fourth; all the sons and
brethren of Hosah *were* thirteen.
12 Among these *were* the divisions of the
gatekeepers, among the chief men, *having* du-
ties just like their brethren, to serve in the
house of the LORD.
13 And they [R]cast lots for each gate, the
small as well as the great, according to their
father's house. 1 Chr. 24:5, 31; 25:8
14 The lot for the East *Gate* fell to
Shelemiah. Then they cast lots *for* his son
Zechariah, a wise counselor, and his lot came
out for the North Gate;
15 to Obed-Edom the South Gate, and to his
sons the storehouse.*
16 To Shuppim and Hosah *the lot came out*
for the West Gate, with the Shallecheth Gate
on the [R]ascending highway—watchman oppo-
site watchman. 1 Kin. 10:5
17 On the east were *six* Levites, on the north
four each day, on the south four each day, and
for the storehouse* two by two.
18 As for the Parbar* on the west, *there were*
four on the highway *and* two at the Parbar.
19 These were the divisions of the gatekeep-
ers among the sons of Korah and among the
sons of Merari.

Organization of the Treasuries of the Temple

20 Of the Levites, Ahijah *was* over the trea-
suries of the house of God and over the trea-
suries of the dedicated things.
21 The sons of [T]Laadan, the descendants of
the Gershonites of Laadan, heads of their fa-
thers' *houses,* of Laadan the Gershonite: [T]Je-
hieli. *Libni,* 1 Chr. 6:17 • *Jehiel,* 1 Chr. 23:8; 29:8
22 The sons of Jehieli, Zetham and Joel his
brother, *were* over the treasuries of the house
of the LORD.
23 Of the [R]Amramites, the Izharites, the He-
bronites, and the Uzzielites: Ex. 6:18
24 Shebuel the son of Gershom, the son of
Moses, *was* overseer of the treasuries.
25 And his brethren by Eliezer *were* Re-
habiah his son, Jeshaiah his son, Joram his
son, Zichri his son, and Shelomith his son.
26 This Shelomith and his brethren *were*
over all the treasuries of the dedicated things
[R]which King David and the heads of fathers'
houses, the captains over thousands and hun-
dreds, and the captains of the army, had dedi-
cated. 2 Sam. 8:11
27 Some of the spoils won in battles they
dedicated to maintain the house of the LORD.
28 And all that Samuel [R]the seer, Saul the
son of Kish, Abner the son of Ner, and Joab
the son of Zeruiah had dedicated, every dedi-
cated *thing,* was under the hand of Shelo-
mith and his brethren. 1 Sam. 9:9

Organization of the Officers Outside of the Temple

29 Of the Izharites, Chenaniah and his sons
performed duties as officials and judges over
Israel outside Jerusalem.
30 Of the Hebronites, Hashabiah and his
brethren, one thousand seven hundred able
men, had the oversight of Israel on the west
side of the Jordan for all the business of the
LORD, and in the service of the king.
31 Among the Hebronites, [R]Jerijah *was* head
of the Hebronites according to his genealogy
of the fathers. In the fortieth year of the reign
of David they were sought, and there were
found among them capable men [R]at Jazer of
Gilead. 1 Chr. 23:19 • Josh. 21:39
32 And his brethren *were* two thousand
seven hundred able men, heads of fathers'
houses, whom King David made officials over
the Reubenites, the Gadites, and the half-tribe
of Manasseh, for every matter pertaining to
God and the affairs of the king.

CHAPTER 27

The Twelve Captains of Israel

AND the children of Israel, according to
their number, the heads of fathers'
houses, the captains of thousands and hun-
dreds and their officers, served the king in
every matter of the *military* divisions. *These*
divisions came in and went out month by
month throughout all the months of the year,
each division *having* twenty-four thousand.
2 Over the first division for the first month
was Jashobeam the son of Zabdiel, and in his
division *were* twenty-four thousand;
3 *he was* of the children of Perez, and the
chief of all the captains of the army for the
first month.
4 Over the division of the second month
was Dodai* an Ahohite, and of his division
Mikloth also *was* the leader; in his division
were twenty-four thousand.
5 The third captain of the army for the third
month *was* Benaiah, the son of Jehoiada the
priest, who was chief; in his division *were*
twenty-four thousand.
6 This was the Benaiah *who was* mighty
among the thirty, and was over the thirty; in
his division *was* Ammizabad his son.
7 The fourth *captain* for the fourth month
was [R]Asahel the brother of Joab, and Zeba-
diah his son after him; in his division *were*
twenty-four thousand. 1 Chr. 11:26
8 The fifth *captain* for the fifth month *was*

26:15 Heb. *asuppim* **26:17** Heb. *asuppim*
26:18 Probably a court or colonnade extending west of the temple **27:4** Heb. *Dodai,* usually spelled *Dodo,* 2 Sam. 23:9

Shamhuth* the Izrahite; in his division were twenty-four thousand.

9 The sixth *captain* for the sixth month *was* Ira the son of Ikkesh the Tekoite; in his division *were* twenty-four thousand.

10 The seventh *captain* for the seventh month *was* [R]Helez the Pelonite, of the children of Ephraim; in his division *were* twenty-four thousand. 1 Chr. 11:27

11 The eighth *captain* for the eighth month *was* [R]Sibbechai the Hushathite, of the Zarhites; in his division *were* twenty-four thousand. 2 Sam. 21:18

12 The ninth *captain* for the ninth month *was* [R]Abiezer the Anathothite, of the Benjamites; in his division *were* twenty-four thousand. 1 Chr. 11:28

13 The tenth *captain* for the tenth month *was* [R]Maharai the Netophathite, of the Zarhites; in his division *were* twenty-four thousand. 1 Chr. 11:30

14 The eleventh *captain* for the eleventh month *was* [R]Benaiah the Pirathonite, of the children of Ephraim; in his division *were* twenty-four thousand. 1 Chr. 11:31

15 The twelfth *captain* for the twelfth month *was* Heldai* the Netophathite, of Othniel; in his division *were* twenty-four thousand.

The Leaders of the Twelve Tribes

16 Furthermore, over the tribes of Israel: the officer over the Reubenites *was* Eliezer the son of Zichri; over the Simeonites, Shephatiah the son of Maachah;

17 *over* the Levites, Hashabiah the son of Kemuel; over the Aaronites, Zadok;

18 *over* Judah, [R]Elihu, *one* of David's brothers; *over* Issachar, Omri the son of Michael; 1 Sam. 16:6

19 *over* Zebulun, Ishmaiah the son of Obadiah; *over* Naphtali, Jerimoth the son of Azriel;

20 *over* the children of Ephraim, Hoshea the son of Azaziah; *over* the half-tribe of Manasseh, Joel the son of Pedaiah;

21 *over* the half-*tribe* of Manasseh in Gilead, Iddo the son of Zechariah; *over* Benjamin, Jaasiel the son of Abner;

22 *over* Dan, Azarel the son of Jeroham. These *were* the leaders of the tribes of Israel.

23 But David did not take the number of those twenty years old and under, because [R]the LORD had said He would multiply Israel like the stars of the heavens. [Deut. 6:3]

24 Joab the son of Zeruiah began a census, but he did not finish, for [R]wrath came upon Israel because of this census; nor was the number recorded in the account of the chronicles of King David. 1 Chr. 21:1–7

The Royal Officers of David

25 And Azmaveth the son of Adiel *was* over the king's treasuries; and Jehonathan the son of Uzziah was over the storehouses in the field, in the cities, in the villages, and in the fortresses.

26 Ezri the son of Chelub was over those who did the work of the field for tilling the ground.

27 And Shimei the Ramathite *was* over the vineyards, and Zabdi the Shiphmite was over the produce of the vineyards for the supply of wine.

28 Baal-Hanan the Gederite was over the olive trees and the sycamore trees that *were* in the lowlands, and Joash *was* over the store of oil.

29 And Shitrai the Sharonite *was* over the herds that fed in Sharon, and Shaphat the son of Adlai was over the herds *that were* in the valleys.

30 Obil the Ishmaelite *was* over the camels, Jehdeiah the Meronothite *was* over the donkeys,

31 and Jaziz the [R]Hagrite *was* over the flocks. All these *were* the officials over King David's property. 1 Chr. 5:10

The Counselors of David

32 Also Jehonathan, David's uncle, *was* a counselor, a wise man, and a [T]scribe; and Jehiel the [T]son of Hachmoni *was* with the king's sons. *secretary* • Or *Hachmonite*

33 [R]Ahithophel *was* the king's counselor, and [R]Hushai the Archite *was* the king's companion. 2 Sam. 15:12 • 2 Sam. 15:32–37

34 After Ahithophel *was* Jehoiada the son of Benaiah, then [R]Abiathar. And the general of the king's army *was* Joab. 1 Kin. 1:7

CHAPTER 28

Charge to Israel

NOW David assembled at Jerusalem all [R]the leaders of Israel: the officers of the tribes and [R]the captains of the divisions who served the king, the captains over thousands and captains over hundreds, and [R]the stewards over all the substance and possessions of the king and of his sons, with the officials, the valiant men, and all the mighty men of valor. 1 Chr. 27:16 • 1 Chr. 27:1, 2 • 1 Chr. 27:25

2 Then King David rose to his feet and said, "Hear me, my brethren and my people: [R]I *had* it in my heart to build a house of rest for the ark of the covenant of the LORD, and for [R]the footstool of our God, and had made preparations to build it. 2 Sam. 7:2 • Ps. 99:5

3 "But God said to me, [R]'You shall not build a house for My name, because you *have been* a man of war and have shed [R]blood.' 2 Sam. 7:5, 13 • [1 Chr. 17:4; 22:8]

27:8 *Shammah,* 2 Sam. 23:11, or *Shammoth,* 1 Chr. 11:27 **27:15** *Heleb,* 2 Sam. 23:29, or *Heled,* 1 Chr. 11:30

4 "However the LORD God of Israel chose
me above all the house of my father to be king
over Israel forever, for He has chosen Judah
to be the ruler. And of the house of Judah, the
house of my father, and among the sons of my
father, He was pleased with me to make *me*
king over all Israel.
5 "And of all my sons (for the LORD has
given me many sons) [R]He has chosen my son
Solomon to sit on the throne of the kingdom
of the LORD over Israel. 1 Chr. 22:9; 29:1
6 "Now He said to me, 'It is [R]your son Sol-
omon *who* shall build My house and My
courts; for I have chosen him *to be* My son,
and I will be his Father. 2 Sam. 7:13, 14
7 'Moreover [R]I will establish his kingdom
forever, [R]if he is steadfast to observe My com-
mandments and My judgments, as it is this
day.' Matt. 1:6☆ • 1 Chr. 22:13
8 "Now therefore, in the sight of all Israel,
the assembly of the LORD, and in the hearing
of our God, be careful to seek out all the com-
mandments of the LORD your God, that you
may possess this good land, and leave *it* as an
inheritance for your children after you for-
ever.

Charge to Solomon

9 "As for you, my son Solomon, know the
God of your father, and serve Him with a loyal
heart and with a willing mind; for the LORD
searches all hearts and understands all the in-
tent of the thoughts. If you seek Him, He will
be found by you; but if you forsake Him, He
will cast you off forever.
10 "Consider now, [R]for the LORD has chosen
you to build a house for the sanctuary; be
strong, and do it." 1 Chr. 22:13; 28:6

Pattern for the Temple

11 Then David gave his son Solomon the
plans for the vestibule, its houses, its treasur-
ies, its upper chambers, its inner chambers,
and the place of the mercy seat;
12 and the [R]plans for all that he had by the
Spirit, of the courts of the house of the LORD,
of all the chambers all around, of the treasur-
ies of the house of God, and of the treasuries
for the dedicated things; Heb. 8:5
13 also for the division of the priests and the
Levites, for all the work of the service of the
house of the LORD, and for all the articles of
service in the house of the LORD.
14 *He gave* gold by weight for *things* of gold,
for all articles used in every kind of service;
also *silver* for all articles of silver by weight,
for all articles used in every kind of service;
15 the weight for the [R]lampstands of gold,
and their lamps of gold, by weight for each
lampstand and its lamps; for the lampstands
of silver by weight, for the lampstand and its
lamps, according to the use of each lamp-
stand. Ex. 25:31–39
16 And by weight *he gave* gold for the tables
of the showbread, for each [R]table, and silver
for the tables of silver; 1 Kin. 7:48
17 also pure gold for the forks, the basins,
the pitchers of pure gold, and the golden
bowls—*he gave gold* by weight for every
bowl; and for the silver bowls, *silver* by
weight for every bowl;
18 and refined gold by weight for the [R]altar
of incense, and for the construction of the

28:4–6 Government of Israel—The government of Israel may be considered under two important headings: the laws, and the leaders.

The laws:

a. The "commandments," especially the Ten Commandments, revealed God's holiness and set up a divine standard of righteousness for the people to follow (Page 74—Ex. 20:1–17).
b. The judgments governed the social life of the people and concerned masters and servants (Page 75—Ex. 21:1–11), physical injuries (Page 75—Ex. 21:12–36), protection of property rights (Page 76—Ex. 22:1–15), and so on.
c. The ordinances included the sacrifices that showed that blood must be shed for sinners to be forgiven (Page 99—Lev. 1—17).

The leaders: At first Moses was the sole leader; then he was replaced by Joshua. After Joshua's death the nation was governed for many years by judges, who were usually raised up by God to oppose a specific enemy. Finally, at the people's request, God granted them a king, thus establishing the monarchy (Page 279—1 Sam. 8:5, 22). Under the monarchy there were four key leaders:

a. The *king* was the Lord's representative who ruled the people, but only as the Lord's servant. He led in war (Page 279—1 Sam. 8:20) and made judicial decisions (Page 319—2 Sam. 15:2); but he could not make law, since he himself was under the law (Page 192—Deut. 17:19). His relationship was so close to the Lord that he was adopted by the Lord (Page 312—2 Sam. 7:14; Page 546—Ps. 2:7).
b. The *priest* taught the Lord's laws and officiated at the offering of the sacrifices (Page 99—Lev. 1:5; Page 767—Jer. 18:18).
c. The *prophet* was the man of God who spoke for God and gave divine pronouncements for the present (forthtelling) or for the future (foretelling).
d. The *wise man* produced literary works stressing practical wisdom (Page 629—Prov. 1:1), taught discipline of character to the young (Page 649—Prov. 22:17), and gave counsel to the king (Page 321— 2 Sam. 16:20). The choice of these men indicates an important biblical principle: God uses people to reach other people, a principle that is also evident in the Great Commission given to Christians (Page 1011—Matt. 28:19, 20).

Now turn to Page 559—Ps. 29:2: Worship by Israel.

chariot, that is, the gold cherubim that spread
their wings and overshadowed the ark of the
covenant of the LORD. Ex. 30:1–10
19 "All *this," said David,* "the LORD made me
understand in writing, by *His* hand upon me,
all the [T]works of these plans." *details*
20 And David said to his son Solomon, [R]"Be
strong and of good courage, and do *it;* do not
fear nor be dismayed, for the LORD God—my
God—*will be* with you. [R]He will not leave you
nor forsake you, until you have finished all
the work for the service of the house of the
LORD. 1 Chr. 22:13 • Josh. 1:5
21 "*Here are* [R]the divisions of the priests and
the Levites for all the service of the house of
God; and [R]every willing craftsman *will be*
with you for all manner of workmanship, for
every kind of service; also the leaders and all
the people *will be* completely at your com-
mand." 1 Chr. 24—26 • Ex. 35:25–35

CHAPTER 29

Provisions of David for the Temple

FURTHERMORE King David said to all
the assembly: "My son Solomon, whom
alone God has [R]chosen, *is* [R]young and inex-
perienced; and the work *is* great, because
the temple* *is* not for man but for the LORD
God. 1 Chr. 28:5 • 1 Kin. 3:7
2 "Now for the house of my God I have pre-
pared with all my might: gold for *things to be
made of* gold, silver for *things of* silver, bronze
for *things of* bronze, iron for *things of* iron,
wood for *things of* wood, [R]onyx stones, *stones*
to be set, glistening stones of various colors,
all kinds of precious stones, and marble slabs
in abundance. Is. 54:11, 12
3 "Moreover, because I have set my affec-
tion on the house of my God, I have given to
the house of my God, over and above all that
I have prepared for the holy house, my own
special treasure of gold and silver:
4 "three thousand talents of gold, of the
gold of [R]Ophir, and seven thousand talents
of refined silver, to overlay the walls of the
houses; 1 Kin. 9:28
5 "the gold for *things of* gold and the silver
for *things of* silver, and for all kinds of work
to be done by the hands of craftsmen. Who
then is [R]willing to consecrate himself this day
to the LORD?" [2 Cor. 8:5, 12]

Provisions of Israel for the Temple

6 Then the leaders of the fathers' *houses,*
leaders of the tribes of Israel, the captains of
thousands and of hundreds, with the officers
over the king's work, offered willingly.
7 They gave for the work of the house of
God five thousand talents and ten thousand
darics of gold, ten thousand talents of silver,
eighteen thousand talents of bronze, and one
hundred thousand talents of iron.
8 And whoever had *precious* stones gave
them to the treasury of the house of the
LORD, into the hand of [R]Jehiel* the Gershon-
ite. 1 Chr. 23:8
9 Then the people rejoiced, for they had of-
fered willingly, because with a loyal heart
they had [R]offered willingly to the LORD; and
King David also rejoiced greatly. 2 Cor. 9:7

David's Final Prayer of Thanksgiving

10 Therefore David blessed the LORD before
all the assembly; and David said:

"Blessed are You, LORD God of Israel, our
    Father, forever and ever.
11 [R]Yours, O LORD, *is* the greatness,
The power and the glory, 1 Tim. 1:17
The victory and the majesty;
For all *that is* in heaven and in earth *is*
    Yours;
Yours *is* the kingdom, O LORD,
And You are exalted as head over all.
12 [R]Both riches and honor *come* from You,
And You reign over all. Rom. 11:36
In Your hand *is* power and might;
In Your hand *it is* to make great
And to give strength to all.

13 "Now therefore, our God,
We thank You
And praise Your glorious name.
14 But who *am* I, and who *are* my people,
That we should be able to offer so
    willingly as this?
For all things *come* from You,
And of Your own we have given You.
15 For [R]we *are* aliens and pilgrims before
    You, Heb. 11:13, 14
As *were* all our fathers;
[R]Our days on earth *are* as a shadow,
And without hope. Job 14:2

16 "O LORD our God, all this abundance that
we have prepared to build You a house for
Your holy name is from Your hand, and *is* all
Your own.
17 "I know also, my God, that You test the
heart and have pleasure in uprightness. As for
me, in the uprightness of my heart I have will-
ingly offered all these *things;* and now with
joy I have seen Your people, who are present
here to offer willingly to You.
18 "O LORD God of Abraham, Isaac, and Is-
rael, our fathers, keep this forever in the in-
tent of the thoughts of the heart of Your
people, and fix their heart toward You.
19 "And [R]give my son Solomon a loyal heart
to keep Your commandments and Your testi-
monies and Your statutes, to do all *these*

29:1 Lit. *palace* **29:8** Possibly the same as *Jehieli,*
1 Chr. 26:21, 22

things, and to build the temple* for which [R]I
have made provision." [1 Chr. 28:9] • 1 Chr. 29:1, 2

Coronation of Solomon—1 Kin. 1:38–40; 2:12

20 Then David said to all the assembly,
"Now bless the LORD your God." So all the assembly blessed the LORD God of their fathers,
and bowed their heads and prostrated themselves before the LORD and the king.
21 And they made sacrifices to the LORD
and offered burnt offerings to the LORD on
the next day: a thousand bulls, a thousand
rams, a thousand lambs, with their drink offerings, and [R]sacrifices in abundance for all
Israel. 1 Kin. 8:62, 63
22 So they ate and drank before the LORD
with great gladness on that day. And they
made Solomon the son of David king the second time, and anointed *him* before the LORD
to be the leader, and Zadok *to be* priest.
23 Then Solomon sat on the throne of the
LORD as king instead of David his father, and
prospered; and all Israel obeyed him.
24 All the leaders and the mighty men, and
also all the sons of King David, [R]submitted
themselves to King Solomon. Eccl. 8:2
25 So the LORD exalted Solomon exceedingly in the sight of all Israel, and [R]bestowed
on him *such* royal majesty as had not been on
any king before him in Israel. 1 Kin. 3:13

Death of King David

26 Thus David the son of Jesse reigned over
all Israel.
27 [R]And the period that he reigned over Israel *was* forty years; [R]seven years he reigned
in Hebron, and thirty-three *years* he reigned
in Jerusalem. 1 Kin. 2:11 • 2 Sam. 5:5
28 So he [R]died in a good old age, full of days
and riches and honor; and Solomon his son
reigned in his place. Gen. 25:8
29 Now the acts of King David, first and last,
indeed they *are* written in the book of Samuel
the seer, in the book of Nathan the prophet,
and in the book of Gad the seer,
30 with all his reign and his might, and the
events that happened to him, to Israel, and to
all the kingdoms of the lands.

29:19 Lit. *palace*

THE SECOND BOOK OF THE
CHRONICLES

THE BOOK OF 2 CHRONICLES

The Book of 2 Chronicles parallels 1 and 2 Kings but virtually ignores the northern kingdom of Israel because of its false worship and refusal to acknowledge the temple in Jerusalem. Chronicles focuses on those kings who pattern their lives and reigns after the life and reign of godly King David. It gives extended treatment to such zealous reformers as Asa, Jehoshaphat, Joash, Hezekiah, and Josiah.

The temple and temple worship, central throughout the book, befit a nation whose worship of God is central to its very survival. The book begins with Solomon's glorious temple and concludes with Cyrus's edict to rebuild the temple more than four hundred years later.

See "The Book of 1 Chronicles" for more detail on the title.

THE AUTHOR OF 2 CHRONICLES

For a discussion of the author of 1 and 2 Chronicles, see "The Author of 1 Chronicles." The sources of 1 and 2 Chronicles include official and prophetic records: (1) The Book of the Kings of Israel and Judah (or Judah and Israel) (1 Chr. 9:1; 2 Chr. 16:11; 20:34; 25:26; 27:7; 28:26; 32:32; 35:27; 36:8), (2) A Commentary on the Book of the Kings (2 Chr. 24:27), (3) Chronicles of Samuel the Seer (1 Chr. 29:29), (4) Chronicles of Nathan the Prophet (1 Chr. 29:29; 2 Chr. 9:29), (5) Chronicles of Gad the Seer (1 Chr. 29:29), (6) The Prophecy of Ahijah the Shilonite (2 Chr. 9:29), (7) The Visions of Iddo the Seer (2 Chr. 9:29; 12:15; 13:22), (8) Records of Shemaiah the Prophet (2 Chr. 12:15), (9) Records of Iddo the Prophet on Genealogies (2 Chr. 12:15), (10) Treatise of the Prophet Iddo (2 Chr. 13:22), (11) The Annals of Jehu the Son of Hanani (2 Chr. 20:34), (12) The Acts of Uzziah by Isaiah the Prophet (2 Chr. 26:22), (13) The Vision of Isaiah the Prophet (2 Chr. 32:32), (14) The Records of the Hozai (2 Chr. 33:19), (15) The Account of the Chronicles of King David (1 Chr. 27:24), (16) The Writing of David and His Son Solomon (2 Chr. 35:4). In addition to these, the author-compiler had access to genealogical lists and documents, such as the message and letters of Sennacherib (2 Chr. 32:10–17).

THE TIME OF 2 CHRONICLES

See "The Time of 1 Chronicles" for the background of 1 and 2 Chronicles. Chapters 1—9 cover the forty years from 971 B.C. to 931 B.C., and chapters 10—36 cover the 393 years from 931 B.C. to 538 B.C. Jeremiah's prediction of a seventy-year captivity in Babylon (36:21; Jer. 29:10) is fulfilled in two ways: (1) a political captivity in which Jerusalem is overcome from 605 B.C. to 536 B.C., and (2) a religious captivity involving the destruction of the temple in 586 B.C. and the completion of the new temple in 516 or 515 B.C.

THE CHRIST OF 2 CHRONICLES

The throne of David has been destroyed, but the line of David remains. Murders, treachery, battles, and captivity all threaten the messianic line; but it remains clear and unbroken from Adam to Zerubbabel. The fulfillment in Christ can be seen in the genealogies of Matthew 1 and Luke 3.

The temple also prefigures Christ. Jesus says, "in this place there is *One* greater than the temple" (Matt. 12:6). He also likens His body to the temple: "Destroy this temple, and in three days I will raise it up" (John 2:19). In Revelation 21:22 He replaces the temple: "But I saw no temple in it, for the Lord God Almighty and the Lamb are its temple."

KEYS TO 2 CHRONICLES

Key Word: Priestly View of Judah—The Book of 2 Chronicles provides topical histories of the end of the united kingdom (Solomon) and the kingdom of Judah. More than historical annals, Chronicles is a divine editorial on the spiritual characteristics of the Davidic dynasty. This is why it focuses on the southern rather than the northern kingdom. Most of the kings fail to realize that apart from the true mission as a covenant nation called to bring others to Yahweh, Judah has no calling, no destiny, and no hope of becoming great on her own. Only what is done in accordance with God's will has any lasting value. Chronicles concentrates on the kings who are concerned with maintaining the proper service of God and the times of spiritual reform. However, growing apostasy inevitably leads to judgment.

The temple in Jerusalem is the major unifying theme of 1 and 2 Chronicles. Much of the material found in 2 Samuel to 2 Kings is omitted from Chronicles because it does not develop this theme. In 1 Chronicles 11—29, the central message is David's preparation for the construction and service of the temple. Most of 2 Chronicles 1—9 is devoted to the building and consecration of the temple. Chapters 10—36 omit the kings of Israel in the north because they have no ties with the temple. Prominence is given to the reigns of Judah's temple restorers (Asa, Jehoshaphat, Joash, Hezekiah, and Josiah). The temple symbolizes God's presence among His people and reminds them of their high calling. It provides the spiritual link between their past and future. Thus, Ezra wrote this book to encourage the people to accept the new temple raised on the site of the old and to remind them of their true calling and God's faithfulness despite their low circumstances. The Davidic line, temple, and priesthood are still theirs.

Key Verses: 2 Chronicles 7:14; 16:9—"If My people who are called by My name will humble themselves, and pray and seek My face, and turn from their wicked ways, then I will hear from heaven, and will forgive their sin and heal their land" (7:14).

"For the eyes of the LORD run to and fro throughout the whole earth, to show Himself strong on behalf of *those* whose heart *is* loyal to Him. In this you have done foolishly; therefore from now on you shall have wars" (16:9).

Key Chapter: 2 Chronicles 34—Second Chronicles records the reforms and revivals under such kings as Asa, Jehoshaphat, Joash, Hezekiah, and Josiah. Chapter 34 traces the dramatic revival that takes place under Josiah when the "Book of the Law" is found, read, and obeyed.

SURVEY OF 2 CHRONICLES

This book repeatedly teaches that whenever God's people forsake Him, He withdraws His blessings, but trust in and obedience to the Lord bring victory. Since everything in Chronicles is related to the temple, it is not surprising that this concludes with Cyrus's edict to rebuild it. Solomon's glory is seen in chapters 1—9, and Judah's decline and deportation in chapters 10—36.

Solomon's Reign (1—9): The reign of Solomon brings in Israel's golden age of peace, prosperity, and temple worship. The kingdom is united and its boundaries extend to their greatest point. Solomon's wealth, wisdom, palace, and temple become legendary. His mighty spiritual, political, and architectural feats raise Israel to her zenith. However, it is in keeping with the purpose of Chronicles that six of these nine chapters concern the construction and dedication of the temple.

The Reign of Judah's Kings (10—36): Unfortunately, Israel's glory is short-lived. Soon after Solomon's death the nation is divided, and both kingdoms begin a downward spiral that can only be delayed by the religious reforms. The nation generally forsakes the temple and the worship of Yahweh, and is soon torn by warfare and unrest. The reformation efforts on the part of some of Judah's kings are valiant, but never last beyond one generation. Nevertheless, about seventy percent of chapters 10—36 deals with the eight good kings, leaving only thirty percent to cover the twelve evil rulers. Each king is seen with respect to his relationship to the temple as the center of worship and spiritual strength. When the king serves Yahweh, Judah is blessed with political and economic prosperity.

Here is a brief survey of Judah's twenty rulers: (1) *Rehoboam*—Although he is not righteous, he humbles himself before God and averts His wrath (12:12). (2) *Abijah*—He enjoys a short and evil reign, but he conquers Israel because "the children of Judah . . . . relied on the LORD God" (13:18). (3) *Asa*—Although he destroys foreign altars and idols, conquers Ethiopia against great odds through his trust in God, and restores the altar of the Lord, yet he fails to trust God when threatened by Israel. (4) *Jehoshaphat*—He brings in a great revival; "his heart took delight in the ways of the LORD" (17:6). Jehoshaphat overthrows idols, teaches God's Word

FOCUS	REIGN OF SOLOMON			REIGNS OF THE KINGS OF JUDAH		
REFERENCE	1:1——2:1	——8:1	——	10:1——14:1	——	36:1—36:23
DIVISION	INAUGURATION OF SOLOMON	COMPLETION OF THE TEMPLE	THE GLORY OF SOLOMON'S REIGN	THE DIVISION OF THE KINGDOM	THE REFORMS UNDER ASA, JEHOSHAPHAT, JOASH, HEZEKIAH, AND JOSIAH	THE FALL OF JUDAH
TOPIC	THE TEMPLE IS CONSTRUCTED			THE TEMPLE IS DESTROYED		
	SPLENDOR			DISASTER		
LOCATION	JUDAH					
TIME	c. 40 YEARS			c. 393 YEARS		

to the people, and trusts in God before battle. (5) *Jehoram*—A wicked king, he follows the ways of Ahab and marries his daughter. He leads Judah into idolatry and when he dies in pain, departs "to no one's sorrow" (21:20). (6 and 7) *Ahaziah* and *Athaliah*—Ahaziah is as wicked as his father, as is his mother Athaliah. Both are murdered. (8) *Joash*—Although he repairs the temple and restores the worship of God, when Jehoiada the priest dies, Joash allows the people to abandon the temple and return to idolatry. (9) *Amaziah*—Mixed in his relationship to God, he later forsakes the Lord for the gods of Edom. He is defeated by Israel and later murdered. (10) *Uzziah*—He begins well with the Lord and is blessed with military victories. However, when he becomes strong, he proudly and presumptuously plays the role of a priest by offering incense in the temple and therefore is struck with leprosy. (11) *Jotham*—Because he rebuilds the gate of the temple and reveres God, the Lord blesses him with prosperity and victory. (12) *Ahaz*—A wicked king and an idolater, he is oppressed by his enemies and forced to give tribute to the Assyrians from the temple treasures. (13) *Hezekiah*—He repairs and reopens the temple and puts away the altars and idols set up by his father, Ahaz. Judah is spared destruction by Assyria because of his righteousness. His reforms are given only a few verses in Kings but three chapters in Chronicles. (14 and 15) *Manasseh* and *Amon*—Manasseh is Judah's most wicked king. He sets up idols and altars all over the land. However, he repents when he is carried away by Assyria. God brings him back to Judah and he makes a halfway reform, but it comes too late. Amon follows in his father's wickedness. Both kings are murdered. (16) *Josiah*—A leader in reforms and spiritual revival, he centers worship around the temple, finds the law and obeys it, and reinstitutes the Passover. (17, 18, and 19) *Jehoahaz, Jehoiakim, Jehoiachin*—Their relentless evil finally brings the downfall of Judah. The temple is ravaged in each of their reigns. (20) *Zedekiah*—Judah's last king is also wicked. Jerusalem and the temple are destroyed, and the captivity begins. Second Chronicles nevertheless ends on a note of hope at the end of the captivity, when Cyrus issues the decree for the restoration of Judah: "Who *is* among you of all His people? May the LORD his God *be* with him, and let him go up!" (36:23).

OUTLINE OF 2 CHRONICLES

Part One: The Reign of Solomon (1:1—9:31)

I. The Inauguration of Solomon as King 1:1–17

A. The Worship of Solomon 1:1–6
B. The Petition for Wisdom 1:7–10
C. The Provision of Wisdom 1:11, 12
D. The Wealth of Solomon 1:13–17

II. The Completion of the Temple ..... 2:1—7:22

A. Preparation to Build the Temple 2:1–18
  1. Selection of the Temple Builders ... 2:1, 2
  2. Selection of the Temple Materials 2:3–18
B. Construction of the Temple .... 3:1—5:1
C. Dedication of the Temple .... 5:2—7:22
  1. The Installation of the Ark 5:2–12
  2. The Glory of the Lord Fills the Temple 5:13, 14
  3. The Sermon of Solomon 6:1–11
  4. The Prayer of Solomon 6:12–42
  5. The Fire of the Lord Consumes the Sacrifices 7:1–3
  6. The Nation Offers Sacrifices 7:4–7
  7. The Nation Celebrates the Feasts of Tabernacles 7:8–11
  8. The Lord Confirms the Covenant 7:12–22

III. The Glory of the Reign of Solomon 8:1—9:28

A. Enlargement of Solomon's Territory ... 8:1–6
B. Subjugation of the Enemies of Solomon 8:7–10
C. Religious Practices of Solomon 8:11–16
D. Economic Operations of Solomon 8:17, 18
E. The Queen of Sheba Visits 9:1–12
F. Solomon's Wealth 9:13–28

IV. The Death of Solomon 9:29–31

Part Two: The Reigns of the Kings of Judah (10:1—36:23)

I. The Reign of Rehoboam .... 10:1—12:16

A. Division of the Kingdom 10:1–19
B. Kingdom of Judah Is Strengthened 11:1–23
C. Kingdom of Judah Is Weakened 12:1–12
D. Death of Rehoboam 12:13–16

II. The Reign of Abijah 13:1–22

A. War of Abijah and Jeroboam 13:1–20
B. Death of Abijah 13:21, 22

III. The Reign of Asa .... 14:1—16:14

A. Evaluation of Asa 14:1–8
B. Victory over the Ethiopians 14:9–15
C. Exhortation of Azariah 15:1–7
D. Reforms of Asa 15:8–19
E. Victory over the Syrians 16:1–6

CHAPTER 1

The Worship of Solomon—1 Kin. 3:4

NOW [R]Solomon the son of David was
strengthened in his kingdom, and [R]the
LORD his God *was* with him and [R]exalted him
exceedingly. 1 Kin. 2:46 • Gen. 39:2 • 1 Chr. 29:25
2 And Solomon spoke to all Israel, to the
captains of thousands and of hundreds, to the
judges, and to every leader in all Israel, the
heads of the fathers' *houses*.
3 Then Solomon, and all the assembly
with him, went to [T]the high place that *was*
at [R]Gibeon; for the tabernacle of meeting
with God was there, which Moses the servant of the LORD had made in the wilderness. Place for worship • 1 Kin. 3:4
4 [R]But David had brought up the ark of God
from Kirjath Jearim to *the place* David had
prepared for it, for he had pitched a tent for it
at Jerusalem. 2 Sam. 6:2–17
5 Now the bronze altar that Bezalel the
son of Uri, the son of Hur, had made, he put*

1:5 Some authorities *it was there*

before the tabernacle of the LORD; Solomon
and the assembly sought Him *there.*
6 And Solomon went up there to the bronze
altar before the LORD, which *was* at the taber-
nacle of meeting, and [R]offered a thousand
burnt offerings on it. 1 Kin. 3:4

The Petition for Wisdom—1 Kin. 3:5–9

7 [R]On that night God appeared to Sol-
omon, and said to him, "Ask! What shall I
give you?" 1 Kin. 3:5–14; 9:2
8 And Solomon said to God: "You have
shown great [R]mercy to David my father, and
have made me king in his place. Ps. 18:50
9 "Now, O LORD God, let Your promise to
David my father be established, for You have
made me king over a people like the [R]dust of
the earth in multitude. Gen. 13:16
10 [R]"Now give me wisdom and knowledge,
that I may [R]go out and come in before this
people; for who can judge this great people of
Yours?" 1 Kin. 3:9 • Deut. 31:2

The Provision of Wisdom—1 Kin. 3:10–14

11 [R]Then God said to Solomon: "Because
this was in your heart, and you have not asked
riches or wealth or honor or the life of your
enemies, nor have you asked long life—but
have asked wisdom and knowledge for your-
self, that you may judge My people over
whom I have made you king— 1 Kin. 3:11–13
12 "wisdom and knowledge *are* granted to
you; and I will give you riches and wealth and
honor, such as [R]none of the kings have had
who *were* before you, nor shall any after you
have the like." 2 Chr. 9:22

The Wealth of Solomon
1 Kin. 10:26–29; 2 Chr. 9:25–28

13 So Solomon came to Jerusalem from [T]the
high place that *was* at Gibeon, from before
the tabernacle of meeting, and reigned over
Israel. Place for worship
14 And Solomon gathered chariots and
horsemen; he had one thousand four hundred
chariots and twelve thousand horsemen,
whom he stationed in the chariot cities and
with the king in Jerusalem.
15 [R]Also the king made silver and gold as
common in Jerusalem as stones, and he made
cedars as abundant as the sycamores which
are in the lowland. 2 Chr. 9:27
16 And Solomon had horses imported from
Egypt and Keveh; the king's merchants
bought them in Keveh at the *current* price.
17 They also acquired and imported from
Egypt a chariot for six hundred *shekels* of sil-
ver, and a horse for one hundred and fifty;
thus, through their agents,* they exported
them to all the kings of the Hittites and the
kings of Syria.

CHAPTER 2

Selection of the Temple Builders
1 Kin. 5:15, 16

THEN Solomon [R]determined to build a tem-
ple for the name of the LORD, and a royal
house for himself. 1 Kin. 5:5
2 Solomon selected seventy thousand men
to bear burdens, eighty thousand to quarry
stone in the mountains, and three thousand
six hundred to oversee them.

Selection of the Temple Materials

3 Then Solomon sent to Hiram* king of
Tyre, saying:

As you have dealt with David my father,
and sent him cedars to build himself a
house to dwell in, *so deal with me.*
4 Behold, [R]I am building a temple for the
name of the LORD my God, to dedicate *it*
to Him, [R]to burn before Him sweet
incense, for the continual showbread, for
the burnt offerings morning and
evening, on the Sabbaths, on the New
Moons, and on the set feasts of the LORD
our God. This *is an ordinance* forever to
Israel. 2 Chr. 2:1 • Ex. 30:7
5 And the temple which I build *will be*
great, for [R]our God is greater than all
gods. Ps. 135:5
6 [R]But who is able to build Him a temple,
since heaven and the heaven of heavens
cannot contain Him? Who *am* I then, that
I should build Him a temple, except to
burn sacrifice before Him? 1 Kin. 8:27
7 Therefore send me at once a man skillful
to work in gold and silver, in bronze and
iron, in purple and crimson and blue,
who has skill to engrave with the skillful
men who are with me in Judah and
Jerusalem, [R]whom David my father
provided. 1 Chr. 22:15
8 Also send me cedar and cypress and
algum logs from Lebanon, for I know
that your servants have skill to cut
timber in Lebanon; and indeed my
servants *will be* with your servants,
9 to prepare timber for me in abundance,
for the temple which I am about to build
shall be great and wonderful.
10 [R]And indeed I will give to your servants,
the woodsmen who cut timber, twenty
thousand kors of ground wheat, twenty
thousand kors of barley, twenty
thousand baths of wine, and twenty
thousand baths of oil. 1 Kin. 5:11

11 Then Hiram king of Tyre answered in
writing, which he sent to Solomon:

1:17 Lit. *by their hands* **2:3** Heb. *Huram;* cf. 1 Kin.
5:1

[R]Because the LORD loves His people, He
has made you king over them. 2 Chr. 9:8
12 Hiram* also said:

Blessed *be* the LORD God of Israel, [R]who
made heaven and earth, for He has given
King David a wise son, endowed with
prudence and understanding, who will
build a temple for the LORD and a royal
house for himself! Rev. 10:6
13 And now I have sent a skillful man,
endowed with understanding, Huram*
my master* *craftsman*
14 [R](the son of a woman of the daughters
of Dan, and his father was a man of
Tyre), skilled to work in gold and silver,
bronze and iron, stone and wood, purple
and blue, fine linen and crimson, and to
make any engraving and to accomplish
any plan which may be given to him,
with your skillful men and with the
skillful men of my lord David your
father. 1 Kin. 7:13, 14
15 Now therefore, the wheat, the barley, the
oil, and the wine which my lord has
spoken of, let him send to his servants.
16 [R]And we will cut wood from Lebanon, as
much as you need; we will bring it to you
in rafts by sea to Joppa, and you will
carry it up to Jerusalem. 1 Kin. 5:8, 9

17 [R]Then Solomon numbered all the aliens
who *were* in the land of Israel, after the cen-
sus in which [R]David his father had num-
bered them; and there were found to be one
hundred and fifty-three thousand six hun-
dred. 1 Kin. 5:13; 2 Chr. 8:7, 8 • 1 Chr. 22:2
18 And he made [R]seventy thousand of them
bearers of burdens, eighty thousand stone-
cutters in the mountain, and three thousand
six hundred overseers to make the people
work. 2 Chr. 2:2

CHAPTER 3

Construction of the Temple—1 Kin. 6:1—7:51

NOW [R]Solomon began to build the house
of the LORD at [R]Jerusalem on Mount Mo-
riah, where *the LORD** had appeared to his fa-
ther David, at the place that David had
prepared on the threshing floor of Ornan* the
Jebusite. 1 Kin. 6:1 • Gen. 22:2–14
2 And he began to build on the second *day*
of the second month in the fourth year of his
reign.
3 This is the foundation [R]which Solomon
laid for building the house of God: The length
was sixty cubits (by cubits according to the
former measure) and the width twenty cu-
bits. 1 Kin. 6:2
4 And the vestibule that *was* in front *of the*
*sanctuary** was twenty cubits long across the
width of the house, and the height *was* one
hundred and* twenty. He overlaid the inside
with pure gold.
5 The larger room* he paneled with cypress
which he overlaid with fine gold, and he
carved palm trees and chainwork on it.
6 And he decorated the house with pre-
cious stones for beauty, and the gold *was* gold
from Parvaim.
7 He also overlaid the house—the beams
and doorposts, its walls and doors—with gold;
and he carved cherubim on the walls.
8 And he made the [R]Most Holy Place. Its
length was according to the width of the
house, twenty cubits, and its width twenty cu-
bits. He overlaid it with six hundred talents of
fine gold. Ex. 26:33
9 The weight of the nails *was* fifty shekels
of gold; and he overlaid the upper [R]area with
gold. 1 Chr. 28:11
10 [R]In the Most Holy Place he made two
cherubim, fashioned by carving, and overlaid
them with gold. 1 Kin. 6:23–28
11 The wings of the cherubim *were* twenty
cubits in *overall* length: one wing *of the one*
cherub was five cubits, touching the wall of
the room, and the other wing *was* five cubits,
touching the wing of the other cherub;
12 *one* wing of the other cherub *was* five cu-
bits, touching the wall of the room, and the
other wing *also was* five cubits, touching the
wing of the other cherub.
13 The wings of these cherubim spanned
twenty cubits overall. They stood on their feet,
and they faced inward.
14 And he made the [R]veil of blue, purple,
crimson, and fine linen, and wove cherubim
into it. Ex. 26:31
15 Also he made in front of the temple* [R]two
pillars thirty-five* cubits [T]high, and the capi-
tal that *was* on the top of each of *them* was
five cubits. 1 Kin. 7:15–20 • Lit. *long*
16 He made wreaths of chainwork, as in the
inner sanctuary, and put *them* on top of the
pillars; and he made [R]one hundred pomegran-
ates, and put *them* on the wreaths of chain-
work. 1 Kin. 7:20
17 Then he [R]set up the pillars before the tem-
ple, one on the right hand and the other on the
left; he called the name of the one on the right
hand Jachin, and the name of the one on the
left Boaz. 1 Kin. 7:21

2:12 Heb. *Huram;* cf. 1 Kin. 5:1 **2:13** *Hiram,* 1 Kin. 7:13 • Lit. *father,* 1 Kin. 7:13, 14 **3:1** Lit. *He,* following MT, Vg.; LXX *the LORD;* Tg. *the Angel of the LORD* • *Araunah,* 2 Sam. 24:16 **3:4** The holy place, the main room of the temple, 1 Kin. 6:3 • So with MT, LXX, Vg.; Arab., some LXX mss., Syr. *twenty* **3:5** Lit. *house* **3:15** Lit. *house* • *eighteen,* 1 Kin. 7:15; 2 Kin. 25:17; Jer. 52:21

CHAPTER 4

MOREOVER he made a bronze altar: twenty cubits was its length, twenty cubits its width, and ten cubits its height.

2 [R]Then he made the [T]Sea of cast *bronze,* ten cubits from one brim to the other; *it was* completely round. Its height *was* five cubits, and a line of thirty cubits measured its circumference. 1 Kin. 7:23–26 • Great laver or basin

3 [R]And under it *was* the likeness of oxen encircling it all around, ten to a cubit, all the way around the Sea. The oxen *were* cast in two rows, when it was cast. 1 Kin. 7:24–26

4 It stood on twelve [R]oxen: three looking toward the north, three looking toward the west, three looking toward the south, and three looking toward the east; the Sea *was set* upon them, and all their back parts *pointed* inward. 1 Kin. 7:25

5 It *was* a handbreadth thick; and its brim was shaped like the brim of a cup, *like* a lily blossom. It contained three thousand *baths.

6 He also made ten lavers, and put five on the right side and five on the left, to wash in them; such things as they offered for the burnt offering they would wash in them, but the Sea *was* for the priests to wash in.

7 [R]And he made ten lampstands of gold [R]according to their design, and set *them* in the temple, five on the right side and five on the left. 1 Kin. 7:49 • Ex. 25:31

8 [R]He also made ten tables, and placed *them* in the temple, five on the right side and five on the left. And he made one hundred [R]bowls of gold. 1 Kin. 7:48 • 1 Chr. 28:17

9 Furthermore [R]he made the court of the priests, and the [R]great court and doors for the court; and he overlaid these doors with bronze. 1 Kin. 6:36 • 2 Kin. 21:5

10 [R]He set the Sea on the right side, toward the southeast. 1 Kin. 7:39

11 Then Huram made the pots and the shovels and the bowls. So Huram finished doing the work that he was to do for King Solomon for the house of God:

12 the two pillars and [R]the bowl-shaped capitals *that were* on top of the two pillars; the two networks covering the two bowl-shaped capitals which *were* on top of the pillars; 1 Kin. 7:41

13 four hundred pomegranates for the two networks (two rows of pomegranates for each network, to cover the two bowl-shaped capitals that *were* on the pillars);

14 he also made [R]carts and the lavers on the carts; 1 Kin. 7:27, 43

15 one Sea and twelve oxen under it;

16 also the pots, the shovels, the forks—and all their articles Huram his master* *craftsman* made of burnished bronze for King Solomon for the house of the LORD.

17 In the plain of Jordan the king had them cast in clay molds, between Succoth and Zeredah.*

18 And Solomon had all these articles made in such great abundance that the weight of the bronze was not determined.

19 Thus [R]Solomon had all the furnishings made for the house of God: the altar of gold and the tables on which *was* [R]the showbread; 1 Kin. 7:48–50 • Ex. 25:30

20 the lampstands with their lamps of pure gold, to burn [R]in the prescribed manner in front of the inner sanctuary, Ex. 27:20, 21

21 with the flowers and the lamps and the wick-trimmers of gold, of purest gold;

22 the trimmers, the bowls, the ladles, and the censers of pure gold. As for the entry of the [T]sanctuary, its inner doors to the Most Holy *Place,* and the doors of the main hall of the temple, *were* gold. Lit. *house*

CHAPTER 5

SO [R]all the work that Solomon had done for the house of the LORD was finished; and Solomon brought in the things which his father David had dedicated: the silver and the gold and all the furnishings. And he put *them* in the treasuries of the house of God. 1 Kin. 7:51

The Installation of the Ark—1 Kin. 8:1–9

2 [R]Now Solomon assembled the elders of Israel and all the heads of the tribes, the chief fathers of the children of Israel, in Jerusalem, that they might bring the ark of the covenant of the LORD up [R]from the City of David, which *is* Zion. 1 Kin. 8:1–9 • 2 Sam. 6:12

3 [R]Therefore all the men of Israel assembled with the king [R]at the feast, which *was* in the seventh month. 1 Kin. 8:2 • 2 Chr. 7:8–10

4 So all the elders of Israel came, and the [R]Levites took up the ark. 1 Chr. 15:2, 15

5 Then they brought up the ark, the tabernacle of meeting, and all the holy furnishings that *were* in the tabernacle. The priests and the Levites brought them up.

6 Also King Solomon, and all the congregation of Israel who were assembled with him before the ark, were sacrificing sheep and oxen that could not be counted or numbered for multitude.

7 Then the priests brought in the ark of the covenant of the LORD to its place, into the [R]inner sanctuary of the temple,* to the Most Holy *Place,* under the wings of the cherubim. 2 Chr. 4:20

8 For the cherubim spread *their* wings over the place of the ark, and the cherubim overshadowed the ark and its poles.

9 The poles extended so that the ends of the [R]poles of the ark could be seen from *the holy*

4:5 About 8,000 gallons; *two thousand,* 1 Kin. 7:26
4:16 Lit. *father* **4:17** *Zaretan,* 1 Kin. 7:46 **5:7** Lit. *house*

place, in front of the inner sanctuary; but they
could not be seen from outside. And they are
there to this day. Ex. 25:13–15
10 Nothing was in the ark except the two
tablets which Moses [R]put *there* at Horeb,
[T]when the LORD made *a covenant* with the
children of Israel, when they had come out of
Egypt. Deut. 10:2, 5 • Or *where*
11 And it came to pass when the priests
came out of the *Most* Holy *Place* (for all the
priests who *were* present had [T]sanctified
themselves, without keeping to their [R]divi-
sions), *consecrated* • 1 Chr. 24:1–5
12 [R]and the Levites *who were* the singers,
all those of Asaph and Heman and Je-
duthun, with their sons and their brethren,
stood at the east end of the altar, clothed in
white linen, having cymbals, stringed instru-
ments and harps, [R]and with them one hun-
dred and twenty priests sounding with
trumpets— 1 Chr. 25:1–7 • 1 Chr. 13:8; 15:16, 24

The Glory of the Lord Fills the Temple *1 Kin. 8:10, 11*

13 indeed it came to pass, when the trum-
peters and singers *were* as one, to make one
sound to be heard in praising and thanking
the LORD, and when they lifted up their voice
with the trumpets and cymbals and instru-
ments of music, and praised the LORD, *saying:*

[R]"*For He is* good,
For His mercy *endures* forever,"*

that the house, the house of the LORD, was
filled with a cloud, 1 Chr. 16:34, 41; Ps. 100:5
14 so that the priests could not continue min-
istering because of the cloud; for the glory of
the LORD filled the house of God.

CHAPTER 6

The Sermon of Solomon—1 Kin. 8:12–21

THEN [R]Solomon spoke:

"The LORD said He would dwell in the
[R]dark cloud. 1 Kin. 8:12–21 • [Lev. 16:2]
2 I have surely built You an exalted house,
And a place for You to dwell in forever."

3 Then the king turned around and blessed
the whole assembly of Israel, while all the as-
sembly of Israel was standing.
4 And he said: "Blessed *be* the LORD God of
Israel, who has fulfilled with His hands *what*
He spoke with His mouth to my father David,
[R]saying, 1 Chr. 17:5
5 'Since the day that I brought My people out
of the land of Egypt, I have chosen no city from
any tribe of Israel *in which* to build a house,
that My name might be there, nor did I choose
any man to be a ruler over My people Israel.
6 [R]'Yet I have chosen Jerusalem, that My
name may be there, and I have chosen David
to be over My people Israel.' Deut. 12:5–7
7 "Now [R]it was in the heart of my father Da-
vid to build a temple* for the name of the
LORD God of Israel. 2 Sam. 7:2
8 "But the LORD said to my father David,
'Whereas it was in your heart to build a tem-
ple for My name, you did well in that it was in
your heart.
9 'Nevertheless you shall not build the tem-
ple, but your son who will come from your
body, he shall build the temple for My
[R]name.' 1 Chr. 28:3–6
10 "So the LORD has fulfilled His word which
He spoke, and I have filled the position of my
father David, and [R]sit on the throne of Israel,
as the LORD promised; and I have built the
temple for the name of the LORD God of Is-
rael. 1 Kin. 2:12; 10:9
11 "And there I have put the ark, [R]in which *is*
the covenant of the LORD which He made with
the children of Israel." 2 Chr. 5:7–10

The Prayer of Solomon—1 Kin. 8:22–53

12 Then *Solomon** stood before the altar of
the LORD in the presence of all the assembly
of Israel, and spread out his hands
13 (for Solomon had made a bronze plat-
form five cubits long, five cubits wide, and
three cubits high, and had set it in the midst of
the court; and he stood on it, knelt down on
his knees before all the assembly of Israel,
and spread out his hands toward heaven);
14 and he said: "LORD God of Israel, [R]*there is*
no God in heaven or on earth like You, who
keep *Your* [R]covenant and mercy with Your ser-
vants who walk before You with all their
hearts. [Ex. 15:11] • [Deut. 7:9]
15 [R]"You have kept what You promised Your
servant David my father; You have both spo-
ken with Your mouth and fulfilled *it* with Your
hand, as *it is* this day. 1 Chr. 22:9, 10
16 "Therefore, LORD God of Israel, now keep
what You promised Your servant David my fa-
ther, saying, [R]'You shall not fail to have a
man sit before Me on the throne of Israel,
[R]only if your sons take heed to their way, that
they walk in My law as you have walked be-
fore Me.' 2 Chr. 7:18 • Ps. 132:12
17 "And now, O LORD God of Israel, let Your
word come true, which You have spoken to
Your servant David.
18 "But will God indeed dwell with men on
the earth? Behold, heaven and the heaven of
heavens cannot contain You. How much less
this temple* which I have built!
19 "Yet regard the prayer of Your servant and
his supplication, O LORD my God, and listen to
the cry and the prayer which Your servant is
praying before You:

5:13 Cf. Ps. 106:1 **6:7** Lit. *house,* and so in vv. 8–10
6:12 Lit. *he* **6:18** Lit. *house*

20 "that Your eyes may be open toward this
temple day and night, toward the place where
You said *You would* put Your name, that You
may hear the prayer which Your servant
makes toward this place.
21 "And may You hear the supplications of
Your servant and of Your people Israel, when
they pray toward this place. Hear from
heaven Your dwelling place, and when You
hear, [R]forgive. [Mic. 7:18]
22 "If anyone sins against his neighbor, and
is forced to take an [R]oath, and comes *and*
takes an oath before Your altar in this tem-
ple, Ex. 22:8–11
23 "then hear from heaven, and act, and
judge Your servants, bringing retribution on
the wicked by bringing his way on his own
head, and justifying the righteous by giving
him according to his righteousness.
24 "Or if Your people Israel are defeated be-
fore an [R]enemy because they have sinned
against You, and return and confess Your
name, and pray and make supplication before
You in this temple, 2 Kin. 21:14, 15
25 "then hear from heaven and forgive the
sin of Your people Israel, and bring them back
to the land which You gave to them and their
fathers.
26 "When the heavens are shut up and there
is no rain because they have sinned against
You, when they pray toward this place and
confess Your name, and turn from their sin be-
cause You afflict them,
27 "then hear *in* heaven, and forgive the sin
of Your servants, Your people Israel, that You
may teach them the good way in which they
should walk; and send rain on Your land
which You have given to Your people as an in-
heritance.
28 "When there is famine in the land, pesti-
lence or blight or mildew, locusts or grasshop-
pers; when their enemies besiege them in the
land of their cities; whatever plague or what-
ever sickness *there is;*
29 "whatever prayer, whatever supplication
is *made* by anyone, or by all Your people Is-
rael, when each one knows his own burden
and his own grief, and spreads out his hands
to this temple:
30 "then hear from heaven Your dwelling
place, and forgive, and give to everyone ac-
cording to all his ways, whose heart You know
(for You alone [R]know the [R]hearts of the sons of
men), [1 Chr. 28:9] • [1 Sam. 16:7]
31 "that they may fear You, to walk in Your
ways as long as they live in the land which
You gave to our fathers.
32 "Moreover, concerning a foreigner, [R]who
is not of Your people Israel, but has come
from a far country for the sake of Your great
name and Your mighty hand and Your out-
stretched arm, when they come and pray in
this temple; John 12:20
33 "then hear from heaven Your dwelling
place, and do according to all for which the
foreigner calls to You, that all peoples of the
earth may know Your name and fear You, as
do Your people Israel, and that they may know
that this temple which I have built is called by
Your name.
34 "When Your people go out to battle
against their enemies, wherever You send
them, and when they pray to You toward this
city which You have chosen and the temple
which I have built for Your name,
35 "then hear from heaven their prayer and
their supplication, and maintain their cause.
36 "When they sin against You (for *there is*
[R]no one who does not sin), and You become
angry with them and deliver them to the
enemy, and they take them [R]captive to a land
far or near; [Rom. 3:9, 19; 5:12] • Deut. 28:63–68
37 "*yet* when they [T]come to themselves in
the land where they were carried captive, and
repent, and make supplication to You in the
land of their captivity, saying, 'We have
sinned, we have done wrong, and have com-
mitted wickedness'; Lit. *bring back to their hearts*
38 "and *when* they return to You with all
their heart and with all their soul in the land
of their captivity, where they have been car-
ried captive, and pray toward their land which
You gave to their fathers, the city which You
have chosen, and toward the temple which I
have built for Your name:
39 "then hear from heaven Your dwelling
place their prayer and their supplications, and
maintain their cause, and forgive Your people
who have sinned against You.
40 "Now, my God, I pray, let Your eyes be
[R]open and *let* Your ears *be* attentive to the
prayer *made* in this place. 2 Chr. 6:20

41 "Now[R] therefore, Ps. 132:8–10, 16
Arise, O LORD God, to Your [R]resting
place, 1 Chr. 28:2
You and the ark of Your strength.
Let Your priests, O LORD God, be clothed
with salvation,
And let Your saints rejoice in goodness.
42 "O LORD God, do not turn away the face
of Your Anointed;
[R]Remember the mercies of Your servant
David."* Ps. 89:49; 132:1, 8–10

CHAPTER 7

The Fire of the Lord Consumes the Sacrifices

WHEN Solomon had finished praying,
fire came down from heaven and con-
sumed the burnt offering and the sacrifices;
and the glory of the LORD filled the temple.*
2 And the priests could not enter the house

6:42 Cf. Ps. 132:8–10 **7:1** Lit. *house*

of the LORD, because the glory of the LORD
had filled the LORD's house.

3 When all the children of Israel saw how
the fire came down, and the glory of the LORD
on the temple, they bowed their faces to the
ground on the pavement, and worshiped and
praised the LORD, *saying:*

[R]"For *He is* good, Ps. 106:1; 136:1
For His mercy *endures* forever."*

The Nation Offers Sacrifices—1 Kin. 8:62–64

4 [R]Then the king and all the people offered
sacrifices before the LORD. 1 Kin. 8:62, 63
5 King Solomon offered a sacrifice of
twenty-two thousand bulls and one hundred
and twenty thousand sheep. So the king and
all the people dedicated the house of God.
6 [R]And the priests attended to their ser-
vices; the Levites also with instruments of the
music of the LORD, which King David had
made to praise the LORD, saying, "For His
mercy *endures* forever,"* whenever David of-
fered praise by their [T]ministry. [R]The priests
sounded trumpets opposite them, while all Is-
rael stood. 1 Chr. 15:16 • Lit. *hand* • 2 Chr. 5:12
7 Furthermore Solomon consecrated the
middle of the court that *was* in front of the
house of the LORD; for there he offered burnt
offerings and the fat of the peace offerings,
because the bronze altar which Solomon had
made was not able to receive the burnt offer-
ings, the grain offerings, and the fat.

The Nation Celebrates
the Feast of Tabernacles
1 Kin. 8:65—9:1

8 At that time Solomon kept the feast seven
days, and all Israel with him, a very great as-
sembly from the entrance of Hamath to the
Brook of Egypt.*
9 And on the eighth day they held a [R]sa-
cred assembly, for they observed the dedica-
tion of the altar seven days, and the feast
seven days. Lev. 23:36
10 [R]On the twenty-third day of the seventh
month he sent the people away to their tents,
joyful and glad of heart for the good that the
LORD had done for David, for Solomon, and
for His people Israel. 1 Kin. 8:66
11 Thus [R]Solomon finished the house of the
LORD and the king's house; and Solomon suc-
cessfully accomplished all that came into his
heart to make in the house of the LORD and in
his own house. 1 Kin. 9:1

The Lord Confirms the Covenant
1 Kin. 9:2–9

12 Then the LORD [R]appeared to Solomon by
night, and said to him: "I have heard your
prayer, and have chosen this place for Myself
as a house of sacrifice. 1 Kin. 3:5; 11:9
13 [R]"When I shut up heaven and there is
no rain, or command the locusts to devour
the land, or send pestilence among My peo-
ple, 2 Chr. 6:26–28
14 "if My people who are called by My name
will humble themselves, and pray and seek
My face, and turn from their wicked ways,
then I will hear from heaven, and will forgive
their sin and heal their land.
15 "Now My eyes will be open and My ears
attentive to prayer *made* in this place.
16 "For now [R]I have chosen and [T]sanctified
this house, that My name may be there for-
ever; and My eyes and My heart will be there
perpetually. 2 Chr. 6:6 • *set apart*
17 "As for you, if you walk before Me as your
father David walked, and do according to all
that I have commanded you, and if you keep
My statutes and My judgments,
18 "then I will establish the throne of your
kingdom, as I covenanted with David your

7:3 Cf. Ps. 106:1 **7:6** Cf. Ps. 106:1 **7:8** The Shihor, 1 Chr. 13:5

7:3 The Reasons for Worship—The first reason for worship is simply that God commands it (Page 416—1 Chr. 16:29; Page 980—Matt. 4:10). The first four of the Ten Commandments, which are also the longest, clearly charge men to worship the one true God and Him alone (Page 74—Ex. 20:3–10). To allow any person or thing to usurp the position of lordship over us constitutes gross disobedience to the will of God and incurs His terrible wrath (Page 74—Ex. 20:5; Page 199—Deut. 27:15). All people are destined to pay homage to God anyway, even if unwillingly (Page 1214—Phil. 2:10).

An equally important reason for worship is that God deserves our worship. He alone possesses the attributes that merit our worship and service. Among these are goodness (Page 599—Ps. 100:4, 5), mercy (Page 59—Ex. 4:31), holiness (Page 598—Ps. 99:5, 9), and creative power (Page 1315—Rev. 4:11). When people of biblical times clearly saw the unveiled glory of God, they could not help but fall prostrate in worship. Examples of this response can be seen in the actions of Moses (Page 88—Ex. 34:5–8), Paul (Page 1121—Acts 9:3–6), and John (Page 1312—Rev. 1:9–17).

A final reason for worship is that we need to give it. People cannot find personal fulfillment apart from the glad submission of themselves in worshipful obedience to God. He is the Creator and we are the creatures (Page 1315—Rev. 4:11). People who adopt as their master anything less than God are building their lives on quicksand. They will be no stronger than the object they worship (Page 608—Ps. 115:4–8). One who worships God, however, not only participates in the occupation of heaven (Page 1317—Rev. 7:9–12), but finds joyful satisfaction for the present (Page 1159—Rom. 12:2; Page 1222—Col. 3:24).

Now turn to Page 1162—Rom. 16:5: Definition of the Local Church.

father, saying, [R]'You shall not fail *to have* a man as ruler in Israel.' 2 Chr. 6:16

19 [R]"But if you turn away and forsake My statutes and My commandments which I have set before you, and go and serve other gods, and worship them, Lev. 26:14, 33

20 "then I will uproot them from My land which I have given them; and this house which I have sanctified for My name I will cast out of My sight, and will make it a proverb and a byword among all peoples.

21 "And *as for* this house, which [T]is exalted, everyone who passes by it will be astonished and say, 'Why has the LORD done thus to this land and this house?' Or *was*

22 "Then they will answer, 'Because they forsook the LORD God of their fathers, who brought them out of the land of Egypt, and embraced other gods, and worshiped them and served them; therefore He has brought all this calamity on them.' "

CHAPTER 8

Enlargement of Solomon's Territory
1 Kin. 9:10–19

IT came to pass at the end of twenty years, when Solomon had built the house of the LORD and his own house,

2 that the cities which Hiram* had given to Solomon, Solomon built them; and he settled the children of Israel there.

3 And Solomon went to Hamath Zobah and seized it.

4 [R]He also built Tadmor in the wilderness, and all the storage cities which he built in [R]Hamath. 1 Kin. 9:17, 18 • 1 Chr. 18:3, 9

5 He built Upper Beth Horon and [R]Lower Beth Horon, fortified cities *with* walls, gates, and bars, 1 Chr. 7:24

6 also Baalath and all the storage cities that Solomon had, and all the chariot cities and the cities of the cavalry, and all that Solomon desired to build in Jerusalem, in Lebanon, and in all the land of his dominion.

Subjugation of the Enemies of Solomon
1 Kin. 9:20–23

7 [R]All the people *who were* left of the Hittites, Amorites, Perizzites, Hivites, and Jebusites, who *were* not of Israel— 1 Kin. 9:20

8 that is, their descendants who were left in the land after them, whom the children of Israel did not destroy—from these Solomon raised forced labor, as it is to this day.

9 But Solomon did not make the children of Israel [T]servants for his work. Some *were* men of war, captains of his officers, captains of his chariots, and his cavalry. *slaves*

10 And others *were* chiefs of the officials of King Solomon: [R]two hundred and fifty, who ruled over the people. 1 Kin. 9:23

Religious Practices of Solomon
1 Kin. 9:24, 25

11 Now Solomon brought the daughter of Pharaoh up from the City of David to the house he had built for her, for he said, "My wife shall not dwell in the house of David king of Israel, because *the places* to which the ark of the LORD has come are holy."

12 Then Solomon offered burnt offerings to the LORD on the altar of the LORD which he had built before the vestibule,

13 according to the daily rate, offering according to the commandment of Moses, for the Sabbaths, the New Moons, and the three appointed yearly [R]feasts—the Feast of Unleavened Bread, the Feast of Weeks, and the Feast of Tabernacles. Lev. 23:1–44

14 And, according to the [T]order of David his father, he appointed the [R]divisions of the priests for their service, [R]the Levites for their duties (to praise and serve before the priests) as the duty of each day required, and the gatekeepers by their divisions at each gate; for so David the man of God had commanded. *ordinance* • 1 Chr. 24:3 • 1 Chr. 25:1

15 They did not depart from the command of the king to the priests and Levites concerning any matter or concerning the [R]treasuries. 1 Chr. 26:20–28

16 Now all the work of Solomon was well-ordered from* the day of the foundation of the house of the LORD until it was finished. So the house of the LORD was completed.

Economic Operations of Solomon
1 Kin. 9:26–28

17 Then Solomon went to Ezion Geber and Elath* on the seacoast, in the land of Edom.

18 [R]And Hiram sent him ships by the hand of his servants, and servants who knew the sea. They went with the servants of Solomon to [R]Ophir, and acquired four hundred and fifty talents of gold from there, and brought it to King Solomon. 2 Chr. 9:10, 13 • 1 Chr. 29:4

CHAPTER 9

The Queen of Sheba Visits—1 Kin. 10:1–13

NOW [R]when the queen of Sheba heard of the fame of Solomon, she came to Jerusalem to test Solomon with hard questions, *having* a very great retinue, camels that bore spices, gold in abundance, and precious stones; and when she came to Solomon, she spoke with him about all that was in her heart. [Matt. 12:42]

2 So Solomon answered all her questions; there was nothing so difficult for Solomon that he could not explain it to her.

8:2 Heb. *Huram,* 2 Chr. 2:3 **8:16** So with LXX, Syr., Vg.; MT *as far as* **8:17** Heb. *Eloth,* 2 Kin. 14:22

3 And when the queen of Sheba had seen the wisdom of Solomon, the house that he had built,

4 the food on his table, the seating of his servants, the service of his waiters and their apparel, his [R]cupbearers and their apparel, and his entryway by which he went up to the house of the LORD, there was no more spirit in her. Neh. 1:11

5 Then she said to the king: "*It was* a true report which I heard in my own land about your words and your wisdom.

6 "However I did not believe their words until I came and saw with my own eyes; and indeed the half of the greatness of your wisdom was not told me. You exceed the fame of which I heard.

7 "Happy *are* your men and happy *are* these your servants, who stand continually before you and hear your wisdom!

8 "Blessed be the LORD your God, who delighted in you, setting you on His throne *to be* king for the LORD your God! Because your God has [R]loved Israel, to establish them forever, therefore He made you king over them, to do justice and righteousness." Deut. 7:8

9 And she gave the king one hundred and twenty talents of gold, spices in great abundance, and precious stones; there never were any spices such as those the queen of Sheba gave to King Solomon.

10 Also, the servants of Hiram and the servants of Solomon, [R]who brought gold from Ophir, brought algum* wood and precious stones. 2 Chr. 8:18

11 And the king made walkways *of* the algum* wood for the house of the LORD and for the king's house, also harps and stringed instruments for singers; and there were none such *as these* seen before in the land of Judah.

12 Now King Solomon gave to the queen of Sheba all she desired, whatever she asked, *much more* than she had brought to the king. So she turned and went to her own country, she and her servants.

Solomon's Wealth
1 Kin. 10:14–29; 2 Chr. 1:14–17

13 [R]The weight of gold that came to Solomon yearly was six hundred and sixty-six talents of gold, 1 Kin. 10:14–29

14 besides *what* the traveling merchants and traders brought. And all the kings of Arabia and governors of the country brought gold and silver to Solomon.

15 And King Solomon made two hundred large shields of hammered gold; six hundred *shekels* of hammered gold went into each shield.

16 *He* also *made* three hundred shields of hammered gold; three hundred *shekels** of gold went into each shield. The king put them in the House of the Forest of Lebanon.

17 Moreover the king made a great throne of ivory, and overlaid it with pure gold.

18 The throne *had* six steps, with a footstool of gold, *which were* fastened to the throne; there were [T]armrests on either side of the place of the seat, and two lions stood beside the armrests. Lit. *hands*

19 Twelve lions stood there, one on each side of the six steps; nothing like *this* had been made for any *other* kingdom.

20 All King Solomon's drinking vessels *were* gold, and all the vessels of the House of the Forest of Lebanon *were* pure gold. Not *one was* silver, for this was accounted as nothing in the days of Solomon.

21 For the king's ships went to [R]Tarshish with the servants of Hiram.* Once every three years the merchant ships* came, bringing gold, silver, ivory, apes, and monkeys.* 2 Chr. 20:36, 37

22 So King Solomon surpassed all the kings of the earth in riches and wisdom.

23 And all the kings of the earth sought the presence of Solomon to hear his wisdom, which God had put in his heart.

24 Each man brought his present: articles of silver and gold, garments, armor, spices, horses, and mules, at a set rate year by year.

25 Solomon had four thousand stalls for horses and chariots, and twelve thousand horsemen whom he stationed in the chariot cities and with the king at Jerusalem.

26 [R]So he reigned over all the kings from the River* to the land of the Philistines, as far as the border of Egypt. 1 Kin. 4:21

27 [R]The king made silver *as common* in Jerusalem as stones, and he made cedar trees [R]as abundant as the sycamores which *are* in the lowland. 1 Kin. 10:27 • 2 Chr. 1:15–17

28 [R]And they brought horses to Solomon from Egypt and from all lands. 2 Chr. 1:16

The Death of Solomon—1 Kin. 11:41–43

29 [R]Now the rest of the acts of Solomon, first and last, *are* they not written in the book of Nathan the prophet, in the prophecy of [R]Ahijah the Shilonite, and in the visions of Iddo the seer concerning Jeroboam the son of Nebat? 1 Kin. 11:41 • 1 Kin. 11:29

30 [R]Solomon reigned in Jerusalem over all Israel forty years. 1 Kin. 4:21; 11:42, 43

31 Then Solomon [T]rested with his fathers, and was buried in the City of David his father. And Rehoboam his son reigned in his place. Died and joined his ancestors

9:10 *almug,* 1 Kin. 10:11, 12 **9:11** *almug,* 1 Kin. 10:11, 12 **9:16** *three minas,* 1 Kin. 10:17 **9:21** Heb. *Huram;* cf. 1 Kin. 10:22 • Lit. *ships of Tarshish,* deep-sea vessels • Or *peacocks* **9:26** The Euphrates

CHAPTER 10

Division of the Kingdom—1 Kin. 12:1–19

AND [R]Rehoboam went to Shechem, for all Israel had gone to Shechem to make him king. 1 Kin. 12:1–20

2 So it happened, when Jeroboam the son of Nebat heard *it* (he was in Egypt, where he had fled from the presence of King Solomon), that Jeroboam returned from Egypt.

3 Then they sent for him and called him. And Jeroboam and all Israel came and spoke to Rehoboam, saying,

4 "Your father made our yoke heavy; now therefore, lighten the burdensome service of your father and his heavy yoke which he put on us, and we will serve you."

5 So he said to them, "Come back to me after three days." And the people departed.

6 Then King Rehoboam consulted the elders who stood before his father Solomon while he still lived, saying, "How do you advise *me* to answer these people?"

7 And they spoke to him, saying, "If you are kind to these people, and please them, and speak good words to them, they will be your servants forever."

8 [R]But he rejected the advice which the elders had given him, and consulted the young men who had grown up with him, who stood before him. 1 Kin. 12:8–11

9 And he said to them, "What advice do you give? How should we answer this people who have spoken to me, saying, 'Lighten the yoke which your father put on us'?"

10 Then the young men who had grown up with him spoke to him, saying, "Thus you should speak to the people who have spoken to you, saying, 'Your father made our yoke heavy, but you make *it* lighter on us'—thus you shall say to them: 'My little *finger* shall be thicker than my father's waist!

11 'And now, whereas my father put a heavy yoke on you, I will add to your yoke; my father chastised you with whips, but I *will chastise you* with scourges!' "*

12 So [R]Jeroboam and all the people came to Rehoboam on the third day, as the king had directed, saying, "Come back to me the third day." 1 Kin. 12:12–14

13 Then the king answered them roughly. King Rehoboam rejected the advice of the elders,

14 and he spoke to them according to the advice of the young men, saying, "My father* made your yoke heavy, but I will add to it; my father chastised you with whips, but I *will chastise you* with scourges!"*

15 So the king did not listen to the people; for the turn *of events* was from God, that the LORD might fulfill His word, which He had spoken by the hand of Ahijah the Shilonite to Jeroboam the son of Nebat.

16 Now when all Israel *saw* that the king did not listen to them, the people answered the king, saying:

"What share have we in David?
We have no inheritance in the son of Jesse.
Every man to your tents, O Israel!
Now see to your own house, O David!"

So all Israel departed to their tents.

17 But Rehoboam reigned over the children of Israel who dwelt in the cities of Judah.

18 Then King Rehoboam sent Hadoram, who *was* in charge of revenue; but the children of Israel stoned him with stones, and he died. Therefore King Rehoboam mounted *his* chariot in haste to flee to Jerusalem.

19 [R]So Israel has been in rebellion against the house of David to this day. 1 Kin. 12:19

CHAPTER 11

Kingdom of Judah Is Strengthened
1 Kin. 12:21–24

NOW [R]when Rehoboam came to Jerusalem, he assembled from the house of Judah and Benjamin one hundred and eighty thousand chosen *men* who were warriors, to fight against Israel, that he might restore the kingdom to Rehoboam. 1 Kin. 12:21–24

2 But the word of the LORD came [R]to Shemaiah the man of God, saying, 1 Chr. 12:5

3 "Speak to Rehoboam the son of Solomon, king of Judah, and to all Israel in Judah and Benjamin, saying,

4 'Thus says the LORD: "You shall not go up or fight against your brethren! Let every man return to his house, for this thing is from Me." ' " Therefore they obeyed the words of the LORD, and turned back from attacking Jeroboam.

5 So Rehoboam dwelt in Jerusalem, and built cities for defense in Judah.

6 And he built Bethlehem, Etam, Tekoa,

7 Beth Zur, Sochoh, Adullam,

8 Gath, Mareshah, Ziph,

9 Adoraim, Lachish, Azekah,

10 Zorah, Aijalon, and Hebron, which are in Judah and Benjamin, fortified cities.

11 And he fortified the strongholds, and put captains in them, and stores of food, oil, and wine.

12 Also in every city *he put* shields and spears, and made them very strong, having Judah and Benjamin on his side.

13 And from all their territories the priests and the Levites who *were* in all Israel took their stand with him.

10:11 Scourges with points or barbs, lit. *scorpions*
10:14 So with many Heb. mss., LXX, Syr., Vg. (cf. v. 10; 1 Kin. 12:14); MT *I* • Lit. *scorpions*

14 For the Levites left [R]their common-lands and their possessions and came to Judah and Jerusalem, for [R]Jeroboam and his sons had rejected them from serving as priests to the LORD. Num. 35:2–5 • 2 Chr. 13:9

15 Then he appointed for himself priests for the high places, for the demons, and the calf idols which he had made.

16 [R]And after *the Levites left*,* those from all the tribes of Israel, such as set their heart to seek the LORD God of Israel, [R]came to Jerusalem to sacrifice to the LORD God of their fathers. 2 Chr. 14:7 • 2 Chr. 15:9, 10

17 So they [R]strengthened the kingdom of Judah, and made Rehoboam the son of Solomon strong for three years, because they walked in the way of David and Solomon for three years. 2 Chr. 12:1, 13

18 Then Rehoboam took for himself as wife Mahalath the daughter of Jerimoth the son of David, *and of* Abihail the daughter of [R]Eliah the son of Jesse. 1 Sam. 16:6

19 And she bore him children: Jeush, Shamariah, and Zaham.

20 After her he took Maachah the granddaughter* of Absalom; and she bore him Abijah, Attai, Ziza, and Shelomith.

21 Now Rehoboam loved Maachah the granddaughter of Absalom more than all his wives and his concubines; for he took eighteen wives and sixty concubines, and begot twenty-eight sons and sixty daughters.

22 And Rehoboam [R]appointed [R]Abijah the son of Maachah as chief, *to be* leader among his brothers; for he *intended* to make him king. Deut. 21:15–17 • 2 Chr. 13:1

23 He dealt wisely, and dispersed some of his sons throughout all the territories of Judah and Benjamin, to every fortified city; and he gave them provisions in abundance. He also sought many wives *for them*.

CHAPTER 12

Kingdom of Judah Is Weakened
1 Kin. 14:25–28

NOW [R]it came to pass, when Rehoboam had established the kingdom and had strengthened himself, that [R]he forsook the law of the LORD, and all Israel along with him. 2 Chr. 11:17 • 1 Kin. 14:22–24

2 And it happened in the fifth year of King Rehoboam *that* Shishak king of Egypt came up against Jerusalem, because they had transgressed against the LORD,

3 with twelve hundred chariots, sixty thousand horsemen, and people without number who came with him out of Egypt—[R]the Lubim and the Sukkiim and the Ethiopians. 2 Chr. 16:8

4 And he took the fortified cities of Judah and came to Jerusalem.

5 Then [R]Shemaiah the prophet came to Rehoboam and the leaders of Judah, who were gathered together in Jerusalem because of Shishak, and said to them, "Thus says the LORD: 'You have forsaken Me, and therefore I also have left you in the hand of Shishak.' " 2 Chr. 11:2

6 So the leaders of Israel and the king [R]humbled themselves; and they said, [R]"The LORD *is* righteous." [James 4:10] • Ex. 9:27

7 Now when the LORD saw that they humbled themselves, [R]the word of the LORD came to Shemaiah, saying, "They have humbled themselves; *therefore* I will not destroy them, but I will grant them some deliverance. My wrath shall not be poured out on Jerusalem by the hand of Shishak. 1 Kin. 21:28, 29

8 "Nevertheless they will be his servants, that they may distinguish My service from the service of the kingdoms of the nations."

9 [R]So Shishak king of Egypt came up against Jerusalem, and took away the treasures of the house of the LORD and the treasures of the king's house; he took everything. He also carried away the gold shields which Solomon had made. 1 Kin. 14:25, 26

10 Then King Rehoboam made bronze shields in their place, and committed *them* [R]to the hands of the captains of the guard, who guarded the doorway of the king's house. 1 Kin. 14:27

11 And whenever the king entered the house of the LORD, the guard would go and bring them out; then they would take them back into the guardroom.

12 When he humbled himself, the wrath of the LORD turned from him, so as not to destroy *him* completely; and things also went well in Judah.

Death of Rehoboam—1 Kin. 14:21, 22, 29–31

13 Thus King Rehoboam strengthened himself in Jerusalem and reigned. Now [R]Rehoboam *was* forty-one years old when he became king; and he reigned seventeen years in Jerusalem, the city which the LORD had chosen out of all the tribes of Israel, to put His name there. His mother's name *was* Naamah, an Ammonitess. 1 Kin. 14:21

14 And he did evil, because he did not prepare his heart to seek the LORD.

15 The acts of Rehoboam, first and last, *are* they not written in the book of Shemaiah the prophet, and of Iddo the seer concerning genealogies? And *there were* wars between Rehoboam and Jeroboam all their days.

16 So Rehoboam rested with his fathers, and was buried in the City of David. Then Abijah* his son reigned in his place.

11:16 Lit. *after them* **11:20** Lit. *daughter*, but in the broader sense of granddaughter **12:16** *Abijam*, 1 Kin. 14:31

CHAPTER 13

War of Abijah and Jeroboam
1 Kin. 15:1, 2, 7

IN the eighteenth year of King Jeroboam, Abijah became king over Judah.

2 He reigned three years in Jerusalem. His mother's name *was* Michaiah* the daughter of Uriel of Gibeah. And there was war between Abijah and Jeroboam.

3 Abijah set the battle in order with an army of valiant warriors, four hundred thousand choice men. Jeroboam also drew up in battle formation against him with eight hundred thousand choice men, mighty men of valor.

4 Then Abijah stood on Mount [R]Zemaraim, which *is* in the mountains of Ephraim, and said, "Hear me, Jeroboam and all Israel: Josh. 18:22

5 "Should you not know that the LORD God of Israel [R]gave the dominion over Israel to David forever, to him and his sons, [R]by a covenant of salt? 2 Sam. 7:8–16 • Num. 18:19

6 "Yet Jeroboam the son of Nebat, the servant of Solomon the son of David, rose up and [R]rebelled against his lord. 1 Kin. 11:28

7 "Then [R]worthless rogues gathered to him, and strengthened themselves against Rehoboam the son of Solomon, when Rehoboam was young and inexperienced and could not withstand them. Judg. 9:4

8 "And now you think to withstand the kingdom of the LORD, which is in the hand of the sons of David; and you *are* a great multitude, and with you are the gold calves which Jeroboam made for you as gods.

9 [R]"Have you not cast out the priests of the LORD, the sons of Aaron, and the Levites, and made for yourselves priests, like the peoples of *other* lands, so that whoever comes to consecrate himself with a young bull and seven rams may be a priest of *things that are* not gods? 2 Chr. 11:13–15

10 "But as for us, the LORD *is* our [R]God, and we have not forsaken Him; and the priests who minister to the LORD *are* the sons of Aaron, and the Levites *attend* to *their* duties. Josh. 24:15

11 [R]"And they burn to the LORD every morning and every evening burnt sacrifices and sweet incense; *they* also *set* the [R]showbread *in order on* the pure *gold* table, and the lampstand of gold with its lamps [R]to burn every evening; for we keep the command of the LORD our God, but you have forsaken Him. 2 Chr. 2:4 • Lev. 24:5–9 • Ex. 27:20, 21

12 "Now look, God Himself is with us as *our* [R]head, [R]and His priests with sounding trumpets to sound the alarm against you. O children of Israel, do not fight against the LORD God of your fathers, for you shall not prosper!" [Heb. 2:10] • [Num. 10:8–10]

13 But Jeroboam caused an ambush to go around behind them; so they were in front of Judah, and the ambush *was* behind them.

14 And when Judah looked around, to their surprise the battle line *was* at both front and rear; and they cried out to the LORD, and the priests sounded the trumpets.

15 Then the men of Judah gave a shout; and as the men of Judah shouted, it happened that God [R]struck Jeroboam and all Israel before Abijah and Judah. 2 Chr. 14:12

16 And the children of Israel fled before Judah, and God delivered them into their hand.

17 Then Abijah and his people struck them with a great slaughter; so five hundred thousand choice men of Israel fell slain.

18 Thus the children of Israel were subdued at that time; and the children of Judah prevailed, [R]because they relied on the LORD God of their fathers. 2 Chr. 14:11

19 And Abijah pursued Jeroboam and took cities from him: Bethel with its villages, Jeshanah with its villages, and [R]Ephrain* with its villages. Josh. 15:9

20 So Jeroboam did not recover strength again in the days of Abijah; and the LORD [R]struck him, and he died. 1 Sam. 2:6; 25:38

Death of Abijah

21 But Abijah grew mighty, married fourteen wives, and begot twenty-two sons and sixteen daughters.

22 Now the rest of the acts of Abijah, his ways, and his sayings *are* written in [R]the annals of the prophet Iddo. 2 Chr. 9:29

CHAPTER 14

Evaluation of Asa—1 Kin. 15:8–12

SO Abijah rested with his fathers, and they buried him in the City of David. Then Asa his son reigned in his place. In his days the land was quiet for ten years.

2 Asa did *what was* good and right in the eyes of the LORD his God,

3 for he removed the altars of the foreign *gods* and [R]the high places, and [R]broke down the *sacred* pillars [R]and cut down the wooden images. 1 Kin. 15:14 • [Ex. 34:13] • 1 Kin. 11:7

4 He commanded Judah to [R]seek the LORD God of their fathers, and to observe the law and the commandment. [2 Chr. 7:14]

5 He also removed the high places and the incense altars from all the cities of Judah, and the kingdom was quiet under him.

6 And he built fortified cities in Judah, for the land had rest; he had no war in those years, because the LORD had given him rest.

7 Therefore he said to Judah, "Let us build these cities and make walls around *them*, and towers, gates, and bars, *while* the land is yet

13:2 *Maachah*, 1 Kin. 15:2; 2 Chr. 11:20, 21 **13:19** Or *Ephron*

before us, because we have sought the LORD
our God; we have sought *Him*, and He has
given us rest on every side." So they built and
prospered.
8 And Asa had an army of three hundred
thousand from Judah who carried shields and
spears, and from Benjamin two hundred and
eighty thousand men who carried shields
and drew [R]bows; all these *were* mighty men
of [R]valor. 1 Chr. 12:2 • 2 Chr. 13:3

Victory over the Ethiopians

9 [R]Then Zerah the Ethiopian came out
against them with an army of a million men
and three hundred chariots, and he came to
[R]Mareshah. 2 Chr. 12:2, 3; 16:8 • Josh. 15:44
10 So Asa went out against him, and they set
the troops in battle array in the Valley of
Zephathah at Mareshah.
11 And Asa cried out to the LORD his God,
and said, "LORD, *it is* nothing for You to help,
whether with many or with those who have
no power; help us, O LORD our God, for we
rest on You, and in Your name we go against
this multitude. O LORD, You *are* our God; do
not let man prevail against You!"
12 So the LORD struck the Ethiopians before
Asa and Judah, and the Ethiopians fled.
13 And Asa and the people who *were* with
him pursued them to [R]Gerar. So the Ethio-
pians were overthrown, and they could not re-
cover, for they were broken before the LORD
and His army. And they carried away very
much [T]spoil. Gen. 10:19; 20:1 • *plunder*
14 Then they defeated all the cities around
Gerar, for the fear of the LORD came upon
them; and they plundered all the cities, for
there was exceedingly much spoil in them.
15 They also attacked the livestock enclo-
sures, and carried off sheep and camels in
abundance, and returned to Jerusalem.

CHAPTER 15

Exhortation of Azariah

NOW [R]the Spirit of God came upon
Azariah the son of Oded. 2 Chr. 20:14
2 And he went out to meet Asa, and said to
him: "Hear me, Asa, and all Judah and Benja-
min. [R]The LORD *is* with you while you are with
Him. [R]If you seek Him, He will be found by
you; but if you forsake Him, He will forsake
you. [James 4:8] • [1 Chr. 28:9]
3 [R]"For a long time Israel *has been* without
the true God, without a [R]teaching priest, and
without law; Hos. 3:4 • 2 Kin. 12:2
4 "but [R]when in their trouble they turned to
the LORD God of Israel, and sought Him, He
was found by them. [Deut. 4:29]
5 "And in those times *there was* no peace to
the one who went out, nor to the one who
came in, but great turmoil *was* on all the in-
habitants of the lands.
6 [R]"So nation was [T]destroyed by nation, and
city by city, for God troubled them with every
adversity. Matt. 24:7 • Lit. *beaten in pieces*
7 "But you, be strong and do not let your
hands be weak, for your work shall be re-
warded!"

Reforms of Asa—1 Kin. 15:13–15

8 And when Asa heard these words and the
prophecy of Oded* the prophet, he took
courage, and removed the abominable idols
from all the land of Judah and Benjamin and
from the cities [R]which he had taken in the
mountains of Ephraim; and he restored the
altar of the LORD that *was* before the vestibule
of the LORD. 2 Chr. 13:19
9 Then he gathered all Judah and Benja-
min, and [R]those who dwelt with them from
Ephraim, Manasseh, and Simeon, for they
came over to him in great numbers from Is-
rael when they saw that the LORD his God was
with him. 2 Chr. 11:16
10 So they gathered together at Jerusalem in
the third month, in the fifteenth year of the
reign of Asa.
11 [R]And they offered to the LORD [T]at that
time seven hundred bulls and seven thou-
sand sheep from the [T]spoil they had
brought. 2 Chr. 14:13–15 • Lit. *in that day* • *plunder*
12 Then they entered into a covenant to seek
the LORD God of their fathers with all their
heart and with all their soul;
13 [R]and whoever would not seek the LORD
God of Israel [R]was to be put to death,
whether small or great, whether man or
woman. Ex. 22:20 • Deut. 13:5–15
14 Then they took an oath before the LORD
with a loud voice, with shouting and trumpets
and rams' horns.
15 And all Judah rejoiced at the oath, for
they had sworn with all their heart and
[R]sought Him with all their soul; and He was
found by them, and the LORD gave them [R]rest
all around. 2 Chr. 15:2 • 2 Chr. 14:7
16 Also he removed [R]Maachah, the [T]mother
of Asa the king, from *being* queen mother, be-
cause she had made an obscene image of
Asherah;* and Asa cut down her obscene
image, then crushed and burned *it* by the
Brook Kidron. 1 Kin. 15:2, 10, 13 • Or *grandmother*
17 But [R]the high places were not removed
from Israel. Nevertheless the heart of Asa was
loyal all his days. 1 Kin. 15:14
18 He also brought into the house of God the
things that his father had dedicated and that
he himself had dedicated: silver and gold and
utensils.
19 And there was no war until the thirty-fifth
year of the reign of Asa.

15:8 So with MT, LXX; Syr., Vg. *Azariah the son of Oded* (cf. v. 1) **15:16** A Canaanite deity

CHAPTER 16

Victory over the Syrians—1 Kin. 15:16–22

IN the thirty-sixth year of the reign of Asa, Baasha king of Israel came up against Judah and built Ramah, that he might let none go out or come in to Asa king of Judah.

2 Then Asa brought silver and gold from the treasuries of the house of the LORD and of the king's house, and sent to Ben-Hadad king of Syria, who dwelt in Damascus, saying,

3 "*Let there be* a treaty between you and me, as there was between my father and your father. See, I have sent you silver and gold; come, break your treaty with Baasha king of Israel, so that he will withdraw from me."

4 So Ben-Hadad heeded King Asa, and sent the captains of his armies against the cities of Israel. They attacked Ijon, Dan, Abel Maim, and all the storage cities of Naphtali.

5 Now it happened, when Baasha heard *it*, that he stopped building Ramah and ceased his work.

6 Then King Asa took all Judah, and they carried away the stones and timber of Ramah, which Baasha had used for building; and with them he built Geba and Mizpah.

Rebuke of Hanani

7 And at that time [R]Hanani the seer came to Asa king of Judah, and said to him: "Because you have relied on the king of Syria, and have not relied on the LORD your God, therefore the army of the king of Syria has escaped from your hand. 2 Chr. 19:2

8 "Were the Ethiopians and the Lubim not a huge army with very many chariots and horsemen? Yet, because you relied on the LORD, He delivered them into your hand.

9 [R]"For the eyes of the LORD run to and fro throughout the whole earth, to show Himself strong on behalf of *those* whose heart *is* loyal to Him. In this [R]you have done foolishly; therefore from now on [R]you shall have wars." Zech. 4:10 • 1 Sam. 13:13 • 1 Kin. 15:32

10 Then Asa was angry with the seer, and [R]put him in prison, for *he was* enraged at him because of this. And Asa oppressed *some* of the people at that time. Jer. 20:2

Death of Asa—1 Kin. 15:23, 24

11 [R]Note that the acts of Asa, first and last, are indeed written in the book of the kings of Judah and Israel. 1 Kin. 15:23, 24

12 And in the thirty-ninth year of his reign, Asa became diseased in his feet, and his malady was severe; yet in his disease he did not seek the LORD, but the physicians.

13 So Asa rested with his fathers; he died in the forty-first year of his reign.

14 They buried him in his own tomb, which he had made for himself in the City of David; and they laid him in the bed which was filled with spices and various ingredients prepared in a mixture of ointments. They made a very great burning for him.

CHAPTER 17

Evaluation of Jehoshaphat

THEN [R]Jehoshaphat his son reigned in his place, and strengthened himself against Israel. 1 Kin. 15:24

2 And he placed troops in all the fortified cities of Judah, and set garrisons in the land of Judah and in the cities of Ephraim which Asa his father had taken.

3 Now the LORD was with Jehoshaphat, because he walked in the former ways of his father David; he did not seek the Baals,

4 but sought the God* of his father, and walked in His commandments and not according to [R]the acts of Israel. 1 Kin. 12:28

5 Therefore the LORD established the kingdom in his hand; and all Judah gave presents to Jehoshaphat, [R]and he had riches and honor in abundance. 2 Chr. 18:1

6 And his heart took delight in the ways of the LORD; moreover he removed the high places and wooden images from Judah.

Instruction by the Priests and Levites

7 Also in the third year of his reign he sent his leaders, Ben-Hail, Obadiah, Zechariah, Nethanel, and Michaiah, [R]to teach in the cities of Judah. 2 Chr. 15:3; 35:3

8 And with them *he sent* Levites: Shemaiah, Nethaniah, Zebadiah, Asahel, Shemiramoth, Jehonathan, Adonijah, Tobijah, and Tobadonijah—the Levites; and with them Elishama and Jehoram, the priests.

9 [R]So they taught in Judah, and *had* the Book of the Law of the LORD with them; they went throughout all the cities of Judah and taught the people. Neh. 8:3, 7

Expansion of the Kingdom

10 And [R]the fear of the LORD fell on all the kingdoms of the lands that *were* around Judah, so that they did not make war against Jehoshaphat. 2 Chr. 14:14

11 Also *some* of the Philistines brought Jehoshaphat presents and silver as tribute; and the Arabians brought him flocks, seven thousand seven hundred rams and seven thousand seven hundred male goats.

12 So Jehoshaphat became increasingly powerful, and he built fortresses and storage cities in Judah.

13 He had much property in the cities of Judah; and the men of war, mighty men of valor, *were* in Jerusalem.

14 These *are* their numbers, according to their fathers' houses. Of Judah, the captains

17:4 LXX *the* LORD God

of thousands: Adnah the captain, and with him three hundred thousand mighty men of valor;

15 and next to him *was* Jehohanan the captain, and with him two hundred and eighty thousand;

16 and next to him *was* Amasiah the son of Zichri, [R]who willingly offered himself to the LORD, and with him two hundred thousand mighty men of valor. Judg. 5:2, 9

17 Of Benjamin: Eliada a mighty man of valor, and with him two hundred thousand men armed with bow and shield;

18 and next to him *was* Jehozabad, and with him one hundred and eighty thousand prepared for war.

19 These served the king, besides [R]those the king put in the fortified cities throughout all Judah. 2 Chr. 17:2

CHAPTER 18

Alliance with Ahab—1 Kin. 22:2–35

JEHOSHAPHAT [R]had riches and honor in abundance; and by marriage he [R]allied himself with Ahab. 2 Chr. 17:5 • 2 Kin. 8:18

2 After some years he went down to *visit* Ahab in Samaria; and Ahab killed sheep and oxen in abundance for him and the people who were with him, and persuaded him to go up *with him* to Ramoth Gilead.

3 So Ahab king of Israel said to Jehoshaphat king of Judah, "Will you go with me *against* Ramoth Gilead?" And he answered him, "I *am* as you *are*, and my people as your people; *we will be* with you in the war."

4 Also Jehoshaphat said to the king of Israel, [R]"Please inquire for the word of the LORD today." 2 Sam. 2:1

5 Then the king of Israel gathered the prophets together, four hundred men, and said to them, "Shall we go to war against Ramoth Gilead, or shall I refrain?" So they said, "Go up, for God will deliver it into the king's hand."

6 But Jehoshaphat said, "*Is there* not still a prophet of the LORD here, that we may inquire of [R]Him?"* 2 Kin. 3:11

7 So the king of Israel said to Jehoshaphat, "*There is* still one man by whom we may inquire of the LORD; but I hate him, because he never prophesies good concerning me, but always evil. He *is* Micaiah the son of Imla." And Jehoshaphat said, "Let not the king say such things!"

8 Then the king of Israel called one *of his* officers and said, "Bring Micaiah the son of Imla quickly!"

9 The king of Israel and Jehoshaphat king of Judah, clothed in *their* robes, sat each on his throne; and they sat at a threshing floor at the entrance of the gate of Samaria; and all the prophets prophesied before them.

10 Now Zedekiah the son of Chenaanah had made [R]horns of iron for himself; and he said, "Thus says the LORD: 'With these you shall gore the Syrians until they are destroyed.' " Zech. 1:18–21

11 And all the prophets prophesied so, saying, "Go up to Ramoth Gilead and prosper, for the LORD will deliver *it* into the king's hand."

12 Then the messenger who had gone to call Micaiah spoke to him, saying, "Now listen, the words of the prophets with one accord encourage the king. Therefore please let your word be like *the word of* one of them, and speak encouragement."

13 And Micaiah said, "*As* the LORD lives, whatever my God says, that I will speak."

14 Then he came to the king; and the king said to him, "Micaiah, shall we go to war against Ramoth Gilead, or shall I refrain?" And he said, "Go and prosper, and they shall be delivered into your hand!"

15 So the king said to him, "How many times shall I make you swear that you tell me nothing but the truth in the name of the LORD?"

16 Then he said, "I saw all Israel [R]scattered on the mountains, as sheep that have no [R]shepherd. And the LORD said, 'These have no master. Let each return to his house in peace.' " [Jer. 23:1–8; 31:10] • Matt. 9:36

17 And the king of Israel said to Jehoshaphat, "Did I not tell you he would not prophesy good concerning me, but evil?"

18 Then *Micaiah* said, "Therefore hear the word of the LORD: I saw the LORD sitting on His throne, and all the host of heaven standing on His right hand and His left.

19 "And the LORD said, 'Who will persuade Ahab king of Israel to go up, that he may fall at Ramoth Gilead?' So one spoke in this manner, and another spoke in that manner.

20 "Then a spirit came forward and stood before the LORD, and said, 'I will persuade him.' The LORD said to him, 'In what way?'

21 "So he said, 'I will go out and be a lying spirit in the mouth of all his prophets.' And *the LORD* said, 'You shall persuade *him* and also prevail; go out and do so.'

22 "Therefore look! [R]The LORD has put a lying spirit in the mouth of these prophets of yours, and the LORD has declared disaster against you." Ezek. 14:9

23 Then Zedekiah the son of Chenaanah went near and struck Micaiah on the cheek, and said, "Which way did the spirit from the LORD go from me to speak to you?"

24 And Micaiah said, "Indeed you shall see on that day when you go into an inner chamber to hide!"

25 Then the king of Israel said, "Take Micaiah, and return him to Amon the governor of the city and to Joash the king's son;

18:6 Or *him*

26 "and say, 'Thus says the king: [R]"Put this *fellow* in prison, and feed him with bread of affliction and water of affliction, until I return in peace." ' " 2 Chr. 16:10

27 But Micaiah said, "If you ever return in peace, the LORD has not spoken by me." And he said, "Take heed, all you people!"

28 So the king of Israel and Jehoshaphat the king of Judah went up to Ramoth Gilead.

29 And the king of Israel said to Jehoshaphat, "I will [R]disguise myself and go into battle; but you put on your robes." So the king of Israel disguised himself, and they went into battle. 2 Chr. 35:22

30 Now the king of Syria had commanded the captains of the chariots who *were* with him, saying, "Fight with no one small or great, but only with the king of Israel."

31 So it was, when the captains of the chariots saw Jehoshaphat, that they said, "It *is* the king of Israel!" Therefore they surrounded him to attack; but Jehoshaphat cried out, and the LORD helped him, and God diverted them from him.

32 For so it was, when the captains of the chariots saw that it was not the king of Israel, that they turned back from pursuing him.

33 Now a certain man drew a bow at random, and struck the king of Israel between the joints of his armor. So he said to the driver of his chariot, "Turn around and take me out of the battle, for I am wounded."

34 The battle increased that day, and the king of Israel propped *himself* up in *his* chariot facing the Syrians until evening; and about the time of sunset he died.

CHAPTER 19

THEN Jehoshaphat the king of Judah returned safely to his house in Jerusalem.

2 And Jehu the son of Hanani [R]the seer went out to meet him, and said to King Jehoshaphat, "Should you help the wicked and love those who hate the LORD? Therefore the wrath of the LORD *is* upon you. 1 Kin. 16:1

3 "Nevertheless [R]good things are found in you, in that you have removed the wooden images from the land, and have prepared your heart to seek God." 2 Chr. 17:4, 6

4 So Jehoshaphat dwelt at Jerusalem; and he went out again among the people from Beersheba to the mountains of Ephraim, and brought them back to the LORD God of their [R]fathers. 2 Chr. 15:8–13

Organization of the Kingdom

5 Then he set [R]judges in the land throughout all the fortified cities of Judah, city by city, [Deut. 16:18–20]

6 and said to the judges, "Take heed to what you are doing, for [R]you do not judge for man but for the LORD, [R]who *is* with you in the judgment. [Deut. 1:17] • Ps. 82:1

7 "Now therefore, let the fear of the LORD be upon you; take care and do *it*, for [R]*there is* no iniquity with the LORD our God, no partiality, nor taking of bribes." [Deut. 32:4]

8 Moreover in Jerusalem, for the judgment of the LORD and for controversies, Jehoshaphat appointed some of the Levites and priests, and some of the chief fathers of Israel, when they returned to Jerusalem.*

9 And he commanded them, saying, "Thus you shall act [R]in the fear of the LORD, faithfully and with a loyal heart: [2 Sam. 23:3]

10 [R]"Whatever case comes to you from your brethren who dwell in their cities, whether of bloodshed or offenses against law or commandment, against statutes or ordinances, you shall warn them, lest they trespass against the LORD and [R]wrath come upon [R]you and your brethren. Do this, and you will not be guilty. Deut. 17:8 • Num. 16:46 • [Ezek. 3:18]

11 "And take notice: [R]Amariah the chief priest *is* over you [R]in all matters of the LORD; and Zebadiah the son of Ishmael, the ruler of the house of Judah, for all the king's matters; also the Levites *will be* officials before you. Behave courageously, and the LORD will be with the good." Ezra 7:3 • 1 Chr. 26:30

CHAPTER 20

Victory over Moab and Ammon

IT happened after this *that* the people of Moab with the people of Ammon, and *others* with them besides the Ammonites,* came to battle against Jehoshaphat.

2 Then some came and told Jehoshaphat, saying, "A great multitude is coming against you from beyond the sea, from Syria;* and they are [R]in Hazazon Tamar" (which *is* [R]En Gedi). Gen. 14:7 • Josh. 15:62

3 And Jehoshaphat feared, and set himself to [R]seek the LORD, and [R]proclaimed a fast throughout all Judah. 2 Chr. 19:3 • Ezra 8:21

4 So Judah gathered together to ask *help* from the LORD; and from all the cities of Judah they came to seek the LORD.

5 Then Jehoshaphat stood in the assembly of Judah and Jerusalem, in the house of the LORD, before the new court,

6 and said: "O LORD God of our fathers, *are* You not [R]God in heaven, and [R]do You *not* rule over all the kingdoms of the nations, and [R]in Your hand *is there not* power and might, so that no one is able to withstand You? Deut. 4:39 • Dan. 4:17, 25, 32 • 1 Chr. 29:12

7 "*Are* You not [R]our God, *who* drove out the inhabitants of this land before Your people Is-

19:8 LXX, Vg. *for the inhabitants of Jerusalem*
20:1 So with MT, Vg.; LXX *Meunites* (cf. 2 Chr. 26:7)
20:2 So with MT, LXX, Vg.; Heb. mss., Old Lat. *Edom*

rael, and gave it to the descendants of Abra-
ham Your friend forever? Ex. 6:7
8 "And they dwell in it, and have built You a
sanctuary in it for Your name, saying,
9 [R]'If disaster comes upon us—sword, judg-
ment, pestilence, or famine—we will stand
before this temple and in Your presence (for
Your [R]name *is* in this temple), and cry out to
You in our affliction, and You will hear and
save.' 2 Chr. 6:28–30 • 2 Chr. 6:20
10 "And now, here are the people of Ammon,
Moab, and Mount Seir—whom You would not
let Israel invade when they came out of the
land of Egypt, but they turned from them and
did not destroy them—
11 "here they are, rewarding us [R]by coming
to throw us out of Your possession which You
have given us to inherit. Ps. 83:1–18
12 "O our God, will You not [R]judge them?
For we have no power against this great mul-
titude that is coming against us; nor do we
know what to do, but [R]our eyes *are* upon
You." Judg. 11:27 • Ps. 25:15; 121:1, 2; 123:1, 2
13 Now all Judah, with their little ones, their
wives, and their children, stood before the
LORD.
14 Then [R]the Spirit of the LORD came upon
Jahaziel the son of Zechariah, the son of Be-
naiah, the son of Jeiel, the son of Mattaniah, a
Levite of the sons of Asaph, in the midst of the
assembly. 2 Chr. 15:1; 24:20
15 And he said, "Listen, all you of Judah and
you inhabitants of Jerusalem, and you, King
Jehoshaphat! Thus says the LORD to you: 'Do
not be afraid nor dismayed because of this
great multitude, [R]for the battle *is* not yours,
but God's. 1 Sam. 17:47
16 'Tomorrow go down against them. They
will surely come up by the Ascent of Ziz, and
you will find them at the end of the brook be-
fore the Wilderness of Jeruel.
17 [R]'You will not *need* to fight in this *battle*.
Position yourselves, stand still and see the sal-
vation of the LORD, who is with you, O Judah
and Jerusalem!' Do not fear or be dismayed;
tomorrow go out against them, [R]for the LORD
is with you." Ex. 14:13, 14 • Num. 14:9
18 And Jehoshaphat [R]bowed his head with
his face to the ground, and all Judah and the
inhabitants of Jerusalem bowed before the
LORD, worshiping the LORD. Ex. 4:31
19 Then the Levites of the children of the Ko-
hathites and of the children of the Korahites
stood up to praise the LORD God of Israel with
voices loud and high.
20 So they rose early in the morning and
went out into the Wilderness of Tekoa; and as
they went out, Jehoshaphat stood and said,
"Hear me, O Judah and you inhabitants of Je-
rusalem: Believe in the LORD your God, and
you shall be established; believe His prophets,
and you shall prosper."
21 And when he had consulted with the peo-
ple, he appointed those who should sing to the
LORD, [R]and who should praise the beauty of
holiness, as they went out before the army
and were saying: 1 Chr. 16:29

[R]"Praise the LORD, Ps. 106:1; 136:1
For His mercy *endures* forever."*

22 Now when they began to sing and to
praise, [R]the LORD set ambushes against the
people of Ammon, Moab, and Mount Seir,
who had come against Judah; and they were
defeated. Judg. 7:22
23 For the people of Ammon and Moab
stood up against the inhabitants of Mount
Seir to utterly kill and destroy *them*. And
when they [T]had made an end of the inhab-
itants of Seir, [R]they helped to destroy one an-
other. *had finished* • 1 Sam. 14:20
24 So when Judah came to a place overlook-
ing the wilderness, they looked toward the
multitude; and there *were* their dead bodies,
fallen on the earth. No one had escaped.
25 When Jehoshaphat and his people came to
take away their spoil, they found among them
an abundance of valuables on the dead bod-
ies,* and precious jewelry, which they stripped
off for themselves, more than they could carry
away; and they were three days gathering the
spoil because there was so much.
26 And on the fourth day they assembled in
the Valley of Berachah, for there they blessed
the LORD; therefore the name of that place
was called The Valley of Berachah* until this
day.
27 Then they returned, every man of Judah
and Jerusalem, with Jehoshaphat in front of
them, to go back to Jerusalem with joy, for the
LORD had [R]made them rejoice over their ene-
mies. Neh. 12:43
28 So they came to Jerusalem, with stringed
instruments and harps and trumpets, to the
house of the LORD.
29 And [R]the fear of God was on all the king-
doms of *those* countries when they heard that
the LORD had fought against the enemies of
Israel. 2 Chr. 14:14; 17:10
30 Then the realm of Jehoshaphat was quiet,
for his God gave him rest all around.

Summary of the Reign of Jehoshaphat
1 Kin. 22:41–45

31 [R]So Jehoshaphat was king over Judah. *He*
was thirty-five years old when he became
king, and he reigned twenty-five years in Je-
rusalem. His mother's name *was* Azubah the
daughter of Shilhi. [1 Kin. 22:41–43]
32 And he walked in the way of his father
Asa, and did not turn aside from it, doing
what was right in the sight of the LORD.

20:21 Cf. Ps. 106:1 **20:25** A few Heb. mss., Old Lat., Vg. *garments;* LXX *armor* **20:26** Lit. *Blessing*

33 Nevertheless [R]the high places were not taken away, for as yet the people had not [R]directed their hearts to the God of their fathers. 2 Chr. 15:17; 17:6 • 2 Chr. 12:14; 19:3

34 Now the rest of the acts of Jehoshaphat, first and last, indeed they *are* written in the book of Jehu the son of Hanani, which *is* mentioned in the book of the kings of Israel.

The Sin and Death of Jehoshaphat
1 Kin. 22:48

35 After this [R]Jehoshaphat king of Judah allied himself with Ahaziah king of Israel, who acted very wickedly. 2 Chr. 18:1

36 And he allied himself with him [R]to make ships to go to Tarshish, and they made the ships in Ezion Geber. 1 Kin. 9:26; 10:22

37 But Eliezer the son of Dodavah of Mareshah prophesied against Jehoshaphat, saying, "Because you have allied yourself with Ahaziah, the LORD has destroyed your works." Then the ships were wrecked, so that they were not able to go to Tarshish.

CHAPTER 21

Evaluation of Jehoram
1 Kin. 22:50; 2 Kin. 8:17–19

AND [R]Jehoshaphat rested with his fathers, and was buried with his fathers in the City of David. Then Jehoram his son reigned in his place. 1 Kin. 22:50

2 He had brothers, the sons of Jehoshaphat: Azariah, Jehiel, Zechariah, Azaryahu, Michael, and Shephatiah; all these *were* the sons of Jehoshaphat king of Israel.

3 Their father gave them great gifts of silver and gold and precious things, with fortified cities in Judah; but he gave the kingdom to Jehoram, because he *was* the firstborn.

4 Now when Jehoram [T]was established over the kingdom of his father, he strengthened himself and killed all his brothers with the sword, and also *others* of the princes of Israel. Lit. *arose*

5 [R]Jehoram *was* thirty-two years old when he became king, and he reigned eight years in Jerusalem. 2 Kin. 8:17–22

6 And he walked in the way of the kings of Israel, just as the house of Ahab had done, for he had the daughter of Ahab as a wife; and he did evil in the sight of the LORD.

7 Yet the LORD would not destroy the house of David, because of the [R]covenant that He had made with David, and since He had promised to give a lamp to him and to his [R]sons forever. 2 Sam. 7:8–17 • 1 Kin. 11:36

Revolt by Edom and Libnah—2 Kin. 8:20–22

8 [R]In his days Edom revolted against Judah's authority, and made a king over themselves. 2 Kin. 8:20; 14:7, 10

9 So Jehoram went out with his officers, and all his chariots with him. And he rose by night and attacked the Edomites who had surrounded him and the captains of the chariots.

10 Thus Edom has been in revolt against Judah's authority to this day. At that time Libnah revolted against his rule, because he had forsaken the LORD God of his fathers.

11 Moreover he made high places in the mountains of Judah, and caused the inhabitants of Jerusalem to [R]commit harlotry, and led Judah astray. [Lev. 20:5]

Warning of Elijah

12 And a letter came to him from Elijah the prophet, saying,

Thus says the LORD God of your father
David:
Because you have not walked in the
ways of Jehoshaphat your father, or in
the ways of Asa king of Judah,
13 but have walked in the way of the kings
of Israel, and have made Judah and the
inhabitants of Jerusalem to play the
harlot like the [R]harlotry of the house of
Ahab, and also have killed your brothers,
those of your father's household, *who*
were better than yourself, 2 Kin. 9:22
14 behold, the LORD will strike your people
with a serious affliction—your children,
your wives, and all your possessions;
15 and you *will become* very sick with a
[R]disease of your intestines, until your
intestines come out by reason of the
sickness, day by day. 2 Chr. 21:18, 19

Invasion by Philistia and Arabia

16 Moreover the LORD stirred up against Jehoram the spirit of the Philistines and the Arabians who *were* near the Ethiopians.

17 And they came up into Judah and invaded it, and carried away all the possessions that were found in the king's house, and also his sons and his wives, so that there was not a son left to him except Jehoahaz,* the youngest of his sons.

Death of Jehoram

18 After all this the LORD struck him in his intestines with an incurable disease.

19 Then it happened in the course of time, after the end of two years, that his intestines came out because of his sickness; so he died in severe pain. And his people made no [T]burning for him, like [R]the burning for his fathers. Burning of spices • 2 Chr. 16:14

20 He was thirty-two years old when he became king. He reigned in Jerusalem eight years and, to no one's sorrow, departed. However they buried him in the City of David, but not in the tombs of the kings.

21:17 *Ahaziah* or *Azariah,* 2 Chr. 22:1

CHAPTER 22

The Reign of Ahaziah
2 Kin. 8:27–29; 9:15, 16, 27, 28; 10:12–14

THEN the inhabitants of Jerusalem made [R]Ahaziah his youngest son king in his place, for the raiders who came with the Arabians into the camp had killed all the older *sons.* So Ahaziah the son of Jehoram, king of Judah, reigned. 2 Chr. 21:17; 22:6

2 Ahaziah *was* forty-two* years old when he became king, and he reigned one year in Jerusalem. His mother's name *was* Athaliah the granddaughter of Omri.

3 He also walked in the ways of the house of Ahab, for his mother advised him to do wickedly.

4 Therefore he did evil in the sight of the LORD, like the house of Ahab; for they were his counselors after the death of his father, to his destruction.

5 He also followed their advice, and went with Jehoram* the son of Ahab king of Israel to war against Hazael king of Syria at Ramoth Gilead; and the Syrians wounded Joram.

6 [R]Then he returned to Jezreel to recover from the wounds which he had received at Ramah, when he fought against Hazael king of Syria. And Azariah* the son of Jehoram, king of Judah, went down to see Jehoram the son of Ahab in Jezreel, because he was sick. 2 Kin. 9:15

7 His going to Joram was God's occasion for Ahaziah's downfall; for when he arrived, he went out with Jehoram against Jehu the son of Nimshi, whom the LORD had anointed to cut off the house of Ahab.

8 And it happened, when Jehu was [R]executing judgment on the house of Ahab, and [R]found the princes of Judah and the sons of Ahaziah's brothers who served Ahaziah, that he killed them. 2 Kin. 9:22–24 • 2 Kin. 10:10–14

9 [R]Then he searched for Ahaziah; and they caught him (he was hiding in Samaria), and brought him to Jehu. When they had killed him, they buried him, "because," they said, "he is the son of [R]Jehoshaphat, who sought the LORD with all his heart." So the house of Ahaziah had no one to assume power over the kingdom. [2 Kin. 9:27] • 1 Kin. 15:24

The Reign of Athaliah—2 Kin. 11:1–16

10 [R]Now when Athaliah the mother of Ahaziah saw that her son was dead, she arose and destroyed all the royal heirs of the house of Judah. 2 Kin. 11:1–3

11 But Jehoshabeath,* the daughter of the king, took [R]Joash the son of Ahaziah, and stole him away from among the king's sons who were being murdered, and put him and his nurse in a bedroom. So Jehoshabeath, the daughter of King Jehoram, the wife of Jehoiada the priest (for she was the sister of Ahaziah), hid him from Athaliah so that she did not kill him. 2 Kin. 12:18

12 And he was hidden with them in the house of God for six years, while Athaliah reigned over the land.

CHAPTER 23

IN the seventh year Jehoiada strengthened himself, *and made a* covenant with the captains of hundreds: Azariah the son of Jeroham, Ishmael the son of Jehohanan, Azariah the son of Obed, Maaseiah the son of Adaiah, and Elishaphat the son of Zichri.

2 And they went throughout Judah and gathered the Levites from all the cities of Judah, and the [R]chief fathers of Israel, and they came to Jerusalem. Ezra 1:5

3 Then all the assembly made a covenant with the king in the house of God. And he said to them, "Behold, the king's son shall reign, as the LORD has [R]said of the sons of David. 2 Sam. 7:12

4 "This *is* what you shall do: One-third of you [R]entering on the Sabbath, of the priests and the Levites, *shall be* keeping watch over the doors; 1 Chr. 9:25

5 "one-third *shall be* at the king's house; and one-third at the Gate of the Foundation. All the people *shall be* in the courts of the house of the LORD.

6 "But let no one come into the house of the LORD except the priests and [R]those of the Levites who serve. They may go in, for they *are* holy; but all the people shall keep the watch of the LORD. 1 Chr. 23:28–32

7 "And the Levites shall surround the king on all sides, every man with his weapons in his hand; and whoever comes into the house, let him be put to death. You are to be with the king when he comes in and when he goes out."

8 So the Levites and all Judah did according to all that Jehoiada the priest commanded. And each man took his men who were to be on duty on the Sabbath, with those who were going *off duty* on the Sabbath; for Jehoiada the priest had not dismissed [R]the divisions. 1 Chr. 24:1–31

9 And Jehoiada the priest gave to the captains of hundreds the spears and the large and small shields which *had belonged* to King David, that *were* in the temple of God.

10 Then he set all the people, every man with his weapon in his hand, from the right side of the temple to the left side of the temple, along by the altar and by the temple, all around the king.

11 And they brought out the king's son, put

22:2 *twenty-two,* 2 Kin. 8:26 **22:5** *Joram,* v. 7; 2 Kin. 8:28 **22:6** Heb. mss., LXX, Syr., Vg. *Ahaziah* and 2 Kin. 8:29 **22:11** *Jehosheba,* 2 Kin. 11:2

the crown on him, [R]*gave him* the Testimony,*
and made him king. Then Jehoiada and his
sons anointed him, and said, "*Long* live the
king!" Deut. 17:18
12 Now when [R]Athaliah heard the noise of
the people running and praising the king,
she came to the people *in* the temple of the
LORD. 2 Chr. 22:10
13 When she looked, there was the king
standing by his pillar at the entrance; and the
leaders and the trumpeters *were* by the king.
All the people of the land were rejoicing and
blowing trumpets, also the singers with musi-
cal instruments, and [R]those who led in praise.
So Athaliah tore her clothes and said, "Trea-
son! Treason!" 1 Chr. 25:6–8
14 And Jehoiada the priest brought out the
captains of hundreds who were set over the
army, and said to them, "Take her outside
under guard, and slay with the sword whoever
follows her." For the priest had said, "Do not
kill her in the house of the LORD."
15 So they seized her; and she went by way
of the entrance of the Horse Gate *into* the
king's house, and they killed her there.

Revival of Jehoiada—2 Kin. 11:17–20

16 Then Jehoiada made a covenant between
himself, the people, and the king, that they
should be the LORD's people.
17 And all the people went to the temple* of
Baal, and tore it down. They broke in pieces
its altars and images, and killed Mattan the
priest of Baal before the altars.
18 Also Jehoiada appointed the oversight of
the house of the LORD to the hand of the
priests, the Levites, whom David had assigned
in the house of the LORD, to offer the burnt of-
ferings of the LORD, as *it is* written in the Law
of Moses, with rejoicing and with singing, *as
it was established* by David.
19 And he set the gatekeepers at the gates of
the house of the LORD, so that no one *who was*
in any way unclean should enter.
20 [R]Then he took the captains of hundreds,
the nobles, the governors of the people, and
all the people of the land, and brought the
king down from the house of the LORD; and
they went through the Upper Gate to the
king's house, and set the king on the throne of
the kingdom. 2 Kin. 11:19
21 So all the people of the land rejoiced; and
the city was quiet, for they had slain Athaliah
with the sword.

CHAPTER 24

Evaluation of Joash—2 Kin. 11:21—12:2

JOASH [R]*was* seven years old when he be-
came king, and he reigned forty years in
Jerusalem. His mother's name *was* Zibiah of
Beersheba. 2 Kin. 11:21; 12:1–15
2 Joash [R]did *what was* right in the sight
of the LORD all the days of Jehoiada the
priest. 2 Chr. 26:4, 5
3 And Jehoiada took two wives for him,
and he had sons and daughters.

Repair of the Temple—2 Kin. 12:4–16

4 Now it happened after this *that* Joash set
his heart on repairing the house of the LORD.
5 Then he gathered the priests and the
Levites, and said to them, "Go out to the cities
of Judah, and gather from all Israel money to
repair the house of your God from year to
year, and see that you do it quickly." However
the Levites did not do it quickly.
6 [R]So the king called Jehoiada the chief
priest, and said to him, "Why have you not re-
quired the Levites to bring in from Judah and
from Jerusalem the collection, *according to
the commandment* of Moses the servant of
the LORD and of the assembly of Israel, for the
tabernacle of witness?" 2 Kin. 12:7
7 For the sons of Athaliah, that wicked
woman, had broken into the house of God,
and had also presented all the dedicated
things of the house of the LORD to the Baals.
8 Then at the king's command [R]they made
a chest, and set it outside at the gate of the
house of the LORD. 2 Kin. 12:9
9 And they made a proclamation throughout
Judah and Jerusalem to bring to the LORD [R]the
collection *that* Moses the servant of God *had
imposed* on Israel in the wilderness. 2 Chr. 24:6
10 Then all the leaders and all the people re-
joiced, brought their contributions, and put
them into the chest until all had given.
11 So it was, at that time, when the chest was
brought to the king's official by the hand of
the Levites, and [R]when they saw that *there
was* much money, that the king's scribe and
the high priest's officer came and emptied the
chest, and took it and returned it to its place.
Thus they did day by day, and gathered
money in abundance. 2 Kin. 12:10
12 The king and Jehoiada gave it to those
who did the work of the service of the house
of the LORD; and they hired masons and
carpenters to repair the house of the LORD,
and also those who worked in iron and
bronze to restore the house of the LORD.
13 So the workmen labored, and the work
was completed by them; they restored the
house of God to its original condition and re-
inforced it.
14 When they had finished, they brought the
rest of the money before the king and Je-
hoiada; [R]they made from it articles for the
house of the LORD, articles for serving and of-
fering, spoons and vessels of gold and silver.
And they offered burnt offerings in the house
of the LORD continually all the days of Je-
hoiada. 2 Kin. 12:13

23:11 Law, Ex. 25:16, 21; 31:18 **23:17** Lit. *house*

Death of Jehoiada

15 But Jehoiada grew old and was full of days, and he died; *he was* one hundred and thirty years old when he died.

16 And they buried him in the City of David among the kings, because he had done good in Israel, both toward God and His house.

Murder of Jehoiada's Son

17 Now after the death of Jehoiada the leaders of Judah came and bowed down to the king. And the king listened to them.

18 Therefore they left the house of the LORD God of their fathers, and served [R]wooden images and idols; and [R]wrath came upon Judah and Jerusalem because of their trespass. 1 Kin. 14:23 • [Ex. 34:12–14]

19 Yet He sent prophets to them, to bring them back to the LORD; and they testified against them, but they would not listen.

20 Then the Spirit of God came upon [R]Zechariah the son of Jehoiada the priest, who stood above the people, and said to them, "Thus says God: [R]'Why do you transgress the commandments of the LORD, so that you cannot prosper? [R]Because you have forsaken the LORD, He also has forsaken you.' " Matt. 23:35 • Num. 14:41 • [2 Chr. 15:2]

21 So they conspired against him, and at the command of the king they [R]stoned him with stones in the court of the house of the LORD. [Neh. 9:26]

22 Thus Joash the king did not remember the kindness which Jehoiada his [T]father had done to him, but killed his son; and as he died, he said, "The LORD look on *it,* and [R]repay!" Foster father • [Gen. 9:5]

Destruction of Judah by Syria

23 So it happened in the spring of the year *that* [R]the army of Syria came up against him; and they came to Judah and Jerusalem, and destroyed all the leaders of the people from among the people, and sent all their [T]spoil to the king of Damascus. 2 Kin. 12:17 • *plunder*

24 For the army of the Syrians [R]came with a small company of men; but the LORD [R]delivered a very great army into their hand, because they had forsaken the LORD God of their fathers. So they executed judgment against Joash. Lev. 26:8; Is. 30:17 • Lev. 26:25

Death of Joash—2 Kin. 12:20, 21

25 And when they had withdrawn from him (for they left him severely wounded), [R]his own servants conspired against him because of the blood of the sons* of Jehoiada the priest, and killed him on his bed. So he died. And they buried him in the City of David, but they did not bury him in the tombs of the kings. 2 Kin. 12:20, 21

26 These are the ones who conspired against him: Zabad* the son of Shimeath the Ammonitess, and Jehozabad the son of Shimrith* the Moabitess.

27 Now *concerning* his sons, and the many oracles about him, and the repairing of the house of God, indeed they *are* written in the annals of the book of the kings. Then Amaziah his son reigned in his place.

CHAPTER 25

Evaluation of Amaziah—2 Kin. 14:1–6

AMAZIAH [R]*was* twenty-five years old *when* he became king, and he reigned twenty-nine years in Jerusalem. His mother's name *was* Jehoaddan of Jerusalem. 2 Kin. 14:1–6

2 And he did *what was* right in the sight of the LORD, but not with a loyal heart.

3 [R]Now it happened, as soon as the kingdom was established for him, that he executed his servants who had murdered his father the king. 2 Kin. 14:5

4 However he did not execute their children, but *did* as *it is* written in the Law in the Book of Moses, where the LORD commanded, saying, "The fathers shall not be put to death for their children, nor shall the children be put to death for their fathers; but a person shall die for his own sin."*

Victory over Edom

5 Moreover Amaziah gathered Judah together and set over them captains of thousands and captains of hundreds, according to *their* fathers' houses, throughout all Judah and Benjamin; and he numbered them [R]from twenty years old and above, and found them to be three hundred thousand choice *men, able* to go to war, who could handle spear and shield. Num. 1:3

6 He also hired one hundred thousand mighty men of valor from Israel for one hundred talents of silver.

7 But a [R]man of God came to him, saying, "O king, do not let the army of Israel go with you, for the LORD *is* not with Israel—*not with* any of the children of Ephraim. 2 Chr. 11:2

8 "But if you go, be gone! Be strong in battle! *Even so,* God shall make you fall before the enemy; for God has [R]power to help and to overthrow." 2 Chr. 14:11; 20:6

9 Then Amaziah said to the man of God, "But what *shall we* do about the hundred talents which I have given to the troops of Israel?" And the man of God answered, [R]"The LORD is able to give you much more than this." [Deut. 8:18]

10 So Amaziah discharged the troops that had come to him from Ephraim, to go back

24:25 LXX, Vg. *son* and vv. 20–22 **24:26** *Jozachar,* 2 Kin. 12:21 • *Shomer,* 2 Kin. 12:21 **25:4** Deut. 24:16

home. Therefore their anger was greatly aroused against Judah, and they returned home in great anger.

11 Then Amaziah strengthened himself, and leading his people, he went to [R]the Valley of Salt and killed ten thousand of the people of Seir. 2 Kin. 14:7

12 Also the children of Judah took captive ten thousand alive, brought them to the top of the rock, and cast them down from the top of the rock, so that they all were dashed in pieces.

13 But as for the soldiers of the army which Amaziah had discharged, so that they would not go with him to battle, they raided the cities of Judah from Samaria to Beth Horon, killed three thousand in them, and took much [T]spoil. *plunder*

Idolatry of Amaziah

14 Now it was so, after Amaziah came from the slaughter of the Edomites, that he brought the gods of the people of Seir, set them up *to be* his gods, and bowed down before them and burned incense to them.

15 Therefore the anger of the LORD was aroused against Amaziah, and He sent him a prophet who said to him, "Why have you sought [R]the gods of the people, which [R]could not rescue their own people from your hand?" [Ps. 96:5] • 2 Chr. 25:11

16 So it was, as he talked with him, that *the king* said to him, "Have we made you the king's counselor? Cease! Why should you be killed?" Then the prophet ceased, and said, "I know that God has [R]determined to destroy you, because you have done this and have not heeded my advice." [1 Sam. 2:25]

Defeat of Judah by Israel—2 Kin. 14:8–14

17 Now Amaziah king of Judah asked advice and sent to Joash* the son of Jehoahaz, the son of Jehu, king of Israel, saying, "Come, let us face one another *in battle*."

18 And Joash king of Israel sent to Amaziah king of Judah, saying, "The thistle that *was* in Lebanon sent to the cedar that was in Lebanon, saying, 'Give your daughter to my son as wife'; and a wild beast that *was* in Lebanon passed by and trampled the thistle.

19 "Indeed you say that you have defeated the Edomites, and your heart is lifted up to [R]boast. Stay at home now; why should you meddle with trouble, that you should fall—you and Judah with you?" 2 Chr. 26:16; 32:25

20 But Amaziah would not heed, for it *came* from God, that He might give them into the hand *of their enemies*, because they [R]sought the gods of Edom. 2 Chr. 25:14

21 So Joash king of Israel went out; and he and Amaziah king of Judah faced one another at [R]Beth Shemesh, which *belongs* to Judah. Josh. 19:38

22 And Judah was defeated by Israel, and every man fled to his tent.

23 Then Joash the king of Israel captured Amaziah king of Judah, the son of Joash, the son of [R]Jehoahaz, at Beth Shemesh; and he brought him to Jerusalem, and broke down the wall of Jerusalem from the Gate of Ephraim to the Corner Gate—four hundred cubits. 2 Chr. 21:17; 22:1, 6

24 And *he took* all the gold and silver, all the articles that were found in the house of God with Obed-Edom, the treasures of the king's house, and hostages, and returned to Samaria.

Death of Amaziah—2 Kin. 14:17–20

25 Amaziah the son of Joash, king of Judah, lived fifteen years after the death of Joash the son of Jehoahaz, king of Israel.

26 Now the rest of the acts of Amaziah, from first to last, indeed *are* they not written in the book of the kings of Judah and Israel?

27 After the time that Amaziah turned away from following the LORD, they made a conspiracy against him in Jerusalem, and he fled to Lachish; but they sent after him to Lachish and killed him there.

28 Then they brought him on horses and buried him with his fathers in [T]the City of Judah. The City of David

CHAPTER 26

Evaluation of Uzziah
2 Kin. 14:21, 22; 15:1–3

NOW all the people of Judah took Uzziah,* who *was* sixteen years old, and made him king instead of his father Amaziah.

2 He built Elath* and restored it to Judah, after the king rested with his fathers.

3 Uzziah *was* sixteen years old when he became king, and he reigned fifty-two years in Jerusalem. His mother's name was Jecholiah of Jerusalem.

4 And he did *what was* [R]right in the sight of the LORD, according to all that his father Amaziah had done. 2 Chr. 24:2

5 He sought God in the days of Zechariah, who had understanding in the visions* of God; and as long as he sought the LORD, God made him prosper.

Victories of Uzziah

6 Now he went out and [R]made war against the Philistines, and broke down the wall of Gath, the wall of Jabneh, and the wall of Ashdod; and he built cities *around* Ashdod and among the Philistines. Is. 14:29

7 God helped him against [R]the Philistines,

25:17 *Jehoash*, 2 Kin. 14:8ff. **26:1** *Azariah*, 2 Kin. 14:21ff. **26:2** Heb. *Eloth* **26:5** Heb. mss., LXX, Syr., Tg., Arab. *fear*

against the Arabians who lived in Gur Baal,
and against the Meunites. 2 Chr. 21:16
8 Also the Ammonites [R]brought tribute to
Uzziah. His fame spread as far as the en-
trance of Egypt, for he became exceedingly
strong. 2 Chr. 17:11
9 And Uzziah built towers in Jerusalem at
the [R]Corner Gate, at the Valley Gate, and at
the corner buttress of the wall; then he forti-
fied them. Neh. 3:13, 19, 32
10 Also he built towers in the desert. He
dug many wells, for he had much livestock,
both in the lowlands and in the plains; *he*
also had farmers and vinedressers in the
mountains and in [T]Carmel, for he loved the
soil. Or *the fertile fields*
11 Moreover Uzziah had an army of fighting
men who went out to war by companies, ac-
cording to the number on their roll as pre-
pared by Jeiel the scribe and Maaseiah the
officer, under the hand of Hananiah, *one* of
the king's captains.
12 The total number of chief officers* of the
mighty men of valor *was* two thousand six
hundred.
13 And under their authority *was* an army of
three hundred and seven thousand five hun-
dred, that made war with mighty power, to
help the king against the enemy.
14 Then Uzziah prepared for them, for the
entire army, shields, spears, helmets, body
armor, bows, and slings *to cast* stones.
15 And he made devices in Jerusalem, in-
vented by [R]skillful men, to be on the towers
and the corners, to shoot arrows and large
stones. So his fame spread far and wide, for
he was marvelously helped till he became
strong. Ex. 39:3, 8

Sinful Offering of Uzziah

16 But [R]when he was strong his heart was
lifted up, to *his* destruction, for he trans-
gressed against the LORD his God by entering
the temple of the LORD to burn incense on the
altar of incense. [Deut. 32:15]
17 So [R]Azariah the priest went in after him,
and with him were eighty priests of the
LORD—valiant men. 1 Chr. 6:10
18 And they withstood King Uzziah, and
said to him, "*It is* not for you, Uzziah, to burn
incense to the LORD, but for the priests, the
sons of Aaron, who are consecrated to burn
incense. Get out of the sanctuary, for you have
trespassed! You *shall have* no honor from the
LORD God."
19 Then Uzziah became furious; and he *had*
a censer in his hand to burn incense. And
while he was angry with the priests, [R]leprosy
broke out on his forehead, before the priests
in the house of the LORD, beside the incense
altar. 2 Kin. 5:25–27
20 And Azariah the chief priest and all the
priests looked at him, and there, on his fore-
head, he *was* leprous; so they thrust him out
of that place. Indeed he also hurried to get
out, because the LORD had struck him.
21 [R]King Uzziah was a leper until the day of
his death. He dwelt in an [R]isolated house, be-
cause he was a leper; for he was cut off from
the house of the LORD. Then Jotham his son
was over the king's house, judging the people
of the land. 2 Kin. 15:5 • [Lev. 13:46]

Death of Uzziah—2 Kin. 15:7

22 Now the rest of the acts of Uzziah, from
first to last, the prophet [R]Isaiah the son of
Amoz wrote. Is. 1:1
23 [R]So Uzziah rested with his fathers, and
they buried him with his fathers in the field of
burial which *belonged* to the kings, for they
said, "He is a leper." Then Jotham his son
reigned in his place. Is. 6:1

CHAPTER 27

The Reign of Jotham—2 Kin. 15:33–38

JOTHAM *was* twenty-five years old when
he became king, and he reigned sixteen
years in Jerusalem. His mother's name *was*
Jerushah* the daughter of Zadok.
2 And he did *what was* right in the sight of
the LORD, according to all that his father
Uzziah had done (although he did not enter
the temple of the LORD). But still [R]the people
acted corruptly. 2 Kin. 15:35
3 He built the Upper Gate of the house of
the LORD, and he built extensively on the wall
of [R]Ophel. 2 Chr. 33:14
4 Moreover he built cities in the mountains
of Judah, and in the forests he built fortresses
and towers.
5 He also fought with the king of the [R]Am-
monites and defeated them. And the people of
Ammon gave him in that year one hundred
talents of silver, ten thousand kors of wheat,
and ten thousand of barley. The people of
Ammon paid this to him in the second and
third years also. 2 Chr. 26:8
6 So Jotham became mighty, because he
prepared his ways before the LORD his God.
7 Now the rest of the acts of Jotham, and all
his wars and his ways, indeed they *are* written
in the book of the kings of Israel and Judah.
8 He was twenty-five years old when he be-
came king, and he reigned sixteen years in Je-
rusalem.
9 So Jotham rested with his fathers, and
they buried him in the City of David. Then
[R]Ahaz his son reigned in his place. Is. 1:1

CHAPTER 28

Evaluation of Ahaz—2 Kin. 16:1–4

AHAZ [R]*was* twenty years old when he be-
came king, and he reigned sixteen years

26:12 Lit. *chief fathers* **27:1** *Jerusha*, 2 Kin. 15:33

in Jerusalem; and he did not do *what was* right in the sight of the LORD, as his father David *had done.* 2 Kin. 16:2–4

2 For he walked in the ways of the kings of Israel, and made [R]molded images for [R]the Baals. Ex. 34:17 • Judg. 2:11

3 He burned incense in [R]the Valley of the Son of Hinnom, and burned his children in the fire, according to the abominations of the nations whom the LORD had cast out before the children of Israel. Josh. 15:8

4 And he sacrificed and burned incense on the [T]high places, on the hills, and under every green tree. Places for pagan worship

Defeat of Judah—2 Kin. 16:5–8; Is. 7:1

5 Therefore [R]the LORD his God delivered him into the hand of the king of Syria. They defeated him, and carried away a great multitude of them as captives, and brought *them* to Damascus. Then he was also delivered into the hand of the king of Israel, who defeated him with a great slaughter. [Is. 10:5]

6 For Pekah the son of Remaliah killed one hundred and twenty thousand in Judah in one day, all valiant men, because they had forsaken the LORD God of their fathers.

7 Zichri, a mighty man of Ephraim, killed Maaseiah the king's son, Azrikam the officer over the house, and Elkanah *who was* second to the king.

8 And the children of Israel carried away captive of their [R]brethren two hundred thousand women, sons, and daughters; and they also took away much spoil from them, and brought the spoil to Samaria. Deut. 28:25, 41

9 But a [R]prophet of the LORD was there, whose name *was* Oded; and he went out before the army that came to Samaria, and said to them: "Look, [R]because the LORD God of your fathers was angry with Judah, He has delivered them into your hand; but you have killed them in a rage *that* [R]reaches up to heaven. 2 Chr. 25:15 • [Is. 10:5; 47:6] • Rev. 18:5

10 "And now you propose to force the children of Judah and Jerusalem to be your male and female slaves; *but are* you not also guilty before the LORD your God?

11 "Now hear me, therefore, and return the captives, whom you have taken captive from your brethren, [R]for the fierce wrath of the LORD *is* upon you." James 2:13

12 Then some of the heads of the children of Ephraim, Azariah the son of Johanan, Berechiah the son of Meshillemoth, Jehizkiah the son of Shallum, and Amasa the son of Hadlai, stood up against those who came from the war,

13 and said to them, "You shall not bring the captives here, for we *already* have offended the LORD. You intend to add to our sins and to our guilt; for our guilt is great, and *there is* fierce wrath against Israel."

14 So the armed men left the captives and the [T]spoil before the leaders and all the assembly. *plunder*

15 Then the men who were designated by name rose up and took the captives, and from the spoil they clothed all who were naked among them, dressed them and gave them sandals, gave them food and drink, and anointed them; and they let all the feeble ones ride on donkeys. So they brought them to their brethren at Jericho, the city of palm trees. Then they returned to Samaria.

16 [R]At the same time King Ahaz sent to the kings* of Assyria to help him. 2 Kin. 16:7

17 For again the Edomites had come, attacked Judah, and carried away captives.

18 [R]The Philistines also had invaded the cities of the lowland and of the South of Judah, and had taken Beth Shemesh, Aijalon, Gederoth, Sochoh with its villages, Timnah with its villages, and Gimzo with its villages; and they dwelt there. Ezek. 16:27, 57

19 For the LORD brought Judah low because of Ahaz king of Israel, for he had encouraged moral decline in Judah and had been continually unfaithful to the LORD.

20 Also [R]Tiglath-Pileser* king of Assyria came to him and distressed him, and did not assist him. 1 Chr. 5:26

21 For Ahaz took part *of the treasures* from the house of the LORD, from the house of the king, and from the leaders, and he gave *it* to the king of Assyria; but he did not help him.

Idolatry of Ahaz—2 Kin. 16:12

22 Now in the time of his distress King Ahaz became increasingly unfaithful to the LORD. This *is that* King Ahaz.

23 For [R]he sacrificed to the gods of Damascus which had defeated him, saying, "Because the gods of the kings of Syria help them, I will sacrifice to them [R]that they may help me." But they were the ruin of him and of all Israel. 2 Chr. 25:14 • Jer. 44:17, 18

24 So Ahaz gathered the articles of the house of God, cut in pieces the articles of the house of God, shut up the doors of the house of the LORD, and made for himself altars in every corner of Jerusalem.

25 And in every single city of Judah he made [T]high places to burn incense to other gods, and provoked to anger the LORD God of his fathers. Places for pagan worship

Death of Ahaz—2 Kin. 16:20

26 [R]Now the rest of his acts and all his ways, from first to last, indeed they *are* written in the book of the kings of Judah and Israel. 2 Kin. 16:19, 20

27 So Ahaz rested with his fathers, and they

28:16 LXX, Syr., Vg. *king* (cf. v. 20) **28:20** Heb. *Tilgath-Pilneser*

buried him in the city, in Jerusalem; but they [R]did not bring him into the tombs of the kings of Israel. Then Hezekiah his son reigned in his place. 2 Chr. 21:20; 24:25

CHAPTER 29

Evaluation of Hezekiah—2 Kin. 18:2, 3

HEZEKIAH [R]became king *when he was* twenty-five years old, and he reigned twenty-nine years in Jerusalem. His mother's name *was* Abijah* the daughter of Zechariah. 2 Kin. 18:1

2 And he did *what was* right in the sight of the LORD, according to all that his father David had done.

Purification of the Temple

3 In the first year of his reign, in the first month, he [R]opened the doors of the house of the LORD and repaired them. 2 Chr. 28:24

4 Then he brought in the priests and the Levites, and gathered them in the East Square,

5 and said to them: "Hear me, Levites! Now sanctify yourselves, sanctify the house of the LORD God of your fathers, and carry out the rubbish from the holy *place*.

6 "For our fathers have trespassed and done evil in the eyes of the LORD our God; they have forsaken Him, have turned their faces away from the dwelling place of the LORD, and turned *their* backs *on Him*.

7 "They have also shut up the doors of the vestibule, put out the lamps, and have not burned incense or offered burnt offerings in the holy *place* to the God of Israel.

8 "Therefore the wrath of the LORD fell upon Judah and Jerusalem, and He has given them up to trouble, to desolation, and to jeering, as you see with your eyes.

9 "For indeed, because of this our fathers have fallen by the sword; and our sons, our daughters, and our wives *are* in captivity.

10 "Now *it is* in my heart to make a covenant with the LORD God of Israel, that His fierce wrath may turn away from us.

11 "My sons, do not be negligent now, for the LORD has [R]chosen you to stand before Him, to serve Him, and that you should minister to Him and burn incense." Num. 3:6

12 Then these Levites arose: [R]Mahath the son of Amasai and Joel the son of Azariah, of the sons of the [R]Kohathites; of the sons of Merari, Kish the son of Abdi and Azariah the son of Jehallelel; of the Gershonites, Joah the son of Zimmah and Eden the son of Joah; 2 Chr. 31:13 • Num. 3:19, 20

13 of the sons of Elizaphan, Shimri and Jeiel; of the sons of Asaph, Zechariah and Mattaniah;

14 of the sons of Heman, Jehiel and Shimei; and of the sons of Jeduthun, Shemaiah and Uzziel.

15 And they gathered their brethren, sanctified themselves, and went according to the commandment of the king, at the words of the LORD, to cleanse the house of the LORD.

16 Then the priests went into the inner part of the house of the LORD to cleanse *it*, and brought out all the debris that they found in the temple of the LORD to the court of the house of the LORD. And the Levites took *it* out and carried *it* to the Brook [R]Kidron. 2 Chr. 15:16; 30:14

17 Now they began to sanctify on the first *day* of the first month, and on the eighth day of the month they came to the vestibule of the LORD. So they sanctified the house of the LORD in eight days, and on the sixteenth day of the first month they finished.

18 Then they went in to King Hezekiah and said, "We have cleansed all the house of the LORD, the altar of burnt offerings with all its articles, and the table of the showbread with all its articles.

19 "Moreover all the articles which King Ahaz in his reign had [R]cast aside in his transgression we have prepared and [T]sanctified; and there they *are*, before the altar of the LORD." 2 Chr. 28:24 • *consecrated*

Restoration of Temple Worship

20 Then King Hezekiah rose early, gathered the rulers of the city, and went up to the house of the LORD.

21 And they brought seven bulls, seven rams, seven lambs, and seven male goats for a [R]sin offering for the kingdom, for the sanctuary, and for Judah. Then he commanded the priests, the sons of Aaron, to offer *them* on the altar of the LORD. Lev. 4:3–14

22 So they killed the bulls, and the priests received the blood and [R]sprinkled *it* on the altar. Likewise they killed the rams and sprinkled the blood on the altar. They also killed the lambs and sprinkled the blood on the altar. Lev. 8:14, 15, 19, 24

23 Then they brought out the male goats *for* the sin offering before the king and the assembly, and they laid their [R]hands on them. Lev. 4:15, 24; 8:14

24 And the priests killed them; and they presented their blood on the altar as a sin offering [R]to make an atonement for all Israel, for the king commanded *that* the burnt offering and the sin offering *be made* for all Israel. Lev. 14:20

25 [R]And he stationed the Levites in the house of the LORD with cymbals, with stringed instruments, and with harps, according to the commandment of David, of Gad the king's seer, and of Nathan the prophet; for thus *was* the commandment of the LORD by His prophets. 1 Chr. 16:4; 25:6

29:1 *Abi*, 2 Kin. 18:2

26 The Levites stood with the instruments [R]of David, and the priests with [R]the trumpets. 1 Chr. 23:5 • 2 Chr. 5:12

27 Then Hezekiah commanded *them* to offer the burnt offering on the altar. And when the burnt offering began, the song of the LORD *also* began, with the trumpets and with the instruments of David king of Israel.

28 So all the assembly worshiped, the singers sang, and the trumpeters sounded; all *this continued* until the burnt offering was finished.

29 And when they had finished offering, [R]the king and all who were present with him bowed and worshiped. 2 Chr. 20:18

30 Moreover King Hezekiah and the leaders commanded the Levites to sing praise to the LORD with the words of David and of Asaph the seer. So they sang praises with gladness, and they bowed their heads and worshiped.

31 Then Hezekiah answered and said, "Now *that* you have consecrated yourselves to the LORD, come near, and bring sacrifices and thank offerings into the house of the LORD." So the assembly brought in sacrifices and thank offerings, and as many as were of a willing heart *brought* burnt offerings.

32 And the number of the burnt offerings which the assembly brought was seventy bulls, one hundred rams, *and* two hundred lambs; all these *were* for a burnt offering to the LORD.

33 The consecrated things *were* six hundred bulls and three thousand sheep.

34 But the priests were too few, so that they could not skin all the burnt offerings; therefore their brethren the Levites helped them until the work was ended and until the *other* priests had sanctified themselves, for the Levites were [R]more diligent in sanctifying themselves than the priests. Ps. 7:10

35 Also the burnt offerings *were* in abundance, with [R]the fat of the peace offerings and *with* the drink offerings for *every* burnt offering. So the service of the house of the LORD was set in order. Lev. 3:15, 16

36 Then Hezekiah and all the people rejoiced that God had prepared the people, since the events took place so suddenly.

CHAPTER 30

Celebration of the Passover

AND Hezekiah sent to all Israel and Judah, and also wrote letters to Ephraim and Manasseh, that they should come to the house of the LORD at Jerusalem, to keep the Passover to the LORD God of Israel.

2 For the king and his leaders and all the assembly in Jerusalem had agreed to keep the Passover in the second month.

3 For they could not keep it [R]at the regular time,* [R]because a sufficient number of priests had not consecrated themselves, nor had the people gathered together at Jerusalem. Ex. 12:6, 18 • 2 Chr. 29:17, 34

4 And the matter pleased the king and all the assembly.

5 So they resolved to make a proclamation throughout all Israel, from Beersheba to Dan, that they should come to keep the Passover to the LORD God of Israel at Jerusalem, since they had not done *it* for a long *time* in the *prescribed* manner.

6 Then the [R]runners went throughout all Israel and Judah with the letters from the king and his leaders, and spoke according to the command of the king: "Children of Israel, [R]return to the LORD God of Abraham, Isaac, and Israel; then He will return to the remnant of you who have escaped from the hand of the kings of Assyria. Esth. 8:14 • [Jer. 4:1]

7 "And do not be like your fathers and your brethren, who trespassed against the LORD God of their fathers, so that He gave them up to desolation, as you see.

8 "Now do not be [R]stiff-necked, as your fathers *were, but* yield yourselves to the LORD; and enter His sanctuary, which He has sanctified forever, and serve the LORD your God, [R]that the fierceness of His wrath may turn away from you. Ex. 32:9 • 2 Chr. 29:10

9 "For if you return to the LORD, your brethren and your children *will be treated* with [R]compassion by those who lead them captive, so that they may come back to this land; for the LORD your God *is* [R]gracious and merciful, and will not turn *His* face from you if you return to Him." Ps. 106:46 • [Ex. 34:6]

10 So the runners passed from city to city through the country of Ephraim and Manasseh, as far as Zebulun; but [R]they laughed at them and mocked them. 2 Chr. 36:16

11 Nevertheless [R]some from Asher, Manasseh, and Zebulun humbled themselves and came to Jerusalem. 2 Chr. 11:16

12 Also [R]the hand of God was on Judah to give them singleness of heart to obey the command of the king and the leaders, [R]at the word of the LORD. [Phil. 2:13] • 2 Chr. 29:25

13 Now many people, a very great assembly, gathered at Jerusalem to keep the Feast of Unleavened Bread in the second month.

14 They arose and took away the [R]altars that *were* in Jerusalem, and they took away all the incense altars and cast *them* into the Brook [R]Kidron. 2 Chr. 28:24 • 2 Chr. 29:16

15 Then they slaughtered the Passover *lambs* on the fourteenth *day* of the second month. The priests and the Levites [T]were [R]ashamed, and sanctified themselves, and brought the burnt offerings to the house of the LORD. *humbled themselves* • 2 Chr. 29:34

16 They stood in their place according to

30:3 The first month, Lev. 23:5; lit. *that time*

their custom, according to the Law of Moses
the man of God; the priests sprinkled the
blood *received* from the hand of the Levites.
17 For *there were* many in the assembly who
had not sanctified themselves; therefore the
Levites had charge of the slaughter of the
Passover *lambs* for everyone *who was* not
clean, to sanctify *them* to the LORD.
18 For a multitude of the people, [R]many
from Ephraim, Manasseh, Issachar, and Zeb-
ulun, had not cleansed themselves, [R]yet they
ate the Passover contrary to what was writ-
ten. But Hezekiah prayed for them, saying,
"May the good LORD provide atonement for
everyone 2 Chr. 30:1, 11, 25 • [Num. 9:10]
19 "*who* [R]prepares his heart to seek God, the
LORD God of his fathers, though *he is* not
cleansed according to the purification of the
sanctuary." 2 Chr. 19:3
20 And the LORD listened to Hezekiah and
healed the people.
21 So the children of Israel who were pres-
ent at Jerusalem kept [R]the Feast of Unleav-
ened Bread seven days with great gladness;
and the Levites and the priests praised the
LORD day by day, *singing* to the LORD, accom-
panied by loud instruments. Ex. 12:15; 13:6
22 And Hezekiah gave encouragement to all
the Levites [R]who taught the good knowledge
of the LORD; and they ate throughout the feast
seven days, offering peace offerings and
[R]making confession to the LORD God of their
fathers. 2 Chr. 17:9; 35:3 • Ezra 10:11

Extra Feast Days

23 Then the whole assembly agreed to keep
the feast another seven days, and they kept it
another seven days with gladness.
24 For Hezekiah king of Judah [R]gave to the
assembly a thousand bulls and seven thou-
sand sheep, and the leaders gave to the as-
sembly a thousand bulls and ten thousand
sheep; and a great number of priests [R]sancti-
fied themselves. 2 Chr. 35:7, 8 • 2 Chr. 29:34
25 The whole assembly of Judah rejoiced,
also the priests and Levites, all the assembly
that came from Israel, the sojourners [R]who
came from the land of Israel, and those who
dwelt in Judah. 2 Chr. 30:11, 18
26 So there was great joy in Jerusalem, for
since the time of [R]Solomon the son of David,
king of Israel, *there had* been nothing like this
in Jerusalem. 2 Chr. 7:8–10
27 Then the priests, the Levites, arose and
[R]blessed the people, and their voice was
heard; and their prayer came *up* to His holy
dwelling place, to heaven. Num. 6:23

CHAPTER 31

Destruction of the Idols—2 Kin. 18:4

NOW when all this was finished, all Israel
who were present went out to the cities
of Judah and [R]broke the sacred pillars in
pieces, cut down the wooden images, and
threw down the [T]high places and the altars—
from all Judah, Benjamin, Ephraim, and
Manasseh—until they had utterly destroyed
them all. Then all the children of Israel re-
turned to their own cities, every man to his
possession. 2 Kin. 18:4 • Places for pagan worship

Contribution for the Priests and Levites

2 And Hezekiah appointed [R]the divisions of
the priests and the Levites according to their
divisions, each man according to his service,
the priests and Levites for burnt offerings and
peace offerings, to serve, to give thanks, and
to praise in the gates of the camp* of the
LORD. 1 Chr. 23:6; 24:1
3 The king also *appointed* a portion of his
[R]possessions for the burnt offerings: for the
morning and evening burnt offerings, the
burnt offerings for the Sabbaths and the New
Moons and the set feasts, as *it is* written in the
Law of the LORD. 2 Chr. 35:7
4 Moreover he commanded the people who
dwelt in Jerusalem to contribute [R]support[T]
for the priests and the Levites, that they
might devote themselves to [R]the Law of the
LORD. Num. 18:8 • *the portion due* • Mal. 2:7
5 As soon as the commandment was circu-
lated, the children of Israel brought in abun-
dance [R]the firstfruits of grain and wine, oil
and honey, and of all the produce of the field;
and they brought in abundantly the [R]tithe of
everything. Ex. 22:29 • [Lev. 27:30]
6 And the children of Israel and Judah, who
dwelt in the cities of Judah, brought the tithe
of oxen and sheep; also the tithe of holy
things which were consecrated to the LORD
their God they laid in heaps.
7 In the third month they began laying
them in heaps, and they finished in the sev-
enth month.
8 And when Hezekiah and the leaders
came and saw the heaps, they blessed the
LORD and His people Israel.
9 Then Hezekiah questioned the priests
and the Levites concerning the heaps.
10 And Azariah the chief priest, from the
[R]house of Zadok, answered him and said,
"Since *the people* began to bring the offerings
into the house of the LORD, we have had
enough to eat and have plenty left, for the
LORD has blessed His people; and what is left
is this great abundance." 1 Chr. 6:8, 9

Reorganization of the Priests and Levites

11 Now Hezekiah commanded *them* to pre-
pare [R]rooms[T] in the house of the LORD, and
they prepared them. 1 Kin. 6:5–8 • *storerooms*
12 Then they faithfully brought in the offer-
ings, the tithes, and the dedicated things;

31:2 Temple

Cononiah the Levite had charge of them, and Shimei his brother *was* the next.

13 Jehiel, Azaziah, Nahath, Asahel, Jerimoth, Jozabad, Eliel, Ismachiah, Mahath, and Benaiah *were* overseers under the hand of Cononiah and Shimei his brother, at the commandment of Hezekiah the king and Azariah the ruler of the house of God.

14 Kore the son of Imnah the Levite, the keeper of the East Gate, *was* over the freewill offerings to God, to distribute the offerings of the LORD and the most holy things.

15 And under him *were* [R]Eden, Miniamin, Jeshua, Shemaiah, Amariah, and Shecaniah, *his* faithful assistants in [R]the cities of the priests, to distribute allotments to their brethren by divisions, to the great as well as the small. 2 Chr. 29:12 • Josh. 21:1–3, 9

16 Besides those males from three years old and up who were written in the genealogy, they distributed to everyone who entered the house of the LORD his daily portion for the work of his service, by his division,

17 and to the priests who were written in the genealogy according to their father's house, and to the Levites [R]from twenty years old and up according to their work, by their divisions, 1 Chr. 23:24, 27

18 and to all who were written in the genealogy—their little ones and their wives, their sons and daughters, the whole company of them—for in their faithfulness they sanctified themselves in holiness.

19 Also for the sons of Aaron the priests, *who were* in [R]the fields of the common-lands of their cities, in every single city, *there were* men who were designated by name to distribute portions to all the males among the priests and to all who were listed by genealogies among the Levites. Lev. 25:34

20 Thus Hezekiah did throughout all Judah, and he did what *was* good and right and true before the LORD his God.

21 And in every work that he began in the service of the house of God, in the law and in the commandment, to seek his God, he did *it* with all his heart. So he prospered.

CHAPTER 32

Invasion by Assyria
2 Kin. 18:17—19:37; Is. 36:2—37:38

AFTER [R]these deeds of faithfulness, Sennacherib king of Assyria came and entered Judah; he encamped against the fortified cities, thinking to win them over to himself. 2 Kin. 18:13—19:37

2 And when Hezekiah saw that Sennacherib had come, and that his purpose was to make war against Jerusalem,

3 he consulted with his leaders and commanders* to stop the water from the springs which *were* outside the city; and they helped him.

4 Thus many people gathered together who stopped all the [R]springs and the brook that ran through the land, saying, "Why should the kings* of Assyria come and find much water?" 2 Kin. 20:20

5 And [R]he strengthened himself, [R]built up all the wall that was broken, raised *it* up to the towers, and *built* another wall outside; also he repaired the Millo* *in* the City of David, and made weapons and shields in abundance. Is. 22:9, 10 • 2 Chr. 25:23

6 Then he set military captains over the people, gathered them together to him in the open square of the city gate, and [R]gave them encouragement, saying, 2 Chr. 30:22

7 [R]"Be strong and courageous; [R]do not be afraid nor dismayed before the king of Assyria, nor before all the multitude that *is* with him; for [R]*there are* more with us than with him. [Deut. 31:6] • 2 Chr. 20:15 • 2 Kin. 6:16

8 "With him *is* an [R]arm of flesh; but [R]with us *is* the LORD our God, to help us and to fight our battles." And the people were strengthened by the words of Hezekiah king of Judah. [Jer. 17:5] • [Rom. 8:31]

9 After this Sennacherib king of Assyria sent his servants to Jerusalem (but he and all the forces with him *laid siege* against Lachish), to Hezekiah king of Judah, and to all Judah who *were* in Jerusalem, saying,

10 [R]"Thus says Sennacherib king of Assyria: 'In what do you trust, that you remain under siege in Jerusalem? 2 Kin. 18:19

11 'Does not Hezekiah persuade you to give yourselves over to die by famine and by thirst, saying, [R]"The LORD our God will deliver us from the hand of the king of Assyria"? 2 Kin. 18:30

12 [R]'Has not the same Hezekiah taken away His high places and His altars, and commanded Judah and Jerusalem, saying, "You shall worship before one altar and burn incense on [R]it"? 2 Kin. 18:22 • 2 Chr. 31:1, 2

13 'Do you not know what I and my fathers have done to all the peoples of *other* lands? [R]Were the gods of the nations of those lands in any way able to deliver their lands out of my hand? 2 Kin. 18:33–35

14 'Who *was there* among all the gods of those nations that my fathers utterly destroyed that could deliver his people from my hand, that your God should be able to deliver you from my [R]hand? [Is. 10:5–12]

15 'Now therefore, [R]do not let Hezekiah deceive you or persuade you like this, and do not believe him; for no god of any nation or kingdom was able to deliver his people from my hand or the hand of my fathers. How much

32:3 Lit. *mighty men* **32:4** So with MT, Vg.; Arab., LXX, Syr. *king* **32:5** Lit. *The Landfill*

less will your God deliver you from my
hand?' " 2 Kin. 18:29
16 Furthermore, his servants spoke against
the LORD God and against His servant Hez-
ekiah.
17 He also wrote letters to revile the LORD
God of Israel, and to speak against Him, say-
ing, [R]"As the gods of the nations of *other* lands
have not delivered their people from my hand,
so the God of Hezekiah will not deliver His
people from my hand." 2 Kin. 19:9
18 Then they called out with a loud voice in
Hebrew* to the people of Jerusalem who *were*
on the wall, to frighten them and trouble
them, that they might take the city.
19 And they spoke against the God of Jeru-
salem, as against the gods of the people of the
earth—the work of men's hands.
20 [R]Now because of this King Hezekiah and
the prophet Isaiah, the son of Amoz, prayed
and cried out to heaven. 2 Kin. 19:15
21 [R]Then the LORD sent an angel who cut
down every mighty man of valor, leader, and
captain in the camp of the king of Assyria. So
he returned shamefaced to his own land. And
when he had gone into the temple of his god,
some of his own offspring struck him down
with the sword there. Zech. 14:3
22 Thus the LORD saved Hezekiah and the in-
habitants of Jerusalem from the hand of Sen-
nacherib the king of Assyria, and from the
hand of all *others*, and guided them* on every
side.

Restoration of Hezekiah 2 Kin. 20:1–11; Is. 38:1–8

23 And many brought gifts to the LORD at Je-
rusalem, and [R]presents to Hezekiah king of
Judah, so that he was exalted in the sight of
all nations thereafter. 2 Sam. 8:10
24 In those days Hezekiah was sick and near
death, and he prayed to the LORD; and He
spoke to him and gave him a sign.
25 But Hezekiah did not repay according to
the favor *shown* him, for his heart was lifted
up; therefore wrath was looming over him
and over Judah and Jerusalem.
26 [R]Then Hezekiah humbled himself for the
pride of his heart, he and the inhabitants of
Jerusalem, so that the wrath of the LORD did
not come upon them [R]in the days of Heze-
kiah. Jer. 26:18, 19 • 2 Kin. 20:19

Wealth of Hezekiah

27 Hezekiah had very great riches and
honor. And he made himself treasuries for sil-
ver, for gold, for precious stones, for spices, for
shields, and for all kinds of desirable items;
28 storehouses for the harvest of grain,
wine, and oil; and stalls for all kinds of live-
stock, and folds for flocks.*
29 Moreover he provided cities for himself,
and possessions of flocks and herds in abun-
dance; for [R]God had given him very much
property. 1 Chr. 29:12
30 [R]This same Hezekiah also stopped the
water outlet of Upper Gihon, and brought the
water by tunnel* to the west side of the City
of David. Hezekiah [R]prospered in all his
works. Is. 22:9–11 • 2 Chr. 31:21

Sin of Hezekiah—2 Kin. 20:12–19; Is. 39:1–8

31 However, *regarding* the ambassadors of
the princes of Babylon, whom they [R]sent to
him to inquire about the wonder that was
done in the land, God withdrew from him, in
order to [R]test him, that He might know all
that was in his heart. Is. 39:1 • [Deut. 8:2, 16]

Death of Hezekiah—2 Kin. 20:20, 21

32 Now the rest of the acts of Hezekiah, and
his goodness, indeed they *are* written in [R]the
vision of Isaiah the prophet, the son of Amoz,
and in the [R]book of the kings of Judah and Is-
rael. Is. 36—39 • 2 Kin. 18—20
33 [R]So Hezekiah rested with his fathers,
and they buried him in the upper tombs of
the sons of David; and all Judah and the in-
habitants of Jerusalem [R]honored him at his
death. Then Manasseh his son reigned in his
place. 2 Kin. 20:21 • Prov. 10:7

CHAPTER 33

The Reign of Manasseh—2 Kin. 21:1–9, 17, 18

MANASSEH [R]*was* twelve years old when
he became king, and he reigned fifty-
five years in Jerusalem. 2 Kin. 21:1–9
2 But he did evil in the sight of the LORD, ac-
cording to the [R]abominations of the nations
whom the LORD had cast out before the chil-
dren of Israel. 2 Chr. 28:3
3 For he rebuilt the high places which
Hezekiah his father had broken down; he
raised up altars for the Baals, and made
wooden images; and he worshiped all the host
of heaven* and served them.
4 He also built altars in the house of the
LORD, of which the LORD had said, [R]"In Jerusa-
lem shall My name be forever." 2 Chr. 6:6
5 And he built altars for all the host of
heaven [R]in the two courts of the house of the
LORD. 2 Chr. 4:9
6 Also he caused his sons to pass through
the fire in the Valley of the Son of Hinnom; he
practiced soothsaying, used witchcraft and
sorcery, and consulted mediums and spirit-
ists. He did much evil in the sight of the LORD,
to provoke Him to anger.
7 He even set a carved image, the idol

32:18 Lit. *Judean* **32:22** LXX *gave them rest;* Vg. *gave them treasures* **32:28** So with LXX, Vg.; Arab., Syr. omit *folds for flocks;* MT *flocks for sheepfolds*
32:30 Lit. *brought it straight to* (cf. 2 Kin. 20:20)
33:3 The gods of the Assyrians

which he had made, in the house of God, of which God had said to David and to Solomon his son, "In this house and in Jerusalem, which I have chosen out of all the tribes of Israel, I will put My name forever;

8 "and I will not again remove the foot of Israel from the land which I have appointed for your fathers—only if they are careful to do all that I have commanded them, according to the whole law and the statutes and the ordinances by the hand of Moses."

9 So Manasseh seduced Judah and the inhabitants of Jerusalem to do more evil than the nations whom the LORD had destroyed before the children of Israel.

10 And the LORD spoke to Manasseh and his people, but they would not listen.

11 [R]Therefore the LORD brought upon them the captains of the army of the king of Assyria, who took Manasseh with hooks,* [R]bound him with bronze *fetters,* and carried him off to Babylon. Deut. 28:36 • 2 Chr. 36:6

12 Now when he was in affliction, he implored the LORD his God, and humbled himself greatly before the God of his fathers,

13 and prayed to Him; and He [R]received his entreaty, heard his supplication, and brought him back to Jerusalem into his kingdom. Then Manasseh [R]knew that the LORD *was* God. Ezra 8:23 • Dan. 4:25

14 After this he built a wall outside the City of David on the west side of Gihon, in the valley, as far as the entrance of the Fish Gate; and *it* enclosed Ophel, and he raised it to a very great height. Then he put military captains in all the fortified cities of Judah.

15 He took away [R]the foreign gods and the idol from the house of the LORD, and all the altars that he had built in the mount of the house of the LORD and in Jerusalem; and he cast *them* out of the city. 2 Chr. 33:3, 5, 7

16 He also repaired the altar of the LORD, sacrificed peace offerings and [R]thank offerings on it, and commanded Judah to serve the LORD God of Israel. Lev. 7:12

17 [R]Nevertheless the people still sacrificed on the [T]high places, *but* only to the LORD their God. 2 Chr. 32:12 • Places for pagan worship

18 Now the rest of the acts of Manasseh, his prayer to his God, and the words of [R]the seers who spoke to him in the name of the LORD God of Israel, indeed they *are written* in the book* of the kings of Israel. 1 Sam. 9:9

19 Also his prayer and *how God* received his entreaty, and all his sin and trespass, and the sites where he built high places and set up wooden images and carved images, before he was humbled, indeed they *are* written among the sayings of Hozai.*

20 So Manasseh rested with his fathers, and they buried him in his own house. Then his son Amon reigned in his place.

The Reign of Amon—2 Kin. 21:19–26

21 [R]Amon *was* twenty-two years old when he became king, and he reigned two years in Jerusalem. 2 Kin. 21:19–24

22 But he did evil in the sight of the LORD, as his father Manasseh had done; for Amon sacrificed to all the carved images which his father Manasseh had made, and served them.

23 And he did not humble himself before the LORD, [R]as his father Manasseh had humbled himself; but Amon trespassed more and more. 2 Chr. 33:12, 19

24 Then his servants conspired against him, and killed him in his own house.

25 But the people of the land executed all those who had conspired against King Amon. Then the people of the land made his son Josiah king in his place.

CHAPTER 34

Evaluation of Josiah—2 Kin. 22:1, 2

JOSIAH [R]*was* eight years old when he became king, and he reigned thirty-one years in Jerusalem. 2 Kin. 22:1, 2

2 And he did *what was* right in the sight of the LORD, and walked in the ways of his father David; *he* did *not* turn aside to the right hand or to the left.

Early Reforms of Josiah

3 For in the eighth year of his reign, while he was still young, he began to seek the God of his father David; and in the twelfth year he began to purge Judah and Jerusalem of the high places, the wooden images, the carved images, and the molded images.

4 They broke down the altars of the Baals in his presence, and the incense altars which *were* above them he cut down; and the wooden images, the carved images, and the molded images he broke in pieces, and made dust of them and scattered *it* on the graves of those who had sacrificed to them.

5 He also [R]burned the bones of the priests on their [R]altars, and cleansed Judah and Jerusalem. 1 Kin. 13:2 • 2 Kin. 23:20

6 And *so he did* in the cities of Manasseh, Ephraim, and Simeon, as far as Naphtali and all around, with [T]axes.* Lit. *swords*

7 When he had broken down the altars and the wooden images, had [R]beaten the carved images into powder, and cut down all the incense altars throughout all the land of Israel, he returned to Jerusalem. Deut. 9:21

Repair of the Temple—2 Kin. 22:3–7

8 [R]In the eighteenth year of his reign, when he had purged the land and the temple,* he

33:11 Nose hooks, 2 Kin. 19:28 **33:18** Lit. *words* **33:19** LXX *the seers* **34:6** Lit. *swords* **34:8** Lit. *house*

sent Shaphan the son of Azaliah, Maaseiah
the governor of the city, and Joah the son of
Joahaz the recorder, to repair the house of the
LORD his God. 2 Kin. 22:3–20
9 When they came to Hilkiah the high
priest, they delivered [R]the money that was
brought into the house of God, which the
Levites who kept the doors had gathered from
the hand of Manasseh and Ephraim, from all
the remnant of Israel, from all Judah and Ben-
jamin, and *which* they had brought back to Je-
rusalem. 2 Kin. 12:4
10 Then they put *it* in the hand of the fore-
men who had the oversight of the house of the
LORD; and they gave it to the workmen who
worked in the house of the LORD, to repair and
restore the house.
11 They gave *it* to the craftsmen and
builders to buy hewn stone and timber for
beams, and to floor the houses which the
kings of Judah had destroyed.
12 And the men did the work faithfully.
Their overseers *were* Jahath and Obadiah the
Levites, of the sons of Merari, and Zechariah
and Meshullam, of the sons of the Kohath-
ites, to supervise. *Others of* the Levites, all of
whom were skillful with instruments of
music,
13 *were* over the burden bearers and *were*
overseers of all who did work in any kind of
service. And *some* of the Levites *were* scribes,
officers, and gatekeepers.

Discovery of the Law—2 Kin. 22:8—23:20

14 Now when they brought out the money
that was brought into the house of the LORD,
Hilkiah the priest [R]found the Book of the Law
of the LORD *given* by Moses. 2 Kin. 22:8
15 Then Hilkiah answered and said to
Shaphan the scribe, "I have found the Book of
the Law in the house of the LORD." And
Hilkiah gave the book to Shaphan.
16 So Shaphan carried the book to the king,
bringing the king word, saying, "All that was
committed to your servants they are doing.
17 "And they have [T]gathered the money that
was found in the house of the LORD, and have
delivered it into the hand of the overseers and
the workmen." Lit. *poured out*
18 Then Shaphan the scribe told the king,
saying, "Hilkiah the priest has given me a
book." And Shaphan read it before the king.
19 Thus it happened, when the king heard
the words of the Law, that he tore his clothes.
20 Then the king commanded Hilkiah,
[R]Ahikam the son of Shaphan, Abdon* the son
of Micah, Shaphan the scribe, and Asaiah a
servant of the king, saying, Jer. 26:24
21 "Go, inquire of the LORD for me, and for
those who are left in Israel and Judah, con-
cerning the words of the book that is found;
for great *is* the wrath of the LORD that is
poured out on us, because our fathers have
not kept the word of the LORD, to do according
to all that is written in this book."
22 So Hilkiah and those the king *had ap-
pointed* went to Huldah the prophetess, the
wife of Shallum the son of Tokhath,* the son
of Hasrah,* keeper of the wardrobe. (She
dwelt in Jerusalem in the Second Quarter.)
And they spoke to her to that *effect*.
23 Then she answered them, "Thus says the
LORD God of Israel, 'Tell the man who sent
you to Me,
24 "Thus says the LORD: 'Behold, I will
[R]bring calamity on this place and on its in-
habitants, all the curses that are written in the
[R]book which they have read before the king of
Judah, 2 Chr. 36:14–20 • Deut. 28:15–68
25 'because they have forsaken Me and
burned incense to other gods, that they might
provoke Me to anger with all the works of
their hands. Therefore My wrath will be
poured out on this place, and not be
quenched.' " '
26 "But as for the king of Judah, who sent
you to inquire of the LORD, in this manner you
shall speak to him, 'Thus says the LORD God
of Israel: "*Concerning* the words which you
have heard—
27 "because your heart was tender, and you
humbled yourself before God when you heard
His words against this place and against its
inhabitants, and you humbled yourself before
Me, and you tore your clothes and wept be-
fore Me, I also have heard *you*," says the
[R]LORD. 2 Chr. 12:7; 30:6
28 "Surely I will gather you to your fathers,
and you shall be gathered to your grave in
peace; and your eyes shall not see all the
calamity which I will bring on this place and
its inhabitants." ' " So they brought back word
to the king.
29 Then the king sent and gathered all the
elders of Judah and Jerusalem.
30 The king went up to the house of the
LORD, with all the men of Judah and the in-
habitants of Jerusalem—the priests and the
Levites, and all the people, great and small.
And he [R]read in their hearing all the words of
the Book of the Covenant which had been
found in the house of the LORD. Neh. 8:1–3
31 Then the king [R]stood in [R]his place and
made a covenant before the LORD, to follow
the LORD, and to keep His commandments
and His testimonies and His statutes with all
his heart and all his soul, to perform the
words of the covenant that were written in
this book. 2 Chr. 6:13 • 2 Kin. 11:14; 23:3
32 And he made all who were present in Je-
rusalem and Benjamin take a stand. So the in-
habitants of Jerusalem did according to the
covenant of God, the God of their fathers.

34:20 *Achbor the son of Michaiah,* 2 Kin. 22:12
34:22 *Tikvah,* 2 Kin. 22:14 • *Harhas,* 2 Kin. 22:14

33 Thus Josiah removed all the abomina-
tions from all the country that *belonged* to the
children of Israel, and made all who were
present in Israel diligently serve the LORD
their God. All his days they did not depart
from following the LORD God of their fathers.

CHAPTER 35

Celebration of the Passover—2 Kin. 23:21–23

NOW [R]Josiah kept a Passover to the LORD
in Jerusalem, and they slaughtered the
Passover *lambs* on the [R]fourteenth *day* of the
first month. 2 Kin. 23:21, 22 • Ex. 12:6
2 And he set the priests in their [R]duties and
[R]encouraged them for the service of the house
of the LORD. 2 Chr. 23:18 • 2 Chr. 29:5–15
3 Then he said to the Levites [R]who taught
all Israel, who were holy to the LORD: [R]"Put
the holy ark in the house which Solomon the
son of David, king of Israel, built. *It shall* no
longer *be* a burden on *your* shoulders. Now
serve the LORD your God and His people Is-
rael. Deut. 33:10 • 2 Chr. 34:14
4 "Prepare *yourselves* [R]according to your
fathers' houses, according to your divisions,
following the written instruction of David
king of Israel and the [R]written instruction of
Solomon his son. 1 Chr. 9:10–13 • 2 Chr. 8:14
5 "And stand in the holy *place* according to
the divisions of the fathers' houses of your
brethren the *lay* people, and *according to* the
division of the father's house of the Levites.
6 "So slaughter the Passover *offerings*,
[R]consecrate yourselves, and prepare *them*
for your brethren, that *they* may do accord-
ing to the word of the LORD by the hand of
Moses." 2 Chr. 29:5, 15
7 Then Josiah [R]gave the *lay* people lambs
and young goats from the flock, all for
Passover *offerings* for all who were present, to
the number of thirty thousand, as well as
three thousand cattle; these *were* from the
king's [R]possessions. 2 Chr. 30:24 • 2 Chr. 31:3
8 And his leaders gave willingly to the peo-
ple, to the priests, and to the Levites. Hilkiah,
Zechariah, and Jehiel, rulers of the house of
God, gave to the priests for the Passover *offer-
ings* two thousand six hundred *from the flock*,
and three hundred cattle.
9 Also Conaniah, his brothers Shemaiah
and Nethanel, and Hashabiah and Jeiel and
Jozabad, chief of the Levites, gave to the
Levites for Passover *offerings* five thousand
from the flock and five hundred cattle.
10 So the service was prepared, and the
priests [R]stood in their places, and the Levites
in their divisions, according to the king's com-
mand. Ezra 6:18
11 And they slaughtered the Passover *offer-
ings;* and the priests [R]sprinkled *the blood* with
their hands, while the Levites [R]skinned *the
animals*. 2 Chr. 29:22 • 2 Chr. 29:34
12 Then they removed the burnt offerings
that *they* might give them to the divisions of
the fathers' houses of the *lay* people, to offer
to the LORD, as *it is* written in the Book of Mo-
ses. And so *they did* with the cattle.
13 Also they roasted the Passover *offerings*
with fire according to the ordinance; but the
other holy *offerings* they boiled in pots, in cal-
drons, and in pans, and divided *them* quickly
among all the *lay* people.
14 Then afterward they prepared portions
for themselves and for the priests, because the
priests, the sons of Aaron, *were busy* in of-
fering burnt offerings and fat until night;
therefore the Levites prepared portions for
themselves and for the priests, the sons of
Aaron.
15 And the singers, the sons of Asaph, *were*
in their places, according to the command of
David, Asaph, Heman, and Jeduthun the
king's seer. Also the gatekeepers were at each
gate; they did not have to leave their position,
because their brethren the Levites prepared
portions for them.
16 So all the service of the LORD was pre-
pared the same day, to keep the Passover and
to offer burnt offerings on the altar of the
LORD, according to the command of King
Josiah.
17 And the children of Israel who were pres-
ent kept the Passover at that time, and the
Feast of Unleavened Bread for seven days.
18 [R]There had been no Passover kept in Is-
rael like that since the days of Samuel the
prophet; and none of the kings of Israel had
kept such a Passover as Josiah kept, with the
priests and the Levites, all Judah and Israel
who were present, and the inhabitants of Je-
rusalem. 2 Kin. 23:22, 23
19 In the eighteenth year of the reign of
Josiah this Passover was kept.

Death of Josiah—2 Kin. 23:28–30

20 After all this, when Josiah had prepared
the temple, Necho king of Egypt came up to
fight against Carchemish by the Euphrates;
and Josiah went out against him.
21 But he sent messengers to him, saying,
"What have I to do with you, king of Judah? *I
have* not *come* against you this day, but
against the house with which I have war; for
God commanded me to make haste. Refrain
from meddling with God, who *is* with me, lest
He destroy you."
22 Nevertheless Josiah would not turn his
face from him, but disguised himself so that
he might fight with him, and did not heed the
words of Necho from the mouth of God. So he
came to fight in the Valley of Megiddo.
23 And the archers shot King Josiah; and the
king said to his servants, "Take me away, for I
am severely wounded."
24 His servants therefore took him out of

that chariot and put him in the second chariot
that he had, and they brought him to Jerusa-
lem. So he died, and was buried in *one of* the
tombs of his fathers. And all Judah and Jeru-
salem mourned for Josiah.
25 Jeremiah also [R]lamented for [R]Josiah. And
to this day [R]all the singing men and the
singing women speak of Josiah in their
lamentations. They made it a custom in Is-
rael; and indeed they *are* written in the
Laments. Lam. 4:20 • Jer. 22:10, 11 • Matt. 9:23
26 Now the rest of the acts of Josiah and his
goodness, according to *what was* written in
the Law of the LORD,
27 and his deeds from first to last, indeed
they *are* written in the book of the kings of Is-
rael and Judah.

CHAPTER 36

The Reign of Jehoahaz—2 Kin. 23:30–33

THEN the people of the land took Jehoahaz
the son of Josiah, and made him king in
his father's place in Jerusalem.
2 Jehoahaz* *was* twenty-three years old
when he became king, and he reigned three
months in Jerusalem.
3 Now the king of Egypt deposed him at Je-
rusalem; and he imposed on the land a tribute
of one hundred talents of silver and a talent of
gold.

The Reign of Jehoiakim—2 Kin. 23:24—24:6

4 Then the king of Egypt made *Jehoahaz's**
brother Eliakim king over Judah and Jerusa-
lem, and changed his name to Jehoiakim. And
Necho took Jehoahaz* his brother and carried
him off to Egypt.
5 [R]Jehoiakim *was* twenty-five years old
when he became king, and he reigned eleven
years in Jerusalem. And he did evil in the
sight of the LORD his God. 2 Kin. 23:36, 37
6 Nebuchadnezzar king of Babylon came
up against him, and bound him in [T]bronze *fet-
ters* to carry him off to Babylon. *chains*
7 [R]Nebuchadnezzar also carried off *some*
of the articles from the house of the LORD to
Babylon, and put them in his temple at Bab-
ylon. Dan. 1:1, 2
8 Now the rest of the acts of Jehoiakim, the
abominations which he did, and what was
found against him, indeed they *are* written in
the book of the kings of Israel and Judah.
Then [T]Jehoiachin his son reigned in his
place. Or *Jeconiah*

The Reign of Jehoiachin
2 Kin. 24:8–17; Jer. 37:1

9 [R]Jehoiachin *was* eight* years old when he
became king, and he reigned in Jerusalem
three months and ten days. And he did evil in
the sight of the LORD. 2 Kin. 24:8–17
10 At the turn of the year [R]King Nebuchad-
nezzar summoned *him* and took him to Bab-
ylon, [R]with the costly articles from the house
of the LORD, and made [R]Zedekiah, *Je-
hoiakim's** brother, king over Judah and Jeru-
salem. 2 Kin. 24:10–17 • Dan. 1:1, 2 • Jer. 37:1

Evaluation of Zedekiah
2 Kin. 24:18, 19; Jer. 52:1, 2

11 [R]Zedekiah *was* twenty-one years old
when he became king, and he reigned eleven
years in Jerusalem. Jer. 52:1
12 He did evil in the sight of the LORD his
God, *and* [R]did not humble himself before
Jeremiah the prophet, *who spoke* from the
mouth of the LORD. Jer. 21:3–7; 44:10

Destruction of Jerusalem
2 Kin. 24:20—25:21; Jer. 52:3–27

13 And he also [R]rebelled against King Nebu-
chadnezzar, who had made him swear *an
oath* by God; but he [R]stiffened his neck and
hardened his heart against turning to the
LORD God of Israel. Ezek. 17:15 • 2 Kin. 17:14
14 Moreover all the leaders of the priests
and the people transgressed more and more,
according to all the abominations of the na-
tions, and defiled the house of the LORD which
He had consecrated in Jerusalem.
15 [R]And the LORD God of their fathers sent
warnings to them by His messengers, rising
up early and sending *them,* because He had
compassion on His people and on His
dwelling place. Jer. 7:13; 25:3, 4
16 But [R]they mocked the messengers of
God, [R]despised His words, and [R]scoffed at
His prophets, until the wrath of the LORD
arose against His people, till *there was* no
remedy. Jer. 5:12, 13 • [Prov. 1:24–32] • Jer. 38:6
17 Therefore He brought against them the
king of the Chaldeans, who killed their young
men with the sword in the house of their sanc-
tuary, and had no compassion on young man
or virgin, on the aged or the weak; He gave
them all into his hand.
18 [R]And all the articles from the house of
God, great and small, the treasures of the
house of the LORD, and the treasures of the
king and of his leaders, all *these* he took to
Babylon. 2 Kin. 25:13–15
19 [R]Then they burned the house of God,
broke down the wall of Jerusalem, burned all
its palaces with fire, and destroyed all its pre-
cious possessions. 2 Kin. 25:9
20 And [R]those who escaped from the sword
he carried away to Babylon, where they be-
came servants to him and his sons until the
rule of the kingdom of Persia, 2 Kin. 25:11
21 to fulfill the word of the LORD by the
mouth of [R]Jeremiah, until the land [R]had

36:2 MT *Joahaz* **36:4** Lit. *his* • MT *Joahaz*
36:9 Heb. mss., LXX, Syr., *eighteen* and 2 Kin. 24:8
36:10 Lit. *his brother,* 2 Kin. 24:17

enjoyed her Sabbaths. As long as she lay
desolate she kept Sabbath, to fulfill seventy
years. Jer. 25:9–12; 27:6–8; 29:10 • Lev. 26:34–43

The Proclamation by Cyrus to Return to Jerusalem—Ezra 1:1–3

22 [R]Now in the first year of Cyrus king of
Persia, that the word of the LORD by the mouth
of [R]Jeremiah might be fulfilled, the LORD
stirred up the spirit of Cyrus king of Persia, so
that he made a proclamation throughout all
his kingdom, and also *put it* in writing, say-
ing, Ezra 1:1–3 • Jer. 29:10

23 [R]Thus says Cyrus king of Persia: All the
kingdoms of the earth the LORD God of
heaven has given me. And He has
commanded me to build Him a [T]house at
Jerusalem which is in Judah. Who *is*
among you of all His people? May the
LORD his God *be* with him, and let him
go up! Ezra 1:2, 3 • Temple

THE BOOK OF
EZRA

THE BOOK OF EZRA

Ezra continues the Old Testament narrative of 2 Chronicles by showing how God fulfills His promise to return His people to the land of promise after seventy years of exile. Israel's "second exodus," this one from Babylon, is less impressive than the return from Egypt because only a remnant chooses to leave Babylon.

Ezra relates the story of two returns from Babylon—the first led by Zerubbabel to rebuild the temple (1—6) and the second under the leadership of Ezra to rebuild the spiritual condition of the people (7—10). Sandwiched between these two accounts is a gap of nearly six decades, during which Esther lives and rules as queen in Persia.

Ezra is the Aramaic form of the Hebrew word *ezer*, "help," and perhaps means "Yahweh helps." Ezra and Nehemiah were originally bound together as one book because Chronicles, Ezra, and Nehemiah were viewed as one continuous history. The Septuagint, a Greek-language version of the Old Testament translated in the third century B.C., calls Ezra-Nehemiah, *Esdras Deuteron,* "Second Esdras." First Esdras is the name of the apocryphal book of Esdras. The Latin title is *Liber Primus Esdrae,* "First Book of Ezra." In the Latin Bible, Ezra is called 1 Ezra and Nehemiah is called 2 Ezra.

THE AUTHOR OF EZRA

Although Ezra is not specifically mentioned as the author, he is certainly the best candidate. Jewish tradition (the Talmud) attributes the book to Ezra; and portions of the book (7:28—9:15) are written in the first person, from Ezra's point of view. The vividness of the details and descriptions favors an author who was an eyewitness of the later events of the book. As in Chronicles, there is a strong priestly emphasis, and Ezra was a direct priestly descendant of Aaron through Eleazar, Phinehas, and Zadok (7:1–5). He studied, practiced, and taught the law of the Lord as an educated scribe (7:1–12). Also, according to 2 Maccabees 2:13–15, he had access to the library of written documents gathered by Nehemiah. Ezra no doubt used this material in writing Ezra 1—6 as he did in writing Chronicles. Some think that Ezra composed Nehemiah as well by making use of Nehemiah's personal diary.

Ezra was a godly man marked by strong trust in the Lord, moral integrity, and grief over sin. He was a contemporary of Nehemiah (Neh. 8:1–9; 12:36) who arrived in Jerusalem in 444 B.C. Tradition holds that Ezra was the founder of the Great Synagogue where the canon of Old Testament Scripture was settled. Another tradition says that he collected the biblical books into a unit and that he originated the synagogue form of worship.

Ezra wrote this book probably between 457 B.C. (the events of Ezra 7—10) and 444 B.C. (Nehemiah's arrival in Jerusalem). During the period covered by the Book of Ezra, Gautama Buddha (c. 560–480 B.C.) is in India, Confucius (551–479 B.C.) is in China, and Socrates (470–399 B.C.) is in Greece.

THE TIME OF EZRA

The following table shows the chronological relationship of the books of Ezra, Nehemiah, and Esther:

538–515 B.C.	483–473 B.C.
Zerubbabel	Esther
Ezra 1—6	Book of Esther
First Return	—

457 B.C.	444–c. 425 B.C.
Ezra	Nehemiah
Ezra 7—10	Book of Nehemiah
Second Return	Third Return

These books fit against the background of these Persian kings

Cyrus	(559–530 B.C.)
Cambyses	(530–522 B.C.)
Smerdis	(522 B.C.)
Darius I	(521–486 B.C.)
Ahasuerus	(486–464 B.C.)
Artaxerxes I	(464–423 B.C.)
Darius II	(423–404 B.C.)

Cyrus the Persian overthrows Babylon in October 539 B.C. and issues his decree allowing the Jews to return in 538 B.C. The temple is begun in 536 B.C. The exile lasts only fifty years after 586 B.C., but the seventy-year figure for the captivity is taken from a beginning date of 606 B.C. when the first deportation to Babylon takes place. The rebuilding of the temple is discontinued in 534 B.C., resumed in 520 B.C., and completed in 515 B.C. It is begun under Cyrus and finished under Darius I. The two intervening kings, Cambyses and Smerdis, are not mentioned in any of these books. The prophets Haggai and Zechariah minister during Zerubbabel's time, about 520 B.C. and following years. Esther's story fits entirely in the reign of Xerxes, and Ezra ministers during the reign of Artaxerxes I, as does Nehemiah. There were three waves of deportation to Babylon (606, 597, and 586 B.C.) and three returns from Babylon: 538 B.C. (Zerubbabel), 457 B.C. (Ezra), and 444 B.C. (Nehemiah).

THE CHRIST OF EZRA

Ezra reveals God's continued fulfillment of His promise to keep David's descendants alive. Zerubbabel himself is part of the messianic line as the grandson of Jeconiah (Jehoiachin, 1 Chr. 3:17–19; see Matt. 1:12, 13). There is a positive note of hope in Ezra and Nehemiah because the remnant has returned to the land of promise. In this land the messianic promises will be fulfilled, because they are connected with such places as Bethlehem, Jerusalem, and Zion. Christ will be born in Bethlehem (Mic. 5:2), not in Babylon.

The Book of Ezra as a whole also typifies Christ's work of forgiveness and restoration.

KEYS TO EZRA

Key Word: Temple—The basic theme of Ezra is the restoration of the temple and the spiritual, moral, and social restoration of the returned remnant in Jerusalem under the leadership of Zerubbabel and Ezra. Israel's worship is revitalized and the people are purified. God's faithfulness is seen in the way He sovereignly protects His people through a powerful empire while they are in captivity. They prosper in their exile, and God raises up pagan kings who are sympathetic to their cause and encourage them to rebuild their homeland. God also provides zealous and capable spiritual leaders who direct the return and the rebuilding. He keeps His promise: "I will be found by you, says the LORD, and I will bring you back from your captivity; I will gather you from all the nations and from all the places where I have driven you, says the LORD, and I will bring you to the place from which I cause you to be carried away captive" (Jer. 29:14).

Key Verses: Ezra 1:3; 7:10—"Who *is there* among you of all His people? May his God be with him, and let him go up to Jerusalem which *is* in Judah, and build the house of the LORD God of Israel (He *is* God), which *is* in Jerusalem" (1:3).

"For Ezra had prepared his heart to seek the Law of the LORD, and to do *it*, and to teach statutes and ordinances in Israel" (7:10).

Key Chapter: Ezra 6—Ezra 6 records the completion and dedication of the temple, which stimulates the obedience of the remnant to keep the Passover and separate themselves from the "filth of the nations of the land" (6:21).

SURVEY OF EZRA

Ezra continues the story exactly where 2 Chronicles ends and shows how God's promise to bring His people back to their land is fulfilled (Jer. 29:10–14). God is with these people; and although their days of glory seem over, their spiritual heritage still remains and God's rich promises will be fulfilled. Ezra relates the story of the first two returns from Babylon, the first led by Zerubbabel and the second led decades later by Ezra. Its two divisions are the restoration of the temple (1—6) and the reformation of the people (7—10), and they are separated by a fifty-eight-year gap during which the story of Esther takes place.

The Restoration of the Temple (1—6): King Cyrus of Persia overthrows Babylon in 539 B.C. and issues a decree in 538 B.C. that allows the exiled Jews to return to their homeland. Isaiah prophesied two centuries before that the

FOCUS	RESTORATION OF THE TEMPLE		REFORMATION OF THE PEOPLE	
REFERENCE	1:1——3:1——		7:1——9:1——10:44	
DIVISION	FIRST RETURN TO JERUSALEM	CONSTRUCTION OF THE TEMPLE	SECOND RETURN TO JERUSALEM	RESTORATION OF THE PEOPLE
TOPIC	ZERUBBABEL		EZRA	
	FIRST RETURN OF 49,897		SECOND RETURN OF 1,754	
LOCATION	PERSIA TO JERUSALEM		PERSIA TO JERUSALEM	
TIME	22 YEARS (538–516 B.C.)		1 YEAR (458–457 B.C.)	

temple would be rebuilt and actually named Cyrus as the one who would bring it about (Is. 44:28—45:4). Cyrus may have read and responded to this passage.

Out of a total Jewish population of perhaps 2 or 3 million, only 49,897 choose to take advantage of this offer. Only the most committed are willing to leave a life of relative comfort in Babylon, endure a trek of nine hundred miles, and face further hardship by rebuilding a destroyed temple and city. Zerubbabel, a "prince" of Judah (a direct descendant of King David), leads the faithful remnant back to Jerusalem. Those who return are from the tribes of Judah, Benjamin, and Levi; but it is evident that representatives from the other ten tribes eventually return as well. The ten "lost tribes" are not entirely lost.

Zerubbabel's priorities are in the right place: he first restores the altar and the religious feasts before beginning work on the temple itself. The foundation of the temple is laid in 536 B.C., but opposition arises and the work ceases from 534 to 520 B.C. While Ezra 4:1–5, 24 concerns Zerubbabel, 4:6–23 concerns opposition to the building of the wall of Jerusalem some time between 464 and 444 B.C. These verses may have been placed here to illustrate the antagonism to the work of rebuilding. The prophets Haggai and Zechariah exhort the people to get back to building the temple (5:1, 2), and the work begins again under Zerubbabel and Joshua the high priest. Tattenai, a Persian governor, protests to King Darius I about the temple building and challenges their authority to continue. King Darius finds the decree of Cyrus and confirms it, even forcing Tattenai to provide whatever is needed to complete the work. It is finished in 515 B.C.

The Reformation of the People (7—10): A smaller return under Ezra takes place in 457 B.C., eighty-one years after the first return under Zerubbabel. Ezra the priest is given authority by King Artaxerxes I to bring people and contributions for the temple in Jerusalem. God protects this band of less than two thousand men and they safely reach Jerusalem with their valuable gifts from Persia. Many priests but few Levites return with Zerubbabel and Ezra (2:36–42; 8:15–19). God uses Ezra to rebuild the people spiritually and morally. When Ezra discovers that the people and the priests have intermarried with foreign women, he identifies with the sin of his people and offers a great intercessory prayer on their behalf. During the gap of fifty-eight years between Ezra 6 and 7, the people fall into a confused spiritual state and Ezra is alarmed. They quickly respond to Ezra's confession and weeping by making a covenant to put away their foreign wives and to live in accordance with God's law. This confession and response to the Word of God brings about a great revival and changes lives.

OUTLINE OF EZRA

Part One: The Restoration of the Temple of God (1:1—6:22)

I. The First Return to Jerusalem Under Zerubbabel .... 1:1—2:70

A. Decree of Cyrus 1:1–4
B. Gifts from Israel and Cyrus 1:5–11
C. Census of the Returning People 2:1–63
1. The People of Known Descent 2:1–58
2. The People of Unknown Descent ... 2:59–63
D. The Return Completed 2:64–70
1. The People Who Returned 2:64–67
2. The Gifts the People Gave 2:68–70

II. The Construction of the Temple .... 3:1—6:22

A. Construction of the Temple Foundation 3:1–13
1. Spiritual Preparation of the People ... 3:1–6
2. Completion of the Temple Foundation 3:7–13
B. Interruption of the Temple Construction 4:1–24
1. Present Opposition Under Cyrus 4:1–5
2. Later Opposition Under Ahasuerus 4:6
3. Later Opposition Under Artaxerxes 4:7–23
4. Present Interruption of Construction Under Darius 4:24
C. Completion of the Temple .... 5:1—6:18
1. Resumption of the Temple Construction 5:1, 2
2. Opposition to the Construction 5:3–17
3. Confirmation of the Temple Construction 6:1–12
4. Completion of the Temple 6:13–15
5. Dedication of the Temple 6:16–18
D. Celebration of the Passover 6:19–22

Part Two: The Reformation of the People of God (7:1—10:44)

I. The Second Return to Jerusalem Under Ezra .... 7:1—8:36

A. The Decree of Artaxerxes 7:1–28
1. Ezra's Qualifications 7:1–10
2. Artaxerxes' Letter 7:11–26
3. Ezra's Response 7:27, 28
B. Census of the Returning Israelites 8:1–14
C. Spiritual Preparation for the Return .. 8:15–23
1. Acquisition of Temple Leadership 8:15–20

CHAPTER 1

Decree of Cyrus—2 Chr. 36:22, 23

NOW in the first year of Cyrus king of Persia, that the word of the LORD [R]by the mouth of Jeremiah might be fulfilled, the LORD stirred up the spirit of Cyrus king of Persia, [R]so that he made a proclamation throughout all his kingdom, and also *put it* in writing, saying, 2 Chr. 36:22, 23 • Ezra 5:13, 14

2 Thus says Cyrus king of Persia: All the
kingdoms of the earth the LORD God of
heaven has given me. And He has
[R]commanded me to build Him a house at
Jerusalem which *is* in Judah. Is. 44:28
3 Who *is* among you of all His people? May
his God be with him, and let him go up to
Jerusalem which *is* in Judah, and build
the house of the LORD God of Israel [R](He
is God), which *is* in Jerusalem. Dan. 6:26
4 And whoever is left in any place where he
dwells, let the men of his place help him
with silver and gold, with goods and
livestock, besides the freewill offerings for
the house of God which *is* in Jerusalem.

Gifts from Israel and Cyrus

5 Then the heads of the fathers' *houses* of Judah and Benjamin, and the priests and the Levites, with all whose spirits God had moved, arose to go up and build the house of the LORD which *is* in Jerusalem.

6 And all those who *were* around them [T]encouraged them with articles of silver and gold, with goods and livestock, and with precious things, besides all *that* was [R]willingly offered. Lit. *strengthened their hands* • Ezra 2:68

7 King Cyrus also brought out the articles of the house of the LORD, which Nebuchadnezzar had taken from Jerusalem and put in the temple of his gods;

8 and Cyrus king of Persia brought them out by the hand of Mithredath the treasurer, and counted them out to [R]Sheshbazzar the prince of Judah. Ezra 5:14, 16

9 This *is* the number of them: thirty gold platters, one thousand silver platters, twenty-nine knives,

10 thirty gold basins, four hundred and ten silver basins of a similar *kind, and* one thousand other articles.

11 All the articles of gold and silver *were* five thousand four hundred. All *these* Sheshbazzar took with the captives who were brought from Babylon to Jerusalem.

CHAPTER 2

The Leaders

NOW* these *are* the people of the province who came back from the captivity, of those who had been carried away, [R]whom Nebuchadnezzar the king of Babylon had carried away to Babylon, and who returned to Jerusalem and Judah, everyone to his *own* city. 2 Kin. 24:14–16; 25:11

2 *Those* who came with Zerubbabel *were* Jeshua, Nehemiah, [T]Seraiah, Reelaiah, Mordecai, Bilshan, Mispar,* Bigvai, Rehum,* *and* Baanah. The number of the men of the people of Israel: *Azariah,* Neh. 7:7

The People

3 the people of Parosh, two thousand one hundred and seventy-two;

4 the people of Shephatiah, three hundred and seventy-two;

5 the people of Arah, [R]seven hundred and seventy-five; Neh. 7:10

6 the people of [R]Pahath-Moab, of the people of Jeshua *and* Joab, two thousand eight hundred and twelve; Neh. 7:11

7 the people of Elam, one thousand two hundred and fifty-four;

8 the people of Zattu, nine hundred and forty-five;

9 the people of Zaccai, seven hundred and sixty;

10 the people of Bani,* six hundred and forty-two;

11 the people of Bebai, six hundred and twenty-three;

12 the people of Azgad, one thousand two hundred and twenty-two;

13 the people of Adonikam, six hundred and sixty-six;

14 the people of Bigvai, two thousand and fifty-six;

15 the people of Adin, four hundred and fifty-four;

16 the people of Ater of Hezekiah, ninety-eight;

2:1 *Cf. Ezra 2 with* Neh. 7:6–73 **2:2** *Mispereth,* Neh. 7:7 • *Nehum,* Neh. 7:7 **2:10** *Binnui,* Neh. 7:15

17 the people of Bezai, three hundred and twenty-three;
18 the people of Jorah,* one hundred and twelve;
19 the people of Hashum, two hundred and twenty-three;
20 the people of Gibbar,* ninety-five;
21 the people of Bethlehem, one hundred and twenty-three;
22 the men of Netophah, fifty-six;
23 the men of Anathoth, one hundred and twenty-eight;
24 the people of Azmaveth,* forty-two;
25 the people of Kirjath Arim,* Chephirah, and Beeroth, seven hundred and forty-three;
26 the people of Ramah and Geba, six hundred and twenty-one;
27 the men of Michmas, one hundred and twenty-two;
28 the men of Bethel and Ai, two hundred and twenty-three;
29 the people of Nebo, fifty-two;
30 the people of Magbish, one hundred and fifty-six;
31 the people of the other [R]Elam, one thousand two hundred and fifty-four; Ezra 2:7
32 the people of Harim, three hundred and twenty;
33 the people of Lod, Hadid, and Ono, seven hundred and twenty-five;
34 the people of Jericho, three hundred and forty-five;
35 the people of Senaah, three thousand six hundred and thirty.

The Priests

36 The priests: the sons of [R]Jedaiah, of the house of Jeshua, nine hundred and seventy-three; 1 Chr. 24:7–18
37 the sons of [R]Immer, one thousand and fifty-two; 1 Chr. 24:14
38 the sons of [R]Pashhur, one thousand two hundred and forty-seven; 1 Chr. 9:12
39 the sons of [R]Harim, one thousand and seventeen. 1 Chr. 24:8

The Levites

40 The Levites: the sons of Jeshua and Kadmiel, of the sons of Hodaviah,* seventy-four.
41 The singers: the sons of Asaph, one hundred and twenty-eight.
42 The sons of the gatekeepers: the sons of Shallum, the sons of Ater, the sons of Talmon, the sons of Akkub, the sons of Hatita, and the sons of Shobai, one hundred and thirty-nine *in* all.

The Servants

43 The Nethinim: the sons of Ziha, the sons of Hasupha, the sons of Tabbaoth,
44 the sons of Keros, the sons of Siaha,* the sons of Padon,
45 the sons of Lebanah, the sons of Hagabah, the sons of Akkub,
46 the sons of Hagab, the sons of Shalmai, the sons of Hanan,
47 the sons of Giddel, the sons of Gahar, the sons of Reaiah,
48 the sons of Rezin, the sons of Nekoda, the sons of Gazzam,
49 the sons of Uzza, the sons of Paseah, the sons of Besai,
50 the sons of Asnah, the sons of Meunim, the sons of Nephusim,*
51 the sons of Bakbuk, the sons of Hakupha, the sons of Harhur,
52 the sons of Bazluth,* the sons of Mehida, the sons of Harsha,
53 the sons of Barkos, the sons of Sisera, the sons of Tamah,
54 the sons of Neziah, and the sons of Hatipha.
55 The sons of [R]Solomon's servants: the sons of Sotai, the sons of [R]Sophereth, the sons of Peruda,* 1 Kin. 9:21 • Neh. 7:57–60
56 the sons of Jaala, the sons of Darkon, the sons of Giddel,
57 the sons of Shephatiah, the sons of Hattil, the sons of Pochereth of Zebaim, and the sons of Ami.*
58 All the [R]Nethinim and the children of [R]Solomon's servants were three hundred and ninety-two. 1 Chr. 9:2 • 1 Kin. 9:21

The People

59 And these *were* the ones who came up from Tel Melah, Tel Harsha, Cherub, Addan,* and Immer; but they could not [T]identify their father's house or their genealogy,* whether they *were* of Israel: Lit. *tell*
60 the sons of Delaiah, the sons of Tobiah, and the sons of Nekoda, six hundred and fifty-two;

The Priests

61 and of the sons of the priests: the sons of [R]Habaiah, the sons of Koz,* and the sons of [R]Barzillai, who took a wife of the daughters of Barzillai the Gileadite, and was called by their name. Neh. 7:63 • 2 Sam. 17:27
62 These sought their listing *among* those who were registered by genealogy, but they were not found; therefore they *were excluded* from the priesthood as defiled.
63 And the governor* said to them that they [R]should not eat of the most holy things till a

2:18 *Hariph*, Neh. 7:24 **2:20** *Gibeon*, Neh. 7:25 **2:24** *Beth Azmaveth*, Neh. 7:28 **2:25** *Kirjath Jearim*, Neh. 7:29 **2:40** *Judah*, Ezra 3:9, or *Hodevah*, Neh. 7:43 **2:44** *Sia*, Neh. 7:47 **2:50** *Nephishesim*, Neh. 7:52 **2:52** *Bazlith*, Neh. 7:54 **2:55** *Perida*, Neh. 7:57 **2:57** *Amon*, Neh. 7:59 **2:59** *Addon*, Neh. 7:61 • Lit. *seed* **2:61** Or *Hakkoz* **2:63** Heb. *Tirshatha*

priest could consult with the [R]Urim and Thummim. Lev. 22:2, 10, 15, 16 • Ex. 28:30

The People Who Returned

64 The whole assembly together *was* forty-two thousand three hundred *and* sixty,

65 besides their male and female servants, of whom *there were* seven thousand three hundred and thirty-seven; and they had two hundred men and women singers.

66 Their horses *were* seven hundred and thirty-six, their mules two hundred and forty-five,

67 their camels four hundred and thirty-five, and *their* donkeys six thousand seven hundred and twenty.

The Gifts the People Gave

68 *Some* of the heads of the fathers' *houses,* when they came to the house of the LORD which *is* in Jerusalem, offered freely for the house of God, to erect it in its place:

69 According to their ability, they gave to the treasury for the work sixty-one thousand gold drachmas, five thousand minas of silver, and one hundred priestly garments.

70 [R]So the priests and the Levites, *some* of the people, the singers, the gatekeepers, and the Nethinim, dwelt in their cities, and all Israel in their cities. Neh. 7:73

CHAPTER 3

Spiritual Preparation of the People

AND when the [R]seventh month had come, and the children of Israel *were* in the cities, the people gathered together as one man to Jerusalem. Neh. 7:73; 8:1, 2

2 Then Jeshua the son of Jozadak* and his brethren the priests, and Zerubbabel the son of Shealtiel and his brethren, arose and built the altar of the God of Israel, to offer burnt offerings on it, as *it is* written in the Law of Moses the man of God.

3 Though fear *had come* upon them because of the people of those countries, they set the altar on its bases; and they offered burnt offerings on it to the LORD, *both* the morning and evening burnt offerings.

4 [R]They also kept the Feast of Tabernacles, as *it is* written, and *offered* the daily burnt offerings in the number required by ordinance for each day. Neh. 8:14–18

5 Afterwards *they offered* the [R]regular burnt offering, and *those* for New Moons and for all the appointed feasts of the LORD that were consecrated, and *those* of everyone who willingly offered a freewill offering to the LORD. Ex. 29:38

6 From the first day of the seventh month they began to offer burnt offerings to the LORD, although the foundation of the temple of the LORD had not been laid.

Completion of the Temple Foundation

7 They also gave money to the masons and the carpenters, and food, drink, and oil to the people of Sidon and Tyre to bring cedar logs from Lebanon to the sea, to Joppa, according to the permission which they had from Cyrus king of Persia.

8 Now in the second month of the second year of their coming to the house of God at Jerusalem, [R]Zerubbabel the son of Shealtiel, Jeshua the son of Jozadak,* and the rest of their brethren the priests and the Levites, and all those who had come out of the captivity to Jerusalem, began *work* [R]and appointed the Levites from twenty years old and above to oversee the work of the house of the LORD. Ezra 3:2; 4:3 • 1 Chr. 23:4, 24

9 Then Jeshua *with* his sons and brothers, Kadmiel *with* his sons, and the sons of Judah,* arose as one to oversee those working on the house of God: the sons of Henadad *with* their sons and their brethren the Levites.

10 When the builders laid the foundation of the temple of the LORD, [R]the priests stood* in their apparel with trumpets, and the Levites, the sons of Asaph, with cymbals, to praise the LORD, according to the ordinance of David king of Israel. 1 Chr. 16:5, 6

11 [R]And they sang responsively, praising and giving thanks to the LORD: Neh. 12:24

[R]"For *He is* good,
[R]For His mercy *endures* forever toward
Israel."* Ps. 136:1 • Jer. 33:11

Then all the people shouted with a great shout, when they praised the LORD, because the foundation of the house of the LORD was laid.

12 But many of the priests and Levites and [R]heads of the fathers' *houses,* old men who had seen the first temple, wept with a loud voice when the foundation of this temple was laid before their eyes. Yet many shouted aloud for joy, Ezra 2:68

13 so that the people could not discern the noise of the shout of joy from the noise of the weeping of the people, for the people shouted with a loud shout, and the sound was heard afar off.

CHAPTER 4

Present Opposition Under Cyrus

NOW when [R]the [T]adversaries of Judah and Benjamin heard that the descendants of the captivity were building the temple of the LORD God of Israel, Ezra 4:7–9 • *enemies*

3:2 *Jehozadak,* 1 Chr. 6:14 **3:8** *Jehozadak,* 1 Chr. 6:14 **3:9** *Hodaviah,* Ezra 2:40 **3:10** So with LXX, Syr., Vg.; MT *they stationed the priests* **3:11** *Cf. Psalm* 136:1

2 they came to Zerubbabel and the heads of
the fathers' *houses*, and said to them, "Let us
build with you, for we seek your God as you
do; and we have sacrificed to Him [R]since the
days of Esarhaddon king of Assyria, who
brought us here." 2 Kin. 17:24; 19:37
3 But Zerubbabel and Jeshua and the rest
of the heads of the fathers' *houses* of Israel
said to them, [R]"You may do nothing with us
to build a [T]house for our God; but we alone
will build to the LORD God of Israel, as [R]King
Cyrus the king of Persia has commanded
us." Neh. 2:20 • Temple • Ezra 1:1–4
4 Then [R]the people of the land tried to dis-
courage the people of Judah. They troubled
them in building, Ezra 3:3
5 and hired counselors against them to
frustrate their purpose all the days of Cyrus
king of Persia, even until the reign of [R]Darius
king of Persia. Ezra 5:5; 6:1

Later Opposition Under Ahasuerus

6 In the reign of Ahasuerus, in the beginning
of his reign, they wrote an accusation against
the inhabitants of Judah and Jerusalem.

Later Opposition Under Artaxerxes

7 In the days of [R]Artaxerxes also, [T]Bish-
lam, Mithredath, Tabel, and the rest of their
companions wrote to Artaxerxes king of Per-
sia; and the letter *was* written in [R]Aramaic
script, and translated into the Aramaic lan-
guage. Ezra 7:1, 7, 21 • Or *in peace* • 2 Kin. 18:26
8 Rehum* the commander and Shimshai
the scribe wrote a letter against Jerusalem to
King Artaxerxes in this fashion:

9 From* Rehum the commander, Shimshai
the scribe, and the rest of their
companions—*representatives* of [R]the
Dinaites, the Apharsathchites, the
Tarpelites, the people of Persia and
Erech and Babylon and Shushan,* the
Dehavites, the Elamites, 2 Kin. 17:30, 31
10 [R]and the rest of the nations whom the
great and noble Osnapper took captive
and settled in the cities of Samaria and
the remainder beyond the River*—[R]and
so forth.* 2 Kin. 17:24 • Ezra 4:11, 17; 7:12

11 (This *is* a copy of the letter that they sent
him)

To King Artaxerxes from your servants,
the men *of the region* beyond the River,
and so forth:*

12 Let it be known to the king that the
Jews who came up from you have come
to us at Jerusalem, and are building the
[R]rebellious and evil city, and are
finishing *its* [R]walls and repairing the
foundations. 2 Chr. 36:13 • Ezra 5:3, 9
13 Let it now be known to the king that, if this
city is built and the walls completed, they
will not pay tax, tribute, or custom, and
the king's treasury will be diminished.
14 Now because we receive support from
the palace, it was not proper for us to see
the king's dishonor; therefore we have
sent and informed the king,
15 that search may be made in the book of
the records of your fathers. And you will
find in the book of the records and know
that this city *is* a rebellious city, harmful
to kings and provinces, and that they
have incited sedition within the city in
former times, for which cause this city
was destroyed.
16 We inform the king that if this city is
rebuilt and its walls are completed, the
result will be that you will have no
dominion beyond the River.

17 The king sent an answer:

To Rehum the commander, *to* Shimshai
the scribe, *to* the rest of their
companions who dwell in Samaria, and
to the remainder beyond the River:

Peace, and so forth.*

18 The letter which you sent to us has been
clearly read before me.
19 And I gave the command, and a search
has been made, and it was found that
this city in former times has revolted
against kings, and rebellion and sedition
have been fostered in it.
20 There have also been mighty kings over
Jerusalem, who have ruled over all *the
region* beyond the River; and tax, tribute,
and custom were paid to them.
21 Now give the command to make these
men cease, that this city may not be built
until the command is given by me.
22 Take heed now that you do not fail to do
this. Why should damage increase to the
hurt of the kings?

23 Now when the copy of King Artaxerxes'
letter *was* read before Rehum, Shimshai the
scribe, and their companions, they went up in
haste to Jerusalem against the Jews, and by
force of arms made them cease.

Present Interruption of Construction Under Darius

24 Thus the work of the house of God
which *is* at Jerusalem ceased, and it was

4:8 The original language of Ezra 4:8 through 6:18 is Aramaic. **4:9** Lit. *Then* • Or *Susa* **4:10** The Euphrates • Lit. *and now* **4:11** Lit. *and now* **4:17** Lit. *and now*

discontinued until the second year of the
reign of Darius king of Persia.

CHAPTER 5

Resumption of the Temple Construction
Hag. 1:1; Zech. 1:1

THEN the prophet [R]Haggai and [R]Zechariah
the son of Iddo, prophets, prophesied to
the Jews who *were* in Judah and Jerusalem, in
the name of the God of Israel, *who was* over
them. Hag. 1:1 • Zech. 1:1
2 So [R]Zerubbabel the son of Shealtiel and
Jeshua the son of Jozadak* rose up and began
to build the house of God which *is* in Jerusa-
lem; and [R]the prophets of God *were* with
them, helping them. Ezra 3:2 • Hag. 2:4

Opposition by Tattenai

3 At the same time [R]Tattenai the governor
of *the region* beyond the River* and Shethar-
Boznai and their companions came to them
and spoke thus to them: [R]"Who has com-
manded you to build this temple and finish
this wall?" Ezra 5:6; 6:6 • Ezra 1:3; 5:9
4 [R]Then, accordingly, we told them the
names of the men who were constructing this
building. Ezra 5:10
5 But [R]the eye of their God was upon the
elders of the Jews, so that they could not
make them cease till a report could go to Da-
rius. Then a written answer was returned con-
cerning this *matter.* Ps. 33:18

The Letter to Darius

6 This is a copy of the letter that Tattenai
sent:

The governor of *the region* beyond the
River, and Shethar-Boznai, [R]and his
companions, the Persians who *were in
the region* beyond the River, to Darius
the king. Ezra 4:7–10

7 (They sent a letter to him, in which was
written thus)

To Darius the king:

All peace.

8 Let it be known to the king that we
went into the province of Judea, to the
[T]temple of the great God, which is being
built with heavy stones, and timber is
being laid in the walls; and this work
goes on diligently and prospers in their
hands. Lit. *house*
9 Then we asked those elders, *and* spoke
thus to them: [R]"Who commanded you to
build this temple and to finish these
walls?" Ezra 5:3, 4
10 We also asked them their names to
inform you, that we might write the names
of the men who *were* chief among them.
11 And thus they returned us an answer,
saying: "We are the servants of the God
of heaven and earth, and we are
rebuilding the temple that was built
many years ago, which a great king of
Israel built [R]and completed. 1 Kin. 6:1, 38
12 "But because our fathers provoked the
God of heaven to wrath, He gave them
into the hand of Nebuchadnezzar king of
Babylon, the Chaldean, *who* destroyed
this temple and [R]carried the people away
to Babylon. Jer. 13:19
13 "However, in the first year of Cyrus king
of Babylon, King Cyrus issued a decree
to build this house of God.
14 "Also, the gold and silver articles of the
house of God, which Nebuchadnezzar
had taken from the temple that *was* in
Jerusalem and carried into the temple of
Babylon—those King Cyrus took from
the temple of Babylon, and they were
given to one named Sheshbazzar, whom
he had made governor.
15 "And he said to him, 'Take these articles;
go, carry them to the temple *site* that *is*
in Jerusalem, and let the house of God
be rebuilt on its former site.'
16 "Then the same Sheshbazzar came *and*
laid the foundation of the house of God
which *is* in Jerusalem; but from that time
even until now it has been under
construction, and it is not finished."
17 Now therefore, if *it seems* good to the
king, [R]let a search be made in the king's
treasure house, which *is* there in
Babylon, whether it is *so* that a decree
was issued by King Cyrus to build this
house of God at Jerusalem, and let the
king send us his pleasure concerning
this *matter.* Ezra 6:1, 2

CHAPTER 6

Confirmation of the Temple Construction

THEN King Darius issued a decree, and a
search was made in the archives,* where
the treasures were stored in Babylon.
2 And at Achmetha,* in the palace that *is* in
the province of Media, a scroll was found, and
in it a record *was* written thus:

3 In the first year of King Cyrus, King
Cyrus issued a [R]decree *concerning* the
house of God at Jerusalem: "Let the
house be rebuilt, the place where they
offered sacrifices; and let the foundations

5:2 *Jehozadak,* 1 Chr. 6:14 **5:3** The Euphrates
6:1 Lit. *house of the scrolls* **6:2** Probably *Ecbatana,*
the ancient capital of Media

of it be firmly laid, its height sixty cubits
and its width sixty cubits, Ezra 1:1; 5:13
4 [R]*with* three rows of heavy stones and
one row of new timber. Let the
[R]expenses be paid from the king's
treasury. 1 Kin. 6:36 • Ezra 3:7
5 Also let [R]the gold and silver articles of
the house of God, which
Nebuchadnezzar took from the temple
which *is* in Jerusalem and brought to
Babylon, be restored and taken back to
the temple which *is* in Jerusalem, *each*
to its place; and deposit *them* in the
house of God"— Ezra 1:7, 8; 5:14
6 [R]Now *therefore,* Tattenai, governor of
the region beyond the River, and
Shethar-Boznai, and your companions
the Persians who *are* beyond the River,
keep yourselves far from there. Ezra 5:3, 6
7 Let the work of this house of God alone;
let the governor of the Jews and the
elders of the Jews build this house of
God on its site.
8 Moreover I issue a decree *as to* what
you shall do for the elders of these Jews,
for the building of this [T]house of God:
Let the cost be paid at the king's
expense from taxes *on the region*
beyond the River; this is to be given
immediately to these men, so that they
are not hindered. Temple
9 And whatever they need—young bulls,
rams, and lambs for the burnt offerings
of the God of heaven, wheat, salt, wine,
and oil, according to the request of the
priests who *are* in Jerusalem—let it be
given them day by day without fail,
10 that they may offer sacrifices of sweet
aroma to the God of heaven, and pray
for the life of the king and his sons.
11 Also I issue a decree that whoever alters
this edict, let a timber be pulled from his
house and erected, and let him be
hanged on it; and let his house be made
a refuse heap because of this.
12 And may the God who causes His [R]name
to dwell there destroy any king or people
who put their hand to alter it, or to
destroy this [T]house of God which is in
Jerusalem. I Darius issue a decree; let it
be done diligently. 1 Kin. 9:3 • Temple

Completion of the Temple

13 Then Tattenai, governor of *the region* be-
yond the River, Shethar-Boznai, and their
companions diligently did according to what
King Darius had sent.
14 [R]So the elders of the Jews built, and they
prospered through the prophesying of Hag-
gai the prophet and Zechariah the son of
Iddo. And they built and finished *it,* accord-
ing to the commandment of the God of Is-
rael, and according to the command of
[R]Cyrus, Darius, and [R]Artaxerxes king of Per-
sia. Ezra 5:1, 2 • Ezra 1:1; 5:13; 6:3 • Ezra 7:1, 11
15 Now the temple was finished on the third
day of the month of Adar, which was in the
sixth year of the reign of King Darius.

Dedication of the Temple

16 Then the children of Israel, the priests
and the Levites and the rest of the descen-
dants of the captivity, celebrated the dedica-
tion of this house of God with joy.
17 And they [R]offered sacrifices at the dedi-
cation of this house of God, one hundred
bulls, two hundred rams, four hundred lambs,
and as a sin offering for all Israel twelve male
goats, according to the number of the tribes of
Israel. Ezra 8:35
18 They assigned the priests to their [R]divi-
sions and the Levites to their divisions, over
the service of God in Jerusalem, as it is writ-
ten in the Book of Moses. 1 Chr. 24:1

Celebration of the Passover

19 And the descendants of the captivity kept
the Passover [R]on the fourteenth *day* of the
first month. Ex. 12:6
20 For the priests and the Levites had [R]puri-
fied themselves; all of them *were ritually*
clean. And they [R]slaughtered the Passover
lambs for all the descendants of the captivity,
for their brethren the priests, and for them-
selves. 2 Chr. 29:34; 30:15 • 2 Chr. 35:11
21 Then the children of Israel who had re-
turned from the captivity ate together with all
who had separated themselves from the [R]filth
of the nations of the land in order to seek the
LORD God of Israel. Ezra 9:11
22 And they kept the Feast of Unleavened
Bread seven days with joy; for the LORD made
them joyful, and turned the heart [R]of the king
of Assyria toward them, to strengthen their
hands in the work of the house of God, the
God of Israel. Ezra 1:1; 6:1

CHAPTER 7

Ezra's Qualifications

NOW after these things, in the reign of [R]Ar-
taxerxes king of Persia, Ezra the [R]son of
Seraiah, [R]the son of Azariah, the son of
Hilkiah, Neh. 2:1 • 1 Chr. 6:14 • Jer. 52:24
2 the son of Shallum, the son of Zadok, the
son of Ahitub,
3 the son of Amariah, the son of Azariah,
the son of Meraioth,
4 the son of Zerahiah, the son of Uzzi, the
son of Bukki,
5 the son of Abishua, the son of Phinehas,
the son of Eleazar, the son of Aaron the chief
priest—
6 this Ezra came up from Babylon; and he
was a skilled scribe in the Law of Moses,
which the LORD God of Israel had given. The

king granted him all his request, according to
the hand of the LORD his God upon him.
7 [R]*Some* of the children of Israel, the
priests, [R]the Levites, the singers, the gate-
keepers, and [R]the Nethinim came up to
Jerusalem in the seventh year of King Artax-
erxes. Ezra 8:1–14 • Ezra 8:15 • Ezra 2:43; 8:20
8 And Ezra came to Jerusalem in the fifth
month, which *was* in the seventh year of the
king.
9 On the first *day* of the first month he
began *his* journey from Babylon, and on the
first *day* of the fifth month he came to Jerusa-
lem, [R]according to the good hand of his God
upon him. Neh. 2:8, 18
10 For Ezra had prepared his heart to seek
the Law of the LORD, and to do *it*, and to teach
statutes and ordinances in Israel.

Artaxerxes' Letter

11 This *is* a copy of the letter that King Ar-
taxerxes gave Ezra the priest, the scribe, ex-
pert in the words of the commandments of the
LORD, and of His statutes to Israel:

12 Artaxerxes,* [R]king of kings, Dan. 2:37

To Ezra the priest, a scribe of the Law of
the God of heaven:

Perfect *peace*, and so forth.*

13 I issue a decree that all those of the
people of Israel and the priests and
Levites in my realm, who volunteer to go
up to Jerusalem, may go with you.
14 And whereas you are being sent by the
king and his seven counselors to inquire
concerning Judah and Jerusalem, with
regard to the Law of your God which *is*
in your hand;
15 and *whereas you are* to carry the
silver and gold which the king and his
counselors have freely offered to the
God of Israel, [R]whose dwelling *is* in
Jerusalem; Ezra 6:12
16 [R]and *whereas* all the silver and gold that
you may find in all the province of
Babylon, along with the freewill offering
of the people and the priests, *are to be*
freely offered for the house of their God
in Jerusalem— Ezra 8:25
17 now therefore, be careful to buy with
this money bulls, rams, and lambs, with
their grain offerings and their drink
offerings, and offer them on the altar of
the house of your God in Jerusalem.
18 And whatever seems good to you and
your brethren to do with the rest of the
silver and the gold, do it according to the
will of your God.
19 Also the articles that are given to you for
the service of the house of your God,
deliver in full before the God of Jerusalem.
20 And whatever more may be needed for
the house of your God, which you may
have occasion to provide, pay *for it* from
the king's treasury.
21 And I, *even* I, Artaxerxes the king, issue
a decree to all the treasurers who *are in
the region* beyond the River, that
whatever Ezra the priest, the scribe of
the Law of the God of heaven, may
require of you, let it be done diligently,
22 up to one hundred talents of silver, one
hundred kors of wheat, one hundred
baths of wine, one hundred baths of oil,
and salt without prescribed limit.
23 Whatever is commanded by the God of
heaven, let it diligently be done for the
[T]house of the God of heaven. For why
should there be wrath against the realm
of the king and his sons? Temple
24 Also we inform you that it shall not be
lawful to impose tax, tribute, or custom
on any of the priests, Levites, singers,

7:12 The original language of Ezra 7:12–26 is Aramaic. • Lit. *and now*

7:10 Sharing Our Faith: How to Prepare—In order to share our faith successfully, we must keep the following rules in mind.

a. First, we must be clean vessels. God reminds Isaiah the prophet of this, "Be clean, you who bear the vessels of the LORD" (Page 730—Is. 52:11). David the sinner prays for forgiveness and cleansing. Upon receiving this he states, "*Then* I will teach transgressors Your ways, and sinners shall be converted to You" (Page 573—Ps. 51:13). While God does not demand golden or silver vessels, He does require clean ones.
b. We must be able to clearly give out the simple facts of the gospel without getting bogged down with profound theological concepts. Philip the evangelist demonstrated how to do this when he dealt with a sinner in the desert. "Then Philip opened his mouth, and beginning at this Scripture, preached Jesus to him" (Page 1121—Acts 8:35).
c. We must avoid arguments and stick to the basic issues of man's sin and Christ's blood. Often unbelievers will attempt to sidestep the gospel by asking unrelated questions, such as "Where did Cain get his wife?"
d. We must use the Word of God. Paul's tremendous success as an evangelist can be linked directly to his constant use of God's Word. See Page 1132—Acts 17:2; 18:28; Page 1244—2 Tim. 2:15; 3:14–17.
e. We must depend upon the Spirit of God. See Page 1083—John 3:15; Page 1118—Acts 6:10; Page 1168—1 Cor. 2:4.

Now turn to Page 1226—1 Thess. 1:5: Sharing Our Faith: How to Do It.

gatekeepers, Nethinim, or servants of
this house of God.
25 And you, Ezra, according to your
God-given wisdom, set magistrates and
judges who may judge all the people
who *are in the region* beyond the River,
all such as know the laws of your God;
and teach those who do not know *them.*
26 Whoever will not observe the law of
your God and the law of the king, let
judgment be executed speedily on him,
whether *it be* death, or banishment, or
confiscation of goods, or imprisonment.

Ezra's Response

27 [R]Blessed *be* the LORD God of our fathers,
who has put *such a thing* as this in the king's
heart, to beautify the house of the LORD which
is in Jerusalem, 1 Chr. 29:10
28 and [R]has extended mercy to me before
the king and his counselors, and before all the
king's mighty princes. Ezra 9:9
So I was encouraged, as the hand of the
LORD my God *was* upon me; and I gathered
leading men of Israel to go up with me.

CHAPTER 8

Census of the Returning Israelites

THESE *are* the heads of their fathers'
houses, and *this is* the genealogy of those
who went up with me from Babylon, in the
reign of King Artaxerxes:
2 of the sons of Phinehas, Gershom; of the
sons of Ithamar, Daniel; of the sons of David,
[R]Hattush; 1 Chr. 3:22
3 of the sons of Shecaniah, of the sons of
[R]Parosh, Zechariah; and registered with him
were one hundred and fifty males; Ezra 2:3
4 of the sons of [R]Pahath-Moab, Eliehoenai
the son of Zerahiah, and with him two hun-
dred males; Ezra 10:30
5 of the sons of Shechaniah,* Ben-Jahaziel,
and with him three hundred males;
6 of the sons of Adin, Ebed the son of Jona-
than, and with him fifty males;
7 of the sons of Elam, Jeshaiah the son of
Athaliah, and with him seventy males;
8 of the sons of Shephatiah, Zebadiah the
son of Michael, and with him eighty males;
9 of the sons of Joab, Obadiah the son of Je-
hiel, and with him two hundred and eighteen
males;
10 of the sons of Shelomith,* Ben-Josiphiah,
and with him one hundred and sixty males;
11 of the sons of Bebai, Zechariah the son of
Bebai, and with him twenty-eight males;
12 of the sons of Azgad, Johanan [T]the son of
Hakkatan, and with him one hundred and ten
males; Or *the youngest son,*
13 of the last sons of Adonikam, whose
names *are* these—Eliphelet, Jeiel, and Shema-
iah—and with them sixty males;
14 also of the sons of Bigvai, Uthai and Zab-
bud, and with them seventy males.

Acquisition of Temple Leadership

15 Now I gathered them by the river that
flows to Ahava, and we camped there three
days. And I looked among the people and the
priests, and found none of the [R]sons of Levi
there. Ezra 7:7; 8:2
16 Then I sent for Eliezer, Ariel, Shemaiah,
Elnathan, Jarib, Elnathan, Nathan, Zechariah,
and [R]Meshullam, leaders; also for Joiarib and
Elnathan, men of understanding. Ezra 10:15
17 And I gave them a command for Iddo the
chief man at the place Casiphia, and I told
them what they should say to Iddo *and* his
brethren* the Nethinim at the place Casiphia—
that they should bring us servants for the
house of our God.
18 Then, by the good hand of our God upon
us, they brought us a man of understanding,
of the sons of Mahli the son of Levi, the son of
Israel, namely Sherebiah, with his sons and
brothers, eighteen men;
19 and [R]Hashabiah, and with him Jeshaiah
of the sons of Merari, his brothers and their
sons, twenty men; Neh. 12:24
20 [R]also of the Nethinim, whom David and
the leaders had appointed for the service of
the Levites, two hundred and twenty
Nethinim. All of them were designated by
name. Ezra 2:43; 7:7

Proclamation of a Fast

21 Then I [R]proclaimed a fast there at the
river of Ahava, that we might [R]humble our-
selves before our God, to seek from Him the
[R]right way for us and our little ones and all
our possessions. 1 Sam. 7:6 • Is. 58:3, 5 • Ps. 5:8
22 For [R]I was ashamed to request of the
king an escort of soldiers and horsemen to
help us against the enemy on the road, be-
cause we had spoken to the king, saying,
[R]"The hand of our God *is* upon all those for
[R]good who seek Him, but His power and His
wrath *are* against all those who forsake
Him." 1 Cor. 9:15 • Ezra 7:6, 9, 28 • [Rom. 8:28]
23 So we fasted and entreated our God for
this, and He answered our prayer.

The Return Is Completed

24 And I separated twelve of the leaders of
the priests—Sherebiah, Hashabiah, and ten of
their brethren with them—
25 and weighed out to them [R]the silver, the
gold, and the articles, the offering for the
house of our God which the king and his

8:5 So with MT, Vg.; LXX *the sons of Zatho, Shechaniah* **8:10** So with MT, Vg.; LXX *the sons of Banni, Shelomith* **8:17** So with Vg.; MT *to Iddo his brother;* LXX *to their brethren*

counselors and his princes, and all Israel *who*
were present, had offered. Ezra 7:15, 16
26 I weighed into their hand six hundred and
fifty talents of silver, silver articles *weighing*
one hundred talents, one hundred talents of
gold,
27 twenty gold basins *worth* a thousand
drachmas, and two vessels of fine polished
bronze, precious as gold.
28 And I said to them, "You *are* [R]holy to the
LORD; the articles *are* holy also; and the silver
and the gold *are* a freewill offering to the
LORD God of your fathers. Lev. 21:6–9
29 "Watch and keep *them* until you weigh
them before the leaders of the priests and the
Levites and [R]heads of the fathers' *houses* of
Israel in Jerusalem, *in* the chambers of the
house of the LORD." Ezra 4:3
30 So the priests and the Levites received
the silver and the gold and the articles by
weight, to bring *them* to Jerusalem to the
house of our God.
31 Then we departed from the river of
Ahava on the twelfth *day* of the first month, to
go to Jerusalem. And [R]the hand of our God
was upon us, and He delivered us from the
hand of the enemy and from ambush along
the road. Ezra 7:6, 9, 28
32 So we [R]came to Jerusalem, and stayed
there three days. Neh. 2:11
33 Now on the fourth day the silver and the
gold and the articles were weighed in the
house of our God by the hand of Meremoth
the son of Uriah the priest, and with him *was*
Eleazar the son of Phinehas; with them *were*
the Levites, [R]Jozabad the son of Jeshua and
Noadiah the son of Binnui, Neh. 11:16
34 with the number *and* weight of every-
thing. All the weight was written down at that
time.
35 The children of those who had been [R]car-
ried away captive, who had come from the
captivity, offered burnt offerings to the God of
Israel: twelve bulls for all Israel, ninety-six
rams, seventy-seven lambs, and twelve male
goats *as* a sin offering. All *this was* a burnt of-
fering to the LORD. Ezra 2:1
36 And they delivered the king's orders to
the king's satraps and the governors *in the re-*
gion beyond the River. So they gave support
to the people and the house of God.

CHAPTER 9

Israel Intermarries

WHEN these things were done, the lead-
ers came to me, saying, "The people of
Israel and the priests and the Levites have
not separated themselves from the peoples of
the lands, with respect to the abominations
of the Canaanites, the Hittites, the Perizzites,
the Jebusites, the Ammonites, the Moabites,
the Egyptians, and the Amorites.
2 "For they have taken some of their
daughters *as wives* for themselves and their
sons, so that the [R]holy seed is [R]mixed with the
peoples of *those* lands. Indeed, the hand of
the leaders and rulers has been foremost in
this trespass." Ex. 22:31 • [2 Cor. 6:14]

Lamentation of Ezra

3 So when I heard this thing, [R]I tore my gar-
ment and my robe, and plucked out some of
the hair of my head and beard, and sat down
[R]astonished. Job 1:20 • Ps. 143:4
4 Then everyone who trembled at the
words of the God of Israel assembled to me,
because of the transgression of those who had
been carried away captive, and I sat aston-
ished until the evening sacrifice.

God's Faithfulness

5 At the evening sacrifice I arose from my
fasting; and having torn my garment and
my robe, I fell on my knees and [R]spread out
my hands to the LORD my God. Ex. 9:29
6 And I said: "O my God, I am too ashamed
and humiliated to lift up my face to You, my
God; for our iniquities have risen higher than
our heads, and our guilt has [R]grown up to the
heavens. Rev. 18:5
7 "Since the days of our fathers to this
day [R]we *have been* very guilty, and for our
iniquities [R]we, our kings, *and* our priests
have been delivered into the hand of the
kings of the lands, to the [R]sword, to captiv-
ity, to plunder, and to humiliation, as *it is*
this day. Dan. 9:5, 6 • Deut. 28:36 • Deut. 32:25
8 "And now for a little while grace has been
shown from the LORD our God, to leave us a
remnant to escape, and to give us a peg in His
holy place, that our God may [R]enlighten our
eyes and give us a measure of revival in our
bondage. Ps. 34:5
9 [R]"For we *were* slaves. Yet our God did not
forsake us in our bondage; but He extended
mercy to us in the sight of the kings of Persia,
to revive us, to repair the house of our God, to
rebuild its ruins, and to give us a wall in Judah
and Jerusalem. Neh. 9:36

Israel's Unfaithfulness

10 "And now, O our God, what shall we say
after this? For we have forsaken Your com-
mandments,
11 "which You commanded by Your servants
the prophets, saying, 'The land which you
are entering to possess is an unclean land,
with the [R]uncleanness of the peoples of the
lands, with their abominations which have
filled it from one end to another with their
impurity. Ezra 6:21
12 'Now therefore, [R]do not give your daugh-
ters as wives for their sons, nor take their
daughters to your sons; and [R]never seek
their peace or prosperity, that you may be

strong and eat the good of the land, and [R]leave *it* as an inheritance to your children forever.' [Deut. 7:3, 4] • Deut. 23:6 • [Prov. 13:22]

13 "And after all that has come upon us for our evil deeds and for our great guilt, since You our God [R]have punished us less than our iniquities *deserve,* and have given us *such* deliverance as this, [Ps. 103:10]

14 "should we [R]again break Your commandments, and [R]join in marriage with the people *committing* these abominations? Would You not be angry with us until You had consumed *us,* so that *there would be* no remnant or survivor? [John 5:14] • Neh. 13:23

15 "O LORD God of Israel, You *are* righteous, for we are left as a remnant, as *it is* this day. [R]Here we *are* before You, [R]in our guilt, though no one can stand before You because of this!" [Rom. 3:19] • 1 Cor. 15:17

CHAPTER 10

Israel Laments

NOW [R]while Ezra was praying, and while he was confessing, weeping, and bowing down [R]before the house of God, a very large assembly of men, women, and children gathered to him from Israel; for the people wept very bitterly. Dan. 9:4, 20 • 2 Chr. 20:9

2 And Shechaniah the son of Jehiel, *one* of the sons of Elam, spoke up and said to Ezra, "We have [R]trespassed against our God, and have taken pagan wives from the peoples of the land; yet now there is hope in Israel in spite of this. Neh. 13:23–27

The Covenant Is Instituted

3 "Now therefore, let us make a covenant with our God to put away all these wives and those who have been born to them, according to the advice of my master and of those who tremble at the commandment of our God; and let it be done according to the law.

4 "Arise, for *this* matter *is* your *responsibility.* We also *are* with you. [R]Be of good courage, and do *it.*" 1 Chr. 28:10

5 Then Ezra arose, and made the leaders of the priests, the Levites, and all Israel swear an oath that they would do according to this word. So they swore an oath.

Separation Is Accepted

6 Then Ezra rose up from before the house of God, and went into the chamber of Jehohanan the son of Eliashib; and *when* he came there, he [R]ate no bread and drank no water, for he mourned because of the guilt of those from the captivity. Deut. 9:18

7 And they issued a proclamation throughout Judah and Jerusalem to all the descendants of the captivity, that they must gather at Jerusalem,

8 and that whoever would not come within three days, according to the instructions of the leaders and elders, all his property would be confiscated, and he himself would be separated from the assembly of those from the captivity.

9 So all the men of Judah and Benjamin gathered at Jerusalem within three days. It *was* the ninth month, on the twentieth of the month; and [R]all the people sat in the open square of the house of God, trembling because of *this* matter and because of heavy rain. 1 Sam. 12:18

10 Then Ezra the priest stood up and said to them, "You have [T]transgressed and have taken pagan wives, adding to the guilt of Israel. *acted unfaithfully*

11 "Now therefore, make confession to the LORD God of your fathers, and do His will; [R]separate yourselves from the peoples of the land, and from the pagan wives." Ezra 10:3

12 Then all the assembly answered and said with a loud voice, "Yes! As you have said, so we must do.

13 "But *there are* many people; *it is* the season for heavy rain, and we are not able to stand outside. Nor *is this* the work of one or two days, for *there are* many of us who have transgressed in this matter.

14 "Please, let the leaders of our entire assembly stand; and let all those in our cities who have taken pagan wives come at appointed times, together with the elders and judges of their cities, until [R]the fierce wrath of our God is turned away from us in this matter." 2 Chr. 28:11–13; 29:10; 30:8

15 Only Jonathan the son of Asahel and Jahaziah the son of Tikvah opposed this, and [R]Meshullam and Shabbethai the Levite gave them support. Neh. 3:4

16 Then the descendants of the captivity did so. And Ezra the priest, *with* certain [R]heads of the fathers' *households,* were set apart by the fathers' *households,* each of them by name; and they sat down on the first day of the tenth month to examine the matter. Ezra 4:3

17 By the first day of the first month they finished *questioning* all the men who had taken pagan wives.

Separation of Priests

18 And among the sons of the priests who had taken pagan wives *the following* were found of the sons of [R]Jeshua the son of Jozadak,* and his brothers: Maaseiah, Eliezer, Jarib, and Gedaliah. Ezra 5:2

19 And they [R]gave their promise that they would put away their wives; and *being* guilty, *they presented* a ram of the flock as their trespass offering. 2 Kin. 10:15

20 Also of the sons of Immer: Hanani and Zebadiah;

10:18 *Jehozadak,* 1 Chr. 6:14

21 of the sons of Harim: Maaseiah, Elijah,
Shemaiah, Jehiel, and Uzziah;
22 of the sons of Pashhur: Elioenai, Maa-
seiah, Ishmael, Nethanel, Jozabad, and
Elasah.

Separation of Levites

23 Also of the Levites: Jozabad, Shimei, Ke-
laiah (the same *is* Kelita), Pethahiah, Judah,
and Eliezer.
24 Also of the singers: Eliashib; and of the
gatekeepers: Shallum, Telem, and Uri.

Separation of People

25 And others of Israel: of the [R]sons of
Parosh: Ramiah, Jeziah, Malchiah, Mijamin,
Eleazar, Malchijah, and Benaiah; Ezra 2:3
26 of the sons of Elam: Mattaniah,
Zechariah, Jehiel, Abdi, Jeremoth, and Eliah;
27 of the sons of Zattu: Elioenai, Eliashib,
Mattaniah, Jeremoth, Zabad, and Aziza;
28 of the [R]sons of Bebai: Jehohanan, Hana-
niah, Zabbai, *and* Athlai; Ezra 8:11
29 of the sons of Bani: Meshullam, Malluch,
Adaiah, Jashub, Sheal, *and* Ramoth;*
30 of the [R]sons of Pahath-Moab: Adna,
Chelal, Benaiah, Maaseiah, Mattaniah, Beza-
lel, Binnui, and Manasseh; Ezra 8:4
31 *of* the sons of Harim: Eliezer, Ishijah,
Malchijah, Shemaiah, Shimeon,
32 Benjamin, Malluch, *and* Shemariah;
33 of the sons of Hashum: Mattenai, Mattat-
tah, Zabad, Eliphelet, Jeremai, Manasseh, *and*
Shimei;
34 of the sons of Bani: Maadai, Amram, Uel,
35 Benaiah, Bedeiah, Cheluh,*
36 Vaniah, Meremoth, Eliashib,
37 Mattaniah, Mattenai, Jaasai,*
38 Bani, Binnui, Shimei,
39 Shelemiah, Nathan, Adaiah,
40 Machnadebai, Shashai, Sharai,
41 Azarel, Shelemiah, Shemariah,
42 Shallum, Amariah, *and* Joseph;
43 of the sons of Nebo: Jeiel, Mattithiah,
Zabad, Zebina, Jaddai,* Joel, *and* Benaiah.
44 All these had taken pagan wives, and
some of them had wives *by whom* they had
children.

10:29 Or *Jeremoth* **10:35** Or *Cheluhi,* or *Cheluhu*
10:37 Or *Jaasu* **10:43** Or *Jaddu*

Measures of Length

Unit	*Length*	*Equivalents*	*Translations*
Day's journey	c. 20 miles		day's journey
Roman mile	4,854 feet	8 stadia	mile
Sabbath day's journey	3,637 feet	6 stadia	Sabbath day's journey
Stadion	606 feet	⅛ Roman mile	furlong
Rod	9 feet (10.5 feet in Ezekiel)	3 paces; 6 cubits	measuring reed, reed
Fathom	6 feet	4 cubits	fathom
Pace	3 feet	⅓ rod; 2 cubits	pace
Cubit	18 inches	½ pace; 2 spans	cubit
Span	9 inches	½ cubit; 3 handbreadths	span
Handbreadth	3 inches	⅓ span; 4 fingers	handbreadth
Finger	.75 inches	¼ handbreadth	finger

THE BOOK OF

NEHEMIAH

THE BOOK OF NEHEMIAH

Nehemiah, contemporary of Ezra and cupbearer to the king in the Persian palace, leads the third and last return to Jerusalem after the Babylonian exile. His concern for the welfare of Jerusalem and its inhabitants prompts him to take bold action. Granted permission to return to his homeland, Nehemiah challenges his countrymen to arise and rebuild the shattered wall of Jerusalem. In spite of opposition from without and abuse from within, the task is completed in only fifty-two days, a feat even the enemies of Israel must attribute to God's enabling. By contrast, the task of reviving and reforming the people of God within the rebuilt wall demands years of Nehemiah's godly life and leadership.

The Hebrew for Nehemiah is *Nehemyah,* "Comfort of Yahweh." The book is named after its chief character, whose name appears in the opening verse. The combined book of Ezra-Nehemiah is given the Greek title *Esdras Deuteron,* "Second Esdras" (see "The Book of Ezra") in the Septuagint, a third-century B.C. Greek language translation of the Hebrew Old Testament. The Latin title of Nehemiah is *Liber Secundus Esdrae,* "Second Book of Ezra" (Ezra was the first). At this point, it is considered a separate book from Ezra, and is later called *Liber Nehemiae,* "Book of Nehemiah."

THE AUTHOR OF NEHEMIAH

Clearly, much of this book came from Nehemiah's personal memoirs. The reporting is remarkably candid and vivid. Certainly 1:1—7:5; 12:27–43; and 13:4–31 are the "words of Nehemiah" (1:1). Some scholars think that Nehemiah composed those portions and compiled the rest. Others think that Ezra wrote 7:6—12:26 and 12:44—13:3, and that he compiled the rest making use of Nehemiah's diary. A third view that neither wrote it seems least likely from the evidence. Nehemiah 7:5–73 is almost the same as Ezra 2:1–70, and both lists may have been taken from another record of the same period.

As cupbearer to Artaxerxes I, Nehemiah holds a position of great responsibility. His role of tasting the king's wine to prevent him from being poisoned places Nehemiah in a position of trust and confidence as one of the king's advisors. As governor of Jerusalem from 444 to 432 B.C. (5:14; 8:9; 10:1; 13:6), Nehemiah demonstrates courage, compassion for the oppressed, integrity, godliness, and selflessness. He is willing to give up the luxury and ease of the palace to help his people. He is a dedicated layman who has the right priorities and is concerned for God's work, who is able to encourage and rebuke at the right times, who is strong in prayer, and who gives all glory and credit to God.

THE TIME OF NEHEMIAH

See "The Time of Ezra," because both Ezra and Nehemiah share the same historical background. The Book of Nehemiah fits within the reign of Artaxerxes I of Persia (464–423 B.C.). Esther is Artaxerxes' stepmother, and it is possible that she is instrumental in Nehemiah's appointment as the king's cupbearer. Nehemiah leaves Persia in the twentieth year of Artaxerxes (2:1), returns to Persia in the thirty-second year of Artaxerxes (13:6), and leaves again for Jerusalem "after certain days" (13:6), perhaps about 425 B.C. This book could not have been completed until after his second visit to Jerusalem.

The historical reliability of this book is supported by the Elephantine papyri. These ancient documents mention Sanballat (2:19) and Jehohanan (6:18; 12:23) and indicate that Bigvai replaces Nehemiah as governor of Judah by 410 B.C.

Malachi lives and ministers during Nehemiah's time, and a comparison of the books shows that many of the evils encountered by Nehemiah are specifically denounced by Malachi. The cold-hearted indifference toward God described in both books remains a problem in Israel during the four hundred years before Christ, during which there is no revelation from God.

THE CHRIST OF NEHEMIAH

Like Ezra, Nehemiah portrays Christ in His ministry of restoration. Nehemiah illustrates Christ in that he gives up a high position in order to identify with the plight of his people; he comes with a specific mission and fulfills it; and his life is characterized by prayerful dependence upon God.

In this book, everything is restored except the king. The temple is rebuilt, Jerusalem is reconstructed, the covenant is renewed, and the people are reformed. The messianic line is intact, but the King is yet to come. The decree of Artaxerxes in his twentieth year (2:2) marks the beginning point of Daniel's prophecy of the seventy weeks (see Dan. 9:25–27). "Know therefore and understand, *that* from the going forth of the command to restore and build Jerusalem until

Messiah the Prince, *there shall be* seven weeks and sixty-two weeks; the street shall be built again, and the wall, even in troublesome times" (Dan. 9:25). The Messiah will come at the end of the sixty-nine weeks, and this is exactly fulfilled in A.D. 33 (see "The Christ of Daniel").

KEYS TO NEHEMIAH

Key Word: Jerusalem Walls—While Ezra deals with the religious restoration of Judah, Nehemiah is primarily concerned with Judah's political and geographical restoration. The first seven chapters are devoted to the rebuilding of Jerusalem's walls, because Jerusalem was the spiritual and political center of Judah. Without walls, Jerusalem could hardly be considered a city at all. As governor, Nehemiah also establishes firm civil authority. Ezra and Nehemiah work together to build the people spiritually and morally so that the restoration will be complete.

Key Verses: Nehemiah 6:15, 16; 8:8—"So the wall was finished on the twenty-fifth *day* of Elul, in fifty-two days. And it happened, when all our enemies heard *of it,* and all the nations around us saw *these things,* that they were very disheartened in their own eyes; for they perceived that this work was done by our God" (6:15, 16).

"So they read distinctly from the book, in the Law of God; and they gave the sense, and helped *them* to understand the reading" (8:8).

Key Chapter: Nehemiah 9—The key to the Old Testament is the covenant, which is its theme and unifying factor. Israel's history can be divided according to the nation's obedience or disobedience to God's conditional covenant: blessings from obedience and destruction from disobedience. Nehemiah 9 records that upon completion of the Jerusalem wall the nation reaffirmed its loyalty to the covenant.

SURVEY OF NEHEMIAH

Nehemiah is closely associated with the ministry of his contemporary, Ezra. Ezra is a priest who brings spiritual revival; Nehemiah is a governor who brings physical and political reconstruction and leads the people in moral reform. They combine to make an effective team in rebuilding the postexilic remnant. Malachi, the last Old Testament prophet, also ministers during this time to provide additional moral and spiritual direction. The Book of Nehemiah takes us to the end of the historical account in the Old Testament, about four hundred years before the birth of the promised Messiah. Its two divisions are: the reconstruction of the wall (1—7), and the restoration of the people (8—13).

The Reconstruction of the Wall (1—7): Nehemiah's great concern for his people and the welfare of Jerusalem leads him to take bold action. The walls of Jerusalem, destroyed by Nebuchadnezzar in 586 B.C., evidently have been almost rebuilt after 464 B.C. when Artaxerxes I took the throne of Persia (see Ezra 4:6–23). When he hears that opposition led to their second destruction, Nehemiah prays on behalf of his people and then secures Artaxerxes' permission, provision, and protection for the massive project of rebuilding the walls.

The return under Nehemiah in 444 B.C. takes place thirteen years after the return led by Ezra, and ninety-four years after the return led by Zerubbabel. Nehemiah inspects the walls and challenges the people to "rise up and build" (2:18). Work begins immediately on the wall and its gates, with people building portions corresponding to where they are living.

However, opposition quickly arises, first in the form of mockery, then in the form of conspiracy when the work is progressing at an alarming rate. Nehemiah overcomes threats of force by setting half of the people on military watch and

FOCUS	RECONSTRUCTION OF THE WALL		RESTORATION OF THE PEOPLE	
REFERENCE	1:1	3:1	8:1	11:1 — 13:31
DIVISION	PREPARATION TO RECONSTRUCT THE WALL	RECONSTRUCTION OF THE WALL	RENEWAL OF THE COVENANT	OBEDIENCE TO THE COVENANT
TOPIC	POLITICAL		SPIRITUAL	
	CONSTRUCTION		INSTRUCTION	
LOCATION	JERUSALEM			
TIME	19 YEARS (444–425 B.C.)			

half on construction. While the external opposition continues to mount, internal opposition also surfaces. The wealthier Jews are abusing and oppressing the people, forcing them to mortgage their property and sell their children into slavery. Nehemiah again deals with the problem by the twin means of prayer and action. He also leads by example when he sacrifices his governor's salary. In spite of deceit, slander, and treachery, Nehemiah continues to trust in God and to press on with singleness of mind until the work is completed. The task is accomplished in an incredible fifty-two days, and even the enemies recognize that it can only have been accomplished with the help of God (6:16).

The Restoration of the People (8—13): The construction of the walls is followed by consecration and consolidation of the people. Ezra the priest is the leader of the spiritual revival (8—10), reminiscent of the reforms he led thirteen years earlier (Ezra 9 and 10). Ezra stands on a special wooden podium after the completion of the walls and gives the people a marathon reading of the law, translating from the Hebrew into Aramaic so they can understand. They respond with weeping, confession, obedience, and rejoicing. The Levites and priests lead them in a great prayer that surveys God's past work of deliverance and loyalty on behalf of His people, and magnifies God's attributes of holiness, justice, mercy, and love. The covenant is then renewed with God as the people commit themselves to separate from the Gentiles in marriage and to obey God's commandments.

Lots are drawn to determine who will remain in Jerusalem and who will return to the cities of their inheritance. One-tenth are required to stay in Jerusalem, and the rest of the land is resettled by the people and priests. The walls of Jerusalem are dedicated to the Lord in a joyful ceremony accompanied by instrumental and vocal music.

Unfortunately, Ezra's revival is short-lived; and Nehemiah, who returned to Persia in 432 B.C. (13:6), makes a second trip to Jerusalem about 425 B.C. to reform the people. He cleanses the temple, enforces the Sabbath, and requires the people to put away all foreign wives.

OUTLINE OF NEHEMIAH

Part One: The Reconstruction of the Wall (1:1—7:73)

I. The Preparation to Reconstruct the Wall .... 1:1—2:20

A. Discovery of the Broken Wall 1:1–3
B. Intercession of Nehemiah .... 1:4—2:8
1. Nehemiah Intercedes with God 1:4–11
2. Nehemiah Intercedes with Artaxerxes 2:1–8
C. Arrival of Nehemiah in Jerusalem 2:9–11
D. Preparation to Reconstruct the Wall ... 2:12–20
1. Nehemiah Inspects the Broken Walls 2:12–16
2. Nehemiah Exhorts the People 2:17, 18
3. Nehemiah Answers the Enemies ... 2:19, 20

II. The Reconstruction of the Wall .... 3:1—7:73

A. Record of the Builders 3:1–32
B. Opposition to the Reconstruction ...... 4:1—6:14
1. Opposition Through Ridicule 4:1–6
2. Opposition Through Threat of Attack 4:7–9
3. Opposition Through Discouragement 4:10–23
4. Opposition Through Extortion 5:1–13
5. Nehemiah's Unselfish Example 5:14–19
6. Opposition Through Compromise 6:1–4
7. Opposition Through Slander 6:5–9
8. Opposition Through Treachery 6:10–14
C. Completion of the Reconstruction 6:15–19
D. Organization of Jerusalem 7:1–4
E. Registration of Jerusalem 7:5–73
1. The Plan 7:5, 6
2. The Remnant of Known Descent 7:7–60
3. The Remnant of Unknown Descent 7:61–65
4. The Total of the Remnant 7:66–69
5. The Gifts of the Remnant for the Temple 7:70–73

Part Two: The Restoration of the People (8:1—13:31)

I. The Renewal of the Covenant .... 8:1—10:39

A. Interpretation of the Law 8:1–18
1. Reading of the Law 8:1–8
2. Response to the Reading 8:9–18
B. Reaffirmation of the Covenant .... 9:1—10:39
1. Spiritual Preparation of Israel 9:1–3
2. Reiteration of the Acts of Parties of the Covenant 9:4–31
3. Renewal of the Covenant 9:32–38
4. Ratifiers of the Covenant 10:1–27
5. Stipulations of the Covenant 10:28–39

II. The Obedience to the Covenant ... 11:1—13:31

A. Resettlement of the People 11:1–36
1. Plan for the Resettlement 11:1, 2
2. Resettlement Within Jerusalem 11:3–24
3. Resettlement Outside of Jerusalem 11:25–36
B. Register of the Priests and the Levites 12:1–26

CHAPTER 1

Discovery of the Broken Wall

THE words of [R]Nehemiah the son of Hachaliah. Neh. 10:1

It came to pass in the month of Chislev, *in* the [R]twentieth year, as I was in [R]Shushan* the citadel, Neh. 2:1 • Esth. 1:1, 2, 5

2 that [R]Hanani one of my brethren came with men from Judah; and I asked them concerning the Jews who had escaped, who had survived the captivity, and concerning Jerusalem. Neh. 7:2

3 And they said to me, "The survivors who are left from the captivity in the province *are* there in great distress and reproach. The wall of Jerusalem *is* also broken down, and its gates *are* burned with fire."

Nehemiah Intercedes with God

4 So it was, when I heard these words, that I sat down and wept, and mourned *for many* days; I was fasting and praying before the God of heaven.

5 And I said: "I pray, [R]LORD God of heaven, O great and [R]awesome God, [R]*You* who keep *Your* covenant and mercy with those who love You* and observe Your* commandments, Dan. 9:4 • Neh. 4:14 • [Ex. 20:6; 34:6, 7]

6 "please let Your ear be attentive and [R]Your eyes open, that You may hear the prayer of Your servant which I pray before You now, day and night, for the children of Israel Your servants, and [R]confess the sins of the children of Israel which we have sinned against You. Both my father's house and I have sinned. 2 Chr. 6:40 • Dan. 9:20

7 [R]"We have acted very corruptly against You, and have not kept the commandments, the statutes, nor the ordinances which You commanded Your servant Moses. Dan. 9:5

8 "Remember, I pray, the word that You commanded Your servant Moses, saying, '*If* you [T]are unfaithful, I will scatter you among the nations;* *act treacherously*

9 'but *if* you return to Me, and keep My commandments and do them, though some of you were cast out to the farthest part of the heavens, *yet* I will gather them from there, and bring them to the place which I have chosen as a dwelling for My name.'*

10 "Now these *are* Your servants and Your people, whom You have redeemed by Your great power, and by Your strong hand.

11 "O Lord, I pray, please [R]let Your ear be attentive to the prayer of Your servant, and to the prayer of Your servants who [R]desire to fear Your name; and let Your servant prosper this day, I pray, and grant him mercy in the sight of this man." For I was the king's [R]cupbearer. Neh. 1:6 • Is. 26:8 • Neh. 2:1

CHAPTER 2

Nehemiah Intercedes with Artaxerxes

AND it came to pass in the month of Nisan, in the twentieth year of King Artaxerxes, *when* wine *was* before him, that I took the wine and gave it to the king. Now I had never been sad in his presence before.

2 Therefore the king said to me, "Why *is* your face sad, since you *are* not sick? This *is* nothing but [R]sorrow of heart." So I became [T]dreadfully afraid, Prov. 15:13 • Lit. *very much*

3 and said to the king, [R]"May the king live forever! Why should my face not be sad, when [R]the city, the place of my fathers' tombs, *lies* waste, and its gates are burned with fire?" Dan. 2:4; 5:10; 6:6, 21 • 2 Chr. 36:19

4 Then the king said to me, "What do you request?" So I prayed to the God of heaven.

5 And I said to the king, "If it pleases the king, and if your servant has found favor in your sight, I ask that you send me to Judah, to the city of my fathers' tombs, that I may rebuild it."

6 Then the king said to me (the queen also sitting beside him), "How long will your journey be? And when will you return?" So it pleased the king to send me; and I set him [R]a time. Neh. 5:14; 13:6

7 Furthermore I said to the king, "If it pleases the king, let letters be given to me for the [R]governors *of the region* beyond the River,* that they must permit me to pass through till I come to Judah, Ezra 7:21; 8:36

8 "and a letter to Asaph the keeper of the king's forest, that he must give me timber to make beams for the gates of the citadel which *pertains* to the temple,* for the city wall, and for the house that I will occupy." And the king granted *them* to me according to the good hand of my God upon me.

Arrival of Nehemiah in Jerusalem

9 Then I went to the governors *in the region* beyond the River, and gave them the king's

1:1 Or *Susa* **1:5** Lit. *Him* • Lit. *His* **1:8** Lev. 26:33
1:9 Deut. 30:2–5 **2:7** The Euphrates **2:8** Lit. *house*

letters. Now the king had sent captains of the
army and horsemen with me.
10 When [R]Sanballat the Horonite and To-
biah the Ammonite official* heard *of it,* they
were deeply disturbed that a man had come
to seek the well-being of the children of Is-
rael. Neh. 2:19; 4:1
11 So I [R]came to Jerusalem and was there
three days. Ezra 8:32

Nehemiah Inspects the Broken Walls

12 Then I arose in the night, I and a few men
with me; I told no one what my God had put
in my heart to do at Jerusalem; nor was there
any animal with me, except the one on which
I rode.
13 And I went out by night [R]through the Val-
ley Gate to the Serpent Well and the Refuse
Gate, and viewed the walls of Jerusalem
which were broken down and its gates which
were burned with fire. Neh. 3:13
14 Then I went on to the Fountain Gate and
to the King's Pool, but *there was* no room for
the animal under me to pass.
15 So I went up in the night by the valley,
and viewed the wall; then I turned back and
entered by the Valley Gate, and so returned.
16 And the officials did not know where I
had gone or what I had done; I had not yet
told the Jews, the priests, the nobles, the offi-
cials, or the others who did the work.

Nehemiah Exhorts the People

17 Then I said to them, "You see the distress
that we *are* in, how Jerusalem *lies* waste, and
its gates are burned with fire. Come and let us
build the wall of Jerusalem, that we may no
longer be a reproach."
18 And I told them of [R]the hand of my God
which had been good upon me, and also of
the king's words that he had spoken to me.
So they said, "Let us rise up and build."
Then they [R]set[T] their hands to *this* good
work. Neh. 2:8 • 2 Sam. 2:7 • Lit. *strengthened*

Nehemiah Answers the Enemies

19 But when Sanballat the Horonite, To-
biah the Ammonite official, and Geshem the
Arab heard *of it,* they laughed at us and de-
spised us, and said, "What *is* this thing that
you are doing? [R]Will you rebel against the
king?" Neh. 6:6
20 So I answered them, and said to them,
"The God of heaven Himself will prosper us;
therefore we His servants will arise and build,
[R]but you have no heritage or right or memo-
rial in Jerusalem." Ezra 4:3

CHAPTER 3

Record of the Builders

THEN Eliashib the high priest rose up with
his brethren the priests and built the
Sheep Gate; they consecrated it and hung its
doors. They built as far as the Tower of the
Hundred,* *and* consecrated it, then as far as
the Tower of Hananel.
2 Next to *Eliashib** [R]the men of Jericho
built. And next to them Zaccur the son of Imri
built. Neh. 7:36
3 Also the sons of Hassenaah built [R]the
Fish Gate; they laid its beams and hung its
doors with its bolts and bars. Zeph. 1:10
4 And next to them Meremoth the son of
Urijah, the son of Koz,* made repairs. Next to
them Meshullam the son of Berechiah, the
son of Meshezabel, made repairs. Next to
them Zadok the son of Baana made repairs.
5 Next to them the Tekoites made repairs;
but their nobles did not put their shoulders* to
[R]the work of their Lord. [Judg. 5:23]
6 Moreover Jehoiada the son of Paseah and
Meshullam the son of Besodeiah repaired the
Old Gate; they laid its beams and hung its
doors, with its bolts and bars.
7 And next to them Melatiah the
Gibeonite, Jadon the Meronothite, the [R]men
of Gibeon and Mizpah, repaired the [R]resi-
dence* of the governor *of the region* beyond
the River. Neh. 7:25 • Neh. 2:7–9
8 Next to him Uzziel the son of Harhaiah,
one of the goldsmiths, made repairs. Also
next to him Hananiah, one* of the perfumers,
made repairs; and they fortified Jerusalem as
far as the [R]Broad Wall. Neh. 12:38
9 And next to them Rephaiah the son of
Hur, leader of half the district of Jerusalem,
made repairs.
10 Next to them Jedaiah the son of Ha-
rumaph made repairs in front of his house.
And next to him Hattush the son of Hashab-
niah made repairs.
11 Malchijah the son of Harim and Hashub
the son of Pahath-Moab repaired another sec-
tion, as well as the Tower of the Ovens.
12 And next to him was Shallum the son of
Hallohesh, leader of half the district of Jeru-
salem; he and his daughters made repairs.
13 Hanun and the inhabitants of Zanoah re-
paired [R]the Valley Gate. They built it, hung its
doors with its bolts and bars, and *repaired* a
thousand cubits of the wall as far as [R]the
Refuse Gate. Neh. 2:13, 15 • Neh. 2:13
14 Malchijah the son of Rechab, leader of
the district of [R]Beth Haccerem, repaired the
Refuse Gate; he built it and hung its doors
with its bolts and bars. Jer. 6:1
15 Shallun the son of Col-Hozeh, leader of
the district of Mizpah, repaired [R]the Fountain
Gate; he built it, covered it, hung its doors
with its bolts and bars, and repaired the wall
of the Pool of [R]Shelah by the King's Garden,

2:10 Lit. *servant* **3:1** Heb. *Hammeah* **3:2** Lit. *On his hand* **3:4** Or *Hakkoz* **3:5** Lit. *necks* **3:7** Lit. *throne* **3:8** Lit. *the son*

as far as the stairs that go down from the City of David. Neh. 2:14 • Is. 8:6

16 After him Nehemiah the son of Azbuk, leader of half the district of Beth Zur, made repairs as far as *the place* in front of the tombs* of David, to the man-made pool, and as far as the House of the Mighty.

17 After him the Levites, *under* Rehum the son of Bani, made repairs. Next to him Hashabiah, leader of half the district of Keilah, made repairs for his district.

18 After him their brethren, *under* Bavai* the son of Henadad, leader of the *other* half of the district of Keilah, made repairs.

19 And next to him Ezer the son of Jeshua, the leader of Mizpah, repaired another section in front of the Ascent to the Armory at the [R]buttress.[T] 2 Chr. 26:9 • Lit. *turning*

20 After him Baruch the son of Zabbai* carefully repaired the other section, from the [T]buttress to the door of the house of Eliashib the high priest. Lit. *turning*

21 After him Meremoth the son of Urijah, the son of Koz,* repaired another section, from the door of the house of Eliashib to the end of the house of Eliashib.

22 And after him the priests, the men of the plain, made repairs.

23 After him Benjamin and Hasshub made repairs opposite their house. After them Azariah the son of Maaseiah, the son of Ananiah, made repairs by his house.

24 After him [R]Binnui the son of Henadad repaired another section, from the house of Azariah to [R]the [T]buttress, even as far as the corner. Ezra 8:33 • Neh. 3:19 • Lit. *turning*

25 Palal the son of Uzai *made repairs* opposite the buttress, and on the tower which projects from the king's upper house that *was* by the court of the prison. After him Pedaiah the son of Parosh *made repairs.*

26 Moreover [R]the Nethinim who dwelt in Ophel *made repairs* as far as *the place* in front of the Water Gate toward the east, and on the projecting tower. Neh. 11:21

27 After them the Tekoites repaired another section, next to the great projecting tower, and as far as the wall of Ophel.

28 Beyond the [R]Horse Gate the priests made repairs, each in front of his *own* house. 2 Chr. 23:15

29 After them Zadok the son of Immer made repairs in front of his *own* house. After him Shemaiah the son of Shechaniah, the keeper of the East Gate, made repairs.

30 After him Hananiah the son of Shelemiah, and Hanun, the sixth son of Zalaph, repaired another section. After him Meshullam the son of Berechiah made repairs in front of his [T]dwelling. Lit. *room*

31 After him Malchijah, one of the goldsmiths, made repairs as far as the house of the Nethinim and of the merchants, in front of the Miphkad* Gate, and as far as the upper room at the corner.

32 And between the upper room at the corner, as far as the Sheep Gate, the goldsmiths and the merchants made repairs.

CHAPTER 4

Opposition Through Ridicule

BUT it so happened, [R]when Sanballat heard that we were rebuilding the wall, that he was furious and very indignant, and mocked the Jews. Neh. 2:10, 19

2 And he spoke before his brethren and the army of Samaria, and said, "What are these feeble Jews doing? Will they fortify themselves? Will they offer sacrifices? Will they complete it in a day? Will they revive the stones from the heaps of rubbish—*stones* that are burned?"

3 Now [R]Tobiah the Ammonite *was* beside him, and he said, "Whatever they build, if even a fox goes up *on it,* he will break down their stone wall." Neh. 2:10, 19

4 [R]Hear, O our God, for we are despised; [R]turn their reproach on their own heads, and give them as plunder to a land of captivity! Ps. 123:3, 4 • Ps. 79:12

5 [R]Do not cover their iniquity, and do not let their sin be blotted out from before You; for they have provoked *You* to anger before the builders. Jer. 18:23

6 So we built the wall, and the entire wall was joined together up to half its *height,* for the people had a mind to work.

Opposition Through Threat of Attack

7 Now it happened, [R]when Sanballat, Tobiah, [R]the Arabs, the Ammonites, and the Ashdodites heard that the walls of Jerusalem were being restored and the [T]gaps were beginning to be closed, that they became very angry, Neh. 4:1 • Neh. 2:19 • Lit. *breaks*

8 and all of them [R]conspired together to come *and* attack Jerusalem and create confusion. Ps. 83:3–5

9 Nevertheless [R]we made our prayer to our God, and because of them we set a watch against them day and night. [Ps. 50:15]

Opposition Through Discouragement

10 Then Judah said, "The strength of the laborers is failing, and *there is* so much rubbish that we are not able to build the wall."

11 And our adversaries said, "They will neither know nor see anything, till we come into their midst and kill them and cause the work to cease."

3:16 LXX, Syr., Vg. *tomb* **3:18** So with MT, Vg.; some Heb. mss., LXX, Syr. *Binnui* (cf. v. 24) **3:20** A few Heb. mss., Syr., Vg. *Zaccai* **3:21** Or *Hakkoz* **3:31** Lit. *Inspection* or *Recruiting*

12 So it was, when the Jews who dwelt near
them came, that they told us ten times, "From
whatever place you turn, *they will be* upon
us."
13 Therefore I positioned *men* behind the
lower parts of the wall, at the openings; and I
set the people according to their families, with
their swords, their spears, and their bows.
14 And I looked, and arose and said to the
nobles, to the leaders, and to the rest of the
people, "Do not be afraid of them. Remember
the Lord, great and awesome, and fight for
your brethren, your sons, your daughters,
your wives, and your houses."
15 And it happened, when our enemies
heard that it was known to us, and [R]*that*
God had brought their plot to nothing, that
all of us returned to the wall, everyone to his
work. Job 5:12
16 So it was, from that time on, *that* half of
my servants worked at construction, while the
other half held the spears, the shields, the
bows, and *wore* armor; and the leaders *were*
behind all the house of Judah.
17 Those who built on the wall, and those
who carried burdens, loaded themselves so
that with one hand they worked at construc-
tion, and with the other held a weapon.
18 Every one of the builders had his sword
girded at his side as he built. And the one who
sounded the trumpet *was* beside me.
19 Then I said to the nobles, the rulers, and
the rest of the people, "The work *is* great and
extensive, and we are separated far from one
another on the wall.
20 "Wherever you hear the sound of the
trumpet, rally to us there. [R]Our God will fight
for us." Ex. 14:14, 25
21 So we labored in the work, and half of *the
men** held the spears from daybreak until the
stars appeared.
22 At the same time I also said to the people,
"Let each man and his servant stay at night in
Jerusalem, that they may be our guard by
night and a working party by day."
23 So neither I, my brethren, my servants,
nor the men of the guard who followed me
took off our clothes, *except* that everyone
took them off for washing.

CHAPTER 5

Opposition Through Extortion

AND there was a great [R]outcry of the peo-
ple and their wives against their [R]Jewish
brethren. Neh. 5:7, 8 • Deut. 15:7
2 For there were those who said, "We, our
sons, and our daughters *are* many; therefore
let us get grain, that we may eat and live."
3 There were also *some* who said, "We have
mortgaged our lands and vineyards and
houses, that we might buy grain because of
the famine."
4 There were also those who said, "We have
borrowed money for the king's tax *on* our
lands and vineyards.
5 "Yet now our flesh *is* as the flesh of our
brethren, our children as their children; and
indeed we are forcing our sons and our
daughters to be slaves, and *some* of our
daughters have been brought into slavery. *It is*
not in our power *to redeem them,* for other
men have our lands and vineyards."
6 And I became very angry when I heard
their outcry and these words.
7 After serious thought, I rebuked the no-
bles and rulers, and said to them, "Each of you
is exacting usury from his brother." So I called
a great assembly against them.
8 And I said to them, "According to our
ability we have redeemed our Jewish brethren
who were sold to the nations. Now indeed,
will you even sell your brethren? Or should
they be sold to us?" Then they were silenced
and found nothing *to say.*
9 Then I said, "What you are doing *is* not
good. Should you not walk [R]in the fear of our
God [R]because of the reproach of the nations,
our enemies? Lev. 25:36 • 2 Sam. 12:14
10 "I also, *with* my brethren and my ser-
vants, am lending them money and grain.
Please, let us stop this [T]usury! *interest*
11 "Restore now to them, even this day, their
lands, their vineyards, their olive groves, and
their houses, also a hundredth of the money
and the grain, the new wine and the oil, that
you have charged them."
12 So they said, "We will restore *it,* and will
require nothing from them; we will do as you
say." Then I called the priests, [R]and required
an oath from them that they would do accord-
ing to this promise. Ezra 10:5
13 Then I shook out the fold of my garment*
and said, "So may God shake out each man
from his house, and from his property, who
does not perform this promise. Even thus may
he be shaken out and emptied." And all the as-
sembly said, "Amen!" and praised the LORD.
Then the people did according to this prom-
ise.

Nehemiah's Unselfish Example

14 Moreover, from the time that I was ap-
pointed to be their governor in the land of Ju-
dah, from the twentieth year until the
thirty-second year of King Artaxerxes, twelve
years, neither I nor my brothers [R]ate the gov-
ernor's provisions. [1 Cor. 9:4–15]
15 But the former governors who *were* be-
fore me laid burdens on the people, and took
from them bread and wine, besides forty
shekels of silver. Yes, even their servants bore
rule over the people, but [R]I did not do so, be-
cause of the fear of God. 2 Cor. 11:9

4:21 Lit. *them* **5:13** Lit. *my lap*

16 Indeed, I also continued the [R]work on this wall, and we* did not buy any land. All my servants *were* gathered there for the work. Neh. 4:1; 6:1

17 And at my table *were* one hundred and fifty Jews and rulers, besides those who came to us from the nations around us.

18 Now *that* [R]which was prepared daily *was* one ox *and* six choice sheep. Also fowl were prepared for me, and once every ten days an abundance of all kinds of wine. Yet in spite of this [R]I did not demand the governor's provisions, because the bondage was heavy on this people. 1 Kin. 4:22 • Neh. 5:14, 15

19 Remember me, my God, for good, *according to* all that I have done for this people.

CHAPTER 6

Opposition Through Compromise

NOW it happened [R]when Sanballat, Tobiah, Geshem the Arab, and the rest of our enemies heard that I had rebuilt the wall, and *that* there were no breaks left in it (though at that time I had not hung the doors in the gates), Neh. 2:10, 19; 4:1, 7; 13:28

2 that Sanballat and Geshem sent to me, saying, "Come, let us meet together among the villages in the plain of [R]Ono." But they thought to do me harm. 1 Chr. 8:12

3 So I sent messengers to them, saying, "I *am* doing a great work, so that I cannot come down. Why should the work cease while I leave it and go down to you?"

4 But they sent me this message four times, and I answered them in the same manner.

Opposition Through Slander

5 Then Sanballat sent his servant to me as before, the fifth time, with an open letter in his hand.

6 In it *was* written:

> It is reported among the nations, and Geshem* says, *that* you and the Jews plan to rebel; therefore, according to these rumors, you are rebuilding the wall, that you may be their king.

> 7 And you have also appointed prophets to proclaim concerning you at Jerusalem, saying, "*There is* a king in Judah!" Now these matters will be reported to the king. So come, therefore, and let us consult together.

8 Then I sent to him, saying, "No such things as you say are being done, but you invent them in your own heart."

9 For they all *were trying to* make us afraid, saying, "Their hands will be weakened in the work, and it will not be done."

Now therefore, *O God,* strengthen my hands.

Opposition Through Treachery

10 Afterward I came to the house of Shemaiah the son of Delaiah, the son of Mehetabel, who *was* a secret informer; and he said, "Let us meet together in the house of God, within the [T]temple, and let us close the doors of the temple, for they are coming to kill you; indeed, at night they will come to kill you." Lit. *house*

11 And I said, "Should such a man as I flee? And who *is there* such as I who would go into the temple to save his life? I will not go in!"

12 Then I perceived that God had not sent him at all, but that [R]he pronounced *this* prophecy against me because Tobiah and Sanballat had hired him. Ezek. 13:22

13 For this reason he *was* hired, that I should be afraid and act that way and sin, so *that* they might have *cause* for an evil report, that they might reproach me.

14 My God, remember Tobiah and Sanballat, according to these their works, and the prophetess Noadiah and the rest of the prophets who would have made me afraid.

Completion of the Reconstruction

15 So the wall was finished on the twenty-fifth *day* of Elul, in fifty-two days.

16 And it happened, when all our enemies heard *of it,* and all the nations around us saw *these things,* that they were very disheartened in their own eyes; for they perceived that this work was done by our God.

17 Also in those days the nobles of Judah sent many letters to Tobiah, and *the letters of* Tobiah came to them.

18 For many in Judah were pledged to him, because he was the [R]son-in-law of Shechaniah the son of Arah, and his son Jehohanan had married the daughter of Meshullam the son of Berechiah. Neh. 13:4, 28

19 Also they reported his good deeds before me, and reported my [T]words to him. Tobiah sent letters to frighten me. Or *affairs*

CHAPTER 7

Organization of Jerusalem

THEN it was, when the wall was built and I had [R]hung the doors, when the gatekeepers, the singers, and the Levites had been appointed, Neh. 6:1, 15

2 that I gave the charge of Jerusalem to my brother Hanani, and Hananiah the leader of the citadel, for he *was* a faithful man and feared God more than many.

3 And I said to them, "Do not let the gates of Jerusalem be opened until the sun is hot; and while they stand *guard,* let them shut and bar the doors; and appoint guards from among the inhabitants of Jerusalem, one at

5:16 So with MT; LXX, Syr., Vg. *I* **6:6** Heb. *Gashmu*

his watch station and another in front of his
own house."
4 Now the city *was* large and spacious, but
the people in it *were* [R]few, and the houses
were not rebuilt. Deut. 4:27

The Plan

5 Then my God put it into my heart to
gather the nobles, the rulers, and the people,
that they might be registered by genealogy.
And I found a register of the genealogy of
those who had come up in the first *return,* and
found written in it:

6 These* *are* the people of the province
who came back from the captivity, of
those who had been carried away, whom
Nebuchadnezzar the king of Babylon
had carried away, and who returned to
Jerusalem and Judah, everyone to his
city.

The Leaders

7 Those who came with [R]Zerubbabel
were Jeshua, Nehemiah, [T]Azariah,
Raamiah, Nahamani, Mordecai, Bilshan,
Mispereth,* Bigvai, Nehum, and
Baanah. Ezra 5:2 • *Seraiah,* Ezra 2:2
The number of the men of the people
of Israel:

The Men of Israel

8 the sons of Parosh, two thousand one hundred and seventy-two;
9 the sons of Shephatiah, three hundred and seventy-two;
10 the sons of Arah, six hundred and fifty-two;
11 the sons of Pahath-Moab, of the sons of Jeshua and Joab, two thousand eight hundred and eighteen;
12 the sons of Elam, one thousand two hundred and fifty-four;
13 the sons of Zattu, eight hundred and forty-five;
14 the sons of Zaccai, seven hundred and sixty;
15 the sons of Binnui,* six hundred and forty-eight;
16 the sons of Bebai, six hundred and twenty-eight;
17 the sons of Azgad, two thousand three hundred and twenty-two;
18 the sons of Adonikam, six hundred and sixty-seven;
19 the sons of Bigvai, two thousand and sixty-seven;
20 the sons of Adin, six hundred and fifty-five;
21 the sons of Ater of Hezekiah, ninety-eight;
22 the sons of Hashum, three hundred and twenty-eight;
23 the sons of Bezai, three hundred and twenty-four;
24 the sons of Hariph,* one hundred and twelve;
25 the sons of Gibeon,* ninety-five;
26 the men of Bethlehem and Netophah, one hundred and eighty-eight;
27 the men of Anathoth, one hundred and twenty-eight;
28 the men of Beth Azmaveth,* forty-two;
29 the men of [T]Kirjath Jearim, Chephirah, and Beeroth, seven hundred and forty-three; *Kirjath Arim,* Ezra 2:25
30 the men of Ramah and Geba, six hundred and twenty-one;
31 the men of Michmas, one hundred and twenty-two;
32 the men of Bethel and Ai, one hundred and twenty-three;
33 the men of the other Nebo, fifty-two;
34 the sons of the other Elam, one thousand two hundred and fifty-four;
35 the sons of Harim, three hundred and twenty;
36 the sons of Jericho, three hundred and forty-five;
37 the sons of Lod, Hadid, and Ono, seven hundred and twenty-one;
38 the sons of Senaah, three thousand nine hundred and thirty.

The Priests

39 The priests: the sons of [R]Jedaiah, of the house of Jeshua, nine hundred and seventy-three; 1 Chr. 24:7
40 the sons of [R]Immer, one thousand and fifty-two; 1 Chr. 9:12
41 the sons of Pashhur, one thousand two hundred and forty-seven;
42 the sons of [R]Harim, one thousand and seventeen. 1 Chr. 24:8

The Levites

43 The Levites: the sons of Jeshua, of Kadmiel, *and* of the sons of Hodevah,* seventy-four.
44 The singers: the sons of Asaph, one hundred and forty-eight.
45 The gatekeepers: the sons of Shallum, the sons of Ater, the sons of Talmon, the sons of Akkub, the sons of Hatita, the sons of Shobai, one hundred and thirty-eight.

The Servants

46 The Nethinim: the sons of Ziha, the sons of Hasupha, the sons of Tabbaoth,

7:6 Cf. vv. 6–72 with Ezra 2:1–70 **7:7** *Mispar,* Ezra 2:2 **7:15** *Bani,* Ezra 2:10 **7:24** *Jorah,* Ezra 2:18 **7:25** *Gibbar,* Ezra 2:20 **7:28** *Azmaveth,* Ezra 2:24 **7:43** *Hodaviah,* Ezra 2:40; or *Judah,* Ezra 3:9

47 the sons of Keros, the sons of Sia,* the
sons of Padon,
48 the sons of Lebana,* the sons of
Hagaba,* the sons of Salmai,*
49 the sons of Hanan, the sons of Giddel,
the sons of Gahar,
50 the sons of Reaiah, the sons of Rezin, the
sons of Nekoda,
51 the sons of Gazzam, the sons of Uzza,
the sons of Paseah,
52 the sons of Besai, the sons of Meunim,
the sons of Nephishesim,*
53 the sons of Bakbuk, the sons of
Hakupha, the sons of Harhur,
54 the sons of Bazlith,* the sons of Mehida,
the sons of Harsha,
55 the sons of Barkos, the sons of Sisera,
the sons of Tamah,
56 the sons of Neziah, and the sons of
Hatipha.
57 The sons of Solomon's servants: the sons
of Sotai, the sons of Sophereth, the sons
of Perida,*
58 the sons of Jaala, the sons of Darkon, the
sons of Giddel,
59 the sons of Shephatiah, the sons of
Hattil, the sons of Pochereth of Zebaim,
and the sons of Amon.*
60 All the Nethinim, and the sons of
Solomon's servants, *were* three hundred
and ninety-two.

The Men of Israel

61 And these *were* the ones who came up
from Tel Melah, Tel Harsha, Cherub,
Addon,* and Immer, but they could not
identify their father's house nor their
lineage, whether they *were* of Israel:
62 the sons of Delaiah, the sons of Tobiah,
the sons of Nekoda, six hundred and
forty-two;

The Priests

63 and of the priests: the sons of Habaiah,
the sons of Koz,* the sons of Barzillai,
who took a wife of the daughters of
Barzillai the Gileadite, and was called by
their name.
64 These sought their listing *among* those
who were registered by genealogy, but it
was not found; therefore they were
excluded from the priesthood as defiled.
65 And the governor* said to them that they
should not eat of the most holy things till
a priest could consult with the Urim and
Thummim.

The Total of the Remnant

66 Altogether the whole assembly *was*
forty-two thousand three hundred and
sixty,
67 besides their male and female servants,
of whom *there were* seven thousand
three hundred and thirty-seven; and they
had two hundred and forty-five men and
women singers.
68 Their horses were seven hundred and
thirty-six, their mules two hundred and
forty-five,
69 *their* camels four hundred and thirty-
five, *and* donkeys six thousand seven
hundred and twenty.

The Gifts of the Remnant for the Temple

70 And some of the heads of the fathers'
houses gave to the work. [R]The governor*
gave to the treasury one thousand gold
drachmas, fifty basins, and five hundred
and thirty priestly garments. Neh. 8:9
71 Some of the heads of the fathers' *houses*
gave to the treasury of the work twenty
thousand gold drachmas, and two
thousand two hundred silver minas.
72 And that which the rest of the people
gave *was* twenty thousand gold
drachmas, two thousand silver minas,
and sixty-seven priestly garments.

73 So the priests, the Levites, the gate-
keepers, the singers, *some* of the people, the
Nethinim, and all Israel dwelt in their cities.
[R]When the seventh month came, the children
of Israel *were* in their cities. Ezra 3:1

CHAPTER 8

Reading of the Law

NOW all [R]the people gathered together as
one man in the open square that *was* [R]in
front of the Water Gate; and they told Ezra
the [R]scribe to bring the Book of the Law of
Moses, which the LORD had commanded Is-
rael. Ezra 3:1 • Neh. 3:26 • Ezra 7:6
2 So Ezra the priest brought the Law before
the assembly of men and women and all who
could hear with understanding [R]on the first
day of the seventh month. [Lev. 23:24

3 Then he [R]read from it in the open square
that *was* in front of the Water Gate from
morning until midday, before the men and
women and those who could understand; and
the ears of all the people *were attentive* to the
Book of the Law. 2 Kin. 23:2

4 So Ezra the scribe stood on a platform of
wood which they had made for the purpose;
and beside him, at his right hand, stood Mat-
tithiah, Shema, Anaiah, Urijah, Hilkiah, and
Maaseiah; and at his left hand Pedaiah,

7:47 *Siaha,* Ezra 2:44 **7:48** MT *Lebanah* • MT *Hogabah* • *Shalmai,* Ezra 2:46; or *Shamlai* **7:52** *Nephusim,* Ezra 2:50 **7:54** *Bazluth,* Ezra 2:52 **7:57** *Peruda,* Ezra 2:55 **7:59** *Ami,* Ezra 2:57 **7:61** *Addan,* Ezra 2:59 **7:63** Or *Hakkoz* **7:65** Heb. *Tirshatha* **7:70** Heb. *Tirshatha*

Mishael, Malchijah, Hashum, Hashbadana,
Zechariah, *and* Meshullam.
5 And Ezra opened the book in the sight of
all the people, for he was *standing* above all
the people; and when he opened it, all the
people [R]stood up. Judg. 3:20
6 And Ezra blessed the LORD, the great
God. Then all the people answered, "Amen,
Amen!" while lifting up their hands. And they
bowed their heads and worshiped the LORD
with *their* faces to the ground.
7 Also Jeshua, Bani, Sherebiah, Jamin,
Akkub, Shabbethai, Hodijah, Maaseiah, Kel-
ita, Azariah, Jozabad, Hanan, Pelaiah, and
the Levites, [R]helped the people to understand
the Law; and the people [R]*stood* in their
place. [Mal. 2:7] • Neh. 9:3
8 So they read distinctly from the book, in
the Law of God; and they gave the sense, and
helped *them* to understand the reading.

Israel Celebrates Her Understanding of the Law

9 [R]And Nehemiah, who *was* the governor,*
Ezra the priest *and* scribe, and the Levites
who taught the people said to all the people,
[R]"This day *is* holy to the LORD your God; do
not mourn nor weep." For all the people
wept, when they heard the words of the
Law. Neh. 7:65, 70; 10:1 • Num. 29:1
10 Then he said to them, "Go your way, eat
the fat, drink the sweet, and send portions to
those for whom nothing is prepared; for *this*
day *is* holy to our Lord. Do not sorrow, for the
joy of the LORD is your strength."
11 So the Levites quieted all the people, say-
ing, "Be still, for the day *is* holy; do not be
grieved."
12 And all the people went their way to eat
and drink, to [R]send portions and rejoice
greatly, because they understood the words
that were declared to them. Neh. 8:10

Israel Obeys the Law

13 Now on the second day the heads of the
fathers' *houses* of all the people, with the
priests and Levites, were gathered to Ezra

8:9 Heb. *Tirshatha*

8:3 Reading God's Word—The person who can read well has a much better opportunity of knowing and understanding God's Word than the person who has to rely upon what others tell him about the Word of God. Reading the Word of God is a very important part of communicating God's Word to God's people. Public Scripture reading was a regular part of the worship services in Israel and in the early church. Today we are blessed above all people in history, for not only does nearly everyone know how to read, but there also are enough copies of the Bible available so that everyone may have a personal copy. Here are some suggestions to aid you in receiving the greatest benefit from reading the Bible:

a. Read the Bible prayerfully. Ask the Spirit of God to meet your heart's need as you read (Page 610—Ps. 119:18).
b. Read the Bible thoughtfully. Think about the meaning and implications of what you are reading.
c. Read the Bible carefully. Take careful note not only of the words that are used but also of how they relate to one another.
d. Read the Bible repeatedly. It may be of great help to read the same portion over daily for a month's time. This is a good way for its words to take root in your heart. If you are reading a short book, read it every day. Divide longer books into manageable portions of two or three chapters and read that portion through every day.
e. Read the Bible extensively. Sometimes it is of great help to read large portions of the Word of God through at one sitting. If you do this, do it at a time when you are alert and not likely to be disturbed during your reading.
f. Read the Bible regularly. It is good to have a particular time every day when you habitually give yourself to the reading of the Word of God.
g. Read the Bible faithfully. Inevitably there will be days when you will fail to read the Bible. Do not let your momentary lapse discourage you. Faithfully resume your practice of reading God's Word.
h. Read the Bible obediently. Because the Bible is God's Word written to you, it is essential to obey it (Page 78—Ex. 24:3).

Now turn to Page 527—Job 22:22: Memorizing God's Word.

8:9 God's Word Convicts—One of the great proofs that the Bible is really God's inspired Word is its unique ability to convict men and women of their sins. Let us consider but a few OT and NT examples that demonstrate the lifesaving power of the Scriptures.

OT examples:

a. Josiah, a young and godly Judean king who ruled the Lord's people more than six centuries before Christ, succeeds a wicked ruler who hated righteousness. At the beginning of Josiah's rule a copy of God's Word is found in the temple. When it is read to the king, both he and his people are convicted of their sins in not keeping God's law. A great revival takes place (Page 463—2 Chr. 34:18–21).
b. Nehemiah returns to help the returning Jews rebuild the gates in the Jerusalem wall. This great wall builder thinks the Word of God to be so important that he assembles the people and has the Scriptures read to them for three hours per day. This soon causes them to confess their sins (Page 492—Neh. 9:3).

NT examples: Before Jesus left this earth He promised that the Holy Spirit would soon come upon the apostles. "And when He has come, He will convict the world of sin, and of righteousness, and of judgment" (Page 1101—John 16:8). There are many instances in the NT where we see the Holy Spirit using God's Word to convict people of their sin. At Pentecost Peter uses the Scriptures to rebuke Israel for crucifying its Messiah. This sermon results in three thousand souls being convicted and accepting Christ (Page 1114—Acts 2:37, 41).

Now turn to Page 552—Ps. 17:4: God's Word Corrects.

the scribe, in order to understand the words of
the Law.
14 And they found written in the Law,
which the LORD had commanded by Moses,
that the children of Israel should dwell in
[R]booths[T] during the feast of the seventh
month, Lev. 23:34, 40, 42 • Temporary shelters
15 and [R]that they should announce and
proclaim in all their cities and [R]in Jerusa-
lem, saying, "Go out to the mountain, and
[R]bring olive branches, branches of oil trees,
myrtle branches, palm branches, and
branches of leafy trees, to make booths, as *it*
is written." Lev. 23:4 • Deut. 16:16 • Lev. 23:40
16 Then the people went out and brought
them and made themselves booths, each one
on the roof of his house, or in their courtyards
or the courts of the house of God, and in the
open square of the Water Gate and in the open
square of the Gate of Ephraim.
17 So the whole assembly of those who had
returned from the captivity made booths and
sat under the booths; for since the days of
Joshua the son of Nun until that day the chil-
dren of Israel had not done so. And there was
very [R]great gladness. 2 Chr. 30:21
18 Also [R]day by day, from the first day until
the last day, he read from the Book of the
Law of God. And they kept the feast [R]seven
days; and on the [R]eighth day *there was* a sa-
cred assembly, according to the *prescribed*
manner. Deut. 31:11 • Lev. 23:36 • Num. 29:35

CHAPTER 9

Spiritual Preparation of Israel

NOW on the twenty-fourth day of [R]this
month the children of Israel were assem-
bled with fasting, in sackcloth, [R]and with dust
on their heads.* Neh. 8:2 • 1 Sam. 4:12
2 Then [R]those of Israelite lineage separated
themselves from all foreigners; and they
stood and confessed their sins and the iniqui-
ties of their fathers. Neh. 13:3, 30
3 And they stood up in their place and
[R]read from the Book of the Law of the LORD
their God *for one*-fourth of the day; and *for*
another fourth they confessed and worshiped
the LORD their God. Neh. 8:7, 8

The Great Deliverances of God

4 Then Jeshua, Bani, Kadmiel, Shebaniah,
Bunni, Sherebiah, Bani, *and* Chenani stood on
the stairs of the Levites and cried out with a
loud voice to the LORD their God.
5 And the Levites, Jeshua, Kadmiel, Bani,
Hashabniah, Sherebiah, Hodijah, Shebaniah,
and Pethahiah, said:

"Stand up *and* bless the LORD your God
Forever and ever!

"Blessed be [R]Your glorious name,
Which is exalted above all blessing and
praise! 1 Chr. 29:13
6 [R]You alone *are* the LORD; 2 Kin. 19:15, 19
[R]You have made heaven, Rev. 14:7
[R]The heaven of heavens, with [R]all their
host, [Deut. 10:14] • Gen. 2:1
The earth and everything on it,
The seas and all that is in them,
And You preserve them all.
The host of heaven worships You.

7 "You *are* the LORD God,
Who chose [R]Abram, Gen. 11:31
And brought him out of Ur of the
Chaldeans,
And gave him the name Abraham;
8 You found his heart faithful before You,
And made a [R]covenant with him
To give the land of the Canaanites,
The Hittites, the Amorites, Gen. 15:18
The Perizzites, the Jebusites,
And the Girgashites—
To give *it* to his descendants.
You [R]have performed Your words,
For You *are* righteous. Josh. 23:14

9 "You[R] saw the affliction of our fathers in
Egypt, Ex. 2:25; 3:7
And heard their cry by the Red Sea.
10 You [R]showed signs and wonders against
Pharaoh, Ex. 7—14
Against all his servants,
And against all the people of his land.
For You knew that they [R]acted proudly
against them. Ex. 18:11
So You [R]made a name for Yourself, as *it*
is this day. Jer. 32:20
11 [R]And You divided the sea before them,
So that they went through the midst of
the sea on the dry land; Ex. 14:20–28
And their persecutors You threw into the
deep,
As a stone into the mighty waters.
12 Moreover You [R]led them by day with a
cloudy pillar, Ex. 13:21, 22
And by night with a pillar of fire,
To give them light on the road
Which they should travel.

13 "You[R] came down also on Mount Sinai,
And spoke with them from heaven,
And gave them [R]just ordinances and true
laws, Ex. 20:1–18 • [Rom. 7:12]
Good statutes and commandments.
14 You made known to them Your [R]holy
Sabbath, Gen. 2:3
And commanded them precepts, statutes
and laws,
By the hand of Moses Your servant.

9:1 Lit. *earth on them*

15 You [R]gave them bread from heaven for
their hunger, Ex. 16:14–17
And [R]brought them water out of the rock
for their thirst, Ex. 17:6
And told them to [R]go in to possess the
land Deut. 1:8
Which You had sworn to give them.

The Great Sins of Israel

16 "But[R] they and our fathers acted
[T]proudly, Ps. 106:6 • *presumptuously*
[R]Hardened their necks, Deut. 1:26–33; 31:27
And did not heed Your commandments.
17 They refused to obey,
And [R]they were not mindful of Your
wonders Ps. 78:11, 42–45
That You did among them.
But they hardened their necks,
And in their rebellion*
They appointed [R]a leader Num. 14:4
To return to their bondage.
But You *are* God,
Ready to pardon,
[R]Gracious and merciful, Joel 2:13
Slow to anger,
Abundant in kindness,
And did not forsake them.

18 "Even [R]when they made a molded calf for
themselves, Ex. 32:4–8, 31
And said, 'This *is* your god
That brought you up out of Egypt,'
And worked great provocations,
19 Yet in Your [R]manifold mercies
You did not forsake them in the
wilderness. Ps. 106:45
The [R]pillar of the cloud did not depart
from them by day, 1 Cor. 10:1
To lead them on the road;
Nor the pillar of fire by night,
To show them light,
And the way they should go.
20 You also gave Your [R]good Spirit to
instruct them, Num. 11:17
And did not withhold Your [R]manna from
their mouth, Ex. 16:14–16
And gave them water for their thirst.
21 [R]Forty years You sustained them in the
wilderness; Deut. 2:7
They lacked nothing;
Their clothes did not wear out*
And their feet did not swell.

22 "Moreover You gave them kingdoms and
nations,
And divided them into districts.*
So they took possession of the land of
[R]Sihon, Num. 21:21–35
The land of* the king of Heshbon,
And the land of Og king of Bashan.
23 You also multiplied [R]their children as the
stars of heaven, Gen. 15:5; 22:17
And brought them into the land
Which You had told their fathers
To go in and possess.
24 So [R]the people went in Josh. 1:2–4
And possessed the land;
You subdued before them the inhabitants
of the land,
The Canaanites,
And gave them into their hands,
With their kings
And the people of the land,
That they might do with them as they
wished.
25 And they took strong cities and a [R]rich
land, Num. 13:27
And possessed [R]houses full of all goods,
Cisterns *already* dug, vineyards, olive
groves, Deut. 6:11
And fruit trees in abundance.
So they ate and were filled and [R]grew
fat, [Deut. 32:15]
And delighted themselves in Your great
[R]goodness. Hos. 3:5

26 "Nevertheless they were disobedient
And rebelled against You,
Cast Your law behind their backs
And killed Your [R]prophets, who testified
against them 1 Kin. 18:4; 19:10
To turn them to Yourself;
And they worked great provocations.
27 [R]Therefore You delivered them into the
hand of their enemies, Judg. 2:14
Who oppressed them;
And in the time of their trouble,
When they cried to You,
You [R]heard from heaven;
And according to Your abundant
mercies Ps. 106:44
[R]You gave them deliverers who saved
them Judg. 2:18
From the hand of their enemies.

28 "But after they had rest,
[R]They again did evil before You.
Therefore You left them in the hand of
their enemies, Judg. 3:12
So that they had dominion over them;
Yet when they returned and cried out to
You,
You heard from heaven;
And many times You delivered them
according to Your mercies,
29 And testified against them,
That You might bring them back to Your
law.
Yet they acted [T]proudly, *presumptuously*
And did not heed Your commandments,
But sinned against Your judgments,
'Which if a man does, he shall live by
them.'*

9:17 So with MT, Vg.; LXX *in Egypt* **9:21** Cf. Deut. 29:5 **9:22** Lit. *corners* • So with MT, Vg.; LXX omits *The land of* **9:29** Lev. 18:5

And they shrugged their shoulders,
Stiffened their necks,
And would not hear.
30 Yet for many years You had patience
with them,
And testified against them by Your Spirit
[R]in Your prophets.
Yet they would not listen; [Acts 7:51]
[R]Therefore You gave them into the hand
of the peoples of the lands. Is. 5:5
31 Nevertheless in Your great mercy
[R]You did not utterly consume them nor
forsake them; Jer. 4:27
For You *are* God, gracious and merciful.

Renewal of the Covenant

32"Now therefore, our God,
The great, the [R]mighty, and awesome
God, [Ex. 34:6, 7]
Who keeps covenant and mercy:
Do not let all the [T]trouble seem small
before You *hardship*
That has come upon us,
Our kings and our princes,
Our priests and our prophets,
Our fathers and on all Your people,
[R]From the days of the kings of Assyria
until this day. 2 Kin. 15:19; 17:3–6
33 However [R]You *are* just in all that has
befallen us; [Dan. 9:14]
For You have dealt faithfully,
But we have done wickedly.
34 Neither our kings nor our princes,
Our priests nor our fathers,
Have kept Your law,
Nor heeded Your commandments and
Your testimonies,
With which You testified against them.
35 For they have [R]not served You in their
kingdom, Deut. 28:47
Or in the many good *things* that You
gave them,
Or in the large and rich land which You
set before them;
Nor did they turn from their wicked
works.

36"Here [R]we *are*, servants today!
And the land that You gave to our
fathers, Deut. 28:48
To eat its fruit and its bounty,
Here we *are*, servants in it!
37 And [R]it yields much increase to the
kings Deut. 28:33, 51
You have set over us,
Because of our sins;
Also they have [R]dominion over our
bodies and our cattle
At their pleasure; Deut. 28:48
And we *are* in great distress.

38"And because of all this,
We [R]make a sure *covenant* and write *it;*
Our leaders, our Levites, *and* our priests
[R]seal *it*." 2 Kin. 23:3 • Neh. 10:1

CHAPTER 10

Ratifiers of the Covenant

NOW those who placed *their* seal on *the document were:*
Nehemiah the [T]governor, [R]the son of Hac-
aliah, and Zedekiah, Heb. *Tirshatha* • Neh. 1:1
2 Seraiah, Azariah, Jeremiah,
3 Pashhur, Amariah, Malchijah,
4 Hattush, Shebaniah, Malluch,
5 Harim, Meremoth, Obadiah,
6 Daniel, Ginnethon, Baruch,
7 Meshullam, Abijah, Mijamin,
8 Maaziah, Bilgai, *and* Shemaiah. These
were the priests.
9 The Levites: Jeshua the son of Azaniah,
Binnui of the sons of Henadad, *and* Kadmiel.
10 Their brethren: Shebaniah, Hodijah, Kel-
ita, Pelaiah, Hanan,
11 Micha, Rehob, Hashabiah,
12 Zaccur, Sherebiah, Shebaniah,
13 Hodijah, Bani, *and* Beninu.
14 The leaders of the people: [R]Parosh,
Pahath-Moab, Elam, Zattu, Bani, Ezra 2:3
15 Bunni, Azgad, Bebai,
16 Adonijah, Bigvai, Adin,
17 Ater, Hezekiah, Azzur,
18 Hodijah, Hashum, Bezai,
19 Hariph, Anathoth, Nebai,
20 Magpiash, Meshullam, Hezir,
21 Meshezabel, Zadok, Jaddua,
22 Pelatiah, Hanan, Anaiah,
23 Hoshea, Hananiah, Hasshub,
24 Hallohesh, Pilha, Shobek,
25 Rehum, Hashabnah, Maaseiah,
26 Ahijah, Hanan, Anan,
27 Malluch, Harim, *and* Baanah.

Stipulations of the Covenant

28 [R]Now the rest of the people—the priests,
the Levites, the gatekeepers, the singers, the
Nethinim, and all those who had separated
themselves from the peoples of the lands to
the Law of God, their wives, their sons, and
their daughters, everyone who had knowl-
edge and understanding— Ezra 2:36–43
29 these joined with their brethren, their no-
bles, [R]and entered into a curse and an oath
[R]to walk in God's Law, which was given by
Moses the servant of God, and to observe
and do all the commandments of the LORD
our Lord, and His ordinances and His
statutes: Deut. 29:12 • 2 Kin. 23:3
30 We would not give [R]our daughters as
wives to the peoples of the land, nor take their
daughters for our sons; Ex. 34:16
31 [R]*if* the peoples of the land brought wares
or any grain to sell on the Sabbath day, we
would not buy it from them on the Sabbath, or
on a holy day; and we would forego the [R]sev-

enth year's *produce* and the exacting of every
debt. Ex. 20:10 • Lev. 25:4
32 Also we made ordinances for ourselves,
to exact from ourselves yearly [R]one-third of a
shekel for the service of the house of our
God: Matt. 17:24
33 for [R]the showbread, for the regular grain
offering, for the regular burnt offering of the
Sabbaths, the New Moons, and the set feasts;
for the holy things, for the sin offerings to
make atonement for Israel, and all the work
of the house of our God. Lev. 24:5
34 We cast lots among the priests, the
Levites, and the people, [R]for *bringing* the
wood offering into the house of our God, ac-
cording to our fathers' houses, at the ap-
pointed times year by year, to burn on the
altar of the LORD our God [R]as *it is* written in
the Law. Neh. 13:31 • Lev. 6:12
35 And *we made ordinances* [R]to bring the
firstfruits of our ground and the firstfruits of
all fruit of all trees, year by year, to the house
of the LORD; Ex. 23:19; 34:26
36 to bring the firstborn of our sons and our
cattle, as *it is* written in the Law, and the first-
born of our herds and our flocks, to the house
of our God, to the priests who minister in the
house of our God;
37 [R]to bring the firstfruits of our dough, our
offerings, the fruit from all kinds of trees, *the*
new wine and oil, to the priests, to the store-
rooms of the [T]house of our God; and to bring
the tithes of our land to the Levites, for the
Levites should receive the tithes in all our
farming communities. Lev. 23:17 • Temple
38 And the priest, the descendant of Aaron,
shall be with the Levites [R]when the Levites re-
ceive tithes; and the Levites shall bring up a
tenth of the tithes to the house of our God, to
the rooms of the storehouse. Num. 18:26
39 For the children of Israel and the children
of Levi shall bring the offering of the grain, of
the new wine and the oil, to the storerooms
where the articles of the sanctuary *are, where*
the priests who minister and the gatekeepers
and the singers *are;* and we will not neglect
the house of our God.

CHAPTER 11

Plan for the Resettlement

NOW the leaders of the people dwelt at
Jerusalem; the rest of the people cast lots
to bring one out of ten to dwell in Jerusalem,
[R]the holy city, and nine-tenths *were to dwell*
in *other* cities. Matt. 4:5; 5:35; 27:53
2 And the people blessed all the men who
[R]willingly offered themselves to dwell at Jeru-
salem. Judg. 5:9

Resettlement Within Jerusalem

3 [R]These *are* the heads of the province
who dwelt in Jerusalem. (But in the cities of
Judah everyone dwelt in his own possession
in their cities—Israelites, priests, Levites,
[R]Nethinim, and [R]descendants of Solomon's
servants.) 1 Chr. 9:2, 3 • Ezra 2:43 • Ezra 2:55
4 Also [R]in Jerusalem dwelt *some* of the
children of Judah and of the children of Ben-
jamin. 1 Chr. 9:3
The children of Judah: Athaiah the son
of Uzziah, the son of Zechariah, the son of
Amariah, the son of Shephatiah, the son of
Mahalalel, of the children of Perez;
5 and Maaseiah the son of Baruch, the son
of Col-Hozeh, the son of Hazaiah, the son of
Adaiah, the son of Joiarib, the son of
Zechariah, the son of Shiloni.
6 All the sons of Perez who dwelt at Jerusa-
lem *were* four hundred and sixty-eight valiant
men.
7 And these are the sons of Benjamin: Sallu
the son of Meshullam, the son of Joed, the son
of Pedaiah, the son of Kolaiah, the son of Maa-
seiah, the son of Ithiel, the son of Jeshaiah;
8 and after him Gabbai *and* Sallai, nine
hundred and twenty-eight.
9 Joel the son of Zichri *was* their overseer,
and Judah the son of Senuah* *was* second
over the city.
10 [R]Of the priests: Jedaiah the son of Joiarib,
and Jachin; 1 Chr. 9:10
11 Seraiah the son of Hilkiah, the son of
Meshullam, the son of Zadok, the son of
Meraioth, the son of Ahitub, *was* the leader
of the house of God.
12 Their brethren who did the work of the
house *were* eight hundred and twenty-two;
and Adaiah the son of Jeroham, the son of
Pelaliah, the son of Amzi, the son of Zecha-
riah, the son of Pashhur, the son of Malchijah,
13 and his brethren, heads of the fathers'
houses, were two hundred and forty-two; and
Amashai the son of Azarel, the son of Ahzai,
the son of Meshillemoth, the son of Immer,
14 and their brethren, mighty men of valor,
were one hundred and twenty-eight. Their
overseer *was* Zabdiel the son of *one of* the
great men.*
15 Also of the Levites: Shemaiah the son of
Hasshub, the son of Azrikam, the son of
Hashabiah, the son of Bunni;
16 Shabbethai and Jozabad, of the heads of
the Levites, *had* the oversight of the business
outside of the [T]house of God; Temple
17 Mattaniah the son of Micha,* the son of
Zabdi, the son of Asaph, the leader *who* began
the thanksgiving with prayer; Bakbukiah, the
second among his brethren; and Abda the son
of Shammua, the son of Galal, the son of Je-
duthun.
18 All the Levites in [R]the holy city *were* two
hundred and eighty-four. Neh. 11:1

11:9 Or *Hassenuah* **11:14** Or *the son of Haggedolim*
11:17 Or *Michah*

19 Moreover the gatekeepers, Akkub, Talmon, and their brethren who kept the gates, *were* one hundred and seventy-two.

20 And the rest of Israel, of the priests *and* Levites, *were* in all the cities of Judah, everyone in his inheritance.

21 But the Nethinim dwelt in Ophel. And Ziha and Gishpa *were* over the Nethinim.

22 Also the overseer of the Levites at Jerusalem *was* Uzzi the son of Bani, the son of Hashabiah, the son of Mattaniah, the son of Micha, of the sons of Asaph, the singers in charge of the service of the house of God.

23 For *it was* the king's command concerning them that a certain portion should be for the singers, a quota day by day.

24 Pethahiah the son of Meshezabel, of the children of [R]Zerah the son of Judah, *was* [R]the king's deputy* in all matters concerning the people. Gen. 38:30 • 1 Chr. 18:17

Resettlement Outside of Jerusalem

25 And as for the villages with their fields, *some* of the children of Judah dwelt in [R]Kirjath Arba and its villages, Dibon and its villages, Jekabzeel and its villages; Josh. 14:15

26 in Jeshua, Moladah, Beth Pelet,

27 Hazar Shual, and Beersheba and its villages;

28 in Ziklag and Meconah and its villages;

29 in En Rimmon, Zorah, Jarmuth,

30 Zanoah, Adullam, and their villages; in Lachish and its fields; in Azekah and its villages. They dwelt from Beersheba to the Valley of Hinnom.

31 Also the children of Benjamin from Geba *dwelt* in Michmash, Aija, and Bethel, and their villages;

32 in Anathoth, Nob, Ananiah;

33 in Hazor, Ramah, Gittaim;

34 in Hadid, Zeboim, Neballat;

35 in Lod, Ono, *and* [R]the Valley of Craftsmen. 1 Chr. 4:14

36 Some of the Judean divisions of Levites *were* in Benjamin.

CHAPTER 12

Register of the Priests and the Levites

NOW these *are* the [R]priests and the Levites who came up with [R]Zerubbabel the son of Shealtiel, and Jeshua: Seraiah, Jeremiah, Ezra, Ezra 2:1, 2; 7:7 • Neh. 7:7

2 Amariah, [T]Malluch, Hattush, *Melichu*, v. 14

3 Shechaniah, Rehum, Meremoth,

4 Iddo, Ginnethoi,* [R]Abijah, Luke 1:5

5 Mijamin, Maadiah, Bilgah,

6 Shemaiah, Joiarib, Jedaiah,

7 Sallu, Amok, Hilkiah, *and* Jedaiah.

These *were* the heads of the priests and their brethren in the days of Jeshua.

8 Moreover the Levites *were* Jeshua, Binnui, Kadmiel, Sherebiah, Judah, *and* Mattaniah [R]*who led* the thanksgiving *psalms*, he and his brethren. Neh. 11:17

9 Also Bakbukiah and Unni, their brethren, *stood* across from them in *their* duties.

10 Jeshua begot Joiakim, Joiakim begot Eliashib, Eliashib begot Joiada,

11 Joiada begot Jonathan, and Jonathan begot Jaddua.

12 Now in the days of Joiakim, the priests, the heads of the fathers' *houses were:* of Seraiah, Meraiah; of Jeremiah, Hananiah;

13 of Ezra, Meshullam; of Amariah, Jehohanan;

14 of Melichu,* Jonathan; of Shebaniah,* Joseph;

15 of Harim,* Adna; of Meraioth,* Helkai;

16 of Iddo, Zechariah; of Ginnethon, Meshullam;

17 of Abijah, Zichri; *the son* of Minjamin;* of Moadiah,* Piltai;

18 of Bilgah, Shammua; of Shemaiah, Jehonathan;

19 of Joiarib, Mattenai; of Jedaiah, Uzzi;

20 of Sallai,* Kallai; of Amok, Eber;

21 of Hilkiah, Hashabiah; *and* of Jedaiah, Nethanel.

22 During the reign of Darius the Persian, a record *was also kept* of the Levites and priests *who had been* [R]heads of their fathers' *houses* in the days of Eliashib, Joiada, Johanan, and Jaddua. 1 Chr. 24:6

23 The sons of Levi, the heads of the fathers' *houses* until the days of Johanan the son of Eliashib, *were* written in the book of the [R]chronicles. 1 Chr. 9:14–22

24 And the heads of the Levites *were* Hashabiah, Sherebiah, and Jeshua the son of Kadmiel, with their brothers across from them, to [R]praise *and* give thanks, group alternating with group, according to the command of David the man of God. Neh. 11:17

25 Mattaniah, Bakbukiah, Obadiah, Meshullam, Talmon, and Akkub *were* gatekeepers keeping the watch at the storerooms of the gates.

26 These *lived* in the days of Joiakim the son of Jeshua, the son of Jozadak,* and in the days of Nehemiah [R]the governor, and of Ezra the priest, the scribe. Neh. 8:9

Dedication of the Jerusalem Wall

27 Now at the dedication of the wall of Jerusalem they sought out the Levites in all their places, to bring them to Jerusalem to celebrate the dedication with gladness, both with thanksgivings and singing, *with* cymbals and stringed instruments and harps.

11:24 Lit. *at the king's hand* **12:4** *Ginnethon*, v. 16 **12:14** *Malluch*, v. 2 • *Shechaniah*, v. 3 **12:15** *Rehum*, v. 3 • *Meremoth*, v. 3 **12:17** *Mijamin*, v. 5 • *Maadiah*, v. 5 **12:20** *Sallu*, v. 7 **12:26** *Jehozadak*, 1 Chr. 6:14

28 And the sons of the singers gathered together from the countryside around Jerusalem, from the villages of the Netophathites,
29 from the house of Gilgal, and from the fields of Geba and Azmaveth; for the singers had built themselves villages all around Jerusalem.
30 Then the priests and Levites [R]purified themselves, and purified the people, the gates, and the wall. Neh. 13:22, 30
31 So I brought the leaders of Judah up on the wall, and appointed two large thanksgiving choirs. *One* went to the right hand on the wall toward the Refuse Gate.
32 After them went Hoshaiah and half of the leaders of Judah,
33 and Azariah, Ezra, Meshullam,
34 Judah, Benjamin, Shemaiah, Jeremiah,
35 and some of the priests' sons [R]with trumpets—Zechariah the son of Jonathan, the son of Shemaiah, the son of Mattaniah, the son of Michaiah, the son of Zaccur, the son of Asaph, Num. 10:2, 8
36 and his brethren, Shemaiah, Azarel, Milalai, Gilalai, Maai, Nethanel, Judah, *and* Hanani, with [R]the musical [R]instruments of David the man of God. Ezra the scribe *went* before them. 1 Chr. 23:5 • 2 Chr. 29:26, 27
37 [R]By the Fountain Gate, in front of them, they went up [R]the stairs of the [R]City of David, on the stairway of the wall, beyond the house of David, as far as the Water Gate eastward. Neh. 2:14; 3:15 • Neh. 3:15 • 2 Sam. 5:7–9
38 [R]The other thanksgiving choir went the opposite *way,* and I *was* behind them with half of the people on the wall, going past the [R]Tower of the Ovens as far as [R]the Broad Wall, Neh. 12:31 • Neh. 3:11 • Neh. 3:8
39 and above the Gate of Ephraim, above the Old Gate, above the Fish Gate, [R]the Tower of Hananel, the Tower of the Hundred, as far as the Sheep Gate; and they stopped by the Gate of the Prison. Neh. 3:1
40 So the two thanksgiving choirs stood in the house of God, likewise I and the half of the rulers with me;
41 and the priests, Eliakim, Maaseiah, Minjamin,* Michaiah, Elioenai, Zechariah, *and* Hananiah, with trumpets;
42 also Maaseiah, Shemaiah, Eleazar, Uzzi, Jehohanan, Malchijah, Elam, and Ezer. The singers [T]sang loudly with Jezrahiah the director. Lit. *made their voice to be heard*
43 Also that day they offered great sacrifices, and rejoiced, for God had made them rejoice with great joy; the women and the children also rejoiced, so that the joy of Jerusalem was heard [R]afar off. Ezra 3:13
44 And at the same time some were appointed over the rooms of the storehouse for the offerings, the firstfruits, and the tithes, to gather into them from the fields of the cities the portions specified by the Law for the priests and Levites; for Judah rejoiced over the priests and Levites who ministered.
45 Both the singers and the gatekeepers kept the charge of their God and the charge of the purification, according to the command of David *and* Solomon his son.
46 For in the days of David and Asaph of old *there were* chiefs of the singers, and songs of praise and thanksgiving to God.
47 In the days of Zerubbabel and in the days of Nehemiah all Israel gave the portions for the singers and the gatekeepers, a portion for each day. They also consecrated *holy things* for the Levites, and the Levites consecrated *them* for the children of Aaron.

CHAPTER 13

Separation from the Heathen

ON that day [R]they read from the Book of Moses in the hearing of the people, and in it was found written [R]that no Ammonite or Moabite should ever come into the assembly of God, Neh. 8:3, 8; 9:3 • Deut. 23:3, 4
2 because they had not met the children of Israel with bread and water, but [R]hired Balaam against them to curse them. [R]However, our God turned the curse into a blessing. Num. 22:5 • Num. 23:1; 24:10
3 So it was, when they had heard the Law, [R]that they separated all the mixed multitude from Israel. Neh. 9:2; 10:28
4 Now before this, Eliashib the priest, having authority over the storerooms of the house of our God, *was* allied with Tobiah.
5 And he had prepared for him a large room, [R]where previously they had stored the grain offerings, the frankincense, the articles, the tithes of grain, the new wine and oil, which were commanded *to be given* to the Levites and singers and gatekeepers, and the offerings for the priests. Neh. 12:44
6 But during all this I was not in Jerusalem, [R]for in the thirty-second year of Artaxerxes king of Babylon I had returned to the king. Then after certain days I obtained leave from the king, Neh. 5:14–16
7 and I came to Jerusalem and discovered the evil that Eliashib had done for Tobiah, in [R]preparing a room for him in the courts of the [T]house of God. Neh. 13:1, 5 • Temple
8 And it grieved me bitterly; therefore I threw all the household goods of Tobiah out of the room.
9 Then I commanded them to [R]cleanse the rooms; and I brought back into them the articles of the house of God, with the grain offering and the frankincense. 2 Chr. 29:5, 15, 16

12:41 *Mijamin,* v. 5

Restoration of Levitical Support

10 I also realized that the portions for the Levites had [R]not been given *them;* for each of the Levites and the singers who did the work had gone back to his field. Neh. 10:37

11 So [R]I contended with the rulers, and said, [R]"Why is the house of God forsaken?" And I gathered them together and set them in their place. Neh. 13:17, 25 • Neh. 10:39

12 [R]Then all Judah brought the tithe of the grain and the new wine and the oil to the storehouse. Neh. 10:38; 12:44

13 [R]And I appointed as treasurers over the storehouse Shelemiah the priest and Zadok the scribe, and of the Levites, Pedaiah; and next to them *was* Hanan the son of Zaccur, the son of Mattaniah; for they were considered [R]faithful, and their task *was* to distribute to their brethren. 2 Chr. 31:12 • 1 Cor. 4:2

14 [R]Remember me, O my God, concerning this, and do not wipe out my good deeds that I have done for the house of my God, and for its services! Neh. 5:19; 13:22, 31

Restoration of the Sabbath

15 In those days I saw *people* in Judah treading wine presses [R]on the Sabbath, and bringing in sheaves, and loading donkeys with wine, grapes, figs, and all *kinds of* burdens, [R]which they brought into Jerusalem on the Sabbath day. And I warned *them* about the day on which they were selling provisions. [Ex. 20:10] • [Jer. 17:21]

16 Men of Tyre dwelt there also, who brought in fish and all kinds of goods, and sold *them* on the Sabbath to the children of Judah, and in Jerusalem.

17 Then I contended with the nobles of Judah, and said to them, "What evil thing *is* this that you do, by which you profane the Sabbath day?

18 [R]"Did not your fathers do thus, and did not our God bring all this disaster on us and on this city? Yet you bring added wrath on Israel by profaning the Sabbath." [Jer. 17:21]

19 So it was, at the gates of Jerusalem, as it began to be dark before the Sabbath, that I commanded the gates to be shut, and charged that they must not be opened till after the Sabbath. Then I posted *some* of my servants at the gates, *so that* no burdens would be brought in on the Sabbath day.

20 Now the merchants and sellers of all kinds of [T]wares [T]lodged outside Jerusalem once or twice. *merchandise • spent the night*

21 Then I warned them, and said to them, "Why do you spend the night [T]around the wall? If you do *so* again, I will lay hands on you!" From that time on they came no *more* on the Sabbath. Lit. *before*

22 And I commanded the Levites that [R]they should cleanse themselves, and that they should go and guard the gates, to sanctify the Sabbath day. Neh. 12:30

Remember me, O my God, *concerning* this also, and spare me according to the greatness of Your mercy!

Restoration from Mixed Marriages

23 In those days I also saw Jews *who* [R]had married women of [R]Ashdod, Ammon, *and* Moab. Ezra 9:2 • Neh. 4:7

24 And half of their children spoke the language of Ashdod, and could not speak the language of Judah, but spoke according to the language of one or the other people.

25 So I [R]contended with them and cursed them, struck some of them and pulled out their hair, and made them swear by God, *saying,* "You shall not give your daughters as wives to their sons, nor take their daughters for your sons or yourselves. Prov. 28:4

26 [R]"Did not Solomon king of Israel sin by these things? Yet among many nations there was no king like him, [R]who was beloved of his God; and God made him king over all Israel. Nevertheless pagan women caused even him to sin. 1 Kin. 11:1, 2 • 2 Sam. 12:24, 25

27 "Should we then hear of your doing all this great evil, [R]transgressing against our God by marrying pagan women?" [Ezra 10:2]

28 And *one* of the sons [R]of Joiada, the son of Eliashib the high priest, *was* a son-in-law of [R]Sanballat the Horonite; therefore I drove him from me. Neh. 12:10, 12 • Neh. 4:1, 7; 6:1, 2

29 Remember them, O my God, because they have defiled the priesthood and the covenant of the priesthood and the Levites.

Restoration in Summary

30 Thus I cleansed them of everything pagan. I also assigned duties to the priests and the Levites, each to his service,

31 and *to bringing* the wood offering and the firstfruits at appointed times.

Remember me, O my God, for good!

THE BOOK OF
ESTHER

THE BOOK OF ESTHER

God's hand of providence and protection on behalf of His people is evident throughout the Book of Esther, though His name does not appear once. Haman's plot brings grave danger to the Jews and is countered by the courage of beautiful Esther and the counsel of her wise cousin Mordecai, resulting in a great deliverance. The Feast of Purim becomes an annual reminder of God's faithfulness on behalf of His people.

Esther's Hebrew name was *Hadassah,* "Myrtle" (2:7), but her Persian name *Ester* was derived from the Persian word for "Star" (*stara*). The Greek title for this book is *Esther,* and the Latin title is *Hester.*

THE AUTHOR OF ESTHER

While the author's identity is not indicated in the text, the evident knowledge of Persian etiquette and customs, the palace in Susa, and details of the events in the reign of Ahasuerus indicate that the author lived in Persia during this period. The obvious Jewish nationalism and knowledge of Jewish customs further suggest that the author was Jewish. If this Persian Jew was not an eyewitness, he probably knew people who were. The book must have been written soon after the death of King Ahasuerus (464 B.C.), because 10:2, 3 speak of his reign in the past tense. Some writers suggest that Mordecai himself wrote the book; this seems unlikely, for although Mordecai did keep records (9:20), 10:2, 3 imply that his career was already over. Nevertheless, the author certainly made use of Mordecai's records and may have had access to the Book of the Chronicles of the Kings of Media and Persia (2:23; 10:2). Ezra and Nehemiah have also been suggested for authorship, but the vocabulary and style of Esther is dissimilar to that found in their books. It seems likely that a younger contemporary of Mordecai composed the book.

THE TIME OF ESTHER

Ahasuerus is the Hebrew name and Xerxes the Greek name of Khshayarsh, king of Persia in 486–464 B.C. According to 1:3, the feast of Xerxes took place in his third year, or 483 B.C. The historian Herodotus refers to this banquet as the occasion of Xerxes' planning for a military campaign against Greece. But in 479 B.C. he was defeated by the Greeks at Salamis, and Herodotus tells us that he sought consolation in his harem. This corresponds to the time when he held a "contest" and crowned Esther queen of Persia (2:16, 17). Since the events of the rest of the book took place in 473 B.C. (3:7–12), the chronological span is ten years (483–473 B.C.). The probable time of authorship was between 464 B.C. (the end of Xerxes' reign; see 10:2, 3) and about 435 B.C. (the palace at Susa was destroyed by fire during that period, and such an event would probably have been mentioned). The historical and linguistic features of Esther do not support a date later than 400 B.C., as there is no trace of Greek influence.

Xerxes was a boisterous man of emotional extremes, whose actions were often strange and contradictory. This fact sheds light on his ability to sign a decree for the annihilation of the Jews, and two months later to sign a second decree allowing them to overthrow their enemies.

Esther was addressed to the many Jews who did not return to their homeland. Not all the godly people left—some did not return for legitimate reasons. Most were disobedient in staying in Persia. Nevertheless, God continued to care for His people in voluntary exile.

THE CHRIST OF ESTHER

Esther, like Christ, puts herself in the place of death for her people but receives the approval of the king. She also portrays Christ's work as Advocate on our behalf. This book reveals another satanic threat to destroy the Jewish people and thus, the messianic line. God continues to preserve His people in spite of opposition and danger, and nothing can prevent the coming of the Messiah.

KEYS TO ESTHER

Key Word: Providence—The Book of Esther was written to show how the Jewish people were protected and preserved by the gracious hand of God from the threat of annihilation. Although God disciplines His covenant people, He never abandons them. The God of Israel is the sovereign controller of history, and His providential care can be seen throughout this book: He raises a Jewish girl out of obscurity to become the queen of the most powerful empire in the world; He ensures that Mordecai's loyal deed is recorded in the palace records; He guides Esther's admission to the king's court; He superintends the timing of Esther's two feasts; He is involved in Ahasuerus's insomnia and the cure he uses for it; He sees that Haman's gallows will be utilized in an unexpected way; He gives Esther great favor in the sight of the king; and He brings about the new decree and the eventual victory of the Jews.

Key Verses: Esther 4:14; 8:17—"For if you remain completely silent at this time, relief and deliverance will arise for the Jews from another place, but you and your father's house will perish. Yet who knows whether you have come to the kingdom for *such* a time as this?" (4:14).

"And in every province and city, wherever the king's command and decree came, the Jews had joy and gladness, a feast and a holiday. Then many of the people of the land became Jews, because fear of the Jews fell upon them" (8:17).

Key Chapter: Esther 8—According to the Book of Esther, the salvation of the Jews is accomplished through the second decree of King Ahasuerus, allowing the Jews to defend themselves against their enemies. Chapter 8 records this pivotal event with the accompanying result that "many of the people of the land became Jews" (8:17).

SURVEY OF ESTHER

The story of Esther fits between chapters 6 and 7 of Ezra, between the first return led by Zerubbabel and the second return led by Ezra. It provides the only biblical portrait of the vast majority of Jews who choose to remain in Persia rather than return to Palestine. God's guiding and protective hand on behalf of His people is evident throughout this book, even though His name does not appear in it. The clearly emerging message is that God uses ordinary men and women to overcome impossible circumstances to accomplish His gracious purposes. Chapters 1—4 describe the threat to the Jews, and chapters 5—10 describe the triumph of the Jews.

The Threat to the Jews (1—4): The story begins in Ahasuerus's winter palace at Susa. The king provides a lavish banquet and display of royal glory for the people of Susa, and proudly seeks to make Queen Vashti's beauty a part of the program. When she refuses to appear, the king is counseled to depose her and seek another queen, because it is feared that the other women will become insolent if Vashti goes unpunished. Esther later finds favor in the eyes of Ahasuerus and wins the royal "beauty pageant." At her cousin Mordecai's instruction, she does not reveal that she is Jewish. With her help, Mordecai is able to warn the king of an assassination plot, and his deed is recorded in the palace records. Meanwhile, Haman becomes captain of the princes, but Mordecai refuses to bow to him. When he learns that Mordecai is Jewish, Haman plots for a year to eliminate all Jews, as his rage and hatred grow. He casts lots (purim) daily during this period until he determines the best day to have them massacred. Through bribery and lies he convinces Ahasuerus to issue an edict that all Jews in the empire will be slain eleven months hence in a single day. Haman conceives his plot in envy and a vengeful spirit, and he executes it with malicious craft. The decree creates a state of confusion, and Mordecai asks Esther to appeal to the king to spare the Jews. At the peril of her life, Esther decides to see the king and reveal her nationality in a desperate attempt to dissuade Ahasuerus. Mordecai convinces her that she has been called to her high position for this purpose.

The Triumph of the Jews (5—10): After fasting, Esther appears before the king and wisely invites him to a banquet along with Haman. At the banquet she requests that they attend a second banquet, as she seeks the right moment to divulge her request. Haman is flattered but later enraged when he sees Mordecai. He takes his wife's suggestion to build a large gallows for Mordecai (he cannot wait the eleven months for Mordecai to be slain). That night

FOCUS	THREAT TO THE JEWS		TRIUMPH OF THE JEWS	
REFERENCE	1:1——————2:21	——————5:1	——————8:4	——————10:3
DIVISION	SELECTION OF ESTHER AS QUEEN	FORMULATION OF THE PLOT BY HAMAN	TRIUMPH OF MORDECAI OVER HAMAN	TRIUMPH OF ISRAEL OVER HER ENEMIES
TOPIC	FEASTS OF AHASUERUS		FEASTS OF ESTHER AND PURIM	
	GRAVE DANGER		GREAT DELIVERANCE	
LOCATION	PERSIA			
TIME	10 YEARS (483–473 B.C.)			

Ahasuerus decides to treat his insomnia by reading the palace records. Reading about Mordecai's deed, he wants him to be honored. Haman, mistakenly thinking the king wants to honor him, tells the king how the honor should be bestowed, only to find out that the reward is for Mordecai. He is humbled and infuriated by being forced to honor the man he loathes. At Esther's second banquet Ahasuerus offers her as much as half of his kingdom for the third time. She then makes her plea for her people and accuses Haman of his treachery. The infuriated king has Haman hanged on the gallows that Haman intended for Mordecai. The gallows, seventy-five feet high, was designed to make Mordecai's downfall a city-wide spectacle, but it ironically provides Haman with unexpected public attention—posthumously.

Persian law sealed with the king's ring (3:12) cannot be revoked, but at Esther's request the king issues a new decree to all the provinces that the Jews may assemble and defend themselves on the day when they are attacked by their enemies. This decree changes the outcome intended by the first order and produces great joy. Mordecai is also elevated and set over the house of Haman. When the fateful day of the two decrees arrives, the Jews defeat their enemies in their cities throughout the Persian provinces, but do not take the plunder. The next day becomes a day of celebration and an annual Jewish holiday called the Feast of Purim. The word is derived from the Assyrian *puru,* meaning "lot," referring to the lots cast by Haman to determine the day decreed for the Jewish annihilation. The narrative closes with the advancement of Mordecai to a position second only to the king.

OUTLINE OF ESTHER

Part One: The Threat to the Jews (1:14:17)

Part Two: The Triumph of the Jews (5:1—10:3)

CHAPTER 1

The Feasts of Ahasuerus

NOW it came to pass in the days of Ahas-
uerus* (this *was* the Ahasuerus who
reigned over one hundred and twenty-seven
provinces, from India to Ethiopia),
2 in those days when King Ahasuerus [R]sat
on the throne of his kingdom, which *was* in
[R]Shushan* the citadel, 1 Kin. 1:46 • Neh. 1:1
3 *that* in the third year of his reign he
[R]made a feast for all his officials and ser-
vants—the powers of Persia and Media, the
nobles, and the princes of the provinces *being*
before him— Gen. 40:20
4 when he showed the riches of his glorious
kingdom and the splendor of his excellent
majesty for many days, one hundred and
eighty days *in all.*
5 And when these days were completed, the
king made a feast lasting seven days for all
the people who were present in Shushan the
[T]citadel, from great to small, in the court of
the garden of the king's palace. palace
6 *There were* white and blue linen *curtains*
fastened with cords of fine linen and purple
on silver rods and marble pillars; *and the*
[R]couches *were* of gold and silver on a *mosaic*
pavement of alabaster, turquoise, and white
and black marble. Amos 2:8; 6:4
7 And they served drinks in golden vessels,
each vessel being different from the other,
with royal wine in abundance, according to
the generosity of the king.
8 In accordance with the law, the drinking
was not compulsory; for so the king had or-
dered all the officers of his household, that
they should do according to each man's pleas-
ure.

Refusal of Queen Vashti

9 Queen Vashti also made a feast for the
women *in* the royal palace which *belonged* to
King Ahasuerus.
10 On the seventh day, when the heart of the
king was merry with wine, he commanded
Mehuman, Biztha, [R]Harbona, Bigtha, Abagtha,
Zethar, and Carcas, seven eunuchs who served
in the presence of King Ahasuerus, Esth. 7:9
11 to bring Queen Vashti before the king,
wearing her royal crown, in order to show her
beauty to the people and the officials, for she
was beautiful to behold.
12 But Queen Vashti refused to come at the
king's command *brought* by *his* eunuchs;
therefore the king was furious, and his anger
burned within him.

Counsel to King Ahasuerus

13 Then the king said to the [R]wise men
[R]who understood the times (for this *was* the
king's manner toward all who knew law and
justice, Dan. 2:12 • 1 Chr. 12:32
14 those closest to him *being* Carshena,
Shethar, Admatha, Tarshish, Meres, Marsena,
and Memucan, the [R]seven princes of Persia
and Media, [R]who had access to the king's
presence, *and* who ranked highest in the king-
dom): Ezra 7:14 • 2 Kin. 25:19
15 "What *shall we* do to Queen Vashti, ac-
cording to law, because she did not obey the
command of King Ahasuerus *brought to her*
by the eunuchs?"
16 And Memucan answered before the king
and the princes: "Queen Vashti has not only
wronged the king, but also all the princes, and
all the people who *are* in all the provinces of
King Ahasuerus.
17 "For the queen's behavior will become
known to all women, so that they will [R]despise
their husbands in their eyes, when they re-
port, 'King Ahasuerus commanded Queen
Vashti to be brought in before him, but she did
not come.' [Eph. 5:33]
18 "This very day the *noble* ladies of Persia
and Media will say to all the king's officials
that they have heard of the behavior of the
queen. Thus *there will be* excessive contempt
and wrath.

Commandment of King Ahasuerus

19 "If it pleases the king, let a royal [T]decree
go out from him, and let it be recorded in the
laws of the Persians and the Medes, so that it
will [R]not be altered, that Vashti shall come no
more before King Ahasuerus; and let the king
give her royal position to another who is bet-
ter than she. Lit. *word* • Esth. 8:8
20 "When the king's decree which he will
make is proclaimed throughout all his empire
(for it is great), all wives will [R]honor their
husbands, both great and small." [Col. 3:18]
21 And the reply pleased the king and the
princes, and the king did according to the
word of Memucan.
22 Then he sent letters to all the king's
provinces, [R]to each province in its own script,
and to every people in their own language,
that each man should [R]be master in his own
house, and speak in the language of his own
people. Esth. 3:12; 8:9 • [Eph. 5:22–24]

CHAPTER 2

Decree to Search for Vashti's Replacement

AFTER these things, when the wrath of
King Ahasuerus subsided, he remem-
bered Vashti, [R]what she had done, and what
had been decreed against her. Esth. 1:19, 20
2 Then the king's servants who attended
him said: "Let beautiful young virgins be
sought for the king;
3 "and let the king appoint officers in all the

1:1 Generally identified with Xerxes I (485–464 B.C.)
1:2 Or *Susa*

provinces of his kingdom, that they may
gather all the beautiful young virgins to
Shushan the citadel, into the women's quar-
ters, under the custody of Hegai* the king's
eunuch, custodian of the women. And let
beauty preparations be given *them*.
4 "Then let the young woman who pleases
the king be queen instead of Vashti." This
thing pleased the king, and he did so.

Preparation of Esther

5 In [T]Shushan the [T]citadel there was a cer-
tain Jew whose name *was* Mordecai the son
of Jair, the son of Shimei, the son of [R]Kish, a
Benjamite. Or *Susa* • *palace* • 1 Sam. 9:1
6 [R]*Kish** had been carried away from Jeru-
salem with the captives who had been cap-
tured with Jeconiah* king of Judah, whom
Nebuchadnezzar the king of Babylon had car-
ried away. 2 Kin. 24:14, 15
7 And *Mordecai* had brought up Hadassah,
that *is*, Esther, [R]his uncle's daughter, for she
had neither father nor mother. The young
woman *was* lovely and beautiful. When her
father and mother died, Mordecai took her as
his own daughter. Esth. 2:15
8 So it was, when the king's command
and decree were heard, and when many
young women were [R]gathered at [T]Shushan
the [T]citadel, *under* the custody of Hegai, that
Esther also was taken to the king's palace,
into the care of Hegai the custodian of the
women. Esth. 2:3 • Or *Susa* • *palace*
9 Now the young woman pleased him, and
she obtained his favor; so he readily gave
beauty preparations to her, besides her al-
lowance. Then seven choice maidservants
were provided for her from the king's palace,
and he moved her and her maidservants to
the best *place* in the house of the women.
10 [R]Esther had not [T]revealed her people or
family, for Mordecai had charged her not to
reveal *it*. Esth. 2:20 • Revealed the identity of
11 And every day Mordecai paced in front of
the court of the women's quarters, to learn of
Esther's welfare and what was happening to
her.
12 Each young woman's turn came to go in
to King Ahasuerus after she had completed
twelve months' preparation, according to the
regulations for the women, for thus were the
days of their preparation apportioned: six
months with oil of myrrh, and six months
with perfumes and preparations for beautify-
ing women.
13 Thus *prepared, each* young woman went
to the king, and she was given whatever she
desired to take with her from the women's
quarters to the king's palace.
14 In the evening she went, and in the morn-
ing she returned to the second house of the
women, to the custody of Shaashgaz, the
king's eunuch who kept the concubines. She
would not go in to the king again unless the
king delighted in her and called for her by
name.

Selection of Queen Esther

15 Now when the turn came for Esther the
daughter of Abihail the uncle of Mordecai,
who had taken her as his daughter, to go in to
the king, she requested nothing but what
Hegai the king's eunuch, the custodian of the
women, advised. And Esther obtained favor in
the sight of all who saw her.
16 So Esther was taken to King Ahasuerus,
into his royal palace, in the tenth month,
which *is* the month of Tebeth, in the seventh
year of his reign.
17 The king loved Esther more than all the
other women, and she obtained grace and
favor in his sight more than all the virgins; so
he set the royal [R]crown upon her head and
made her queen instead of Vashti. Esth. 1:11
18 Then the king [R]made a great feast, the
Feast of Esther, for all his officials and ser-
vants; and he proclaimed a holiday in the
provinces and gave gifts according to the
[T]generosity of a king. Esth. 1:3 • Lit. *hand*
19 When virgins were gathered together a
second time, Mordecai sat within the king's
gate.
20 [R]*Now* Esther had not revealed her family
and her people, just as Mordecai had charged
her, for Esther obeyed the command of
Mordecai as when she was brought up by
him. Esth. 2:10

Mordecai Reveals the Plot to Murder the King

21 In those days, while Mordecai sat within
the king's gate, two of the king's eunuchs,
[T]Bigthan and Teresh, doorkeepers, became
furious and sought to lay hands on King
Ahasuerus. *Bigthana*, Esth. 6:2
22 So the matter became known to Morde-
cai, who told Queen Esther, and Esther in-
formed the king in Mordecai's name.
23 And when an inquiry was made into the
matter, it was confirmed, and both were
hanged on a gallows; and it was written in
[R]the book of the chronicles in the presence of
the king. Esth. 6:1

CHAPTER 3

Haman Is Promoted

AFTER these things King Ahasuerus pro-
moted Haman, the son of Hammedatha
the [R]Agagite, and [R]advanced him and set his
seat above all the princes who *were* with
him. Num. 24:7 • Esth. 5:11

2:3 Heb. *Hege* **2:6** Lit. *Who* • *Jehoiachin*, 2 Kin. 24:6

The Reason for Haman's Plot

2 And all the king's servants who *were* within the king's gate bowed and paid homage to Haman, for so the king had commanded concerning him. But Mordecai [R]would not bow or pay homage. Ps. 15:4

3 Then the king's servants who *were* within the king's gate said to Mordecai, "Why do you transgress the [R]king's command?" Esth. 3:2

4 Now it happened, when they spoke to him daily and he would not listen to them, that they told *it* to Haman, to see whether Mordecai's words would stand; for *Mordecai* had told them that he *was* a Jew.

5 When Haman saw that Mordecai [R]did not bow or pay him homage, Haman was [R]filled with wrath. Esth. 3:2; 5:9 • Dan. 3:19

6 But he disdained to lay hands on Mordecai alone, for they had told him of the people of Mordecai. Instead, Haman [R]sought to destroy all the Jews who *were* throughout the whole kingdom of Ahasuerus—the people of Mordecai. Ps. 83:4

Presentation of the Plot

7 In the first month, which is the month of Nisan, in the twelfth year of King Ahasuerus, [R]they cast Pur (that *is,* the lot), before Haman to determine the day and the month,* until *it fell on the* twelfth *month,** which *is* the month of Adar. Esth. 9:24–26

8 Then Haman said to King Ahasuerus, "There is a certain people scattered and dispersed among the people in all the provinces of your kingdom; [R]their laws *are* different from all *other* people's, and they do not keep the king's laws. Therefore it *is* not fitting for the king to let them remain. Acts 16:20, 21

9 "If it pleases the king, let *a decree* be written that they be destroyed, and I will pay ten thousand talents of silver into the hands of those who do the work, to bring *it* into the king's treasuries."

Publication of the Decree

10 So the king [R]took [R]his signet ring from his hand and gave it to Haman, the son of Hammedatha the Agagite, the [R]enemy of the Jews. Gen. 41:42 • Esth. 8:2, 8 • Esth. 7:6

11 And the king said to Haman, "The money and the people *are* given to you, to do with them as seems good to you."

12 [R]Then the king's scribes were called on the thirteenth day of the first month, and *a decree* was written according to all that Haman commanded—to the king's satraps, to the governors who *were* over each province, to the officials of all people, to every province according to its script, and to every people in their language. In the name of King Ahasuerus it was written, and sealed with the king's signet ring. Esth. 8:9

13 And the letters were sent by couriers into all the king's provinces, to destroy, to kill, and to annihilate all the Jews, both young and old, little children and women, in one day, on the thirteenth *day* of the twelfth *month,* which *is* the month of Adar, and to plunder their possessions.*

14 [R]A copy of the document was to be issued as law in every province, being published for all people, that they should be ready for that day. Esth. 8:13, 14

15 The couriers went out, hastened by the king's command; and the decree was proclaimed in Shushan the citadel. So the king and Haman sat down to drink, but [R]the city of Shushan was perplexed. Esth. 8:15

CHAPTER 4

The Lamentation of the Jews

WHEN Mordecai learned all that had happened, he [R]tore his clothes and put on sackcloth [R]and ashes, and went out into the midst of the city. He cried out with a loud and bitter cry. 2 Sam. 1:11 • Josh. 7:6

2 He went as far as the front of the king's gate, for no one *might* enter the king's gate clothed with sackcloth.

3 And in every province where the king's command and decree arrived, *there was* great mourning among the Jews, with fasting, weeping, and wailing; and many lay in sackcloth and ashes.

The Plan of Mordecai

4 So Esther's maids and eunuchs came and told her, and the queen was deeply distressed. Then she sent garments to clothe Mordecai and take his sackcloth away from him, but he would not accept *them.*

5 Then Esther called Hathach, *one* of the king's eunuchs whom he had appointed to attend her, and she gave him a command concerning Mordecai, to learn what and why this *was.*

6 So Hathach went out to Mordecai in the city square that *was* in front of the king's gate.

7 And Mordecai told him all that had happened to him, and [R]the sum of money that Haman had promised to pay into the king's treasuries to destroy the Jews. Esth. 3:9

8 He also gave him [R]a copy of the written decree for their destruction, which was given at [T]Shushan, that he might show it to Esther and explain it to her, and that he might command her to go in to the king to make suppli-

3:7 LXX adds *to destroy the people of Mordecai in one day;* Vg. adds *the nation of the Jews should be destroyed* • So with MT, Vg.; LXX *and the lot fell on the fourteenth of the month* **3:13** LXX adds the text of the letter here

cation to him and plead before him for her
people. Esth. 3:14, 15 • Or *Susa*
9 So Hathach returned and told Esther the
words of Mordecai.
10 Then Esther spoke to Hathach, and gave
him a command for Mordecai:
11 "All the king's servants and the people
of the king's provinces know that any man
or woman who goes into [R]the inner court to
the king, who has not been called, [R]*he has*
but one law: put *all* to death, except the one
to whom the king holds out the golden
scepter, that he may live. Yet I myself have
not been [R]called to go in to the king these
thirty days." Esth. 5:1; 6:4 • Dan. 2:9 • Esth. 2:14
12 So they told Mordecai Esther's words.
13 And Mordecai told *them* to answer Es-
ther: "Do not think in your heart that you will
escape in the king's palace any more than all
the other Jews.
14 "For if you remain completely silent at
this time, relief and deliverance will arise for
the Jews from another place, but you and
your father's house will perish. Yet who
knows whether you have come to the king-
dom for *such* a time as this?"

The Promise of Queen Esther

15 Then Esther told *them* to reply to Morde-
cai:
16 "Go, gather all the Jews who are present
in [T]Shushan, and fast for me; neither eat nor
drink for [R]three days, night or day. My maids
and I will fast likewise. And so I will go to the
king, which *is* against the law; [R]and if I perish,
I perish!" Or *Susa* • Esth. 5:1 • Gen. 43:14
17 So Mordecai went his way and did ac-
cording to all that Esther commanded him.*

CHAPTER 5

Esther's First Feast

NOW it happened on the third day that Es-
ther put on *her* royal *robes* and stood in
the inner court of the king's palace, across
from the king's house, while the king sat on
his royal throne in the royal house, facing the
entrance of the house.*
2 So it was, when the king saw Queen Es-
ther standing in the court, *that* [R]she found
favor in his sight, and [R]the king held out to Es-
ther the golden scepter that *was* in his hand.
Then Esther went near and touched the top of
the scepter. [Prov. 21:1] • Esth. 4:11
3 And the king said to her, "What do you
wish, Queen Esther? What *is* your request? [R]It
shall be given to you—up to half the king-
dom!" Mark 6:23
4 So Esther answered, "If it pleases the
king, let the king and Haman come today to
the banquet that I have prepared for him."
5 Then the king said, "Bring Haman
quickly, that he may do as Esther has said." So
the king and Haman went to the banquet that
Esther had prepared.
6 At the banquet of wine the king said to
Esther, "What *is* your petition? It shall be
granted you. What *is* your request, up to half
the kingdom? It shall be done!"
7 Then Esther answered and said, "My peti-
tion and request *is this:*
8 "If I have found favor in the sight of the
king, and if it pleases the king to grant my pe-
tition and fulfill my request, then let the king
and Haman come to the [R]banquet which I will
prepare for them, and tomorrow I will do as
the king has said." Esth. 6:14

Haman Plots to Kill Mordecai

9 So Haman went out that day joyful and
with a glad heart; but when Haman saw
Mordecai in the king's gate, and that he did
not stand or tremble before him, he was filled
with indignation against Mordecai.
10 Nevertheless Haman restrained himself
and went home, and he sent and called for his
friends and his wife Zeresh.
11 Then Haman told them of his great
riches, [R]the multitude of his children, every-
thing in which the king had promoted him,
and how he had advanced him above the offi-
cials and servants of the king. Esth. 9:7–10
12 Moreover Haman said, "Besides, Queen
Esther invited no one but me to come in with
the king to the banquet that she prepared; and
tomorrow I am again invited by her, along
with the king.
13 "Yet all this avails me nothing, so long as
I see Mordecai the Jew sitting at the king's
gate."
14 Then his wife Zeresh and all his friends
said to him, "Let a [R]gallows be made, fifty cu-
bits high, and in the morning [R]suggest to the
king that Mordecai be hanged on it; then go
merrily with the king to the banquet." And the
thing pleased Haman; so he had the gallows
made. Esth. 7:9 • Esth. 6:4

CHAPTER 6

King Ahasuerus's Plan to Honor Mordecai

THAT night the king could not sleep. So
one was commanded to bring [R]the book of
the records of the chronicles; and they were
read before the king. Esth. 2:23; 10:2
2 And it was found written that Mordecai
had told of Bigthana and Teresh, two of the
king's eunuchs, the doorkeepers who had
sought to lay hands on King Ahasuerus.
3 Then the king said, "What honor or dig-
nity has been bestowed on Mordecai for this?"
And the king's servants who attended him
said, "Nothing has been done for him."

4:17 LXX adds a prayer of Mordecai here **5:1** LXX adds many extra details in vv. 1, 2

Haman's Plan to Honor Himself

4 So the king said, "Who *is* in the court?" Now Haman had *just* entered [R]the outer court of the king's palace [R]to suggest that the king hang Mordecai on the gallows that he had prepared for him. Esth. 5:1 • Esth. 5:14

5 The king's servants said to him, "Haman is there, standing in the court." And the king said, "Let him come in."

6 So Haman came in, and the king asked him, "What shall be done for the man whom the king delights to honor?" Now Haman thought in his heart, "Whom would the king delight to honor more than me?"

7 And Haman answered the king, "*For* the man whom the king delights to honor,

8 "let a royal robe be brought which the king has worn, and [R]a horse on which the king has ridden, which has a royal [T]crest placed on its head. 1 Kin. 1:33 • *crown*

9 "Then let this robe and horse be delivered to the hand of one of the king's most noble princes, that he may array the man whom the king delights to honor. Then parade him on horseback through the city square, [R]and proclaim before him: 'Thus shall it be done to the man whom the king delights to honor!' " Gen. 41:43

Haman Is Forced to Honor Mordecai

10 Then the king said to Haman, "Hurry, take the robe and the horse, as you have suggested, and do so for Mordecai the Jew who sits within the king's gate! Leave nothing undone of all that you have spoken."

11 So Haman took the robe and the horse, arrayed Mordecai and led him on horseback through the city square, and proclaimed before him, "Thus shall it be done to the man whom the king delights to honor!"

12 Afterward Mordecai went back to the king's gate. But Haman [R]hurried to his house, mourning [R]and with his head covered. 2 Chr. 26:20 • 2 Sam. 15:30

13 When Haman told his wife Zeresh and all his friends everything that had happened to him, his wise men and his wife Zeresh said to him, "If Mordecai, before whom you have begun to fall, is of Jewish descent, you will not prevail against [R]him but will surely fall before him." Zech. 2:8

14 While they *were* still talking with him, the king's eunuchs came, and hastened to bring Haman to [R]the banquet which Esther had prepared. Esth. 5:8

CHAPTER 7

Esther's Second Feast

SO the king and Haman went to dine with Queen Esther.

2 And on the second day, at the banquet of wine, the king again said to Esther, "What *is* your petition, Queen Esther? It shall be granted you. And what *is* your request, up to half the kingdom? It shall be done!"

3 Then Queen Esther answered and said, "If I have found favor in your sight, O king, and if it pleases the king, let my life be given me at my petition, and my people at my request.

4 "For we have been [R]sold, my people and I, to be destroyed, to be killed, and to be annihilated. Had we been sold as [R]male and female slaves, I would have held my tongue, although the enemy could never compensate for the king's loss." Esth. 3:9; 4:7 • Deut. 28:68

Haman Is Indicted

5 So King Ahasuerus answered and said to Queen Esther, "Who is he, and where is he, who would dare presume in his heart to do such a thing?"

6 And Esther said, "The adversary and enemy *is* this wicked Haman!" So Haman was terrified before the king and queen.

7 Then the king arose in his wrath from the banquet of wine *and went* into the palace garden; but Haman stood before Queen Esther, pleading for his life, for he saw that evil was determined against him by the king.

8 When the king returned from the palace garden to the place of the banquet of wine, Haman had fallen across [R]the couch where Esther *was.* Then the king said, "Will he also assault the queen while I *am* in the house?" As the word left the king's mouth, they [R]covered Haman's face. Esth. 1:6 • Job 9:24

Haman Is Hanged

9 Now Harbonah, one of the eunuchs, said to the king, "Look! [R]The gallows, fifty cubits high, which Haman made for Mordecai, who spoke good on the king's behalf, is standing at the house of Haman." Then the king said, "Hang him on it!" Esth. 5:14

10 So [R]they hanged Haman on the gallows that he had prepared for Mordecai. Then the king's wrath subsided. [Ps. 7:16; 94:23]

CHAPTER 8

Mordecai Is Given Haman's House

ON that day King Ahasuerus gave Queen Esther the house of Haman, the [R]enemy of the Jews. And Mordecai came before the king, for Esther had told [R]how he *was related* to her. Esth. 7:6 • Esth. 2:7, 15

2 So the king took off [R]his signet ring, which he had taken from Haman, and gave it to Mordecai; and Esther appointed Mordecai over the house of Haman. Esth. 3:10

3 Now Esther spoke again to the king, fell down at his feet, and implored him with tears to counteract the evil of Haman the Agagite,

and the scheme which he had devised against
the Jews.

Esther's Petition to King Ahasuerus

4 And [R]the king held out the golden scepter
toward Esther. So Esther arose and stood be-
fore the king, Esth. 4:11; 5:2
5 and said, "If it pleases the king, and if I
have found favor in his sight and the thing
seems right to the king and I am pleasing in his
eyes, let it be written to revoke the [R]letters de-
vised by Haman, the son of Hammedatha the
Agagite, which he wrote to annihilate the Jews
who *are* in all the king's provinces. Esth. 3:13
6 "For how can I endure to see [R]the evil that
will come to my people? Or how can I endure to
see the destruction of my countrymen?" Neh. 2:3

King Ahasuerus's Counter-Decree

7 Then King Ahasuerus said to Queen Es-
ther and Mordecai the Jew, "Indeed, I have
given Esther the house of Haman, and they
have hanged him on the gallows because he
tried to lay his hand on the Jews.
8 "You yourselves write *a decree* concern-
ing the Jews, as you please, in the king's
name, and seal *it* with the king's signet ring;
for whatever is written in the king's name and
sealed with the king's signet ring [R]no one can
revoke." Dan. 6:8, 12, 15
9 [R]So the king's scribes were called at that
time, in the third month, which *is* the month of
Sivan, on the twenty-third *day;* and it was
written, according to all that Mordecai com-
manded, to the Jews, the satraps, the gover-
nors, and the princes of the provinces [R]from
India to Ethiopia, one hundred and twenty-
seven provinces *in all,* to every province in its
own script, to every people in their own lan-
guage, and to the Jews in their own script and
language. Esth. 3:12 • Esth. 1:1
10 [R]And he wrote in the name of King
Ahasuerus, sealed *it* with the king's signet
ring, and sent letters by couriers on horse-
back, riding on royal horses bred from swift
steeds.* 1 Kin. 21:8
11 By these letters the king permitted the
Jews who *were* in every city to [R]gather to-
gether and protect their lives—to destroy, kill,
and annihilate all the forces of any people or
province that would assault them, *both* little
children and women, and to plunder their
possessions, Esth. 9:2
12 on one day in all the provinces of King
Ahasuerus, on the thirteenth *day* of the
twelfth month, which *is* the month of Adar.*
13 [R]A copy of the document was to be issued
as a decree in every province and published
for all people, so that the Jews would be ready
on that day to avenge themselves on their en-
emies. Esth. 3:14, 15
14 The couriers who rode on royal horses
went out, hastened and pressed on by the
king's command. And the decree was issued
in [T]Shushan the [T]citadel. Or *Susa* • *palace*

Many Gentiles Are Converted

15 So Mordecai went out from the presence
of the king in royal apparel of [T]blue and
white, with a great crown of gold and a gar-
ment of fine linen and purple; and the city of
Shushan rejoiced and was glad. *violet*
16 The Jews had [R]light and gladness, joy and
honor. Ps. 97:11; 112:4
17 And in every province and city, wherever
the king's command and decree came, the
Jews had joy and gladness, a feast [R]and a hol-
iday. Then many of the people of the land [R]be-
came Jews, because [R]fear of the Jews fell
upon them. Esth. 9:19 • Ps. 18:43 • Gen. 35:5

CHAPTER 9

Victories on the First Day

NOW [R]in the twelfth month, that *is,* the
month of Adar, on the thirteenth day,
[R]*the time* came for the king's command and
his decree to be executed. On the day that the
enemies of the Jews had hoped to overpower
them, the opposite occurred, in that the Jews
themselves overpowered those who hated
them. Esth. 8:12 • Esth. 3:13
2 The Jews [R]gathered together in their
cities throughout all the provinces of King
Ahasuerus to lay hands on those who [R]sought
their harm. And no one could withstand
them, because fear of them fell upon all peo-
ple. Esth. 8:11; 9:15–18 • Ps. 71:13, 14
3 And all the officials of the provinces, the
satraps, the governors, and all those doing the
king's work, helped the Jews, because the fear
of Mordecai fell upon them.
4 For Mordecai *was* great in the king's
palace, and his fame spread throughout all
the provinces; for this man Mordecai [R]became
increasingly prominent. 2 Sam. 3:1
5 Thus the Jews defeated all their enemies
with the stroke of the sword, with slaughter
and destruction, and did what they pleased
with those who hated them.
6 And in Shushan the citadel the Jews
killed and destroyed five hundred men.
7 Also Parshandatha, Dalphon, Aspatha,
8 Poratha, Adalia, Aridatha,
9 Parmashta, Arisai, Aridai, and Vajeza-
tha—
10 [R]the ten sons of Haman the son of
Hammedatha, the enemy of the Jews—they
killed; [R]but they did not lay a hand on the
[T]plunder. Esth. 5:11; 9:7–10 • Esth. 8:11 • *spoil*
11 On that day the number of those who
were killed in [T]Shushan the [T]citadel [T]was
brought to the king. Or *Susa* • *palace* • Lit. *came*

8:10 Lit. *sons of the swift horses* **8:12** LXX adds the text of the letter here

Victories on the Second Day

12 And the king said to Queen Esther, "The Jews have killed and destroyed five hundred men in Shushan the citadel, and the ten sons of Haman. What have they done in the rest of the king's provinces? Now [R]what *is* your petition? It shall be granted to you. Or what *is* your further request? It shall be done." Esth. 5:6; 7:2

13 Then Esther said, "If it pleases the king, let it be granted to the Jews who *are* in Shushan to do again tomorrow [R]according to today's decree, and let Haman's ten sons be hanged on the gallows." Esth. 8:11; 9:15

14 So the king commanded this to be done; the decree was issued in Shushan, and they hanged Haman's ten sons.

15 And the Jews who *were* in Shushan [R]gathered together again on the fourteenth day of the month of Adar and killed three hundred men at Shushan; but they did not lay a hand on the plunder. Esth. 8:11; 9:2

16 The remainder of the Jews in the king's provinces [R]gathered together and protected their lives, had rest from their enemies, and killed seventy-five thousand of their enemies; [R]but they did not lay a hand on the plunder. Esth. 9:2 • Esth. 8:11

The Feast of Purim

17 *This was* on the thirteenth day of the month of Adar. And on the fourteenth of *the month** they rested and made it a day of feasting and gladness.

18 But the Jews who *were* at [T]Shushan assembled together on the thirteenth *day*, as well as on the fourteenth; and on the fifteenth of *the month** they rested, and made it a day of feasting and gladness. Or *Susa*

19 Therefore the Jews of the villages who dwelt in the unwalled towns celebrated the fourteenth day of the month of Adar *with* gladness and feasting, as a holiday, and for sending presents to one another.

20 And Mordecai wrote these things and sent letters to all the Jews, near and far, who *were* in all the provinces of King Ahasuerus,

21 to establish among them that they should celebrate yearly the fourteenth and fifteenth days of the month of Adar,

22 as the days on which the Jews had rest from their enemies, as the month which was turned from sorrow to joy for them, and from mourning to a holiday; that they should make them days of feasting and joy, of [R]sending presents to one another and gifts to the [R]poor. Neh. 8:10 • [Deut. 15:7–11]

23 So the Jews accepted the custom which they had begun, as Mordecai had written to them,

24 because Haman, the son of Hammedatha the Agagite, the enemy of all the Jews, had plotted against the Jews to annihilate them, and had cast Pur (that *is*, the lot), to consume them and destroy them;

25 but when *Esther** came before the king, he commanded by letter that this* wicked plot which *Haman* had devised against the Jews should [R]return on his own head, and that he and his sons should be hanged on the gallows. Esth. 7:10

26 So they called these days Purim, after the name [T]Pur. Therefore, because of all the words of [R]this letter, what they had seen concerning this matter, and what had happened to them, Lit. *Lot* • Esth. 9:20

27 the Jews established and imposed it upon themselves and their descendants and all who would join them, that without fail they should celebrate these two days every year, according to the written *instructions* and according to the *prescribed* time,

28 *that* these days *should be* remembered and kept throughout every generation, every family, every province, and every city, that these days of Purim should not fail *to be observed* among the Jews, and *that* the memory of them should not perish among their descendants.

29 Then Queen Esther, [R]the daughter of Abihail, with Mordecai the Jew, wrote with full authority to confirm this [R]second letter about Purim. Esth. 2:15 • Esth. 8:10; 9:20, 21

30 And *Mordecai* sent letters to all the Jews, to [R]the one hundred and twenty-seven provinces of the kingdom of Ahasuerus, *with* words of peace and truth, Esth. 1:1

31 to confirm these days of Purim at their *appointed* time, as Mordecai the Jew and Queen Esther had prescribed for them, and as they had decreed for themselves and their descendants concerning matters of their [R]fasting and lamenting. Esth. 4:3, 16

32 So the decree of Esther confirmed these matters of Purim, and it was written in the book.

CHAPTER 10

The Fame of Mordecai

AND King Ahasuerus imposed tribute on the land and *on* the islands of the sea.

2 Now all the acts of his power and his might, and the account of the greatness of Mordecai, to which the king advanced him, *are* they not written in the book of the chronicles of the kings of Media and Persia?

3 For Mordecai the Jew *was* second to King Ahasuerus, and was great among the Jews and well received by the multitude of his brethren, seeking the good of his people and speaking peace to all his countrymen.*

9:17 Lit. *it* **9:18** Lit. *it* **9:25** Lit. *she* or *it* • Lit. *his*
10:3 Lit. *seed*. LXX, Vg. add a dream of Mordecai here; Vg. adds six more chapters

THE BOOK OF

JOB

THE BOOK OF JOB

Job is perhaps the earliest book of the Bible. Set in the period of the patriarchs (Abraham, Isaac, Jacob, and Joseph), it tells the story of a man who loses everything—his wealth, his family, his health—and wrestles with the question, Why?

The book begins with a heavenly debate between God and Satan, moves through three cycles of earthly debates between Job and his friends, and concludes with a dramatic "divine diagnosis" of Job's problem. In the end, Job acknowledges the sovereignty of God in his life and receives back more than he had before his trials.

Iyyōb is the Hebrew title for this book, and the name has two possible meanings. If derived from the Hebrew word for persecution, it means "Persecuted One." It is more likely that it comes from the Arabic word meaning "To Come Back" or "Repent." If so, it may be defined "Repentant One." Both meanings apply to the book. The Greek title is *Iob,* and the Latin title is *Iob.*

THE AUTHOR OF JOB

The author of Job is unknown, and there are no textual hints as to his identity. Commentators, however, have been generous with suggestions: Job, Elihu, Moses, Solomon, Isaiah, Hezekiah, Jeremiah, Baruch, and Ezra have all been nominated. The non-Hebraic cultural background of this book may point to Gentile authorship. The rabbinic traditions are inconsistent, but one talmudic tradition suggests that Moses wrote the book. The land of Uz (1:1) is adjacent to Midian, where Moses lived for forty years, and it is conceivable that Moses obtained a record of the dialogue left by Job or Elihu.

THE TIME OF JOB

Lamentations 4:21 locates Uz in the area of Edom, southeast of the Dead Sea. This is also in the region of northern Arabia, and Job's friends come from nearby countries.

It is important to distinguish the date of the events in Job from the date of its writing. Accurate dating of the events is difficult because there are no references to contemporary historical occurrences. However, a number of facts indicate a patriarchal date for Job, perhaps between Genesis 11 and 12 or not long after the time of Abraham: (1) Job lived 140 years *after* the events in the book (42:16), his life span must have been close to 200 years. This fits the patriarchal period (Abraham lived 175 years, Gen. 25:7). (2) Job's wealth is measured in terms of livestock (1:3; 42:12) rather than gold and silver. (3) Like Abraham, Isaac, and Jacob, Job is the priest of his family and offers sacrifices. (4) There are no references to Israel, the Exodus, the Mosaic Law, or the tabernacle. (5) Fitting Abraham's time, the social unit in Job is the patriarchal family clan. (6) The Chaldeans who murder Job's servants (1:17) are nomads and have not yet become city-dwellers. (7) Job uses the characteristic patriarchal name for God, *Shaddai* ("the Almighty"), thirty-one times. This early term is found only seventeen times in the rest of the Old Testament. The rare use of Yahweh "the LORD" also suggests a pre-Mosaic date. Ezekiel 14:14, 20 and James 5:11 show that Job was a historical person.

Several theories have been advanced for the date of writing: (1) It was written shortly after the events occurred, perhaps by Job or Elihu. (2) It was written by Moses in Midian (1485–1445 B.C.). (3) It was written in the time of Solomon (c. 950 B.C.). (Job is similar to other wisdom literature of this time; compare the praises of wisdom in Job 28 and Proverbs 8. The problem here is the great time lag of about a thousand years.) (4) It was written during or after the Babylonian captivity.

THE CHRIST OF JOB

Job acknowledges a Redeemer (see 19:25–27) and cries out for a mediator (9:33; 25:4; 33:23). The book raises problems and questions which are answered perfectly in Christ who identifies with our sufferings (Heb. 4:15). Christ is the believer's Life, Redeemer, Mediator, and Advocate.

KEYS TO JOB

Key Word: Sovereignty—The basic question of the book is, "Why do the righteous suffer if God is loving and all-powerful?" Suffering itself is not the central theme; rather, the focus is on what Job *learns* from his suffering—the sovereignty of God over all creation. The debate in chapters 3—37 regards whether God would allow this suffering to happen to a person who is innocent. The over-simplified solutions offered by Job's three friends are simply inadequate. Elihu's claim that God can use suffering to purify the righteous is closer to the mark. The conclusion at the whirlwind is that God is sovereign and worthy of worship in *whatever* He chooses to do. Job must learn to trust in the goodness and power of God in adversity by enlarging his concept of God. Even this "blameless" man (1:1) needs to repent when he becomes proud and self-righteous. He has to come to the end of his own resources, humble himself, and acknowledge the greatness and majesty of the Lord. Job teaches that God is Lord "of those in heaven, and of those on earth, and of those under the earth" (Phil. 2:10). He is omniscient, omnipotent, and good. As such, His ways are sometimes incomprehensible to men and women, but He can always be trusted. Without the divine perspective in chapters 1 and 2 and in 38—42, chapters 3—37 are a mystery. Job does not have access to chapters 1 and 2, but he is responsible to trust God when all appearances are contrary. Suffering is not always associated with sin; God often sovereignly uses it to test and teach.

Key Verses: Job 13:15; 37:23, 24—"Though He slay me, yet will I trust Him. Even so, I will defend my own ways before Him" (13:15).

"*As for* the Almighty, we cannot find Him; *He is* excellent in power, *in* judgment and abundant justice; He does not oppress. Therefore men fear Him; He shows no partiality to any *who are* wise of heart" (37:23, 24).

Key Chapter: Job 42—The last chapter of the book records the climax of the long and difficult struggle Job has with himself, his wife, his friends, and even his God. Upon Job's full recognition of the utter majesty and sovereignty of the Lord, he repents and no longer demands an answer as to the "why" of his plight.

SURVEY OF JOB

The Book of Job concerns the transforming crisis in the life of a great man who lived perhaps four thousand years ago. Job's trust in God (1 and 2) changes to complaining and growing self-righteousness (3—31; see 32:1 and 40:8), but his repentance (42:1–6) leads to his restoration (42:7–17). The trials bring about an important transformation: The man after the process is different from the man before the process. The Book of Job divides into three parts: the dilemma of Job (1 and 2), the debates of Job (3—37), and the deliverance of Job (38—42).

The Dilemma of Job (1 and 2): Job is not a logical candidate for disaster (see 1:1, 8). His moral integrity and his selfless service to God heighten the dilemma. Behind the scene, Satan ("Accuser") charges that no one loves God from pure motives, but only for material blessings (1:10). To refute Satan's accusations, God allows him to strike Job with two series of assaults. In his sorrow Job laments the day of his birth but does not deny God (1:21; 2:10).

The Debates of Job (3—37): Although Job's "comforters" reach wrong conclusions, they are his friends: of all who know Job, they are the only ones who come; they mourn with him in seven days of silent sympathy; they confront Job without talking behind his back. However, after Job breaks the silence, a three-round debate follows in which his friends say Job must be suffering because of his sin. Job's responses to their simplistic assumptions make the debate cycles increase in emotional fervor. He first accuses his friends of judging him, and later appeals to the Lord as his judge and refuge.

Job makes three basic complaints: (1) God does not hear me (13:3, 24; 19:7; 23:3–5; 30:20); (2) God is punishing me (6:4; 7:20; 9:17); and (3) God allows the wicked to prosper (21:7). His defenses are much longer than his friends' accusations; in the process of defending his innocence, he becomes guilty of self-righteousness.

After Job's five-chapter closing monologue (27—31), Elihu freshens the air with a more perceptive and accurate view than those offered by Eliphaz, Bildad, or Zophar (32—37). He tells Job

FOCUS	DILEMMA OF JOB	DEBATES OF JOB					DELIVERANCE OF JOB
REFERENCE	1:1—	3:1—	15:1—	22:1—	27:1—	32:1—	38:1—42:17
DIVISION	CONTROVERSY OF GOD AND SATAN	FIRST CYCLE OF DEBATE	SECOND CYCLE OF DEBATE	THIRD CYCLE OF DEBATE	FINAL DEFENSE OF JOB	SOLUTION OF ELIHU	CONTROVERSY OF GOD WITH JOB
TOPIC	CONFLICT	DEBATE					REPENTANCE
	PROSE	POETRY					PROSE
LOCATION	LAND OF UZ (NORTH ARABIA)						
TIME	PATRIARCHAL PERIOD (c. 2000 B.C.)						

that he needs to humble himself before God and submit to God's process of purifying his life through trials.

The Deliverance of Job (38—42): After Elihu's preparatory discourse, God Himself ends the debate by speaking to Job from the whirlwind. In His first speech God reveals His power and wisdom as Creator and Preserver of the physical and animal world. Job responds by acknowledging his own ignorance and insignificance; he can offer no rebuttal (40:3–5). In His second speech God reveals His sovereign authority and challenges Job with two illustrations of His power to control the uncontrollable. This time Job responds by acknowledging his error with a repentant heart (42:1–6). If Job cannot understand God's ways in the realm of nature, how then can he understand God's ways in the spiritual realm? God makes no reference to Job's personal sufferings and hardly touches on the real issue of the debate. However, Job catches a glimpse of the divine perspective; and when he acknowledges God's sovereignty over his life, his worldly goods are restored twofold. Job prays for his three friends who have cut him so deeply, but Elihu's speech is never rebuked. Thus, Satan's challenge becomes God's opportunity to build up Job's life. "Indeed we count them blessed who endure. You have heard of the perseverance of Job and seen the end *intended by* the Lord—that the Lord is very compassionate and merciful" (James 5:11; see James 1:12).

OUTLINE OF JOB

Part One: The Dilemma of Job (1:1—2:13)

I. The Circumstances of Job........................1:1–5

II. The First Assault of Satan....................1:6–22

III. The Second Assault of Satan.................2:1–10

IV. The Arrival of Job's Friends................2:11–13

Part Two: The Debates of Job (3:1—37:24)

I. The First Cycle of Debate ....3:1—14:22

A. Job's First Speech...............................3:1–26
B. Eliphaz's First Speech ....4:1—5:27
1. Eliphaz Believes the Innocent Do Not Suffer...4:1–21
2. Eliphaz Calls Job Foolish 5:1–7
3. Eliphaz Encourages Job to Appeal to God 5:8–16
4. Eliphaz Encourages Job to Not Despise God's Discipline...............5:17–27
C. Job's Reply to Eliphaz.......................6:1—7:21
1. Job's Deep Anguish............................6:1–13
2. Job Seeks His Friends' Sympathy...6:14–30
3. Job Questions God's Continuing Trials...7:1–21
D. Bildad's First Speech..............................8:1–22
E. Job's Response to Bildad ....9:1—10:22
1. Job Argues His Case............................9:1–35
2. Job Questions His Oppression.......10:1–22
F. Zophar's First Speech..........................11:1–20
G. Job's Response to Zophar.............12:1—14:22
1. Job Tells His Friends Only God Knows 12:1–25
2. Job Begs God to Speak to Him 13:1–28
3. Job Mourns That Man Has Only One Life 14:1–22

II. The Second Cycle of Debate.........15:1—21:34

A. Eliphaz's Second Speech 15:1–35
1. Job's Mouth Condemns Him 15:1–13
2. The Wicked Suffer........................15:14–35
B. Job's Response to Eliphaz.............16:1—17:16
1. Job Calls His Friends Miserable Comforters...16:1–5
2. Job Laments His Situation 16:6–14
3. Job Defends His Innocence 16:15–22
4. God Makes Job a Byword................17:1–16
C. Bildad's Second Speech 18:1–21
D. Job's Response to Bildad 19:1–29
E. Zophar's Second Speech 20:1–29
F. Job's Response to Zophar 21:1–34

III. The Third Cycle of Debate............22:1—26:14

A. Eliphaz's Third Speech..........................22:1–30
B. Job's Response to Eliphaz............23:1—24:25
1. Job Will Come Forth as Gold 23:1–17
2. God Seems Indifferent to the Wicked 24:1–25
C. Bildad's Third Speech............................25:1–6
D. Job's Response to Bildad.......................26:1–14

IV. The Final Defense of Job ....27:1—31:40

A. Job's First Monologue....................27:1—28:28
1. Job Affirms His Righteousness 27:1–23
2. Job Observes That Man Cannot Discover Wisdom..........................28:1–28
B. Job's Second Monologue ....29:1—31:40
1. Job Remembers His Happy Past .. 29:1–25
2. Job Describes His Present Humiliation..30:1–31
3. Job Defends His Innocency 31:1–34
4. Job Pleads to Meet God and Defend Himself...................................31:35–40

V. The Solution of Elihu ....32:1—37:24

A. Elihu Intervenes in the Debate 32:1–22
B. Elihu's First Rebuttal............................33:1–33
1. Elihu Challenges Job to Debate.......33:1–7
2. Elihu Quotes Job's Complaints......33:8–11
3. Elihu Answers Job's Complaints 33:12–33
C. Elihu's Second Rebuttal 34:1–37

1. Elihu Challenges Job to Debate Again 34:1–4
2. Elihu Quotes Job's Complaints 34:5–9
3. Elihu Answers Job's Complaints 34:10–37

D. Elihu's Third Rebuttal 35:1–16

E. Elihu's Conclusion ....36:1—37:24
1. Elihu Believes That God Is Disciplining Job 36:1–21
2. Elihu Reminds Job of the Greatness of God ....36:22—37:24

Part Three: The Deliverance of Job (38:1—42:17)

I. The First Controversy of God with Job ....38:1—40:5

A. God's First Challenge to Job ....38:1—40:2
1. God Questions Job from the Realm of Creation 38:1–38
2. God Questions Job from the Realm of Animals ....38:39—39:30
3. God Demands an Answer to His Questions 40:1, 2

B. Job's First Answer to God 40:3–5

II. The Second Controversy of God with Job ....40:6—42:6

A. God's Second Challenge to Job..... 40:6—41:34
1. God Tells Job to Save Himself 40:6–14
2. God Compares the Power of Job with That of the Behemoth 40:15–24
3. God Compares the Power of Job with That of the Leviathan 41:1–34

B. Job's Second Answer to God 42:1–6
1. Job Confesses Lack of Understanding 42:1–3
2. Job Repents of His Rebellion 42:4–6

III. The Deliverance of Job and His Friends 42:7–17

CHAPTER 1

The Circumstances of Job

THERE was a man [R]in the land of Uz,
whose name *was* Job; and that man was
blameless and upright, and one who feared
God and shunned evil. 1 Chr. 1:17
2 And seven sons and three daughters were
born to him.
3 Also, his possessions were seven thou-
sand sheep, three thousand camels, five hun-
dred yoke of oxen, five hundred female
donkeys, and a very large household, so that
this man was the greatest of all the [T]people of
the East. Lit. *sons*
4 And his sons would go and feast *in their*
houses, each on his *appointed* day, and would
send and invite their three sisters to eat and
drink with them.
5 So it was, when the days of feasting had
run their course, that Job would send and
sanctify them, and he would rise early in the
morning [R]and offer burnt offerings *according*
to the number of them all. For Job said, "It
may be that my sons have sinned and
[R]cursed* God in their hearts." Thus Job did
regularly. [Job 42:8] • 1 Kin. 21:10, 13

The First Assault of Satan

6 Now there was a day when the sons of
God came to present themselves before the
LORD, and Satan* also came among them.
7 And the LORD said to [T]Satan, "From
where do you come?" So Satan answered the
LORD and said, "From [R]going to and fro on
the earth, and from walking back and forth
on it." Lit. *the Adversary* • [1 Pet. 5:8]
8 Then the LORD said to Satan, "Have you
[T]considered My servant Job, that *there is*
none like him on the earth, a blameless and
upright man, one who fears God and [T]shuns
evil?" Lit. *set your heart on* • Lit. *turns away from*
9 So Satan answered the LORD and said,
"Does Job fear God for nothing?
10 [R]"Have You not made a hedge around him,
around his household, and around all that he
has on every side? You have blessed the work
of his hands, and his possessions have in-
creased in the land. Ps. 34:7
11 [R]"But now, stretch out Your hand and
touch all that he has, and he will surely curse
You to Your face!" Job 2:5; 19:21
12 And the LORD said to Satan, "Behold, all
that he has *is* in your [T]power; only do not lay
a hand on his *person*." So Satan went out
from the presence of the LORD. Lit. *hand*
13 Now there was a day when his sons and
daughters *were* eating and drinking wine in
their oldest brother's house;
14 and a messenger came to Job and said,
"The oxen were plowing and the donkeys
feeding beside them,
15 "when the Sabeans* [T]raided *them* and
took them away—indeed they have killed the
servants with the edge of the sword; and I
alone have escaped to tell you!" Lit. *fell upon*
16 While he *was* still speaking, another also
came and said, "The fire of God fell from
heaven and burned up the sheep and the ser-
vants, and [T]consumed them; and I alone have
escaped to tell you!" *destroyed*
17 While he *was* still speaking, another also
came and said, "The Chaldeans formed three
bands, raided the camels and took them away,
yes, and killed the servants with the edge of the
sword; and I alone have escaped to tell you!"

1:5 Lit. *blessed,* but in an evil sense; cf. Job 1:11; 2:5, 9
1:6 Lit. *the Adversary* **1:15** Lit. *Sheba;* cf. Job 6:19

18 While he *was* still speaking, another also came and said, [R]"Your sons and daughters *were* eating and drinking wine in their oldest brother's house, Job 1:4, 13
19 "and suddenly a great wind came from across* the wilderness and struck the four corners of the house, and it fell on the young people, and they are dead; and I alone have escaped to tell you!"
20 Then Job arose, [R]tore his robe, and shaved his head; and he [R]fell to the ground and worshiped. Gen. 37:29, 34 • [1 Pet. 5:6]

21 And he said:

"Naked I came from my mother's womb,
And naked shall I return there.
The LORD [R]gave, and the LORD has
[R]taken away; [James 1:17] • Gen. 31:16
Blessed be the name of the LORD."

22 [R]In all this Job did not sin nor charge God with wrong. Job 2:10

CHAPTER 2

The Second Assault of Satan

AGAIN there was a day when the sons of God came to present themselves before the LORD, and Satan came also among them to present himself before the LORD.
2 And the LORD said to Satan, "From where do you come?" So [R]Satan answered the LORD and said, "From going to and fro on the earth, and from walking back and forth on it." Job 1:7
3 Then the LORD said to Satan, "Have you considered My servant Job, that *there is* none like him on the earth, [R]a blameless and upright man, one who fears God and shuns evil? And still he holds fast to his integrity, although you incited Me against him, to destroy him without cause." Job 1:1, 8
4 So Satan answered the LORD and said, "Skin for skin! Yes, all that a man has he will give for his life.
5 [R]"But stretch out Your hand now, and touch his bone and his flesh, and he will surely curse You to Your face!" Job 1:11
6 And the LORD said to Satan, "Behold, he *is* in your hand, but spare his life."

7 So Satan went out from the presence of the LORD, and struck Job with painful boils [R]from the sole of his foot to the crown of his head. Is. 1:6

8 And he took for himself a potsherd with which to scrape himself [R]while he sat in the midst of the ashes. Ezek. 27:30
9 Then his wife said to him, "Do you still hold fast to your integrity? [T]Curse God and die!" Lit. *Bless*, but in an evil sense; cf. Job 1:5
10 But he said to her, "You speak as one of the foolish women speaks. [R]Shall we indeed accept good from God, and shall we not accept adversity?" [R]In all this Job did not [R]sin with his lips. Job 1:21, 22 • Job 1:22 • Ps. 39:1

The Arrival of Job's Friends

11 Now when Job's three friends heard of all this adversity that had come upon him, each one came from his own place—Eliphaz the Temanite, Bildad the Shuhite, and Zophar the Naamathite. For they had made an appointment together to come and mourn with him, and to comfort him.

1:19 LXX omits *across*

1:21 Responses to Suffering—In the hour of suffering the Christian should attempt to determine first of all just why he may be suffering. One can suffer because of his position or his disposition. Peter brings this truth out in his first epistle: "Servants, *be* submissive to *your* masters with all fear, not only to the good and gentle, but also to the harsh. For this *is* commendable, if because of conscience toward God one endures grief, suffering wrongfully" (Page 1281—1 Pet. 2:18, 19).

Suffering is often a two-sided coin. On the one side suffering may be viewed as coming from God to bring out the best in us. See Gen. 22:1, 2, 15–18; Heb. 11:17. On the other side Satan attempts to use the same temptation and suffering to bring out the worst in us (Page 1272—James 1:13, 14). Finally, the believer can react to suffering in three different ways:

a. Despise it, that is, treat it too lightly, as did Esau his birthright (Page 1267—Heb. 12:5, 16).
b. Faint under it, that is, treat it too seriously (Page 1267—Heb. 12:5).
c. Be exercised by it, that is, receive instruction from it. This is the reaction desired by God (Page 1267—Heb. 12:11–13).

During this time both Peter and Paul advise us to commit our pain and suffering to God, realizing He is faithful to work out all things for our good and God's glory (Page 1155—Rom. 8:28; Page 1283—1 Pet. 4:19). James tells us to count it all joy when we experience these dark hours (Page 1272—James 1:2).

Now turn to Page 788—Jer. 37:15: Examples of Suffering.

2:7 Purposes of Suffering—Perhaps the most painful question confronting the believer is the problem of suffering. Why does a loving and wise God permit His children to suffer? The Scriptures offer a number of reasons for this.

a. To produce fruit. If we allow suffering to accomplish its purpose, it can bring forth patience (Page 1265—Heb. 10:36; Page 1272—James 1:3), joy (Page 559—Ps. 30:5; 126:6), knowledge (Page 597—Ps. 94:12), and maturity (Page 1283—1 Pet. 5:10).
b. To silence the devil. Satan once accused Job of merely serving God for the material blessings involved. But the Lord allowed the devil to torment Job to demonstrate that His servant loved God because of who He was, and not for what he could get from Him (Page 512—Job 1:9–12; 2:3–7).

(continued on next page)

12 And when they raised their eyes from
afar, and did not recognize him, they lifted
their voices and wept; and each one tore his
robe and [R]sprinkled dust on his head toward
heaven. Neh. 9:1
13 So they sat down with him on the ground
[R]seven days and seven nights, and no one
spoke a word to him, for they saw that *his*
grief was very great. Gen. 50:10

CHAPTER 3

Job's First Speech

AFTER this Job opened his mouth and
cursed the day of his *birth*.
2 And Job [T]spoke, and said: Lit. *answered*

3 "May[R] the day perish on which I was
born, Jer. 20:14–18
And the night *in which* it was said,
'A male child is conceived.'
4 May that day be darkness;
May God above not seek it,
Nor the light shine upon it.
5 May darkness and [R]the shadow of death
claim it; Jer. 13:16
May a cloud settle on it;
May the blackness of the day terrify it.
6 *As for* that night, may darkness seize it;
May it not rejoice* among the days of
the year,
May it not come into the number of the
months.
7 Oh, may that night be barren!
May no joyful shout come into it!
8 May those curse it who curse the day,
Those [R]who are ready to arouse
Leviathan. Jer. 9:17
9 May the stars of its morning be dark;
May it look for light, but *have* none,
And not see the dawning of the day;
10 Because it did not shut up the doors of
my *mother's* womb,
Nor hide sorrow from my eyes.

11 "Why[R] did I not die at birth? Job 10:18, 19
Why did I *not* [T]perish when I came from
the womb? *expire*
12 [R]Why did the knees receive me?
Or why the breasts, that I should
nurse? Gen. 30:3
13 For now I would have lain still and been
quiet,
I would have been asleep;
Then I would have been at rest
14 With kings and counselors of the earth,
Who built ruins for themselves,
15 Or with princes who had gold,
Who filled their houses *with* silver;
16 Or *why* was I not hidden [R]like a stillborn
child, Ps. 58:8
Like infants who never saw light?
17 There the wicked cease *from* troubling,
And there the weary are at rest.
18 *There* the prisoners [T]rest together;
[R]They do not hear the voice of the
oppressor. *are at ease* • Job 39:7
19 The small and great are there,
And the servant *is* free from his master.

20 "Why[R] is light given to him who is in
misery, Jer. 20:18
And life to the bitter of soul,
21 Who [R]long[T] for death, but it does not
come, Rev. 9:6 • Lit. *wait*
And search for it more than [R]hidden
treasures; Prov. 2:4
22 Who rejoice exceedingly,
And are glad when they can find the
[R]grave? Job 7:15, 16
23 *Why is light given* to a man whose way
is hidden,
And whom God has hedged in?
24 For my sighing comes before I eat,*
And my groanings pour out like water.
25 For the thing I greatly [R]feared has come
upon me, [Job 9:28; 30:15]
And what I dreaded has happened to me.
26 I am not at ease, nor am I quiet;
I have no rest, for trouble comes."

CHAPTER 4

Eliphaz Believes the Innocent Do Not Suffer

THEN Eliphaz the Temanite answered and
said:

2 "*If* one attempts a word with you, will you
become weary?

3:6 LXX, Syr., Tg., Vg. *be joined* **3:24** Lit. *my bread*

(continued from previous page)

c. To glorify God (Page 1092—John 9:1–3; 11:1–4).
d. To make us like Jesus. "That I may know Him and the power of His resurrection, and the fellowship of His sufferings, being conformed to His death" (Page 1215—Phil. 3:10).
e. To teach us dependence. This is brought out by both Christ (Page 1100—John 15:1–5) and the apostle Paul (Page 1191—2 Cor. 12:1–10).
f. To refine our lives (Page 579—Ps. 66:10–12; Page 643—Prov. 17:3; Page 1279—1 Pet. 1:6, 7).
g. To rebuke our sin (Page 1281—1 Pet. 2:20; 3:17; 4:15). As a faithful earthly father must in love punish his erring child, so does our heavenly Father (Page 1267—Heb. 12:5–9).
h. To enlarge our ministry toward others (Page 1184—2 Cor. 1:3–7). It has been observed that he who has suffered much speaks many languages (understands others).

Now turn to Page 513—Job 1:21: Responses to Suffering.

But who can withhold himself from
speaking?
3 Surely you have instructed many,
And you [R]have strengthened weak
hands. Is. 35:3
4 Your words have upheld him who was
stumbling,
And you [R]have strengthened the [T]feeble
knees; Is. 35:3 • Lit. *bending*
5 But now it comes upon you, and you are
weary;
It touches you, and you are troubled.
6 *Is* not [R]your reverence [R]your confidence?
And the integrity of your ways your
hope? Job 1:1 • Prov. 3:26

7 "Remember now, [R]who *ever* perished
being innocent? [Ps. 37:25]
Or where were the upright *ever* cut off?
8 Even as I have seen,
[R]Those who plow iniquity [Prov. 22:8]
And sow trouble reap the same.
9 By the blast of God they perish,
And by the breath of His anger they are
consumed.
10 The roaring of the lion,
The voice of the fierce lion,
And [R]the teeth of the young lions are
broken. Ps. 58:6
11 [R]The old lion perishes for lack of prey,
And the cubs of the lioness are
scattered. Ps. 34:10

12 "Now a word was secretly brought to me,
And my ear received a whisper of it.
13 [R]In disquieting thoughts from the visions
of the night, Job 33:15
When deep sleep falls on men,
14 Fear came upon me, and trembling,
Which made all my bones shake.
15 Then a spirit passed before my face;
The hair on my body stood up.
16 It stood still,
But I could not discern its appearance.
A form *was* before my eyes;
There was silence;
Then I heard a voice *saying*:
17 'Can a mortal be more righteous than
God?
Can a man be more pure than his
Maker?
18 If He puts no trust in His servants,
If He charges His angels with error,
19 How much more those who dwell in
houses of clay,
Whose foundation is in the dust,
Who are crushed before a moth?
20 [R]They are broken in pieces from morning
till evening; Ps. 90:5, 6
They perish forever, with no one
regarding.
21 Does not their own excellence go away?
They die, even without wisdom.'

CHAPTER 5

Eliphaz Calls Job Foolish

"CALL out now;
Is there anyone who will answer you?
And to which of the holy ones will you
turn?
2 For wrath kills a foolish man,
And envy slays a simple one.
3 [R]I have seen the foolish taking root,
But suddenly I cursed his dwelling
place. Jer. 12:1–3
4 His sons are far from safety,
They are crushed in the gate,
And [R]*there is* no deliverer. Ps. 109:12
5 Because the hungry eat up his harvest,
Taking it even from the thorns,*
And a snare snatches their substance.*
6 For affliction does not come from the dust,
Nor does trouble spring from the
ground;
7 Yet man is [R]born to [T]trouble, Job 14:1
As the sparks fly upward. *labor*

Eliphaz Encourages Job to Appeal to God

8 "But as for me, I would seek God,
And to God I would commit my cause—
9 Who does great things, and
unsearchable,
Marvelous things without number.
10 He gives rain on the earth,
And sends waters on the fields.
11 [R]He sets on high those who are lowly,
And those who mourn are lifted to
safety. Ps. 113:7
12 [R]He frustrates the devices of the crafty,
So that their hands cannot carry out
their plans. Neh. 4:15
13 He catches the [R]wise in their own
craftiness, [1 Cor. 3:19]
And the counsel of the cunning comes
quickly upon them.
14 They meet with darkness in the daytime,
And grope at noontime as in the night.
15 But [R]He saves the needy from the
sword, Ps. 35:10
From the mouth of the mighty,
And from their hand.
16 [R]So the poor have hope, 1 Sam. 2:8
And injustice shuts her mouth.

Eliphaz Encourages Job to Not Despise God's Discipline

17 "Behold,[R] happy *is* the man whom God
corrects; Ps. 94:12
Therefore do not despise the chastening
of the Almighty.
18 For He bruises, but He binds up;

5:5 LXX *They shall not be taken from evil men;* Vg. *And the armed man shall take him by violence* • LXX *The might shall draw them off;* Vg. *And the thirsty shall drink up their riches*

He wounds, but His hands make whole.
19 He shall deliver you in six troubles,
Yes, in seven no evil shall touch you.
20[R] In famine He shall redeem you from death, Ps. 33:19, 20; 37:19
And in war from the [T]power of the sword. Lit. *hand*
21[R] You shall be hidden from the scourge of the tongue, Ps. 31:20
And you shall not be afraid of destruction when it comes.
22 You shall laugh at destruction and famine,
And [R]you shall not be afraid of the beasts of the earth. Ezek. 34:25
23[R] For you shall have a covenant with the stones of the field, Ps. 91:12
And the beasts of the field shall be at peace with you.
24 You shall know that your tent *is* in peace;
You shall visit your dwelling and find nothing amiss.
25 You shall also know that [R]your descendants *shall be* many,
And your offspring [R]like the grass of the earth. Ps. 112:2 • Ps. 72:16
26 You shall come to the grave at a full age,
As a sheaf of grain ripens in its season.
27 Behold, this we have [R]searched out;
It *is* true. Ps. 111:2
Hear it, and know for yourself."

CHAPTER 6

Job's Deep Anguish

THEN Job answered and said:

2 "Oh, that my grief were fully weighed,
And my calamity laid with it on the scales!
3 For then it would be heavier than the sand of the sea—
Therefore my words have been rash.
4[R] For the arrows of the Almighty *are* within me; Ps. 38:2
My spirit drinks in their poison;
[R]The terrors of God are arrayed [R]against me. Ps. 88:15, 16 • Job 30:15
5 Does the [R]wild donkey bray when it has grass, Job 39:5–8
Or does the ox low over its fodder?
6 Can flavorless food be eaten without salt?
Or is there *any* taste in the white of an egg?
7 My soul refuses to touch them;
They *are* as loathsome food to me.

8 "Oh, that I might have my request,
That God would grant *me* the thing that I long for!
9 That it would please God to crush me,
That He would loose His hand and [R]cut me off! Job 7:16; 9:21; 10:1
10 Then I would still have comfort;
Though in anguish I would exult,
He will not spare;
For [R]I have not concealed the words of [R]the Holy One. Acts 20:20 • [Is. 57:15]

11 "What strength do I have, that I should hope?
And what *is* my end, that I should prolong my life?
12 *Is* my strength the strength of stones?
Or is my flesh bronze?
13 *Is* my help not within me?
And is success driven from me?

Job Seeks His Friends' Sympathy

14 "To[R] him who is [T]afflicted, kindness *should be shown* by his friend,
Even though he forsakes the fear of the Almighty. [Prov. 17:17] • Or *despairing*
15[R] My brothers have dealt deceitfully like a brook, Ps. 38:11
[R]Like the streams of the brooks that pass away, Jer. 15:18
16 Which are dark because of the ice,
And into which the snow vanishes.
17 When it is warm, they cease to flow;
When it is hot, they vanish from their place.
18 The paths of their way turn aside,
They go nowhere and perish.
19 The caravans of [R]Tema look, Gen. 25:15
The travelers of Sheba hope for them.
20 They are [R]disappointed[T] because they were confident; Jer. 14:3 • Lit. *ashamed*
They come there and are confused.
21 For now [R]you are nothing, Job 13:4
You see terror and are afraid.
22 Did I ever say, 'Bring *something* to me'?
Or, 'Offer a bribe for me from your wealth'?
23 Or, 'Deliver me from the enemy's hand'?
Or, 'Redeem me from the hand of oppressors'?

24 "Teach me, and I will hold my tongue;
Cause me to understand wherein I have erred.
25 How forceful are right words!
But what does your arguing prove?
26 Do you intend to rebuke *my* words,
And the speeches of a desperate one, *which are* as wind?
27 Yes, you overwhelm the fatherless,
And you undermine your friend.
28 Now therefore, be pleased to look at me;
For I would never lie to your face.
29[R] Yield now, let there be no injustice!
Yes, concede, my [R]righteousness still stands! Job 17:10 • Job 27:5, 6; 34:5
30 Is there injustice on my tongue?
Cannot my taste discern the unsavory?

CHAPTER 7

Job Questions God's Continuing Trials

"*IS there* not [R]a time of hard service for
man on earth? [Job 14:5, 13, 14]
Are not his days also like the days of a
hired man?
2 Like a servant who [T]earnestly desires the
shade, Lit. *pants for*
And like a hired man who eagerly looks
for his wages,
3 So I have been allotted [R]months of
futility, [Job 15:31]
And wearisome nights have been
appointed to me.
4[R] When I lie down, I say, 'When shall I
arise, Deut. 28:67
And the night be ended?'
For I have had my fill of tossing till
dawn.
5 My flesh is [R]caked with worms and dust,
My skin is cracked and breaks out
afresh. Is. 14:11

6 "My[R] days are swifter than a weaver's
shuttle, Job 9:25; 16:22; 17:11
And are spent without hope.
7 Oh, remember that my life *is* a breath!
My eye will never again see good.
8[R] The eye of him who sees me will see me
no *more;* Job 8:18; 20:9
While your *eyes* are upon me, I shall no
longer *be.*
9 *As* the cloud disappears and vanishes
away,
So [R]he who goes down to the grave does
not come up. 2 Sam. 12:23
10 He shall never return to his house,
Nor shall his place know him anymore.

11 "Therefore I will [R]not restrain my mouth;
I will speak in the anguish of my spirit;
I will [R]complain in the bitterness of my
soul. Ps. 39:1, 9 • 1 Sam. 1:10
12 *Am* I a sea, or a sea serpent,
That You set a guard over me?
13 When I say, 'My bed will comfort me,
My couch will ease my complaint,'
14 Then You scare me with dreams
And terrify me with visions,
15 So that my soul chooses strangling
And death rather than my body.*
16[R] I loathe *my life;* Job 10:1
I would not live forever.
[R]Let me alone, Job 14:6
For my days *are but* a breath.

17 "What[R] *is* man, that You should exalt
him, Ps. 8:4; 144:3
That You should set Your heart on him,
18 That You should [T]visit him every
morning, *attend to*
And test him every moment?
19 How long?
Will You not look away from me,
And let me alone till I swallow my
saliva?
20 Have I sinned?
What have I done to You, [R]O watcher of
men? Ps. 36:6
Why have You set me as Your target,
So that I am a burden to myself?*
21 Why then do You not pardon my
transgression,
And take away my iniquity?
For now I will lie down in the dust,
And You will seek me diligently,
But I *will* no longer *be.*"

CHAPTER 8

Bildad's First Speech

THEN Bildad the Shuhite answered and
said:

2 "How long will you speak these *things,*
And the words of your mouth *be like* a
strong wind?
3[R] Does God subvert judgment? [Deut. 32:4]
Or does the Almighty pervert justice?
4 If [R]your sons have sinned against Him,
He has cast them away for their
transgression. Job 1:5, 18, 19
5[R] If you would earnestly seek God
And make your supplication to the
Almighty, [Job 5:17–27; 11:13]
6 If you *were* pure and upright,
Surely now He would [T]awake for you,
And prosper your rightful dwelling
place. *arise*
7 Though your beginning was small,
Yet your latter end would [R]increase
abundantly. Job 42:12

8 "For[R] inquire, please, of the former age,
And consider the things discovered by
their fathers; Deut. 4:32; 32:7
9 For [R]we *were born* yesterday, and know
[T]nothing, Gen. 47:9 • Lit. *not*
Because our days on earth *are* a shadow.
10 Will they not teach you and tell you,
And utter words from their heart?

11 "Can the papyrus grow up without a
marsh?
Can the reeds flourish without water?
12 While it *is* yet green *and* not cut down,
It withers before any *other* plant.
13 So *are* the paths of all who [R]forget God;
And the hope of the [R]hypocrite shall
perish, Ps. 9:17 • Job 11:20; 18:14; 27:8
14 Whose confidence shall be cut off,
And whose trust *is* a spider's web.

7:15 Lit. *my bones* **7:20** So with MT, Tg., Vg.; LXX, Jewish tradition *to You*

15[R] He leans on his house, but it does not stand. Job 8:22; 27:18
He holds it fast, but it does not endure.
16 He grows green in the sun,
And his branches spread out in his garden.
17 His roots wrap around the rock heap,
And look for a place in the stones.
18[R] If he is destroyed from his place,
Then *it* will deny him, *saying*, 'I have not seen you.' Job 7:10

19 "Behold, this is the joy of His way,
And out of the earth others will grow.
20 Behold, [R]God will not [T]cast away the blameless, Job 4:7 • *reject*
Nor will He uphold the evildoers.
21 He will yet fill your mouth with laughing,
And your lips with rejoicing.
22 Those who hate you will be [R]clothed with shame, Ps. 35:26; 109:29
And the dwelling place of the wicked will come to nothing."*

CHAPTER 9

Job Argues His Case

THEN Job answered and said:

2 "Truly I know *it is* so,
But how can a [R]man be righteous before God? [Job 4:17; 15:14–16]
3 If one wished to [T]contend with Him,
He could not answer Him one time out of a thousand. *argue*
4[R] *God is* wise in heart and mighty in strength. Job 36:5
Who has hardened *himself* against Him and prospered?
5 He removes the mountains, and they do not know
When He overturns them in His anger;
6 He [R]shakes the earth out of its place,
And its pillars tremble; Heb. 12:26
7 He commands the sun, and it does not rise;
He seals off the stars;
8 He alone spreads out the heavens,
And treads on the waves of the sea;
9[R] He made the Bear, Orion, and the Pleiades, Amos 5:8
And the chambers of the south;
10[R] He does great things past finding out,
Yes, wonders without number. Job 5:9
11 If He goes by me, I do not see *Him;*
If He moves past, I do not perceive Him;
12[R] If He takes away, who can hinder Him?
Who can say to Him, 'What are You doing?' [Is. 45:9]
13 God will not withdraw His anger,
[R]The allies of the proud* lie prostrate beneath Him. Job 26:12

14 "How then can I answer Him,
And choose my words *to reason* with Him?
15[R] For though I were righteous, I could not answer Him; Job 10:15; 23:1–7
I would beg mercy of my Judge.
16 If I called and He answered me,
I would not believe that He was listening to my voice.
17 For He crushes me with a tempest,
And multiplies my wounds [R]without cause. Job 2:3
18 He will not allow me to catch my breath,
But fills me with bitterness.
19 If *it is a matter* of strength, indeed *He is* strong;
And if of justice, who will appoint my day *in* court?
20 Though I were righteous, my own mouth would condemn me;
Though I *were* blameless, it would prove me perverse.

21 "I am blameless, yet I do not know myself;
I despise my life.
22 It *is* all one *thing;*
Therefore I say, 'He destroys the blameless and the wicked.'
23 If the scourge slays suddenly,
He laughs at the plight of the innocent.
24 The earth is given into the hand of the wicked.
He covers the faces of its judges.
If it is not *He*, who else could it be?

25 "Now my days are swifter than a runner;
They flee away, they see no good.
26 They pass by like swift ships,
Like an eagle swooping on its prey.
27[R] If I say, 'I will forget my complaint,
I will put off my sad face and wear a smile,' Job 7:13
28[R] I am afraid of all my sufferings;
I know that You [R]will not hold me innocent. Ps. 119:120 • Ex. 20:7
29 *If* I am condemned,
Why then do I labor in vain?
30 If I wash myself with snow water,
And cleanse my hands with [T]soap, *lye*
31 Yet You will plunge me into the pit,
And my own clothes will abhor me.

32 "For [R]*He is* not a man, as I *am*, [Is. 45:9]
That I may answer Him,
And that we should go to court together.
33 Nor is there any mediator between us,
Who may lay his hand on us both.
34 Let Him take His rod away from me,
And do not let dread of Him terrify me.
35 *Then* I would speak and not fear Him,
But it is not so with me.

8:22 Lit. *will not be* **9:13** Heb. *rahab*

CHAPTER 10

Job Questions His Oppression

"MY [R]soul loathes my life; Job 7:16
I will give free course to my complaint,
I will speak in the bitterness of my soul.
2 I will say to God, 'Do not condemn me;
Show me why You contend with me.
3 *Does it* seem good to You that You should oppress,
That You should despise the work of Your hands,
And smile on the counsel of the wicked?
4 Do You have eyes of flesh?
Or do You see as man sees?
5 *Are* Your days like the days of a mortal man?
Are Your years like the days of a mighty man,
6 That You should seek for my iniquity
And search out my sin,
7 Although You know that I am not wicked,
And *there is* no one who can deliver from Your hand?

8 'Your[R] hands have made me and fashioned me, Ps. 119:73
An intricate unity;
Yet You would [R]destroy me. [Job 9:22]
9 Remember, I pray, [R]that You have made me like clay. Gen. 2:7
And will You turn me into dust again?
10 Did You not pour me out like milk,
And curdle me like cheese,
11 Clothe me with skin and flesh,
And knit me together with bones and sinews?
12 You have granted me life and favor,
And Your care has preserved my spirit.
13 'And these *things* You have hidden in Your heart;
I know that this *was* with You:
14 If I sin, then [R]You mark me, Ps. 139:1
And will not acquit me of my iniquity.
15 If I am wicked, [R]woe to me; Is. 3:11
[R]Even *if* I am righteous, I [T]cannot lift up my head. [Job 9:12, 15] • Lit. *will not*
I am full of disgrace;
[R]See my misery! Ps. 25:18
16 If *my head* is exalted,
[R]You hunt me like a fierce lion, Is. 38:13
And again You show Yourself awesome against me.
17 You renew Your witnesses against me,
And increase Your indignation toward me;
Changes and war are *ever* with me.

18 'Why[R] then have You brought me out of the womb? Job 3:11–13
Oh, that I had perished and no eye had seen me!
19 I would have been as though I had not been.
I would have been carried from the womb to the grave.
20 [R]Are not my days few? Ps. 39:5
Cease! [R]Leave me alone, that I may take a little comfort, Job 7:16, 19
21 Before I go *to the place from which* I shall not return,
[R]To the land of darkness [R]and the shadow of death, Ps. 88:12 • Ps. 23:4
22 A land as dark as darkness *itself*,
As the shadow of death, without any order,
Where even the light *is* like darkness.' "

CHAPTER 11

Zophar's First Speech

THEN Zophar the Naamathite answered and said:

2 "Should not the multitude of words be answered?
And should [T]a man full of talk be vindicated? Lit. *a man of lips*
3 Should your empty talk make men [T]hold their peace? *be silent*
And when you mock, should no one rebuke you?
4 For you have said,
[R]'My doctrine *is* pure, Job 6:30
And I am clean in your eyes.'
5 But oh, that God would speak,
And open His lips against you,
6 That He would show you the secrets of wisdom!
For *they would* double *your* prudence.
Know therefore that [R]God exacts from you [Ezra 9:13]
Less than your iniquity *deserves*.

7 "Can[R] you search out the deep things of God? [Eccl. 3:11]
Can you find out the limits of the Almighty?
8 *They are* higher than heaven—what can you do?
Deeper than [T]Sheol—what can you know? The abode of the dead
9 Their measure *is* longer than the earth
And broader than the sea.

10 If[R] He passes by, imprisons, and gathers *to judgment*, [Rev. 3:7]
Then who can [T]hinder Him? *restrain*
11 For [R]He knows deceitful men; [Ps. 10:14]
He sees wickedness also.
Will He not then consider *it*?
12 For an [R]empty-headed man will be wise,

When a wild donkey's colt is born a
man. Rom. 1:22

13"If you would [R]prepare your heart,
And [R]stretch out your hands toward
Him; [1 Sam. 7:3] • Ps. 88:9
14 If iniquity *were* in your hand, *and you*
put it far away,
And [R]would not let wickedness dwell in
your tents; Ps. 101:3
15[R]Then surely you could lift up your face
without spot; Ps. 119:6
Yes, you could be steadfast, and not fear;
16 Because you would [R]forget *your* misery,
And remember *it* as waters *that have*
passed away, Is. 65:16
17 And *your* life [R]would be brighter than
noonday. Is. 58:8, 10
Though you were dark, you would be
like the morning.
18 And you would be secure, because there
is hope;
Yes, you would dig *around you, and*
[R]take your rest in safety. Lev. 26:5, 6
19 You would also lie down, and no one
would make *you* afraid;
Yes, many would court your favor.
20 But [R]the eyes of the wicked will fail,
And they shall not escape, Deut. 28:65
And their hope—loss of life!"

CHAPTER 12

Job Tells His Friends Only God Knows

THEN Job answered and said:

2"No doubt you *are* the people,
And wisdom will die with you!
3 But I have [T]understanding as well as
you; Lit. *a heart*
I *am* not [R]inferior to you. Job 13:2
Indeed, who does not *know* such things
as these?

4"I[R] am one mocked by his friends,
Who [R]called on God, and He answered
him, Job 21:3 • Ps. 91:15
The just and blameless *who is* ridiculed.
5 A lamp* is despised in the thought of
one who is at ease;
It is made ready for [R]those whose feet
slip. Prov. 14:2
6[R]The tents of robbers prosper,
And those who provoke God are
secure— [Job 9:24; 21:6–16]
In what God provides by His hand.

7"But now ask the beasts, and they will
teach you;
And the birds of the air, and they will tell
you;
8 Or speak to the earth, and it will teach
you;
And the fish of the sea will explain to
you.
9 Who among all these does not know
That the hand of the LORD has done this,
10[R]In whose hand *is* the [T]life of every living
thing, [Acts 17:28] • Or *soul*
And the breath of all mankind?
11 Does not the ear test words
And the [T]mouth taste its food? *palate*
12 Wisdom *is* with aged men,
And with [T]length of days,
understanding. Long life

13"With Him *are* wisdom and strength,
He has counsel and understanding.
14 If [R]He breaks *a thing* down, it cannot be
rebuilt; Job 11:10
If He imprisons a man, there can be no
release.
15 If He [R]withholds the waters, they dry up;
If He [R]sends them out, they overwhelm
the earth. [1 Kin. 8:35, 36] • Gen. 7:11–24
16 With Him *are* strength and prudence.
The deceived and the deceiver *are* His.
17 He leads counselors away plundered,
And makes fools of the judges.
18 He loosens the bonds of kings,
And binds their waist with a belt.
19 He leads princes* away plundered,
And overthrows the mighty.
20[R]He deprives the trusted ones of speech,
And takes away the discernment of the
elders. Job 32:9
21[R]He pours contempt on princes,
And disarms the mighty. Ps. 107:40
22 He [R]uncovers deep things out of
darkness, [1 Cor. 4:5]
And brings the shadow of death to light.
23[R]He makes nations great, and destroys
them; Is. 9:3; 26:15
He enlarges nations, and guides them.
24 He takes away the understanding* of the
chiefs of the people of the earth,
And [R]makes them wander in a pathless
wilderness. Ps. 107:4
25 They grope in the dark without light,
And He makes them [R]stagger like a
drunken *man.* Ps. 107:27

CHAPTER 13

Job Begs God to Speak to Him

"BEHOLD, my eye has seen all *this,*
My ear has heard and understood it.
2[R]What you know, I also know; Job 12:3
I *am* not inferior to you.
3 But I would speak to the Almighty,
And I desire to reason with God.
4 But you forgers of lies,
You *are* all worthless physicians.

12:5 Or *disaster* **12:19** Lit. *priests,* but not in a technical sense **12:24** Lit. *heart*

5 Oh, that you would be silent,
And it would be your wisdom!
6 Now hear my reasoning,
And heed the pleadings of my lips.
7 Will you speak wickedly for God,
And talk deceitfully for Him?
8 Will you show partiality for Him?
Will you contend for God?
9 Will it be well when He searches you out?
Or can you mock Him as one mocks a man?
10 He will surely rebuke you
If you secretly show partiality.
11 Will not His excellence make you afraid,
And the dread of Him fall upon you?
12 Your platitudes *are* proverbs of ashes,
Your defenses are defenses of clay.

13 "Hold[T] your peace with me, and let me speak, *Be silent*
Then let come on me what *may!*
14 Why [R]do I take my flesh in my teeth,
And put my life in my hands? Job 18:4
15 [R]Though He slay me, yet will I trust Him.
[R]Even so, I will defend my own ways before Him. Ps. 23:4 • Job 27:5
16 He also *shall* be my salvation,
For a [R]hypocrite could not come before Him. Job 8:13
17 Listen carefully to my speech,
And to my declaration with your ears.
18 See now, I have prepared *my* case,
I know that I shall be vindicated.
19 Who *is* he *who* will contend with me?
If now I hold my tongue, I perish.

20 "Only two *things* do not do to me,
Then I will not hide myself from You:
21 [R]Withdraw Your hand far from me,
And let not the dread of You make me afraid. Ps. 39:10
22 Then call, and I will [R]answer;
Or let me speak, then You respond to me. Job 9:16; 14:15
23 How many *are* my iniquities and sins?
Make me know my transgression and my sin.
24 Why do You hide Your face,
And regard me as Your enemy?
25 [R]Will You frighten a leaf driven to and fro? Is. 42:3
And will You pursue dry stubble?
26 For You write bitter things against me,
And [R]make me inherit the iniquities of my youth. Job 20:11
27 You put my feet in the stocks,
And watch closely all my paths.
You set a limit* for the soles of my feet.

28 "*Man** decays like a rotten thing,
Like a garment that is moth-eaten.

CHAPTER 14

Job Mourns That Man Has Only One Life

"MAN *who is* born of woman
Is of few days and full of trouble.
2 [R]He comes forth like a flower and fades away; Job 8:9
He flees like a shadow and does not continue.
3 And [R]do You open Your eyes on such a one, Ps. 8:4; 144:3
And [R]bring me* to judgment with Yourself? [Ps. 143:2]
4 Who [R]can bring a clean *thing* out of an unclean? [Ps. 51:2, 5, 10]
No one!
5 [R]Since his days *are* determined,
The number of his months *is* with You;
You have appointed his limits, so that he cannot pass. Job 7:1; 21:21
6 [R]Look away from him that he may [T]rest,
Till [R]like a hired man he finishes his day. Ps. 39:13 • Lit. *cease* • Job 7:1

7 "For there is hope for a tree,
If it is cut down, that it will sprout again,
And that its tender shoots will not cease.
8 Though its root may grow old in the earth,
And its stump may die in the ground,
9 *Yet* at the scent of water it will bud
And bring forth branches like a plant.
10 But man dies and is laid away;
Indeed he [T]breathes his last *expires*
And where *is* [R]he? Job 10:21, 22
11 *As* water disappears from the sea,
And a river becomes parched and dries up,
12 So man lies down and does not rise.
[R]Till the heavens *are* no more,
They will not awake [Is. 51:6; 65:17; 66:22]
Nor be roused from their sleep.

13 "Oh, that You would hide me in the grave,
That You would conceal me until Your wrath is past,
That You would appoint me a set time, and remember me!
14 If a man dies, shall he live *again?*
All the days of my hard service [R]I will wait, Job 13:15
Till my change comes.
15 You shall call, and I will answer You;
You shall desire the work of Your hands.
16 For now You number my steps,
But do not watch over my sin.
17 My transgression *is* sealed up in a bag,
And You cover* my iniquity.

18 "But *as* a mountain falls *and* crumbles away,

13:27 Lit. *inscribe a print* **13:28** Lit. *He* **14:3** LXX, Syr., Vg. *him* **14:17** Lit. *plaster over*

And *as* a rock is moved from its place;
19 *As* water wears away stones,
And as torrents wash away the soil of the earth;
So You destroy the hope of man.
20 You prevail forever against him, and he passes on;
You change his countenance and send him away.
21 His sons come to honor, and [R]he does not know *it;* Eccl. 9:5
They are brought low, and he does not perceive *it*.
22 But his flesh will be in pain over it,
And his soul will mourn over it."

CHAPTER 15

Job's Mouth Condemns Him

THEN [R]Eliphaz the Temanite answered and said: Job 4:1

2 "Should a wise man answer with empty knowledge,
And fill himself with the east wind?
3 Should he reason with unprofitable talk,
Or by speeches with which he can do no good?
4 Yes, you cast off fear,
And restrain prayer before God.
5 For your iniquity teaches your mouth,
And you choose the tongue of the crafty.
6 [R]Your own mouth condemns you, and not I; [Luke 19:22]
Yes, your own lips testify against you.

7 "*Are* you the first man *who* was born?
Or were you made before the hills?
8 Have you heard the counsel of God?
Do you limit wisdom to yourself?
9 [R]What do you know that we do not know? Job 12:3; 13:2
What do you understand that *is* not in us?
10 [R]Both the gray-haired and the aged *are* among us, Job 8:8–10; 12:12; 32:6, 7
Much older than your father.
11 *Are* the consolations of God too small for you,
And the word *spoken* gently* with you?
12 Why does your heart carry you away,
And what do your eyes wink at,
13 That you turn your spirit against God,
And let *such* words go out of your mouth?

The Wicked Suffer

14 "What[R] *is* man, that he could be pure?
And *he who is* born of a woman, that he could be righteous? Prov. 20:9
15 [R]If *God* puts no trust in His saints,
And the heavens are not pure in His sight, Job 4:18; 25:5
16 [R]How much less man, *who is* abominable and filthy, Ps. 14:3; 53:3
Who drinks iniquity like water!

17 "I will tell you, hear me;
What I have seen I will declare,
18 What wise men have told,
Not hiding *anything received* [R]from their fathers, Job 8:8; 20:4
19 To whom alone the land was given,
And no alien passed among them:
20 The wicked man writhes with pain all *his* days,
[R]And the number of years is hidden from the oppressor. Ps. 90:12
21 [T]Dreadful sounds *are* in his ears;
[R]In prosperity the destroyer comes upon him. *Terrifying* • 1 Thess. 5:3
22 He does not believe that he will [R]return from darkness, Job 14:10–12
For a sword is waiting for him.
23 He [R]wanders about for bread, *saying,* 'Where *is it?*' Ps. 59:15; 109:10
He knows [R]that a day of darkness is ready at his hand. Job 18:12
24 Trouble and anguish make him afraid;
They overpower him, like a king ready for [T]battle. *attack*
25 For he stretches out his hand against God,
And acts defiantly against the Almighty,
26 Running stubbornly against Him
With his strong, embossed shield.

27 "Though[R] he has covered his face with his fatness, Ps. 17:10; 73:7; 119:70
And made *his* waist heavy with fat,
28 He dwells in desolate cities,
In houses which no one inhabits,
Which are destined to become ruins.
29 He will not be rich,
Nor will his wealth [R]continue,
Nor will his possessions overspread the earth. Job 20:28; 27:16, 17
30 He will not depart from darkness;
The flame will dry out his branches,
And [R]by the breath of His mouth he will go away. Job 4:9
31 Let him not [R]trust in futile *things,* deceiving himself, Is. 59:4
For futility will be his reward.
32 It will be accomplished before his time,
And his branch will not be green.
33 He will shake off his unripe grape like a vine,
And cast off his blossom like an olive tree.
34 For the company of hypocrites *will be* barren,
And fire will consume the tents of bribery.

15:11 Or *a secret thing*

35[R] They conceive trouble and bring forth
futility; Is. 59:4
Their womb prepares deceit."

CHAPTER 16

Job Calls His Friends Miserable Comforters

THEN Job answered and said:

2 "I have heard many such things;
Miserable comforters *are* you all!
3 Shall words of wind have an end?
Or what provokes you that you answer?
4 I also could speak as you *do,*
If your soul were in my soul's place.
I could heap up words against you,
And [R]shake my head at you; Ps. 22:7
5 *But* I would strengthen you with my
mouth,
And the comfort of my lips would relieve
your grief.

Job Laments His Situation

6 "Though I speak, my grief is not relieved;
And *if* I remain silent, how am I eased?
7 But now He has [R]worn me out; Job 7:3
You [R]have made desolate all my
company. Job 16:20; 19:13–15
8 You have shriveled me up,
And it is a witness *against me;*
My leanness rises up against me
And bears witness to my face.
9 He tears *me* in His wrath, and hates me;
He gnashes at me with His teeth;
My adversary sharpens His gaze on me.
10 They [R]gape at me with their mouth,
They [R]strike me reproachfully on the
cheek, Ps. 22:13; 35:21 • Lam. 3:30
They gather together against me.
11 God [R]has delivered me to the ungodly,
And turned me over to the hands of the
wicked. Job 1:15, 17
12 I was at ease, but He has [R]shattered me;
He also has taken *me* by my neck, and
shaken me to pieces; Job 9:17
He has set me up for His target,
13 His archers surround me.
He pierces my heart* and does not pity;
He pours out my gall on the ground.
14 He breaks me with wound upon wound;
He runs at me like a warrior.*

Job Defends His Innocence

15 "I have sewn sackcloth over my skin,
And laid my head* in the dust.
16 My face is [T]flushed from weeping,
And on my eyelids *is* the shadow of
death; Lit. *red*
17 Although no violence *is* in my hands,
And my prayer *is* pure.

18 "O earth, do not cover my blood,
And let my cry have no *resting* place!
19 Surely even now [R]my witness *is* in
heaven, Rom. 1:9
And my evidence *is* on high.
20 My friends scorn me;
My eyes pour out *tears* to God.
21[R] Oh, that one might plead for a man with
God, Job 31:35
As a man *pleads* for his neighbor!
22 For when a few years are finished,
I shall go the way of no return.

CHAPTER 17

God Makes Job a Byword

"MY spirit is broken,
My days are extinguished,
[R]The grave *is ready* for me. Ps. 88:3, 4
2 *Are* not mockers with me?
And does not my eye [T]dwell on their
provocation? Lit. *lodge*

3 "Now put down a pledge for me with
Yourself.
Who *is* he *who* [R]will shake hands with
me? Prov. 6:1; 17:18; 22:26
4 For You have hidden their heart from
[R]understanding; Job 12:20; 32:9
Therefore You will not exalt *them.*
5 He who speaks flattery to *his* friends,
Even the eyes of his children will fail.

6 "But He has made me [R]a byword of the
people, Job 30:9
And I have become one in whose face
men spit.
7[R] My eye has also grown dim because of
sorrow, Ps. 6:7; 31:9
And all my members *are* like shadows.
8 Upright *men* are astonished at this,
And the innocent stirs himself up against
the hypocrite.
9 Yet the righteous will hold to his way,
And he who has [R]clean hands will be
stronger and stronger. Ps. 24:4

10 "But please, [R]come back again, all of
you,* Job 6:29
For I shall not find *one* wise *man* among
you.
11[R] My days are past, Job 7:6
My purposes are broken off,
Even the thoughts of my heart.
12 They change the night into day;
'The light *is* near,' *they say,* in the face of
darkness.
13 If I wait *for* the grave *as* my house,
If I make my bed in the darkness,
14 If I say to corruption, 'You *are* my father,'

16:13 Lit. *kidneys* **16:14** Vg. *giant* **16:15** Lit. *horn* **17:10** So with some Heb. mss., LXX, Syr., Vg.; MT, Tg. *all of them*

And to the worm, 'You *are* my mother
and my sister,'
15 Where then *is* my [R]hope? Job 7:6; 14:19
As for my hope, who can see it?
16 *Will* they go down [R]to the gates of
[T]Sheol? Jon. 2:6 • The abode of the dead
Shall *we have* [R]rest together in the
dust?" Job 3:17–19; 21:33

CHAPTER 18

Bildad's Second Speech

THEN [R]Bildad the Shuhite answered and
said: Job 8:1

2 "How long *till* you put an end to words?
Gain understanding, and afterward we
will speak.
3 Why are we counted as beasts,
And regarded as stupid in your sight?
4 [R]You[T] who tear yourself in anger,
Shall the earth be forsaken for you?
Or shall the rock be removed from its
place? Job 13:14 • Lit. *one who tears his soul*

5 "The light of the wicked indeed goes out,
And the flame of his fire does not shine.
6 The light is dark in his tent,
And his lamp beside him is put out.
7 The steps of his strength are shortened,
And his own counsel casts him down.
8 For [R]he is cast into a net by his own
feet, Job 22:10
And he walks into a snare.
9 The net takes *him* by the heel,
And [R]a snare lays hold of him. Job 5:5
10 A noose *is* hidden for him on the ground,
And a trap for him in the road.
11 [R]Terrors frighten him on every side,
And drive him to his feet. Jer. 6:25
12 His strength is starved,
And destruction *is* ready at his side.
13 It devours patches of his skin;
The firstborn of death devours his
[T]limbs. *parts*
14 He is uprooted from [R]the shelter of his
tent, Job 11:20
And they parade him before the king of
terrors.
15 They dwell in his tent *who are* none of
his;
Brimstone is scattered on his dwelling.
16 His roots are dried out below,
And his branch withers above.
17 [R]The memory of him perishes from the
earth, [Ps. 34:16]
And he has no name among the
renowned.*
18 He is driven from light into darkness,
And chased out of the world.
19 [R]He has neither son nor posterity among
his people, Is. 14:22
Nor any remaining in his dwellings.
20 Those [T]in the west are astonished [R]at his
day, Lit. *who came after* • Ps. 37:13
As those in the east are frightened.
21 Surely such *are* the dwellings of the
wicked,
And this *is* the place *of him who* [R]does
not know God." Jer. 9:3

CHAPTER 19

Job's Response to Bildad

THEN Job answered and said:
2 "How long will you torment my soul,
And break me in pieces with words?
3 These ten times you have [T]reproached
me; *shamed* or *disgraced*
You are not ashamed *that* you have
wronged me.*
4 And if indeed I have erred,
My error remains with me.
5 If indeed you [R]exalt *yourselves* against
me, Ps. 35:26; 38:16; 55:12, 13
And plead my disgrace against me,
6 Know then that God has wronged me,
And has surrounded me with His net.

7 "If I cry out concerning [T]wrong, I am not
heard. *violence*
If I cry aloud, *there is* no justice.
8 [R]He has [T]fenced up my way, so that I
cannot pass; Job 3:23 • *walled off my way*
And He has set darkness in my paths.
9 He has stripped me of my glory,
And taken the crown *from* my head.
10 He breaks me down on every side,
And I am gone;
My hope He has uprooted like a tree.
11 He has also kindled His wrath against
me,
And [R]He counts me as *one* of His
enemies. Job 13:24; 33:10
12 His troops come together
And build up their road against me;
They encamp all around my tent.

13 "He[R] has removed my brothers far from
me, Ps. 31:11; 38:11; 69:8; 88:8, 18
And my acquaintances are completely
estranged from me.
14 My relatives have failed,
And my close friends have forgotten me.
15 Those who dwell in my house, and my
maidservants,
Count me as a stranger;
I am an alien in their sight.
16 I call my servant, but he gives no
answer;
I beg him with my mouth.

18:17 Lit. *before the outside,* i.e., the distinguished or famous **19:3** A Jewish tradition *make yourselves strange to me*

17 My breath is offensive to my wife,
And I am [T]repulsive to the children of my own body. Lit. *strange*
18 Even young children despise me;
I arise, and they speak against me.
19[R] All my close friends abhor me,
And those whom I love have turned against me. Ps. 38:11; 55:12, 13
20[R] My bone clings to my skin and to my flesh, Ps. 102:5
And I have escaped by the skin of my teeth.

21 "Have pity on me, have pity on me, O you my friends,
For the hand of God has struck me!
22 Why do you persecute me as God *does*,
And are not satisfied with my flesh?

23 "Oh, that my words were written!
Oh, that they were inscribed in a book!
24 That they were engraved on a rock
With an iron pen and lead, forever!
25 For I know *that* my Redeemer lives,
And He shall stand at last on the earth;
26 And after my skin is [T]destroyed, this *I know*, Lit. *struck off*
That in my flesh I shall see God,
27 Whom I shall see for myself,
And my eyes shall behold, and not another.
How my heart yearns within me!
28 If you should say, 'How shall we persecute him?'—
Since the root of the matter is found in me,
29 Be afraid of the sword for yourselves;
For wrath *brings* the punishment of the sword,
That you may know *there is* a judgment."

CHAPTER 20

Zophar's Second Speech

THEN [R]Zophar the Naamathite answered and said: Job 11:1

2 "Therefore my anxious thoughts make me answer,
Because of the turmoil within me.
3 I have heard the rebuke that reproaches me,
And the spirit of my understanding causes me to answer.

4 "Do you *not* know this of [R]old, Job 8:8
Since man was placed on earth,
5[R] That the triumphing of the wicked is short, Ps. 37:35, 36
And the joy of the hypocrite is *but* for a [R]moment? [Job 8:13; 13:16; 15:34; 27:8]
6[R] Though his haughtiness mounts up to the heavens, Is. 14:13, 14
And his head reaches to the clouds,
7 *Yet* he will perish forever like his own refuse;
Those who have seen him will say, 'Where is he?'
8 He will fly away [R]like a dream, and not be found; Ps. 73:20; 90:5
Yes, he [R]will be chased away like a vision of the night. Job 18:18; 27:21–23
9 The eye *that* saw him will *see him* no more,
Nor will his place behold him anymore.
10 His children will seek the favor of the poor,
And his hands will restore his wealth.
11 His bones are full of his youthful vigor,
But it will lie down with him in the dust.

12 "Though evil is sweet in his mouth,
And he hides it under his tongue,
13 *Though* he spares it and does not forsake it,
But still keeps it in his mouth,
14 *Yet* his food in his stomach turns sour;
It becomes cobra venom within him.
15 He swallows down riches
And vomits them up again;
God casts them out of his belly.
16 He will suck the poison of cobras;
The viper's tongue will slay him.
17 He will not see [R]the streams, Jer. 17:8
The rivers flowing with honey and cream.
18 He will restore that for which he labored,
And will not swallow *it* down;
From the proceeds of business
He will get no enjoyment.
19 For he has [T]oppressed *and* forsaken the poor, *crushed*
He has violently seized a house which he did not build.

20 "Because[R] he knows no quietness in his heart,* Eccl. 5:13–15
He will not save anything he desires.
21 Nothing is left for him to eat;
Therefore his well-being will not last.
22 In his self-sufficiency he will be in distress;
Every hand of [T]misery will come against him. Or *the wretched* or *sufferer*
23 *When* he is about to fill his stomach,
God will cast on him the fury of His wrath,
And will rain *it* on him while he is eating.
24 He will flee from the iron weapon;
A bronze bow will pierce him through.
25 It is drawn, and comes out of the body;
Yes, [R]the glittering *point comes* out of his [T]gall. Job 16:13 • Gallbladder

20:20 Lit. *belly*

[R]Terrors *come* upon him; Job 18:11, 14
26 Total darkness *is* reserved for his
treasures.
[R]An unfanned fire will consume him;
It shall go ill with him who is left in his
tent. Ps. 21:9
27 The heavens will reveal his iniquity,
And the earth will rise up against him.
28 The increase of his house will depart,
And his goods will flow away in the day
of His [R]wrath. Job 20:15; 21:30
29[R]This *is* the portion from God for a
wicked man, Job 27:13; 31:2, 3
The heritage appointed to him by God."

CHAPTER 21

Job's Response to Zophar

THEN Job answered and said:
2"Listen carefully to my speech,
And let this be your consolation.
3 Bear with me that I may speak,
And after I have spoken, keep mocking.

4"As for me, *is* my complaint against
man?
And if *it were*, why should I not be
impatient?
5 Look at me and be astonished;
Put *your* hand over *your* mouth.
6 Even when I remember I am terrified,
And trembling takes hold of my flesh.
7 Why do the wicked live *and* become
old,
Yes, become mighty in power?
8 Their descendants are established with
them in their sight,
And their offspring before their eyes.
9 Their houses *are* safe from fear,
Neither *is* the rod of God upon them.
10 Their bull breeds without failure;
Their cow calves without miscarriage.
11 They send forth their little ones like a
flock,
And their children dance.
12 They sing to the tambourine and harp,
And rejoice to the sound of the flute.
13 They [R]spend their days in wealth,
And in a moment go down to the
grave.* Job 21:23; 36:11
14[R]Yet they say to God, 'Depart from us,
For we do not desire the knowledge of
Your ways. Job 22:17
15[R]Who *is* the Almighty, that we should
serve Him? Ex. 5:2
And [R]what profit do we have if we pray
to Him?' Mal. 3:14
16 Indeed [T]their prosperity *is* not in their
hand; Lit. *their goal*
[R]The counsel of the wicked is far from
me. Prov. 1:10
17"How often is the lamp of the wicked put
out?
How often does their destruction come
upon them,
The sorrows *God* [R]distributes in His
anger? [Luke 12:46]
18[R]They are like straw before the wind,
And like chaff that a storm [T]carries
away. Ps. 1:4; 35:5 • *steals away*
19 *They say,* 'God [T]lays up one's* iniquity
[R]for his children'; *stores up* • [Ex. 20:5]
Let Him recompense him, that he may
know *it.*
20 Let his eyes see his destruction,
And [R]let him drink of the wrath of the
Almighty. Is. 51:17
21 For what does he care about his
household after him,
When the number of his months is cut in
half?

22"Can *anyone* teach God knowledge,
Since He judges those on high?
23 One dies in his full strength,
Being wholly at ease and secure;
24 His pails* are full of milk,
And the marrow of his bones is moist.
25 Another man dies in the bitterness of his
soul,
Never having eaten with pleasure.
26 They [R]lie down alike in the dust,
And worms cover them. Eccl. 9:2

27"Look, I know your thoughts,
And the schemes *with which* you would
wrong me.
28 For you say,
'Where *is* the house of the prince?
And where *is* the tent,*
The dwelling place of the wicked?'
29 Have you not asked those who travel the
road?
And do you not know their signs?
30[R]For the wicked are reserved for the day
of doom; [Prov. 16:4]
They shall be brought out on the day of
wrath.
31 Who condemns his way to his face?
And who repays him *for what* he has
done?
32 Yet he shall be brought to the grave,
And a vigil kept over the tomb.
33 The clods of the valley shall be sweet to
him;
[R]Everyone shall follow him, Heb. 9:27
As countless *have gone* before him.
34 How then can you comfort me with
empty words,
Since [T]falsehood remains in your
answers?" *faithlessness*

21:13 Or *Sheol* **21:19** Lit. *his* **21:24** LXX, Vg. *bowels;* Syr. *sides;* Tg. *breasts* **21:28** Vg. omits *the tent*

CHAPTER 22

Eliphaz's Third Speech

THEN [R]Eliphaz the Temanite answered and
said: Job 4:1; 15:1; 42:9

2 "Can[R] a man be profitable to God,
Though he who is wise may be profitable
to himself? [Luke 17:10]
3 *Is it* any pleasure to the Almighty that
you are righteous?
Or *is it* gain *to Him* that you make your
ways blameless?

4 "Is it because of your fear of Him that He
corrects you,
And enters into judgment with you?
5 *Is* not your wickedness great,
And your iniquity without end?
6 For you have [R]taken pledges from your
brother for no reason, [Ex. 22:26, 27]
And stripped the naked of their
clothing.
7 You have not given the weary water to
drink,
And you [R]have withheld bread from the
hungry. Deut. 15:7
8 But the [T]mighty man possessed the
land, Lit. *man of arm*
And the honorable man dwelt in it.
9 You have sent widows away empty,
And the [T]strength of the fatherless was
crushed. Lit. *arms*
10 Therefore snares *are* all around you,
And sudden fear troubles you,
11 Or darkness *so that* you cannot see;
And an abundance of water covers you.

12 "Is not God in the height of heaven?
And see the highest stars, how lofty they
are!
13 And you say, [R]'What does God know?
Can He judge through the deep
darkness? Ps. 73:11
14 [R]Thick clouds cover Him, so that He
cannot see, Ps. 139:11, 12
And He walks above the circle of
heaven.'
15 Will you keep to the old way
Which wicked men have trod,
16 Who [R]were cut down before their time,
Whose foundations were swept away by
a flood? Job 14:19; 15:32
17 They said to God, 'Depart from us!
What can the Almighty do to them?'*
18 Yet He filled their houses with good
things;
But the counsel of the wicked is far from
me.

19 "The righteous see *it* and are glad,
And the innocent laugh at them:
20 'Surely our adversaries* are cut down,
And the fire consumes their remnant.'

21 "Now acquaint yourself with Him, and
[R]be at peace; Is. 27:5
Thereby good will come to you.
22 Receive, please, [R]instruction from His
mouth, Prov. 2:6
And lay up His words in your heart.
23 If you return to the Almighty, you will be
built up;
You will remove iniquity far from your
tents.
24 Then you will [R]lay your gold in the dust,
And the *gold* of Ophir among the stones
of the brooks. 2 Chr. 1:15
25 Yes, the Almighty will be your gold*
And your precious silver;
26 For then you will have your [R]delight in
the Almighty, Job 27:10; Ps. 37:4
And lift up your face to God.
27 [R]You will make your prayer to Him,
He will hear you, [Is. 58:9–11]
And you will pay your vows.
28 You will also declare a thing,
And it will be established for you;
So light will shine on your ways.
29 When they cast *you* down, and you say,
'Exaltation *will come!*'
Then He will save the humble *person.*
30 He will *even* deliver one who is not
innocent;
Yes, he will be delivered by the purity of
your hands."

22:17 LXX, Syr. *us* **22:20** LXX *substance is* **22:25** Ancient vss. suggest *defense;* MT *gold,* as in v. 24

22:22 Memorizing God's Word—You are not always able to study the Bible by reading it. If you have memorized a portion of the Word of God, you are able to gain insights into its meaning at times when a Bible is not readily available. The Bible recognizes the importance of Scripture memorization. The following benefits can be cited:

a. It keeps the child of God from sinning (Page 610—Ps. 119:11).
b. It provides comfort in times of trouble (Page 611—Ps. 119:52, 92).
c. It stays your mind upon God (Page 568—Ps. 43:3).
d. It provides daily sustenance for the spiritual life (Page 183—Deut. 8:3).
e. It provides continual and ready guidance in all the situations of life (Page 633—Prov. 6:20–23).
f. It provides the basis for formal and informal instruction of your children (Page 181—Deut. 6:6, 7).

Now turn to Page 214—Josh. 1:8: Meditating upon God's Word.

CHAPTER 23

Job Will Come Forth as Gold

THEN Job answered and said:

2 "Even today my [R]complaint is bitter;
My* hand is listless because of my
groaning. Job 7:11
3 Oh, that I knew where I might find Him,
That I might come to His seat!
4 I would present *my* case before Him,
And fill my mouth with arguments.
5 I would know the words *which* He would
answer me,
And understand what He would say to
me.
6 [R]Would He contend with me in His great
power? Is. 57:16
No! But He would take *note* of me.
7 There the upright could reason with
Him,
And I would be delivered forever from
my Judge.

8 "Look,[R] I go forward, but He is not *there*,
And backward, but I cannot perceive
Him; Job 9:11; 35:14
9 When He works on the left hand, I
cannot behold *Him;*
When He turns to the right hand, I
cannot see *Him.*
10 But He knows the way that I take;
When [R]He has tested me, I shall come
forth as gold. [James 1:12]
11 [R]My foot has held fast to His steps;
I have kept His way and not turned
aside. Ps. 17:5
12 I have not departed from the
commandment of His lips;
[R]I have treasured the words of His mouth
More than my necessary *food.* Ps. 44:18

13 "But He *is* unique, and who can make
Him change?
And *whatever* [R]His soul desires, *that* He
does. [Ps. 115:3]
14 For He performs *what is* [R]appointed for
me, [1 Thess. 3:2–4]
And many such *things are* with Him.
15 Therefore I am terrified at His presence;
When I consider *this,* I am afraid of Him.
16 For God made my heart weak,
And the Almighty terrifies me;
17 Because I was not [R]cut off [T]from the
presence of darkness, Job 10:18, 19
And He did *not* hide deep darkness from
my face. Or *by* or *before*

CHAPTER 24

God Seems Indifferent to the Wicked

"SINCE [R]times are not hidden from the
Almighty, [Acts 1:7]
Why do those who know Him see not
His [R]days? [Is. 2:12]

2 "*Some* remove [R]landmarks;
They seize flocks violently and feed *on
them;* [Deut. 19:14; 27:17]
3 They drive away the donkey of the
fatherless;
They take the widow's ox as a pledge.
4 They push the needy off the road;
All the [R]poor of the land are forced to
hide. Prov. 28:28
5 Indeed, *like* wild donkeys in the desert,
They go out to their work, searching for
food.
The wilderness *yields* food for them *and*
for *their* children.
6 They gather their fodder in the field
And glean in the vineyard of the wicked.
7 They [R]spend the night naked, without
clothing, Ex. 22:26, 27
And have no covering in the cold.
8 They are wet with the showers of the
mountains,
And [R]huddle around the rock for want of
shelter. Lam. 4:5

9 "*Some* snatch the fatherless from the
breast,
And take a pledge from the poor.
10 They cause *the poor* to go naked,
without [R]clothing; Job 31:19
And they take away the sheaves from the
hungry.
11 They press out oil within their walls,
And tread winepresses, yet suffer thirst.
12 The dying groan in the city,
And the souls of the wounded cry out;
Yet God does not charge *them* with
wrong.

13 "There are those who rebel against the
light;
They do not know its ways
Nor abide in its paths.
14 [R]The murderer rises with the light;
He kills the poor and needy; Ps. 10:8
And in the night he is like a thief.
15 [R]The eye of the adulterer waits for the
twilight, Prov. 7:7–10
[R]Saying, 'No eye will see me'; Ps. 10:11
And he disguises *his* face.
16 In the dark they break into houses
Which they marked for themselves in
the daytime;
[R]They do not know the light. [John 3:20]
17 For the morning is the same to them as
the shadow of death;
If *someone* recognizes *them,*
They are in the terrors of the shadow of
death.

23:2 So with MT, Tg., Vg.; LXX, Syr. *His*

18"They *should be* swift on the face of the waters,
Their portion *should be* cursed in the earth,
So that no *one would* turn into the way of their vineyards.
19 As drought and heat [T]consume the snow waters, Lit. *seize*
So the grave* *consumes those who* have sinned.
20 The womb *should* forget him,
The worm *should* feed sweetly on him;
[R]He *should* be remembered no more,
And wickedness *should* be broken like a tree. Prov. 10:7
21 For he [T]preys on the barren *who* do not bear, Lit. *feeds on*
And does no good for the widow.

22"But *God* draws the mighty away with His power;
He rises up, but no *man* is sure of life.
23 He gives them security, and they rely *on it;*
Yet His eyes *are* on their ways.
24 They are exalted for a little while,
Then they are gone.
They are brought low;
They are [T]taken out of the way like all *others;* Lit. *gathered up*
They dry out like the heads of grain.

25"Now if *it is* not so, who will prove me a liar,
And make my speech worth nothing?"

CHAPTER 25

Bildad's Third Speech

THEN [R]Bildad the Shuhite answered and said: Job 8:1; 18:1

2"Dominion and fear *belong* to Him;
He makes peace in His high places.
3 Is there any number to His armies?
Upon whom does His light not rise?
4[R]How then can man be righteous before God? Job 4:17; 15:14
Or how can he be [R]pure *who is* born of a woman? [Job 14:4]
5 If even the moon does not shine,
And the stars are not pure in His sight,
6 How much less man, *who is* a maggot,
And a son of man, *who is* a worm?"

CHAPTER 26

Job's Response to Bildad

BUT Job answered and said:

2"How have you helped *him who is* without power?
How have you saved the arm *that has* no strength?
3 How have you counseled *one* who has no wisdom?
And *how* have you declared sound advice to many?
4 To whom have you uttered words?
And whose spirit came from you?

5"The dead tremble,
Those under the waters and those inhabiting them.
6[R]Sheol *is* naked before Him, Prov. 15:11
And Destruction has no covering.
7[R]He stretches out the north over empty space; Job 9:8
He hangs the earth on nothing.
8[R]He binds up the water in His thick clouds, Prov. 30:4
Yet the clouds are not broken under it.
9 He covers the face of *His* throne,
And spreads His cloud over it.
10[R]He drew a circular horizon on the face of the waters, Prov. 8:29
At the boundary of light and darkness.
11 The pillars of heaven tremble,
And are astonished at His rebuke.
12[R]He stirs up the sea with His power,
And by His understanding He breaks up [T]the storm. Is. 51:15 • Heb. *rahab*
13 By His Spirit He adorned the heavens;
His hand pierced the fleeing serpent.
14 Indeed these *are* the mere edges of His ways,
And how small a whisper we hear of Him!
But the thunder of His power who can understand?"

CHAPTER 27

Job Affirms His Righteousness

MOREOVER Job continued his discourse, and said:

2"*As* God lives, [R]*who* has taken away my justice, Job 34:5
And the Almighty, *who* has made my soul bitter,
3 As long as my breath *is* in me,
And the breath of God in my nostrils,
4 My lips will not speak wickedness,
Nor my tongue utter deceit.
5 Far be it from me
That I should say you are right;
Till I die [R]I will not put away my integrity from me. Job 2:9; 13:15
6 My righteousness I [R]hold fast, and will not let it go; Job 2:3; 33:9
[R]My heart shall not [T]reproach *me* as long as I live. Acts 24:16 • *reprove*

24:19 Or *Sheol*

7 "May my enemy be like the wicked,
And he who rises up against me like the unrighteous.
8 [R]For what is the hope of the hypocrite,
Though he may gain *much*, Matt. 16:26
If God takes away his life?
9 [R]Will God hear his cry Jer. 14:12
When trouble comes upon him?
10 [R]Will he delight himself in the Almighty?
Will he always call on God? Job 22:26, 27

11 "I will teach you [T]about the hand of God;
What *is* with the Almighty I will not conceal. Or *by*
12 Surely all of you have seen *it;*
Why then do you behave with complete nonsense?

13 "This[R] is the portion of a wicked man with God, Job 20:29
And the heritage of oppressors, received from the Almighty:
14 [R]If his children are multiplied, *it is* for the sword; Deut. 28:41
And his offspring shall not be satisfied with bread.
15 Those who survive him shall be buried in death,
And their* widows shall not weep,
16 Though he heaps up silver like dust,
And piles up clothing like clay—
17 He may pile *it* up, but [R]the just will wear *it,* Prov. 28:8
And the innocent will divide the silver.
18 He builds his house like a moth,*
Like a booth *which* a watchman makes.
19 The rich man will lie down,
But not be gathered *up;**
He opens his eyes,
And he *is* [R]no more. Job 7:8, 21; 20:7
20 Terrors overtake him like a flood;
A tempest steals him away in the night.
21 The east wind carries him away, and he is gone;
It sweeps him out of his place.
22 It hurls against him and does not [R]spare; Jer. 13:14
He flees desperately from its power.
23 *Men* shall clap their hands at him,
And shall hiss him out of his place.

CHAPTER 28

Job Observes That Man Cannot Discover Wisdom

"SURELY there is a mine for silver,
And a place *where* gold is refined.
2 Iron is taken from the [T]earth, Lit. *dust*
And copper *is* smelted *from* ore.
3 *Man* puts an end to darkness,
And searches every recess
For ore in the darkness and the shadow of death.
4 He breaks open a shaft away from people;
In places forgotten by feet
They hang far away from men;
They swing to and fro.
5 *As for* the earth, from it comes bread,
But underneath it is turned up as by fire;
6 Its stones *are* the source of sapphires,
And it contains gold dust.
7 *That* path no bird knows,
Nor has the falcon's eye seen it.
8 The proud lions* have not trodden it,
Nor has the fierce lion passed over it.
9 He puts his hand on the flint;
He overturns the mountains [T]at the roots. At the base
10 He cuts out channels in the rocks,
And his eye sees every precious thing.
11 He dams up the streams from trickling;
What is hidden he brings forth to light.

12 "But[R] where can wisdom be found?
And where *is* the place of understanding? Eccl. 7:24
13 Man does not know its value,
Nor is it found in the land of the living.
14 The deep says, '*It is* not in me';
And the sea says, '*It is* not with me.'
15 It cannot be purchased for gold,
Nor can silver be weighed *for* its price.
16 It cannot be valued in the gold of Ophir,
In precious onyx or sapphire.
17 Neither gold nor crystal can equal it,
Nor can it be exchanged for [T]jewelry of fine gold. *vessels*
18 No mention shall be made of [T]coral or quartz, Heb. *ramoth*
For the price of wisdom *is* above rubies.
19 The topaz of Ethiopia cannot equal it,
Nor can it be valued in pure gold.

20 "From[R] where then does wisdom come?
And where *is* the place of understanding? Job 28:12
21 It is hidden from the eyes of all living,
And concealed from the birds of the air.
22 [R]Destruction[T] and Death say, Job 28:14
'We have heard a report about it with our ears.' Heb. *Abaddon*
23 God understands its way,
And He knows its place.
24 For He looks to the ends of the earth,
And sees under the whole heavens,
25 To establish a weight for the wind,
And apportion the waters by measure.
26 When He made a law for the rain,
And a path for the thunderbolt,

27:15 Lit. *his* **27:18** So with MT, Vg.; LXX, Syr. *spider* (cf. Job 8:14); Tg. *decay* **27:19** So with MT, Tg.; LXX, Syr. *But shall not add* (i.e., do it again); Vg. *But take away nothing* **28:8** Lit. *sons of pride,* figurative of the great lions

27 Then He saw *wisdom** and declared it;
He prepared it, indeed, He searched it out.
28 And to man He said,
'Behold, [R]the fear of the Lord, that *is* wisdom, [Prov. 1:7; 9:10]
And to depart from evil *is* understanding.' "

CHAPTER 29

Job Remembers His Happy Past

JOB further continued his discourse, and said:

2 "Oh, that I were as *in* months [R]past,
As *in* the days *when* God [R]watched over me; Job 1:1–5 • Job 1:10
3 [R]When His lamp shone upon my head,
And when by His light I walked *through* darkness; Job 18:6
4 Just as I was in the days of my prime,
When [R]the friendly counsel of God *was* over my tent; [Ps. 25:14]
5 When the Almighty *was* yet with me,
When my children *were* around me;
6 When [R]my steps were bathed with cream,* Deut. 32:14; Job 20:17
And [R]the rock poured out rivers of oil for me! Ps. 81:16

7 "When I went out to the gate by the city,
When I took my seat in the open square,
8 The young men saw me and hid,
And the aged arose *and* stood;
9 The princes refrained from talking,
And put *their* hand on their mouth;
10 The voice of nobles was hushed,
And their [R]tongue stuck to the roof of their mouth. Ps. 137:6
11 When the ear heard, then it blessed me,
And when the eye saw, then it approved me;
12 Because [R]I delivered the poor who cried out, [Ps. 72:12]
The fatherless and *the one who* had no helper.
13 The blessing of a perishing *man* came upon me,
And I caused the widow's heart to sing for joy.
14 [R]I put on righteousness, and it clothed me; [Is. 59:17; 61:10]
My justice *was* like a robe and a turban.
15 I *was* [R]eyes to the blind, Num. 10:31
And I *was* feet to the lame.
16 I *was* a father to the poor,
And [R]I searched out the case *that* I did not know. Prov. 29:7
17 I broke the fangs of the wicked,
And plucked the victim from his teeth.

18 "Then I said, 'I shall die in my nest,
And multiply *my* days as the sand.
19 My root *is* spread out to the waters,
And the dew lies all night on my branch.
20 My glory *is* fresh within me,
And my bow is renewed in my hand.'

21 "*Men* listened to me and waited,
And kept silence for my counsel.
22 After my words they did not speak again,
And my speech settled on them *as dew*.
23 They waited for me *as* for the rain,
And they opened their mouth wide *as* for [R]the spring rain. [Zech. 10:1]
24 *If* I mocked at them, they did not believe *it*,
And the light of my countenance they did not cast down.
25 I chose the way for them, and sat as chief;
So I dwelt as a king in the army,
As one *who* comforts mourners.

CHAPTER 30

Job Describes His Present Humiliation

"BUT now they mock at me, *men*
[T]younger than I, Lit. *of fewer days*
Whose fathers I disdained to put with the dogs of my flock.
2 Indeed, what *profit* is the strength of their hands to me?
Their vigor has perished.
3 *They are* gaunt from want and famine,
Fleeing late to the wilderness, desolate and waste,
4 Who pluck mallow by the bushes,
And broom tree roots *for* their food.
5 They were driven out from among *men*,
They shouted at them as *at* a thief.
6 *They had* to live in the clefts of the [T]valleys, *wadis*
In caves of the earth and the rocks.
7 Among the bushes they brayed,
Under the nettles they nestled.
8 *They were* sons of fools,
Yes, sons of vile men;
They were scourged from the land.

9 "And[R] now I am their taunting song;
Yes, I am their byword. Job 17:6
10 They abhor me, they keep far from me;
They do not hesitate to spit in my face.
11 Because [R]He has loosed my* bowstring and afflicted me, Job 12:18
They have cast off restraint before me.
12 At *my* right *hand* the rabble arises;
They push away my feet,
And [R]they raise against me their ways of destruction. Job 19:12

28:27 Lit. *it* **29:6** So with ancient vss. and a few Heb. mss. (cf. Job 20:17); MT *wrath* **30:11** So with MT, Syr., Tg.; LXX, Vg. *His*

13 They break up my path,
They promote my calamity;
They have no helper.
14 They come as broad breakers;
Under the ruinous storm they roll along.
15 Terrors are turned upon me;
They pursue my honor as the wind,
And my prosperity has passed like a cloud.

16 "And[R] now my soul is poured out because of my *plight;* Ps. 42:4
The days of affliction take hold of me.
17 My bones are pierced in me at night,
And my gnawing pains take no rest.
18 By great force my garment is disfigured;
It binds me about as the collar of my coat.
19 He has cast me into the mire,
And I have become like dust and ashes.

20 "I [R]cry out to You, but You do not answer me; Job 19:7
I stand up, and You regard me.
21 *But* You have become cruel to me;
With the strength of Your hand You [R]oppose me. Job 10:3; 16:9, 14; 19:6, 22
22 You lift me up to the wind and cause me to ride *on it;*
You spoil my success.
23 For I know *that* You will bring me *to* death,
And *to* the house [R]appointed for all living. [Heb. 9:27]

24 "Surely He would not stretch out *His* hand against a heap of ruins,
If they cry out when He destroys *it.*
25 [R]Have I not wept for him who was in trouble? Ps. 35:13, 14
Has *not* my soul grieved for the poor?
26 [R]But when I looked for good, evil came *to me;* Jer. 8:15
And when I waited for light, then came darkness.
27 My heart is in turmoil and cannot rest;
Days of affliction confront me.
28 [R]I go about mourning, but not in the sun; Ps. 38:6; 42:9; 43:2
I stand up in the assembly *and* cry out for help.
29 [R]I am a brother of jackals, Mic. 1:8
And a companion of ostriches.
30 My skin grows black and falls from me;
[R]My bones burn with fever. Ps. 102:3
31 My harp is *turned* to mourning,
And my flute to the voice of those who weep.

CHAPTER 31

Innocent of Sensual Sins

1 "I HAVE made a covenant with my eyes;
Why then should I [T]look upon a [R]young woman? *look intently* or *gaze* • [Matt. 5:28]
2 For what *is* the [R]allotment of God from above, Job 20:29
And the inheritance of the Almighty from on high?
3 *Is* it not destruction for the wicked,
And disaster for the workers of iniquity?
4 [R]Does He not see my ways, [2 Chr. 16:9]
And count all my steps?

5 "If I have walked with falsehood,
Or if my foot has hastened to deceit,
6 Let me be weighed on honest scales,
That God may know my integrity.
7 If my step has turned from the way,
Or my heart walked after my eyes,
Or if any spot adheres to my hands,
8 *Then* let me sow, and another eat;
Yes, let my harvest be rooted out.

9 "If my heart has been enticed by a woman,
Or *if* I have lurked at my neighbor's door,
10 *Then* let my wife grind for another,
And let others bow down over her.
11 For that *would be* wickedness;
Yes, [R]it *would be* iniquity *deserving of* judgment. Gen. 38:24
12 For that *would be* a fire *that* consumes to destruction,
And would root out all my increase.

Innocent of Abusing His Power

13 "If I have [R]despised the cause of my male or female servant [Deut. 24:14, 15]
When they complained against me,
14 What then shall I do when [R]God rises up? [Ps. 44:21]
When He punishes, how shall I answer Him?
15 [R]Did not He who made me in the womb make them? Job 34:19
Did not the same One fashion us in the womb?

16 "If I have kept the poor from *their* desire,
Or caused the eyes of the widow to fail,
17 Or eaten my morsel by myself,
So that the fatherless could not eat of it
18 (But from my youth I reared him as a father,
And from my mother's womb I guided *the widow**);
19 If I have seen anyone perish for lack of clothing,
Or any poor *man* without covering;
20 If his heart* has not [R]blessed me,
And *if* he was *not* warmed with the fleece of my sheep; [Deut. 24:13]
21 If I have raised my hand [R]against the fatherless, Job 22:9

31:18 Lit. *her* **31:20** Lit. *loins*

When I saw I had help in the gate;
22 *Then* let my arm fall from my shoulder,
Let my arm be torn from the socket.
23 For [R]destruction *from* God *is* a terror to
me, Is. 13:6
And because of His magnificence I
cannot endure.

Innocent of Trusting in His Wealth

24 "If[R] I have made gold my hope,
Or said to fine gold, '*You are* my
confidence'; [Mark 10:23–25]
25[R] If I have rejoiced because my wealth *was*
great, Ps. 62:10
And because my hand had gained much;
26[R] If I have observed the sun* when it
shines, Ezek. 8:16
Or the moon moving *in* brightness,
27 So that my heart has been secretly
enticed,
And my mouth has kissed my hand;
28 This also *would be* an iniquity *deserving*
of judgment,
For I would have denied God *who is*
above.

Innocent of Not Caring for His Enemies

29 "If[R] I have rejoiced at the destruction of
him who hated me, [Prov. 17:5; 24:17]
Or lifted myself up when evil found him
30[R] (Indeed I have not allowed my mouth to
sin [Matt. 5:44]
By asking for a curse on his soul);
31 If the men of my tent have not said,
'Who is there that has not been satisfied
with his meat?'
32[R] (*But* no sojourner had to lodge in the
street, Gen. 19:2, 3
For I have opened my doors to the
traveler*);
33 If I have covered my transgressions [R]as[T]
Adam, [Prov. 28:13] • Or *as men do*
By hiding my iniquity in my bosom,
34 Because I feared the great [R]multitude,
And dreaded the contempt of families,
So that I kept silence Ex. 23:2
And did not go out of the door—

Job Pleads to Meet God and Defend Himself

35[R] Oh, that I had one to hear me!
Here is my mark. Job 19:7; 30:20, 24, 28
Oh, [R]*that* the Almighty would answer
me, Job 13:22, 24; 33:10
That my Prosecutor had written a book!
36 Surely I would carry it on my shoulder,
And bind it on me *like* a crown;
37 I would declare to Him the number of
my steps;
Like a prince I would approach Him.

38 "If my land cries out against me,
And its furrows weep together;
39 If [R]I have eaten its fruit* without
money, Job 24:6, 10–12
Or caused its owners to lose their lives;
40 *Then* let [R]thistles grow instead of wheat,
And weeds instead of barley." Gen. 3:18

The words of Job are ended.

CHAPTER 32

Elihu Intervenes in the Debate

SO these three men ceased answering Job,
because he *was* [R]righteous in his own
eyes. Job 6:29; 31:6; 33:9
2 Then the wrath of Elihu, the son of
Barachel the [R]Buzite, of the family of Ram,
was aroused against Job; his wrath was
aroused because he [R]justified himself rather
than God. Gen. 22:21 • Job 27:5, 6
3 Also against his three friends his wrath
was aroused, because they had found no an-
swer, and *yet* had condemned Job.
4 Now because they *were* years older than
he, Elihu had waited to speak to Job.*
5 When Elihu saw that *there was* no an-
swer in the mouth of these three men, his
wrath was aroused.
6 So Elihu, the son of Barachel the Buzite,
answered and said:

"I *am* [R]young in years, and you *are* very
old; Lev. 19:32
Therefore I was afraid,
And dared not declare my opinion to
you.
7 I said, 'Age* should speak,
And multitude of years should teach
wisdom.'
8 But *there is* a spirit in man,
And [R]the breath of the Almighty gives
him understanding. [Prov. 2:6]
9[R] Great men* are not *always* wise,
Nor do the aged *always* understand
justice. [1 Cor. 1:26]

10 "Therefore I say, 'Listen to me,
I also will declare my opinion.'
11 Indeed I waited for your words,
I listened to your reasonings, while you
searched out what to say.
12 I paid close attention to you;
And surely not one of you convinced Job,
Or answered his words—
13[R] Lest you say, [Jer. 9:23]
'We have found wisdom';
God will vanquish him, not man.
14 Now he has not [T]directed *his* words
against me; *ordered*

31:26 Lit. *light* **31:32** So with LXX, Syr., Tg., Vg.; MT *road* **31:39** Lit. *strength* **32:4** Vg. *till Job had spoken* **32:7** Lit. *Days,* i.e., years **32:9** Or *Men of many years*

So I will not answer him with your
words.
15 "They are dismayed and answer no more;
Words escape them.
16 And I have waited, because they did not
speak,
Because they stood still *and* answered no
more.
17 I also will answer my part,
I too will declare my opinion.
18 For I am full of words;
The spirit within me compels me.
19 Indeed my [T]belly *is* like wine *that* has no
[T]vent; *bosom* • *opening*
It is ready to burst like new wineskins.
20 I will speak, that I may find relief;
I must open my lips and answer.
21 Let me not, I pray, show partiality to
anyone;
Nor let me flatter any man.
22 For I do not know how to flatter,
Else my Maker would soon take me
[R]away. Job 27:8

CHAPTER 33

Elihu Challenges Job to Debate

"BUT please, Job, hear my speech,
And listen to all my words.
2 Now, I open my mouth;
My tongue speaks in my mouth.
3 My words *come* from my upright heart;
My lips utter pure knowledge.
4 [R]The Spirit of God has made me,
And the breath of the Almighty gives me
life. [Gen. 2:7]
5 If you can answer me,
Set *your words* in order before me;
Take your stand.
6 [R]Truly I *am* as your spokesman* before
God; Job 4:19
I also have been formed out of clay.
7 Surely no fear of me will terrify you,
Nor will my hand be heavy on you.

Elihu Quotes Job's Complaints

8 "Surely you have spoken [T]in my hearing,
And I have heard the sound of *your*
words, *saying*, Lit. *in my ears*
9 'I[R] *am* pure, without transgression;
I *am* innocent, and *there is* no iniquity in
me. Job 10:7
10 Yet He finds occasions against me,
He counts me as His enemy;
11 [R]He puts my feet in the stocks,
He watches all my paths.' Job 13:27

Elihu Answers Job's Complaints

12 "Look, *in* this you are not righteous.
I will answer you,
For God is greater than man.
13 Why do you [R]contend with Him?
For He does not give an accounting of
any of His words. [Is. 45:9]
14 [R]For God may speak in one way, or in
another, Ps. 62:11
Yet man does not perceive it.
15 In a dream, in a vision of the night,
When deep sleep falls upon men,
While slumbering on their beds,
16 [R]Then He opens the ears of men,
And seals their instruction. [Job 36:10, 15]
17 In order to turn man *from his* deed,
And conceal pride from man,
18 He keeps back his soul from the Pit,
And his life from [T]perishing by the
sword. Lit. *passing*

19 "*Man* is also chastened with pain on his
[R]bed, Job 30:17
And with strong *pain* in many of his
bones,
20 [R]So that his life abhors bread,
And his soul succulent food. Ps. 107:18
21 His flesh wastes away from sight,
And his bones stick out *which once* were
not seen.
22 Yes, his soul draws near the Pit,
And his life to the executioners.

23 "If there is a messenger for him,
A mediator, one among a thousand,
To show man His uprightness,
24 Then He is gracious to him, and says,
'Deliver him from going down to the Pit;
I have found [T]a ransom'; *an atonement*
25 His flesh shall be young like a child's,
He shall return to the days of his youth.
26 He shall pray to God, and He will delight
in him,
He shall see His face with joy,
For He restores to man His righteousness.
27 Then he looks at men and [R]says,
'I have sinned, and perverted *what was*
right, [Luke 15:21]
And it [R]did not profit me.' [Rom. 6:21]
28 He will [R]redeem his* soul from going
down to the Pit, Is. 38:17
And his* life shall see the light.

29 "Behold, God works all these *things*,
Twice, *in fact*, three *times* with a man,
30 [R]To bring back his soul from the Pit,
That he may be enlightened with the
light of life. Ps. 56:13

31 "Give ear, Job, listen to me;
Hold your peace, and I will speak.
32 If you have anything to say, answer me;
Speak, for I desire to justify you.
33 If not, [R]listen to me; Ps. 34:11
[T]Hold your peace, and I will teach you
wisdom." *Keep silent*

33:6 Lit. *as your mouth* **33:28** Kt. *my* • Kt. *my*

CHAPTER 34

Elihu Challenges Job to Debate Again

ELIHU further answered and said:

2 "Hear my words, you wise *men;*
Give ear to me, you who have knowledge.
3 [R]For the ear tests words Job 6:30; 12:11
As the palate tastes food.
4 Let us choose justice for ourselves;
Let us know among ourselves what *is* good.

Elihu Quotes Job's Complaints

5 "For Job has said, 'I am righteous,
But God has taken away my justice;
6 [R]Should I lie concerning my right?
My wound *is* incurable, *though I am* without transgression.' Job 6:4; 9:17
7 What man *is* like Job,
Who drinks [T]scorn like water, *derision*
8 Who goes in company with the workers of iniquity,
And walks with wicked men?
9 For [R]he has said, 'It profits a man nothing Mal. 3:14
That he should delight in God.'

Elihu Answers Job's Complaints

10 "Therefore listen to me, you [T]men of understanding: *men of heart*
[R]Far be it from God *to do* wickedness,
And *from* the Almighty to *commit* iniquity. Job 8:3; 36:23
11 [R]For He repays man *according to* his work, Ps. 62:12
And makes man to find a reward according to *his* way.
12 Surely God will never do wickedly,
Nor will the Almighty pervert justice.
13 Who gave Him charge over the earth?
Or who appointed *Him over* the whole world?
14 If He should set His heart on it,
If He should [R]gather to Himself His Spirit and His breath, Ps. 104:29
15 All flesh would perish together,
And man would return to dust.

16 "If *you have* understanding, hear this;
Listen to the sound of my words:
17 [R]Should one who hates justice govern?
Will you [R]condemn *Him who is* most just? 2 Sam. 23:3 • Job 40:8
18 [R]*Is it fitting* to say to a king, '*You are* worthless,' Ex. 22:28
And to nobles, '*You are* wicked'?
19 Yet He [R]is not partial to princes,
Nor does He regard the rich more than the poor; [Deut. 10:17]
For they *are* all the work of His hands.
20 In a moment they die, [R]in the middle of the night; Ex. 12:29
The people are shaken and pass away;
The mighty are taken away without a hand.

21 "For[R] His eyes *are* on the ways of man,
And He sees all his steps. Job 31:4
22 [R]There is no darkness nor shadow of death [Amos 9:2, 3]
Where the workers of iniquity may hide themselves.
23 For He need not further consider a man,
That he should go before God in judgment.
24 [R]He breaks in pieces mighty men without inquiry, [Dan. 2:21]
And sets others in their place.
25 Therefore He knows their works;
He overthrows *them* in the night,
And they are crushed.
26 He strikes them as wicked *men*
In the open sight of others,
27 Because they [R]turned back from Him,
And [R]would not consider any of His ways, 1 Sam. 15:11 • Is. 5:12
28 So that they [R]caused the cry of the poor to come to Him; Job 35:9
For He hears the cry of the afflicted.
29 When He gives quietness, who then can make trouble?
And when He hides *His* face, who then can see Him,
Whether *it is* against a nation or a man alone?—
30 That the hypocrite should not reign,
Lest the people be ensnared.

31 "For has *anyone* said to God,
'I have borne *chastening;*
I will offend no more;
32 Teach me *what* I do not see;
If I have done iniquity, I will do no more'?
33 Should He repay *it* according to your *terms,*
Just because you disavow it?
You must choose, and not I;
Therefore speak what you know.

34 "Men of understanding say to me,
Wise men who listen to me:
35 'Job speaks without knowledge,
His words *are* without wisdom.'
36 Oh, that Job were tried to the utmost,
Because *his* answers *are like* those of wicked men!
37 For he adds rebellion to his sin;
He claps *his hands* among us,
And multiplies his words against God."

CHAPTER 35

Elihu's Third Rebuttal

MOREOVER Elihu answered and said:

2 "Do you think this is right?
Do you say,
'My righteousness is more than God's'?
3 For [R]you say, Job 21:15; 34:9
'What advantage will it be to You?
What profit shall I have, more than *if* I
had sinned?'

4 "I will answer you,
And your companions with you.
5 [R]Look to the heavens and see;
And behold the clouds—
They are higher than you. [Job 22:12]
6 If you sin, what do you accomplish
[R]against Him? [Jer. 7:19]
Or, *if* your transgressions are multiplied,
what do you do to Him?
7 [R]If you are righteous, what do you give
Him? Prov. 9:12
Or what does He receive from your hand?
8 Your wickedness affects a man such as
you,
And your righteousness a son of man.

9 "Because[R] of the multitude of oppressions
they cry out; Job 34:28
They cry out for help because of the arm
of the mighty.
10 But no one says, [R]'Where *is* God my
Maker, Is. 51:13
Who gives songs in the night,
11 Who [R]teaches us more than the beasts of
the earth, Ps. 94:12
And makes us wiser than the birds of
heaven?'
12 [R]There they cry out, but He does not
answer, Prov. 1:28
Because of the pride of evil men.
13 [R]Surely God will not listen to empty *talk*,
Nor will the Almighty regard it. [Is. 1:15]
14 [R]Although you say you do not see Him,
Yet justice *is* before Him, and [R]you must
wait for Him. Job 9:11 • [Ps. 37:5, 6]
15 And now, because He has not [R]punished
in His anger, Ps. 89:32
Nor taken much notice of folly,
16 [R]Therefore Job opens his mouth in vain;
He multiplies words without
knowledge." Job 34:35; 38:2

CHAPTER 36

Elihu Believes That God Is Disciplining Job

ELIHU also proceeded and said:
2 "Bear with me a little, and I will show you
That *there are* yet words to speak on
God's behalf.
3 I will fetch my knowledge from afar;
I will ascribe righteousness to my Maker.
4 For truly my words *are* not false;
One who is perfect in knowledge *is* with
you.

5 "Behold, God *is* mighty, but despises *no
one*;
[R]*He is* mighty in strength of
understanding. Job 12:13, 16; 37:23
6 He does not preserve the life of the
wicked,
But gives justice to the oppressed.
7 [R]He does not withdraw His eyes from the
righteous; [Ps. 33:18; 34:15]
But [R]*they are* on the throne with kings,
For He has seated them forever,
And they are exalted. Ps. 113:8
8 And if *they are* bound in [T]fetters, chains
Held in the cords of affliction,
9 Then He tells them their work and their
transgressions—
That they have acted defiantly.
10 [R]He also opens their ear to [T]instruction,
And commands that they turn from
iniquity. Job 33:16; 36:15 • *discipline*
11 If they obey and serve *Him*,
They shall [R]spend their days in
prosperity, [Is. 1:19, 20]
And their years in pleasures.
12 But if they do not obey,
They shall perish by the sword,
And they shall die without knowledge.*

13 "But the hypocrites in heart [R]store up
wrath; [Rom. 2:5]
They do not cry for help when He binds
them.
14 [R]They[T] die in youth, Ps. 55:23
And their life *ends* among the perverted
persons.* Lit. *Their soul dies*
15 He delivers the poor in their affliction,
And opens their ears in oppression.

16 "Indeed He would have brought you out
of dire distress,
[R]*Into* a broad place where *there is* no
restraint; Ps. 18:19; 31:8; 118:5
And [R]what is set on your table *would be*
full of [R]richness. Ps. 23:5 • Ps. 36:8
17 But you are filled with the judgment due
the [R]wicked; Job 22:5, 10, 11
Judgment and justice take hold *of you*.
18 Because *there is* wrath, *beware* lest He
take you away with *one* blow;
For [R]a large ransom would not help you
avoid *it*. Ps. 49:7
19 [R]Will your riches, [Prov. 11:4]
Or all the mighty forces,
Keep you from distress?
20 Do not desire the night,
When people are cut off in their place.
21 Take heed, [R]do not turn to iniquity,
For [R]you have chosen this rather than
affliction. [Ps. 31:6; 66:18] • [Heb. 11:25]

36:12 MT *as one without knowledge* **36:14** Heb. *qedeshim*, those practicing sodomy or prostitution in religious rituals

Elihu Reminds Job of the Greatness of God

22"Behold, God is exalted by His power;
Who teaches like Him?
23 [R]Who has assigned Him His way,
Or who has said, 'You have done
[R]wrong'? Job 34:13; [Is. 40:13, 14] • Job 8:3

24"Remember to [R]magnify His work,
Of which men have sung. [Rev. 15:3]
25 Everyone has seen it;
Man looks on *it* from afar.

26"Behold, God *is* great, and we [R]do not
know *Him;* [1 Cor. 13:12]
[R]Nor can the number of His years *be*
discovered. Heb. 1:12
27 For He draws up drops of water,
Which distill as rain from the mist,
28 Which the clouds drop down
And pour abundantly on man.
29 Indeed, can *anyone* understand the
spreading of clouds,
The thunder from His canopy?
30 Look, He scatters His light upon it,
And covers the depths of the sea.
31 For [R]by these He judges the peoples;
He gives food in abundance. [Acts 14:17]
32 [R]He covers *His* hands with lightning,
And commands it to strike. Ps. 147:8
33 [R]His thunder declares it, 1 Kin. 18:41
The cattle also, concerning [T]the rising
storm. Lit. *what is rising*

CHAPTER 37

"AT this also my heart trembles,
And leaps from its place.
2 Hear attentively the thunder of His voice,
And the rumbling *that* comes from His
mouth.
3 He sends it forth under the whole
heaven,
His lightning to the ends of the earth.
4 After it [R]a voice roars; Ps. 29:3
He thunders with His majestic voice,
And He does not restrain them when His
voice is heard.
5 God thunders marvelously with His
voice;
[R]He does great things which we cannot
comprehend. Job 5:9; 9:10; 36:26
6 For [R]He says to the snow, 'Fall *on* the
earth'; Ps. 147:16, 17
Likewise to the gentle rain and the
heavy rain of His strength.
7 He seals the hand of every man,
That all men may know His work.
8 The beasts [R]go into dens, Ps. 104:21, 22
And remain in their lairs.
9 From the chamber *of the south* comes
the whirlwind,
And cold from the scattering winds *of
the north.*
10 By the breath of God ice is given,
And the broad waters are frozen.
11 Also with moisture He saturates the
thick clouds;
He scatters His bright clouds.
12 And they swirl about, being turned by
His guidance,
That they may [R]do whatever He
commands them Job 36:32
On the face of the whole earth.*
13 [R]He causes it to come, Ex. 9:18, 23
Whether for [T]correction, Lit. *a rod*
Or [R]for His land, Job 38:26, 27
Or [R]for mercy. 1 Kin. 18:41–46

14"Listen to this, O Job;
Stand still and [R]consider the wondrous
works of God. Ps. 111:2
15 Do you know when God [T]dispatches
them, *places them*
And causes the light of His cloud to
shine?
16 [R]Do you know how the clouds are
balanced, Job 36:29
Those wondrous works of [R]Him who is
perfect in knowledge? Job 36:4
17 Why *are* your garments hot,
When He quiets the earth by the south
wind?
18 With Him, have you [R]spread out the
[R]skies, [Is. 44:24] • Ps. 104:2
Strong as a cast metal mirror?

19"Teach us what we should say to Him,
For we can prepare nothing because of
the darkness.
20 Should He be told that I *wish to* speak?
If a man were to speak, surely he would
be swallowed up.
21 Even now *men* cannot look at the light
when it is bright in the skies,
When the wind has passed and cleared
them.
22 He comes from the north *as* golden
splendor;
With God *is* awesome majesty.
23 *As for* the Almighty, [R]we cannot find
Him; [1 Tim. 6:16]
[R]*He is* excellent in power, [Job 9:4; 36:5]
In judgment and abundant justice;
He does not oppress.
24 Therefore men [R]fear Him; [Matt. 10:28]
He shows no partiality to any *who are*
[R]wise of heart." [Matt. 11:25]

CHAPTER 38

God Questions Job from the Realm of Creation

THEN the LORD answered Job [R]out of the
whirlwind, and said: Ex. 19:16

37:12 Lit. *the world of the earth*

2 "Who *is* this who darkens counsel
By words without knowledge?
3 [R]Now prepare yourself like a man;
I will question you, and you shall answer
Me. Job 40:7

4 "Where[R] were you when I laid the
foundations of the earth? Ps. 104:5
Tell *Me*, if you have understanding.
5 Who determined its measurements?
Surely you know!
Or who stretched the line upon it?
6 To what were its foundations fastened?
Or who laid its cornerstone,
7 When the morning stars sang together,
And all [R]the sons of God shouted for
joy? Job 1:6

8 "Or[R] *who* shut in the sea with doors,
When it burst forth *and* issued from the
womb; Gen. 1:9
9 When I made the clouds its garment,
And thick darkness its swaddling band;
10 When [R]I fixed My limit for it, Job 26:10
And set bars and doors;
11 When I said,
'This far you may come, but no farther,
And here your proud waves must stop!'

12 "Have you [R]commanded the morning
since your days *began*, [Ps. 74:16]
And caused the dawn to know its
place,
13 That it might take hold of the ends of the
earth,
And the wicked be shaken out of it?
14 It takes on form like clay *under* a seal,
And stands out like a garment.
15 From the wicked their light is withheld,
And the upraised arm is broken.

16 "Have you [R]entered the springs of the
sea? [Ps. 77:19]
Or have you walked in search of the
depths?
17 Have [R]the gates of death been [T]revealed
to you? Ps. 9:13 • Lit. *opened*
Or have you seen the doors of the
shadow of death?
18 Have you comprehended the breadth of
the earth?
Tell *Me*, if you know all this.

19 "Where *is* the way *to* the dwelling of
light?
And darkness, where *is* its place,
20 That you may take it to its territory,
That you may know the paths *to* its
home?
21 Do you know *it*, because you were born
then,
Or *because* the number of your days *is*
great?

22 "Have you entered the treasury of snow,
Or have you seen the treasury of hail,
23 [R]Which I have reserved for the time of
trouble, Is. 30:30
For the day of battle and war?
24 By what way is light [T]diffused,
Or the east wind scattered over the
earth? Lit. *divided*

25 "Who [R]has divided a channel for the
overflowing *water*, Job 28:26
Or a path for the thunderbolt,
26 To cause it to rain on a land *where there*
is no one,
A wilderness in which *there is* no man;
27 [R]To satisfy the desolate waste,
And cause to spring forth the growth of
tender grass? Ps. 104:13, 14; 107:35
28 [R]Has the rain a father? Job 36:27, 28
Or who has begotten the drops of dew?
29 From whose womb comes the ice?
And the [R]frost of heaven, who gives it
birth? Ps. 147:16, 17
30 The waters harden like stone,
And the surface of the deep is frozen.

31 "Can you bind the cluster of the
[R]Pleiades,[T] Amos 5:8 • Or *the Seven Stars*
Or loose the belt of Orion?
32 Can you bring out Mazzaroth* in its
season?
Or can you guide [T]the Great Bear with
its cubs? Or *Arcturus*
33 Do you know [R]the ordinances of the
heavens? Jer. 31:35, 36
Can you set their dominion over the
earth?

34 "Can you lift up your voice to the clouds,
That an abundance of water may cover
you?
35 Can you send out lightnings, that they
may go,
And say to you, 'Here we *are!*'?
36 [R]Who has put wisdom in the mind?*
Or who has given understanding to the
heart? [Ps. 51:6]
37 Who can number the clouds by wisdom?
Or who can pour out the bottles of
heaven,
38 When the dust hardens in clumps,
And the clods cling together?

God Questions Job from the Realm of Animals

39 "Can[R] you hunt the prey for the lion,
Or satisfy the appetite of the young
lions, Ps. 104:21
40 When they crouch in *their* dens,
Or lurk in their lairs to lie in wait?
41 Who provides food for the raven,

38:32 Lit. *Constellations* **38:36** Lit. *the inward parts*

When its young ones cry to God,
And wander about for lack of food?

CHAPTER 39

"DO you know the time when the wild
[R]mountain goats bear young?
Or can you mark when [R]the deer gives
birth? Ps. 104:18 • Ps. 29:9
2 Can you number the months *that* they
fulfill?
Or do you know the time when they bear
young?
3 They bow down,
They bring forth their young,
They deliver their offspring.*
4 Their young ones are healthy,
They grow strong with grain;
They depart and do not return to them.

5 "Who set the wild donkey free?
Who loosed the bonds of the onager,
6 [R]Whose home I have made the
wilderness, Jer. 2:24
And the barren land his dwelling?
7 He scorns the tumult of the city;
He does not heed the shouts of the
driver.
8 The range of the mountains *is* his pasture,
And he searches after [R]every green
thing. Gen. 1:29

9 "Will the [R]wild ox be willing to serve you?
Will he bed by your manger? Num. 23:22
10 Can you bind the wild ox in the furrow
with ropes?
Or will he plow the valleys behind you?
11 Will you trust him because his strength
is great?
Or will you leave your labor to him?
12 Will you trust him to bring home your
[T]grain, Lit. *seed*
And gather it to your threshing floor?

13 "The wings of the ostrich wave proudly,
But are her wings and pinions *like the*
kindly stork's?
14 For she leaves her eggs on the ground,
And warms them in the dust;
15 She forgets that a foot may crush them,
Or that a wild beast may break them.
16 She [R]treats her young harshly, as though
they were not hers; Lam. 4:3
Her labor is in vain, without concern,
17 Because God deprived her of wisdom,
And did not [R]endow her with
understanding. Job 35:11
18 When she lifts herself on high,
She scorns the horse and its rider.

19 "Have you given the horse strength?
Have you clothed his neck with
thunder?*
20 Can you frighten him like a locust?
His majestic snorting strikes terror.
21 He paws in the valley, and rejoices in *his*
strength;
He gallops into the clash of arms.
22 He mocks at fear, and is not frightened;
Nor does he turn back from the sword.
23 The quiver rattles against him,
The glittering spear and javelin.
24 He devours the distance with fierceness
and rage;
Nor does he come to a halt because the
trumpet *has* sounded.
25 At *the blast of* the trumpet he says,
'Aha!'
He smells the battle from afar,
The thunder of captains and shouting.

26 "Does the hawk fly by your wisdom,
And spread its wings toward the south?
27 Does the [R]eagle mount up at your
command, Prov. 30:18, 19
And [R]make its nest on high? Jer. 49:16
28 On the rock it dwells and resides,
On the crag of the rock and the
stronghold.
29 From there it spies out the prey;
Its eyes observe from afar.
30 Its young ones suck up blood;
And where the slain *are*, there it *is*."

CHAPTER 40

God Demands an Answer to His Questions

MOREOVER the LORD [R]answered Job, and
said: Job 38:1

2 "Shall [R]the one who contends with the
Almighty correct *Him*? Job 9:3; 10:2
He who [R]rebukes God, let him answer
it." Job 13:3; 23:4

Job's First Answer to God

3 Then Job answered the LORD and said:

4 "Behold,[R] I am vile; Ezra 9:6
What shall I answer You?
I lay my hand over my mouth.
5 Once I have spoken, but I will not
answer;
Yes, twice, but I will proceed no further."

God Tells Job to Save Himself

6 [R]Then the LORD answered Job out of the
whirlwind, and said: Job 38:1

7 "Now[R] prepare yourself like a man;
[R]I will question you, and you shall answer
Me: Job 38:3 • Job 42:4

39:3 Lit. *pangs* **39:19** Or *a mane*

8 "Would[R] you indeed [T]annul My
judgment? [Rom. 3:4] • *nullify*
Would you condemn Me that you may be
justified?
9 Have you an arm like God?
Or can you thunder with [R]a voice like
His? [Ps. 29:3, 4]
10 [R]Then adorn yourself *with* majesty and
splendor, Ps. 93:1; 104:1
And array yourself with glory and
beauty.
11 Disperse the rage of your wrath;
Look on everyone *who is* proud, and
humble him.
12 Look on everyone *who is* [R]proud, *and*
bring him low; Dan. 4:37
Tread down the wicked in their place.
13 Hide them in the dust together,
Bind their faces in hidden *darkness*.
14 Then I will also confess to you
That your own right hand can save you.

God Compares the Power of Job with That of the Behemoth

15 "Look now at the behemoth,* which I
made *along* with you;
He eats grass like an ox.
16 See now, his strength *is* in his hips,
And his power *is* in his stomach muscles.
17 He moves his tail like a cedar;
The sinews of his thighs are tightly knit.
18 His bones *are like* beams of bronze,
His ribs like bars of iron.
19 He *is* the first of the [R]ways of God;
Only He who made him can bring near
His sword. Job 26:14
20 Surely the mountains [R]yield food for
him, Ps. 104:14
And all the beasts of the field play there.
21 He lies under the lotus trees,
In a covert of reeds and marsh.
22 The lotus trees cover him *with* their
shade;
The willows by the brook surround him.
23 Indeed the river may rage,
Yet he is not disturbed;
He is confident, though the Jordan
gushes into his mouth,
24 *Though* he takes it in his eyes,
Or one pierces *his* nose with a snare.

CHAPTER 41

God Compares the Power of Job with That of the Leviathan

"CAN you draw out [R]Leviathan* with a
hook, Is. 27:1
Or *snare* his tongue with a line *which*
you lower?
2 Can you [R]put a reed through his nose,
Or pierce his jaw with a hook? Is. 37:29
3 Will he make many supplications to you?
Will he speak softly to you?
4 Will he make a covenant with you?
Will you take him as a servant forever?
5 Will you play with him as *with* a bird,
Or will you leash him for your maidens?
6 Will *your* companions make a banquet*
of him?
Will they apportion him among the
merchants?
7 Can you fill his skin with harpoons,
Or his head with fishing spears?
8 Lay your hand on him;
Remember the battle—
Never do it again!
9 Indeed, *any* hope of *overcoming* him is
false;
Shall *one not* be overwhelmed at the
sight of him?
10 No one *is so* fierce that he would dare
stir him up.
Who then is able to stand against Me?
11 [R]Who has preceded Me, that I should pay
him? [Rom. 11:35]
Everything under heaven is Mine.

12 "I will not conceal* his limbs,
His mighty power, or his graceful
proportions.
13 Who can [T]remove his outer coat?
Who can approach *him* with a double
bridle? Lit. *take off the face of his garment*
14 Who can open the doors of his face,
With his terrible teeth all around?
15 *His* rows of scales are *his* pride,
Shut up tightly *as with* a seal;
16 One is so near another
That no air can come between them;
17 They are joined one to another,
They stick together and cannot be
parted.
18 His sneezings flash forth light,
And his eyes *are* like the eyelids of the
morning.
19 Out of his mouth go burning lights;
Sparks of fire shoot out.
20 Smoke goes out of his nostrils,
As *from* a boiling pot and burning
rushes.
21 His breath kindles coals,
And a flame goes out of his mouth.
22 Strength dwells in his neck,
And sorrow dances before him.
23 The folds of his flesh are joined together;
They are firm on him and cannot be
moved.
24 His heart is as hard as stone,
Even as hard as the lower *millstone*.
25 When he raises himself up, the mighty
are afraid;

40:15 A large animal, exact identity unknown
41:1 A large sea creature, exact identity unknown
41:6 Or *bargain over him* **41:12** Lit. *keep silent about*

Because of his crashings they are
beside* themselves.
26 *Though* the sword reaches him, it cannot
avail;
Nor does spear, dart, or javelin.
27 He regards iron as straw,
And bronze as rotten wood.
28 The arrow cannot make him flee;
Slingstones become like stubble to him.
29 Darts are regarded as straw;
He laughs at the threat of javelins.
30 His undersides *are* like sharp potsherds;
He spreads pointed *marks* in the mire.
31 He makes the deep boil like a pot;
He makes the sea like a pot of ointment.
32 He leaves a shining wake behind him;
One would think the deep had white hair.
33 On earth there is nothing like him,
Which is made without fear.
34 He beholds every high *thing;*
He *is* king over all the children of pride."

CHAPTER 42

Job Confesses Lack of Understanding

THEN Job answered the LORD and said:

2 "I know that You [R]can do everything,
And that no purpose *of Yours* can be
withheld from You. [Matt. 19:26]
3 *You asked,* [R]'Who *is* this who hides
counsel without knowledge?'
Therefore I have uttered what I did not
understand, Job 38:2
[R]Things too wonderful for me, which I did
not know. Ps. 40:5; 131:1; 139:6

Job Repents of His Rebellion

4 Listen, please, and let me speak;
You said, [R]'I will question you, and you
shall answer Me.' Job 38:3; 40:7

5 "I have [R]heard of You by the hearing of
the ear, Job 26:14
But now my eye sees You.
6 Therefore I [R]abhor[T] *myself,* Ezra 9:6
And repent in dust and ashes." *despise*

The Deliverance of Job and His Friends

7 And so it was, after the LORD had spoken
these words to Job, that the LORD said to Eli-
phaz the Temanite, "My wrath is aroused
against you and your two friends, for you
have not spoken of Me *what is* right, as My
servant Job *has.*
8 "Now therefore, take for yourselves
[R]seven bulls and seven rams, [R]go to My ser-
vant Job, and offer up for yourselves a burnt
offering; and My servant Job shall pray for
you. For I will accept him, lest I deal with you
according to your folly; because you have not
spoken of Me *what is* right, as My servant Job
has." Num. 23:1 • [Matt. 5:24]
9 So Eliphaz the Temanite and Bildad the
Shuhite *and* Zophar the Naamathite went and
did as the LORD commanded them; for the
LORD had accepted Job.
10 [R]And the LORD restored Job's losses*
when he prayed for his friends. Indeed the
LORD gave Job [R]twice as much as he had be-
fore. Deut. 30:3 • Is. 40:2
11 Then [R]all his brothers, all his sisters, and
all those who had been his acquaintances be-
fore, came to him and ate food with him in his
house; and they consoled him and comforted
him for all the adversity that the LORD had
brought upon him. Each one gave him a piece
of silver and each a ring of gold. Job 19:13
12 Now the LORD blessed [R]the latter *days* of
Job more than his beginning; for he had four-
teen thousand sheep, six thousand camels,
one thousand yoke of oxen, and one thousand
female donkeys. James 5:11
13 [R]He also had seven sons and three daugh-
ters. Job 1:2
14 And he called the name of the first
Jemimah, the name of the second Keziah, and
the name of the third Keren-Happuch.
15 In all the land were found no women *so*
beautiful as the daughters of Job; and their fa-
ther gave them an inheritance among their
brothers.
16 After this Job lived one hundred and forty
years, and saw his children and grandchil-
dren *for* four generations.
17 So Job died, old and full of days.

41:25 Or *purify themselves* **42:10** Lit. *turned the captivity of Job,* what was captured from Job

THE BOOK OF PSALMS

THE BOOK OF PSALMS

The Book of Psalms is the largest and perhaps most widely used book in the Bible. It explores the full range of human experience in a very personal and practical way. Its 150 "songs" run from the Creation through the patriarchal, theocratic, monarchical, exilic, and postexilic periods. The tremendous breadth of subject matter in the Psalms includes diverse topics, such as jubilation, war, peace, worship, judgment, messianic prophecy, praise, and lament. The Psalms were set to the accompaniment of stringed instruments and served as the temple hymnbook and devotional guide for the Jewish people.

The Book of Psalms was gradually collected and originally unnamed, perhaps due to the great variety of material. It came to be known as *Sepher Tehillim*—"Book of Praises"—because almost every psalm contains some note of praise to God. The Septuagint uses the Greek word *Psalmoi* as its title for this book, meaning poems sung to the accompaniment of musical instruments. It also calls it the *Psalterium* ("a collection of songs"), and this word is the basis for the term *Psalter*. The Latin title is *Liber Psalmorum*, "Book of Psalms."

THE AUTHOR OF PSALMS

Although critics have challenged the historical accuracy of the superscriptions regarding authorship, the evidence is strongly in their favor. Almost half (seventy-three) of the psalms are designated as Davidic: 3—9; 11—32; 34—41; 51—65; 68—70; 86; 101; 103; 108—110; 122; 124; 131; 133; and 138—145. David's wide experience as shepherd, musician, warrior, and king (1011–971 B.C.) is reflected in these psalms. The New Testament reveals that the anonymous psalms 2 and 95 were also written by this king whose name means "Beloved of Yahweh" (Acts 4:25; Heb. 4:7). In addition to the seventy-five by David, twelve were by Asaph, "Collector," a priest who headed the service of music (50; 73—83; Ezra 2:41); ten were by the sons of Korah, "Bald," a guild of singers and composers (42; 44—49; 84; 85; 87; Num. 26:9–11); two were by Solomon, "Peaceful," Israel's most powerful king (72; 127); one was by Moses, "Son of the Water," a prince, herdsman, and deliverer (90); one was by Heman, "Faithful," a wise man (88; 1 Kin. 4:31; 1 Chr. 15:19); and one was by Ethan, "Enduring," a wise man (89; 1 Kin. 4:31; 1 Chr. 15:19). The remaining fifty psalms are anonymous: 1; 2; 10; 33; 43; 66; 67; 71; 91—100; 102; 104—107; 111—121; 123; 125; 126; 128—130; 132; 134—137; and 146—150. Some of the anonymous psalms are traditionally attributed to Ezra.

THE TIME OF PSALMS

The psalms cover a wide time span from Moses (c. 1410 B.C.) to the postexilic community under Ezra and Nehemiah (c. 430 B.C.). Because of their broad chronological and thematic range, the psalms were written to different audiences under many conditions. They therefore reflect a multitude of moods and as such are relevant to every reader.

The five books were compiled over several centuries. As individual psalms were written, some were used in Israel's worship. A number of small collections were independently made, like the pilgrimage songs and groups of Davidic psalms (1—41; 51—70; 138—145). These smaller anthologies were gradually collected into the five books. The last stage was the uniting and editing of the five books themselves. David (1 Chr. 15:16), Hezekiah (2 Chr. 29:30; Prov. 25:1), and Ezra (Neh. 8) were involved in various stages of collecting the psalms. David was the originator of the temple liturgy of which his psalms were a part. The superscriptions of thirteen psalms specify key events in his life: 1 Samuel 19:11 (Ps. 59); 21:11 (Ps. 56); 21:13 (Ps. 34); 22:1 (Ps. 142); 22:9 (Ps. 52); 23:19 (Ps. 54); 24:3 (Ps. 57); 2 Samuel 8:13 (Ps. 60); 12:13 (Ps. 51); 15:16 (Ps. 3); 15:23 (Ps. 63); 16:5 (Ps. 7); 22:2–51 (Ps. 18).

Here are four things to remember when interpreting the psalms: (1) When the superscription gives the historical event, the psalm should be interpreted in that light. When it is not given, there is little hope in reconstructing the historical occasion. Assuming occasions will probably hurt more than help the interpretive process. (2) Some of the psalms are associated with definite aspects of Israel's worship (e.g., 5:7; 66:13; 68:24, 25), and this can help in understanding those psalms. (3) Many of the psalms use definite structure and motifs. (4) Many psalms anticipate Israel's Messiah and are fulfilled in Christ. However, care must be taken not to allegorize them and forget the grammatical-historical method of interpretation.

THE CHRIST OF PSALMS

Many of the psalms specifically anticipated the life and ministry of Jesus Christ, the One who came centuries later as the promised Messiah ("Anointed One").

There are five different kinds of messianic psalms: (1) *Typical Messianic*—The subject of the psalm is in some respects a type of Christ (see 34:20; 69:4, 9). (2) *Typical Prophetic*—The psalmist uses language to describe his present experience, which points beyond his own life and becomes historically true only in Christ (see 22). (3) *Indirectly Messianic*—At the time of composition the psalm refers to a king or the house of David in general, but awaits final fulfillment in Christ (see 2; 45; 72). (4) *Purely Prophetic*—Refers solely to Christ without reference to any other son of David (see 110). (5) *Enthronement*—Anticipates the coming of Yahweh and the consummation of His kingdom, which will be fulfilled in the Person of Christ (see 96—99).

Some of the specific messianic prophecies in the Book of Psalms include:

	Prophecy	***Fulfillment***
2:7	God will declare Him to be His Son.	Matthew 3:17
8:6	All things will be put under His feet.	Hebrews 2:8
16:10	He will be resurrected from the dead.	Mark 16:6, 7
22:1	God will forsake Him in His hour of need.	Matthew 27:46
22:7, 8	He will be scourned and mocked.	Luke 23:35
22:16	His hands and feet will be pierced.	John 20:25, 27
22:18	Others will gamble for His clothes.	Matthew 27:35, 36
34:20	Not one of His bones will be broken.	John 19:32, 33, 36
35:11	He will be accused by false witnesses.	Mark 14:57
35:19	He will be hated without a cause.	John 15:25
40:7, 8	He will come to do God's will.	Hebrews 10:7
41:9	He will be betrayed by a friend.	Luke 22:47
45:6	His throne will be forever.	Hebrews 1:8
68:18	He will ascend to God's right hand.	Mark 16:19
69:9	Zeal for God's house will consume Him.	John 2:17
69:21	He will be given vinegar and gall to drink.	Matthew 27:34
109:4	He will pray for His enemies.	Luke 23:34
109:8	His betrayer's office will be fulfilled by another.	Acts 1:20
110:1	His enemies will be made subject to Him.	Matthew 22:44
110:4	He will be a priest like Melchizedek.	Hebrews 5:6
118:22	He will be the chief cornerstone.	Matthew 21:42
118:26	He will come in the name of the Lord.	Matthew 21:9

KEYS TO PSALMS

Key Word: Worship—The central theme of the Book of Psalms is worship—God is worthy of all praise because of who He is, what He has done, and what He will do. His goodness extends through all time and eternity. The psalms present personal responses to God as they reflect on His program for His people. There is a keen desire to see His program fulfilled and His name extolled. Many of the psalms survey the Word of God and the attributes of God, especially during difficult times. This kind of faith produces confidence in His power in spite of circumstances.

The psalms were used in the two temples and some were part of the liturgical service. They also served as an individual and communal devotional guide.

Key Verses: Psalm 19:14; 145:21—"Let the words of my mouth and the meditation of my heart be acceptable in Your sight, O LORD, my strength and my Redeemer" (19:14).

"My mouth shall speak the praise of the LORD, and all flesh shall bless His holy name forever and ever" (145:21).

Key Chapter: Psalm 100—So many of the favorite chapters of the Bible are contained in the Book of Psalms that it is difficult to select the key chapter among such psalms as Psalms 1; 22; 23; 24; 37; 72; 100; 101; 119; 121; and 150. The two central themes of worship and praise are beautifully wed in Psalm 100.

SURVEY OF PSALMS

The Psalter is really five books in one, and each book ends with a doxology (see chart). The last psalm is the closing doxology for Book 5 and for the Psalter as a whole. After the psalms were written, editorial superscriptions or instructions were added to 116 of them. These superscriptions are historically accurate and are even numbered as the first verses in the Hebrew text. They designate fifty-seven psalms as *mizmor,* "psalm"—a song accompanied by a stringed instrument. Another twenty-nine are called *shir,* "song," and thirteen are called *maschil,* "contemplative poem." Six are called *miktam,* perhaps meaning "epigram" or "inscription poem." Five are termed *tepillah,* "prayer" (see Hab. 3), and only one is called *tehillah,* "praise" (145). In addition to these technical terms, the psalms can be classified according to certain themes: Creation psalms (8; 19), Exodus psalm (78), penitence psalm (6), pilgrimage psalms (120—134), and messianic psalms (see "The Christ of Psalms"). There are even nine acrostic psalms in which the first verse or line begins with the first letter of the Hebrew alphabet, the next begins with the second, and so on (9; 10; 25; 34; 37; 111; 112; 119; 145).

First Chronicles 16:4 supports another approach to classification: "to commemorate, to thank, and to praise the LORD God of Israel." This leads to three basic types—lament, thanksgiving, and praise psalms. The following classification further divides the psalms into ten types: (1) *Individual Lament Psalms:* Directly addressed to God, these psalms petition Him to rescue and defend an individual. They have these elements: (a) an introduction (usually a cry to God), (b) the lament, (c) a confession of trust in God, (d) the petition, (e) a declaration or vow of praise. Most psalms are of this type (e.g., 3—7; 12; 13; 22; 25—28; 35; 38—40; 42; 43; 51; 54—57; 59; 61; 63; 64; 69—71; 86; 88; 102; 109; 120; 130; 140—143). (2) *Communal Lament Psalms:* The only difference is that the nation rather than an individual makes the lament (e.g., 44; 60; 74; 79; 80; 83; 85; 90; and 123). (3) *Individual Thanksgiving Psalms:* The psalmist publicly acknowledges God's activity on his behalf. These psalms thank God for something He has already done or express confidence in what He will yet do. They have these elements: (a) a proclamation to praise God, (b) a summary statement, (c) a report of deliverance, and (d) a renewed vow of praise (e.g., 18; 30; 32; 34; 40; 41; 66; 106; 116; and 138). (4) *Communal Thanksgiving Psalms:* In these psalms the acknowledgment is made by the nation rather than by an individual (see 124 and 129). (5) *General Praise Psalms:* These psalms are more general than the thanksgiving psalms. The psalmist attempts to magnify the name of God and boast about His greatness (see 8; 19; 29; 103; 104; 139; 148; 150). The joyous exclamation "hallelujah" ("praise the LORD!") is found in several of these psalms. (6) *Descriptive Praise Psalms:* These psalms praise God for His attributes and acts (e.g., 33; 36; 105; 111; 113; 117; 135; 136; 146; 147). (7) *Enthronement Psalms:* These psalms describe Yahweh's sovereign reign over all (see 47; 93; 96—99). Some anticipate the kingdom rule of Christ. (8) *Pilgrimage Songs:* Also known as Songs of Zion, these psalms were sung by pilgrims traveling up to Jerusalem for the three annual religious feasts of Passover, Pentecost, and Tabernacles (see 43; 46; 48; 76; 84; 87; 120—134). (9) *Royal Psalms:* The reigns of the earthly king and the heavenly King are portrayed in most of these psalms (e.g., 2; 18; 20; 21; 45; 72; 89; 101; 110; 132; and 144). (10) *Wisdom and Didactic Psalms:* The reader is exhorted and instructed in the way of righteousness (see 1; 37; 119).

There is a problem with the so-called imprecatory ("to call down a curse") psalms. These psalms invoke divine judgment on one's enemies (see 7; 35; 40; 55; 58; 59; 69; 79; 109; 137; 139; and 144). Although some of them seem unreasonably harsh, a few things should be kept in mind: (1) they call for divine justice rather than human vengeance; (2) they ask for God to punish the wicked and thus vindicate His righteousness; (3) they condemn sin (in Hebrew thinking no sharp distinction exists between a sinner and his sin); and (4) even Jesus calls down a curse on several cities and tells His disciples to curse cities that do not receive the gospel (Matt. 10:14, 15).

A number of special musical terms (some obscure) are used in the superscriptions of the psalms. "To the Chief Musician" appears in fifty-five psalms indicating that there is a collection of psalms used by the conductor of music in the temple, perhaps for special occasions. "Selah" is used seventy-one times in the psalms and three times in Habakkuk 3. This word may mark a pause, a musical interlude, or a crescendo.

BOOK	BOOK I (1–41)	BOOK II (42–72)	BOOK III (73–89)	BOOK IV (90–106)	BOOK V (107–150)
CHIEF AUTHOR	DAVID	DAVID AND KORAH	ASAPH	ANONYMOUS	DAVID AND ANONYMOUS
NUMBER OF PSALMS	41	31	17	17	44
BASIC CONTENT	SONGS OF WORSHIP	HYMNS OF NATIONAL INTEREST		ANTHEMS OF PRAISE	
TOPICAL LIKENESS TO PENTATEUCH	GENESIS: MAN AND CREATION	EXODUS: DELIVERANCE AND REDEMPTION	LEVITICUS: WORSHIP AND SANCTUARY	NUMBERS: WILDERNESS AND WANDERING	DEUTERONOMY: SCRIPTURE AND PRAISE
CLOSING DOXOLOGY	41:13	72:18, 19	89:52	106:48	150:1–6
POSSIBLE COMPILER	DAVID	HEZEKIAH OR JOSIAH		EZRA OR NEHEMIAH	
POSSIBLE DATES OF COMPILATION	c. 1020–970 B.C.	c. 970–610 B.C.		UNTIL c. 430 B.C.	
SPAN OF AUTHORSHIP	ABOUT 1,000 YEARS (c. 1410–430 B.C.)				

OUTLINE OF PSALMS

Book One: Psalms 1—41

1. Two Ways of Life Contrasted
2. Coronation of the Lord's Anointed
3. Victory in the Face of Defeat
4. Evening Prayer for Deliverance
5. Morning Prayer for Guidance
6. Prayer for God's Mercy
7. Wickedness Justly Rewarded
8. God's Glory and Human Dominion
9. Praise for Victory over Enemies
10. Petition for God's Judgment
11. God Tests the Sons of Men
12. The Pure Words of the Lord
13. The Prayer for God's Answer—Now
14. The Characteristics of the Godless
15. The Characteristics of the Godly
16. Eternal Life for One Who Trusts
17. "Hide Me Under the Shadow of Your Wings"
18. Thanksgiving for Deliverance by God
19. The Works and Words of God
20. Trust Not in Chariots and Horses but in God
21. Triumph of the King
22. Psalm of the Cross
23. Psalm of the Divine Shepherd
24. Psalm of the King of Glory
25. Acrostic Prayer for Instruction
26. "Examine Me, O LORD, and Prove Me"
27. Trust in the Lord and Be Not Afraid
28. Rejoice Because of Answered Prayer
29. The Powerful Voice of God
30. Praise for Dramatic Deliverance
31. "Be of Good Courage"
32. The Blessedness of Forgiveness
33. God Considers All Human Works
34. Seek the Lord
35. Petition for God's Intervention
36. The Excellent Lovingkindness of God
37. "Rest in the LORD"
38. The Heavy Burden of Sin
39. Know the Measure of Human Days
40. Delight to Do God's Will
41. The Blessedness of Helping the Poor

Book Two: Psalms 42—72

42. Seek After the Lord
43. "Hope in God"
44. Prayer for Deliverance by God
45. The Psalm of the Great King
46. "God Is Our Refuge and Strength"
47. The Lord Shall Subdue All Nations
48. The Praise of Mount Zion
49. Riches Cannot Redeem
50. The Lord Shall Judge All People
51. Confession and Forgiveness of Sin
52. The Lord Shall Judge the Deceitful
53. A Portrait of the Godless
54. The Lord Is Our Helper
55. "Cast Your Burden on the LORD"
56. Fears in the Midst of Trials
57. Prayers in the Midst of Perils
58. Wicked Judges Will Be Judged
59. Petition for Deliverance from Enemies
60. A Prayer for Deliverance of the Nation
61. A Prayer When Overwhelmed
62. Wait for God
63. Thirst for God
64. A Prayer for God's Protection
65. God's Provision Through Nature
66. Remember What God Has Done
67. God Shall Govern the Earth
68. God Is the Father of the Fatherless
69. Petition for God to Draw Near
70. Prayer for the Poor and Needy
71. Prayer for the Aged
72. The Reign of the Messiah

Book Three: Psalms 73—89

73. The Perspective of Eternity
74. Request for God to Remember His Covenant
75. "God Is the Judge"
76. The Glorious Might of God
77. When Overwhelmed, Remember God's Greatness
78. God's Continued Guidance in Spite of Unbelief
79. Avenge the Defilement of Jerusalem
80. Israel's Plea for God's Mercy
81. God's Plea for Israel's Obedience
82. Rebuke of Israel's Unjust Judges
83. Plea for God to Destroy Israel's Enemies
84. The Joy of Dwelling with God
85. Prayer for Revival
86. "Teach Me Your Way, O LORD"
87. Glorious Zion, City of God
88. Crying from Deepest Affliction
89. Claiming God's Promises in Affliction

Book Four: Psalms 90—106

90. "Teach Us to Number Our Days"
91. Abiding in "the Shadow of the Almighty"
92. It Is Good to Praise the Lord
93. The Majesty of God
94. Vengeance Belongs Only to God
95. Call to Worship the Lord
96. Declare the Glory of God
97. Rejoice! The Lord Reigns!
98. Sing a New Song to the Lord
99. "Exalt the LORD Our God"
100. "Serve the LORD with Gladness"
101. Commitments of a Holy Life
102. Prayer of an Overwhelmed Saint
103. "Bless the LORD"
104. Psalm Rehearsing Creation
105. Remember, God Keeps His Promises
106. "We Have Sinned"

Book Five: Psalms 107—150

107. God Satisfies the Longing Soul
108. Awake Early and Praise the Lord
109. Song of the Slandered
110. The Coming of the Priest-King-Judge
111. Praise for God's Tender Care
112. The Blessings of Those Who Fear God
113. The Condescending Grace of God
114. In Praise for the Exodus
115. To God Alone Be the Glory
116. Love the Lord for What He Has Done

BOOK ONE

Psalms 1—41

PSALM 1

Two Ways of Life Contrasted

BLESSED [R]*is* the man — Prov. 4:14
Who walks not in the counsel of the
[T]ungodly, — *wicked*
Nor stands in the path of sinners,
Nor sits in the seat of the scornful;
2 But [R]his delight *is* in the law of the
LORD, — Ps. 119:14, 16, 35
[R]And in His law he meditates day and
night. — [Josh. 1:8]
3 He shall be like a tree
[R]Planted by the [T]rivers of water,
That brings forth its fruit in its
season, — Jer. 17:8 • *channels*
Whose leaf also shall not wither;
And whatever he does shall prosper.

4 The ungodly *are* not so,
But *are* [R]like the chaff which the wind
drives away. — Job 21:18
5 Therefore the ungodly shall not stand in
the judgment,
Nor sinners in the congregation of the
righteous.

6 For [R]the LORD knows the way of the
righteous, — Ps. 37:18
But the way of the ungodly shall perish.

PSALM 2

Coronation of the Lord's Anointed

WHY [R]do the nations rage, — [Acts 4:25–28]☆
And the people plot a vain thing?
2 The kings of the earth set themselves,
And the rulers take counsel together,
Against the LORD and against His
[R]Anointed, *saying*, — [John 1:41]☆
3 "Let us break Their bonds in pieces
And cast away Their cords from us."
4 He who sits in the heavens shall laugh;
The LORD shall hold them in derision.
5 Then He shall speak to them in His wrath,
And distress them in His deep displeasure:
6 "Yet I have [T]set My King — Lit. *installed*
On My holy hill of Zion."

7 "I will declare the decree:
The LORD has said to Me,
[R]'You *are* My Son, — [Luke 1:35]☆
Today I have begotten You.
8 Ask of Me, and I will give *You*
The nations *for* Your inheritance,
And the ends of the earth *for* Your
possession.
9 [R]You shall break* them with a rod of
iron; — Ps. 89:23; 110:5, 6☆
You shall dash them to pieces like a
potter's vessel.' "

10 Now therefore, be wise, O kings;
Be instructed, you judges of the earth.
11 Serve the LORD with fear,
And rejoice with trembling.
12 Kiss the Son,* lest* He be angry,
And you perish *in* the way,
When [R]His wrath is kindled but a little.
[R]Blessed *are* all those who put their trust
in Him. — [Rev. 6:16, 17] • [Ps. 5:11; 34:22]

PSALM 3

Victory in the Face of Defeat

A Psalm of David [R]when he fled
from Absalom his son. — 2 Sam. 15:13–17

LORD, how they have increased who
trouble me!

2:9 So with MT, Tg.; LXX, Syr., Vg. *rule* (cf. Rev. 2:27)
2:12 LXX, Vg. *Embrace discipline;* Tg. *Receive instruction* • LXX *the LORD*

Many *are* they who rise up against me.
2 Many *are* they who say of me,
"There is no help for him in God." Selah

3 But You, O LORD, *are* [R]a shield for me,
My glory and [R]the One who lifts up my
head. Ps. 5:12; 28:7 • Ps. 9:13; 27:6
4 I cried to the LORD with my voice,
And [R]He heard me from His [R]holy hill.
Selah Ps. 4:3; 34:4 • Ps. 2:6; 15:1; 43:3

5 [R]I lay down and slept; Lev. 26:6
I awoke, for the LORD sustained me.
6 [R]I will not be afraid of ten thousands of
people Ps. 23:4; 27:3
Who have set *themselves* against me all
around.

7 Arise, O LORD;
Save me, O my God!
[R]For You have struck all my enemies on
the cheekbone; Job 16:10
You have broken the teeth of the
ungodly.
8 [R]Salvation *belongs* to the LORD.
Your blessing *is* upon Your people.
Selah [Is. 43:11]

PSALM 4

Evening Prayer for Deliverance

To the [T]Chief Musician. With stringed instruments.
A Psalm of David. *Choir Director*

HEAR me when I call, O God of my
righteousness!
You have relieved me in *my* distress;
Have mercy on me, and hear my prayer.

2 How long, O you sons of men,
Will you turn my glory to shame?
How long will you love worthlessness
And seek falsehood? Selah
3 But know that the LORD has set apart*
for Himself him who is godly;
The LORD will hear when I call to Him.

4 [R]Be angry, and do not sin. [Eph. 4:26]
[R]Meditate within your heart on your bed,
and be still. Selah Ps. 77:6
5 Offer the sacrifices of righteousness,
And put your trust in the LORD.

6 *There are* many who say,
"Who will show us *any* good?"
[R]LORD, lift up the light of Your
countenance upon us. Num. 6:26
7 You have put [R]gladness in my heart,
More than in the season that their grain
and wine increased. Is. 9:3
8 [R]I will both lie down in peace, and sleep;
[R]For You alone, O LORD, make me dwell in
safety. Ps. 3:5 • [Lev. 25:18]

PSALM 5

Morning Prayer for Guidance

To the Chief Musician. With flutes.*
A Psalm of David.

GIVE [R]ear to my words, O LORD, Ps. 4:1
Consider my [T]meditation. Lit. *groaning*
2 Give heed to the voice of my cry,
My King and my God,
For to You I will pray.
3 My voice You shall hear in the morning,
O LORD;
[R]In the morning I will direct *it* to You,
And I will look up. Ps. 55:17; 88:13

4 For You *are* not a God who takes
pleasure in wickedness,
Nor shall evil [T]dwell with You. Lit. *sojourn*
5 The [R]boastful shall not [R]stand in Your
sight; [Hab. 1:13] • Ps. 1:5
You hate all workers of iniquity.
6 You shall destroy those who speak
falsehood;
The LORD abhors the [R]bloodthirsty and
deceitful man. Ps. 55:23

7 But as for me, I will come into Your
house in the multitude of Your
mercy;
In fear of You I will worship toward Your
holy temple.
8 [R]Lead me, O LORD, in Your righteousness
because of my enemies; Ps. 25:4, 5
Make Your way straight before my face.

9 For *there is* no [T]faithfulness in their
mouth; *uprightness*
Their inward part *is* destruction;
Their throat *is* an open tomb;
They flatter with their tongue.
10 Pronounce them guilty, O God!
Let them fall by their own counsels;
Cast them out in the multitude of their
transgressions,
For they have rebelled against You.

11 But let all those rejoice who put their
trust in You;
Let them ever shout for joy, because You
[T]defend them; *protect*, lit. *cover*
Let those also who love Your name
Be joyful in You.
12 For You, O LORD, will bless the
righteous;
With favor You will surround him as *with*
a shield.

4:3 Many Heb. mss., LXX, Tg., Vg. *made wonderful*
5:title Heb. *nehiloth*

PSALM 6

Prayer for God's Mercy

To the Chief Musician. With stringed instruments. On an eight-stringed harp.* A Psalm of David.

O LORD, [R]do not rebuke me in Your
anger, Ps. 38:1; 118:18
Nor chasten me in Your hot displeasure.
2 Have mercy on me, O LORD, for I *am*
weak;
O LORD, [R]heal me, for my bones are
troubled. [Hos. 6:1]
3 My soul also is greatly [R]troubled; Ps. 88:3
But You, O LORD—how long?

4 Return, O LORD, deliver me!
Oh, save me for Your mercies' sake!
5 [R]For in death *there is* no remembrance of
You; [Eccl. 9:10]
In the grave who will give You thanks?

6 I am weary with my groaning;
All night I make my bed swim;
I drench my couch with my tears.
7 My eye wastes away because of grief;
It grows old because of all my enemies.

8 [R]Depart from me, all you workers of
iniquity; [Matt. 25:41]
For the LORD has [R]heard the voice of my
weeping. Ps. 3:4; 28:6
9 The LORD has heard my supplication;
The LORD will receive my prayer.
10 Let all my enemies be ashamed and
greatly troubled;
Let them turn back *and* be ashamed
suddenly.

PSALM 7

Wickedness Justly Rewarded

A Meditation* of David, which he sang to the LORD concerning the words of Cush, a Benjamite.

O LORD my God, in You I put my trust;
[R]Save me from all those who persecute
me; Ps. 31:15
And deliver me,
2 [R]Lest they tear me like a lion, Is. 38:13
[R]Rending *me* in pieces, while *there is*
none to deliver. Ps. 50:22

3 O LORD my God, if I have done this:
If there is iniquity in my hands,
4 If I have repaid evil to him who was at
peace with me,
Or [R]have plundered my enemy without
cause, 1 Sam. 24:7; 26:9
5 Let the enemy pursue me and overtake
me;
Yes, let him trample my life to the earth,
And lay my honor in the dust. Selah

6 Arise, O LORD, in Your anger;
[R]Lift Yourself up because of the rage of
my enemies; Ps. 94:2
[R]Rise up for me* *to* the judgment You
have commanded! Ps. 35:23; 44:23
7 So the congregation of the peoples shall
surround You;
For their sakes, therefore, return on high.
8 The LORD shall judge the peoples;
[R]Judge me, O LORD, [R]according to my
righteousness, Ps. 26:1; 35:24; 43:1
And according to my integrity within
me. Ps. 18:20; 35:24

9 Oh, let the wickedness of the wicked
come to an end,
But establish the just;
[R]For the righteous God tests the hearts
and minds. [1 Sam. 16:7]
10 My defense *is* of God,
Who saves the upright in heart.

11 God *is* a just judge,
And God is angry *with the wicked* every
day.
12 If he does not turn back,
He will [R]sharpen His sword; Deut. 32:41
He bends His bow and makes it ready.
13 He also prepares for Himself
instruments of death;
He makes His arrows into fiery shafts.

14 [R]Behold, *the wicked* brings forth iniquity;
Yes, he conceives trouble and brings
forth falsehood. Is. 59:4
15 He made a pit and dug it out,
[R]And has fallen into the ditch *which* he
made. [Job 4:8]
16 [R]His trouble shall return upon his own
head, Esth. 9:25
And his violent dealing shall come down
on his own crown.

17 I will praise the LORD according to His
righteousness,
And will sing praise to the name of the
LORD Most High.

PSALM 8

God's Glory and Human Dominion

To the Chief Musician. On the instrument of Gath.* A Psalm of David.

O LORD, our Lord,
How [R]excellent *is* Your name in all the
earth, Ps. 148:13
Who have [R]set Your glory above the
heavens! Ps. 113:4

6:title Heb. *sheminith* **7:title** Heb. *Shiggaion*
7:6 So with MT, Tg., Vg.; LXX *O LORD my God*
8:title Heb. *Al Gittith*

2 [R]Out of the mouth of babes and nursing infants Matt. 21:15, 16☆
You have [T]ordained strength, *established*
Because of Your enemies,
That You may silence [R]the enemy and the avenger. Ps. 44:16

3 When I [R]consider Your heavens, the work of Your fingers, Ps. 111:2
The moon and the stars, which You have ordained,
4 [R]What is man that You are mindful of him, Job 7:17, 18
And the son of man that You visit him?
5 For You have made him a little lower than the angels,*
And You have crowned him with glory and honor.

6 You have made him to have dominion over the works of Your hands;
You have put all *things* under his feet,
7 All sheep and oxen—
Even the beasts of the field,
8 The birds of the air,
And the fish of the sea
That pass through the paths of the seas.

9 [R]O LORD, our Lord, Ps. 8:1
How excellent *is* Your name in all the earth!

PSALM 9

Praise for Victory over Enemies

To the Chief Musician. To *the tune of* "Death of the Son."* A Psalm of David.

I WILL praise *You,* O LORD, with my whole heart;
I will tell of all Your marvelous works.
2 I will be glad and [R]rejoice in You;
I will sing praise to Your name, [R]O Most High. Ps. 5:11; 104:34 • [Ps. 83:18; 92:1]

3 When my enemies turn back,
They shall fall and perish at Your presence.
4 For You have maintained my right and my cause;
You sat on the throne judging in righteousness.
5 You have rebuked the [T]nations, *Gentiles*
You have destroyed the wicked;
You have [R]blotted out their name forever and ever. Prov. 10:7

6 O enemy, destructions are finished forever!
And you have destroyed cities;
Even their memory has perished.
7 [R]But the LORD shall endure forever;
He has prepared His throne for judgment. Heb. 1:11
8 [R]He shall judge the world in righteousness, [Ps. 96:13; 98:9]
And He shall administer judgment for the peoples in uprightness.

9 The LORD also will be a [R]refuge for the oppressed, Ps. 32:7; 46:1; 91:2
A refuge in times of trouble.
10 And those who [R]know Your name will put their trust in You; Ps. 91:14
For You, LORD, have not forsaken those who seek You.

11 Sing praises to the LORD, who dwells in Zion!
Declare His deeds among the people.
12 [R]When He avenges blood, He remembers them; [Ps. 72:14]
He does not forget the cry of the [T]humble. *afflicted*

13 Have mercy on me, O LORD!
Consider my trouble from those who hate me,
You who lift me up from the gates of death,
14 That I may tell of all Your praise
In the gates of the daughter of Zion.
I will [R]rejoice in Your salvation. Ps. 13:5

15 [R]The [T]nations have sunk down in the pit *which* they made; Ps. 7:15, 16 • *Gentiles*
In the net which they hid, their own foot is caught.
16 The LORD is [R]known *by* the judgment He executes; Ex. 7:5
The wicked is snared in the work of his own hands.
[R]Meditation.* Selah Ps. 92:3

17 The wicked shall be turned into hell,
And all the nations that forget God.
18 [R]For the needy shall not always be forgotten; Ps. 9:12; 12:5
[R]The expectation of the poor shall *not* perish forever. Prov. 23:18

19 Arise, O LORD,
Do not let man prevail;
Let the nations be judged in Your sight.
20 Put them in fear, O LORD,
That the [T]nations may know themselves *to be but* men. Selah *Gentiles*

PSALM 10

Petition for God's Judgment

WHY do You stand afar off, O LORD?
Why do You hide in times of trouble?

8:5 Heb. *Elohim, God;* LXX, Syr., Tg., Jewish tradition *angels* **9:title** Heb. *Muth Labben* **9:16** Heb. *Higgaion*

2 The wicked in *his* pride [T]persecutes the
poor; *hotly pursues*
[R]Let them be caught in the plots which
they have devised. Ps. 7:16; 9:16

3 For the wicked [R]boasts of his heart's
desire; Ps. 49:6; 94:3, 4
He [R]blesses the greedy *and* renounces
the LORD. Prov. 28:4
4 The wicked in his proud countenance
does not seek *God;*
God *is* in none of his thoughts.

5 His ways [T]are always prospering;
Your judgments *are* far above, out of his
sight; Lit. *are strong*
As for all his enemies, he sneers at them.
6[R] He has said in his heart, "I shall not be
moved; [Eccl. 8:11]
[R]I shall never be in adversity." Rev. 18:7
7[R] His mouth is full of cursing and [R]deceit
and oppression; [Rom. 3:14] • Ps. 55:10, 11
Under his tongue *is* trouble and iniquity.

8 He sits in the lurking places of the
villages;
In the secret places he murders the
innocent;
His eyes are secretly fixed on the
helpless.
9 He lies in wait secretly, as a lion in his
den;
He lies in wait to catch the poor;
He catches the poor when he draws him
into his net.
10 So he crouches, he lies low,
That the helpless may fall by his
[T]strength. Or *mighty ones*
11 He has said in his heart,
"God has forgotten;
He hides His face;
He will never see."

12 Arise, O LORD!
O God, [R]lift up Your hand! Mic. 5:9
Do not forget the [R]humble. Ps. 9:12
13 Why do the wicked renounce God?
He has said in his heart,
"You will not require *an account.*"
14 But You have [R]seen, for You observe
trouble and grief, [Ps. 11:4]
To repay *it* by Your hand.
The helpless commits himself to You;
You are the helper of the fatherless.
15 Break the arm of the wicked and the evil
man;
Seek out his wickedness *until* You find
none.

16[R] The LORD *is* King forever and ever;
The nations have perished out of His
land. Ps. 29:10
17 LORD, You have heard the desire of the
humble;
You will prepare their heart;
You will cause Your ear to hear,
18 To [T]do justice to the fatherless and the
oppressed, *vindicate*
That the man of the earth may [T]oppress
no more. *terrify*

PSALM 11

God Tests the Sons of Men

To the Chief Musician. A Psalm of David.

IN [R]the LORD I put my trust; Ps. 56:11
How can you say to my soul,
"Flee *as* a bird to your mountain"?
2 For look! [R]The wicked bend *their* bow,
They make ready their arrow on the
string, Ps. 64:3, 4
That they may shoot [T]secretly at the
upright in heart. Lit. *in darkness*
3 If the foundations are destroyed,
What can the righteous do?

4 The LORD *is* in His holy temple,
The LORD's throne *is* in heaven;
[R]His eyes behold, [Ps. 33:18; 34:15, 16]
His eyelids test the sons of men.
5 The LORD [R]tests the righteous,
But the wicked and the one who loves
violence His soul hates. Gen. 22:1
6 Upon the wicked He will rain coals;
Fire and brimstone and a burning wind
Shall be the portion of their cup.

7 For the LORD *is* righteous,
He [R]loves righteousness; Ps. 33:5; 45:7
His countenance beholds the upright.*

PSALM 12

The Pure Words of the Lord

To the Chief Musician. [R]On an eight-stringed harp.*
A Psalm of David. Ps. 6:title

HELP,[T] LORD, for the godly man [R]ceases!
For the faithful disappear from among
the sons of men. *Save* • [Is. 57:1]
2[R] They speak idly everyone with his
neighbor; Ps. 10:7; 41:6
With flattering lips *and* [T]a double heart
they speak. *An inconsistent mind*

3 May the LORD [T]cut off all flattering lips,
And the tongue that speaks [T]proud
things, *destroy* • *great*
4 Who have said,
"With our tongue we will prevail;
Our lips *are* our own;
Who *is* lord over us?"

11:7 Or *The upright beholds His countenance*
12:title Heb. *sheminith*

5 "For the oppression of the poor, for the
sighing of the needy,
Now I will arise," says the LORD;
"I will set *him* in the safety for which he
yearns."

6 The words of the LORD *are* [R]pure words,
Like silver tried in a furnace of earth,
Purified seven times. 2 Sam. 22:31
7 You shall keep them, O LORD,
You shall preserve them from this
generation forever.

8 The wicked prowl on every side,
When vileness is exalted among the sons
of men.

PSALM 13

The Prayer for God's Answer—Now

To the Chief Musician. A Psalm of David.

HOW long, O LORD? Will You forget me
forever?
[R]How long will You hide Your face from
me? Job 13:24
2 How long shall I take counsel in my soul,
Having sorrow in my heart daily?
How long will my enemy be exalted over
me?

3 Consider *and* hear me, O LORD my God;
[R]Enlighten my eyes, Ezra 9:8
[R]Lest I sleep the *sleep of* death; Jer. 51:39
4 Lest my enemy say,
"I have prevailed against him";
Lest those who trouble me rejoice when
I am moved.

5 But I have trusted in Your mercy;
My heart shall rejoice in Your salvation.
6 I will sing to the LORD,
Because He has dealt bountifully with
me.

PSALM 14

The Characteristics of the Godless

To the Chief Musician. A Psalm of David.

THE [R]fool has said in his heart,
"*There is* no God." Ps. 10:4; 53:1
They are corrupt,
They have done abominable works,
There is none who does good.

2 [R]The LORD looks down from heaven upon
the children of men, Ps. 33:13, 14; 102:19
To see if there are any who understand,
who seek God.
3 [R]They have all turned aside, Rom. 3:12
They have together become corrupt;
There is none who does good,
No, not one.

4 Have all the workers of iniquity no
knowledge,
Who eat up my people *as* they eat bread,
And [R]do not call on the LORD? Is. 64:7
5 There they are in great fear,
For God *is* with the generation of the
righteous.
6 You shame the counsel of the poor,
But the LORD *is* his [R]refuge. Ps. 9:9; 40:17

7 [R]Oh, that the salvation of Israel *would
come* out of Zion! Ps. 53:6
[R]When the LORD brings back the captivity
of His people, Job 42:10
Let Jacob rejoice *and* Israel be glad.

PSALM 15

The Characteristics of the Godly

A Psalm of David.

LORD, [R]who may [T]abide in Your
tabernacle? Ps. 24:3–5 • *sojourn*
Who may dwell in Your holy hill?

2 He who walks uprightly,
And works righteousness,
And speaks the truth in his heart;
3 He *who* [R]does not backbite with his
tongue, [Lev. 19:16–18]
Nor does evil to his neighbor,
[R]Nor does he [T]take up a reproach
against his friend; Ex. 23:1 • *receive*
4 [R]In whose eyes a vile person is despised,
But he honors those who fear the
LORD; Esth. 3:2
He *who* [R]swears to his own hurt and
does not change; Lev. 5:4
5 He *who* does not put out his money at
usury,
Nor does he take a bribe against the
innocent.

He who does these *things* [R]shall never be
moved. 2 Pet. 1:10

PSALM 16

Eternal Life for One Who Trusts

A [R]Michtam of David. Ps. 56—60

PRESERVE[T] me, O God, for in You I put
my trust. *Watch over*

2 O *my soul,* you have said to the LORD,
"You *are* my Lord,
My goodness is nothing apart from You."
3 As for the saints who *are* on the earth,
"They are the excellent ones, in [R]whom is
all my delight." Ps. 119:63

4 Their sorrows shall be multiplied who
hasten *after* another *god;*

Their drink offerings of [R]blood I will not
offer, Ps. 106:37, 38
Nor take up their names on my lips.

5 O LORD, *You are* the portion of my
inheritance and my cup;
You [T]maintain my lot. Lit. *uphold*
6 The lines have fallen to me in pleasant
places;
Yes, I have a good inheritance.

7 I will bless the LORD who has given me
counsel;
My [T]heart also instructs me in the night
seasons. Mind, lit. *kidneys*
8 [R]I have set the LORD always before me;
Because *He is* at my right hand I shall
not be moved. [Acts 2:25–28]

9 Therefore my heart is glad, and my glory
rejoices;
My flesh also will rest in hope.
10 [R]For You will not leave my soul in Sheol,
Nor will You allow Your Holy One to [T]see
corruption. [Ps. 49:15; Acts 2:31, 32☆ • *undergo*
11 You will show me the [R]path of life;
In Your presence *is* fullness of joy;
At Your right hand *are* pleasures
forevermore. [Matt. 7:14]

PSALM 17

"Hide Me Under the Shadow of Your Wings"

A Prayer of David.

HEAR a just cause, O LORD,
Attend to my cry;
Give ear to my prayer *which is* not from
deceitful lips.
2 Let my vindication come from Your
presence;
Let Your eyes look on the things that are
upright.

3 You have tested my heart;
You have visited *me* in the night;
[R]You have [T]tried me and have found
[T]nothing; Job 23:10 • *examined* • Nothing evil
I have purposed that my mouth shall not
[R]transgress. Ps. 39:1

4 Concerning the works of men,
By the word of Your lips,
I have kept away from the paths of the
destroyer.

5 Uphold my steps in Your paths,
That my footsteps may not slip.

6 [R]I have called upon You, for You will hear
me, O God; Ps. 86:7; 116:2
Incline Your ear to me, *and* hear my
speech.
7 Show Your marvelous lovingkindness by
Your right hand,
O You who save those who trust *in You*
From those who rise up *against them.*
8 Keep me as the [T]apple of Your eye;
Hide me under the shadow of Your
wings, *pupil*
9 From the wicked who oppress me,
From my deadly enemies who surround
me.

10 They have closed up their fat *hearts;*
With their mouths they speak proudly.
11 They have now surrounded us in our steps;
They have set their eyes, crouching
down to the earth,
12 As a lion is eager to tear his prey,
And like a young lion lurking in secret
places.

13 Arise, O LORD,
Confront him, cast him down;
Deliver my life from the wicked with
Your sword,
14 With Your hand from men, O LORD,
From men of the world *who have* their
portion in *this* life,
And whose belly You fill with Your
hidden treasure.

17:4 God's Word Corrects—There are many symbols for God's Word that can be found in the Bible itself. It can be thought of as a mirror (Page 1272—James 1:23–25), a seed (Page 1280—1 Pet. 1:23), a lamp (Page 612—Ps. 119:105), a sword (Page 1209—Eph. 6:17), and even as food (Page 1261—Heb. 5:12–14). But the Bible also serves as a measuring rod or ruler. Many teachers have used wooden rulers in their classes not only to give the right measurement but, on occasion, to correct a misbehaving pupil. God's Word likewise can do both of these things. It should be used as a standard against which to measure our beliefs. What about certain religious groups that claim Christ was not God, or that the Bible is filled with silly tales? Immediately we can reject such claims by using our divine written ruler to discover that such arguments simply do not measure up.

Sometimes our heavenly Teacher uses His written ruler to correct us when we are in the wrong. Israel's great king David once experienced this. "You have dealt well with Your servant, O LORD, according to Your word. . . . Before I was afflicted I went astray, but now I keep Your word" (Page 611—Ps. 119:65, 67).

There are times when God's Word can correct believers when they are in honest and unintentional error. Aquila and Priscilla, a godly Christian couple, use the Scriptures to help a powerful young preacher named Apollos (Page 1134—Acts 18:24–26). Paul does the same thing for some former disciples of John the Baptist he meets in the city of Ephesus (Page 1134—Acts 19:1–7).

Now turn to Page 610—Ps. 119:9: God's Word Cleanses.

They are satisfied with children,
And leave the rest of their *possession* for
their babes.

15 As for me, [R]I will see Your face in
righteousness; [1 John 3:2]
[R]I shall be satisfied when I [R]awake in Your
likeness. Ps. 4:6, 7; 16:11 • [Is. 26:19]

PSALM 18

Thanksgiving for Deliverance by God

To the Chief Musician. A Psalm of David [R]the servant of the LORD, who spoke to the LORD the words of this song on the day that the LORD delivered him from the hand of all his enemies and from the hand of Saul. And he said: Ps. 36:title

I WILL love You, O LORD, my strength.
2 The LORD is my rock and my fortress
and my deliverer;
My God, my [T]strength, [R]in whom I will
trust; Lit. *rock* • Heb. 2:13
My shield and the [T]horn of my salvation,
my stronghold. Strength
3 I will call upon the LORD, [R]*who is worthy*
to be praised; Rev. 5:12
So shall I be saved from my enemies.

4 [R]The pangs of death surrounded me,
And the floods of [T]ungodliness made me
afraid. Ps. 116:3 • Lit. *Belial*
5 The sorrows of Sheol surrounded me;
The snares of death confronted me.
6 In my distress I called upon the LORD,
And cried out to my God;
He heard my voice from His temple,
And my cry came before Him, *even* to
His ears.

7 [R]Then the earth shook and trembled;
The foundations of the hills also quaked
and were shaken,
Because He was angry. Acts 4:31
8 Smoke went up from His nostrils,
And devouring fire from His mouth;
Coals were kindled by it.
9 [R]He bowed the heavens also, and came
down Ps. 144:5
With darkness under His feet.
10 And He rode upon a cherub, and flew;
He flew upon the wings of the wind.
11 He made darkness His secret place;
[R]His canopy around Him *was* dark
waters Ps. 97:2
And thick clouds of the skies.
12 [R]From the brightness before Him,
His thick clouds passed with hailstones
and coals of fire. Ps. 97:3; 140:10

13 The LORD thundered from heaven,
And the Most High uttered His voice,
Hailstones and coals of fire.*

14 [R]He sent out His arrows and scattered
[T]the foe, Ps. 144:6 • Lit. *them*
Lightnings in abundance, and He
vanquished them.
15 Then the channels of the sea were seen,
The foundations of the world were
uncovered
At Your rebuke, O LORD,
At the blast of the breath of Your
nostrils.

16 He sent from above, He took me;
He drew me out of many waters.
17 He delivered me from my strong enemy,
From those who hated me,
For they were too strong for me.
18 They confronted me in the day of my
calamity,
But the LORD was my support.
19 [R]He also brought me out into a broad
place; Ps. 4:1; 31:8; 118:5
He delivered me because He delighted in
me.

20 [R]The LORD rewarded me according to my
righteousness; 1 Sam. 24:19
According to the cleanness of my hands
He has recompensed me.
21 For I have kept the ways of the LORD,
And have not wickedly departed from
my God.
22 For all His judgments *were* before me,
And I did not put away His statutes from
me.
23 I was also blameless [T]before Him, with
And I kept myself from my iniquity.
24 [R]Therefore the LORD has recompensed me
according to my righteousness,
According to the cleanness of my hands
in His sight. 1 Sam. 26:23

25 [R]With the merciful You will show Yourself
merciful; [1 Kin. 8:32]
With a blameless man You will show
Yourself blameless;
26 With the pure You will show Yourself
pure;
And [R]with the devious You will show
Yourself shrewd. [Lev. 26:23–28]
27 For You will save the humble people,
But will bring down haughty looks.

28 [R]For You will light my lamp; Job 18:6
The LORD my God will enlighten my
darkness.
29 For by You I can run against a troop,
By my God I can leap over a wall.
30 *As for* God, [R]His way *is* perfect; Rev. 15:3
[R]The word of the LORD is proven; Ps. 12:6
He *is* a shield to all who trust in Him.

18:13 So with MT, Tg., Vg.; a few Heb. mss., LXX omit *Hailstones and coals of fire*

31 For who *is* God, except the LORD?
And who *is* a rock, except our God?
32 *It is* God who [R]arms me with strength,
And makes my way perfect. [Ps. 91:2]
33 He makes my feet like the *feet of* deer,
And sets me on my high places.
34[R] He teaches my hands to make war,
So that my arms can bend a bow of bronze. Ps. 144:1

35 You have also given me the shield of Your salvation;
Your right hand has held me up,
Your gentleness has made me great.
36 You enlarged my path under me,
[R] So my feet did not slip. Prov. 4:12

37 I have pursued my enemies and overtaken them;
Neither did I turn back again till they were destroyed.
38 I have wounded them,
So that they could not rise;
They have fallen under my feet.
39 For You have armed me with strength for the battle;
You have [T]subdued under me those who rose up against me. Lit. *caused to bow*
40 You have also given me the necks of my enemies,
So that I destroyed those who hated me.
41 They cried out, but *there was* none to save;
[R] *Even* to the LORD, but He did not answer them. Job 27:9
42 Then I beat them as fine as the dust before the wind;
I cast them out like dirt in the streets.
43 You have delivered me from the strivings of the people;
[R] You have made me the head of the [T]nations; 2 Sam. 8 • *Gentiles*
[R] A people I have not known shall serve me. Is. 52:15
44 As soon as they hear of me they obey me;
The foreigners submit to me.
45[R] The foreigners fade away, Mic. 7:17
And come frightened from their hideouts.

46 The LORD lives!
Blessed *be* my Rock!
Let the God of my salvation be exalted.
47 *It is* God who avenges me,
And subdues the peoples under me;
48 He delivers me from my enemies.
[R] You also lift me up above those who rise against me; Ps. 27:6; 59:1
You have delivered me from the violent man.
49 Therefore I will give thanks to You,
O LORD, among the [T]Gentiles, *nations*
And sing praises to Your name.
50[R] Great deliverance He gives to His king,
And shows mercy to His anointed,
To David and his [T]descendants forevermore. Ps. 21:1; 144:10 • Lit. *seed*

PSALM 19

The Works and Words of God

To the Chief Musician. A Psalm of David.

THE [R]heavens declare the glory of God;
And the [R]firmament shows His handiwork. Is. 40:22 • Gen. 1:6, 7
2 Day unto day utters speech,
And night unto night reveals knowledge.
3 *There is* no speech nor language
Where their voice is not heard.
4[R] Their line* has gone out through all the earth, Rom. 10:18
And their words to the end of the world.

In them He has set a [T]tabernacle for the sun, *tent*
5 Which *is* like a bridegroom coming out of his chamber,
[R] *And* rejoices like a strong man to run its race. Eccl. 1:5
6 Its rising *is* from one end of heaven,
And its circuit to the other end;
And there is nothing hidden from its heat.

7[R] The law of the LORD *is* perfect, [T]converting the soul; Ps. 111:7 • *restoring*
The testimony of the LORD *is* sure, making [R]wise the simple; Ps. 119:130
8 The statutes of the LORD *are* right, rejoicing the heart;
The commandment of the LORD *is* pure, enlightening the eyes;
9 The fear of the LORD *is* clean, enduring forever;
The judgments of the LORD *are* true *and* righteous altogether.
10 More to be desired *are they* than [R]gold,
Yea, than much fine gold; Ps. 119:72, 127
Sweeter also than honey and the [T]honeycomb. *honey in the combs*
11 Moreover by them Your servant is warned,
And in keeping them *there is* great reward.

12 Who can understand *his* errors?
Cleanse me from secret *faults.*
13 Keep back Your servant also from [R]presumptuous *sins;* Num. 15:30
Let them not have [R]dominion over me.
Then I shall be blameless, Ps. 119:133
And I shall be innocent of [T]great transgression. Or *much*

19:4 LXX, Syr., Vg. *sound;* Tg. *business*

14[R] Let the words of my mouth and the
meditation of my heart Ps. 51:15
Be acceptable in Your sight,
O LORD, my [T]strength and my
[R]Redeemer. Lit. *rock* • Is. 47:4

PSALM 20

Trust Not in Chariots and Horses but in God

To the Chief Musician. A Psalm of David.

MAY the LORD answer you in the day of
trouble;
May the name of the God of Jacob
[T]defend you; Lit. *set you on high*
2 May He send you help from the
sanctuary,
And strengthen you out of Zion;
3 May He remember all your offerings,
And accept your burnt sacrifice. Selah

4 May He grant you according to your
heart's *desire,*
And [R]fulfill all your purpose. Ps. 21:2
5 We will rejoice in your salvation,
And in the name of our God we will set
up *our* banners!
May the LORD fulfill all your petitions.

6 Now I know that the LORD saves His
[T]anointed; Commissioned one, Heb. *messiah*
He will answer him from His holy heaven
With the saving strength of His right
hand.

7 Some *trust* in chariots, and some in
[R]horses; Ps. 33:16, 17
But we will remember the name of the
LORD our God.
8 They have bowed down and fallen;
But we have risen and stand upright.

9 Save, LORD!
May the King answer us when we call.

PSALM 21

Triumph of the King

To the Chief Musician. A Psalm of David.

THE king shall have joy in Your strength,
O LORD;
And in Your salvation how greatly shall
he rejoice!
2 You have given him his heart's desire,
And have not withheld the [R]request of
his lips. Selah 2 Sam. 7:26–29

3 For You meet him with the blessings of
goodness;
You set a crown of pure gold upon his
head.
4[R] He asked life from You, *and* You gave *it*
to him— Ps. 61:5, 6; 133:3
Length of days forever and ever.
5 His glory *is* great in Your salvation;
Honor and majesty You have placed
upon him.
6 For You have made him most blessed
forever;
[R] You have made him exceedingly glad
with Your presence. Ps. 16:11; 45:7
7 For the king trusts in the LORD,
And through the mercy of the Most High
he shall not be [T]moved. *shaken*

8 Your hand will find all Your enemies;
Your right hand will find those who hate
You.
9 You shall make them as a fiery oven in
the time of Your anger;
The LORD shall swallow them up in His
wrath,
And the fire shall devour them.
10 Their offspring You shall destroy from
the earth,
And their [T]descendants from among the
sons of men. Lit. *seed*
11 For they intended evil against You;
They devised a plot *which* they are not
able *to* [R]*perform.* Ps. 2:1–4
12 Therefore You will make them turn their
back;
You will make ready *Your arrows* on
Your string toward their faces.

13 Be exalted, O LORD, in Your own
strength!
We will sing and praise Your power.

PSALM 22

Psalm of the Cross

To the Chief Musician. Set to "The Deer
of the Dawn."* A Psalm of David.

MY [R]God, My God, why have You
forsaken Me? [Mark 15:34]☆
Why are You so far from helping Me,
And from the words of My groaning?
2 O My God, I cry in the daytime, but You
do not hear;
And in the night season, and am not
silent.

3 But You *are* holy,
Enthroned in the praises of Israel.
4 Our fathers trusted in You;
They trusted, and You delivered them.
5 They cried to You, and were delivered;
[R] They trusted in You, and were not
ashamed. Is. 49:23

6 But I *am* [R]a worm, and no man; Is. 41:14
[R] A reproach of men, and despised by the
people. [Is. 53:3]

22:title Heb. *Aijeleth Hashahar*

7[R] All those who see Me ridicule Me;
They shoot out the lip, they shake the head, *saying*, Matt. 27:39☆
8 "He[R] trusted* in the LORD, let Him rescue Him; Ps. 91:14; Matt. 27:43☆
[R] Let Him deliver Him, since He delights in Him!" Ps. 91:14

9[R] But You *are* He who took Me out of the womb; [Ps. 71:5, 6]
You made Me trust *while* on My mother's breasts.
10 I was cast upon You from birth.
From My mother's womb
[R] You *have been* My God. [Is. 46:3; 49:1]
11 Be not far from Me,
For trouble *is* near;
For *there is* none to help.

12[R] Many bulls have surrounded Me;
Strong *bulls* of [R]Bashan have encircled Me. Ps. 22:21; 68:30 • Deut. 32:14
13 They gape at Me *with* their mouths,
Like a raging and roaring lion.

14 I am poured out like water,
[R] And all My bones are out of joint;
My heart is like wax; Dan. 5:6
It has melted within Me.
15[R] My strength is dried up like a potsherd,
And [R]My tongue clings to My jaws;
You have brought Me to the dust of death. Prov. 17:22 • John 19:28

16 For dogs have surrounded Me;
The congregation of the wicked has enclosed Me.
They pierced* My hands and My feet;
17 I can count all My bones.
They look *and* stare at Me.
18 They divide My garments among them,
And for My clothing they cast lots.

19 But You, O LORD, do not be far from Me;
O My Strength, hasten to help Me!
20 Deliver Me from the sword,
[R] My[T] precious *life* from the power of the dog. Ps. 35:17 • Lit. *My only one*
21 Save Me from the lion's mouth
And from the horns of the wild oxen!

[R] You have answered Me. Is. 34:7

22[R] I will declare Your name to [R]My brethren; Heb. 2:12☆ • [Rom. 8:29]
In the midst of the assembly I will praise You.
23[R] You who fear the LORD, praise Him!
All you [T]descendants of Jacob, glorify Him, Ps. 135:19, 20 • Lit. *seed*
And fear Him, all you offspring of Israel!
24 For He has not despised nor abhorred
the affliction of the afflicted;
Nor has He hidden His face from Him;
But when He cried to Him, He heard.

25[R] My praise *shall be* of You in the great assembly; Ps. 35:18; 40:9, 10
[R] I will pay My vows before those who fear Him. Eccl. 5:4
26 The poor shall eat and be satisfied;
Those who seek Him will praise the LORD.
Let your heart live forever!

27 All the ends of the world
Shall remember and turn to the LORD,
And all the families of the nations
Shall worship before You.*
28 For the kingdom *is* the LORD's,
And He rules over the nations.

29[R] All the prosperous of the earth
Shall eat and worship; Ps. 17:10; 45:12
[R] All those who go down to [T]the dust
Shall bow before Him, [Is. 26:19] • Death
Even he who cannot keep himself alive.

30 A posterity shall serve Him.
It will be recounted of the Lord to the *next* generation,
31 They will come and declare His righteousness to a people who will be born,
That He has done *this*.

PSALM 23

Psalm of the Divine Shepherd

A Psalm of David.

THE LORD *is* [R]my shepherd; [Is. 40:11]
[R] I shall not [T]want. [Phil. 4:19] • *lack*
2[R] He makes me to lie down in green pastures; Ezek. 34:14
He leads me beside the still waters.
3 He restores my soul;
[R] He leads me in the paths of righteousness Ps. 5:8; 31:3
For His name's sake.

4 Yea, though I walk through the valley of [R]the shadow of death, Job 3:5
[R] I will fear no evil; [Ps. 3:6; 27:1]
[R] For You *are* with me; [Is. 43:2]
Your rod and Your staff, they comfort me.

5 You [R]prepare a table before me in the presence of my enemies; Ps. 104:15
You [R]anoint my head with oil; Ps. 92:10
My cup runs over.

22:8 LXX, Syr., Vg. *hoped;* Tg. *praised* **22:16** So with some Heb. mss., LXX, Syr., Vg.; MT *Like a lion* instead of *They pierced* **22:27** So with MT, LXX, Tg.; Arab., Syr., Vg. *Him*

6 Surely goodness and mercy shall follow me
All the days of my life;
And I will dwell* in the house of the LORD
Forever.

PSALM 24

Psalm of the King of Glory

A Psalm of David.

THE [R]earth *is* the LORD's, and all its fullness, 1 Cor. 10:26, 28
The world and those who dwell therein.
2 For He has founded it upon the seas,
And established it upon the waters.

3 [R]Who may ascend into the hill of the LORD? Ps. 15:1–5
Or who may stand in His holy place?
4 He who has [R]clean hands and [R]a pure heart, [Job 17:9] • [Matt. 5:8]
Who has not lifted up his soul to an idol,
Nor [R]sworn deceitfully. Ps. 15:4
5 He shall receive blessing from the LORD,
And righteousness from the God of his salvation.
6 This *is* Jacob, the generation of those who [R]seek Him, Ps. 27:4, 8
Who seek Your face. Selah

7 [R]Lift up your heads, O you gates! Is. 26:2
And be lifted up, you everlasting doors!
And the King of glory shall come in.
8 Who *is* this King of glory?
The LORD strong and mighty,
The LORD mighty in [R]battle. Rev. 19:13–16
9 Lift up your heads, O you gates!
Lift up, you everlasting doors!
And the King of glory shall come in.
10 Who is this King of glory?
The LORD of hosts,
He *is* the King of glory. Selah

PSALM 25

Acrostic Prayer for Instruction

A Psalm of David.

TO You, O LORD, I lift up my soul.
2 O my God, I [R]trust in You; Ps. 34:8
Let me not be ashamed;
Let not my enemies triumph over me.
3 Indeed, let no one who [T]waits on You be ashamed; Waits for You in faith
Let those be ashamed who deal treacherously without cause.

4 [R]Show me Your ways, O LORD; Ex. 33:13
Teach me Your paths.
5 Lead me in Your truth and teach me,
For You *are* the God of my salvation;
On You I wait all the day.
6 Remember, O LORD, [R]Your tender mercies and Your lovingkindnesses,
For they *are* from of old. Ps. 103:17; 106:1
7 Do not remember [R]the sins of my youth, nor my transgressions; [Jer. 3:25]
According to Your mercy remember me,
For Your goodness' sake, O LORD.

8 Good and upright *is* the LORD;
Therefore He teaches sinners in the way.
9 The humble He guides in justice,
And the humble He teaches His way.
10 All the paths of the LORD *are* mercy and truth,
To such as keep His covenant and His testimonies.
11 [R]For Your name's sake, O LORD, Ps. 31:3
Pardon my iniquity, for it *is* great.

12 Who *is* the man that fears the LORD?
[R]Him shall He* teach in the way He* chooses. [Ps. 25:8; 37:23]
13 [R]He himself shall dwell in [T]prosperity,
And [R]his descendants shall inherit the earth. [Prov. 19:23] • Lit. *goodness* • Matt. 5:5
14 [R]The secret of the LORD *is* with those who fear Him, [John 7:17]
And He will show them His covenant.
15 [R]My eyes *are* ever toward the LORD,
For He shall [T]pluck my feet out of the net. [Ps. 123:2; 141:8] • Lit. *bring out*

16 [R]Turn Yourself to me, and have mercy on me, Ps. 69:16
For I *am* [T]desolate and afflicted. *lonely*
17 The troubles of my heart have enlarged;
Bring me out of my distresses!
18 [R]Look on my affliction and my pain,
And forgive all my sins. 2 Sam. 16:12
19 Consider my enemies, for they are many;
And they hate me with cruel hatred.
20 Keep my soul, and deliver me;
Let me not be ashamed, for I put my trust in You.
21 Let integrity and uprightness preserve me,
For I wait for You.

22 [R]Redeem Israel, O God, [Ps. 130:8]
Out of all their troubles!

PSALM 26

"Examine Me, O LORD, and Prove Me"

A Psalm of David.

VINDICATE [R]me, O LORD, Ps. 7:8
For I have [R]walked in my integrity.
[R]I have also trusted in the LORD;
I shall not slip. 2 Kin. 20:3 • [Ps. 13:5; 28:7]

23:6 So with LXX, Syr., Tg., Vg.; MT *return* **25:12** Or *he* • Or *he*

2 [R]Examine me, O LORD, and prove me;
Try my mind and my heart. Ps. 17:3
3 For Your lovingkindness *is* before my eyes,
And I have walked in Your truth.
4 I have not [R]sat with idolatrous mortals,
Nor will I go in with hypocrites. Ps. 1:1
5 I have hated the assembly of evildoers,
And will not sit with the wicked.
6 I will wash my hands in innocence;
So I will go about Your altar, O LORD,
7 That I may proclaim with the voice of thanksgiving,
And tell of all Your wondrous works.
8 LORD, [R]I have loved the habitation of Your house, Ps. 27:4; 84:1–4, 10
And the place where Your glory dwells.

9 Do not gather my soul with sinners,
Nor my life with bloodthirsty men,
10 In whose hands *is* a sinister scheme,
And whose right hand is full of bribes.
11 But as for me, I will walk in my integrity;
Redeem me and be merciful to me.
12 [R]My foot stands in an even place; Ps. 40:2
In the congregations I will bless the LORD.

PSALM 27

Trust in the Lord and Be Not Afraid

A Psalm of David.

THE LORD *is* my [R]light and my salvation;
Whom shall I fear? [Mic. 7:8]
The [R]LORD *is* the strength of my life;
Of whom shall I be afraid? Ps. 62:7
2 When the wicked came against me
To [R]eat[T] up my flesh, Ps. 14:4 • *devour*
My enemies and foes,
They [R]stumbled and fell. John 18:6☆
3 [R]Though an army may encamp against me, Ps. 3:6
My heart shall not fear;
Though war may rise against me,
In this I *will be* confident.

4 [R]One *thing* I have desired of the LORD,
That will I seek: Ps. 26:8; 65:4
That I may [R]dwell in the house of the LORD Luke 2:37
All the days of my life,
To behold the beauty of the LORD,
And to inquire in His temple.
5 For [R]in the time of trouble Ps. 31:20; 91:1
He shall hide me in His pavilion;
In the secret place of His tabernacle
He shall hide me;
He shall set me high upon a rock.

6 And now [R]my head shall be lifted up above my enemies all around me;
Therefore I will offer sacrifices of [T]joy in His tabernacle; Ps. 3:3 • *joyous shouts*
I will sing, yes, I will sing praises to the LORD.

7 Hear, O LORD, *when* I cry with my voice!
Have mercy also upon me, and answer me.
8 *When You said,* "Seek My face,"
My heart said to You, "Your face, LORD, I will seek."
9 [R]Do not hide Your face from me;
Do not turn Your servant away in anger;
You have been my help;
Do not leave me nor forsake me,
O God of my salvation. Ps. 69:17; 143:7
10 [R]When my father and my mother forsake me, Is. 49:15
Then the LORD will take care of me.

11 [R]Teach me Your way, O LORD,
And lead me in a smooth path, because of my enemies. Ps. 25:4; 86:11; 119:33
12 Do not deliver me to the will of my adversaries;
For [R]false witnesses have risen against me, Ps. 35:11; Matt. 26:60, 61☆
And such as breathe out violence.
13 *I would have lost heart,* unless I had believed
That I would see the goodness of the LORD
[R]In the land of the living. Ezek. 26:20

14 [R]Wait[T] on the LORD; Is. 25:9 • Wait in faith
Be of good courage,
And He shall strengthen your heart;
Wait, I say, on the LORD!

PSALM 28

Rejoice Because of Answered Prayer

A Psalm of David.

TO You I will cry, O LORD my Rock:
[R]Do not be silent to me, Ps. 35:22; 39:12
[R]Lest, if You *are* silent to me,
I become like those who go down to the pit. Ps. 88:4; 143:7
2 Hear the voice of my supplications
When I cry to You,
[R]When I lift up my hands [R]toward Your holy sanctuary. Ps. 5:7 • Ps. 138:2

3 Do not [T]take me away with the wicked
And with the workers of iniquity, *drag*
[R]Who speak peace to their neighbors,
But evil *is* in their hearts. Ps. 12:2
4 [R]Give them according to their deeds,
And according to the wickedness of their endeavors; [Rev. 18:6; 22:12]
Give them according to the work of their hands;

Render to them what they deserve.
5 Because [R]they do not regard the works
of the LORD, Is. 5:12
Nor the operation of His hands,
He shall destroy them
And not build them up.

6 Blessed *be* the LORD,
Because He has heard the voice of my
supplications!
7 The LORD *is* [R]my strength and my shield;
My heart [R]trusted in Him, and I am
helped; Ps. 18:2; 59:17 • Ps. 13:5; 112:7
Therefore my heart greatly rejoices,
And with my song I will praise Him.

8 The LORD *is* their strength,*
And He *is* the [R]saving refuge of His
anointed. Ps. 20:6
9 Save Your people,
And bless [R]Your inheritance;
Shepherd them also, [Deut. 9:29; 32:9]
[R]And bear them up forever. Deut. 1:31

PSALM 29

The Powerful Voice of God

A Psalm of David.

GIVE unto the LORD, O you mighty
ones,
Give unto the LORD glory and strength.

2 [T]Give unto the LORD the glory [T]due to His
name; *Ascribe* • Lit. *of His name*
Worship the LORD in [R]the [T]beauty of
holiness. 2 Chr. 20:21 • *majesty*

3 The voice of the LORD *is* over the waters;
[R]The God of glory thunders; [Job 37:4, 5]
The LORD *is* over many waters.
4 The voice of the LORD *is* powerful;
The voice of the LORD *is* full of majesty.

5 The voice of the LORD breaks [R]the
cedars, Is. 2:13; 14:8
Yes, the LORD splinters the cedars of
Lebanon.
6 [R]He makes them also skip like a calf,
Lebanon and [R]Sirion like a young wild
ox. Ps. 114:4 • Deut. 3:9
7 The voice of the LORD [T]divides the
flames of fire. *stirs up,* lit. *hews out*

8 The voice of the LORD shakes the
wilderness;
The LORD shakes the Wilderness of
[R]Kadesh. Num. 13:26
9 The voice of the LORD makes the [R]deer
give birth, Job 39:1
And strips the forests bare;
And in His temple everyone says, "Glory!"

10 The LORD sat *enthroned* at the Flood,
And the LORD sits as King forever.
11 [R]The LORD will give strength to His
people; Ps. 28:8; 68:35
The LORD will bless His people with
peace.

PSALM 30

Praise for Dramatic Deliverance

A Psalm. A Song [R]at the dedication
of the house of David. Deut. 20:5

I WILL extol You, O LORD, for You have
[R]lifted me up, Ps. 28:9
And have not let my foes [R]rejoice over
me. Ps. 25:2
2 O LORD my God, I cried out to You,
And You [R]healed me. Ps. 6:2; 103:3
3 O LORD, [R]You brought my soul up from
the grave; Ps. 86:13
You have kept me alive, that I should not
go down to the pit.*

4 [R]Sing praise to the LORD, you saints of
His, Ps. 97:12
And give thanks at the remembrance of
His holy name.*
5 For [R]His anger *is but for* a moment,
[R]His favor *is for* life; Ps. 103:9 • Ps. 63:3

28:8 So with MT, Tg.; LXX, Syr., Vg. *the strength of His people* **30:3** So with Qr., Tg.; Kt., LXX, Syr., Vg. *from those who descend to the pit* **30:4** Or *His holiness*

29:2 Worship by Israel—The central aspect of Israel's worship was the object of their worship, the Lord. While other nations paid homage to many gods (Page 203—Deut. 29:18), only Israel worshiped the one true God (Page 74—Ex. 20:3). This worship could be private (Page 88—Ex. 34:8), as a family (Page 22—Gen. 22:5), or corporate (Page 429—1 Chr. 29:20), as a congregation.

Since so much of the Bible is devoted to Israel's public worship, it deserves special notice. It included offering sacrifices (Page 272—1 Sam. 1:3), adopting a reverent posture (Page 439—2 Chr. 7:6), verbal praise—either spoken (Page 417—1 Chr. 16:36) or sung (Page 575—Ps. 57:7), instrumental praise (Page 625—Ps. 150:3–5), prayer (Page 437—2 Chr. 6:14–42), and the great feasts (Page 120—Lev. 23; 25). One need only read the Psalms to see the excellent form and spirit in which the godly of Israel worshiped.

The first place of worship for the people of Israel was the tabernacle constructed by Moses (Page 122—Ex. 25—27; 30; 31; 35—40) and later the magnificent temple constructed by Solomon (Page 421—1 Chr. 22:5). These structures served to localize the worship of the entire nation. This geographic limitation stands in bold contrast to the privilege of immediate and direct access to God now available to the NT believer who himself is the temple of God (Page 1260—Heb. 4:16; Page 1170—1 Cor. 6:19).

Now turn to Page 1119—Acts 7:38: The Meaning of the Church.

Weeping may endure for a night,
But joy *comes* in the morning.

6 Now in my prosperity I said,
"I shall never be [T]moved." *shaken*
7 LORD, by Your favor You have made my
mountain stand strong;
You hid Your face, *and* I was troubled.

8 I cried out to You, O LORD;
And to the LORD I made supplication:
9 "What profit *is there* in my blood,
When I go down to the pit?
[R]Will the dust praise You? [Ps. 6:5]
Will it declare Your truth?
10 Hear, O LORD, and have mercy on me;
LORD, be my helper!"
11 [R]You have turned for me my mourning
into dancing; Jer. 31:4
You have put off my sackcloth and
clothed me with gladness,
12 To the end that *my* [T]glory may sing
praise to You and not be silent. *soul*
O LORD my God, I will give thanks to You
forever.

PSALM 31

"Be of Good Courage"

To the Chief Musician. A Psalm of David.

IN [R]You, O LORD, I put my trust;
Let me never be ashamed; Ps. 22:5
Deliver me in Your righteousness.
2 [R]Bow down Your ear to me, Ps. 17:6; 71:2
Deliver me speedily;
Be my rock of [T]refuge, *strength*
A fortress of defense to save me.

3 For You *are* my rock and my fortress;
Therefore, [R]for Your name's sake,
Lead me and guide me. Ps. 23:3; 25:11
4 Pull me out of the net which they have
secretly laid for me,
For You *are* my strength.
5 [R]Into Your hand I commit my spirit;
You have redeemed me, O LORD God of
[R]truth. Luke 23:46 • [Deut. 32:4]

6 I have hated those [R]who regard useless
idols; Jon. 2:8
But I trust in the LORD.
7 I will be glad and rejoice in Your mercy,
For You have considered my trouble;
You have [R]known my soul in
[T]adversities, [John 10:27] • *troubles*
8 And have not [R]shut me up into the hand
of the enemy; [Deut. 32:30]
You have set my feet in a wide place.

9 Have mercy on me, O LORD, for I am in
trouble;
[R]My eye wastes away with grief, Ps. 6:7
Yes, my soul and my [T]body! Lit. *belly*
10 For my life is spent with grief,
And my years with sighing;
My strength fails because of my
iniquity,
And my bones waste away.
11 I am a reproach among all my enemies,
But especially among my neighbors,
And *am* repulsive to my acquaintances;
Those who see me outside flee from me.
12 [R]I am forgotten like a dead man, out of
mind; Ps. 88:4, 5
I am like a [T]broken vessel. Lit. *perishing*
13 [R]For I hear the slander of many;
[R]Fear *is* on every side; Jer. 20:10 • Lam. 2:22
While they [R]take counsel together
against me, Matt. 27:1
They scheme to take away my life.

14 But as for me, I trust in You, O LORD;
I say, "You *are* my God."
15 My times *are* in Your [R]hand;
Deliver me from the hand of my
enemies, [Job 14:5; 24:1]
And from those who persecute me.
16 [R]Make Your face shine upon Your
servant; Ps. 4:6; 80:3
Save me for Your mercies' sake.
17 [R]Do not let me be ashamed, O LORD, for I
have called upon You; Ps. 25:2, 20
Let the wicked be ashamed;
Let them be silent in the grave.
18 [R]Let the lying lips be put to silence,
Which [R]speak insolent things proudly
and contemptuously against the
righteous. Ps. 109:2; 120:2 • Ps. 94:4

19 [R]Oh, how great *is* Your goodness,
Which You have laid up for those who
fear You, [Rom. 2:4; 11:22]
Which You have prepared for those who
trust in You
In the presence of the sons of men!
20 [R]You shall hide them in the secret place of
Your presence [Ps. 27:5; 32:7]
From the plots of man;
[R]You shall keep them secretly in a
[T]pavilion Job 5:21 • *shelter*
From the strife of tongues.

21 Blessed *be* the LORD,
For [R]He has shown me His marvelous
kindness in a strong city! [Ps. 17:7]
22 For I said in my haste,
"I am cut off from before Your eyes";
Nevertheless You heard the voice of my
supplications
When I cried out to You.

23 Oh, love the LORD, all you His saints!
For the LORD preserves the faithful,
And fully repays the proud person.

24 [R]Be of good courage, [Ps. 27:14]
And He shall strengthen your heart,
All you who hope in the LORD.

PSALM 32

The Blessedness of Forgiveness

A Psalm of David. A Contemplation.*

BLESSED *is he whose* [R]transgression *is* forgiven, [Ps. 85:2; 103:3]
Whose sin *is* covered.
2 Blessed *is* the man to whom the LORD does not impute iniquity,
And in whose spirit *there is* no deceit.

3 When I kept silent, my bones grew old
Through my groaning all the day long.
4 For day and night Your [R]hand was heavy upon me; 1 Sam. 5:6
My vitality was turned into the drought of summer. Selah

5 I acknowledged my sin to You,
And my iniquity I have not hidden.
[R]I said, "I will confess my transgressions to the LORD," [Prov. 28:13]
And You forgave the iniquity of my sin. Selah

6 [R]For this cause everyone who is godly shall [R]pray to You [1 Tim. 1:16] • Is. 55:6
In a time when You may be found;
Surely in a flood of great waters
They shall not come near him.
7 [R]You *are* my hiding place; Ps. 9:9
You shall preserve me from trouble;
You shall surround me with [R]songs of deliverance. Selah Ex. 15:1

8 I will instruct you and teach you in the way you should go;
I will guide you with My eye.
9 Do not be like the [R]horse *or* like the mule, Prov. 26:3
Which have no understanding,
Which must be harnessed with bit and bridle,
Else they will not come near you.

10 [R]Many sorrows *shall be* to the wicked;
But he who trusts in the LORD, mercy shall surround him. [Rom. 2:9]
11 [R]Be glad in the LORD and rejoice, you righteous; Ps. 64:10; 68:3; 97:12
And shout for joy, all *you* upright in heart!

PSALM 33

God Considers All Human Works

REJOICE in the LORD, O you righteous!
For praise from the upright is beautiful.
2 Praise the LORD with the harp;
[T]Make melody to Him with an instrument of ten strings. Lit. *Sing to Him*
3 Sing to Him a new song;
Play skillfully with a shout of joy.

4 For the word of the LORD *is* right,
And all His work *is done* in truth.
5 He loves righteousness and justice;
The earth is full of the goodness of the LORD.

6 [R]By the word of the LORD the heavens were made, [Heb. 11:3]
And all the [R]host of them [R]by the breath of His mouth. Gen. 2:1 • [Job 26:13]
7 [R]He gathers the waters of the sea together as a heap;* Job 26:10; 38:8
He lays up the deep in storehouses.

8 Let all the earth fear the LORD;
Let all the inhabitants of the world stand in awe of Him.
9 For He spoke, and it was *done;*
He commanded, and it stood fast.

10 [R]The LORD brings the counsel of the nations to nothing; Is. 8:10; 19:3
He makes the plans of the peoples of no effect.
11 [R]The counsel of the LORD stands forever,
The plans of His heart to all generations. [Job 23:13]
12 Blessed *is* the nation whose God *is* the LORD,

32:title Heb. *Maschil* **33:7** LXX, Tg., Vg. *in a vessel*

32:5 What Should Be Done About Sin—The believer should never condone or attempt to excuse his sin. There are only two things that should be done about sin: confess it and forsake it. The Old Testament and New Testament are agreed on this. David confessed his sin and experienced the Lord's forgiveness. John agrees as he points out: "If we confess our sins, He is faithful and just to forgive us *our* sins and to cleanse us from all unrighteousness" (Page 1293—1 John 1:9). To "confess" means "to acknowledge" or "to say the same thing as." Believers are instructed to say the same thing God says about sin, "It is sin." When believers confess their sin, they have the assurance that God "is faithful" (He can be counted upon to keep His word) and "just" (He is just in dealing with our sins because He paid the price for them) "to forgive us *our* sins and to cleanse us from all unrighteousness." There is no sin too great and no sin too small—God is able to cleanse us completely from anything that is inconsistent with His own moral character. Having received forgiveness and cleansing, believers are to forsake their sin and yield themselves completely to God. In doing this believers are restored to full fellowship with God.

Now turn to Page 1294—1 John 2:15: Temptation by the World.

The people He has [R]chosen as His own
inheritance. [Ex. 19:5]

13[R] The LORD looks from heaven; Job 28:24
He sees all the sons of men.
14 From the place of His dwelling He looks
On all the inhabitants of the earth;
15 He fashions their hearts individually;
He considers all their works.

16[R] No king *is* saved by the multitude of an
army; Ps. 44:6; 60:11
A mighty man is not delivered by great
strength.
17[R] A horse *is* a [T]vain hope for safety;
Neither shall it deliver *any* by its great
strength. [Prov. 21:31] • *false*

18[R] Behold, the eye of the LORD *is* on those
who fear Him, [Job 36:7]
On those who hope in His mercy,
19 To deliver their soul from death,
And to keep them alive in famine.

20 Our soul waits for the LORD;
He *is* our help and our shield.
21 For our heart shall rejoice in Him,
Because we have trusted in His holy
name.
22 Let Your mercy, O LORD, be upon us,
Just as we hope in You.

PSALM 34

Seek The Lord

A Psalm of David [R]when he pretended madness
before Abimelech, who drove him away,
and he departed. 1 Sam. 21:10–15

I WILL [R]bless the LORD at all times;
His praise *shall* continually *be* in my
mouth. [Eph. 5:20]
2 My soul shall make its boast in the LORD;
The humble shall hear *of it* and be glad.
3 Oh, magnify the LORD with me,
And let us exalt His name together.

4 I sought the LORD, and He heard me,
And delivered me from all my fears.
5 They looked to Him and were radiant,
And their faces were not ashamed.
6 This poor man cried out, and the LORD
heard *him*,
And saved him out of all his troubles.
7[R] The angel* of the LORD [R]encamps all
around those who fear Him,
And delivers them. Dan. 6:22 • 2 Kin. 6:17

8 Oh, taste and see that the LORD *is* good;
Blessed *is* the man *who* trusts in Him!
9 Oh, fear the LORD, you His saints!
There is no want to those who fear Him.
10 The young lions lack and suffer hunger;
[R]But those who seek the LORD shall not
lack any good *thing*. [Ps. 84:11]

11 Come, you children, listen to me;
I will teach you the fear of the LORD.
12[R] Who *is* the man *who* desires life,
And loves *many* days, that he may see
good? [1 Pet. 3:10–12]
13 Keep your tongue from evil,
And your lips from speaking deceit.
14[R] Depart from evil and do good; Ps. 37:27
[R]Seek peace and pursue it. [Rom. 14:19]

15[R] The eyes of the LORD *are* on the
righteous, Job 36:7
And His ears *are open* to their cry.
16[R] The face of the LORD *is* against those
who do evil, Lev. 17:10
[R]To [T]cut off the remembrance of them
from the earth. [Prov. 10:7] • *destroy*

17 *The righteous* cry out, and [R]the LORD
hears, Ps. 34:6; 145:19
And delivers them out of all their
troubles.
18[R] The LORD *is* near [R]to those who have a
broken heart, [Ps. 145:18] • [Is. 57:15]
And saves such as [T]have a contrite
spirit. *are crushed in spirit*

19[R] Many *are* the afflictions of the righteous,
[R]But the LORD delivers him out of them
all. Prov. 24:16 • Ps. 34:4, 6, 17
20 He guards all his bones;
[R]Not one of them is broken. John 19:33, 36☆
21[R] Evil shall slay the wicked, Ps. 94:23
And those who hate the righteous shall
be [T]condemned. *held guilty*
22 The LORD [R]redeems the soul of His
servants, 1 Kin. 1:29
And none of those who trust in Him
shall be condemned.

PSALM 35

Petition for God's Intervention

A Psalm of David.

PLEAD[T] *my cause,* O LORD, with those
who strive with me; *Contend for me*
Fight against those who fight against me.
2 Take hold of shield and [T]buckler,
And stand up for my help. A small shield
3 Also draw out the spear,
And stop those who pursue me.
Say to my soul,
"I *am* your salvation."

4[R] Let those be put to shame and brought to
dishonor Ps. 40:14, 15; 70:2, 3
Who seek after my life;

34:7 Or *Angel*

Let those be [R]turned back and brought to
confusion Ps. 129:5
Who plot my hurt.
5[R]Let them be like chaff before the wind,
And let the angel* of the LORD chase
them. Job 21:18
6 Let their way be [R]dark and slippery,
And let the angel of the LORD pursue
them. Ps. 73:18
7 For without cause they have [R]hidden
their net for me *in* a pit, Ps. 9:15
Which they have dug without cause for
my life.
8 Let [R]destruction come upon him
unexpectedly, [1 Thess. 5:3]
And let his net that he has hidden catch
himself;
Into that very destruction let him fall.

9 And my soul shall be joyful in the LORD;
It shall rejoice in His salvation.
10[R]All my bones shall say, Ps. 51:8
"LORD, [R]who *is* like You, [Ex. 15:11]
Delivering the poor from him who is too
strong for him,
Yes, the poor and the needy from him
who plunders him?"

11[R]Fierce witnesses rise up; Mark 14:57, 58☆
They ask me *things* that I do not know.
12[R]They reward me evil for good, John 10:32
To the sorrow of my soul.
13 But as for me, [R]when they were sick,
My clothing *was* sackcloth; Job 30:25
I humbled myself with fasting;
And my prayer would return to my own
[T]heart. Lit. *bosom*
14 I paced about as though *he were* my
friend *or* brother;
I bowed down [T]heavily, as one who
mourns *for his* mother. *in mourning*

15 But in my adversity they rejoiced
And gathered together;
Attackers gathered against me,
And I did not know *it;*
They tore *at me* and did not cease;
16 With ungodly mockers at feasts
They gnashed at me with their teeth.

17 Lord, how long will You look on?
Rescue me from their destructions,
My precious *life* from the lions.
18 I will give You thanks in the great
assembly;
I will praise You among many people.

19[R]Let them not rejoice over me who are
wrongfully my enemies; Ps. 69:4; 109:3
Nor let them wink with the eye who
[R]hate me without a cause. John 15:24, 25☆
20 For they do not speak peace,
But they devise deceitful matters
Against *the* quiet ones in the land.
21 They also opened their mouth wide
against me,
And said, "Aha, aha!
Our eyes have seen *it.*"
22 *This* You have seen, O LORD;
Do not keep silence.
O Lord, do not be far from me.
23 Stir up Yourself, and awake to my
vindication,
To my cause, my God and my Lord.
24 Vindicate me, O LORD my God, according
to Your righteousness;
And let them not rejoice over me.
25 Let them not say in their hearts, "Ah, so
we would have it!"
Let them not say, "We have swallowed
him up."

26 Let them be ashamed and brought to
mutual confusion
Who rejoice at my hurt;
Let them be [R]clothed with shame and
dishonor Ps. 109:29
Who exalt themselves against me.

27[R]Let them shout for joy and be glad,
Who favor my righteous cause;
And let them say continually,
"Let the LORD be magnified,
Who has pleasure in the prosperity of
His servant." Rom. 12:15
28 And my tongue shall speak of Your
righteousness
And of Your praise all the day long.

PSALM 36

The Excellent Lovingkindness of God

To the Chief Musician. A Psalm of David
the servant of the LORD.

AN oracle within my heart concerning the
transgression of the wicked:
There is no fear of God before his eyes.
2 For he flatters himself in his own eyes,
When he finds out his iniquity *and* when
he hates.
3 The words of his mouth *are* wickedness
and deceit;
[R]He has ceased to be wise *and* to do
good. Jer. 4:22
4[R]He devises wickedness on his bed;
He sets himself [R]in a way *that is* not
good; Prov. 4:16 • Is. 65:2
He does not abhor [R]evil. [Rom. 12:9]

5 Your mercy, O LORD, *is* in the heavens;
Your faithfulness *reaches* to the clouds.
6 Your righteousness *is* like the [T]great
mountains; Lit. *mountains of God*

35:5 Or *Angel*

Your judgments *are* a great deep;
O LORD, You preserve man and beast.

7 How precious *is* Your lovingkindness,
O God!
Therefore the children of men put their
trust under the shadow of Your wings.
8[R] They are abundantly satisfied with the
fullness of Your house, Ps. 63:5; 65:4
And You give them drink from [R]the river
of Your pleasures. Rev. 22:1
9 For with You *is* the fountain of life;
[R]In Your light we see light. [1 Pet. 2:9]

10 Oh, continue Your lovingkindness to
those who know You,
And Your righteousness to the upright in
heart.
11 Let not the foot of pride come against
me,
And let not the hand of the wicked drive
me away.
12 There the workers of iniquity have
fallen;
They have been cast down and are not
able to rise.

PSALM 37

"Rest in the LORD"

A Psalm of David.

DO[R] not fret because of evildoers, Ps. 73:3
Nor be envious of the workers of iniquity.
2 For they shall soon be cut down [R]like the
grass, Ps. 90:5, 6; 92:7
And wither as the green herb.

3 Trust in the LORD, and do good;
Dwell in the land, and feed on His
faithfulness.
4[R] Delight yourself also in the LORD,
And He shall give you the desires of
your [R]heart. Is. 58:14 • Ps. 21:2; 145:19

5[R] Commit your way to the LORD,
Trust also in Him, [Ps. 55:22]
And He shall bring *it* to pass.
6[R] He shall bring forth your righteousness
as the light, Job 11:17
And your justice as the noonday.

7 Rest in the LORD, [R]and wait patiently for
Him; [Lam. 3:26]
Do not fret because of him who
[R]prospers in his way, [Ps. 73:3–12]
Because of the man who brings wicked
schemes to pass.
8 Cease from anger, and forsake wrath;
Do not fret—*it* only *causes* harm.

9 For evildoers shall be [T]cut off; *destroyed*
But those who wait on the LORD,
They shall [R]inherit the earth. [Is. 57:13]
10 For [R]yet a little while and the wicked
shall be no *more;* [Heb. 10:37]
Indeed, [R]you will look carefully for his
place, Job 7:10
But it *shall be* no *more.*
11[R] But the meek shall inherit the earth,
And shall delight themselves in the
abundance of peace. [Matt. 5:5]

12 The wicked plots against the just,
And gnashes at him with his teeth.
13[R] The Lord laughs at him, Ps. 2:4; 59:8
For He sees that his day is coming.
14 The wicked have drawn the sword
And have bent their bow,
To cast down the poor and needy,
To slay those who are of upright
conduct.
15 Their sword shall enter their own heart,
And their bows shall be broken.

16[R] A little that a righteous man has
Is better than the riches of many
wicked. Prov. 15:16; 16:8
17 For the arms of the wicked shall be
broken,
But the LORD upholds the righteous.

18 The LORD knows the days of the
upright,
And their inheritance shall be forever.
19 They shall not be ashamed in the evil
time,
And in the days of famine they shall be
satisfied.
20 But the wicked shall perish;
And the enemies of the LORD,
Like the splendor of the meadows, shall
vanish.
Into smoke they shall vanish away.

21 The wicked borrows and does not repay,
But [R]the righteous shows mercy and
gives. Ps. 112:5, 9
22[R] For *those* blessed by Him shall inherit
the earth, [Prov. 3:33]
But *those* cursed by Him shall be [T]cut
off. *destroyed*

23[R] The steps of a *good* man are [T]ordered by
the LORD, [1 Sam. 2:9] • *established*
And He delights in his way.
24[R] Though he fall, he shall not be utterly
cast down; Prov. 24:16
For the LORD upholds *him with* His hand.

25 I have been young, and *now* am old;
Yet I have not seen the righteous
forsaken,
Nor his descendants begging bread.
26 *He is* ever merciful, and lends;
And his descendants *are* blessed.

27 Depart from evil, and do good;
And dwell forevermore.
28 For the LORD loves justice,
And does not forsake His saints;
They are preserved forever,
But the descendants of the wicked shall be cut off.
29 [R]The righteous shall inherit the land,
And dwell in it forever. Prov. 2:21

30 [R]The mouth of the righteous speaks wisdom, [Matt. 12:35]
And his tongue talks of justice.
31 The law of his God *is* in his heart;
None of his steps shall [T]slide. slip

32 The wicked [R]watches the righteous,
And seeks to slay him. Ps. 10:8; 17:11
33 The LORD [R]will not leave him in his hand, [2 Pet. 2:9]
Nor condemn him when he is judged.

34 [R]Wait on the LORD, Ps. 27:14; 37:9
And keep His way,
And He shall exalt you to inherit the land;
When the wicked are cut off, you shall see *it*.
35 I have seen the wicked in great power,
And spreading himself like a native green tree.
36 Yet he passed away,* and behold, he *was* no *more;*
Indeed I sought him, but he could not be found.

37 Mark the blameless *man,* and observe the upright;
For the future of *that* man *is* peace.
38 [R]But the transgressors shall be destroyed together; [Ps. 1:4–6; 37:20, 28]
The future of the wicked shall be cut off.

39 But the salvation of the righteous *is* from the LORD;
He is their strength [R]in the time of trouble. Ps. 9:9; 37:19
40 And [R]the LORD shall help them and deliver them; Is. 31:5
He shall deliver them from the wicked,
And save them,
[R]Because they trust in Him. 1 Chr. 5:20

PSALM 38

The Heavy Burden of Sin

A Psalm of David. To bring to remembrance.

O LORD, do not [R]rebuke me in Your wrath, Ps. 6:1
Nor chasten me in Your hot displeasure!
2 For Your arrows pierce me deeply,
And Your hand presses me down.

3 *There is* no soundness in my flesh
Because of Your anger,
Nor *any* health in my bones
Because of my sin.
4 For my iniquities have gone over my head;
Like a heavy burden they are too heavy for me.
5 My wounds are foul *and* festering
Because of my foolishness.

6 I am [T]troubled, I am bowed down greatly; Lit. *bent down*
I go mourning all the day long.
7 For my loins are full of inflammation,
And *there is* no soundness in my flesh.
8 I am feeble and severely broken;
I groan because of the turmoil of my heart.

9 Lord, all my desire *is* before You;
And my sighing is not hidden from You.
10 My heart pants, my strength fails me;
As for the light of my eyes, it also has gone from me.

11 My loved ones and my friends [R]stand aloof from my plague, Ps. 31:11; 88:18
And my relatives stand afar off.
12 Those also who seek my life lay snares *for me;*
Those who seek my hurt speak of destruction,
And plan deception all the day long.

13 But I, like a deaf *man,* do not hear;
And *I am* like a [R]mute *who* does not open his mouth. Matt 27:12–14☆
14 Thus I am like a man who does not hear,
And in whose mouth *is* no response.

15 For in You, O LORD, [R]I hope; [Ps. 39:7]
You will [T]hear, O Lord my God. answer
16 For I said, "*Hear me,* lest they rejoice over me,
Lest, when my foot slips, they exalt *themselves* against me."

17 [R]For I *am* ready to fall, Ps. 51:3
And my sorrow *is* continually before me.
18 For I will [R]declare my iniquity; Ps. 32:5
I will be in anguish over my sin.
19 But my enemies *are* vigorous, *and* they are strong;
And those who hate me wrongfully have multiplied.
20 Those also [R]who render evil for good,
They are my adversaries, because I follow *what is* good. Ps. 35:12

21 Do not forsake me, O LORD;
O my God, be not far from me!
22 Make haste to help me,
O Lord, my salvation!

37:36 So with MT, LXX, Tg.; Syr., Vg. *I passed by*

PSALM 39

Know the Measure of Human Days

To the Chief Musician. To Jeduthun. A Psalm of David.

I SAID, "I will guard my ways,
Lest I sin with my [R]tongue; [James 3:5–12]
I will restrain my mouth with a muzzle,
While the wicked are before me."
2 [R]I was mute with silence, Ps. 38:13
I held my peace *even* from good;
And my sorrow was stirred up.
3 My heart was hot within me;
While I was [T]musing, the fire burned.
Then I spoke with my tongue: *meditating*

4 "LORD, make me to know my end,
And what *is* the measure of my days,
That I may know how frail I *am*.
5 Indeed, You have made my days *as* handbreadths,
And my age *is* as nothing before You;
Certainly every man at his best state *is* but [R]vapor. Selah Ps. 62:9
6 Surely every man walks about like a shadow;
Surely they [T]busy themselves in vain;
He heaps up *riches*,
And does not know who will gather them. *make an uproar for nothing*

7 "And now, Lord, what do I wait for?
My [R]hope *is* in You. Ps. 38:15
8 Deliver me from all my transgressions;
Do not make me [R]the reproach of the foolish. Ps. 44:13; 79:4; 119:22
9 I was mute, I did not open my mouth,
Because it was [R]You who did *it*. Job 2:10
10 [R]Remove Your plague from me;
I am consumed by the blow of Your hand. Job 9:34; 13:21
11 When with rebukes You correct man for iniquity,
You make his beauty [R]melt away like a moth; Job 13:28
Surely every man *is* vapor. Selah

12 "Hear my prayer, O LORD,
And give ear to my cry;
Do not be silent at my tears;
For I *am* a stranger with You,
A sojourner, as all my fathers *were*.
13 [R]Remove Your gaze from me, that I may regain strength, Job 7:19; 10:20, 21; 14:6
Before I go away and am no more."

PSALM 40

Delight to Do God's Will

To the Chief Musician. A Psalm of David.

I [R]WAITED patiently for the LORD;
And He inclined to me,
And heard my cry. Ps. 25:5; 27:14; 37:7
2 He also brought me up out of a horrible pit,
Out of [R]the miry clay, Ps. 69:2, 14
And [R]set my feet upon a rock, Ps. 27:5
And established my steps.
3 [R]He has put a new song in my mouth—
Praise to our God;
Many will see *it* and fear,
And will trust in the LORD. Ps. 32:7; 33:3

4 [R]Blessed *is* that man who makes the LORD his trust, Ps. 34:8; 84:12
And does not respect the proud, nor such as turn aside to lies.
5 [R]Many, O LORD my God, *are* Your wonderful works Job 9:10
Which You have done;
[R]And Your thoughts toward us [Is. 55:8]
Cannot be recounted to You in order;
If I would declare and speak *of them*,
They are more than can be numbered.

6 [R]Sacrifice and offering You did not desire;
My ears You have opened.
Burnt offering and sin offering You did not require. [Heb. 10:5–9]
7 Then I said, "Behold, I come;
In the scroll of the book *it is* written of me.

8 I delight to do Your will, O my God,
And Your law *is* within my heart."

9 [R]I have proclaimed the good news of righteousness Ps. 22:22, 25
In the great assembly;
Indeed, [R]I do not restrain my lips,
O LORD, You Yourself know. Ps. 119:13

40:8 We Know God's Will Through His Word—Knowing the will of God must not be thought of merely as finding a certain vocation in life. That aspect represents only a small part of God's will. Rather, the will of God is for everyone to live in conformity to His revealed will in His Word.

a. First of all, and most important, the will of God means believing Christ (Page 1088—John 6:40). If we do not take this first step in doing God's will, we will not be saved from judgment (Page 984—Matt. 7:21; 12:50); if we do, we will live forever (Page 1294—1 John 2:17).
b. Second, there are clear statements of Scripture teaching that God's will for every Christian includes sanctification (Page 1228—1 Thess. 4:3), giving thanks to God (Page 1229—1 Thess. 5:18), doing good (Page 1281—1 Pet. 2:15), and suffering for doing the right thing (Page 1282—1 Pet. 3:17).
c. Third, the Bible is God's will and must be applied to our lives (Page 203—Deut. 29:29). This fact involves commands to be obeyed, principles to be followed, prohibitions of things to be avoided, and living examples to be imitated or shunned. An attitude of delightful desire should fill all attempts to do God's will (Page 566—Ps. 40:8). God takes great joy in those who cheerfully do His will.

10 [R]I have not hidden Your righteousness
within my heart; Acts 20:20, 27
I have declared Your faithfulness and
Your salvation;
I have not concealed Your lovingkindness
and Your truth
From the great assembly.

11 Do not withhold Your tender mercies
from me, O LORD;
[R]Let Your lovingkindness and Your truth
continually preserve me. Ps. 61:7
12 For innumerable evils have surrounded me;
[R]My iniquities have overtaken me, so that
I am not able to look up; Ps. 38:4; 65:3
They are more than the hairs of my head;
Therefore my heart fails me.

13 [R]Be pleased, O LORD, to deliver me;
O LORD, make haste to help me! Ps. 70:1
14 [R]Let them be ashamed and brought to
mutual confusion Ps. 35:4, 26; 70:2
Who seek to destroy my [T]life; Lit. *soul*
Let them be driven backward and
brought to dishonor
Who wish me evil.
15 Let them be [R]confounded because of
their shame, Ps. 73:19
Who say to me, "Aha, aha!"

16 [R]Let all those who seek You rejoice and be
glad in You; Ps. 70:4
Let such as love Your salvation [R]say
continually, Ps. 35:27
"The LORD be magnified!"
17 [R]But I *am* poor and needy; Ps. 70:5; 86:1
[R]*Yet* the LORD thinks upon me. 1 Pet. 5:7
You *are* my help and my deliverer;
Do not delay, O my God.

PSALM 41

The Blessedness of Helping the Poor

To the Chief Musician. A Psalm of David.

BLESSED *is* he who considers the [T]poor;
The LORD will deliver him in time of
trouble. *helpless* or *powerless*
2 The LORD will preserve him and keep
him alive,
And he will be blessed on the earth;
[R]You will not deliver him to the will of his
enemies. Ps. 27:12
3 The LORD will strengthen him on his bed
of illness;
You will sustain him on his sickbed.

4 I said, "LORD, be merciful to me;
[R]Heal my soul, for I have sinned against
You." Ps. 6:2; 103:3; 147:3
5 My enemies speak evil of me:
"When will he die, and his name perish?"
6 And if he comes to see *me*, he speaks
[T]lies; *empty words*
His heart gathers iniquity to itself;
When he goes out, he tells *it*.

7 All who hate me whisper together
against me;
Against me they [T]devise my hurt. *plot*
8 "An[T] evil disease," *they say*, "clings to
him. Lit. *A thing of Belial*
And *now* that he lies down, he will rise
up no more."
9 [R]Even my own familiar friend in whom I
trusted, 2 Sam. 15:12
[R]Who ate my bread, John 13:18, 21–30☆
Has lifted up *his* heel against me.

10 But You, O LORD, be merciful to me, and
raise me up,
That I may repay them.
11 By this I know that You are well pleased
with me,
Because my enemy does not triumph
over me.
12 As for me, You uphold me in my integrity,
And set me before Your face forever.

13 [R]Blessed *be* the LORD God of Israel
From everlasting to everlasting!
Amen and Amen. Ps. 72:18, 19

BOOK TWO
Psalms 42—72

PSALM 42

Seek After the Lord

To the Chief Musician. A Contemplation* of the sons of Korah.

AS the deer pants for the water brooks,
So pants my soul for You, O God.

42:title Heb. *Maschil*

Although the Bible is a complete revelation of God's will, there are always decisions we must make that are not covered by specific statements of Scripture. In order to know God's will in such instances we must be in fellowship with the Lord (Page 1293—1 John 1:6, 7), seek principles from the Word (Page 1174—1 Cor. 10:6), obtain advice from godly counselors (Page 637—Prov. 11:14; 15:22; 24:6), use common sense, and remember that God works through our own minds and desires to do His will (Page 1214—Phil. 2:13). When none of these principles seem to work, we must simply make the best possible decision, realizing that God will shut the door if it is not His will. Paul, for example, planned to go and see the Roman Christians, although not knowing if God would actually permit it in His will (Page 1161—Rom. 15:22–32). In most cases, however, the believer who thoroughly searches the Word will find the basis for an intelligent decision.

Now turn to Page 206—Deut. 32:7: God's Work in the Past.

2 [R]My soul thirsts for God, for the [R]living
God. Ps. 63:1; 84:2; 143:6 • 1 Thess. 1:9
When shall I come and appear before
God?*
3 [R]My tears have been my food day and
night, Ps. 80:5; 102:9
While they continually say to me,
[R]"Where *is* your God?" Ps. 79:10; 115:2
4 When I remember these *things*,
[R]I pour out my soul within me. Job 30:16
For I used to go with the multitude;
[R]I went with them to the house of God,
With the voice of joy and praise,
With a multitude that kept a pilgrim
feast. Is. 30:29

5 Why are you cast down, O my soul?
And *why* are you disquieted within me?
Hope in God, for I shall yet praise Him
For the help of His countenance.*

6 O my God,* my soul is cast down within
me;
Therefore I will remember You from the
land of the Jordan,
And from the heights of Hermon,
From [T]the Hill Mizar. Or *Mount*
7 Deep calls unto deep at the noise of Your
waterfalls;
[R]All Your waves and billows have gone
over me. Ps. 69:1, 2; 88:7
8 The LORD will [R]command His
lovingkindness in the daytime,
And [R]in the night His song *shall be* with
me— Deut. 28:8 • Job 35:10
A prayer to the God of my life.

9 I will say to God my Rock,
[R]"Why have You forgotten me? Ps. 38:6
Why do I go mourning because of the
oppression of the enemy?"
10 *As* with a breaking of my bones,
My enemies [T]reproach me, *revile*
[R]While they say to me all day long,
"Where *is* your God?" Joel 2:17

11 [R]Why are you cast down, O my soul?
And why are you disquieted within me?
Hope in God; Ps. 43:5
For I shall yet praise Him,
The [T]help of my countenance and my
God. Lit. *salvation*

PSALM 43

"Hope in God"

VINDICATE [R]me, O God, [Ps. 26:1; 35:24]
And [R]plead my cause against an ungodly
nation; Ps. 35:1
Oh, deliver me from the deceitful and
unjust man!
2 For You *are* the God of my strength;
Why do You cast me off?
[R]Why do I go mourning because of the
oppression of the enemy? Ps. 42:9

3 [R]Oh, send out Your light and Your truth!
Let them lead me; [Ps. 40:11]
Let them bring me to Your holy hill
And to Your [T]tabernacle. *dwelling places*
4 Then I will go to the altar of God,
To God my exceeding joy;
And on the harp I will praise You,
O God, my God.

5 [R]Why are you cast down, O my soul?
And why are you disquieted within me?
Hope in God; Ps. 42:5, 11
For I shall yet praise Him,
The [T]help of my countenance and my
God. Lit. *salvation*

PSALM 44

Prayer for Deliverance by God

To the Chief Musician. A [R]Contemplation*
of the sons of Korah. Ps. 42:title

WE have heard with our ears, O God,
[R]Our fathers have told us,
The deeds You did in their days,
In days of old: [Ex. 12:26, 27]
2 [R]You drove out the [T]nations with Your
hand, Ex. 15:17 • *Gentiles, heathen*
But them You planted;
You afflicted the peoples, and cast them
out.
3 For [R]they did not gain possession of the
land by their own sword, [Deut. 8:17, 18]
Nor did their own arm save them;
But it was Your right hand, Your arm, and
the light of Your countenance,
[R]Because You favored them. [Deut. 4:37]

4 [R]You are my King, O God;* [Ps. 74:12]
Command* victories for Jacob.
5 Through You [R]we will push down our
enemies; [Dan. 8:4]
Through Your name we will trample
those who rise up against us.
6 For [R]I will not trust in my bow, Ps. 33:16
Nor shall my sword save me.
7 But You have saved us from our enemies,
And have put to shame those who hated
us.
8 [R]In God we boast all day long, Ps. 34:2
And praise Your name forever. Selah

42:2 So with MT, Vg.; some Heb. mss., LXX, Syr., Tg. *I see the face of God* **42:5** So with MT, Tg.; a few Heb. mss., LXX, Syr., Vg. *The help of my countenance, my God* **42:6** So with MT, Tg.; a few Heb. mss., LXX, Syr., Vg. put *my God* at the end of v. 5 **44:title** Heb. *Maschil* **44:4** So with MT, Tg.; LXX, Vg. *and my God* • So with MT, Tg.; LXX, Syr., Vg. *Who commands*

9 But [R]You have cast *us* off and put us to shame, Ps. 60:1
And You do not go out with our armies.
10 You make us [R]turn back from the enemy, Lev. 26:17
And those who hate us have taken [T]spoil for themselves. *plunder*
11[R] You have given us up like sheep *intended* for food, Rom. 8:36
And have [R]scattered us among the nations. Deut. 4:27; 28:64
12 You sell Your people for *next to* nothing,
And are not enriched by selling them.

13[R] You make us a reproach to our neighbors, Jer. 24:9
A scorn and a derision to those all around us.
14[R] You make us a byword among the nations, Deut. 28:37
[R]A shaking of the head among the peoples. Job 16:4
15 My dishonor *is* continually before me,
And the shame of my face has covered me,
16 Because of the voice of him who reproaches and reviles,
Because of the enemy and the avenger.

17[R] All this has come upon us; Dan. 9:13
But we have not forgotten You,
Nor have we dealt falsely with Your covenant.
18 Our heart has not turned back,
[R]Nor have our steps departed from Your way; Job 23:11
19 But You have severely broken us in [R]the place of jackals, Is. 34:13
And covered us [R]with the shadow of death. [Ps. 23:4]

20 If we had forgotten the name of our God,
Or [R]stretched[T] out our hands to a foreign god, [Deut. 6:14] • Worshiped
21 Would not God search this out?
For He knows the secrets of the heart.
22[R] Yet for Your sake we are killed all day long; Rom. 8:36
We are accounted as sheep for the slaughter.

23[R] Awake! Why do You sleep, O Lord?
Arise! Do not cast *us* off forever. Ps. 7:6
24[R] Why do You hide Your face, Job 13:24
And forget our affliction and our oppression?
25 For [R]our soul is bowed down to the [T]dust; Ps. 119:25 • Ground, in humiliation
Our body clings to the ground.
26 Arise for our help,
And redeem us for Your mercies' sake.

PSALM 45

The Psalm of the Great King

To the Chief Musician. [R]Set to "The Lilies."*
A Contemplation* of the sons of Korah.
A Song of Love. Ps. 69:title

MY heart is overflowing with a good theme;
I recite my composition concerning the King;
My tongue *is* the pen of a ready writer.

2 You are fairer than the sons of men;
Grace is poured upon Your lips;
Therefore God has blessed You forever.
3 Gird Your [R]sword upon *Your* thigh,
[R]O Mighty One, [Heb. 4:12] • [Is. 9:6]
With Your glory and Your majesty.
4[R] And in Your majesty ride prosperously because of truth, humility, *and* righteousness; Rev. 6:2
And Your right hand shall teach You awesome things.
5 Your arrows *are* sharp in the heart of the King's enemies;
The peoples fall under You.

6[R] Your throne, O God, *is* forever and ever; Heb. 1:8☆
A [R]scepter of righteousness *is* the scepter of Your kingdom. [Num. 24:17]
7 You love righteousness and hate wickedness;
Therefore God, Your God, has [R]anointed You Ps. 2:2
With the oil of [R]gladness more than Your companions. Ps. 21:6
8 All Your garments are [R]scented with myrrh and aloes *and* cassia,
Out of the ivory palaces, by which they have made You glad. Song 1:2, 13
9[R] Kings' daughters *are* among Your honorable women; Song 6:8
[R]At Your right hand stands the queen in gold from Ophir. 1 Kin. 2:19

10 Listen, O daughter,
Consider and incline your ear;
[R]Forget your own people also, and your father's house; Deut. 21:13
11 So the King will greatly desire your beauty;
Because He *is* your Lord, worship Him.
12 And the daughter of Tyre *will come* with a gift;
[R]The rich among the people will seek your favor. Is. 49:23

13 The royal daughter *is* all glorious within *the palace;*
Her clothing *is* woven with gold.

45:title Heb. *Shoshannim* • Heb. *Maschil*

14[R] She shall be brought to the King in robes
of many colors; Song 1:4
The virgins, her companions who follow
her, shall be brought to You.
15 With gladness and rejoicing they shall
be brought;
They shall enter the King's palace.

16 Instead of Your fathers shall be Your
sons,
[R] Whom You shall make princes in all the
earth. [1 Pet. 2:9]
17[R] I will make Your name to be remembered
in all generations;
Therefore the people shall praise You
forever and ever. Mal. 1:11

PSALM 46

"God Is Our Refuge and Strength"

To the Chief Musician. A Psalm of the sons of
Korah. A Song [R]for Alamoth. 1 Chr. 15:20

GOD *is* our [R]refuge and strength, Ps. 62:7, 8
A very present help in trouble.
2 Therefore we will not fear,
Even though the earth be removed,
And though the mountains be carried
into the [T]midst of the sea; Lit. *heart*
3[R] *Though* its waters roar *and* be troubled,
Though the mountains shake with its
swelling. Selah [Ps. 93:3, 4]

4 *There is* a [R]river whose streams shall
make glad the [R]city of God,
The holy *place* of the tabernacle of the
Most High. [Ezek. 47:1–12] • Is. 60:14
5 God *is* [R]in the midst of her, she shall not
be [T]moved; [Zeph. 3:15] • *shaken*
God shall help her, just [T]at the break of
dawn. Lit. *at the turning of the morning*
6[R] The nations raged, the kingdoms were
moved; Ps. 2:1, 2
He uttered His voice, the earth melted.

7 The [R]LORD of hosts *is* with us; Num. 14:9
The God of Jacob *is* our refuge. Selah

8 Come, behold the works of the LORD,
Who has made desolations in the earth.
9[R] He makes wars cease to the end of the
earth; Is. 2:4
[R] He breaks the bow and cuts the spear in
two; Ps. 76:3
He burns the chariot in the fire.

10 Be still, and know that I *am* God;
I will be exalted among the nations,
I will be exalted in the earth!

11 The LORD of hosts *is* with us;
The God of Jacob *is* our refuge. Selah

PSALM 47

The Lord Shall Subdue All Nations

To the Chief Musician.
A Psalm of the sons of Korah.

OH, clap your hands, all you peoples!
Shout to God with the voice of triumph!
2 For the LORD Most High *is* awesome;
He is a great King over all the earth.
3 He will subdue the peoples under us,
And the nations under our feet.
4 He will choose our inheritance for us,
The excellence of Jacob whom He loves.
Selah

5 God has gone up with a shout,
The LORD with the sound of a trumpet.
6 Sing praises to God, sing praises!
Sing praises to our King, sing praises!
7 For God *is* the King of all the earth;
Sing praises with understanding.

8[R] God reigns over the nations; 1 Chr. 16:31
God [R]sits on His holy throne. Ps. 97:2
9 The princes of the people have gathered
together,
[R] The people of the God of Abraham.
[R] For the shields of the earth *belong* to
God; [Rom. 4:11, 12] • [Ps. 89:18]
He is greatly exalted.

PSALM 48

The Praise of Mount Zion

A Song. A Psalm of the sons of Korah.

GREAT *is* the LORD, and greatly to be
praised
In the [R]city of our God, Ps. 46:4; 87:3
In His holy mountain.
2[R] Beautiful in [T]elevation, Ps. 50:2 • *height*
The joy of the whole earth,
Is Mount Zion *on* the sides of the north,
The city of the great King.
3 God *is* in her palaces;
He is known as her refuge.

4 For behold, [R]the kings assembled,
They passed by together. 2 Sam. 10:6, 14
5 They saw *it, and* so they marveled;
They were troubled, they hastened
away.
6 Fear [R]took hold of them there, Ex. 15:15
And pain, as of a woman in birth pangs,
7 *As when* You break the [R]ships of
Tarshish Ezek. 27:25
With an east wind.

8 As we have heard,
So we have seen
In the city of the LORD of hosts,
In the city of our God:
God will establish it forever. Selah

9 We have thought, O God, on [R]Your lovingkindness, Ps. 26:3
In the midst of Your temple.
10 According to [R]Your name, O God,
So *is* Your praise to the ends of the earth; Mal. 1:11
Your right hand is full of righteousness.
11 Let Mount Zion rejoice,
Let the daughters of Judah be glad,
Because of Your judgments.

12 Walk about Zion,
And go all around her.
Count her towers;
13 Mark well her bulwarks;
Consider her palaces;
That you may [R]tell *it* to the generation following. [Ps. 78:5–7]
14 For this *is* God,
Our God forever and ever;
[R]He will be our guide Is. 58:11
Even to death.*

PSALM 49

Riches Cannot Redeem

To the Chief Musician.
A Psalm of the sons of Korah.

HEAR this, all peoples;
Give ear, all inhabitants of the world,
2 Both low and high,
Rich and poor together.
3 My mouth shall speak wisdom,
And the meditation of my heart *shall give* understanding.
4 I will incline my ear to a proverb;
I will disclose my [T]dark saying on the harp. *riddle*

5 Why should I fear in the days of evil,
When the iniquity at my heels surrounds me?
6 Those who [R]trust in their wealth
And boast in the multitude of their riches, [Mark 10:23, 24]
7 None *of them* can by any means redeem *his* brother,
Nor give to God a ransom for him—
8 For [R]the redemption of their souls *is* costly, [Matt. 16:26]
And it shall cease forever—
9 That he should continue to live eternally,
And [R]not see the Pit. Ps. 89:48

10 For he sees wise men die;
Likewise the fool and the senseless person perish,
And leave their wealth to others.
11 Their inner thought *is that* their houses *will last* forever,*
Their dwelling places to all generations;
They [R]call *their* lands after their own names. Gen. 4:17
12 Nevertheless man, *though* in honor, does not remain;*
He is like the beasts *that* perish.

13 This is the way of those who *are* [R]foolish, [Luke 12:20]
And of their posterity who approve their sayings. Selah
14 Like sheep they are laid in the grave;
Death shall feed on them;
[R]The upright shall have dominion over them in the morning; [Dan. 7:18]
And their beauty shall be consumed in the grave, far from their dwelling.
15 But God [R]will redeem my soul from the power of the grave, Acts 2:31, 32☆
For He shall receive me. Selah

16 Do not be afraid when one becomes rich,
When the glory of his house is increased;
17 For when he dies he shall carry nothing away;
His glory shall not descend after him.
18 Though while he lives [R]he blesses himself Deut. 29:19
(For *men* will praise you when you do well for yourself),
19 He shall go to the generation of his fathers;
They shall never see [R]light. Job 33:30
20 A man *who is* in honor, yet does not understand,
[R]Is like the beasts *that* perish. Eccl. 3:19

PSALM 50

The Lord Shall Judge All People

A Psalm of Asaph.

THE [R]Mighty One, God the LORD, Is. 9:6
Has spoken and called the earth
From the rising of the sun to its going down.
2 Out of Zion, the perfection of beauty,
[R]God will shine forth. Ps. 80:1
3 Our God shall come, and shall not keep silent;
[R]A fire shall devour before Him, [Ps. 97:3]
And it shall be very tempestuous all around Him.

4 [R]He shall call to the heavens from above,
And to the earth, that He may judge His people: Is. 1:2
5 "Gather [R]My saints together to Me,
[R]Those who have made a covenant with Me by sacrifice." Deut. 33:3 • Ex. 24:7

48:14 So with MT, Syr.; LXX, Vg. *Forever* **49:11** LXX, Syr., Tg., Vg. *Their graves shall be their houses forever* **49:12** So with MT, Tg.; LXX, Syr., Vg. *understand* (cf. v. 20)

6 Let the [R]heavens declare His
righteousness, [Ps. 97:6]
For God Himself *is* Judge. Selah

7 "Hear, O My people, and I will speak,
O Israel, and I will testify against you;
[R]I *am* God, your God! Ex. 20:2
8 I will not [T]rebuke you [R]for your
sacrifices
Or your burnt offerings, *reprove* • [Hos. 6:6]
Which are continually before Me.
9 [R]I will not take a bull from your house,
Nor goats out of your folds. Ps. 69:31
10 For every beast of the forest *is* Mine,
And the cattle on a thousand hills.
11 I know all the birds of the mountains,
And the wild beasts of the field *are*
Mine.

12 "If I were hungry, I would not tell you;
[R]For the world *is* Mine, and all its
fullness. Ex. 19:5
13 [R]Will I eat the flesh of bulls, [Ps. 51:15–17]
Or drink the blood of goats?
14 [R]Offer to God thanksgiving, Heb. 13:15
And pay your vows to the Most High.
15 [R]Call upon Me in the day of trouble;
I will deliver you, and you shall glorify
Me." [Zech. 13:9]

16 But to the wicked God says:
"What *right* have you to declare My
statutes,
Or take My covenant in your mouth,
17 [R]Seeing you hate instruction Rom. 2:21
And cast My words behind you?
18 When you saw a thief, you [R]consented*
with him, [Rom. 1:32]
And have been a [R]partaker with
adulterers. 1 Tim. 5:22
19 You give your mouth to evil,
And [R]your tongue frames deceit. Ps. 52:2
20 You sit *and* speak against your brother;
You slander your own mother's son.
21 These *things* you have done, and I kept
silent;
[R]You thought that I was altogether like
you; [Rom. 2:4]
But I will rebuke you,
And set *them* in order before your eyes.

22 "Now consider this, you who [R]forget God,
Lest I tear *you* in pieces,
And *there be* none to deliver: [Job 8:13]
23 Whoever offers praise glorifies Me;
And [R]to him who orders *his* conduct
aright Gal. 6:16
I will show the salvation of God."

PSALM 51

Confession and Forgiveness of Sin

To the Chief Musician. A Psalm of David [R]when
Nathan the prophet went to him, after he had
gone in to Bathsheba. 2 Sam. 12:1

HAVE mercy upon me, O God,
According to Your lovingkindness;
According to the multitude of Your
tender mercies,
[R]Blot out my transgressions. [Is. 43:25]

2 [R]Wash me thoroughly from my iniquity,
And cleanse me from my sin. [Heb. 9:14]

3 For I acknowledge my transgressions,
And my sin *is* always before me.
4 Against You, You only, have I sinned,
And done *this* evil in Your sight—
[R]That You may be found just when You
speak,* Rom. 3:4
And blameless when You judge.

5 Behold, I was brought forth in iniquity,
And in sin my mother conceived me.
6 Behold, You desire truth in the inward
parts,
And in the hidden *part* You will make me
to know wisdom.

7 [R]Purge me with hyssop, and I shall be
clean; Heb. 9:19
Wash me, and I shall be [R]whiter than
snow. [Is. 1:18]
8 Make me hear joy and gladness,
That the bones You have broken [R]may
rejoice. [Matt. 5:4]
9 Hide Your face from my sins,
And blot out all my iniquities.

10 Create in me a clean heart, O God,
And renew a steadfast spirit within me.
11 Do not cast me away from Your
presence,

50:18 LXX, Syr., Tg., Vg. *ran* **51:4** LXX, Tg., Vg. *in Your words*

51:2 What Sin Is—In dealing with sin it is important to know what sin is. If asked to define sin, people will come up with many different definitions as to what sin is—usually the things that the individual does not like. One of the most common definitions of sin is *missing the mark*—a failure to live up to an expected standard. The problem with this definition is that it fails to take into account that when the mark is missed, something is hit. Another definition of sin is found in 1 John 3:4, "sin is lawlessness." Put simply according to this verse, sin is anything that is contrary to what the Word of God commands or forbids. This definition, however, does not take into account those things about which the Word of God is silent. The best definition for sin is found in 1 John 5:17, "All unrighteousness is sin."

Now turn to Page 736—Is. 59:2: What Sin Does.

And do not take Your [R]Holy Spirit from
me. [Luke 11:13]

12 Restore to me the joy of Your salvation,
And uphold me *by Your* [R]generous
Spirit. [2 Cor. 3:17]
13 *Then* I will teach transgressors Your
ways,
And sinners shall be converted to You.

14 Deliver me from the guilt of bloodshed,
O God,
The God of my salvation,
And my tongue shall sing aloud of Your
righteousness.
15 O Lord, open my lips,
And my mouth shall show forth Your
praise.
16 For [R]You do not desire sacrifice, or else I
would give *it;* [1 Sam. 15:22]
You do not delight in burnt offering.
17 The sacrifices of God *are* a broken spirit,
A broken and a contrite heart—
These, O God, You will not despise.

18 Do good in Your good pleasure to Zion;
Build the walls of Jerusalem.
19 Then You shall be pleased with [R]the
sacrifices of righteousness, Ps. 4:5
With burnt offering and whole burnt
offering;
Then they shall offer bulls on Your altar.

PSALM 52

The Lord Shall Judge the Deceitful

To the Chief Musician. A Contemplation* of David [R]when Doeg the Edomite went and [R]told Saul, and said to him, "David has gone to the house of Ahimelech." 1 Sam. 22:9 • Ezek. 22:9

WHY do you boast in evil, O mighty
man?
The goodness of God *endures*
continually.
2 Your tongue devises destruction,
Like a sharp razor, working deceitfully.
3 You love evil more than good,
Lying rather than speaking
righteousness. Selah
4 You love all devouring words,
You deceitful tongue.

5 God shall likewise destroy you forever;
He shall take you away, and pluck you
out of *your* dwelling place,
And uproot you from the land of the
living. Selah
6 The righteous also shall see and fear,
And shall laugh at him, *saying,*
7 "Here is the man *who* did not make God
his strength,
But trusted in the abundance of his
riches,
And strengthened himself in his
[T]wickedness." Lit. *desire,* in evil sense
8 But I *am* [R]like a green olive tree in the
house of God; Jer. 11:16
I trust in the mercy of God forever and
ever.
9 I will praise You forever,
Because You have done *it;*
And in the presence of Your saints
I will wait on Your name, for *it is* good.

PSALM 53

A Portrait of the Godless

To the Chief Musician. Set to "Mahalath." A Contemplation* of David.

THE [R]fool has said in his heart, Ps. 10:4
"*There is* no God."
They are corrupt, and have done
abominable iniquity;
There is none who does good.

2 God looks down from heaven upon the
children of men,
To see if there are *any* who understand,
who [R]seek God. [2 Chr. 15:2]
3 Every one of them has turned aside;
They have together become corrupt;
There is none who does good,
No, not one.

4 Have the workers of iniquity [R]no
knowledge, Jer. 4:22
Who eat up my people *as* they eat bread,
And do not call upon God?
5 [R]There they are in great fear Prov. 28:1
Where no fear was,
For God has scattered the bones of him
who encamps against you;
You have put *them* to shame,
Because God has despised them.

6 [R]Oh, that the salvation of Israel would
come out of Zion! Ps. 14:7
When God brings back [T]the captivity of
His people, Or *His captive people*
Let Jacob rejoice *and* Israel be glad.

PSALM 54

The Lord Is Our Helper

To the Chief Musician. With stringed instruments.* A Contemplation* of David [R]when the Ziphites went and said to Saul, "Is David not hiding with us?" 1 Sam. 23:19

SAVE me, O God, by Your name,
And vindicate me by Your strength.
2 Hear my prayer, O God;
Give ear to the words of my mouth.

52:title Heb. *Maschil* **53:title** Heb. *Maschil*
54:title Heb. *neginoth* • Heb. *Maschil*

3 For strangers have risen up against me,
And oppressors have sought after my life;
They have not set God before them.
Selah

4 Behold, God *is* my helper;
The Lord *is* with those who [T]uphold my
life. *sustain my soul*
5 He will repay my enemies for their evil.
Cut them off in Your truth.

6 I will freely sacrifice to You;
I will praise Your name, O LORD, for *it is*
good.
7 For He has delivered me out of all
trouble;
[R]And my eye has seen *its desire* upon my
enemies. Ps. 59:10

PSALM 55

"Cast Your Burden on the LORD"

To the Chief Musician. With stringed instruments.* A Contemplation* of David.

GIVE ear to my prayer, O God,
And do not hide Yourself from my
supplication.
2 Attend to me, and hear me;
I [R]am[T] restless in my complaint, and
moan noisily, Is. 38:14; 59:11 • *wander*
3 Because of the voice of the enemy,
Because of the oppression of the wicked;
For they bring down trouble upon me,
And in wrath they hate me.

4[R] My heart is severely pained within me,
And the terrors of death have fallen
upon me. Ps. 116:3
5 Fearfulness and trembling have come
upon me,
And horror has overwhelmed me.
6 So I said, "Oh, that I had wings like a dove!
I would fly away and be at rest.
7 Indeed, I would wander far off,
And remain in the wilderness. Selah
8 I would hasten my escape
From the windy storm *and* tempest."

9 Destroy, O Lord, *and* divide their
[T]tongues, *speech*, their counsel
For I have seen [R]violence and strife in
the city. Jer. 6:7
10 Day and night they go around it on its
walls;
[R]Iniquity and trouble *are* also in the midst
of it. Ps. 10:7
11 Destruction *is* in its midst;
[R]Oppression and deceit do not depart
from its streets. Ps. 10:7

12[R] For *it is* not an enemy *who* reproaches
me; Ps. 41:9
Then I could bear *it*.
Nor *is it* one *who* hates me who has
[R]exalted *himself* against me;
Then I could hide from him. Ps. 35:26
13 But *it was* you, a man my equal,
My companion and my acquaintance.
14 We took sweet counsel together,
And [R]walked to the house of God in the
throng. Ps. 42:4

15 Let death seize them;
Let them [R]go down alive into [T]hell,
For wickedness *is* in their dwellings *and*
among them. Num. 16:30, 33 • Or *Sheol*

16 As for me, I will call upon God,
And the LORD shall save me.
17[R] Evening and morning and at noon
I will pray, and cry aloud,
And He shall hear my voice. Dan. 6:10
18 He has redeemed my soul in peace from
the battle *that was* against me,
For there were many against me.
19 God will hear, and afflict them,
Even He who abides from of old. Selah
Because they do not change,
Therefore they do not fear God.

20 He has [R]put forth his hands against
those who were at peace with him;
He has broken his covenant. Acts 12:1
21[R] *The words* of his mouth were smoother
than butter, Ps. 28:3; 57:4
But war *was* in his heart;
His words were softer than oil,
Yet they *were* drawn swords.

22[R] Cast your burden on the LORD, [Ps. 37:5]
And [R]He shall sustain you; Ps. 37:24
He shall never permit the righteous to be
[T]moved. *shaken*

23 But You, O God, shall bring them down
to the pit of destruction;
[R]Bloodthirsty and deceitful men [R]shall not
live out half their days; Ps. 5:6
But I will trust in You. Prov. 10:27

PSALM 56

Fears in the Midst of Trials

To the Chief Musician. Set to "The Silent Dove in Distant Lands."* A Michtam of David when the [R]Philistines captured him in Gath. 1 Sam. 21:11

BE [R]merciful to me, O God, for man would
swallow me up; Ps. 57:1
Fighting all day he oppresses me.
2 My enemies would [R]hound *me* all day,
For *there are* many who fight against
me, O Most High. Ps. 57:3

55:title Heb. *neginoth* • Heb. *Maschil* **56:title** Heb. *Jonath Elem Rechokim*

3 Whenever I am afraid,
I will trust in You.
4 In God (I will praise His word),
In God I have put my trust;
[R]I will not fear. Ps. 118:6
What can flesh do to me?
5 All day they twist my words;
All their thoughts *are* against me for
evil.
6 They gather together,
They hide, they mark my steps,
When they lie in wait for my life.
7 Shall they escape by iniquity?
In anger cast down the peoples, O God!

8 You number my wanderings;
Put my tears into Your bottle;
[R]*Are they* not in Your book? [Mal. 3:16]
9 When I cry out *to You,*
Then my enemies will turn back;
This I know, because God *is* for me.
10 In God (I will praise *His* word),
In the LORD (I will praise *His* word),
11 In God I have put my trust;
I will not be afraid.
What can man do to me?

12 Vows *made* to You *are binding* upon me,
O God;
I will render praises to You,
13[R] For You have delivered my soul from
death. Ps. 116:8, 9
Have You not *kept* my feet from falling,
That I may walk before God
In the [R]light of the living? Job 33:30

PSALM 57

Prayers in the Midst of Perils

To the Chief Musician. Set to "Do Not Destroy."*
A Michtam of David [R]when he fled from Saul
into the cave. 1 Sam. 22:1

BE merciful to me, O God, be merciful to
me!
For my soul trusts in You;
[R]And in the shadow of Your wings I will
make my refuge, Ps. 17:8; 63:7
Until *these* calamities have passed by.

2 I will cry out to God Most High,
To God who performs *all things* for me.
3[R] He shall send from heaven and save me;
He reproaches the one who would
swallow me up. Selah Ps. 144:5, 7
God [R]shall send forth His mercy and His
truth. Ps. 43:3

4 My soul *is* among lions;
I lie *among* the sons of men
Who are set on fire,
Whose teeth *are* spears and arrows,
And their tongue a sharp sword.
5 Be exalted, O God, above the heavens;
Let Your glory *be* above all the earth.

6[R] They have prepared a net for my steps;
My soul is bowed down;
They have dug a pit before me; Ps. 9:15
Into the midst of it they *themselves* have
fallen. Selah

7[R] My heart is steadfast, O God, my heart is
steadfast; Ps. 108:1–5
I will sing and give praise.
8 Awake, [R]my glory! Ps. 16:9
Awake, lute and harp!
I will awaken the dawn.

9[R] I will praise You, O Lord, among the
peoples; Ps. 108:3
I will sing to You among the nations.
10[R] For Your mercy reaches unto the
heavens, Ps. 103:11
And Your truth unto the clouds.

11 Be exalted, O God, above the heavens;
Let Your glory *be* above all the earth.

PSALM 58

Wicked Judges Will Be Judged

To the Chief Musician. Set to "Do Not Destroy."*
A Michtam of David.

DO you indeed speak righteousness, you
silent ones?
Do you judge uprightly, you sons of
men?
2 No, in heart you work wickedness;
You weigh out the violence of your
hands in the earth.

3[R] The wicked are estranged from the
womb; [Is. 48:8]
They go astray as soon as they are born,
speaking lies.
4[R] Their poison *is* like the poison of a
serpent; Eccl. 10:11
They are like the deaf cobra *that* stops
its ear,
5 Which will not [R]heed the voice of
charmers, Jer. 8:17
Charming ever so skillfully.

6[R] Break[T] their teeth in their mouth,
O God! Job 4:10 • *Break away*
Break out the fangs of the young lions,
O LORD!
7[R] Let them flow away as waters *which* run
continually; Josh. 2:11; 7:5
When he bends *his bow,*
Let his arrows be as if cut in pieces.

57:title Heb. *Al Tashcheth* **58:title** Heb. *Al Tashcheth*

8 *Let them be* like a snail which melts
away as it goes,
[R] *Like* a stillborn child of a woman, that
they may not see the sun. Job 3:16
9 Before your [R]pots can feel *the burning*
thorns, Eccl. 7:6
He shall take them away [R]as with a
whirlwind, Prov. 10:25
As in His living and burning wrath.
10 The righteous shall rejoice when he sees
the [R]vengeance; Jer. 11:20
[R] He shall wash his feet in the blood of the
wicked, Ps. 68:23
11 [R] So that men will say, Ps. 92:15
"Surely *there is* a reward for the
righteous;
Surely He is God who [R]judges in the
earth." Ps. 50:6; 75:7

PSALM 59

Petition for Deliverance from Enemies

To the Chief Musician. Set to "Do Not Destroy."*
A Michtam of David when Saul sent men, and
they watched the house in order to kill him.

DELIVER me from my enemies, O my
God;
[T] Defend me from those who rise up
against me. Lit. *Set me on high*
2 Deliver me from the workers of iniquity,
And save me from bloodthirsty men.

3 For look, they lie in wait for my life;
[R] The mighty gather against me, Ps. 56:6
Not *for* my transgression nor *for* my sin,
O LORD.
4 They run and prepare themselves
through no fault *of mine*.

Awake to help me, and behold!
5 You therefore, O LORD God of hosts, the
God of Israel,
Awake to punish all the [T]nations;
Do not be merciful to any wicked
transgressors. Selah Gentiles

6 [R] At evening they return, Ps. 59:14
They growl like a dog,
And go all around the city.
7 Indeed, they belch with their mouth;
[R] Swords *are* in their lips; Prov. 12:18
For *they say*, [R]"Who hears?" Ps. 10:11

8 But [R]You, O LORD, shall laugh at them;
You shall have all the [T]nations in
derision. Prov. 1:26 • *Gentiles*
9 I will wait for You, O You his Strength;*
[R] For God *is* my defense. [Ps. 62:2]
10 My God of mercy* shall [R]come to meet
me; Ps. 21:3
God shall let [R]me see *my desire* on my
enemies. Ps. 54:7

11 Do not slay them, lest my people forget;
Scatter them by Your power,
And bring them down,
O Lord our shield.
12 [R] *For* the sin of their mouth *and* the words
of their lips, Prov. 12:13
Let them even be taken in their pride,
And for the cursing and lying *which* they
speak.
13 [R] Consume *them* in wrath, consume *them*,
That they *may* not *be*; Ps. 104:35
And [R]let them know that God rules in
Jacob Ps. 83:18
To the ends of the earth. Selah

14 And [R]at evening they return, Ps. 59:6
They growl like a dog,
And go all around the city.
15 They wander up and down for food,
And howl* if they are not satisfied.

16 But I will sing of Your power;
Yes, I will sing aloud of Your mercy in
the morning;
For You have been my defense
And refuge in the day of my trouble.
17 To You, [R]O my Strength, I will sing
praises; Ps. 18:1
For God *is* my defense,
My God of mercy.

PSALM 60

A Prayer for Deliverance of the Nation

To the Chief Musician. [R]Set to "Lily of the
Testimony."* A Michtam of David. For teaching.
When he fought against Mesopotamia and Syria of
Zobah, and Joab returned and killed twelve
thousand Edomites in the Valley of Salt. Ps. 80

O GOD, [R]You have cast us off; Ps. 44:9
You have broken us down;
You have been displeased;
Oh, restore us again!
2 You have made the earth tremble;
You have broken it;
Heal its breaches, for it is shaking.
3 [R] You have shown Your people hard
things; Ps. 71:20
[R] You have made us drink the wine of
[T]confusion. Jer. 25:15 • *staggering*

4 [R] You have given a banner to those who
fear You, Ps. 20:5
That it may be displayed because of the
truth. Selah
5 [R] That Your beloved may be delivered,

59:title Heb. *Al Tashcheth* **59:9** So with MT, Syr.; some Heb. mss., LXX, Tg., Vg. *my Strength* **59:10** So with Qr.; some Heb. mss., LXX, Vg. *My God, His mercy;* Kt., some Heb. mss., Tg. *O God, my mercy;* Syr. *O God, Your mercy* **59:15** So with LXX, Vg.; MT, Syr., Tg. *spend the night* **60:title** Heb. *Shushan Eduth*

Save *with* Your right hand, and hear
me.[60:12] Ps. 108:6–13

6 God has [R]spoken in His holiness:
"I will rejoice; Ps. 89:35
I will [R]divide [R]Shechem Josh. 1:6 • Gen. 12:6
And measure out the Valley of Succoth.
7 Gilead *is* Mine, and Manasseh *is* Mine;
[R]Ephraim also *is* the [T]helmet for My
head; Deut. 33:17 • Lit. *protection*
[R]Judah *is* My lawgiver. [Gen. 49:10]
8 [R]Moab *is* My washpot; 2 Sam. 8:2
[R]Over Edom I will cast My shoe;
[R]Philistia, shout in triumph because of
Me." 2 Sam. 8:14 • 2 Sam. 8:1

9 Who will bring me *to* the strong city?
Who will lead me to Edom?
10 *Is it* not You, O God, [R]*who* cast us off?
And You, O God, *who* did [R]not go out
with our armies? Ps. 108:11 • Josh. 7:12
11 Give us help from trouble,
For the help of man *is* useless.
12 Through God [R]we will do valiantly,
For *it is* He *who* shall tread down our
enemies.* Num. 24:18

PSALM 61

A Prayer When Overwhelmed

To the Chief Musician. On a stringed instrument.*
A Psalm of David.

HEAR my cry, O God;
Attend to my prayer.
2 From the end of the earth I will cry to You,
When my heart is overwhelmed;
Lead me to the rock that is higher than I.

3 For You have been a shelter for me,
A strong tower from the enemy.
4 I will abide in Your [T]tabernacle forever;
[R]I will trust in the shelter of Your wings.
Selah tent • Ps. 91:4

5 For You, O God, have heard my vows;
You have given *me* the heritage of those
who fear Your name.
6 You will prolong the king's life,
His years as many generations.
7 He shall abide before God forever.
Oh, prepare mercy [R]and truth, *which*
may preserve him! Ps. 40:11

8 So I will sing praise to Your name forever,
That I may daily perform my vows.

PSALM 62

Wait for God

To the Chief Musician. To [R]Jeduthun.
A Psalm of David. 1 Chr. 25:1

TRULY [R]my soul silently *waits* for God;
From Him *comes* my salvation. Ps. 33:20
2 He only *is* my rock and my salvation;
He is my [T]defense; *strong tower*
I shall not be greatly [R]moved. Ps. 55:22

3 How long will you attack a man?
You shall be slain, all of you,
Like a leaning wall and a tottering fence.
4 They only consult to cast *him* down from
his high position;
They [R]delight in lies; Ps. 28:3
They bless with their mouth,
But they curse inwardly. Selah

5 My soul, wait silently for God alone,
For my [T]expectation *is* from Him. *hope*
6 He only *is* my rock and my salvation;
He is my defense;
I shall not be [T]moved. *shaken*
7 [R]In God *is* my salvation and my glory;
The rock of my strength,
And my refuge, *is* in God. [Jer. 3:23]

8 Trust in Him at all times, you people;
Pour out your heart before Him;
God *is* a refuge for us. Selah

9 [R]Surely men of low degree *are* a vapor,
Men of high degree *are* a lie; Is. 40:17
If they are weighed on the scales,
They *are* altogether *lighter* than vapor.
10 Do not trust in oppression,
Nor vainly hope in robbery;
[R]If riches increase, [Luke 12:15]
Do not set *your* heart *on them*.

11 God has spoken once,
Twice I have heard this:
That power *belongs* to God.
12 Also to You, O Lord, *belongs* mercy;
For [R]You [T]render to each one according
to his work. [Matt. 16:27] • *reward*

PSALM 63

Thirst for God

A Psalm of David [R]when he was in the
wilderness of Judah. 1 Sam. 22:5

O GOD, You *are* my God;
Early will I seek You;
[R]My soul thirsts for You; Ps. 42:2
My flesh longs for You
In a dry and thirsty land
Where there is no water.
2 So I have looked for You in the
sanctuary,
To see Your power and Your glory.

3 [R]Because Your lovingkindness *is* better
than life, Ps. 138:2
My lips shall praise You.

60:12 Cf. vv. 5–12 with 108:6–13 **61:title** Heb. *neginah*

4 Thus I will bless You while I live;
I will lift up my hands in Your name.
5 My soul shall be satisfied as with
[T]marrow and [T]fatness,
And my mouth shall praise *You* with
joyful lips. Lit. *fat* • Abundance
6 When I remember You on my bed,
I meditate on You in the *night* watches.
7 Because You have been my help,
Therefore in the shadow of Your wings I
will rejoice.
8 My soul follows close behind You;
Your right hand upholds me.
9 But those *who* seek my life, to destroy
it,
Shall go into the lower parts of the earth.
10 They shall fall by the sword;
They shall be a portion for jackals.
11 But the king shall rejoice in God;
[R]Everyone who swears by Him shall
glory; Deut. 6:13
But the mouth of those who speak lies
shall be stopped.

PSALM 64

A Prayer for God's Protection

To the Chief Musician. A Psalm of David.

HEAR my voice, O God, in my
[T]meditation; *complaint*
Preserve my life from fear of the enemy.
2 Hide me from the secret plots of the
wicked,
From the rebellion of the workers of
iniquity,
3 Who sharpen their tongue like a sword,
[R]And bend *their bows to shoot* their
arrows—bitter words, Ps. 58:7
4 That they may shoot in secret at the
blameless;
Suddenly they shoot at him and do not
fear.
5 They encourage themselves *in* an evil
matter;
They talk of laying snares secretly;
They say, "Who will see them?"
6 They devise iniquities:
"We have perfected a shrewd scheme."
Both the inward thought and the heart of
man are deep.
7 But God shall shoot at them *with* an
arrow;
Suddenly they shall be wounded.
8 So He will make them stumble over their
own tongue;
All who see them shall flee away.
9 All men shall fear,
And shall declare the work of God;
For they shall wisely consider His
doing.
10 [R]The righteous shall be glad in the LORD,
and trust in Him. Ps. 32:11
And all the upright in heart shall glory.

PSALM 65

God's Provision Through Nature

To the Chief Musician. A Psalm of David. A Song.

PRAISE is awaiting You, O God, in Zion;
And to You the vow shall be performed.
2 O You who hear prayer,
[R]To You all flesh will come. [Is. 66:23]
3 Iniquities prevail against me;
As for our transgressions,
You will provide atonement for them.
4 Blessed *is the man* You choose,
And cause to approach *You,*
That he may dwell in Your courts.
[R]We shall be satisfied with the goodness
of Your house, Ps. 36:8
Of Your holy temple.
5 *By* awesome deeds in righteousness You
will answer us,
O God of our salvation,
You who are the confidence of all the
ends of the earth,
And of the far-off seas;
6 Who established the mountains by His
strength,
[R]*Being* clothed with power; Ps. 93:1
7 [R]You who still the noise of the seas,
The noise of their waves, Matt. 8:26
And the tumult of the peoples.
8 They also who dwell in the farthest parts
are afraid of Your signs;
You make the outgoings of the morning
and evening [T]rejoice. *shout for joy*
9 You visit the earth and [R]water it,
You greatly enrich it; Jer. 5:24
The river of God is full of water;
You provide their grain,
For so You have prepared it.
10 You water its ridges abundantly,
You settle its furrows;
You make it soft with showers,
You bless its growth.
11 You crown the year with Your goodness,
And Your paths drip *with* abundance.
12 They drop *on* the pastures of the
wilderness,
And the little hills rejoice on every side.
13 The pastures are clothed with flocks;
The valleys also are covered with grain;
They shout for joy, they also sing.

PSALM 66

Remember What God Has Done

To the Chief Musician. A Song. A Psalm.

MAKE [R]a joyful shout to God, all the earth! Ps. 100:1
2 Sing out the honor of His name;
Make His praise glorious.
3 Say to God,
"How [R]awesome are Your works! Ps. 65:5
[R]Through the greatness of Your power
Your enemies shall submit themselves to You. Ps. 18:44
4 [R]All the earth shall worship You Ps. 117:1
And sing praises to You;
They shall sing praises *to* Your name."
Selah

5 Come and see the works of God;
He is awesome *in His* doing toward the sons of men.
6 [R]He turned the sea into dry *land;*
They went through the river on foot.
There we will rejoice in Him. Ex. 14:21
7 He rules by His power forever;
His eyes observe the nations;
Do not let the rebellious exalt themselves. Selah

8 Oh, bless our God, you peoples!
And make the voice of His praise to be heard,
9 Who keeps our soul among the living,
And does not allow our feet to [T]be moved. *slip*
10 For You, O God, have tested us;
You have refined us as silver is refined.
11 [R]You brought us into the net; Lam. 1:13
You laid affliction on our backs.
12 [R]You have caused men to ride over our heads; Is. 51:23
[R]We went through fire and through water; Is. 43:2
But You brought us out to [T]rich *fulfillment.* *abundance*

13 [R]I will go into Your house with burnt offerings; Ps. 100:4; 116:14, 17–19
[R]I will pay You my vows, [Eccl. 5:4]
14 Which my lips have uttered
And my mouth has spoken when I was in trouble.
15 I will offer You burnt sacrifices of fat animals,
With the sweet aroma of rams;
I will offer bulls with goats. Selah

16 Come *and* hear, all you who fear God,
And I will declare what He has done for my soul.
17 I cried to Him with my mouth,
And He was extolled with my tongue.
18 [R]If I regard iniquity in my heart, Is. 1:15
The Lord will not hear.
19 *But* certainly God [R]has heard *me;*
He has attended to the voice of my prayer. Ps. 116:1, 2

20 Blessed *be* God,
Who has not turned away my prayer,
Nor His mercy from me!

PSALM 67

God Shall Govern the Earth

To the Chief Musician. On stringed instruments.* A Psalm. A Song.

GOD be merciful to us and bless us,
And [R]cause His face to shine upon us,
Selah Num. 6:25
2 That Your way may be known on earth,
Your salvation among all nations.

3 Let the peoples praise You, O God;
Let all the peoples praise You.
4 Oh, let the nations be glad and sing for joy!
For [R]You shall judge the people righteously, [Ps. 96:10, 13; 98:9]
And govern the nations on earth. Selah

5 Let the peoples praise You, O God;
Let all the peoples praise You.
6 *Then* the earth shall yield her increase;
God, our own God, shall bless us.
7 God shall bless us,
And all the ends of the earth shall fear Him.

PSALM 68

God Is the Father of the Fatherless

To the Chief Musician. A Psalm of David. A Song.

LET [R]God arise, Num. 10:35
Let His enemies be scattered;
Let those also who hate Him flee before Him.
2 [R]As smoke is driven away, [Is. 9:18]
So drive *them* away;
[R]As wax melts before the fire, Mic. 1:4
So let the wicked perish at the presence of God.
3 But [R]let the righteous be glad; Ps. 32:11
Let them rejoice before God;
Yes, let them rejoice exceedingly.

4 Sing to God, sing praises to His name;
Extol Him who rides on the clouds,*
[R]By His name YAH, [Ex. 6:3]
And rejoice before Him.

67:title Heb. *neginoth* **68:4** MT *deserts;* Tg. *heavens* (cf. v. 34 and Is. 19:1)

5 [R]A father of the fatherless, a defender of
widows, [Ps. 10:14, 18; 146:9]
Is God in His holy habitation.
6 [R]God sets the solitary in families;
[R]He brings out those who are bound into
prosperity; Ps. 107:4–7 • Acts 12:6–11
But the rebellious dwell in a dry *land.*

7 O God, [R]when You went out before Your
people, Ex. 13:21
When You marched through the
wilderness, Selah
8 The earth shook;
The heavens also dropped *rain* at the
presence of God;
Sinai itself *was moved* at the presence of
God, the God of Israel.
9 [R]You, O God, sent a plentiful rain,
Whereby You confirmed Your
inheritance,
When it was weary. Deut. 11:11
10 Your congregation dwelt in it;
[R]You, O God, provided from Your
goodness for the poor. Deut. 26:5

11 The Lord gave the word;
Great *was* the [T]company of those who
proclaimed *it:* *host*
12 "Kings[R] of armies flee, they flee,
And she who remains at home divides
the [T]spoil. Josh. 10:16 • *plunder*
13 [R]Though you lie down among the
[T]sheepfolds, Ps. 81:6 • Or *saddlebags*
[R]*You will be* like the wings of a dove
covered with silver, Ps. 105:37
And her feathers with yellow gold."
14 When the Almighty scattered kings in it,
It was *white* as snow in Zalmon.

15 A mountain of God *is* the mountain of
Bashan;
A mountain *of many* peaks *is* the
mountain of Bashan.
16 Why do you [T]fume with envy, you
mountains of *many* peaks? Lit. *stare*
[R]*This is* the mountain *which* God desires
to dwell in; [Deut. 12:5]
Yes, the LORD will dwell *in it* forever.

17 [R]The chariots of God *are* twenty
thousand, Deut. 33:2
Even thousands of thousands;
The Lord is among them *as in* Sinai, in
the Holy *Place.*
18 [R]You have ascended on high, Eph. 4:8
[R]You have led captivity captive; Judg. 5:12
You have received gifts among men,
Even *from* [R]the rebellious, [1 Tim. 1:13]
That the LORD God might dwell *there.*

19 Blessed *be* the Lord,
Who daily loads us *with benefits,*
The God of our salvation! Selah

20 Our God *is* the God of salvation;
And [R]to GOD the Lord *belong* escapes
from death. [Deut. 32:39]

21 But [R]God will wound the head of His
enemies, Hab. 3:13
[R]The hairy scalp of the one who still goes
on in his trespasses. Ps. 55:23
22 The Lord said, "I will bring [R]back from
Bashan, Num. 21:33
I will bring *them* back [R]from the depths
of the sea, Ex. 14:22
23 [R]That your foot may crush *them** in
blood, Ps. 58:10
And the tongues of your dogs *may have*
their portion from *your* enemies."

24 They have seen Your [T]procession,
O God, Lit. *goings*
The procession of my God, my King, into
the sanctuary.
25 [R]The singers went before, the players on
instruments *followed* after; 1 Chr. 13:8
Among *them were* the maidens playing
timbrels.
26 Bless God in the congregations,
The Lord, from the fountain of Israel.
27 [R]There *is* little Benjamin, their leader,
The princes of Judah *and* their
[T]company, 1 Sam. 9:21 • *throng*
The princes of Zebulun *and* the princes
of Naphtali.

28 Your God has [R]commanded* your
strength; Is. 26:12
Strengthen, O God, what You have done
for us.
29 Because of Your temple at Jerusalem,
Kings will bring presents to You.
30 Rebuke the beasts of the reeds,
[R]The herd of bulls with the calves of the
peoples, Ps. 22:12
Till everyone [R]submits himself with
pieces of silver. 2 Sam. 8:2
Scatter the peoples *who* delight in war.
31 Envoys will come out of Egypt;
[R]Ethiopia will quickly [R]stretch out her
hands to God. Is. 45:14 • Ps. 44:20

32 Sing to God, you [R]kingdoms of the
earth; [Ps. 67:3, 4]
Oh, sing praises to the Lord, Selah
33 To Him [R]who rides on the heaven of
heavens, *which were* of old!
Indeed, He sends out His voice, a
[R]mighty voice. Ps. 18:10 • Ps. 46:6
34 [R]Ascribe strength to God; Ps. 29:1
His excellence *is* over Israel,
And His strength *is* in the clouds.

68:23 LXX, Syr. Tg., Vg. *you may dip your foot*
68:28 LXX, Syr. Tg., Vg. *Command, O God*

35 O God, [R]*You are* more awesome than
Your holy places. Ps. 76:12
The God of Israel *is* He who gives
strength and power to *His* people.

Blessed *be* God!

PSALM 69

Petition for God to Draw Near

To the Chief Musician. Set to "The Lilies."*
A Psalm of David.

SAVE me, O God!
For [R]the waters have come up to *my*
[T]neck. Jon. 2:5 • Lit. *soul*
2 [R]I sink in deep mire, Ps. 40:2
Where *there is* no standing;
I have come into deep waters,
Where the floods overflow me.
3 [R]I am weary with my crying; Ps. 6:6
My throat is dry;
My eyes fail while I wait for my God.

4 Those who [R]hate me without a cause
Are more than the hairs of my head;
They are mighty who would destroy me,
Being my enemies wrongfully;
Though I have stolen nothing,
I *still* must restore *it*. John 15:25☆

5 O God, You know my foolishness;
And my sins are not hidden from You.
6 Let not those who [T]wait for You, O Lord
GOD of hosts, be ashamed because of
me; Wait in faith
Let not those who seek You be
[T]confounded because of me, O God of
Israel. *dishonored*
7 Because [R]for Your sake I have borne
reproach; Rom. 15:3☆
Shame has covered my face.
8 [R]I have become a stranger to my
brothers, Is. 53:3; Mark 3:21☆
And an alien to my mother's children;
9 [R]Because zeal for Your house has eaten
me up, John 2:17
And the reproaches of those who
reproach You have fallen on me.
10 When I wept *and chastened* my soul
with fasting,
That became my reproach.
11 I also made sackcloth my garment;
I became a byword to them.
12 Those who [T]sit in the gate speak against
me, Sit as judges
And I *am* the song of the drunkards.

13 But as for me, my prayer *is* to You,
O LORD, *in* the acceptable time;
O God, in the multitude of Your mercy,
Hear me in the truth of Your salvation.
14 Deliver me out of the mire,
And let me not sink;
Let me be delivered from those who hate
me,
And out of the deep waters.
15 Let not the floodwater overflow me,
Nor let the deep swallow me up;
And let not the pit shut its mouth on me.

16 Hear me, O LORD, for Your
lovingkindness *is* good;
Turn to me according to the multitude of
Your tender mercies.
17 And do not hide Your face from Your
servant,
For I am in trouble;
Hear me speedily.
18 Draw near to my soul, *and* redeem it;
Deliver me because of my enemies.

19 You know [R]my reproach, my shame, and
my dishonor; Ps. 22:6, 7
My adversaries *are* all before You.
20 [R]Reproach has broken my heart,
And I am full of heaviness; Rom. 15:3☆
[R]I looked *for someone* to take pity, but
there was none; Is. 63:5
And for comforters, but I found none.
21 They also gave me gall for my food,
[R]And for my thirst they gave me vinegar
to drink. Matt. 27:34, 48☆

22 [R]Let their table become a snare before
them, Rom. 11:9, 10
And their well-being a trap.
23 [R]Let their eyes be darkened, so that they
do not see; Is. 6:9, 10
And make their loins shake continually.
24 [R]Pour out Your indignation upon them,
And let Your wrathful anger take hold of
them. [1 Thess. 2:16]
25 [R]Let their dwelling place be desolate;
Let no one live in their tents. Matt. 23:38
26 For they persecute the *ones* [R]You have
struck, [Is. 53:4]
And talk of the grief of those You have
wounded.
27 [R]Add iniquity to their iniquity,
[R]And let them not come into Your
righteousness. [Rom. 1:28] • [Is. 26:10]
28 Let them [R]be blotted out of the book of
the living, [Ex. 32:32]
And not be written with the righteous.

29 But I *am* poor and sorrowful;
Let Your salvation, O God, set me up on
high.
30 [R]I will praise the name of God with a
song, [Ps. 28:7]
And will magnify Him with thanksgiving.
31 [R]*This* also shall please the LORD better
than an ox *or* bull, Ps. 50:13, 14, 23

69:title Heb. *Shoshannim*

Which has horns and hooves.
32 [R]The humble shall see *this and* be glad;
And you who seek God, [R]your hearts
shall live. Ps. 34:2 • Ps. 22:26
33 For the LORD hears the poor,
And does not despise His prisoners.

34 [R]Let heaven and earth praise Him,
The seas [R]and everything that moves in
them. Ps. 96:11 • Is. 55:12
35 [R]For God will save Zion Is. 44:26
And build the cities of Judah,
That they may dwell there and possess
it.
36 Also, [R]the [T]descendants of His servants
shall inherit it, Ps. 102:28 • Lit. *seed*
And those who love His name shall
dwell in it.

PSALM 70

Prayer for the Poor and Needy

To the Chief Musician. *A Psalm* of David.
[R]To bring to remembrance. Ps. 38:title

MAKE *haste*, O God, to deliver me!
Make haste to help me, O LORD!

2 [R]Let them be ashamed and confounded
Who seek my life; Ps. 35:4, 26
Let them be turned back* and confused
Who desire my hurt.
3 [R]Let them be turned back because of their
shame, Ps. 40:15
Who say, "Aha, aha!"

4 Let all those who seek You rejoice and be
glad in You;
And let those who love Your salvation
say continually,
"Let God be magnified!"

5 [R]But I *am* poor and needy; Ps. 72:12, 13
[R]Make haste to me, O God! Ps. 141:1
You *are* my help and my deliverer;
O LORD, do not delay.

PSALM 71

Prayer for the Aged

IN [R]You, O LORD, I put my trust; Ps. 25:2, 3
Let me never be put to shame.
2 [R]Deliver me in Your righteousness, and
cause me to escape; Ps. 31:1
Incline Your ear to me, and save me.
3 [R]Be my strong refuge, Ps. 31:2, 3
To which I may resort continually;
You have given the [R]commandment to
save me, Ps. 44:4
For You *are* my rock and my fortress.
4 [R]Deliver me, O my God, out of the hand of
the wicked, Ps. 140:1, 3
Out of the hand of the unrighteous and
cruel man.
5 For You are my hope, O Lord GOD;
You are my trust from my youth.
6 [R]By You I have been upheld from birth;
You are He who took me out of my
mother's womb. Ps. 22:9, 10
My praise *shall be* continually of You.

7 [R]I have become as a wonder to many,
But You *are* my strong refuge. Is. 8:18
8 Let my mouth be filled *with* Your praise
And with Your glory all the day.

9 Do not cast me off in the time of old age;
Do not forsake me when my strength
fails.
10 For my enemies speak against me;
And those who lie in wait for my life
[R]take counsel together, 2 Sam. 17:1
11 Saying, "God has forsaken him;
Pursue and take him, for *there is* none to
deliver *him*."

12 [R]O God, do not be far from me; Ps. 35:22
O my God, make haste to help me!
13 Let them be [T]confounded *and* consumed
Who are adversaries of my life; *ashamed*
Let them be covered *with* reproach and
dishonor
Who seek my hurt.

14 But I will hope continually,
And will praise You yet more and more.
15 My mouth shall tell of Your
righteousness
And Your salvation all the day,
For I do not know *their* limits.
16 I will go in the strength of the Lord GOD;
I will make mention of Your
righteousness, of Yours only.

17 O God, You have taught me from my
[R]youth; Deut. 4:5; 6:7
And to this *day* I declare Your wondrous
works.
18 Now also [R]when *I am* old and
grayheaded, [Is. 46:4]
O God, do not forsake me,
Until I declare Your strength to *this*
generation,
Your power to everyone *who* is to come.

19 Also [R]Your righteousness, O God, *is* very
high, Ps. 57:10
You who have done great things;
[R]O God, who *is* like You? Ps. 35:10
20 [R]*You*, who have shown me great and
severe troubles, Ps. 60:3
[R]Shall revive me again, Hos. 6:1, 2

70:2 So with MT, LXX, Tg., Vg.; some Heb. mss., Syr. *appalled* (cf. 40:15)

And bring me up again from the depths
of the earth.
21 You shall increase my greatness,
And comfort me on every side.

22 Also with the lute I will praise You—
And Your faithfulness, O my God!
To You I will sing with the harp,
O [R]Holy One of Israel. 2 Kin. 19:22
23 My lips shall greatly rejoice when I sing
to You,
And [R]my soul, which You have
redeemed. Ps. 103:4
24 My tongue also shall talk of Your
righteousness all the day long;
For they are confounded,
For they are brought to shame
Who seek my hurt.

PSALM 72

The Reign of the Messiah

A Psalm [R]of Solomon. Ps. 127:title

GIVE the king Your judgments, O God,
And Your righteousness to the king's Son.
2 [R]He will judge Your people with
righteousness, [Is. 9:7; 11:2–5; 32:1]☆
And Your poor with justice.
3 [R]The mountains will bring peace to the
people, Ps. 85:10
And the little hills, by righteousness.
4 [R]He will bring justice to the poor of the
people; Is. 11:4☆
He will save the children of the needy,
And will break in pieces the oppressor.

5 They shall fear You*
[R]As long as the sun and moon endure,
Throughout all generations. Ps. 89:36☆
6 [R]He shall come down like rain upon the
grass before mowing, Hos. 6:3
Like showers *that* water the earth.
7 In His days the righteous shall flourish,
[R]And abundance of peace, Is. 2:4☆
Until the moon is no more.

8 [R]He shall have dominion also from sea to
sea, Ex. 23:31
And from the River to the ends of the
earth.
9 [R]Those who dwell in the wilderness will
bow before Him, Is. 23:13
[R]And His enemies will lick the
dust. Is. 49:23☆
10 [R]The kings of Tarshish and of the isles
Will bring presents; 2 Chr. 9:21
The kings of Sheba and Seba
Will offer gifts.
11 [R]Yes, all kings shall fall down before Him;
All nations shall serve Him. Is. 49:23☆

12 For He [R]will deliver the needy when he
cries, Job 29:12
The [R]poor also, and *him* who has no
helper. [Ps. 72:4]☆
13 He will spare the poor and needy,
And will save the souls of the needy.
14 He will redeem their life from
oppression and violence;
And [R]precious shall be their blood in His
sight. [Ps. 116:15]☆

15 And He shall live;
And the gold of [R]Sheba will be given to
Him; Is. 60:6☆
Prayer also will be made for Him
continually,
And daily He shall be praised.

16 There will be an abundance of grain in
the earth,
On the top of the mountains;
Its fruit shall wave like Lebanon;
[R]And *those* of the city shall flourish like
grass of the earth. 1 Kin. 4:20
17 [R]His name shall endure forever;
His name shall continue as long as the
sun. [Ps. 89:36]☆
And *men* shall be blessed in Him;
All nations shall call Him blessed.
18 [R]Blessed *be* the LORD God, the God of
Israel, 1 Chr. 29:10
Who only does wondrous things!
19 And [R]blessed *be* His glorious name
forever! [Neh. 9:5]
[R]And let the whole earth be filled *with*
His glory. Num. 14:21
Amen and Amen.

20 The prayers of David the son of Jesse are
ended.

BOOK THREE
Psalms 73—89

PSALM 73

The Perspective of Eternity

A Psalm of [R]Asaph. Ps. 50:title

TRULY God *is* good to Israel,
To such as are pure in heart.

2 But as for me, my feet had almost
stumbled;
My steps had nearly [R]slipped. Job 12:5
3 [R]For I *was* envious of the boastful,
When I saw the prosperity of the
[R]wicked. Ps. 37:1, 7 • Job 21:5–16

72:5 So with MT, Tg.; LXX, Vg. *They shall continue*

4 For *there are* no [T]pangs in their death,
But their strength *is* firm. *pains*
5 They *are* not in trouble *as other* men,
Nor are they plagued like *other* men.
6 Therefore pride serves as their necklace;
Violence covers them *like* a garment.
7 Their eyes bulge* with abundance;
They have more than heart could wish.
8 [R]They scoff and speak wickedly
concerning oppression; Ps. 53:1
They [R]speak [T]loftily. 2 Pet. 2:18 • Proudly
9 They set their mouth [R]against the heavens, Rev. 13:6
And their tongue walks through the earth.

10 Therefore his people return here,
[R]And waters of a full *cup* are drained by them. [Ps. 75:8]
11 And they say, [R]"How does God know?
And is there knowledge in the Most High?" Job 22:13
12 Behold, these *are* the ungodly,
Who are always at ease;
They increase *in* riches.
13 Surely I have cleansed my heart *in* [R]vain, Job 21:15; 35:3
And washed my hands in innocence.
14 For all day long I have been plagued,
And chastened every morning.

15 If I had said, "I will speak thus,"
Behold, I would have been untrue to the generation of Your children.
16 When I thought *how* to understand this,
It *was* too painful for me—
17 Until I went into the sanctuary of God;
Then I understood their end.

18 Surely You set them in slippery places;
You cast them down to destruction.
19 Oh, how they are *brought* to desolation, as in a moment!
They are utterly consumed with terrors.
20 As a dream when *one* awakes,
So, Lord, when You awake,
You shall despise their image.

21 Thus my heart was grieved,
And I was vexed in my mind.
22 [R]I *was* so foolish and ignorant; Ps. 92:6
I was *like* a beast before You.
23 Nevertheless I *am* continually with You;
You hold *me* by my right hand.
24 You will guide me with Your counsel,
And afterward receive me *to* glory.

25 [R]Whom have I in heaven *but You*?
And *there is* none upon earth *that* I desire besides You. [Phil. 3:8]
26 [R]My flesh and my heart fail; Ps. 84:2
But God *is* the [T]strength of my heart and my [R]portion forever. Lit. *rock* • Ps. 16:5

27 For indeed, [R]those who are far from You shall perish; [Ps. 119:155]
You have destroyed all those who desert You for harlotry.
28 But *it is* good for me to [R]draw near to God; [Heb. 10:22]
I have put my trust in the Lord GOD,
That I may declare all Your works.

PSALM 74

Request for God to Remember His Covenant

A Contemplation* of Asaph.

O GOD, why have You cast *us* off forever?
Why does Your anger smoke against the sheep of Your pasture?
2 Remember Your congregation, *which* You have purchased of old,
The tribe of Your inheritance, *which* You have redeemed—
This Mount Zion where You have dwelt.
3 Lift up Your feet to the perpetual desolations.
The enemy has damaged everything in the sanctuary.
4 [R]Your enemies roar in the midst of Your meeting place; Lam. 2:7

73:7 Tg. *face bulges;* LXX, Syr., Vg. *iniquity bulges*
74:title Heb. *Maschil*

73:1 Walking in the Spirit: Confession—An important prerequisite to walking in the Spirit is the confession of sin. Sin must be confessed in order to restore fellowship and to continue receiving God's power (Page 1293—1 John 1:5–10). Confession means that we agree with God about our sin. This involves much more than simply acknowledging the sin. Confession requires an attitude of sorrow for the sin and a willingness to turn from it. It does not mean that we will never commit the same sin again, but it does mean that the attitude of repentance is present.

Confession should be made at the moment the Christian becomes aware of sin. Apart from this rule, moreover, the Scriptures mention two specific times for confession: before the close of the day (Page 1207—Eph. 4:26) and before the Lord's Supper is observed (Page 1175—1 Cor. 11:27–32). Failure to do the latter is a special cause for discipline from the Lord.

Confession of sin should normally involve only those who have knowledge of the sin. This means that private sins should be confessed privately (Page 1293—1 John 1:9); sins between individuals confessed between those involved (Page 981—Matt. 5:23, 24); and public sins confessed publicly (Page 996—Matt. 18:17). Public confession normally is made for the edification of the church (Page 1177— 1 Cor. 14:26).

Now turn to Page 1158—Rom. 12:1, 2: Walking in the Spirit: Yielding.

They set up their banners *for* signs.
5 They seem like men who lift up
Axes among the thick trees.
6 And now they break down its carved
work, all at once,
With axes and hammers.
7 They have set fire to Your sanctuary;
They have defiled the dwelling place of
Your name to the ground.
8 [R]They said in their hearts, Ps. 83:4
"Let us [T]destroy them altogether."
They have burned up all the meeting
places of God in the land. *oppress*

9 We do not see our signs;
[R]*There is* no longer any prophet;
Nor *is there* any among us who knows
how long. Amos 8:11
10 O God, how long will the adversary
[T]reproach? *revile*
Will the enemy blaspheme Your name
forever?
11 [R]Why do You withdraw Your hand, even
Your right hand? Lam. 2:3
Take it out of Your bosom and destroy
them.
12 For [R]God *is* my King from of old,
Working salvation in the midst of the
earth. Ps. 44:4
13 [R]You divided the sea by Your strength;
You broke the heads of the [T]sea serpents
in the waters. Ex. 14:21 • *sea monsters*
14 You broke the heads of Leviathan in
pieces,
And gave him *as* food to the people
inhabiting the wilderness.
15 [R]You broke open the fountain and the
flood; Ex. 17:5, 6
[R]You dried up mighty rivers. Josh. 2:10
16 The day *is* Yours, the night also *is*
[R]Yours; Job 38:12
[R]You have prepared the light and the
sun. Gen. 1:14–18
17 You have [R]set all the borders of the
earth; Acts 17:26
You have made summer and winter.

18 Remember this, *that* the enemy has
reproached, O LORD,
And *that* a foolish people has
blasphemed Your name.
19 Oh, do not deliver the life of Your
turtledove to the wild beast!
Do not forget the life of Your poor
forever.
20 Have respect to the covenant;
For the dark places of the earth are full
of the [T]haunts of cruelty. *homes*
21 Oh, do not let the oppressed return
ashamed!
Let the poor and needy praise Your
name.

22 Arise, O God, plead Your own cause;
Remember how the foolish man
[T]reproaches You daily. *reviles* or *taunts*
23 Do not forget the voice of Your enemies;
The tumult of those who rise up against
You increases continually.

PSALM 75

"God Is the Judge"

To the Chief Musician. Set to [R]"Do Not Destroy."*
A Psalm of Asaph. A Song. Ps. 57:title

WE give thanks to You, O God, we give
thanks!
For Your wondrous works declare *that*
Your name is near.

2 "When I choose the [T]proper time,
I will judge uprightly. *appointed*
3 The earth and all its inhabitants are
dissolved;
I set up its pillars firmly. Selah

4 "I said to the boastful, 'Do not deal
boastfully,'
And to the wicked, [R]'Do not lift up the
horn. [1 Sam. 2:3]
5 Do not lift up your horn on high;
Do *not* speak with a stiff neck.' "

6 For exaltation *comes* neither from the
east
Nor from the west nor from the south.
7 But [R]God *is* the Judge: Ps. 50:6
[R]He puts down one, 1 Sam. 2:7
And exalts another.
8 For [R]in the hand of the LORD *there is* a
cup, Jer. 25:15
And the wine is red;
It is fully mixed, and He pours it out;
Surely its dregs shall all the wicked of
the earth
Drain *and* drink down.

9 But I will declare forever,
I will sing praises to the God of Jacob.

10 "All[R] the [T]horns of the wicked I will also
cut off, Jer. 48:25 • Strength
But [R]the horns of the righteous shall be
[R]exalted." Ps. 89:17; 148:14 • 1 Sam. 2:1

PSALM 76

The Glorious Might of God

To the Chief Musician. On stringed instruments.*
A Psalm of Asaph. A Song.

IN [R]Judah God *is* known; Ps. 48:1, 3
His name *is* great in Israel.
2 In Salem* also is His tabernacle,

75:title Heb. *Al Tashcheth* **76:title** Heb. *neginoth*
76:2 Jerusalem

And His dwelling place in Zion.
3 There He broke the arrows of the bow,
The shield and sword of battle. Selah

4 You *are* more glorious and excellent
[R]*Than* the mountains of prey. Ezek. 38:12
5 The stouthearted were plundered;
[R]They have sunk into their sleep;
And none of the mighty men have found
the use of their hands. Ps. 13:3
6[R] At Your rebuke, O God of Jacob,
Both the chariot and horse were cast
into a dead sleep. Ex. 15:1–21

7 You, Yourself, *are* to be feared;
And [R]who may stand in Your presence
When once You are angry? [Nah. 1:6]
8[R] You caused judgment to be heard from
heaven; Ex. 19:9
The earth feared and was still,
9 When God [R]arose to judgment, [Ps. 9:7–9]
To deliver all the oppressed of the earth.
Selah

10[R] Surely the wrath of man shall praise
You; Rom. 9:17
With the remainder of wrath You shall
gird Yourself.

11[R] Make vows to the LORD your God, and
pay *them;* [Eccl. 5:4–6]
[R]Let all who are around Him bring
presents to Him who ought to be
feared. 2 Chr. 32:22, 23
12 He shall cut off the spirit of princes;
He is awesome to the kings of the earth.

PSALM 77

When Overwhelmed, Remember God's Greatness

To the Chief Musician. [R]To Jeduthun.
A Psalm of Asaph. Ps. 39:title

I CRIED out to God with my voice—
To God with my voice;
And He gave ear to me.
2 In the day of my trouble I sought the Lord;
My hand was stretched out in the night
without ceasing;
My soul refused to be comforted.
3 I remembered God, and was troubled;
I complained, and my spirit was
overwhelmed. Selah

4 You hold my eyelids *open;*
I am so troubled that I cannot speak.
5 I have considered the days of old,
The years of ancient times.
6 I call to remembrance my song in the
night;
I meditate within my heart,
And my spirit makes diligent search.

7 Will the Lord cast off forever?
And will He be favorable no more?
8 Has His mercy ceased forever?
Has *His* promise failed forevermore?
9 Has God forgotten to be gracious?
Has He in anger shut up His tender
mercies? Selah

10 And I said, "This *is* my anguish;
But I will remember the years of the
right hand of the Most High."
11 I will remember the works of the LORD;
Surely I will remember Your wonders of
old.
12 I will also meditate on all Your work,
And talk of Your deeds.
13 Your way, O God, *is* in the sanctuary;
Who *is* so great a God as *our* God?
14 You *are* the God who does wonders;
You have declared Your strength among
the peoples.
15 You have with *Your* arm redeemed Your
people,
The sons of Jacob and Joseph. Selah

16 The waters saw You, O God;
The waters saw You, they were [R]afraid;
The depths also trembled. Ex. 14:21
17 The clouds poured out water;
The skies sent out a sound;
Your arrows also flashed about.
18 The voice of Your thunder *was* in the
whirlwind;
The lightnings lit up the world;
The earth trembled and shook.
19 Your way *was* in the sea,
Your path in the great waters,
And Your footsteps were not known.
20 You led Your people like a flock
By the hand of Moses and Aaron.

PSALM 78

God's Continued Guidance in Spite of Unbelief

A [R]Contemplation* of Asaph. Ps. 74:title

GIVE ear, O my people, *to* my law;
Incline your ears to the words of my
mouth.
2 I will open my mouth in a parable;
I will utter dark sayings of old,
3 Which we have heard and known,
And our fathers have told us.

4[R] We will not hide *them* from their
children, Deut. 4:9; 6:7
[R]Telling to the generation to come the
praises of the LORD, Ex. 13:8, 14
And His strength and His wonderful
works that He has done.

78:title Heb. *Maschil*

5 For [R]He established a testimony in
Jacob, Ps. 147:19
And appointed a law in Israel,
Which He commanded our fathers,
That [R]they should make them known to
their children; Deut. 4:9; 11:19
6 [R]That the generation to come might know
them, Ps. 102:18
The children *who* would be born,
That they may arise and declare *them* to
their children,
7 That they may set their hope in God,
And not forget the works of God,
But keep His commandments;
8 And [R]may not be like their fathers,
[R]A stubborn and rebellious generation,
A generation [R]*that* did not set its heart
aright,
And whose spirit was not faithful to
God. 2 Kin. 17:14 • Ex. 32:9 • Ps. 78:37

9 The children of Ephraim, *being* armed
and [T]carrying bows, Lit. *bow shooters*
Turned back in the day of battle.
10 They did not keep the covenant of God;
They refused to walk in His law,
11 And [R]forgot His works Ps. 106:13
And His wonders that He had shown
them.

12 [R]Marvelous things He did in the sight of
their fathers, Ex. 7—12
In the land of Egypt, [R]*in* the field of
Zoan. Num. 13:22
13 [R]He divided the sea and caused them to
pass through; Ex. 14:21
And [R]He made the waters stand up like a
heap. Ex. 15:8
14 [R]In the daytime also He led them with the
cloud, Ex. 13:21
And all the night with a light of fire.
15 [R]He split the rocks in the wilderness,
And gave *them* drink in abundance like
the depths. Num. 20:11
16 He also brought [R]streams out of the
rock, Num. 20:8, 10, 11
And caused waters to run down like
rivers.

17 But they sinned even more against Him
By [R]rebelling against the Most High in
the wilderness. Heb. 3:16
18 And they tested God in their heart
By asking for the food of their fancy.
19 [R]Yes, they spoke against God:
They said, "Can God prepare a table in
the wilderness? Num. 11:4; 20:3; 21:5
20 [R]Behold, He struck the rock, Num. 20:11
So that the waters gushed out,
And the streams overflowed.
Can He give bread also?
Can He provide meat for His people?"

21 Therefore the LORD heard *this* and [R]was
furious; Num. 11:1
So a fire was kindled against Jacob,
And anger also came up against Israel,
22 Because they did not believe in God,
And did not trust in His salvation.
23 Yet He had commanded the clouds
above,
And opened the doors of heaven,
24 Had rained down manna on them to eat,
And given them of the bread of heaven.
25 Men ate angels' food;
He sent them food to [T]the full. *satiation*

26 [R]He caused an east wind to blow in the
heavens; Num. 11:31
And by His power He brought in the
south wind.
27 He also rained meat on them like the
dust,
Feathered fowl like the sand of the seas;

78:4 History of Israel—The biblical history of Israel covers 1,800 years and represents a marvelous panorama of God's gracious working through promise, miracle, blessing, and judgment. Israel begins as only a promise to Abraham (Page 14—Gen. 12:2). For over four hundred years the people of Israel rely on that promise, especially during the period of bondage to Egypt. Finally, in God's perfect timing, He brings the nation out of Egypt with the greatest series of miracles known in the entire OT (Page 61—Ex. 7—15). This event is called the Exodus, meaning "a going out." Since it constitutes the miraculous birth of the nation, it is to this great act of redemption that the nation always looks back as the foremost example of God's care for His people (Page 586—Ps. 77:14–20; 78:12–55; Page 897—Hos. 11:1).

Once God has redeemed Israel He establishes His covenant with them at Mount Sinai (Page 73—Ex.19:5–8). From that point forward the nation is truly the Lord's possession, and He is their God. The covenant foretells gracious blessings for obedience and severe judgments for disobedience. The rest of Israel's history demonstrates the certainty of that prophecy. Through the periods of conquest, judges, monarchy, exile, restoration, and Gentile domination, Israel is blessed when she obeys and judged when she disobeys. The nation is finally destroyed in A.D. 70, although this event is not described in the New Testament. Many prophecies, however, promise a future redemption for Israel (Page 1158—Rom. 11:26).

The practical value of studying Israel's history is threefold:

a. It sets forth examples to be followed or avoided (Page 1174—1 Cor. 10:6).
b. It shows God's control of all historical events, in that He was able to deal with Israel as He chose (Page 586—Ps. 78).
c. It serves as a model for all ages of God's kindness and mercy toward His people (Page 600—Ps. 103:14).

Now turn to page 189—Deut. 14:2: Purpose of Israel.

28 And He let *them* fall in the midst of their
camp,
All around their dwellings.
29 So they ate and were well filled,
For He gave them their own desire.
30 They were not [T]deprived of their craving;
But [R]while their food *was* still in their
mouths, Lit. *separated* • Num. 11:33
31 The wrath of God came against them,
And slew the stoutest of them,
And struck down the choice *men* of Israel.

32 In spite of this [R]they still sinned,
And [R]did not believe in His wondrous
works. Num. 14:16, 17 • Num. 14:11
33[R] Therefore their days He consumed in
futility, Num. 14:29, 35
And their years in fear.

34[R] When He slew them, then they sought
Him; [Hos. 5:15]
And they returned and sought earnestly
for God.
35 Then they remembered that [R]God *was*
their rock, [Deut. 32:4, 15]
And the Most High God their Redeemer.
36 Nevertheless they [R]flattered Him with
their mouth, Ezek. 33:31
And they lied to Him with their tongue;
37 For their heart was not steadfast with
Him,
Nor were they faithful in His covenant.
38[R] But He, *being* full of [R]compassion,
forgave *their* iniquity, [Num. 14:18–20]
And did not destroy *them*. Ex. 34:6
Yes, many a time [R]He turned His anger
away, [Is. 48:9]
And did not stir up all His wrath;
39 For [R]He remembered [R]that they *were but*
flesh, Job 10:9 • John 3:6
[R] A breath that passes away and does not
come again. [Job 7:7, 16]

40 How often they [R]provoked Him in the
wilderness, Heb. 3:16
And grieved Him in the desert!
41 Yes, again and again they tempted God,
And limited the Holy One of Israel.
42 They did not remember His [T]power:
The day when He redeemed them from
the enemy, Lit. *hand*
43 When He worked His signs in Egypt,
And His wonders in the field of Zoan;
44[R] Turned their rivers into blood, Ex. 7:20
And their streams, that they could not
drink.
45[R] He sent swarms of flies among them,
which devoured them, Ex. 8:24
And frogs, which destroyed them.
46 He also gave their crops to the caterpillar,
And their labor to the locust.
47 He destroyed their vines with hail,
And their sycamore trees with frost.
48 He also gave up their cattle to the hail,
And their flocks to fiery lightning.
49 He cast on them the fierceness of His
anger,
Wrath, indignation, and trouble,
By sending angels of destruction *among
them*.
50 He made a path for His anger;
He did not spare their soul from death,
But gave their life over to the plague,
51 And destroyed all the [R]firstborn in
Egypt, Ex. 12:29, 30
The first of *their* strength in the tents of
Ham.
52 But He [R]made His own people go forth
like sheep, Ps. 77:20
And guided them in the wilderness like a
flock;
53 And He [R]led them on safely, so that they
did not fear; Ex. 14:19, 20
But the sea [R]overwhelmed their
enemies. Ex. 14:27, 28
54 And He brought them to His [R]holy
border, Ex. 15:17
This mountain [R]*which* His right hand
had acquired. Ps. 44:3
55[R] He also drove out the nations before
them, Ps. 44:2
[R] Allotted them an inheritance by survey,
And made the tribes of Israel dwell in
their tents. Josh. 13:7; 19:51; 23:4

56[R] Yet they tested and provoked the Most
High God, Judg. 2:11–13
And did not keep His testimonies,
57 But [R]turned back and acted unfaithfully
like their fathers; Ezek. 20:27, 28
They were turned aside [R]like a deceitful
bow. Hos. 7:16
58[R] For they provoked Him to anger with
their [R]high places,
And moved Him to jealousy with their
carved images. Judg. 2:12 • Deut. 12:2
59 When God heard *this*, He was furious,
And greatly abhorred Israel,
60[R] So that He forsook the tabernacle of
Shiloh, 1 Sam. 4:11
The tent He had placed among men,
61[R] And delivered His strength into
captivity, Judg. 18:30
And His glory into the enemy's hand.
62[R] He also gave His people over to the
sword, 1 Sam. 4:10
And was furious with His inheritance.
63 The fire consumed their young men,
And [R]their maidens were not given in
marriage. Jer. 7:34; 16:9; 25:10
64 Their priests fell by the sword,
And their widows made no lamentation.

65 Then the Lord awoke as *from* sleep,
[R] Like a mighty man who shouts because
of wine. Is. 42:13

66 And He beat back His enemies;
He put them to a perpetual reproach.
67 Moreover He rejected the tent of Joseph,
And did not choose the tribe of Ephraim,
68 But chose the tribe of Judah,
Mount Zion Rwhich He loved. [Ps. 87:2]
69 And He built His Rsanctuary like the heights, 1 Kin. 6:1–38
Like the earth which He has established forever.
70 He also chose David His servant,
And took him from the sheepfolds;
71 From following Rthe ewes that had young
He brought him, [Is. 40:11]
RTo shepherd Jacob His people,
And Israel His inheritance. 2 Sam. 5:2
72 So he shepherded them according to the
Rintegrity of his heart, 1 Kin. 9:4
And guided them by the skillfulness of his hands.

PSALM 79

Avenge the Defilement of Jerusalem

A Psalm of Asaph.

O GOD, the Tnations have come into RYour inheritance; *Gentiles* • Ps. 74:2
Your holy temple they have defiled;
They have laid Jerusalem in heaps.
2 RThe dead bodies of Your servants
They have given *as* food for the birds of the heavens, Jer. 7:33; 19:7; 34:20
The flesh of Your saints to the beasts of the earth.
3 Their blood they have shed like water all around Jerusalem,
And *there was* no one to bury *them*.
4 We have become a reproach to our
Rneighbors, Ps. 44:13
A scorn and derision to those who are around us.

5 RHow long, LORD? Ps. 74:1, 9
Will You be angry forever?
Will Your jealousy burn like fire?
6 RPour out Your wrath on the nations that do not know You, Jer. 10:25
And on the kingdoms that Rdo not call on Your name. Ps. 53:4
7 For they have devoured Jacob,
And laid waste his dwelling place.

8 ROh, do not remember former iniquities against us! Is. 64:9
Let Your tender mercies come speedily to meet us,
For we have been brought very low.
9 Help us, O God of our salvation,
For the glory of Your name;
And deliver us, and provide atonement for our sins,
RFor Your name's sake! Jer. 14:7, 21
10 RWhy should the Tnations say,
"Where *is* their God?" Ps. 42:10 • *Gentiles*
Let there be known among the nations in our sight
The avenging of the blood of Your servants *which has been* shed.

11 Let Rthe groaning of the prisoner come before You; Ps. 102:20
According to the greatness of Your
Tpower Lit. *arm*
Preserve those who are appointed to die;
12 And return to our neighbors Rsevenfold into their bosom Gen. 4:15
Their reproach with which they have reproached You, O Lord.

13 So Rwe, Your people and sheep of Your pasture, Ps. 74:1; 95:7
Will give You thanks forever;
RWe will show forth Your praise to all generations. Is. 43:21

PSALM 80

Israel's Plea for God's Mercy

To the Chief Musician. RSet to "The Lilies."*
A Testimony* of Asaph. A Psalm. Ps. 45:title

GIVE ear, O Shepherd of Israel,
You who lead Joseph Rlike a flock;
You who dwell *between* the cherubim,
Rshine forth! Ps. 77:20 • Deut. 33:2
2 Before REphraim, Benjamin, and Manasseh, Ps. 78:9, 67
Stir up Your strength,
And come *and* save us!

3 RRestore us, O God; Lam. 5:21
RCause Your face to shine, Num. 6:25
And we shall be saved!

4 O LORD God of hosts,
RHow long will You be angry Ps. 79:5
Against the prayer of Your people?
5 RYou have fed them with the bread of tears, Is. 30:20
And given them tears to drink in great measure.
6 You have made us a strife to our neighbors,
And our enemies laugh among themselves.

7 Restore us, O God of hosts;
Cause Your face to shine,
And we shall be saved!

8 You have brought Ra vine out of Egypt;
RYou have cast out the Tnations, and planted it. [Is. 5:1, 7] • Ps. 44:2 • *Gentiles*

80:title Heb. *Shoshannim* • Heb. *Eduth*

9 You prepared *room* for it,
And caused it to take deep root,
And it filled the land.
10 The hills were covered with its shadow,
And the [T]mighty cedars with its
[R]boughs. Lit. *cedars of God* • Lev. 23:40
11 She sent out her boughs to the Sea,*
And her branches to the River.*

12 Why have You [R]broken down her
[T]hedges, Is. 5:5 • *walls or fences*
So that all who pass by the way pluck
her *fruit?*
13 The boar out of the woods uproots it,
And the wild beast of the field devours
it.

14 Return, we beseech You, O God of hosts;
[R]Look down from heaven and see,
And visit this vine Is. 63:15
15 And the vineyard which Your right hand
has planted,
And the branch *that* You made strong
[R]for Yourself. [Is. 49:5]
16 *It is* burned with fire, *it is* cut down;
[R]They perish at the rebuke of Your
countenance. [Ps. 39:11]
17 [R]Let Your hand be upon the man of Your
right hand, Ps. 89:21
Upon the son of man *whom* You made
strong for Yourself.
18 Then we will not turn back from You;
Revive us, and we will call upon Your
name.

19 Restore us, O LORD God of hosts;
Cause Your face to shine,
And we shall be saved!

PSALM 81

God's Plea for Israel's Obedience

To the Chief Musician. [R]On an instrument of Gath.*
A Psalm of Asaph. Ps. 8:title

SING aloud to God our strength;
Make a joyful shout to the God of Jacob.
2 Raise a song and strike the timbrel,
The pleasant harp with the lute.

3 Blow the trumpet at the time of the New
Moon,
At the full moon, on our solemn feast
day.
4 For [R]this *is* a statute for Israel,
A law of the God of Jacob. Num. 10:10
5 This He established in Joseph *as* a
testimony,
When He went throughout the land of
Egypt,
[R]*Where* I heard a language I did not
understand. Ps. 114:1

6 "I removed his shoulder from the burden;
His hands were freed from the baskets.
7 [R]You called in trouble, and I delivered
you; Ex. 2:23; 14:10
[R]I answered you in the secret place of
thunder; Ex. 19:19; 20:18
I [R]tested you at the waters of [T]Meribah.
Selah Ex. 17:6, 7 • Lit. *Strife* or *Contention*

8 "Hear,[R] O My people, and I will admonish
you! [Ps. 50:7]
O Israel, if you will listen to Me!
9 There shall be no [R]foreign god among
you; [Is. 43:12]
Nor shall you worship any foreign god.
10 [R]I *am* the LORD your God, Ex. 20:2
Who brought you out of the land of
Egypt;
Open your mouth wide, and I will fill it.

11 "But My people would not heed My voice,
And Israel would *have* none of Me.
12 [R]So I gave them over to their own
stubborn heart, [Acts 7:42]
To walk in their own counsels.

13 "Oh, that My people would listen to Me,
That Israel would walk in My ways!
14 I would soon subdue their enemies,
And turn My hand against their
adversaries.
15 [R]The haters of the LORD would pretend
submission to Him, Rom. 1:30
But their fate would endure forever.
16 He would [R]have fed them also with the
finest of wheat; Deut. 32:14
And with honey [R]from the rock I would
have satisfied you." Job 29:6

PSALM 82

Rebuke of Israel's Unjust Judges

A Psalm of Asaph.

GOD [R]stands in the congregation of [T]the
mighty; [2 Chr. 19:6] • Heb. *El*, lit. *God*
He judges among [R]the gods.* Ps. 82:6
2 How long will you judge unjustly,
And [R]show partiality to the wicked?
Selah [Deut. 1:17]
3 Defend the poor and fatherless;
Do justice to the afflicted and needy.
4 Deliver the poor and needy;
Free *them* from the hand of the wicked.

5 They do not know, nor do they
understand;
They walk about in darkness;
All the [R]foundations of the earth are
[T]unstable. Ps. 11:3 • *moved*

80:11 The Mediterranean • The Euphrates
81:title Heb. *Al Gittith* **82:1** Judges; Heb. *elohim*, lit. *mighty ones* or *gods*

6 I said, [R]"You *are* gods,* John 10:34
And all of you *are* children of the Most
High.
7 But you shall die like men,
And fall like one of the princes."

8 Arise, O God, judge the earth;
For You shall inherit all nations.

PSALM 83

Plea for God to Destroy Israel's Enemies

A Song. A Psalm of Asaph.

DO[R] not keep silent, O God! Ps. 28:1
Do not hold Your peace,
And do not be still, O God!
2 For behold, [R]Your enemies make a
[T]tumult; Ps. 81:15 • *uproar*
And those who hate You have [T]lifted up
their head. Exalted themselves
3 They have taken crafty counsel against
Your people,
And consulted together [R]against Your
sheltered ones. [Ps. 27:5]
4 They have said, "Come, and [R]let us cut
them off from *being* a nation,
That the name of Israel may be
remembered no more." Jer. 11:19; 31:36

5 For they have consulted together with
one [T]consent; Lit. *heart*
They form a confederacy against You:
6[R] The tents of Edom and the Ishmaelites;
Moab and the Hagrites; 2 Chr. 20:1, 10, 11
7 Gebal, Ammon, and Amalek;
Philistia with the inhabitants of Tyre;
8 Assyria also has joined with them;
They have helped the children of Lot.
Selah

9 Deal with them as *with* Midian,
As *with* [R]Sisera, Judg. 4:15–24; 5:20, 21
As *with* Jabin at the Brook Kishon,
10 Who perished at En Dor,
Who became *as* refuse on the earth.
11 Make their nobles like [R]Oreb and like
Zeeb, Judg. 7:25
Yes, all their princes like [R]Zebah and
Zalmunna, Judg. 8:12–21
12 Who said, "Let us take for ourselves
The pastures of God for a possession."

13[R] O my God, make them like the whirling
dust, Is. 17:13
[R]Like the chaff before the wind! Ps. 35:5
14 As the fire burns the woods,
And as the flame [R]sets the mountains on
fire, Deut. 32:22
15 So pursue them with Your tempest,
And frighten them with Your storm.
16 Fill their faces with shame,
That they may seek Your name, O LORD.
17 Let them be [T]confounded and dismayed
forever; *ashamed*
Yes, let them be put to shame and perish,
18 That they may know that You, whose
[R]name alone *is* the LORD, Ex. 6:3
Are the Most High over all the earth.

PSALM 84

The Joy of Dwelling with God

To the Chief Musician. [R]On an instrument of Gath.*
A Psalm of the sons of Korah. Ps. 8:title

HOW [R]lovely *is* Your tabernacle,
O LORD of hosts! Ps. 27:4; 46:4, 5
2[R] My soul longs, yes, even faints
For the courts of the LORD; Ps. 42:1, 2
My heart and my flesh cry out for the
living God.

3 Even the sparrow has found a home,
And the swallow a nest for herself,
Where she may lay her young—
Even Your altars, O LORD of hosts,
My King and my God.
4 Blessed *are* those who dwell in Your
[R]house; [Ps. 65:4]
They will still be praising You. Selah

5 Blessed *is* the man whose strength *is* in
You,
Whose heart *is* set on pilgrimage.
6 *As they* pass through the Valley [R]of
[T]Baca, 2 Sam. 5:22–25 • Lit. *Weeping*
They make it a spring;
The rain also covers it with pools.
7 They go from strength to strength;
Each one appears before God in Zion.*

8 O LORD God of hosts, hear my prayer;
Give ear, O God of Jacob! Selah
9[R] O God, behold our shield, Gen. 15:1
And look upon the face of Your anointed.

10 For a day in Your courts *is* better than a
thousand.
I would rather [T]be a doorkeeper in the
house of my God *stand at the threshold*
Than dwell in the tents of wickedness.
11 For the LORD God *is* a sun and shield;
The LORD will give grace and glory;
No good *thing* will He withhold
From those who walk uprightly.

12 O LORD of hosts,
Blessed *is* the man who trusts in You!

82:6 Judges; Heb. *elohim*, lit. *mighty ones* or *gods*
84:title Heb. *Al Gittith* **84:7** LXX, Syr., Vg. *The God of gods shall be seen*

PSALM 85

Prayer for Revival

To the Chief Musician. A Psalm [R]of the sons of Korah. Ps. 42:title

LORD, You have been favorable to Your land;
You have [R]brought back the captivity of Jacob. Joel 3:1
2 You have forgiven the iniquity of Your people;
You have covered all their sin. Selah
3 You have taken away all Your wrath;
You have turned from the fierceness of Your anger.

4 [R]Restore us, O God of our salvation,
And cause Your anger toward us to cease. Ps. 80:3, 7
5 [R]Will You be angry with us forever?
Will You prolong Your anger to all generations? Ps. 79:5
6 Will You not [R]revive us again, Hab. 3:2
That Your people may rejoice in You?
7 Show us Your mercy, LORD,
And grant us Your salvation.

8 I will hear what God the LORD will speak,
For He will speak peace
To His people and to His saints;
But let them not turn back to folly.
9 Surely [R]His salvation *is* near to those who fear Him, Is. 46:13
That glory may dwell in our land.

10 Mercy and truth have met together;
Righteousness and peace have kissed.
11 Truth shall spring out of the earth,
And righteousness shall look down from heaven.
12 Yes, the LORD will give *what is* good;
And our land will yield its increase.
13 Righteousness will go before Him,
And shall make His footsteps *our* pathway.

PSALM 86

"Teach Me Your Way, O LORD"

A Prayer of David.

BOW down Your ear, O LORD, hear me;
For I *am* poor and needy.
2 Preserve my [T]life, for I *am* holy; Lit. *soul*
You are my God;
Save Your servant who trusts in You!
3 Be merciful to me, O Lord,
For I cry to You all day long.
4 Rejoice the soul of Your servant,
For to You, O Lord, I lift up my soul.
5 For [R]You, Lord, *are* good, and ready to forgive, [Joel 2:13]
And abundant in mercy to all those who call upon You.
6 Give ear, O LORD, to my prayer;
And attend to the voice of my supplications.
7 In the day of my trouble I will call upon You,
For You will answer me.

8 [R]Among the gods *there is* none like You, O Lord; [Ex. 15:11]
Nor *are there any works* like Your works.
9 All nations whom You have made
Shall come and worship before You, O Lord,
And shall glorify Your name.
10 For You *are* great, and [R]do wondrous things; [Ex. 15:11]
[R]You alone *are* God. Deut. 6:4

11 [R]Teach me Your way, O LORD; Ps. 27:11
I will walk in Your truth;
Unite my heart to fear Your name.
12 I will praise You, O Lord my God, with all my heart,
And I will glorify Your name forevermore.
13 For great *is* Your mercy toward me,
And You have delivered my soul from the depths of Sheol.

14 O God, the proud have risen against me,
And a mob of violent *men* have sought my life,
And have not set You before them.
15 But [R]You, O Lord, *are* a God full of compassion, and gracious, Ex. 34:6
Longsuffering and abundant in mercy and truth.

16 Oh, turn to me, and have mercy on me!
Give Your strength to Your servant,
And save the son of Your maidservant.
17 Show me a sign for good,
That those who hate me may see *it* and be ashamed,
Because You, LORD, have helped me and comforted me.

PSALM 87

Glorious Zion, City of God

A Psalm of the sons of Korah. A Song.

HIS foundation *is* in the holy mountains.
2 The LORD loves the gates of Zion
More than all the dwellings of Jacob.
3 [R]Glorious things are spoken of you,
O city of God! Selah Is. 60:1

4 "I will make mention of [T]Rahab and Babylon to those who know Me;

Behold, O Philistia and Tyre, with
Ethiopia: Egypt
'This *one* was born there.'"

5 And of Zion it will be said,
"This *one* and that *one* were born in her;
And the Most High Himself shall
establish her."
6 The LORD will record,
When He [R]registers the peoples: Is. 4:3
"This *one* was born there." Selah

7 Both the singers and the players on
instruments *say,*
"All my springs *are* in you."

PSALM 88

Crying from Deepest Affliction

A Song. A Psalm of the sons of Korah.
To the Chief Musician. Set to "Mahalath Leannoth."
A Contemplation* of [R]Heman
the Ezrahite. 1 Kin. 4:31

O LORD, [R]God of my salvation, Ps. 27:9
I have cried out day and night before
You.
2 Let my prayer come before You;
[T]Incline Your ear to my cry. Listen to
3 For my soul is full of troubles,
And my life draws near to the grave.
4 I am counted with those who [R]go[T] down
to the pit; [Ps. 28:1] • Die
I am like a man *who has* no strength,
5 [T]Adrift among the dead, Lit. *Free*
Like the slain who lie in the grave,
Whom You remember no more,
And who are cut off from Your hand.

6 You have laid me in the lowest pit,
In darkness, in the depths.
7 Your wrath lies heavy upon me,
And You have afflicted *me* with all [R]Your
waves. Selah Ps. 42:7
8 [R]You have [T]put away my acquaintances
far from me; Job 19:13, 19
You have made me an abomination to
them; *taken away my friends*
I am shut up, and I cannot get out;
9 My eye wastes away because of
affliction.

LORD, I have called daily upon You;
I have stretched out my hands to You.
10 Will You work wonders for the dead?
Shall [T]the dead arise *and* praise You?
Selah *shades, ghosts*
11 Shall Your lovingkindness be declared in
the grave?
Or Your faithfulness in the place of
destruction?
12 Shall Your wonders be known in the
dark?
And Your righteousness in the land of
forgetfulness?

13 But to You I have cried out, O LORD,
And in the morning my prayer comes
before You.
14 LORD, why do You cast off my soul?
Why do You hide Your face from me?
15 I *have been* afflicted and ready to die
from *my* youth;
I suffer Your terrors;
I am distraught.
16 Your fierce wrath has gone over me;
Your terrors have cut me off.
17 They came around me all day long like
water;
They engulfed me altogether.
18 [R]Loved one and friend You have put far
from me, Ps. 31:11; 38:11
And my acquaintances into darkness.

PSALM 89

Claiming God's Promises in Affliction

A Contemplation* of Ethan the Ezrahite.

I WILL sing of the mercies of the LORD
forever;
With my mouth will I make known Your
faithfulness to all generations.
2 For I have said, "Mercy shall be built up
forever;
[R]Your faithfulness You shall establish in
the very heavens." [Ps. 119:89, 90]

3 "I[R] have made a covenant with My
chosen, 1 Kin. 8:16
I have sworn to My servant David:
4 'Your seed I will establish forever,
And build up your throne [R]to all
generations.'" Selah [Luke 1:33]

5 And [R]the heavens will praise Your
wonders, O LORD; [Ps. 19:1]
Your faithfulness also in the assembly of
the saints.
6 [R]For who in the heavens can be compared
to the LORD? Ps. 86:8; 113:5
Who among the sons of the mighty can
be likened to the LORD?
7 [R]God is greatly to be feared in the
assembly of the saints, Ps. 76:7, 11
And to be held in reverence by all *those*
around Him.
8 O LORD God of hosts,
Who *is* mighty like You, O LORD?
Your faithfulness also surrounds You.
9 [R]You rule the raging of the sea; Ps. 65:7
When its waves rise, You still them.
10 [R]You have broken [T]Rahab in pieces, as
one who is slain; Ps. 87:4 • Egypt

88:title Heb. *Maschil* **89:title** Heb. *Maschil*

You have scattered Your enemies with
Your mighty arm.

11[R] The heavens *are* Yours, the earth also *is*
Yours; [Gen. 1:1]
The world and all its fullness, You have
founded them.
12 The north and the south, You have
created them;
[R]Tabor and [R]Hermon rejoice in Your
name. Josh. 19:22 • Josh. 11:17; 12:1
13 You have a mighty arm;
Strong is Your hand, *and* high is Your
right hand.
14 Righteousness and justice *are* the
foundation of Your throne;
Mercy and truth go before Your face.
15 Blessed *are* the people who know the
[R]joyful sound! Ps. 98:6
They walk, O LORD, in the light of Your
countenance.
16 In Your name they rejoice all day long,
And in Your righteousness they are
exalted.
17 For You *are* the glory of their strength,
And in Your favor our horn is exalted.
18 For our shield *belongs* to the LORD,
And our king to the Holy One of Israel.

19 Then You spoke in a vision to Your holy
one,*
And said: "I have given help to *one who
is* mighty;
I have exalted one [R]chosen from the
people. 1 Kin. 11:34
20 I have found My servant David;
With My holy oil I have anointed him,
21[R] With whom My hand shall be
established; Ps. 80:17
Also My arm shall strengthen him.
22 The enemy shall not outwit him,
Nor the son of wickedness afflict him.
23 I will beat down his foes before his face,
And plague those who hate him.

24 "But My faithfulness and My mercy *shall
be* with him,
And in My name his horn shall be exalted.
25 Also I will set his hand over the sea,
And his right hand over the rivers.
26 He shall cry to Me, 'You *are* my Father,
My God, and the rock of my salvation.'
27 Also I will make him *My* firstborn,
The highest of the kings of the earth.
28[R] My mercy I will keep for him forever,
And My covenant shall stand firm with
him. Is. 55:3
29 His seed also I will make *to endure*
forever,
And his throne as the days of heaven.

30 "If his sons forsake My law
And do not walk in My judgments,
31 If they [T]break My statutes *profane*
And do not keep My commandments,
32 Then I will punish their transgression
with the rod,
And their iniquity with stripes.
33 Nevertheless My lovingkindness I will
not utterly take from him,
Nor allow My faithfulness to fail.
34 My covenant I will not break,
Nor [R]alter the word that has gone out of
My lips. Jer. 33:20–22
35 Once I have sworn [R]by My holiness;
I will not lie to David: Amos 4:2
36[R] His seed shall endure forever, [Luke 1:33]
And his throne as the sun before Me;
37 It shall be established forever like the
moon,
Even *like* the faithful witness in the sky."
Selah

38 But You have [R]cast off and [R]abhorred,
You have been furious with Your
anointed. [1 Chr. 28:9] • Deut. 32:19
39 You have renounced the covenant of
Your servant;
[R]You have [T]profaned his crown *by casting
it* to the ground. Lam. 5:16 • *defiled*
40 You have broken down all his hedges;
You have brought his [T]strongholds to
ruin. *fortresses*
41 All who pass by the way plunder him;
He is a reproach to his neighbors.
42 You have exalted the right hand of his
adversaries;
You have made all his enemies rejoice.
43 You have also turned back the edge of
his sword,
And have not sustained him in the battle.
44 You have made his glory cease,
And cast his throne down to the ground.
45 The days of his youth You have
shortened;
You have covered him with shame. Selah

46 How long, LORD?
Will You hide Yourself forever?
Will Your wrath burn like fire?
47 Remember how short my time [R]is;
For what [R]futility have You created all the
children of men? Ps. 90:9 • Ps. 62:9
48 What man can live and not see [R]death?
Can he deliver his life from the power of
the grave? Selah [Eccl. 3:19]

49 Lord, where *are* Your former
lovingkindnesses,
Which You [R]swore to David [R]in Your
truth? [2 Sam. 7:15] • Ps. 54:5
50 Remember, Lord, the reproach of Your
servants—

89:19 So with many Heb. mss.; MT, LXX, Tg., Vg. *holy ones*

[R]*How* I bear in my bosom *the reproach of*
all the many peoples, Ps. 69:9, 19
51[R] With which Your enemies have
reproached, O LORD, Ps. 74:10, 18, 22
With which they have reproached the
footsteps of Your anointed.

52[R] Blessed *be* the LORD forevermore!
Amen and Amen. Ps. 41:13

BOOK FOUR
Psalms 90—106

PSALM 90

"Teach Us to Number Our Days"

A Prayer [R]of Moses the man of God. Deut. 33:1

LORD, [R]You have been our dwelling place*
in all generations. [Ezek. 11:16]
2[R] Before the mountains were brought
forth, [Prov. 8:25, 26]
Or ever You [T]had formed the earth and
the world, Lit. *gave birth to*
Even from everlasting to everlasting, You
are God.

3 You turn man to destruction,
And say, "Return, O children of men."
4[R] For a thousand years in Your sight
Are like yesterday when it is past,
And *like* a watch in the night. 2 Pet. 3:8
5 You carry them away *like* a flood;
[R]*They are* like a sleep. Ps. 73:20
In the morning [R]they are like grass
which grows up: Is. 40:6
6 In the morning it flourishes and grows
up;
In the evening it is cut down and withers.

7 For we have been consumed by Your
anger,
And by Your wrath we are terrified.
8[R] You have set our iniquities before You,
Our [R]secret *sins* in the light of Your
countenance. Ps. 50:21 • Ps. 19:12
9 For all our days have passed away in
Your wrath;
We finish our years like a sigh.
10 The days of our lives *are* seventy years;
And if by reason of strength *they are*
eighty years,
Yet their boast *is* only labor and sorrow;
For it is soon cut off, and we fly away.
11 Who knows the power of Your anger?
For as the fear of You, *so is* Your wrath.
12 So teach *us* to number our days,
That we may gain a heart of wisdom.

13 Return, O LORD!
How long?
And [R]have compassion on Your
servants. Deut. 32:36
14 Oh, satisfy us early with Your mercy,
[R]That we may rejoice and be glad all our
days! Ps. 85:6
15 Make us glad according to the days *in
which* You have afflicted us,
The years *in which* we have seen evil.
16 Let Your work appear to Your servants,
And Your glory to their children.
17[R] And let the beauty of the LORD our God
be upon us, Ps. 27:4
And [R]establish the work of our hands for
us; Is. 26:12
Yes, establish the work of our hands.

PSALM 91

Abiding in "the Shadow of the Almighty"

HE [R]who dwells in the secret place of the
Most High Ps. 27:5; 31:20; 32:7
Shall abide [R]under the shadow of the
Almighty. Ps. 17:8
2[R] I will say of the LORD, "He is my refuge
and my fortress; Ps. 142:5
My God, in Him I will trust."

3 Surely [R]He shall deliver you from the
snare of the fowler* Ps. 124:7
And from the perilous pestilence.
4[R] He shall cover you with His feathers,
And under His wings you shall take
refuge; Ps. 17:8
His truth *shall be your* shield and
[T]buckler. A small shield
5[R] You shall not be afraid of the terror by
night, [Job 5:19]
Nor of the arrow *that* flies by day,
6 *Nor* of the pestilence *that* walks in
darkness,
Nor of the destruction *that* lays waste at
noonday.

7 A thousand may fall at your side,
And ten thousand at your right hand;
But it shall not come near you.
8 Only with your eyes shall you look,
And see the reward of the wicked.

9 Because you have made the LORD, *who is*
[R]my refuge, Ps. 91:2
Even the Most High, [R]your dwelling
place, Ps. 90:1
10[R] No evil shall befall you, [Prov. 12:21]
Nor shall any plague come near your
dwelling;
11[R] For He shall give His angels charge over
you, [Heb. 1:14]
To keep you in all your ways.
12 In *their* hands they shall [T]bear you up,

90:1 LXX, Tg., Vg. *refuge* **91:3** One who catches birds in a trap or snare

[R]Lest you [T]dash your foot against a stone. *lift* • Matt. 4:6 • *strike*
13 You shall tread upon the lion and the cobra,
The young lion and the serpent you shall trample underfoot.

14 "Because he has set his love upon Me, therefore I will deliver him;
I will [T]set him on high, because he has [R]known My name. *exalt him* • [Ps. 9:10]
15 He shall [R]call upon Me, and I will answer him; Ps. 50:15
I *will be* [R]with him in trouble; Is. 43:2
I will deliver him and honor him.
16 With long life I will satisfy him,
And show him My salvation."

PSALM 92

It Is Good to Praise the Lord

A Psalm. A Song for the Sabbath day.

IT *is* [R]good to give thanks to the LORD,
And to sing praises to Your name, O Most High; Ps. 147:1
2 To [R]declare Your lovingkindness in the morning, Ps. 89:1
And Your faithfulness every night,
3 [R]On an instrument of ten strings,
On the lute, 1 Chr. 23:5
And on the harp,
With harmonious sound.
4 For You, LORD, have made me glad through Your work;
I will triumph in the works of Your hands.

5 O LORD, how great are Your works!
[R]Your thoughts are very deep. [Is. 28:29]
6 A senseless man does not know,
Nor does a fool understand this.
7 When [R]the wicked [T]spring up like grass,
And when all the workers of iniquity flourish, Job 12:6 • *sprout*
It is that they may be destroyed forever.

8 But You, LORD, *are* on high forevermore.
9 For behold, Your enemies, O LORD,
For behold, Your enemies shall perish;
All the workers of iniquity shall [R]be scattered. Ps. 68:1

10 But [R]my [T]horn You have exalted like a wild ox; Ps. 89:17 • Strength
I have been anointed with fresh oil.
11 [R]My eye also has seen *my desire* on my enemies; Ps. 54:7
My ears hear *my desire* on the wicked
Who rise up against me.

12 [R]The righteous shall flourish like a palm tree, Ps. 52:8
He shall grow like a cedar in Lebanon.
13 Those who are planted in the house of the LORD
Shall flourish in the courts of our God.
14 They shall still bear fruit in old age;
They shall be fresh and flourishing,
15 To declare that the LORD is upright;
He is my rock, and [R]*there is* no unrighteousness in Him. [Rom. 9:14]

PSALM 93

The Majesty of God

THE [R]LORD reigns, He is clothed with majesty; Ps. 96:10
The LORD is clothed,
[R]He has girded Himself with strength.
Surely the world is established, so that it cannot be [T]moved. Ps. 65:6 • *shaken*
2 [R]Your throne *is* established from of old;
You *are* from everlasting. Ps. 45:6

3 The floods have lifted up, O LORD,
The floods have lifted up their voice;
The floods lift up their waves.
4 [R]The LORD on high *is* mightier Ps. 65:7
Than the noise of many waters,
Than the mighty waves of the sea.

5 Your testimonies are very sure;
Holiness adorns Your house,
O LORD, [T]forever. Lit. *for length of days*

PSALM 94

Vengeance Belongs Only to God

O LORD God, [R]to whom vengeance belongs— [Nah. 1:2]
O God, to whom vengeance belongs, shine forth!
2 Rise up, O Judge of the earth;
Render punishment to the proud.
3 LORD, how long will the wicked,
How long will the wicked triumph?

4 They [R]utter speech, *and* speak insolent things; Ps. 31:18
All the workers of iniquity boast in themselves.
5 They break in pieces Your people, O LORD,
And afflict Your heritage.
6 They slay the widow and the stranger,
And murder the fatherless.
7 [R]Yet they say, "The LORD does not see,
Nor does the God of Jacob [T]understand." Ps. 10:11 • *pay attention*

8 Understand, you senseless among the people;
And *you* fools, when will you be wise?
9 [R]He who planted the ear, shall He not hear? [Ex. 4:11]

He who formed the eye, shall He not
see?
10 He who [T]instructs the [T]nations, shall He
not correct, *disciplines • Gentiles*
He who teaches man knowledge?
11 The LORD [R]knows the thoughts of man,
That they *are* futile. 1 Cor. 3:20
12 Blessed *is* the man whom You [R]instruct,
O LORD, [Heb. 12:5, 6]
And teach out of Your law,
13 That You may give him [T]rest from the
days of adversity, *relief*
Until the pit is dug for the wicked.
14 For the LORD will not [T]cast off His
people, *abandon*
Nor will He forsake His inheritance.
15 But judgment will return to
righteousness,
And all the upright in heart will follow it.
16 Who will rise up for me against the
evildoers?
Who will stand up for me against the
workers of iniquity?
17 Unless the LORD *had been* my help,
My soul would soon have settled in
silence.
18 If I say, "My foot slips,"
Your mercy, O LORD, will hold me up.
19 In the multitude of my anxieties within
me,
Your comforts delight my soul.
20 Shall [R]the throne of iniquity, which
devises evil by law, Amos 6:3
Have fellowship with You?
21 They gather together against the life of
the righteous,
And condemn [R]innocent blood. [Ex. 23:7]
22 But the LORD has been my defense,
And my God the rock of my refuge.
23 He has brought on them their own
iniquity,
And shall [T]cut them off in their own
wickedness; *destroy them*
The LORD our God shall cut them off.

PSALM 95

Call to Worship the Lord

OH come, let us sing to the LORD!
Let us shout joyfully to the Rock of our
salvation.
2 Let us come before His presence with
thanksgiving;
Let us shout joyfully to Him with
[R]psalms. James 5:13
3 For [R]the LORD *is* the great God, [Ps. 96:4]
And the great King above all gods.
4 [T]In His hand *are* the deep places of the
earth; *In His possession*
The heights of the hills *are* His also.
5 The sea *is* His, for He made it;
And His hands formed the dry *land.*
6 Oh come, let us worship and bow down;
Let us kneel before the LORD our Maker.
7 For He *is* our God,
And [R]we *are* the people of His pasture,
And the sheep of His hand. Ps. 79:13

Today, if you will hear His voice:
8 "Do not harden your hearts, as in the
rebellion,*
As *in* the day of trial* in the wilderness,
9 When [R]your fathers tested Me;
They tried Me, though they [R]saw My
work. Ps. 78:18 • Num. 14:22
10 For [R]forty years I was [T]grieved with *that*
generation, Heb. 3:10, 17 • *disgusted*
And said, 'It *is* a people who go astray in
their hearts,
And they do not know My ways.'
11 So [R]I swore in My wrath, Heb. 4:3, 5
'They shall not enter My rest.' "

PSALM 96

Declare the Glory of God

OH, sing to the LORD a new song!
Sing to the LORD, all the earth.
2 Sing to the LORD, bless His name;
Proclaim the good news of His salvation
from day to day.
3 Declare His glory among the [T]nations,
His wonders among all peoples. *Gentiles*
4 For [R]the LORD *is* great and [R]greatly to be
praised; Ps. 145:3 • Ps. 18:3
He *is* to be feared above all gods.
5 For all the gods of the peoples *are* idols,
But the LORD made the heavens.
6 Honor and majesty *are* before Him;
Strength and [R]beauty *are* in His
sanctuary. Ps. 29:2

7 [R]Give[T] to the LORD, O families of the
peoples, Ps. 29:1, 2 • *Ascribe*
Give to the LORD glory and strength.
8 [T]Give to the LORD the glory *due* His
name; *Ascribe*
Bring an offering, and come into His
courts.
9 Oh, worship the LORD [R]in the beauty of
holiness! Ps. 29:2
Tremble before Him, all the earth.

10 Say among the [T]nations, [R]"The LORD
reigns; *Gentiles* • Ps. 93:1; 97:1
The world also is firmly established,
It shall not be [T]moved; *shaken*
He shall judge the peoples righteously."

95:8 Or *Meribah,* lit. *Strife, Contention* • Or *Massah,*
lit. *Trial, Testing*

11[R] Let the heavens rejoice, and let the earth
be glad; Ps. 69:34
Let the sea roar, and all its fullness;
12 Let the field be joyful, and all that *is* in it.
Then all the trees of the woods will
rejoice before the LORD.
13 For He is coming, for He is coming to
judge the earth.
[R] He shall judge the world with
righteousness, [Rev. 19:11]
And the peoples with His truth.

PSALM 97
Rejoice! The Lord Reigns!

THE LORD [R]reigns; [Ps. 96:10]
Let the earth rejoice;
Let the multitude of isles be glad!

2 Clouds and darkness surround Him;
[R] Righteousness and justice *are* the
foundation of His throne. [Ps. 89:14]
3[R] A fire goes before Him, Ps. 18:8
And burns up His enemies round about.
4 His lightnings light the world;
The earth sees and trembles.
5[R] The mountains melt like wax at the
presence of the LORD, Mic. 1:4
At the presence of the Lord of the whole
earth.
6 The heavens declare His righteousness,
And all the peoples see His glory.

7[R] Let all be put to shame who serve carved
images, [Ex. 20:4]
Who boast of idols.
[R] Worship Him, all *you* gods. [Heb. 1:6]
8 Zion hears and is glad,
And the daughters of Judah rejoice
Because of Your judgments, O LORD.
9 For You, LORD, *are* [R]most high above all
the earth; Ps. 83:18
You are exalted far above all gods.

10 You who love the LORD, [R]hate evil!
[R] He preserves the souls of His saints;
[R] He delivers them out of the hand of the
wicked. [Ps. 34:14] • Prov. 2:8 • Ps. 37:40
11 Light is sown for the righteous,
And gladness for the upright in heart.
12[R] Rejoice in the LORD, you righteous,
[R] And give thanks at the remembrance of
His holy name.* Ps. 33:1 • Ps. 30:4

PSALM 98
Sing a New Song to the Lord

A Psalm.

OH, [R]sing to the LORD a new song! Is. 42:10
For He has [R]done marvelous things;
His right hand and His holy arm have
gained Him the victory. Ex. 15:11
2[R] The LORD has made known His
salvation; Is. 52:10
[R] His righteousness He has revealed in the
sight of the nations. Is. 62:2
3 He has remembered His mercy and His
faithfulness to the house of Israel;
[R] All the ends of the earth have seen the
salvation of our God. Luke 3:6

4 Shout joyfully to the LORD, all the earth;
Break forth in song, rejoice, and sing
praises.
5 Sing to the LORD with the harp,
With the harp and the sound of a psalm,
6 With trumpets and the sound of a horn;
Shout joyfully before the LORD, the King.

7 Let the sea roar, and all its fullness,
The world and those who dwell in it;
8 Let the rivers clap *their* hands;
Let the hills be joyful together before the
LORD,
9[R] For He is coming to judge the earth.
With righteousness He shall judge the
world, [Ps. 96:10, 13]
And the peoples with equity.

PSALM 99
"Exalt the LORD Our God"

THE LORD reigns;
Let the peoples tremble!
[R] He dwells *between* the cherubim;
Let the earth be moved! Ex. 25:22
2 The LORD *is* great in Zion,
And He *is* high above all the peoples.
3 Let them praise Your great and awesome
name—
[T] He *is* holy. Or *It*
4 The King's strength also loves justice;
You have established equity;
You have executed justice and
righteousness in Jacob.
5 Exalt the LORD our God,
And worship at His footstool—
He *is* holy.

6 Moses and Aaron were among His priests,
And Samuel was among those who
[R]called upon His name; 1 Sam. 7:9
They called upon the LORD, and He
answered them.
7 He spoke to them in the cloudy pillar;
They kept His testimonies and the
[T]ordinance He gave them. *statute*

8 You answered them, O LORD our God;
You were to them God-Who-Forgives,
Though You took vengeance on their
deeds.

97:12 Or *His holiness*

9 Exalt the LORD our God,
And worship at His holy hill;
For the LORD our God *is* holy.

PSALM 100

"Serve the LORD with Gladness"

[R]A Psalm of Thanksgiving. Ps. 145:title

MAKE [R]a joyful shout to the LORD, [T]all
you lands! Ps. 95:1 • Lit. *all the earth*
2 Serve the LORD with gladness;
Come before His presence with singing.
3 Know that the LORD, He *is* God;
[R]*It is* He *who* has made us, and not we
ourselves;* [Eph. 2:10]
[R]*We are* His people and the sheep of His
pasture. Ezek. 34:30, 31

4[R]Enter into His gates with thanksgiving,
And into His courts with praise.
Be thankful to Him, *and* bless His
name. Ps. 66:13; 116:17–19
5 For the LORD *is* good;
[R]His mercy *is* everlasting, Ps. 136:1
And His truth *endures* to all generations.

PSALM 101

Commitments of a Holy Life

A Psalm of David.

I WILL sing of mercy and justice;
To You, O LORD, I will sing praises.

2 I will behave wisely in a [T]perfect way.
Oh, when will You come to me?
I will [R]walk within my house with a
perfect heart. *blameless* • 1 Kin. 11:4

3 I will set nothing [T]wicked before my
eyes; *worthless*
I hate the work of those [R]who fall away;
It shall not cling to me. Josh. 23:6
4 A perverse heart shall depart from me;
I will not know wickedness.

5 Whoever secretly slanders his neighbor,
Him I will destroy;
[R]The one who has a haughty look and a
proud heart, Prov. 6:17
Him I will not endure.

6 My eyes *shall be* on the faithful of the
land,
That they may dwell with me;
He who walks in a [T]perfect way,
He shall serve me. *blameless*
7 He who works deceit shall not dwell
within my house;
He who tells lies shall not [T]continue in
my presence. Lit. *be established*
8[R]Early I will destroy all the wicked of the
land, Jer. 21:12
That I may cut off all the evildoers [R]from
the city of the LORD. Ps. 48:2, 8

PSALM 102

Prayer of an Overwhelmed Saint

A Prayer of the afflicted, when he is overwhelmed
and pours out his complaint before the LORD.

HEAR my prayer, O LORD,
And let my cry come to You.
2[R]Do not hide Your face from me in the day
of my trouble; Ps. 27:9; 69:17
Incline Your ear to me;
In the day that I call, answer me
speedily.

3 For my days are consumed like smoke,
And my bones are burned like a hearth.
4 My heart is stricken and withered like
grass,
So that I forget to eat my bread.
5 Because of the sound of my groaning
My bones cling to my [T]skin. *flesh*
6 I am like a pelican of the wilderness;
I am like an owl of the desert.
7 I lie awake,
And am like a sparrow alone on the
housetop.

8 My enemies reproach me all day long;
Those who deride me swear an oath
against me.
9 For I have eaten ashes like bread,
And mingled my drink with weeping,
10 Because of Your indignation and Your
wrath;
For You have lifted me up and cast me
away.
11 My days *are* like a shadow that
lengthens,
And I wither away like grass.

12 But You, O LORD, shall endure forever,
And the remembrance of Your name to
all generations.
13 You will arise *and* have mercy on Zion;
For the time to favor her,
Yes, the set time, has come.
14 For Your servants take pleasure in her
stones,
And show favor to her dust.
15 So the [T]nations shall [R]fear the name of
the LORD, Gentiles • 1 Kin. 8:43
And all the kings of the earth Your glory.
16 For the LORD shall build up Zion;
[R]He shall appear in His glory. [Is. 60:1, 2]
17[R]He shall regard the prayer of the
destitute, Neh. 1:6
And shall not despise their prayer.

100:3 So with Kt., LXX, Vg.; Qr., many Heb. mss., Tg. *we are His*

18 This will be [R]written for the generation
to come, [Rom. 15:4]
That [R]a people yet to be created may
praise the LORD. Ps. 22:31
19 For He [R]looked down from the height of
His sanctuary; Deut. 26:15
From heaven the LORD viewed the earth,
20 To hear the groaning of the prisoner,
To release those appointed to death,
21 To [R]declare the name of the LORD in
Zion, Ps. 22:22
And His praise in Jerusalem,
22 When the peoples are gathered together,
And the kingdoms, to serve the LORD.

23 He weakened my strength in the way;
He [R]shortened my days. Job 21:21
24 [R]I said, "O my God, Is. 38:10
Do not take me away in the midst of my
days;
[R]Your years *are* throughout all
generations. [Ps. 90:2]
25 [R]Of old You laid the foundation of the
earth, [Heb. 1:10–12]
And the heavens *are* the work of Your
hands.
26 [R]They will perish, but You will [T]endure;
Yes, they will all grow old like a
garment; Is. 34:4; 51:6 • *continue*
Like a cloak You will change them,
And they will be changed.
27 But [R]You *are* the same, [Mal. 3:6]
And Your years will have no end.
28 [R]The children of Your servants will
continue, Ps. 69:36
And their descendants will be
established before You."

PSALM 103

"Bless the LORD"

A Psalm of David.

BLESS [R]the LORD, O my soul; Ps. 104:1, 35
And all that is within me, *bless* His holy
name!
2 Bless the LORD, O my soul,
And forget not all His benefits:
3 Who forgives all your iniquities,
Who heals all your diseases,
4 Who redeems your life from destruction,
[R]Who crowns you with lovingkindness
and tender mercies, [Ps. 5:12]
5 Who satisfies your mouth with good
things,
So that [R]your youth is renewed like the
eagle's. [Is. 40:31]

6 The LORD executes righteousness
And justice for all who are oppressed.
7 He made known His ways to Moses,
His acts to the children of Israel.
8 The LORD *is* merciful and gracious,
Slow to anger, and abounding in mercy.
9 He will not always strive *with us*,
Nor will He keep *His anger* forever.
10 [R]He has not dealt with us according to
our sins, [Ezra 9:13]
Nor punished us according to our
iniquities.

11 For as the heavens are high above the
earth,
So great is His mercy toward those who
fear Him;
12 As far as the east is from the west,
So far has He [R]removed our
transgressions from us. [Is. 38:17]
13 As a father pities *his* children,
So the LORD pities those who fear Him.
14 For He knows our frame;
He remembers that we *are* dust.

15 *As for* man, his days *are* like grass;
As a flower of the field, so he flourishes.
16 [R]For the wind passes over it, and it is
[T]gone, [Is. 40:7] • *not*
And its place remembers it no more.*
17 But the mercy of the LORD *is* from
everlasting to everlasting
On those who fear Him,
And His righteousness to children's
children,
18 To such as keep His covenant,
And to those who remember His
commandments to do them.

19 The LORD has established His throne in
heaven,
And His kingdom rules over all.
20 [R]Bless the LORD, you His angels,
Who excel in strength, who [R]do His
word, Ps. 148:2 • [Matt. 6:10]
Heeding the voice of His word.
21 Bless the LORD, all *you* His hosts,
[R]*You* [T]ministers of His, who do His
pleasure. [Heb. 1:14] • *servants*
22 Bless the LORD, all His works,
In all places of His dominion.

Bless the LORD, O my soul!

PSALM 104

Psalm Rehearsing Creation

BLESS [R]the LORD, O my soul! Ps. 103:1

O LORD my God, You are very great:
You are clothed with honor and majesty,
2 Who cover *Yourself* with light as *with* a
garment,
Who stretch out the heavens like a
curtain.

103:16 Cf. Job 7:10

3 [R]He lays the beams of His upper
chambers in the waters, [Amos 9:6]
Who makes the clouds His chariot,
Who walks on the wings of the wind,

4 Who makes His angels spirits,
His [T]ministers a flame of fire. *servants*

5 *You who* [T]laid the foundations of the
earth, Lit. *founded the earth upon her bases*
So *that* it should not be moved forever,
6 You [R]covered it with the deep as *with* a
garment; Gen. 1:6
The waters stood above the mountains.
7 At Your rebuke they fled;
At the voice of Your thunder they
hastened away.
8 They went up over the mountains;
They went down into the valleys,
To the place which You founded for them.
9 You have [R]set a boundary that they may
not pass over, [Jer. 5:22]
[R]That they may not return to cover the
earth. Gen. 9:11–15

10 He sends the springs into the valleys;
They flow among the hills.
11 They give drink to every beast of the
field;
The wild donkeys quench their thirst.
12 By them the birds of the heavens have
their home;
They sing among the branches.
13 [R]He waters the hills from His upper
chambers; Ps. 147:8
The earth is satisfied with [R]the fruit of
Your works. Jer. 10:13

14 [R]He causes the grass to grow for the
cattle, Gen. 1:29
And vegetation for the service of man,
That he may bring forth [R]food from the
earth, Job 28:5
15 And [R]wine *that* makes glad the heart of
man, Judg. 9:13
Oil to make *his* face shine,
And bread *which* strengthens man's
heart.
16 The trees of the LORD are full *of sap,*
The cedars of Lebanon which He
planted,
17 Where the birds make their nests;
The stork has her home in the fir trees.
18 The high hills *are* for the wild goats;
The cliffs are a refuge for the rock
badgers.*

19 He appointed the moon for seasons;
The [R]sun knows its going down. Ps. 19:6
20 [R]You make darkness, and it is night,
In which all the beasts of the forest
creep about. [Is. 45:7]
21 [R]The young lions roar after their prey,
And seek their food from God. Job 38:39
22 *When* the sun rises, they gather together
And lie down in their dens.
23 Man goes out to [R]his work Gen. 3:19
And to his labor until the evening.

24 O LORD, how manifold are Your works!
In wisdom You have made them all.
The earth is full of Your possessions—
25 This great and wide sea,
In which *are* innumerable teeming things,
Living things both small and great.
26 There the ships sail about;
There is that [R]Leviathan Job 41:1
Which You have made to play there.

27 [R]These all wait for You, Ps. 136:25
That You may give *them* their food in
due season.
28 *What* You give them they gather in;
You open Your hand, they are filled with
good.
29 You hide Your face, they are troubled;
[R]You take away their breath, they die and
return to their dust. Job 34:15

104:18 Or *rock hyraxes* (cf. Lev. 11:5)

104:4 Angels: Spirit Beings—The term "angel" denotes a class of beings who are not usually perceived by human senses. Angels were created at some point before the physical universe (Page 624—Ps. 148:2, 5). They apparently do not age or die. They are compared to spirit and fire because they have no bodies (Page 601—Ps. 104:4; Page 1258—Heb. 1:7). However, angels do appear in some sort of visible bodies frequently in the pages of Scripture to serve as God's messengers (Page 1043—Luke 2:8–14) or to intervene in human events on behalf of God or His people (Page 374—2 Kin. 6:13–17). They always appear as males. They do not marry or reproduce (Page 1001—Matt. 22:30). They are wiser and stronger than humans (Page 1004—Matt. 24:36; Page 1232—2 Thess. 1:7), but they cannot comprehend redemption (Page 1279—1 Pet. 1:12). People do not become angels when they die (Page 1267—Heb. 12:22, 23). Humans were created lower than the angels (Page 549—Ps. 8:5) but will judge angels in the age to come (Page 1170—1 Cor. 6:3).

All angels are not alike. There seems to be rank among angels. Satan was an exalted angel before he rebelled against God (Page 695—Is. 14:12–15). A few angels are called archangels or identified with personal names (Page 883—Dan. 9:21; 10:13; Page 1041—Luke 1:19; Page 1228—1 Thess. 4:16; Page 1306—Jude 9). The seraphim and cherubim probably are angelic beings of rank (Page 687—Is. 6:2–7; Page 826—Ezek. 10). When they are visible, their appearance is distinctive from humankind and radiantly glorious. Cherubim and seraphim are the only angelic beings described as having wings, although Gabriel was said to fly (Page 883—Dan. 9:21).

Now turn to Page 1258—Heb. 1:14: Angels: Messengers and Servants.

30[R] You send forth Your Spirit, they are
created; Is. 32:15
And You renew the face of the earth.

31 May the glory of the LORD endure forever;
May the LORD rejoice in His works.
32 He looks on the earth, and it trembles;
He touches the hills, and they smoke.

33[R] I will sing to the LORD as long as I live;
I will sing praise to my God while I have
my being. Ps. 63:4
34 May my [R]meditation be sweet to Him;
I will be glad in the LORD. Ps. 19:14
35 May [R]sinners be consumed from the
earth, Ps. 37:38
And the wicked be no more.

Bless the LORD, O my soul!
[T]Praise the LORD! Heb. *Hallelujah*

PSALM 105

Remember, God Keeps His Promises

OH, [R]give thanks to the LORD! Is. 12:4
Call upon His name;
[R]Make known His deeds among the
peoples! Ps. 145:12
2 Sing to Him, sing psalms to Him;
Talk of all His wondrous works!
3 Glory in His holy name;
Let the hearts of those rejoice who seek
the LORD!
4 Seek the LORD and His strength;
[R]Seek His face evermore! Ps. 27:8
5[R] Remember His marvelous works which
He has done, Ps. 77:11
His wonders, and the judgments of His
mouth,
6 O seed of Abraham His servant,
You children of Jacob, His chosen ones!

7 He *is* the LORD our God;
His judgments *are* in all the earth.
8 He [R]remembers His covenant forever,
The word *which* He commanded, for a
thousand generations, Luke 1:72
9[R] *The covenant* which He made with
Abraham, Gen. 17:2
And His oath to Isaac,
10 And confirmed it to Jacob for a statute,
To Israel *as* an everlasting covenant,
11 Saying, [R]"To you I will give the land of
Canaan Gen. 13:15; 15:18
As the allotment of your inheritance,"
12 When they were few in number,
Indeed very few, and strangers in it.

13 When they went from one nation to
another,
From *one* kingdom to another people,
14 He permitted no one to do them wrong;
Yes, He rebuked kings for their sakes,
15 *Saying*, "Do not touch My anointed ones,
And do My prophets no harm."

16 Moreover [R]He called for a famine in the
land; Gen. 41:54
He destroyed all the provision of bread.
17 He sent a man before them—
Joseph—*who* was sold as a slave.
18[R] They hurt his feet with fetters,
He was laid in irons. Gen. 40:15
19 Until the time that his word came to pass,
The word of the LORD tested him.
20 The king sent and released him,
The ruler of the people let him go free.
21 He made him lord of his house,
And ruler of all his possessions,
22 To bind his princes at his pleasure,
And teach his elders wisdom.

23[R] Israel also came into Egypt, Gen. 46:6
And Jacob dwelt in the land of Ham.
24[R] He increased His people greatly,
And made them stronger than their
enemies. Ex. 1:7, 9
25[R] He turned their heart to hate His
people, Ex. 1:8–10; 4:21
To deal craftily with His servants.

26[R] He sent Moses His servant, Ex. 3:10
And Aaron whom He had chosen.
27 They performed His signs among them,
And wonders in the land of Ham.
28 He sent darkness, and made *it* dark;
And they did not rebel against His word.
29[R] He turned their waters into blood,
And killed their fish. Ex. 7:20, 21
30[R] Their land abounded with frogs, Ex. 8:6
Even in the chambers of their kings.
31[R] He spoke, and there came swarms of
flies, Ex. 8:16, 17
And lice in all their territory.
32[R] He gave them hail for rain, Ex. 9:23–25
And flaming fire in their land.
33[R] He struck their vines also, and their fig
trees, Ps. 78:47
And splintered the trees of their
territory.
34[R] He spoke, and locusts came, Ex. 10:4
Young locusts without number,
35 And ate up all the vegetation in their
land,
And devoured the fruit of their ground.
36[R] He also destroyed all the firstborn in
their land, Ex. 12:29; 13:15
[R]The first of all their strength. Gen. 49:3

37[R] He also brought them out with silver and
gold, Ex. 12:35, 36
And *there was* none feeble among His
tribes.
38[R] Egypt was glad when they departed,
For the fear of them had fallen upon
them. Ex. 12:33

39 He spread a cloud for a covering,
And fire to give light in the night.
40[R] *The people* asked, and He brought quail,
And [R]satisfied them with the bread of heaven. Ex. 16:12 • Ps. 78:24
41[R] He opened the rock, and water gushed out; Ex. 17:6
It ran in the dry places *like* a river.

42 For He remembered [R]His holy promise,
And Abraham His servant. Gen. 15:13, 14
43 He brought out His people with joy,
His chosen ones with gladness.
44[R] He gave them the lands of the [T]Gentiles,
And they inherited the labor of the nations, Josh. 11:16–23; 13:7 • *nations*
45[R] That they might observe His statutes
And keep His laws. [Deut. 4:1, 40]

[T]Praise the LORD! Heb. *Hallelujah*

PSALM 106

"We Have Sinned"

PRAISE[T] the LORD! Heb. *Hallelujah*
[R]Oh, give thanks to the LORD, for *He is* good! 1 Chr. 16:34, 41
For His mercy *endures* forever.

2 Who can [T]utter the mighty acts of the LORD? *express*
Who can declare all His praise?
3 Blessed *are* those who keep justice,
And he who [R]does* righteousness at [R]all times! Ps. 15:2 • [Gal. 6:9]

4 Remember me, O LORD, with the favor
You have toward Your people.
Oh, visit me with Your salvation,
5 That I may see the benefit of Your chosen ones,
That I may rejoice in the gladness of Your nation,
That I may glory with Your inheritance.

6[R] We have sinned with our fathers,
We have committed iniquity, [Dan. 9:5]
We have done wickedly.
7 Our fathers in Egypt did not understand Your wonders;
They did not remember the multitude of Your mercies,
But rebelled by the sea—the Red Sea.

8 Nevertheless He saved them for His name's sake,
[R]That He might make His mighty power known. Ex. 9:16
9[R] He rebuked the Red Sea also, and it dried up; Ex. 14:21
So [R]He led them through the depths,
As through the wilderness. Is. 63:11–13
10 He [R]saved them from the hand of him who hated *them*, Ex. 14:30
And redeemed them from the hand of the enemy.
11 The waters covered their enemies;
There was not one of them left.
12[R] Then they believed His words;
They sang His praise. Ex. 15:1–21

13[R] They soon forgot His works; Ex. 15:24
They did not wait for His counsel,
14[R] But lusted exceedingly in the wilderness, 1 Cor. 10:6
And tested God in the desert.
15 And He gave them their request,
But sent leanness into their soul.

16 When they envied Moses in the camp,
And Aaron the saint of the LORD,
17[R] The earth opened up and swallowed Dathan, Deut. 11:6
And covered the faction of Abiram.
18 A fire was kindled in their company;
The flame burned up the wicked.

19[R] They made a calf in Horeb, Ex. 32:1–4
And worshiped the molded image.
20 Thus they changed their glory
Into the image of an ox that eats grass.
21 They forgot God their Savior,
Who had done great things in Egypt,
22 Wondrous works in the land of Ham,
Awesome things by the Red Sea.
23[R] Therefore He said that He would destroy them, Ex. 32:10
Had not Moses His chosen one [R]stood before Him in the breach, Ezek. 22:30
To turn away His wrath, lest He destroy *them*.

24 Then they despised the pleasant land;
They did not believe His word,
25 But complained in their tents,
And did not heed the voice of the LORD.
26[R] Therefore He raised up His hand *in an oath* against them, Ezek. 20:15, 16
To overthrow them in the wilderness,
27[R] To overthrow their descendants among the [T]nations, Lev. 26:33 • *Gentiles*
And to scatter them in the lands.

28[R] They joined themselves also to Baal of Peor, Hos. 9:10
And ate sacrifices made to the dead.
29 Thus they provoked *Him* to anger with their deeds,
And the plague broke out among them.
30 Then Phinehas stood up and intervened,
And the plague was stopped.
31 And that was accounted to him [R]for righteousness Num. 25:11–13
To all generations forevermore.

106:3 LXX, Syr., Tg., Vg. *those who do*

32 [R]They angered *Him* also at the waters of strife,* Num. 20:3–13
[R]So that it went ill with Moses on account of them; Deut. 1:37; 3:26
33 Because they rebelled against His Spirit,
So that he spoke rashly with his lips.

34 They did not destroy the peoples,
[R]Concerning whom the LORD had commanded them, [Deut. 7:2, 16]
35 [R]But they mingled with the Gentiles
And learned their works; Judg. 3:5, 6
36 [R]They served their idols, Judg. 2:12
Which became a snare to them.
37 They even sacrificed their sons
And their daughters to demons,
38 And shed innocent blood,
The blood of their sons and daughters,
Whom they sacrificed to the idols of Canaan;
And the land was polluted with blood.
39 Thus they [T]were [R]defiled by their own works, *became unclean* • Ezek. 20:18
And [R]played[T] the harlot by their own deeds. [Lev. 17:7] • Were unfaithful

40 Therefore [R]the wrath of the LORD was kindled against His people, Judg. 2:14
So that He abhorred [R]His own inheritance. [Deut. 9:29; 32:9]
41 And [R]He gave them into the hand of the Gentiles, Judg. 2:14
And those who hated them ruled over them.
42 Their enemies also oppressed them,
And they were brought into subjection under their hand.
43 Many times He delivered them;
But they rebelled in their counsel,
And were brought low for their iniquity.

44 Nevertheless He regarded their affliction,
When [R]He heard their cry; Judg. 3:9
45 [R]And for their sake He remembered His covenant, [Lev. 26:41, 42]
And [R]relented according to the multitude of His mercies. Judg. 2:18
46 [R]He also made them to be pitied Ezra 9:9
By all those who carried them away captive.

47 Save us, O LORD our God,
And gather us from among the Gentiles,
To give thanks to Your holy name,
To triumph in Your praise.

48 Blessed *be* the LORD God of Israel
From everlasting to everlasting!
And let all the people say, "Amen!"

[T]Praise the LORD! Heb. *Hallelujah*

BOOK FIVE
Psalms 107—150

PSALM 107

God Satisfies the Longing Soul

OH, [R]give thanks to the LORD, for *He is* good! Ps. 106:1
For His mercy *endures* forever.
2 Let the redeemed of the LORD say *so,*
Whom He has redeemed from the hand of the enemy,
3 And gathered out of the lands,
From the east and from the west,
From the north and from the south.

4 They wandered in [R]the wilderness in a desolate way; [Deut. 2:7; 32:10]
They found no city to dwell in.
5 Hungry and thirsty,
Their soul fainted in them.
6 [R]Then they cried out to the LORD in their trouble, Ps. 50:15
And He delivered them out of their distresses.
7 And He led them forth by the [R]right way,
That they might go to a city for a dwelling place. Ezra 8:21
8 [R]Oh, that *men* would give thanks to the LORD *for* His goodness, Ps. 107:15, 21
And *for* His wonderful works to the children of men!
9 For He satisfies the longing soul,
And fills the hungry soul with goodness.

10 Those who [R]sat in darkness and in the shadow of death, [Luke 1:79]
Bound in affliction and irons—
11 Because they [R]rebelled against the words of God, Lam. 3:42
And [T]despised [R]the counsel of the Most High, *scorned* • [Ps. 73:24]
12 Therefore He brought down their heart with labor;
They fell down, and *there was* [R]none to help. Ps. 22:11
13 Then they cried out to the LORD in their trouble,
And He saved them out of their distresses.
14 [R]He brought them out of darkness and the shadow of death, Ps. 68:6
And broke their chains in pieces.
15 Oh, that *men* would give thanks to the LORD *for* His goodness,
And *for* His wonderful works to the children of men!
16 For He has broken the gates of bronze,
And cut the bars of iron in two.

106:32 Or *Meribah*

17 Fools, [R]because of their transgression,
And because of their iniquities, were afflicted. Lam. 3:39
18 [R]Their soul abhorred all manner of food,
And they [R]drew near to the gates of death. Job 33:20 • Job 33:22
19 Then they cried out to the LORD in their trouble,
And He saved them out of their distresses.
20 [R]He sent His word and healed them,
And [R]delivered *them* from their destructions. Matt. 8:8 • Job 33:28, 30
21 Oh, that *men* would give thanks to the LORD *for* His goodness,
And *for* His wonderful works to the children of men!
22 [R]Let them sacrifice the sacrifices of thanksgiving, Lev. 7:12
And declare His works with rejoicing.

23 Those who go down to the sea in ships,
Who do business on great waters,
24 They see the works of the LORD,
And His wonders in the deep.
25 For He commands and [R]raises the stormy wind, Jon. 1:4
Which lifts up the waves of the sea.
26 They mount up to the heavens,
They go down again to the depths;
Their soul melts because of trouble.
27 They reel to and fro, and stagger like a drunken man,
And are at their wits' end.
28 Then they cry out to the LORD in their trouble,
And He brings them out of their distresses.
29 [R]He calms the storm, Ps. 89:9
So that its waves are still.
30 Then they are glad because they are quiet;
So He guides them to their desired haven.
31 [R]Oh, that *men* would give thanks to the LORD *for* His goodness, Ps. 107:8, 15, 21
And *for* His wonderful works to the children of men!
32 Let them exalt Him also [R]in the assembly of the people, Ps. 22:22, 25
And praise Him in the company of the elders.

33 He turns rivers into a wilderness,
And the watersprings into dry ground;
34 A [R]fruitful land into [T]barrenness,
For the wickedness of those who dwell in it. Gen. 13:10 • Lit. *a salty waste*
35 [R]He turns a wilderness into pools of water, Ps. 114:8
And dry land into watersprings.
36 There He makes the hungry dwell,
That they may establish a city for a dwelling place,
37 And sow fields and plant vineyards,
That they may yield a fruitful harvest.
38 [R]He also blesses them, and they multiply greatly; Gen. 12:2; 17:16, 20
And He does not let their cattle [R]decrease. [Deut. 7:14]

39 When they are [R]diminished and brought low 2 Kin. 10:32
Through oppression, affliction and sorrow,
40 He pours contempt on princes,
And causes them to wander in the wilderness *where there is* no way;
41 [R]Yet He sets the poor on high, far from affliction, 1 Sam. 2:8
And makes *their* families like a flock.
42 The righteous see *it* and rejoice,
And all iniquity stops its mouth.

43 [R]Whoever *is* wise will observe these *things*, Jer. 9:12
And they will understand the lovingkindness of the LORD.

PSALM 108

Awake Early and Praise the Lord

A Song. A Psalm of David.

O [R]GOD, my heart is steadfast; Ps. 57:7–11
I will sing and give praise, even with my glory.
2 [R]Awake, lute and harp! Ps. 57:8–11
I will awaken the dawn.
3 I will praise You, O LORD, among the peoples,
And I will sing praises to You among the nations.
4 For Your mercy *is* great above the [T]heavens, *skies*
And Your truth *reaches* to the clouds.

5 Be exalted, O God, above the heavens,
And Your glory above all the earth;
6 [R]That Your beloved may be delivered,
Save *with* Your right hand, and [T]hear me. Ps. 60:5–12 • Lit. *answer*

7 God has spoken in His holiness:
"I will rejoice;
I will divide Shechem
And measure out the Valley of Succoth.
8 Gilead *is* Mine; Manasseh *is* Mine;
Ephraim also *is* the [T]helmet for My head; Lit. *protection*
[R]Judah *is* My lawgiver. [Gen. 49:10]
9 Moab *is* My washpot;
Over Edom I will cast My shoe;
Over Philistia I will triumph."

10 [R]Who will bring me *into* the strong city?
Who will lead me to Edom? Ps. 60:9

11 *Is it* not *You,* O God, *who* cast us off?
And *You,* O God, *who* did not go out with our armies?
12 Give us help from trouble,
For the help of man is useless.
13 Through God we will do valiantly,[R]
For *it is* He *who* shall tread down our enemies.*

PSALM 109

Song of the Slandered

To the Chief Musician. A Psalm of David.

DO[R] not keep silent, Ps. 83:1
O God of my praise!
2 For the mouth of the wicked and the mouth of the deceitful
Have opened against me;
They have spoken against me with a [R]lying tongue. Ps. 27:12
3 They have also surrounded me with words of hatred,
And fought against me [R]without a cause. John 15:23–25☆
4 In return for my love they are my accusers,
But I *give myself to* prayer.
5 Thus [R]they have rewarded me evil for good, Ps. 35:7, 12; 38:20
And hatred for my love.
6 Set a wicked man over him,
And let [R]an accuser* stand at his right hand. Zech. 3:1
7 When he is judged, let him be found guilty,
And let his prayer become sin.
8 Let his days be [R]few, [Ps. 55:23]
And [R]let another take his office. Acts 1:20☆
9[R] Let his children be fatherless,
And his wife a widow. Ex. 22:24
10 Let his children continually be vagabonds, and beg;
Let them seek *their bread** also from their desolate places.
11 Let the creditor seize all that he has,
And let strangers plunder his labor.
12 Let there be none to extend mercy to him,
Nor let there be any to favor his fatherless children.
13 Let his posterity be cut off,
And in the generation following let their [R]name be blotted out. Prov. 10:7

14[R] Let the iniquity of his fathers be remembered before the LORD,
And let not the sin of his mother [R]be blotted out. [Ex. 20:5] • Neh. 4:5
15 Let them be continually before the LORD,
That He may [R]cut off the memory of them from the earth; Job 18:17
16 Because he did not remember to show mercy,
But persecuted the poor and needy man,
That he might even slay the [R]broken in heart. [Ps. 34:18]
17[R] As he loved cursing, so let it come to him; Prov. 14:14
As he did not delight in blessing, so let it be far from him.
18 As he clothed himself with cursing as with his garment,
So let it [R]enter his body like water,
And like oil into his bones. Num. 5:22
19 Let it be to him like the garment which covers him,
And for a belt with which he girds himself continually.
20 *Let* this *be* the LORD's reward to my accusers,
And to those who speak evil against my person.

21 But You, O GOD the Lord,
Deal with me for Your name's sake;
Because Your mercy *is* good, deliver me.
22 For I *am* poor and needy,
And my heart is wounded within me.
23 I am gone [R]like a shadow when it lengthens; Ps. 102:11
I am shaken off like a locust.
24 My [R]knees are weak through fasting,
And my flesh is feeble from lack of fatness. Heb. 12:12
25 I also have become [R]a reproach to them;
When they look at me, [R]they shake their heads. Ps. 22:7 • Matt. 27:39

26 Help me, O LORD my God!
Oh, save me according to Your mercy,
27[R] That they may know that this *is* Your hand— Job 37:7
That You, LORD, have done it!
28 Let them curse, but You bless;
When they arise, let them be ashamed,
But let [R]Your servant rejoice. Is. 65:14
29 Let my accusers be clothed with shame,
And let them cover themselves with their own disgrace as with a mantle.

30 I will greatly praise the LORD with my mouth;
Yes, [R]I will praise Him among the multitude. Ps. 35:18; 111:1
31 For [R]He shall stand at the right hand of the poor, [Ps. 16:8]
To save *him* from those [T]who condemn him. Lit. *judging his soul*

108:13 Cf. vv. 6–13 with 60:5–12 **109:6** Heb. *satan*
109:10 So with MT, Tg.; LXX, Vg. *be cast out*

PSALM 110

The Coming of the Priest-King-Judge

A Psalm of David.

THE [R]LORD said to my Lord, Matt. 22:44☆
"Sit at My right hand,
Till I make Your enemies Your
[R]footstool." [1 Cor. 15:25]
2 The LORD shall send the rod of Your
strength [R]out of Zion. [Rom. 11:26, 27]
Rule in the midst of Your enemies!

3 [R]Your people *shall be* volunteers
In the day of Your power; Judg. 5:2
[R]In the beauties of holiness, from the
womb of the morning, Ps. 96:9
You have the dew of Your youth.
4 The LORD has sworn
And [R]will not relent, [Num. 23:19]
"You *are* a [R]priest forever [Zech. 6:13]
According to the order of
[R]Melchizedek." [Heb. 5:6, 10; 6:20]☆

5 The Lord *is* [R]at Your right hand;
He shall execute kings [R]in the day of His
wrath. [Ps. 16:8] • Ps. 2:5, 12
6 He shall judge among the nations,
He shall fill *the places* with dead bodies,
[R]He shall [T]execute the heads of many
countries. Ps. 68:21 • Lit. *break in pieces*
7 He shall drink of the brook by the
wayside;
Therefore He shall lift up the head.

PSALM 111

Praise for God's Tender Care

PRAISE[T] the LORD! Heb. *Hallelujah*

[R]I will praise the LORD with *my* whole
heart, Ps. 35:18
In the assembly of the upright and *in* the
congregation.

2 [R]The works of the LORD *are* great,
[R]Studied by all who have pleasure in
them. Ps. 92:5 • Ps. 143:5
3 His work *is* honorable and glorious,
And His righteousness endures forever.
4 He has made His wonderful works to be
remembered;
[R]The LORD *is* gracious and full of
compassion. [Ps. 86:5]
5 He has given food to those who fear Him;
He will ever be mindful of His covenant.
6 He has declared to His people the power
of His works,
In giving them the [T]heritage of the
nations. *inheritance*

7 The works of His hands *are* [R]verity[T] and
justice; [Rev. 15:3] • *truth*
All His precepts *are* sure.
8 [R]They stand fast forever and ever, Is. 40:8
And are done in truth and uprightness.
9 [R]He has sent redemption to His people;
He has commanded His covenant
forever: Luke 1:68
Holy and awesome *is* His name.

10 [R]The fear of the LORD *is* the beginning of
wisdom; Eccl. 12:13
A good understanding have all those
who do *His commandments*.
His praise endures forever.

PSALM 112

The Blessings of Those Who Fear God

PRAISE[T] the LORD! Heb. *Hallelujah*

Blessed *is* the man *who* fears the LORD,
Who [R]delights greatly in His
commandments. Ps. 128:1

2 [R]His descendants will be mighty on
earth; [Ps. 102:28]
The generation of the upright will be
blessed.
3 Wealth and riches *will be* in his house,
And his righteousness endures forever.
4 [R]Unto the upright there arises light in the
darkness; Job 11:17
He is gracious, and full of compassion,
and righteous.
5 A good man deals graciously and lends;
He will guide his affairs with discretion.
6 Surely he will never be shaken;
[R]The righteous will be in everlasting
remembrance. Prov. 10:7
7 [R]He will not be afraid of evil tidings;
His heart is steadfast, trusting in the
LORD. [Prov. 1:33]
8 His [R]heart *is* established; Heb. 13:9
[R]He will not be afraid, Prov. 1:33; 3:24
Until he [R]sees *his desire* upon his
enemies. Ps. 59:10

9 He has dispersed abroad,
He has given to the poor;
His righteousness endures forever;
His horn will be exalted with honor.
10 The wicked will see *it* and be grieved;
He will gnash his teeth and melt away;
The desire of the wicked shall perish.

PSALM 113

The Condescending Grace of God

PRAISE[T] the LORD! Heb. *Hallelujah*

[R]Praise, O servants of the LORD,
Praise the name of the LORD! Ps. 135:1
2 Blessed be the name of the LORD
From this time forth and forevermore!

3[R] From the rising of the sun to its going
down Is. 59:19
The LORD's name *is* to be praised.

4 The LORD *is* high above all nations,
[R] His glory above the heavens. [Ps. 8:1]
5[R] Who *is* like the LORD our God,
Who dwells on high, [Is. 57:15]
6[R] Who humbles Himself to behold
The things that are in the heavens and
in the earth? [Ps. 11:4]

7 He raises the poor out of the dust,
And lifts the needy out of the ash heap,
8 That He may [R]seat *him* with princes—
With the princes of His people. [Job 36:7]
9 He grants the barren woman a home,
Like a joyful mother of children.

Praise the LORD!

PSALM 114

In Praise for the Exodus

WHEN Israel went out of Egypt,
The house of Jacob [R]from a people of
strange language, Ps. 81:5
2[R] Judah became His sanctuary, Ex. 6:7
And Israel His dominion.

3[R] The sea saw *it* and fled; Ex. 14:21
[R] Jordan turned back. Josh. 3:13–16
4[R] The mountains skipped like rams,
The little hills like lambs. Ps. 29:6
5 What ails you, O sea, that you fled?
O Jordan, *that* you turned back?
6 O mountains, *that* you skipped like
rams?
O little hills, like lambs?

7 Tremble, O earth, at the presence of the
Lord,
At the presence of the God of Jacob,
8[R] Who turned the rock *into* a pool of
water, Ex. 17:6
The flint into a fountain of waters.

PSALM 115

To God Alone Be the Glory

NOT [R]unto us, O LORD, not unto us,
But to Your name give glory, [Is. 48:11]
Because of Your mercy,
Because of Your truth.
2 Why should the [T]Gentiles say, *nations*
[R]"So where *is* their God?" Ps. 42:3, 10

3[R] But our God *is* in heaven; [1 Chr. 16:26]
He does whatever He pleases.
4[R] Their idols *are* silver and gold,
The work of men's hands. Jer. 10:3
5 They have mouths, but they do not
speak;
Eyes they have, but they do not see;
6 They have ears, but they do not hear;
Noses they have, but they do not smell;
7 They have hands, but they do not handle;
Feet they have, but they do not walk;
Nor do they mutter through their throat.
8 Those who make them are like them;
So is everyone who trusts in them.

9[R] O Israel, trust in the LORD; Ps. 118:2, 3
He *is* their help and their shield.
10 O house of Aaron, trust in the LORD;
He *is* their help and their shield.
11 You who fear the LORD, trust in the LORD;
He *is* their help and their shield.

12 The LORD [T]has been mindful of *us;*
He will bless us; *has remembered us*
He will bless the house of Israel;
He will bless the house of Aaron.
13[R] He will bless those who fear the LORD,
Both small and great. Ps. 128:1, 4

14 May the LORD give you increase more
and more,
You and your children.
15 *May* you *be* blessed by the LORD,
[R] Who made heaven and earth. Gen. 1:1

16 The heaven, *even* the heavens, *are* the
LORD's;
But the earth He has given to the
children of men.
17 The dead do not praise the LORD,
Nor any who go down into silence.
18[R] But we will bless the LORD Dan. 2:20
From this time forth and forevermore.

Praise the LORD!

PSALM 116

Love the Lord for What He Has Done

I [R]LOVE the LORD, because He has heard
My voice *and* my supplications. Ps. 18:1
2 Because He has inclined His ear to me,
Therefore I will call *upon Him* as long as
I live.

3[R] The pains of death surrounded me,
And the pangs of Sheol laid hold of me;
I found trouble and sorrow. Ps. 18:4–6
4 Then I called upon the name of the
LORD:
"O LORD, I implore You, deliver my soul!"
5 Gracious *is* the LORD, and [R]righteous;
Yes, our God *is* merciful. [Ezra 9:15]
6 The LORD preserves the simple;
I was brought low, and He saved me.
7 Return to your [R]rest, O my soul,
For [R]the LORD has dealt bountifully with
you. [Jer. 6:16] • Ps. 13:6

8 [R]For You have delivered my soul from death, Ps. 56:13
My eyes from tears,
And my feet from falling.
9 I will walk before the LORD
[R]In the land of the living. Ps. 27:13
10 [R]I believed, therefore I spoke, 2 Cor. 4:13
"I am greatly afflicted."
11 [R]I said in my haste, Ps. 31:22
[R]"All men *are* liars." Rom. 3:4

12 What shall I render to the LORD
For all His benefits toward me?
13 I will take up the cup of salvation,
And call upon the name of the LORD.
14 I will pay my vows to the LORD
Now in the presence of all His people.

15 [R]Precious in the sight of the LORD
Is the death of His saints. Ps. 72:14

16 O LORD, truly [R]I *am* Your servant;
I *am* Your servant, [R]the son of Your maidservant; Ps. 119:125 • Ps. 86:16
You have loosed my bonds.
17 I will offer to You [R]the sacrifice of thanksgiving, Lev. 7:12
And will call upon the name of the LORD.

18 I will pay my vows to the LORD
Now in the presence of all His people,
19 In the courts of the LORD's house,
In the midst of you, O Jerusalem.

[T]Praise the LORD! Heb. *Hallelujah*

PSALM 117

The Praise of All Peoples

PRAISE [R]the LORD, all you Gentiles!
Laud Him, all you peoples! Rom. 15:11
2 For His merciful kindness is great toward us,
And [R]the truth of the LORD *endures* forever. [Ps. 100:5]

Praise the LORD!

PSALM 118

Better to Trust God than People

OH, [R]give thanks to the LORD, for *He is* good! 1 Chr. 16:8, 34
For His mercy *endures* forever.
2 [R]Let Israel now say, [Ps. 115:9]
"His mercy *endures* forever."
3 Let the house of Aaron now say,
"His mercy *endures* forever."
4 Let those who fear the LORD now say,
"His mercy *endures* forever."
5 [R]I called on the LORD in distress; Ps. 120:1
The LORD answered me *and* [R]*set me* in a broad place. Ps. 18:19
6 [R]The LORD *is* on my side; Ps. 27:1; 56:9
I will not fear.
What can man do to me?
7 [R]The LORD is for me among those who help me; Ps. 54:4
Therefore [R]I shall see *my desire* on those who hate me. Ps. 59:10
8 [R]*It is* better to trust in the LORD Ps. 40:4
Than to put confidence in man.
9 [R]*It is* better to trust in the LORD Ps. 146:3
Than to put confidence in princes.

10 All nations surrounded me,
But in the name of the LORD I will destroy them.
11 They [R]surrounded me, Ps. 88:17
Yes, they surrounded me;
But in the name of the LORD I will destroy them.
12 They surrounded me [R]like bees;
They were quenched [R]like a fire of thorns; Deut. 1:44 • Nah. 1:10
For in the name of the LORD I will [T]destroy them. *cut them off*
13 You pushed me violently, that I might fall,
But the LORD helped me.
14 The LORD *is* my strength and song,
And He has become my salvation.*

15 The voice of rejoicing and salvation
Is in the tents of the righteous;
The right hand of the LORD does valiantly.
16 [R]The right hand of the LORD is exalted;
The right hand of the LORD does valiantly. Ex. 15:6
17 [R]I shall not die, but live, Hab. 1:12
And declare the works of the LORD.
18 The LORD has chastened me severely,
But He has not given me over to death.

19 [R]Open to me the gates of righteousness;
I will go through them, Is. 26:2
And I will praise the LORD.
20 [R]This is the gate of the LORD, Ps. 24:7
[R]Through which the righteous shall enter. Is. 35:8

21 I will praise You,
For You have [R]answered me, Ps. 116:1
And have become my salvation.

22 The stone *which* the builders rejected
Has become the chief cornerstone.
23 This was the LORD's doing;
It *is* marvelous in our eyes.
24 This *is* the day the LORD has made;
We will rejoice and be glad in it.

118:14 Cf. Ex. 15:2

25 Save now, I pray, O LORD;
O LORD, I pray, send now prosperity.
26[R] Blessed *is* he who comes in the name of the LORD! Mark 11:9; Luke 19:38☆
We have blessed you from the house of the LORD.
27 God *is* the LORD,
And He has given us [R]light; [1 Pet. 2:9]
Bind the sacrifice with cords to the horns of the altar.
28 You *are* my God, and I will praise You;
[R] *You are* my God, I will exalt You. Is. 25:1
29 Oh, give thanks to the LORD, for *He is* good!
For His mercy *endures* forever.

PSALM 119

An Acrostic in Praise of the Scriptures

א ALEPH

BLESSED *are* the undefiled in the way,
Who walk in the law of the LORD!
2 Blessed *are* those who keep His testimonies,
Who seek Him with the whole heart!
3[R] They also do no iniquity; [1 John 3:9]
They walk in His ways.
4 You have commanded *us*
To keep Your precepts diligently.
5 Oh, that my ways were directed
To keep Your statutes!
6[R] Then I would not be ashamed,
When I look into all Your commandments. Job 22:26
7 I will praise You with uprightness of heart,
When I learn Your righteous judgments.
8 I will keep Your statutes;
Oh, do not forsake me utterly!

ב BETH

9 How can a young man cleanse his way?
By taking heed according to Your word.
10 With my whole heart I have [R]sought You;
Oh, let me not wander from Your commandments! 2 Chr. 15:15
11 Your word I have hidden in my heart,
That I might not sin against You.
12 Blessed *are* You, O LORD!
Teach me Your statutes.
13 With my lips I have [R]declared Ps. 34:11
All the judgments of Your mouth.
14 I have rejoiced in the way of Your testimonies,
As *much as* in all riches.
15 I will meditate on Your precepts,
And [T]contemplate Your ways. *look into*
16 I will [R]delight myself in Your statutes;
I will not forget Your word. Ps. 1:2

ג GIMEL

17 Deal bountifully with Your servant,
That I may live and keep Your word.
18 Open my eyes, that I may see
Wondrous things from Your law.
19[R] I *am* a stranger in the earth; Heb. 11:13
Do not hide Your commandments from me.
20 My soul breaks with longing
For Your judgments at all times.
21 You rebuke the proud—the cursed,
Who stray from Your commandments.
22[R] Remove from me reproach and contempt, Ps. 39:8
For I have kept Your testimonies.
23 Princes also sit *and* speak against me,
But Your servant meditates on Your statutes.
24 Your testimonies also *are* my delight
And my counselors.

119:9 God's Word Cleanses—One of the pieces of furniture in the Old Testament tabernacle was called the bronze laver (Page 92—Ex. 38:8). It consisted of a huge upright bronze bowl filled with water, resting upon a pedestal. The priests would often stop at this laver and wash. The Word of God may be thought of in terms of that laver, for it too has the power to cleanse. The Old Testament laver could only remove the physical dirt from human hands, but the Scriptures possess the ability to take away our moral filth (Page 1280—1 Pet. 1:22).

"If we confess our sins, He is faithful and just to forgive us *our* sins and to cleanse us from all unrighteousness" (Page 1293—1 John 1:9). What areas of my life can the Bible cleanse?

It can cleanse me from wrong thoughts. Sometimes we are tempted to think critically of others; God's Word can prevent this (Page 546—Ps. 1:2). On other occasions fearful thoughts may race through our minds; the Scriptures will prevent this also (Page 214—Josh. 1:8). In fact, the Bible will establish our total thought-life if we but allow it to do so (Page 1216—Phil. 4:8, 9; Page 1287—2 Pet. 1:5–10).

It can cleanse me from wrong words. Of all the Bible authors, James seems to be God's expert on the sins of the human tongue. In the first chapter of his book, he deals with this very thing and shows the absolute necessity of dependence upon the Scriptures to keep our words true (Page 1272—James 1:22–26). See also Ps. 119:172.

It can cleanse me from wrong actions. Jesus promised us this would be the case: "You are already clean because of the word which I have spoken to you" (Page 1100—John 15:3).

Finally, God's Word will keep us from wrong thoughts, words, and actions; or else wrong thoughts, words, and actions will keep us from God's Word.

Now turn to Page 1091—John 8:31: God's Word Confirms.

ד DALETH

25[R] My soul clings to the dust; Ps. 44:25
Revive me according to Your word.
26 I have declared my ways, and You answered me;
[R]Teach me Your statutes. Ps. 25:4; 27:11
27 Make me understand the way of Your precepts;
So [R]shall I meditate on Your wonderful works. Ps. 145:5, 6
28 My soul melts from [T]heaviness; *grief*
Strengthen me according to Your word.
29 Remove from me the way of lying,
And grant me Your law graciously.
30 I have chosen the way of truth;
Your judgments I have laid *before me.*
31 I cling to Your testimonies;
O LORD, do not put me to shame!
32 I will run the course of Your commandments,
For You shall enlarge my heart.

ה HE

33[R] Teach me, O LORD, the way of Your statutes, [Rev. 2:26]
And I shall keep it *to* the end.
34[R] Give me understanding, and I shall keep Your law; [Prov. 2:6]
Indeed, I shall observe it with *my* whole heart.
35 Make me walk in the path of Your commandments,
For I delight in it.
36 Incline my heart to Your testimonies,
And not to [R]covetousness. Ezek. 33:31
37[R] Turn away my eyes from [R]looking at worthless things, Is. 33:15 • Prov. 23:5
And revive me in Your way.*
38 Establish Your word to Your servant,
Who *is devoted* to fearing You.
39 Turn away my reproach which I dread,
For Your judgments *are* good.
40 Behold, I long for Your precepts;
Revive me in Your righteousness.

ו WAW

41 Let Your mercies come also to me, O LORD—
Your salvation according to Your word.
42 So shall I have an answer for him who [T]reproaches me, *taunts*
For I trust in Your word.
43 And take not the word of truth utterly out of my mouth,
For I have hoped in Your ordinances.
44 So shall I keep Your law continually,
Forever and ever.
45 And I will walk at [R]liberty, Prov. 4:12
For I seek Your precepts.
46[R] I will speak of Your testimonies also before kings, Matt. 10:18
And will not be ashamed.
47 And I will delight myself in Your commandments,
Which I love.
48 My hands also I will lift up to Your commandments,
Which I love,
And I will meditate on Your statutes.

ז ZAYIN

49 Remember the word to Your servant,
Upon which You have caused me to hope.
50 This *is* my comfort in my affliction,
For Your word has given me life.
51 The proud have me in great derision,
Yet I do not turn aside from Your law.
52 I remembered Your judgments of old, O LORD,
And have comforted myself.
53[R] Indignation has taken hold of me
Because of the wicked, who forsake Your law. Ezra 9:3
54 Your statutes have been my songs
In the house of my pilgrimage.
55[R] I remember Your name in the night, O LORD, Ps. 63:6
And I keep Your law.
56 This has become mine,
Because I kept Your precepts.

ח HETH

57[R] *You are* my portion, O LORD; Jer. 10:16
I have said that I would keep Your words.
58 I entreated Your favor with *my* whole heart;
Be merciful to me according to Your word.
59 I [R]thought about my ways, Luke 15:17
And turned my feet to Your testimonies.
60 I made haste, and did not delay
To keep Your commandments.
61 The cords of the wicked have bound me,
But I have not forgotten Your law.
62[R] At midnight I will rise to give thanks to You, Acts 16:25
Because of Your righteous judgments.
63 I *am* a companion of all who fear You,
And of those who keep Your precepts.
64[R] The earth, O LORD, is full of Your mercy;
Teach me Your statutes. Ps. 33:5

ט TETH

65 You have dealt well with Your servant,
O LORD, according to Your word.
66 Teach me good judgment and [R]knowledge, Phil. 1:9

119:37 So with MT, LXX, Vg.; Tg. *Your words*

For I believe Your commandments.
67 Before I was [R]afflicted I went astray,
But now I keep Your word. [Heb. 12:5–11]
68 You *are* [R]good, and do good; [Matt. 19:17]
Teach me Your statutes.
69 The proud have [R]forged[T] a lie against
me, Job 13:4 • Lit. *smeared me with a lie*
But I will keep Your precepts with *my*
whole heart.
70[R] Their heart is as fat as grease,
But I delight in Your law. Acts 28:27
71 *It is* good for me that I have been
afflicted,
That I may learn Your statutes.
72[R] The law of Your mouth *is* better to me
Than thousands of *coins of* gold and
silver. Ps. 19:10

י YOD

73[R] Your hands have made me and fashioned
me; Job 10:8; 31:15
Give me understanding, that I may learn
Your commandments.
74[R] Those who fear You will be glad when
they see me, Ps. 34:2
Because I have hoped in Your word.
75 I know, O LORD, [R]that Your judgments *are*
[T]right, [Heb. 12:10] • Lit. *righteous*
And *that* in faithfulness You have
afflicted me.
76 Let, I pray, Your merciful kindness be for
my comfort,
According to Your word to Your servant.
77 Let Your tender mercies come to me, that
I may live;
For Your law *is* my delight.
78 Let the proud [R]be ashamed, Ps. 25:3
For they treated me wrongfully with
falsehood;
But I will meditate on Your precepts.
79 Let those who fear You turn to me,
Those who know Your testimonies.
80 Let my heart be blameless regarding
Your statutes,
That I may not be ashamed.

כ KAPH

81[R] My soul faints for Your salvation,
But I hope in Your word. Ps. 73:26; 84:2
82 My eyes fail *from searching* Your word,
Saying, "When will You comfort me?"
83 For [R]I have become like a wineskin in
smoke, Job 30:30
Yet I do not forget Your statutes.
84 How many *are* the days of Your servant?
[R]When will You execute judgment on
those who persecute me? Rev. 6:10
85 The proud have dug pits for me,
Which *is* not according to Your law.
86 All Your commandments *are* faithful;
They persecute me [R]wrongfully;
Help me! Ps. 35:19
87 They almost made an end of me on
earth,
But I did not forsake Your precepts.
88 Revive me according to Your
lovingkindness,
So that I may keep the testimony of Your
mouth.

ל LAMED

89[R] Forever, O LORD, Matt. 24:35
Your word is settled in heaven.
90 Your faithfulness *endures* to all
generations;
You established the earth, and it
[T]abides. Lit. *stands*
91 They continue this day according to
[R]Your ordinances, Jer. 33:25
For all *are* Your servants.
92 Unless Your law *had been* my delight,
I would then have perished in my
affliction.
93 I will never forget Your precepts,
For by them You have given me life.
94 I *am* Yours, save me;
For I have sought Your precepts.
95 The wicked wait for me to destroy me,
But I will consider Your testimonies.
96[R] I have seen the consummation of all
perfection, Matt. 5:18
But Your commandment *is* exceedingly
broad.

מ MEM

97 Oh, how I love Your law!
[R]It *is* my meditation all the day. Ps. 1:2
98 You, through Your commandments, make
me [R]wiser than my enemies;
For they *are* ever with me. Deut. 4:6
99 I have more understanding than all my
teachers,
For Your testimonies *are* my meditation.
100 I understand more than the [T]ancients,
Because I keep Your precepts. *aged*
101 I have restrained my feet from every evil
way,
That I may keep Your word.
102 I have not departed from Your
judgments,
For You Yourself have taught me.
103 How sweet are Your words to my taste,
Sweeter than honey to my mouth!
104 Through Your precepts I get
understanding;
Therefore I hate every false way.

נ NUN

105[R] Your word *is* a lamp to my feet
And a light to my path. Prov. 6:23
106[R] I have sworn and confirmed Neh. 10:29

That I will keep Your righteous
judgments.
107 I am afflicted very much;
Revive me, O LORD, according to Your
word.
108 Accept, I pray, [R]the freewill offerings of
my mouth, O LORD, Hos. 14:2
And teach me Your judgments.
109[R] My life *is* continually in my hand,
Yet I do not forget Your law. Job 13:14
110[R] The wicked have laid a snare for me,
Yet I have not strayed from Your
precepts. Ps. 140:5
111[R] Your testimonies I have taken as a
[T]heritage forever, Deut. 33:4 • *inheritance*
For they *are* the rejoicing of my heart.
112 I have inclined my heart to perform Your
statutes
Forever, to the very end.

ס SAMEK

113 I hate the double-minded,
But I love Your law.
114[R] You *are* my hiding place and my shield;
I hope in Your word. [Ps. 32:7]
115[R] Depart from me, you evildoers,
For I will keep the commandments of my
God! Matt. 7:23
116 Uphold me according to Your word, that I
may live;
And do not let me [R]be ashamed of my
hope. [Rom. 5:5; 9:33; 10:11]
117[T] Hold me up, and I shall be safe,
And I shall observe Your statutes
continually. *Uphold me*
118 You reject all those who stray from Your
statutes,
For their deceit *is* falsehood.
119 You put away all the wicked of the earth
[R]*like* dross; Ezek. 22:18, 19
Therefore I love Your testimonies.
120 My flesh trembles for fear of You,
And I am afraid of Your judgments.

ע AYIN

121 I have done justice and righteousness;
Do not leave me to my oppressors.
122 Be surety for Your servant for good;
Do not let the proud oppress me.
123 My eyes fail *from seeking* Your salvation
And Your righteous word.
124 Deal with Your servant according to Your
mercy,
And teach me Your statutes.
125[R] I *am* Your servant; Ps. 116:16
Give me understanding,
That I may know Your testimonies.
126 *It is* time for *You* to act, O LORD,
For they have [T]regarded Your law as
void. *broken Your law*
127 Therefore I love Your commandments
More than gold, yes, than fine gold!
128 Therefore all *Your* precepts *concerning*
all *things*
I consider *to be* right;
I hate every false way.

פ PE

129 Your testimonies are wonderful;
Therefore my soul keeps them.
130 The entrance of Your words gives light;
It gives understanding to the simple.
131 I opened my mouth and panted,
For I longed for Your commandments.
132 Look upon me and be merciful to me,
[R]As Your custom *is* toward those who love
Your name. [2 Thess. 1:6]
133[R] Direct my steps by Your word, Ps. 17:5
And [R]let no iniquity have dominion over
me. [Rom. 6:12]
134 Redeem me from the oppression of man,
That I may keep Your precepts.
135[R] Make Your face shine upon Your
servant, Ps. 4:6
And teach me Your statutes.
136 Rivers of water run down from my eyes,
Because *men* do not keep Your law.

צ TSADDE

137[R] Righteous *are* You, O LORD, Neh. 9:33
And upright *are* Your judgments.
138[R] Your testimonies, *which* You have
commanded, [Ps. 19:7–9]
Are righteous and very faithful.
139[R] My zeal has [T]consumed me, John 2:17
Because my enemies have forgotten Your
words. put an end to
140[R] Your word *is* very pure; Ps. 12:6
Therefore Your servant loves it.
141 I *am* small and despised,
Yet I do not forget Your precepts.
142 Your righteousness *is* an everlasting
righteousness,
And Your law *is* [R]truth. [John 17:17]
143 Trouble and anguish have [T]overtaken
me, Lit. *found*
Yet Your commandments *are* my
delights.
144 The righteousness of Your testimonies *is*
everlasting;
Give me understanding, and I shall live.

ק QOPH

145 I cry out with *my* whole heart;
Hear me, O LORD!
I will keep Your statutes.
146 I cry out to You;
Save me, and I will keep Your
testimonies.
147[R] I rise before the dawning of the
morning, Ps. 5:3

And cry for help;
I hope in Your word.
148[R] My eyes are awake through the *night* watches, Ps. 63:1, 6
That I may meditate on Your word.
149 Hear my voice according to Your lovingkindness;
O LORD, revive me according to Your justice.
150 They draw near who follow after wickedness;
They are far from Your law.
151 You *are* [R]near, O LORD, [Ps. 145:18]
And all Your commandments *are* truth.
152 Concerning Your testimonies,
I have known of old that You have founded them [R]forever. Luke 21:33

ר RESH

153[R] Consider my affliction and deliver me,
For I do not forget Your law. Lam. 5:1
154 Plead my cause and redeem me;
Revive me according to Your word.
155 Salvation *is* far from the wicked,
For they do not seek Your statutes.
156 Great *are* Your tender mercies, O LORD;
Revive me according to Your judgments.
157 Many *are* my persecutors and my enemies,
Yet I do not turn from Your testimonies.
158 I see the treacherous, and [R]am disgusted, Ezek. 9:4
Because they do not keep Your word.
159 Consider how I love Your precepts;
Revive me, O LORD, according to Your lovingkindness.
160 The entirety of Your word *is* truth,
And every one of Your righteous judgments *endures* forever.

ש SHIN

161[R] Princes persecute me without a cause,
But my heart stands in awe of Your word. 1 Sam. 24:11; 26:18
162 I rejoice at Your word
As one who finds great treasure.
163 I hate and abhor lying,
But I love Your law.
164 Seven times a day I praise You,
Because of Your righteous judgments.
165[R] Great peace have those who love Your law, Prov. 3:2
And nothing causes them to stumble.
166 LORD, I hope for Your salvation,
And I do Your commandments.
167 My soul keeps Your testimonies,
And I love them exceedingly.
168 I keep Your precepts and Your testimonies,
For all my ways *are* before You.

ת TAU

169 Let my cry come before You, O LORD;
[R]Give me understanding according to Your word. Ps. 119:27, 144
170 Let my supplication come before You;
Deliver me according to Your word.
171[R] My lips shall utter praise, Ps. 119:7
For You teach me Your statutes.
172 My tongue shall speak of Your word,
For all Your commandments *are* righteousness.
173 Let Your hand become my help,
For I have chosen Your precepts.
174 I long for Your salvation, O LORD,
And [R]Your law *is* my delight. Ps. 119:16, 24
175 Let my soul live, and it shall praise You;
And let Your judgments help me.
176[R] I have gone astray like a lost sheep;
Seek Your servant, [Is. 53:6]
For I do not forget Your commandments.

PSALM 120

A Cry in Distress

A Song of Ascents.

IN [R]my distress I cried to the LORD, Jon. 2:2
And He heard me.
2 Deliver my soul, O LORD, from lying lips
And from a deceitful tongue.

3 What shall be given to you,
Or what shall be done to you,
You false tongue?
4 Sharp arrows of the [T]warrior, *mighty one*
With coals of the broom tree!

5 Woe is me, that I dwell in Meshech,
That I dwell among the tents of Kedar!
6 My soul has dwelt too long
With one who hates peace.
7 I *am for* peace;
But when I speak, they *are* for war.

PSALM 121

God Is Our Keeper

A Song of Ascents.

I WILL lift up my eyes to the hills—
From whence comes my help?
2 My help *comes* from the LORD,
Who made heaven and earth.

3 He will not allow your foot to be moved;
He who keeps you will not slumber.
4 Behold, He who keeps Israel
Shall neither slumber nor sleep.

5 The LORD *is* your [T]keeper; *protector*
The LORD *is* [R]your shade [R]at your right hand. Is. 25:4 • Ps. 16:8

6[R] The sun shall not strike you by day,
Nor the moon by night. Is. 49:10

7 The LORD shall [T]preserve you from all evil; *keep*
He shall [R]preserve your soul. Ps. 41:2
8 The LORD shall [R]preserve[T] your going out and your coming in Deut. 28:6 • *keep*
From this time forth, and even forevermore.

PSALM 122

"Pray for the Peace of Jerusalem"

A Song of Ascents. Of David.

I WAS glad when they said to me,
"Let us go into the house of the LORD."
2 Our feet have been standing
Within your gates, O Jerusalem!

3 Jerusalem is built
As a city that is compact together,
4[R] Where the tribes go up, Deut. 16:16
The tribes of the LORD,
To [R]the Testimony of Israel, Ex. 16:34
To give thanks to the name of the LORD.
5 For thrones are set there for judgment,
The thrones of the house of David.

6 Pray for the peace of Jerusalem:
"May they prosper who love you.
7 Peace be within your walls,
Prosperity within your palaces."
8 For the sake of my brethren and companions,
I will now say, "Peace *be* within you."
9 Because of the house of the LORD our God
I will [R]seek your good. Neh. 2:10

PSALM 123

Plea for the Mercy of God

A Song of Ascents.

UNTO You [R]I lift up my eyes, Ps. 121:1
O You who dwell in the heavens.
2 Behold, as the eyes of servants *look* to the hand of their masters,
As the eyes of a maid to the hand of her mistress,
[R] So our eyes *look* to the LORD our God,
Until He has mercy on us. Ps. 25:15

3 Have mercy on us, O LORD, have mercy on us!
For we are exceedingly filled with contempt.
4 Our soul is exceedingly filled
With the scorn of those who are at ease,
With the contempt of the proud.

PSALM 124

God Is on Our Side

A Song of Ascents. Of David.

"IF it had not been the LORD who was on our [R]side," [Rom. 8:31]
[R] Let Israel now say— Ps. 129:1
2 "If it had not been the LORD who was on our side,
When men rose up against us,
3 Then they would have [R]swallowed us alive, Prov. 1:12
When their wrath was kindled against us;
4 Then the waters would have overwhelmed us,
The stream would have [T]gone over our soul; *swept over*
5 Then the swollen waters
Would have gone over our soul."

6 Blessed *be* the LORD,
Who has not given us *as* prey to their teeth.
7[R] Our soul has escaped [R]as a bird from the snare of the fowlers;* Ps. 91:3
The snare is broken, and we have escaped. Prov. 6:5
8 Our help *is* in the name of the LORD,
[R] Who made heaven and earth. Gen. 1:1

PSALM 125

Trust in the Lord and Abide Forever

A Song of Ascents.

THOSE who trust in the LORD
Are like Mount Zion,
Which cannot be moved, *but* abides forever.
2 As the mountains surround Jerusalem,
So the LORD surrounds His people
From this time forth and forever.

3 For [R]the scepter of wickedness shall not rest Prov. 22:8
On the land allotted to the righteous,
Lest the righteous reach out their hands to iniquity.

4 Do good, O LORD, to *those who are* good,
And to *those who are* upright in their hearts.

5 As for such as turn aside to their [R]crooked ways, Prov. 2:15
The LORD shall lead them away
With the workers of iniquity.

[R] Peace *be* upon Israel! [Gal. 6:16]

124:7 Persons who catch birds in a trap or snare

PSALM 126

"Sow in Tears . . . Reap in Joy"

A Song of Ascents.

WHEN [R]the LORD brought back the
captivity of Zion, Hos. 6:11
We were like those who dream.
2 Then [R]our mouth was filled with
laughter, Job 8:21
And our tongue with singing.
Then they said among the [T]nations,
"The LORD has done great things for
them." *Gentiles*
3 The LORD has done great things for us,
And we are glad.

4 Bring back our captivity, O LORD,
As the streams in the South.

5[R] Those who sow in tears Jer. 31:9
Shall reap in joy.
6 He who continually goes [T]forth weeping,
Bearing seed for sowing, *to and fro*
Shall doubtless come again [T]with
[R]rejoicing, *with shouts of joy* • Is. 61:3
Bringing his sheaves *with him.*

PSALM 127

Children Are God's Heritage

A Song of Ascents. Of Solomon.

UNLESS the LORD builds the house,
They labor in vain who build it;
Unless the LORD guards the city,
The watchman stays awake in vain.
2 *It is* vain for you to rise up early,
To sit up late,
To eat the bread of sorrows;
For so He gives His beloved sleep.

3 Behold, [R]children *are* a heritage from the
LORD, [Josh. 24:3, 4]
The fruit of the womb *is* a reward.
4 Like arrows in the hand of a warrior,
So *are* the children of one's youth.
5[R] Happy *is* the man who has his quiver full
of them; Ps. 128:2, 3
[R]They shall not be ashamed, Prov. 27:11
But shall speak with their enemies in the
gate.

PSALM 128

Blessing on the House of the God-Fearing

A Song of Ascents.

BLESSED [R]*is* every one who fears the
LORD, Ps. 119:1
Who walks in His ways.

2[R] When you eat the labor of your hands,
You *shall be* happy, and *it shall be* [R]well
with you. Is. 3:10 • Deut. 4:40
3 Your wife *shall be* like a fruitful vine
In the very heart of your house,
Your children like olive plants
All around your table.
4 Behold, thus shall the man be blessed
Who fears the LORD.

5[R] The LORD bless you out of Zion,
And may you see the good of Jerusalem
All the days of your life. Ps. 134:3
6 Yes, may you [R]see your children's
children. Job 42:16

[R]Peace *be* upon Israel! Ps. 125:5

PSALM 129

Plea of the Persecuted

A Song of Ascents.

"MANY a time they have [R]afflicted me
from my youth," [Jer. 1:19; 15:20]
[R]Let Israel now say— Ps. 124:1
2 "Many a time they have afflicted me from
my youth;
Yet they have not prevailed against me.
3 The plowers plowed on my back;
They made their furrows long."
4 The LORD *is* righteous;
He has cut in pieces the cords of the
wicked.

5 Let all those who hate Zion
Be put to shame and turned back.
6 Let them be as the [R]grass *on* the
housetops, Ps. 37:2
Which withers before it grows up,
7 With which the reaper does not fill his
hand,
Nor he who binds sheaves, his arms.
8 Neither let those who pass by them say,
"The blessing of the LORD *be* upon you;
We bless you in the name of the LORD!"

PSALM 130

"My Soul Waits for the Lord"

A Song of Ascents.

OUT [R]of the depths I have cried to You,
O LORD; Lam. 3:55
2 Lord, hear my voice!
Let Your ears be attentive
To the voice of my supplications.

3 If You, LORD, should mark iniquities,
O Lord, who could [R]stand? [Nah. 1:6]
4 But *there is* forgiveness with You,
That [R]You may be feared. [1 Kin. 8:39, 40]

5 I wait for the LORD, my soul waits,
And [R]in His word I do hope. Ps. 119:81
6[R] My soul *waits* for the Lord Ps. 119:147

More than those who watch for the
morning—
Yes, more than those who watch for the
morning.

7 [R]O Israel, hope in the LORD; Ps. 131:3
For with the LORD *there is* mercy,
And with Him *is* abundant redemption.
8 And [R]He shall redeem Israel [Ps. 103:3, 4]
From all his iniquities.

PSALM 131

A Childlike Faith

A Song of Ascents. Of David.

LORD, my heart is not [T]haughty, Proud
Nor my eyes [T]lofty. Arrogant
[R]Neither do I [T]concern myself with great
matters, [Rom. 12:16] • Lit. *walk in*
Nor with things too profound for me.

2 Surely I have calmed and quieted my
soul,
[R]Like a weaned child with his mother;
Like a weaned child *is* my soul within
me. [Matt. 18:3]

3 [R]O Israel, hope in the LORD [Ps. 130:7]
From this time forth and forever.

PSALM 132

Trust in the God of David

A Song of Ascents.

LORD, remember David
And all his afflictions;
2 How he swore to the LORD,
And vowed to the Mighty One of Jacob:
3 "Surely I will not go into the chamber of
my house,
Or go up to the comfort of my bed;
4 I will [R]not give sleep to my eyes
Or slumber to my eyelids, Prov. 6:4
5 Until I [R]find a place for the LORD,
A dwelling place for the Mighty One of
Jacob." Acts 7:46

6 Behold, we heard of it in Ephrathah;
We found it in the fields of the woods.*
7 Let us go into His tabernacle;
Let us worship at His footstool.
8 Arise, O LORD, to Your resting place,
You and the ark of Your strength.
9 Let Your priests [R]be clothed with
righteousness, Job 29:14
And let Your saints shout for joy.

10 For Your servant David's sake,
Do not turn away the face of Your
Anointed.

11 The LORD has sworn *in* truth to David;
He will not turn from it:
"I will set upon your throne [R]the [T]fruit of
your body. 2 Sam. 7:12 • *offspring*
12 If your sons will keep My covenant
And My testimony which I shall teach
them,
Their sons also shall sit upon your
throne forevermore."

13 For the LORD has chosen Zion;
He has desired *it* for His dwelling place:
14 "This *is* My resting place forever;
Here I will dwell, for I have desired it.
15 I will abundantly bless her provision;
I will satisfy her poor with bread.
16 [R]I will also clothe her priests with
salvation, 2 Chr. 6:41
And her saints shall shout aloud for joy.
17 [R]There I will make the [T]horn of David
grow; Ezek. 29:21 • Government
I will prepare a lamp for My Anointed.
18 His enemies I will [R]clothe with shame,
But upon Himself His crown shall
flourish." Ps. 35:26

PSALM 133

Beauty of the Unity of the Brethren

A Song of Ascents. Of David.

BEHOLD, how good and how pleasant
it is
For brethren to dwell together in unity!

2 *It is* like the precious oil upon the head,
Running down on the beard,
The beard of Aaron,
Running down on the edge of his
garments.
3 *It is* like the dew of [R]Hermon, Deut. 4:48
Descending upon the mountains of Zion;
For [R]there the LORD commanded the
blessing— Lev. 25:21
Life forevermore.

PSALM 134

Praise the Lord in the Evening

A Song of Ascents.

BEHOLD, bless the LORD,
All *you* servants of the LORD,
Who by night stand in the house of the
LORD!
2 [R]Lift up your hands *in* the sanctuary,
And bless the LORD. [1 Tim. 2:8]

3 The LORD who made heaven and earth
Bless you from Zion!

132:6 Heb. *Jaar*, lit. *Woods*

PSALM 135

God Has Done Great Things!

PRAISE the LORD!

Praise the name of the LORD;
Praise *Him*, O you servants of the LORD!
2 You who stand in the house of the LORD,
In the courts of the house of our God,
3 Praise the LORD, for [R]the LORD *is* good;
Sing praises to His name, [R]for *it is* pleasant. [Ps. 119:68] • Ps. 147:1
4 For [R]the LORD has chosen Jacob for Himself, [Ex. 19:5]
Israel for His special treasure.

5 For I know that the LORD *is* great,
And our Lord *is* above all gods.
6[R] Whatever the LORD pleases He does,
In heaven and in earth, Ps. 115:3
In the seas and in all deep places.
7[R] He causes the vapors to ascend from the ends of the earth; Jer. 10:13
He makes lightning for the rain;
He brings the wind out of His [R]treasuries. Jer. 51:16

8[R] He destroyed the firstborn of Egypt,
Both of man and beast. Ex. 12:12
9[R] He sent signs and wonders into the midst of you, O Egypt, Ex. 7:10
Upon Pharaoh and all his servants.
10[R] He defeated many nations Num. 21:24
And slew mighty kings—
11 Sihon king of the Amorites,
Og king of Bashan,
And all the kingdoms of Canaan—
12 And gave their land *as* a heritage,
A heritage to Israel His people.

13[R] Your name, O LORD, *endures* forever,
Your fame, O LORD, throughout all generations. [Ex. 3:15]
14[R] For the LORD will judge His people,
And He will have compassion on His servants. Deut. 32:36

15[R] The idols of the nations *are* silver and gold, [Ps. 115:4–8]
The work of men's hands.
16 They have mouths, but they do not speak;
Eyes they have, but they do not see;
17 They have ears, but they do not hear;
Nor is there *any* breath in their mouths.
18 Those who make them are like them;
So is everyone who trusts in them.

19 Bless the LORD, O house of Israel!
Bless the LORD, O house of Aaron!
20 Bless the LORD, O house of Levi!
You who fear the LORD, bless the LORD!
21 Blessed be the LORD [R]out of Zion,
Who dwells in Jerusalem! Ps. 134:3

Praise the LORD!

PSALM 136

God's Mercy Endures Forever

OH, [R]give thanks to the LORD, for *He is* good! Ps. 106:1
For His mercy *endures* forever.
2 Oh, give thanks to the God of gods!
For His mercy *endures* forever.
3 Oh, give thanks to the Lord of lords!
For His mercy *endures* forever:

4 To Him who alone does great wonders,
For His mercy *endures* forever;
5[R] To Him who by wisdom made the heavens, Jer. 51:15
For His mercy *endures* forever;
6[R] To Him who laid out the earth above the waters, Jer. 10:12
For His mercy *endures* forever;
7 To Him who made great lights,
For His mercy *endures* forever—
8[R] The sun to rule by day, Gen. 1:16
For His mercy *endures* forever;
9 The moon and stars to rule by night,
For His mercy *endures* forever.

10[R] To Him who struck Egypt in their firstborn, Ex. 12:29
For His mercy *endures* forever;
11[R] And brought out Israel from among them, Ex. 12:51; 13:3, 16
For His mercy *endures* forever;
12[R] With a strong hand, and with an outstretched arm, Ex. 6:6
For His mercy *endures* forever;
13 To Him who divided the Red Sea in two,
For His mercy *endures* forever;
14 And made Israel pass through the midst of it,
For His mercy *endures* forever;
15[R] But overthrew Pharaoh and his army in the Red Sea, Ex. 14:27
For His mercy *endures* forever;
16[R] To Him who led His people through the wilderness, Ex. 13:18; 15:22
For His mercy *endures* forever;
17 To Him who struck down great kings,
For His mercy *endures* forever;
18[R] And slew famous kings, Deut. 29:7
For His mercy *endures* forever—
19[R] Sihon king of the Amorites, Num. 21:21
For His mercy *endures* forever;
20[R] And Og king of Bashan, Num. 21:33
For His mercy *endures* forever—
21 And gave their land as a heritage,
For His mercy *endures* forever;
22 A heritage to Israel His servant,
For His mercy *endures* forever.

23 Who remembered us in our lowly state,
For His mercy *endures* forever;
24 And rescued us from our enemies,
For His mercy *endures* forever;
25[R] Who gives food to all flesh, Ps. 104:27
For His mercy *endures* forever.

26 Oh, give thanks to the God of heaven!
For His mercy *endures* forever.

PSALM 137

Tears in Exile

BY the rivers of Babylon,
There we sat down, yea, we wept
When we remembered Zion.
2 We hung our harps
Upon the willows in the midst of it.
3 For there those who carried us away
captive asked of us a song,
And those who [R]plundered us *requested*
mirth, Ps. 79:1
Saying, "Sing us *one* of the songs of
Zion!"

4 How shall we sing the LORD's song
In a foreign land?
5 If I forget you, O Jerusalem,
Let my right hand forget *its skill!*
6 If I do not remember you,
Let my [R]tongue cling to the roof of my
mouth— Ezek. 3:26
If I do not exalt Jerusalem
Above my chief joy.

7 Remember, O LORD, against [R]the sons of
Edom Jer. 49:7–22
The day of Jerusalem,
Who said, [T]"Raze *it*, raze *it*, Lit. *Make bare*
To its very foundation!"

8 O daughter of Babylon, [R]who are to be
destroyed, Is. 13:1–6; 47:1
Happy the one [R]who repays you as you
have served us! Jer. 50:15
9 Happy the one who takes and dashes
Your little ones against the rock!

PSALM 138

God Answered My Prayer

A Psalm of David.

I WILL praise You with my whole heart;
[R]Before the gods I will sing praises to
You. Ps. 119:46
2[R] I will worship [R]toward Your holy temple,
And praise Your name Ps. 28:2 • 1 Kin. 8:29
For Your lovingkindness and Your truth;
For You have [R]magnified Your word
above all Your name. Is. 42:21
3 In the day when I cried out, You
answered me,
And made me bold *with* strength in my
soul.

4[R] All the kings of the earth shall praise
You, O LORD, Ps. 102:15
When they hear the words of Your
mouth.
5 Yes, they shall sing of the ways of the
LORD,
For great *is* the glory of the LORD.
6 Though the LORD *is* on high,
Yet [R]He regards the lowly; [James 4:6]
But the proud He knows from afar.

7[R] Though I walk in the midst of trouble,
You will revive me; [Ps. 23:3, 4]
You will stretch out Your hand
Against the wrath of my enemies,
And Your right hand will save me.
8[R] The LORD will [T]perfect *that which*
concerns me; Ps. 57:2 • *complete*
Your mercy, O LORD, *endures* forever;
Do not forsake the works of Your hands.

PSALM 139

"Search Me, O God"

For the Chief Musician. A Psalm of David.

O LORD, [R]You have searched me and
known *me*. Ps. 17:3
2[R] You know my sitting down and my rising
up; 2 Kin. 19:27
You understand my thought afar off.
3[R] You [T]comprehend my path and my lying
down, Job 14:16; 31:4 • Lit. *winnow*
And are acquainted with all my ways.
4 For *there is* not a word on my tongue,
But behold, O LORD, [R]You know it
altogether. [Heb. 4:13]
5 You have [T]hedged me behind and before,
And laid Your hand upon me. *enclosed*
6[R] *Such* knowledge *is* too wonderful for me;
It is high, I cannot *attain* it. Job 42:3

7 Where can I go from Your Spirit?
Or where can I flee from Your presence?
8 If I ascend into heaven, You *are* there;
[R]If I make my bed in [T]hell, behold, You *are*
there. [Job 26:6] • Or *Sheol*
9 *If* I take the wings of the morning,
And dwell in the uttermost parts of the
sea,
10 Even there Your hand shall lead me,
And Your right hand shall hold me.
11 If I say, "Surely the darkness shall fall*
on me,"
Even the night shall be light about me;
12 Indeed, [R]the darkness [T]shall not hide
from You, Job 26:6; 34:22 • Lit. *is not dark*
But the night shines as the day;

139:11 Vg., Symmachus *cover*

The darkness and the light *are* both alike
to You.

13 For You formed my inward parts;
You covered me in my mother's womb.

14 I will praise You, for I am fearfully *and*
wonderfully made;*
Marvelous are Your works,
And *that* my soul knows very well.

15[R] My frame was not hidden from You,
When I was made in secret,
And skillfully wrought in the lowest
parts of the earth. Job 10:8, 9
16 Your eyes saw my substance, being yet
unformed.
And in Your book they all were written,
The days fashioned for me,
When *as yet there were* none of them.

17[R] How precious also are Your thoughts to
me, O God! [Ps. 40:5]
How great is the sum of them!
18 *If* I should count them, they would be
more in number than the sand;
When I awake, I am still with You.

19 Oh, that You would [R]slay the wicked,
O God! [Is. 11:4]
[R]Depart from me, therefore, you
bloodthirsty men. Ps. 119:115
20 For they speak against You wickedly;
Your enemies take *Your name* in vain.*
21[R] Do I not hate them, O LORD, who hate
You? 2 Chr. 19:2
And do I not loathe those who rise up
against You?
22 I hate them with [T]perfect hatred;
I count them my enemies. *complete*

23 Search me, O God, and know my heart;
Try me, and know my anxieties;
24 And see if *there is any* wicked way in me,
And lead me in the way everlasting.

PSALM 140

Preserve Me from Violence

To the Chief Musician. A Psalm of David.

DELIVER me, O LORD, from evil men;
Preserve me from violent men,
2 Who plan evil things in *their* hearts;
They continually gather together *for* war.
3 They sharpen their tongues like a
serpent;
The [R]poison of asps *is* under their lips.
Selah Ps. 58:4

4[R] Keep me, O LORD, from the hands of the
wicked; Ps. 71:4
Preserve me from violent men,
Who have purposed to make my steps
stumble.
5 The proud have hidden a [R]snare for me,
and cords; Jer. 18:22
They have spread a net by the wayside;
They have set traps for me. Selah

6 I said to the LORD: "You *are* my God;
Hear the voice of my supplications,
O LORD.
7 O GOD the Lord, the strength of my
salvation,
You have [T]covered my head in the day of
battle. *sheltered*
8 Do not grant, O LORD, the desires of the
wicked;
Do not further his *wicked* scheme,
[R]*Lest* they be exalted. Selah Deut. 32:27

9 "*As for* the head of those who surround
me,
Let the evil of their lips cover them;
10[R] Let burning coals fall upon them;
Let them be cast into the fire,

139:14 So with MT, Tg.; LXX, Syr., Vg. *You are fearfully wonderful* **139:20** LXX, Vg. *They take your cities in vain*

139:14 God's Work in Our Lives—All people possess an inward desire that their work should have meaning and permanence (Page 595—Ps. 90:16, 17). If such work is not to be lost in the vastness of eternity, however, it must conform to the work God has designed. This work for the present day can be known only from God's Word.

According to the Word of God, the initial work of God is for us to believe in Jesus Christ (Page 1088—John 6:29; Page 1153—Rom. 6:17, 18). Apart from entering into this vital relationship with God, man cannot even begin to work for God. After coming to know Christ, the new Christian discovers God's program for the present from the Scriptures. It is, first of all, His work in the Christian himself. Regeneration is only the beginning of God's work in the believer. It actually introduces a process of becoming like Christ which God promises ultimately to bring to perfection (Page 1213—Phil. 1:6). The Christian's cheerful obedience to God's will as revealed in His Word helps speed this work along.

Second, no Christian can overlook God's work in the world. Jesus' command to spread the good news of the gospel to all people appears near the end of all four Gospels and at the beginning of the Book of Acts. God's method is that people proclaim the gospel and that the Holy Spirit convict (Page 1101—John 16:8–11).

Finally, God's work is in and through the church, the organism ordained by Christ for this age (Page 994—Matt. 16:18). God works in the church through the Spirit and through spiritually gifted people to strengthen and bless it (Page 1207—Eph. 4:11–13).

Now turn to Page 1204—Eph. 1:22, 23: God's Work in the Church.

Into deep pits, that they rise not up
again. Ps. 11:6
11 Let not a slanderer be established in the
earth;
Let evil hunt the violent man to
overthrow *him*."

12 I know that the LORD will [R]maintain
The cause of the afflicted,
And justice for the poor. 1 Kin. 8:45
13 Surely the righteous shall give thanks to
Your name;
The upright shall dwell in Your presence.

PSALM 141

"Set a Guard, O LORD, over My Mouth"

A Psalm of David.

LORD, I cry out to You;
Make haste to me!
Give ear to my voice when I cry out to
You.
2 Let my prayer be set before You [R]*as*
incense, [Rev. 5:8; 8:3, 4]
[R]The lifting up of my hands *as* the
evening sacrifice. [1 Tim. 2:8]

3 Set a guard, O LORD, over my mouth;
Keep watch over the door of my lips.
4 Do not incline my heart to any evil
thing,
To practice wicked works
With men who work iniquity;
And do not let me eat of their delicacies.

5 [R]Let the righteous strike me; [Prov. 9:8]
It shall be a kindness.
And let him rebuke me;
It shall be as excellent oil;
Let my head not refuse it.

For still my prayer *is* against the deeds of
the wicked.
6 Their judges are overthrown by the sides
of the [T]cliff, rock
And they hear my words, for they are
sweet.
7 Our bones are scattered at the mouth of
the grave,
As when one plows and breaks up the
earth.

8 But [R]my eyes *are* upon You, O GOD the
Lord; Ps. 25:15
In You I take refuge;
Do not leave my soul destitute.
9 Keep me from [R]the snares they have laid
for me, Ps. 119:110
And from the traps of the workers of
iniquity.
10 [R]Let the wicked fall into their own nets,
While I escape safely. Ps. 35:8

PSALM 142

"No One Cares for My Soul"

A [R]Contemplation* of David.
A Prayer [R]when he was in
the cave. Ps. 32:title • 1 Sam. 22:1

I CRY out to the LORD with my voice;
With my voice to the LORD I make my
supplication.
2 I pour out my complaint before Him;
I declare before Him my trouble.

3 When my spirit [T]was [R]overwhelmed
within me, Lit. *fainted* • Ps. 77:3
Then You knew my path.
In the way in which I walk
They have secretly set a snare for me.
4 Look on *my* right hand and see,
For *there is* no one who acknowledges
me;
Refuge has failed me;
No one cares for my soul.

5 I cried out to You, O LORD:
I said, "You *are* my refuge,
My portion in the land of the living.
6 [T]Attend to my cry, *Give heed*
For I am brought very low;
Deliver me from my persecutors,
For they are stronger than I.
7 Bring my soul out of prison,
That I may praise Your name;
The righteous shall surround me,
For You shall deal bountifully with me."

PSALM 143

"Teach Me to Do Your Will"

A Psalm of David.

HEAR my prayer, O LORD,
Give ear to my supplications!
In Your faithfulness answer me,
And in Your righteousness.
2 Do not enter into judgment with Your
servant,
[R]For in Your sight no one living is
righteous. [Gal. 2:16]

3 For the enemy has persecuted my soul;
He has crushed my life to the ground;
He has made me dwell in darkness,
Like those who have long been dead.
4 [R]Therefore my spirit is overwhelmed
within me; Ps. 77:3
My heart within me is distressed.

5 I remember the days of old;
I meditate on all Your works;
I muse on the work of Your hands.
6 I spread out my hands to You;

142:title Heb. *Maschil*

[R]My soul *longs* for You like a thirsty land.
Selah Ps. 63:1

7 Answer me speedily, O LORD;
My spirit fails!
Do not hide Your face from me,
[R]Lest I [T]be like those who [T]go down into the pit. Ps. 28:1 • *become* • Die
8 Cause me to hear Your lovingkindness
[R]in the morning, Ps. 46:5
For in You do I trust;
[R]Cause me to know the way in which I should walk, Ps. 5:8
For [R]I lift up my soul to You. Ps. 25:1

9 Deliver me, O LORD, from my enemies;
In You I take shelter.*
10 [R]Teach me to do Your will, Ps. 25:4, 5
For You *are* my God;
[R]Your Spirit *is* good. Neh. 9:20
Lead me in the land of uprightness.

11 [R]Revive me, O LORD, for Your name's sake! Ps. 119:25
For Your righteousness' sake bring my soul out of trouble.
12 In Your mercy [R]cut[T] off my enemies,
And destroy all those who afflict my soul; Ps. 54:5 • *put an end to*
For I *am* Your servant.

PSALM 144

"What Is Man?"

A Psalm of David.

BLESSED *be* the LORD my Rock,
[R]Who trains my hands for war,
And my fingers for battle— 2 Sam. 22:35
2 My lovingkindness and my fortress,
My high tower and my deliverer,
My shield and *the One* in whom I take refuge,
Who subdues my people* under me.

3 [R]LORD, what *is* man, that You take knowledge of him? Heb. 2:6
Or the son of man, that You are mindful of him?
4 [R]Man is like a breath; Ps. 39:11
His days *are* like a passing shadow.

5 [R]Bow down Your heavens, O LORD, and come down; Ps. 18:9
[R]Touch the mountains, and they shall smoke. Ps. 104:32
6 [R]Flash forth lightning and scatter them;
Shoot out Your arrows and destroy them. Ps. 18:13, 14
7 Stretch out Your hand from above;
Rescue me and deliver me out of great waters,
From the hand of foreigners,
8 Whose mouth [R]speaks [T]lying words,
And whose right hand *is* a right hand of falsehood. Ps. 12:2 • *empty* or *worthless*

9 I will [R]sing a new song to You, O God;
On a harp of ten strings I will sing praises to You, Ps. 33:2, 3; 40:3
10 *The One* who gives salvation to kings,
[R]Who delivers David His servant
From the deadly sword. Ps. 18:50
11 Rescue me and deliver me from the hand of foreigners,
Whose mouth speaks lying words,
And whose right hand *is* a right hand of falsehood—
12 That our sons *may be* [R]as plants grown up in their youth; Ps. 128:3
That our daughters *may be* as [T]pillars,
Sculptured in palace style; *corner pillars*
13 *That* our barns *may be* full,
Supplying all kinds of produce;
That our sheep may bring forth thousands
And ten thousands in our fields;
14 *That* our oxen *may be* well laden;
That there be no [T]breaking in or going out; Lit. *breach*
That there be no outcry in our streets.
15 [R]Happy *are* the people who are in such a state; [Ps. 33:12]
Happy *are* the people whose God *is* the LORD!

PSALM 145

Testify to God's Great Acts

[R]A Praise of David. Ps. 100:title

I WILL [T]extol You, my God, O King; *praise*
And I will bless Your name forever and ever.
2 Every day I will bless You,
And I will praise Your name forever and ever.
3 [R]Great *is* the LORD, and greatly to be praised; [Ps. 147:5]
And His greatness *is* unsearchable.

4 [R]One generation shall praise Your works to another, Is. 38:19
And shall declare Your mighty acts.
5 I* will meditate on the glorious splendor of Your majesty,
And on Your wondrous works.*
6 *Men* shall speak of the might of Your awesome acts,
And I will declare Your greatness.

143:9 LXX, Vg. *To You I flee* **144:2** So with MT, LXX, Vg.; Syr., Tg. *the peoples* (cf. 18:47) **145:5** So with MT, Tg.; DSS, LXX, Syr., Vg. *They* • Lit. *on the words of Your wondrous works*

7 They shall utter the memory of Your
great goodness,
And shall sing of Your righteousness.

8[R] The LORD *is* gracious and full of
compassion, [Num. 14:18]
Slow to anger and great in mercy.
9[R] The LORD *is* good to all, Nah. 1:7
And His tender mercies *are* over all His
works.

10[R] All Your works shall praise You, O LORD,
And Your saints shall bless You. Ps. 19:1
11 They shall speak of the glory of Your
kingdom,
And talk of Your power,
12 To make known to the sons of men His
mighty acts,
And the glorious majesty of His
kingdom.
13[R] Your kingdom *is* an everlasting
kingdom, [1 Tim. 1:17]
And Your dominion *endures* throughout
all generations.*

14 The LORD upholds all who fall,
And raises up all *who are* bowed down.
15[R] The eyes of all look expectantly to You,
And [R]You give them their food in due
season. Ps. 104:27 • Ps. 136:25
16 You open Your hand
[R]And satisfy the desire of every living
thing. Ps. 104:21, 28

17 The LORD *is* righteous in all His ways,
Gracious in all His works.
18[R] The LORD *is* near to all who call upon
Him, [Deut. 4:7]
To all who call upon Him in truth.
19 He will fulfill the desire of those who
fear Him;
He also will hear their cry and save
them.
20 The LORD preserves all who love Him,
But all the wicked He will destroy.
21 My mouth shall speak the praise of the
LORD,
And all flesh shall bless His holy name
Forever and ever.

PSALM 146

"Do Not Put Your Trust in Princes"

PRAISE[T] the LORD! Heb. *Hallelujah*

[R]Praise the LORD, O my soul! Ps. 103:1
2[R] While I live I will praise the LORD;
I will sing praises to my God while I
have my being. Ps. 104:33

3[R] Do not put your trust in princes,
Nor in a son of man, in whom *there is* no
[T]help. [Is. 2:22] • *salvation*
4[R] His spirit departs, he returns to his
earth; [Eccl. 12:7]
In that very day his plans perish.

5[R] Happy *is he* who *has* the God of Jacob
for his help, Jer. 17:7
Whose hope *is* in the LORD his God,
6[R] Who made heaven and earth, Rev. 14:7
The sea, and all that *is* in them;
Who keeps truth forever,
7 Who executes justice for the oppressed,
[R]Who gives food to the hungry. Ps. 107:9
The LORD gives freedom to the prisoners.

8[R] The LORD opens *the eyes of* the blind;
[R]The LORD raises those who are bowed
down; Matt. 9:30 • Luke 13:13
The LORD loves the righteous.
9[R] The LORD watches over the strangers;
He relieves the fatherless and widow;
[R]But the way of the wicked He turns
upside down. Deut. 10:18 • Ps. 147:6
10[R] The LORD shall reign forever—
Your God, O Zion, to all generations.

Praise the LORD! Ex. 15:18

PSALM 147

God Heals the Brokenhearted

PRAISE[T] the LORD! Heb. *Hallelujah*
For [R]*it is* good to sing praises to our
God; Ps. 92:1
[R]For *it is* pleasant, *and* [R]praise is
beautiful. Ps. 135:3 • Ps. 33:1

2 The LORD [R]builds up Jerusalem;
[R]He gathers together the outcasts of
Israel. Ps. 102:16 • Deut. 30:3
3[R] He heals the brokenhearted [Ps. 51:17]
And binds up their [T]wounds. Lit. *sorrows*
4[R] He counts the number of the stars;
He calls them all by name. Is. 40:26
5 Great *is* our Lord, and mighty in power;
[R]His understanding *is* infinite. Is. 40:28
6[R] The LORD lifts up the humble;
He casts the wicked down to the
ground. Ps. 146:8, 9

7 Sing to the LORD with thanksgiving;
Sing praises on the harp to our God,
8[R] Who covers the heavens with clouds,
Who prepares rain for the earth,
Who makes grass to grow on the
mountains. Job 38:26
9[R] He gives to the beast its food, Job 38:41
And to the young ravens that cry.

145:13 So with MT, Tg.; DSS, LXX, Syr., Vg. add *The LORD is faithful in all His words, And holy in all His works*

10[R] He does not delight in the strength of the horse; Ps. 33:16, 17
He takes no pleasure in the legs of a man.
11 The LORD takes pleasure in those who fear Him,
In those who hope in His mercy.

12 Praise the LORD, O Jerusalem!
Praise your God, O Zion!
13 For He has strengthened the bars of your gates;
He has blessed your children within you.
14 He makes peace *in* your borders,
And fills you with the finest wheat.

15[R] He sends out His command *to the* earth;
His word runs very swiftly. [Ps. 107:20]
16[R] He gives snow like wool; Job 37:6
He scatters the frost like ashes;
17 He casts out His hail like morsels;
Who can stand before His cold?
18[R] He sends out His word and melts them;
He causes His wind to blow, *and* the waters flow. Job 37:10

19[R] He declares His word to Jacob,
[R] His statutes and His judgments to Israel. Deut. 33:4 • Mal. 4:4
20[R] He has not dealt thus with any nation;
And *as for His* judgments, they have not known them. [Rom. 3:1, 2]

[T] Praise the LORD! Heb. *Hallelujah*

PSALM 148

All Creation Praises the LORD

PRAISE[T] the LORD! Heb. *Hallelujah*

Praise the LORD from the heavens;
Praise Him in the heights!
2 Praise Him, all His angels;
Praise Him, all His hosts!
3 Praise Him, sun and moon;
Praise Him, all you stars of light!
4 Praise Him, you heavens of heavens,
And you waters above the heavens!

5 Let them praise the name of the LORD,
For [R]He commanded and they were created. Gen. 1:1, 6
6[R] He also established them forever and ever; Ps. 89:37
He made a decree which shall not pass away.

7 Praise the LORD from the earth,
[R] You great sea creatures and all the depths; Is. 43:20
8 Fire and hail, snow and clouds;
Stormy wind, fulfilling His word;
9[R] Mountains and all hills; Is. 44:23; 49:13
Fruitful trees and all cedars;
10 Beasts and all cattle;
Creeping things and flying fowl;
11 Kings of the earth and all peoples;
Princes and all judges of the earth;
12 Both young men and maidens;
Old men and children.

13 Let them praise the name of the LORD,
For His [R]name alone is exalted; Ps. 8:1
His glory *is* above the earth and heaven.
14 And He [R]has exalted the [T]horn of His people, Ps. 75:10 • *Strength or dominion*
The praise of [R]all His saints— Ps. 149:9
Of the children of Israel,
[R] A people near to Him. Eph. 2:17

[T] Praise the LORD! Heb. *Hallelujah*

PSALM 149

"The LORD Takes Pleasure in His People"

PRAISE[T] the LORD! Heb. *Hallelujah*

[R] Sing to the LORD a new song, Ps. 33:3
And His praise in the assembly of saints.

2 Let Israel rejoice in their Maker;
Let the children of Zion be joyful in their [R]King. Zech. 9:9
3[R] Let them praise His name with the dance; Ps. 81:2
Let them sing praises to Him with the timbrel and harp.
4 For [R]the LORD takes pleasure in His people; Ps. 35:27
[R] He will beautify the [T]humble with salvation. Ps. 132:16 • *meek*

5 Let the saints be joyful in glory;
Let them sing aloud on their beds.
6 *Let* the high praises of God *be* in their mouth,
And a two-edged sword in their hand,
7 To execute vengeance on the nations,
And punishments on the peoples;
8 To bind their kings with chains,
And their nobles with fetters of iron;
9[R] To execute on them the written judgment— Deut. 7:1, 2
This honor have all His saints.

[T] Praise the LORD! Heb. *Hallelujah*

PSALM 150

"Praise the LORD!"

PRAISE[R] the LORD! Ps. 145:5, 6

Praise God in His sanctuary;
Praise Him in His mighty firmament!

2 Praise Him for His mighty acts;
Praise Him according to His excellent
[R]greatness! Deut. 3:24

3 Praise Him with the sound of the
[T]trumpet; cornet
Praise Him with the lute and harp!
4 Praise Him with the timbrel and
dance;
Praise Him with stringed instruments
and flutes!
5 Praise Him with loud cymbals;
Praise Him with clashing cymbals!

6 Let everything that has breath praise the
LORD.

[T]Praise the LORD! Heb. *Hallelujah*

150:1 Praise—To praise God is to acknowledge the glories of His excellent Person. It differs somewhat from thanksgiving, which describes what God has done rather than what He is. Here are some facts about praise.

a. God alone is worthy of our praise (Page 553—Ps. 18:3; 113:3).
b. It is His will for us that we praise Him (Page 572—Ps. 50:23; Page 721—Is. 43:21).
c. This praise should be continuous (Page 562—Ps. 34:1; 71:6) and also public (Page 556—Ps. 22:25).
d. We are to praise God for His holiness (Page 449—2 Chr. 20:21), grace (Page 1204—Eph. 1:6), goodness (Page 618—Ps. 135:3), and kindness (Page 619—Ps. 138:2).
e. All nature praises God (Page 624—Ps. 148:7–10).
f. The sun, moon, and stars praise Him (Page 554—Ps. 19:1; 148:3).
g. The angels praise Him (Page 624—Ps. 148:2).

In fact, we are told that on occasion God uses even the wrath of men to praise Him (Page 586—Ps. 76:10). An example of this is seen in the selling of Joseph by his brothers into slavery (Page 39—Gen. 37:28). God later uses this cruel act to promote Joseph as second ruler over all Egypt. As Joseph would remind his brothers: "But as for you, you meant evil against me; *but* God meant it for good, in order to bring it about as *it is* this day, to save many people alive" (Page 52—Gen. 50:20).

Now turn to Page 1293—1 John 1:9: Confession.

THE BOOK OF

PROVERBS

THE BOOK OF PROVERBS

The key word in Proverbs is *wisdom,* "the ability to live life skillfully." A godly life in an ungodly world, however, is no simple assignment. Proverbs provides God's detailed instructions for His people to deal successfully with the practical affairs of everyday life: how to relate to God, parents, children, neighbors, and government. Solomon, the principal author, uses a combination of poetry, parables, pithy questions, short stories, and wise maxims to give in strikingly memorable form the common sense and divine perspective necessary to handle life's issues.

Because Solomon, the pinnacle of Israel's wise men, was the principal contributor, the Hebrew title of this book is *Mishle Shelomoh,* "Proverbs of Solomon" (1:1). The Greek title is *Paroimiai Salomontos,* "Proverbs of Solomon." The Latin title *Liber Proverbiorum,* "Book of Proverbs," combines the words *pro* ("for") and *verba* ("words") to describe the way the proverbs concentrate many words into a few. The Rabbinical writings called Proverbs *Sepher Hokhmah,* "Book of Wisdom."

THE AUTHOR OF PROVERBS

Solomon's name appears at the beginning of the three sections he wrote: 1:1 for chapters 1—9, 10:1 for chapters 10:1—22:16, and 25:1 for chapters 25—29. According to 1 Kings 4:32, he spoke 3,000 proverbs and 1,005 songs. Only about 800 of his 3,000 proverbs are included in the two Solomonic collections in this book. No man was better qualified than Solomon to be the principal contributor. He asked for wisdom (1 Kin. 3:5–9) and God granted it to him (1 Kin. 4:29–31) to such a degree that people from foreign lands came to hear him speak (1 Kin. 4:34; 10:1–13, 24). His breadth of knowledge, aptitude, skill, and perception were extraordinary. In every area Solomon brought prosperity and glory to Israel until his latter years (cf. 1 Kin. 11:4).

It is likely that Solomon collected and edited proverbs other than his own. According to Ecclesiastes 12:9, "he pondered and sought out *and* set in order many proverbs." The second collection of Solomonic proverbs in 25—29 was assembled by the scribes of King Hezekiah because of his interest in spiritually benefiting his subjects with the Word of God. The prophets Isaiah and Micah ministered during Hezekiah's time, and it has been suggested that they also might have been involved in this collection.

Proverbs 22:17—24:34 consists of "the words of the wise" (22:17; 24:23). Some of these sayings are quite similar to those found in The Wisdom of Amenemope, a document of teachings on civil service by an Egyptian who probably lived between 1000 B.C. and 600 B.C. Wise men of this period went to hear one another, and it is probable that Amenemope borrowed certain aphorisms from Hebrew literature. If the *hakhamim* ("wise men") lived before Solomon's time, he may have been the collector and editor of this series of wise sayings.

There is no biblical information about Agur (30) or Lemuel (31). Agur ben Jakeh (30:1) is simply called an oracle, and Lemuel is called a king and an oracle (31:1). Both have been identified with Solomon, but there is no basis for this suggestion.

THE TIME OF PROVERBS

Proverbs is a collection of topical maxims and is not a historical book. It is a product of the wisdom school in Israel. According to Jeremiah 18:18 and Ezekiel 7:26, three groups communicated to the people on behalf of God: the priests imparted the Law; the prophets communicated the divine word and visions; and the elders gave counsel to the people. The elders provided the practical application of godly wisdom to specific problems and decisions. The "Preacher" of Ecclesiastes is a good example of the wisdom school (Eccl. 1:1, 12; 7:27; 12:8–10). *Qoheleth,* or "Preacher," meant "one who addresses an assembly": he presided over a "school" of wise men and "taught the people knowledge" (Eccl. 12:9). "My son" in Proverbs and Ecclesiastes evidently refers to the pupil. This was parallel to Samuel's role of heading Israel's school of prophets.

Wisdom literature is also found in other countries of the ancient Near East. In Egypt, written examples can be found as early as 2700 B.C. Although the style was similar to Israel's wisdom literature, the proverbs and sayings of these countries differed from those of Israel in content because they lacked the character of the righteous standards of the Lord.

Solomon's proverbs were written by 931 B.C., and his proverbs in chapters 25—29 were collected by Hezekiah about 230 years later (Hezekiah reigned from 715 to 686 B.C.). Under Solomon, Israel was at its spiritual, political, and economic summit. Solomon probably wrote his proverbs in his middle years, before his character began to decline into carnality, materialism, and idolatry.

THE CHRIST OF PROVERBS

In Proverbs 8, wisdom is personified and seen in its perfection. It is divine (8:22–31), it is the source of biological and spiritual life (3:18; 8:35), it is righteous and moral (8:8, 9), and it is available to all who will receive it (8:1–6, 32–35). This wisdom became incarnate in Christ "in whom are hidden all the treasures of wisdom and knowledge" (Col. 2:3). "But of Him you are in Christ Jesus, who became for us wisdom from God—and righteousness and sanctification and redemption" (1 Cor. 1:30; cf. 1 Cor. 1:22–24).

KEYS TO PROVERBS

Key Word: Wisdom—Proverbs is one of the few biblical books that clearly spells out its purpose. The purpose statement in 1:2–6 is twofold: (1) to impart moral discernment and discretion (1:3–5), and (2) to develop mental clarity and perception (1:2, 6). The words "wisdom and instruction" in 1:2 complement each other because "wisdom" (*hokhmah*) means "skill" and "instruction" (*musar*) means "discipline." No skill is perfected without discipline, and when a person has skill he has freedom to create something beautiful. Proverbs deals with the most fundamental skill of all: practical righteousness before God in every area of life. This requires knowledge, experience, and a willingness to put God first (see 3:5–7). Chapters 1—9 are designed to create a felt need for wisdom, and Proverbs as a whole is designed both to prevent and to remedy ungodly lifestyles. The book served as a manual to impart the legacy of wisdom, prudence, understanding, discretion, knowledge, guidance, competence, correction, counsel, and truth—from generation to generation.

Key Verses: Proverbs 1:5–7 and 3:5, 6—"A wise *man* will hear and increase learning, and a man of understanding will attain wise counsel, to understand a proverb and an enigma, the words of the wise and their riddles. The fear of the LORD *is* the beginning of knowledge, *but* fools despise wisdom and instruction" (1:5–7).

"Trust in the LORD with all your heart, and lean not on your own understanding; in all your ways acknowledge Him, and He shall direct your paths" (3:5, 6).

Key Chapter: Proverbs 31—The last chapter of Proverbs is unique in ancient literature, as it reveals a very high and noble view of women. The woman in these verses is: (1) a good woman (31:13, 15, 16, 19, 25), (2) a good wife (31:11, 12, 23, 24), (3) a good mother (31:14, 15, 18, 21, 27), and (4) a good neighbor (31:20–26). Her conduct, concern, speech, and life stand in sharp contrast to the woman pictured in Proverbs 7.

SURVEY OF PROVERBS

Proverbs is the most intensely practical book in the Old Testament because it teaches skillful living in the multiple aspects of everyday life. Its specific precepts include instruction on wisdom and folly, the righteous and the wicked, the tongue, pride and humility, justice and vengeance, the family, laziness and work, poverty and wealth, friends and neighbors, love and lust, anger and strife, masters and servants, life and death. Proverbs touches upon every facet of human relationships, and its principles transcend the bounds of time and culture.

The Hebrew word for "proverb" (*mashal*) means "comparison, similar, parallel." A proverb uses a comparison or figure of speech to make a pithy but poignant observation. Proverbs have been defined as simple illustrations that expose fundamental realities of life. These maxims are not theoretical but practical; they are easily memorized, based on real-life experience, and designed for use in the mainstream of life. The proverbs are general statements and illustrations of timeless

FOCUS	PURPOSE OF PROVERBS	PROVERBS TO YOUTH	PROVERBS OF SOLOMON	PROVERBS OF SOLOMON (HEZEKIAH)	WORDS OF AGUR	WORDS OF LEMUEL
REFERENCE	1:1	1:8	10:1	25:1	30:1	31:1—31:31
DIVISION	PURPOSE AND THEME	FATHER'S EXHORTATIONS	FIRST COLLECTION OF SOLOMON	SECOND COLLECTION OF SOLOMON	NUMERICAL PROVERBS	VIRTUOUS WIFE
TOPIC	PROLOGUE	PRINCIPLES OF WISDOM			EPILOGUE	
	COMMENDATION OF WISDOM	COUNSEL OF WISDOM			COMPARISONS OF WISDOM	
LOCATION	JUDAH					
TIME	c. 950–700 B.C.					

truth, which allow for, but do not condone, exceptions to the rule. The key word is *hokhmah*, "wisdom": it literally means "skill" (in living). Wisdom is more than shrewdness or intelligence. Instead, it relates to practical righteousness and moral acumen. The Book of Proverbs may be divided into six segments: the purpose of Proverbs (1:1–7), the proverbs to the youth (1:8—9:18), the proverbs of Solomon (10:1—24:34), the proverbs of Solomon copied by Hezekiah's men (25:1—29:27), the words of Agur (30:1–33), and the words of King Lemuel (31:1–31).

The Purpose of Proverbs (1:1–7): The brief prologue states the author, theme, and purpose of the book.

The Proverbs to the Youth (1:8—9:18): Following the introduction, there is a series of ten exhortations, each beginning with "My son" (1:8—9:18). These messages introduce the concept of wisdom in the format of a father's efforts to persuade his son to pursue the path of wisdom in order to achieve godly success in life. Wisdom rejects the invitation of crime and foolishness, rewards seekers of wisdom on every level, and wisdom's discipline provides freedom and safety (1—4). Wisdom protects one from illicit sensuality and its consequences, from foolish practices and laziness, and from adultery and the lure of the harlot (5—7). Wisdom is to be preferred to folly because of its divine origin and rich benefits (8 and 9). There are four kinds of fools, ranging from those who are naive and uncommitted to scoffers who arrogantly despise the way of God. The fool is not mentally deficient; he is self-sufficient, ordering his life as if there were no God.

The Proverbs of Solomon (10:1—24:34): There is a minimal amount of topical arrangement in these chapters. There are some thematic clusters (e.g., 26:1–12, 13–16, 20–22), but the usual units are one-verse maxims. It is helpful to assemble and organize these proverbs according to such specific themes as money and speech. This Solomonic collection consists of 375 proverbs of Solomon. Chapters 10—15 contrast right and wrong in practice, and all but nineteen proverbs use antithetic parallelism, that is, parallels of paired opposite principles. Chapters 16:1—22:16 offer a series of self-evident moral truths and all but eighteen proverbs use synonymous parallelism, that is, parallels of paired identical or similar principles. The words of wise men (22:17—24:34) are given in two groups. The first group includes thirty distinct sayings (22:17—24:22), and six more are found in the second group (24:23–34).

The Proverbs of Solomon Copied by Hezekiah's Men (25:1—29:27): This second Solomonic collection was copied and arranged by "the men of Hezekiah" (25:1). These proverbs in chapters 25—29 further develop the themes in the first Solomonic collection.

The Words of Agur (30:1–33): The last two chapters of Proverbs form an appendix of sayings by two otherwise unknown sages, Agur and Lemuel. Most of Agur's material is given in clusters of numerical proverbs.

The Words of King Lemuel (31:1–31): The last chapter includes an acrostic of twenty-two verses (the first letter of each verse consecutively follows the complete Hebrew alphabet) portraying a virtuous wife (31:10–31).

OUTLINE OF PROVERBS

I. The Purpose of Proverbs....................1:1–7

II. Proverbs to the Youth....................1:8—9:18

A. Obey Parents....................1:8, 9
B. Avoid Bad Company....................1:10–19
C. Seek Wisdom....................1:20—2:22
D. Benefits of Wisdom....................3:1–26
E. Be Kind to Others....................3:27–35
F. Father Says Get Wisdom....................4:1–13
G. Avoid the Wicked....................4:14–22
H. Keep Your Heart....................4:23–27
I. Do Not Commit Adultery....................5:1–14
J. Do Be Faithful to Your Spouse....................5:15–23
K. Avoid Surety....................6:1–5
L. Do Not Be Lazy....................6:6–19
M. Do Not Commit Adultery....................6:20—7:27
N. Praise of Wisdom....................8:1—9:12
O. Foolish Woman....................9:13–18

III. Proverbs of Solomon....................10:1—24:34

A. Proverbs Contrasting the Godly and the Wicked....................10:1—15:33
B. Proverbs Encouraging Godly Lives 16:1—22:16
C. Proverbs Concerning Various Situations....................22:17—24:34

IV. Proverbs of Solomon Copied by Hezekiah's Men....................25:1—29:27

A. Proverbs Regulating Relationships with Others....................25:1—26:28
1. Relationships with Kings....................25:1–7
2. Relationships with Neighbors....................25:8–20
3. Relationships with Enemies....................25:21–24
4. Relationships with Yourself....................25:25–28
5. Relationships with Fools....................26:1–12
6. Relationships with Lazy People.. 26:13–16
7. Relationships with Gossips....................26:17–28
B. Proverbs Regulating Various Activities....................27:1—29:27

V. The Words of Agur....................30:1–33

VI. The Words of King Lemuel....................31:1–31

A. Wisdom for Leaders....................31:1–9
B. Wise Woman....................31:10–31

CHAPTER 1

The Purpose of Proverbs

THE [R]proverbs of Solomon the son of David, king of Israel: 1 Kin. 4:32

2 To know wisdom and instruction,
To [T]perceive the words of
understanding, *understand* or *discern*
3 To receive the instruction of wisdom,
Justice, judgment, and equity;
4 To give prudence to the [R]simple,
To the young man knowledge and
discretion— Prov. 9:4
5 [R]A wise *man* will hear and increase
learning, Prov. 9:9
And a man of understanding will [T]attain
wise counsel, *acquire*
6 To understand a proverb and an enigma,
The words of the wise and their riddles.

7 [R]The fear of the LORD *is* the beginning of
knowledge, Job 28:28
But fools despise wisdom and instruction.

Obey Parents

8 [R]My son, hear the instruction of your
father, Prov. 4:1
And do not forsake the law of your
mother;

9 For they *will be* a [R]graceful ornament on
your head, Prov. 3:22
And chains about your neck.

Avoid Bad Company

10 My son, if sinners entice you,
[R]Do not consent. Gen. 39:7–10
11 If they say, "Come with us,
Let us [R]lie in wait to *shed* blood;
Let us lurk secretly for the innocent
without cause; Jer. 5:26
12 Let us swallow them alive like Sheol,*
And whole, [R]like those who go down to
the Pit; Ps. 28:1
13 We shall find all *kinds* of precious
[T]possessions, Lit. *wealth*
We shall fill our houses with spoil;
14 Cast in your lot among us,
Let us all have one purse"—
15 My son, [R]do not walk in the way with
them, Ps. 1:1
Keep your foot from their path;
16 [R]For their feet run to evil, [Is. 59:7]
And they make haste to shed blood.
17 Surely, in [T]vain the net is spread
In the sight of any bird; *futility*
18 But they lie in wait for their *own* blood,
They lurk secretly for their *own* lives.
19 [R]So *are* the ways of everyone who is
greedy for gain; [1 Tim. 6:10]
It takes away the life of its owners.

Seek Wisdom

20 [R]Wisdom calls aloud [T]outside;
She raises her voice in the open
squares. [John 7:37] • *in the street*
21 She cries out in the chief concourses,*
At the openings of the gates in the city
She speaks her words:
22 "How long, you [T]simple ones, will you
love [T]simplicity? *naive* • *naivete*
For scorners delight in their scorning,
And fools hate knowledge.
23 Turn at my rebuke;
Surely I will pour out my spirit on you;
I will make my words known to you.
24 [R]Because I have called and you refused,
I have stretched out my hand and no one
regarded, Jer. 7:13
25 Because you disdained all my counsel,

1:12 Or *the grave* **1:21** LXX, Syr., Tg. *top of the walls;* Vg. *the head of multitudes*

1:8 The Role of Children—Both the Old Testament and the New Testament agree that children have only one responsibility in the family—to obey their parents. The admonition of Solomon is more fully explained by Paul in Ephesians 6:1–3: "Children, obey your parents in the Lord, for this is right. 'Honor your father and mother,' which is the first commandment with promise: 'that it may be well with you and you may live long on the earth.' " "Children" is an inclusive term. It is not a matter of either sex or age that is involved.

Twice in Scripture God has intervened and directly stated what He would have children do. The last time was nearly two thousand years ago when He gave a revelation to Paul for the church. The first time was nearly thirty-four hundred years ago when He gave a revelation to Moses and Israel in which He commanded, "Honor your father and your mother." God's will for children is that they are to obey their parents. The expression "in the Lord" does not limit the responsibility only to the circumstances where the parents are believers. Col. 3:20 clearly points out that children are to obey their parents "in all things," not just in those things pertaining to Christian living. "In the Lord" more properly is understood to mean by the Lord or because it is the Lord's directive (this is what God says children are to do). "For this is right" indicates that for children to obey their parents is righteous or Godlike. Such obedience is perfectly illustrated by God the Son who was completely obedient to God the Father, even though that obedience resulted in His death (Page 1214—Phil. 2:6–8).

Two things are promised to children who obey their parents: it will be well with them—they will have a happy life; and they will have a long life. These are the two things that children want most, and obedience to parents is the only way to assure them. That is why this is the first commandment with promise; from it springs all the other important issues of life. Children who have not learned to obey their parents, who are God's representatives in the family, will not learn to obey God.

Now turn to Page 1209—Eph. 6:4: The Role of the Parents.

And would have none of my rebuke,
26 I also will laugh at your calamity;
I will mock when your terror comes,
27 When [R]your terror comes like a storm,
And your destruction comes like a
whirlwind, [Prov. 10:24, 25]
When distress and anguish come upon
you.
28 "Then[R] they will call on me, but I will not
answer; Is. 1:15
They will seek me diligently, but they
will not find me.
29 Because they [R]hated knowledge
And did not [R]choose the fear of the
LORD, Job 21:14 • Ps. 119:173
30 [R]They would have none of my counsel
And despised my every rebuke. Ps. 81:11
31 Therefore [R]they shall eat the fruit of
their own way, Job 4:8
And be filled to the full with their own
fancies.
32 For the [T]turning away of the simple will
slay them, *waywardness*
And the complacency of fools will
destroy them;
33 But whoever listens to me will dwell
[R]safely, Prov. 3:24–26
And [R]will be [T]secure, without fear of
evil." Ps. 112:7 • *at ease*

CHAPTER 2

MY son, if you receive my words,
And [R]treasure my commands within
you, [Prov. 4:21]
2 So that you incline your ear to wisdom,
And apply your heart to understanding;
3 Yes, if you cry out for discernment,
And lift up your voice for understanding,
4 [R]If you seek her as silver, [Prov. 3:14]
And search for her as *for* hidden
treasures;
5 [R]Then you will understand the fear of the
LORD, [James 1:5, 6]
And find the knowledge of God.
6 [R]For the LORD gives wisdom; 1 Kin. 3:9, 12
From His mouth *come* knowledge and
understanding;
7 He stores up sound wisdom for the
upright;
[R]*He is* a shield to those who walk
uprightly; [Ps. 84:11]
8 He guards the paths of justice,
And preserves the way of His saints.
9 Then you will understand righteousness
and justice,
Equity *and* every good path.

10 When wisdom enters your heart,
And knowledge is pleasant to your soul,
11 Discretion will preserve you;
[R]Understanding will keep you, Prov. 4:6
12 To deliver you from the way of evil,
From the man who speaks perverse
things,
13 From those who leave the paths of
uprightness
To walk in the ways of darkness;
14 [R]Who rejoice in doing evil, [Rom. 1:32]
And delight in the perversity of the
wicked;
15 [R]Whose ways *are* crooked, Ps. 125:5
And *who are* devious in their paths;
16 To deliver you from [R]the immoral
woman, Prov. 5:20; 6:24; 7:5
[R]From the seductress *who* flatters with
her words, Prov. 5:3
17 Who forsakes the companion of her
youth,
And forgets the covenant of her God.
18 For [R]her house leads down to death,
And her paths to the dead; Prov. 7:27
19 None who go to her return,
Nor do they regain the paths of life—
20 So you may walk in the way of goodness,
And keep *to* the paths of righteousness.
21 For the upright will dwell in the land,
And the blameless will remain in it;
22 But the wicked will be [T]cut off from the
[T]earth, *destroyed* • *land*
And the unfaithful will be uprooted from
it.

CHAPTER 3

Benefits of Wisdom

MY son, do not forget my law,
[R]But let your heart keep my
commands; Deut. 8:1
2 For length of days and long life
And peace they will add to you.

3 Let not mercy and truth forsake you;
Bind them around your neck,
Write them on the tablet of your heart,
4 [R]*And* so find favor and high esteem
In the sight of God and man. Rom. 14:18

5 Trust in the LORD with all your heart,
[R]And lean not on your own
understanding; [Jer. 9:23, 24]
6 In all your ways acknowledge Him,
And He shall direct* your paths.

7 Do not be wise in your own eyes;
Fear the LORD and depart from evil.
8 It will be health to your flesh,*
And strength* to your bones.

9 [R]Honor the LORD with your possessions,
And with the firstfruits of all your
increase; Ex. 22:29

3:6 Or *make smooth* or *straight* 3:8 Body, lit. *navel* • Lit. *drink* or *refreshment*

10[R] So your barns will be filled with plenty,
And your vats will overflow with new wine. Deut. 28:8

11[R] My son, do not despise the chastening of the LORD, Job 5:17
Nor detest His correction;
12 For whom the LORD loves He corrects,
[R] Just as a father the son *in whom* he delights. Deut. 8:5

13 Happy *is* the man *who* finds wisdom,
And the man *who* gains understanding;
14[R] For her proceeds *are* better than the profits of silver, Job 28:13
And her gain than fine gold.
15 She *is* more precious than rubies,
And [R]all the things you may desire cannot compare with her. Matt. 13:44
16 Length of days *is* in her right hand,
In her left hand riches and honor.
17[R] Her ways *are* ways of pleasantness,
And all her paths *are* peace. [Matt. 11:29]
18 She *is* [R]a tree of life to those who take hold of her, Gen. 2:9
And happy *are all* who retain her.

19[R] The LORD by wisdom founded the earth;
By understanding He established the heavens; Ps. 104:24
20 By His knowledge the depths were [R]broken up, Gen. 7:11
And clouds drop down the dew.

21 My son, let them not depart from your eyes—
Keep sound wisdom and discretion;
22 So they will be life to your soul
And grace to your neck.
23 Then you will walk safely in your way,
And your foot will not stumble.
24 When you lie down, you will not be afraid;
Yes, you will lie down and your sleep will be sweet.
25[R] Do not be afraid of sudden terror,
Nor of trouble from the wicked when it comes; Ps. 91:5
26 For the LORD will be your confidence,
And will keep your foot from being caught.

Be Kind to Others

27[R] Do not withhold good from [T]those to whom it is due, Rom. 13:7
When it is in the power of your hand to do *so*. *Lit.* its owners
28[R] Do not say to your neighbor, Lev. 19:13
"Go, and come back,
And tomorrow I will give *it*,"
When *you have* it with you.
29 Do not devise evil against your neighbor,
For he dwells by you for safety's sake.
30[R] Do not strive with a man without cause,
If he has done you no harm. [Rom. 12:18]

31[R] Do not envy the oppressor, Ps. 37:1
And choose none of his ways;
32 For the perverse *person is* an abomination to the LORD,
[R] But His secret counsel *is* with the upright. Ps. 25:14
33[R] The curse of the LORD *is* on the house of the wicked, Zech. 5:3, 4
But He blesses the home of the just.
34 Surely He scorns the scornful,
But gives grace to the humble.
35 The wise shall inherit glory,
But shame shall be the legacy of fools.

CHAPTER 4

Father Says Get Wisdom

HEAR, [R]*my* children, the instruction of a father, Ps. 34:11
And give attention to know understanding;
2 For I give you good doctrine:
Do not forsake my law.
3 When I was my father's son,
[R] Tender and the only one in the sight of my mother, 1 Chr. 29:1
4 He also taught me, and said to me:
"Let your heart retain my words;
[R] Keep my commands, and live. Prov. 7:2
5[R] Get wisdom! Get understanding!
Do not forget, nor turn away from the words of my mouth. Prov. 2:2, 3
6 Do not forsake her, and she will preserve you;
Love her, and she will keep you.
7[R] Wisdom *is* the principal thing;
Therefore get wisdom. Matt. 13:44
And in all your getting, get understanding.
8[R] Exalt her, and she will promote you;
She will bring you honor, when you embrace her. 1 Sam. 2:30
9 She will place on your head [R]an ornament of grace; Prov. 3:22
A crown of glory she will deliver to you."

10 Hear, my son, and receive my sayings,
And the years of your life will be many.
11 I have [R]taught you in the way of wisdom; 1 Sam. 12:23
I have led you in right paths.
12 When you walk, [R]your steps will not be hindered, Ps. 18:36
[R] And when you run, you will not stumble. [Ps. 91:11]
13 Take firm hold of instruction, do not let go;
Keep her, for she *is* your life.

Avoid the Wicked

14 Do not enter the path of the wicked,
And do not walk in the way of evil.
15 Avoid it, do not travel on it;
Turn away from it and pass on.
16[R] For they do not sleep unless they have
done evil; Ps. 36:4
And their sleep is [T]taken away unless
they make *someone* fall. Lit. *robbed*
17 For they eat the bread of wickedness,
And drink the wine of violence.

18[R] But the path of the just *is* like the
shining sun,* Matt. 5:14, 45
That shines ever brighter unto the
perfect day.
19[R] The way of the wicked *is* like darkness;
They do not know what makes them
stumble. [Is. 59:9, 10]

20 My son, give attention to my words;
Incline your ear to my sayings.
21 Do not let them depart from your eyes;
Keep them in the midst of your heart;
22 For they *are* life to those who find them,
And health to all their flesh.

Keep Your Heart

23 Keep your heart with all diligence,
For out of it *spring* the issues of life.
24 Put away from you a deceitful mouth,
And put perverse lips far from you.
25 Let your eyes look straight ahead,
And your eyelids look right before you.
26 Ponder the path of your feet,
And let all your ways be established.
27 Do not turn to the right or the left;
Remove your foot from evil.

CHAPTER 5

Do Not Commit Adultery

MY son, pay attention to my wisdom;
Lend your ear to my understanding,
2 That you may preserve discretion,
And your lips may keep knowledge.
3[R] For the lips of [T]an immoral woman drip
honey, Prov. 2:16 • Lit. *a strange*
And her mouth *is* smoother than oil;
4 But in the end she is bitter as
wormwood,
Sharp as a two-edged sword.
5 Her feet go down to death,
[R]Her steps lay hold of hell.* Prov. 7:27
6 Lest you ponder *her* path of life—
Her ways are unstable;
You do not know *them.*

7 Therefore hear me now, *my* children,
And do not depart from the words of my
mouth.
8 Remove your way far from her,
And do not go near the door of her
house,
9 Lest you give your [T]honor to others,
And your years to the cruel *one;* *vigor*
10 Lest aliens be filled with your [T]wealth,
And your labors *go* to the house of a
foreigner; Lit. *strength*
11 And you mourn at last,
When your flesh and your body are
consumed,
12 And say:
"How I have hated instruction,
And my heart despised correction!
13 I have not obeyed the voice of my
teachers,
Nor inclined my ear to those who
instructed me!
14 I was on the verge of total ruin,
In the midst of the assembly and
congregation."

Be Faithful to Your Spouse

15 Drink water from your own cistern,
And running water from your own well.
16 Should your fountains be dispersed
abroad,
Streams of water in the streets?
17 Let them be only your own,
And not for strangers with you.
18 Let your fountain be blessed,
And rejoice with the wife of your youth.
19[R] *As a* loving deer and a graceful doe,
Let her breasts satisfy you at all times;
And always be [T]enraptured with her
love. Song 2:9 • Lit. *intoxicated*
20 For why should you, my son, be
enraptured by [R]an immoral woman,
And be embraced in the arms of a
seductress? Prov. 2:16
21[R] For the ways of man *are* before the eyes
of the LORD, Hos. 7:2
And He ponders all his paths.
22[R] His own iniquities entrap the wicked
man, Num. 32:23
And he is caught in the cords of his sin.
23[R] He shall die for lack of instruction,
And in the greatness of his folly he shall
go astray. Job 4:21

CHAPTER 6

Avoid Surety

MY son, [R]if you become [T]surety for your
friend, Prov. 11:15 • *guaranty or collateral*
If you have [T]shaken hands in pledge for
a stranger, Lit. *struck*
2 You are snared by the words of your
mouth;
You are taken by the words of your
mouth.

4:18 Lit. *light* **5:5** Or *Sheol*

3 So do this, my son, and deliver yourself;
For you have come into the hand of your friend:
Go and humble yourself;
Plead with your friend.
4[R] Give no sleep to your eyes, Ps. 132:4
Nor slumber to your eyelids.
5 Deliver yourself like a gazelle from the hand *of the hunter,*
And like a bird from the hand of the fowler.*

Do Not Be Lazy

6[R] Go to the ant, you sluggard! Job 12:7
Consider her ways and be wise,
7 Which, having no [T]captain, Lit. *leader*
Overseer or ruler,
8 Provides her supplies in the summer,
And gathers her food in the harvest.
9 How long will you slumber, O sluggard?
When will you rise from your sleep?
10 A little sleep, a little slumber,
A little folding of the hands to sleep—
11[R] So shall your poverty come on you like a prowler, Prov. 10:4
And your need like an armed man.

12 A worthless person, a wicked man,
Walks with a perverse mouth;
13[R] He winks with his eyes, Job 15:12
He shuffles his feet,
He points with his fingers;
14 Perversity *is* in his heart,
[R]He devises evil continually,
[R]He sows discord. Mic. 2:1 • Prov. 6:19
15 Therefore his calamity shall come [R]suddenly; Is. 30:13
Suddenly he shall [R]be broken [R]without remedy. Jer. 19:11 • 2 Chr. 36:16

16 These six *things* the LORD hates,
Yes, seven *are* an abomination to Him:
17[R] A[T] proud look, Ps. 101:5 • Lit. *Haughty eyes*
[R]A lying tongue, Ps. 120:2
Hands that shed innocent blood,
18 A heart that devises wicked plans,
Feet that are swift in running to evil,
19[R] A false witness *who* speaks lies,
And one who [R]sows discord among brethren. Ps. 27:12 • Prov. 6:14

Do Not Commit Adultery

20[R] My son, keep your father's command,
And do not forsake the law of your mother. Eph. 6:1
21[R] Bind them continually upon your heart;
Tie them around your neck. Prov. 3:3
22[R] When you roam, they* will lead you;
When you sleep, [R]they will keep you;
And *when* you awake, they will speak with you. [Prov. 3:23] • Prov. 2:11

23[R] For the commandment *is* a lamp,
And the law a light; Ps. 19:8
Reproofs of instruction *are* the way of life,

24[R] To keep you from the evil woman,
From the flattering tongue of a seductress. Prov. 2:16
25[R] Do not lust after her beauty in your heart, Matt. 5:28
Nor let her allure you with her eyelids.
26 For [R]by means of a harlot Prov. 29:3
A man is reduced to a crust of bread;
[R]And an adulteress* will [R]prey upon his precious life. Gen. 39:14 • Ezek. 13:18
27 Can a man take fire to his bosom,
And his clothes not be burned?
28 Can one walk on hot coals,
And his feet not be seared?
29 So *is* he who goes in to his neighbor's wife;
Whoever touches her shall not be innocent.

30 *People* do not despise a thief
If he steals to satisfy himself when he is starving.

6:5 One who catches birds in a trap or snare
6:22 Lit. *it* **6:26** Wife of another, lit. *a man's wife*

6:23 Illumination of God's Word—Illumination is the last of three important steps taken by God in communicating His Word to us. The first step was revelation which occurred when God spoke to the Bible authors. The second step was inspiration, that process whereby God guided them in correctly writing or uttering His message. But now a third step is needed to provide understanding for men and women as they hear God's revealed and inspired message. This vital step is illumination, that divine process whereby God causes the written revelation to be understood by the human heart.

This third step is needed because unsaved people are blinded both by their fallen, fleshly nature (Page 1168—1 Cor. 2:14) and by Satan himself (Page 1186—2 Cor. 4:3, 4).

The Person behind this illumination is the Holy Spirit. Just prior to His crucifixion, Christ promised to send the Holy Spirit, who would illuminate both unsaved people (Page 1101—John 16:8–11) and Christians (Page 1100—John 14:26; 16:13, 14).

An important example of the Holy Spirit's using God's Word to illuminate sinners is seen at Pentecost, where three thousand people are saved after hearing Simon Peter preach about Christ and the Cross (Page 1114—Acts 2:36–41).

But Christians also need this illumination to help them fully grasp the marvelous message in God's Word. Paul tells us that the Holy Spirit will show these tremendous truths to us as we read the Scriptures (Page 1168—1 Cor. 2:10; Page 1186—2 Cor. 4:6).

Now turn to Page 491—Neh. 8:9: God's Word Convicts.

31 Yet *when* he is found, [R]he must restore
sevenfold; Ex. 22:1–4
He may have to give up all the substance
of his house.
32 Whoever commits adultery with a
woman lacks understanding;
He *who* does so destroys his own soul.
33 Wounds and dishonor he will get,
And his reproach will not be wiped away.
34 For [R]jealousy *is* a husband's fury;
Therefore he will not spare in the day of
vengeance. Song 8:6
35 He will [T]accept no recompense,
Nor will he be appeased though you give
many gifts. Lit. *lift up the face of any*

CHAPTER 7

MY son, keep my words,
And [R]treasure my commands within
you. Prov. 2:1
2 [R]Keep my commands and live, Lev. 18:5
And my law as the apple of your eye.
3 [R]Bind them on your fingers; Deut. 6:8
Write them on the tablet of your heart.
4 Say to wisdom, "You *are* my sister,"
And call understanding *your* nearest kin,
5 [R]That they may keep you from the
immoral woman, Prov. 2:16; 5:3
From the seductress *who* flatters with
her words.

6 For at the window of my house
I looked through my lattice,
7 And saw among the simple,
I perceived among the youths,
A young man devoid of understanding,
8 Passing along the street near her corner;
And he took the path to her house
9 [R]In the twilight, in the evening,
In the black and dark night. Job 24:15
10 And there a woman met him,
With the attire of a harlot, and a crafty
heart.
11 She *was* loud and rebellious,
Her feet would not stay at home.
12 At times *she was* outside, at times in the
open square,
Lurking at every corner.
13 So she caught him and kissed him;
With an impudent face she said to him:
14 "*I* have peace offerings with me;
Today I have paid my vows.
15 So I came out to meet you,
Diligently to seek your face,
And I have found you.
16 I have spread my bed with tapestry,
Colored coverings of Egyptian linen.
17 I have perfumed my bed
With myrrh, aloes, and cinnamon.
18 Come, let us take our fill of love until
morning;
Let us delight ourselves with love.
19 For my husband *is* not at home;
He has gone on a long journey;
20 He has taken a bag of money [T]with him,
And will come home [T]on the appointed
day." Lit. *in his hand* • *at the full moon*

21 [T]With [R]her enticing speech she caused
him to yield, *By the greatness of her words*
[R]With her flattering lips she [T]seduced
him. Prov. 5:3 • Ps. 12:2 • *compelled*
22 Immediately he went after her, as an ox
goes to the slaughter,
Or as a fool to the correction of the
[T]stocks,* *shackles*
23 Till an arrow struck his liver.
As a bird hastens to the snare,
He did not know it *would cost* his life.

24 Now therefore, listen to me, my children;
Pay attention to the words of my mouth:
25 Do not let your heart turn aside to her
ways,
Do not stray into her paths;
26 For she has cast down many wounded,
And [R]all who were slain by her were
strong *men*. Neh. 13:26
27 Her house *is* the way to hell,*
Descending to the chambers of death.

CHAPTER 8

Praise of Wisdom

DOES not [R]wisdom cry out, Prov. 1:20, 21; 9:3
And understanding lift up her voice?
2 She takes her stand on the top of the
[T]high hill, Lit. *heights*
Beside the way, where the paths meet.
3 She cries out by the gates, at the entry of
the city,
At the entrance of the doors:
4 "To you, O men, I call,
And my voice *is* to the sons of men.
5 O you [T]simple ones, understand
prudence, *naive*
And you fools, be of an understanding
heart.
6 Listen, for I will speak of [R]excellent
things, Prov. 22:20
And from the opening of my lips will
come right things;
7 For my mouth will speak truth;
Wickedness *is* an abomination to my
lips.
8 All the words of my mouth *are* with
righteousness;
Nothing crooked or perverse *is* in them.
9 They *are* all plain to him who
understands,
And right to those who find knowledge.

7:22 LXX, Syr., Tg. *as a dog to bonds;* Vg. *as a lamb . . . to bonds* **7:27** Or *Sheol*

10 Receive my instruction, and not silver,
And knowledge rather than choice gold;
11 For wisdom *is* better than rubies,
And all the things one may desire cannot be compared with her.

12"I, wisdom, dwell with prudence,
And find out knowledge *and* discretion.
13 The fear of the LORD *is* to hate evil;
Pride and arrogance and the evil way
And the perverse mouth I hate.
14 Counsel *is* mine, and sound wisdom;
I *am* understanding, I have strength.
15[R]By me kings reign, Rom. 13:1
And rulers decree justice.
16 By me princes rule, and nobles,
All the judges of the earth.*
17[R]I love those who love me, [John 14:21]
And [R]those who seek me diligently will find me. James 1:5
18 Riches and honor *are* with me,
Enduring riches and righteousness.
19 My fruit *is* better than gold, yes, than fine gold,
And my revenue than choice silver.
20 I traverse the way of righteousness,
In the midst of the paths of justice,
21 That I may cause those who love me to inherit wealth,
That I may fill their treasuries.

22"The[R] LORD possessed me at the beginning of His way, Prov. 3:19
Before His works of old.
23[R]I have been established from everlasting, [Ps. 2:6]
From the beginning, before there was ever an earth.
24 When *there were* no depths I was brought forth,
When *there were* no fountains abounding with water.
25 Before the mountains were settled,
Before the hills, I was brought forth;
26 While as yet He had not made the earth or the [T]fields, *outer places*
Or the primal dust of the world.
27 When He prepared the heavens, I *was* there,
When He drew a circle on the face of the deep,
28 When He established the clouds above,
When He strengthened the fountains of the deep,
29[R]When He assigned to the sea its limit,
So that the waters would not transgress His command, Gen. 1:9, 10
When [R]He marked out the foundations of the earth, Job 38:4, 6
30[R]Then I was beside Him as a master craftsman;* [John 1:1–3, 18]
[R]And I was daily *His* delight, [Matt. 3:17]
Rejoicing always before Him,
31 Rejoicing in His inhabited world,
And [R]my delight *was* with the sons of men. Ps. 16:3

32"Now therefore, listen to me, my children,
For [R]blessed *are those who* keep my ways. Luke 11:28
33 Hear instruction and be wise,
And do not disdain *it*.
34[R]Blessed is the man who listens to me,
Watching daily at my gates, Prov. 3:13, 18
Waiting at the posts of my doors.
35 For whoever finds me finds life,
And obtains favor from the LORD;
36 But he who sins against me [R]wrongs his own soul; Prov. 20:2
All those who hate me love death."

CHAPTER 9

WISDOM has built her house,
She has hewn out her seven pillars;
2[R]She has slaughtered her meat,
She has mixed her wine, Matt. 22:4
She has also furnished her table.
3 She has sent out her maidens,
She cries out from the highest places of the city,
4"Whoever[R] *is* simple, let him turn in here!" Ps. 19:7
As for him who lacks understanding, she says to him,
5"Come,[R] eat of my bread Is. 55:1
And drink of the wine I have mixed.
6 Forsake foolishness and live,
And go in the way of understanding.

7"He who corrects a scoffer gets shame for himself,
And he who rebukes a wicked *man* only harms himself.
8[R]Do not correct a scoffer, lest he hate you; Matt. 7:6
[R]Rebuke a wise *man*, and he will love you. Ps. 141:5
9 Give *instruction* to a wise *man*, and he will be still wiser;
Teach a just *man*, [R]and he will increase in learning. [Matt. 13:12]

10"The[R] fear of the LORD *is* the beginning of wisdom, Job 28:28
And the knowledge of the Holy One is understanding.
11 For by me your days will be multiplied,
And years of life will be added to you.
12[R]If you are wise, you are wise for yourself, Job 35:6, 7
And *if* you scoff, you will bear *it* alone."

8:16 MT, Syr., Tg., Vg. *righteousness;* LXX, Bg., some mss. and editions *earth* **8:30** A Jewish tradition *one brought up*

Foolish Woman

13 A foolish woman is clamorous;
She is simple, and knows nothing.
14 For she sits at the door of her house,
On a seat [R]*by* the highest places of the city, Prov. 9:3
15 To call to those who pass by,
Who go straight on their way:
16 "Whoever[R] *is* [T]simple, let him turn in here"; Prov. 7:7, 8 • *naive*
And *as for* him who lacks understanding, she says to him,
17 "Stolen[R] water is sweet, Prov. 20:17
And bread *eaten* in secret is pleasant."
18 But he does not know that [R]the dead *are* there, Prov. 2:18; 7:27
That her guests *are* in the depths of hell.*

CHAPTER 10

Proverbs Contrasting the Godly and the Wicked

THE proverbs of [R]Solomon: Prov. 1:1; 25:1

A wise son makes a glad father,
But a foolish son *is* the grief of his mother.

2 Treasures of wickedness profit nothing,
But righteousness delivers from death.
3 [R]The LORD will not allow the righteous soul to famish, Ps. 34:9, 10; 37:25
But He casts away the desire of the wicked.

4 [R]He who has a slack hand becomes poor,
But [R]the hand of the diligent makes rich. Prov. 19:15 • Prov. 12:24; 13:4; 21:5
5 He who gathers in [R]summer is a wise son; Prov. 6:8
He who sleeps in harvest is [R]a son who causes shame. Prov. 19:26

6 Blessings *are* on the head of the righteous,
But violence covers the mouth of the wicked.
7 The memory of the righteous *is* blessed,
But the name of the wicked will rot.

8 The wise in heart will receive commands,
[R]But a prating fool will fall. Prov. 10:10

9 [R]He who walks with integrity walks securely, [Ps. 23:4]
But he who perverts his ways will become known.

10 He who winks with the eye causes trouble,
But a prating fool will fall.

11 The mouth of the righteous *is* a well of life,
But violence covers the mouth of the wicked.

12 Hatred stirs up strife,
But [R]love covers all sins. [1 Cor. 13:4–7]

13 Wisdom is found on the lips of him who has understanding,
But [R]a rod *is* for the back of him who is devoid of understanding. Prov. 26:3

14 Wise *people* store up knowledge,
But [R]the mouth of the foolish *is* near destruction. Prov. 18:7

15 The [R]rich man's wealth *is* his strong city; Job 31:24
The destruction of the poor *is* their poverty.

16 The labor of the righteous *leads* to life,
The wages of the wicked to sin.

17 He who keeps instruction *is in* the way of life,
But he who refuses correction [T]goes astray. *leads*

18 Whoever hides hatred *has* lying lips,
And whoever spreads slander *is* a fool.

19 [R]In the multitude of words sin is not lacking, Eccl. 5:3
But he who restrains his lips *is* wise.
20 The tongue of the righteous *is* choice silver;
The heart of the wicked *is worth* little.
21 The lips of the righteous feed many,
But fools die for lack of wisdom.*

22 [R]The blessing of the LORD makes *one* rich, Gen. 24:35; 26:12
And He adds no sorrow with it.

23 [R]To do evil *is* like sport to a fool,
But a man of understanding has wisdom. Prov. 2:14; 15:21
24 [R]The fear of the wicked will come upon him, Job 15:21
And [R]the desire of the righteous will be granted. Ps. 145:19
25 When the whirlwind passes by, [R]the wicked *is* no *more*, Ps. 37:9, 10
But [R]the righteous *has* an everlasting foundation. Ps. 15:5

26 As vinegar to the teeth and smoke to the eyes,
So *is* the lazy *man* to those who send him.

9:18 Or *Sheol* **10:21** Lit. *heart*

27 [R]The fear of the LORD prolongs days,
But [R]the years of the wicked will be shortened. Prov. 9:11 • Job 15:32
28 The hope of the righteous *will be* gladness,
But the [R]expectation of the wicked will perish. Job 8:13
29 The way of the LORD *is* strength for the upright,
But [R]destruction *will come* to the workers of iniquity. Ps. 1:6

30 [R]The righteous will never be removed,
But the wicked will not inhabit the [T]earth. Ps. 37:22 • land
31 [R]The mouth of the righteous brings forth wisdom, Ps. 37:30
But the perverse tongue will be cut out.
32 The lips of the righteous know what is acceptable,
But the mouth of the wicked *what is* perverse.

CHAPTER 11

DISHONEST[RT] scales *are* an abomination to the LORD, Lev. 19:35, 36 • *deceptive*
But a just weight *is* His delight.

2 When pride comes, then comes shame;
But with the humble *is* wisdom.

3 The integrity of the upright will guide [R]them, Prov. 13:6
But the perversity of the unfaithful will destroy them.
4 Riches do not profit in the day of wrath,
But righteousness delivers from death.
5 The righteousness of the blameless will direct* his way aright,
But the wicked will fall by his own [R]wickedness. Prov. 5:22
6 The righteousness of the upright will deliver them,
But the unfaithful will be caught by *their* lust.

7 When a wicked man dies, his expectation will [R]perish, Prov. 10:28
And the hope of the unjust perishes.
8 The righteous is delivered from trouble,
And it comes to the wicked instead.
9 The hypocrite with *his* mouth destroys his neighbor,
But through knowledge the righteous will be delivered.
10 [R]When it goes well with the righteous, the city rejoices; Prov. 28:12
And when the wicked perish, there is jubilation.
11 By the blessing of the upright the city is [R]exalted, Prov. 14:34
But it is overthrown by the mouth of the wicked.

12 He who [T]is devoid of wisdom despises his neighbor, Lit. *lacks heart*
But a man of understanding holds his peace.

13 [R]A talebearer reveals secrets, Lev. 19:16
But he who is of a faithful spirit [R]conceals a matter. Prov. 19:11

14 [R]Where *there is* no counsel, the people fall; 1 Kin. 12:1
But in the multitude of counselors *there is* safety.

15 He who is [R]surety[T] for a stranger will suffer, Prov. 6:1, 2 • *guaranty*
But one who hates being surety is secure.

16 A gracious woman retains honor,
But ruthless *men* retain riches.
17 [R]The merciful man does good for his own soul, [Matt. 5:7; 25:34–36]
But *he who is* cruel troubles his own flesh.
18 The wicked *man* does deceptive work,
But [R]he who sows righteousness *will have* a sure reward. Hos. 10:12
19 As righteousness *leads* to [R]life,
So he who pursues evil *pursues it* to his own [R]death. Prov. 10:16 • [Rom. 6:23]
20 Those who are of a perverse heart *are* an abomination to the LORD,
But *the* blameless in their ways *are* His delight.
21 [R]*Though they* join forces,* the wicked will not go unpunished; Prov. 16:5
But [R]the posterity of the righteous will be delivered. Ps. 112:2

22 *As* a ring of gold in a swine's snout,
So is a lovely woman who lacks [T]discretion. *taste*

23 The desire of the righteous *is* only good,
But the expectation of the wicked [R]*is* wrath. Rom. 2:8, 9

24 There is *one* who [R]scatters, yet increases more; Ps. 112:9
And there is *one* who withholds more than is right,
But it *leads* to poverty.
25 [R]The generous soul will be made rich,
[R]And he who waters will also be watered himself. [2 Cor. 9:6, 7] • [Matt. 5:7]
26 The people will curse [R]him who withholds grain, Amos 8:5, 6

11:5 Or *make smooth* or *straight* **11:21** Lit. *hand to hand*

But [R]blessing *will be* on the head of him who sells *it*. Job 29:13

27 He who earnestly seeks good [T]finds favor, Lit. *seeks*
[R]But trouble will come to him who seeks *evil*. Esth. 7:10

28[R] He who trusts in his riches will fall,
But [R]the righteous will flourish like foliage. Job 31:24 • Ps. 1:3

29 He who troubles his own house [R]will inherit the wind, Eccl. 5:16
And the fool *will be* [R]servant to the wise of heart. Prov. 14:19

30 The fruit of the righteous *is a* tree of life,
And he who wins souls *is* wise.
31[R] If the righteous will be [T]recompensed on the earth, Jer. 25:29 • *rewarded*
How much more the ungodly and the sinner.

CHAPTER 12

WHOEVER loves instruction loves knowledge,
But he who hates correction *is* stupid.

2 A good *man* obtains favor from the LORD,
But a man of wicked intentions He will condemn.

3 A man is not established by wickedness,
But the [R]root of the righteous cannot be moved. [Prov. 10:25]

4[R] An excellent* wife *is* the crown of her husband, 1 Cor. 11:7
But she who causes shame *is* [R]like rottenness in his bones. Prov. 14:30

5 The thoughts of the righteous *are* right,
But the counsels of the wicked *are* deceitful.
6[R] The words of the wicked *are*, "Lie in wait for blood," Prov. 1:11, 18
[R]But the mouth of the upright will deliver them. Prov. 14:3

7[R] The wicked are overthrown and *are* no more, Matt. 7:24–27
But the house of the righteous will stand.

8 A man will be commended according to his wisdom,
[R]But he who is of a perverse heart will be despised. 1 Sam. 25:17

9[R] Better *is the one* who is [T]slighted but has a servant, Prov. 13:7
Than he who honors himself but lacks bread. *lightly esteemed*

10[R] A righteous *man* regards the life of his animal, Deut. 25:4
But the tender mercies of the wicked *are* cruel.

11[R] He who tills his land will be satisfied with [R]bread, Gen. 3:19 • Prov. 28:19
But he who follows frivolity [R]*is* devoid of understanding. Prov. 6:32

12 The wicked covet the catch of evil *men*,
But the root of the righteous yields *fruit*.
13[R] The wicked is ensnared by the transgression of *his* lips, Prov. 18:7
[R]But the righteous will come through trouble. [2 Pet. 2:9]
14[R] A man will be satisfied with good by the fruit of *his* mouth, Prov. 13:2; 15:23
[R]And the recompense of a man's hands will be rendered to him. [Is. 3:10, 11]

15[R] The way of a fool *is* right in his own eyes, Luke 18:11
But he who heeds counsel *is* wise.
16 A fool's wrath is known at once,
But a prudent *man* covers shame.

17[R] He *who* speaks truth declares righteousness, Prov. 14:5
But a false witness, deceit.
18[R] There is one who speaks like the piercings of a sword, Ps. 57:4
But the tongue of the wise *promotes* health.
19 The truthful lip shall be established forever,
But a lying tongue *is* but for a moment.
20 Deceit is in the heart of those who devise evil,
But counselors of peace have joy.
21[R] No grave [T]trouble will overtake the righteous, 1 Pet. 3:13 • *harm*
But the wicked shall be filled with evil.
22[R] Lying lips *are* an abomination to the LORD, Rev. 22:15
But those who deal truthfully *are* His delight.

23[R] A prudent man conceals knowledge,
But the heart of fools proclaims foolishness. Prov. 13:16

24[R] The hand of the diligent will rule,
But the lazy *man* will be put to forced labor. Prov. 10:4

25[R] Anxiety in the heart of man causes depression, Prov. 15:13
But a good word makes it glad.

12:4 Lit. *A wife of valor* **12:11** Lit. *heart*

26 The righteous should choose his friends carefully,
For the way of the wicked leads them astray.

27 The lazy *man* does not roast what he took in hunting,
But diligence *is* man's precious possession.

28 In the way of righteousness *is* life,
And in *its* pathway *there is* no death.

CHAPTER 13

A WISE son *heeds* his father's instruction,
But a scoffer does not listen to rebuke.

2[R] A man shall eat well by the fruit of *his* mouth, Prov. 12:14
But the soul of the unfaithful feeds on violence.
3[R] He who guards his mouth preserves his life, Prov. 21:23
But he who opens wide his lips shall have destruction.

4[R] The soul of a lazy *man* desires, and *has* nothing; Prov. 10:4
But the soul of the diligent shall be made rich.

5 A righteous *man* hates lying,
But a wicked *man* is loathsome and comes to shame.
6[R] Righteousness guards *him whose* way is blameless, Prov. 11:3, 5, 6
But wickedness overthrows the sinner.

7[R] There is one who makes himself rich, yet *has* nothing; [Prov. 11:24; 12:9]
And one who makes himself poor, yet *has* great riches.

8 The ransom of a man's life *is* his riches,
But the poor does not hear rebuke.

9 The light of the righteous rejoices,
[R] But the lamp of the wicked will be put out. Prov. 24:20

10 By pride comes nothing but strife,
But with the well-advised *is* wisdom.

11[R] Wealth *gained by* dishonesty will be diminished, Prov. 10:2; 20:21
But he who gathers by labor will increase.

12 Hope deferred makes the heart sick,
But [R]*when* the desire comes, it is a tree of life. Prov. 13:19

13 He who [R]despises the word will be destroyed, Num. 15:31
But he who fears the commandment will be rewarded.
14[R] The law of the wise *is* a fountain of life,
To turn *one* away from [R]the snares of death. Prov. 6:22; 10:11; 14:27 • 2 Sam. 22:6

15 Good understanding gains favor,
But the way of the unfaithful *is* hard.
16[R] Every prudent *man* acts with knowledge, Prov. 12:23
But a fool lays open *his* folly.

17 A wicked messenger falls into trouble,
But [R]a faithful ambassador *brings* health. Prov. 25:13

18 Poverty and shame *will come* to him who [T]disdains correction, Lit. *ignores*
But [R]he who regards a rebuke will be honored. Prov. 15:5, 31, 32

19 A desire accomplished is sweet to the soul,
But *it is* an abomination to fools to depart from evil.

20 He who walks with wise *men* will be wise,
But the companion of fools will be destroyed.

21[R] Evil pursues sinners, Ps. 32:10
But to the righteous, good shall be repaid.

22 A good *man* leaves an inheritance to his children's children,
But [R]the wealth of the sinner is stored up for the righteous. [Eccl. 2:26]

23[R] Much food *is in* the [T]fallow *ground* of the poor, Prov. 12:11 • *uncultivated*
And for lack of justice there is waste.*

24[R] He who spares his rod hates his son,
But he who loves him disciplines him [T]promptly. Prov. 19:18 • *early*

25[R] The righteous eats to the satisfying of his soul, Ps. 34:10
But the stomach of the wicked shall be in want.

CHAPTER 14

THE wise woman builds her house,
But the foolish pulls it down with her hands.

13:23 Lit. *what is swept away*

2 He who walks in his uprightness fears
the LORD,
[R]But *he who is* perverse in his ways
despises Him. [Rom. 2:4]

3 In the mouth of a fool *is* a rod of pride,
[R]But the lips of the wise will preserve
them. Prov. 12:6

4 Where no oxen *are*, the [T]trough *is* clean;
But much increase *comes* by the
strength of an ox. *manger or feed trough*

5 A faithful witness does not lie,
But a false witness will utter lies.

6 A scoffer seeks wisdom and does not
find it,
But [R]knowledge *is* easy to him who
understands. Prov. 8:9; 17:24

7 Go from the presence of a foolish man,
When you do not perceive *in him* the lips
of [R]knowledge. Prov. 23:9

8 The wisdom of the prudent *is* to
understand his way,
But the folly of fools *is* deceit.

9[R] Fools mock at [T]sin, Prov. 10:23 • Lit. *guilt*
But among the upright *there is* favor.

10 The heart knows its own bitterness,
And a stranger does not share its joy.

11[R] The house of the wicked will be
overthrown, Job 8:15
But the tent of the upright will flourish.

12[R] There is a way *that seems* right to a
man, Prov. 16:25
But its end *is* the way of death.

13 Even in laughter the heart may sorrow,
And the end of mirth *may be* grief.

14 The backslider in heart will be [R]filled
with his own ways, Prov. 1:31; 12:15
But a good man *will be satisfied* from
[R]above.* Prov. 13:2; 18:20

15 The simple believes every word,
But the prudent considers well his
steps.

16 A wise *man* fears and departs from evil,
But a fool rages and is self-confident.

17 A quick-tempered *man* acts foolishly,
And a man of wicked intentions is
hated.

18 The simple inherit folly,
But the prudent are crowned with
knowledge.

19 The evil will bow before the good,
And the wicked at the gates of the
righteous.

20[R] The poor *man* is hated even by his own
neighbor, Prov. 19:7
But the rich *has* many friends.

21 He who despises his neighbor sins;
[R]But he who has mercy on the poor,
happy *is* he. Ps. 112:9

22 Do they not go astray who devise evil?
But mercy and truth *belong* to those who
devise good.

23 In all labor there is profit,
But idle chatter* *leads* only to poverty.

24 The crown of the wise is their riches,
But the foolishness of fools *is* folly.

25 A true witness delivers souls,
But a deceitful *witness* speaks lies.

26 In the fear of the LORD *there is* strong
confidence,
And His children will have a place of
refuge.

27[R] The fear of the LORD *is* a fountain of life,
To turn *one* away from the snares of
death. Prov. 13:14

28 In a multitude of people *is* a king's
honor,
But in the lack of people *is* the downfall
of a prince.

29[R] *He who is* slow to wrath has great
understanding, James 1:19
But *he who is* impulsive* exalts folly.

30 A sound heart *is* life to the body,
But envy *is* rottenness to the bones.

31[R] He who oppresses the poor reproaches
[R]his Maker, Matt. 25:40 • [Prov. 22:2]
But he who honors Him has mercy on
the needy.

32 The wicked is banished in his
wickedness,
But [R]the righteous has a refuge in his
death. Job 13:15

33 Wisdom rests in the heart of him who
has understanding,
But [R]*what is* in the heart of fools is made
known. Prov. 12:16

34 Righteousness exalts a nation,
But sin *is* a reproach to *any* people.

35[R] The king's favor *is* toward a wise
servant, Matt. 24:45–47

14:14 Lit. *from above himself* **14:23** Lit. *talk of the lips* **14:29** Lit. *short of spirit*

But his wrath *is against* him who causes
shame.

CHAPTER 15

A SOFT answer turns away wrath,
But a harsh word stirs up anger.
2 The tongue of the wise uses knowledge rightly,
[R]But the mouth of fools pours forth foolishness. Prov. 12:23

3 The eyes of the LORD *are* in every place,
Keeping watch on the evil and the good.

4 A wholesome tongue *is* a tree of life,
But perverseness in it breaks the spirit.

5 A fool despises his father's instruction,
[R]But he who [T]receives correction is prudent. Prov. 13:18 • Lit. *keeps*

6 *In* the house of the righteous there is much treasure,
But in the revenue of the wicked is trouble.

7 The lips of the wise disperse knowledge,
But the heart of the fool *does* not *do* so.

8 [R]The sacrifice of the wicked *is* an abomination to the LORD, Is. 1:11
But the prayer of the upright *is* His delight.
9 The way of the wicked *is* an abomination to the LORD,
But He loves him who [R]follows righteousness. Prov. 21:21

10 [R]Harsh discipline *is* for him who forsakes the way, 1 Kin. 22:8
And he who hates correction will die.

11 [R]Hell* and Destruction* *are* before the LORD; Job 26:6
So how much more [R]the hearts of the sons of men. 2 Chr. 6:30

12 [R]A scoffer does not love one who corrects him, Amos 5:10
Nor will he go to the wise.

13 [R]A merry heart makes a cheerful [T]countenance, Prov. 12:25 • *face*
But [R]by sorrow of the heart the spirit is broken. Prov. 17:22

14 The heart of him who has understanding seeks knowledge,
But the mouth of fools feeds on foolishness.

15 All the days of the afflicted *are* evil,
[R]But he who is of a merry heart *has* a continual feast. Prov. 17:22

16 [R]Better *is* a little with the fear of the LORD, Ps. 37:16
Than great treasure with trouble.
17 [R]Better *is* a dinner of herbs* where love is, Prov. 17:1
Than a fatted calf with hatred.

18 [R]A wrathful man stirs up strife,
But *he who is* slow to anger allays contention. Prov. 26:21

19 [R]The way of the lazy *man* is like a hedge of thorns, Prov. 22:5
But the way of the upright *is* a highway.

20 A wise son makes a father glad,
But a foolish man despises his mother.

21 [R]Folly *is* joy *to him who is* destitute of [T]discernment, Prov. 10:23 • Lit. *heart*
[R]But a man of understanding walks uprightly. Eph. 5:15

22 [R]Without counsel, plans go awry,
But in the multitude of counselors they are established. Prov. 11:14

23 A man has joy by the answer of his mouth,
And [R]a word *spoken* [T]in due season, how good *it is!* Prov. 25:11 • Lit. *in its time*

24 [R]The way of life *winds* upward for the wise, Phil. 3:20
That he may [R]turn away from hell* below. Prov. 14:16

25 [R]The LORD will destroy the house of the proud, Prov. 12:7
But [R]He will establish the boundary of the widow. Ps. 68:5, 6

26 The thoughts of the wicked *are* an abomination to the LORD,
But *the words* of the pure *are* pleasant.

27 [R]He who is greedy for gain troubles his own house, Is. 5:8
But he who hates bribes will live.

28 The heart of the righteous [R]studies how to answer, 1 Pet. 3:15
But the mouth of the wicked pours forth evil.

15:11 Or *Sheol* • Heb. *Abaddon* **15:17** Or *vegetables*
15:24 Or *Sheol*

29[R] The LORD *is* far from the wicked,
But [R]He hears the prayer of the righteous. Ps. 10:1; 34:16 • Ps. 145:18

30 The light of the eyes rejoices the heart,
And a good report makes the bones healthy.*

31 The ear that hears the rebukes of life
Will abide among the wise.
32 He who disdains instruction despises his own soul,
But he who heeds rebuke gets understanding.
33[R] The fear of the LORD *is* the instruction of wisdom, Prov. 1:7
And before honor *is* humility.

CHAPTER 16

Proverbs Encouraging Godly Lives

THE [R]preparations[T] of the heart *belong* to man, Jer. 10:23 • *plans*
[R]But the answer of the tongue *is* from the LORD. Matt. 10:19

2 All the ways of a man *are* pure in his own [R]eyes, Prov. 21:2
But the LORD weighs the spirits.

3 Commit your works to the LORD,
And your thoughts will be established.

4 The [R]LORD has made all for Himself,
[R]Yes, even the wicked for the day of [T]doom. Is. 43:7 • [Rom. 9:22] • Lit. *evil*

5[R] Everyone proud in heart *is* an abomination to the LORD;
Though they join forces,* none will go unpunished. Prov. 6:17; 8:13

6[R] In mercy and truth Dan. 4:27
Atonement is provided for iniquity;
And [R]by the fear of the LORD *one* departs from evil. Prov. 8:13; 14:16

7 When a man's ways please the LORD,
He makes even his enemies to be at peace with him.

8 Better *is* a little with righteousness,
Than vast revenues without justice.

9 A man's heart plans his way,
But the LORD directs his steps.

10 Divination *is* on the lips of the king;
His mouth must not transgress in judgment.
11[R] Honest weights and scales *are* the LORD's; Lev. 19:36
All the weights in the bag *are* His work.
12 *It is* an abomination for kings to commit wickedness,
For [R]a throne is established by righteousness. Prov. 25:5
13[R] Righteous lips *are* the delight of kings,
And they love him who speaks *what is* right. Prov. 14:35
14 As messengers of death *is* the king's wrath,
But a wise man will appease it.
15 In the light of the king's face *is* life,
And his favor *is* like a [R]cloud of the latter rain. Zech. 10:1

16[R] How much better to get wisdom than gold! Prov. 8:10, 11, 19
And to get understanding is to be chosen rather than silver.

17 The highway of the upright *is* to depart from evil;
He who keeps his way preserves his soul.

18 Pride *goes* before destruction,
And a haughty spirit before a fall.
19 Better *to be* of a humble spirit with the lowly,
Than to divide the spoil with the proud.

20 He who heeds the word wisely will find good,
And whoever [R]trusts in the LORD, happy *is* he. Ps. 34:8

15:30 Lit. *fat* **16:5** Lit. *hand to hand*

16:3 Commitment—Dedication is the foundation of commitment. Without it the believer is unable to offer God anything else. Paul explains this dedication process in Rom. 12:1 and 2. He emphasizes three things. First, it is our body that is to be dedicated as a living sacrifice to God. Second, we are to avoid being conformed to this world, but are to strive to be transformed by the Word. Finally, by doing this we can discover God's perfect will for our lives.

After the dedication of our bodies, what are we to commit? We are to commit our salvation to God (Page 1243—2 Tim. 1:12). Second, we are to commit our works (Prov. 16:3). Then, our goals in life are to be given to Him (Page 515—Job 5:8; Page 564—Ps. 37:5). It is difficult but vital to commit our suffering experiences to God (Page 1283—1 Pet. 4:19). Our Lord Jesus did this very thing when He was on earth (Page 1281—1 Pet. 2:23). Finally, in the hour of death we can with confidence commit our very souls to God (Page 560—Ps. 31:5). Paul the apostle assures us that any and all such commitments to the Lord will be accepted and honored. See 1 Cor. 15:58.

Now turn to Page 1175—1 Cor. 12:1–10: Using Spiritual Gifts.

21 The wise in heart will be called prudent,
And sweetness of the lips increases
learning.

22 Understanding *is* a wellspring of life to
him who has it.
But the correction of fools *is* folly.

23 The heart of the wise teaches his
mouth,
And adds learning to his lips.

24 Pleasant words *are like* a honeycomb,
Sweetness to the soul and health to the
bones.

25 There is a way *that seems* right to a
man,
But its end *is* the way of death.

26 The person who labors, labors for
himself,
For his *hungry* mouth drives him *on*.

27 An ungodly man digs up evil,
And *it is* on his lips like a burning fire.

28 A perverse man sows strife,
And [R]a whisperer separates the best of
friends. Prov. 17:9

29 A violent man entices his neighbor,
And leads him in a way *that is* not
good.

30 He winks his eye to devise perverse
things;
He [T]purses his lips *and* brings about
evil. Lit. *compresses*

31[R]The silver-haired head *is* a crown of
glory, Prov. 20:29
If it is found in the way of righteousness.

32[R]*He who is* slow to anger *is* better than
the mighty, Prov. 14:29; 19:11
And he who rules his spirit than he who
takes a city.

33 The lot is cast into the lap,
But its every decision *is* from the LORD.

CHAPTER 17

BETTER *is* [R]a dry morsel with quietness,
Than a house full of feasting* *with*
strife. Prov. 15:17

2 A wise servant will rule over [R]a son who
causes shame, Prov. 10:5
And will share an inheritance among the
brothers.

3 The refining pot *is* for silver and the
furnace for gold,
But the LORD tests the hearts.

4 An evildoer gives heed to false lips;
A liar listens eagerly to a [T]spiteful
tongue. Lit. *destructive*

5[R]He who mocks the poor reproaches his
Maker; Prov. 14:31
[R]He who is glad at calamity will not go
unpunished. Job 31:29

6[R]Children's children *are* the crown of old
men, [Ps. 127:3; 128:3]
And the glory of children *is* their father.

7 Excellent speech is not becoming to a
fool,
Much less lying lips to a prince.

8 A present *is* a precious stone in the eyes
of its possessor;
Wherever he turns, he prospers.

9[R]He who covers a transgression seeks
love, [Prov. 10:12]
But [R]he who repeats a matter separates
friends. Prov. 16:28

10 Rebuke is more effective for a wise *man*
Than a hundred blows on a fool.

11 An evil *man* seeks only rebellion;
Therefore a cruel messenger will be sent
against him.

12 Let a man meet [R]a bear robbed of her
cubs, Hos. 13:8
Rather than a fool in his folly.

13 Whoever rewards evil for good,
Evil will not depart from his house.

14 The beginning of strife *is like* releasing
water;
Therefore [R]stop contention before a
quarrel starts. [Prov. 20:3]

15[R]He who justifies the wicked, and he who
condemns the just, Ex. 23:7
Both of them alike *are* an abomination to
the LORD.

16 Why *is there* in the hand of a fool the
purchase price of wisdom,
Since *he has* no heart *for it*?

17[R]A friend loves at all times, Ruth 1:16
And a brother is born for adversity.

18[R]A man devoid of [T]understanding shakes
hands in a pledge, Prov. 6:1 • Lit. *heart*
And becomes surety for his friend.

17:1 Or *sacrificial meals*

19 He who loves transgression loves strife,
And [R]he who exalts his gate seeks destruction. Prov. 16:18

20 He who has a [T]deceitful heart finds no good, crooked
And he who has [R]a perverse tongue falls into evil. James 3:8

21 He who begets a scoffer *does so* to his sorrow,
And the father of a fool has no joy.

22 A [R]merry heart does good, like medicine,* Prov. 12:25; 15:13, 15
But a broken spirit dries the bones.

23 A wicked *man* accepts a bribe behind the back*
To pervert the ways of justice.

24 [R]Wisdom *is* in the sight of him who has understanding, Eccl. 2:14
But the eyes of a fool *are* on the ends of the earth.

25 A foolish son *is* a grief to his father,
And bitterness to her who bore him.

26 Also, to punish the righteous *is* not good,
Nor to strike princes for *their* uprightness.

27 [R]He who has knowledge spares his words, James 1:19
And a man of understanding is of a calm spirit.

28 [R]Even a fool is counted wise when he holds his peace; Job 13:5
When he shuts his lips, *he is considered* perceptive.

CHAPTER 18

A MAN who isolates himself seeks his own desire;
He rages against all wise judgment.

2 A fool has no delight in understanding,
But in expressing his own heart.

3 When the wicked comes, contempt comes also;
And with dishonor *comes* reproach.

4 [R]The words of a man's mouth *are* deep waters; Prov. 10:11
[R]The wellspring of wisdom *is* a flowing brook. [James 3:17]

5 *It is* not good to show partiality to the wicked,
Or to overthrow the righteous in [R]judgment. Prov. 17:15

6 A fool's lips enter into contention,
And his mouth calls for blows.

7 A fool's mouth *is* his destruction,
And his lips *are* the snare of his soul.

8 [R]The words of a [T]talebearer *are* like tasty trifles,* Prov. 12:18 • *gossip* or *slanderer*
And they go down into the inmost body.

9 He who is slothful in his work
Is a brother to him who is a great destroyer.

10 The name of the LORD *is* a strong [R]tower; 2 Sam. 22:2, 3, 33
The righteous run to it and are safe.

11 The rich man's wealth *is* his strong city,
And like a high wall in his own esteem.

12 [R]Before destruction the heart of a man is haughty, Prov. 15:33; 16:18
And before honor *is* humility.

13 He who answers a matter before he hears *it*,
It *is* folly and shame to him.

14 The spirit of a man will sustain him in sickness,
But who can bear a broken spirit?

15 The heart of the prudent acquires knowledge,
And the ear of the wise seeks knowledge.

16 A man's gift makes room for him,
And brings him before great men.

17 The first *one* to plead his cause *seems* right,
Until his neighbor comes and examines him.

18 Casting [R]lots causes contentions to cease, [Prov. 16:33]
And keeps the mighty apart.

19 A brother offended *is harder to win* than a strong city,
And contentions *are* like the bars of a castle.

20 [R]A man's stomach shall be satisfied from the fruit of his mouth; Prov. 12:14
From the produce of his lips he shall be filled.

21 [R]Death and life *are* in the power of the tongue, Matt. 12:37
And those who love it will eat its fruit.

17:22 Or *makes medicine even better* **17:23** Under cover, lit. *from the bosom* **18:8** A Jewish tradition *wounds*

22 *He who* finds a wife finds a good *thing*,
And obtains favor from the LORD.

23 The poor *man* uses entreaties,
But the rich answers roughly.

24 A man *who has* friends must himself be
friendly,*
[R]But there is a friend *who* sticks closer
than a brother. Prov. 17:17

CHAPTER 19

BETTER [R]*is* the poor who walks in his
integrity Prov. 28:6
Than *one who is* perverse in his lips, and
is a fool.

2 Also it is not good *for* a soul *to be*
without knowledge,
And he sins who hastens with *his* feet.

3 The foolishness of a man twists his
way,
And his heart frets against the LORD.

4[R]Wealth makes many friends,
But the poor is separated from his
friend. Prov. 14:20

5 A false witness will not go unpunished,
And *he who* speaks lies will not
escape.

6 Many entreat the favor of the nobility,
And every man *is* a friend to one who
gives gifts.

7[R]All the brothers of the poor hate him;
How much more do his friends go [R]far
from him! Prov. 14:20 • Ps. 38:11
He may pursue *them with* words, yet
they [T]abandon *him*. Lit. *are not*

8 He who gets [T]wisdom loves his own
soul;
He who keeps understanding [R]will find
good. Lit. *heart* • Prov. 16:20

9 A false witness will not go unpunished,
And *he who* speaks lies shall perish.

10 Luxury is not fitting for a fool,
Much less [R]for a servant to rule over
princes. Prov. 30:21, 22

11[R]The discretion of a man makes him slow
to anger, James 1:19
[R]And his glory *is* to overlook a
transgression. Eph. 4:32

12[R]The king's wrath *is* like the roaring of a
lion, Prov. 16:14
But his favor *is* like dew on the grass.

13 A foolish son *is* the ruin of his father,
[R]And the contentions of a wife *are* a
continual dripping. Prov. 21:9, 19

14[R]Houses and riches *are* an inheritance
from fathers, 2 Cor. 12:14
But a prudent wife *is* from the LORD.

15 Laziness casts *one* into a deep sleep,
And an idle person will suffer hunger.

16[R]He who keeps the commandment keeps
his soul, Luke 10:28; 11:28
But he who is careless* of his ways will die.

17[R]He who has pity on the poor lends to the
LORD, [2 Cor. 9:6–8]
And He will pay back what he has given.

18[R]Chasten your son while there is hope,
And do not set your heart on his
destruction.* Prov. 13:24

19 *A man of* great wrath will suffer
punishment;
For if you rescue *him*, you will have to
do it again.

20 Listen to counsel and receive instruction,
That you may be wise [R]in your latter
days. Ps. 37:37

21 There are many plans in a man's heart,
[R]Nevertheless the LORD's counsel—that
will stand. Heb. 6:17

22 What is desired in a man is kindness,
And a poor man is better than a liar.

23[R]The fear of the LORD *leads* to life,
And *he who has it* will abide in
satisfaction; [1 Tim. 4:8]
He will not be visited with evil.

24[R]A lazy *man* buries his hand in the
bowl,* Prov. 15:19
And will not so much as bring it to his
mouth again.

25 Strike a scoffer, and the simple [R]will
become wary; Deut. 13:11
Rebuke one who has understanding, *and*
he will discern knowledge.

26 He who mistreats *his* father *and* chases
away *his* mother
Is [R]a son who causes shame and brings
reproach. Prov. 17:2

18:24 So with Gr. mss., Syr., Tg., Vg.; MT *may come to ruin* **19:16** Is reckless, lit. *despises* **19:18** Lit. *to put him to death*; a Jewish tradition *on his crying* **19:24** LXX, Syr. *bosom*; Tg., Vg. *armpit*

27 Cease listening to instruction, my son,
And you will stray from the words of knowledge.

28 A disreputable witness scorns justice,
And [R]the mouth of the wicked devours iniquity. Job 15:16

29 Judgments are prepared for scoffers,
And beatings for the backs of fools.

CHAPTER 20

WINE [R]*is* a mocker, Gen. 9:21
Strong drink *is* a brawler,
And whoever is led astray by it is not wise.

2 The wrath* of a king *is* like the roaring of a lion;
Whoever provokes him to anger sins *against* his own life.

3 [R]*It is* honorable for a man to stop striving, Prov. 17:14
Since any fool can start a quarrel.

4 [R]The lazy *man* will not plow because of winter; Prov. 10:4
[R]He will beg during harvest and *have* nothing. Prov. 19:15

5 Counsel in the heart of man *is like* deep water,
But a man of understanding will draw it out.

6 Most men will proclaim each his own [T]goodness, Lit. *mercy*
But who can find a faithful man?

7 [R]The righteous *man* walks in his integrity; 2 Cor. 1:12
His children *are* blessed after him.

8 A king who sits on the throne of judgment
Scatters all evil with his eyes.

9 [R]Who can say, "I have made my heart clean, [1 Kin. 8:46]
I am pure from my sin"?

10 [R]Diverse weights *and* diverse measures,
They *are* both alike, an abomination to the LORD. Deut. 25:13

11 Even a child is known by his deeds,
Whether what he does *is* pure and right.

12 The hearing ear and the seeing eye,
The LORD has made them both.

13 [R]Do not love sleep, lest you come to poverty; Rom. 12:11
Open your eyes, *and* you will be satisfied with bread.

14 "*It is* good for nothing,"* cries the buyer;
But when he has gone his way, then he boasts.

15 There is gold and a multitude of rubies,
But [R]the lips of knowledge *are* a precious jewel. [Prov. 3:13–15]

16 [R]Take the garment of one who is surety *for* a stranger, Prov. 22:26
And hold it as a pledge *when it* is for a seductress.

17 [R]Bread gained by deceit *is* sweet to a man, Prov. 9:17
But afterward his mouth will be filled with gravel.

18 Plans are established by counsel;
[R]By wise counsel wage war. Luke 14:31

19 [R]He who goes about *as* a talebearer reveals secrets; Prov. 11:13
Therefore do not associate with one who flatters with his lips.

20 [R]Whoever curses his father or his mother, Matt. 15:4
[R]His lamp will be put out in deep darkness. Job 18:5, 6

21 [R]An inheritance gained hastily at the beginning Prov. 28:20
[R]Will not be blessed at the end. Hab. 2:6

22 Do not say, "I will recompense evil";
Wait for the LORD, and He will save you.

23 Diverse weights *are* an abomination to the LORD,
And dishonest scales *are* not good.

24 A man's steps *are* of the LORD;
How then can a man understand his own way?

25 *It is* a snare for a man to devote rashly *something as* holy,
And afterward to reconsider *his* vows.

26 [R]A wise king sifts out the wicked,
And brings the threshing wheel over them. Ps. 101:8

20:2 Lit. *fear* or *terror*, produced by the king's wrath
20:14 Lit. *evil, evil*

27[R] The spirit of a man *is* the lamp of the LORD,
Searching all the inner depths of his heart.*
1 Cor. 2:11

28[R] Mercy and truth preserve the king,
And by [T]lovingkindness he upholds his throne.
Prov. 21:21 • *mercy*

29 The glory of young men *is* their strength,
And [R]the splendor of old men *is* their gray head.
Prov. 16:31

30 Blows that hurt cleanse away evil,
As *do* stripes the inner depths of the heart.*

CHAPTER 21

THE king's heart *is* in the hand of the LORD,
Like the [T]rivers of water;
He turns it wherever He wishes.
channels

2[R] Every way of a man *is* right in his own eyes,
But the LORD weighs the hearts.
Prov. 16:2

3[R] To do righteousness and justice
Is more acceptable to the LORD than sacrifice.
1 Sam. 15:22

4 A haughty look, a proud heart,
And the plowing* of the wicked *are* sin.

5[R] The plans of the diligent *lead* surely to plenty,
But *those of* everyone *who is* hasty, surely to poverty.
Prov. 10:4

6[R] Getting treasures by a lying tongue
Is the fleeting fantasy of those who seek death.*
2 Pet. 2:3

7 The violence of the wicked will destroy them,*
Because they refuse to do justice.

8 The way of a guilty man *is* perverse;*
But *as for* the pure, his work *is* right.

9 Better to dwell in a corner of a housetop,
Than in a house shared with [R]a contentious woman.
Prov. 19:13

10 The soul of the wicked desires evil;
His neighbor finds no favor in his eyes.

11 When the scoffer is punished, the simple is made wise;
But when the [R]wise is instructed, he receives knowledge.
Prov. 19:25

12 The righteous *God* wisely considers the house of the wicked,
Overthrowing the wicked for *their* wickedness.

13[R] Whoever shuts his ears to the cry of the poor
Will also cry himself and not be heard.
[Matt. 7:2; 18:30–34]

14 A gift in secret pacifies anger,
And a bribe behind the back,* strong wrath.

15 *It is* a joy for the just to do justice,
But destruction *will come* to the workers of iniquity.

16 A man who wanders from the way of understanding
Will rest in the assembly of the dead.

17 He who loves pleasure *will be* a poor man;
He who loves wine and oil will not be rich.

18 The wicked *shall be* a ransom for the righteous,
And the unfaithful for the upright.

19 Better to dwell [T]in the wilderness,
Than with a contentious and angry woman.
Lit. *in the land of the desert*

20[R] *There is* desirable treasure,
And oil in the dwelling of the wise,
But a foolish man squanders it.
Ps. 112:3

21[R] He who follows righteousness and mercy
Finds life, righteousness and honor.
Matt. 5:6

22 A [R]wise *man* [T]scales the city of the mighty,
And brings down the trusted stronghold.
Prov. 24:5 • Climbs over the walls of

23[R] Whoever guards his mouth and tongue
Keeps his soul from troubles.
[James 3:2]

24 A proud *and* haughty *man*—"Scoffer" *is* his name;
He acts with arrogant pride.

25 The [R]desire of the lazy *man* kills him,
For his hands refuse to labor.
Prov. 13:4

20:27 Lit. *rooms of the belly* **20:30** Lit. *rooms of the belly* **21:4** Or *lamp* **21:6** LXX *Pursue vanity on the snares of death;* Vg. *Is vain and foolish, and shall stumble on the snares of death;* Tg. *They shall be destroyed, and they shall fall who seek death* **21:7** Lit. *drag them away* **21:8** Or *The way of a man is perverse and strange;* **21:14** Under cover, lit. *in the bosom*

26 He covets greedily all day long,
But the righteous [R]gives and does not spare. [Prov. 22:9]

27[R] The sacrifice of the wicked *is* an abomination; Jer. 6:20
How much more *when* he brings it with wicked intent!

28 A false witness shall perish,
But the man who hears *him* will speak endlessly.

29 A wicked man hardens his face,
But *as for* the upright, he establishes* his way.

30 *There is* no wisdom or understanding
Or counsel against the LORD.

31 The horse *is* prepared for the day of battle,
But [R]deliverance *is* of the LORD. Ps. 3:8

CHAPTER 22

A [R]*GOOD* name is to be chosen rather than great riches, Eccl. 7:1
Loving favor rather than silver and gold.

2 The [R]rich and the poor have this in common, Prov. 29:13
The LORD *is* the maker of them all.

3 A prudent *man* foresees evil and hides himself,
But the simple pass on and are [R]punished. Prov. 27:12

4 By humility *and* the fear of the LORD
Are riches and honor and life.

5 Thorns *and* snares *are* in the way of the perverse;
He who guards his soul will be far from them.

6[R] Train up a child in the way he should go, Eph. 6:4
[T]And when he is old he will not depart from it. Even

7 The [R]rich rules over the poor,
And the borrower *is* servant to the lender. James 2:6

8 He who sows iniquity will reap sorrow,
And the rod of his anger will fail.

9[R] He who has a generous eye will be [R]blessed, 2 Cor. 9:6 • [Prov. 19:17]
For he gives of his bread to the poor.

10[R] Cast out the scoffer, and contention will leave; Ps. 101:5
Yes, strife and reproach will cease.

11[R] He who loves purity of heart Ps. 101:6
And has grace on his lips,
The king *will be* his friend.

21:29 Qr., LXX *understands*

22:6 A Prescription for Rearing Children—This proverb sets out two stages in the process of godly child rearing: first, the method, "Train up a child in the way he should go"; and second, the result, "when he is old he will not depart from it."

The method involves three parts:

a. The concept of training—"Train up." This does not denote corporal punishment but rather includes three ideas: *Dedication*—this is the consistent meaning of the word in its other OT occurrences (Page 194—Deut. 20:5; Page 346—1 Kin. 8:63; Page 439—2 Chr. 7:5). Child training must begin with dedication of the child to God; the parent must realize that the child belongs exclusively to God and is given to the parent only as a stewardship. *Instruction*—this is the meaning of this word as it is used in the Jewish writings; the parents are to instruct or cause their children to learn everything essential in pleasing God. *Motivation*—this is the meaning of the word in Arabic, as it is used to describe the action of a midwife who stimulates the palate of the newborn babe so it will take nourishment. Parents are to create a taste or desire within the child so that he is internally motivated (rather than externally compelled) to do what God wants him to do.
b. The recipient of training—"a child." This is one of seven Hebrew words translated by the English word "child" and would better be translated by our word "dependent." As long as the child is dependent on his parents he is to be the recipient of training, regardless of his age.
c. The content of the training—"in the way that he should go." The thought is that at each stage of development the parents or guardians are to dedicate, instruct, and motivate the child to do what God evidently has best equipped the child to do for Him. This is graphically illustrated by Joshua when he said, "But as for me and my house, we will serve the LORD" (Page 236—Josh. 24:15).

Proverbs are wisdom statements: general truths about the most important issues of life. If God's process has been followed, the desired results usually occur. A child can reject the training of godly parents, but usually godly parenting results in godly adult offspring. The result includes the time of realization—"when he is old"—this is best understood as being parallel with "a child," hence, "when he is independent," that is, no longer economically dependent upon parents, referring to the time when the child leaves the parents' home to establish another home. The result includes the nature of realization—"he will not depart from it." Persistent, careful, godly parenting produces adult children whose Christian faith and commitment are unwavering.

Now turn to Page 12—Gen. 9:5: The Origin of Human Government.

12 The eyes of the LORD preserve knowledge,
But He overthrows the words of the faithless.

13[R] The lazy *man* says, "*There is* a lion outside! Prov. 26:13
I shall be slain in the streets!"

14[R] The mouth of an immoral woman *is* a deep pit; Prov. 2:16; 5:3; 7:5
[R] He who is abhorred by the LORD will fall there. Eccl. 7:26

15 Foolishness *is* bound up in the heart of a child;
[R] The rod of correction will drive it far from him. Prov. 13:24; 23:13, 14

16 He who oppresses the poor to increase his *riches,*
And he who gives to the rich, will surely *come* to poverty.

Proverbs Concerning Various Situations

17 Incline your ear and hear the words of the wise,
And apply your heart to my knowledge;
18 For *it is* a pleasant thing if you keep them within you;
Let them all be fixed upon your lips,
19 So that your trust may be in the LORD;
I have instructed you today, even you.
20 Have I not written to you excellent things
Of counsels and knowledge,

21 That I may make you know the certainty of the words of truth,
[R] That you may answer words of truth
To those who send to you? 1 Pet. 3:15

22 Do not rob the poor because he *is* poor,
Nor oppress the afflicted at the gate;
23[R] For the LORD will plead their cause,
And plunder the soul of those who plunder them. 1 Sam. 24:12

24 Make no friendship with an angry man,
And with a furious man do not go,
25 Lest you learn his ways
And set a snare for your soul.

26[R] Do not be one of those who shakes hands in a pledge, Prov. 11:15
One of those who is surety for debts;
27 If you have nothing *with which* to pay,
Why should he take away your bed from under you?

28 Do not remove the ancient [T]landmark
Which your fathers have set. *boundary*

29 Do you see a man *who* [T]excels in his work? *is prompt in his business*
He will stand before kings;
He will not stand before unknown *men.*

CHAPTER 23

WHEN you sit down to eat with a ruler,
Consider carefully what *is* before you;
2 And put a knife to your throat
If you *are* a man given to appetite.
3 Do not desire his delicacies,
For they *are* deceptive food.

4[R] Do not overwork to be rich;
[R] Because of your own understanding, cease! [1 Tim. 6:9, 10] • Rom. 12:16
5 Will you set your eyes on that which is not?
For *riches* certainly make themselves wings;
They fly away like an eagle *toward* heaven.

6 Do not eat the bread of [R]a miser,*
Nor desire his delicacies; Deut. 15:9
7 For as he thinks in his heart, so *is* he.
"Eat and drink!" [R]he says to you,
But his heart is not with you. Prov. 12:2

23:6 Lit. *one who has an evil eye*

22:21 God's Word Equips—In a general sense it can be said that the Bible was written to convict sinners of sin and to equip believers for service.

a. It equips for evangelism. Philip the evangelist uses Isaiah 53 to point the Ethiopian eunuch to Christ in Acts 8:26–35.
b. It equips for counseling others. In his two letters to Timothy, Paul constantly urges this young man to preach the Word of God (Page 1237—1 Tim. 1:3, 18; 4:13–15; Page 1244—2 Tim. 2:1, 2, 15). "If you instruct the brethren in these things, you will be a good minister of Jesus Christ, nourished in the words of faith and of the good doctrine which you have carefully followed" (Page 1239—1 Tim. 4:6).
c. It equips for using one's spiritual gifts from God. A spiritual gift is an ability given by the Holy Spirit to the believer for the purpose of edifying the church and glorifying God. In Eph. 1:17–19 and 4:7, 11–14 Paul says a knowledge of God's Word will provide us with the maturity we need to use our gifts in the most effective way.
d. It equips us for doing battle with Satan. In Ephesians 6:10–17 Paul likens the believers' armor to that used by Roman foot soldiers. In this comparison the Word of God is likened to the soldier's sword (Page 1209—Eph. 6:17).

Now turn to Page 886—Dan. 11:32: We Know God Through His Word.

8 The morsel you have eaten, you will
vomit up,
And waste your pleasant words.

9[R] Do not speak in the hearing of a fool,
For he will despise the wisdom of your
words. Matt. 7:6

10 Do not remove the ancient landmark,
Nor enter the fields of the fatherless;
11 For their Redeemer *is* mighty;
He will plead their cause against you.

12 Apply your heart to instruction,
And your ears to words of knowledge.

13[R] Do not withhold correction from a child,
For *if* you beat him with a rod, he will
not die. Prov. 13:24
14 You shall beat him with a rod,
And deliver his soul from hell.*

15 My son, if your heart is wise,
My heart will rejoice—indeed, I myself;
16 Yes, my inmost being will rejoice
When your lips speak right things.

17[R] Do not let your heart envy sinners,
But [R]*be zealous* for the fear of the LORD
all the day; Ps. 37:1 • Prov. 28:14
18 For surely there is a hereafter,
And your hope will not be cut off.

19 Hear, my son, and be wise;
And guide your heart in the way.
20[R] Do not mix with winebibbers, Is. 5:22
Or with gluttonous eaters of meat;
21 For the drunkard and the glutton will
come to poverty,
And drowsiness will clothe *a man* with
rags.

22[R] Listen to your father who begot you,
And do not despise your mother when
she is old. Prov. 1:8

23[R] Buy the truth, and do not sell *it*,
Also wisdom and instruction and
understanding. [Matt. 13:44]

24[R] The father of the righteous will greatly
rejoice, Prov. 10:1
And he who begets a wise *child* will
delight in him.
25 Let your father and your mother be glad,
And let her who bore you rejoice.

26 My son, give me your heart,
And let your eyes observe my ways.
27[R] For a harlot *is* a deep pit, Prov. 22:14
And a seductress *is* a narrow well.
28[R] She also lies in wait as *for* a victim,
And increases the unfaithful among
men. Prov. 7:12

29[R] Who has woe? Is. 5:11, 22
Who has sorrow?
Who has contentions?
Who has complaints?
Who has wounds without cause?
Who [R]has redness of eyes? Gen. 49:12
30 Those who linger long at the wine,
Those who go in search of mixed wine.
31 Do not look on the wine when it is red,
When it sparkles in the cup,
When it swirls around smoothly;
32 At the last it bites like a serpent,
And stings like a viper.
33 Your eyes will see strange things,
And your heart will utter perverse things.
34 Yes, you will be like one who lies down
in the [T]midst of the sea, Lit. *heart*
Or like one who lies at the top of the
mast, *saying:*
35 "They[R] have struck me, but I was not
hurt; Jer. 5:3
They have beaten me, but I did not feel
it.
When shall [R]I awake, that I may seek
another *drink*?" Eph. 4:19

CHAPTER 24

DO not be [R]envious of evil men, Ps. 37:1
Nor desire to be with them;
2 For their heart devises violence,
And their lips talk of troublemaking.

3 Through wisdom a house is built,
And by understanding it is established;
4 By knowledge the rooms are filled
With all precious and pleasant riches.

5[R] A wise man *is* strong, Prov. 21:22
Yes, a man of knowledge increases
strength;

6[R] For by wise counsel you will wage your
own war, Luke 14:31
And in a multitude of counselors *there is*
safety.

23:14 Or *Sheol*

24:6 Knowing the Will of God Through Circumstances and Counsel—While the Christian is to live above his circumstances, he is not to be unaware of them. God often works through circumstances in revealing His perfect will for us. Certainly Paul's wonderful statement, "all things work together for good to those who love God" (Page 1155—Rom. 8:28) takes into account our circumstances. A number of biblical examples can be given to illustrate this.

7[R] Wisdom *is* too lofty for a fool; Ps. 10:5
He does not open his mouth in the gate.

8 He who [R]plots to do evil Rom. 1:30
Will be called a schemer.
9 The devising of foolishness *is* sin,
And the scoffer *is* an abomination to men.

10 *If* you [R]faint in the day of adversity,
Your strength *is* small. Heb. 12:3

11[R] Deliver *those who* are drawn toward death, Ps. 82:4
And hold back *those* stumbling to the slaughter.
12 If you say, "Surely we did not know this,"
Does not [R]He who weighs the hearts consider *it?* Prov. 21:2
He who keeps your soul, does He *not* know *it?*
And will He *not* render to *each* man [R]according to his deeds? Ps. 62:12

13 My son, [R]eat honey because *it is* good,
And the honeycomb *which is* sweet to your taste; Song 5:1
14[R] So *shall* the knowledge of wisdom be to your soul; Ps. 19:10; 58:11
If you have found *it*, there is a prospect,
And your hope will not be cut off.

15 Do not lie in wait, O wicked *man*, against the dwelling of the righteous;
Do not plunder his resting place;
16[R] For a righteous *man* may fall seven times [Mic. 7:8]
And rise again,
But the wicked shall fall by calamity.

17[R] Do not rejoice when your enemy falls,
And do not let your heart be glad when he stumbles; Obad. 12
18 Lest the LORD see *it*, and [T]it displease Him, Lit. *it be evil in His eyes*
And He turn away His wrath from him.

19[R] Do not fret because of evildoers,
Nor be envious of the wicked; Ps. 37:1
20 For there will be no prospect for the evil *man;*
The lamp of the wicked will be put out.

21 My son, [R]fear the LORD and the king;
Do not associate with those given to change; [1 Pet. 2:17]
22 For their calamity will rise suddenly,
And who knows the ruin those two can bring?

23 These *things* also *belong* to the wise:

[R]*It is* not good to [T]show partiality in judgment. Lev. 19:15 • Lit. *recognize faces*
24[R] He who says to the wicked, "You *are* righteous," Is. 5:23
Him the people will curse;
Nations will abhor him.
25 But those who rebuke *the wicked* will have [R]delight, Prov. 28:23
And a good blessing will come upon them.

26 He who gives a right answer kisses the lips.

27 Prepare your outside work,
Make it fit for yourself in the field;
And afterward build your house.

28[R] Do not be a witness against your neighbor without cause, Eph. 4:25
For would you deceive* with your lips?
29[R] Do not say, "I will do to him just as he has done to me; [Prov. 20:22]
I will render to the man according to his work."

30 I went by the field of the lazy *man*,
And by the vineyard of the man devoid of understanding;

24:28 LXX, Vg. *Do not deceive*

---

a. God directed Abraham to substitute a ram, whose horns had somehow become entangled in a thicket, for the life of Isaac (Page 23—Gen. 22:13).
b. God arranged for Pharaoh's daughter to be bathing in the river Nile at the exact time the baby Moses floated by in a little ark of bulrushes (Page 56—Ex. 2:1–10).
c. Paul's young nephew happened to overhear a plot to kill his famous uncle. He then reported it to the authorities, thus saving the apostle's life (Page 1139—Acts 23:12–22).

Surely the above circumstances were providentially arranged. So the Christian should ask, when attempting to discover God's will, Is the Lord showing me something through my circumstances?

Counselors also play an important role in finding God's will. "In a multitude of counselors *there is* safety" (Page 650—Prov. 24:6). However, three things must be kept in mind at this point:

a. Counsel must come from a godly source. "Confidence in an unfaithful man in time of trouble *is like* a bad tooth and a foot out of joint" (Page 652—Prov. 25:19).
b. Sometimes even the godliest person can unknowingly give us wrong advice. Nathan the prophet did this when he encouraged David to build the temple (Page 311—2 Sam. 7:1–13).
c. In the final analysis, each person is responsible for knowing God's revealed purpose for his or her own life.

Now turn to Page 28—THE CHRISTIAN'S GUIDE: Recognizing God's Institutions.

31 And there it was, [R]all overgrown with
thorns; Gen. 3:18
Its surface was covered with nettles;
Its stone wall was broken down.
32 When I saw *it*, I considered *it* well;
I looked on *it and* received instruction:
33 A little sleep, a little slumber,
A little folding of the hands to rest;
34[R] So shall your poverty come *like* a
prowler, Prov. 6:9–11
And your need like an armed man.

CHAPTER 25

Relationships with Kings

THESE[R] also *are* proverbs of Solomon
which the men of Hezekiah king of Judah
copied: 1 Kin. 4:32

2[R] *It is* the glory of God to conceal a
matter,
But the glory of kings *is* to search out a
matter. Deut. 29:29

3 *As* the heavens for height and the earth
for depth,
So the heart of kings *is* unsearchable.

4[R] Take away the dross from silver,
And it will go to the silversmith *for*
jewelry. 2 Tim. 2:21
5 Take away the wicked from before the
king,
And his throne will be established in
[R]righteousness. Prov. 16:12; 20:8

6 Do not exalt yourself in the presence of
the king,
And do not stand in the place of the
great;
7[R] For *it is* better that he say to you,
"Come up here," Luke 14:7–11
Than that you should be put lower in the
presence of the prince,
Whom your eyes have seen.

Relationships with Neighbors

8[R] Do not go hastily to [T]court; Matt. 5:25
For what will you do in the end,
When your neighbor has put you to
shame? Lit. *contend* or *bring a lawsuit*
9[R] Debate your case with your neighbor,
And do not disclose the secret to
another; [Matt. 18:15]
10 Lest he who hears *it* expose your shame,
And your reputation be ruined.

11 A word fitly [R]spoken *is like* apples of
gold Prov. 15:23
In settings of silver.
12 *Like* an earring of gold and an ornament
of fine gold
Is a wise rebuker to an obedient ear.

13[R] Like the cold of snow in time of harvest
Is a faithful messenger to those who
send him, Prov. 13:17
For he refreshes the soul of his masters.

14 Whoever falsely boasts of giving
Is like clouds and wind without rain.

15[R] By long forbearance a ruler is
persuaded, Prov. 15:1
And a gentle tongue breaks a bone.

16 Have you found honey?
Eat only as much as you need,
Lest you be filled with it and vomit.

17 Seldom set foot in your neighbor's
house,
Lest he become weary of you and hate
you.

18[R] A man who bears false witness against
his neighbor Ps. 57:4
Is like a club, a sword, and a sharp
arrow.

19 Confidence in an unfaithful *man* in time
of trouble
Is like a bad tooth and a foot out of joint.

20 *Like* one who takes away a garment in
cold weather,
And like vinegar on soda,
Is one who [R]sings songs to a heavy
heart. Dan. 6:18

Relationships with Enemies

21[R] If your enemy is hungry, give him bread
to eat; Rom. 12:20
And if he is thirsty, give him water to
drink;
22 For *so* you will heap coals of fire on his
head,
And the LORD will reward you.

23 The north wind brings forth rain,
And [R]a backbiting tongue an angry
countenance. Ps. 101:5

24[R] *It is* better to dwell in a corner of a
housetop, Prov. 19:13
Than in a house shared with a
contentious woman.

Relationships with Yourself

25 *As* cold water to a weary soul,
So *is* good news from a far country.

26 A righteous *man* who falters before the
wicked
Is like a murky spring and a [T]polluted
well. *ruined*

27 *It is* not good to eat much honey;
So to seek one's own glory *is not* glory.

28[R] Whoever *has* no rule over his own spirit
Is like a city broken down, without
walls. Prov. 16:32

CHAPTER 26

Relationships with Fools

AS snow in summer and rain in harvest,
So honor is not fitting for a fool.

2 Like a flitting sparrow, like a flying
swallow,
So [R]a curse without cause shall not
alight. Deut. 23:5

3[R] A whip for the horse, Ps. 32:9
A bridle for the donkey,
And a rod for the fool's back.
4 Do not answer a fool according to his
folly,
Lest you also be like him.
5 Answer a fool according to his folly,
Lest he be wise in his own eyes.
6 He who sends a message by the hand of
a fool
Cuts off *his own* feet *and* drinks violence.
7 *Like* the legs of the lame that hang limp
Is a proverb in the mouth of fools.
8 Like one who binds a stone in a sling
Is he who gives honor to a fool.
9 *Like* a thorn *that* goes into the hand of a
drunkard
Is a proverb in the mouth of fools.
10 The great *God* who formed everything
Gives the fool *his* hire and the
transgressor *his* wages.*
11[R] As a dog returns to his own vomit,
So a fool repeats his folly. 2 Pet. 2:22
12[R] Do you see a man wise in his own eyes?
There is more hope for a fool than for
him. [Rev. 3:17]

Relationships with Lazy People

13 The lazy *man* says, "*There is* a lion in the
road!
A fierce lion *is* in the streets!"
14 *As* a door turns on its hinges,
So *does* the lazy *man* on his bed.
15 The lazy *man* buries his hand in the
[T]bowl;* LXX, Syr. *bosom;* Tg., Vg. *armpit*
It wearies him to bring it back to his
mouth.
16 The lazy *man is* wiser in his own eyes
Than seven men who can answer
sensibly.

Relationships with Gossips

17 He who passes by *and* meddles in a
quarrel not his own
Is like one who takes a dog by the ears.
18 Like a madman who throws firebrands,
arrows, and death,
19 *Is* the man *who* deceives his neighbor,
And says, [R]"I was only joking!" Eph. 5:4
20 Where *there is* no wood, the fire goes
out;
And where *there is* no [T]talebearer, strife
ceases. *gossip* or *slanderer,* lit. *whisperer*
21[R] *As* charcoal *is* to burning coals, and
wood to fire, Prov. 15:18
So *is* a contentious man to kindle strife.
22 The words of a [T]talebearer *are* like tasty
trifles, *gossip* or *slanderer*
And they go down into the inmost body.

23 Fervent lips with a wicked heart
Are like earthenware covered with silver
dross.

24 He who hates, disguises *it* with his lips,
And lays up deceit within himself;
25[R] When [T]he speaks kindly, do not believe
him, Ps. 28:3 • Lit. *his voice is gracious*
For *there are* seven abominations in his
heart;
26 *Though his* hatred is covered by deceit,
His wickedness will be revealed before
the assembly.

27[R] Whoever digs a pit will fall into it,
And he who rolls a stone will have it roll
back on him. Ps. 7:15

28 A lying tongue hates *those who are*
crushed by it,
And a flattering mouth works ruin.

CHAPTER 27

Proverbs Regulating Various Activities

DO[R] not boast about tomorrow,
For you do not know what a day may
bring forth. James 4:13–16

2[R] Let another man praise you, and not
your own mouth; Prov. 25:27
A stranger, and not your own lips.

3 A stone *is* heavy and sand *is* weighty,
But a fool's wrath *is* heavier than both of
them.

4 Wrath *is* cruel and anger a torrent,
But [R]who *is* able to stand before
jealousy? 1 John 3:12

5[R] Open rebuke *is* better [Prov. 28:23]
Than love carefully concealed.

26:10 Heb. difficult in v. 10; ancient and modern translators differ greatly **26:15** Cf. 19:24

6 Faithful *are* the wounds of a friend,
But the kisses of an enemy *are*
[R]deceitful. Matt. 26:49

7 A satisfied soul [T]loathes the honeycomb,
But to a hungry soul every bitter thing *is*
sweet. *tramples on*

8 Like a bird that wanders from its nest
Is a man who wanders from his place.

9 Ointment and perfume delight the heart,
And the sweetness of a man's friend
gives delight by hearty counsel.

10 Do not forsake your own friend or your
father's friend,
Nor go to your brother's house in the
day of your calamity;
[R]Better *is* a neighbor nearby than a
brother far away. Prov. 17:17; 18:24

11 My son, be wise, and make my heart glad,
[R]That I may answer him who reproaches
me. Prov. 10:1; 23:15–26

12 A prudent *man* foresees evil *and* hides
himself;
The simple pass on *and* are punished.

13 Take the garment of him who is surety
for a stranger,
And hold it in pledge *when* he is surety
for a seductress.

14 He who blesses his friend with a loud
voice, rising early in the morning,
It will be counted a curse to him.

15 A [R]continual dripping on a very rainy
day Prov. 19:13
And a contentious woman are alike;
16 Whoever [T]restrains her restrains the
wind, Lit. *hides*
And grasps oil with his right hand.

17 *As* iron sharpens iron,
So a man sharpens the countenance of
his friend.

18 [R]Whoever [T]keeps the fig tree will eat its
fruit; [1 Cor. 3:8; 9:7–13] • *protects* or *tends*
So he who waits on his master will be
honored.

19 As in water face *reflects* face,
So a man's heart *reveals* the man.

20 Hell* and Destruction* are never full;
So the eyes of man are never satisfied.

21 [R]The refining pot *is* for silver and the
furnace for gold, Prov. 17:3
And a man *is valued* by what others say
of him.

22 [R]Though you grind a fool in a mortar
with a pestle along with crushed
grain, Jer. 5:3
Yet his foolishness will not depart from
him.

23 Be diligent to know the state of your
[R]flocks, Prov. 24:27
And attend to your herds;
24 For riches *are* not forever,
Nor does a crown *endure* to all
generations.
25 [R]*When* the hay is removed, and the tender
grass shows itself, Ps. 104:14
And the herbs of the mountains are
gathered in,
26 The lambs *will provide* your clothing,
And the goats the price of a field;
27 *You shall have* enough goats' milk for
your food,
For the food of your household,
And the nourishment of your
maidservants.

CHAPTER 28

THE wicked flee when no one pursues,
But the righteous are bold as a lion.

2 Because of the transgression of a land,
many *are* its princes;
But by a man of understanding *and*
knowledge
Right will be prolonged.

3 [R]A poor man who oppresses the poor
Is like a driving rain [T]which leaves no
food. Matt. 18:28 • Lit. *and there is no bread*

4 [R]Those who forsake the law praise the
wicked, Ps. 49:18
[R]But such as keep the law contend with
them. 1 Kin. 18:18

5 [R]Evil men do not understand justice,
But [R]those who seek the LORD
understand all. Ps. 92:6 • John 17:17

6 Better *is* the poor who walks in his
integrity
Than one perverse *in his* ways, though
he *be* rich.

7 Whoever keeps the law *is* a discerning
son,
But a companion of gluttons shames his
father.

27:20 Or *Sheol* • Heb. *Abaddon*

8 One who increases his possessions by
usury and extortion
Gathers it for him who will pity the poor.

9 One who turns away his ear from
hearing the law,
Even his prayer *is* an abomination.

10[R] Whoever causes the upright to go astray
in an evil way, Prov. 26:27
He himself will fall into his own pit;
But the blameless will inherit good.

11 The rich man *is* wise in his own eyes,
But the poor who has understanding
searches him out.

12 When the righteous rejoice, *there is*
great [R]glory; Prov. 11:10; 29:2
But when the wicked arise, men [T]hide
themselves. Lit. *will be searched for*

13[R] He who covers his sins will not prosper,
But whoever confesses and forsakes
them will have mercy. Ps. 32:3–5

14 Happy *is* the man who is always reverent,
But he who hardens his heart will fall
into calamity.

15 *Like* a roaring lion and a charging bear
Is a wicked ruler over poor people.

16 A ruler who lacks understanding *is* a
great [R]oppressor, Eccl. 10:16
But he who hates covetousness will
prolong *his* days.

17[R] A man burdened with bloodshed will
flee into a pit; Gen. 9:6
Let no one help him.

18 Whoever walks blamelessly will be
[T]saved, *delivered*
But *he who is* perverse *in his* ways will
suddenly fall.

19[R] He who tills his land will have plenty of
bread, Prov. 12:11; 20:13
But he who follows frivolity will have
poverty enough!

20 A faithful man will abound with
blessings,
[R]But he who hastens to be rich will not go
unpunished. 1 Tim. 6:9

21[R] To show partiality *is* not good,
[R]Because for a piece of bread a man will
transgress. Prov. 18:5 • Ezek. 13:19

22 A man with an evil eye hastens after
riches,
And does not consider that [R]poverty will
come upon him. Prov. 21:5

23[R] He who rebukes a man will find more
favor afterward Prov. 27:5, 6
Than he who flatters with the tongue.

24 Whoever robs his father or his mother,
And says, "*It is* no transgression,"
The same *is* companion to a destroyer.

25[R] He who is of a proud heart stirs up
strife, Prov. 13:10
[R]But he who trusts in the LORD will be
prospered. 1 Tim. 6:6

26 He who [R]trusts in his own heart is a
fool, Prov. 3:5
But whoever walks wisely will be
delivered.

27[R] He who gives to the poor will not lack,
But he who hides his eyes will have
many curses. Deut. 15:7

28 When the wicked arise, [R]men hide
themselves; Job 24:4
But when they perish, the righteous
increase.

CHAPTER 29

HE[R] who is often rebuked, *and* hardens
his neck, 2 Chr. 36:16
Will suddenly be destroyed, and that
without remedy.

2 When the righteous are in authority, the
[R]people rejoice; Prov. 28:12
But when a wicked *man* rules, [R]the
people groan. Esth. 4:3

3 Whoever loves wisdom makes his father
rejoice,
But a companion of harlots wastes *his*
wealth.

4 The king establishes the land by justice,
But he who receives bribes overthrows it.

5 A man who [R]flatters his neighbor
Spreads a net for his feet. Prov. 26:28

6 By transgression an evil man is snared,
But the righteous sings and rejoices.

7 The righteous [R]considers the cause of the
poor, Job 29:16
But the wicked does not understand
such knowledge.

8 Scoffers [R]set a city aflame, Prov. 11:11
But wise *men* turn away wrath.

9 *If* a wise man contends with a foolish man,
[R]Whether *the fool* rages or laughs, *there is* no peace. Matt. 11:17

10 The bloodthirsty hate the blameless,
But the upright seek his well-being.*

11 A fool vents all his feelings,*
But a wise *man* holds them back.

12 If a ruler pays attention to lies,
All his servants *become* wicked.

13 The poor *man* and the oppressor have this in common:
The LORD gives light to the eyes of both.

14 The king who judges the [R]poor with truth, Is. 11:4
His throne will be established forever.

15 The rod and rebuke give [R]wisdom,
But a child left *to himself* brings shame to his mother. Prov. 22:15

16 When the wicked are multiplied, transgression increases;
But the righteous will see their fall.

17 Correct your son, and he will give you rest;
Yes, he will give delight to your soul.

18[R] Where *there is* no revelation,* the people cast off restraint; 1 Sam. 3:1
But happy *is* he who keeps the law.

19 A servant will not be corrected by mere words;
For though he understands, he will not respond.

20 Do you see a man hasty in his words?
[R]*There is* more hope for a fool than for him. Prov. 26:12

21 He who pampers his servant from childhood
Will have him as a son in the end.

22[R] An angry man stirs up strife,
And a furious man abounds in transgression. Prov. 26:21

23[R] A man's pride will bring him low,
But the humble in spirit will retain honor. Is. 66:2

24 Whoever is a partner with a thief hates his own life;
[R]He swears to tell the truth,* but reveals nothing. Lev. 5:1

25 The fear of man brings a snare,
But whoever trusts in the LORD shall be [T]safe. *secure,* lit. *set on high*

26[R] Many seek the ruler's [T]favor, Ps. 20:9
But justice for man *comes* from the LORD. Lit. *face*

27 An unjust man *is* an abomination to the righteous,
And *he who is* upright in the way *is* an abomination to the wicked.

CHAPTER 30

The Words of Agur

THE words of Agur the son of Jakeh, *his* utterance. This man declared to Ithiel—to Ithiel and Ucal:

2[R] Surely I *am* more stupid than *any* man,
And do not have the understanding of a man. Ps. 73:22

3 I neither learned wisdom
Nor have knowledge of the Holy One.

4[R] Who has ascended into heaven, or descended? [John 3:13]
[R]Who has gathered the wind in His fists?
Who has bound the waters in a garment? Job 38:4
Who has established all the ends of the earth?
What *is* His name, and what *is* His Son's name,
If you know?

5[R] Every word of God *is* pure; Ps. 12:6
[R]He *is* a shield to those who put their trust in Him. Ps. 18:30; 84:11; 115:9–11

6[R] Do not add to His words,
Lest He rebuke you, and you be found a liar. Deut. 4:2; 12:32

7 Two *things* I request of You
(Deprive me not before I die):

8 Remove falsehood and lies far from me;
Give me neither poverty nor riches—
Feed me with the food allotted to me;

9 Lest I be full and deny *You,*
And say, "Who *is* the LORD?"
Or lest I be poor and steal,
And profane the name of my God.

10 Do not malign a servant to his master,
Lest he curse you, and you be found guilty.

11 *There is* a generation *that* curses its [R]father, Ex. 21:17

29:10 Lit. *soul* or *life* **29:11** Lit. *spirit* **29:18** Or *prophetic vision* **29:24** Lit. *hears the adjuration* or *oath*

And does not bless its mother.
12 *There is* a generation [R]*that is* pure in its
own eyes, Luke 18:11
Yet is not washed from its filthiness.
13 *There is* a generation—oh, how [R]lofty are
their eyes! Prov. 6:17
And their eyelids are lifted up.
14[R] *There is* a generation whose teeth *are*
like swords, Job 29:17
And whose fangs *are like* knives,
To devour the poor from off the earth,
And the needy from *among* men.

15 The leech has two daughters—
Give *and* Give!

There are three *things that* are never
satisfied,
Four never say, "Enough!":
16[R] The grave,* Prov. 27:20
The barren womb,
The earth *that* is not satisfied with water—
And the fire never says, "Enough!"

17 The eye *that* mocks *his* father,
And scorns obedience to *his* mother,
The ravens of the valley will pick it out,
And the young eagles will eat it.

18 There are three *things which* are too
wonderful for me,
Yes, four *which* I do not understand:
19 The way of an eagle in the air,
The way of a serpent on a rock,
The way of a ship in the [T]midst of the
sea, Lit. *heart*
And the way of a man with a virgin.

20 This *is* the way of an adulterous woman:
She eats and wipes her mouth,
And says, "I have done no wickedness."

21 For three *things* the earth is perturbed,
Yes, for four it cannot bear up:
22 For a servant when he reigns,
A fool when he is filled with food,
23 A [T]hateful *woman* when she is married,
And a maidservant who succeeds her
mistress. Or *hated*

24 There are four *things which* are little on
the earth,
But they *are* exceedingly wise:
25[R] The ants *are* a people not strong,
Yet they prepare their food in the
summer; Prov. 6:6
26 The rock badgers* are a feeble folk,
Yet they make their homes in the crags;
27 The locusts have no king,
Yet they all advance in ranks;
28 The spider* skillfully grasps with its
hands,
And it is in kings' palaces.

29 There are three *things which* are
majestic in pace,
Yes, four *which* are stately in walk:
30 A lion, *which is* mighty among beasts
And does not turn away from any;
31 A greyhound,*
A male goat also,
And a king *whose* troops *are* with him.*

32 If you have been foolish in exalting
yourself,
Or if you have devised evil, [R]*put your*
hand on *your* mouth. Mic. 7:16
33 For *as* the churning of milk produces
butter,
And wringing the nose produces blood,
So the forcing of wrath produces strife.

CHAPTER 31

Wisdom for Leaders

THE words of King Lemuel, the utterance
which his mother taught him:

2 What, my son?
And what, son of my womb?
And what, [R]son of my vows? Is. 49:15
3[R] Do not give your strength to women,
Nor your ways [R]to that which destroys
kings. Prov. 5:9 • Deut. 17:17

4 *It is* not for kings, O Lemuel,
It is not for kings to drink wine,
Nor for princes intoxicating drink;
5[R] Lest they drink and forget the law,
And pervert the justice of all [T]the
afflicted. Hos. 4:11 • Lit. *sons of affliction*
6[R] Give strong drink to him who is
perishing, Ps. 104:15
And wine to those who are bitter of
heart.
7 Let him drink and forget his poverty,
And remember his misery no more.

8[R] Open your mouth for the speechless,
In the cause of all *who are* appointed to
die.* Job 29:15, 16
9 Open your mouth, [R]judge righteously,
And [R]plead the cause of the poor and
needy. Lev. 19:15 • Jer. 22:16

Wise Woman

10 Who* can find a virtuous* wife?
For her worth *is* far above rubies.
11 The heart of her husband safely trusts
her;

30:16 Or *Sheol* **30:26** Or *rock hyraxes* **30:28** Or *lizard* **30:31** Or perhaps *strutting rooster,* lit., *girded of waist* • A Jewish tradition *a king against whom there is no uprising* **31:8** Lit. *sons of passing away* **31:10** Vv. 10–31 are an alphabetic acrostic in Hebrew; cf. Ps. 119 • Lit. *a wife of valor,* in the sense of all forms of excellence

So he will have no lack of gain.
12 She does him good and not evil
All the days of her life.
13 She seeks wool and flax,
And willingly works with her hands.
14 She is like the merchant ships,
She brings her food from afar.
15 She also rises while it is yet night,
And provides food for her household,
And a portion for her maidservants.
16 She considers a field and buys it;
From her profits she plants a vineyard.
17 She girds herself with strength,
And strengthens her arms.
18 She perceives that her merchandise *is*
good,
And her lamp does not go out by night.
19 She stretches out her hands to the
distaff,
And her hand holds the spindle.
20[R] She extends her hand to the poor,
Yes, she reaches out her hands to the
needy. Eph. 4:28
21 She is not afraid of snow for her
household,
For all her household *is* clothed with
scarlet.
22 She makes tapestry for herself;
Her clothing *is* fine linen and purple.
23[R] Her husband is known in the gates,
When he sits among the elders of the
land. Prov. 12:4
24 She makes linen garments and sells
them,
And supplies sashes for the merchants.
25 Strength and honor *are* her clothing;
She shall rejoice in time to come.
26 She opens her mouth with wisdom,
And on her tongue *is* the law of
kindness.
27 She watches over the ways of her
household,
And does not eat the bread of idleness.
28 Her children rise up and call her
blessed;
Her husband *also,* and he praises her:
29 "Many daughters have done well,
But you excel them all."
30 Charm *is* deceitful and beauty *is* passing,
But a woman *who* fears the LORD, she
shall be praised.
31 Give her of the fruit of her hands,
And let her own works praise her in the
gates.

THE BOOK OF

ECCLESIASTES

THE BOOK OF ECCLESIASTES

The key word in Ecclesiastes is *vanity,* the futile emptiness of trying to be happy apart from God. The Preacher (traditionally taken to be Solomon—1:1, 12—the wisest, richest, most influential king in Israel's history) looks at life "under the sun" (1:9) and, from the human perspective, declares it all to be empty. Power, popularity, prestige, pleasure—nothing can fill the God-shaped void in man's life but God Himself! But once seen from God's perspective, life takes on meaning and purpose, causing Solomon to exclaim, "Eat . . . drink . . . rejoice . . . do good . . . live joyfully . . . fear God . . . keep His commandments!" Skepticism and despair melt away when life is viewed as a daily gift from God.

The Hebrew title *Qoheleth* is a rare term, found only in Ecclesiastes (1:1, 2, 12; 7:27; 12:8–10). It comes from the word *qahal,* "to convoke an assembly, to assemble." Thus, it means "one who addresses an assembly, a preacher." The Septuagint used the Greek word *Ekklesiastes* as its title for this book. Derived from the word *ekklesia,* "assembly, congregation, church," it simply means "preacher." The Latin *Ecclesiastes* means "speaker before an assembly."

THE AUTHOR OF ECCLESIASTES

There are powerful arguments that the author of Ecclesiastes was Solomon.

External Evidence: Jewish talmudic tradition attributes the book to Solomon but suggests that Hezekiah's scribes may have edited the text (see Prov. 25:1). Solomonic authorship of Ecclesiastes is the standard Christian position, although some scholars, along with the Talmud, believe the work was later edited during the time of Hezekiah or possibly Ezra.

Internal Evidence: The author calls himself "the son of David, king in Jerusalem" in 1:1, 12. Solomon was the best qualified Davidic descendant for the quest in this book. He was the wisest man who ever taught in Jerusalem (see 1:16; 1 Kin. 4:29, 30). The descriptions of Qoheleth's exploration of pleasure (2:1–3), impressive accomplishments (2:4–6), and unparalleled wealth (2:7–10) were fulfilled only by King Solomon. The proverbs in this book are similar to those in the Book of Proverbs (e.g., Eccl. 7; 10). According to 12:9, Qoheleth collected and arranged many proverbs, perhaps referring to the two Solomonic collections in Proverbs. The unity of authorship of Ecclesiastes is supported by the seven references to Qoheleth.

THE TIME OF ECCLESIASTES

Some scholars argue that the literary forms in Ecclesiastes are postexilic, but they are, in fact, unique, and cannot be used in dating this book. The phrase "all who were before me in Jerusalem" in 1:16 has been used to suggest a date after Solomon's time, but there were many kings and wise men in Jerusalem before the time of Solomon. However, Solomon was the only son of David who reigned over Israel from Jerusalem (1:12).

Ecclesiastes was probably written late in Solomon's life, about 935 B.C. If this is so, the great glory that Solomon ushered in early in his reign was already beginning to fade; and the disruption of Israel into two kingdoms would soon take place. Jewish tradition asserts that Solomon wrote Song of Solomon in his youthful years, Proverbs in his middle years, and Ecclesiastes in his latter years. This book may be expressing his regret for his folly and wasted time due to carnality and idolatry (cf. 1 Kin. 11).

There are no references to historical events other than to personal aspects of Qoheleth's life. The location was Jerusalem (1:1, 12, 16), the seat of Israel's rule and authority.

THE CHRIST OF ECCLESIASTES

Ecclesiastes convincingly portrays the emptiness and perplexity of life without a relationship with the Lord. Each person has eternity in his heart (3:11), and only Christ can provide ultimate satisfaction, joy, and wisdom. Man's highest good is found in the "one Shepherd" (12:11) who offers abundant life (John 10:9, 10).

KEYS TO ECCLESIASTES

Key Word: Vanity—Ecclesiastes reports the results of a diligent quest for purpose, meaning, and satisfaction in human life. The Preacher poignantly sees the emptiness and futility of power, popularity, prestige, and pleasure apart from God. The word "vanity" appears thirty-seven times to express the many things that cannot be understood about life. All earthly goals and ambitions when pursued as ends in themselves lead to dissatisfaction and frustration. Life "under the sun" (used twenty-nine times) seems to be filled with inequities, uncertainties, changes in fortune, and violations of justice. But Ecclesiastes does not give an answer of atheism or skepticism; God is referred to throughout. In fact, it claims that the search for man's *summum bonum* must end in God.

Satisfaction in life can be found only by looking beyond this world. Ecclesiastes gives an analysis of negative themes, but it also develops the positive theme of overcoming the vanities of life by fearing a God who is good, just, and sovereign (12:13, 14). Wisdom involves seeing life from a divine perspective and trusting God in the face of apparent futility and lack of purpose. Life is a daily gift from God and it should be enjoyed as much as possible (see 2:24–26; 3:12, 13, 22; 5:18–20; 8:15; 9:7–10; 11:8, 9). Our comprehension is indeed limited, but there are many things we can understand. Qoheleth recognized that ultimately God will judge all people. Therefore he exhorted: "Fear God and keep His commandments" (12:13).

Key Verses: Ecclesiastes 2:24 and 12:13, 14—"Nothing is better for a man *than* that he should eat and drink, and *that* his soul should enjoy good in his labor. This also, I saw, was from the hand of God" (2:24).

"Let us hear the conclusion of the whole matter: Fear God and keep His commandments, for this is man's all. For God will bring every work into judgment, including every secret thing, whether good or evil" (12:13, 14).

Key Chapter: Ecclesiastes 12—At the end of the Book of Ecclesiastes, the Preacher looks at life through "binoculars." On the other hand, from the perspective of the natural man who only sees life "under the sun," the conclusion is, "All *is* vanity." Life's every activity, even though pleasant for the moment, becomes purposeless and futile when viewed as an end in itself.

The Preacher carefully documents the latter view with a long list of his own personal pursuits in life. No amount of activities or possessions has satisfied the craving of his heart. Every earthly prescription for happiness has left the same bitter aftertaste. Only when the Preacher views his life from God's perspective "above the sun" does it take on meaning as a precious gift "from the hand of God" (2:24).

Chapter 12 resolves the book's extensive inquiry into the meaning of life with the single conclusion, "Fear God and keep His commandments, for this is man's all" (12:13).

SURVEY OF ECCLESIASTES

Ecclesiastes is a profound and problematic book. It is the record of an intense search for meaning and satisfaction in life on this earth, especially in view of all the iniquities and apparent absurdities that surround us. It takes the perspective of the greatest answers that wisdom under the sun can produce. If the Preacher is identified as Solomon, Ecclesiastes was written from a unique vantage point. Possessing the greatest mental, material, and political resources ever combined in one man, he was qualified beyond all others to write this book. Ecclesiastes is extremely difficult to synthesize, and several alternate approaches have been used. The one used here is: the thesis that "all *is* vanity" (1:1–11), the proof that "all *is* vanity" (1:12—6:12), the counsel for living with vanity (7:1—12:14).

The Thesis That "All Is Vanity" (1:1–11): After a one-verse introduction, the Preacher states his theme: "Vanity of vanities, all *is* vanity" (1:2). Life under the sun appears to be futile and perplexing. Verses 3–11 illustrate this theme in the endless and apparently meaningless cycles found in nature and history.

The Proof That "All Is Vanity" (1:12—6:12): The Preacher describes his multiple quest for meaning and satisfaction as he explores his vast personal resources. He begins with wisdom (1:12–18) but finds that "he who increases knowledge increases sorrow." Due to his intense perception of reality he experiences just the re-

FOCUS	THESIS: "ALL IS VANITY"		PROOF: "LIFE IS VAIN"		COUNSEL: "FEAR GOD"		
REFERENCE	1:1———1:4———	1:12———3:1———		7:1———10:1———12:9———12:14			
DIVISION	INTRODUCTION OF VANITY	ILLUSTRATIONS OF VANITY	PROOF FROM SCRIPTURE	PROOF FROM OBSERVATIONS	COPING IN A WICKED WORLD	COUNSEL FOR UNCERTAINTY	CONCLUSION: FEAR AND OBEY GOD
TOPIC	DECLARATION OF VANITY		DEMONSTRATION OF VANITY		FROM VANITY		
	SUBJECT		SERMONS		SUMMARY		
LOCATION	UNIVERSE: "UNDER THE SUN"						
TIME	c. 935 B.C.						

verse of "ignorance is bliss." The Preacher moves from wisdom to laughter, hedonism, and wine (2:1–3) and then turns to works, women, and wealth (2:4–11); but all lead to emptiness. He realizes that wisdom is far greater than foolishness, but both seem to lead to futility in view of the brevity of life and universality of death (2:12–17). He concludes by acknowledging that contentment and joy are found only in God.

At this point, Ecclesiastes turns from his situation in life to a philosophical quest; but the conclusion remains the same. The Preacher considers the unchanging order of events and the fixed laws of God. Time is short, and there is no eternity on earth (3:1–15). The futility of death seems to cancel the difference between righteousness and wickedness (3:16–22). Chapters 4 and 5 explore the futility in social relationships (oppression, rivalry, covetousness, power) and in religious relationships (formalism, empty prayer, vows). In addition, the world's offerings produce disappointment, not satisfaction. Ultimate meaning can be found only in God.

The Counsel for Living with Vanity (7:1—12:14): A series of lessons on practical wisdom is given in 7:1—9:12. Levity and pleasure-seeking are seen as superficial and foolish; it is better to have sober depth of thought. Wisdom and self-control provide perspective and strength in coping with life. One should enjoy prosperity and consider in adversity that God made both. Avoid the twin extremes of self-righteousness and immorality. Sin invades all men, and wisdom is cut short by evil and death. The human mind cannot grasp ultimate meaning. Submission to authority helps one avoid unnecessary hardship, but real justice is often lacking on earth. The uncertainties of life and certainty of the grave show that God's purposes and ways often cannot be grasped. One should, therefore, magnify opportunities while they last, because fortune can change suddenly.

Observations on wisdom and folly are found in 9:13—11:6. Wisdom, the most powerful human resource, is contrasted with the meaningless talk and effort of fools. In view of the unpredictability of circumstances, wisdom is the best course to follow in order to minimize grief and misfortune. Wisdom involves discipline and diligence. In 11:7—12:7 the Preacher offers exhortations on using life well. Youth is too brief and precious to be squandered in foolishness or evil. A person should live well in the fullness of each day before God and acknowledge Him early in life. This section closes with an exquisite allegory of old age (12:1–7).

The Preacher concludes that the "good life" is only attained by revering God. Those who fail to take God and His will seriously into account are doomed to lives of foolishness and futility. Life will not wait upon the solution of all its problems; nevertheless, real meaning can be found by looking not "under the sun" but beyond the sun to the "one Shepherd" (12:11).

OUTLINE OF ECCLESIASTES

Part One: The Thesis That "All Is Vanity" (1:1–11)

I. Introduction of Vanity 1:1–3

II. Illustrations of Vanity 1:4–11

Part Two: The Proof That "All Is Vanity" (1:12—6:12)

I. Proof of "All Is Vanity" from Experience .... 1:12—2:26

A. Vanity of Striving After Wisdom 1:12–18
B. Vanity of Striving After Pleasure 2:1–3
C. Vanity of Great Accomplishments 2:4–17
D. Vanity of Hard Labor 2:18–23
E. Conclusion: Be Content 2:24–26

II. Proof of "All Is Vanity" from Observation .... 3:1—6:12

A. Immutability of God's Program 3:1–22
1. God Predetermines the Events of Life 3:1–9
2. God Predetermines the Conditions of Life 3:10–15
3. God Judges All 3:16–22

B. Inequalities of Life 4:1–16
1. Evil Oppression 4:1–3
2. Folly of Hard Work 4:4–12
3. Transience of Popularity 4:13–16

C. Insufficiencies of Human Religion 5:1–7

D. Insufficiencies of Wealth 5:8–20
1. Wealth Does Not Satisfy 5:8–12
2. Wealth Brings Difficulties 5:13–17
3. Wealth Comes Ultimately from God 5:18–20

E. Inescapable Vanity of Life 6:1–12
1. No Satisfaction in Wealth 6:1, 2
2. No Satisfaction in Children 6:3–6
3. No Satisfaction in Labor 6:7, 8
4. No Satisfaction in the Future 6:9–12

Part Three: The Counsel for Living with Vanity (7:1—12:14)

CHAPTER 1

Introduction of Vanity

THE words of the Preacher, the son of David, [R]king in Jerusalem. Prov. 1:1

2 "Vanity* of vanities," says the Preacher;
"Vanity of vanities, all *is* vanity."

3 What profit has a man from all his labor
In which he toils under the sun?

Illustrations of Vanity

4 *One* generation passes away, and
another generation comes;
[R]But the earth abides forever. Ps. 104:5
5 [R]The sun also rises, and the sun goes
down, Ps. 19:4–6
And [T]hastens to the place where it
arose. Is eager for, lit. *panting*
6 The wind goes toward the south,
And turns around to the north;
The wind whirls about continually,
And comes again on its circuit.
7 [R]All the rivers run into the sea,
Yet the sea *is* not full; [Jer. 5:22]
To the place from which the rivers come,
There they return again.
8 All things *are* [T]full of labor; *wearisome*
Man cannot express *it*.
The eye is not satisfied with seeing,
Nor the ear filled with hearing.

9 That which has been *is* what will be,
That which *is* done is what will be done,
And *there is* nothing new under the sun.
10 Is there anything of which it may be
said,
"See, this *is* new"?
It has already been in ancient times
before us.
11 *There is* [R]no remembrance of former
things, Eccl. 2:16
Nor will there be any remembrance of
things that are to come
By *those* who will come after.

Vanity of Striving After Wisdom

12 I, the Preacher, was king over Israel in Je-
rusalem.
13 And I set my heart to seek and search out
by wisdom concerning all that is done under
heaven; [R]this burdensome task God has given
to the sons of man, by which they may be [T]ex-
ercised. Eccl. 3:10 • Or *afflicted*
14 I have seen all the works that are done
under the sun; and indeed, all *is* vanity and
grasping for the wind.

15 [R]*What is* crooked cannot be made
straight, Eccl. 7:13
And what is lacking cannot be
numbered.

16 I communed with my heart, saying,
"Look, I have attained greatness, and have
gained more wisdom than all who were be-
fore me in Jerusalem. My heart has under-
stood great wisdom and knowledge."
17 And I set my heart to know wisdom and
to know madness and folly. I perceived that
this also is grasping for the wind.

18 For [R]in much wisdom *is* much grief,
And he who increases knowledge
increases sorrow. Eccl. 12:12

CHAPTER 2

Vanity of Striving After Pleasure

I SAID in my heart, "Come now, I will test
you with mirth; therefore enjoy pleasure";
but surely, this also *was* vanity.
2 I said of laughter—"Madness!"; and of
mirth, "What does it accomplish?"
3 [R]I searched in my heart *how* to gratify my
flesh with wine, while guiding my heart with
wisdom, and how to lay hold on folly, till I
might see what *was* [R]good for the sons of

1:2 Or *Absurdity, Frustration, Futility, Nonsense;* and so throughout the book

men to do under heaven all the days of their
lives. Eccl. 1:17 • [Eccl. 3:12, 13; 5:18; 6:12]

Vanity of Great Accomplishments

4 I made my works great, I built myself
houses, and planted myself vineyards.
5 I made myself gardens and orchards, and
I planted all *kinds* of fruit trees in them.
6 I made myself water pools from which to
water the growing trees of the grove.
7 I acquired male and female servants, and
had servants born in my house. Yes, I had
greater possessions of herds and flocks than
all who were in Jerusalem before me.
8 I also gathered for myself silver and gold
and the special treasures of kings and of the
provinces. I acquired male and female
singers, the delights of the sons of men, *and*
musical instruments* of all kinds.
9 So I became great and excelled more than
all who were before me in Jerusalem. Also my
wisdom remained with me.

10 Whatever my eyes desired I did not keep
from them.
I did not withhold my heart from any
pleasure,
For my heart rejoiced in all my labor;
And [R]this was my [T]reward from all my
labor. Eccl. 3:22; 5:18; 9:9 • Lit. *portion*
11 Then I looked on all the works that my
hands had done
And on the labor in which I had toiled;
And indeed all *was* [R]vanity and grasping
for the wind. Eccl. 1:3, 14
There was no profit under the sun.

12 Then I turned myself to consider wisdom
[R]and madness and folly;
For what *can* the man *do* who succeeds
the king?— Eccl. 1:17; 7:25
Only what he has already done.
13 Then I saw that wisdom [R]excels folly
As light excels darkness. Eccl. 7:11, 14, 19
14[R] The wise man's eyes *are* in his head,
But the fool walks in darkness.
Yet I myself perceived
That [R]the same event happens to them
all. Prov. 17:24 • Ps. 49:10

15 So I said in my heart,
"As it happens to the fool,
It also happens to me,
And why was I then more wise?"
Then I said in my heart,
"This also *is* vanity."
16 For *there is* [R]no more remembrance of
the wise than of the fool forever,
Since all that now *is* will be forgotten in
the days to come.
And how does a wise *man* die?
As the fool! Eccl. 1:11; 4:16

17 Therefore I hated life because the work
that was done under the sun *was* distressing
to me, for all *is* vanity and grasping for the
wind.

Vanity of Hard Labor

18 Then I hated all my labor in which I had
toiled under the sun, because I must leave it to
the man who will come after me.
19 And who knows whether he will be wise
or a fool? Yet he will rule over all my labor in
which I toiled and in which I have shown my-
self wise under the sun. This also *is* vanity.
20 Therefore I turned my heart and de-
spaired of all the labor in which I had toiled
under the sun.
21 For there is a man whose labor *is* with
wisdom, knowledge, and skill; yet he must
leave his [T]heritage to a man who has not la-
bored for it. This also *is* vanity and a great
evil. Lit. *portion*
22 [R]For what has man for all his labor, and
for the striving of his heart with which he has
toiled under the sun? Eccl. 1:3; 3:9
23 For all his days *are* sorrowful, and his
work burdensome; even in the night his heart
takes no rest. This also is vanity.

Conclusion: Be Content

24 Nothing *is* better for a man *than* that he
should eat and drink, and *that* his soul should
enjoy good in his labor. This also, I saw, was
from the hand of God.
25 For who can eat, or who can have enjoy-
ment, more than I?*
26 For *God* gives [R]wisdom and knowledge
and joy to a man who *is* good in His sight; but
to the sinner He gives the work of gathering
and collecting, that he may give to *him who is*
good before God. This also *is* vanity and
grasping for the wind. Prov. 2:6

CHAPTER 3

God Predetermines the Events of Life

TO everything *there is* a season,
A time for every purpose under heaven:

2 A time [T]to be born, Lit. *to bear*
And [R]a time to die; Heb. 9:27
A time to plant,
And a time to pluck *what is* planted;
3 A time to kill,
And a time to heal;
A time to break down,
And a time to build up;
4 A time to [R]weep, Rom. 12:15
And a time to laugh;
A time to mourn,
And a time to dance;

2:8 Exact meaning unknown **2:25** So with MT, Tg., Vg.; some Heb. mss., LXX, Syr. *without Him*

5 A time to cast away stones,
And a time to gather stones;
[R]A time to embrace, Joel 2:16
And a time to refrain from embracing;
6 A time to gain,
And a time to lose;
A time to keep,
And a time to throw away;
7 A time to tear,
And a time to sew;
[R]A time to keep silence, Amos 5:13
And a time to [R]speak; Prov. 25:11
8 A time to love,
And a time to [R]hate; Luke 14:26
A time of war,
And a time of peace.

9 [R]What profit has the worker from that in
which he labors? Eccl. 1:3

God Predetermines the Conditions of Life

10 I have seen the God-given task with
which the sons of men are to be occupied.
11 He has made everything beautiful in its
time. Also He has put eternity in their hearts,
except that no one can find out the work that
God does from beginning to end.
12 I know that nothing *is* better for them
than to rejoice, and to do good in their lives,
13 and also that [R]every man should eat and
drink and enjoy the good of all his labor—it *is*
the gift of God. Eccl. 2:24

14 I know that whatever God does,
It shall be forever.
[R]Nothing can be added to it, James 1:17
And nothing taken from it.
God does *it*, that men should fear before
Him.
15[R] That which is has already been,
And what is to be has already been;
And God [T]requires an account of what is
past. Eccl. 1:9 • Lit. *seeks*

God Judges All

16 Moreover I saw under the sun:

In the place of [T]judgment, *justice*
Wickedness *was* there;
And *in* the place of righteousness,
[T]Iniquity *was* there. *Wickedness*

17 I said in my heart,

[R]"God shall judge the righteous and the
wicked, [Rom. 2:6–10]
For *there is* a time there for every
[T]purpose and for every work." *desire*

18 I said in my heart, "Concerning the condi-
tion of the sons of men, God tests them, that
they may see that they themselves are *like* an-
imals."
19 For what happens to the sons of men also
happens to animals; one thing befalls them:
as one dies, so dies the other. Surely, they all
have one breath; man has no advantage over
animals, for all *is* vanity.
20 All go to one place: [R]all are from the dust,
and all return to dust. Gen. 3:19
21 Who knows the spirit of the sons of men,
which goes upward, and the spirit of the ani-
mal, which goes down to the earth?*
22 [R]So I perceived that nothing *is* better
than that a man should rejoice in his own
works, for [R]that *is* his heritage. [R]For who can
bring him to see what will happen after
him? Eccl. 2:24; 5:18 • Eccl. 2:10 • Eccl. 6:12; 8:7

CHAPTER 4

Evil Oppression

THEN I returned and considered all the
[R]oppression that is done under the sun:

And look! The tears of the oppressed,
But they have no comforter—
[T]On the side of their oppressors *there is*
power, Eccl. 3:16; 5:8 • Lit. *At the hand*
But they have no comforter.
2[R] Therefore I praised the dead who were
already dead, Job 3:17, 18
More than the living who are still alive.
3[R] Yet, better than both *is he* who has never
existed, Job 3:11–22
Who has not seen the evil work that is
done under the sun.

Folly of Hard Work

4 Again, I saw that for all toil and every
skillful work a man is envied by his neighbor.
This also *is* vanity and grasping for the wind.

5[R] The fool folds his hands Prov. 6:10; 24:33
And consumes his own flesh.
6 Better a handful *with* quietness
Than both hands full, *together with* toil
and grasping for the wind.

7 Then I returned, and I saw vanity under
the sun:

8 There is one alone, without companion:
He has neither son nor brother.
Yet *there is* no end to all his labors,
Nor is his eye satisfied with riches.
But [R]*he never asks,* Ps. 39:6
"For whom do I toil and deprive myself of
[R]good?" Eccl. 2:18–21
This also *is* vanity and a [T]grave
misfortune. Lit. *evil task*

3:21 LXX, Syr., Tg., Vg. *Who knows whether the spirit . . . goes upward, and whether . . . goes downward to the earth?*

9 Two *are* better than one,
Because they have a good reward for their labor.
10 For if they fall, one will lift up his companion.
But woe to him *who is* alone when he falls,
For *he has* no one to help him up.
11 Again, if two lie down together, they will keep warm;
But how can one be warm *alone*?
12 Though one may be overpowered by another, two can withstand him.
And a threefold cord is not quickly broken.

Transience of Popularity

13 Better a poor and wise youth
Than an old and foolish king who will be admonished no more.
14 For he comes out of prison to be king,
Although [T]he was born poor in his kingdom. The youth
15 I saw all the living who walk under the sun;
They were with the second youth who stands in his place.
16 *There was* no end of all the people over whom he was made king;
Yet those who come afterward will not rejoice in him.
Surely this also *is* vanity and grasping for the wind.

CHAPTER 5

Insufficiencies of Human Religion

WALK [R]prudently when you go to the
house of God; and draw near to hear
rather than to give the sacrifice of fools, for
they do not know that they do evil. Ex. 3:5

2 Do not be [R]rash with your mouth,
And let not your heart utter anything hastily before God. Prov. 20:25
For God *is* in heaven, and you on earth;
Therefore let your words be few.
3 For a dream comes through much activity,
And [R]a fool's voice *is known* by *his* many words. Prov. 10:19

4[R] When you make a vow to God, do not delay to pay it; Num. 30:2
For *He has* no pleasure in fools.
Pay what you have vowed—
5[R] Better not to vow than to vow and not pay. Acts 5:4

6 Do not let your [R]mouth cause your flesh
to sin, [R]nor say before the messenger *of God*
that it *was* an error. Why should God be angry
at your excuse* and destroy the work of your
hands? Prov. 6:2 • 1 Cor. 11:10

7 For in the multitude of dreams and
many words *there is* also vanity. But [R]fear
God. [Eccl. 12:13]

Wealth Does Not Satisfy

8 If you [R]see the oppression of the poor,
and the violent [T]perversion of justice and
righteousness in a province, do not marvel at
the matter; for [R]high official watches over
high official, and higher officials are over
them. Eccl. 3:16 • *wresting* • [Ps. 12:5; 58:11; 82:1]
9 Moreover the profit of the land is for all;
even the king is served from the field.

10 He who loves silver will not be satisfied with silver;
Nor he who loves abundance, with increase.
This also *is* vanity.

11 When goods increase,
They increase who eat them;
So what profit have the owners
Except to see *them* with their eyes?
12 The sleep of a laboring man *is* sweet,
Whether he eats little or much;
But the abundance of the rich will not permit him to sleep.

Wealth Brings Difficulties

13[R] There is a severe evil *which* I have seen under the sun: Eccl. 6:1, 2
Riches kept for their owner to his hurt.
14 But those riches perish through [T]misfortune; Lit. *bad business*
When he begets a son, *there is* nothing in his hand.
15[R] As he came from his mother's womb, naked shall he return, 1 Tim. 6:7
To go as he came;
And he shall take nothing from his labor
Which he may carry away in his hand.

16 And this also *is* a severe evil—
Just exactly as he came, so shall he go.
And what profit has he [R]who has labored for the wind? Prov. 11:29
17 All his days [R]he also eats in darkness,
And *he has* much sorrow and sickness and anger. Ps. 127:2

Wealth Comes Ultimately from God

18 Here is what I have seen: [R]*It is* good and
fitting *for one* to eat and drink, and to enjoy
the good of all his labor in which he toils un-
der the sun all the days of his life which God
gives him; for it *is* his heritage. [1 Tim. 6:17]
19 As for every man to whom God has given
riches and wealth, and given him power to eat

5:6 Lit. *voice*

of it, to receive his heritage and rejoice in his
labor—this *is* the gift of God.
20 For he will not dwell unduly on the days
of his life, because God keeps *him* busy with
the joy of his heart.

CHAPTER 6

No Satisfaction in Wealth

THERE is an evil which I have seen under
the sun, and it *is* common among men:
2 A man to whom God has given riches and
wealth and honor, [R]so that he lacks nothing
for himself of all he desires; [R]yet God does not
give him power to eat of it, but a foreigner
consumes it. This *is* vanity, and it *is* an evil af-
fliction. Job 21:10 • Luke 12:20

No Satisfaction in Children

3 If a man begets a hundred *children* and
lives many years, so that the days of his
years are many, but his soul is not satisfied
with goodness, or [R]indeed he has no burial, I
say *that* [R]a [T]stillborn child *is* better than
he— Is. 14:19, 20 • Job 3:16 • Or *miscarriage*
4 for it comes in vanity and departs in
darkness, and its name is covered with dark-
ness.
5 Though it has not seen the sun or known
anything, this has more rest than that man,
6 even if he lives a thousand years twice—
but has not seen goodness. Do not all go to
one [R]place? Eccl. 2:14, 15

No Satisfaction in Labor

7 All the labor of man *is* for his mouth,
And yet the soul is not satisfied.
8 For what more has the wise *man* than
the fool?
What does the poor man have,
Who knows *how* to walk before the
living?

No Satisfaction in the Future

9 Better *is* [T]the [R]sight of the eyes than the
wandering of [T]desire. What the eyes see
This also *is* vanity and grasping for the
wind. Eccl. 11:9 • Lit. *soul*

10 Whatever one is, he has been named
[R]already, Eccl. 1:9; 3:15
For it is known that he *is* man;
[R]And he cannot contend with Him who is
mightier than he. Job 9:32
11 Since there are many things that
increase vanity,
How *is* man the better?

12 For who knows what *is* good for man in
life, all the days of his vain life which he
passes like a shadow? Who can tell a man
what will happen after him under the sun?

CHAPTER 7

Wisdom and Folly Contrasted

A [R]GOOD name *is* better than precious
ointment, Prov. 22:1
And the day of death than the day of
one's [R]birth; Eccl. 4:2
2 Better to go to the house of mourning
Than to go to the house of feasting,
For that *is* the end of all men;
And the living will take *it* to heart.
3 Sorrow *is* better than laughter,
[R]For by a sad countenance the heart is
made better. [2 Cor. 7:10]
4 The heart of the wise *is* in the house of
mourning,
But the heart of fools *is* in the house of
mirth.

5 [R]*It is* better to [T]hear the rebuke of the
wise Ps. 141:5 • *listen to*
Than for a man to hear the song of
fools.
6 [R]For like the [T]crackling of thorns under a
pot, Eccl. 2:2 • Lit. *sound*
So *is* the laughter of the fool.
This also is vanity.
7 Surely oppression destroys a wise *man's*
reason,
And a bribe debases the heart.

8 The end of a thing *is* better than its
beginning;
[R]The patient in spirit *is* better than the
proud in spirit. Prov. 14:29
9 Do not hasten in your spirit to be
angry,
For anger rests in the bosom of fools.
10 Do not say,
"Why were the former days better than
these?"
For you do not inquire wisely concerning
this.

11 Wisdom *is* good with an inheritance,
And profitable [R]to those who see the
sun. Eccl. 11:7
12 For wisdom *is* a [R]defense *as* money *is* a
defense, Eccl. 9:18
But the [T]excellence of knowledge *is that*
wisdom gives [R]life to those who have
it. *advantage* or *profit* • Prov. 3:18

13 Consider the work of God;
For [R]who can make straight what He has
made crooked? Job 12:14
14 [R]In the day of prosperity be joyful,
But in the day of adversity consider:
Surely God has appointed the one [T]as
well as the other, Deut. 28:47 • *alongside*
So that man can find out nothing *that*
will come after him.

Wisdom of Moderation

15 I have seen everything in my days of vanity:

[R]There is a just *man* who perishes in his
righteousness, Eccl. 8:12–14
And there is a wicked *man* who prolongs
life in his wickedness.

16[R] Do not be overly righteous, Prov. 25:16
[R]Nor be overly wise: Rom. 12:3
Why should you destroy yourself?
17 Do not be overly wicked,
Nor be foolish:
Why should you die before your time?
18 *It is* good that you grasp this,
And also not remove your hand from the
other;
For he who [R]fears God will escape them
all. Eccl. 3:14; 5:7; 8:12, 13

Strength of Wisdom

19 Wisdom strengthens the wise
More than ten rulers of the city.

20[R] For *there is* not a just man on earth who
does good 1 John 1:8
And does not sin.

21 Also do not take to heart everything
people say,
Lest you hear your servant cursing you.
22 For many times, also, your own heart has
known
That even you have cursed others.

23 All this I have [T]proved by wisdom.
[R]I said, "I will be wise"; *tested* • Rom. 1:22
But it *was* far from me.
24[R] As for that which is far off and
[R]exceedingly deep, 1 Tim. 6:16
Who can find it out? Rom. 11:33
25[R] I applied my heart to know, Eccl. 1:17
To search and seek out wisdom and the
reason *of things,*
To know the wickedness of folly,
Even of foolishness *and* madness.
26[R] And I find more bitter than death
The woman whose heart *is* snares and
nets, Prov. 5:3, 4
Whose hands *are* fetters.
[T]He who pleases God shall escape from
her, Lit. *He who is good before God*
But the sinner shall be trapped by her.

27 "Here is what I have found," says [R]the
Preacher, Eccl. 1:1, 2
"*Adding* one thing to the other to find out
the reason,
28 Which my soul still seeks but I cannot
find:
[R]One man among a thousand I have
found, Job 33:23
But a woman among all these I have not
found.
29 Truly, this only I have found:
[R]That God made man upright, Gen. 1:27
But [R]they have sought out many
schemes." Gen. 3:6, 7

CHAPTER 8

Submit to Authority

WHO *is* like a wise *man?*
And who knows the interpretation of a
thing?
[R]A man's wisdom makes his face shine,
And [R]the sternness of his face is
changed. Acts 6:15 • Deut. 28:50

2 I *say,* "Keep the king's commandment for
the sake of your oath to God.
3 "Do not be hasty to go from his presence.
Do not take your stand for an evil thing, for he
does whatever pleases him."

4 Where the word of a king *is,* there is
power;
And [R]who may say to him, "What are
you doing?" Job 34:18
5 He who keeps his command will
experience nothing harmful;
And a wise man's heart [T]discerns both
time and judgment, Lit. *knows*
6 Because [R]for every matter there is a time
and judgment, Eccl. 3:1, 17
Though the misery of man [T]increases
greatly. *is great upon him*
7 For he does not know what will happen;
So who can tell him when it will occur?
8[R] No one has power over the spirit to
retain the spirit, Ps. 49:6, 7

7:20 Individual Sin—Each individual man, woman, and child who composes humankind is a sinner. Paul points out in Romans 3:13–16 that "their throat *is* an open tomb . . . the poison of asps [a small, deadly poisonous snake] *is* under their lips; whose mouth *is* full of cursing and bitterness. Their feet *are* swift to shed blood [consider the high incidence of violent crime, murder, and abortion that infects our society]; destruction and misery *are* in their ways [whatever man touches he corrupts]." All of this shows that there is no person who seeks after God and no person does what is right (Page 1150—Rom. 3:10, 11). Each individual man, woman, and child needs the righteousness of God. Without God's righteousness no one can ever enter or stand in God's presence. Plainly, every man, woman, and child needs to have a new life because each is a sinner.

Now turn to Page 1153—Rom. 6:23: New Life: A Free Gift.

And no one has power in the day of death.
There is [R]no release from that war,
And wickedness will not deliver those
who are given to it. Deut. 20:5–8

9 All this I have seen, and applied my heart
to every work that is done under the sun:
There is a time in which one man rules over
another to his own hurt.

Inability to Understand All God's Doing

10 Then I saw the wicked buried, who had
come and gone from the place of holiness,
and they were forgotten* in the city where
they had so done. This also *is* vanity.
11 [R]Because the sentence against an evil
work is not executed speedily, therefore the
heart of the sons of men is fully set in them to
do evil. Is. 26:10
12 Though a sinner does evil a hundred
times, and his *days* are prolonged, yet I surely
know that it will be well with those who fear
God, who fear before Him.
13 But it will not be well with the wicked;
nor will he prolong *his* days, *which are* as a
shadow, because he does not fear before God.
14 There is a vanity which occurs on earth,
that there are just *men* to whom it [R]happens
according to the work of the wicked; again,
there are wicked *men* to whom it happens ac-
cording to the work of the righteous. I said
that this also *is* vanity. Ps. 73:14
15 So I commended enjoyment, because a
man has nothing better under the sun than to
eat, drink, and be merry; for this will remain
with him in his labor *all* the days of his life
which God gives him under the sun.
16 When I applied my heart to know wisdom
and to see the business that is done on earth,
even though one sees no sleep day or night,
17 then I saw all the work of God, that [R]a
man cannot find out the work that is done
under the sun. For though a man labors to dis-
cover *it,* yet he will not find *it;* moreover,
though a wise *man* attempts to know *it,* he
will not be able to find *it.* Rom. 11:33

CHAPTER 9

Judgment Comes to All

FOR I [T]considered all this in my heart, so
that I could declare it all: [R]that the righ-
teous and the wise and their works *are* in
the hand of God. People know neither love
nor hatred *by* anything *they see* before
them. Lit. *put* • Eccl. 8:14
2 [R]All things *come* alike to all: Mal. 3:15

One event *happens* to the righteous and
the wicked;
To the good,* the clean, and the unclean;
To him who sacrifices and him who does
not sacrifice.
As is the good, so *is* the sinner;
He who takes an oath as *he* who fears an
oath.

3 This *is* an evil in all that is done under the
sun: that one thing *happens* to all. Truly the
hearts of the sons of men are full of evil; mad-
ness *is* in their hearts while they live, and
after that *they go* to the dead.
4 But for him who is joined to all the living
there is hope, for a living dog is better than a
dead lion.

5 For the living know that they will die;
But [R]the dead know nothing, Is. 63:16
And they have no more reward,
For the memory of them is forgotten.
6 Also their love, their hatred, and their
envy have now perished;
Nevermore will they have a share
In anything done under the sun.

Enjoy Life While You Have It

7 Go, [R]eat your bread with joy, Eccl. 8:15
And drink your wine with a merry heart;
For God has already accepted your
works.
8 Let your garments always be white,
And let your head lack no oil.

9 [T]Live joyfully with the wife whom you
love all the days of your vain life which He
has given you under the sun, all your days of
vanity; [R]for that *is* your portion in life, and
in the labor which you perform under the
sun. Lit. *See life* • Eccl. 2:10
10 [R]Whatever your hand finds to do, do *it*
with your [R]might; for *there is* no work or de-
vice or knowledge or wisdom in the grave
where you are going. [Col. 3:17] • Rom. 12:11
11 I returned [R]and saw under the sun
that— Amos 2:14, 15

The race *is* not to the swift,
Nor the battle to the strong,
Nor bread to the wise,
Nor riches to men of understanding,
Nor favor to men of skill;
But time and [R]chance happen to them
all. 1 Sam. 6:9
12 For [R]man also does not know his time:
Like fish taken in a cruel net,
Like birds caught in a snare,
So the sons of men *are* [R]snared in an evil
time, Eccl. 8:7 • Prov. 29:6
When it falls suddenly upon them.

Value of Wisdom

13 This wisdom I have also seen under the
sun, and it *seemed* great to me:

8:10 Some Heb. mss., LXX, Vg. *praised* **9:2** LXX, Syr., Vg. *good and bad,*

14 *There was* a little city with few men in it;
and a great king came against it, besieged it,
and built great snares* around it.
15 Now there was found in it a poor wise
man, and he by his wisdom delivered the city.
Yet no one remembered that same poor man.
16 Then I said:

"Wisdom *is* better than [R]strength.
Nevertheless [R]the poor man's wisdom *is* despised, Eccl. 7:12, 19 • Mark 6:2, 3
And his words are not heard.
17 Words of the wise, *spoken* quietly, *should be* heard
Rather than the shout of a ruler of fools.
18 Wisdom *is* better than weapons of war;
But one sinner destroys much good."

CHAPTER 10

Wisdom's Characteristics

DEAD[T] flies putrefy* the perfumer's ointment, Lit. *Flies of death*
And cause it to give off a foul odor;
So does a little folly to one respected for wisdom *and* honor.
2 A wise man's heart *is* at his right hand,
But a fool's heart at his left.
3 Even when a fool walks along the way,
He lacks wisdom,
And he shows everyone *that* he *is* a fool.
4 If the spirit of the ruler rises against you,
[R]Do not leave your post; Eccl. 8:3
For conciliation pacifies great offenses.

5 There is an evil I have seen under the sun,
As an error proceeding from the ruler:
6[R] Folly is set in great dignity, Esth. 3:1
While the rich sit in a lowly place.
7 I have seen servants [R]on horses,
While princes walk on the ground like servants. Prov. 19:10; 30:22
8[R] He who digs a pit will fall into it,
And whoever breaks through a wall will be bitten by a serpent. Prov. 26:27
9 He who quarries stones may be hurt by them,
And he who splits wood may be endangered by it.
10 If the ax is dull,
And one does not sharpen the edge,
Then he must use more strength;
But wisdom brings success.

11 A serpent may bite [R]when *it is* not charmed; Jer. 8:17
The babbler is no different.
12[R] The words of a wise man's mouth *are* gracious, Prov. 10:32
But [R]the lips of a fool shall swallow him up; Prov. 10:14
13 The words of his mouth begin with foolishness,
And the end of his talk *is* raving madness.
14[R] A fool also multiplies words. [Prov. 15:2]
No man knows what is to be;
Who can tell him [R]what will be after him? Eccl. 3:22; 8:7
15 The labor of fools wearies them,
For they do not even know how to go to the city!

Wisdom Related to the King

16[R] Woe to you, O land, when your king *is* a child, Is. 3:4, 5; 5:11
And your princes feast in the morning!
17 Blessed *are* you, O land, when your king *is* the son of nobles,
And your [R]princes feast at the proper time— Prov. 31:4
For strength and not for drunkenness!
18 Because of laziness the [T]building decays, Lit. *rafters sink*
And [R]through idleness of hands the house leaks. Prov. 24:30–34
19 A feast is made for laughter,
And [R]wine makes merry; Ps. 104:15
But money answers everything.

20[R] Do not curse the king, even in your thought; Acts 23:5
Do not curse the rich, even in your bedroom;
For a bird of the air may carry your voice,
And a bird in flight may tell the matter.

CHAPTER 11

Wisdom Related to Business

CAST your bread upon the waters,
For you will find it after many days.
2[R] Give a serving [R]to seven, and also to eight, [1 Tim. 6:18, 19] • Mic. 5:5
[R]For you do not know what evil will be on the earth. Eph. 5:16

3 If the clouds are full of rain,
They empty *themselves* upon the earth;
And if a tree falls to the south or the north,
In the place where the tree falls, there it shall lie.
4 He who observes the wind will not sow,
And he who regards the clouds will not reap.

5 As [R]you do not know what *is* the way of the wind,* John 3:8
[R]*Or* how the bones *grow* in the womb of her who is with child, Ps. 139:14

9:14 LXX, Syr., Vg. *bulwarks* **10:1** Tg., Vg. omit *putrefy* **11:5** Or *spirit*

So you do not know the works of God
who makes everything.
6 In the morning sow your seed,
And in the evening do not withhold your
hand;
For you do not know which will prosper,
Either this or that,
Or whether both alike *will be* good.

Rejoice in Your Youth

7 Truly the light is sweet,
And *it is* pleasant for the eyes [R]to behold
the sun; Eccl. 7:11
8 But if a man lives many years
And [R]rejoices in them all, Eccl. 9:7
Yet let him [R]remember the days of
darkness, Eccl. 12:1
For they will be many.
All that is coming *is* vanity.

9 Rejoice, O young man, in your youth,
And let your heart cheer you in the days
of your youth;
Walk in the ways of your heart,
And in the sight of your eyes;
But know that for all these
God will bring you into judgment.
10 Therefore remove [T]sorrow from your
heart, *vexation*
And put away evil from your flesh,
For childhood and youth *are* vanity.

CHAPTER 12

Remember God in Your Youth

REMEMBER[R] now your Creator in the
days of your youth, Lam. 3:27
Before the [T]difficult days come, Lit. *evil*
And the years draw near [R]when you say,
"I have no pleasure in them": 2 Sam. 19:35
2 While the sun and the light,
The moon and the stars,
Are not darkened,
And the clouds do not return after the
rain;
3 In the day when the keepers of the house
tremble,
And the strong men bow down;
When the grinders cease because they
are few,
And those that look through the
windows grow dim;
4 When the doors are shut in the streets,
And the sound of grinding is low;
When one rises up at the sound of a bird,
And all [R]the daughters of music are
brought low. 2 Sam. 19:35
5 Also they are afraid of height,
And of terrors in the way;
When the almond tree blossoms,
The grasshopper is a burden,
And desire fails.
For man goes to his eternal home,
And the mourners go about the streets.

6 *Remember your Creator* before the silver
cord is loosed,*
Or the golden bowl is broken,
Or the pitcher shattered at the fountain,
Or the wheel broken at the well.
7 [R]Then the dust will return to the earth as
it was, Gen. 3:19
[R]And the spirit will return to God [R]who
gave it. Eccl. 3:21 • Job 34:14

8 "Vanity[R] of vanities," says the Preacher,
"All *is* vanity." Ps. 62:9

"Fear God and Keep His Commandments"

9 And moreover, because the Preacher was
wise, he still taught the people knowledge;
yes, he pondered and sought out *and* [R]set in
order many proverbs. 1 Kin. 4:32
10 The Preacher sought to find [T]acceptable
words; and *what was* written *was* upright—
words of truth. Lit. *delightful*
11 The words of the wise are like goads, and
the words of scholars* are like well-driven
nails, given by one Shepherd.
12 And further, my son, be admonished by
these. Of making many books there is no
end, and [R]much study *is* wearisome to the
flesh. Eccl. 1:18
13 Let us hear the conclusion of the whole
matter:

[R]Fear God and keep His commandments,
For this is man's all. [Deut. 6:2; 10:12]
14 For [R]God will bring every work into
judgment, Matt. 12:36
Including every secret thing,
Whether good or evil.

12:6 So with Qr., Tg.; Kt. *removed;* LXX, Vg. *broken*
12:11 Lit. *masters of assemblies*

THE

SONG OF SOLOMON

THE BOOK OF SONG OF SOLOMON

The Song of Solomon is a love song written by Solomon and abounding in metaphors and oriental imagery. Historically, it depicts the wooing and wedding of a shepherdess by King Solomon, and the joys and heartaches of wedded love.

Allegorically, it pictures Israel as God's espoused bride (Hos. 2:19, 20), and the church as the bride of Christ. As human life finds its highest fulfillment in the love of man and woman, so spirtual life finds its highest fulfillment in the love of God for His people and Christ for His church.

The book is arranged like scenes in a drama with three main speakers: the bride (Shulamite), the king (Solomon), and a chorus (daughters of Jerusalem).

The Hebrew title *Shir Hashirim* comes from 1:1, "The song of songs." This is in the superlative and speaks of Solomon's most exquisite song. The Greek title *Asma Asmaton* and the Latin *Canticum Canticorum* also mean "Song of Songs" or "The Best Song." The name *Canticles* ("Songs") is derived from the Latin title. Because Solomon is mentioned in 1:1, the book is also known as the Song of Solomon.

THE AUTHOR OF SONG OF SOLOMON

Solomonic authorship is rejected by critics who claim it is a later collection of songs. Many take 1:1 to mean "which is about or concerning Solomon." But the internal evidence of the book strongly favors the traditional position that Solomon is its author. Solomon is specifically mentioned seven times (1:1, 5; 3:7, 9, 11; 8:11, 12), and he is identified as the groom. There is evidence of royal luxury and rich imported goods (e.g., 3:6–11). The king by this time also had sixty queens and eighty concubines (6:8). Solomon's harem at its fullest extent reached seven hundred queens and three hundred concubines (1 Kin. 11:3).

In 1 Kings 4:32, 33 we read that Solomon composed 1,005 songs and had intimate knowledge of the plant and animal world. This greatest of his songs alludes to twenty-one species of plants and fifteen species of animals. It cites geographical locations in the north and in the south, indicating that they were still one kingdom. For example, 6:4 mentions both Tirzah and Jerusalem, the northern and southern capitals (after Solomon's time, Samaria became the northern capital). Because of the poetic imagery, the Song of Solomon uses forty-nine words that occur nowhere else in Scripture.

THE TIME OF SONG OF SOLOMON

This song was written primarily from the point of view of the Shulamite, but Solomon was its author, probably early in his reign, about 965 B.C. There is a problem regarding how a man with a harem of 140 women (6:8) could extol the love of the Shulamite as though she were his only bride. It may be that Solomon's relationship with the Shulamite was the only pure romance he ever experienced. The bulk of his marriages were political arrangements. It is significant that the Shulamite was a vineyard keeper of no great means. This book was also written before Solomon plunged into gross immorality and idolatry. "For it was so, when Solomon was old, that his wives turned his heart after other gods; and his heart was not loyal to the LORD his God" (1 Kin. 11:4).

The Shulamite addresses the king as "my beloved," and the king addresses his bride as "my love." The daughters of Jerusalem were probably attendants to the Shulamite. The term *Shulamite* appears only in 6:13; and it may be derived from the town of Shunem, which was southwest of the Sea of Galilee in the tribal area of Issachar. The song refers to fifteen geographic locations from Lebanon in the north to Egypt in the south: Kedar (1:5), Egypt (1:9), En Gedi (1:14), Sharon (2:1), Jerusalem (2:7), Lebanon (3:9), Mount Gilead (4:1), Amana (4:8), Senir (4:8), Hermon (4:8), Tirzah (6:4), Heshbon (7:4), Damascus (7:4), Carmel (7:5), and Baal Hamon (8:11).

THE CHRIST OF SONG OF SOLOMON

In the Old Testament, Israel is regarded as the bride of Yahweh (see Is. 54:5, 6; Jer. 2:2; Ezek. 16:8–14; Hos. 2:16–20). In the New Testament, the church is seen as the bride of Christ (see 2 Cor. 11:2; Eph. 5:23–25; Rev. 19:7–9; 21:9). The Song of Solomon illustrates the former and anticipates the latter.

KEYS TO SONG OF SOLOMON

Key Word: Love in Marriage—The purpose of this book depends on the viewpoint taken as to its primary thrust. Is it fictional, allegorical, or historical?

(1) *Fictional:* Some hold that this song is a fictional drama that portrays Solomon's attraction and marriage to a poor but beautiful girl from

the country. However, the book gives every indication that the story really happened.

(2) *Allegorical:* In this view, the primary purpose of the Song is to illustrate the truth of God's love for His people whether the events were fictional or not. Some commentators insist that the book is indeed historical, but its primary purpose is typical, that is, to present God's love for His bride Israel or Christ's love for His church. However, this interpretation is subjective and lacking in evidence. In other scriptures the husband and wife relationship is used symbolically (cf. Ezek. 16; 23; Hos. 1—3), but these are always indicated as symbols. This may be an application of the book, but it should not be the primary interpretation.

(3) *Historical:* The Song of Solomon is a poetic record of Solomon's actual romance with a Shulamite woman. The various scenes in the book exalt the joys of love in courtship and marriage and teach that physical beauty and sexuality in marriage should not be despised as base or unspiritual. It offers a proper perspective of human love and avoids the extremes of lust and asceticism. Only when sexuality is viewed in the wrong way, as something akin to evil, is an attempt made to allegorize the book. But this is part of God's creation with its related desires and pleasures, and it is reasonable that He would provide us with a guide to a pure sexual relationship between a husband and wife. In fact, the union of the two sexes was originally intended to illustrate the oneness of the Godhead (see Gen. 1:27; 2:24; 1 Cor. 6:16–20). Thus, the Song is a bold and positive endorsement by God of marital love in all its physical and emotional beauty. This interpretation does not mean that the book has no spiritual illustrations and applications. It certainly illustrates God's love for His covenant people Israel, and it anticipates Christ's love for His bride, the church.

Key Verses: Song of Solomon 7:10 and 8:7—"I *am* my beloved's, and his desire *is* toward me" (7:10).

"Many waters cannot quench love, nor can the floods drown it. If a man would give for love all the wealth of his house, it would be utterly despised" (8:7).

Key Chapter: Song of Solomon—Since the whole book is a unity, there is no key chapter; rather, all eight chapters beautifully depict the love of a married couple.

SURVEY OF SONG OF SOLOMON

Solomon wrote 1,005 songs (1 Kin. 4:32), but this beautiful eulogy of love stood out among them as the "song of songs" (1:1). The great literary value of this song can be seen in its rich use of metaphor and oriental imagery as it extols the purity, beauty, and satisfaction of love. It is never crass, but often intimate, as it explores the dimensions of the relationship between two lovers: attraction, desire, companionship, pleasure, union, separation, faithfulness, and praise. Like Ecclesiastes, this little book is not easily outlined, and various schemes can be used. It abounds with sudden changes of speakers. The beginning of love is seen in 1:1—5:1, and the broadening of love is found in 5:2—8:14.

The Beginning of Love (1:1—5:1): King Solomon has a vineyard in the country of the Shulamite (6:13; 8:11). The Shulamite must work in the vineyard with her brothers (1:6; 8:11, 12); and when Solomon visits the area, he wins her heart and eventually takes her to the palace in Jerusalem as his bride. She is tanned from hours of work outside in the vineyard, but she is "fairest among women" (1:6, 8).

This song is arranged like scenes in a one-act drama with three main speakers—the bride (the Shulamite), the king (Solomon), and a chorus

FOCUS	BEGINNING OF LOVE		BROADENING OF LOVE	
REFERENCE	1:1—3:6	3:6—5:2	5:2—7:11	7:11—8:14
DIVISION	FALLING IN LOVE	UNITED IN LOVE	STRUGGLING IN LOVE	GROWING IN LOVE
TOPIC	COURTSHIP	WEDDING	PROBLEM	PROGRESS
	FOSTERING OF LOVE	FULFILLMENT OF LOVE	FRUSTRATION OF LOVE	FAITHFULNESS OF LOVE
LOCATION	ISRAEL			
TIME	c. 1 YEAR			

(the daughters of Jerusalem). It is not always clear who is speaking, but this is a likely arrangement:

The bride: 1:2–4, 5–7, 12–14, 16, 17; 2:1, 3–14, 16, 17; 3:1–11; 4:16; 5:2–8, 10–16; 6:2, 3, 11–13; 7:9–13; 8:1–4, 6, 7, 10–12, 14
The groom: 1:8–10, 15; 2:2; 4:1–15; 5:1; 6:4–10, 13; 7:1–9; 8:13
The chorus or relatives: 1:4, 11; 2:15; 5:9; 6:1; 8:5, 8, 9

Chapters 1—3 give a series of recollections of the courtship: (1) the bride's longing for affection at the palace before the wedding (1:2–8), (2) expressions of mutual love in the banquet hall (1:9—2:7), (3) a springtime visit of the king to the bride's home in the country (2:8–17), (4) the Shulamite's dream of separation from her beloved (3:1–5), and (5) the ornate wedding procession from the bride's home to Jerusalem (3:6–11).

In 4:1—5:1, Solomon praises his bride from head to foot with a superb chain of similes and metaphors. Her virginity is compared to "a garden enclosed" (4:12), and the garden is entered when the marriage is consummated (4:16—5:1). The union is commended, possibly by God, in 5:1.

The Broadening of Love (5:2—8:14): Some time after the wedding, the Shulamite has a troubled dream (5:2) in the palace while Solomon is away. In her dream Solomon comes to her door, but she answers too late—he is gone. She panics and searches for him late at night in Jerusalem. Upon his return, Solomon assures her of his love and praises her beauty (6:4—7:10). The Shulamite begins to think of her country home and tries to persuade her beloved to return there with her (7:11—8:4). The journey takes place in 8:5–7 and their relationship continues to deepen. Their love will not be overthrown by jealousy or circumstances. At her homecoming (8:8–14) the Shulamite reflects on her brothers' care for her when she was young (8:8, 9). She remains virtuous ("I *am* a wall," 8:10) and is now in a position to look out for her brothers' welfare (8:11, 12). The song concludes with a dual invitation of lover and beloved (8:13, 14).

OUTLINE OF SONG OF SOLOMON

I. The Beginning of Love .... 1:1—5:1
- A. Falling in Love .... 1:1—3:5
  - 1. Bride's Longing for Affection 1:1–8
  - 2. Expressions of Mutual Love .... 1:9—2:7
  - 3. Visit of the King to the Bride's Home 2:8–17
  - 4. Bride's Dream of Separation 3:1–5
- B. United in Love .... 3:6—5:1
  - 1. Wedding Procession 3:6–11
  - 2. Bride's Beauty Is Praised 4:1–15
  - 3. The Marriage Is Consummated .. 4:16—5:1

II. Broadening of Love .... 5:2—8:14
- A. Struggling in Love .... 5:2—7:10
  - 1. Bride's Second Dream of Separation 5:2–7
  - 2. Bridegroom's Handsomeness Is Praised .... 5:8—6:3
  - 3. Bride's Beauty Is Praised .... 6:4—7:10
- B. Growing in Love .... 7:11—8:14
  - 1. Bride's Desire to Visit Her Home .... 7:11—8:4
  - 2. Journey and Homecoming 8:5–14

CHAPTER 1

Bride's Longing for Affection

THE song of songs, which *is* Solomon's

THE SHULAMITE*

2 Let him kiss me with the kisses of his mouth—
For your* love *is* better than wine.
3 Because of the fragrance of your good ointments,
Your name *is* ointment poured forth;
Therefore the virgins love you.
4 [R]Draw me away! Hos. 11:4

THE DAUGHTERS OF JERUSALEM

[R]We will run after you.* Phil. 3:12–14

THE SHULAMITE

The king [R]has brought me into his chambers. Ps. 45:14, 15

THE DAUGHTERS OF JERUSALEM

We will be glad and rejoice in you.*
We will remember your* love more than wine.

THE SHULAMITE

Rightly do they love you.*

1:2 A Palestinian young woman, Song 6:13. The speaker and audience are identified according to the number, gender, and person of the Hebrew words. Occasionally the identity is not certain. • Masc. sing.: the Beloved **1:4** Masc. sing.: the Beloved • Fem. sing.: the Shulamite • Masc. sing.: the Beloved • Masc. sing.: the Beloved

5 I *am* dark, but lovely,
O daughters of Jerusalem,
Like the tents of Kedar,
Like the curtains of Solomon.
6 Do not look upon me, because I *am* dark,
Because the sun has [T]tanned me.
My mother's sons were angry with me;
They made me the keeper of the
vineyards, Lit. *looked upon me*
But my own vineyard I have not kept.

(TO HER BELOVED)

7 Tell me, O you whom I love,
Where you feed *your flock,*
Where you make *it* rest at noon.
For why should I be as one who veils
herself*
By the flocks of your companions?

THE BELOVED

8 If you do not know, [R]O fairest among
women, Song 5:9
[T]Follow in the footsteps of the flock,
And feed your little goats Lit. *Go out*
Beside the shepherds' tents.

Expressions of Mutual Love

9 I have compared you, my love,
To my filly among Pharaoh's chariots.
10 Your cheeks are lovely with ornaments,
Your neck with chains *of gold.*

THE DAUGHTERS OF JERUSALEM

11 We will make you* ornaments of gold
With studs of silver.

THE SHULAMITE

12 While the king *is* at his table,
My spikenard sends forth its fragrance.
13 A bundle of myrrh *is* my beloved to me,
That lies all night between my breasts.
14 My beloved *is* to me a cluster of henna
blooms
In the vineyards of En Gedi.

THE BELOVED

15[R] Behold, you *are* fair, my love!
Behold, you *are* fair! Song 4:1; 5:12
You *have* dove's eyes.

THE SHULAMITE

16 Behold, you *are* [R]handsome, my beloved!
Yes, pleasant! Song 5:10–16
Also our [T]bed *is* green. *couch*
17 The beams of our houses *are* cedar,
And our rafters of fir.

CHAPTER 2

I *AM* the rose of Sharon,
And the lily of the valleys.

THE BELOVED

2 Like a lily among thorns,
So is my love among the daughters.

THE SHULAMITE

3 Like an apple tree among the trees of the
woods,
So *is* my beloved among the sons.
I sat down in his shade with great
delight,
And his fruit *was* sweet to my taste.

THE SHULAMITE TO THE DAUGHTERS OF JERUSALEM

4 He brought me to the [T]banqueting
house, Lit. *house of wine*
And his banner over me *was* love.
5 Sustain me with cakes of raisins,
Refresh me with apples,
For I *am* lovesick.

6 His left hand *is* under my head,
And his right hand embraces me.
7[R] I [T]charge you, O daughters of
Jerusalem, Song 3:5; 8:4 • *adjure*
By the gazelles or by the does of the field,
Do not stir up nor awaken love
Until it pleases.

Visit of the King to the Bride's Home

THE SHULAMITE

8 The voice of my beloved!
Behold, he comes
Leaping upon the mountains,
Skipping upon the hills.
9[R] My beloved is like a gazelle or a young
stag. Song 2:17
Behold, he stands behind our wall;
He is looking through the windows,
Gazing through the lattice.

10 My beloved spoke, and said to me:
"Rise up, my love, my fair one,
And come away.
11 For lo, the winter is past,
The rain is over *and* gone.
12 The flowers appear on the earth;
The time of singing has come,
And the voice of the turtledove
Is heard in our land.
13 The fig tree puts forth her green figs,
And the vines *with* the tender grapes
Give a good smell.
Rise up, my love, my fair one,
And come away!

14 "O my [R]dove, in the clefts of the rock,
In the secret *places* of the cliff,

1:7 LXX, Syr., Vg. *wanders* **1:11** Fem. sing.: the Shulamite

Let me see your face, Song 5:2
[R]Let me hear your voice; Song 8:13
For your voice *is* sweet,
And your face *is* lovely."

HER BROTHERS

15 Catch us [R]the foxes, Ezek. 13:4
The little foxes that spoil the vines,
For our vines *have* tender grapes.

THE SHULAMITE

16 My beloved *is* mine, and I *am* his.
He feeds *his flock* among the lilies.

(TO HER BELOVED)

17[R]Until the day breaks Song 4:6
And the shadows flee away,
Turn, my beloved,
And be [R]like a gazelle Song 8:14
Or a young stag
Upon the mountains of Bether.*

CHAPTER 3

Bride's Dream of Separation

THE SHULAMITE

BY [R]night on my bed I sought the one I love; Is. 26:9
I sought him, but I did not find him.
2"I will rise now," *I said,*
"And go about the city;
In the streets and in the squares
I will seek the one I love."
I sought him, but I did not find him.
3[R]The watchmen who go about the city found me; Song 5:7
I said,
"Have you seen the one I love?"

4 Scarcely had I passed by them,
When I found the one I love.
I held him and would not let him go,
Until I had brought him to the [R]house of my mother, Song 8:2
And into the [T]chamber of her who conceived me. room

5[R]I [T]charge you, O daughters of Jerusalem, Song 2:7; 8:4 • adjure
By the gazelles or by the does of the field,
Do not stir up nor awaken love
Until it pleases.

Wedding Procession

THE SHULAMITE

6[R]Who *is* this coming out of the wilderness Song 8:5
Like pillars of smoke,
Perfumed with myrrh and frankincense,
With all the merchant's fragrant powders?
7 Behold, it *is* Solomon's couch,
With sixty valiant men around it,
Of the valiant of Israel.
8 They all hold swords,
Being expert in war.
Every man *has* his sword on his thigh
Because of fear in the night.

9 Of the wood of Lebanon
Solomon the King
Made himself a palanquin:*
10 He made its pillars *of* silver,
Its support *of* gold,
Its seat *of* purple,
Its interior paved *with* love
By the daughters of Jerusalem.
11 Go forth, O daughters of Zion,
And see King Solomon with the crown
With which his mother crowned him
On the day of his wedding,
The day of the gladness of his heart.

CHAPTER 4

Bride's Beauty Is Praised

THE BELOVED

BEHOLD, [R]you *are* fair, my love!
Behold, you *are* fair! Song 1:15; 5:12
You *have* dove's eyes behind your veil.
Your hair *is* like a flock of goats,
Going down from Mount Gilead.
2[R]Your teeth *are* like a flock of shorn *sheep* Song 6:6
Which have come up from the washing,
Every one of which bears twins,
And none *is* barren among them.
3 Your lips *are* like a strand of scarlet,
And your mouth is lovely.
[R]Your temples behind your veil Song 6:7
Are like a piece of pomegranate.
4[R]Your neck *is* like the tower of David,
Built [R]for an armory, Song 7:4 • Neh. 3:19
On which hang a thousand [T]bucklers,
All shields of mighty men. Small shields
5[R]Your two breasts *are* like two fawns,
Twins of a gazelle, Song 7:3
Which feed among the lilies.

6[R]Until the day breaks Song 2:17
And the shadows flee away,
I will go my way to the mountain of myrrh
And to the hill of frankincense.

7[R]You *are* all fair, my love, Eph. 5:27
And *there is* no spot in you.
8 Come with me from Lebanon, *my* spouse,
With me from Lebanon.

2:17 Lit. *Separation* **3:9** A portable enclosed chair

Look from the top of Amana,
From the top of Senir [R]and Hermon,
From the lions' dens, Deut. 3:9
From the mountains of the leopards.

9 You have ravished my heart,
My sister, *my* spouse;
You have ravished my heart
With one *look* of your eyes,
With one link of your necklace.
10 How fair is your love,
My sister, *my* spouse!
[R]How much better than wine is your love,
And the [T]scent of your perfumes
Than all spices! Song 1:2, 4 • *fragrance*
11 Your lips, O *my* spouse,
Drip as the honeycomb;
Honey and milk *are* under your tongue;
And the fragrance of your garments
Is like the fragrance of Lebanon.

12 A garden [T]enclosed *locked* or *barred*
Is my sister, *my* spouse,
A spring shut up,
A fountain sealed.
13 Your plants *are* an orchard of
pomegranates
With pleasant fruits,
Fragrant henna with spikenard,
14 Spikenard and saffron,
Calamus and cinnamon,
With all trees of frankincense,
Myrrh and aloes,
With all the chief spices—
15 A fountain of gardens,
A well of [R]living waters, Zech. 14:8
And streams from Lebanon.

The Marriage Is Consummated

THE SHULAMITE

16 Awake, O north *wind*,
And come, O south!
Blow upon my garden,
That its spices may flow out.
Let my beloved come to his garden
And eat its pleasant [R]fruits. Song 7:13

CHAPTER 5

THE BELOVED

I [R]HAVE come to my garden, my [R]sister, *my*
spouse; Song 4:16 • Song 4:9
I have gathered my myrrh with my spice;
[R]I have eaten my honeycomb with my
honey; Song 4:11
I have drunk my wine with my milk.

(TO HIS FRIENDS)

Eat, O [R]friends! Luke 15:7, 10
Drink, yes, drink deeply,
O beloved ones!

Bride's Second Dream of Separation

THE SHULAMITE

2 I sleep, but my heart is awake;
It is the voice of my beloved!
[R]He knocks, *saying*, Rev. 3:20
"Open for me, my sister, my love,
My dove, my perfect one;
For my head is covered with dew,
My locks with the drops of the night."

3 I have taken off my robe;
How can I put it on *again*?
I have washed my feet;
How can I [T]defile them? *dirty*
4 My beloved put his hand
By the [T]latch *of the door*, *opening*
And my heart yearned for him.
5 I arose to open for my beloved,
And my hands dripped *with* myrrh,
My fingers with liquid myrrh,
On the handles of the lock.

6 I opened for my beloved,
But my beloved had turned away *and*
was gone.
My heart leaped up when he spoke.
I sought him, but I could not find him;
I called him, but he gave me no answer.
7 [R]The watchmen who went about the city
found me, Song 3:3
They struck me, they wounded me;
The keepers of the walls
Took my veil away from me.

Bridegroom's Handsomeness Is Praised

8 I charge you, O daughters of Jerusalem,
If you find my beloved,
That you tell him I *am* lovesick!

THE DAUGHTERS OF JERUSALEM

9 What *is* your beloved
More than *another* beloved,
[R]O fairest among women? Song 1:8; 6:1
What *is* your beloved
More than *another* beloved,
That you so [T]charge us? *adjure*

THE SHULAMITE

10 My beloved *is* white and ruddy,
Chief among ten thousand.
11 His head *is like* the finest gold;
His locks *are* wavy,
And black as a raven.
12 [R]His eyes *are* like doves Song 1:15; 4:1
By the rivers of waters,
Washed with milk,
And [T]fitly set. *sitting in a setting*
13 His cheeks *are* like a bed of spices,
Banks of scented herbs.
His lips *are* lilies,
Dripping liquid myrrh.

14 His hands *are* rods of gold
Set with beryl.
His body *is* carved ivory
Inlaid *with* sapphires.
15 His legs *are* pillars of marble
Set on bases of fine gold.
His countenance *is* like Lebanon,
Excellent as the cedars.
16 His mouth *is* most sweet,
Yes, he *is* altogether lovely.
This *is* my beloved,
And this *is* my friend,
O daughters of Jerusalem!

CHAPTER 6

THE DAUGHTERS OF JERUSALEM

WHERE has your beloved gone,
[R]O fairest among women? Song 1:8; 5:9
Where has your beloved turned aside,
That we may seek him with you?

THE SHULAMITE

2 My beloved has gone to his [R]garden,
To the beds of spices, Song 4:16; 5:1
To feed *his flock* in the gardens,
And to gather lilies.
3[R] I *am* my beloved's, Song 2:16; 7:10
And my beloved *is* mine.
He feeds *his flock* among the lilies.

Bride's Beauty Is Praised

THE BELOVED

4 O my love, you *are as* beautiful as Tirzah,
Lovely as Jerusalem,
Awesome as *an army* with banners!
5 Turn your eyes away from me,
For they have overcome me.
Your hair *is* [R]like a flock of goats
Going down from Gilead. Song 4:1
6[R] Your teeth *are* like a flock of sheep
Which have come up from the washing;
Every one bears twins, Song 4:2
And none *is* barren among them.
7[R] Like a piece of pomegranate Song 4:3
Are your temples behind your veil.

8 There are sixty queens
And eighty concubines,
And [R]virgins without number. Song 1:3
9 My dove, my [R]perfect one, Song 2:14; 5:2
Is the only one,
The only one of her mother,
The favorite of the one who bore her.
The daughters saw her
And called her blessed,
The queens and the concubines,
And they praised her.

10 Who is she who looks forth as the morning,
Fair as the moon,
Clear as the sun,
Awesome as *an army* with banners?

THE SHULAMITE

11 I went down to the garden of nuts
To see the verdure of the valley,
To see whether the vine had budded
And the pomegranates had bloomed.
12 Before I was even aware,
My soul had made me
As the chariots of my noble people.*

THE BELOVED AND HIS FRIENDS

13 Return, return, O Shulamite;
Return, return, that we may look upon you!

THE SHULAMITE

What would you see in the Shulamite—
As it were, the dance of the two camps?*

CHAPTER 7

THE BELOVED

HOW beautiful are your feet in sandals,
[R]O prince's daughter! Ps. 45:13
The curves of your thighs *are* like jewels,
The work of the hands of a skillful workman.
2 Your navel *is* a rounded goblet;
It lacks no blended beverage.
Your waist *is* a heap of wheat
Set about with lilies.
3[R] Your two breasts *are* like two fawns,
Twins of a gazelle. Song 4:5
4[R] Your neck *is* like an ivory tower,
Your eyes *like* the pools in Heshbon
By the gate of Bath Rabbim. Song 4:4
Your nose *is* like the tower of Lebanon
Which looks toward Damascus.
5 Your head *crowns* you like *Mount* Carmel,
And the hair of your head *is* like purple;
A king *is* held captive by *your* tresses.

6 How fair and how pleasant you are,
O love, with your delights!
7 This stature of yours is like a palm tree,
And your breasts *like* its clusters.
8 I said, "I will go up to the palm tree,
I will take hold of its branches."
Let now your breasts be like clusters of the vine,
The fragrance of your [T]breath like apples, Lit. *nose*
9 And the roof of your mouth like the best wine.

6:12 Heb. *Ammi Nadib* **6:13** Heb. *Mahanaim*

THE SHULAMITE

The wine goes *down* smoothly for my
beloved,
Moving gently the lips of sleepers.*
10[R] I *am* my beloved's, Song 2:16; 6:3
And [R]his desire *is* toward me. Ps. 45:11

Bride's Desire to Visit Her Home

11 Come, my beloved,
Let us go forth to the field;
Let us lodge in the villages.
12 Let us get up early to the vineyards;
Let us [R]see if the vine has budded,
Whether the grape blossoms are open,
And the pomegranates are in bloom.
There I will give you my love. Song 6:11
13 The [R]mandrakes give off a fragrance,
And at our gates [R]*are* pleasant *fruits*,
All manner, new and old,
Which I have laid up for you, my
beloved. Gen. 30:14 • Matt. 13:52

CHAPTER 8

OH, that you were like my brother,
Who nursed at my mother's breasts!
If I should find you outside,
I would kiss you;
I would not be despised.
2 I would lead you *and* bring you
Into the [R]house of my mother, Song 3:4
She *who* used to instruct me.
I would cause you to drink of [R]spiced
wine, Prov. 9:2
Of the juice of my pomegranate.

(TO THE DAUGHTERS OF JERUSALEM)

3 His left hand *is* under my head,
And his right hand embraces me.
4[R] I charge you, O daughters of Jerusalem,
Do not stir up nor awaken love
Until it pleases. Song 2:7; 3:5

Journey and Homecoming

A RELATIVE

5[R] Who *is* this coming up from the
wilderness, Song 3:6
Leaning upon her beloved?

I awakened you under the apple tree.
There your mother brought you forth;
There she *who* bore you brought *you*
forth.

THE SHULAMITE TO HER BELOVED

6[R] Set me as a seal upon your heart,
As a seal upon your arm; Jer. 22:24
For love *is as* strong as death,
[R]Jealousy *as* cruel as the grave;*
Its flames *are* flames of fire,
A most vehement* flame. Prov. 6:34, 35
7 Many waters cannot quench love,
Nor can the floods drown it.
[R]If a man would give for love Prov. 6:35
All the wealth of his house,
It would be utterly despised.

THE SHULAMITE'S BROTHERS

8[R] We have a little sister, Ezek. 23:33
And she has no breasts.
What shall we do for our sister
In the day when she is spoken for?
9 If she *is* a wall,
We will build upon her
A battlement of silver;
And if she *is* a door,
We will enclose her
With boards of cedar.

THE SHULAMITE

10 I *am* a wall,
And my breasts like towers;
Then I became in his eyes
As one who found peace.
11 Solomon had a vineyard at Baal
Hamon;
[R]He leased the vineyard to keepers;
Everyone was to bring for its fruit
A thousand silver coins. Matt. 21:33

(TO SOLOMON)

12 My own vineyard *is* before me.
You, O Solomon, *may have* a thousand,
And those who tend its fruit two
hundred.

THE BELOVED

13 You who dwell in the gardens,
The companions listen for your voice—
[R]Let me hear it! Song 2:14

THE SHULAMITE

14[R] Make haste, my beloved, Rev. 22:17, 20
And [R]be like a gazelle Song 2:7, 9, 17
Or a young stag
On the mountains of spices.

7:9 LXX, Syr., Vg. *lips and teeth.* **8:6** Or *Sheol* • Lit. *A flame of YAH*, a poetic form of *YHWH, the LORD*

THE BOOK OF
ISAIAH

THE BOOK OF ISAIAH

Isaiah is like a miniature Bible. The first thirty-nine chapters (like the thirty-nine books of the Old Testament) are filled with judgment upon immoral and idolatrous men. Judah has sinned; the surrounding nations have sinned; the whole earth has sinned. Judgment must come, for God cannot allow such blatant sin to go unpunished forever. But the final twenty-seven chapters (like the twenty-seven books of the New Testament) declare a message of hope. The Messiah is coming as a Savior and a Sovereign to bear a cross and to wear a crown.

Isaiah's prophetic ministry, spanning the reigns of four kings of Judah, covers at least forty years.

Yesha'yahu and its shortened form *yeshaiah* mean "Yahweh Is Salvation." This name is an excellent summary of the contents of the book. The Greek form in the Septuagint is *Hesaias,* and the Latin form is *Esaias* or *Isaias.*

THE AUTHOR OF ISAIAH

Isaiah, the "St. Paul of the Old Testament," was evidently from a distinguished Jewish family. His education is evident in his impressive vocabulary and style. His work is comprehensive in scope and beautifully communicated. Isaiah maintained close contact with the royal court, but his exhortations against alliances with foreign powers were not always well received. This great poet and prophet was uncompromising, sincere, and compassionate. His wife was a prophetess, and he fathered at least two sons (7:3; 8:3). He spent most of his time in Jerusalem, and talmudic tradition says his persecutors sawed him in two during the reign of Manasseh (cf. Heb. 11:37).

The unity of this book has been challenged by critics who hold that a "Deutero-Isaiah" wrote chapters 40—66 after the Babylonian captivity. They argue that 1—39 have an Assyrian background, while 40—66 are set against a Babylonian background. But Babylon is mentioned more than twice as often in 1—39 as in 40—66. The only shift is one of perspective from present time to future time. Critics also argue that there are radical differences in the language, style, and theology of the two sections. Actually, the resemblances between 1—39 and 40—66 are greater than the differences. These include similarities in thoughts, images, rhetorical ornaments, characteristic expressions, and local coloring. It is true that the first section is more terse and rational, while the second section is more flowing and emotional, but much of this is caused by the different subject matter, condemnation versus consolation. Critics often forget that content, time, and circumstances typically affect any author's style. In addition, there is no theological contradiction between the emphasis on the Messiah as King in 1—39 and as Suffering Servant in 40—66. While the thrust is different, the Messiah is seen in both sections as Servant and King. Another critical argument is that Isaiah could not have predicted the Babylonian captivity and the return under Cyrus (mentioned by name in 44 and 45) 150 years in advance. This view is based on the mere assumption that divine prophecy is impossible, rejecting the predictive claims of the book (see 42:9). The theory cannot explain the amazing messianic prophecies of Isaiah that were literally fulfilled in the life of Christ (see "The Christ of Isaiah").

The unity of Isaiah is supported by the book of Ecclesiasticus, the Septuagint, and the Talmud. The New Testament also claims that Isaiah wrote both sections. John 12:37–41 quotes from Isaiah 6:9, 10 and 53:1 and attributes it all to Isaiah. In Romans 9:27 and 10:16–21, Paul quotes from Isaiah 10, 53, and 65 and gives the credit to Isaiah. The same is true of Matthew 3:3 and 12:17–21, Luke 3:4–6, and Acts 8:28.

If 40—66 was written by another prophet after the events took place, it is a misleading and deceptive work. Furthermore, it would lead to the strange conclusion that Israel's greatest prophet is the only writing prophet of the Old Testament to go unnamed.

THE TIME OF ISAIAH

Isaiah's long ministry ranged from about 740 to 680 B.C. (1:1). He began his ministry near the end of Uzziah's reign (790–739 B.C.) and continued through the reigns of Jotham (739–731 B.C.), Ahaz (731–715 B.C.), and Hezekiah (715–686 B.C.). Assyria was growing in power under Tiglath-Pileser who turned toward the west after his conquests in the east. He plucked up the small nations that dotted the Mediterranean coast including Israel and much of Judah. Isaiah lived during this time of military threat to Judah, and warned its kings against trusting in alliances with other countries rather than the power of Yahweh. As a contemporary of Hosea and Micah, he prophesied during the last years of the northern kingdom but ministered to the southern kingdom of Judah who was following the sins of her sister

Israel. After Israel's demise in 722 B.C., he warned Judah of judgment not by Assyria but by Babylon, even though Babylon had not yet risen to power.

Isaiah ministered from the time of Tiglath-Pileser (745–727 B.C.) to the time of Sennacherib (705–681 B.C.) of Assyria. He outdated Hezekiah by a few years because 37:38 records the death of Sennacherib in 681 B.C. Hezekiah was succeeded by his wicked son Manasseh who overthrew the worship of Yahweh and no doubt opposed the work of Isaiah.

THE CHRIST OF ISAIAH

When he speaks about Christ, Isaiah sounds more like a New Testament writer than an Old Testament prophet. His messianic prophecies are clearer and more explicit than those in any other Old Testament book. They describe many aspects of the Person and work of Christ in His first and second advents, and often blend the two together. Here are a few of the Christological prophecies with their New Testament fulfillments: 7:14 (Matt. 1:22, 23); 9:1, 2 (Matt. 4:12–16); 9:6 (Luke 2:11; Eph. 2:14–18); 11:1 (Luke 3:23, 32; Acts 13:22, 23); 11:2 (Luke 3:22); 28:16 (1 Pet. 2:4–6); 40:3–5 (Matt. 3:1–3); 42:1–4 (Matt. 12:15–21); 42:6 (Luke 2:29–32); 50:6 (Matt. 26:67; 27:26, 30); 52:14 (Phil. 2:7–11); 53:3 (Luke 23:18; John 1:11; 7:5); 53:4, 5 (Rom. 5:6, 8); 53:7 (Matt. 27:12–14; John 1:29; 1 Pet. 1:18, 19); 53:9 (Matt. 27:57–60); 53:12 (Mark 15:28); 61:1, 2 (Luke 4:17–19, 21). The Old Testament has over three hundred prophecies about the first advent of Christ, and Isaiah contributes a number of them. The odds that even ten of them could be fulfilled by one person is a statistical marvel. Isaiah's messianic prophecies that await fulfillment in the Lord's second advent include: 4:2; 11:2–6, 10; 32:1–8; 49:7; 52:13, 15; 59:20, 21; 60:1–3; 61:2, 3.

Isaiah 52:13—53:12 is the central passage of the consolation section (40—66). Its five stanzas present five different aspects of the saving work of Christ: (1) 52:13–15—His wholehearted sacrifice (burnt offering); (2) 53:1–3—His perfect character (meal offering); (3) 53:4–6—He brought atonement that issues in peace with God (peace offering); (4) 53:7–9—He paid for the transgression of the people (sin offering); (5) 53:10–12—He died for the effects of sin (trespass offering).

KEYS TO ISAIAH

Key Word: Salvation Is of the Lord—The basic theme of this book is found in Isaiah's name: "Salvation Is of the Lord." The word "salvation" appears twenty-six times in Isaiah but only seven times in all the other prophets combined. Chapters 1—39 portray man's great need for salvation, and chapters 40—66 reveal God's great provision of salvation. Salvation is of God, not man; and He is seen as the supreme Ruler, the sovereign Lord of history, and the only Savior. Isaiah solemnly warns Judah of approaching judgment because of moral depravity, political corruption, social injustice, and especially spiritual idolatry. Because the nation does not turn away from its sinful practice, Isaiah announces the ultimate overthrow of Judah. Nevertheless, God will remain faithful to His covenant by preserving a godly remnant and promises salvation and deliverance through the coming Messiah. The Savior will come out of Judah and accomplish the dual work of redemption and restoration. The Gentiles will come to His light and universal blessing will finally take place.

Key Verses: Isaiah 9:6, 7 and 53:6—"For unto us a Child is born, unto us a Son is given; and the government will be upon His shoulder. And His name will be called Wonderful, Coun-

FOCUS	PROPHECIES OF CONDEMNATION				HISTORICAL PARENTHESIS	PROPHECIES OF COMFORT		
REFERENCE	1:1—	13:1—	24:1—	28:1—	36:1—	40:1—	49:1—	58:1—66:24
DIVISION	PROPHECIES AGAINST		PROPHECIES OF		HEZEKIAH'S SALVATION, SICKNESS, AND SIN	ISRAEL'S DELIVERANCE	ISRAEL'S DELIVERER	ISRAEL'S GLORIOUS FUTURE
	JUDAH	THE NATIONS	DAY OF LORD	JUDGMENT & BLESSING				
TOPIC	PROPHETIC				HISTORIC	MESSIANIC		
	JUDGMENT				TRANSITION	HOPE		
LOCATION	ISRAEL AND JUDAH							
TIME	c. 740–680 B.C.							

selor, Mighty God, Everlasting Father, Prince of Peace. Of the increase of *His* government and peace *there will be* no end, upon the throne of David and over His kingdom, to order it and establish it with judgment and justice from that time forward, even forever. The zeal of the LORD of hosts will perform this" (9:6, 7).

"All we like sheep have gone astray; we have turned, every one, to his own way; and the LORD has laid on Him the iniquity of us all" (53:6).

Key Chapter: Isaiah 53—Along with Psalm 22, Isaiah 53 lists the most remarkable and specific prophecies of the atonement of the Messiah. Fulfilling each clear prophecy, the Jewish nation later proved the messiahship of Jesus.

SURVEY OF ISAIAH

Isaiah, the "Shakespeare of the prophets" has often been called the "evangelical prophet" because of his incredibly clear and detailed messianic prophecies. The "gospel according to Isaiah" has three major sections: prophecies of condemnation (1—35), historical parenthesis (36—39), and prophecies of comfort (40—66).

Prophecies of Condemnation (1—35): Isaiah's first message of condemnation is aimed at his own countrymen in Judah (1—12). Chapter 1 is a capsulized message of the entire book. Judah is riddled with moral and spiritual disease; the people are neglecting God as they bow to ritualism and selfishness. But Yahweh graciously invites them to repent and return to Him because this is their only hope of avoiding judgment. Isaiah's call to proclaim God's message is found in chapter 6, and this is followed by the book of Immanuel (7—12). These chapters repeatedly refer to the Messiah (see 7:14; 8:14; 9:2, 6, 7; 11:1, 2) and anticipate the blessing of His future reign.

The prophet moves from local to regional judgment as he proclaims a series of oracles against the surrounding nations (13—23). The eleven nations are Babylon, Assyria, Philistia, Moab, Damascus (Syria), Ethiopia, Egypt, Babylon (again), Edom, Arabia, Jerusalem (Judah), and Tyre. Isaiah's little apocalypse (24—27) depicts universal tribulation followed by the blessings of the kingdom. Chapters 28—33 pronounce six woes on Israel and Judah for specific sins. Isaiah's prophetic condemnation closes with a general picture of international devastation that will precede universal blessing (34 and 35).

Historical Parenthesis (36—39): This historical parenthesis looks back to the Assyrian invasion of Judah in 701 B.C. and anticipates the coming Babylonian invasion of Judah. Judah escapes captivity by Assyria (36 and 37; 2 Kin. 18 and 19), but they will not escape from the hands of Babylon (38 and 39; 2 Kin. 20). God answers King Hezekiah's prayers and delivers Judah from Assyrian destruction by Sennacherib. Hezekiah also turns to the Lord in his illness and is granted a fifteen-year extension of his life. But he foolishly shows all his treasures to the Babylonian messengers, and Isaiah tells him that the Babylonians will one day carry his treasure and descendants to their land.

Prophecies of Comfort (40—66): Having pronounced Judah's divine condemnation, Isaiah comforts them with God's promises of hope and restoration. The basis for this hope is the sovereignty and majesty of God (40—48). Of the 216 verses in these nine chapters, 115 speak of God's greatness and power. The Creator is contrasted with idols, the creations of men. His sovereign character is Judah's assurance of future restoration. Babylon will indeed carry them off; but Babylon will finally be judged and destroyed, and God's people will be released from captivity.

Chapters 49—57 concentrate on the coming Messiah who will be their Savior and Suffering Servant. This rejected but exalted One will pay for their iniquities and usher in a kingdom of peace and righteousness throughout the earth. All who acknowledge their sins and trust in Him will be delivered (58—66). In that day Jerusalem will be rebuilt, Israel's borders will be enlarged, and the Messiah will reign in Zion. God's people will confess their sins and His enemies will be judged. Peace, prosperity, and justice will prevail; and God will make all things new.

OUTLINE OF ISAIAH

Part One: Prophecies of Condemnation (1:1—35:10)

I. Prophecies Against Judah ....1:1—12:6

- A. The Judgment of Judah 1:1–31
- B. The Day of the Lord............................2:1—4:6
- C. The Parable of the Vineyard.................5:1–30
- D. The Commission of Isaiah....................6:1–13
- E. The Destruction of Israel by Assyria .7:1—10:4
  1. Sign of Immanuel...............................7:1–25
  2. Sign of Maher-Shalal-Hash-Baz 8:1–22
  3. Prophecy of the Messiah's Birth 9:1–7
  4. Judgment on Ephraim ....9:8—10:4
- F. The Destruction of Assyria by God ..10:5—12:6
  1. Destruction of Assyria 10:5–19
  2. Remnant of Israel 10:20–34
  3. Restoration of the Messiah's Kingdom 11:1–16
  4. Thanksgiving in the Messiah's Kingdom 12:1–6

Part Two: The Historical Parenthesis (36:1—39:8)

Part Three: The Prophecies of Comfort (40:1—66:24)

CHAPTER 1

The Judgment of Judah

THE vision of Isaiah the son of Amoz,
which he saw concerning Judah and Jeru-
salem in the days of Uzziah, Jotham, Ahaz,
and Hezekiah, kings of Judah.

2 [R]Hear, O heavens, and give ear, O earth! Jer. 2:12
For the LORD has spoken:
"I have nourished and brought up
children,
And they have rebelled against Me;
3 [R]The ox knows its owner Jer. 8:7
And the donkey its master's crib;
But Israel [R]does not know, Jer. 9:3, 6
My people do not [T]consider." *understand*
4 Alas, sinful nation,
A people laden with iniquity,

R A brood of evildoers, Matt. 3:7
Children who are corrupters!
They have forsaken the LORD,
They have provoked to anger
The Holy One of Israel,
They have turned away backward.

5 R Why should you be stricken again?
You will revolt more and more.
The whole head is sick,
And the whole heart faints. Jer. 5:3
6 From the sole of the foot even to the head,
There is no soundness in it,
But wounds and bruises and putrefying sores;
They have not been closed or bound up,
Or soothed with ointment.

7 R Your country *is* desolate, Deut. 28:51, 52
Your cities *are* burned with fire;
Strangers devour your land in your presence;
And *it is* desolate, as overthrown by strangers.
8 So the daughter of Zion is left R as a
T booth in a vineyard, Job 27:18 • *shelter*
As a hut in a garden of cucumbers,
R As a besieged city. Jer. 4:17
9 R Unless the LORD of hosts Lam. 3:22
Had left to us a very small remnant,
We would have become like R Sodom,
We would have been made like Gomorrah. Gen. 19:24

10 Hear the word of the LORD,
You rulers R of Sodom; Deut. 32:32
Give ear to the law of our God,
You people of Gomorrah:
11 "To what purpose *is* the multitude of your
R sacrifices to Me?" [1 Sam. 15:22]
Says the LORD.
"I have had enough of burnt offerings of rams
And the fat of fed cattle.
I do not delight in the blood of bulls,
Or of lambs or goats.

12 "When you come R to appear before Me,
Who has required this from your hand,
To trample My courts? Ex. 23:17
13 Bring no more R futile sacrifices;
Incense is an abomination to Me.
The New Moons, the Sabbaths, and R the calling of assemblies—
I cannot endure iniquity and the sacred meeting. Matt. 15:9 • Joel 1:14
14 Your R New Moons and your R appointed feasts Num. 28:11 • Lam. 2:6
My soul hates;
They are a trouble to Me,
I am weary of bearing *them*.
15 R When you T spread out your hands,
I will hide My eyes from you;
R Even though you make many prayers,
I will not hear. Prov. 1:28 • Pray • Mic. 3:4
Your hands are full of blood.

16 "Wash R yourselves, make yourselves clean; Jer. 4:14
Put away the evil of your doings from before My eyes.
R Cease to do evil, Rom. 12:9
17 Learn to do good;
Seek justice,
Rebuke the oppressor;*
T Defend the fatherless, *Vindicate*
Plead for the widow.

18 "Come now, and let us R reason together,"
Says the LORD, Is. 43:26
"Though your sins are like scarlet,
R They shall be as white as snow; Ps. 51:7
Though they are red like crimson,
They shall be as wool.
19 If you are willing and obedient,
You shall eat the good of the land;
20 But if you refuse and rebel,
You shall be devoured by the sword";
For the mouth of the LORD has spoken.

21 R How the faithful city has become a
T harlot! Jer. 2:20 • Unfaithful
It was full of justice;
Righteousness lodged in it,
But now R murderers. Mic. 3:1–3
22 R Your silver has become dross, Jer. 6:28
Your wine mixed with water.
23 R Your princes *are* rebellious, Hos. 9:15
And R companions of thieves; Prov. 29:24
R Everyone loves bribes, Jer. 22:17
And follows after rewards.
They R do not defend the fatherless,
Nor does the cause of the widow come before them. Jer. 5:28

24 Therefore the Lord says,
The LORD of hosts, the Mighty One of Israel,
"Ah, I will rid Myself of My adversaries,
And take vengeance on My enemies.
25 I will turn My hand against you,
And R thoroughly T purge away your dross, Mal. 3:3 • *refine with lye*
And take away all your alloy.
26 I will restore your judges R as at the first,
And your counselors as at the beginning. Jer. 33:7–11
Afterward you shall be called the city of righteousness, the faithful city."

27 Zion shall be redeemed with justice,
And her penitents with righteousness.
28 The R destruction of transgressors and of sinners *shall be* together,

1:17 Some ancient vss. *the oppressed*

And those who forsake the LORD shall be
consumed. [2 Thess. 1:8, 9]
29 For they* shall be ashamed of the
[T]terebinth trees Sites of pagan worship
Which you have desired;
And you shall be embarrassed because
of the gardens
Which you have chosen.
30 For you shall be as a terebinth whose
leaf fades,
And as a garden that has no water.
31[R]The strong shall be as tinder,
And the work of it as a spark;
Both will burn together, Ezek. 32:21
And no one shall quench *them.*

CHAPTER 2

The Day of the Lord

THE word that Isaiah the son of Amoz saw
concerning Judah and Jerusalem.

2 Now [R]it shall come to pass [R]in the latter
days Mic. 4:1–3☆ • Gen. 49:1
[R]*That* the mountain of the LORD's house
Shall be established on the top of the
mountains, Ps. 68:15
And shall be exalted above the hills;
And all nations shall flow to it.
3 Many people shall come and say,
[R]"Come, and let us go up to the mountain
of the LORD, Jer. 50:5☆
To the house of the God of Jacob;
He will teach us His ways,
And we shall walk in His paths."
[R]For out of Zion shall go forth the law,
And the word of the LORD from
Jerusalem. Is. 51:4, 5; Luke 24:47☆
4 He shall judge between the nations,
And rebuke many people;
They shall beat their swords into
plowshares,
And their spears into pruning [T]hooks;
Nation shall not lift up sword against
nation, *knives*
Neither shall they learn war anymore.

5 O house of Jacob, come and let us [R]walk
In the light of the LORD. Eph. 5:8

6 For You have forsaken Your people, the
house of Jacob,
Because they are filled [R]with eastern
ways; Num. 23:7
They *are* [R]soothsayers like the
Philistines, Deut. 18:14
[R]And they are pleased with the children
of foreigners. Ps. 106:35
7 Their land is also full of silver and gold,
And there is no end to their treasures;
Their land is also full of horses,
And there is no end to their chariots.
8[R]Their land is also full of idols; Jer. 2:28
They worship the work of their own
hands,
That which their own fingers have made.
9 People bow down,
And each man humbles himself;
Therefore do not forgive them.

10[R]Enter into the rock, and hide in the
dust, Rev. 6:15, 16
From the terror of the LORD
And the glory of His majesty.
11 The [T]lofty looks of man shall be
[R]humbled, *proud* • Prov. 16:5
The haughtiness of men shall be bowed
down,
And the LORD alone shall be exalted [R]in
that day. Hos. 2:16

12 For the day of the LORD of hosts
Shall come upon everything proud and
lofty,
Upon everything lifted up—
And it shall be brought low—
13 Upon all [R]the cedars of Lebanon *that are*
high and lifted up, Zech. 11:1, 2
And upon all the oaks of Bashan;
14[R]Upon all the high mountains, Is. 30:25
And upon all the hills *that are* lifted up;
15 Upon every high tower,
And upon every fortified wall;
16 Upon all the ships of Tarshish,
And upon all the beautiful sloops.
17 The [T]loftiness of man shall be bowed
down, *pride*
And the haughtiness of men shall be
brought low;
The LORD alone will be exalted in that
day,
18 But the idols He shall utterly abolish.
19 They shall go into the [R]holes of the
rocks, Hos. 10:8
And into the caves of the [T]earth, Lit. *dust*
[R]From the terror of the LORD [2 Thess. 1:9]
And the glory of His majesty,
When He arises [R]to shake the earth
mightily. Hag. 2:6, 7

20 In that day a man will cast away his
idols of silver
And his idols of gold,
Which they made, *each* for himself to
worship,
To the moles and bats,
21 To go into the clefts of the rocks,
And into the crags of the rugged rocks,
From the terror of the LORD
And the glory of His majesty,
When He arises to shake the earth
mightily.

1:29 So with MT, LXX, Vg.; some Heb. mss., Tg. *you*

22 [R]Sever yourselves from such a man,
Whose breath *is* in his nostrils;
For of what account is he? Jer. 17:5

CHAPTER 3

FOR behold, the Lord, the LORD of hosts,
[R]Takes away from Jerusalem and from Judah Jer. 37:21
[R]The stock and the store, Lev. 26:26
The whole supply of bread and the whole supply of water;
2 [R]The mighty man and the man of war,
The judge and the prophet, 2 Kin. 24:14
And the diviner and the elder;
3 The captain of fifty and the [T]honorable man, Eminent looking men
The counselor and the skillful artisan,
And the expert enchanter.

4 "I will give children[T] *to be* their princes,
And babes shall rule over them. *boys*
5 The people will be oppressed,
Every one by another and every one by his neighbor;
The child will be insolent toward the [T]elder, *aged*
And the base toward the honorable."

6 When a man takes hold of his brother
In the house of his father, *saying,*
"You have clothing;
You be our ruler,
And *let* these ruins *be* under your power,"*
7 In that day he will protest, saying,
"I cannot cure *your* ills,
For in my house *is* neither food nor clothing;
Do not make me a ruler of the people."

8 For [R]Jerusalem stumbled, Mic. 3:12
And Judah is fallen,
Because their tongue and their doings
Are against the LORD,
To provoke the eyes of His glory.
9 The look on their countenance witnesses against them,
And they declare their sin as [R]Sodom;
They do not hide *it*.
Woe to their soul!
For they have brought evil upon themselves. Gen. 13:13

10 "Say to the righteous [R]that *it shall be* well *with them,* [Eccl. 8:12]
[R]For they shall eat the fruit of their doings. Ps. 128:2
11 Woe to the wicked! [R]*It shall be* ill *with him,* [Ps. 11:6]
For the reward of his hands shall be [T]given him. *done to him*
12 *As for* My people, children *are* their oppressors,
And women rule over them.
O My people! [R]Those who lead you cause *you* to err, Is. 9:16
And destroy the way of your paths."

13 The LORD stands up [R]to plead, Mic. 6:2
And stands to judge the people.
14 The LORD will enter into judgment
With the elders of His people
And His princes:
"For you have [T]eaten up [R]the vineyard;
The plunder of the poor *is* in your houses. *burned* • Matt. 21:33
15 What do you mean by [R]crushing My people Mic. 3:2, 3
And grinding the faces of the poor?"
Says the Lord GOD of hosts.

16 Moreover the LORD says:

"Because the daughters of Zion are haughty,
And walk with outstretched necks
And [T]wanton eyes, *seductive, ogling*
Walking and mincing *as* they go,
Making a jingling with their feet,
17 Therefore the Lord will strike with [R]a scab Deut. 28:27
The crown of the head of the daughters of Zion,
And the LORD will [R]uncover their secret parts." Jer. 13:22

18 In that day the Lord will take away the finery:
The jingling anklets, the scarves, and the [R]crescents; Judg. 8:21, 26
19 The pendants, the bracelets, and the veils;
20 The headdresses, the leg ornaments, and the headbands;
The perfume boxes, the charms,
21 and the rings;
The nose jewels,
22 the festal apparel, and the mantles;
The outer garments, the purses,
23 and the mirrors;
The fine linen, the turbans, and the robes.

24 And so it shall be:

Instead of a sweet smell there will be a stench;
Instead of a sash, a rope;
Instead of well-set hair, [R]baldness;
Instead of a rich robe, a girding of sackcloth; Is. 22:12
And branding instead of beauty.
25 Your men shall fall by the sword,
And your [T]mighty in the war. Lit. *strength*

3:6 Lit. *hand*

26[R] Her gates shall lament and mourn,
And she *being* desolate [R]shall sit on the ground. Jer. 14:2 • Lam. 2:10

CHAPTER 4

AND [R]in that day seven women shall take hold of one man, saying, Is. 2:11, 17
"We will [R]eat our own food and wear our own apparel; 2 Thess. 3:12
Only let us be called by your name,
To take away [R]our reproach." Luke 1:25

2 In that day [R]the Branch of the LORD shall be beautiful and glorious;
And the fruit of the earth *shall be* excellent and appealing [Jer. 23:5]
For those of Israel who have escaped.

3 And it shall come to pass that *he who is*
left in Zion and remains in Jerusalem will be
called holy—everyone who is [R]recorded
among the living in Jerusalem. Phil. 4:3
4 When [R]the Lord has washed away the
filth of the daughters of Zion, and purged the
[T]blood of Jerusalem from her midst, by the
spirit of judgment and by the spirit of burn-
ing, Mal. 3:2, 3 • *bloodshed*
5 then the LORD will create above every
dwelling place of Mount Zion, and above her
assemblies, a cloud and smoke by day and the
shining of a flaming fire by night. For over all
the glory there *will be* a covering.
6 And there will be a tabernacle for shade
in the daytime from the heat, [R]for a place of
refuge, and for a shelter from storm and
rain. Is. 25:4

CHAPTER 5

The Parable of the Vineyard

NOW let me sing to my Well-beloved
A song of my Beloved [R]regarding His vineyard: Matt. 21:33

My Well-beloved has a vineyard
On a very fruitful hill.
2 He dug it up and cleared out its stones,
And planted it with the choicest vine.
He built a tower in its midst,
And also [T]made a winepress in it;
[R]So He expected *it* to bring forth *good* grapes, Lit. *hewed out* • Deut. 32:6
But it brought forth wild grapes.

3 "And now, O inhabitants of Jerusalem and men of Judah,
[R]Judge, please, between Me and My vineyard. [Rom. 3:4]
4 What more could have been done to My vineyard
That I have not done in [R]it?
Why then, when I expected *it* to bring forth *good* grapes, 2 Chr. 36:15, 16
Did it bring forth wild grapes?
5 And now, please let Me tell you what I will do to My vineyard:
[R]I will take away its hedge, and it shall be burned; Ps. 80:12; 89:40, 41
And break down its wall, and it shall be trampled down.
6 I will lay it [R]waste; 2 Chr. 36:19–21
It shall not be pruned or [T]dug, *hoed*
But there shall come up briers and [R]thorns. Is. 7:19–25
I will also command the clouds
That they rain no rain on it."

7 For the vineyard of the LORD of hosts *is* the house of Israel,
And the men of Judah are His pleasant plant.
He looked for justice, but behold, oppression;
For righteousness, but behold, [T]a cry *for help*. *wailing*

8 Woe to those who join [R]house to house;
They add field to field,
Till *there is* no place
Where they may dwell alone in the midst of the land! Mic. 2:2
9[R] In my hearing the LORD of hosts *said*,
"Truly, many houses shall be desolate,
Great and beautiful ones, without inhabitant. Is. 22:14
10 For ten acres of vineyard shall yield one [R]bath,[T] Ezek. 45:11 • 1 bath=1/10 homer
And a homer of seed shall yield one [T]ephah." 1 homer=1/10 ephah

11[R] Woe to those who rise early in the morning, Prov. 23:29, 30
That they may [T]follow intoxicating drink;
Who continue until night, *till* wine inflames them! *pursue*
12[R] The harp and the strings, Amos 6:5
The tambourine and flute,
And wine are in their feasts;
But [R]they do not regard the work of the LORD, Job 34:27
Nor consider the operation of His hands.

13[R] Therefore my people have gone into captivity, 2 Kin. 24:14–16
Because *they have* no [R]knowledge;
Their honorable men *are* famished,
And their multitude dried up with thirst. Hos. 4:6
14 Therefore Sheol has enlarged itself
And opened its mouth beyond measure;
Their glory and their multitude and their pomp,
And he who is jubilant, shall descend into it.

15 People shall be brought down,
[R]Each man shall be humbled, Is. 2:9, 11
And the eyes of the lofty shall be humbled.
16 But the LORD of hosts shall be [R]exalted
in judgment, Is. 2:11
And God who is holy shall be hallowed
in righteousness.
17 Then the lambs shall feed in their
pasture,
And in the waste places of [R]the fat ones
strangers shall eat. Is. 10:16

18 Woe to those who [T]draw iniquity with
cords of vanity, *drag*
And sin as if with a cart rope;
19[R] That say, "Let Him make speed *and*
hasten His work, Jer. 17:15
That we may see *it;*
And let the counsel of the Holy One of
Israel draw near and come,
That we may know *it.*"

20 Woe to those who call evil good, and
good evil;
Who put darkness for light, and light for
darkness;
Who put bitter for sweet, and sweet for
bitter!

21 Woe to *those who are* [R]wise in their own
eyes, Rom. 1:22; 12:16
And prudent in their own sight!

22 Woe to men mighty at drinking wine,
Woe to men valiant for mixing
intoxicating drink,
23 Who [R]justify the wicked for a bribe,
And take away justice from the righteous
man! Prov. 17:15

24 Therefore, [R]as the [T]fire devours the
stubble, Ex. 15:7 • Lit. *tongue of fire*
And the flame consumes the chaff,
So [R]their root will be as rottenness,
And their blossom will ascend like dust;
Because they have rejected the law of
the LORD of hosts, Job 18:16
And despised the word of the Holy One
of Israel.
25[R] Therefore the anger of the LORD is
aroused against His people;
He has stretched out His hand against
them 2 Kin. 22:13, 17
And stricken them,
And [R]the hills trembled. Jer. 4:24
Their carcasses *were* as refuse in the
midst of the streets.
[R]For all this His anger is not turned
away, Is. 9:12, 17
But His hand *is* stretched out still.

26[R] He will lift up a banner to the nations
from afar, Is. 11:10, 12
And will [R]whistle to them from [R]the end
of the earth; Is. 7:18 • Mal. 1:11
Surely [R]they shall come with speed,
swiftly. Joel 2:7
27 No one will be weary or stumble among
them,
No one will slumber or sleep;
Nor [R]will the belt on their loins be
loosed, Dan. 5:6
Nor the strap of their sandals be broken;
28[R] Whose arrows *are* sharp, Jer. 5:16
And all their bows bent;
Their horses' hooves will seem like
flint,
And their wheels like a whirlwind.
29 Their roaring *will be* like a lion,
They will roar like young lions;
Yes, they will roar
And lay hold of the prey;
They will carry *it* away safely,
And no one will deliver.
30 In that day they will roar against them
Like the roaring of the sea.
And if *one* [R]looks to the land, Is. 8:22
Behold, darkness *and* [T]sorrow; *distress*
And the light is darkened by the clouds.

CHAPTER 6

The Commission of Isaiah

IN the year that [R]King Uzziah died, I [R]saw
the Lord sitting on a throne, high and lifted
up, and the train of His *robe* filled the tem-
ple. 2 Kin. 15:7 • John 12:41
2 Above it stood seraphim; each one had
six wings: with two he covered his face,
[R]with two he covered his feet, and with two
he flew. Ezek. 1:11

3 And one cried to another and said:

"Holy, holy, holy *is* the LORD of hosts;
The whole earth *is* full of His glory!"

6:3 Holiness of God—Our greatest failing is in not realizing who God is and what His character is like. God is NOT human. He is God, and as such there is an infinite gap between the highest in us and the lowest in God. The gap between God and us is unbridgeable from our side. If the gap is to be bridged, it must be from God's side—for God is holy. To be holy means "to be set apart." God is set apart from the power, practice, and presence of sin, and is set apart to absolute righteousness and goodness. There is no sin in God and God can have nothing to do with sin. If we are to approach God, we must do so on God's terms. Somehow, we must be made holy—just as holy as God is. Any holiness that falls short of God's holiness will not be able to stand in the presence of God. Therefore, because of the holiness of God, we must have

(continued on next page)

4 And the posts of the door were shaken by
the voice of him who cried out, and the house
was filled with smoke.

5 So I said:

"Woe *is* me, for I am undone!
Because I *am* a man of [R]unclean lips,
And I dwell in the midst of a people of
unclean lips; Ex. 6:12, 30
For my eyes have seen the King,
The LORD of hosts."

6 Then one of the seraphim flew to me, hav-
ing in his hand a live coal *which* he had taken
with the tongs from [R]the altar. Rev. 8:3
7 And he [R]touched my mouth *with it,* and
said: Jer. 1:9

"Behold, this has touched your lips;
Your iniquity is taken away,
And your sin [T]purged." *atoned for*

8 Also I heard the voice of the Lord, saying:

"Whom shall I send,
And who will go for [R]Us?" Gen. 1:26

Then I said, "Here *am* I! Send me."

9 And He said, "Go, and tell this people:

[R]'Keep on hearing, but do not
understand; Matt. 13:14, 15☆
Keep on seeing, but do not perceive.'

10 "Make [R]the heart of this people dull,
And their ears heavy,
And shut their eyes; Mark. 6:1–6☆
[R]Lest they see with their eyes, Jer. 5:21
And hear with their ears,
And understand with their heart,
And return and be healed."

11 Then I said, "Lord, how long?" And He an-
swered:

[R]"Until the cities are laid waste and
without inhabitant, Mic. 3:12
The houses are without a man,
The land is utterly desolate,
12 [R]The LORD has removed men far away,
And the forsaken places *are* many in the
midst of the land. 2 Kin. 25:21
13 But yet a tenth *will be* in it,
And will return and be for consuming,
As a terebinth tree or as an oak,
Whose stump *remains* when it is cut
down.
So the holy seed *shall be* its stump."

CHAPTER 7

Sign of Immanuel—2 Kin. 16:5; 2 Chr. 28:5–15

NOW it came to pass in the days of Ahaz
the son of Jotham, the son of Uzziah,
king of Judah, *that* Rezin king of Syria and
Pekah the son of Remaliah, king of Israel,
went up to Jerusalem to *make* war against it,
but could not prevail against it.
2 And it was told to the house of David,
saying, "Syria's forces are [T]deployed in
Ephraim." So his heart and the heart of his
people were moved as the trees of the woods
are moved with the wind. Lit. *settled upon*
3 Then the LORD said to Isaiah, "Go out now

(continued from previous page)
a new life in which our sins have been forgiven and done away with so that we actually can be as separated from sin as God is. This is the good news of the gospel—that Christ died for our sins, having taken them upon Himself, and has set us apart from them. This is our position before God, which will never change. Because of what God has done, we can enter boldly into the presence of God.

Now turn to Page 6—Gen. 3:6, 7: Adam's Sin.

6:8 Knowing the Will of God Through Submission to the Spirit—The moment a repenting sinner receives Christ by faith into his or her heart the Holy Spirit immediately does five things:

a. He regenerates the believer, that is, He gives the believer a new nature (Page 1083—John 3:5, 6; Page 1250—Titus 3:5).
b. He baptizes the believer into the body of Christ (Page 1176—1 Cor. 12:13).
c. He indwells the believer (Page 1154—Rom. 8:9; Page 1171—1 Cor. 6:19).
d. He seals the believer (Page 1204—Eph. 1:13; 4:30).
e. He fills the believer (Page 1113—Acts 2:4; 4:8; 7:55; 13:52).

All five of these ministries often occur at conversion. The fifth ministry, however, should be asked for as needed. See Ephesians 5:18; Galatians 5:16. Actually the word *"control"* is a better term than *"fill"* in describing this fifth ministry. It does not mean that we get more of the Spirit, but rather that He gets more of us. The fifth ministry is lost when the believer either quenches (Page 1229—1 Thess. 5:19) or grieves (Page 1207—Eph. 4:30) the Holy Spirit. The fifth ministry can be regained by following the command of 1 John 1:9, "If we confess our sins, He is faithful and just to forgive us *our* sins and to cleanse us from all unrighteousness."

How can a Christian be certain that he or she is indeed controlled by the Holy Spirit on a daily basis? First, the believer must consecrate his or her body as a living sacrifice to the Holy Spirit (Page 1158—Rom. 12:1, 2). Second, the believer must depend upon the Holy Spirit to convict him of sin (Page 620—Ps. 139:23, 24; 19:12–14). Finally, the believer must look to the Holy Spirit for divine power in serving Christ (Page 1112—Acts 1:8; Page 1200—Gal. 5:16, 17; Page 1206—Eph. 3:16).

Now turn to Page 650—Prov. 24:6: Knowing the Will of God Through Circumstances and Counsel.

to meet Ahaz, you and Shear-Jashub* your
son, at the end of the aqueduct from the upper
pool, on the highway to the Fuller's Field,
4 "and say to him: [T]'Take heed, and [T]be
[R]quiet; do not fear or be fainthearted for these
two stubs of smoking firebrands, for the fierce
anger of Rezin and Syria, and the son of Rem-
aliah. *Be careful* • *be calm* • Is. 30:15
5 'Because Syria, Ephraim, and the son of
Remaliah have plotted evil against you, say-
ing,
6 "Let us go up against Judah and [T]trouble
it, and let us make a gap in its wall for our-
selves, and set a king over them, the son of
Tabel"— *cause a sickening dread*
7 'thus says the Lord GOD:

[R]"It shall not stand, Is. 8:10
Nor shall it come to pass.
8 [R]For the head of Syria *is* Damascus,
And the head of Damascus *is* Rezin.
Within sixty-five years Ephraim will be
[T]broken, 2 Sam. 8:6 • Lit. *shattered*
So that it will not *be* a people.
9 The head of Ephraim *is* Samaria,
And the head of Samaria *is* Remaliah's
son.
[R]If you will not believe, 2 Chr. 20:20
Surely you shall not be established." ' "

10 Moreover the LORD spoke again to Ahaz,
saying,
11 [R]"Ask a sign for yourself from the LORD
your God; ask it either in the depth or in the
height above." Matt. 12:38
12 But Ahaz said, "I will not ask, nor will I
test the LORD!"
13 Then he said, "Hear now, O house of Da-
vid! *Is it* a small thing for you to weary men,
but will you weary my God also?
14 "Therefore the Lord Himself will give you
a sign: [R]Behold, the virgin shall conceive and
bear a Son, and shall call His name Im-
manuel.* Matt. 1:23; Luke 1:31, 34, 35☆
15 "Curds and honey He shall eat, that He
may know to refuse the evil and choose the
good.
16 [R]"For before the Child shall know to re-
fuse the evil and choose the good, the land
that you dread will be forsaken by [R]both her
kings. Is. 8:4 • 2 Kin. 15:30
17 "The LORD will bring the king of Assyria
upon you and your people and your father's
house—days that have not come since the day
that Ephraim departed from Judah."

18 And it shall come to pass in that day
That the LORD [R]will whistle for the fly
That *is* in the farthest part of the rivers
of Egypt,
And for the bee that *is* in the land of
Assyria. Is. 5:26
19 They will come, and all of them will rest
In the desolate valleys and in [R]the clefts
of the rocks, Jer. 16:16
And on all thorns and in all pastures.

20 In the same day the Lord will shave with
a [R]hired [R]razor, Is. 10:5, 15 • 2 Kin. 16:7
With those from beyond the River,* with
the king of Assyria,
The head and the hair of the legs,
And will also remove the beard.

21 It shall be in that day
That a man will keep alive a young cow
and two sheep;
22 So it shall be, from the abundance of
milk they give,
That he will eat curds;
For curds and honey everyone will eat
who is left in the land.

23 It shall happen in that day,
That wherever there could be a
thousand vines
Worth a thousand *shekels* of silver,
[R]It will be for briers and thorns. Is. 5:6
24 With arrows and bows men will come
there,
Because all the land will become briers
and thorns.

25 And to any hill which could be dug with
the hoe,
You will not go there for fear of briers
and thorns;
But it will become a range for oxen
And a place for sheep to roam.

CHAPTER 8

Sign of Maher-Shalal-Hash-Baz

MOREOVER the LORD said to me, "Take a
large scroll, and [R]write on it with a
man's pen concerning Maher-Shalal-Hash-
Baz.* Hab. 2:2
2 "And I will take for Myself faithful wit-
nesses to record, Uriah the priest and
Zechariah the son of Jeberechiah."
3 Then I went to the prophetess, and she
conceived and bore a son. Then the LORD said
to me, "Call his name Maher-Shalal-Hash-Baz;
4 [R]"for before the child shall have knowl-
edge to cry 'My father' and 'My mother,' [R]the
riches of Damascus and the spoil of Samaria
will be taken away before the king of As-
syria." 2 Kin. 17:6; Is. 7:16 • 2 Kin. 15:29
5 The LORD also spoke to me again, saying:

6 "Inasmuch as these people refused
The waters of [R]Shiloah that flow softly,

7:3 Lit. *A Remnant Shall Return* **7:14** Lit. *God-With-Us* **7:20** The Euphrates **8:1** Lit. *Speed the Spoil, Hasten the Booty*

And rejoice [R]in Rezin and in Remaliah's
son; John 9:7 • Is. 7:1, 2
7 Now therefore, behold, the Lord brings
up over them
The waters of the River,* strong and
mighty—
The king of Assyria and all his glory;
He will go up over all his channels
And go over all his banks.
8 He will pass through Judah,
He will overflow and pass over,
[R]He will reach up to the neck; Is. 30:28
And the stretching out of his wings
Will fill the breadth of Your land, O
[R]Immanuel.* Is. 7:14

9 "Be[R] shattered, O you peoples, and be
broken in pieces! Joel 3:9
Give ear, all you from far countries.
Gird yourselves, but be broken in pieces;
Gird yourselves, but be broken in pieces.
10 [R]Take counsel together, but it will come to
nothing; Is. 7:7
Speak the word, [R]but it will not stand,
[R]For God *is* with us."* Is. 7:14 • Rom. 8:31

11 For the LORD spoke thus to me with [T]a
strong hand, and instructed me that I
should not walk in the way of this people,
saying: Mighty power

12 "Do not say, 'A conspiracy,'
Concerning all that this people call a
conspiracy,
Nor be afraid of their [T]threats, nor be
[T]troubled. Lit. *fear* or *terror* • Lit. *in dread*
13 The LORD of hosts, Him you shall hallow;
Let Him *be* your fear,
And *let* Him *be* your dread.
14 [R]He will be as a sanctuary, Ezek. 11:16
But [R]a stone of stumbling and a rock of
[T]offense Luke 2:34; 20:17☆ • *stumbling over*
To both the houses of Israel,
As a trap and a snare to the inhabitants
of Jerusalem.
15 And many among them shall [R]stumble;
They shall fall and be broken, Matt. 21:44
Be snared and [T]taken." *captured*

16 Bind up the testimony,
Seal the law among my disciples.
17 And I will wait on the LORD,
Who [R]hides His face from the house of
Jacob; Is. 54:8
And I [R]will hope in Him. Hab. 2:3
18 [R]Here am I and the children whom the
LORD has given me! Heb. 2:13
We [R]*are* for signs and wonders in Israel
From the LORD of hosts, Ps. 71:7
Who dwells in Mount Zion.

19 And when they say to you, [R]"Seek those
who are mediums and wizards, [R]who whisper
and mutter," should not a people seek their
God? *Should they seek* the dead on behalf of
the living? 1 Sam. 28:8 • Is. 29:4
20 [R]To the law and to the testimony! If they
do not speak according to this word, *it is* be-
cause *there is* no light in them. Luke 16:29
21 They will pass through it hard-pressed
and hungry; and it shall happen, when they
are hungry, that they will be enraged and
[R]curse their king and their God, and look up-
ward. Rev. 16:11
22 Then they will look to the earth, and see
trouble and darkness, gloom of anguish; and
they will be driven into darkness.

CHAPTER 9

Prophecy of the Messiah's Birth

NEVERTHELESS [R]the gloom *will* not *be*
upon her who *is* distressed, Is. 8:22
As when at [R]first He lightly esteemed
The land of Zebulun and the land of
Naphtali, 2 Kin. 15:29
And [R]afterward more heavily oppressed
her, Matt. 4:13–16☆
By the way of the sea, beyond the
Jordan,
In Galilee of the Gentiles.
2 The [R]people who walked in darkness
Have seen a great light; Luke 1:79☆
Those who dwelt in the land of the
shadow of death,
Upon them a light has shined.

3 You have multiplied the nation
And increased its joy;*
They rejoice before You
According to the joy of harvest,
As *men* rejoice [R]when they divide the
spoil. Judg. 5:30
4 For You have broken the yoke of his
burden
And the staff of his shoulder,
The rod of his oppressor,
As in the day of [R]Midian. Judg. 7:22
5 For every warrior's [T]sandal from the
noisy battle, *boot*
And garments rolled in blood,
[R]Will be used for burning *and* fuel [T]of
fire. Is. 66:15 • *for the fire*

6 [R]For unto us a Child is born, [Luke 2:11]☆
Unto us a [R]Son is given; [John 3:16]
And [R]the government will be upon His
shoulder. [Matt. 28:18]
And His name will be called
Wonderful, Counselor, Mighty God,
Everlasting Father, Prince of Peace.

8:7 The Euphrates **8:8** Lit. *God-With-Us* **8:10** Heb. *Immanuel* **9:3** So with Qr., Tg.; Kt., Vg. *not increased joy;* LXX *Most of the people You brought down in Your joy*

7 Of the increase of *His* government and
peace
[R] *There will be* no end,
Upon the throne of David and over His
kingdom, Dan. 2:44; Luke 1:32, 33☆
To order it and establish it with
judgment and justice
From that time forward, even forever.
The [R]zeal of the LORD of hosts will
perform this. Is. 37:32

Judgment on Ephraim

8 The Lord sent a word against [R]Jacob,
And it has fallen on Israel. Gen. 32:28
9 All the people will know—
Ephraim and the inhabitant of Samaria—
Who say in pride and arrogance of heart:
10 "The bricks have fallen down,
But we will rebuild with hewn stones;
The sycamores are cut down,
But we will replace *them* with cedars."
11 Therefore the LORD shall set up
The adversaries of Rezin against him,
And spur his enemies on,
12 The Syrians before and the Philistines
behind;
And they shall devour Israel with an
open mouth.

For all this His anger is not turned away,
But His hand *is* stretched out still.

13 For the people do not turn to Him who
strikes them,
Nor do they seek the LORD of hosts.
14 Therefore the LORD will cut off head and
tail from Israel,
Palm branch and bulrush in one day.
15 The elder and honorable, he *is* the head;
The prophet who teaches lies, he *is* the
tail.
16 For [R]the leaders of this people cause
them to err, Is. 3:12
And *those who are* led by them are
destroyed.
17 Therefore the Lord [R]will have no joy in
their young men, Ps. 147:10
Nor have mercy on their fatherless and
widows;
For everyone *is* a hypocrite and an
evildoer,
And every mouth speaks folly.

[R]For all this His anger is not turned
away, Is. 5:25
But His hand *is* stretched out still.

18 For wickedness burns as the fire;
It shall devour the briers and thorns,
And kindle in the thickets of the forest;
They shall mount up *like* rising smoke.
19 Through the wrath of the LORD of hosts
[R]The land is burned up, Is. 8:22
And the people shall be as fuel for the
fire;
No man shall spare his brother.
20 And he shall [T]snatch on the right hand
And be hungry; *slice off* or *tear*

9:6 The Person of the Son of God—It is crucial to remember that the existence of the Son of God did not commence with His birth in Bethlehem. He is spoken of as the Son before He became a Man (Page 690—Is. 9:6; Page 1198—Gal. 4:4). Micah prophesies of His birth, but yet states that His "goings forth *are* from of old, from everlasting" (Page 930—Mic. 5:2). John says that He existed "in the beginning" before anything was created (Page 1081—John 1:1–3).

Even before He was born of Mary, He appeared to men in the Old Testament as the "Angel of the LORD." It is clear that this Angel is no ordinary angel because He is identified as God (Page 57—Ex. 3:1, 4); He pardons sin (Page 77—Ex. 23:20, 21); and He is worshiped (Page 218—Josh. 5:13–15). While these passages do not say that this member of the Godhead was the preincarnate Christ, we may conclude that they are the same Person since their work is the same.

While Christ was preexistent and appeared occasionally to men in the Old Testament, He took on a body permanently when He was conceived in Mary's womb. This incomparable event of God's becoming man in Jesus Christ is called the Incarnation. This miracle was prophesied hundreds of years previously (Page 689—Is. 7:14) and was fulfilled historically in Mary in whose womb the Holy Spirit's power conceived a child (Page 978—Matt. 1:23; Page 1042—Luke 1:35). Thus Christ, the sinless God-Man, was qualified to become our Redeemer (Page 1187—2 Cor. 5:21).

Having been born of a woman, Jesus Christ was fully man apart from sin (Page 1081—John 1:14). As a man He experienced the normal physical, mental, social, and spiritual growth as others did (Page 1044—Luke 2:52). He suffered pain, hunger, thirst, fatigue, temptation, pleasure, and rest. Because of His complete humanity He can be sympathetic and compassionate toward us (Page 1260—Heb. 4:15).

While Christ was fully man He was also fully God, as these facts indicate: He is called God (Page 1081—John 1:1; Page 1258—Heb. 1:8); He did works that only God could do, such as forgive sins (Page 1015—Mark 2:7) and create (Page 1220—Col. 1:16); He had attributes that only God could have, such as truth (Page 1099—John 14:6) and omniscience, all-knowing (Page 1083—John 2:24, 25); and He claimed equality with God (Page 1095—John 10:30).

The question may then be raised as to whether Christ lost any aspect of deity when He became a man (Page 1214—Phil. 2:6–8). While there is an inscrutable mystery involved in this unparalleled act of condescension, one can be certain that He lost none of God's attributes, because He was still God (Page 1106—John 20:28). He was fully God and fully man united in one Person forever. Even now, at the right hand of God, He is the God-Man (Page 1237—1 Tim. 2:5). The great condescension of the Son of God's becoming a man serves eternally as a perfect model of humility and self-giving love (Page 1214—Phil. 2:5).

Now turn to Page 1094—John 10:10: The Earthly Life of the Son of God.

He shall devour on the left hand
[R]And not be satisfied; Lev. 26:26
[R]Every man shall eat the flesh of his own arm. Jer. 19:9
21 Manasseh *shall devour* Ephraim, and Ephraim Manasseh;
Together they *shall be* [R]against Judah.

[R]For all this His anger is not turned away, 2 Chr. 28:6, 8 • Is. 9:12, 17
But His hand *is* stretched out still.

CHAPTER 10

"WOE to those who [R]decree unrighteous decrees, Ps. 58:2
Who write misfortune,
Which they have prescribed
2 To rob the needy of justice,
And to take what is right from the poor of My people,
That widows may be their prey,
And *that* they may rob the fatherless.
3[R] What will you do in [R]the day of punishment, Job 31:14 • Hos. 9:7
And in the desolation *which* will come from [R]afar? Is. 5:26
To whom will you flee for help?
And where will you leave your glory?
4 Without Me they shall bow down among the [R]prisoners, Is. 24:22
And they shall fall among the slain."

[R]For all this His anger is not turned away, Is. 5:25
But His hand *is* stretched out still.

Destruction of Assyria

5"Woe to Assyria, [R]the rod of My anger
And the staff in whose hand is My indignation. Jer. 51:20
6 I will send him against [R]an ungodly nation, Is. 9:17
And against the people of My wrath
I will [R]give him charge, Jer. 34:22
To seize the spoil, to take the prey,
And to tread them down like the mire of the streets.
7[R] Yet he does not mean so, Gen. 50:20
Nor does his heart think so;
But *it is* in his heart to destroy,
And cut off not a few nations.
8[R] For he says, 2 Kin. 19:10
'*Are* not my princes altogether kings?
9 *Is* not [R]Calno like Carchemish?
Is not Hamath like Arpad? Amos 6:2
Is not Samaria like Damascus?
10 As my hand has found the kingdoms of the idols,
Whose carved images excelled those of Jerusalem and Samaria,
11 As I have done to Samaria and her idols,
Shall I not do also to Jerusalem and her idols?' "

12 Therefore it shall come to pass, when the
Lord has performed all His work [R]on Mount
Zion and on Jerusalem, *that He will say,* [R]"I
will punish the fruit of the arrogant heart of
the king of Assyria, and the glory of his
haughty looks." 2 Kin. 19:31 • Jer. 50:18
13 [R]For he says: Is. 37:24–27

"By the strength of my hand I have done *it*,
And by my wisdom, for I am prudent;
Also I have removed the boundaries of the people,
And have robbed their treasuries;
So I have put down the inhabitants like a [T]valiant *man*. mighty
14[R] My hand has found like a nest the riches of the people, Job 31:25
And as one gathers eggs *that are* left,
I have gathered all the earth;
And there was no one who moved *his* wing,
Nor opened *his* mouth with even a peep."

15 Shall [R]the ax boast itself against him who chops with it? Jer. 51:20
Or shall the saw exalt itself against him who saws with it?
As if a rod could wield *itself* against those who lift it up,
Or as if a staff could lift up, *as if it were* not wood!
16 Therefore the Lord, the Lord* of hosts,
Will send leanness among his fat ones;
And under his glory
He will kindle a burning
Like the burning of a fire.
17 So the Light of Israel will be for a fire,
And his Holy One for a flame;
[R]It will burn and devour Is. 9:18
His thorns and his briers in one day.
18 And it will consume the glory of his forest and of [R]his fruitful field,
Both soul and body; 2 Kin. 19:23
And they will be as when a sick man wastes away.
19 Then the rest of the trees of his forest
Will be so few in number
That a child may write them.

Remnant of Israel

20 And it shall come to pass in that day
That the remnant of Israel,
And such as have escaped of the house of Jacob,
[R]Will never again depend on him who [T]defeated them, 2 Kin. 16:7 • Lit. *struck*
But will depend on the LORD, the Holy One of Israel, in truth.

10:16 So with Bg.; MT, DSS *YHWH* (*the* LORD)

21 The remnant will return, the remnant of
Jacob,
To the [R]Mighty God. [Is. 9:6]
22[R] For though your people, O Israel, be as
the sand of the sea, Rom. 9:27, 28
[R] A remnant of them will return; Is. 6:13
The destruction decreed shall overflow
with righteousness.
23[R] For the Lord GOD of hosts Dan. 9:27
Will make a determined end
In the midst of all the land.

24 Therefore thus says the Lord GOD of
hosts: "O My people, who dwell in Zion, [R]do
not be afraid of the Assyrian. He shall strike
you with a rod and lift up his staff against
you, in the manner of Egypt. Is. 7:4; 12:2
25 "For yet a very little while [R]and the
indignation will cease, as will My anger in
their destruction." Dan. 11:36
26 And the LORD of hosts will [T]stir up [R]a
scourge for him like the slaughter of [R]Midian
at the rock of Oreb; [R]*as* His rod was on the
sea, so will He lift it up in the manner of
Egypt. *arouse* • 2 Kin. 19:35 • Is. 9:4 • Ex. 14:26, 27

27 It shall come to pass in that day
That his burden will be taken away from
your shoulder,
And his yoke from your neck,
And the yoke will be destroyed because
of [R]the anointing oil. Ps. 105:15

28 He has come to Aiath,
He has passed Migron;
At Michmash he has attended to his
equipment.
29 They have gone along [R]the ridge,
They have taken up lodging at Geba.
Ramah is afraid, 1 Sam. 13:23
[R] Gibeah of Saul has fled. 1 Sam. 11:4
30[T] Lift up your voice, Or *Cry shrilly*
O daughter [R]of Gallim! 1 Sam. 25:44
Cause it to be heard as far as [R]Laish—
O poor Anathoth!* Judg. 18:7
31[R] Madmenah has fled, Josh. 15:31
The inhabitants of Gebim seek refuge.
32 As yet he will remain at Nob that day;
He will [R]shake his fist at the mount of
[R]the daughter of Zion,
The hill of Jerusalem. Is. 13:2 • Is. 37:22

33 Behold, the Lord,
The LORD of hosts,
Will lop off the bough with terror;
[R] Those of high stature *will be* hewn
down, Amos 2:9
And the haughty will be humbled.
34 He will cut down the thickets of the
forest with iron,
And Lebanon will fall by the Mighty
One.

CHAPTER 11

Restoration of the Messiah's Kingdom

THERE [R]shall come forth a Rod from the
stem of [R]Jesse, [Zech. 6:12] • [Acts 13:23]☆
And [R]a Branch shall [T]grow out of his
roots. Is. 4:2 • *be fruitful*
2[R] The Spirit of the LORD shall rest upon
Him, [John 1:32]☆
The Spirit of wisdom and understanding,
The Spirit of counsel and might,
The Spirit of knowledge and of the fear
of the LORD.

3 His delight *is* in the fear of the LORD,
[R]And He shall not judge by the sight of
His eyes, John 2:25☆
Nor decide by the hearing of His ears;
4 But [R]with righteousness He shall judge
the poor, Rev. 19:11☆
And decide with equity for the meek of
the earth;
He shall [R]strike the earth with the rod of
His mouth, Job 4:9
And with the breath of His lips He shall
slay the wicked.
5 Righteousness shall be the belt of His
loins,
And faithfulness the belt of His waist.

6 "The[R] wolf also shall dwell with the lamb,
The leopard shall lie down with the
young goat, Hos. 2:18
The calf and the young lion and the
fatling together;
And a little child shall lead them.
7 The cow and the bear shall graze;
Their young ones shall lie down
together;
And the lion shall eat straw like the ox.
8 The nursing child shall play by the
cobra's hole,
And the weaned child shall put his hand
in the viper's den.
9[R] They shall not hurt nor destroy in all My
holy mountain, Job 5:23
For [R]the earth shall be full of the
knowledge of the LORD Hab. 2:14
As the waters cover the sea.

10 "And[R] in that day [R]there shall be a [R]Root of
Jesse, Is. 2:11 • Rom. 15:12 • Is. 11:1☆
Who shall stand as a [R]banner to the
people; Is. 27:12, 13
For the Gentiles shall seek Him,
And His resting place shall be glorious."

11 It shall come to pass in that day
That the Lord shall set His hand again
the second time

10:30 So with MT, Tg., Vg.; LXX, Syr. *Listen to her, O Anathoth*

To recover the remnant of His people
who are left,
[R]From Assyria and Egypt, Zech. 10:10
From Pathros and Cush,
From Elam and Shinar,
From Hamath and the [T]islands of the
sea. Or *coastlands*

12 He will set up a banner for the nations,
And will [T]assemble the outcasts of
Israel, *gather*
And gather together [R]the dispersed of
Judah John 7:35
From the four corners of the earth.
13 Also [R]the envy of Ephraim shall depart,
And the adversaries of Judah shall be
cut off; Jer. 3:18
Ephraim shall not envy Judah,
And Judah shall not harass Ephraim.
14 But they shall fly down upon the
shoulder of the Philistines toward the
west;
Together they shall plunder the [T]people
of the East; Lit. *sons*
[R]They shall lay their hand on Edom and
Moab; Dan. 11:41
And the people of Ammon shall obey
them.
15 The LORD [R]will utterly destroy* the
tongue of the Sea of Egypt;
With His mighty wind He will shake His
fist over the River,* Zech. 10:10, 11
And strike it in the seven streams,
And make *men* cross over dryshod.
16 [R]There will be a highway for the remnant
of His people Is. 19:23
Who will be left from Assyria,
[R]As it was for Israel Ex. 14:29
In the day that he came up from the land
of Egypt.

CHAPTER 12

Thanksgiving in the Messiah's Kingdom

AND [R]in that day you will say: Is. 2:11

"O LORD, I will praise You;
Though You were angry with me,
Your anger is turned away, and You
comfort me.
2 Behold, God *is* my salvation,
I will trust and not be afraid;
[R]'For YAH, the LORD, *is* my strength and
song; Ps. 83:18
He also has become my salvation.' "*
3 Therefore with joy you will draw water
From the wells of salvation.

4 And in that day you will say:

[R]"Praise the LORD, call upon His name;
[R]Declare His deeds among the peoples,
Make mention that His [R]name is
exalted. 1 Chr. 16:8 • Ps. 145:4–6 • Ps. 34:3
5 [R]Sing to the LORD, Ex. 15:1
For He has done excellent things;
This *is* known in all the earth.
6 [R]Cry out and shout, O inhabitant of Zion,
For great *is* [R]the Holy One of Israel in
your midst!" Zeph. 3:14, 15 • Ps. 89:18

CHAPTER 13

Prophecies Against Babylon

THE [R]burden against Babylon which Isaiah
the son of Amoz saw. Jer. 50; 51

2 "Lift[R] up a banner [R]on the high
mountain, Is. 18:3 • Jer. 51:25
Raise your voice to them;
[R]Wave your hand, that they may enter the
gates of the nobles. Is. 10:32
3 I have commanded My sanctified ones;
I have also called [R]My mighty ones for
My anger— Joel 3:11
Those who rejoice in My exaltation."

4 The [R]noise of a multitude in the
mountains, Is. 17:12
Like that of many people!
A tumultuous noise of the kingdoms of
nations gathered together!
The LORD of hosts musters
The army for battle.
5 They come from a far country,
From the end of heaven—
The [R]LORD and His [T]weapons of
indignation, Is. 42:13 • Or *instruments*
To destroy the whole [R]land. Is. 24:1

6 Wail, [R]for the day of the LORD *is* at hand!
[R]It will come as destruction from the
Almighty. Zeph. 1:7 • Joel 1:15
7 Therefore all hands will be limp,
Every man's heart will melt,
8 And they will be afraid.
[R]Pangs[T] and sorrows will take hold of
them; Ps. 48:6 • *Sharp pains*
They will be in pain as a woman in
childbirth;
They will be amazed at one another;
Their faces *will be like* flames.

9 Behold, [R]the day of the LORD comes,
Cruel, with both wrath and fierce anger,
To lay the land desolate; Mal. 4:1
And He will destroy its sinners from it.
10 For the stars of heaven and their
constellations
Will not give their light;
The sun will be [R]darkened in its going
forth, Joel 2:31

11:15 So with MT, Vg.; LXX, Syr., Tg. *dry up* • The Euphrates **12:2** Ex. 15:2

And the moon will not cause its light to
shine.
11 "I will [R]punish the world for *its* evil,
And the wicked for their iniquity;
[R]I will halt the arrogance of the proud,
And will lay low the haughtiness of the
[T]terrible. Is. 26:21 • [Is. 2:17] • Or *tyrants*
12 I will make a mortal more rare than fine
gold,
A man more than the golden wedge of
Ophir.
13 Therefore I will shake the heavens,
And the earth will move out of her place,
In the wrath of the LORD of hosts
And in the day of His fierce anger.
14 It shall be as the hunted gazelle,
And as a sheep that no man takes up;
Every man will turn to his own people,
And everyone will flee to his own land.
15 Everyone who is found will be thrust
through,
And everyone who is captured will fall
by the sword.
16 Their children also will be [R]dashed to
pieces before their eyes; Nah. 3:10
Their houses will be plundered
And their wives [R]ravished. Zech. 14:2

17 "Behold,[R] I will stir up the Medes against
them, Dan. 5:28, 31
Who will not [T]regard silver; *esteem*
And *as for* gold, they will not delight in
it.
18 Also *their* bows will dash the young men
to pieces,
And they will have no pity on the fruit of
the womb;
Their eye will not spare children.
19 [R]And Babylon, the glory of kingdoms,
The beauty of the Chaldeans' pride,
Will be as when God overthrew [R]Sodom
and Gomorrah. Is. 14:4 • Gen. 19:24
20 [R]It will never be inhabited, Jer. 50:3
Nor will it be settled from generation to
generation;
Nor will the Arabian pitch tents there,
Nor will the shepherds make their
sheepfolds there.
21 [R]But wild beasts of the desert will lie
there, Is. 34:11–15
And their houses will be full of owls;
Ostriches will dwell there,
And wild goats will caper there.
22 The hyenas will howl in their citadels,
And jackals in their pleasant palaces.
[R]Her time *is* near to come, Jer. 51:33
And her days will not be prolonged."

CHAPTER 14

FOR the LORD [R]will have mercy on Jacob,
and [R]will still choose Israel, and settle
them in their own land. The strangers will be
joined with them, and they will cling to the
house of Jacob. Ps. 102:13 • Zech. 1:17; 2:12
2 Then people will take them [R]and bring
them to their place, and the house of Israel
will possess them for servants and maids in
the land of the LORD; they will take them cap-
tive whose captives they were, and rule over
their oppressors. Is. 49:22; 60:9; 66:20
3 It shall come to pass in the day the LORD
gives you rest from your sorrow, and from
your fear and the hard bondage in which you
were made to serve,
4 that you will take up this proverb against
the king of Babylon, and say:

"How the oppressor has ceased,
The [R]golden* city ceased! Rev. 18:16
5 The LORD has broken [R]the staff of the
wicked, Ps. 125:3
The scepter of the rulers;
6 He who struck the people in wrath with
a continual stroke,
He who ruled the nations in anger,
Is persecuted *and* no one hinders.
7 The whole earth is at rest *and* quiet;
They break forth into singing.
8 [R]Indeed the cypress trees rejoice over
you, Ezek. 31:16
And the cedars of Lebanon,
Saying, 'Since you were cut down,
No woodsman has come up against us.'

9 "Hell[RT] from beneath is excited about
you, Ezek. 32:21 • Or *Sheol*
To meet *you* at your coming;
It stirs up the dead for you,
All the chief ones of the earth;
It has raised up from their thrones
All the kings of the nations.
10 They all shall [R]speak and say to you:
'Have you also become as weak as we?
Have you become like us? Ezek. 32:21
11 Your pomp is brought down to Sheol,
And the sound of your stringed
instruments;
The maggot is spread under you,
And worms cover you.'

12 "How you are fallen from heaven,
O Lucifer,* son of the morning!
How you are cut down to the ground,
You who weakened the nations!
13 For you have said in your heart:
[R]'I will ascend into heaven, Ezek. 28:2
[R]I will exalt my throne above the stars of
God; Dan. 8:10
I will also sit on the [R]mount of the
congregation Ezek. 28:14
On the farthest sides of the north;

14:4 Or *insolent* **14:12** Lit. *Day Star*

14 I will ascend above the heights of the clouds,
[R]I will be like the Most High.' 2 Thess. 2:4
15 Yet you shall be brought down to Sheol,
To the lowest depths of the Pit.

16 "Those who see you will gaze at you,
And consider you, *saying*:
'*Is* this the man who made the earth tremble,
Who shook kingdoms,
17 Who made the world as a wilderness
And destroyed its cities,
Who [T]did not open the house of his prisoners?' Would not release

18 "All the kings of the nations,
All of them, sleep in glory,
Everyone in his own house;
19 But you are cast out of your grave
Like an [T]abominable branch, *despised*
Like the garment of those who are slain,
[T]Thrust through with a sword, *Pierced*
Who go down to the stones of the pit,
Like a corpse trodden underfoot.
20 You will not be joined with them in burial,
Because you have destroyed your land
And slain your people.
[R]The brood of evildoers shall never be named. Ps. 21:10; 109:13
21 Prepare slaughter for his children
Because of the iniquity of their fathers,
Lest they rise up and possess the land,
And fill the face of the world with cities."

22 "For I will rise up against them," says the LORD of hosts,
"And cut off from Babylon [R]the name and [R]remnant, Prov. 10:7 • 1 Kin. 14:10
[R]And offspring and posterity," says the LORD. Job 18:19
23 "I will also make it a possession for the [R]porcupine, Zeph. 2:14
And marshes of muddy water;
I will sweep it with the broom of destruction," says the LORD of hosts.

Prophecies Against Assyria

24 The LORD of hosts has sworn, saying,
"Surely, as I have thought, so it shall come to pass,
And as I have purposed, *so* it shall [R]stand: Is. 43:13
25 That I will break the [R]Assyrian in My land, Mic. 5:5, 6
And on My mountains tread him underfoot.
Then [R]his yoke shall be removed from them, Is. 10:27
And his burden removed from their shoulders.
26 This *is* the [R]purpose that is purposed against the whole earth, Is. 23:9
And this *is* the hand that is stretched out over all the nations.
27 For the LORD of hosts has [R]purposed,
And who will annul *it*? Dan. 4:31, 35
His hand *is* stretched out,
And who will turn it back?"

Prophecies Against Philistia

28 This is the burden which came in the year
that [R]King Ahaz died. 2 Kin. 16:20

29 "Do not rejoice, all you of Philistia,
[R]Because the rod that struck you is broken; 2 Chr. 26:6
For out of the serpent's roots will come forth a viper,
[R]And its offspring *will be* a fiery flying serpent. 2 Kin. 18:8
30 The firstborn of the poor will feed,
And the needy will lie down in safety;
I will kill your roots with famine,
And it will slay your remnant.
31 Wail, O gate! Cry, O city!
All you of Philistia *are* dissolved;
For smoke will come from the north,
And no one *will be* alone in his [T]appointed times." Or *ranks*

32 What will they answer the messengers of the nation?
That [R]the LORD has founded Zion,

14:12–15 Satan: Fall of Satan—Biblical information about Satan is brief because he is incidental to the revelation of God and His redemption of sinful humans that occupies the focus of Scripture. The serpent appears in the first pages (Page 6—Gen. 3:1), but his identity as Satan is not explicit until the end (Page 1320—Rev. 12:9). In the OT Satan is named only in three books (Page 420—1 Chr. 21:1; Page 512—Job 1:6–12; 2:1–7; Page 956—Zech. 3:1, 2). The name "Satan" means "adversary," and the OT occurrences vividly show him opposing God's purposes in the lives of His people. In the NT the descriptive noun "the devil" means a "slanderer" or "accuser."

Apparently Satan was created one of the mightiest angels named Lucifer, meaning "light bearer" (Page 695—Is. 14:12). At some indeterminate point before the creation of the heavens and the earth, Lucifer coveted the glory and power of God and tried to usurp divine authority (vv. 13, 14). A subsequent war in heaven led to Lucifer's expulsion from heaven along with the other angels who rebelled against God by joining Lucifer (Page 1320—Rev. 12:4, 7–9). Unable to defy God to His face in heaven, Satan attempts to disrupt the purposes of God on earth among God's imagebearers, human beings.

Now turn to Page 1092—John 8:44: Satan: Role in Fall of Humans.

And [R]the poor of His people shall take
refuge in it. Ps. 87:1, 5 • Zech. 11:11

CHAPTER 15

Prophecies Against Moab

THE [R]burden against Moab. 2 Kin. 3:4
Because in the night [R]Ar of [R]Moab is laid
waste Deut. 2:9 • Amos 2:1–3
And destroyed,
Because in the night Kir of Moab is laid
waste
And destroyed,
2 He has gone up to the temple* and Dibon,
To the high places to weep.
Moab will wail over Nebo and over
Medeba;
[R]On all their heads *will be* baldness,
And every beard cut off. Lev. 21:5
3 In their streets they will clothe
themselves with sackcloth;
On the tops of their houses
And in their streets
Everyone will wail, weeping bitterly.
4 Heshbon and Elealeh will cry out,
Their voice shall be heard as far as
[R]Jahaz; Jer. 48:34
Therefore the armed soldiers* of Moab
will cry out;
His life will be burdensome to him.

5 "My[R] heart will cry out for Moab; Jer. 48:31
His fugitives *shall flee* to Zoar,
Like a three-year-old heifer.*
For [R]by the Ascent of Luhith Jer. 48:5
They will go up with weeping;
For in the way of Horonaim
They will raise up a cry of destruction,
6 For the waters [R]of Nimrim will be
desolate, Num. 32:36
For the green grass has withered away;
The grass fails, there is nothing green.
7 Therefore the abundance they have
gained,
And what they have laid up,
They will carry away to the Brook of the
Willows.
8 For the cry has gone all around the
borders of Moab,
Its wailing to Eglaim
And its wailing to Beer Elim.
9 For the waters of Dimon* will be full of
blood;
Because I will bring more upon Dimon,*
[R]Lions upon him who escapes from
Moab, 2 Kin. 17:25
And on the remnant of the land."

CHAPTER 16

SEND the lamb to the ruler of the land,
From [T]Sela to the wilderness, Lit. *Rock*
To the mount of the daughter of Zion.
2 For it shall be as a [R]wandering bird
thrown out of the nest; Prov. 27:8
So shall be the daughters of Moab at the
fords of the [R]Arnon. Num. 21:13

3 "Take counsel, execute judgment;
Make your shadow like the night in the
middle of the day;
Hide the outcasts,
Do not betray him who escapes.
4 Let My outcasts dwell with you, O Moab;
Be a shelter to them from the face of the
[T]spoiler. *devastator*
For the extortioner is at an end,
Devastation ceases,
The oppressors are consumed out of the
land.
5 In mercy [R]the throne will be established;
And One will sit on it in truth, in the
tabernacle of David, [Dan. 7:14]
[R]Judging and seeking justice and
hastening righteousness." Ps. 72:2

6 We have heard of the [R]pride of Moab—
He is very proud— Jer. 48:29
Of his haughtiness and his pride and his
wrath;
[R]*But* his lies *shall* not *be* so. Is. 28:15
7 Therefore Moab shall [R]wail for Moab;
Everyone shall wail. Jer. 48:20
For the foundations [R]of Kir Hareseth you
shall mourn; 2 Kin. 3:25
Surely *they are* stricken.

8 For the fields of Heshbon languish,
And [R]the vine of Sibmah; Is. 16:9
The lords of the nations have broken
down its choice plants,
Which have reached to Jazer
And wandered through the wilderness.
Her branches are stretched out,
They are gone over the [R]sea. Jer. 48:32
9 Therefore I will bewail the vine of
Sibmah,
With the weeping of Jazer;
I will drench you with my tears,
[R]O Heshbon and Elealeh; Is. 15:4
For [T]battle cries have fallen
Over your summer fruits and your
harvest. Or *shouting has*

10 [R]Gladness is taken away, Is. 24:8
And joy from the plentiful field;
In the vineyards there will be no singing,
Nor will there be shouting;
No treaders will tread out wine in the
presses;

15:2 Heb. *bayith*, lit. *house* **15:4** So with MT, Tg., Vg.; LXX, Syr. *loins* **15:5** Or *The Third Eglath*, an unknown city, Jer. 48:34 **15:9** So with MT, Tg.; DSS, Vg. *Dibon*; LXX *Rimon* • See preceding note

I have made their shouting cease.
11 Therefore [R]my [T]heart shall resound like
a harp for Moab, Jer. 48:36 • Lit. *belly*
And my inner being for Kir Heres.

12 And it shall come to pass,
When it is seen that Moab is weary on
[R]the high place, Is. 15:2
That he will come to his sanctuary to
pray;
But he will not prevail.

13 This *is* the word which the LORD has spo-
ken concerning Moab since that time.
14 But now the LORD has spoken, saying,
"Within three years, [R]as the years of a hired
man, the glory of Moab will be despised with
all that great multitude, and the remnant *will
be* very small *and* feeble." Is. 21:16

CHAPTER 17

Prophecies Against Damascus and Samaria

THE burden against Damascus.
"Behold, Damascus will cease from *being*
a city,
And it will be a ruinous heap.
2 The cities of [R]Aroer *are* forsaken;*
They will be for flocks Num. 32:34
Which lie down, and [R]no one will make
them afraid. Jer. 7:33
3 [R]The fortress also will cease from
Ephraim, Is. 7:16; 8:4
The kingdom from Damascus,
And the remnant of Syria;
They will be as the glory of the children
of Israel,"
Says the LORD of hosts.

4 "In that day it shall come to pass
That the glory of Jacob will wane,
And the fatness of his flesh grow lean.
5 [R]It shall be as when the harvester gathers
the grain, Jer. 51:33
And reaps the heads with his arm;
It shall be as he who gathers heads of
grain
In the Valley of Rephaim.
6 [R]Yet gleaning grapes will be left in it,
Like the shaking of an olive tree,
Two *or* three olives at the top of the
uppermost bough, Is. 24:13
Four *or* five in its most fruitful
branches,"
Says the LORD God of Israel.

7 In that day a man will [R]look to his
Maker, Mic. 7:7
And his eyes will have respect for the
Holy One of Israel.
8 He will not look to the altars,
The work of his hands;
He will not respect what his [R]fingers
have made, Is. 2:8; 31:7
Nor the wooden images* nor the incense
altars.

9 In that day his strong cities will be as a
forsaken bough*
And an uppermost branch,*
Which they left because of the children
of Israel;
And there will be desolation.

10 Because you have forgotten [R]the God of
your salvation, Ps. 68:19
And have not been mindful of the Rock
of your [T]stronghold, *refuge*
Therefore you will plant pleasant plants
And set out foreign seedlings;
11 In the day you will make your plant to
grow,
And in the morning you will make your
seed to flourish;
But the harvest *will be* a heap of ruins
In the day of grief and desperate
sorrow.

12 Woe to the multitude of many people
Who make a noise [R]like the roar of the
seas, Jer. 6:23
And to the rushing of nations
That make a rushing like the rushing of
mighty waters!
13 The nations will rush like the rushing of
many waters;
But *God* will [R]rebuke them and they will
flee far away, Ps. 9:5
And [R]be chased like the chaff of the
mountains before the wind, Hos. 13:3
Like a rolling thing before the
whirlwind.
14 Then behold, at eventide, trouble!
And before the morning, he *is* no more.
This *is* the portion of those who plunder
us,
And the lot of those who rob us.

CHAPTER 18

Prophecies Against Ethiopia

WOE [R]to the land shadowed with
buzzing wings, Zeph. 2:12; 3:10
Which *is* beyond the rivers of Ethiopia,
2 Which sends ambassadors by sea,
Even in vessels of reed on the waters,
saying,
"Go, swift messengers, to a nation tall and
smooth *of skin*,

17:2 So with MT, Vg.; LXX *It shall be forsaken forever;* Tg. *Its cities shall be forsaken and desolate*
17:8 Heb. *Asherim*, Canaanite deities **17:9** LXX *Hivites;* Tg. *laid waste;* Vg. *as the plows* • LXX *Amorites;* Tg. *in ruins;* Vg. *corn*

To a people terrible from their beginning
onward,
A nation powerful and treading down,
Whose land the rivers divide."

3 All inhabitants of the world and dwellers
on the earth:
[R]When he lifts up a banner on the
mountains, you see *it;* Is. 5:26
And when he blows a trumpet, you hear
it.

4 For so the LORD said to me,
"I will take My rest,
And I will [T]look from My dwelling place
Like clear heat in sunshine, *watch*
Like a cloud of dew in the heat of harvest."

5 For before the harvest, when the bud is
perfect
And the sour grape is ripening in the
flower,
He will both cut off the sprigs with
pruning hooks
And take away *and* cut down the
branches.

6 They will be left together for the
mountain birds of prey
And for the beasts of the earth;
The birds of prey will summer on them,
And all the beasts of the earth will
winter on them.

7 In that time [R]a present will be brought to
the LORD of hosts Zeph. 3:10
From* a people tall and smooth *of skin,*
And from a people terrible from their
beginning onward,
A nation powerful and treading down,
Whose land the rivers divide—
To the place of the name of the LORD of
hosts,
To Mount Zion.

CHAPTER 19

Prophecies Against Egypt

THE [R]burden against Egypt. Joel 3:19

Behold, the LORD [R]rides on a swift cloud,
And will come into Egypt; Ps. 18:10; 104:3
[R]The idols of Egypt will [T]totter at His
presence, Jer. 43:12 • Lit. *shake*
And the heart of Egypt will melt in its
midst.

2 "I will [R]set Egyptians against Egyptians;
Everyone will fight against his brother,
And everyone against his neighbor,
City against city, kingdom against
kingdom. Judg. 7:22

3 The spirit of Egypt will fail in its midst;
I will destroy their counsel,
And they will [R]consult the idols and the
charmers, Is. 8:19; 47:12
The mediums and the sorcerers.

4 And the Egyptians I will give
Into the hand of a cruel master,
And a fierce king will rule over them,"
Says the Lord, the LORD of hosts.

5 [R]The waters will fail from the sea,
And the river will be wasted and dried
up. Jer. 51:36

6 The rivers will turn foul;
The brooks [R]of defense will be emptied
and dried up; 2 Kin. 19:24
The reeds and rushes will wither.

7 The papyrus reeds by the River, by the
mouth of the River,
And everything sown by the River,*
Will wither, be driven away, and be no
more.

8 The fishermen also will mourn;
All those will lament who cast hooks
into the River,
And they will languish who spread nets
on the waters.

9 Moreover those who work in [R]fine flax
And those who weave fine fabric will be
ashamed; Prov. 7:16

10 And its foundations will be broken.
All who make wages *will be* troubled of
soul.

11 Surely the princes of [R]Zoan *are* fools;
Pharaoh's wise counselors give foolish
counsel. Num. 13:22
[R]How do you say to Pharaoh, "I *am* the
son of the wise, 1 Kin. 4:29, 30
The son of ancient kings?"

12 [R]Where *are* they? 1 Cor. 1:20
Where are your wise men?
Let them tell you now,
And let them know what the LORD of
hosts has purposed against Egypt.

13 The princes of Zoan have become fools;
[R]The princes of Noph* are deceived;
They have also deluded Egypt, Jer. 2:16
Those who are the [T]mainstay of its
tribes. *cornerstone*

14 The LORD has mingled [R]a perverse spirit
in her midst; Is. 29:10
And they have caused Egypt to err in all
her work,
As a drunken man staggers in his vomit.

15 Neither will there be *any* work for Egypt,
Which the head or tail,
Palm branch or bulrush, may do.*

16 In that day Egypt will [R]be like women,
and will be afraid and fear because of the
waving of the hand of the LORD of hosts,
[R]which He waves over it. Nah. 3:13 • Is. 11:15

18:7 So with DSS, LXX, Vg.; MT omits *From;* Tg. *To*
19:7 The Nile **19:13** Ancient Memphis **19:15** Cf. Is.
9:14–16

17 And the land of Judah will be a terror to Egypt; everyone who makes mention of it will be afraid in himself, because of the counsel of the LORD of hosts which He has [R]determined against it. Dan. 4:35

18 In that day five cities in the land of Egypt will [R]speak the language of Canaan and swear by the LORD of hosts; one will be called the City of Destruction.* Zeph. 3:9

19 In that day [R]there will be an altar to the LORD in the midst of the land of Egypt, and a pillar to the LORD at its border. Ex. 24:4

20 And [R]it will be for a sign and for a witness to the LORD of hosts in the land of Egypt; for they will cry to the LORD because of the oppressors, and He will send them a [R]Savior and a Mighty One, and He will deliver them. Josh. 4:20; 22:27 • Is. 43:11

21 Then the LORD will be known to Egypt, and the Egyptians will [R]know the LORD in that day, and [R]will make sacrifice and offering; yes, they will make a vow to the LORD and perform *it*. [Is. 2:3, 4; 11:9] • Mal. 1:11

22 And the LORD will strike Egypt, He will strike and [R]heal *it;* they will return to the LORD, and He will be entreated by them and heal them. Deut. 32:39

23 In that day [R]there will be a highway from Egypt to Assyria, and the Assyrian will come into Egypt and the Egyptian into Assyria, and the Egyptians will [R]serve with the Assyrians. Is. 11:16; 35:8; 49:11; 62:10 • Is. 27:13

24 In that day Israel will be one of three with Egypt and Assyria—a blessing in the midst of the land,

25 whom the LORD of hosts shall bless, saying, "Blessed *is* Egypt My people, and Assyria [R]the work of My hands, and Israel My inheritance." Is. 29:23

CHAPTER 20

IN the year that [R]Tartan* came to Ashdod, when Sargon the king of Assyria sent him, and he fought against Ashdod and took it, 2 Kin. 18:17

2 at the same time the LORD spoke by Isaiah the son of Amoz, saying, "Go, and remove [R]the sackcloth from your body, and take your sandals off your feet." And he did so, walking naked and barefoot. Zech. 13:4

3 Then the LORD said, "Just as My servant Isaiah has walked naked and barefoot three years [R]*for* a sign and a wonder against Egypt and Ethiopia, Is. 8:18

4 "so shall the [R]king of Assyria lead away the Egyptians as prisoners and the Ethiopians as captives, young and old, naked and barefoot, [R]with their buttocks uncovered, to the shame of Egypt. Is. 19:4 • Jer. 13:22

5 [R]"Then they shall be afraid and ashamed of Ethiopia their expectation and Egypt their glory. 2 Kin. 18:21

6 "And the inhabitant of this territory will say in that day, 'Surely such *is* our expectation, wherever we flee for [R]help to be delivered from the king of Assyria; and how shall we escape?' " Is. 30:5, 7

CHAPTER 21

Prophecies Against Babylon

THE [T]burden against the Wilderness of the Sea. *oracle, prophecy*

As [R]whirlwinds in the South pass
through, Zech. 9:14
So it comes from the desert, from a
terrible land.
2 A distressing vision is declared to me;
[R]The treacherous dealer deals
treacherously, Is. 33:1
And the plunderer plunders.
[R]Go up, O Elam! Jer. 49:34
Besiege, O Media!
All its sighing I have made to cease.

3 Therefore my loins are filled with pain;
[R]Pangs have taken hold of me, like the
pangs of a woman in labor. Is. 13:8
I was distressed when *I* heard *it;*
I was dismayed when *I* saw *it*.
4 My heart wavered, fearfulness frightened
me;
[R]The night for which I longed He turned
into fear for me. Deut. 28:67
5 [R]Prepare the table, Dan. 5:5
Set a watchman in the tower,
Eat and drink.
Arise, you princes,
Anoint the shield!

6 For thus has the Lord said to me:

"Go, set a watchman,
Let him declare what he sees."
7 And he saw a chariot *with* a pair of
horsemen,
A chariot of donkeys, *and* a chariot of
camels,
And he listened earnestly with great
care.
8 Then he cried, "A lion,* my Lord!
I stand continually on the [R]watchtower
in the daytime; Hab. 2:1
I have sat at my post every night.
9 And look, here comes a chariot of men
with a pair of horsemen!"
Then he answered and said,
[R]"Babylon is fallen, is fallen! Jer. 51:8
And [R]all the carved images of her gods
He has broken to the ground." Is. 46:1

19:18 Some Heb. mss., Arab., DSS, Tg., Vg. *Sun;* LXX *Asedek*, lit. *Righteousness* **20:1** Or *the Commander in Chief* **21:8** DSS *Then the observer cried*

10[R] Oh, my threshing and the grain of my
floor! Jer. 51:33
That which I have heard from the LORD
of hosts,
The God of Israel,
I have declared to you.

Prophecies Against Dumah (Edom)

11 The burden against Dumah.

He calls to me out of [R]Seir, Gen. 32:3
"Watchman, what of the night?
Watchman, what of the night?"
12 The watchman said,
"The morning comes, and also the night.
If you will inquire, inquire;
Return! Come back!"

Prophecies Against Arabia

13 The burden against Arabia.

In the forest in Arabia you will lodge,
O you traveling companies [R]of
Dedanites. 1 Chr. 1:9, 32
14 O inhabitants of the land of Tema,
Bring water to him who is thirsty;
With their bread they met him who fled.
15 For they fled from the swords, from the
drawn sword,
From the bent bow, and from the distress
of war.

16 For thus the LORD has said to me: "Within
a year, according to the year of a hired man,
all the glory of Kedar will fail;
17 "and the remainder of the number of
archers, the mighty men of the people of
Kedar, will be diminished; for the LORD God of
Israel has spoken *it*."

CHAPTER 22

Prophecies Against Jerusalem

THE burden against the Valley of Vision.

What ails you now, that you have all
gone up to the housetops,
2 You who are full of noise,
A [T]tumultuous city, [R]a joyous city?
Your slain *men are* not slain with the
sword, *boisterous* • Is. 32:13
Nor dead in battle.
3 All your rulers have fled together;
They are captured by the archers.
All who are found in you are bound
together;
They have fled from afar.
4 Therefore I said, "Look away from me,
[R]I will weep bitterly; Jer. 4:19
Do not labor to comfort me
Because of the plundering of the
daughter of my people."

5[R] For *it is* a day of trouble and treading
down and perplexity Is. 37:3
[R]By the Lord GOD of hosts Lam. 1:5; 2:2
In the Valley of Vision—
Breaking down the walls
And of crying to the mountain.
6[R] Elam bore the quiver Jer. 49:35
With chariots of men *and* horsemen,
And [R]Kir uncovered the shield. Is. 15:1
7 It shall come to pass *that* your choicest
valleys
Shall be full of chariots,
And the horsemen shall set themselves
in array at the gate.

8 He removed the protection of Judah.
You looked in that day to the armor [R]of
the House of the Forest; 1 Kin. 7:2
9[R] You also saw the damage to the city of
David, 2 Kin. 20:20
That it was great;
And you gathered together the waters of
the lower pool.
10 You numbered the houses of
Jerusalem,
And the houses you broke down
To fortify the wall.
11[R] You also made a reservoir between the
two walls Neh. 3:16
For the water of the old pool.
But you did not look to its Maker,
Nor did you have respect for Him who
fashioned it long ago.

12 And in that day the Lord GOD of hosts
[R]Called for weeping and for mourning,
[R]For baldness and for girding with
sackcloth. Joel 1:13; 2:17 • Mic. 1:16
13 But instead, joy and gladness,
Slaying oxen and killing sheep,
Eating meat and [R]drinking wine:
[R]"Let us eat and drink, for tomorrow we
die!" Luke 17:26–29 • 1 Cor. 15:32

14[R] Then it was revealed in my hearing by
the LORD of hosts, Is. 5:9
"Surely for this iniquity there [R]will be no
atonement for you, Ezek. 24:13
Even to your death," says the Lord GOD
of hosts.

15 Thus says the Lord GOD of hosts:

"Go, proceed to this steward,
To [R]Shebna, who *is* over the house, *and*
say: Is. 36:3
16 'What have you here, and whom have
you here,
That you have hewn a sepulcher here,
As he [R]who hews himself a sepulcher on
high, Matt. 27:60
Who carves a tomb for himself in a
rock?

17 Indeed, the LORD will throw you away
violently,
O mighty man,
[R]And will surely seize you. Esth. 7:8
18 He will surely turn violently and toss
you like a ball
Into a large country;
There you shall die, and there [R]your
glorious chariots Is. 2:7
Shall be the shame of your master's
house.
19 So I will drive you out of your office,
And from your position he will pull you
down.*

20 'Then it shall be in that day,
That I will call My servant [R]Eliakim the
son of Hilkiah; 2 Kin. 18:18
21 I will clothe him with your robe
And strengthen him with your belt;
I will commit your responsibility into his
hand.
He shall be a father to the inhabitants of
Jerusalem
And to the house of Judah.
22 The key of the house of David
I will lay on his [R]shoulder; Is. 9:6
So he shall [R]open, and no one shall
shut; Job 12:14; Rev. 3:7☆
And he shall shut, and no one shall
open.
23 I will fasten him *as* [R]a peg in a secure
place, Ezra 9:8
And he will become a glorious throne to
his father's house.

24 'They will hang on him all the glory of his
father's house, the offspring and the posterity,
all vessels of small quantity, from the cups to
all the pitchers.
25 'In that day,' says the LORD of hosts, 'the
peg that is fastened in the secure place will be
removed and be cut down and fall, and the
burden that *was* on it will be cut off; for the
LORD has spoken.' "

CHAPTER 23

Prophecies Against Tyre

THE [R]burden against Tyre. Zech. 9:2, 4

Wail, you ships of Tarshish!
For it is laid waste,
So that there is no house, no harbor;
From the land of Cyprus* it is revealed
to them.
2 Be still, you inhabitants of the coastland,
You merchants of Sidon,
Whom those who cross the sea have
filled.*
3 And on great waters the grain of Shihor,
The harvest of the River,* *is* her revenue;
And [R]she is a marketplace for the
nations. Ezek. 27:3–23
4 Be ashamed, O Sidon;
For the sea has spoken,
The strength of the sea, saying,
"I do not labor, nor bring forth children;
Neither do I rear young men,
Nor bring up virgins."
5 [R]When the report *reaches* Egypt, Is. 19:16
They also will be in agony at the report
of Tyre.

6 Cross over to Tarshish;
Wail, you inhabitants of the coastland!
7 *Is* this your [R]joyous *city,* Is. 22:2; 32:13
Whose antiquity *is* from ancient days,
Whose feet carried her far off to dwell?
8 Who has taken this counsel against Tyre,
[R]the crowning *city,* Ezek. 28:2, 12
Whose merchants *are* princes,
Whose traders *are* the honorable of the
earth?
9 The LORD of hosts has [R]purposed it,
To [T]bring to dishonor the [R]pride of all
glory, Is. 14:26 • *pollute* • Dan. 4:37
To bring into contempt all the honorable
of the earth.

10 Overflow through your land like the
River,*
O daughter of Tarshish;
There is no more strength.
11 He stretched out His hand over the sea,
He shook the kingdoms;
The LORD has given a commandment
[R]against Canaan Zech. 9:2–4
To destroy its strongholds.
12 And He said, "You will rejoice no more,
O you oppressed virgin daughter of
Sidon.
Arise, [R]cross over to Cyprus; Rev. 18:22
There also you will have no rest."

13 Behold, the land of the [R]Chaldeans,
This people *which* was not; Is. 47:1
Assyria founded it for [R]wild beasts of the
desert. Ps. 72:9
They set up its towers,
They raised up its palaces,
And brought it to ruin.

14 Wail, you ships of Tarshish!
For your strength is laid waste.

15 Now it shall come to pass in that day that
Tyre will be forgotten seventy years, accord-

22:19 LXX omits *he will pull you down;* Syr., Tg., Vg. *I will pull you down* **23:1** Heb. *Kittim,* western lands, especially Cyprus **23:2** So with MT, Vg.; LXX, Tg. *Passing over the water;* DSS *Your messengers passing over the sea* **23:3** The Nile **23:10** The Nile

ing to the days of one king. At the end of seventy years it will happen to Tyre as *in* the song of the harlot:

16 "Take a harp, go about the city,
You forgotten harlot;
Make sweet melody, sing many songs,
That you may be remembered."

17 And it shall be, at the end of seventy years, that the LORD will deal with Tyre. She will return to her hire, and [R]commit fornication with all the kingdoms of the world on the face of the earth. Rev. 17:2
18 Her gain and her pay [R]will be set apart for the LORD; it will not be treasured nor laid up, for her gain will be for those who dwell before the LORD, to eat sufficiently, and for [T]fine clothing. Zech. 14:20, 21 • *choice*

CHAPTER 24

Judgments of the Tribulation

BEHOLD, the LORD makes the earth
empty and makes it waste,
Distorts its surface
And scatters abroad its inhabitants.
2 And it shall be:
As with the people, so with the [R]priest;
As with the servant, so with his master;
As with the maid, so with her mistress;
[R]As with the buyer, so with the seller;
As with the lender, so with the
borrower; Hos. 4:9 • Ezek. 7:12, 13
As with the creditor, so with the debtor.
3 The land shall be entirely emptied and
utterly plundered,
For the LORD has spoken this word.

4 The earth mourns *and* fades away,
The world languishes *and* fades away;
The [R]haughty[T] people of the earth
languish. Is. 25:11 • *proud*
5 [R]The earth is also defiled under its
inhabitants, Num. 35:33
Because they have [R]transgressed the
laws, Is. 59:12
Changed the ordinance,
Broken the everlasting covenant.
6 Therefore [R]the curse has devoured the
earth, Mal. 4:6
And those who dwell in it are [T]desolate.
Therefore the inhabitants of the earth
are [R]burned, Or *held guilty* • Is. 9:19
And few men *are* left.

7 [R]The new wine fails, the vine languishes,
All the merry-hearted sigh. Joel 1:10, 12
8 The mirth [R]of the tambourine ceases,
The noise of the jubilant ends,
The joy of the harp ceases. Ezek. 26:13
9 They shall not drink wine with a song;
Strong drink is bitter to those who drink
it.
10 The city of confusion is broken down;
Every house is shut up, so that none may
go in.
11 *There is* a cry for wine in the streets,
All joy is darkened,
The mirth of the land is gone.
12 In the city desolation is left,
And the gate is stricken with
destruction.
13 When it shall be thus in the midst of the
land among the people,
[R]*It shall be* like the shaking of an olive
tree, [Is. 17:5, 6; 27:12]
Like the gleaning of grapes when the
vintage is done.

14 They shall lift up their voice, they shall
sing;
For the majesty of the LORD
They shall cry aloud from the sea.
15 Therefore [R]glorify the LORD in the
dawning light, Is. 25:3
[R]The name of the LORD God of Israel in
the coastlands of the sea. Mal. 1:11
16 From the ends of the earth we have
heard songs:
"Glory to the righteous!"
But I said, "I am ruined, ruined!
Woe to me!
[R]The treacherous dealers have dealt
treacherously, Jer. 3:20; 5:11
Indeed, the treacherous dealers have
dealt very treacherously."

17 Fear and the pit and the snare
Are upon you, O inhabitant of the earth.
18 And it shall be
That he who flees from the noise of the
fear
Shall fall into the pit,
And he who comes up from the midst of
the pit
Shall be [T]caught in the snare;
For [R]the windows from on high are
open, Lit. *taken* • Gen. 7:11
And [R]the foundations of the earth are
shaken. Ps. 18:7; 46:2

19 [R]The earth is violently broken, Jer. 4:23
The earth is split open,
The earth is shaken exceedingly.
20 The earth shall [R]reel[T] to and fro like a
drunkard, Is. 19:14; 24:1; 28:7 • *stagger*
And shall totter like a hut;
Its transgression shall be heavy upon it,
And it will fall, and not rise again.

21 It shall come to pass in that day
That the LORD will punish on high the
host of exalted ones,
And on the earth the kings of the earth.

22 They will be gathered together,
As prisoners are gathered in the pit,
And will be shut up in the prison;
After many days they will be punished.
23 Then the [R]moon will be disgraced
And the sun ashamed; Is. 13:10; 60:19
For the LORD of hosts will reign
On Mount Zion and in Jerusalem
And before His elders, gloriously.

CHAPTER 25

Israel's Praise for Kingdom Blessings

O LORD, You *are* my God.
[R]I will exalt You, Ex. 15:2
I will praise Your name,
[R]For You have done wonderful *things;*
[R]*Your* counsels of old *are* faithfulness *and* truth. Ps. 98:1 • Num. 23:19
2 For You have made [R]a city a ruin,
A fortified city a ruin, Jer. 51:37
A palace of foreigners to be a city no more;
It will never be rebuilt.
3 Therefore the strong people will [R]glorify You; Is. 24:15
The city of the [T]terrible nations will fear You. *terrifying*
4 For You have been a strength to the poor,
A strength to the needy in his distress,
[R]A refuge from the storm, Is. 4:6
A shade from the heat;
For the blast of the terrible ones *is* as a storm *against* the wall.
5 You will reduce the noise of aliens,
As heat in a dry place;
As heat in the shadow of a cloud,
The song of the terrible ones will be [T]diminished. *humbled*

6 And in [R]this mountain [Is. 2:2–4; 56:7]
[R]The LORD of hosts will make for [R]all people Prov. 9:2 • [Dan. 7:14]
A feast of [T]choice pieces, Lit. *fat things*
A feast of wines on the lees,
Of fat things full of marrow,
Of well-refined wines on the lees.
7 And He will destroy on this mountain
The surface of the covering cast over all people,
And [R]the veil that is spread over all nations. [Eph. 4:18]
8 He will swallow up death forever,
And the Lord GOD will [R]wipe away tears from all faces; Rev. 7:17; 21:4
The rebuke of His people
He will take away from all the earth;
For the LORD has spoken.

9 And it will be said in that day:
"Behold, this *is* our God;
[R]We have waited for Him, and He will save us. Gen. 49:18
This *is* the LORD;
We have waited for Him;
[R]We will be glad and rejoice in His salvation." Ps. 20:5
10 For on this mountain the hand of the LORD will rest,
And [R]Moab shall be trampled down under Him, Amos 2:1–3
As straw is trampled down for the refuse heap.
11 And He will spread out His hands in their midst
As a swimmer reaches out to swim,
And He will bring down their [R]pride
Together with the trickery of their hands. Is. 24:4; 26:5
12 The [R]fortress of the high fort of your walls Is. 26:5
He will bring down, lay low,
And bring to the ground, down to the dust.

CHAPTER 26

Israel's Kingdom Song

IN [R]that day this song will be sung in the land of Judah: Is. 2:11; 12:1

"We have a strong city;
[R]*God* will appoint salvation *for* walls and bulwarks. Is. 60:18
2 [R]Open the gates, Ps. 118:19, 20
That the righteous nation which keeps the truth may enter in.
3 You will keep *him* in perfect [R]peace,
Whose mind *is* stayed *on You,*
Because he trusts in You. Is. 57:19
4 Trust in the LORD forever,
[R]For in YAH, the LORD, *is* everlasting strength.* Is. 12:2; 45:17
5 For He brings [T]down those who dwell on high, *low*
[R]The lofty city; Is. 25:11, 12
He lays it low,
He lays it low to the ground,
He brings it down to the dust.
6 The foot shall [T]tread it down— *trample*
The feet of the poor
And the steps of the needy."

7 The way of the just *is* uprightness;
[R]O Most Upright, Ps. 37:23
You weigh the path of the just.
8 Yes, in the way of Your judgments,
O LORD, we have waited for You;
The desire of *our* soul *is* for Your name
And for the remembrance of You.
9 [R]With my soul I have desired You in the night, Ps. 63:6
Yes, by my spirit within me I will seek You early;

26:4 Or *Rock of Ages*

For when Your judgments *are* in the
earth,
The inhabitants of the world will learn
righteousness.

10 Let grace be shown to the wicked,
Yet he will not learn righteousness;
In [R]the land of uprightness he will deal
unjustly, [Rom. 2:4] • Ps. 143:10
And will not behold the majesty of the
LORD.
11 LORD, *when* Your hand is lifted up, [R]they
will not see. Is. 5:12
But they will see and be ashamed
For [T]*their* envy of people;
Yes, the fire of Your enemies shall devour
them. Or *Your zeal for the people*

12 LORD, You will establish peace for us,
For You have also done all our works [T]in
us. Or *for us*
13 O LORD our God, [R]masters besides You
Have had dominion over us; 2 Chr. 12:8
But by You only we make mention of
Your name.
14 *They are* dead, they will not live;
They are deceased, they will not rise.
Therefore You have punished and
destroyed them,
And made all their memory to perish.
15 You have increased the nation, O LORD,
You have [R]increased the nation; Is. 9:3
You are glorified;
You have expanded all the [T]borders of
the land. Or *ends*
16 LORD, [R]in trouble they have visited You,
They poured out a prayer *when* Your
chastening *was* upon them. Hos. 5:15
17 As [R]a woman with child [John 16:21]
Is in pain and cries out in her [T]pangs,
When she draws near the time of her
delivery, *sharp pains*
So have we been in Your sight, O LORD.
18 We have been with child, we have been
in pain;
We have, as it were, [T]brought forth wind;
We have not accomplished any
deliverance in the earth,
Nor have [R]the inhabitants of the world
fallen. *given birth to* • Ps. 17:14

19 [R]Your dead shall live; [Ezek. 37:1–14]☆
Together with my dead body* they shall
arise.
Awake and sing, you who dwell in dust;
For your dew *is like* the dew of herbs,
And the earth shall cast out the dead.

20 Come, my people, [R]enter your chambers,
And shut your doors behind you;
Hide yourself, as it were, [R]for a little
moment, Ex. 12:22, 23 • [Ps. 30:5]
Until the indignation is past.
21 For behold, the LORD [R]comes out of His
place Mic. 1:3
To punish the inhabitants of the earth for
their iniquity;
The earth will also disclose her blood,
And will no more cover her slain.

CHAPTER 27

Israel Blossoms in the Kingdom

IN that day the LORD with His severe sword,
great and strong,
Will punish Leviathan the fleeing
serpent,
[R]Leviathan that twisted serpent;
And He will slay [R]the reptile that *is* in
the sea. Ps. 74:13, 14 • Is. 51:9

2 In that day [R]sing to her, Is. 5:1
[R]"A vineyard of red wine!* Is. 5:7
3 [R]I, the LORD, keep it, Is. 31:5
I water it every moment;
Lest any hurt it,
I keep it night and day.
4 Fury *is* not in Me.
Who would set [R]briers *and* thorns
Against Me in battle? 2 Sam. 23:6
I would go through them,
I would burn them together.
5 Or let him take hold of My strength,
That he may make peace with Me;
And he shall make peace with Me."

6 Those who come He shall cause [R]to take
root in Jacob; Is. 37:31
Israel shall blossom and bud,
And fill the face of the world with fruit.

7 [R]Has He struck Israel as He struck those
who struck him? Is. 10:12, 17; 30:30–33
Or has He been slain according to the
slaughter of those who were slain by
Him?
8 [R]In measure, by sending it away, Job 23:6
You contended with it.
[R]He removes *it* by His rough wind
In the day of the east wind. [Ps. 78:38]
9 Therefore by this the iniquity of Jacob
will be covered;
And this *is* all the fruit of taking away
his sin:
When he makes all the stones of the altar
Like chalkstones that are beaten to dust,
Wooden images* and incense altars shall
not stand.

26:19 So with MT, Vg.; Syr., Tg. *their dead bodies;* LXX *those in the tombs* **27:2** So with MT (Kittel's *Biblia Hebraica*), Bg., Vg.; MT (*Biblia Hebraica Stuttgartensia*), some Heb. mss., LXX *delight;* Tg. *choice vineyard* **27:9** Heb. *Asherim,* Canaanite deities

10 Yet the fortified city *will be* [R]desolate,
The habitation forsaken and left like a
wilderness; Is. 5:6, 17; 32:14
There the calf will feed, and there it will
lie down
And consume its branches.
11 When its boughs are withered, they will
be broken off;
The women come *and* set them on fire.
For it *is* a people of no understanding;
Therefore He who made them will [R]not
have mercy on them, Is. 9:17
And [R]He who formed them will show
them no favor. Deut. 32:18

12 And it shall come to pass in that day
That the LORD will thresh,
From the channel of the River* to the
Brook of Egypt;
And you will be [R]gathered one by one,
O you children of Israel. [Is. 11:11; 56:8]

13 [R]So it shall be in that day: Is. 2:11
[R]The great trumpet will be blown;
They will come, who are about to perish
in the land of Assyria, Rev. 11:15
And they who are outcasts in the land of
[R]Egypt, Is. 19:21, 22
And shall [R]worship the LORD in the holy
mount at Jerusalem. Zech. 14:16

CHAPTER 28

Woe to Ephraim

WOE to the crown of pride, to the
drunkards of Ephraim,
Whose glorious beauty *is* a fading flower
Which *is* at the head of the [T]verdant
valleys, Lit. *valleys of fatness*
To those who are overcome with wine!
2 Behold, the Lord has a mighty and
strong one,
[R]Like a tempest of hail and a destroying
storm, Ezek. 13:11
Like a flood of mighty waters
overflowing,
Who will bring *them* down to the earth
with *His* hand.
3 The crown of pride, the drunkards of
Ephraim,
Will be trampled underfoot;
4 And the glorious beauty is a fading
flower
Which *is* at the head of the [T]verdant
valley, Lit. *valley of fatness*
Like the first fruit before the summer,
Which an observer sees;
He eats it up while it is still in his hand.

5 In that day the LORD of hosts will be
For a crown of glory and a diadem of
beauty
To the remnant of His people,
6 For a spirit of justice to him who sits in
judgment,
And for strength to those who turn back
the battle at the gate.

7 But they also [R]have erred through wine,
And through intoxicating drink are out
of the way; Hos. 4:11
[R]The priest and the prophet have erred
through intoxicating drink,
They are swallowed up by wine,
They are out of the way through
intoxicating drink;
They err in vision, they stumble *in*
judgment. Is. 56:10, 12
8 For all tables are full of vomit *and* filth;
No place *is clean*.

9 "Whom[R] will he teach knowledge?
And whom will he make to understand
the message? Jer. 6:10
Those *just* weaned from milk?
Those *just* drawn from the breasts?
10 [R]For precept *must be* upon precept,
precept upon precept, [2 Chr. 36:15]
Line upon line, line upon line,
Here a little, there a little."

11 For with [R]stammering lips and another
tongue 1 Cor. 14:21
He will speak to this people,
12 To whom He said, "This *is* the [R]rest *with
which* Is. 30:15
You may cause the weary to rest,"
And, "This *is* the refreshing";
Yet they would not hear.
13 But the word of the LORD was to them,
"Precept upon precept, precept upon
precept,
Line upon line, line upon line,
Here a little, there a little,"
That they might go and fall backward,
and be broken
And snared and caught.

14 Therefore hear the word of the LORD,
you scornful men,
Who rule this people who *are* in
Jerusalem,
15 Because you have said, "We have made a
covenant with death,
And with Sheol we are in agreement.
When the overflowing scourge passes
through,
It will not come to us,
[R]For we have made lies our refuge,
And under falsehood we have hidden
ourselves." Is. 9:15

27:12 The Euphrates

16 Therefore thus says the Lord GOD:

"Behold, I lay in Zion [R]a stone for a
foundation, Matt. 21:42; 1 Pet. 2:6–8☆
A tried stone, a precious cornerstone, a
sure foundation;
Whoever believes will not act hastily.
17 Also I will make justice the measuring
line,
And righteousness the plummet;
The hail will sweep away the refuge of
lies,
And the waters will overflow the hiding
place.
18 Your covenant with death will be
annulled,
And your agreement with Sheol will not
stand;
When the overflowing scourge passes
through,
Then you will be trampled down by it.
19 As often as it goes out it will take you;
For morning by morning it will pass
over,
And by day and by night;
It will be a terror just to understand the
report."

20 For the bed is too short to stretch out *on*,
And the covering so narrow that one
cannot wrap himself *in it*.
21 For the LORD will rise up as *at* Mount
[R]Perazim, 2 Sam. 5:20
He will be angry as in the Valley of
[R]Gibeon— Josh. 10:10, 12
That He may do His work, [R]His awesome
work, [Lam. 3:33]
And bring to pass His act, His [T]unusual
act. Lit. *foreign*
22 Now therefore, do not be mockers,
Lest your bonds be made strong;
For I have heard from the Lord GOD of
hosts,
[R]A destruction determined even upon the
whole earth. Is. 10:22

23 Give ear and hear my voice,
Listen and hear my speech.
24 Does the plowman keep plowing all day
to sow?
Does he keep turning his soil and
breaking the clods?
25 When he has leveled its surface,
Does he not sow the black cummin
And scatter the cummin,
Plant the wheat in rows,
The barley in the appointed place,
And the [T]spelt in its place? *rye*
26 For He instructs him in right judgment,
His God teaches him.

27 For the black cummin is not threshed
with a threshing sledge,
Nor is a cartwheel rolled over the
cummin;
But the black cummin is beaten out with
a stick,
And the cummin with a rod.
28 Bread *flour* must be ground;
Therefore he does not thresh it forever,
Break *it with* his cartwheel,
Or crush it *with* his horsemen.
29 This also comes from the LORD of hosts,
[R]*Who* is wonderful in counsel *and*
excellent in guidance. Ps. 92:5

CHAPTER 29

Woe to Ariel (Jerusalem)

"WOE [R]to Ariel,* to Ariel, the city
[R]*where* David dwelt! Ezek. 24:6, 9
Add year to year;
Let feasts come around. 2 Sam. 5:9
2 Yet I will distress Ariel;
There shall be heaviness and sorrow,
And it shall be to Me as Ariel.
3 I will encamp against you all around,
I will lay siege against you with a
mound,
And I will raise siegeworks against you.
4 You shall be brought down,
You shall speak out of the ground;
Your speech shall be low, out of the dust;
Your voice shall be like a medium's, [R]out
of the ground; Is. 8:19
And your speech shall whisper out of the
dust.

5 "Moreover the multitude of your [R]foes
Shall be like fine dust, Is. 25:5
And the multitude of the terrible ones
Like [R]chaff that passes away; Job 21:18
Yes, it shall be in an instant, suddenly.
6 [R]You will be punished by the LORD of
hosts Is. 28:2; 30:30
With thunder and [R]earthquake and great
noise, Rev. 16:18, 19
With storm and tempest
And the flame of devouring fire.
7 [R]The multitude of all the nations who
fight against [T]Ariel, Mic. 4:11, 12
Even all who fight against her and her
fortress, Jerusalem
And distress her,
Shall be as a dream of a night vision.
8 [R]It shall even be as when a hungry man
dreams, Ps. 73:20
And look—he eats;
But he awakes, and his soul is still
empty;
Or as when a thirsty man dreams,
And look—he drinks;
But he awakes, and indeed *he is* faint,
And his soul still craves:

29:1 Jerusalem, lit. *Lion of God*

So the multitude of all the nations shall be,
Who fight against Mount Zion."

9 Pause and wonder!
Blind yourselves and be blind!
[R]They are drunk, [R]but not with wine;
They stagger, but not with intoxicating drink. Is. 28:7, 8 • Is. 51:21
10 For [R]the LORD has poured out on you
The spirit of deep sleep, Rom. 11:8
And has [R]closed your eyes, namely, the prophets; Ps. 69:23
And He has covered your heads, *namely,*
[R]the seers. Is. 44:18

11 The whole vision has become to you like
the words of a [T]book [R]that is sealed, which
men deliver to one who is literate, saying,
"Read this, please." [R]And he says, "I cannot,
for it *is* sealed." *scroll* • Is. 8:16 • Dan. 12:4, 9
12 Then the book is delivered to one who is
illiterate, saying, "Read this, please." And he
says, "I am not literate."
13 Therefore the Lord said:

[R]"Inasmuch as these people draw near with their mouths Ezek. 33:31
And honor Me [R]with their lips,
But have removed their hearts far from Me, Col. 2:22
And their fear toward Me is taught by the commandment of men,
14 [R]Therefore, behold, I will again do a marvelous work Hab. 1:5
Among this people,
A marvelous work and a wonder;
[R]For the wisdom of their wise *men* shall perish, Jer. 49:7
And the understanding of their prudent *men* shall be hidden."

15 [R]Woe to those who seek deep to hide their counsel far from the LORD,
And their works are in the dark;
[R]They say, "Who sees us?" and, "Who knows us?" Is. 30:1 • Ps. 10:11; 94:7
16 Surely you have things turned around!
Shall the potter be esteemed as the clay;
For shall the [R]thing made say of him who made it, Is. 45:9
"He did not make me"?
Or shall the thing formed say of him who formed it,
"He has no understanding"?

17 *Is* it not yet a very little while
Till [R]Lebanon shall be turned into a fruitful field, Is. 32:15
And the fruitful field be esteemed as a forest?
18 [R]In that day the deaf shall hear the words of the book, Is. 35:5
And the eyes of the blind shall see out of obscurity and out of darkness.
19 [R]The humble also shall increase *their* joy in the LORD, [Is. 11:4; 61:1]
And [R]the poor among men shall rejoice
In the Holy One of Israel. [James 2:5]
20 For the [T]terrible one is brought to nothing, *terrifying*
[R]The scornful one is consumed, Is. 28:14
And all who [R]watch for iniquity are cut off— Mic. 2:1
21 Who make a man an offender by a word,
And [R]lay a snare for him who reproves in the gate, Amos 5:10, 12
And turn aside the just [R]by empty words. Prov. 28:21

22 Therefore thus says the LORD, [R]who re-
deemed Abraham, concerning the house of
Jacob: Josh. 24:3

"Jacob shall not now be ashamed,
Nor shall his face now grow pale;
23 But when he sees his children,
The work of My hands, in his midst,
They will hallow My name,
And hallow the Holy One of Jacob,
And fear the God of Israel.
24 These also [R]who erred in spirit will come to understanding, Is. 28:7
And those who complained will learn doctrine."

CHAPTER 30

Woe to Egyptian Alliance

"WOE to the rebellious children," says the LORD,
[R]"Who take counsel, but not of Me,
And who [T]devise plans, but not of My Spirit, Is. 29:15 • Lit. *weave a web*
That they may add sin to sin;
2 [R]Who walk to go down to Egypt, Is. 31:1
And [R]have not asked My advice,
To strengthen themselves in the strength of Pharaoh, Josh. 9:14
And to trust in the shadow of Egypt!
3 [R]Therefore the strength of Pharaoh
Shall be your shame, Is. 20:5
And trust in the shadow of Egypt
Shall be *your* humiliation.
4 For his princes were at [R]Zoan, Is. 19:11
And his ambassadors came to Hanes.
5 [R]They were all ashamed of a people *who* could not benefit them, Jer. 2:36
Or be help or benefit,
But a shame and also a reproach."

6 [R]The [T]burden against the beasts of the
South. Is. 57:9 • *oracle, prophecy*

Through a land of trouble and anguish,
From which *came* the lioness and lion,

[R]The viper and fiery flying serpent,
They will carry their riches on the backs of young donkeys, Deut. 8:15
And their treasures on the humps of camels,
To a people *who* shall not profit;
7 [R]For the Egyptians shall help in vain and to no purpose. Jer. 37:7
Therefore I have called her Rahab-Hem-Shebeth.*
8 Now go, [R]write it before them on a tablet, Hab. 2:2
And note it on a scroll,
That it may be for time to come,
Forever and ever:
9 That [R]this *is* a rebellious people, Lying children, Is. 1:2, 4; 65:2
Children *who* will not hear the law of the LORD;
10 [R]Who say to the seers, "Do not see,"
And to the prophets, "Do not prophesy to us right things; Jer. 11:21
[R]Speak to us smooth things, prophesy deceits. 1 Kin. 22:8, 13
11 Get out of the way,
Turn aside from the path,
Cause the Holy One of Israel
To cease from before us."

12 Therefore thus says the Holy One of Israel:

"Because you [R]despise this word, Is. 5:24
And trust in oppression and perversity,
And rely on them,
13 Therefore this iniquity shall be to you
[R]Like a breach ready to fall, Ps. 62:3, 4
A bulge in a high wall,
Whose breaking [R]comes suddenly, in an instant. Is. 29:5
14 And [R]He shall break it like the breaking of the potter's vessel, Jer. 19:11
Which is broken in pieces;
He shall not spare.
So there shall not be found among its fragments
A shard to take fire from the hearth,
Or to take water from the cistern."

15 For thus says the Lord GOD, the Holy One of Israel:

[R]"In returning and rest you shall be saved; Is. 7:4; 28:12
In quietness and confidence shall be your strength."
[R]But you would not, Matt. 23:37
16 And you said, "No, for we will flee on horses"—
Therefore you shall flee!
And, "We will ride on swift *horses*"—
Therefore those who pursue you shall be swift!
17 [R]One thousand *shall flee* at the threat of one, Josh. 23:10
At the threat of five you shall flee,
Till you are left as a [T]pole on top of a mountain A tree stripped of branches
And as a banner on a hill.

18 Therefore the LORD will wait, that He may be [R]gracious to you; Is. 33:2
And therefore He will be exalted, that He may have mercy on you.
For the LORD *is* a God of justice;
[R]Blessed *are* all those who [R]wait for Him. Jer. 17:7 • Is. 26:8
19 For the people [R]shall dwell in Zion at Jerusalem; Is. 65:9
You shall [R]weep no more. Is. 25:8
He will be very gracious to you at the sound of your cry;
When He hears it, He will answer you.
20 And *though* the Lord gives you
[R]The bread of adversity and the water of [T]affliction, 1 Kin. 22:27 • *oppression*
Yet [R]your teachers will not be moved into a corner anymore, Amos 8:11
But your eyes shall see your teachers.
21 Your ears shall hear a word behind you, saying,
"This *is* the way, walk in it,"
Whenever you turn to the right hand
Or whenever you turn to the left.
22 [R]You will also defile the covering of your images of silver, Is. 2:20; 31:7
And the ornament of your molded images of gold.
You will throw them away as an unclean thing;
You will say to them, "Get away!"

23 Then He will give the rain for your seed
With which you sow the ground,
And bread of the increase of the earth;
It will be [T]fat and plentiful. *rich*
In that day your cattle will feed
In large pastures.
24 Likewise the oxen and the young donkeys that work the ground
Will eat cured fodder,
Which has been winnowed with the shovel and fan.
25 There will be [R]on every high mountain
And on every high hill Is. 2:14, 15
Rivers *and* streams of waters,
In the day of the [R]great slaughter,
When the towers fall. Is. 2:10–21; 34:2
26 Moreover [R]the light of the moon will be as the light of the sun, [Is. 60:19, 20]
And the light of the sun will be sevenfold,
As the light of seven days,

30:7 Lit. *Rahab Sits Idle*

In the day that the LORD binds up the bruise of His people
And heals the stroke of their wound.

27 Behold, the name of the LORD comes from afar,
Burning *with* His anger,
And *His* burden *is* heavy;
His lips are full of indignation,
And His tongue like a devouring fire.
28 His breath is like an overflowing stream,
[R]Which reaches up to the neck, Is. 8:8
To sift the nations with the sieve of futility;
And *there shall be* [R]a bridle in the jaws of the people, Is. 37:29
Causing *them* to err.

29 You shall have a song
As in the night *when* a holy festival is kept,
And gladness of heart as when one goes with a flute,
To come into [R]the mountain of the LORD,
To the Mighty One of Israel. [Is. 2:3]
30 [R]The LORD will cause His glorious voice to be heard, Is. 29:6
And show the descent of His arm,
With the indignation of *His* anger
And the flame of a devouring fire,
With scattering, tempest, [R]and hailstones. Is. 28:2
31 For through the voice of the LORD
Assyria will be beaten down,
As He strikes with the [R]rod. Is. 10:5, 24
32 And *in* every place where the staff of punishment passes,
Which the LORD lays on him,
It will be with tambourines and harps;
And in battles of [R]brandishing He will fight with it. Is. 11:15
33 [R]For Tophet *was* established of old,
Yes, for the king it is prepared. Jer. 7:31
He has made *it* deep and large;
Its pyre *is* fire with much wood;
The breath of the LORD, like a stream of brimstone,
Kindles it.

CHAPTER 31

WOE to those [R]who go down to Egypt for help, Is. 30:1, 2
And [R]rely on horses, Ps. 20:7
Who trust in chariots because *they are* many,
And in horsemen because they are very strong,
But who do not look to the Holy One of Israel,
[R]Nor seek the LORD! Dan. 9:13
2 Yet He also *is* wise and will bring disaster,
And [R]will not [T]call back His words,
But will arise against the house of evildoers,
And against the help of those who work iniquity. Num. 23:19 • *retract*
3 Now the Egyptians *are* men, and not God;
And their horses are flesh, and not spirit.
When the LORD stretches out His hand,
Both he who helps will fall,
And he who is helped will fall down;
They all will perish [R]together. Is. 20:6

4 For thus the LORD has spoken to me:

[R]"As a lion roars, Hos. 11:10
And a young lion over his prey
(When a multitude of shepherds is summoned against him,
He will not be afraid of their voice
Nor be disturbed by their noise),
So the LORD of hosts will come down
To fight for Mount Zion and for its hill.
5 [R]Like birds flying about, Deut. 32:11
So will the LORD of hosts defend Jerusalem.
Defending, He will also deliver *it;*
Passing over, He will preserve *it.*"

6 Return *to Him* against whom the children
of Israel have [R]deeply revolted. Hos. 9:9
7 For in that day every man shall [R]throw
away his idols of silver and his idols of gold—
sin, which your own hands have made for
yourselves. Is. 2:20; 30:22

8 "Then Assyria shall [R]fall by a sword not of man, 2 Kin. 19:35, 36
And a sword not of mankind shall [R]devour him. Is. 37:36
But he shall flee from the sword,
And his young men shall become forced labor.
9 [R]He shall cross over to his stronghold for fear, Is. 37:37
And his princes shall be afraid of the banner,"
Says the LORD,
Whose fire *is* in Zion
And whose furnace *is* in Jerusalem.

CHAPTER 32

Behold the Coming King

BEHOLD, [R]a king will reign in righteousness, Ps. 45:1
And princes will rule with justice.
2 A man will be as a hiding place from the wind,
And [R]a cover from the tempest, Is. 4:6
As rivers of water in a dry place,
As the shadow of a great rock in a weary land.

3 [R]The eyes of those who see will not be
dim, Is. 29:18; 35:5
And the ears of those who hear will
listen.
4 Also the heart of the rash will
[R]understand knowledge, Is. 29:24
And the tongue of the stammerers will
be ready to speak plainly.

5 The foolish person will no longer be
called [T]generous, *noble*
Nor the miser said *to be* bountiful;
6 For the foolish person will speak
foolishness,
And his heart will work [R]iniquity:
To practice ungodliness, Prov. 24:7–9
To utter error against the LORD,
To keep the hungry unsatisfied,
And he will cause the drink of the thirsty
to fail.
7 Also the schemes of the schemer *are*
evil;
He devises wicked plans
To destroy the poor with lying words,
Even when the needy speaks justice.
8 But a [T]generous man devises generous
things, *noble*
And by generosity he shall stand.

9 Rise up, you women [R]who are at ease,
Hear my voice;
You complacent daughters,
Give ear to my speech. Amos 6:1
10 In a year and *some* days
You will be troubled, you complacent
women;
For the vintage will fail,
The gathering will not come.
11 Tremble, you *women* who are at ease;
Be troubled, you complacent ones;
Strip yourselves, make yourselves bare,
And gird *sackcloth* on *your* waists.

12 People shall mourn upon their breasts
For the pleasant fields, for the fruitful
vine.
13 [R]On the land of my people will come up
thorns *and* briers, Hos. 9:6
Yes, on all the happy homes *in* [R]the
joyous city; Is. 22:2
14 [R]Because the palaces will be forsaken,
The bustling city will be deserted.
The forts and towers will become lairs
forever,
A joy of wild donkeys, a pasture of
flocks— Is. 27:10
15 Until [R]the Spirit is poured upon us from
on high, [Joel 2:28]
And [R]the wilderness becomes a fruitful
field, Is. 29:17
And the fruitful field is counted as a
forest.

16 Then justice will dwell in the wilderness,
And righteousness remain in the fruitful
field.
17 The work of righteousness will be peace,
And the effect of righteousness,
quietness and assurance forever.
18 My people will dwell in a peaceful
habitation,
In secure dwellings, and in quiet [R]resting
places, [Zech. 2:5; 3:10]
19 [R]Though hail comes down [R]on the forest,
And the city is brought low in
humiliation. Is. 30:30 • Zech. 11:2

20 Blessed *are* you who sow beside all
waters,
Who send out freely the feet of [R]the ox
and the donkey. Is. 30:23, 24

CHAPTER 33

Woe to the Spoiler of Jerusalem (Assyria)

WOE to you [R]who plunder, though you
have not *been* plundered; Hab. 2:8
And you who deal treacherously, though
they have not dealt treacherously with
you!
[R]When you cease plundering, Rev. 13:10
You will be [R]plundered;
When you make an end of dealing
treacherously, Is. 10:12; 14:25; 31:8
They will deal treacherously with you.

2 O LORD, be gracious to us;
[R]We have waited for You. Is. 25:9; 26:8
Be their* arm every morning,
Our salvation also in the time of trouble.
3 At the noise of the tumult the people
[R]shall flee; Is. 17:13
When You lift Yourself up, the nations
shall be scattered;
4 And Your plunder shall be gathered
Like the gathering of the caterpillar;
As the running to and fro of locusts,
He shall run upon them.

5 [R]The LORD is exalted, for He dwells on
high; Ps. 97:9
He has filled Zion with justice and
righteousness.
6 Wisdom and knowledge will be the
stability of your times,
And the strength of salvation;
The fear of the LORD *is* His treasure.

7 Surely their valiant ones shall cry
outside,
[R]The ambassadors of peace shall weep
bitterly. 2 Kin. 18:18, 37
8 [R]The highways lie waste, Judg. 5:6
The traveling man ceases.

33:2 LXX omits *their;* Syr., Tg., Vg. *our*

[R]He has broken the covenant,
He has despised the cities,*
He regards no man. 2 Kin. 18:13–17
9[R]The earth mourns *and* languishes,
Lebanon is shamed *and* shriveled;
Sharon is like a wilderness,
And Bashan and Carmel shake off *their* *fruits.* Is. 24:4

10"Now[R] I will rise," says the LORD; Ps. 12:5
"Now I will be exalted,
Now I will lift Myself up.
11[R]You shall conceive chaff, [Ps. 7:14]
You shall bring forth stubble;
Your breath, *as* fire, shall devour you.
12 And the people shall be *like* the burnings of lime;
[R]*Like* thorns cut up they shall be burned in the fire. Is. 9:18
13 Hear, [R]you *who are* afar off, what I have done; Is. 49:1
And you *who are* near, acknowledge My might."

14 The sinners in Zion are afraid;
Fearfulness has seized the hypocrites:
"Who among us shall dwell with the devouring [R]fire? Heb. 12:29
Who among us shall dwell with everlasting burnings?"
15 He who [R]walks righteously and speaks uprightly, Ps. 15:2; 24:3, 4
He who despises the gain of oppressions,
Who gestures with his hands, refusing bribes,
Who stops his ears from hearing of bloodshed,
And shuts his eyes from seeing evil:
16 He will dwell on [T]high; Lit. *heights*
His place of defense *will be* the fortress of rocks;
Bread will be given him,
His water *will be* sure.

17 Your eyes will see the King in His [R]beauty; Ps. 27:4
They will see the land that is very far off.
18 Your heart will meditate on terror:
[R]"Where *is* the scribe? 1 Cor. 1:20
Where *is* he who weighs?
Where *is* he who counts the towers?"
19[R]You will not see a fierce people,
[R]A people of obscure speech, beyond perception, 2 Kin. 19:32 • Jer. 5:15
Of a stammering tongue *that you* cannot understand.

20 Look upon Zion, the city of our appointed feasts; Ps. 48:12
Your eyes will see [R]Jerusalem, a quiet home, Ps. 46:5; 125:1
A tabernacle *that* will not be taken down;
[R]Not one of [R]its stakes will ever be removed, Is. 37:33 • Is. 54:2
Nor will any of its cords be broken.
21 But there the majestic LORD *will be* for us
A place of broad rivers *and* streams,
In which no [T]galley with oars will sail, *ship*
Nor majestic ships pass by
22 (For the LORD *is* our Judge,
The LORD *is* our [R]Lawgiver, James 4:12
[R]The LORD *is* our King; Ps. 89:18
He will save us);
23 Your tackle is loosed,
They could not strengthen their mast,
They could not spread the sail.

Then the prey of great plunder is divided;
The lame take the prey.
24 And the inhabitant will not say, "I am sick";
[R]The people who dwell in it *will be* forgiven *their* iniquity. Is. 40:2

CHAPTER 34

Woe to the Nations

COME [R]near, you nations, to hear;
And heed, you people!
[R]Let the earth hear, and all that is in it,
The world and all things that come forth from it. Ps. 49:1 • Deut. 32:1
2 For the indignation of the LORD *is* against all nations,
And *His* fury against all their armies;
He has utterly destroyed them,
He has given them over to the [R]slaughter. Is. 13:5
3 Also their slain shall be thrown out;
[R]Their stench shall rise from their corpses, Joel 2:20
And the mountains shall be melted with their blood.
4[R]All the host of heaven shall be dissolved,
And the heavens shall be rolled up like a scroll; Is. 13:13
[R]All their host shall fall down Is. 14:12
As the leaf falls from the vine,
And as *fruit* falling from a fig tree.

5"For [R]My sword shall be bathed in heaven; Jer. 46:10
Indeed it [R]shall come down on Edom,
And on the people of My curse, for judgment. Mal. 1:4
6 The [R]sword of the LORD is filled with blood, Is. 66:16
It is made [T]overflowing with fatness,
With the blood of lambs and goats,
With the fat of the kidneys of rams.
For [R]the LORD has a sacrifice in Bozrah,

33:8 So with MT, Vg.; DSS *witnesses;* LXX omits *cities;* Tg. *They have been removed from their cities*

And a great slaughter in the land of
Edom. Lit. *fat* • Zeph. 1:7
7 The wild oxen shall come down with
them,
And the young bulls with the mighty
bulls;
Their land shall be soaked with blood,
And their dust saturated with fatness."

8 For *it is* the day of the LORD's
[R]vengeance, Is. 63:4
The year of recompense for the cause of
Zion.
9 [R]Its streams shall be turned into pitch,
And its dust into brimstone; Deut. 29:23
Its land shall become burning pitch.
10 It shall not be quenched night or day;
[R]Its smoke shall ascend forever.
[R]From generation to generation it shall lie
waste; Rev. 14:11; 18:18 • Mal. 1:3, 4
No one shall pass through it forever and
ever.
11 [R]But the [T]pelican and the [T]porcupine shall
possess it,
Also the owl and the raven shall dwell in
it. Zeph. 2:14 • Or *owl* • Or *hedgehog*
And [R]He shall stretch out over it
The line of confusion and the stones of
emptiness. Lam. 2:8
12 They shall call its nobles to the kingdom,
But none *shall be* there, and all its
princes shall be nothing.

13 And [R]thorns shall come up in its
palaces, Is. 32:13
Nettles and brambles in its fortresses;
[R]It shall be a habitation of jackals,
A courtyard for ostriches. Is. 13:21
14 The wild beasts of the desert shall also
meet with the [T]jackals,
And the wild goat shall bleat to its
companion; Lit. *howling creatures*
Also the night creature shall rest there,
And find for herself a place of rest.
15 There the arrow snake shall make her
nest and lay *eggs*
And hatch, and gather *them* under her
shadow;
There also shall the hawks be gathered,
Every one with her mate.

16 "Search from [R]the book of the LORD, and
read: [Mal. 3:16]
Not one of these shall fail;
Not one shall lack her mate.
For My mouth has commanded it, and
His Spirit has gathered them.
17 He has cast the lot for them,
And His hand has divided it among them
with a measuring line.
They shall possess it forever;
From generation to generation they shall
dwell in it."

CHAPTER 35

Behold the Coming Kingdom

THE [R]wilderness and the [T]wasteland shall
be glad for them, Is. 32:15; 55:12 • *desert*
And the [R]desert shall rejoice and
blossom as the rose; Is. 41:19; 51:3
2 [R]It shall blossom abundantly and rejoice,
Even with joy and singing. Is. 32:15
The glory of Lebanon shall be given to it,
The excellence of Carmel and Sharon.
They shall see the [R]glory of the LORD,
The excellency of our God. Is. 40:5

3 Strengthen the weak hands,
And make firm the feeble knees.
4 Say to those *who are* fearful-hearted,
"Be strong, do not fear!
Behold, your God will come *with*
[R]vengeance, Is. 34:8
With the recompense of God;
He will come and [R]save you." Is. 33:22☆

5 Then the [R]eyes of the blind shall be
opened, Is. 29:18; John 9:6, 7☆
And [R]the ears of the deaf shall be
unstopped. [Matt. 11:5]
6 Then the [R]lame shall leap like a deer,
And the tongue of the dumb sing.
For [R]waters shall burst forth in the
wilderness, Matt. 15:30☆ • [John 7:38]
And streams in the desert.
7 The parched ground shall become a pool,
And the thirsty land springs of water;
In [R]the habitation of jackals, where each
lay, Is. 34:13
There shall be grass with reeds and
rushes.

8 A [R]highway shall be there, and a road,
And it shall be called the Highway of
Holiness. Is. 19:23
[R]The unclean shall not pass over it,
But it *shall be* for others. Joel 3:17
Whoever walks the road, although a fool,
Shall not go astray.
9 [R]No lion shall be there, Lev. 26:6
Nor shall *any* ravenous beast go up on it;
It shall not be found there.
But the redeemed shall walk *there*,
10 And the [R]ransomed of the LORD shall
return, Is. 51:11
And come to Zion with singing,
With everlasting joy on their heads.
They shall obtain joy and gladness,
And sorrow and sighing shall flee away.

CHAPTER 36

Assyria Challenges God
2 Kin. 18:13–37; 2 Chr. 32:1–19

NOW it came to pass in the fourteenth year
of King Hezekiah *that* Sennacherib king

of Assyria came up against all the fortified cities of Judah and took them.

2 Then the king of Assyria sent *the* Rabshakeh* with a great army from Lachish to King Hezekiah at Jerusalem. And he stood by the aqueduct from the upper pool, on the highway to the Fuller's Field.

3 And [R]Eliakim the son of Hilkiah, who was over the household, [R]Shebna the scribe, and Joah the son of Asaph, the recorder, came out to him. Is. 22:20 • Is. 22:15

4 [R]Then *the* Rabshakeh said to them, "Say now to Hezekiah, 'Thus says the great king, the king of Assyria: "What confidence is this in which you trust? 2 Kin. 18:19

5 "I say you speak of having plans and power for war; but *they are* [T]mere words. Now in whom do you trust, that you rebel against me? Lit. *a word of the lips*

6 "Look! You are trusting in the [R]staff of this broken reed, Egypt, on which if a man leans, it will go into his hand and pierce it. So *is* Pharaoh king of Egypt to all who [R]trust in him. Ezek. 29:6 • Ps. 146:3

7 "But if you say to me, 'We trust in the LORD our God,' *is it* not He whose high places and whose altars Hezekiah has taken away, and said to Judah and Jerusalem, 'You shall worship before this altar'?" '

8 "Now therefore, I urge you, give a pledge to my master the king of Assyria, and I will give you two thousand horses—if you are able on your part to put riders on them!

9 "How then will you repel one captain of the least of my master's servants, and put your trust in Egypt for chariots and horsemen?

10 "Have I now come up without the LORD against this land to destroy it? The LORD said to me, 'Go up against this land, and destroy it.' "

11 Then Eliakim, Shebna, and Joah said to *the* Rabshakeh, "Please speak to your servants in Aramaic, for we understand *it;* and do not speak to us in Hebrew* in the hearing of the people who *are* on the wall."

12 But *the* Rabshakeh said, "Has my master sent me to your master and to you to speak these words, and not to the men who sit on the wall, who will eat and drink their own waste with you?"

13 Then *the* Rabshakeh stood and called out with a loud voice in Hebrew, and said, "Hear the words of the great king, the king of Assyria!

14 "Thus says the king: 'Do not let Hezekiah deceive you, for he will not be able to deliver you;

15 'nor let Hezekiah make you trust in the LORD, saying, "The LORD will surely deliver us; this city will not be given into the hand of the king of Assyria." '

16 "Do not listen to Hezekiah; for thus says the king of Assyria: 'Make *peace* with me *by a* present and come out to me; and every one of you eat from his own vine and every one from his own fig tree, and every one of you drink the waters of his own cistern;

17 'until I come and take you away to a land like your own land, a land of grain and new wine, a land of bread and vineyards.

18 '*Beware* lest Hezekiah persuade you, saying, "The LORD will deliver us." Has any one of the gods of the nations delivered its land from the hand of the king of Assyria?

19 'Where *are* the gods of Hamath and Arpad? Where *are* the gods of Sepharvaim? Indeed, have they delivered [R]Samaria from my hand? 2 Kin. 17:6

20 'Who among all the gods of these lands have delivered their countries from my hand, that the LORD should deliver Jerusalem from my hand?' "

21 But they [T]held their peace and answered him not a word; for the king's commandment was, "Do not answer him." *were silent*

22 Then Eliakim the son of Hilkiah, who *was* over the household, Shebna the scribe, and Joah the son of Asaph, the recorder, came to Hezekiah with *their* clothes torn, and told him the words of *the* Rabshakeh.

CHAPTER 37

God Destroys Assyria—2 Kin. 19:1–37

AND [R]so it was, when King Hezekiah heard *it,* that he tore his clothes, covered himself with sackcloth, and went into the house of the LORD. 2 Kin. 19:1–37

2 Then he sent Eliakim, who *was* over the household, Shebna the scribe, and the elders of the priests, covered with sackcloth, to Isaiah the prophet, the son of Amoz.

3 And they said to him, "Thus says Hezekiah: 'This day *is* a day of [R]trouble and rebuke and blasphemy; for the children have come to birth, but *there is* no strength to bring them forth. Is. 22:5; 26:16; 33:2

4 'It may be that the LORD your God will hear the words of *the* Rabshakeh, whom his master the king of Assyria has sent to [R]reproach the living God, and will rebuke the words which the LORD your God has heard. Therefore lift up *your* prayer for the remnant that is left.' " Is. 36:15, 18, 20

5 So the servants of King Hezekiah came to Isaiah.

6 And Isaiah said to them, "Thus you shall say to your master, 'Thus says the LORD: "Do not be afraid of the words which you have heard, with which the servants of the king of Assyria have blasphemed Me.

7 "Surely I will send a spirit upon him, and

36:2 A title, probably *Chief of Staff* or *Governor*
36:11 Lit. *Judean*

he shall hear a rumor and return to his own
land; and I will cause him to fall by the sword
in his own land." ' "
8 Then *the* Rabshakeh returned, and found
the king of Assyria warring against Libnah,
for he heard that he had departed from
Lachish.
9 And the king heard concerning Tirhakah
king of Ethiopia, "He has come out to make
war with you." So when he heard *it*, he sent
messengers to Hezekiah, saying,
10 "Thus you shall speak to Hezekiah king
of Judah, saying: 'Do not let your God in
whom you trust deceive you, saying, "Jerusa-
lem shall not be given into the hand of the
king of Assyria."
11 'Look! You have heard what the kings of
Assyria have done to all lands by utterly de-
stroying them; and shall you be delivered?
12 'Have the gods of the nations delivered
those whom my fathers have destroyed,
Gozan and Haran and Rezeph, and the people
of Eden who *were* in Telassar?
13 'Where *is* the king of [R]Hamath, the king
of Arpad, and the king of the city of Sephar-
vaim, Hena, and Ivah?' " Is. 49:23
14 And Hezekiah received the letter from
the hand of the messengers, and read it; and
Hezekiah went up to the house of the LORD,
and spread it before the LORD.
15 Then Hezekiah prayed to the LORD, saying:
16 "O LORD of hosts, God of Israel, *the One*
who dwells *between* the cherubim, You *are*
God, You alone, of all the kingdoms of the
earth. You have made heaven and earth.
17 [R]"Incline Your ear, O LORD, and hear; open
Your eyes, O LORD, and see; and hear all the
words of Sennacherib, which he has sent to
reproach the living God. Dan. 9:18
18 "Truly, LORD, the kings of Assyria have
laid waste all the nations and their lands,
19 "and have cast their gods into the fire; for
they *were* [R]not gods, but the work of men's
hands—wood and stone. Therefore they de-
stroyed them. Is. 40:19, 20
20 "Now therefore, O LORD our God, [R]save us
from his hand, that all the kingdoms of the
earth may [R]know that You *are* the LORD, You
alone." Is. 33:22 • Ps. 83:18
21 Then Isaiah the son of Amoz sent to
Hezekiah, saying, "Thus says the LORD God of
Israel, 'Because you have prayed to Me
against Sennacherib king of Assyria,
22 'this *is* the word which the LORD has spo-
ken concerning him:

"The virgin, the daughter of Zion,
Has despised you, laughed you to scorn;
The daughter of Jerusalem
Has shaken *her* head behind your back!

23 "Whom have you reproached and
blasphemed?
Against whom have you raised *your*
voice,
And lifted up your eyes on high?
Against the Holy One of Israel.
24 By your servants you have reproached
the Lord,
And said, 'By the multitude of my
chariots
I have come up to the height of the
mountains,
To the limits of Lebanon;
I will cut down its tall cedars
And its choice cypress trees;
I will enter its farthest height,
To its fruitful forest.
25 I have dug and drunk water,
And with the soles of my feet I have
dried up
All the brooks of defense.'

26 "Did you not hear [R]long ago Is. 25:1
How I made it,
From ancient times that I formed it?
Now I have brought it to pass,
That you should be
For crushing fortified cities *into* heaps of
ruins.
27 Therefore their inhabitants *had* little
power;
They were dismayed and confounded;
They were *as* the grass of the field
And the green herb,
As the grass on the housetops
And *grain* blighted before it is grown.

28 "But I know your dwelling place,
Your going out and your coming in,
And your rage against Me.
29 Because your rage against Me and your
tumult
Have come up to My ears,
Therefore [R]I will put My hook in your
nose Is. 30:28
And My bridle in your lips,
And I will turn you back
By the way which you came." '

30 "This *shall be* a sign to you:

You shall eat this year such as grows of
itself,
And the second year what springs from
the same;
Also in the third year sow and reap,
Plant vineyards and eat the fruit of them.
31 And the remnant who have escaped of
the house of Judah
Shall again take root downward,
And bear fruit upward.
32 For out of Jerusalem shall go a remnant,
And those who escape from Mount Zion.
The [R]zeal of the LORD of hosts will do
this. 2 Kin. 19:31

33 "Therefore thus says the LORD concerning
the king of Assyria:

'He shall not come into this city,
Nor shoot an arrow there,
Nor come before it with shield,
Nor build a siege mound against it.
34 By the way that he came,
By the same shall he return;
And he shall not come into this city,'
Says the LORD.
35 'For I will [R]defend this city, to save it
For My own sake and for My servant
[R]David's sake.'" Is. 31:5 • 1 Kin. 11:13

36 Then the angel* of the LORD went out, and
killed in the camp of the Assyrians one hun-
dred and eighty-five thousand; and when *peo-
ple* arose early in the morning, there were the
corpses—all dead.
37 So Sennacherib king of Assyria departed
and went away, returned *home,* and remained
at Nineveh.
38 Now it came to pass, as he was worship-
ing in the house of Nisroch his god, that his
sons Adrammelech and Sharezer struck him
down with the sword; and they escaped into
the land of Ararat. Then [R]Esarhaddon his son
reigned in his place. Ezra 4:2

CHAPTER 38

Hezekiah's Salvation from Sickness

IN [R]those days Hezekiah was sick and near
death. And Isaiah the prophet, the son of
Amoz, went to him and said to him, "Thus
says the LORD: 'Set your house in order, for
you shall die and not live.'" 2 Chr. 32:24
2 Then Hezekiah turned his face toward the
wall, and prayed to the LORD,
3 and said, [R]"Remember now, O LORD, I
pray, how I have walked before You in truth
and with a loyal heart, and have done *what is*
good in Your [R]sight." And Hezekiah wept bit-
terly. Neh. 13:14 • 2 Kin. 18:5, 6
4 And the word of the LORD came to Isaiah,
saying,
5 "Go and tell Hezekiah, 'Thus says the
LORD, the God of David your father: "I have
heard your prayer, I have seen your tears;
surely I will add to your days fifteen years.
6 "I will deliver you and this city from the
hand of the king of Assyria, and [R]I will defend
this city."' Is. 31:5; 37:35
7 "And this *is* [R]the sign to you from the
LORD, that the LORD will do this thing which
He has spoken: Is. 7:11
8 "Behold, I will bring the shadow on the
sundial, which has gone down with the sun on
the sundial of Ahaz, ten degrees backward."
So the sun returned ten degrees on the dial by
which it had gone down.
9 This is the writing of Hezekiah king of Ju-
dah, when he had been sick and had recov-
ered from his sickness:

10 I said,
"In the prime of my life
I shall go to the gates of Sheol;
I am deprived of the remainder of my
years."
11 I said,
"I shall not see YAH,
The LORD* in the land of the living;
I shall observe man no more among the
inhabitants of the world.*
12 [R]My life span is gone, Job 7:6
Taken from me like a shepherd's tent;
I have cut off my life like a weaver.
He cuts me off from the loom;
From day until night You make an end of
me.
13 I have considered until morning—
Like a lion,
So He breaks all my bones;
From day until night You make an end of
me.
14 Like a crane *or* a swallow, so I chattered;
[R]I mourned like a dove; Is. 59:11
My eyes fail *from looking* upward.
O LORD,* I am oppressed;
[T]Undertake for me! *Be my surety*

15 "What shall I say?
He has both spoken to me,*
And He Himself has done *it.*
I shall walk carefully all my years
[R]In the bitterness of my soul. Job 7:11
16 O Lord, by these *things men* live;
And in all these *things is* the life of my
spirit;
So You will restore me and make me live.
17 Indeed *it was* for *my own* peace
That I had great bitterness;
But You have lovingly *delivered* my soul
from the pit of corruption,
For You have cast all my sins behind Your
back.
18 For [R]Sheol cannot thank You, Ps. 6:5
Death cannot praise You;
Those who go down to the pit cannot
hope for Your truth.
19 The living, the living man, he shall
praise You,
As I *do* this day;
[R]The father shall make known Your truth
to the children. Deut. 4:9; 6:7

20 "The LORD *was ready* to save me;
Therefore we will sing my songs with
stringed instruments

37:36 Or *Angel* **38:11** Heb. YAH, YAH • So with some Heb. mss.; MT, Vg. *rest;* LXX omits *among the inhabitants of the world;* Tg. *land* **38:14** So with Bg.; MT, DSS *Lord* **38:15** So with MT, Vg.; DSS, Tg. *And shall I say to Him;* LXX omits first half of this verse

All the days of our life, in the house of
the LORD."

21 Now [R]Isaiah had said, "Let them take a
lump of figs, and apply *it* as a poultice on the
boil, and he shall recover." 2 Kin. 20:7
22 And [R]Hezekiah had said, "What *is* the
sign that I shall go up to the house of the
LORD?" 2 Kin. 20:8

CHAPTER 39

Hezekiah's Sin

AT that time Merodach-Baladan* the son
of Baladan, king of Babylon, sent letters
and a present to Hezekiah, for he heard that
he had been sick and had recovered.
2 And Hezekiah was pleased with them,
and showed them the house of his treasures—
the silver and gold, the spices and precious
ointment, and all his armory—all that was
found among his treasures. There was noth-
ing in his house or in all his dominion that
Hezekiah did not show them.
3 Then Isaiah the prophet went to King
Hezekiah, and said to him, "What did these
men say, and from where did they come to
you?" So Hezekiah said, "They came to me
from a far country, from Babylon."
4 And he said, "What have they seen in
your house?" So Hezekiah answered, "They
have seen all that *is* in my house; there is
nothing among my treasures that I have not
shown them."
5 Then Isaiah said to Hezekiah, "Hear the
word of the LORD of hosts:
6 'Behold, the days are coming [R]when all
that *is* in your house, and what your fathers
have accumulated until this day, shall be car-
ried to Babylon; nothing shall be left,' says the
LORD. Jer. 20:5
7 'And they shall take away *some* of your
[R]sons who will descend from you, whom you
will beget; and they shall be eunuchs in the
palace of the king of Babylon.' " Dan. 1:1–7
8 So Hezekiah said to Isaiah, [R]"The word of
the LORD which you have spoken *is* good!" For
he said, "At least there will be peace and truth
in my days." 1 Sam. 3:18

CHAPTER 40

Comfort Because of Israel's Deliverance

"COMFORT, yes, comfort My people!"
Says your God.
2 "Speak [T]comfort to Jerusalem, and cry
out to her, Lit. *to the heart of*
That her warfare is ended,
That her iniquity is pardoned;
[R]For she has received from the LORD's
hand Is. 61:7
Double for all her sins."

3 [R]The voice of one crying in the
wilderness: Matt. 3:3☆
[R]"Prepare the way of the LORD; [Mal. 3:1]
[R]Make straight in the desert* Ps. 68:4
A highway for our God.
4 Every valley shall be exalted
And every mountain and hill brought low;
[R]The crooked places shall be made
[T]straight Is. 45:2 • Or *a plain*
And the rough places smooth;
5 The glory of the LORD shall be revealed,
And all flesh shall see *it* together;
For the mouth of the LORD has spoken."

6 The voice said, "Cry out!"
And he* said, "What shall I cry?"

[R]"All flesh *is* grass, Job 14:2
And all its loveliness *is* like the flower of
the field.
7 The grass withers, the flower fades,
Because the breath of the LORD blows
upon it;
Surely the people *are* grass.
8 The grass withers, the flower fades,
But [R]the word of our God stands
forever." [John 12:34]

9 O Zion,
You who bring good tidings,
Get up into the high mountain;
O Jerusalem,
You who bring good tidings,
Lift up your voice with strength,
Lift *it* up, be not afraid;
Say to the cities of Judah, "Behold your
God!"

10 Behold, the Lord GOD shall come [T]with a
strong *hand*, *in strength*
And His arm shall rule for Him;
Behold, [R]His reward *is* with Him,
And His work before Him. Is. 62:11
11 He will [R]feed His flock like a shepherd;
He will gather the lambs with His arm,
And carry *them* in His bosom,
And gently lead those who are with
young. Mic. 5:4; [John 10:11, 14–16]☆

Comfort Because of God's Character

12 [R]Who has measured the waters* in the
hollow of His hand, Prov. 30:4
Measured heaven with a span
And calculated the dust of the earth in a
measure?
Weighed the mountains in scales
And the hills in a balance?

39:1 *Berodach-Baladan,* 2 Kin. 20:12 **40:3** So with MT, Tg., Vg.; LXX omits *in the desert* **40:6** So with MT, Tg.; DSS, LXX, Vg. *I* **40:12** So with MT, LXX, Vg.; DSS read *waters of the sea;* Tg. reads *waters of the world*

13 Who has directed the Spirit of the LORD,
Or *as* His counselor has taught Him?
14 With whom did He take counsel, and
who instructed Him,
And [R]taught Him in the path of justice?
Who taught Him knowledge,
And showed Him the way of
understanding? Job 36:22, 23

15 Behold, the nations *are* as a drop in a
bucket,
And are counted as the small dust on the
scales;
Look, He lifts up the isles as a very little
thing.
16 And Lebanon *is* not sufficient to burn,
Nor its beasts sufficient for a burnt
offering.
17 All nations before Him *are* as nothing,
And [R]they are counted by Him less than
nothing and worthless. Ps. 62:9

18 To whom then will you [R]liken God?
Or what likeness will you compare to
Him? Is. 46:5
19 The workman molds an image,
The goldsmith overspreads it with gold,
And the silversmith casts silver chains.
20 Whoever *is* too impoverished for *such* [T]a
contribution *an offering*
Chooses a tree *that* will not rot;
He seeks for himself a skillful
workman
[R]To prepare a carved image *that* will not
totter. Is. 41:7; 46:7

21[R] Have you not known? Rom. 1:19
Have you not heard?
Has it not been told you from the
beginning?
Have you not understood from the
foundations of the earth?
22 *It is* He who sits above the circle of the
earth,
And its inhabitants *are* like
grasshoppers,
Who [R]stretches out the heavens like a
curtain, Jer. 10:12
And spreads them out like a [R]tent to
dwell in. Ps. 19:4
23 He [T]brings the [R]princes to nothing;
He makes the judges of the earth
useless. *reduces* • Ps. 107:40

24 Scarcely shall they be planted,
Scarcely shall they be sown,
Scarcely shall their stock take root in the
earth,
When He will also blow on them,
And they will wither,
And the whirlwind will take them away
like stubble.

25 "To[R] whom then will you liken Me,
Or *to whom* shall I be equal?" says the
Holy One. Is. 40:18
26 Lift up your eyes on high,
And see who has created these *things*,
Who brings out their host by number;
[R]He calls them all by name, Ps. 147:4
By the greatness of His might
And the strength of *His* power;
Not one is missing.

27[R] Why do you say, O Jacob, Is. 54:7, 8
And speak, O Israel:
"My way is hidden from the LORD,
And my just claim is passed over by my
God"?
28 Have you not known?
Have you not heard?
The everlasting God, the LORD,
The Creator of the ends of the earth,
Neither faints nor is weary.
His understanding is unsearchable.
29 He gives power to the weak,
And to *those who have* no might He
increases strength.
30 Even the youths shall faint and be weary,
And the young men shall utterly fall,
31 But those who [R]wait on the LORD
[R]Shall renew *their* strength;
They shall mount up with wings like
eagles, Is. 30:15 • Ps. 103:5
They shall run and not be weary,
They shall walk and not faint.

CHAPTER 41

Comfort Because of God's Greatness

"KEEP [R]silence before Me, O coastlands,
And let the people renew *their*
strength!
Let them come near, then let them
speak; Zech. 2:13
Let us [R]come near together for
judgment. Is. 1:18

2 "Who raised up one [R]from the east?
Who in righteousness called him to His
feet? Is. 46:11
Who gave the nations before him,
And made *him* rule over kings?
Who gave *them* as the dust *to* his sword,
As driven stubble to his bow?
3 Who pursued them, *and* passed [T]safely
By the way *that* he had not gone with
his feet? Lit. *in peace*
4[R] Who has performed and done *it*,
Calling the generations from the
beginning? Is. 41:26
'I, the LORD, am [R]the first; Rev. 1:8, 17
And with the last I *am* [R]He.' " Is. 43:10

5 The coastlands saw *it* and feared,
The ends of the earth were afraid;

They drew near and came.
6 [R]Everyone helped his neighbor, Is. 40:19
And said to his brother,
[T]"Be of good courage!" Lit. *Be strong*
7 [R]So the craftsman encouraged the
[R]goldsmith;[T] Is. 44:13 • Is. 40:19 • *refiner*
He who smooths *with* the hammer
inspired him who strikes the anvil,
Saying, "It *is* ready for the soldering";
Then he fastened it with pegs,
[R]*That* it might not totter. Is. 40:20

8 "But you, Israel, *are* My servant,
Jacob whom I have [R]chosen, Deut. 7:6
The descendants of Abraham My
[R]friend. James 2:23
9 *You* whom I have taken from the ends of
the earth,
And called from its farthest regions,
And said to you,
'You *are* My servant,
I have chosen you and have not cast you
away:
10 [R]Fear not, [R]for I *am* with you; Is. 43:5
Be not dismayed, for I *am* your God.
I will strengthen you, [Deut. 31:6]
Yes, I will help you,
I will uphold you with My righteous
right hand.'

11 "Behold, all those who were incensed
against you
Shall be [R]ashamed and disgraced;
They shall be as nothing,
And those who strive with you shall
perish. Zech. 12:3
12 You shall seek them and not find them—
Those who contended with you.
Those who war against you
Shall be as nothing,
As a nonexistent thing.
13 For I, the LORD your God, will hold your
right hand,
Saying to you, 'Fear not, I will help you.'

14 "Fear not, you [R]worm Jacob, Job 25:6
You men of Israel!
I will help you," says the LORD
And your Redeemer, the Holy One of
Israel.
15 "Behold, [R]I will make you into a new
threshing sledge with sharp teeth;
You shall thresh the mountains and beat
them small,
And make the hills like chaff. Mic. 4:13
16 You shall [R]winnow them, the wind shall
carry them away, Jer. 51:2
And the whirlwind shall scatter them;
You shall [R]rejoice in the LORD, Is. 25:9☆
And glory in the Holy One of Israel.

17 "The poor and needy seek water, but
there is none,
Their tongues fail for thirst.
I, the LORD, will hear them;
I, the God of Israel, will not [R]forsake
them. Rom. 11:2
18 I will open [R]rivers in desolate heights,
And fountains in the midst of the
valleys; Is. 35:6, 7; 43:19; 44:3
I will make the [R]wilderness a pool of
water, Ps. 107:35
And the dry land springs of water.
19 I will plant in the wilderness the cedar
and the acacia tree,
The myrtle and the oil tree;
I will set in the [R]desert the cypress tree
and the pine Is. 35:1
And the box tree together,
20 [R]That they may see and know, Job 12:9
And consider and understand together,
That the hand of the LORD has done this,
And the Holy One of Israel has created it.

21 "Present your case," says the LORD.
"Bring forth your strong *reasons*," says
the [R]King of Jacob. Is. 43:15
22 "Let[R] them bring forth and show us what
will happen; Is. 45:21
Let them show the [R]former things, what
they *were*, Is. 43:9
That we may consider them,
And know the latter end of them;
Or declare to us things to come.
23 [R]Show the things that are to come
hereafter, [John 13:19]
That we may know that you *are* gods;
Yes, [R]do good or do evil, Jer. 10:5
That we may be dismayed and see *it*
together.
24 Indeed [R]you *are* nothing, [1 Cor. 8:4]
And your work *is* nothing;
He who chooses you *is* an abomination.

25 "I have raised up one from the north,
And he shall come;
From the [T]rising of the sun [R]he shall call
on My name; East • Ezra 1:2
[R]And he shall come against princes as
though mortar, Is. 41:2
As the potter treads clay.
26 [R]Who has declared from the beginning,
that we may know? Is. 43:9
And former times, that we may say, '*He*
is righteous'?
Surely *there is* no one who shows,
Surely *there is* no one who declares,
Surely *there is* no one who hears your
words.
27 [R]The first time [R]*I said* to Zion,
'Look, there they are!' Is. 41:4 • Is. 40:9
And I will give to Jerusalem one who
brings good tidings.
28 [R]For I looked, and *there was* no man;
I looked among them, but *there was* no
counselor,

Who, when I asked of them, could
answer a word. Is. 63:5
29[R] Indeed they *are* all worthless;*
Their works *are* nothing;
Their molded images *are* wind and
confusion. Is. 41:24

CHAPTER 42

Comfort Because of God's Servant

"BEHOLD! [R]My Servant whom I uphold,
My Elect One *in whom* My soul
[R]delights! Luke 3:22☆ • Matt. 3:17; 17:5
[R]I have put My Spirit upon Him; [Is. 11:2]
He will bring forth justice to the
Gentiles.
2 He will not cry out, nor raise *His voice*,
Nor cause His voice to be heard in the
street.
3 A bruised reed He will not break,
And smoking flax He will not quench;
He will bring forth justice for truth.
4 He will not fail nor be discouraged,
Till He has established justice in the
earth;
[R]And the coastlands shall wait for His
law." [Gen. 49:10]☆

5 Thus says God the LORD,
[R]Who created the heavens and stretched
them out, Zech. 12:1
Who spread forth the earth and that
which comes from it,
Who gives breath to the people on it,
And spirit to those who walk on it:
6 "I,[R] the LORD, have called You in
[R]righteousness, Is. 43:1 • Jer. 23:5, 6☆
And will hold Your hand;
I will keep You [R]and give You as a
covenant to the people, Is. 49:8
As [R]a light to the Gentiles, Luke 2:32
7[R] To open blind eyes, Is. 35:5☆
To [R]bring out prisoners from the prison,
Those who sit in [R]darkness from the
prison house. Luke 4:18 • Is. 9:2
8 I *am* the LORD, that *is* My name;
And My glory I will not give to another,
Nor My praise to carved images.
9 Behold, the former things have come to
pass,
And new things I declare;
Before they spring forth I tell you of
them."

10[R] Sing to the LORD a new song,
And His praise from the ends of the
earth, Ps. 33:3; 40:3; 98:1
[R]You who go down to the sea, and [T]all
that is in it, Ps. 107:23 • Lit. *its fullness*
You coastlands and you inhabitants of
them!
11 Let the wilderness and its cities lift up
their voice,
The villages *that* Kedar inhabits.
Let the inhabitants of Sela sing,
Let them shout from the top of the
mountains.
12 Let them give glory to the LORD,
And declare His praise in the coastlands.
13 The LORD shall go forth like a mighty
man;
He shall stir up *His* zeal like a man of
war.
He shall cry out, yes, shout aloud;
He shall prevail against His enemies.

14 "I have held My peace a long time,
I have been still and restrained Myself.
Now I will cry like a woman in [T]labor,
I will pant and gasp at once. *childbirth*
15 I will lay waste the mountains and hills,
And dry up all their vegetation;
I will make the rivers coastlands,
And I will dry up the pools.
16 I will bring the blind by a way they did
not know;
I will lead them in paths they have not
known.
I will make darkness light before them,
And crooked places straight.
These things I will do for them,
And not forsake them.
17 They shall be [R]turned back, Ps. 97:7
They shall be greatly ashamed,
Who trust in carved images,
Who say to the molded images,
'You *are* our gods.'

18 "Hear, you deaf;
And look, you blind, that you may see.
19 Who *is* blind but My servant,
Or deaf as My messenger *whom* I send?
Who *is* blind as *he who is* perfect,
And blind as the LORD's servant?
20 Seeing many things, [R]but you do not
observe; Rom. 2:21
Opening the ears, but he does not hear."

21 The LORD is well pleased for His
righteousness' sake;
He will exalt the law and make *it*
honorable.
22 But this *is* a people robbed and plundered;
All of them are snared in holes,
And they are hidden in prison houses;
They are for prey, and no one delivers;
For plunder, and no one says, "Restore!"

23 Who among you will give ear to this?
Who will listen and hear for the time to
come?
24 Who gave Jacob for plunder, and Israel
to the robbers?

41:29 So with MT, Vg.; DSS, Syr., Tg. *nothing;* LXX omits first line

Was it not the LORD,
He against whom we have sinned?
For they would not walk in His ways,
Nor were they obedient to His law.
25 Therefore He has poured on him the fury of His anger
And the strength of battle;
It has set him on fire all around,
[R]Yet he did not know; Hos. 7:9
And it burned him,
Yet he did not take *it* to [R]heart. Is. 29:13

CHAPTER 43

Comfort Because of Israel's Restoration

BUT now, thus says the LORD, who created you, O Jacob,
And He who formed you, O Israel:
"Fear not, [R]for I have redeemed you;
[R]I have called *you* by your name;
You *are* Mine. Is. 43:5; 44:6 • Is. 42:6; 45:4
2 [R]When you pass through the waters, [R]I *will be* with you; [Ps. 66:12; 91:3]
And through the rivers, they shall not overflow you. [Deut. 31:6]
When you [R]walk through the fire, you shall not be burned, Dan. 3:25
Nor shall the flame scorch you.
3 For I *am* the LORD your God,
The Holy One of Israel, your Savior;
I gave Egypt for your ransom,
Ethiopia and Seba in your place.
4 Since you were precious in My sight,
You have been honored,
And I have [R]loved you; Is. 63:9
Therefore I will give men for you,
And people for your life.
5 [R]Fear not, for I *am* with you; Is. 41:10
I will bring your descendants from the east,
And [R]gather you from the west; Is. 54:7
6 I will say to the [R]north, 'Give them up!'
And to the south, 'Do not keep them back!' Is. 49:12
Bring My sons from afar,
And My daughters from the ends of the earth—
7 Everyone who is [R]called by My name,
Whom [R]I have created for My glory;
I have formed him, yes, I have made him." James 2:7 • [2 Cor. 5:17]

8 [R]Bring out the blind people who have eyes, Ezek. 12:2
And the [R]deaf who have ears. Is. 29:18
9 Let all the nations be gathered together,
And let the people be assembled.
Who among them can declare this,
And show us former things?
Let them bring out their witnesses, that they may be justified;
Or let them hear and say, "*It is* truth."
10 "You[R] *are* My witnesses," says the LORD,
"And My servant whom I have chosen,
That you may know and believe Me,
And understand that I *am* He. Is. 44:8
Before Me there was no God formed,
Nor shall there be after Me.
11 I, *even* I, [R]*am* the LORD, Hos. 13:4
And besides Me *there is* no savior.
12 I have declared and saved,
I have proclaimed,
And *there was* no [R]foreign *god* among you; Deut. 32:16
[R]Therefore you *are* My witnesses," Is. 44:8
Says the LORD, "that I *am* God.
13 [R]Indeed before the day *was*, I *am* He;
And *there is* no one who can deliver out of My hand; Ps. 90:2
I work, and who will reverse it?"

14 Thus says the LORD, your Redeemer,
The Holy One of Israel:
"For your sake I will send to Babylon,
And bring them all down as fugitives—
The Chaldeans, who rejoice in their ships.
15 I *am* the LORD, your Holy One,
The Creator of Israel, your King."

16 Thus says the LORD, who [R]makes a way in the sea Ex. 14:16, 21, 22
And a path through the mighty waters,
17 Who [R]brings forth the chariot and horse,
The army and the power Ex. 14:4–9, 25
(They shall lie down together, they shall not rise;
They are extinguished, they are quenched like a wick):
18 "Do[R] not remember the former things,
Nor consider the things of old. Jer. 16:14
19 Behold, I will do a [R]new thing,
Now it shall spring forth;
Shall you not know it? [2 Cor. 5:17]
[R]I will even make a road in the wilderness Ex. 17:6
And rivers in the desert.
20 The beast of the field will honor Me,
The jackals and the ostriches,
Because [R]I give waters in the wilderness
And rivers in the desert, Is. 48:21
To give drink to My people, My chosen.
21 This people I have formed for Myself;
They shall declare My [R]praise. Jer. 13:11

22 "But you have not called upon Me, O Jacob;
And you [R]have been weary of Me, O Israel. Mal. 1:13; 3:14
23 [R]You have not brought Me the sheep for your burnt offerings, Amos 5:25
Nor have you honored Me with your sacrifices.
I have not caused you to serve with grain offerings,
Nor wearied you with incense.

24 You have bought Me no sweet cane with
money,
Nor have you satisfied Me with the fat of
your sacrifices;
But you have burdened Me with your
sins,
You have [R]wearied Me with your
iniquities. Is. 1:14; 7:13

25 "I, *even* I, *am* He who blots out your
transgressions for My own sake;
And I will not remember your sins.
26 Put Me in remembrance;
Let us contend together;
State your *case*, that you may be
[T]acquitted. *justified*
27 Your first father sinned,
And your [T]mediators have transgressed
against Me. *interpreters*
28 Therefore I will profane the princes of
the sanctuary;
[R]I will give Jacob to the curse, Dan. 9:11
And Israel to reproaches.

CHAPTER 44

"YET hear now, O Jacob My servant,
And Israel whom I have chosen.
2 Thus says the LORD who made you
And formed you from the womb, *who*
will help you:
'Fear not, O Jacob My servant;
And you, Jeshurun, whom I have chosen.
3 For I will pour water on him who is
thirsty,
And floods on the dry ground;
I will pour My Spirit on your
descendants,
And My blessing on your offspring;
4 They will spring up among the grass
Like willows by the watercourses.'
5 One will say, 'I *am* the LORD's';
Another will call *himself* by the name of
Jacob;
Another will write *with* his hand, 'The
LORD's,'
And name *himself* by the name of Israel.

6 "Thus says the LORD, the King of Israel,
And his Redeemer, the LORD of hosts:
[R]'I *am* the First and I *am* the Last; Is. 41:4
Besides Me *there is* no God.
7 And [R]who can proclaim as I do?
Then let him declare it and set it in order
for Me, Is. 41:4, 22, 26
Since I appointed the ancient people.
And the things that are coming and shall
come,
Let them show these to them.
8 Do not fear, nor be afraid;
[R]Have I not told you from that time, and
declared *it?* Is. 41:22
[R]You *are* My witnesses. Is. 43:10, 12
Is there a God besides Me?
Indeed [R]*there is* no other Rock;
I know not *one*.'" 1 Sam. 2:2

9 [R]Those who make an image, all of them
are useless, Is. 41:24
And their precious things shall not
profit;
They *are* their own witnesses;
[R]They neither see nor know, that they
may be ashamed. Ps. 115:4
10 Who would form a god or mold an
image
[R]*That* profits him nothing? Hab. 2:18
11 Surely all his companions would be
[R]ashamed; Ps. 97:7
And the workmen, they *are* mere men.
Let them all be gathered together,
Let them stand up;
Yet they shall fear,
They shall be ashamed together.

12 [R]The blacksmith with the tongs works
one in the coals, Jer. 10:3–5
Fashions it with hammers,
And works it with the strength of his
arms.
Even so, he is hungry, and his strength
fails;
He drinks no water and is faint.

13 The craftsman stretches out *his* rule,
He marks one out with chalk;
He fashions it with a plane,
He marks it out with the compass,
And makes it like the figure of a man,
According to the beauty of a man, that it
may remain in the house.
14 He cuts down cedars for himself,
And takes the cypress and the oak;
He [T]secures *it* for himself among the
trees of the forest. Lit. *appropriates*
He plants a pine, and the rain nourishes
it.

15 Then it shall be for a man to burn,
For he will take some of it and warm
himself;
Yes, he kindles *it* and bakes bread;
Indeed he makes a god and worships *it;*
He makes it a carved image, and falls
down to it.
16 He burns half of it in the fire;
With this half he eats meat;
He roasts a roast, and is satisfied.
He even warms *himself* and says,
"Ah! I am warm,
I have seen the fire."
17 And the rest of it he makes into a god,
His carved image.
He falls down before it and worships *it*,
Prays to it and says,
"Deliver me, for you *are* my god!"

18 They do not know nor understand;
For [R]He has shut their eyes, so that they cannot see, Is. 6:9, 10; 29:10
And their hearts, so that they cannot [R]understand. Jer. 10:14
19 And no one [R]considers in his heart,
Nor *is there* knowledge nor understanding to say,
"I have burned half of it in the fire,
Yes, I have also baked bread on its coals;
I have roasted meat and eaten *it;*
And shall I make the rest of it an abomination?
Shall I fall down before a block of wood?" Is. 46:8
20 He feeds on ashes;
[R]A deceived heart has turned him aside;
And he cannot deliver his soul,
Nor say, "*Is there* not a [R]lie in my right hand?" 2 Thess. 2:11 • Rom. 1:25

21 "Remember these, O Jacob,
And Israel, for you *are* My servant;
I have formed you, you *are* My servant;
O Israel, you will not be [R]forgotten by Me! Is. 49:15
22 [R]I have blotted out, like a thick cloud, your transgressions, Is. 43:25
And like a cloud, your sins.
Return to Me, for [R]I have redeemed you." 1 Cor. 6:20

23 Sing, O heavens, for the LORD has done *it!* Ps. 69:34
Shout, you lower parts of the earth;
Break forth into singing, you mountains,
O forest, and every tree in it!
For the LORD has redeemed Jacob,
And glorified Himself in Israel

24 Thus says the LORD, [R]your Redeemer,
And [R]He who formed you from the womb: Is. 43:14 • Is. 43:1
"I *am* the LORD, who makes all *things,*
[R]Who stretches out the heavens [T]all alone, Job 9:8 • By Himself
Who spreads abroad the earth by Myself;
25 Who [R]frustrates the signs [R]of the babblers, Is. 47:13 • Jer. 50:36
And drives diviners mad;
Who turns wise men backward,
And makes their knowledge foolishness;
26 [R]Who confirms the word of His servant,
And performs the counsel of His messengers; Zech. 1:6
Who says to Jerusalem, 'You shall be inhabited,'
To the cities of Judah, 'You shall be built,'
And I will raise up her waste places;
27 Who says to the deep, 'Be dry!
And I will dry up your rivers';
28 Who says of [R]Cyrus, '*He is* My shepherd,
And he shall perform all My pleasure,
Saying to Jerusalem, [R]"You shall be built," Ezra 1:1 • Ezra 6:7
And to the temple, "Your foundation shall be laid." '

CHAPTER 45

Comfort Because of God's Use of Cyrus

"THUS says the LORD to His anointed,
To [R]Cyrus, whose [R]right hand I have held— Is. 44:28 • Is. 41:13
[R]To subdue nations before him Dan. 5:30
And [R]loose the armor of kings, Job 12:21
To open before him the double doors,
So that the gates will not be shut:
2 'I will go before you
[R]And make the crooked places* straight; Is. 40:4
[R]I will break in pieces the gates of bronze
And cut the bars of iron. Ps. 107:16
3 I will give you the treasures of darkness
And hidden riches of secret places,
That you may know that I, the LORD,
Who [R]call *you* by your name, Ex. 33:12
Am the God of Israel.
4 For [R]Jacob My servant's sake, Is. 44:1
And Israel My elect,
I have even called you by your name;
I have named you, though you have not known Me.
5 I *am* the LORD, and [R]*there is* no other;
There is no God besides Me. Is. 45:14, 18
[R]I will gird you, though you have not known Me, Ps. 18:32
6 [R]That they may know from the rising of the sun to its setting Mal. 1:11
That *there is* none besides Me.
I *am* the LORD, and *there is* no other;
7 I form the light and create darkness,
I make peace and create calamity;
I, the LORD, do all these *things.*'

8 "Rain[R] down, you heavens, from above,
And let the skies pour down righteousness; Ps. 85:11
Let the earth open, let them bring forth salvation,
And let righteousness spring up together.
I, the LORD, have created it.

9 "Woe to him who strives with [R]his Maker!
Let the potsherd *strive* with the potsherds of the earth! Is. 64:8
[R]Shall the clay say to him who forms it,
'What are you making?' Jer. 18:6
Or shall your handiwork *say,* 'He has no hands'?

45:2 DSS, LXX *mountains;* Tg. *I will trample down the walls;* Vg. *I will humble the great ones of the earth*

10 Woe to him who says to *his* father, 'What
are you begetting?'
Or to the woman, 'What have you
brought forth?' "

11 Thus says the LORD,
The Holy One of Israel, and his Maker:
R"Ask Me of things to come concerning
RMy sons; Is. 8:19 • Jer. 31:9
And concerning Rthe work of My hands,
you command Me. Is. 29:23; 60:21; 64:8
12 RI have made the earth, Is. 42:5
And Rcreated man on it. Gen. 1:26
I—My hands—stretched out the
heavens,
And all their host I have commanded.
13 RI have raised him up in righteousness,
And I will direct all his ways; Is. 41:2
He shall Rbuild My city 2 Chr. 36:22
And let My exiles go free,
RNot for price nor reward," [Rom. 3:24]
Says the LORD of hosts.

14 Thus says the LORD:
R"The labor of Egypt and merchandise of
Cush Zech. 8:22, 23
And of the Sabeans, men of stature,
Shall come over to you, and they shall be
yours;
They shall walk behind you,
They shall come over in chains;
And they shall bow down to you.
They will make supplication to you,
saying, R'Surely God *is* in you,
And *there is* no other; 1 Cor. 14:25
R*There is* no other God.' " Is. 45:5

15 Truly You *are* God, Rwho hide Yourself,
O God of Israel, the Savior! Ps. 44:24
16 They shall be Rashamed Is. 44:11
And also disgraced, all of them;
They shall go in confusion together,
Who are makers of idols.
17 *But* Israel shall be saved by the LORD
With an Reverlasting salvation; Is. 51:6
You shall not be ashamed or Rdisgraced
Forever and ever. Is. 29:22

18 For thus says the LORD,
RWho created the heavens, Is. 42:5
Who is God,
Who formed the earth and made it,
Who has established it,
Who did not create it in vain,
Who formed it to be inhabited:
"I *am* the LORD, and *there is* no other.
19 I have not spoken in secret,
In a dark place of the earth;
I did not say to the seed of Jacob,
'Seek Me Tin vain'; Or *in a waste place*
I, the LORD, speak righteousness,
I declare things that are right.

20 "Assemble yourselves and come;
Draw near together,
You *who have* escaped from the nations.
RThey have no knowledge, Is. 44:9; 46:7
Who carry the wood of their carved
image,
And pray to a god *that* cannot save.
21 Tell and bring forth *your case;*
Yes, let them take counsel together.
RWho has declared this from ancient
time? Is. 41:22; 43:9
Who has told it from that time?
Have not I, the LORD?
RAnd *there is* no other God besides Me,
A just God and a Savior; Is. 44:8
There is none besides Me.

22 "Look to Me, and be saved,
RAll you ends of the earth! Ps. 22:27; 65:5
For I *am* God, and *there is* no other.
23 RI have sworn by Myself; [Heb. 6:13]
The word has gone out of My mouth *in*
righteousness,
And shall not return,
That to Me every knee shall bow,
Every tongue shall take an oath.
24 He shall say,
'Surely in the LORD I have Rrighteousness
and strength. [1 Cor. 1:30]
To Him *men* shall come,
And Rall shall be ashamed Is. 41:11
Who are incensed against Him.
25 In the LORD all the descendants of Israel
Shall be justified, and shall glory.' "

CHAPTER 46

Destruction of Babylon's Idols

BEL Rbows down, Nebo stoops; Jer. 50:2
Their idols were on the beasts and on
the cattle.
Your carriages *were* heavily loaded,
RA burden to the weary *beast*. Jer. 10:5
2 They stoop, they bow down together;
They could not deliver the burden,
But have themselves gone into captivity.

3 "Listen to Me, O house of Jacob,
And all the remnant of the house of
Israel,
RWho have been upheld *by Me* from
Tbirth, Ps. 71:6 • Lit. *the belly*
Who have been carried from the womb:
4 Even to *your* old age, I *am* He,
And *even* to gray hairs RI will carry *you!*
I have made, and I will bear; Ps. 48:14
Even I will carry, and will deliver *you*.

5 "ToR whom will you liken Me, and make
Me equal Is. 40:18, 25
And compare Me, that we should be
alike?
6 RThey lavish gold out of the bag,

And weigh silver on the scales;
They hire a [R]goldsmith, and he makes it
a god; Is. 40:19; 41:6 • Is. 44:12
They prostrate themselves, yes, they
worship.
7[R] They bear it on the shoulder, they carry
it Jer. 10:5
And set it in its place, and it stands;
From its place it shall not move.
Though [R]*one* cries out to it, yet it cannot
answer Is. 45:20
Nor save him out of his trouble.

8 "Remember this, and [T]show yourselves
men; *be men, take courage*
Recall to mind, O you transgressors.
9 Remember the former things of old
For I *am* God, and *there is* no other;
I am God, and *there is* none like Me,
10[R] Declaring the end from the beginning,
And from ancient times *things* that are
not *yet* done, Is. 45:21; 48:3
Saying, 'My counsel shall stand,
And I will do all My pleasure,'
11 Calling a bird of prey from the east,
The man [R]who executes My counsel,
from a far country. Is. 44:28
Indeed [R]I have spoken *it;* Num. 23:19
I will also bring it to pass.
I have purposed *it;*
I will also do it.

12 "Listen to Me, you [R]stubborn-hearted,
Who *are* far from righteousness: Ps. 76:5
13[R] I bring My righteousness near, it shall
not be far off; [Rom. 1:17]
My salvation [R]shall not linger.
And I will place [R]salvation in Zion,
For Israel My glory. Hab. 2:3 • Is. 62:11

CHAPTER 47

Destruction of Babylon

"COME down and sit in the dust,
O virgin daughter of Babylon;
Sit on the ground without a throne,
O daughter of the Chaldeans!
For you shall no more be called
Tender and [T]delicate. *dainty*
2[R] Take the millstones and grind meal.
Remove your veil,
Take off the skirt,
Uncover the thigh,
Pass through the rivers. Ex. 11:5
3 Your nakedness shall be uncovered,
Yes, your shame will be seen;
[R]I will take vengeance, [Rom. 12:19]
And I will not arbitrate with a man."

4 *As for* [R]our Redeemer, the LORD of hosts
is His name, Jer. 50:34
The Holy One of Israel.

5 "Sit in [R]silence, and go into darkness,
O daughter of the Chaldeans; 1 Sam. 2:9
[R]For you shall no longer be called
The Lady of Kingdoms. [Dan. 2:37]
6 I was angry with My people;
I have profaned My inheritance,
And given them into your hand.
You showed them no mercy;
[R]On the elderly you laid your yoke very
heavily. Deut. 28:49, 50
7 And you said, 'I shall be [R]a lady forever,'
So that you did not [R]take these *things* to
heart, Rev. 18:7 • Is. 42:25; 46:8
Nor remember the latter end of them.

8 "Therefore hear this now, *you who are*
given to pleasures,
Who dwell securely,
Who say in your heart,
'I *am*, and *there is* no one else besides
me;
I shall not sit *as* a widow,
Nor shall I know the loss of children';
9 But these two *things* shall come to you
[R]In a moment, in one day: 1 Thess. 5:3
The loss of children, and widowhood.
They shall come upon you in their
fullness
Because of the multitude of your
sorceries,
For the great abundance of your
enchantments.

10 "For you have trusted in your wickedness;
You have said, 'No one [R]sees me';
Your wisdom and your knowledge have
[T]warped you; Is. 29:15 • *led you astray*
And you have said in your heart,
'I *am*, and *there is* no one else besides
me.'
11 Therefore evil shall come upon you;
You shall not know from where it arises.
And trouble shall fall upon you;
You will not be able to put it off.
And [R]desolation shall come upon you
[R]suddenly, 1 Thess. 5:3 • Is. 29:5
Which you shall not know.

12 "Stand now with your enchantments
And the multitude of your sorceries,
In which you have labored from your
youth—
Perhaps you will be able to profit,
Perhaps you will prevail.
13[R] You are wearied in the multitude of your
counsels; Is. 57:10
Let now [R]the astrologers, the
stargazers, Dan. 2:2, 10
And the monthly prognosticators
Stand up and save you
From what shall come upon you.
14 Behold, they shall be as stubble,
The fire shall [R]burn them; Jer. 51:58

They shall not deliver themselves
From the power of the flame;
It shall not *be* a coal to be warmed by,
Nor a fire to sit before!
15 Thus shall they be to you
With whom you have labored,
[R]Your merchants from your youth;
They shall wander each one to his
[T]quarter. Rev. 18:11 • *own side* or *way*
No one shall save you.

CHAPTER 48

Declaration of Judah's Chastening

"HEAR this, O house of Jacob,
Who are called by the name of Israel,
And have come forth from the
wellsprings of Judah;
Who swear by the name of the LORD,
And make mention of the God of Israel,
But not in truth or in righteousness;
2 For they call themselves [R]after the holy
city, Is. 52:1; 64:10
And [R]lean on the God of Israel; Mic. 3:11
The LORD of hosts *is* His name:

3 "I have [R]declared the former things from
the beginning; Is. 44:7, 8; 46:10
They went forth from My mouth, and I
caused them to hear it.
Suddenly I did *them,* [R]and they came to
pass. Josh. 21:45
4 Because I knew that you *were*
[T]obstinate, Heb. *hard*
And [R]your neck *was* an iron sinew,
And your brow bronze, Deut. 31:27
5 Even from the beginning I have declared
it to you;
Before it came to pass I proclaimed *it* to
you,
Lest you should say, 'My idol has done
them,
And my carved image and my molded
image
Have commanded them.'

6 "You have heard;
See all this.
And will you not declare *it?*
I have made you hear new things from
this time,
Even hidden things, and you did not
know them.
7 They are created now and not from the
beginning;
And before this day you have not heard
them,
Lest you should say, 'Of course I knew
them.'
8 Surely you did not hear,
Surely you did not know;
Surely from long ago your ear was not
opened.
For I knew that you would deal very
treacherously,
And were called [R]a transgressor from
the womb. Ps. 58:3

9 "For[R] My name's sake [R]I will defer My
anger, Ezek. 20:9, 14, 22, 44 • Ps. 78:38
And *for* My praise I will restrain it from
you,
So that I do not cut you off.
10 Behold, [R]I have refined you, but not as
silver; Ps. 66:10
I have tested you in the [R]furnace of
affliction. Deut. 4:20
11 For My own sake, for My own sake, I
will do *it;*
For how should *My name* be profaned?
And I will not give My glory to another

12 "Listen to Me, O Jacob,
And Israel, My called:
I *am* He, [R]I *am* the [R]First, Deut. 32:39
I *am* also the Last. [Rev. 22:13]
13 Indeed [R]My hand has laid the foundation
of the earth, Ps. 102:25
And My right hand has stretched out the
heavens;
When [R]I call to them, Is. 40:26
They stand up together.

14 "All of you, assemble yourselves, and
hear!
Who among them has declared these
things?
[R]The LORD loves him; Is. 45:1
[R]He shall do His pleasure on Babylon,
And His arm *shall be against* the
Chaldeans. Is. 44:28; 47:1–15
15 I, *even* I, have spoken;
Yes, [R]I have called him, Is. 45:1, 2
I have brought him, and his way will
prosper.

16 "Come near to Me, hear this:
[R]I have not spoken in secret from the
beginning; Is. 45:19
From the time that it was, I *was* there.
And now [R]the Lord GOD and His Spirit
Have* sent Me." Zech. 2:8, 9, 11

17 Thus says [R]the LORD, your Redeemer,
The Holy One of Israel:
"I *am* the LORD your God,
Who teaches you to profit,
[R]Who leads you by the way you should
go. Is. 43:14 • Ps. 32:8
18 [R]Oh, that you had heeded My
commandments! Ps. 81:13
[R]Then your peace would have been like a
river, Ps. 119:165

48:16 Heb. verb is sing.; or *Has sent Me and His Spirit*

And your righteousness like the waves of the sea.
19[R] Your descendants also would have been like the sand, Gen. 22:17
And the offspring of your body like the grains of sand;
His name would not have been cut off
Nor destroyed from before Me."

20[R] Go forth from Babylon! Zech. 2:6, 7
Flee from the Chaldeans!
With a voice of singing,
Declare, proclaim this,
Utter it to the end of the earth;
Say, "The LORD has [R]redeemed
His servant Jacob!" [Ex. 19:4–6]
21 And they [R]did not thirst [Is. 41:17, 18]
When He led them through the deserts;
He [R]caused the waters to flow from the rock for them; Ex. 17:6
He also split the rock, and the waters gushed out.

22 "*There*[R] *is* no peace," says the LORD, "for the wicked." [Is. 57:21]

CHAPTER 49

The Messiah's Mission

"LISTEN, [R]O coastlands, to Me, Is. 41:1
And take heed, you peoples from afar!
[R]The LORD has called Me from the womb;
From the matrix of My mother He has made mention of My name. Jer. 1:5
2 And He has made [R]My mouth like a sharp sword; Rev. 1:16; 2:12☆
[R]In the shadow of His hand He has hidden Me, Is. 51:16
And made Me [R]a polished shaft; Ps. 45:5
In His quiver He has hidden Me."

3 "And He said to me,
[R]'You *are* My servant, O Israel, [Zech. 3:8]
[R]In whom I will be glorified.' Is. 44:23
4[R] Then I said, 'I have labored in vain,
I have spent my strength for nothing and in vain; [Ezek. 3:19]
Yet surely my [T]just reward *is* with the LORD, *justice*
And my work with my God.'"

5 "And now the LORD says,
Who formed Me from the womb *to be* His Servant,
To bring Jacob back to Him,
So that Israel [R]is gathered to Him*
(For I shall be glorious in the eyes of the LORD, Matt. 23:37☆
And My God shall be My strength),
6 Indeed He says,
'It is too small a thing that You should be My Servant
To raise up the tribes of Jacob,
And to restore the preserved ones of Israel;
I will also give You as a [R]light to the Gentiles, [Luke 2:32]; Acts 13:47☆
That You should be My salvation to the ends of the earth.'"

7 Thus says the LORD,
The Redeemer of Israel, their Holy One,
[R]To Him whom man despises,
To Him whom the nation abhors,
To the Servant of rulers: [Ps. 22:6–8]☆
[R]"Kings shall see and arise, [Is. 52:15]
Princes also shall worship,
Because of the LORD who is faithful,
The Holy One of Israel;
And He has chosen You."

8 Thus says the LORD:

"In an [R]acceptable[T] time I have heard You, 2 Cor. 6:2☆ • *favorable*
And in the day of salvation I have helped You;
I will [T]preserve You [R]and give You *keep*
As a covenant to the people, Is. 42:6
To restore the earth,
To cause them to inherit the desolate [T]heritages; *inheritances*
9 That You may say [R]to the prisoners, 'Go forth,' Is. 61:1; Luke 4:18☆
To those who *are* in darkness, 'Show yourselves.'

"They shall feed along the roads,
And their pastures *shall be* on all desolate heights.
10 They shall neither [R]hunger nor thirst,
Neither heat nor sun shall strike them;
For He who has mercy on them [R]will lead them, Rev. 7:16☆ • Ps. 23:2
Even by the springs of water He will guide them.
11[R] I will make each of My mountains a road, Is. 40:4
And My highways shall be elevated.
12 Surely [R]these shall come from afar;
Look! Those from the north and the west, Is. 43:5, 6
And these from the land of Sinim."

13[R] Sing, O heavens! Is. 44:23
Be joyful, O earth!
And break out in singing, O mountains!
For the LORD has comforted His people,
And will have mercy on His afflicted.

14[R] But Zion said, "The LORD has forsaken me, Is. 40:27
And my Lord has forgotten me."

49:5 Qr., DSS, LXX *is gathered to Him;* Kt. *is not gathered*

15 "Can[R] a woman forget her nursing child,
And not have compassion on the son of her womb? Ps. 103:13
Surely they may forget,
[R]Yet I will not forget you. Rom. 11:29
16 See, [R]I have inscribed you on the palms *of My hands;* Song 8:6
Your walls *are* continually before Me.
17 Your sons* shall make haste;
Your destroyers and those who laid you waste
Shall go away from you.
18 [R]Lift up your eyes, look around and see;
All these gather together *and* come to you. Is. 60:4
As I live," says the LORD,
"You shall surely clothe yourselves with them all [R]as an ornament, Prov. 17:6
And bind them *on you* as a bride *does.*

19 "For your waste and desolate places,
And the land of your destruction,
[R]Will even now be too small for the inhabitants; Zech. 10:10
And those who swallowed you up will be far away.
20 [R]The children you will have, Is. 60:4
After you have lost the others,
Will say again in your ears,
'The place *is* too small for me;
Give me a place where I may dwell.'
21 Then you will say in your heart,
'Who has begotten these for me,
Since I have lost my children and am desolate,
A captive, and wandering to and fro?
And who has brought these up?
There I was, left alone;
But these, where *were* they?'"

22 [R]Thus says the Lord GOD: Is. 60:4

"Behold, I will lift My hand in an oath to the nations,
And set up My [T]standard for the peoples; *banner*
They shall bring your sons in *their* [T]arms, *Lit. bosom*
And your daughters shall be carried on *their* shoulders;
23 [R]Kings shall be your foster fathers,
And their queens your nursing mothers;
They shall bow down to you with *their* faces to the earth, Is. 52:15
And [R]lick up the dust of your feet.
Then you will know that I *am* the LORD,
[R]For they shall not be ashamed who wait for Me." Ps. 72:9 • [Rom. 5:5]

24 [R]Shall the prey be taken from the mighty,
Or the captives of the righteous* be delivered? Luke 11:21, 22

25 But thus says the LORD:

"Even the captives of the mighty shall be taken away,
And the prey of the terrible be delivered;
For I will contend with him who contends with you,
And I will save your children.
26 I will [R]feed those who oppress you with their own flesh, Is. 9:20
And they shall be drunk with their own [R]blood as with sweet wine. Rev. 14:20
All flesh [R]shall know Ps. 9:16
That I, the LORD, *am* your Savior,
And your Redeemer, the Mighty One of Jacob."

CHAPTER 50

The Messiah's Obedience

THUS says the LORD:

"Where *is* [R]the certificate of your mother's divorce, Deut. 24:1
Whom I have put away?
Or which of My [R]creditors *is it* to whom I have sold you? Deut. 32:30; 2 Kin. 4:1
For your iniquities [R]you have sold yourselves, Is. 52:3
And for your transgressions your mother has been put away.
2 Why, when I came, *was there* no man?
Why, when I called, *was there* none to answer?
Is My hand shortened at all that it cannot redeem?
Or have I no power to deliver?
Indeed with My [R]rebuke I dry up the sea, Nah. 1:4
I make the rivers a wilderness;
Their fish stink because *there is* no water,
And die of thirst.
3 I clothe the heavens with blackness,
And I make sackcloth their covering."

4 "The[R] Lord GOD has given Me Ex. 4:11
The tongue of the learned,
That I should know how to speak
A word in season to *him who is* [R]weary.
He awakens Me morning by morning,
He awakens My ear
To hear as the learned. Matt. 11:28
5 The Lord GOD has opened My ear;
And I was not [R]rebellious,
Nor did I turn away. Matt. 26:39; John 14:31☆
6 I gave My back to those who struck *Me,*
And [R]My cheeks to those who plucked out the beard; Matt. 26:67; 27:30☆
I did not hide My face from shame and [R]spitting. Lam. 3:30

49:17 DSS, LXX, Tg., Vg. *builders* **49:24** So with MT, Tg.; DSS, Syr., Vg. *the mighty;* LXX *unjustly*

7 "For the Lord GOD will help Me;
Therefore I will not be disgraced;
Therefore [R]I have set My face like a
flint, Luke 9:51☆
And I know that I will not be ashamed.
8 [R]*He is* near who justifies Me;
Who will contend with Me?
Let us stand together. [Rom. 8:32–34]
Who *is* My adversary?
Let him come near Me.
9 Surely the Lord GOD [R]will help Me;
Who *is* he *who* will condemn Me?
[R]Indeed they will all grow old like a
garment; Acts 2:24☆ • Job 13:28
[R]The moth will eat them up. Is. 51:6, 8

10 "Who among you fears the LORD?
Who obeys the voice of His Servant?
Who [R]walks in darkness Ps. 23:4
And has no light?
[R]Let him trust in the name of the LORD
And rely upon his God. 2 Chr. 20:20
11 Look, all you who kindle a fire,
Who encircle *yourselves* with sparks:
Walk in the light of your fire and in the
sparks you have kindled—
This you shall have from My hand:
You shall lie down [R]in torment. Ps. 16:4

CHAPTER 51

The Messiah's Encouragement to Israel

"LISTEN to Me, [R]you who [T]follow after
righteousness, [Rom. 9:30–32] • *pursue*
You who seek the LORD:
Look to the rock *from which* you were
hewn,
And to the hole of the pit *from which*
you were dug.
2 [R]Look to Abraham your father, Heb. 11:11
And to Sarah *who* bore you;
[R]For I called him alone, Gen. 12:1
And blessed him and increased him."

3 For the LORD will [R]comfort Zion,
He will comfort all her waste places;
He will make her wilderness like Eden,
And her desert [R]like the garden of the
LORD; Is. 40:1; 52:9 • Gen. 13:10
Joy and gladness will be found in it,
Thanksgiving and the voice of melody.

4 "Listen to Me, My people;
And give ear to Me, O My nation:
[R]For law will proceed from Me, Is. 2:3
And I will make My justice rest
[R]As a light of the peoples. Is. 42:6
5 [R]My righteousness *is* near, Is. 46:13
My salvation has gone forth,
And My arms will judge the peoples;
The coastlands will wait upon Me,
And on My arm they will trust.
6 [R]Lift up your eyes to the heavens,
And look on the earth beneath.
For [R]the heavens will vanish away like
smoke, Is. 40:26 • Matt. 24:35
[R]The earth will grow old like a garment,
And those who dwell in it will die in like
manner; Is. 24:19, 20; 50:9
But My salvation will be [R]forever,
And My righteousness will not be
[T]abolished. Is. 45:17 • *broken*

7 "Listen to Me, you who know
righteousness,
You people in whose heart *is* My law:
Do not fear the reproach of men,
Nor be afraid of their insults.
8 For [R]the moth will eat them up like a
garment, Is. 50:9
And the worm will eat them like wool;
But My righteousness will be forever,
And My salvation from generation to
generation."

9 [R]Awake, awake, [R]put on strength,
O arm of the LORD! Ps. 44:23 • Ps. 93:1
Awake [R]as in the ancient days, Ps. 44:1
In the generations of old.
[R]*Are* You not *the arm* that cut [R]Rahab
apart, Job 26:12 • Ps. 87:4
And wounded the [R]serpent? Ps. 74:13

10 *Are* You not *the One* who [R]dried up the
sea, Ex. 14:21
The waters of the great deep;
That made the depths of the sea a road
For the redeemed to cross over?
11 So [R]the ransomed of the LORD shall
return, Is. 35:10
And come to Zion with singing,
With everlasting joy on their heads.
They shall obtain joy and gladness;
Sorrow and sighing shall flee away.

12 "I, *even* I, *am* He [R]who comforts you.
Who *are* you that you should be afraid
Of a man *who* will die, 2 Cor. 1:3
And of the son of a man *who* will be
made [R]like grass? Is. 40:6, 7
13 And [R]you forget the LORD your Maker,
Who stretched out the heavens Is. 17:10
And laid the foundations of the earth;
You have feared continually every day
Because of the fury of the oppressor,
When *he has* prepared to destroy.
And where *is* the fury of the oppressor?
14 The captive exile hastens, that he may be
loosed,
That he should not die in the pit,
And that his bread should not fail.
15 But I *am* the LORD your God,
Who [R]divided the sea whose waves
roared— Job 26:12
The LORD of hosts *is* His name.

16 And [R]I have put My words in your
mouth; Deut. 18:18
[R]I have covered you with the shadow of
My hand, Is. 49:2
That I may plant the heavens,
Lay the foundations of the earth,
And say to Zion, 'You *are* My people.' "

17[R] Awake, awake! Is. 52:1
Stand up, O Jerusalem,
You who [R]have drunk at the hand of the
LORD Job 21:20
The cup of His fury;
You have drunk the dregs of the cup of
trembling,
And drained *it* out.
18 *There is* no one to guide her
Among all the sons she has brought forth;
Nor *is there any* who takes her by the
hand
Among all the sons she has brought up.
19[R] These two *things* have come to you;
Who will be sorry for you?— Is. 47:9
Desolation and destruction, famine and
sword—
[R]By whom will I comfort you? Amos 7:2
20[R] Your sons have fainted, Lam. 2:11
They lie at the head of all the streets,
Like an antelope in a net;
They are full of the fury of the LORD,
The rebuke of your God.

21 Therefore please hear this, you afflicted,
And drunk [R]but not with wine. Lam. 3:15
22 Thus says your Lord,
The LORD and your God,
Who [R]pleads the cause of His people:
"See, I have taken out of your hand
The cup of trembling,
The dregs of the cup of My fury;
You shall no longer drink it. Jer. 50:34
23[R] But I will put it into the hand of those
who afflict you, Zech. 12:2
Who have said to you,*
'Lie down, that we may walk over you.'
And you have laid your body like the
ground,
And as the street, for those who walk
over."

CHAPTER 52

AWAKE, awake!
Put on your strength, O Zion;
Put on your beautiful garments,
O Jerusalem, the holy city!
For the uncircumcised and the unclean
Shall no longer come to you.
2[R] Shake yourself from the dust, arise;
Sit down, O Jerusalem! Is. 3:26
[R]Loose yourself from the bonds of your
neck, Zech. 2:7
O captive daughter of Zion!

3 For thus says the LORD:
[R]"You have sold yourselves for nothing,
And you shall be redeemed [R]without
money." Ps. 44:12 • Is. 45:13
4 For thus says the Lord GOD:
"My people went down at first
Into [R]Egypt to [T]dwell there; Gen. 46:6
Then the Assyrian oppressed them
without cause. As resident aliens
5 Now therefore, what have I here," says
the LORD,
"That My people are taken away for
nothing?
Those who rule over them
Make them wail,"* says the LORD,
"And My name *is* [R]blasphemed
continually every day. Ezek. 36:20, 23
6 Therefore My people shall know My
name;
Therefore *they shall know* in that day
That I *am* He who speaks:
'Behold, *it is* I.' "

7[R] How beautiful upon the mountains
Are the feet of him who brings good
news, Rom. 10:15
Who proclaims peace,
Who brings glad tidings of good *things*,
Who proclaims salvation,
Who says to Zion,
[R]"Your God reigns!" Ps. 93:1
8 Your watchmen shall lift up *their* voices,
With their voices they shall sing
together;
For they shall see eye to eye
When the LORD brings back Zion.
9 Break forth into joy, sing together,
You waste places of Jerusalem!
For the LORD has comforted His people,
He has redeemed Jerusalem.
10 The LORD has made bare His holy arm
In the eyes of [R]all the nations; Luke 3:6
And all the ends of the earth shall see
The salvation of our God.

11[R] Depart! Depart! Go out from there,
Touch no unclean *thing;*
Go out from the midst of her,
[R]Be clean, Is. 48:20 • Lev. 22:2
You who bear the vessels of the LORD.
12 For [R]you shall not go out with haste,
Nor go by flight; Ex. 12:11, 33
[R]For the LORD will go before you, Mic. 2:13
[R]And the God of Israel *will* be your rear
guard. Ex. 14:19, 20

51:23 Lit. *your soul* **52:5** DSS *Mock;* LXX *Marvel and wail;* Tg. *Boast themselves;* Vg. *Treat them unjustly*

The Messiah's Atonement

13 Behold, [R]My Servant shall [T]deal
prudently; Is. 42:1 • *prosper*
[R]He shall be exalted and [T]extolled and be
very high. Phil. 2:9☆ • Lit. *be lifted up*
14 Just as many were astonished at you,
So His [R]visage[T] was marred more than
any man, Ps. 22:6, 7; Is. 53:2, 3☆
And His form more than the sons of
men; *appearance*
15[R] So shall He sprinkle* many nations.
Kings shall shut their mouths at Him;
For [R]what had not been told them they
shall see, 1 Pet. 1:2☆ • Rom. 15:21☆
And what they had not heard they shall
consider.

CHAPTER 53

WHO [R]has believed our report? And to
whom has the arm of the LORD been
revealed? John 12:38; Rom. 10:16☆
2 For He shall grow up before Him as a
tender plant,
And as a root out of dry ground.
He has no form or comeliness;
And [R]when we see Him, Mark 15:32☆
There is no [T]beauty that we should
desire Him. Lit. *appearance*
3[R] He is despised and rejected by men,
A Man of sorrows and acquainted with
grief. Ps. 22:6; [Is. 49:7]☆
And we hid, as it were, *our* faces from
Him;
He was despised, and [R]we did not esteem
Him. [John 1:10, 11]☆

4 Surely [R]He has borne our griefs
And carried our sorrows; [Matt. 8:17]☆
Yet we esteemed Him stricken,
Smitten by God, and afflicted.
5 But He *was* [R]wounded for our
transgressions, [Rom. 4:25; 1 Pet. 2:24, 25]☆
He was [T]bruised for our iniquities;
The chastisement for our peace *was*
upon Him, *crushed*
And by His stripes we are healed.
6 All we like sheep have gone astray;
We have turned, every one, to his own
way;
And the LORD has laid on Him the
iniquity of us all.

7 He was oppressed and He was afflicted,
Yet [R]He opened not His mouth;
[R]He was led as a lamb to the slaughter,
And as a sheep before its shearers is
silent, Matt. 26:63; Mark 15:4, 5☆ • Acts 8:32☆
So He opened not His mouth.

8 He was [R]taken from [T]prison and from
judgment, Luke 23:1–25 • *confinement*
And who will declare His generation?
For [R]He was cut off from the land of the
living; [Dan. 9:26]
[R]For the transgressions of My people He
was stricken. 1 Cor. 15:3☆
9[R] And they* made His grave with the
wicked— Matt. 27:38, 57–60☆
But with the rich at His death,
Because He had done no violence,
Nor *was any* deceit in His mouth.

10 Yet it pleased the LORD to [T]bruise Him;
He has put *Him* to grief. *crush*
When You make His soul [R]an offering for
sin, [John 1:29; 2 Cor. 5:21]☆
He shall see *His* seed, [R]He shall prolong
His days, Acts 2:24☆
And the pleasure of the LORD shall
prosper in His hand.
11 He shall see the labor of His soul,* *and*
be satisfied.
[R]By His knowledge My righteous
Servant shall justify many, [Rom. 5:15–18]☆
For He shall bear their iniquities.
12[R] Therefore I will divide Him a portion
with the great, Ps. 2:8
[R]And He shall divide the [T]spoil with the
strong, Col. 2:15 • *plunder*
Because He [R]poured out His soul unto
death, Is. 50:6
And He was [R]numbered with the
transgressors, Matt. 27:38; Luke 22:37☆
And He bore the sin of many,
And [R]made intercession for the
transgressors. Luke 23:34☆

52:15 Or *startle* **53:9** Lit. *he* or *He* **53:11** So with MT, Tg., Vg.; DSS, LXX *From the labor of His soul He shall see light*

53:7 The Lamb of God—The imagery of Jesus as a lamb invokes the rich significance of the OT sacrificial system. Jesus suffered and died to fulfill the spiritual significance God had built into those sacrifices when He instituted the Levitical rituals.

a. *The Passover lamb.* Jesus died as an unblemished lamb in the place of those who by faith apply His blood to the doorposts of their hearts. The death angel has no claim on them (Page 1170—1 Cor. 5:7; see Ex. 12).

b. *The Day of Atonement.* The New Testament looks at Jesus fulfilling the Day of Atonement imagery primarily through His activity as High Priest (Page 1263—Heb. 9:11, 12) because the offerings that day were of a bull and two goats. However, it was His own blood that Jesus offered to God as High Priest (v. 14).

Jesus was "the Lamb of God who takes away the sin of the world" (Page 1082—John 1:29) because He died in the place of sinful humans. His death was a substitutionary sacrifice (Page 1028—Mark 10:45; Page 1094—John 10:11; Page 1187—2 Cor. 5:21; Page 1281—1 Pet. 2:24; 3:18).

Now turn to Page 1206—Eph. 4:3: The Person of the Holy Spirit.

CHAPTER 54

The Messiah's Promise of Israel's Restoration

"SING, O [R]barren, Gal. 4:27
You *who* have not borne!
Break forth into singing, and cry aloud,
You *who* have not labored with child!
For more *are* the children of the desolate
Than the children of the married woman," says the LORD.
2 "Enlarge[R] the place of your tent,
And let them stretch out the curtains of your dwellings; Is. 49:19, 20
Do not spare;
Lengthen your cords,
And strengthen your stakes.
3 For you shall expand to the right and to the left,
And your descendants will [R]inherit the nations, Is. 14:2; 49:22, 23; 60:9
And make the desolate cities inhabited.

4 "Do[R] not fear, for you will not be ashamed; Is. 41:10
Neither be disgraced, for you will not be put to shame;
For you will forget the shame of your youth,
And will not remember the reproach of your widowhood anymore.
5 [R]For your Maker *is* your husband,
The LORD of hosts *is* His name;
And your Redeemer *is* the Holy One of Israel; Jer. 3:14
He is called the God of the whole earth.
6 For the LORD [R]has called you Is. 62:4
Like a woman forsaken and grieved in spirit,
Like a youthful wife when you were refused,"
Says your God.
7 "For[R] a mere moment I have forsaken you, Is. 26:20; 60:10
But with great mercies [R]I will gather you. [Is. 43:5; 56:8]
8 With a little wrath I hid My face from you for a moment;
[R]But with everlasting kindness I will have mercy on you," Jer. 31:3
Says the LORD, your Redeemer.

9 "For this *is* like the waters of [R]Noah to Me; Gen. 8:21; 9:11
For as I have sworn
That the waters of Noah would no longer cover the earth,
So have I sworn
That I would not be angry with [R]you, nor rebuke you. Ezek. 39:29
10 For [R]the mountains shall depart Is. 51:6
And the hills be removed,
[R]But My kindness shall not depart from you, Ps. 89:33, 34
Nor shall My covenant of peace be removed,"
Says the LORD, who has mercy on you.

11 "O you afflicted one,
Tossed with tempest, *and* not comforted,
Behold, I will lay your stones with [R]colorful gems, Rev. 21:18, 19
And lay your foundations with sapphires.
12 I will make your pinnacles of rubies,
Your gates of crystal,
And all your walls of precious stones.
13 All your children *shall be* [R]taught by the LORD, [John 6:45]
And [R]great *shall be* the peace of your children. Ps. 119:165
14 In righteousness you shall be established;
You shall be far from oppression, for you shall not fear;
And from terror, for it shall not come near you.
15 Indeed they shall surely assemble, *but* not because of Me.
Whoever assembles against you shall [R]fall for your sake. Is. 41:11–16

16 "Behold, I have created the blacksmith
Who blows the coals in the fire,
Who brings forth an [T]instrument for his work; Or *weapon*
And I have created the [T]spoiler to destroy. *destroyer*
17 No weapon formed against you shall [R]prosper, Is. 17:12–14; 29:8
And every tongue *which* rises against you in judgment
You shall condemn.
This *is* the heritage of the servants of the LORD,
[R]And their righteousness *is* from Me,"
Says the LORD. Is. 45:24, 25; 54:14

CHAPTER 55

The Messiah's Invitation to the World

"HO! [R]Everyone who thirsts,
Come to the waters; [John 4:14; 7:37]
And you who have no money,
[R]Come, buy and eat. [Rev. 3:18]
Yes, come, buy wine and milk
Without money and without price.
2 Why do you [T]spend money for *what is* not bread, Lit. *weigh out silver*
And your wages for *what* does not satisfy?
Listen carefully to Me, and eat *what is* good,
And let your soul delight itself in abundance.

3 Incline your ear, and [R]come to Me.
Hear, and your soul shall live;
[R]And I will make an everlasting covenant with you— Matt. 11:28 • Jer. 32:40
The [R]sure mercies of David. 2 Sam. 7:8
4 Indeed I have given him *as* [R]a witness to the people, [Rev. 1:5]
A leader and commander for the people.
5 [R]Surely you shall call a nation you do not know, Is. 52:15; Eph. 2:11, 12☆
[R]And nations *who* do not know you shall run to you, Is. 60:5
Because of the LORD your God,
And the Holy One of Israel;
[R]For He has glorified you." Is. 60:9

6 Seek the LORD while He may be [R]found,
Call upon Him while He is near. Ps. 32:6
7 Let the wicked forsake his way,
And the unrighteous man [R]his thoughts;
Let him return to the LORD, Zech. 8:17
[R]And He will have mercy on him;
And to our God, Jer. 3:12
For He will abundantly pardon.

8 "For[R] My thoughts *are* not your thoughts,
Nor *are* your ways My ways," says the LORD. 2 Sam. 7:19
9 "For[R] *as* the heavens are higher than the earth, Ps. 103:11
So are My ways higher than your ways,
And My thoughts than your thoughts.

10 "For [R]as the rain comes down, and the snow from heaven, Deut. 32:2
And do not return there,
But water the earth,
And make it bring forth and bud,
That it may give seed to the sower
And bread to the eater,
11 [R]So shall My word be that goes forth from My mouth; Is. 45:23
It shall not return to Me void,
But it shall accomplish what I please,
And it shall [R]prosper *in the thing* for which I sent it. Is. 46:9–11

12 "For[R] you shall go out with joy, Is. 35:10
And be led out with peace;
The mountains and the hills
Shall [R]break forth into singing before you, Ps. 98:8
And [R]all the trees of the field shall clap *their* hands. 1 Chr. 16:33
13 [R]Instead of [R]the thorn shall come up the cypress tree, Is. 41:19 • Mic. 7:4
And instead of the brier shall come up the myrtle tree;
And it shall be to the LORD [R]for a name,
For an everlasting sign *that* shall not be cut off." Jer. 13:11

CHAPTER 56

THUS says the LORD:

"Keep justice, and do righteousness,
For My salvation *is* about to come,
And My righteousness to be revealed.
2 Blessed *is* the man *who* does this,
And the son of man *who* lays hold on it;
[R]Who keeps from defiling the Sabbath,
And keeps his hand from doing any evil." Is. 58:13

3 Do not let [R]the son of the foreigner
Who has joined himself to the LORD
Speak, saying, [Eph. 2:12–19]
"The LORD has utterly separated me from His people";
Nor let the [R]eunuch say, Acts 8:27
"Here I am, a dry tree."
4 For thus says the LORD:
"To the eunuchs who keep My Sabbaths,
And choose what pleases Me,
And hold fast My covenant,
5 Even to them I will give in [R]My house
And within My walls a place [R]and a name 1 Tim. 3:15 • [1 John 3:1, 2]
Better than that of sons and daughters;
I will give them* an everlasting name
That shall not be cut off.

6 "Also the sons of the foreigner
Who join themselves to the LORD, to serve Him,
And to love the name of the LORD, to be His servants—
Everyone who keeps from defiling the Sabbath,
And holds fast My covenant—
7 Even them I will [R]bring to My holy mountain, [Is. 2:2, 3; 60:11]
And make them joyful in My [R]house of prayer. Mark 11:17
[R]Their burnt offerings and their sacrifices
Will be accepted on My altar; [Rom. 12:1]
For [R]My house shall be called a house of prayer for all nations." Matt. 21:13
8 The Lord GOD, [R]who gathers the outcasts of Israel, says, Is. 11:12
[R]"Yet I will gather to him [John 10:16]
Others besides those who are gathered to him."

The Messiah's Rebuke of the Wicked

9 [R]All you beasts of the field, come to devour, Jer. 12:9
All you beasts in the forest.
10 His watchmen *are* [R]blind, Matt. 15:14
They are all ignorant;
[R]They *are* all dumb dogs, Phil. 3:2
They cannot bark;

56:5 Lit. *him*

Sleeping, lying down, loving to slumber.
11 Yes, *they are* [R]greedy dogs [Mic. 3:5, 11]
Which never have enough.
And they *are* shepherds
Who cannot understand;
They all look to their own way,
Every one for his own gain,
From his *own* territory.
12 "Come," *one says,* "I will bring wine,
And we will fill ourselves with
intoxicating [R]drink; Is. 28:7
[R]Tomorrow will be [R]as today, Luke 12:19
And much more abundant." 2 Pet. 3:4

CHAPTER 57

THE righteous perishes,
And no man takes *it* to heart;
[R]Merciful men *are* taken away, Ps. 12:1
[R]While no one considers 1 Kin. 14:13
That the righteous is taken away from
[T]evil. Lit. *the face of evil*
2 He shall enter into peace;
They shall rest in their beds,
Each one walking *in* his uprightness.

3 "But come here,
[R]You sons of the sorceress, Matt. 16:4
You offspring of the adulterer and the
harlot!
4 Whom do you ridicule?
Against whom do you make a wide
mouth
And stick out the tongue?
Are you not children of transgression,
Offspring of falsehood,
5 Inflaming yourselves with gods [R]under
every green tree, 2 Kin. 16:4
[R]Slaying the children in the valleys
Under the clefts of the rocks? Jer. 7:31
6 Among the smooth [R]*stones* of the stream
Is your portion;
They, they, *are* your lot! Jer. 3:9
Even to them you have poured a drink
offering,
You have offered a grain offering.
Should I receive comfort in these?

7 "On a lofty and high mountain
You have set [R]your bed; Ezek. 23:41
Even there you went up
To offer sacrifice.
8 Also behind the doors and their posts
You have set up your remembrance;
For you have uncovered yourself *to
those other* than Me,
And have gone up to them;
You have enlarged your bed
And made *a covenant* with them;
[R]You have loved their bed, Ezek. 16:26
Where you saw *their* nudity.*
9 [R]You went to the king with ointment,
And increased your perfumes;
You sent your messengers far off,
And *even* descended to Sheol. Hos. 7:11
10 You are wearied in the length of your
way;
Yet you did not say, 'There is no hope.'
You have found the life of your hand;
Therefore you were not grieved.

11 "And [R]of whom have you been afraid, or
feared, Is. 51:12, 13
That you have lied
And not remembered Me,
Nor taken *it* to your heart?
Is it not because [R]I have [T]held My peace
from of old Ps. 50:21 • *remained silent*
That you do not fear Me?
12 I will declare your righteousness
And your works,
For they will not profit you.
13 When you cry out,
Let your collection *of idols* deliver you.
But the wind will carry them all away,
A breath will take *them.*
But he who puts his trust in Me shall
possess the land,
And shall inherit My holy mountain."

14 And one shall say,
[R]"Heap it up! Heap it up! Is. 40:3; 62:10
Prepare the way,
Take the stumbling block out of the way
of My people."
15 For thus says the High and Lofty One
Who inhabits eternity, [R]whose name *is*
Holy: Job 6:10
"I dwell in the high and holy *place,*
[R]With him *who* has a contrite and humble
spirit, Ps. 34:18; 51:17
[R]To revive the spirit of the humble,
And to revive the heart of the contrite
ones. Is. 61:1–3
16 [R]For I will not contend forever, [Mic. 7:18]
Nor will I always be angry;
For the spirit would fail before Me,
And the souls *which* I have made.
17 For the iniquity of [R]his covetousness
I was angry and struck him; Jer. 6:13
[R]I hid and was angry, Is. 8:17; 45:15; 59:2
[R]And he went on [T]backsliding in the way
of his heart. Is. 9:13 • Or *turning back*
18 I have seen his ways, and [R]will heal him;
I will also lead him,
And restore comforts to him Jer. 3:22
And to [R]his mourners. Is. 61:2

19 "I create [R]the fruit of the lips: Heb. 13:15
Peace, peace [R]to *him who is* far off and
to *him who is* near," Eph. 2:17
Says the LORD,
"And I will heal him."

57:8 Lit. *hand,* a euphemism

20[R] But the wicked *are* like the troubled sea,
When it cannot rest, Job 15:20
Whose waters cast up mire and dirt.

21 "*There*[R] *is* no peace," Is. 48:22
Says my God, "for the wicked."

CHAPTER 58

Blessings of True Worship

"CRY aloud, [T]spare not; *do not hold back*
Lift up your voice like a trumpet;
Tell My people their transgression,
And the house of Jacob their sins.
2 Yet they seek Me daily,
And delight to know My ways,
As a nation that did righteousness,
And did not forsake the ordinance of their God.
They ask of Me the ordinances of justice;
They take delight in approaching God.
3 'Why[R] have we fasted,' *they say,* 'and You have not seen? Mal. 3:13–18
Why have we [R]afflicted our souls, and You take no notice?' Lev. 16:29; 23:27

"In fact, in the day of your fast you find pleasure,
And exploit all your laborers.
4[R] Indeed you fast for strife and debate,
And to strike with the fist of wickedness. 1 Kin. 21:9
You will not fast as *you do* this day,
To make your voice heard on high.
5 Is [R]it a fast that I have chosen, Zech. 7:5
[R]A day for a man to afflict his soul?
Is it to bow down his head like a bulrush, Lev. 16:29
And [R]to spread out sackcloth and ashes? Esth. 4:3
Would you call this a fast,
And an acceptable day to the LORD?

6 "*Is* this not the fast that I have chosen:
To loose the bonds of wickedness,
To undo the heavy burdens,
[R]To let the oppressed go free, Jer. 34:9
And that you break every yoke?
7 *Is it* not [R]to share your bread with the hungry, Ezek. 18:7
And that you bring to your house the poor who are [T]cast out; *wandering*
[R]When you see the naked, that you cover him, Job 31:19–22
And not hide yourself from [R]your own flesh? Neh. 5:5
8[R] Then your light shall break forth like the morning, Job 11:17
Your healing shall spring forth speedily,
And your righteousness shall go before you;
[R]The glory of the LORD shall be your rear guard. Ex. 14:19
9 Then you shall call, and the LORD will answer;
You shall cry, and He will say, 'Here I *am.*'

"If you take away the yoke from your midst,
The pointing of the finger, and [R]speaking wickedness, Ps. 12:2
10 *If* you extend your soul to the hungry
And satisfy the afflicted soul,
Then your light shall dawn in the darkness,
And your [T]darkness shall *be* as the noonday. *Or gloom*
11 The LORD will guide you continually,
And satisfy your soul in drought,
And strengthen your bones;
You shall be like a watered garden,
And like a spring of water, whose waters do not fail.
12 Those from among you
[R]Shall build the old waste places;
You shall raise up the foundations of many generations; Is. 61:4
And you shall be called the Repairer of the Breach,
The Restorer of Streets to Dwell In.

13 "If [R]you turn away your foot from the Sabbath, Is. 56:2, 4, 6
From doing your pleasure on My holy day,
And call the Sabbath a delight,
The holy *day* of the LORD honorable,
And shall honor Him, not doing your own ways,
Nor finding your own pleasure,
Nor speaking *your own* words,
14[R] Then you shall delight yourself in the LORD; Job 22:26
And I will cause you to [R]ride on the high hills of the earth, Deut. 32:13; 33:29
And feed you with the heritage of Jacob your father.
The mouth of the LORD has spoken."

CHAPTER 59

Sins of Israel

BEHOLD, the LORD's hand is not [R]shortened, Num. 11:23
That it cannot save;
Nor His ear heavy,
That it cannot hear.

2 But your iniquities have separated you from your God;
And your sins have hidden *His* face from you,
So that He will [R]not hear. Is. 1:15

3 For [R]your hands are defiled with blood,
And your fingers with iniquity;

Your lips have spoken lies, Ezek. 7:23
Your tongue has muttered perversity.
4 No one calls for justice,
Nor does *any* plead for truth.
They trust in [R]empty words and speak
lies; Jer. 7:4
[R]They conceive [T]evil and bring forth
iniquity. Job 15:35 • *trouble*
5 They hatch vipers' eggs and weave the
spider's web;
He who eats of their eggs dies,
And *from* that which is crushed a viper
breaks out.

6[R] Their webs will not become garments,
Nor will they cover themselves with their
works; Job 8:14
Their works *are* works of iniquity,
And the act of violence *is* in their hands.
7[R] Their feet run to evil, Rom. 3:15
And they make haste to shed [R]innocent
blood; Prov. 6:17
[R]Their thoughts *are* thoughts of iniquity;
Wasting and [R]destruction *are* in their
paths. Is. 55:7 • Rom. 3:16, 17
8 The way of [R]peace they have not known,
And *there is* no justice in their ways;
[R]They have made themselves crooked
paths; Is. 57:20, 21 • Prov. 2:15
Whoever takes that way shall not know
peace.

9 Therefore justice is far from us,
Nor does righteousness overtake us;
[R]We look for light, but there is darkness!
For brightness, *but* we walk in
blackness! Jer. 8:15
10 We grope for the wall like the blind,
And we grope as if *we had* no eyes;
We stumble at noonday as at twilight;
We are as dead *men* in desolate places.
11 We all growl like bears,
And [R]moan sadly like doves; Ezek. 7:16
We look for justice, but *there is* none;
For salvation, *but* it is far from us.
12 For our [R]transgressions are multiplied
before You, Is. 24:5; 58:1
And our sins testify against us;
For our transgressions *are* with us,
And *as for* our iniquities, we know them:
13 In transgressing and lying against the
LORD,
And departing from our God,
Speaking oppression and revolt,
Conceiving and uttering [R]from the heart
words of falsehood. Matt. 12:34
14 Justice is turned back,
And righteousness stands afar off;
For truth is fallen in the street,
And equity cannot enter.
15 So truth fails,
And he *who* departs from evil makes
himself a [R]prey. Is. 5:23; 10:2; 29:21; 32:7

Then the LORD saw *it*, and [T]it displeased
Him Lit. *it was evil in His eyes*
That *there was* no justice.
16[R] He saw that *there was* no man,
And [R]wondered that *there was* no
intercessor; Ezek. 22:30 • Mark 6:6
[R]Therefore His own arm brought
salvation for Him; Ps. 98:1
And His own righteousness, it sustained
Him.
17[R] For He put on righteousness as a
breastplate, Eph. 6:14, 17
And a helmet of salvation on His head;
He put on the garments of vengeance for
clothing,
And was clad with zeal as a cloak.
18[R] According to *their* deeds, accordingly He
will repay, Is. 63:6
Fury to His adversaries,
Recompense to His enemies;
The coastlands He will fully repay.
19[R] So shall they fear Mal. 1:11
The name of the LORD from the west,
And His glory from the rising of the
sun;
When the enemy comes in [R]like a flood,
The Spirit of the LORD will lift up a
standard against him. Rev. 12:15

20 "The[R] Redeemer will come to Zion,
And to those who turn from
transgression in Jacob,"
Says the LORD. Rom. 11:26☆

59:2 What Sin Does—Sin, regardless of its degree, always has an effect—separation. Sin separates one from God. This separation from God is death. Adam was told that if he ate of the tree of the knowledge of good and evil that he would die (Page 6—Gen. 3:3). Adam ate of the tree and immediately died spiritually—his soul was separated from God—and he began to die physically. The entrance of sin into the human race brought with it death (Page 1152—Rom. 5:12; 6:23). That man is a sinner is proven by the fact that he dies—where there is death, there is sin. Sin's penalty, death, can be remedied by life—union with God. This is achieved by belief in Jesus, who died to pay the penalty of man's sin (Page 1152—Rom. 5:21). For the one who believes in Jesus, the penalty of sin is broken. Yes, he will die physically (unless he is alive when Jesus returns to take all believers to heaven with Himself, Page 1228—1 Thess. 4:14–18), but physical death for him is only the doorway into the presence of God. Sin, however, does have an effect upon the believer, for it mars his fellowship with God. Sin in the believer's life is a terrible thing and is not to be tolerated. While it is probable that the believer will sin, it is never necessary for him to do so (Page 1293—1 John 2:1).

Now turn to Page 561—Ps. 32:5: What Should Be Done About Sin.

21 "As[R] for Me," says the LORD, "this *is* My covenant with them: My Spirit who *is* upon you, and My words which I have put in your mouth, shall not depart from your mouth, nor from the mouth of your descendants, nor from the mouth of your descendants' descendants," says the LORD, "from this time and forevermore." [Heb. 8:10; 10:16]

CHAPTER 60

Glory of Israel in the Kingdom

ARISE, [R]shine; Eph. 5:14
For your light has come!
And [R]the glory of the LORD is risen upon
you. Mal. 4:2
2 For behold, the darkness shall cover the
earth,
And deep darkness the people;
But the LORD will arise over you,
And His glory will be seen upon you.
3 The [R]Gentiles shall come to your light,
And kings to the brightness of your
rising. Is. 49:6, 23; Rev. 21:24☆

4 "Lift[R] up your eyes all around, and see:
They all gather together, [R]they come to
you; Is. 49:18 • Is. 49:20–22
Your sons shall come from afar,
And your daughters shall be nursed at
your side.
5 Then you shall see and become radiant,
And your heart shall swell with joy;
Because [R]the abundance of the sea shall
be turned to you, [Rom. 11:25–27]
The wealth of the Gentiles shall come to
you.
6 The multitude of camels shall cover your
land,
The dromedaries of Midian and Ephah;
All those from [R]Sheba shall come;
They shall bring [R]gold and incense,
And they shall proclaim the praises of
the LORD. Ps. 72:10 • Matt. 2:11
7 All the flocks of [R]Kedar shall be
gathered together to you, Gen. 25:13
The rams of Nebaioth shall minister to
you;
They shall ascend with [R]acceptance on
My altar, Is. 56:7
And I will glorify the house of My glory.

8 "Who *are* these *who* fly like a cloud,
And like doves to their roosts?
9 [R]Surely the coastlands shall wait for Me;
And the ships of Tarshish *will come*
first, Ps. 72:10
[R]To bring your sons from afar, [Gal. 4:26]
[R]Their silver and their gold with them,
To the name of the LORD your God,
And to the Holy One of Israel, Jer. 3:17
[R]Because He has glorified you. Is. 55:5

10 "The[R] sons of foreigners shall build up
your walls, Zech. 6:15
And their kings shall minister to you;
For [R]in My wrath I struck you, Is. 57:17
[R]But in My favor I have had mercy on
you. Is. 54:7, 8
11 Therefore your gates [R]shall be open
continually; Rev. 21:25, 26
They shall not be shut day or night,
That *men* may bring to you the wealth of
the Gentiles,
And their kings in procession.
12 [R]For the nation and kingdom which will
not serve you shall perish, Zech. 14:17
And *those* nations shall be utterly ruined.

13 "The[R] glory of Lebanon shall come to you,
The cypress, the pine, and the box tree
together, Is. 35:2
To beautify the place of My sanctuary;
And I will make [R]the place of My feet
glorious. 1 Chr. 28:2
14 Also the sons of those who afflicted you
Shall come [R]bowing to you, Is. 45:14
And all those who despised you shall
[R]fall prostrate at the soles of your feet;
And they shall call you The City of the
LORD, Rev. 3:9
Zion of the Holy One of Israel.

59:21 Inspiration of God's Word—The word "inspiration" is found but once in the New Testament. This occurs in Second Timothy 3:16, where Paul writes, "All Scripture *is* given by inspiration of God," literally "God-breathed." Divine inspiration logically follows divine revelation. In revelation God speaks to man's ear while by inspiration He guides the pen to ensure that the imparted message is correctly written down.

There are several ideas about the process of inspiration. One is called the natural theory. This says that the Bible authors were inspired in the same sense that William Shakespeare was inspired. Another theory, called the content theory, suggests that God merely gave the writer the main content or idea, allowing him to choose his own words to express that concept. In contrast Jesus Himself said that the very letters of the words were also chosen by God (Page 981—Matt. 5:18). This position is referred to as the plenary-verbal view, which says that all (plenary) the very words (verbal) of the Bible are inspired by God. Jesus once told the devil that the Christian is to live by each of these inspired words (Page 980—Matt. 4:4). The Bible authors understood that their writings were being guided by the Spirit of God, even as they wrote them. Peter said this was true of the Old Testament authors (Page 1287—2 Pet. 1:20, 21). He then stated that his own letters (Page 1288—1 and 2 Pet.) were inspired by God (Page 1288—2 Pet. 3:1, 2). Finally, he pointed out that this was also true concerning Paul's writings (Page 1289—2 Pet. 3:15, 16).

One final thing should be said about inspiration. Plenary-verbal inspiration does not guarantee the inspiration of any translation, but only of the original Hebrew and Greek manuscripts.

Now turn to Page 633—Prov. 6:23: Illumination of God's Word.

15 "Whereas you have been forsaken and
hated,
So that no one went through *you,*
I will make you an eternal excellence,
A joy of many generations.
16 You shall drink the milk of the Gentiles,
[R]And milk the breast of kings; Is. 49:23
You shall know that [R]I, the LORD, *am*
your Savior Is. 43:3
And your Redeemer, the Mighty One of
Jacob.

17 "Instead of bronze I will bring gold,
Instead of iron I will bring silver,
Instead of wood, bronze,
And instead of stones, iron.
I will also make your officers peace,
And your magistrates righteousness.
18 Violence shall no longer be heard in your
land,
Neither [T]wasting nor destruction within
your borders; *devastation*
But you shall call [R]your walls Salvation,
And your gates Praise. Is. 26:1

19 "The [R]sun shall no longer be your light by
day, Rev. 21:23; 22:5
Nor for brightness shall the moon give
light to you;
But the LORD will be to you an
everlasting light,
And [R]your God your glory. Zech. 2:5
20 [R]Your sun shall no longer go down,
Nor shall your moon withdraw itself;
For the LORD will be your everlasting light,
And the days of your mourning shall be
ended. Amos 8:9
21 Also your people *shall* all *be* righteous;
They shall inherit the land forever,
[R]The branch of My planting, Is. 61:3
[R]The work of My hands, [Eph. 2:10]
That I may be glorified.
22 A little one shall become a thousand,
And a small one a strong nation.
I, the LORD, will hasten it in its time."

CHAPTER 61

Advents of the Messiah

"THE [R]Spirit of the Lord GOD *is* upon Me,
Because the LORD has anointed Me
To preach good tidings to the poor;
He has sent Me to heal the
brokenhearted,
To proclaim [R]liberty to the captives,
And the opening of the prison to *those*
who are bound; Luke 4:18, 19☆ • Is. 42:7☆
2 [R]To proclaim the acceptable year of the
LORD, Lev. 25:9
And the day of vengeance of our God;
[R]To comfort all who mourn, Matt. 5:4
3 To console those who mourn in Zion,
[R]To give them beauty for ashes,
The oil of joy for mourning, Ps. 30:11
The garment of praise for the spirit of
heaviness;
That they may be called trees of
righteousness,
[R]The planting of the LORD, [R]that He may
be glorified." Is. 60:21 • [John 15:8]

4 And they shall [R]rebuild the old ruins,
They shall raise up the former
desolations, Ezek. 36:33
And they shall repair the ruined cities,
The desolations of many generations.
5 [R]Strangers shall stand and feed your
flocks, [Eph. 2:12]
And the sons of the foreigner
Shall be your plowmen and your
vinedressers.
6 [R]But you shall be named the priests of the
LORD, Ex. 19:6
They shall call you the servants of our
God.
You shall eat the riches of the Gentiles,
And in their glory you shall boast.
7 [R]Instead of your shame *you shall have*
double *honor,* Zech. 9:12
And *instead of* confusion they shall
rejoice in their portion.
Therefore in their land they shall
possess double;
Everlasting joy shall be theirs.
8 "For [R]I, the LORD, love justice; Ps. 11:7
[R]I hate robbery [T]for burnt offering;
I will direct their work in truth,
[R]And will make with them an everlasting
covenant. Is. 1:11, 13 • Or *in* • Is. 55:3
9 Their descendants shall be known
among the Gentiles,
And their offspring among the people.
All who see them shall acknowledge
them,
[R]That they *are* the posterity *whom* the
LORD has blessed." Is. 65:23

10 [R]I will greatly rejoice in the LORD,
My soul shall be joyful in my God;
For He has clothed me with the garments
of salvation, Hab. 3:18
He has covered me with the robe of
righteousness,
[R]As a bridegroom decks *himself* with
ornaments, Is. 49:18
And as a bride adorns *herself* with her
jewels.

61:10 Christ's Righteousness—One of the most awesome requirements of God made upon men and women is that they be righteous, that is, conform to His ethical and moral standards (Page 551—Ps. 15:2;

11 For as the earth brings forth its bud,
As the garden causes the things that are sown in it to spring forth,
So the Lord GOD will cause [R]righteousness and praise to spring forth before all the nations. Ps. 72:3

CHAPTER 62

Future of Jerusalem

FOR Zion's sake I will not [T]hold My peace,
And for Jerusalem's sake I will not rest,
Until her righteousness goes forth as brightness, *keep silent*
And her salvation as a lamp *that* burns.
2 [R]The Gentiles shall see your righteousness, Is. 60:3
And all [R]kings your glory. Ps. 102:15, 16
You shall be called by a new name,
Which the mouth of the LORD will name.
3 You shall also be [R]a crown of glory
In the hand of the LORD, Zech. 9:16
And a royal diadem
In the hand of your God.
4 [R]You shall no longer be termed
[R]Forsaken, Hos. 1:10 • Is. 49:14; 54:6, 7
Nor shall your land any more be termed
[R]Desolate;[T] Is. 54:1 • Heb. *Shemamah*
But you shall be called Hephzibah,* and your land Beulah;*
For the LORD delights in you,
And your land shall be married.
5 For *as* a young man marries a virgin,
So shall your sons marry you;
And *as* the bridegroom rejoices over the bride,
So shall your God rejoice over you.

6 [R]I have set watchmen on your walls,
O Jerusalem; Ezek. 3:17; 33:7
They shall [T]never hold their peace day or night. *not be silent*
You who [T]make mention of the LORD, do not keep silent, *remember*
7 And give Him no rest till He establishes
And till He makes Jerusalem [R]a praise in the earth. Zeph. 3:19, 20
8 The LORD has sworn by His right hand
And by the arm of His strength:
"Surely I will no longer [R]give your grain
As food for your enemies; Deut. 28:31, 33
And the sons of the foreigner shall not drink your new wine,
For which you have labored.
9 But those who have gathered it shall eat it,
And praise the LORD;
Those who have brought it together shall drink it in My holy courts."

10 Go through,
Go through the gates!
[R]Prepare the way for the people;
Build up,
Build up the highway! Is. 40:3; 57:14
Take out the stones,
Lift up a banner for the peoples!

11 Indeed the LORD has proclaimed
To the end of the world:
[R]"Say to the daughter of Zion, Zech. 9:9☆
'Surely your salvation is coming;
Behold, His reward *is* with Him,
And His work before Him.' "
12 And they shall call them The Holy People,
The Redeemed of the LORD;
And you shall be called Sought Out,
A City Not Forsaken.

CHAPTER 63

Vengeance of God

WHO *is* this who comes from Edom,
With dyed garments from Bozrah,
This *One who is* [T]glorious in His apparel,
Traveling in the greatness of His strength?— Or *adorned*

"I who speak in righteousness, mighty to save."

2 Why [R]*is* Your apparel red,
And Your garments like one who treads in the winepress? [Rev. 19:13, 15]☆

62:4 Lit. *My Delight Is in Her* • Lit. *Married*

Page 931—Mic. 6:8). Since God is holy, He cannot allow sinners into His presence (Page 687—Is. 6:3–5). Since all persons are sinners, they could not be saved apart from the supernatural intervention of God (Page 1150—Rom 3:10, 23). The righteous demands of God coupled with the inability of man might present an insoluble dilemma. God Himself, however, has graciously solved the problem. He sent Christ, who never sinned, to die for our sins and thus satisfy His own wrath toward us. Simply put, it means that God, at the Cross, treated Christ as though He had committed our sins even though He was righteous. On the other hand, when we believe in Christ, He treats us as though we were as righteous as Christ (Page 1187—2 Cor. 5:21). The Bible calls this type of righteousness "imputed righteousness" (Page 1151—Rom. 4:6). That simply means that God puts to our spiritual account the very worth of Christ, much as though He were a banker adding an inexhaustible deposit to our bank account. There are, sadly, many people who still refuse to believe that such an abundant blessing can be theirs as a free gift (Page 1205—Eph. 2:8, 9). Nevertheless, the Bible clearly urges all people to trust in Jesus Christ as Savior and thus be reckoned as righteous by God (Page 1152—Rom. 4:24).

Now turn to Page 1295—1 John 3:2: Placed into God's Family.

3 "I have [R]trodden the winepress alone,
And from the peoples no one *was* with
Me. Rev. 14:19, 20; 19:15☆
For I have trodden them in My anger,
And trampled them in My fury;
Their blood is sprinkled upon My
garments,
And I have stained all My robes.
4 For the [R]day of vengeance *is* in My
heart, Is. 34:8; 35:4; 61:2
And the year of My redeemed has come.
5 I looked, but [R]*there was* no one to help,
And I wondered [John 16:32]
That *there was* no one to uphold;
Therefore My own [R]arm brought
salvation for Me; Ps. 98:1
And My own fury, it sustained Me.
6 I have trodden down the peoples in My
anger,
Made them drunk in My fury,
And brought down their strength to the
earth."

Prayer of the Remnant

7 I will mention the lovingkindnesses of
the LORD
And the praises of the LORD,
According to all that the LORD has
bestowed on us,
And the great goodness toward the
house of Israel,
Which He has bestowed on them
according to His mercies,
According to the multitude of His
lovingkindnesses.
8 For He said, "Surely they *are* My
people,
Children *who* will not lie."
So He became their [R]Savior. Is. 60:16☆
9 [R]In all their affliction He was afflicted,
[R]And the Angel of His Presence saved
them; Judg. 10:16 • Ex. 14:19
[R]In His love and in His pity He redeemed
them; Deut. 7:7
And [R]He bore them and carried them
All the days of old. Ex. 19:4
10 But they [R]rebelled and [R]grieved His Holy
Spirit; Ex. 15:24 • Ps. 78:40
[R]So He turned Himself against them as an
enemy, Ex. 23:21
And He fought against them.

11 Then he [R]remembered the days of old,
Moses *and* his people, *saying:*
"Where *is* He who [R]brought them up out
of the sea Ps. 106:44, 45 • Ex. 14:30
With the shepherd of His flock?
[R]Where *is* He who put His Holy Spirit
within them, Num. 11:17, 25, 29
12 Who led *them* by the right hand of
Moses,
[R]With His glorious arm, Ex. 15:6
[R]Dividing the water before them
To make for Himself an everlasting
name, Ex. 14:21, 22
13 [R]Who led them through the deep,
As a horse in the wilderness, Ps. 106:9
That they might not stumble?"

14 As a beast goes down into the valley,
And the Spirit of the LORD causes him to
rest,
So You lead Your people,
To make Yourself a glorious name.

15 [R]Look down from heaven, Deut. 26:15
And see [R]from Your habitation, holy and
glorious. Ps. 33:14
Where *are* Your zeal and Your strength,
The yearning [R]of Your heart and Your
mercies toward me? Jer. 31:20
Are they restrained?
16 Doubtless You *are* our Father,
Though Abraham [R]was ignorant of us,
And Israel does not acknowledge us.
You, O LORD, *are* our Father; Job 14:21
Our Redeemer from Everlasting *is* Your
name.
17 O LORD, why have You [R]made us stray
from Your ways, John 12:40
And hardened our heart from Your fear?
Return for Your servants' sake,
The tribes of Your inheritance.
18 [R]Your holy people have possessed *it* but a
little while; Deut. 7:6
[R]Our adversaries have trodden down Your
sanctuary. Ps. 74:3–7
19 We have become *like* those of old, over
whom You never ruled,
Those who were never called by Your
name.

CHAPTER 64

OH, that You would [T]rend the heavens!
That You would come down! *tear open*
That the mountains might shake at Your
[R]presence— Mic. 1:3, 4
2 As fire burns brushwood,
As fire causes water to boil—
To make Your name known to Your
adversaries,
That the nations may tremble at Your
presence!
3 When [R]You did awesome things *for
which* we did not look, Ex. 34:10
You came down,
The mountains shook at Your presence.
4 For since the beginning of the world
[R]*Men* have not heard nor perceived by the
ear, Ps. 31:19
Nor has the eye seen any God besides
You,
Who acts for the one who waits for Him.
5 You meet him who rejoices and does
righteousness,

Who remembers You in Your ways.
You are indeed angry, for we have
sinned—
[R]In these ways we continue; Mal. 3:6
And we need to be saved.
6 But we are all like an unclean *thing,*
And all [R]our righteousnesses *are* like
[T]filthy rags; [Phil. 3:9] • Lit. *a filthy garment*
We all [R]fade as a leaf, Ps. 90:5, 6
And our iniquities, like the wind,
Have taken us away.
7 And *there is* no one who calls on Your
name,
Who stirs himself up to take hold of
You;
For You have hidden Your face from us,
And have [T]consumed us because of our
iniquities. Lit. *caused us to melt*

8 But now, O LORD,
You *are* our Father;
We *are* the clay, and You our potter;
And all we *are* the work of Your hand.
9 Do not be furious, O LORD,
Nor remember iniquity forever;
Indeed, please look—we all *are* Your
people!
10 Your holy cities are a wilderness,
Zion is a wilderness,
Jerusalem a desolation.
11 Our holy and beautiful [T]temple,
Where our fathers praised You,
Is burned up with fire; Lit. *house*
And all [R]our pleasant things [T]are laid
waste. Ezek. 24:21 • *have become a ruin*
12 [R]Will You restrain Yourself because of
these *things,* O LORD? Is. 42:14
[R]Will You [T]hold Your peace, and afflict us
very severely? Ps. 83:1 • *keep silent*

CHAPTER 65

The Lord's Answer to the Remnant

"I WAS [R]sought by *those who* did not ask
for Me; Rom. 9:24; 10:20
I was found by *those who* did not seek
Me.
I said, 'Here I am, here I am,'
To a nation *that* [R]was not called by My
name. Is. 63:19
2 [R]I have stretched out My hands all day
long to a [R]rebellious
people, Rom. 10:21 • Is. 1:2, 23☆
Who walk in a way *that is* not good,
According to their own thoughts;
3 A people [R]who provoke Me to anger
continually to My face; Deut. 32:21
[R]Who sacrifice in gardens, Is. 1:29
And burn incense on altars of brick;
4 [R]Who sit among the graves, Deut. 18:11
And spend the night in the tombs;
[R]Who eat swine's flesh, Is. 66:17
And the broth of abominable things is *in*
their vessels;
5 [R]Who say, 'Keep to yourself, Matt. 9:11
Do not come near me,
For I am holier than you!'
These *are* smoke in My nostrils,
A fire that burns all the day.

6 "Behold, *it is* written before Me:
I will not keep silence, [R]but will repay—
Even repay into their bosom— Ps. 79:12
7 Your iniquities and [R]the iniquities of
your fathers together," Ex. 20:5
Says the LORD,
[R]"Who have burned incense on the
mountains Ezek. 18:6
And blasphemed Me on the hills;
Therefore I will measure their former
work into their bosom."

8 Thus says the LORD:

"As the new wine is found in the cluster,
And *one* says, 'Do not destroy it,
For [R]a blessing *is* in it,' Joel 2:14
So will I do for My servants' sake,
That I may not destroy them [R]all. Is. 1:9
9 I will bring forth descendants from
Jacob,
And from Judah an heir of My
mountains;
My [R]elect shall inherit it, Matt. 24:22
And My servants shall dwell there.
10 [R]Sharon shall be a fold of flocks, Is. 33:9
And [R]the Valley of Achor a place for
herds to lie down, Josh. 7:24
For My people who have sought Me.

11 "But you *are* those who forsake the LORD,
Who forget [R]My holy mountain, Is. 56:7
Who prepare [R]a table for Gad,*
And who furnish a drink offering for
Meni.* Ezek. 23:41
12 Therefore I will number you for the
sword,
And you shall all bow down to the
slaughter;
[R]Because, when I called, you did not
answer; Prov. 1:24
When I spoke, you did not hear,
But did evil before My eyes,
And chose *that* in which I do not
delight."

13 Therefore thus says the Lord GOD:

"Behold, My servants shall eat,
But you shall be hungry;
Behold, My servants shall drink,
But you shall be thirsty;

65:11 Lit. *Troop* or *Fortune;* a pagan deity • Lit. *Number* or *Destiny;* a pagan deity

Behold, My servants shall rejoice,
But you shall be ashamed;
14 Behold, My servants shall sing for joy of heart,
But you shall cry for sorrow of heart,
And [R]wail for grief of spirit. Matt. 8:12
15 You shall leave your name [R]as a curse to [R]My chosen; Jer. 29:22 • Is. 65:9, 22
For the Lord GOD will slay you,
And call His servants by another name;
16 [R]So that he who blesses himself in the earth Jer. 4:2
Shall bless himself in the God of truth;
And [R]he who swears in the earth
Shall swear by the God of truth;
Because the former troubles are forgotten, Zeph. 1:5
And because they are hidden from My eyes.

Glorious Consummation of History

17 "For behold, I create [R]new heavens and a new earth; Rev. 21:1
And the former shall not be remembered or come to mind.
18 But be glad and rejoice forever in what I create;
For behold, I create Jerusalem *as* a rejoicing,
And her people a joy.
19 [R]I will rejoice in Jerusalem, Is. 62:4, 5
And joy in My people;
The [R]voice of weeping shall no longer be heard in her, Rev. 7:17; 21:4
Nor the voice of crying.

20 "No more shall an infant from there *live but a few* days,
Nor an old man who has not fulfilled his days;
For the child shall die one hundred years old,
[R]But the sinner *being* one hundred years old shall be accursed. Eccl. 8:12, 13
21 [R]They shall build houses and inhabit *them;* Amos 9:14
They shall plant vineyards and eat their fruit.
22 They shall not build and another inhabit;
They shall not plant and another eat;
For [R]as the days of a tree, *so shall be* the days of My people, Ps. 92:12
And [R]My elect shall long enjoy the work of their hands. Is. 65:9, 15
23 They shall not labor in vain,
Nor bring forth children for trouble;
For [R]they *shall be* the descendants of the blessed of the LORD, Is. 61:9
And their offspring with them.

24 "It shall come to pass
That [R]before they call, I will answer;
And while they are still speaking, I will [R]hear. Is. 58:9 • Dan. 9:20–23
25 The [R]wolf and the lamb shall feed together, Is. 11:6–9
The lion shall eat straw like the ox,
[R]And dust *shall be* the serpent's food.
They shall not hurt nor destroy in all My holy mountain," Gen. 3:14
Says the LORD.

CHAPTER 66

THUS says the LORD:

[R]"Heaven *is* My throne, 1 Kin. 8:27
And earth *is* My footstool.
Where *is* the house that you will build Me?
And where *is* the place of My rest?
2 For all those *things* My hand has made,
And all those *things* exist,"
Says the LORD.
[R]"But on this *one* will I look:
[R]On *him who is* poor and of a contrite spirit, [Is. 57:15; 61:1] • Ps. 34:18; 51:17
And who trembles at My word.

3 "He[R] who kills a bull *is as if* he slays a man; [Is. 1:10–17; 58:1–7]
He who sacrifices a lamb, *as if* he [R]breaks a dog's neck; Deut. 23:18
He who offers a grain offering, *as if he offers* swine's blood;
He who burns incense, *as if* he blesses an idol.
Just as they have chosen their own ways,
And their soul delights in their abominations,
4 So will I choose their delusions,
And bring their fears on them;
[R]Because, when I called, no one answered, Is. 65:12
When I spoke they did not hear;
But they did evil before My eyes,
And chose *that* in which I do not delight."

5 Hear the word of the LORD,
You who tremble at His word:
"Your brethren who [R]hated you, Is. 60:15
Who cast you out for My name's sake, said,
[R]'Let the LORD be glorified, Is. 5:19
That [R]we may see your joy.' [Titus 2:13]
But they shall be ashamed."

6 The sound of noise from the city!
A voice from the temple!
The voice of the LORD,
Who fully repays His enemies!

7 "Before she was in labor, she gave birth;
Before her pain came,

She delivered a male child.
8 Who has heard such a thing?
Who has seen such things?
Shall the earth be made to give birth in
one day?
Or shall a nation be born at once?
For as soon as Zion was in labor,
She gave birth to her children.
9 Shall I bring to the time of birth, and not
cause delivery?" says the LORD.
"Shall I who cause delivery shut up *the*
womb?" says your God.
10"Rejoice with Jerusalem,
And be glad with her, all you who love
her;
Rejoice for joy with her, all you who
mourn for her;
11 That you may feed and be satisfied
With the consolation of her bosom,
That you may drink deeply and be
delighted
With the abundance of her glory."

12 For thus says the LORD:

"Behold, [R]I will extend peace to her like a
river, Is. 48:18; 60:5
And the glory of the Gentiles like a
flowing stream.
Then you shall [R]feed; Is. 60:16
On *her* sides shall you be carried,
And be dandled on *her* knees.
13 As one whom his mother comforts,
So I will [R]comfort you; Is. 51:3
And you shall be comforted in
Jerusalem."

14 When you see *this,* your heart shall
rejoice,
And [R]your bones shall flourish like
grass; Ezek. 37:1
The hand of the LORD shall be known to
His servants,
And *His* indignation to His enemies.
15[R] For behold, the LORD will come with fire
And with His chariots, like a whirlwind,
To render His anger with fury, Is. 9:5
And His rebuke with flames of fire.
16 For by fire and by [R]His sword Is. 27:1
The LORD will judge all flesh;
And the slain of the LORD shall be
[R]many. Is. 34:6

17"Those[R] who sanctify themselves and
purify themselves, Is. 65:3–8
To go to the gardens
[T]After an *idol* in the midst, Lit. *After one*
Eating swine's flesh and the abomination
and the mouse,
Shall [T]be consumed together," says the
LORD. *come to an end*

18 "For I *know* their works and their
[R]thoughts. It shall be that I will [R]gather all na-
tions and tongues; and they shall come and
see My glory. Is. 59:7 • Jer. 3:17
19 "I will set a sign among them; and those
among them who escape I will send to the na-
tions: *to* Tarshish and Pul* and Lud, who draw
the bow, and Tubal and Javan, *to* the coast-
lands afar off who have not heard My fame
nor seen My glory. And they shall declare My
glory among the Gentiles.
20 "Then they shall bring all your brethren
[R]for an offering to the LORD out of all nations,
on horses and in chariots and in litters, on
mules and on camels, to My holy mountain
Jerusalem," says the LORD, "as the children of
Israel bring an offering in a clean vessel into
the house of the LORD. [Rom. 15:16]
21 "And I will also take some of them for
[R]priests *and* Levites," says the LORD. Ex. 19:6

22"For as [R]the new heavens and the new
earth Rev. 21:1
Which I will make shall remain before
Me," says the LORD,
"So shall your descendants and your
name remain.
23 And [R]it shall come to pass Zech. 14:16
That from one New Moon to another,
And from one Sabbath to another,
[R]All flesh shall come to worship before
Me," says the LORD. Zech. 14:17–21

24"And they shall go forth and look
Upon the corpses of the men
Who have transgressed against Me.
For their [R]worm does not die,
And their fire is not quenched.
They shall be an abhorrence to all
flesh." Mark 9:44, 46, 48

66:19 So with MT, Tg.; LXX *Put* (cf. Jer. 46:9)

THE BOOK OF JEREMIAH

THE BOOK OF JEREMIAH

The Book of Jeremiah is the prophecy of a man divinely called in his youth from the priest-city of Anathoth. A heartbroken prophet with a heartbreaking message, Jeremiah labors for more than forty years proclaiming a message of doom to the stiff-necked people of Judah. Despised and persecuted by his countrymen, Jeremiah bathes his harsh prophecies in tears of compassion. His broken heart causes him to write a broken book, which is difficult to arrange chronologically or topically. But through his sermons and signs he faithfully declares that surrender to God's will is the only way to escape calamity.

Yirmeyahu or *Yirmeyah* literally means "Yahweh Throws," perhaps in the sense of laying a foundation. It may effectively mean "Yahweh establishes, appoints, or sends." The Greek form of the Hebrew name in the Septuagint is *Hieremias,* and the Latin form is *Jeremias.*

THE AUTHOR OF JEREMIAH

Jeremiah was the son of Hilkiah the priest and lived just over two miles north of Jerusalem in Anathoth. As an object lesson to Judah he was not allowed to marry (16:2). Because of his radical message of God's judgment through the coming Babylonian invasion, he led a life of conflict. He was threatened in his hometown of Anathoth, tried for his life by the priests and prophets of Jerusalem, put in stocks, forced to flee from King Jehoiakim, publicly humiliated by the false prophet Hananiah, and thrown into a cistern.

The book clearly states that Jeremiah is its author (1:1). Jeremiah dictated all his prophecies to his secretary Baruch from the beginning of his ministry until the fourth year of Jehoiakim. After this scroll was destroyed by the king, Jeremiah dictated a more complete edition to Baruch (see 36—38), and later sections were also composed. Only chapter 52 was evidently not written by Jeremiah. This supplement is almost identical to 2 Kings 24:18—25:30, and it may have been added by Baruch.

Daniel alludes to Jeremiah's prophecy of the seventy-year captivity (25:11–14; 29:10; Dan. 9:2), and Jeremiah's authorship is also confirmed by Ecclesiasticus, Josephus, and the Talmud. The New Testament makes explicit and implicit references to Jeremiah's prophecy: Matthew 2:17, 18 (31:15); Matthew 21:13; Mark 11:17; Luke 19:4 (7:11); Romans 11:27 (31:33); and Hebrews 8:8–13 (31:31–34).

THE TIME OF JEREMIAH

Jeremiah was a contemporary of Zephaniah, Habakkuk, Daniel, and Ezekiel. His ministry stretched from 627 to about 580 B.C. Josiah, Judah's last good king (640–609 B.C.), instituted spiritual reforms when the Book of the Law was discovered in 622 B.C. Jeremiah was on good terms with Josiah and lamented when he was killed in 609 B.C. by Pharaoh Necho of Egypt. By this time, Babylon had already overthrown Nineveh, the capital city of Assyria (612 B.C.). Jehoahaz replaced Josiah as king of Judah, but reigned only three months before he was deposed and taken to Egypt by Necho. Jehoiakim (609–597 B.C.) was Judah's next king, but he reigned as an Egyptian vassal until 605 B.C., when Egypt was defeated by Babylon at Carchemish. Nebuchadnezzar took Palestine and deported key persons such as Daniel to Babylon. Judah's King Jehoiakim was now a Babylonian vassal, but he rejected Jeremiah's warnings in 601 B.C. and rebelled against Babylon. Jehoiachin became Judah's next king in 597 B.C., but was replaced by Zedekiah three months later when Nebuchadnezzar captured Jerusalem and deported Jehoiachin to Babylon. Zedekiah was the last king of Judah; his attempted alliance with Egypt led to Nebuchadnezzar's occupation and overthrow of Jerusalem in 586 B.C.

Thus, there were three stages in Jeremiah's ministry: (1) From 627 to 605 B.C. he prophesied while Judah was threatened by Assyria and Egypt. (2) From 605 to 586 B.C. he proclaimed God's judgment while Judah was threatened and besieged by Babylon. (3) From 586 to about 580 B.C. he ministered in Jerusalem and Egypt after Judah's downfall.

THE CHRIST OF JEREMIAH

The Messiah is clearly seen in 23:1–8 as the coming Shepherd and righteous Branch who "shall reign and prosper, and execute judgment and righteousness in the earth. In His days Judah will be saved, and Israel will dwell safely; now this *is* His name by which He will be called: THE LORD OUR RIGHTEOUSNESS (23:5, 6). He will bring in the new covenant (31:31–34), which will fulfill God's covenants with Abraham (Gen. 12:1–3; 17:1–8), Moses and the people (Deut. 28—30), and David (2 Sam. 7:1–17).

The curse on Jehoiachin (Jeconiah, Coniah) in 22:28–30 meant that no physical descendant would succeed him to the throne. Matthew

1:1–17 traces the genealogy of Christ through Solomon and Jeconiah to His legal (but not His physical) father, Joseph. However, no son of Joseph could sit upon the throne of David, for he would be under the curse of Jehoiachin. Luke 3:23–38 traces Christ's lineage backward from Mary (His physical parent) through David's other son, Nathan (3:31), thereby avoiding the curse. The righteous Branch will indeed reign on the throne of David.

KEYS TO JEREMIAH

Key Word: Judah's Last Hour—In Jeremiah, God is seen as patient and holy: He delays judgment and appeals to His people to repent before it is too late. As the object lesson at the potter's house demonstrates, a ruined vessel can be repaired while still wet (18:1–4); but once dried, a marred vessel is fit only for the garbage heap (19:10, 11). God's warning is clear: Judah's time for repentance will soon pass. Because they defy God's words and refuse to repent, the Babylonian captivity is inevitable. Jeremiah lists the moral and spiritual causes for their coming catastrophe, but he also proclaims God's gracious promise of hope and restoration. There will always be a remnant, and God will establish a new covenant.

Key Verses: Jeremiah 7:23, 24 and 8:11, 12—"But this is what I commanded them, saying, 'Obey My voice, and I will be your God, and you shall be My people. And walk in all the ways that I have commanded you, that it may be well with you.' Yet they did not obey or incline their ear, but followed the counsels *and* the dictates of their evil hearts, and went backward and not forward" (7:23, 24).

"For they have healed the hurt of the daughter of My people slightly, saying, 'Peace, peace!' when *there is* no peace. Were they ashamed when they had committed abomination? No! They were not at all ashamed, nor did they know how to blush. Therefore they shall fall among those who fall; in the time of their punishment they shall be cast down, says the LORD" (8:11, 12).

Key Chapter: Jeremiah 31—Amid all the judgment and condemnation by Jeremiah are the wonderful promises of Jeremiah 31. Even though Judah has broken the covenants of her great King, God will make a new covenant when He will "put My law in their minds, and write it on their hearts; and I will be their God, and they shall be My people" (31:33). The Messiah instituted that new covenant with His death and resurrection (cf. Matt. 26:26–29).

SURVEY OF JEREMIAH

Jeremiah is a record of the ministry of one of Judah's greatest prophets during its darkest days. He is called as a prophet during the reign of Josiah, the last of Judah's good kings. But even Josiah's well-intentioned reforms cannot stem the tide of apostasy. The downhill slide of the nation continues virtually unabated through a succession of four godless kings during Jeremiah's ministry. The people wallow in apostasy and idolatry and grow even more treacherous than Israel was before its captivity (3:11). They pervert the worship of the true God and give themselves over to spiritual and moral decay. Because they refuse to repent or even listen to God's prophet, the divine cure requires radical surgery. Jeremiah proclaims an approaching avalanche of judgment. Babylon will be God's instrument of judgment, and this book refers to that nation 164 times, more references than the rest of the Bible.

Jeremiah faithfully proclaims the divine condemnation of rebellious Judah for forty years and is rewarded with opposition, beatings, isolations, and imprisonment. His sympathy and sensitivity cause him to grieve over the

FOCUS	CALL OF JEREMIAH	PROPHECIES TO JUDAH				PROPHECIES TO THE GENTILES	FALL OF JERUSALEM
REFERENCE	1:1—	2:1—	26:1—	30:1—	34:1—	46:1—	52:1—52:34
DIVISION	PROPHETIC COMMISSION	CONDEMNATION OF JUDAH	CONFLICTS OF JEREMIAH	FUTURE RESTORATION OF JERUSALEM	PRESENT FALL OF JERUSALEM	CONDEMNATION OF NINE NATIONS	HISTORIC CONCLUSION
TOPIC	BEFORE THE FALL				THE FALL	AFTER THE FALL	
	CALL	MINISTRY					RETROSPECT
LOCATION	JUDAH					SURROUNDING NATIONS	BABYLON
TIME	c. 627–580 B.C.						

rebelliousness and imminent doom of his nation. He often desires to resign from his prophetic office because of the harshness of his message and his reception, but he perseveres to Judah's bitter end. He is the weeping prophet (9:1; 13:17)—lonely, rejected, and persecuted.

Although Jeremiah is not easily arranged chronologically or thematically, its basic message is clear: surrender to God's will is the only way to escape calamity. Judgment cannot be halted, but promises of restoration are sprinkled throughout the book. Its divisions are: the call of Jeremiah (1); the prophecies to Judah (2—45); the prophecies to the Gentiles (46—51); and the fall of Jerusalem (52).

The Call of Jeremiah (1): Jeremiah is called and sanctified before birth to be God's prophet. This introductory chapter surveys the identification, inauguration, and instructions of the prophet.

The Prophecies to Judah (2—45): Jeremiah's message is communicated through a variety of parables, sermons, and object lessons. The prophet's life becomes a daily illustration to Judah, and most of the book's object lessons are found in this section (13:1–14; 14:1–9; 16:1–9; 18:1–8; 19:1–13; 24:1–10; 27:1–11; 32:6–15; 43:8–13). In a series of twelve graphic messages, Jeremiah lists the causes of Judah's coming judgment. The Gentile nations are more faithful to their false gods than Judah is to God. They become a false vine by following idols and are without excuse. The people are condemned for their empty profession, disobedience to God's covenant, and spiritual harlotry. God has bound Judah to Himself; but like a rotten waistband, they have become corrupt and useless. Jeremiah offers a confession for the people, but their sin is too great; the prophet can only lament for them. As a sign of imminent judgment Jeremiah is forbidden to marry and participate in the feasts. Because the nation does not trust God or keep the Sabbath, the land will receive a sabbath rest when they are in captivity. Jerusalem will be invaded and the rulers and people will be deported to Babylon. Restoration will only come under the new Shepherd, the Messiah, the nation's future King. Jeremiah announces the duration of the captivity as seventy years, in contrast to the messages of the false prophets who insist it will not happen.

Because of his message (2:25), Jeremiah suffers misery and opposition (26—45). He is rejected by the prophets and priests who call for his death, but he is spared by the elders and officials. In his sign of the yoke he proclaims the unpopular message that Judah must submit to divine discipline. But he assures the nation of restoration and hope under a new covenant (30—33). A remnant will be delivered and there will be a coming time of blessing. Jeremiah's personal experiences and sufferings are the focal point of 34—45 as opposition against the prophet mounts. Since he is no longer allowed in the temple, he sends his assistant Baruch to read his prophetic warnings. His scroll is burned by Jehoiakim, and Jeremiah is imprisoned. After the destruction of the city, Jeremiah is taken to Egypt by fleeing Jews, but he prophesies that Nebuchadnezzar will invade Egypt as well.

The Prophecies to the Gentiles (46—51): These chapters are a series of prophetic oracles against nine nations: Egypt, Philistia, Moab, Ammon, Edom, Damascus (Syria), Arabia, Elam, and Babylon. Only Egypt, Moab, Ammon, and Elam are given a promise of restoration.

The Fall of Jerusalem (52): Jeremiah's forty-year declaration of doom was finally vindicated in an event so significant that it is recorded in detail four times in the Scriptures (2 Kin. 25; 2 Chr. 36; Jer. 39; 52). In this historical supplement, Jerusalem is captured, destroyed, and plundered. The leaders are killed and the captives taken to Babylon.

OUTLINE OF JEREMIAH

Part One: The Call of Jeremiah (1:1–19)

I. Jeremiah's Call 1:1–10

II. Jeremiah's Signs......................................1:11–16

III. Jeremiah's Assurance 1:17–19

Part Two: The Prophecies to Judah (2:1—45:5)

I. The Condemnation of Judah..........2:1—25:38

A. Jeremiah's First Sermon: Judah Sinned Willfully.........................2:1—3:5

B. Jeremiah's Second Sermon: Judah to Be Judged ....3:6—6:30

1. Judah Ignores Israel's Example.......3:6–10
2. Judah Is Called from Backsliding ....3:11—4:4
3. Judah's Destruction from the North 4:5–31
4. Judah's Sins 5:1–31
5. Jerusalem to Be Destroyed 6:1–30

C. Jeremiah's Third Sermon: Judah's Hypocrisy in Worship......................7:1—10:25

Part Three: The Prophecies to the Gentiles (46:1—51:64)

Part Four: The Fall of Jerusalem (52:1–34)

CHAPTER 1

Jeremiah's Call

THE words of Jeremiah the son of Hilkiah,
of the priests who *were* [R]in Anathoth in
the land of Benjamin, Josh. 21:18
2 to whom the word of the LORD came in
the days of Josiah the son of Amon, king of
Judah, in the thirteenth year of his reign.
3 It came also in the days of [R]Jehoiakim
the son of Josiah, king of Judah, [R]until the
end of the eleventh year of Zedekiah the
son of Josiah, king of Judah, [R]until the car-
rying away of Jerusalem captive in the fifth
month. 2 Kin. 23:34 • Jer. 39:2 • Jer. 52:12
4 Then the word of the LORD came to me,
saying:

5 "Before I [R]formed you in the womb [R]I
knew you; Is. 49:1, 5 • Ex. 33:12
Before you were born I [R]sanctified you;
I [T]ordained you a prophet to the
nations." [Luke 1:15] • *appointed*

6 Then said I:

[R]"Ah, Lord GOD! Ex. 4:10; 6:12, 30
Behold, I cannot speak, for I *am* a
youth."

7 But the LORD said to me:

"Do not say, 'I *am* a youth,'
For you shall go to all to whom I send
you,
And [R]whatever I command you, you
shall speak. Num. 22:20, 38
8 [R]Do not be afraid of their faces,
For [R]I *am* with you to deliver you," says
the LORD. Ezek. 2:6; 3:9 • Ex. 3:12

9 Then the LORD put forth His hand and
[R]touched my mouth, and the LORD said to
me: Is. 6:7

"Behold, I have [R]put My words in your
mouth. Is. 51:16
10 See, I have this day set you over the
nations and over the kingdoms,
To [R]root out and to pull down,
To destroy and to throw down,
To build and to plant." [2 Cor. 10:4, 5]

Jeremiah's Signs

11 Moreover the word of the LORD came to
me, saying, "Jeremiah, what do you see?"
And I said, "I see a [T]branch of an almond
tree." Lit. *rod*
12 Then the LORD said to me, "You have
seen well, for I am [T]ready to perform My
word." Lit. *watching*
13 And the word of the LORD came to me the
second time, saying, "What do you see?" And
I said, "I see [R]a boiling pot, and it is facing
away from the north." Ezek. 11:3; 24:3
14 Then the LORD said to me:

"Out of the [R]north calamity shall break
forth Jer. 6:1
On all the inhabitants of the land.
15 For behold, I am [R]calling Jer. 6:22; 25:9
All the families of the kingdoms of the
north," says the LORD;
"They shall come and [R]each one set his
throne Jer. 39:3
At the entrance of the gates of
Jerusalem,
Against all its walls all around,
And against all the cities of Judah.
16 I will utter My judgments
Against them concerning all their
wickedness,
Because they have forsaken Me,
Burned [R]incense to other gods, Jer. 7:9
And worshiped the works of their own
[R]hands. Is. 37:19

Jeremiah's Assurance

17 "Therefore [R]prepare yourself and arise,
And speak to them all that I command
you. Job 38:3
[R]Do not be dismayed before their faces,
Lest I dismay you before them. Ezek. 2:6
18 For behold, I have made you this day
[R]A fortified city and an iron pillar,
And bronze walls against the whole
land— Is. 50:7
Against the kings of Judah,
Against its princes,
Against its priests,
And against the people of the land.
19 They will fight against you,
But they shall not prevail against you.
For I *am* with you," says the LORD, "to
deliver you."

CHAPTER 2

Jeremiah's First Sermon: Judah Sinned Willfully

MOREOVER the word of the LORD came to
me, saying,
2 "Go and cry in the hearing of Jerusalem,
saying, 'Thus says the LORD:

"I remember you,
The kindness of your [R]youth, Ezek. 16:8
The love of your betrothal,
[R]When you [T]went after Me in the
wilderness, Deut. 2:7 • *followed*
In a land not sown.
3 Israel *was* holiness to the LORD,
[R]The firstfruits of His increase.
All that devour him will offend;
Disaster will [R]come upon them," says
the LORD.'" Rev. 14:4 • Is. 41:11

4 Hear the word of the LORD, O house of Jacob and all the families of the house of Israel.
5 Thus says the LORD:

R"What injustice have your fathers found
in Me, Is. 5:4
That they have gone far from Me,
RHave followed idols, 2 Kin. 17:15
And have become idolaters?
6 Neither did they say, 'Where *is* the LORD,
Who Rbrought us up out of the land of
Egypt, Is. 63:11
Who led us through Rthe wilderness,
Through a land of deserts and pits,
Through a land of drought and the
shadow of death, Deut. 8:15; 32:10
Through a land that no one crossed
And where no one dwelt?'
7 I brought you into Ra bountiful country,
To eat its fruit and its goodness.
But when you entered, you Rdefiled My
land Num. 13:27 • Num. 35:33
And made My heritage an abomination.
8 The priests did not say, 'Where *is* the
LORD?'
And those who handle the Rlaw did not
know Me; Rom. 2:20
The rulers also transgressed against Me;
RThe prophets prophesied by Baal,
And walked after *things that* do not
profit. Jer. 23:13

9"Therefore RI will yet Tbring charges
against you," says the LORD, Mic. 6:2
"And against your children's children I
will bring charges. *contend with*
10 For pass beyond the coasts of Cyprus*
and see,
Send to Kedar* and consider diligently,
And see if there has been such *a thing*.
11RHas a nation changed *its* gods,
Which *are* Rnot gods? Mic. 4:5 • Is. 37:19
RBut My people have changed their Glory
For *what* does not profit. Rom. 1:23
12 Be astonished, O heavens, at this,
And be horribly afraid;
Be very desolate," says the LORD.
13"For My people have committed two
evils:
They have forsaken Me, the Rfountain of
living waters, Ps. 36:9
And hewn themselves cisterns—broken
cisterns that can hold no water.

14"*Is* Israel Ra servant? [Ex. 4:22]
Is he a homeborn *slave*?
Why is he plundered?
15RThe young lions roared at him, *and*
growled; Is. 1:7
They made his land waste;
His cities are burned, without inhabitant.
16 Also the people of Noph* and
RTahpanhes Jer. 43:7–9
Have broken the crown of your head.
17RHave you not brought this on yourself,
In that you have forsaken the LORD your
God Jer. 4:18
When He led you in the way?
18 And now why take the road to Egypt,
To drink the waters of Sihor?
Or why take the road to Assyria,
To drink the waters of the River?*
19 Your own wickedness will Rcorrect you,
And your backslidings will rebuke you.
Know therefore and see that *it is* an evil
and bitter *thing* Jer. 4:18
That you have forsaken the LORD your
God,
And the Tfear of Me *is* not in you,"
Says the Lord GOD of hosts. *dread*

20"For of old I have Rbroken your yoke *and*
burst your bonds; Lev. 26:13
And you said, 'I will not Ttransgress,'
When Ron every high hill and under
every green tree Kt. *serve* • Deut. 12:2
You lay down, playing the harlot.
21 Yet I had Rplanted you a noble vine, a
seed of highest quality. Ex. 15:17
How then have you turned before Me
Into Rthe degenerate plant of an alien
vine? Is. 5:4
22 For though you wash yourself with lye,
and use much soap,
Yet your iniquity is Rmarked before Me,"
says the Lord GOD. Job 14:16, 17

23"HowR can you say, 'I am not Tpolluted,
I have not gone after the Baals'?
See your way in the valley;
Know what you have done:
You are a swift dromedary breaking
loose in her ways, Prov. 30:12 • *defiled*
24 A wild donkey used to the wilderness,
That sniffs at the wind in her desire;
In her time of mating, who can turn her
away?
All those who seek her will not weary
themselves;
In her month they will find her.
25 Withhold your foot from being unshod,
and your throat from thirst.
But you said, R'There is no hope.
No! For I have loved Raliens, and after
them I will go.' Jer. 18:12 • Jer. 3:13

26"As the thief is ashamed when he is found
out,
So is the house of Israel ashamed;
They and their kings and their princes,
and their priests and their prophets,

2:10 Heb. *Kittim*, representative of western cultures • In northern Arabian desert, representative of eastern cultures **2:16** Memphis in ancient Egypt **2:18** The Euphrates

27 Saying to a tree, 'You *are* my father,'
And to a [R]stone, 'You gave birth to me.'
For they have turned *their* back to Me,
and not *their* face. Jer. 3:9
But in the time of their trouble
They will say, 'Arise and save us.'
28 But [R]where *are* your gods that you have
made for yourselves? Judg. 10:14
Let them arise,
If they [R]can save you in the time of your
[T]trouble; Is. 45:20 • Or *evil*
For [R]*according to* the number of your
cities Jer. 11:13
Are your gods, O Judah.

29 "Why will you plead with Me?
You all have transgressed against Me,"
says the LORD.
30 "In vain I have [R]chastened your children;
They received no correction. Is. 9:13
Your sword has [R]devoured your
prophets Neh. 9:26
Like a destroying lion.

31 "O generation, see the word of the LORD!
Have I been a wilderness to Israel,
Or a land of darkness?
Why do My people say, 'We are lords;
We will come no more to You'?
32 Can a virgin forget her ornaments,
Or a bride her attire?
Yet My people [R]have forgotten Me days
without number. Ps. 106:21

33 "Why do you beautify your way to seek
love?
Therefore you have also taught
The wicked women your ways.
34 Also on your skirts is found
[R]The blood of the lives of the poor
innocents. Ps. 106:38
I have not found it by [T]secret search,
But plainly on all these things. *digging*
35 [R]Yet you say, 'Because I am innocent,
Surely His anger shall turn from me.'
Behold, [R]I will plead My case against
you, Jer. 2:23, 29 • Jer. 2:9
Because you say, 'I have not sinned.'
36 [R]Why do you gad about so much to
change your way? Hos. 5:13; 12:1
Also you shall be ashamed of Egypt as
you were ashamed of Assyria.
37 Indeed you will go forth from him
With your hands on [R]your head;
For the LORD has rejected your trusted
allies, 2 Sam. 13:19
And you will not prosper by them.

CHAPTER 3

"THEY say, 'If a man divorces his wife,
And she goes from him
And becomes another man's,
[R]May he return to her again?'
Would not that [R]land be greatly
polluted? Deut. 24:1–4 • Jer. 2:7
But you have [R]played the harlot with
many lovers; Ezek. 16:26
Yet return to Me," says the LORD.
2 "Lift up your eyes to [R]the desolate
heights and see: Deut. 12:2
Where have you not lain *with men*?
By the road you have sat for them
Like an Arabian in the wilderness;
[R]And you have polluted the land
With your harlotries and your
wickedness. Jer. 2:7
3 Therefore the [R]showers have been
withheld, Lev. 26:19
And there has been no latter rain.
You have had a [R]harlot's forehead;
You refuse to be ashamed. Zeph. 3:5
4 Will you not from this time cry to Me,
'My Father, You *are* [R]the guide of [R]my
youth? Prov. 2:17 • Jer. 2:2
5 [R]Will He remain angry forever?
Will He keep it to the end?'
Behold, you have spoken and done evil
things,
As you were able." [Is. 57:16]

Judah Ignores Israel's Example

6 The LORD said also to me in the days of
Josiah the king: "Have you seen what [R]back-
sliding Israel has done? She has gone up on
every high mountain and under every green
tree, and there played the harlot. Jer. 7:24
7 [R]"And I said, after she had done all these
things, 'Return to Me.' But she did not re-
turn. And her treacherous [R]sister Judah saw
it. 2 Kin. 17:13 • Ezek. 16:47, 48
8 "Then I saw that [R]for all the causes for
which backsliding Israel had committed adul-
tery, I had [R]put her away and given her a cer-
tificate of divorce; yet her treacherous sister
Judah did not fear, but went and played the
harlot also. Ezek. 23:9 • 2 Kin. 17:6
9 "So it came to pass, through her casual
harlotry, that she defiled the land and com-
mitted adultery with stones and trees.
10 "And yet for all this her treacherous sister
Judah has not turned to Me with her whole
heart, but in pretense," says the LORD.

Judah Is Called from Backsliding

11 Then the LORD said to me, [R]"Backsliding
Israel has shown herself more righteous than
treacherous Judah. Ezek. 16:51, 52
12 "Go and proclaim these words toward
[R]the north, and say: 2 Kin. 17:6

'Return, backsliding Israel,' says the
LORD;
'I will not cause My anger to fall on you.
For I *am* merciful,' says the LORD;
'I will not remain angry forever.

13[R]Only acknowledge your iniquity,
That you have transgressed against the
LORD your God, Deut. 30:1, 2
And have scattered your charms
To [R]alien deities [R]under every green tree,
And you have not obeyed My voice,'
says the LORD. Jer. 2:25 • Deut. 12:2

14 "Return, O backsliding children," says the
LORD; "for I am married to you. I will take you,
one from a city and two from a family, and I
will bring you to Zion.
15 "And I will give you [R]shepherds according
to My heart, who will feed you with knowl-
edge and understanding. Eph. 4:11
16 "Then it shall come to pass, when you are
multiplied and [R]increased in the land in those
days," says the LORD, "that they will say no
more, 'The ark of the covenant of the LORD.'
[R]It shall not come to mind, nor shall they re-
member it, nor shall they visit *it*, nor shall it
be made anymore. Is. 49:19 • Is. 65:17
17 "At that time Jerusalem shall be called
The Throne of the LORD, and all the nations
shall be gathered to it, to the name of the
LORD, to Jerusalem. No more shall they follow
the dictates of their evil hearts.
18 "In those days [R]the house of Judah shall
walk with the house of Israel, and they shall
come together out of the land of [R]the north to
the land that I have given as an inheritance to
your fathers. Is. 11:13 • Jer. 31:8
19 "But I said:

'How can I put you among the children
And give you [R]a pleasant land,
A beautiful heritage of the hosts of
nations?' Ps. 106:24

"And I said:

'You shall call Me, [R]"My Father,"
And not turn away from Me.' Is. 63:16
20 Surely, *as* a wife treacherously departs
from her [T]husband, Lit. *companion*
So [R]have you dealt treacherously with
Me, Is. 48:8
O house of Israel," says the LORD.

21 A voice was heard on [R]the desolate
heights, Is. 15:2
Weeping *and* supplications of the
children of Israel.
For they have perverted their way;
They have forgotten the LORD their God.

22 "Return, you backsliding children,
And I will [R]heal your backslidings."

"Indeed we do come to You, Hos. 6:1; 14:4
For You are the LORD our God.
23[R]Truly, in vain *is salvation hoped for*
from the hills, Ps. 121:1, 2
And from the multitude of mountains;
[R]Truly, in the LORD our God Ps. 3:8
Is the salvation of Israel.
24[R]For shame has devoured Hos. 9:10
The labor of our fathers from our
youth—
Their flocks and their herds,
Their sons and their daughters.
25 We lie down in our shame,
And our [T]reproach covers us. *disgrace*
[R]For we have sinned against the LORD
our God, Ezra 9:6, 7
We and our fathers,
From our youth even to this day,
And [R]have not obeyed the voice of the
LORD our God." Jer. 22:21

CHAPTER 4

"IF you will return, O Israel," says the
LORD,
[R]"Return to Me; Joel 2:12
And if you will put away your
abominations out of My sight,
Then you shall not be moved.
2 And you shall swear, 'The LORD lives,'
[R]In truth, in [T]judgment, and in
righteousness; Zech. 8:8 • *justice*
[R]The nations shall bless themselves in
Him, [Gen. 22:18]
And in Him they shall glory."

3 For thus says the LORD to the men of Ju-
dah and Jerusalem:

"Break up your [T]fallow ground, *untilled*
And do not sow among thorns.
4[R]Circumcise yourselves to the LORD,
And take away the foreskins of your
hearts, Deut. 10:16; 30:6
You men of Judah and inhabitants of
Jerusalem,
Lest My fury come forth like fire,
And burn so that no one can quench *it*,
Because of the evil of your doings."

Judah's Destruction from the North

5 Declare in Judah and proclaim in Jerusa-
lem, and say:

[R]"Blow the trumpet in the land; Hos. 8:1
Cry, 'Gather together,'
And say, 'Assemble yourselves,
And let us go into the fortified cities.'
6 Set up the [T]standard toward Zion.
Take refuge! Do not delay! *banner*
For I will bring disaster from the [R]north,
And great destruction." Jer. 1:13–15

7[R]The lion has come up from his thicket,
And [R]the destroyer of nations is on his
way. Dan. 7:4 • Jer. 25:9
He has gone forth from his place

[R]To make your land desolate.
Your cities will be laid waste,
Without inhabitant. Is. 1:7; 6:11
8 For this, [R]clothe yourself with sackcloth,
Lament and wail. Is. 22:12
For the fierce anger of the LORD
Has not turned back from us.

9 "And it shall come to pass in that day,"
says the LORD,
"*That* the heart of the king shall perish,
And the heart of the princes;
The priests shall be astonished,
And the prophets shall wonder."

10 Then I said, "Ah, Lord GOD!
[R]Surely You have greatly deceived this
people and Jerusalem, Ezek. 14:9
[R]Saying, 'You shall have peace,'
Whereas the sword reaches to the
[T]heart." Jer. 5:12; 14:13 • Lit. *soul*

11 At that time it will be said
To this people and to Jerusalem,
[R]"A dry wind of the desolate heights *blows*
in the wilderness Hos. 13:15
Toward the daughter of My people—
Not to fan or to cleanse—
12 A wind too strong for these will come for
Me;
Now [R]I will also speak judgment against
them." Jer. 1:16

13 "Behold, he shall come up like clouds,
And his chariots like a whirlwind.
His horses are swifter than eagles.
Woe to us, for we are plundered!"

14 O Jerusalem, [R]wash your heart from
wickedness, James 4:8
That you may be saved.
How long shall your evil thoughts lodge
within you?
15 For a voice declares [R]from Dan
And proclaims [T]affliction from Mount
Ephraim: Jer. 8:16; 50:17 • Or *wickedness*
16 "Make mention to the nations,
Yes, proclaim against Jerusalem,
That watchers come from a [R]far country
And raise their voice against the cities
of Judah. Is. 39:3
17 [R]Like keepers of a field they are against
her all around, 2 Kin. 25:1, 4
Because she has been rebellious against
Me," says the LORD.
18 "Your[R] ways and your doings Is. 50:1
Have procured these *things* for you.
This *is* your wickedness,
Because it is bitter,
Because it reaches to your heart."

19 O my [R]soul, my soul! Is. 15:5; 16:11; 21:3
I am pained in my very heart!
My heart makes a noise in me;
I cannot hold my peace,
Because you have heard, O my soul,
The sound of the trumpet,
The alarm of war.
20 Destruction upon destruction is cried,
For the whole land is plundered.
Suddenly my tents are plundered,
And my curtains in a moment.
21 How long will I see the standard,
And hear the sound of the trumpet?

22 "For My people *are* foolish,
They have not known Me.
They *are* [T]silly children, *foolish*
And they have no understanding.
[R]They *are* wise to do evil, Rom. 16:19
But to do good they have no knowledge."

23 [R]I beheld the earth, and indeed *it was*
without form, and void; Is. 24:19
And the heavens, they *had* no light.
24 [R]I beheld the mountains, and indeed they
trembled, Ezek. 38:20
And all the hills moved back and forth.
25 I beheld, and indeed *there was* no man,
And [R]all the birds of the heavens had
fled. Zeph. 1:3
26 I beheld, and indeed the fruitful land
was a [R]wilderness, Jer. 9:10
And all its cities were broken down
At the presence of the LORD,
By His fierce anger.

27 For thus says the LORD:

"The whole land shall be desolate;
Yet I will not make a full end.
28 For this shall the earth mourn,
And [R]the heavens above be black,
Because I have spoken. Is. 5:30; 50:3
I have purposed and [R]will not relent,
Nor will I turn back from it. [Num. 23:19]
29 The whole city shall flee from the noise
of the horsemen and bowmen.
They shall go into thickets and climb up
on the rocks.
Every city *shall be* forsaken,
And not a man shall dwell in it.

30 "And *when* you *are* plundered,
What will you do?
Though you clothe yourself with crimson,
Though you adorn *yourself* with
ornaments of gold,
[R]Though you enlarge your eyes with
paint, 2 Kin. 9:30
In vain you will make yourself fair;
[R]*Your* lovers will despise you;
They will seek your life. Jer. 22:20, 22

31 "For I have heard a voice as of a woman
in [T]labor, *childbirth*

The anguish as of her who brings forth
her first child,
The voice of the daughter of Zion
bewailing herself;
She [R]spreads her hands, *saying*,
'Woe *is* me now, for my soul is weary
Because of murderers!' Lam. 1:17

CHAPTER 5

Judah's Sins

"RUN to and fro through the streets of
Jerusalem;
See now and know;
And seek in her open places
[R]If you can find a man, Ezek. 22:30
[R]If there is *anyone* who executes
[T]judgment, Gen. 18:23–32 • *justice*
Who seeks the truth,
[R]And I will pardon her. Gen. 18:26
2 [R]Though they say, '*As* the LORD lives,'
Surely they swear falsely." Titus 1:16

3 O LORD, *are* not Your eyes on the truth?
You have [R]stricken them, Is. 1:5; 9:13
But they have not grieved;
You have consumed them,
But [R]they have refused to receive
correction. Zeph. 3:2
They have made their faces harder than
rock;
They have refused to return.

4 Therefore I said, "Surely these *are*
poor.
They are foolish;
For [R]they do not know the way of the
LORD, Jer. 8:7
The judgment of their God.
5 I will go to the great men and speak to
them,
For [R]they have known the way of the
LORD, Mic. 3:1
The judgment of their God."

But these have altogether [R]broken the
yoke Ps. 2:3
And burst the bonds.
6 Therefore [R]a lion from the forest shall
slay them, Jer. 4:7
[R]A wolf of the deserts shall destroy
them;
[R]A leopard will watch over their cities.
Everyone who goes out from there shall
be torn in pieces, Zeph. 3:3 • Hos. 13:7
Because their transgressions are many;
Their backslidings have increased.

7 "How shall I pardon you for this?
Your children have forsaken Me
And sworn by *those that are* not gods.
[R]When I had fed them to the full,
Then they committed adultery
And assembled themselves by troops in
the harlots' houses. Deut. 32:15
8 [R]They were *like* well-fed lusty stallions;
Every one neighed after his neighbor's
wife. Ezek. 22:11
9 Shall I not punish *them* for these
things?" says the LORD.
"And shall I not [R]avenge Myself on such a
nation as this? Jer. 9:9

10 "Go up on her walls and destroy,
But do not make a [R]complete end.
Take away her branches,
For they *are* not the LORD's. Jer. 4:27
11 For [R]the house of Israel and the house of
Judah Jer. 3:6, 7, 20
Have dealt very treacherously with Me,"
says the LORD.

12 They have lied about the LORD,
And said, [R]"*It is* not He. Jer. 23:17
Neither will evil come upon us,
Nor shall we see sword or famine.
13 And the prophets become wind,
For the word *is* not in them.
Thus shall it be done to them."

14 Therefore thus says the LORD God of
hosts:

"Because you speak this word,
[R]Behold, I will make My words in your
mouth fire, Jer. 1:9; 23:29
And this people wood,
And it shall devour them.
15 Behold, I will bring a [R]nation against you
[R]from afar, Deut. 28:49 • Jer. 4:16
O house of Israel," says the LORD.
"It *is* a mighty nation,
It *is* an ancient nation,
A nation whose language you do not
know,
Nor can you understand what they say.
16 Their quiver *is* like an open tomb;
They *are* all mighty men.
17 And they shall eat up your [R]harvest and
your bread, Lev. 26:16
Which your sons and daughters should
eat.
They shall eat up your flocks and your
herds;
They shall eat up your vines and your fig
trees;
They shall destroy your fortified cities,
In which you trust, with the sword.

18 "Nevertheless in those days," says the
LORD, "I [R]will not [T]make a complete end of
you. Jer. 30:11 • *completely destroy*
19 "And it will be when you say, [R]'Why does
the LORD our God do all these *things* to us?'
then you shall answer them, 'Just as you have
forsaken Me and served foreign gods in your

land, so you shall serve aliens in a land *that is* not yours.' Deut. 29:24–29

20"Declare this in the house of Jacob
And proclaim it in Judah, saying,
21 'Hear this now, O [R]foolish people,
Without understanding, Matt. 13:14
Who have eyes and see not,
And who have ears and hear not:
22[R] Do you not fear Me?' says the LORD.
'Will you not tremble at My presence,
Who have placed the sand as the [R]bound of the sea, [Rev. 15:4] • Job 26:10
By a perpetual decree, that it cannot pass beyond it?
And though its waves toss to and fro,
Yet they cannot prevail;
Though they roar, yet they cannot pass over it.
23 But this people has a defiant and rebellious heart;
They have revolted and departed.
24 They do not say in their heart,
"Let us now fear the LORD our God,
[R]Who gives rain, both the [R]former and the latter, in its season. Acts 14:17 • Joel 2:23
[R]He reserves for us the appointed weeks of the harvest." [Gen. 8:22]
25[R] Your iniquities have turned these *things* away, Jer. 3:3
And your sins have withheld good from you.

26 'For among My people are found wicked *men;*
They [R]lie in wait as one who sets snares;
They set a trap;
They catch men. Hab. 1:15
27 As a cage is full of birds,
So their houses *are* full of deceit.
Therefore they have become great and grown rich.
28 They have grown [R]fat, they are sleek;
Yes, they surpass the deeds of the wicked; Deut. 32:15
They do not plead [R]the cause,
The cause of the fatherless; Zech. 7:10
[R]Yet they prosper, Job 12:6
And the right of the needy they do not defend.
29[R] Shall I not punish *them* for these *things?*' says the LORD. Mal. 3:5
'Shall I not avenge Myself on such a nation as this?'

30"An astonishing and horrible thing
Has been committed in the land:
31 The prophets prophesy falsely,
And the priests rule by their *own* power;
And My people love *to have it* so.
But what will you do in the end?

CHAPTER 6

Jerusalem to Be Destroyed

"O YOU children of Benjamin,
Gather yourselves to flee from the midst of Jerusalem!
Blow the trumpet in Tekoa,
And set up a signal-fire in [R]Beth Haccerem; Neh. 3:14
[R]For disaster appears out of the north,
And great destruction. Jer. 4:6
2 I have likened the daughter of Zion
To a lovely and delicate woman.
3 The [R]shepherds with their flocks shall come to her. 2 Kin. 25:1–4
They shall pitch *their* tents against her all around.
Each one shall pasture in his own place."

4"Prepare[R] war against her; Joel 3:9
Arise, and let us go up [R]at noon.
Woe to us, for the day goes away,
For the shadows of the evening are lengthening. Jer. 15:8
5 Arise, and let us go by night,
And let us destroy her palaces."

6 For thus has the LORD of hosts said:

"Cut down trees,
And build a mound against Jerusalem.
This *is* the city to be punished.
She *is* full of oppression in her midst.
7[R] As a fountain [T]wells up with water,
So she wells up with her wickedness.
[R]Violence and plundering are heard in her. Is. 57:20 • *gushes* • Ps. 55:9
Before Me continually *are* [T]grief and wounds. *sickness*
8 Be instructed, O Jerusalem,
Lest [R]My soul depart from you;
Lest I make you desolate,
A land not inhabited." Hos. 9:12

9 Thus says the LORD of hosts:

"They shall thoroughly glean as a vine the remnant of Israel;
As a grape-gatherer, put your hand back into the branches."

10 To whom shall I speak and give warning,
That they may hear?
Indeed their [R]ear *is* uncircumcised,
And they cannot give heed. [Acts 7:51]
Behold, [R]the word of the LORD is a reproach to them; Jer. 8:9; 20:8
They have no delight in it.
11 Therefore I am full of the fury of the LORD.
[R]I am weary of holding *it* in. Jer. 20:9
"I will pour it out [R]on the children outside, Jer. 9:21

And on the assembly of young men
together;
For even the husband shall be taken with
the wife,
The aged with *him who is* full of days.
12 And [R]their houses shall be turned over to
others, Deut. 28:30
Fields and wives together;
For I will stretch out My hand
Against the inhabitants of the land," says
the LORD.
13 "Because from the least of them even to
the greatest of them,
Everyone *is* given to [R]covetousness;
And from the prophet even to the
[R]priest, Is. 56:11 • Jer. 5:31; 23:11
Everyone deals falsely.
14 They have also [R]healed the hurt of My
people slightly, Jer. 8:11–15
[R]Saying, 'Peace, peace!' Jer. 4:10; 23:17
When *there is* no peace.
15 Were they [R]ashamed when they had
committed abomination?
No! They were not at all ashamed;
Nor did they know how to blush.
Therefore they shall fall among those
who fall; Jer. 3:3; 8:12
At the time I punish them,
They shall be cast down," says the LORD.

16 Thus says the LORD:

"Stand in the ways and see,
And ask for the [R]old paths, where the
good way *is*, Jer. 18:15
And walk in it;
Then you will find rest for your souls.
But they said, 'We will not walk *in it.*'
17 Also, I set watchmen over you, *saying*,
'Listen to the sound of the trumpet!'
But they said, 'We will not listen.'
18 Therefore hear, you nations,
And know, O congregation, what *is*
among them.
19 [R]Hear, O earth! Is. 1:2
Behold, I will certainly bring [R]calamity
on this people— Jer. 19:3, 15
[R]The fruit of their thoughts, Prov. 1:31
Because they have not heeded My words
Nor My law, but rejected it.
20 [R]For what purpose to Me Mic. 6:6, 7
Comes frankincense from Sheba,
And sweet cane from a far country?
Your burnt offerings *are* not acceptable,
Nor your sacrifices sweet to Me."

21 Therefore thus says the LORD:

"Behold, I will lay stumbling blocks
before this people,
And the fathers and the sons together
shall fall on them.
The neighbor and his friend shall perish."

22 Thus says the LORD:

"Behold, a people comes from the [R]north
country, Jer. 1:15; 10:22; 50:41–43
And a great nation will be raised from
the farthest parts of the earth.
23 They will lay hold on bow and spear;
They *are* cruel and have no mercy;
Their voice [R]roars like the sea; Is. 5:30
And they ride on horses,
As men of war set in array against you,
O daughter of Zion."

24 We have heard the report of it;
Our hands grow feeble.
Anguish has taken hold of us,
Pain as of a woman in [T]labor. *childbirth*
25 Do not go out into the field,
Nor walk by the way.
Because of the sword of the enemy,
Fear *is* on every side.
26 O daughter of my people,
[R]Dress in sackcloth Jer. 4:8
[R]And roll about in ashes! Mic. 1:10
[R]Make mourning *as for* an only son, most
bitter lamentation; [Zech. 12:10]
For the plunderer will suddenly come
upon us.

27 "I have set you *as* an assayer *and* [R]a
fortress among My people, Jer. 1:18
That you may know and test their way.
28 [R]They *are* all stubborn rebels, [R]walking as
slanderers. Jer. 5:23 • Jer. 9:4
They are [R]bronze and iron, Ezek. 22:18
They *are* all corrupters;
29 The bellows blow fiercely,
The lead is consumed by the fire;
The smelter refines in vain,
For the wicked are not drawn off.
30 *People* will call them rejected silver,
Because the LORD has rejected them."

CHAPTER 7

Judah's Sin of External Religion

THE word that came to Jeremiah from the
LORD, saying,
2 [R]"Stand in the gate of the LORD's house,
and proclaim there this word, and say, 'Hear
the word of the LORD, all *you of* Judah who
enter in at these gates to worship the
LORD!' " Jer. 17:19; 26:2
3 Thus says the LORD of hosts, the God of
Israel: "Amend your ways and your doings,
and I will cause you to dwell in this place.
4 "Do not trust in these lying words, saying,
'The temple of the LORD, the temple of the
LORD, the temple of the LORD *are* these.'
5 "For if you thoroughly amend your ways
and your doings, if you thoroughly execute
judgment between a man and his neighbor,
6 "*if* you do not oppress the stranger, the

fatherless, and the widow, and do not shed in-
nocent blood in this place, [R]or walk after
other gods to your hurt, Deut. 6:14, 15
7 [R]"then I will cause you to dwell in this
place, in [R]the land that I gave to your fathers
forever and ever. Deut. 4:40 • Jer. 3:18
8 "Behold, you trust in [R]lying words that
cannot profit. Jer. 5:31; 14:13, 14
9 [R]"Will you steal, murder, commit adul-
tery, swear falsely, burn incense to Baal, and
[R]walk after other gods whom you do not
know, 1 Kin. 18:21 • Ex. 20:3
10 [R]"and *then* come and stand before Me in
this house [R]which is called by My name, and
say, 'We are delivered to do all these abomina-
tions'? Ezek. 23:39 • Jer. 7:11, 14; 32:34
11 "Has [R]this house, which is called by My
name, become a [R]den of thieves in your eyes?
Behold, I, even I, have seen *it*," says the
LORD. Is. 56:7 • Matt. 21:13
12 "But go now to [R]My place which *was* in
Shiloh, where I set My name at the first, and
see what I did to it because of the wickedness
of My people Israel. Josh. 18:1
13 "And now, because you have done all
these works," says the LORD, "and I spoke to
you, [R]rising up early and speaking, but you
did not hear, and I [R]called you, but you did not
answer, 2 Chr. 36:15 • Prov. 1:24
14 "therefore I will do to the house which is
called by My name, in which you trust, and to
this place which I gave to you and your fa-
thers, as I have done to Shiloh.
15 "And I will cast you out of My sight, [R]as I
have cast out all your brethren—[R]the whole
posterity of Ephraim. 2 Kin. 17:23 • Ps. 78:67
16 "Therefore [R]do not pray for this people,
nor lift up a cry or prayer for them, nor
make intercession to Me; [R]for I will not hear
you. Ex. 32:10; Jer. 11:14 • Jer. 15:1
17 "Do you not see what they do in the cities
of Judah and in the streets of Jerusalem?
18 "The children gather wood, the fathers
kindle the fire, and the women knead dough,
to make cakes for the queen of heaven; and
they pour out drink offerings to other gods,
that they may provoke Me to anger.
19 "Do they provoke Me to anger?" says the
LORD. "*Do they* not *provoke* themselves, to the
shame of their own faces?"
20 Therefore thus says the Lord GOD: "Be-
hold, My anger and My fury will be poured
out on this place—on man and on beast,
on the trees of the field and on the fruit of
the ground. And it will burn and not be
quenched."
21 Thus says the LORD of hosts, the God of
Israel: [R]"Add your burnt offerings to your sac-
rifices and eat meat. Jer. 6:20
22 [R]"For I did not speak to your fathers, or
command them in the day that I brought them
out of the land of Egypt, concerning burnt of-
ferings or sacrifices. [Hos. 6:6]
23 "But this is what I commanded them, say-
ing, [R]'Obey My voice, and I will be your God,
and you shall be My people. And walk in all
the ways that I have commanded you, that it
may be well with you.' Deut. 6:3
24 [R]"Yet they did not obey or incline their
ear, but [R]followed the counsels *and* the dic-
tates of their evil hearts, and went backward
and not forward. Ps. 81:11 • Deut. 29:19
25 "Since the day that your fathers came
out of the land of Egypt until this day, I have
even [R]sent to you all My servants the
prophets, daily rising up early and sending
them. 2 Chr. 36:15
26 [R]"Yet they did not obey Me or incline their
ear, but [R]stiffened their neck. They did worse
than their fathers. Jer. 11:8 • Neh. 9:17
27 "Therefore [R]you shall speak all these
words to them, but they will not obey you. You
shall also call to them, but they will not an-
swer you. Ezek. 2:7
28 "So you shall say to them, 'This *is* a na-
tion that does not obey the voice of the LORD
their God [R]nor receive correction. [R]Truth has
perished and has been cut off from their
mouth. Jer. 5:3 • Jer. 9:3
29 'Cut off your hair and cast *it* away, and
take up a lamentation on the desolate heights;
for the LORD has rejected and forsaken the
generation of His wrath.'
30 "For the children of Judah have done evil
in My sight," says the LORD. [R]"They have set
their abominations in the house which is
called by My name, to pollute it. Dan. 9:27
31 "And they have built the high places of
Tophet, which *is* in the Valley of the Son of
Hinnom, to burn their sons and their daugh-
ters in the fire, which I did not command, nor
did it come into My heart.
32 "Therefore behold, [R]the days are coming,"
says the LORD, "when it will no more be called
Tophet, or the Valley of the Son of Hinnom, but
the Valley of Slaughter; [R]for they will bury in
Tophet until there is no room. Jer. 19:6 • 2 Kin. 23:10
33 "The [R]corpses of this people will be food
for the birds of the heaven and for the beasts
of the earth. And no one will frighten *them*
away. Jer. 9:22; 19:11
34 "Then I will cause to [R]cease from the
cities of Judah and from the streets of Jerusa-
lem the voice of mirth and the voice of glad-
ness, the voice of the bridegroom and the
voice of the bride. For [R]the land shall be deso-
late. Is. 24:7, 8 • Lev. 26:33

CHAPTER 8

"AT that time," says the LORD, "they shall
bring out the bones of the kings of Ju-
dah, and the bones of its princes, and the
bones of the priests, and the bones of the
prophets, and the bones of the inhabitants of
Jerusalem, out of their graves.

2 "They shall spread them before the sun
and the moon and all the host of heaven,
which they have loved and which they have
served and after which they have walked,
which they have sought and [R]which they have
worshiped. They shall not be gathered [R]nor
buried; they shall be like refuse on the face of
the earth. 2 Kin. 23:5 • Jer. 22:19
3 "Then [R]death shall be chosen rather than
life by all the [T]residue of those who remain of
this evil family, who remain in all the places
where I have driven them," says the LORD of
hosts. Rev. 9:6 • *remnant*

Judah's Judgment Imminent

4 "Moreover you shall say to them, 'Thus
says the LORD:

"Will they fall and not rise?
Will one turn away and not return?
5 Why has this people slidden back,
Jerusalem, in a perpetual backsliding?
[R]They hold fast to deceit, Jer. 9:6
[R]They refuse to return. Jer. 5:3
6 [R]I listened and heard, Ps. 14:2
But they do not speak aright.
[R]No man repented of his wickedness,
Saying, 'What have I done?' Mic. 7:2
Everyone turned to his own course,
As the horse rushes into the battle.

7 "Even [R]the stork in the heavens
Knows her appointed times;
And the turtledove, the swift, and the
swallow Song 2:12
Observe the time of their coming.
But [R]My people do not know the
judgment of the LORD. Jer. 5:4; 9:3

8 "How can you say, 'We *are* wise,
[R]And the law of the LORD *is* with us'?
Look, the false pen of the scribe
certainly works falsehood. Rom. 2:17
9 [R]The wise men are ashamed, Jer. 6:15
They are dismayed and taken.
Behold, they have rejected the word of
the LORD;
So what wisdom do they have?
10 Therefore [R]I will give their wives to
others, Deut. 28:30
And their fields to those who will inherit
them;
Because from the least even to the
greatest
Everyone is given to [R]covetousness;
From the prophet even to the priest
Everyone deals falsely. Is. 56:11; 57:17
11 For they have healed the hurt of the
daughter of My people slightly,
Saying, [R]'Peace, peace!' Ezek. 13:10
When *there is* no peace.
12 Were they [R]ashamed when they had
committed abomination? Jer. 3:3
No! They were not at all ashamed,
Nor did they know how to blush.
Therefore they shall fall among those
who fall;
In the time of their punishment
They shall be cast down," says the LORD.

13 "I will surely [T]consume them," says the
LORD. Or *take them away*
"No grapes *shall be* on the vine,
Nor figs on the [R]fig tree, Matt. 21:19
And the leaf shall fade;
And *the things* I have given them shall
pass away from them." ' "

14 "Why do we sit still?
[R]Assemble yourselves, Jer. 4:5
And let us enter the fortified cities,
And let us be silent there.
For the LORD our God has put us to
silence
And given us [R]water[T] of gall to drink,
Because we have sinned against the
LORD. Jer. 9:15 • Bitter or poisonous water

15 "*We* [R]looked for peace, but no good *came;*
And for a time of health, and there was
trouble! Jer. 14:19
16 The snorting of His horses was heard
from [R]Dan. Jer. 4:15
The whole land trembled at the sound of
the neighing of His [R]strong ones;
For they have come and devoured the
land and all that is in it, Jer. 47:3
The city and those who dwell in it."

17 "For behold, I will send serpents among
you,
Vipers which cannot be charmed,
And they shall bite you," says the LORD.

Jeremiah's Lament for Judah

18 I would comfort myself in sorrow;
My heart *is* faint in me.
19 Listen! The voice,
The cry of the daughter of my people
From [R]a far country: Is. 39:3
"*Is* not the LORD in Zion?
Is not her King in her?"

"Why have they provoked Me to anger
With their carved images—
With foreign idols?"

20 "The harvest is past,
The summer is ended,
And we are not saved!"

21 [R]For the hurt of the daughter of my
people I am hurt. Jer. 9:1
I am [R]mourning; Joel 2:6
Astonishment has taken hold of me.
22 *Is there* no [R]balm in Gilead, Jer. 46:11

Is there no physician there?
Why then is there no recovery
For the health of the daughter of my people?

CHAPTER 9

OH, [R]that my head were waters, Is. 22:4
And my eyes a fountain of tears,
That I might weep day and night
For the slain of the daughter of my people!
2 Oh, that I had in the wilderness
A lodging place for travelers;
That I might leave my people,
And go from them!
For [R]they *are* all adulterers, Jer. 5:7, 8
An assembly of treacherous men.

3 "And *like* their bow [R]they have bent their tongues *for* lies. Ps. 64:3
They are not valiant for the truth on the earth.
For they proceed from [R]evil to evil,
And they [R]do not know Me," says the LORD. Jer. 4:22; 13:23 • 1 Sam. 2:12
4 "Everyone[R] take heed to his [T]neighbor,
And do not trust any brother;
For every brother will utterly supplant,
And every neighbor will [R]walk with slanderers. Mic. 7:5, 6 • *friend* • Jer. 6:28
5 Everyone will [R]deceive his neighbor,
And will not speak the truth; Is. 59:4
They have taught their tongue to speak lies;
They weary themselves to commit iniquity.
6 Your dwelling place *is* in the midst of deceit;
Through deceit they refuse to know Me," says the LORD.

Judah's Judgment Is Described

7 Therefore thus says the LORD of hosts:

"Behold, [R]I will refine them and [T]try them; Is. 1:25 • *test*
[R]For how shall I deal with the daughter of My people? Hos. 11:8
8 Their tongue *is* an arrow shot out;
It speaks [R]deceit; Ps. 12:2
One speaks [R]peaceably to his neighbor with his mouth, Ps. 55:21
But in his heart he lies in wait.
9 [R]Shall I not punish them for these *things?*" says the LORD. Jer. 5:9, 29
"Shall I not avenge Myself on such a nation as this?"

10 I will take up a weeping and wailing for the mountains,
And [R]for the dwelling places of the wilderness a lamentation, Hos. 4:3
Because they are burned up,
So that no one can pass through;
Nor can *men* hear the voice of the cattle.
[R]Both the birds of the heavens and the beasts have fled; Jer. 4:25
They are gone.

11 "I will make Jerusalem [R]a heap of ruins,
[R]a den of jackals. Is. 25:2 • Is. 13:22
I will make the cities of Judah desolate, without an inhabitant."

12 [R]Who *is* the wise man who may under-
stand this? And *who is he* to whom the mouth
of the LORD has spoken, that he may declare
it? Why does the land perish *and* burn up
like a wilderness, so that no one can pass
through? Hos. 14:9
13 And the LORD said, "Because they have
forsaken My law which I set before them, and
have [R]not obeyed My voice, nor walked ac-
cording to it, Jer. 3:25; 7:24
14 "but they have walked according to the
dictates of their own hearts and after the
Baals, which their fathers taught them,"
15 therefore thus says the LORD of hosts, the
God of Israel: "Behold, I will [R]feed them, this
people, [R]with wormwood, and give them wa-
ter of gall to drink. Ps. 80:5 • Lam. 3:15
16 "I will scatter them also among the Gen-
tiles, whom neither they nor their fathers have
known. And I will send a sword after them
until I have consumed them."

17 Thus says the LORD of hosts:

"Consider and call for [R]the mourning women, 2 Chr. 35:25
That they may come;
And send for skillful wailing women,
That they may come.
18 Let them make haste
And take up a wailing for us,
That our eyes may run with tears,
And our eyelids gush with water.
19 For a voice of wailing is heard from Zion:
'How we are plundered!
We are greatly ashamed,
Because we have forsaken the land,
Because we have been cast out of [R]our dwellings.' " Lev. 18:28

20 Yet hear the word of the LORD, O women,
And let your ear receive the word of His mouth;
Teach your daughters wailing,
And everyone her neighbor a lamentation.
21 For death has come through our windows,
Has entered our palaces,
To kill off [R]the children—[T]*no longer to be* outside! Jer. 6:11; 18:21 • Lit. *from outside*

And the young men—[T]*no longer* on the
streets! Lit. *from the square*

22 Speak, "Thus says the LORD:

'Even the carcasses of men shall fall [R]as
refuse on the open field, Jer. 8:1, 2
Like cuttings after the harvester,
And no one shall gather *them*.'"

23 Thus says the LORD:

[R]"Let not the wise *man* glory in his
wisdom, [Eccl. 9:11]
Let not the mighty *man* glory in his
[R]might, Ps. 33:16–18
Nor let the rich *man* glory in his riches;
24 But [R]let him who glories glory in this,
That he understands and knows Me,
That I *am* the LORD, exercising 1 Cor. 1:31
lovingkindness, [T]judgment, and
righteousness in the earth. *justice*
For in these I delight," says the LORD.

25 "Behold, the days are coming," says the
LORD, "that I will punish all *who are* circum-
cised with the uncircumcised—
26 "Egypt, Judah, Edom, the people of
Ammon, Moab, and all *who are* in the [R]far-
thest corners, who dwell in the wilderness.
For all *these* nations *are* uncircumcised, and
all the house of Israel *are* [R]uncircumcised in
the heart." Jer. 25:23 • [Rom. 2:28]

CHAPTER 10

Judah's Futile Idolatry

HEAR the word which the LORD speaks to
you, O house of Israel.
2 Thus says the LORD:

[R]"Do not learn the way of the Gentiles;
Do not be dismayed at the signs of
heaven, [Lev. 18:3; 20:23]
For the Gentiles are dismayed at them.
3 For the customs of the peoples *are*
[T]futile; Lit. *vanity*
For [R]*one* cuts a tree from the forest,
The work of the hands of the workman,
with the ax. Is. 40:19; 45:20
4 They decorate it with silver and gold;
They [R]fasten it with nails and hammers
So that it will not topple. Is. 41:7
5 They *are* upright, like a palm tree,
And [R]they cannot speak; Ps. 115:5
They must be [R]carried, Ps. 115:7
Because they cannot go *by themselves*.
Do not be afraid of them,
For [R]they cannot do evil, Is. 41:23, 24
Nor can they do any good."

6 Inasmuch as *there is* none [R]like You,
O LORD Ex. 15:11
(You *are* great, and Your name *is* great in
might),
7 [R]Who would not fear You, O King of the
nations? Rev. 15:4
For this is Your rightful due.
For [R]among all the wise *men* of the
nations, Ps. 89:6
And in all their kingdoms,
There is none like You.
8 But they are altogether [R]dull-hearted
and foolish; Hab. 2:18
A wooden idol *is* a worthless doctrine.
9 Silver is beaten into plates;
It is brought from Tarshish,
And [R]gold from Uphaz, Dan. 10:5
The work of the craftsman
And of the hands of the metalsmith;
Blue and purple *are* their clothing;
They *are* all the work of skillful *men*.
10 But the LORD *is* the true God;
He *is* [R]the living God and the
[R]everlasting King. 1 Tim. 6:17 • Ps. 10:16
At His wrath the earth will tremble,
And the nations will not be able to
endure His indignation.

11 Thus you shall say to them: [R]"The gods
that have not made the heavens and the earth
[R]shall perish from the earth and from under
these heavens." Ps. 96:5 • Zeph. 2:11

12 He [R]has made the earth by His power,
He has [R]established the world by His
wisdom, Jer. 51:15 • Ps. 93:1
And [R]has stretched out the heavens at
His discretion. Job 9:8
13 [R]When He utters His voice, Job 38:34
There is a [T]multitude of waters in the
heavens: Or *noise*
"And He causes the vapors to ascend
from the ends of the earth.
He makes lightning for the rain,
He brings the wind out of His treasuries."*

14 [R]Everyone is [R]dull-hearted, without
knowledge; Jer. 51:17 • Prov. 30:2
[R]Every metalsmith is put to shame by an
image; Is. 42:17; 44:11
For his molded image *is* falsehood,
And *there is* no breath in them.
15 They *are* futile, a work of errors;
In the time of their punishment they
shall perish.
16 [R]The Portion of Jacob *is* not like them,
For He *is* the Maker of all *things*,
And [R]Israel *is* the tribe of His
inheritance; Lam. 3:24 • Deut. 32:9
[R]The LORD of hosts *is* His name. Is. 47:4

17 [R]Gather up your wares from the land,
O inhabitant of the fortress! Jer. 6:1

10:13 Ps. 135:7

18 For thus says the LORD:

"Behold, I will [R]throw out at this time
The inhabitants of the land, 1 Sam. 25:29
And will distress them,
[R]That they may find *it so*." Ezek. 6:10

Jeremiah's Prayer for Correction

19[R] Woe is me for my hurt! Jer. 8:21
My wound is severe.
But I say, [R]"Truly this *is* an infirmity,
And [R]I must bear it." Ps. 77:10 • Mic. 7:9
20[R] My tent is plundered, Jer. 4:20
And all my cords are broken;
My children have gone from me,
And they *are* [R]no more. Jer. 31:15
There is no one to pitch my tent
anymore,
Or set up my curtains.

21 For the shepherds have become
dull-hearted,
And have not sought the LORD;
Therefore they shall not prosper,
And all their flocks shall be scattered.
22 Behold, the noise of the report has
come,
And a great commotion out of the [R]north
country, Jer. 5:15
To make the cities of Judah desolate, a
[R]den of jackals. Jer. 9:11

23 O LORD, I know the [R]way of man *is* not in
himself; Prov. 16:1; 20:24
It is not in man who walks to direct his
own steps.
24 O LORD, [R]correct me, but with justice;
Not in Your anger, lest You bring me to
nothing. Jer. 30:11
25[R] Pour out Your fury on the Gentiles, [R]who
do not know You, Ps. 79:6, 7 • Job 18:21
And on the families who do not call on
Your name;
For they have eaten up Jacob,
Devoured him and consumed him,
And made his dwelling place desolate.

CHAPTER 11

Judah's Curse Because of the Broken Covenant

THE word that came to Jeremiah from the
LORD, saying,
2 "Hear the words of this covenant, and
speak to the men of Judah and to the inhabi-
tants of Jerusalem;
3 "and say to them, 'Thus says the LORD
God of Israel: "Cursed *is* the man who does
not obey the words of this covenant
4 "which I commanded your fathers in the
day I brought them out of the land of Egypt,
[R]from the iron furnace, saying, [R]'Obey My
voice, and do according to all that I command
you; so shall you be My people, and I will be
your God,' Deut. 4:20 • Lev. 26:3
5 "that I may establish the [R]oath which I
have sworn to your fathers, to give them 'a
land flowing with milk and honey,'* as *it is*
this day." ' " And I answered and said, [T]"So be
it, LORD." Ps. 105:9 • Heb. *Amen*
6 Then the LORD said to me, "Proclaim all
these words in the cities of Judah and in the
streets of Jerusalem, saying: 'Hear the words
of this covenant [R]and do them. [Rom. 2:13]
7 'For I earnestly exhorted your fathers in
the day I brought them up out of the land of
Egypt, until this day, [R]rising early and exhort-
ing, saying, "Obey My voice." Jer. 35:15
8 [R]'Yet they did not obey or incline their
ear, but [R]everyone followed the dictates of his
evil heart; therefore I will bring upon them all
the words of this covenant, which I com-
manded *them* to do, but *which* they have not
done.' " Jer. 7:26 • Jer. 13:10
9 And the LORD said to me, "A conspiracy
has been found among the men of Judah and
among the inhabitants of Jerusalem.
10 "They have turned back to the iniquities
of their forefathers who refused to hear My
words, and they have gone after other gods to
serve them; the house of Israel and the house
of Judah have broken My covenant which I
made with their fathers."
11 Therefore thus says the LORD: "Behold, I
will surely bring calamity on them which they
will not be able to escape; and though they
cry out to Me, I will not listen to them.
12 "Then the cities of Judah and the inhabi-
tants of Jerusalem will go and [R]cry out to the
gods to whom they offer incense, but they will
not save them at all in the time of their trou-
ble. Deut. 32:37
13 "For *according to* the number of your cit-
ies were your gods, O Judah; and *according to*
the number of the streets of Jerusalem you
have set up altars to *that* shameful thing, al-
tars to burn incense to Baal.
14 "So [R]do not pray for this people, or lift up
a cry or prayer for them; for I will not hear
them in the time that they cry out to Me be-
cause of their trouble. Ex. 32:10

15 "What[R] has My beloved to do in My
house, Ps. 50:16
Having [R]done lewd deeds with many?
And [R]the holy flesh has passed from
you. Ezek. 16:25 • [Titus 1:15]
When you do evil, then you rejoice.
16 The LORD called your name,
[R]Green Olive Tree, Lovely *and* of Good
Fruit. Ps. 52:8
With the noise of a great tumult
He has kindled fire on it,
And its branches are broken.

11:5 Ex. 3:8

17 “For the LORD of hosts, [R]who planted you,
has pronounced doom against you for the evil
of the house of Israel and of the house of Ju-
dah, which they have done against themselves
to provoke Me to anger in offering incense to
Baal.” Is. 5:2

Anathoth's Conspiracy Against Jeremiah

18 Now the LORD gave me knowledge *of it*,
and I know *it;* for You showed me their doings.
19 But I *was* like a docile lamb brought to the
slaughter; and I did not know that they had de-
vised schemes against me, *saying*, “Let us de-
stroy the tree with its fruit, [R]and let us cut him
off from [R]the land of the living, that his name
may be remembered no more.” Ps. 83:4 • Ps. 27:13

20 But, O LORD of hosts,
You who judge righteously,
Testing the mind and the heart,
Let me see Your vengeance on them,
For to You I have revealed my cause.

21 “Therefore thus says the LORD concerning
the men of Anathoth who seek your life, say-
ing, [R]‘Do not prophesy in the name of the
LORD, lest you die by our hand’— Mic. 2:6
22 “therefore thus says the LORD of hosts:
‘Behold, I will punish them. The young men
shall die by the sword, their sons and their
daughters shall [R]die by famine; Jer. 9:21
23 ‘and there shall be no remnant of them,
for I will bring catastrophe on the men of
Anathoth, *even* [R]the year of their punish-
ment.’ ” Jer. 23:12

CHAPTER 12

Jeremiah's Complaint to God

RIGHTEOUS [R]*are* You, O LORD, when I
plead with You; Ps. 51:4
Yet let me talk with You about *Your*
judgments.
[R]Why does the way of the wicked
prosper? Mal. 3:15
Why are those happy who deal so
treacherously?
2 You have planted them, yes, they have
taken root;
They grow, yes, they bear fruit.
[R]You *are* near in their mouth Matt. 15:8
But far from their mind.

3 But You, O LORD, [R]know me; Ps. 17:3
You have seen me,
And You have [R]tested my heart toward
You. Jer. 11:20
Pull them out like sheep for the slaughter,
And prepare them for [R]the day of
slaughter. James 5:5
4 How long will [R]the land mourn,
And the herbs of every field wither?
[R]The beasts and birds are consumed,
[R]For the wickedness of those who dwell
there, Hos. 4:3 • Jer. 9:10 • Ps. 107:34
Because they said, “He will not see our
final end.”

God's Reply to Jeremiah

5 “If you have run with the footmen, and
they have wearied you,
Then how can you contend with horses?
And *if* in the land of peace,
In which you trusted, *they wearied you*,
Then how will you do in [R]the floodplain*
of the Jordan? Josh. 3:15
6 For even [R]your brothers, the house of
your father, Jer. 9:4, 5
Even they have dealt treacherously with
you;
Yes, they have called [T]a multitude after
you. Or *abundantly*
[R]Do not believe them, Prov. 26:25
Even though they speak [T]smooth words
to you. Lit. *good*

7 “I have forsaken My house, I have left My
heritage;
I have given the dearly beloved of My
soul into the hand of her enemies.
8 My heritage is to Me like a lion in the
forest;
It cries out against Me;
Therefore I have [R]hated it. Hos. 9:15
9 My [T]heritage *is* to Me *like* a speckled
vulture; *inheritance*
The vultures all around *are* against her.
Come, assemble all the beasts of the field,
[R]Bring them to devour! Lev. 26:22

10 “Many [R]rulers* have destroyed [R]My
vineyard, Jer. 6:3; 23:1 • Is. 5:1–7
They have [R]trodden My portion
underfoot; Is. 63:18
They have made My pleasant portion a
desolate wilderness.
11 They have made it [R]desolate; Jer. 10:22
Desolate, it mourns to Me;
The whole land is made desolate,
Because no one takes *it* to heart.
12 The plunderers have come
On all the desolate heights in the
wilderness,
For the sword of the LORD shall devour
From *one* end of the land to the *other*
end of the land;
No flesh shall have peace.
13 [R]They have sown wheat but reaped
thorns; Hag. 1:6
They have [T]put themselves to pain *but*
do not profit. Or *strained*
But be ashamed of your harvest
Because of the fierce anger of the LORD.”

12:5 Or *thicket* **12:10** Lit. *shepherds* or *pastors*

14 Thus says the LORD: "Against all My evil neighbors who [R]touch the inheritance which I have caused My people Israel to inherit—behold, I will [R]pluck them out of their land and pluck out the house of Judah from among them. Zech. 2:8 • Deut. 30:3

15 [R]"Then it shall be, after I have plucked them out, that I will return and have compassion on them [R]and bring them back, everyone to his heritage and everyone to his land. Ezek. 28:25 • Amos 9:14

16 "And it shall be, if they will learn carefully the ways of My people, to swear by My name, 'As the LORD lives,' as they taught My people to swear by Baal, then they shall be established in the midst of My people.

17 "But if they do not [R]obey, I will utterly pluck up and destroy that nation," says the LORD. Is. 60:12

CHAPTER 13

Sign of the Ruined Sash

THUS the LORD said to me: "Go and get yourself a linen sash, and put it around your waist, but do not put it in water."

2 So I got a sash according to the word of the LORD, and put *it* around my waist.

3 And the word of the LORD came to me the second time, saying,

4 "Take the [T]sash that you acquired, which *is* [T]around your waist, and arise, go to the Euphrates,* and hide it there in a hole in the rock." *waistband* • Lit. *upon your loins*

5 So I went and hid it by the Euphrates, as the LORD commanded me.

6 Now it came to pass after many days that the LORD said to me, "Arise, go to the Euphrates, and take from there the sash which I commanded you to hide there."

7 Then I went to the Euphrates and dug, and I took the sash from the place where I had hidden it; and there was the sash, ruined. It was profitable for nothing.

8 Then the word of the LORD came to me, saying,

9 "Thus says the LORD: 'In this manner [R]I will ruin the pride of Judah and the great [R]pride of Jerusalem. Lev. 26:19 • Zeph. 3:11

10 'This evil people, who refuse to hear My words, who follow the dictates of their hearts, and walk after other gods to serve them and worship them, shall be just like this sash which is profitable for nothing.

11 'For as the sash clings to the waist of a man, so I have caused the whole house of Israel and the whole house of Judah to cling to Me,' says the LORD, 'that they may become My people, for renown, for praise, and for glory; but they would not hear.'

Sign of the Wine Bottles

12 "Therefore you shall speak to them this word: 'Thus says the LORD God of Israel: "Every bottle shall be filled with wine." ' And they will say to you, 'Do we not certainly know that every bottle will be filled with wine?'

13 "Then you shall say to them, 'Thus says the LORD: "Behold, I will fill all the inhabitants of this land—even the kings who sit on David's throne, the priests, the prophets, and all the inhabitants of Jerusalem—[R]with drunkenness! Is. 51:17; 63:6

14 "And [R]I will dash them [T]one against another, even the fathers and the sons together," says the LORD. "I will not pity nor spare nor have mercy, but will destroy them." ' " Jer. 19:9–11 • Lit. *a man against his brother*

15 Hear and give ear:
Do not be proud,
For the LORD has spoken.
16 Give glory to the LORD your God
Before He causes [R]darkness, Amos 8:9
And before your feet stumble
On the dark mountains,
And while you are looking for light,
He turns it into [R]the shadow of death
And makes *it* dense darkness. Ps. 44:19
17 But if you will not hear it,
My soul will [R]weep in secret for *your*
pride; Jer. 9:1; 14:17
My eyes will weep bitterly
And run down with tears,
Because the LORD's flock has been taken
captive.

18 Say to [R]the king and to the queen
mother, Jer. 22:26
"Humble yourselves;
Sit down,
For your rule shall collapse, the crown of
your glory."
19 The cities of the South shall be shut up,
And no one shall open *them;*
Judah shall be carried away captive, all
of it;
It shall be wholly carried away captive.

20 Lift up your eyes and see
Those who come from the [R]north.
Where *is* the flock *that* was given to you,
Your beautiful sheep? Jer. 10:22; 46:20
21 What will you say when He punishes you?
For you have taught them
To be chieftains, to be head over you.
Will not [R]pangs seize you, Jer. 6:24
Like a woman in [T]labor? *childbirth*
22 And if you say in your heart,
[R]"Why have these things come upon me?"
For the greatness of your iniquity
[R]Your skirts have been uncovered,
Your heels made bare. Jer. 16:10 • Is. 47:2

13:4 Heb. *Perath*

23 Can the Ethiopian change his skin or the
leopard its spots?
Then may you also do good who are
accustomed to do evil.

24 "Therefore I will [R]scatter them [R]like
stubble Jer. 9:16 • Hos. 13:3
That passes away by the wind of the
wilderness.
25 [R]This is your lot, Job 20:29
The portion of your measures from Me,"
says the LORD,
"Because you have forgotten Me
And trusted in [R]falsehood. Jer. 10:14
26 Therefore [R]I will uncover your skirts
over your face, Lam. 1:8
That your shame may appear.
27 I have seen your adulteries
And your *lustful* [R]neighings, Jer. 5:7, 8
The lewdness of your harlotry,
Your abominations [R]on the hills in the
fields. Is. 65:7; Ezek. 6:13
Woe to you, O Jerusalem!
Will you still not be made clean?"

CHAPTER 14

Judah's Drought Is Described

THE word of the LORD that came to Jeremiah concerning the droughts.

2 "Judah mourns,
And [R]her gates languish; Is. 3:26
They [R]mourn for the land, Jer. 8:21
And the cry of Jerusalem has gone up.
3 Their nobles have sent their lads for
water;
They went to the cisterns *and* found no
water.
They returned with their vessels empty;
They were ashamed and confounded
[R]And covered their heads. 2 Sam. 15:30
4 Because the ground is parched,
For there was [R]no rain in the land,
The plowmen were ashamed;
They covered their heads. Jer. 3:3
5 Yes, the deer also gave birth in the field,
But left because there was no grass.
6 And [R]the wild donkeys stood in the
desolate heights; Jer. 2:24
They sniffed at the wind like jackals;
Their eyes failed because *there was* no
grass."

Jeremiah's First Intercession

7 O LORD, though our iniquities testify
against us,
Do it [R]for Your name's sake; Ps. 25:11
For our backslidings are many,
We have sinned against You.
8 [R]O the Hope of Israel, his Savior in time
of trouble, Jer. 17:13
Why should You be like a stranger in the
land,
And like a traveler *who* turns aside to
tarry for a night?
9 Why should You be like a man
astonished,
Like a mighty one [R]*who* cannot save?
Yet You, O LORD, [R]*are* in our midst,
And we are called by Your name;
Do not leave us! Is. 59:1 • Ex. 29:45

10 Thus says the LORD to this people:

[R]"Thus they have loved to wander;
They have not restrained their feet.
Therefore the LORD does not accept
them; Jer. 2:23–25
[R]He will remember their iniquity now,
And punish their sins." Hos. 8:13

11 Then the LORD said to me, [R]"Do not pray
for this people, for *their* good. Ex. 32:10
12 [R]"When they fast, I will not hear their cry;
and when they offer burnt offering and grain
offering, I will not accept them. But I will consume them by the sword, by the famine, and
by the pestilence." Ezek. 8:18

Jeremiah's Second Intercession

13 Then I said, "Ah, Lord GOD! Behold, the
prophets say to them, 'You shall not see the
sword, nor shall you have famine, but I will
give you assured peace in this place.' "
14 And the LORD said to me, [R]"The prophets
prophesy lies in My name. [R]I have not sent
them, commanded them, nor spoken to them;
they prophesy to you a false vision, divination, a worthless thing, and the deceit of their
heart. Jer. 27:10 • Jer. 29:8, 9
15 "Therefore thus says the LORD concerning
the prophets who prophesy in My name,
whom I did not send, [R]and who say, 'Sword
and famine shall not be in this land'—'By
sword and famine those prophets shall be
consumed! Ezek. 14:10
16 'And the people to whom they prophesy
shall be cast out in the streets of Jerusalem
because of the famine and the sword; they
will have no one to bury them—them nor their
wives, their sons nor their daughters—for I
will pour their wickedness on them.'
17 "Therefore you shall say this word to
them:

[R]'Let my eyes flow with tears night and
day, Jer. 9:1; 13:17
And let them not cease;
[R]For the virgin daughter of my people
Has been broken with a mighty stroke,
with a very severe blow. Jer. 8:21
18 If I go out to [R]the field, Ezek. 7:15
Then behold, those slain with the sword!
And if I enter the city,

Then behold, those sick from famine!
Yes, both prophet and priest go about in
a land they do not know.' "

Jeremiah's Third Intercession

19[R] Have You utterly rejected Judah?
Has Your soul loathed Zion? Lam. 5:22
Why have You stricken us so that [R]*there*
is no healing for us? Jer. 15:18
[R]We looked for peace, but *there was* no
good; Jer. 8:15
And for the time of healing, and there
was trouble.
20 We acknowledge, O LORD, our
wickedness
And the iniquity of our fathers,
For we have sinned against You.
21 Do not abhor *us*, for Your name's sake;
Do not disgrace the throne of Your glory.
[R]Remember, do not break Your covenant
with us. Ps. 106:45
22 Are there any among the idols of the
nations that can cause rain?
Or can the heavens give showers?
Are You not He, O LORD our God?
Therefore we will wait for You,
Since You have made all these.

CHAPTER 15

THEN the LORD said to me, [R]"*Even* if [R]Mo-
ses and Samuel stood before Me, My mind
would not *be* favorable toward this people.
Cast *them* out of My sight, and let them go
forth. Ezek. 14:14 • Ex. 32:11–14
2 "And it shall be, if they say to you, 'Where
should we go?' then you shall tell them, 'Thus
says the LORD:

[R]"Such as *are* for death, to death;
And such as *are* for the sword, to the
sword; Zech. 11:9
And such as *are* for the famine, to the
famine;
And such as *are* for the [R]captivity, to the
captivity." ' Jer. 9:16; 16:13

3 "And I will [R]appoint over them four forms
of destruction," says the LORD: "the sword to
slay, the dogs to drag, [R]the birds of the heav-
ens and the beasts of the earth to devour and
destroy. Ezek. 14:21 • Jer. 7:33
4 "I will hand them over to trouble, to all
kingdoms of the earth, because of Manasseh
the son of Hezekiah, king of Judah, for what
he did in Jerusalem.

5"For who will have pity on you,
O Jerusalem?
Or who will bemoan you?
Or who will turn aside to ask how you
are doing?
6 You have forsaken Me," says the LORD,
"You have [R]gone backward. Jer. 7:24
Therefore I will stretch out My hand
against you and destroy you;
[R]I am [T]weary of relenting! Jer. 20:16 • *tired*
7 And I will winnow them with a
winnowing fan in the gates of the land;
I will [R]bereave *them* of children;
I will destroy My people, Jer. 18:21
Since they [R]do not return from their
ways. Is. 9:13
8 Their widows will be increased to Me
more than the sand of the seas;
I will bring against them,
Against the mother of the young men,
A plunderer at noonday;
I will cause anguish and terror to fall on
them [R]suddenly. Is. 29:5

9"She[R] languishes who has borne seven;
She has breathed her last; 1 Sam. 2:5
[R]Her sun has gone down Amos 8:9
While *it was* yet day;
She has been ashamed and confounded.
And the remnant of them I will deliver to
the sword
Before their enemies," says the LORD.

God Encourages Jeremiah

10[R] Woe is me, my mother, Job 3:1
That you have borne me,
A man of strife and a man of contention
to the whole [T]earth! Or *land*
I have neither lent for interest,
Nor have men lent to me for interest.
Every one of them curses me.

11 The LORD said:

"Surely it will be well with your remnant;
Surely I will cause [R]the enemy to
intercede with you Jer. 40:4, 5
In the time of adversity and in the time
of affliction.
12 Can anyone break iron,
The northern iron and the bronze?
13 Your wealth and your treasures
I will give as [R]plunder without price,
Because of all your sins, Ps. 44:12
Throughout your territories.
14 And I will make *you* cross over with*
your enemies
[R]Into a land *which* you do not know;
For a fire is kindled in My anger,
Which shall burn upon you." Jer. 16:13

15 O LORD, [R]You know; Jer. 12:3
Remember me and [T]visit me, *attend to*
And [R]take vengeance for me on my
persecutors. Jer. 20:12

15:14 So with MT, Vg.; LXX, Syr., Tg. *cause you to serve* (cf. 17:4)

In Your enduring patience, do not take
me away.
Know that [R]for Your sake I have suffered
rebuke. Ps. 69:7–9
16 Your words were found, and I ate them,
And [R]Your word was to me the joy and
rejoicing of my heart; [Job 23:12]
For I am called by Your name,
O LORD God of hosts.
17 [R]I did not sit in the assembly of the
mockers, Ps. 26:4, 5
Nor did I rejoice;
I sat alone because of Your hand,
For You have filled me with indignation.
18 Why is my [R]pain perpetual Jer. 10:19
And my wound incurable,
Which refuses to be healed?
Will You surely be to me [R]like an
unreliable stream, Job 6:15
As waters *that* [T]fail? Or *cannot be trusted*

19 Therefore thus says the LORD:

[R]"If you return, Zech. 3:7
Then I will bring you back;
You shall [R]stand before Me; Jer. 15:1
If you [R]take out the precious from the
vile, Ezek. 22:26; 44:23
You shall be as My mouth.
Let them return to you,
But you must not return to them.
20 And I will make you to this people a
fortified bronze [R]wall; Ezek. 3:9
And they will fight against you,
But they shall not prevail against you;
For I *am* with you to save you
And deliver you," says the LORD.
21 "I will deliver you from the hand of the
wicked,
And I will redeem you from the grip of
the terrible."

CHAPTER 16

Jeremiah Is Not to Marry

THE word of the LORD also came to me,
saying,
2 "You shall not take a wife, nor shall you
have sons or daughters in this place."
3 For thus says the LORD concerning the
sons and daughters who are born in this
place, and concerning their mothers who bore
them and their fathers who begot them in this
land:
4 "They shall die [R]gruesome deaths; they
shall not be lamented nor shall they be bur-
ied, *but* they shall be like refuse on the face of
the earth. They shall be consumed by the
sword and by famine, and their [R]corpses shall
be meat for the birds of heaven and for the
beasts of the earth." Jer. 15:2 • Ps. 79:2
5 For thus says the LORD: "Do not enter the
house of mourning, nor go to lament or be-
moan them; for I have taken away My peace
from this people," says the LORD, "lovingkind-
ness and mercies.
6 "Both the great and the small shall die in
this land. They shall not be buried; neither
shall men lament for them, cut themselves,
nor make themselves bald for them.
7 "Nor shall *men* break *bread* in mourning
for them, to comfort them for the dead; nor
shall *men* give them the cup of consolation to
drink for their father or their mother.
8 "Also you shall not go into the house of
feasting to sit with them, to eat and drink."
9 For thus says the LORD of hosts, the God
of Israel: "Behold, [R]I will cause to cease from
this place, before your eyes and in your days,
the voice of [T]mirth and the voice of gladness,
the voice of the bridegroom and the voice of
the bride. Rev. 18:23 • *rejoicing*

Judah's Idolatry

10 "And it shall be, when you show this peo-
ple all these words, and they say to you, [R]'Why
has the LORD pronounced all this great disas-
ter against us? Or what *is* our iniquity? Or
what *is* our sin that we have committed
against the LORD our God?' Deut. 29:24
11 "then you shall say to them, 'Because
your fathers have forsaken Me,' says the
LORD; 'they have walked after other gods and
have served them and worshiped them, and
have forsaken Me and not kept My law.
12 'And you have done [R]worse than your fa-
thers, for behold, [R]each one follows the dic-
tates of his own evil heart, so that no one
listens to Me. Jer. 7:26 • Jer. 3:17; 18:12
13 [R]'Therefore I will cast you out of this land
into a land that you do not know, neither you
nor your fathers; and there you shall serve
other gods day and night, where I will not
show you favor.' Deut. 4:26; 28:36, 63

God's Promise of Judah's Restoration

14 "Therefore behold, the days are coming,"
says the LORD, "that it shall no more be said,
'The LORD lives who brought up the children
of Israel from the land of Egypt,'
15 "but, 'The LORD lives who brought up the
children of Israel from the land of the north
and from all the lands where He had driven
them.' For I will bring them back into their
land which I gave to their fathers.
16 "Behold, I will send for many [R]fishermen,"
says the LORD, "and they shall fish them; and
afterward I will send for many hunters, and
they shall hunt them from every mountain
and every hill, and out of the holes of the
rocks. Amos 4:2
17 "For My [R]eyes *are* on all their ways; they
are not hidden from My face, nor is their iniq-
uity hidden from My eyes. Heb. 4:13
18 "And first I will repay [R]double for their
iniquity and their sin, because [R]they have

defiled My land; they have filled My inheritance with the carcasses of their detestable and abominable idols." Jer. 17:18 • [Ezek. 43:7]

19 O LORD, my strength and my fortress,
My refuge in the day of affliction,
The Gentiles shall come to You
From the ends of the earth and say,
"Surely our fathers have inherited lies,
Worthlessness and unprofitable *things*."
20 Will a man make gods for himself,
[R]Which *are* not gods? Gal. 4:8

21 "Therefore behold, I will this once cause them to know,
I will cause them to know
My hand and My might;
And they shall know that [R]My name *is* the LORD. Amos 5:8

CHAPTER 17

Judah's Sins Are Listed

"THE sin of Judah *is* [R]written with a [R]pen of iron; Jer. 2:22 • Job 19:24
With the point of a diamond *it is* [R]engraved 2 Cor. 3:3
On the tablet of their heart,
And on the horns of your altars,
2 While their children remember
Their altars and their wooden images*
By the green trees on the high hills.
3 O My mountain in the field,
I will give as plunder your wealth, all your treasures,
And your high places of sin within all your borders.
4 And you, even yourself,
Shall let go of your heritage which I gave you;
And I will cause you to serve your enemies
In the land which you do not know;
For [R]you have kindled a fire in My anger *which* shall burn forever." Jer. 15:14

5 Thus says the LORD:

"Cursed *is* the man who trusts in man
And makes flesh his strength,
Whose heart departs from the LORD.
6 For he shall be [R]like a shrub in the desert, Jer. 48:6
And [R]shall not see when good comes,
But shall inhabit the parched places in the wilderness, Job 20:17
In a salt land *which is* not inhabited.

7 "Blessed[R] *is* the man who trusts in the LORD, [Is. 30:18]
And whose hope is the LORD.
8 For he shall be [R]like a tree planted by the waters, [Ps. 1:3]
Which spreads out its roots by the river,
And will not fear* when heat comes;
But its leaf will be green,
And will not be anxious in the year of drought,
Nor will cease from yielding fruit.

9 "The [R]heart *is* deceitful above all *things*,
And desperately wicked; [Eccl. 9:3]
Who can know it?
10 I, the LORD, [R]search the heart,
I test the mind, Rev. 2:23
[R]Even to give every man according to his ways, Rom. 2:6
According to the fruit of his doings.

11 "*As* a partridge that [T]broods but does not hatch, Sits on eggs
So is he who gets riches, but not by right;
It [R]will leave him in the midst of his days, Ps. 55:23
And at his end he will be a fool."

12 A glorious high throne from the beginning
Is the place of our sanctuary.
13 O LORD, [R]the hope of Israel, Jer. 14:8
All who forsake You shall be ashamed.

"Those who depart from Me
Shall be written in the earth,
Because they have forsaken the LORD,
The fountain of living waters."

14 Heal me, O LORD, and I shall be healed;
Save me, and I shall be saved,
For [R]You *are* my praise. Deut. 10:21
15 Indeed they say to me,
[R]"Where *is* the word of the LORD? Is. 5:19
Let it come now!"
16 As for me, I have not hurried away from *being* a shepherd *who* follows You,
Nor have I desired the woeful day;
You know what came out of my lips;
It was right there before You.
17 Do not be a terror to me;
You *are* my hope in the day of doom.
18 [R]Let them be ashamed who persecute me, Ps. 35:4; 70:2
But [R]do not let me be put to shame;
Let them be dismayed, Ps. 25:2
But do not let me be dismayed.
Bring on them the day of doom,
And [R]destroy[T] them with double destruction! Jer. 11:20 • Lit. *crush*

Jeremiah's Call for Sabbath Observance

19 Thus the LORD said to me: "Go and stand
in the gate of the children of the people, by

17:2 Heb. *Asherim*, Canaanite deities **17:8** Qr., Tg. *see*

which the kings of Judah come in and by
which they go out, and in all the gates of Jeru-
salem;
20 "and say to them, [R]'Hear the word of the
LORD, you kings of Judah, and all Judah, and
all the inhabitants of Jerusalem, who enter by
these gates. Jer. 19:3, 4
21 'Thus says the LORD: [R]"Take heed to
yourselves, and bear no burden on the Sab-
bath day, nor bring *it* in by the gates of Jeru-
salem; Neh. 13:19
22 "nor carry a burden out of your houses on
the Sabbath day, nor do any work, but hallow
the Sabbath day, as I [R]commanded your fa-
thers. Ex. 20:8; 31:13
23 "But they did not obey nor incline their
ear, but made their neck stiff, that they might
not hear nor receive instruction.
24 "And it shall be, [R]if you heed Me care-
fully," says the LORD, "to bring no burden
through the gates of this city on the [R]Sabbath
day, but hallow the Sabbath day, to do no
work in it, Jer. 11:4; 26:3 • Ex. 16:23–30
25 [R]"then shall enter the gates of this city
kings and princes sitting on the throne of Da-
vid, riding in chariots and on horses, they and
their princes, accompanied by the men of Ju-
dah and the inhabitants of Jerusalem; and
this city shall remain forever. Jer. 22:4
26 "And they shall come from the cities of
Judah and from [R]the places around Jerusa-
lem, from the land of Benjamin and from
[R]the lowland, from the mountains and from
[R]the South, bringing burnt offerings and
sacrifices, grain offerings and incense,
bringing sacrifices of praise to the house of
the LORD. Jer. 33:13 • Zech. 7:7 • Judg. 1:9
27 "But if you will not heed Me to hallow
the Sabbath day, such as not carrying a
burden when entering the gates of Jerusa-
lem on the Sabbath day, then [R]I will kindle
a fire in its gates, [R]and it shall devour the
palaces of Jerusalem, and it shall not be
[R]quenched." ' " Lam. 4:11 • 2 Kin. 25:9 • Jer. 7:20

CHAPTER 18

Sign of the Potter

THE word which came to Jeremiah from
the LORD, saying:
2 "Arise and go down to the potter's house,
and there I will cause you to hear My words."
3 Then I went down to the potter's house,
and there he was, making something at the
[T]wheel. Potter's wheel
4 And the vessel that he made of clay was
[T]marred in the hand of the potter; so he made
it again into another vessel, as it seemed good
to the potter to make. *ruined*
5 Then the word of the LORD came to me,
saying:
6 "O house of Israel, can I not do with you
as this potter?" says the LORD. "Look, [R]as the
clay *is* in the potter's hand, so *are* you in My
hand, O house of Israel! Is. 64:8
7 "The instant I speak concerning a nation
and concerning a kingdom, to pluck up, to
pull down, and to destroy *it*,
8 "if that nation against whom I have spo-
ken turns from its evil, I will relent of the di-
saster that I thought to bring upon it.
9 "And the instant I speak concerning a na-
tion and concerning a kingdom, to build and
to plant *it*,
10 "if it does evil in My sight so that it does
not obey My voice, then I will relent concern-
ing the good with which I said I would benefit
it.
11 "Now therefore, speak to the men of Ju-
dah and to the inhabitants of Jerusalem, say-
ing, 'Thus says the LORD: "Behold, I am
fashioning a disaster and devising a plan
against you. [R]Return now every one from his
evil way, and make your ways and your do-
ings [R]good." ' " 2 Kin. 17:13 • Jer. 7:3–7
12 And they said, [R]"That is hopeless! So we
will walk according to our own plans, and we
will every one [T]obey the [R]dictates of his evil
heart." Jer. 2:25 • Lit. *do* • Jer. 3:17; 23:17
13 Therefore thus says the LORD:

[R]"Ask now among the Gentiles,
Who has heard such things?
The virgin of Israel has done [R]a very
horrible thing. Jer. 2:10, 11 • Jer. 5:30
14 Will *a man* [T]leave the snow water of
Lebanon, *forsake*
Which comes from the rock of the field?
Will the cold flowing waters be forsaken
for strange waters?

15 "Because My people have forgotten [R]Me,
They have burned incense to worthless
idols. Jer. 2:13, 32
And they have caused themselves to
stumble in their ways,
From the [R]ancient paths, Jer. 6:16
To walk in pathways and not on a
highway,
16 To make their land [R]desolate *and* a
perpetual [R]hissing; Jer. 19:8 • 1 Kin. 9:8
Everyone who passes by it will be
astonished
And shake his head.
17 [R]I will scatter them [R]as with an east wind
before the enemy; Jer. 13:24 • Ps. 48:7
[R]I will show them* the back and not the
face Jer. 2:27
In the day of their calamity."

18 Then they said, [R]"Come and let us de-
vise plans against Jeremiah; [R]for the law
shall not perish from the priest, nor counsel
from the wise, nor the word from the

18:17 So with LXX, Syr., Tg., Vg.; MT *look them in*

prophet. Come and let us attack him with the tongue, and let us not give heed to any of his words." Jer. 11:19 • Lev. 10:11

19 Give heed to me, O LORD,
And listen to the voice of those who
contend with me!
20[R] Shall evil be repaid for good? Ps. 109:4
For they have dug a pit for my life.
Remember that I [R]stood before You
To speak good for them, Jer.14:7—15:1
To turn away Your wrath from them.
21 Therefore [R]deliver up their children to
the famine, Ps. 109:9–20
And pour out their *blood*
By the force of the sword;
Let their wives *become* widows
And [R]bereaved of their children.
Let their men be put to death,
Their young men *be* slain
By the sword in battle. Jer. 15:7, 8
22 Let a cry be heard from their houses,
When You bring a troop suddenly upon
them;
For they have dug a pit to take me,
And hidden snares for my feet.
23 Yet, LORD, You know all their counsel
Which is against me, to slay *me*.
[R] Provide no atonement for their iniquity,
Nor blot out their sin from Your sight;
But let them be overthrown before You.
Deal *thus* with them Ps. 35:14; 109:14
In the time of Your [R]anger. Jer. 7:20

CHAPTER 19

Sign of the Broken Flask

THUS says the LORD: "Go and get a potter's earthen flask, and *take* some of the elders of the people and some of the elders of the priests.

2 "And go out to [R]the Valley of the Son of Hinnom, which *is* by the entry of the Potsherd Gate; and proclaim there the words that I will tell you, Josh. 15:8

3 [R]"and say, 'Hear the word of the LORD, O kings of Judah and inhabitants of Jerusalem. Thus says the LORD of hosts, the God of Israel: "Behold, I will bring such a catastrophe on this place, that whoever hears of it, his ears will [R]tingle. Jer. 17:20 • 1 Sam. 3:11

4 "Because they [R]have forsaken Me and made this an alien place, because they have burned incense in it to other gods whom neither they, their fathers, nor the kings of Judah have known, and have filled this place with the blood of the innocents Is. 65:11

5 "(they have also built the high places of Baal, to burn their sons with fire *for* burnt offerings to Baal, which I did not command or speak, nor did it come into My mind),

6 "therefore behold, the days are coming," says the LORD, "that this place shall no more be called Tophet or the Valley of the Son of Hinnom, but the Valley of Slaughter.

7 "And I will make void the counsel of Judah and Jerusalem in this place, [R]and I will cause them to fall by the sword before their enemies and by the hands of those who seek their lives; their [R]corpses I will give as meat for the birds of the heaven and for the beasts of the earth. Lev. 26:17 • Ps. 79:2

8 "I will make this city [R]desolate and a hissing; everyone who passes by it will be astonished and hiss because of all its plagues. Jer. 18:16; 49:13; 50:13

9 "And I will cause them to eat the flesh of their sons and the flesh of their daughters, and everyone shall eat the flesh of his friend in the siege and in the desperation with which their enemies and those who seek their lives shall drive them to despair." '

10 "Then you shall break the flask in the sight of the men who go with you,

11 "and say to them, 'Thus says the LORD of hosts: [R]"Even so I will break this people and this city, as *one* breaks a potter's vessel, which cannot be [T]made whole again; and they shall [R]bury *them* in Tophet till *there is* no place to bury. Is. 30:14 • *restored* • Jer. 7:32

12 "Thus I will do to this place," says the LORD, "and to its inhabitants, and make this city like Tophet.

13 "And the houses of Jerusalem and the houses of the kings of Judah shall be defiled like the place of Tophet, because of all the houses on whose roofs they have burned incense to all the host of heaven, and poured out drink offerings to other gods." ' "

14 Then Jeremiah came from Tophet, where the LORD had sent him to prophesy; and he stood in [R]the court of the Lord's house and said to all the people, 2 Chr. 20:5

15 "Thus says the LORD of hosts, the God of Israel: 'Behold, I will bring on this city and on all her towns all the doom that I have pronounced against it, because [R]they have stiffened their necks that they might not hear My words.' " Neh. 9:17, 29

CHAPTER 20

Jeremiah Is Persecuted by Pashhur

NOW [R]Pashhur the son of Immer, the priest who *was* also chief governor in the house of the LORD, heard that Jeremiah prophesied these things. Ezra 2:37, 38

2 Then Pashhur struck Jeremiah the prophet, and put him in the stocks that *were* in the high [R]gate of Benjamin, which *was* by the house of the LORD. Jer. 37:13

3 And it happened on the next day that Pashhur brought Jeremiah out of the stocks. Then Jeremiah said to him, "The LORD has

not called your name Pashhur, but Magor-Missabib.*

4 "For thus says the LORD: 'Behold, I will make you a terror to yourself and to all your friends; and they shall fall by the sword of their enemies, and your eyes shall see *it*. I will give all Judah into the hand of the king of Babylon, and he shall carry them captive to Babylon and slay them with the sword.

5 'Moreover I [R]will deliver all the wealth of this city, all its produce, and all its precious things; all the treasures of the kings of Judah I will give into the hand of their enemies, who will plunder them, seize them, and carry them to Babylon. 2 Kin. 20:17

6 'And you, Pashhur, and all who dwell in your house, shall go into captivity. You shall go to Babylon, and there you shall die, and be buried there, you and all your friends, to whom you have prophesied lies.' "

Jeremiah Complains to God

7 O LORD, You [T]induced me, and I was
persuaded; *enticed* or *persuaded*
[R]You are stronger than I, and have
prevailed. Jer. 1:6, 7
[R]I am in derision daily; Lam. 3:14
Everyone mocks me.
8 For when I spoke, I cried out;
[R]I shouted, "Violence and plunder!"
Because the word of the LORD was made
to me Jer. 6:7
A reproach and a derision daily.
9 Then I said, "I will not make mention of
Him,
Nor speak anymore in His name."
But *His word* was in my heart like a
[R]burning fire Ps. 39:3
Shut up in my bones;
I was weary of holding *it* back,
And [R]I could not. Job 32:18
10 [R]For I heard many mocking: Ps. 31:13
"Fear on every side!"
"Report," *they say,* "and we will report it!"
[R]All my acquaintances watched for my
stumbling, *saying,* Ps. 41:9; 55:13, 14
"Perhaps he can be induced;
Then we will prevail against him,
And we will take our revenge on him."

11 But the LORD *is* [R]with me as a mighty,
awesome One. Jer. 1:18, 19
Therefore my persecutors will stumble,
and will not [R]prevail. Jer. 15:20; 17:18
They will be greatly ashamed, for they
will not prosper.
Their [R]everlasting confusion will never
be forgotten. Jer. 23:40
12 But, O LORD of hosts,
You who [R]test the righteous, [Jer. 11:20]
And see the mind and heart,
Let me see Your vengeance on them;
For I have pleaded my cause before You.

13 Sing to the LORD! Praise the LORD!
For He has delivered the life of the poor
From the hand of evildoers.

14 [R]Cursed *be* the day in which I was born!
Let the day not be blessed in which my
mother bore me! Job 3:3
15 Let the man *be* cursed
Who brought news to my father, saying,
"A male child has been born to you!"
Making him very glad.
16 And let that man be like the cities
Which the LORD [R]overthrew, and did not
relent; Gen. 19:25
Let him [R]hear the cry in the morning
And the shouting at noon, Jer. 18:22
17 [R]Because he did not kill me from the
womb, Job 3:10, 11
That my mother might have been my
grave,
And her womb always enlarged *with me*.
18 [R]Why did I come forth from the womb to
[R]see [T]labor and sorrow, Job 3:20
That my days should be consumed with
shame? Lam. 3:1 • *toil*

CHAPTER 21

Message Against Zedekiah

THE word which came to Jeremiah from the LORD when [R]King Zedekiah sent to him [R]Pashhur the son of Melchiah, and [R]Zephaniah the son of Maaseiah, the priest, saying, 2 Kin. 24:17, 18 • Jer. 38:1 • 2 Kin. 25:18

2 "Please inquire of the LORD for us, for Nebuchadnezzar* king of Babylon makes war against us. Perhaps the LORD will deal with us according to all His wonderful works, that *the king* may go away from us."

3 Then Jeremiah said to them, "Thus you shall say to Zedekiah,

4 'Thus says the LORD God of Israel: "Behold, I will turn back the weapons of war that *are* in your hands, with which you fight against the king of Babylon and the Chaldeans* who besiege you outside the walls; and [R]I will assemble them in the midst of this city. Is. 13:4

5 "I Myself will fight against you with an outstretched hand and with a strong arm, even in anger and fury and great wrath.

6 "I will strike the inhabitants of this city, both man and beast; they shall die of a great pestilence.

7 "And afterward," says the LORD, "I will deliver Zedekiah king of Judah, his servants and the people, and such as are left in this city from the pestilence and the sword and the famine, into the hand of Nebuchadnezzar

20:3 Lit. *Fear on Every Side* **21:2** Heb. *Nebuchadrezzar,* and so elsewhere in the book
21:4 Or *Babylonians,* and so elsewhere in the book

king of Babylon, into the hand of their ene-
mies, and into the hand of those who seek
their life; and he shall strike them with the
edge of the sword. [R]He shall not spare them,
or have pity or mercy." ' 2 Chr. 36:17
8 "Now you shall say to this people, 'Thus
says the LORD: "Behold, I set before you the
way of life and the way of death.
9 "He who remains in this city shall die by
the sword, by famine, and by pestilence; but
he who goes out and defects to the Chaldeans
who besiege you, he shall live, and his life
shall be as a prize to him.
10 "For I have [R]set My face against this city
for adversity and not for good," says the
LORD. [R]"It shall be given into the hand of the
king of Babylon, and he shall [R]burn it with
fire." ' Amos 9:4 • Jer. 38:3 • Jer. 34:2, 22; 37:10
11 "And concerning the house of the king of
Judah, *say*, 'Hear the word of the LORD,
12 'O house of David! Thus says the LORD:

"Execute judgment in the morning;
And deliver *him who is* plundered
Out of the hand of the oppressor,
Lest My fury go forth like fire
And burn so that no one can quench *it*,
Because of the evil of your doings.

13 "Behold, [R]I *am* against you, O [T]inhabitant
of the valley, [Ezek. 13:8] • *dweller*
And rock of the plain," says the LORD,
"Who say, [R]'Who shall come down against
us? Jer. 49:4
Or who shall enter our dwellings?'
14 But I will punish you according to the
[R]fruit of your [T]doings," says the LORD;
"I will kindle a fire in its forest,
And [R]it shall devour all things around
it." ' " Is. 3:10, 11 • *deeds* • 2 Chr. 36:19

CHAPTER 22

THUS says the LORD: "Go down to the
house of the king of Judah, and there
speak this word,
2 "and say, [R]'Hear the word of the LORD, O
king of Judah, you who sit on the throne of
David, you and your servants and your people
who enter these gates! Jer. 17:20
3 'Thus says the LORD: "Execute judgment
and righteousness, and deliver the plundered
out of the hand of the oppressor. Do no wrong
and do no violence to the stranger, the [R]fa-
therless, or the widow, nor shed innocent
blood in this place. Jer. 7:6
4 "For if you indeed do this thing, [R]then
shall enter the gates of this house, riding on
horses and in chariots, accompanied by ser-
vants and people, kings who sit on the throne
of David. Jer. 17:25
5 "But if you will not [T]hear these words, I
swear by Myself," says the LORD, "that this
house shall become a desolation." ' " Obey
6 For thus says the LORD to the house of the
king of Judah:

"You *are* [R]Gilead to Me, Song 4:1
The head of Lebanon;
Yet I surely will make you a wilderness,
Cities *which* are not inhabited.
7 I will prepare destroyers against you,
Everyone with his weapons;
They shall cut down your choice cedars
[R]And cast *them* into the fire. Jer. 21:14

8 "And many nations will pass by this
city; and everyone will say to his neighbor,
[R]'Why has the LORD done so to this great
city?' Deut. 29:24–26
9 "Then they will answer, [R]'Because they
have forsaken the covenant of the LORD their
God, and worshiped other gods and served
them.' " 2 Chr. 34:25

Message Against Shallum

10 Weep not for [R]the dead, nor bemoan
him; 2 Kin. 22:20
Weep bitterly for him who goes away,
For he shall return no more,
Nor see his native country.

11 For thus says the LORD concerning [R]Shal-
lum* the son of Josiah, king of Judah, who
reigned instead of Josiah his father, [R]who
went from this place: "He shall not return
here anymore, 1 Chr. 3:15 • 2 Kin. 23:34
12 "but he shall die in the place where they
have led him captive, and shall see this land
no more.

Message Against Jehoiakim

13 "Woe[R] to him who builds his house by
unrighteousness 2 Kin. 23:35
And his chambers by injustice,
[R]*Who* uses his neighbor's service without
wages James 5:4
And gives him nothing for his work,
14 Who says, 'I will build myself a wide
house with spacious chambers,
And cut out windows for it,
Paneling *it* with cedar
And painting *it* with vermilion.'

15 "Shall you reign because you enclose
yourself in cedar?
Did not your father eat and drink,
And do justice and righteousness?
Then [R]*it was* well with him. Ps. 128:2
16 He [T]judged the cause of the poor and
needy; Defended
Then *it was* well.

22:11 Or *Jehoahaz*

Was not this knowing Me?" says the
LORD.
17 "Yet[R] your eyes and your heart *are* for
nothing but your covetousness,
For shedding innocent blood,
And practicing oppression and
violence." Ezek. 19:6

18 Therefore thus says the LORD concerning
Jehoiakim the son of Josiah, king of Judah:

[R]"They shall not lament for him,
Saying, [R]'Alas, my brother!' or 'Alas, my
sister!' Jer. 16:4, 6 • 1 Kin. 13:30
They shall not lament for him,
Saying, 'Alas, master!' or 'Alas, his
glory!'
19 [R]He shall be buried with the burial of a
donkey, Jer. 36:30
Dragged and cast out beyond the gates
of Jerusalem.

20 "Go up to Lebanon, and cry out,
And lift up your voice in Bashan;
Cry from Abarim,
For all your lovers are destroyed.
21 I spoke to you in your prosperity,
But you said, 'I will not hear.'
[R]This *has been* your manner from your
youth, Jer. 3:24, 25; 32:30
That you did not obey My voice.
22 The wind shall eat up all [R]your [T]rulers,
And your lovers shall go into captivity;
Surely then you will be ashamed and
humiliated Jer. 23:1 • Lit. *shepherds*
For all your wickedness.
23 O inhabitant of Lebanon,
Making your nest in the cedars,
How gracious will you be when pangs
come upon you,
Like the pain of a woman in labor?

Message Against Coniah (Jehoiachin)

24 "*As* I live," says the LORD, [R]"though Co-
niah* the son of Jehoiakim, king of Judah,
[R]were the signet on My right hand, yet I would
pluck you off; 2 Kin. 24:6, 8 • Hag. 2:23
25 [R]"and I will give you into the hand of
those who seek your life, and into the hand *of*
those whose face you fear—the hand of Neb-
uchadnezzar king of Babylon and the hand of
the Chaldeans. Jer. 34:20
26 "So I will cast you out, and your mother
who bore you, into another country where
you were not born; and there you shall die.
27 "But to the land to which they desire to
return, there they shall not return.

28 "Is this man [T]Coniah a despised, broken
idol— See note at v. 24
[R]A vessel in which *is* no pleasure?
Why are they cast out, he and his
descendants, Hos. 8:8
And cast into a land which they do not
know?
29 [R]O earth, earth, earth, Deut. 32:1
Hear the word of the LORD!
30 Thus says the LORD:
'Write this man down as [R]childless,
A man *who* shall not prosper in his
days; Matt. 1:12
For [R]none of his descendants shall
prosper, Jer. 36:30
Sitting on the throne of David,
And ruling anymore in Judah.' "

CHAPTER 23

Message of the Righteous King

"WOE [R]to the shepherds who destroy
and scatter the sheep of My pasture!"
says the LORD. Jer. 10:21
2 Therefore thus says the LORD God of Is-
rael against the shepherds who feed My peo-
ple: "You have scattered My flock, driven
them away, and not attended to them. [R]Be-
hold, I will attend to you for the evil of your
doings," says the LORD. Ex. 32:34
3 "But I will gather the remnant of My flock
out of all countries where I have driven them,
and bring them back to their folds; and they
shall be fruitful and increase.
4 "I will set up [R]shepherds over them who
will feed them; and they shall fear no more,
nor be dismayed, nor shall they be lacking,"
says the LORD. Jer. 3:15

5 "Behold, [R]*the* days are coming," says the
LORD, Jer. 33:14
"That I [R]will raise to David a Branch of
righteousness; Matt. 1:1, 6☆
A King shall reign and prosper,
[R]And execute judgment and
righteousness in the earth. Ps. 72:2
6 In His days Judah will be saved,
And Israel [R]will dwell safely; Jer. 32:37
Now [R]this *is* His name by which He will
be called: [1 Cor. 1:30]☆

THE LORD OUR RIGHTEOUSNESS.*

7 "Therefore, behold, [R]*the* days are com-
ing," says the LORD, "that they shall no
longer say, 'As the LORD lives who brought
up the children of Israel from the land of
Egypt,' Jer. 16:14
8 "but, 'As the LORD lives who brought up
and led the descendants of the house of Israel
from the north country and from all the coun-
tries where I had driven them.' And they shall
dwell in their own land."

22:24 Or *Jeconiah* or *Jehoiachin* **23:6** Heb. *YHWH Tsidkenu*

Jeremiah's Tenth Sermon: Against Judah's False Prophets

9 My heart within me is broken
Because of the prophets;
[R]All my bones shake. Hab. 3:16
I am like a drunken man,
And like a man whom wine has
overcome,
Because of the LORD,
And because of His holy words.
10 For [R]the land is full of adulterers;
For [R]because of a curse the land
mourns. Jer. 9:2 • Hos. 4:2
[R]The pleasant places of the wilderness
are dried up. Jer. 9:10
Their course of life is evil,
And their might *is* not right.

11"For [R]both prophet and priest are
profane; Zeph. 3:4
Yes, in My house I have found their
wickedness," says the LORD.
12"Therefore[R] their way shall be to them
Like slippery *ways;* [Prov. 4:19]
In the darkness they shall be driven on
And fall in them;
For I [R]will bring disaster on them,
The year of their punishment," says the
LORD. Jer. 11:23
13"And I have seen [T]folly in the prophets of
Samaria: Lit. *distastefulness*
[R]They prophesied by Baal Jer. 2:8
And caused My people Israel to err.
14 Also I have seen a horrible thing in the
prophets of Jerusalem:
[R]They commit adultery and walk in lies;
They also [R]strengthen the hands of
evildoers, Jer. 29:23 • Ezek. 13:22, 23
So that no one turns back from his
wickedness.
All of them are like Sodom to Me,
And her inhabitants like Gomorrah.

15 "Therefore thus says the LORD of hosts
concerning the prophets:

'Behold, I will feed them with
[R]wormwood, Jer. 9:15
And make them drink the water of gall;
For from the prophets of Jerusalem
[T]Profaneness has gone out into all the
land.' " Or *Pollution*

16 Thus says the LORD of hosts:
"Do not listen to the words of the
prophets who prophesy to you.
They make you worthless;
They speak a vision of their own heart,
Not from the mouth of the LORD.
17 They continually say to those who
despise Me,
'The LORD has said, [R]"You shall have
peace" '; Ezek. 13:10
And *to* everyone who [R]walks according
to the dictates of his own heart, they
say, Deut. 29:19; Jer. 3:17
'No evil shall come upon you.' "

18 For [R]who has stood in the counsel of the
LORD, [1 Cor. 2:16]
And has perceived and heard His word?
Who has marked His word and heard *it?*
19 Behold, a [R]whirlwind of the LORD has
gone forth in fury— Amos 1:14
A violent whirlwind!
It will fall violently on the head of the
wicked.
20 The [R]anger of the LORD will not turn
back Jer. 30:24
Until He has executed and performed
the thoughts of His heart.
[R]In the latter days you will understand it
perfectly. Gen. 49:1

21"I[R] have not sent these prophets, yet they
ran. Jer. 14:14; 23:32; 27:15
I have not spoken to them, yet they
prophesied.
22 But if they had stood in My counsel,
And had caused My people to hear My
words,
Then they would have [R]turned them
from their evil way Jer. 25:5
And from the evil of their doings.

23"*Am* I a God near at hand," says the LORD,
"And not a God afar off?
24 Can anyone [R]hide himself in secret
places, [Ps. 139:7]
So I shall not see him?" says the LORD;
[R]"Do I not fill heaven and earth?" says the
LORD. [1 Kin. 8:27]

25 "I have heard what the prophets have said
who prophesy lies in My name, saying, 'I have
dreamed, I have dreamed!'
26 "How long will *this* be in the heart of the
prophets who prophesy lies? Indeed *they are*
prophets of the deceit of their own heart,
27 "who try to make My people forget My
name by their dreams which everyone tells
his neighbor, [R]as their fathers forgot My name
for Baal. Judg. 3:7

28"The prophet who has a dream, let him
tell a dream;
And he who has My word, let him speak
My word faithfully.
What *is* the chaff to the wheat?" says the
LORD.
29"*Is* not My word like a [R]fire?" says the
LORD, Jer. 5:14
"And like a hammer *that* breaks the rock
in pieces?

30 "Therefore behold, I *am* against the
prophets," says the LORD, "who steal My
words every one from his neighbor.
31 "Behold, I *am* [R]against the prophets," says
the LORD, "who use their tongues and say, 'He
says.' Ezek. 13:9
32 "Behold, I *am* against those who proph-
esy false dreams," says the LORD, "and tell
them, and cause My people to err by their
[R]lies and by [R]their recklessness. Yet I did not
send them or command them; therefore they
shall not [R]profit this people at all," says the
LORD. Lam. 2:14; 3:37 • Zeph. 3:4 • Jer. 7:8
33 "So when these people or the prophet or
the priest ask you, saying, 'What is [R]the [T]ora-
cle of the LORD?' you shall then say to them,
'What oracle?'* I will even forsake you," says
the LORD. Mal. 1:1 • *burden, prophecy*
34 "And *as for* the prophet and the priest
and the people who say, 'The [T]oracle of the
LORD!' I will even punish that man and his
house. *burden, prophecy*
35 "Thus every one of you shall say to his
neighbor, and every one to his brother, 'What
has the LORD answered?' and, 'What has the
LORD spoken?'
36 "And the [T]oracle of the LORD you shall
mention no more. For every man's word will
be his oracle, for you have [R]perverted the
words of the living God, the LORD of hosts, our
God. *burden, prophecy* • Deut. 4:2
37 "Thus you shall say to the prophet, 'What
has the LORD answered you?' and, 'What has
the LORD spoken?'
38 "But since you say, 'The oracle of the
LORD!' therefore thus says the LORD: 'Because
you say this word, "The oracle of the LORD!"
and I have sent to you, saying, "Do not say,
'The oracle of the LORD!' "
39 'therefore behold, I, even I, [R]will utterly
forget you and forsake you, and the city that I
gave you and your fathers, and *will cast you*
out of My presence. Hos. 4:6
40 'And I will bring [R]an everlasting reproach
upon you, and a perpetual shame, which shall
not be forgotten.' " Jer. 20:11

CHAPTER 24

Jeremiah's Eleventh Sermon: The Two Baskets of Figs

THE [R]LORD showed me, and there were two
baskets of figs set before the temple of
the LORD, after Nebuchadnezzar king of
Babylon had carried away captive Jeconiah
the son of Jehoiakim, king of Judah, and the
princes of Judah with the craftsmen and
smiths, from Jerusalem, and had brought
them to Babylon. Amos 7:1, 4; 8:1
2 One basket *had* very good figs, like the
figs *that are* first ripe; and the other basket
had very bad figs which could not be eaten,
they were so [R]bad. Jer. 29:17
3 Then the LORD said to me, "What do you
see, Jeremiah?" And I said, "Figs, the good
figs, very good; and the bad, very bad, which
cannot be eaten, they are so bad."
4 Again the word of the LORD came to me,
saying,
5 "Thus says the LORD, the God of Israel:
'Like these good figs, so will I [T]acknowledge
those who are carried away captive from
Judah, whom I have sent out of this place
for *their own* good, into the land of the
Chaldeans. *regard*
6 'For I will set My eyes on them for good,
and I will bring them back to this land; I will
build them and not pull *them* down, and I will
plant them and not pluck *them* up.
7 'Then I will give them a heart to know
Me, that I *am* the LORD; and they shall be My
people, and I will be their God, for they shall
return to Me with their whole heart.
8 'And as the bad [R]figs which cannot be
eaten, they are so bad'—surely thus says the
LORD—'so will I give up Zedekiah the king of
Judah, his princes, the residue of Jerusalem
who remain in this land, and those who dwell
in the land of Egypt. Jer. 29:17
9 'I will deliver them to trouble into all the
kingdoms of the earth, for *their* harm, *to be* a
reproach and a byword, a taunt and a curse, in
all places where I shall drive them.
10 'And I will send the sword, the famine,
and the pestilence among them, till they are
[T]consumed from the land that I gave to them
and their fathers.' " *destroyed*

CHAPTER 25

Jeremiah's Twelfth Sermon: The Seventy-Year Captivity

THE word that came to Jeremiah concern-
ing all the people of Judah, [R]in the fourth
year of Jehoiakim the son of Josiah, king of
Judah (which *was* the first year of Nebu-
chadnezzar king of Babylon), Jer. 36:1
2 which Jeremiah the prophet spoke to all
the people of Judah and to all the inhabitants
of Jerusalem, saying:
3 [R]"From the thirteenth year of Josiah the
son of Amon, king of Judah, even to this day,
this *is* the twenty-third year in which the word
of the LORD has come to me; and I have spo-
ken to you, rising early and speaking, but you
have not listened. Jer. 1:2
4 "And the LORD has sent to you all His ser-
vants the prophets, [R]rising early and sending
them, but you have not listened nor inclined
your ear to hear. Jer. 7:13, 25
5 "They said, [R]'Repent now everyone of his
evil way and his evil doings, and dwell in the
land that the LORD has given to you and your
fathers forever and ever. Jer. 18:11

23:33 LXX, Tg., Vg. *'You are the burden.'*

6 'Do not go after other gods to serve them and worship them, and do not provoke Me to anger with the works of your hands; and I will not harm you.'

7 "Yet you have not listened to Me," says the LORD, "that you might [R]provoke Me to anger with the works of your hands to your own hurt. Deut. 32:21

8 "Therefore thus says the LORD of hosts: 'Because you have not heard My words,

9 'behold, I will send and take all the families of the north,' says the LORD, 'and Nebuchadnezzar the king of Babylon, My servant, and will bring them against this land, against its inhabitants, and against these nations all around, and will utterly destroy them, and make them an astonishment, a hissing, and perpetual desolations.

10 'Moreover I will take from them the [R]voice of mirth and the voice of gladness, the voice of the bridegroom and the voice of the bride, [R]the sound of the millstones and the light of the lamp. Rev. 18:23 • Eccl. 12:4

11 'And this whole land shall be a desolation *and* an astonishment, and these nations shall serve the king of Babylon seventy [R]years. Jer. 29:10

12 'Then it will come to pass, [R]when seventy years are completed, *that* I will punish the king of Babylon and that nation, the land of the Chaldeans, for their iniquity,' says the LORD; [R]'and I will make it a perpetual desolation. Ezra 1:1 • Is. 13:20

13 'So I will bring on that land all My words which I have pronounced against it, all that is written in this book, which Jeremiah has prophesied concerning all the nations.

14 '(For many nations and great kings shall be served by them also; and I will repay them according to their deeds and according to the works of their own hands.)' "

15 For thus says the LORD God of Israel to me: "Take this [R]wine cup of [T]fury from My hand, and cause all the nations, to whom I send you, to drink it. Rev. 14:10 • *wrath*

16 "And [R]they will drink and stagger and go mad because of the sword that I will send among them." Nah. 3:11

17 Then I took the cup from the LORD's hand, and made all the nations drink, to whom the LORD had sent me:

18 Jerusalem and the cities of Judah, its kings and its princes, to make them [R]a desolation, an astonishment, a hissing, and [R]a curse, as *it is* this day; Jer. 25:9, 11 • Jer. 24:9

19 Pharaoh king of Egypt, his servants, his princes, and all his people;

20 all the mixed multitude, all the kings of the land of Uz, all the kings of the land of the Philistines (namely, Ashkelon, Gaza, Ekron, and the remnant of Ashdod);

21 [R]Edom, Moab, and the people of Ammon; Jer. 49:7

22 all the kings of [R]Tyre, all the kings of Sidon, and the kings of the coastlands which *are* across the [R]sea; Jer. 47:4 • Jer. 49:23

23 [R]Dedan, Tema, Buz, and all *who are* in the farthest corners; Jer. 49:7, 8

24 all the kings of Arabia and all the kings of the [R]mixed multitude who dwell in the desert; Ezek. 30:5

25 all the kings of Zimri, all the kings of Elam, and all the kings of the Medes;

26 [R]all the kings of the north, far and near, one with another; and all the kingdoms of the world which *are* on the face of the earth. Also the king of Sheshach* shall drink after them. Jer. 50:9

27 "Therefore you shall say to them, 'Thus says the LORD of hosts, the God of Israel: [R]"Drink, [R]be drunk, and vomit! Fall and rise no more, because of the sword which I will send among you." ' Hab. 2:16 • Is. 63:6

28 "And it shall be, if they refuse to take the cup from your hand to drink, then you shall say to them, 'Thus says the LORD of hosts: "You shall certainly drink!

29 "For behold, [R]I begin to bring calamity on the city [R]which is called by My name, and should you be utterly unpunished? You shall not be unpunished, for I will call for a sword on all the inhabitants of the earth," says the LORD of hosts.' Ezek. 9:6 • Dan. 9:18

30 "Therefore prophesy against them all these words, and say to them:

'The LORD will [R]roar from on high,
And utter His voice from [R]His holy
habitation; Amos 1:2 • Ps. 11:4
He will roar mightily against [R]His fold.
He will give [R]a shout, as those who tread
the grapes, 1 Kin. 9:3 • Is. 16:9
Against all the inhabitants of the earth.
31 A noise will come to the ends of the
earth—
For the LORD has [R]a controversy with the
nations; Mic. 6:2
[R]He will plead His case with all flesh.
He will give those *who are* wicked to the
sword,' says the LORD." Is. 66:16

32 Thus says the LORD of hosts:

"Behold, disaster shall go forth
From nation to nation,
And [R]a great whirlwind shall be raised
up Jer. 23:19; 30:23
From the farthest parts of the earth.

33 "And at that day the slain of the LORD shall be from *one* end of the earth even to the *other* end of the earth. They shall not be lamented, [R]or gathered, or buried; they shall become refuse on the ground. Ps. 79:3

25:26 A code word for Babylon, Jer. 51:41

34 "Wail,[R] shepherds, and cry! Jer. 4:8; 6:26
Roll about *in the ashes,*
You leaders of the flock!
For the days of your slaughter and your
dispersions are fulfilled;
You shall fall like a precious vessel.
35 And the shepherds will have no [T]way to
flee, Or *refuge*
Nor the leaders of the flock to escape.
36 A voice of the cry of the shepherds,
And a wailing of the leaders to the flock
will be heard.
For the LORD has plundered their
pasture,
37 And the peaceful dwellings are cut down
Because of the fierce anger of the LORD.
38 He has left His lair like the lion;
For their land is desolate
Because of the fierceness of the
Oppressor,
And because of His fierce anger."

CHAPTER 26

Conflict with the Nation

IN the beginning of the reign of Jehoiakim the son of Josiah, king of Judah, this word came from the LORD, saying,

2 "Thus says the LORD: 'Stand in the court of the LORD's house, and speak to all the cities of Judah, which come to worship *in* the LORD's house, [R]all the words that I command you to speak to them. [R]Do not diminish a word. Matt. 28:20 • Acts 20:27

3 [R]'Perhaps everyone will listen and turn from his evil way, that I may [R]relent concerning the calamity which I purpose to bring on them because of the evil of their doings.' Jer. 36:3–7 • Jer. 18:8

4 "And you shall say to them, 'Thus says the LORD: "If you will not listen to Me, to walk in My law which I have set before you,

5 "to heed the words of My servants the prophets [R]whom I sent to you, both rising up early and sending *them* (but you have not heeded), Jer. 25:4; 29:19

6 "then I will make this house like Shiloh, and will make this city [R]a curse to all the nations of the earth." ' " Is. 65:15

7 So the priests and the prophets and all the people heard Jeremiah speaking these words in the house of the LORD.

8 Now it happened, when Jeremiah had made an end of speaking all that the LORD had commanded *him* to speak to all the people, that the priests and the prophets and all the people seized him, saying, "You will surely die!

9 "Why have you prophesied in the name of the LORD, saying, 'This house shall be like Shiloh, and this city shall be [R]desolate, without an inhabitant'?" And all the people were gathered against Jeremiah in the house of the LORD. Jer. 9:11

10 When the princes of Judah heard these things, they came up from the king's house to the house of the LORD and sat down in the entry of the New Gate of the LORD's *house.*

11 And the priests and the prophets spoke to the princes and all the people, saying, "This man deserves to [R]die! For he has prophesied against this city, as you have heard with your ears." Jer. 38:4

12 Then Jeremiah spoke to all the princes and all the people, saying: "The LORD sent me to prophesy against this house and against this city with all the words that you have heard.

13 "Now therefore, [R]amend your ways and your doings, and obey the voice of the LORD your God; then the LORD will relent concerning the doom that He has pronounced against you. Jer. 7:3

14 "As for me, here I am, in your hand; do with me as seems good and proper to you.

15 "But know for certain that if you put me to death, you will surely bring innocent blood on yourselves, on this city, and on its inhabitants; for truly the LORD has sent me to you to speak all these words in your hearing."

16 So the princes and all the people said to the priests and the prophets, "This man does not deserve to die. For he has spoken to us in the name of the LORD our God."

17 [R]Then certain of the elders of the land rose up and spoke to all the assembly of the people, saying: Acts 5:34

18 [R]"Micah of Moresheth prophesied in the days of Hezekiah king of Judah, and spoke to all the people of Judah, saying, 'Thus says the LORD of hosts: Mic. 1:1

"Zion shall be plowed *like* a field,
Jerusalem shall become heaps of ruins,
And the mountain of the temple*
Like the bare hills of the forest." '*

19 "Did Hezekiah king of Judah and all Judah ever put him to death? Did he not fear the LORD and seek the LORD's favor? And the LORD relented concerning the doom which He had pronounced against them. But we are doing great evil against ourselves."

20 Now there was also a man who prophesied in the name of the LORD, Urijah the son of Shemaiah of Kirjath Jearim, who prophesied against this city and against this land according to all the words of Jeremiah.

21 And when Jehoiakim the king, with all his mighty men and all the princes, heard his words, the king sought to put him to death; but when Urijah heard *it,* he was afraid and fled, and went to Egypt.

22 Then Jehoiakim the king sent men to Egypt: Elnathan the son of Achbor, and *other* men *who went* with him to Egypt.

26:18 Lit. *house* • Cf. Mic. 3:12

23 And they brought Urijah from Egypt and brought him to Jehoiakim the king, who killed him with the sword and cast his dead body into the graves of the common people.

24 Nevertheless the hand of Ahikam the son of Shaphan was with Jeremiah, so that they should not give him into the hand of the people to put him to death.

CHAPTER 27

Conflict with the False Prophets

IN the beginning of the reign of Jehoiakim* the son of Josiah, [R]king of Judah, this word came to Jeremiah from the LORD, saying,* Jer. 27:3, 12, 20; 28:1

2 "Thus says the LORD to me: 'Make for yourselves bonds and yokes, [R]and put them on your neck, Jer. 28:10, 12

3 'and send them to the king of Edom, the king of Moab, the king of the Ammonites, the king of Tyre, and the king of Sidon, by the hand of the messengers who come to Jerusalem to Zedekiah king of Judah.

4 'And command them to say to their masters, "Thus says the LORD of hosts, the God of Israel—thus you shall say to your masters:

5 [R]'I have made the earth, the man and the beast that *are* on the ground, by My great power and by My outstretched arm, and [R]have given it to whom it seemed proper to Me. Is. 45:12 • Dan. 4:17, 25, 32

6 'And now I have given all these lands into the hand of Nebuchadnezzar the king of Babylon, My servant; and the beasts of the field I have also given him to serve him.

7 'So all nations shall serve him and his son and his son's son, until the time of his land comes; and then many nations and great kings shall make him serve them.

8 'And it shall be, *that* the nation and kingdom which will not serve Nebuchadnezzar the king of Babylon, and which will not put its neck under the yoke of the king of Babylon, that nation I will punish,' says the LORD, 'with the sword, the famine, and the pestilence, until I have consumed them by his hand.

9 'Therefore do not listen to your prophets, your diviners, your [T]dreamers, your soothsayers, or your sorcerers, who speak to you, saying, "You shall not serve the king of Babylon." Lit. *dreams*

10 'For they prophesy a [R]lie to you, to remove you far from your land; and I will drive you out, and you will perish. Jer. 23:16, 32

11 'But the nations that bring their necks under the yoke of the king of Babylon and serve him, I will let them remain in their own land,' says the LORD, 'and they shall till it and dwell in it.' " ' "

12 I also spoke to [R]Zedekiah king of Judah according to all these words, saying, "Bring your necks under the yoke of the king of Babylon, and serve him and his people, and live! Jer. 28:1; 38:17

13 [R]"Why will you die, you and your people, by the sword, by the famine, and by the pestilence, as the LORD has spoken against the nation that will not serve the king of Babylon? [Ezek. 18:31]

14 "Therefore [R]do not listen to the words of the prophets who speak to you, saying, 'You shall not serve the king of Babylon,' for they prophesy [R]a lie to you; Jer. 23:16 • Jer. 14:14

15 "for I have [R]not sent them," says the LORD, "yet they prophesy a lie in My name, that I may drive you out, and that you may perish, you and the prophets who prophesy to you." Jer. 23:21; 29:9

16 Also I spoke to the priests and to all this people, saying, "Thus says the LORD: 'Do not listen to the words of your prophets who prophesy to you, saying, "Behold, [R]the vessels of the LORD's house will now shortly be brought back from Babylon"; for they prophesy a lie to you. Dan. 1:2

17 'Do not listen to them; serve the king of Babylon, and live! Why should this city be laid waste?

18 'But if they *are* prophets, and if the word of the LORD is with them, let them now make intercession to the LORD of hosts, that the vessels which are left in the house of the LORD, *in* the house of the king of Judah, and at Jerusalem, do not go to Babylon.'

19 "For thus says the LORD of hosts [R]concerning the pillars, concerning the Sea, concerning the carts, and concerning the remainder of the vessels that remain in this city, 2 Kin. 25:13–17

20 "which Nebuchadnezzar king of Babylon did not take, when he carried away [R]captive Jeconiah the son of Jehoiakim, king of Judah, from Jerusalem to Babylon, and all the nobles of Judah and Jerusalem— Jer. 24:1

21 "yes, thus says the LORD of hosts, the God of Israel, concerning the [R]vessels that remain in the house of the LORD, and in the house of the king of Judah and of Jerusalem: Jer. 20:5

22 'They shall be carried to Babylon, and there they shall be until the day that I visit them,' says the LORD. 'Then I will bring them up and restore them to this place.' "

CHAPTER 28

Conflict with Hananiah

AND it happened in the same year, at the beginning of the reign of Zedekiah king of Judah, in the fourth year *and* in the fifth month, *that* Hananiah the son of Azur the prophet, who *was* from Gibeon, spoke to me

27:1 So with MT, Tg., Vg.; some Heb. mss., Arab., Syr. *Zedekiah* (cf. 27:3, 12; 28:1) • LXX omits v. 1.

in the house of the LORD in the presence of the
priests and of all the people, saying,
2 "Thus speaks the LORD of hosts, the God
of Israel, saying: 'I have broken [R]the yoke of
the king of Babylon. Jer. 27:12
3 [R]'Within two full years I will bring back
to this place all the vessels of the LORD's
house, that Nebuchadnezzar king of Babylon
[R]took away from this place and carried to
Babylon. Jer. 27:16 • Dan. 1:2
4 'And I will bring back to this place Jeco-
niah the son of Jehoiakim, king of Judah, with
all the captives of Judah who went to Bab-
ylon,' says the LORD, 'for I will break the yoke
of the king of Babylon.' "
5 Then the prophet Jeremiah spoke to the
prophet Hananiah in the presence of the
priests and in the presence of all the people
who stood in the house of the LORD,
6 and the prophet Jeremiah said, [R]"Amen!
The LORD do so; the LORD perform your words
which you have prophesied, to bring back the
vessels of the LORD's house and all who were
carried away captive, from Babylon to this
place. 1 Kin. 1:36
7 "Nevertheless hear now this word that I
speak in your hearing and in the hearing of all
the people:
8 "The prophets who have been before me
and before you of old prophesied against
many countries and great kingdoms—of war
and disaster and pestilence.
9 "As for [R]the prophet who prophesies of
peace, when the word of the prophet comes to
pass, the prophet will be known *as* one whom
the LORD has truly sent." Deut. 18:22
10 Then Hananiah the prophet took the
[R]yoke off the prophet Jeremiah's neck and
broke it. Jer. 27:2
11 And Hananiah spoke in the presence of
all the people, saying, "Thus says the LORD:
'Even so I will break the yoke of Nebu-
chadnezzar king of Babylon from the neck of
all nations within the space of two full years.' "
And the prophet Jeremiah went his way.
12 Now the word of the LORD came to Jere-
miah, after Hananiah the prophet had broken
the yoke from the neck of the prophet Jere-
miah, saying,
13 "Go and tell Hananiah, saying, 'Thus says
the LORD: "You have broken the yokes of
wood, but you have made in their place yokes
of iron."
14 'For thus says the LORD of hosts, the God
of Israel: [R]"I have put a yoke of iron on the
neck of all these nations, that they may serve
Nebuchadnezzar king of Babylon; and they
shall serve him. I have given him the beasts of
the field also." ' " Deut. 28:48
15 Then the prophet Jeremiah said to Hana-
niah the prophet, "Hear now, Hananiah, the
LORD has not sent you, but [R]you make this
people trust in a lie. Ezek. 13:22
16 "Therefore thus says the LORD: 'Behold, I
will cast you from the face of the earth. This
year you shall [R]die, because you have taught
rebellion against the LORD.' " Jer. 20:6
17 So Hananiah the prophet died the same
year in the seventh month.

CHAPTER 29

First Letter to the Exiles

NOW these *are* the words of the letter that
Jeremiah the prophet sent from Jerusa-
lem to the remainder of the elders who were
[R]carried away captive—to the priests, the
prophets, and all the people whom Nebuchad-
nezzar had carried away captive from Jerusa-
lem to Babylon. Jer. 27:20
2 (This happened after [R]Jeconiah the
king, the [R]queen mother, the [T]eunuchs, the
princes of Judah and Jerusalem, the crafts-
men, and the smiths had departed from Je-
rusalem.) 2 Kin. 24:12–16 • Jer. 13:18 • Or *officers*
3 *The letter was sent* by the hand of Elasah
the son of [R]Shaphan, and Gemariah the son of
Hilkiah, whom Zedekiah king of Judah sent
to Babylon, to Nebuchadnezzar king of Bab-
ylon, saying, 2 Chr. 34:8

4 Thus says the LORD of hosts, the God of
Israel, to all who were carried away
captive, whom I have caused to be
carried away from Jerusalem to Babylon:
5 Build houses and dwell *in them;* plant
gardens and eat their fruit.
6 Take wives and beget sons and
daughters; and take wives for your sons
and give your daughters to husbands, so
that they may bear sons and daughters—
that you may be increased there, and not
diminished.
7 And seek the peace of the city where I
have caused you to be carried away
captive, and pray to the LORD for it; for
in its peace you will have peace.
8 For thus says the LORD of hosts, the God
of Israel: Do not let your prophets and
your diviners who are in your midst
deceive you, nor listen to your dreams
which you cause to be dreamed.
9 For they prophesy [R]falsely to you in My
name; I have not sent them, says the
LORD. Jer. 28:15; 37:19
10 For thus says the LORD: After [R]seventy
years are completed at Babylon, I will
visit you and perform My good word
toward you, and cause you to [R]return to
this place. Dan. 9:2 • [Jer. 24:6, 7]
11 For I know the thoughts that I think
toward you, says the LORD, thoughts of
peace and not of evil, to give you a
future and a hope.
12 Then you will call upon Me and go and
pray to Me, and I will listen to you.

13 And [R]you will seek Me and find *Me*,
when you search for Me [R]with all your
heart. Deut. 30:1–3 • Jer. 24:7
14 I will be found by you, says the LORD,
and I will bring you back from your
captivity; I will gather you from all the
nations and from all the places where I
have driven you, says the LORD, and I
will bring you to the place from which I
cause you to be carried away captive.
15 Because you have said, "The LORD has
raised up prophets for us in Babylon"—
16 therefore thus says the LORD concerning
the king who sits on the throne of David,
concerning all the people who dwell in
this city, and concerning your brethren
who have not gone out with you into
captivity—
17 thus says the LORD of hosts: Behold, I
will send on them the sword, the famine,
and the pestilence, and will make them
like rotten figs that cannot be eaten, they
are so bad.
18 And I will pursue them with the sword,
with famine, and with pestilence; and I
[R]will deliver them to trouble among all
the kingdoms of the earth—to be [R]a
curse, an astonishment, a hissing, and a
reproach among all the nations where I
have driven them, Deut. 28:25 • Jer. 26:6
19 because they have not heeded My words,
says the LORD, which I sent to them by
My servants the prophets, rising up early
and sending *them;* neither would you
heed, says the LORD.
20 Therefore hear the word of the LORD, all
you of the captivity, whom I have sent
from Jerusalem to Babylon.
21 Thus says the LORD of hosts, the God of
Israel, concerning Ahab the son of
Kolaiah, and Zedekiah the son of
Maaseiah, who prophesy a [R]lie to you in
My name: Behold, I will deliver them
into the hand of Nebuchadnezzar king
of Babylon, and he shall slay them
before your eyes. Lam. 2:14
22 [R]And because of them a curse shall be
taken up by all the captivity of Judah
who *are* in Babylon, saying, "The LORD
make you like Zedekiah and Ahab,
[R]whom the king of Babylon roasted in
the fire"; Is. 65:15 • Dan. 3:6, 21
23 because [R]they have done disgraceful
things in Israel, have committed
adultery with their neighbors' wives,
and have spoken lying words in My
name, which I have not commanded
them. Indeed I know, and *am* a witness,
says the LORD. Jer. 23:14

Letter for Shemaiah

24 You shall also speak to Shemaiah the
Nehelamite, saying,
25 Thus speaks the LORD of hosts, the God
of Israel, saying: You have sent letters in
your name to all the people who *are* at
Jerusalem, [R]to Zephaniah the son of
Maaseiah the priest, and to all the
priests, saying, Jer. 21:1
26 "The LORD has made you priest instead
of Jehoiada the priest, so that there
should be [R]officers *in* the house of the
LORD over every man *who* is [R]demented
and considers himself a prophet, that
you should put him in prison and in the
stocks. Jer. 20:1 • John 10:20
27 Now therefore, why have you not
rebuked Jeremiah of Anathoth who
makes himself a prophet to you?
28 For he has sent to us *in* Babylon, saying,
'This *captivity is* long; build houses and
dwell *in them,* and plant gardens and eat
their fruit.' "
29 Now Zephaniah the priest read this
letter in the hearing of Jeremiah the
prophet.

Second Letter to the Exiles

30 Then the word of the LORD came to
Jeremiah, saying:
31 Send to all those in captivity, saying,
Thus says the LORD concerning
Shemaiah the Nehelamite: Because
Shemaiah has prophesied to you, [R]and I
have not sent him, and he has caused
you to trust in a lie— Jer. 28:15
32 therefore thus says the LORD: Behold, I
will punish Shemaiah the Nehelamite
and his family: he shall not have anyone
to dwell among this people, nor shall he
see the good that I will do for My people,
says the LORD, because he has taught
rebellion against the LORD.

CHAPTER 30

Restoration to the Land

THE word that came to Jeremiah from the
LORD, saying,
2 "Thus speaks the LORD God of Israel, say-
ing: 'Write in a book for yourself all the words
that I have spoken to you.
3 'For behold, the days are coming,' says
the LORD, 'that [R]I will bring back from captiv-
ity My people Israel and Judah,' says the
LORD. [R]'And I will cause them to return to the
land that I gave to their fathers, and they shall
possess it.' " Ezek. 39:25 • Jer. 16:15
4 Now these *are* the words that the LORD
spoke concerning Israel and Judah.
5 "For thus says the LORD:

'We have heard a voice of trembling,
Of [T]fear, and not of peace. *dread*
6 Ask now, and see,

Whether a [T]man is ever in [T]labor with
child? Lit. *male can give birth* • *childbirth*
So why do I see every man *with* his
hands on his loins
[R]Like a woman in labor, Jer. 4:31; 6:24
And all faces turned pale?
7 [R]Alas! For that day *is* great, Amos 5:18
[R]So that none *is* like it; Dan. 9:12; 12:1
And it *is* the time of Jacob's trouble,
But he shall be saved out of it.

8 'For it shall come to pass in that day,'
Says the LORD of hosts,
'*That* I will break his yoke from your neck,
And will burst your bonds;
Foreigners shall no more enslave them.
9 But they shall serve the LORD their God,
And [R]David their king, Hos. 3:5
Whom I will [R]raise up for them. [Luke 1:69]☆
10 'Therefore [R]do not fear, O My servant
Jacob,' says the LORD, Is. 41:13; 43:5
'Nor be dismayed, O Israel;
For behold, I will save you from afar,
And your seed [R]from the land of their
captivity. Jer. 3:18
Jacob shall return, have rest and be quiet,
And no one shall make *him* afraid.
11 For I *am* with [R]you,' says the LORD, 'to
save you; [Is. 43:2–5]
[R]Though I make a full end of all nations
where I have scattered you, Amos 9:8
[R]Yet I will not make a complete end of
you. Jer. 4:27; 46:27, 28
But I will correct you [R]in justice,
And will not let you go altogether
unpunished.' Ps. 6:1

12 "For thus says the LORD:

[R]'Your affliction *is* incurable, Jer. 15:18
Your wound *is* severe.
13 *There is* no one to plead your cause,
That you may be bound up;
You have no healing medicines.
14 [R]All your lovers have forgotten you;
They do not seek you; Lam. 1:2
For I have wounded you with the wound
[R]of an enemy, Job 13:24; 16:9; 19:11
With the chastisement of a cruel one,
For the multitude of your iniquities,
Because your sins have increased.
15 Why [R]do you cry about your affliction?
Your sorrow *is* incurable. Jer. 15:18
Because of the multitude of your iniquities,
Because your sins have increased,
I have done these things to you.

16 'Therefore all those who devour you
[R]shall be devoured; Jer. 10:25
And all your adversaries, every one of
them, shall go into [R]captivity;
Those who plunder you shall become
[R]plunder, Is. 14:2 • Ezek. 39:10
And all who prey upon you I will make a
[R]prey. Jer. 2:3
17 [R]For I will restore health to you
And heal you of your wounds,' says the
LORD, Jer. 33:6
'Because they called you an outcast
saying:
"This *is* Zion;
No one seeks her." '

18 "Thus says the LORD:

'Behold, I will bring back the captivity of
Jacob's tents,
And [R]have mercy on his dwelling places;
The city shall be built upon its own
[T]mound, Ps. 102:13 • *ruins*
And the palace shall remain according to
its own plan.
19 Then [R]out of them shall proceed
thanksgiving Is. 51:11
And the voice of those who make merry;
[R]I will multiply them, and they shall not
diminish; Zech. 10:8
I will also glorify them, and they shall
not be small.
20 Their children also shall be [R]as before,
And their congregation shall be
established before Me; Is. 1:26
And I will punish all who oppress them.
21 Their nobles shall be from among them,
[R]And their governor shall come from
their midst; Gen. 49:10
Then I will [R]cause him to draw near,
And he shall approach Me; Num. 16:5
For who *is* this who pledged his heart to
approach Me?' says the LORD.
22 'You shall be [R]My people, Ezek. 36:28
And I will be your God.' "

23 Behold, the [R]whirlwind of the LORD
Goes forth with fury, Jer. 23:19, 20; 25:32
A [T]continuing whirlwind; Or *sweeping*
It will fall violently on the head of the
wicked.
24 The fierce anger of the LORD will not
return until He has done it,
And until He has performed the intents
of His heart.

In the latter days you will consider it.

CHAPTER 31

Israel Is Restored

"AT the same time," says the LORD, "I will
be the God of all the families of Israel,
and they shall be My people."
2 Thus says the LORD:

"The people who survived the sword
Found grace in the wilderness—
Israel, when I went to give him rest."

3 The LORD has appeared [T]of old to me,
saying: Lit. *from afar*
"Yes, [R]I have loved you with [R]an
everlasting love; Mal. 1:2 • Rom. 11:28
Therefore with lovingkindness I have
[R]drawn you. Hos. 11:4
4 Again [R]I will build you, and you shall be
rebuilt, Jer. 33:7
O virgin of Israel!
You shall again be adorned with your
[R]tambourines, Judg. 11:34
And shall go forth in the dances of those
who rejoice.
5 [R]You shall yet plant vines on the
mountains of Samaria; Amos 9:14
The planters shall plant and eat *them* as
ordinary food.
6 For there shall be a day
When the watchmen will cry on Mount
Ephraim,
[R]'Arise, and let us go up *to* Zion,
To the LORD our God.'" [Mic. 4:2]

7 For thus says the LORD:

[R]"Sing with gladness for Jacob,
And shout among the chief of the
nations; Is. 12:5, 6
Proclaim, give praise, and say,
'O LORD, save Your people,
The remnant of Israel!'
8 Behold, I will bring them [R]from the north
country, Jer. 3:12, 18; 23:8
And [R]gather them from the ends of the
earth, Ezek. 20:34, 41; 34:13
Among them the blind and the lame,
The woman with child
And the one who labors with child,
together;
A great throng shall return there.
9 They shall come with weeping,
And with supplications I will lead them.
I will cause them to walk [R]by the rivers
of waters, Is. 35:8; 43:19; 49:10, 11
In a straight way in which they shall not
stumble;
For I am a Father to Israel,
And Ephraim *is* My [R]firstborn. Ex. 4:22

10 "Hear the word of the LORD, O nations,
And declare *it* in the [T]isles afar off, and
say, Or *coastlands*
'He who scattered Israel [R]will gather him,
And keep him as a shepherd *does* his
flock.' Is. 40:11
11 For the LORD has redeemed Jacob,
And ransomed him [R]from the hand of
one stronger than he. Is. 49:24
12 Therefore they shall come and sing in
[R]the height of Zion, Ezek. 17:23
Streaming to [R]the goodness of the
LORD— Hos. 3:5
For wheat and new wine and oil,
For the young of the flock and the herd;
Their souls shall be like a [R]well-watered
garden, Is. 58:11
And they shall sorrow no more at all.

13 "Then shall the virgin rejoice in the
dance,
And the young men and the old,
together;
For I will turn their mourning to joy,
Will comfort them,
And make them rejoice rather than
sorrow.
14 I will [T]satiate the soul of the priests with
abundance, Fill to the full
And My people shall be satisfied with
My goodness, says the LORD."

15 Thus says the LORD:

[R]"A voice was heard in [R]Ramah,
Lamentation *and* bitter weeping,
Rachel weeping for her children,
Refusing to be comforted for her
children, Matt. 2:17, 18☆ • Josh. 18:25
Because [R]they *are* no more." Jer. 10:20

16 Thus says the LORD:

"Refrain your voice from [R]weeping,
And your eyes from tears;
For your work shall be rewarded, says
the LORD, [Is. 25:8; 30:19]
And they shall come back from the land
of the enemy.
17 There is [R]hope in your future, says the
LORD, Jer. 29:11
That *your* children shall come back to
their own border.

18 "I have surely heard Ephraim bemoaning
himself:
'You have [R]chastised me, and I was
chastised, Ps. 94:12
Like an untrained bull;
Restore me, and I will return,
For You *are* the LORD my God.
19 Surely, [R]after my turning, I repented;
And after I was instructed, I struck
myself on the thigh; Deut. 30:2
I was [R]ashamed, yes, even humiliated,
Because I bore the reproach of my
youth.' Ezek. 36:31
20 *Is* Ephraim My dear son?
Is he a pleasant child?
For though I spoke against him,
I earnestly remember him still;
[R]Therefore My heart yearns for him;
[R]I will surely have mercy on him, says the
LORD. Is. 63:15 • [Hos. 14:4]

21 "Set up signposts,
Make landmarks;

[R]Set your heart toward the highway,
The way in *which* you went. Jer. 50:5
[T]Turn back, O virgin of Israel, Or *Return*
Turn back to these your cities.

Judah Is Restored

22 How long will you gad about,
O you [R]backsliding daughter?
For the LORD has created a new thing in
the earth— Jer. 3:6, 8, 11, 12, 14, 22
A woman shall encompass a man."

23 Thus says the LORD of hosts, the God of
Israel: "They shall again use this speech in
the land of Judah and in its cities, when I
bring back their captivity: [R]'The LORD bless
you, O home of justice, *and* [R]mountain of ho-
liness!' Is. 1:26 • [Zech. 8:3]
24 "And there shall dwell in Judah itself, and
[R]in all its cities together, farmers and those
going out with flocks. Jer. 33:12
25 "For I have satiated the weary soul, and I
have replenished every sorrowful soul."
26 After this I awoke and looked around,
and my sleep was [R]sweet to me. Prov. 3:24
27 "Behold, the days are coming, says the
LORD, that [R]I will sow the house of Israel and
the house of Judah with the seed of man and
the seed of beast. Ezek. 36:9–11
28 "And it shall come to pass, *that* as I have
[R]watched over them to pluck up, to break
down, to throw down, to destroy, and to afflict,
so I will watch over them to build and to plant,
says the LORD. Jer. 44:27
29 [R]"In those days they shall say no more:

'The fathers have eaten sour grapes,
And the children's teeth are set on
edge.' Ezek. 18:2, 3

30 [R]"But every one shall die for his own iniq-
uity; every man who eats the sour grapes, his
teeth shall be set on edge. [Gal. 6:5, 7]
31 "Behold, the [R]days are coming, says the
LORD, when I will make a [R]new covenant with
the house of Israel and with the house of Ju-
dah— Heb. 8:8–12; 10:16, 17 • [Luke 22:20]☆
32 "not according to the covenant that I
made with their fathers in the day *that* [R]I took
them by the hand to lead them out of the land
of Egypt, My covenant which they broke,
though I was a husband to them,* says the
LORD. Deut. 1:31
33 [R]"But this *is* the covenant that I will
make with the house of Israel after those
days, says the LORD: [R]I will put My law in
their minds, and write it on their hearts;
[R]and I will be their God, and they shall be
My people. Jer. 32:40 • Ps. 40:8 • Heb. 10:15–17☆
34 "No more shall every man teach his
neighbor, and every man his brother, saying,
'Know the LORD,' for [R]they all shall know Me,
from the least of them to the greatest of
them, says the LORD. For [R]I will forgive their
iniquity, and their sin I will remember no
more." [John 6:45] • [Rom. 11:27]☆

35 Thus says the LORD,
[R]Who gives the sun for a light by day,
The ordinances of the moon and the
stars for a light by night, Gen. 1:14–18
Who disturbs [R]the sea, Is. 51:15
And its waves roar
(The LORD of hosts *is* His name):

36 "If [R]those ordinances depart Ps. 148:6
From before Me, says the LORD,
Then the seed of Israel shall also cease
From being a nation before Me forever."

37 Thus says the LORD:

[R]"If heaven above can be measured,
And the foundations of the earth
searched out beneath, Jer. 33:22
I will also [R]cast off all the seed of Israel
For all that they have done, says the
LORD. [Rom. 11:2–5, 26, 27]

38 "Behold, the days are coming, says the
LORD, that the city shall be built for the LORD
[R]from the Tower of Hananel to the Corner
Gate. Zech. 14:10
39 [R]"The surveyor's line shall again extend
straight forward over the hill Gareb; then it
shall turn toward Goath. Zech. 2:1, 2
40 "And the whole valley of the dead bodies
and of the ashes, and all the fields as far as the

31:32 So with MT, Tg., Vg.; LXX, Syr. *and I turned away from them*

31:31–34 The New Covenant—The New Covenant is the fifth and last of the theocratic covenants (pertaining to the rule of God). Four provisions are made in this covenant: (1) regeneration—God will put His law in their inward parts and write it in their hearts, 31:33; (2) a national restoration—Yahweh will be their God and the nation will be His people, 31:33; (3) personal ministry of the Holy Spirit—they will all be taught individually by God, 31:34; and (4) full justification—their sins will be forgiven and completely removed, 31:34. The New Covenant is made sure by the blood that Jesus shed on Calvary's cross. That blood which guarantees to Israel its New Covenant also provides for the forgiveness of sins for the believers who comprise the church. Jesus' payment for sins is more than adequate to pay for the sins of all who will believe in Him. The New Covenant is called "new" in contrast to the covenant with Moses which is called "old" (Jer. 31:32; Page 1263—Heb. 8:6–13) because it actually accomplishes what the Mosaic covenant could only point to, that is, the child of God living in a manner that is consistent with the character of God.

Now turn to Page 25—THE CHRISTIAN'S GUIDE: Understanding God's Being.

Brook Kidron, [R]to the corner of the Horse
Gate toward the east, [R]*shall be* holy to the
LORD. It shall not be plucked up or thrown
down anymore forever." Neh. 3:28 • [Joel 3:17]

CHAPTER 32

Rebuilding of Jerusalem

THE word that came to Jeremiah from the
LORD [R]in the tenth year of Zedekiah king
of Judah, which was the eighteenth year of
Nebuchadnezzar. Jer. 39:1, 2
2 For then the king of Babylon's army be-
sieged Jerusalem, and Jeremiah the prophet
was shut up in the court of the prison, which
was in the king of Judah's house.
3 For Zedekiah king of Judah had shut him
up, saying, "Why do you [R]prophesy and say,
'Thus says the LORD: "Behold, I will give this
city into the hand of the king of Babylon, and
he shall take it; Jer. 26:8, 9
4 "and Zedekiah king of Judah shall not es-
cape from the hand of the Chaldeans, but
shall surely be delivered into the hand of the
king of Babylon, and shall speak with him
face to face,* and see him eye to eye;
5 "then he shall lead Zedekiah to Babylon,
and there he shall be until I visit him," says
the LORD; "though you fight with the Chal-
deans, you shall not succeed" '?"
6 And Jeremiah said, "The word of the
LORD came to me, saying,
7 'Behold, Hanamel the son of Shallum
your uncle will come to you, saying, "Buy my
field which *is* in Anathoth, for the [R]right of re-
demption *is* yours to buy *it*." ' Ruth 4:4
8 "Then Hanamel my uncle's son came to
me in the court of the prison according to the
word of the LORD, and said to me, 'Please buy
my field that *is* in Anathoth, which *is* in the
country of Benjamin; for the right of inheri-
tance *is* yours, and the redemption yours; buy
it for yourself.' Then I knew that this was the
word of the LORD.
9 "So I bought the field from Hanamel, the
son of my uncle who *was* in Anathoth, and
[R]weighed *out to* him the money—seventeen
shekels of silver. Zech. 11:12
10 "And I signed the [T]deed and sealed *it*,
took witnesses, and weighed the money on
the scales. Lit. *book*
11 "So I took the purchase deed, *both* that
which was sealed *according* to the law and
custom, and that which was open;
12 "and I gave the purchase deed to Baruch
the son of Neriah, son of Mahseiah, in the
presence of Hanamel my uncle's *son*, and in
the presence of the witnesses who signed the
purchase deed, before all the Jews who sat in
the court of the prison.
13 "Then I charged [R]Baruch before them,
saying, Jer. 36:4
14 'Thus says the LORD of hosts, the God of
Israel: "Take these deeds, both this purchase
deed which is sealed and this deed which is
open, and put them in an earthen vessel, that
they may last many days."
15 'For thus says the LORD of hosts, the
God of Israel: "Houses and fields and vine-
yards shall be [R]possessed again in this
land." ' [Jer. 31:5, 12, 14]
16 "Now when I had delivered the purchase
deed to Baruch the son of Neriah, I prayed to
the LORD, saying:
17 'Ah, Lord GOD! Behold, [R]You have made
the heavens and the earth by Your great power
and outstretched arm. [R]There is nothing too
hard for You. 2 Kin. 19:15 • Luke 18:27
18 '*You* show [R]lovingkindness to thousands,
and repay the iniquity of the fathers into the
bosom of their children after them—the Great,
[R]the Mighty God, whose name *is* the LORD of
hosts. Deut. 5:9, 10 • [Is. 9:6]
19 '*You are* [R]great in counsel and mighty in
[T]work, for your [R]eyes *are* open to all the ways
of the sons of men, [R]to give everyone accord-
ing to his ways and according to the fruit of
his doings. Is. 28:29 • *deed* • Prov. 5:21 • Jer. 17:10
20 'You have set signs and wonders in the
land of Egypt, to this day, and in Israel and
among *other* men; and You have made Your-
self [R]a name, as it is this day. Is. 63:12
21 'You have brought Your people Israel out
of the land of Egypt with signs and wonders,
with a strong hand and an outstretched arm,
and with great terror;
22 'You have given them this land, of which
You swore to their fathers to give them—"a
land flowing with milk and honey."*
23 'And they came in and took possession of
it, but [R]they have not obeyed Your voice or
walked in Your law. They have done nothing
of all that You commanded them to do; there-
fore You have caused all this calamity to come
upon them. [Neh. 9:26]
24 'Look, the siege mounds! They have come
to the city to take it; and the city has been
given into the hand of the Chaldeans who
fight against it, because of the sword and
famine and pestilence. What You have spoken
has happened; there You see *it!*
25 'And You have said to me, O Lord GOD,
"Buy the field for money, and take wit-
nesses"!—yet the city has been given into the
hand of the Chaldeans.' "
26 Then the word of the LORD came to Jere-
miah, saying,
27 "Behold, I *am* the LORD, the God of all
flesh. Is there anything too hard for Me?
28 "Therefore thus says the LORD: 'Behold, I
will give this city into the hand of the
Chaldeans, into the hand of Nebuchadnezzar
king of Babylon, and he shall take it.
29 'And the Chaldeans who fight against this

32:4 Lit. *mouth to mouth* **32:22** Ex. 3:8

city shall come and [R]set fire to this city and
burn it, with the houses [R]on whose roofs they
have offered incense to Baal and poured out
drink offerings to other gods, to provoke Me
to anger; 2 Chr. 36:19 • Jer. 19:13
30 'because the children of Israel and the
children of Judah have done only evil before
Me from their youth. For the children of Israel
have provoked Me only to anger with the
work of their hands,' says the LORD.
31 'For this city has been to Me *a provocation of* My anger and My fury from the day
that they built it, even to this day; [R]so I will remove it from before My face 2 Kin. 23:27
32 'because of all the evil of the children of
Israel and the children of Judah, which they
have done to provoke Me to anger—[R]they,
their kings, their princes, their priests, [R]their
prophets, the men of Judah, and the inhabitants of Jerusalem. Dan. 9:8 • Jer. 23:14
33 'And they have turned to Me the back, and
not the face; though I taught them, rising up
early and teaching *them*, yet they have not listened to receive instruction.
34 'But they [R]set their abominations in [T]the
house which is called by My name, to defile
it. Jer. 7:10–12, 30; 23:11 • The temple
35 'And they built the high places of Baal
which *are* in the Valley of the Son of Hinnom,
to cause their sons and their daughters to
pass through *the fire* to Molech, which I did
not command them, nor did it come into My
mind that they should do this abomination, to
cause Judah to sin.'
36 "Now therefore, thus says the LORD, the
God of Israel, concerning this city of which
you say, 'It shall be delivered into the hand of
the king of Babylon by the sword, by the
famine, and by the pestilence':
37 'Behold, I will [R]gather them out of all
countries where I have driven them in My
anger, in My fury, and in great wrath; I will
bring them back to this place, and I will cause
them to dwell safely. Deut. 30:3
38 'They shall be [R]My people, and I will be
their God; [Jer. 24:7; 30:22; 31:33]
39 'then I will give them one heart and one
way, that they may fear Me forever, for the
good of them and their children after them.
40 'And [R]I will make an everlasting covenant
with them, that I will not turn away from
doing them good; but [R]I will put My fear in
their hearts so that they will not depart from
Me. Is. 55:3 • [Jer. 31:33]
41 'Yes, [R]I will rejoice over them to do them
good, and [R]I will [T]assuredly plant them in
this land, with all My heart and with all My
soul.' Deut. 30:9 • Amos 9:15 • *truly*
42 "For thus says the LORD: [R]'Just as I have
brought all this great calamity on this people,
so I will bring on them all the good that I have
promised them. Jer. 31:28
43 'And fields will be bought in this land [R]of
which you say, "*It is* desolate, without man or
beast; it has been given into the hand of the
Chaldeans." Jer. 33:10
44 'Men will buy fields for money, sign
deeds and seal *them*, and take witnesses, in
[R]the land of Benjamin, in the places around
Jerusalem, in the cities of Judah, in the cities
of the mountains, in the cities of the lowland, and in the cities of the South; for [R]I
will cause their captives to return,' says the
LORD." Jer. 17:26 • Jer. 33:7, 11

CHAPTER 33

Reconfirming the Covenant

MOREOVER the word of the LORD came
to Jeremiah a second time, while he
was still [R]shut up in the court of the prison,
saying, Jer. 32:2, 3
2 "Thus says the LORD [R]who made it, the
LORD who formed it to establish it [R](the[T] LORD
is His name): Is. 37:26 • Ex. 15:3 • Heb. *YHWH*
3 [R]'Call to Me, and I will answer you, and
show you great and [T]mighty things, which
you do not know.' Jer. 29:12 • *inaccessible*
4 "For thus says the LORD, the God of Israel,
concerning the houses of this city and the
houses of the kings of Judah, which have been
pulled down *to fortify** against the siege
mounds and the sword:
5 'They come to fight with the Chaldeans,
but *only* to fill their places* with the dead bodies of men whom I will slay in My anger and
My fury, all for whose wickedness I have hidden My face from this city.
6 'Behold, [R]I will bring it health and healing; I will heal them and reveal to them the
abundance of peace and truth. Jer. 30:17
7 'And I will cause the captives of Judah
and the captives of Israel to return, and will
rebuild those places [R]as at the first. Is. 1:26
8 'I will [R]cleanse them from all their iniquity by which they have sinned against Me,
and I will pardon all their iniquities by which
they have sinned and by which they have
transgressed against Me. Zech. 13:1
9 [R]'Then it shall be to Me a name of joy, a
praise, and an honor before all nations of the
earth, who shall hear all the good that I do to
them; they shall [R]fear and tremble for all the
goodness and all the prosperity that I provide
for it.' Is. 62:7 • Is. 60:5
10 "Thus says the LORD: 'Again there shall be
heard in this place—of which you say, "It *is*
desolate, without man and without beast"—in
the cities of Judah, in the streets of Jerusalem
that are desolate, without man and without
inhabitant and without beast,
11 'the [R]voice of joy and the voice of gladness,
the voice of the bridegroom and the voice of the
bride, the voice of those who will say: Rev. 18:23

33:4 Cf. Is. 22:10 **33:5** Cf. 2 Kin. 23:14

[R]"Praise the LORD of hosts, Is. 12:4
For the LORD *is* good,
For His mercy *endures* forever"—

and of those *who will* bring [R]the sacrifice of
praise into the house of the LORD. For I will
cause the captives of the land to return as at
the first,' says the LORD. Lev. 7:12
12 "Thus says the LORD of hosts: [R]'In this
place which is desolate, without man and
without beast, and in all its cities, there shall
again be a dwelling place of shepherds caus-
ing *their* flocks to lie down. Is. 65:10
13 [R]'In the cities of the mountains, in the
cities of the lowland, in the cities of the
South, in the land of Benjamin, in the places
around Jerusalem, and in the cities of Ju-
dah, the flocks shall again [R]pass under the
hands of him who counts *them*,' says the
LORD. Jer. 17:26; 32:44 • Lev. 27:32
14 'Behold, the days are coming,' says the
LORD, 'that [R]I will perform that good thing
which I have promised to the house of Israel
and to the house of Judah: Jer. 29:10; 32:42

15 'In those days and at that time
I will cause to grow up to David
A [R]Branch of righteousness; Zech. 6:12, 13☆
He shall execute judgment and
righteousness in the earth.
16 In those days [R]Judah will be saved,
And Jerusalem will dwell safely.
And this *is the name* by which she will
be called: Is. 45:17, 22☆

THE LORD OUR RIGHTEOUSNESS.'*

17 "For thus says the LORD: 'David shall
never [R]lack a man to sit on the throne of the
house of Israel; 2 Sam. 7:16
18 'nor shall the [R]priests, the Levites, lack a
man to [R]offer burnt offerings before Me, to
[T]kindle grain offerings, and to sacrifice con-
tinually.'" Ezek. 44:15 • [1 Pet. 2:5, 9] • *burn*
19 And the word of the LORD came to Jere-
miah, saying,
20 "Thus says the LORD: 'If you can break My
covenant with the day and My covenant with
the night, so that there will not be day and
night in their season,
21 'then My covenant may also be broken
with David My servant, so that he shall not
have a son to reign on his throne, and with the
Levites, the priests, My ministers.
22 'As [R]the host of heaven cannot be num-
bered, nor the sand of the sea measured, so
will I [R]multiply the descendants of David My
servant and the [R]Levites who minister to
Me.'" Gen. 15:5; 22:17 • Jer. 30:19 • Is. 66:21
23 Moreover the word of the LORD came to
Jeremiah, saying,
24 "Have you not considered what these peo-
ple have spoken, saying, 'The two families
which the LORD has chosen, He has also cast
them off'? Thus they have [R]despised My peo-
ple, as if they should no more be a nation be-
fore them. Esth. 3:6–8
25 "Thus says the LORD: 'If [R]My covenant
is not with day and night, *and if* I have not
[R]appointed the ordinances of heaven and
earth, Gen. 8:22 • Ps. 74:16; 104:19
26 'then I will cast away the descendants of
Jacob and David My servant, *so* that I will not
take *any* of his descendants *to be* rulers over
the descendants of Abraham, Isaac, and Ja-
cob. For I will cause their captives to return,
and will have mercy on them.'"

CHAPTER 34

Message to Zedekiah

THE word which came to Jeremiah from
the LORD, [R]when Nebuchadnezzar king of
Babylon and all his army, [R]all the kingdoms of
the earth under his dominion, and all the peo-
ple, fought against Jerusalem and all its cities,
saying, 2 Kin. 25:1 • Jer. 1:15; 25:9
2 "Thus says the LORD, the God of Israel:
'Go and speak to Zedekiah king of Judah and
tell him, "Thus says the LORD: 'Behold, I will
give this city into the hand of the king of
Babylon, and he shall burn it with fire.
3 'And [R]you shall not escape from his hand,
but shall surely be taken and delivered into
his hand; your eyes shall see the eyes of the
king of Babylon, he shall speak with you
[R]face to face,* and you shall go to Bab-
ylon.'"' 2 Kin. 25:4, 5 • Jer. 32:4; 39:5, 6
4 "Yet hear the word of the LORD, O
Zedekiah king of Judah! Thus says the LORD
concerning you: 'You shall not die by the
sword.
5 'You shall die in peace; as in [R]the cere-
monies of your fathers, the former kings who
were before you, [R]so they shall burn incense
for you and lament for you, *saying*, "Alas,
lord!" For I have pronounced the word, says
the LORD.'" 2 Chr. 16:14; 21:19 • Dan. 2:46
6 Then Jeremiah the prophet spoke all
these words to Zedekiah king of Judah in Je-
rusalem,
7 when the king of Babylon's army fought
against Jerusalem and all the cities of Judah
that were left, against Lachish and Azekah;
for *only* [R]these fortified cities remained of the
cities of Judah. 2 Kin. 18:13

Message to the People

8 *This is* the word that came to Jeremiah
from the LORD, after King Zedekiah had made
a covenant with all the people who *were* at Je-
rusalem to proclaim [R]liberty to them: Ex. 21:2
9 [R]that every man should set free his male

33:16 Heb. *YHWH Tsidkenu;* cf. Jer. 23:5, 6 **34:3** Lit. *mouth to mouth*

and female slave—a Hebrew man or
woman—[R]that no one should keep a Jewish
brother in bondage. Neh. 5:11 • Lev. 25:39–46
10 Now when all the princes and all the peo-
ple, who had entered into the covenant, heard
that everyone should set free his male and fe-
male slaves, that no one should keep them in
bondage anymore, they obeyed and let *them*
go.
11 But afterward they changed their minds
and made the male and female slaves return,
whom they had set free, and brought them
into subjection as male and female slaves.
12 Therefore the word of the LORD came to
Jeremiah from the LORD, saying,
13 "Thus says the LORD, the God of Israel: 'I
made a covenant with your fathers in the day
that I brought them out of the land of Egypt,
out of the house of bondage, saying,
14 "At the end of [R]seven years let every man
set free his Hebrew brother, who [T]has been
sold to him; and when he has served you six
years, you shall let him go free from you." But
your fathers did not obey Me nor incline their
ear. Deut. 15:12 • Or *sold himself*
15 'Then you recently turned and did what
was right in My sight—every man proclaim-
ing liberty to his neighbor; and you [R]made a
covenant before Me [R]in the house which is
called by My name. Neh. 10:29 • Jer. 7:10
16 'Then you turned around and [R]profaned
My name, and every one of you brought back
his male and female slaves, whom he had set
at liberty, at their pleasure, and brought them
back into subjection, to be your male and fe-
male slaves.' Ex. 20:7
17 "Therefore thus says the LORD: 'You have
not obeyed Me in proclaiming liberty, every
one to his brother and every one to his
neighbor. [R]Behold, I proclaim liberty to you,'
says the LORD—[R]'to the sword, to pestilence,
and to famine! And I will deliver you to
[R]trouble among all the kingdoms of the
earth. [Matt. 7:2] • Jer. 32:24, 36 • Deut. 28:25, 64
18 'And I will give the men who have trans-
gressed My covenant, who have not per-
formed the words of the covenant which they
made before Me, when they cut the calf in two
and passed between the parts of it—
19 'the princes of Judah, the princes of Jeru-
salem, the [T]eunuchs, the priests, and all the
people of the land who passed between the
parts of the calf— Or *officers*
20 'I will [R]give them into the hand of their
enemies and into the hand of those who seek
their life. Their [R]dead bodies shall be for meat
for the birds of the heaven and the beasts of
the earth. Jer. 22:25 • Jer. 7:33; 16:4
21 'And I will give Zedekiah king of Judah
and his princes into the hand of their enemies,
into the hand of those who seek their life, and
into the hand of the king of Babylon's army
which has gone back from you.
22 'Behold, I will command,' says the LORD,
'and cause them to return to this city. They
will fight against it and take it and burn it
with fire; and I will make the cities of Judah a
desolation without inhabitant.' "

CHAPTER 35

Message to the Rechabites

THE word which came to Jeremiah from
the LORD in the days of Jehoiakim the son
of Josiah, king of Judah, saying,
2 "Go to the house of the Rechabites, speak
to them, and bring them into the house of the
LORD, into one of the chambers, and give them
wine to drink."
3 Then I took Jaazaniah the son of Jere-
miah, the son of Habazziniah, his brothers
and all his sons, and the whole house of the
Rechabites,
4 and I brought them into the house of the
LORD, into the chamber of the sons of Hanan
the son of Igdaliah, a man of God, which *was*
by the chamber of the princes, above the
chamber of Maaseiah the son of Shallum, the
keeper of the door.
5 Then I set before the sons of the house of
the Rechabites bowls full of wine, and cups;
and I said to them, "Drink wine."
6 But they said, "We will drink no wine, for
Jonadab the son of Rechab, our father, com-
manded us, saying, 'You shall drink [R]no wine,
you nor your sons, forever. Luke 1:15
7 'You shall not build a house, sow seed,
plant a vineyard, nor have *any of these;* but all
your days you shall dwell in tents, [R]that you
may live many days in the land where you are
sojourners.' Ex. 20:12
8 "Thus we have [R]obeyed the voice of Jon-
adab the son of Rechab, our father, in all
that he charged us, to drink no wine all our
days, we, our wives, our sons, or our daugh-
ters, [Col. 3:20]
9 "nor to build ourselves houses to dwell in;
nor do we have vineyard, field, or seed.
10 "But we have dwelt in tents, and have
obeyed and done according to all that Jon-
adab our father commanded us.
11 "But it came to pass, when Nebuchadnez-
zar king of Babylon came up into the land,
that we said, 'Come, let us [R]go to Jerusalem
for fear of the army of the Chaldeans and for
fear of the army of the Syrians.' So we dwell
at Jerusalem." Jer. 4:5–7; 8:14
12 Then came the word of the LORD to Jere-
miah, saying,
13 "Thus says the LORD of hosts, the God of
Israel: 'Go and tell the men of Judah and the
inhabitants of Jerusalem, "Will you not [R]re-
ceive instruction to [T]obey My words?" says
the LORD. Jer. 6:10; 17:23; 32:33 • *listen to*
14 "The words of Jonadab the son of Rechab,
which he commanded his sons, not to drink

wine, are performed; for to this day they drink none, and obey their father's commandment. [R]But although I have spoken to you, [R]rising early and speaking, you did not obey Me. 2 Chr. 36:15 • Jer. 7:13; 25:3

15 "I have also sent to you all My [R]servants the prophets, rising up early and sending *them*, saying, 'Turn now everyone from his evil way, amend your doings, and do not go after other gods to serve them; then you will dwell in the land which I have given you and your fathers.' But you have not inclined your ear, nor obeyed Me. Jer. 26:4, 5; 29:19

16 "Surely the sons of Jonadab the son of Rechab have performed the commandment of their father, which he commanded them, but this people has not obeyed Me." '

17 "Therefore thus says the LORD God of hosts, the God of Israel: 'Behold, I will bring on Judah and on all the inhabitants of Jerusalem all the doom that I have pronounced against them; [R]because I have spoken to them but they have not heard, and I have called to them but they have not answered.' " Prov. 1:24

18 And Jeremiah said to the house of the Rechabites, "Thus says the LORD of hosts, the God of Israel: 'Because you have obeyed the commandment of Jonadab your father, and kept all his precepts and done according to all that he commanded you,

19 'therefore thus says the LORD of hosts, the God of Israel: "Jonadab the son of Rechab shall not lack a man to [R]stand before Me forever." ' " Jer. 15:19

CHAPTER 36

Message of the Scroll

NOW it came to pass in the [R]fourth year of Jehoiakim the son of Josiah, king of Judah, *that* this word came to Jeremiah from the LORD, saying: Jer. 25:1, 3; 45:1

2 "Take a scroll of a book and write on it all the words that I have spoken to you against Israel, against Judah, and against all the nations, from the day I spoke to you, from the days of Josiah even to this day.

3 "It [R]may be that the house of Judah will hear all the adversities which I purpose to bring upon them, that everyone may [R]turn from his evil way, that I may forgive their iniquity and their sin." Jer. 26:3 • Jon. 3:8

4 Then Jeremiah [R]called Baruch the son of Neriah; and [R]Baruch wrote on a scroll of a book, at the instruction of Jeremiah,* all the words of the LORD which He had spoken to him. Jer. 32:12 • Jer. 45:1

5 And Jeremiah commanded Baruch, saying, "I *am* confined, I cannot go into the house of the LORD.

6 "You go, therefore, and read from the scroll which you have written at my instruction,* the words of the LORD, in the hearing of the people in the LORD's house on [R]the day of fasting. And you shall also read them in the hearing of all Judah who come from their cities. Acts 27:9

7 "It may be that they will present their supplication before the LORD, and everyone will turn from his evil way. For great *is* the anger and the fury that the LORD has pronounced against this people."

8 And Baruch the son of Neriah did according to all that Jeremiah the prophet commanded him, reading from the book the words of the LORD in the LORD's house.

9 Now it came to pass in the fifth year of Jehoiakim the son of Josiah, king of Judah, in the ninth month, *that* they proclaimed a fast before the LORD to all the people in Jerusalem, and to all the people who came from the cities of Judah to Jerusalem.

10 Then Baruch read from the book the words of Jeremiah in the house of the LORD, in the chamber of Gemariah the son of Shaphan the scribe, in the upper court at the entry of the New Gate of the LORD's house, in the hearing of all the people.

11 When Michaiah the son of Gemariah, the son of Shaphan, heard all the words of the LORD from the book,

12 he then went down to the king's house, into the scribe's chamber; and there all the princes were sitting—[R]Elishama the scribe, Delaiah the son of Shemaiah, [R]Elnathan the son of Achbor, Gemariah the son of Shaphan, Zedekiah the son of Hananiah, and all the princes. Jer. 41:1 • Jer. 26:22

13 Then Michaiah declared to them all the words that he had heard when Baruch read the book in the hearing of the people.

14 Therefore all the princes sent Jehudi the son of Nethaniah, the son of Shelemiah, the son of Cushi, to Baruch, saying, "Take in your hand the scroll from which you have read in the hearing of the people, and come." So Baruch the son of Neriah took the scroll in his hand and came to them.

15 And they said to him, "Sit down now, and read it in our hearing." So Baruch read *it* in their hearing.

16 Now it happened, when they had heard all the words, that they looked in fear from one to another, and said to Baruch, "We will surely tell the king of all these words."

17 And they asked Baruch, saying, "Tell us now, how did you write all these words—at his instruction?"*

18 So Baruch answered them, "He proclaimed with his mouth all these words to me, and I wrote *them* with ink in the book."

36:4 Lit. *from Jeremiah's mouth* **36:6** Lit. *from my mouth* **36:17** Lit. *with his mouth*

19 Then the princes said to Baruch, "Go and
hide, you and Jeremiah; and let no one know
where you are."
20 And they went to the king, into the court;
but they stored the scroll in the chamber of
Elishama the scribe, and told all the words in
the hearing of the king.
21 So the king sent Jehudi to bring the scroll,
and he took it from Elishama the scribe's
chamber. And Jehudi read it in the hearing of
the king and in the hearing of all the princes
who stood beside the king.
22 Now the king was sitting in [R]the winter
house in the ninth month, with *a fire* burning
on the hearth before him. Amos 3:15
23 And it happened, when Jehudi had read
three or four columns, *that the king* cut it
with the scribe's knife and cast *it* into the fire
that *was* on the hearth, until all the scroll was
consumed in the fire that *was* on the hearth.
24 Yet they were not afraid, nor did they tear
their garments, the king nor any of his ser-
vants who heard all these words.
25 Nevertheless Elnathan, Delaiah, and
Gemariah implored the king not to burn the
scroll; but he would not listen to them.
26 And the king commanded Jerahmeel the
king's* son, Seraiah the son of Azriel, and
Shelemiah the son of Abdeel, to seize Baruch
the scribe and Jeremiah the prophet, but the
LORD hid them.
27 Now after the king had burned the scroll
with the words which Baruch had written at
the instruction of Jeremiah,* the word of the
LORD came to Jeremiah, saying:
28 "Take yet another scroll, and write on it
all the former words that were in the first
scroll which Jehoiakim the king of Judah has
burned.
29 "And you shall say to Jehoiakim king of
Judah, 'Thus says the LORD: "You have burned
this scroll, saying, 'Why have you written in it
that the king of Babylon will certainly come
and destroy this land, and cause man and
beast to cease from here?' "
30 'Therefore thus says the LORD concerning
Jehoiakim king of Judah: "He shall have no
one to sit on the throne of David, and his dead
body shall be cast out to the heat of the day
and the frost of the night.
31 "I will punish him, his [T]family, and his
servants for their iniquity; and I will bring on
them, on the inhabitants of Jerusalem, and on
the men of Judah all the doom that I have pro-
nounced against them; but they did not
heed." ' " Lit. *seed*
32 Then Jeremiah took another scroll and
gave it to Baruch the scribe, the son of Neriah,
who wrote on it at the instruction of Jere-
miah* all the words of the book which Je-
hoiakim king of Judah had burned in the fire.
And besides, there were added to them many
similar words.

CHAPTER 37

First Interview with Zedekiah
2 Kin. 24:17; 2 Chr. 36:10

NOW King Zedekiah the son of Josiah
reigned instead of Coniah the son of Je-
hoiakim, whom Nebuchadnezzar king of
Babylon made king in the land of Judah.
2 [R]But neither he nor his servants nor the
people of the land gave heed to the words of
the LORD which He spoke by the prophet
Jeremiah. 2 Chr. 36:12–16
3 And Zedekiah the king sent Jehucal the
son of Shelemiah, and [R]Zephaniah the son of
Maaseiah, the priest, to the prophet Jeremiah,
saying, [R]"Pray now to the LORD our God for
us." Jer. 21:1, 2; 29:25; 52:24 • Jer. 42:2
4 Now Jeremiah was coming and going
among the people, for they had not *yet* put
him in prison.
5 Then [R]Pharaoh's army came up from
Egypt; and when the Chaldeans who were be-
sieging Jerusalem heard news of them, they
departed from Jerusalem. Ezek. 17:15
6 Then the word of the LORD came to the
prophet Jeremiah, saying,
7 "Thus says the LORD, the God of Israel,
'Thus you shall say to the king of Judah,
[R]who sent you to Me to inquire of Me: "Be-
hold, Pharaoh's army which has come up to
help you will return to Egypt, to their own
land. Jer. 21:2
8 [R]"And the Chaldeans shall come back and
fight against this city, and take it and burn it
with fire." ' Jer. 34:22
9 "Thus says the LORD: 'Do not deceive
yourselves, saying, "The Chaldeans will
surely depart from us," for they will not de-
part.
10 'For though you had defeated the whole
army of the Chaldeans who fight against you,
and there remained *only* wounded men
among them, they would rise up, every man in
his tent, and burn the city with fire.' "

Jeremiah Is Imprisoned in a Dungeon

11 And it happened, when the army of the
Chaldeans left *the siege* of Jerusalem for fear
of Pharaoh's army,
12 that Jeremiah went out of Jerusalem to go
into the land of Benjamin to claim his prop-
erty there among the people.
13 And when he was in the Gate of Benja-
min, a captain of the guard *was* there whose
name *was* Irijah the son of Shelemiah, the son
of Hananiah; and he seized Jeremiah the
prophet, saying, "You are defecting to the
Chaldeans!"
14 Then Jeremiah said, [T][R]"False! I am not de-
fecting to the Chaldeans." But he did not

36:26 Or *son of Hammelech* **36:27** Lit. *from Jeremiah's mouth* **36:32** Lit. *from Jeremiah's mouth*

listen to him. So Irijah seized Jeremiah and brought him to the princes. *a lie*

15 Therefore the princes were angry with Jeremiah, and they struck him and put him in prison in the house of Jonathan the scribe. For they had made that the prison.

16 When Jeremiah entered [R]the dungeon and the cells, and Jeremiah had remained there many days, Jer. 38:6

Second Interview of Zedekiah

17 then Zedekiah the king sent and took him *out*. The king asked him secretly in his house, and said, "Is there *any* word from the LORD?" And Jeremiah said, "There is." Then he said, "You shall be [R]delivered into the hand of the king of Babylon!" Jer. 21:7

18 Moreover Jeremiah said to King Zedekiah, "What offense have I committed against you, against your servants, or against this people, that you have put me in prison?

19 "Where now *are* your prophets who prophesied to you, saying, 'The king of Babylon will not come against you or against this land'?

20 "Therefore please hear now, O my lord the king. Please, let my petition be accepted before you, and do not make me return to the house of Jonathan the scribe, lest I die there."

21 Then Zedekiah the king commanded that they should commit Jeremiah [R]to the court of the prison, and that they should give him daily a piece of bread from the bakers' street, [R]until all the bread in the city was gone. Thus Jeremiah remained in the court of the prison. Jer. 32:2; 38:13, 28 • Jer. 38:9; 52:6

CHAPTER 38

Jeremiah Is Imprisoned in a Cistern

NOW Shephatiah the son of Mattan, Gedaliah the son of Pashhur, Jucal* the son of Shelemiah, and Pashhur the son of Malchiah heard the words that Jeremiah had spoken to all the people, saying,

2 "Thus says the LORD: 'He who remains in this city shall die by the sword, by famine, and by pestilence; but he who goes over to the Chaldeans shall live; his life shall be as a prize to him, and he shall live.'*

3 "Thus says the LORD: 'This city shall surely be given into the hand of the king of Babylon's army, which shall take it.' "

4 Therefore the princes said to the king, "Please, let this man be put to death, for thus he weakens the hands of the men of war who remain in this city, and the hands of all the people, by speaking such words to them. For this man does not seek the welfare of this people, but their harm."

5 Then Zedekiah the king said, "Look, he *is* in your hand. For the king can *do* nothing against you."

6 So they took Jeremiah and cast him into the dungeon of Malchiah the king's* son, which *was* in the court of the prison, and they let Jeremiah down with ropes. And in the dungeon *there was* no water, but mire. So Jeremiah sank in the mire.

7 [R]Now Ebed-Melech the Ethiopian, one of the [T]eunuchs, who was in the king's house, heard that they had put Jeremiah in the dungeon. When the king was sitting at the Gate of Benjamin, Jer. 39:16 • Or *officers*

8 Ebed-Melech went out of the king's house and spoke to the king, saying:

9 "My lord the king, these men have done evil in all that they have done to Jeremiah the prophet, whom they have cast into the dungeon, and he is likely to die from hunger in the place where he is. For *there is* [R]no more bread in the city." Jer. 37:21

10 Then the king commanded Ebed-Melech

38:1 *Jehucal,* Jer. 37:3 **38:2** Cf. 21:9 **38:6** Heb. *Hammelech*

37:15 Examples of Suffering—In the Word of God there are four great examples of believers suffering for the sake of righteousness. These are: Joseph, Job, Jeremiah, and Paul.

The sufferings of Joseph: he was hated by his brothers (Page 39—Gen. 37:4, 5, 8); he was sold into slavery (Page 39—Gen. 37:28); he was severely tempted (Page 41—Gen. 39:7); and he was imprisoned (Page 41—Gen. 39:20).

The sufferings of Job: His oxen and donkeys were stolen and his farmhands killed (Page 512—Job 1:14, 15); his sheep and herdsmen were burned by a fire (Page 512—Job 1:16); his camels were stolen and his servants killed (Page 512—Job 1:17); his sons and daughters died in a windstorm (Page 513—Job 1:18, 19); and he was struck with boils (Page 513—Job 2:7).

The sufferings of Jeremiah: He was persecuted by his own family (Page 761—Jer. 12:6); he was plotted against by his own hometown (Page 760—Jer. 11:18–23); he was rejected and ridiculed by his religious peers (Page 768—Jer. 20:1–3, 7–9); and he was arrested, beaten, and accused of treason (Page 787—Jer. 37:11–16).

The sufferings of Paul: He was plotted against (Page 1122—Acts 9:23, 29; 20:3; 21:30; 23:10, 12; 25:3); he was stoned and left for dead (Page 1128—Acts 14:19); he was subjected to satanic pressure (Page 1227—1 Thess. 2:18); he was beaten and jailed at Philippi (Page 1131—Acts 16:19–24); he was ridiculed (Page 1132—Acts 17:16–18; 26:24); he was falsely accused (Page 1137—Acts 21:21, 28; 24:5–9); he endured a number of violent storms at sea (Page 1191—2 Cor. 11:25; Page 1143—Acts 27:14–20); he was bitten by a serpent (Acts 28:3, 4); and he was forsaken by all (Page 1245—2 Tim. 4:10, 16).

Now turn to Page 393—2 Kin. 23:3: Knowing the Will of God Through the Scriptures.

the Ethiopian, saying, "Take from here thirty men with you, and lift Jeremiah the prophet out of the dungeon before he dies."

11 So Ebed-Melech took the men with him and went into the house of the king under the treasury, and took from there old clothes and old rags, and let them down by ropes into the dungeon to Jeremiah.

12 Then Ebed-Melech the Ethiopian said to Jeremiah, "Please put these old clothes and rags under your armpits, under the ropes." And Jeremiah did so.

13 So they pulled Jeremiah up with ropes and lifted him out of the dungeon. And Jeremiah remained in the court of the prison.

Third Interview of Zedekiah

14 Then Zedekiah the king sent and had Jeremiah the prophet brought to him at the third entrance of the house of the LORD. And the king said to Jeremiah, "I will ask you something. Hide nothing from me."

15 Jeremiah said to Zedekiah, "If I declare *it* to you, will you not surely put me to death? And if I give you advice, you will not listen to me."

16 So Zedekiah the king swore secretly to Jeremiah, saying, "*As* the LORD lives, [R]who made our very souls, I will not put you to death, nor will I give you into the hand of these men who seek your life." Is. 57:16

17 Then Jeremiah said to Zedekiah, "Thus says the LORD, the God of hosts, the God of Israel: 'If you surely surrender to the king of Babylon's princes, then your soul shall live; this city shall not be burned with fire, and you and your house shall live.

18 'But if you do not surrender to the king of Babylon's princes, then this city shall be given into the hand of the Chaldeans; they shall burn it with fire, and [R]you shall not escape from their hand.' " Jer. 32:4; 34:3

19 And Zedekiah the king said to Jeremiah, "I am afraid of the Jews who have [R]defected to the Chaldeans, lest they deliver me into their hand, and they abuse me." Jer. 39:9

20 But Jeremiah said, "They shall not deliver *you*. Please, obey the voice of the LORD which I speak to you. So it shall be [R]well with you, and your soul shall live. Jer. 40:9

21 "But if you refuse to surrender, this *is* the word that the LORD has shown me:

22 'Now behold, all the [R]women who are left in the king of Judah's house *shall be* surrendered to the king of Babylon's princes, and those *women* shall say: Jer. 8:10

"Your close friends have [T]set upon you
And prevailed against you; Or *misled*
Your feet have sunk in the mire,
And they have turned away again."

23 'So they shall surrender all your wives and [R]children to the Chaldeans. [R]You shall not escape from their hand, but shall be taken by the hand of the king of Babylon. And you shall cause this city to be burned with fire.' " Jer. 39:6; 41:10 • Jer. 39:5

24 Then Zedekiah said to Jeremiah, "Let no one know of these words, and you shall not die.

25 "But if the princes hear that I have talked with you, and they come to you and say to you, 'Declare to us now what you have said to the king, and also what the king said to you; do not hide *it* from us, and we will not put you to death,'

26 "then you shall say to them, [R]'I presented my request before the king, that he would not make me return [R]to Jonathan's house to die there.' " Jer. 37:20 • Jer. 37:15

27 Then all the princes came to Jeremiah and asked him. And he told them according to all these words that the king had commanded. So they stopped speaking with him, for the conversation had not been heard.

28 Now [R]Jeremiah remained in the court of the prison until the day that Jerusalem was taken. And he was *there* when Jerusalem was taken. Jer. 37:21; 39:14

CHAPTER 39

Jerusalem Falls—2 Kin. 25:1–12; Jer. 52:4–14

IN the ninth year of Zedekiah king of Judah, in the tenth month, Nebuchadnezzar king of Babylon and all his army came against Jerusalem, and besieged it.

2 In the [R]eleventh year of Zedekiah, in the fourth month, on the ninth *day* of the month, the city was penetrated. Jer. 1:3

3 [R]Then all the princes of the king of Babylon came in and sat in the Middle Gate: Nergal-Sharezer, Samgar-Nebo, Sarsechim, Rabsaris,* Nergal-Sarezer, Rabmag,* with the rest of the princes of the king of Babylon. Jer. 1:15; 38:17

4 [R]So it was, when Zedekiah the king of Judah and all the men of war saw them, that they fled and went out of the city by night, by way of the king's garden, by the gate between the two walls. And he went out by way of the plain.* Jer. 52:7

5 But the Chaldean army pursued them and overtook Zedekiah in the plains of Jericho. And when they had captured him, they brought him up to Nebuchadnezzar king of Babylon, to Riblah in the land of Hamath, where he pronounced judgment on him.

6 Then the king of Babylon killed the sons of Zedekiah before his [R]eyes in Riblah; the king of Babylon also killed all the [R]nobles of Judah. Deut. 28:34 • Jer. 34:19–21

39:3 A title, probably *Chief Officer;* also v. 13 • A title, probably *Troop Commander;* also v. 13 **39:4** Or *the Arabah;* the Jordan Valley

7 Moreover [R]he put out Zedekiah's eyes, and bound him with bronze [T]fetters to carry him off to Babylon. Ezek. 12:13 • *chains*

8 [R]And the Chaldeans burned the king's house and the houses of the people with [R]fire, and broke down the [R]walls of Jerusalem. 2 Kin. 25:9 • Jer. 21:10 • Neh. 1:3

9 Then Nebuzaradan the captain of the guard carried away captive to Babylon the remnant of the people who remained in the city and those who defected to him, with the rest of the people who remained.

10 But Nebuzaradan the captain of the guard left in the land of Judah the poor people, who had nothing, and gave them vineyards and fields at the same time.

Jeremiah Is Released

11 Now Nebuchadnezzar king of Babylon gave charge concerning Jeremiah to Nebuzaradan the captain of the guard, saying,

12 "Take him and look after him, and do him no [R]harm; but do to him just as he says to you." Jer. 1:18, 19; 15:20, 21

13 So Nebuzaradan the captain of the guard sent Nebushasban, Rabsaris, Nergal-Sharezer, Rabmag, and all the king of Babylon's chief officers;

14 then they sent *someone* to take Jeremiah from the court of the prison, and committed him to Gedaliah the son of Ahikam, the son of Shaphan, that he should take him home. So he dwelt among the people.

Ebed-Melech Is Rewarded

15 Meanwhile the word of the LORD had come to Jeremiah while he was shut up in the court of the prison, saying,

16 "Go and speak to [R]Ebed-Melech the Ethiopian, saying, 'Thus says the LORD of hosts, the God of Israel: "Behold, [R]I will bring My words upon this city for adversity and not for good, and they shall be *performed* in that day before you. Jer. 38:7, 12 • [Dan. 9:12]

17 "But I will deliver you in that day," says the LORD, "and you shall not be given into the hand of the men of whom you *are* afraid.

18 "For I will surely deliver you, and you shall not fall by the sword; but your life shall be as a prize to you, because you have put your trust in Me," says the LORD.' "

CHAPTER 40

Ministry to the Remnant in Judah

THE word that came to Jeremiah from the LORD [R]after Nebuzaradan the captain of the guard had let him go from Ramah, when he had taken him bound in chains among all who were carried away captive from Jerusalem and Judah, who were carried away captive to Babylon. Jer. 39:9, 11

2 And the captain of the guard took Jeremiah and said to him: "The LORD your God has pronounced this doom on this place.

3 "Now the LORD has brought *it*, and has done just as He said. [R]Because you *people* have sinned against the LORD, and not obeyed His voice, therefore this thing has come upon you. Dan. 9:11

4 "And now look, I free you this day from the chains that *were* on your hand. If it seems good to you to come with me to Babylon, come, and I will look after you. But if it seems wrong for you to come with me to Babylon, remain here. See, [R]all the land *is* before you; wherever it seems good and convenient for you to go, go there." Gen. 20:15

5 Now while Jeremiah had not yet gone back, *Nebuzaradan said,* "Go back to [R]Gedaliah the son of Ahikam, the son of Shaphan, whom the king of Babylon has made governor over the cities of Judah, and dwell with him among the people. Or go wherever it seems convenient for you to go." So the captain of the guard gave him rations and a gift and let him go. Jer. 39:14

6 [R]Then Jeremiah went to Gedaliah the son of Ahikam, to [R]Mizpah, and dwelt with him among the people who were left in the land. Jer. 39:14 • Judg. 20:1

7 [R]And when all the captains of the armies who *were* in the fields, they and their men, heard that the king of Babylon had made Gedaliah the son of Ahikam governor in the land, and had committed to him men, women, children, and [R]the poorest of the land who had not been carried away captive to Babylon, 2 Kin. 25:23, 24 • Jer. 39:10

8 then they came to Gedaliah at Mizpah—Ishmael the son of Nethaniah, Johanan and Jonathan the sons of Kareah, Seraiah the son of Tanhumeth, the sons of Ephai the Netophathite, and [R]Jezaniah* the son of a Maachathite, they and their men. Jer. 42:1

9 And Gedaliah the son of Ahikam, the son of Shaphan, took an oath before them and their men, saying, "Do not be afraid to serve the Chaldeans. Dwell in the land and serve the king of Babylon, and it shall be [R]well with you. Jer. 27:11; 38:17–20

10 "As for me, I will indeed dwell at Mizpah and serve the Chaldeans who come to us. But you, gather wine and summer fruit and oil, put *them* in your vessels, and dwell in your cities that you have taken."

11 Likewise, when all the Jews who *were* in Moab, among the Ammonites, in Edom, and who *were* in all the countries, heard that the king of Babylon had left a remnant of Judah, and that he had set over them Gedaliah the son of Ahikam, the son of Shaphan,

12 then all the Jews [R]returned out of all places where they had been driven, and came

40:8 *Jaazaniah*, 2 Kin. 25:23

to the land of Judah, to Gedaliah at Mizpah,
and gathered wine and summer fruit in abun-
dance. Jer. 43:5
13 Moreover Johanan the son of Kareah and
all the captains of the forces that *were* in the
fields came to Gedaliah at Mizpah,
14 and said to him, "Do you certainly know
that [R]Baalis the king of the Ammonites has
sent Ishmael the son of Nethaniah to murder
you?" But Gedaliah the son of Ahikam did not
believe them. Jer. 41:10
15 Then Johanan the son of Kareah spoke
secretly to Gedaliah in Mizpah, saying, "Let
me go, please, and I will kill Ishmael the son
of Nethaniah, and no one will know *it*. Why
should he murder you, so that all the Jews
who are gathered to you would be scattered,
and the remnant in Judah perish?"
16 But Gedaliah the son of Ahikam said to
Johanan the son of Kareah, "You shall not do
this thing, for you speak falsely concerning
Ishmael."

CHAPTER 41

NOW it came to pass in the seventh
month [R]*that* Ishmael the son of Netha-
niah, the son of Elishama, of the royal [T]fam-
ily and of the officers of the king, came with
ten men to Gedaliah the son of Ahikam, at
[R]Mizpah. And there they ate bread together
in Mizpah. 2 Kin. 25:25 • Lit. *seed* • Jer. 40:6, 10
2 Then Ishmael the son of Nethaniah, and
the ten men who were with him, arose and
[R]struck Gedaliah the son of Ahikam, the son
of Shaphan, with the sword, and killed him
whom the king of Babylon had made gover-
nor over the land. 2 Kin. 25:25
3 Ishmael also struck down all the Jews
who were with him, *that is*, with Gedaliah at
Mizpah, and the Chaldeans who were found
there, the men of war.
4 And it happened, on the second day after
he had killed Gedaliah, when as yet no one
knew *it*,
5 that certain men came from Shechem,
from Shiloh, and from Samaria, eighty men
[R]with their beards shaved and their clothes
torn, having cut themselves, with offerings
and incense in their hand, to bring *them* to
[R]the house of the LORD. Deut. 14:1 • 1 Sam. 1:7
6 Now Ishmael the son of Nethaniah went
out from Mizpah to meet them, weeping as he
went along; and it happened as he met them
that he said to them, "Come to Gedaliah the
son of Ahikam!"
7 So it was, when they came into the
midst of the city, that Ishmael the son of
Nethaniah [R]killed them *and cast them* into
the midst of a [T]pit, he and the men who were
with him. Ps. 55:23 • Or *cistern*
8 But ten men were found among them who
said to Ishmael, "Do not kill us, for we have
treasures of wheat, barley, oil, and honey in
the field." So he desisted and did not kill them
among their brethren.
9 Now the pit into which Ishmael had cast
all the dead bodies of the men whom he had
slain, because of Gedaliah, *was* [R]the same one
Asa the king had made for fear of Baasha
king of Israel. Ishmael the son of Nethaniah
filled it with *the* slain. 1 Kin. 15:22
10 Then Ishmael carried away captive all
the [R]rest of the people who *were* in Mizpah,
[R]the king's daughters and all the people who
remained in Mizpah, [R]whom Nebuzaradan
the captain of the guard had committed to
Gedaliah the son of Ahikam. And Ishmael
the son of Nethaniah carried them away cap-
tive and departed to go over to the Am-
monites. Jer. 40:11, 12 • Jer. 43:6 • Jer. 40:7
11 But when Johanan the son of Kareah and
all the captains of the forces that *were* with
him heard of all the evil that Ishmael the son
of Nethaniah had done,
12 they took all the men and went to fight
with Ishmael the son of Nethaniah; and they
found him by [R]the great pool that *is* in
Gibeon. 2 Sam. 2:13
13 So it was, when all the people who *were*
with Ishmael saw Johanan the son of Kareah,
and all the captains of the forces who *were*
with him, that they were glad.
14 Then all the people whom Ishmael had
carried away captive from Mizpah turned
around and came back, and went to Johanan
the son of Kareah.
15 But Ishmael the son of Nethaniah es-
caped from Johanan with eight men and went
to the Ammonites.
16 Then Johanan the son of Kareah, and all
the captains of the forces that were with him,
took from Mizpah all the [R]rest of the people
whom he had recovered from Ishmael the son
of Nethaniah after he had murdered Gedaliah
the son of Ahikam—the mighty men of war
and the women and the children and the eu-
nuchs, whom he had brought back from
Gibeon. Jer. 40:11, 12; 43:4–7
17 And they departed and dwelt in the habi-
tation of Chimham, which is near Bethlehem,
as they went on their way to Egypt,
18 because of the Chaldeans; for they were
afraid of them, because Ishmael the son of
Nethaniah had murdered Gedaliah the son
of Ahikam, [R]whom the king of Babylon had
made governor in the land. Jer. 40:5

CHAPTER 42

NOW all the captains of the forces, [R]Jo-
hanan the son of Kareah, Jezaniah the
son of Hoshaiah, and all the people, from the
least to the greatest, came near Jer. 41:11
2 and said to Jeremiah the prophet,
[R]"Please, let our petition be acceptable to you,

and pray for us to the LORD your God, for all this remnant (since we are left *but* a few of many, as you can see), Jer. 15:11

3 "that the LORD your God may show us [R]the way in which we should walk and the thing we should do." Ezra 8:21

4 Then Jeremiah the prophet said to them, "I have heard. Indeed, I will pray to the LORD your God according to your words, and it shall be, *that* [R]whatever the LORD answers you, I will declare *it* to you. I will keep nothing back from you." 1 Kin. 22:14

5 So they said to Jeremiah, "Let the LORD be a true and faithful witness between us, if we do not do according to everything which the LORD your God sends us by you.

6 "Whether *it is* [T]pleasing or [T]displeasing, we will [R]obey the voice of the LORD our God to whom we send you, [R]that it may be well with us when we obey the voice of the LORD our God." Lit. *good* • Lit. *evil* • Ex. 24:7 • Jer. 7:23

7 And it happened after ten days that the word of the LORD came to Jeremiah.

8 Then he called Johanan the son of Kareah, all the captains of the forces which *were* with him, and all the people from the least even to the greatest,

9 and said to them, "Thus says the LORD, the God of Israel, to whom you sent me to present your petition before Him:

10 'If you will still remain in this land, then [R]I will build you and not pull *you* down, and I will plant you and not pluck *you* up. For I relent concerning the disaster that I have brought upon you. Jer. 24:6; 31:28; 33:7

11 'Do not be afraid of the king of Babylon, of whom you are afraid; do not be afraid of him,' says the LORD, 'for I *am* with you, to save you and deliver you from his hand.

12 'And [R]I will show you mercy, that he may have mercy on you and cause you to return to your own land.' Ps. 106:46

13 "But if [R]you say, 'We will not dwell in this land,' disobeying the voice of the LORD your God, Jer. 44:16

14 "saying, 'No, but we will go to the land of [R]Egypt where we shall see no war, nor hear the sound of the trumpet, nor be hungry for bread, and there we will dwell'— Jer. 41:17

15 "Then hear now the word of the LORD, O remnant of Judah! Thus says the LORD of hosts, the God of Israel: 'If you [R]wholly[T] set [R]your faces to enter Egypt, and go to dwell there, Deut. 17:16 • Or *surely* • Luke 9:51

16 'then it shall be *that* the [R]sword which you feared shall overtake you there in the land of Egypt; the famine of which you were afraid shall follow close after you there *in* Egypt; and there you shall die. Ezek. 11:8

17 'So shall it be with all the men who set their faces to go to Egypt to dwell there. They shall die by the sword, by famine, and by pestilence. And [R]none of them shall remain or escape from the disaster that I will bring upon them.' Jer. 44:14, 28

18 "For thus says the LORD of hosts, the God of Israel: 'As My anger and My fury have been [R]poured out on the inhabitants of Jerusalem, so will My fury be poured out on you when you enter Egypt. And [R]you shall be an oath, an astonishment, a curse, and a reproach; and you shall see this place no more.' Jer. 7:20 • Is. 65:15

19 "The LORD has said concerning you, O remnant of Judah, [R]'Do not go to Egypt!' Know certainly that I have [T]admonished you this day. Deut. 17:16 • *warned*

20 "For you were hypocrites in your hearts when you sent me to the LORD your God, saying, 'Pray for us to the LORD our God, and according to all that the LORD your God says, so declare to us and we will do *it*.'

21 "And I have this day declared *it* to you, but you have [R]not obeyed the voice of the LORD your God, or anything which He has sent you by me. Is. 30:1–7

22 "Now therefore, know certainly that you [R]shall die by the sword, by famine, and by pestilence in the place where you desire to go to dwell." Ezek. 6:11

CHAPTER 43

Ministry to Remnant in Egypt

NOW it happened, when Jeremiah had stopped speaking to all the people all the [R]words of the LORD their God, for which the LORD their God had sent him to them, all these words, Jer. 42:9–18

2 that Azariah the son of Hoshaiah, Johanan the son of Kareah, and all the proud men spoke, saying to Jeremiah, "You speak falsely! The LORD our God has not sent you to say, 'Do not go to Egypt to dwell there.'

3 "But Baruch the son of Neriah has set you against us, to deliver us into the hand of the Chaldeans, that they may put us to death or carry us away captive to Babylon."

4 So Johanan the son of Kareah, all the captains of the forces, and all the people would [R]not obey the voice of the LORD, to remain in the land of Judah. 2 Kin. 25:26

5 But Johanan the son of Kareah and all the captains of the forces took [R]all the remnant of Judah who had returned to dwell in the land of Judah, from all nations where they had been driven— Jer. 40:11, 12

6 men, women, children, [R]the king's daughters, and every person whom Nebuzaradan the captain of the guard had left with Gedaliah the son of Ahikam, the son of Shaphan, and Jeremiah the prophet and Baruch the son of Neriah. Jer. 41:10

7 [R]So they went to the land of Egypt, for they did not obey the voice of the LORD. And they went as far as Tahpanhes. Jer. 42:19

8 Then the word of the LORD came to Jere-
miah in Tahpanhes, saying,
9 "Take large stones in your hand, and
hide them in the sight of the men of Judah, in
the [T]clay in the brick courtyard which *is* at
the entrance to Pharaoh's house in Tahpan-
hes; Or *mortar*
10 "and say to them, 'Thus says the LORD of
hosts, the God of Israel: "Behold, I will send
and bring Nebuchadnezzar the king of Bab-
ylon, My servant, and will set his throne
above these stones that I have hidden. And he
will spread his royal pavilion over them.
11 "When he comes, he shall strike the land
of Egypt *and deliver* to death [R]*those ap-*
pointed for death, and to captivity *those ap-*
pointed for captivity, and to the sword *those*
appointed for the sword. Jer. 15:2
12 "I* will kindle a fire in the houses of [R]the
gods of Egypt, and he shall burn them and
carry them away captive. And he shall array
himself with the land of Egypt, as a shepherd
puts on his garment, and he shall go out from
there in peace. Jer. 46:25
13 "He shall also break the sacred pillars of
Beth Shemesh* that *are* in the land of Egypt;
and the houses of the gods of the Egyptians
he shall burn with fire." ' "

CHAPTER 44

THE word that came to Jeremiah concern-
ing all the Jews who dwell in the land of
Egypt, who dwell at [R]Migdol, at [R]Tahpanhes,
at [R]Noph,* and in the country of Pathros, say-
ing, Jer. 46:14 • Jer. 43:7 • Is. 19:13
2 "Thus says the LORD of hosts, the God of
Israel: 'You have seen all the calamity that I
have brought on Jerusalem and on all the
cities of Judah; and behold, this day they *are*
a desolation, and no one dwells in them,
3 'because of their wickedness which they
have committed to provoke Me to anger, in
that they went [R]to burn incense *and* to serve
other gods whom they did not know, they nor
you nor your fathers. Jer. 19:4
4 'However [R]I have sent to you all My ser-
vants the prophets, rising early and sending
them, saying, "Oh, do not do this abominable
thing that I hate!" Jer. 7:25; 25:4; 26:5
5 'But they did not listen or incline their ear
to turn from their wickedness, to burn no in-
cense to other gods.
6 'So My fury and My anger were poured
out and kindled in the cities of Judah and in
the streets of Jerusalem; and they are wasted
and desolate, as it is this day.'
7 "Now therefore, thus says the LORD, the
God of hosts, the God of Israel: 'Why do you
commit *this* great evil against yourselves, to
cut off from you man and woman, child and
infant, out of Judah, leaving none to remain,
8 'in that you provoke Me to wrath with the
works of your hands, burning incense to other
gods in the land of Egypt where you have
gone to dwell, that you may cut yourselves off
and be a curse and a reproach among all the
nations of the earth?
9 'Have you forgotten the wickedness of
your fathers, the wickedness of the kings of
Judah, the wickedness of their wives, your
own wickedness, and the wickedness of your
wives, which they committed in the land of
Judah and in the streets of Jerusalem?
10 'They have not been [R]humbled, to this
day, nor have they feared; they have not
walked in My law or in My statutes that I set
before you and your fathers.' Jer. 6:15; 8:12
11 "Therefore thus says the LORD of hosts,
the God of Israel: 'Behold, [R]I will set My face
against you for catastrophe and for [T]cutting
off all Judah. Amos 9:4 • *destroying*
12 'And I will take the remnant of Judah who
have set their faces to go into the land of
Egypt to dwell there, and [R]they shall all be
consumed *and* fall in the land of Egypt. They
shall be consumed by the sword *and* by
famine. They shall die, from the least to the
greatest, by the sword and by famine; and
they shall be an oath, an astonishment, a
curse and a reproach! Jer. 42:15–17, 22
13 [R]'For I will punish those who dwell in
the land of Egypt, as I have punished Jerusa-
lem, by the sword, by famine, and by pesti-
lence, Jer. 43:11
14 'so that none of the remnant of Judah
who have gone into the land of Egypt to dwell
there shall escape or survive, lest they return
to the land of Judah, to which they desire to
return and dwell. For none shall return except
those who escape.' "
15 Then all the men who knew that their
wives had burned incense to other gods, with
all the women who stood by, a great multitude,
and all the people who dwelt in the land of
Egypt, in Pathros, answered Jeremiah, saying:
16 "*As for* the word that you have spoken to
us in the name of the LORD, [R]we will not listen
to you! Jer. 6:16
17 "But we will certainly do whatever has
gone out of our own mouth, to burn incense to
the [R]queen of heaven and pour out drink of-
ferings to her, as we have done, we and our fa-
thers, our kings and our princes, in the cities
of Judah and in the streets of Jerusalem. For
then we had plenty of food, were well-off, and
saw no trouble. Jer. 7:18
18 "But since we stopped burning incense to
the queen of heaven and pouring out drink of-
ferings to her, we have lacked everything and
have been consumed by the sword and by
famine."

43:12 So with MT, Tg.; LXX, Syr., Vg. *He* **43:13** Lit. *House of the Sun,* ancient On; later called Heliopolis
44:1 Ancient Memphis

19 *The women also said,* [R]"And when we
burned incense to the queen of heaven and
poured out drink offerings to her, did we
make cakes for her, to worship her, and pour
out drink offerings to her without our hus-
bands' *permission?*" Jer. 7:18
20 Then Jeremiah spoke to all the people—
the men, the women, and all the people who
had given him *that* answer—saying:
21 "The incense that you burned in the cities
of Judah and in the streets of Jerusalem, you
and your fathers, your kings and your princes,
and the people of the land, did not the LORD
remember them, and did it *not* come into His
mind?
22 "So the LORD could no longer bear *it*, be-
cause of the evil of your doings *and* because
of the abominations which you committed.
Therefore your land is a desolation, an aston-
ishment, a curse, and without an inhabitant,
[R]as *it is* this day. Jer. 25:11, 18, 38
23 "Because you have burned incense and
because you have sinned against the LORD,
and have not obeyed the voice of the LORD or
walked in His law, in His statutes or in His tes-
timonies, therefore this calamity has hap-
pened to you, as *at* this day."
24 Moreover Jeremiah said to all the people
and to all the women, "Hear the word of the
LORD, all Judah who *are* in the land of Egypt!
25 "Thus says the LORD of hosts, the God of
Israel, saying: 'You and your wives have spo-
ken with your mouths and fulfilled with your
hands, saying, "We will surely keep our vows
that we have made, to burn incense to the
queen of heaven and pour out drink offerings
to her." You will surely keep your vows and
perform your vows!'
26 "Therefore hear the word of the LORD, all
Judah who dwell in the land of Egypt: 'Be-
hold, [R]I have sworn by My [R]great name,' says
the LORD, 'that [R]My name shall no more be
named in the mouth of any man of Judah in
all the land of Egypt, saying, "The Lord GOD
lives."' Heb. 6:13 • Jer. 10:6 • Ezek. 20:39
27 'Behold, I will watch over them for adver-
sity and not for good. And all the men of Ju-
dah who *are* in the land of Egypt [R]shall be
consumed by the sword and by famine, until
there is an end to them. Ezek. 7:6
28 'Yet [R]a small number who escape the
sword shall return from the land of Egypt to
the land of Judah; and all the remnant of Ju-
dah, who have gone to the land of Egypt to
dwell there, shall know whose words will
stand, Mine or theirs. Is. 10:19; 27:12, 13
29 'And this *shall be* a sign to you,' says the
LORD, 'that I will punish you in this place, that
you may know that My words will surely
stand against you for adversity.'
30 "Thus says the LORD: 'Behold, [R]I will give
Pharaoh Hophra king of Egypt into the hand
of his enemies and into the hand of those
who seek his life, as I gave [R]Zedekiah king
of Judah into the hand of Nebuchadnezzar
king of Babylon, his enemy who sought his
life.'" Ezek. 29:3; 30:21 • Jer. 39:5

CHAPTER 45

Message to Baruch

THE [R]word that Jeremiah the prophet
spoke to Baruch the son of Neriah, when
he had written these words in a book at the in-
struction of Jeremiah,* in the fourth year of
Jehoiakim the son of Josiah, king of Judah,
saying, Jer. 36:1, 4, 32
2 "Thus says the LORD, the God of Israel, to
you, O Baruch:
3 'You said, "Woe is me now! For the LORD
has added grief to my sorrow. I [R]fainted in my
sighing, and I find no rest."' Ps. 6:6
4 "Thus you shall say to him, 'Thus says the
LORD: "Behold, [R]what I have built I will break
down, and what I have planted I will pluck up,
that is, this whole land. Is. 5:5
5 "And do you seek great things for your-
self? Do not seek *them;* for behold, [R]I will
bring adversity on all flesh," says the LORD.
"But I will give your life to you as a prize in all
places, wherever you go."'" Jer. 25:17–26

CHAPTER 46

Prophecies Against Egypt

THE word of the LORD which came to Jere-
miah the prophet against the nations.
2 Against [R]Egypt. Jer. 25:17–19
[R]Concerning the army of Pharaoh Necho,
king of Egypt, which was by the River Eu-
phrates in Carchemish, and which Nebu-
chadnezzar king of Babylon defeated in the
fourth year of Jehoiakim the son of Josiah,
king of Judah: 2 Kin. 23:33–35

3 "Order the [T]buckler and shield,
And draw near to battle! A small shield
4 Harness the horses,
And mount up, you horsemen!
Stand forth with *your* helmets,
Polish the spears,
[R]Put on the armor! Jer. 51:11, 12
5 Why have I seen them dismayed *and*
turned back?
Their mighty ones are beaten down;
They have speedily fled,
And did not look back,
For [R]fear *was* all around," says the
LORD. Jer. 49:29
6 "Do not let the swift flee away,
Nor the mighty man escape;
They will [R]stumble and fall Dan. 11:19
Toward the north, by the River
Euphrates.

45:1 Lit. *from Jeremiah's mouth*

7 "Who *is* this coming up like a flood,
Whose waters move like the rivers?
8 Egypt rises up like a flood,
And *its* waters move like the rivers;
And he says, 'I will go up *and* cover the earth,
I will destroy the city and its inhabitants.'
9 Come up, O horses, and rage, O chariots!
And let the mighty men come forth:
[T]The Ethiopians and [T]the Libyans who handle the shield, Heb. *Cush* • Heb. *Put*
And the Lydians [R]who handle *and* bend the bow. Is. 66:19
10 For this *is* [R]the day of the Lord GOD of hosts, Joel 1:15
A day of vengeance,
That He may avenge Himself on His adversaries.
[R]The sword shall devour; Deut. 32:42
It shall be [T]satiated and made drunk with their blood; Filled to the full
For the Lord GOD of hosts [R]has a sacrifice Is. 34:6
In the north country by the River Euphrates.

11 "Go up to Gilead and take balm,
[R]O virgin, the daughter of Egypt; Is. 47:1
In vain you will use many medicines;
[R]You shall not be cured. Ezek. 30:21
12 The nations have heard of your [R]shame,
And your cry has filled the land;
For the mighty man has stumbled against the mighty; Jer. 2:36
They both have fallen together."

13 The word that the LORD spoke to Jere-
miah the prophet, how Nebuchadnezzar king
of Babylon would come *and* [R]strike the land of
Egypt. Is. 19:1

14 "Declare in Egypt, and proclaim in [R]Migdol; Jer. 44:1
Proclaim in Noph* and in Tahpanhes;
Say, 'Stand fast and prepare yourselves,
For the sword devours all around you.'
15 Why are your valiant *men* swept away?
They did not stand
Because the LORD drove them away.
16 He made many fall;
Yes, [R]one fell upon another.
And they said, 'Arise! Lev. 26:36, 37
[R]Let us go back to our own people
And to the land of our nativity
From the oppressing sword.' Jer. 51:9
17 They cried there,
'Pharaoh, king of Egypt, *is but* a noise.
He has passed by the appointed time!'

18 "*As* I live," says the King,
[R]Whose name *is* the LORD of hosts,
"Surely as Tabor *is* among the mountains Jer. 48:15
And as Carmel by the sea, *so* he shall come.
19 O you daughter dwelling in Egypt,
Prepare yourself [R]to go into captivity!
For Noph* shall be waste and desolate, without inhabitant. Is. 20:4

20 "Egypt *is* a very pretty [R]heifer,
But destruction comes, it comes [R]from the north. Hos. 10:11 • Jer. 1:14
21 Also her mercenaries are in her midst like [T]fat bulls, Lit. *calves of the stall*
For they also are turned back,
They have fled away together.
They did not stand,
For [R]the day of their calamity had come upon them, [Ps. 37:13]
The time of their punishment.
22 [R]Her noise shall go like a serpent,
For they shall march with an army
And come against her with axes,
Like those who chop wood. [Is. 29:4]
23 "They shall [R]cut down her forest," says the LORD, Is. 10:34
"Though it cannot be searched,
Because they *are* innumerable,
And more numerous than [R]grasshoppers. Judg. 6:5; 7:12
24 The daughter of Egypt shall be ashamed;
She shall be delivered into the hand
Of [R]the people of the north." Jer. 1:15

25 The LORD of hosts, the God of Israel, says:
"Behold, I will bring punishment on Amon* of
[R]No,* and Pharaoh and Egypt, with their gods
and their kings—Pharaoh and those who trust
in him. Ezek. 30:14–16
26 [R]"And I will deliver them into the hand of
those who seek their lives, into the hand of
Nebuchadnezzar king of Babylon and the
hand of his servants. [R]Afterward it shall be
inhabited as in the days of old," says the
LORD. Ezek. 32:11 • Ezek. 29:8–14

27 "But do not fear, O My servant Jacob,
And do not be dismayed, O Israel!
For behold, I will [R]save you from afar,
And your offspring from the land of their captivity; Is. 11:11
Jacob shall return, have rest and be at ease;
No one shall make *him* afraid.
28 Do not fear, O Jacob My servant," says the LORD,
"For I *am* with you;
For I will make a complete end of all the nations
To which I have driven you,

46:14 Ancient Memphis **46:19** Ancient Memphis
46:25 A sun god • Ancient Thebes

But I will not make [R]a complete end of
you. Amos 9:8, 9
I will rightly [R]correct you, Jer. 30:11
For I will not leave you wholly
unpunished."

CHAPTER 47

Prophecies Against Philistia

THE word of the LORD that came to Jere-
miah the prophet [R]against the Philistines,
before Pharaoh attacked Gaza. Zeph. 2:4, 5
2 Thus says the LORD:

"Behold, [R]waters rise [R]out of the north,
And shall be an overflowing flood;
They shall overflow the land and all that
is in it, Is. 8:7, 8 • Jer. 1:14
The city and those who dwell within;
Then the men shall cry,
And all the inhabitants of the land shall
wail.
3 At the [R]noise of the stamping hooves of
his strong horses, Jer. 8:16
At the rushing of his chariots,
At the rumbling of his wheels,
The fathers will not look back for *their*
children,
[T]Lacking courage, Lit. *From sinking hands*
4 Because of the day that comes to plunder
all the Philistines,
To cut off from [R]Tyre and Sidon every
helper who remains; Jer. 25:22
For the LORD shall plunder the Philistines,
[R]The remnant of the country of
[R]Caphtor. Ezek. 25:16 • Gen. 10:14
5 [R]Baldness has come upon Gaza,
[R]Ashkelon is cut off Mic. 1:16 • Jer. 25:20
With the remnant of their valley.
How long will you cut yourself?

6 "O you [R]sword of the LORD, Ezek. 21:3–5
How long until you are quiet?
Put yourself up into your scabbard,
Rest and be still!
7 How can [T]it be quiet, Lit. *you*
Seeing the LORD has [R]given it a charge
Against Ashkelon and against the
seashore? Ezek. 14:17
There He has [R]appointed it." Mic. 6:9

CHAPTER 48

Prophecies Against Moab

AGAINST [R]Moab. Is. 15:1—16:14; 25:10
Thus says the LORD of hosts, the God of
Israel:

"Woe to [R]Nebo! Is. 15:2
For it is plundered,
[R]Kirjathaim is shamed *and* taken;
The high stronghold* is shamed and
dismayed— Num. 32:37

2 [R]No more praise of Moab. Is. 16:14
In [R]Heshbon they have devised evil
against her: Jer. 49:3
'Come, and let us cut her off as a nation.'
You also shall be cut down,
O [R]Madmen!* Is. 10:31
The sword shall pursue you;
3 A voice of crying *shall be* from
[R]Horonaim: Is. 15:5
'Plundering and great destruction!'

4 "Moab is destroyed;
Her little ones have caused a cry to be
heard;*
5 [R]For in the Ascent of Luhith they ascend
with continual weeping; Is. 15:5
For in the descent of Horonaim the
enemies have heard a cry of
destruction.

6 "Flee, save your lives!
And be like the [R]juniper* in the
wilderness. Jer. 17:6
7 For because you have trusted in your
works and your [R]treasures, Jer. 9:23
You also shall be taken.
And [R]Chemosh shall go forth into
captivity, Jer. 48:13
His priests and his princes together.
8 And [R]the plunderer shall come against
every city; Jer. 6:26
No one shall escape.
The valley also shall perish,
And the plain shall be destroyed,
As the LORD has spoken.

9 "Give[R] wings to Moab, Ps. 55:6
That she may flee and get away;
For her cities shall be desolate,
Without any to dwell in them.
10 [R]Cursed *is* he who does the work of the
LORD deceitfully, 1 Sam. 15:3, 9
And cursed *is* he who keeps back his
sword from blood.

11 "Moab has been at ease from his* youth;
He [R]has settled on his dregs, Zeph. 1:12
And has not been emptied from vessel to
vessel,
Nor has he gone into captivity.
Therefore his taste remained in him,
And his scent has not changed.

12 "Therefore behold, the days are coming,"
says the LORD,
"That I shall send him wine-workers
Who will tip him over
And empty his vessels

48:1 Heb. *Misgab* **48:2** A city of Moab **48:4** So with MT, Tg., Vg.; LXX *Proclaim it in Zoar* **48:6** Or *Aroer*, a city of Moab **48:11** Heb. uses masc. and fem. pronouns interchangeably in this chapter.

And break the bottles.
13 Moab shall be ashamed of Chemosh,
As the house of Israel [R]was ashamed of
Bethel, their confidence. Hos. 10:6

14 "How can you say, [R]'We *are* mighty
And strong men for the war'? Is. 16:6
15 Moab is plundered and gone up *from* her
cities;
Her chosen young men have gone down
to the slaughter," says the King,
Whose name *is* the LORD of hosts.

16 "The calamity of Moab *is* near at hand,
And his affliction comes quickly.
17 Bemoan him, all you who are around him;
And all you who know his name,
Say, [R]'How the strong staff is broken,
The beautiful rod!' Is. 9:4; 14:4, 5

18 "O [R]daughter inhabiting [R]Dibon,
Come down from *your* glory,
And sit in thirst;
For the plunderer of Moab has come
against you, Is. 47:1 • Is. 15:2
He has destroyed your strongholds.
19 O inhabitant of [R]Aroer, Deut. 2:36
[R]Stand by the way and watch;
Ask him who flees
And her who escapes; 1 Sam. 4:13, 14, 16
Say, 'What has happened?'
20 Moab is shamed, for he is broken down.
[R]Wail and cry! Is. 16:7
Tell it in [R]Arnon, that Moab is
plundered. Num. 21:13

21 "And judgment has come on the plain
country:
On Holon and Jahzah and Mephaath,
22 On Dibon and Nebo and Beth
Diblathaim,
23 On Kirjathaim and Beth Gamul and Beth
Meon,
24 On [R]Kerioth and Bozrah, Amos 2:2
On all the cities of the land of Moab,
Far or near.
25 [R]The horn of Moab is cut off, Ps. 75:10
And his arm is broken," says the LORD.

26 "Make[R] him drunk, Jer. 25:15
Because he exalted *himself* against the
LORD.
Moab shall wallow in his vomit,
And he shall also be in derision.
27 For was not Israel a derision to you?
[R]Was he found among thieves? Jer. 2:26
For whenever you speak of him,
You shake *your head in scorn.*
28 You who dwell in Moab,
Leave the cities and [R]dwell in the rock,
And be like [R]the dove *which* makes her
nest Ps. 55:6, 7 • Song 2:14
In the sides of the cave's mouth.

29 "We have heard the [R]pride of Moab
(He *is* exceedingly proud), Is. 16:6
Of his loftiness and arrogance and
[R]pride, Jer. 49:16
And of the haughtiness of his heart."

30 "I know his wrath," says the LORD,
"But it *is* not right;
His lies have made nothing right.
31 Therefore [R]I will wail for Moab, Is. 15:5
And I will cry out for all Moab;
I* will mourn for the men of Kir Heres.
32 [R]O vine of Sibmah! I will weep for you
with the weeping of Jazer. Is. 16:8, 9
Your plants have gone over the sea,
They reach to the sea of Jazer.
The plunderer has fallen on your
summer fruit and your vintage.
33 [R]Joy and gladness are taken Joel 1:12
From the plentiful field
And from the land of Moab;
I have caused wine to [T]fail from the
winepresses; *cease*
No one will tread with joyous shouting—
Not joyous shouting!

34 "From[R] the cry of Heshbon to [R]Elealeh
and to Jahaz Is. 15:4–6 • Num. 32:3, 37
They have uttered their voice,
[R]From Zoar to Horonaim, Is. 15:5, 6
Like a three-year-old heifer;*
For the waters of Nimrim also shall be
desolate.

35 "Moreover," says the LORD,
"I will cause to cease in Moab
[R]The one who offers *sacrifices* in the high
places Is. 15:2; 16:12
And burns incense to his gods.
36 Therefore [R]My heart shall wail like flutes
for Moab, Is. 15:5; 16:11
And like flutes My heart shall wail
For the men of Kir Heres.
Therefore [R]the riches they have acquired
have perished. Is. 15:7

37 "For [R]every head *shall be* bald, and every
beard clipped; Is. 15:2, 3
On all the hands *shall be* cuts, and [R]on
the loins sackcloth— Gen. 37:34
38 A general lamentation
On all the [R]housetops of Moab, Is. 15:3
And in its streets;
For I have broken Moab like a vessel in
which *is* no pleasure," says the LORD.
39 "They shall wail:
'How she is broken down!
How Moab has turned her back with
shame!'

48:31 So with DSS, LXX, Vg.; MT *He* **48:34** Or *The Third Eglath,* an unknown city, Is. 15:5

So Moab shall be a derision
And a dismay to all those about her."

40 For thus says the LORD:

"Behold, one shall fly like an eagle,
And spread his wings over Moab.
41 Kerioth is taken,
And the strongholds are surprised;
[R]The mighty men's hearts in Moab on
that day shall be Is. 13:8; 21:3
Like the heart of a woman in birth
pangs.
42 And Moab shall be destroyed [R]as a
people, Ps. 83:4
Because he exalted *himself* against the
LORD.
43 [R]Fear and the pit and the snare *shall be*
upon you, Is. 24:17, 18
O inhabitant of Moab," says the LORD.
44 "He who flees from the fear shall fall into
the pit,
And he who gets out of the pit shall be
caught in the [R]snare. Is. 24:18
For upon Moab, upon it [R]I will bring
The year of their punishment," says the
LORD. Jer. 11:23

45 "Those who fled stood under the shadow
of Heshbon
Because of exhaustion.
But a fire shall come out of Heshbon,
A flame from the midst of [R]Sihon,
And [R]shall devour the brow of Moab,
The crown of the head of the sons of
tumult. Ps. 135:11 • Num. 24:17
46 [R]Woe to you, O Moab! Num. 21:29
The people of Chemosh perish;
For your sons have been taken captive,
And your daughters captive.

47 "Yet I will bring back the captives of
Moab
In the latter days," says the LORD.

Thus far *is* the judgment of Moab.

CHAPTER 49

Prophecies Against Ammon

AGAINST the [R]Ammonites. Ezek. 21:28–32
Thus says the LORD:

"Has Israel no sons?
Has he no heir?
Why *then* does Milcom* inherit Gad,
And his people dwell in its cities?
2 [R]Therefore behold, the days are coming,"
says the LORD, Amos 1:13–15
"That I will cause to be heard an alarm of
war
In [R]Rabbah of the Ammonites;
It shall be a desolate mound,
And her [T]villages shall be burned with
fire. Ezek. 25:5 • Lit. *daughters*
Then Israel shall take possession of his
inheritance," says the LORD.

3 "Wail, O Heshbon, for Ai is plundered!
Cry, you daughters of Rabbah,
Gird yourselves with sackcloth!
Lament and run to and fro by the walls;
For Milcom shall go into captivity
With his [R]priests and his princes
together. Jer. 48:7
4 Why [R]do you boast in the valleys,
Your flowing valley, O [R]backsliding
daughter? Jer. 9:23 • Jer. 3:14
Who trusted in her [R]treasures, *saying,*
'Who will come against me?' Jer. 48:7
5 Behold, I will bring fear upon you,"
Says the Lord GOD of hosts,
"From all those who are around you;
You shall be driven out, everyone
headlong,
And no one will gather those who
wander off.
6 But [R]afterward I will bring back
The captives of the people of Ammon,"
says the LORD. Jer. 48:47

Prophecies Against Edom

7 [R]Against Edom. Ezek. 25:12–14; 35:1–15
Thus says the LORD of hosts:
"*Is* wisdom no more in Teman?
Has counsel perished from the prudent?
Has their wisdom [R]vanished? Jer. 8:9
8 Flee, turn back, dwell in the depths,
O inhabitants of [R]Dedan! Jer. 25:23
For I will bring the calamity of Esau
upon him,
The time *that* I will punish him.
9 If grape-gatherers came to you,
Would they not leave *some* gleaning
grapes?
If thieves by night,
Would they not destroy until they have
enough?
10 [R]But I have made Esau bare; Mal. 1:3
I have uncovered his secret places,*
And he shall not be able to hide himself.
His descendants are plundered,
His brethren and his neighbors,
And [R]he *is* no more. Is. 17:14
11 Leave your fatherless children,
I will preserve *them* alive;
And let your widows trust in Me."

12 For thus says the LORD: "Behold, [R]those
whose judgment *was* not to drink of the cup
have assuredly drunk. And *are* you the one
who will altogether go unpunished? You shall

49:1 Heb. *Malcam,* lit. *their king;* an Ammonite god, 1 Kin. 11:5; *Molech,* Lev. 18:21 **49:10** Cf. Obad. 5, 6

not go unpunished, but you shall surely drink *of it*. Jer. 25:29

13 "For I have sworn by Myself," says the LORD, "that Bozrah shall become a desolation, a reproach, a waste, and a curse. And all its cities shall be perpetual wastes."

14[R] I have heard a message from the LORD,
And an ambassador has been sent to the nations: Obad. 1–4
"Gather together, come against her,
And rise up to battle!

15 "For indeed, I will make you small among nations,
Despised among men.
16 Your fierceness has deceived you,
The [R]pride of your heart, Jer. 48:29
O you who dwell in the clefts of the rock,
Who hold the height of the hill!
Though you make your [R]nest as high as the eagle, Job 39:27
[R]I will bring you down from there," says the LORD.* Amos 9:2

17 "Edom also shall be an astonishment;
[R]Everyone who goes by it will be astonished Jer. 18:16; 49:13; 50:13
And will hiss at all its plagues.
18[R] As in the overthrow of Sodom and Gomorrah Deut. 29:23
And their neighbors," says the LORD,
"No one shall remain there,
Nor shall a son of man dwell in it.

19 "Behold,[R] he shall come up like a lion
from [R]the floodplain* of the Jordan
Against the dwelling place of the strong;
But I will suddenly make him run away from her. Jer. 50:44 • Jer. 12:5
And who *is* a chosen *man that* I may appoint over her?
For [R]who *is* like Me? Ex. 15:11
Who will arraign Me?
And [R]who *is* that shepherd Job 41:10
Who will withstand Me?"

20[R] Therefore hear the counsel of the LORD
that He has taken against Edom,
And His purposes that He has proposed
against the inhabitants of Teman:
Surely the least of the flock shall [T]draw them out; Jer. 50:45 • Or *drag them away*
Surely He shall make their dwelling places desolate with them.
21[R] The earth shakes at the noise of their fall; Jer. 50:46
At the cry its noise is heard at the Red Sea.
22 Behold, [R]He shall come up and fly like the eagle, Jer. 48:40, 41
And spread His wings over Bozrah;
The heart of the mighty men of Edom in that day shall be
Like the heart of a woman in birth pangs.

Prophecies Against Damascus

23 [R]Against Damascus. Amos 1:3, 5

[R]"Hamath and Arpad are shamed,
For they have heard bad news.
They are fainthearted; Jer. 39:5
[R]*There is* [T]trouble on the sea; [Is. 57:20]
It cannot be quiet. *anxiety*
24 Damascus has grown feeble;
She turns to flee,
And fear has seized *her*.
[R]Anguish and sorrows have taken her like a woman in labor. Is. 13:8
25 Why is [R]the city of praise not deserted, the city of My joy? Jer. 33:9
26[R] Therefore her young men shall fall in her streets, Jer. 50:30
And all the men of war shall be cut off in that day," says the LORD of hosts.
27 "I will kindle a fire in the wall of Damascus,
And it shall consume the palaces of Ben-Hadad."*

Prophecies Against Kedar and Hazor

28 [R]Against Kedar and against the kingdoms
of Hazor, which Nebuchadnezzar king of
Babylon shall strike. Ezek. 27:21
Thus says the LORD:

"Arise, go up to Kedar,
And devastate the men of the East!
29 Their [R]tents and their flocks they shall take away. Ps. 120:5
They shall take for themselves their curtains,
All their vessels and their camels;
And they shall cry out to them,
[R]'Fear *is* on every side!' Jer. 46:5

30 "Flee, get far away! Dwell in the depths,
O inhabitants of Hazor!" says the LORD.
"For Nebuchadnezzar king of Babylon
has taken counsel against you,
And has conceived a plan against you.

31 "Arise, go up to [R]the wealthy nation that dwells securely," says the LORD,
"Which has neither gates nor bars,
[R]Dwelling alone. Ezek. 38:11 • Num. 23:9
32 Their camels shall be for booty,
And the multitude of their cattle for plunder.
I will [R]scatter to all winds those in the farthest corners, Ezek. 5:10
And I will bring their calamity from all its sides," says the LORD.

49:16 Cf. Obad. 3, 4 **49:19** Or *thicket* **49:27** Cf. Amos 1:4

33 "Hazor [R]shall be a dwelling for jackals,
a desolation forever; Mal. 1:3
No one shall reside there,
Nor son of man dwell in it."

Prophecies Against Elam

34 The word of the LORD that came to Jere-
miah the prophet against [R]Elam, in the [R]be-
ginning of the reign of Zedekiah king of
Judah, saying, Jer. 25:25 • 2 Kin. 24:17, 18
35 "Thus says the LORD of hosts:

'Behold, I will break [R]the bow of Elam,
The foremost of their might. Is. 22:6
36 Against Elam I will bring the four winds
From the four quarters of heaven,
And scatter them toward all those winds;
There shall be no nations where the
outcasts of Elam will not go.
37 For I will cause Elam to be dismayed
before their enemies
And before those who seek their life.
I will bring disaster upon them,
My fierce anger,' says the LORD;
'And I will send the sword after them
Until I have consumed them.
38 I will set My throne in Elam,
And will destroy from there the king and
the princes,' says the LORD.
39 'But it shall come to pass [R]in the latter
days: Jer. 48:47
I will bring back the captives of Elam,'
says the LORD."

CHAPTER 50

Babylon's Defeat

THE word that the LORD spoke against
Babylon *and* against the land of the
Chaldeans by Jeremiah the prophet.

2 "Declare among the nations,
Proclaim, and [T]set up a standard; lift
Proclaim—do not conceal *it*—
Say, 'Babylon is [R]taken, Bel is shamed.
Merodach* is broken in pieces; Is. 21:9
[R]Her idols are humiliated, Jer. 43:12, 13
Her images are broken in pieces.'
3 [R]For out of the north [R]a nation comes up
against her, Jer. 51:48 • Is. 13:17, 18, 20
Which shall make her land desolate,
And no one shall dwell therein.
They shall [T]move, they shall depart,
Both man and beast. Or *wander*

4 "In those days and in that time," says the
LORD,
"The children of Israel shall come,
[R]They and the children of Judah
together; Hos. 1:11
With continual weeping they shall come,
[R]And seek the LORD their God. Hos. 3:5
5 They shall ask the way to Zion,
With their faces toward it, *saying,*
'Come and let us join ourselves to the
LORD
In [R]a perpetual covenant Jer. 31:31
That will not be forgotten.'

6 "My people have been [R]lost sheep.
Their shepherds have led them astray;
They have turned them away *on* [R]the
mountains. Is. 53:6 • [Jer. 2:20; 3:6, 23]
They have gone from mountain to hill;
They have forgotten their resting place.
7 All who found them have [R]devoured
them; Ps. 79:7
And [R]their adversaries said, [R]'We have
not offended, Zech. 11:5 • Jer. 2:3
Because they have sinned against the
LORD, the habitation of justice,
The LORD, the hope of their fathers.'

8 "Move from the midst of Babylon,
Go out of the land of the Chaldeans;
And be like the rams before the flocks.
9 [R]For behold, I will raise and cause to
come up against Babylon
An assembly of great nations from the
north country, Jer. 15:14; 51:27
And they shall array themselves against
her;
From there she shall be captured.
Their arrows *shall be* like *those* of an
expert warrior;*
[R]None shall return in vain. 2 Sam. 1:22
10 And Chaldea shall become plunder;
[R]All who plunder her shall be satisfied,"
says the LORD. [Rev. 17:16]

11 "Because[R] you were glad, because you
rejoiced, Is. 47:6
You destroyers of My heritage,
Because you have grown fat [R]like a
heifer threshing grain, Hos. 10:11
And you bellow like bulls,
12 Your mother shall be deeply ashamed;
She who bore you shall be ashamed.
Behold, the least of the nations *shall be* a
[R]wilderness, Jer. 51:43
A dry land and a desert.
13 Because of the wrath of the LORD
She shall not be inhabited,
[R]But she shall be wholly desolate.
[R]Everyone who goes by Babylon shall be
horrified Jer. 25:12 • Jer. 49:17
And hiss at all her plagues.

14 "Put[R] yourselves in array against Babylon
all around, Jer. 51:2
All you who bend the bow;

50:2 Or *Marduk;* a Babylonian god **50:9** So with some Heb. mss., LXX, Syr.; MT, Tg., Vg. *a warrior who makes childless*

Shoot at her, spare no arrows,
For she has sinned against the LORD.
15 Shout against her all around;
She has [R]given her hand, Lam. 5:6
Her foundations have fallen,
[R]Her walls are thrown down; Jer. 51:58
For [R]it *is* the vengeance of the LORD.
Take vengeance on her. Jer. 51:6, 11
As she has done, so do to her.
16 Cut off the sower from Babylon,
And him who handles the sickle at
harvest time.
For fear of the oppressing sword
Everyone shall turn to his own people,
And everyone shall flee to his own land.

17"Israel *is* like scattered sheep;
The lions have driven *him* away.
First the king of Assyria devoured him;
Now at last this Nebuchadnezzar king of
Babylon has broken his bones."

18 Therefore thus says the LORD of hosts, the God of Israel:

"Behold, I will punish the king of Babylon
and his land,
As I have punished the king of Assyria.
19[R]But I will bring back Israel to his home,
And he shall feed on Carmel and
Bashan; Is. 65:10
His soul shall be satisfied on Mount
Ephraim and Gilead.
20 In those days and in that time," says the
LORD,
[R]"The iniquity of Israel shall be sought, but
there shall be none; [Jer. 31:34]
And the sins of Judah, but they shall not
be found;
For I will pardon those [R]whom I
preserve. Is. 1:9

Babylon's Desolation

21"Go up against the land of Merathaim,
against it,
And against the inhabitants of [R]Pekod.
Waste and utterly destroy them," says
the LORD, Ezek. 23:23
"And do [R]according to all that I have
commanded you. 2 Sam. 16:11
22[R]A sound of battle *is* in the land,
And of great destruction. Jer. 51:54
23 How [R]the hammer of the whole earth
has been cut apart and broken!
How Babylon has become a desolation
among the nations! Jer. 51:20–24
I have laid a snare for you;
24 You have indeed been [R]trapped,
O Babylon, Dan. 5:30
And you were not aware;
You have been found and also caught,
Because you have [R]contended against
the LORD. [Is. 45:9]
25 The LORD has opened His armory,
And has brought out [R]the weapons of
His indignation; Is. 13:5
For this *is* the work of the Lord GOD of
hosts
In the land of the Chaldeans.
26 Come against her from the farthest
border;
Open her storehouses;
Cast her up as heaps of ruins,
And destroy her utterly;
Let nothing of her be left.
27 Slay all her [R]bulls, Is. 34:7
Let them go down to the slaughter.
Woe to them!
For their day has come, the time of
[R]their punishment. Jer. 48:44
28 The voice of those who flee and escape
from the land of Babylon
[R]Declares in Zion the vengeance of the
LORD our God, Jer. 51:10
The vengeance of His temple.

29"Call together the archers against
Babylon.
All you who bend the bow, encamp
against it all around;
Let none of them escape.*
[R]Repay her according to her work;
According to all she has done, do to her;
[R]For she has been proud against the
LORD, Jer. 51:56 • [Is. 47:10]
Against the Holy One of Israel.
30[R]Therefore her young men shall fall in
the streets, Jer. 49:26; 51:4
And all her men of war shall be cut off
in that day," says the LORD.
31"Behold, I *am* against you,
O most haughty one!" says the Lord GOD
of hosts;
"For your day has come,
The time *that* I will punish you.*
32 The most [R]proud shall stumble and fall,
And no one will raise him up; Mal. 4:1
I will kindle a fire in his cities,
And it will devour all around him."

33 Thus says the LORD of hosts:

"The children of Israel *were* oppressed,
Along with the children of Judah;
All who took them captive have held
them fast;
They have refused to let them go.
34[R]Their Redeemer *is* strong; Rev. 18:8
[R]The LORD of hosts *is* His name. Is. 47:4
He will thoroughly plead their case,
That He may give rest to the land,
And disquiet the inhabitants of Babylon.

50:29 Qr., some Heb. mss., LXX, Tg. add *to her*
50:31 So with MT, Tg.; LXX, Vg. *The time of your punishment*

35 "A sword *is* against the Chaldeans," says the LORD,
"Against the inhabitants of Babylon,
And [R]against her princes and [R]her wise men. Dan. 5:30 • Is. 47:13
36 A sword *is* [R]against the soothsayers, and they will be fools. Is. 44:25
A sword *is* against her mighty men, and they will be dismayed.
37 A sword *is* against their horses,
Against their chariots,
And against all [R]the mixed peoples who *are* in her midst; Jer. 25:20
And [R]they will become like women.
A sword *is* against her treasures, and they will be robbed. Jer. 51:30
38 [R]A drought* *is* against her waters, and they will be dried up. Rev. 16:12
For it *is* the land of carved images,
And they are insane with *their* idols.

39 "Therefore[R] the wild desert beasts shall dwell *there* with the jackals,
And the ostriches shall dwell in it.
[R]It shall be inhabited no more forever,
Nor shall it be dwelt in from generation to generation. Rev. 18:2 • Is. 13:20
40 [R]As God overthrew Sodom and Gomorrah
And their neighbors," says the LORD,
"*So* no one shall reside there, Is. 13:19
Nor son of man [R]dwell in it. Is. 13:20

41 "Behold,[R] a people shall come from the north, Jer. 6:22; 25:14; 51:27
And a great nation and many kings
Shall be raised up from the ends of the earth.
42 [R]They shall hold the bow and the lance;
[R]They *are* cruel and shall not show mercy. Jer. 6:23 • Is. 13:18
[R]Their voice shall roar like the sea;
They shall ride on horses, Is. 5:30
Set in array, like a man for the battle,
Against you, O daughter of Babylon.

43 "The king of Babylon has [R]heard the report about them, Jer. 51:31
And his hands grow feeble;
Anguish has taken hold of him,
Pangs as of a woman in childbirth.

44 "Behold,[R] he shall come up like a lion from the floodplain* of the Jordan
Against the dwelling place of the strong;
But I will make them suddenly run away from her. Jer. 49:19–21
And who *is* a chosen *man that* I may appoint over her?
For who *is* like Me?
Who will arraign Me?
And [R]who *is* that shepherd Job 41:10
Who will withstand Me?"

45 Therefore hear [R]the counsel of the LORD that He has taken against Babylon,
And His [R]purposes that He has proposed against the land of the Chaldeans: Jer. 51:10, 11 • Jer. 51:29
[R]Surely the least of the flock shall draw them out; Jer. 49:19, 20
Surely He will make their dwelling place desolate with them.
46 [R]At the noise of the taking of Babylon
The earth trembles, Rev. 18:9
And the cry is heard among the nations.

CHAPTER 51

Babylon's Destiny

THUS says the LORD:
"Behold, I will raise up against [R]Babylon,
Against those who dwell in Leb Kamai,*
[R]A destroying wind. Is. 47:1 • Jer. 4:11
2 And I will send [R]winnowers to Babylon,
Who shall winnow her and empty her land. Jer. 15:7
[R]For in the day of doom Jer. 50:14
They shall be against her all around.
3 Against *her* [R]let the archer bend his bow, Jer. 50:14, 29
And lift himself up against *her* in his armor.
Do not spare her young men;
[R]Utterly destroy all her army. Jer. 50:21
4 Thus the slain shall fall in the land of the Chaldeans,
And *those* thrust through in her streets.
5 For Israel is not forsaken, nor Judah,
By his God, the LORD of hosts,
Though their land was filled with sin against the Holy One of Israel."

6 [R]Flee from the midst of Babylon,
And every one save his life!
Do not be cut off in her iniquity,
For [R]this *is* the time of the LORD's vengeance; Rev. 18:4 • Jer. 50:15
[R]He shall recompense her. Jer. 25:14
7 [R]Babylon *was* a golden cup in the LORD's hand, Rev. 17:4
That made all the earth drunk.
[R]The nations drank her wine; Rev. 14:8
Therefore the nations are deranged.
8 Babylon has suddenly [R]fallen and been destroyed. Is. 21:9
[R]Wail for her! Rev. 18:9, 11, 19
[R]Take balm for her pain; Jer. 46:11
Perhaps she may be healed.

50:38 So with MT, Tg., Vg.; Syr. *sword;* LXX omits *A drought is* **50:44** Or *thicket* **51:1** Lit. *The Midst of Those Who Rise Up Against Me;* a code word for Chaldea (Babylonia)

9 We would have healed Babylon,
But she is not healed.
Forsake her, and [R]let us go everyone to
his own country; Is. 13:14
[R]For her judgment reaches to heaven and
is lifted up to the skies. Rev. 18:5
10 The LORD has [R]revealed our
righteousness. Ps. 37:6
Come and let us [R]declare in Zion the
work of the LORD our God. Jer. 50:28

11[R]Make the arrows bright! Jer. 46:4, 9
Gather the shields!
[R]The LORD has raised up the spirit of the
kings of the Medes. Is. 13:17
[R]For His plan *is* against Babylon to
destroy it, Jer. 50:45
Because it *is* [R]the vengeance of the
LORD, Jer. 50:28
The vengeance for His temple.
12[R]Set up the standard on the walls of
Babylon; Nah. 2:1; 3:14
Make the guard strong,
Set up the watchmen,
Prepare the ambushes.
For the LORD has both devised and done
What He spoke against the inhabitants
of Babylon.
13[R]O you who dwell by many waters,
Abundant in treasures, Rev. 17:1, 15
Your end has come,
The measure of your covetousness.
14[R]The LORD of hosts has sworn by Himself:
"Surely I will fill you with men, [R]as with
locusts, Jer. 49:13 • Nah. 3:15
And they shall lift [R]up a shout against
you." Jer. 50:15

15[R]He has made the earth by His power;
He has established the world by His
wisdom, Gen. 1:1, 6
And [R]stretched out the heaven by His
understanding. Job 9:8
16 When He utters *His* voice—
There is a multitude of waters in the
heavens:
"He causes the vapors to ascend from the
ends of the earth;
He makes lightnings for the rain;
He brings the wind out of His
treasuries."*

17[R]Everyone is dull-hearted, without
knowledge; Jer. 10:14
Every metalsmith is put to shame by the
carved image;
For his molded image *is* falsehood,
And *there is* no breath in them.
18 They *are* futile, a work of errors;
In the time of their punishment they
shall perish.
19 The Portion of Jacob *is* not like them,
For He *is* the Maker of all things;
And *Israel is* the tribe of His inheritance.
The LORD of hosts *is* His name.

20"You[R] *are* My battle-ax *and* weapons of
war: Is. 10:5, 15
For with you I will break the nation in
pieces;
With you I will destroy kingdoms;
21 With you I will break in pieces the horse
and its rider;
With you I will break in pieces the
chariot and its rider;
22 With you also I will break in pieces man
and woman;
With you I will break in pieces [R]old and
young; 2 Chr. 36:17
With you I will break in pieces the young
man and the maiden;
23 With you also I will break in pieces the
shepherd and his flock;
With you I will break in pieces the
farmer and his yoke of oxen;
And with you I will break in pieces
governors and rulers.

24"And[R] I will repay Babylon Jer. 50:15, 29
And all the inhabitants of Chaldea
For all the evil they have done
In Zion in your sight," says the LORD.

25"Behold, I *am* against you, [R]O destroying
mountain, Zech. 4:7
Who destroys all the earth," says the
LORD.
"And I will stretch out My hand against
you,
Roll you down from the rocks,
And make you a burnt mountain.
26 They shall not take from you a stone for
a corner
Nor a stone for a foundation,
[R]But you shall be desolate forever," says
the LORD. Jer. 50:26, 40

27[R]Set up a banner in the land, Is. 13:2
Blow the trumpet among the nations!
Prepare the nations against her,
Call [R]the kingdoms together against her:
Ararat, Minni, and Ashkenaz.
Appoint a general against her;
Cause the horses to come up like the
bristling locusts. Jer. 50:41, 42
28 Prepare against her the nations,
With the kings of the Medes,
Its governors and all its rulers,
All the land of his dominion.
29 And the land will tremble and sorrow;
For every purpose of the LORD shall be
performed against Babylon,
To make the land of Babylon a
desolation without inhabitant.

51:16 Ps. 135:7

30 The mighty men of Babylon have ceased
fighting,
They have remained in their strongholds;
Their might has failed,
[R]They became *like* women; Is. 19:16
They have burned her dwelling places,
The bars of her *gate* are broken.
31[R]One runner will run to meet another
And one messenger to meet another,
To show the king of Babylon that his city
is taken on *all* sides; Jer. 50:24
32[R]The passages are blocked, Jer. 50:38
The reeds they have burned with fire,
And the men of war are terrified.

33 For thus says the LORD of hosts, the God
of Israel:

"The daughter of Babylon *is* [R]like a
threshing floor Is. 21:10
When [R]*it is* time to thresh her;
Yet a little while Hab. 3:12
And the time of her harvest will come."

34"Nebuchadnezzar the king of Babylon
Has [R]devoured me, he has crushed me;
He has made me an [R]empty vessel,
He has swallowed me up like a monster;
He has filled his stomach with my
delicacies, Jer. 50:17 • Is. 24:1–3
He has spit me out.
35 Let the violence *done* to me and my flesh
be upon Babylon,"
The inhabitant of Zion will say;
"And my blood be upon the inhabitants
of Chaldea!"
Jerusalem will say.

36 Therefore thus says the LORD:

"Behold, [R]I will plead your case and take
vengeance for you. Jer. 50:34
[R]I will dry up her sea and make her
springs dry. Jer. 50:38
37[R]Babylon shall become a heap, Is. 13:22
A dwelling place for jackals,
[R]An astonishment and a hissing,
Without an inhabitant. Jer. 25:9, 11
38 They shall roar together like lions,
They shall growl like lions' whelps.
39 In their excitement I will prepare their
feasts;
[R]I will make them drunk, Jer. 51:57
That they may rejoice,
And sleep a perpetual sleep
And not awake," says the LORD.
40"I will bring them down
Like lambs to the slaughter,
Like rams with male goats.

41"Oh, how [R]Sheshach* is taken!
Oh, how [R]the praise of the whole earth
is seized! Jer. 25:26 • Is. 13:19
How Babylon has become desolate
among the nations!
42[R]The sea has come up over Babylon;
She is covered with the multitude of its
waves. Is. 8:7, 8
43 Her cities are a desolation,
A dry land and a wilderness,
A land where [R]no one dwells, Is. 13:20
Through which no son of man passes.
44 I will punish [R]Bel in Babylon, Jer. 50:2
And I will bring out of his mouth what
he has swallowed;
And the nations shall not stream to him
anymore.
Yes, the wall of Babylon shall fall.

45"My[R] people, go out of the midst of her!
And let everyone deliver himself from
the fierce anger of the LORD. [Rev. 18:4]
46 And lest your heart faint,
And you fear [R]for the rumor that *will be*
heard in the land 2 Kin. 19:7
(A rumor will come *one* year,
And after that, in *another* year
A rumor *will come,*
And violence in the land,
Ruler against ruler),
47 Therefore behold, the days are coming
That I will bring judgment on the carved
images of Babylon;
Her whole land shall be ashamed,
And all her slain shall fall in her midst.
48 Then [R]the heavens and the earth and all
that *is* in them Is. 44:23; 48:20; 49:13
Shall sing joyously over Babylon;
For the plunderers shall come to her
from the north," says the LORD.

49 As Babylon *has caused* the slain of Israel
to fall,
So at Babylon the slain of all the earth
shall fall.
50[R]You who have escaped the sword,
Get away! Do not stand still! Jer. 44:28
Remember the LORD afar off,
And let Jerusalem come to your mind.

51[R]We are ashamed because we have heard
reproach. Ps. 44:15; 79:4
Shame has covered our faces,
For strangers have come into the
sanctuaries of the LORD's house.

52"Therefore behold, the days are coming,"
says the LORD,
"That I will bring judgment on her carved
images,
And throughout all her land the
wounded shall groan.
53[R]Though Babylon were to [T]mount up to
heaven, Amos 9:2 • *ascend*

51:41 A code word for Babylon, Jer. 25:26

And though she were to fortify the
height of her strength,
Yet from Me plunderers would come to
her," says the LORD.

54[R] The sound of a cry *comes* from
Babylon,
And great destruction from the land of
the Chaldeans, Jer. 50:22
55 Because the LORD is plundering Babylon
And silencing her loud voice,
Though her waves roar like great
waters,
And the noise of their voice is uttered,
56 Because the plunderer comes against
her, against Babylon,
And her mighty men are taken.
Every one of their bows is broken;
[R] For the LORD *is* the God of recompense,
He will surely repay. Jer. 50:29

57 "And I will make drunk
Her princes and [R]wise men, Jer. 50:35
Her governors, her deputies, and her
mighty men.
And they shall sleep a perpetual sleep
And not awake," says the King,
Whose name *is* the LORD of hosts.

58 Thus says the LORD of hosts:

"The broad walls of Babylon shall be
utterly [R]broken,[T]
And her high gates shall be burned with
fire; Jer. 50:15 • Lit. *laid utterly bare*
[R] The people will labor in vain, Hab. 2:13
And the nations, because of the fire;
And they shall be weary."

59 The word which Jeremiah the prophet
commanded Seraiah the son of [R]Neriah, the
son of Mahseiah, when he went with Zede-
kiah the king of Judah to Babylon in the
fourth year of his reign. And Seraiah *was* the
quartermaster. Jer. 32:12
60 So Jeremiah wrote in a book all the evil
that would come upon Babylon, all these
words that are written against Babylon.
61 And Jeremiah said to Seraiah, "When you
arrive in Babylon and see it, and read all these
words,
62 "then you shall say, 'O LORD, You have
spoken against this place to cut it off, so that
none shall remain in it, neither man nor beast,
but it shall be desolate forever.'
63 "Now it shall be, when you have finished
reading this book, *that* you shall tie a stone to
it and throw it out into the Euphrates.
64 "Then you shall say, 'Thus Babylon shall
sink and not rise from the catastrophe that I
will bring upon her. And they shall be
weary.' " Thus far *are* the words of Jeremiah.

CHAPTER 52

The Capture of Jerusalem
2 Kin. 24:18—25:30; 2 Chr. 36:11–20; Jer. 39:1–8

ZEDEKIAH *was* [R]twenty-one years old
when he became king, and he reigned
eleven years in Jerusalem. His mother's name
was Hamutal the daughter of Jeremiah of
[R]Libnah. 2 Kin. 24:18 • Josh. 10:29
2 He also did evil in the sight of the LORD,
according to all that Jehoiakim had done.
3 For because of the anger of the LORD *this*
happened in Jerusalem and Judah, till He fi-
nally cast them out from His presence. Then
Zedekiah [R]rebelled against the king of Bab-
ylon. 2 Chr. 36:13
4 Now it came to pass in the ninth year of
his reign, in the tenth month, on the tenth *day*
of the month, *that* Nebuchadnezzar king of
Babylon and all his army came against Jeru-
salem and encamped against it; and *they* built
a siege wall against it all around.
5 So the city was besieged until the
eleventh year of King Zedekiah.
6 By the fourth month, on the ninth day of
the month, the famine had become so severe
in the city that there was no food for the peo-
ple of the land.
7 Then the city wall was broken through,
and all the men of war fled and went out of the
city at night by way of the gate between the
two walls, which *was* by the king's garden,
even though the Chaldeans *were* near the city
all around. And they went by way of the plain.*
8 But the army of the Chaldeans pursued
the king, and they overtook Zedekiah in the
plains of Jericho. All his army was scattered
from him.
9 [R]So they took the king and brought him
up to the king of Babylon at Riblah in the land
of Hamath, and he pronounced judgment on
him. Jer. 32:4; 39:5
10 Then the king of Babylon killed the sons
of Zedekiah before his eyes. And he killed all
the princes of Judah in Riblah.
11 He also put out the eyes of Zedekiah; and
the king of Babylon bound him in bronze fet-
ters, took him to Babylon, and put him in
prison till the day of his death.

The Destruction of Jerusalem

12 [R]Now in the fifth month, on the tenth *day*
of the month ([R]which *was* the nineteenth year
of King Nebuchadnezzar king of Babylon),
Nebuzaradan, the captain of the guard, *who*
served the king of Babylon, came to Jerusa-
lem. 2 Kin. 25:8–21 • Jer. 52:29
13 He burned the house of the LORD and the
king's house; all the houses of Jerusalem, that
is, all the houses of the great, he burned with
fire.

52:7 Or *the Arabah;* the Jordan Valley

14 And all the army of the Chaldeans who *were* with the captain of the guard broke down all the walls of Jerusalem all around.

15 [R]Then Nebuzaradan the captain of the guard carried away captive *some* of the poor people, the rest of the people who remained in the city, the defectors who had deserted to the king of Babylon, and the rest of the craftsmen. Jer. 39:9

16 But Nebuzaradan the captain of the guard left *some* of the poor of the land as vinedressers and farmers.

17 The bronze pillars that *were* in the house of the LORD, and the carts and the bronze Sea that *were* in the house of the LORD, the Chaldeans broke in pieces, and carried all their bronze to Babylon.

18 They also took away [R]the pots, the shovels, the trimmers, the [T]bowls, the spoons, and all the bronze utensils with which the priests ministered. Ex. 27:3 • *basins*

19 The basins, the firepans, the bowls, the pots, the lampstands, the spoons, and the cups, whatever *was* solid gold and whatever *was* solid silver, the captain of the guard took away.

20 The two pillars, one Sea, the twelve bronze bulls which *were* under *it, and* the carts, which King Solomon had made for the house of the LORD—[R]the bronze of all these articles was beyond measure. 1 Kin. 7:47

21 Now *concerning* the [R]pillars: the height of one pillar *was* eighteen cubits, a measuring line of twelve cubits could measure its circumference, and its thickness *was* [T]four fingers; *it was* hollow. 2 Kin. 25:17 • 3 inches

22 A capital of bronze *was* on it; and the height of one capital *was* five cubits, with a network and pomegranates all around the capital, all of bronze. The second pillar, with pomegranates was the same.

23 There were ninety-six pomegranates on the sides; all the pomegranates, all around on the network, *were* one hundred.

The Exile to Babylon

24 The captain of the guard took Seraiah the chief priest, Zephaniah the second priest, and the three doorkeepers.

25 He also took out of the city an officer who had charge of the men of war, seven men of the king's close associates who were found in the city, the principal scribe of the army who mustered the people of the land, and sixty men of the people of the land who were found in the midst of the city.

26 And Nebuzaradan the captain of the guard took these and brought them to the king of Babylon at Riblah.

27 Then the king of Babylon struck them and put them to death at Riblah in the land of Hamath. Thus Judah was carried away captive from its own land.

28 [R]These *are* the people whom Nebuchadnezzar carried away captive: [R]in the seventh year, [R]three thousand and twenty-three Jews; 2 Kin. 24:2 • 2 Kin. 24:12 • 2 Kin. 24:14

29 in the eighteenth year of Nebuchadnezzar he carried away captive from Jerusalem eight hundred and thirty-two persons;

30 in the twenty-third year of Nebuchadnezzar, Nebuzaradan the captain of the guard carried away captive of the Jews seven hundred and forty-five persons. All the persons *were* four thousand six hundred.

The Liberation of Jehoiachin

31 [R]Now it came to pass in the thirty-seventh year of the captivity of Jehoiachin king of Judah, in the twelfth month, on the twenty-fifth *day* of the month, *that* Evil-Merodach* king of Babylon, in the first *year* of his reign, [R]lifted up the head of Jehoiachin king of Judah and brought him out of prison. 2 Kin. 25:27–30 • Gen. 40:13, 20

32 And he spoke kindly to him and gave him a more prominent seat than those of the kings who *were* with him in Babylon.

33 So Jehoiachin changed from his prison garments, [R]and he ate bread regularly before the king all the days of his life. 2 Sam. 9:7, 13

34 And as for his provisions, there was a regular ration given him by the king of Babylon, a portion for each day until the day of his death, all the days of his life.

52:31 Or *Awil-Marduk;* lit. *The Man of Marduk*

THE BOOK OF

LAMENTATIONS

THE BOOK OF LAMENTATIONS

Lamentations describes the funeral of a city. It is a tearstained portrait of the once proud Jerusalem, now reduced to rubble by the invading Babylonian hordes. In a five-poem dirge, Jeremiah exposes his emotions. A death has occurred; Jerusalem lies barren.

Jeremiah writes his lament in acrostic or alphabetical fashion. Beginning each chapter with the first letter *A* (aleph) he progresses verse by verse through the Hebrew alphabet, literally weeping from *A* to *Z*. And then, in the midst of this terrible holocaust, Jeremiah triumphantly cries out, "Great *is* Your faithfulness" (3:23). In the face of death and destruction, with life seemingly coming apart, Jeremiah turns tragedy into a triumph of faith. God has never failed him in the past. God has promised to remain faithful in the future. In the light of the God he knows and loves, Jeremiah finds hope and comfort.

The Hebrew title of this book comes from the first word of chapters 1, 2, and 4: *Ekah,* "Ah, how!" Another Hebrew word *Ginoth* ("Elegies" or "Lamentations") has also been used as the title because it better represents the contents of the book. The Greek title *Threnoi* means "Dirges" or "Laments," and the Latin title *Threni* ("Tears" or "Lamentations") was derived from this word. The subtitle in Jerome's Vulgate reads: *"Id est lamentationes Jeremiae prophetae,"* and this became the basis for the English title "The Lamentations of Jeremiah."

THE AUTHOR OF LAMENTATIONS

The author of Lamentations is unnamed in the book, but internal and external evidence consistently favors Jeremiah.

External Evidence: The universal consensus of early Jewish and Christian tradition attributes this book to Jeremiah. The superscription to Lamentations in the Septuagint says: "And it came to pass, after Israel had been carried away captive, and Jerusalem had become desolate, that Jeremiah sat weeping, and lamented with this lamentation over Jerusalem, saying. . . ." This is also the position of the Talmud, the Aramaic Targum of Jonathan, and early Christian writers, such as Origen and Jerome. In addition, 2 Chronicles 35:25 says that "Jeremiah also lamented for Josiah." This was an earlier occasion, but Jeremiah was obviously familiar with the lament form.

Internal Evidence: The scenes in this graphic book were clearly portrayed by an eyewitness to Jerusalem's siege and fall soon after the destruction took place (cf. 1:13–15; 2:6, 9; 4:1–12). Jeremiah witnessed the fall of Jerusalem and remained behind after the captives were deported (see Jer. 39). Although some critics claim that the style of Lamentations is different from the Book of Jeremiah, the similarities are, in fact, striking and numerous, especially in the poetic sections of Jeremiah. Compare these passages from Lamentations and Jeremiah: 1:2 (Jer. 30:14); 1:15 (Jer. 8:21); 1:16 and 2:11 (Jer. 9:1, 18); 2:22 (Jer. 6:25); 4:21 (Jer. 49:12). The same compassion, sympathy, and grief over Judah's downfall are evident in both books.

THE TIME OF LAMENTATIONS

The historical background of Lamentations can be found in "The Time of Jeremiah." The book was written soon after Jerusalem's destruction (Jer. 39; 52) at the beginning of the Exile. Nebuchadnezzar laid siege to Jerusalem from January 588 B.C. to July 586 B.C. It fell on July 19, and the city and temple were burned on August 15. Jeremiah probably wrote these five elegies before he was taken captive to Egypt by his disobedient countrymen not long after the destruction (Jer. 43:1–7).

THE CHRIST OF LAMENTATIONS

The weeping prophet Jeremiah is a type of Christ, the Prophet who wept over the same city six centuries later. "O Jerusalem, Jerusalem, the one who kills the prophets and stones those who are sent to her! How often I wanted to gather your children together, as a hen gathers her chicks under *her* wings, but you were not willing! See! Your house is left to you desolate" (Matt. 23:37, 38). Like Christ, Jeremiah identified himself personally with the plight of Jerusalem and with human suffering caused by sin.

Lamentations also includes elements that typify Christ's life and ministry as the man of sorrows who was acquainted with grief. He was afflicted (1:12; 3:19), despised, and derided by His enemies (2:15, 16; 3:14, 30).

KEYS TO LAMENTATIONS

Key Word: Lamentations—Three themes run through the five laments of Jeremiah. The most prominent is the theme of mourning over Jerusalem's holocaust. The Holy City has been laid waste and desolate: God's promised judgment for sin has come. In his sorrow, Jeremiah speaks for himself, for the captives, and sometimes for the personified city. The second theme is a confession of sin and an acknowledgment of God's righteous and holy judgment upon Judah. The third theme is least prominent but very important: it is a note of hope in God's future restoration of His people. Yahweh has poured out His wrath, but in His mercy He will be faithful to His covenant promises.

Key Verses: Lamentations 2:5, 6 and 3:22, 23—"The Lord was like an enemy. He has swallowed up Israel, He has swallowed up all her palaces; He has destroyed her strongholds, and has increased mourning and lamentation in the daughter of Judah. He has done violence to His tabernacle, *as if it were* a garden; He has destroyed His place of assembly; the LORD has caused the appointed feasts and Sabbaths to be forgotten in Zion. In His burning indignation He has spurned the king and the priest" (2:5, 6).

"*Through* the LORD's mercies we are not consumed, because His compassions fail not. *They are* new every morning; great *is* Your faithfulness" (3:22, 23).

Key Chapter: Lamentations 3—In the midst of five chapters of ruin, destruction, and utter hopelessness, Jeremiah rises and grasps with strong faith the promises and character of God.

Lamentations 3:22–25 expresses a magnificent faith in the mercy of God—especially when placed against the dark backdrop of chapters 1, 2, 4, and 5.

SURVEY OF LAMENTATIONS

For forty years Jeremiah suffers rejection and abuse for his warnings of coming judgment. When Nebuchadnezzar finally comes and destroys Jerusalem in 586 B.C., a lesser man might say, "I told you so!" But Jeremiah compassionately identifies with the tragic overthrow of Jerusalem and composes five beautiful and emotional lament poems as a requiem for the once proud city. These dirges reflect the tender heart of the man who was divinely commissioned to communicate a harsh message to a sinful and stiff-necked people. The city, the temple, the palace, and the walls have been reduced to rubble and its inhabitants have been deported to distant Babylon. Jeremiah's five mournful poems can be entitled: the destruction of Jerusalem (1), the anger of Yahweh (2), the prayer for mercy (3), the siege of Jerusalem (4), and the prayer for restoration (5).

The Destruction of Jerusalem (1): This poem consists of a lamentation by Jeremiah (1:1–11) and a lamentation by the personified Jerusalem (1:12–22). The city has been left desolate because of its grievous sins, and her enemies "mocked at her downfall" (1:7). Jerusalem pleads with God to regard her misery and repay her adversaries.

The Anger of Yahweh (2): In his second elegy, Jeremiah moves from Jerusalem's desolation to a description of her destruction. Babylon has destroyed the city, but only as the Lord's instrument of judgment. Jeremiah presents an eyewitness account of the thoroughness and severity of Jerusalem's devastation. Through the Babylonians, God has terminated all religious observances, removed the priests, prophets, and kings, and razed the temple and palaces. Jeremiah grieves over the suffering the people brought on themselves through rebellion against God, and Jerusalem's supplications complete the lament.

The Prayer for Mercy (3): In the first eighteen verses, Jeremiah enters into the miseries and despair of his people and makes them his own. However, there is an abrupt turn in verses 19–39 as the prophet reflects on the faithfulness and loyal love of the compassionate God of Israel. These truths enable him to find comfort and hope in spite of his dismal circumstances.

FOCUS	DESTRUCTION OF JERUSALEM	ANGER OF JEHOVAH	PRAYER FOR MERCY	SIEGE OF JERUSALEM	PRAYER FOR RESTORATION
REFERENCE	1:1—	2:1—	3:1—	4:1—	5:1—5:22
DIVISION	MOURNING CITY	BROKEN PEOPLE	SUFFERING PROPHET	RUINED KINGDOM	PENITENT NATION
TOPIC	GRIEF	CAUSE	HOPE	REPENTANCE	PRAYER
LOCATION	JERUSALEM				
TIME	c. 586 B.C.				

Jeremiah expresses his deep sorrow and petitions God for deliverance and for God to avenge Jerusalem's misery.

The Siege of Jerusalem (4): The prophet rehearses the siege of Jerusalem and remembers the suffering and starvation of rich and poor. He also reviews the causes of the siege, especially the sins of the prophets and priests and their foolish trust in human aid. This poem closes with a warning to Edom of future punishment and a glimmer of hope for Jerusalem.

Prayer for Restoration (5): Jeremiah's last elegy is a melancholy description of his people's lamentable state. Their punishment is complete, and Jeremiah prayerfully desires the restoration of his nation.

OUTLINE OF LAMENTATIONS

I. The Destruction of Jerusalem 1:1–22

A. The Lament of the Prophet Jeremiah ..1:1–11
  1. The Desolation of Jerusalem............1:1–7
  2. The Cause of Jerusalem's Desolation............1:8–11

B. The Lament of the City Jerusalem 1:12–22
  1. The Contrition of Jerusalem 1:12–19
  2. The Confession of Jerusalem 1:20–22

II. The Anger of God 2:1–22

A. The Anger of God............2:1–9
B. The Agony of Jerusalem............2:10–17
C. The Appeal of Jerusalem............2:18–22

III. The Prayer for Mercy............3:1–66

A. Jeremiah's Cry of Despair............3:1–18
B. Jeremiah's Confession of Faith............3:19–39
C. Jeremiah's Condition of Need............3:40–54
D. Jeremiah's Confidence in God............3:55–66

IV. The Siege of Jerusalem............4:1–22

A. The Conditions During the Siege 4:1–10
B. The Cause of the Siege............4:11–20
C. The Consequences of the Siege............4:21, 22

V. The Prayer for Restoration 5:1–22

A. The Review of the Need for Restoration............5:1–15
B. The Repentance of Sin 5:16–18
C. The Request for Restoration............5:19–22

CHAPTER 1

The Desolation of Jerusalem

HOW lonely sits the city
That was full of people!
[R]*How* like a widow is she, Is. 47:7–9
Who *was* great among the nations!
The [R]princess among the provinces
Has become a slave! Ezra 4:20

2 She [R]weeps bitterly in the [R]night,
Her tears *are* on her cheeks;
Among all her lovers Jer. 13:17 • Job 7:3
She has none to comfort *her.*
All her friends have dealt treacherously with her;
They have become her enemies.

3 [R]Judah has gone into captivity, Jer. 52:27
Under affliction and hard servitude;
[R]She dwells among the nations,
She finds no [R]rest; Lam. 2:9 • Deut. 28:65
All her persecutors overtake her in dire straits.

4 The roads to Zion mourn
Because no one comes to the set feasts.
All her gates are [R]desolate; Is. 27:10
Her priests sigh,
Her virgins are afflicted,
And she *is* in bitterness.

5 Her adversaries [R]have become [T]the master, Deut. 28:43 • Lit. *her head*
Her enemies prosper;
For the LORD has afflicted her
[R]Because of the multitude of her transgressions. Dan. 9:7, 16
Her [R]children have gone into captivity before the enemy. Jer. 52:28

6 And from the daughter of Zion
All her splendor has departed.
Her princes have become like deer
That find no pasture,
That [T]flee without strength Lit. *are gone*
Before the pursuer.

7 In the days of her affliction and roaming,
Jerusalem [R]remembers all her pleasant things Ps. 137:1
That she had in the days of old.
When her people fell into the hand of the enemy,
With no one to help her,
The adversaries saw her
And mocked at her downfall.*

The Cause of Jerusalem's Desolation

8 Jerusalem has sinned gravely,
Therefore she has become vile.*
All who honored her despise her
Because they have seen her nakedness;
Yes, she sighs and turns away.

1:7 Vg. *her Sabbaths* 1:8 LXX, Vg. *moved* or *removed*

9 Her uncleanness *is* in her skirts;
She [R]did not consider her destiny;
Therefore her collapse was awesome;
She had no comforter. Is. 47:7
"O LORD, behold my affliction,
For *the* enemy is exalted!"

10 The adversary has spread his hand
Over all her [T]pleasant things; *desirable*
For she has seen [R]the nations enter her sanctuary, Jer. 51:51
Those whom You commanded
[R]Not to enter Your assembly. Deut. 23:3

11 All her people sigh,
[R]They [T]seek bread; Jer. 38:9; 52:6 • *hunt food*
They have given their [T]valuables for food to restore life. *desirable things*
"See, O LORD, and consider,
For I am scorned."

The Contrition of Jerusalem

12 "*Is it* nothing to you, all you who [T]pass by? Lit. *pass by this way*
Behold and see
[R]If there is any sorrow like my sorrow,
Which has been brought on me,
Which the LORD has inflicted
In the day of His fierce anger. Dan. 9:12

13 "From above He has sent fire into my bones,
And it overpowered them;
He has [R]spread a net for my feet
And turned me back;
He has made me desolate
And faint all the day. Ezek. 12:13; 17:20

14 "The[R] yoke of my transgressions was bound;* Deut. 28:48
They were woven together by His hands,
And thrust upon my neck.
He made my strength fail;
The Lord delivered me into the hands of *those whom* I am not able to withstand.

15 "The Lord has trampled underfoot all my mighty *men* in my midst;
He has called an assembly against me
To crush my young men;
The Lord trampled *as* in a winepress
The virgin daughter of Judah.

16 "For these *things* I weep;
My eye, [R]my eye overflows with water;
Because the comforter, who should restore my life,
Is far from me. Eccl. 4:1
My children are desolate
Because the enemy prevailed."

17 [R]Zion [T]spreads out her hands, Jer. 4:31 • Prays
But no one comforts her;
The LORD has commanded concerning Jacob
That those [R]around him *become* his adversaries; 2 Kin. 24:2–4
Jerusalem has become an unclean thing among them.

18 "The LORD is [R]righteous, Dan. 9:7, 14
For I [R]rebelled against His [T]commandment. 1 Sam. 12:14, 15 • Lit. *mouth*
Hear now, all peoples,
And behold my sorrow;
My virgins and my young men
Have gone into captivity.

19 "I called for my lovers,
But they deceived me;
My priests and my elders
Breathed their last in the city,
While they sought food
To restore their life.

The Confession of Jerusalem

20 "See, O LORD, that I *am* in distress;
My [R]soul is troubled; Is. 16:11
My heart is overturned within me,
For I have been very rebellious.
[R]Outside the sword bereaves, Ezek. 7:15
At home *it is* like death.

21 "They have heard that I sigh,
But no one comforts me.
All my enemies have heard of my trouble;
They are glad that You have done *it*.
Bring on the day You have announced,
That they may become like me.

22 "Let[R] all their wickedness come before You, Ps. 109:15; 137:7, 8
And do to them as You have done to me
For all my transgressions;
For my sighs *are* many,
And my heart *is* faint."

CHAPTER 2

The Anger of God

HOW the Lord has covered the daughter of Zion
With a [R]cloud in His anger! [Lam. 3:44]
He cast down from heaven to the earth
[R]The beauty of Israel, 2 Sam. 1:19
And did not remember [R]His footstool
In the day of His anger. Ps. 99:5

2 The Lord has swallowed up and has [R]not pitied Lam. 3:43
All the dwelling places of Jacob.

1:14 So with MT, Tg.; LXX, Syr., Vg. *watched over*

He has thrown down in His wrath
The strongholds of the daughter of
Judah;
He has brought *them* down to the ground;
[R]He has profaned the kingdom and its
princes. Ps. 89:39, 40

3 He has cut off in fierce anger
Every [T]horn of Israel; Strength
[R]He has drawn back His right hand
From before the enemy. Ps. 74:11
[R]He has blazed against Jacob like a
flaming fire Ps. 89:46
Devouring all around.

4 [R]Standing like an enemy, He has bent His
bow; Is. 63:10
With His right hand, like an adversary,
He has slain [R]all *who were* pleasing to
His eye; Ezek. 24:25
On the tent of the daughter of Zion,
He has poured out His fury like fire.

5 [R]The Lord was like an enemy. Jer. 30:14
He has swallowed up Israel,
He has swallowed up all her palaces;
[R]He has destroyed her strongholds,
And has increased mourning and
lamentation
In the daughter of Judah. Jer. 52:13

6 He has done violence [R]to His
[T]tabernacle, Ps. 80:12; 89:40 • Lit. *booth*
[R]*As if it were* a garden; Is. 1:8
He has destroyed His place of assembly;
The LORD has caused
The appointed feasts and Sabbaths to be
forgotten in Zion.
In His burning indignation He has
spurned the king and the priest.

7 The Lord has spurned His altar,
He has [R]abandoned His sanctuary;
He has [T]given up the walls of her
palaces Ezek. 24:21 • *delivered*
Into the hand of the enemy.
[R]They have made a noise in the house of
the LORD Ps. 74:3–8
As on the day of a set feast.

8 The LORD has purposed to destroy
The [R]wall of the daughter of Zion.
[R]He has stretched out a line;
He has not withdrawn His hand from
destroying; Jer. 52:14 • [Is. 34:11]
Therefore He has caused the rampart
and wall to lament;
They languished together.

9 Her gates have sunk into the ground;
He has destroyed and [R]broken her bars.
[R]Her king and her princes *are* among the
[T]nations; Jer. 51:30 • Deut. 28:36 • *Gentiles*
[R]The Law *is* no *more*, 2 Chr. 15:3
And her [R]prophets find no [T]vision from
the LORD. Ps. 74:9 • Prophetic revelation

The Agony of Jerusalem

10 The elders of the daughter of Zion
Sit on the ground *and* keep silence;
They throw dust on their heads
And [R]gird themselves with sackcloth.
The virgins of Jerusalem
Bow their heads to the ground. Is. 15:3

11 [R]My eyes fail with tears, Lam. 3:48
My [T]heart is troubled; Lit. *inward parts*
[R]My bile is poured on the ground
Because of the destruction of the
daughter of my people, Job 16:13
Because [R]the children and the infants
Faint in the streets of the city. Lam. 4:4

12 They say to their mothers,
"Where *is* grain and wine?"
As they swoon like the wounded
In the streets of the city,
As their life is poured out
In their mothers' bosom.

13 How shall I [R]console you? Lam. 1:12
To what shall I liken you,
O daughter of Jerusalem?
What shall I compare with you, that I
may comfort you,
O virgin daughter of Zion?
For your ruin *is* spread wide as the sea;
Who can heal you?

14 Your prophets have seen for you
False and deceptive visions;
They have not [R]uncovered your iniquity,
To bring back your captives,
But have envisioned for you false
prophecies and delusions. Is. 58:1

15 All who [T]pass by [R]clap *their* hands at
you; Lit. *pass by this way* • Ezek. 25:6
They hiss [R]and shake their heads
At the daughter of Jerusalem:
"*Is* this the city that is called Ps. 44:14
[R]'The perfection of beauty, [Ps. 48:2; 50:2]
The joy of the whole earth'?"

16 [R]All your enemies have opened their
mouth against you; Job 16:9, 10
They hiss and gnash *their* teeth.
They say, [R]"We have swallowed *her* up!
Surely this *is* the [R]day we have waited
for; Ps. 56:2; 124:3 • Lam. 1:21
We have found *it*, we have seen *it!*"

17 The LORD has done what He [R]purposed;
He has fulfilled His word Lev. 26:16
Which He commanded in days of old.
He has thrown down and has not pitied,

And He has caused an enemy to [R]rejoice
over you; Ps. 38:16
He has exalted the [T]horn of your
adversaries. Strength

The Appeal of Jerusalem

18 Their heart cried out to the Lord,
"O wall of the daughter of Zion,
[R]Let tears run down like a river day and
night; Jer. 14:17
Give yourself no relief;
Give your eyes no rest.

19 "Arise, [R]cry out in the night, Ps. 119:147
At the beginning of the watches;
[R]Pour out your heart like water before the
face of the Lord. Ps. 42:4; 62:8
Lift your hands toward Him
For the life of your young children,
Who faint from hunger [R]at the head of
every street." Is. 51:20

20 "See, O LORD, and consider!
To whom have You done this?
[R]Should the women eat their offspring,
The children they have cuddled?*
Should the priest and prophet be slain
In the sanctuary of the Lord? Lev. 26:29

21 "Young[R] and old lie 2 Chr. 36:17
On the ground in the streets;
My virgins and my young men
Have fallen by the [R]sword; Jer. 18:21
You have slain *them* in the day of Your
anger,
You have slaughtered *and* not pitied.

22 "You have invited as to a feast day
[R]The terrors that surround me. Ps. 31:13
In the day of the LORD's anger
There was no refugee or survivor.
[R]Those whom I have borne and brought
up Hos. 9:12
My enemies have [R]destroyed." Jer. 44:7

CHAPTER 3

Jeremiah's Cry of Despair

I *AM* the man *who* has seen affliction by
the rod of His wrath.
2 He has led me and made *me* walk
In darkness and not *in* light.
3 Surely He has turned His hand against
me
Time and time again throughout the day.

4 He has aged [R]my flesh and my skin,
And [R]broken my bones. Job 16:8 • Ps. 51:8
5 He has besieged me
And surrounded *me* with bitterness and
[T]woe. *hardship* or *weariness*
6 [R]He has set me in dark places
Like the dead of long ago. [Ps. 88:5, 6]

7 [R]He has hedged me in so that I cannot get
out; Hos. 2:6
He has made my chain heavy.
8 Even [R]when I cry and shout, Job 30:20
He shuts out my prayer.
9 He has blocked my ways with hewn stone;
He has made my paths crooked.

10 [R]He *has been* to me a bear lying in wait,
Like a lion in ambush. Is. 38:13
11 He has turned aside my ways and [R]torn
me in pieces; Hos. 6:1
He has made me desolate.
12 He has bent His bow
And [R]set me up as a target for the
arrow. Job 7:20; 16:12

13 He has caused [R]the [T]arrows of His
quiver Job 6:4 • Lit. *sons of*
To pierce my loins.*
14 I have become the [R]ridicule of all my
people— Jer. 20:7
[R]Their taunting song all the day. Job 30:9
15 He has filled me with bitterness,
He has made me drink wormwood.

16 He has also broken my teeth [R]with
gravel, [Prov. 20:17]
And covered me with ashes.
17 You have moved my soul far from peace;
I have forgotten [T]prosperity. Lit. *good*
18 [R]And I said, "My strength and my hope
Have perished from the LORD." Ps. 31:22

Jeremiah's Confession of Faith

19 Remember my affliction and roaming,
[R]The wormwood and the gall. Jer. 9:15
20 My soul still remembers
And [T]sinks within me. Lit. *bowed down*
21 This I recall to my mind,
Therefore I have [R]hope. Ps. 130:7

22 [R]*Through* the LORD's mercies we are not
consumed, [Mal. 3:6]
Because His compassions fail not.
23 *They are* new [R]every morning; Is. 33:2
Great *is* Your faithfulness.
24 "The LORD *is* my portion," says my soul,
"Therefore I [R]hope in Him!" Mic. 7:7

25 The LORD *is* good to those who [R]wait for
Him, Is. 30:18
To the soul *who* seeks Him.
26 *It is* good that *one* should [R]hope [R]and
wait quietly [Rom. 4:16–18] • Ps. 37:7
For the salvation of the LORD.
27 [R]*It is* good for a man to bear Ps. 94:12
The yoke in his youth.

28 Let him sit alone and keep silent,
Because *God* has laid *it* on him;

2:20 Vg. *a span long* **3:13** Lit. *kidneys*

29[R] Let him put his mouth in the dust—
There may yet be hope. Job 42:6
30[R] Let him give *his* cheek to the one who
strikes him, Is. 50:6
And be full of reproach.

31 For the Lord will not cast off forever.
32 Though He causes grief,
Yet He will show compassion
According to the multitude of His
mercies.
33 For He does not afflict willingly,
Nor grieve the children of men.

34 To crush under one's feet
All the prisoners of the earth,
35 To turn aside the justice *due* a man
Before the face of the Most High,
36 Or subvert a man in his cause—
[R] The Lord does not approve. [Hab. 1:13]

37 Who *is* he [R]*who* speaks and it comes to
pass, [Ps. 33:9–11]
When the Lord has not commanded *it*?
38 *Is it* not from the mouth of the Most High
That woe and well-being proceed?
39 Why should a living man complain,
A man for the punishment of his sins?

Jeremiah's Condition of Need

40 Let us search out and examine our ways,
And turn back to the LORD;
41[R] Let us lift our hearts and hands
To God in heaven. Ps. 86:4
42[R] We have transgressed and rebelled;
You have not pardoned. Dan. 9:5

43 You have covered *Yourself* with anger
And pursued us;
You have slain *and* not pitied.
44 You have covered Yourself with a cloud,
That prayer should not pass through.
45 You have made us an [R]offscouring and
refuse 1 Cor. 4:13
In the midst of the peoples.

46[R] All our enemies Lam. 2:16
Have opened their mouths against us.
47 Fear and a snare have come upon us,
[R] Desolation and destruction. Is. 51:19
48[R] My eyes overflow with rivers of water
For the destruction of the daughter of my
people. Jer. 4:19; 14:17

49[R] My eyes flow and do not cease, Jer. 14:17
Without interruption,
50 Till the LORD from heaven
[R] Looks down and sees. Is. 63:15
51 My eyes bring suffering to my soul
Because of all the daughters of my city.

52 My enemies [R]without cause Ps. 35:7, 19
Hunted me down like a bird.
53 They silenced* my life in the pit
And [R]threw stones at me. Dan. 6:17
54[R] The waters flowed over my head;
[R] I said, "I am cut off!" Ps. 69:2 • Is. 38:10

Jeremiah's Confidence in God

55[R] I called on Your name, O LORD, Ps. 130:1
From the lowest [R]pit. Jer. 38:6–13
56[R] You have heard my voice: Ps. 3:4
"Do not hide Your ear
From my sighing, from my cry for help."
57 You [R]drew near on the day I called on
You, James 4:8
And said, [R]"Do not fear!" Is. 41:10, 14

58 O Lord, You have [R]pleaded the case for
my soul; Jer. 51:36
[R] You have redeemed my life. Ps. 71:23
59 O LORD, You have seen [T]*how* I am
wronged; Lit. *my wrong*
[R] Judge my case. Ps. 9:4
60 You have seen all their vengeance,
All their [R]schemes against me. Jer. 11:19

61 You have heard their reproach, O LORD,
All their schemes against me,
62 The lips of my enemies
And their whispering against me all the
day.
63 Look at their [R]sitting down and their
rising up; Ps. 139:2
I *am* their taunting song.

64[R] Repay them, O LORD, Ps. 28:4
According to the work of their hands.
65 Give them a veiled* heart;
Your curse *be* upon them!
66 In Your anger,
Pursue and destroy them
From under the heavens of the LORD.

CHAPTER 4

The Conditions During the Siege

HOW the gold has become dim!
How changed the fine gold!
The stones of the sanctuary are
[T]scattered Lit. *poured out*
At the head of every street.

2 The precious sons of Zion,
[T] Valuable as fine gold, Lit. *Weighed against*
How they are regarded as clay pots,
The work of the hands of the potter!

3 Even the jackals present their breasts
To nurse their young;
But the daughter of my people *is* cruel,
Like ostriches in the wilderness.

3:53 LXX *put to death* **3:65** A Jewish tradition *sorrow of*

4 The tongue of the infant clings
To the roof of its mouth for thirst;
The young children ask for bread,
But no one breaks *it* for them.

5 Those who ate delicacies
Are desolate in the streets;
Those who were brought up in scarlet
[R]Embrace ash heaps. Job 24:8

6 The punishment of the iniquity of the
daughter of my people
Is greater than the punishment of the
[R]sin of Sodom, Ezek. 16:48
Which was [R]overthrown in a moment,
With no hand to help her! Gen. 19:25

7 Her Nazirites* were [T]brighter than
snow
And whiter than milk; Or *purer*
They were more ruddy in body than
rubies,
Like sapphire in their appearance.

8 *Now* their appearance is blacker than
soot;
They go unrecognized in the streets;
[R]Their skin clings to their bones,
It has become as dry as wood. Ps. 102:5

9 *Those* slain by the sword are better off
Than *those* who die of hunger;
For these [R]pine away, Lev. 26:39
Stricken *for lack* of the fruits of the
[R]field. Jer. 16:4

10 The hands of the [R]compassionate
women Lam. 2:20
Have cooked their [R]own children;
They became [R]food for them
In the destruction of the daughter of my
people. Is. 49:15 • Deut. 28:57

The Cause of the Siege

11 The LORD has fulfilled His fury,
He has poured out His fierce anger.
[R]He kindled a fire in Zion, Deut. 32:22
And it has devoured its foundations.

12 The kings of the earth,
And all inhabitants of the world,
Would not have believed
That the adversary and the enemy
Could enter the gates of Jerusalem—

13 Because of the sins of her prophets
And the iniquities of her priests,
[R]Who shed in her midst Matt. 23:31
The blood of the just.

14 They wandered blind in the streets;
[R]They have defiled themselves with
blood, Jer. 2:34
[R]So that no one would touch their
garments. Num. 19:16

15 They cried out to them,
"Go away, [R]unclean! Lev. 13:45, 46
Go away, go away,
Do not touch us!"
When they fled and wandered,
Those among the nations said,
"They shall no longer dwell *here*."

16 The face* of the LORD scattered them;
He no longer regards them.
[R]*The people* do not respect the priests
Nor show favor to the elders. Lam. 5:12

17 Still [R]our eyes failed us, 2 Kin. 24:7
Watching vainly for our help;
In our watching we watched
For a nation *that* could not save *us*.

18 [R]They tracked our steps 2 Kin. 25:4
So that we could not walk in our streets.
[R]Our end was near; Ezek. 7:2, 3, 6
Our days were over,
For our end had come.

19 Our pursuers were [R]swifter Deut. 28:49
Than the eagles of the heavens.
They pursued us on the mountains
And lay in wait for us in the wilderness.

20 The [R]breath of our nostrils, the anointed
of the LORD, Gen. 2:7
[R]Was caught in their pits, Jer. 52:9
Of whom we said, "Under his shadow
We shall live among the nations."

The Consequences of the Siege

21 Rejoice and be glad, O daughter of
[R]Edom, Ps. 83:3–6
You who dwell in the land of Uz!
[R]The cup shall also pass over to you
And you shall become drunk and make
yourself naked. Jer. 25:15

22 [R]*The punishment of* your iniquity is
accomplished, [Is. 40:2]
O daughter of Zion;
He will no longer send you into captivity.
[R]He will punish your iniquity, Ps. 137:7
O daughter of Edom;
He will uncover your sins!

CHAPTER 5

The Review of the Need for Restoration

REMEMBER, [R]O LORD, what has come
upon us; Ps. 89:50
Look, and behold our reproach!

4:7 Or *nobles* **4:16** Tg. *anger*

2 [R]Our inheritance has been turned over to
aliens, Ps. 79:1
And our houses to foreigners.
3 We have become orphans and waifs,
Our mothers *are* like widows.
4 We pay for the water we drink,
And our wood comes at a price.
5 [R]*They* pursue at our heels;* Jer. 28:14
We labor *and* have no rest.
6 [R]We have given our hand [R]*to* the
Egyptians Gen. 24:2 • Hos. 9:3; 12:1
And the [R]Assyrians, to be satisfied with
bread. Hos. 5:13
7 [R]Our fathers sinned *and are* no more,
But we bear their iniquities. Jer. 31:29
8 Servants rule over us;
There is none to deliver *us* from their
hand.
9 We get our bread *at the risk* of our
lives,
Because of the sword in the wilderness.
10 Our skin is hot as an oven,
Because of the fever of famine.
11 They ravished the women in Zion,
The maidens in the cities of Judah.
12 Princes were hung up by their hands,
And elders were not respected.
13 Young men ground at the millstones;
Boys staggered under *loads of* wood.
14 The elders have ceased *gathering at* the
gate,
And the young men from their music.
15 The joy of our heart has ceased;
Our dance has turned into mourning.

The Repentance of Sin

16 [R]The crown has fallen *from* our head.
Woe to us, for we have sinned! Ps. 89:39
17 Because of this our heart is faint;
[R]Because of these *things* our eyes grow
dim; Ps. 6:7
18 Because of Mount Zion which is
[R]desolate, Is. 27:10
With foxes walking about on it.

The Request for Restoration

19 You, O LORD, [R]remain forever; Ps. 9:7
[R]Your throne from generation to
generation. Ps. 45:6
20 [R]Why do You forget us forever, Ps. 13:1
And forsake us for so long a time?
21 [R]Turn us back to You, O LORD, and we will
be [T]restored; Jer. 31:18 • *returned*
Renew our days as of old,
22 Unless You have utterly rejected us,
And are very angry with us!

5:5 Lit. *necks*

5:20 Occasions of Doubt—Doubt may be defined as an uncertainty of belief or lack of confidence in something. Applied to the Christian life, doubt refers to the unbelief in God and His Word that Christians occasionally exhibit. It is possible that in a moment of infirmity a Christian may doubt the existence of God in spite of the fact that it is not reasonable for a person to disbelieve this obvious truth (Page 551—Ps. 14:1). A Christian is more likely to doubt his salvation after sinning or after a spiritual defeat. A misunderstanding of such verses as 1 John 3:9 contributes to this doubt: "Whoever has been born of God does not sin." It is crucial to note that this verse speaks of a lifestyle of sin, not instances of sin.

A Christian may also doubt God's sovereignty or His goodness. In such circumstances as sickness, suffering, injustice, opposition, economic problems, family problems, national calamity, or apparently unanswered prayer, a Christian may be tempted to doubt the goodness of God. One must remember that it is not always possible to discern God's good hand in the affairs of life. The person of faith believes God even when circumstances appear to the contrary.

All doubt may be traced ultimately to unbelief in the Word of God, which affirms beyond question the existence and character of God. To regard doubt as the sin of unbelief and then confess it to God as sin is therefore the first step toward conquering it.

Now turn to Page 940—Hab. 1:2: Sources of Doubt.

THE BOOK OF

EZEKIEL

THE BOOK OF EZEKIEL

Ezekiel, a priest and a prophet, ministers during the darkest days of Judah's history: the seventy-year period of Babylonian captivity. Carried to Babylon before the final assault on Jerusalem, Ezekiel uses prophecies, parables, signs, and symbols to dramatize God's message to His exiled people. Though they are like dry bones in the sun, God will reassemble them and breathe life into the nation once again. Present judgment will be followed by future glory so that "you shall know that *I am* the LORD" (6:7).

The Hebrew name *Yeheze'l* means "God Strengthens" or "Strengthened by God." Ezekiel is indeed strengthened by God for the prophetic ministry to which he is called (3:8, 9). The name occurs twice in this book and nowhere else in the Old Testament. The Greek form in the Septuagint is *Iezekiel* and the Latin form in the Vulgate is *Ezechiel*.

THE AUTHOR OF EZEKIEL

Ezekiel, the son of Buzi (1:3), had a wife who died as a sign to Judah when Nebuchadnezzar began his final siege on Jerusalem (24:16–24). Like Jeremiah, he was a priest who was called to be a prophet of the Lord. His prophetic ministry shows a priestly emphasis in his concern with the temple, priesthood, sacrifices, and Shekinah (the glory of God). Ezekiel was privileged to receive a number of visions of the power and plan of God, and he was careful and artistic in his written presentation.

Some objections have been raised, but there is not a good reason to overthrow the strong evidence in favor of Ezekiel's authorship. The first person singular is used throughout the book, indicating that it is the work of a single personality. This person is identified as Ezekiel in 1:3 and 24:24, and internal evidence supports the unity and integrity of Ezekiel's prophetic record. The style, language, and thematic development are consistent throughout the book; and several distinctive phrases are repeated throughout, such as, "they shall know that I *am* the LORD," "Son of man," "the word of the LORD came to me," and the "glory of the LORD."

THE TIME OF EZEKIEL

Nebuchadnezzar destroyed Jerusalem in three stages. First, in 605 B.C., he overcame Jehoiakim and carried off key hostages including Daniel and his friends. Second, in 597 B.C., the rebellion of Jehoiakim and Jehoiachin brought further punishment; and Nebuchadnezzar made Jerusalem submit a second time. He carried off ten thousand hostages including Jehoiachin and Ezekiel. Third, in 586 B.C., Nebuchadnezzar destroyed the city after a long siege and disrupted all of Judah. If "thirtieth year" in 1:1 refers to Ezekiel's age, he was twenty-five years old when he was taken to Babylon and thirty years old when he received his prophetic commission (1:2, 3). This means he was about seventeen when Daniel was deported in 605 B.C., so that Ezekiel and Daniel were about the same age. Both men were about twenty years younger than Jeremiah who was ministering in Jerusalem. According to this chronology, Ezekiel was born in 622 B.C., deported to Babylon in 597 B.C., prophesied from 592 B.C. to at least 570 B.C., and died about 560 B.C. Thus, he overlapped the end of Jeremiah's ministry and the beginning of Daniel's ministry. By the time Ezekiel arrived in Babylon, Daniel was already well known; and he is mentioned three times in Ezekiel's prophecy (14:14, 20; 28:3). Ezekiel's Babylonian home was at Tel Abib, the principal colony of Jewish exiles along the River Chebar, Nebuchadnezzar's "Grand Canal" (1:1; 3:15, 23).

From 592 to 586 B.C., Ezekiel found it necessary to convince the disbelieving Jewish exiles that there was no hope of immediate deliverance. But it was not until they heard that Jerusalem was destroyed that their false hopes of returning were abandoned.

Ezekiel no doubt wrote this book shortly after the incidents recorded in it occurred. His active ministry lasted for at least twenty-two years (1:2; 29:17), and his book was probably completed by 565 B.C.

THE CHRIST OF EZEKIEL

Ezekiel 17:22–24 depicts the Messiah as a tender twig that becomes a stately cedar on a lofty mountain, as He is similarly called the Branch in Isaiah (11:1), Jeremiah (23:5; 33:15), and Zechariah (3:8; 6:12). The Messiah is the King who has the right to rule (21:26, 27), and He is the true Shepherd who will deliver and feed His flock (34:11–31).

KEYS TO EZEKIEL

Key Word: The Future Restoration of Israel—The broad purpose of Ezekiel is to remind the generation born during the Babylonian exile of the cause of Israel's current destruction, of the coming judgment on the Gentile nations, and of the coming national restoration of Israel. Central to that hope is the departure of the glory of God from Israel and the prediction of its ultimate return (43:2).

Key Verses: Ezekiel 36:24–26 and 36:33–35—"For I will take you from among the nations, gather you out of all countries, and bring you into your own land. Then I will sprinkle clean water on you, and you shall be clean; I will cleanse you from all your filthiness and from all your idols. I will give you a new heart and put a new spirit within you; I will take the heart of stone out of your flesh and give you a heart of flesh" (36:24–26).

"Thus says the Lord GOD: 'On the day that I cleanse you from all your iniquities, I will also enable *you* to dwell in the cities, and the ruins shall be rebuilt. The desolate land shall be tilled instead of lying desolate in the sight of all who pass by. So they will say, "This land that was desolate has become like the garden of Eden; and the wasted, desolate, and ruined cities *are now* fortified *and* inhabited" ' " (36:33–35).

Key Chapter: Ezekiel 37—Central to the hope of the restoration of Israel is the vision of the valley of the dry bones. Ezekiel 37 outlines with clear steps Israel's future.

SURVEY OF EZEKIEL

Ezekiel prophesies among the Jewish exiles in Babylon during the last days of Judah's decline and downfall. His message of judgment is similar to that of his older contemporary Jeremiah, who has remained in Jerusalem. Judah will be judged because of her unfaithfulness, but God promises her future restoration and blessing. Like Isaiah and Jeremiah, Ezekiel proclaims a message of horror and hope, of condemnation and consolation. But Ezekiel places special emphasis on the glory of Israel's sovereign God who says, "They shall know that I *am* the LORD." The book breaks into four sections: the commission of Ezekiel (1—3), the judgment on Judah (4—24), the judgment on the Gentiles (25—32), and the restoration of Israel (33—48).

The Commission of Ezekiel (1—3): God gives Ezekiel an overwhelming vision of His divine glory and commissions him to be His prophet (cf. the experiences of Moses in Ex. 3:1–10, Isaiah in 6:1–10, Daniel in 10:5–14, and John in Rev. 1:12–19). Ezekiel is given instruction, enablement, and responsibility.

The Judgment on Judah (4—24): Ezekiel directs his prophecies against the nation God chose for Himself. The prophet's signs and sermons (4—7) point to the certainty of Judah's judgment. In 8—11, Judah's past sins and coming doom are seen in a series of visions of the abominations in the temple, the slaying of the wicked, and the departing glory of God. The priests and princes are condemned as the glory leaves the temple, moves to the Mount of Olives, and disappears in the east. Chapters 12—24 speak of the causes and extent of Judah's coming judgment through dramatic signs, powerful sermons, and parables. Judah's prophets are counterfeits and her elders are idolators. They have become a fruitless vine and an adulterous wife. Babylon will swoop down like an eagle and pluck them up, and they will not be aided by Egypt. The people are responsible for their own sins, and they are not being unjustly judged for the sins of their ancestors. Judah has been unfaithful, but God promises that her judgment ultimately will be followed by restoration.

The Judgment on the Gentiles (25—32): Judah's nearest neighbors may gloat over her destruction, but they will be next in line. They too will suffer the fate of siege and destruction by Babylon. Ezekiel shows the full circle of judgment on the nations that surround Judah by

FOCUS	COMMISSION OF EZEKIEL		JUDGMENT ON JUDAH	JUDGMENT ON GENTILES	RESTORATION OF ISRAEL	
REFERENCE	1:1——2:1——4:1——25:1——33:1——40:1——48:35					
DIVISION	EZEKIEL SEES THE GLORY	EZEKIEL IS COMMISSIONED TO THE WORK	SIGNS, MESSAGES, VISIONS, AND PARABLES OF JUDGMENT	JUDGMENT ON SURROUNDING NATIONS	RETURN OF ISRAEL TO THE LORD	RESTORATION OF ISRAEL IN THE KINGDOM
TOPIC	BEFORE THE SIEGE (c. 592–587 B.C.)			DURING THE SIEGE (c. 586 B.C.)	AFTER THE SIEGE (c. 585–570 B.C.)	
	JUDAH'S FALL			JUDAH'S FOES	JUDAH'S FUTURE	
LOCATION	BABYLON					
TIME	c. 592–570 B.C.					

following them in a clockwise circuit: Ammon, Moab, Edom, Philistia, Tyre, and Sidon (25—28). He spends a disproportionate amount of time on Tyre, and many scholars believe that the "king of Tyre" in 28:11–19 may be Satan, the real power behind the nation. Chapters 29—32 contain a series of oracles against Egypt. Unlike the nations in chapters 25—28 that were destroyed by Nebuchadnezzar, Egypt will continue to exist, but as "the lowliest of kingdoms" (29:15). Since that time it has never recovered its former glory or influence.

The Restoration of Israel (33—48): The prophecies in these chapters were given after the overthrow of Jerusalem. Now that the promised judgment has come, Ezekiel's message no longer centers on coming judgment but on the positive theme of comfort and consolation. Just as surely as judgment has come, blessing will also come; God's people will be regathered and restored. The mouth of Ezekiel, God's watchman, is opened when he is told that Jerusalem has been taken. Judah has had false shepherds (rulers), but the true Shepherd will lead them in the future. The vision of the valley of dry bones pictures the reanimation of the nation by the Spirit of God. Israel and Judah will be purified and reunited. There will be an invasion by the northern armies of Gog, but Israel will be saved because the Lord will destroy the invading forces.

In 572 B.C., fourteen years after the destruction of Jerusalem, Ezekiel returns in a vision to the fallen city and is given detailed specifications for the reconstruction of the temple, the city, and the land (40—48). After an intricate description of the new outer court, inner court, and temple (40—42), Ezekiel views the return of the glory of the Lord to the temple from the east. Regulations concerning worship in the coming temple (43—46) are followed by revelations concerning the new land and city (47 and 48).

OUTLINE OF EZEKIEL

Part One: The Commission of Ezekiel (1:1—3:27)

I. Ezekiel Sees the Glory of God 1:1–28

- A. Time of the Vision 1:1–3
- B. The Four Living Creatures 1:4–14
- C. The Four Wheels 1:15–21
- D. The Firmament 1:22–25
- E. The Appearance of a Man 1:26–28

II. Ezekiel Is Commissioned to the Word of God .... 2:1—3:27

- A. Ezekiel Is Sent to Israel .... 2:1—3:3
- B. Ezekiel Is Instructed About His Ministry 3:4–27

Part Two: Judgment on Judah (4:1—24:27)

I. Four Signs of Coming Judgment ...... 4:1—5:17

- A. Sign of the Clay Tablet 4:1–3
- B. Sign of Ezekiel's Lying on His Side 4:4–8
- C. Sign of the Defiled Bread 4:9–17
- D. Sign of the Razor and Hair 5:1–4
- E. Explanation of the Signs 5:5–17

II. Two Messages of Coming Judgment .... 6:1—7:27

- A. Destruction Because of Idolatry 6:1–14
  1. Destruction of High Places 6:1–7
  2. Salvation of the Remnant 6:8–10
  3. Desolation of the Land 6:11–14
- B. Description of the Babylonian Conquest 7:1–27

III. Four-Part Vision of Coming Judgment .... 8:1—11:25

- A. Vision of the Glory of God 8:1–4
- B. Vision of the Abominations in the Temple 8:5–18
  1. Image of Jealousy 8:5, 6
  2. Paintings on the Wall 8:7–12
  3. Weeping for Tammuz 8:13, 14
  4. Sun Worship 8:15–18
- C. Vision of the Slaying in Jerusalem 9:1–11
  1. Call to the Six Men 9:1–3
  2. Command to Slay the Wicked 9:4–7
  3. Weeping of Ezekiel 9:8–11
- D. Departure of the Glory of God to the Threshold 10:1–8
- E. Vision of the Wheels and Cherubim ... 10:9–22
- F. Vision of the Twenty-five Wicked Rulers 11:1–12
- G. Promise of the Restoration of the Remnant 11:13–21
- H. Departure of the Glory of God from the Mount of Olives 11:22–25

IV. Signs, Parables, and Messages of Judgment .... 12:1—24:27

- A. Sign of Belongings for Removing 12:1–16
- B. Sign of Trembling 12:17–28
- C. Message Against the False Prophets 13:1–23
  1. Judgment upon False Prophets 13:1–16
  2. Judgment upon False Prophetesses 13:17–23
- D. Message Against the Elders 14:1–23
  1. Idolatry of the Elders 14:1–11
  2. Jerusalem to Be Destroyed 14:12–23
- E. Parable of the Vine 15:1–8
- F. Parable of Israel's Marriage 16:1–63

Part Three: Judgment on Gentiles (25:1—32:32)

Part Four: Restoration of Israel (33:1—48:35)

CHAPTER 1

Time of the Vision

NOW it came to pass in the thirtieth year,
in the fourth *month*, on the fifth *day* of
the month, as I *was* among the captives by the
River Chebar, *that* the heavens were opened
and I saw visions* of God.
2 On the fifth *day* of the month, which *was*
in the fifth year of King Jehoiachin's captivity,
3 the word of the LORD came expressly to
Ezekiel the priest, the son of Buzi, in the
land of the Chaldeans* by the River Chebar;
and [R]the hand of the LORD was upon him
there. Ezek. 3:14, 22

1:1 So with MT, LXX, Vg.; Syr., Tg. *a vision* **1:3** Or *Babylonians*, and so elsewhere in the book

The Four Living Creatures

4 Then I looked, and behold, [R]a whirlwind was coming [R]out of the north, a great cloud with raging fire engulfing itself; and brightness *was* all around it and radiating out of its midst like the color of amber, out of the midst of the fire. Jer. 23:19; 25:32 • Jer. 1:14

5 Also from within it *came* the likeness of four living creatures. And this *was* their appearance: they had the likeness of a man.

6 Each one had four faces, and each one had four wings.

7 Their [T]legs *were* straight, and the soles of their feet *were* like the soles of calves' feet. They sparkled [R]like the color of burnished bronze. Lit. *feet* • Dan. 10:6

8 [R]The hands of a man *were* under their wings on their four sides; and each of the four had faces and wings. Ezek. 10:8, 21

9 Their wings touched one another. *The creatures* did not turn when they went, but each one went straight [R]forward. Ezek. 1:12

10 As for the likeness of their faces, *each* [R]had the face of a man; each of the four had [R]the face of a lion on the right side, [R]each of the four had the face of an ox on the left side, [R]and each of the four had the face of an eagle. Num. 2:10 • Num. 2:3 • Num. 2:18 • Num. 2:25

11 Thus *were* their faces. Their wings stretched upward; two *wings* of each one touched one another, and [R]two covered their bodies. Is. 6:2

12 And each one went straight forward; they went wherever the spirit wanted to go, and they did not turn when they went.

13 As for the likeness of the living creatures, their appearance *was* like burning coals of fire, [R]like the appearance of torches going back and forth among the living creatures. The fire was bright, and out of the fire went lightning. Rev. 4:5

14 And the living creatures ran back and forth, [R]in appearance like a flash of lightning. [Matt. 24:27]

The Four Wheels

15 Now as I looked at the living creatures, behold, a wheel *was* on the earth beside each living creature with its four faces.

16 The appearance of the wheels and their workings *was* [R]like the color of beryl, and all four had the same likeness. The appearance of their workings *was*, as it were, a wheel in the middle of a wheel. Dan. 10:6

17 When they moved, they went toward any one of four directions; they did not turn aside when they went.

18 As for their rims, they were so high they were awesome; and their rims *were* full of eyes, all around the four of them.

19 [R]When the living creatures went, the wheels went beside them; and when the living creatures were lifted up from the earth, the wheels were lifted up. Ezek. 10:16, 17

20 Wherever the spirit wanted to go, they went, *because* there the spirit went; and the wheels were lifted together with them, [R]for the spirit of the living creatures* *was* in the wheels. Ezek. 10:17

21 When those went, *these* went; when those stood, *these* stood; and when those were lifted up from the earth, the wheels were lifted up together with them, for the spirit of the living creatures* *was* in the wheels.

The Firmament

22 [R]The likeness of the firmament above the heads of the living creatures* *was* like the color of an awesome [R]crystal, stretched out over their heads. Ezek. 10:1 • Rev. 4:6

23 And under the firmament their wings *spread out* straight, one toward another. Each one had two which covered one side, and each one had two which covered the other side of the body.

24 When they went, I heard the noise of their wings, [R]like the noise of many waters, like the voice of the Almighty, a tumult like the noise of an army; and when they stood still, they let down their wings. Rev. 1:15

25 A voice came from above the firmament that *was* over their heads; whenever they stood, they let down their wings.

The Appearance of a Man

26 And above the firmament over their heads *was* the likeness of a throne, in appearance like a sapphire stone; on the likeness of the throne *was* a likeness with the appearance of a man high above it.

27 Also from the appearance of His waist and upward [R]I saw, as it were, the color of amber with the appearance of fire all around within it; and from the appearance of His waist and downward I saw, as it were, the appearance of fire with brightness all around. Ezek. 8:2

28 [R]Like the appearance of a rainbow in a cloud on a rainy day, so *was* the appearance of the brightness all around it. [R]This *was* the appearance of the likeness of the glory of the LORD. Rev. 4:3; 10:1 • Ezek. 3:23; 8:4

So when I saw *it*, [R]I fell on my face, and I heard a voice of One speaking. Dan. 8:17

CHAPTER 2

Ezekiel Is Sent to Israel

AND He said to me, "Son of man, stand on your feet, and I will speak to you."

1:20 Lit. *living creature;* LXX, Vg. *spirit of life;* Tg. *creatures* **1:21** Lit. *living creature;* LXX, Vg. *spirit of life;* Tg. *creatures* **1:22** So with LXX, Tg., Vg.; MT *living creature*

2 Then [R]the Spirit entered me when He
spoke to me, and set me on my feet; and I
heard Him who spoke to me. Ezek. 3:24
3 And He said to me: "Son of man, I am
sending you to the children of Israel, to a re-
bellious nation that has rebelled against Me;
they and their fathers have transgressed
against Me to this very day.
4 "For *they are* impudent and stubborn chil-
dren. I am sending you to them, and you shall
say to them, 'Thus says the Lord GOD.'
5 "As for them, whether they hear or
whether they refuse—for they *are* a [R]rebel-
lious house—yet they will know that a
prophet has been among them. Ezek. 3:26
6 "And you, son of man, do not be afraid of
them nor be afraid of their words, though
briers and thorns *are* with you and you dwell
among scorpions; do not be afraid of their
words or dismayed by their looks, though
they *are* a rebellious house.
7 [R]"You shall speak My words to them,
whether they hear or whether they refuse, for
they *are* rebellious. Jer. 1:7, 17
8 "But you, son of man, hear what I say to
you. Do not be rebellious like that rebellious
house; open your mouth and [R]eat what I give
you." Rev. 10:9
9 Now when I looked, there was [R]a hand
stretched out to me; and behold, [R]a scroll of a
book *was* in it. [Ezek. 8:3] • Ezek. 3:1
10 Then He spread it before me; and *there
was* writing on the inside and on the outside,
and written on it *were* lamentations and
mourning and woe.

CHAPTER 3

MOREOVER He said to me, "Son of man,
eat what you find; [R]eat this scroll, and
go, speak to the house of Israel." Ezek. 2:8, 9
2 So I opened my mouth, and He caused me
to eat that scroll.
3 And He said to me, "Son of man, feed
your belly, and fill your stomach with this
scroll that I give you." So I ate, and it was in
my mouth like honey in sweetness.

Ezekiel Is Instructed About His Ministry

4 Then He said to me: "Son of man, go to
the house of Israel and speak with My words
to them.
5 "For you *are* not sent to a people of unfa-
miliar speech and of hard language, *but* to the
house of Israel,
6 "not to many people of unfamiliar speech
and of hard language, whose words you cannot
understand. Surely, [R]had I sent you to them,
they would have listened to you. Matt. 11:21
7 "But the house of Israel will not listen to
you, [R]because they will not listen to Me; [R]for
all the house of Israel *are* impudent and hard-
hearted. John 15:20, 21 • Ezek. 2:4
8 "Behold, I have made your face strong
against their faces, and your forehead strong
against their foreheads.
9 "Like adamant stone, harder than flint, I
have made your forehead; do not be afraid of
them, nor be dismayed at their looks, though
they *are* a rebellious house."
10 Moreover He said to me: "Son of man, re-
ceive into your heart all My words that I
speak to you, and hear with your ears.
11 "And go, get to the captives, to the chil-
dren of your people, and speak to them and
tell them, 'Thus says the Lord GOD,' whether
they hear, or whether they refuse."
12 Then [R]the Spirit lifted me up, and I heard
behind me a great thunderous voice:
"Blessed *is* the [R]glory of the LORD from His
place!" Acts 8:39 • Ezek. 1:28; 8:4
13 *I* also *heard* the noise of the wings of the
living creatures that touched one another, and
the noise of the wheels beside them, and a
great thunderous noise.
14 So the Spirit lifted me up and took me
away, and I went in bitterness, in the [T]heat of
my spirit; but [R]the hand of the LORD was
strong upon me. Or *anger* • 2 Kin. 3:15
15 Then I came to the captives at Tel Abib,
who dwelt by the River Chebar; and [R]I sat
where they sat, and remained there aston-
ished among them seven days. Job 2:13
16 Now it [R]came to pass at the end of seven
days that the word of the LORD came to me,
saying, Jer. 42:7
17 [R]"Son of man, I have made you [R]a watch-
man for the house of Israel; therefore hear a
word from My mouth, and give them warning
from Me: Ezek. 33:7–9 • Jer. 6:17
18 "When I say to the wicked, 'You shall
surely die,' and you give him no warning, nor
speak to warn the wicked from his wicked
way, to save his life, that same wicked *man*
shall die in his iniquity; but his blood I will re-
quire at your hand.
19 "Yet, if you warn the wicked, and he does
not turn from his wickedness, nor from his
wicked way, he shall die in his iniquity; but
you have delivered your soul.
20 "Again, when a [R]righteous *man* turns from
his righteousness and commits iniquity, and I
lay a stumbling block before him, he shall die;
because you did not give him warning, he shall
die in his sin, and his righteousness which he
has done shall not be remembered; but his blood
I will require at your hand. Ezek. 18:24; 33:18
21 "Nevertheless if you warn the righteous
man that the righteous should not sin, and he
does not sin, he shall surely live because he
took warning; also you will have delivered
your soul."
22 [R]Then the hand of the LORD was upon
me there, and He said to me, "Arise, go out
[R]into the plain, and there I shall talk with
you." Ezek. 1:3 • Ezek. 8:4

23 So I arose and went out into the plain, and
behold, the glory of the LORD stood there, like
the glory which I saw by the River Chebar;
and I fell on my face.
24 Then the Spirit entered me and set me on
my feet, and spoke with me and said to me:
"Go, shut yourself inside your house.
25 "And you, O son of man, surely [R]they will
put ropes on you and bind you with them, so
that you cannot go out among them. Ezek. 4:8
26 [R]"I will make your tongue cling to the roof
of your mouth, so that you shall be mute and
not be one to rebuke them, for they *are* a rebellious house. Luke 1:20, 22
27 "But when I speak with you, I will open
your mouth, and you shall say to them, 'Thus
says the Lord GOD.' He who hears, let him
hear; and he who refuses, let him refuse; for
they *are* a rebellious house.

CHAPTER 4

Sign of the Clay Tablet

"YOU also, son of man, take a clay tablet and lay it before you, and portray on it a city, Jerusalem.
2 [R]"Lay siege against it, build a siege wall
against it, and heap up a mound against it; set
camps against it also, and place battering
rams against it all around. Jer. 6:6
3 "Moreover take for yourself an iron
plate, and set it *as* an iron wall between you
and the city. Set your face against it, and it
shall be [R]besieged, and you shall lay siege
against it. [R]This *will be* a sign to the house of
Israel. Jer. 39:1, 2 • Ezek. 12:6, 11; 24:24, 27

Sign of Ezekiel's Lying on His Side

4 "Lie also on your left side, and lay the iniquity of the house of Israel upon it. *According* to the number of the days that you lie on
it, you shall bear their iniquity.
5 "For I have laid on you the years of their
iniquity, according to the number of the
days, three hundred and ninety days; [R]so
you shall bear the iniquity of the house of Israel. Num. 14:34
6 "And when you have completed them, lie
again on your right side; then you shall bear
the iniquity of the house of Judah forty days.
I have laid on you a day for each year.
7 "Therefore you shall set your face toward
the siege of Jerusalem; your arm *shall be*
uncovered, and you shall prophesy against it.
8 "And surely I will restrain you so that you
cannot turn from one side to another till you
have ended the days of your siege.

Sign of the Defiled Bread

9 "Also take for yourself wheat, barley,
beans, lentils, millet, and spelt; put them into
one vessel, and make bread of them for yourself. *During* the number of days that you lie on
your side, three hundred and ninety days, you
shall eat it.
10 "And your food which you eat *shall be* by
weight, twenty shekels a day; from time to
time you shall eat it.
11 "You shall also drink water by measure,
one-sixth of a hin; from time to time you shall
drink.
12 "And you shall eat it *as* barley cakes; and
bake it using fuel of human waste in their
sight."
13 Then the LORD said, "So shall the children
of Israel eat their defiled bread among the
Gentiles, where I will drive them."
14 So I said, [R]"Ah, Lord GOD! Indeed I have
never defiled myself from my youth till now; I
have never eaten what died of itself or was
torn by beasts, nor has abominable flesh ever
come into my mouth." Acts 10:14
15 Then He said to me, "See, I am giving you
cow dung instead of human waste, and you
shall prepare your bread over it."
16 Moreover He said to me, "Son of man,
surely I will cut off the [R]supply of bread in Jerusalem; they shall eat bread by weight and
with anxiety, and shall [R]drink water by measure and with dread, Is. 3:1 • Ezek. 4:11
17 "that they may lack bread and water, and
be dismayed with one another, and waste
away because of their iniquity.

CHAPTER 5

Sign of the Razor and the Hair

"AND you, son of man, take a sharp sword, take it as a barber's razor, and pass *it* over your head and your beard; then take scales to weigh and divide the hair.
2 "You shall burn with fire one-third in the
midst of the city, when the days of the siege
are finished; then you shall take one-third and
strike around *it* with the sword, and one-third
you shall scatter in the wind: I will draw out a
sword after them.
3 [R]"You shall also take a small number of
them and bind them in the edge of your *garment*. Jer. 40:6; 52:16
4 "Then take some of them again and throw
them into the midst of the fire, and burn them
in the fire. From there a fire will go out into all
the house of Israel.

Explanation of the Signs

5 "Thus says the Lord GOD: 'This *is* Jerusalem; I have set her in the midst of the nations
and the countries all around her.
6 'She has rebelled against My judgments
by doing wickedness more than the nations,
and against My statutes more than the countries that *are* all around her; for they have refused My judgments, and they have not
walked in My statutes.'
7 "Therefore thus says the Lord GOD: 'Be-

cause you have [T]multiplied *disobedience* more
than the nations that *are* all around you, have
not walked in My statutes [R]nor kept My judg-
ments, nor even done* according to the judg-
ments of the nations that *are* all around
you'— Or *raged* • Jer. 2:10, 11
8 "therefore thus says the Lord GOD: 'In-
deed I, even I, *am* against you and will execute
judgments in your midst in the sight of the na-
tions.
9 'And I will do among you what I have
never done, and the like of which I will never
do again, because of all your abominations.
10 'Therefore fathers [R]shall eat *their* sons in
your midst, and sons shall eat their fathers;
and I will execute judgments among you, and
all of you who remain I will [R]scatter to all the
winds. Jer. 19:9 • Zech. 2:6; 7:14
11 'Therefore, *as* I live,' says the Lord GOD,
'surely, because you have [R]defiled My sanctu-
ary with all your detestable things and with
all your abominations, therefore I will also di-
minish *you;* My eye will not spare, nor will I
have any pity. [Jer. 7:9–11]
12 [R]'One-third of you shall die of the pesti-
lence, and be consumed with famine in your
midst; and one-third shall fall by the sword all
around you; and [R]I will scatter another third
to all the winds, and I will draw out a sword
after them. Ezek. 6:12 • Jer. 9:16
13 'Thus shall My anger be spent, and I will
cause My fury to rest upon them, [R]and I will
be avenged; and they shall know that I, the
LORD, have spoken *it* in My zeal, when I have
spent My fury upon them. Is. 1:24
14 'Moreover I will make you a waste and a
reproach among the nations that *are* all
around you, in the sight of all who pass by.
15 'So it* shall be a [R]reproach, a taunt, a
[R]lesson, and an astonishment to the nations
that *are* all around you, when I execute judg-
ments among you in anger and in fury and
in [R]furious rebukes. I, the LORD, have spo-
ken. Jer. 24:9 • [Is. 26:9] • Ezek. 5:8; 25:17
16 'When I [R]send against them the terrible
arrows of famine which shall be for destruc-
tion, which I will send to destroy you, I will in-
crease the famine upon you and cut off your
[R]supply of bread. Deut. 32:23 • Lev. 26:26
17 'So I will send against you famine and
[R]wild beasts, and they will bereave you. [R]Pes-
tilence and blood shall pass through you, and
I will bring the sword against you. I, the LORD,
have spoken.'" Lev. 26:22 • Ezek. 38:22

CHAPTER 6

Destruction of High Places

NOW the word of the LORD came to me,
saying:
2 "Son of man, [R]set your face toward the
[R]mountains of Israel, and prophesy against
them, Ezek. 20:46; 21:2; 25:2 • Ezek. 36:1
3 "and say, 'O mountains of Israel, hear the
word of the Lord GOD! Thus says the Lord
GOD to the mountains, to the hills, to the
ravines, and to the valleys: "Indeed I, *even* I,
will bring a sword against you, and [R]I will de-
stroy your high places. Lev. 26:30
4 "Then your altars shall be desolate, your
incense altars shall be broken, and I will cast
down your slain *men* before your idols.
5 "And I will lay the corpses of the children
of Israel before their idols, and I will scatter
your bones all around your altars.
6 "In all your dwelling places the cities
shall be laid waste, and the high places shall
be desolate, so that your altars may be laid
waste and made desolate, your idols may be
broken and made to cease, your incense altars
may be cut down, and your works may be
abolished.
7 "The slain shall fall in your midst, and
you shall know that I *am* the LORD.

Salvation of the Remnant

8 [R]"Yet I will leave a remnant, so that you
may have *some* who escape the sword among
the nations, when you are [R]scattered through
the countries. Jer. 44:28 • Ezek. 5:12
9 "Then those of you who escape will re-
member Me among the nations where they
are carried captive, because I was crushed by
their adulterous heart which has departed
from Me, and by their eyes which play the
harlot after their idols; they will loathe them-
selves for the evils which they committed in
all their abominations.
10 "And they shall know that I *am* the LORD;
I have not said in vain that I would bring this
calamity upon them."

Desolation of the Land

11 'Thus says the Lord GOD: [R]"Pound your
fists and stamp your feet, and say, 'Alas, for all
the evil abominations of the house of Israel!
For they shall fall by the sword, by famine,
and by pestilence. Ezek. 21:14
12 'He who is far off shall die by the pesti-
lence, he who is near shall fall by the sword,
and he who remains and is besieged shall die
by the famine. [R]Thus will I spend My fury
upon them. Ezek. 5:13
13 'Then you shall know that I *am* the LORD,
when their slain are among their idols all
around their altars, on every high hill, on all
the mountaintops, under every green tree, and
under every thick oak, wherever they offered
sweet incense to all their idols.
14 'So I will [R]stretch out My hand against
them and make the land desolate, yes, more
desolate than the wilderness toward Diblah,

5:7 So with MT, LXX, Tg., Vg.; many Heb. mss., Syr. *but have done* (cf. 11:12) **5:15** LXX, Syr., Tg., Vg. *you*

in all their dwelling places. Then they shall know that I *am* the LORD.' " ' " Is. 5:25

CHAPTER 7

Description of the Babylonian Conquest

MOREOVER the word of the LORD came to me, saying,
2 "And you, son of man, thus says the Lord GOD to the land of Israel:

R'An end! The end has come upon the
four corners of the land. Amos 8:2, 10
3 Now the end *has come* upon you,
And I will send My anger against you;
I will judge you Raccording to your ways,
And I will repay you for all your
abominations. [Rom. 2:6]
4RMy eye will not spare you, Ezek. 5:11
Nor will I have pity;
But I will repay your ways,
And your abominations will be in your
midst;
RThen you shall know that I *am* the
LORD!' Ezek. 12:20

5 "Thus says the Lord GOD:

'A disaster, a singular Rdisaster;
Behold, it has come! 2 Kin. 21:12, 13
6 An end has come,
The end has come;
It has dawned for you;
Behold, it has come!
7RDoom has come to you, you who dwell
in the land; Ezek. 7:10
RThe time has come, Zeph. 1:14, 15
A day of trouble *is* near,
And not of rejoicing in the mountains.
8 Now upon you I will soon Rpour out My
fury, Ezek. 20:8, 21
And spend My anger upon you;
I will judge you according to your ways,
And I will repay you for all your
abominations.

9 'My eye will not spare,
Nor will I have pity;
I will Trepay you according to your ways,
And your abominations will be in your
midst. Lit. *give*
Then you shall know that I *am* the LORD
who strikes.

10 'Behold, the day!
Behold, it has come!
RDoom has gone out; Ezek. 7:7
The rod has blossomed,
Pride has budded.
11RViolence has risen up into a rod of
wickedness; Jer. 6:7
None of them *shall remain,*
None of their multitude,
None of Tthem; Or *their wealth*
Nor *shall there be* wailing for them.
12 The time has come,
The day draws near.

'Let not the buyer Rrejoice, Prov. 20:14
Nor the seller Rmourn, Is. 24:2
For wrath *is* on their whole multitude.
13 For the seller shall not return to what
has been sold,
Though he may still be alive;
For the vision concerns the whole
multitude,
And it shall not turn back;
No one will strengthen himself
Who lives in iniquity.

14 'They have blown the trumpet and made
everyone ready,
But no one goes to battle;
For My wrath *is* on all their multitude.
15RThe sword *is* outside, Jer. 14:18
And the pestilence and famine within.
Whoever *is* in the field
Will die by the sword;
And whoever *is* in the city,
Famine and pestilence will devour him.

16 'Those who Rsurvive will escape and be
on the mountains Ezek. 6:8; 14:22
Like doves of the valleys,
All of them mourning,
Each for his iniquity.
17 Every Rhand will be feeble, Is. 13:7
And every knee will be *as* weak *as*
water.
18 They will also Rbe girded with sackcloth;
Horror will cover them; Amos 8:10
Shame *will be* on every face,
Baldness on all their heads.

19 'They will throw their silver into the
streets,
And their gold will be like refuse;
Their Rsilver and their gold will not be
able to deliver them Zeph. 1:18
In the day of the wrath of the LORD;
They will not satisfy their souls,
Nor fill their stomachs,
Because it became their stumbling block
of iniquity.

20 'As for the beauty of his ornaments,
He set it in majesty;
RBut they made from it Jer. 7:30
The images of their abominations—
Their detestable things;
Therefore I have made it
Like refuse to them.
21 I will give it as Rplunder 2 Kin. 24:13
Into the hands of strangers,
And to the wicked of the earth as spoil;
And they shall defile it.

22 I will turn My face from them,
And they will defile My secret place;
For robbers shall enter it and defile it.

23 'Make a chain,
For [R]the land is filled with crimes of blood, 2 Kin. 21:16
And the city is full of violence.
24 Therefore I will bring the [R]worst of the Gentiles, Ezek. 21:31; 28:7
And they will possess their houses;
I will cause the pomp of the strong to cease,
And their holy places shall be defiled.
25 [T]Destruction comes; Lit. *Shuddering*
They will seek peace, but *there shall be* none.
26 [R]Disaster will come upon disaster,
And rumor will be upon rumor.
[R]Then they will seek a vision from a prophet; Jer. 4:20 • Ps. 74:9
But the law will perish from the priest,
And counsel from the elders.

27 'The king will mourn,
The prince will be clothed with desolation,
And the hands of the common people will tremble.
I will do to them according to their way,
And according to what they deserve I will judge them;
Then they shall know that I *am* the LORD!' "

CHAPTER 8

Vision of the Glory of God

AND it came to pass in the sixth year, in
the sixth *month,* on the fifth *day* of the
month, as I sat in my house with the elders of
Judah sitting before me, that the hand of the
Lord GOD fell upon me there.
2 [R]Then I looked, and there was a likeness,
like the appearance of fire—from the appearance of His waist and downward, fire;
and from His waist and upward, like the appearance of brightness, [R]like the color of
amber. Ezek. 1:26, 27 • Ezek. 1:4, 27
3 He [R]stretched out the form of a hand,
and took me by a lock of my hair; and [R]the
Spirit lifted me up between earth and
heaven, and [R]brought me in visions of God
to Jerusalem, to the door of the north gate
of the inner *court,* where the seat of the
image of jealousy *was,* which provokes to
jealousy. Dan. 5:5 • Ezek. 3:14 • Ezek. 11:1, 24; 40:2
4 And behold, the [R]glory of the God of Israel *was* there, like the vision that I [R]saw in
the plain. Ezek. 3:12; 9:3 • Ezek. 1:28; 3:22, 23

Image of Jealousy

5 Then He said to me, "Son of man, lift your
eyes now toward the north." So I lifted my
eyes toward the north, and there, north of the
altar gate, was this image of jealousy in the
entrance.
6 Furthermore He said to me, "Son of man,
do you see what they are doing, the great
[R]abominations that the house of Israel commits here, to make Me go far away from My
sanctuary? Now turn again, you will see
greater abominations." 2 Kin. 23:4, 5

Paintings on the Wall

7 So He brought me to the door of the
court; and when I looked, there was a hole in
the wall.
8 Then He said to me, "Son of man, dig into
the wall"; and when I dug into the wall, there
was a door.
9 And He said to me, "Go in, and see the
wicked abominations which they are doing
there."
10 So I went in and saw, and there—every
sort of [R]creeping thing, abominable beasts,
and all the idols of the house of Israel, portrayed all around on the walls. Rom. 1:23
11 And there stood before them seventy men
of the elders of the house of Israel, and in
their midst stood Jaazaniah the son of
Shaphan. Each man had a censer in his hand,
and a thick cloud of incense went up.
12 Then He said to me, "Son of man, have
you seen what the elders of the house of Israel
do in the dark, every man in the room of his
idols? For they say, 'The LORD does not see us,
the LORD has forsaken the land.' "

Weeping for Tammuz

13 And He said to me, "Turn again, *and* you
will see greater abominations that they are
doing."
14 So He brought me to the door of the north
gate of the LORD's house; and to my dismay,
women were sitting there weeping for Tammuz.

Sun Worship

15 Then He said to me, "Have you seen *this,*
O son of man? Turn again, you will see greater
abominations than these."
16 So He brought me into the inner court of
the LORD's house; and there, at the door of
the temple of the LORD, [R]between the porch
and the altar, [R]*were* about twenty-five men
[R]with their backs toward the temple of the
LORD and their faces toward the east, and
they were worshiping the sun toward the
east. Joel 2:17 • Ezek. 11:1 • Jer. 2:27; 32:33
17 And He said to me, "Have you seen *this,*
O son of man? Is it a trivial thing to the house
of Judah to commit the abominations which
they commit here? For they have [R]filled the
land with violence; then they have returned to
provoke Me to anger. Indeed they put the
branch to their nose. Ezek. 9:9

18 "Therefore I also will act in fury. My eye will not spare nor will I have pity; and though they [R]cry in My ears with a loud voice, I will not hear them." Mic. 3:4

CHAPTER 9

Call to the Six Men

THEN He called out in my hearing with a loud voice, saying, "Let those who have charge over the city draw near, each *with* a [T]deadly weapon in his hand." Or *destroying*

2 And suddenly six men came from the direction of the upper gate, which faces north, each with his battle-ax in his hand. One man among them *was* clothed with linen and had a writer's inkhorn at his side. They went in and stood beside the bronze altar.

3 Now the glory of the God of Israel had gone up from the cherub, where it had been, to the threshold of the temple.* And He called to the man clothed with linen, who *had* the writer's inkhorn at his side;

Command to Slay the Wicked

4 and the LORD said to him, "Go through the midst of the city, through the midst of Jerusalem, and put a mark on the foreheads of the men who sigh and cry over all the abominations that are done within it."

5 To the others He said in my hearing, "Go after him through the city and kill; do not let your eye spare, nor have any pity.

6 [R]"Utterly slay old *and* young men, maidens and little children and women; but [R]do not come near anyone on whom *is* the mark; and [R]begin at My sanctuary." So they began with the elders who *were* before the temple. 2 Chr. 36:17 • Rev. 9:4 • Jer. 25:29

7 Then He said to them, "Defile the [T]temple, and fill the courts with the slain. Go out!" And they went out and killed in the city. Lit. *house*

Weeping of Ezekiel

8 So it was, that while they were killing them, I was left *alone;* and I fell on my face and cried out, and said, "Ah, Lord GOD! Will You destroy all the remnant of Israel in pouring out Your fury on Jerusalem?"

9 Then He said to me, "The iniquity of the house of Israel and Judah *is* exceedingly great, and [R]the land is full of bloodshed, and the city full of perversity; for they say, [R]'The LORD has forsaken the land, and [R]the LORD does not see!' 2 Kin. 21:16 • Ezek. 8:12 • Is. 29:15

10 "And as for Me also, My eye will neither spare, nor will I have pity, *but* I will recompense their deeds on their own head."

11 Just then, the man clothed with linen, who *had* the inkhorn at his side, reported back and said, "I have done as You commanded me."

CHAPTER 10

Departure of the Glory of God to the Threshold

AND I looked, and there in the [R]firmament[T] that was above the head of the cherubim, there appeared something like a sapphire stone, having the appearance of the likeness of a throne. Ezek. 1:22, 26 • *expanse*

2 [R]Then He spoke to the man clothed with linen, and said, "Go in among the wheels, under the cherub, fill your hands with [R]coals of fire from among the cherubim, and [R]scatter *them* over the city." And he went in as I watched. Dan. 10:5 • Ezek. 1:13 • Rev. 8:5

3 Now the cherubim were standing on the [T]south side of the temple* when the man went in, and the [R]cloud filled the inner court. Lit. *right* • 1 Kin. 8:10, 11

4 Then the glory of the LORD went up from the cherub, *and paused* over the threshold of the temple; and the house was filled with the cloud, and the court was full of the brightness of the LORD's glory.

5 And the [R]sound of the wings of the cherubim was heard *even* in the outer court, like [R]the voice of Almighty God when He speaks. Ezek. 1:24 • [Ps. 29:3]

6 Then it happened, when He commanded the man clothed in linen, saying, "Take fire from among the wheels, from among the cherubim," that he went in and stood beside the wheels.

7 And the cherub stretched out his hand from among the cherubim to the fire that *was* among the cherubim, and took *some of it* and put *it* into the hands of the *man* clothed with linen, who took *it* and went out.

8 The cherubim appeared to have the form of a man's hand under their wings.

Vision of the Wheels and Cherubim

9 [R]And when I looked, there were four wheels by the cherubim, one wheel by one cherub and another wheel by each other cherub; the wheels appeared *to have* the color of a [R]beryl stone. Ezek. 1:15 • Ezek. 1:16

10 *As for* their appearance, all four looked alike—as it were, a wheel in the middle of a wheel.

11 [R]When they went, they went toward *any of* their four directions; they did not turn aside when they went, but followed in the direction the head was facing. They did not turn aside when they went. Ezek. 1:17

12 And their whole body, with their back, their hands, their wings, and the wheels that the four had, *were* full of eyes all around.

13 As for the wheels, they were called in my [T]hearing, "Wheel." Lit. *ears*

14 Each one had four faces: the first face

9:3 Lit. *house* **10:3** Lit. *house*, also in vv. 4 and 18 *was* the face of a cherub, the second face the face of a man, the third the face of a lion, and the fourth the face of an eagle.

15 And the cherubim were lifted up. This *was* [R]the living creature I saw by the River Chebar. Ezek. 1:3, 5

16 [R]When the cherubim went, the wheels went beside them; and when the cherubim lifted their wings to mount up from the earth, the same wheels also did not turn from beside them. Ezek. 1:19

17 When *the cherubim** stood still, *the wheels* stood still, and when *one** was lifted up, *the other** lifted itself up, for the spirit of the living creature *was* in them.

18 Then [R]the glory of the LORD [R]departed from the threshold of the temple and stood over the cherubim. Ezek. 10:4 • Hos. 9:12

19 And [R]the cherubim lifted their wings and mounted up from the earth in my sight. When they went out, the wheels *were* beside them; and they stood at the door of the east gate of the LORD's house, and the glory of the God of Israel *was* above them. Ezek. 11:22

20 [R]This *is* the living creature I saw under the God of Israel by the River Chebar, and I knew they *were* cherubim. Ezek. 1:22

21 [R]Each one had four faces and each one four wings, and the likeness of the hands of a man *was* under their wings. Ezek. 1:6, 8

22 And the likeness of their faces *was* the same *as* the faces which I had seen by the River Chebar, their appearance and their persons. They each went straight forward.

CHAPTER 11

Vision of the Twenty-five Wicked Rulers

THEN [R]the Spirit lifted me up and brought me to [R]the East Gate of the LORD's house, which faces eastward; and there [R]at the door of the gate were twenty-five men, among whom I saw Jaazaniah the son of Azzur, and Pelatiah the son of Benaiah, princes of the people. Ezek. 3:12, 14 • Ezek. 10:19 • Ezek. 8:16

2 And He said to me: "Son of man, these *are* the men who devise iniquity and give wicked [T]counsel in this city, Advice

3 "who say, '*The time is* not [R]near to build houses; [R]this *city is* the [T]caldron, and we *are* the meat.' 2 Pet. 3:4 • Jer. 1:13 • Pot

4 "Therefore prophesy against them, prophesy, O son of man!"

5 Then [R]the Spirit of the LORD fell upon me, and said to me, "Speak! 'Thus says the LORD: "Thus you have said, O house of Israel; for [R]I know the things that come into your mind. Ezek. 2:2; 3:24 • [Jer. 16:17; 17:10]

6 [R]"You have multiplied your slain in this city, and you have filled its streets with the slain." Ezek. 7:23; 22:2–6, 9, 12, 27

7 'Therefore thus says the Lord GOD: [R]"Your slain whom you have laid in its midst, they *are* the meat, and this *city is* the caldron; [R]but I shall bring you out of the midst of it. Mic. 3:2, 3 • Ezek. 11:9

8 "You have feared the sword; and I will bring a sword upon you," says the Lord GOD.

9 "And I will bring you out of its midst, and deliver you into the hands of strangers, and [R]execute judgments on you. Ezek. 5:8

10 [R]"You shall fall by the sword. I will judge you at the border of Israel. Then you shall know that I *am* the LORD. Jer. 39:6; 52:10

11 "This *city* shall not be your [T]caldron, nor shall you be the meat in its midst. I will judge you at the border of Israel. Pot

12 "And you shall know that I *am* the LORD; for you have not walked in My statutes nor executed My judgments, but [R]have done according to the customs of the Gentiles which *are* all around you." ' " Deut. 12:30, 31

Promise of the Restoration of the Remnant

13 Now it happened, while I was prophesying, that [R]Pelatiah the son of Benaiah died. Then [R]I fell on my face and cried with a loud voice, and said, "Ah, Lord GOD! Will You make a complete end of the remnant of Israel?" Acts 5:5 • Ezek. 9:8

14 Again the word of the LORD came to me, saying,

15 "Son of man, your brethren, your relatives, your countrymen, and all the house of Israel in its entirety, *are* those about whom the inhabitants of Jerusalem have said, 'Get far away from the LORD; this land has been given to us as a possession.'

16 "Therefore say, 'Thus says the Lord GOD: "Although I have cast them far off among the Gentiles, and although I have scattered them among the countries, [R]yet I shall be a little [T]sanctuary for them in the countries where they have gone." ' Is. 8:14 • *holy place*

17 "Therefore say, 'Thus says the Lord GOD: [R]"I will gather you from the peoples, assemble you from the countries where you have been scattered, and I will give you the land of Israel." ' Jer. 3:12, 18; 24:5

18 "And they will go there, and they will take away all its [R]detestable things and all its abominations from there. Ezek. 37:23

19 "Then [R]I will give them one heart, and I will put a new spirit within them,* and take the stony heart out of their flesh, and give them a heart of flesh, Jer. 32:39

20 "that they may walk in My statutes and keep My judgments and do them; and they shall be My people, and I will be their God.

21 "But *as for those* whose hearts follow the desire for their detestable things and their abominations, [R]I will recompense their

10:17 Lit. *they* • Lit. *they* • Lit. *they* **11:19** Lit. *you* (pl.)

deeds on their own heads," says the Lord GOD. Ezek. 9:10

Departure of the Glory of God from the Mount of Olives

22 So the cherubim lifted up their wings, with the wheels beside them, and the glory of the God of Israel *was* high above them.

23 And [R]the glory of the LORD went up from the midst of the city and stood [R]on the mountain, [R]which *is* on the east side of the city. Ezek. 8:4; 9:3 • Zech. 14:4 • Ezek. 43:2

24 Then the Spirit took me up and brought me in a vision by the Spirit of God into Chaldea,* to those in captivity. And the vision that I had seen went up from me.

25 So I spoke to those in captivity of all the things the LORD had shown me.

CHAPTER 12

Sign of Belongings for Removing

NOW the word of the LORD came to me, saying:

2 "Son of man, you dwell in the midst of a rebellious house, which has eyes to see but does not see, and ears to hear but does not hear; for they *are* a rebellious house.

3 "Therefore, son of man, prepare your belongings for captivity, and go into captivity by day in their sight. You shall go from your place into captivity to another place in their sight. It may be that they will consider, though they *are* a rebellious house.

4 "By day you shall bring out your belongings in their sight, as though going into captivity; and at evening you shall go in their sight, like those who go into captivity.

5 "Dig through the wall in their sight, and carry your belongings out through it.

6 "In their sight you shall bear *them* on *your* shoulders *and* carry *them* out at twilight; you shall cover your face, so that you cannot see the ground, [R]for I have made you a sign to the house of Israel." Ezek. 4:3

7 So I did as I was commanded. I brought out my belongings by day, as though going into captivity, and at evening I dug through the wall with my hand. I brought *them* out at twilight, *and* I bore *them* on *my* shoulder in their sight.

8 And in the morning the word of the LORD came to me, saying,

9 "Son of man, has not the house of Israel, [R]the rebellious house, said to you, 'What are you doing?' Ezek. 2:5

10 "Say to them, 'Thus says the Lord GOD: "This [R]burden[T] *concerns* the prince in Jerusalem and all the house of Israel who are among them." ' Mal. 1:1 • *oracle, prophecy*

11 "Say, [R]'I *am* a sign to you. As I have done, so shall it be done to them; they shall be carried away into captivity.' Ezek. 12:6

12 "And [R]the prince who *is* among them shall bear *his belongings* on *his* shoulder at twilight and go out. They shall dig through the wall to carry *them* out through it. He shall cover his face, so that he cannot see the ground with *his* eyes. Jer. 39:4; 52:7

13 "I will also spread My [R]net over him, and he shall be caught in My snare. [R]I will bring him to Babylon, *to* the land of the Chaldeans; yet he shall not see it, though he shall die there. Jer. 52:9 • Jer. 52:11

14 "I will scatter to every wind all who *are* around him to help him, and all his troops; and I will draw out the sword after them.

15 [R]"Then they shall know that I *am* the LORD, when I scatter them among the nations and disperse them throughout the countries. Ezek. 6:7, 14; 12:16, 20

16 [R]"But I will spare a few of their men from the sword, from famine, and from pestilence, that they may declare all their abominations among the Gentiles wherever they go. Then they shall know that I *am* the LORD." Ezek. 6:8–10

Sign of Trembling

17 Moreover the word of the LORD came to me, saying,

18 "Son of man, [R]eat your bread with [T]quaking, and drink your water with trembling and anxiety. Ezek. 4:16 • *shaking*

19 "And say to the people of the land, 'Thus says the Lord GOD to the inhabitants of Jerusalem *and* to the land of Israel: "They shall eat their bread with anxiety, and drink their water with dread, so that her land may be emptied of all who are in it, because of the violence of all those who dwell in it.

20 "Then the cities that are inhabited shall be laid waste, and the land shall become desolate; and you shall know that I *am* the LORD." ' "

21 And the word of the LORD came to me, saying,

22 "Son of man, what *is* this proverb *that* you *people* have about the land of Israel, which says, [R]'The days are prolonged, and every vision fails'? Ezek. 11:3; 12:27

23 "Tell them therefore, 'Thus says the Lord GOD: "I will lay this proverb to rest, and they shall no more use it as a proverb in Israel." But say to them, "The days are at hand, and the fulfillment of every vision.

24 "For [R]no more shall there be any [R]false[T] vision or flattering divination within the house of Israel. Ezek. 13:6 • Lam. 2:14 • Lit. *vain*

25 "For I *am* the LORD. I speak, and the word which I speak will come to pass; it will no more be postponed; for in your days, O rebellious house, I will say the word and perform it," says the Lord GOD.' "

26 Again the word of the LORD came to me, saying,

11:24 Or *Babylon,* and so elsewhere in the book

27 [R]"Son of man, look, the house of Israel is
saying, 'The vision that he sees *is* [R]for many
days *from now,* and he prophesies of times far
off.' Ezek. 12:22 • Dan. 10:14
28 "Therefore say to them, 'Thus says the
Lord GOD: "None of My words will be post-
poned any more, but the word which I speak
will be done," says the Lord GOD.' "

CHAPTER 13

Judgment upon False Prophets

AND the word of the LORD came to me,
saying,
2 "Son of man, prophesy against the
prophets of Israel who prophesy, and say to
those who prophesy out of their own heart,
'Hear the word of the LORD!' "
3 Thus says the Lord GOD: "Woe to the fool-
ish prophets, who follow their own spirit and
have seen [T]nothing! No vision
4 "O Israel, your prophets are [R]like foxes in
the deserts. Song 2:15
5 "You [R]have not gone up into the gaps to
build a wall for the house of Israel to stand in
battle on the day of the LORD. Ps. 106:23
6 "They have envisioned futility and false
divination, saying, 'Thus says the LORD!' But
the LORD has not sent them; yet they hope that
the word may be confirmed.
7 "Have you not seen a futile vision, and
have you not spoken false divination? You say,
'The LORD says,' but I have not spoken."
8 Therefore thus says the Lord GOD: "Be-
cause you have spoken nonsense and envi-
sioned lies, therefore I *am* indeed against
you," says the Lord GOD.
9 "My hand will be [R]against the prophets
who envision futility and who [R]divine lies;
they shall not be in the assembly of My peo-
ple, nor be written in the record of the house
of Israel, nor shall they enter into the land of
Israel. Then you shall know that I *am* the Lord
GOD. Jer. 23:30 • Jer. 20:3–6
10 "Because, indeed, because they have se-
duced My people, saying, [R]'Peace!' when
there is no peace—and one builds a wall,
and they [R]plaster it with untempered *mor-*
tar— Jer. 6:14; 8:11 • Ezek. 22:28
11 "say to those who plaster *it* with untem-
pered *mortar,* that it will fall. [R]There will be
flooding rain, and you, O great hailstones,
shall fall; and a stormy wind shall tear *it*
down. Ezek. 38:22
12 "Surely, when the wall has fallen, will it
not be said to you, 'Where *is* the mortar with
which you plastered *it?*' "
13 Therefore thus says the Lord GOD: "I will
cause a stormy wind to break forth in My
fury; and there shall be a flooding rain in My
anger, and great hailstones in fury to consume
it.
14 "So I will break down the wall you have
plastered with untempered *mortar,* and bring
it down to the ground, so that its foundation
will be uncovered; it will fall, and you shall be
consumed in the midst of it. Then you shall
know that I *am* the LORD.
15 "Thus will I accomplish My wrath on the
wall and on those who have plastered it with
untempered *mortar;* and I will say to you,
'The wall *is* no *more,* nor those who plastered
it,
16 '*that is,* the prophets of Israel who proph-
esy concerning Jerusalem, and who see vi-
sions of peace for her when *there is* no
peace,' " says the Lord GOD.

Judgment upon False Prophetesses

17 "Likewise, son of man, [R]set your face
against the daughters of your people, [R]who
prophesy out of their own heart; prophesy
against them, Ezek. 20:46; 21:2 • Ezek. 13:2
18 "and say, 'Thus says the Lord GOD: "Woe
to the *women* who sew *magic* charms on their
sleeves* and make veils for the heads of peo-
ple of every height to hunt souls! Will you
[R]hunt the souls of My people, and keep your-
selves alive? [2 Pet. 2:14]
19 "And will you profane Me among My
people [R]for handfuls of barley and for pieces
of bread, killing people who should not die,
and keeping people alive who should not live,
by your lying to My people who listen to
lies?" Mic. 3:5
20 'Therefore thus says the Lord GOD: "Be-
hold, I *am* against your *magic* charms by
which you hunt souls there like birds. I will
tear them from your arms, and let the souls
go, the souls you hunt like birds.
21 "I will also tear off your veils and deliver
My people out of your hand, and they shall no
longer be as prey in your hand. Then you shall
know that I *am* the LORD.
22 "Because with lies you have made the
heart of the righteous sad, whom I have not
made sad; and you have strengthened the
hands of the wicked, so that he does not turn
from his wicked way to save his life.
23 "Therefore [R]you shall no longer envision
futility nor practice divination; for I will de-
liver My people out of your hand, and you
shall know that I *am* the LORD." ' " Mic. 3:5, 6

CHAPTER 14

Idolatry of the Elders

NOW [R]some of the elders of Israel came to
me and sat before me. Ezek. 8:1; 20:1
2 And the word of the LORD came to me,
saying,
3 "Son of man, these men have set up their
idols in their hearts, and put before them [R]that

13:18 Lit. *over all the joints of My hands;* Vg. *under every elbow;* LXX, Tg. *on all elbows of the hands*

which causes them to stumble into iniquity.
[R]Should I let Myself be inquired of at all by
them? Ezek. 7:19 • Ezek. 20:3, 31
4 "Therefore speak to them, and say to
them, 'Thus says the Lord GOD: "Everyone of
the house of Israel who sets up his idols in his
heart, and puts before him what causes him to
stumble into iniquity, and then comes to the
prophet, I the LORD will answer him who
comes, according to the multitude of his idols,
5 "that I may seize the house of Israel by
their heart, because they are all estranged
from Me by their idols." '
6 "Therefore say to the house of Israel,
'Thus says the Lord GOD: "Repent, turn away
from your idols, and [R]turn your faces away
from all your abominations. Is. 2:20; 30:22
7 "For anyone of the house of Israel, or of
the strangers who dwell in Israel, who sepa-
rates himself from Me and sets up his idols in
his heart and puts before him what causes
him to stumble into iniquity, then comes to a
prophet to inquire of him concerning Me, I the
LORD will answer him by Myself.
8 "I will set My face against that man and
make him a sign and a proverb, and I will cut
him off from the midst of My people. Then
you shall know that I *am* the LORD.
9 "And if the prophet is induced to speak
anything, I the LORD [R]have induced that
prophet, and I will stretch out My hand
against him and destroy him from among My
people Israel. 2 Thess. 2:11
10 "And they shall bear their iniquity; the
punishment of the prophet shall be the same
as the punishment of the one who inquired,
11 "that the house of Israel may [R]no longer
stray from Me, nor be profaned anymore with
all their transgressions, [R]but that they may be
My people and I may be their God," says the
Lord GOD.' " 2 Pet. 2:15 • Ezek. 11:20

Jerusalem to Be Destroyed

12 The word of the LORD came again to me,
saying:
13 "Son of man, when a land sins against Me
by persistent unfaithfulness, I will stretch out
My hand against it; I will cut off its [R]supply of
bread, send famine on it, and cut off man and
beast from it. Is. 3:1
14 [R]"Even *if* these three men, Noah, Daniel,
and Job, were in it, they would deliver *only*
themselves [R]by their righteousness," says the
Lord GOD. Jer. 15:1 • [Prov. 11:4]
15 "If I cause [R]wild beasts to pass through
the land, and they empty it, and make it so
desolate that no man may pass through be-
cause of the beasts, Lev. 26:22
16 "*even* [R]*though* these three men *were* in it,
as I live," says the Lord GOD, "they would de-
liver neither sons nor daughters; only they
would be delivered, and the land would be
[R]desolate. Ezek. 14:14, 18, 20 • Ezek. 15:8; 33:28, 29
17 "Or *if* [R]I bring a sword on that land, and
say, 'Sword, go through the land,' and I cut off
man and beast from it, Lev. 26:25
18 "even *though* these three men *were* in it,
as I live," says the Lord GOD, "they would de-
liver neither sons nor daughters, but only they
themselves would be delivered.
19 "Or *if* I send [R]a pestilence into that land
and pour out My fury on it in blood, and cut
off from it man and beast, 2 Sam. 24:15
20 "even [R]*though* Noah, Daniel, and Job
were in it, *as* I live," says the Lord GOD, "they
would deliver neither son nor daughter; they
would deliver *only* themselves by their righ-
teousness." Ezek. 14:14
21 For thus says the Lord GOD: "How much
more it shall be when [R]I send My four severe
judgments on Jerusalem—the sword and
famine and wild beasts and pestilence—to cut
off man and beast from it? Ezek. 5:17
22 "Yet behold, there shall be left in it a rem-
nant who will be brought out, *both* sons and
daughters; surely they will come out to you,
and you will see their ways and their doings.
Then you will be comforted concerning the
disaster that I have brought upon Jerusalem,
all that I have brought upon it.
23 "And they will comfort you, when you see
their ways and their doings; and you shall
know that I have done nothing [R]without
cause that I have done in it," says the Lord
GOD. Jer. 22:8, 9

CHAPTER 15

Parable of the Vine

THEN the word of the LORD came to me,
saying:
2 "Son of man, how is the wood of the vine
better than any other wood, the vine branch
which is among the trees of the forest?
3 "Is wood taken from it to make any ob-
ject? Or can *men* make a peg from it to hang
any vessel on?
4 "Instead, it is thrown into the fire for fuel;
the fire devours both ends of it, and its middle
is burned. Is it useful for *any* work?
5 "Indeed, when it was whole, no object
could be made from it. How much less will it
be useful for *any* work when the fire has de-
voured it, and it is burned?
6 "Therefore thus says the Lord GOD: 'Like
the wood of the vine among the trees of the
forest, which I have given to the fire for fuel,
so I will give up the inhabitants of Jerusalem;
7 'and [R]I will set My face against them.
[R]They will go out from *one* fire, but *another*
fire shall devour them. [R]Then you shall know
that I *am* the LORD, when I set My face against
them. Ezek. 14:8 • Is. 24:18 • Ezek. 7:4
8 'Thus I will make the land desolate, be-
cause they have persisted in unfaithfulness,'
says the Lord GOD."

CHAPTER 16

God Has Mercy on Israel

AGAIN the word of the LORD came to me,
saying,
2 "Son of man, [R]cause Jerusalem to know
her abominations, Ezek. 20:4; 22:2
3 "and say, 'Thus says the Lord GOD to Jeru-
salem: "Your birth and your nativity *are* from
the land of Canaan; your father *was* an Amo-
rite and your mother a Hittite.
4 "*As for* your nativity, [R]on the day you
were born your navel cord was not cut, nor
were you washed in water to cleanse *you;* you
were not rubbed with salt nor wrapped in
swaddling cloths. Hos. 2:3
5 "No eye pitied you, to do any of these
things for you, to have compassion on you;
but you were thrown out into the open field,
when you yourself were [T]loathed on the day
you were born. *abhorred*
6 "And when I passed by you and saw you
struggling in your own blood, I said to you in
your blood, 'Live!' Yes, I said to you in your
blood, 'Live!'
7 [R]"I made you [T]thrive like a plant in the
field; and you grew, matured, and became
very beautiful. *Your* breasts were formed,
your hair grew, but you *were* naked and
bare. Ex. 1:7 • Lit. *a myriad*
8 "When I passed by you again and looked
upon you, indeed your time *was* the time of
love; [R]so I spread My wing over you and
covered your nakedness. Yes, I [R]swore an
oath to you and entered into a [R]covenant
with you, and you became Mine," says the
Lord GOD. Ruth 3:9 • Gen. 22:16–18 • Ex. 24:6–8
9 "Then I washed you in water; yes, I thor-
oughly washed off your blood, and I anointed
you with oil.
10 "I clothed you in embroidered cloth and
gave you sandals of [T]badger skin; I clothed
you with fine linen and covered you with
silk. Or *dolphin* or *dugong*
11 "I adorned you with ornaments, [R]put
bracelets on your wrists, [R]and a chain on your
neck. Gen. 24:22, 47 • Prov. 1:9
12 "And I put a [T]jewel in your nose, earrings
in your ears, and a beautiful crown on your
head. Lit. *ring*
13 "Thus you were adorned with gold and sil-
ver, and your clothing *was of* fine linen, silk, and
embroidered cloth. [R]You ate *pastry of* fine flour,
honey, and oil. You were exceedingly [R]beautiful,
and succeeded to royalty. Deut. 32:13, 14 • Ps. 48:2
14 [R]"Your fame went out among the nations
because of your beauty, for it *was* perfect
through My splendor which I had bestowed
on you," says the Lord GOD. Lam. 2:15

Israel Rejects God

15 [R]"But you trusted in your own beauty,
[R]played the harlot because of your fame, and
poured out your harlotry on everyone passing
by who *would have* it. Mic. 3:11 • Is. 1:21
16 "You took some of your garments and
adorned multicolored high places for your-
self, and played the harlot on them. *Such*
things should not happen, nor be.
17 "You have also taken your beautiful jew-
elry from My gold and My silver, which I had
given you, and made for yourself male images
and played the harlot with them.
18 "You took your embroidered garments
and covered them, and you set My oil and My
incense before them.
19 "Also My food which I gave you—the pas-
try of fine flour, oil, and honey *which* I fed
you—you set it before them as sweet incense;
and *so* it was," says the Lord GOD.
20 "Moreover you took your sons and your
daughters, whom you bore to Me, and these
you sacrificed to them to be devoured. *Were*
your *acts* of harlotry a small matter,
21 "that you have slain My children and of-
fered them up to them by causing them to
pass through *the* [R]*fire?* Jer. 19:5
22 "And in all your abominations and acts of
harlotry you did not remember the days of
your [R]youth, when you were naked and bare,
struggling in your blood. Jer. 2:2
23 "Then it was so, after all your wicked-
ness—'Woe, woe to you!' says the Lord GOD—
24 "*that* [R]you also built for yourself a shrine,
and [R]made a high place for yourself in every
street. Jer. 11:13 • Jer. 2:20; 3:2
25 "You built your high places [R]at the head of
every road, and made your beauty to be ab-
horred. You offered yourself to everyone who
passed by, and multiplied your acts of har-
lotry. Prov. 9:14
26 "You also committed harlotry with [R]the
Egyptians, your very fleshly neighbors, and
increased your acts of harlotry to [R]provoke
Me to anger. Ezek. 16:26; 20:7, 8 • Deut. 31:20
27 "Behold, therefore, I stretched out My
hand against you, diminished your [T]allot-
ment, and gave you up to the will of those
who hate you, [R]the daughters of the
Philistines, who were ashamed of your lewd
behavior. Allowance of food • Ezek. 16:57
28 "You also played the harlot with the [R]As-
syrians, because you were insatiable; indeed
you played the harlot with them and still were
not satisfied. Jer. 2:18, 36
29 "Moreover you multiplied your acts of
harlotry as far as the land of the trader,
[R]Chaldea; and even then you were not satis-
fied. Ezek. 23:14–17
30 "How degenerate is your heart!" says the
Lord GOD, "seeing you do all these *things,* the
deeds of a brazen harlot.
31 "You erected your shrine at the head of
every road, and built your high place in every
street. Yet you were not like a harlot, because
you scorned [R]payment. Is. 52:3

32 "*You are* an adulterous wife, *who* takes strangers instead of her husband.

33 "Men make payment to all harlots, but [R]you made your payments to all your lovers, and hired them to come to you from all around for your harlotry. Hos. 8:9, 10

34 "You are the opposite of *other* women in your harlotry, because no one solicited you to be a harlot. In that you gave payment but no payment was given you, therefore you are the opposite."

God Punishes Israel

35 'Now then, O harlot, hear the word of the LORD!

36 'Thus says the Lord GOD: "Because your filthiness was poured out and your nakedness uncovered in your harlotry with your lovers, and with all your abominable idols, and because of [R]the blood of your children which you gave to them, Jer. 2:34

37 "surely, therefore, I will gather all your lovers with whom you took pleasure, all those you loved, *and* all those you hated; I will gather them from all around against you and will uncover your nakedness to them, that they may see all your nakedness.

38 "And I will judge you as [R]women who break wedlock or [R]shed blood are judged; I will bring blood upon you in fury and jealousy. Lev. 20:10 • Gen. 9:6

39 "I will also give you into their hand, and they shall throw down your shrines and break down [R]your high places. [R]They shall also strip you of your clothes, take your beautiful jewelry, and leave you naked and bare. Ezek. 16:24, 31 • Hos. 2:3

40 [R]"They shall also bring up an assembly against you, [R]and they shall stone you with stones and thrust you through with their swords. Ezek. 23:45–47 • John 8:5, 7

41 "They shall [R]burn your houses with fire, and [R]execute judgments on you in the sight of many women; and I will make you cease playing the harlot, and you shall no longer hire lovers. Deut. 13:16 • Ezek. 5:8; 23:10, 48

42 "So I will lay to rest My fury toward you, and My jealousy shall depart from you. I will be quiet, and be angry no more.

43 "Because [R]you did not remember the days of your youth, but agitated Me* with all these *things*, surely [R]I will also recompense your deeds on *your own* head," says the Lord GOD. "And you shall not commit lewdness in addition to all your abominations. Ps. 78:42 • Ezek. 9:10; 11:21; 22:31

44 "Indeed everyone who quotes proverbs will use *this* proverb against you: 'Like mother, like daughter!'

45 "You *are* your mother's daughter, loathing husband and children; and you *are* the sister of your sisters, who loathed their husbands and children; your mother *was* a Hittite and your father an Amorite.

46 "Your elder sister *is* Samaria, who dwells with her daughters to the north of you; and [R]your younger sister, who dwells to the south of you, *is* Sodom and her daughters. Is. 1:10

47 "You did not walk in their ways nor act according to their abominations; but, as *if that were* too little, [R]you became more corrupt than they in all your ways. Ezek. 5:6, 7

48 "*As* I live," says the Lord GOD, "neither your sister Sodom nor her daughters have done as you and your daughters have done.

49 "Look, this was the iniquity of your sister Sodom: She and her daughter had pride, [R]fullness of food, and abundance of idleness; neither did she strengthen the hand of the poor and needy. Gen. 13:10

50 "And they were haughty and committed abomination before Me; therefore [R]I took them away as I saw *fit*.* Gen. 19:24

51 "Samaria did not commit [R]half of your sins; but you have multiplied your abominations more than they, and [R]have justified your sisters by all the abominations which you have done. Ezek. 23:11 • Jer. 3:8–11

52 "You who judged your sisters, bear your own shame also, because the sins which you committed were more abominable than theirs; they are more righteous than you. Yes, be disgraced also, and bear your own shame, because you justified your sisters.

53 [R]"When I bring back their captives, the captives of Sodom and her daughters, and the captives of Samaria and her daughters, then *I will also bring back* [R]the captives of your captivity among them, Is. 1:9 • Jer. 20:16

54 "that you may bear your own shame and be disgraced by all that you did when [R]you comforted them. Ezek. 14:22

55 "When your sisters, Sodom and her daughters, return to their former state, and Samaria and her daughters return to their former state, then you and your daughters will return to your former state.

56 "For your sister Sodom was not a byword in your mouth in the days of your pride,

57 "before your wickedness was uncovered. It was like the time of the [R]reproach of the daughters of Syria* and all *those* around her, and of the daughters of the Philistines, who despise you everywhere. 2 Kin. 16:5

58 "You have paid for your lewdness and your abominations," says the LORD.

59 'For thus says the Lord GOD: "I will deal with you as you have done, who despised the oath by breaking the covenant.

16:43 So with LXX, Syr., Tg., Vg.; MT *were agitated with Me* **16:50** Vg. *you saw;* LXX *he saw;* Tg. *as was revealed to Me* **16:57** Heb. *Aram;* so with MT, LXX, Tg., Vg.; many Heb. mss., Syr. *Edom*

God Remembers His Covenant

60 "Nevertheless I will [R]remember My
covenant with you in the days of your youth,
and I will establish [R]an everlasting covenant
with you. Ps. 106:45 • Is. 55:3
61 "Then you will remember your ways and
be ashamed, when you receive your older and
your younger sisters; for I will give them to
you for [R]daughters, [R]but not because of My
covenant with you. [Gal. 4:26] • Jer. 31:31
62 [R]"And I will establish My covenant with
you. Then you shall know that I *am* the
LORD, Hos. 2:19, 20
63 "that you may remember and be
ashamed, [R]and never open your mouth any-
more because of your shame, when I provide
you an atonement for all you have done," says
the Lord GOD.'" [Rom. 3:19]

CHAPTER 17

Parable of the Two Eagles

AND the word of the LORD came to me,
saying,
2 "Son of man, pose a riddle, and speak a
[R]parable to the house of Israel, Ezek. 20:49
3 "and say, 'Thus says the Lord GOD:

[R]"A great eagle with large wings and long
pinions, Ezek. 17:12
Full of feathers of various colors,
Came to Lebanon
And [R]took from the cedar the highest
branch. 2 Kin. 24:12
4 He cropped off its topmost young twig
And carried it to a land of trade;
He set it in a city of merchants.
5 Then he took some of the seed of the
land
And planted it in a fertile field;
He placed *it* by abundant waters
And set it [R]like a willow tree. Is. 44:4
6 And it grew and became a spreading
vine [R]of low stature; Ezek. 17:14
Its branches turned toward him,
But its roots were under it.
So it became a vine,
Brought forth branches,
And put forth shoots.

7 "But there was another* great eagle with
large wings and many feathers;
And behold, [R]this vine bent its roots
toward him, Ezek. 17:15
And stretched its branches toward him,
From the garden terrace where it had
been planted,
That he might water it.
8 It was planted in [T]good soil by many
waters, Lit. *a good field*
To bring forth branches, bear fruit,
And become a majestic vine."'

9 "Say, 'Thus says the Lord GOD:
"Will it thrive?
[R]Will he not pull up its roots, 2 Kin. 25:7
Cut off its fruit,
And leave it to wither?
All of its spring leaves will wither,
And no great power or many people
Will be needed to pluck it up by its roots.
10 Behold, *it is* planted,
Will it thrive?
[R]Will it not utterly wither when the east
wind touches it? Hos. 13:15
It will wither in the garden terrace where
it grew."'"

11 Moreover the word of the LORD came to
me, saying,
12 "Say now to the rebellious house: 'Do you
not know what these *things mean?*' Tell *them,*
'Indeed the king of Babylon went to Jerusa-
lem and took its king and princes, and led
them with him to Babylon.
13 [R]'And he took the king's offspring, made
a covenant with him, [R]and put him under
oath. He also took away the mighty of the
land, 2 Kin. 24:17 • 2 Chr. 36:13
14 'that the kingdom might be [R]brought low
and not lift itself up, *but* that by keeping his
covenant it might stand. Ezek. 29:14
15 'But [R]he rebelled against him by sending
his ambassadors to Egypt, [R]that they might
give him horses and many people. [R]Will he
prosper? Will he who does such *things* es-
cape? Can he break a covenant and still be de-
livered? 2 Kin. 24:20 • Deut. 17:16 • Ezek. 17:9
16 '*As* I live,' says the Lord GOD, 'surely [R]in
the place *where* the king *dwells* who made
him king, whose oath he despised and whose
covenant he broke—with him in the midst of
Babylon he shall die. Ezek. 12:13
17 'Nor will Pharaoh with *his* mighty army
and great company do anything in the war,
when they heap up a siege mound and build a
wall to cut off many persons.
18 'Since he despised the oath by breaking
the covenant, and in fact [R]gave[T] his hand and
still did all these *things,* he shall not es-
cape.'" 1 Chr. 29:24 • Took an oath
19 Therefore thus says the Lord GOD: "*As* I
live, surely My oath which he despised, and
My covenant which he broke, I will recom-
pense on his own head.
20 "I will spread My net over him, and he
shall be taken in My snare. I will bring him to
Babylon and try him there for the treason
which he committed against Me.
21 [R]"All his fugitives* with all his troops
shall fall by the sword, and those who remain

17:7 So with LXX, Syr., Vg.; MT, Tg. *one* **17:21** So with MT, Vg.; many Heb. mss., Syr. *choice men;* Tg. *mighty men;* LXX omits *All his fugitives*

shall be [R]scattered to every wind; and you
shall know that I, the LORD, have spoken."
Ezek. 12:14 • Ezek. 12:15; 22:15

22 Thus says the Lord GOD: "I will take also
one of the highest [R]branches of the high
cedar and set *it* out. I will crop off from the
topmost of its young twigs [R]a tender one, and
will [R]plant *it* on a high and prominent moun-
tain. [Zech. 3:8] • Is. 53:2 • [Ps. 2:6]
23 [R]"On the mountain height of Israel I will
plant it; and it will bring forth boughs, and
bear fruit, and be a majestic cedar. Under it
will dwell birds of every sort; in the shadow of
its branches they will dwell. [Is. 2:2, 3]
24 "And all the trees of the field shall know
that I, the LORD, [R]have brought down the
high tree and exalted the low tree, dried up
the green tree and made the dry tree flour-
ish; [R]I, the LORD, have spoken and have done
it." Amos 9:11 • Ezek. 22:14

CHAPTER 18

Message of Personal Judgment for Personal Sin

THE word of the LORD came to me again,
saying,
2 "What do you mean when you use this
proverb concerning the land of Israel, saying:

'The [R]fathers have eaten sour grapes,
And the children's teeth are set on
edge'? Lam. 5:7

3 "*As* I live," says the Lord GOD, "you shall
no longer use this proverb in Israel.

4 "Behold, all souls are [R]Mine;
The soul of the father Num. 16:22; 27:16
As well as the soul of the son is Mine;
[R]The soul who sins shall die. [Rom. 6:23]
5 But if a man is just
And does what is lawful and right;
6 [R]If he has not eaten on the mountains,
Nor lifted up his eyes to the idols of the
house of Israel, Ezek. 22:9
Nor [R]defiled his neighbor's wife,
Nor approached [R]a woman during her
impurity; Lev. 18:20; 20:10 • Lev. 18:19
7 If he has not [R]oppressed anyone,
But has restored to the debtor his
[R]pledge; Ex. 22:21 • Deut. 24:12
Has robbed no one by violence,
But has given his bread to the hungry
And covered the naked with clothing;
8 If he has not [T]exacted [R]usury
Nor taken any increase,
But has withdrawn his hand from
iniquity Lent money at interest • Ex. 22:25
And [R]executed true [T]judgment between
man and man; Zech. 8:16 • *justice*
9 *If* he has walked in My statutes
And kept My judgments faithfully—
He *is* just;
He shall surely [R]live!" Amos 5:4
Says the Lord GOD.

10 "If he begets a son *who is* a robber
Or [R]a shedder of blood, Num. 35:31
Who does any of these *things*
11 And does none of those *duties,*
But has eaten on the mountains
Or defiled his neighbor's wife;
12 If he has oppressed the poor and needy,
Robbed by violence,
Not restored the pledge,
Lifted his eyes to the idols,
Or committed abomination;
13 If he has exacted usury
Or taken increase—
Shall he then live?
He shall not live!
If he has done any of these
abominations,
He shall surely die;
His blood shall be upon him.

14 "*If,* however, he begets a son
Who sees all the sins which his father
has done,
And considers but does not do likewise;
15 [R]*Who* has not eaten on the mountains,
Nor lifted his eyes to the idols of the
house of Israel, Ezek. 18:6
Nor defiled his neighbor's wife;
16 Has not oppressed anyone,
Nor withheld a pledge,
Nor robbed by violence,
But has given his bread to the hungry
And covered the naked with clothing;
17 *Who* has withdrawn his hand from the
poor*
And not received usury or increase,
But has executed My judgments
And walked in My statutes—
He shall not die for the iniquity of his
father;
He shall surely live!

18 "*As for* his father,
Because he cruelly oppressed,
Robbed his brother by violence,
And did what *is* not good among his
people,
Behold, he shall die for his iniquity.

19 "Yet you say, 'Why [R]should the son not
bear the guilt of the father?' Because the son
has done what is lawful and right, and has
kept all My statutes and observed them, he
shall surely live. Ex. 20:5
20 [R]"The soul who sins shall die. The son
shall not bear the guilt of the father, nor the
father bear the guilt of the son. The righ-

18:17 So with MT, Tg., Vg.; LXX *iniquity* (cf. v. 8)

teousness of the righteous shall be upon him-
self, [R]and the wickedness of the wicked shall
be upon himself. Ezek. 18:4 • Rom. 2:6–9
21 "But if a wicked man turns from all his
sins which he has committed, keeps all My
statutes, and does what is lawful and right, he
shall surely live; he shall not die.
22 [R]"None of the transgressions which he
has committed shall be remembered against
him; because of the righteousness which he
has done, he shall live. Ezek. 18:24; 33:16
23 [R]"Do I have any pleasure at all that the
wicked should die?" says the Lord GOD, "*and*
not that he should turn from his ways and
live? [Ezek. 18:32; 33:11]
24 "But when a righteous man turns away
from his righteousness and commits iniquity,
and does according to all the abominations
that the wicked *man* does, shall he live? [R]All
the righteousness which he has done shall not
be remembered; because of the unfaithful-
ness of which he is guilty and the sin which
he has committed, because of them he shall
die. [2 Pet. 2:20]
25 "Yet you say, [R]'The way of the Lord is not
fair.' Hear now, O house of Israel, is it not My
way which is fair, and your ways which are
not fair? Ezek. 18:29; 33:17, 20
26 [R]"When a righteous *man* turns away from
his righteousness, commits iniquity, and dies
in it, it is because of the iniquity which he has
done that he dies. Ezek. 18:24
27 "Again, [R]when a wicked *man* turns away
from the wickedness which he committed,
and does what is lawful and right, he pre-
serves himself alive. Ezek. 18:21
28 "Because he considers and turns away
from all the transgressions which he commit-
ted, he shall surely live; he shall not die.
29 [R]"Yet the house of Israel says, 'The way of
the Lord is not fair.' O house of Israel, is it not
My ways which are fair, and your ways which
are not fair? Ezek. 18:25
30 [R]"Therefore I will judge you, O house of
Israel, every one according to his ways," says
the Lord GOD. [R]"Repent, and turn from all
your transgressions, so that iniquity will not
be your ruin. Ezek. 7:3; 33:20 • Matt. 3:2
31 "Cast away from you all the transgres-
sions which you have committed, and get
yourselves a new heart and a new spirit. For
why should you die, O house of Israel?
32 "For [R]I have no pleasure in the death of
one who dies," says the Lord GOD. "Therefore
turn and [R]live!" Lam. 3:33 • [Prov. 4:2, 5, 6]

CHAPTER 19

Lament for the Princes of Israel

"MOREOVER [R]take up a lamentation for
the princes of Israel, Ezek. 26:17; 27:2
2 "and say:
'What *is* your mother? A lioness:
She lay down among the lions;
Among the young lions she nourished
her cubs.
3 She brought up one of her cubs,
And [R]he became a young lion;
He learned to catch prey,
And he devoured men. 2 Kin. 23:31, 32
4 The nations also heard of him;
He was trapped in their pit,
And they brought him with chains to the
land of [R]Egypt. 2 Kin. 23:33, 34
5 'When she saw that she waited, *that* her
hope was lost,
She took [R]another of her cubs *and* made
him a young lion. 2 Kin. 23:34
6 [R]He roved among the lions, 2 Kin. 24:8, 9
And [R]became a young lion; Ezek. 19:3
He learned to catch prey;
He devoured men.
7 He knew their desolate places,*
And laid waste their cities;
The land with its fullness was desolated
By the noise of his roaring.
8 Then the nations set against him from
the provinces on every side,
And spread their net over him;
[R]He was trapped in their pit. Ezek. 19:4
9 They put him in a cage with chains,
And brought him to the king of Babylon;
They brought him in nets,
That his voice should no longer be heard
on the mountains of Israel.

Parable of the Withered Vine

10 'Your mother *was* [R]like a vine in your
bloodline,* Ezek. 17:6
Planted by the waters,
[R]Fruitful and full of branches Deut. 8:7–9
Because of many waters.
11 She had strong branches for scepters of
rulers.
[R]She towered in stature above the thick
branches, Dan. 4:11
And was seen in her height amid the
[T]dense foliage. Or *many branches*
12 But she was [R]plucked up in fury,
She was cast down to the ground,
And the [R]east wind dried her fruit.
Her strong branches were broken and
withered; Jer. 31:27, 28 • Hos. 13:5
The fire consumed them.
13 And now she *is* planted in the
wilderness,
In a dry and thirsty land.
14 [R]Fire has come out from a rod of her
branches Judg. 9:15

19:7 LXX *He stood in insolence;* Tg. *He destroyed its palaces;* Vg. *He learned to make widows* **19:10** Lit. *blood,* so with MT, Syr., Vg.; LXX *like a flower on a pomegranate tree;* Tg. *in your likeness*

And devoured her fruit,
So that she has no strong branch—a
scepter for ruling.' "

[R]This *is* a lamentation, and has become a
lamentation. Lam. 2:5

CHAPTER 20

In Egypt

IT came to pass in the seventh year, in the
fifth *month,* on the tenth *day* of the
month, *that* [R]certain of the elders of Israel
came to inquire of the LORD, and sat before
me. Ezek. 8:1, 11, 12; 14:1
2 Then the word of the LORD came to me,
saying,
3 "Son of man, speak to the elders of Israel,
and say to them, 'Thus says the Lord GOD:
"Have you come to inquire of Me? *As* I live,"
says the Lord GOD, [R]"I will not be inquired of
by you." ' Ezek. 7:26; 14:3
4 "Will you judge them, son of man, will
you judge *them?* Then make known to them
the abominations of their fathers.
5 "Say to them, 'Thus says the Lord GOD:
"On the day when I chose Israel and raised
My hand in an oath to the descendants of the
house of Jacob, and made Myself [R]known to
them in the land of Egypt, I raised My hand in
an oath to them, saying, [R]'I *am* the LORD your
God.' Deut. 4:34 • Ex. 20:2
6 "On that day I raised My hand in an oath
to them, [R]to bring them out of the land of
Egypt into a land that I had searched out for
them, 'flowing with milk and honey,'* [R]the
glory of all lands. Jer. 32:22 • Jer. 11:5
7 "Then I said to them, 'Each of you,
[R]throw away [R]the abominations which are be-
fore his eyes, and do not defile yourselves
with [R]the idols of Egypt. I *am* the LORD your
God.' Ezek. 18:31 • 2 Chr. 15:8 • Lev. 18:3
8 "But they rebelled against Me and would
not [T]obey Me. They did not all cast away the
abominations which were before their eyes,
nor did they forsake the idols of Egypt. Then
I said, 'I will [R]pour out My fury on them and
fulfill My anger against them in the midst of
the land of Egypt.' Lit. *listen to* • Ezek. 7:8
9 [R]"But I acted for My name's sake, that it
should not be profaned before the Gentiles
among whom they *were,* in whose sight I had
made Myself known to them, to bring them
out of the land of Egypt. Num. 14:13

In the Wilderness

10 "Therefore I [R]made them go out of the
land of Egypt and brought them into the
wilderness. Ex. 13:18
11 [R]"And I gave them My statutes and
showed them My judgments, 'which, *if* a man
does, he shall live by them.'* Neh. 9:13
12 "Moreover I also gave them My [R]Sab-
baths, to be a sign between them and Me, that
they might know that I *am* the LORD who
sanctifies them. Deut. 5:12
13 "Yet the house of Israel [R]rebelled
against Me in the wilderness; they did not
walk in My statutes; they [R]despised My
judgments, 'which, *if* a man does, he shall
live by them';* and they greatly [R]defiled My
Sabbaths. Then I said I would pour out My
fury on them in the wilderness, to consume
them. Num. 14:22 • Prov. 1:25 • Ex. 16:27
14 "But I acted for My name's sake, that it
should not be profaned before the Gentiles, in
whose sight I had brought them out.
15 "So [R]I also raised My hand in an oath to
them in the wilderness, that I would not bring
them into the land which I had given *them,*
'flowing with milk and honey,'* [R]the glory of
all lands, Num. 14:28 • Ezek. 20:6
16 [R]"because they despised My judgments
and did not walk in My statutes, but profaned
My Sabbaths; for [R]their heart went after their
idols. Ezek. 20:13, 24 • Amos 5:25
17 [R]"Nevertheless My eye spared them from
destruction. I did not make an end of them in
the wilderness. [Ps. 78:38]
18 "But I said to their children in the wilder-
ness, 'Do not walk in the statutes of your fa-
thers, nor observe their judgments, nor defile
yourselves with their idols.
19 'I *am* the LORD your God: Walk in My
statutes, keep My judgments, and do them;
20 'hallow My Sabbaths, and they will be a
sign between Me and you, that you may know
that I *am* the LORD your God.'
21 "Notwithstanding, [R]the children rebelled
against Me; they did not walk in My statutes,
and were not careful to observe My judg-
ments, 'which, *if* a man does, he shall live by
them';* but they profaned My Sabbaths. Then
I said I would pour out My fury on them and
fulfill My anger against them in the wilder-
ness. Num. 25:1
22 "Nevertheless I withdrew My hand and
acted for My name's sake, that it should not
be profaned in the sight of the Gentiles, in
whose sight I had brought them out.
23 "Also I raised My hand in an oath to those
in the wilderness, that [R]I would scatter them
among the Gentiles and disperse them
throughout the countries, Lev. 26:33
24 [R]"because they had not executed My
judgments, but had despised My statutes, pro-
faned My Sabbaths, and their eyes were fixed
on their fathers' idols. Ezek. 20:13, 16
25 "Therefore [R]I also gave them up to
statutes *that were* not good, and judgments
by which they could not live; Rom. 1:24
26 "and I pronounced them unclean be-
cause of their ritual gifts, in that they

20:6 Ex. 3:8 **20:11** Lev. 18:5 **20:13** Lev. 18:5
20:15 Ex. 3:8 **20:21** Lev. 18:5

caused all their firstborn to pass [R]through
the fire, that I might make them desolate
and that they [R]might know that I am the
LORD." ' Jer. 32:35 • Ezek. 6:7; 20:12, 20

In Canaan

27 "Therefore, son of man, speak to the
house of Israel, and say to them, 'Thus says
the Lord GOD: "In this too your fathers have
blasphemed Me, by being unfaithful to Me.
28 "When I brought them into the land *con-
cerning* which I had raised My hand in an
oath to give them, and [R]they saw all the high
hills and all the thick trees, there they offered
their sacrifices and provoked Me with their
offerings. There they also sent up their
[R]sweet aroma and poured out their drink of-
ferings. Ezek. 6:13 • Ezek. 16:19

In Ezekiel's Time

29 "Then I said to them, 'What *is* this [T]high
place to which you go?' So its name is called
Bamah* to this day." ' Place for pagan worship
30 "Therefore say to the house of Israel,
'Thus says the Lord GOD: "Are you defiling
yourselves in the manner of your [R]fathers,
and committing harlotry according to their
[R]abominations? Judg. 2:19 • Jer. 7:26; 16:12
31 "For when you offer your gifts and make
your sons pass through the fire, you defile
yourselves with all your idols, even to this
day. So shall I be inquired of by you, O house
of Israel? *As* I live," says the Lord GOD, "I will
not be inquired of by you.
32 [R]"What you have in your mind shall never
be, when you say, 'We will be like the Gentiles,
like the families in other countries, serving
wood and stone.' Ezek. 11:5

Message of God's Future Restoration of Israel

33 "*As* I live," says the Lord GOD, "surely
with a mighty hand, [R]with an outstretched
arm, and with fury poured out, I will rule over
you. Jer. 21:5
34 "I will bring you out from the peoples and
gather you out of the countries where you are
scattered, with a mighty hand, with an out-
stretched arm, and with fury poured out.
35 "And I will bring you into the wilderness
of the peoples, and there [R]I will plead My case
with you face to face. Jer. 2:9, 35
36 [R]"Just as I pleaded My case with your fa-
thers in the wilderness of the land of Egypt, so
I will plead My case with you," says the Lord
GOD. Num. 14:21–23, 28
37 "I will make you [R]pass under the rod, and
I will bring you into the bond of the
[R]covenant; Lev. 27:32 • Ps. 89:30–34
38 [R]"I will purge the rebels from among
you, and those who transgress against Me; I
will bring them out of the country where
they dwell, but [R]they shall not enter the land
of Israel. Then you will know that I *am* the
LORD. Ezek. 34:17 • Jer. 44:14
39 "As for you, O house of Israel," thus says
the Lord GOD: "Go, serve every one of you his
idols—and hereafter—if you will not obey Me;
but profane My holy name no more with your
gifts and your idols.
40 "For [R]on My holy mountain, on the moun-
tain height of Israel," says the Lord GOD,
"there all the house of Israel, all of them in the
land, shall serve Me; there I will accept them,
and there I will require your offerings and the
firstfruits of your sacrifices, together with all
your holy things. Is. 2:2, 3
41 "I will accept you as a [R]sweet aroma when
I bring you out from the peoples and gather
you out of the countries where you have been
scattered; and I will be hallowed in you before
the Gentiles. Phil. 4:18
42 "Then you shall know that I *am* the LORD,
when I bring you into the land of Israel, into
the country *for* which I raised My hand in an
oath to give to your fathers.
43 "And [R]there you shall remember your
ways and all your doings with which you were
defiled; and you shall loathe yourselves in
your own sight because of all the evils that
you have committed. Ezek. 16:61
44 "Then you shall know that I *am* the LORD,
when I have dealt with you for My name's
sake, not according to your wicked ways nor
according to your corrupt doings, O house of
Israel," says the Lord GOD.' "

Sign of the Forest Fire

45 Furthermore the word of the LORD came
to me, saying,
46 "Son of man, set your face toward the
south; preach against the south and prophesy
against the forest land, the South,*
47 "and say to the forest of the South,
'Hear the word of the LORD! Thus says the
Lord GOD: "Behold, [R]I will kindle a fire in
you, and it shall devour [R]every green tree
and every dry tree in you; the blazing flame
shall not be quenched, and all faces [R]from
the south to the north shall be scorched by
it. Jer. 21:14 • Luke 23:31 • Ezek. 21:4
48 "All flesh shall see that I, the LORD, have
kindled it; it shall not be quenched." ' "
49 Then I said, "Ah, Lord GOD! They say of
me, 'Does he not speak parables?' "

CHAPTER 21

Sign of the Drawn Sword

AND the word of the LORD came to me,
saying,
2 "Son of man, set your face toward Jerusa-
lem, preach against the holy places, and
prophesy against the land of Israel;

20:29 Lit. *High Place* **20:46** Heb. *Negev*

3 “and say to the land of Israel, ‘Thus says
the LORD: “Behold, I *am* against you, and I will
draw My sword out of its sheath and cut off
both righteous and wicked from you.
4 “Because I will cut off both righteous and
wicked from you, therefore My sword shall go
out of its sheath against all flesh [R]from south
to north, Ezek. 20:47
5 “that all flesh may know that I, the LORD,
have drawn My sword out of its sheath; it
shall not return anymore.” ’
6 [R]“Sigh therefore, son of man, with a
breaking heart, and sigh with bitterness be-
fore their eyes. Is. 22:4
7 “And it shall be when they say to you,
‘Why are you sighing?’ that you shall answer,
‘Because of the news; when it comes, every
heart will melt, [R]all hands will be feeble, every
spirit will faint, and all knees will be weak *as*
water. Behold, it is coming and shall be
brought to pass,’ says the Lord GOD.” Ezek. 7:17
8 Again the word of the LORD came to me,
saying,
9 “Son of man, prophesy and say, ‘Thus
says the LORD!’ Say:

[R]‘A sword, a sword is sharpened
And also polished! Deut. 32:41
10 Sharpened to make a dreadful
slaughter,
Polished to flash like lightning!
Should we then make mirth?
It despises the scepter of My son,
As it does all wood.
11 And He has given it to be polished,
That it may be handled;
This sword is sharpened, and it is
polished
To be given into the hand of the slayer.’

12 “Cry and wail, son of man;
For it will be against My people,
Against all the princes of Israel.
Terrors including the sword will be
against My people;
Therefore [R]strike *your* thigh. Jer. 31:19

13 “Because *it is* [R]a testing, Job 9:23
And what if *the sword* despises even the
scepter?
The scepter shall be no *more,*”

says the Lord GOD.

14 “You therefore, son of man, prophesy,
And [R]strike *your* hands together.
The third time let the sword do double
damage. Num. 24:10
It *is* the sword *that* slays,
The sword that slays the great *men,*
That enters their private chambers.
15 I have set the point of the sword against
all their gates,
That the heart may melt and many may
stumble.
Ah! [R]*It is* made bright; Ezek. 21:10, 28
It is grasped for slaughter:

16 “Swords[R] at the ready! Ezek. 14:17
Thrust right!
Set your blade!
Thrust left—
Wherever your [T]edge is ordered! Lit. *face*

17 “I also will [R]beat My fists together,
And I will cause My fury to rest;
I, the LORD, have spoken.” Ezek. 22:13

Sign of the Double Stroke of the Sword

18 The word of the LORD came to me again,
saying:
19 “And son of man, appoint for yourself two
ways for the sword of the king of Babylon to
go; both of them shall go from the same land.
Make a sign; put *it* at the head of the road to
the city.
20 “Appoint a road for the sword to go to
[R]Rabbah of the Ammonites, and to Judah, into
fortified Jerusalem. Jer. 49:2
21 “For the king of Babylon stands at the
parting of the road, at the fork of the two
roads, to use divination: he shakes the ar-
rows, he consults the [T]images, he looks at the
liver. Heb. *teraphim*
22 “In his right hand is the divination for
Jerusalem: to set up battering rams, to call
for a slaughter, to [R]lift the voice with shout-
ing, [R]to set battering rams against the gates,
to heap up a *siege* mound, and to build a
wall. Jer. 51:14 • Ezek. 4:2
23 “And it will be to them like a false
divination in the eyes of those who [R]have
sworn oaths with them; but he will bring
their iniquity to remembrance, that they may
be taken. Ezek. 17:16, 18
24 “Therefore thus says the Lord GOD: ‘Be-
cause you have made your iniquity to be re-
membered, in that your transgressions are
uncovered, so that in all your doings your sins
appear—because you have come to remem-
brance, you shall be taken in hand.
25 ‘Now to you, O [R]profane, wicked prince of
Israel, [R]whose day has come, whose iniquity
shall end, Jer. 52:2 • Ezek. 21:29
26 ‘thus says the Lord GOD:

“Remove the turban, and take off the
crown;
Nothing *shall remain* the same.
[R]Exalt the humble, and humble the
exalted. Luke 1:52
27 Overthrown, overthrown,
I will make it overthrown!
[R]It shall be no *longer,* [Luke 1:32, 33]
Until He comes whose right it is,
And I will give it *to* [R]*Him.*” ’ [Jer. 23:5, 6]

28 "And you, son of man, prophesy and say,
'Thus says the Lord GOD [R]concerning the Am-
monites and concerning their reproach,' and
say: Ezek. 25:1–7

'A sword, a sword *is* drawn,
Polished for slaughter,
For consuming, for flashing—
29 While they [R]see false visions for you,
While they divine a lie to you,
To bring you on the necks of the wicked,
the slain Ezek. 12:24; 13:6–9; 22:28
[R]Whose day has come, Job 18:20
Whose iniquity *shall* end.

30 'Return[R] *it* to its sheath. Jer. 47:6, 7
[R]I will judge you Gen. 15:14
In the place where you were created,
[R]In the land of your nativity. Ezek. 16:3
31 I will [R]pour out My indignation on you;
I will [R]blow against you with the fire of
My wrath, Ezek. 7:8 • Ezek. 22:20, 21
And deliver you into the hands of brutal
men *who are* skillful to destroy.
32 You shall be fuel for the fire;
Your blood shall be in the midst of the
land.
You shall not be remembered,
For I the LORD have spoken.' "

CHAPTER 22

Message of Judgment on Jerusalem

MOREOVER the word of the LORD came to
me, saying,
2 "Now, son of man, [R]will you judge, will
you judge [R]the bloody city? Yes, show her all
her abominations! Ezek. 20:4 • Nah. 3:1
3 "Then say, 'Thus says the Lord GOD: "The
city sheds [R]blood in her own midst, that her
time may come; and she makes idols within
herself to defile herself. Ezek. 24:6, 7
4 "You have become guilty by the blood
which you have [R]shed, and have defiled your-
self with the idols which you have made. You
have caused your days to draw near, and have
come to *the end of* your years; [R]therefore I have
made you a reproach to the nations, and a
mockery to all countries. 2 Kin. 21:16 • Deut. 28:37
5 "*Those* near and *those* far from you will
mock you as infamous *and* full of tumult.
6 "Look, the princes of Israel: each one has
used his power to shed blood in you.
7 "In you they have made light of father and
mother; in your midst they have oppressed
the stranger; in you they have mistreated the
fatherless and the widow.
8 "You have despised My holy things and
[R]profaned My Sabbaths. Lev. 19:30
9 "In you are [R]men who slander to cause
bloodshed; [R]in you are those who eat on the
mountains; in your midst they commit lewd-
ness. Lev. 19:16 • Ezek. 18:6, 11
10 "In you men uncover their fathers' naked-
ness; in you they violate women who are set
apart during their impurity.
11 "One commits abomination with his
neighbor's wife; another lewdly defiles his
daughter-in-law; and another in you violates
his sister, his father's [R]daughter. Lev. 18:9
12 "In you [R]they take bribes to shed blood;
[R]you take usury and increase; you have
made profit from your neighbors by extor-
tion, and [R]have forgotten Me," says the Lord
GOD. Ex. 23:8 • Ex. 22:25 • Ezek. 23:35
13 "Behold, therefore, I [R]beat My fists at the
dishonest profit which you have made, and
at the bloodshed which has been in your
midst. Ezek. 21:17
14 [R]"Can your heart endure, or can your
hands remain strong, in the days when I shall
deal with you? [R]I, the LORD, have spoken, and
will do *it*. Ezek. 21:7 • Ezek. 17:24
15 "I will scatter you among the nations, dis-
perse you throughout the countries, and re-
move your filthiness completely from you.
16 "You shall defile yourself in the sight of
the nations; then [R]you shall know that I *am*
the LORD." ' " Ps. 9:16
17 The word of the LORD came to me, saying,
18 "Son of man, the house of Israel has be-
come dross to Me; they *are* all bronze, tin,
iron, and lead, in the midst of a furnace; they
have become dross from silver.
19 "Therefore thus says the Lord GOD: 'Be-
cause you have all become dross, therefore
behold, I will gather you into the midst of Je-
rusalem.
20 '*As men* gather silver, bronze, iron, lead,
and tin into the midst of a furnace, to blow fire
on it, to [R]melt *it*; so I will gather *you* in My
anger and in My fury, and I will leave *you*
there and melt you. Is. 1:25
21 'Yes, I will gather you and blow on you
with the fire of My wrath, and you shall be
melted in its midst.
22 'As silver is melted in the midst of a fur-
nace, so shall you be melted in its midst; then
you shall know that I, the LORD, have [R]poured
out My fury on you.' " Ezek. 20:8, 33
23 And the word of the LORD came to me,
saying,
24 "Son of man, say to her: 'You *are* a land
that is [R]not cleansed* or rained on in the day
of indignation.' Ezek. 24:13
25 "The conspiracy of her prophets* in her
midst is like a roaring lion tearing the prey;
they have devoured people; they have taken
treasure and precious things; they have made
many widows in her midst.
26 [R]"Her priests have violated My law and
profaned My holy things; they have not distin-
guished between the holy and unholy, nor

22:24 So with MT, Syr., Vg.; LXX *showered upon*
22:25 So with MT, Vg.; LXX *princes;* Tg. *scribes*

have they made known *the difference* be-
tween the unclean and the clean; and they
have hidden their eyes from My Sabbaths, so
that I am profaned among them. Mal. 2:8
27 "Her princes in her midst *are* like wolves
tearing the prey, to shed blood, to destroy peo-
ple, and to get dishonest gain.
28 [R]"Her prophets plastered them with un-
tempered *mortar,* [R]seeing false visions, and
divining [R]lies for them, saying, 'Thus says
the Lord GOD,' when the LORD had not spo-
ken. Ezek. 13:10 • Ezek. 13:6, 7 • Jer. 23:25–32
29 "The people of the land have used op-
pressions, committed robbery, and mistreated
the poor and needy; and they wrongfully [R]op-
press the stranger. Ex. 23:9
30 "So I sought for a man among them who
would make a wall, and stand in the gap be-
fore Me on behalf of the land, that I should
not destroy it; but I found no one.
31 "Therefore I have [R]poured out My
indignation on them; I have consumed them
with the fire of My wrath; and I have recom-
pensed [R]their deeds on their own heads," says
the Lord GOD. Ezek. 22:22 • Ezek. 9:10

CHAPTER 23

Parable of Two Sisters

THE word of the LORD came again to me,
saying:

2 "Son of man, there were two women,
The daughters of one mother.
3 They committed harlotry in Egypt,
They committed harlotry in their youth;
Their breasts were there embraced,
Their virgin bosom was there pressed.
4 Their names: Oholah* the elder and
Oholibah* [R]her sister; Jer. 3:6, 7
[R]They were Mine, Ezek. 16:8, 20
And they bore sons and daughters.
As for their names,
Samaria *is* Oholah, and Jerusalem *is*
Oholibah.

5 "Oholah played the harlot even though
she was Mine;
And she lusted for her lovers, the
neighboring Assyrians,
6 *Who were* clothed in purple,
Captains and rulers,
All of them desirable young men,
Horsemen riding on horses.
7 Thus she committed her harlotry with
them,
All of them choice men of Assyria;
And with all for whom she lusted,
With all their idols, she defiled herself.
8 She has never given up her harlotry
brought [R]from Egypt, Ezek. 23:3, 19
For in her youth they had lain with her,
Pressed her virgin bosom,
And poured out their immorality upon
her.
9 "Therefore I have delivered her
Into the hand of her lovers,
Into the hand of the [R]Assyrians,
For whom she lusted. 2 Kin. 17:3
10 They uncovered her nakedness,
Took away her sons and daughters,
And slew her with the sword;
She became a byword among women,
For they had executed judgment on her.

11 "Now [R]although her sister Oholibah saw
this, [R]she became more corrupt in her lust
than she, and in her harlotry more corrupt
than her sister's harlotry. Jer. 3:8 • Jer. 3:8–11

12 "She lusted for the neighboring
[R]Assyrians, 2 Kin. 16:7, 8
[R]Captains and rulers, Ezek. 23:6, 23
Clothed most gorgeously,
Horsemen riding on horses,
All of them desirable young men.
13 Then I saw that she was defiled;
Both *took* the same way.
14 But she increased her harlotry;
She looked at men portrayed on the wall,
Images of [R]Chaldeans portrayed in
vermilion, Ezek. 8:10; 16:29
15 Girded with belts around their waists,
Flowing turbans on their heads,
All of them looking like captains,
In the manner of the Babylonians of
Chaldea,
The land of their nativity.
16 [R]As soon as her eyes saw them,
She lusted for them
And sent [R]messengers to them in
Chaldea. 2 Kin. 24:1 • Is. 57:9

17 "Then the [T]Babylonians came to her, into
the bed of love, Lit. *sons of Babel*
And they defiled her with their
immorality;
So she was defiled by them, and
alienated herself from them.
18 She revealed her harlotry and uncovered
her nakedness.
Then [R]I [R]alienated Myself from her,
As I had alienated Myself from her
sister. Jer. 6:8 • Jer. 12:8

19 "Yet she multiplied her harlotry
In calling to remembrance the days of
her youth,
[R]When she had played the harlot in the
land of Egypt. Ezek. 23:2
20 For she lusted for her [T]paramours,
Whose flesh *is like* the flesh of donkeys,

23:4 Lit. *Her Own Tabernacle* • Lit. *My Tabernacle Is in Her*

And whose issue *is like* the issue of
horses. Illicit lovers
21 Thus you called to remembrance the
lewdness of your youth,
When the [R]Egyptians pressed your
bosom Ezek. 16:26
Because of your youthful breasts.

22 "Therefore, Oholibah, thus says the Lord
GOD:

[R]'Behold, I will stir up your lovers against
you, Ezek. 16:37–41; 23:28
From whom you have alienated yourself,
And I will bring them against you from
every side:
23 The Babylonians,
All the Chaldeans,
[R]Pekod, Shoa, Koa, Jer. 50:21
[R]All the Assyrians with them, Ezek. 23:12
All of them desirable young men,
Governors and rulers,
Captains and men of renown,
All of them riding on horses.
24 And they shall come against you
With chariots, wagons, and war-horses,
With a horde of people.
They shall array against you
Buckler, shield, and helmet all around.

'I will delegate judgment to them,
And they shall judge you according to
their judgments.
25 I will set My [R]jealousy against you,
And they shall deal furiously with you;
They shall remove your nose and your
ears, Ex. 34:14
And your remnant shall fall by the
sword;
They shall take your sons and your
daughters,
And your remnant shall be devoured by
fire.
26 They shall also strip you of your clothes
And take away your beautiful jewelry.

27 'Thus [R]I will make you cease your
lewdness and your [R]harlotry
Brought from the land of Egypt,
So that you will not lift your eyes to
them, Ezek. 16:41; 22:15 • Ezek. 23:3, 19
Nor remember Egypt anymore.'

28 "For thus says the Lord GOD: 'Surely I will
deliver you into the hand of [R]those you hate,
into the hand *of those* [R]from whom you alien-
ated yourself. Ezek. 16:37–41 • Ezek. 23:17
29 [R]'They will deal hatefully with you, take
away all you have worked for, and [R]leave you
naked and bare. The nakedness of your har-
lotry shall be uncovered, both your lewdness
and your harlotry. Deut. 28:48 • Ezek. 16:39
30 'I will do these *things* to you because
you have [R]gone as a harlot after the Gentiles,
because you have become defiled by their
idols. Ezek. 6:9
31 'You have walked in the way of your sis-
ter; therefore I will put her [R]cup in your
hand.' Jer. 7:14, 15; 25:15
32 "Thus says the Lord GOD:

'You shall drink of your sister's cup,
The deep and wide one;
[R]You shall be laughed to scorn
And held in derision; Ezek. 22:4, 5
It contains much.
33 You will be filled with drunkenness and
sorrow,
The cup of horror and desolation,
The cup of your sister Samaria.
34 You shall [R]drink and drain it, Is. 51:17
You shall break its [T]shards,
And tear at your own breasts;
For I have spoken,' Earthenware fragments
Says the Lord GOD.

35 "Therefore thus says the Lord GOD:

'Because you have forgotten Me and cast
Me behind your back,
Therefore you shall bear the *penalty*
Of your lewdness and your harlotry.' "

36 The LORD also said to me: "Son of man,
will you judge Oholah and Oholibah? Then
declare to them their abominations.
37 "For they have committed adultery, and
[R]blood *is* on their hands. They have commit-
ted adultery with their idols, and even sacri-
ficed their sons [R]whom they bore to Me,
passing them through *the fire,* to devour
them. Ezek. 16:38 • Ezek. 16:20, 21, 36, 45; 20:26, 31
38 "Moreover they have done this to Me:
They have defiled My sanctuary on the same
day and profaned My Sabbaths.
39 "For after they had slain their children
for their idols, on the same day they came
into My sanctuary to profane it; and indeed
[R]thus they have done in the midst of My
house. 2 Kin. 21:2–8
40 "Furthermore you sent for men to come
from afar, [R]to whom a messenger *was* sent;
and there they came. And you washed your-
self for them, painted your eyes, and adorned
yourself with ornaments. Is. 57:9
41 "You sat on a stately [R]couch, with a table
prepared before it, on which you had set My
incense and My oil. Is. 57:7
42 "The sound of a carefree multitude *was*
with her, and Sabeans *were* brought from the
wilderness with men of the common sort, who
put bracelets on their [T]wrists and beautiful
crowns on their heads. Lit. *hands*
43 "Then I said concerning *her who had*
grown old in adulteries, 'Will they commit
harlotry with her now, and she *with them?*'

44 "Yet they went in to her, as men go in to
a woman who plays the harlot; thus they
went in to Oholah and Oholibah, the lewd
women.
45 "But righteous men will [R]judge them after
the manner of adulteresses, and after the
manner of women who shed blood, because
they *are* adulteresses, and [R]blood *is* on their
hands. Ezek. 16:38 • Ezek. 23:37
46 "For thus says the Lord GOD: [R]'Bring up
an assembly against them, give them up to
trouble and plunder. Ezek. 16:40
47 'The assembly shall stone them with
stones and execute them with their swords;
they shall slay their sons and their daughters,
and burn their houses with fire.
48 'Thus I will cause lewdness to cease from
the land, that all women may be taught not to
practice your lewdness.
49 'They shall repay you for your lewdness,
and you shall [R]pay for your idolatrous sins.
[R]Then you shall know that I *am* the Lord
GOD.'" Ezek. 23:35 • Ezek. 20:38, 42, 44; 25:5

CHAPTER 24

Parable of the Boiling Pot

AGAIN, in the ninth year, in the tenth
month, on the tenth *day* of the month, the
word of the LORD came to me, saying,
2 "Son of man, write down the name of the
day, this very day—the king of Babylon
started his siege against Jerusalem [R]this very
day. 2 Kin. 25:1
3 [R]"And utter a parable to the rebellious
house, and say to them, 'Thus says the Lord
GOD: Ezek. 17:12

[R]"Put on a pot, set *it* on, Jer. 1:13
And also pour water into it.
4 Gather pieces *of meat* in it,
Every good piece,
The thigh and the shoulder.
Fill *it* with choice [T]cuts; Lit. *bones*
5 Take the choice of the flock.
Also pile *fuel* bones under it,
Make it boil well,
And let the cuts simmer in it."

6 'Therefore thus says the Lord GOD:

"Woe to [R]the bloody city, Ezek. 22:2, 3, 27
To the pot whose scum *is* in it,
And whose scum is not gone from it!
Bring it out piece by piece,
On which no [R]lot has fallen. Nah. 3:10
7 For her blood is in her midst;
She set it on top of a rock;
[R]She did not pour it on the ground,
To cover it with dust. Lev. 17:13
8 That it may raise up fury and take
vengeance,
[R]I have set her blood on top of a rock,
That it may not be covered." [Matt. 7:2]

9 'Therefore thus says the Lord GOD:

[R]"Woe to the bloody city! Hab. 2:12
I too will make the pyre great.
10 Heap on the wood,
Kindle the fire;
Cook the meat well,
Mix in the spices,
And let the cuts be burned up.

11 "Then set the pot empty on the coals,
That it may become hot and its bronze
may burn,
That its filthiness may be melted in it,
That its scum may be consumed.
12 She has [T]grown weary with [T]lies,
And her great scum has not gone from
her. Or *wearied Me* • Or *toil*
Let her scum *be* in the fire!
13 In your [R]filthiness *is* lewdness.
Because I have cleansed you, and you
were not cleansed, Ezek. 23:36–48
You will [R]not be cleansed of your
filthiness anymore, Jer. 6:28–30
[R]Till I have caused My fury to rest upon
you. Ezek. 5:13; 8:18; 16:42
14 [R]I, the LORD, have spoken *it;*
[R]It shall come to pass, and I will do *it;*
I will not hold back, [1 Sam. 15:29] • Is. 55:11
[R]Nor will I spare, Ezek. 5:11
Nor will I relent;
According to your ways
And according to your deeds
They* will judge you,"
Says the Lord GOD.'"

Sign Through the Death of Ezekiel's Wife

15 Also the word of the LORD came to me,
saying,
16 "Son of man, behold, I take away from
you the desire of your eyes with one stroke;
yet you shall [R]neither mourn nor weep, nor
shall your tears run down. Jer. 16:5
17 "Sigh in silence, [R]make no mourning for
the dead; [R]bind your turban on your head, and
put your sandals on your feet; [R]do not cover
your lips, and do not eat man's bread *of sor-*
row." Jer. 16:5 • Lev. 10:6; 21:10 • Mic. 3:7
18 So I spoke to the people in the morning,
and at evening my wife died; and the next
morning I did as I was commanded.
19 And the people said to me, [R]"Will you not
tell us what these *things signify* to us, that you
behave so?" Ezek. 12:9; 37:18
20 Then I answered them, "The word of the
LORD came to me, saying,
21 'Speak to the house of Israel, "Thus says

24:14 LXX, Syr., Tg., Vg. *I*

the Lord GOD: 'Behold, [R]I will profane My
sanctuary, your arrogant boast, the desire of
your eyes, the delight of your soul; and your
sons and daughters whom you left behind
shall fall by the sword. Jer. 7:14
22 'And you shall do as I have done; [R]you
shall not cover *your* [T]lips nor eat man's bread
of sorrow. Jer. 16:6, 7 • Lit. *moustache*
23 'Your turbans shall be on your heads
and your sandals on your feet; [R]you shall
neither mourn nor weep, but [R]you shall pine
away in your iniquities and mourn with one
another. Job 27:15 • Lev. 26:39
24 'Thus [R]Ezekiel is a sign to you; according
to all that he has done you shall do; [R]and
when this comes, [R]you shall know that I *am*
the Lord GOD.' " Is. 20:3 • Jer. 17:15 • Ezek. 6:7
25 'And you, son of man—*will it* not *be* in the
day when I take from them their stronghold,
their joy and their glory, the desire of their
eyes, and that on which they set their minds,
their sons and their daughters:
26 'on that day one who escapes will come to
you to let *you* hear *it* with *your* ears;
27 [R]'on that day your mouth will be opened
to him who has escaped; you shall speak and
no longer be mute. Thus you will be a sign to
them, and they shall know that I *am* the
LORD.' " Ezek. 3:26; 33:22

CHAPTER 25

Judgment on Ammon

THE word of the LORD came to me, saying,
2 "Son of man, set your face against the
Ammonites, and prophesy against them.
3 "Say to the Ammonites, 'Hear the word
of the Lord GOD! Thus says the Lord GOD:
[R]"Because you said, 'Aha!' against My sanctu-
ary when it was profaned, and against the
land of Israel when it was desolate, and
against the house of Judah when they went
into captivity, Ezek. 26:2
4 "indeed, therefore, I will deliver you as a
possession to the [T]men of the East, and they
shall set their encampments among you and
make their dwellings among you; they shall
eat your fruit, and they shall drink your
milk. Lit. *sons*
5 "And I will make [R]Rabbah [R]a stable for
camels and Ammon a resting place for
flocks. [R]Then you shall know that I *am* the
LORD." Ezek. 21:20 • Is. 17:2 • Ezek. 24:24
6 'For thus says the Lord GOD: "Because
you [R]clapped *your* hands, stamped your feet,
and [R]rejoiced in heart with all your disdain
for the land of Israel, Job 27:23 • Ezek. 36:5
7 "indeed, therefore, I will [R]stretch out My
hand against you, and give you as plunder to
the nations; I will cut you off from the peo-
ples, and I will cause you to perish from the
countries; I will destroy you, and you shall
know that I *am* the LORD." Ezek. 35:3

Judgment on Moab

8 'Thus says the Lord GOD: "Because [R]Moab
and Seir say, 'Look! The house of Judah *is* like
all the nations,' Amos 2:1, 2
9 "therefore, behold, I will clear the terri-
tory of Moab of cities, of the cities on its fron-
tier, the glory of the country, Beth Jeshimoth,
Baal Meon, and Kirjathaim.
10 [R]"To the men of the East I will give it as a
possession, together with the Ammonites, that
the Ammonites may not be remembered
among the nations. Ezek. 25:4
11 "And I will execute judgments upon Moab,
and they shall know that I *am* the LORD."

Judgment on Edom

12 'Thus says the Lord GOD: "Because of
what Edom did against the house of Judah by
taking vengeance, and has greatly offended
by avenging itself on them,"
13 'therefore thus says the Lord GOD: "I will
also stretch out My hand against Edom, cut
off man and beast from it, and make it deso-
late from Teman; [T]Dedan shall fall by the
sword. Or *even to Dedan they shall fall*
14 [R]"I will lay My vengeance on Edom by the
hand of My people Israel, that they may do in
Edom according to My anger and according
to My fury; and they shall know My ven-
geance," says the Lord GOD. Is. 11:14

Judgment on Philistia

15 'Thus says the Lord GOD: [R]"Because the
Philistines dealt vengefully and took ven-
geance with a spiteful heart, to destroy be-
cause of the old hatred," Jer. 25:20
16 'therefore thus says the Lord GOD: "I will
stretch out My hand against the Philistines,
and I will cut off the Cherethites and destroy
the remnant of the seacoast.
17 "I will [R]execute great vengeance on them
with furious rebukes; [R]and they shall know
that I *am* the LORD, when I lay My vengeance
upon them." ' " Ezek. 5:15 • Ps. 9:16

CHAPTER 26

Destruction of Tyre

AND it came to pass in the eleventh year,
on the first *day* of the month, *that* the
word of the LORD came to me, saying,
2 "Son of man, [R]because Tyre has said
against Jerusalem, [R]'Aha! She is broken who
was the gateway of the peoples; now she is
turned over to me; I shall be filled; she is laid
waste.' Jer. 25:22 • Ezek. 25:3
3 "Therefore thus says the Lord GOD: 'Be-
hold, I *am* against you, O Tyre, and will cause
many nations to come up against you, as the
sea causes its waves to come up.
4 'And they shall destroy the walls of Tyre
and break down her towers; I will also scrape

her dust from her, and [R]make her like the top of a rock. Ezek. 26:14

5 'It shall be *a place for* spreading nets [R]in the midst of the sea, for I have spoken,' says the Lord GOD; 'it shall become plunder for the nations. Ezek. 27:32

6 'Also her daughter *villages* which *are* in the fields shall be slain by the sword. Then they shall know that I am the LORD.'

7 "For thus says the Lord GOD: 'Behold, I will bring against Tyre from the north Nebuchadnezzar* king of Babylon, king of kings, with horses, with chariots, and with horsemen, and an army with many people.

8 'He will slay with the sword your daughter *villages* in the fields; he will [R]heap up a siege mound against you, build a wall against you, and raise a [T]defense against you. Ezek. 21:22 • Lit. *a large shield*

9 'He will direct his battering rams against your walls, and with his axes he will break down your towers.

10 'Because of the abundance of his horses, their dust will cover you; your walls will shake at the noise of the horsemen, the wagons, and the chariots, when he enters your gates, as men enter a city that has been breached.

11 'With the hooves of his [R]horses he will trample all your streets; he will slay your people by the sword, and your strong pillars will fall to the ground. Hab. 1:8

12 'They will plunder your riches and pillage your merchandise; they will break down your walls and destroy your pleasant houses; they will lay your stones, your timber, and your soil in the midst of the water.

13 [R]'I will put an end to the sound of [R]your songs, and the sound of your harps shall be heard no more. Is. 14:11; 24:8 • Rev. 18:22

14 'I will make you like the top of a rock; you shall be *a place for* spreading nets, and you shall never be rebuilt, for I the LORD have spoken,' says the Lord GOD.

15 "Thus says the Lord GOD to Tyre: 'Will the coastlands not shake at the sound of your fall, when the wounded cry, when slaughter is made in the midst of you?

16 'Then all the [R]princes of the sea will [R]come down from their thrones, lay aside their robes, and take off their embroidered garments; they will clothe themselves with trembling; [R]they will sit on the ground, [R]tremble *every* moment, and be astonished at you. Is. 23:8 • Jon. 3:6 • Job 2:13 • Ezek. 32:10

17 'And they will take up a [R]lamentation for you, and say to you: Ezek. 27:2–36

"How you have perished,
O one inhabited by seafaring men,
O renowned city,
Who was [R]strong at sea, Is. 23:4
She and her inhabitants,
Who caused their terror *to be* on all her
inhabitants!
18 Now [R]the coastlands tremble on the day
of your fall; Ezek. 26:15
Yes, the coastlands by the sea are
troubled at your departure." '

19 "For thus says the Lord GOD: 'When I make you a desolate city, like cities that are not inhabited, when I bring the deep upon you, and great waters cover you,

20 'then I will bring you down with those who descend into the Pit, to the people of old, and I will make you dwell in the lowest part of the earth, in places desolate from antiquity, with those who go down to the Pit, so that you may never be inhabited; and I shall establish glory in the land of the living.

21 [R]'I will make you a terror, and you *shall be* no *more;* [R]though you are sought for, you will never be found again,' says the Lord GOD." Ezek. 27:36; 28:19 • Ps. 37:10, 36

CHAPTER 27

Lament over Tyre

THE word of the LORD came again to me, saying,

2 "Now, son of man, [R]take up a lamentation for Tyre, Ezek. 26:17

3 "and say to Tyre, [R]'You who are situated at the entrance of the sea, [R]merchant of the peoples on many coastlands, thus says the Lord GOD: Ezek. 26:17; 28:2 • Is. 23:3

"O Tyre, you have said,
[R]'I *am* perfect in beauty.' Ezek. 28:12
4 Your borders *are* in the midst of the
seas.
Your builders have perfected your
beauty.
5 They [T]made all *your* planks of fir trees
from [R]Senir; *built* • Deut. 3:9
They took a cedar from Lebanon to
make you a mast.
6 *Of* [R]oaks from Bashan they made your
oars; Is. 2:12, 13
The company of Ashurites have inlaid
your planks
With ivory from the coasts of Cyprus.*
7 Fine embroidered linen from Egypt was
what you spread for your sail;
Blue and purple from the coasts of
Elishah was what covered you.

8 "Inhabitants of Sidon and Arvad were
your oarsmen;
Your wise men, O Tyre, were in you;
They became your pilots.

26:7 Heb. *Nebuchadrezzar,* and so elsewhere in the book **27:6** Heb. *Kittim,* western lands, especially Cyprus

9 Elders of [R]Gebal and its wise men
Were in you to caulk your seams;
All the ships of the sea 1 Kin. 5:18
And their oarsmen were in you
To market your merchandise.

10 "Those from Persia, Lydia,* and Libya*
Were in your army as men of war;
They hung shield and helmet in you;
They gave splendor to you.
11 Men of Arvad with your army *were* on
your walls *all* around,
And the men of Gammad were in your
towers;
They hung their shields on your walls *all*
around;
They made your beauty perfect.

12 "Tarshish *was* your merchant because of
your many luxury goods. They gave you sil-
ver, iron, tin, and lead for your goods.
13 "Javan, Tubal, and Meshech *were* your
traders. They bartered human lives and ves-
sels of bronze for your merchandise.
14 "Those from the house of [R]Togarmah
traded for your wares with horses, steeds, and
mules. Gen. 10:3
15 "The men of [R]Dedan *were* your traders;
many isles *were* the market of your hand.
They brought you ivory tusks and ebony as
payment. Gen. 10:7
16 "Syria *was* your merchant because of the
abundance of goods you made. They gave you
for your wares emeralds, purple, embroidery,
fine linen, corals, and rubies.
17 "Judah and the land of Israel *were* your
traders. They traded for your merchandise
wheat of [R]Minnith, millet, honey, oil, and
[R]balm. Judg. 11:33 • Jer. 8:22
18 "Damascus *was* your merchant because
of the abundance of goods you made, because
of your many luxury items, with the wine of
Helbon and with white wool.
19 "Dan and Javan paid for your wares,
[T]traversing back and forth. Wrought iron,
cassia, and cane were among your merchan-
dise. LXX, Syr. *from Uzal*
20 [R]"Dedan *was* your merchant in saddle-
cloths for riding. Gen. 25:3
21 "Arabia and all the princes of Kedar *were*
your regular merchants. They traded with you
in lambs, rams, and goats.
22 "The merchants of [R]Sheba and Raamah
were your merchants. They traded for your
wares the choicest spices, all kinds of pre-
cious stones, and gold. Gen. 10:7
23 [R]"Haran, Canneh, Eden, the merchants of
[R]Sheba, Assyria, *and* Chilmad *were* your mer-
chants. 2 Kin. 19:12 • Gen. 25:3
24 "These *were* your merchants in choice
items—in purple clothes, in embroidered gar-
ments, in chests of multicolored apparel, in
sturdy woven cords, which were in your mar-
ketplace.

25 "The [R]ships of Tarshish were carriers of
your merchandise. Is. 2:16
You were filled and very glorious [R]in the
midst of the seas. Ezek. 27:4
26 Your oarsmen brought you into many
waters,
But [R]the east wind broke you in the
midst of the seas. Ps. 48:7

27 "Your [R]riches, wares, and merchandise,
Your mariners and pilots, [Prov. 11:4]
Your caulkers and merchandisers,
All your men of war who *are* in you,
And the entire company which *is* in your
midst,
Will fall into the midst of the seas on the
day of your ruin.
28 The common-land will shake at the
sound of the cry of your pilots.

29 "All [R]who handle the oar, Rev. 18:17
The mariners,
All the pilots of the sea
Will come down from their ships *and*
stand on the [T]shore. Lit. *land*
30 They will make their voice heard
because of you;
They will cry bitterly and [R]cast dust on
their heads; Rev. 18:19
They [R]will roll about in ashes; Jer. 6:26
31 They will [R]shave themselves completely
bald because of you, Ezek. 29:18
Gird themselves with sackcloth,
And weep for you
With bitterness of heart *and* bitter wailing.
32 In their wailing for you
They will [R]take up a lamentation,
And lament for you: Ezek. 26:17
[R]'What *city is* like Tyre, Rev. 18:18
Destroyed in the midst of the sea?

33 'When[R] your wares went out by sea,
You satisfied many people; Rev. 18:19
You enriched the kings of the earth
With your many luxury goods and your
merchandise.
34 But [R]you are broken by the seas in the
depths of the waters; Ezek. 26:19
Your merchandise and the entire
company will fall in your midst.
35 [R]All the inhabitants of the isles will be
astonished at you; Ezek. 26:15, 16
Their kings will be greatly afraid,
And *their* countenance will be troubled.
36 The merchants among the peoples [R]will
hiss at you; Jer. 18:16
You will become a horror, and *be* no
[R]more forever.' " ' " Ps. 37:10, 36

27:10 Heb. *Lud* • Heb. *Put*

CHAPTER 28

Fall of the Prince of Tyre

THE word of the LORD came to me again, saying,
2 "Son of man, say to the prince of Tyre, 'Thus says the Lord GOD:

"Because your heart *is* lifted up,
And [R]you say, 'I *am* a god, Ezek. 28:9
I sit *in* the seat of gods,
[R]In the midst of the seas,' Ezek. 27:3, 4
[R]Yet you *are* a man, and not a god,
Though you set your heart as the heart of a god Is. 31:3
3 (Behold, [R]you *are* wiser than Daniel!
There is no secret that can be hidden from you! Dan. 1:20; 2:20–23, 28; 5:11, 12
4 With your wisdom and your understanding
You have gained [R]riches for yourself,
And gathered gold and silver into your treasuries; Zech. 9:1–3
5 [R]By your great wisdom in trade you have increased your riches, Ps. 62:10
And your heart is lifted up because of your riches),"
6 'Therefore thus says the Lord GOD:

"Because you have set your heart as the heart of a god,
7 Behold, therefore, I will bring [R]strangers against you, Ezek. 26:7
[R]The most terrible of the nations;
And they shall draw their swords against the beauty of your wisdom,
And defile your splendor. Ezek. 7:24
8 They shall throw you down into the [R]Pit,
And you shall die the death of the slain
In the midst of the seas. Is. 14:15
9 "Will you still [R]say before him who slays you, Ezek. 28:2
'I *am* a god'?
But you *shall be* a man, and not a god,
In the hand of him who slays you.
10 You shall die the death of [R]the uncircumcised Ezek. 31:18
By the hand of aliens;
For I have spoken," says the Lord GOD.' "

11 Moreover the word of the LORD came to me, saying,
12 "Son of man, [R]take up a lamentation for the king of Tyre, and say to him, 'Thus says the Lord GOD: Ezek. 27:2

"You *were* the seal of perfection,
Full of wisdom and perfect in beauty.
13 You were in [R]Eden, the garden of God;
Every precious stone *was* your covering:
The sardius, topaz, and diamond,
Beryl, onyx, and jasper,
Sapphire, turquoise, and emerald with gold. Ezek. 31:8, 9; 36:35
The workmanship of [R]your timbrels and pipes Ezek. 26:13
Was prepared for you on the day you were created.

14 "You *were* the anointed [R]cherub who covers; Ex. 25:20
I established you;
You were on [R]the holy mountain of God;
You walked back and forth in the midst of fiery stones. Ezek. 20:40
15 You *were* perfect in your ways from the day you were created,
Till [R]iniquity was found in you. [Is. 14:12]

16 "By the abundance of your trading
You became filled with violence within,
And you sinned;
Therefore I cast you as a profane thing
Out of the mountain of God;
And I destroyed you, [R]O covering cherub, Ezek. 28:14
From the midst of the fiery stones.

17 "Your [R]heart was [T]lifted up because of your beauty; Ezek. 28:2, 5 • Proud
You corrupted your wisdom for the sake of your splendor;
I cast you to the ground,
I laid you before kings,
That they might gaze at you.

18 "You defiled your sanctuaries
By the multitude of your iniquities,
By the iniquity of your trading;
Therefore I brought fire from your midst;
It devoured you,
And I turned you to ashes upon the earth
In the sight of all who saw you.
19 All who knew you among the peoples are astonished at you;
[R]You have become a horror, Ezek. 26:21
And *shall be* no more forever." ' "

Judgment on Sidon

20 Then the word of the LORD came to me, saying,
21 "Son of man, [R]set your face toward Sidon, and prophesy against her, Ezek. 6:2
22 "and say, 'Thus says the Lord GOD:

[R]"Behold, I *am* against you, O Sidon;
I will be glorified in your midst;
And [R]they shall know that I *am* the LORD, Ex. 14:4, 17 • Ps. 9:16
When I execute judgments in her and am [R]hallowed in her. Ezek. 28:25
23 [R]For I will send pestilence upon her,
And blood in her streets;

The wounded shall be judged in her
midst Ezek. 38:22
By the sword against her on every side;
Then they shall know that I *am* the
LORD.

24 "And there shall no longer be a pricking
brier or [R]a painful thorn for the house of Is-
rael from among all *who are* around them,
who despise them. Then they shall know that
I *am* the Lord GOD." Josh. 23:13
25 'Thus says the Lord GOD: "When I have
gathered the house of Israel from the peoples
among whom they are scattered, and am hal-
lowed in them in the sight of the Gentiles,
then they will dwell in their own land which I
gave to My servant Jacob.
26 "And they will [R]dwell safely there, [R]build
houses, and [R]plant vineyards; yes, they will
dwell securely, when I execute judgments on
all those around them who despise them.
Then they shall know that I *am* the LORD their
God." ' " Jer. 23:6 • Amos 9:13, 14 • Jer. 31:5

CHAPTER 29

Egypt to Be Desolate

IN the tenth year, in the tenth *month,* on the
twelfth *day* of the month, the word of the
LORD came to me, saying,
2 "Son of man, [R]set your face against
Pharaoh king of Egypt, and prophesy against
him, and against all Egypt. Ezek. 28:21
3 "Speak, and say, 'Thus says the Lord GOD:

[R]"Behold, I *am* against you, Jer. 44:30
O Pharaoh king of Egypt,
O great [R]monster who lies in the midst
of his rivers, Ps. 74:13, 14
[R]Who has said, 'My River* *is* my own;
I have made *it* for myself.' Ezek. 28:2
4 But [R]I will put hooks in your jaws,
And cause the fish of your rivers to
stick to your scales; Ezek. 38:4
I will bring you up out of the midst of
your rivers,
And all the fish in your rivers will stick
to your scales.
5 I will leave you in the wilderness,
You and all the fish of your rivers;
You shall fall on the open field;
[R]You shall not be picked up or
gathered.* Jer. 8:2; 16:4; 25:33
[R]I have given you as food Jer. 7:33; 34:20
To the beasts of the field
And to the birds of the heavens.

6 "Then all the inhabitants of Egypt
Shall know that I *am* the LORD,
Because they have been a [R]staff of reed
to the house of Israel. Is. 36:6
7 [R]When they took hold of you with the
hand, Ezek. 17:17
You broke and tore all their shoulders;*
When they leaned on you,
You broke and made all their backs
quiver."

8 'Therefore thus says the Lord GOD:
"Surely I will bring a sword upon you and cut
off from you man and beast.
9 "And the land of Egypt shall become des-
olate and waste; then they will know that I *am*
the LORD, because he said, 'The River *is* mine,
and I have made *it*.'
10 "Indeed, therefore, I *am* against you and
against your rivers, [R]and I will make the land
of Egypt utterly waste and desolate, [R]from
Migdol* *to* Syene, as far as the border of Ethi-
opia. Ezek. 30:12 • Ezek. 30:6
11 "Neither foot of man shall pass through it
nor foot of beast pass through it, and it shall
be uninhabited forty years.
12 [R]"I will make the land of Egypt desolate
in the midst of the countries *that are* deso-
late; and among the cities *that are* laid
waste, her cities shall be desolate forty years;
and I will scatter the Egyptians among the
nations and disperse them throughout the
countries." Ezek. 30:7, 26
13 'Yet, thus says the Lord GOD: "At the [R]end
of forty years I will gather the Egyptians from
the peoples among whom they were scat-
tered. Jer. 46:26
14 "I will bring back the captives of Egypt
and cause them to return to the land of
Pathros, to the land of their origin, and there
they shall be a lowly kingdom.
15 "It shall be the lowliest of kingdoms; it
shall never again exalt itself above the na-
tions, for I will diminish them so that they will
not rule over the nations anymore.
16 "No longer shall it be [R]the confidence of
the house of Israel, but will remind them of
their iniquity when they turned to follow
them. Then they shall know that I *am* the Lord
GOD." ' " Is. 30:2, 3; 36:4, 6

Egypt to Be Taken by Babylon

17 And it came to pass in the twenty-seventh
year, in the first *month,* on the first *day* of the
month, *that* the word of the LORD came to me,
saying,
18 "Son of man, [R]Nebuchadnezzar king of
Babylon caused his army to labor strenu-
ously against Tyre; every head *was* made
[R]bald, and every shoulder rubbed raw; yet
neither he nor his army received wages from
Tyre, for the labor which they expended on
it. Jer. 25:9; 27:6 • Ezek. 27:31
19 "Therefore thus says the Lord GOD:
'Surely I will give the land of Egypt to

29:3 The Nile **29:5** So with MT, LXX, Vg.; some Heb. mss., Tg. *buried* **29:7** So with MT, Vg.; LXX, Syr. *hand* **29:10** Or *the tower*

[R]Nebuchadnezzar king of Babylon; he shall
take away her wealth, carry off her spoil, and
remove her pillage; and that will be the wages
for his army. Jer. 43:10–13
20 'I have given him the land of Egypt *for* his
labor, because they [R]worked for Me,' says the
Lord GOD. Jer. 25:9
21 'In that day I will cause the horn of the
house of Israel to spring forth, and I will open
your mouth to speak in their midst. Then they
shall know that I *am* the LORD.' "

CHAPTER 30

Egypt to Be Destroyed

THE word of the LORD came to me again,
saying,
2 "Son of man, prophesy and say, 'Thus
says the Lord GOD:

[R]"Wail, 'Woe to the day!' Is. 13:6; 15:2
3 For [R]the day *is* near, Joel 2:1
Even the day of the LORD *is* near;
It will be a day of clouds, the time of the
Gentiles.
4 The sword shall come upon Egypt,
And great anguish shall be in Ethiopia,
When the slain fall in Egypt,
And they take away her wealth,
And her foundations are broken down.

5 "Ethiopia, Libya,* Lydia,* [R]all the min-
gled people, Chub, and the men of the lands
who are allied, shall fall with them by the
sword." Jer. 25:20, 24
6 'Thus says the LORD:

"Those who uphold Egypt shall fall,
And the pride of her power shall come
down.
[R]From [T]Migdol *to* Syene
Those within her shall fall by the
sword," Ezek. 29:10 • Or *the tower*
Says the Lord GOD.

7 "They[R] shall be desolate in the midst of
the desolate countries, Ezek. 29:12
And her cities shall be in the midst of
the cities *that are* laid waste.
8 Then they will know that I *am* the
LORD,
When I have set a fire in Egypt
And all her helpers are destroyed.
9 On that day [R]messengers shall go forth
from Me in ships Is. 18:1, 2
To make the [T]careless Ethiopians
afraid,
And great anguish shall come upon
them, Or *secure*
As on the day of Egypt;
For indeed it is coming!"

10 'Thus says the Lord GOD:

[R]"I will also make a multitude of Egypt to
cease Ezek. 29:19
By the hand of Nebuchadnezzar king of
Babylon.
11 He and his people with him, [R]the most
terrible of the nations, Ezek. 28:7
Shall be brought to destroy the land;
They shall draw their swords against
Egypt,
And fill the land with the slain.
12[R] I will make the rivers dry, Is. 19:5, 6
And [R]sell the land into the hand of the
wicked; Is. 19:4
I will make the land waste, and all that
is in it,
By the hand of aliens.
I, the LORD, have spoken."

13 'Thus says the Lord GOD:

"I will also [R]destroy the idols, Is. 19:1
And cause the images to cease from
Noph;*
[R]There shall no longer be princes from
the land of Egypt; Zech. 10:11
I will put fear in the land of Egypt.
14 I will make [R]Pathros desolate,
Set fire to [R]Zoan, Ezek. 29:14 • Ps. 78:12, 43
And execute judgments in No.*
15 I will pour My fury on Sin,* the strength
of Egypt;
I will cut off the multitude of No,
16 And [R]set a fire in Egypt; Ezek. 30:8
Sin shall have great pain,
No shall be split open,
And Noph *shall be in* distress daily.
17 The young men of Aven* and Pi Beseth
shall fall by the sword,
And these *cities* shall go into captivity.
18[R] At Tehaphnehes* the day shall also be
darkened,* Jer. 2:16
When I break the yokes of Egypt there.
And her arrogant strength shall cease in
her;
As for her, a cloud shall cover her,
And her daughters shall go into
captivity.
19 Thus I will [R]execute judgments on
Egypt, [Ps. 9:16]
Then they shall know that I *am* the
LORD." ' "

20 And it came to pass in the eleventh year,
in the first *month*, on the seventh *day* of the
month, *that* the word of the LORD came to me,
saying,
21 "Son of man, I have [R]broken the arm of

30:5 Heb. *Put* • Heb. *Lud* **30:13** Ancient Memphis
30:14 Ancient Thebes **30:15** Ancient Pelusium
30:17 Ancient On, Heliopolis **30:18** *Tahpanhes*, Jer. 43:7 • So with many Heb. mss., Bg., LXX, Syr., Tg., Vg.; MT *refrained*

Pharaoh king of Egypt; and see, [R]it has not
been bandaged for healing, nor a [T]splint put
on to bind it, to make it strong enough to hold
a sword. Jer. 48:25 • Jer. 46:11 • Lit. *bandage*
22 "Therefore thus says the Lord God:
'Surely I *am* against Pharaoh king of Egypt,
and will break his arms, both the strong one
and the one that was broken; and I will make
the sword fall out of his hand.
23 [R]'I will scatter the Egyptians among the
nations, and disperse them throughout the
countries. Ezek. 29:12; 30:17, 18, 26
24 'I will strengthen the arms of the king of
Babylon and put My sword in his hand; but I
will break Pharaoh's arms, and he will groan
before him with the groanings of a mortally
wounded *man.*
25 'Thus I will strengthen the arms of the
king of Babylon, but the arms of Pharaoh
shall fall down; [R]they shall know that I *am* the
LORD, when I put My sword into the hand of
the king of Babylon and he stretches it out
against the land of Egypt. Ps. 9:16
26 [R]'I will scatter the Egyptians among the na-
tions and disperse them throughout the coun-
tries. Then they shall know that I *am* the
LORD.' " Ezek. 29:12

CHAPTER 31

Egypt Is Cut Down Like Assyria

NOW it came to pass in the [R]eleventh year,
in the third *month,* on the first *day* of the
month, *that* the word of the LORD came to me,
saying, Ezek. 30:20; 32:1
2 "Son of man, say to Pharaoh king of
Egypt and to his multitude:

'Whom are you like in your greatness?
3 [R]Indeed Assyria *was* a cedar in Lebanon,
With fine branches that shaded the
forest, Dan. 4:10, 20–23
And of high stature;
And its top was among the thick boughs.
4 [R]The waters made it grow; Jer. 51:36
Underground waters gave it height,
With their rivers running around the
place where it was planted,
And sent out [T]rivulets to all the trees of
the field. Or *channels*

5 'Therefore [R]its height was exalted above
all the trees of the field; Dan. 4:11
Its boughs were multiplied,
And its branches became long because
of the abundance of water,
As it sent them out.
6 All the [R]birds of the heavens made their
nests in its boughs; Dan. 4:12, 21
Under its branches all the beasts of the
field brought forth their young;
And in its shadow all great nations
[T]made their home. Lit. *dwelled*

7 'Thus it was beautiful in greatness and in
the length of its branches,
Because its roots reached to abundant
waters.
8 The cedars in the [R]garden of God could
not hide it; Gen. 2:8, 9; 13:10
The fir trees were not like its boughs,
And the chestnut* trees were not like its
branches;
No tree in the garden of God was like it
in beauty.
9 I made it beautiful with a multitude of
branches,
So that all the trees of Eden envied it,
That *were* in the garden of God.'

10 "Therefore thus says the Lord GOD: 'Be-
cause you have increased in height, and it set
its top among the thick boughs, and its heart
was [T]lifted up in its height, Proud
11 'therefore I will deliver it into the hand of
the [R]mighty one of the nations, and he shall
surely deal with it; I have driven it out for its
wickedness. Ezek. 30:10
12 'And aliens, [R]the most terrible of the na-
tions, have cut it down and left it; its
branches have fallen on the mountains and in
all the valleys; its boughs lie broken by all the
rivers of the land; and all the peoples of the
earth have gone from under its shadow and
left it. Ezek. 28:7; 30:11; 32:12

13 'On [R]its ruin will remain all the birds of
the heavens, Is. 18:6
And all the beasts of the field will come
to its branches—

14 'So that no trees by the waters may ever
again exalt themselves for their height, nor
set their tops among the thick boughs, that no
tree which drinks water may ever be high
enough to reach up to them.

'For [R]they have all been delivered to
death, Ps. 82:7
[R]To the depths of the earth, Ezek. 32:18
Among the children of men who go
down to the Pit.'

15 "Thus says the Lord GOD: 'In the day
when it [R]went down to [T]hell, I caused mourn-
ing. I covered the deep because of it. I re-
strained its rivers, and the great waters were
held back. I caused Lebanon to mourn for it,
and all the trees of the field wilted because of
it. Ezek. 32:22, 23 • Or *Sheol*
16 'I made the nations shake at the sound
of its fall, when I cast it down to hell to-
gether with those who descend into the Pit;
and all the trees of Eden, the choice and best

31:8 Or *plane,* Heb. *armon*

of Lebanon, all that drink water, were com-
forted in the depths of the earth.
17 'They also went down to hell with it, with
those *slain* by the sword; and *those who were*
its *strong* arm [R]dwelt in its shadows among
the nations. Lam. 4:20
18 'To which of the trees in Eden will you
then be likened in glory and greatness? Yet
you shall be brought down with the trees of
Eden to the depths of the earth; you shall lie
in the midst of the uncircumcised, with *those*
slain by the sword. This *is* Pharaoh and all his
multitude,' says the Lord GOD."

CHAPTER 32

Egypt Is Lamented

AND it came to pass in the twelfth year, in
the [R]twelfth *month,* on the first *day* of the
month, *that* the word of the LORD came to me,
saying, Ezek. 31:1; 33:21
2 "Son of man, take up a lamentation for
Pharaoh king of Egypt, and say to him:

[R]'You are like a young lion among the
nations, Ezek. 19:2–6
And you *are* like a monster in the seas,
Bursting forth in your rivers,
Troubling the waters with your feet,
And [R]fouling their rivers.' Ezek. 34:18

3 "Thus says the Lord GOD:

'I will therefore spread My net over you
with a company of many people,
And they will draw you up in My net.
4 Then [R]I will leave you on the land;
I will cast you out on the open fields,
[R]And cause to settle on you all the birds
of the heavens. Ezek. 29:5 • Is. 18:6
And with you I will fill the beasts of the
whole earth.
5 I will lay your flesh on the mountains,
And fill the valleys with your carcass.

6 'I will also water the land with the flow of
your blood,
Even to the mountains;
And the riverbeds will be full of you.
7 When *I* put out your light,
[R]I will cover the heavens, and make its
stars dark; Rev. 6:12, 13; 8:12
I will cover the sun with a cloud,
And the moon shall not give her light.
8 All the [T]bright lights of the heavens I will
make dark over you, Or *shining*
And bring darkness upon your land,'
Says the Lord GOD.

9 'I will also trouble the hearts of many
peoples, when I bring your destruction among
the nations, into the countries which you have
not known.
10 'Yes, I will make many peoples aston-
ished at you, and their kings shall be horribly
afraid of you when I brandish My sword be-
fore them; and [R]they shall tremble *every* mo-
ment, every man for his own life, in the day of
your fall.' Ezek. 26:16
11 [R]"For thus says the Lord GOD: 'The
sword of the king of Babylon shall come
upon you. Jer. 46:26
12 'By the swords of the mighty warriors, all
of them the most terrible of the nations, I will
cause your multitude to fall.

'They shall plunder the pomp of Egypt,
And all its multitude shall be destroyed.
13 Also I will destroy all its animals
From beside its great waters;
[R]The foot of man shall muddy them no
more, Ezek. 29:11
Nor shall the hooves of animals muddy
them.
14 Then I will make their waters clear,
And make their rivers run like oil,'
Says the Lord GOD.

15 'When I make the land of Egypt desolate,
And the country is destitute of all that
once filled it,
When I strike all who dwell in it,
[R]Then they shall know that I *am* the
LORD. Ps. 9:16

16 'This *is* the [R]lamentation Ezek. 26:17
With which they shall lament her;
The daughters of the nations shall
lament her;
They shall lament for her, for Egypt,
And for all her multitude,'
Says the Lord GOD."

Egypt in Sheol

17 It came to pass also in the twelfth year, on
the fifteenth *day* of the month, *that* the word
of the LORD came to me, saying:

18 "Son of man, wail over the multitude of
Egypt,
And [R]cast them down to the depths of
the earth, Ezek. 26:20; 31:14
Her and the daughters of the famous
nations,
With those who go down to the Pit:
19 'Whom do you surpass in beauty?
[R]Go down, be placed with the
uncircumcised.' Ezek. 28:10

20 "They shall fall in the midst of *those* slain
by the sword;
She is delivered to the sword,
Drawing her and all her multitudes.
21 [R]The strong among the mighty
Shall speak to him out of the midst of
hell Is. 1:31; 14:9, 10

With those who help him:
'They have [R]gone down, Ezek. 32:19, 25
They lie with the uncircumcised, slain
by the sword.'

22 "Assyria *is* there, and all her company,
With their graves all around her,
All of them slain, fallen by the sword.
23 [R]Her graves are set in the recesses of the
Pit, Is. 14:15
And her company is all around her
grave,
All of them slain, fallen by the sword,
Who [R]caused terror in the land of the
living. Ezek. 32:24–27, 32

24 "There *is* [R]Elam and all her multitude,
All around her grave, Jer. 25:25; 49:34–39
All of them slain, fallen by the sword,
Who have gone down uncircumcised to
the lower parts of the earth,
[R]Who caused their terror in the land of
the living; Ezek. 32:23
Now they bear their shame with those
who go down to the Pit.
25 They have set her [R]bed in the midst of
the slain, Ps. 139:8
With all her multitude,
With her graves all around it,
All of them uncircumcised, slain by the
sword;
Though their terror was caused
In the land of the living,
Yet they bear their shame
With those who go down to the Pit;
It was put in the midst of the slain.

26 "There *are* [R]Meshech and Tubal and all
their multitudes, Gen. 10:2
With all their graves around it,
All of them [R]uncircumcised, slain by the
sword, Ezek. 32:19
Though they caused their terror in the
land of the living.
27 [R]They do not lie with the mighty
Who are fallen of the uncircumcised,
Who have gone down to hell with their
weapons of war; Is. 14:18, 19
They have laid their swords under their
heads,
But their iniquities will be on their
bones,
Because of the terror of the mighty in
the land of the living.
28 Yes, you shall be broken in the midst of
the uncircumcised,
And lie with *those* slain by the sword.

29 "There *is* [R]Edom, Ezek. 25:12–14
Her kings and all her princes,
Who despite their might
Are laid beside *those* slain by the sword;
They shall lie with the uncircumcised,
And with those who go down to the Pit.
30 There *are* the princes of the north,
All of them, and all the [R]Sidonians,
Who have gone down with the slain
In shame at the terror which they
caused by their might; Ezek. 28:21–23
They lie uncircumcised with *those* slain
by the sword,
And bear their shame with those who go
down to the Pit.

31 "Pharaoh will see them
And be [R]comforted over all his
multitude, Ezek. 14:22; 31:16
Pharaoh and all his army,
Slain by the sword,"
Says the Lord GOD.

32 "For I have caused My terror in the land
of the living;
And he shall be placed in the midst of
the uncircumcised
With *those* slain by the sword,
Pharaoh and all his multitude,"
Says the Lord GOD.

CHAPTER 33

The Appointment of Ezekiel as Watchman

AGAIN the word of the LORD came to me,
saying,
2 "Son of man, speak to [R]the children of
your people, and say to them: 'When I bring
the sword upon a land, and the people of the
land take a man from their territory and make
him their watchman, Ezek. 3:11
3 'when he sees the sword coming upon the
land, if he blows the trumpet and warns the
people,
4 'then whoever hears the sound of the
trumpet and does not take warning, if the
sword comes and takes him away, [R]his blood
shall be on his *own* head. [Acts 18:6]
5 'He heard the sound of the trumpet, but
did not take warning; his blood shall be upon
himself. But he who takes warning will [T]save
his life. Or *deliver his soul*
6 'But if the watchman sees the sword com-
ing and does not blow the trumpet, and the
people are not warned, and the sword comes
and takes *any* person from among them, [R]he
is taken away in his iniquity; but his blood I
will require at the watchman's hand.' Ezek. 33:8
7 [R]"So you, son of man: I have made you a
watchman for the house of Israel; therefore
you shall hear a word from My mouth and
warn them for Me. Is. 62:6
8 "When I say to the wicked, 'O wicked
man, you shall surely die!' and you do not
speak to warn the wicked from his way, that
wicked *man* shall die in his iniquity; but his
blood I will require at your hand.
9 "Nevertheless if you warn the wicked to

turn from his way, and he does not turn from his way, he shall die in his iniquity; but you have delivered your soul.

10 "Therefore you, O son of man, say to the house of Israel: 'Thus you say, "If our transgressions and our sins *lie* upon us, and we [R]pine[T] away in them, [R]how can we then live?" ' Ezek. 24:23 • Or *waste away* • Is. 49:14

11 "Say to them: '*As* I live,' says the Lord GOD, [R]'I have no pleasure in the death of the wicked, but that the wicked [R]turn from his way and live. Turn, turn from your evil ways! For [R]why should you die, O house of Israel?' [2 Sam. 14:14] • [Acts 3:19] • Ezek. 18:30, 31

12 "Therefore you, O son of man, say to the children of your people: 'The [R]righteousness of the righteous man shall not deliver him in the day of his transgression; as for the wickedness of the wicked, he shall not fall because of it in the day that he turns from his wickedness; nor shall the righteous be able to live because of *his righteousness* in the day that he sins.' Ezek. 3:20; 18:24, 26

13 "When I say to the righteous *that* he shall surely live, [R]but he trusts in his own righteousness and commits iniquity, none of his righteous works shall be remembered; but because of the iniquity that he has committed, he shall die. Ezek. 3:20; 18:24

14 "Again, when I say to the wicked, 'You shall surely die,' if he turns from his sin and does [T]what is lawful and right, *justice*

15 "*if* the wicked restores the pledge, gives back what he has stolen, and walks in the statutes of life without committing iniquity, he shall surely live; he shall not die.

16 [R]"None of his sins which he has committed shall be remembered against him; he has done what is lawful and right; he shall surely live. [Is. 1:18; 43:25]

17 [R]"Yet the children of your people say, 'The way of the LORD is not fair.' But it is their way which is not fair! Ezek. 18:25, 29

18 [R]"When the righteous turns from his righteousness and commits iniquity, he shall die because of it. Ezek. 18:26

19 "But when the wicked turns from his wickedness and does what is lawful and right, he shall live because of it.

20 "Yet you say, 'The way of the LORD is not fair.' O house of Israel, I will judge every one of you according to his own ways."

21 And it came to pass in the twelfth year [R]of our captivity, in the tenth *month*, on the fifth *day* of the month, *that* one who had escaped from Jerusalem came to me and said, "The city has been captured!" Ezek. 1:2

22 Now [R]the hand of the LORD had been upon me the evening before the man came who had escaped. And He had [R]opened my mouth; so when he came to me in the morning, my mouth was opened, and I was no longer mute. Ezek. 1:3; 8:1; 37:1 • Ezek. 24:27

23 Then the word of the LORD came to me, saying:

24 "Son of man, they who inhabit those ruins in the land of Israel are saying, [R]'Abraham was only one, and he inherited the land. But we *are* many; the land has been given to us as a possession.' Is. 51:2

25 "Therefore say to them, 'Thus says the Lord GOD: [R]"You eat *meat* with blood, you [R]lift up your eyes toward your idols, and shed blood. Should you then possess the land? Lev. 3:17; 7:26; 17:10–14; 19:26 • Ezek. 18:6

26 "You rely on your sword, you commit abominations, and you defile one another's wives. Should you then possess the land?" '

27 "Say thus to them, 'Thus says the Lord GOD: "*As* I live, surely [R]those who *are* in the ruins shall fall by the sword, and the one who *is* in the open field [R]I will give to the beasts to be devoured, and those who *are* in the strongholds and [R]caves shall die of the pestilence. Ezek. 33:24 • Ezek. 39:4 • 1 Sam. 13:6

28 [R]"For I will make the land most desolate, her arrogant strength shall cease, and the mountains of Israel shall be so desolate that no one will pass through. Jer. 44:2, 6, 22

29 "Then they shall know that I *am* the LORD, when I have made the land most desolate because of all their abominations which they have committed." '

30 "As for you, son of man, the children of your people are talking about you beside the walls and in the doors of the houses; and they speak to one another, everyone saying to his brother, 'Please come and hear what the word is that comes from the LORD.'

31 "So they come to you as people do, they sit before you *as* My people, and they [R]hear your words, but they do not do them; for with their mouth they show much love, *but* their hearts pursue their *own* gain. Is. 58:2

32 "Indeed you *are* to them as a very lovely song of one who has a pleasant voice and can play well on an instrument; for they hear your words, but they do not do them.

33 [R]"And when this comes to pass—surely it will come—then they will know that a prophet has been among them." 1 Sam. 3:20

CHAPTER 34

The False Shepherds

AND the word of the LORD came to me, saying,

2 "Son of man, prophesy against the shepherds of Israel, prophesy and say to them, 'Thus says the Lord GOD to the shepherds: [R]"Woe to the shepherds of Israel who feed themselves! Should not the shepherds feed the flocks? Zech. 11:17

3 [R]"You eat the fat and clothe yourselves with the wool; you slaughter the fatlings, *but* you do not feed the flock. Zech. 11:16

4 [R]"The weak you have not strengthened, nor have you healed those who were sick, nor bound up the broken, nor brought back what was driven away, nor [R]sought what was lost; but with [R]force and cruelty you have ruled them. Zech. 11:16 • Luke 15:4 • [1 Pet. 5:3]

5 [R]"So they were [R]scattered because *there was* no shepherd; [R]and they became food for all the beasts of the field when they were scattered. Ezek. 33:21 • Matt. 9:36 • Is. 56:9

6 "My sheep [R]wandered through all the mountains, and on every high hill; yes, My flock was scattered over the whole face of the earth, and no one was seeking or searching *for them.*" 1 Pet. 2:25

7 'Therefore, you shepherds, hear the word of the LORD:

8 "*As* I live," says the Lord GOD, "surely because My flock became a prey, and My flock [R]became food for every beast of the field, because *there was* no shepherd, nor did My shepherds search for My flock, [R]but the shepherds fed themselves and did not feed My flock"— Ezek. 34:5, 6 • Ezek. 34:2, 10

9 'therefore, O shepherds, hear the word of the LORD!

10 'Thus says the Lord GOD: "Behold, I *am* against the shepherds, and [R]I will require My flock at their hand; I will cause them to cease feeding the sheep, and the shepherds shall feed themselves no more; for I will deliver My flock from their mouths, that they may no longer be food for them." Heb. 13:17

The True Shepherd

11 'For thus says the Lord GOD: "Indeed I Myself will search for My sheep and seek them out.

12 "As a [R]shepherd seeks out his flock on the day he is among his scattered sheep, so will I seek out My sheep and deliver them from all the places where they were scattered on a cloudy and dark day. Jer. 31:10

13 "And [R]I will bring them out from the peoples and gather them from the countries, and will bring them to their own land; I will feed them on the mountains of Israel, [T]in the valleys and in all the inhabited places of the country. Jer. 23:3 • Or *by the streams*

14 [R]"I will feed them in good pasture, and their fold shall be on the high mountains of Israel. [R]There they shall lie down in a good fold and feed in rich pasture on the mountains of Israel. [John 10:9] • Jer. 33:12

15 "I will feed My flock, and I will make them lie down," says the Lord GOD.

16 [R]"I will seek what was lost and bring back what was driven away, bind up the broken and strengthen what was sick; but I will destroy [R]the fat and the strong, and feed them in judgment." Mic. 4:6 • Is. 10:16

17 'And *as for* you, O My flock, thus says the Lord GOD: [R]"Behold, I shall judge between sheep and sheep, between rams and goats. [Matt. 25:32]

18 "*Is it* too little for you to have eaten up the good pasture, that you must tread down with your feet the residue of your pasture—and to have drunk of the clear waters, that you must foul the residue with your feet?

19 "And *as for* My flock, they eat what you have trampled with your feet, and they drink what you have fouled with your feet."

20 'Therefore thus says the Lord GOD to them: [R]"Behold, I Myself will judge between the fat and the lean sheep. Ezek. 34:17

21 "Because you have pushed with side and shoulder, butted all the weak ones with your horns, and scattered them abroad,

22 "therefore I will save My flock, and they shall no longer be a prey; and I will judge between sheep and sheep.

23 "I will establish one [R]shepherd over them, and he shall feed them—[R]My servant David. He shall feed them and be their shepherd. [Is. 40:11] • Jer. 30:9

24 "And [R]I, the LORD, will be their God, and My servant David a prince among them; I, the LORD, have spoken. Ex. 29:45

25 "I will make a covenant of peace with them, and cause wild beasts to cease from the land; and they [R]will dwell safely in the wilderness and sleep in the woods. Jer. 23:6

26 "I will make them and the places all around [R]My hill a blessing; and I will cause showers to come down in their season; there shall be showers of blessing. Is. 56:7

27 "Then [R]the trees of the field shall yield their fruit, and the earth shall yield her increase. They shall be safe in their land; and they shall know that I *am* the LORD, when I have [R]broken the bands of their yoke and delivered them from the hand of those who [R]enslaved them. Is. 4:2 • Jer. 2:20 • Jer. 25:14

28 "And they shall no longer be a prey for the nations, nor shall beasts of the land devour them; but [R]they shall dwell safely, and no one shall make *them* afraid. Jer. 30:10

29 "I will raise up for them a garden of renown, and they shall no longer be consumed with hunger in the land, nor bear the shame of the Gentiles anymore.

30 "Thus they shall know that [R]I, the LORD their God, *am* with them, and they, the house of Israel, *are* [R]My people," says the Lord GOD.' " Ezek. 34:24 • Ezek. 14:11; 36:28

31 "You are My [R]flock, the flock of My pasture; you *are* men, *and* I *am* your God," says the Lord GOD. Ps. 100:3

CHAPTER 35

The Judgment of Edom

MOREOVER the word of the LORD came to me, saying,

2 "Son of man, set your face against Mount Seir and prophesy against it,

3 "and say to it, 'Thus says the Lord GOD:

"Behold, O Mount Seir, I *am* against you;
I will stretch out My hand against you,
And make you most desolate;
4 I shall lay your cities waste,
And you shall be desolate.
Then you shall know that I *am* the LORD.

5 [R]"Because you have had an ancient hatred, and have shed *the blood of* the children of Israel by the power of the sword at the time of their calamity, [R]*when* their iniquity *came to an* end, Ezek. 25:12 • Ps. 137:7

6 "therefore, *as* I live," says the Lord GOD, "I will prepare you for blood, and blood shall pursue you; since you have not hated blood, therefore blood shall pursue you.

7 "Thus I will make Mount Seir most desolate, and cut off from it the [R]one who leaves and the one who returns. Judg. 5:6

8 "And I will fill its mountains with the slain; on your hills and in your valleys and in all your ravines those who are slain by the sword shall fall.

9 "I will make you perpetually desolate, and your cities shall be uninhabited; then you shall know that I *am* the LORD.

10 "Because you have said, 'These two nations and these two countries shall be mine, and we will [R]possess them,' although [R]the LORD was there, Ps. 83:4–12 • [Ps. 48:1–3]

11 "therefore, *as* I live," says the Lord GOD, "I will do [R]according to your anger and according to the envy which you showed in your hatred against them; and I will make Myself known among them when I judge you. [James 2:13]

12 [R]"Then you shall know that I *am* the LORD. I have heard all your blasphemies which you have spoken against the mountains of Israel, saying, 'They are desolate; they are given to us to consume.' Ps. 9:16

13 "Thus with your mouth you have boasted against Me and multiplied your words against Me; I have heard *them.*"

14 'Thus says the Lord GOD: "The whole earth will rejoice when I make you desolate.

15 "As you rejoiced because the inheritance of the house of Israel was desolate, so I will do to you; you shall be desolate, O Mount Seir, as well as all of Edom—all of it! Then they shall know that I *am* the LORD." '

CHAPTER 36

Judgment on the Nations

"AND you, son of man, prophesy to the [R]mountains of Israel, and say, 'O mountains of Israel, hear the word of the LORD! Ezek. 6:2, 3

2 'Thus says the Lord GOD: "Because the enemy has said of you, 'Aha! The ancient heights have become our possession,' " '

3 "therefore prophesy, and say, 'Thus says the Lord GOD: "Because they made *you* desolate and swallowed you up on every side, so that you became the possession of the rest of the nations, [R]and you are taken up by the lips of [R]talkers and slandered by the people"— Deut. 28:37 • Ezek. 35:13

4 'therefore, O mountains of Israel, hear the word of the Lord GOD! Thus says the Lord GOD to the mountains, the hills, the rivers, the valleys, the desolate wastes, and the cities that have been forsaken, which became plunder and [R]mockery to the rest of the nations all around— Ps. 79:4

5 'therefore thus says the Lord GOD: [R]"Surely I have spoken in My burning jealousy against the rest of the nations and against all Edom, who gave My land to themselves as a possession, with wholehearted joy *and* spiteful minds, in order to plunder its open country." ' Deut. 4:24

6 "Therefore prophesy concerning the land of Israel, and say to the mountains, the hills, the rivers, and the valleys, 'Thus says the Lord GOD: "Behold, I have spoken in My jealousy and My fury, because you have [R]borne the shame of the nations." Ps. 74:10

7 'Therefore thus says the Lord GOD: "I have [R]raised My hand in an oath that surely the nations that *are* around you shall [R]bear their own shame. Ezek. 20:5 • Jer. 25:9, 15, 29

Israel Returns to the Lord

8 "But you, O mountains of Israel, you shall shoot forth your branches and yield your fruit to My people Israel, for they are about to come.

9 "For indeed I *am* for you, and I will turn to you, and you shall be tilled and sown.

10 "I will multiply men upon you, all the house of Israel, all of it; and the cities shall be inhabited and the ruins rebuilt.

11 [R]"I will multiply upon you man and beast; and they shall increase and bear young; I will make you inhabited as in former times, and do [R]better *for you* than at your beginnings. Then you shall know that I *am* the LORD. Jer. 31:27; 33:12 • Is. 51:3

12 "Yes, I will cause men to walk on you, My people Israel; [R]they shall take possession of you, and you shall be their inheritance; no more shall you [R]bereave them *of children.*" Obad. 17 • Jer. 15:7

13 'Thus says the Lord GOD: "Because they say to you, [R]'You devour men and bereave your nation *of children,*' Num. 13:32

14 "therefore you shall devour men no more, nor bereave your nation anymore," says the Lord GOD.

15 [R]"Nor will I let you hear the taunts of the

nations anymore, nor bear the reproach of the
peoples anymore, nor shall you cause your
nation to stumble anymore," says the Lord
GOD.' " Ezek. 34:29
16 Moreover the word of the LORD came to
me, saying:
17 "Son of man, when the house of Israel
dwelt in their own land, [R]they defiled it by
their own ways and deeds; to Me their way
was like [R]the uncleanness of a woman in her
customary impurity. Jer. 2:7 • Lev. 15:19
18 "Therefore I poured out My fury on them
[R]for the blood they had shed on the land,
and for their idols *with which* they had de-
filed it. Ezek. 16:36, 38; 23:37
19 "So I scattered them among the nations,
and they were dispersed throughout the coun-
tries; I judged them [R]according to their ways
and their deeds. [Rom. 2:6]
20 "When they came to the nations, wher-
ever they went, they [R]profaned My holy
name—when they said of them, 'These *are* the
people of the LORD, *and* yet they have gone
out of His land.' Rom. 2:24
21 "But I had concern for My holy name,
which the house of Israel had profaned
among the nations wherever they went.
22 "Therefore say to the house of Israel,
'Thus says the Lord GOD: "I do not do *this* for
your sake, O house of Israel, but for My holy
name's sake, which you have profaned among
the nations wherever you went.
23 "And I will sanctify My great name, which
has been profaned among the nations, which
you have profaned in their midst; and the na-
tions shall know that I *am* the LORD," says the
Lord GOD, "when I am hallowed in you be-
fore their eyes.
24 "For [R]I will take you from among the na-
tions, gather you out of all countries, and
bring you into your own land. Ezek. 34:13
25 [R]"Then I will sprinkle clean water on you,
and you shall be clean; I will cleanse you
[R]from all your filthiness and from all your
idols. Heb. 9:13, 19; 10:22 • Jer. 33:8
26 "I will give you a [R]new heart and put a
new spirit within you; I will take the heart of
stone out of your flesh and give you a heart of
flesh. Ezek. 11:19
27 "I will put My Spirit within you and cause
you to walk in My statutes, and you will keep
My judgments and do *them*.
28 [R]"Then you shall dwell in the land that I
gave to your fathers; you shall be My people,
and I will be your God. Ezek. 28:25; 37:25
29 "I will deliver you from all your unclean-
nesses. I will call for the grain and multiply it,
and bring no famine upon you.
30 [R]"And I will multiply the fruit of your
trees and the increase of your fields, so that
you need never again bear the reproach of
famine among the nations. Ezek. 34:27
31 "Then you will remember your evil ways
and your deeds that *were* not good; and you
will loathe yourselves in your own sight, for
your iniquities and your abominations.
32 [R]"Not for your sake do I do *this*," says
the Lord GOD, "let it be known to you. Be
ashamed and confounded for your own ways,
O house of Israel!" Deut. 9:5
33 'Thus says the Lord GOD: "On the day that
I cleanse you from all your iniquities, I will
also enable *you* to dwell in the cities, [R]and the
ruins shall be rebuilt. Ezek. 36:10
34 "The desolate land shall be tilled instead
of lying desolate in the sight of all who pass
by.
35 "So they will say, 'This land that was des-
olate has become like the garden of Eden; and
the wasted, desolate, and ruined cities *are
now* fortified *and* inhabited.'
36 "Then the nations which are left all
around you shall know that I, the LORD, have
rebuilt the ruined places *and* planted what
was desolate. [R]I, the LORD, have spoken *it*, and
I will do *it*." Ezek. 17:24; 22:14; 37:14
37 'Thus says the Lord GOD: [R]"I will also let
the house of Israel inquire of Me to do this
for them: I will [R]increase their men like a
flock. Ezek. 14:3; 20:3, 31 • Ezek. 36:10
38 "Like a [T]flock *offered as* holy *sacrifices*,
like the flock at Jerusalem on its [T]feast days,
so shall the ruined cities be filled with flocks
of men. Then they shall know that I *am* the
LORD." ' " Lit. *holy flock* • *appointed feasts*

CHAPTER 37

Vision of Dry Bones

THE [R]hand of the LORD came upon me and
brought me out [R]in the Spirit of the LORD,
and set me down in the midst of the valley;
and it *was* full of bones. Ezek. 1:3 • Ezek. 3:14
2 Then He caused me to pass by them all
around, and behold, *there were* very many in
the open valley; and indeed *they were* very dry.
3 And He said to me, "Son of man, can
these bones live?" So I answered, "O Lord
GOD, [R]You know." [1 Sam. 2:6]
4 Again He said to me, "Prophesy to these
bones, and say to them, 'O dry bones, hear the
word of the LORD!
5 'Thus says the Lord GOD to these bones:
"Surely I will [R]cause breath to enter into you,
and you shall live. Ps. 104:29, 30
6 "I will put sinews on you and bring flesh
upon you, cover you with skin and put breath
in you; and you shall live. Then you shall
know that I *am* the LORD." ' "
7 So I prophesied as I was commanded; and
as I prophesied, there was a noise, and sud-
denly a rattling; and the bones came together,
bone to bone.
8 Indeed, as I looked, the sinews and the
flesh came upon them, and the skin covered
them over; but *there was* no breath in them.

9 Also He said to me, "Prophesy to the breath, prophesy, son of man, and say to the breath, 'Thus says the Lord GOD: "Come from the four winds, O breath, and breathe on these slain, that they may live." ' "

10 So I prophesied as He commanded me, [R]and [T]breath came into them, and they lived, and stood upon their feet, an exceedingly great army. Rev. 11:11 • Breath of life

11 Then He said to me, "Son of man, these bones are the whole house of Israel. They indeed say, 'Our bones are dry, our hope is lost, and we ourselves are cut off!'

12 "Therefore prophesy and say to them, 'Thus says the Lord GOD: "Behold, [R]O My people, I will open your graves and cause you to come up from your graves, and bring you into the land of Israel. Is. 26:19; 66:14

13 "Then you shall know that I *am* the LORD, when I have opened your graves, O My people, and brought you up from your graves.

14 "I [R]will put My Spirit in you, and you shall live, and I will place you in your own land. Then you shall know that I, the LORD, have spoken *it* and performed *it*," says the LORD.' " Ezek. 36:27

Sign of the Two Sticks

15 Again the word of the LORD came to me, saying,

16 "As for you, son of man, take a stick for yourself and write on it: 'For Judah and for the children of Israel, his companions.' Then take another stick and write on it, 'For Joseph, the stick of Ephraim, and *for* all the house of Israel, his companions.'

17 "Then [R]join them one to another for yourself into one stick, and they will become one in your hand. Hos. 1:11

18 "And when the children of your people speak to you, saying, [R]'Will you not show us what you *mean* by these?'— Ezek. 12:9; 24:19

19 [R]"say to them, 'Thus says the Lord GOD: "Surely I will take [R]the stick of Joseph, which *is* in the hand of Ephraim, and the tribes of Israel, his companions; and I will join them with it, with the stick of Judah, and make them one stick, and they will be one in My hand." ' Zech. 10:6 • Ezek. 37:16, 17

20 "And the sticks on which you write will be in your hand before their eyes.

21 "Then say to them, 'Thus says the Lord GOD: "Surely I will take the children of Israel from among the nations, wherever they have gone, and will gather them from every side and bring them into their own land;

22 "and I will make them one nation in the land, on the mountains of Israel; and one king shall be king over them all; they shall no longer be two nations, nor shall they ever be divided into two kingdoms again.

23 "They shall not defile themselves anymore with their idols, nor with their detestable things, nor with any of their transgressions; but I will deliver them from all their dwelling places in which they have sinned, and will cleanse them. Then they shall be My people, and I will be their God.

24 [R]"David My servant *shall be* king over them, and they shall all have one shepherd; they shall also walk in My judgments and observe My statutes, and do them. Is. 11:1☆

25 "Then they shall dwell in the land that I have given to Jacob My servant, where your fathers dwelt; and they shall dwell there, they, their children, and their children's children, forever; and [R]My servant David *shall be* their prince forever. John 12:34☆

26 "Moreover I will make [R]a covenant of peace with them, and it shall be an everlasting covenant with them; I will establish them and multiply them, and I will set My sanctuary in their midst forevermore. Is. 55:3

27 [R]"My tabernacle also shall be with them; indeed I will be [R]their God, and they shall be My people. [John 1:14] • Ezek. 11:20

28 [R]"The nations also will know that I, the LORD, sanctify Israel, when My sanctuary is in their midst forevermore." ' " Ezek. 36:23

CHAPTER 38

Attack by Gog

NOW the word of the LORD came to me, saying,

2 [R]"Son of man, [R]set your face against [R]Gog, of the land of Magog, the prince of Rosh,* Meshech, and Tubal, and prophesy against him, Ezek. 39:1 • Ezek. 35:2, 3 • Rev. 20:8

3 "and say, 'Thus says the Lord GOD: "Behold, I *am* against you, O Gog, the prince of Rosh, Meshech, and Tubal.

4 "I will turn you around, put hooks into your jaws, and lead you out, with all your army, horses, and horsemen, all splendidly clothed, a great company *with* bucklers and shields, all of them handling swords.

5 "Persia, Ethiopia,* and Libya* are with them, all of them *with* shield and helmet;

6 "Gomer and all its troops; the house of Togarmah *from* the far north and all its troops—many people *are* with you.

7 "Prepare yourself and be ready, you and all your companies that are gathered about you; and be a guard for them.

8 [R]"After many days you will be visited. In the latter years you will come into the land of those brought back from the sword *and* gathered from many people on the mountains of Israel, which had long been desolate; they were brought out of the nations, and now all of them dwell safely. Is. 24:22

9 "You will ascend, coming like a storm,

38:2 Tg., Vg., Aquila *the chief prince of Meshech,* also v. 3 **38:5** Heb. *Cush* • Heb. *Put*

covering the land like a cloud, you and all
your troops and many peoples with you."
10 'Thus says the Lord GOD: "On that day it
shall come to pass *that* thoughts will arise in
your mind, and you will make an evil plan:
11 "You will say, 'I will go up against a land
of [R]unwalled villages; I will [R]go to a peaceful
people, who dwell [T]safely, all of them dwelling
without walls, and having neither bars nor
gates'— Zech. 2:4 • Jer. 49:31 • *securely*
12 "to take plunder and to take booty, to
stretch out your hand against the waste
places *that are again* inhabited, [R]and against
a people gathered from the nations, who have
acquired livestock and goods, who dwell in
the midst of the land. Ezek. 38:8
13 [R]"Sheba, [R]Dedan, the merchants of
Tarshish, and all their young lions will say to
you, 'Have you come to take plunder? Have
you gathered your army to take booty, to
carry away silver and gold, to take away
livestock and goods, to take great plun-
der?' " ' Ezek. 27:22 • Ezek. 27:15, 20
14 "Therefore, son of man, prophesy and say
to Gog, 'Thus says the Lord GOD: [R]"On that
day when My people Israel [R]dwell safely, will
you not know *it?* Is. 4:1 • Ezek. 38:8, 11
15 "Then you will come from your place out
of the far north, you and many peoples with
you, all of them riding on horses, a great com-
pany and a mighty army.
16 "You will come up against My people Is-
rael like a cloud, to cover the land. It will be in
the latter days that I will bring you against My
land, so that the nations may [R]know Me, when
I am hallowed in you, O Gog, before their
eyes." Ezek. 35:11

Judgment of God

17 'Thus says the Lord GOD: "Are *you* he of
whom I have spoken in former days by My
servants the prophets of Israel, who prophe-
sied for years in those days that I would bring
you against them?
18 "And it will come to pass at the same time,
when Gog comes against the land of Israel,"
says the Lord GOD, "*that* My fury will show in
My face.
19 "For [R]in My jealousy [R]*and* in the fire of
My wrath I have spoken: [R]'Surely in that day
there shall be a great earthquake in the land
of Israel, Ezek. 36:5, 6 • Ps. 89:46 • Rev. 16:18
20 'so that the fish of the sea, the birds of the
heavens, the beasts of the field, all creeping
things that creep on the earth, and all men
who *are* on the face of the earth shall shake at
My presence. The mountains shall be thrown
down, the steep places shall fall, and every
wall shall fall to the ground.'
21 "I will [R]call for [R]a sword against Gog
throughout all My mountains," says the Lord
GOD. "Every man's sword will be against his
brother. Ps. 105:16 • Ezek. 14:17
22 "And I will bring him to judgment with
pestilence and bloodshed; I will rain down on
him, on his troops, and on the many peoples
who *are* with him, flooding rain, [R]great hail-
stones, fire, and brimstone. Rev. 16:21
23 "Thus I will magnify Myself and [R]sanctify
Myself, [R]and I will be known in the eyes of
many nations. Then they shall know that I *am*
the LORD." ' Ezek. 36:23 • Ezek. 37:28; 38:16

CHAPTER 39

"AND you, son of man, prophesy against
Gog, and say, 'Thus says the Lord GOD:
"Behold, I *am* against you, O Gog, the prince
of Rosh,* Meshech, and Tubal;
2 "and I will [R]turn you around and lead
you on, [R]bringing you up from the far north,
and bring you against the mountains of Is-
rael. Ezek. 38:8 • Ezek. 38:15
3 "Then I will knock the bow out of your
left hand, and cause the arrows to fall out of
your right hand.
4 [R]"You shall fall upon the mountains of Is-
rael, you and all your troops and the peoples
who *are* with you; I will give you to birds of
prey of every sort and *to* the beasts of the field
to be devoured. Ezek. 38:4, 21
5 "You shall [T]fall on the open field; for I
have spoken," says the Lord GOD. Be slain
6 [R]"And I will send fire on Magog and on
those who live in security in [R]the coast-
lands. Then they shall know that I *am* the
LORD. Amos 1:4, 7, 10 • Ps. 72:10
7 [R]"So I will make My holy name known in
the midst of My people Israel, and I will not
let them profane My holy name anymore.
Then the nations shall know that *I am* the
LORD, the Holy One in Israel. Ezek. 39:25
8 [R]"Surely it is coming, and it shall be
done," says the Lord GOD. "This *is* the day of
which I have spoken. Rev. 16:17; 21:6
9 "Then those who dwell in the cities of Is-
rael will go out and set on fire and burn the
weapons, both the shields and bucklers, the
bows and arrows, the [T]javelins and spears;
and they will make fires with them for seven
years. Lit. *hand staffs*
10 "They will not take wood from the field
nor cut down *any* from the forests, because
they will make fires with the weapons; [R]and
they will plunder those who plundered them,
and pillage those who pillaged them," says the
Lord GOD. Is. 14:2; 33:1
11 "It will come to pass in that day *that* I will
give Gog a burial place there in Israel, the val-
ley of those who pass by east of the sea; and it
will obstruct travelers, because there they will
bury Gog and all his multitude. Therefore
they will call *it* the Valley of Hamon Gog.*

39:1 Tg., Vg., Aquila *the chief prince of Meshech*
39:11 Lit. *The Multitude of Gog*

12 "For seven months the house of Israel will
be burying them, [R]in order to cleanse the
land. Deut. 21:23
13 "Indeed all the people of the land will be
burying, and they will gain [R]renown for it on
the day that [R]I am glorified," says the Lord
GOD. Zeph. 3:19, 20 • Ezek. 28:22
14 "They will set apart men regularly em-
ployed, with the help of a search party,* to
pass through the land and bury those bodies
remaining on the ground, in order [R]to cleanse
it. At the end of seven months they will make
a search. Ezek. 39:12
15 "The search party will pass through the
land; and *when anyone* sees a man's bone, he
shall [T]set up a marker by it, till the buriers have
buried it in the Valley of Hamon Gog. *build*
16 "*The* name of *the* city *will* also *be* Ha-
monah. Thus they shall cleanse the land." '
17 "And as for you, son of man, thus says the
Lord GOD, [R]'Speak to every sort of bird and to
every beast of the field: Rev. 19:17, 18

[R]" Assemble yourselves and come;
Gather together from all sides to My
[R]sacrificial meal Is. 18:6 • Zeph. 1:7
Which I am sacrificing for you,
A great sacrificial meal [R]on the
mountains of Israel, Ezek. 39:4
That you may eat flesh and drink blood.
18 [R]You shall eat the flesh of the mighty,
Drink the blood of the princes of the
earth, Rev. 19:18
Of rams and lambs,
Of goats and bulls,
All of them fatlings of Bashan.
19 You shall eat fat till you are full,
And drink blood till you are drunk,
At My sacrificial meal
Which I am sacrificing for you.
20 [R]You shall be filled at My table
With horses and riders, Ps. 76:5, 6
[R]With mighty men Rev. 19:18
And with all the men of war," says the
Lord GOD.

21 [R]"I will set My glory among the nations;
all the nations shall see My judgment which I
have executed, and [R]My hand which I have
laid on them. Ezek. 36:23; 38:23 • Ex. 7:4
22 [R]"So the house of Israel shall know that I
am the LORD their God from that day for-
ward. Ex. 39:7, 28
23 [R]"The Gentiles shall know that the house
of Israel went into captivity for their iniquity;
because they were unfaithful to Me, therefore
I hid My face from them. I gave them into the
hand of their enemies, and they all fell by the
sword. Ezek. 36:18–20, 23
24 [R]"According to their uncleanness and
according to their transgressions I have
dealt with them, and hidden My face from
them." ' Ezek. 36:19

25 "Therefore thus says the Lord GOD:
[R]'Now I will bring back the captives of Jacob,
and have mercy on the [R]whole house of
Israel; and I will be jealous for My holy
name— Ezek. 34:13; 36:24 • Hos. 1:11
26 [R]'after they have borne their shame, and
all their unfaithfulness in which they were
unfaithful to Me, when they [R]dwelt safely
in their *own* land and no one made *them*
afraid. Dan. 9:16 • Lev. 26:5, 6
27 [R]'When I have brought them back from
the peoples and gathered them out of their en-
emies' lands, and I am hallowed in them in the
sight of many nations, Ezek. 28:25, 26
28 [R]'then they shall know that I *am* the LORD
their God, who sent them into captivity
among the nations, but also brought them
back to their land, and left none of them [T]cap-
tive any longer. Ezek. 34:30 • Lit. *there*
29 [R]'And I will not hide My face from them
anymore; for I shall have [R]poured out My
Spirit on the house of Israel,' says the Lord
GOD." Is. 54:8, 9 • [Joel 2:28]

CHAPTER 40

Vision of the Man with the Measuring Rod

IN the twenty-fifth year of our captivity, at
the beginning of the year, on the tenth *day*
of the month, in the fourteenth year after [R]the
city was [T]captured, on the very same day the
hand of the LORD was upon me; and He took
me there. Ezek. 33:21 • Lit. *struck*
2 In the visions of God He took me into the
land of Israel and [R]set me on a very high
mountain; on it toward the south *was* some-
thing like the structure of a city. Rev. 21:10
3 He took me there, and behold, *there was*
a man whose appearance *was* [R]like the ap-
pearance of bronze. He had a line of flax [R]and
a measuring rod in his hand, and he stood in
the gateway. Dan. 10:6 • Rev. 11:1; 21:15
4 And the man said to me, [R]"Son of man,
look with your eyes and hear with your ears,
and fix your mind on everything I show you;
for you *were* brought here so that I might
show *them* to you. Declare to the house of Is-
rael everything you see." Ezek. 44:5

The Outer Court

5 Now there was a wall all around the out-
side of the temple.* In the man's hand was a
measuring rod six cubits *long, each being a*
cubit and a handbreadth; and he measured
the width of the wall structure, one rod; and
the height, one rod.
6 Then he went to the gateway which faced
[R]east; and he went up its stairs and measured
the threshold of the gateway, *which was* one
rod wide, and the other threshold *was* one rod
wide. Ezek. 43:1

39:14 Lit. *those who pass through* **40:5** Lit. *house*

7 Each gate chamber *was* one rod long and one rod wide; between the gate chambers *was a space of* five cubits; and the threshold of the gateway by the vestibule of the inside gate *was* one rod.

8 He also measured the vestibule of the inside gate, one rod.

9 Then he measured the vestibule of the gateway, eight cubits; and the gateposts, two cubits. The vestibule of the gate *was* on the inside.

10 In the eastern gateway *were* three gate chambers on one side and three on the other; the three *were* all the same size; also the gateposts were of the same size on this side and that side.

11 He measured the width of the entrance to the gateway, ten cubits; *and* the length of the gate, thirteen cubits.

12 *There was* a [T]space in front of the gate chambers, one cubit *on this side* and one cubit on that side; the gate chambers *were* six cubits on this side and six cubits on that side. Lit. *border*

13 Then he measured the gateway from the roof of *one* gate chamber to the roof of the other; the width *was* twenty-five cubits, as door faces door.

14 He measured the gateposts, sixty cubits high, and the court all around the gateway *extended* to the gatepost.

15 *From* the front of the entrance gate to the front of the vestibule of the inner gate *was* fifty cubits.

16 *There were* beveled window *frames* in the gate chambers and in their intervening archways on the inside of the gateway all around, and likewise in the vestibules. *There were* windows all around on the inside. And on each gatepost *were* palm trees.

17 Then he brought me into [R]the outer court; and *there were* chambers and a pavement made all around the court; thirty chambers faced the pavement. Rev. 11:2

18 The pavement was by the side of the gateways, corresponding to the length of the gateways; *this was* the lower pavement.

19 Then he measured the width from the front of the lower gateway to the front of the inner court exterior, one hundred cubits toward the east and the north.

20 On the outer court was also a gateway facing north, and he measured its length and its width.

21 Its gate chambers, three on this side and three on that side, its gateposts and its archways, had the same measurements as the first gate; its length *was* fifty cubits and its width twenty-five cubits.

22 Its windows and those of its archways, and also its palm trees, *had* the same measurements as the gateway facing east; it was ascended by seven steps, and its archway *was* in front of it.

23 A gate of the inner court was opposite the northern gateway, just as the eastern *gateway;* and he measured from gateway to gateway, one hundred cubits.

24 After that he brought me toward the south, and there a gateway was facing south; and he measured its gateposts and archways according to these same measurements.

25 *There were* windows in it and in its archways all around like those windows; its length *was* fifty cubits and its width twenty-five cubits.

26 Seven steps led up to it, and its archway *was* in front of them; and it had palm trees on its gateposts, one on this side and one on that side.

27 *There was* also a gateway on the inner court, facing south; and he measured from gateway to gateway toward the south, one hundred cubits.

The Inner Court

28 Then he brought me to the inner court through the southern gateway; he measured the southern gateway according to these same measurements.

29 Also its gate chambers, its gateposts, and its archways *were* according to these same measurements; *there were* windows in it and in its archways all around; *it was* fifty cubits long and twenty-five cubits wide.

30 *There were* archways all around, twenty-five cubits long and five cubits wide.

31 Its archways faced the outer court, palm trees *were* on its gateposts, and going up to it *were* eight steps.

32 And he brought me into the inner court facing east; he measured the gateway according to these same measurements.

33 Also its gate chambers, its gateposts, and its archways *were* according to these same measurements; and *there were* windows in it and in its archways all around; *it was* fifty cubits long and twenty-five cubits wide.

34 Its archways faced the outer court, and palm trees *were* on its gateposts on this side and on that side; and going up to it *were* eight steps.

35 Then he brought me to the north gateway and measured *it* according to these same measurements—

36 also its gate chambers, its gateposts, and its archways. It had windows all around; its length *was* fifty cubits and its width twenty-five cubits.

37 Its gateposts faced the outer court, palm trees *were* on its gateposts on this side and on that side, and going up to it *were* eight steps.

38 *There was* a chamber and its entrance by the gateposts of the gateway, where they [R]washed the burnt offering. 2 Chr. 4:6

39 In the vestibule of the gateway *were* two tables on this side and two tables on that side,

on which to slay the burnt offering, the sin offering, and the trespass offering.

40 At the outer side of the vestibule, as one goes up to the entrance of the northern gateway, *were* two tables; and on the other side of the vestibule of the gateway *were* two tables.

41 Four tables *were* on this side and four tables on that side, by the side of the gateway, eight tables on which they slaughtered *the sacrifices.*

42 *There were* also four tables of hewn stone for the burnt offering, one cubit and a half long, one cubit and a half wide, and one cubit high; on these they laid the instruments with which they slaughtered the burnt offering and the sacrifice.

43 Inside *were* hooks, a handbreadth wide, fastened all around; and the flesh of the sacrifices *was* on the tables.

44 Outside the inner gate *were* the chambers for [R]the singers in the inner court, one facing south at the side of the northern gateway, and the other facing north at the side of the southern gateway. 1 Chr. 6:31, 32

45 Then he said to me, "This chamber which faces south *is* for [R]the priests who have charge of the temple. Lev. 8:35

46 "The chamber which faces north *is* for the priests [R]who have charge of the altar; these *are* the sons of [R]Zadok, from the sons of Levi, who come near the LORD to minister to Him." Num. 18:5 • 1 Kin. 2:35

47 And he measured the court, one hundred cubits long and one hundred cubits wide, foursquare. The altar *was* in front of the temple.

The Temple Vestibule

48 Then he brought me to the [R]vestibule of the temple and measured the doorposts of the vestibule, five cubits on this side and five cubits on that side; and the width of the gateway was three cubits on this side and three cubits on that side. 1 Kin. 6:3

49 [R]The length of the vestibule *was* twenty cubits, and the width eleven cubits; and by the steps which led up to it *there were* [R]pillars by the doorposts, one on this side and another on that side. 1 Kin. 6:3 • 1 Kin. 7:15–22

CHAPTER 41

The Temple Itself

THEN he brought me into the sanctuary* and measured the doorposts, six cubits wide on one side and six cubits wide on the other side—the width of the tabernacle.

2 The width of the entryway *was* ten cubits, and the side walls of the entrance *were* five cubits on this side and five cubits on the other side; and he measured its length, forty cubits, and its width, twenty cubits.

3 Also he went inside and measured the doorposts, two cubits; and the entrance, six cubits *high;* and the width of the entrance, seven cubits.

4 [R]He measured the length, twenty cubits; and the width, twenty cubits, beyond the sanctuary; and he said to me, "This *is* the Most Holy *Place.*" 1 Kin. 6:20

5 Next, he measured the wall of the [T]temple, six cubits. The width of each side chamber all around the temple *was* four cubits on every side. Lit. *house*

6 [R]The side chambers *were* in three stories, one above the other, thirty chambers in each story; they rested on ledges which *were* for the side chambers all around, that they might be supported, but not fastened to the wall of the temple. 1 Kin. 6:5–10

7 As one went up from story to story, the side chambers [R]became wider all around, because their supporting ledges in the wall of the temple ascended like steps; therefore the width of the structure increased as one went up *from* the lowest *story* to the highest by way of the middle one. 1 Kin. 6:8

8 I also saw an elevation all around the temple; it was the foundation of the side chambers, a full rod, *that is,* six cubits *high.*

9 The thickness of the outer wall of the side chambers *was* five cubits, and so also the remaining terrace by the place of the side chambers of the [T]temple. Lit. *house*

10 And between *it and* the *wall* chambers was a width of twenty cubits all around the temple on every side.

11 The doors of the side chambers opened on the terrace, one door toward the north and another toward the south; and the width of the terrace *was* five cubits all around.

12 The building that faced the separating courtyard at its western end *was* seventy cubits wide; the wall of the building *was* five cubits thick all around, and its length ninety cubits.

13 So he measured the temple, one [R]hundred cubits long; and the separating courtyard with the building and its walls *was* one hundred cubits long; Ezek. 40:47

14 also the width of the eastern face of the temple, including the separating courtyard, *was* one hundred cubits.

15 He measured the length of the building behind it, facing the separating courtyard, with its [R]galleries on the one side and on the other side, one hundred cubits, as well as the inner [T]temple and the porches of the court, Ezek. 42:3, 5 • Or *sanctuary*

16 their doorposts and the beveled window frames. And the galleries all around their three stories opposite the threshold were paneled with wood from the ground to the windows—the windows were covered—

41:1 Heb. *heykal;* the main room in the temple, the holy place, Ex. 26:33

17 from the space above the door, even to the
inner room,* as well as outside, and on every
wall all around, inside and outside, by measure.
18 And *it was* made with cherubim and palm
trees, a palm tree between cherub and cherub.
Each cherub had two faces,
19 [R]so that the face of a man *was* toward a
palm tree on one side, and the face of a young
lion toward a palm tree on the other side; thus
it was made throughout the temple all
around. Ezek. 1:10; 10:14
20 From the floor to the space above the
door, and on the wall of the sanctuary, cherubim and palm trees *were* carved.
21 The [R]doorposts of the temple *were*
square, *as was* the front of the sanctuary;
their appearance was similar. 1 Kin. 6:33
22 [R]The altar *was* of wood, three cubits high,
and its length two cubits. Its corners, its
length, and its sides *were* of wood; and he said
to me, "This *is* [R]the table that *is* before the
LORD." Ex. 30:1–3 • Ex. 25:23, 30
23 [R]The temple and the sanctuary had two
doors. 1 Kin. 6:31–35
24 The doors had two [R]panels *apiece,* two
folding panels: two *panels* for one door and
two panels for the other *door.* 1 Kin. 6:34
25 Cherubim and palm trees *were* carved on
the doors of the temple just as they *were*
carved on the walls. A wooden canopy *was* on
the front of the vestibule outside.
26 *There were* beveled window *frames* and
palm trees on one side and on the other, on
the sides of the vestibule—also on the side
chambers of the temple and on the canopies.

CHAPTER 42

The Chamber in the Outer Court

THEN he [R]brought me out into the outer
court, by the way toward the [R]north; and
he brought me into [R]the chamber which *was*
opposite the separating courtyard, and
which *was* opposite the building toward the
north. Ezek. 41:1 • Ezek. 40:20 • Ezek. 41:12, 15
2 Facing the length, *which was* one hundred cubits (the width was fifty cubits), was
the north door.
3 Opposite the inner court of twenty *cubits,*
and opposite the [R]pavement of the outer
court, *was* [R]gallery against gallery in three
stories. Ezek. 40:17 • Ezek. 41:15, 16; 42:5
4 In front of the chambers, toward the inside, *was* a walk ten cubits wide, at a distance
of one cubit; and their doors faced north.
5 Now the upper chambers *were* shorter,
because the galleries took away *space* from
them more than from the lower and middle
stories of the building.
6 For they *were* in three *stories* and did not
have pillars like the pillars of the courts;
therefore *the upper level* was [T]shortened
more than the lower and middle levels from
the ground up. Or *narrowed*
7 And a wall which *was* outside ran parallel to the chambers, at the front of the chambers, toward the outer court; its length *was*
fifty cubits.
8 The length of the chambers toward the
outer court *was* fifty cubits, whereas that facing the temple *was* one hundred cubits.
9 At the lower chambers *was* the entrance
on the east side, as one goes into them from
the outer court.
10 Also *there were* chambers in the thickness of the wall of the court toward the east,
opposite the separating courtyard and opposite the building.
11 *There was* a walk in front of them also,
and their appearance *was* like the chambers
which *were* toward the north; they *were* as
long and as wide as the others, and all their
exits and entrances *were* according to plan.
12 And corresponding to the doors of the
chambers that *were* facing south, as one enters them, *there was* a door in front of the
walk, the way directly in front of the wall toward the east.
13 Then he said to me, "The north chambers *and* the south chambers, which *are* opposite the separating courtyard, *are* the holy
chambers where the priests who approach
the LORD [R]shall eat the most holy offerings.
There they shall lay the most holy offerings—[R]the grain offering, the sin offering,
and the trespass offering—for the place *is*
holy. Lev. 6:16, 26; 24:9 • Lev. 2:3, 10; 6:14, 17, 25
14 [R]"When the priests enter them, they shall
not go out of the holy *chamber* into the outer
court; but there they shall leave their garments in which they minister, for they *are*
holy. They shall put on other garments; then
they may approach *that* which *is* for the people." Ezek. 44:19

The Place of Separation

15 Now when he had finished measuring the
inner temple, he brought me out through the
gateway that faces toward the east, and measured it all around.
16 He measured the east side with the measuring rod,* five hundred rods by the measuring rod all around.
17 He measured the north side, five hundred
rods by the measuring rod all around.
18 He measured the south side, five hundred
rods by the measuring rod.
19 He came around to the west side *and*
measured five hundred rods by the measuring
rod.
20 He measured it on the four sides; [R]it had
a wall all around, five hundred *cubits* long

41:17 Lit. *house;* the Most Holy Place **42:16** About 10.5 feet, Ezek. 40:5

and five hundred wide, to separate the holy areas from the common. Ezek. 40:5

CHAPTER 43

The Return of the Glory of God to the Temple

AFTERWARD he brought me to the gate, the gate that faces toward the east.

2 And behold, the glory of the God of Israel came from the way of the east. His voice *was* like the sound of many waters; and the earth shone with His glory.

3 *It was* like the appearance of the vision which I saw—like the vision which I saw when I* came to destroy the city. The visions *were* like the vision which I saw by the River Chebar; and I fell on my face.

4 [R]And the glory of the LORD came into the [T]temple by way of the gate which faces toward the east. Ezek. 10:19; 11:23 • Lit. *house*

5 The Spirit lifted me up and brought me into the inner court; and behold, [R]the glory of the LORD filled the temple. 1 Kin. 8:10, 11

6 Then I heard *Him* speaking to me from the temple, while a man stood beside me.

7 And He said to me, "Son of man, *this is* [R]the place of My throne and [R]the place of the soles of My feet, [R]where I will dwell in the midst of the children of Israel forever. No more shall the house of Israel defile My holy name, they nor their kings, by their harlotry or with the carcasses of their kings on their high places. Ps. 99:1 • 1 Chr. 28:2 • Joel 3:17

8 [R]"When they set their threshold by My threshold, and their doorpost by My doorpost, with a wall between them and Me, they defiled My holy name by the abominations which they committed; therefore I have consumed them in My anger. Ezek. 8:3; 23:39

9 "Now let them put their harlotry and the carcasses of their kings far away from Me, and I will dwell in their midst forever.

10 "Son of man, [R]describe the [T]temple to the house of Israel, that they may be ashamed of their iniquities; and let them measure the pattern. Ezek. 40:4 • Lit. *house*

11 "And if they are ashamed of all that they have done, make known to them the design of the temple and its arrangement, its exits and its entrances, its entire design and all its [R]ordinances, all its forms and all its laws. Write *it* down in their sight, so that they may keep its whole design and all its ordinances, and [R]perform them. Ezek. 44:5 • Ezek. 11:20

12 "This *is* the law of the [T]temple: The whole area surrounding [R]the mountaintop *is* most holy. Behold, this *is* the law of the temple. Lit. *house* • Ezek. 40:2

The Altar of Burnt Offerings

13 "These are the measurements of the [R]altar in cubits [R](the *cubit is* one cubit and a handbreadth): the base one cubit high and one cubit wide, with a rim all around its edge of one span. This *is* the height of the altar: Ex. 27:1–8 • Ezek. 41:8

14 "from the base on the ground to the lower ledge, two cubits; the width of the ledge, one cubit; from the smaller ledge to the larger ledge, four cubits; and the width of the ledge, *one* cubit.

15 "The altar hearth *is* four cubits high, with four [R]horns extending upward from the [T]hearth. Ex. 27:2 • Heb. *ariel*

16 "The altar hearth *is* twelve cubits long, twelve wide, square at its four corners;

17 "the ledge, fourteen *cubits* long and fourteen wide on its four sides, with a rim of half a cubit around it; its base, one cubit all around; and its steps face toward the east."

18 And He said to me, "Son of man, thus says the Lord GOD: 'These *are* the ordinances for the altar on the day when it is made, for sacrificing [R]burnt offerings on it, and for sprinkling blood on it. Ex. 40:29

19 'You shall give a young bull for a sin offering to the priests, the Levites, who are of the seed of Zadok, who approach Me to minister to Me,' says the Lord GOD.

20 'You shall take some of its blood and put *it* on the four horns of the altar, on the four corners of the ledge, and on the rim around it; thus you shall cleanse it and make atonement for it.

21 'Then you shall also take the bull of the sin offering, and burn it in the appointed place of the temple, outside the sanctuary.

22 'On the second day you shall offer a kid of the goats without blemish for a sin offering; and they shall cleanse the altar, as they cleansed *it* with the bull.

23 'When you have finished cleansing *it*, you shall offer a young bull without blemish, and a ram from the flock without blemish.

24 'When you offer them before the LORD, [R]the priests shall throw salt on them, and they will offer them up *as* a burnt offering to the LORD. Lev. 2:13

25 'Every day for [R]seven days you shall prepare a goat *for* a sin offering; they shall also prepare a young bull and a ram from the flock, both without blemish. Ex. 29:35

26 'Seven days they shall make atonement for the altar and purify it, and so [T]consecrate [T]*it*. Lit. *fill its hands* • LXX, Syr. *themselves*

27 [R]'When these days are over it shall be, on the eighth day and thereafter, that the priests shall offer your burnt offerings and your peace offerings on the altar; and I will accept you,' says the Lord GOD." Lev. 9:1–4

43:3 Some Heb. mss., Vg. *He*

CHAPTER 44

Duties of Temple Priests

THEN He brought me back to the outer gate of the sanctuary [R]which faces toward the east, but it *was* shut. Ezek. 43:1

2 And the LORD said to me, "This gate shall be shut; it shall not be opened, and no man shall enter by it, [R]because the LORD God of Israel has entered by it; therefore it shall be shut. Ezek. 43:2–4

3 "*As for* the [R]prince, *because* he *is* the prince, he may sit in it to [R]eat bread before the LORD; he shall enter by way of the vestibule of the gateway, and go out the same way." Gen. 31:54 • Ezek. 46:2, 8

4 Also He brought me by way of the north gate to the front of the temple; so I looked, and behold, the glory of the LORD filled the house of the LORD; and I fell on my face.

5 And the LORD said to me, [R]"Son of man, [T]mark well, see with your eyes and hear with your ears, all that I say to you concerning all the [R]ordinances of the house of the LORD and all its laws. Mark well who may enter the house and all who go out from the sanctuary. Ezek. 40:4 • Lit. *set your heart* • Ezek. 43:10, 11

6 "Now say to the [R]rebellious, to the house of Israel, 'Thus says the Lord GOD: "O house of Israel, [R]let Us have no more of all your abominations. Ezek. 2:5 • 1 Pet. 4:3

7 "When you brought in foreigners, uncircumcised in heart and uncircumcised in flesh, to be in My sanctuary to defile it—My house—and when you offered My food, the fat and the blood, then they broke My covenant because of all your abominations.

8 "And you have not [R]kept charge of My holy things, but you have set *others* to keep charge of My sanctuary for you." Lev. 22:2

9 'Thus says the Lord GOD: [R]"No foreigner, uncircumcised in heart or uncircumcised in flesh, shall enter My sanctuary, including any foreigner who *is* among the children of Israel. Ezek. 44:7

10 [R]"And the Levites who went far from Me, when Israel went astray, who strayed away from Me after their idols, they shall bear their iniquity. 2 Kin. 23:8

11 "Yet they shall be ministers in My sanctuary, [R]*as* gatekeepers of the house and ministers of the house; they shall slay the burnt offering and the sacrifice for the people, and [R]they shall stand before them to minister to them. 1 Chr. 26:1–19 • Num. 16:9

12 "Because they ministered to them before their idols and [R]caused the house of Israel to fall into iniquity, therefore I have [R]raised My hand in an oath against them," says the Lord GOD, "that they shall bear their iniquity. Is. 9:16 • Ps. 106:26

13 [R]"And they shall not come near Me to minister to Me as priest, nor come near any of My holy things, nor into the Most Holy *Place;* but they shall [R]bear their shame and their abominations which they have committed. 2 Kin. 23:9 • Ezek. 32:30

14 "Nevertheless I will make them [R]keep charge of the temple, for all its work, and for all that has to be done in it. Num. 18:4

15 [R]"But the priests, the Levites, [R]the sons of Zadok, who kept charge of My sanctuary [R]when the children of Israel went astray from Me, they shall come near Me to minister to Me; and they shall stand before Me to offer to Me the fat and the blood," says the Lord GOD. Ezek. 40:46 • [1 Sam. 2:35] • Ezek. 44:10

16 "They shall enter My sanctuary, and they shall come near My table to minister to Me, and they shall keep My charge.

17 "And it shall be, whenever they enter the gates of the inner court, that they shall put on linen garments; no wool shall come upon them while they minister within the gates of the inner court or within the house.

18 [R]"They shall have linen turbans on their heads and linen trousers on their bodies; they shall not clothe themselves with *anything that causes* sweat. Ex. 28:40; 39:28

19 "When they go out to the outer court, to the *outer* court to the people, they shall take off their garments in which they have ministered, leave them in the holy chambers, and put on other garments; and in their holy garments they shall not sanctify the people.

20 [R]"They shall neither shave their heads nor let their hair grow long, but they shall keep their hair well trimmed. Lev. 21:5

21 [R]"No priest shall drink wine when he enters the inner court. Lev. 10:9

22 "They shall not take as wife a [R]widow or a divorced woman, but take virgins of the descendants of the house of Israel, or widows of priests. Lev. 21:7, 13, 14

23 "And [R]they shall teach My people *the difference* between the holy and the unholy, and cause them to [R]discern between the unclean and the clean. Mal. 2:6–8 • Lev. 20:25

24 "In controversy they shall stand as judges, *and* judge it according to My judgments. They shall keep My laws and My statutes in all My appointed meetings, [R]and they shall hallow My Sabbaths. Ezek. 22:26

25 "They shall not defile *themselves* by coming near a dead person. Only for father or mother, for son or daughter, for brother or unmarried sister may they defile themselves.

26 [R]"After he is cleansed, they shall count seven days for him. Num. 6:10; 19:11, 13–19

27 "And on the day that he goes to the sanctuary to minister in the sanctuary, [R]he must offer his sin offering in the inner court," says the Lord GOD. Lev. 5:3, 6

28 "It shall be, in regard to their inheritance, *that* I [R]*am* their inheritance. You shall give them no [R]possession in Israel, for I *am* their possession. Num. 18:20 • Ezek. 45:4

29 "They shall eat the grain offering, the sin offering, and the trespass offering; every dedicated thing in Israel shall be theirs.

30 "The [R]best of all firstfruits of any kind, and every sacrifice of any kind from all your sacrifices, shall be the priest's; also you [R]shall give to the priest the first of your ground meal, to cause a blessing to rest on your house. Num. 3:13; 18:12 • Neh. 10:37

31 "The priests shall not eat anything, bird or beast, that [R]died naturally or was torn *by wild beasts.* Lev. 22:8

CHAPTER 45

Land of the Temple Priests

"MOREOVER, when you [R]divide the land by lot into inheritance, you shall [R]set apart a district for the LORD, a holy section of the land; its length *shall be* twenty-five thousand *cubits,* and the width ten thousand. It *shall be* holy throughout its territory all around. Ezek. 47:22 • Ezek. 48:8, 9

2 "Of this there shall be a square plot for the sanctuary, [R]five hundred by five hundred *rods,* with fifty cubits around it for an open space. Ezek. 42:20

3 "So this is the district you shall measure: twenty-five thousand *cubits* long and ten thousand wide; [R]in it shall be the sanctuary, the Most Holy *Place.* Ezek. 48:10

4 "It shall be a holy *section* of the land, belonging to the priests, the ministers of the sanctuary, who come near to minister to the LORD; it shall be a place for their houses and a holy place for the sanctuary.

5 [R]"*An area* twenty-five thousand *cubits* long and ten thousand wide shall belong to the Levites, the ministers of the [T]temple; they shall have [R]twenty chambers as a possession.* Ezek. 48:13 • Lit. *house* • Ezek. 40:17

6 [R]"You shall appoint as the property of the city *an area* five thousand *cubits* wide and twenty-five thousand long, adjacent to the district of the holy *section;* it shall belong to the whole house of Israel. Ezek. 48:15

7 [R]"The prince shall have *a section* on one side and the other of the holy district and the city's property; and bordering on the holy district and the city's property, extending westward on the west side and eastward on the east side, the length *shall be* side by side with one of the *tribal* portions, from the west border to the east border. Ezek. 48:21

8 "The land shall be his possession in Israel; and [R]My princes shall no more oppress My people, but they shall give *the rest of* the land to the house of Israel, according to their tribes." Ezek. 22:27

Offerings of the Temple Priests

9 'Thus says the Lord GOD: [R]"Enough, O princes of Israel! [R]Remove violence and plundering, execute justice and righteousness, and stop dispossessing My people," says the Lord GOD. Ezek. 44:6 • Jer. 22:3

10 "You shall have [R]honest scales, an honest ephah, and an honest bath. Lev. 19:36

11 "The ephah and the bath shall be of the same measure, so that the bath contains one-tenth of a homer, and the ephah one-tenth of a homer; their measure shall be according to the homer.

12 "The [R]shekel *shall be* twenty gerahs; twenty shekels, twenty-five shekels, *and* fifteen shekels shall be your mina. Ex. 30:13

13 "This *is* the offering which you shall offer: you shall give one-sixth of an ephah from a homer of wheat, and one-sixth of an ephah from a homer of barley.

14 "The ordinance concerning oil, the bath of oil, *is* one-tenth of a bath from a kor. A kor *is* a homer or ten baths, for ten baths *are* a homer.

15 "And one lamb shall be given from a flock of two hundred, from the rich pastures of Israel. These shall be for grain offerings, burnt offerings, and peace offerings, [R]to make atonement for them," says the Lord GOD. Lev. 1:4; 6:30

16 "All the people of the land shall give this offering for the prince in Israel.

17 "Then it shall be the [R]prince's part *to give* burnt offerings, grain offerings, and drink offerings, at the feasts, the New Moons, the Sabbaths, and at all the appointed seasons of the house of Israel. He shall prepare the sin offering, the grain offering, the burnt offering, and the peace offerings to make atonement for the house of Israel." Ezek. 46:4–12

18 'Thus says the Lord GOD: "In the first *month,* on the first *day* of the month, you shall take a young bull without blemish and [R]cleanse the sanctuary. Lev. 16:16, 33

19 [R]"The priest shall take some of the blood of the sin offering and put *it* on the doorposts of the temple, on the four corners of the ledge of the altar, and on the gateposts of the gate of the inner court. Ezek. 43:20

20 "And so you shall do on the seventh *day* of the month for everyone who has sinned unintentionally or in ignorance. Thus you shall make atonement for the temple.

21 [R]"In the first *month,* on the fourteenth day of the month, you shall observe the Passover, a feast of seven days; unleavened bread shall be eaten. Ex. 12:18

22 "And on that day the prince shall prepare for himself and for all the people of the land [R]a bull *for* a sin offering. Lev. 4:14

23 "On the [R]seven days of the feast he shall

45:5 So with MT, Tg., Vg.; LXX *a possession, cities of dwelling*

prepare a burnt offering to the LORD, seven
bulls and seven rams without blemish, daily
for seven days, [R]and a kid of the goats daily
for a sin offering. Lev. 23:8 • Num. 28:15, 22, 30
24 [R]"And he shall prepare a grain offering of
one ephah for each bull and one ephah for
each ram, together with a hin of oil for each
ephah. Ezek. 46:5, 7
25 "In the seventh *month*, on the fifteenth
day of the month, at the [R]feast, he shall do
likewise for seven days, according to the sin
offering, the burnt offering, the grain offering,
and the oil." Num. 29:12

CHAPTER 46

'THUS says the Lord GOD: "The gateway of
the inner court that faces toward the east
shall be shut the six working days; but on the
Sabbath it shall be opened, and on the day of
the New Moon it shall be opened.
2 [R]"The prince shall enter by way of the
vestibule of the gateway from the outside, and
stand by the gatepost. The priests shall pre-
pare his burnt offering and his peace offer-
ings. He shall worship at the threshold of the
gate. Then he shall go out, but the gate shall
not be shut until evening. Ezek. 44:3
3 "Likewise the people of the land shall
worship at the entrance to this gateway before
the LORD on the Sabbaths and the New Moons.
4 "The burnt offering that [R]the prince offers
to the LORD on the [R]Sabbath day *shall be* six
lambs without blemish, and a ram without
blemish; Ezek. 45:17 • Num. 28:9, 10
5 "and the grain offering *shall be one* ephah
for a ram, and the grain offering for the
lambs, as much as he wants to give, as well as
a hin of oil with every ephah.
6 "On the day of the New Moon *it shall be* a
young bull without blemish, six lambs, and a
ram; they shall be without blemish.
7 "He shall prepare a grain offering of an
ephah for a bull, an ephah for a ram, as much
as he wants to give for the lambs, and a hin of
oil with every ephah.
8 [R]"When the prince enters, he shall go in
by way of the vestibule of the gateway, and go
out the same way. Ezek. 44:3; 46:2
9 "But when the people of the land come
before the LORD on the appointed feast days,
whoever enters by way of the north [R]gate to
worship shall go out by way of the south gate;
and whoever enters by way of the south gate
shall go out by way of the north gate. He shall
not return by way of the gate through which
he came, but shall go out through the opposite
gate. Ezek. 48:31, 33
10 "The prince shall then be in their midst.
When they go in, he shall go in; and when
they go out, he shall go out.
11 "At the festivals and the appointed feast
days [R]the grain offering shall be an ephah for
a bull, an ephah for a ram, as much as he
wants to give for the lambs, and a hin of oil
with every ephah. Ezek. 46:5, 7
12 "Now when the prince makes a voluntary
burnt offering or voluntary peace offering to
the LORD, the gate that faces toward the east
shall then be opened for him; and he shall
prepare his burnt offering and his peace of-
ferings as he did on the Sabbath day. Then he
shall go out, and after he goes out the gate
shall be shut.
13 [R]"You shall daily make a burnt offering
to the LORD *of* a lamb of the first year with-
out blemish; you shall prepare it [T]every
morning. Num. 28:3–5 • Lit. *morning by morning*
14 "And you shall prepare a grain offering
with it every morning, a sixth of an ephah,
and a third of a hin of oil to moisten the fine
flour. This grain offering is a perpetual ordi-
nance, to be made regularly to the LORD.
15 "Thus they shall prepare the lamb, the
grain offering, and the oil, *as* a [R]regular burnt
offering every morning." Ex. 29:42
16 'Thus says the Lord GOD: "If the prince
gives a gift *of some* of his inheritance to any
of his sons, it shall belong to his sons; it is
their possession by inheritance.
17 "But if he gives a gift of some of his inher-
itance to one of his servants, it shall be his until
[R]the year of liberty, after which it shall return
to the prince. But his inheritance shall belong
to his sons; it shall become theirs. Lev. 25:10
18 "Moreover [R]the prince shall not take any
of the people's inheritance by evicting them
from their property; he shall provide an in-
heritance for his sons from his own property,
so that none of My people may be scattered
from his property." ' " Ezek. 45:8
19 Now he brought me through the entrance,
which *was* at the side of the gate, into the holy
chambers of the priests which face toward the
north; and there a place *was* situated at their
extreme western end.
20 And he said to me, "This *is* the place
where the priests shall [R]boil the trespass of-
fering and the sin offering, *and* where they
shall bake the grain offering, so that they do
not bring *them* out into the outer court to
sanctify the people." 2 Chr. 35:13
21 Then he brought me out into the outer
court and caused me to pass by the four cor-
ners of the court; and in fact, in every corner
of the court *there was another* court.
22 In the four corners of the court *were* en-
closed courts, forty *cubits* long and thirty
wide; all four corners *were* the same size.
23 *There was* a row *of building stones* all
around in them, all around the four of them;
and [T]cooking hearths were made under the
rows of stones all around. Lit. *boiling places*
24 And he said to me, "These *are* the
kitchens where the ministers of the temple
shall boil the sacrifices of the people."

CHAPTER 47

River from the Temple

THEN he brought me back to the door of the
[T]temple; and there was [R]water, flowing from
under the threshold of the temple toward the
east, for the front of the temple faced east; the
water was flowing from under the right side of
the temple, south of the altar. Lit. *house* • Joel 3:18
2 He brought me out by way of the north
gate, and led me around on the outside to the
outer gateway that faces east; and there was
water, running out on the right side.
3 And when [R]the man went out to the east
with the line in his hand, he measured one thou-
sand cubits, and he brought me through the wa-
ters; the water *came up to my* ankles. Ezek. 40:3
4 Again he measured one thousand and
brought me through the waters; the water
came up to my knees. Again he measured one
thousand and brought me through; the water
came up to my waist.
5 Again he measured one thousand, *and it
was* a river that I could not cross; for the
water was too deep, water in which one must
swim, a river that could not be crossed.
6 He said to me, "Son of man, have you
seen *this?*" Then he brought me and returned
me to the bank of the river.
7 When I returned, there, along the bank of
the river, *were* very many [R]trees on one side
and the other. [Rev. 22:2]
8 Then he said to me: "This water flows to-
ward the eastern region, goes down into the
valley, and enters the sea. *When it* reaches the
sea, *its* waters are healed.
9 "And it shall be *that* every living thing
that moves, wherever [T]the rivers go, will live.
There will be a very great multitude of fish,
because these waters go there; for they will be
healed, and everything will live wherever the
river goes. Lit. *two rivers*
10 "It shall be *that* fishermen will stand by it
from En Gedi to En Eglaim; they will be
places for spreading their nets. Their fish will
be of the same kinds as the fish [R]of the Great
Sea, exceedingly many. Num. 34:3
11 "But its swamps and marshes will not be
healed; they will be given over to salt.
12 "Along the bank of the river, on this side
and that, will grow all *kinds of* trees used for
food; their leaves will not wither, and their
fruit will not fail. They will bear fruit every
month, because their water flows from the
sanctuary. Their fruit will be for food, and
their leaves for medicine."

Boundaries of the Land

13 Thus says the Lord GOD: "These *are* the
borders by which you shall divide the land as
an inheritance among the twelve tribes of Is-
rael. Joseph *shall have two* portions.
14 "You shall inherit it equally with one an-
other; for I raised My hand in an oath to give
it to your fathers, and this land shall [R]fall to
you as your inheritance. Ezek. 48:29
15 "This *shall be* the border of the land on
the north: from the Great Sea, *by* the road to
Hethlon, as one goes to Zedad,
16 [R]"Hamath, Berothah, Sibraim (which *is*
between the border of Damascus and the bor-
der of Hamath), to Hazar Hatticon (which *is*
on the border of Hauran). Num. 34:8
17 "Thus the boundary shall be from the Sea
to Hazar Enan, the border of Damascus; and
as for the north, northward, it is the border of
Hamath. *This is* the north side.
18 "On the east side you shall mark out the
border from between Hauran and Damascus,
and between Gilead and the land of Israel,
along the Jordan, and along the eastern side
of the sea. *This is* the east side.
19 "The south side, toward the South,* *shall
be* from Tamar to [R]the waters of [T]Meribah
by Kadesh, along the brook to the Great
Sea. *This is* the south side, toward the
South. Ps. 81:7 • Lit. *Strife*
20 "The west side *shall be* the Great Sea, from
the *southern* boundary until one comes to a
point opposite Hamath. This *is* the west side.
21 "Thus you shall divide this land among
yourselves according to the tribes of Israel.
22 "It shall be that you will divide it by lot as
an inheritance for yourselves, [R]and for the
strangers who dwell among you and who bear
children among you. [R]They shall be to you as
native-born among the children of Israel; they
shall have an inheritance with you among the
tribes of Israel. [Eph. 3:6] • [Col. 3:11]
23 "And it shall be *that* in whatever tribe the
stranger dwells, there you shall give *him* his
inheritance," says the Lord GOD.

CHAPTER 48

Divisions of the Land

"NOW these *are* the names of the tribes:
[R]From the northern border along the
road to Hethlon at the entrance of Hamath, to
Hazar Enan, the border of Damascus north-
ward, in the direction of Hamath, *there shall
be* one *section for* [R]Dan from its east to its
west side; Ezek. 47:15 • Josh. 19:40–48
2 "by the border of Dan, from the east side
to the west, one *section for* Asher;
3 "by the border of Asher, from the east side
to the west, one *section for* Naphtali;
4 "by the border of Naphtali, from the east
side to the west, one *section for* Manasseh;
5 "by the border of Manasseh, from the
east side to the west, one *section for*
[R]Ephraim; Josh. 16:5–10; 17:8–10, 14–18
6 "by the border of Ephraim, from the east
side to the west, one *section for* Reuben;

47:19 Heb. *Negev*

7 "by the border of Reuben, from the east side to the west, one *section for* Judah;

8 "by the border of Judah, from the east side to the west, shall be the district which you shall set apart, twenty-five thousand *cubits* in width, and *in* length the same as one of the *other* portions, from the east side to the west, with the sanctuary in the center.

9 "The district that you shall set apart for the LORD *shall be* twenty-five thousand *cubits* in length and ten thousand in width.

10 "To these—to the priests—the holy district shall belong: on the north twenty-five thousand *cubits in length,* on the west ten thousand in width, on the east ten thousand in width, and on the south twenty-five thousand in length. The sanctuary of the LORD shall be in the center.

11 [R]"*It shall be* for the priests of the sons of Zadok, who are sanctified, who have kept My charge, who did not go astray when the children of Israel went astray, [R]as the Levites went astray. Ezek. 40:46; 44:15 • Ezek. 44:10, 12

12 "And *this* district of land that is set apart shall be to them a thing most [R]holy by the border of the Levites. Ezek. 45:4

13 "Opposite the border of the priests, the Levites *shall have an area* twenty-five thousand *cubits* in length and ten thousand in width; its entire length *shall be* twenty-five thousand and its width ten thousand.

14 "And they shall not sell or exchange any of it; they may not alienate this best *part* of the land, for *it is* holy to the LORD.

15 [R]"The five thousand *cubits* in width that remain, along the edge of the twenty-five thousand, shall be for general use by the city, for dwellings and common-land; and the city shall be in the center. Ezek. 45:6

16 "These *shall be* its measurements: the north side four thousand five hundred *cubits,* the south side four thousand five hundred, the east side four thousand five hundred, and the west side four thousand five hundred.

17 "The common-land of the city shall be: to the north two hundred and fifty *cubits,* to the south two hundred and fifty, to the east two hundred and fifty, and to the west two hundred and fifty.

18 "The rest of the length, alongside the district of the holy *section, shall be* ten thousand *cubits* to the east and ten thousand to the west. It shall be adjacent to the district of the holy *section,* and its produce shall be food for the workers of the city.

19 [R]"The workers of the city, from all the tribes of Israel, shall cultivate it. Ezek. 45:6

20 "The entire district *shall be* twenty-five thousand *cubits* by twenty-five thousand *cubits,* foursquare. You shall set apart the holy district with the property of the city.

21 "The rest *shall belong* to the prince, on one side and on the other of the holy district and of the city's property, next to the twenty-five thousand *cubits* of the *holy* district as far as the eastern border, and westward next to the twenty-five thousand as far as the western border, adjacent to the *tribal* portions; *it shall belong* to the prince. It shall be the holy district, and the sanctuary of the [T]temple *shall be* in the center. Lit. *house*

22 "Moreover, apart from the possession of the Levites and the possession of the city *which are* in the midst of what *belongs* to the prince, *the area* between the border of Judah and the border of [R]Benjamin shall belong to the prince. Josh. 18:21–28

23 "As for the rest of the tribes, from the east side to the west, Benjamin *shall have* one *section;*

24 "by the border of Benjamin, from the east side to the west, [R]Simeon *shall have* one *section;* Josh. 19:1–9

25 "by the border of Simeon, from the east side to the west, [R]Issachar *shall have* one *section;* Josh. 19:17–23

26 "by the border of Issachar, from the east side to the west, [R]Zebulun *shall have* one *section;* Josh. 19:10–16

27 "by the border of Zebulun, from the east side to the west, Gad *shall have* one *section;*

28 "by the border of Gad, on the south side, toward the South,* the border shall be from Tamar *to* the waters of Meribah *by* Kadesh, along the brook to the Great Sea.

29 [R]"This *is* the land which you shall divide by lot as an inheritance among the tribes of Israel, and these *are* their portions," says the Lord GOD. Ezek. 47:14, 21, 22

Gates of the City

30 "These *are* the exits of the city. On the north side, measuring four thousand five hundred *cubits*

31 [R]"(the gates of the city *shall be* named after the tribes of Israel), the three gates northward: one gate for Reuben, one gate for Judah, and one gate for Levi; [Rev. 21:10–14]

32 "on the east side, four thousand five hundred *cubits,* three gates: one gate for Joseph, one gate for Benjamin, and one gate for Dan;

33 "on the south side, measuring four thousand five hundred *cubits,* three gates: one gate for Simeon, one gate for Issachar, and one gate for Zebulun;

34 "on the west side, four thousand five hundred *cubits* with their three gates: one gate for Gad, one gate for Asher, and one gate for Naphtali.

Name of the City

35 "All the way around *shall be* eighteen thousand *cubits;* [R]and the name of the city from *that* day *shall be:* [R]THE LORD *IS* THERE."* Jer. 23:6; 33:16 • Joel 3:21

48:28 Heb. *Negev* **48:35** Heb. *YHWH Shammah*

THE BOOK OF

DANIEL

THE BOOK OF DANIEL

Daniel's life and ministry bridge the entire seventy-year period of Babylonian captivity. Deported to Babylon at the age of sixteen, and handpicked for government service, Daniel becomes God's prophetic mouthpiece to the Gentile and Jewish world declaring God's present and eternal purpose. Nine of the twelve chapters in his book revolve around dreams, including God-given visions involving trees, animals, beasts, and images. In both his personal adventures and prophetic visions, Daniel shows God's guidance, intervention, and power in the affairs of men.

The name *Daniye'l* or *Dani'el* means "God Is My Judge"; and the book is, of course, named after the author and principal character. The Greek form *Daniel* in the Septuagint is the basis for the Latin and English titles.

THE AUTHOR OF DANIEL

Daniel and his three friends were evidently born into noble Judean families and were "young men in whom *there was* no blemish, but good-looking, gifted in all wisdom, possessing knowledge and quick to understand" (1:4). He was given three years of training in the best of Babylon's schools (1:5). As part of the reidentification process, he was given a new name that honored one of the Babylonian deities: *Belteshazzar* meant "Bel Protect His Life" (see 1:7; 4:8; Jer. 51:44). Daniel's wisdom and divinely given interpretive abilities brought him into a position of prominence, especially in the courts of Nebuchadnezzar and Darius. He is one of the few well-known Bible characters about whom nothing negative is ever written. His life was characterized by faith, prayer, courage, consistency, and lack of compromise. This "greatly beloved" man (9:23; 10:11, 19) was mentioned three times by his sixth-century B.C. contemporary Ezekiel as an example of righteousness.

Daniel claimed to write this book (12:4), and he used the autobiographical first person from 7:2 onward. The Jewish Talmud agrees with this testimony, and Christ attributed a quote from 9:27 to "Daniel the prophet" (Matt. 24:15).

THE TIME OF DANIEL

Babylon rebelled against the Assyrian Empire in 626 B.C. and overthrew the Assyrian capital of Nineveh in 612 B.C. Babylon became the master of the Middle East when it defeated the Egyptian armies in 605 B.C. Daniel was among those taken captive to Babylon that year when Nebuchadnezzar subdued Jerusalem. He ministered for the full duration of the Babylonian captivity as a prophet and a government official and continued on after Babylon was overcome by the Medes and Persians in 539 B.C. His prophetic ministry was directed to the Gentile courts of Babylon (Nebuchadnezzar and Belshazzar) and Persia (Darius and Cyrus), as well as to his Jewish countrymen. Zerubbabel led a return of the Jews to Jerusalem in the first year of Cyrus, and Daniel lived and ministered at least until the third year of Cyrus (536 B.C., 10:1). Daniel's book was no doubt written by Cyrus's ninth year (c. 530 B.C.). As he predicted, the Persian Empire continued until Alexander the Great (11:2, 3), who extended the boundaries of the Greek Empire as far east as India. The Romans later displaced the Greeks as rulers of the Middle East.

For various reasons, many critics have argued that Daniel is a fraudulent book that was written in the time of the Maccabees in the second century B.C., not the sixth century B.C. as it claims. But their arguments are not compelling:

(1) *The prophetic argument* holds that Daniel could not have made such accurate predictions; it must be a "prophecy after the events." Daniel 11 alone contains over one hundred specific prophecies of historical events that literally came true. The author, the critics say, must have lived at the time of Antiochus Epiphanes (175–163 B.C.) and probably wrote this to strengthen the faith of the Jews. But this argument was developed out of a theological bias that assumes true prophecy cannot take place. It also implies that the work was intentionally deceptive.

(2) *The linguistic argument* claims that the book uses a late Aramaic in 2—7 and that the Persian and Greek words also point to a late date. But recent discoveries show that Daniel's Aramaic is actually a form of the early Imperial Aramaic. Daniel's use of some Persian words is no argument for a late date since he continued living in the Persian period under Cyrus. The only Greek words are names of musical instruments in chapter 3, and this comes as no surprise since there were Greek mercenaries in the Assyrian and Babylonian armies. Far more Greek words would be expected if the book were written in the second century B.C.

(3) *The historical argument* asserts that Daniel's historical blunders argue for a late date. But recent evidence has demonstrated the historical accuracy of Daniel. Inscriptions found at Haran show that Belshazzar reigned in Bab-

ylon while his father Nabonidus was fighting the invading Persians. And Darius the Mede (5:31; 6:1) has been identified as Gubaru, a governor appointed by Cyrus.

THE CHRIST OF DANIEL

Christ is the Great Stone who will crush the kingdoms of this world (2:34, 35, 44), the Son of Man who is given dominion by the Ancient of Days (7:13, 14), and the coming Messiah who will be cut off (9:25, 26). It is likely that Daniel's vision in 10:5–9 was an appearance of Christ (cf. Rev. 1:12–16).

The vision of the sixty-nine weeks in 9:25, 26 pinpoints the coming of the Messiah. The decree of 9:25 took place on March 4, 444 B.C. (Neh. 2:1–8). The sixty-nine weeks of seven years equals 483 years, or 173,880 days (using 360-day prophetic years). This leads to March 29, A.D. 33, the date of the Triumphal Entry. This is checked by noting that 444 B.C. to A.D. 33 is 476 years, and 476 times 365.24219 days per year equals 173,855 days. Adding twenty-five days for the difference between March 4 and March 29 gives 173,880 days.

KEYS TO DANIEL

Key Word: God's Program for Israel—Daniel was written to encourage the exiled Jews by revealing God's sovereign program for Israel during and after the period of Gentile domination. The "Times of the Gentiles" began with the Babylonian captivity, and Israel would suffer under Gentile powers for many years. But this period is not permanent, and a time will come when God will establish the messianic kingdom, which will last forever. Daniel repeatedly emphasizes the sovereignty and power of God over human affairs. "The Most High rules in the kingdom of men, and gives it to whomever He chooses" (4:25). The God who directs the forces of history has not deserted His people. They must continue to trust in Him, because His promises of preservation and ultimate restoration are as sure as the coming of the Messiah.

Key Verses: Daniel 2:20–22 and Daniel 2:44—"Daniel answered and said: 'Blessed be the name of God forever and ever, for wisdom and might are His. And He changes the times and the seasons; He removes kings and raises up kings; He gives wisdom to the wise and knowledge to those who have understanding. He reveals deep and secret things; He knows what *is* in the darkness, and light dwells with Him'" (2:20–22).

"And in the days of these kings the God of heaven will set up a kingdom which shall never be destroyed; and the kingdom shall not be left to other people; it shall break in pieces and consume all these kingdoms, and it shall stand forever" (2:44).

Key Chapter: Daniel 9—Daniel's prophecy of the seventy weeks (9:24–27) provides the chronological frame for messianic prediction from the time of Daniel to the establishment of the kingdom on earth. It is clear that the first sixty-nine weeks were fulfilled at Christ's first coming. Some scholars affirm that the last week has not yet been fulfilled because Christ relates its main events to His second coming (Matt. 24:6, 15). Others perceive these words of Christ as applying to the Roman desecration of the temple in A.D. 70.

SURVEY OF DANIEL

Daniel, the "Apocalypse of the Old Testament," presents a surprisingly detailed and comprehensive sweep of prophetic history. After an introductory chapter in Hebrew, Daniel switches to Aramaic in chapters 2—7 to describe the future course of the Gentile

FOCUS	HISTORY OF DANIEL	PROPHETIC PLAN FOR THE GENTILES				PROPHETIC PLAN OF ISRAEL		
REFERENCE	1:1—	2:1—	5:1—	6:1—	7:1—	8:1—	9:1—	10:1—12:13
DIVISION	PERSONAL LIFE OF DANIEL	VISIONS OF NEBUCHADNEZZAR	VISIONS OF BELSHAZZAR	DECREE OF DARIUS	FOUR BEASTS	VISION OF RAM AND HE-GOAT	VISION OF SEVENTY WEEKS	VISION OF ISRAEL'S FUTURE
TOPIC	DANIEL'S BACKGROUND	DANIEL INTERPRETS OTHERS' DREAMS				ANGEL INTERPRETS DANIEL'S DREAMS		
	HEBREW	ARAMAIC				HEBREW		
LOCATION	BABYLON OR PERSIA							
TIME	c. 605–536 B.C.							

world powers. Then in 8—12, Daniel reverts back to his native language to survey the future of the Jewish nation under Gentile dominion. The theme of God's sovereign control in the affairs of world history clearly emerges and provides comfort to the future church, as well as to the Jews whose nation was destroyed by the Babylonians. The Babylonians, Persians, Greeks, and Romans will come and go, but God will establish His kingdom through His redeemed people forever. Daniel's three divisions are: the personal history of Daniel (1), the prophetic plan for the Gentiles (2—7), and the prophetic plan for Israel (8—12).

The Personal History of Daniel (1): This chapter introduces the book by giving the background and preparation of the prophet. Daniel is deported along with other promising youths and placed in an intensive training program in Nebuchadnezzar's court. Their names and diets are changed so that they will lose their Jewish identification, but Daniel's resolve to remain faithful to the Lord is rewarded. He and his friends are granted wisdom and knowledge.

The Prophetic Plan for the Gentiles (2—7): Only Daniel can relate and interpret Nebuchadnezzar's disturbing dream of the great statue (2). God empowers Daniel to foretell the way in which He will sovereignly raise and depose four Gentile empires. The Messiah's kingdom will end the times of the Gentiles. Because of his position revealed in the dream, Nebuchadnezzar erects a golden image and demands that all bow to it (3). The persecution and preservation of Daniel's friends in the fiery furnace again illustrate the power of God. After Nebuchadnezzar refuses to respond to the warning of his vision of the tree (4), he is humbled until he acknowledges the supremacy of God and the foolishness of his pride. The feast of Belshazzar marks the end of the Babylonian kingdom (5). Belshazzar is judged because of his arrogant defiance of God. In the reign of Darius, a plot against Daniel backfires when he is divinely delivered in the den of lions (6). Daniel's courageous faith is rewarded, and Darius learns a lesson about the might of the God of Israel. The vision of the four beasts (7) supplements the four-part statue vision of chapter 2 in its portrayal of the Babylonian, Persian, Greek, and Roman empires. But once again, "the saints of the Most High shall receive the kingdom, and possess the kingdom forever" (7:18).

The Prophetic Plan for Israel (8—12): The focus in chapter 8 narrows to a vision of the ram and goat that shows Israel under the Medo-Persian and Grecian empires. Alexander the Great is the large horn of 8:21 and Antiochus Epiphanes is the little horn of 8:9. After Daniel's prayer of confession for his people, he is privileged to receive the revelation of the seventy weeks, including the Messiah's atoning death (9). This gives the chronology of God's perfect plan for the redemption and deliverance of His people. Following is a great vision that gives amazing details of Israel's future history (10 and 11). Chapter 11 chronicles the coming kings of Persia and Greece, the wars between the Ptolemies of Egypt and the Seleucids of Syria, and the persecution led by Antiochus. God's people will be saved out of tribulation and resurrected (12).

OUTLINE OF DANIEL

Part One: The Personal History of Daniel (1:1–21)

I. The Deportation of Daniel to Babylon...1:1–7

II. The Faithfulness of Daniel in Babylon 1:8–16

III. The Reputation of Daniel in Babylon.........1:17–21

Part Two: The Prophetic Plan for the Gentiles (2:1—7:28)

I. Nebuchadnezzar's Dream of the Great Image.........2:1–49

A. Nebuchadnezzar Conceals His Dream ..2:1–13
B. God Reveals the Dream 2:14–23
C. Daniel Interprets the Dream.........2:24–45
D. Nebuchadnezzar Promotes Daniel 2:46–49

II. Nebuchadnezzar's Image of Gold.........3:1–30

A. Nebuchadnezzar's Image Is Erected 3:1–7
B. Daniel's Friends Refuse to Worship 3:8–12
C. Daniel's Friends Trust God.........3:13–18
D. Daniel's Friends Are Protected in the Furnace 3:19–25
E. Daniel's Friends Are Promoted.........3:26–30

III. Nebuchadnezzar's Vision of a Great Tree.........4:1–37

A. Nebuchadnezzar's Proclamation.........4:1–3
B. Nebuchadnezzar's Vision.........4:4–18
C. Daniel's Interpretation of the Vision...4:19–27
D. Nebuchadnezzar's Humiliation.........4:28–33
E. Nebuchadnezzar's Restoration 4:34–37

IV. Belshazzar and the Handwriting on the Wall 5:1–31

A. Belshazzar Defiles the Temple Vessels ...5:1–4

Part Three: The Prophetic Plan for Israel (8:1—12:13)

CHAPTER 1

The Deportation of Daniel to Babylon

IN the third year of the reign of Jehoiakim
king of Judah, Nebuchadnezzar king of
Babylon came to Jerusalem and besieged it.
2 And the Lord gave Jehoiakim king of Ju-
dah into his hand, with [R]some of the articles
of the house of God, which he carried into the
land of Shinar to the house of his god; and he
brought the articles into the treasure house of
his god. Jer. 27:19, 20
3 Then the king instructed Ashpenaz, the
master of his eunuchs, to bring [R]some of the
children of Israel and some of the king's de-
scendants and some of the nobles, Is. 39:7
4 young men [R]in whom *there was* no
blemish, but good-looking, gifted in all wis-
dom, possessing knowledge and quick to
understand, who *had* ability to serve in the
king's palace, and [R]whom they might teach
the language and literature of the Chal-
deans. Lev. 24:19, 20 • Acts 7:22
5 And the king appointed for them a daily
provision of the king's delicacies and of the
wine which he drank, and three years of train-
ing for them, so that at the end of *that time*
they might serve before the king.
6 Now from among those of the sons of Ju-
dah were Daniel, Hananiah, Mishael, and
Azariah.
7 To them the chief of the eunuchs gave
names: he gave Daniel *the name* Belteshaz-
zar; to Hananiah, Shadrach; to Mishael, Me-
shach; and to Azariah, Abed-Nego.

The Faithfulness of Daniel in Babylon

8 But Daniel purposed in his heart that he
would not defile himself [R]with the portion of
the king's delicacies, nor with the wine which
he drank; therefore he requested of the chief
of the eunuchs that he might not defile him-
self. Hos. 9:3
9 Now [R]God had brought Daniel into the
favor and [T]goodwill of the chief of the eu-
nuchs. Gen. 39:21 • *kindness*
10 And the chief of the eunuchs said to Dan-
iel, "I fear my lord the king, who has ap-
pointed your food and drink. For why should
he see your faces looking worse than the

young men who *are* your age? Then you
would endanger my head before the king."
11 So Daniel said to the steward* whom the
chief of the eunuchs had set over Daniel,
Hananiah, Mishael, and Azariah,
12 "Please test your servants for ten days,
and let them give us vegetables to eat and
water to drink.
13 "Then let our appearance be examined
before you, and the appearance of the young
men who eat the portion of the king's delica-
cies; and as you see fit, *so* deal with your ser-
vants."
14 So he consented with them in this matter,
and tested them ten days.
15 And at the end of ten days their features
appeared better and fatter in flesh than all the
young men who ate the portion of the king's
delicacies.
16 Thus the steward took away their portion
of delicacies and the wine that they were to
drink, and gave them vegetables.

The Reputation of Daniel in Babylon

17 As for these four young men, God gave
them [R]knowledge and skill in all literature
and wisdom; and Daniel had understanding
in all visions and dreams. Acts 7:22
18 Now at the end of the days, when the king
had said that they should be brought in, the
chief of the eunuchs brought them in before
Nebuchadnezzar.
19 Then the king interviewed* them, and
among them all none was found like Daniel,
Hananiah, Mishael, and Azariah; therefore
[R]they served before the king. Gen. 41:46
20 [R]And in all matters of wisdom *and* under-
standing about which the king examined
them, he found them ten times better than all
the magicians *and* astrologers who *were* in all
his realm. 1 Kin. 10:1
21 [R]Thus Daniel continued until the first
year of King Cyrus. Dan. 6:28; 10:1

CHAPTER 2

Nebuchadnezzar Conceals His Dream

NOW in the second year of Nebuchad-
nezzar's reign, Nebuchadnezzar had
dreams; [R]and his spirit was *so* troubled that
his sleep left him. Gen. 40:5–8; 41:1, 8
2 [R]Then the king gave the command to call
the magicians, the astrologers, the sorcerers,
and the Chaldeans to tell the king his
dreams. So they came and stood before the
king. Ex. 7:11
3 And the king said to them, "I have had a
dream, and my spirit is anxious to [T]know the
dream." Or *understand*
4 Then the Chaldeans spoke to the king in
Aramaic,* [R]"O king, live forever! Tell your ser-
vants the dream, and we will give the inter-
pretation." Dan. 3:9; 5:10; 6:6, 21
5 The king answered and said to the
Chaldeans, "My decision is firm: if you do not
make known the dream to me, and its inter-
pretation, you shall be cut in pieces, and your
houses shall be made an ash heap.
6 "However, if you tell the dream and its in-
terpretation, you shall receive from me gifts,
rewards, and great honor. Therefore tell me
the dream and its interpretation."
7 They answered again and said, "Let the
king tell his servants the dream, and we will
give its interpretation."
8 The king answered and said, "I know for
certain that you would gain time, because you
see that my decision is firm:
9 "if you do not make known the dream to
me, *there is only* one decree for you! For you
have agreed to speak lying and corrupt
words before me till the [T]time has changed.
Therefore tell me the dream, and I shall
know that you can [T]give me its interpreta-
tion." Situation • Or *declare to me*
10 The Chaldeans answered the king, and
said, "There is not a man on earth who can tell
the king's matter; therefore no king, lord, or
ruler has *ever* asked such things of any magi-
cian, astrologer, or Chaldean.
11 "*It is* a [T]difficult thing that the king re-
quests, and there is no other who can tell it to
the king [R]except the gods, whose dwelling is
not with flesh." Or *rare* • Dan. 5:11
12 For this reason the king was angry and
very furious, and gave the command to de-
stroy all the wise *men* of Babylon.
13 So the decree went out, and they began
killing the wise *men;* and they sought Daniel
and his companions, to kill *them.*

God Reveals the Dream

14 Then with counsel and wisdom Daniel
answered Arioch, the captain of the king's
guard, who had gone out to kill the wise *men*
of Babylon;
15 he answered and said to Arioch the king's
captain, "Why is the decree from the king so
[T]urgent?" Then Arioch made the decision
known to Daniel. Or *harsh*
16 So Daniel went in and asked the king to
give him time, that he might tell the king the
interpretation.
17 Then Daniel went to his house, and made
the decision known to Hananiah, Mishael,
and Azariah, his companions,
18 [R]that they might seek mercies from the
God of heaven concerning this secret, so
that Daniel and his companions might not
perish with the rest of the wise *men* of
Babylon. [Matt. 18:19]
19 Then the secret was revealed to Daniel

1:11 Or *Melzar,* also in v. 16 **1:19** Lit. *talked with them* **2:4** The original language of Dan. 2:4b through 7:28 is Aramaic.

[R]in a night vision. So Daniel blessed the God
of heaven. Job 33:15
20 Daniel answered and said:

[R]"Blessed be the name of God forever and
ever, Ps. 113:2
For wisdom and might are His.
21 And He changes [R]the times and the
seasons; Esth. 1:13
[R]He removes kings and raises up kings;
[R]He gives wisdom to the wise
And knowledge to those who have
understanding. [Ps. 75:6, 7] • [James 1:5]
22 He reveals deep and secret things;
[R]He knows what *is* in the darkness,
And light dwells with Him. [Heb. 4:13]

23 "I thank You and praise You,
O God of my fathers;
You have given me wisdom and might,
And have now made known to me what
we [R]asked of You, Dan. 2:18, 29, 30
For You have made known to us the
king's [T]demand." Lit. *word*

Daniel Interprets the Dream

24 Therefore Daniel went to Arioch, whom
the king had appointed to destroy the wise
men of Babylon. He went and said thus to
him: "Do not destroy the wise *men* of Bab-
ylon; take me before the king, and I will tell
the king the interpretation."
25 Then Arioch quickly brought Daniel be-
fore the king, and said thus to him, "I have
found a man of the captives* of Judah, who
will make known to the king the interpreta-
tion."
26 The king answered and said to Daniel,
whose name *was* Belteshazzar, "Are you able
to make known to me the dream which I have
seen, and its interpretation?"
27 Daniel answered in the presence of the
king, and said, "The secret which the king has
demanded, the wise *men*, the astrologers, the
magicians, and the soothsayers cannot de-
clare to the king.
28 "But there is a God in heaven who reveals
secrets, and He has made known to King Neb-
uchadnezzar what will be in the latter days.
Your dream, and the visions of your head
upon your bed, were these:
29 "As for you, O king, thoughts came *to*
your *mind while* on your bed, *about* what
would come to pass after this; [R]and He who
reveals secrets has made known to you what
will be. [Dan. 2:22, 28]
30 [R]"But as for me, this secret has not been
revealed to me because I have more wisdom
than anyone living, but for *our* sakes who
make known the interpretation to the king,
[R]and that you may [T]know the thoughts of your
heart. Acts 3:12 • Dan. 2:47 • Understand
31 "You, O king, were watching; and behold,
a great image! This great image, whose splen-
dor *was* excellent, stood before you; and its
form *was* awesome.
32 [R]"This image's head *was* of fine gold, its
chest and arms of silver, its belly and thighs*
of bronze, Dan. 2:38, 45
33 "its legs of iron, its feet partly of iron and
partly of clay.*
34 "You watched while a stone was cut out
[R]without hands, which struck the image on its
feet of iron and clay, and broke them in
pieces. [Zech. 4:6]
35 "Then the iron, the clay, the bronze, the
silver, and the gold were crushed together,
and became like chaff from the summer
threshing floors; the wind carried them away
so that no trace of them was found. And the
stone that struck the image became a great
mountain and filled the whole earth.
36 "This *is* the dream. Now we will tell the
interpretation of it before the king.
37 [R]"You, O king, *are* a king of kings. For the
God of heaven has given you a kingdom,
power, strength, and glory; Jer. 27:6, 7
38 [R]"and wherever the children of men
dwell, or the beasts of the field and the birds
of the heaven, He has given *them* into your
hand, and has made you ruler over them all—
you *are* this head of gold. Dan. 4:21, 22
39 "But after you shall arise [R]another king-
dom [R]inferior to yours; then another, a third
kingdom of bronze, which shall rule over all
the earth. Dan. 5:28, 31 • Dan. 2:32
40 "And [R]the fourth kingdom shall be as
strong as iron, inasmuch as iron breaks in
pieces and shatters everything; and like iron
that crushes, *that kingdom* will break in
pieces and crush all the others. Dan. 7:7, 23
41 "Whereas you saw the feet and toes,
partly of potter's clay and partly of iron, the
kingdom shall be divided; yet the strength of
the iron shall be in it, just as you saw the iron
mixed with ceramic clay.
42 "And *as* the toes of the feet *were* partly of
iron and partly of clay, *so* the kingdom shall
be partly strong and partly fragile.
43 "As you saw iron mixed with ceramic
clay, they will mingle with the seed of men;
but they will not adhere to one another, just as
iron does not mix with clay.
44 "And in the days of these kings the God of
heaven will [R]set up a kingdom which shall
never be destroyed; and the kingdom shall not
be left to other people; it shall break in pieces
and consume all these kingdoms, and it shall
stand forever. Is. 9:7☆
45 "Inasmuch as you saw that the stone was
cut out of the mountain without hands, and
that it broke in pieces the iron, the bronze, the
clay, the silver, and the gold—the great God

2:25 Lit. *of the sons of the captivity* **2:32** Or *sides*
2:33 Or *baked clay*, also vv. 34, 35, 42

has made known to the king what will come to pass after this. The dream is certain, and its interpretation is sure."

Nebuchadnezzar Promotes Daniel

46 [R]Then King Nebuchadnezzar fell on his face, prostrate before Daniel, and commanded that they should present an offering and incense to him. Acts 10:25; 14:13

47 The king answered Daniel, and said, "Truly your God *is* the God of gods, the Lord of kings, and a revealer of secrets, since you could reveal this secret."

48 [R]Then the king promoted Daniel [R]and gave him many great gifts; and he made him ruler over the whole province of Babylon, and chief administrator over all the wise *men* of Babylon. [Prov. 14:35; 21:1] • Dan. 2:6

49 Also Daniel petitioned the king, and he set Shadrach, Meshach, and Abed-Nego over the affairs of the province of Babylon; but Daniel *sat* in the gate* of the king.

CHAPTER 3

Nebuchadnezzar's Image Is Erected

NEBUCHADNEZZAR the king made an image of gold, whose height *was* [T]sixty cubits *and* its width six cubits. He set it up in the plain of Dura, in the province of Babylon. About 90 feet

2 And King Nebuchadnezzar sent *word* to gather together the satraps, the administrators, the governors, the counselors, the treasurers, the judges, the magistrates, and all the officials of the provinces, to come to the dedication of the image which King Nebuchadnezzar had set up.

3 So the satraps, the administrators, the governors, the counselors, the treasurers, the judges, the magistrates, and all the officials of the provinces gathered together for the dedication of the image that King Nebuchadnezzar had set up; and they stood before the image that Nebuchadnezzar had set up.

4 Then a herald cried [T]aloud: "To you it is commanded, [R]O peoples, nations, and languages, Lit. *with strength* • Dan. 4:1; 6:25

5 "*that* at the time you hear the sound of the horn, flute, harp, lyre, *and* psaltery, in symphony with all kinds of music, you shall fall down and worship the gold image that King Nebuchadnezzar has set up;

6 "and whoever does not fall down and worship shall [R]be cast immediately into the midst of a burning fiery furnace." Jer. 29:22

7 So at that time, when all the people heard the sound of the horn, flute, harp, *and* lyre, in symphony with all kinds of music, all the people, nations, and languages fell down *and* worshiped the gold image which King Nebuchadnezzar had set up.

Daniel's Friends Refuse to Worship

8 Therefore at that time certain Chaldeans came forward and accused the Jews.

9 They spoke and said to King Nebuchadnezzar, [R]"O king, live forever! Dan. 2:4; 5:10

10 "You, O king, have made a decree that everyone who hears the sound of the horn, flute, harp, lyre, *and* psaltery, in symphony with all kinds of music, shall fall down and worship the gold image;

11 "and whoever does not fall down and worship shall be cast into the midst of a burning fiery furnace.

12 [R]"There are certain Jews whom you have set over the affairs of the province of Babylon: Shadrach, Meshach, and Abed-Nego; these men, O king, have [R]not paid due regard to you. They do not serve your gods or worship the gold image which you have set up." Dan. 2:49 • Dan. 1:8; 6:12, 13

Daniel's Friends Trust God

13 Then Nebuchadnezzar, in [R]rage and fury, gave the command to bring Shadrach, Meshach, and Abed-Nego. So they brought these men before the king. Dan. 2:12; 3:19

14 Nebuchadnezzar spoke, saying to them, "*Is it* true, Shadrach, Meshach, and Abed-Nego, *that* you do not serve my gods or worship the gold image which I have set up?

15 "Now if you are ready at the time you hear the sound of the horn, flute, harp, lyre, *and* psaltery, in symphony with all kinds of music, and you fall down and worship the image which I have made, [R]*good!* But if you do not worship, you shall be cast immediately into the midst of a burning fiery furnace. [R]And who *is* the god who will deliver you from my hands?" Luke 13:9 • Ex. 5:2

16 Shadrach, Meshach, and Abed-Nego answered and said to the king, "O Nebuchadnezzar, [R]we have no need to answer you in this matter. [Matt. 10:19]

17 "If that *is the case,* our [R]God whom we serve is able to [R]deliver us from the burning fiery furnace, and He will deliver *us* from your hand, O king. [Is. 26:3, 4] • 1 Sam. 17:37

18 "But if not, let it be known to you, O king, that we do not serve your gods, nor will we [R]worship the gold image which you have set up." Job 13:15

Daniel's Friends Are Protected in the Furnace

19 Then Nebuchadnezzar was full of fury, and the expression on his face changed toward Shadrach, Meshach, and Abed-Nego. He spoke and commanded that they heat the furnace seven times more than it was usually heated.

20 And he commanded certain mighty men of valor who *were* in his army to bind

2:49 The king's court

Shadrach, Meshach, and Abed-Nego, *and* cast
them into the burning fiery furnace.
21 Then these men were bound in their
coats, their trousers, their turbans, and their
other garments, and were cast into the midst
of the burning fiery furnace.
22 Therefore, because the king's command
was [T]urgent, and the furnace exceedingly hot,
the flame of the fire killed those men who took
up Shadrach, Meshach, and Abed-Nego. Or *harsh*
23 And these three men, Shadrach, Me-
shach, and Abed-Nego, fell down bound into
the midst of the burning fiery furnace.
24 Then King Nebuchadnezzar was aston-
ished; and he rose in haste *and* spoke, saying
to his [T]counselors, "Did we not cast three
men bound into the midst of the fire?" They
answered and said to the king, "True, O
king." High officials
25 "Look!" he answered, "I see four men
loose, [R]walking in the midst of the fire; and
they are not hurt, and the form of the fourth is
like [R]the Son of God."* Is. 43:2 • [Ps. 34:7]

Daniel's Friends Are Promoted

26 Then Nebuchadnezzar went near the
[T]mouth of the burning fiery furnace *and*
spoke, saying, "Shadrach, Meshach, and
Abed-Nego, servants of the [R]Most High God,
come out, and come *here.*" Then Shadrach,
Meshach, and Abed-Nego came from the
midst of the fire. Lit. *door* • [Dan. 4:2, 3, 17, 34, 35]
27 And the satraps, administrators, gover-
nors, and the king's counselors gathered to-
gether, and they saw these men [R]on whose
bodies the fire had no power; the hair of their
head was not singed nor were their garments
affected, and the smell of fire was not on
them. Heb. 11:34
28 Nebuchadnezzar spoke, saying, "Blessed
be the God of Shadrach, Meshach, and Abed-
Nego, who sent His [R]Angel* and delivered His
servants who trusted in Him, and they have
frustrated the king's word, and yielded their
bodies, that they should not serve nor worship
any god except their own God! [Ps. 34:7, 8]
29 "Therefore I make a decree that any peo-
ple, nation, or language which speaks anything
amiss against the God of Shadrach, Meshach,
and Abed-Nego shall be cut in pieces, and their
houses shall be made an ash heap; because
there is no other God who can deliver like this."
30 Then the king [T]promoted Shadrach, Me-
shach, and Abed-Nego in the province of
Babylon. Lit. *caused to prosper*

CHAPTER 4

Nebuchadnezzar's Proclamation

NEBUCHADNEZZAR the king,

[R]To all peoples, nations, and languages
that dwell in all the earth: Dan. 3:4; 6:25

Peace be multiplied to you.
2 I thought it good to declare the signs and
wonders [R]that the Most High God has
worked for me. Dan. 3:26

3 [R]How great *are* His signs, 2 Sam. 7:16
And how mighty His wonders!
His kingdom *is* [R]an everlasting kingdom,
And His dominion *is* from generation to
generation. [Dan. 2:44; 4:34; 6:26]

Nebuchadnezzar's Vision

4 I, Nebuchadnezzar, was at rest in my
house, and flourishing in my palace.
5 I saw a dream which made me afraid,
and the thoughts on my bed and the
visions of my head troubled me.
6 Therefore I issued a decree to bring in
all the wise *men* of Babylon before me,
that they might make known to me the
interpretation of the dream.
7 [R]Then the magicians, the astrologers, the
Chaldeans, and the soothsayers came in,
and I told them the dream; but they did
not make known to me its
interpretation. Dan. 2:2
8 But at last Daniel came before me [R](his
name *is* Belteshazzar, according to the
name of my god; in him *is* the Spirit of
the Holy God), and I told the dream
before him, *saying:* Dan. 1:7
9 "Belteshazzar, [R]chief of the magicians,
because I know that the Spirit of the
Holy God *is* in you, and no secret
troubles you, explain to me the visions of
my dream that I have seen, and its
interpretation. Dan. 2:48; 5:11
10 "These *were* the visions of my head
while on my bed:

I was looking, and behold,
[R]A tree in the midst of the earth,
And its height was great. Ezek. 31:3
11 The tree grew and became strong;
Its height reached to the heavens,
And it could be seen to the ends of all
the earth.
12 Its leaves *were* lovely,
Its fruit abundant,
And in it *was* food for all.
[R]The beasts of the field found shade
under it, Lam. 4:20
The birds of the heavens dwelt in its
branches,
And all flesh was fed from it.

13 "I saw in the visions of my head *while* on
my bed, and there was a watcher, a holy
one, coming down from heaven.
14 He cried aloud and said thus:

3:25 Or *a son of the gods* **3:28** Or *angel*

[R]'Chop down the tree and cut off its
branches, Ezek. 31:10–14
Strip off its leaves and scatter its fruit.
Let the beasts get out from under it,
And the birds from its branches.
15 Nevertheless leave the stump and roots
in the earth,
Bound with a band of iron and bronze,
In the tender grass of the field.
Let it be wet with the dew of heaven,
And *let* him graze with the beasts
On the grass of the earth.
16 Let his heart be changed from *that of* a
man,
Let him be given the heart of a beast,
And let seven times* pass over him.

17 'This decision *is* by the decree of the
watchers,
And the sentence by the word of the holy
ones,
In order that the living may know
[R]That the Most High rules in the
kingdom of men, Dan. 2:21; 4:25, 32; 5:21
[R]Gives it to whomever He will, Jer. 27:5–7
And sets over it the lowest of men.'

18 "This dream I, King Nebuchadnezzar,
have seen. Now you, Belteshazzar,
declare its interpretation, [R]since all the
wise *men* of my kingdom are not able to
make known to me the interpretation;
but you *are* able, for the Spirit of the
Holy God *is* in you." Gen. 41:8, 15

Daniel's Interpretation of the Vision

19 Then Daniel, whose name was
Belteshazzar, was astonished for a time,
and his thoughts troubled him. *So* the
king spoke, and said, "Belteshazzar, do
not let the dream or its interpretation
trouble you." Belteshazzar answered and
said, "My lord, *may* the dream concern
those who hate you, and its
interpretation concern your enemies!
20 [R]The tree that you saw, which grew and
became strong, whose height reached to
the heavens and which *could be seen* by
all the earth, Dan. 4:10–12
21 whose leaves *were* lovely and its fruit
abundant, in which *was* food for all,
under which the beasts of the field dwelt,
and in whose branches the birds of the
heaven had their home—
22 it *is* you, O king, who have grown and
become strong; for your greatness has
grown and reaches to the heavens, and
your dominion to the end of the earth.
23 [R]And inasmuch as the king saw a
watcher, a holy one, coming down from
heaven and saying, 'Chop down the tree
and destroy it, but leave its stump and
roots in the earth, *bound* with a band of
iron and bronze in the tender grass of
the field; let it be wet with the dew of
heaven, [R]and let him graze with the
beasts of the field, till seven times pass
over him'; Dan. 4:13–15 • Dan. 5:21
24 this is the interpretation, O king, and this
is the decree of the Most High, which
has come upon my lord the king:
25 They shall drive you from men, your
dwelling shall be with the beasts of the
field, and they shall make you eat grass
like oxen. They shall wet you with the
dew of heaven, and seven times shall
pass over you, till you know that the
Most High rules in the kingdom of men,
and gives it to whomever He chooses.
26 And inasmuch as they gave the
command to leave the stump *and* roots
of the tree, your kingdom shall be
assured to you, after you come to know
that [R]Heaven[T] rules. Matt. 21:25 • God
27 Therefore, O king, let my advice be
acceptable to you; [R]break off your sins
by *being* righteous, and your iniquities
by showing mercy to *the* poor. [R]Perhaps
there may be a lengthening of your
prosperity." [1 Pet. 4:8] • [Ps. 41:1–3]

Nebuchadnezzar's Humiliation

28 All *this* came upon King
Nebuchadnezzar.
29 At the end of the twelve months he was
walking [T]about the royal palace of
Babylon. Or *upon*
30 The king spoke, saying, "Is not this great
Babylon, that I have built for a royal
dwelling by my mighty power and for
the honor of my majesty?"
31 While the word *was still* in the king's
mouth, a voice fell from heaven: "King
Nebuchadnezzar, to you it is spoken: the
kingdom has departed from you!
32 And they shall drive you from men, and
your dwelling *shall be* with the beasts of
the field. They shall make you eat grass
like oxen; and seven times shall pass
over you, until you know that the Most
High rules in the kingdom of men, and
gives it to whomever He chooses."
33 That very hour the word was fulfilled
concerning Nebuchadnezzar; he was
driven from men and ate grass like oxen;
his body was wet with the dew of heaven
till his hair had grown like eagles'
feathers and his nails like birds' *claws*.

Nebuchadnezzar's Restoration

34 And at the end of the time* I,
Nebuchadnezzar, lifted my eyes to heaven,
and my understanding returned to me;

4:16 Possibly *seven years*, and so in vv. 23, 25, and 32
4:34 Lit. *days*

and I blessed the Most High and praised
and honored Him [R]who lives forever:

For His dominion *is* [R]an everlasting
dominion,
And His kingdom *is* from generation to
generation. [Rev. 4:10] • [Luke 1:33]

35 [R]All the inhabitants of the earth *are*
reputed as nothing; Is. 40:15, 17
[R]He does according to His will in the
army of heaven Ps. 115:3; 135:6
And *among* the inhabitants of the earth.
[R]No one can restrain His hand Job 34:29
Or say to Him, "What have You done?"

36 At the same time my reason returned to
me, and for the glory of my kingdom, my
honor and splendor returned to me. My
counselors and nobles resorted to me,
I was restored to my kingdom, and
excellent majesty was added to me.

37 Now I, Nebuchadnezzar, praise and extol
and honor the King of heaven, [R]all of
whose works *are* truth, and His ways
justice. [R]And those who walk in pride He
is able to put down. [Ps. 33:4] • Ex. 18:11

CHAPTER 5

Belshazzar Defiles the Temple Vessels

BELSHAZZAR the king made a great feast for a thousand of his lords, and drank wine in the presence of the thousand.

2 While he tasted the wine, Belshazzar gave the command to bring the gold and silver vessels [R]which his [T]father Nebuchadnezzar had taken from the temple which *had been* in Jerusalem, that the king and his lords, his wives, and his concubines might drink from them. Dan. 1:2 • Or *ancestor*

3 Then they brought the gold [R]vessels that had been taken from the temple of the house of God which *had been* in Jerusalem; and the king and his lords, his wives, and his concubines drank from them. 2 Chr. 36:10

4 They drank wine, [R]and praised the gods of gold and silver, bronze and iron, wood and stone. Rev. 9:20

Belshazzar Sees the Handwriting

5 [R]In the same hour the fingers of a man's hand appeared and wrote opposite the lampstand on the plaster of the wall of the king's palace; and the king saw the part of the hand that wrote. Dan. 4:31

6 Then the king's countenance changed, and his thoughts troubled him, so that the joints of his hips were loosened and his knees knocked against each other.

7 The king cried aloud to bring in [R]the astrologers, the Chaldeans, and the soothsayers. The king spoke, saying to the wise *men* of Babylon, "Whoever reads this writing, and tells me its interpretation, shall be clothed with purple and *have* a chain of gold around his neck; [R]and he shall be the third ruler in the kingdom." Is. 47:13 • Dan. 6:2, 3

8 Now all the king's wise *men* came, but they could not read the writing, or make known to the king its interpretation.

9 Then King Belshazzar was greatly [R]troubled, his countenance was changed, and his lords were astonished. Dan. 2:1; 5:6

Daniel Interprets the Handwriting

10 The queen, because of the words of the king and his lords, came to the banquet hall. The queen spoke, saying, "O king, live forever! Do not let your thoughts trouble you, nor let your countenance change.

11 "There is a man in your kingdom in whom *is* the Spirit of the Holy God. And in the days of your father, light and understanding and wisdom, like the wisdom of the gods, were found in him; and King Nebuchadnezzar your father—your father the king—made him chief of the magicians, astrologers, Chaldeans, *and* soothsayers.

12 "Inasmuch as an excellent spirit, knowledge, understanding, interpreting dreams, solving riddles, and explaining enigmas* were found in this Daniel, whom the king named Belteshazzar, now let Daniel be called, and he will give the interpretation."

13 Then Daniel was brought in before the king. The king spoke, and said to Daniel, "*Are* you that Daniel who is one of the captives* from Judah, whom my [T]father the king brought from Judah? Or *ancestor*

14 "I have heard of you, that [R]the [T]Spirit of God *is* in you, and *that* light and understanding and excellent wisdom are found in you. Dan. 4:8, 9, 18; 5:11, 12 • Or *spirit of the gods*

15 "Now [R]the wise *men,* the astrologers, have been brought in before me, that they should read this writing and make known to me its interpretation, but they could not give the interpretation of the thing. Dan. 5:7, 8

16 "And I have heard of you, that you can give interpretations and explain enigmas. [R]Now if you can read the writing and make known to me its interpretation, you shall be clothed with purple and *have* a chain of gold around your neck, and shall be the third ruler in the kingdom." Dan. 5:7, 29

17 Then Daniel answered, and said before the king, "Let your gifts be for yourself, and give your rewards to another; yet I will read the writing to the king, and make known to him the interpretation.

18 "O king, [R]the Most High God gave Nebuchadnezzar your father a kingdom and majesty, glory and honor. Dan. 2:37, 38

5:12 Lit. *untying knots,* and so in v. 16 **5:13** Lit. *of the sons of the captivity*

19 "And because of the majesty that He gave
him, all peoples, nations, and languages trem-
bled and feared before him. Whomever he
wished, he executed; whomever he wished, he
kept alive; whomever he wished, he set up;
and whomever he wished, he put down.
20 [R]"But when his heart was lifted up, and
his spirit was hardened in pride, he was de-
posed from his kingly throne, and they took
his glory from him. Dan. 4:30, 37
21 "Then he was driven from the sons of
men, his heart was made like the beasts, and
his dwelling *was* with the wild donkeys. They
fed him with grass like oxen, and his body
was wet with the dew of heaven, [R]till he [T]knew
that the Most High God rules in the kingdom
of men, and appoints over it whomever He
chooses. Ezek. 17:24 • Recognized
22 "But you his son, Belshazzar, [R]have not
humbled your heart, although you knew all
this. 2 Chr. 33:23; 36:12
23 "And you have lifted yourself up against
the Lord of heaven. They have brought the
[R]vessels of His house before you, and you and
your lords, your wives and your concubines,
have drunk wine from them. And you have
praised the gods of silver and gold, bronze and
iron, wood and stone, [R]which do not see or hear
or know; and the God who *holds* your breath in
His hand [R]and owns all your ways, you have
not glorified. Ex. 40:9 • Ps. 115:5, 6 • [Jer. 10:23]
24 "Then the fingers* of the hand were sent
from Him, and this writing was written.
25 "And this is the inscription that was writ-
ten:

MENE,* MENE, TEKEL,* UPHARSIN.*

26 "This *is* the interpretation of *each* word.
MENE: God has numbered your kingdom, and
finished it;
27 "TEKEL: [R]You have been weighed in the
balances, and found wanting; Ps. 62:9
28 "PERES: Your kingdom has been divided,
and given to the Medes and Persians."*
29 Then Belshazzar gave the command, and
they clothed Daniel with purple and *put* a
chain of gold around his neck, and made a
proclamation concerning him that he should
be the third ruler in the kingdom.

Belshazzar Is Killed

30 [R]That very night Belshazzar, king of the
Chaldeans, was slain. Jer. 51:31, 39, 57
31 And Darius the Mede received the king-
dom, *being* about sixty-two years old.

CHAPTER 6

Daniel Is Promoted

IT pleased Darius to set over the kingdom
one hundred and twenty satraps, to be over
the whole kingdom;
2 and over these, three governors, of whom
Daniel *was* one, that the satraps might give
account to them, so that the king would suffer
no loss.
3 Then this Daniel distinguished himself
above the governors and satraps, [R]because
an excellent spirit *was* in him; and the king
gave thought to setting him over the whole
realm. Dan. 5:12

Darius Signs the Foolish Decree

4 So the governors and satraps sought to
find *some* charge against Daniel concerning
the kingdom; but they could find no charge or
fault, because he *was* faithful; nor was there
any error or fault found in him.
5 Then these men said, "We shall not find
any charge against this Daniel unless we find
it against him concerning the law of his God."
6 So these governors and satraps thronged
before the king, and said thus to him: [R]"King
Darius, live forever! Neh. 2:3
7 "All the governors of the kingdom, the ad-
ministrators and satraps, the counselors and
advisors, have [R]consulted together to estab-
lish a royal statute and to make a firm decree,
that whoever petitions any god or man for
thirty days, except you, O king, shall be cast
into the den of lions. Ps. 59:3
8 "Now, O king, establish the decree and
sign the writing, so that it cannot be changed,
according to the law of the Medes and Per-
sians, which does not alter."
9 Therefore King Darius signed the written
decree.

Daniel Prays Faithfully

10 Now when Daniel knew that the writing
was signed, he went home. And in his upper
room, with his windows open [R]toward Jeru-
salem, he knelt down on his knees [R]three
times that day, and prayed and gave thanks
before his God, as was his custom since early
days. Jon. 2:4 • Ps. 55:17
11 Then these men assembled and found
Daniel praying and making supplication be-
fore his God.
12 [R]And they went before the king, and
spoke concerning the king's decree: "Have
you not signed a decree that every man
who petitions any god or man within thirty
days, except you, O king, shall be cast into
the den of lions?" The king answered and
said, "The thing *is* true, [R]according to the
law of the Medes and Persians, which does
not alter." Dan. 3:8–12 • Dan. 6:8, 15
13 So they answered and said before the

5:24 Lit. *palm* **5:25** Lit. *a mina* (50 shekels) from the verb "to number" • Lit. *a shekel* from the verb "to weigh" • Lit. *and half-shekels* from the verb "to divide"; pl. of *Peres*, v. 28 **5:28** Aram. *Paras*, consonant with *Peres*

king, "That Daniel, [R]who is one of the captives* from Judah, [R]does not show due regard for you, O king, or for the decree that you have signed, but makes his petition three times a day." Dan. 1:6; 5:13 • Dan. 3:12
14 And the king, when he heard *these* words, [R]was greatly displeased with himself, and set *his* heart on Daniel to deliver him; and he [T]labored till the going down of the sun to deliver him. Mark 6:26 • *strove*
15 Then these men approached the king, and said to the king, "Know, O king, that *it is* [R]the law of the Medes and Persians that no decree or statute which the king establishes may be changed." Dan. 6:8, 12

Daniel Is Saved in the Lions' Den

16 So the king gave the command, and they brought Daniel and cast *him* into the den of lions. *But* the king spoke, saying to Daniel, "Your God, whom you serve continually, He will deliver you."
17 Then a stone was brought and laid on the mouth of the den, [R]and the king sealed it with his own signet ring and with the signets of his lords, that the purpose concerning Daniel might not be changed. Matt. 27:66
18 Now the king went to his palace and spent the night fasting; and no musicians* were brought before him. [R]Also his sleep [T]went from him. Dan. 2:1 • Or *fled*
19 Then the [R]king arose very early in the morning and went in haste to the den of lions. Dan. 3:24
20 And when he came to the den, he cried out with a [T]lamenting voice to Daniel. The king spoke, saying to Daniel, "Daniel, servant of the living God, [R]has your God, whom you serve continually, been able to deliver you from the lions?" Or *grieved* • Dan. 3:17
21 Then Daniel said to the king, [R]"O king, live forever! Dan. 2:4; 6:6
22 [R]"My God sent His angel and [R]shut the lions' mouths, so that they have not hurt me, because I was found innocent before Him; and also, O king, I have done no wrong before you." Dan. 3:28 • Heb. 11:33
23 Now the king was exceedingly glad for him, and commanded that they should take Daniel up out of the den. So Daniel was taken up out of the den, and no injury whatever was found on him, [R]because he believed in his God. Heb. 11:33
24 And the king gave the command, and they brought those men who had accused Daniel, and they cast *them* into the den of lions—them, [R]their children, and their wives; and the lions overpowered them, and broke all their bones in pieces before they ever came to the bottom of the den. Deut. 24:16

Darius's Wise Decree

25 [R]Then King Darius wrote: Dan. 4:1

To all peoples, nations, and languages
that dwell in all the earth:

Peace be multiplied to you.

26 I make a decree that in every dominion
of my kingdom *men must* [R]tremble and
fear before the God of Daniel. Ps. 99:1

[R]For He *is* the living God,
And steadfast forever; Dan. 4:34, 6:20
His kingdom *is the one* which shall not
be [R]destroyed,
And His dominion *shall endure* to the
end. Dan. 2:44; 4:3; 7:14, 27
27 He delivers and rescues,
[R]And He works signs and wonders
In heaven and on earth, Dan. 4:2, 3
Who has delivered Daniel from the
[T]power of the lions. Lit. *hand*

28 So this Daniel prospered in the reign of Darius [R]and in the reign of [R]Cyrus the Persian. Dan. 1:21 • Ezra 1:1, 2

CHAPTER 7

Four Beasts

IN the first year of Belshazzar king of Babylon, Daniel had a dream and visions of his

6:13 Lit. *of the sons of the captivity* **6:18** Exact meaning unknown

6:22 Angels: Interaction with Humans—One of the primary functions of angels is to minister to believers in Jesus Christ (Page 1258—Heb. 1:14). Sometimes in the pages of the Bible the ministry of angels is overt and visible (Page 1010—Matt. 28:2–7). Other times angels deal with people in dreams or visions (Page 978—Matt. 1:20; 2:13). Still other angelic ministries occur without the people affected knowing it (Page 1268—Heb. 13:2).

It would appear that some angels have more or less fixed assignments of oversight, protection, and guidance. Powerful angels may involve themselves in the affairs of certain nations (Page 884—Dan. 10:13, 18–20; 12:1). Angels may be assigned to oversee churches (Page 1313—Rev. 1:20; 2:1, 8, 12, 18; 3:1, 7, 14). Other angels may be "guardian angels" to individuals (Page 996—Matt. 18:10).

Angels are worshipers, not objects of worship or idolatrous fascination (see Page 254—Judg. 13:15, 16). Whenever people get overly fascinated with angels, their attention is diverted from God. Satan is pleased by excessive attention to angels or anything other than God. Angels always try to direct our attention and praise toward God Himself (Page 1316—Rev. 5:11, 12).

Now turn to Page 1320—Rev. 12:9: Demons: Fallen Angels.

head *while* on his bed. Then he wrote down
the dream, telling the main facts.*
2 Daniel spoke, saying, "I saw in my vision
by night, and behold, the four winds of heaven
were stirring up the Great Sea.
3 "And four great beasts came up from the
sea, each different from the other.
4 "The first *was* like a lion, and had eagle's
wings. I watched till its wings were plucked
off; and it was lifted up from the earth and
made to stand on two feet like a man, and a
man's heart was given to it.
5 [R]"And suddenly another beast, a second,
like a bear. It was raised up on one side, and
had three ribs in its mouth between its teeth.
And they said thus to it: 'Arise, devour much
flesh!' Dan. 2:39
6 "After this I looked, and there was an-
other, like a leopard, which had on its back
four wings of a bird. The beast also had four
heads, and dominion was given to it.
7 "After this I saw in the night visions, and
behold, [R]a fourth beast, dreadful and terrible,
exceedingly strong. It had huge iron teeth; it
was devouring, breaking in pieces, and tram-
pling the residue with its feet. It *was* different
from all the beasts that *were* before it, and it
had ten horns. Dan. 2:40
8 "I was considering the horns, and [R]there
was another horn, a little one, coming up
among them, before whom three of the first
horns were plucked out by the roots. And
there, in this horn, *were* eyes like the eyes
[R]of a man, [R]and a mouth speaking pompous
words. Dan. 8:9 • Rev. 9:7 • Rev. 13:5, 6

"Ancient of Days"

9"I[R] watched till thrones were [T]put in
place, [Rev. 20:4] • Or *set up*
And [R]the Ancient of Days was seated;
[R]His garment *was* white as snow,
And the hair of His head *was* like pure
wool. Ps. 90:2 • Rev. 1:14
His throne *was* a fiery flame,
[R]Its wheels a burning fire; Ezek. 1:15
10[R] A fiery stream issued Is. 30:33; 66:15
And came forth from before Him.
[R]A thousand thousands ministered to
Him; Rev. 5:11
Ten thousand times ten thousand stood
before Him.
[R]The court* was seated, [Rev. 20:11–15]
And the books were opened.

11 "I watched then because of the sound of
the [T]pompous words which the horn was
speaking; [R]I watched till the beast was slain,
and its body destroyed and given to the burn-
ing flame. Lit. *great* • [Rev. 19:20; 20:10]
12 "As for the rest of the beasts, they had
their dominion taken away, yet their lives
were prolonged for a season and a time.

13"I was watching in the night visions,
And behold, *One* like the Son of Man,
Coming with the clouds of heaven!
He came to the Ancient of Days,
And they brought Him near before Him.
14[R] Then to Him was given dominion and
glory and a kingdom, [John 3:35, 36]
That all peoples, nations, and languages
should serve Him.
His dominion *is* [R]an everlasting
dominion, Mic. 4:7; [Luke 1:33]☆
Which shall not pass away,
And His kingdom *the one*
Which shall not be destroyed.

Interpretation of the Four Beasts

15 "I, Daniel, was grieved in my spirit
[T]within *my* body, and the visions of my head
troubled me. Lit. *in the midst of its sheath*
16 "I came near to one of those who stood by,
and asked him the truth of all this. So he told
me and made known to me the interpretation
of these things:
17 'Those great beasts, which are four, *are*
four kings* *which* arise out of the earth.
18 'But the saints of the Most High shall re-
ceive the kingdom, and possess the kingdom
forever, even forever and ever.'
19 "Then I wished to know the truth about
the fourth beast, which was different from all
the others, exceedingly dreadful, *with* its
teeth of iron and its nails of bronze, *which* de-
voured, broke in pieces, and trampled the
residue with its feet;
20 "and the ten horns that *were* on its head,
and the other *horn* which came up, before
which three fell, namely, that horn which had
eyes and a mouth which spoke [T]pompous
words, whose appearance *was* greater than
his fellows. Lit. *great things*
21 "I was watching; [R]and the same horn was
making war against the saints, and prevailing
against them, Rev. 11:7; 13:7; 17:14
22 "until the Ancient of Days came, [R]and a
judgment was made *in favor* of the saints of
the Most High, and the time came for the
saints to possess the kingdom. [Rev. 1:6]

Interpretation of the Fourth Beast

23 "Thus he said:

'The fourth beast shall be
[R]A fourth kingdom on earth, Dan. 2:40
Which shall be different from all *other*
kingdoms,
And shall devour the whole earth,
Trample it and break it in pieces.
24[R] The ten horns *are* ten kings Rev. 13:1
Who shall arise from this kingdom.
And another shall rise after them;

7:1 Lit. *the head* (or *chief*) *of the words* **7:10** Or *judgment* **7:17** Representing their kingdoms, v. 23

He shall be different from the first *ones*,
And shall subdue three kings.
25 [R]He shall speak *pompous* words against
the Most High, Rev. 13:1–6
Shall [R]persecute* the saints of the Most
High, Rev. 17:6
And shall [R]intend to change times and
law. Dan. 2:21
Then [R]*the saints* shall be given into his
hand Rev. 13:7; 18:2
For a time and times and half a time.

26 'But the court shall be seated,
And they shall take away his dominion,
To consume and destroy *it* forever.
27 Then the [R]kingdom and dominion,
And the greatness of the kingdoms
under the whole heaven,
Shall be given to the people, the saints of
the Most High. Dan. 7:14, 18, 22
[R]His kingdom *is* an everlasting kingdom,
[R]And all dominions shall serve and obey
Him.' [Luke 1:33, 34] • Is. 60:12

28 "This *is* the end of the account.* As for me, Daniel, [R]my thoughts greatly troubled me, and my countenance changed; but I kept the matter in my heart." Dan. 8:27

CHAPTER 8

The Ram

IN the third year of the reign of King Belshazzar a vision appeared *to* me—to me, Daniel—after the one that appeared to me [R]the first time. Dan. 7:1

2 I saw in the vision, and it so happened while I was looking, that I *was* in [R]Shushan,[T] the citadel, which *is* in the province of Elam; and I saw in the vision that I was by the River Ulai. Esth. 1:2; 2:8 • Or *Susa*

3 Then I lifted my eyes and saw, and there, standing beside the river, was a ram which had two horns, and the two horns *were* high; but one *was* higher than the other, and the higher *one* came up last.

4 I saw the ram pushing westward, northward, and southward, so that no animal could withstand him; nor *was there any* that could deliver from his hand, but he did according to his will and became great.

The Male Goat

5 And as I was considering, suddenly a male goat came from the west, across the surface of the whole earth, without touching the ground; and the goat *had* a notable [R]horn between his eyes. Dan. 8:8, 21; 11:3

6 Then he came to the ram that had two horns, which I had seen standing beside the river, and ran at him with furious power.

7 And I saw him confronting the ram; he was moved with rage against him, attacked the ram, and broke his two horns. There was no power in the ram to withstand him, but he cast him down to the ground and trampled him; and there was no one that could deliver the ram from his hand.

8 Therefore the male goat grew very great; but when he became strong, the large horn was broken, and in place of it [R]four notable ones came up toward the four winds of heaven. Dan. 7:6; 8:22; 11:4

The Little Horn

9 [R]And out of one of them came a little horn which grew exceedingly great toward the south, [R]toward the east, and toward the [R]Glorious *Land*. Dan. 11:21 • Dan. 11:25 • Ps. 48:2

10 [R]And it grew up to [R]the host of heaven; and [R]it cast down *some* of the host and *some* of the stars to the ground, and trampled them. Dan. 11:28 • Is. 14:13 • Rev. 12:4

11 He even exalted *himself* as high as the Prince of the host; and by him [R]the daily *sacrifices* were taken away, and the place of His sanctuary was cast down. Ex. 29:38

12 Because of transgression, an army was given over *to the horn* to oppose the daily *sacrifices;* and he cast truth down to the ground. He did *all this* and prospered.

The Length of the Vision

13 Then I heard [R]a holy one speaking; and *another* holy one said to that certain *one* who was speaking, "How long *will* the vision *be, concerning* the daily *sacrifices* and the transgression of desolation, the giving of both the sanctuary and the host to be trampled underfoot?" Dan. 4:13, 23

14 And he said to me, "For two thousand three hundred days;* then the sanctuary shall be cleansed."

Interpretation of the Vision

15 Then it happened, when I, Daniel, had seen the vision and was seeking the meaning, that suddenly there stood before me one having the appearance of a man.

16 And I heard a man's voice [R]between *the banks of* the Ulai, who called, and said, [R]"Gabriel, make this *man* understand the vision." Dan. 12:6, 7 • Luke 1:19, 26

17 So he came near where I stood, and when he came I was afraid and [R]fell on my face; but he said to me, "Understand, son of man, that the vision *refers* to the time of the end." Rev. 1:17

18 [R]Now, as he was speaking with me, I was in a deep sleep with my face to the ground; [R]but he touched me, and stood me upright. Luke 9:32 • Ezek. 2:2

19 And he said, "Look, I am making known

7:25 Lit. *wear out* **7:28** Lit. *the word* **8:14** Lit. *evening-mornings*

to you what shall happen in the latter time of the indignation; [R]for at the appointed time the end *shall be.* Hab. 2:3

Interpretation of the Ram

20 "The ram which you saw, having the two horns—*they are* the kings of Media and Persia.

Interpretation of the Male Goat

21 "And the [T]male goat *is* the kingdom* of Greece. The large horn that *is* between its eyes [R]*is* the first king. *shaggy male* • Dan. 11:3
22 [R]"As for the broken *horn* and the four that stood up in its place, four kingdoms shall arise out of that nation, but not with its power. Dan. 11:4

Interpretation of the Little Horn

23 "And in the latter time of their kingdom,
When the transgressors have reached
their fullness,
A king shall arise,
[R]Having fierce features, Deut. 28:50
Who understands sinister schemes.
24 His power shall be mighty, [R]but not by
his own power; Rev. 17:13
He shall destroy fearfully,
[R]And shall prosper and thrive; Dan. 11:36
[R]He shall destroy the mighty, and *also*
the holy people. Dan. 7:25

25 "Through[R] his cunning Dan. 11:21
He shall cause deceit to prosper under
his rule;*
[R]And he shall exalt *himself* in his heart.
He shall destroy many in *their*
prosperity. Dan. 8:11–13; 11:36; 12:7
[R]He shall even rise against the Prince of
princes; Rev. 19:19, 20
But he shall be [R]broken without *human*
means.* Job 34:20

26 "And the vision of the evenings and
mornings
Which was told is true;
[R]Therefore seal up the vision, Ezek. 12:27
For *it refers* to many days *in the future.*"

Response of Daniel

27 And I, Daniel, fainted and was sick for days; afterward I arose and went about the king's business. I was [T]astonished by the vision, but no one understood it. *amazed*

CHAPTER 9

The Understanding of Daniel

IN the first year [R]of Darius the son of Ahasuerus, of the lineage of the Medes, who was made king over the realm of the Chaldeans— Dan. 1:21
2 in the first year of his reign I, Daniel, understood by the books the number of the years *specified* by the word of the LORD through [R]Jeremiah the prophet, that He would accomplish seventy years in the desolations of Jerusalem. 2 Chr. 36:21

The Intercession of Daniel

3 Then I set my face toward the Lord God to make request by prayer and supplications, with fasting, sackcloth, and ashes.
4 And I prayed to the LORD my God, and made confession, and said, "O Lord, great and awesome God, who keeps His covenant and mercy with those who love Him, and with those who keep His commandments,

5 [R]"we have sinned and committed iniquity, we have done wickedly and rebelled, even by departing from Your precepts and Your judgments. 1 Kin. 8:47, 48
6 [R]"Neither have we heeded Your servants the prophets, who spoke in Your name to our kings and our princes, to our fathers and all the people of the land. 2 Chr. 36:15

8:21 Lit. *king,* representing his kingdom, Dan. 7:17, 23
8:25 Lit. *hand* • Lit. *hand*

9:3, 4 Knowing the Will of God Through Prayer and Fasting—Soon after Israel had invaded Palestine in the days of Joshua, the Israelites were tricked into signing an unscriptural peace treaty with a group of deceitful pagans. The cause for this tragic error is clearly stated in God's Word, "Then the men . . . did not ask counsel of the LORD" (Page 222—Josh. 9:14). These pagans, the Gibeonites, brought only trouble to Israel. See Josh. 10:4–15; 2 Sam. 21:1–14.

It therefore becomes immediately obvious that one of the most important factors in knowing God's will for our lives is to pray. "If any of you lacks wisdom, let him ask of God, who gives to all liberally and without reproach, and it will be given to him" (Page 1272—James 1:5). See also Ps. 143:8, 10; James 4:2.

In the light of these passages it is evident a Christian must pray to know God's will. In other Bible verses fasting is linked with prayer.

a. Meaning of fasting: to fast is to abstain for a period of time from some important and necessary activity in our lives.
b. Purpose of fasting: this is done that we might spend that time in prayer before God.
c. Kinds of fasting: one may, for a time, refrain from sleep (Page 1187—2 Cor. 6:5; 11:27), marital sex (Page 1171—1 Cor. 7:1–5), or food (Page 979—Matt. 4:1, 2).
d. Examples of biblical fasting: Moses (Page 184—Deut. 9:9, 18, 25–29); Elijah (Page 359—1 Kin. 19:8); Daniel (Page 882—Dan. 9:3; 10:3); Ezra (Page 479—Ezra 10:6); Nehemiah (Page 484—Neh. 1:4); and Paul (Page 1187—2 Cor. 6:5; 11:27).

Now turn to Page 688—Is. 6:8: Knowing the Will of God Through Submission to the Spirit.

7 "O Lord, righteousness *belongs* to You, but to us shame of face, as *it is* this day—to the men of Judah, to the inhabitants of Jerusalem and all Israel, those near and those far off in all the countries to which You have driven them, because of the unfaithfulness which they have committed against You.

8 "O Lord, to us *belongs* shame of face, to our kings, our princes, and our fathers, because we have sinned against You.

9 [R]"To the Lord our God *belong* mercy and forgiveness, though we have rebelled against Him. [Ps. 130:4, 7]

10 "We have not obeyed the voice of the LORD our God, to walk in His laws, which He set before us by His servants the prophets.

11 "Yes, [R]all Israel has transgressed Your law, and has departed so as not to obey Your voice; therefore the curse and the oath written in the [R]Law of Moses the servant of God have been poured out on us, because we have sinned against Him. Is. 1:3–6 • Lev. 26:14

12 "And He has [R]confirmed His words, which He spoke against us and against our judges who judged us, by bringing upon us a great disaster; [R]for under the whole heaven such has never been done as what has been done to Jerusalem. Zech. 1:6 • Lam. 1:12; 2:13

13 [R]"As *it is* written in the Law of Moses, all this disaster has come upon us; yet we have not made our prayer before the LORD our God, that we might turn from our iniquities and understand Your truth. Deut. 28:15–68

14 "Therefore the LORD has [R]kept the disaster in mind, and brought it upon us; for [R]the LORD our God *is* righteous in all the works which He does, though we have not obeyed His voice. Jer. 31:28; 44:27 • Neh. 9:33

15 "And now, O Lord our God, [R]who brought Your people out of the land of Egypt with a mighty hand, and made Yourself [R]a name, as *it is* this day—we have sinned, we have done wickedly! Neh. 1:10 • Neh. 9:10

16 "O Lord, [R]according to all Your righteousness, I pray, let Your anger and Your fury be turned away from Your city Jerusalem, [R]Your holy mountain; because for our sins, and for the iniquities of our fathers, Jerusalem and Your people *are* a reproach to all *those* around us. 1 Sam. 12:7 • Zech. 8:3

17 "Now therefore, our God, hear the prayer of Your servant, and his supplications, [R]and [R]for the Lord's sake cause Your face to shine on Your sanctuary, [R]which is desolate. Num. 6:24–26 • Lam. 5:18 • [John 16:24]

18 [R]"O my God, incline Your ear and hear; open Your eyes and see our desolations, and the city which is called by Your name; for we do not present our supplications before You because of our righteous deeds, but because of Your great mercies. Is. 37:17

19 "O Lord, hear! O Lord, forgive! O Lord, listen and act! Do not delay for Your own sake, my God, for Your city and Your people are called by Your name."

The Intervention of Gabriel

20 Now while I *was* speaking, praying, and confessing my sin and the sin of my people Israel, and presenting my supplication before the LORD my God for the holy mountain of my God,

21 yes, while I *was* speaking in prayer, the man [R]Gabriel, whom I had seen in the vision at the beginning, [T]being caused to fly swiftly, reached me about the time of the evening offering. Dan. 8:16 • Or *being weary with weariness*

22 And he informed *me*, and talked with me, and said, "O Daniel, I have now come forth to give you skill to understand.

23 "At the beginning of your supplications the [T]command went out, and I have come to tell *you*, for you *are* greatly [R]beloved; therefore [R]consider the matter, and understand the vision: Lit. *word* • Dan. 10:11, 19 • Matt. 24:15

The Revelation of the Seventy Weeks

24 "Seventy weeks* are determined
For your people and for your holy city,
To finish the transgression,
To make an end of* sins,
To make reconciliation for iniquity,
To bring in everlasting righteousness,
To seal up vision and prophecy,
And to anoint the Most Holy.

25 "Know therefore and understand,
That from the going forth of the
command
To restore and build Jerusalem
Until [R]Messiah [R]the Prince,
There shall be seven weeks and sixty-
two weeks; John 1:41; 4:25☆ • Is. 55:4
The street* shall be built again, and the
wall,*
Even in troublesome times.

26 "And after the sixty-two weeks
[R]Messiah shall be cut off, [R]but not for
Himself; [Is. 53:8]; Matt. 27:50☆ • [1 Pet. 2:21]
And [R]the people of the prince who is to
come Matt. 22:7
[R]Shall destroy the city and the
sanctuary. Luke 19:43, 44
The end of it *shall be* with a flood,
And till the end of the war desolations
are determined.

27 Then he shall confirm [R]a [T]covenant with
[R]many for one week; Is. 42:6 • Or *treaty*
But in the middle of the week
He shall bring an end to sacrifice and
offering. [Matt. 26:28]

9:24 Lit. *sevens*, and so throughout the chapter • So with Qr., LXX, Syr., Vg.; Kt., Theodotion *To seal up*
9:25 Or *open square* • Or *moat*

And on the wing of abominations shall
be one who makes desolate,
[R]Even until the consummation, which is
determined, Dan. 11:36
Is poured out on the desolate."

CHAPTER 10

Time of the Vision

IN the third year of Cyrus king of Persia a message was revealed to Daniel, whose [R]name was called Belteshazzar. The message *was* true, but the appointed time *was* long;* and he understood the message, and had understanding of the vision. Dan. 1:7

2 In those days I, Daniel, was mourning three full weeks.

3 I ate no pleasant food, no meat or wine came into my mouth, nor did I anoint myself at all, till three whole weeks were fulfilled.

4 Now on the twenty-fourth day of the first month, as I was by the side of the great river, that *is*, the Tigris,*

Vision of the Heavenly Messenger

5 I lifted my eyes and looked, and behold, a certain man clothed in linen, whose waist *was* [R]girded with gold of Uphaz! Rev. 1:13

6 His body *was* like beryl, his face like the appearance of lightning, his eyes like torches of fire, his arms and feet like burnished bronze in color, [R]and the sound of his words like the voice of a multitude. [Rev. 1:15]

7 And I, Daniel, alone saw the vision, for the men who were with me did not see the vision; but a great terror fell upon them, so that they fled to hide themselves.

8 Therefore I was left alone when I saw this great vision, and no strength remained in me; for my [T]vigor was turned to frailty in me, and I retained no strength. Lit. *splendor*

9 Yet I heard the sound of his words; and while I heard the sound of his words I was in a deep sleep on my face, with my face to the ground.

Touch of the Heavenly Messenger

10 [R]Suddenly, a hand touched me, which made me tremble on my knees and *on* the palms of my hands. Dan. 9:21

11 And he said to me, "O Daniel, man greatly beloved, understand the words that I speak to you, and stand upright, for I have now been sent to you." While he was speaking this word to me, I stood trembling.

12 Then he said to me, "Do not fear, Daniel, for from the first day that you set your heart to understand, and to humble yourself before your God, your words were heard; and I have come because of your words.

13 [R]"But the prince of the kingdom of Persia withstood me twenty-one days; and behold, Michael, one of the chief princes, came to help me, for I had been left alone there with the kings of Persia. Dan. 10:20

14 "Now I have come to make you understand what will happen to your people [R]in the latter days, [R]for the vision *refers* to *many* days yet *to come*." Dan. 2:28 • Dan. 8:26; 10:1

15 When he had spoken such words to me, [R]I [T]turned my face toward the ground and became speechless. Dan. 8:18; 10:9 • Lit. *set*

16 And suddenly, *one* having the likeness of the sons* of men touched my lips; then I opened my mouth and spoke, saying to him who stood before me, "My lord, because of the vision my sorrows have overwhelmed me, and I have retained no strength.

17 "For how can this servant of my lord talk with you, my lord? As for me, no strength remains in me now, nor is any breath left in me."

Strengthening by the Heavenly Messenger

18 Then again, *the one* having the likeness of a man touched me and strengthened me.

19 And he said, "O man greatly beloved, [R]fear not! Peace *be* to you; be strong, yes, be strong!" So when he spoke to me I was strengthened, and said, "Let my lord speak, for you have strengthened me." Judg. 6:23

20 Then he said, "Do you know why I have come to you? And now I must return to fight [R]with the prince of Persia; and when I have gone forth, indeed the prince of Greece will come. Dan. 10:13

21 "But I will tell you what is noted in the Scripture of Truth. (No one upholds me against these, except Michael your prince.

CHAPTER 11

The Rule of Persia

"ALSO [R]in the first year of [R]Darius the Mede, I, *even* I, stood up to confirm and strengthen him.) Dan. 9:1 • Dan. 5:31

2 "And now I will tell you the truth: Behold, three more kings will arise in Persia, and the fourth shall be far richer than *them* all; by his strength, through his riches, he shall stir up all against the realm of Greece.

The Rule of Greece

3 "Then [R]a mighty king shall arise, who shall rule with great dominion, and [R]do according to his will. Dan. 7:6; 8:5 • Dan. 8:4

4 "And when he has arisen, his kingdom shall be broken up and divided toward the four winds of heaven, but not among his posterity nor according to his dominion with which he ruled; for his kingdom shall be uprooted, even for others besides these.

5 "Also the king of the South shall become strong, as well as *one* of his princes; and he

10:1 Or *and of great conflict;* **10:4** Heb. *Hiddekel*
10:16 Theodotion, Vg. *the son;* LXX *a hand*

shall gain power over him and have dominion. His dominion *shall be* a great dominion.

6 "And at the end of *some* years they shall join forces, for the daughter of the king of the South shall go to the king of the North to make an agreement; but she shall not retain the power of her authority,* and neither he nor his authority* shall stand; but she shall be given up, with those who brought her, and with him who begot her, and with him who strengthened her in *those* times.

7 "But from a branch of her roots *one* shall arise in his place, who shall come with an army, enter the fortress of the king of the North, and deal with them and prevail.

8 "And he shall also carry their gods captive to Egypt, with their princes* *and* their precious articles of silver and gold; and he shall continue *more* years than the king of the North.

9 "Also *the king of the North* shall come to the kingdom of the king of the South, but shall return to his own land.

10 "However his sons shall stir up strife, and assemble a multitude of great forces; and *one* shall certainly come and overwhelm and pass through; then he shall return to his fortress and stir up strife.

11 "And the king of the South shall be moved with rage, and go out and fight with him, with the king of the North, who shall muster a great multitude; but the multitude shall be given into the hand of his *enemy*.

12 "When he has taken away the multitude, his heart will be [T]lifted up; and he will cast down tens of thousands, but he will not prevail. Proud

13 "For the king of the North will return and muster a multitude greater than the former, and shall certainly come at the end of some years with a great army and much equipment.

14 "Now in those times many shall rise up against the king of the South. Also, violent men* of your people shall exalt themselves [T]in fulfillment of the vision, but they shall [R]fall. Lit. *to establish* • Job 9:13

15 "So the king of the North shall come and [R]build a siege mound, and take a fortified city; and the forces* of the South shall not withstand *him*. Even his choice troops *shall have* no strength to resist. Ezek. 4:2; 17:17

16 "But he who comes against him [R]shall do according to his own will, and [R]no one shall stand against him. He shall stand in the Glorious Land with destruction in his power.* Dan. 8:4, 7 • Josh. 1:5

17 "He shall also [R]set his face to enter with the strength of his whole kingdom, and upright ones* with him; thus shall he do. And he shall give him the daughter of women to destroy it; but she shall not stand *with him*, [R]or be for him. 2 Chr. 20:3 • Dan. 9:26

18 "After this he shall turn his face to the coastlands, and shall take many. But a ruler shall bring the reproach against them to an end; and with the reproach removed, he shall turn back on him.

19 "Then he shall turn his face toward the fortress of his own land; but he shall [R]stumble and fall, and not be found. Jer. 46:6

20 "There shall arise in his place one who imposes taxes *on* the glorious kingdom; but within a few days he shall be destroyed, but not in anger or in battle.

21 "And in his place [R]shall arise a vile person, to whom they will not give the honor of royalty; but he shall come in peaceably, and seize the kingdom by intrigue. Dan. 7:8

22 "With the force* of a flood they shall be swept away from before him and be broken, and also the prince of the covenant.

23 "And after the league *is made* with him [R]he shall act deceitfully, for he shall come up and become strong with a small *number of* people. Dan. 8:25

24 "He shall enter peaceably, even into the richest places of the province; and he shall do *what* his fathers have not done, nor his forefathers: he shall disperse among them the plunder, [T]spoil, and riches; and he shall devise his plans against the strongholds, but *only* for a time. *booty*

25 "He shall stir up his power and his courage against the king of the South with a great army. And the king of the South shall be stirred up to battle with a very great and mighty army; but he shall not stand, for they shall devise plans against him.

26 "Yes, those who eat of the portion of his delicacies shall destroy him; his army shall [T]be swept away, and many shall fall down slain. Or *overflow*

27 "Both these kings' hearts *shall be* bent on evil, and they shall speak lies at the same table; but it shall not prosper, for the end *will* still *be* at the [R]appointed time. Hab. 2:3

28 "While returning to his land with great riches, his heart shall be *moved* against the holy covenant; so he shall do *damage* and return to his own land.

29 "At the appointed time he shall return and go toward the south; but it shall not be like the former or the latter.

30 [R]"For ships from Cyprus* shall come against him; therefore he shall be grieved, and return in rage against the holy covenant, and do *damage*. So he shall return and show regard for those who forsake the holy covenant. Jer. 2:10

31 "And forces* shall be mustered by him, [R]and they shall defile the sanctuary fortress;

11:6 Lit. *arm* • Lit. *arm* **11:8** Or *molded images* **11:14** Or *robbers*, lit. *sons of breakage* **11:15** Lit. *arms* **11:16** Lit. *hand* **11:17** Or *bring equitable terms* **11:22** Lit. *arms* **11:30** Heb. *Kittim*, western lands, especially Cyprus **11:31** Lit. *arms*

then they shall take away the daily *sacrifices*,
and place *there* the abomination of desola-
tion. Dan. 8:11–13; 12:11

32 "Those who do wickedly against the
covenant he shall [T]corrupt with flattery; but
the people who know their God shall be
strong, and carry out *great exploits.* pollute
33 "And those of the people who understand
shall instruct many; yet *for many* days they
shall fall by sword and flame, by captivity and
plundering.
34 "Now when they fall, they shall be aided
with a little help; but many shall join with
them by [T]intrigue. Or *slipperiness, flattery*
35 "And *some* of those of understanding
shall fall, to refine them, purify *them,* and
make *them* white, *until* the time of the end;
because *it is* still for the appointed time.

Prophecy of the Willful King

36 "Then the king shall do according to his
own will: he shall exalt and magnify himself
above every god, shall speak blasphemies
against the God of gods, and shall prosper till
the wrath has been accomplished; for what
has been determined shall be done.
37 "He shall regard neither the God* of his
fathers nor the desire of women, [R]nor regard
any god; for he shall exalt himself above *them*
all. Is. 14:13
38 "But in their place he shall honor a god of
fortresses; and a god which his fathers did not
know he shall honor with gold and silver, with
precious stones and pleasant things.
39 "Thus he shall act against the strongest
fortresses with a foreign god, which he shall
acknowledge, *and* advance *its* glory; and he
shall cause them to rule over many, and divide
the land for [T]gain. profit
40 "At the time of the end the king of the
South shall attack him; and the king of the
North shall come against him like a whirl-
wind, with chariots, horsemen, and with
many ships; and he shall enter the countries,
overwhelm *them,* and pass through.
41 "He shall also enter the Glorious Land,
and many *countries* shall be overthrown; but
these shall escape from his hand: Edom,
Moab, and the prominent people of Ammon.
42 "He shall stretch out his hand against the
countries, and the land of [R]Egypt shall not es-
cape. Joel 3:19
43 "He shall have power over the treasures
of gold and silver, and over all the precious
things of Egypt; also the Libyans and Ethio-
pians *shall follow* [R]at his heels. Ex. 11:8
44 "But news from the east and the north
shall trouble him; therefore he shall go out
with great fury to destroy and annihilate many.
45 "And he shall plant the tents of his palace
between the seas and the glorious holy moun-
tain; [R]yet he shall come to his end, and no one
will help him. Rev. 19:20

CHAPTER 12

Prophecy of the Great Time of Trouble

"AT that time Michael shall stand up,
The great prince who stands *watch*
over the sons of your people;
[R]And there shall be a time of trouble,
Such as never was since there was a
nation,
Even to that time.

11:37 Or *gods*

11:32 We Know God Through His Word—One of the most vital teachings of Scripture is that God can be known. The highest knowledge to which men and women can attain is a personal knowledge of God (Page 759—Jer. 9:24). People do not naturally possess this knowledge (Page 1150—Rom. 3:10, 11), even though they know that He exists (Page 551—Ps. 14:1; Page 1149—Rom. 1:19, 20). Knowing that God exists is not the same as knowing God personally, just as knowing about the President does not mean that you necessarily know him personally. This knowledge of God is crucial, however, since to know God personally is to be saved and have eternal life (Page 1102—John 17:3). People should rejoice in the fact that God earnestly wants them to attain this knowledge. That is why He has spoken to us in His Word, revealing Himself and disclosing the means by which we may know Him.

While God surely can be known, there is always more to be learned about Him. There are many Scriptures that teach that our knowledge of God is partial. It is said to be "too wonderful" (Page 620—Ps. 139:6), "unsearchable" (Page 622—Ps. 145:3; Page 1158—Rom. 11:33), and "infinite" (Page 623—Ps. 147:5). Since our knowledge of God is incomplete, we must increase it through spiritual growth. Paul, for example, prays to know God better (Page 1215—Phil. 3:10). We are even commanded to grow in the knowledge of Christ (Page 1289—2 Pet. 3:18). The development of one's intimate knowledge of God constitutes one of the greatest delights of the Christian life.

The Bible also reveals that God cannot be known personally apart from His Word. It contains the gospel that must be believed (Page 1204—Eph. 1:13), and the gospel brings forth saving faith in itself (Page 1157—Rom. 10:17). The gospel can therefore be called "the power of God to salvation" (Page 1149—Rom. 1:16). The part that the Scriptures and the gospel contained within them play in bringing people to know God is described in three important illustrations: the gospel is the agent of the new birth (Page 1272—James 1:18), that is, it is like the implanted seed without which the conception of new life cannot occur; it is also a cleansing agent through which God gives the believing sinner a spiritual bath that results in salvation (Page 1208—Eph. 5:26); the Scriptures are like an educator bringing the wisdom that leads to salvation (Page 1245—2 Tim. 3:15).

Now turn to Page 566—Ps. 40:8: We Know God's Will Through His Word.

And at that time your people [R]shall be
delivered,
Every one who is found [R]written in the
book. Jer. 30:7 • Rom. 11:26 • Ex. 32:32

Prophecy of the Resurrections

2 And many of those who sleep in the
dust of the earth shall awake,
[R]Some to everlasting life, [John 5:28, 29]
Some to shame [R]*and* everlasting
[T]contempt. [Is. 66:24] • Lit. *abhorrence*
3 Those who are wise shall shine
Like the brightness of the firmament,
[R]And those who turn many to
righteousness [James 5:19, 20]
Like the stars forever and ever.

Sealing of the Book

4 "But you, Daniel, [R]shut up the words, and
seal the book until the time of the end; many
shall [R]run to and fro, and knowledge shall in-
crease." Rev. 22:10 • Amos 8:12

Questions Regarding the Great Time of Trouble

5 Then I, Daniel, looked; and there stood
two others, one on this riverbank and the
other on that [R]riverbank. Dan. 10:4
6 And *one* said to the man clothed in [R]linen,
who *was* above the waters of the river, [R]"How
long shall the fulfillment of these wonders
be?" Ezek. 9:2 • Dan. 8:13; 12:8
7 Then I heard the man clothed in linen,
who *was* above the waters of the river, when
he held up his right hand and his left hand to
heaven, and swore by Him who lives forever,
that *it shall be* for a time, times, and half *a
time;* [R]and when the power of the holy people
has been completely shattered, all these
things shall be finished. Luke 21:24
8 Although I heard, I did not understand.
Then I said, "My lord, what *shall be* the end of
these *things?"*
9 And he said, "Go *your way,* Daniel, for the
words *are* closed up and sealed till the time of
the end.
10 "Many shall be purified, made white, and
refined, but the wicked shall do wickedly; and
none of the wicked shall understand, but the
wise shall understand.
11 "And from the time *that* the daily *sacri-
fice* is taken away, and the abomination of
desolation is set up, *there shall be* one thou-
sand two hundred and ninety days.
12 "Blessed *is* he who waits, and comes to
the one thousand three hundred and thirty-
five days.
13 "But you, go *your way* till the end; [R]for
you shall rest, and will arise to your inheri-
tance at the end of the days." Rev. 14:13

THE BOOK OF
HOSEA

THE BOOK OF HOSEA

Hosea, whose name means "Salvation," ministers to the northern kingdom of Israel (also called Ephraim, after its largest tribe). Outwardly, the nation is enjoying a time of prosperity and growth; but inwardly, moral corruption and spiritual adultery permeate the people. Hosea, instructed by God to marry a woman named Gomer, finds his domestic life to be an accurate and tragic dramatization of the unfaithfulness of God's people. During his half century of prophetic ministry, Hosea repeatedly echoes his threefold message: God abhors the sins of His people; judgment is certain; but God's loyal love stands firm.

The names "Hosea," "Joshua," and "Jesus" are all derived from the same Hebrew root word. The word *Hoshea* means "Salvation," but "Joshua" and "Jesus" include an additional idea: "Yahweh Is Salvation" (see "The Book of Joshua"). As God's messenger, Hosea offers the possibility of salvation if only the nation will turn from idolatry back to God.

Israel's last king, Hoshea, has the same name as the prophet even though the English Bible spells them differently. "Hosea" in the Greek and Latin is *Osee.*

THE AUTHOR OF HOSEA

Few critics refute the claim in 1:1 that Hosea is the author of this book. His place of birth is not given, but his familiarity and obvious concern with the northern kingdom indicate that he lived in Israel, not Judah. This is also seen when he calls the king of Samaria "our king" (7:5). Hosea was the son of Beeri (1:1), husband of Gomer (1:3), and father of two sons and a daughter (1:4, 6, 9). Nothing more is known of him since he is not mentioned elsewhere in the Bible.

Hosea has a real compassion for his people, and his personal suffering because of Gomer gives him some understanding of God's grief over their sin. Thus, his words of coming judgment are passionately delivered but tempered with a heart of tenderness. He upbraids his people for their lying, murder, insincerity, ingratitude, idolatry, and covetousness with cutting metaphors and images; but his messages are punctuated with consolation and future hope.

THE TIME OF HOSEA

Hosea addressed the northern kingdom of Israel (5:1), often called Ephraim after the largest tribe (5:3, 5, 11, 13). According to 1:1, he ministered during the reigns of Uzziah (767–739 B.C.), Jotham (739–731 B.C.), Ahaz (731–715 B.C.), and Hezekiah (715–686 B.C.), kings of Judah. When Hosea began his ministry, Jeroboam II (782–753 B.C.) was still reigning in Israel. This makes Hosea a younger contemporary of Amos, another prophet to the northern kingdom. Hosea was also a contemporary of Isaiah and Micah who ministered to the southern kingdom. Hosea's long career continued after the time of Jeroboam II and spanned the reigns of the last six kings of Israel from Zechariah (753–752 B.C.) to Hoshea (732–722 B.C.). Hosea evidently compiled this book during the early years of Hezekiah, and his ministry stretched from about 755 B.C. to about 710 B.C. The Book of Hosea represents approximately forty years of prophetic ministry.

When Hosea began his ministry, Israel was enjoying a temporary period of political and economic prosperity under Jeroboam II. However, the nation began to crumble after Tiglath-Pileser III (745–727 B.C.) strengthened Assyria. The reigns of Israel's last six kings were relatively brief since four were murdered and a fifth was carried captive to Assyria. Confusion and decline characterized the last years of the northern kingdom, and her people refused to heed Hosea's warning of imminent judgment. The people were in a spiritual stupor, riddled with sin and idolatry.

THE CHRIST OF HOSEA

Matthew 2:15 applies Hosea 11:1 to Christ in Egypt: "When Israel *was* a child, I loved him, and out of Egypt I called My son." Matthew quotes the second half of this verse to show that the Exodus of Israel from Egypt as a new nation was a prophetic type of Israel's Messiah who was also called out of Egypt in His childhood. Both Israel and Christ left Palestine to take refuge in Egypt.

Christ's identification with our plight and His loving work of redemption can be seen in Hosea's redemption of Gomer from the slave market.

KEYS TO HOSEA

Key Word: The Loyal Love of God for Israel—The themes of chapters 1—3 echo throughout the rest of the book. The adultery of Gomer (1) illustrates the sin of Israel (4—7); the degradation of Gomer (2) represents the judgment of Israel (8—10); and Hosea's redemption of Gomer (3) pictures the restoration of Israel (11—14). More than any other Old Testament prophet, Hosea's personal experiences illustrate his prophetic message. In his relationship to Gomer, Hosea portrays God's faithfulness, justice, love, and forgiveness toward His people. The theme of God's holiness is developed in contrast to Israel's corruption and apostasy. Hosea utters about 150 statements concerning the sins of Israel, and more than half deal specifically with idolatry. The theme of God's justice is contrasted with Israel's lack of justice. There has never been a good king in Israel, and judgment is long overdue. The theme of God's love is seen in contrast to Israel's hardness and empty ritual. God's loyal love is unconditional and ceaseless; in spite of Israel's manifold sins, God tries every means to bring His people back to Himself. He pleads with the people to return to Him, but they will not. "O Israel, return to the LORD your God, for you have stumbled because of your iniquity" (14:1).

Key Verses: Hosea 4:1; 11:7–9—"Hear the word of the LORD, you children of Israel, for the LORD *brings* a charge against the inhabitants of the land: there is no truth or mercy or knowledge of God in the land" (4:1).

"My people are bent on backsliding from Me. Though they call to the Most High, none at all exalt *Him.* How can I give you up, Ephraim? *How* can I hand you over, Israel? How can I make you like Admah? *How* can I set you like Zeboiim? My heart churns within Me; My sympathy is stirred. I will not execute the fierceness of My anger; I will not again destroy Ephraim. For I *am* God, and not man, the Holy One in your midst; and I will not come with terror" (11:7–9).

Key Chapter: Hosea 4—The nation of Israel has left the knowledge of the truth and followed the idolatrous ways of their pagan neighbors. Central to the book is Hosea 4:6—"My people are destroyed for lack of knowledge. Because you have rejected knowledge, I also will reject you from being priest for Me; because you have forgotten the law of your God, I also will forget your children."

SURVEY OF HOSEA

Hosea is called by God to prophesy during Israel's last hours, just as Jeremiah will prophesy years later to the crumbling kingdom of Judah. As one commentator has noted, "What we see in the prophecy of Hosea are the last few swirls as the kingdom of Israel goes down the drain." This book represents God's last gracious effort to plug the drain. Hosea's personal tragedy is an intense illustration of Israel's national tragedy. It is a story of one-sided love and faithfulness that represents the relationship between Israel and God. As Gomer is married to Hosea, so Israel is betrothed to God. Both relationships gradually disintegrate—Gomer runs after other men, and Israel runs after other gods. Israel's spiritual adultery is illustrated in Gomer's physical adultery. The development of the book can be traced in two parts: the adulterous wife and faithful husband (1—3) and the adulterous Israel and faithful Lord (4—14).

The Adulterous Wife and Faithful Husband (1—3): Hosea marries a woman named Gomer who bears him three children appropriately named by God as signs to Israel. "Jezreel," "Lo-Ruhamah," and "Lo-Ammi" mean "God Scatters," "Not Pitied," and "Not My People." Similarly, God will judge and scatter Israel because of her sin.

Gomer seeks other lovers and deserts Hosea. In spite of the depth to which Gomer's sin carries her, Hosea redeems her from the slave market and restores her.

The Adulterous Israel and Faithful Lord (4—14): Because of his own painful experience,

FOCUS	ADULTEROUS WIFE AND FAITHFUL HUSBAND			ADULTEROUS ISRAEL AND FAITHFUL LORD			
REFERENCE	1:1———2:2———3:1———4:1———6:4———9:1———11:1———14:9						
DIVISION	PROPHETIC MARRIAGE	APPLICATION OF GOMER TO ISRAEL	RESTORATION OF GOMER	SPIRITUAL ADULTERY OF ISRAEL	REFUSAL OF ISRAEL TO REPENT	JUDGMENT OF ISRAEL BY GOD	RESTORATION OF ISRAEL TO GOD
TOPIC	MARRIAGE OF HOSEA			MESSAGE OF HOSEA			
	PERSONAL			NATIONAL			
LOCATION	NORTHERN KINGDOM OF ISRAEL						
TIME	c. 755–710 B.C.						

Hosea can feel some of the sorrow of God over the sinfulness of His people. His loyal love for Gomer is a reflection of God's concern for Israel. However, Israel has fallen into the dregs of sin and is hardened against God's gracious last appeal to return. The people have flagrantly violated all of God's commandments, and they are indicted by the holy God for their crimes. Even now God wants to heal and redeem them (7:1, 13), but in their arrogance and idolatry they rebel.

Chapters 9 and 10 give the verdict of the case God has just presented. Israel's disobedience will lead to her dispersion. "They sow the wind" (4—7), "and reap the whirlwind" (8—10). Israel spurns repentance, and the judgment of God can no longer be delayed.

God is holy (4—7) and just (8—10), but He is also loving and gracious (11—14). God must discipline, but because of His endless love, He will ultimately save and restore His wayward people. "How can I give you up, Ephraim?. . . I will heal their backsliding, I will love them freely, for My anger has turned away from him" (11:8; 14:4).

OUTLINE OF HOSEA

I. The Adulterous Wife and Faithful Husband .... 1:1—3:5

A. The Introduction to the Book of Hosea 1:1
B. The Prophetic Marriage of Hosea to Gomer .... 1:2—2:1
  1. Hosea's Marriage to Gomer 1:2
  2. The Children of Hosea and Gomer 1:3–9
  3. The Application of Future Restoration .... 1:10—2:1
C. The Application of the Adultery of Gomer 2:2–23
  1. Israel's Sin of Spiritual Adultery 2:2–5
  2. Judgment of God 2:6–13
  3. Restoration of Israel 2:14–23
D. The Restoration of Gomer to Hosea 3:1–5

II. The Adulterous Israel and Faithful Lord .... 4:1—14:9

A. The Spiritual Adultery of Israel .... 4:1—6:3
  1. The Sins of Israel 4:1–19
  2. Judgment on Israel 5:1–14
  3. Eventual Restoration of Israel .... 5:15—6:3
B. The Refusal of Israel to Repent of Her Adultery .... 6:4—8:14
  1. Willful Transgression of the Covenant 6:4–11
  2. Willful Refusal to Return to the Lord 7:1–16
  3. Willful Idolatry 8:1–14
C. The Judgment of Israel by God .... 9:1—10:15
  1. Judgment of Dispersion 9:1–9
  2. Judgment of Barrenness 9:10–17
  3. Judgment of Destruction 10:1–15
D. The Restoration of Israel to the Lord .... 11:1—14:9
  1. God's Love for Israel 11:1–12
  2. Israel's Continuing Sin .... 12:1—13:16
  3. God's Promise to Restore Israel 14:1–9

CHAPTER 1

The Introduction to the Book of Hosea

THE word of the LORD that came to Hosea the son of Beeri, in the days of [R]Uzziah, [R]Jotham, Ahaz, *and* Hezekiah, kings of Judah, and in the days of Jeroboam the son of Joash, king of Israel. Amos 1:1 • 2 Chr. 27

Hosea's Marriage to Gomer

2 When the LORD began to speak by Hosea, the LORD said to Hosea:

[R]"Go, take yourself a wife of harlotry
And children of harlotry, Hos. 3:1
For [R]the land has committed great
[T]harlotry Jer. 2:13 • Spiritual adultery
By departing from the LORD."

The Children of Hosea and Gomer

3 So he went and took Gomer the daughter of Diblaim, and she conceived and bore him a son.

4 Then the LORD said to him:

"Call his name Jezreel,
For in a little *while*
[R]I will avenge the bloodshed of Jezreel on
the house of Jehu, 2 Kin. 10:11
[R]And bring an end to the kingdom of the
house of Israel. 2 Kin.15:8–10; 17:6, 23
5 [R]It shall come to pass in that day
That I will break the bow of Israel in the
Valley of Jezreel." 2 Kin. 15:29

6 And she conceived again and bore a daughter. Then *God* said to him:

"Call her name Lo-Ruhamah,*
[R]For I will no longer have mercy on the
house of Israel, 2 Kin. 17:6
But I will utterly take them away.*
7 [R]Yet I will have mercy on the house of
Judah, 2 Kin. 19:29–35
Will save them by the LORD their God,
And [R]will not save them by bow,
Nor by sword or battle,
By horses or horsemen." [Zech. 4:6]

1:6 Lit. *No-Mercy* • Or *That I may forgive them at all*

8 Now when she had weaned Lo-Ruhamah, she conceived and bore a son.
9 Then *God* said:

"Call his name Lo-Ammi,*
For you *are* not My people,
And I will not be your *God.*

The Application of Future Restoration

10 "Yet [R]the number of the children of Israel
Shall be as the sand of the sea,
Which cannot be measured or numbered. Gen. 22:17; 32:12
[R]And it shall come to pass 1 Pet. 2:10
In the place where it was said to them,
'You *are* not My [R]people,'* Rom. 9:26
There it shall be said to them,
'*You are* sons of the living God.'
11 [R]Then the children of Judah and the children of Israel Is. 11:11–13
Shall be gathered together,
And appoint for themselves one head;
And they shall come up out of the land,
For great *will be* the day of Jezreel!

CHAPTER 2

SAY to your brethren, 'My people,'*
And to your sisters, 'Mercy* *is shown.*'

Israel's Sin of Spiritual Adultery

2 "Bring[T] charges against your mother, bring charges; Or *Contend with*
For [R]she *is* not My wife, nor *am* I her Husband! Is. 50:1
Let her put away her [R]harlotries from her sight, Ezek. 16:25
And her adulteries from between her breasts;
3 Lest [R]I strip her naked Jer. 13:22, 26
And expose her, as in the day she was [R]born, Ezek. 16:4–7, 22
And make her like a wilderness,
And set her like a dry land,
And slay her with [R]thirst. Amos 8:11–13

4 "I will not have mercy on her children,
For they *are* the children of harlotry.
5 For their mother has played the harlot;
She who conceived them has behaved shamefully.
For she said, 'I will go after my lovers,
[R]Who give *me* my bread and my water,
My wool and my linen,
My oil and my drink.' Hos. 2:8, 12

Judgment of God

6 "Therefore, behold,
[R]I will hedge up your way with thorns,
And wall her in, Lam. 3:7, 9
So that she cannot find her paths.
7 She will [T]chase her lovers, Or *pursue*
But not overtake them;
Yes, she will seek them, but not find *them.*
Then she will say,
[R]'I will go and return to my [R]first husband, Luke 15:17, 18 • Ezek. 16:8; 23:4
For then *it was* better for me than now.'
8 For she did not [R]know Is. 1:3
That I gave her grain, new wine, and oil,
And multiplied her silver and gold—
Which they prepared for Baal.

9 "Therefore I will return and take away
My grain in its time
And My new wine in its season,
And will take back My wool and My linen,
Given to cover her nakedness.
10 Now [R]I will uncover her lewdness in the sight of her lovers, Ezek. 16:37
And no one shall deliver her from My hand.
11 [R]I will also cause all her mirth to cease,
Her feast days,
Her New Moons,
Her Sabbaths—
All her appointed feasts. Amos 5:21; 8:10

12 "And I will destroy her vines and her fig trees,
Of which she has said,
'These *are* my wages that my lovers have given me.'
So I will make them a forest,
And the beasts of the field shall eat them.
13 I will punish her
For the days of the Baals to which she burned incense.
She decked herself with her earrings and jewelry,
And went after her lovers;
But Me she forgot," says the LORD.

Restoration of Israel

14 "Therefore, behold, I will allure her,
Will bring her into the wilderness,
And speak comfort to her.
15 I will give her her vineyards from there,
And [R]the Valley of Achor as a door of hope; Josh. 7:26
She shall sing there,
As in [R]the days of her youth,
[R]As in the day when she came up from the land of Egypt. Ezek.16:8–14 • Ex. 15:1

16 "And it shall be, in that day,"
Says the LORD,
"*That* you will call Me 'My Husband,'*
And no longer call Me 'My Master,'*

1:9 Lit. *Not-My-People* **1:10** Heb. *lo-ammi,* v. 9
2:1 Heb. *Ammi,* Hos. 1:9, 10 • Heb. *Ruhamah,* Hos. 1:6
2:16 Heb. *Ishi* • Heb. *Baali*

17 For [R]I will take from her mouth the
names of the Baals, Ex. 23:13
And they shall be remembered by their
name no more.
18 In that day I will make a [R]covenant for
them Job 5:23
With the beasts of the field,
With the birds of the air,
And *with* the creeping things of the
ground.
Bow and sword of battle [R]I will shatter
from the earth, Is. 2:4
To make them [R]lie down safely. Lev. 26:5

19 "I will betroth you to Me forever;
Yes, I will betroth you to Me
In righteousness and justice,
In lovingkindness and mercy;
20 I will betroth you to Me in faithfulness,
And you shall know the LORD.

21 "It shall come to pass in that day
That [R]I will answer," says the LORD;
"I will answer the heavens, Zech. 8:12
And they shall answer the earth.
22 The earth shall answer
With grain,
With new wine,
And with oil;
They shall answer Jezreel.*
23 Then [R]I will sow her for Myself in the
earth, Jer. 31:27
[R]And I will have mercy on *her who had*
not obtained mercy;* Hos. 1:6
Then [R]I will say to *those who were* not
My people,* Hos. 1:10
'You *are* [T]My people!' Heb. *ammi*
And they shall say, '*You are* my God!' "

CHAPTER 3

The Restoration of Gomer to Hosea

THEN the LORD said to me, "Go again, love
a woman *who is* loved by a [R]lover* and is
committing adultery, just like the love of the
LORD for the children of Israel, who look to
other gods and love *the* raisin cakes *of the pa-
gans.*" Jer. 3:20
2 So I bought her for myself for fifteen
shekels of silver, and one and one-half homers
of barley.
3 And I said to her, "You shall [R]stay with me
many days; you shall not play the harlot, nor
shall you have a man—so, too, *will* I *be* toward
you." Deut. 21:13
4 For the children of Israel shall abide
many days [R]without king or prince, without
sacrifice or sacred pillar, without [R]ephod or
[R]teraphim. Hos. 10:3 • Ex. 28:4–12 • Judg. 17:5
5 Afterward the children of Israel shall re-
turn and [R]seek the LORD their God and David
their king. They shall fear the LORD and His
goodness in the latter days. Jer. 50:4

CHAPTER 4

Rejection of the Knowledge of God

HEAR the word of the LORD,
You children of Israel,
For the LORD *brings* a [R]charge against
the inhabitants of the land: Is. 1:18

"There is no truth or mercy
Or knowledge of God in the land.
2 *By* swearing and lying,
Killing and stealing and committing
adultery,
They break all restraint,
With bloodshed upon bloodshed.
3 Therefore [R]the land will mourn;
And [R]everyone who dwells there will
waste away Amos 5:16; 8:8 • Zeph. 1:3
With the beasts of the field
And the birds of the air;
Even the fish of the sea will be taken
away.

4 "Now let no man contend, or rebuke
another;
For your people *are* like those [R]who
contend with the priest. Deut. 17:12
5 Therefore you shall stumble [R]in the day;
The prophet also shall stumble with you
in the night; Jer. 15:8
And I will destroy your mother.
6 [R]My people are destroyed for lack of
knowledge. Is. 5:13
Because you have rejected knowledge,
I also will reject you from being priest
for Me;
[R]Because you have forgotten the law of
your God, Ezek. 22:26
I also will forget your children.

7 "The more they increased,
The more they sinned against Me;
I will change* their glory* into shame.
8 They eat up the sin of My people;
They set their heart on their iniquity.
9 And it shall be: like people, like priest.
So I will punish them for their ways,
And reward them for their deeds.
10 For [R]they shall eat, but not have
enough; Lev. 26:26
They shall commit harlotry, but not
increase;
Because they have ceased obeying the
LORD.

11 "Harlotry, wine, and new wine [R]enslave
the heart. Is. 5:12; 28:7

2:22 Lit. *God Will Sow* **2:23** Heb. *lo-ruhamah* • Heb. *lo-ammi* **3:1** Lit. *friend* or *husband* **4:7** So with MT, LXX, Vg.; scribal tradition, Syr., Tg. *They will change* • So with MT, LXX, Syr., Tg., Vg.; scribal tradition *My glory*

Idolatry of Israel

12 My people ask counsel from their
[R]wooden *idols*, Jer. 2:27
And their staff informs them.
For [R]the spirit of harlotry has caused
them to stray, Is. 44:19, 20
And they have played the harlot against
their God.
13[R]They offer sacrifices on the
mountaintops, Is. 1:29; 57:5, 7
And burn incense on the hills,
Under oaks, poplars, and terebinths,
Because their shade *is* good.
[R]Therefore your daughters commit
harlotry, Amos 7:17
And your brides commit adultery.

14"I will not punish your daughters when
they commit harlotry,
Nor your brides when they commit
adultery;
For *the men* themselves go apart with
harlots,
And offer sacrifices with a ritual harlot.*
Therefore people *who* do not understand
will be trampled.

15"Though you, Israel, play the harlot,
Let not Judah offend.
[R]Do not come up to Gilgal, Hos. 9:15
Nor go up to [R]Beth Aven, 1 Kin. 12:29
[R]Nor swear an oath, *saying*, 'As the LORD
lives'— Amos 8:14

16"For Israel [R]is stubborn Jer. 3:6; 7:24; 8:5
Like a stubborn calf;
Now the LORD will let them forage
Like a lamb in open country.

17"Ephraim *is* joined to idols,
[R]Let him alone. Matt. 15:14
18 Their drink is rebellion,
They commit harlotry continually.
Her rulers dearly* love dishonor.
19[R]The wind has wrapped her up in its
wings, Jer. 51:1
And [R]they shall be ashamed because of
their sacrifices. Is. 1:29

CHAPTER 5

Judgment on Israel

"HEAR this, O priests!
Take heed, O house of Israel!
Give ear, O house of the king!
For [T]yours *is* the judgment, Or *to you*
Because [R]you have been a snare to
Mizpah Hos. 6:9
And a net spread on Tabor.
2 The revolters are [R]deeply involved in
slaughter, Is. 29:15
Though I rebuke them all.

3[R]I know Ephraim, Amos 3:2; 5:12
And Israel is not hidden from Me;
For now, O Ephraim, [R]you commit
harlotry; Hos. 4:17
Israel is defiled.

4"They do not direct their deeds
Toward turning to their God,
For [R]the spirit of harlotry is in their
midst, Hos. 4:12
And they do not know the LORD.
5 The [R]pride of Israel testifies to his face;
Therefore Israel and Ephraim stumble in
their iniquity; Hos. 7:10
Judah also stumbles with them.

6"With their flocks and herds
[R]They shall go to seek the LORD,
But they will not find *Him*; Prov. 1:28
He has withdrawn Himself from them.
7 They have [R]dealt treacherously with the
LORD, Jer. 3:20
For they have begotten [T]pagan children.
Now a New Moon shall devour them and
their heritage. Lit. *strange*

8"Blow[R] the ram's horn in Gibeah, Joel 2:1
The trumpet in Ramah!
[R]Cry aloud *at* Beth Aven, Is. 10:30
'*Look* behind you, O Benjamin!'
9 Ephraim shall be desolate in the day of
rebuke;
Among the tribes of Israel I make known
what is sure.

10"The princes of Judah are like those who
[R]remove a landmark;
I will pour out My wrath on them like
water. Deut. 19:14; 27:17
11 Ephraim is [R]oppressed *and* broken in
judgment, Deut. 28:33
Because he willingly walked by [R]*human*
precept. Mic. 6:16
12 Therefore I *will be* to Ephraim like a
moth,
And to the house of Judah [R]like
rottenness. Prov. 12:4

13"When Ephraim saw his sickness,
And Judah *saw* his wound,
Then Ephraim went [R]to Assyria
And sent to King Jareb; 2 Kin. 15:19
Yet he cannot cure you,
Nor heal you of your wound.
14 For [R]I *will be* like a lion to Ephraim,
And like a young lion to the house of
Judah. Lam. 3:10
[R]I, *even* I, will tear *them* and go away;
I will take *them* away, and no one shall
rescue. Ps. 50:22

4:14 Cf. Deut. 23:18 **4:18** Heb. difficult; a Jewish tradition *Her rulers shamefully love, 'Give!'*

Eventual Restoration of Israel

15 I will return again to My place
Till they acknowledge their offense.
Then they will seek My face;
In their affliction they will earnestly seek
Me."

CHAPTER 6

COME, and let us return to the LORD;
For [R]He has torn, but [R]He will heal us;
He has stricken, but He will [T]bind us
up. Deut. 32:39 • Jer. 30:17 • Bandage
2[R] After two days He will revive us; [1 Cor. 15:4]☆
On the third day He will raise us up,
That we may live in His sight.
3[R] Let us know, Is. 54:13
Let us pursue the knowledge of the LORD.
His going forth is established [R]as the
morning; 2 Sam. 23:4
[R]He will come to us [R]like the rain,
Like the latter *and* former rain to the
earth. Ps. 72:6 • Job 29:23

Willful Transgression of the Covenant

4 "O Ephraim, what shall I do to you?
O Judah, what shall I do to you?
For your faithfulness is like a morning
cloud,
And like the early dew it goes away.
5 Therefore I have hewn *them* by the
prophets,
I have slain them by [R]the words of My
mouth; [Jer. 23:29]
And [T]your judgments *are like* light *that*
goes forth. Or *the judgments on you*
6 For I desire mercy and [R]not sacrifice,
And the [R]knowledge of God more than
burnt offerings. [Mic. 6:6–8] • [John 17:3]

7 "But like men* they transgressed the
covenant;
There they dealt treacherously with Me.
8[R] Gilead *is* a city of evildoers Hos. 12:11
And [T]defiled with blood. Lit. *foot-tracked*
9 As bands of robbers lie in wait for a man,
So the company of priests [R]murder on
the way to Shechem; Jer. 7:9, 10
Surely they commit lewdness.
10 I have seen a horrible thing in the house
of Israel:
There *is* the [T]harlotry of Ephraim;
Israel is defiled. Spiritual adultery
11 Also, O Judah, a harvest is appointed for
you,
When I return the captives of My people.

CHAPTER 7

Willful Refusal to Return to the Lord

"WHEN I would have healed Israel,
Then the iniquity of Ephraim was
uncovered,
And the wickedness of Samaria.
For [R]they have committed fraud;
A thief comes in; Hos. 5:1
A band of robbers takes spoil outside.
2 They [T]do not consider in their hearts
That [R]I remember all their wickedness;
Now their own deeds have surrounded
them; Lit. *do not say to* • Jer. 14:10; 17:1
They are before My face.
3 They make a [R]king glad with their
wickedness, Hos. 1:1
And princes [R]with their lies. [Rom. 1:32]

4 "They[R] *are* all adulterers. Jer. 9:2; 23:10
Like an oven heated by a baker—
He ceases stirring *the fire* after kneading
the dough,
Until it is leavened.
5 In the day of our king
Princes have made *him* sick, [T]inflamed
with [R]wine; Lit. *with the heat of* • Is. 28:1, 7
He stretched out his hand with scoffers.
6 They prepare their heart like an oven,
While they lie in wait;
Their baker* sleeps all night;
In the morning it burns like a flaming
fire.
7 They are all hot, like an oven,
And have devoured their judges;
All their kings have fallen.
[R]None among them calls upon Me. Is. 64:7

8 "Ephraim [R]has mixed himself among the
peoples; Ps. 106:35
Ephraim is a cake unturned.
9[R] Aliens have devoured his strength,
But he does not know *it;* Hos. 8:7
Yes, gray hairs are here and there on
him,
Yet he does not know *it.*
10 And the [R]pride of Israel testifies to his
face, Hos. 5:5
But [R]they do not return to the LORD their
God, Is. 9:13
Nor seek Him for all this.

11 "Ephraim[R] also is like a silly dove,
without [T]sense— Hos. 11:11 • Lit. *heart*
[R]They call to Egypt, Is. 30:3
They go to [R]Assyria. Hos. 5:13; 8:9
12 Wherever they go, I will [R]spread My net
on them; Ezek. 12:13
I will bring them down like birds of the
air;
I will chastise them
[R]According to what their congregation
has heard. Lev. 26:14

13 "Woe to them, for they have fled from Me!
Destruction to them,

6:7 Or *like Adam* **7:6** So with MT, Vg.; Syr., Tg. *Their anger;* LXX *Ephraim*

Because they have transgressed against
Me!
Though [R]I redeemed them, Mic. 6:4
Yet they have spoken lies against Me.
14 [R]They did not cry out to Me with their
heart Job 35:9, 10
When they wailed upon their beds.

"They assemble together for* grain and
new [R]wine, Amos 2:8
They rebel against Me;*
15 Though I disciplined *and* strengthened
their arms,
Yet they devise evil against Me;
16 They return, *but* not to the Most High;*
They are like a treacherous bow.
Their princes shall fall by the sword
For the [R]cursings of their tongue.
This *shall be* their derision [R]in the land
of Egypt. Ps. 73:9 • Hos. 8:13; 9:3

CHAPTER 8

Willful Idolatry

"SET the trumpet* to your mouth!
He shall come [R]like an eagle against
the house of the LORD, Deut. 28:49
Because they have transgressed My
covenant
And rebelled against My law.
2 [R]Israel will cry to Me, Ps. 78:34
'My God, [R]we know You!' Titus 1:16
3 Israel has rejected the good;
The enemy will pursue him.

4 "They[R] set up kings, but not by Me;
They made princes, but I did not
acknowledge *them.* 2 Kin. 15:23, 25
From their silver and gold
They made idols for themselves—
That they might be cut off.
5 Your calf is rejected, O Samaria!
My anger is aroused against them—
How long until they attain to innocence?
6 For from Israel *is* even this:
A [R]workman made it, and it *is* not God;
But the calf of Samaria shall be broken
to pieces. Is. 40:19

7 "They[R] sow the wind, Prov. 22:8
And reap the whirlwind.
The stalk has no bud;
It shall never produce meal.
If it should produce,
[R]Aliens would swallow it up. Hos. 7:9
8 [R]Israel is swallowed up; 2 Kin. 17:6
Now they are among the Gentiles
Like a vessel in which *is* no pleasure.
9 For they have gone up to Assyria,
Like [R]a wild donkey alone by itself;
Ephraim has hired lovers. Jer. 2:24
10 Yes, though they have hired among the
nations,
Now [R]I will gather them; Ezek. 16:37
And they shall sorrow a little,*
Because of the burden* of [R]the king of
princes. Is. 10:8

11 "Because Ephraim has made many altars
for sin,
They have become for him altars for
sinning.
12 I have written for him [R]the great things
of My law, [Deut. 4:6–8]
But they were considered a strange thing.
13 *For* the sacrifices of My offerings [R]they
sacrifice flesh and eat *it,* Zech. 7:6
[R]*But* the LORD does not accept them.
[R]Now He will remember their iniquity
and punish their sins. Jer. 14:10 • Amos 8:7
They shall return to Egypt.

14 "For Israel has forgotten [R]his Maker,
And has built temples;* Is. 29:23
Judah also has multiplied [R]fortified
cities; Num. 32:17
But I will send fire upon his cities,
And it shall devour his palaces."

CHAPTER 9

Judgment of Dispersion

DO[R] not rejoice, O Israel, with joy like
other peoples, Is. 22:12, 13
For you have played the harlot against
your God.
You have made love *for* [R]hire on every
threshing floor. Jer. 44:17
2 The threshing floor and the winepress
Shall not feed them,
And the new wine shall fail in her.

3 They shall not dwell in the LORD's land,
But Ephraim shall return to Egypt,
And shall eat unclean *things* in Assyria.
4 They shall not offer wine *offerings* to the
LORD,
Nor [R]shall their [R]sacrifices be pleasing to
Him. Jer. 6:20 • Hos. 8:13
It shall be like bread of mourners to
them;
All who eat it shall be defiled.
For their bread *shall be* for their *own*
life;
It shall not come into the house of the
LORD.

5 What will you do in the appointed day,
And in the day of the feast of the LORD?

7:14 So with MT, Tg.; Vg. *thought upon;* LXX *slashed themselves for* (cf. 1 Kin. 18:28) • So with MT, Syr., Tg.; LXX omits *They rebel against Me;* Vg. *They departed from Me* **7:16** Or *upward* **8:1** ram's horn, Heb. *shophar* **8:10** Or *begin to diminish* • Or *oracle* or *proclamation* **8:14** Or *palaces*

6 For indeed they are gone because of
destruction.
Egypt shall gather them up;
Memphis shall bury them.
[R]Nettles shall possess their valuables of
silver; Is. 5:6; 7:23
Thorns *shall be* in their tents.

7 The [R]days of punishment have come;
The days of recompense have come.
Israel knows! Is. 10:3
The prophet *is* a [R]fool, Lam. 2:14
[R]The spiritual man *is* insane, Mic. 2:11
Because of the greatness of your iniquity
and great enmity.
8 The [R]watchman of Ephraim *is* with my
God; Ezek. 3:17; 33:7
But the prophet *is* a fowler's* snare in all
his ways—
Enmity in the house of his God.
9 [R]They are deeply corrupted, Hos. 10:9
As in the days of [R]Gibeah. Judg. 19:22
He will remember their iniquity;
He will punish their sins.

Judgment of Barrenness

10 "I found Israel
Like grapes in the [R]wilderness; Jer. 2:2
I saw your fathers
As the [R]firstfruits on the fig tree in its
first season. Is. 28:4
But they went to [R]Baal Peor, Num. 25:3
And [T]separated themselves *to that*
shame; Or *dedicated*
[R]They became an abomination like the
thing they loved. Ps. 81:12
11 *As for* Ephraim, their glory shall fly
away like a bird—
No birth, no pregnancy, and no
conception!
12 Though they bring up their children,
Yet I will bereave them to the last man.
Yes, [R]woe to them when I depart from
them! Deut. 31:17
13 Just [R]as I saw Ephraim like Tyre, planted
in a pleasant place,
So Ephraim will bring out his children to
the murderer." Ezek. 26—28

14 Give them, O LORD—
What will You give?
Give them [R]a miscarrying womb
And dry breasts! Luke 23:29

15 "All their wickedness *is* in [R]Gilgal,
For there I hated them.
Because of the evil of their deeds
I will drive them from My house;
I will love them no more. Hos. 4:15
[R]All their princes *are* rebellious. Is. 1:23
16 Ephraim is [R]stricken, Hos. 5:11
Their root is dried up;
They shall bear no fruit.
Yes, were they to bear children,
I would kill the darlings of their womb."
17 My God will [R]cast them away,
Because they did not obey Him;
And they shall be [R]wanderers among the
nations. [Zech. 10:6] • Lev. 26:33

CHAPTER 10

Judgment of Destruction

1 ISRAEL [R]empties *his* vine; Nah. 2:2
He brings forth fruit for himself.
According to the multitude of his fruit
[R]He has increased the altars; Jer. 2:28
According to the bounty of his land
They have embellished *his* sacred pillars.
2 Their heart is [R]divided; 1 Kin. 18:21
Now they are held guilty.
He will break down their altars;
He will ruin their sacred pillars.

3 For now they say,
"We have no king,
Because we did not fear the LORD.
And as for a king, what would he do for
us?"
4 They have spoken words,
Swearing falsely in making a covenant.
Thus judgment springs up [R]like hemlock
in the furrows of the field. Amos 5:7

5 The inhabitants of Samaria fear
Because of the calf* of Beth Aven.
For its people mourn for it,
And its priests shriek for it—
Because its glory has departed from it.
6 *The idol* also shall be carried to Assyria
As a present for King [R]Jareb. Hos. 5:13
Ephraim shall receive shame,
And Israel shall be ashamed of his own
counsel.

7 *As for* Samaria, her king is cut off
Like a twig on the water.
8 Also the [R]high places of Aven, [R]the sin of
Israel, Hos. 4:15 • 1 Kin. 13:34
Shall be destroyed.
The thorn and thistle shall grow on their
altars;
[R]They shall say to the mountains, "Cover
us!" Luke 23:30
And to the hills, "Fall on us!"

9 "O Israel, you have sinned from the days
of [R]Gibeah; Hos. 9:9
There they stood.
The [R]battle in Gibeah against the
children of iniquity* Judg. 20

9:8 One who catches birds in a trap or snare
10:5 Lit. *calves,* images **10:9** So with many Heb. mss., LXX, Vg.; MT *unruliness*

Did not [T]overtake them. Or *overcome*
10 When *it is* My desire, I will chasten them.
[R]Peoples shall be gathered against them
When I bind them for their two
transgressions.* Jer. 16:16
11 Ephraim *is* [R]a trained heifer [Mic. 4:13]
That loves to thresh *grain;*
But I harnessed her fair neck,
I will make Ephraim [T]pull *a plow.*
Judah shall plow; Lit. *to ride*
Jacob shall break his clods."

12 Sow for yourselves righteousness;
Reap in mercy;
[R]Break up your fallow ground, Jer. 4:3
For *it is* time to seek the LORD,
Till He [R]comes and rains righteousness
on you. Hos. 6:3

13 [R]You have plowed wickedness; [Prov. 22:8]
You have reaped iniquity.
You have eaten the fruit of lies,
Because you trusted in your own way,
In the multitude of your mighty men.
14 Therefore tumult shall arise among your
people,
And all your fortresses shall be
plundered
As Shalman plundered Beth Arbel in the
day of battle—
A mother dashed in pieces upon *her*
children.
15 Thus it shall be done to you, O Bethel,
Because of your great wickedness.
At dawn the king of Israel
Shall be cut off utterly.

CHAPTER 11

God's Love for Israel

"WHEN Israel *was* a child, I loved him,
And out of Egypt I called My son.
2 *As* they called them,*
So they went from them;*
They sacrificed to the Baals,
And burned incense to carved images.

3 "I[R] taught Ephraim to walk, Deut. 1:31
Taking them by their arms;*
But they did not know that [R]I healed
them. Ex. 15:26
4 I drew them with gentle cords,*
With bands of love,
And I was to them as those who take the
yoke from their neck.*
[R]I stooped *and* fed them. Ps. 78:25

5 "He shall not return to the land of Egypt;
But the Assyrian shall be his king,
Because they refused to repent.
6 And the sword shall slash in his cities,
Devour his districts,
And consume *them,*
Because of their own counsels.
7 My people are bent on [R]backsliding from
Me. Jer. 3:6, 7; 8:5
Though [T]they call to the Most High,*
None at all exalt *Him.* The prophets

8 "How[R] can I give you up, Ephraim?
How can I hand you over, Israel?
How can I make you like Admah?
How can I set you like Zeboiim?
My heart churns within Me;
My sympathy is stirred. Jer. 9:7

9 I will not execute the fierceness of My
anger;
I will not again destroy Ephraim.
For I *am* God, and not man,
The Holy One in your midst;
And I will not come with terror.*

10 "They shall walk after the LORD.
[R]He will roar like a lion. [Joel 3:16]
When He roars,
Then *His* sons shall come trembling
from the west;
11 They shall come trembling like a bird
from Egypt,
Like a dove from the land of Assyria.
[R]And I will let them dwell in their
houses," Ezek. 28:25, 26; 34:27, 28
Says the LORD.

12 "Ephraim has encircled Me with lies,
And the house of Israel with deceit;
But Judah still walks with God,
Even with the Holy One* *who is* faithful.

CHAPTER 12

Israel's Continuing Sin

"EPHRAIM [R]feeds on the wind, Job 15:2, 3
And pursues the east wind;
He daily increases lies and [T]desolation.
[R]Also they make a [T]covenant with the
Assyrians, *ruin* • 2 Kin. 17:4 • Or *treaty*
And [R]oil is carried to Egypt. Is. 30:6

2 "The[R] LORD also *brings* a [T]charge against
Judah, Mic. 6:2 • A legal complaint
And will punish Jacob according to his
ways;
According to his deeds He will
recompense him.
3 He took his brother [R]by the heel in the
womb, Gen. 25:26

10:10 Or *in their two habitations* **11:2** So with MT, Vg.; LXX *Just as I called them;* Tg. interprets as *I sent prophets to a thousand of them.* • So with MT, Tg., Vg.; LXX *from My face* **11:3** Some Heb. mss., LXX, Syr., Vg. *My arms* **11:4** Lit. *cords of a man* • Lit. *jaws* **11:7** Or *upward* **11:9** Or *I will not enter a city* **11:12** Or *holy ones*

And in his strength he struggled with
God.*
4 Yes, he struggled with the Angel and
prevailed;
He wept, and sought favor from Him.
He found Him *in* Bethel,
And there He spoke to us—
5 That is, the LORD God of hosts.
The LORD *is* His memorable name.
6[R] So you, by *the help of* your God, return;
Observe mercy and justice, Mic. 6:8
And wait on your God continually.

7 "A cunning [T]Canaanite! Or *merchant*
[R]Deceitful scales *are* in his hand;
He loves to oppress. Amos 8:5
8 And Ephraim said,
[R]'Surely I have become rich, Rev. 3:17
I have found wealth for myself;
In all my labors
They shall find in me no iniquity that *is*
sin.'

9 "But I *am* the LORD your God,
Ever since the land of Egypt;
I will again make you dwell in tents,
As in the days of the appointed feast.
10[R] I have also spoken by the prophets,
And have multiplied visions; 2 Kin. 17:13
I have given [T]symbols through the
witness of the prophets." Or *parables*

11 Though [R]Gilead *has* idols— Hos. 6:8
Surely they are [T]vanity— *worthless*
Though they sacrifice bulls in [R]Gilgal,
Indeed their altars *shall be* heaps in the
furrows of the field. Hos. 9:15

12 Jacob fled to the country of Syria;
[R]Israel served for a spouse, Gen. 29:20, 28
And for a wife he tended *sheep.*
13[R] By a prophet the LORD brought Israel out
of Egypt, Ex. 12:50, 51; 13:3
And by a prophet he was preserved.
14 Ephraim [R]provoked *Him* to anger most
bitterly; Ezek. 18:10–13
Therefore his Lord will leave the guilt of
his bloodshed upon him,
And return his reproach upon him.

CHAPTER 13

WHEN Ephraim spoke, trembling,
He exalted *himself* in Israel;
But when he offended through Baal
worship, he died.
2 Now they sin more and more,
And have made for themselves molded
images,
Idols of their silver, according to their
skill;
All of it *is* the work of craftsmen.
They say of them,
"Let the men who sacrifice* [T]kiss the
calves!" Worship with kisses
3 Therefore they shall be like the morning
cloud
And like the early dew that passes
away,
[R]Like chaff blown off from a threshing
floor Dan. 2:35
And like smoke from a chimney.

4 "Yet [R]I *am* the LORD your God Is. 43:11
Ever since the land of Egypt,
And you shall know no God but Me;
For *there is* no savior besides Me.
5 I knew you in the wilderness,
[R]In the land of great drought. Deut. 8:15
6[R] When they had pasture, they were filled;
They were filled and their heart was
exalted; Deut. 8:12, 14; 32:13–15
Therefore they forgot Me.

7 "So I will be to them like a lion;
Like a leopard by the road I will lurk;
8 I will meet them [R]like a bear deprived *of
her cubs;* 2 Sam. 17:8
I will tear open their rib cage,
And there I will devour them like a lion.
The wild beast shall tear them.

9 "O Israel, you are destroyed,*
But your help* *is* from Me.
10 I will be your King;*
[R]Where *is any other,* Deut. 32:38
That he may save you in all your cities?
And your judges to whom you said,
'Give me a king and princes'?
11 I gave you a king in My anger,
And took *him* away in My wrath.

12 "The[R] iniquity of Ephraim *is* bound up;
His sin *is* stored up. Deut. 32:34, 35
13[R] The sorrows of a woman in childbirth
shall come upon him. Is. 13:8
He *is* an unwise son,
For he should not stay long where
children are born.

14 "I will ransom them from the [T]power of
the grave;* Lit. *hand*
I will redeem them from death.
O Death, I will be your plagues!*
O Grave,* I will be your destruction!*
[R]Pity is hidden from My eyes." Jer. 15:6

15 Though he is fruitful among *his*
brethren,
[R]An east wind shall come; Jer. 4:11, 12

12:3 Cf. Gen. 32:28 **13:2** Or *those who offer human sacrifice* **13:9** Lit. *it* or *he destroyed you* • Lit. *in your help* **13:10** LXX, Syr., Tg., Vg. *Where is your king?* **13:14** Or *Sheol* • LXX *where is your punishment?* • Or *Sheol* • LXX *where is your sting?*

The wind of the LORD shall come up
from the wilderness.
Then his spring shall become dry,
And his fountain shall be dried up.
He shall plunder the treasury of every
desirable prize.
16 Samaria is held guilty,*
For she has [R]rebelled against her God.
They shall fall by the sword, 2 Kin. 18:12
Their infants shall be dashed in pieces,
And their women with child [R]ripped
open. 2 Kin. 15:16

CHAPTER 14

God's Promise to Restore Israel

O ISRAEL, [R]return to the LORD your
God,
For you have stumbled because of your
iniquity; [Joel 2:13]
2 Take words with you,
And return to the LORD.
Say to Him,
"Take away all iniquity;
Receive *us* graciously,
For we will offer the [R]sacrifices* of our
lips. [Heb. 13:15]
3 Assyria shall [R]not save us, Hos. 7:11
[R]We will not ride on horses, [Ps. 33:17]
Nor will we say anymore to the work of
our hands,
'*You are* our gods.'
For in You the fatherless finds mercy."

4 "I will heal their [R]backsliding, Jer. 14:7
I will [R]love them freely, [Eph. 1:6]
For My anger has turned away from him.
5 I will be like the [R]dew to Israel;
He shall grow like the lily, Prov. 19:12
And lengthen his roots like Lebanon.
6 His branches shall [T]spread; Lit. *go*
His beauty shall be like an olive tree,
And his fragrance like Lebanon.
7 [R]Those who dwell under his shadow shall
return; Dan. 4:12
They shall be revived *like* grain,
And [T]grow like a vine. Lit. *bud* or *sprout*
Their scent* *shall be* like the wine of
Lebanon.

8 "Ephraim *shall say,*
'What have I to do anymore with idols?'
I have heard and observed him.
I *am* like a green cypress tree;
[R]Your fruit is found in Me." [John 15:4]

9 Who *is* wise?
Let him understand these things.
Who is prudent?
Let him know them.
For the ways of the LORD *are* right;
The righteous walk in them,
But transgressors stumble in them.

13:16 LXX *shall be disfigured* **14:2** Lit. *bull calves;* LXX *fruit* **14:7** Lit. *remembrance*

THE BOOK OF
JOEL

THE BOOK OF JOEL

Disaster strikes the southern kingdom of Judah without warning. An ominous black cloud descends upon the land—the dreaded locusts. In a matter of hours, every living green thing has been stripped bare. Joel, God's spokesman during the reign of Joash (835–796 B.C.), seizes this occasion to proclaim God's message. Although the locust plague has been a terrible judgment for sin, God's future judgments during the day of the Lord will make that plague pale by comparison. In that day, God will destroy His enemies, but bring unparalleled blessing to those who faithfully obey Him.

The Hebrew name *Yo'el* means "Yahweh Is God." This name is appropriate to the theme of the book, which emphasizes God's sovereign work in history. The courses of nature and nations are in His hand. The Greek equivalent is *Ioel,* and the Latin is *Joel.*

THE AUTHOR OF JOEL

Although there are several other Joels in the Bible, the prophet Joel is known only from this book. In the introductory verse, Joel identifies himself as the son of Pethuel (1:1), meaning "Persuaded of God." His frequent references to Zion and the house of the Lord (1:9, 13, 14; 2:15–17, 23, 32; 3:1, 5, 6, 16, 17, 20, 21) suggest that he probably lived not far from Jerusalem. Because of his statements about the priesthood in 1:13, 14 and 2:17, some think Joel was a priest as well as a prophet. In any case, Joel was a clear, concise, and uncompromising preacher of repentance.

THE TIME OF JOEL

Since this book includes no explicit time references, it cannot be dated with certainty. Some commentators assign a late date (usually postexilic) to Joel for these reasons: (1) It does not mention the northern kingdom and indicates it was written after the 722 B.C. demise of Israel. (2) The references to priests but not kings fit the postexilic period. (3) Joel does not refer to Assyria, Syria, or Babylon, perhaps because these countries have already been overthrown. (4) If Joel 3:2 refers to the Babylonian captivity, this also supports the postexilic date. (5) The mention of the Greeks in 3:6 argues for a late date.

Commentators who believe Joel was written in the ninth century B.C. answer the above arguments in this way: (1) Joel's failure to mention the northern kingdom is an argument from silence. His prophecy was directed to Judah, not Israel. (2) Other early prophets omit references to a king (Obadiah, Jonah, Nahum, and Habakkuk). This also fits the political situation during 841–835 B.C. when Athaliah usurped the throne upon the death of her son Ahaziah. Joash, the legitimate heir to the throne, was a minor and protected by the high priest Jehoiada. When Athaliah was removed from power in 835, Joash came to the throne but ruled under the regency of Jehoiada. Thus, the prominence of the priests and lack of reference to a king in Joel fit this historical context. (3) It is true that Joel does not refer to Assyria or Babylon, but the countries Joel mentions are more crucial. They include Phoenicia, Philistia, Egypt, and Edom—countries prominent in the ninth century but not later. Assyria and Babylon are not mentioned because they had not yet reached a position of power. Also, if Joel was postexilic, a reference to Persia would be expected. (4) Joel 3:2 does not refer to the Babylonian captivity but to an event that has not yet occurred. (5) Greeks are mentioned in Assyrian records from the eighth century B.C. It is just an assumption to state that the Hebrews had no knowledge of the Greeks at an early time.

Evidence also points to a sharing of material between Joel and Amos (cf. Joel 3:16 and Amos 1:2; Joel 3:18 and Amos 9:13). The context of the books suggests that Amos, an eighth-century prophet, borrowed from Joel. Also, Joel's style is more like that of Hosea and Amos than of the postexilic writers. The evidence seems to favor a date of about 835 B.C. for Joel. Since Joel does not mention idolatry, it may have been written after the purge of Baal worship and most other forms of idolatry in the early reign of Joash under Jehoiada the priest. As an early prophet of Judah, Joel would have been a contemporary of Elisha in Israel.

THE CHRIST OF JOEL

Christ promised to send the Holy Spirit after His ascension to the Father (John 16:7–15; Acts 1:8). When this was fulfilled on the Day of Pentecost, Peter said, "This is what was spoken by the prophet Joel" (Joel 2:28–32; Acts 2:16–21). Joel also portrays Christ as the One who will judge the nations in the Valley of Jehoshaphat in 3:2, 12.

KEYS TO JOEL

Key Word: The Great and Terrible Day of the Lord—The key theme of Joel is the day of the Lord in retrospect and prospect. Joel uses the terrible locust plague that has recently occurred in Judah to illustrate the coming day of judgment when God will directly intervene in human history to vindicate His righteousness. This will be a time of unparalleled retribution upon Israel (2:1–11) and the whole nation (3:1–17), but this time will culminate in great blessing and salvation for all who trust in the Lord (2:18–32; 3:18–21). "And it shall come to pass *that* whoever calls on the name of the LORD shall be saved" (2:32).

Joel is written as a warning to the people of Judah of their need to turn humbly to the Lord with penitent hearts (2:12–17) so that God can bless rather than buffet them. If they continue to spurn God's gracious call to repentance, judgment will be inevitable. Joel stresses the sovereign power of God over nature and nations, and points out how God uses nature to get the attention of people.

Key Verses: Joel 2:11, 28, 29—"The LORD gives voice before His army, for His camp is very great; for strong *is the One* who executes His word. For the day of the LORD *is* great and very terrible; who can endure it?" (2:11).

"And it shall come to pass afterward that I will pour out My Spirit on all flesh; your sons and your daughters shall prophesy, your old men shall dream dreams, your young men shall see visions. And also on *My* menservants and on *My* maidservants I will pour out My Spirit in those days" (2:28, 29).

Key Chapter: Joel 2—The prophet calls for Judah's repentance and promises God's repentance (2:13,14) from His planned judgment upon Judah if they do indeed turn to Him. Though the offer is clearly given, Judah continues to rebel against the Lord, and judgment is to follow. In that judgment, however, is God's promise of His later outpouring, fulfilled initially on the Day of Pentecost (Acts 2:16ff.) and ultimately when Christ returns for the culmination of the day of the Lord.

SURVEY OF JOEL

This brief book develops the crucial theme of the coming day of the Lord (1:15; 2:1, 2, 11, 31; 3:14, 18). It is a time of awesome judgment upon people and nations that have rebelled against God. But it is also a time of future blessing upon those who have trusted in Him. The theme of disaster runs throughout the book (locust plagues, famine, raging fires, invading armies, celestial phenomena), but promises of hope are interspersed with the pronouncements of coming judgment. The basic outline of Joel is: the day of the Lord in retrospect (1:1–20) and the day of the Lord in prospect (2:1—3:21).

The Day of the Lord in Retrospect (1:1–20): Joel begins with an account of a recent locust plague that has devastated the land. The black cloud of insects has stripped the grapevines and fruit trees and ruined the grain harvest. The economy has been brought to a further standstill by a drought and the people are in a desperate situation.

The Day of the Lord in Prospect (2:1—3:21): Joel makes effective use of this natural catastrophe as an illustration of a far greater judgment to come. Compared to the terrible day of the Lord, the destruction by the locusts will seem insignificant. The land will be invaded by a swarming army; like locusts they will be speedy and voracious. The desolation caused by this army will be dreadful: "The day of the LORD *is* great and very terrible; who can endure it?" (2:11).

Even so, it is not too late for the people to avert disaster. The prophetic warning is designed to bring them to the point of repentance (2:12–17). " 'Now, therefore,' says the LORD, 'turn

FOCUS	DAY OF THE LORD IN RETROSPECT		DAY OF THE LORD IN PROSPECT	
REFERENCE	1:1——1:13——	2:1——	2:28——	3:21
DIVISION	PAST DAY OF THE LOCUST	PAST DAY OF THE DROUGHT	IMMINENT DAY OF THE LORD	ULTIMATE DAY OF THE LORD
TOPIC	HISTORICAL INVASION		PROPHETIC INVASION	
	PAST JUDGMENT OF JUDAH		FUTURE JUDGMENT AND RESTORATION OF JUDAH	
LOCATION	SOUTHERN KINGDOM OF JUDAH			
TIME	C. 835 B.C.			

to Me with all your heart, with fasting, with weeping, and with mourning' " (2:12). But God's gracious offer falls on deaf ears.

Ultimately, the swarming, creeping, stripping, and gnawing locusts (1:4; 2:25) will come again in a fiercer form. But God promises that judgment will be followed by great blessing in a material (2:18–27) and spiritual (2:28–32) sense.

These rich promises are followed by a solemn description of the judgment of all nations in the valley of decision (3:14) in the end times. The nations will give an account of themselves to the God of Israel who will judge those who have rebelled against Him. God alone controls the course of history. "So you shall know that I *am* the LORD your God, dwelling in Zion My holy mountain" (3:17). Joel ends with the kingdom blessings upon the remnant of faithful Judah: "But Judah shall abide forever, and Jerusalem from generation to generation" (3:20).

OUTLINE OF JOEL

I. The Day of the Lord in Retrospect.......1:1–20

A. The Past Day of the Locust....................1:1–12
B. The Past Day of the Drought...............1:13–20

II. The Day of the Lord in Prospect......2:1—3:21

A. The Imminent Day of the Lord.............2:1–27
1. Prophecy of the Imminent Invasion of Judah...2:1–11
2. Conditional Promise of the Salvation of Judah...2:12–27
B. The Ultimate Day of the Lord.........2:28—3:21
1. Last Events Before the Terrible Day of the Lord 2:28–32
2. Events of the Terrible Day of the Lord...3:1–21

CHAPTER 1

The Past Day of the Locust

THE word of the LORD that came to [R]Joel
the son of Pethuel. Acts 2:16

2 Hear this, you elders,
And give ear, all you inhabitants of the
land!
[R]Has *anything like* this happened in your
days, Joel 2:2
Or even in the days of your fathers?
3[R] Tell your children about it, Ps. 78:4
Let your children *tell* their children,
And their children another generation.

4 What the chewing locust* left, the
swarming locust has eaten;
What the swarming locust left, the
crawling locust has eaten;
And what the crawling locust left, the
consuming locust has eaten.

5 Awake, you [R]drunkards, and weep;
And wail, all you drinkers of wine,
Because of the new wine, Is. 5:11; 28:1
For it has been cut off from your mouth.
6 For [R]a nation has come up against My
land, Joel 2:2, 11, 25
Strong, and without number;
[R]His teeth *are* the teeth of a lion, Rev. 9:8
And he has the fangs of a fierce lion.
7 He has [R]laid waste My vine, Is. 5:6
And [T]ruined My fig tree; Or *splintered*
He has stripped it bare and thrown *it*
away;
Its branches are made white.

8[R] Lament like a virgin girded with
sackcloth Is. 22:12
For [R]the husband of her youth. Jer. 3:4
9[R] The grain offering and the drink
offering
Have been cut off from the house of the
LORD; Joel 1:13; 2:14
The priests [R]mourn, who minister to the
LORD. Joel 2:17
10 The field is wasted,
[R]The land mourns; Jer. 12:11
For the grain is ruined,
[R]The new wine is dried up, Is. 24:7
The oil fails.

11[R] Be ashamed, you farmers, Jer. 14:3, 4
Wail, you vinedressers,
For the wheat and the barley;
Because the harvest of the field has
perished.
12[R] The vine has dried up, Joel 1:10
And the fig tree has withered;
The pomegranate tree,
The palm tree also,
And the apple tree—
All the trees of the field are withered;
Surely [R]joy has withered away from the
sons of men. Jer. 48:33

The Past Day of the Drought

13[R] Gird yourselves and lament, you priests;
Wail, you who minister before the altar;
Come, lie all night in sackcloth,
You who minister to my God; Jer. 4:8
For the grain offering and the drink
offering

1:4 Exact identity of these locusts unknown

Are withheld from the house of your
God.
14[R] Consecrate a fast, Joel 2:15, 16
Call [R]a sacred assembly; Lev. 23:36
Gather the elders
And [R]all the inhabitants of the land
Into the house of the LORD your God,
And cry out to the LORD. 2 Chr. 20:13

15[R] Alas for the day! [Jer. 30:7]
For [R]the day of the LORD *is* at hand;
It shall come as destruction from the
Almighty. Is. 13:6
16 Is not the food [R]cut off before our eyes,
[R]Joy and gladness from the house of our
God? Is. 3:1 • Deut. 12:7
17 The seed shrivels under the clods,
Storehouses are in shambles;
Barns are broken down,
For the grain has withered.
18 How [R]the animals groan! Hos. 4:3
The herds of cattle are restless,
Because they have no pasture;
Even the flocks of sheep suffer
punishment.*

19 O LORD, [R]to You I cry out; [Ps. 50:15]
For [R]fire has devoured the [T]open
pastures, Jer. 9:10
And a flame has burned all the trees of
the field. Lit. *pastures of the wilderness*
20 The beasts of the field also [R]cry out to
You, Ps. 104:21; 147:9
For [R]the water brooks are dried up,
And fire has devoured the open
pastures. 1 Kin. 17:7; 18:5

CHAPTER 2

Prophecy of the Imminent Invasion of Judah

BLOW [R]the [T]trumpet in Zion, Jer. 4:5
And [R]sound an alarm in My holy
mountain! *ram's horn* • Num. 10:5
Let all the inhabitants of the land
tremble;
For [R]the day of the LORD is coming,
For it is at hand: [Obad. 15]
2[R] A day of darkness and gloominess,
A day of clouds and thick darkness,
Like the morning *clouds* spread over the
mountains. Amos 5:18
[R]A people *come,* great and strong,
[R]The like of whom has never been;
Nor will there ever be any *such* after
them, Joel 1:6; 2:11, 25 • Dan. 9:12; 12:1
Even for many successive generations.

3 A fire devours before them,
And behind them a flame burns;
The land *is* like [R]the Garden of Eden
before them, Is. 51:3
And behind them a desolate wilderness;
Surely nothing shall escape them.

4[R] Their appearance is like the appearance
of horses; Rev. 9:7
And like swift steeds, so they run.
5[R] With a noise like chariots Rev. 9:9
Over mountaintops they leap,
Like the noise of a flaming fire that
devours the stubble,
Like a strong people set in battle array.

6 Before them the people writhe in pain;
All faces are drained of color.*
7 They run like mighty men,
They climb the wall like men of war;
Every one marches in formation,
And they do not break ranks.
8 They do not push one another;
Every one marches in his own column.*
Though they lunge between the
weapons,
They are not cut down.*
9 They run to and fro in the city,
They run on the wall;
They climb into the houses,
They enter at the windows like a thief.

10[R] The earth quakes before them, Ps. 18:7
The heavens tremble;
The sun and moon grow dark,
And the stars diminish their brightness.
11[R] The LORD gives voice before His army,
For His camp is very great; Jer. 25:30
[R]For strong *is the One* who executes His
word. Rev. 18:8
For the [R]day of the LORD *is* great and
very terrible; Amos 5:18
[R]Who can endure it? [Mal. 3:2]

Conditional Promise of the Salvation of Judah

12 "Now, therefore," says the LORD,
[R]"Turn to Me with all your heart, Jer. 4:1
With fasting, with weeping, and with
mourning."
13 So [R]rend your heart, and not [R]your
garments; [Ps. 34:18; 51:17] • Gen. 37:34
Return to the LORD your God,
For He *is* gracious and merciful,
Slow to anger, and of great kindness;
And He relents from doing harm.
14 Who knows *if* He will turn and relent,
And leave [R]a blessing behind Him—
A grain offering and a drink offering
For the LORD your God? Hag. 2:19

15[R] Blow the [T]trumpet in Zion, Num. 10:3
[R]Consecrate a fast, *ram's horn* • Joel 1:14
Call a sacred assembly;
16 Gather the people,
[R]Sanctify the congregation, Ex. 19:10

1:18 LXX, Vg. *are made desolate* **2:6** LXX, Tg., Vg. *gather blackness* **2:8** Lit. *his own highway* • That is, they are not halted by losses

Assemble the elders,
Gather the children and nursing babes;
[R]Let the bridegroom go out from his chamber, Ps. 19:5
And the bride from her dressing room.
17 Let the priests, who minister to the LORD,
Weep [R]between the porch and the altar;
Let them say, [R]"Spare Your people, O LORD, Matt. 23:35 • Ex. 32:11, 12
And do not give Your heritage to reproach,
That the nations should rule over them.
[R]Why should they say among the peoples, Ps. 42:10
'Where *is* their God?' "

18 Then the LORD will [R]be zealous for His land, [Is. 60:10; 63:9, 15]
And pity His people.
19 The LORD will answer and say to His people,
"Behold, I will send you [R]grain and new wine and oil, [Mal. 3:10]
And you will be satisfied by them;
I will no longer make you a reproach among the nations.

20"But [R]I will remove far from you [R]the northern *army*, Ex. 10:19 • Jer. 1:14, 15
And will drive him away into a barren and desolate land,
With his face toward the eastern sea
And his back [R]toward the western sea;
His stench will come up,
And his foul odor will rise, Deut. 11:24
Because he has done [T]monstrous things." Lit. *great*

21 Fear not, O land;
Be glad and rejoice,
For the LORD has done [T]marvelous things! Lit. *great*
22 Do not be afraid, you beasts of the field;
For [R]the open pastures are springing up,
And the tree bears its fruit; Joel 1:19
The fig tree and the vine yield their strength.
23 Be glad then, you children of Zion,
And [R]rejoice in the LORD your God;
For He has given you the former rain faithfully,* Is. 41:16
And He [R]will cause the rain to come down for you— Lev. 26:4
The former rain,
And the latter rain in the first *month*.
24 The threshing floors shall be full of wheat,
And the vats shall overflow with new wine and oil.

25"So I will restore to you the years that the swarming locust has eaten,
The crawling locust,
The consuming locust,
And the chewing locust,*
My great army which I sent among you.
26 You shall [R]eat in plenty and be satisfied,
And praise the name of the LORD your God, Lev. 26:5
Who has dealt wondrously with you;
And My people shall never be put to [R]shame. Is. 45:17
27 Then you shall know that I *am* [R]in the midst of Israel: Lev. 26:11, 12
[R]I *am* the LORD your God [Is. 45:5, 6]
And there is no other.
My people shall never be put to shame.

Last Events Before the Terrible Day of the Lord

28"And[R] it shall come to pass afterward
That [R]I will pour out My Spirit on all flesh; Ezek. 39:29 • Zech. 12:10
[R]Your sons and your [R]daughters shall prophesy, Is. 54:13 • Acts 21:9
Your old men shall dream dreams,
Your young men shall see visions.
29 And also on *My* [R]menservants and on *My* maidservants [Gal. 3:28]
I will pour out My Spirit in those days.

30"And [R]I will show wonders in the heavens and in the earth: Matt. 24:29
Blood and fire and pillars of smoke.
31[R]The sun shall be turned into darkness,
And the moon into blood, Is. 13:9, 10; 34:4
Before the coming of the great and awesome day of the LORD.
32 And it shall come to pass
That [R]whoever calls on the name of the LORD Rom. 10:13
Shall be [T]saved. Or *delivered*
For [R]in Mount Zion and in Jerusalem there shall be [T]deliverance, Is. 46:13
As the LORD has said, Or *salvation*
Among [R]the remnant whom the LORD calls. [Mic. 4:7]

CHAPTER 3

Judgment on the Gentiles

"FOR behold, [R]in those days and at that time, Jer. 30:3
When I bring back the captives of Judah and Jerusalem,
2[R]I will also gather all nations, Zech. 14:2
And bring them down to the Valley of Jehoshaphat;
And I [R]will enter into judgment with them there Is. 66:16
On account of My people, My heritage Israel,
Whom they have scattered among the nations;

2:23 Or *the teacher of righteousness* **2:25** Cf. 1:4

They have also divided up My land.
3 They have [R]cast lots for My people,
Have given a boy *as payment* for a
harlot, Nah. 3:10
And sold a girl for wine, that they may
drink.

4"Indeed, what have you to do with Me,
[R]O Tyre and Sidon, and all the coasts of
Philistia? Amos 1:6–8
Will you retaliate against Me?
But if you retaliate against Me,
Swiftly and speedily I will return your
retaliation upon your own head;
5 Because you have taken My silver and
My gold,
And have carried into your temples My
prized possessions.
6 Also the people of Judah and the people
of Jerusalem
You have sold to the Greeks,
That you may remove them far from
their borders.

7"Behold, [R]I will raise them Jer. 23:8
Out of the place to which you have sold
them,
And will return your [T]retaliation upon
your own head. Or *repayment*
8 I will sell your sons and your daughters
Into the hand of the people of Judah,
And they will sell them to the
[R]Sabeans,* Ezek. 23:42
To a people [R]far off; Jer. 6:20
For the LORD has spoken."

9[R] Proclaim this among the nations:
"Prepare for war! Ezek. 38:7
Wake up the mighty men,
Let all the men of war draw near,
Let them come up.
10 Beat your plowshares into swords
And your pruning hooks into spears;
Let the weak say, 'I *am* strong.' "
11 Assemble and come, all you nations,
And gather together all around.
Cause [R]Your mighty ones to go down
there, O LORD. Is. 13:3

12"Let the nations be wakened, and come
up to the Valley of Jehoshaphat;
For there I will sit to [R]judge all the
surrounding nations. Is. 2:4
13[R] Put in the sickle, for [R]the harvest is ripe.
Come, go down; Rev. 14:15 • Jer. 51:33
For the [R]winepress is full, [Is. 63:3]
The vats overflow—
For their wickedness *is* great."

14 Multitudes, multitudes in the valley of
decision!
For [R]the day of the LORD *is* near in the
valley of decision. Joel 2:1
15 The sun and moon will grow dark,
And the stars will diminish their
brightness.

Restoration of Judah

16 The LORD also will roar from Zion,
And utter His voice from Jerusalem;
The heavens and earth will shake;
[R]But the LORD will be a shelter for His
people, [Is. 51:5, 6]
And the strength of the children of
Israel.

17"So you shall know that I *am* the LORD
your God,
Dwelling in Zion My [R]holy mountain.
Then Jerusalem shall be holy, Zech. 8:3
And no aliens shall ever pass through
her again."

18 And it will come to pass in that day
That the mountains shall drip with new
wine,
The hills shall flow with milk,
And all the brooks of Judah shall be
flooded with water;
A [R]fountain shall flow from the house of
the LORD Ezek. 47:1
And water the Valley of Acacias.

19"Egypt shall be a desolation,
And Edom a desolate wilderness,
Because of violence *against* the people
of Judah,
For they have shed innocent blood in
their land.
20 But Judah shall abide forever,
And Jerusalem from generation to
generation.
21 For I will [R]acquit them of the guilt of
bloodshed, whom I had not acquitted;
For the LORD dwells in Zion." Is. 4:4

3:8 Lit. *Shebaites*, Is. 60:6; Ezek. 27:22

THE BOOK OF
AMOS

THE BOOK OF AMOS

Amos prophesies during a period of national optimism in Israel. Business is booming and boundaries are bulging. But below the surface, greed and injustice are festering. Hypocritical religious motions have replaced true worship, creating a false sense of security and a growing callousness to God's disciplining hand. Famine, drought, plagues, death, destruction—nothing can force the people to their knees.

Amos, the farmer-turned-prophet, lashes out at sin unflinchingly, trying to visualize the nearness of God's judgment and mobilize the nation to repentance. The nation, like a basket of rotting fruit, stands ripe for judgment because of its hypocrisy and spiritual indifference.

The name "Amos" is derived from the Hebrew root *amas,* "to lift a burden, to carry." Thus, his name means "Burden" or "Burden-Bearer." Amos lives up to the meaning of his name by bearing up under his divinely given burden of declaring judgment to rebellious Israel. The Greek and Latin titles are both trans-literated in English as *Amos.*

THE AUTHOR OF AMOS

The only Old Testament appearance of the name "Amos" is in this book. (He should not be confused with Amoz, the father of Isaiah.) Concerning his background, Amos said, 'I *was* no prophet, nor *was* I a son of a prophet, but I *was* a sheepbreeder and a tender of sycamore fruit" (7:14). But he was gripped by God and divinely commissioned to bring his prophetic burden to Israel (3:8; 7:15). He came from the rural area of Tekoa in Judah, twelve miles south of Jerusalem, where he tended a special breed of small sheep that produced wool of the best quality. As a grower of sycamore figs, he had to puncture the fruit before it ripened to allow the insects inside to escape. Amos lived a disciplined life, and his knowledge of the wilderness often surfaces in his messages (cf. 3:4, 5, 12; 5:8, 19; 9:9). Amos was from the country, but he was well educated in the Scriptures. His keen sense of morality and justice is obvious; and his objective appraisal of Israel's spiritual condition was not well received, especially since he was from Judah. He delivered his message in Bethel because it was the residence of the king of Israel and a center of idolatry. His frontal attack on the greed, injustice, and self-righteousness of the people of the northern kingdom made his words unpopular.

THE TIME OF AMOS

Amos prophesied "in the days of Uzziah king of Judah, and in the days of Jeroboam the son of Joash, king of Israel, two years before the earthquake" (1:1). Uzziah reigned from 767 to 739 B.C. and Jeroboam II reigned from 782 to 753 B.C., leaving an overlap from 767 to 753 B.C. Over two hundred years later, Zechariah referred to this earthquake in Uzziah's reign (Zech. 14:5). Amos 7:11 anticipates the 722 B.C. Assyrian captivity of Israel and indicates that at the time of writing, Jeroboam II was not yet dead. Thus, Amos prophesied in Bethel about 755 B.C. Astronomical calculations indicate that a solar eclipse took place in Israel on June 15, 763 B.C. This event was probably fresh in the minds of Amos's hearers (see 8:9).

Amos ministered after the time of Obadiah, Joel, and Jonah and just before Hosea, Micah, and Isaiah. At this time Uzziah reigned over a prosperous and militarily successful Judah. He fortified Jerusalem and subdued the Philistines, the Ammonites, and the Edomites. In the north, Israel was ruled by the capable King Jeroboam II. Economic and military circumstances were almost ideal, but prosperity only increased the materialism, immorality, and injustice of the people (2:6–8; 3:10; 4:1; 5:10–12; 8:4–6). During these years, Assyria, Babylon, Syria, and Egypt were relatively weak. Thus, the people of Israel found it hard to imagine the coming disaster predicted by Amos. However, it was only three decades until the downfall of Israel.

THE CHRIST OF AMOS

The clearest anticipation of Christ in Amos is found at the end of the book. He has all authority to judge (1:1—9:10), but He will also restore His people (9:11–15).

KEYS TO AMOS

Key Word: The Judgment of Israel— The basic theme of Amos is the coming judgment of Israel because of the holiness of Yahweh and the sinfulness of His covenant people. Amos unflinchingly and relentlessly visualizes the causes and course of Israel's quickly approaching doom. God is gracious and patient, but His justice and righteousness will not allow sin to go unpunished indefinitely. The sins of Israel are heaped as high as heaven: empty ritualism, oppression of the poor, idolatry, deceit, self-righteousness, arrogance, greed, materialism, and callousness. The people have repeatedly broken every aspect of their covenant relationship with God. Nevertheless, God's mercy and love are evident in His offer of deliverance if the people will only turn back to Him. God graciously sends Amos as a reformer to warn the people of Israel of their fate if they refuse to repent. But they reject his plea, and the course of judgment cannot be altered.

Key Verses: Amos 3:1, 2; 8:11, 12—"Hear this word that the LORD has spoken against you, O children of Israel, against the whole family which I brought up from the land of Egypt, saying: 'You only have I known of all the families of the earth; therefore I will punish you for all your iniquities'" (3:1, 2).

"'Behold, the days are coming,' says the Lord GOD, 'that I will send a famine on the land, not a famine of bread, nor a thirst for water, but of hearing the words of the LORD; they shall wander from sea to sea, and from north to east; they shall run to and fro, seeking the word of the LORD, but shall not find *it*'" (8:11, 12).

Key Chapter: Amos 9—Set in the midst of the harsh judgments of Amos are some of the greatest prophecies of restoration of Israel anywhere in Scripture. Within the scope of just five verses the future of Israel becomes clear, as the Abrahamic, Davidic, and Palestinian covenants are focused on their climactic fulfillment in the return of the Messiah.

SURVEY OF AMOS

Amos's message of the coming doom of the northern kingdom of Israel seems preposterous to the people. Unsurprisingly, Amos's earnest and forceful message against Israel's sins and abuses is poorly received. The prophet of Israel's Indian summer presents a painfully clear message: "prepare to meet your God, O Israel" (4:12). The four divisions of Amos are: the eight prophecies (1:1—2:16), the three sermons (3:1—6:14), the five visions (7:1—9:10), and the five promises (9:11–15).

The Eight Prophecies (1:1—2:16): Amos is called by God to the unenviable task of leaving his homeland in Judah to preach a harsh message of judgment to Israel. Each of his eight oracles in chapters 1 and 2 begins with the statement "For three transgressions of . . . and for four." The fourth transgression is equivalent to the last straw; the iniquity of each of the eight countries is full. Amos begins with the nations that surround Israel as his catalog of catastrophes gradually spirals in on Israel herself. Seven times God declares, "I will send a fire" (1:4, 7, 10, 12, 14; 2:2, 5), a symbol of judgment.

The Three Sermons (3:1—6:14): In these chapters, Amos delivers three sermons, each beginning with the phrase "Hear this word" (3:1; 4:1; 5:1). The first sermon (3) is a general pronouncement of judgment because of Israel's iniquities. The second sermon (4) exposes the crimes of the people and describes the ways God has chastened them in order to draw them back to Himself. Five times He says, "Yet you have not returned to Me" (4:6, 8, 9, 10, 11). The third sermon (5 and 6) lists the sins of the house of Israel and calls the people to repent. But they hate integrity, justice, and compassion, and their refusal to turn to Yahweh will lead to their exile. Although they arrogantly wallow in luxury, their time of prosperity will suddenly come to an end.

The Five Visions (7:1—9:10): Amos's three sermons are followed by five visions of coming judgment upon the northern kingdom. The first two judgments of locusts and fire do not come to pass because of Amos's intercession. The third vision of the plumb line is followed by the only narrative section in the book (7:10–17). Amaziah, the priest of Bethel, wants Amos to go back to Judah. The fourth vision pictures Israel

FOCUS	EIGHT PROPHECIES	THREE SERMONS	FIVE VISIONS	FIVE PROMISES
REFERENCE	1:1—	3:1—	7:1—	9:11—9:15
DIVISION	JUDGMENT OF ISRAEL AND SURROUNDING NATIONS	SIN OF ISRAEL PRESENT, PAST, AND FUTURE	PICTURES OF THE JUDGMENT OF ISRAEL	RESTORATION OF ISRAEL
TOPIC	PRONOUNCEMENTS OF JUDGMENT	PROVOCATIONS FOR JUDGMENT	FUTURE OF JUDGMENT	PROMISES AFTER JUDGMENT
	JUDGMENT			HOPE
LOCATION	SURROUNDING NATIONS	NORTHERN KINGDOM OF ISRAEL		
TIME	c. 760–753 B.C.			

as a basket of rotten fruit, overripe for judgment. The fifth vision is a relentless portrayal of Israel's unavoidable judgment.

The Five Promises (9:11–15): Amos has hammered upon the theme of divine retribution with oracles, sermons, and visions. Nevertheless, he ends his book on a note of consolation, not condemnation. God promises to reinstate the Davidic line, to renew the land, and to restore the people.

OUTLINE OF AMOS

CHAPTER 1

Introduction to Amos

THE words of Amos, who was among the sheepbreeders* of [R]Tekoa, which he saw concerning Israel in the days of [R]Uzziah king of Judah, and in the days of Jeroboam the son of Joash, king of Israel, two years before the earthquake. 2 Sam. 14:2 • 2 Chr. 26:1–23

2 And he said:

"The LORD [R]roars from Zion, Joel 3:16
And utters His voice from Jerusalem;
The pastures of the shepherds mourn,
And the top of Carmel withers."

Judgment on Damascus

3 Thus says the LORD:

"For three transgressions of [R]Damascus,
and for four, Is. 8:4; 17:1–3
I will not turn away its *punishment*,
Because they have threshed Gilead with
implements of iron.
4 [R]But I will send a fire into the house of
Hazael, Jer. 49:27; 51:30
Which shall devour the palaces of
[R]Ben-Hadad. 2 Kin. 6:24
5 I will also break the *gate* [R]bar of
Damascus, Jer. 51:30
And cut off the inhabitant from the
Valley of Aven,
And the one who [T]holds the scepter from
[T]Beth Eden. Rules • Lit. *House of Eden*
The people of Syria shall go captive to Kir,"
Says the LORD.

Judgment on Gaza

6 Thus says the LORD:

"For three transgressions of [R]Gaza, and
for four, Jer. 47:1, 5
I will not turn away its *punishment*,
Because they took captive the whole
captivity
To deliver *them* up to Edom.
7 [R]But I will send a fire upon the wall of
Gaza, Jer. 47:1
Which shall devour its palaces.
8 I will cut off the inhabitant [R]from
Ashdod, Zeph. 2:4
And the one who holds the scepter from
Ashkelon;
I will [R]turn My hand against Ekron,
And [R]the remnant of the Philistines shall
perish," Ps. 81:14 • Ezek. 25:16
Says the Lord GOD.

Judgment on Tyre

9 Thus says the LORD:

"For three transgressions of [R]Tyre, and for
four, Is. 23:1–18
I will not turn away its *punishment*,
Because they delivered up the whole
captivity to Edom,

1:1 Cf. 2 Kin. 3:4

And did not remember the covenant of
brotherhood.
10 But I will send a fire upon the wall of Tyre,
Which shall devour its palaces."

Judgment on Edom

11 Thus says the LORD:

"For three transgressions of [R]Edom, and
for four, Is. 21:11
I will not turn away its *punishment*,
Because he pursued his [R]brother with
the sword, Obad. 10–12
And cast off all pity;
His anger tore perpetually,
And he kept his wrath forever.
12 But [R]I will send a fire upon Teman,
Which shall devour the palaces of
Bozrah." Obad. 9, 10

Judgment on Ammon

13 Thus says the LORD:

"For three transgressions of [R]the people
of Ammon, and for four, Ezek. 25:2
I will not turn away its *punishment*,
Because they ripped open the women
with child in Gilead,
That they might enlarge their territory.
14 But I will kindle a fire in the wall of
[R]Rabbah, Deut. 3:11
And it shall devour its palaces,
[R]Amid shouting in the day of battle,
And a tempest in the day of the
whirlwind. Amos 2:2
15 [R]Their king shall go into captivity,
He and his princes together,"
Says the LORD. Jer. 49:3

CHAPTER 2

Judgment on Moab

THUS says the LORD:
[R]"For three transgressions of Moab, and
for four, Zeph. 2:8–11
I will not turn away its *punishment*,
Because he [R]burned the bones of the
king of Edom to lime. 2 Kin. 3:26, 27
2 But I will send a fire upon Moab,
And it shall devour the palaces of
[R]Kerioth; Jer. 48:24, 41
Moab shall die with tumult,
With shouting *and* trumpet sound.
3 And I will cut off [R]the judge from its
midst, Num. 24:17
And slay all its princes with him,"
Says the LORD.

Judgment on Judah

4 Thus says the LORD:

"For three transgressions of [R]Judah, and
for four, Hos. 12:2
I will not turn away its *punishment*,
[R]Because they have despised the law of
the LORD, Lev. 26:14
And have not kept His commandments.
[R]Their lies lead them astray, Jer. 16:19
Lies which their fathers followed.
5 [R]But I will send a fire upon Judah,
And it shall devour the palaces of
Jerusalem." Hos. 8:14

Judgment on Israel

6 Thus says the LORD:

"For three transgressions of [R]Israel, and
for four, 2 Kin. 17:7–18; 18:12
I will not turn away its *punishment*,
Because [R]they sell the righteous for
silver, Is. 29:21
And the poor for a pair of sandals.
7 They pant after* the dust of the earth
which is on the head of the poor,
And [R]pervert the way of the humble.
[R]A man and his father go in to the *same*
girl, Amos 5:12 • Ezek. 22:11
[R]To defile My holy name. Lev. 20:3
8 They lie down [R]by every altar on clothes
[R]taken in pledge, 1 Cor. 8:10 • Ex. 22:26
And drink the wine of the condemned *in*
the house of their god.

9 "Yet *it was* I *who* destroyed the [R]Amorite
before them, Num. 21:25
Whose height *was* like the [R]height of the
cedars, Ezek. 31:3
And he *was as* strong as the oaks;
Yet I [R]destroyed his fruit above [Mal. 4:1]
And his roots beneath.
10 Also *it was* [R]I *who* brought you up from
the land of Egypt, Ex. 12:51
And [R]led you forty years through the
wilderness, Deut. 2:7
To possess the land of the Amorite.
11 I raised up some of your sons as
[R]prophets, Num. 12:6
And some of your young men as
[R]Nazirites. Num. 6:2, 3
Is it not so, O you children of Israel?"
Says the LORD.
12 "But you gave the Nazirites wine to drink,
And commanded the prophets [R]saying,
'Do not prophesy!' Is. 30:10

13 "Behold,[R] I am [T]weighed down by you,
As a cart full of sheaves [T]is weighed
down. Is. 1:14 • Or *tottering under* • Or *totters*
14 [R]Therefore [T]flight shall perish from the
swift, Jer. 46:6 • Or *the place of refuge*
The strong shall not strengthen his
power,
Nor shall the mighty deliver himself;
15 He shall not stand who handles the bow,

2:7 Or *trample on*

The swift of foot shall not [T]escape,
Nor shall he who rides a horse deliver
himself. Or *save*
16 The most courageous men of might
Shall flee naked in that day,"
Says the LORD.

CHAPTER 3

Israel's Judgment Is Deserved (Present)

HEAR this word that the LORD has spoken against you, O children of Israel, against the whole family which I brought up from the land of Egypt, saying:

2 "You[R] only have I known of all the families of the earth; [Deut. 7:6]
[R]Therefore I will punish you for all your iniquities." [Rom. 2:9]

3 Can two walk together, unless they are agreed?
4 Will a lion roar in the forest, when he has no prey?
Will a young lion cry out of his den, if he has caught nothing?
5 Will a bird fall into a snare on the earth, where there is no trap for it?
Will a snare spring up from the earth, if it has caught nothing at all?
6 If a [T]trumpet is blown in a city, will not the people be afraid? *ram's horn*
[R]If there is calamity in a city, will not the LORD have done *it*? Is. 45:7

7 Surely the Lord GOD does nothing,
Unless [R]He reveals His secret to His servants the prophets. [John 15:15]
8 A lion has roared!
Who will not fear?
The Lord GOD has spoken!
[R]Who can but prophesy? Acts 4:20

9 "Proclaim in the palaces at Ashdod,*
And in the palaces in the land of Egypt, and say:
'Assemble on the mountains of Samaria;
See great tumults in her midst,
And the oppressed within her.
10 For they [R]do not know to do right,'
Says the LORD, Jer. 4:22
'Who store up violence and [T]robbery in their palaces.' " Or *devastation*

Israel's Judgment Is Described (Present)

11 Therefore thus says the Lord GOD:

"An adversary *shall be* all around the land;
He shall sap your strength from you,
And your palaces shall be plundered."

12 Thus says the LORD:

"As a shepherd [T]takes from the mouth of a lion Or *snatches*
Two legs or a piece of an ear,
So shall the children of Israel be taken out
Who dwell in Samaria—
In the corner of a bed and on the edge*
of a couch!
13 Hear and testify against the house of Jacob,"
Says the Lord GOD, the God of hosts,
14 "That in the day I punish Israel for their transgressions,
I will also visit *destruction* on the altars of [R]Bethel; Amos 4:4
And the horns of the altar shall be cut off
And fall to the ground.
15 I will [T]destroy the winter house along with the summer house; Lit. *strike*
The [R]houses of ivory shall perish,
And the great houses shall have an end," 1 Kin. 22:39
Says the LORD.

CHAPTER 4

Israel's Judgment Is Deserved (Past)

HEAR this word, you cows of Bashan,
who *are* on the mountain of Samaria,
Who oppress the [R]poor, Amos 2:6
Who crush the needy,
Who say to your husbands,* "Bring *wine*,
let us [R]drink!" Prov. 23:20

3:9 So with MT; LXX *Assyria* **3:12** Heb. uncertain, possibly *on the cover* **4:1** Lit. *their masters* or *their lords*

3:2 Selection of Israel—The selection of Israel as a special nation to God was part of God's plan (Page 1158—Rom. 11:2). Historically, the selection of Israel began with the Lord's promise to Abraham, "I will make you a great nation" (Page 14—Gen. 12:2). The name *Israel* actually is from the new name which God gave to Abraham's grandson, Jacob. It was occasioned by Jacob's spiritual victory at the ford of Jabbok (Page 35—Gen. 32:28). This fact explains why his descendants are often called the children of Israel.

The motivation for the Lord's choice of Israel as His select nation did not lie in any special attraction it possessed. Its people were, in fact, the least in number among all the nations (Page 182—Deut. 7:6–8). Rather, the Lord chose them because of His love for them and because of His covenant with Abraham. This fact does not mean that God did not love other nations, because it was through Israel that He intended to bring forth the Savior and to bless the entire world (Page 14—Gen. 12:3).

Now turn to Page 587—Ps. 78:4: History of Israel.

2[R] The Lord GOD has sworn by His
holiness: Ps. 89:35
"Behold, the days shall come upon you
When He will take you away [R]with
fishhooks, Jer. 16:16
And your posterity with fishhooks.
3[R] You will go out *through* broken
walls,
Each one straight ahead of her,
And you will [T]be cast into Harmon,"
Says the LORD. Ezek. 12:5 • Or *cast them*

4"Come to Bethel and transgress,
At Gilgal multiply transgression;
Bring your sacrifices every morning,
Your tithes every three days.*
5[R] Offer a sacrifice of thanksgiving with
leaven, Lev. 7:13
Proclaim *and* announce [R]the freewill
offerings; Lev. 22:18
For this you love,
You children of Israel!"
Says the Lord GOD.

Israel's Judgment Is Demonstrated (Past)

6"Also I gave you [T]cleanness of teeth in all
your cities. Hunger
And lack of bread in all your places;
[R]Yet you have not returned to Me,"
Says the LORD. Jer. 5:3

7"I also withheld rain from you,
When *there were* still three months to
the harvest.
I made it rain on one city,
I withheld rain from another city.
One part was rained upon,
And where it did not rain the part
withered.
8 So two *or* three cities wandered to
another city to drink water,
But they were not satisfied;
Yet you have not returned to Me,"
Says the LORD.

9"I[R] blasted you with blight and mildew.
When your gardens increased, Hag. 2:17
Your vineyards,
Your fig trees,
And your olive trees,
[R]The locust devoured *them;* Joel 1:4, 7
Yet you have not returned to Me,"
Says the LORD.

10"I sent among you a plague [R]after the
manner of Egypt; Ps. 78:50
Your young men I killed with a sword,
Along with your captive horses;
I made the stench of your camps come
up into your nostrils;
Yet you have not returned to Me,"
Says the LORD.

11"I overthrew *some* of you,
As God overthrew [R]Sodom and
Gomorrah, Is. 13:19
And you were like a firebrand plucked
from the burning;
Yet you have not returned to Me,"
Says the LORD.

Israel's Judgment Is Described (Past)

12"Therefore thus will I do to you, O Israel;
Because I will do this to you,
Prepare to meet your God, O Israel!"

13 For behold,
He who forms mountains,
And creates the [T]wind, Or *spirit*
[R]Who declares to man what his* thought
is, Ps. 139:2
And makes the morning darkness,
[R]Who treads the high places of the
earth— Mic. 1:3
The LORD God of hosts *is* His name.

CHAPTER 5

Israel's Judgment Is Deserved (Future)

HEAR this word which I take up against
you, a lamentation, O house of Israel:

2 The virgin of Israel has fallen;
She will rise no more.
She lies forsaken on her land;
There is no one to raise her up.

3 For thus says the Lord GOD:

"The city that goes out by a thousand
Shall have a hundred left,
And that which goes out by a hundred
Shall have ten left to the house of Israel."

4 For thus says the LORD to the house of Israel:

[R]"Seek Me [R]and live; [Jer. 29:13] • [Is. 55:3]
5 But do not seek [R]Bethel, Amos 4:4
Nor enter Gilgal,
Nor pass over to [R]Beersheba; Amos 8:14
For Gilgal shall surely go into captivity,
And Bethel shall come to nothing.
6[R] Seek the LORD and live, [Is. 55:3, 6, 7]
Lest He break out like fire *in* the house
of Joseph,
And devour *it,*
With no one to quench *it* in Bethel—
7 You who [R]turn justice to wormwood,
And lay righteousness to rest in the
earth!" Amos 6:12

8 He made the [R]Pleiades and Orion;
He turns the shadow of death into
morning Job 9:9; 38:31

4:4 Or *years,* Deut. 14:28 **4:13** Or *His*

[R]And makes the day dark as night;
He [R]calls for the waters of the sea
And pours them out on the face of the
earth; Ps. 104:20 • Job 38:34
[R]The LORD *is* His name. [Amos 4:13]
9 He rains ruin upon the strong,
So that fury comes upon the fortress.

10[R]They hate the one who rebukes in the
gate, Is. 29:21; 66:5
And they [R]abhor the one who speaks
uprightly. 1 Kin. 22:8
11[R]Therefore, because you [T]tread down the
poor Amos 2:6 • *trample*
And take grain [T]taxes from him,
Though [R]you have built houses of hewn
stone, Or *tribute* • Mic. 6:15
Yet you shall not dwell in them;
You have planted pleasant vineyards,
But you shall not drink wine from them.
12 For I [R]know your manifold
transgressions Hos. 5:3
And your mighty sins:
[R]Afflicting the just *and* taking bribes;
[R]Diverting the poor *from justice* at the
gate. Amos 2:6 • Is. 29:21
13 Therefore [R]the prudent keep silent at
that time, Amos 6:10
For it *is* an evil time.

14 Seek good and not evil,
That you may live;
So the LORD God of hosts will be with you,
[R]As you have spoken. Mic. 3:11
15[R]Hate evil, love good; Rom. 12:9
Establish justice in the gate.
[R]It may be that the LORD God of hosts
Will be gracious to the remnant of
Joseph. Joel 2:14

The First Woe of Judgment

16 Therefore the LORD God of hosts, the
Lord, says this:

"*There shall be* wailing in all streets,
And they shall say in all the highways,
'Alas! Alas!'
They shall call the farmer to mourning,
And skillful lamenters to wailing.
17 In all vineyards *there shall be* wailing,
For [R]I will pass through you," Ex. 12:12
Says the LORD.

18[R]Woe to you who desire the day of the
LORD! Is. 5:19
For what good *is* [R]the day of the LORD to
you? Joel 2:2
It *will be* darkness, and not light.
19 It *will be* [R]as though a man fled from a
lion, Jer. 48:44
And a bear met him!
Or *as though* he went into the house,
Leaned his hand on the wall,
And a serpent bit him!
20 *Is* not the day of the LORD darkness, and
not light?
Is it not very dark, with no brightness in
it?

21"I[R] hate, I despise your feast days,
And [R]I do not savor your sacred
assemblies. Is. 1:11–16 • Lev. 26:31
22[R]Though you offer Me burnt offerings and
your grain offerings, Mic. 6:6, 7
I will not accept *them*,
Nor will I regard your fattened peace
offerings.
23 Take away from Me the noise of your
songs,
For I will not hear the melody of your
stringed instruments.
24 But let justice run down like water,
And righteousness like a mighty stream.

25"Did[R] you offer Me sacrifices and
offerings Deut. 32:17
In the wilderness forty years, O house of
Israel?
26 You also carried Sikkuth* [R]your king*
And Chiun,* your idols, 1 Kin. 11:33
The star of your gods,
Which you made for yourselves.
27 Therefore I will send you into captivity
[R]beyond Damascus," 2 Kin. 17:6
Says the LORD, [R]whose name *is* the God
of hosts. Amos 4:13

CHAPTER 6

The Second Woe of Judgment

WOE to you *who are* at ease in Zion,
And [R]trust in Mount Samaria, Is. 31:1
Notable persons in the chief nation,
To whom the house of Israel comes!
2[R]Go over to Calneh and see; Jer. 2:10
And from there go to Hamath the great;
Then go down to Gath of the Philistines.
[R]*Are you* better than these kingdoms?
Or is their territory greater than your
territory? Nah. 3:8

3 *Woe to* you who [R]put far off the day of
[R]doom, Is. 56:12 • Amos 5:18
[R]Who cause [R]the seat of violence to come
near; Amos 5:12 • Ps. 94:20
4 Who lie on beds of ivory,
Stretch out on your couches,
Eat lambs from the flock
And calves from the midst of the stall;
5[R]Who sing idly to the sound of stringed
instruments, Is. 5:12; Amos 5:23
And invent for yourselves musical
instruments [R]like David; 1 Chr. 23:5

5:26 A pagan deity • LXX, Vg. *tabernacle of Moloch* •
A pagan deity

6 Who [R]drink wine from bowls,
And anoint yourselves with the best
ointments, Amos 2:8; 4:1
[R]But are not grieved for the affliction of
Joseph. Gen. 37:25
7 Therefore they shall now go [R]captive as
the first of the captives, Amos 5:27
And those who recline at banquets shall
be removed.

8 [R]The Lord GOD has sworn by Himself,
The LORD God of hosts says: Jer. 51:14
"I abhor [R]the pride of Jacob, Amos 8:7
And hate his palaces;
Therefore I will deliver up *the* city
And all that is in it."

9 Then it shall come to pass, that if ten men
remain in one house, they shall die.
10 And when a relative *of the dead,* with
one who will burn *the bodies,* picks up the
bodies* to take them out of the house, he will
say to one inside the house, "*Are there* any
more with you?" Then someone will say,
"None." And he will say, [R]"Hold your tongue!
[R]For we dare not mention the name of the
LORD." Amos 5:13 • Amos 8:3

11 For behold, the LORD gives a command:
He will break the great house into bits,
And the little house into pieces.

12 Do horses run on rocks?
Does *one* plow *there* with oxen?
Yet [R]you have turned justice into gall,
And the fruit of righteousness into
wormwood, Hos. 10:4
13 You who rejoice over Lo Debar,*
Who say, "Have we not taken Karnaim*
for ourselves
By our own strength?"

14 "But, behold, [R]I will raise up a nation
against you, Jer. 5:15
O house of Israel,"
Says the LORD God of hosts;
"And they will afflict you from the
[R]entrance of Hamath 1 Kin. 8:65
To the Valley of the Arabah."

CHAPTER 7

Vision of the Locusts

THUS the Lord GOD showed me: Behold,
He formed locust swarms at the beginning
of the late crop; indeed *it was* the late crop
after the king's mowings.
2 And so it was, when they had finished
eating the grass of the land, that I said:

"O Lord GOD, forgive, I pray!
[R]Oh,[T] that Jacob may stand, Is. 51:19
For he *is* small!" Or *How shall Jacob stand*

3 *So* [R]the LORD relented concerning this.
"It shall not be," said the LORD. Jon. 3:10

Vision of the Fire

4 Thus the Lord GOD showed me: Behold,
the Lord GOD called [T]for conflict by fire, and it
consumed the great deep and devoured the
[T]territory. *to contend* • Lit. *portion*
5 Then I said:

"O Lord GOD, cease, I pray!
[R]Oh, that Jacob may stand, Amos 7:2, 3
For he *is* small!"
6 *So* the LORD relented concerning this.
"This also shall not be," said the Lord GOD.

Vision of the Plumb Line

7 Thus He showed me: Behold, the Lord
stood on a wall *made* with a plumb line, with
a plumb line in His hand.
8 And the LORD said to me, "Amos, what do
you see?" And I said, "A plumb line." Then the
Lord said:

"Behold, I am setting a plumb line
In the midst of My people Israel;
I will not pass by them anymore.
9 [R]The high places of Isaac shall be
desolate, Gen. 46:1
And the [T]sanctuaries of Israel shall be
laid waste. Or *holy places*
[R]I will rise with the sword against the
house of Jeroboam." 2 Kin. 15:8–10

Opposition of Amaziah (Historical Parenthesis)

10 Then Amaziah the [R]priest of Bethel sent
to Jeroboam king of Israel, saying, "Amos has
conspired against you in the midst of the
house of Israel. The land is not able to bear all
his words. 1 Kin. 12:31, 32; 13:33
11 "For thus Amos has said:

'Jeroboam shall die by the sword,
And Israel shall surely be led away
[R]captive Amos 5:27; 6:7
From their own land.' "

12 Then Amaziah said to Amos:

"Go, you seer!
Flee to the land of Judah.
There eat bread,
And there prophesy.
13 But never again prophesy at Bethel,
For it *is* the king's sanctuary,
And it *is* the royal residence."

14 Then Amos answered, and said to
Amaziah:

6:10 Lit. *bones* **6:13** Lit. *Nothing* • Lit. *Horns*, a symbol of strength

"I *was* no prophet,
Nor *was* I a son of a prophet,
But I *was* a [R]sheepbreeder* Zech. 13:5
And a tender of sycamore fruit.
15 Then the LORD took me [T]as I followed
the flock, Lit. *from behind*
And the LORD said to me,
'Go, prophesy to My people Israel.'
16 Now therefore, hear the word of the LORD:
You say, 'Do not prophesy against Israel,
And [R]do not [T]spout against the house of
Isaac.' Ezek. 21:2 • Lit. *drip*

17 "Therefore thus says the LORD:

[R]'Your wife shall be a harlot in the city;
Your sons and daughters shall fall by the
sword; Zech. 14:2
Your land shall be divided by *survey* line;
You shall die in a [R]defiled land;
And Israel shall surely be led away
captive Hos. 9:3
From his own land.' "

CHAPTER 8

Vision of the Summer Fruit

THUS the Lord GOD showed me: Behold, a
basket of summer fruit.
2 And He said, "Amos, what do you see?"
So I said, "A basket of summer fruit." Then the
LORD said to me:

[R]"The end has come upon My people
Israel; Ezek. 7:2
I will not pass by them anymore.
3 And [R]the songs of the temple Amos 5:23
Shall be wailing in that day,"
Says the Lord GOD—
"Many dead bodies everywhere,
They shall be thrown out in silence."

4 Hear this, you who swallow up* the
needy,
And make the poor of the land fail,

5 Saying:

"When will the New Moon be past,
That we may sell grain?
And [R]the Sabbath, Neh. 13:15
That we may [T]trade wheat? Lit. *open*
[R]Making the ephah small and the shekel
large, Mic. 6:10, 11
Falsifying the scales by deceit,
6 That we may buy the poor for [R]silver,
And the needy for a pair of sandals—
Even sell the bad wheat?" Amos 2:6

7 The LORD has sworn by [R]the pride of
Jacob: Amos 6:8
"Surely [R]I will never forget any of their
works. Hos. 7:2; 8:13

8 Shall the land not tremble for this,
And everyone mourn who dwells in it?
All of it shall swell like the River,*
Heave and subside
[R]Like the River of Egypt. Amos 9:5

9 "And it shall come to pass in that day,"
says the Lord GOD,
[R]"That I will make the sun go down at
noon, Job 5:14
And I will darken the earth in [T]broad
daylight; Lit. *a day of light*
10 I will turn your feasts into mourning,
[R]And all your songs into lamentation;
[R]I will bring sackcloth on every waist,
And baldness on every head;
I will make it like mourning for an only
son, Ezek. 27:31 • [Zech. 12:10]
And its end like a bitter day.

11 "Behold, the days are coming," says the
Lord GOD,
"That I will send a famine on the land,
Not a famine of bread,
Nor a thirst for water,
But of hearing the words of the LORD.
12 They shall wander from sea to sea,
And from north to east;
They shall run to and fro, seeking the
word of the LORD,
But shall [R]not find *it*. Hos. 5:6

13 "In that day the fair virgins
And strong young men
Shall faint from thirst.
14 Those who [R]swear by [R]the sin* of
Samaria, Hos. 4:15 • Deut. 9:21
Who say,
'As your god lives, O Dan!'
And, 'As the way of Beersheba lives!'
They shall fall and never rise again."

CHAPTER 9

Vision of the Stricken Doorposts

I SAW the Lord standing by the altar, and
He said:

"Strike the [T]doorposts, that the thresholds
may shake,
And [R]break them on the heads of them
all. Capitals of the pillars • Hab. 3:13
I will slay the last of them with the
sword.
[R]He who flees from them shall not get
away, Amos 2:14
And he who escapes from them shall not
be delivered.

7:14 Cf. 2 Kin. 3:4 **8:4** Or *trample on,* Amos 2:7
8:8 The Nile; some Heb. mss., LXX, Syr., Tg., Vg.
River (cf. Amos 9:5); MT *the light* **8:14** Or *Ashima,* a
Syrian goddess

2"Though[R] they dig into hell,* Ps. 139:8
From there My hand shall take them;
Though they climb up to heaven,
From there I will bring them down;
3 And though they [R]hide themselves on
top of Carmel, Jer. 23:24
From there I will search and take them;
Though they hide from My sight at the
bottom of the sea,
From there I will command the serpent,
and it shall bite them;
4 Though they go into captivity before
their enemies,
From there [R]I will command the sword,
And it shall slay them. Lev. 26:33
[R]I will set My eyes on them for harm and
not for good." Jer. 21:10; 39:16; 44:11

5 The Lord GOD of hosts,
He who touches the earth and it [R]melts,
And all who dwell there mourn; Mic. 1:4
All of it shall swell like the River,*
And subside like the River of Egypt.
6 He who builds His layers in the sky,
And has founded His strata in the earth;
Who [R]calls for the waters of the sea,
And pours them out on the face of the
earth— Amos 5:8
[R]The LORD *is* His name. Amos 4:13; 5:27

7"*Are* you not like the [T]people of Ethiopia
to Me, Lit. *sons of the Ethiopians*
O children of Israel?" says the LORD.
"Did I not bring up Israel from the land of
Egypt,
The Philistines from [T]Caphtor, Crete
And the Syrians from [R]Kir? Amos 1:5

8"Behold, [R]the eyes of the Lord GOD *are* on
the sinful kingdom, Amos 9:4
And I [R]will destroy it from the face of the
earth; Jer. 5:10; 30:11
Yet I will not utterly destroy the house of
Jacob,"
Says the LORD.

9"For surely I will command,
And will [T]sift the house of Israel among
all nations, *shake*
As *grain* is sifted in a sieve;
[R]Yet not the smallest [T]grain shall fall to
the ground. [Is. 65:8–16] • Lit. *pebble*
10 All the sinners of My people shall die by
the sword,
[R]Who say, 'The calamity shall not
overtake nor confront us.' Amos 6:3

The Five Promises of the Restoration of Israel

11"On[R] that day I will raise up
The tabernacle* of David, which has
fallen down, Acts 15:16–18
And repair its damages;
I will raise up its ruins,
And rebuild it as in the days of old;
12[R]That they may possess the remnant of
[R]Edom,* Obad. 19 • Num. 24:18
And all the Gentiles who are called by
My name,"
Says the LORD who does this thing.

13"Behold, [R]the days are coming," says the
LORD, Lev. 26:5
"When the plowman shall overtake the
reaper,
And the treader of grapes him who sows
seed;
[R]The mountains shall drip with sweet
wine, Joel 3:18
And all the hills shall flow *with it.*
14[R]I will bring back the captives of My
people Israel; Jer. 30:3, 18
[R]They shall build the waste cities and
inhabit *them;* Is. 61:4
They shall plant vineyards and drink
wine from them;
They shall also make gardens and eat
fruit from them.
15 I will plant them in their land,
[R]And no longer shall they be pulled up
From the land I have given them,"
Says the LORD your God. Ezek. 34:28

9:2 Or *Sheol* **9:5** The Nile **9:11** Lit. *booth;* a figure of a deposed dynasty **9:12** LXX *mankind*

THE BOOK OF

OBADIAH

THE BOOK OF OBADIAH

A struggle that began in the womb between twin brothers, Esau and Jacob, eventuates in a struggle between their respective descendants, the Edomites and the Israelites. For the Edomites' stubborn refusal to aid Israel, first during the time of wilderness wandering (Num. 20:14–21) and later during a time of invasion, they are roundly condemned by Obadiah. This little-known prophet describes their crimes, tries their case, and pronounces their judgment: total destruction.

The Hebrew name *Obadyah* means "Worshiper of Yahweh" or "Servant of Yahweh." The Greek title in the Septuagint is *Obdiou,* and the Latin title in the Vulgate is *Abdias.*

THE AUTHOR OF OBADIAH

Obadiah was an obscure prophet who probably lived in the southern kingdom of Judah. Nothing is known of his hometown or family, but it is not likely that he came out of the kingly or priestly line, because his father is not mentioned (1:1). There are thirteen Obadiahs in the Old Testament, and some scholars have attempted to identify the author of this book with one of the other twelve. Four of the better prospects are: (1) the officer in Ahab's palace who hid God's prophets in a cave (1 Kin. 18:3); (2) one of the officials sent out by Jehoshaphat to teach the law in the cities of Judah (2 Chr. 17:7); (3) one of the overseers who took part in repairing the temple under Josiah (2 Chr. 34:12); or (4) a priest in the time of Nehemiah (Neh. 10:5).

THE TIME OF OBADIAH

Obadiah mentions no kings, so verses 10–14 provide the only historical reference point to aid in determining the book's time and setting. However, scholars disagree about which invasion of Jerusalem Obadiah had in mind. There are four possibilities: (1) In 926 B.C. Shishak of Egypt plundered the temple and palace of Jerusalem in the reign of Rehoboam (1 Kin. 14:25, 26). At this time, Edom was still subject to Judah. This does not fit Obadiah 10–14, which indicates that Edom was independent of Judah. (2) During the reign of Jehoram (848–841 B.C.), the Philistines and Arabians invaded Judah and looted the palace (2 Chr. 21:16, 17). Edom revolted during the reign of Jehoram and became a bitter antagonist (2 Kin. 8:20–22; 2 Chr. 21:8–20). This fits the description of Obadiah. (3) In 790 B.C. King Jehoash of Israel invaded Judah (2 Kin. 14; 2 Chr. 25). However, Obadiah in verse 11 calls the invaders "strangers." This would be an inappropriate term for describing the army of the northern kingdom. (4) In 586 B.C. Nebuchadnezzar of Babylon defeated and destroyed Jerusalem (2 Kin. 24 and 25).

The two best candidates are (2) and (4). Obadiah 10–14 seems to fit (2) better than (4) because it does not indicate the total destruction of the city, which took place when Nebuchadnezzar burned the palace and temple and razed the walls. And Nebuchadnezzar certainly would not have "cast lots for Jerusalem" (11) with anyone. Also, all of the other prophets who speak of the destruction of 586 B.C. identify Nebuchadnezzar and the Babylonians as the agents; but Obadiah leaves the enemy unidentified. For these and other reasons, it appears likely that the plundering of Jerusalem written of in Obadiah was by the Philistines between 848 and 841 B.C. This would make the prophet a contemporary of Elisha, and Obadiah would be the earliest of the writing prophets, predating Joel by a few years.

The history of Edom began with Esau who was given the name "Edom" ("Red") because of the red stew for which he traded his birthright. Esau moved to the mountainous area of Seir and absorbed the Horites, the original inhabitants. Edom refused to allow Israel to pass through their land on the way to Canaan. The Edomites opposed Saul and were subdued under David and Solomon. They fought against Jehoshaphat and successfully rebelled against Jehoram. They were again conquered by Judah under Amaziah, but they regained their freedom during the reign of Ahaz. Edom was later controlled by Assyria and Babylon; and in the fifth century B.C. the Edomites were forced by the Nabateans to leave their territory. They moved to the area of southern Palestine and became known as Idumeans. Herod the Great, an Idumean, became king of Judea under Rome in 37 B.C. In a sense, the enmity between Esau and Jacob was continued in Herod's attempt to murder Jesus. The Idumeans participated in the rebellion of Jerusalem against Rome and were defeated along with the Jews by Titus in A.D. 70. Ironically, the Edomites applauded the destruction of Jerusalem in 586 B.C. (see Ps. 137:7) but died trying to defend it in A.D. 70. After that time they were never heard of again. As Obadiah predicted, they would be "cut off forever" (10); "and no survivor shall *remain* of the house of Esau" (18).

THE CHRIST OF OBADIAH

Christ is seen in Obadiah as the Judge of the nations (15–16), the Savior of Israel (17–20), and the Possessor of the kingdom (21).

KEYS TO OBADIAH

Key Word: The Judgment of Edom—The major theme of Obadiah is a declaration of Edom's coming doom because of its arrogance and cruelty to Judah: "I will make you small among the nations" (2); "the pride of your heart has deceived you" (3); "how you will be cut off!" (5); "how Esau shall be searched out!" (6); "your mighty men, O Teman, shall be dismayed" (9); "shame shall cover you" (10); "you shall be cut off forever" (10); "as you have done, it shall be done to you" (15). Even the last few verses, which primarily deal with Israel, speak of Edom's downfall (17–21). The secondary theme of Obadiah is the future restoration of Israel and faithfulness of Yahweh to His covenant promises. God's justice will ultimately prevail.

Key Verses: Obadiah 10 and 21—"For violence against your brother Jacob, shame shall cover you, and you shall be cut off forever" (10).

"Then saviors shall come to Mount Zion to judge the mountains of Esau, and the kingdom shall be the LORD's" (21).

SURVEY OF OBADIAH

Obadiah is the shortest book in the Old Testament (twenty-one verses), but it carries one of the strongest messages of judgment in the Old Testament. For Edom there are no pleas to return, no words of consolation or hope. Edom's fate is sealed, and there are no conditions for possible deliverance. God will bring total destruction upon Edom, and there will be no remnant. Obadiah is Edom's day in court, complete with Edom's arraignment, indictment, and sentence. This prophet of poetic justice describes how the Judge of the earth will overthrow the pride of Edom and restore the house of Jacob. The two sections of Obadiah are: the judgment of Edom (1–18) and the restoration of Israel (19–21).

The Judgment of Edom (1–18): The first section of Obadiah makes it clear that the coming overthrow of Edom is a certainty, not a condition. Edom is arrogant (3) because of its secure position in Mount Seir, a mountainous region south of the Dead Sea. Its capital city of Sela (Petra) is protected by a narrow canyon that prevents invasion by an army. But God says this will make no difference. Even a thief does not take everything, but when God destroys Edom it will be totally ransacked. Nothing will avert God's complete judgment. Verses 10–14 describe Edom's major crime of gloating over the invasion of Jerusalem. Edom rejoiced when foreigners plundered Jerusalem, and became as one of them. On the day when she should have been allies with Judah, she instead became an aggressor against Judah. Edom will eventually be judged during the coming day of the Lord when Israel "shall be a fire, . . . but the house of Esau *shall be* stubble" (18).

The Restoration of Israel (19–21): The closing verses give hope to God's people that they will possess not only their own land, but also that of Edom and Philistia.

FOCUS	JUDGMENT OF EDOM			RESTORATION OF ISRAEL
REFERENCE	1——10——	15——	——19	——21
DIVISION	PREDICTIONS OF JUDGMENT	REASONS FOR JUDGMENT	RESULTS OF JUDGMENT	POSSESSION OF EDOM BY ISRAEL
TOPIC	DEFEAT OF ISRAEL			VICTORY OF ISRAEL
	PREDICTION OF JUDGMENT			PREDICTION OF POSSESSION
LOCATION	EDOM AND ISRAEL			
TIME	c. 840 B.C.			

OUTLINE OF OBADIAH

The Predictions of Judgment on Edom

THE vision of Obadiah.
Thus says the Lord GOD [R]concerning
Edom Is. 21:11
[R](We have heard a report from the LORD,
And a messenger has been sent among
the nations, *saying*, Jer. 49:14–16
"Arise, and let us rise up against her for
battle"):

2 "Behold, I will make you small among the
nations;
You shall be greatly despised.
3 The [R]pride of your heart has deceived
you, Jer. 49:16
You who dwell in the clefts of the rock,
Whose habitation is high;
[R]*You* who say in your heart, Rev. 18:7
'Who will bring me down to the ground?'
4 [R]Though you ascend *as* high as the
eagle, Job 20:6
And though you [R]set your nest among
the stars, Hab. 2:9
From there I will bring you down," says
the LORD.

5 "If [R]thieves had come to you, Jer. 49:9
If robbers by night—
Oh, how you will be cut off!—
Would they not have stolen till they had
enough?
If grape-gatherers had come to you,
[R]Would they not have left *some*
gleanings? Deut. 24:21

6 "Oh, how Esau shall be searched out!
How his hidden treasures shall be
sought after!
7 All the men in your confederacy
Shall force you to the border;
[R]The men at peace with you Jer. 38:22
Shall deceive you *and* prevail against
you.
Those who eat your bread shall lay a
trap* for you.
[R]No one is aware of it. Is. 19:11

8 "Will[R] I not in that day," says the LORD,
"Even destroy the wise *men* from Edom,
And understanding from the mountains
of Esau? [Job 5:12–14]
9 Then your [R]mighty men, O [R]Teman, shall
be dismayed, Ps. 76:5 • Jer. 49:7
To the end that everyone from the
mountains of Esau
May be cut off by slaughter.

The Reasons for the Judgment on Edom

10 "For [R]violence against your brother
Jacob, Gen. 27:41
Shame shall cover you,
And you shall be cut off forever.
11 In the day that you [R]stood on the other
side— Ps. 83:5–8
In the day that strangers carried captive
his forces,
When foreigners entered his gates
And [R]cast lots for Jerusalem— Nah. 3:10
Even you *were* as one of them.

12 "But you should not have [R]gazed[T] on the
day of your brother Mic. 4:11; 7:10
In the day of his captivity;* Gloated over
Nor should you have [R]rejoiced over the
children of Judah [Prov. 17:5]
In the day of their destruction;
Nor should you have spoken proudly
In the day of distress.
13 You should not have entered the gate of
My people
In the day of their calamity.
Indeed, you should not have [T]gazed on
their affliction Gloated over
In the day of their calamity,
Nor laid *hands* on their substance
In the day of their calamity.
14 You should not have stood at the
crossroads
To cut off those among them who
escaped;
Nor should you have delivered up those
among them who remained
In the day of distress.

The Results of the Judgment on Edom

15 "For[R] the day of the LORD upon all the
nations *is* near; Ezek. 30:3
[R]As you have done, it shall be done to
you; Hab. 2:8
Your [T]reprisal shall return upon your
own head. Or *reward*
16 [R]For as you drank on My holy mountain,
So shall all the nations drink Joel 3:17
continually;
Yes, they shall drink, and swallow,
And they shall be as though they had
never been.

17 "But on Mount Zion there [R]shall be
[T]deliverance, Amos 9:8 • Or *salvation*
And there shall be holiness;
The house of Jacob shall possess their
possessions.
18 The house of Jacob shall be a fire,
And the house of Joseph [R]a flame;
But the house of Esau *shall be* stubble;
They shall kindle them and devour
them, Zech. 12:6
And no survivor shall *remain* of the
house of Esau,"
For the LORD has spoken.

7 Or *wound or plot* **12** Lit. *On the day he became a foreigner*

The Possession of Edom by Israel

19 The South* [R]shall possess the mountains
of Esau, Is. 11:14
[R]And the Lowland shall possess Philistia.
They shall possess the fields of Ephraim
And the fields of Samaria. Zeph. 2:7
Benjamin *shall possess* Gilead.
20 And the captives of this host of the
children of Israel
Shall possess the land of the Canaanites
As [R]far as Zarephath. 1 Kin. 17:9
The captives of Jerusalem who are in
Sepharad
Shall possess the cities of the South.*
21 Then [R]saviors* shall come to Mount
Zion [James 5:20]
To judge the mountains of Esau,
And the kingdom shall be the LORD's.

19 Heb. *Negev* **20** Heb. *Negev* **21** Or *deliverers*

THE BOOK OF

JONAH

THE BOOK OF JONAH

Nineveh is northeast; Tarshish is west. When God calls Jonah to preach repentance to the wicked Ninevites, the prophet knows that God's mercy may follow. He turns down the assignment and heads for Tarshish instead. But once God has dampened his spirits (by tossing him out of the boat and into the water) and has demonstrated His protection (by moving him out of the water and into the fish), Jonah realizes God is serious about His command. Nineveh must hear the word of the Lord; therefore Jonah goes. Although the preaching is a success, the preacher comes away angry and discouraged. He must learn firsthand of God's compassion for sinful men.

Yonah is the Hebrew word for "dove." The Septuagint hellenized this word into *Ionas,* and the Latin Vulgate used the title *Jonas.*

THE AUTHOR OF JONAH

The first verse introduces Jonah as "the son of Amittai." Nothing more would be known about him were it not for another reference to him in 2 Kings 14:25 as a prophet in the reign of Jeroboam II of Israel. Under Jeroboam, the borders of Israel were expanded "according to the word of the LORD God of Israel, which He had spoken through His servant Jonah the son of Amittai, the prophet who *was* from Gath Hepher." Gath Hepher was three miles north of Nazareth in lower Galilee, making Jonah a prophet of the northern kingdom. The Pharisees were wrong when they said, "Search and look, for no prophet has arisen out of Galilee" (John 7:52), because Jonah was a Galilean. One Jewish tradition says that Jonah was the son of the widow of Zarephath whom Elijah raised from the dead (1 Kin. 17:8–24).

Some critics claim that Jonah was written during the fifth to third centuries B.C. as a historical fiction to oppose the "narrow nationalism" of Ezra and Nehemiah by introducing universalistic ideas. They say an anonymous writer created this work to counteract the Jewish practice of excluding the Samaritans from worship and of divorcing foreign wives. To support this view, it is noted that the book is written in the third person with no claim that Jonah wrote it. The use of Aramaic words and the statement that "Nineveh was an exceedingly great city" (3:3) indicate a late date after Nineveh's fall in 612 B.C.

Conservative scholars refute this claim with these arguments: (1) The idea of God's inclusion of the Gentiles in His program is found elsewhere in the Scripture (cf. Gen. 9:27; 12:3; Lev. 19:33, 34; 1 Sam. 2:10; Is. 2:2; Joel 2:28–32). (2) Aramaic words occur in early as well as late Old Testament books. Aramaic is found in Near Eastern texts as early as 1500 B.C. (3) The fact that the book does not explicitly say that it was written by Jonah is an argument from silence. (4) Use of the third-person style was common among biblical writers. (5) The text in 3:3 literally means "had become." At the time of the story, Nineveh had already become a very large city. (6) Jonah was a historical prophet (2 Kin. 14:25), and there are no hints that the book is fictional or allegorical. (7) Christ supported the historical accuracy of the book (Matt. 12:39–41).

THE TIME OF JONAH

Jonah was a contemporary of Jeroboam II of Israel (782–753 B.C.) who ministered after the time of Elisha and just before the time of Amos and Hosea. Israel under Jeroboam II was enjoying a period of resurgence and prosperity (see "The Time of Amos"). Conditions looked promising after many bleak years, and nationalistic fervor was probably high. During these years, Assyria was in a period of mild decline. Weak rulers had ascended the throne, but Assyria remained a threat. By the time of Jonah, Assyrian cruelty had become legendary. Graphic accounts of their cruel treatment of captives have been found in ancient Assyrian records, especially from the ninth and seventh centuries B.C. The repentance of Nineveh probably occurred in the reign of Ashurdan III (773–755 B.C.). Two plagues (765 and 759 B.C.) and a solar eclipse (763 B.C.) may have prepared the people for Jonah's message of judgment.

THE CHRIST OF JONAH

Jonah is the only prophet whom Jesus likened to Himself. "But He answered and said to them, 'An evil and adulterous generation seeks after a sign, and no sign will be given to it except the sign of the prophet Jonah. For as Jonah was three days and three nights in the belly of the great fish, so will the Son of Man be three days and three nights in the heart of the earth. The men of Nineveh will rise in the judgment with this generation and condemn it, because they repented at the preaching of Jonah; and indeed a greater than Jonah *is* here' " (Matt. 12:39–41). Jonah's experience is a type of the death, burial, and resurrection of Christ. (The Hebrew idiom, "three days and three nights," only requires a portion of the first and third days.)

KEYS TO JONAH

Key Word: The Revival in Nineveh—God's loving concern for the Gentiles is not a truth disclosed only in the New Testament. More than seven centuries before Christ, God commissioned the Hebrew prophet Jonah to proclaim a message of repentance to the Assyrians. Jewish nationalism, however, blinded both God's prophets and covenant people to God's worldwide purposes of salvation. The story of Jonah is one of the clearest demonstrations of God's love and mercy for all humankind in the entire Scriptures.

Key Verses: Jonah 2:8, 9; 4:2—"Those who regard worthless idols forsake their own Mercy. But I will sacrifice to You with the voice of thanksgiving; I will pay what I have vowed. Salvation *is* of the LORD" (2:8, 9).

"So he prayed to the LORD, and said, 'Ah, LORD, was not this what I said when I was still in my country? Therefore I fled previously to Tarshish; for I know that You *are* a gracious and merciful God, slow to anger and abundant in lovingkindness, One who relents from doing harm'" (4:2).

Key Chapter: Jonah 3—The third chapter of Jonah records perhaps the greatest revival of all time as the entire city of Nineveh "[believes] God, and [proclaims] a fast," and cries out to God.

SURVEY OF JONAH

Jonah is an unusual book because of its message and messenger. Unlike other Old Testament books, it revolves exclusively around a Gentile nation. God is concerned for the Gentiles as well as for His covenant people Israel. But God's messenger is a reluctant prophet who does not want to proclaim his message for fear that the Assyrians will respond and be spared by the compassionate God of Israel. Of all the people and things mentioned in the book—the storm, the lots, the sailors, the fish, the Ninevites, the plant, the worm, and the east wind—only the prophet himself fails to obey God. All these were used to teach Jonah a lesson in compassion and obedience. The four chapters divide: the first commission of Jonah (1 and 2) and the second commission of Jonah (3 and 4).

The First Commission of Jonah (1 and 2): This chapter records the commission of Jonah (1:1, 2), the disobedience of Jonah (1:3), and the judgment on Jonah (1:4–17). Jonah does not want to see God spare the notoriously cruel Assyrians. To preach a message of repentance to them would be like helping Israel's enemy. In his patriotic zeal, Jonah puts his country before his God and refuses to represent Him in Nineveh. Instead of going five hundred miles northeast to Nineveh, Jonah attempts to go two thousand miles west to Tarshish (Spain). But the Lord uses a creative series of counter-measures to accomplish His desired result. Jonah's efforts to thwart God's plan are futile.

God prepares a "great fish" to preserve Jonah and deliver him on dry land. The fish's divinely appointed rendezvous with the sinking prophet becomes a powerful reminder to Jonah of the sovereignty of God in every circumstance. While inside the fish (2), Jonah utters a declarative praise psalm, alluding to several psalms that were racing through his mind (Ps. 3:8; 31:22; 42:7; 69:1). In his unique "prayer closet," Jonah offers thanksgiving for his deliverance from drowning. When he acknowledges that "salvation *is* of the LORD" (2:9), he is finally willing to obey and be used by God. After he is cast up on the shore, Jonah has a long time to reflect on his experiences during his eastward trek of five hundred miles to Nineveh.

FOCUS	FIRST COMMISSION OF JONAH				SECOND COMMISSION OF JONAH			
REFERENCE	1:1——1:4——2:1——2:10——3:1——3:5——4:1——4:4——4:11							
DIVISION	DISOBEDIENCE TO THE FIRST CALL	JUDGMENT ON JONAH EXACTED	PRAYER OF JONAH IN THE FISH	DELIVERANCE OF JONAH FROM THE FISH	OBEDIENCE TO THE SECOND CALL	JUDGMENT ON NINEVEH AVERTED	PRAYER OF JONAH	REBUKE OF JONAH
TOPIC	GOD'S MERCY UPON JONAH				GOD'S MERCY UPON NINEVEH			
	"I WON'T GO."		"I WILL GO."		"I'M HERE."		"I SHOULDN'T HAVE COME."	
LOCATION	THE GREAT SEA				THE GREAT CITY			
TIME	c. 760 B.C.							

The Second Commission of Jonah (3 and 4): Jonah obeys his second commission to go to Nineveh (3:1–4) where he becomes "a sign to the Ninevites" (Luke 11:30). The prophet is a walking object lesson from God, his skin no doubt bleached from his stay in the fish. As he proceeds through the city, his one-sentence sermon brings incredible results: it is the most responsive evangelistic effort in history. Jonah's words of coming judgment are followed by a proclamation by the king of the city to fast and repent. Because of His great mercy, God "relented from the disaster that He had said He would bring upon them" (3:10).

In the final chapter, God's love and grace are contrasted with Jonah's anger and lack of compassion. Jonah is unhappy with the good results of his message because he knows God will now spare Nineveh. God uses a plant, a worm, and a wind to teach Jonah a lesson in compassion. Jonah's emotions shift from fierce anger (4:1), to despondency (4:3), then to great joy (4:6), and finally to despair (4:8). In a humorous but meaningful account, Jonah is forced to see that he has more concern for a plant than for hundreds of thousands of people (if 120,000 children are in mind in 4:11, the population of the area may have been 600,000). Jonah's lack of a divine perspective makes his repentance a greater problem than the repentance of Nineveh.

OUTLINE OF JONAH

I. The First Commission of Jonah........1:1—2:10

- A. The Disobedience to the First Call..........1:1–3
- B. The Judgment on Jonah Is Exacted......1:4–17
  - 1. The Great Storm..............................1:4–16
  - 2. The Great Salvation of Jonah by the Fish..1:17
- C. The Prayer of Jonah..............................2:1–9
- D. The Deliverance of Jonah.......................2:10

II. The Second Commission of Jonah...3:1—4:11

- A. The Obedience to the Second Call...........3:1–4
- B. The Judgment of Nineveh Averted........3:5–10
  - 1. The Great Fast....................................3:5–9
  - 2. The Great Salvation of Nineveh by God...3:10
- C. The Prayer of Jonah..............................4:1–3
- D. The Rebuke of Jonah by God...............4:4–11

CHAPTER 1

The Disobedience to the First Call

NOW the word of the LORD came to [R]Jonah
the son of Amittai, saying, 2 Kin. 14:25
2 "Arise, go to [R]Nineveh, that great city, and
cry out against it; for their wickedness has
come up before Me." Is. 37:37
3 But Jonah arose to flee to Tarshish from
the presence of the LORD. He went down to
[R]Joppa, and found a ship going to Tarshish; so
he paid the fare, and went down into it, to go
with them to [R]Tarshish from the presence of
the LORD. Josh. 19:46 • Is. 23:1

The Great Storm

4 But [R]the LORD [T]sent out a great wind on
the sea, and there was a mighty tempest on
the sea, so that the ship was about to be bro-
ken up. Ps. 107:25 • Lit. *hurled*
5 Then the mariners were afraid; and every
man cried out to his god, and threw the cargo
that *was* in the ship into the sea, to lighten the
load.* But Jonah had gone down [R]into the
lowest parts of the ship, had lain down, and
was fast asleep. 1 Sam. 24:3
6 So the captain came to him, and said to
him, "What do you mean, sleeper? Arise, call
on your God; perhaps your God will consider
us, so that we may not perish."
7 And they said to one another, "Come, let
us cast lots, that we may know for whose
cause this trouble *has come* upon us." So they
cast lots, and the lot fell on Jonah.
8 Then they said to him, [R]"Please tell us!
For whose cause *is* this trouble upon us? What
is your occupation? And where do you come
from? What is your country? And of what peo-
ple are you?" Josh. 7:19
9 So he said to them, "I *am* a Hebrew; and I
fear the LORD, the God of heaven, [R]who made
the sea and the dry *land*." [Neh. 9:6]
10 Then the men were exceedingly afraid,
and said to him, "Why have you done this?"
For the men knew that he fled from the pres-
ence of the LORD, because he had told them.
11 Then they said to him, "What shall we do
to you that the sea may be calm for us?"—for
the sea was growing more tempestuous.
12 And he said to them, [R]"Pick me up and
throw me into the sea; then the sea will be-
come calm for you. For I know that this great
tempest *is* because of me." John 11:50
13 Nevertheless the men rowed hard to re-
turn to land, [R]but they could not, for the sea
continued to grow more tempestuous against
them. [Prov. 21:30]
14 Therefore they cried out to the LORD and
said, "We pray, O LORD, please do not let us
perish for this man's life, and [R]do not charge
us with innocent blood; for You, O LORD, have
done as it pleased You." Deut. 21:8

1:5 Lit. *from upon them*

15 So they picked up Jonah and threw him
into the sea, [R]and the sea ceased from its rag-
ing. [Ps. 89:9; 107:29]
16 Then the men [R]feared the LORD exceed-
ingly, and offered a sacrifice to the LORD and
took vows. Acts 5:11

The Great Salvation of Jonah by the Fish

17 Now the LORD had prepared a great fish
to swallow Jonah. And Jonah was in the belly
of the fish three days and three nights.

CHAPTER 2

The Prayer of Jonah

THEN Jonah prayed to the LORD his God
from the fish's belly.
2 And he said:

"I [R]cried out to the LORD because of my
affliction, Ps. 120:1
[R]And He answered me. Ps. 65:2

"Out of the belly of Sheol I cried,
And You heard my voice.
3 [R]For You cast me into the deep, Ps. 88:6
Into the heart of the seas,
And the floods surrounded me;
[R]All Your billows and Your waves passed
over me. Ps. 42:7
4 [R]Then I said, 'I have been cast out of Your
sight; Ps. 31:22
Yet I will look again [R]toward Your holy
temple.' 1 Kin. 8:38
5 The [R]waters surrounded me, *even* to my
soul; Lam. 3:54
The deep closed around me;
Weeds were wrapped around my head.
6 I went down to the [T]moorings of the
mountains; *foundations* or *bases*
The earth with its bars *closed* behind me
forever;
Yet You have brought up my [R]life from
the pit, [Ps. 16:10]
O LORD, my God.

7 "When my soul fainted within me,
I remembered the LORD;
[R]And my prayer went *up* to You,
Into Your holy temple. Ps. 18:6

8 "Those who regard [R]worthless idols
Forsake their own Mercy. Jer. 10:8
9 But I will [R]sacrifice to You Hos. 14:2
With the voice of thanksgiving;
I will pay what I have [R]vowed. [Eccl. 5:4, 5]
[R]Salvation *is* of the LORD." Ps. 3:8

The Deliverance of Jonah

10 So the LORD spoke to the fish, and it vom-
ited Jonah onto dry *land*.

CHAPTER 3

The Obedience to the Second Call

NOW the word of the LORD came to Jonah
the second time, saying,
2 "Arise, go to Nineveh, that great city, and
preach to it the message that I tell you."
3 So Jonah arose and went to Nineveh, ac-
cording to the word of the LORD. Now Nineveh
was an exceedingly great city, a three-day
journey* *in extent*.
4 And Jonah began to enter the city on the
first day's walk. Then [R]he cried out and said,
"Yet forty days, and Nineveh shall be over-
thrown!" [Deut. 18:22]

The Great Fast

5 So the people of Nineveh believed God,
proclaimed a fast, and put on sackcloth, from
the greatest to the least of them.
6 Then word came to the king of Nineveh;
and he arose from his throne and laid aside
his robe, covered *himself* with sackcloth [R]and
sat in ashes. Job 2:8
7 [R]And he caused *it* to be proclaimed and
published throughout Nineveh by the decree
of the king and his [T]nobles, saying,

Let neither man nor beast, herd nor
flock, taste anything; do not let them eat,
or drink water. 2 Chr. 20:3 • Lit. *great ones*
8 But let man and beast be covered with
sackcloth, and cry mightily to God; yes,
let every one turn from his evil way and
from the violence that is in his hands.
9 [R]Who can tell *if* God will turn and relent,
and turn away from His fierce anger, so
that we may not perish? Joel 2:14

The Great Salvation of Nineveh by God

10 Then God saw their works, that they
turned from their evil way; and God relented
from the disaster that He had said He would
bring upon them, and He did not do it.

CHAPTER 4

The Prayer of Jonah

BUT it displeased Jonah exceedingly, and
he became angry.
2 So he prayed to the LORD, and said, "Ah,
LORD, was not this what I said when I was still
in my country? Therefore I [R]fled previously to
Tarshish; for I know that You *are* a [R]gracious
and merciful God, slow to anger and abun-
dant in lovingkindness, One who relents from
doing harm. Jon. 1:3 • Joel 2:13
3 [R]"Therefore now, O LORD, please take my
life from me, for [R]*it is* better for me to die than
to live!" 1 Kin. 19:4 • Jon. 4:8

3:3 Exact meaning unknown

The Rebuke of Jonah by God

4 Then the LORD said, "*Is it* right for you to be angry?"

5 So Jonah went out of the city and sat on the east side of the city. There he made himself a shelter and sat under it in the shade, till he might see what would become of the city.

6 And the LORD God prepared a plant* and made it come up over Jonah, that it might be shade for his head to deliver him from his misery. So Jonah [T]was very grateful for the plant. Lit. *rejoiced with great joy*

7 But as morning dawned the next day God prepared a worm, and it *so* damaged the plant that it withered.

8 And it happened, when the sun arose, that God prepared a vehement east wind; and the sun beat on Jonah's head, so that he grew faint. Then he wished death for himself, and said, [R]"*It is* better for me to die than to live." Jon. 4:3

9 Then God said to Jonah, "*Is it* right for you to be angry about the plant?" And he said, "*It is* right for me to be angry, even to death!"

10 But the LORD said, "You have had pity on the plant for which you have not labored, nor made it grow, which came up in a night and perished in a night.

11 "And should I not pity Nineveh, [R]that great city, in which are more than one hundred and twenty thousand persons who cannot discern between their right hand and their left—and much livestock?" Jon. 1:2

4:6 Heb. *kikayon,* exact identity unknown

THE BOOK OF

MICAH

THE BOOK OF MICAH

Micah, called from his rustic home to be a prophet, leaves his familiar surroundings to deliver a stern message of judgment to the princes and people of Jerusalem. Burdened by the abusive treatment of the poor by the rich and influential, the prophet turns his verbal rebukes upon any who would use their social or political power for personal gain. One-third of Micah's book exposes the sins of his countrymen; another third pictures the punishment God is about to send; and the final third holds out the hope of restoration once that discipline has ended. Through it all, God's righteous demands upon His people are clear: "to do justly, to love mercy, and to walk humbly with your God" (6:8).

The name *Michayahu* ("Who Is Like Yahweh?") is shortened to *Michaia.* In 7:18 Micah hints at his own name with the phrase "Who *is* a God like You?" The Greek and Latin titles of this book are *Michaias* and *Micha.*

THE AUTHOR OF MICAH

Micah's hometown of Moresheth Gath (1:14) was located about twenty-five miles southwest of Jerusalem on the border of Judah and Philistia, near Gath. Like Amos, Micah was from the country. His family and occupation are unknown, but Moresheth was in a productive agricultural belt. Micah was not as aware of the political situation as Isaiah or Daniel, but he showed a profound concern for the sufferings of the people. His clear sense of prophetic calling is seen in 3:8: "But truly I am full of power by the Spirit of the LORD, and of justice and might, to declare to Jacob his transgression and to Israel his sin."

THE TIME OF MICAH

The first verse indicates that Micah prophesied in the days of Jotham (739–731 B.C.), Ahaz (731–715 B.C.), and Hezekiah (715–686 B.C.), kings of Judah. Although Micah deals primarily with Judah, he also addresses the northern kingdom of Israel and predicts the fall of Samaria (1:6). Much of his ministry, therefore, took place before the Assyrian captivity of Israel in 722 B.C. His strong denunciations of idolatry and immorality also suggest that his ministry largely preceded the sweeping religious reforms of Hezekiah. Thus, Micah's prophecies ranged from about 735 to 710 B.C. He was a contemporary of Hosea in the northern kingdom and of Isaiah in the court of Jerusalem.

After the prosperous reign of Uzziah in Judah (767–739 B.C.), his son, Jotham, came to power and followed the same policies (739–731 B.C.). He was a good king, although he failed to remove the idolatrous high places. Under the wicked King Ahaz (731–715 B.C.), Judah was threatened by the forces of Assyria and Syria. Hezekiah (715–686 B.C.) opposed the Assyrians and successfully withstood an Assyrian siege with the help of God. He was an unusually good king who guided the people of Judah back to a proper course in their walk with God.

During the ministry of Micah, the kingdom of Israel continued to crumble inwardly and outwardly until its collapse in 722 B.C. The Assyrian Empire under Tiglath-Pileser III (745–727 B.C.), Shalmaneser V (727–722 B.C.), Sargon II (722–705 B.C.), and Sennacherib (705–681 B.C.) reached the zenith of its power and became a constant threat to Judah. Babylon was still under Assyrian domination, and Micah's prediction of future Babylonian captivity for Judah (4:10) must have seemed unlikely.

THE CHRIST OF MICAH

Micah 5:2 is one of the clearest and most important of all Old Testament prophecies: "But you, Bethlehem Ephrathah, *though* you are little among the thousands of Judah, *yet* out of you shall come forth to Me the One to be Ruler in Israel, whose goings forth *are* from of old, from everlasting." This prophecy about the birthplace and eternity of the Messiah was made seven hundred years before His birth. The chief priests and scribes paraphrased this verse in Matthew 2:5, 6 when questioned about the birthplace of the Messiah. Micah 2:12, 13; 4:1–8; and 5:4, 5 offer some of the best Old Testament descriptions of the righteous reign of Christ over the whole world.

KEYS TO MICAH

Key Word: The Judgment and Restoration of Judah—Micah exposes the injustice of Judah and the righteousness and justice of Yahweh. About one-third of the book indicts Israel and Judah for specific sins, including oppression; bribery among judges, prophets, and priests; exploitation of the powerless; covetousness; cheating; violence; and pride. Another third of Micah predicts the judgment that will come as a result of those sins. The remaining third of the book is a message of hope and consolation. God's justice will triumph and the divine Deliverer will come. True peace and justice will prevail only when the Messiah reigns. The "goodness and severity of God" (Rom. 11:22) are illustrated in Micah's presentation of divine judgment and pardon. This book emphasizes the integral relationship between true spirituality and social ethics. Micah 6:8 summarizes what God wants to see in His people: justice and equity tempered with mercy and compassion, as the result of a humble and obedient relationship with Him.

Key Verses: Micah 6:8; 7:18—"He has shown you, O man, what is good; and what does the LORD require of you but to do justly, to love mercy, and to walk humbly with your God?" (6:8).

"Who *is* a God like You, pardoning iniquity and passing over the transgression of the remnant of His heritage? He does not retain His anger forever, because He delights *in* mercy" (7:18).

Key Chapters: Micah 6; 7—The closing section of Micah describes a courtroom scene. God has a controversy against His people, and He calls the mountains and hills together to form the jury as He sets forth His case. The people have replaced heartfelt worship with empty ritual, thinking that this is all God demands. They have divorced God's standards of justice from their daily dealings in order to cover their unscrupulous practices. They have failed to realize what the Lord requires of man. There can only be one verdict: guilty.

Nevertheless, the book closes on a note of hope. The same God who executes judgment also delights to extend mercy (7:18). No wonder the prophet exclaims, "Therefore I will look to the LORD; I will wait for the God of my salvation; my God will hear me" (7:7).

SURVEY OF MICAH

Micah is the prophet of the downtrodden and exploited people of Judean society. He prophesies during a time of great social injustice and boldly opposes those who impose their power upon the poor and weak for selfish ends. Corrupt rulers, false prophets, and ungodly priests all become targets for Micah's prophetic barbs. Micah exposes judges who are bought by bribes and merchants who use deceptive weights. The pollution of sin has permeated every level of society in Judah and Israel. The whole earth is called to witness God's indictment against His people (1:2; 6:1, 2), and the guilty verdict leads to a sentence of destruction and captivity. However, while the three major sections begin with condemnation (1:2—2:11; 3:6), they all end on a clear note of consolation (2:12, 13; 4; 5; 7). After sin is punished and justice is established, "He will again have compassion on us, and will subdue our iniquities. You will cast all our sins into the depths of the sea" (7:19). The three sections of Micah are: the prediction of judgment (1—3), the prediction of restoration (4 and 5), and the plea for repentance (6 and 7).

The Prediction of Judgment (1—3): Micah begins by launching into a general declaration of the condemnation of Israel (Samaria) and Judah (Jerusalem). Both kingdoms will be overthrown because of their rampant treachery. Micah uses a series of wordplays on the names of several cities of Judah in his lamentation over Judah's coming destruction (1:10–16). This is followed by some of the specific causes for judgment: premeditated schemes, covetousness, and cruelty. Nevertheless, God will regather a remnant of His people (2:12, 13). The prophet then systematically condemns the princes (3:1–4) and the prophets (3:5–8) and concludes with a warning of coming judgment (3:9–12).

The Prediction of Restoration (4 and 5): Micah then moves into a two-chapter message of hope, which describes the reinstitution of the

FOCUS	PREDICTION OF JUDGMENT		PREDICTION OF RESTORATION			PLEA FOR REPENTANCE		
REFERENCE	1:1—	3:1—	4:1—	4:6—	5:2—	6:1—	6:10—	7:7—7:20
DIVISION	JUDGMENT OF PEOPLE	JUDGMENT OF LEADERSHIP	PROMISE OF COMING KINGDOM	PROMISE OF COMING CAPTIVITIES	PROMISE OF COMING KING	FIRST PLEA OF GOD	SECOND PLEA OF GOD	PROMISE OF FINAL SALVATION
TOPIC	PUNISHMENT RETRIBUTION		PROMISE RESTORATION			PARDON REPENTANCE		
LOCATION	JUDAH—ISRAEL							
TIME	c. 735–710 B.C.							

kingdom (4:1–5) and the intervening captivity of the kingdom (4:6—5:1), concluding with the coming Ruler of the Kingdom (5:2–15). The prophetic focus gradually narrows from the nations to the remnant to the King.

The Plea for Repentance (6 and 7): In His two controversies with His people, God calls them into court and presents an unanswerable case against them. The people have spurned God's grace, choosing instead to revel in wickedness. Micah concludes with a sublime series of promises that the Lord will pardon their iniquity and renew their nation in accordance with His covenant.

OUTLINE OF MICAH

CHAPTER 1

Introduction to the Book of Micah

THE word of the LORD that came to Micah of Moresheth in the days of Jotham, Ahaz, *and* Hezekiah, kings of Judah, which he saw concerning Samaria and Jerusalem.

Judgment on Samaria

2 Hear, all you peoples!
Listen, O earth, and all that is in it!
Let the Lord GOD be a witness against you,
The Lord from [R]His holy temple. [Ps. 11:4]

3 For behold, the LORD is coming out of His place;
He will come down
And tread on the high places of the earth.
4 [R]The mountains will melt under Him,
And the valleys will split Amos 9:5
Like wax before the fire,
Like waters poured down a steep place.
5 All this is for the transgression of Jacob
And for the sins of the house of Israel.
What *is* the transgression of Jacob?
Is it not Samaria?
And what *are* the [R]high places of Judah?
Are they not Jerusalem? Deut. 32:13

6 "Therefore I will make Samaria [R]a heap of ruins in the field, 2 Kin. 19:25
Places for planting a vineyard;
I will pour down her stones into the valley,
And I will uncover her foundations.
7 All her carved images shall be beaten to pieces,
And all her [R]pay as a harlot shall be burned with the fire; Hos. 2:5
All her idols I will lay desolate,
For she gathered *it* from the pay of a harlot,
And they shall return to the [R]pay of a harlot." Deut. 23:18

8 Therefore I will wail and howl,
I will go stripped and naked;
I will make a wailing like the jackals
And a mourning like the ostriches,

Judgment on Judah

9 For her wounds *are* incurable.
For [R]it has come to Judah; 2 Kin. 18:13
It has come to the gate of My people—
To Jerusalem.

10 [R]Tell *it* not in Gath, 2 Sam. 1:20
Weep not at all;
In Beth Aphrah*
Roll yourself in the dust.
11 Pass by in naked shame, you inhabitant of [T]Shaphir; Lit. *Beautiful*
The inhabitant of Zaanan* does not go out.
Beth Ezel mourns;
Its place to stand is taken away from you.

1:10 Lit. *House of Dust* **1:11** Lit. *Going Out*

12 For the inhabitant of [T]Maroth pined* for
good, Lit. *Bitterness*
But [R]disaster came down from the LORD
To the gate of Jerusalem. Is. 59:9–11
13 O inhabitant of [R]Lachish, Is. 36:2
Harness the chariot to the swift steeds
(She *was* the beginning of sin to the
daughter of Zion),
For the transgressions of Israel were
[R]found in you. Ezek. 23:11

14 Therefore you shall [R]give presents to
Moresheth Gath;* 2 Sam. 8:2
The houses of [R]Achzib* *shall be* a lie to
the kings of Israel. Josh. 15:44
15 I will yet bring an heir to you, O
inhabitant of Mareshah;*
The glory of Israel shall come to
[R]Adullam.[T] 2 Chr. 11:7 • Lit. *Refuge*
16 Make yourself [R]bald and cut off your
hair, Job 1:20
Because of your [R]precious children;
Enlarge your baldness like an eagle,
For they shall go from you into
[R]captivity. Lam. 4:5 • Amos 7:11, 17

CHAPTER 2

Cause of the Judgment

WOE to those who devise iniquity,
And [T]work out evil on their beds! Plan
At morning light they practice it,
Because it is in the power of their
hand.
2 They [R]covet fields and take *them* by
violence, Is. 5:8
Also houses, and seize *them*.
So they oppress a man and his house,
A man and his inheritance.

3 Therefore thus says the LORD:

"Behold, against this [R]family I am
devising [R]disaster, Jer. 8:3 • Amos 5:13
From which you cannot remove your
necks;
Nor shall you walk haughtily,
For this *is* an evil time.
4 In that day *one* shall take up a proverb
against you,
And [R]lament with a bitter lamentation,
saying: 2 Sam. 1:17
'We are utterly destroyed!
He has changed the [T]heritage of my
people; Lit. *portion*
How He has removed *it* from me!
To [T]a turncoat He has divided our
fields.' " Lit. *one turning back,* an apostate

5 Therefore you will have no one to
determine boundaries* by lot
In the assembly of the LORD.

6 "Do not prattle," *you say to those* who
[T]prophesy. Or *preach,* lit. *drip* words
So they shall not prophesy to you;*
They shall not return insult for insult.*
7 *You who are* named the house of Jacob:
"Is the Spirit of the LORD restricted?
Are these His doings?
Do not My words do good
To him who walks uprightly?

8 "Lately My people have risen up as an
enemy—
You pull off the robe with the garment
From those who trust *you,* as they pass
by,
Like men returned from war.
9 The women of My people you cast out
From their pleasant houses;
From their children
You have taken away My glory forever.

10 "Arise and depart,
For this *is* not *your* [R]rest; Deut. 12:9
Because it is [R]defiled, it shall destroy,
Yes, with utter destruction. Lev. 18:25
11 If a man should walk in a false spirit
And speak a lie, *saying,*
'I will [T]prophesy to you [T]of wine and
drink,' Or *preach,* lit. *drip* • *concerning*
Even he would be the [R]prattler of this
people. Is. 30:10

Promise of Future Restoration

12 "I[R] will surely assemble all of you,
O Jacob, [Mic. 4:6, 7]
I will surely gather the remnant of Israel;
I will put them together [R]like sheep of
the fold,* Jer. 31:10
Like a flock in the midst of their pasture;
[R]They shall make a loud noise because of
so many people. Ezek. 33:22; 36:37
13 The one who breaks open will come up
before them;
They will break out,
Pass through the gate,
And go out by it;
Their king will pass before them,
[R]With the LORD at their head." Is. 52:12

CHAPTER 3

Judgment on Princes

AND I said:

"Hear now, O heads of Jacob,
And you rulers of the house of Israel:
Is it not for you to know justice?

1:12 Lit. *was sick* **1:14** Lit. *Possession of Gath* • Lit. *Lie* **1:15** Lit. *Inheritance* **2:5** Lit. *one casting a surveyor's line* **2:6** Lit. *to these* • Vg. *He shall not take shame* **2:12** Heb. *Bozrah*

2 You who hate good and love evil;
Who strip the skin from My people,*
And the flesh from their bones;
3 Who also [R]eat the flesh of My people,
Flay their skin from them, Ps. 14:4; 27:2
Break their bones,
And chop *them* in pieces
Like *meat* for the pot,
[R]Like flesh in the caldron." Ezek. 11:3, 6, 7

4 Then [R]they will cry to the LORD,
But He will not hear them;
He will even hide His face from them at that time,
Because they have been evil in their deeds. Jer. 11:11

Judgment on Prophets

5 Thus says the LORD [R]concerning the prophets Ezek. 13:10, 19
Who make my people stray;
Who chant [T]"Peace" All is well
While they chew with their teeth,
But who prepare war against him
Who puts nothing into their mouths:
6 "Therefore[R] you shall have night without [T]vision, Is. 8:20–22; 29:10–12
And you shall have darkness without divination; Prophetic revelation
The sun shall go down on the prophets,
And the day shall be dark for them.
7 So the seers shall be ashamed,
And the diviners abashed;
Indeed they shall all cover their lips;
For *there is* no answer from God."

8 But truly I am full of power by the Spirit of the LORD,
And of justice and might,
[R]To declare to Jacob his transgression
And to Israel his sin. Is. 58:1

Promise of Future Judgment

9 Now hear this,
You heads of the house of Jacob
And rulers of the house of Israel,
Who abhor justice
And [T]pervert all equity, Lit. *twist*
10 Who build up Zion with [R]bloodshed
And Jerusalem with iniquity: Hab. 2:12
11 [R]Her heads judge for a bribe, Is. 1:23
[R]Her priests teach for pay, Jer. 6:13
And her prophets divine for [T]money.
[R]Yet they lean on the LORD, and say,
"Is not the LORD among us? Lit. *silver*
No harm can come upon us." Is. 48:2
12 Therefore because of you
Zion shall be plowed *like* a field,
Jerusalem shall become heaps of ruins,
And [R]the mountain of the temple*
Like the bare hills of the forest. Mic. 4:1, 2

CHAPTER 4

The Promise of the Coming Kingdom

NOW [R]it shall come to pass in the latter days Is. 2:2–4
That the mountain of the LORD's house
Shall be established on the top of the mountains,
And shall be exalted above the hills;
And peoples shall flow to it.
2 Many nations shall come and say,
"Come, and let us go up to the mountain of the LORD,
To the house of the God of Jacob;
He will teach us His ways,
And we shall walk in His paths."
For out of Zion the law shall go forth,
And the word of the LORD from Jerusalem.
3 He shall judge between many peoples,
And rebuke strong nations afar off;
They shall beat their swords into plowshares,
And their spears into [T]pruning hooks;
Nation shall not lift up sword against nation, *pruning knives*
Neither shall they learn war anymore.*

4 [R]But everyone shall sit under his vine and under his fig tree, Zech. 3:10
And no one shall make *them* afraid;
For the mouth of the LORD of hosts has spoken.
5 For all people walk each in the name of his god,
But [R]we will walk in the name of the LORD our God Zech. 10:12
Forever and ever.

The Promise of the Coming Captivities

6 "In that day," says the LORD,
[R]"I will assemble the lame, Ezek. 34:16
[R]I will gather the outcast Ps. 147:2
And those whom I have afflicted;
7 I will make the lame a remnant,
And the outcast a strong nation;
So the LORD [R]will reign over them in Mount Zion [Is. 9:6; 24:23]
From now on, even forever.
8 And you, O tower of the flock,
The stronghold of the daughter of Zion,
To you shall it come,
Even the former dominion shall come,
The kingdom of the daughter of Jerusalem."

9 Now why do you cry aloud?
[R]*Is there* no king in your midst? Jer. 8:19
Has your counselor perished?
For [R]pangs have seized you like a woman in [T]labor. Is. 13:8 • *childbirth*

3:2 Lit. *them* **3:12** Lit. *house* **4:3** Cf. Is. 2:2–4

10 Be in pain, and labor to bring forth,
O daughter of Zion,
Like a woman in birth pangs.
For now you shall go forth from the city,
You shall dwell in the field,
And to Babylon you shall go.
There you shall be delivered;
There the LORD will redeem you
From the hand of your enemies.

11 [R]Now also many nations have gathered
against you, Lam. 2:16
Who say, "Let her be defiled,
And let our eye look upon Zion."
12 But they do not know [R]the thoughts of
the LORD, [Is. 55:8, 9]
Nor do they understand His counsel;
For He will gather them [R]like sheaves to
the threshing floor. Is. 21:10

13 "Arise and thresh, O daughter of Zion;
For I will make your horn iron,
And I will make your hooves bronze;
You shall beat in pieces many peoples;
[R]I will consecrate their gain to the LORD,
And their substance to [R]the Lord of the
whole earth." Is. 18:7 • Zech. 4:14

CHAPTER 5

NOW gather yourself in troops,
O daughter of troops;
He has laid siege against us;
They will [R]strike the judge of Israel with
a rod on the cheek. Mark 15:19☆

Birth of the Messiah

2 "But you, [R]Bethlehem Ephrathah,
Though you are little among the
thousands of Judah, Luke 2:4–7☆
Yet out of you shall come forth to Me
The One to be [R]Ruler in Israel, [Is. 9:6]
[R]Whose goings forth *are* from of old,
From everlasting." Ps. 90:2

Rejection of the Messiah

3 Therefore He shall give them up,
Until the time *that* [R]she who is in labor
has given birth; Mic. 4:10
Then the remnant of His brethren
Shall return to the children of Israel.

Work of the Messiah

4 And He shall stand and [R]feed[T] *His flock*
In the strength of the LORD,
In the majesty of the name of the LORD
His God; [Is. 40:11; 49:9] • *shepherd*
And they shall abide,
For now He [R]shall be great Ps. 72:8
To the ends of the earth;
5 And this *One* [R]shall be peace. [Is. 9:6]
When the Assyrian comes into our land,
And when he treads in our palaces,
Then we will raise against him
Seven shepherds and eight princely men.
6 They shall [T]waste with the sword the
land of Assyria, *devastate*
And the land of [R]Nimrod at its
entrances; Gen. 10:8–11
Thus He shall [R]deliver *us* from the
Assyrian, Is. 14:25
When he comes into our land
And when he treads within our borders.

7 Then [R]the remnant of Jacob Mic. 5:3
Shall be in the midst of many peoples,
[R]Like dew from the LORD, Deut. 32:2
Like showers on the grass,
That [T]tarry for no man *wait*
Nor [T]wait for the sons of men. *delay*
8 And the remnant of Jacob
Shall be among the Gentiles,
In the midst of many peoples,
Like a [R]lion among the beasts of the
forest, Num. 24:9
Like a young lion among flocks of sheep,
Who, if he passes through,
Both treads down and tears in pieces,
And none can deliver.
9 Your hand shall be lifted against your
adversaries,
And all your enemies shall be cut off.

10 "And it shall be in that day," says the
LORD,
"That I will [R]cut off your [R]horses from
your midst Zech. 9:10 • Deut. 17:16
And destroy your [R]chariots. Is. 2:7
11 I will cut off the cities of your land
And throw down all your strongholds.
12 I will cut off sorceries from your hand,
And you shall have no soothsayers.
13 [R]Your carved images I will also cut off,
And your sacred pillars from your
midst; Zech. 13:2
You shall [R]no more worship the work of
your hands; Is. 2:8
14 I will pluck your wooden images* from
your midst;
Thus I will destroy your cities.
15 And I will [R]execute vengeance in anger
and fury [2 Thess. 1:8]
On the nations that have not heard."*

CHAPTER 6

God Pleads

HEAR now what the LORD says:
"Arise, plead your case before the
mountains,
And let the hills hear your voice.
2 [R]Hear, O you mountains, [R]the LORD's
complaint, Ps. 50:1, 4 • Hos. 12:2

5:14 Heb. *Asherim,* Canaanite deities **5:15** obeyed

And you strong foundations of the earth;
For [R]the LORD has a complaint against
His people, [Is. 1:18]
And He will contend with Israel.

3 "O My people, what [R]have I done to you?
And how have I wearied you?
Testify against Me. Jer. 2:5, 31
4 [R]For I brought you up from the land of
Egypt, [Deut. 4:20]
I redeemed you from the house of
bondage;
And I sent before you Moses, Aaron, and
Miriam.
5 O My people, remember now
What [R]Balak king of Moab counseled,
And what Balaam the son of Beor
answered him, Num. 22:5, 6
From Acacia Grove* to Gilgal,
That you may know [R]the righteousness
of the LORD." Judg. 5:11

Micah Replies

6 With what shall I come before the LORD,
And bow myself before the High God?
Shall I come before Him with burnt
offerings,
With calves a year old?
7 [R]Will the LORD be pleased with thousands
of rams, Is. 1:11
Ten thousand [R]rivers of oil? Job 29:6
[R]Shall I give my firstborn *for* my
transgression, 2 Kin. 16:3
[T]The fruit of my body *for* the sin of my
soul? My own child

8 He has [R]shown you, O man, what *is*
good; [Deut. 10:12]
And what does the LORD require of you
But [R]to do justly, Gen. 18:19
To love [T]mercy, Or *lovingkindness*
And to walk humbly with your God?

9 The LORD's voice cries to the city—
Wisdom shall see Your name:

"Hear the rod!
Who has appointed it?

God Pleads

10 Are there yet the treasures of
wickedness
In the house of the wicked,
And the short measure *that is* an
abomination?
11 Shall I count pure *those* with [R]the
wicked scales, Hos. 12:7
And with the bag of deceitful weights?
12 For her rich men are full of [R]violence,
Her inhabitants have spoken lies,
And [R]their tongue is deceitful in their
mouth. Mic. 2:1, 2 • Jer. 9:2–6, 8

13 "Therefore I will also [R]make *you* sick by
striking you, Lev. 26:16
By making *you* desolate because of your
sins.
14 [R]You shall eat, but not be satisfied;
Hunger* *shall be* in your midst.
*You may carry *some* away, but shall not
save *them;*
And what you do rescue I will give over
to the sword. Lev. 26:26

15 "You shall [R]sow, but not reap; Amos 5:11
You shall tread the olives, but not anoint
yourselves with oil;
And *make* sweet wine, but not drink
wine.
16 For the statutes of Omri are [R]kept;
All the works of Ahab's house *are done;*
And you walk in their counsels,
That I may make you a desolation,
And your inhabitants a hissing.
Therefore you shall bear the [R]reproach
of My people."* Hos. 5:11 • Is. 25:8

CHAPTER 7

Micah Replies

WOE is me!
For I am like those who gather summer
fruits,
Like those who [R]glean vintage grapes;
There is no cluster to eat Is. 17:6
Of the first-ripe fruit *which* [R]my soul
desires. Is. 28:4
2 The [R]faithful[T] *man* has perished from the
earth, Is. 57:1 • Or *loyal*
And *there is* no one upright among men.
They all lie in wait for blood;
Every man hunts his brother with a net.

3 That they may successfully do evil with
both hands—
The prince asks *for gifts,*
The judge *seeks* a [R]bribe, Mic. 3:11
And the great *man* utters his evil desire;
So they scheme together.
4 The best of them *is* [R]like a brier;
The most upright *is sharper* than a thorn
hedge; Ezek. 2:6
The day of your watchman and your
punishment comes;
Now shall be their perplexity.

5 [R]Do not trust in a friend; Jer. 9:4
Do not put your confidence in a
companion;
Guard the doors of your mouth
From her who lies in your bosom.
6 For [R]son dishonors father, Matt. 10:36

6:5 Heb. *Shittim,* Num. 25:1; Josh. 2:1; 3:1 **6:14** Or *Emptiness* or Humiliation • Tg., Vg. *You shall take hold* **6:16** So with MT, Tg., Vg.; LXX *of nations*

Daughter rises against her mother,
Daughter-in-law against her
mother-in-law;
A man's enemies *are* the men of his own
household.

The Promise of Final Salvation

7 Therefore I will look to the LORD;
I will [R]wait for the God of my salvation;
My God will hear me. Is. 25:9

8 Do not rejoice over me, my enemy;
[R]When I fall, I will arise; [Prov. 24:16]
When I sit in darkness,
The LORD *will be* a light to me.
9 I will bear the indignation of the LORD,
Because I have sinned against Him,
Until He pleads my [R]case Jer. 50:34
And executes justice for me.
He will bring me forth to the light;
I will see His righteousness.
10 Then *she who is* my enemy will see,
And [R]shame will cover her who said to
me, Ps. 35:26
[R]"Where is the LORD your God?" Ps. 42:3
My eyes will see her;
Now she will be trampled down
Like mud in the streets.

11 *In* the day when your [R]walls are to be
built, [Amos 9:11]
In that day the decree shall go far and
wide.*
12 *In* that day [R]they* shall come to you
From Assyria and the fortified cities,*
From the fortress* to the River,*
From sea to sea, [Is. 11:16; 19:23–25]
And mountain *to* mountain.
13 Yet the land shall be desolate
Because of those who dwell in it,
And for the fruit of their deeds.

14 Shepherd Your people with Your staff,
The flock of Your heritage,
Who dwell solitarily *in* a [R]woodland,
In the midst of Carmel; Is. 37:24
Let them feed *in* Bashan and Gilead,
As in days of old.

15 "As[R] in the days when you came out of
the land of Egypt, Ps. 68:22; 78:12
I will show them* [R]wonders." Ex. 34:10

16 The nations [R]shall see and be ashamed
of all their might; Is. 26:11
[R]They shall put *their* hand over *their*
mouth; Job 21:5
Their ears shall be deaf.
17 They shall lick the dust like a serpent;
[R]They shall crawl from their holes like
snakes of the earth. Ps. 18:45
[R]They shall be afraid of the LORD our
God, Jer. 33:9
And shall fear because of You.
18 [R]Who *is* a God like You, Ex. 15:11
[R]Pardoning iniquity Ex. 34:6, 7, 9
And passing over the transgression of
[R]the remnant of His heritage? Mic. 4:7

He does not retain His anger forever,
Because He delights *in* mercy.
19 He will again have compassion on us,
And will subdue our iniquities.

You will cast all our* sins
Into the depths of the sea.
20 [R]You will give truth to Jacob
And mercy to Abraham, Luke 1:72, 73☆
[R]Which You have sworn to our fathers
From days of old. Ps. 105:9

7:11 Or *the boundary shall be extended* **7:12** Lit. *he,* collective of the captives • Heb. *arey mazor,* possibly *cities of Egypt* • Heb. *mazor,* possibly *Egypt* • The Euphrates **7:15** Lit. *him,* collective for the captives **7:19** Lit. *their*

THE BOOK OF

NAHUM

THE BOOK OF NAHUM

"For everyone to whom much is given, from him much will be required" (Luke 12:48). Nineveh had been given the privilege of knowing the one true God. Under Jonah's preaching this great Gentile city had repented, and God had graciously stayed His judgment. However, a hundred years later, Nahum proclaims the downfall of this same city. The Assyrians have forgotten their revival and have returned to their habits of violence, idolatry, and arrogance. As a result, Babylon will so destroy the city that no trace of it will remain—a prophecy fulfilled in painful detail.

The Hebrew word *nahum* ("comfort, consolation") is a shortened form of "Nehemiah" ("Comfort of Yahweh"). The destruction of the capital city of Assyria is a message of comfort and consolation to Judah and all who live in fear of the cruelty of the Assyrians. The title of this book in the Greek and Latin Bibles is *Naoum* and *Nahum*.

THE AUTHOR OF NAHUM

The only mention of Nahum in the Old Testament is found in 1:1 where he is called an Elkoshite. At least four locations have been proposed for Elkosh: (1) a sixteenth-century tradition identifies Elkosh with Al-Qush in Iraq, north of the site of Nineveh on the Tigris River. (2) Jerome believed that Elkesi, a city near Ramah in Galilee, was Elkosh because of the similarity of the consonants. (3) "Capernaum" means "City of Nahum" (*Kephar-Nahum*), and many believe that the name "Elkosh" was changed to "Capernaum" in Nahum's honor. (4) Most conservative scholars believe that Elkosh was a city of southern Judah (later called Elcesei) between Jerusalem and Gaza. This would make Nahum a prophet of the southern kingdom and may explain his interest in the triumph of Judah (1:15; 2:2).

THE TIME OF NAHUM

The fall of Nineveh to the Babylonians in 612 B.C. is seen by Nahum as a future event. Critics who deny predictive prophecy naturally date Nahum after 612 B.C., but this is not based upon exegetical or historical considerations. Nahum 3:8–10 refers to the fall of Thebes as a recent event, so this book must be dated after 664 B.C., the year when this took place. Thus, Nahum can safely be placed between 663 and 612 B.C. Thebes was restored a decade after its defeat, and Nahum's failure to mention this restoration has led several scholars to the conclusion that Nahum was written before 654 B.C. The fact that Nahum mentions no king in the introduction to his book (1:1) may point to the reign of the wicked King Manasseh (686–642 B.C.).

The conversion of the Ninevites in response to Jonah's message of judgment took place about 760 B.C. The revival was evidently short-lived, because the Assyrians soon returned to their ruthless practices. In 722 B.C. Sargon II of Assyria destroyed Samaria, the capital of the northern kingdom of Israel, and scattered the ten tribes. Led by Sennacherib, the Assyrians also came close to capturing Jerusalem in the reign of King Hezekiah in 701 B.C. By the time of Nahum (c. 660 B.C.), Assyria reached the peak of its prosperity and power under Ashurbanipal (669–633 B.C.). This king extended Assyria's influence farther than had any of his predecessors. Nineveh became the mightiest city on earth with walls 100 feet high and wide enough to accommodate three chariots riding abreast. Dotted around the walls were huge towers that stretched an additional 100 feet above the top of the walls. In addition, the walls were surrounded by a moat 150 feet wide and 60 feet deep. Nineveh appeared impregnable and could withstand a twenty-year siege. Thus, Nahum's prophecy of Nineveh's overthrow seemed unlikely indeed.

Assyrian power faded under Ashurbanipal's sons, Ashuretililani (633–629 B.C.) and Sinsharishkun (629–612 B.C.). Nahum predicted that Nineveh would end "with an overflowing flood" (1:8), and this is precisely what occurred. The Tigris River overflowed its banks and the flood destroyed part of Nineveh's wall. The Babylonians invaded through this breach in the wall, plundered the city, and set it on fire. Nahum also predicted that Nineveh would "be hidden" (3:11). After its destruction in 612 B.C. the site was not discovered until A.D. 1842.

THE CHRIST OF NAHUM

While there are no direct messianic prophecies in Nahum, the divine attributes in 1:2–8 are consistent with Christ's work as the Judge of the nations in His second advent.

KEYS TO NAHUM

Key Word: The Judgment of Nineveh—If ever a city deserved the title "Here to Stay," Nineveh was that city. The great city appeared invincible. But into the scene steps Nahum—a prophet of God's judgment—to declare that Nineveh will fall. Less than half a century later the prediction of God's spokesman comes true as the great city topples before the Babylonian onslaught, never again to be rebuilt.

Key Verses: Nahum 1:7, 8, 3:5–7—"The LORD *is* good, a stronghold in the day of trouble; and He knows those who trust in Him. But with an overflowing flood He will make an utter end of its place, and darkness will pursue His enemies" (1:7, 8).

"Behold, I *am* against you," says the LORD of hosts; "I will lift your skirts over your face, I will show the nations your nakedness, and the kingdoms your shame. I will cast abominable filth upon you, make you vile, and make you a spectacle. It shall come to pass *that* all who look upon you will flee from you, and say, 'Nineveh is laid waste! Who will bemoan her?' Where shall I seek comforters for you?" (3:5–7).

Key Chapter: Nahum 1—The first chapter of Nahum records the principles of divine judgment resulting in the decree of the destruction of Nineveh and the deliverance and celebration of Judah. Beginning with 1:9, the single thrust of Nahum's prophecy is the retribution of God upon the wickedness of Nineveh. Nineveh's judgment is irreversibly decreed by the righteous God who will no longer delay His wrath. Assyria's arrogance and cruelty to other nations will come to a sudden end: her power will be useless against the mighty hand of Yahweh.

Nahum 1:2–8 portrays the patience, power, holiness, and justice of the living God. He is slow to wrath, but God settles His accounts in full. This book concerns the downfall of Assyria, but it is written for the benefit of the surviving kingdom of Judah. (Israel had already been swallowed up by Assyria.) The people in Judah who trust in the Lord will be comforted to hear of God's judgment upon the proud and brutal Assyrians (1:15; 2:2).

SURVEY OF NAHUM

When God finally convinces His prophet Jonah to preach to the people of Nineveh, the whole city responds with repentance and Nineveh escapes destruction. The people humble themselves before the one true God, but their humility soon changes to arrogance as Assyria reaches its zenith as the most powerful empire in the world. About a century after the preaching of Jonah, God calls Nahum to proclaim the coming destruction of Nineveh. This time there will be no escape, because their measure of wickedness is full. Unlike Jonah, Nahum does not go to the city but declares his oracle from afar. There is no hope of repentance. Nineveh's destruction is decreed (1), described (2), and deserved (3).

The Destruction of Nineveh Is Decreed (1): Nahum begins with a very clear description of the character of Yahweh. Because of His righteousness, He is a God of vengeance (1:2). God is also characterized by patience (1:3) and power (1:3–6). He is gracious to all who respond to Him, but those who rebel against Him will be overthrown (1:7, 8). God is holy, and Nineveh stands condemned because of her sins (1:9–14). Nothing can stand in the way of judgment, and this is a message of comfort to the people of Judah (1:15). The threat of Assyrian invasion will soon be over.

The Destruction of Nineveh Is Described (2): Assyria will be conquered, but Judah will be restored (2:1, 2). Nahum's description of the siege of Nineveh (2:3–7) and the sack of Nineveh (2:8–13) is one of the most vivid portraits of battle in Scripture. The storming warriors and chariots can almost be seen as they enter the city through a breach in the wall. As the Ninevites flee in terror, the invading army plunders the treasures of the city. Nineveh is burned and cut off forever.

FOCUS	DESTRUCTION OF NINEVAH DECREED		DESTRUCTION OF NINEVAH DESCRIBED		DESTRUCTION OF NINEVAH DESERVED	
REFERENCE	1:1—	—1:9—	—2:1—	—2:3—	—3:1—	—3:12——3:19
DIVISION	GENERAL PRINCIPLES OF DIVINE JUDGMENT	DESTRUCTION OF NINEVAH AND DELIVERANCE OF JUDAH	THE CALL TO BATTLE	DESCRIPTION OF THE DESTRUCTION OF NINEVAH	REASONS FOR THE DESTRUCTION OF NINEVAH	INEVITABLE DESTRUCTION OF NINEVAH
TOPIC	VERDICT OF VENGEANCE		VISION OF VENGEANCE		VINDICATION OF VENGEANCE	
	WHAT GOD WILL DO		HOW GOD WILL DO IT		WHY GOD WILL DO IT	
LOCATION	IN JUDAH AGAINST NINEVAH, CAPITAL OF ASSYRIA					
TIME	c. 660 B.C.					

The Destruction of Nineveh Is Deserved (3): Nahum closes his brief book of judgment with God's reasons for Nineveh's coming overthrow. The city is characterized by cruelty and corruption (3:1–7). Just as Assyria crushed the Egyptian capital city of Thebes (No Amon), Assyria's capital city will also be destroyed (3:8–10). Nineveh is fortified so well that defeat seems impossible, but God proclaims that its destruction is inevitable (3:11–19). None of its resources can deter divine judgment.

OUTLINE OF NAHUM

CHAPTER 1

God's Vengeance in Judgment

THE burden* against Nineveh. The book of the vision of Nahum the Elkoshite.

2 God *is* [R]jealous, and the LORD avenges;
The LORD avenges and *is* furious.
The LORD will take vengeance on His adversaries, Ex. 20:5
And He reserves *wrath* for His enemies;

God's Power in Judgment

3 The LORD *is* [R]slow to anger and [R]great in power, Ex. 34:6, 7 • [Job 9:4]
And will not at all acquit *the wicked.*

[R]The LORD has His way Ps. 18:17
In the whirlwind and in the storm,
And the clouds *are* the dust of His feet.
4 [R]He rebukes the sea and makes it dry,
And dries up all the rivers. Matt. 8:26
[R]Bashan and Carmel wither, Is. 33:9
And the flower of Lebanon wilts.
5 The mountains quake before Him,
The hills melt,
And the earth heaves* at His presence,
Yes, the world and all who dwell in it.

6 Who can stand before His indignation?
And [R]who can endure the fierceness of His anger? [Mal. 3:2]
His fury is poured out like fire,
And the rocks are thrown down by Him.

7 [R]The LORD *is* good, [Jer. 33:11]
A stronghold in the day of trouble;
And He knows those who trust in Him.
8 But with an overflowing flood
He will make an utter end of its place,
And darkness will pursue His enemies.

The Destruction of Nineveh and Deliverance of Judah

9 [R]What do you [T]conspire against the LORD? Ps. 2:1 • Or *devise*
He will make an utter end *of it.*
Affliction will not rise up a second time.
10 For while tangled [R]*like* thorns,
[R]And while drunken *like* drunkards,
[R]They shall be devoured like stubble fully dried. 2 Sam. 23:6 • Nah. 3:11 • Mal. 4:1
11 From you comes forth *one*
Who plots evil against the LORD,
A wicked counselor.

12 Thus says the LORD:

"Though *they are* [T]safe, and likewise many, Or *at peace or complete*
Yet in this manner they will be [R]cut down [Is. 10:16–19, 33, 34]
When he passes through.
Though I have afflicted you,
I will afflict you no more;
13 For now I will break off his yoke from you,
And burst your bonds apart."

14 The LORD has given a command concerning you:
"Your name shall be perpetuated no longer.

1:1 Or *oracle, prophecy* **1:5** Tg. *burns*

Out of the house of your gods
I will cut off the carved image and the molded image.
I will dig your [R]grave, Ezek. 32:22, 23
For you are [R]vile." Nah. 3:6

15 Behold, on the mountains
The [R]feet of him who brings good tidings, Rom. 10:15
Who proclaims peace!
O Judah, keep your appointed feasts,
Perform your vows,
For the [T]wicked one shall no more pass through you; Lit. *one of Belial*
He is [R]utterly cut off. Is. 29:7, 8

CHAPTER 2

The Call to Battle

HE who scatters* has come up before your face.
Man the fort!
Watch the road!
Strengthen *your* flanks!
Fortify *your* power mightily.

2 For the LORD will restore the excellence of Jacob
Like the excellence of Israel,
For the emptiers have emptied them out
And ruined their vine branches.

The Destruction of Nineveh

3 The shields of his mighty men *are* made red,
The valiant men *are* in scarlet.
The chariots *come* with flaming torches
In the day of his preparation,
And the spears are brandished.*
4 The chariots rage in the streets,
They jostle one another in the broad roads;
They seem like torches,
They run like lightning.

5 He remembers his nobles;
They stumble in their walk;
They make haste to her walls,
And the defense is prepared.
6 The gates of the rivers are opened,
And the palace is dissolved.
7 It is decreed:*
She shall be led away captive,
She shall be brought up;
And her maidservants shall lead *her* as with the voice of doves,
Beating their breasts.

8 Though Nineveh of old *was* like a pool of water,
Now they flee away.
[T]"Halt! Halt!" *they cry;* Lit. *Stand*
But no one turns back.
9 [T]Take spoil of silver! *Plunder*
Take spoil of [R]gold! Zeph. 1:18
There is no end of treasure,
Or wealth of every desirable prize.
10 She is empty, desolate, and waste!
The heart melts, and the knees shake;
Much pain *is* in every side,
And all their faces are drained of color.*

11 Where *is* the dwelling of the [R]lions,
And the feeding place of the young lions,
Where the lion walked, the lioness *and* lion's cub, Job 4:10, 11
And no one made *them* afraid?
12 The lion tore in pieces enough for his cubs,
[T]Killed for his lionesses, Lit. *Strangled*
[R]Filled his caves with prey, Jer. 51:34
And his dens with [T]flesh. Torn flesh

13 "Behold, [R]I *am* against you," says the
LORD of hosts, "I will burn your* chariots in
smoke, and the sword shall devour your
young lions; I will cut off your prey from the
earth, and the voice of your messengers shall
be heard no more." Nah. 3:5

CHAPTER 3

Nineveh's Great Ungodliness

WOE to the [R]bloody city! Hab. 2:12
It *is* all full of lies *and* robbery.
Its [T]victim never departs. Lit. *prey*
2 The noise of a whip
And the noise of rattling wheels,
Of galloping horses,
Of [T]clattering chariots! *bounding* or *jolting*
3 Horsemen charge with bright sword and glittering spear.
There is a multitude of slain,
A great number of bodies,
Countless corpses—
They stumble over the corpses—
4 Because of the multitude of harlotries of the seductive harlot,
[R]The mistress of sorceries, Is. 47:9–12
Who sells nations through her harlotries,
And families through her sorceries.

5 "Behold, I *am* [R]against you," says the LORD of hosts; Nah. 2:13
"I will lift your skirts over your face,
I will show the nations your nakedness,
And the kingdoms your shame.
6 I will cast abominable filth upon you,
Make you [R]vile,[T] Nah. 1:14 • *despicable*
And make you [R]a spectacle. Heb. 10:33

2:1 Vg. *He who destroys* **2:3** Lit. *the cypresses are shaken;* LXX, Syr. *the horses rush about;* Vg. *the drivers are stupefied* **2:7** Heb. *Huzzab* **2:10** LXX, Tg., Vg. *gather blackness;* Joel 2:6 **2:13** Lit. *her*

7 It shall come to pass *that* all who look
upon you
[R]Will flee from you, and say, Rev. 18:10
[R]'Nineveh is laid waste! Jon. 3:3; 4:11
[R]Who will bemoan her?' Jer. 15:5
Where shall I seek comforters for you?"

Comparison of Nineveh to No Amon

8[R] Are you better than No Amon*
That was situated by the River,*
That had the waters around her,
Whose rampart *was* the sea,
Whose wall *was* the sea? Amos 6:2
9 Ethiopia and Egypt *were* her strength,
And *it was* boundless;
Put and Lubim were your* helpers.
10 Yet she *was* carried away,
She went into captivity;
[R]Her young children also were dashed to
pieces Hos. 13:16
[R]At the head of every street; Lam. 2:19
They [R]cast lots for her honorable men,
And all her great men were bound in
chains. Joel 3:3
11 You also will be [R]drunk; Nah. 1:10
You will be hidden;
You also will seek refuge from the
enemy.

Nineveh's Strongholds Are Weak

12 All your strongholds *are* [R]fig trees with
ripened figs: Rev. 6:12, 13
If they are shaken,
They fall into the mouth of the eater.
13 Surely, [R]your people in your midst *are*
women! Is. 19:16
The gates of your land are wide open for
your enemies;
Fire shall devour the [R]bars of your
gates. Jer. 51:30
14 Draw your water for the siege!
[R]Fortify your strongholds! Nah. 2:1
Go into the clay and tread the mortar!
Make strong the brick kiln!
15 There the fire will devour you,
The sword will cut you off;
It will eat you up like a [R]locust. Joel 1:4

Make yourself many—like the locust!
Make yourself many— like the *swarming*
locusts!

Nineveh's Leaders Are Weak

16 You have multiplied your merchants
more than the stars of heaven.
The locust plunders and flies away.
17[R] Your commanders *are* like *swarming*
locusts, Rev. 9:7
And your generals like great grasshoppers,
Which camp in the hedges on a cold day;
When the sun rises they flee away,
And the place where they *are* is not
known.

18[R] Your shepherds slumber, O [R]king of
Assyria; Ps. 76:5, 6 • Jer. 50:18
Your nobles rest *in the dust*.
Your people are [R]scattered on the
mountains, 1 Kin. 22:17
And no one gathers them.
19 Your injury *has* no healing,
[R]Your wound is severe. Mic. 1:9
[R]All who hear news of you Lam. 2:15
Will clap *their* hands over you,
For upon whom has not your wickedness
passed continually?

3:8 Ancient Thebes; Tg., Vg. *populous Alexandria* • Lit. *rivers*, the Nile and the surrounding canals
3:9 LXX *her*

THE BOOK OF

HABAKKUK

THE BOOK OF HABAKKUK

Habakkuk ministers during the "death throes" of the nation of Judah. Although repeatedly called to repentance, the nation stubbornly refuses to change her sinful ways. Habakkuk, knowing the hardheartedness of his countrymen, asks God how long this intolerable condition can continue. God replies that the Babylonians will be His chastening rod upon the nation—an announcement that sends the prophet to his knees. He acknowledges that the just in any generation shall live by faith (2:4), not by sight. Habakkuk concludes by praising God's wisdom even though he does not fully understand God's ways.

Habaqquq is an unusual Hebrew name derived from the verb *habaq,* "embrace." Thus his name probably means "One Who Embraces" or "Clings." At the end of his book this name becomes appropriate because Habakkuk chooses to cling firmly to God regardless of what happens to his nation (3:16–19). The Greek title in the Septuagint is *Ambakouk,* and the Latin title in Jerome's Vulgate is *Habacuc.*

THE AUTHOR OF HABAKKUK

In the introduction to the book (1:1) and in the closing psalm (3:1), the author identifies himself as Habakkuk the prophet. This special designation seems to indicate that Habakkuk was a professional prophet. The closing statement at the end of the psalm "To the Chief Musician. With my stringed instruments" suggests that Habakkuk may have been a priest connected with the temple worship in Jerusalem. He mentions nothing of his genealogy or location, but speculative attempts have been made to identify him with certain unnamed Old Testament characters. In the apocryphal book of Bel and the Dragon, Daniel is rescued a second time by the prophet Habakkuk.

THE TIME OF HABAKKUK

The only explicit time reference in Habakkuk is to the Babylonian invasion as an imminent event (1:6; 2:1; 3:16). Some scholars suggest Habakkuk was written during the reign of Manasseh (686–642 B.C.) or Amon (642–640 B.C.) because of the list of Judah's sins in 1:2–4. However, the descriptions of the Chaldeans indicate that Babylon had become a world power; and this was not true in the time of Manasseh when Babylon was under the thumb of Assyria. It is also unlikely that this prophecy took place in the time of King Josiah (640–609 B.C.), because the moral and spiritual reforms of Josiah do not fit the situation in 1:2–4. The most likely date for the book is in the early part of Jehoiakim's reign (609–597 B.C.). Jehoiakim was a godless king who led the nation down the path of destruction (cf. 2 Kin. 23:34—24:5; Jer. 22:17).

The Babylonians began to rise in power during the reign of Nabopolassar (626–605 B.C.), and in 612 B.C. they destroyed the Assyrian capital of Nineveh. By the time of Jehoiakim, Babylon was the uncontested world power. Nabopolassar's successor, Nebuchadnezzar, came to power in 605 B.C. and carried out successful military expeditions in the west, advancing into Palestine and Egypt. Nebuchadnezzar's first invasion of Judah occurred in his first year, when he deported ten thousand of Jerusalem's leaders to Babylon. The nobles who oppressed and extorted from the poor were the first to be carried away. Since Habakkuk prophesied prior to the Babylonian invasion, the probable date for this book is about 607 B.C.

THE CHRIST OF HABAKKUK

The word "salvation" appears three times in 3:13, 18 and is the root word from which the name "Jesus" *is* derived (cf. Matt. 1:21). When He comes again, "the earth will be filled with the knowledge of the glory of the LORD, as the waters cover the sea" (2:14).

KEYS TO HABAKKUK

Key Word: "The Just Shall Live by His Faith"—The circumstances of life sometimes appear to contradict God's revelation concerning His power and purposes. Habakkuk struggles in his faith when he sees men flagrantly violate God's law and distort justice on every level, without fear of divine intervention. He wants to know why God allows this growing iniquity to go unpunished. When God reveals His intention to use Babylon as His rod of judgment, Habakkuk is even more troubled, because that nation is more corrupt than Judah. God's answer satisfies Habakkuk that he can trust Him even in the worst of circumstances because of His matchless wisdom, goodness, and power. God's plan is perfect, and nothing is big enough to stand in the way of its ultimate fulfillment. In spite of appearances to the contrary, God is still on the throne as the Lord of history and the Ruler of the nations. God may be slow to wrath, but all iniquity will be punished eventually. He is the worthiest object of faith, and the righteous man will trust in Him at all times.

Key Verses: Habakkuk 2:4; 3:17–19—"Behold the proud, his soul is not upright in him; but the just shall live by his faith" (2:4).

"Though the fig tree may not blossom, nor fruit be on the vines; though the labor of the olive may fail, and the fields yield no food; though the flock may be cut off from the fold, and there be no herd in the stalls—yet I will rejoice in the LORD, I will joy in the God of my salvation. The LORD God is my strength; He will make my feet like deer's *feet,* and He will make me walk on my high hills. To the Chief Musician. With my stringed instruments" (3:17–19).

Key Chapter: Habakkuk 3—The Book of Habakkuk builds to a triumphant climax reached in the last three verses (3:17–19). The beginning of the book and the ending stand in stark contrast: mystery to certainty, questioning to affirming, and complaint to confidence. Chapter 3 is one of the most majestic of all Scripture and records the glory of God in past history and in future history (prophecy).

SURVEY OF HABAKKUK

Habakkuk is a freethinking prophet who is not afraid to wrestle with issues that test his faith. He openly and honestly directs his problems to God and waits to see how He will respond to his probing questions. After two rounds of dialogue with the Lord, Habakkuk's increased understanding of the Person, power, and plan of God cause him to conclude with a psalm of unqualified praise. The more he knows about the Planner, the more he can trust His plans. No matter what God brings to pass, "the just shall live by his faith" (2:4). The two divisions of this book are: the problems of Habakkuk (1 and 2) and the praise of Habakkuk (3).

The Problems of Habakkuk (1 and 2): Habakkuk's first dialogue with God takes place in 1:1–11. In 1:1–4 the prophet asks God how long He will allow the wickedness of Judah to go unpunished. The people of Judah sin with impunity, and justice is perverted. God's startling answer is given in 1:5–11: He is raising up the fierce Babylonians as His rod of judgment upon sinful Judah. The Chaldeans will come against Judah swiftly, violently, and completely. The coming storm from the east will be God's answer to Judah's crimes.

This answer leads to Habakkuk's second dialogue with God (1:12—2:20). The prophet is more perplexed than ever and asks how the righteous God can punish Judah with a nation that is even more wicked (1:12—2:1). Will the God whose eyes are too pure to approve evil reward the Babylonians for their cruelty and idolatry? Habakkuk stands upon a watchtower to wait for God's reply. The Lord answers with a series of five woes—of greed and aggression (2:5–8), exploitation and extortion (2:9–11), violence (2:12–14), immorality (2:15–17), and idolatry (2:18–20). God is aware of the sins of the Babylonians, and they will not escape His terrible judgment. But Judah is guilty of the same offenses and stands under the same condemnation. Yahweh concludes His answer with a statement of His sovereign majesty: "But the LORD is in His holy temple. Let all the earth keep silence before Him" (2:20).

The Praise of Habakkuk (3): Habakkuk begins by questioning God, but he concludes his book with a psalm of praise for the Person (3:1–3), power (3:4–12), and plan (3:13–19) of God. He now acknowledges God's wisdom in the coming invasion of Judah; and although it terrifies him, he will trust the Lord. God's creative and redemptive work in the past gives the prophet confidence in the divine purposes, and hope at a time when he would otherwise despair. "Yet I will rejoice in the LORD, I will joy in the God of my salvation" (3:18).

FOCUS	PROBLEMS OF HABAKKUK				PRAISE OF HABAKKUK
REFERENCE	1:1	1:5	1:12	2:2	3:1—3:19
DIVISION	FIRST PROBLEM OF HABAKKUK	FIRST REPLY OF GOD	SECOND PROBLEM OF HABAKKUK	SECOND REPLY OF GOD	PRAYER OF PRAISE OF HABAKKUK
TOPIC	FAITH TROUBLED				FAITH TRIUMPHANT
	WHAT GOD IS DOING				WHO GOD IS
LOCATION	THE NATION OF JUDAH				
TIME	c. 607 B.C.				

OUTLINE OF HABAKKUK

CHAPTER 1

The First Problem of Habakkuk

THE burden* which the prophet Habakkuk saw.

2 O LORD, how long shall I cry,
[R]And You will not hear? Lam. 3:8
Even cry out to You, "Violence!"
And You will [R]not save. [Job 21:5–16]

3 Why do You show me iniquity,
And cause *me* to see [T]trouble? Or *toil*
For plundering and violence *are* before me;
There is strife, and contention arises.
4 Therefore the law is powerless,
And justice never goes forth.
For the wicked surround the righteous;
Therefore perverse judgment proceeds.

God's First Reply

5 "Look[R] among the nations and watch—
Be utterly astounded! Is. 29:14
For *I will* work a work in your days
Which you would not believe, though it were told *you.*
6 For indeed I am [R]raising up the Chaldeans, 2 Kin. 24:2
A bitter and hasty [R]nation
Which marches through the breadth of the earth, Ezek. 7:24; 21:31
To possess dwelling places *that are* not theirs.
7 They are terrible and dreadful;
Their judgment and their dignity proceed from themselves.
8 Their horses also are [R]swifter than leopards, Jer. 4:13
And more fierce than evening wolves.
Their [T]chargers [T]charge ahead;
Their cavalry comes from afar;
They fly as the [R]eagle *that* hastens to eat. Lit. *horsemen* • Lit. *spring about* • Hos. 8:1

9 "They all come for violence;
Their faces are set *like* the east wind.
They gather captives like sand.
10 They scoff at kings,
And princes are scorned by them.
They deride every stronghold,
For they heap up earthen *mounds* and seize it.
11 Then *his* mind* changes, and he transgresses;
He commits offense,
[R]*Ascribing* this power to his god." Dan. 5:4

The Second Problem of Habakkuk

12 Are You not [R]from everlasting,
O LORD my God, my Holy One?
We shall not die. Ps. 90:2; 93:2

1:1 Or *oracle, prophecy* **1:11** Lit. *spirit* or *wind*

1:2 Sources of Doubt—One of the most potent sources of doubt is introduced in the early chapters of Genesis. It is Satan himself who causes Eve to doubt God by questioning His Word: "Has God indeed said, 'You shall not eat of every tree of the garden?'" (Page 6—Gen. 3:1). Satan even tries to get the long-suffering Job to curse God (Page 572—Job 1:11). Satan is said to be seeking to devour Christians (Page 1283—1 Pet. 5:8). This statement must not be taken literally, but means that Satan wants to devour the Christian's commitment to God and testimony before others. One way he does this is by introducing doubt into the mind.

The world system is another source of doubt. Since it has its own set of values and objectives that are opposed to God, it also has its own worldly wisdom (Page 1168—1 Cor. 2:6). This wisdom stands in direct opposition to the wisdom of God taught by the Holy Spirit (Page 1168—1 Cor. 2:13). It is clearly revealed, for example, in the opposition of the evolutionary theory to the truth of the creation of man (Page 1240—1 Tim. 6:20).

Probably the greatest source of doubt Christians face is simply their own spiritual immaturity. James traces doubting in prayer to double-mindedness and instability (Page 1272—James 1:8). Paul explains that when Christians doubt sound doctrine, it is because they are children in the faith and thus are easily deceived (Page 1207—Eph. 4:14). Conquering this kind of doubt demands a growing, obedient relationship with God.

Now turn to Page 357—1 Kin. 18:21: Cure for Doubt.

O LORD, [R]You have appointed them for
judgment; Is. 10:5–7
O Rock, You have marked them for
[R]correction. Jer. 25:9
13 *You are* of purer eyes than to behold evil,
And cannot look on wickedness.
Why do You look on those who deal
treacherously,
And hold Your tongue when the wicked
devours
A *person* more righteous than he?
14 *Why* do You make men like fish of the sea,
Like creeping things *that have* no ruler
over them?

15 They take up all of them with a hook,
They catch them in their net,
And gather them in their dragnet.
Therefore they rejoice and are glad.
16 Therefore [R]they sacrifice to their net,
And burn incense to their dragnet;
Because by them their share *is*
[T]sumptuous Deut. 8:17 • Lit. *fat*
And their food plentiful.
17 Shall they therefore empty their net,
And continue to slay nations without
pity?

CHAPTER 2

I WILL [R]stand my watch Is. 21:8, 11
And set myself on the rampart,
And watch to see what He will say to me,
And what I will answer when I am
corrected.

God's Second Reply

2 Then the LORD answered me and said:
[R]"Write the vision Is. 8:1
And make *it* plain on tablets,
That he may run who reads it.
3 For [R]the vision *is* yet for an appointed
time; Dan. 8:17, 19; 10:14
But at the end it will speak, and it will
[R]not lie. Ezek. 12:24, 25
Though it tarries, wait for it;
Because it will [R]surely come, [2 Pet. 3:9]
It will not tarry.

4 "Behold the proud,
His soul is not upright in him;
But the just shall live by his faith.

5 "Indeed, because he transgresses by wine,
He is a proud man,
And he does not stay at home.
Because he [R]enlarges his desire as
hell,* Is. 5:11–15
And he *is* like death, and cannot be
satisfied,
He gathers to himself all nations
And heaps up for himself all peoples.

6 "Will not all these [R]take up a proverb
against him, Mic. 2:4
And a taunting riddle against him, and
say,
'Woe to him who increases
What is not his—how long?
And to him who loads himself with
many pledges'?*
7 Will not your creditors* rise up
suddenly?
Will they not awaken who oppress you?
And you will become their booty.
8 [R]Because you have plundered many
nations, Is. 33:1
All the remnant of the people shall
plunder you,
Because of men's [T]blood Or *bloodshed*
And the violence of the land *and* the city,
And of all who dwell in it.

9 "Woe to him who covets evil gain for his
house,
That he may [R]set his nest on high,
That he may be delivered from the
power of disaster! Obad. 4
10 You give shameful counsel to your house,
Cutting off many peoples,
And sin *against* your soul.
11 For the stone will cry out from the wall,
And the beam from the timbers will
answer it.

12 "Woe to him who builds a town with
bloodshed,
Who establishes a city by iniquity!
13 Behold, *is it* not of the LORD of hosts
That the peoples labor to feed the fire,*
And nations weary themselves in vain?
14 For the earth will be filled
With the knowledge of the glory of the
LORD,
As the waters cover the sea.

15 "Woe to him who gives drink to his
neighbor,
Pressing* *him to* your [R]bottle, Hos. 7:5
Even to make *him* drunk,
That you may look on his nakedness!
16 You are filled with shame instead of glory.
You also—drink!
And be exposed as uncircumcised!*
The cup of the LORD's right hand *will be*
turned against you,
And utter shame will be on your glory.
17 For the violence *done to* Lebanon will
cover you,
And the plunder of beasts *which* made
them afraid,

2:5 Or *Sheol* **2:6** Syr., Vg. *thick clay* **2:7** Lit. *those who bite you* **2:13** Lit. *for what satisfies fire*, for what is of no lasting value **2:15** Lit. *Attaching* or *Joining* **2:16** DSS, LXX *And reel!*; Syr., Vg. *And fall fast asleep!*

Because of men's blood
And the violence of the land *and* the city,
And of all who dwell in it.

18 "What profit is the image, that its maker should carve it,
The molded image, a teacher of lies,
That the maker of its mold should trust in it,
To make mute idols?
19 Woe to him who says to wood, 'Awake!'
To silent stone, 'Arise! It shall teach!'
Behold, it is overlaid with gold and silver,
Yet in it there is no breath at all.

20 "But[R] the LORD is in His holy temple.
Let all the earth keep silence before Him." Zeph. 1:7

CHAPTER 3

Habakkuk Prays for God's Mercy

A PRAYER of Habakkuk the prophet, on Shigionoth.*

2 O LORD, I have heard Your speech *and* was afraid;
O LORD, revive Your work in the midst of the years!
In the midst of the years make *it* known;
In wrath remember mercy.

The Glory of the Person of God

3 God came from Teman,
The Holy One from Mount Paran. Selah

His glory covered the heavens,
And the earth was full of His praise.
4 *His* brightness was like the light;
He had rays *flashing* from His hand,
And there His power *was* hidden.

The Power of the Saving Acts of God

5 Before Him went pestilence,
And fever followed at His feet.

6 He stood and measured the earth;
He looked and startled the nations.
[R]And the everlasting mountains were scattered, Nah. 1:5
The perpetual hills bowed.
His ways *are* everlasting.
7 I saw the tents of Cushan in affliction;
The curtains of the land of Midian trembled.

8 O LORD, were *You* displeased with the rivers,
Was Your anger against the rivers,
Was Your wrath against the sea,
That You rode on Your horses,
Your chariots of salvation?
9 Your bow was made quite ready;
Oaths were sworn over *Your* arrows.* Selah

You divided the earth with rivers.
10 The mountains saw You *and* trembled;
The overflowing of the water passed by.
The deep uttered its voice,
And [R]lifted its hands on high. Ex. 14:22
11 The [R]sun and moon stood still in their habitation; Josh. 10:12–14
At the light of Your arrows they went,
At the shining of Your glittering spear.

12 You marched through the land in indignation;
You trampled the nations in anger.
13 You went forth for the salvation of Your people,
For salvation with Your Anointed.
You struck the head from the house of the wicked,
By laying bare from foundation to neck. Selah

14 You thrust through with his own arrows
The head of his villages.
They came out like a whirlwind to scatter me;
Their rejoicing was like feasting on the poor in secret.
15 [R]You walked through the sea with Your horses, Ps. 77:19
Through the heap of great waters.

Habakkuk Trusts in God's Salvation

16 When I heard, [R]my body trembled;
My lips quivered at *the* voice;
Rottenness entered my bones;
And I trembled in myself, Ps. 119:120
That I might rest in the day of trouble.
When he comes up to the people,
He will invade them with his troops.

17 Though the fig tree may not blossom,
Nor fruit be on the vines;
Though the labor of the olive may fail,
And the fields yield no food;
Though the flock may be cut off from the fold,
And there be no herd in the stalls—
18 Yet I will rejoice in the LORD,
I will joy in the God of my salvation.

19 The LORD God* is my strength;
He will make my feet like [R]deer's *feet*,
And He will make me [R]walk on my high hills. 2 Sam. 22:34 • Deut. 32:13; 33:29

To the Chief Musician. With my stringed instruments.

3:1 Exact meaning unknown **3:9** Lit. *tribes* or *rods*, cf. v. 14 **3:19** Heb. *YHWH Adonai*

THE BOOK OF
ZEPHANIAH

THE BOOK OF ZEPHANIAH

During Judah's hectic political and religious history, reform comes from time to time. Zephaniah's forceful prophecy may be a factor in the reform that occurs during Josiah's reign—a "revival" that produces outward change, but does not fully remove the inward heart of corruption that characterizes the nation. Zephaniah hammers home his message repeatedly that the day of the Lord, judgment day, is coming when the malignancy of sin will be dealt with. Israel and her Gentile neighbors will soon experience the crushing hand of God's wrath. But after the chastening process is complete, blessing will come in the Person of the Messiah, who will be the cause for praise and singing.

Tsephan-yah means "Yahweh Hides" or "Yahweh Has Hidden." Zephaniah was evidently born during the latter part of the reign of King Manasseh. His name may mean that he was "hidden" from Manasseh's atrocities. The Greek and Latin title is *Sophonias.*

THE AUTHOR OF ZEPHANIAH

The first verse is very unusual in that Zephaniah traces his lineage back four generations to Hezekiah. This is probably Hezekiah the king of Judah, since this would best explain the genealogy. If Zephaniah was the great-great-grandson of the godly King Hezekiah, he was the only prophet of royal descent. This may have given the prophet freer access to the court of King Josiah in whose reign he ministered. Because Zephaniah used the phrase "this place" (1:4) to refer to Jerusalem and was quite familiar with its features (cf. 1:9, 10; 3:1–7), he was probably an inhabitant of Judah's royal city.

THE TIME OF ZEPHANIAH

Zephaniah solves the dating problem by fixing his prophecy "in the days of Josiah the son of Amon, king of Judah" (1:1). Josiah reigned from 640 to 609 B.C., and 2:13 indicates that the destruction of Nineveh (612 B.C.) was still a future event. Thus, Zephaniah's prophecy can be dated between 640 and 612 B.C.

However, the sins cataloged in 1:3–13 and 3:1–7 indicate a date prior to Josiah's reforms when the sins from the reigns of Manasseh and Amon still predominated. It is therefore likely that Zephaniah's ministry played a significant role in preparing Judah for the revivals that took place in the reign of the nation's last righteous king. Josiah became king of Judah at the age of eight, and by the age of sixteen his heart had already begun to turn toward God. His first reform took place in the twelfth year of his reign (628 B.C.; 2 Chr. 34:3–7) when he tore down all the altars of Baal, destroyed the foreign incense altars, burned the bones of the false prophets on their altars, and broke the Asherim (carved images) and molten images in pieces. Six years later (622 B.C.), Josiah's second reform was kindled when Hilkiah the priest found the Book of the Law in the temple (2 Chr. 34:8—35:19). Thus, Zephaniah's prophecy can be dated more precisely as occurring between 630 and 625 B.C.

The evil reigns of Manasseh and Amon (a total of fifty-five years) had such a profound effect upon Judah that it never recovered. Josiah's reforms were too little and too late, and the people reverted to their crass idolatry and teaching soon after Josiah was gone. As a contemporary of Jeremiah and Habakkuk, Zephaniah was one of the eleventh-hour prophets to Judah.

THE CHRIST OF ZEPHANIAH

Jesus alluded to Zephaniah on two occasions (cf. Zeph. 1:3; Matt. 13:41 and cf. Zeph. 1:15; Matt. 24:29). Both of these passages about the day of the Lord are associated with Christ's second advent. Although the Messiah is not specifically mentioned in Zephaniah, it is clear that He is the One who will fulfill the great promises of 3:9–20. He will gather His people and reign in victory: "The LORD has taken away your judgments, He has cast out your enemy. The King of Israel, the LORD, *is* in your midst; you shall see disaster no more" (3:15).

KEYS TO ZEPHANIAH

Key Word: The Day of the Lord—Zephaniah discusses the day of the Lord and describes the coming day of judgment upon Judah and the nations. God is holy and must vindicate His righteousness by calling all the nations of the world into account before Him. The sovereign God will judge not only His own people but also the whole world: no one escapes from His authority and dominion. The day of the Lord will have universal impact. To some degree, that day has already come for Judah and all the nations mentioned in 2:4–15, but there is also a future aspect, when all the earth will be judged. Zephaniah 3:9–20 speaks of another side of the day of the Lord: it will be a day of blessing after the judgment is complete. A righteous remnant will survive and all who call upon Him, Jew or Gentile, will be blessed. God will regather and restore His people, and there will be worldwide rejoicing.

Zephaniah is also written as a warning to Judah and as a call to repentance (2:1–3). God wants to spare the people, but they ultimately reject Him. His judgment will be great; but God promises His people a future day of hope and joy. Wrath and mercy, severity and kindness, cannot be separated in the character of God.

Key Verses: Zephaniah 1:14, 15; 2:3—"The great day of the LORD *is* near; *it is* near and hastens quickly. The noise of the day of the LORD is bitter; there the mighty men shall cry out. That day *is* a day of wrath, a day of trouble and distress, a day of devastation and desolation, a day of darkness and gloominess, a day of clouds and thick darkness" (1:14, 15).

"Seek the LORD, all you meek of the earth, who have upheld His justice. Seek righteousness, seek humility. It may be that you will be hidden in the day of the LORD's anger" (2:3).

Key Chapter: Zephaniah 3—The last chapter of Zephaniah records the two distinct parts of the day of the Lord: judgment and restoration. Following the conversion of the nation, Israel finally is fully restored. Under the righteous rule of God, Israel fully inherits the blessings contained in the biblical covenants.

SURVEY OF ZEPHANIAH

On the whole, Zephaniah is a fierce and grim book of warning about the coming day of the Lord. Desolation, darkness, and ruin will strike Judah and the nations because of the wrath of God upon sin. Zephaniah looks beyond judgment, however, to a time of joy when God will cleanse the nations and restore the fortunes of His people Israel. The book begins with God's declaration, "I will utterly consume everything from the face of the land" (1:2); but it ends with this promise, "At that time I will bring you back" and "return your captives before your eyes" (3:20). Zephaniah moves three times from the general to the specific: (1) from universal judgment (1:1–3) to judgment upon Judah (1:4—2:3); (2) from judgment upon surrounding nations (2:4–15) to judgment upon Jerusalem (3:1–7); (3) from judgment and cleansing of all nations (3:8–10) to restoration of Israel (3:11–20). The two broad divisions of the book are: the judgment in the day of the Lord (1:1—3:8) and the salvation in the day of the Lord (3:9–20).

The Judgment in the Day of the Lord (1:1—3:8): The prophetic oracle begins with an awesome statement of God's coming judgment upon the entire earth because of the sins of men (1:2, 3). Zephaniah then concentrates on the judgment of Judah (1:4–18), listing some of the offenses that will cause it to come. Judah is polluted with idolatrous priests who promote the worship of Baal and nature, and her officials and princes are completely corrupt. Therefore, the day of the Lord is imminent; and it will be characterized by terror, desolation, and distress. However, by His grace, Yahweh appeals to His people to repent and humble themselves to avert the coming disaster before it is too late (2:1–3).

Zephaniah pronounces God's coming judgment upon the nations that surround Judah (2:4–15). He looks in all four directions: Philistia (west), Moab and Ammon (east), Ethiopia (south), and Assyria (north). Then he focuses on Jerusalem, the center of God's dealings (3:1–7). Jerusalem is characterized by spiritual rebellion and moral treachery. "She has not obeyed *His* voice, she has not received correction; she has not trusted in the LORD, she has not drawn near to her God" (3:2).

The Salvation in the Day of the Lord (3:9–20): After a broad statement of the judgment of all nations (3:8), Zephaniah changes the tone of the remainder of his book to blessing; for

FOCUS	JUDGMENT IN THE DAY OF THE LORD					SALVATION IN THE DAY OF THE LORD	
REFERENCE	1:1—	1:4—	2:4—	3:1—	3:8—	3:9—	3:14—3:20
DIVISION	JUDGMENT ON THE WHOLE EARTH	JUDGMENT ON THE NATION OF JUDAH	JUDGMENT ON THE NATIONS SURROUNDING JUDAH	JUDGMENT ON THE CITY OF JERUSALEM	JUDGMENT ON THE WHOLE EARTH	PROMISE OF CONVERSION	PROMISE OF RESTORATION
TOPIC	DAY OF WRATH					DAY OF JOY	
	JUDGMENT ON JUDAH					RESTORATION FOR JUDAH	
LOCATION	JUDAH AND THE NATIONS						
TIME	c. 630 B.C.						

this, too, is an aspect of the day of the Lord. The nation will be cleansed and will call on the name of the Lord (3:9, 10). The remnant of Israel will be regathered, redeemed, and restored (3:11–20). They will rejoice in their Redeemer, and He will be in their midst. Zephaniah opens with idolatry, wrath, and judgment, but closes with true worship, rejoicing, and blessing.

OUTLINE OF ZEPHANIAH

I. The Judgment in the Day of the Lord ....1:1—3:8

A. The Judgment on the Whole Earth 1:1–3
B. The Judgment on the Nation of Judah ....1:4—2:3
1. Causes of the Judgment 1:4–13
2. Description of the Judgment 1:14–18
3. Call to Repentance 2:1–3
C. The Judgment on the Nations Surrounding Judah 2:4–15
1. Judgment Against Philistia (West) 2:4–7
2. Judgment Against Moab and Ammon (East) 2:8–11
3. Judgment Against Ethiopia (South) 2:12
4. Judgment Against Assyria (North) 2:13–15
D. The Judgment on Jerusalem 3:1–7
1. Jerusalem's Injustice 3:1–4
2. The Lord's Justice 3:5–7
E. The Judgment on the Whole Earth 3:8

II. The Salvation in the Day of the Lord 3:9–20

A. The Promise of Conversion 3:9–13
B. The Promise of Restoration 3:14–20

CHAPTER 1

The Judgment on the Whole Earth

THE word of the LORD which came to
Zephaniah the son of Cushi, the son of
Gedaliah, the son of Amariah, the son of
Hezekiah, in the days of [R]Josiah the son of
Amon, king of Judah. 2 Kin. 22:1, 2

2 "I will utterly consume everything
From the face of the land,"
Says the LORD;
3 "I[R] will consume man and beast; Hos. 4:3
I will consume the birds of the heavens,
The fish of the sea,
And the stumbling blocks* along with the wicked.
I will cut off man from the face of the [T]land," *ground*
Says the LORD.

Causes of the Judgment

4 "I will stretch out My hand against Judah,
And against all the inhabitants of Jerusalem.
[T]I will cut off every trace of Baal from this place, Fulfilled in 2 Kin. 23:4, 5
The names of the [R]idolatrous priests* with the *pagan* priests— Hos. 10:5
5 Those [R]who worship the host of heaven on the housetops; 2 Kin. 23:12
Those who worship and swear *oaths* by the LORD,
But who *also* swear by Milcom;*
6 [R]Those who have turned back from *following* the LORD, Is. 1:4
And [R]have not sought the LORD, nor inquired of Him." Hos. 7:7

7 [R]Be silent in the presence of the Lord GOD; Zech. 2:13
For the day of the LORD *is* at hand
For [R]the LORD has prepared a sacrifice;
He has invited* His guests. Jer. 46:10

8 "And it shall be,
In the day of the LORD's sacrifice,
That I will punish [R]the princes and the king's children, Jer. 39:6
And all such as are clothed with foreign apparel.
9 In the same day I will punish
All those who leap over the threshold,*
Who fill their masters' houses with violence and deceit.

10 "And there shall be on that day," says the LORD,
"The sound of a mournful cry from [R]the Fish Gate, 2 Chr. 33:14
A wailing from the Second Quarter,
And a loud crashing from the hills.
11 [R]Wail, you inhabitants of Maktesh!*
For all the merchant people are cut down; James 5:1
All those who handle money are cut off.

12 "And it shall come to pass at that time
That I will search Jerusalem with lamps,
And punish the men
Who are settled in complacency,*

1:3 Idols **1:4** Heb. *chemarim* **1:5** Or *Malcam*, an Ammonite god, 1 Kin. 11:5; Jer. 49:1; *Molech*, Lev. 18:21 **1:7** Lit. *set apart, consecrated* **1:9** Cf. 1 Sam. 5:5 **1:11** A market district of Jerusalem, lit. *Mortar* **1:12** Lit. *on their lees;* settled like the dregs of wine

[R]Who say in their heart, Ps. 94:7
'The LORD will not do good,
Nor will He do evil.'
13 Therefore their goods shall become
booty,
And their houses a desolation;
They shall build houses, but not inhabit
them;
They shall plant vineyards, but [R]not
drink their wine." Deut. 28:39

Description of the Judgment

14[R]The great day of the LORD *is* near;
It is near and hastens quickly.
The noise of the day of the LORD is
bitter; Joel 2:1, 11
There the mighty men shall cry out.
15[R]That day *is* a day of wrath, Is. 22:5
A day of trouble and distress,
A day of devastation and desolation,
A day of darkness and gloominess,
A day of clouds and thick darkness,
16 A day of [R]trumpet and alarm Jer. 4:19
Against the fortified cities
And against the high towers.

17"I will bring distress upon men,
And they shall [R]walk like blind men,
Because they have sinned against the
LORD; Deut. 28:29
Their blood shall be poured out like dust,
And their flesh like refuse."

18 Neither their silver nor their gold
Shall be able to deliver them
In the day of the LORD's wrath;
But the whole land shall be devoured
By the fire of His jealousy,
For He will make speedy riddance
Of all those who dwell in the land.

CHAPTER 2

Call to Repentance

GATHER[R] yourselves together, yes, gather
together, Joel 1:14; 2:16
O undesirable* nation,
2 Before the decree is issued,
Or the day passes like chaff,
Before the LORD's fierce anger comes
upon you,
Before the day of the LORD's anger
comes upon you!
3[R] Seek the LORD, [R]all you meek of the
earth, Amos 5:6 • Ps. 76:9
Who have upheld His justice.
Seek righteousness, seek humility.
It may be that you will be hidden
In the day of the LORD's anger.

Judgment Against Philistia (West)

4 For [R]Gaza shall be forsaken, Zech. 9:5
And Ashkelon desolate;
They shall drive out Ashdod [R]at
noonday, Jer. 6:4
And Ekron shall be uprooted.
5 Woe to the inhabitants of the seacoast,
The nation of the Cherethites!
The word of the LORD *is* against you,
O [R]Canaan, land of the Philistines:
"I will destroy you; Josh. 13:3
So there shall be no inhabitant."

6 The seacoast shall be pastures,
With shelters* for shepherds [R]and folds
for flocks. Is. 17:2
7 The coast shall be for [R]the remnant of
the house of Judah; [Mic. 5:7, 8]
They shall feed *their* flocks there;
In the houses of Ashkelon they shall lie
down at evening.
For the LORD their God will [R]intervene[T]
for them, Luke 1:68 • Lit. *visit them*
And [R]return their captives. Jer. 29:14

Judgment Against Moab and Ammon (East)

8"I[R] have heard the reproach of Moab,
And [R]the insults of the people of
Ammon, Jer. 48:27 • Ezek. 25:3
With which they have reproached My
people,
And [R]made arrogant threats against
their borders. Jer. 49:1
9 Therefore, as I live,"
Says the LORD of hosts, the God of Israel,
"Surely [R]Moab shall be like Sodom,
And [R]the people of Ammon like
Gomorrah— Is. 15:1–9 • Amos 1:13
[R]Overrun with weeds and saltpits,
And a perpetual desolation. Deut. 29:23
The residue of My people shall plunder
them,
And the remnant of My people shall
possess them."

10 This they shall have [R]for their pride,
Because they have reproached and made
arrogant threats Is. 16:6
Against the people of the LORD of hosts.
11 The LORD *will be* awesome to them,
For He will reduce to nothing all the
gods of the earth;
[R]*People* shall worship Him, Mal. 1:11
Each one from his place,
Indeed all the shores of the nations.

Judgment Against Ethiopia (South)

12"You[R] Ethiopians also, Is. 18:1–7
You shall be slain by My sword."

Judgment Against Assyria (North)

13 And He will stretch out His hand against
the north,

2:1 Or *shameless* **2:6** Underground huts or cisterns, lit. *excavations*

[R]Destroy Assyria, Is.10:5–27; 14:24–27
And make Nineveh a desolation,
As dry as the wilderness.
14 The herds shall lie down in her midst,
[R]Every beast of the nation. Is. 13:21
Both the pelican and the bittern
Shall lodge on the capitals *of* her
pillars;
Their voice shall sing in the windows;
Desolation *shall be* at the threshold;
For He will lay bare the cedar work.
15 This is the rejoicing city
[R]That dwelt securely, Is. 47:8
[R]That said in her heart, Rev. 18:7
"I *am it,* and *there is* none besides me."
How has she become a desolation,
A place for beasts to lie down!
Everyone who passes by her
Shall hiss and shake his fist.

CHAPTER 3

Jerusalem's Injustice

WOE to her who is rebellious and
polluted,
To the oppressing city!
2 She has not obeyed *His* voice,
She has not received correction;
She has not trusted in the LORD,
She has not drawn near to her God.

3[R]Her princes in her midst *are* roaring
lions; Ezek. 22:27
Her judges *are* evening wolves
That leave not a bone till morning.
4 Her [R]prophets are insolent, treacherous
people; Hos. 9:7
Her priests have [T]polluted the
sanctuary, Or *profaned*
They have done violence to the law.

The Lord's Justice

5 The LORD *is* righteous in her midst,
He will do no unrighteousness.
[T]Every morning He brings His justice to
light; Lit. *Morning by morning*
He never fails,
But the unjust knows no shame.

6"I have cut off nations,
Their fortresses are devastated;
I have made their streets desolate,
With none passing by.
Their cities are destroyed;
There is no one, no inhabitant.
7[R]I said, 'Surely you will fear Me, Jer. 8:6
You will receive instruction'—
So that her dwelling would not be cut
off,
Despite everything for which I punished
her.
But [T]they rose early and [R]corrupted all
their deeds. They were eager • Gen. 6:12

The Judgment on the Whole Earth

8"Therefore [R]wait for Me," says the LORD,
"Until the day I rise up for plunder;*
My determination *is* to [R]gather the
nations Hab. 2:3 • Joel 3:2
To My assembly of kingdoms,
To pour on them My indignation,
All My fierce anger;
All the earth shall be devoured
With the fire of My jealousy.

The Promise of Conversion

9"For then I will restore to the peoples [R]a
pure [T]language, Is. 19:18; 57:19 • Lit. *lip*
That they all may call on the name of the
LORD,
To serve Him with one accord.
10[R]From beyond the rivers of Ethiopia
My worshipers, Ps. 68:31
The daughter of My dispersed ones,
Shall bring My offering.
11 In that day you shall not be shamed for
any of your deeds
In which you transgress against Me;
For then I will take away from your
midst
Those who [R]rejoice in your pride,
And you shall no longer be haughty
In My holy mountain. Is. 2:12; 5:15
12 I will leave in your midst
[R]A meek and humble people, Is. 14:32
And they shall trust in the name of the
LORD.
13[R]The remnant of Israel [R]shall do no
unrighteousness [Mic. 4:7] • Is. 60:21
[R]And speak no lies, Rev. 14:5
Nor shall a deceitful tongue be found in
their mouth;
For [R]they shall feed *their* flocks and lie
down, Ezek. 34:13–15, 28
And no one shall make *them* afraid."

The Promise of Restoration

14 Sing, O daughter of Zion! Is. 12:6
Shout, O Israel!
Be glad and rejoice with all *your* heart,
O daughter of Jerusalem!
15 The LORD has taken away your
judgments,
He has cast out your enemy.
[R]The King of Israel, the LORD, [R]*is* in your
midst; [John 1:49] • Ezek. 48:35
You shall see* disaster no more.

16 In that day [R]it shall be said to
Jerusalem: Is. 35:3, 4
"Do not fear;
Zion, let not your hands be weak.

3:8 LXX, Syr. *for witness;* Tg. *for the day of My revelation for judgment;* Vg. *for the day of My resurrection that is to come* **3:15** So with Heb. mss., LXX, Bg. *see;* MT, Vg. *fear*

17 The LORD your God [R]in your midst,
The Mighty One, will save; Zeph. 3:5, 15
He will rejoice over you with gladness,
He will quiet *you* with His love,
He will rejoice over you with singing."

18 "I will gather those who [R]sorrow over the appointed assembly, Lam. 2:6
Who are among you,
To whom its reproach *is* a burden.
19 Behold, at that time
I will deal with all who afflict you;
I will save the [R]lame, [Mic. 4:6, 7]
And gather those who were driven out;
I will appoint them for praise and fame
In every land where they were put to shame.
20 At that time [R]I will bring you back,
Even at the time I gather you;
For I will give you [T]fame and praise
Among all the peoples of the earth,
When I return your captives before your eyes," Is. 11:12 • Lit. *a name*
Says the LORD.

THE BOOK OF

HAGGAI

THE BOOK OF HAGGAI

With the Babylonian exile in the past, and a newly returned group of Jews back in the land, the work of rebuilding the temple can begin. However, sixteen years after the process is begun, the people have yet to finish the project, for their personal affairs have interfered with God's business. Haggai preaches a fiery series of sermonettes designed to stir up the nation to finish the temple. He calls the builders to renewed courage in the Lord, renewed holiness of life, and renewed faith in God who controls the future.

The etymology and meaning of *haggay* is uncertain, but it is probably derived from the Hebrew word *hag* "festival." It may also be an abbreviated form of *haggiah,* "festival of Yahweh." Thus, Haggai's name means "Festal" or "Festive," possibly because he was born on the day of a major feast, such as Tabernacles (Haggai's second message takes place during that feast, 2:1). The title in the Septuagint is *Aggaios,* and in the Vulgate it is *Aggaeus.*

THE AUTHOR OF HAGGAI

Haggai's name is mentioned nine times (1:1, 3, 12, 13; 2:1, 10, 13, 14, 20); the authorship and date of the book are virtually uncontested. The unity of theme, style, and dating is obvious. Haggai is known only from this book and from two references to him in Ezra 5:1 and 6:14. There he is seen working alongside the younger prophet Zechariah in the ministry of encouraging the rebuilding of the temple. Haggai returned from Babylon with the remnant under Zerubbabel and evidently lived in Jerusalem. Some think 2:3 may mean that he was born in Judah before the 586 B.C. captivity and was one of the small company who could remember the former temple before its destruction. This would mean Haggai was about seventy-five when he prophesied in 520 B.C. It is equally likely, however, that he was born in Babylon during the captivity.

THE TIME OF HAGGAI

In 538 B.C. Cyrus of Persia issued a decree allowing the Jews to return to their land and rebuild their temple. The first return was led by Zerubbabel, and in 536 B.C. work on the temple began. Ezra 4—6 gives the background to the Book of Haggai and describes how the Samaritans hindered the building of the temple and wrote a letter to the Persian king. This opposition only added to the growing discouragement of the Jewish remnant. Their initial optimism upon returning to their homeland was dampened by the desolation of the land, crop failure, hard work, hostility, and other hardships. They gave up the relative comfort of Babylonian culture to pioneer in a land that seemed unproductive and full of enemies. Finding it easier to stop building than to fight their neighbors, the work on the temple ceased in 534 B.C. The pessimism of the people led to spiritual lethargy, and they became preoccupied with their own building projects. They used political opposition and a theory that the temple was not to be rebuilt until some later time (perhaps after Jerusalem was rebuilt) as excuses for neglecting the house of the Lord.

It was in this context that God called His prophets Haggai and Zechariah to the same task of urging the people to complete the temple. Both books are precisely dated: Haggai 1:1, September 1, 520 B.C.; Haggai 1:15, September 24, 520 B.C.; Haggai 2:1, October 21, 520 B.C.; Zechariah 1:1, November, 520 B.C.; Haggai 2:10, 20, December 24, 520 B.C.; Zechariah 1:7, February 24, 519 B.C.; Zechariah 7:1, December 4, 518 B.C. Zechariah's prophecy commenced between Haggai's second and third messages. Thus, after fourteen years of neglect, work of the temple was resumed in 520 B.C. and was completed in 516 B.C. (Ezra 6:15). The Talmud indicates that the ark of the covenant, the Shekinah glory, and the Urim and Thummim were not in the rebuilt temple.

Darius I (521–486 B.C.) was king of Persia during the ministries of Haggai and Zechariah. He was a strong ruler who consolidated his kingdom by defeating a number of revolting nations.

THE CHRIST OF HAGGAI

The promise of Haggai 2:9 points ahead to the crucial role the second temple is to have in God's redemptive plan. Herod the Great later spent a fortune on the project of enlarging and enriching this temple, and it was filled with the glory of God incarnate every time Christ came to Jerusalem.

The Messiah is also portrayed in the person of Zerubbabel: " 'I will take you, Zerubbabel . . . and will make you like a signet *ring;* for I have chosen you' " (2:23). Zerubbabel becomes the center of the messianic line and is like a signet ring, sealing both branches together.

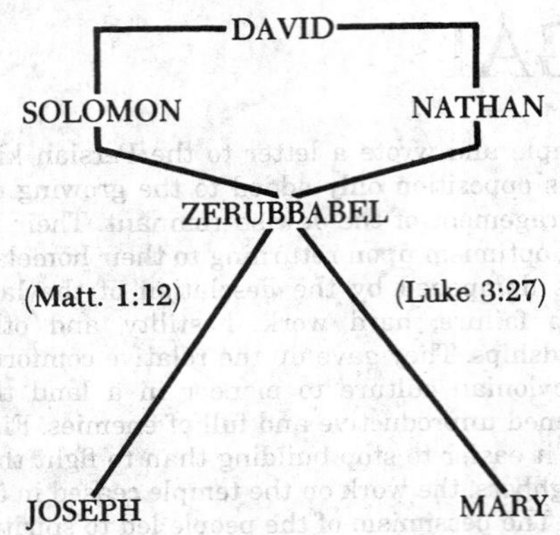

KEYS TO HAGGAI

Key Word: The Reconstruction of the Temple—Haggai's basic theme is clear: the remnant must reorder its priorities and complete the temple before it can expect the blessing of God upon its efforts. Because of spiritual indifference the people fail to respond to God's attempts to get their attention. In their despondency they do not realize that their hardships are divinely given symptoms of their spiritual disease. Haggai brings them to an understanding that circumstances become difficult when people place their own selfish interests before God's. When they put God first and seek to do His will, He will bring His people joy and prosperity.

Key Verses: Haggai 1:7, 8; 2:7–9—"Thus says the LORD of hosts: 'Consider your ways! Go up to the mountains and bring wood and build the temple, that I may take pleasure in it and be glorified, says the LORD' " (1:7, 8).

" 'And I will shake all nations, and they shall come to the Desire of All Nations, and I will fill this temple with glory,' says the LORD of hosts. 'The silver *is* Mine, and the gold *is* Mine,' says the LORD of hosts. 'The glory of this latter temple shall be greater than the former,' says the LORD of hosts. 'And in this place I will give peace,' says the LORD of hosts" (2:7–9).

Key Chapter: Haggai 2—Verses 6–9 record some of the most startling prophecies in Scripture: "I will shake heaven and earth, the sea and dry land" (the tribulation) and "they shall come to the Desire of All Nations" and "in this place I will give peace" (the second coming of the Messiah).

SURVEY OF HAGGAI

Haggai is second only to Obadiah in brevity among Old Testament books, but this strong and frank series of four terse sermons accomplishes its intended effect. The work on the temple has ceased, and the people have become more concerned with the beautification of their own houses than with the building of the central sanctuary of God. Because of their misplaced priorities, their labor is no longer blessed by God. Only when the people put the Lord first by completing the task He has set before them will His hand of blessing once again be upon them. Haggai acts as God's man in God's hour, and his four messages are: the completion of the latter temple (1:1–15), the glory of the latter temple (2:1–9), the present blessings of obedience (2:10–19), and the future blessings of promise (2:20–23).

The Completion of the Latter Temple (1:1–15): When the remnant returns from Babylon under Zerubbabel, they begin to rebuild the temple of the Lord. However, the work soon stops and the people find excuses to ignore it as the years pass. They have no problem in building rich dwellings for themselves ("paneled houses," 1:4) while they claim that the time for building the temple has not yet come (1:2). God withdraws His blessing and they sink into an economic depression. However, they do not recognize what is happening because of their indif-

FOCUS	COMPLETION OF THE LATTER TEMPLE	GLORY OF THE LATTER TEMPLE	PRESENT BLESSING OF OBEDIENCE	FUTURE BLESSING THROUGH PROMISE
REFERENCE	1:1—	2:1—	2:10—	2:20—2:23
DIVISION	"CONSIDER YOUR WAYS . . . MY HOUSE THAT IS IN RUINS."	"THE GLORY OF THIS LATTER TEMPLE SHALL BE GREATER."	"FROM THIS DAY FORWARD I WILL BLESS YOU."	"I WILL SHAKE HEAVEN AND EARTH."
TOPIC	THE TEMPLE OF GOD		THE BLESSINGS OF GOD	
	FIRST REBUKE (PRESENT)	FIRST ENCOURAGEMENT (FUTURE)	SECOND REBUKE (PRESENT)	SECOND ENCOURAGEMENT (FUTURE)
LOCATION	JERUSALEM			
TIME	SEPTEMBER 1 520 B.C.	OCTOBER 21 520 B.C.	DECEMBER 24 520 B.C.	DECEMBER 24 520 B.C.

ference to God and indulgence of self; so God communicates directly to the remnant through His prophet Haggai. Zerubbabel the governor, Joshua the high priest, and all the people respond; and twenty-three days later they again begin to work on the temple.

The Glory of the Latter Temple (2:1–9): In a few short weeks, the enthusiasm of the people sours into discouragement; the elders remember the glory of Solomon's temple and bemoan the puniness of the present temple (see Ezra 3:8–13). Haggai's prophetic word of encouragement reminds the people of God's covenant promises in the past (2:4, 5), and of His confident plans for the future (2:6–9): "The glory of this latter temple shall be greater than the former" (2:9).

The Present Blessings of Obedience (2:10–19): Haggai's message to the priests illustrates the concept of contamination (2:11–13) and applies it to the nation (2:14–19). The Lord requires holiness and obedience, and the contamination of sin blocks the blessing of God. Because the people have obeyed God in building the temple, they will be blessed from that day forward.

The Future Blessings of Promise (2:20–23): On the same day that Haggai addresses the priests, he gives a second message to Zerubbabel. God will move in judgment, and in His power He will overthrow the nations of the earth (2:21, 22). At that time, Zerubbabel, a symbol of the Messiah to come, will be honored.

OUTLINE OF HAGGAI

I. The Completion of the Latter Temple 1:1–15
- A. The Temple Is Not Complete 1:1–6
- B. The Temple Must Be Completed 1:7–15

II. The Glory of the Latter Temple 2:1–9
- A. The Latter Temple Is Not as Glorious as the First 2:1–3
- B. The Latter Temple Will Be More Glorious than the First 2:4–9

III. The Present Blessings of Obedience ..2:10–19
- A. The Disobedience of the Remnant 2:10–14
- B. The Solution: The Obedience of the Remnant 2:15–19

IV. The Future Blessings Through Promise 2:20–23
- A. The Future Destruction of the Nations 2:20–22
- B. The Future Recognition of Zerubbabel 2:23

CHAPTER 1

The Temple Is Not Complete—Ezra 5:1

IN [R]the second year of King Darius, in the
sixth month, on the first day of the
month, the word of the LORD came by [R]Haggai the prophet to [R]Zerubbabel the son of
Shealtiel, governor of Judah, and to [R]Joshua
the son of Jehozadak, the high priest, saying,
Ezra 4:24 • Ezra 5:1; 6:14 • Ezra 2:2 • Ezra 5:2, 3
2 "Thus speaks the LORD of hosts, saying:
'This people says, "The time has not come, the
time that the LORD's house should be built." ' "
3 Then the word of the LORD [R]came by Haggai the prophet, saying,
Ezra 5:1
4 *"Is it* [R]time for you yourselves to dwell in
your paneled houses, and this temple* *to lie* in
ruins?"
2 Sam. 7:2
5 Now therefore, thus says the LORD of
hosts: [R]"Consider your ways!
Lam. 3:40

6 "You have [R]sown much, and bring in
little;
Deut. 28:38–40
You eat, but do not have enough;
You drink, but you are not filled with
drink;
You clothe yourselves, but no one is warm;
And [R]he who earns wages,
Earns wages *to put* into a bag with
holes."
Zech. 8:10

The Temple Must Be Completed

7 Thus says the LORD of hosts: "Consider
your ways!
8 "Go up to the [R]mountains and bring
wood and build the [T]temple, that I may take
pleasure in it and be glorified," says the
LORD.
Ezra 3:7 • Lit. *house*
9 [R]"*You* looked for much, but indeed *it
came to* little; and when you brought it
home, [R]I blew it away. Why?" says the LORD
of hosts. "Because of My house that *is in*
ruins, while every one of you runs to his own
house.
Hag. 2:16 • Hag. 2:17
10 "Therefore [R]the heavens above you withhold the dew, and the earth withholds its
fruit.
Deut. 28:23
11 "For I called for a drought on the land and
the mountains, on the grain and the new wine
and the oil, on whatever the ground brings
forth, on men and livestock, and on all the
labor of *your* hands."
12 [R]Then Zerubbabel the son of Shealtiel,
and Joshua the son of Jehozadak, the high

1:4 Lit. *house*, and so in v. 8

priest, with all the remnant of the people,
obeyed the voice of the LORD their God, and
the words of Haggai the prophet, as the LORD
their God had sent him; and the people feared
the presence of the LORD. Ezra 5:2
13 Then Haggai, the LORD's messenger,
spoke the LORD's message to the people, say-
ing, "I *am* with you, says the LORD."
14 So [R]the LORD stirred up the spirit of Ze-
rubbabel the son of Shealtiel, [R]governor of
Judah, and the spirit of Joshua the son of Je-
hozadak, the high priest, and the spirit of all
the remnant of the people; and they came and
worked on the house of the LORD of hosts,
their God, Ezra 1:1 • Hag. 2:21
15 on the twenty-fourth day of the sixth
month, in the second year of King Darius.

CHAPTER 2

The Latter Temple Is Not as Glorious as the First

In the seventh *month,* on the twenty-first of
the month, the word of the LORD came [T]by
Haggai the prophet, saying: Lit. *by the hand of*
2 "Speak now to Zerubbabel the son of
Shealtiel, governor of Judah, and to Joshua
the son of Jehozadak, the high priest, and to
the remnant of the people, saying:
3 [R]'Who is left among you who saw this
temple* in its former glory? And how do you
see it now? In comparison with it, *is this* not
in your eyes as nothing? Ezra 3:12, 13

The Latter Temple Will Be More Glorious than the First

4 'Yet now [R]be strong, Zerubbabel,' says the
LORD; 'and be strong, Joshua, son of Jehozadak,
the high priest; and be strong, all you people of
the land,' says the LORD, 'and work; for I *am*
with you,' says the LORD of hosts. Zech. 8:9
5 [R]'*According to* the word that I cov-
enanted with you when you came out of
Egypt, so [R]My Spirit remains among you; do
not fear!' Ex. 29:45, 46 • [Neh. 9:20]
6 "For thus says the LORD of hosts: [R]'Once
more (it *is* a little while) I will shake heaven
and earth, the sea and dry land; Heb. 12:26
7 'and I will shake all nations, and they
shall come to [R]the Desire of All Nations,* and
I will fill this temple with [R]glory,' says the
LORD of hosts. Gen. 49:10 • Is. 60:7
8 'The silver *is* Mine, and the gold *is* Mine,'
says the LORD of hosts.
9 [R]'The glory of this latter temple shall be
greater than the former,' says the LORD of
hosts. 'And in this place I will give [R]peace,'
says the LORD of hosts." [John 1:14] • Ps. 85:8, 9

The Disobedience of the Remnant

10 On the twenty-fourth *day* of the ninth
month, in the second year of Darius, the word of
the LORD came by Haggai the prophet, saying,
11 "Thus says the LORD of hosts: 'Now, ask
the priests *concerning the* law, saying,
12 "If one carries holy meat in the fold of his
garment, and with the edge he touches bread
or stew, wine or oil, or any food, will it become
holy?" ' " Then the priests answered and said,
"No."
13 And Haggai said, "If *one who is* unclean
because of a dead body touches any of these,
will it be unclean?" So the priests answered
and said, "It shall be unclean."
14 Then Haggai answered and said, [R]" 'So
is this people, and so is this nation before
Me,' says the LORD, 'and so is every work of
their hands; and what they offer there is un-
clean. [Titus 1:15]

The Obedience of the Remnant

15 'And now, carefully consider from this
day forward: from before stone was laid upon
stone in the temple of the LORD—
16 'since those *days,* [R]when *one* came to a
heap of twenty ephahs, there were *but* ten;
when *one* came to the wine vat to draw out
fifty baths from the press, there were *but*
twenty. Zech. 8:10
17 'I struck you with blight and mildew and
hail in all the labors of your hands; yet you
did not *turn* to Me,' says the LORD.
18 'Consider now from this day forward,
from the twenty-fourth day of the ninth
month, from the day that the foundation of the
LORD's temple was laid—consider it:
19 [R]'Is the seed still in the barn? As yet the
vine, the fig tree, the pomegranate, and the
olive tree have not yielded *fruit. But* from this
day I will [R]bless *you.*' " Zech. 8:12 • [Mal. 3:10]

The Future Destruction of the Nations

20 And again the word of the LORD came to
Haggai on the twenty-fourth day of the
month, saying,
21 "Speak to Zerubbabel, [R]governor of Ju-
dah, saying: Zech. 4:6–10

[R]'I will shake heaven and earth. Hag. 2:6, 7
22 [R]I will overthrow the throne of kingdoms;
I will destroy the strength of the Gentile
kingdoms. [Dan. 2:44]
[R]I will overthrow the chariots Mic. 5:10
And those who ride in them;
The horses and their riders shall come
down,
Every one by the sword of his brother.

The Future Recognition of Zerubbabel

23 'In that day,' says the LORD of hosts, 'I will
take you, Zerubbabel My servant, the son of
Shealtiel,' says the LORD, [R]'and will make you
like a signet *ring;* for I have chosen you,' says
the LORD of hosts." Song 8:6

2:3 Lit. *house,* and so on in vv. 7 and 9 **2:7** Or *the desire of all nations*

THE BOOK OF ZECHARIAH

THE BOOK OF ZECHARIAH

For a dozen years or more, the task of rebuilding the temple has been half completed. Zechariah is commissioned by God to encourage the people in their unfinished responsibility. Rather than exhorting them to action with strong words of rebuke, Zechariah seeks to encourage them to action by reminding them of the future importance of the temple. The temple must be built, for one day the Messiah's glory will inhabit it. But future blessing is contingent upon present obedience. The people are not merely building a building; they are building the future. With that as their motivation, they can enter into the building project with wholehearted zeal, for their Messiah is coming.

Zekar-yah means "Yahweh Remembers" or "Yahweh Has Remembered." This theme dominates the whole book: Israel will be blessed because Yahweh remembers the covenant He made with the fathers. The Greek and Latin version of his name is *Zacharias.*

THE AUTHOR OF ZECHARIAH

"Zechariah" ("Yahweh Remembers") was a popular name shared by no fewer than twenty-nine Old Testament characters. It may have been given out of gratitude for God's gift of a baby boy. Like his predecessors, Jeremiah and Ezekiel, Zechariah was of priestly lineage as the son of Berechiah and grandson of Iddo (1:1, 7; Ezra 5:1; 6:14; Neh. 12:4, 16). He was born in Babylon and was brought by his grandfather to Palestine when the Jewish exiles returned under Zerubbabel and Joshua the high priest. If he was the "young man" of 2:4, he was called to prophesy at an early age in 520 B.C. According to Jewish tradition, Zechariah was a member of the Great Synagogue that collected and preserved the canon of revealed Scripture. Matthew 23:35 indicates he was "murdered between the temple and the altar" in the same way that an earlier Zechariah was martyred (see 2 Chr. 24:20, 21). The universal testimony of Jewish and Christian tradition affirms Zechariah as the author of the entire book.

THE TIME OF ZECHARIAH

Zechariah was a younger contemporary of Haggai the prophet, Zerubbabel the governor, and Joshua the high priest. The historical setting for chapters 1—8 (520–518 B.C.) is identical to that of Haggai (see "The Time of Haggai"). Work was resumed on the temple in 520 B.C., and the project was completed in 516 B.C. Chapters 9—14 are undated, but stylistic differences and references to Greece indicate a date of between 480 and 470 B.C. This would mean that Darius I (521–486 B.C.) had passed from the scene and had been succeeded by Xerxes (486–464 B.C.), the king who deposed Queen Vashti and made Esther queen of Persia.

THE CHRIST OF ZECHARIAH

Very clear messianic passages abound in this book. Christ is portrayed in His two advents as both Servant and King, Man and God. The following are a few of Zechariah's explicit anticipations of Christ: the angel of the Lord (3:1, 2); the righteous Branch (3:8; 6:12, 13), the stone with seven eyes (3:9); the King-Priest (6:13); the humble King (9:9, 10); the cornerstone, tent peg, and battle bow (10:4); the good Shepherd who is rejected and sold for thirty shekels of silver, the price of a slave (11:4–13); the pierced One (12:10); the cleansing fountain (13:1); the smitten Shepherd who is abandoned (13:7); the coming Judge and righteous King (14).

KEYS TO ZECHARIAH

Key Word: Prepare for the Messiah—The first eight chapters frequently allude to the temple and encourage the people to complete their great work on the new sanctuary. As they build the temple, they are building their future, because that very structure will be used by the Messiah when He comes to bring salvation. Zechariah eloquently attests to Yahweh's covenant faithfulness toward Israel through the work of the Messiah, especially in chapters 9—14. This book outlines God's program for His people during the times of the Gentiles until the Messiah comes to deliver them and reign upon the earth. This hope of glory provides a source of reassurance to the Jewish remnant at a time when circumstances are trying. Zechariah also seeks to promote spiritual revival so that the people will call upon the Lord with humble hearts and commit their ways to Him.

Key Verses: Zechariah 8:3; 9:9—"Thus says the LORD: 'I will return to Zion, and dwell in the midst of Jerusalem. Jerusalem shall be called the City of Truth, the Mountain of the LORD of hosts, the Holy Mountain' " (8:3).

"Rejoice greatly, O daughter of Zion! Shout, O daughter of Jerusalem! Behold, your King is coming to you; He *is* just and having salvation, lowly and riding on a donkey, a colt, the foal of a donkey" (9:9).

Key Chapter: Zechariah 14—Zechariah builds to a tremendous climax in the fourteenth chapter where he discloses the last siege of Jerusalem, the initial victory of the enemies of Israel, the cleaving of the Mount of Olives, the Lord's defense of Jerusalem with His visible appearance on Olivet, judgment on the confederated nations, the topographical changes in the land of Israel, the Feast of Tabernacles, and the ultimate holiness of Jerusalem and her people.

SURVEY OF ZECHARIAH

Zechariah uses a series of eight visions, four messages, and two burdens to portray God's future plans for His covenant people. The first eight chapters were written to encourage the remnant while they were rebuilding the temple; the last six chapters were written after the completion of the temple to anticipate Israel's coming Messiah. Zechariah moves from Gentile domination to messianic rule, from persecution to peace, and from uncleanness to holiness. The book divides into: the eight visions (1—6), the four messages (7 and 8), and the two burdens (9—14).

The Eight Visions (1—6): The book opens with an introductory appeal to the people to repent and return to God, unlike their fathers who rejected the warnings of the prophets (1:1–6). A few months later, Zechariah has a series of eight night visions, evidently in one troubled night (Feb. 15, 519 B.C.; 1:7). The angel who speaks with him interprets the visions, but some of the symbols are not explained. The visions mix the work of the Messiah in both advents; and like the other prophets, Zechariah sees only the peaks of God's program without the intervening valleys. The first five are visions of comfort, and the last three are visions of judgment: (1) The horseman among the myrtle trees—God will rebuild Zion and His people (1:7–17). (2) The four horns and craftsmen—Israel's oppressors will be judged (1:18–21). (3) The man with a measuring line—God will protect and glorify Jerusalem (2:1–13). (4) The cleansing of Joshua the high priest—Israel will be cleansed and restored by the coming Branch (3:1–10). (5) The golden lampstand—God's Spirit is empowering Zerubbabel and Joshua (4:1–14). (6) The flying scroll—individual sin will be judged (5:1–4). (7) The woman in the basket—national sin will be removed (5:5–11). (8) The four chariots—God's judgment will descend on the nations (6:1–8). The crowning of Joshua (6:9–15) anticipates the coming of the Branch who will be King and Priest (the composite crown).

The Four Messages (7 and 8): In response to a question about the continuation of the fasts (7:1–3), God gives Zechariah a series of four messages: (1) a rebuke of empty ritualism (7:4–7); (2) a reminder of past disobedience (7:8–14); (3) the restoration and consolation of Israel (8:1–17); and (4) the recovery of joy in the kingdom (8:18–23).

The Two Burdens (9—14): The first burden (9—11) concerns the first advent and rejection of Israel's coming King. Alexander the Great will conquer Israel's neighbors, but will spare Jerusalem (9:1–8), which will be preserved for her King (the Messiah; 9:9, 10). Israel will succeed against Greece (the Maccabean revolt; 9:11–17); and although they will later be scattered, the Messiah will bless them and bring them back (10:1—11:3). Israel will reject her Shepherd-King and be led astray by false shepherds (11:4–17). The second burden (12—14) concerns the second advent of Christ and the acceptance of Israel's King. The nations will attack Jerusalem, but the Messiah will come and deliver His people (12). They will be cleansed of impurity and falsehood (13), and the Messiah will come in power to judge the nations and reign in Jerusalem over the whole earth (14).

FOCUS	EIGHT VISIONS			FOUR MESSAGES	TWO BURDENS	
REFERENCE	1:1—1:7	—6:9		—7:1	—9:1	—12:1—14:21
DIVISION	CALL TO REPENTANCE	EIGHT VISIONS	CROWNING OF JOSHUA	QUESTION OF THE FASTS	FIRST BURDEN: REJECTION OF THE MESSIAH	SECOND BURDEN: REIGN OF THE MESSIAH
TOPIC	PICTURES			PROBLEM	PREDICTION	
	ISRAEL'S FORTUNE			ISRAEL'S FASTINGS	ISRAEL'S FUTURE	
LOCATION	JERUSALEM					
TIME	WHILE BUILDING THE TEMPLE (520–518 B.C.)				AFTER BUILDING THE TEMPLE (c. 480–470 B.C.)	

OUTLINE OF ZECHARIAH

CHAPTER 1

The Call to Repentance—Ezra 5:1

IN the eighth month of the second year of
Darius, the word of the LORD came [R]to
Zechariah the son of Berechiah, the son of
Iddo the prophet, saying, Matt. 23:35
2 "The LORD has been very angry with your
fathers.
3 "Therefore say to them, 'Thus says the
LORD of hosts: "Return [R]to Me," says the LORD
of hosts, "and I will return to you," says the
LORD of hosts. [Mal. 3:7–10]
4 "Do not be like your fathers, [R]to whom
the former prophets preached, saying, 'Thus
says the LORD of hosts: [R]"Turn now from
your evil ways and your evil deeds." ' But
they did not hear nor heed Me," says the
LORD. 2 Chr. 36:15, 16 • Is. 31:6

5 "Your fathers, where *are* they?
And the prophets, do they live forever?
6 Yet surely [R]My words and My statutes,
Which I commanded My servants the
prophets, [Is. 55:11]
Did they not overtake your fathers?

"So they returned and said:

[R]'Just as the LORD of hosts determined to
do to us, Lam. 1:18; 2:17
According to our ways and according to
our deeds,
So He has dealt with us.' " ' "

The Horses Among the Myrtle Trees

7 On the twenty-fourth day of the eleventh
month, which is the month Shebat, in the sec-
ond year of Darius, the word of the LORD
came to Zechariah the son of Berechiah, the
son of Iddo the prophet:
8 I saw by night, and behold, a man riding
on a red horse, and it stood among the myrtle
trees in the hollow; and behind him *were*
horses: red, sorrel, and white.
9 Then I said, [R]"My lord, what *are* these?"
So the angel who talked with me said to me,
"I will show you what they *are*." Zech. 6:4
10 And the man who stood among the myr-
tle trees answered and said, [R]"These *are the
ones* whom the LORD has sent to walk to and
fro throughout the earth." [Heb. 1:14]
11 [R]So they answered the Angel of the LORD,
who stood among the myrtle trees, and said,
"We have walked to and fro throughout the
earth, and behold, all the earth is resting qui-
etly." [Ps. 103:20, 21]
12 Then the Angel of the LORD answered and
said, "O LORD of hosts, [R]how long will You not
have mercy on Jerusalem and on the cities of
Judah, against which You were angry these
seventy years?" Ps. 74:10
13 And the LORD answered the angel who
talked to me, *with* [R]good *and* comforting
words. Jer. 29:10
14 So the angel who spoke with me said to
me, [T]"Proclaim, saying, 'Thus says the LORD of
hosts: Lit. *Cry out*

"I am [R]zealous for Jerusalem Zech. 8:2
And for Zion with great zeal.
15 I am exceedingly angry with the nations
at ease;
For [R]I was a little angry, Is. 47:6
And they helped—*but* with evil *intent*."

16 'Therefore thus says the LORD:

"I am returning to Jerusalem with
mercy;
My [R]house [R]shall be built in it," says the
LORD of hosts, Ezra 6:14, 15 • Is. 44:28

"And [R]a *surveyor's* line shall be stretched
out over Jerusalem." ' Zech. 2:1–3

17 "Again proclaim, saying, 'Thus says the
LORD of hosts:

"My cities shall again [T]spread out through
prosperity; Or *overflow with good*
The LORD will again comfort Zion,
And will again choose Jerusalem." ' "

The Four Horns and Four Craftsmen

18 Then I raised my eyes and looked, and
there *were* four [R]horns. [Lam. 2:17]
19 And I said to the angel who talked with
me, "What *are* these?" So he answered me,
[R]"These *are* the horns that have scattered Ju-
dah, Israel, and Jerusalem." Ezra 4:1, 4, 7
20 Then the LORD showed me four craftsmen.
21 And I said, "What are these coming to
do?" So he said, "These *are* the horns that
scattered Judah, so that no one could lift up
his head; but the craftsmen* are coming to
terrify them, to cast out the horns of the na-
tions that [R]lifted up *their* horn against the
land of Judah to scatter it." Ps. 75:4, 5

CHAPTER 2

The Man with the Measuring Line

THEN I raised my eyes and looked, and be-
hold, [R]a man with a measuring line in his
hand. Jer. 31:39
2 So I said, "Where are you going?" And he
said to me, "To measure Jerusalem, to see
what *is* its width and what *is* its length."
3 And there *was* the angel who talked with
me, going out; and another angel was coming
out to meet him,
4 who said to him, "Run, speak to this
young man, saying: 'Jerusalem shall be in-
habited *as* towns without walls, because of
the multitude of men and livestock in it.
5 'For I,' says the LORD, 'will be [R]a wall of
fire all around her, [R]and I will be the glory in
her midst.' " [Is. 26:1] • [Is. 60:19]
6 "Up, up! Flee [R]from the land of the
north," says the LORD; "for I have [R]spread you
abroad like the four winds of heaven," says
the LORD. Is. 48:20 • Deut. 28:64
7 "Up, Zion! [R]Escape, you who dwell with
the daughter of Babylon." Is. 48:20
8 For thus says the LORD of hosts: "He sent
Me after glory, to the nations which plunder
you; for he who [R]touches you touches the ap-
ple of His eye. Deut. 32:10
9 "For surely I will [R]shake My hand against
them, and they shall become spoil for their
servants. Then you will know that the LORD of
hosts has sent Me. Is. 19:16
10 [R]"Sing and rejoice, O daughter of Zion!
For behold, I am coming and I will dwell in
your midst," says the LORD. Is. 12:6
11 [R]"Many nations shall be joined to the
LORD [R]in that day, and they shall become My
people. And I will dwell in your midst. Then
you will know that the LORD of hosts has sent
Me to you. [Is. 2:2, 3] • Zech. 3:10
12 "And the LORD will take possession of Ju-
dah as His inheritance in the Holy Land, and
will again choose Jerusalem.
13 "Be silent, all flesh, before the LORD, for
He is aroused from His holy habitation!"

CHAPTER 3

The Cleansing of Joshua, the High Priest

THEN he showed me [R]Joshua the high
priest standing before the Angel of the
LORD, and [R]Satan standing at his right hand to
oppose him. Hag. 1:1 • Ps. 109:6
2 And the LORD said to Satan, [R]"The LORD
rebuke you, Satan! The LORD who has chosen
Jerusalem rebuke you! *Is* this not a brand
plucked from the fire?" [Jude 9]
3 Now Joshua was clothed with [R]filthy
garments, and was standing before the
Angel. Is. 64:6
4 Then He answered and spoke to those
who stood before Him, saying, "Take away the
filthy garments from him." And to him He said,
"See, I have removed your iniquity from you,
[R]and I will clothe you with rich robes." Is. 61:10
5 And I said, "Let them put a clean turban
on his head." So they put a clean turban on his
head, and they put the clothes on him. And
the Angel of the LORD stood by.
6 Then the Angel of the LORD admonished
Joshua, saying,
7 "Thus says the LORD of hosts:

'If you will walk in My ways,
And if you will keep My command,
Then you shall also judge My house,
And likewise have charge of My courts;
I will give you places to walk
Among these who [R]stand here. Zech. 3:4

8 'Hear, O Joshua, the high priest,
You and your companions who sit before
you,
For they are a wondrous sign;
For behold, I am bringing forth [R]My
Servant the BRANCH. Is. 42:1☆
9 For behold, the stone
That I have laid before Joshua:
Upon the stone *are* [R]seven eyes.
Behold, I will engrave its inscription,'
Says the LORD of hosts, Ps. 118:22
'And [R]I will remove the iniquity of that
land in one day. Jer. 31:34; 50:20
10 In that day,' says the LORD of hosts,
'Everyone will invite his neighbor
Under his vine and under his fig tree.' "

1:21 Lit. *these*

CHAPTER 4

The Golden Lampstand and Olive Trees

NOW the angel who talked with me came
back and wakened me, [R]as a man who is
wakened out of his sleep. Dan. 8:18
2 And he said to me, "What do you see?" So
I said, "I am looking, and there *is* [R]a lamp-
stand of solid gold with a bowl on top of it,
[R]and on the *stand* seven lamps with seven
pipes to the seven lamps. Rev. 1:12 • [Rev. 4:5]
3 "Two olive trees *are* by it, one at the right
of the bowl and the other at its left."
4 So I answered and spoke to the angel who
talked with me, saying, "What *are* these, my
lord?"
5 Then the angel who talked with me an-
swered and said to me, "Do you not know
what these are?" And I said, "No, my lord."
6 So he answered and said to me:

"This *is* the word of the LORD to
[R]Zerubbabel: Hag. 1:1
[R]'Not by might nor by power, but by My
Spirit,' Hos. 1:7
Says the LORD of hosts.
7 'Who *are* you, [R]O great mountain?
Before Zerubbabel *you shall become* a
plain! Jer. 51:25
And he shall bring forth the capstone
With shouts of "Grace, grace to it!" ' "

8 Moreover the word of the LORD came to
me, saying:

9 "The hands of Zerubbabel
[R]Have laid the foundation of this
temple;* Ezra 3:8–10; 5:16
His hands shall also finish *it.*
Then [R]you will know Zech. 2:9, 11; 6:15
That the [R]LORD of hosts has sent Me to
you. [Is. 43:16]
10 For who has despised the day of [R]small
things? Hag. 2:3
For these seven rejoice to see
The [T]plumb line in the hand of
Zerubbabel. Lit. *plummet stone*
[R]They are the eyes of the LORD,
Which scan to and fro throughout the
whole earth." 2 Chr. 16:9

11 Then I answered and said to him, "What
are these [R]two olive trees—at the right of the
lampstand and at its left?" Zech. 4:3
12 And I further answered and said to him,
"What *are these* two olive branches that *drip*
into the receptacles* of the two gold pipes
from which the golden *oil* drains?"
13 Then he answered me and said, "Do you not
know what these *are?*" And I said, "No, my lord."
14 So he said, [R]"These *are* the two anointed
ones, [R]who stand beside the Lord of the whole
earth." Rev. 11:4 • Zech. 3:1–7

CHAPTER 5

The Flying Scroll

THEN I turned and raised my eyes, and saw
there a flying [R]scroll. Ezek. 2:9
2 And he said to me, "What do you see?" So
I answered, "I see a flying scroll. Its length *is*
twenty cubits and its width ten cubits."
3 Then he said to me, "This *is* the [R]curse
that goes out over the face of the whole earth:
'Every thief shall be expelled,' according *to*
this side of *the scroll;* and, 'Every perjurer
shall be expelled,' according *to* that side of
it." Mal. 4:6

4 "I will send out *the curse,*" says the LORD
of hosts;
"It shall enter the house of the thief
And the house of [R]the one who swears
falsely by My name. Lev. 19:12
It shall remain in the midst of his house
And consume [R]it, with its timber and
stones." Lev. 14:34, 35

The Woman in the Basket

5 Then the angel who talked with me came
out and said to me, "Lift your eyes now, and
see what this *is* that goes forth."
6 So I asked, "What *is* it?" And he said, "It *is*
a basket* that is going forth." He also said,
"This *is* their resemblance throughout the
earth:
7 "Here *is* a lead disc lifted up, and this *is* a
woman sitting inside the basket";
8 then he said, "This *is* Wickedness!" And
he thrust her down into the basket, and threw
the lead cover* over its mouth.
9 Then I raised my eyes and looked, and
there *were* two women, coming with the wind
in their wings; for they had wings like the
wings of a stork, and they lifted up the basket
between earth and heaven.
10 So I said to the angel who talked with me,
"Where are they carrying the basket?"
11 And he said to me, "To [R]build a house
for it in [R]the land of Shinar;* when it is
ready, *the basket* will be set there on its
base." Jer. 29:5, 28 • Gen. 10:10

CHAPTER 6

The Four Chariots

THEN I turned and raised my eyes and
looked, and behold, four chariots *were*
coming from between two mountains, and the
mountains *were* mountains of bronze.
2 With the first chariot *were* red horses,
with the second chariot black horses,

4:9 Lit. *house* **4:12** Lit. *into the hands of* **5:6** Heb. *ephah,* a measuring container, and so elsewhere **5:8** Lit. *stone* **5:11** Babylon

3 with the third chariot white horses, and
with the fourth chariot dappled horses—
strong *steeds*.
4 Then I answered [R]and said to the angel
who talked with me, "What *are* these, my
lord?" Zech. 5:10
5 And the angel answered and said to me,
[R]"These *are* four spirits of heaven, who go out
from *their* [R]station before the Lord of all the
earth. [Heb. 1:7, 14] • Dan. 7:10
6 [T]"The one with the black horses is going
to [R]the north country, the white are going
after them, and the dappled are going toward
the south country." The chariot • Jer. 1:14
7 Then the strong *steeds* went out, eager to
go, that they might walk to and fro throughout
the earth. And He said, "Go, walk to and fro
throughout the earth." So they walked to and
fro throughout the earth.
8 And He called to me, and spoke to me,
saying, "See, those who go toward the north
country have given rest to My [R]Spirit in the
north country." Eccl. 10:4

The Crowning of Joshua

9 Then the word of the LORD came to me,
saying:
10 "Receive *the gift* from the captives—from
Heldai, Tobijah, and Jedaiah, who have come
from Babylon—and go the same day and
enter the house of Josiah the son of Zepha-
niah.
11 "Take the silver and gold, make [R]an[T] elab-
orate crown, and set *it* on the head of
[R]Joshua the son of Jehozadak, the high
priest. Ex. 29:6 • Lit. *crowns* • Hag. 1:1
12 "Then speak to him, saying, 'Thus says
the LORD of hosts, saying:

"Behold, [R]the Man whose name *is* the
[R]BRANCH! John 1:45 • Is. 11:1☆
From His place He shall [T]branch out,
[R]And He shall build the temple of the
LORD; Lit. *sprout up* • [Eph. 2:20]
13 Yes, He shall build the temple of the
LORD.
He [R]shall bear the glory, Is. 22:24
And shall sit and rule on His throne;
So He shall be a priest on His throne,
And the counsel of peace shall be
between [T]them both." ' Both offices

14 "Now the [T]elaborate crown shall be [R]for a
memorial in the temple of the LORD for
Helem,* Tobijah, Jedaiah, and Hen the son of
Zephaniah. Lit. *crowns* • Ex. 12:14
15 "Even those from afar shall come and
build the temple of the LORD. Then you shall
know that the LORD of hosts has sent Me to
you. And *this* shall come to pass if you dili-
gently obey the voice of the LORD your
God."

CHAPTER 7

The Question of Fasting

NOW in the fourth year of King Darius it
came to pass *that* the word of the LORD
came to Zechariah, on the fourth day of the
ninth month, Chislev,
2 when *the people** sent Sherezer,* with
Regem-Melech and his men, *to* the house of
God,* to pray before the LORD,
3 *and* to [R]ask the priests who *were* in the
house of the LORD of hosts, and the
prophets, saying, "Should I weep in [R]the fifth
month and [T]fast as I have done for so many
years?" Mal. 2:7 • Zech. 8:19 • Lit. *consecrate myself*

Rebuke of Hypocrisy

4 Then the word of the LORD of hosts came
to me, saying,
5 "Say to all the people of the land, and to
the priests: 'When you [R]fasted and mourned
in the fifth and seventh *months* [R]during those
seventy years, did you really fast [R]for Me—for
Me? [Is. 58:1–9] • Zech. 1:12 • [Rom. 14:6]
6 'When you eat and when you drink, do
you not eat and drink *for yourselves*?
7 '*Should you* not *have obeyed* the words
which the LORD proclaimed through the [R]for-
mer prophets when Jerusalem and the cities
around it were inhabited and prosperous, and
[R]the South* and the Lowland were inhab-
ited?' " Zech. 1:4 • Jer. 17:26

Repent of Disobedience

8 Then the word of the LORD came to
Zechariah, saying,
9 "Thus says the LORD of hosts:

[R]'Execute true justice, Jer. 7:28
Show [T]mercy and compassion
Everyone to his brother. Or *lovingkindness*
10 [R]Do not oppress the widow or the
fatherless, Ex. 22:22
The alien or the poor.
[R]Let none of you plan evil in his heart
Against his brother.' Mic. 2:1

11 "But they refused to heed, [R]shrugged their
shoulders, and [R]stopped their ears so that
they could not hear. Neh. 9:29 • Jer. 17:23
12 "Yes, they made their hearts like flint, re-
fusing to hear the law and the words which
the LORD of hosts had sent by His Spirit
through the former prophets. Thus great
wrath came from the LORD of hosts.
13 "Therefore it happened, *that* just as He
proclaimed and they would not hear, so [R]they
called out and I would not listen," says the
LORD of hosts. Prov. 1:24–28

6:14 So with MT, Tg., Vg.; Syr. *for Heldai* (cf. v. 10); LXX *for the patient ones* **7:2** Lit. *they*, cf. v. 5 • Or *Sar-Ezer* • Heb. *Bethel* **7:7** Heb. *Negev*

14 "But [R]I scattered them with a whirlwind
among all the nations which they had not
known. Thus the land became desolate after
them, so that no one passed through or re-
turned; for they made the pleasant land deso-
late." Deut. 4:27; 28:64

CHAPTER 8

Restoration of Israel

AGAIN the word of the LORD of hosts came, saying,
2 "Thus says the LORD of hosts:

'I am zealous for Zion with great zeal;
With great fervor I am zealous for her.'

3 "Thus says the LORD:

[R]'I will return to Zion, Zech. 1:16
And [R]dwell in the midst of Jerusalem.
Jerusalem [R]shall be called the City of
Truth, Zech. 2:10, 11 • Is. 1:21
[R]The Mountain of the LORD of hosts,
[R]The Holy Mountain.' [Is. 2:2, 3] • Jer. 31:23

4 "Thus says the LORD of hosts:

[R]'Old men and old women shall again sit
In the streets of Jerusalem, Is. 65:20
Each one with his staff in his hand
Because of [T]great age. Lit. *many days*
5 The streets of the city
Shall be [R]full of boys and girls
Playing in its streets.' Jer. 30:19, 20

6 "Thus says the LORD of hosts:

'If it is marvelous in the eyes of the
remnant of this people in these days,
[R]Will it also be marvelous in My eyes?'
Says the LORD of hosts. [Luke 1:37]

7 "Thus says the LORD of hosts:

'Behold, [R]I will save My people from the
land of the [T]east Is. 11:11 • Lit. *rising sun*
And from the land of the west;
8 I will [R]bring them *back,* Zeph. 3:20
And they shall dwell in the midst of
Jerusalem.
They shall be My people
And I will be their God,
[R]In truth and righteousness.' Jer. 4:2

9 "Thus says the LORD of hosts:

[R]'Let your hands be strong, Hag. 2:4
You who have been hearing in these days
These words by the mouth of [R]the
prophets, Ezra 5:1, 2; 6:14
Who *spoke* in [R]the day the foundation
was laid Hag. 2:18
For the house of the LORD of hosts,
That the temple might be built.
10 For before these days
There were no [R]wages for man nor any
hire for beast; Hag. 1:6, 9
There was no peace from the enemy for
whoever went out or came in;
For I set all men, everyone, against his
neighbor.

11 [R]'But now I *will* not *treat* the remnant of
this people as in the former days,' says the
LORD of hosts. Hag. 2:15–19

12 'For[R] the seed *shall be* prosperous,
The vine shall give its fruit, Joel 2:22
[R]The ground shall give her increase,
And [R]the heavens shall give their dew—
I will cause the remnant of this people
To possess all these. Ps. 67:6 • Hag. 1:10
13 And it shall come to pass
That just as you were [R]a curse among
the nations, Jer. 42:18
O house of Judah and house of Israel,
So I will save you, and [R]you shall be a
blessing. Gen. 12:2
Do not fear,
Let your hands be strong.'

14 "For thus says the LORD of hosts:

[R]'Just as I determined to [T]punish you
When your fathers provoked Me to
wrath,' Jer. 31:28 • Lit. *bring calamity to you*
Says the LORD of hosts,
[R]'And I would not relent, [2 Chr. 36:16]
15 So again in these days
I am determined to do good
To Jerusalem and to the house of Judah.
Do not fear.
16 These *are* the things you shall [R]do:
[R]Speak each man the truth to his
neighbor; Zech. 7:9, 10 • [Eph. 4:25]
Give judgment in your gates for truth,
justice, and peace;
17 [R]Let none of you think evil in your* heart
against your neighbor;
And do not love a false oath.
For all these *are things* that I hate,'
Says the LORD." Prov. 3:29

Rejoice in Israel's Future

18 Then the word of the LORD of hosts came
to me, saying,
19 "Thus says the LORD of hosts:

[R]'The fast of the fourth *month,* Jer. 52:6
[R]The fast of the fifth, Jer. 52:12
[R]The fast of the seventh, 2 Kin. 25:25
[R]And the fast of the tenth, Jer. 52:4

8:17 Lit. *his*

Shall be [R]joy and gladness and cheerful feasts Esth. 8:17
For the house of Judah.
Therefore love truth and peace.'

20 "Thus says the LORD of hosts:

'Peoples shall yet come,
Inhabitants of many cities;
21 The inhabitants of one *city* shall go to another, saying,
[R]"Let us continue to go and pray before the LORD, [Is. 2:2, 3]
And seek the LORD of hosts.
I myself will go also."
22 Yes, [R]many peoples and strong nations
Shall come to seek the LORD of hosts in Jerusalem, Is. 60:3; 66:23
And to pray before the LORD.'

23 "Thus says the LORD of hosts: 'In those
days ten men from every language of the na-
tions shall grasp the sleeve of a Jewish man,
saying, "Let us go with you, for we have heard
that God *is* with you." ' "

CHAPTER 9

Judgment on Surrounding Nations

THE burden* of the word of the LORD
Against the land of Hadrach,
And [R]Damascus its resting place
(For [R]the eyes of men
And all the tribes of Israel
Are on the LORD); Is. 17:1 • Amos 1:3–5
2 Also *against* [R]Hamath, *which* borders on it, Jer. 49:23
And *against* [R]Tyre and [R]Sidon, though they are very wise. Is. 23 • 1 Kin. 17:9

3 For Tyre built herself a tower,
Heaped up silver like the dust,
And gold like the mire of the streets.
4 Behold, the LORD will cast her out;
He will destroy her power in the sea,
And she will be devoured by fire.

5 Ashkelon shall see *it* and fear;
Gaza also shall be very sorrowful;
And [R]Ekron, for He dried up her expectation. Zeph. 2:4, 5
The king shall perish from Gaza,
And Ashkelon shall not be inhabited.

6 "A mixed race shall settle [R]in Ashdod,
And I will cut off the pride of the [R]Philistines. Amos 1:8 • Ezek. 25:15–17
7 I will take away the blood from his mouth,
And the abominations from between his teeth.
But he who remains, even he *shall be* for our God,
And shall be like a leader in Judah,
And Ekron like a Jebusite.
8 [R]I will camp around My house [Ps. 34:7]
Because of the army,
Because of him who passes by and him who returns.
No more shall an oppressor pass through them,
For now I have seen with My eyes.

First Coming of the Messiah

9 "Rejoice [R]greatly, O daughter of Zion!
Shout, O daughter of Jerusalem!
Behold, your King is coming to you;
He *is* just and having salvation,
Lowly and riding on a donkey,
A colt, the foal of a donkey. Matt. 21:4, 5☆

Second Coming of the Messiah

10 I will cut off the chariot from Ephraim
And the horse from Jerusalem;
The [R]battle bow shall be cut off.
He shall speak [R]peace to the nations;
His dominion *shall be* 'from sea to sea,
And from the River to the ends of the earth.'* Hos. 2:18 • Mic. 4:2–4☆

11 "As for you also,
Because of the blood of your covenant,
I will set your [R]prisoners free from the waterless pit. Is. 42:7
12 Return to the stronghold,
[R]You prisoners of hope. Is. 49:9
Even today I declare
That I will restore double to you.
13 For I have bent Judah, My *bow,*
Fitted the bow with Ephraim,
And raised up your sons, O Zion,
Against your sons, O Greece,
And made you like the sword of a mighty man."

14 Then the LORD will be seen over them,
And [R]His arrow will go forth like lightning. Ps. 18:14
The Lord GOD will blow the trumpet,
And go with whirlwinds from the south.
15 The LORD of hosts will [R]defend them;
They shall devour and subdue with slingstones. Zech. 12:8
They shall drink *and* roar as if with wine;
They shall be filled *with blood* like [T]basins, Sacrificial basins
Like the corners of the altar.
16 The LORD their God will [R]save them in that day, Jer. 31:10, 11
As the flock of His people.
For [R]they *shall be like* the [T]jewels of a crown, Is. 62:3 • Lit. *stones*
Lifted like a banner over His land—
17 For [R]how great is its* goodness

9:1 Or *oracle, prophecy* **9:10** Ps. 72:8 **9:17** Or *His*

And how great its* beauty! [Ps. 31:19]
Grain shall make the young men thrive,
And new wine the young women.

CHAPTER 10

ASK Rthe LORD for rain [Jer. 14:22]
In the time of the latter rain.*
The LORD will make flashing clouds;
He will give them showers of rain,
Grass in the field for everyone.

2 For the idols* speak delusion;
The diviners envision Rlies, Jer. 27:9
And tell false dreams;
They Rcomfort in vain. Job 13:4
Therefore *the people* wend their way like
Rsheep; Jer. 50:6, 17
They are Tin trouble Rbecause *there is* no
shepherd. *afflicted* • Ezek. 34:5–8

3 "My anger is kindled against the
Rshepherds, Jer. 25:34–36
RAnd I will punish the Tgoatherds.
For the LORD of hosts Rwill visit His
flock, Ezek. 34:17 • Leaders • Luke 1:68
The house of Judah,
And Rwill make them as His royal horse
in the battle. Song 1:9
4 From him comes the cornerstone,
From him Rthe tent peg, Is. 22:23
From him the battle bow,
From him every ruler* together.
5 They shall be like mighty men,
Who Rtread down *their enemies*
In the mire of the streets in the battle.
They shall fight because the LORD is with
them, Ps. 18:42
And the riders on horses shall be put to
shame.

6 "I will strengthen the house of Judah,
And I will save the house of Joseph.
RI will bring them back, Jer. 3:18
Because I Rhave mercy on them.
They shall be as though I had not cast
them aside; Hos. 1:7
For I *am* the LORD their God,
And I Rwill hear them. Zech. 13:9
7 *Those of* Ephraim shall be like a mighty
man,
And their Rheart shall rejoice as if with
wine. Ps. 104:15
Yes, their children shall see *it* and be glad;
Their heart shall rejoice in the LORD.
8 I will Rwhistle for them and gather them,
For I will redeem them; Is. 5:26
RAnd they shall increase as they once
increased. Ezek. 36:37

9 "IR will sow them among the peoples,
And they shall Rremember Me in far
countries; Hos. 2:23 • Deut. 30:1
They shall live, together with their
children,
And they shall return.
10 RI will also bring them back from the land
of Egypt, Is. 11:11
And gather them from Assyria.
I will bring them into the land of Gilead
and Lebanon,
Until no *more room* is found for them.
11 RHe shall pass through the sea with
affliction, Is. 11:15
And strike the waves of the sea:
All the depths of the River* shall dry up.
Then Rthe pride of Assyria shall be
brought down, Zeph. 2:13
And the scepter of Egypt shall depart.

12 "So I will strengthen them in the LORD,
And Rthey shall walk up and down in His
name," Mic. 4:5
Says the LORD.

CHAPTER 11

Rejection of the Messiah

OPEN your doors, O Lebanon,
That fire may devour your cedars.
2 Wail, O cypress, for the Rcedar has
fallen, Ezek. 31:3
Because the mighty *trees* are ruined.
Wail, O oaks of Bashan,
For the thick forest has come down.
3 *There is* the sound of wailing
Rshepherds! Jer. 25:34–36
For their glory is in ruins.
There is the sound of roaring lions!
For the pride* of the Jordan is in ruins.

4 Thus says the LORD my God, "Feed the
flock for slaughter,
5 "whose owners slaughter them and Rfeel
no guilt; those who sell them say, 'Blessed be
the LORD, for I am rich'; and their shepherds
do not pity them. [Jer. 2:3]; 50:7
6 "For I will no longer pity the inhabitants
of the land," says the LORD. "But indeed I will
give everyone into his neighbor's hand and
into the hand of his king. They shall Tattack
the land, and I will not deliver *them* from their
hand." Lit. *strike*
7 So I fed the flock for slaughter, in par-
ticular Rthe poor of the flock.* I took for my-
self two staffs: the one I called Beauty,* and
the other I called Bonds;* and I fed the
flock. Zeph. 3:12
8 I dismissed the three shepherds Rin one
month. My soul loathed them, and their soul
also abhorred me. Hos. 5:7

9:17 Or *His* **10:1** Spring rain **10:2** Heb. *teraphim* **10:4** Or *despot* **10:11** The Nile **11:3** Or *floodplain, thicket* **11:7** So with MT, Tg., Vg.; LXX *for the Canaanites* • Or *Grace* • Or *Unity*, and so in v. 14

9 Then I said, "I will not feed you. [R]Let what is dying die, and what is perishing perish. Let those that are left eat each other's flesh." Jer. 15:2

10 And I took my staff, Beauty, and cut it in two, that I might break the covenant which I had made with all the peoples.

11 So it was broken on that day. Thus the poor* of the flock, who were watching me, knew that it *was* the word of the LORD.

12 Then I said to them, "If it is agreeable to you, give *me* my wages; and if not, refrain." So they [R]weighed out for my wages thirty *pieces* of silver. Matt. 27:9☆

13 And the LORD said to me, "Throw it to the [R]potter"—that princely price they set on me. So I took the thirty *pieces* of silver and threw them into the house of the LORD for the potter. Matt. 27:3–10☆

14 Then I cut in two my other staff, [T]Bonds, that I might break the brotherhood between Judah and Israel. Or *Unity*

15 And the LORD said to me, [R]"Next, take for yourself the implements of a foolish shepherd. Is. 56:11

16 "For indeed I will raise up a shepherd in the land *who* will not care for those who are cut off, nor seek the young, nor heal those that are broken, nor feed those that still stand. But he will eat the flesh of the fat and tear their hooves in [R]pieces. Ezek. 34:1–10

17 "Woe[R] to the worthless shepherd,
Who leaves the flock! Jer. 23:1
A sword *shall be* against his arm
And against his right eye;
His arm shall completely wither,
And his right eye shall be totally
blinded."

CHAPTER 12

Physical Salvation of Judah

THE burden* of the word of the LORD against Israel. Thus says the LORD, [R]who stretches out the heavens, lays the foundation of the earth, and [R]forms the spirit of man within him: Is. 42:5; 44:24 • [Is. 57:16]

2 "Behold, I will make Jerusalem [R]a cup of [T]drunkenness to all the surrounding peoples, when they lay siege against Judah and Jerusalem. Is. 51:17 • Lit. *reeling*

3 "And it shall happen in that day that I will make Jerusalem [R]a very heavy stone for all peoples; all who would heave it away will surely be cut in pieces, though all nations of the earth are gathered against it. Matt. 21:44

4 "In that day," says the LORD, "I will strike every horse with confusion, and its rider with madness; I will open My eyes on the house of Judah, and will strike every horse of the peoples with blindness.

5 "And the governors of Judah shall say in their heart, 'The inhabitants of Jerusalem *are* my strength in the LORD of hosts, their God.'

6 "In that day I will make the governors of Judah [R]like a firepan in the woodpile, and like a fiery torch in the sheaves; they shall devour all the surrounding peoples on the right hand and on the left, but Jerusalem shall be inhabited again in her own place—Jerusalem. Obad. 18

7 "The LORD will save the tents of Judah first, so that the glory of the house of David and the glory of the inhabitants of Jerusalem shall not become greater than that of Judah.

8 "In that day the LORD will defend the inhabitants of Jerusalem; the one who is feeble among them in that day shall be like David, and the house of David *shall be* like God, like the Angel of the LORD before them.

9 "It shall be in that day *that* I will seek to [R]destroy all the nations that come against Jerusalem. Hag. 2:22

Spiritual Salvation of Judah

10 "And I will pour on the house of David and on the inhabitants of Jerusalem the Spirit of grace and supplication; then they will [R]look on Me whom they pierced. Yes, they will mourn for Him as one mourns for *his* only *son*, and grieve for Him as one grieves for a firstborn. John 19:34, 37; 20:27☆

11 "In that day there shall be a great mourning in Jerusalem, like the mourning at Hadad Rimmon in the plain of Megiddo.*

12 "And the land shall mourn, every family by itself: the family of the house of David by itself, and their wives by themselves; the family of the house of [R]Nathan by itself, and their wives by themselves; Luke 3:31

13 "the family of the house of Levi by itself, and their wives by themselves; the family of Shimei by itself, and their wives by themselves;

14 "all the families that remain, every family by itself, and their wives by themselves.

CHAPTER 13

"IN that [R]day [R]a fountain shall be opened for the house of David and for the inhabitants of Jerusalem, for sin and for [R]uncleanness. [Rev. 21:6, 7] • [Heb. 9:14] • Ezek. 36:25

2 "It shall be in that day," says the LORD of hosts, "*that* I will [R]cut off the names of the idols from the land, and they shall no longer be remembered. I will also cause [R]the prophets and the unclean spirit to depart from the land. Ex. 23:13 • Jer. 23:14, 15

3 "It shall come to pass *that* if anyone still prophesies, then his father and mother who begot him will say to him, 'You shall [R]not live,

11:11 So with MT, Tg., Vg.; LXX *the Canaanites*
12:1 Or *oracle, prophecy* **12:11** Heb. *Megiddon*

because you have spoken lies in the name of
the LORD.' And his father and mother who
begot him shall thrust him through when he
prophesies. Deut. 18:20
4 "And it shall be in that day *that* [R]every
prophet will be ashamed of his vision when
he prophesies; they will not wear [R]a robe of
coarse hair to deceive. [Mic. 3:6, 7] • 2 Kin. 1:8
5 [R]"But he will say, 'I *am* no prophet, I *am* a
farmer; for a man taught me to keep cattle
from my youth.' Amos 7:14
6 "And *one* will say to him, [R]'What are these
wounds between your arms?'* Then he will
answer, '*Those* with which I was wounded in
the house of my friends.' John 20:25, 27☆

7 "Awake, O sword, against [R]My Shepherd,
Against the Man [R]who is My
Companion," Is. 40:11 • [John 10:30]
Says the LORD of hosts.
[R]"Strike the Shepherd, Matt. 26:31, 56, 67☆
And the sheep will be scattered;
Then I will turn My hand against [R]the
little ones. Luke 12:32
8 And it shall come to pass in all the land,"
Says the LORD,
"*That* [R]two-thirds in it shall be cut off *and*
die, Ezek. 5:2, 4, 12
But *one*-third shall be left in it:
9 I will bring the *one*-third [R]through the
fire, Is. 48:10
Will refine them as silver is refined,
And test them as gold is tested.
[R]They will call on My name, Ps. 50:15
And I will answer them.
[R]I will say, 'This *is* My people';
And each one will say, 'The LORD *is* my
God.'" Hos. 2:23

CHAPTER 14

Final Siege of Jerusalem

BEHOLD, [R]the day of the LORD is coming,
And your [T]spoil will be divided in your
midst. [Is. 13:6, 9] • *plunder* or *booty*
2 For [R]I will gather all the nations to battle
against Jerusalem; Zech. 12:2, 3
The city shall be taken,
The houses [T]rifled, Or *plundered*
And the women ravished.
Half of the city shall go into captivity,
But the remnant of the people shall not
be cut off from the city.

Second Coming of the Messiah

3 Then the LORD will go forth
And fight against those nations,
As He fights in the day of battle.
4 And in that day His feet will stand [R]on
the Mount of Olives, Ezek. 11:23
Which faces Jerusalem on the east.
And the Mount of Olives shall be split in
two,
From east to west,
[R]*Making* a very large valley; Joel 3:12
Half of the mountain shall move toward
the north
And half of it toward the south.
5 Then you shall flee *through* My
mountain valley,
For the mountain valley shall reach to
Azal.
Yes, you shall flee
As you fled from the earthquake
In the days of Uzziah king of Judah.

Thus the LORD my God will come,
And all the saints with You.*

6 It shall come to pass in that day
That there will be no light;
The lights will diminish.
7 It shall be one day
[R]Which is known to the LORD—
Neither day nor night. Matt. 24:36
But at [R]evening time it shall happen
That it will be light. Is. 30:26
8 And in that day it shall be
That living [R]waters shall flow from
Jerusalem, Ezek. 47:1–12
Half of them toward [T]the eastern sea
And half of them toward [T]the western
sea; The Dead Sea • The Mediterranean Sea
In both summer and winter it shall occur.

Kingdom of the Messiah

9 And the LORD shall be [R]King over all the
earth. [Rev. 11:15]
In that day it shall be—
"The LORD *is* one,"*
And His name one.

10 All the land shall be turned into a plain
from Geba to Rimmon south of Jerusalem. *Je-
rusalem** shall be raised up and [R]inhabited in
her place from Benjamin's Gate to the place
of the First Gate and the Corner Gate, [R]and
from the Tower of Hananel to the king's wine-
presses. Zech. 12:6 • Jer. 31:38

11 *The people* shall dwell in it;
And [R]no longer shall there be utter
destruction, Jer. 31:40
But Jerusalem shall be safely inhabited.

12 And this shall be the plague with which
the LORD will strike all the people who fought
against Jerusalem:

Their flesh shall [T]dissolve while they
stand on their feet, Lit. *decay*

13:6 Or *hands* **14:5** Or *you;* LXX, Tg., Vg. *Him*
14:9 Cf. Deut. 6:4 **14:10** Lit. *She*

Their eyes shall dissolve in their sockets,
And their tongues shall dissolve in their
mouths.

13 It shall come to pass in that day
That [R]a great panic from the LORD will
be among them. 1 Sam. 14:15, 20
Everyone will seize the hand of his
neighbor,
And raise [R]his hand against his
neighbor's hand; Judg. 7:22
14 Judah also will fight at Jerusalem.
[R]And the wealth of all the surrounding
nations Ezek. 39:10, 17
Shall be gathered together:
Gold, silver, and apparel in great
abundance.

15 [R]Such also shall be the plague
On the horse *and* the mule,
On the camel and the donkey,
And on all the cattle that will be in those
camps. Zech. 14:12
So *shall* this plague *be*.

16 And it shall come to pass *that* everyone
who is left of all the nations which came
against Jerusalem shall go up from year to
year to worship the King, the LORD of hosts,
and to keep the Feast of Tabernacles.
17 And it shall be *that* whichever of the fam-
ilies of the earth do not come up to Jerusalem
to worship the King, the LORD of hosts, on
them there will be no rain.
18 If the family of [R]Egypt will not come up
and enter in, they *shall have* no *rain;* they
shall receive the plague with which the LORD
strikes the nations who do not come up to
keep the Feast of Tabernacles. Is. 19:21
19 This shall be the [T]punishment of Egypt
and the punishment of all the nations that do
not come up to keep the Feast of Taberna-
cles. Lit. *sin*
20 In that day [R]"HOLINESS TO THE LORD"
shall be *engraved* on the bells of the horses.
The pots in the LORD's house shall be like the
bowls before the altar. Is. 23:18
21 Yes, every pot in Jerusalem and Judah
shall be holiness to the LORD of hosts.* Every-
one who sacrifices shall come and take them
and cook in them. In that day there shall no
longer be a Canaanite [R]in the house of the
LORD of hosts. [Eph. 2:19–22]

14:21 Or *on every pot . . . shall be engraved "HOLINESS TO THE LORD OF HOSTS"*

THE BOOK OF

MALACHI

THE BOOK OF MALACHI

Malachi, a prophet in the days of Nehemiah, directs his message of judgment to a people plagued with corrupt priests, wicked practices, and a false sense of security in their privileged relationship with God. Using the question-and-answer method, Malachi probes deeply into their problems of hypocrisy, infidelity, mixed marriages, divorce, false worship, and arrogance. So sinful has the nation become that God's words to the people no longer have any impact. For four hundred years after Malachi's ringing condemnations, God remains silent. Only with the coming of John the Baptist (3:1) does God again communicate to His people through a prophet's voice.

The meaning of the name *Mal'aki* ("My Messenger") is probably a shortened form of *Mal'akya*, "Messenger of Yahweh"; and it is appropriate to the book, which speaks of the coming of the "messenger of the covenant" ("messenger" is mentioned three times in 2:7; 3:1). The Septuagint used the title *Malachias* even though it also translated it "by the hand of his messenger." The Latin title is *Maleachi*.

THE AUTHOR OF MALACHI

The only Old Testament mention of Malachi is in 1:1. The authorship, date, and unity of Malachi have never been seriously challenged. The unity of the book can be seen in the dialectic style that binds it together. Nothing is known of Malachi (not even his father's name), but a Jewish tradition says that he was a member of the Great Synagogue (see "The Author of Zechariah").

THE TIME OF MALACHI

Although an exact date cannot be established for Malachi, internal evidence can be used to deduce an approximate date. The Persian term for governor, *pechah* (1:8; cf. Neh. 5:14; Hag. 1:1, 14; 2:21), indicates that this book was written during the Persian domination of Israel (539–333 B.C.). Sacrifices were being offered in the temple (1:7–10; 3:8), which was rebuilt in 516 B.C. Evidently many years had passed since the offerings were instituted, because the priests had grown tired of them and corruptions had crept into the system. In addition, Malachi's oracle was inspired by the same problems that Nehemiah faced: corrupt priests (1:6—2:9; Neh. 13:1–9), neglect of tithes and offerings (3:7–12; Neh. 13:10–13), and intermarriage with pagan wives (2:10–16; Neh. 13:23–28). Nehemiah came to Jerusalem in 444 B.C. to rebuild the city walls, thirteen years after Ezra's return and reforms (457 B.C.). Nehemiah returned to Persia in 432 B.C., but came back to Palestine about 425 B.C. and dealt with the sins described in Malachi. It is therefore likely that Malachi proclaimed his message while Nehemiah was absent between 432 B.C. and 425 B.C., almost a century after Haggai and Zechariah began to prophesy (520 B.C.).

THE CHRIST OF MALACHI

The Book of Malachi is the prelude to four hundred years of prophetic silence, broken finally by the words of the next prophet, John the Baptist: "Behold! The Lamb of God who takes away the sin of the world!" (John 1:29). Malachi predicts the coming of the messenger who will clear the way before the Lord (3:1; cf. Is. 40:3). John the Baptist later fulfills this prophecy, but the next few verses (3:2–5) jump ahead to Christ in His second advent. This is also true of the prophecy of the appearance of "Elijah the prophet" (4:5). John the Baptist was this Elijah (Matt. 3:3; 11:10–14; 17:9–13; Mark 1:3; 9:10, 11; Luke 1:17; 3:4; John 1:23), but Elijah will also appear before the second coming of Christ.

KEYS TO MALACHI

Key Word: An Appeal to Backsliders—The divine dialogue in Malachi's prophecy is designed as an appeal to break through the barrier of Israel's disbelief, disappointment, and discouragement. The promised time of prosperity has not yet come, and the prevailing attitude that it is not worth serving God becomes evident in their moral and religious corruption. However, God reveals His continuing love in spite of Israel's lethargy. His appeal in this oracle is for the people and priests to stop and realize that their lack of blessing is not caused by God's lack of concern, but by their disobedience of the covenant law. When they repent and return to God with sincere hearts, the obstacles to the flow of divine blessing will be removed. Malachi also reminds the people that a day of reckoning will surely come when God will judge the righteous and the wicked.

Key Verses: Malachi 2:17—3:1; 4:5, 6—"You have wearied the LORD with your words; yet you say, 'In what way have we wearied *Him?*' In that you say, 'Everyone who does evil *is* good in the sight of the LORD, and He delights in them' or, 'Where *is* the God of justice?' "

"'Behold, I send My messenger, and he will prepare the way before Me. And the Lord, whom you seek, will suddenly come to His temple, even the Messenger of the covenant, in whom you delight. Behold, He is coming,' says the LORD of hosts" (2:17—3:1).

"Behold, I will send you Elijah the prophet before the coming of the great and dreadful day of the LORD. And he will turn the hearts of the fathers to the children, and the hearts of the children to their fathers, lest I come and strike the earth with a curse" (4:5, 6).

Key Chapter: Malachi 3—The last book of the Old Testament concludes with a dramatic prophecy of the coming of the Lord and John the Baptist: "I send My messenger, and he will prepare the way before Me" (3:1). Israel flocked to the Jordan four hundred years later when "the voice of one crying in the wilderness: 'Prepare the way of the LORD'" (Matt. 3:3) was heard, breaking the long silence of prophetic revelation. Malachi 3 and 4 record the coming of the Messiah and His forerunner.

SURVEY OF MALACHI

The great prophecies of Haggai and Zechariah are not yet fulfilled, and the people of Israel become disillusioned and doubtful. They begin to question God's providence as their faith imperceptibly degenerates into cynicism. Internally, they wonder whether it is worth serving God after all. Externally, these attitudes surface in mechanical observances, empty ritual, cheating on tithes and offerings, and crass indifference to God's moral and ceremonial law. Their priests are corrupt and their practices wicked, but they are so spiritually insensitive that they wonder why they are not being blessed by God.

Using a probing series of questions and answers, God seeks to pierce their hearts of stone. In each case the divine accusations are denied: How has God loved us? (1:2–5); How have we (priests) despised God's name? (1:6—2:9); How have we (people) profaned the covenant? (2:10–16); How have we wearied God? (2:17—3:6); How have we robbed God? (3:7–12); How have we spoken against God? (3:13–15). In effect, the people sneer, "Oh, come on now: it's not that bad!" However, their rebellion is quiet, not open. As their perception of God grows dim, the resulting materialism and externalism become settled characteristics that later grip the religious parties of the Pharisees and Sadducees. In spite of all this, God still loves His people and once again extends His grace to any who will humbly turn to Him. Malachi explores: the privilege of the nation (1:1–5), the pollution of the nation (1:6—3:15), and the promise to the nation (3:16—4:6).

The Privilege of the Nation (1:1–5): The Israelites blind themselves to God's love for them. Wallowing in the problems of the present, they are forgetful of God's works for them in the past. God gives them a reminder of His special love by contrasting the fates of Esau (Edom) and Jacob (Israel).

The Pollution of the Nation (1:6—3:15): The priests have lost all respect for God's name and in their greed offer only diseased and imperfect animals on the altar. They have more respect for the Persian governor than they do for the living God. Moreover, God is withholding His blessings from them because of their disobedience to God's covenant and because of their insincere teaching.

The people are indicted for their treachery in divorcing the wives of their youth in order to marry foreign women (2:10–16). In response to their questioning the justice of God, they receive a promise of the Messiah's coming but also a warning of the judgment that He will bring (2:17—3:6). The people have robbed God of the

FOCUS	PRIVILEGE OF THE NATION	POLLUTION OF THE NATION		PROMISE TO THE NATION		
REFERENCE	1:1—	1:6—	2:10—	3:16—	4:1—	4:4—4:6
DIVISION	LOVE OF GOD FOR THE NATION	SIN OF THE PRIESTS	SIN OF THE PEOPLE	BOOK OF REMEMBRANCE	COMING OF CHRIST	COMING OF ELIJAH
TOPIC	PAST	PRESENT		FUTURE		
	CARE OF GOD	COMPLAINT OF GOD		COMING OF GOD		
LOCATION	JERUSALEM					
TIME	c. 432–425 B.C.					

tithes and offerings due Him, but God is ready to bless them with abundance if they will put Him first (3:7–12). The final problem is the arrogant challenge to the character of God (3:13–15), and this challenge is answered in the remainder of the book.

The Promise to the Nation (3:16—4:6): The Lord assures His people that a time is coming when the wicked will be judged and those who fear Him will be blessed. The day of the Lord will reveal that it is not "useless to serve God" (3:14).

Malachi ends on the bitter word "curse." Although the people are finally cured of idolatry, there is little spiritual progress in Israel's history. Sin abounds, and the need for the coming Messiah is greater than ever.

OUTLINE OF MALACHI

CHAPTER 1

The Privilege of the Nation

THE burden* of the word of the LORD to Israel [T]by Malachi. Lit. *by the hand of*

2 "I[R] have loved you," says the LORD.
"Yet you say, 'In what way have You loved us?' Deut. 4:37; 7:8; 23:5
Was not Esau Jacob's brother?"
Says the LORD.
"Yet [R]Jacob I have loved; Rom. 9:13
3 But Esau I have hated,
And [R]laid waste his mountains and his heritage Jer. 49:18
For the jackals of the wilderness."

4 Even though Edom has said,
"We have been impoverished,
But we will return and build the desolate places,"

Thus says the LORD of hosts:

"They may build, but I will [R]throw down;
They shall be called the Territory of Wickedness, Jer. 49:16–18
And the people against whom the LORD will have indignation forever.
5 Your eyes shall see,
And you shall say,
[R]'The LORD is magnified beyond the border of Israel.' Ps. 35:27

The Priests Despise the Name of the Lord

6 "A son [R]honors *his* father, [Ex. 20:12]
And a servant *his* master.
[R]If then I am the Father, Luke 6:46
Where *is* My honor?
And if I *am* a Master,
Where *is* My reverence?
Says the LORD of hosts
To you priests who despise My name.
[R]Yet you say, 'In what way have we despised Your name?' Mal. 2:14

7 "You offer [R]defiled food on My altar,
But say, Deut. 15:21
'In what way have we defiled You?'
By saying,
'The table of the LORD is contemptible.'
8 And [R]when you offer the blind as a sacrifice, Lev. 22:22
Is it not evil?
And when you offer the lame and sick,
Is it not evil?
Offer it then to your governor!
Would he be pleased with you?
Would he [R]accept you favorably?"
Says the LORD of hosts. [Job 42:8]

9 "But now entreat God's favor,
That He may be gracious to us.
[R]*While* this is being *done* by your hands,
Will He accept you favorably?" Hos. 13:9
Says the LORD of hosts.
10 "Who *is there* even among you who would shut the doors,
[R]So that you would not kindle fire *on* My altar in vain? 1 Cor. 9:13
I have no pleasure in you,"
Says the LORD of hosts,

1:1 Or *oracle, prophecy*

R"Nor will I accept an offering from your
hands. Is. 1:11
11 For Rfrom the rising of the sun, even to
its going down, Is. 59:19
My name *shall be* great Ramong the
Gentiles; Is. 60:3, 5
RIn every place Rincense *shall be* offered
to My name, 1 Tim. 2:8 • Rev. 8:3
And a pure offering;
RFor My name shall be great among the
nations," Is. 66:18, 19
Says the LORD of hosts.

12"But you profane it,
In that you say,
'The table of the LORD* is defiled;
And its fruit, its food, *is* contemptible.'
13 You also say,
'Oh, what a Rweariness!' Is. 43:22
And you sneer at it,"
Says the LORD of hosts.
"And you bring the stolen, the lame, and
the sick;
Thus you bring an offering!
RShould I accept this from your hand?"
Says the LORD. Lev. 22:20
14"But cursed *be* Rthe deceiver Mal. 1:8
Who has in his flock a male,
And takes a vow,
But sacrifices to the Lord Rwhat is
blemished— Lev. 22:18–20
For RI *am* a great King," Ps. 47:2
Says the LORD of hosts,
"And My name *is to be* feared among the
nations.

CHAPTER 2

The Lord Curses the Priests

"AND now, O Rpriests, this
commandment is for you. Mal. 1:6
2RIf you will not hear, [Deut. 28:15]
And if you will not take *it* to heart,
To give glory to My name,"
Says the LORD of hosts,
"I will send a curse upon you,
And I will curse your blessings.
Yes, I have cursed them already,
Because you do not take *it* to heart.

3"Behold, I will rebuke your descendants
And spread refuse on your faces,
The refuse of your solemn feasts;
And *one* will take you away with it.
4 Then you shall know that I have sent this
commandment to you,
That My covenant with Levi may
continue,"
Says the LORD of hosts.
5"MyR covenant was with him, *one* of life
and peace, Num. 25:12
And I gave them to him R*that he might*
fear *Me;* Deut. 33:9
So he feared Me
And was reverent before My name.
6 The law of truth* was in his mouth,
And injustice was not found on his lips.
He walked with Me in peace and equity,
And turned many away from iniquity.

7"ForR the lips of a priest should keep
knowledge, Deut. 17:8–11
And *people* should seek the law from his
mouth;
RFor he is the messenger of the LORD of
hosts. [Gal. 4:14]
8 But you have departed from the way;
You Rhave caused many to stumble at the
law. Jer. 18:15
RYou have corrupted the covenant of
Levi," Neh. 13:29
Says the LORD of hosts.
9"Therefore RI also have made you
contemptible and base 1 Sam. 2:30
Before all the people,
Because you have not kept My ways
But have shown partiality in the law."

The People Commit Idolatry

10RHave we not all one Father? 1 Cor. 8:6
RHas not one God created us? Job 31:15
Why do we deal treacherously with one
another
By profaning the covenant of the fathers?

11 Judah has dealt treacherously,
And an abomination has been
committed in Israel and in Jerusalem,

1:12 So with Bg.; MT *Lord* **2:6** Or *True instruction*

2:10 God the Father of All—The Fatherhood of God applies in a general sense to everyone since all men and women are created by God in His image. Thus their creaturehood is derived from His Fatherhood. This fact is demonstrated by Hebrews 12:9, which speaks of God as "the Father of spirits" (cf. Page 150—Num. 16:22; Page 670—Eccl. 12:7). Paul even agrees with a heathen poet that all people are God's offspring (Page 1133—Acts 17:28). He does not mean, of course, that everyone will have eternal life but that all men and women are the offspring of God in their created natures. James says that people still bear this image (Page 1273—James 3:9).

God is also the Father of all as sustainer of life. Every person is an object of His fatherly care (Page 996—Matt. 18:10) and a candidate for His kingdom (Page 1066—Luke 18:16). Furthermore, God is not willing that any should perish (Page 996—Matt. 18:14; Page 1237—1 Tim. 2:4). Even when men and women reject God He still provides for them as He does believers with rain, fruitful seasons, food, and gladness (Page 982—Matt. 5:45; Page 1128—Acts 14:17).

Now turn to Page 979—Matt. 3:17: God the Father of Christ.

For Judah has [R]profaned Ezra 9:1, 2
The LORD's holy *institution* which He
loves:
He has married the daughter of a foreign
god.
12 May the LORD cut off from the tents of
Jacob
The man who does this, being awake and
aware,*
Yet [R]who brings an offering to the LORD
of hosts! Neh. 13:29

13 And this is the second thing you do:
You cover the altar of the LORD with tears,
With weeping and crying;
So He does not regard the offering
anymore,
Nor receive *it* with goodwill from your
hands.

The People Divorce

14 Yet you say, "For what reason?"
Because the LORD has been witness
Between you and [R]the wife of your
youth, Mal. 3:5
With whom you have dealt
treacherously;
[R]Yet she is your companion Prov. 2:17
And your wife by covenant.
15 But [R]did He not make *them* one,
Having a remnant of the Spirit?
And why one? Matt. 19:4, 5
He seeks [R]godly offspring. [1 Cor. 7:14]
Therefore take heed to your spirit,
And let none deal treacherously with the
wife of his youth.

16 "For [R]the LORD God of Israel says
That He hates divorce,
For it covers one's garment with
violence," [Matt. 5:31; 19:6–8]
Says the LORD of hosts.
"Therefore take heed to your spirit,
That you do not deal treacherously."

The Lord Will Judge at His Coming

17 [R]You have wearied the LORD with your
words; Is. 43:22, 24
Yet you say,
"In what way have we wearied *Him?*"
In that you say,
[R]"Everyone who does evil Is. 5:20
Is good in the sight of the LORD,
And He delights in them,"
Or, "Where *is* the God of justice?"

CHAPTER 3

"BEHOLD, [R]I send My messenger,
And he will [R]prepare the way
before Me. Matt. 11:10☆ • [Is. 40:3]
And the Lord, whom you seek,
Will suddenly come to His temple,
[R]Even the Messenger of the covenant,
In whom you delight. Is. 63:9
Behold, [R]He is coming," Hab. 2:7
Says the LORD of hosts.

2 "But who can endure [R]the day of His
coming? [Mal. 4:1]
And [R]who can stand when He appears?
For He *is* like a refiner's fire Rev. 6:17
And like launderers' soap.
3 [R]He will sit as a refiner and a purifier of
silver; Is. 1:25
He will purify the sons of Levi,
And purge them as gold and silver,
That they may [R]offer to the LORD
An offering in righteousness. [1 Pet. 2:5]

4 "Then [R]the offering of Judah and
Jerusalem Mal. 1:11
Will be [T]pleasant to the LORD, *pleasing*
As in the days of old,
As in former years.
5 And I will come near you for judgment;
I will be a swift witness
Against sorcerers,
Against adulterers,
[R]Against perjurers, Zech. 5:4
Against those who [R]exploit wage earners
and [R]widows and orphans, James 5:4
And against those who turn away an
alien— Ex. 22:22
Because they do not fear Me,"
Says the LORD of hosts.

The People Rob God

6 "For I *am* the LORD, [R]I do not change;
[R]Therefore you are not consumed, O sons
of Jacob. [Rom. 11:29] • [Lam. 3:22]
7 Yet from the days of [R]your fathers
You have gone away from My
ordinances Acts 7:51
And have not kept *them*.
[R]Return to Me, and I will return to you,"
Says the LORD of hosts. Zech. 1:3
[R]"But you said, Mal. 1:6
'In what way shall we return?'

8 "Will a man rob God?
Yet you have robbed Me!
But you say,
'In what way have we robbed You?'
[R]In tithes and offerings. Neh. 13:10–12
9 You are cursed with a curse,
For you have robbed Me,
Even this whole nation.
10 [R]Bring all the tithes into the [R]storehouse,
That there may be food in My house,
And try Me now in this," Prov. 3:9, 10
Says the LORD of hosts, 1 Chr. 26:20
"If I will not open for you the [R]windows
of heaven Gen. 7:11

2:12 Talmud, Vg. *teacher and student*

And [R]pour out for you *such* blessing
That *there will* not *be room* enough *to*
receive it. 2 Chr. 31:10

11 "And I will rebuke [R]the devourer for your
sakes, Amos 4:9
So that he will not destroy the fruit of
your ground,
Nor shall the vine fail to bear fruit for
you in the field,"
Says the LORD of hosts;
12 "And all nations will call you blessed,
For you will be [R]a delightful land,"
Says the LORD of hosts. Dan. 8:9

The People Doubt the Character of God

13 "Your[R] words have been [T]harsh against
Me," Mal. 2:17 • Lit. *strong*
Says the LORD,
"Yet you say,
'What have we spoken against You?'
14 [R]You have said, Job 21:14
'It is useless to serve God;
What profit *is it* that we have kept His
ordinance,
And that we have walked as mourners
Before the LORD of hosts?
15 So now [R]we call the proud blessed,
For those who do wickedness are [T]raised
up; Ps. 73:12 • Lit. *built*
They even tempt God and go free.' "

The Rewards of the Book of Remembrance

16 Then those [R]who feared the LORD [R]spoke
to one another, Ps. 66:16 • Heb. 3:13
And the LORD listened and heard *them;*
So [R]a book of remembrance was written
before Him Ps. 56:8
For those who fear the LORD
And who meditate on His name.

17 "They[R] shall be Mine," says the LORD of
hosts, Ex. 19:5
"On the day that I make them My
[R]jewels.* Is. 62:3
And [R]I will spare them Ps. 103:13
As a man spares his own son who serves
him."
18 [R]Then you shall again discern [Ps. 58:11]
Between the righteous and the wicked,
Between one who serves God
And one who does not serve Him.

CHAPTER 4

The Rewards of the Coming of Christ

"FOR behold, [R]the day is coming,
Burning like an oven, [2 Pet. 3:7]
And all [R]the proud, yes, all who do
wickedly will be [R]stubble.
And the day which is coming shall burn
them up," Mal. 3:18 • Obad. 18
Says the LORD of hosts,
"That will [R]leave them neither root nor
branch. Amos 2:9
2 But to you who [R]fear My name Mal. 3:16
The [R]Sun of Righteousness shall arise
With healing in His wings; Luke 1:78
And you shall go out
And grow fat like stall-fed calves.
3 [R]You shall trample the wicked, Mic. 7:10
For they shall be ashes under the soles
of your feet
On the day that I do *this*,"
Says the LORD of hosts.

The Prophecy of the Coming of Elijah

4 "Remember the [R]Law of Moses, My
servant, Ex. 20:3
Which I commanded him in Horeb for
all Israel,
With the statutes and judgments.
5 Behold, I will send you [R]Elijah the
prophet [Matt. 11:14; 17:10–13]☆
[R]Before the coming of the great and
dreadful day of the LORD. Joel 2:31
6 And he will turn
The hearts of the fathers to the children,
And the hearts of the children to their
fathers,
Lest I come and [R]strike the earth with
[R]a curse." Is. 11:4☆ • Zech. 5:3

3:17 Lit. *special treasure*

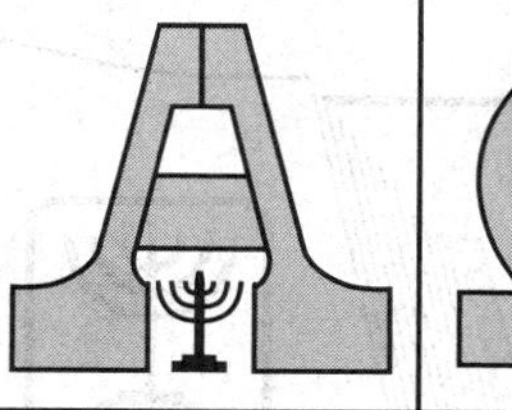

Introduction to the Visual Survey of the Bible

The book introductions in *The Open Bible®* provide background information and a survey of each book. But the "Visual Survey of the Bible" takes a further step by giving a perspective on the whole of Scripture.

Take a moment to familiarize yourself with the first chart, which compares the Old and New Testaments. Note particularly the time-line at the bottom of the page. This time line divides the Old Testament into five periods and the New Testament into two. It is the key to the rest of the charts.

As you look through the following pages, notice that each chart has its own time-line containing both biblical and extrabiblical events. The maps portray the major movement of each period; the boxes present key topics. The charts also summarize the themes of the Old Testament poetic and prophetic books and the themes of the New Testament epistles.

The ten Life Applications are an important part of this Survey. Based on the flow of each period, they crystallize the central spiritual truths of Scripture. Each principle leads into the next, and all of them relate to your own life.

VISUAL SURVEY . . .

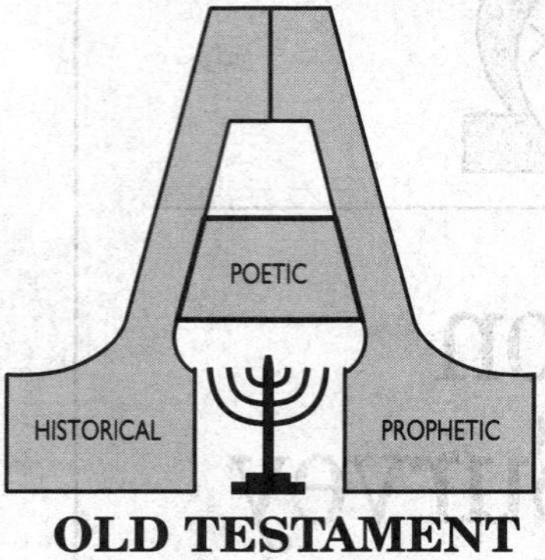

THE OLD TESTAMENT

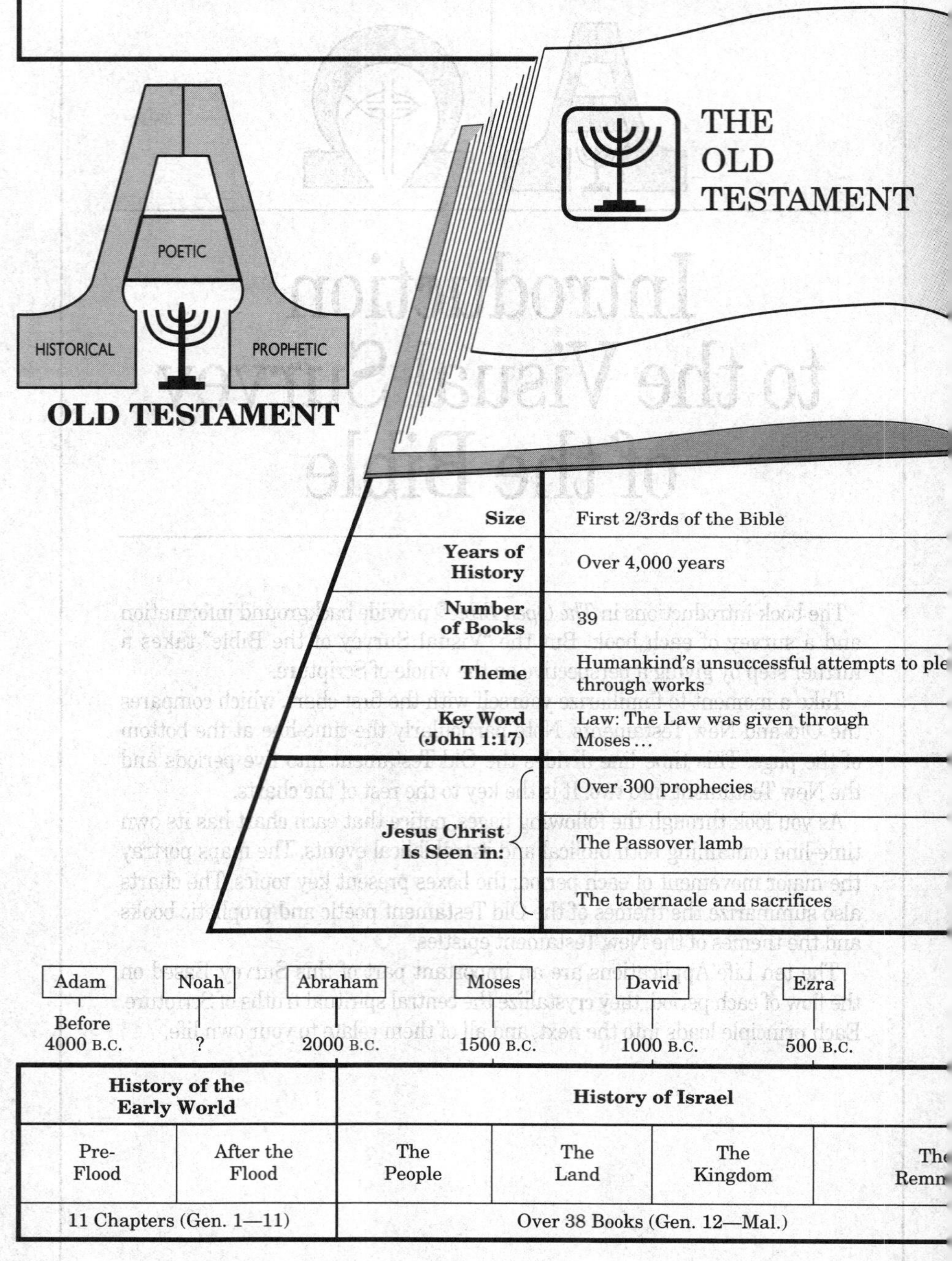

Size	First 2/3rds of the Bible
Years of History	Over 4,000 years
Number of Books	39
Theme	Humankind's unsuccessful attempts to ple through works
Key Word (John 1:17)	Law: The Law was given through Moses . . .
Jesus Christ Is Seen in:	Over 300 prophecies
	The Passover lamb
	The tabernacle and sacrifices

Adam	Noah	Abraham	Moses	David	Ezra
Before 4000 B.C.	?	2000 B.C.	1500 B.C.	1000 B.C.	500 B.C.

History of the Early World		**History of Israel**			
Pre-Flood	After the Flood	The People	The Land	The Kingdom	The Remn
11 Chapters (Gen. 1—11)		Over 38 Books (Gen. 12—Mal.)			

. . . OF THE BIBLE

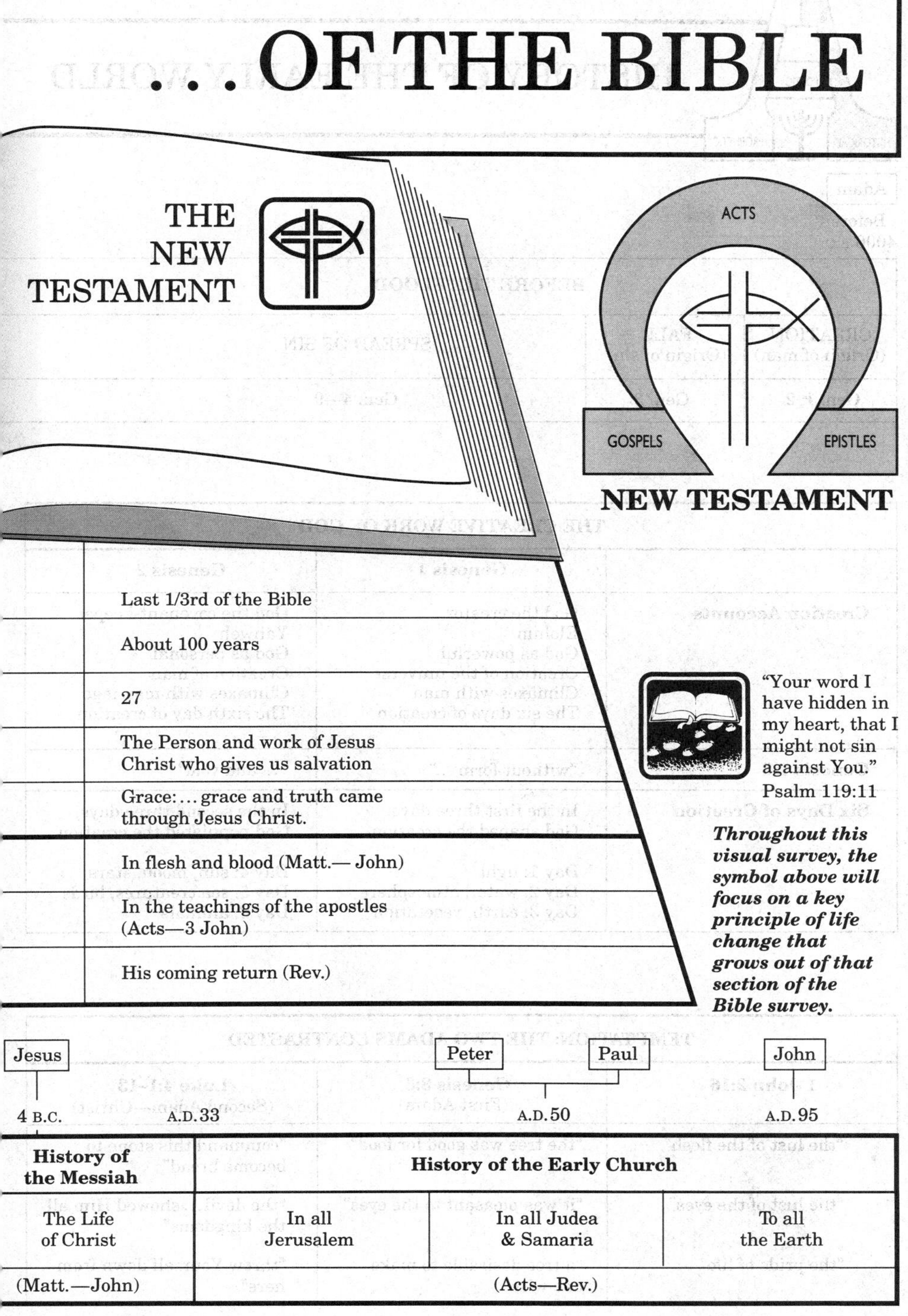

"Your word I have hidden in my heart, that I might not sin against You."
Psalm 119:11

Throughout this visual survey, the symbol above will focus on a key principle of life change that grows out of that section of the Bible survey.

Jesus — 4 B.C. — A.D. 33 — Peter, Paul — A.D. 50 — John — A.D. 95

History of the Messiah	**History of the Early Church**		
The Life of Christ	In all Jerusalem	In all Judea & Samaria	To all the Earth
(Matt.—John)	(Acts—Rev.)		

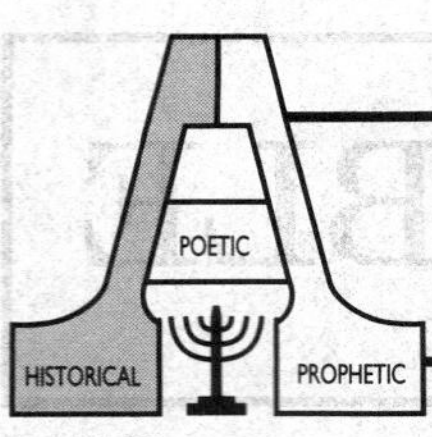

HISTORY OF THE EARLY WORLD

Adam

Before
4000 B.C.

BEFORE THE FLOOD		
CREATION (Origin of man)	FALL (Origin of sin)	SPREAD OF SIN
Gen. 1; 2	Gen. 3	Gen. 4—9

THE CREATIVE WORK OF GOD		
	Genesis 1	**Genesis 2**
Creation Accounts	God the creator Elohim God as powerful Creation of the universe Climaxes with man The six days of creation	God the covenant-keeper Yahweh God as personal Creation of man Climaxes with marriage The sixth day of creation
Genesis 1:2	"without form …"	"… and void"
Six Days of Creation	In the first three days, God shaped the creation Day 1: light Day 2: water, atmosphere Day 3: earth, vegetation	In the second three days, God populated the creation Day 4: sun, moon, stars Day 5: sea creatures, birds Day 6: animals

TEMPTATION: THE TWO ADAMS CONTRASTED		
1 John 2:16	**Genesis 3:6** (First Adam)	**Luke 4:1–13** (Second Adam—Christ)
"the lust of the flesh"	"the tree was good for food"	"command this stone to become bread"
"the lust of the eyes"	"it was pleasant to the eyes"	"the devil … showed Him all the kingdoms"
"the pride of life"	"a tree desirable to make one wise"	"throw Yourself down from here"

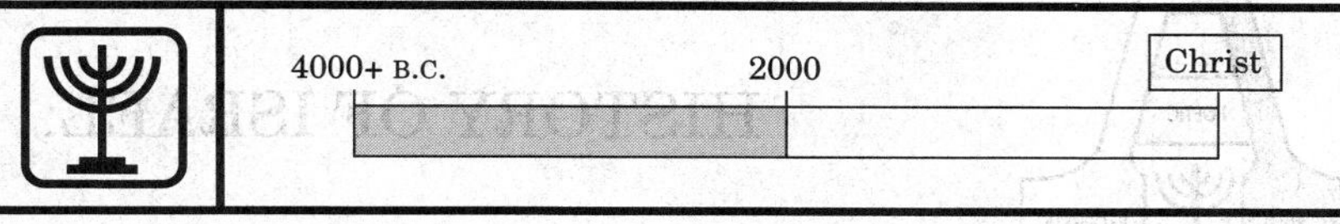

Noah		Abraham
2500 B.C.?		2000 B.C.

AFTER THE FLOOD	
FLOOD (Judgment of sin)	SPREAD OF NATIONS
Gen. 6—9	Gen. 10; 11

AGES OF THE PATRIARCHS
(Before and after the Flood)

The patriarchs who lived before the Flood had an average life span of about 900 years (Gen. 5). The ages of post-Flood patriarchs dropped rapidly and gradually leveled off (Gen. 11). Some suggest that this is due to major environmental changes brought about by the Flood.

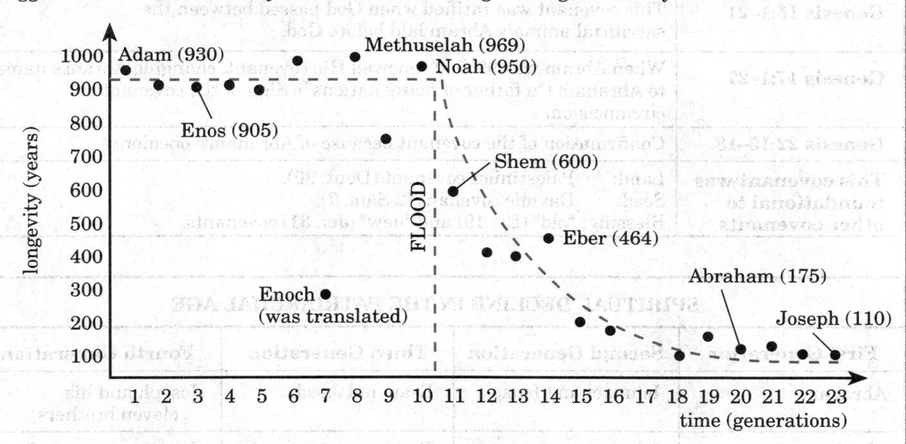

Principle: Rigteousness is creative; sin is destructive (Gen. 2:17; Rom. 6:23).

Practice: Genesis 1—11, the prologue not only to Genesis, but to the entire Bible, begins with the ordered and life-giving activity of the holy Creator. The fall of man and the consequent spread of sin stand in stark contrast to the work of God and illustrate the disorder and death that always accompany rebellion against the purposes of the Lord. God is not mocked; in a moral and spiritual universe, sin must be judged. What must you do, according to Romans 3:21–26, to escape the condemnation of your Creator?

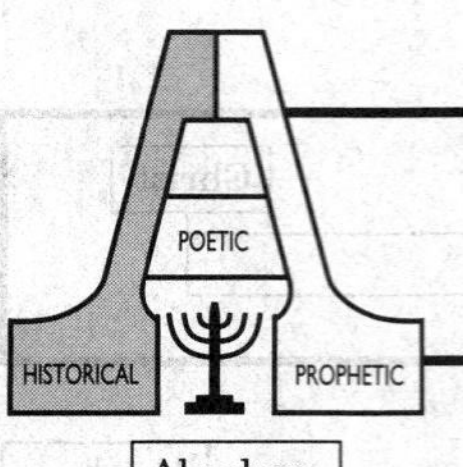

HISTORY OF ISRAEL:

Abraham 2000 B.C.	Joseph 1914 B.C.	
		THE PEOPLE
THE PATRIARCHS	BONDAGE IN EGYPT	

2165 Birth of Abraham	1991 Beginning of Egyptian Middle Kingdom	Jacob Enters Egypt with His Family	1790 Code of Hammurabi

THE ABRAHAMIC COVENANT	
Genesis 12:1–3	God initiated His covenant with Abram when he was living in Ur of the Chaldeans, promising a land, descendants, and blessing.
Genesis 12:4, 5	Abram went with his family to Haran, lived there for a time, and left at the age of 75.
Genesis 13:14–17	After Lot separated from Abram, God again promised the land to him and his descendants.
Genesis 15:1–21	This covenant was ratified when God passed between the sacrificial animals Abram laid before God.
Genesis 17:1–27	When Abram was 99 God renewed His covenant, changing Abram's name to Abraham ("a father of many nations"). Sign of the covenant: circumcision.
Genesis 22:15–18	Confirmation of the covenant because of Abraham's obedience.
This covenant was foundational to other covenants.	Land: Palestinian covenant (Deut. 30). Seed: Davidic covenant (2 Sam. 7). Blessing: "old" (Ex. 19) and "new" (Jer. 31) covenants.

SPIRITUAL DECLINE IN THE PATRIARCHAL AGE			
First Generation	**Second Generation**	**Third Generation**	**Fourth Generation**
Abraham	Ishmael and Isaac	Esau and Jacob	Joseph and his eleven brothers
Abraham: man of faith believed God	Ishmael: not son of promise Isaac: called on God believed God	Esau: unspiritual little faith Jacob: at first compromised, later turned to the Lord	Joseph: man of God showed faith Brothers: treachery, immorality, lack of separation from Canaanites
Abraham: built altars to God (Gen. 12:7, 8; 13:4, 18; 22:9)	Isaac: built an altar to God (Gen. 26:25)	Jacob: built altars to God (Gen. 33:20; 35:1, 3, 7)	No altars were built to God in the fourth generation

THE PEOPLE

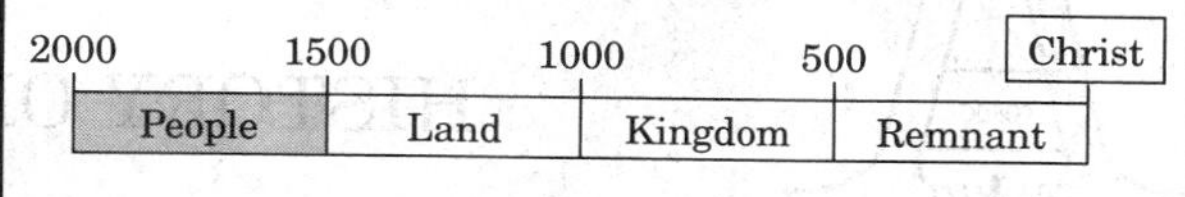

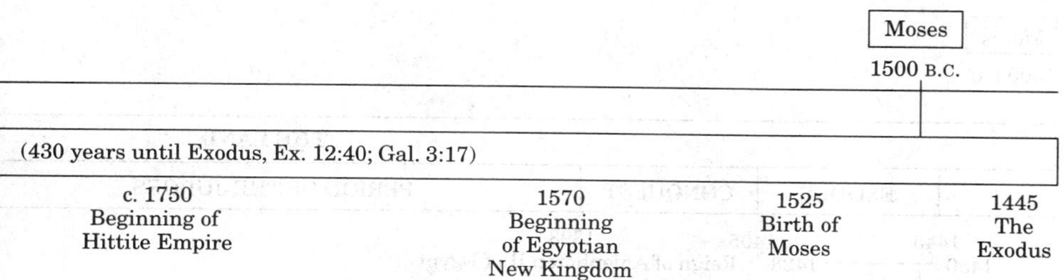

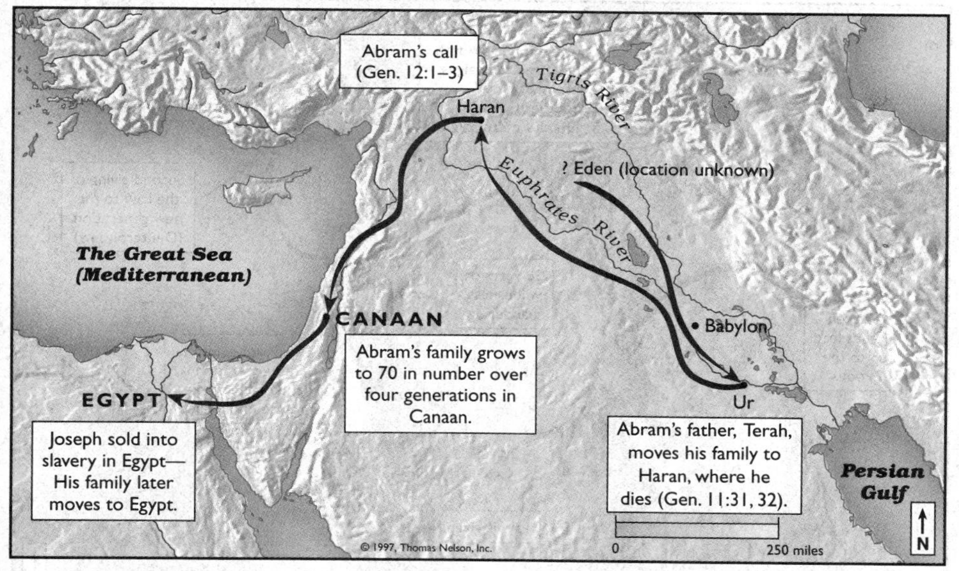

Principle: The destructiveness of sin is overcome by a faith that takes God at His word in spite of appearances and circumstances to the contrary (Gen. 15:6; John 3:16; Heb. 11:8–22).

Practice: Beginning in Genesis 12, God drew forth a man who would be the father of the people from whom and to whom the Messiah would come. Abraham became a friend of God through faith. In spite of appearances to the contrary, he went to a land he had not seen, believed God's promise of a son, and offered up that son at the same area where God's own Son would be crucified. Because he believed God, his faith was accounted to him for righteousness. In the same way, you can enter into a relationship with God by placing your trust in the Person and work of His Son. Have you made that decision?

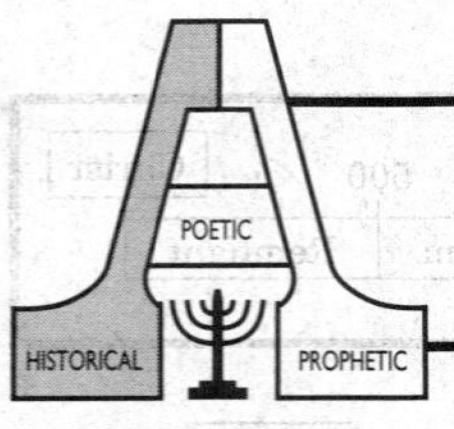

HISTORY OF ISRAEL:

Moses

1500 B.C.

			THE LAND
	EXODUS	CONQUEST	PERIOD OF THE JUDGES

1445 1405 1398
1450 ——— 1423 Reign of Amenhotep II of Egypt

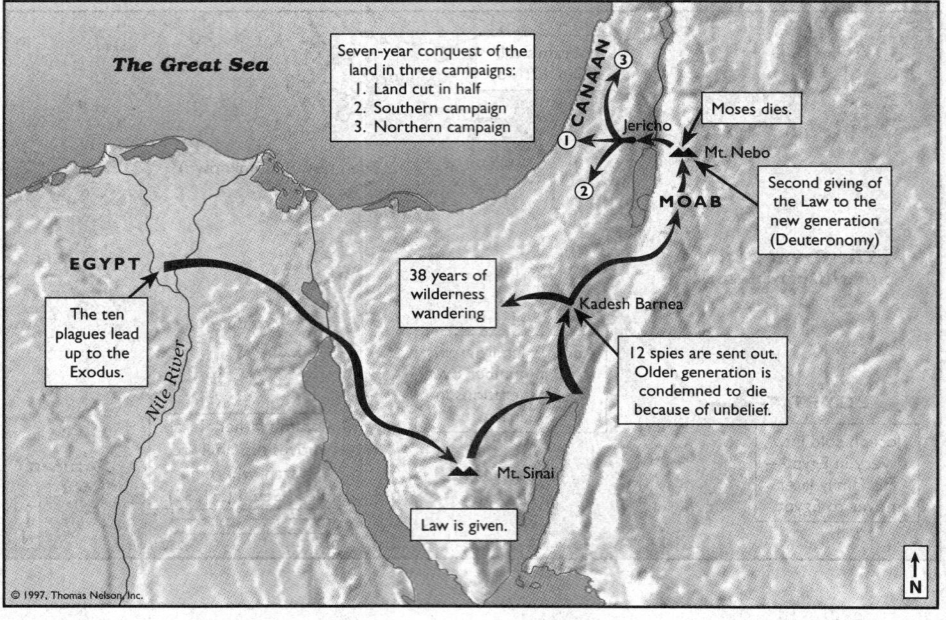

Principle: Revelation demands obedience, and obedience brings blessing (Deut. 6:1–15; Josh. 1:8; John 15:12–17).

Practice: After redeeming His people from bondage, the Lord spoke to them in power and glory at Mt. Sinai. The revelation of the Mosaic law required a response of obedience. Their success as individuals and as a nation would depend on the degree of their conformity to God's moral, civil, and ceremonial law. Likewise, disobedience would lead to disaster (e.g., the wilderness wandering and servitude in the time of the Judges). As believers in Christ, our success is measured by the degree of our conformity to His character. To what extent is Christ the Lord of your life?

THE LAND

2000 | 1500 | 1000 | 500 | Christ

People | **Land** | Kingdom | Remnant

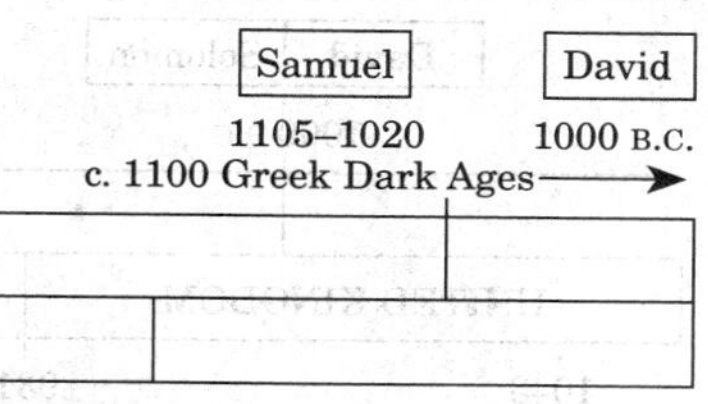

1191
Gideon beats Midianites

1043
Saul anointed King

THE LAW

After their deliverance from Egyptian bondage, the children of Israel needed to learn to walk with their God. The Law was given to instruct the people about the person and the ways of their Redeemer so that they could be set apart to a life of holiness and obedience, not to save anyone but to reveal the people's need to trust in the Lord. As Paul told the Galatians, "Therefore the law was our tutor *to bring us* to Christ, that we might be justified by faith" (Gal. 3:24).

The Law combines poetry, salvation history, legislation, and exhortation. The three major divisions of the Law (Deut. 4:44) are the testimonies (moral duties), the statutes (ceremonial duties), and the judgments or ordinances (civil and social duties). The moral portion of the Law is summarized in the Ten Commandments (Ex. 20:1–17; Deut. 5:6–21):

THE TEN COMMANDMENTS (Moral Law)		
1–4	Duties to God	"You shall love the LORD your God" (Matt. 22:37).
5–10	Duties to others	"You shall love your neighbor" (Matt. 22:39).

THE JUDGES: A CASE STUDY IN DISOBEDIENCE

Each of the seven cycles found in Judges 3:5—16:31 has five steps: sin, servitude, supplication, salvation, and silence. The cycles connect as a descending spiral of sin (2:19), with Israel vacillating between obedience and apostasy.

Cycle	Oppressor	Years of Oppression	Judge/Deliverer	Years of Peace
1. (3:7–11)	Mesopotamians	8	Othniel	40
2. (3:12–30)	Moabites	18	Ehud	80
(3:31)	Philistines		Shamgar	
3. (4:1—5:31)	Canaanites	20	Deborah/Barak	40
4. (6:1—8:32)	Midianites	7	Gideon	40
5. (8:33—10:5)	Abimelech	3	Tola/Jair	45
6. (10:6—12:15)	Ammonites	18	Jephthah/Ibzan/Elon/Abdon	6/7/10/8
7. (13:1—16:31)	Philistines	40	Samson	20

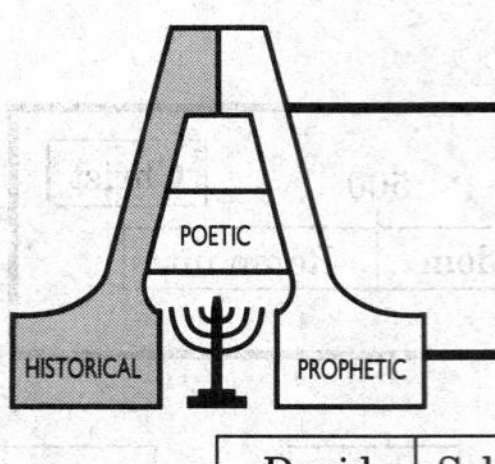

HISTORY OF ISRAEL:

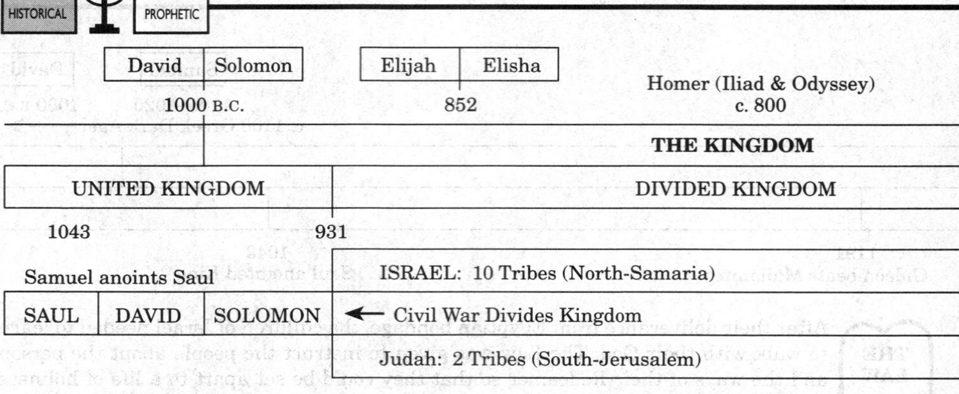

THE LIFE OF DAVID: A Man After God's Own Heart								
1041 B.C.				1011				971 B.C.
DAVID'S 70 YEARS								
David as Subject (30 Years)				David as King (40 Years)				
As a son to his father	As a servant to King Saul			King over the South		King over all 12 tribes		
	His rise over Saul 17—18	Rejected by Saul 19—26	Refuge with Philistines 27—31	Success	Growing	Growing		Crisis
Psalms	1 Samuel			2 Samuel				1 Kings
23	17	19:1–10	31	7	11	14—18	24	2:10
David the Shepherd	Kills Goliath	Protected by Jonathan	Saul and Jonathan Killed at Gilboa	Promise of Christ	Sins with Bathsheba	Absalom's Rebellion	David's Census	David Dies

Principle: Obedience grows out of a heart for God (Deut. 6:5; 1 Sam 13:14; 1 Chr. 28:9; Acts 13:22).

Practice: Saul and David are a study in contrasts. The key to Saul's failure was his lack of a heart for God; the key to David's greatness was his obvious love for the Lord. David's relationship with God became the standard by which all the kings of Judah would be measured. To know God is to love Him, and to love Him is to desire to obey Him. Read Psalm 23 as a model of a man who was intimate with God. What are the things that may be hindering your growth in the knowledge of God?

THE KINGDOM

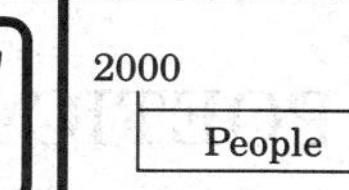

2000	1500	1000	500	Christ
People	Land	Kingdom	Remnant	

Rome Founded 753

Births of Buddha, Confucius 563 551

Ezra 500 B.C.

EXILE 586 — RETURN 516

722 ← Assyria Conquers Israel

Babylon Conquers Judah →

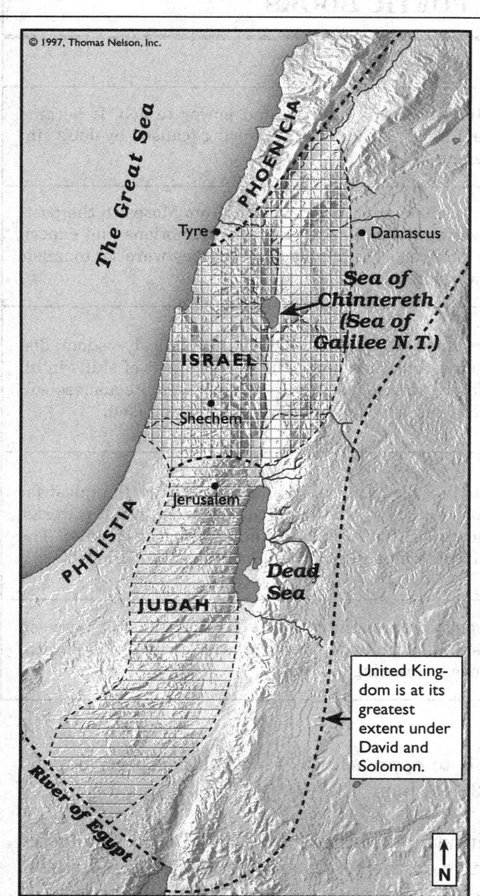

KINGS OF ISRAEL	KINGS OF JUDAH
1. Jeroboam I	1. Rehoboam
2. Nadab	2. Abijam
3. Baasha	3. Asa
4. Elah	4. Jehoshaphat
5. Zimri	5. Jehoram
6. Omri	6. Ahaziah
7. Ahab	7. Athaliah
8. Ahaziah	8. Joash
9. Jehoram	9. Amaziah
10. Jehu	10. Azariah
11. Jehoahaz	11. Jotham
12. Jehoash	12. Ahaz
13. Jeroboam II	13. Hezekiah
14. Zechariah	14. Manasseh
15. Shallum	15. Amon
16. Menahem	16. Josiah
17. Pekahiah	17. Jehoahaz
18. Pekah	18. Jehoiakim
19. Hoshea	19. Jehoiachin
	20. Zedekiah

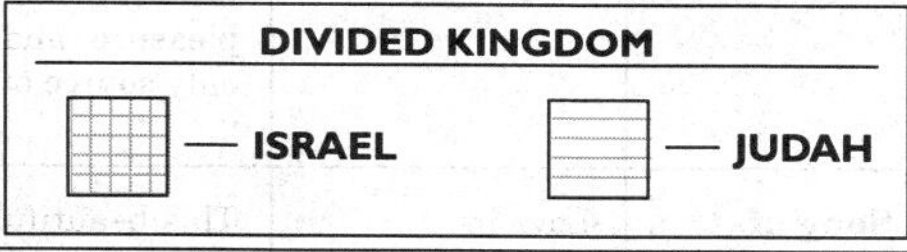

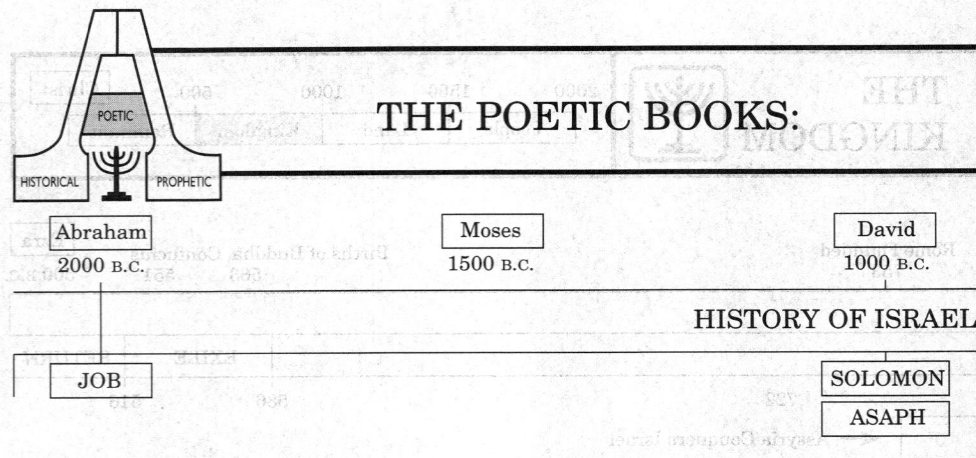

THEMES OF THE POETIC BOOKS		
BOOK	**KEY WORD**	**THEME**
Job	Sovereignty	God revealed Himself in His majesty and power to Job. It became clear that the real issue was not Job's suffering (caused by Job's sin) but God's sovereignty.
Psalms	Worship	The five books of psalms span the centuries from Moses to the post-exilic period, covering the full range of human emotions and experiences. Suited for service as the temple hymnal, they were set to music and focused on worship.
Proverbs	Wisdom	Proverbs was designed to equip the reader in practical wisdom, discernment, discipline, and discretion. The development of skills in all the details of life are stressed, so that beauty and righteousness will replace foolishness and evil through dependence upon God.
Ecclesiastes	Vanity	The Preacher applied his great mind and resources to the quest for meaning and purpose in life. He found that wisdom, wealth, works, pleasure, and power all led to futility and striving after wind. The only source of ultimate meaning and fulfillment is God Himself.
Song of Solomon	Love in Marriage	This beautiful song portrays the intimate love relationship between Solomon and his Shulamite bride. It magnifies the virtues of physical and emotional love in marriage.

Principle: To have a heart for God is to approach life from His perspective (Job 42:1–6; Ps. 1; 19; 63; 73; 119; Prov. 2:1–9; Rom. 12:1–3).

Practice: The poetic books record the struggles of men like Job, David, Solomon, and Asaph to gain a divine perspective on their lives and circumstances. As they learned to set their minds on the Person, powers, and perfections of God, their wills and emotions came into alignment with His truth. True wisdom is seeing life from God's side, and this is rooted in setting our minds (meditating) on the things above (Col. 3:1–3). Try dipping into the Psalms and Proverbs on a daily basis and prayerfully ponder what you read.

THE HEART OF THE JEWS

Ezra	Christ
500 B.C.	4 B.C.

THE PATH TO TRUE SUCCESS

Question	Principle
1. What is wisdom?	Wisdom is the key to a life of beauty, fulfillment, and purpose (Prov. 3:15–18). Wisdom is the skill in the art of living life with every area under the dominion of God. It is the ability to use the best means at the best time to accomplish the best ends.
2. How do we pursue wisdom?	The treasure of wisdom rests in the hands of God. Since it comes from above (Prov. 2:6; cf. James 3:17), we cannot attain it apart from Him.
3. What are the conditions for attaining wisdom?	True wisdom can only be gained by cultivating the fear of the Lord (Job 28:28; Ps. 86:11; 111:10; Prov. 1:7; 9:10).
4. What is the fear of the Lord?	To fear God is to have an attitude of awe and humility before Him (Prov. 15:33). It is to recognize Him as our Creator and our complete dependence upon Him in every activity of our lives.
5. Why have so few people developed this fear of God?	The temporal value system of this world is based on what is seen, while the eternal value system of Scripture is based on what is unseen (2 Cor. 4:16–18; 5:7). The former exerts a powerful influence upon us, and we struggle with giving up the seen for the unseen.
6. What can enable us to choose the eternal value system?	This choice is based on faith (believing God in spite of appearances and circumstances), and faith is based on trust.
7. How do we grow in faith?	Our ability to trust God is directly proportional to our knowledge of God. The better we know Him, the more we can trust Him.
8. How can we increase in our knowledge of God?	We become intimate with God as we talk with Him in prayer and listen to His voice in Scripture. The better we know God, the more we love Him and want to respond to His desires for our lives. Faith in God is simply trusting Him as a person, and trust is manifested in action.

THE PROPHETIC BOOKS:

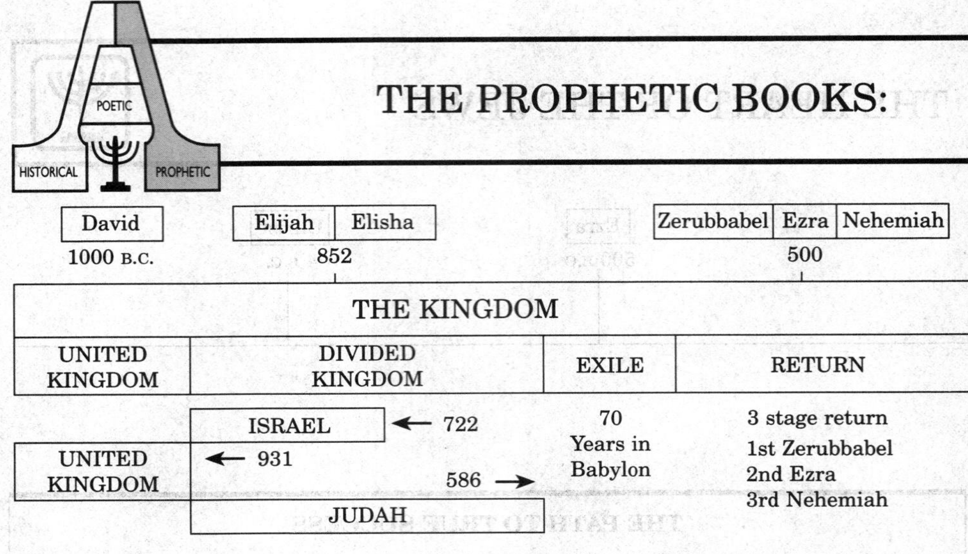

PROPHETS BEFORE THE EXILE		EXILE PROPHETS	PROPHETS AFTER THE EXILE
To Israel: Amos (760) Hosea (755) To Nineveh: Jonah (760) Nahum (660)	To Judah: Joel (835) Isaiah (740) Micah (735) Zephaniah (630) Jeremiah (627) Habakkuk (607) Lamentations (586)	To Jews in Babylon: Daniel (605) Ezekiel (592)	To the Remnant after returning: Haggai (520) Zechariah (520) Malachi (432)
To Edom: Obadiah (840)			

Principle: God's disciplines are designed to restore a heart for Himself (Jer. 17:5, 7; Joel 2:12, 13; Heb. 12:5–11).

Practice: God had to discipline His people because of their moral and spiritual rebellion and their refusal to heed the warnings of His prophets. Reproof is designed to bring repentance, and repentance brings restoration. The same prophets who pronounced the condemnation of God also announced the consolation of God. Similarly, because God loves us, He must sometimes chasten us as His children to train us in the ways of righteousness. How do you respond during these times? Are you teachable or intractable?

THE HOPE OF THE JEWS

Christ

4 B.C.

THE REMNANT

400 YEARS UNTIL CHRIST

415

THEMES OF THE PROPHETIC BOOKS

The Major Prophets

BOOK	KEY WORD	THEME
Isaiah	Salvation Is of the Lord	Twofold message of condemnation (1—39) and consolation (40—66). God's judgment on the sins of Judah, the surrounding nations, and the world, followed by future salvation and restoration.
Jeremiah	Judah's Last Hour	Declaration of certain judgment of God against Judah. God promises to establish a new covenant with His people.
Lamentations	Lamentations	This beautifully structured series of five lament poems is a funeral dirge for the fallen city of Jerusalem.
Ezekiel	Future Restoration	Ministry to the Jewish captives in Babylon before and after the fall of Jerusalem. The fate of Judah's foes and an apocalyptic vision of Judah's future.
Daniel	God's Program for Israel	Outlines God's plan for the Gentile nations (2—7) and portrays Israel during the time of Gentile domination (8—12).

The Minor Prophets

BOOK	KEY WORD	THEME
Hosea	God's Love for Israel	The story of Hosea and his faithless wife illustrates the loyal love of God and the spiritual adultery of Israel.
Joel	Day of the Lord	A recent locust plague illustrates the far more terrifying day of the Lord. God appeals to the people to repent in order to avert the coming disaster.
Amos	Judgment of Israel	In eight pronouncements of judgment, Amos spirals around the surrounding countries before landing on Israel. He lists the sins of Israel and calls for repentance.
Obadiah	Judgment of Edom	Condemns the nation of Edom (descended from Esau) for refusing to act as a brother toward Judah (descended from Jacob).
Jonah	Revival in Nineveh	The repentant response of the people of Nineveh to Jonah's one-line prophetic message caused the God of mercy to spare the city.
Micah	Judgment and Restoration of Judah	In spite of divine retribution against the corruption of Israel and Judah. God's covenant with them will be fulfilled in Messiah's future kingdom.
Nahum	Judgment of Nineveh	About 125 years after Nineveh repented under the preaching of Jonah, Micah predicted the destruction of the city because of its idolatry and brutality.
Habakkuk	Live by Faith	Troubled with God's plan to use the Babylonians as His rod of judgment of Judah, Habakkuk praises the Lord after gaining a better pespective on His power and purposes.
Zephaniah	Day of the Lord	The coming day of the Lord is a time of awesome judgment followed by great blessing. Judah stands condemned, but God will restore the fortunes of the remnant.
Haggai	Reconstruction of the Temple	After the Babylonian exile, Haggai urges the Jews to put God first and finish the temple they had begun so that they can enjoy God's blessing.
Zechariah	Prepare for the Messiah	Like Haggai, Zechariah exhorts the Jews to complete the construction of the temple. He relates it to the coming of Messiah in a series of visions and messianic prophecies.
Malachi	Appeal to Backsliders	The spiritual climate of the people had grown cold, and Malachi rebukes them for their religious and social compromise. If they return to God with sincere hearts, they will be blessed.

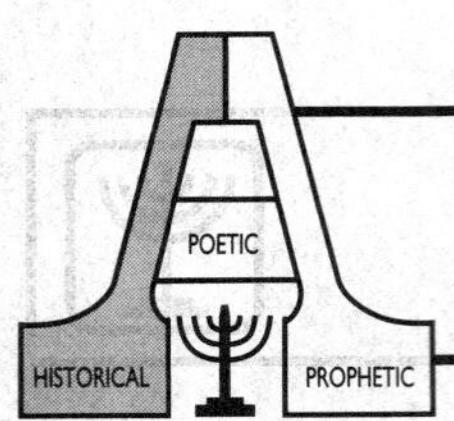

HISTORY OF ISRAEL: THE REMNANT

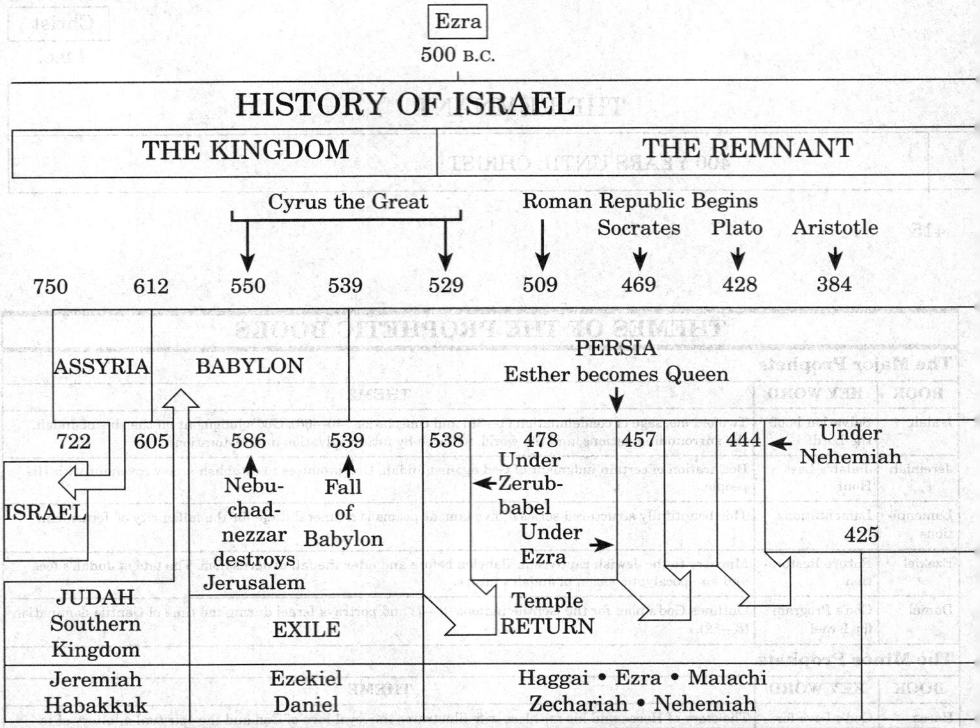

Ezra
500 B.C.

HISTORY OF ISRAEL

THE KINGDOM | THE REMNANT

Cyrus the Great
Roman Republic Begins
Socrates
Plato
Aristotle

750 612 550 539 529 509 469 428 384

ASSYRIA
BABYLON
PERSIA
Esther becomes Queen

722 605 586 539 538 478 457 444 425

Under Zerubbabel
Under Ezra
Under Nehemiah

ISRAEL

Nebuchadnezzar destroys Jerusalem

Fall of Babylon

JUDAH
Southern Kingdom

EXILE

Temple
RETURN

Jeremiah
Habakkuk

Ezekiel
Daniel

Haggai • Ezra • Malachi
Zechariah • Nehemiah

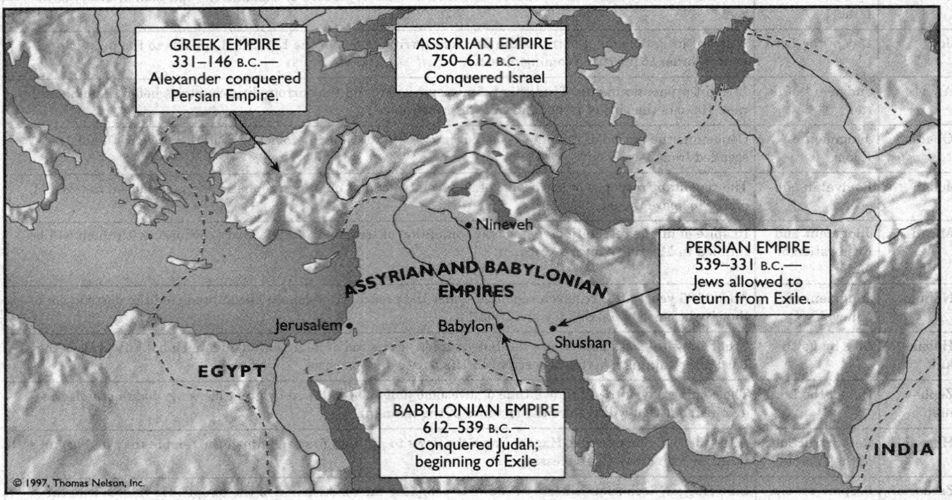

GREEK EMPIRE
331–146 B.C.—
Alexander conquered Persian Empire.

ASSYRIAN EMPIRE
750–612 B.C.—
Conquered Israel

Nineveh

ASSYRIAN AND BABYLONIAN EMPIRES

PERSIAN EMPIRE
539–331 B.C.—
Jews allowed to return from Exile.

Jerusalem
Babylon
Shushan
EGYPT

BABYLONIAN EMPIRE
612–539 B.C.—
Conquered Judah; beginning of Exile

INDIA

Bridging the Testaments

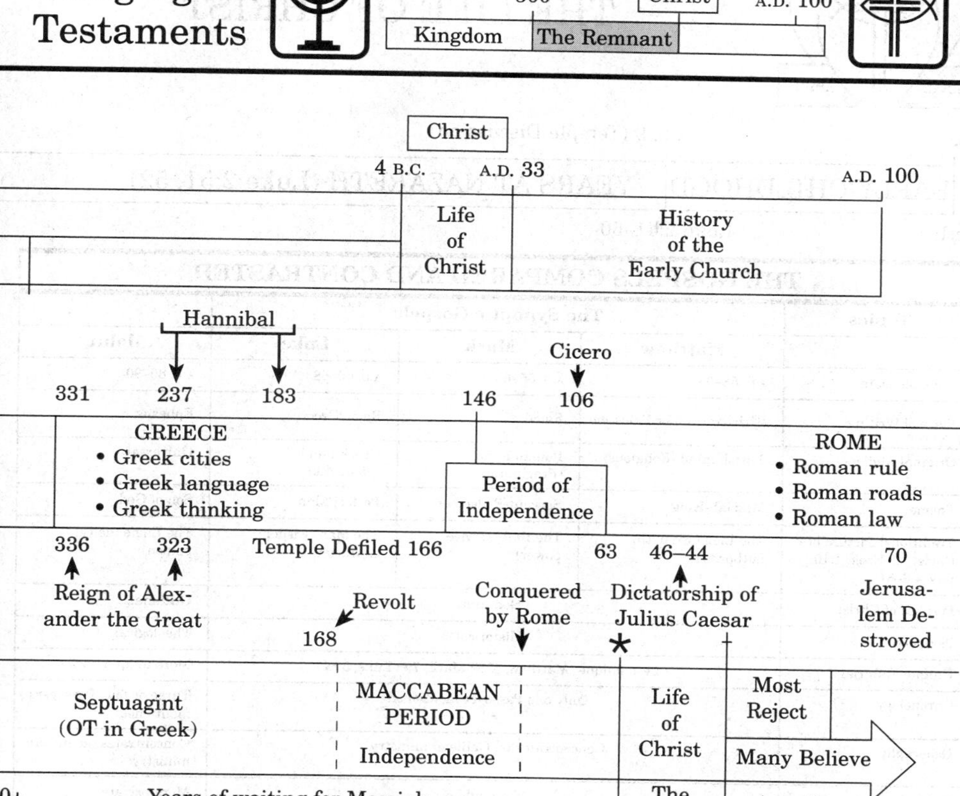

Principle: True restoration results from being molded by the Word within rather than by the world without (Ezra 7:10; 9:10–15; Is. 46:3, 4; Acts 7:51–53).

Practice: Even after the chastening of the Exile, most of the returning Jews became enmeshed once again in the affairs of the world and neglected their relationship with God. For some, the problem was external religiosity without internal reality; for others, the problem was being more influenced by culture than by Scripture. God has always had to work with a faithful minority who love Him enough to stand against the tide of the world system. Is your quality of life different from that of those who love the world more than they love the Lord?

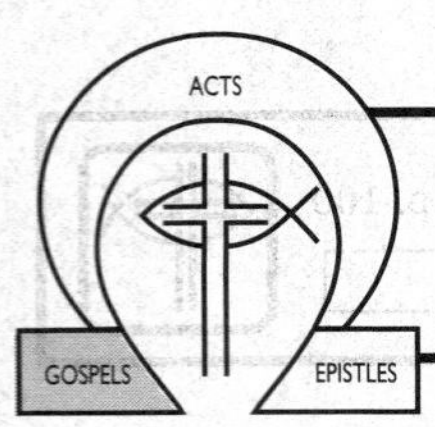

THE LIFE OF CHRIST

4 B.C. A.D. 9 (Temple Discussion)

EARLY CHILDHOOD	YEARS AT NAZARETH (Luke 2:51, 52)

Birth Luke 2:41–50

THE GOSPELS COMPARED AND CONTRASTED

Topics	The Synoptic Gospels			
	Matthew	**Mark**	**Luke**	**John**
Probable Date	A.D. 58–68	A.D. 55–65	A.D. 60–68	A.D. 80–90
Place of Writing	Syria Antioch or Palestine	Rome	Rome/Greece	Ephesus
Original Audience	Jewish mind (Religious)	Roman mind (Pragmatic)	Greek mind (Idealistic)	Universal
Theme	Messiah-King	Servant-Redeemer	Perfect Man	Son of God
Traditional Picture of Christ (cf. Ezek. 1:10; Rev. 4:6–8)	The Lion (strength, authority)	The Bull (service, power)	The Man (wisdom, character)	The Eagle (deity, person)
Portrait of Christ	God-**man**			**God**-man
Perspective	Historical			Theological
Unique Material	Less unique (Matthew, 42%; Mark, 7%; Luke, 59%)			More unique (92%)
Chronology	Only one Passover mentioned			Three or four Passovers mentioned
Geography	Concentrates on Galilean ministry			Concentrates on Judean ministry
Discourse Material	More public			More private
Teaching Method	Parables			Allegories
Teaching Emphasis	More on ethical, practical teachings			More on the Person of Christ
Relationship to Other Gospels	Complementary			Supplementary

CHRIST'S PUBLIC MINISTRY

Masses drawn to His miracles and teachings

Popularity peaks
Leaders attribute His miracles

A.D. 29	30	31
Opening events	Early Judean ministry	Great Galilean ministry
Year of curious acceptance		Year of growing hostility

Baptized by John Matt. 3 — First miracle John 2 — Nicodemus learns of new birth John 3 — Woman at well John 4 — Rejected at Nazareth Luke 4 — Apostles selected Mark 3 — Sermon on Mount Matt. 5—7

History of Israel	Life of Christ	History of Early Church
	4 B.C.	A.D. 33

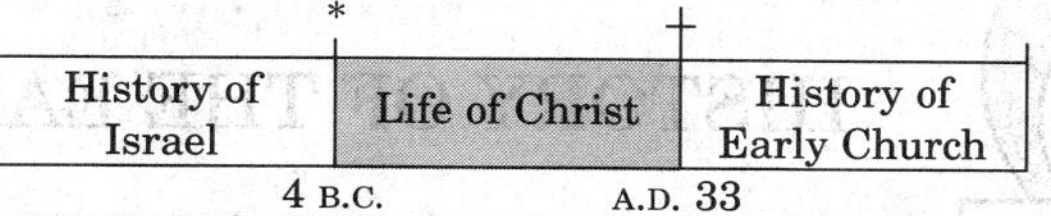

A.D. 29 A.D. 33

PUBLIC MINISTRY

Principle: Jesus, the living Word, lives His life in and through us as we walk in dependence upon Him (John 1:11, 12; 10:10; 15:4, 5; Gal. 2:20).

ractice: In Christ, God personally re-
ealed Himself in human flesh: to see Him
s to see God (John 12:45; 14:9), to know
Iim is to know God (John 8:19), to receive
Iim is to receive God (Mark 9:37), to honor
Iim is to honor God (John 5:23), and to re-
ect Him is to reject God (Luke 10:16). He is
he vine, the source of life; we are the
ranches, the channels of life. It is only as
ve draw our life from Him that we bear
asting fruit. To what extent are you look-
ng to Jesus as the true source of your se-
urity, significance, and fulfillment?

to Satan (Matt. 12:24)

Masses fall away in face of "official" rejection

	32	A.D. 33

	Later Judean ministry	Perean ministry
Years of training the apostles to carry on	Period of intense struggle leading to the Cross	

- Rejection by leaders Matt. 12
- Begin teaching in parables Matt. 13
- 12 sent out Matt. 10
- 5000 fed Mark 6
- 4000 fed Mark 8
- Transfiguration Luke 9
- 70 sent out Luke 10
- Lazarus raised John 11

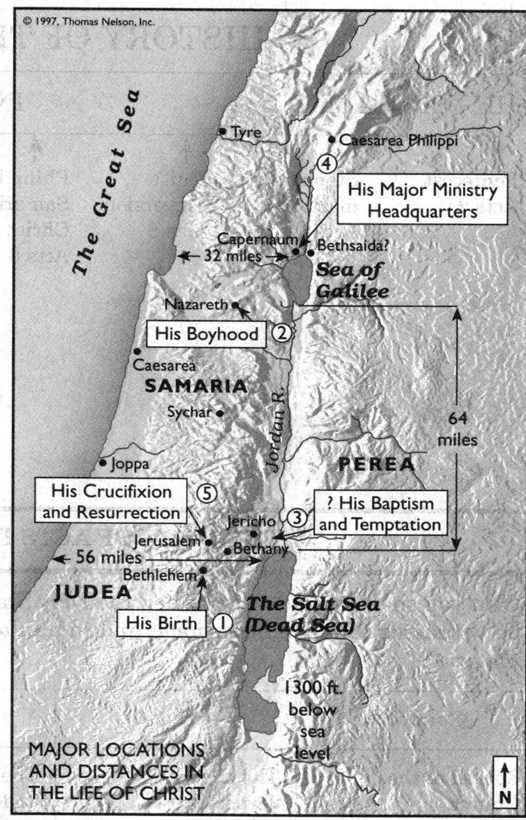

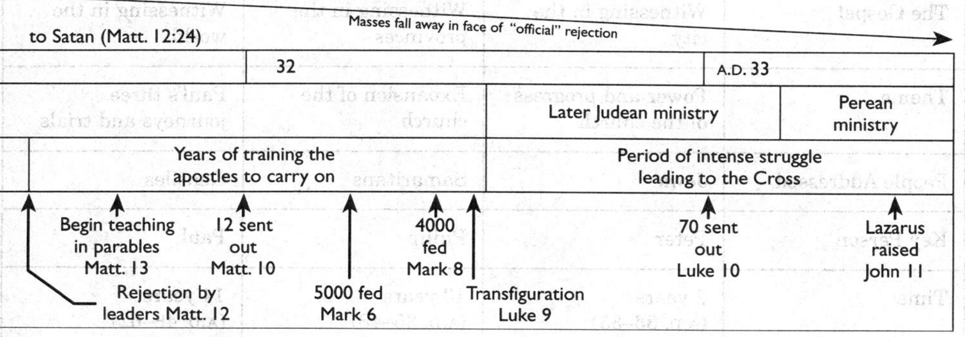

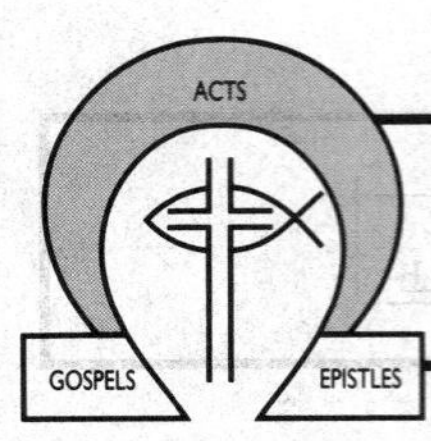

HISTORY OF THE EARLY CHURCH

A.D. 33 — 35

HISTORY OF THE EARLY CHURCH

IN JERUSALEM	IN ALL JUDEA AND SAMARIA

- Pentecost Acts 2
- Stephen martyred Acts 6
- Paul's conversion Acts 9
- Philip brings Samaritans to Christ Acts 8
- Peter brings Gentiles to Christ Acts 10

THE BOOK OF ACTS IN OVERVIEW

"But you shall receive power when the Holy Spirit has come upon you; and you shall be witnesses to Me in *Jerusalem*, and in all *Judea*, and *Samaria*, and to the *end of the earth*." (Acts 1:8).

Chapters	Acts 1–7	Acts 8–12	Acts 13–28
Spread of the Church	The church in Jerusalem	The church in all Judea and Samaria	The church to all the earth
The Gospel	Witnessing in the city	Witnessing in the provinces	Witnessing in the world
Theme	Power and progress of the church	Expansion of the church	Paul's three journeys and trials
People Addressed	Jews	Samaritans	Gentiles
Key Person	Peter	Philip	Paul
Time	2 years (A.D. 33–35)	13 years (A.D. 35–48)	14 years (A.D. 48–62)
Development	Triumph	Transition	Travels and trials

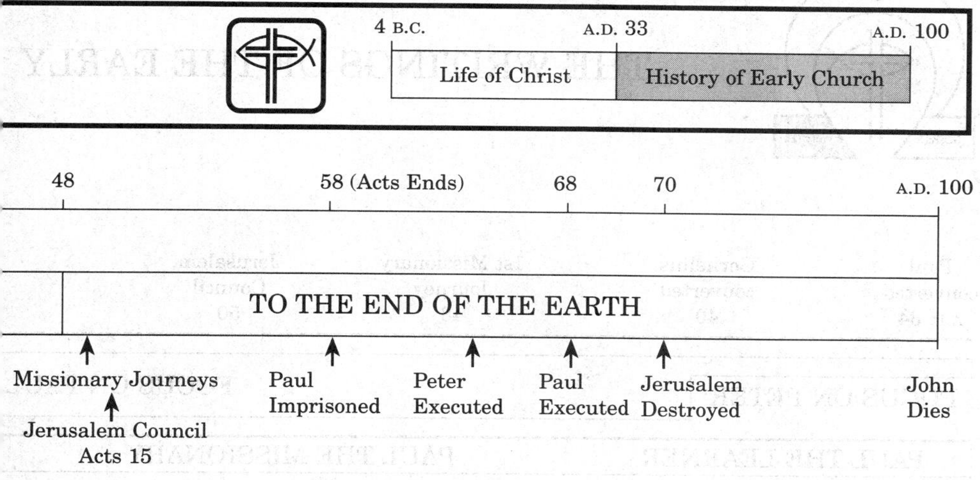

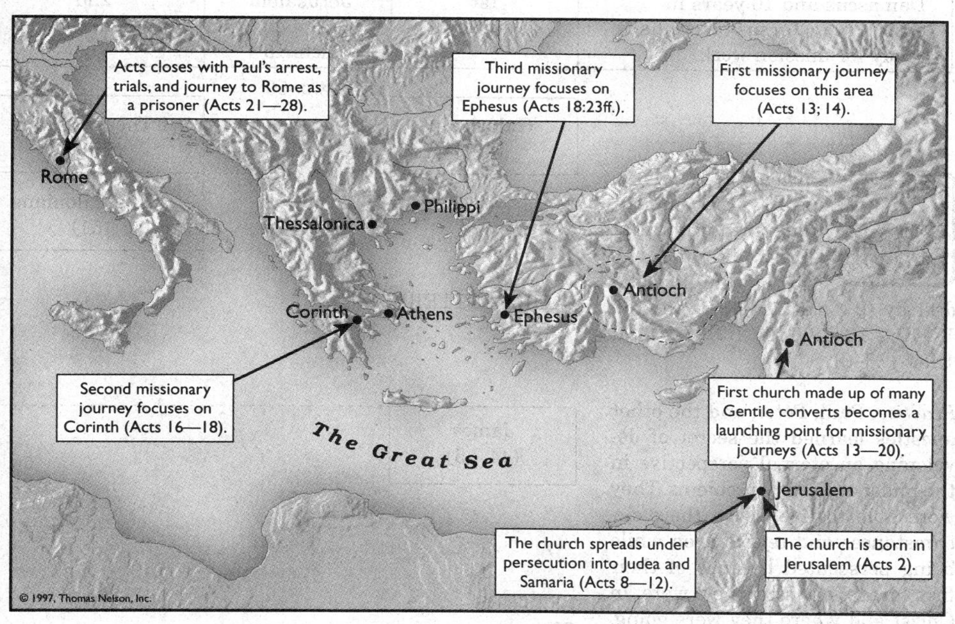

Principle: Christ's life is reproduced in others when we take the initiative to witness in the power of the Holy Spirit (Matt. 28:18–20; Acts 1:8; Col. 4:2–6).

Practice: The Book of Acts records the spread of the gospel from the city of Jerusalem to the whole province of Judea and Samaria, and ultimately through the Roman Empire and beyond. These first-century Christians were sold out for the cause of Christ and transformed their world as their lives became living epistles of the Good News. God has called us to a lifestyle of evangelism in which we build relationships with non-Christians. These friendships in turn become natural bridges for communicating the gospel. Take a close look at Colossians 4:2–6 to learn how to become more effective as an instrument of the Holy Spirit to reproduce the life of Christ in others.

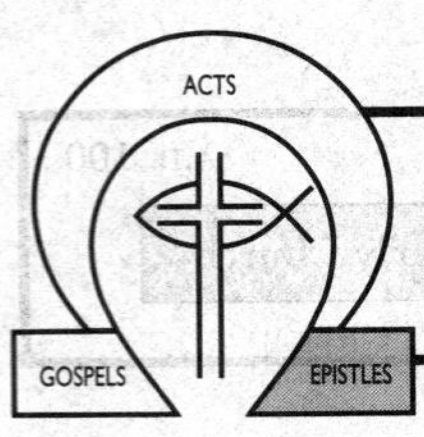

THE WRITINGS OF THE EARLY

Paul converted A.D. 34	Cornelius converted 40	1st Missionary Journey 48	Jerusalem Council 50

FOCUS ON PETER

FOCUS ON PAUL

PAUL THE LEARNER	PAUL THE MISSIONARY		
Paul spends nearly 3 years at Damascus and 10 years in obscurity in Tarsus before he is ready for mission work.	1st Journey	The Jerusalem Council Acts 15	2nd Journey

A.D. 50

PAUL'S LETTERS

Galatians (49)

1 Thessalonians (51)

2 Thessalonians (51)

LETTERS BY OTHERS

James (44, 45)

GOSPELS & ACTS

Matthew (c. 40's)

Principle: God wants us to grow in our understanding that Christ's life and destiny are our life and destiny (2 Cor. 4:16–18; Eph. 1:3, 17–19; 3:16–19; Phil. 1:21; 3:20, 21; 1 Pet. 1:3–9).

Practice: Paul, Peter, and the other apostles learned the secret of developing an eternal perspective in the midst of earthly problems. They were able to live above their circumstances and rejoice even while being persecuted because of their firm grasp on who they were in Christ and where they were going. In spite of his imprisonment, Paul could write, "For to me, to live *is* Christ, and to die *is* gain" (Phil. 1:21). Are you looking more at "the things which are seen" or at "the things which are not seen"? The former are temporary, but the latter are eternal (2 Cor. 4:18).

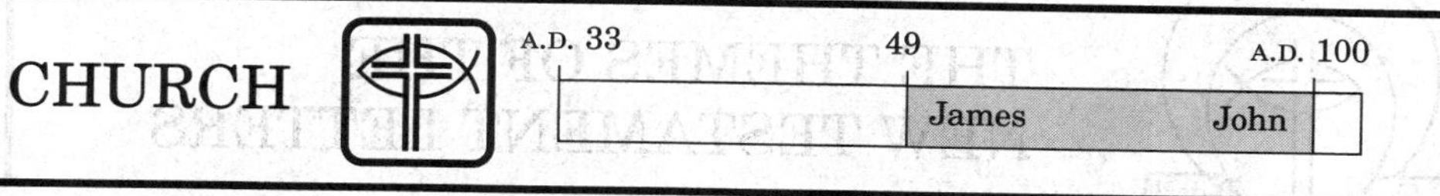

Paul imprisoned 58	Peter executed 64	Paul executed 68	Jerusalem destroyed 70	John dies A.D. 100

PAUL THE PRISONER				FOCUS ON JOHN
3rd Journey	1st Imprisonment	Freedom	2nd Imprisonment	JOHN'S WRITINGS
1 Corinthians (56)	Ephesians (60)	1 Timothy (62)	2 Timothy (67)	
2 Corinthians (56)	Colossians (61)	Titus (66)		
Romans (56, 57)	Philemon (61)			
	Philippians (62)			
		1 Peter (64)	Hebrews (66–69)	1 John (85–90)
		2 Peter (64)	Jude (75)	2 John (85–90)
				3 John (85–90)
				Revelation (95–96)
	Acts (62)			
	Luke (58–60)	Mark (60)		John (65–70)

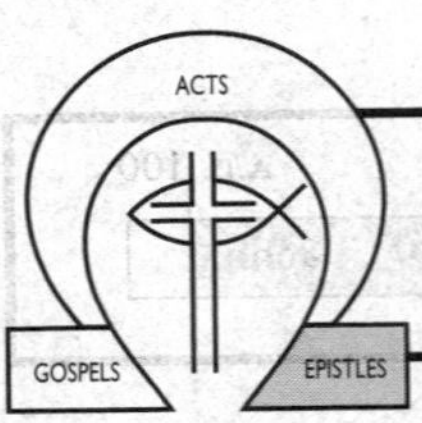

THE THEMES OF THE NEW TESTAMENT LETTERS

PAUL'S LETTERS TO CHURCHES

BOOK	KEY WORD	THEME
Romans	Righteousness of God	Portrays the gospel from condemnation to justification to sanctification to glorification (1—8). Presents God's program for Jews and Gentiles (9—11) and practical exhortations for believers (12—16).
1 Corinthians	Correction of Carnal Living	Corrects problems of factions, immorality, lawsuits, and abuse of the Lord's Supper (1—6). Replies to questions concerning marriage, meat offered to idols, public worship, and the Resurrection (7—16).
2 Corinthians	Paul Defends His Ministry	Defends Paul's apostolic character, call, and credentials. The majority had repented of their rebellion against Paul, but there was still an unrepentant minority.
Galatians	Freedom from the Law	Refutes the error of legalism that had ensnared the churches of Galatia. Demonstrates the superiority of grace over law, and magnifies the life of liberty over legalism and license.
Ephesians	Building the Body of Christ	Extols the believer's position in Christ (1—3), and exhorts the readers to maintain a spiritual walk that is based upon their spiritual wealth (4—6).
Philippians	To Live Is Christ	Paul speaks of the latest developments in his imprisonment and urges his readers to a lifestyle of unity, humility, and godliness.
Colossians	The Preeminence of Christ	Demonstrates the preeminence of Christ in creation, redemption, and the relationships of life. The Christian is complete in Christ and needs nothing else.
1 Thessalonians	Holiness in Light of Christ's Return	Paul commends the Thessalonians for their faith and reminds them of his motives and concerns on their behalf. He exhorts them to purity of life and teaches them about the coming of the Lord.
2 Thessalonians	Understanding the Day of the Lord	Paul corrects false conclusions about the day of the Lord, explains what must precede this awesome event, and exhorts his readers to remain diligent.

PAUL'S LETTERS TO PEOPLE

BOOK	KEY WORD	THEME
1 Timothy	Leadership Manual for Churches	Paul counsels Timothy on the problems of false teachers, public prayer, the role of women, and the requirements for elders and deacons.
2 Timothy	Endurance in Ministry	A combat manual designed to build up and encourage Timothy to boldness and steadfastness in view of the hardships of the spiritual warfare.
Titus	Conduct Manual for Churches	Lists the requirements for elders and instructs Titus in his duties relative to the various groups in the churches.
Philemon	Forgiveness from Slavery	Paul appeals to Philemon to forgive Onesimus and to regard him no longer as a slave but as a brother in Christ.

LETTERS FROM OTHERS

BOOK	KEY WORD	THEME
Hebrews	Superiority of Christ	Demonstrates the superiority of Christ's Person, priesthood, and power over all that preceded Him to encourage the readers to mature and to become stable in their faith.
James	Faith that Works	A practical catalog of the characteristics of true faith written to exhort James's Hebrew-Christian readers to examine the reality of their own faith.
1 Peter	Suffering for Christ	Comfort and counsel to those who were being maligned for their faith in Christ. They are encouraged to develop an attitude of submission in view of their suffering.
2 Peter	Guard Against False Prophets	Copes with internal opposition in the form of false teachers who were enticing believers into their errors of belief and conduct. Appeals for growth in the true knowledge of Christ.
1 John	Fellowship with God	Explores the dimensions of fellowship between redeemed people and God. Believers must walk in His light, manifest His love, and abide in His life.
2 John	Avoid Fellowship with False Teachers	John commends his readers for remaining steadfast in apostolic truth and reminds them to walk in love and avoid false teachers.
3 John	Enjoy Fellowship with the Brethren	John thanks Gaius for his support of traveling teachers of the truth, in contrast to Diotrephes, who rejected them and told others to do the same.
Jude	Contend for the Faith	This exposé of false teachers reveals their conduct and character and predicts their judgment. Jude encourages his readers to build themselves up in the truth and contend earnestly for the faith.
Revelation	Revelation of the Coming Christ	The glorified Christ gives seven messages to the church (1—3). Visions of unparalleled judment upon rebellious humankind are followed by the Second Advent (4—19). The Apocalypse concludes with a description of the new heaven and new earth and the marvels of the New Jerusalem (20—22).

The

New Testament

of

The Open Bible®

Expanded Edition

The New King James Version

THE GOSPEL ACCORDING TO

MATTHEW

THE BOOK OF MATTHEW

Matthew is the gospel written by a Jew to Jews about a Jew. Matthew is the writer, his countrymen are the readers, and Jesus Christ is the subject. Matthew's design is to present Jesus as the King of the Jews, the long-awaited Messiah. Through a carefully selected series of Old Testament quotations, Matthew documents Jesus Christ's claim to be the Messiah. His genealogy, baptism, messages, and miracles all point to the same inescapable conclusion: Christ is King. Even in His death, seeming defeat is turned to victory by the Resurrection, and the message again echoes forth: the King of the Jews lives.

At an early date this gospel was given the title *Kata Matthaion,* "According to Matthew." As this title suggests, other gospel accounts were known at that time (the word "gospel" was added later). Matthew ("Gift of the Lord") was also surnamed Levi (Mark 2:14; Luke 5:27).

THE AUTHOR OF MATTHEW

The early church uniformly attributed this gospel to Matthew, and no tradition to the contrary ever emerged. This book was known early and accepted quickly. In his Ecclesiastical History (A.D. 323), Eusebius quoted a statement by Papias (c. A.D. 140) that Matthew wrote *logia* ("sayings") in Aramaic. No Aramaic gospel of Matthew has been found, and it is evident that Matthew is not a Greek translation of an Aramaic original. Some believe that Matthew wrote an abbreviated version of Jesus' sayings in Aramaic before writing his gospel in Greek for a larger circle of readers.

Matthew, the son of Alphaeus (Mark 2:14), occupied the unpopular post of tax collector in Capernaum for the Roman government. As a publican he was no doubt disliked by his Jewish countrymen. When Jesus called him to discipleship (9:9–13; Mark 2:14; Luke 5:27, 28), his quick response probably meant that he had already been stirred by Jesus' public preaching. He gave a large reception for Jesus in his house so that his associates could meet Jesus. He was chosen as one of the twelve apostles, and the last appearance of his name in the Bible is in Acts 1:13. Matthew's life from that point on is veiled in tradition.

THE TIME OF MATTHEW

Like all the gospels, Matthew is not easy to date: suggestions have ranged from A.D. 40 to 140. The two expressions "to this day" (27:8) and "until this day" (28:15) indicate that a substantial period of time has passed since the events described in the book, but they also point to a date prior to the destruction of Jerusalem in A.D. 70. The Olivet Discourse (24 and 25) also anticipates this event. The strong Jewish flavor of this gospel is another argument for a date prior to A.D. 70. If Matthew depended on Mark's gospel as a source, the date of Mark would determine the earliest date for Matthew. The likely time frame for this book is A.D. 58–68. It may have been written in Palestine or Syrian Antioch.

THE CHRIST OF MATTHEW

Matthew presents Jesus as Israel's promised messianic King (1:23; 2:2, 6; 3:17; 4:15–17; 21:5, 9; 22:44, 45; 26:64; 27:11, 27–37). The phrase "the kingdom of heaven" appears thirty-two times in Matthew but nowhere else in the New Testament. To show that Jesus fulfills the qualifications for the Messiah, Matthew uses more Old Testament quotations and allusions than any other book (almost 130). Often used in this gospel is the revealing phrase "that what was spoken through the prophet might be fulfilled," which does not appear even once in the other gospels. Jesus is the climax of the prophets (12:39, 40; 13:13–15, 35; 17:5–13), "the Son of Man" (24:30ff.), the "Servant" of the Lord (12:17–21), and the "Son of David" (the Davidic reference occurs nine times in Matthew, but only six times in all of the other gospels).

KEYS TO MATTHEW

Key Word: Jesus the King—A Jewish tax collector named Matthew writes to a Jewish audience to convince them that the King of Jews has come. By quoting repeatedly from the Old Testament, Matthew validates Christ's claims that He is, in fact, the prophesied Messiah (the Anointed One) of Israel. Everything about this King is unique: His miraculous birth and obscure yet carefully prophesied birthplace, His flight into Egypt, His announcement by John, His battle with Satan in the wilderness, all support the only possible conclusion—Jesus is the culmination of promises delivered by the prophets over a period of a thousand years. Thus God's redemptive plan is alive and well, even after four hundred years of prophetic silence.

Key Verses: Matthew 16:16–19 and 28:18–20—"Simon Peter answered and said, 'You are the Christ, the Son of the living God.' Jesus answered and said to him, 'Blessed are you, Simon Bar-Jonah, for flesh and blood has not revealed *this* to you, but My Father who is in heaven. And I also say to you that you are Peter, and on this rock I will build My church, and the gates of Hades shall not prevail against it. And I will give you the keys of the kingdom of heaven, and whatever you bind on earth will be bound in heaven, and whatever you loose on earth will be loosed in heaven' " (16:16–19).

"And Jesus came and spoke to them, saying, 'All authority has been given to Me in heaven and on earth. Go therefore and make disciples of all the nations, baptizing them in the name of the Father and of the Son and of the Holy Spirit, teaching them to observe all things that I have commanded you; and lo, I am with you always, *even* to the end of the age.' Amen" (28:18–20).

Key Chapter: Matthew 12—The turning point of Matthew comes in the twelfth chapter when the Pharisees, acting as the leadership of the nation of Israel, formally reject Jesus Christ as the Messiah, saying that His power comes not from God but from Satan. Christ's ministry changes immediately with His new teaching of parables, increased attention given to His disciples, and His repeated statement that His death is now near.

SURVEY OF MATTHEW

The Old Testament prophets predicted and longed for the coming of the Anointed One who would enter history to bring redemption and deliverance. The first verse of Matthew succinctly announces the fulfillment of Israel's hope in the coming of Christ: "The book of the genealogy of Jesus Christ, the Son of David, the Son of Abraham." Matthew was placed first in the canon of New Testament books by the early church because it is a natural bridge between the Testaments. This gospel describes the Person and work of Israel's messianic King. An important part of Matthew's structure is revealed in the phrase "when Jesus had ended [finished]" (7:28; 11:1; 13:53; 19:1; 26:1), which is used to conclude the five key discourses of the book: the Sermon on the Mount (5:3—7:27), Instruction of the Disciples (10:5–42), Parables of the Kingdom (13:3–52), Terms of Discipleship (18:3–35), and the Olivet Discourse (24:4—25:46). Matthew can be outlined as follows: the presentation of the King (1:1—4:11); the proclamation of the King (4:12—7:29); the power of the King (8:1—11:1); the progressive rejection of the King (11:2—16:12); the preparation of the King's disciples (16:13—20:28); the presentation and rejection of the King (20:29—27:66); the proof of the King (28:1–20).

The Presentation of the King (1:1—4:11): The promise to Abraham was that "in you all the families of the earth shall be blessed" (Gen. 12:3). Jesus Christ, the Savior of the world, is "the Son of Abraham" (1:1). However, He is also "the Son of David"; and as David's direct descendant, He is qualified to be Israel's King. The Magi know that the "King of the Jews" (2:2) has been born and come to worship Him. John the Baptist, the messianic forerunner who breaks the four hundred years of prophetic silence, also bears witness of Him (cf. Mal. 3:1). The sinlessness of the King is proved when He overcomes the satanic temptations to disobey the will of the Father.

The Proclamation of the King (4:12—7:29): In this section, Matthew uses a topical rather than a chronological arrangement of his material in order to develop a crucial pattern in Christ's ministry. The words of the Lord are found in the Sermon on the Mount (5—7). This discourse requires less than fifteen minutes to read, but its brevity has not diminished its profound influence on the world. The Sermon on the

FOCUS	OFFER OF THE KING			REJECTION OF THE KING			
REFERENCE	1:1——4:12	——8:1	——11:2	——16:13	——20:29	——28:1	——28:20
DIVISION	PRESENTATION OF THE KING	PROCLAMATION OF THE KING	POWER OF THE KING	PROGRESSIVE REJECTION OF THE KING	PREPARATION OF THE KING'S DISCIPLES	PRESENTATION AND REJECTION OF THE KING	PROOF OF THE KING
TOPIC	TEACHING THE THRONGS				TEACHING THE TWELVE		
	CHRONOLOGICAL	THEMATIC		CHRONOLOGICAL			
LOCATION	BETHLEHEM AND NAZARETH	GALILEE				JUDEA	
TIME	C. 4 B.C.–A.D. 33						

Mount presents new laws and standards for God's people.

The Power of the King (8:1—11:1): The works of the Lord are presented in a series of ten miracles (8 and 9) that reveal His authority over every realm (disease, demons, death, and nature). Thus, the words of the Lord are supported by His works; His claims are verified by His credentials.

The Progressive Rejection of the King (11:2—16:12): Here we note a series of reactions to Christ's words and works. Because of increasing opposition, Jesus begins to spend proportionately more time with His disciples as He prepares them for His coming death and departure.

The Preparation of the King's Disciples (16:13—20:28): In a series of discourses, Jesus communicates the significance of accepting or rejecting His offer of righteousness. His teaching in 16:13—21:11 is primarily directed to those who accept Him.

The Presentation and Rejection of the King (20:29—27:66): The majority of Christ's words in this section are aimed at those who reject their King. The Lord predicts the terrible judgment that will fall on Jerusalem, resulting in the dispersion of the Jewish people. Looking beyond these events (fulfilled in A.D. 70), He also describes His second coming as the Judge and Lord of the earth.

The Proof of the King (28): Authenticating His words and works are the empty tomb, resurrection, and appearances, all proving that Jesus Christ is indeed the prophesied Messiah, the very Son of God.

Christ's final ministry in Judea (beginning in 19:1) reaches a climax at the Cross as the King willingly gives up His life to redeem sinful persons. Jesus endures awesome human hatred in this great demonstration of divine love (cf. Rom. 5:7, 8). His perfect sacrifice is acceptable, and this gospel concludes with His glorious resurrection.

OUTLINE OF MATTHEW

Part One: The Presentation of the King (1:1—4:11)

I. The Advent of the King ....1:1—2:23

- A. Genealogy of Christ 1:1–17
- B. Birth of Christ 1:18–25
- C. Visit of Wise Men 2:1–12
- D. Flight into Egypt 2:13–15
- E. Herod Kills the Children 2:16–18
- F. Jesus Returns to Nazareth 2:19–23

II. The Announcer of the King 3:1–12

- A. The Person of John the Baptist 3:1–6
- B. The Preaching of John the Baptist 3:7–12

III. The Approval of the King ....3:13—4:11

- A. Baptism of Jesus 3:13–17
- B. Temptation of Jesus 4:1–11
  - 1. First Temptation 4:1–4
  - 2. Second Temptation 4:5–7
  - 3. Third Temptation 4:8–11

Part Two: The Proclamation of the King (4:12—7:29)

I. The Background for the Sermon 4:12–25

- A. Jesus Begins His Ministry 4:12–17
- B. Jesus Calls His First Disciples 4:18–22
- C. Jesus Ministers in Galilee 4:23–25

II. The Sermon on the Mount ....5:1—7:29

- A. The Subjects of the Kingdom 5:1–16
  - 1. The Beatitudes 5:1–12
  - 2. The Similitudes 5:13–16
- B. The Relationship of Jesus to the Law ....5:17—7:6
  - 1. Jesus Fulfills the Law 5:17–19
  - 2. Jesus Rejects Pharisaic Interpretation 5:20–48
  - 3. Jesus Rejects Pharisaic Practices ....6:1—7:6
- C. Jesus Instructs on Entering the Kingdom 7:7–27
  - 1. "Ask, and It Will Be Given" 7:7–11
  - 2. Golden Rule 7:12
  - 3. Two Ways of Life 7:13, 14
  - 4. False and True Teaching 7:15–20
  - 5. True Way into the Kingdom 7:21–23
  - 6. Parable of the Two Builders 7:24–27
- D. Response to the Sermon 7:28, 29

Part Three: The Power of the King (8:1—11:1)

I. The Demonstration of the King's Power ....8:1—9:34

- A. Miracles of Healing 8:1–17
  - 1. The Leper Is Cleansed 8:1–4
  - 2. The Centurion's Servant Is Healed 8:5–13
  - 3. Peter's Mother-in-Law Is Healed ...8:14–17
- B. Demands of Discipleship 8:18–22
- C. Miracles of Power ....8:23—9:8
  - 1. The Sea Is Stilled 8:23–27
  - 2. Demons Are Cast into Swine 8:28–34
  - 3. The Paralytic Is Forgiven 9:1–8

Part Four: The Progressive Rejection of the King (11:2—16:12)

Part Five: The Preparation of the King's Disciples (16:13—20:28)

Part Six: The Presentation and Rejection of the King (20:29—27:66)

C. Conflict with Pharisees and Herodians 22:15–22
D. Conflict with Sadducees 22:23–33
E. Conflict with Pharisees 22:34–46
1. The Greatest Commandment 22:34–40
2. The Son of David 22:41–46

IV. The King Rejects the Nation 23:1–39

A. Jesus Characterizes the Pharisees......23:1–12
B. Jesus Condemns the Pharisees 23:13–36
C. Jesus Laments over Jerusalem 23:37–39

V. The Predictions of the King's Second Coming ....24:1—25:46

A. The Temple to Be Destroyed 24:1, 2
B. The Disciples' Two Questions: "When?" and "What?" 24:3
C. Jesus Answers the "What?" 24:4–31
1. The Tribulation 24:4–26
2. The Second Coming 24:27–31
D. Jesus Answers the "When?" 24:32–51
1. Parable of the Fig Tree 24:32–35
2. Illustration of the Days of Noah ..24:36–44
3. Illustration of the Two Servants ..24:45–51
E. Jesus Predicts Judgment at His Coming 25:1–46
1. Parable of the Ten Virgins 25:1–13
2. Parable of the Talents 25:14–30
3. Judgment of the Gentiles 25:31–46

VI. The Passion of the King ....26:1—27:66

A. The Religious Leaders Plot to Kill Jesus 26:1–5
B. Mary Anoints Jesus for Burial 26:6–13
C. Judas Agrees to Betray Jesus 26:14–16
D. The Disciples Celebrate the Passover 26:17–35
1. The Passover Is Prepared 26:17–19
2. The Passover Is Celebrated 26:20–25
3. The Lord's Supper Is Instituted ...26:26–29
4. Peter's Denial Is Predicted 26:30–35
E. Jesus Is Arrested in Gethsemane 26:36–56
1. Jesus' Three Prayers 26:36–46
2. Jesus' Betrayal and Arrest 26:47–56
F. Jesus Is Tried ....26:57—27:25
1. The Trial Before Caiaphas 26:57–75
2. The Trial Before Pilate 27:1–25
G. Jesus Is Crucified 27:26–56
1. Jesus Is Scourged 27:26–28
2. Jesus Is Led to Golgotha 27:29–33
3. Jesus Is Crucified 27:34–44
4. Jesus Dies 27:45–50
5. Signs Accompanying Jesus' Death 27:51–56
H. Jesus Is Buried 27:57–66

Part Seven: The Proof of the King (28:1–20)

I. The Empty Tomb 28:1–8

II. The Appearance of Jesus to the Women 28:9, 10

III. The Bribery of the Soldiers 28:11–15

IV. The Appearance of Jesus to the Disciples 28:16, 17

V. The Great Commission 28:18–20

CHAPTER 1

Genealogy of Christ—Ruth 4:18–22; 1 Chr. 1:34; 2:1–15; Luke 3:31–34

THE book of the [R]genealogy of Jesus
Christ, [R]the Son of David, the Son of Abra-
ham: Luke 3:23 • Ps. 132:11; Jer. 23:5★
2 [R]Abraham begot Isaac, [R]Isaac begot Ja-
cob, and Jacob begot Judah and his broth-
ers. Gen. 21:2, 12 • Gen. 25:26; 28:14
3 [R]Judah begot Perez and Zerah by Tamar,
[R]Perez begot Hezron, and Hezron begot
Ram. Gen. 38:27; 49:10 • Ruth 4:18–22
4 Ram begot Amminadab, Amminadab
begot Nahshon, and Nahshon begot Salmon.
5 Salmon begot Boaz by Rahab, Boaz begot
Obed by Ruth, Obed begot Jesse,
6 and [R]Jesse begot David the king.
David the king begot Solomon by her
*who had been the wife** of Uriah. Is. 11:1, 10★
7 Solomon begot Rehoboam, Rehoboam
begot Abijah, and Abijah begot Asa.*
8 Asa begot Jehoshaphat, Jehoshaphat
begot Joram, and Joram begot Uzziah.
9 Uzziah begot Jotham, Jotham begot
Ahaz, and Ahaz begot Hezekiah.
10 Hezekiah begot Manasseh, Manasseh
begot Amon,* and Amon begot Josiah.
11 [R]Josiah begot Jeconiah and his brothers
about the time they were carried away to
Babylon. 1 Chr. 3:15, 16
12 And after they were brought to Babylon,
[R]Jeconiah begot Shealtiel, and Shealtiel begot
[R]Zerubbabel. 1 Chr. 3:17 • Ezra 3:2
13 Zerubbabel begot Abiud, Abiud begot Eli-
akim, and Eliakim begot Azor.
14 Azor begot Zadok, Zadok begot Achim,
and Achim begot Eliud.
15 Eliud begot Eleazar, Eleazar begot
Matthan, and Matthan begot Jacob.
16 And Jacob begot Joseph the husband of
[R]Mary, of whom was born Jesus who is called
Christ. Matt. 13:55
17 So all the generations from Abraham to

1:6 Words in italic type have been added for clarity. They are not found in the original Greek. **1:7** NU *Asaph* **1:10** NU *Amos*

David *are* fourteen generations, from David until the captivity in Babylon *are* fourteen generations, and from the captivity in Babylon until the Christ *are* fourteen generations.

Birth of Christ

18 Now the [R]birth of Jesus Christ was as follows: After His mother Mary was betrothed to Joseph, [R]before they came together, she was found with child [R]of the Holy Spirit. Luke 1:27 • Is. 7:14; 49:1, 5★ • Luke 1:35

19 Then Joseph her husband, being [T]a just *man,* and not wanting [R]to make her a public example, was minded to put her away secretly. *an upright* • Deut. 24:1

20 But while he thought about these things, behold, an angel of the Lord appeared to him in a dream, saying, "Joseph, son of David, do not be afraid to take to you Mary your wife, [R]for that which is conceived in her is of the Holy Spirit. Luke 1:35

21 "And she will bring forth a Son, and you shall call His name JESUS, for He [R]will save His people from their sins." Rom. 5:18, 19☆

22 So all this was done that it might be fulfilled which was spoken by the Lord through the prophet, saying:

23 [R]*"Behold, the virgin shall be with child, and bear a Son, and they shall call His name Immanuel,"** which is translated, "God with us." Is. 7:14★

24 Then Joseph, being aroused from sleep, did as the angel of the Lord commanded him and took to him his wife,

25 and did not know her till she had brought forth [R]her firstborn Son.* And he called His name JESUS. Luke 2:7, 21★

CHAPTER 2

Visit of Wise Men

NOW after [R]Jesus was [R]born in Bethlehem of Judea in the days of Herod the king, behold, wise men [R]from the East came to Jerusalem, Luke 2:4–7 • Mic. 5:2★ • Gen. 25:6

2 saying, [R]"Where is He who has been born King of the Jews? For we have seen [R]His star in the East and have come to worship Him." Luke 2:11 • [Num. 24:17]

3 When Herod the king heard *this,* he was troubled, and all Jerusalem with him.

4 And when he had gathered all [R]the chief priests and [R]scribes of the people together, [R]he inquired of them where the Christ was to be born. 2 Chr. 36:14 • 2 Chr. 34:13 • Mal. 2:7

5 So they said to him, "In Bethlehem of Judea, for thus it is written by the prophet:

6 *'But you, Bethlehem, in the land of*
Judah,
Are not the least among the rulers of
Judah;
For out of you shall come a Ruler
*Who will shepherd My people Israel.' "**

7 Then Herod, when he had secretly called the wise men, determined from them what time the [R]star appeared. Num. 24:17

8 And he sent them to Bethlehem and said, "Go and search carefully for the young Child, and when you have found *Him,* bring back word to me, that I may come and worship Him also."

9 When they heard the king, they departed; and behold, the star which they had seen in the East went before them, till it came and stood over where the young Child was.

10 When they saw the star, they rejoiced with exceedingly great joy.

11 And when they had come into the house, they saw the young Child with Mary His mother, and fell down and worshiped Him. And when they had opened their treasures, [R]they presented gifts to Him: gold, frankincense, and myrrh. Is. 60:6

12 Then, being divinely warned in a dream that they should not return to Herod, they departed for their own country another way.

Flight into Egypt

13 Now when they had departed, behold, an angel of the Lord appeared to Joseph in a dream, saying, "Arise, take the young Child and His mother, flee to Egypt, and stay there until I bring you word; for [R]Herod will seek the young Child to destroy Him." Matt. 2:16☆

14 When he arose, he took the young Child and His mother by night and departed for Egypt,

15 and was there until the death of Herod, that it might be fulfilled which was spoken by the Lord through the prophet, saying, *"Out of Egypt I called My Son."**

Herod Kills the Children

16 Then Herod, when he saw that he was deceived by the wise men, was exceedingly angry; and he sent forth and put to death all the male children who were in Bethlehem and in all its districts, from two years old and under, according to the time which he had determined from the wise men.

17 Then was fulfilled what was spoken by Jeremiah the prophet, saying:

18 *"A voice was heard in Ramah,*
Lamentation, weeping, and great
mourning,
Rachel weeping for her children,
Refusing to be comforted,
*Because they are no more."**

1:23 Words in oblique type in the New Testament are quoted from the Old Testament. **1:25** NU *a Son*
2:6 Mic. 5:2★ **2:15** Hos. 11:1★ **2:18** Jer. 31:15★

Jesus Returns to Nazareth—Luke 2:39

19 Now when Herod was dead, behold, an
angel of the Lord appeared in a dream to Jo-
seph in Egypt,
20 [R]saying, "Arise, take the young Child and
His mother, and go to the land of Israel, for
those who [R]sought the young Child's life are
dead." Luke 2:39 • Matt. 2:16
21 Then he arose, took the young Child and
His mother, and came into the land of Israel.
22 But when he heard that Archelaus was
reigning over Judea instead of his father
Herod, he was afraid to go there. And being
warned by God in a [R]dream, he turned aside
into the region of Galilee. Matt. 2:12, 13, 19
23 And he came and dwelt in a city called
[R]Nazareth, that it might be fulfilled [R]which
was spoken by the prophets, "He shall be
called a Nazarene." John 1:45, 46 • Judg. 13:5★

CHAPTER 3

The Person of John the Baptist
Mark 1:2–6; Luke 3:3–6

IN those days John the Baptist came
preaching in the wilderness of Judea,
2 and saying, "Repent, for [R]the kingdom of
heaven is at hand!" Dan. 2:44; Mal. 4:5, 6★
3 For this is he who was spoken of by the
prophet Isaiah, saying:

"*The voice of one crying in the*
wilderness:
[R]'*Prepare the way of the* LORD; Luke 1:76
Make His paths straight.' "*

4 Now [R]John himself was clothed in
camel's hair, with a leather belt around his
waist; and his food was [R]locusts and [R]wild
honey. Mark 1:6 • Lev. 11:22 • 1 Sam. 14:25, 26
5 Then Jerusalem, all Judea, and all the re-
gion around the Jordan went out to him
6 [R]and were baptized by him in the Jordan,
confessing their sins. Acts 19:4, 18

The Preaching of John the Baptist
Mark 1:7, 8; Luke 3:7–9, 16, 17

7 But when he saw many of the Pharisees
and Sadducees coming to his baptism, he said
to them, "Brood of vipers! Who warned you to
flee from the wrath to come?
8 "Therefore bear fruits worthy of repen-
tance,
9 "and do not think to say to yourselves,
[R]'We have Abraham as *our* father.' For I say to
you that God is able to raise up children to
Abraham from these stones. John 8:33
10 "And even now the ax is laid to the root of
the trees. [R]Therefore every tree which does
not bear good fruit is cut down and thrown
into the fire. Matt. 7:19
11 [R]"I indeed baptize you with water unto re-
pentance, but He who is coming after me is
mightier than I, whose sandals I am not wor-
thy to carry. He will baptize you with the Holy
Spirit and fire.* Acts 2:4, 33☆
12 [R]"His winnowing fan *is* in His hand, and
He will thoroughly clean out His threshing
floor, and gather His wheat into the barn; but
He will [R]burn up the chaff with unquenchable
fire." Mal. 3:3 • Matt. 13:30

Baptism of Jesus—Mark 1:9–11;
Luke 3:21–23

13 Then Jesus came from Galilee to John at
the Jordan to be baptized by him.
14 And John *tried to* prevent Him, saying, "I
need to be baptized by You, and are You com-
ing to me?"
15 But Jesus answered and said to him, "Per-
mit *it to be so* now, for thus it is fitting for us to
fulfill all righteousness." Then he allowed Him.
16 When He had been baptized, Jesus came
up immediately from the water; and behold,
the heavens were opened to Him, and He* saw
[R]the Spirit of God descending like a dove and
alighting upon Him. Is. 11:2; 42:1★
17 [R]And suddenly a voice *came* from
heaven, saying, [R]"This is My beloved Son, in
whom I am well pleased." John 12:28 • Ps. 2:7

CHAPTER 4

First Temptation—Mark 1:12, 13; Luke 4:1–4

THEN [R]Jesus was led up by [R]the Spirit
into the wilderness to be tempted by the
devil. Mark 1:12 • Ezek. 3:14
2 And when He had fasted forty days and
forty nights, afterward He was hungry.

3:3 Is. 40:3★ **3:11** M omits *and fire* **3:16** Or *he*

3:17 God the Father of Christ—Every new Christian eventually wonders in what sense God may be called the Father of Christ and Christ the Son of God. The answer to this question is not a simple one. First, one must recognize that the title "Son of God" does not speak of physical nature, for God is spirit (Page 1085—John 4:24), and Christ was the Son of God before He assumed a human body in Bethlehem (Page 1083—John 3:16; Page 1198—Gal. 4:4). Passages which use terms implying physical origin must be taken in a figurative sense (Page 1258—Heb. 1:5).

Second, the title expresses a unique relationship. Christ distinguished His sonship from that of His disciples (Page 1105—John 20:17). He is begotten of God in a sense that no one else is (Page 1081—John 1:14; 3:16). Some call it "eternal generation," signifying the timelessness of this "God from God" relationship.

(continued on next page)

3 Now when the tempter came to Him, he said, "If You are the Son of God, command that these stones become bread."

4 But He answered and said, "It is written, *'Man shall not live by bread alone, but by every word that proceeds from the mouth of God.'*"*

Second Temptation—Luke 4:9–12

5 Then the devil took Him up [R]into the holy city, set Him on the pinnacle of the temple, Neh. 11:1, 18

6 and said to Him, "If You are the Son of God, throw Yourself down. For it is written:

'He shall give His angels charge over
you,'

and,

'In their hands they shall bear you up,
Lest you dash your foot against a
stone.'"*

7 Jesus said to him, "It is written again, *'You shall not tempt the LORD your God.'*"*

Third Temptation—Mark 1:13; Luke 4:5–8, 13

8 Again, the devil took Him up on an exceedingly high mountain, and [R]showed Him all the kingdoms of the world and their glory. [1 John 2:15–17]

9 And he said to Him, "All these things I will give You if You will fall down and worship me."

10 Then Jesus said to him, "Away with you,* Satan! For it is written, *'You shall worship the LORD your God, and Him only you shall serve.'*"*

11 Then the devil left Him, and behold, angels came and ministered to Him.

Jesus Begins His Ministry
Mark 1:14, 15; Luke 4:14, 31

12 Now when Jesus heard that John had been put in prison, He departed to Galilee.

13 And leaving Nazareth, He came and dwelt in Capernaum, which is by the sea, in the regions of Zebulun and Naphtali,

14 that it might be fulfilled which was spoken by Isaiah the prophet, saying:

15 "*The land of Zebulun and the land of*
Naphtali,
By the way of the sea, beyond the
Jordan,
Galilee of the Gentiles:
16 *The people who sat in darkness have*
seen a great light,
And upon those who sat in the region
and shadow of death
Light has dawned."*

17 [R]From that time Jesus began to preach and to say, "Repent, for the kingdom of heaven is at hand." Mark 1:14, 15

Jesus Calls His First Disciples—Mark 1:16–20

18 And Jesus, walking by the Sea of Galilee, saw two brothers, Simon called Peter, and Andrew his brother, casting a net into the sea; for they were fishermen.

19 Then He said to them, "Follow Me, and [R]I will make you fishers of men." Luke 5:10

20 [R]They immediately left *their* nets and followed Him. Mark 10:28

21 [R]Going on from there, He saw two other brothers, James *the son* of Zebedee, and John his brother, in the boat with Zebedee their father, mending their nets. He called them, Mark 1:19

22 and immediately they left the boat and their father, and followed Him.

Jesus Ministers in Galilee
Mark 1:39; Luke 4:44

23 And Jesus went about all Galilee, [R]teaching in their synagogues, preaching [R]the gospel of the kingdom, and healing all kinds of sickness and all kinds of disease among the people. Ps. 22:22★ • [Matt. 24:14]

24 Then [T]His fame went throughout all Syria; and they [R]brought to Him all sick people who were afflicted with various diseases and torments, and those who were demon-possessed, epileptics, and paralytics; and He healed them. Lit. *the report of Him* • Luke 4:40

25 [R]Great multitudes followed Him—from Galilee, and *from* Decapolis, Jerusalem, Judea, and beyond the Jordan. Mark 3:7, 8

4:4 Deut. 8:3 **4:6** Ps. 91:11, 12★ **4:7** Deut. 6:16
4:10 M *Get behind Me* • Deut. 6:13 **4:16** Is. 9:1, 2★

(continued from previous page)

Third, the title describes a relationship of equality. The Son of God is no less than God. When Jesus claimed to be "one" with the Father, He was speaking of a unity of "substance" with the Father and thus equality in all the attributes of deity (Page 1095—John 10:30). The Jews certainly understood this claim, for they took up stones to stone Him, protesting that "You . . . make Yourself God" (Page 1095—John 10:33).

Fourth, the title especially emphasizes Christ's role as the revealer of God. He alone possesses the knowledge of the Father (Page 1099—John 14:6–9; Page 1293—1 John 1:2), and He is the sole mediator of that knowledge (Page 1237—1 Tim. 2:5). Therefore no one can know the Father except through the Son (Page 1099—John 14:6). The narrowness of this way to God should be a sober incentive to take to all the world the message that the Son of God has come to impart to every person the life of the Father.

Now turn to Page 1154—Rom. 8:15: God the Father of Believers.

CHAPTER 5

The Beatitudes—Luke 6:20–26

AND seeing the multitudes, He went up on a mountain, and when He was seated His disciples came to Him.
2 Then He opened His mouth and [R]taught them, saying: [Matt. 7:29]

3 "Blessed *are* the poor in spirit,
For theirs is the kingdom of heaven.
4 Blessed *are* those who mourn,
For they shall be comforted.
5 [R]Blessed *are* the meek, Ps. 37:11
For they shall inherit the earth.
6 Blessed *are* those who [R]hunger and
thirst for righteousness, Luke 1:53
[R]For they shall be filled. [Is. 55:1; 65:13]
7 Blessed *are* the merciful,
[R]For they shall obtain mercy. Ps. 41:1
8 [R]Blessed *are* the pure in heart, Ps. 15:2
For [R]they shall see God. 1 Cor. 13:12
9 Blessed *are* the peacemakers,
For they shall be called sons of God.
10 [R]Blessed *are* those who are persecuted
for righteousness' sake, 1 Pet. 3:14
For theirs is the kingdom of heaven.

11 [R]"Blessed are you when they revile and
persecute you, and say all kinds of evil
against you falsely for My sake. Luke 6:22
12 [R]"Rejoice and be exceedingly glad, for
great *is* your reward in heaven, for [R]so they
persecuted the prophets who were before
you. 1 Pet. 4:13, 14 • Acts 7:52

The Similitudes

13 "You are the salt of the earth; but if the
salt loses its flavor, how shall it be seasoned?
It is then good for nothing but to be thrown
out and trampled underfoot by men.
14 "You are the light of the world. A city that
is set on a hill cannot be hidden.
15 "Nor do they light a lamp and put it under
a basket, but on a lampstand, and it gives light
to all *who are* in the house.
16 "Let your light so shine before men, [R]that
they may see your good works and glorify
your Father in heaven. 1 Pet. 2:12

Jesus Fulfills the Law

17 [R]"Do not think that I came to destroy the
Law or the Prophets. I did not come to destroy
but to fulfill. Rom. 10:4
18 "For assuredly, I say to you, [R]till heaven
and earth pass away, one jot or one tittle will
by no means pass from the law till all is ful-
filled. Luke 16:17
19 [R]"Whoever therefore breaks one of the
least of these commandments, and teaches
men so, shall be called least in the kingdom of
heaven; but whoever does and teaches *them*,
he shall be called great in the kingdom of
heaven. [James 2:10]

Murder

20 "For I say to you, that unless your righ-
teousness exceeds [R]*the righteousness* of the
scribes and Pharisees, you will by no means
enter the kingdom of heaven. [Rom. 10:3]
21 "You have heard that it was said to
those [T]of old, '*You shall not murder*,* and
whoever murders will be in danger of the
judgment.' *in ancient times*
22 "But I say to you that whoever is angry
with his brother without a cause* shall be in
danger of the judgment. And whoever says to
his brother, 'Raca!' shall be in danger of the
council. But whoever says, 'You fool!' shall be
in danger of hell fire.
23 "Therefore [R]if you bring your gift to the
altar, and there remember that your brother
has something against you, Matt. 8:4
24 "leave your gift there before the altar, and
go your way. First be reconciled to your
brother, and then come and offer your gift.
25 "Agree with your adversary quickly,
[R]while you are on the way with him, lest your
adversary deliver you to the judge, the judge
hand you over to the officer, and you be
thrown into prison. [Is. 55:6]
26 "Assuredly, I say to you, you will by no
means get out of there till you have paid the
last penny.

Adultery

27 "You have heard that it was said to those
of old,* '*You shall not commit adultery*.'*
28 "But I say to you that whoever looks at a
woman to lust for her has already committed
adultery with her in his heart.
29 [R]"If your right eye causes you to sin,
[R]pluck it out and cast *it* from you; for it is
more profitable for you that one of your
members perish, than for your whole body to
be cast into hell. Mark 9:43 • [Col. 3:5]
30 "And if your right hand causes you to [T]sin,
cut it off and cast *it* from you; for it is more
profitable for you that one of your members
perish, than for your whole body to be cast
into hell. Lit. *stumble* or *offend*

Divorce

31 "Furthermore it has been said, [R]'Whoever
divorces his wife, let him give her a certificate
of divorce.' Deut. 24:1
32 "But I say to you that [R]whoever divorces
his wife for any reason except sexual im-
morality* causes her to commit adultery; and
whoever marries a woman who is divorced
commits adultery. [Luke 16:18]

5:21 Ex. 20:13; Deut. 5:17 **5:22** NU omits *without a cause* **5:27** NU, M omit *to those of old* • Ex. 20:14; Deut. 5:18 **5:32** Or *fornication*

Oaths

33 "Again you have heard that it was said to those of old, 'You shall not swear falsely, but shall perform your oaths to the Lord.'

34 "But I say to you, do not swear at all: neither by heaven, for it is God's throne;

35 "nor by the earth, for it is His footstool; nor by Jerusalem, for it is the city of [R]the great King. Ps. 48:2

36 "Nor shall you swear by your head, because you cannot make one hair white or black.

37 [R]"But let your 'Yes' be 'Yes,' and your 'No,' 'No.' For whatever is more than these is from the evil one. [Col. 4:6]

Retaliation

38 "You have heard that it was said, *'An eye for an eye and a tooth for a tooth.'**

39 "But I tell you not to resist an evil person. [R]But whoever slaps you on your right cheek, turn the other to him also. Is. 50:6

40 "If anyone wants to sue you and take away your tunic, let him have *your* cloak also.

41 "And whoever [R]compels you to go one mile, go with him two. Matt. 27:32

42 "Give to him who asks you, and [R]from him who wants to borrow from you do not turn away. Luke 6:30–34

Love—Luke 6:27, 32

43 "You have heard that it was said, *'You shall love your neighbor** [R]and hate your enemy.' Deut. 23:3–6

44 "But I say to you, [R]love your enemies, bless those who curse you, do good to those who hate you, and pray for those who spitefully use you and persecute you,* Luke 6:27

45 "that you may be sons of your Father in heaven; for [R]He makes His sun rise on the evil and on the good, and sends rain on the just and on the unjust. Job 25:3

46 [R]"For if you love those who love you, what reward have you? Do not even the tax collectors do the same? Luke 6:32

47 "And if you greet your brethren* only, what do you do more *than others?* Do not even the tax collectors* do so?

48 "Therefore you shall be perfect, just [R]as your Father in heaven is perfect. Eph. 5:1

CHAPTER 6

Charitable Deeds

"TAKE heed that you do not do your charitable deeds before men, to be seen by them. Otherwise you have no reward from your Father in heaven.

2 "Therefore, [R]when you do a charitable deed, do not sound a trumpet before you as the hypocrites do in the synagogues and in the streets, that they may have glory from men. Assuredly, I say to you, they have their reward. Rom. 12:8

3 "But when you do a charitable deed, do not let your left hand know what your right hand is doing,

4 "that your charitable deed may be in secret; and your Father who sees in secret [R]will Himself reward you openly.* Luke 14:12–14

Prayer—Luke 11:2–4

5 "And when you pray, you shall not be like the [T]hypocrites. For they love to pray standing in the synagogues and on the corners of the streets, that they may be seen by men. Assuredly, I say to you, they have their reward. *pretenders*

6 "But you, when you pray, [R]go into your room, and when you have shut your door, pray to your Father who *is* in the secret *place;* and your Father who sees in secret will reward you openly.* 2 Kin. 4:33

7 "And when you pray, [R]do not use vain repetitions as the heathen *do.* [R]For they think that they will be heard for their many words. Eccl. 5:2 • 1 Kin. 18:26

8 "Therefore do not be like them. For your Father [R]knows the things you have need of before you ask Him. [Rom. 8:26, 27]

9 "In this manner, therefore, pray:

[R]Our Father in heaven, [Matt. 5:9, 16]
Hallowed be Your [R]name. Mal. 1:11
10 Your kingdom come.
[R]Your will be done Matt. 26:42
On earth [R]as *it is* in heaven. Ps. 103:20
11 Give us this day our daily bread.
12 And forgive us our debts,
As we forgive our debtors.
13 And do not lead us into temptation,
But deliver us from the evil one.
For Yours is the kingdom and the power
and the glory forever. Amen.*

14 "For if you forgive men their trespasses, your heavenly Father will also forgive you.

15 "But [R]if you do not forgive men their trespasses, neither will your Father forgive your trespasses. Matt. 18:35

Fasting

16 "Moreover, [R]when you fast, do not be like the hypocrites, with a sad countenance. For they disfigure their faces that they may appear to men to be fasting. Assuredly, I say to you, they have their reward. Is. 58:3–7

17 "But you, when you fast, [R]anoint your head and wash your face, Ruth 3:3

5:38 Ex. 21:24; Lev. 24:20; Deut. 19:21 **5:43** Cf. Lev. 19:18 **5:44** NU *But I say to you, love your enemies and pray for those who persecute you* **5:47** M *friends* • NU *Gentiles* **6:4** NU omits *openly* **6:6** NU omits *openly* **6:13** NU omits *For Yours* through *Amen.*

18 "so that you do not appear to men to be fasting, but to your Father who *is* in the secret *place;* and your Father who sees in secret will reward you openly.*

Wealth—Luke 11:34–36; 12:22–34

19 [R]"Do not lay up for yourselves treasures on earth, where moth and rust destroy and where thieves break in and steal; Prov. 23:4

20 [R]"but lay up for yourselves treasures in heaven, where neither moth nor rust destroys and where thieves do not break in and steal. Matt. 19:21

21 "For where your treasure is, there your heart will be also.

22 [R]"The lamp of the body is the eye. If therefore your eye is good, your whole body will be full of light. Luke 11:34, 35

23 "But if your eye is [T]bad, your whole body will be full of darkness. If therefore the light that is in you is darkness, how great *is* that darkness! Evil, or unhealthy

24 [R]"No one can serve two masters; for either he will hate the one and love the other, or else he will be loyal to the one and despise the other. [R]You cannot serve God and mammon. Luke 16:9, 11, 13 • [Gal. 1:10]

25 "Therefore I say to you, do not worry about your life, what you will eat or what you will drink; nor about your body, what you will put on. Is not life more than food and the body more than clothing?

26 "Look at the birds of the air, for they neither sow nor reap nor gather into barns; yet your heavenly Father feeds them. Are you not of more value than they?

27 "Which of you by worrying can add one [T]cubit to his [T]stature? About 18 inches • *height*

28 "So why do you worry about clothing? Consider the lilies of the field, how they grow: they neither toil nor spin;

29 "and yet I say to you that even Solomon in all his glory was not [T]arrayed like one of these. *dressed*

30 "Now if God so clothes the grass of the field, which today is, and tomorrow is thrown into the oven, *will He* not much more *clothe* you, O you of little faith?

31 "Therefore do not worry, saying, 'What shall we eat?' or 'What shall we drink?' or 'What shall we wear?'

32 "For after all these things the Gentiles seek. For your heavenly Father knows that you need all these things.

33 "But [R]seek first the kingdom of God and His righteousness, and all these things shall be added to you. [1 Tim. 4:8]

34 "Therefore do not worry about tomorrow, for tomorrow will worry about its own things. Sufficient for the day *is* its own trouble.

CHAPTER 7

Judging—Luke 6:37–42

"JUDGE not, that you be not judged.

2 "For with what judgment you judge, you will be judged; and with the measure you use, it will be measured back to you.

3 [R]"And why do you look at the speck in your brother's eye, but do not consider the plank in your own eye? Luke 6:41

4 "Or how can you say to your brother, 'Let me remove the speck from your eye'; and look, a plank *is* in your own eye?

5 "Hypocrite! First remove the plank from your own eye, and then you will see clearly to remove the speck from your brother's eye.

6 [R]"Do not give what is holy to the dogs; nor cast your pearls before swine, lest they trample them under their feet, and turn and tear you in pieces. Prov. 9:7, 8

"Ask, and It Will Be Given"—Luke 11:9–13

7 [R]"Ask, and it will be given to you; seek, and you will find; knock, and it will be opened to you. [Mark 11:24]

8 "For [R]everyone who asks receives, and he who seeks finds, and to him who knocks it will be opened. Prov. 8:17

9 [R]"Or what man is there among you who, if his son asks for bread, will give him a stone? Luke 11:11

10 "Or if he asks for a fish, will he give him a serpent?

11 "If you then, being evil, know how to give good gifts to your children, how much more will your Father who is in heaven give good things to those who ask Him!

Golden Rule—Luke 6:31

12 "Therefore, [R]whatever you want men to do to you, do also to them, for [R]this is the Law and the Prophets. Luke 6:31 • Gal. 5:14

Two Ways of Life

13 [R]"Enter by the narrow gate; for wide *is* the gate and broad *is* the way that leads to destruction, and there are many who go in by it. Luke 13:24

14 "Because* narrow *is* the gate and [T]difficult *is* the way which leads to life, and there are few who find it. *confined*

False and True Teaching—Luke 6:43–45

15 [R]"Beware of false prophets, [R]who come to you in sheep's clothing, but inwardly they are ravenous wolves. Jer. 23:16 • Mic. 3:5

16 [R]"You will know them by their fruits. [R]Do men gather grapes from thornbushes or figs from thistles? Matt. 7:20; 12:33 • Luke 6:43

17 "Even so, every good tree bears good fruit, but a bad tree bears bad fruit.

6:18 NU, M omit *openly* **7:14** NU, M *How narrow . . . !*

18 "A good tree cannot bear bad fruit, nor *can* a bad tree bear good fruit.

19 "Every tree that does not bear good fruit is cut down and thrown into the fire.

20 "Therefore by their fruits you will know them.

True Way into the Kingdom—Luke 6:46

21 "Not everyone who says to Me, [R]'Lord, Lord,' shall enter the kingdom of heaven, but he who [R]does the will of My Father in heaven. Luke 6:46 • Rom. 2:13

22 "Many will say to Me in that day, 'Lord, Lord, have we [R]not prophesied in Your name, cast out demons in Your name, and done many wonders in Your name?' Num. 24:4

23 "And [R]then I will declare to them, 'I never knew you; [R]depart from Me, you who practice lawlessness!' [2 Tim. 2:19] • Ps. 5:5; 6:8☆

Parable of the Two Builders—Luke 6:47–49

24 "Therefore whoever hears these sayings of Mine, and does them, I will liken him to a wise man who built his house on the rock:

25 "and the rain descended, the floods came, and the winds blew and beat on that house; and it did not fall, for it was founded on the rock.

26 "But everyone who hears these sayings of Mine, and does not do them, will be like a foolish man who built his house on the sand:

27 "and the rain descended, the floods came, and the winds blew and beat on that house; and it fell. And great was its fall."

Response to the Sermon

28 And so it was, when Jesus had ended these sayings, that [R]the people were astonished at His teaching, Matt. 13:54

29 [R]for He taught them as one having authority, and not as the scribes. [John 7:46]

CHAPTER 8

The Leper Is Cleansed *Mark 1:40–44; Luke 5:12–14*

WHEN He had come down from the mountain, great multitudes followed Him.

2 [R]And behold, a leper came and worshiped Him, saying, "Lord, if You are willing, You can make me clean." Mark 1:40–45

3 Then Jesus put out *His* hand and touched him, saying, "I am willing; be cleansed." Immediately his leprosy [R]was cleansed. Luke 4:27

4 And Jesus said to him, "See that you tell no one; but go your way, show yourself to the priest, and offer the gift that Moses commanded, as a testimony to them."

The Centurion's Servant Is Healed *Luke 7:1–10*

5 [R]Now when Jesus had entered Capernaum, a [R]centurion came to Him, pleading with Him, Luke 7:1–3 • Matt. 27:54

6 saying, "Lord, my servant is lying at home paralyzed, dreadfully tormented."

7 And Jesus said to him, "I will come and heal him."

8 The centurion answered and said, "Lord, I am not worthy that You should come under my roof. But only speak a word, and my servant will be healed.

9 "For I also am a man under authority, having soldiers under me. And I say to this *one*, 'Go,' and he goes; and to another, 'Come,' and he comes; and to my servant, 'Do this,' and he does *it*."

10 When Jesus heard *it*, He marveled, and said to those who followed, "Assuredly, I say to you, I have not found such great faith, not even in Israel!

11 "And I say to you that [R]many will come from east and west, and sit down with Abraham, Isaac, and Jacob in the kingdom of heaven. Is. 49:12; 59:19; Mal. 1:11; Eph. 3:6☆

12 "But the sons of the kingdom [R]will be cast out into outer darkness. There will be weeping and gnashing of teeth." Luke 13:28

13 Then Jesus said to the centurion, "Go your way; and as you have believed, *so* let it be done for you." And his servant was healed that same hour.

Peter's Mother-in-Law Is Healed *Mark 1:29–34; Luke 4:38–41*

14 [R]Now when Jesus had come into Peter's house, He saw [R]his wife's mother lying sick with a fever. Mark 1:29–31 • 1 Cor. 9:5

15 So He touched her hand, and the fever left her. And she arose and served them.*

16 [R]When evening had come, they brought to Him many who were demon-possessed. And He cast out the spirits with a word, and healed all who were sick, Luke 4:40, 41

17 that it might be fulfilled which was spoken by Isaiah the prophet, saying:

"He Himself took our infirmities
*And bore our sicknesses."**

Demands of Discipleship—Luke 9:57–62

18 And when Jesus saw great multitudes about Him, He gave a command to depart to the other side.

19 [R]Then a certain scribe came and said to Him, "Teacher, I will follow You wherever You go." Luke 9:57, 58

20 And Jesus said to him, "Foxes have holes and birds of the air *have* nests, but the Son of Man has nowhere to lay *His* head."

21 [R]Then another of His disciples said to Him, "Lord, [R]let me first go and bury my father." Luke 9:59, 60 • 1 Kin. 19:20

22 But Jesus said to him, "Follow Me, and let the dead bury their own dead."

8:15 NU, M *Him* **8:17** Is. 53:4★

The Sea Is Stilled
Mark 4:35–41; Luke 8:22–25

23 Now when He got into a boat, His disciples followed Him.

24 [R]And suddenly a great tempest arose on the sea, so that the boat was covered with the waves. But He was asleep. Mark 4:37

25 Then His disciples came to *Him* and awoke Him, saying, "Lord, save us! We are perishing!"

26 But He said to them, "Why are you fearful, O you of little faith?" Then [R]He arose and rebuked the winds and the sea, and there was a great calm. Ps. 65:7; 89:9; 107:29

27 So the men marveled, saying, [T]"Who can this be, that even the winds and the sea obey Him?" Lit. *What sort of man is this*

Demons Are Cast into Swine
Mark 5:1–17; Luke 8:26–37

28 [R]When He had come to the other side, to the country of the Gergesenes,* there met Him two demon-possessed *men,* coming out of the tombs, exceedingly fierce, so that no one could pass that way. Mark 5:1–4

29 And suddenly they cried out, saying, "What have we to do with You, Jesus, You Son of God? Have You come here to torment us before the time?"

30 Now a good way off from them there was a herd of many swine feeding.

31 So the demons begged Him, saying, "If You cast us out, permit us to go away* into the herd of swine."

32 And He said to them, "Go." So when they had come out, they went into the herd of swine. And suddenly the whole herd of swine ran violently down the steep place into the sea, and perished in the water.

33 Then those who kept *them* fled; and they went away into the city and told everything, including what *had happened* to the demon-possessed *men.*

34 And behold, the whole city came out to meet Jesus. And when they saw Him, they begged *Him* to depart from their region.

CHAPTER 9

The Paralytic Is Forgiven
Mark 2:1–12; Luke 5:17–26

SO He got into a boat, crossed over, [R]and came to His own city. Matt. 4:13; 11:23

2 Then behold, they brought to Him a paralytic lying on a bed. When Jesus saw their faith, He said to the paralytic, "Son, be of good cheer; your sins are forgiven you."

3 And at once some of the scribes said within themselves, "This Man blasphemes!"

4 But Jesus, knowing their thoughts, said, "Why do you think evil in your hearts?

5 "For which is easier, to say, '*Your* sins are forgiven you,' or to say, 'Arise and walk'?

6 "But that you may know that the Son of Man has power on earth to forgive sins"—then He said to the paralytic, "Arise, take up your bed, and go to your house."

7 And he arose and departed to his house.

8 Now when the multitudes saw *it,* they [R]marveled* and glorified God, who had given such power to men. John 7:15

Matthew Is Called—Mark 2:14; Luke 5:27, 28

9 [R]As Jesus passed on from there, He saw a man named Matthew sitting at the tax office. And He said to him, "Follow Me." So he arose and followed Him. Luke 5:27

The Disciples Eat with Sinners
Mark 2:15–17; Luke 5:29–32

10 [R]Now it happened, as Jesus sat at the table in the house, *that* behold, many tax collectors and sinners came and sat down with Him and His disciples. Mark 2:15

11 And when the Pharisees saw *it,* they said to His disciples, "Why does your Teacher eat with [R]tax collectors and [R]sinners?" Matt. 11:19 • [Gal. 2:15]

12 When Jesus heard *that,* He said to them, "Those who are well have no need of a physician, but those who are sick.

13 "But go and learn what *this* means: *'I desire mercy and not sacrifice.'** For I did not come to call the righteous, [R]but sinners, to repentance."* 1 Tim. 1:15

The Disciples Do Not Fast
Mark 2:18–22; Luke 5:33–39

14 Then the disciples of John came to Him, saying, "Why do we and the Pharisees fast often,* but Your disciples do not fast?"

15 And Jesus said to them, "Can the friends of the bridegroom mourn as long as the bridegroom is with them? But the days will come when the bridegroom will be taken away from them, and then they will fast.

16 "No one puts a piece of unshrunk cloth on an old garment; for [T]the patch pulls away from the garment, and the tear is made worse. Lit. *that which is put on*

17 "Nor do they put new wine into old wineskins, or else the wineskins [T]break, the wine is spilled, and the wineskins are ruined. But they put new wine into new wineskins, and both are preserved." *burst*

Life Is Restored—Mark 5:21–43; Luke 8:40–56

18 [R]While He spoke these things to them, behold, a ruler came and worshiped Him, saying,

8:28 NU *Gadarenes* **8:31** NU *send us* **9:8** NU *were afraid* **9:13** Hos. 6:6 • NU omits *to repentance*
9:14 NU brackets *often* as disputed.

"My daughter has just died, but come and lay Your hand on her and she will live." Luke 8:41–56

19 So Jesus arose and followed him, and so *did* His [R]disciples. Matt. 10:2–4

20 And suddenly, a woman who had a flow of blood for twelve years came from behind and touched the hem of His garment.

21 For she said to herself, "If only I may touch His garment, I shall be made well."

22 But Jesus turned around, and when He saw her He said, "Be of good cheer, daughter; your faith has made you well." And the woman was made well from that hour.

23 [R]When Jesus came into the ruler's house, and saw [R]the flute players and the noisy crowd wailing, Mark 5:38 • 2 Chr. 35:25

24 He said to them, [R]"Make room, for the girl is not dead, but sleeping." And they ridiculed Him. Acts 20:10

25 But when the crowd was put outside, He went in and [R]took her by the hand, and the girl arose. Mark 1:31

26 And the [R]report of this went out into all that land. Matt. 4:24

Sight Is Restored

27 When Jesus departed from there, two blind men followed Him, crying out and saying, "Son of David, have mercy on us!"

28 And when He had come into the house, the blind men came to Him. And Jesus said to them, "Do you believe that I am able to do this?" They said to Him, "Yes, Lord."

29 Then He touched their eyes, saying, "According to your faith let it be to you."

30 And their eyes were opened. And Jesus sternly warned them, saying, [R]"See *that* no one knows *it*." Matt. 8:4

31 [R]But when they had departed, they [T]spread the news about Him in all that country. Mark 7:36 • Lit. *made Him known*

Speech Is Restored

32 As they went out, behold, they brought to Him a man, mute and demon-possessed.

33 And when the demon was cast out, the mute spoke. And the multitudes marveled, saying, "It was never seen like this in Israel!"

34 But the Pharisees said, "He casts out demons by the ruler of the demons."

The Need for Delegation of Power

35 Then Jesus went about all the cities and villages, [R]teaching in their synagogues, preaching the gospel of the kingdom, and healing every sickness and every disease among the people.* Matt. 4:23

36 [R]But when He saw the multitudes, He was moved with compassion for them, because they were weary* and scattered, like sheep having no shepherd. Mark 6:34

37 Then He said to His disciples, [R]"The harvest truly *is* plentiful, but the laborers *are* few. Luke 10:2

38 "Therefore pray the Lord of the harvest to send out laborers into His harvest."

CHAPTER 10

The Twelve Apostles Are Sent
Mark 6:7; Luke 9:1

AND [R]when He had called His twelve disciples to *Him,* He gave them power *over* unclean spirits, to cast them out, and to heal all kinds of sickness and all kinds of disease. Luke 6:13

2 Now the names of the twelve apostles are these: first, Simon, [R]who is called Peter, and Andrew his brother; James the *son* of Zebedee, and John his brother; John 1:42

3 Philip and Bartholomew; Thomas and Matthew the tax collector; James the *son* of Alphaeus, and Lebbaeus, whose surname was* Thaddaeus;

4 [R]Simon the Cananite,* and Judas Iscariot, who also betrayed Him. Acts 1:13

The Twelve Apostles Are Instructed
Mark 6:8–13; Luke 9:2–6; 12:2–10

5 These twelve Jesus sent out and commanded them, saying: [R]"Do not go into the way of the Gentiles, and do not enter a city of [R]the Samaritans. Matt. 4:15 • John 4:9

6 [R]"But go rather to the [R]lost sheep of the house of Israel. Matt. 15:24 • Jer. 50:6

7 [R]"And as you go, preach, saying, 'The kingdom of heaven is at hand.' Luke 9:2

8 "Heal the sick, cleanse the lepers, raise the dead,* cast out demons. [R]Freely you have received, freely give. [Acts 8:18]

9 [R]"Provide neither gold nor silver nor copper in your money belts, 1 Sam. 9:7

10 "nor bag for *your* journey, nor two tunics, nor sandals, nor staffs; [R]for a worker is worthy of his food. 1 Tim. 5:18

11 [R]"Now whatever city or town you enter, inquire who in it is worthy, and stay there till you go out. Luke 10:8

12 "And when you go into a household, greet it.

13 "If the household is worthy, let your peace come upon it. [R]But if it is not worthy, let your peace return to you. Ps. 35:13

14 [R]"And whoever will not receive you nor hear your words, when you depart from that house or city, [R]shake off the dust from your feet. Mark 6:11 • Acts 13:51

15 "Assuredly, I say to you, it will be more tolerable for the land of Sodom and Gomorrah in the day of judgment than for that city!

9:35 NU omits *among the people* **9:36** NU, M *harassed* **10:3** NU omits *Lebbaeus, whose surname was* **10:4** NU *Cananaean* **10:8** NU *raise the dead, cleanse the lepers;* M omits *raise the dead*

16 [R]"Behold, I send you out as sheep in the
midst of wolves. Therefore be wise as serpents and harmless as doves. Luke 10:3
17 "But beware of men, for [R]they will deliver
you up to councils and [R]scourge you in their
synagogues. Mark 13:9 • Acts 5:40; 22:19
18 [R]"You will be brought before governors
and kings for My sake, as a testimony to them
and to the Gentiles. 2 Tim. 4:16
19 "But when they deliver you up, do not
worry about how or what you should speak.
For [R]it will be given to you in that hour what
you should speak; Ex. 4:12
20 "for it is not you who speak, but the Spirit
of your Father who speaks in you.
21 [R]"Now brother will deliver up brother to
death, and a father *his* child; and children will
rise up against parents and cause them to be
put to death. Mic. 7:6
22 "And [R]you will be hated by all for My
name's sake. [R]But he who endures to the end
will be saved. Luke 21:17 • Mark 13:13
23 "When they persecute you in this city, flee
to another. For assuredly, I say to you, you will
not have gone through the cities of Israel before the Son of Man comes.
24 [R]"A disciple is not above *his* teacher, nor a
servant above his master. John 15:20
25 "It is enough for a disciple that he be like
his teacher, and a servant like his master. If
they have called the master of the house
Beelzebub,* how much more *will they call*
those of his household!
26 "Therefore do not fear them. For there is
nothing covered that will not be revealed, and
hidden that will not be known.
27 "Whatever I tell you in the dark, [R]speak in
the light; and what you hear in the ear, preach
on the housetops. Acts 5:20
28 [R]"And do not fear those who kill the body
but cannot kill the soul. But rather [R]fear Him
who is able to destroy both soul and body in
hell. Luke 12:4 • Luke 12:5
29 "Are not two sparrows sold for a copper
coin? And not one of them falls to the ground
apart from your Father's will.
30 [R]"But the very hairs of your head are all
numbered. Luke 21:18
31 "Do not fear therefore; you are of more
value than many sparrows.
32 [R]"Therefore whoever confesses Me before
men, [R]him I will also confess before My Father who is in heaven. Luke 12:8 • [Rev. 3:5]
33 [R]"But whoever denies Me before men,
him I will also deny before My Father who is
in heaven. 2 Tim. 2:12
34 [R]"Do not think that I came to bring peace
on earth. I did not come to bring peace but a
sword. [Luke 12:49]
35 "For I have come to [T]*'set a man against
his father, a daughter against her mother,
and a daughter-in-law against her mother-in-law'*; *alienate a man from*
36 "and [R]*'a man's enemies will be those of
his own household.'** Ps. 41:9; John 13:18★
37 [R]"He who loves father or mother more
than Me is not worthy of Me. And he who
loves son or daughter more than Me is not
worthy of Me. Luke 14:26
38 "And he who does not take his cross and
follow after Me is not worthy of Me.
39 "He who finds his life will lose it, and he
who loses his life for My sake will find it.
40 [R]"He who receives you receives Me, and
he who receives Me receives Him who sent
Me. Luke 9:48
41 [R]"He who receives a prophet in the name
of a prophet shall receive a prophet's reward.
And he who receives a righteous man in the
name of a righteous man shall receive a righteous man's reward. 1 Kin. 17:10
42 [R]"And whoever gives one of these little
ones only a cup of cold *water* in the name of
a disciple, assuredly, I say to you, he shall by
no means lose his reward." Mark 9:41

CHAPTER 11

Now it came to pass, when Jesus finished
commanding His twelve disciples, that
He departed from there to [R]teach and to
preach in their cities. Luke 23:5

Rejection of John the Baptist—Luke 7:19–30

2 [R]And when John had heard [R]in prison
about the works of Christ, he sent two of* his
disciples Luke 7:18–35 • Matt. 4:12; 14:3
3 and said to Him, "Are You [R]the Coming
One, or do we look for another?" John 6:14
4 Jesus answered and said to them, "Go
and tell John the [R]things which you hear and
see: Is. 29:18, 19; 35:4–6★
5 "*The* blind see and *the* lame walk; *the* lepers are cleansed and *the* deaf hear; *the* dead
are raised up and [R]*the* poor have the gospel
preached to them. Is. 61:1
6 "And blessed is he who is not [R]offended
because of Me." [Rom. 9:32]
7 [R]As they departed, Jesus began to say to
the multitudes concerning John: "What did
you go out into the wilderness to see? A reed
shaken by the wind? Luke 7:24
8 "But what did you go out to see? A man
clothed in soft garments? Indeed, those who
wear soft *clothing* are in kings' houses.
9 "But what did you go out to see? A
prophet? Yes, I say to you, [R]and more than a
prophet. Luke 1:76; 20:6
10 "For this is *he* of whom it is written:

*'Behold, I send My messenger before
Your face,
Who will prepare Your way before You.'**

10:25 NU, M *Beelzebul;* a Philistine deity, 2 Kin. 1:2, 3
10:36 Mic. 7:6★ **11:2** NU *by* for *two of* **11:10** Mal. 3:1★

11 "Assuredly, I say to you, among those born of women there has not risen one greater than John the Baptist; but he who is least in the kingdom of heaven is greater than he.

12 "And from the days of John the Baptist until now the kingdom of heaven suffers violence, and the violent take it by force.

13 [R]"For all the prophets and the law prophesied until John. Mal. 4:4–6

14 "And if you are willing to receive *it*, he is [R]Elijah who is to come. Luke 1:17

15 "He who has ears to hear, let him hear!

Rejection by Jesus' Generation *Luke 7:31–35*

16 "But to what shall I liken this generation? It is like children sitting in the marketplaces and calling to their companions,

17 "and saying:

'We played the flute for you,
  And you did not dance;
We mourned to you,
  And you did not lament.'

18 "For John came neither eating nor drinking, and they say, 'He has a demon.'

19 "The Son of Man came eating and drinking, and they say, 'Look, a glutton and a [T]winebibber, [R]a friend of tax collectors and sinners!' [R]But wisdom is justified by her children."* *wine drinker* • Matt. 9:10 • Luke 7:35

Rejection of Chorazin, Bethsaida, and Capernaum—Luke 10:12–15

20 Then He began to rebuke the cities in which most of His mighty works had been done, because they did not repent:

21 "Woe to you, Chorazin! Woe to you, Bethsaida! For if the mighty works which were done in you had been done in Tyre and Sidon, they would have repented long ago [R]in sackcloth and ashes. Jon. 3:6–8

22 "But I say to you, [R]it will be more tolerable for Tyre and Sidon in the day of judgment than for you. Matt. 10:15; 11:24

23 "And you, Capernaum, who are exalted to heaven, will be* brought down to Hades; for if the mighty works which were done in you had been done in Sodom, it would have remained until this day.

24 "But I say to you [R]that it shall be more tolerable for the land of Sodom in the day of judgment than for you." Matt. 10:15

Invitation to Come to Jesus

25 [R]**At that time Jesus answered and said,** "I thank You, Father, Lord of heaven and earth, that [R]You have hidden these things from *the* wise and prudent and have revealed them to babes. Luke 10:21, 22 • Ps. 8:2

26 "Even so, Father, for so it seemed good in Your sight.

27 [R]"All things have been delivered to Me by My Father, and no one knows the Son except the Father. Nor does anyone know the Father except the Son, and *the one* to whom the Son wills to reveal *Him.* Matt. 28:18

28 "Come to Me, all *you* who labor and are heavy laden, and I will give you rest.

29 "Take My yoke upon you and learn from Me, for I am gentle and lowly in heart, and you will find rest for your souls.

30 [R]"For My yoke *is* easy and My burden is light." [1 John 5:3]

CHAPTER 12

Controversy over Sabbath-Labor *Mark 2:23–28; Luke 6:1–5*

AT that time Jesus went through the grainfields on the Sabbath. And His disciples were hungry, and began to [R]pluck heads of grain and to eat. Deut. 23:25

2 And when the Pharisees saw *it*, they said to Him, "Look, Your disciples are doing what is not lawful to do on the Sabbath!"

3 But He said to them, "Have you not read [R]what David did when he was hungry, he and those who were with him: 1 Sam. 21:6

4 "how he entered the house of God and ate [R]the showbread which was not lawful for him to eat, nor for those who were with him, [R]but only for the priests? Lev. 24:5 • Ex. 29:32

5 "Or have you not read in the law that on the Sabbath the priests in the temple profane the Sabbath, and are blameless?

6 "Yet I say to you that in this place there is [R]*One* greater than the temple. [Is. 66:1, 2]

7 "But if you had known what *this* means, *'I desire mercy and not sacrifice,'** you would not have condemned the guiltless.

8 "For the Son of Man is Lord even* of the Sabbath."

Controversy over Sabbath-Healing *Mark 3:1–5; Luke 6:6–10*

9 [R]Now when He had departed from there, He went into their synagogue. Mark 3:1–6

10 And behold, there was a man who had a withered hand. And they asked Him, saying, [R]"Is it lawful to heal on the Sabbath?"—that they might accuse Him. John 9:16

11 Then He said to them, "What man is there among you who has one sheep, and if it falls into a pit on the Sabbath, will not lay hold of it and lift *it* out?

12 "Of how much more value then is a man than a sheep? Therefore it is lawful to do good on the Sabbath."

13 Then He said to the man, "Stretch out

11:19 NU *works* **11:23** NU *will you be exalted to heaven? No, you will be* **12:7** Hos. 6:6 **12:8** NU, M omit *even*

your hand." And he stretched *it* out, and it was
restored as whole as the other.

Pharisees Plan to Destroy Christ
Mark 3:6–12; Luke 6:11

14 Then [R]the Pharisees went out and plot-
ted against Him, how they might destroy
Him. Mark 3:6
15 But when Jesus knew *it,* [R]He withdrew
from there. And great multitudes* followed
Him, and He healed them all. Mark 3:7
16 Yet He [R]warned them not to make Him
known, Matt. 8:4; 9:30; 17:9
17 that it might be fulfilled which was spo-
ken by Isaiah the prophet, saying:

18*"Behold! My Servant whom I have*
chosen,
My Beloved [R]in whom My soul is well
pleased! Matt. 3:17; 17:5
I will put My Spirit upon Him,
And He will declare justice to the
Gentiles.
19 *He will not quarrel nor cry out,*
Nor will anyone hear His voice in the
streets.
20 *A bruised reed He will not break,*
And smoking flax He will not quench,
Till He sends forth justice to victory;
21 *And in His name Gentiles will trust."**

Pharisees Blaspheme the Holy Spirit
Mark 3:22–27; Luke 11:14–23

22 [R]Then one was brought to Him who was
demon-possessed, blind and mute; and He
healed him, so that the blind and* mute man
both spoke and saw. Luke 11:14
23 And all the multitudes were amazed and
said, "Could this be the Son of David?"

24 [R]Now when the Pharisees heard *it* they
said, "This *fellow* does not cast out demons
except by Beelzebub,* the ruler of the
demons." Matt. 9:34

25 But Jesus [R]knew their thoughts, and said to
them: "Every kingdom divided against itself is
brought to desolation, and every city or house
divided against itself will not stand. Matt. 9:4
26 "If Satan casts out Satan, he is divided
against himself. How then will his kingdom
stand?
27 "And if I cast out demons by Beelzebub,
by whom do your sons cast *them* out? There-
fore they shall be your judges.
28 "But if I cast out demons by the Spirit of
God, [R]surely the kingdom of God has come
upon you. [Dan. 2:44; 7:14]
29 [R]"Or how can one enter a strong man's
house and plunder his goods, unless he first
binds the strong man? And then he will plun-
der his house. Is. 49:24
30 "He who is not with Me is against Me, and
he who does not gather with Me scatters
abroad.

Pharisees Commit the Unpardonable Sin
Mark 3:28, 29

31 "Therefore I say to you, [R]every sin and
blasphemy will be forgiven men, [R]but the
blasphemy *against* the Spirit will not be for-
given men. Mark 3:28–30 • Acts 7:51
32 "Anyone who [R]speaks a word against the
Son of Man, [R]it will be forgiven him; but who-
ever speaks against the Holy Spirit, it will not
be forgiven him, either in this age or in the
age to come. John 7:12, 52 • 1 Tim. 1:13
33 "Either make the tree good and its fruit
good, or else make the tree bad and its fruit
bad; for a tree is known by *its* fruit.
34 "Brood of vipers! How can you, being evil,
speak good things? For out of the abundance
of the heart the mouth speaks.
35 "A good man out of the good treasure of
his heart* brings forth good things, and an
evil man out of the evil treasure brings forth
evil things.
36 "But I say to you that for every idle word
men may speak, they will give account of it in
the day of judgment.
37 "For by your words you will be justified,
and by your words you will be condemned."

Pharisees Demand a Sign
Luke 11:24–26, 29–32

38 [R]Then some of the scribes and Pharisees
answered, saying, "Teacher, we want to see a
sign from You." Mark 8:11
39 But He answered and said to them, "An

12:15 NU brackets *multitudes* as disputed. **12:21** Is. 42:1–4★ **12:22** NU omits *blind and* **12:24** NU, M *Beelzebul,* a Philistine deity **12:35** NU, M omit *of his heart*

12:24 Demons: Relation to Satan—The relation of the fallen angels to Satan is presented in the Bible under two figures of speech:

a. He is their ruler. Satan is "the ruler of the demons" (Matt. 12:24) and "the prince of the power of the air" (Page 1205—Eph. 2:2). "Principalities or powers" is biblical shorthand for organized spiritual forces (Page 1220—Col. 1:16).
b. He is their captain. The fallen angels function as an army under the control of Satan opposing the hosts of heaven (Page 1209—Eph. 6:12; Page 1320—Rev. 12:7–9).

Nowhere in the Bible do fallen angels worship Satan. They are not said to love him, which is impossible, or to fear him, although that seems likely. Someday they will reluctantly bow before the Lord Jesus (Page 1214—Phil. 2:10, 11).

Now turn to Page 1057—Luke 11:24–26: Demons: Interaction with Humans.

evil and [R]adulterous generation seeks after a
sign, and no sign will be given to it except the
sign of the prophet Jonah. Matt. 16:4
40 [R]"For as Jonah was three days and three
nights in the belly of the great fish, so will the
Son of Man be three days and three nights in
the heart of the earth. Jon. 1:17☆
41 "The men of Nineveh will rise up in the
judgment with this generation and [R]condemn
it, [R]because they repented at the preaching of
Jonah; and indeed a greater than Jonah *is*
here. Jer. 3:11 • Jon. 3:5
42 "The queen of the South will rise up in the
judgment with this generation and condemn
it, for she came from the ends of the earth to
hear the wisdom of Solomon; and indeed a
greater than Solomon *is* here.
43 [R]"When an unclean spirit goes out of a
man, he goes through dry places, seeking rest,
and finds none. Luke 11:24–26
44 "Then he says, 'I will return to my house
from which I came.' And when he comes, he
finds *it* empty, swept, and put in order.
45 "Then he goes and takes with him seven
other spirits more wicked than himself, and
they enter and dwell there; and the last *state*
of that man is worse than the first. So shall it
also be with this wicked generation."

Jesus and the True Brethren—Mark 3:31–35

**46 While He was still talking to the multi-
tudes, behold, His mother and brothers stood
outside, seeking to speak with Him.**
**47 Then one said to Him, "Look, Your mother
and Your brothers are standing outside, seek-
ing to speak with You."**
**48 But He answered and said to the one who
told Him,** "Who is My mother and who are My
brothers?"
**49 And He stretched out His hand toward
His disciples and said,** "Here are My mother
and My [R]brothers! John 20:17
50 "For [R]whoever does the will of My Father
in heaven is My brother and sister and
mother." John 15:14

CHAPTER 13

Parable of the Soils
Mark 4:1–20; Luke 8:4–15

**ON the same day Jesus went out of the
house and sat by the sea.**
**2 [R]And great multitudes were gathered to-
gether to Him, so that [R]He got into a boat and
sat; and the whole multitude stood on the
shore.** Luke 8:4 • Luke 5:3
**3 Then He spoke many things to them in
parables, saying:** [R]"Behold, a sower went out
to sow. Luke 8:5
4 "And as he sowed, some *seed* fell by the
wayside; and the birds came and devoured
them.
5 "Some fell on stony places, where they
did not have much earth; and they immedi-
ately sprang up because they had no depth of
earth.
6 "But when the sun was up they were
scorched, and because they had no root they
withered away.
7 "And some fell among thorns, and the
thorns sprang up and choked them.
8 "But others fell on good ground and
yielded a crop: some [R]a hundredfold, some
sixty, some thirty. Gen. 26:12
9 "He who has ears to hear, let him hear!"
**10 And the disciples came and said to Him,
"Why do You speak to them in parables?"**
11 He answered and said to them, "Because
[R]it has been given to you to know the myster-
ies of the kingdom of heaven, but to them it
has not been given. Mark 4:10, 11
12 [R]"For whoever has, to him more will be
given, and he will have abundance; but who-
ever does not have, even what he has will be
taken away from him. Matt. 25:29
13 "Therefore I speak to them in parables,
because seeing they do not see, and hearing
they do not hear, nor do they understand.
14 "And in them the prophecy of Isaiah is
fulfilled, which says:

'Hearing you will hear and shall not
understand,
And seeing you will see and not
[R]*perceive;* [John 3:36]
15 *For the hearts of this people have grown*
dull.
Their ears are hard of hearing,
And their eyes they have [R]*closed*
Lest they should see with their eyes and
hear with their ears, Luke 19:42
Lest they should understand with their
hearts and turn,
So that I should heal them.'**

16 "But [R]blessed *are* your eyes for they see,
and your ears for they hear; Luke 10:23, 24
17 "for assuredly, I say to you that many
prophets and righteous *men* desired to see
what you see, and did not see *it*, and to hear
what you hear, and did not hear *it*.
18 [R]"Therefore hear the parable of the
sower: Mark 4:13–20
19 "When anyone hears the word [R]of the
kingdom, and does not understand *it*, then the
wicked *one* comes and snatches away what
was sown in his heart. This is he who received
seed by the wayside. Matt. 4:23
20 "But he who received the seed on stony
places, this is he who hears the word and im-
mediately [R]receives it with joy; Is. 58:2
21 "yet he has no root in himself, but endures
only for a while. For when tribulation or per-

13:15 NU, M *would* • Is. 6:9, 10★

secution arises because of the word, immedi-
ately [R]he stumbles. Matt. 11:6
22 "Now [R]he who received seed [R]among the
thorns is he who hears the word, and the
cares of this world and the deceitfulness of
riches choke the word, and he becomes un-
fruitful. 1 Tim. 6:9 • Jer. 4:3
23 "But he who received seed on the good
ground is he who hears the word and under-
stands *it,* who indeed bears [R]fruit and pro-
duces: some a hundredfold, some sixty, some
thirty." Col. 1:6

Parable of the Wheat and Tares

**24 Another parable He put forth to them,
saying:** "The kingdom of heaven is like a man
who sowed good seed in his field;
25 "but while men slept, his enemy came and
sowed tares among the wheat and went his
way.
26 "But when the grain had sprouted and
produced a crop, then the tares also appeared.
27 "So the servants of the owner came and
said to him, 'Sir, did you not sow good seed in
your field? How then does it have tares?'
28 "He said to them, 'An enemy has done
this.' The servants said to him, 'Do you want
us then to go and gather them up?'
29 "But he said, 'No, lest while you gather up
the tares you also uproot the wheat with
them.
30 'Let both grow together until the harvest,
and at the time of harvest I will say to the
reapers, "First gather together the tares and
bind them in bundles to burn them, but gather
the wheat into my barn." ' "

Parable of the Mustard Seed
Mark 4:30–32; Luke 13:18, 19

**31 Another parable He put forth to them,
saying:** [R]"The kingdom of heaven is like a
mustard seed, which a man took and sowed in
his field, Luke 13:18, 19
32 "which indeed is the least of all the
seeds; but when it is grown it is greater than
the herbs and becomes a [R]tree, so that the
birds of the air come and nest in its
branches." Ezek. 17:22–24; 31:3–9

Parable of the Leaven—Luke 13:20, 21

33 Another parable He spoke to them: "The
kingdom of heaven is like leaven, which a
woman took and hid in three measures* of
meal till [R]it was all leavened." [1 Cor. 5:6]
**34 [R]All these things Jesus spoke to the mul-
titude in parables; and without a parable He
did not speak to them,** Mark 4:33, 34
**35 that it might be fulfilled which was spo-
ken by the prophet, saying:**

"I will open My mouth in parables;
[R]*I will utter things kept secret from the*
*foundation of the world."** Eph. 3:9

Parable of the Tares Explained

**36 Then Jesus sent the multitude away and
went into the house. And His disciples came
to Him, saying, "Explain to us the parable of
the tares of the field."**
37 He answered and said to them: "He who
sows the good seed is the Son of Man.
38 [R]"The field is the world, the good seeds
are the sons of the kingdom, but the tares are
the sons of the wicked *one.* Rom. 10:18
39 "The enemy who sowed them is the devil,
[R]the harvest is the end of the age, and the
reapers are the angels. Rev. 14:15
40 "Therefore as the tares are gathered and
burned in the fire, so it will be at the end of
this age.
41 "The Son of Man will send out His angels,
[R]and they will gather out of His kingdom all
things that offend, and those who practice
lawlessness, Matt. 18:7
42 [R]"and will cast them into the furnace of
fire. [R]There will be wailing and gnashing of
teeth. Rev. 19:20; 20:10 • Matt. 8:12; 13:50
43 "Then the righteous will shine forth as the
sun in the kingdom of their Father. He who
has ears to hear, let him hear!

Parable of the Hidden Treasure

44 "Again, the kingdom of heaven is like
treasure hidden in a field, which a man
found and hid; and for joy over it he goes
and [R]sells all that he has and [R]buys that
field. Phil. 3:7, 8 • [Is. 55:1]

Parable of the Pearl of Great Price

45 "Again, the kingdom of heaven is like a
merchant seeking beautiful pearls,
46 "who, when he had found [R]one pearl of
great price, went and sold all that he had and
bought it. Prov. 2:4; 3:14, 15; 8:10, 19

Parable of the Dragnet

47 "Again, the kingdom of heaven is like a
dragnet that was cast into the sea and [R]gath-
ered some of every kind, Matt. 22:9, 10
48 "which, when it was full, they drew to
shore; and they sat down and gathered the
good into vessels, but threw the bad away.
49 "So it will be at the end of the age. The
angels will come forth, [R]separate the wicked
from among the just, Matt. 25:32
50 "and cast them into the furnace of fire.
There will be wailing and gnashing of teeth."

Parable of the Householder

51 Jesus said to them,* "Have you under-
stood all these things?" **They said to Him,
"Yes, Lord."***
52 Then He said to them, "Therefore every

13:33 Gr. *sata,* same as a Heb. *seah;* approximately 2 pecks in all **13:35** Ps. 78:2★ **13:51** NU omits *Jesus said to them* • NU omits *Lord*

scribe instructed concerning* the kingdom of heaven is like a householder who brings out of his treasure *things* new and old."

53 Now it came to pass, when Jesus had finished these parables, that He departed from there.

Rejection at Nazareth—Mark 6:1–6

54 [R]When He had come to His own country, He [R]taught them in their synagogue, so that they were astonished and said, "Where did this *Man* get this wisdom and *these* mighty works? Luke 4:16 • Ps. 22:22★

55 "Is this not the carpenter's son? Is not His mother called Mary? And His brothers James, Joses,* Simon, and Judas?

56 "And His sisters, are they not all with us? Where then did this *Man* get all these things?"

57 So they [R]were offended at Him. But Jesus said to them, [R]"A prophet is not without honor except in his own country and in his own house." Matt. 11:6 • Luke 4:24

58 Now [R]He did not do many mighty works there because of their unbelief. Mark 6:5, 6

CHAPTER 14

Present Response to Jesus Mark 6:14–16; Luke 9:7–9

At that time [R]Herod the tetrarch heard the report about Jesus Mark 6:14–29

2 and said to his servants, "This is John the Baptist; he is risen from the dead, and therefore these powers are at work in him."

Recount of the Murder of John the Baptist Mark 6:17–29

3 For Herod had laid hold of John and bound him, and put *him* in prison for the sake of Herodias, his brother Philip's wife.

4 Because John had said to him, [R]"It is not lawful for you to have her." Lev. 18:16

5 And although he wanted to put him to death, he feared the multitude, [R]because they counted him as a prophet. Luke 20:6

6 But when Herod's birthday was celebrated, the daughter of Herodias danced before them and pleased Herod.

7 Therefore he promised with an oath to give her whatever she might ask.

8 So she, having been prompted by her mother, said, "Give me John the Baptist's head here on a platter."

9 And the king was sorry; nevertheless, because of the oaths and because of those who sat with him, he commanded *it* to be given to *her*.

10 So he sent and had John beheaded in prison.

11 And his head was brought on a platter and given to the girl, and she brought *it* to her mother.

12 Then his disciples came and took away the body and buried it, and went and told Jesus.

Jesus Feeds 5,000 Mark 6:31–44; Luke 9:11–17; John 6:1–13

13 When Jesus heard *it*, He departed from there by boat to a deserted place by Himself. But when the multitudes heard it, they followed Him on foot from the cities.

14 And when Jesus went out He saw a great multitude; and He was moved with compassion for them, and healed their sick.

15 When it was evening, His disciples came to Him, saying, "This is a deserted place, and the hour is already late. Send the multitudes away, that they may go into the villages and buy themselves food."

16 But Jesus said to them, "They do not need to go away. You give them something to eat."

17 And they said to Him, "We have here only five loaves and two fish."

18 He said, "Bring them here to Me."

19 Then He commanded the multitudes to sit down on the grass. And He took the five loaves and the two fish, and looking up to heaven, [R]He blessed and broke and gave the loaves to the disciples; and the disciples gave to the multitudes. Matt. 15:36; 26:26

20 So they all ate and were filled, and they took up twelve baskets full of the fragments that remained.

21 Now those who had eaten were about five thousand men, besides women and children.

Jesus Walks on Water Mark 6:45–52; John 6:14–21

22 Immediately Jesus [T]made His disciples get into the boat and go before Him to the other side, while He sent the multitudes away. *invited, strongly urged*

23 [R]And when He had sent the multitudes away, He went up on the mountain by Himself to pray. [R]Now when evening came, He was alone there. Mark 6:46 • John 6:16

24 But the boat was now in the middle of the sea,* tossed by the waves, for the wind was contrary.

25 Now in the fourth watch of the night Jesus went to them, walking on the sea.

26 And when the disciples saw Him walking on the sea, they were troubled, saying, "It is a ghost!" And they cried out for fear.

27 But immediately Jesus spoke to them, saying, [T]"Be of good [R]cheer! It is I; do not be afraid." *Take courage* • Acts 23:11; 27:22, 25, 36

28 And Peter answered Him and said, "Lord, if it is You, command me to come to You on the water."

29 So He said, "Come." And when Peter had come down out of the boat, he walked on the water to go to Jesus.

30 But when he saw that the wind *was* bois-

13:52 Or *for* **13:55** NU *Joseph* **14:24** NU *many furlongs away from the land*

terous,* he was afraid; and beginning to sink he cried out, saying, "Lord, save me!"
31 And immediately Jesus stretched out *His* hand and caught him, and said to him, "O you of little faith, why did you doubt?"
32 And when they got into the boat, the wind ceased.
33 Then those who were in the boat came and* worshiped Him, saying, "Truly [R]You are the Son of God." Ps. 2:7

Jesus Heals Many—Mark 6:53–56

34 [R]When they had crossed over, they came to the land of* Gennesaret. Mark 6:53
35 And when the men of that place recognized Him, they sent out into all that surrounding region, brought to Him all who were sick,
36 and begged Him that they might only touch the hem of His garment. And as many as touched *it* were made perfectly well.

CHAPTER 15

Debate over Tradition—Mark 7:1–23

THEN [R]the scribes and Pharisees who were from Jerusalem came to Jesus, saying, Mark 7:1
2 [R]"Why do Your disciples transgress the tradition of the elders? For they do not wash their hands when they eat bread." Mark 7:5
3 He answered and said to them, "Why do you also transgress the commandment of God because of your tradition?
4 "For God commanded, saying, *'Honor your father and your mother';** and, *'He who curses father or mother, let him be put to death.'**
5 "But you say, 'Whoever says to his father or mother, [R]"Whatever profit you might have received from me *is a gift to God*"— Mark 7:11, 12
6 'then he need not honor his father or mother.'* Thus you have made the commandment* of God of no effect by your tradition.
7 [R]"Hypocrites! Well did Isaiah prophesy about you, saying: Mark 7:6

8 *'These people draw near to Me with their*
mouth,
And honor Me with their lips,*
But their heart is far from Me.
9 *And in vain they worship Me,*
Teaching as doctrines the
commandments of men.' "*

10 [R]When He had called the multitude to *Himself,* He said to them, "Hear and understand: Mark 7:14
11 [R]"Not what goes into the mouth defiles a man; but what comes out of the mouth, this defiles a man." [Acts 10:15]
12 Then His disciples came and said to Him, "Do You know that the Pharisees were offended when they heard this saying?"
13 But He answered and said, [R]"Every plant which My heavenly Father has not planted will be uprooted. [John 15:2]
14 "Let them alone. [R]They are blind leaders of the blind. And if the blind leads the blind, both will fall into a ditch." Luke 6:39
15 [R]Then Peter answered and said to Him, "Explain this parable to us." Mark 7:17
16 So Jesus said, [R]"Are you also still without understanding? Matt. 16:9
17 "Do you not yet understand that [R]whatever enters the mouth goes into the stomach and is eliminated? [1 Cor. 6:13]
18 "But [R]those things which proceed out of the mouth come from the heart, and they defile a man. [James 3:6]
19 "For out of the heart proceed evil thoughts, murders, adulteries, fornications, thefts, false witness, blasphemies.
20 "These are *the things* which defile a man, but to eat with unwashed hands does not defile a man."

Jesus Heals the Gentile Woman's Daughter Mark 7:24–30

21 Then Jesus went out from there and departed to the region of Tyre and Sidon.
22 And behold, a woman of Canaan came from that region and cried out to Him, saying, "Have mercy on me, O Lord, [R]Son of David! My daughter is severely demon-possessed." Matt. 1:1; 22:41, 42
23 But He answered her not a word. And His disciples came and urged Him, saying, "Send her away, for she cries out after us."
24 But He answered and said, [R]"I was not sent except to the lost sheep of the house of Israel." Matt. 10:5, 6
25 Then she came and worshiped Him, saying, "Lord, help me!"
26 But He answered and said, "It is not good to take the children's bread and throw *it* to the little [R]dogs." Matt. 7:6
27 And she said, "Yes, Lord, yet even the little dogs eat the crumbs which fall from their masters' table."
28 Then Jesus answered and said to her, "O woman, [R]great *is* your faith! Let it be to you as you desire." And her daughter was healed from that very hour. Luke 7:9

Jesus Heals Many—Mark 7:31–37

29 [R]Jesus departed from there, [R]skirted the Sea of Galilee, and went up on the mountain and sat down there. Mark 7:31–37 • Matt. 4:18
30 [R]Then great multitudes came to Him, having with them *the* lame, blind, mute,

14:30 NU brackets *that* and *boisterous* as disputed. **14:33** NU omits *came and* **14:34** NU *to land at* **15:4** Ex. 20:12; Deut. 5:16 • Ex. 21:17 **15:6** NU omits *or mother* • NU *word* **15:8** NU omits *draw near to Me with their mouth, And* **15:9** Is. 29:13

[T]maimed, and many others; and they laid
them down at Jesus' [R]feet, and He healed
them. Is. 35:5, 6 • *crippled* • Luke 7:38; 8:41; 10:39
31 So the multitude marveled when they saw
the mute speaking, *the* maimed made whole,
the lame walking, and *the* blind seeing; and
they glorified the God of Israel.

Jesus Feeds 4,000—Mark 8:1–10

32 [R]Now Jesus called His disciples to *Him-*
self and said, "I have compassion on the mul-
titude, because they have now continued with
Me three days and have nothing to eat. And I
do not want to send them away hungry, lest
they faint on the way." Mark 8:1–10
33 [R]Then His disciples said to Him, "Where
could we get enough bread in the wilderness
to fill such a great multitude?" 2 Kin. 4:43
34 Jesus said to them, "How many loaves do
you have?" And they said, "Seven, and a few
little fish."
35 So He commanded the multitude to sit
down on the ground.
36 And [R]He took the seven loaves and the
fish and [R]gave thanks, broke *them* and gave
them to His disciples; and the disciples *gave*
to the multitude. Matt. 14:19; 26:27 • Luke 22:19
37 So they all ate and were filled, and they
took up seven large baskets full of the frag-
ments that were left.
38 Now those who ate were four thousand
men, besides women and children.
39 [R]And He sent away the multitude, got
into the boat, and came to the region of Mag-
dala.* Mark 8:10

CHAPTER 16

Debate over a Sign from Heaven
Mark 8:11, 12

THEN the Pharisees and Sadducees came,
and testing Him asked that He would
show them a sign from heaven.
2 He answered and said to them, "When it
is evening you say, '*It will be* fair weather, for
the sky is red';
3 "and in the morning, '*It will be* foul
weather today, for the sky is red and threat-
ening.' Hypocrites!* You know how to discern
the face of the sky, but you cannot *discern* the
signs of the times.
4 [R]"A wicked and adulterous generation
seeks after a sign, and no sign shall be given
to it except the sign of the prophet* Jonah."
And He left them and departed. Matt. 12:39

Withdrawal of Jesus—Mark 8:13–21

5 Now [R]when His disciples had come to
the other side, they had forgotten to take
bread. Mark 8:14
6 Then Jesus said to them, [R]"Take heed and
beware of the [T]leaven of the Pharisees and the
Sadducees." Luke 12:1 • *yeast*
7 And they reasoned among themselves,
saying, "*It is* because we have taken no bread."
8 But Jesus, being aware of *it*, said to them,
"O you of little faith, why do you reason
among yourselves because you have brought
no bread?*
9 "Do you not yet understand, or remember
the five loaves of the five thousand and how
many baskets you took up?
10 [R]"Nor the seven loaves of the four thou-
sand and how many large baskets you took
up? Matt. 15:32–38
11 "How is it you do not understand that I
did not speak to you concerning bread?—*but*
to beware of the [T]leaven of the Pharisees and
Sadducees." *yeast*
12 Then they understood that He did not tell
them to beware of the leaven of bread, but of
the [T]doctrine of the Pharisees and Sad-
ducees. *teaching*

Revelation of the Person of the King
Mark 8:27–30; Luke 9:18–21

13 When Jesus came into the region of
Caesarea Philippi, He asked His disciples,
saying, [R]"Who do men say that I, the Son of
Man, am?" Luke 9:18
14 So they said, [R]"Some *say* John the Bap-
tist, some Elijah, and others Jeremiah or [R]one
of the prophets." Matt. 14:2 • Matt. 21:11
15 He said to them, "But who do [R]you say
that I am?" John 6:67
16 Simon Peter answered and said, "You are
the Christ, the Son of the living God."
17 Jesus answered and said to him, "Blessed
are you, Simon Bar-Jonah, for flesh and blood
has not revealed *this* to you, but [R]My Father
who is in heaven. Gal. 1:16

Revelation of the Church

18 "And I also say to you that [R]you are Pe-
ter, and [R]on this rock I will [R]build My church,
and the gates of Hades shall not prevail
against it. John 1:42 • [Eph. 2:20] • Acts 2:41, 47☆

15:39 NU *Magadan* **16:3** NU omits *Hypocrites*
16:4 NU omits *the prophet* **16:8** NU *have no bread*

16:18 The Origin of the Church—The church was a mystery (that is, hidden, not revealed) in the Old Testament. It was first prophesied in these words spoken to Peter, "on this rock I will build My church." In this prophecy there is a play on the word "rock" which also happens to be Peter's name. Jesus said, "you are Peter" (masculine, *petros*) and "on this rock [feminine, *petra*] I will build My church." But when did the church actually begin? Again, many suggestions are offered for varying reasons. The simplest view is to understand the New Testament church as beginning on the Day of Pentecost in response to Peter's Pen-

19 R"And I will give you the keys of the
kingdom of heaven, and whatever you bind
on earth will be bound in heaven, and what-
ever you loose on earth will be loosed* in
heaven." Matt. 18:18
20 RThen He commanded His disciples that
they should tell no one that He was Jesus the
Christ. Luke 9:21

Revelation of Jesus' Death
Mark 8:31–33; Luke 9:22

21 From that time Jesus began to show to
His disciples that He must go to Jerusalem,
and suffer many things from the elders and
chief priests and scribes, and be killed, and be
Rraised the third day. Acts 10:40; 1 Cor. 15:4☆
22 Then Peter took Him aside and began to
rebuke Him, saying, "Far be it from You, Lord;
this shall not happen to You!"
23 But He turned and said to Peter, "Get be-
hind Me, RSatan! You are an offense to Me, for
you are not mindful of the things of God, but
the things of men." Matt. 4:10

Revelation of Jesus' Reward
Mark 8:34–37; Luke 9:23–25

24 RThen Jesus said to His disciples, "If any-
one desires to come after Me, let him deny
himself, and take up his cross, and Rfollow
Me. [2 Tim. 3:12] • [1 Pet. 2:21]
25 "For Rwhoever desires to save his life will
lose it, but whoever loses his life for My sake
will find it. John 12:25
26 "For what Rprofit is it to a man if he gains
the whole world, and loses his own soul? Or
Rwhat will a man give in exchange for his
soul? Luke 12:20, 21 • Ps. 49:7, 8

The Prophecy of the Second Coming
Mark 8:38—9:1; Luke 9:26, 27

27 "For Rthe Son of Man will come in the
glory of His Father Rwith His angels, Rand
then He will reward each according to his
works. Mark 8:38 • [Dan. 7:10] • Rom. 2:6
28 "Assuredly, I say to you, Rthere are some
standing here who shall not taste death till
they see the Son of Man coming in His king-
dom." Luke 9:27

CHAPTER 17

The Transfiguration
Mark 9:2–13; Luke 9:28–36; 2 Pet. 1:17, 18

NOW after six days Jesus took Peter,
James, and John his brother, led them up
on a high mountain by themselves;
2 and He was transfigured before them. His
face shone like the sun, and His clothes be-
came as white as the light.
3 And behold, Moses and Elijah appeared
to them, talking with Him.
4 Then Peter answered and said to Jesus,
"Lord, it is good for us to be here; if You wish,
let us* make here three tabernacles: one for
You, one for Moses, and one for Elijah."
5 While he was still speaking, behold, a
bright cloud overshadowed them; and sud-
denly a voice came out of the cloud, saying,
R"This is My beloved Son, in whom I am well
pleased. Hear Him!" Is. 42:1; 2 Pet. 1:17★
6 And when the disciples heard *it*, they fell
on their faces and were greatly afraid.
7 But Jesus came and touched them and
said, "Arise, and do not be afraid."
8 When they had lifted up their eyes, they
saw no one but Jesus only.
9 Now as they came down from the moun-
tain, Jesus commanded them, saying, "Tell the
vision to no one until the Son of Man is risen
from the dead."
10 And His disciples asked Him, saying,
R"Why then do the scribes say that Elijah
must come first?" Mal. 4:5
11 Jesus answered and said to them, "In-
deed, Elijah is coming first* and will Rrestore
all things. [Mal. 4:6]
12 R"But I say to you that Elijah has come
already, and they Rdid not know him but did
to him whatever they wished. Likewise Rthe
Son of Man is also about to suffer at their
hands." Mark 9:12, 13 • Matt. 14:3, 10 • Matt. 16:21
13 Then the disciples understood that He
spoke to them of John the Baptist.

Instruction About Faith
Mark 9:14–29; Luke 9:37–42

14 RAnd when they had come to the multi-
tude, a man came to Him, kneeling down to
Him and saying, Mark 9:14–28
15 "Lord, have mercy on my son, for he is an
epileptic* and suffers severely; for he often
falls into the fire and often into the water.
16 "So I brought him to Your disciples, but
they could not cure him."
17 Then Jesus answered and said, "O faith-
less and Rperverse generation, how long shall
I be with you? How long shall I bear with you?
Bring him here to Me." Phil. 2:15
18 And Jesus Rrebuked the demon, and it

16:19 Or *will have been bound . . . will have been loosed* **17:4** NU *I will* **17:11** NU omits *first* **17:15** Lit. *moonstruck*

---

tecostal sermon when "that day about three thousand souls were added *to them* [that is, the apostles]" (Page 1114—Acts 2:41). This group for the first time is called "the church" in Acts 2:47, and God added to their number daily those who were saved.

Now turn to Page 1206—Eph. 3:21: The Purpose of the Church.

came out of him; and the child was cured from
that very hour. Luke 4:41
19 Then the disciples came to Jesus privately
and said, "Why could we not cast it out?"
20 So Jesus said to them, "Because of your
unbelief;* for assuredly, I say to you, [R]if you
have faith as a mustard seed, you will say to
this mountain, 'Move from here to there,' and
it will move; and nothing will be impossible
for you. Luke 17:6
21 "However, this kind does not go out ex-
cept by prayer and fasting."*

Instruction About Jesus' Death
Mark 9:30–32; Luke 9:43–45

22 Now while they were staying* in Galilee,
Jesus said to them, "The Son of Man is about
to be betrayed into the hands of men,
23 "and they will [R]kill Him, and the third day
He will be raised up." And they were exceed-
ingly sorrowful. Mark 15:37; Acts 10:40☆

Instruction About Taxes

24 [R]When they had come to Capernaum,*
those who received the [T]*temple* tax came to
Peter and said, "Does your Teacher not pay
the *temple* tax?" Mark 9:33 • Lit. *double drachma*
25 He said, "Yes." And when he had come into
the house, Jesus anticipated him, saying,
"What do you think, Simon? From whom do the
kings of the earth take customs or taxes, from
their sons or from [R]strangers?" [Is. 60:10–17]
26 Peter said to Him, "From strangers." Jesus
said to him, "Then the sons are free.
27 "Nevertheless, lest we offend them, go to
the sea, cast in a hook, and take the fish that
comes up first. And when you have opened its
mouth, you will find a piece of money;* take
that and give it to them for Me and you."

CHAPTER 18

Instruction About Humility
Mark 9:33–37; Luke 9:46–48

AT [R]that time the disciples came to Jesus,
saying, "Who then is greatest in the king-
dom of heaven?" Luke 9:46–48; 22:24–27
2 Then Jesus called a little [R]child to Him,
set him in the midst of them, Matt. 19:14
3 and said, "Assuredly, I say to you, [R]unless
you are converted and become as little chil-
dren, you will by no means enter the kingdom
of heaven. Luke 18:16
4 [R]"Therefore whoever humbles himself as
this little child is the greatest in the kingdom
of heaven. [Matt. 20:27; 23:11]
5 [R]"Whoever receives one little child like
this in My name receives Me. [Matt. 10:42]

Punishment of Offenders—Mark 9:42–48

6 [R]"But whoever causes one of these little
ones who believe in Me to sin, it would be bet-
ter for him if a millstone were hung around
his neck, and he were drowned in the depth of
the sea. Mark 9:42
7 "Woe to the world because of offenses!
For offenses must come, but woe to that man
by whom the offense comes!
8 [R]"If your hand or foot causes you to sin,
cut it off and cast *it* from you. It is better for
you to enter into life lame or maimed, rather
than having two hands or two feet, to be cast
into the everlasting fire. Matt. 5:29, 30
9 "And if your eye causes you to sin, pluck it
out and cast *it* from you. It is better for you to
enter into life with one eye, rather than having
two eyes, to be cast into [T]hell fire. Gr. *Gehenna*
10 "Take heed that you do not despise one of
these little ones, for I say to you that in heaven
their angels always [R]see the face of My Father
who is in heaven. Luke 1:19

Parable of the Lost Sheep—Luke 15:4–7

11 [R]"For the Son of Man has come to save
that which was lost.* Luke 9:56
12 [R]"What do you think? If a man has a
hundred sheep, and one of them goes astray,
does he not leave the ninety-nine and go to
the mountains to seek the one that is stray-
ing? Luke 15:4–7
13 "And if he should find it, assuredly, I say
to you, he rejoices more over that *sheep* than
over the ninety-nine that did not go astray.
14 "Even so it is not the [R]will of your Father
who is in heaven that one of these little ones
should perish. [1 Tim. 2:4]

The Offended Brother

15 "Moreover [R]if your brother sins against
you, go and tell him his fault between you and
him alone. If he hears you, [R]you have gained
your brother. Lev. 19:17 • [James 5:20]
16 "But if he will not hear, take with you one
or two more, that [R]'*by the mouth of two or
three witnesses every word may be estab-
lished.*'* Deut. 17:6
17 "And if he refuses to hear them, tell *it* to
the church. But if he refuses even to hear the
church, let him be to you like a [R]heathen and
a tax collector. [2 Thess. 3:6, 14]
18 "Assuredly, I say to you, [R]whatever you
bind on earth will be bound in heaven, and
whatever you loose on earth will be loosed in
heaven. [John 20:22, 23]
19 [R]"Again I say* to you that if two of you
agree on earth concerning anything that they
ask, [R]it will be done for them by My Father in
heaven. [1 Cor. 1:10] • [1 John 3:22; 5:14]
20 "For where two or three are gathered [R]to-

17:20 NU *little faith* **17:21** NU omits v. 21.
17:22 NU *gathering together* **17:24** NU
Capharnaum, here and elsewhere **17:27** Gr. *stater*,
the exact amount to pay the temple tax (didrachma)
for two **18:11** NU omits v. 11. **18:16** Deut. 19:15
18:19 NU, M *Again, assuredly, I say*

gether in My name, I am there in the midst of them." Acts 20:7

Instruction About Forgiveness

21 Then Peter came to Him and said, "Lord, how often shall my brother sin against me, and I forgive him? Up to seven times?"

22 Jesus said to him, "I do not say to you, [R]up to seven times, but up to seventy times seven. Col. 3:13

23 "Therefore the kingdom of heaven is like a certain king who wanted to settle accounts with his servants.

24 "And when he had begun to settle accounts, one was brought to him who owed him ten thousand talents.

25 "But as he was not able to pay, his master commanded [R]that he be sold, with his wife and children and all that he had, and that payment be made. 2 Kin. 4:1

26 "The servant therefore fell down before him, saying, 'Master, have patience with me, and I will pay you all.'

27 "Then the master of that servant was moved with compassion, released him, and forgave him the debt.

28 "But that servant went out and found one of his fellow servants who owed him a hundred denarii; and he laid hands on him and took *him* by the throat, saying, 'Pay me what you owe!'

29 "So his fellow servant fell down at his feet* and begged him, saying, 'Have patience with me, and I will pay you all.'*

30 "And he would not, but went and threw him into prison till he should pay the debt.

31 "So when his fellow servants saw what had been done, they were very grieved, and came and told their master all that had been done.

32 "Then his master, after he had called him, said to him, 'You wicked servant! I forgave you [R]all that debt because you begged me. Luke 7:41–43

33 'Should you not also have had compassion on your fellow servant, just as I had pity on you?'

34 "And his master was angry, and delivered him to the torturers until he should pay all that was due to him.

35 "So My heavenly Father also will do to you if each of you, from his heart, does not forgive his brother his trespasses."*

CHAPTER 19

Instruction About Divorce
Mark 10:1–16; Luke 18:15–17

NOW it came to pass, [R]when Jesus had finished these sayings, *that* He departed from Galilee and came to the region of Judea beyond the Jordan. Mark 10:1–12

2 [R]And great multitudes followed Him, and He healed them there. Matt. 12:15

3 The Pharisees also came to Him, testing Him, and saying to Him, "Is it lawful for a man to divorce his wife for *just* any reason?"

4 And He answered and said to them, "Have you not read that He who made* *them* at the beginning *'made them male and female,'**

5 "and said, *'For this reason a man shall leave his father and mother and be joined to his wife, and* [R]*the two shall become one flesh'?** [1 Cor. 6:16; 7:2]

6 "So then, they are no longer two but one flesh. Therefore what God has joined together, let not man separate."

7 They said to Him, [R]"Why then did Moses command to give a certificate of divorce, and to put her away?" Deut. 24:1–4

8 He said to them, "Moses, because of the [R]hardness of your hearts, permitted you to divorce your [R]wives, but from the beginning it was not so. Heb. 3:15 • Mal. 2:16

9 [R]"And I say to you, whoever divorces his wife, except for sexual immorality,* and marries another, commits adultery; and whoever marries her who is divorced commits adultery." [Matt. 5:32]

10 His disciples said to Him, [R]"If such is the case of the man with *his* wife, it is better not to marry." [Prov. 21:19]

11 But He said to them, [R]"All cannot accept this saying, but only *those* to whom it has been given: [1 Cor. 7:2, 7, 9, 17]

12 "For there are [T]eunuchs who were born thus from *their* mother's womb, and [R]there are eunuchs who were made eunuchs by men, and there are eunuchs who have made themselves eunuchs for the kingdom of heaven's sake. He who is able to accept *it*, let him accept *it*." Emasculated men • [1 Cor. 7:32]

13 Then little children were brought to Him that He might put *His* hands on them and pray, but the disciples rebuked them.

14 But Jesus said, "Let the little children come to Me, and do not forbid them; for of such is the kingdom of heaven."

15 And He laid *His* hands on them and departed from there.

Rich Young Ruler
Mark 10:17–27; Luke 18:18–27

16 [R]Now behold, one came and said to Him, "Good* Teacher, what good thing shall I do that I may have eternal life?" Mark 10:17–30

17 So He said to him, "Why do you call Me good?* No one *is* [R]good but One, *that is*, God.* But if you want to enter into life, [R]keep the commandments." Nah. 1:7 • Lev. 18:5

18:29 NU omits *at his feet* • NU, M omit *all*
18:35 NU omits *his trespasses* **19:4** NU *created* • Gen. 1:27; 5:2 **19:5** Gen. 2:24 **19:9** Or *fornication*
19:16 NU omits *Good* **19:17** NU *Why do you ask Me about what is good?* • NU *There is One who is good.*

18 He said to Him, "Which ones?" Jesus said, [R]"'*You shall not murder,' 'You shall not commit adultery,' 'You shall not steal,' 'You shall not bear false witness,'* Ex. 20:13–16

19 *'Honor your father and your mother,'** and, *'You shall love your neighbor as yourself.'* "*

20 The young man said to Him, "All these things I have [R]kept from my youth.* What do I still lack?" [Phil. 3:6, 7]

21 Jesus said to him, "If you want to be perfect, [R]go, sell what you have and give to the poor, and you will have treasure in heaven; and come, follow Me." Acts 2:45

22 But when the young man heard that saying, he went away sorrowful, for he had great possessions.

23 Then Jesus said to His disciples, "Assuredly, I say to you that it is hard for a rich man to enter the kingdom of heaven.

24 "And again I say to you, it is easier for a camel to go through the eye of a needle than for a rich man to enter the kingdom of God."

25 When His disciples heard *it,* they were greatly astonished, saying, "Who then can be saved?"

26 But Jesus looked at *them* and said to them, "With men this is impossible, but with God all things are possible."

The Apostles' Reward
Mark 10:28–30; Luke 18:28–30

27 Then Peter answered and said to Him, "See, [R]we have left all and followed You. Therefore what shall we have?" Deut. 33:9

28 So Jesus said to them, "Assuredly I say to you, that in the regeneration, when the Son of Man sits on the throne of His glory, [R]you who have followed Me will also sit on twelve thrones, judging the twelve tribes of Israel. Luke 22:28–30

29 [R]"And everyone who has left houses or brothers or sisters or father or mother or wife* or children or [T]lands, for My name's sake, shall receive a hundredfold, and inherit eternal life. Mark 10:29, 30 • Lit. *fields*

30 [R]"But many *who are* first will be last, and the last first. Luke 13:30

CHAPTER 20

Parable of the Laborers—Mark 10:31

"FOR the kingdom of heaven is like a landowner who went out early in the morning to hire laborers for his vineyard.

2 "Now when he had agreed with the laborers for a denarius a day, he sent them into his vineyard.

3 "And he went out about the third hour and saw others standing idle in the marketplace,

4 "and said to them, 'You also go into the vineyard, and whatever is right I will give you.' So they went.

5 "Again he went out about the sixth and the ninth hour, and did likewise.

6 "And about the eleventh hour he went out and found others standing idle,* and said to them, 'Why have you been standing here idle all day?'

7 "They said to him, 'Because no one hired us.' He said to them, 'You also go into the vineyard, and whatever is right you will receive.'*

8 "So when evening had come, the owner of the vineyard said to his steward, 'Call the laborers and give them *their* wages, beginning with the last to the first.'

9 "And when those came who *were hired* about the eleventh hour, they each received a denarius.

10 "But when the first came, they supposed that they would receive more; and they likewise received each a denarius.

11 "And when they had received *it,* they complained against the landowner,

12 "saying, 'These last *men* have worked *only* one hour, and you made them equal to us who have borne the burden and the heat of the day.'

13 "But he answered one of them and said, 'Friend, I am doing you no wrong. Did you not agree with me for a denarius?

14 'Take *what is* yours and go your way. I wish to give to this last man *the same* as to you.

15 [R]'Is it not lawful for me to do what I wish with my own things? Or [R]is your eye evil because I am good?' [Rom. 9:20, 21] • Deut. 15:9

16 "So the last will be first, and the first last. For many are called, but few chosen."*

Instruction About Jesus' Death
Mark 10:32–34; Luke 18:31–34

17 [R]Now Jesus, going up to Jerusalem, took the twelve disciples aside on the road and said to them, Mark 10:32–34

18 [R]"Behold, we are going up to Jerusalem, and the Son of Man will be betrayed to the chief priests and to the scribes; and they will condemn Him to death, Matt. 16:21; 26:47–57☆

19 [R]"and deliver Him to the Gentiles to mock and to scourge and to crucify. And the third day He will rise again."* Acts 2:23, 24☆

Instruction About Ambition—Mark 10:35–45

20 Then the mother of Zebedee's sons came to Him with her sons, kneeling down and asking something from Him.

21 And He said to her, "What do you wish?" She said to Him, "Grant that these two sons of

19:19 Ex. 20:12–16; Deut. 5:16–20 • Lev. 19:18 **19:20** NU omits *from my youth* **19:29** NU omits *or wife* **20:6** NU omits *idle* **20:7** NU omits the last clause of this verse. **20:16** NU omits the last sentence of this verse.

mine may sit, one on Your right hand and the other on the left, in Your kingdom."

22 But Jesus answered and said, "You do not know what you ask. Are you able to drink [R]the cup that I am about to drink, and be baptized with [R]the baptism that I am baptized with?"* They said to Him, "We are able." Luke 22:42 • Luke 12:50

23 So He said to them, [R]"You will indeed drink My cup, and be baptized with the baptism that I am baptized with;* but to sit on My right hand and on My left is not Mine to give, but *it is for those* for whom it is prepared by My Father." [Acts 12:2]

24 And when the ten heard *it*, they were greatly displeased with the two brothers.

25 But Jesus called them to *Himself* and said, "You know that the rulers of the Gentiles lord it over them, and those who are great exercise authority over them.

26 "Yet it shall not be so among you; but [R]whoever desires to become great among you, let him be your servant. Matt. 23:11

27 [R]"And whoever desires to be first among you, let him be your slave— [Matt. 18:4]

28 "just as the Son of Man did not come to be served, but to serve, and [R]to give His life a ransom for many." Is. 53:12★

The Blind Men Recognize the King
Mark 10:46–52; Luke 18:35–43

29 [R]Now as they went out of Jericho, a great multitude followed Him. Mark 10:46–52

30 And behold, [R]two blind men sitting by the road, when they heard that Jesus was passing by, cried out, saying, "Have mercy on us, O Lord, Son of David!" Matt. 9:27

31 Then the multitude [R]warned them that they should be quiet; but they cried out all the more, saying, "Have mercy on us, O Lord, Son of David!" Matt. 19:13

32 So Jesus stood still and called them, and said, "What do you want Me to do for you?"

33 They said to Him, "Lord, that our eyes may be opened."

34 So Jesus had compassion and touched their eyes. And immediately their eyes received sight, and they followed Him.

CHAPTER 21

The Triumphal Entry
Mark 11:1–10; Luke 19:29–38; John 12:12–15

NOW when they drew near Jerusalem, and came to Bethphage,* at the Mount of Olives, then Jesus sent two disciples,

2 saying to them, "Go into the village opposite you, and immediately you will find a donkey tied, and a colt with her. Loose *them* and bring *them* to Me.

3 "And if anyone says anything to you, you shall say, 'The Lord has need of them,' and immediately he will send them."

4 All* this was done that it might be fulfilled which was spoken by the prophet, saying:

5" *Tell the daughter of Zion,*
'Behold, your King is coming to you,
Lowly, and sitting on a donkey,
*A colt, the foal of a donkey.' "**

6 [R]So the disciples went and did as Jesus commanded them. Mark 11:4

7 They brought the donkey and the colt, [R]laid their clothes on them, and set *Him** on them. 2 Kin. 9:13

8 And a very great multitude spread their clothes on the road; [R]others cut down branches from the trees and spread *them* on the road. Lev. 23:40

9 Then the multitudes who went before and those who followed cried out, saying:

"Hosanna to the Son of David!
[R]*'Blessed is He who comes in the name of the LORD!'** Matt. 23:39
Hosanna in the highest!"

10 [R]And when He had come into Jerusalem, all the city was moved, saying, "Who is this?" John 2:13, 15

11 So the multitudes said, "This is Jesus, the prophet from Nazareth of Galilee."

The Cleansing of the Temple
Mark 11:15–17; Luke 19:45, 46

12 [R]Then Jesus went into the temple of God* and drove out all those who bought and sold in the temple, and overturned the tables of the [R]money changers and the seats of those who sold doves. Mal. 3:1★ • Deut. 14:25

13 And He said to them, "It is written, *'My house shall be called a house of prayer,'** but you have made it a *'den of thieves.'* "*

14 Then *the* blind and *the* lame came to Him in the temple, and He healed them.

15 But when the chief priests and scribes saw the wonderful things that He did, and the children crying out in the temple and saying, "Hosanna to the [R]Son of David!" they were [T]indignant John 7:42 • *angry*

16 and said to Him, "Do You hear what these are saying?" And Jesus said to them, "Yes. Have you never read,

'Out of the mouth of babes and nursing infants
*You have perfected praise' ?"**

20:22 NU omits *and be baptized with the baptism that I am baptized with* **20:23** NU omits *and be baptized with the baptism that I am baptized with* **21:1** M *Bethsphage* **21:4** NU omits *All* **21:5** Zech. 9:9★ **21:7** NU *and He sat* **21:9** Ps. 118:26★ **21:12** NU omits *of God* **21:13** Is. 56:7 • Jer. 7:11 **21:16** Ps. 8:2★

17 Then He left them and went out of the city to Bethany, and He lodged there.

Cursing of the Fig Tree
Mark 11:11–14, 20–24

18 Now in the morning, as He returned to the city, He was hungry.

19 [R]And seeing a fig tree by the road, He came to it and found nothing on it but leaves, and said to it, "Let no fruit grow on you ever again." Immediately the fig tree withered away. Mark 11:13

20 [R]And when the disciples saw *it*, they marveled, saying, "How did the fig tree wither away so soon?" Mark 11:20

21 So Jesus answered and said to them, "Assuredly, I say to you, [R]if you have faith and do not doubt, you will not only do what was done to the fig tree, but also if you say to this mountain, 'Be removed and be cast into the sea,' it will be done. Matt. 17:20

22 "And whatever things you ask in prayer, believing, you will receive."

Question of Jesus' Authority
Mark 11:27–33; Luke 20:1–8

23 [R]Now when He came into the temple, the chief priests and the elders of the people confronted Him as He was teaching, and [R]said, "By what authority are You doing these things? And who gave You this authority?" Luke 20:1–8 • Ex. 2:14

24 But Jesus answered and said to them, "I also will ask you one thing, which if you tell Me, I likewise will tell you by what authority I do these things:

25 "The baptism of John—where was it from? From heaven or from men?" And they reasoned among themselves, saying, "If we say, 'From heaven,' He will say to us, 'Why then did you not believe him?'

26 "But if we say, 'From men,' we fear the multitude, for all count John as a prophet."

27 So they answered Jesus and said, "We do not know." And He said to them, "Neither will I tell you by what authority I do these things.

Parable of the Two Sons

28 "But what do you think? A man had two sons, and he came to the first and said, 'Son, go, work today in my vineyard.'

29 "He answered and said, 'I will not,' but afterward he regretted it and went.

30 "Then he came to the second and said likewise. And he answered and said, 'I *go*, sir,' but he did not go.

31 "Which of the two did the will of *his* father?" They said to Him, "The first." Jesus said to them, [R]"Assuredly, I say to you that tax collectors and harlots enter the kingdom of God before you. Luke 7:29, 37–50

32 "For [R]John came to you in the way of righteousness, and you did not believe him; but tax collectors and harlots believed him; and when you saw *it*, you did not afterward relent and believe him. Luke 3:1–12; 7:29

Parable of the Landowner
Mark 12:1–12; Luke 20:9–19

33 "Hear another parable: There was a certain landowner who planted a vineyard and set a hedge around it, dug a winepress in it and built a tower. And he leased it to vinedressers and went into a far country.

34 "Now when vintage-time drew near, he sent his servants to the vinedressers, that they might receive its fruit.

35 [R]"And the vinedressers took his servants, beat one, killed one, and stoned another. [1 Thess. 2:15]

36 "Again he sent other servants, more than the first, and they did likewise to them.

37 "Then last of all he sent his son to them, saying, 'They will respect my son.'

38 "But when the vinedressers saw the son, they said among themselves, [R]'This is the heir. [R]Come, let us kill him and seize his inheritance.' [Heb. 1:2] • John 11:53

39 [R]"So they took him and cast *him* out of the vineyard and killed *him*. [Acts 2:23]

40 "Therefore, when the owner of the vineyard comes, what will he do to those vinedressers?"

41 They said to Him, "He will destroy those wicked men miserably, and lease *his* vineyard to other vinedressers who will render to him the fruits in their seasons."

42 Jesus said to them, "Have you never read in the Scriptures:

'The stone which the builders rejected
Has become the chief cornerstone.
This was the LORD's doing,
And it is marvelous in our eyes' ?*

43 "Therefore I say to you, [R]the kingdom of God will be taken from you and given to a nation bearing the fruits of it. [Matt. 8:12]

44 "And [R]whoever falls on this stone will be broken; but on whomever it falls, [R]it will grind him to powder." Is. 8:14, 15★ • [Dan. 2:44]

45 Now when the chief priests and Pharisees heard His parables, they [T]perceived that He was speaking of them. *knew*

46 But when they sought to lay hands on Him, they [R]feared the multitudes, because they took Him for a prophet. Matt. 21:26

CHAPTER 22

Parable of the Marriage Feast

AND Jesus answered and spoke to them again by parables and said:

21:42 Ps. 118:22, 23★

2 "The kingdom of heaven is like a certain king who arranged a marriage for his son,

3 "and sent out his servants to call those who were invited to the wedding; and they were not willing to come.

4 "Again, he sent out other servants, saying, 'Tell those who are invited, "See, I have prepared my dinner; [R]my oxen and fatted cattle *are* killed, and all things *are* ready. Come to the wedding." ' Prov. 9:2

5 "But they made light of it and went their ways, one to his own farm, another to his business.

6 "And the rest seized his servants, treated *them* spitefully, and killed *them*.

7 "But when the king heard *about it*, he was furious. And he sent out [R]his armies, destroyed those murderers, and burned up their city. [Dan. 9:26]

8 "Then he said to his servants, 'The wedding is ready, but those who were invited were not [R]worthy. Matt. 10:11

9 'Therefore go into the highways, and as many as you find, invite to the wedding.'

10 "So those servants went out into the highways and gathered together all whom they found, both bad and good. And the wedding *hall* was filled with guests.

11 "But when the king came in to see the guests, he saw a man there [R]who did not have on a wedding garment. [Col. 3:10, 12]

12 "So he said to him, 'Friend, how did you come in here without a wedding garment?' And he was [R]speechless. [Rom. 3:19]

13 "Then the king said to the servants, 'Bind him hand and foot, take him away, and* cast *him* into outer darkness; there will be weeping and gnashing of teeth.'

14 [R]"For many are called, but few *are* chosen." Matt. 20:16

Conflict with Pharisees and Herodians
Mark 12:13–17; Luke 20:20–26

15 Then the Pharisees went and plotted how they might entangle Him in *His* talk.

16 And they sent to Him their disciples with the [R]Herodians, saying, "Teacher, we know that You are true, and teach the way of God in truth; nor do You care about anyone, for You do not [T]regard the person of men. Mark 3:6; 8:15; 12:13 • Lit. *look at the face of*

17 "Tell us, therefore, what do You think? Is it lawful to pay taxes to Caesar, or not?"

18 But Jesus [T]perceived their wickedness, and said, "Why do you test Me, *you* hypocrites? *knew*

19 "Show Me the tax money." **So they brought Him a denarius.**

20 And He said to them, "Whose image and inscription *is* this?"

21 They said to Him, "Caesar's." And He said to them, [R]"Render[T] therefore to Caesar the things that are Caesar's, and to God the things that are God's." Matt. 17:25 • *Pay*

22 When they had heard *these words*, they marveled, and left Him and went their way.

Conflict with the Sadducees
Mark 12:18–27; Luke 20:27–40

23 [R]The same day the Sadducees, [R]who say there is no resurrection, came to Him and asked Him, Luke 20:27–40 • Acts 23:8

24 saying: "Teacher, [R]Moses said that if a man dies, having no children, his brother shall marry his wife and raise up offspring for his brother. Deut. 25:5

25 "Now there were with us seven brothers. The first died after he had married, and having no offspring, left his wife to his brother.

26 "Likewise the second also, and the third, even to the seventh.

27 "Last of all the woman died also.

28 "Therefore, in the resurrection, whose wife of the seven will she be? For they all had her."

29 Jesus answered and said to them, "You are [T]mistaken, [R]not knowing the Scriptures nor the power of God. *deceived* • John 20:9

30 "For in the resurrection they neither marry nor are given in marriage, but [R]are like angels of God* in heaven. [1 John 3:2]

31 "But concerning the resurrection of the dead, have you not read what was spoken to you by God, saying,

32 *'I am the God of Abraham, the God of Isaac, and the God of Jacob'* ?* God is not the God of the dead, but of the living."

33 And when the multitudes heard *this*, they were astonished at His teaching.

The Greatest Commandment—Mark 12:28–34

34 [R]But when the Pharisees heard that He had silenced the Sadducees, they gathered together. Mark 12:28–31

35 Then one of them, a lawyer, asked Him *a question*, testing Him, and saying,

36 "Teacher, which *is* the great commandment in the law?"

37 Jesus said to him, "*'You shall love the* LORD *your God with all your heart, with all your soul, and with all your mind.'**

38 "This is *the* first and great commandment.

39 "And *the* second *is* like it: *'You shall love your neighbor as yourself.'**

40 [R]"On these two commandments hang all the Law and the Prophets." [Matt. 7:12]

The Son of David
Mark 12:35–37; Luke 20:41–44

41 [R]While the Pharisees were gathered together, Jesus asked them, Luke 20:41–44

22:13 NU omits *take him away, and* **22:30** NU omits *of God* **22:32** Ex. 3:6, 15 **22:37** Deut. 6:5 **22:39** Lev. 19:18

42 **saying,** "What do you think about the
Christ? Whose Son is He?" **They said to Him,**
"*The* [R]*Son* of David." Matt. 1:1; 21:9
43 **He said to them,** "How then does David in
the Spirit call Him *'Lord,'* saying:

44 *'The* LORD *said to my Lord,*
"Sit at My right hand,
Till I make Your enemies Your
footstool" ' ?*

45 "If David then calls Him *'Lord,'* how is He
his Son?"
46 [R]**And no one was able to answer Him a**
word, [R]nor from that day on did anyone dare
question Him anymore. Luke 14:6 • Mark 12:34

CHAPTER 23

Jesus Characterizes the Pharisees
Mark 12:38–40; Luke 20:45–47

THEN Jesus spoke to the multitudes and to
His disciples,
2 **saying:** [R]"The scribes and the Pharisees
sit in Moses' seat. Neh. 8:4, 8
3 "Therefore whatever they tell you to ob-
serve,* *that* observe and do, but do not do ac-
cording to their works; for [R]they say, and do
not do. [Rom. 2:19]
4 [R]"For they bind heavy burdens, hard to
bear, and lay *them* on men's shoulders; but
they *themselves* will not move them with one
of their fingers. Luke 11:46
5 "But all their works they do to be seen by
men. They make their phylacteries broad and
enlarge the borders of their garments.
6 "They love the best places at feasts, the
best seats in the synagogues,
7 "greetings in the marketplaces, and to be
called by men, 'Rabbi, Rabbi.'
8 [R]"But you, do not be called 'Rabbi'; for
One is your [T]Teacher, the Christ,* and you are
all brethren. [James 3:1] • *Leader*
9 "Do not call anyone on earth your fa-
ther; [R]for One is your Father, He who is in
heaven. [Mal. 1:6]
10 "And do not be called teachers; for One is
your Teacher, the Christ.
11 "But [R]he who is greatest among you shall
be your servant. Matt. 20:26, 27
12 [R]"And whoever exalts himself will be
[T]humbled, and he who humbles himself will
be [T]exalted. Luke 14:11; 18:14 • *put down* • *lifted up*

Jesus Condemns the Pharisees

13 "But [R]woe to you, scribes and Pharisees,
hypocrites! For you shut up the kingdom of
heaven against men; for you neither go in
yourselves, nor do you allow those who are
entering to go in. Luke 11:52
14 "Woe to you, scribes and Pharisees, hyp-
ocrites! For you devour widows' houses, and
for a pretense make long prayers. Therefore
you will receive greater condemnation.*
15 "Woe to you, scribes and Pharisees, hyp-
ocrites! For you travel land and sea to win
one proselyte, and when he is won, you make
him twice as much a son of [T]hell as your-
selves. Gr. *Gehenna*
16 "Woe to you, blind guides, who say, 'Who-
ever swears by the temple, it is nothing; but
whoever swears by the gold of the temple, he
is obliged *to perform it.'*
17 "Fools and blind! For which is greater,
the gold [R]or the temple that sanctifies* the
gold? Ex. 30:29
18 "And, 'Whoever swears by the altar, it is
nothing; but whoever swears by the gift that is
on it, he is obliged *to perform it.'*
19 "Fools and blind! For which is greater, the
gift or the altar that sanctifies the gift?
20 "Therefore he who swears by the altar,
swears by it and by all things on it.
21 "He who swears by the temple, swears by
it and by Him who dwells* in it.
22 "And he who swears by heaven, swears
by [R]the throne of God and by Him who sits on
it. Matt. 5:34
23 "Woe to you, scribes and Pharisees, hyp-
ocrites! For you pay tithe of mint and anise
and cummin, and have neglected the weight-
ier *matters* of the law: justice and mercy and
faith. These you ought to have done, without
leaving the others undone.
24 "Blind guides, who strain out a gnat and
swallow a camel!
25 "Woe to you, scribes and Pharisees, hyp-
ocrites! [R]For you cleanse the outside of the
cup and dish, but inside they are full of extor-
tion and self-indulgence.* Luke 11:39
26 "Blind Pharisee, first cleanse the inside of
the cup and dish, that the outside of them may
be clean also.
27 "Woe to you, scribes and Pharisees, hyp-
ocrites! [R]For you are like whitewashed tombs
which indeed appear beautiful outwardly, but
inside are full of dead *men's* bones and all
uncleanness. Acts 23:3
28 "Even so you also outwardly appear
righteous to men, but inside you are full of
hypocrisy and lawlessness.
29 [R]"Woe to you, scribes and Pharisees, hyp-
ocrites! Because you build the tombs of the
prophets and [T]adorn the monuments of the
righteous, Luke 11:47, 48 • *decorate*
30 "and say, 'If we had lived in the days of
our fathers, we would not have been partak-
ers with them in the blood of the prophets.'
31 "Therefore you are witnesses against
yourselves that [R]you are sons of those who
murdered the prophets. [Acts 7:51, 52]

22:44 Ps. 110:1 **23:3** NU omits *to observe* **23:8** NU omits *the Christ* **23:14** NU omits v. 14. **23:17** NU *sanctified* **23:21** M *dwelt* **23:25** M *unrighteousness*

32 [R]"Fill up, then, the measure of your fa-
thers' *guilt*. [1 Thess. 2:16]
33 "Serpents, brood of vipers! How can you
escape the condemnation of hell?
34 [R]"Therefore, indeed, I send you prophets,
wise men, and scribes: *some* of them you will
kill and crucify, and *some* of them you will
scourge in your synagogues and persecute
from city to city, Luke 11:49
35 "that on you may come all the righteous
blood shed on the earth, from the blood of
righteous Abel to the blood of Zechariah, son
of Berechiah, whom you murdered between
the temple and the altar.
36 "Assuredly, I say to you, all these things
will come upon this generation.

Jesus Laments over Jerusalem

37 "O Jerusalem, Jerusalem, the one who
kills the prophets and stones those who are
sent to her! How often I wanted to gather
your children together, as a hen gathers her
chicks [R]under *her* wings, but you [R]were not
willing! Deut. 32:11, 12 • Is. 49:5★
38 "See! Your house is left to you desolate;
39 "for I say to you, you shall see Me no
more till you say, *'Blessed is He who comes in
the name of the LORD!'* "*

CHAPTER 24

The Temple to Be Destroyed
Mark 13:1, 2; Luke 21:5, 6

**THEN Jesus went out and departed from
the temple, and His disciples came up to
show Him the buildings of the temple.**
2 And Jesus said to them, "Do you not see
all these things? Assuredly, I say to you, not
one stone shall be left here upon another, that
shall not be thrown down."

The Disciples' Two Questions
Mark 13:3, 4; Luke 21:7

3 Now as He sat on the Mount of Olives,
[R]the disciples came to Him privately, saying,
[R]"Tell us, when will these things be? And what
will be the sign of Your coming, and of the end
of the age?" Mark 13:3 • [1 Thess. 5:1–3]

The Tribulation—Mark 13:5–23; Luke 21:8–24

4 And Jesus answered and said to them:
"Take heed that no one deceives you.
5 "For [R]many will come in My name, say-
ing, 'I am the Christ,' [R]and will deceive
many. John 5:43 • Matt. 24:11
6 "And you will hear of [R]wars and rumors
of wars. See that you are not troubled; for all*
these things must come to pass, but the end is
not yet. [Rev. 6:2–4]
7 "For [R]nation will rise against nation, and
kingdom against kingdom. And there will be
[R]famines, pestilences,* and earthquakes in
various places. Hag. 2:22 • Rev. 6:5, 6
8 "All these *are* the beginning of sorrows.
9 [R]"Then they will deliver you up to tribula-
tion and kill you, and you will be hated by all
nations for My name's sake. Matt. 10:17
10 "And then many will be offended, will be-
tray one another, and will hate one another.
11 "Then [R]many false prophets will rise up
and [R]deceive many. 2 Pet. 2:1 • [1 Tim. 4:1]
12 "And because lawlessness will abound,
the love of many will grow cold.
13 [R]"But he who endures to the end shall be
saved. Matt. 10:22
14 "And this gospel of the kingdom will be
preached in all the world as a witness to all
the nations, and then the end will come.
15 "Therefore when you see the *'abomina-
tion of desolation,'** spoken of by Daniel the
prophet, standing in the holy place" [R]**(who-
ever reads, let him understand),** Dan. 9:23
16 "then let those who are in Judea flee to
the mountains.
17 "Let him who is on the housetop not go
down to take anything out of his house.
18 "And let him who is in the field not go
back to get his clothes.
19 "But [R]woe to those who are pregnant and
to those who are nursing babies in those
days! Luke 23:29
20 "And pray that your flight may not be in
winter or on the Sabbath.
21 "For [R]then there will be great tribulation,
such as has not been since the beginning of
the world until this time, no, nor ever shall
be. Dan. 9:26
22 "And unless those days were shortened,
no flesh would be saved; but for the elect's
sake those days will be shortened.
23 "Then if anyone says to you, 'Look, here *is*
the Christ!' or 'There!' do not believe *it*.
24 "For false christs and false prophets will
rise and show great signs and wonders to de-
ceive, if possible, even the elect.
25 "See, I have told you beforehand.
26 "Therefore if they say to you, 'Look, He is
in the desert!' do not go out; *or* 'Look, *He is* in
the inner rooms!' do not believe *it*.

The Second Coming
Mark 13:24–27; Luke 21:25–28

27 [R]"For as the lightning comes from the east
and flashes to the west, so also will the com-
ing of the Son of Man be. Luke 17:24
28 [R]"For wherever the carcass is, there the
eagles will be gathered together. Luke 17:37
29 "Immediately after the tribulation of
those days [R]the sun will be darkened, and the
moon will not give its light; the stars will fall
from heaven, and the powers of the heavens
will be shaken. Ezek. 32:7
30 "Then the sign of the Son of Man will

23:39 Ps. 118:26 **24:6** NU omits *all* **24:7** NU omits *pestilences* **24:15** Dan. 11:31; 12:11

appear in heaven, [R]and then all the tribes of the earth will mourn, and they will see the Son of Man coming on the clouds of heaven with power and great glory. Rev. 1:7☆

31 "And He will send His angels with a great sound of a trumpet, and they will gather together His elect from the four winds, from one end of heaven to the other.

Parable of the Fig Tree
Mark 13:28–31; Luke 21:29–33

32 "Now learn [R]this parable from the fig tree: When its branch has already become tender and puts forth leaves, you know that summer *is* near. Luke 21:29

33 "So you also, when you see all these things, know that it* is near—at the doors!

34 "Assuredly, I say to you, [R]this generation will by no means pass away till all these things take place. [Matt. 10:23; 16:28; 23:36]

35 "Heaven and earth will pass away, but My words will by no means pass away.

Illustration of the Days of Noah
Mark 13:32–37; Luke 21:34–36

36 [R]"But of that day and hour no one knows, not even the angels of heaven,* [R]but My Father only. Acts 1:7 • Zech. 14:7

37 "But as the days of Noah *were,* so also will the coming of the Son of Man be.

38 [R]"For as in the days before the flood, they were eating and drinking, marrying and giving in marriage, until the day that Noah entered the ark, [Gen. 6:3–5]

39 "and did not know until the flood came and took them all away, so also will the coming of the Son of Man be.

40 [R]"Then two *men* will be in the field: one will be taken and the other left. Luke 17:34

41 "Two *women will be* grinding at the mill: one will be taken and the other left.

42 "Watch therefore, for you do not know what hour* your Lord is coming.

43 "But know this, that if the master of the house had known what hour the thief would come, he would have watched and not allowed his house to be broken into.

44 [R]"Therefore you also be ready, for the Son of Man is coming at an hour you do not expect. [1 Thess. 5:6]

Illustration of the Two Servants
Luke 12:41–48

45 "Who then is a faithful and wise servant, whom his master made ruler over his household, to give them food in due season?

46 "Blessed *is* that servant whom his master, when he comes, will find so doing.

47 "Assuredly, I say to you that he will make him ruler over all his goods.

48 "But if that evil servant says in his heart, 'My master is delaying his coming,'*

49 "and begins to beat *his* fellow servants, and to eat and drink with the drunkards,

50 "the master of that servant will come on a day when he is not looking for *him* and at an hour that he is not aware of,

51 "and will cut him in two and appoint *him* his portion with the hypocrites. There shall be weeping and gnashing of teeth.

CHAPTER 25

Parable of the Ten Virgins

"THEN the kingdom of heaven shall be likened to ten virgins who took their lamps and went out to meet [R]the bridegroom. [Eph. 5:29, 30]

2 [R]"Now five of them were wise, and five *were* foolish. Matt. 13:47; 22:10

3 "Those who *were* foolish took their lamps and took no oil with them,

4 "but the wise took oil in their vessels with their lamps.

5 "But while the bridegroom was delayed, [R]they all slumbered and slept. 1 Thess. 5:6

6 "And at midnight [R]a cry was *heard:* 'Behold, the bridegroom is coming;* go out to meet him!' [1 Thess. 4:16]

7 "Then all those virgins arose and [R]trimmed their lamps. Luke 12:35

8 "And the foolish said to the wise, 'Give us *some* of your oil, for our lamps are going out.'

9 "But the wise answered, saying, '*No,* lest there should not be enough for us and you; but go rather to those who sell, and buy for yourselves.'

10 "And while they went to buy, the bridegroom came, and those who were ready went in with him to the wedding; and [R]the door was shut. Luke 13:25

11 "Afterward the other virgins came also, saying, 'Lord, Lord, open to us!'

12 "But he answered and said, 'Assuredly, I say to you, [R]I do not know you.' [Hab. 1:13]

13 [R]"Watch therefore, for you [R]know neither the day nor the hour* in which the Son of Man is coming. Mark 13:35 • Matt. 24:36, 42

Parable of the Talents

14 [R]"For *the kingdom of heaven is* [R]like a man traveling to a far country, *who* called his own servants and delivered his goods to them. Luke 19:12–27 • Matt. 21:33

15 "And to one he gave five talents, to another two, and to another one, [R]to each according to his own ability; and immediately he went on a journey. [Rom. 12:6]

16 "Then he who had received the five talents went and traded with them, and made another five talents.

24:33 Or *He* **24:36** NU adds *nor the Son* **24:42** NU *day* **24:48** NU omits *his coming* **25:6** NU omits *is coming* **25:13** NU omits the rest of v. 13.

17 "And likewise he who *had received* two gained two more also.

18 "But he who had received one went and dug in the ground, and hid his lord's money.

19 "After a long time the lord of those servants came and settled accounts with them.

20 "So he who had received five talents came and brought five other talents, saying, 'Lord, you delivered to me five talents; look, I have gained five more talents besides them.'

21 "His lord said to him, 'Well *done,* good and faithful servant; you were [R]faithful over a few things, [R]I will make you ruler over many things. Enter into the joy of your lord.' **[1 Cor. 4:2] • [Luke 12:44; 22:29, 30]**

22 "He also who had received two talents came and said, 'Lord, you delivered to me two talents; look, I have gained two more talents besides them.'

23 "His lord said to him, [R]'Well *done,* good and faithful servant; you have been faithful over a few things, I will make you ruler over many things. Enter into [R]the joy of your lord.' **Matt. 24:45, 47; 25:21 • [Ps. 16:11]**

24 "Then he who had received the one talent came and said, 'Lord, I knew you to be a hard man, reaping where you have not sown, and gathering where you have not scattered seed.

25 'And I was afraid, and went and hid your talent in the ground. Look, *there* you have *what is* yours.'

26 "But his lord answered and said to him, 'You wicked and lazy servant, you knew that I reap where I have not sown, and gather where I have not scattered seed.

27 'So you ought to have deposited my money with the bankers, and at my coming I would have received back my own with interest.

28 'Therefore take the talent from him, and give *it* to him who has ten talents.

29 [R]'For to everyone who has, more will be given, and he will have abundance; but from him who does not have, even what he has will be taken away. **Matt. 13:12**

30 'And cast the unprofitable servant [R]into the outer darkness. There will be weeping and gnashing of teeth.' **Matt. 8:12; 22:13**

Judgment of the Gentiles

31 "When the Son of Man comes in His glory, and all the holy* angels with Him, then He will sit on the throne of His glory.

32 [R]"All the nations will be gathered before Him, and [R]He will separate them one from another, as a shepherd divides *his* sheep from the goats. **[2 Cor. 5:10] • Ezek. 20:38**

33 "And He will set the sheep on His right hand, but the goats on the left.

34 "Then the King will say to those on His right hand, 'Come, you blessed of My Father, inherit the kingdom [R]prepared for you from the foundation of the world: **Mark 10:40**

35 [R]'for I was hungry and you gave Me food; I was thirsty and you gave Me drink; I was a stranger and you took Me in; **Is. 58:7**

36 'I *was* [R]naked and you clothed Me; I was sick and you visited Me; [R]I was in prison and you came to Me.' **[James 2:15, 16] • 2 Tim. 1:16**

37 "Then the righteous will answer Him, saying, 'Lord, when did we see You hungry and feed *You,* or thirsty and give *You* drink?

38 'When did we see You a stranger and take *You* in, or naked and clothe *You?*

39 'Or when did we see You sick, or in prison, and come to You?'

40 "And the King will answer and say to them, 'Assuredly, I say to you, [R]inasmuch as you did *it* to one of the least of these My brethren, you did *it* to Me.' **Mark 9:41**

41 "Then He will also say to those on the left hand, [R]'Depart from Me, you cursed, [R]into the everlasting fire prepared for the devil and his angels: **Matt. 7:23 • Matt. 13:40, 42**

25:31 NU omits *holy*

25:31, 32 God's Work in the Future—When the Bible was written fully one-fourth of it predicted events future to its writers. Both the OT and the NT contain a great deal of information about still-future events surrounding the return of Christ and subsequent events. Christians may differ about how to interpret details of the Bible's information about the future, but they agree that it is important and that we should live lives of expectation and preparedness for the Lord's return.

a. The Second Coming. Jesus promised that He would return for His followers (Page 1099—John 14:3). His return will set in motion the culminating events of time and history (Page 1003—Matt. 24:3).
b. The Great Tribulation. The end of time is characterized as an era of increasing wickedness culminating in a period of intense evil and opposition to the truth of Christ (Page 1003—Matt. 24:21–28; Page 1244—2 Tim. 3:1, 13)
c. The millennial reign of Christ. Rev. pictures Christ reigning from Jerusalem over the whole earth for a thousand years. The redeemed through the ages participate with Him in a golden age of peace and prosperity before a final rebellion led by Satan (Page 1326—Rev. 20:4–6).
d. Final judgments. Among the events surrounding the return of Christ are judgments by the Lord that identify the redeemed (Page 1327—Rev. 21:27), evaluate the faithfulness of their lives (Page 1168—1 Cor. 3:11–15), and condemn the unredeemed (Page 1326—Rev. 20:11–15).
e. Eternal rewards and punishment. Believers in Jesus will enjoy the presence of the Lord forever (Page 1327—Rev. 22:3–5), while unbelievers will suffer eternally with Satan and His angels (Page 1005—Matt. 25:41).

Now turn to Page 5—Gen. 2:15–17: The Edenic Covenant.

42 'for I was hungry and you gave Me no
food; I was thirsty and you gave Me no drink;
43 'I was a stranger and you did not take Me
in, naked and you did not clothe Me, sick and
in prison and you did not visit Me.'
44 "Then they also will answer Him,* saying,
'Lord, when did we see You hungry or thirsty
or a stranger or naked or sick or in prison,
and did not minister to You?'
45 "Then He will answer them, saying, 'As-
suredly, I say to you, [R]inasmuch as you did not
do *it* to one of the least of these, you did not
do *it* to Me.' Prov. 14:31
46 "And [R]these will go away into everlasting
punishment, but the righteous into eternal
life." [Dan. 12:2]

CHAPTER 26

The Religious Leaders Plot to Kill Jesus
Mark 14:1, 2; Luke 22:1, 2

NOW it came to pass, when Jesus had fin-
ished all these sayings, *that* He said to
His disciples,
2 [R]"You know that after two days is the
Passover, and the Son of Man will be deliv-
ered up to be crucified." Luke 22:1, 2
3 [R]Then the chief priests, the scribes,* and
the elders of the people assembled at the
palace of the high priest, who was called Ca-
iaphas, John 11:47
4 and [R]plotted to take Jesus by [T]trickery
and kill *Him*. Acts 4:25–28 • *deception*
5 But they said, "Not during the feast, lest
there be an uproar among the people."

Mary Anoints Jesus for Burial
Mark 14:3–9; John 12:2–8

6 And when Jesus was in [R]Bethany at the
house of Simon the leper, Mark 14:3–9
7 a woman came to Him having an alabaster
flask of very costly fragrant oil, and she
poured *it* on His head as He sat *at the table*.
8 But when His disciples saw *it*, they were
indignant, saying, "Why this waste?
9 "For this fragrant oil might have been
sold for much and given to *the* poor."
10 But when Jesus was aware of *it*, He said
to them, "Why do you trouble the woman? For
she has done a good work for Me.
11 "For you have the poor with you always,
but Me you do not have always.
12 "For in pouring this fragrant oil on My
body, she did *it* for My burial.
13 "Assuredly, I say to you, wherever this
gospel is preached in the whole world, what
this woman has done will also be told as a me-
morial to her."

Judas Agrees to Betray Jesus
Mark 14:10, 11; Luke 22:3–6

14 Then one of the twelve, called [R]Judas Is-
cariot, went to the chief priests Matt. 10:4
15 and said, "What are you willing to give
me if I deliver Him to you?" And they counted
out to him thirty pieces of silver.
16 So from that time he sought opportunity
to betray Him.

The Passover Is Prepared
Mark 14:12–16; Luke 22:7–13

17 Now on the first *day of the Feast* of Un-
leavened Bread the disciples came to Jesus,
saying to Him, "Where do You want us to pre-
pare for You to eat the Passover?"
18 And He said, "Go into the city to a certain
man, and say to him, 'The Teacher says, "My
time is at hand; I will keep the Passover at
your house with My disciples."'"
19 So the disciples did as Jesus had directed
them; and they prepared the Passover.

The Passover Is Celebrated
Mark 14:17–21; Luke 22:14, 21–23; John 13:21, 22

20 [R]When evening had come, He sat down
with the twelve. Mark 14:17–21
21 Now as they were eating, He said, "As-
suredly, I say to you, one of you will [R]betray
Me." John 6:70, 71; 13:21
22 And they were exceedingly sorrowful,
and each of them began to say to Him, "Lord,
is it I?"
23 He answered and said, [R]"He who dipped
his hand with Me in the dish will betray
Me. Ps. 41:9★
24 "The Son of Man indeed goes just [R]as it is
written of Him, but [R]woe to that man by whom
the Son of Man is betrayed! [R]It would have
been good for that man if he had not been
born." 1 Cor. 15:3 • Luke 17:1 • John 17:12
25 Then Judas, who was betraying Him, an-
swered and said, "Rabbi, is it I?" He said to
him, "You have said it."

25:44 NU, M omit *Him* **26:3** NU omits *the scribes*

25:41 Satan: Destiny of Satan—Jesus said that a place of everlasting fire awaits the devil and his angels at the end of the age. The Scriptures say that Satan will be bound for a thousand years in the bottomless pit during the millennial reign of Christ (Page 1326—Rev. 20:1–4). After he has been bound for a thousand years, Satan will be loosed briefly and he will gather a new army of the nations against the Lord (vv. 7, 8). Fire from the Lord will consume Satan's last grasp at power on earth (v. 9), and he will be cast into "the lake of fire and brimstone" forever (v. 10). The fate of Satan will also be the fate of all the fallen angels (Matt. 25:41).

Now turn to Page 26—THE CHRISTIAN'S GUIDE: Beginning the New Life.

The Lord's Supper Is Instituted
Mark 14:22–25; Luke 22:19, 20; 1 Cor. 11:23–26

26 [R]And as they were eating, [R]Jesus took bread, blessed* and broke *it,* and gave *it* to the disciples and said, "Take, eat; this is My body." Mark 14:22–25 • 1 Cor. 11:23–25

27 Then He took the cup, and gave thanks, and gave *it* to them, saying, [R]"Drink from it, all of you. Mark 14:23

28 "For [R]this is My blood [R]of the new* covenant, which is shed for many for the remission of sins. [Ex. 24:8] • Jer. 31:31

29 "But [R]I say to you, I will not drink of this fruit of the vine from now on [R]until that day when I drink it new with you in My Father's kingdom." Mark 14:25 • Acts 10:41

Peter's Denial Is Predicted
Mark 14:26–31; Luke 22:34, 39; John 13:37, 38

30 And when they had sung a hymn, they went out to the Mount of Olives.

31 Then Jesus said to them, [R]"All of you will [R]be made to stumble because of Me this night, for it is written: John 16:32 • [Matt. 11:6]

'I will strike the Shepherd,
And the sheep of the flock will be
*scattered.'**

32 "But after I have been raised, [R]I will go before you to Galilee." Matt. 28:7, 10, 16☆

33 Peter answered and said to Him, "Even if all are made to stumble because of You, I will never be made to stumble."

34 Jesus said to him, [R]"Assuredly, I say to you that this night, before the rooster crows, you will deny Me three times." John 13:38☆

35 Peter said to Him, "Even if I have to die with You, I will not deny You!" And so said all the disciples.

Jesus' Three Prayers
Mark 14:32–42; Luke 22:40–46

36 [R]Then Jesus came with them to a place called Gethsemane, and said to the disciples, "Sit here while I go and pray over there." Mark 14:32–35

37 And He took with Him Peter and [R]the two sons of Zebedee, and He began to be sorrowful and deeply distressed. Matt. 4:21

38 Then He said to them, [R]"My soul is exceedingly sorrowful, even to death. Stay here and watch with Me." John 12:27

39 He went a little farther and fell on His face, and prayed, saying, "O My Father, if it is possible, let this cup pass from Me; nevertheless, not as I will, but as You *will.*"

40 Then He came to the disciples and found them sleeping, and said to Peter, "What? Could you not watch with Me one hour?

41 [R]"Watch and pray, lest you enter into temptation. [R]The spirit indeed *is* willing, but the flesh *is* weak." Luke 22:40, 46 • [Gal. 5:17]

42 Again, a second time, He went away and prayed, saying, "O My Father, if this cup cannot pass away from Me unless* I drink it, [R]Your will be done." Is. 50:5★

43 And He came and found them asleep again, for their eyes were heavy.

44 So He left them, went away again, and prayed the third time, saying the same words.

45 Then He came to His disciples and said to them, "Are *you* still sleeping and resting? Behold, the hour [T]is at hand, and the Son of Man is being [R]betrayed into the hands of sinners. *has drawn near* • Matt. 17:22, 23; 20:18, 19

46 "Rise, let us be going. See, My [R]betrayer is at hand." Matt. 20:18; 26:21★

Jesus' Betrayal and Arrest
Mark 14:43–52; Luke 22:47–53; John 18:1–11

47 And while He was still speaking, behold, Judas, one of the twelve, with a great multitude with swords and clubs, came from the chief priests and elders of the people.

48 Now His betrayer had given them a sign, saying, "Whomever I kiss, He is the One; seize Him."

49 Immediately he went up to Jesus and said, "Greetings, Rabbi!" and kissed Him.

50 But Jesus said to him, [R]"Friend, why have you come?" Then they came and laid hands on Jesus and took Him. Ps. 41:9

51 And suddenly, [R]one of those *who were* with Jesus stretched out *his* hand and drew his sword, struck the servant of the high priest, and cut off his ear. John 18:10

52 But Jesus said to him, "Put your sword in its place, [R]for all who take the sword will perish* by the sword. Rev. 13:10

53 "Or do you think that I cannot now pray to My Father, and He will provide Me with more than twelve legions of angels?

54 "How then could the Scriptures be fulfilled, [R]that it must happen thus?" Is. 50:6

55 In that hour Jesus said to the multitudes, "Have you come out, as against a robber, with swords and clubs to take Me? I sat daily with you, teaching in the temple, and you did not seize Me.

56 "But all this was done that the Scriptures of the prophets might be fulfilled." Then all the disciples forsook Him and fled.

Two False Witnesses
Mark 14:53–65; Luke 22:54, 55, 63–65; John 18:12, 18, 24

57 [R]And those who had laid hold of Jesus led *Him* away to Caiaphas the high priest, where the scribes and the elders were assembled. John 18:12, 19–24

26:26 M *gave thanks for* **26:28** NU omits *new* **26:31** Zech. 13:7★ **26:42** NU *if this may not pass away unless* **26:52** M *die*

58 But Peter followed Him at a distance to
the high priest's courtyard. And he went in
and sat with the servants to see the end.
59 Now the chief priests, the elders,* and all
the council sought [R]false testimony against
Jesus to put Him to death, Ps. 35:11
60 but found none. Even though [R]many false
witnesses came forward, they found none.*
But at last [R]two false witnesses* came for-
ward Ps. 27:12★ • Deut. 19:15
61 and said, "This *fellow* said, [R]'I am able to
destroy the temple of God and to build it in
three days.'" John 2:19
62 [R]And the high priest arose and said to
Him, "Do You answer nothing? What *is it*
these men testify against You?" Mark 14:60
63 But [R]Jesus kept silent. And the high priest
answered and said to Him, "I put You under
oath by the living God: Tell us if You are the
Christ, the Son of God!" Is. 53:7★
64 Jesus said to him, "*It is as* you said. Nev-
ertheless, I say to you, [R]hereafter you will see
the Son of Man [R]sitting at the right hand of
the Power, and coming on the clouds of
heaven." Dan. 7:13 • [Acts 7:55]
65 Then the high priest tore his clothes, say-
ing, "He has spoken blasphemy! What further
need do we have of witnesses? Look, now you
have heard His blasphemy!
66 "What do you think?" They answered and
said, "He is deserving of death."
67 [R]Then they spat in His face and beat Him;
and [R]others struck *Him* with the palms of
their hands, Is. 50:6; 53:3★ • Luke 22:63–65
68 saying, [R]"Prophesy to us, Christ! Who is
the one who struck You?" Mark 14:65

Three Denials of Peter
Mark 14:66–72; Luke 22:55–62; John 18:15–18, 25–27

69 Now Peter sat outside in the courtyard.
And a servant girl came to him, saying, "You
also were with Jesus of Galilee."
70 But he denied it before *them* all, saying, "I
do not know what you are saying."
71 And when he had gone out to the gate-
way, another *girl* saw him and said to those
who were there, "This *fellow* also was with Je-
sus of Nazareth."
72 But again he denied with an oath, "I do
not know the Man!"
73 And a little later those who stood by
came up and said to Peter, "Surely you also
are *one* of them, for your [R]speech betrays
you." Luke 22:59
74 Then [R]he began to curse and swear, *say-
ing*, "I do not know the Man!" Immediately a
rooster crowed. Matt. 26:34★
75 And Peter remembered the word of Jesus
who had said to him, "Before the rooster
crows, you will deny Me three times." So he
went out and wept bitterly.

CHAPTER 27

Jesus Is Delivered to Pilate
Mark 15:1; Luke 22:66; 23:1; John 18:28

WHEN morning came, all the chief priests
and elders of the people plotted against
Jesus to put Him to death.
2 And when they had bound Him, they led
Him away and [R]delivered Him to Pontius* Pi-
late the governor. Acts 3:13★

Judas Repents—Acts 1:18, 19

3 [R]Then Judas, His betrayer, seeing that He
had been condemned, was remorseful and
brought back the thirty pieces of silver to the
chief priests and elders, Matt. 26:14
4 saying, "I have sinned by betraying inno-
cent blood." And they said, "What *is that* to
us? You see *to it!*"
5 Then he threw down the pieces of silver
in the temple and [R]departed, and went and
hanged himself. Matt. 18:7; 26:24★
6 But the chief priests took the silver pieces
and said, "It is not lawful to put them into the
treasury, because they are the price of blood."
7 And they consulted together and bought
with them the potter's field, to bury strangers
in.
8 Therefore that field has been called [R]the
Field of Blood to this day. Acts 1:19
9 Then was fulfilled what was spoken by
Jeremiah the prophet, saying, [R]"*And they
took the thirty pieces of silver, the value of
Him who was priced,* whom they of the chil-
dren of Israel priced, Zech. 11:12★
10 "*and* [R]*gave them for the potter's field, as
the* LORD *directed me.*"* Zech. 11:12, 13★

Jesus Is Examined
Mark 15:2–5; Luke 23:2–5; John 18:29–38

11 Now Jesus stood before the governor.
[R]And the governor asked Him, saying, "Are
You the King of the Jews?" Jesus said to him,
"*It is as* you say." Mark 15:2–5
12 And while He was being accused by the
chief priests and elders, [R]He answered noth-
ing. John 19:9
13 Then Pilate said to Him, [R]"Do You not
hear how many things they testify against
You?" Matt. 26:62
14 But He answered him not one word, so
that the governor marveled greatly.

Barabbas Is Freed
Mark 15:6–14; Luke 23:17–23; John 18:39, 40

15 Now at the feast the governor was accus-
tomed to releasing to the multitude one pris-
oner whom they wished.

26:59 NU omits *the elders* **26:60** NU puts a comma after *but found none*, does not capitalize *Even*, and omits *they found none*. • NU omits *false witnesses* **27:2** NU omits *Pontius* **27:10** Jer. 32:6–9

16 And at that time they had a notorious prisoner called Barabbas.*

17 Therefore, when they had gathered together, Pilate said to them, "Whom do you want me to release to you? Barabbas, or Jesus who is called Christ?"

18 For he knew that they had handed Him over because of [R]envy. Matt. 21:38

19 While he was sitting on the judgment seat, his wife sent to him, saying, "Have nothing to do with that just Man, for I have suffered many things today in a dream because of Him."

20 [R]But the chief priests and elders persuaded the multitudes that they should ask for Barabbas and destroy Jesus. Acts 3:14

21 The governor answered and said to them, "Which of the two do you want me to release to you?" They said, "Barabbas!"

22 Pilate said to them, "What then shall I do with Jesus who is called Christ?" *They* all said to him, "Let Him be crucified!"

23 Then the governor said, "Why, what evil has He done?" But they cried out all the more, saying, "Let Him be crucified!"

24 When Pilate saw that he could not prevail at all, but rather *that* a [T]tumult was rising, he [R]took water and washed *his* hands before the multitude, saying, "I am innocent of the blood of this just Person.* You see *to it.*" *an uproar* • Deut. 21:6–8

25 And all the people answered and said, "His blood *be* on us and on our children."

Jesus Is Scourged
Mark 15:15–17; Luke 23:24, 25; John 19:16

26 Then he released Barabbas to them; and when [R]he had scourged Jesus, he delivered *Him* to be crucified. [Is. 50:6; 53:5]★

27 [R]Then the soldiers of the governor took Jesus into the Praetorium and gathered the whole garrison around Him. Mark 15:16–20

28 And they [R]stripped Him and [R]put a scarlet robe on Him. John 19:2 • Luke 23:11

Jesus Is Led to Golgotha
Mark 15:18–22; Luke 23:26–33; John 19:17

29 [R]When they had [T]twisted a crown of thorns, they put *it* on His head, and a reed in His right hand. And they bowed the knee before Him and mocked Him, saying, "Hail, King of the Jews!" Is. 53:3★ • Lit. *woven*

30 Then [R]they spat on Him, and took the reed and struck Him on the head. Is. 50:6★

31 And when they had mocked Him, they took the robe off Him, put His *own* clothes on Him, and led Him away to be crucified.

32 [R]Now as they came out, they found a man of Cyrene, Simon by name. Him they compelled to bear His cross. Heb. 13:12

33 [R]And when they had come to a place called Golgotha, that is to say, Place of a Skull, John 19:17

Jesus Is Crucified
Mark 15:23–32; Luke 23:33–43; John 19:18–24

34 [R]they gave Him sour* wine mingled with gall to drink. But when He had tasted *it,* He would not drink. Ps. 69:21★

35 Then they crucified Him, and divided His garments, casting lots,* that it might be fulfilled which was spoken by the prophet:

> *"They divided My garments among them,*
> *And for My clothing they cast lots."**

36 [R]Sitting down, they kept watch over Him there. Ps. 22:17; Matt. 27:54★

37 And they [R]put up over His head the accusation written against Him: John 19:19

THIS IS JESUS THE KING OF THE JEWS.

38 [R]Then two robbers were crucified with Him, one on the right and another on the left. Is. 53:9, 12

39 And [R]those who passed by blasphemed Him, wagging their heads Ps. 22:7★

40 and saying, [R]"You who destroy the temple and build *it* in three days, save Yourself! [R]If You are the Son of God, come down from the cross." John 2:19 • Matt. 26:63

41 Likewise the chief priests also, [R]mocking with the scribes and elders,* said, Matt. 20:19★

42 "He [R]saved others; Himself He cannot save. [R]If He is the King of Israel,* let Him now come down from the cross, and we will believe Him.* [John 3:14, 15] • Ps. 22:6; 69:9★

43 [R]"He trusted in God; let Him deliver Him now if He will have Him; for He said, 'I am the Son of God.'" Ps. 22:8☆

44 Even the robbers who were crucified with Him reviled Him with the same thing.

Jesus Dies
Mark 15:33–37; Luke 23:44–46; John 19:28–30

45 Now from the sixth hour until the ninth hour there was darkness over all the land.

46 And about the ninth hour [R]Jesus cried out with a loud voice, saying, "Eli, Eli, lama sabachthani?" that is, *"My God, My God, why have You forsaken Me?"** [Heb. 5:7]

47 Some of those who stood there, when they heard *that,* said, "This Man is calling for Elijah!"

48 Immediately one of them ran and took a sponge, filled *it* with sour wine and put *it* on a reed, and offered it to Him to drink.

49 The rest said, "Let Him alone; let us see if Elijah will come to save Him."

27:16 NU *Jesus Barabbas* **27:24** NU omits *just* **27:34** NU omits *sour* **27:35** NU, M omit the rest of v. 35. • Ps. 22:18★ **27:41** M *with the scribes, the Pharisees, and the elders* **27:42** NU *He is the King of Israel!* • NU, M *we will believe in Him.* **27:46** Ps. 22:1★

50 And Jesus [R]cried out again with a loud
voice, and yielded up His spirit. Luke 23:46

Signs Accompanying Jesus' Death
Mark 15:38–41; Luke 23:45, 47–49

51 Then, behold, [R]the veil of the temple was
torn in two from top to bottom; and the earth
quaked, and the rocks were split, Zech. 11:10, 11★
52 and the graves were opened; and many
bodies of the saints who had fallen asleep
were raised;
53 and coming out of the graves after His
resurrection, they went into the holy city and
appeared to many.
54 So when the centurion and those with
him, who were guarding Jesus, saw the earth-
quake and the things that had happened, they
feared greatly, saying, [R]"Truly this was the
Son of God!" Matt. 14:33
55 And many women [R]who followed Jesus
from Galilee, ministering to Him, were there
looking on from afar, Luke 8:2, 3
56 [R]among whom were Mary Magdalene,
Mary the mother of James and Joses,* and the
mother of Zebedee's sons. Mark 16:9

Jesus Is Buried
Mark 15:42–47; Luke 23:50–55; John 19:38–42

57 Now [R]when evening had come, there
came a rich man from Arimathea, named Jo-
seph, who himself had also become a disciple
of Jesus. John 19:38–42
58 This man went to Pilate and asked for the
body of Jesus. Then Pilate commanded the
body to be given to him.
59 When Joseph had taken the body, he
wrapped it in a clean linen cloth,
60 and [R]laid it in his new tomb which he had
hewn out of the rock; and he rolled a large
stone against the door of the tomb, and de-
parted. Is. 53:9★
61 And Mary Magdalene was there, and the
other Mary, sitting opposite the tomb.
62 On the next day, which followed the Day
of Preparation, the chief priests and Pharisees
gathered together to Pilate,
63 saying, "Sir, we remember, while He was
still alive, how that deceiver said, [R]'After three
days I will rise.' Mark 8:31; 10:34
64 "Therefore command that the tomb be
made secure until the third day, lest His disci-
ples come by night* and steal Him *away,* and
say to the people, 'He has risen from the
dead.' So the last deception will be worse than
the first."
65 Pilate said to them, "You have a guard; go
your way, make *it* as secure as you know
how."
66 So they went and made the tomb se-
cure, [R]sealing the stone and setting the
guard. Dan. 6:17

CHAPTER 28

The Empty Tomb—Mark 16:1–8; Luke 24:1–11

NOW [R]after the Sabbath, as the first *day* of
the week began to dawn, Mary Magda-
lene [R]and the other Mary came to see the
tomb. Luke 24:1–10 • Matt. 27:56, 61
2 And behold, there was a great earth-
quake; for an angel of the Lord descended
from heaven, and came and rolled back the
stone from the door,* and sat on it.
3 His countenance was like lightning, and
his clothing as white as snow.
4 And the guards shook for fear of him, and
became like [R]dead *men.* Rev. 1:17
5 But the angel answered and said to the
women, "Do not be afraid, for I know that you
seek Jesus who was crucified.
6 "He is not here; for He is risen, [R]as He
said. Come, see the place where the Lord
lay. Matt. 12:40; 16:21; 17:23; 20:19★
7 "And go quickly and tell His disciples that
He is risen from the dead, and indeed He is
going before you into Galilee; there you will
see Him. Behold, I have told you."
8 So they went out quickly from the tomb
with fear and great joy, and ran to bring His
disciples word.

The Appearance of Jesus to the Women

9 And as they went to tell His disciples,* be-
hold, [R]Jesus met them, saying, "Rejoice!" So
they came and held Him by the feet and wor-
shiped Him. John 20:14
10 Then Jesus said to them, "Do not be
afraid. Go *and* tell [R]My brethren to go to Gal-
ilee, and there they will see Me." John 20:17

The Bribery of the Soldiers

11 Now while they were going, behold, some
of the guard came into the city and reported
to the chief priests all the things that had
happened.
12 When they had assembled with the elders
and consulted together, they gave a large sum
of money to the soldiers,
13 saying, "Tell them, 'His disciples came at
night and stole Him *away* while we slept.'
14 "And if this comes to the governor's ears,
we will appease him and make you secure."
15 So they took the money and did as they
were instructed; and this saying is commonly
reported among the Jews until this day.

The Appearance of Jesus to the Disciples

16 Then the eleven disciples went away into
Galilee, to the mountain [R]which Jesus had ap-
pointed for them. Matt. 26:32; 28:7, 10

27:56 NU *Joseph* **27:64** NU omits *by night* **28:2** NU omits *from the door* **28:9** NU omits *as they went to tell His disciples*

17 When they saw Him, they worshiped
Him; but some [R]doubted. John 20:24–29

The Great Commission

18 And Jesus came and spoke to them, say-
ing, [R]"All authority has been given to Me in
heaven and on earth. [Dan. 7:13, 14]

19 [R]"Go therefore* and [R]make disciples of
all the nations, baptizing them in the name of
the Father and of the Son and of the Holy
Spirit, Mark 16:15 • Luke 24:47

20 [R]"teaching them to observe all things that
I have commanded you; and lo, I am [R]with
you always, *even* to the end of the age."
Amen.* [Acts 2:42] • [Acts 4:31; 18:10; 23:11]

28:19 M omits *therefore* **28:20** NU omits *Amen*

28:19 Sharing Our Faith: Why?—There are at least six compelling reasons for sharing our faith in Christ with those who have not experienced new life in Christ.

a. Because God has commanded us to do so. The final words of Jesus while on earth (Page 1112—Acts 1:8) and also the Bible (Page 1328—Rev. 22:17) speak concerning this.
b. Because it demonstrates our love for God. Christ said that if we truly loved Him we would keep His commandments (Page 1099—John 14:15).
c. Because all are lost (Page 1150—Rom. 3:10, 23).
d. Because our sharing is God's chosen method to tell all people. He could have used angels, but He didn't. Only redeemed sinners can tell lost sinners about Christ. See Rom. 10:14–17; Acts 8:3.
e. Because God desires to save all people (Page 1116—Acts 4:12; Page 1288—2 Pet. 3:9; Page 1237—1 Tim. 2:4).
f. Because someone once shared his faith with us. It may have been a faithful Bible teacher, or a godly pastor, or a praying parent. In other words, they have the right to expect that we will do for others what they have done for us.

Now turn to Page 1178—1 Cor. 15:3, 4: Sharing Our Faith: What?

THE GOSPEL ACCORDING TO

MARK

THE BOOK OF MARK

The message of Mark's gospel is captured in a single verse: "For even the Son of Man did not come to be served, but to serve, and to give His life a ransom for many" (10:45). Chapter by chapter, the book unfolds the dual focus of Christ's life: service and sacrifice.

Mark portrays Jesus as a Servant on the move, instantly responsive to the will of the Father. By preaching, teaching, and healing, He ministers to the needs of others even to the point of death. After the Resurrection, He commissions His followers to continue His work in His power—servants following in the steps of the perfect Servant.

The ancient title for this gospel was *Kata Markon,* "According to Mark." The author is best known by his Latin name *Marcus,* but in Jewish circles he was called by his Hebrew name *John.* Acts 12:12, 25 and 15:37 refer to him as "John whose surname was Mark."

THE AUTHOR OF MARK

According to Acts 12:12, Mark's mother Mary had a large house that was used as a meeting place for believers in Jerusalem. Peter apparently went to this house often because the servant girl recognized his voice at the gate (Acts 12:13–16). Barnabas was Mark's cousin (Col. 4:10), but Peter may have been the person who led him to Christ (Peter called him "Mark my son," 1 Pet. 5:13). It was this close association with Peter that lent apostolic authority to Mark's gospel, since Peter was evidently Mark's primary source of information. It has been suggested that Mark was referring to himself in his account of "a certain young man" in Gethsemane (14:51, 52). Since all the disciples had abandoned Jesus (14:50), this little incident may have been a firsthand account.

Barnabas and Saul took Mark along with them when they returned from Jerusalem to Antioch (Acts 12:25) and again when they left on the first missionary journey (Acts 13:5). However, Mark left early and returned to Jerusalem (Acts 13:13). When Barnabas wanted to bring Mark on the second missionary journey, Paul's refusal led to a disagreement. The result was that Barnabas took Mark to Cyprus and Paul took Silas through Syria and Cilicia (Acts 15:36–41). Nevertheless, Paul wrote that Mark was with him during his first Roman imprisonment (Col. 4:10; Philem. 24) about twelve years later, so there must have been a reconciliation. In fact, at the end of his life Paul sent for Mark, saying, "he is useful to me for ministry" (2 Tim. 4:11).

The early church uniformly attested that Mark wrote this gospel. Papias, Irenaeus, Clement of Alexandria, and Origen are among the church fathers who affirmed Marcan authorship.

THE TIME OF MARK

Many scholars believe that Mark was the first of the four gospels, but there is uncertainty over its date. Because of the prophecy about the destruction of the temple (13:2), it should be dated before A.D. 70, but early traditions disagree as to whether it was written before or after the martyrdom of Peter (c. A.D. 64). The probable range for this book is A.D. 55–65.

Mark was evidently directed to a Roman readership and early tradition indicates that it originated in Rome. This may be why Mark omitted a number of items that would not have been meaningful to Gentiles, such as the genealogy of Christ, fulfilled prophecy, references to the Law, and certain Jewish customs that are found in other gospels. Mark interpreted Aramaic words (3:17; 5:41; 7:34; 15:22) and used a number of Latin terms in place of their Greek equivalents (4:21; 6:27; 12:14, 42; 15:15, 16, 39).

THE CHRIST OF MARK

The Lord is presented as an active, compassionate, and obedient Servant who constantly ministers to the physical and spiritual needs of others. Because this is the story of a Servant, Mark omits Jesus' ancestry and birth and moves right into His busy public ministry. The distinctive word of this book is *euthus* (translated "immediately"), and it appears more often in this compact gospel than in the rest of the New Testament. Christ is constantly moving toward a goal that is hidden to almost all. Mark clearly shows the power and authority of this unique Servant, identifying Him as no less than the Son of God (1:1, 11; 3:11; 5:7; 9:7; 13:32; 14:61; 15:39).

KEYS TO MARK

Key Word: Jesus the Servant—Even in the first verse it is obvious that this gospel centers on the Person and mission of the Son of God. Mark's theme is captured well in 10:45 because Jesus is portrayed in this book as a Servant and as the Redeemer of men (cf. Phil. 2:5–11). Like the other gospels, Mark is not a biography but a topical narrative. Mark juxtaposes Christ's teachings and works to show how they authenticate each other. Miracles are predominant in this book (there are eighteen), and they are used to demonstrate Christ's power and His compassion. Mark shows his Gentile readers how the Son of God—rejected by His own people—achieved ultimate victory through apparent defeat. There was no doubt an evangelistic purpose behind this gospel as Mark directed his words to a Gentile audience that knew little about Old Testament theology.

Key Verses: Mark 10:43–45 and 8:34–37—"Yet it shall not be so among you; but whoever desires to become great among you shall be your servant. And whoever of you desires to be first shall be slave of all. For even the Son of Man did not come to be served, but to serve, and to give His life a ransom for many" (10:43–45).

"When He had called the people to *Himself,* with His disciples also, He said to them, 'Whoever desires to come after Me, let him deny himself, and take up his cross, and follow Me. For whoever desires to save his life will lose it, but whoever loses his life for My sake and the gospel's will save it. For what will it profit a man if he gains the whole world, and loses his own soul? Or what will a man give in exchange for his soul?' " (8:34–37).

Key Chapter: Mark 8—As in Matthew, Mark's gospel contains a pivotal chapter showing the change of emphasis in Jesus' ministry. In Matthew it is chapter 12; in Mark it is chapter 8. The pivotal event lies in Peter's confession, "You are the Christ." That faith-inspired response triggers a new phase in both the content and the course of Jesus' ministry. Until this point He has sought to validate His claims as the Messiah. But now He begins to fortify His men for His forthcoming suffering and death at the hands of the religious leaders. Jesus' steps begin to take Him daily closer to Jerusalem—the place where the Perfect Servant will demonstrate the full extent of His servanthood.

SURVEY OF MARK

Mark, the shortest and simplest of the four gospels, gives a crisp and fast-moving look at the life of Christ. With few comments, Mark lets the narrative speak for itself as it tells the story of the Servant who constantly ministers to others through preaching, healing, teaching, and, ultimately, His own death. Mark traces the steady building of hostility and opposition to Jesus as He resolutely moves toward the fulfillment of His earthly mission. Almost forty percent of this gospel is devoted to a detailed account of the last eight days of Jesus' life, climaxing in His resurrection. The Lord is vividly portrayed in this book in two parts: to serve (1—10); to sacrifice (11—16).

To Serve (1—10): Mark passes over the birth and early years of Jesus' life and begins with the events that immediately precede the inauguration of His public ministry—His baptism by John and His temptation by Satan (1:1–13). The first four chapters emphasize the words of the Servant while chapters 5—7 accent His works. However, in both sections there is a frequent alternation between Christ's messages and miracles in order to reveal His Person and power. Though He has come to serve others, Jesus' authority prevails over many realms.

Although Jesus has already been teaching and testing His disciples (see ch. 4), His ministry with them becomes more intense from this point on as He begins to prepare them for His departure. The religious leaders are growing more antagonistic, and Christ's "hour" is only about six months away. Mark 8:31 is the pivotal point in the gospel as the Son of Man speaks clearly to His disciples about His coming death and

FOCUS	TO SERVE			TO SACRIFICE	
REFERENCE	1:1——2:13——8:27——11:1——16:1——16:20				
DIVISION	PRESENTATION OF THE SERVANT	OPPOSITION TO THE SERVANT	INSTRUCTION BY THE SERVANT	REJECTION OF THE SERVANT	RESURRECTION OF THE SERVANT
TOPIC	SAYINGS AND SIGNS			SUFFERINGS	
	c. 3 YEARS		c. 6 MONTHS	8 DAYS	
LOCATION	GALILEE AND PEREA			JUDEA AND JERUSALEM	
TIME	c. A.D. 29–33				

resurrection. The disciples struggle with this difficult revelation, but Jesus' steps head inexorably to Jerusalem.

To Sacrifice (11—16): Mark allots a disproportionate space to the last weeks of the Servant's redemptive ministry. During the last seven days in Jerusalem, hostility from the chief priests, scribes, elders, Pharisees, Herodians, and Sadducees reaches crisis proportions as Jesus publicly refutes their arguments in the temple. After His last supper with the disciples, Jesus offers no resistance to His arrest, abuse, and agonizing crucifixion. His willingness to bear countless human sins is the epitome of servanthood.

OUTLINE OF MARK

Part One: The Presentation of the Servant (1:1—2:12)

I. The Forerunner of the Servant 1:1–8

II. The Baptism of the Servant..................1:9–11

III. The Temptation of the Servant 1:12, 13

IV. The Mission of the Servant.............1:14—2:12

- A. The Work of the Servant 1:14, 15
- B. The First Disciples Are Called...........1:16–20
- C. The First Miracles Are Performed ....1:21—2:12
  1. Demons Are Cast Out.....................1:21–28
  2. Peter's Mother-in-Law Is Healed ...1:29–31
  3. Many Healings..................................1:32–39
  4. A Leper Is Cleansed 1:40–45
  5. A Paralytic Is Healed.........................2:1–12

Part Two: The Opposition to the Servant (2:13—8:26)

I. The Initial Opposition to the Servant...2:13—3:35

- A. Controversy over Jesus' Friendship with Sinners...................................2:13–22
  1. Call of Matthew 2:13–17
  2. Parable of Cloth and Wineskins.....2:18–22
- B. Controversy over Sabbath-Work..........2:23–28
- C. Controversy over Sabbath-Healing 3:1–5
- D. Pharisees Counsel to Destroy Jesus......3:6–12
- E. Selection of the Twelve.......................3:13–19
- F. Opposition of His Friends 3:20, 21
- G. Scribes Commit the Unpardonable Sin..3:22–30
- H. New Relationships Are Defined..........3:31–35

II. The Parables of the Servant..............4:1–34

- A. Parable of the Soils................................4:1–20
- B. Parable of the Lamp 4:21–25
- C. Parable of the Growing Seed 4:26–29
- D. Parable of the Mustard Seed 4:30–34

III. The Miracles of the Servant ....4:35—5:43

- A. The Sea Is Stilled 4:35–41
- B. Demons Are Cast into Swine..................5:1–20
- C. Jairus Pleads for His Daughter 5:21–24
- D. A Woman with Issue Is Healed 5:25–34
- E. Jairus's Daughter Is Healed 5:35–43

IV. The Growing Opposition to the Servant..6:1—8:26

- A. Jesus Is Rejected at Nazareth 6:1–6
- B. Twelve Are Sent to Serve........................6:7–13
- C. John the Baptist Is Murdered 6:14–29
- D. Twelve Return 6:30, 31
- E. Five Thousand Are Fed 6:32–44
- F. Jesus Walks on Water..........................6:45–52
- G. Jesus Heals at Gennesaret 6:53–56
- H. Pharisees and Defilement 7:1–23
- I. Withdrawal to the Gentiles ....7:24—8:9
  1. Syro-Phoenician's Daughter Is Healed..7:24–30
  2. Deaf and Dumb Man Is Healed 7:31–37
  3. Four Thousand Are Fed 8:1–9
- J. Pharisees Seek a Sign 8:10–13
- K. Disciples Do Not Understand 8:14–21
- L. A Blind Man Is Healed 8:22–26

Part Three: The Instruction by the Servant (8:27—10:52)

I. Peter's Confession of Christ 8:27–33

II. Cost of Discipleship..............................8:34–38

III. The Transfiguration 9:1–13

IV. Demon-Possessed Son Is Delivered ...9:14–29

V. Jesus Foretells His Death 9:30–32

VI. Jesus Teaches to Prepare the Disciples ....9:33—10:45

- A. Attitude of Servanthood.......................9:33–41
- B. Warning About Hell...............................9:42–50
- C. Marriage and Divorce..........................10:1–12
- D. Children and the Kingdom 10:13–16
- E. Wealth 10:17–31
  1. Rich Young Ruler 10:17–22
  2. Difficulty of Riches..........................10:23–27
  3. Eternal Reward...............................10:28–31
- F. Coming Crucifixion.............................10:32–34
- G. "Whoever Desires to Become Great" 10:35–45

VII. Blind Bartimaeus Is Healed 10:46–52

Part Four: The Rejection of the Servant (11:1—15:47)

Part Five: The Resurrection of the Servant (16:1–20)

CHAPTER 1

The Forerunner of the Servant
Matt. 3:1–11; Luke 3:3–16; John 1:19–34

THE [R]beginning of the gospel of Jesus
Christ, the Son of God. Luke 3:22
2 As it is written in the Prophets:*

"Behold, I send My messenger before
Your face,
*Who will prepare Your way before You."**
3 *"The voice of one crying in the*
wilderness:
'Prepare the way of the LORD;
*Make His paths straight.'"**

4 [R]John came baptizing in the wilderness
and preaching a [R]baptism of repentance for
the remission of sins. Matt. 3:1 • Mal. 4:6★
5 [R]Then all the land of Judea, and those
from Jerusalem, went out to him and were all
baptized by him in the Jordan River, confess-
ing their sins. Matt. 3:5
6 Now John was clothed with camel's hair
and with a leather belt around his waist, and
he ate locusts and wild honey.
7 And he preached, saying, [R]"There comes
One after me who is mightier than I, whose
sandal strap I am not worthy to stoop down
and loose. John 1:27
8 "I indeed baptized you with water, but He
will baptize you with the Holy Spirit."

The Baptism of the Servant
Matt. 3:13–17; Luke 3:21–23

9 It came to pass in those days *that* Jesus
came from Nazareth of Galilee, and was bap-
tized by John in the Jordan.
10 And immediately, coming up from* the
water, He saw the heavens parting and the
Spirit descending upon Him like a dove.
11 Then a voice came from heaven, [R]"You
are My beloved Son, in whom I am well
pleased." Is. 42:1★

The Temptation of the Servant
Matt. 4:1–11; Luke 4:1–13

12 [R]Immediately the Spirit [T]drove Him into
the wilderness. Matt. 4:1–11 • *sent Him out*
13 And He was there in the wilderness forty
days, tempted by Satan, and was with the
wild beasts; [R]and the angels ministered to
Him. Matt. 4:10, 11

1:2 NU *Isaiah the prophet* • Mal. 3:1★ **1:3** Is. 40:3★
1:10 NU *out of*

The Work of the Servant
Matt. 4:12–17; Luke 4:14, 15

14 [R]Now after John was put in prison, Jesus came to Galilee, preaching the gospel of the kingdom* of God, Matt. 4:12

15 and saying, [R]"The time is fulfilled, and the kingdom of God is at hand. Repent, and believe in the gospel." [Gal. 4:4]

The First Disciples Are Called—Matt. 4:18–22

16 [R]And as He walked by the Sea of Galilee, He saw Simon and Andrew his brother casting a net into the sea; for they were fishermen. Luke 5:2–11

17 Then Jesus said to them, "Follow Me, and I will make you become fishers of men."

18 [R]They immediately left their nets and followed Him. [Luke 14:26]

19 When He had gone a little farther from there, He saw James the *son* of Zebedee, and John his brother, who also *were* in the boat mending their nets.

20 And immediately He called them, and they left their father Zebedee in the boat with the hired servants, and went after Him.

Demons Are Cast Out—Luke 4:31–37

21 [R]Then they went into Capernaum, and immediately on the Sabbath He entered the synagogue and taught. Luke 4:31–37

22 And they were astonished at His teaching, for He taught them as one having authority, and not as the scribes.

23 Now there was a man in their synagogue with an [R]unclean spirit. And he cried out, [Matt. 12:43]

24 saying, "Let *us* alone! [R]What have we to do with You, Jesus of Nazareth? Did You come to destroy us? I know who You are—the [R]Holy One of God!" Matt. 8:28, 29 • Ps. 16:10

25 But Jesus [R]rebuked him, saying, "Be quiet, and come out of him!" [Luke 4:39]

26 And when the unclean spirit [R]had convulsed him and cried out with a loud voice, he came out of him. Mark 9:20

27 Then they were all amazed, so that they questioned among themselves, saying, "What is this? What new doctrine *is* this? For with authority* He commands even the unclean spirits, and they obey Him."

28 And immediately His fame spread throughout all the region around Galilee.

Peter's Mother-in-Law Is Healed
Matt. 8:14, 15; Luke 4:38, 39

29 Now as soon as they had come out of the synagogue, they entered the house of Simon and Andrew, with James and John.

30 But Simon's wife's mother lay sick with a fever, and they told Him about her at once.

31 So He came and took her by the hand and lifted her up, and immediately the fever left her. And she served them.

Many Healings
Matt. 4:23; 8:16, 17; Luke 4:40–44

32 [R]At evening, when the sun had set, they brought to Him all who were sick and those who were demon-possessed. Matt. 8:16, 17

33 And the whole city was gathered together at the door.

34 Then He healed many who were sick with various diseases, and cast out many demons; and He did not allow the demons to speak, because they knew Him.

35 Now [R]in the morning, having risen a long while before daylight, He went out and departed to a solitary place; and there He [R]prayed. Luke 4:42, 43 • Luke 5:16; 6:12; 9:28, 29

36 And Simon and those *who were* with Him searched for Him.

37 When they found Him, they said to Him, [R]"Everyone is looking for You." John 3:26

38 But He said to them, "Let us go into the next towns, that I may preach there also, because for this purpose I have come forth."

39 [R]And He was preaching in their synagogues throughout all Galilee, and [R]casting out demons. Matt. 4:23; 9:35 • Mark 5:8, 13

A Leper Is Cleansed
Matt. 8:1–4; Luke 5:12–16

40 [R]Now a leper came to Him, imploring Him, kneeling down to Him and saying to Him, "If You are willing, You can make me clean." Luke 5:12–14

41 Then Jesus, moved with compassion, stretched out *His* hand and touched him, and said to him, "I am willing; be cleansed."

42 As soon as He had spoken, immediately the leprosy left him, and he was cleansed.

43 And He strictly warned him and sent him away at once,

44 and said to him, "See that you say nothing to anyone; but go your way, show yourself to the priest, and offer for your cleansing those things [R]which Moses commanded, as a testimony to them." Lev. 14:1–32

45 However, he went out and began to proclaim *it* freely, and to spread the matter, so that Jesus could no longer openly enter the city, but was outside in deserted places; and they came to Him from every direction.

CHAPTER 2

A Paralytic Is Healed
Matt. 9:1–8; Luke 5:17–26

AND again [R]He entered Capernaum after *some* days, and it was heard that He was in the house. Matt. 9:1

2 Immediately* many gathered together, so that there was no longer room to receive

1:14 NU omits *of the kingdom* **1:27** NU *What is this? A new doctrine with authority!* **2:2** NU omits *Immediately*

them, not even near the door. And He
preached the word to them.
3 Then they came to Him, bringing a para-
lytic who was carried by four *men.*
4 And when they could not come near Him
because of the crowd, they uncovered the roof
where He was. So when they had broken
through, they let down the bed on which the
paralytic was lying.
5 When Jesus saw their faith, He said to the
paralytic, "Son, your sins are forgiven you."
6 And some of the scribes were sitting there
and reasoning in their hearts,
7 "Why does this *Man* speak blasphemies
like this? [R]Who can forgive sins but God
alone?" Is. 43:25
8 But immediately, when Jesus perceived in
His spirit that they reasoned thus within
themselves, He said to them, "Why do you
reason about these things in your hearts?
9 [R]"Which is easier, to say to the paralytic,
'*Your* sins are forgiven you,' or to say, 'Arise,
take up your bed and walk'? Matt. 9:5
10 "But that you may know that the Son of
Man has [T]power on earth to forgive sins"—He
said to the paralytic, *authority*
11 "I say to you, arise, take up your bed, and
go to your house."
12 Immediately he arose, took up the bed,
and went out in the presence of them all, so
that all were amazed and glorified God, say-
ing, "We never saw *anything* like this!"

Call of Matthew—Matt. 9:9–13; Luke 5:27–32

13 [R]Then He went out again by the sea; and
all the multitude came to Him, and He taught
them. Matt. 9:9
14 [R]As He passed by, He saw Levi the *son* of
Alphaeus sitting at the tax office. And He said
to him, "Follow Me." So he arose and [R]fol-
lowed Him. Luke 5:27–32 • Luke 18:28
15 [R]Now it happened, as He was dining in
Levi's house, that many tax collectors and sin-
ners also sat together with Jesus and His dis-
ciples; for there were many, and they followed
Him. Matt. 9:10
16 And when the scribes and* Pharisees saw
Him eating with the tax collectors and sin-
ners, they said to His disciples, "How *is it* that
He eats and drinks with tax collectors and
sinners?"
17 When Jesus heard *it,* He said to them,
[R]"Those who are well have no need of a physi-
cian, but those who are sick. I did not come to
call *the* righteous, but sinners, to repen-
tance."* Matt. 9:12, 13; 18:11

Parable of Cloth and Wineskins
Matt. 9:14–17; Luke 5:33–39

18 [R]The disciples of John and of the Phar-
isees were fasting. Then they came and said
to Him, "Why do the disciples of John and of
the Pharisees fast, but Your disciples do not
fast?" Luke 5:33–38
19 And Jesus said to them, "Can the
[T]friends of the bridegroom fast while the
bridegroom is with them? As long as they
have the bridegroom with them they cannot
fast. Lit. *sons of the bridechamber*
20 "But the days will come when the bride-
groom will be [R]taken away from them, and
then they will fast in those days. Acts 1:9
21 "No one sews a piece of unshrunk cloth
on an old garment; or else the new piece pulls
away from the old, and the tear is made
worse.
22 "And no one puts new wine into old wine-
skins; or else the new wine bursts the wine-
skins, the wine is spilled, and the wineskins
are ruined. But new wine must be put into
new wineskins."

Controversy over Sabbath-Work
Matt. 12:1–8; Luke 6:1–5

23 [R]Now it happened that He went through
the grainfields on the Sabbath; and as they
went His disciples began [R]to pluck the heads
of grain. Luke 6:1–5 • Deut. 23:25
24 And the Pharisees said to Him, "Look,
why do they do what is [R]not lawful on the
Sabbath?" Ex. 20:10; 31:15
25 But He said to them, "Have you never
read what David did when he was in need and
hungry, he and those with him:
26 "how he went into the house of God *in the
days* of Abiathar the high priest, and ate the
showbread, [R]which is not lawful to eat except
for the priests, and also gave some to those
who were with him?" Lev. 24:5–9
27 And He said to them, "The Sabbath was
made for man, and not man for the [R]Sab-
bath. Deut. 5:14
28 "Therefore [R]the Son of Man is also Lord
of the Sabbath." Matt. 12:8

CHAPTER 3

Controversy over Sabbath-Healing
Matt. 12:9–13; Luke 6:6–10

AND [R]He entered the synagogue again,
and a man was there who had a withered
hand. Luke 6:6–11
2 So they [R]watched Him closely, whether
He would heal him on the Sabbath, so that
they might accuse Him. Luke 14:1; 20:20
3 And He said to the man who had the
withered hand, "Step forward."
4 Then He said to them, "Is it lawful on the
Sabbath to do good or to do evil, to save life or
to kill?" But they kept silent.
5 And when He had looked around at
them with anger, being grieved by the [R]hard-
ness of their hearts, He said to the man,

2:16 NU *of the* **2:17** NU omits *to repentance*

"Stretch out your hand." And he stretched *it* out, and his hand was restored as whole as the other.* Zech. 7:12

Pharisees Counsel to Destroy Jesus
Matt. 12:14–16; Luke 6:11

6 [R]Then the Pharisees went out and immediately plotted with the Herodians against Him, how they might destroy Him. Ps. 2:2★

7 But Jesus withdrew with His disciples to the sea. And a great multitude from Galilee followed Him, and from Judea

8 and Jerusalem and Idumea and beyond the Jordan; and those from Tyre and Sidon, a great multitude, when they heard how many things He was doing, came to Him.

9 So He told His disciples that a small boat should be kept ready for Him because of the multitude, lest they should crush Him.

10 For He healed [R]many, so that as many as had afflictions pressed about Him to [R]touch Him. Luke 7:21 • Matt. 9:21; 14:36

11 And the unclean spirits, whenever they saw Him, fell down before Him and cried out, saying, "You are the Son of God."

12 But [R]He sternly warned them that they should not make Him known. Mark 1:25, 34

Selection of the Twelve—Luke 6:12–16

13 [R]And He went up on the mountain and called to *Him* those He Himself wanted. And they came to Him. Luke 9:1

14 Then He appointed twelve,* that they might be with Him and that He might send them out to preach,

15 and to have [T]power to heal sicknesses and* to cast out demons: *authority*

16 Simon,* [R]to whom He gave the name Peter; John 1:42

17 James the *son* of Zebedee and John the brother of James, to whom He gave the name Boanerges, that is, "Sons of Thunder";

18 Andrew, Philip, Bartholomew, Matthew, Thomas, James the *son* of Alphaeus, Thaddaeus, Simon the Cananite;

19 and Judas Iscariot, who also betrayed Him. And they went into a house.

Opposition of His Friends

20 Then the multitude came together again, [R]so that they could not so much as eat bread. Mark 6:31

21 But when His [R]own people heard *about this,* they went out to lay hold of Him, for they said, "He is out of His mind." Mark 6:3

Scribes Commit the Unpardonable Sin
Matt. 12:24–32; Luke 11:17–23

22 And the scribes who came down from Jerusalem said, [R]"He has Beelzebub," and, "By the [R]ruler of the demons He casts out demons." Matt. 9:34; 10:25 • [John 12:31; 14:30]

23 [R]So He called them to *Himself* and said to them in parables: "How can Satan cast out Satan? Matt. 12:25–29

24 "If a kingdom is divided against itself, that kingdom cannot stand.

25 "And if a house is divided against itself, that house cannot stand.

26 "And if Satan has risen up against himself, and is divided, he cannot stand, but has an end.

27 [R]"No one can enter a strong man's house and plunder his goods, unless he first binds the strong man. And then he will plunder his house. [Is. 49:24, 25]

28 [R]"Assuredly, I say to you, all sins will be forgiven the sons of men, and whatever blasphemies they may utter; Luke 12:10

29 "but he who blasphemes against the Holy Spirit never has forgiveness, but is subject to eternal condemnation"—

30 because they [R]said, "He has an unclean spirit." Matt. 9:34

New Relationships Are Defined
Matt. 12:46–50; Luke 8:19–21

31 [R]Then His brothers and His mother came, and standing outside they sent to Him, calling Him. Matt. 12:46–50

32 And a multitude was sitting around Him; and they said to Him, "Look, Your mother and Your brothers* are outside seeking You."

33 But He answered them, saying, "Who is My mother, or My brothers?"

34 And He looked around in a circle at those who sat about Him, and said, "Here are My mother and My brothers!

35 "For whoever does the will of God is My brother and My sister and mother."

CHAPTER 4

Parable of the Soils
Matt. 13:1–23; Luke 8:4–15

AND [R]again He began to teach by the sea. And a great multitude was gathered to Him, so that He got into a boat and sat *in it* on the sea; and the whole multitude was on the land facing the sea. Luke 8:4–10

2 Then He taught them many things by parables, and said to them in His teaching:

3 "Listen! Behold, a sower went out to sow.

4 "And it happened, as he sowed, *that* some *seed* fell by the wayside; and the birds of the air* came and devoured it.

5 "Some fell on stony ground, where it did not have much earth; and immediately it sprang up because it had no depth of earth.

6 "But when the sun was up it was

3:5 NU omits *as whole as the other* **3:14** NU adds *whom He also named apostles* **3:15** NU omits *to heal sicknesses and* **3:16** NU *and He appointed the twelve: Simon, . . .* **3:32** NU, M add *and Your sisters* **4:4** NU, M omit *of the air*

scorched, and because it had no root it withered away.

7 "And some *seed* fell among thorns; and the thorns grew up and choked it, and it yielded no [T]crop. Lit. *fruit*

8 "But other *seed* fell on good ground and yielded a crop that sprang up, increased and produced: some thirtyfold, some sixty, and some a hundred."

9 **And He said to them,*** "He who has ears to hear, let him hear!"

10 [R]But when He was alone, those around Him with the twelve asked Him about the parable. Luke 8:9

11 **And He said to them,** "To you it has been given to know the mystery of the kingdom of God; but to [R]those who are outside, all things come in parables, [Col. 4:5]

12 "so that

'Seeing they may see and not perceive,
And hearing they may hear and not
understand;
Lest they should turn,
*And their sins be forgiven them.'"**

13 And He said to them, "Do you not understand this parable? How then will you understand all the parables?

14 "The sower sows the word.

15 "And these are the ones by the wayside where the word is sown. When they hear, Satan comes immediately and takes away the word that was sown in their hearts.

16 "These likewise are the ones sown on stony ground who, when they hear the word, immediately receive it with gladness;

17 "and they have no root in themselves, and so endure only for a time. Afterward, when tribulation or persecution arises for the word's sake, immediately they stumble.

18 "Now these are the ones sown among thorns; *they are* the ones who hear the word,

19 "and the [R]cares of this world, the deceitfulness of riches, and the desires for other things entering in choke the word, and it becomes unfruitful. Luke 21:34

20 "But these are the ones sown on good ground, those who hear the word, [T]accept *it*, and bear [R]fruit: some thirtyfold, some sixty, and some a hundred." *receive* • [Rom. 7:4]

Parable of the Lamp—Luke 8:16–18

21 Also He said to them, "Is a lamp brought to be put under a basket or under a bed? Is it not to be set on a lampstand?

22 "For there is nothing hidden which will not be revealed, nor has anything been kept secret but that it should come to light.

23 [R]"If anyone has ears to hear, let him hear." Matt. 11:15; 13:9, 43

24 **Then He said to them,** "Take heed what you hear. [R]With the same measure you use, it will be measured to you; and to you who hear, more will be given. Matt. 7:2

25 "For whoever has, to him more will be given; but whoever does not have, even what he has will be taken away from him."

Parable of the Growing Seed

26 And He said, "The kingdom of God is as if a man should scatter seed on the ground,

27 "and should sleep by night and rise by day, and the seed should sprout and [R]grow, he himself does not know how. [2 Pet. 3:18]

28 "For the earth [R]yields crops by itself: first the blade, then the head, after that the full grain in the head. [John 12:24]

29 "But when the grain ripens, immediately [R]he puts in the sickle, because the harvest has come." Rev. 14:15

Parable of the Mustard Seed—Matt. 13:31–35

30 Then He said, [R]"To what shall we liken the kingdom of God? Or with what parable shall we picture it? Matt. 13:31, 32

31 "*It is* like a mustard seed which, when it is sown on the ground, is smaller than all the seeds on earth;

32 "but when it is sown, it grows up and becomes greater than all herbs, and shoots out large branches, so that the birds of the air may nest under its shade."

33 [R]And with many such parables He spoke the word to them as they were able to hear *it*. Matt. 13:34, 35

34 But without a parable He did not speak to them. And when they were alone, He explained all things to His disciples.

The Sea Is Stilled
Matt. 8:23–27; Luke 8:22–25

35 [R]On the same day, when evening had come, He said to them, "Let us cross over to the other side." Luke 8:22, 25

36 Now when they had left the multitude, they took Him along in the boat as He was. And other little boats were also with Him.

37 And a great windstorm arose, and the waves beat into the boat, so that it was already filling.

38 But He was in the stern, asleep on a pillow. And they awoke Him and said to Him, [R]"Teacher, [R]do You not care that we are perishing?" [Matt. 23:8–10] • Ps. 44:23

39 Then He arose and rebuked the wind, and said to the sea, "Peace, be still!" **And the wind ceased and there was a great calm.**

40 But He said to them, "Why are you so fearful? How *is it* that you have no faith?"*

41 And they feared exceedingly, and said to one another, "Who can this be, that even the wind and the sea obey Him!"

4:9 NU, M omit *to them* **4:12** Is. 6:9, 10 **4:40** NU *Have you still no faith?*

CHAPTER 5

Demons Are Cast into Swine
Matt. 8:28–34; Luke 8:26–39

THEN they came to the other side of the sea, to the country of the Gadarenes.*

2 And when He had come out of the boat, immediately there met Him out of the tombs a man with an [R]unclean spirit, Mark 1:23

3 who had *his* dwelling among the tombs; and no one could bind him,* not even with chains,

4 because he had often been bound with shackles and chains. And the chains had been pulled apart by him, and the shackles broken in pieces; neither could anyone tame him.

5 And always, night and day, he was in the mountains and in the tombs, crying out and cutting himself with stones.

6 When he saw Jesus from afar, he ran and worshiped Him.

7 And he cried out with a loud voice and said, "What have I to do with You, Jesus, Son of the Most High God? I implore You by God that You do not torment me."

8 For He said to him, [R]"Come out of the man, unclean spirit!" Mark 1:25; 9:25

9 Then He asked him, "What *is* your name?" And he answered, saying, "My name *is* Legion; for we are many."

10 Also he begged Him earnestly that He would not send them out of the country.

11 Now a large herd of [R]swine was feeding there near the mountains. Deut. 14:8

12 So all the demons begged Him, saying, "Send us to the swine, that we may enter them."

13 And at once Jesus* gave them permission. Then the unclean spirits went out and entered the swine (there were about two thousand); and the herd ran violently down the steep place into the sea, and drowned in the sea.

14 So those who fed the swine fled, and they told *it* in the city and in the country. And they went out to see what it was that had happened.

15 Then they came to Jesus, and saw the one *who had been* demon-possessed and had the legion, sitting and clothed and in his right mind. And they were afraid.

16 And those who saw it told them how it happened to him *who had been* demon-possessed, and about the swine.

17 Then [R]they began to plead with Him to depart from their region. Acts 16:39

18 And when He got into the boat, [R]he who had been demon-possessed begged Him that he might be with Him. Luke 8:38, 39

19 However, Jesus did not permit him, but said to him, "Go home to your friends, and tell them what great things the Lord has done for you, and how He has had compassion on you."

20 And he departed and began to [R]proclaim in Decapolis all that Jesus had done for him; and all marveled. Ps. 66:16

Jairus Pleads for His Daughter
Matt. 9:18, 19; Luke 8:41, 42

21 [R]Now when Jesus had crossed over again by boat to the other side, a great multitude gathered to Him; and He was by the sea. Luke 8:40

22 [R]And behold, one of the rulers of the synagogue came, Jairus by name. And when he saw Him, he fell at His feet Matt. 9:18–26

23 and begged Him earnestly, saying, "My little daughter lies at the point of death. Come and [R]lay Your hands on her, that she may be healed, and she will live." Acts 9:17

24 So *Jesus* went with him, and a great multitude followed Him and thronged Him.

A Woman with Issue Is Healed
Matt. 9:20–22; Luke 8:43–48

25 Now a certain woman [R]had a flow of blood for twelve years, Lev. 15:19, 25

26 and had suffered many things from many physicians. She had spent all that she had and was no better, but rather grew worse.

27 When she heard about Jesus, she came behind *Him* in the crowd and [R]touched His garment. Matt. 14:35, 36

28 For she said, "If only I may touch His clothes, I shall be made well."

29 Immediately the fountain of her blood was dried up, and she felt in *her* body that she was healed of the [T]affliction. *suffering*

30 And Jesus, immediately knowing in Himself that [R]power had gone out of Him, turned around in the crowd and said, "Who touched My clothes?" Luke 6:19; 8:46

31 But His disciples said to Him, "You see the multitude thronging You, and You say, 'Who touched Me?' "

32 And He looked around to see her who had done this thing.

33 But the woman, [R]fearing and trembling, knowing what had happened to her, came and fell down before Him and told Him the whole truth. [Ps. 89:7]

34 And He said to her, "Daughter, [R]your faith has made you well. Go in peace, and be healed of your affliction." Matt. 9:22

Jairus's Daughter Is Healed
Matt. 9:23–26; Luke 8:49–56

35 [R]While He was still speaking, *some* came from the ruler of the synagogue's *house* who said, "Your daughter is dead. Why trouble the Teacher any further?" Luke 8:49

36 As soon as Jesus heard the word that was spoken, He said to the ruler of the synagogue, "Do not be afraid; only believe."

5:1 NU *Gerasenes* **5:3** NU adds *anymore* **5:13** NU *And He gave*

37 And He permitted no one to follow Him
except Peter, James, and John the brother of
James.
38 Then He came to the house of the ruler of
the synagogue, and saw a tumult and those
who wept and wailed loudly.
39 When He came in, He said to them, "Why
make this commotion and weep? The child is
not dead, but sleeping."
40 And they ridiculed Him. [R]But when He
had put them all outside, He took the father
and the mother of the child, and those *who*
were with Him, and entered where the child
was lying. Acts 9:40
41 Then He took the child by the hand, and
said to her, "Talitha, cumi," which is trans-
lated, "Little girl, I say to you, arise."
42 Immediately the girl arose and walked,
for she was twelve years *of age*. And they
were overcome with great amazement.
43 But [R]He commanded them strictly that no
one should know it, and said that *something*
should be given her to eat. [Matt. 8:4]

CHAPTER 6

Jesus Is Rejected at Nazareth—Matt. 13:54–58

1 THEN [R]He went out from there and came to
His own country, and His disciples fol-
lowed Him. Matt. 13:54
2 And when the Sabbath had come, He
began to teach in the synagogue. And many
hearing *Him* were [R]astonished, saying,
[R]"Where *did* this Man *get* these things? And
what wisdom *is* this which is given to Him,
that such mighty works are performed by His
hands! Matt. 7:28 • John 6:42
3 "Is this not the carpenter, the Son of Mary,
and brother of James, Joses, Judas, and Si-
mon? And are not His sisters here with us?"
So they were offended at Him.
4 But Jesus said to them, [R]"A prophet is not
without honor except in his own country,
among his own relatives, and in his own
house." John 4:44
5 [R]Now He could do no mighty work there,
except that He laid His hands on a few sick
people and healed *them*. Gen. 19:22; 32:25
6 And [R]He marveled because of their unbe-
lief. [R]Then He went about the villages in a cir-
cuit, teaching. Is. 59:16 • Matt. 9:35

Twelve Are Sent to Serve
Matt. 10:1–42; Luke 9:1–6

7 And He called the twelve to *Himself*, and
began to send them out two *by* two, and gave
them power over unclean spirits.
8 He commanded them to take nothing for
the journey except a staff—no bag, no bread,
no copper in *their* money belts—
9 but [R]to wear sandals, and not to put on
two tunics. [Eph. 6:15]
10 [R]Also He said to them, "In whatever place
you enter a house, stay there till you depart
from that place. Matt. 10:11
11 [R]"And whoever* will not receive you nor
hear you, when you depart from there,
[R]shake off the dust under your feet as a testi-
mony against them.* Assuredly, I say to you,
it will be more tolerable for Sodom and Go-
morrah in the day of judgment than for that
city!" Matt. 10:14 • Acts 13:51; 18:6
12 So they went out and preached that *peo-*
ple should repent.
13 And they cast out many demons, [R]and
anointed with oil many who were sick, and
healed *them*. [James 5:14]

John the Baptist Is Murdered
Matt. 14:1–12; Luke 9:7–9

14 [R]Now King Herod heard *of Him*, for His
name had become well known. And he said,
"John the Baptist is risen from the dead,
and therefore [R]these powers are at work in
him." Luke 9:7–9 • Luke 19:37
15 [R]Others said, "It is Elijah." And others
said, "It is the Prophet, [R]or* like one of the
prophets." Mark 8:28 • Matt. 21:11
16 [R]But when Herod heard, he said, "This is
John, whom I beheaded; he has been raised
from the dead!" Luke 3:19
17 For Herod himself had sent and laid hold
of John, and bound him in prison for the sake
of Herodias, his brother Philip's wife; for he
had married her.
18 Because John had said to Herod, [R]"It is
not lawful for you to have your brother's
wife." Lev. 18:16; 20:21
19 Therefore Herodias held it against him
and wanted to kill him, but she could not;
20 for Herod [R]feared John, knowing that he
was a just and holy man, and he protected
him. And when he heard him, he did* many
things, and heard him gladly. Matt. 14:5
21 [R]Then an opportune day came when
Herod [R]on his birthday gave a feast for his no-
bles, the high officers, and the chief *men* of
Galilee. Matt. 14:6 • Gen. 40:20
22 And when Herodias' daughter herself
came in and danced, and pleased Herod and
those who sat with him, the king said to the
girl, "Ask me whatever you want, and I will
give *it* to you."
23 He also swore to her, [R]"Whatever you
ask me, I will give you, up to half my king-
dom." Esth. 5:3, 6; 7:2
24 So she went out and said to her mother,
"What shall I ask?" And she said, "The head of
John the Baptist!"
25 Immediately she came in with haste to
the king and asked, saying, "I want you to give
me at once the head of John the Baptist on a
platter."

6:11 NU *whatever place* • NU omits the rest of v. 11.
6:15 NU, M omit *or* **6:20** NU *was very perplexed, yet*

26 [R]And the king was exceedingly sorry; *yet,*
because of the oaths and because of those
who sat with him, he did not want to refuse
her. Matt. 14:9
27 Immediately the king sent an executioner
and commanded his head to be brought. And
he went and beheaded him in prison,
28 brought his head on a platter, and gave it
to the girl; and the girl gave it to her mother.
29 When his disciples heard *of it,* they came
and [R]took away his corpse and laid it in a
tomb. 1 Kin. 13:29, 30

Twelve Return—Luke 9:10

30 [R]Then the apostles gathered to Jesus and
told Him all things, both what they had done
and what they had taught. Luke 9:10
31 And He said to them, "Come aside by
yourselves to a deserted place and rest a
while." For there were many coming and
going, and they did not even have time to eat.

Five Thousand Are Fed
Matt. 14:13–21; Luke 9:11–17; John 6:1–14

32 [R]So they departed to a deserted place in
the boat by themselves. Matt. 14:13–21
33 But the multitudes* saw them departing,
and many [R]knew Him and ran there on foot
from all the cities. They arrived before them
and came together to Him. [Col. 1:6]
34 And Jesus, when He came out, saw a
great multitude and was moved with compas-
sion for them, because they were like [R]sheep
not having a shepherd. So He began to teach
them many things. Num. 27:17
35 When the day was now far spent, His dis-
ciples came to Him and said, "This is a de-
serted place, and already the hour *is* late.
36 "Send them away, that they may go into
the surrounding country and villages and buy
themselves bread;* for they have nothing to
eat."
37 But He answered and said to them, "You
give them something to eat." And they said to
Him, [R]"Shall we go and buy two hundred
denarii worth of bread and give them *some-
thing* to eat?" 2 Kin. 4:43
38 But He said to them, "How many loaves
do you have? Go and see." And when they
found out they said, "Five, and two fish."
39 Then He [R]commanded them to make
them all sit down in groups on the green
grass. Matt. 15:35
40 So they sat down in ranks, in hundreds
and in fifties.
41 And when He had taken the five loaves
and the two fish, He looked up to heaven,
blessed and broke the loaves, and gave *them*
to His disciples to set before them; and the
two fish He divided among *them* all.
42 So they all ate and were filled.
43 And they took up twelve baskets full of
fragments and of the fish.
44 Now those who had eaten the loaves were
about* five thousand men.

Jesus Walks on Water
Matt. 14:22–33; John 6:15–21

45 [R]Immediately He [T]made His disciples get
into the boat and go before Him to the other
side, to Bethsaida, while He sent the multitude
away. John 6:15–21 • *invited, strongly urged*
46 And when He had sent them away, He de-
parted to the mountain to pray.
47 Now when evening came, the boat was in
the middle of the sea; and He *was* alone on
the land.
48 Then He saw them straining at rowing,
for the wind was against them. Now about the
fourth watch of the night He came to them,
walking on the sea, and [R]would have passed
them by. Luke 24:28
49 And when they saw Him walking on the
sea, they supposed it was a [R]ghost, and cried
out; Matt. 14:26
50 for they all saw Him and were troubled.
But immediately He talked with them and
said to them, [R]"Be[T] of good cheer! It is I; do
not be [R]afraid." Matt. 9:2 • *Take courage* • Is. 41:10
51 Then He went up into the boat to them,
and the wind [R]ceased. And they were greatly
[R]amazed in themselves beyond measure, and
marveled. Ps. 107:29 • Mark 1:27; 2:12; 5:42; 7:37
52 For they had not understood about the
loaves, because their heart was hardened.

Jesus Heals at Gennesaret—Matt. 14:34–36

53 [R]When they had crossed over, they came
to the land of Gennesaret and anchored
there. Matt. 14:34–36
54 And when they came out of the boat, im-
mediately the people recognized Him,
55 ran through that whole surrounding re-
gion, and began to carry about on beds those
who were sick to wherever they heard He
was.
56 Wherever He entered, into villages,
cities, or the country, they laid the sick in the
marketplaces, and begged Him that [R]they
might just touch the [R]hem of His garment.
And as many as touched Him were made
well. Matt. 9:20 • Num. 15:38, 39

CHAPTER 7

Pharisees and Defilement—Matt. 15:1–20

THEN [R]the Pharisees and some of the
scribes came together to Him, having
come from Jerusalem. Matt. 15:1–20
2 Now when* they saw some of His disci-
ples eat bread with defiled, that is, with [R]un-
washed hands, they found fault.* Matt. 15:20

6:33 NU, M *they* **6:36** NU *something to eat* and
omits the rest of v. 36. **6:44** NU, M omit *about*
7:2 NU omits *when* • NU omits *they found fault*

3 For the Pharisees and all the Jews do not eat unless they wash *their* hands [T]in a special way, holding the [R]tradition of the elders. Lit. *with the fist* • Gal. 1:14

4 *When they come* from the marketplace, they do not eat unless they wash. And there are many other things which they have received and hold, *like* the washing of cups, pitchers, copper vessels, and couches.

5 [R]Then the Pharisees and scribes asked Him, "Why do Your disciples not walk according to the tradition of the elders, but eat bread with unwashed hands?" Matt. 15:2

6 He answered and said to them, "Well did Isaiah prophesy of you [R]hypocrites, as it is written: Matt. 23:13–29

'This people honors Me with their lips,
But their heart is far from Me.
7 *And in vain they worship Me,*
Teaching as doctrines the
*commandments of men.'**

8 "For laying aside the commandment of God, you hold the tradition of men*—the washing of pitchers and cups, and many other such things you do."

9 He said to them, "*All too* well [R]you [T]reject the commandment of God, that you may keep your tradition. Prov. 1:25 • *set aside*

10 "For Moses said, *'Honor your father and your mother'*;* and, *'He who curses father or mother, let him be put to death.'**

11 "But you say, 'If a man says to his father or mother, [R]"Whatever profit you might have received from me *is* Corban"—' (that is, a gift *to God*), Matt. 15:5; 23:18

12 "then you no longer let him do anything for his father or his mother,

13 "making the word of God of no effect through your tradition which you have handed down. And many such things you do."

14 [R]When He had called all the multitude to *Himself*, He said to them, "Hear Me, everyone, and understand: Matt. 15:10

15 "There is nothing that enters a man from outside which can defile him; but the things which come out of him, those are the things that [R]defile a man. Is. 59:3

16 [R]"If anyone has ears to hear, let him hear!"* Matt. 11:15

17 [R]When He had entered a house away from the crowd, His disciples asked Him concerning the parable. Matt. 15:15

18 So He said to them, [R]"Are you thus without understanding also? Do you not perceive that whatever enters a man from outside cannot defile him, [Heb. 5:11–14]

19 "because it does not enter his heart but his stomach, and is eliminated, *thus* purifying all foods?"*

20 And He said, [R]"What comes out of a man, that defiles a man. Ps. 39:1

21 [R]"For from within, out of the heart of men, [R]proceed evil thoughts, adulteries, fornications, murders, Gen. 6:5; 8:21 • [Gal. 5:19–21]

22 "thefts, [R]covetousness, wickedness, [R]deceit, lewdness, an evil eye, blasphemy, pride, foolishness. Luke 12:15 • Rom. 1:28, 29

23 "All these evil things come from within and defile a man."

Syro-Phoenician's Daughter Is Healed
Matt. 15:21–28

24 [R]From there He arose and went to the region of Tyre and Sidon.* And He entered a house and wanted no one to know *it*, but He could not be [R]hidden. Matt. 15:21 • Mark 2:1, 2

25 For a woman whose young daughter had an unclean spirit heard about Him, and she came and [R]fell at His feet. John 11:32

26 The woman was a Greek, a Syro-Phoenician by birth, and she kept asking Him to cast the demon out of her daughter.

27 But Jesus said to her, "Let the children be filled first, for it is not good to take the children's bread and throw *it* to the little dogs."

28 And she answered and said to Him, "Yes, Lord, yet even the little dogs under the table eat from the children's crumbs."

29 Then He said to her, "For this saying go your way; the demon has gone out of your daughter."

30 And when she had come to her house, she found the demon gone out, and her daughter lying on the bed.

Deaf and Dumb Man Is Healed

31 [R]Again, departing from the region of Tyre and Sidon, He came through the midst of the region of Decapolis to the Sea of Galilee. Matt. 15:29

32 Then [R]they brought to Him one who was deaf and had an impediment in his speech, and they begged Him to put His hand on him. Luke 11:14

33 And He took him aside from the multitude, and put His fingers in his ears, and He spat and touched his tongue.

34 Then, [R]looking up to heaven, [R]He sighed, and said to him, "Ephphatha," that is, "Be opened." Mark 6:41 • John 11:33, 38

35 [R]Immediately his ears were opened, and the [T]impediment of his tongue was loosed, and he spoke plainly. Is. 35:5, 6 • Lit. *bond*

36 Then [R]He commanded them that they should tell no one; but the more He commanded them, the more widely they proclaimed *it*. Mark 5:43

37 And they were [R]astonished beyond measure, saying, "He has done all things well. He

7:7 Is. 29:13★ **7:8** NU omits the rest of v. 8. **7:10** Ex. 20:12; Deut. 5:16 • Ex. 21:17 **7:16** NU omits v. 16. **7:19** NU sets off the final phrase as Mark's comment that Jesus has declared all foods clean. **7:24** NU omits *and Sidon*

[R]makes both the deaf to hear and the mute to
speak." Mark 6:51; 10:26 • Matt. 12:22

CHAPTER 8

Four Thousand Are Fed—Matt. 15:32–38

IN those days, the multitude being very great
and having nothing to eat, Jesus called His
disciples *to Him* and said to them,
2 "I have compassion on the multitude, be-
cause they have now continued with Me three
days and have nothing to eat.
3 "And if I send them away hungry to their
own houses, they will faint on the way; for
some of them have come from afar."
4 Then His disciples answered Him, "How
can one satisfy these people with bread here
in the wilderness?"
5 He asked them, "How many loaves do you
have?" And they said, "Seven."
6 So He commanded the multitude to sit
down on the ground. And He took the seven
loaves and gave thanks, broke *them* and gave
them to His disciples to set before *them;* and
they set *them* before the multitude.
7 They also had a few small fish; and [R]hav-
ing blessed them, He said to set them also be-
fore *them.* Matt. 14:19
8 So they ate and were filled, and they took
up seven large baskets of leftover fragments.
9 Now those who had eaten were about
four thousand. And He sent them away,
10 [R]immediately got into the boat with His
disciples, and came to the region of Dal-
manutha. Matt. 15:39

Pharisees Seek a Sign—Matt. 15:39—16:4

11 [R]Then the Pharisees came out and began
to dispute with Him, seeking from Him a sign
from heaven, testing Him. Matt. 12:38
12 But He [R]sighed deeply in His spirit, and
said, "Why does this generation seek a sign?
Assuredly, I say to you, no sign shall be given
to this generation." Mark 7:34
13 And He left them, and getting into the
boat again, departed to the other side.

Disciples Do Not Understand—Matt. 16:5–12

14 [R]Now the disciples* had forgotten to take
bread, and they did not have more than one
loaf with them in the boat. Matt. 16:5
15 [R]Then He charged them, saying, "Take
heed, beware of the [T]leaven of the Pharisees
and the leaven of Herod." Luke 12:1 • *yeast*
16 And they reasoned among themselves,
saying, "*It is* because we have no bread."
17 But Jesus, being aware of *it,* said to them,
"Why do you reason because you have no
bread? Do you not yet perceive nor under-
stand? Is your heart still* hardened?
18 "Having eyes, do you not see? And having
ears, do you not hear? And do you not re-
member?
19 [R]"When I broke the five loaves for the five
thousand, how many baskets full of frag-
ments did you take up?" They said to Him,
"Twelve." Matt. 14:20
20 "Also, [R]when I broke the seven for the
four thousand, how many large baskets full of
fragments did you take up?" And they said,
"Seven." Matt. 15:37
21 So He said to them, "How *is it* [R]you do not
understand?" [Mark 6:52]

A Blind Man Is Healed

22 Then He came to Bethsaida; and they
brought a [R]blind man to Him, and begged Him
to [R]touch him. John 9:1 • Luke 18:15
23 So He took the blind man by the hand and
led him out of the town. And when He had spit
on his eyes and put His hands on him, He
asked him if he saw anything.
24 And he looked up and said, "I see men
like trees, walking."
25 Then He put *His* hands on his eyes again
and made him look up. And he was restored
and saw everyone clearly.
26 Then He sent him away to his house, say-
ing, "Neither go into the town, [R]nor tell any-
one in the town."* Mark 5:43; 7:36

Peter's Confession of Christ *Matt. 16:13–23; Luke 9:18–22*

27 [R]Now Jesus and His disciples went out to
the towns of Caesarea Philippi; and on the
road He asked His disciples, saying to them,
"Who do men say that I am?" Luke 9:18–20
28 So they answered, [R]"John the Baptist; but
some *say,* [R]Elijah; and others, one of the
prophets." Matt. 14:2 • Luke 9:7, 8
29 He said to them, "But who do you say that
I am?" Peter answered and said to Him, [R]"You
are the Christ." John 1:41; 4:42; 6:69
30 [R]Then He strictly warned them that they
should tell no one about Him. Matt. 8:4
31 And He began to teach them that the Son
of Man must suffer many things, and be [R]re-
jected by the elders and chief priests and
scribes, and be [R]killed, and after three days
rise again. Mark 10:33 • Mark 9:31; 10:34☆
32 He spoke this word openly. Then Peter
took Him aside and began to rebuke Him.
33 But when He had turned around and
looked at His disciples, He [R]rebuked Peter,
saying, "Get behind Me, Satan! For you are
not [T]mindful of the things of God, but the
things of men." [Rev. 3:19] • *setting your mind on*

Cost of Discipleship *Matt. 16:24–27; Luke 9:23–26*

34 When He had called the people to *Him-
self,* with His disciples also, He said to them,
[R]"Whoever desires to come after Me, let him

8:14 NU, M *they* **8:17** NU omits *still* **8:26** NU "*Do not even go into the town.*"

deny himself, and take up his cross, and follow Me. Luke 14:27

35 "For [R]whoever desires to save his life will lose it, but whoever loses his life for My sake and the gospel's will save it. John 12:25

36 "For what will it profit a man if he gains the whole world, and loses his own soul?

37 "Or what will a man give in exchange for his soul?

38 [R]"For whoever is ashamed of Me and My words in this adulterous and sinful generation, of him the Son of Man also will be ashamed when He comes in the glory of His Father with the holy angels." Matt. 10:33

CHAPTER 9

The Transfiguration
Matt. 16:28—17:13; Luke 9:27–36

AND He said to them, "Assuredly, I say to you that there are some standing here who will not taste death till they see the kingdom of God present with power."

2 [R]Now after six days Jesus took Peter, James, and John, and led them up on a high mountain apart by themselves; and He was transfigured before them. Matt. 17:1–8

3 His clothes became shining, exceedingly [R]white, like snow, such as no launderer on earth can whiten them. Dan. 7:9

4 And Elijah appeared to them with Moses, and they were talking with Jesus.

5 Then Peter answered and said to Jesus, "Rabbi, it is good for us to be here; and let us make three tabernacles: one for You, one for Moses, and one for Elijah"—

6 because he did not know what to say, for they were greatly afraid.

7 And a cloud came and overshadowed them; and a voice came out of the cloud, saying, "This is [R]My beloved Son. Hear Him!" Ps. 2:7; Is. 42:1; Luke 1:35★

8 Suddenly, when they had looked around, they saw no one anymore, but only Jesus with themselves.

9 Now as they came down from the mountain, He commanded them that they should tell no one the things they had seen, till the Son of Man had risen from the dead.

10 So they kept this word to themselves, questioning [R]what the rising from the dead meant. John 2:19–22

11 And they asked Him, saying, "Why do the scribes say [R]that Elijah must come first?" Mal. 4:5

12 Then He answered and told them, "Indeed, Elijah is coming first and restores all things. And [R]how is it written concerning the Son of Man, that He must suffer many things and [R]be treated with contempt? Ps. 22:6; Is. 53:3☆ • Phil. 2:7

13 "But I say to you that [R]Elijah has also come, and they did to him whatever they wished, as it is written of him." Luke 1:17

Demon-Possessed Son Is Delivered
Matt. 17:14–21; Luke 9:37–42

14 [R]And when He came to the disciples, He saw a great multitude around them, and scribes disputing with them. Matt. 17:14–19

15 Immediately, when they saw Him, all the people were greatly amazed, and running to *Him*, greeted Him.

16 And He asked the scribes, "What are you discussing with them?"

17 Then [R]one of the crowd answered and said, "Teacher, I brought You my son, who has a mute spirit. Luke 9:38

18 "And wherever it seizes him, it throws him down; he foams at the mouth, gnashes his teeth, and becomes rigid. So I spoke to Your disciples, that they should cast it out, but they could not."

19 He answered him and said, "O [R]faithless[T] generation, how long shall I be with you? How long shall I [T]bear with you? Bring him to Me." John 4:48 • *unbelieving* • *put up with*

20 Then they brought him to Him. And when he saw Him, immediately the spirit convulsed him, and he fell on the ground and wallowed, foaming at the mouth.

21 So He asked his father, "How long has this been happening to him?" And he said, "From childhood.

22 "And often he has thrown him both into the fire and into the water to destroy him. But if You can do anything, have compassion on us and help us."

23 Jesus said to him, "If you can believe,* all things *are* possible to him who believes."

24 Immediately the father of the child cried out and said with tears, "Lord, I believe; [R]help my unbelief!" Luke 17:5

25 When Jesus saw that the people came running together, He [R]rebuked the unclean spirit, saying to it: "Deaf and dumb spirit, I command you, come out of him and enter him no more!" Mark 1:25

26 Then *the spirit* cried out, convulsed him greatly, and came out of him. And he became as one dead, so that many said, "He is dead."

27 But Jesus took him by the hand and lifted him up, and he arose.

28 [R]And when He had come into the house, His disciples asked Him privately, "Why could we not cast it out?" Matt. 17:19

29 So He said to them, "This kind can come out by nothing but prayer and fasting."*

Jesus Foretells His Death
Matt. 17:22, 23; Luke 9:43–45

30 Then they departed from there and passed through Galilee, and He did not want anyone to know *it*.

9:23 NU "*'If you can!' All things. . . .*" **9:29** NU omits *and fasting*

31 [R]For He taught His disciples and said to them, "The Son of Man is being betrayed into the hands of men, and they will kill Him. And after He is killed, He will [R]rise the third day." Luke 9:44 • Luke 24:46; 1 Cor. 15:4☆

32 But they [R]did not understand this saying, and were afraid to ask Him. Luke 2:50

Attitude of Servanthood
Matt. 18:1–5; Luke 9:46–50

33 [R]Then He came to Capernaum. And when He was in the house He asked them, "What was it you [T]disputed among yourselves on the road?" Matt. 18:1–5 • *discussed*

34 But they kept silent, for on the road they had [R]disputed among themselves who *would be the* greatest. [Prov. 13:10]

35 And He sat down, called the twelve, and said to them, "If anyone desires to be first, he shall be last of all and servant of all."

36 Then He took a little child and set him in the midst of them. And when He had taken him in His arms, He said to them,

37 "Whoever receives one of these little children in My name receives Me; and [R]whoever receives Me, receives not Me but Him who sent Me." Matt. 10:40

38 [R]Now John answered Him, saying, "Teacher, we saw someone who does not follow us casting out demons in Your name, and we forbade him because he does not follow us." Num. 11:27–29

39 But Jesus said, "Do not forbid him, [R]for no one who works a miracle in My name can soon afterward speak evil of Me. 1 Cor. 12:3

40 "For [R]he who is not against us is on our* side. [Matt. 12:30]

41 [R]"For whoever gives you a cup of water to drink in My name, because you belong to Christ, assuredly, I say to you, he will by no means lose his reward. Matt. 10:42

Warning About Hell—Matt. 18:6–9

42 [R]"But whoever causes one of these little ones who believe in Me [T]to stumble, it would be better for him if a millstone were hung around his neck, and he were thrown into the sea. Luke 17:1, 2 • To fall into sin

43 [R]"If your hand causes you to sin, cut it off. It is better for you to enter into life [T]maimed, rather than having two hands, to go to hell, into the fire that shall never be quenched— Matt. 5:29, 30; 18:8, 9 • *crippled*

44 "where

[R]*'Their worm does not die,* Is. 66:24
*And the fire is not quenched.'**

45 "And if your foot causes you to sin, cut it off. It is better for you to enter life lame, rather than having two feet, to be cast into [T]hell, into the fire that shall never be quenched— Gr. *Gehenna*

46 "where

[R]*'Their worm does not die,* Is. 66:24
*And the fire is not quenched.'**

47 "And if your eye causes you to sin, pluck it out. It is better for you to enter the kingdom of God with one eye, rather than having two eyes, to be cast into hell fire—

48 "where

'Their worm does not die,
*And the fire is not quenched.'**

49 "For everyone will be [R]seasoned with fire,* [R]and every sacrifice will be seasoned with salt. [Matt. 3:11] • Lev. 2:13

50 [R]"Salt *is* good, but if the salt loses its flavor, how will you season it? [R]Have salt in yourselves, and [R]have peace with one another." Matt. 5:13 • Col. 4:6 • Rom. 12:18; 14:19

CHAPTER 10

Marriage and Divorce—Matt. 19:1–9

THEN [R]He arose from there and came to the region of Judea by the other side of the Jordan. And multitudes gathered to Him again, and as He was accustomed, He taught them again. Matt. 19:1–9

2 [R]The Pharisees came and asked Him, "Is it lawful for a man to divorce *his* wife?" testing Him. Matt. 19:3

3 And He answered and said to them, "What did Moses command you?"

4 They said, [R]"Moses permitted *a man* to write a certificate of divorce, and to dismiss *her.*" Deut. 24:1–4

5 And Jesus answered and said to them, "Because of the hardness of your heart he wrote you this [T]precept. *command*

6 "But from the beginning of the creation, God *'made them male and female.'**

7 *'For this reason a man shall leave his father and mother and be joined to his wife,*

8 *'and the two shall become one flesh';** so then they are no longer two, but one flesh.

9 "Therefore what God has joined together, let not man separate."

10 In the house His disciples also asked Him again about the same *matter.*

11 So He said to them, [R]"Whoever divorces his wife and marries another commits adultery against her. [Matt. 5:32; 19:9]

12 "And if a woman divorces her husband and marries another, she commits adultery."

9:40 M *against you is on your side.* **9:44** NU omits v. 44. **9:46** NU omits the last clause of v. 45 and all of v. 46. **9:48** Is. 66:24 **9:49** NU omits the rest of v. 49. **10:6** Gen. 1:27; 5:2 **10:8** Gen. 2:24

Children and the Kingdom
Matt. 19:13–15; Luke 18:15–17

13 Then they brought little children to Him, that He might touch them; but the disciples rebuked those who brought *them.*

14 But when Jesus saw *it,* He was greatly displeased and said to them, "Let the little children come to Me, and do not forbid them; for of such is the kingdom of God.

15 "Assuredly, I say to you, whoever does not receive the kingdom of God as a little child will [R]by no means enter it." Luke 13:28

16 And He took them up in His arms, laid *His* hands on them, and blessed them.

Rich Young Ruler
Matt. 19:16–22; Luke 18:18–23

17 Now as He was going out on the road, one came running, knelt before Him, and asked Him, "Good Teacher, what shall I [R]do that I may inherit eternal life?" John 6:28

18 So Jesus said to him, "Why do you call Me good? No one *is* good but One, *that is,* [R]God. 1 Sam. 2:2

19 "You know the commandments: *'Do not commit adultery,' 'Do not murder,' 'Do not steal,' 'Do not bear false witness,'* 'Do not defraud,' *'Honor your father and your mother.'* "*

20 And he answered and said to Him, "Teacher, all these things I have [R]kept from my youth." Phil. 3:6

21 Then Jesus, looking at him, loved him, and said to him, "One thing you lack: Go your way, [R]sell whatever you have and give to the poor, and you will have treasure in heaven; and come, [R]take up the cross, and follow Me." [Luke 12:33; 16:9] • [Mark 8:34]

22 But he was sad at this word, and went away sorrowful, for he had great possessions.

Difficulty of Riches
Matt. 19:23–26; Luke 18:24–27

23 Then Jesus looked around and said to His disciples, "How hard it is for those who have riches to enter the kingdom of God!"

24 And the disciples were astonished at His words. But Jesus answered again and said to them, "Children, how hard it is for those [R]who trust in riches* to enter the kingdom of God! [1 Tim. 6:17]

25 "It is easier for a camel to go through the eye of a needle than for a [R]rich man to enter the kingdom of God." [Matt. 13:22]

26 And they were greatly astonished, saying among themselves, "Who then can be saved?"

27 But Jesus looked at them and said, "With men *it is* impossible, but not with God; for with God all things are possible."

Eternal Reward
Matt. 19:27–30; Luke 18:28–30

28 Then Peter began to say to Him, "See, we have left all and followed You."

29 So Jesus answered and said, "Assuredly, I say to you, there is no one who has left house or brothers or sisters or father or mother or wife* or children or [T]lands, for My sake and the gospel's, Lit. *fields*

30 [R]"who shall not receive a hundredfold now in this time—houses and brothers and sisters and mothers and children and lands, with [R]persecutions—and in the age to come, eternal life. Luke 18:29, 30 • [1 Pet. 4:12, 13]

31 [R]"But many *who are* first will be last, and the last first." Luke 13:30

Coming Crucifixion
Matt. 20:17–19; Luke 18:31–34

32 Now they were on the road, going up to Jerusalem, and Jesus was going before them; and they were amazed. And as they followed they were afraid. Then He took the twelve aside again and began to tell them the things that would happen to Him:

33 "Behold, we are going up to Jerusalem, and the Son of Man will be [R]betrayed to the chief priests and to the scribes; and they will condemn Him to death and deliver Him to the Gentiles; Mark 14:53, 64☆

34 "and [R]they will mock Him, and scourge Him, and spit on Him, and kill Him. And the third day He will rise again." Luke 24:46☆

"Whoever Desires to Become Great"
Matt. 20:20–28

35 Then James and John, the sons of Zebedee, came to Him, saying, "Teacher, we want You to do for us whatever we ask."

36 And He said to them, "What do you want Me to do for you?"

37 They said to Him, "Grant us that we may sit, one on Your right hand and the other on Your left, in Your glory."

38 But Jesus said to them, "You do not know what you ask. Are you able to drink the cup that I drink, and be baptized with the baptism that I am baptized with?"

39 They said to Him, "We are able." So Jesus said to them, "You will indeed drink the cup that I drink, and with the baptism I am baptized with you will be baptized;

40 "but to sit on My right hand and on My left is not Mine to give, but *it is for those* [R]for whom it is prepared." [Heb. 11:16]

41 [R]And when the ten heard *it,* they began to be greatly displeased with James and John. Matt. 20:24

42 But Jesus called them to *Himself* and said to them, [R]"You know that those who are considered rulers over the Gentiles lord it over them, and their great ones exercise authority over them. Luke 22:25

43 [R]"Yet it shall not be so among you; but

10:19 Ex. 20:12–16; Deut. 5:16–20 **10:24** NU omits *for those who trust in riches* **10:29** NU omits *or wife*

whoever desires to become great among you
shall be your servant. Mark 9:35
44 "And whoever of you desires to be first
shall be slave of all.

45 "For even [R]the Son of Man did not come
to be served, but to serve, and [R]to give His life
a ransom for many." [Phil. 2:7, 8] • Is. 53:12☆

Blind Bartimaeus Is Healed
Matt. 20:29–34; Luke 18:35–43

46 Now they came to Jericho. As He went
out of Jericho with His disciples and a great
multitude, blind Bartimaeus, the son of
Timaeus, sat by the road begging.
47 And when he heard that it was Jesus of
Nazareth, he began to cry out and say, "Jesus,
Son of David, have mercy on me!"
48 Then many warned him to be quiet; but
he cried out all the more, "Son of David, have
mercy on me!"
49 So Jesus stood still and commanded him
to be called. Then they called the blind man,
saying to him, "Be of good cheer. Rise, He is
calling you."
50 And throwing aside his garment, he rose
and came to Jesus.
51 So Jesus answered and said to him,
"What do you want Me to do for you?" The
blind man said to Him, [T]"Rabboni, that I may
receive my sight." Lit. *My Great One*
52 Then Jesus said to him, "Go your way;
[R]your faith has [T]made you well." And immedi-
ately he received his sight and followed Jesus
on the road. Matt. 9:22 • Lit. *saved you*

CHAPTER 11

The Triumphal Entry
Matt. 21:1–11; Luke 19:29–40

NOW [R]when they drew near Jerusalem, to
Bethphage* and Bethany, at the Mount of
Olives, He sent two of His disciples; Matt. 21:1–9
2 and He said to them, "Go into the village
opposite you; and as soon as you have entered
it you will find a colt tied, on which no one has
sat. Loose it and bring *it*.
3 "And if anyone says to you, 'Why are you
doing this?' say, 'The Lord has need of it,' and
immediately he will send it here."
4 So they went their way, and found the*
colt tied by the door outside on the street, and
they loosed it.
5 But some of those who stood there said to
them, "What are you doing, loosing the colt?"
6 And they spoke to them just as Jesus had
commanded. So they let them go.
7 Then they brought the colt to Jesus and
threw their clothes on it, and He sat on it.
8 And many spread their clothes on the
road, and others cut down leafy branches
from the trees and spread *them* on the road.
9 Then those who went before and those
who followed [R]cried out, saying: Zech. 9:9★

"Hosanna!
'Blessed is He who comes in the name of
the LORD!' *
10 Blessed *is* the kingdom of our father
David
That comes in the name of the Lord!*
[R]Hosanna in the highest!" Ps. 148:1

11 [R]And Jesus went into Jerusalem and into
the temple. So when He had looked around at
all things, as the hour was already late, He went
out to Bethany with the twelve. Matt. 21:12

A Fig Tree Is Cursed—Matt. 21:18, 19

12 Now the next day, when they had come
out from Bethany, He was hungry.
13 [R]And seeing from afar a fig tree having
leaves, He went to see if perhaps He would
find something on it. When He came to it, He
found nothing but leaves, for it was not the
season for figs. Matt. 21:19
14 In response Jesus said to it, "Let no one
eat fruit from you ever again." And His disci-
ples heard *it*.

11:1 M *Bethsphage* **11:4** NU, M *a* **11:9** Ps. 118:26★
11:10 NU omits *in the name of the Lord*

10:45 The Ministry of the Son of God—The ministry of Christ is threefold:

a. He is Savior. The title *Savior* implies many important and interrelated truths: the need of sinful people to be saved (Page 1237—1 Tim. 1:15); the qualifications of Christ as God-man to be our Savior (Page 1094—John 10:18); the humiliating death He experienced to become our Savior (Page 1104—John 19:18); the victorious, bodily resurrection He experienced as a sure guarantee of our salvation (Page 1178—1 Cor. 15:13–22); and the glorious results of salvation (Page 1086—John 5:24). It is no wonder that in light of these precious realities Paul speaks of Christ as "our great God and Savior" (Page 1250—Titus 2:13).
b. He is High Priest. The high priest was of supreme importance in the Old Testament. It was on the basis of his mediation for the people before God on the Day of Atonement that they were brought near to God and protected from judgment (Page 70—Lev. 16:16). Therefore his qualifications were exacting: appointed by God, physically perfect, ceremonially pure, etc. (Page 75—Lev. 21). Jesus is eminently qualified to be our High Priest: He was appointed by God (Page 1261—Heb. 5:5); He is eternal (Page 1262—Heb. 7:24, 25); He is sinless (Page 1262—Heb. 7:26); His offering was final (Page 1264—Heb. 9:28); and His mediation is effective (Page 1155—Rom. 8:34; Page 1262—Heb. 7:25; Page 1293—1 John 2:1). As the only qualified High Priest for men and women, Jesus Christ thus constitutes the only way to God (Page 1237—1 Tim. 2:5).

The Temple Is Cleansed
Matt. 21:12, 13; Luke 19:45, 46

15 [R]So they came to Jerusalem. Then Jesus
went into the temple and began to drive out
those who bought and sold in the temple,
and overturned the tables of the money
changers and the seats of those who sold
[R]doves. John 2:13–16 • Lev. 14:22
16 And He would not allow anyone to carry
wares through the temple.
17 Then He taught, saying to them, "Is it not
written, *'My house shall be called a house of*
prayer for all nations' ?* But you have made it
a *'den of thieves.'* "*
18 And the scribes and chief priests heard it
and sought how they might destroy Him; for
they feared Him, because all the people were
astonished at His teaching.
19 When evening had come, He went out of
the city.

Power of Faith—Matt. 21:20–22

20 Now in the morning, as they passed by,
they saw the fig tree dried up from the roots.
21 And Peter, remembering, said to Him,
"Rabbi, look! The fig tree which You cursed
has withered away."
22 So Jesus answered and said to them,
"Have faith in God.
23 "For assuredly, I say to you, whoever says
to this mountain, 'Be removed and be cast into
the sea,' and does not doubt in his heart, but
believes that those things he says will be
done, he will have whatever he says.
24 "Therefore I say to you, whatever things
you ask when you pray, believe that you re-
ceive *them,* and you will have *them.*

Necessity of Forgiveness

25 "And whenever you stand praying, [R]if you
have anything against anyone, forgive him,
that your Father in heaven may also forgive
you your trespasses. [Col. 3:13]
26 "But [R]if you do not forgive, neither will
your Father in heaven forgive your tres-
passes."* Matt. 6:15; 18:35

Question of Authority
Matt. 21:23–27; Luke 20:1–8

27 Then they came again to Jerusalem. [R]And
as He was walking in the temple, the chief
priests, the scribes, and the elders came to
Him. Luke 20:1–8
28 And they said to Him, "By what authority
are You doing these things? And who gave You
this authority to do these things?"
29 But Jesus answered and said to them, "I
also will ask you one question; then answer
Me, and I will tell you by what authority I do
these things:
30 "The baptism of John—was it from
heaven or from men? Answer Me."
31 And they reasoned among themselves,
saying, "If we say, 'From heaven,' He will say,
'Why then did you not believe him?'
32 "But if we say, 'From men' "—they feared
the people, for [R]all counted John to have been
a prophet indeed. Matt. 3:5; 14:5
33 So they answered and said to Jesus, "We
do not know." And Jesus answered and said to
them, "Neither will I tell you by what author-
ity I do these things."

CHAPTER 12

Parable of the Vineyard Owner
Matt. 21:33–46; Luke 20:9–19

THEN He began to speak to them in para-
bles: "A man planted a vineyard and set a
hedge around *it,* dug *a place for* the wine vat
and built a tower. And he leased it to vine-
dressers and went into a far country.
2 "Now at vintage-time he sent a servant to
the vinedressers, that he might receive some
of the fruit of the vineyard from the vine-
dressers.
3 "And they took *him* and beat him and sent
him away empty-handed.
4 "Again he sent them another servant, and
at him they threw stones,* wounded *him* in the
head, and sent *him* away shamefully treated.
5 "And again he sent another, and him they
killed; and many others, [R]beating some and
killing some. 2 Chr. 36:16
6 "Therefore still having one son, his
beloved, he also sent him to them last, saying,
'They will respect my son.'
7 "But those vinedressers said among
themselves, 'This is the heir. Come, let us kill
him, and the inheritance will be ours.'
8 "So they took him and [R]killed *him* and
cast *him* out of the vineyard. [Acts 2:23]
9 "Therefore what will the owner of the
vineyard do? He will come and destroy the
vinedressers, and give the vineyard to others.

11:17 Is. 56:7 • Jer. 7:11 **11:26** NU omits v. 26.
12:4 NU omits *and at him they threw stones*

---

c. He is King. The position of king implies sovereign authority and rule over all. The Scriptures clearly teach that this right belongs only to Jesus Christ, who is called "the King of Kings and Lord of Lords" (Page 1325—Rev. 19:16). This title means that He is destined to rule as King and that every knee must ultimately bow and acknowledge His authority (Page 1214—Phil. 2:10). Those who acknowledge Christ as King and Lord in this life will reign with Him; those who do not will be judged by Him (Page 1326—Rev. 20:11–15). The weight of eternity hangs on this solemn decision.

Now turn to Page 731—Is. 53:7: The Lamb of God.

10 "Have you not even read this Scripture:

'The stone which the builders rejected
Has become the chief cornerstone.
11 *This was the* LORD*'s doing,*
And it is marvelous in our eyes'?"*

12 And they sought to lay hands on Him, but feared the multitude, for they knew He had spoken the parable against them. So they left Him and went away.

Question of Taxes
Matt. 22:15–22; Luke 20:20–26

13 [R]Then they sent to Him some of the Pharisees and the Herodians, to catch Him in *His* words. Luke 20:20–26
14 When they had come, they said to Him, "Teacher, we know that You are true, and [T]care about no one; for You do not regard the person of men, but teach the [R]way of God in truth. Is it lawful to pay taxes to Caesar, or not? Court no man's favor • Acts 18:26
15 "Shall we pay, or shall we not pay?" But He, knowing their [R]hypocrisy, said to them, "Why do you test Me? Bring Me a denarius that I may see *it.*" Luke 12:1
16 So they brought *it.* And He said to them, "Whose image and inscription *is* this?" They said to Him, "Caesar's."
17 And Jesus answered and said to them, [T]"Render to Caesar the things that are Caesar's, and to [R]God the things that are God's." And they marveled at Him. *Pay* • [Eccl. 5:4, 5]

Question of the Resurrection
Matt. 22:23–33; Luke 20:27–40

18 [R]Then *some* Sadducees, [R]who say there is no resurrection, came to Him; and they asked Him, saying: Luke 20:27–38 • Acts 23:8
19 "Teacher, [R]Moses wrote to us that if a man's brother dies, and leaves *his* wife behind, and leaves no children, his brother should take his wife and raise up offspring for his brother. Deut. 25:5
20 "Now there were seven brothers. The first took a wife; and dying, he left no offspring.
21 "And the second took her, and he died; nor did he leave any offspring. And the third likewise.
22 "So the seven had her and left no offspring. Last of all the woman died also.
23 "Therefore, in the resurrection, when they rise, whose wife will she be? For all seven had her as wife."
24 Jesus answered and said to them, "Are you not therefore [T]mistaken, because you do not know the Scriptures nor the power of God? Or *deceived*
25 "For when they rise from the dead, they neither marry nor are given in marriage, but are like angels in heaven.
26 "But concerning the dead, that they [R]rise, have you not read in the book of Moses, in the *burning* bush *passage,* how God spoke to him, saying, *'I am the God of Abraham, the God of Isaac, and the God of Jacob'* ?* [Rev. 20:12, 13]
27 "He is not the God of the dead, but the God of the living. You are therefore greatly [T]mistaken." Or *deceived*

Question of the Greatest Commandment
Matt. 22:34–40

28 [R]Then one of the scribes came, and having heard them reasoning together, perceiving* that He had answered them well, asked Him, "Which is the [T]first commandment of all?" Matt. 22:34–40 • *foremost*
29 Jesus answered him, "The first of all the commandments *is:* [R]*'Hear, O Israel, the* LORD *our God, the* LORD *is one.* Deut. 6:4, 5
30 *'And you shall love the* LORD *your God with all your heart, with all your soul, with all your mind, and with all your strength.'** This *is* the first commandment.*
31 "And the second, like *it, is* this: *'You shall love your neighbor as yourself.'** There is no other commandment greater than [R]these." [Rom. 13:9]
32 So the scribe said to Him, "Well *said,* Teacher. You have spoken the truth, for there is one God, [R]and there is no other but He. Deut. 4:39
33 "And to love Him with all the heart, with all the understanding, with all the soul,* and with all the strength, and to love one's neighbor as oneself, is more than all the whole burnt offerings and sacrifices."
34 Now when Jesus saw that he answered wisely, He said to him, "You are not far from the kingdom of God." [R]But after that no one dared question Him. Matt. 22:46

Jesus Questions the Leaders
Matt. 22:41–45; Luke 20:41–44

35 [R]Then Jesus answered and said, while He taught in the temple, "How *is it* that the scribes say that the Christ is the Son of David? Luke 20:41–44
36 "For David himself said [R]by the Holy Spirit: 2 Sam. 23:2

'The LORD *said to my Lord,*
"Sit at My right hand,
*Till I make Your enemies Your footstool."'**

37 "Therefore David himself calls Him *'Lord'*; how is He *then* his Son?" And the common people heard Him gladly.

12:11 Ps. 118:22, 23★ **12:26** Ex. 3:6,15 **12:28** NU *seeing* **12:30** Deut. 6:4, 5 • NU omits this sentence. **12:31** Lev. 19:18 **12:33** NU omits *with all the soul* **12:36** Ps. 110:1

Jesus Condemns the Leaders
Matt. 23:1–14; Luke 20:45—21:4

38 Then [R]He said to them in His teaching, [R]"Beware of the scribes, who desire to go around in long robes, [R]*love* greetings in the marketplaces, Mark 4:2 • Matt. 23:1–7 • Matt. 23:7

39 "the [R]best seats in the synagogues, and the best places at feasts, Luke 14:7

40 [R]"who devour widows' houses, and for a pretense make long prayers. These will receive greater condemnation." Matt. 23:14

41 [R]Now Jesus sat opposite the treasury and saw how the people put money [R]into the treasury. And many *who were* rich put in much. Luke 21:1–4 • 2 Kin. 12:9

42 Then one poor widow came and threw in two mites,* which make a quadrans.

43 So He called His disciples to *Himself* and said to them, "Assuredly, I say to you that this poor widow has put in more than all those who have given to the treasury;

44 "for they all put in out of their abundance, but she out of her poverty put in all that she had, her whole livelihood."

CHAPTER 13

Questions from the Disciples
Matt. 24:1–3; Luke 21:5–7

THEN [R]as He went out of the temple, one of His disciples said to Him, "Teacher, see what manner of stones and what buildings *are here!*" Luke 21:5–36

2 And Jesus answered and said to him, "Do you see these great buildings? [R]Not *one* stone shall be left upon another, that shall not be thrown down." Luke 19:44

3 Now as He sat on the Mount of Olives opposite the temple, Peter, James, John, and Andrew asked Him privately,

4 [R]"Tell us, when will these things be? And what *will be* the sign when all these things will be fulfilled?" Matt. 24:3

The Tribulation—Matt. 24:4–25; Luke 21:8–24

5 And Jesus, answering them, began to say: "Take heed that no one deceives you.

6 "For many will come in My name, saying, 'I am *He,*' and will deceive many.

7 "But when you hear of wars and rumors of wars, do not be troubled; for *such things* must happen, but the end *is* not yet.

8 "For nation will rise against nation, and [R]kingdom against kingdom. And there will be earthquakes in various places, and there will be famines and troubles.* These *are* the beginnings of sorrows. Hag. 2:22

9 "But [R]watch out for yourselves, for they will deliver you up to councils, and you will be beaten in the synagogues. You will be brought* before rulers and kings for My sake, for a testimony to them. Matt. 24:9

10 "And [R]the gospel must first be preached to all the nations. Matt. 24:14

11 [R]"But when they arrest *you* and deliver you up, do not worry beforehand, or premeditate* what you will speak. But whatever is given you in that hour, speak that; for it is not you who speak, [R]but the Holy Spirit. Luke 12:11; 21:12–17 • Acts 2:4; 4:8, 31

12 "Now [R]brother will betray brother to death, and a father *his* child; and children will rise up against parents and cause them to be put to death. Mic. 7:6

13 [R]"And you will be hated by all for My name's sake. But [R]he who endures to the end shall be saved. Luke 21:17 • Matt. 10:22

14 "So when you see the *'abomination of desolation,'** spoken of by Daniel the prophet,* standing where it ought not" **(let the reader understand),** "then let those who are in Judea flee to the mountains.

15 "Let him who is on the housetop not go down into the house, nor enter to take anything out of his house.

16 "And let him who is in the field not go back to get his clothes.

17 [R]"But woe to those who are pregnant and to those who are nursing babies in those days! Luke 21:23

18 "And pray that your flight may not be in winter.

19 [R]"For *in* those days there will be tribulation, such as has not been since the beginning of the creation which God created until this time, nor ever shall be. Dan. 9:26; 12:1

20 "And unless the Lord had shortened those days, no flesh would be saved; but for the elect's sake, whom He chose, He shortened the days.

21 [R]"Then if anyone says to you, 'Look, here *is* the Christ!' or, 'Look, *He is* there!' do not believe it. Luke 17:23; 21:8

22 "For false christs and false prophets will rise and show signs and wonders to deceive, if possible, even the elect.

23 "But [R]take heed; see, I have told you all things beforehand. [2 Pet. 3:17]

The Second Coming
Matt. 24:29–31; Luke 21:25–28

24 [R]"But in those days, after that tribulation, the sun will be darkened, and the moon will not give its light; Zeph. 1:15

25 "the stars of heaven will fall, and the powers in the heavens will be shaken.

26 [R]"Then they will see the Son of Man coming in the clouds with great power and glory. [Dan. 7:13, 14; Matt. 16:27]☆

27 "And then He will send His angels, and

12:42 Gr. *lepta,* very small copper coins **13:8** NU omits *and troubles* **13:9** NU, M *will stand* **13:11** NU omits *or premeditate* **13:14** Dan. 11:31; 12:11 • NU omits *spoken of by Daniel the prophet*

gather together His [T]elect from the four winds, from the farthest part of earth to the farthest part of heaven. *chosen ones*

Parable of the Fig Tree—Matt. 24:32–35

28 [R]"Now learn this parable from the fig tree: When its branch has already become tender, and puts forth leaves, you know that summer is near. Luke 21:29

29 "So you also, when you see these things happening, know that it* is near—at the doors!

30 "Assuredly, I say to you, this generation will by no means pass away till all these things take place.

31 "Heaven and earth will pass away, but My words will by no means pass away.

Exhortation to Watch
Matt. 24:36–51; Luke 21:34–36

32 "But of that day and hour [R]no one knows, not even the angels in heaven, nor the Son, but only the Father. Matt. 25:13

33 [R]"Take heed, watch and pray; for you do not know when the time is. 1 Thess. 5:6

34 "*It is* like a man going to a far country, who left his house and gave authority to his servants, and to each his work, and commanded the doorkeeper to watch.

35 "Watch therefore, for you do not know when the master of the house is coming—in the evening, at midnight, at the crowing of the rooster, or in the morning—

36 "lest, coming suddenly, he find you sleeping.

37 "And what I say to you, I say to all: Watch!"

CHAPTER 14

Leaders Plot to Kill Jesus
Matt. 26:1–5; Luke 22:1, 2

AFTER [R]two days it was the Passover and [R]*the Feast* of Unleavened Bread. And the chief priests and the scribes sought how they might take Him by trickery and put *Him* to death. Luke 22:1, 2 • Ex. 12:1–27

2 But they said, "Not during the feast, lest there be an uproar of the people."

Mary Anoints Jesus
Matt. 26:6–13; John 12:1–8

3 And being in Bethany at the house of Simon the leper, as He sat at the table, a woman came having an alabaster flask of very costly oil of spikenard. Then she broke the flask and poured *it* on His head.

4 But there were some who were indignant among themselves, and said, "Why was this fragrant oil wasted?

5 "For it might have been sold for more than three hundred denarii and given to the poor." And they criticized her sharply.

6 But Jesus said, "Let her alone. Why do you trouble her? She has done a good work for Me.

7 "For you have the poor with you always, and whenever you wish you may do them good; but Me you do not have always.

8 "She has done what she could. She has come beforehand to anoint My body for [R]burial. John 19:40–42☆

9 "Assuredly, I say to you, wherever this gospel is [R]preached in the whole world, what this woman has done will also be told as a memorial to her." Luke 24:47

Judas Plans to Betray Jesus
Matt. 26:14–16; Luke 22:3–6

10 [R]Then Judas Iscariot, one of the twelve, went to the chief priests to betray Him to them. Matt. 10:2–4

11 And when they heard *it*, they were glad, and promised to give him money. So he sought how he might conveniently betray Him.

The Passover Is Prepared
Matt. 26:17–19; Luke 22:7–13

12 [R]Now on the first day of Unleavened Bread, when they [T]killed the Passover *lamb*, His disciples said to Him, "Where do You want us to go and prepare, that You may eat the Passover?" Matt. 26:17–19 • *sacrificed*

13 And He sent out two of His disciples and said to them, "Go into the city, and a man will meet you carrying a pitcher of water; follow him.

14 "Wherever he goes in, say to the master of the house, 'The Teacher says, "Where is the guest room in which I may eat the Passover with My disciples?" '

15 "Then he will show you a large upper room, furnished *and* prepared; there make ready for us."

16 So His disciples went out, and came into the city, and found it just as He had said to them; and they prepared the Passover.

The Passover Is Celebrated
Matt. 26:20–25; Luke 22:14–16; John 13:21–30

17 In the evening He came with the twelve.

18 Now as they sat and ate, Jesus said, "Assuredly, I say to you, [R]one of you who eats with Me will betray Me." Ps. 41:9☆

19 And they began to be sorrowful, and to say to Him one by one, "*Is* it I?" And another *said*, "*Is* it I?"*

20 He answered and said to them, "*It is* one of the twelve, who dips with Me in the dish.

21 [R]"The Son of Man indeed goes just as it is written of Him, but woe to that man by whom the Son of Man is betrayed! It would have been good for that man if he had never been born." Luke 22:22

13:29 Or *He* **14:19** NU omits this sentence.

The Lord's Supper Is Instituted
Matt. 26:26–29; Luke 22:17–23

22 [R]And as they were eating, Jesus took bread, blessed and broke *it*, and gave *it* to them and said, "Take, eat;* this is My [R]body." 1 Cor. 11:23–25 • [1 Pet. 2:24]
23 Then He took the cup, and when He had given thanks He gave *it* to them, and they all drank from it.
24 And He said to them, "This is My blood of the new* covenant, which is shed for many.
25 "Assuredly, I say to you, I will no longer drink of the fruit of the vine until that day when I drink it new in the kingdom of God."

Jesus Predicts Peter's Denial
Matt. 26:30–35; Luke 22:31–38; John 13:36–38

26 [R]And when they had sung a hymn, they went out to the Mount of Olives. Matt. 26:30
27 [R]Then Jesus said to them, "All of you will be made to stumble because of Me this night,* for it is written: Matt. 26:31–35

'I will strike the Shepherd,
*And the sheep will be scattered.'**

28 "But [R]after I have been raised, I will go before you to Galilee." Mark 16:7
29 [R]Peter said to Him, "Even if all are made to stumble, yet I *will* not *be*." John 13:37, 38
30 Jesus said to him, "Assuredly, I say to you [R]that today, *even* this night, before the rooster crows twice, you will deny Me three times." Mark 14:72; Luke 22:61☆
31 But he spoke more vehemently, "If I have to die with You, I will not deny You!" And they all said likewise.

Jesus Prays in Gethsemane
Matt. 26:36–46; Luke 22:39–46

32 [R]Then they came to a place which was named Gethsemane; and He said to His disciples, "Sit here while I pray." Luke 22:40–46
33 And He [R]took Peter, James, and John with Him, and He began to be troubled and deeply distressed. Mark 5:37; 9:2; 13:3
34 Then He said to them, [R]"My soul is exceedingly sorrowful, *even* to death. Stay here and watch." John 12:27
35 He went a little farther, and fell on the ground, and prayed that if it were possible, the hour might pass from Him.
36 And He said, [R]"Abba, Father, [R]all things *are* possible for You. Take this cup away from Me; [R]nevertheless, not what I will, but what You *will*." Gal. 4:6 • [Heb. 5:7] • Is. 50:5★
37 Then He came and found them sleeping, and said to Peter, "Simon, are you sleeping? Could you not watch one hour?

38 [R]"Watch and pray, lest you enter into temptation. The spirit indeed *is* willing, but the flesh *is* weak." Luke 21:36

39 Again He went away and prayed, and spoke the same words.
40 And when He returned, He found them asleep again, for their eyes were heavy; and they did not know what to answer Him.
41 Then He came the third time and said to them, "Are you still sleeping and resting? It is enough! [R]The hour has come; behold, the Son of Man is being betrayed into the hands of sinners. John 13:1; 17:1
42 [R]"Rise, let us be going. See, My [R]betrayer is at hand." John 13:21; 18:1, 2 • Matt. 20:18; 26:21★

Judas Betrays Jesus
Matt. 26:47–56; Luke 22:47–53; John 18:1–11

43 [R]And immediately, while He was still speaking, Judas, one of the twelve, with a great multitude with swords and clubs, came from the chief priests and the scribes and the elders. Luke 22:47–53
44 Now His betrayer had given them a signal, saying, "Whomever I kiss, He is the One; seize Him and lead *Him* away safely."
45 As soon as he had come, immediately he went up to Him and said to Him, "Rabbi, Rabbi!" and kissed Him.
46 Then they laid their hands on Him and took Him.
47 And one of those who stood by drew his sword and struck the servant of the high priest, and cut off his ear.
48 Then Jesus answered and said to them,

14:22 NU omits *eat* **14:24** NU omits *new* **14:27** NU omits *because of Me this night* • Zech. 13:7

14:38 Temptation by the Flesh—"Flesh" in the Bible often means something other than the substance of the human body. It is used constantly to refer to the carnal, sinful principle within man that is opposed to God (Page 1154—Rom. 8:7). The actions produced by the flesh are given in detail in Galatians 5:19–21. Among these are all types of sexual immorality, impurity, hatred, anger, false religions, envy, and drunkenness. A person whose life is characterized by these sins cannot be a true Christian and is under the wrath of God (Page 1200—Gal. 5:21; Page 1205—Eph. 2:3).

Though the flesh is not eradicated for Christians, we do not have to obey it (Page 1154—Rom. 7:15–25). We possess a new nature empowered by the Holy Spirit. Since the flesh and the Spirit are totally opposed to each other, the one whom believers allow to dominate will take charge in life and produce its own fruit. The solution to the urges of the flesh lies in acknowledging that the power of sin was nullified by Jesus' death (Page 1153—Rom. 6:11) and in living under the control of the Spirit's power (Page 1200—Gal. 5:16). The latter is a moment-by-moment dependence in faith on the Spirit's power. We must choose by an act of will to benefit from the Spirit's enablement.

Now turn to Page 420—1 Chr. 21:1: Temptation by Satan.

"Have you come out, as against a robber, with
swords and clubs to take Me?
49 "I was daily with you in the temple teaching, and you did not seize Me. But [R]the Scriptures must be fulfilled." Is. 53:7
50 Then they all forsook Him and fled.
51 Now a certain young man followed Him, having a linen cloth thrown around *his* naked *body.* And the young men laid hold of him,
52 and he left the linen cloth and fled from them naked.

The Sanhedrin Tries Jesus
Matt. 26:57–68; Luke 22:54, 55, 63–65; John 18:12, 18, 24

53 And they led Jesus away to the high priest; and with him were assembled all the chief priests, the elders, and the scribes.
54 But [R]Peter followed Him at a distance, right into the courtyard of the high priest. And he sat with the servants and warmed himself at the fire. John 18:15
55 [R]Now the chief priests and all the council sought testimony against Jesus to put Him to death, but found none. Matt. 26:59
56 For many bore false witness against Him, but their testimonies did not agree.
57 Then [R]some rose up and bore false witness against Him, saying, Ps. 27:12; 35:11★
58 "We heard Him say, [R]'I will destroy this temple made with hands, and within three days I will build another made without hands.'" John 2:19
59 But not even then did their testimony agree.
60 [R]And the high priest stood up in the midst and asked Jesus, saying, "Do You answer nothing? What *is it* these men testify against You?" Matt. 26:62
61 But [R]He kept silent and answered nothing.
[R]Again the high priest asked Him, saying to Him, "Are You the Christ, the Son of the Blessed?" Is. 53:7 • Luke 22:67–71
62 Jesus said, "I am. [R]And you will see the Son of Man sitting at the right hand of the Power, and coming with the clouds of heaven." Luke 22:69
63 Then the high priest tore his clothes and said, "What further need do we have of witnesses?
64 "You have heard the blasphemy! What do you think?" And they all [R]condemned Him to be deserving of death. Matt. 20:18; Mark 10:33★
65 Then some began to [R]spit on Him, and to blindfold Him, and to beat Him, and to say to Him, "Prophesy!" And the officers struck Him with the palms of their hands.* Is. 50:6; 52:14★

Peter Denies Jesus
Matt. 26:69–75; Luke 22:55–62; John 18:15–18, 25–27

66 [R]Now as Peter was below in the courtyard, one of the servant girls of the high priest came. John 18:16–18, 25–27
67 And when she saw Peter warming himself, she looked at him and said, "You also were with [R]Jesus of Nazareth." John 1:45
68 But he denied it, saying, "I neither know nor understand what you are saying." And he went out on the porch, and a rooster crowed.
69 [R]And the servant girl saw him again, and began to say to those who stood by, "This is one of them." Matt. 26:71
70 But he denied it again. And a little later those who stood by said to Peter again, "Surely you are *one* of them; for you are a Galilean, and your speech shows *it.*"*
71 Then he began to curse and swear, "I do not know this Man of whom you speak!"
72 [R]A second time *the* rooster crowed. Then Peter called to mind the word that Jesus had said to him, "Before the rooster crows twice, you will deny Me three times." And when he thought about it, he wept. Matt. 26:75

CHAPTER 15

Pilate Tries Jesus
Matt. 27:1, 2, 11–23; Luke 23:1–5, 13–23; John 18:28—19:15

IMMEDIATELY, [R]in the morning, the chief priests held a consultation with the elders and scribes and the whole council; and they bound Jesus, led *Him* away, and [R]delivered *Him* to Pilate. Ps. 2:2 • Is. 53:7★
2 [R]Then Pilate asked Him, "Are You the King of the Jews?" He answered and said to him, "*It is as* you say." Matt. 27:11–14
3 And the chief priests accused Him of many things, but He answered nothing.
4 Then Pilate asked Him again, saying, "Do You answer nothing? See how many things they testify against You!"*
5 [R]But Jesus still answered nothing, so that Pilate marveled. Ps. 38:13, 14; Is. 53:7★
6 Now [R]at the feast he was accustomed to releasing one prisoner to them, whomever they requested. Matt. 27:15–26
7 And there was one named Barabbas, *who was* chained with his fellow rebels; they had committed murder in the rebellion.
8 Then the multitude, crying aloud,* began to ask *him to do* just as he had always done for them.
9 But Pilate answered them, saying, "Do you want me to release to you the King of the Jews?"
10 For he knew that the chief priests had handed Him over because of envy.
11 But [R]the chief priests stirred up the crowd, so that he should rather release Barabbas to them. Acts 3:14
12 Pilate answered and said to them again,

14:65 NU *received Him with slaps* **14:70** NU omits and *your speech shows it.* **15:4** NU *of which they accuse You* **15:8** NU *going up*

"What then do you want me to do *with Him* whom you call the King of the Jews?"

13 So they cried out again, "Crucify Him!"

14 Then Pilate said to them, "Why, [R]what evil has He done?" But they cried out all the more, "Crucify Him!" 1 Pet. 2:21–23

Jesus Is Beaten
Matt. 27:26–34; Luke 23:24–32; John 19:16–22

15 [R]So Pilate, wanting to gratify the crowd, released Barabbas to them; and he delivered Jesus, after he had scourged *Him*, to be [R]crucified. Matt. 27:26 • [Is. 53:8]

16 [R]Then the soldiers led Him away into the hall called Praetorium, and they called together the whole garrison. Matt. 27:27–31

17 And they clothed Him with purple; and they twisted a crown of thorns, put it on His *head,*

18 and began to salute Him, "Hail, King of the Jews!"

19 Then they [R]struck Him on the head with a reed and spat on Him; and bowing the knee, they worshiped Him. Is. 52:14; Mic. 5:1★

20 And when they had mocked Him, they took the purple off Him, put His own clothes on Him, and led Him out to crucify Him.

21 Then they compelled a certain man, Simon a Cyrenian, the father of Alexander and Rufus, as he was coming out of the country and passing by, to bear His cross.

22 And they brought Him to the place Golgotha, which is translated, Place of a Skull.

23 Then they gave Him wine mingled with myrrh to drink, but He did not take *it.*

Jesus Is Crucified
Matt. 27:35–56; Luke 23:33–49; John 19:18, 23–30

24 And when they crucified Him, they divided His garments, casting lots for them to determine what every man should take.

25 Now [R]it was the third hour, and they crucified Him. John 19:14

26 And [R]the inscription of His [T]accusation was written above: Matt. 27:37 • *crime*

THE KING OF THE JEWS.

27 [R]With Him they also crucified two robbers, one on His right and the other on His left. Luke 22:37

28 So the Scripture was fulfilled* which says, "*And He was numbered with the transgressors.*"*

29 And [R]those who passed by blasphemed Him, [R]wagging their heads and saying, "Aha! *You* who destroy the temple and build *it* in three days, Ps. 22:6, 7; 69:7★ • Ps. 109:25

30 "save Yourself, and come down from the cross!"

31 Likewise the chief priests also, [R]mocking among themselves with the scribes, said, "He saved [R]others; Himself He cannot save. Ps. 69:19★ • John 11:43, 44

32 [R]"Let the Christ, the King of Israel, descend now from the cross, that we may see and believe."* Even those who were crucified with Him reviled Him. Ps. 22:8★

33 Now [R]when the sixth hour had come, there was darkness over the whole land until the ninth hour. Amos 8:9★

34 And at the ninth hour Jesus cried out with a loud voice, saying, "Eloi, Eloi, lama sabachthani?" which is translated, *"My God, My God, why have You forsaken Me?"**

35 Some of those who stood by, when they heard *that,* said, "Look, He is calling for Elijah!"

36 Then [R]someone ran and filled a sponge full of sour wine, put *it* on a reed, and [R]offered *it* to Him to drink, saying, "Let Him alone; let us see if Elijah will come to take Him down." John 19:29 • Ps. 69:21★

37 [R]And Jesus cried out with a loud voice, and breathed His last. Matt. 17:23★

38 Then [R]the veil of the temple was torn in two from top to bottom. Zech. 11:10, 11★

39 So [R]when the centurion, who stood opposite Him, saw that He cried out like this and breathed His last,* he said, "Truly this Man was the Son of God!" Luke 23:47

40 [R]There were also women looking on [R]from afar, among whom were Mary Magdalene, Mary the mother of James the Less and of Joses, and Salome, Matt. 27:55 • Ps. 38:11

41 who also [R]followed Him and ministered to Him when He was in Galilee, and many other women who came up with Him to Jerusalem. Luke 8:2, 3

Jesus Is Buried
Matt. 27:57–61; Luke 23:50–55; John 19:38–42

42 [R]Now when evening had come, because it was the Preparation Day, that is, the day before the Sabbath, John 19:38–42

43 [R]Joseph of Arimathea, a prominent council member, who [R]was himself waiting for the kingdom of God, coming and taking courage, went in to Pilate and asked for the body of Jesus. Is. 53:9★ • Luke 2:25, 38; 23:51

44 Pilate marveled that He was already dead; and summoning the centurion, he asked him if He had been dead for some time.

45 So when he found out from the centurion, he granted the body to Joseph.

46 Then he bought fine linen, took Him down, and wrapped Him in the linen. And he [R]laid Him in a tomb which had been hewn out of the rock, and rolled a stone against the door of the tomb. Matt. 26:12; Mark 14:8★

15:28 Is. 53:12★ • NU omits v. 28. **15:32** M *believe Him* **15:34** Ps. 22:1★ **15:39** NU *He thus breathed His last*

47 And Mary Magdalene and Mary *the mother* of Joses observed where He was laid.

CHAPTER 16

The Resurrection of Jesus
Matt. 28:1–8; Luke 24:1–9

NOW [R]when the Sabbath was past, Mary Magdalene, Mary *the mother* of James, and Salome bought spices, that they might come and anoint Him. John 20:1–8

2 [R]Very early in the morning, on the first *day* of the week, they came to the tomb when the sun had risen. Luke 24:1

3 And they said among themselves, "Who will roll away the stone from the door of the tomb for us?"

4 But when they looked up, they saw that the stone had been rolled away—for it was very large.

5 [R]And entering the tomb, they saw a young man clothed in a long white robe sitting on the right side; and they were alarmed. John 20:11, 12

6 But he said to them, "Do not be alarmed. You seek Jesus of Nazareth, who was crucified. He is [R]risen! He is not here. See the place where they laid Him. Hos. 6:2★

7 "But go, tell His disciples—and Peter—that He is going before you into Galilee; there you will see Him, as He said to you."

8 So they went out quickly* and fled from the tomb, for they trembled and were amazed. [R]And they said nothing to anyone, for they were afraid. Matt. 28:8

The Appearances of Jesus
Luke 24:13–48; John 20:1–10

9 Now when *He* rose early on the first *day* of the week, He appeared first to Mary Magdalene, [R]out of whom He had cast seven demons. Luke 8:2

10 She went and told those who had been with Him, as they mourned and wept.

11 [R]And when they heard that He was alive and had been seen by her, they did not believe. Luke 24:11, 41

12 After that, He appeared in another form [R]to two of them as they walked and went into the country. Luke 24:13–35

13 And they went and told *it* to the rest, *but* they did not believe them either.

14 [R]Later He appeared to the eleven as they sat at the table; and He rebuked their unbelief and hardness of heart, because they did not believe those who had seen Him after He had risen. 1 Cor. 15:5

15 [R]And He said to them, "Go into all the world [R]and preach the gospel to every creature. Matt. 28:19 • [Col. 1:23]

16 [R]"He who believes and is baptized will be saved; [R]but he who does not believe will be condemned. [John 3:18, 36] • [John 12:48]

17 "And these signs will follow those who believe: In My name they will cast out demons; they will speak with new tongues;

18 [R]"they* will take up serpents; and if they drink anything deadly, it will by no means hurt them; they will lay hands on the sick, and they will recover." Acts 28:3–6

The Ascension of Jesus
Luke 24:49–53; Acts 1:9

19 So then, after the Lord had spoken to them, He was [R]received up into heaven, and sat down at the right hand of God. Is. 9:7★

20 And they went out and preached everywhere, the Lord working with *them* [R]and confirming the word through the accompanying signs. Amen.* [Heb. 2:4]

16:8 NU, M omit *quickly* **16:18** NU *and in their hands they will* **16:20** Vv. 9–20 are bracketed in NU as not in the original text. They are lacking in Codex Sinaiticus and Codex Vaticanus, although nearly all other mss. of Mark contain them.

THE GOSPEL ACCORDING TO

LUKE

THE BOOK OF LUKE

Luke, a physician, writes with the compassion and warmth of a family doctor as he carefully documents the perfect humanity of the Son of Man, Jesus Christ. Luke emphasizes Jesus' ancestry, birth, and early life before moving carefully and chronologically through His earthly ministry. Growing belief and growing opposition develop side by side. Those who believe are challenged to count the cost of discipleship. Those who oppose will not be satisfied until the Son of Man hangs lifeless on a cross. But the Resurrection insures that His purpose will be fulfilled: "to seek and to save that which was lost" (19:10).

Kata Loukon, "According to Luke," is the ancient title that was added to this gospel at a very early date. The Greek name *Luke* appears only three times in the New Testament (Col. 4:14; 2 Tim. 4:11; Philem. 24).

THE AUTHOR OF LUKE

It is evident from the prologues to Luke and Acts (Luke 1:1–4; Acts 1:1–5) that both books were addressed to Theophilus as a two-volume work (Luke is called "the former account"). Acts begins with a summary of Luke and continues the story from where the Gospel of Luke concludes. The style and language of both books are quite similar. The "we" portions of Acts (Acts 16:1–17; 20:5—21:18; 27:1—28:16) reveal that the author was a close associate and traveling companion of Paul. Because all but two of Paul's associates are named in the third person, the list can be narrowed to Titus and Luke. Titus has never been seriously regarded as a possible author of Acts, and Luke best fits the requirements. He was with Paul during his first Roman imprisonment, and Paul referred to him as "Luke the beloved physician" (Col. 4:14; cf. Philem. 24). During his second Roman imprisonment, Paul wrote "Only Luke is with me" (2 Tim. 4:11), an evidence of Luke's loyalty to the apostle in the face of profound danger.

Luke may have been a Hellenistic Jew, but it is more likely that he was a Gentile (this would make him the only Gentile contributor to the New Testament). In Colossians 4:10–14, Paul lists three fellow workers who are "of the circumcision" (vv. 10, 11) and then includes Luke's name with two Gentiles (vv. 12–14). Luke's obvious skill with the Greek language and his phrase "their own language" in Acts 1:19 also imply that he was not Jewish. It has been suggested that Luke may have been a Greek physician to a Roman family who at some point was set free and given Roman citizenship. Another guess is that he was the "brother" referred to in 2 Corinthians 8:18, 19. Ancient traditions (including the Muratorian Fragment, Irenaeus, Tertullian, Clement of Alexandria, Origen, Eusebius, and Jerome) strongly support Luke as the author of Luke and Acts. Tradition also says that Luke was from Syrian Antioch, remained unmarried, and died at the age of eighty-four.

THE TIME OF LUKE

Luke was not an eyewitness of the events in his gospel, but he relied on the testimony of eyewitnesses and written sources (1:1–4). He carefully investigated and arranged his material and presented it to Theophilus ("Friend of God"). The title "most excellent," or "most noble" (see Acts 23:26; 24:3; 26:25), indicates that Theophilus was a man of high social standing. He probably assumed responsibility for publishing Luke and Acts so that they would be available to Gentile readers. Luke translates Aramaic terms with Greek words and explains Jewish customs and geography to make his gospel more intelligible to his original Greek readership. During Paul's two-year Caesarean imprisonment, Luke may have traveled in Palestine to gather information from eyewitnesses of Jesus' ministry. The date of this gospel depends on that of Acts since this was the first volume (see "The Time of Acts"). If Luke was written during Paul's first imprisonment in Rome it would be dated in the early 60s. However, it may have been given final form in Greece. In all probability, its publication preceded the destruction of Jerusalem (A.D. 70).

THE CHRIST OF LUKE

The humanity and compassion of Jesus are repeatedly stressed in Luke's gospel. Luke gives the most complete account of Christ's ancestry, birth, and development. He is the ideal Son of Man who identified with the sorrow and plight of sinful men in order to carry our sorrows and offer us the priceless gift of salvation. Jesus alone fulfills the Greek ideal of human perfection.

KEYS TO LUKE

Key Word: Jesus the Son of Man—Luke clearly states his purpose in the prologue of his gospel: "to write to you an orderly account . . . that you may know the certainty of those things in which you were instructed" (1:3, 4). Luke wanted to create an accurate, chronological, and comprehensive account of the unique life of Jesus the Christ to strengthen the faith of Gentile believers and stimulate saving faith among nonbelievers. Luke also had another purpose, and that was to show that Christ was not only divine but also human. Luke portrays Christ in His fullest humanity by devoting more of his writing to Christ's feelings and humanity than any other gospel.

Key Verses: Luke 1:3, 4 and 19:10—"It seemed good to me also, having had perfect understanding of all things from the very first, to write to you an orderly account, most excellent Theophilus, that you may know the certainty of those things in which you were instructed" (1:3, 4).

" 'For the Son of Man has come to seek and to save that which was lost' " (19:10).

Key Chapter: Luke 15—Captured in the three parables of the Lost Sheep, Lost Coin, and Lost Son is the crux of this gospel: that God through Christ has come to seek and to save that which was lost.

SURVEY OF LUKE

Luke builds the gospel narrative on the platform of historical reliability. His emphasis on chronological and historical accuracy makes this the most comprehensive of the four gospels. This is also the longest and most literary gospel, and it presents Jesus Christ as the Perfect Man who came to seek and to save sinful men. This book can be divided into four sections: the introduction of the Son of Man (1:1—4:13); the ministry of the Son of Man (4:14—9:50); the rejection of the Son of Man (9:51—19:27); the crucifixion and resurrection of the Son of Man (19:28—24:53).

The Introduction of the Son of Man (1:1—4:13): Luke places a strong emphasis on the ancestry, birth, and early years of the Perfect Man and of His forerunner John the Baptist. Their infancy stories are intertwined as Luke records their birth announcements, advents, and temple presentations. Jesus prepares over thirty years (summarized in one verse, 2:52) for a public ministry of only three years. The ancestry of the Son of Man is traced back to the first man Adam, and His ministry commences after His baptism and temptation.

The Ministry of the Son of Man (4:14—9:50): The authority of the Son of Man over every realm is demonstrated in 4:14—6:49. In this section His authority over demons, disease, nature, the effects of sin, tradition, and all people is presented as a prelude to His diverse ministry of preaching, healing, and discipling (7:1—9:50).

The Rejection of the Son of Man (9:51—19:27): The dual response of growing belief and growing rejection has already been introduced in the gospel (cf. 4:14 and 6:11), but from this time forward the intensity of opposition to the ministry of the Son of Man increases. When the religious leaders accuse Him of being demonized, Jesus pronounces a series of divine woes upon them (11). Knowing that He is on His last journey to Jerusalem, Jesus instructs His disciples on a number of practical matters including prayer, covetousness, faithfulness, repentance, humility, discipleship, evangelism, money, forgiveness, service, thankfulness, the Second Advent, and salvation (12:1—19:27).

The Crucifixion and Resurrection of the Son of Man (19:28—24:53): After His triumphal entry into Jerusalem, Jesus encounters the opposition of the priests, Sadducees, and scribes and predicts the overthrow of Jerusalem (19:28—21:38). The Son of Man instructs His

FOCUS	INTRODUCTION OF THE SON OF MAN	MINISTRY OF THE SON OF MAN	REJECTION OF THE SON OF MAN	CRUCIFIXION AND RESURRECTION OF THE SON OF MAN
REFERENCE	1:1—	4:14—	9:51—	19:28——24:53
DIVISION	ADVENT	ACTIVITIES	ANTAGONISM AND ADMONITION	APPLICATION AND AUTHENTICATION
TOPIC	SEEKING THE LOST			SAVING THE LOST
	MIRACLES PROMINENT		TEACHING PROMINENT	
LOCATION	ISRAEL	GALILEE	ISRAEL	JERUSALEM
TIME	C. 4 B.C.–A.D. 33			

disciples for the last time before His betrayal in Gethsemane. The three religious and three civil trials culminate in His crucifixion. The glory and foundation of the Christian message is the historical resurrection of Jesus Christ. The Lord conquers the grave as He has promised, and appears on a number of occasions to His disciples before His ascension to the Father.

OUTLINE OF LUKE

Part One: The Introduction of the Son of Man (1:1—4:13)

I. The Purpose and Method of Luke's Gospel **1:1–4**

II. The Events Preceding Christ's Birth ... **1:5–56**

A. John the Baptist's Birth Is Foretold 1:5–25
1. Zacharias Ministers in the Temple 1:5–10
2. An Angel Announces the Birth of John the Baptist 1:11–17
3. Zacharias Is Unable to Speak 1:18–25

B. Jesus the Christ's Birth Is Foretold 1:26–56
1. Gabriel Announces Christ's Birth .. 1:26–33
2. Mary Miraculously Conceives 1:34–38
3. Mary Visits Elizabeth 1:39–56

III. The Events Accompanying Christ's Birth .... **1:57—2:38**

A. The Birth of John the Baptist 1:57–80
1. Elizabeth Gives Birth to John 1:57–66
2. Zacharias Prophesies of John's Ministry 1:67–80

B. The Birth of Jesus the Christ 2:1–38
1. Christ Is Born 2:1–7
2. The Angels Announce Jesus to the Shepherds 2:8–14
3. The Shepherds Visit Jesus 2:15–20
4. Christ Is Presented at the Temple 2:21–38

IV. The Events During Christ's Childhood **2:39–52**

A. Jesus Returns to Nazareth 2:39, 40
B. Jesus Celebrates the Passover 2:41–50
C. Jesus Grows in Wisdom 2:51, 52

V. The Events Preceding Christ's Presentation .... **3:1—4:13**

A. The Ministry of John the Baptist 3:1–20
B. The Baptism of Christ 3:21, 22
C. The Genealogy of Christ Through Mary 3:23–38
D. The Temptation of Christ 4:1–13

Part Two: The Ministry of the Son of Man (4:14—9:50)

I. The Presentation of Christ **4:14–30**

A. Acceptance Throughout Galilee 4:14, 15
B. Rejection at Nazareth 4:16–30

II. The Demonstration of Christ's Powers .... **4:31—5:28**

A. Demons Are Cast Out 4:31–37
B. Peter's Mother-in-Law Is Healed 4:38, 39
C. Jesus Ministers Throughout Galilee ... 4:40–44
D. The First Disciples Are Called 5:1–11
E. A Leper Is Cleansed 5:12–15
F. A Paralytic Is Healed 5:16–26
G. Matthew Is Called 5:27, 28

III. The Explanation of Christ's Program .... **5:29—6:49**

A. Jesus Teaches the Pharisees .... 5:29—6:11
1. Jesus Eats with Sinners 5:29–32
2. Jesus Teaches About Fasting 5:33–35
3. Parable of the Cloth and Wineskins 5:36–39
4. Jesus Works on the Sabbath 6:1–5
5. Jesus Heals on the Sabbath 6:6–11

B. Jesus Teaches the Disciples 6:12–49
1. Selection of the Twelve Apostles 6:12–19
2. The Beatitudes 6:20–26
3. Rules of Kingdom Life 6:27–38
4. Parable of the Blind Leading the Blind 6:39–45
5. Parable of the Two Foundations 6:46–49

IV. The Expansion of Christ's Program 7:1—9:50

A. A Centurion's Servant Is Healed 7:1–10
B. A Widow's Son Is Raised 7:11–16
C. Christ Comments on John the Baptist 7:17–35
1. John's Questions Are Answered 7:17–23
2. Jesus Praises John 7:24–30
3. Jesus Criticizes His Generation 7:31–35

D. Christ Dines at a Pharisee's Home 7:36–50
1. A Woman Anoints Jesus' Feet 7:36–39
2. The Parable of the Two Debtors 7:40–50

E. Certain Women Minister to Christ 8:1–3
F. Parable of the Soils 8:4–15
G. Parable of the Lamp 8:16–18
H. Christ's True Brethren 8:19–21
I. The Storm Is Stilled 8:22–25
J. Demons Are Cast into Swine 8:26–40
K. A Woman Is Healed 8:41–48
L. Jairus's Daughter Is Raised 8:49–56
M. Twelve Are Sent to Preach 9:1–11
N. Five Thousand Are Fed 9:12–17
O. Peter's Confession of Faith 9:18–22
P. True Cost of Discipleship 9:23–26
Q. The Transfiguration 9:27–36
R. Demoniac Son Is Healed 9:37–42
S. Christ Prophesies His Coming Death 9:43–45
T. True Greatness 9:46–50

Part Three: The Rejection of the Son of Man (9:51—19:27)

Part Four: The Crucifixion and Resurrection of the Son of Man (19:28—24:53)

5. Herod Tries Christ 23:8–12
6. Pilate Tries Christ Again 23:13–25
7. Christ Is Crucified 23:26–49
8. Christ Is Buried 23:50–55
F. Saturday: In the Grave 23:56

II. The Authentication of Christ 24:1–53

A. The Resurrection 24:1–12
B. Christ Appears on the Road to Emmaus 24:13–32
C. Christ Appears to the Eleven 24:33–53
1. The Proof of His Resurrection......24:33–43
2. The Great Commission 24:44–48
3. The Ascension 24:49–53

CHAPTER 1

The Purpose and Method of Luke's Gospel

INASMUCH as many have taken in hand to set in order a narrative of those things which have been fulfilled* among us,

2 just as those who [R]from the beginning were eyewitnesses and ministers of the word delivered them to us, Acts 1:21, 22

3 it seemed good to me also, having had perfect understanding of all things from the very first, to write to you an orderly account, [R]most excellent Theophilus, Acts 1:1

4 that you may know the certainty of those things in which you were instructed.

Zacharias Ministers in the Temple

5 There was in the days of Herod, the king of Judea, a certain priest named Zacharias, [R]of the division of [R]Abijah. His wife *was* of the daughters of Aaron, and her name *was* Elizabeth. 1 Chr. 24:1, 10 • Neh. 12:4

6 And they were both righteous before God, walking in all the commandments and ordinances of the Lord blameless.

7 But they had no child, because Elizabeth was barren, and they were both well advanced in years.

8 So it was, that while he was serving as priest before God in the order of his division,

9 according to the custom of the priesthood, his lot fell [R]to burn incense when he went into the temple of the Lord. Ex. 30:7, 8

10 And the whole multitude of the people was praying outside at the hour of incense.

An Angel Announces the Birth of John the Baptist

11 Then an angel of the Lord appeared to him, standing on the right side of [R]the altar of incense. Ex. 30:1

12 And when Zacharias saw *him,* [R]he was troubled, and fear fell upon him. Luke 2:9

13 But the angel said to him, "Do not be afraid, Zacharias, for your prayer is heard; and your wife Elizabeth will bear you a son, and you shall call his name John.

14 "And you will have joy and gladness, and many will rejoice at his birth.

15 "For he will be great in the sight of the Lord, and shall drink neither wine nor strong drink. He will also be filled with the Holy Spirit, even from his mother's womb.

16 "And he will turn many of the children of Israel to the Lord their God.

17 "He will also go before Him in the spirit and power of Elijah, *'to turn the hearts of the fathers to the children,'** and the disobedient to the wisdom of the just, to make ready a people prepared for the Lord."

Zacharias Is Unable to Speak

18 And Zacharias said to the angel, "How shall I know this? For I am an old man, and my wife is well advanced in years."

19 And the angel answered and said to him, "I am Gabriel, who stands in the presence of God, and was sent to speak to you and bring you these glad tidings.

20 "But behold, you will be mute and not able to speak until the day these things take place, because you did not believe my words which will be fulfilled in their own time."

21 And the people waited for Zacharias, and marveled that he lingered so long in the temple.

22 But when he came out, he could not speak to them; and they perceived that he had seen a vision in the temple, for he beckoned to them and remained speechless.

23 So it was, as soon as [R]the days of his service were completed, that he departed to his own house. 2 Kin. 11:5

24 Now after those days his wife Elizabeth conceived; and she hid herself five months, saying,

25 "Thus the Lord has dealt with me, in the days when He looked on *me,* to [R]take away my reproach among people." Gen. 30:23

Gabriel Announces Christ's Birth

26 Now in the sixth month the angel Gabriel was sent by God to a city of Galilee named Nazareth,

27 to a [R]virgin betrothed to a man whose name was Joseph, of the house of David. The virgin's name *was* Mary. Is. 7:14★

28 And having come in, the angel said to her, [R]"Rejoice, highly favored *one,* [R]the Lord *is* with you; blessed *are* you among women!"* Dan. 9:23 • Judg. 6:12

29 But when she saw *him,** [R]she was troubled

1:1 Or *are most surely believed* **1:17** Mal. 4:5, 6☆
1:28 NU omits *blessed are you among women*
1:29 NU omits *when she saw him*

at his saying, and considered what manner of
greeting this was. Luke 1:12
30 Then the angel said to her, "Do not be
afraid, Mary, for you have found [R]favor with
God. Luke 2:52
31 [R]"And behold, you will conceive in your
womb and bring forth a Son, and [R]shall call
His name JESUS. Is. 7:14 • Luke 2:21☆
32 "He will be great, [R]and will be called the
Son of the Highest; and the Lord God will give
Him the throne of His father David. Mark 5:7☆
33 [R]"And He will reign over the house of Ja-
cob [R]forever, and of His kingdom there will be
no end." [Dan. 2:44] • Ps. 89:36, 37☆

Mary Miraculously Conceives

34 Then Mary said to the angel, "How can
this be, since I do not know a man?"
35 And the angel answered and said to her,
"*The* Holy Spirit will come upon you, and the
power of the Highest will overshadow you;
therefore, also, that Holy One who is to be
born will be called the Son of God.
36 "Now indeed, Elizabeth your relative has
also conceived a son in her old age; and this is
now the sixth month for her who was called
barren.
37 "For [R]with God nothing will be impossi-
ble." Jer. 32:17
38 Then Mary said, "Behold the maidservant
of the Lord! Let it be to me according to your
word." And the angel departed from her.

Mary Visits Elizabeth

39 Now Mary arose in those days and went
into the hill country with haste, [R]to a city of
Judah, Josh. 21:9
40 and entered the house of Zacharias and
greeted Elizabeth.
41 And it happened, when Elizabeth heard
the greeting of Mary, that the babe leaped in
her womb; and Elizabeth was [R]filled with the
Holy Spirit. Acts 6:3
42 Then she spoke out with a loud voice and
said, "Blessed *are* you among women, and
blessed *is* the fruit of your womb!
43 "But why *is* this *granted* to me, that the
mother of my Lord should come to me?
44 "For indeed, as soon as the voice of your
greeting sounded in my ears, the babe leaped
in my womb for joy.
45 [R]"Blessed *is* she who believed, for there
will be a fulfillment of those things which
were told her from the Lord." John 20:29
46 And Mary said:

"My soul magnifies the Lord,
47 And my spirit has [R]rejoiced in [R]God my
Savior. Hab. 3:18 • 1 Tim. 1:1; 2:3
48 For [R]He has regarded the lowly state of
His maidservant; Ps. 138:6
For behold, henceforth [R]all generations
will call me blessed. Luke 11:27
49 For He who is mighty [R]has done great
things for me, Ps. 71:19; 126:2, 3
And [R]holy *is* His name. Ps. 111:9
50 And [R]His mercy *is* on those who fear
Him Ps. 103:17
From generation to generation.
51 He has shown strength with His arm;
He has scattered *the* proud in the
imagination of their hearts.
52[R] He has put down the mighty from *their*
thrones, 1 Sam. 2:7, 8
And exalted *the* lowly.
53 He has [R]filled *the* hungry with good
things, [Matt. 5:6]
And *the* rich He has sent away empty.
54 He has helped His servant Israel,
In remembrance of *His* mercy,
55[R] As He spoke to our fathers, Gen. 17:19
To Abraham and to his seed forever."

56 And Mary remained with her about three
months, and returned to her house.

Elizabeth Gives Birth to John

57 Now Elizabeth's full time came for her to
be delivered, and she brought forth a son.
58 When her neighbors and relatives heard
how the Lord had shown great mercy to her,
they [R]rejoiced with her. [Rom. 12:15]
59 So it was, [R]on the eighth day, that they
came to circumcise the child; and they would
have called him by the name of his father,
Zacharias. Gen. 17:12
60 His mother answered and said, [R]"No; he
shall be called John." Luke 1:13, 63
61 But they said to her, "There is no one
among your relatives who is called by this
name."
62 So they made signs to his father—what he
would have him called.
63 And he asked for a writing tablet, and
wrote, saying, "His name is John." So they all
marveled.
64 Immediately his mouth was opened and
his tongue *loosed,* and he spoke, praising
God.
65 Then fear came on all who dwelt around
them; and all these sayings were discussed
throughout all the hill country of Judea.
66 And all those who heard *them* [R]kept *them*
in their hearts, saying, "What kind of child
will this be?" And [R]the hand of the Lord was
with him. Luke 2:19 • Acts 11:21

Zacharias Prophesies of John's Ministry

67 Now his father Zacharias was filled with
the Holy Spirit, and prophesied, saying:

68 "Blessed[R] *is* the Lord God of Israel,
For [R]He has visited and redeemed His
people, 1 Kin. 1:48 • Ex. 3:16
69[R] And has raised up a horn of salvation for
us Ps. 132:17

In the house of His servant David,
70 [R]As He spoke by the mouth of His holy
prophets, Rom. 1:2
Who *have been* since the world began,
71 That we should be saved from our
enemies
And from the hand of all who hate us,
72 [R]To perform the mercy *promised* to our
fathers Lev. 26:42
And to remember His holy covenant,
73 [R]The oath which He swore to our father
Abraham: Gen. 12:3; 22:16–18
74 To grant us that we,
Being delivered from the hand of our
enemies,
Might serve Him without fear,
75 In holiness and righteousness before
Him all the days of our life.

76 "And you, child, will be called the
[R]prophet of the Highest; Matt. 3:3
For [R]you will go before the face of the
Lord to prepare His ways, Is. 40:3
77 To give [R]knowledge of salvation to His
people [Mark 1:4]
By the remission of their sins,
78 Through the tender mercy of our God,
With which the [T]Dayspring from on high
has visited* us; Lit. *Dawn;* the Messiah
79 [R]To give light to those who sit in darkness
and the shadow of death,
To [R]guide our feet into the way of
peace." Is. 9:2 • [John 10:4; 14:27; 16:33]☆

80 So [R]the child grew and became strong in
spirit, and was in the deserts till the day of his
manifestation to Israel. Luke 2:40

CHAPTER 2

Christ Is Born

AND it came to pass in those days *that* a
decree went out from Caesar Augustus
that all the world should be registered.
2 [R]This census first took place while
Quirinius was governing Syria. Acts 5:37
3 So all went to be registered, everyone to
his own city.
4 Joseph also went up from Galilee, out of
the city of Nazareth, into Judea, to [R]the city
of David, which is called [R]Bethlehem, [R]be-
cause he was of the house and lineage of Da-
vid, 1 Sam. 16:1 • Mic. 5:2★ • Matt. 1:16
5 to be registered with Mary, his betrothed
wife,* who was with child.
6 So it was, that while they were there, the
days were completed for her to be delivered.
7 And [R]she brought forth her firstborn Son,
and wrapped Him in swaddling cloths, and
laid Him in a manger, because there was no
room for them in the inn. Matt. 1:25

The Angels Announce Jesus to the Shepherds

8 Now there were in the same country
shepherds living out in the fields, keeping
watch over their flock by night.
9 And behold,* an angel of the Lord stood
before them, and the glory of the Lord shone
around them, and they were greatly afraid.
10 Then the angel said to them, "Do not be
afraid, for behold, I bring you good tidings of
great joy which will be to all people.
11 [R]"For there is born to you this day in the
city of David [R]a Savior, [R]who is Christ the
Lord. Is. 9:6★ • Matt. 1:21 • Acts 2:36
12 "And this *will be* the sign to you: You will
find a Babe wrapped in swaddling cloths,
lying in a [T]manger." *feed trough*
13 [R]And suddenly there was with the angel a
multitude of the heavenly host praising God
and saying: Dan. 7:10

14 "Glory to God in the highest,
And on earth [R]peace, [R]goodwill toward
men!"* Is. 57:19 • [Eph. 2:4, 7]

The Shepherds Visit Jesus

15 So it was, when the angels had gone away
from them into heaven, that the shepherds
said to one another, "Let us now go to Bethle-
hem and see this thing that has come to pass,
which the Lord has made known to us."
16 And they came with haste and found
Mary and Joseph, and the Babe lying in a
manger.
17 Now when they had seen *Him,* they made
widely* known the saying which was told
them concerning this Child.
18 And all those who heard *it* marveled at
those things which were told them by the
shepherds.
19 [R]But Mary kept all these things and pon-
dered *them* in her heart. Gen. 37:11
20 Then the shepherds returned, glorifying
and praising God for all the things that they
had heard and seen, as it was told them.

Christ Is Circumcised

21 And when eight days were completed for
the circumcision of the Child,* His name was
called JESUS, the name given by the angel be-
fore He was conceived in the womb.
22 Now when [R]the days of her purification
according to the law of Moses were com-
pleted, they brought Him to Jerusalem to
present *Him* to the Lord Lev. 12:2–8
23 [R](as it is written in the law of the Lord,
"Every male who opens the womb shall be
called holy to the LORD"),* Deut. 18:4
24 and to offer a sacrifice according to what

1:78 NU *shall visit* **2:5** NU omits *wife* **2:9** NU omits *behold* **2:14** NU *toward men of goodwill* **2:17** NU omits *widely* **2:21** NU *for His circumcision* **2:23** Ex. 13:2, 12, 15

is said in the law of the Lord, *"A pair of
turtledoves or two young pigeons."* *

Simeon's Prophecy

25 And behold, there was a man in Jerusa-
lem whose name was Simeon, and this man
was just and devout, [R]waiting for the Consola-
tion of Israel, and the Holy Spirit was upon
him. Mark 15:43
26 And it had been revealed to him by the
Holy Spirit that he would not see death before
he had seen the Lord's Christ.
27 So he came [R]by the Spirit into the temple.
And when the parents brought in the Child
Jesus, to do for Him according to the custom
of the law, Matt. 4:1
28 he took Him up in his arms and blessed
God and said:

29 "Lord, [R]now You are letting Your servant
depart in peace, Gen. 46:30
According to Your word;
30 For my eyes have seen Your salvation
31 Which You have prepared before the
face of all peoples,
32 [R]A light to *bring* revelation to the
Gentiles, Is. 9:2; 42:6☆
And the glory of Your people Israel."

33 And Joseph and His mother* marveled at
those things which were spoken of Him.
34 Then Simeon blessed them, and said to
Mary His mother, "Behold, this *Child* is des-
tined for the [R]fall and rising of many in Is-
rael, and for [R]a sign which will be spoken
against Is. 8:14; [1 Pet. 2:7, 8]☆ • Acts 4:1–3; 17:32; 28:22
35 "(yes, [R]a sword will pierce through your
own soul also), that the thoughts of many
hearts may be revealed." Ps. 42:10

Anna's Testimony

36 Now there was one, Anna, a prophetess,
the daughter of Phanuel, of the tribe of
[R]Asher. She was of a great age, and had lived
with a husband seven years from her virgin-
ity; Josh. 19:24
37 and this woman *was* a widow of about
eighty-four years,* who did not depart from
the temple, but served *God* with fastings and
prayers [R]night and day. 1 Tim. 5:5
38 And coming in that instant she gave
thanks to the Lord,* and spoke of Him to all
those who [R]looked for redemption in Jerusa-
lem. Mark 15:43

Jesus Returns to Nazareth—Matt. 2:19–23

39 So when they had performed all things
according to the law of the Lord, they re-
turned to Galilee, to their *own* city, Nazareth.
40 [R]And the Child grew and became strong
in spirit,* filled with wisdom; and the grace of
God was upon Him. Luke 1:80; 2:52

Jesus Celebrates the Passover

41 His parents went to [R]Jerusalem every
year at the Feast of the Passover. John 4:20
42 And when He was twelve years old, they
went up to Jerusalem according to the [R]cus-
tom of the feast. Ex. 23:14, 15
43 When they had finished the [R]days, as they
returned, the Boy Jesus lingered behind in Je-
rusalem. And Joseph and His mother* did not
know *it;* Ex. 12:15
44 but supposing Him to have been in the
company, they went a day's journey, and
sought Him among *their* relatives and ac-
quaintances.
45 So when they did not find Him, they re-
turned to Jerusalem, seeking Him.
46 Now so it was *that* after three days they
found Him in the temple, sitting in the midst
of the teachers, both listening to them and
asking them questions.
47 And all who heard Him were astonished
at His understanding and answers.
48 So when they saw Him, they were
amazed; and His mother said to Him, "Son,
why have You done this to us? Look, Your fa-
ther and I have sought You anxiously."
49 And He said to them, "Why did you seek
Me? Did you not know that I must be [R]about
My Father's business?" John 9:4
50 But [R]they did not understand the state-
ment which He spoke to them. John 7:15, 46

Jesus Grows in Wisdom

51 Then He went down with them and came
to Nazareth, and was [T]subject to them, but
His mother [R]kept all these things in her
heart. *obedient* • Dan. 7:28
52 And Jesus increased in wisdom and
stature, and in favor with God and men.

CHAPTER 3

The Ministry of John the Baptist
Matt. 3:1–12; Mark 1:2–8; John 1:19–31

NOW in the fifteenth year of the reign of
Tiberius Caesar, [R]Pontius Pilate being
governor of Judea, Herod being tetrarch of
Galilee, his brother Philip tetrarch of Iturea
and the region of Trachonitis, and Lysanias
tetrarch of Abilene, Matt. 27:2
2 while [R]Annas and Caiaphas were high
priests,* the word of God came to John the
son of Zacharias in the wilderness. Acts 4:6
3 And he went into all the region around
the Jordan, preaching a baptism of repen-
tance [R]for the remission of sins, Luke 1:77★

2:24 Lev. 12:8 **2:33** NU *And His father and mother* **2:37** NU *a widow until she was eighty-four* **2:38** NU *to God* **2:40** NU omits *in spirit* **2:43** NU *And His parents* **3:2** NU, M *in the high priesthood of Annas and Caiaphas*

4 as it is written in the book of the words of
Isaiah the prophet, saying:

"The voice of one crying in the
wilderness:
'Prepare the way of the LORD;
Make His paths straight.
5 *Every valley shall be filled*
And every mountain and hill brought
low;
The crooked places shall be made
straight
And the rough ways smooth;
6 *And* R*all flesh shall see the salvation of*
God.' "* Is. 52:10

7 Then he said to the multitudes that came
out to be baptized by him, R"BroodT of vipers!
Who warned you to flee from the wrath to
come? Matt. 3:7; 12:34; 23:33 • *Offspring*
8 "Therefore bear fruits Rworthy of repen-
tance, and do not begin to say to yourselves,
'We have Abraham as *our* father.' For I say to
you that God is able to raise up children to
Abraham from these stones. [2 Cor. 7:9–11]
9 "And even now the ax is laid to the root of
the trees. Therefore Revery tree which does
not bear good fruit is cut down and thrown
into the fire." Matt. 7:19
10 So the people asked him, saying, R"What
shall we do then?" [Acts 2:37, 38; 16:30, 31]
11 He answered and said to them, R"He who
has two tunics, let him give to him who has
none; and he who has food, Rlet him do like-
wise." 2 Cor. 8:14 • Is. 58:7
12 Then Rtax collectors also came to be bap-
tized, and said to him, "Teacher, what shall we
do?" Luke 7:29
13 And he said to them, R"Collect no more
than what is appointed for you." Luke 19:8
14 Likewise the soldiers asked him, saying,
"And what shall we do?" So he said to them,
"Do not intimidate anyone or accuse falsely,
and be content with your wages."
15 Now as the people were in expectation,
and all reasoned in their hearts about John,
whether he was the Christ *or* not,
16 John answered, saying to all, R"I indeed
baptize you with water; but One mightier than
I is coming, whose sandal strap I am not wor-
thy to loose. He will baptize you with the Holy
Spirit and fire. Matt. 3:11, 12
17 "His winnowing fan *is* in His hand, and
He will thoroughly clean out His threshing
floor, and Rgather the wheat into His barn; but
the chaff He will burn with unquenchable
fire." Matt. 13:24–30
18 And with many other exhortations he
preached to the people.
19 RBut Herod the tetrarch, being rebuked by
him concerning Herodias, his brother Philip's
wife,* and for all the evils which Herod had
done, Mark 6:17
20 also added this, above all, that he shut
John up in prison.

The Baptism of Christ
Matt. 3:13–17; Mark 1:9–11; John 1:32–34

21 When all the people were baptized, Rit came
to pass that Jesus also was baptized; and while
He prayed, the heaven was opened. Matt. 3:13–17
22 And the Holy Spirit descended in bodily
form like a dove upon Him, and a voice came
from heaven which said, "You are My beloved
Son; in You I am well pleased."

The Genealogy of Christ Through Mary
Gen. 5:1–32; 11:10–26; Ruth 4:18–22;
1 Chr. 1:1–4, 24–27, 34; 2:1–15; Matt. 1:2–6

23 Now Jesus Himself began *His ministry*
at Rabout thirty years of age, being (as was
supposed) R*the* son of Joseph, *the son* of
Heli, [Num. 4:3, 35, 39, 43, 47] • John 6:42
24 *the son* of Matthat,* *the son* of Levi, *the*
son of Melchi, *the son* of Janna, *the son* of Jo-
seph,
25 *the son* of Mattathiah, *the son* of Amos,
the son of Nahum, *the son* of Esli, *the son* of
Naggai,
26 *the son* of Maath, *the son* of Mattathiah,
the son of Semei, *the son* of Joseph, *the son* of
Judah,
27 *the son* of Joannas, *the son* of Rhesa, *the*
son of RZerubbabel, *the son* of Shealtiel, *the*
son of Neri, Ezra 2:2; 3:8
28 *the son* of Melchi, *the son* of Addi, *the son*
of Cosam, *the son* of Elmodam, *the son* of Er,
29 *the son* of Jose, *the son* of Eliezer, *the son*
of Jorim, *the son* of Matthat, *the son* of Levi,
30 *the son* of Simeon, *the son* of Judah, *the*
son of Joseph, *the son* of Jonan, *the son* of Eli-
akim,
31 *the son* of Melea, *the son* of Menan, *the*
son of Mattathah, *the son* of RNathan, R*the*
son of David, Zech. 12:12 • Is. 9:7★
32 R*the son* of Jesse, *the son* of Obed, *the son*
of Boaz, *the son* of Salmon, *the son* of
Nahshon, Is. 11:1, 10★
33 *the son* of Amminadab, *the son* of Ram,
the son of Hezron, *the son* of Perez, R*the son*
of Judah, Gen. 49:10★
34 *the son* of Jacob, *the son* of Isaac, *the son*
of Abraham, R*the son* of Terah, *the son* of
Nahor, Gen. 11:24, 26–30; 12:3
35 *the son* of Serug, *the son* of Reu, *the son*
of Peleg, *the son* of Eber, *the son* of Shelah,
36 R*the son* of Cainan, *the son* of Arphaxad,
the son of Shem, *the son* of Noah, *the son* of
Lamech, Gen. 11:12

3:6 Is. 40:3–5★ **3:19** NU *his brother's wife* **3:24** This and several other names in the genealogy are spelled somewhat differently in the NU-Text. Since the New King James Version uses the Old Testament spelling for persons mentioned in the New Testament, these variations, which come from the Greek have not been footnoted.

37 *the son* of Methuselah, *the son* of Enoch, *the son* of Jared, *the son* of Mahalalel, *the son* of Cainan,

38 *the son* of Enosh, *the son* of Seth, *the son* of Adam, [R]*the son* of God. Gen. 5:1, 2

CHAPTER 4

The Temptation of Christ
Matt. 4:1–11; Mark 1:12, 13

THEN Jesus, being filled with the Holy Spirit, returned from the Jordan and was led by the Spirit into* the wilderness,

2 being [T]tempted for forty days by the devil. And [R]in those days He ate nothing, and afterward, when they had ended, He was hungry. *tested* • Ex. 34:28

3 And the devil said to Him, "If You are [R]the Son of God, command this stone to become bread." John 20:31

4 But Jesus answered him, saying,* *"It is written, 'Man shall not live by bread alone, but by every word of God.' "**

5 Then the devil, taking Him up on a high mountain, showed Him* all the kingdoms of the world in a moment of time.

6 And the devil said to Him, "All this authority I will give You, and their glory; for [R]*this* has been delivered to me, and I give it to whomever I wish. [Rev. 13:2, 7]

7 "Therefore, if You will worship before me, all will be Yours."

8 And Jesus answered and said to him, "Get behind Me, Satan!* For* it is written, *'You shall worship the LORD your God, and Him only you shall serve.' "**

9 [R]Then he brought Him to Jerusalem, set Him on the pinnacle of the temple, and said to Him, "If You are the Son of God, throw Yourself down from here. Matt. 4:5–7

10 "For it is written:

'He shall give His angels charge over you,
To keep you,'

11 "and,

'In their hands they shall bear you up,
Lest you dash your foot against a
*stone.' "**

12 And Jesus answered and said to him, "It has been said, *'You shall not [T]tempt the LORD your God.' "** *test*

13 Now when the devil had ended every [T]temptation, he departed from Him [R]until an opportune time. *testing* • [Heb. 4:15]

Acceptance Throughout Galilee
Matt. 4:12; Mark 1:14

14 Then Jesus returned in the power of the Spirit to Galilee, and news of Him went out through all the surrounding region.

15 And He [R]taught in their synagogues, [R]being glorified by all. Matt. 4:23 • Is. 52:13★

Rejection at Nazareth

16 So He came to [R]Nazareth, where He had been brought up. And as His custom was, He went into the synagogue on the Sabbath day, and stood up to read. Mark 6:1

17 And He was handed the book of the prophet Isaiah. And when He had opened the book, He found the place where it was written:

18 *"The Spirit of the LORD is upon Me,*
Because He has anointed Me
To preach the gospel to the poor;
He has sent Me to heal the
*brokenhearted,**
To proclaim liberty to the captives
And recovery of sight to the blind,
To [R]set at liberty those who are
[T]oppressed; [Dan. 9:24] • *downtrodden*
19 *To proclaim the acceptable year of the*
*LORD."**

20 Then He closed the book, and gave *it* back to the attendant and sat down. And the eyes of all who were in the synagogue were fixed on Him.

21 And He began to say to them, "Today this Scripture is fulfilled in your hearing."

22 So all bore witness to Him, and [R]marveled at the gracious words which proceeded out of His mouth. And they said, [R]"Is this not Joseph's son?" [Ps. 45:2] • John 6:42

23 He said to them, "You will surely say this proverb to Me, 'Physician, heal yourself! Whatever we have heard done in Capernaum,* do also here in Your country.' "

24 Then He said, "Assuredly, I say to you, no prophet is accepted in his own country.

25 "But I tell you truly, [R]many widows were in Israel in the days of Elijah, when the heaven was shut up three years and six months, and there was a great famine throughout all the land; 1 Kin. 17:9

26 "but to none of them was Elijah sent except to Zarephath,* *in the region* of Sidon, to a woman *who was* a widow.

27 "And many lepers were in Israel in the time of Elisha the prophet, and none of them was cleansed except Naaman the Syrian."

28 So all those in the synagogue, when they heard these things, were [R]filled with [T]wrath, Luke 6:11 • *rage*

4:1 NU *in* **4:4** Deut. 8:3 • NU omits *but by every word of God* **4:5** NU *And taking Him up, he showed Him* **4:8** NU omits Get behind Me, Satan • NU, M omit *For* • Deut. 6:13 **4:11** Ps. 91:11, 12★ **4:12** Deut. 6:16 **4:18** NU omits *to heal the brokenhearted* **4:19** Is. 61:1, 2★ **4:23** NU *Capharnaum*, here and elsewhere **4:26** Gr. *Sarepta*

29 and rose up and thrust Him out of the
city; and they led Him to the brow of the hill
on which their city was built, that they might
throw Him down over the cliff.
30 Then [R]passing through the midst of them,
He went His way. John 8:59; 10:39

Demons Are Cast Out—Mark 1:21–28

31 Then [R]He went down to Capernaum, a
city of Galilee, and was teaching them on the
Sabbaths. Matt. 4:13
32 And they were astonished at His teach-
ing, for His word was with authority.
33 [R]Now in the synagogue there was a man
who had a spirit of an unclean demon. And he
cried out with a loud voice, Mark 1:23
34 saying, "Let *us* alone! What have we to do
with You, Jesus of Nazareth? Did You come to
destroy us? [R]I know who You are—[R]the Holy
One of God!" Luke 4:41 • Ps. 16:10
35 But Jesus rebuked him, saying, "Be quiet,
and come out of him!" And when the demon
had thrown him in *their* midst, it came out of
him and did not hurt him.
36 Then they were all amazed and spoke
among themselves, saying, "What a word this
is! For with authority and power He com-
mands the unclean spirits, and they come
out."
37 And the report about Him went out into
every place in the surrounding region.

Peter's Mother-in-Law Is Healed
Matt. 8:14, 15; Mark 1:29–31

38 Now He arose from the synagogue and
entered Simon's house. But Simon's wife's
mother was sick with a high fever, and they
made request of Him concerning her.
39 So He stood over her and [R]rebuked the
fever, and it left her. And immediately she
arose and served them. Luke 8:24

Jesus Ministers Throughout Galilee
Matt. 4:23–25; 8:16, 17; Mark 1:32–39

40 [R]When the sun was setting, all those who
had any that were sick with various diseases
brought them to Him; and He laid His hands on
every one of them and healed them. Matt. 8:16, 17
41 And demons also came out of many, cry-
ing out and saying, [R]"You are the Christ,* the
Son of God!" And He, rebuking *them*, did not
allow them to speak, for they knew that He
was the Christ. Mark 8:29
42 [R]Now when it was day, He departed and
went into a deserted place. And the crowd
sought Him and came to Him, and tried to
keep Him from leaving them; Mark 1:35–38
43 but He said to them, "I must preach the
kingdom of God to the other cities also, be-
cause for this purpose I have been sent."
44 [R]And He was preaching in the syna-
gogues of Galilee.* Matt. 4:23; 9:35

CHAPTER 5

The First Disciples Are Called

SO it was, as the multitude pressed about
Him to [R]hear the word of God, that He
stood by the Lake of Gennesaret, Acts 13:44
2 and saw two boats standing by the lake;
but the fishermen had gone from them and
were washing *their* nets.
3 Then He got into one of the boats, which
was Simon's, and asked him to put out a little
from the land. And He sat down and taught
the multitudes from the boat.
4 When He had stopped speaking, He said
to Simon, [R]"Launch out into the deep and let
down your nets for a catch." John 21:6
5 But Simon answered and said to Him,
"Master, we have toiled all night and caught
[R]nothing; nevertheless [R]at Your word I will let
down the net." John 21:3 • Ps. 33:9
6 And when they had done this, they caught
a great number of fish, and their net was
breaking.
7 So they signaled to *their* partners in the
other boat to come and help them. And they
came and filled both the boats, so that they
began to sink.
8 When Simon Peter saw *it*, he fell down at
Jesus' knees, saying, [R]"Depart from me, for I
am a sinful man, O Lord!" 1 Kin. 17:18
9 For he and all who were with him were
[R]astonished at the catch of fish which they
had taken; Mark 5:42; 10:24, 26
10 and so also *were* James and John, the
sons of Zebedee, who were partners with Si-
mon. And Jesus said to Simon, "Do not be
afraid. From now on you will catch men."
11 So when they had brought their boats to
land, they forsook all and followed Him.

A Leper Is Cleansed
Matt. 8:2–4; Mark 1:40–45

12 And it happened when He was in a cer-
tain city, that behold, a man who was full of
[R]leprosy saw Jesus; and he fell on *his* face and
implored Him, saying, "Lord, if You are will-
ing, You can make me clean." Lev. 13:14
13 Then He put out *His* hand and touched
him, saying, "I am willing; be cleansed." [R]Im-
mediately the leprosy left him. John 5:9
14 [R]And He charged him to tell no one,
"But go and show yourself to the priest, and
make an offering for your cleansing, as a
testimony to them, [R]just as Moses com-
manded." Matt. 8:4 • Lev. 13:1–3; 14:2–32
15 However, the report went around con-
cerning Him all the more; and great multi-
tudes came together to hear, and to be healed
by Him of their infirmities.

4:41 NU omits *the Christ* **4:44** NU *Judea*

A Paralytic Is Healed
Matt. 9:1–8; Mark 2:1–12

16 [R]So He Himself *often* withdrew into the
wilderness and prayed. Luke 9:10
17 Now it happened on a certain day, as He
was teaching, that there were Pharisees and
teachers of the law sitting by, who had come
out of every town of Galilee, Judea, and Jeru-
salem. And the power of the Lord was *present*
to heal them.*
18 [R]Then behold, men brought on a bed a
man who was paralyzed, whom they sought
to bring in and lay before Him. Mark 2:3–12
19 And when they could not find how they
might bring him in, because of the crowd,
they went up on the housetop and let him
down with *his* bed through the tiling into the
midst [R]before Jesus. Matt. 15:30
20 When He saw their faith, He said to him,
"Man, your sins are forgiven you."
21 [R]And the scribes and the Pharisees began
to reason, saying, "Who is this who speaks
blasphemies? [R]Who can forgive sins but God
alone?" Mark 2:6, 7 • Is. 43:25
22 But when Jesus perceived their thoughts,
He answered and said to them, "Why are you
reasoning in your hearts?
23 "Which is easier, to say, 'Your sins are for-
given you,' or to say, 'Rise up and walk'?
24 "But that you may know that the Son of
Man has power on earth to forgive sins"—He
said to the man who was paralyzed, [R]"I say to
you, arise, take up your bed, and go to your
house." Luke 7:14
25 Immediately he rose up before them, took
up what he had been lying on, and departed to
his own house, glorifying God.
26 And they were all amazed, and they glori-
fied God and were filled with fear, saying, "We
have seen strange things today!"

Matthew Is Called—Matt. 9:9; Mark 2:13, 14

27 After these things He went out and saw a
tax collector named Levi, sitting at the tax of-
fice. And He said to him, "Follow Me."
28 So he left all, rose up, and [R]followed
Him. Mark 10:28

Jesus Eats with Sinners
Matt. 9:10–13; Mark 2:15–17

29 [R]Then Levi gave Him a great feast in his
own house. And [R]there were a great number
of tax collectors and others who sat down
with them. Matt. 9:9, 10 • Luke 15:1
30 And their scribes and the Pharisees*
[T]complained against His disciples, saying,
[R]"Why do You eat and drink with tax collec-
tors and sinners?" *grumbled* • Luke 15:2
31 Jesus answered and said to them, "Those
who are well have no need of a physician, but
those who are sick.
32 [R]"I have not come to call *the* righteous,
but sinners, to repentance." 1 Tim. 1:15

Jesus Teaches About Fasting
Matt. 9:14, 15; Mark 2:18–20

33 Then they said to Him, [R]"Why do* the dis-
ciples of John fast often and make prayers,
and likewise those of the Pharisees, but Yours
eat and drink?" Matt. 9:14
34 And He said to them, "Can you make the
friends of the bridegroom fast while the
[R]bridegroom is with them? John 3:29
35 "But the days will come when the bride-
groom will be taken away from them; then
they will fast in those days."

Parable of the Cloth and Wineskins
Matt. 9:16, 17; Mark 2:21, 22

36 [R]Then He spoke a parable to them: "No
one puts a piece from a new garment on an
old one;* otherwise the new makes a tear, and
also the piece that was *taken* out of the new
does not match the old. Mark 2:21, 22
37 "And no one puts new wine into old wine-
skins; or else the new wine will burst the
wineskins and be spilled, and the wineskins
will be ruined.
38 "But new wine must be put into new
wineskins, and both are preserved.*
39 "And no one, having drunk old *wine,* im-
mediately* desires new; for he says, 'The old
is better.' "*

CHAPTER 6

Jesus Works on the Sabbath
Matt. 12:1–8; Mark 2:23–28

NOW [R]it happened on the second Sabbath
after the first* that He went through the
grainfields. And His disciples plucked the
heads of grain and ate *them,* rubbing *them* in
their hands. Matt. 12:1–8
2 And some of the Pharisees said to them,
"Why are you doing [R]what is not lawful to do
on the Sabbath?" Ex. 20:10
3 But Jesus answering them said, "Have
you not even read this, [R]what David did when
he was hungry, he and those who were with
him: 1 Sam. 21:6
4 "how he went into the house of God, took
and ate the showbread, and also gave some to
those with him, [R]which is not lawful for any
but the priests to eat?" Lev. 24:9
5 And He said to them, "The Son of Man is
also Lord of the Sabbath."

5:17 NU *present with Him to heal* **5:30** NU *But the Pharisees and their scribes* **5:33** NU omits *Why do,* making the verse a statement. **5:36** NU *No one tears a piece from a new garment and puts it on an old one* **5:38** NU omits *and both are preserved* **5:39** NU omits *immediately* • NU *good* **6:1** NU *on a Sabbath*

Jesus Heals on the Sabbath
Matt. 12:9–14; Mark 3:1–6

6 [R]Now it happened on another Sabbath,
also, that He entered the synagogue and
taught. And a man was there whose right
hand was withered. Mark 3:1–6
7 So the scribes and Pharisees watched
Him closely, whether He would [R]heal on the
Sabbath, that they might find an accusation
against Him. Luke 13:14; 14:1–6
8 But He [R]knew their thoughts, and said to
the man who had the withered hand, "Arise and
stand here." And he arose and stood. Matt. 9:4
9 Then Jesus said to them, "I will ask you
one thing: [R]Is it lawful on the Sabbath to do
good or to do evil, to save life or to de-
stroy?"* John 7:23
10 And when He had looked around at them
all, He said to the man,* "Stretch out your
hand." And he did so, and his hand was re-
stored as whole as the other.*
11 But they were filled with rage, and dis-
cussed with one another what they might do
to Jesus.

Selection of the Twelve Apostles
Mark 3:13–19

12 Now it came to pass in those days that He
went out to the mountain to pray, and contin-
ued all night in prayer to God.
13 And when it was day, He called His disci-
ples to *Himself;* and from them He chose
twelve whom He also named apostles:
14 Simon, [R]whom He also named Peter, and
Andrew his brother; James and John; Philip
and Bartholomew; John 1:42
15 Matthew and Thomas; James the *son* of
Alphaeus, and Simon called the Zealot;
16 Judas [R]*the son* of James, and Judas Iscar-
iot who also became a traitor. Jude 1
17 And He came down with them and stood
on a level place with a crowd of His disciples
and a great multitude of people from all Judea
and Jerusalem, and from the seacoast of Tyre
and Sidon, who came to hear Him and be
healed of their diseases,
18 as well as those who were tormented with
unclean spirits. And they were healed.
19 And the whole multitude [R]sought to touch
Him, for power went out from Him and healed
them all. Matt. 9:21; 14:36

The Beatitudes—Matt. 5:1–12

20 Then He lifted up His eyes toward His dis-
ciples, and said:

[R]"Blessed *are you* poor, Matt. 5:3–12; [11:5]
For yours is the kingdom of God.
21 Blessed *are you* who hunger now,
For you shall be [R]filled. [Rev. 7:16]
Blessed *are you* who weep now,
For you shall [R]laugh. Ps. 126:5
22 Blessed are you when men hate you,
And when they [R]exclude you,
And revile *you,* and cast out your
name as evil, [John 16:2]
For the Son of Man's sake.
23[R] Rejoice in that day and leap for joy!
For indeed your reward *is* great in
heaven, James 1:2
For [R]in like manner their fathers did
to the prophets. Acts 7:51

24 "But woe to you [R]who are rich,
For [R]you have received your
consolation. Luke 12:21 • Luke 16:25
25[R] Woe to you who are full, [Is. 65:13]
For you shall hunger.
Woe to you who laugh now,
For you shall mourn and weep.
26[R] Woe to you* when all* men speak well
of you, [John 15:19]
For so did their fathers to the false
prophets.

Rules of Kingdom Life
Matt. 5:39–48; 7:1, 2, 12

27 "But I say to you who hear: Love your en-
emies, do good to those who hate you,
28 [R]"bless those who curse you, and pray for
those who spitefully use you. Rom. 12:14
29 [R]"To him who strikes you on the *one*
cheek, offer the other also. [R]And from him
who takes away your cloak, do not withhold
your tunic either. Matt. 5:39–42 • [1 Cor. 6:7]
30 [R]"Give to everyone who asks of you. And
from him who takes away your goods do not
ask *them* back. Deut. 15:7, 8
31 "And just as you want men to do to you,
you also do to them likewise.
32 [R]"But if you love those who love you, what
credit is that to you? For even sinners love
those who love them. Matt. 5:46
33 "And if you do good to those who do good
to you, what credit is that to you? For even sin-
ners do the same.
34 [R]"And if you lend *to those* from whom
you hope to receive back, what credit is that
to you? For even sinners lend to sinners to re-
ceive as much back. Matt. 5:42
35 "But [R]love your enemies, [R]do good, and
lend, hoping for nothing in return; and your
reward will be great, and you will be sons of
the Most High. For He is kind to the unthank-
ful and evil. [Rom. 13:10] • Heb. 13:16
36 [R]"Therefore be merciful, just as your Fa-
ther also is merciful. Matt. 5:48
37 [R]"Judge not, and you shall not be
judged. Condemn not, and you shall not be
condemned. [R]Forgive, and you will be for-
given. Matt. 7:1–5 • Matt. 18:21–35
38 "Give, and it will be given to you: good

6:9 M *to kill* **6:10** NU, M *to him* • NU omits *as whole as the other* **6:26** NU, M omit *to you* • M omits *all* measure, pressed down, shaken together, and running over will be put into your bosom. For with the same measure that you use, it will be measured back to you."

Parable of the Blind Leading the Blind
Matt. 7:3–5, 16–18

39 And He spoke a parable to them: [R]"Can the blind lead the blind? Will they not both fall into the ditch? Matt. 15:14; 23:16

40 [R]"A disciple is not above his teacher, but everyone who is perfectly trained will be like his teacher. [John 13:16; 15:20]

41 [R]"And why do you look at the speck in your brother's eye, but do not perceive the plank in your own eye? Matt. 7:3

42 "Or how can you say to your brother, 'Brother, let me remove the speck that *is* in your eye,' when you yourself do not see the plank that *is* in your own eye? Hypocrite! First remove the plank from your own eye, and then you will see clearly to remove the speck that is in your brother's eye.

43 "For a good tree does not bear bad fruit, nor does a bad tree bear good fruit.

44 "For [R]every tree is known by its own fruit. For *men* do not gather figs from thorns, nor do they gather grapes from a bramble bush. Matt. 12:33

45 [R]"A good man out of the good treasure of his heart brings forth good; and an evil man out of the evil treasure of his heart* brings forth evil. For out of the abundance of the heart his mouth speaks. Matt. 12:35

Parable of the Two Foundations
Matt. 7:21–27

46 [R]"But why do you call Me 'Lord, Lord,' and not do the things which I say? Mal. 1:6

47 [R]"Whoever comes to Me, and hears My sayings and does them, I will show you whom he is like: James 1:22–25

48 "He is like a man building a house, who dug deep and laid the foundation on the rock. And when the flood arose, the stream beat vehemently against that house, and could not shake it, for it was founded on the rock.*

49 "But he who heard and did nothing is like a man who built a house on the earth without a foundation, against which the stream beat vehemently; and immediately it fell.* And the ruin of that house was great."

CHAPTER 7

A Centurion's Servant Is Healed—Matt. 8:5–13

NOW when He concluded all His sayings in the hearing of the people, He [R]entered Capernaum. Matt. 8:5–13

2 And a certain centurion's servant, who was dear to him, was sick and ready to die.

3 So when he heard about Jesus, he sent elders of the Jews to Him, pleading with Him to come and heal his servant.

4 And when they came to Jesus, they begged Him earnestly, saying that the one for whom He should do this was deserving,

5 "for he loves our nation, and has built us a synagogue."

6 Then Jesus went with them. And when He was already not far from the house, the centurion sent friends to Him, saying to Him, "Lord, do not trouble Yourself, for I am not worthy that You should enter under my roof.

7 "Therefore I did not even think myself worthy to come to You. But [R]say the word, and my servant will be healed. Ps. 33:9

8 "For I also am a man placed under [R]authority, having soldiers under me. And I say to one, 'Go,' and he goes; and to another, 'Come,' and he comes; and to my servant, 'Do this,' and he does *it*." [Mark 13:34]

9 When Jesus heard these things, He marveled at him, and turned around and said to the crowd that followed Him, "I say to you, I have not found such great faith, not even in Israel!"

10 And those who were sent, returning to the house, found the servant well who had been sick.*

A Widow's Son Is Raised

11 Now it happened, the day after, *that* He went into a city called Nain; and many of His disciples went with Him, and a large crowd.

12 And when He came near the gate of the city, behold, a dead man was being carried out, the only son of his mother; and she was a widow. And a large crowd from the city was with her.

13 When the Lord saw her, He had [R]compassion on her and said to her, [R]"Do not weep." John 11:35 • Luke 8:52

14 Then He came and touched the open coffin, and those who carried *him* stood still. And He said, "Young man, I say to you, [R]arise." Acts 9:40

15 So he who was dead [R]sat up and began to speak. And He [R]presented him to his mother. John 11:44 • 2 Kin. 4:36

16 [R]Then fear came upon all, and they [R]glorified God, saying, [R]"A great prophet has risen up among us"; and, "God has visited His people." Luke 1:65 • Luke 5:26 • Luke 24:19

John's Questions Are Answered—Matt. 11:2–6

17 And this report about Him went throughout all Judea and all the surrounding region.

18 Then the disciples of John reported to him concerning all these things.

19 And John, calling two of his disciples to *him,* sent *them* to Jesus,* saying, "Are You

6:45 NU omits *treasure of his heart* **6:48** NU *for it was well built* **6:49** NU *collapsed* **7:10** NU omits *who had been sick* **7:19** NU *the Lord*

[R]the Coming One, or [T]do we look for another?" [Zech. 9:9] • *should we expect*

20 When the men had come to Him, they said, "John the Baptist has sent us to You, saying, 'Are You the Coming One, or do we look for another?' "

21 And that very hour He cured many of [T]infirmities, afflictions, and evil spirits; and to many blind He gave sight. *illnesses*

22 [R]Jesus answered and said to them, "Go and tell John the things you have seen and heard: that [R]*the* blind see, *the* lame walk, *the* lepers are cleansed, *the* deaf hear, *the* dead are raised, *the* poor have the gospel preached to them. Matt. 11:4 • Is. 35:5; 61:1★

23 "And [R]blessed is *he* who is not [T]offended because of Me." Ps. 2:12★ • *caused to stumble*

Jesus Praises John—Matt. 11:7–15

24 [R]When the messengers of John had departed, He began to speak to the multitudes concerning John: "What did you go out into the wilderness to see? A reed shaken by the wind? Matt. 11:7

25 "But what did you go out to see? A man clothed in soft garments? Indeed those who are gorgeously appareled and live in luxury are in kings' courts.

26 "But what did you go out to see? A prophet? Yes, I say to you, and more than a prophet.

27 "This is *he* of whom it is written:

'Behold, I send My messenger before
Your face,
*Who will prepare Your way before You.'**

28 "For I say to you, among those born of women there is not a greater prophet than John the Baptist;* but he who is least in the kingdom of God is greater than he."

29 And when all the people heard *Him,* even the tax collectors justified God, having been baptized with the baptism of John.

30 But the Pharisees and lawyers rejected [R]the will of God for themselves, not having been baptized by him. Acts 20:27

Jesus Criticizes His Generation Matt. 11:16–19

31 And the Lord said,* [R]"To what then shall I liken the men of this generation, and what are they like? Matt. 11:16

32 "They are like children sitting in the marketplace and calling to one another, saying:

'We played the flute for you,
And you did not dance;
We mourned to you,
And you did not weep.'

33 "For [R]John the Baptist came [R]neither eating bread nor drinking wine, and you say, 'He has a demon.' Matt. 3:1 • Luke 1:15

34 "The Son of Man has come [R]eating and drinking, and you say, 'Look, a glutton and a [T]winebibber, a friend of tax collectors and sinners!' Luke 15:2 • An excessive drinker

35 [R]"But wisdom is justified by all her children." Matt. 11:19

A Woman Anoints Jesus' Feet

36 [R]Then one of the Pharisees asked Him to eat with him. And He went to the Pharisee's house, and sat down to eat. John 11:2

37 And behold, a woman in the city who was a sinner, when she knew that *Jesus* sat at the table in the Pharisee's house, brought an alabaster flask of fragrant oil,

38 and stood at His feet behind *Him* weeping; and she began to wash His feet with her tears, and wiped *them* with the hair of her head; and she kissed His feet and anointed *them* with the fragrant oil.

39 Now when the Pharisee who had invited Him saw *this,* he spoke to himself, saying, "This Man, if He were a prophet, would know who and what manner of woman *this is* who is touching Him, for she is a sinner."

The Parable of the Two Debtors

40 And Jesus answered and said to him, "Simon, I have something to say to you." So he said, "Teacher, say it."

41 "There was a certain creditor who had two debtors. One owed five hundred [R]denarii, and the other fifty. Matt. 18:28

42 "And when they had nothing with which to repay, he freely forgave them both. Tell Me, therefore, which of them will love him more?"

43 Simon answered and said, "I suppose the *one* whom he forgave more." And He said to him, "You have rightly judged."

44 Then He turned to the woman and said to Simon, "Do you see this woman? I entered your house; you gave Me no [R]water for My feet, but she has washed My feet with her tears and wiped *them* with the hair of her head. Gen. 18:4; 19:2; 43:24

45 "You gave Me no [R]kiss, but this woman has not ceased to kiss My feet since the time I came in. Rom. 16:16

46 [R]"You did not anoint My head with oil, but this woman has anointed My feet with fragrant oil. Ps. 23:5

47 [R]"Therefore I say to you, her sins, *which are* many, are forgiven, for she loved much. But to whom little is forgiven, *the same* loves little." [1 Tim. 1:14]

48 Then He said to her, [R]"Your sins are forgiven." Matt. 9:2

49 And those who sat at the table with Him began to say to themselves, [R]"Who is this who even forgives sins?" Luke 5:21

7:27 Mal. 3:1★ **7:28** NU *there is none greater than John;* **7:31** NU, M omit *And the Lord said*

50 Then He said to the woman, [R]"Your faith has saved you. Go in peace." Matt. 9:22

CHAPTER 8

Certain Women Minister to Christ

NOW it came to pass, afterward, that He went through every city and village, preaching and [T]bringing the glad tidings of the kingdom of God. And the twelve *were* with Him, *proclaiming the good news*

2 and [R]certain women who had been healed of evil spirits and infirmities—Mary called Magdalene, [R]out of whom had come seven demons, Matt. 27:55 • Mark 16:9

3 and Joanna the wife of Chuza, Herod's steward, and Susanna, and many others who provided for Him* from their [T]substance. *possessions*

Parable of the Soils
Matt. 13:1–23; Mark 4:1–20

4 [R]And when a great multitude had gathered, and they had come to Him from every city, He spoke by a parable: Mark 4:1–9

5 "A sower went out to sow his seed. And as he sowed, some fell by the wayside; and it was trampled down, and the birds of the air devoured it.

6 "Some fell on rock; and as soon as it sprang up, it withered away because it lacked moisture.

7 "And some fell among thorns, and the thorns sprang up with it and choked it.

8 "But others fell on good ground, sprang up, and yielded a crop a hundredfold." When He had said these things He cried, "He who has ears to hear, let him hear!"

9 Then His disciples asked Him, saying, "What does this parable mean?"

10 And He said, "To you it has been given to know the [T]mysteries of the kingdom of God, but to the rest *it is given* in parables, that *secret* or *hidden truths*

'Seeing they may not see,
*And hearing they may not understand.'**

11 [R]"Now the parable is this: The seed is the [R]word of God. [1 Pet. 1:23] • Luke 5:1; 11:28

12 "Those by the wayside are the ones who hear; then the devil comes and takes away the word out of their hearts, lest they should believe and be saved.

13 "But the ones on the rock *are those* who, when they hear, receive the word with joy; and these have no root, who believe for a while and in time of temptation fall away.

14 "Now the ones *that* fell among thorns are those who, when they have heard, go out and are choked with cares, [R]riches, and pleasures of life, and bring no fruit to maturity. 1 Tim. 6:9, 10

15 "But the ones *that* fell on the good ground are those who, having heard the word with a noble and good heart, keep *it* and bear fruit with [T]patience. *endurance*

Parable of the Lamp—Mark 4:21–25

16 [R]"No one, when he has lit a lamp, covers it with a vessel or puts *it* under a bed, but sets *it* on a lampstand, that those who enter may see the [R]light. Luke 11:33 • Matt. 5:14

17 [R]"For nothing is secret that will not be revealed, nor *anything* hidden that will not be known and come to light. Luke 12:2

18 "Therefore take heed how you hear. For whoever has, to him *more* will be given; and whoever does not have, even what he seems to have will be taken from him."

Christ's True Brethren
Matt. 12:46–50; Mark 3:31–35

19 [R]Then His mother and brothers came to Him, and could not approach Him because of the crowd. Mark 3:31–35

20 And it was told Him *by some,* who said, "Your mother and Your brothers are standing outside, desiring to see You."

21 But He answered and said to them, "My mother and My brothers are these who hear the word of God and do it."

The Storm Is Stilled
Matt. 8:23–27; Mark 4:35–41

22 Now it happened, on a certain day, that He got into a boat with His disciples. And He said to them, "Let us cross over to the other side of the lake." And they launched out.

23 But as they sailed He fell asleep. And a windstorm came down on the lake, and they were filling *with water,* and were in [T]jeopardy. *danger*

24 And they came to Him and awoke Him, saying, "Master, Master, we are perishing!" Then He arose and rebuked the wind and the raging of the water. And they ceased, and there was a calm.

25 But He said to them, [R]"Where is your faith?" And they were afraid, and marveled, saying to one another, [R]"Who can this be? For He commands even the winds and water, and they obey Him!" Luke 9:41 • Luke 4:36; 5:26

Demons Are Cast into Swine
Matt. 8:28–34; Mark 5:1–20

26 Then they sailed to the country of the Gadarenes,* which is opposite Galilee.

27 And when He stepped out on the land, there met Him a certain man from the city who had demons for a long time. And he wore no clothes,* nor did he live in a house but in the tombs.

8:3 NU, M *them* **8:10** Is. 6:9★ **8:26** NU *Gerasenes*
8:27 NU *who had demons and for a long time wore no clothes*

28 When he saw Jesus, he [R]cried out, fell
down before Him, and with a loud voice said,
[R]"What have I to do with You, Jesus, Son of the
Most High God? I beg You, do not torment
me!" Mark 1:26; 9:26 • Mark 1:23, 24
29 For He had commanded the unclean spirit
to come out of the man. For it had often seized
him, and he was kept under guard, bound
with chains and shackles; and he broke the
bonds and was driven by the demon into the
wilderness.
30 Jesus asked him, saying, "What is your
name?" And he said, "Legion," because many
demons had entered him.
31 And they begged Him that He would not
command them to go out into the abyss.
32 Now a herd of many [R]swine was feeding
there on the mountain. So they begged Him
that He would permit them to enter them. And
He permitted them. Lev. 11:7
33 Then the demons went out of the man and
entered the swine, and the herd ran violently
down the steep place into the lake and
drowned.
34 When those who fed *them* saw what had
happened, they fled and told *it* in the city and
in the country.
35 Then they went out to see what had hap-
pened, and came to Jesus, and found the man
from whom the demons had departed, sitting
at the feet of Jesus, clothed and in his right
mind. And they were afraid.
36 They also who had seen *it* told them
by what means he who had been demon-
possessed was [T]healed. *delivered*
37 [R]Then the whole multitude of the sur-
rounding region of the Gadarenes* [R]asked
Him to depart from them, for they were seized
with great fear. And He got into the boat and
returned. Matt. 8:34 • Luke 4:34
38 Now the man from whom the demons had
departed begged Him that he might be with
Him. But Jesus sent him away, saying,
39 "Return to your own house, and tell what
great things God has done for you." And he
went his way and proclaimed throughout the
whole city what great things Jesus had done
for him.
40 So it was, when Jesus returned, that the
multitude welcomed Him, for they were all
waiting for Him.

A Woman Is Healed
Matt. 9:18–22; Mark 5:21–34

41 [R]And behold, there came a man named
Jairus, and he was a ruler of the synagogue.
And he fell down at Jesus' feet and begged
Him to come to his house, Mark 5:22–43
42 for he had an only daughter about twelve
years of age, and she was dying. But as He
went, the multitudes thronged Him.
43 [R]Now a woman, having a [R]flow of blood
for twelve years, who had spent all her liveli-
hood on physicians and could not be healed
by any, Matt. 9:20 • Luke 15:19–22
44 came from behind and [R]touched the bor-
der of His garment. And immediately her flow
of blood stopped. Mark 6:56
45 And Jesus said, "Who touched Me?"
When all denied it, Peter and those with him*
said, "Master, the multitudes throng and press
You, and You say, 'Who touched Me?' "*
46 But Jesus said, "Somebody touched Me,
for I perceived power going out from Me."
47 Now when the woman saw that she was not
hidden, she came trembling; and falling down
before Him, she declared to Him in the presence
of all the people the reason she had touched
Him and how she was healed immediately.
48 And He said to her, "Daughter, be of good
cheer;* [R]your faith has made you well. [R]Go in
peace." Luke 7:50 • John 8:11

Jairus's Daughter Is Raised
Matt. 9:23–26; Mark 5:35–43

49 While He was still speaking, someone
came from the ruler of the synagogue's *house,*
saying to him, "Your daughter is dead. Do not
trouble the Teacher."*
50 But when Jesus heard *it,* He answered
him, saying, "Do not be afraid; [R]only believe,
and she will be made well." [Mark 11:22–24]
51 When He came into the house, He permit-
ted no one to go in* except Peter, James, and
John,* and the father and mother of the girl.
52 Now all wept and mourned for her; but
He said, [R]"Do not weep; she is not dead, [R]but
sleeping." Luke 7:13 • [John 11:11, 13]
53 And they ridiculed Him, knowing that she
was dead.
54 But He put them all outside,* took her by
the hand and called, saying, "Little girl,
[R]arise." John 11:43
55 Then her spirit returned, and she arose
immediately. And He commanded that she be
given *something* to eat.
56 And her parents were astonished, but [R]He
charged them to tell no one what had hap-
pened. Matt. 8:4; 9:30

CHAPTER 9

Twelve Are Sent to Preach
Matt. 10:1–14; 14:1–14; Mark 6:7–16, 30–34

THEN [R]He called His twelve disciples to-
gether and [R]gave them power and au-
thority over all demons, and to cure
diseases. Matt. 10:1, 2 • [John 14:12]
2 [R]He sent them to preach the kingdom of
God and to heal the sick. Matt. 10:7, 8

8:37 NU *Gerasenes* **8:45** NU omits *and those with him* • NU omits *and You say, 'Who touched Me?'* **8:48** NU omits *be of good cheer* **8:49** NU adds *anymore* **8:51** NU adds *with Him* • NU, M *Peter, John, and James* **8:54** NU omits *put them all outside*

3 [R]And He said to them, "Take nothing for the journey, neither staffs nor bag nor bread nor money; and do not have two tunics apiece. Luke 10:4–12; 22:35

4 [R]"Whatever house you enter, stay there, and from there depart. Mark 6:10

5 [R]"And whoever will not receive you, when you go out of that city, [R]shake off the very dust from your feet as a testimony against them." Matt. 10:14 • Acts 13:51

6 [R]So they departed and went through the towns, preaching the gospel and healing everywhere. Mark 6:12

7 [R]Now Herod the tetrarch heard of all that was done by Him; and he was perplexed, because it was said by some that John had risen from the dead, Matt. 14:1, 2

8 and by some that Elijah had appeared, and by others that one of the old prophets had risen again.

9 Herod said, "John I have beheaded, but who is this of whom I hear such things?" [R]So he sought to see Him. Luke 23:8

10 [R]And the apostles, when they had returned, told Him all that they had done. [R]Then He took them and went aside privately into a deserted place belonging to the city called Bethsaida. Mark 6:30 • Matt. 14:13

11 But when the multitudes knew *it*, they followed Him; and He received them and spoke to them about the kingdom of God, and healed those who had need of healing.

Five Thousand Are Fed
Matt. 14:15–21; Mark 6:35–44; John 6:1–14

12 [R]When the day began to wear away, the twelve came and said to Him, "Send the multitude away, that they may go into the surrounding towns and country, and lodge and get provisions; for we are in a deserted place here." John 6:1, 5

13 But He said to them, "You give them something to eat." And they said, "We have no more than five loaves and two fish, unless we go and buy food for all these people."

14 For there were about five thousand men. Then He said to His disciples, "Make them sit down in groups of fifty."

15 And they did so, and made them all sit down.

16 Then He took the five loaves and the two fish, and looking up to heaven, He [R]blessed and broke *them*, and gave *them* to the disciples to set before the multitude. Luke 22:19

17 So they all ate and were [T]filled, and twelve baskets of the leftover fragments were taken up by them. *satisfied*

Peter's Confession of Faith
Matt. 16:13–21; Mark 8:27–31

18 [R]And it happened, as He was alone praying, *that* His disciples joined Him, and He asked them, saying, "Who do the crowds say that I am?" Matt. 16:13–16

19 So they answered and said, [R]"John the Baptist, but some *say* Elijah; and others *say* that one of the old prophets has risen again." Matt. 14:2

20 He said to them, "But who do you say that I am?" [R]Peter answered and said, "The Christ of God." John 6:68, 69

21 And He strictly warned and commanded them to tell this to no one,

22 saying, [R]"The Son of Man must suffer many things, and be rejected by the elders and chief priests and scribes, and be killed, and be raised the third day." John 19:7☆

True Cost of Discipleship
Matt. 16:24–27; Mark 8:34–38

23 Then He said to *them* all, "If anyone desires to come after Me, let him deny himself, and take up his cross daily,* and follow Me.

24 [R]"For whoever desires to save his life will lose it, but whoever loses his life for My sake will save it. [John 12:25]

25 [R]"For what profit is it to a man if he gains the whole world, and is himself destroyed or lost? Mark 8:36

26 "For whoever is ashamed of Me and My words, of him the Son of Man will be ashamed when He comes in His *own* glory, and *in His* Father's, and of the holy angels.

The Transfiguration
Matt. 16:28—17:9; Mark 9:1–9; 2 Pet. 1:17, 18

27 [R]"But I tell you truly, there are some standing here who shall not taste death till they see the kingdom of God." Acts 7:55, 56☆

28 [R]Now it came to pass, about eight days after these sayings, that He took Peter, John, and James and went up on the mountain to pray. Mark 9:2–8

29 As He prayed, the appearance of His face was altered, and His robe *became* white *and* glistening.

30 And behold, two men talked with Him, who were [R]Moses and Elijah, Heb. 11:23–29

31 who appeared in glory and spoke of His [T]decease which He was about to accomplish at Jerusalem. Death, lit. *departure*

32 But Peter and those with him [R]were heavy with sleep; and when they were fully awake, they saw His glory and the two men who stood with Him. Dan. 8:18; 10:9

33 Then it happened, as they were parting from Him, *that* Peter said to Jesus, "Master, it is good for us to be here; and let us make three [T]tabernacles: one for You, one for Moses, and one for Elijah"—not knowing what he said. *tents*

34 While he was saying this, a cloud came and overshadowed them; and they were fearful as they entered the [R]cloud. Ex. 13:21

9:23 M omits *daily*

35 And a voice came out of the cloud, saying,
"This is My beloved Son.* Hear Him!"
36 When the voice had ceased, Jesus was
found alone. [R]But they kept quiet, and told no
one in those days any of the things they had
seen. Matt. 17:9

Demoniac Son Is Healed
Matt. 17:14–18; Mark 9:14–27

37 Now it happened on the next day, when
they had come down from the mountain, that
a great multitude met Him.
38 Suddenly a man from the multitude cried
out, saying, "Teacher, I implore You, look on
my son, for he is my only child.
39 "And behold, a spirit seizes him, and he
suddenly cries out; it convulses him so that he
foams *at the mouth;* and it departs from him
with great difficulty, bruising him.
40 "So I implored Your disciples to cast it out,
but they could not."
41 Then Jesus answered and said, "O [T]faith-
less and perverse generation, how long shall I
be with you and [T]bear with you? Bring your
son here." *unbelieving • put up with*
42 And as he was still coming, the demon
threw him down and convulsed *him.* Then Je-
sus rebuked the unclean spirit, healed the
child, and gave him back to his father.

Christ Prophesies His Coming Death
Matt. 17:22, 23; Mark 9:30–32

43 And they were all amazed at the majesty
of God. But while everyone marveled at all the
things which Jesus did, He said to His disci-
ples,
44 "Let these words sink down into your
ears, for the Son of Man is about to be [R]be-
trayed into the hands of men." Luke 22:54☆
45 [R]But they did not understand this saying,
and it was hidden from them so that they did
not perceive it; and they were afraid to ask
Him about this saying. Mark 9:32

True Greatness—Matt. 18:1–5; Mark 9:33–40

46 Then a dispute arose among them as to
which of them would be greatest.
47 And Jesus, [R]perceiving the thought of
their heart, took a [R]little child and set him by
Him, Matt. 9:4 • Luke 18:17
48 and said to them, [R]"Whoever receives this
little child in My name receives Me; and
[R]whoever receives Me [R]receives Him who sent
Me. For he who is least among you all will be
great." Matt. 18:5 • John 12:44 • John 13:20
49 [R]Now John answered and said, "Master,
we saw someone casting out demons in Your
name, and we forbade him because he does
not follow with us." Mark 9:38–40
50 But Jesus said to him, "Do not forbid
him, for [R]he who is not against us* is on our
side."* Luke 11:23

Samaria Rejects Christ

51 Now it came to pass, when the time had
come for Him to be received up, that He stead-
fastly set His face to go to Jerusalem,
52 and sent messengers before His face. And
as they went, they entered a village of the Sa-
maritans, to prepare for Him.
53 But [R]they did not receive Him, because
His face was *set* for the journey to Jerusa-
lem. John 4:4, 9
54 And when His disciples [R]James and
John saw *this,* they said, "Lord, do You want
us to command fire to come down from
heaven and consume them, just as [R]Elijah
did?"* Mark 3:17 • 2 Kin. 1:10, 12
55 But He turned and rebuked them,* and
said, "You do not know what manner of [R]spirit
you are of. [2 Tim. 1:7]
56 "For [R]the Son of Man did not come to de-
stroy men's lives but to save *them.*"* And they
went to another village. John 3:17; 12:47

True Cost of Discipleship—Matt. 8:18–22

57 Now it happened as they journeyed on
the road, *that* someone said to Him, "Lord, I
will follow You wherever You go."
58 And Jesus said to him, "Foxes have holes
and birds of the air *have* nests, but the Son of
Man has nowhere to lay *His* head."
59 [R]Then He said to another, "Follow Me."
But he said, "Lord, let me first go and bury my
father." Matt. 8:21, 22
60 Jesus said to him, "Let the dead bury their
own dead, but you go and preach the kingdom
of God."
61 And another also said, "Lord, [R]I will fol-
low You, but let me first go *and* bid them
farewell who are at my house." 1 Kin. 19:20
62 But Jesus said to him, "No one, having put
his hand to the plow, and looking back, is [R]fit
for the kingdom of God." 2 Tim. 4:10

CHAPTER 10

Mission of the Seventy

AFTER these things the Lord appointed
seventy others also,* and sent them two
by two before His face into every city and
place where He Himself was about to go.
2 Then He said to them, "The harvest truly
is great, but the laborers *are* few; therefore
pray the Lord of the harvest to send out la-
borers into His harvest.
3 "Go your way; [R]behold, I send you out as
lambs among wolves. Matt. 10:16
4 [R]"Carry neither money bag, knapsack,

9:35 NU *This is My Son, the Chosen One* **9:50** NU *you* • NU *your* **9:54** NU omits *just as Elijah did* **9:55** NU omits the rest of v. 55. **9:56** NU omits the first sentence of this verse. **10:1** NU *seventy-two others*

nor sandals; and [R]greet no one along the
road. Luke 9:3–5 • 2 Kin. 4:29
5 [R]"But whatever house you enter, first say,
'Peace to this house.' Matt. 10:12
6 "And if a son of peace is there, your peace
will rest on it; if not, it will return to you.
7 [R]"And remain in the same house, eating
and drinking such things as they give, for the
laborer is worthy of his wages. Do not go from
house to house. Matt. 10:11
8 "Whatever city you enter, and they re-
ceive you, eat such things as are set before
you.
9 [R]"And heal the sick there, and say to
them, [R]'The kingdom of God has come near to
you.' Mark 3:15 • Matt. 3:2; 10:7
10 "But whatever city you enter, and they do
not receive you, go out into its streets and say,
11 [R]'The very dust of your city which clings
to us* we wipe off against you. Nevertheless
know this, that the kingdom of God has come
near you.' Acts 13:51
12 "But* I say to you that [R]it will be more tol-
erable in that Day for Sodom than for that
city. Matt. 10:15; 11:24
13 "Woe to you, Chorazin! Woe to you, Beth-
saida! [R]For if the mighty works which were
done in you had been done in Tyre and Sidon,
they would have repented long ago, sitting in
sackcloth and ashes. Ezek. 3:6
14 "But it will be more tolerable for Tyre and
Sidon at the judgment than for you.
15 "And you, Capernaum, who are exalted to
heaven, will be brought down to Hades.*
16 [R]"He who hears you hears Me, he who re-
jects you rejects Me, and he who rejects Me
rejects Him who sent Me." John 13:20

Return of the Seventy

17 Then [R]the seventy* returned with joy, say-
ing, "Lord, even the demons are subject to us
in Your name." Luke 10:1
18 And He said to them, [R]"I saw Satan fall
like lightning from heaven. John 12:31
19 "Behold, [R]I give you the authority to tram-
ple on serpents and scorpions, and over all
the power of the enemy, and nothing shall by
any means hurt you. Mark 16:18
20 "Nevertheless do not rejoice in this, that
the spirits are subject to you, but rather* re-
joice because [R]your names are written in
heaven." Is. 4:3
21 In that hour Jesus rejoiced in the Spirit
and said, "I thank You, Father, Lord of heaven
and earth, that You have hidden these things
from *the* wise and prudent and revealed them
to babes. Even so, Father, for so it seemed
good in Your sight.
22 "All* things have been delivered to Me by
My Father, and no one knows who the Son is
except the Father, and who the Father is ex-
cept the Son, and *the one* to whom the Son
wills to reveal *Him*."
23 Then He turned to *His* disciples and said
privately, [R]"Blessed *are* the eyes which see the
things you see; Matt. 13:16, 17
24 "for I tell you [R]that many prophets and
kings have desired to see what you see, and
have not seen *it*, and to hear what you hear,
and have not heard *it*." 1 Pet. 1:10, 11

How to Inherit Eternal Life

25 And behold, a certain lawyer stood up
and tested Him, saying, "Teacher, what shall I
do to inherit eternal life?"
26 He said to him, "What is written in the
law? What is your reading *of it*?"
27 So he answered and said, "*'You shall love*
the L*ORD* *your God with all your heart, with all*
your soul, with all your strength, and with all
*your mind,'** and *'your neighbor as yourself.'* "*
28 And He said to him, "You have answered
rightly; do this and you will live."

Parable of the Good Samaritan

29 But he, wanting to justify himself, said to
Jesus, "And who is my neighbor?"
30 Then Jesus answered and said: "A certain
man went down from Jerusalem to Jericho,
and fell among [T]thieves, who stripped him of
his clothing, wounded *him*, and departed,
leaving *him* half dead. *robbers*
31 "Now by chance a certain priest came
down that road. And when he saw him, [R]he
passed by on the other side. Ps. 38:11
32 "Likewise a Levite, when he arrived at the
place, came and looked, and passed by on the
other side.
33 "But a certain [R]Samaritan, as he jour-
neyed, came where he was. And when he saw
him, he had compassion. John 4:9
34 "So he went to *him* and bandaged his
wounds, pouring on oil and wine; and he set
him on his own animal, brought him to an inn,
and took care of him.
35 "On the next day, when he departed,* he
took out two [R]denarii, gave *them* to the
innkeeper, and said to him, 'Take care of him;
and whatever more you spend, when I come
again, I will repay you.' Matt. 20:2
36 "So which of these three do you think was
neighbor to him who fell among the thieves?"
37 And he said, "He who showed mercy on
him." Then Jesus said to him, [R]"Go and do
likewise." Prov. 14:21

Mary and Martha Are Contrasted

38 Now it happened as they went that He en-
tered a certain village; and a certain woman

10:11 NU *our feet* **10:12** NU, M omit *But* **10:15** NU *will you be exalted to heaven? You will be thrust down to Hades!* **10:17** NU *seventy-two* **10:20** NU, M omit *rather* **10:22** M *And turning to the disciples He said, "All . . .* **10:27** Deut. 6:5 • Lev. 19:18 **10:35** NU omits *when he departed*

named [R]Martha welcomed Him into her
house. John 11:1; 12:2, 3
39 And she had a sister called Mary, who
also sat at Jesus'* feet and heard His word.
40 But Martha was distracted with much
serving, and she approached Him and said,
"Lord, do You not care that my sister has left
me to serve alone? Therefore tell her to help
me."
41 And Jesus* answered and said to her,
"Martha, Martha, you are worried and trou-
bled about many things.
42 "But [R]one thing is needed, and Mary has
chosen that good part, which will not be taken
away from her." [Ps. 27:4]

CHAPTER 11

The Lord's Prayer—Matt. 6:9–13

NOW it came to pass, as He was praying in
a certain place, when He ceased, *that* one
of His disciples said to Him, "Lord, teach us to
pray, as John also taught his disciples."
2 So He said to them, "When you pray, say:

[R]Our Father in heaven,* Matt. 6:9–13
Hallowed be Your name.
Your kingdom come.*
Your will be done
On earth as *it is* in heaven.
3 Give us day by day our daily bread.
4 And [R]forgive us our sins, [Eph. 4:32]
For we also forgive everyone who is
indebted to us.
And do not lead us into temptation,
But deliver us from the evil one."*

Parable of the Persistent Friend

5 And He said to them, "Which of you shall
have a friend, and go to him at midnight and
say to him, 'Friend, lend me three loaves;
6 'for a friend of mine has come to me on
his journey, and I have nothing to set before
him';
7 "and he will answer from within and say,
'Do not trouble me; the door is now shut, and
my children are with me in bed; I cannot rise
and give to you'?
8 "I say to you, [R]though he will not rise and
give to him because he is his friend, yet be-
cause of his persistence he will rise and give
him as many as he needs. [Luke 18:1–5]
9 "So I say to you, ask, and it will be given
to you; [R]seek, and you will find; knock, and it
will be opened to you. Is. 55:6
10 "For everyone who asks receives, and he
who seeks finds, and to him who knocks it
will be opened.

Parable of the Good Father—Matt. 7:7–11

11 [R]"If a son asks for bread* from any father
among you, will he give him a stone? Or if *he
asks* for a fish, will he give him a serpent in-
stead of a fish? Matt. 7:9
12 "Or if he asks for an egg, will he offer him
a scorpion?
13 "If you then, being evil, know how to give
[R]good gifts to your children, how much more
will *your* heavenly Father give the Holy Spirit
to those who ask Him!" James 1:17

Christ Heals the Demoniac

14 [R]And He was casting out a demon, and it
was mute. So it was, when the demon had
gone out, that the mute spoke; and the multi-
tudes marveled. Matt. 9:32–34; 12:22, 24

Christ's Power Not from Satan Matt. 12:25–30, 43–45; Mark 3:22–27

15 But some of them said, [R]"He casts out
demons by Beelzebub,* the ruler of the
demons." Matt. 9:34; 12:24
16 Others, testing *Him,* [R]sought from Him a
sign from heaven. Matt. 12:38; 16:1
17 [R]But He, knowing their thoughts, said to
them: "Every kingdom divided against itself is
brought to desolation, and a house *divided*
against a house falls. Matt. 12:25–29
18 "If Satan also is divided against himself,
how will his kingdom stand? Because you say
I cast out demons by Beelzebub.
19 "And if I cast out demons by Beelzebub,
by whom do your sons cast *them* out? There-
fore they will be your judges.
20 "But if I cast out demons [R]with the finger
of God, surely the kingdom of God has come
upon you. Ex. 8:19
21 [R]"When a strong man, fully armed,
guards his own palace, his goods are in
peace. Mark 3:27
22 "But [R]when a stronger than he comes
upon him and overcomes him, he takes from
him all his armor in which he trusted, and di-
vides his [T]spoils. [Is. 53:12] • *plunder*
23 [R]"He who is not with Me is against Me,
and he who does not gather with Me scat-
ters. Matt. 12:30
24 "When an unclean spirit goes out of a
man, he goes through dry places, seeking rest;
and finding none, he says, 'I will return to my
house from which I came.'

10:39 NU *the Lord's* **10:41** NU *the Lord* **11:2** NU omits *Our* and *in heaven* • NU omits the rest of v. 2. **11:4** NU omits *But deliver us from the evil one* **11:11** NU omits the words from *bread* through *for* in the next sentence. **11:15** NU, M *Beelzebul*

11:24–26 Demons: Interaction with Humans—Few subjects are as volatile as this one because Satan specializes in producing and exploiting human fears. Remember at every point that God and His angels

(continued on next page)

25 "And when he comes, he finds *it* swept
and put in order.
26 "Then he goes and takes with *him* seven
other spirits more wicked than himself, and
they enter and dwell there; and the last *state*
of that man is worse than the first."

27 And it happened, as He spoke these
things, that a certain woman from the crowd
raised her voice and said to Him, [R]"Blessed *is*
the womb that bore You, and *the* breasts
which nursed You!" Luke 1:28, 48
28 **But He said,** [R]"More than that, blessed
are those who hear the word of God and keep
it!" [Luke 8:21]

Christ's Only Sign Is Jonah—Matt. 12:39–42

29 And while the crowds were thickly gath-
ered together, He began to say, "This is an evil
generation. It seeks a sign, and no sign will
be given to it except [R]the sign of Jonah the
prophet.* Luke 24:46; Acts 10:40☆
30 "For as [R]Jonah became a sign to the
Ninevites, [R]so also the Son of Man will be to
this generation. Jon. 1:17; 2:10; 3:3–10 • 1 Cor. 15:4☆
31 [R]"The queen of the South will rise up in
the judgment with the men of this generation
and condemn them, for she came from the
ends of the earth to hear the wisdom of Sol-
omon; and indeed a [R]greater than Solomon *is*
here. 1 Kin. 10:1–9 • [Rom. 9:5]
32 "The men of Nineveh will rise up in the
judgment with this generation and condemn it,
for [R]they repented at the preaching of Jonah;
and indeed a greater than Jonah *is* here. Jon. 3:5

Parable of the Lighted Lamp

33 [R]"No one, when he has lit a lamp, puts *it*
in a secret place or under a [R]basket, but on a
lampstand, that those who come in may see
the light. Mark 4:21 • Matt. 5:15
34 "The lamp of the body is the eye. There-
fore, when your eye is good, your whole body
also is full of light. But when *your eye* is bad,
your body also *is* full of darkness.
35 "Therefore take heed that the light which
is in you is not darkness.
36 "If then your whole body *is* full of light,
having no part dark, *the* whole *body* will be
full of light, as when the bright shining of a
lamp gives you light."

"Woes" on the Pharisees

37 And as He spoke, a certain Pharisee
asked Him to dine with him. So He went in
and sat down to eat.
38 **When the Pharisee saw *it*, he marveled**
that He had not first washed before dinner.
39 [R]**Then the Lord said to him,** "Now you
Pharisees make the outside of the cup and
dish clean, but [R]your inward part is full of
greed and wickedness. Matt. 23:25 • Titus 1:15
40 "Foolish ones! Did not He who made the
outside make the inside also?
41 [R]"But rather give alms of [T]such things as
you have; then indeed all things are clean to
you. [Luke 12:33; 16:9] • Or *what is inside*
42 "But woe to you Pharisees! For you tithe
mint and rue and all manner of herbs, and
[R]pass by justice and the love of God. These
you ought to have done, without leaving the
others undone. [Mic. 6:7, 8]
43 [R]"Woe to you Pharisees! For you love the
best seats in the synagogues and greetings in
the marketplaces. Mark 12:38, 39
44 "Woe to you, scribes and Pharisees, hyp-
ocrites!* [R]For you are like graves which are
not seen, and the men who walk over *them*
are not aware *of them.*" Ps. 5:9

"Woes" on the Lawyers

45 Then one of the lawyers answered and
said to Him, "Teacher, by saying these things
You reproach us also."
46 **And He said,** "Woe to you also, lawyers!
[R]For you load men with burdens hard to bear,

11:29 NU omits *the prophet* **11:44** NU omits *scribes and Pharisees, hypocrites*

(continued from previous page)
are the primary spiritual powers and the only creative ones. What Satan and his minions do is always an attempt to ruin God's purposes. Never let yourself become engrossed with the devil or his angels.

If, as seems likely, the demons of the Gospels, Acts, and Epistles are to be identified with the fallen angels, they can interact with humans in the following ways:

a. They motivate false philosophies of life. Whether religious (Page 1239—1 Tim. 4:1) or secular (Page 1221—Col. 2:8–10), false teachings are prompted at least in part by fallen angels.
b. They can lead people into moral impurity. The result of false philosophies of life is always sin (Page 1239—1 Tim. 4:2; Page 1221—Col. 2:12–15).
c. They oppose spiritual growth. The warfare of the Christian life is a battle against the influences of invisible fallen angels (Page 1209—Eph. 6:12).
d. They can cause disease. In the Gospels some diseases have evil supernatural origins (Page 989—Matt. 12:22).
e. They can cause mental disorders. Jesus healed some mental disorders by casting out demons (Page 1053—Luke 8:29, 35).
f. They can possess people. The Gospels and Acts record instances of demon control of unbelievers' lives (Page 980—Matt. 4:24; Page 1020—Mark 5:8–14; Page 1052—Luke 8:2; Page 1120—Acts 8:7; 16:16).

Now turn to Page 696—Is. 14:12–15: Satan: Fall of Satan.

and you yourselves do not touch the burdens with one of your fingers. Matt. 23:4

47 "Woe to you! For you build the tombs of the prophets, and your fathers killed them.

48 "In fact, you bear witness that you approve the deeds of your fathers; for they indeed killed them, and you build their tombs.

49 "Therefore the wisdom of God also said, 'I will send them prophets and apostles, and *some* of them they will kill and persecute,'

50 "that the blood of all the prophets which was shed from the foundation of the world may be required of this generation,

51 [R]"from the blood of Abel to the blood of Zechariah who perished between the altar and the temple. Yes, I say to you, it shall be required of this generation. Gen. 4:8

52 [R]"Woe to you lawyers! For you have taken away the key of knowledge. You did not enter in yourselves, and those who were entering in you hindered." Matt. 23:13

53 And as He said these things to them,* the scribes and the Pharisees began to assail *Him* vehemently, and to cross-examine Him about many things,

54 lying in wait for Him, and [R]seeking to catch Him in something He might say, that they might accuse Him.* Mark 12:13

CHAPTER 12

Christ Warns About Hypocrisy
Matt. 10:26–33

IN [R]the meantime, when an innumerable multitude of people had gathered together, so that they trampled one another, He began to say to His disciples first *of all*, [R]"Beware of the leaven of the Pharisees, which is hypocrisy. Mark 8:15 • Matt. 16:12

2 [R]"For there is nothing covered that will not be revealed, nor hidden that will not be known. Matt. 10:26; [1 Cor. 4:5]

3 "Therefore whatever you have spoken in the dark will be heard in the light, and what you have spoken in the ear in inner rooms will be proclaimed on the housetops.

4 "And I say to you, My friends, do not be afraid of those who kill the body, and after that have no more that they can do.

5 "But I will show you whom you should fear: Fear Him who, after He has killed, has power to cast into hell; yes, I say to you, [R]fear Him! Ps. 119:120

6 "Are not five sparrows sold for two copper coins?* And [R]not one of them is forgotten before God. Matt. 6:26

7 "But the very hairs of your head are all numbered. Do not fear therefore; you are of more value than many sparrows.

8 "Also I say to you, whoever confesses Me before men, him the Son of Man also will confess before the angels of God.

9 "But he who denies Me before men will be denied before the angels of God.

10 "And anyone who speaks a word against the Son of Man, it will be forgiven him; but to him who blasphemes against the Holy Spirit, it will not be forgiven.

11 [R]"Now when they bring you to the synagogues and magistrates and authorities, do not worry about how or what you should answer, or what you should say. Mark 13:11

12 "For the Holy Spirit will teach you in that very hour what you ought to say."

Parable of the Rich Fool

13 Then one from the crowd said to Him, "Teacher, tell my brother to divide the inheritance with me."

14 But He said to him, "Man, who made Me a judge or an arbitrator over you?"

15 And He said to them, [R]"Take heed and beware of covetousness,* for one's life does not consist in the abundance of the things he possesses." [1 Tim. 6:6–10]

16 Then He spoke a parable to them, saying: "The ground of a certain rich man yielded plentifully.

17 "And he thought within himself, saying, 'What shall I do, since I have no room to store my crops?'

18 "So he said, 'I will do this: I will pull down my barns and build greater, and there I will store all my crops and my goods.

19 'And I will say to my soul, "Soul, you have many goods laid up for many years; take your ease; eat, drink, *and* be merry." '

20 "But God said to him, 'Fool! This night [R]your soul will be required of you; [R]then whose will those things be which you have provided?' Ps. 52:7 • Ps. 39:6

21 "So *is* he who lays up treasure for himself, and is not rich toward God."

Seek the Kingdom of God—Matt. 6:25–33

22 Then He said to His disciples, "Therefore I say to you, [R]do not worry about your life, what you will eat; nor about the body, what you will put on. Matt. 6:25–33

23 "Life is more than food, and the body *is more* than clothing.

24 "Consider the ravens, for they neither sow nor reap, which have neither storehouse nor barn; and God feeds them. Of how much more value are you than the birds?

25 "And which of you by worrying can add one cubit to his stature?

26 "If you then are not able to do *the* least, why are you anxious for the rest?

11:53 NU *And when He left there* **11:54** NU omits *and seeking* and *that they might accuse Him*
12:6 Gr. *assarion*, a coin worth about 1/16 of a denarius
12:15 NU *all covetousness*

27 "Consider the lilies, how they grow: they neither toil nor spin; and yet I say to you, even [R]Solomon in all his glory was not [T]arrayed like one of these. 1 Kin. 10:4–7 • *clothed*

28 "If then God so clothes the grass, which today is in the field and tomorrow is thrown into the oven, how much more *will He clothe* you, O *you* of [R]little faith? Matt. 6:30; 8:26

29 "And do not seek what you should eat or what you should drink, nor have an anxious mind.

30 "For all these things the nations of the world seek after, and your Father [R]knows that you need these things. Matt. 6:31, 32

31 "But seek the kingdom of God, and all these things* shall be added to you.

32 "Do not fear, little [R]flock, for [R]it is your Father's good pleasure to give you the kingdom. Is. 40:11; Zech. 13:7☆ • [Matt. 11:25, 26]

33 [R]"Sell what you have and give [R]alms; provide yourselves money bags which do not grow old, a treasure in the heavens that does not fail, where no thief approaches nor moth destroys. Matt. 19:21 • Luke 11:41

34 "For where your treasure is, there your heart will be also.

Parable of the Expectant Steward

35 [R]"Let your waist be girded and [R]*your* lamps burning; [1 Pet. 1:13] • [Matt. 25:1–13]

36 "and you yourselves be like men who wait for their master, when he will return from the wedding, that when he comes and knocks they may open to him immediately.

37 [R]"Blessed *are* those servants whom the master, when he comes, will find watching. Assuredly, I say to you that he will gird himself and have them sit down *to eat*, and will come and serve them. Matt. 24:46

38 "And if he should come in the second watch, or come in the third watch, and find *them* so, blessed are those servants.

39 "But know this, that if the master of the house had known what hour the thief would come, he would have watched and* not allowed his house to be broken into.

40 [R]"Therefore you also be ready, for the Son of Man is coming at an hour you do not expect." Mark 13:33

Parable of the Faithful Steward
Matt. 24:45–51

41 Then Peter said to Him, "Lord, do You speak this parable *only* to us, or to all *people?*"

42 And the Lord said, "Who then is that faithful and wise steward, whom *his* master will make ruler over his household, to give *them their* portion of food in due season?

43 "Blessed *is* that servant whom his master will find so doing when he comes.

44 [R]"Truly, I say to you that he will make him ruler over all that he has. Matt. 24:47

45 "But if that servant says in his heart, 'My master is delaying his coming,' and begins to beat the male and female servants, and to eat and drink and be drunk,

46 "the master of that servant will come on a [R]day when he is not looking for *him*, and at an hour when he is not aware, and will cut him in two and appoint *him* his portion with the unbelievers. 1 Thess. 5:3

47 "And [R]that servant who [R]knew his master's will, and did not prepare *himself* or do according to his will, shall be beaten with many *stripes*. Deut. 25:2 • [James 4:17]

48 "But he who did not know, yet committed things deserving of stripes, shall be beaten with few. For everyone to whom much is given, from him much will be required; and to whom much has been committed, of him they will ask the more.

Christ Warns of the Costs of Discipleship

49 "I came to send fire on the earth, and how I wish it were already kindled!

50 "But [R]I have a baptism to be baptized with, and how distressed I am till it is [R]accomplished! Mark 10:38 • John 12:27; 19:30

51 [R]"Do *you* suppose that I came to give peace on earth? I tell you, not at all, [R]but rather division. Matt. 10:34–36 • John 7:43; 9:16

52 [R]"For from now on five in one house will be divided: three against two, and two against three. Mark 13:12

53 "Father will be divided against son and son against father, mother against daughter and daughter against mother, mother-in-law against her daughter-in-law and daughter-in-law against her mother-in-law."

Christ Warns of Not Discerning the Times

54 Then He also said to the multitudes, [R]"Whenever you see a cloud rising out of the west, immediately you say, 'A shower is coming'; and so it is. Matt. 16:2, 3

55 "And when you see the [R]south wind blow, you say, 'There will be hot weather'; and there is. Job 37:17

56 "Hypocrites! You can discern the face of the sky and of the earth, but how *is it* you do not discern [R]this time? Luke 19:41–44

57 "Yes, and why, even of yourselves, do you not judge what is right?

58 "When you go with your adversary to the magistrate, make every effort along the way to settle with him, lest he drag you to the judge, the judge deliver you to the officer, and the officer throw you into prison.

59 "I tell you, you shall not depart from there till you have paid the very last mite."

12:31 NU *His kingdom, and these things* **12:39** NU *he would not have allowed*

CHAPTER 13

Christ Teaches on Repentance

THERE were present at that season some who told Him about the Galileans whose blood Pilate had [T]mingled with their sacrifices. *mixed*

2 And Jesus answered and said to them, "Do you suppose that these Galileans were worse sinners than all *other* Galileans, because they suffered such things?

3 "I tell you, no; but unless you repent you will all likewise perish.

4 "Or those eighteen on whom the tower in Siloam fell and killed them, do you think that they were worse sinners than all *other* men who dwelt in Jerusalem?

5 "I tell you, no; but unless you repent you will all likewise perish."

6 He also spoke this parable: [R]"A certain *man* had a fig tree planted in his vineyard, and he came seeking fruit on it and found none. Matt. 21:19

7 "Then he said to the keeper of his vineyard, 'Look, for three years I have come seeking fruit on this fig tree and find none. Cut it down; why does it [T]use up the ground?' *waste*

8 "But he answered and said to him, 'Sir, let it alone this year also, until I dig around it and fertilize *it*.

9 'And if it bears fruit, *well*. But if not, after that* you can [R]cut it down.' " [John 15:2]

10 Now He was teaching in one of the synagogues on the Sabbath.

11 And behold, there was a woman who had a spirit of infirmity eighteen years, and was bent over and could in no way [T]raise *herself* up. *straighten up*

12 But when Jesus saw her, He called *her* to *Him* and said to her, "Woman, you are loosed from your [R]infirmity." Luke 7:21; 8:2

13 [R]And He laid *His* hands on her, and immediately she was made straight, and glorified God. Acts 9:17

14 But the ruler of the synagogue answered with indignation, because Jesus had healed on the Sabbath; and he said to the crowd, "There are six days on which men ought to work; therefore come and be healed on them, and not on the Sabbath day."

15 The Lord then answered him and said, "Hypocrite!* Does not each one of you on the Sabbath loose his ox or donkey from the stall, and lead *it* away to water it?

16 "So ought not this woman, being a daughter of Abraham, whom Satan has bound—think of it—for eighteen years, be loosed from this bond on the Sabbath?"

17 And when He said these things, all His adversaries were put to shame; and all the multitude rejoiced for all the glorious things that were [R]done by Him. Mark 5:19, 20

Parable of the Mustard Seed
Matt. 13:31, 32; Mark 4:30–32

18 Then He said, "What is the kingdom of God like? And to what shall I compare it?

19 "It is like a mustard seed, which a man took and put in his garden; and it grew and became a large* tree, and the birds of the air nested in its branches."

Parable of the Leaven—Matt. 13:33–35

20 And again He said, "To what shall I liken the kingdom of God?

21 "It is like [T]leaven, which a woman took and hid in three [R]measures* of meal till it was all leavened." *yeast* • Matt. 13:33

The Way into the Kingdom

22 [R]And He went through the cities and villages, teaching, and journeying toward Jerusalem. Mark 6:6

23 Then one said to Him, "Lord, are there few who are saved?" And He said to them,

24 [R]"Strive to enter through the narrow gate, for many, I say to you, will seek to enter and will not be able. [Matt. 7:13]

25 [R]"When once the Master of the house has risen up and [R]shut the door, and you begin to stand outside and knock at the door, saying, 'Lord, Lord, open for us,' and He will answer and say to you, 'I do not know you, where you are from,' Is. 55:6 • Matt. 25:10

26 "then you will begin to say, 'We ate and drank in Your presence, and You taught in our streets.'

27 "But He will say, 'I tell you I do not know you, where you are from. [R]Depart from Me, all you workers of iniquity.' Ps. 6:8

28 "There will be weeping and gnashing of teeth, when you see Abraham and Isaac and Jacob and all the prophets in the kingdom of God, and yourselves thrust out.

29 "They will come from the east and the west, from the north and the south, and sit down in the kingdom of God.

30 "And indeed there are last who will be first, and there are first who will be last."

Christ Mourns over Jerusalem

31 On that very day* some Pharisees came, saying to Him, "Get out and depart from here, for Herod wants to kill You."

32 And He said to them, "Go, tell that fox, 'Behold, I cast out demons and perform cures today and tomorrow, and the third *day* [R]I shall be perfected.' [Heb. 2:10; 5:9]

33 "Nevertheless I must journey today, tomorrow, and the *day* following; for it cannot

13:9 NU *And if it bears fruit after that, well. But if not, you can cut it down.* **13:15** NU, M *Hypocrites* **13:19** NU omits *large* **13:21** Gr. *sata*, same as Heb. *seah;* approximately 2 pecks in all **13:31** NU *In that very hour*

be that a prophet should perish outside of Jerusalem.

34 [R]"O Jerusalem, Jerusalem, the one who kills the prophets and stones those who are sent to her! How often I wanted to gather your children together, as a hen *gathers* her brood under *her* wings, but you were not willing! Matt. 23:37–39

35 "See! [R]Your house is left to you desolate; and assuredly,* I say to you, you shall not see Me until *the time* comes when you say, *'Blessed is He who comes in the name of the* LORD!' "* Lev. 26:31, 32; Jer. 22:5☆

CHAPTER 14

Instruction on the Sabbath

NOW it happened, as He went into the house of one of the rulers of the Pharisees to eat bread on the Sabbath, that they watched Him closely.

2 And behold, there was a certain man before Him who had dropsy.

3 And Jesus, answering, spoke to the lawyers and Pharisees, saying, [R]"Is it lawful to heal on the Sabbath?"* Matt. 12:10

4 But they kept silent. And He took *him* and healed him, and let him go.

5 Then He answered them, saying, "Which of you, having a donkey* or an ox that has fallen into a pit, will not immediately pull him out on the Sabbath day?"

6 And they could not answer Him regarding these things.

Parable of the Ambitious Guest

7 So He told a parable to those who were invited, when He noted how they chose the best places, saying to them:

8 "When you are invited by anyone to a wedding feast, do not sit down in the best place, lest one more honorable than you be invited by him;

9 "and he who invited you and him come and say to you, 'Give place to this man,' and then you begin with shame to take the lowest place.

10 [R]"But when you are invited, go and sit down in the lowest place, so that when he who invited you comes he may say to you, 'Friend, go up higher.' Then you will have glory in the presence of those who sit at the table with you. Prov. 25:6, 7

11 [R]"For whoever exalts himself will be [T]humbled, and he who humbles himself will be exalted." Matt. 23:12 • *put down*

12 Then He also said to him who invited Him, "When you give a dinner or a supper, do not ask your friends, your brothers, your relatives, nor rich neighbors, lest they also invite you back, and you be repaid.

13 "But when you give a feast, invite *the* poor, *the* maimed, *the* lame, *the* blind.

14 "And you will be [R]blessed, because they cannot repay you; for you shall be repaid at the resurrection of the just." [Matt. 25:34–40]

Parable of the Great Supper

15 Now when one of those who sat at the table with Him heard these things, he said to Him, [R]"Blessed *is* he who shall eat bread* in the kingdom of God!" Rev. 19:9

16 Then He said to him, "A certain man gave a great supper and invited many,

17 "and [R]sent his servant at supper time to say to those who were invited, 'Come, for all things are now ready.' Prov. 9:2, 5

18 "But they all with one *accord* began to make excuses. The first said to him, 'I have bought a piece of ground, and I must go and see it. I ask you to have me excused.'

19 "And another said, 'I have bought five yoke of oxen, and I am going to test them. I ask you to have me excused.'

20 "Still another said, 'I have married a wife, and therefore I cannot come.'

21 "So that servant came and reported these things to his master. Then the master of the house, being angry, said to his servant, 'Go out quickly into the streets and lanes of the city, and bring in here *the* poor and *the* [T]maimed and *the* lame and *the* blind.' *crippled*

22 "And the servant said, 'Master, it is done as you commanded, and still there is room.'

23 "Then the master said to the servant, 'Go out into the highways and hedges, and compel *them* to come in, that my house may be filled.

24 'For I say to you that none of those men who were invited shall taste my supper.' "

Christ Teaches on Discipleship

25 Now great multitudes went with Him. And He turned and said to them,

26 "If anyone comes to Me and does not hate his father and mother, wife and children, brothers and sisters, yes, and his own life also, he cannot be My disciple.

27 "And whoever does not bear his cross and come after Me cannot be My disciple.

28 "For which of you, intending to build a tower, does not sit down first and count the cost, whether he has *enough* to finish *it*—

29 "lest, after he has laid the foundation, and is not able to finish, all who see *it* begin to mock him,

30 "saying, 'This man began to build and was not able to finish.'

31 "Or what king, going to make war against another king, does not sit down first and consider whether he is able with ten thousand to meet him who comes against him with twenty thousand?

32 "Or else, while the other is still a great

13:35 NU, M omit *assuredly* • Ps. 118:26 **14:3** NU adds *or not* **14:5** NU, M *son* **14:15** M *dinner*

way off, he sends a delegation and asks conditions of peace.

33 "So likewise, whoever of you [R]does not forsake all that he has cannot be My disciple. Matt. 19:27

34 [R]"Salt *is* good; but if the salt has lost its flavor, how shall it be seasoned? [Mark 9:50]

35 "It is neither fit for the land nor for the [T]dunghill, *but* men throw it out. He who has ears to hear, let him hear!" *rubbish heap*

CHAPTER 15

Parable of the Lost Sheep—Matt. 18:12–14

THEN all the tax collectors and the sinners drew near to Him to hear Him.

2 And the Pharisees and scribes complained, saying, "This Man [T]receives sinners [R]and eats with them." *welcomes* • Gal. 2:12

3 So He spoke this parable to them, saying:

4 "What man of you, having a hundred sheep, if he loses one of them, does not leave the ninety-nine in the wilderness, and go after the one which is lost until he finds it?

5 "And when he has found *it,* he lays *it* on his shoulders, rejoicing.

6 "And when he comes home, he calls together *his* friends and neighbors, saying to them, [R]'Rejoice with me, for I have found my sheep which was lost!' [Rom. 12:15]

7 "I say to you that likewise there will be more joy in heaven over one sinner who repents [R]than over ninety-nine [T]just persons who need no repentance. [Luke 5:32] • *upright*

Parable of the Lost Coin

8 "Or what woman, having ten silver coins,* if she loses one coin, does not light a lamp, sweep the house, and search carefully until she finds *it?*

9 "And when she has found *it,* she calls *her* friends and neighbors together, saying, 'Rejoice with me, for I have found the piece which I lost!'

10 "Likewise, I say to you, there is joy in the presence of the angels of God over one sinner who repents."

Parable of the Lost Son

11 Then He said: "A certain man had two sons.

12 "And the younger of them said to *his* father, 'Father, give me the portion of goods that falls *to me.*' So he divided to them [R]*his* livelihood. Mark 12:44

13 "And not many days after, the younger son gathered all together, journeyed to a far country, and there wasted his possessions with [T]prodigal living. *wasteful*

14 "But when he had spent all, there arose a severe famine in that land, and he began to be in want.

15 "Then he went and joined himself to a citizen of that country, and he sent him into his fields to feed swine.

16 "And he would gladly have filled his stomach with the [T]pods that the swine ate, and no one gave him *anything.* *carob pods*

17 "But when he came to himself, he said, 'How many of my father's hired servants have bread enough and to spare, and I perish with hunger!

18 'I will arise and go to my father, and will say to him, "Father, [R]I have sinned against heaven and before you, 2 Sam. 12:13

19 "and I am no longer worthy to be called your son. Make me like one of your hired servants." '

20 "And he arose and came to his father. But when he was still a great way off, his father saw him and had compassion, and ran and fell on his neck and kissed him.

21 "And the son said to him, 'Father, I have sinned against heaven [R]and in your sight, and am no longer worthy to be called your son.' Ps. 51:4

22 "But the father said to his servants, 'Bring* out the best robe and put *it* on him, and put a ring on his hand and sandals on *his* feet.

23 'And bring the fatted calf here and kill *it,* and let us eat and be merry;

24 [R]'for this my son was dead and is alive again; he was lost and is found.' And they began to be merry. Luke 9:60; 15:32

25 "Now his older son was in the field. And as he came and drew near to the house, he heard music and dancing.

26 "So he called one of the servants and asked what these things meant.

27 "And he said to him, 'Your brother has come, and because he has received him safe and sound, your father has killed the fatted calf.'

28 "But he was angry and would not go in. Therefore his father came out and pleaded with him.

29 "So he answered and said to *his* father, 'Lo, these many years I have been serving you; I never transgressed your commandment at any time; and yet you never gave me a young goat, that I might make merry with my friends.

30 'But as soon as this son of yours came, who has devoured your livelihood with harlots, you killed the fatted calf for him.'

31 "And he said to him, 'Son, you are always with me, and all that I have is yours.

32 'It was right that we should make merry and be glad, for your brother was dead and is alive again, and was lost and is found.' "

15:8 Gr. *drachma,* a valuable coin often worn in a ten-piece garland by married women **15:22** NU *Quickly bring*

CHAPTER 16

Parable of the Unjust Servant

HE also said to His disciples: "There was a
certain rich man who had a steward, and
an accusation was brought to him that this
man was wasting his goods.
2 "So he called him and said to him, 'What
is this I hear about you? Give an [R]account of
your stewardship, for you can no longer be
steward.' [Rom. 14:12]
3 "Then the steward said within himself,
'What shall I do? For my master is taking the
stewardship away from me. I cannot dig; I am
ashamed to beg.
4 'I have resolved what to do, that when I
am put out of the stewardship, they may re-
ceive me into their houses.'
5 "So he called every one of his master's
debtors to *him,* and said to the first, 'How
much do you owe my master?'
6 "And he said, 'A hundred measures* of
oil.' So he said to him, 'Take your bill, and sit
down quickly and write fifty.'
7 "Then he said to another, 'And how much
do you owe?' So he said, 'A hundred mea-
sures* of wheat.' And he said to him, 'Take
your bill, and write eighty.'
8 "So the master commended the unjust
steward because he had dealt shrewdly. For
the sons of this world are more shrewd in
their generation than the sons of light.
9 "And I say to you, [R]make friends for your-
selves by unrighteous mammon, that when
you fail,* they may receive you into an ever-
lasting home. Dan. 4:27
10 "He who *is* faithful in *what is* least is
faithful also in much; and he who is unjust in
what is least is unjust also in much.
11 "Therefore if you have not been faithful in
the unrighteous mammon, who will commit to
your trust the true *riches*?
12 "And if you have not been faithful in what
is another man's, who will give you what is
your [R]own? [1 Pet. 1:3, 4]
13 [R]"No servant can serve two masters; for
either he will hate the one and love the other,
or else he will be loyal to the one and despise
the other. You cannot serve God and mam-
mon." Matt. 6:24

Christ Warns the Pharisees

14 Now the Pharisees, [R]who were lovers of
money, also heard all these things, and they
derided Him. Matt. 23:14
15 And He said to them, "You are those who
justify yourselves before men, but [R]God
knows your hearts. For [R]what is highly es-
teemed among men is an abomination in the
sight of God. Ps. 7:9 • 1 Sam. 16:7
16 [R]"The law and the prophets *were* until
John. Since that time the kingdom of God has
been preached, and everyone is pressing into
it. Matt. 3:1–12; 4:17; 11:12, 13
17 [R]"And it is easier for heaven and earth to
pass away than for one [T]tittle of the law to
fail. Is. 40:8; 51:6 • The smallest stroke in a Heb. letter

Christ Teaches on Divorce

18 [R]"Whoever divorces his wife and marries
another commits adultery; and whoever mar-
ries her who is divorced from *her* husband
commits adultery. 1 Cor. 7:10, 11

Parable of the Rich Man and Lazarus

19 "There was a certain rich man who was
clothed in purple and fine linen and [T]fared
sumptuously every day. *lived in luxury*
20 "But there was a certain beggar named
Lazarus, full of sores, who was laid at his gate,
21 "desiring to be fed with the crumbs which
fell* from the rich man's table. Moreover the
dogs came and licked his sores.
22 "So it was that the beggar died, and was
carried by the angels to Abraham's bosom.
The rich man also died and was buried.
23 "And being in torments in Hades, he lifted
up his eyes and saw Abraham afar off, and
Lazarus in his bosom.
24 "Then he cried and said, 'Father Abra-
ham, have mercy on me, and send Lazarus
that he may dip the tip of his finger in water
and [R]cool my tongue; for I [R]am tormented in
this flame.' Zech. 14:12 • [Mark 9:42–48]
25 "But Abraham said, 'Son, remember that
in your lifetime you received your good
things, and likewise Lazarus evil things; but
now he is comforted and you are tormented.
26 'And besides all this, between us and you
there is a great gulf fixed, so that those who
want to pass from here to you cannot, nor can
those from there pass to us.'
27 "Then he said, 'I beg you therefore, father,
that you would send him to my father's house,
28 'for I have five brothers, that he may tes-
tify to them, lest they also come to this place
of torment.'
29 "Abraham said to him, 'They have Moses
and the prophets; let them hear them.'
30 "And he said, 'No, father Abraham; but if
one goes to them from the dead, they will re-
pent.'
31 "But he said to him, [R]'If they do not hear
Moses and the prophets, [R]neither will they
be persuaded though one rise from the
dead.' " [John 5:46] • John 12:10, 11

CHAPTER 17

Christ Teaches on Offenses

THEN He said to the disciples, [R]"It is im-
possible that no [T]offenses should come,

16:6 Gr. *batos,* same as Heb. *bath;* 8 or 9 gallons each **16:7** Gr. *koros,* same as Heb. *kor;* 10 or 12 bushels each **16:9** NU *it fails* **16:21** NU *with what fell*

but [R]woe *to him* through whom they do
come! [1 Cor. 11:19] • *stumbling blocks* • [2 Thess. 1:6]
2 "It would be better for him if a millstone
were hung around his neck, and he were
thrown into the sea, than that he should of-
fend one of these little ones.
3 "Take heed to yourselves. If your brother
sins against you,* [R]rebuke him; and if he re-
pents, forgive him. [Prov. 17:10]
4 "And if he sins against you seven times in
a day, and seven times in a day returns to
you,* saying, 'I repent,' you shall forgive him."
5 **And the apostles said to the Lord, "In-
crease our faith."**
6 **So the Lord said,** "If you have faith as a
mustard seed, you can say to this mulberry
tree, 'Be pulled up by the roots and be planted
in the sea,' and it would obey you.
7 "And which of you, having a servant
plowing or tending sheep, will say to him
when he has come in from the field, 'Come at
once and sit down to eat'?
8 "But will he not rather say to him, 'Prepare
something for my supper, and gird yourself
[R]and serve me till I have eaten and drunk, and
afterward you will eat and drink'? [Luke 12:37]
9 "Does he thank that servant because he
did the things that were commanded him? I
think not.*
10 "So likewise you, when you have done all
those things which you are commanded, say,
'We are [R]unprofitable servants. We have done
what was our duty to do.'" Rom. 3:12

Christ Cleanses Ten Lepers

11 **Now it happened [R]as He went to Jerusa-
lem that He passed through the midst of Sa-
maria and Galilee.** Luke 9:51, 52
12 **Then as He entered a certain village,
there met Him ten men who were lepers, [R]who
stood afar off.** Lev. 13:46
13 **And they lifted up *their* voices and said,
"Jesus, Master, have mercy on us!"**
14 **So when He saw *them,* He said to them,**
"Go, show yourselves to the priests." **And so it
was that as they went, they were cleansed.**
15 **And one of them, when he saw that he
was healed, returned, and with a loud voice
[R]glorified God,** Luke 5:25; 18:43
16 **and fell down on *his* face at His feet, giv-
ing Him thanks. And he was a Samaritan.**
17 **So Jesus answered and said,** "Were there
not ten cleansed? But where *are* the nine?
18 "Were there not any found who returned
to give glory to God except this foreigner?"
19 **And He said to him,** "Arise, go your way.
Your faith has made you well."

Christ Teaches on the Second Coming

20 **Now when He was asked by the Pharisees
when the kingdom of God would come, He
answered them and said,** "The kingdom of
God does not come with observation;
21 [R]"nor will they say, 'See here!' or 'See
there!'* For indeed, [R]the kingdom of God is
within you." Luke 17:23 • [Rom. 14:17]
22 **Then He said to the disciples,** [R]"The days
will come when you will desire to see one of
the days of the Son of Man, and you will not
see *it.* Matt. 9:15
23 [R]"And they will say to you, 'Look here!' or
'Look there!'* Do not go after *them* or follow
them. Matt. 24:23
24 [R]"For as the lightning that flashes out of
one *part* under heaven shines to the other
part under heaven, so also the Son of Man
will be in His day. Matt. 24:27
25 "But first He must suffer many things and
be rejected by this generation.
26 [R]"And as it [R]was in the [R]days of Noah,
so it will be also in the days of the Son of
Man: Matt. 24:37–39 • [Gen. 6:5–7] • [Gen. 6:8–13]
27 "They ate, they drank, they married
wives, they were given in marriage, until the
day that Noah entered the ark, and the flood
came and destroyed them all.
28 [R]"Likewise as it was also in the days of
Lot: They ate, they drank, they bought, they
sold, they planted, they built; Gen. 19
29 "but on the day that Lot went out of
Sodom it rained fire and brimstone from
heaven and destroyed *them* all.
30 "Even so will it be in the day when the
Son of Man [R]is revealed. [2 Thess. 1:7]
31 "In that day, he [R]who is on the housetop,
and his [T]goods *are* in the house, let him not
come down to take them away. And likewise
the one who is in the field, let him not turn
back. Mark 13:15 • *possessions*
32 [R]"Remember Lot's wife. Gen. 19:26
33 "Whoever seeks to save his life will lose
it, and whoever loses his life will preserve it.
34 [R]"I tell you, in that night there will be two
men in one bed: the one will be taken and the
other will be left. [1 Thess. 4:17]
35 "Two *women* will be grinding together:
the one will be taken and the other left.
36 "Two *men* will be in the field: the one will
be taken and the other left."*
37 **And they answered and said to Him,**
[R]"Where, Lord?" **So He said to them,** "Wher-
ever the body is, there the eagles will be gath-
ered together." Matt. 24:28

CHAPTER 18

Parable of the Woman and the Judge

**THEN He spoke a parable to them, that
men [R]always ought to pray and not lose
heart,** Luke 11:5–10

17:3 NU omits *against you* **17:4** M omits *to you*
17:9 NU ends verse with *commanded;* M omits *him*
17:21 NU reverses *here* and *there* **17:23** NU reverses
here and *there* **17:36** NU, M omit v. 36.

2 saying: "There was in a certain city a
judge who did not fear God nor regard man.
3 "Now there was a widow in that city; and
she came to him, saying, [T]'Get justice for me
from my adversary.' *Avenge me on*
4 "And he would not for a while; but after-
ward he said within himself, 'Though I do not
fear God nor regard man,
5 [R]'yet because this widow troubles me I
will [T]avenge her, lest by her continual coming
she weary me.' " Luke 11:8 • *vindicate*
6 Then the Lord said, "Hear what the unjust
judge said.
7 "And [R]shall God not avenge His own elect
who cry out day and night to Him, though He
bears long with them? Rev. 6:10
8 "I tell you [R]that He will avenge them speed-
ily. Nevertheless, when the Son of Man comes,
will He really find faith on the earth?" Heb. 10:37

Parable of the Pharisee and the Tax Collector

9 Also He spoke this parable to some [R]who
trusted in themselves that they were righ-
teous, and despised others: Luke 10:29
10 "Two men went up to the temple to pray,
one a Pharisee and the other a tax collector.
11 "The Pharisee stood and prayed thus with
himself, 'God, I thank You that I am not like
other men—extortioners, unjust, adulterers,
or even as this tax collector.
12 'I fast twice a week; I give tithes of all that
I possess.'
13 "And the tax collector, standing afar off,
would not so much as raise *his* eyes to heaven,
but beat his breast, saying, 'God, be merciful
to me a sinner!'
14 "I tell you, this man went down to his
house justified *rather* than the other; [R]for
everyone who exalts himself will be [T]hum-
bled, and he who humbles himself will be ex-
alted." Luke 14:11 • *put down*

Christ Blesses the Children
Matt. 19:13–15; Mark 10:13–16

15 Then they also brought infants to Him
that He might touch them; but when the disci-
ples saw *it*, they rebuked them.
16 But Jesus called them to *Him* and said,
"Let the little children come to Me, and do not
forbid them; for [R]of such is the kingdom of
God. 1 Pet. 2:2
17 [R]"Assuredly, I say to you, whoever does
not receive the kingdom of God as a little
child will by no means enter it." Mark 10:15

Rich Young Ruler
Matt. 19:16–26; Mark 10:17–27

18 [R]Now a certain ruler asked Him, saying,
"Good Teacher, what shall I do to inherit eter-
nal life?" Matt. 19:16–29
19 So Jesus said to him, "Why do you call
Me good? No one *is* good but [R]One, *that is*,
God. Ps. 86:5; 119:68
20 "You know the commandments: *'Do not*
commit adultery,' 'Do not murder,' 'Do not
steal,' 'Do not bear false witness,' 'Honor your
father and your mother.' "*
21 And he said, "All [R]these things I have kept
from my youth." Phil. 3:6
22 So when Jesus heard these things, He
said to him, "You still lack one thing. [R]Sell all
that you have and distribute to the poor, and
you will have treasure in heaven; and come,
follow Me." Matt. 6:19, 20; 19:21
23 But when he heard this, he became very
sorrowful, for he was very rich.
24 And when Jesus saw that he became very
sorrowful, He said, [R]"How hard it is for those
who have riches to enter the kingdom of
God! Mark 10:23
25 "For it is easier for a camel to go through
the eye of a needle than for a rich man to
enter the kingdom of God."
26 And those who heard it said, "Who then
can be saved?"
27 But He said, "The things which are im-
possible with men are possible with God."

Christ Will Reward Sacrifice
Matt. 19:27–29; Mark 10:28–30

28 [R]Then Peter said, "See, we have left all*
and followed You." Matt. 19:27
29 So He said to them, "Assuredly, I say to
you, [R]there is no one who has left house or
parents or brothers or wife or children, for the
sake of the kingdom of God, Deut. 33:9
30 [R]"who shall not receive many times more
in this present time, and in the age to come
eternal life." Job 42:10

Christ Foretells His Death and Resurrection
Matt. 20:17–19; Mark 10:32–34

31 [R]Then He took the twelve aside and said
to them, "Behold, we are going up to Jerusa-
lem, and all things [R]that are written by the
prophets concerning the Son of Man will be
accomplished. Matt. 16:21; 17:22; 20:17 • Ps. 22
32 "For [R]He will be delivered to the Gentiles
and will be mocked and insulted and spit
upon. Luke 23:1, 11, 36; Mark 15:19☆
33 [R]"They will scourge *Him* and kill
Him. And the third day He will rise
again." Luke 23:46; 24:46; John 19:1☆
34 [R]But they understood none of these
things; this saying was hidden from them, and
they did not know the things which were spo-
ken. Luke 2:50; 9:45

Christ Heals Bartimaeus
Matt. 20:29–34; Mark 10:46–52

35 [R]Then it happened, as He was coming
near Jericho, that a certain blind man sat by
the road begging. Matt. 20:29–34

18:20 Ex. 20:12–16; Deut. 5:16–20 **18:28** NU *our own*

36 And hearing a multitude passing by, he asked what it meant.

37 So they told him that Jesus of Nazareth was passing by.

38 And he cried out, saying, "Jesus, [R]Son of David, have mercy on me!" Matt. 9:27

39 Then those who went before warned him that he should be quiet; but he cried out all the more, "Son of David, have mercy on me!"

40 So Jesus stood still and commanded him to be brought to Him. And when he had come near, He asked him,

41 saying, "What do you want Me to do for you?" He said, "Lord, that I may receive my sight."

42 Then Jesus said to him, "Receive your sight; your faith has made you well."

43 And immediately he received his sight, and followed Him, [R]glorifying God. And all the people, when they saw *it*, gave praise to God. Luke 5:26

CHAPTER 19

Christ Abides with Zacchaeus

THEN *Jesus* entered and passed through [R]Jericho. Josh. 6:26

2 Now behold, *there was* a man named Zacchaeus who was a chief tax collector, and he was rich.

3 And he sought to [R]see who Jesus was, but could not because of the crowd, for he was of short stature. John 12:21

4 So he ran ahead and climbed up into a sycamore tree to see Him, for He was going to pass that *way*.

5 And when Jesus came to the place, He looked up and saw him,* and said to him, "Zacchaeus, [T]make haste and come down, for today I must stay at your house." *hurry*

6 So he [T]made haste and came down, and received Him joyfully. *hurried*

7 But when they saw *it*, they all complained, saying, [R]"He has gone to be a guest with a man who is a sinner." Luke 5:30; 15:2

8 Then Zacchaeus stood and said to the Lord, "Look, Lord, I give half of my goods to the [R]poor; and if I have taken anything from anyone by [R]false accusation, [R]I restore fourfold." [Ps. 41:1] • Luke 3:14 • Ex. 22:1

9 And Jesus said to him, "Today salvation has come to this house, because [R]he also is [R]a son of Abraham; [Gal. 3:7] • [Luke 13:16]

10 "for the Son of Man has come to seek and to save that which was lost."

Christ Gives the Parable of the Ten Minas

11 Now as they heard these things, He spoke another parable, because He was near Jerusalem and because they thought the kingdom of God would appear immediately.

12 [R]Therefore He said: "A certain nobleman went into a far country to receive for himself a kingdom and to return. Matt. 25:14–30

13 "So he called ten of his servants, delivered to them ten minas,* and said to them, 'Do business till I come.'

14 [R]"But his citizens hated him, and sent a delegation after him, saying, 'We will not have this *man* to reign over us.' [John 1:11]

15 "And so it was that when he returned, having received the kingdom, he then commanded these servants, to whom he had given the money, to be called to him, that he might know how much every man had gained by trading.

16 "Then came the first, saying, 'Master, your mina has earned ten minas.'

17 "And he said to him, 'Well *done*, good servant; because you were faithful in a very little, have authority over ten cities.'

18 "And the second came, saying, 'Master, your mina has earned five minas.'

19 "Likewise he said to him, 'You also be over five cities.'

20 "Then another came, saying, 'Master, here is your mina, which I have kept put away in a handkerchief.

21 'For I feared you, because you are an austere man. You collect what you did not deposit, and reap what you did not sow.'

22 "And he said to him, [R]'Out of your own mouth I will judge you, *you* wicked servant. [R]You knew that I was an austere man, collecting what I did not deposit and reaping what I did not sow. Job 15:6 • Matt. 25:26

23 'Why then did you not put my money in the bank, that at my coming I might have collected it with interest?'

24 "And he said to those who stood by, 'Take the mina from him, and give *it* to him who has ten minas.'

25 ("But they said to him, 'Master, he has ten minas.')

26 'For I say to you, [R]that to everyone who has will be given; and from him who does not have, even what he has will be taken away from him. Luke 8:18

27 'But bring here those enemies of mine, who did not want me to reign over them, and slay *them* before me.' "

The Triumphal Entry
Matt. 21:1–9; Mark 11:1–10; John 12:12–19

28 When He had said this, [R]He went on ahead, going up to Jerusalem. Mark 10:32

29 And it came to pass, when He drew near to Bethphage* and [R]Bethany, at the mountain called [R]Olivet, *that* He sent two of His disciples, John 12:1 • Acts 1:12

30 saying, "Go into the village opposite *you*,

19:5 NU omits *and saw him* **19:13** Gr. *mna*, same as Heb. *minah*, each worth about three months' salary **19:29** M *Bethsphage*

where as you enter you will find a colt tied, on
which no one has ever sat. Loose it and bring
it here.
31 "And if anyone asks you, 'Why are you
loosing *it?*' thus you shall say to him, 'Be-
cause the Lord has need of it.' "
32 So those who were sent went their way
and found *it* just as He had said to them.
33 But as they were loosing the colt, the
owners of it said to them, "Why are you loos-
ing the colt?"
34 And they said, "The Lord has need of him."
35 Then they brought him to Jesus. [R]And
they threw their own clothes on the colt, and
they set Jesus on him. 2 Kin. 9:13
36 And as He went, *many* spread their
clothes on the road.
37 Then, as He was now drawing near the
descent of the Mount of Olives, the whole
multitude of the disciples began to [R]rejoice
and praise God with a loud voice for all the
mighty works they had seen, Luke 13:17
38 saying:

" 'Blessed is the King who comes in the
name of the L*ORD*!' *
[R]*Peace in heaven and glory in the*
highest!" [Eph. 2:14]

39 And some of the Pharisees called to Him
from the crowd, "Teacher, rebuke Your disci-
ples."
40 But He answered and said to them, "I tell
you that if these should keep silent, the stones
would immediately cry out."
41 Now as He drew near, He saw the city and
[R]wept over it, John 11:35
42 saying, "If you had known, even you,
especially in this [R]your day, the things *that*
make for your [R]peace! But now they are hid-
den from your eyes. Heb. 3:13 • [Rom. 5:1]
43 "For days will come upon you when your
enemies will [R]build an embankment around
you, surround you and close you in on every
side, Jer. 6:3, 6
44 [R]"and level you, and your children
within you, to the ground; and [R]they will not
leave in you one stone upon another, [R]be-
cause you did not know the time of your vis-
itation." 1 Kin. 9:7, 8 • Matt. 24:2 • [1 Pet. 2:12]

Cleansing the Temple
Matt. 21:12, 13; Mark 11:15–17

45 [R]Then He went into the temple and
began to drive out those who bought and sold
in it,* Mal. 3:1★; Mark 11:11, 15–17
46 saying to them, "It is written, *'My house*
is a house of prayer,'* but you have made it
a *'den of thieves.'* "*
47 And He [R]was teaching daily in the tem-
ple. But [R]the chief priests, the scribes, and
the leaders of the people sought to destroy
Him, Luke 21:37; 22:53 • John 7:19; 8:37
48 and were unable to do anything; for all
the people were very attentive to hear Him.

CHAPTER 20

Religious Leaders Question Christ's
Authority—Matt. 21:23–27; Mark 11:27–33

NOW [R]it happened on one of those days, as
He taught the people in the temple and
preached the gospel, *that* the chief priests
and the scribes, together with the elders, con-
fronted *Him* Matt. 21:23–27
2 and spoke to Him, saying, "Tell us, by
what authority are You doing these things? Or
who is he who gave You this authority?"
3 But He answered and said to them, "I also
will ask you one thing, and answer Me:
4 "The [R]baptism of John—was it from
heaven or from men?" John 1:26, 31
5 And they reasoned among themselves,
saying, "If we say, 'From heaven,' He will say,
'Why then* did you not believe him?'
6 "But if we say, 'From men,' all the people
will stone us, [R]for they are persuaded that
John was a prophet." Luke 7:24–30
7 So they answered that they did not know
where *it was* from.
8 And Jesus said to them, "Neither will I tell
you by what authority I do these things."

Parable of the Vineyard Owner
Matt. 21:33–44; Mark 12:1–11

9 Then He began to tell the people this
parable: [R]"A certain man planted a vineyard,
leased it to vinedressers, and went into a far
country for a long time. Mark 12:1–12
10 "Now at [T]vintage-time he [R]sent a servant
to the vinedressers, that they might give him
some of the fruit of the vineyard. But the vine-
dressers beat him and sent *him* away empty-
handed. Lit. *the season* • [1 Thess. 2:15]
11 "Again he sent another servant; and they
beat him also, treated *him* shamefully, and
sent *him* away empty-handed.
12 "And again he sent a third; and they
wounded him also and cast *him* out.
13 "Then the owner of the vineyard said,
'What shall I do? I will send my beloved son.
Probably they will respect *him* when they see
him.'
14 "But when the vinedressers saw him, they
reasoned among themselves, saying, 'This is
the [R]heir. Come, let us kill him, that the inher-
itance may be ours.' [Heb. 1:1–3]
15 "So they cast him out of the vineyard and
killed *him.* Therefore what will the owner of
the vineyard do to them?
16 "He will come and destroy those vine-
dressers and give the vineyard to [R]others."

19:38 Ps. 118:26★ **19:45** NU *those who were selling,* **19:46** NU *shall be* • Is. 56:7 • Jer. 7:11 **20:5** NU, M omit *then*

And when they heard *it* they said, "Certainly
not!" Rom. 11:1, 11
17 Then He looked at them and said, "What
then is this that is written:

'The stone which the builders rejected
*Has become the chief cornerstone'?**

18 "Whoever falls on that stone will be [R]bro-
ken; but on whomever it falls, it will grind him
to powder." Is. 8:14, 15

Herodians Question Tribute Money
Matt. 21:45, 46; 22:15–22; Mark 12:12–17

19 And the chief priests and the scribes that
very hour sought to lay hands on Him, but
they feared the people*—for they knew He
had spoken this parable against them.
20 [R]So they watched *Him*, and sent spies
who pretended to be righteous, that they
might seize on His words, in order to deliver
Him to the power and the authority of the
governor. Matt. 22:15
21 Then they asked Him, saying, [R]"Teacher,
we know that You say and teach rightly, and
You do not show personal favoritism, but
teach the way of God in truth: Mark 12:14
22 "Is it lawful for us to pay taxes to Caesar
or not?"
23 But He perceived their craftiness, and
said to them, "Why do you test Me?*
24 "Show Me a denarius. Whose image and
inscription does it have?" They answered and
said, "Caesar's."
25 And He said to them, "Render therefore
to Caesar the things that are Caesar's, and to
God the things that are God's."
26 But they could not catch Him in His
words in the presence of the people. And they
marveled at His answer and kept silent.

Sadducees Question Resurrection
Matt. 22:23–32; Mark 12:18–27

27 [R]Then some of the Sadducees, who deny
that there is a resurrection, came to *Him* and
asked Him, Mark 12:18–27
28 saying: "Teacher, Moses wrote to us *that*
if a man's brother dies, having a wife, and he
dies without children, his brother should take
his wife and raise up offspring for his brother.
29 "Now there were seven brothers. And the
first took a wife, and died without children.
30 "And the second* took her as wife, and he
died childless.
31 "Then the third took her, and in like man-
ner the seven also; and they left no children,*
and died.
32 "Last of all the woman died also.
33 "Therefore, in the resurrection, whose
wife does she become? For all seven had her
as wife."
34 Jesus answered and said to them, "The
sons of this age marry and are given in mar-
riage.
35 "But those who are [R]counted worthy to at-
tain that age, and the resurrection from the
dead, neither marry nor are given in mar-
riage; Phil. 3:11
36 "nor can they die anymore, for they are
equal to the angels and are sons of God, [R]be-
ing sons of the resurrection. Rom. 8:23
37 "But even Moses showed in the *burning*
bush *passage* that the dead are raised, when
he called the Lord *'the God of Abraham, the*
God of Isaac, and the God of Jacob.' *
38 "For He is not the God of the dead but of
the living, for all live to Him."

Christ Questions the Scribes
Matt. 22:41—23:14; Mark 12:35–40

39 Then some of the scribes answered and
said, "Teacher, You have spoken well."
40 But after that they dared not question
Him anymore.
41 And He said to them, "How can they say
that the Christ is the Son of David?
42 "Now David himself said in the Book of
Psalms:

'The LORD *said to my Lord,*
"Sit at My right hand,
43 *Till I make Your enemies Your*
*footstool."'**

44 "Therefore David calls Him *'Lord'*; [R]how
is He then his Son?" Rom. 1:3; 9:4, 5
45 [R]Then, in the hearing of all the people, He
said to His disciples, Matt. 23:1–7
46 "Beware of the scribes, who desire to go
around in long robes, love greetings in the
marketplaces, the best seats in the syna-
gogues, and the best places at feasts,
47 [R]"who devour widows' houses, and for a
pretense make long prayers. These will re-
ceive greater condemnation." Matt. 23:14

CHAPTER 21

Christ Teaches on the Widow's Mites
Mark 12:41–44

AND He looked up and saw the rich put-
ting their gifts into the treasury,
2 and He saw also a certain poor widow
putting in two [R]mites. Mark 12:42
3 So He said, "Truly I say to you that this
poor widow has put in more than all;
4 "for all these out of their abundance have
put in offerings for God,* but she out of her
poverty put in [R]all the livelihood that she
had." [2 Cor. 8:12]

20:17 Ps. 118:22★ **20:19** M *but they were afraid* **20:23** NU omits *Why do you test Me?* **20:30** NU omits the rest of v. 30. **20:31** NU, M *the seven also left no children* **20:37** Ex. 3:6, 15 **20:43** Ps. 110:1☆ **21:4** NU omits *for God*

The Disciples' Two Questions
Matt. 24:1–3; Mark 13:1–4

5 [R]Then, as some spoke of the temple, how
it was [T]adorned with beautiful stones and
donations, He said, Mark 13:1 • *decorated*
6 "These things which you see—the days
will come in which [R]not *one* stone shall be
left upon another that shall not be thrown
down." Luke 19:41–44
7 So they asked Him, saying, "Teacher, but
when will these things be? And what sign *will
there be* when these things are about to take
place?"

Signs of Christ's Coming
Matt. 24:4–13; Mark 13:5–13

8 And He said: [R]"Take heed that you not be
deceived. For many will come in My name, say-
ing, 'I am *He,*' and, 'The time has drawn near.'
Therefore* do not [T]go after them. Eph. 5:6 • *follow*
9 "But when you hear of [R]wars and commo-
tions, do not be terrified; for these things must
come to pass first, but the end *will not come*
immediately." Rev. 6:4
10 [R]Then He said to them, "Nation will rise
against nation, and kingdom against king-
dom. Matt. 24:7
11 "And there will be great [R]earthquakes in
various places, and famines and pestilences;
and there will be fearful sights and great
signs from heaven. Rev. 6:12
12 [R]"But before all these things, they will lay
their hands on you and persecute *you,* deliv-
ering *you* up to the synagogues and prisons.
You will be brought before kings and rulers
for My name's sake. [Rev. 2:10]
13 "But [R]it will turn out for you as an occa-
sion for testimony. [Phil. 1:12–14, 28]
14 [R]"Therefore settle *it* in your hearts not to
meditate beforehand on what you will [T]an-
swer; Luke 12:11 • *say in defense*
15 "for I will give you a mouth and wisdom
[R]which all your adversaries will not be able to
contradict or [T]resist. Acts 6:10 • *withstand*
16 [R]"You will be betrayed even by parents
and brothers, relatives and friends; and they
will put *some* of you to death. Mic. 7:6
17 "And [R]you will be hated by all for My
name's sake. Matt. 10:22
18 [R]"But not a hair of your head shall be
lost. Matt. 10:30
19 "By your patience possess your souls.

Destruction of Jerusalem
Matt. 24:15–21; Mark 13:14–19

20 [R]"But when you see Jerusalem sur-
rounded by armies, then know that its desola-
tion is near. Mark 13:14
21 "Then let those who are in Judea flee to
the mountains, let those who are in the midst
of her depart, and let not those who are in the
country enter her.
22 "For these are the days of vengeance,
that [R]all things which are written may be ful-
filled. [Dan. 9:24–27]
23 "But woe to those who are pregnant and
to those who are nursing babies in those days!
For there will be great distress in the land and
wrath upon this people.
24 "And they will fall by the edge of the
sword, and be led away captive into all na-
tions. And Jerusalem will be trampled by
Gentiles [R]until the times of the Gentiles are
fulfilled. [Dan. 9:27; 12:7]

The Second Coming
Matt. 24:29–31; Mark 13:24–27

25 [R]"And there will be signs in the sun, in the
moon, and in the stars; and on the earth dis-
tress of nations, with perplexity, the sea and
the waves roaring; [2 Pet. 3:10–12]
26 "men's hearts failing them from fear and
the expectation of those things which are
coming on the earth, [R]for the powers of the
heavens will be shaken. Matt. 24:29
27 "Then they will see the Son of Man
[R]coming in a cloud with power and great
glory. Rev. 1:7; 14:14
28 "Now when these things begin to happen,
look up and lift up your heads, because your
redemption draws near."

Parable of the Fig Tree
Matt. 24:32–35; Mark 13:28–31

29 Then He spoke to them a parable: "Look
at the fig tree, and all the trees.
30 "When they are already budding, you see
and know for yourselves that summer is now
near.
31 "So you also, when you see these things
happening, know that the kingdom of God is
near.
32 "Assuredly, I say to you, this generation
will by no means pass away till all things take
place.
33 "Heaven and earth will pass away, but My
words will by no means pass away.

Warning to Watch for His Coming
Matt. 24:36–44; Mark 13:32–37

34 "But take heed to yourselves, lest your
hearts be weighed down with carousing,
drunkenness, and cares of this life, and that
Day come on you unexpectedly.
35 "For it will come as a snare on all those
who dwell on the face of the whole earth.
36 "Watch therefore, and pray always that
you may be counted [R]worthy* to escape all
these things that will come to pass, and to
stand before the Son of Man." Luke 20:35
37 And in the daytime He was teaching in

21:8 NU omits *Therefore* **21:36** NU *may have strength* the temple, but at night He went out and stayed on the mountain called Olivet.

38 Then early in the morning all the people came to Him in the temple to hear Him.

CHAPTER 22

Judas Agrees to Betray Christ
Matt. 26:1–5, 14–16; Mark 14:1, 2, 10, 11

NOW the Feast of Unleavened Bread drew near, which is called Passover.

2 And [R]the chief priests and the scribes sought how they might kill Him, for they feared the people. John 11:47

3 [R]Then Satan entered Judas, surnamed Iscariot, who was numbered among the [R]twelve. Mark 14:10, 11 • Matt. 10:2–4

4 So he went his way and conferred with the chief priests and captains, how he might betray Him to them.

5 And they were glad, and [R]agreed to give him money. Zech. 11:12

6 So he promised and sought opportunity to [R]betray Him to them in the absence of the multitude. Ps. 41:9

The Upper Room Is Prepared
Matt. 26:17–19; Mark 14:12–16

7 Then came the Day of Unleavened Bread, when the Passover must be killed.

8 And He sent Peter and John, saying, "Go and prepare the Passover for us, that we may eat."

9 So they said to Him, "Where do You want us to prepare?"

10 And He said to them, "Behold, when you have entered the city, a man will meet you carrying a pitcher of water; follow him into the house which he enters.

11 "Then you shall say to the master of the house, 'The Teacher says to you, "Where is the guest room where I may eat the Passover with My disciples?" '

12 "Then he will show you a large, furnished upper room; there make ready."

13 So they went and [R]found it just as He had said to them, and they prepared the Passover. Luke 19:32

The Passover Is Celebrated
Matt. 26:20, 29; Mark 14:17, 25

14 When the hour had come, He sat down, and the twelve* apostles with Him.

15 Then He said to them, "With *fervent* desire I have desired to eat this Passover with you before I suffer;

16 "for I say to you, I will no longer eat of it until it is fulfilled in the kingdom of God."

17 Then He took the cup, and gave thanks, and said, "Take this and divide *it* among yourselves;

18 "for [R]I say to you,* I will not drink of the fruit of the vine until the kingdom of God comes." Mark 14:25

The Lord's Supper Is Instituted
Matt. 26:26–28; Mark 14:22–24

19 [R]And He took bread, gave thanks and broke *it*, and gave *it* to them, saying, "This is My [R]body which is given for you; do this in remembrance of Me." Matt. 26:26 • [1 Pet. 2:24]

20 Likewise He also *took* the cup after supper, saying, "This cup *is* the new covenant in My blood, which is shed for you.

Christ Predicts His Betrayer
Matt. 26:21–25; Mark 14:18–21; John 13:21–26

21 [R]"But behold, the hand of My betrayer *is* with Me on the table. Ps. 41:9☆

22 [R]"And truly the Son of Man goes as it has been determined, but woe to that man by whom He is betrayed!" Matt. 26:24

23 [R]Then they began to question among themselves, which of them it was who would do this thing. John 13:22, 25

The Disciples Argue over
Who Is the Greatest

24 [R]Now there was also a dispute among them, as to which of them should be considered the greatest. Mark 9:34

25 [R]And He said to them, "The kings of the Gentiles exercise lordship over them, and those who exercise authority over them are called 'benefactors.' Mark 10:42–45

26 [R]"But not so *among* you; on the contrary, [R]he who is greatest among you, let him be as the younger, and he who governs as he who serves. [1 Pet. 5:3] • Luke 9:48

27 [R]"For who *is* greater, he who sits at the table, or he who serves? *Is* it not he who sits at the table? Yet [R]I am among you as the One who serves. [Luke 12:37] • Phil. 2:7

28 "But you are those who have continued with Me in [R]My trials. [Heb. 2:18; 4:15]

29 "And I bestow upon you a kingdom, just as My Father bestowed *one* upon Me,

30 "that you may eat and drink at My table in My kingdom, and sit on thrones judging the twelve tribes of Israel."

Christ Predicts Peter's Denial
Matt. 26:31–35; Mark 14:27–31; John 13:36–38

31 And the Lord said,* "Simon, Simon! Indeed, [R]Satan has asked for you, that he may [R]sift *you* as wheat. 1 Pet. 5:8 • Amos 9:9

32 "But I have prayed for you, that your faith should not fail; and when you have returned to *Me*, strengthen your brethren."

33 But he said to Him, "Lord, I am ready to go with You, both to prison and to death."

34 Then He said, "I tell you, Peter, the rooster

22:14 NU omits *twelve* **22:18** NU adds *from now on*
22:31 NU omits *And the Lord said*

shall not crow this day before you will deny
three times that you know Me."

Christ Predicts Coming Conflict

35 [R]And He said to them, "When I sent you
without money bag, knapsack, and sandals,
did you lack anything?" So they said, "Noth-
ing." Matt. 10:9
36 Then He said to them, "But now, he who
has a money bag, let him take *it*, and likewise
a knapsack; and he who has no sword, let him
sell his garment and buy one.
37 "For I say to you that this which is written
must still be accomplished in Me: *'And He
was numbered with the transgressors.'** For
the things concerning Me have an end."
38 So they said, "Lord, look, here *are* two
swords." And He said to them, "It is enough."

Christ Prays in Gethsemane
Matt. 26:36–46; Mark 14:32–42; John 18:1

39 [R]Coming out, He went to the Mount of
Olives, as He was accustomed, and His disci-
ples also followed Him. John 18:1
40 [R]When He came to the place, He said to
them, "Pray that you may not enter into temp-
tation." Mark 14:32–42
41 [R]And He was withdrawn from them about
a stone's throw, and He knelt down and
prayed, Matt. 26:39
42 saying, "Father, if it is Your will, take this
cup away from Me; nevertheless [R]not My will,
but Yours, be done." Is. 50:5★
43 Then [R]an angel appeared to Him from
heaven, strengthening Him. Matt. 4:11
44 And being in agony, He prayed more
earnestly. Then His sweat became like great
drops of blood falling down to the ground.*
45 When He rose up from prayer, and had
come to His disciples, He found them sleeping
from sorrow.
46 Then He said to them, "Why [R]do you
sleep? Rise and [R]pray, lest you enter into
temptation." Luke 9:32 • Luke 22:40

Judas Betrays Christ
Matt. 26:47–56; Mark 14:43–50; John 18:2–11

47 And while He was still speaking, behold,
a multitude; and he who was called Judas, one
of the twelve, went before them and drew
near to Jesus to kiss Him.
48 But Jesus said to him, "Judas, are you be-
traying the Son of Man with a kiss?"
49 When those around Him saw what was
going to happen, they said to Him, "Lord,
shall we strike with the sword?"
50 And one of them struck the servant of the
high priest and cut off his right ear.
51 But Jesus answered and said, "Permit
even this." And He touched his ear and healed
him.
52 Then Jesus said to the chief priests, cap-
tains of the temple, and the elders who had
come to Him, "Have you come out, as against
a robber, with swords and clubs?
53 "When I was with you daily in the temple,
you did not try to seize Me. But this is your
hour, and the power of darkness."

Peter Denies Christ
Matt. 26:57, 58, 69–75; Mark 14:53, 54, 66–72; John 18:15–18, 25–27

54 Having arrested Him, they led *Him* and
brought Him into the high priest's house. But
Peter followed at a distance.
55 Now when they had kindled a fire in the
midst of the courtyard and sat down together,
Peter sat among them.
56 And a certain servant girl, seeing him as
he sat by the fire, looked intently at him and
said, "This man was also with Him."
57 But he denied Him,* saying, "Woman, I do
not know Him."
58 [R]And after a little while another saw him
and said, "You also are of them." But Peter
said, "Man, I am not!" John 18:25
59 [R]Then after about an hour had passed, an-
other confidently affirmed, saying, "Surely
this *fellow* also was with Him, for he is a [R]Gal-
ilean." Mark 14:70 • Acts 1:11; 2:7
60 But Peter said, "Man, I do not know
what you are saying!" [R]Immediately, while
he was still speaking, the rooster*
crowed. Luke 22:34; John 13:38★
61 And the Lord turned and looked at Peter.
Then [R]Peter remembered the word of the
Lord, how He had said to him, [R]"Before the
rooster crows,* you will deny Me three
times." Matt. 26:75 • John 13:38
62 So Peter went out and wept bitterly.

Christ Is Beaten—Matt. 26:67, 68; Mark 14:65

63 [R]Now the men who held Jesus mocked
Him and beat Him. Ps. 69:19; Is. 50:6; 52:14★
64 And having blindfolded Him, they
[R]struck Him on the face and asked Him,* say-
ing, "Prophesy! Who is the one who struck
You?" Zech. 13:7
65 [R]And many other things they blasphe-
mously spoke against Him. Is. 53:3★

The Sanhedrin Tries Christ
Matt. 27:1; Mark 15:1

66 [R]As soon as it was day, [R]the elders of the
people, both chief priests and scribes, came
together and led Him into their council, say-
ing, Matt. 27:1 • Acts 4:26
67 [R]"If You are the Christ, tell us." But He
said to them, "If I tell you, you will [R]by no
means believe. Matt. 26:63–66 • Luke 20:5–7

22:37 Is. 53:12☆ **22:44** NU brackets vv. 43 and 44 as not in the original text. **22:57** NU *denied it*
22:60 NU, M *a rooster* **22:61** NU adds *today*
22:64 NU *And having blindfolded Him, they asked Him*

68 "And if I also ask *you*, you will by no
means answer Me or let *Me* go.*
69 "Hereafter the Son of Man will sit on the
right hand of the power of God."
70 Then they all said, "Are You then the Son
of God?" So He said to them, [R]"You *rightly* say
that I am." Luke 1:35★
71 [R]And they said, "What further testimony
do we need? For we have heard it ourselves
from His own mouth." Mark 14:63

CHAPTER 23

Pilate Tries Christ
Matt. 27:2, 11–14; Mark 15:1–5; John 18:28–38

THEN [R]the whole multitude of them arose
and led Him to Pilate. Luke 18:32★
2 And they began to accuse Him, saying,
"We found this *fellow* perverting the* nation,
and forbidding to pay taxes to Caesar, saying
that He Himself is Christ, a King."
3 [R]Then Pilate asked Him, saying, "Are You
the King of the Jews?" He answered him and
said, "*It is as* you say." 1 Tim. 6:13
4 So Pilate said to the chief priests and the
crowd, "I find no fault in this Man."
5 But they were the more fierce, saying,
"He stirs up the people, teaching throughout
all Judea, beginning from [R]Galilee to this
place." John 7:41
6 When Pilate heard of Galilee,* he asked if
the Man were a Galilean.
7 And as soon as he knew that He belonged
to [R]Herod's jurisdiction, he sent Him to
Herod, who was also in Jerusalem at that
time. Luke 3:1; 9:7; 13:31

Herod Tries Christ

8 Now when Herod saw Jesus, [R]he was ex-
ceedingly glad; for he had desired for a long
time to see Him, because he had heard many
things about Him, and he hoped to see some
miracle done by Him. Luke 9:9
9 Then he questioned Him with many
words, but He answered him nothing.
10 And the chief priests and scribes stood
and vehemently accused Him.
11 [R]Then Herod, with his [T]men of war,
treated Him with contempt and mocked *Him*,
arrayed Him in a gorgeous robe, and sent Him
back to Pilate. Ps. 69:19; Is. 53:3★ • *troops*
12 That very day Pilate and Herod became
friends with each other, for previously they
had been at enmity with each other.

Pilate Tries Christ Again
Matt. 27:15–26; Mark 15:6–15; John 18:39—19:16

13 [R]Then Pilate, when he had called to-
gether the chief priests, the rulers, and the
people, Mark 15:14
14 said to them, [R]"You have brought this
Man to me, as one who misleads the people.
And indeed, [R]having examined *Him* in your
presence, I have found no fault in this Man
concerning those things of which you accuse
Him; Luke 23:1, 2 • Luke 23:4
15 "no, neither did Herod, for I sent you back
to him;* and indeed nothing deserving of
death has been done by Him.
16 [R]"I will therefore chastise Him and re-
lease *Him*" John 19:1
17 [R](for it was necessary for him to release
one to them at the feast).* John 18:39
18 And [R]they all cried out at once, saying,
"Away with this *Man*, and release to us Barab-
bas"— Is. 53:3; Acts 3:13–15★
19 who had been thrown into prison for a
certain rebellion made in the city, and for
murder.
20 Pilate, therefore, wishing to release Jesus,
again called out to them.
21 But they shouted, saying, "Crucify *Him*,
crucify Him!"
22 Then he said to them the third time, "Why,
what evil has He done? I have found no rea-
son for death in Him. I will therefore chastise
Him and let *Him* go."
23 But they were insistent, demanding with
loud voices that He be crucified. And the
voices of these men and of the chief priests
prevailed.*
24 So [R]Pilate gave sentence that it should be
as they requested. Mark 15:15
25 [R]And he released to them* the one they
requested, who for rebellion and murder had
been thrown into prison; but he delivered Je-
sus to their will. Is. 53:8

Christ Is Crucified
Matt. 27:31–56; Mark 15:20–41; John 19:16–30

26 [R]Now as they led Him away, they laid
hold of a certain man, Simon a Cyrenian, who
was coming from the country, and on him
they laid the cross that he might bear *it* after
Jesus. Matt. 27:32
27 And a great multitude of the people fol-
lowed Him, and women who also mourned
and lamented Him.
28 But Jesus, turning to them, said, "Daugh-
ters of Jerusalem, do not weep for Me, but
weep for yourselves and for your children.
29 [R]"For indeed the days are coming in
which they will say, 'Blessed *are* the barren,
wombs that never bore, and breasts which
never nursed!' Matt. 24:19
30 "Then they will begin [R]'*to say to the
mountains, "Fall on us!" and to the hills,
"Cover us!"*'* Rev. 6:16, 17; 9:6

22:68 NU omits *also* and *Me or let Me go*. **23:2** NU *our* **23:6** NU omits *of Galilee* **23:15** NU *he sent Him back to us* **23:17** NU omits v. 17. **23:23** NU omits *and of the chief priests* **23:25** NU, M omit *to them* **23:30** Hos. 10:8

31 "For if they do these things in the green wood, what will be done in the dry?"

32 [R]There were also two others, criminals, led with Him to be put to death. Is. 53:9, 12

33 And [R]when they had come to the place called Calvary, there they [R]crucified Him, and the criminals, one on the right hand and the other on the left. John 19:17–24 • Ps. 22:16–18★

34 Then Jesus said, "Father, forgive them, for they do not know what they do."* And they divided His garments and cast lots.

35 And [R]the people stood looking on. But even the rulers with them sneered, saying, "He saved others; let Him save Himself if He is the Christ, the chosen of God." Ps. 22:7, 8★

36 The soldiers also mocked Him, coming and offering Him [R]sour wine, Ps. 69:21

37 and saying, "If You are the King of the Jews, save Yourself."

38 [R]And an inscription also was written over Him in letters of Greek, Latin, and Hebrew:* John 19:19

THIS IS THE KING OF THE JEWS.

39 Then one of the criminals who were hanged blasphemed Him, [R]saying, "If You are the Christ,* save Yourself and us." Ps. 22:8★

40 But the other, answering, rebuked him, saying, "Do you not even fear God, seeing you are under the same condemnation?

41 "And we indeed justly, for we receive the due reward of our deeds; but this Man has done [R]nothing wrong." [Heb. 7:26]

42 Then he said to Jesus, "Lord,* remember me when You come into Your kingdom."

43 And Jesus said to him, "Assuredly, I say to you, today you will be with Me in [R]Paradise." [Rev. 2:7]

44 [R]Now it was* about the sixth hour, and there was darkness over all the earth until the ninth hour. Amos 8:9★

45 Then the sun was darkened,* and the veil of the temple was torn in two.

46 And when Jesus had cried out with a loud voice, He said, *"Father, 'into Your hands I commit My spirit.'* "* [R]Having said this, He breathed His last. Matt. 17:23★

47 So when the centurion saw what had happened, he glorified God, saying, "Certainly this was a righteous Man!"

48 And the whole crowd who came together to that sight, seeing what had been done, beat their breasts and returned.

49 But all His acquaintances, and the women who followed Him from Galilee, stood at a distance, watching these things.

Christ Is Buried
Matt. 27:57–61; Mark 15:42–47; John 19:38–42

50 [R]Now behold, *there was* a man named Joseph, a council member, a good and just man. Matt. 27:57–61

51 He had not consented to their decision and deed. *He was* from Arimathea, a city of the Jews, [R]who himself was also waiting* for the kingdom of God. Luke 2:25, 38

52 [R]This man went to Pilate and asked for the body of Jesus. Is. 53:9★

53 [R]Then he took it down, wrapped it in linen, and laid it in a tomb *that was* hewn out of the rock, where no one had ever lain before. Matt. 26:12; Mark 14:8★

54 That day was [R]the Preparation, and the Sabbath drew near. Matt. 27:62

55 And the women [R]who had come with Him from Galilee followed after, and [R]they observed the tomb and how His body was laid. Luke 8:2 • Mark 15:47

In the Grave

56 Then they returned and [R]prepared spices and fragrant oils. And they rested on the Sabbath [R]according to the commandment. Mark 16:1 • Ex. 20:10

CHAPTER 24

The Resurrection
Matt. 28:1–8; Mark 16:1–8; John 20:1–10

NOW [R]on the first *day* of the week, very early in the morning, they, and certain *other women* with them,* came to the tomb [R]bringing the spices which they had prepared. John 20:1–8 • Luke 23:56

2 [R]But they found the stone rolled away from the tomb. Mark 16:4

3 [R]Then they went in and did not find the body of the Lord Jesus. Mark 16:5

4 And it happened, as they were greatly* perplexed about this, that behold, two men stood by them in shining garments.

5 Then, as they were afraid and bowed *their* faces to the earth, they said to them, "Why do you seek the living among the dead?

6 "He is not here, but is risen! [R]Remember how He spoke to you when He was still in Galilee, Matt. 16:21; Mark 8:31; Luke 9:22★

7 "saying, 'The Son of Man must be delivered into the hands of sinful men, and be crucified, and the third day rise again.' "

8 And they remembered His words.

9 [R]Then they returned from the tomb and told all these things to the eleven and to all the rest. Mark 16:10

10 It was Mary Magdalene, [R]Joanna, Mary *the mother* of James, and the other *women* with them, who told these things to the apostles. Luke 8:3

23:34 NU brackets the first sentence as a later addition. **23:38** NU omits *written* and *in letters of Greek, Latin, and Hebrew* **23:39** NU *Are You not the Christ?* **23:42** NU *And he said, "Jesus, remember me* **23:44** NU adds *already* **23:45** NU *obscured* **23:46** Ps. 31:5 **23:51** NU *who was waiting* **24:1** NU omits *and certain other women with them* **24:4** NU omits *greatly*

11 And their words seemed to them like idle
tales, and they did not believe them.
12 But Peter arose and ran to the tomb; and
stooping down, he saw the linen cloths lying*
by themselves; and he departed, marveling to
himself at what had happened.

Christ Appears on the Road to Emmaus *Mark 16:12, 13*

13 Now behold, two of them were traveling
that same day to a village called Emmaus,
which was seven miles* from Jerusalem.
14 And they talked together of all these
things which had happened.
15 So it was, while they conversed and rea-
soned, that [R]Jesus Himself drew near and
went with them. [Matt. 18:20]
16 But [R]their eyes were restrained, so that
they did not know Him. John 20:14; 21:4
17 And He said to them, "What kind of con-
versation *is* this that you have with one an-
other as you walk and are sad?"*
18 Then the one [R]whose name was Cleopas
answered and said to Him, "Are You the only
stranger in Jerusalem, and have You not
known the things which happened there in
these days?" John 19:25
19 And He said to them, "What things?" So
they said to Him, "The things concerning Je-
sus of Nazareth, [R]who was a Prophet [R]mighty
in deed and word before God and all the peo-
ple, Matt. 21:11 • Acts 7:22
20 [R]"and how the chief priests and our rulers
delivered Him to be condemned to death, and
crucified Him. Acts 13:27, 28
21 "But we were hoping [R]that it was He who
was going to redeem Israel. Indeed, besides
all this, today is the third day since these
things happened. Luke 1:68; 2:38
22 "Yes, and [R]certain women of our com-
pany, who arrived at the tomb early, aston-
ished us. Mark 16:10
23 "When they did not find His body, they
came saying that they had also seen a vision
of angels who said He was alive.
24 "And certain of those *who were* with us
went to the tomb and found *it* just as the
women had said; but Him they did not see."
25 Then He said to them, "O foolish ones,
and slow of heart to believe in all that the
prophets have spoken!
26 "Ought not the Christ to have suffered
these things and to enter into His glory?"
27 And beginning at Moses and all the
Prophets, He expounded to them in all the
Scriptures the things concerning Himself.
28 Then they drew near to the village where
they were going, and [R]He indicated that He
would have gone farther. Mark 6:48
29 But [R]they constrained Him, saying,
[R]"Abide with us, for it is toward evening, and
the day is far spent." And He went in to stay
with them. Gen. 19:2, 3 • [John 14:23]
30 Now it came to pass, as He sat at the table
with them, that He took bread, blessed and
broke *it,* and gave it to them.
31 Then their eyes were opened and they
knew Him; and He vanished from their sight.
32 And they said to one another, "Did not
our heart burn within us while He talked with
us on the road, and while He opened the
Scriptures to us?"

The Proof of His Resurrection *Mark 16:4; John 20:19–23; 1 Cor. 15:5*

33 So they rose up that very hour and re-
turned to Jerusalem, and found the eleven and
those *who were* with them gathered together,
34 saying, "The Lord is risen indeed, and
[R]has appeared to Simon!" 1 Cor. 15:5
35 And they told about the things *that had
happened* on the road, and how He was
known to them in the breaking of bread.
36 [R]Now as they said these things, Jesus
Himself stood in the midst of them, and said
to them, "Peace to you." Mark 16:14
37 But they were terrified and frightened,
and supposed they had seen a spirit
38 And He said to them, "Why are you trou-
bled? And why do doubts arise in your hearts?
39 "Behold My hands and My feet, that it is
I Myself. [R]Handle Me and see, for a [R]spirit
does not have flesh and bones as you see I
have." John 20:20, 27 • [1 Cor. 15:50]
40 When He had said this, He showed them
His hands and His feet.*
41 But while they still did not believe [R]for
joy, and marveled, He said to them, [R]"Have
you any food here?" Gen. 45:26 • John 21:5
42 So they gave Him a piece of a broiled fish
and some honeycomb.*
43 [R]And He took *it* and ate in their pres-
ence. Acts 10:39–41

The Great Commission—Acts 1:3–8

44 Then He said to them, [R]"These *are* the
words which I spoke to you while I was still
with you, that all things must be fulfilled
which were written in the Law of Moses and
the Prophets and *the* Psalms concerning
Me." Matt. 16:21; 17:22; 20:18
45 And He opened their understanding, that
they might comprehend the Scriptures.
46 Then He said to them, [R]"Thus it is written,
and thus it was necessary for the Christ to
suffer and to rise* from the dead the third
day, Hos. 6:1, 2; Acts 17:3★
47 "and that repentance and remission of

24:12 NU omits *lying* **24:13** Lit. *60 stadia* **24:17** NU *walk? And they stood still, looking sad.* **24:40** Some printed New Testaments omit v. 40. It is found in nearly all Gr. mss. **24:42** NU omits *and some honeycomb* **24:46** NU *written, that the Christ should suffer and rise*

sins should be preached in His name [R]to all nations, beginning at Jerusalem. [Jer. 31:34]

48 "And you are witnesses of these things.

The Ascension—Mark 16:19; Acts 1:9

49 [R]"Behold, I send the Promise of My Father upon you; but tarry in the city of Jerusalem* until you are endued with power from on high." Is. 44:3; Joel 2:28; Acts 2:4☆

50 And He led them out [R]as far as Bethany, and He lifted up His hands and blessed them. Acts 1:12

51 [R]Now it came to pass, while He blessed them, that He was parted from them and carried up into heaven. Ps. 68:18; 110:1★

52 [R]And they worshiped Him, and returned to Jerusalem with great joy, Matt. 28:9

53 and were continually in the temple praising and* blessing God. Amen.*

24:49 NU omits *of Jerusalem* **24:53** NU omits *praising and* • NU omits *Amen.*

THE GOSPEL ACCORDING TO

JOHN

THE BOOK OF JOHN

Just as a coin has two sides, both valid, so Jesus Christ has two natures, both valid. Luke presents Christ in His humanity as the Son of Man; John portrays Him in His deity as the Son of God. John's purpose is crystal clear: to set forth Christ in His deity in order to spark believing faith in his readers. John's gospel is topical, not primarily chronological, and it revolves around seven miracles and seven "I am" statements of Christ.

Following an extended eyewitness description of the Upper Room meal and Discourse, John records events leading up to the Resurrection, the final climactic proof that Jesus is who He claims to be—the Son of God.

The title of the Fourth Gospel follows the same format as the titles of the synoptic Gospels: *Kata Ioannen,* "According to John." As with the others, the word "Gospel" was later added *Ioannes* is derived from the Hebrew name *Johanan,* "Yahweh Has Been Gracious."

THE AUTHOR OF JOHN

Jesus nicknamed John and his brother, James, "Sons of Thunder" (Mark 3:17). Their father was Zebedee; and their mother Salome, served Jesus in Galilee and was present at His crucifixion (Mark 15:40, 41). John was evidently among the Galileans who followed John the Baptist until they were called to follow Jesus at the outset of His public ministry (1:19–51). These Galileans were later called to become full-time disciples of the Lord (Luke 5:1–11), and John was among the twelve men who were selected to be apostles (Luke 6:12–16). After Christ's ascension, John became one of the "pillars" of the church in Jerusalem along with James and Peter (Gal. 2:9). He is mentioned three times by name in Acts (3:1; 4:13; 8:14), each time in association with Peter. Tradition says that John later went to Ephesus (perhaps just before the destruction of Jerusalem). He was eventually exiled by the Romans for a time to the island of Patmos (Rev. 1:9).

The author of this gospel is identified only as the disciple "whom Jesus loved" (13:23; 19:26; 20:2; 21:7, 20). His knowledge of Palestinian geography and Jewish customs makes it clear that he was a Palestinian Jew, and his meticulous attention to numbers (2:6; 6:13, 19; 21:8, 11) and names (1:45; 3:1; 11:1; 18:10) indicates that he was an eyewitness. This fits his own claim to be a witness of the events he described (1:14; 19:35; 21:24, 25). The disciple "whom Jesus loved" was part of the inner circle of disciples and was closely associated with Peter. The synoptic Gospels name this inner circle as Peter, James, and John. Since Peter is separate from the beloved disciple, only James and John are left. James was martyred too early to be the author (Acts 12:1, 2), so the apostle John was the author of this gospel. This conclusion from internal evidence is consistent with the external testimony of the early church. Irenaeus (c. A.D. 185) was a disciple of Polycarp who was in turn a disciple of the apostle John. In his *Against Heresies,* Irenaeus bore witness to Johannine authorship of this gospel and noted that John lived until the time of the emperor Trajan (A.D. 98–117). Clement of Alexandria, Theophilus of Antioch, Origen, and others also ascribe this book to John.

THE TIME OF JOHN

In spite of the strong internal and external testimony supporting Johannine authorship of this gospel, theological assumptions have motivated a number of critics to deny this claim. Until recently it was popular to propose a second-century date for this book. The discovery of the John Rylands Papyrus 52 containing portions of John 18:31–33, 37, 38 has overthrown this conjecture. This fragment has been dated at about A.D. 135, and a considerable period of time must have been required for John's gospel to be copied and circulated before it reached Egypt, where this papyrus was found.

On the other hand, John was written after the last of the synoptic Gospels (c. A.D. 66–68). His familiarity with the topography of Jerusalem (e.g., 5:2; 19:13) does not necessarily require a date before A.D. 70. Since John's three epistles and Revelation were written after his gospel, the probable range for this work is A.D. 60–90. By this time, John would have been one of the last surviving eyewitnesses of the Lord. According to tradition, John wrote this gospel in Ephesus.

THE CHRIST OF JOHN

This book presents the most powerful case in all the Bible for the deity of the incarnate Son of God. "A Man called Jesus" (9:11) is also "Christ, the Son of the living God" (6:69). The deity of Christ can be seen in His seven "I am" statements: "I am the bread of life" (6:35, 48); "I am the light of the world" (8:12; 9:5); "I am the door" (10:7, 9); "I am the good shepherd" (10:11, 14); "I am the resurrection and the life" (11:25); "I am the way, the truth, and the life" (14:6); "I am the true vine" (15:1–5). The seven signs (1—12) and the five witnesses (5:30–40) also point to His divine character. On certain occasions, Jesus equates Himself with the Old Testament "I AM," or Yahweh (see 4:25, 26; 8:24, 28, 58; 13:19; 18:5, 6, 8). Some of the most crucial affirmations of His deity are in 1:1; 8:58; 10:30; 14:9; 20:28.

"The Word was God" (1:1), but the Word also became flesh (1:14). The humanity of Jesus can be seen in His weariness (4:6), thirst (4:7), dependence (5:19), grief (11:35), troubled soul (12:27), and His anguish and death (19).

KEYS TO JOHN

Key Word: Believe That Jesus Is the Son of God—The fourth Gospel has the clearest statement of purpose in the Bible: "But these are written that you may believe that Jesus is the Christ, the Son of God, and that believing you may have life in His name" (20:31). John selected the signs he used for the specific purpose of creating intellectual ("that you may believe") and spiritual ("that believing you may have life") conviction about the Son of God. The key verb in John is "believe," and requires both knowledge (8:32; 10:38) and volition (1:12; 3:19; 7:17).

The predominant theme of this gospel is the dual response of faith and unbelief to the Person of Jesus Christ. Those who place their faith in the Son of God have eternal life, but those who reject Him are under the condemnation of God (3:36; 5:24–29; 10:27–29): this is the basic issue. John 1:11, 12 summarizes the responses of accepting or rejecting the Son of God that are traced through the rest of the book. The rejection of Jesus by His own people can be seen over and over in chapters 2 through 19 ("His own did not receive Him"), but John also lists a number of men and women who believed in Him ("But as many as received Him").

Key Verses: John 1:11–13 and John 20:30, 31—"He came to His own, and His own did not receive Him. But as many as received Him, to them He gave the right to become children of God, to those who believe in His name: who were born, not of blood, nor of the will of the flesh, nor of the will of man, but of God" (1:11–13).

"And truly Jesus did many other signs in the presence of His disciples, which are not written in this book; but these are written that you may believe that Jesus is the Christ, the Son of God, and that believing you may have life in His name" (20:30, 31).

Key Chapter: John 3—John 3:16 is without doubt the most quoted and preached verse in all of Scripture. Captured in it is the gospel in its clearest and simplest form: that salvation is a gift of God and is obtainable only through belief. The conversation with Nicodemus and the testimony of John the Baptist provide the setting that clearly points out that being "born again" is the only way to find the "kingdom of God."

SURVEY OF JOHN

This most unusual gospel, with its distinct content and style, serves as a supplement to the three Synoptics. It is easily the simplest and yet the most profound of the gospels, and for many people it is the greatest and most powerful. John writes his gospel for the specific purpose of bringing people to spiritual life through belief in the Person and work of Jesus Christ. The five basic sections of this gospel are: the incarnation of the Son of God (1:1–18); the presentation of the Son of God (1:19—4:54); the opposition to the Son of God (5:1—12:50); the preparation of the disciples by the Son of God (13:1—17:26); the crucifixion and resurrection of the Son of God (18:1—21:25).

FOCUS	INCARNATION OF THE SON OF GOD	PRESENTATION OF THE SON OF GOD	OPPOSITION TO THE SON OF GOD	PREPARATION OF THE DISCIPLES	CRUCIFIXION AND RESURRECTION OF THE SON OF GOD
REFERENCE	1:1——	1:19——	5:1——	13:1——	18:1——21:25
DIVISION	INTRODUCTION TO CHRIST	REVELATION OF CHRIST	REJECTION OF CHRIST	REVELATION OF CHRIST	REJECTION OF CHRIST
TOPIC	SEVEN MIRACLES			UPPER ROOM DISCOURSE	SUPREME MIRACLE
	"THAT YOU MIGHT BELIEVE"			"THAT YOU MIGHT HAVE LIFE"	
LOCATION	ISRAEL				
TIME	A FEW YEARS			A FEW HOURS	A FEW WEEKS

The Incarnation of the Son of God (1:1–18): This prologue introduces the rest of the book and gives the background for the historical narrative that follows. It dates the nature of Jesus, introduces His forerunner, clarifies His mission, and notes the rejection and acceptance He will find during His ministry.

The Presentation of the Son of God (1:19—4:54): In this section Christ is under careful consideration and scrutiny by Israel. He is introduced by John the Baptist who directs his own disciples to Christ. Shortly the author begins listing the seven signs, which continue through the next section. John carefully selects seven miracles out of the many that Christ accomplished (cf. John 21:25) in order to build a concise case for His deity. They are called signs because they symbolize the life-changing results of belief in Jesus—(1) water to wine: the ritual of law is replaced by the reality of grace (2:1–11); (2) healing the nobleman's son: the gospel brings spiritual restoration (4:46–54); (3) healing the paralytic: weakness is replaced by strength (5:1–16); (4) feeding the multitude: Christ satisfies spiritual hunger (6:1–13); (5) walking on water: the Lord transforms fear to faith (6:16–21); (6) sight to the man born blind: Jesus overcomes darkness and brings in light (9:1–7); (7) raising of Lazarus: the gospel brings people from death to life (11:1–44). These signs combine to show that Jesus is indeed the Son of God.

The Opposition to the Son of God (5:1—12:50): John's unusual pattern in these chapters is to record the reactions of belief and disbelief after the performance of one miracle before moving to the next. In a series of growing confrontations, John portrays the intense opposition that will culminate in the Lord's final rejection on the cross. Even though many people received Him, the inevitable crucifixion is foreshadowed in several places (2:4, 21, 22; 7:6, 39; 11:51, 52; 12:16).

The Preparation of the Disciples by the Son of God (13:1—17:26): John surveys the incarnation and public ministry of Jesus in twelve chapters, but radically changes the pace in the next five chapters to give a detailed account of a few crucial hours. In this clear and vivid recollection of Jesus' last discourse to His intimate disciples, John captures the Lord's words of comfort and assurance to a group of fearful and confused followers. Jesus knows that in less than twenty-four hours He will be on the cross. Therefore, His last words speak of all the resources that will be at the disciples' disposal after His departure. They will be indwelled and empowered by the triune Godhead. The Upper Room Discourse contains the message of the epistles in capsule form as it reveals God's pattern for Christian living. In it, the key themes of servanthood, the Holy Spirit, and abiding in Christ are developed.

The Crucifixion and Resurrection of the Son of God (18:1—21:25): After recording Christ's High Priestly Prayer on behalf of His disciples and all who believe in Him "through their word" (17:20), John immediately launches into a dramatic description of Christ's arrest and trials before Annas, Caiaphas, and Pilate. In His crucifixion, Jesus willingly fulfills John the Baptist's prophetic words: "Behold! The Lamb of God who takes away the sin of the world!" (1:29). John closes his profound gospel with a particularly detailed account of the post-resurrection appearances of the Lord. The Resurrection is the ultimate sign that points to Jesus as the Son of God.

OUTLINE OF JOHN

Part One: The Incarnation of the Son of God (1:1–18)

I. The Deity of Christ 1:1, 2

II. The Preincarnate Work of Christ 1:3–5

III. The Forerunner of Christ 1:6–8

IV. The Rejection of Christ 1:9–11

V. The Acceptance of Christ 1:12, 13

VI. The Incarnation of Christ 1:14–18

Part Two: The Presentation of the Son of God (1:19—4:54)

I. The Presentation of Christ by John the Baptist 1:19–34

A. John's Witness to the Priests and Levites 1:19–28
B. John's Witness at Christ's Baptism 1:29–34

II. The Presentation of Christ to John's Disciples 1:35–51

A. Andrew and Peter Follow Christ 1:35–42
B. Philip and Nathanael Follow Christ 1:43–51

III. The Presentation of Christ in Galilee 2:1–12

A. First Sign: Christ Changes Water to Wine 2:1–10
B. The Disciples Believe 2:11, 12

IV. The Presentation of Christ in Judea .... 2:13—3:36

A. Christ Cleanses the Temple 2:13–25
B. Christ Witnesses to Nicodemus 3:1–21

C. John the Baptist Witnesses Concerning Christ....................3:22–36

V. The Presentation of Christ in Samaria....................4:1–42

A. Christ Witnesses to the Woman at the Well....................4:1–26
B. Christ Witnesses to the Disciples........4:27–38
C. Christ Witnesses to the Samaritans....................4:39–42

VI. The Presentation of Christ in Galilee....................4:43–54

A. Christ Is Received by the Galileans....4:43–45
B. Second Sign: Christ Heals the Nobleman's Son....................4:46–54

Part Three: The Opposition to the Son of God (5:1—12:50)

I. The Opposition at the Feast in Jerusalem....................5:1–47

A. Third Sign: Christ Heals the Paralytic Man....................5:1–9
B. Jews Reject Christ....................5:10–47
1. Christ Heals on the Sabbath........5:10–16
2. Christ Claims Equality with God..5:17–30
3. Christ Lists Other Witnesses to His Person....................5:31–47

II. The Opposition During Passover Time in Galilee....................6:1–71

A. Fourth Sign: Christ Feeds 5,000............6:1–14
B. Fifth Sign: Christ Walks on the Water....................6:15–21
C. Christ Announces: "I Am the Bread of Life"....................6:22–71
1. To the Crowds....................6:22–40
2. To the Jews....................6:41–59
3. To the Disciples....................6:60–71

III. The Opposition at the Feast of Tabernacles in Jerusalem....................7:1—10:21

A. Before the Feast of Tabernacles..........7:1–13
1. Christ's Brothers Do Not Believe.......7:1–9
2. Christ Secretly Goes to the Feast....................7:10–13
B. In the Middle of the Feast of Tabernacles....................7:14–36
1. Christ's Authority from the Father....................7:14–24
2. Christ's Origin from the Father.....7:25–31
3. Christ's Departure to the Father...7:32–36
C. In the Last Day of the Feast of Tabernacles....................7:37–53
1. Christ Reveals the "Living Water" 7:37–39
2. Israel Is Divided over Christ..........7:40–44
3. The Sanhedrin Is Confused over Christ....................7:45–53
D. After the Feast of Tabernacles ....8:1—10:21
1. A Woman Is Caught in Adultery......8:1–11
2. Christ Announces, "I Am the Light of the World"....................8:12–59
3. Sixth Sign: Christ Heals the Blind Man....................9:1–41
4. Christ Announces, "I Am the Good Shepherd"....................10:1–21

IV. The Opposition at the Feast of Dedication in Jerusalem....................10:22–42

V. The Opposition at Bethany..........11:1—12:11

A. Seventh Sign: Christ Raises Lazarus..11:1–44
B. The Pharisees Plan to Kill Christ.....11:45–57
C. Mary Anoints Christ....................12:1–11

VI. The Opposition at Jerusalem............12:12–50

A. The Triumphal Entry....................12:12–22
B. The Messiah Teaches....................12:23–50

Part Four: The Preparation of the Disciples by the Son of God (13:1—17:26)

I. The Preparation in the Upper Room....................13:1—14:31

A. Christ Washes the Disciples' Feet 13:1–20
B. Christ Announces Judas, the Betrayer....................13:21–30
C. Christ Gives the Upper Room Discourse....................13:31—14:31
1. Christ Announces His Departure 13:31–35
2. Christ Foretells Peter's Denial.....13:36–38
3. Christ Comforts His Disciples..........14:1–4
4. Christ Answers Thomas....................14:5–7
5. Christ Answers Philip....................14:8–21
6. Christ Answers Judas....................14:22–31

II. The Preparation on the Way to the Garden....................15:1—17:26

A. Christ Instructs the Disciples.......15:1—16:33
1. The Relationship of Believers to Christ....................15:1–11
2. The Relationship of Believers to Each Other....................15:12–17
3. The Relationship of Believers to the World....................15:18–25
4. The Promise of the Holy Spirit....................15:26—16:15
5. The Predictions of Christ's Death and Resurrection....................16:16–33
B. Christ Intercedes with the Father.......17:1–26
1. Christ Prays for Himself....................17:1–5
2. Christ Prays for His Disciples.........17:6–19
3. Christ Prays for All Believers......17:20–26

Part Five: The Crucifixion and Resurrection of the Son of God (18:1—21:25)

CHAPTER 1

The Deity of Christ

IN the beginning [R]was the Word, and the
[R]Word was [R]with God, and the Word was
God. 1 John 1:1 • Rev. 19:13 • [John 17:5]
2 He was in the beginning with God.

The Preincarnate Work of Christ

3 [R]All things were made through Him, and
without Him nothing was made that was
made. [Col. 1:16, 17]
4 [R]In Him was life, and [R]the life was the
light of men. [1 John 5:11] • John 8:12; 9:5; 12:46
5 And the light shines in the darkness, and
the darkness did not comprehend* it.

The Forerunner of Christ

6 There was a [R]man sent from God, whose
name *was* John. Matt. 3:1–17
7 This man came for a [R]witness, to bear wit-
ness of the Light, that all through him might
believe. John 3:25–36; 5:33–35
8 He was not that Light, but *was sent* to
bear witness of that [R]Light. Is. 9:2; 49:6

The Rejection of Christ

9 That was the true Light which gives light
to every man coming into the world.*
10 He was in the world, and the world was
made through Him, and [R]the world did not
know Him. Heb. 1:2
11 [R]He came to His own,* and His own* did
not receive Him. [Luke 19:14]☆

The Acceptance of Christ

12 But as many as received Him, to them He
gave the right to become children of God, to
those who believe in His name:
13 [R]who were born, not of blood, nor of the
will of the flesh, nor of the will of man, but of
God. [1 Pet. 1:23]

The Incarnation of Christ

14 [R]And the Word became flesh and dwelt
among us, and [R]we beheld His glory, the glory
as of the only begotten of the Father, full of
grace and truth. Rev. 19:13 • Is. 40:5
15 [R]John bore witness of Him and cried out,
saying, "This was He of whom I said, 'He who
comes after me is preferred before me, for He
was before me.' " John 3:32
16 And* of His [R]fullness we have all re-
ceived, and grace for grace. [Col. 1:19; 2:9]
17 For [R]the law was given through Moses,
but [R]grace and [R]truth came through Jesus
Christ. [Ex. 20:1] • [Rom. 5:21; 6:14] • [John 8:32]
18 No one has seen God at any time. [R]The
only begotten Son,* who is in the bosom of
the Father, He has declared *Him*. Ps. 2:7★

John's Witness to the Priests and Levites
Matt. 3:1–12; Mark 1:2–8; Luke 3:3–16

19 Now this is the testimony of John, when
the Jews sent priests and Levites from Jerusa-
lem to ask him, "Who are you?"
20 [R]He confessed, and did not deny, but con-
fessed, "I am not the Christ." Luke 3:15
21 And they asked him, "What then? Are you
Elijah?" He said, "I am not." "Are you the
Prophet?" And he answered, "No."
22 Then they said to him, "Who are you, that
we may give an answer to those who sent us?
What do you say about yourself?"
23 He said: [R]"I *am* Matt. 3:3

'The voice of one crying in the
wilderness:
*"Make straight the way of the LORD," '**

1:5 Or *overcome* **1:9** Or *That was the true Light which, coming into the world, gives light to every man.* **1:11** That is, His own things or domain • That is, His own people **1:16** NU *For* **1:18** NU *only begotten God* **1:23** Is. 40:3★

as the prophet Isaiah said."
24 Now those who were sent were from the
Pharisees.
25 And they asked him, saying, "Why then
do you baptize if you are not the Christ, nor
Elijah, nor the Prophet?"
26 John answered them, saying, "I baptize
with water, [R]but there stands One among you
whom you do not know. Mal. 3:1
27 [R]"It is He who, coming after me, is pre-
ferred before me, whose sandal strap I am not
worthy to loose." Acts 19:4
28 These things were done [R]in Bethabara*
beyond the Jordan, where John was baptiz-
ing. Judg. 7:24

John's Witness at Christ's Baptism
Matt. 3:13–17; Mark 1:9–11; Luke 3:21, 22

29 The next day John saw Jesus coming to-
ward him, and said, "Behold! The Lamb of
God who takes away the sin of the world!
30 "This is He of whom I said, 'After me
comes a Man who [T]is preferred before me, for
He was before me.' *ranks higher than I*
31 "I did not know Him; but that He should
be revealed to Israel, [R]therefore I came bap-
tizing with water." Matt. 3:6
32 And John bore witness, saying, "I saw the
Spirit descending from heaven like a dove,
and He remained upon Him.
33 "I did not know Him, but He who sent me
to baptize with water said to me, 'Upon whom
you see [R]the Spirit descending, and remaining
on Him, [R]this is He who baptizes with the
Holy Spirit.' Is. 42:1; 61:1★ • Matt. 3:11
34 "And I have seen and testified that [R]this is
the [R]Son of God." Ps. 2:7; Luke 1:35★ • John 11:27

Andrew and Peter Follow Christ

35 Again, the next day, John stood with two
of his disciples.
36 And looking at Jesus as He walked, he
said, [R]"Behold the Lamb of God!" John 1:29
37 The two disciples heard him speak, and
they [R]followed Jesus. Matt. 4:20, 22
38 Then Jesus turned, and seeing them fol-
lowing, said to them, "What do you seek?"
They said to Him, "Rabbi" (which is to say,
when translated, Teacher), "where are You
staying?"
39 He said to them, "Come and see." They
came and saw where He was staying, and re-
mained with Him that day (now it was about
the tenth hour).
40 One of the two who heard John *speak*,
and followed Him, was [R]Andrew, Simon Pe-
ter's brother. Matt. 4:18
41 He first found his own brother Simon,
and said to him, "We have found the Messiah"
(which is translated, the Christ).
42 And he brought him to Jesus. Now when
Jesus looked at him, He said, "You are Simon
the son of Jonah.* [R]You shall be called Cephas"
(which is translated, A Stone). Matt. 16:18

Philip and Nathanael Follow Christ

43 The following day Jesus wanted to go to
Galilee, and He found [R]Philip and said to him,
"Follow Me." John 6:5; 12:21, 22; 14:8, 9
44 Now [R]Philip was from Bethsaida, the city
of Andrew and Peter. John 12:21
45 Philip found Nathanael and said to him,
"We have found Him of whom Moses in the
law, and also the prophets, wrote—Jesus of
Nazareth, the son of Joseph."
46 And Nathanael said to him, "Can any-
thing good come out of Nazareth?" Philip said
to him, "Come and see."
47 Jesus saw Nathanael coming toward Him,
and said of him, "Behold, [R]an Israelite indeed,
in whom is no deceit!" Ps. 32:2; 73:1
48 Nathanael said to Him, "How do You
know me?" Jesus answered and said to him,
"Before Philip called you, when you were
under the fig tree, I saw you."
49 Nathanael answered and said to Him,
"Rabbi, [R]You are the Son of God! You are [R]the
King of Israel!" Ps. 2:7★ • Matt. 21:5
50 Jesus answered and said to him, "Because
I said to you, 'I saw you under the fig tree,' do
you believe? You will see greater things than
these."
51 And He said to him, "Most assuredly, I say
to you, hereafter* you shall see heaven open,
and the angels of God ascending and de-
scending upon the Son of Man."

CHAPTER 2

Christ Changes Water to Wine

ON the third day there was a [R]wedding in
[R]Cana of Galilee, and the mother of Jesus
was there. [Heb. 13:4] • John 4:46
2 Now both Jesus and His disciples were in-
vited to the wedding.
3 And when they ran out of wine, the
mother of Jesus said to Him, "They have no
wine."
4 Jesus said to her, [R]"Woman, [R]what does
your concern have to do with Me? My hour
has not yet come." John 19:26 • 2 Sam. 16:10
5 His mother said to the servants, "What-
ever He says to you, do *it*."
6 Now there were set there six waterpots of
stone, [R]according to the manner of purifica-
tion of the Jews, containing twenty or thirty
gallons apiece. [Mark 7:3]
7 Jesus said to them, "Fill the waterpots with
water." And they filled them up to the brim.
8 And He said to them, "Draw *some* out
now, and take *it* to the master of the feast."
And they took it.

1:28 NU, M *Bethany* **1:42** NU *John* **1:51** NU omits *hereafter*

9 When the master of the feast had tasted the water that was made wine, and did not know where it came from (but the servants who had drawn the water knew), the master of the feast called the bridegroom.

10 And he said to him, "Every man at the beginning sets out the good wine, and when the *guests* have well drunk, then the inferior. You have kept the good wine until now!"

The Disciples Believe

11 This beginning of signs Jesus did in Cana of Galilee, and [T]manifested His glory; and His disciples believed in Him. *revealed*

12 After this He went down to Capernaum, He, His mother, His brothers, and His disciples; and they did not stay there many days.

Christ Cleanses the Temple

13 Now the Passover of the Jews was at hand, and Jesus went up to Jerusalem.

14 [R]And He found in the temple those who sold oxen and sheep and doves, and the money changers doing business. Mal. 3:1★

15 When He had made a whip of cords, He drove them all out of the temple, with the sheep and the oxen, and poured out the changers' money and overturned the tables.

16 And He said to those who sold doves, "Take these things away! Do not make My Father's house a house of merchandise!"

17 Then His disciples remembered that it was written, *"Zeal for Your house has eaten* Me up."**

18 So the Jews answered and said to Him, [R]"What sign do You show to us, since You do these things?" Matt. 12:38

19 Jesus answered and said to them, [R]"Destroy this temple, and in three days I will raise it up." Matt. 26:61; 27:40; Acts 10:40☆

20 Then the Jews said, "It has taken forty-six years to build this temple, and will You raise it up in three days?"

21 But He was speaking [R]of the temple of His body. [1 Cor. 3:16; 6:19]

22 Therefore, when He had risen from the dead, [R]His disciples remembered that He had said this to them;* and they believed the Scripture and the word which Jesus had said. Luke 24:8

23 Now when He was in Jerusalem at the Passover, during the feast, many believed in His name when they saw the [R]signs which He did. [Acts 2:22]

24 But Jesus did not commit Himself to them, because He [R]knew all *men,* Rev. 2:23

25 and had no need that anyone should testify of man, for [R]He knew what was in man. Matt. 9:4

CHAPTER 3

Christ Witnesses to Nicodemus

THERE was a man of the Pharisees named Nicodemus, a ruler of the Jews.

2 [R]This man came to Jesus by night and said to Him, "Rabbi, we know that You are a teacher come from God; for [R]no one can do these signs that You do unless [R]God is with him." John 7:50; 19:39 • John 9:16, 33 • [Acts 10:38]

3 Jesus answered and said to him, "Most assuredly, I say to you, unless one is born again, he cannot see the kingdom of God."

4 Nicodemus said to Him, "How can a man be born when he is old? Can he enter a second time into his mother's womb and be born?"

5 Jesus answered, "Most assuredly, I say to you, unless one is born of water and the Spirit, he cannot enter the kingdom of God.

6 "That which is born of the flesh is flesh, and that which is born of the Spirit is spirit.

7 "Do not marvel that I said to you, 'You must be born again.'

8 "The wind blows where it wishes, and you hear the sound of it, but cannot tell where it comes from and where it goes. So is everyone who is born of the Spirit."

9 Nicodemus answered and said to Him, [R]"How can these things be?" John 6:52, 60

10 Jesus answered and said to him, "Are you the teacher of Israel, and do not know these things?

11 "Most assuredly, I say to you, We speak what We know and testify what We have seen, and you do not receive Our witness.

12 "If I have told you earthly things and you do not believe, how will you believe if I tell you heavenly things?

13 [R]"No one has ascended to heaven but He who came down from heaven, *that is,* the Son of Man who is in heaven.* Eph. 4:9

14 [R]"And as Moses lifted up the serpent in the wilderness, even so [R]must the Son of Man be lifted up, Num. 21:9 • John 8:28; 12:34☆

15 "that whoever believes in Him should not perish but* have eternal life.

16 [R]"For God so loved the world that He gave His only begotten [R]Son, that whoever believes in Him should not perish but have everlasting life. Rom. 5:8 • [Is. 9:6]

17 "For God did not send His Son into the world to condemn the world, but [R]that the world through Him might be saved. Matt. 1:21☆

18 [R]"He who believes in Him is not condemned; but he who does not believe is condemned already, because he has not believed in the name of the only begotten Son of God. John 5:24; 6:40, 47; 20:31

19 "And this is the condemnation, [R]that the light has come into the world, and men loved darkness rather than light, because their deeds were evil. [John 1:4, 9–11]

20 "For [R]everyone practicing evil hates the

2:17 NU, M *will eat* • Ps. 69:9★ **2:22** NU, M omit *to them* **3:13** NU omits *who is in heaven* **3:15** NU omits *not perish but*

light and does not come to the light, lest his
deeds should be exposed. Eph. 5:11, 13
21 "But he who does the truth comes to the
light, that his deeds may be clearly seen, that
they have been done in God."

John the Baptist Witnesses Concerning Christ

22 After these things Jesus and His disciples
came into the land of Judea, and there He re-
mained with them and baptized.
23 Now John also was baptizing in Aenon
near Salim, because there was much water
there. And they came and were baptized.
24 For [R]John had not yet been thrown into
prison. Matt. 4:12; 14:3
25 Then there arose a dispute between *some*
of John's disciples and the Jews about purifi-
cation.
26 And they came to John and said to him,
"Rabbi, He who was with you beyond the
Jordan, [R]to whom you have testified—be-
hold, He is baptizing, and all [R]are coming to
Him!" John 1:7, 15, 27, 34 • Mark 2:2; 3:10; 5:24
27 John answered and said, [R]"A man can re-
ceive nothing unless it has been given to him
from heaven. 1 Cor. 3:5, 6; 4:7
28 "You yourselves bear me witness, that I
said, [R]'I am not the Christ,' but, [R]'I have been
sent before Him.' John 1:19–27 • Mal. 3:1
29 "He who has the bride is the bridegroom;
but [R]the friend of the bridegroom, who stands
and hears him, rejoices greatly because of the
bridegroom's voice. Therefore this joy of mine
is fulfilled. Song 5:1
30 [R]"He must increase, but I *must* de-
crease. [Is. 9:7]
31 [R]"He who comes from above is above all;
he who is of the earth is earthly and speaks of
the earth. He who comes from heaven is
above all. John 3:13; 8:23
32 "And [R]what He has seen and heard, that
He testifies; [R]and no one receives His testi-
mony. John 3:11; 15:15 • Is. 53:1, 3★
33 "He who has received His testimony [R]has
certified that God is true. 1 John 5:10
34 [R]"For He whom God has sent speaks the
words of God, for God does not give the Spirit
[R]by measure. Deut. 18:18★ • John 1:16
35 [R]"The Father loves the Son, and has given
all things into His hand. [Heb. 2:8]
36 [R]"He who believes in the Son has ever-
lasting life; and he who does not believe the
Son shall not see life, but the [R]wrath of God
abides on him." John 3:16, 17; 6:47 • Rom. 1:18

CHAPTER 4

Christ Witnesses to the Woman at the Well

THEREFORE, when the Lord knew that the
Pharisees had heard that Jesus made and
[R]baptized more disciples than John John 3:22, 26
2 (though Jesus Himself did not baptize,
but His disciples),
3 He left Judea and departed again to Gali-
lee.
4 But He needed to go through Samaria.
5 So He came to a city of Samaria which is
called Sychar, near the plot of ground that
[R]Jacob gave to his son Joseph. Gen. 33:19
6 Now Jacob's well was there. Jesus there-
fore, being wearied from *His* journey, sat thus
by the well. It was about the sixth hour.
7 A woman of Samaria came to draw water.
Jesus said to her, "Give Me a drink."
8 For His disciples had gone away into the
city to buy food.
9 Then the woman of Samaria said to Him,
"How is it that You, being a Jew, ask a drink
from me, a Samaritan woman?" For Jews have
no dealings with Samaritans.
10 Jesus answered and said to her, "If you
knew the [R]gift of God, and who it is who says
to you, 'Give Me a drink,' you would have
asked Him, and He would have given you [R]liv-
ing water." [Rom. 5:15] • Is. 12:3; 44:3
11 The woman said to Him, "Sir, You have
nothing to draw with, and the well is deep.
Where then do You get that living water?
12 "Are You greater than our father Jacob,
who gave us the well, and drank from it him-
self, as well as his sons and his livestock?"
13 Jesus answered and said to her, "Whoever
drinks of this water will thirst again,
14 "but [R]whoever drinks of the water that I
shall give him will never thirst. But the water
that I shall give him [R]will become in him a
fountain of water springing up into everlast-
ing life." [John 6:35, 58] • John 7:37, 38
15 [R]The woman said to Him, "Sir, give me
this water, that I may not thirst, nor come here
to draw." John 6:34, 35; 17:2, 3
16 Jesus said to her, "Go, call your husband,
and come here."
17 The woman answered and said, "I have no
husband." Jesus said to her, "You have well
said, 'I have no husband,'
18 "for you have had five husbands, and the
one whom you now have is not your husband;
in that you spoke truly."
19 The woman said to Him, "Sir, [R]I perceive
that You are a prophet. Luke 7:16, 39; 24:19
20 "Our fathers worshiped on this mountain,
and you *Jews* say that in Jerusalem is the
place where one ought to worship."
21 Jesus said to her, "Woman, believe Me, the
hour is coming [R]when you will neither on this
mountain, nor in Jerusalem, worship the Fa-
ther. 1 Tim. 2:8
22 "You worship [R]what you do not know; we
know what we worship, for [R]salvation is of the
Jews. [2 Kin. 17:28–41] • [Rom. 3:1; 9:4, 5]
23 "But the hour is coming, and now is, when
the true worshipers will worship the Father in
[R]spirit and truth; for the Father is seeking
such to worship Him. Phil. 3:3

24 "God *is* Spirit, and those who worship
Him must worship in spirit and truth."
25 The woman said to Him, "I know that
Messiah is coming" (who is called Christ).
"When He comes, He will tell us all things."
26 Jesus said to her, [R]"I who speak to you am
He." Dan. 9:25; Matt. 26:63, 64; Mark 14:61, 62★

Christ Witnesses to the Disciples

27 And at this *point* His disciples came, and
they marveled that He talked with a woman;
yet no one said, "What do You seek?" or, "Why
are You talking with her?"
28 The woman then left her waterpot, went
her way into the city, and said to the men,
29 "Come, see a Man [R]who told me all
things that I ever did. Could this be the
Christ?" John 4:25
30 Then they went out of the city and came
to Him.
31 In the meantime His disciples urged Him,
saying, "Rabbi, eat."
32 But He said to them, "I have food to eat of
which you do not know."
33 Therefore the disciples said to one another,
"Has anyone brought Him *anything* to eat?"
34 Jesus said to them, [R]"My food is to do the
will of Him who sent Me, and to [R]finish His
work. Ps. 40:7, 8 • [John 6:38; 17:4; 19:30]
35 "Do you not say, 'There are still four
months and *then* comes [R]the harvest'? Be-
hold, I say to you, lift up your eyes and look at
the fields, [R]for they are already white for har-
vest! Gen. 8:22 • Matt. 9:37
36 [R]"And he who reaps receives wages, and
gathers fruit for eternal life, that [R]both he
who sows and he who reaps may rejoice to-
gether. Dan. 12:3 • 1 Thess. 2:19
37 "For in this the saying is true: [R]'One sows
and another reaps.' 1 Cor. 3:5–9
38 "I sent you to reap that for which you
have not labored; others have labored, and
you have entered into their labors."

Christ Witnesses to the Samaritans

39 And many of the Samaritans of that city
believed in Him [R]because of the word of the
woman who testified, "He told me all that I
ever did." John 4:29
40 So when the Samaritans had come to
Him, they urged Him to stay with them; and
He stayed there two days.
41 And many more believed because of His
own [R]word. Luke 4:32
42 Then they said to the woman, "Now we
believe, not because of what you said, for [R]we
ourselves have heard *Him* and we know that
this is indeed the Christ,* the Savior of the
world." 1 John 4:14

Christ Is Received by the Galileans

43 Now after the two days He departed from
there and went to Galilee.
44 For Jesus Himself testified that a prophet
has no honor in his own country.
45 So when He came to Galilee, the Gali-
leans received Him, having seen all the things
He did in Jerusalem at the feast; [R]for they also
had gone to the feast. Deut. 16:16

Christ Heals the Nobleman's Son

46 So Jesus came again to Cana of Galilee
[R]where He had made the water wine. And
there was a certain nobleman whose son was
sick at Capernaum. John 2:1, 11
47 When he heard that Jesus had come out
of Judea into Galilee, he went to Him and im-
plored Him to come down and heal his son,
for he was at the point of death.
48 Then Jesus said to him, [R]"Unless you *peo-
ple* see signs and wonders, you will by no
means believe." 1 Cor. 1:22
49 The nobleman said to Him, "Sir, come
down before my child dies!"
50 Jesus said to him, "Go your way; your son
lives." So the man believed the word that Je-
sus spoke to him, and he went his way.
51 And as he was now going down, his ser-
vants met him and told *him*, saying, "Your son
lives!"
52 Then he inquired of them the hour when
he got better. And they said to him, "Yesterday
at the seventh hour the fever left him."
53 So the father knew that *it was* at the same
hour in which Jesus said to him, "Your son
lives." And he himself believed, and his whole
household.
54 This again *is* the second sign Jesus did
when He had come out of Judea into Galilee.

CHAPTER 5

Christ Heals the Paralytic Man

AFTER this there was a feast of the Jews,
and Jesus went up to Jerusalem.
2 Now there is in Jerusalem [R]by the Sheep
Gate a pool, which is called in Hebrew,
Bethesda,* having five porches. Neh. 12:39
3 In these lay a great multitude of sick peo-
ple, blind, lame, [T]paralyzed, waiting for the
moving of the water. *withered*
4 For an angel went down at a certain time
into the pool and stirred up the water; then
whoever stepped in first, after the stirring of
the water, was made well of whatever disease
he had.*
5 Now a certain man was there who had an
infirmity thirty-eight years.
6 When Jesus saw him lying there, and
knew that he already had been *in that condi-
tion* a long time, He said to him, "Do you want
to be made well?"

4:42 NU omits *the Christ* **5:2** NU *Bethzatha*
5:4 NU omits *waiting for the moving of the water* at
the end of v. 3, and all of v. 4

7 The sick man answered Him, "Sir, I have
no man to put me into the pool when the
water is stirred up; but while I am coming, an-
other steps down before me."
8 Jesus said to him, [R]"Rise, take up your
bed and walk." Luke 5:24
9 And immediately the man was made well,
took up his bed, and walked. And [R]that day
was the Sabbath. John 9:14

Christ Heals on the Sabbath

10 The Jews therefore said to him who was
cured, "It is the Sabbath; [R]it is not lawful for
you to carry your bed." Jer. 17:21, 22
11 He answered them, "He who made me
well said to me, 'Take up your bed and walk.'"
12 Then they asked him, "Who is the Man
who said to you, 'Take up your bed and walk'?"
13 But the one who was [R]healed did not
know who it was, for Jesus had withdrawn, a
multitude being in *that* place. Luke 13:14
14 Afterward Jesus found him in the temple,
and said to him, "See, you have been made
well. [R]Sin no more, lest a worse thing come
upon you." John 8:11
15 The man departed and told the Jews that
it was Jesus who had made him well.
16 For this reason the Jews persecuted Je-
sus, and sought to kill Him,* because He had
done these things on the Sabbath.

Equality with God in Nature

17 But Jesus answered them, [R]"My Father
has been working until now, and I have been
working." [John 9:4; 17:4]
18 Therefore the Jews sought all the more to
kill Him, because He not only broke the Sab-
bath, but also said that God was His Father,
making Himself equal with God.

Equality with God in Power

19 Then Jesus answered and said to them,
"Most assuredly, I say to you, [R]the Son can do
nothing of Himself, but what He sees the Fa-
ther do; for whatever He does, the Son also
does in like manner. John 5:30; 6:38
20 "For [R]the Father loves the Son, and shows
Him all things that He Himself does; and He
will show Him greater works than these, that
you may marvel. Matt. 3:17
21 "For as the Father raises the dead and
gives life to *them,* [R]even so the Son gives life
to whom He will. [John 11:25]

Equality with God in Authority

22 "For the Father judges no one, but has
committed all judgment to the Son,
23 "that all should honor the Son just as
they honor the Father. [R]He who does not
honor the Son does not honor the Father who
sent Him. 1 John 2:23

24 "Most assuredly, I say to you, [R]he who
hears My word and believes in Him who sent
Me has everlasting life, and shall not come
into judgment, [R]but has passed from death
into life. John 3:16, 18; 6:47 • [1 John 3:14]

25 "Most assuredly, I say to you, the hour is
coming, and now is, when [R]the dead will hear
the voice of the Son of God; and those who
hear will live. [Col. 2:13]
26 "For [R]as the Father has life in Himself, so
He has granted the Son to have [R]life in Him-
self, Ps. 36:9 • 1 Cor. 15:45
27 "and [R]has given Him authority to execute
judgment also, [R]because He is the Son of
Man. [Acts 10:42; 17:31] • Dan. 7:13
28 "Do not marvel at this; for the hour is
coming in which all who are in the graves will
[R]hear His voice [1 Thess. 4:15–17]
29 [R]"and come forth—[R]those who have done
good, to the resurrection of life, and those
who have done evil, to the resurrection of
condemnation. Is. 26:19 • Dan. 12:2
30 [R]"I can of Myself do nothing. As I hear, I
judge; and My judgment is righteous, because
I do not seek My own will but the will of the
Father who sent Me. John 5:19

Witness of John the Baptist

31 [R]"If I bear witness of Myself, My witness
is not [T]true. John 8:14 • *valid* as testimony
32 [R]"There is another who bears witness of

5:16 NU omits *and sought to kill Him*

5:24 Everlasting Life—One benefit of finding new life in Christ is called in the Bible "everlasting [eternal] life." The character of this great reality may be summarized by carefully looking at each word. The word "life" stresses the quality of this new relationship to God (Page 1094—John 10:10). It does not mean, of course, that we are not physically alive before salvation; it simply stresses the fact that we enter a new, personal relationship with God that gives us a fullness of spiritual vitality that we lacked before (Page 1102—John 17:3).

The word "everlasting" emphasizes life without end. Though it will not be completely fulfilled until our future bodily redemption (Page 1155—Rom. 8:23), it is still a present possession that can never perish (Page 1095—John 10:28).

Everlasting life must not be conceived of as an exclusively future possession. Rather, its possession is clearly seen in our actions. Thus, "no murderer has eternal life abiding in him" (Page 1295—1 John 3:15). Indeed, love is the confirming evidence that we do, in fact, have eternal life (Page 1295—1 John 3:14).

The greatness of this spiritual reality constitutes a wonderful incentive to vigorously proclaim the gospel to those who are still "dead in trespasses and sins" (Page 1205—Eph. 2:1).

Now turn to Page 1187—2 Cor. 5:17: New Nature.

Me, and I know that the witness which He wit-
nesses of Me is true. [Matt. 3:17]
33 "You have sent to John, and he has borne
witness to the truth.
34 "Yet I do not receive testimony from man,
but I say these things that you may be saved.
35 "He was the burning and [R]shining lamp,
and [R]you were willing for a time to rejoice in
his light. 2 Pet. 1:19 • Mark 6:20

Witness of the Works of Christ

36 "But [R]I have a greater witness than
John's; for [R]the works which the Father has
given Me to finish—the very works that I do—
bear witness of Me, that the Father has sent
Me. 1 John 5:9 • John 3:2; 10:25; 17:4

Witness of the Father

37 "And the Father Himself, who sent Me,
has testified of Me. You have neither heard His
voice at any time, nor seen His form.
38 "But you do not have His word abiding in
you, because whom He sent, Him you do not
believe.

Witness of the Scriptures

39 [R]"You search the Scriptures, for in them
you think you have eternal life; and these are
they which testify of Me. Is. 8:20; 34:16
40 [R]"But you are not willing to come to Me
that you may have life. [John 1:11; 3:19]
41 "I do not receive honor from men.
42 "But I know you, that you do not have the
love of God in you.
43 "I have come in My Father's name, and
you do not receive Me; if another comes in his
own name, him you will receive.
44 "How can you believe, who receive honor
from one another, and do not seek the honor
that *comes* from the only God?
45 "Do not think that I shall accuse you to
the Father; [R]there is *one* who accuses you—
Moses, in whom you trust. Rom. 2:12
46 "For if you believed Moses, you would be-
lieve Me; for he wrote about Me.
47 "But if you do not believe his writings,
how will you believe My words?"

CHAPTER 6

Christ Feeds 5,000
Matt. 14:13–21; Mark 6:31–44; Luke 9:11–17

AFTER [R]these things Jesus went over
the Sea of Galilee, which is *the Sea* of
[R]Tiberias. Mark 6:32 • John 6:23; 21:1
2 Then a great multitude followed Him, be-
cause they saw His signs which He performed
on those who were diseased.
3 And Jesus went up on the mountain, and
there He sat with His disciples.
4 [R]Now the Passover, a feast of the Jews,
was near. Deut. 16:1
5 [R]Then Jesus lifted up *His* eyes, and seeing
a great multitude coming toward Him, He said
to Philip, "Where shall we buy bread, that
these may eat?" Matt. 14:14
6 But this He said to test him, for He Him-
self knew what He would do.
7 Philip answered Him, [R]"Two hundred
denarii worth of bread is not sufficient for
them, that every one of them may have a lit-
tle." Num. 11:21, 22
8 One of His disciples, [R]Andrew, Simon Pe-
ter's brother, said to Him, John 1:40
9 "There is a lad here who has five barley
loaves and two small fish, [R]but what are they
among so many?" 2 Kin. 4:43
10 Then Jesus said, "Make the people sit
down." Now there was much grass in the
place. So the men sat down, in number about
five thousand.
11 And Jesus took the loaves, and when He
had given thanks He distributed *them* to the
disciples, and the disciples* to those sitting
down; and likewise of the fish, as much as
they wanted.
12 So when they were filled, He said to His
disciples, "Gather up the fragments that re-
main, so that nothing is lost."
13 Therefore they gathered *them* up, and
filled twelve baskets with the fragments of the
five barley loaves which were left over by
those who had eaten.
14 Then those men, when they had seen the
sign that Jesus did, said, "This is truly the
Prophet who is to come into the world."

Christ Walks on the Water
Matt. 14:22–33; Mark 6:45–52

15 Therefore when Jesus perceived that they
were about to come and take Him by force to
make Him king, He departed again to the
mountain by Himself alone.
16 [R]Now when evening came, His disciples
went down to the sea, Matt. 14:23
17 got into the boat, and went over the sea
toward Capernaum. And it was already dark,
and Jesus had not come to them.
18 Then the sea arose because a great wind
was blowing.
19 So when they had rowed about three or
four miles,* they saw Jesus walking on the sea
and drawing near the boat; and they were
[R]afraid. Matt. 17:6
20 But He said to them, [R]"It is I; do not be
afraid." Is. 43:1, 2
21 Then they willingly received Him into the
boat, and immediately the boat was at the
land where they were going.

"I Am the Bread of Life"

22 On the following day, when the people
who were standing on the other side of the

6:11 NU omits *to the disciples, and the disciples*
6:19 Lit. *25 or 30 stadia*

sea saw that there was no other boat there,
except that one which His disciples had en-
tered,* and that Jesus had not entered the
boat with His disciples, but His disciples had
gone away alone—
23 however, other boats came from Tiberias,
near the place where they ate bread after the
Lord had given thanks—
24 when the people therefore saw that Jesus
was not there, nor His disciples, they also got
into boats and came to Capernaum, [R]seeking
Jesus. Luke 4:42
25 And when they found Him on the other
side of the sea, they said to Him, "Rabbi, when
did You come here?"
26 Jesus answered them and said, "Most as-
suredly, I say to you, you seek Me, not because
you saw the signs, but because you ate of the
loaves and were filled.
27 [R]"Do not labor for the food which per-
ishes, but [R]for the food which endures to ever-
lasting life, which the Son of Man will give
you, because God the Father has set His seal
on Him." Matt. 6:19 • John 4:14
28 Then they said to Him, "What shall we do,
that we may work the works of God?"
29 Jesus answered and said to them, [R]"This
is the work of God, that you believe in Him
whom He sent." [1 John 3:23]
30 Therefore they said to Him, "What sign
will You perform then, that we may see it and
believe You? What work will You do?
31 [R]"Our fathers ate the manna in the desert;
as it is written, *'He gave them bread from
heaven to eat.'* "* Ex. 16:15
32 Then Jesus said to them, "Most assuredly,
I say to you, Moses did not give you the bread
from heaven, but My Father gives you the true
bread from heaven.
33 "For the bread of God is He who comes
down from heaven and gives life to the
world."
34 [R]Then they said to Him, "Lord, give us
this bread always." John 4:15
35 And Jesus said to them, [R]"I am the bread
of life. He who comes to Me shall never
hunger, and he who believes in Me shall never
[R]thirst. John 6:48, 58 • Is. 55:1, 2
36 "But I said to you that you have seen Me
and yet [R]do not believe. John 10:26
37 [R]"All that the Father gives Me will come to
Me, and [R]the one who comes to Me I will by
no means cast out. John 6:45 • 2 Tim. 2:19
38 "For I have come down from heaven, [R]not
to do My own will, [R]but the will of Him who
sent Me. Matt. 26:39 • John 4:34
39 "This is the will of the Father who sent
Me, [R]that of all He has given Me I should
lose nothing, but should raise it up at the last
day. John 10:28; 17:12; 18:9
40 "And this is the will of Him who sent Me,
that everyone who sees the Son and believes
in Him may have everlasting life; and I will
raise him up at the last day."
41 The Jews then [T]complained about Him,
because He said, "I am the bread which came
down from heaven." *grumbled*
42 And they said, [R]"Is not this Jesus, the son
of Joseph, whose father and mother we
know? How is it then that He says, 'I have
come down from heaven'?" Matt. 13:55
43 Jesus therefore answered and said to
them, "Do not murmur among yourselves.
44 [R]"No one can come to Me unless the Fa-
ther who sent Me draws him; and I will raise
him up at the last day. Song 1:4
45 "It is written in the prophets, *'And they
shall all be taught by God.'** [R]Therefore every-
one who has heard and learned* from the Fa-
ther comes to Me. John 6:37
46 [R]"Not that anyone has seen the Father,
[R]except He who is from God; He has seen the
Father. John 1:18 • Matt. 11:27
47 "Most assuredly, I say to you, he who be-
lieves in Me* has everlasting life.
48 [R]"I am the bread of life. John 6:33, 35
49 [R]"Your fathers ate the manna in the
wilderness, and are dead. John 6:31, 58
50 [R]"This is the bread which comes down
from heaven, that one may eat of it and not
die. John 6:51, 58
51 "I am the living bread [R]which came down
from heaven. If anyone eats of this bread, he
will live forever; and the bread that I shall
give is My flesh, which I shall give for the life
of the world." John 3:13
52 The Jews therefore [R]quarreled among
themselves, saying, "How can this Man give
us *His* flesh to eat?" John 7:43; 9:16; 10:19
53 Then Jesus said to them, "Most assuredly,
I say to you, unless [R]you eat the flesh of the
Son of Man and drink His blood, you have no
life in you. Matt. 26:26
54 [R]"Whoever eats My flesh and drinks My
blood has eternal life, and I will raise him up
at the last day. John 4:14; 6:27, 40
55 "For My flesh is food indeed,* and My
blood is drink indeed.
56 "He who eats My flesh and drinks My
blood abides in Me, and I in him.
57 "As the living Father sent Me, and I live
because of the Father, so he who feeds on Me
will live because of Me.
58 "This is the bread which came down from
heaven—not [R]as your fathers ate the manna,
and are dead. He who eats this bread will live
forever." Ex. 16:14–35
59 These things He said in the synagogue as
He taught in Capernaum.

6:22 NU omits *that* and *which His disciples had entered* **6:31** Ex. 16:4; Neh. 9:15; Ps. 78:24 **6:45** Is. 54:13★ • M *hears and has learned* **6:47** NU omits *in Me* **6:55** NU *true food* and *true drink*

Rejection by Many Followers

60 [R]Therefore many of His disciples, when they heard *this*, said, "This is a [T]hard saying; who can understand it?" John 6:66 • *difficult*

61 When Jesus knew in Himself that His disciples [T]complained about this, He said to them, "Does this offend you? *grumbled*

62 [R]"*What* then if you should see the Son of Man ascend where He was before? Acts 1:9☆

63 [R]"It is the Spirit who gives life; the flesh profits nothing. The words that I speak to you are spirit, and *they* are life. 2 Cor. 3:6

64 "But [R]there are some of you who do not believe." For [R]Jesus knew from the beginning who they were who did not believe, and who would betray Him. John 6:36 • John 2:24, 25

65 And He said, "Therefore I have said to you that no one can come to Me unless it has been granted to him by My Father."

66 From that *time* many of His disciples went back and walked with Him no more.

Confession by Peter

67 Then Jesus said to the twelve, "Do you also want to go away?"

68 But Simon Peter answered Him, "Lord, to whom shall we go? You have [R]the words of eternal life. Acts 5:20

69 [R]"Also we have come to believe and know that You are the Christ, the Son of the living God."* Luke 9:20

70 Jesus answered them, [R]"Did I not choose you, the twelve, [R]and one of you is a devil?" Luke 6:13 • [John 13:27]

71 He spoke of [R]Judas Iscariot, *the son* of Simon, for it was he who would betray Him, being one of the twelve. John 12:4; 13:2, 26

CHAPTER 7

Christ's Brothers Do Not Believe

AFTER these things Jesus walked in Galilee; for He did not want to walk in Judea, [R]because the Jews* sought to kill Him. John 5:18; 7:19, 25; 8:37, 40

2 [R]Now the Jews' Feast of Tabernacles was at hand. Lev. 23:34

3 [R]His brothers therefore said to Him, "Depart from here and go into Judea, that Your disciples also may see the works that You are doing. Matt. 12:46

4 "For no one does anything in secret while he himself seeks to be known openly. If You do these things, show Yourself to the world."

5 For [R]even His [R]brothers did not believe in Him. Ps. 69:8 • Mark 3:21

6 Then Jesus said to them, "My time has not yet come, but your time is always ready.

7 [R]"The world cannot hate you, but it hates Me [R]because I testify of it that its works are evil. [John 15:19] • John 3:19

8 "You go up to this feast. I am not yet* going up to this feast, [R]for My time has not yet fully come." John 8:20

9 When He had said these things to them, He remained in Galilee.

Christ Secretly Goes to the Feast

10 But when His brothers had gone up, then He also went up to the feast, not openly, but as it were in secret.

11 Then [R]the Jews sought Him at the feast, and said, "Where is He?" John 11:56

12 And there was much complaining among the people concerning Him. Some said, "He is good"; others said, "No, on the contrary, He deceives the people."

13 However, no one spoke openly of Him [R]for fear of the Jews. [John 9:22; 12:42; 19:38]

Christ's Authority from the Father

14 Now about the middle of the feast [R]Jesus went up into the temple and taught. Ps. 22:22★

15 [R]And the Jews marveled, saying, "How does this Man know letters, having never studied?" Matt. 13:54

16 Jesus* answered them and said, "My doctrine is not Mine, but His who sent Me.

17 [R]"If anyone wills to do His will, he shall know concerning the doctrine, whether it is from God or *whether* I speak on My own *authority*. John 3:21; 8:43

18 [R]"He who speaks from himself seeks his own glory; but He who [R]seeks the glory of the One who sent Him is true, and no unrighteousness is in Him. John 5:41 • John 8:50

19 [R]"Did not Moses give you the law, yet none of you keeps the law? [R]Why do you seek to kill Me?" Deut. 33:4 • Matt. 12:14

20 The people answered and said, "You have a demon. Who is seeking to kill You?"

21 Jesus answered and said to them, "I did one work, and you all marvel.

22 [R]"Moses therefore gave you circumcision (not that it is from Moses, [R]but from the fathers), and you circumcise a man on the Sabbath. Lev. 12:3 • Gen. 17:9–14

23 "If a man receives circumcision on the Sabbath, so that the law of Moses should not be broken, are you angry with Me because [R]I made a man completely well on the Sabbath? John 5:8, 9, 16

24 "Do not judge according to appearance, but judge with righteous judgment."

Christ's Origin from the Father

25 Now some of them from Jerusalem said, "Is this not He whom they seek to kill?

26 "But look! He speaks boldly, and they say nothing to Him. Do the rulers know indeed that this is truly* the Christ?

6:69 NU *You are the Holy One of God.* **7:1** That is, the ruling authorities **7:8** NU omits *yet* **7:16** NU, M *So Jesus* **7:26** NU omits *truly*

27 [R]"However, we know where this Man is from; but when the Christ comes, no one knows where He is from." Luke 4:22

28 Then Jesus cried out, as He taught in the temple, saying, [R]"You both know Me, and you know where I am from; and I have not come of Myself, but He who sent Me is true, whom you do not know. John 8:14

29 "But* [R]I know Him, for I am from Him, and He sent Me." Matt. 11:27

30 Therefore [R]they sought to take Him; but no one laid a hand on Him, because His hour had not yet come. Mark 11:18

31 And [R]many of the people believed in Him, and said, "When the Christ comes, will He do more signs than these which this *Man* has done?" Matt. 12:23

Christ's Departure to the Father

32 The Pharisees heard the crowd murmuring these things concerning Him, and the Pharisees and the chief priests sent officers to take Him.

33 Then Jesus said to them,* [R]"I shall be with you a little while longer, and *then* I go to Him who sent Me. Mark 16:19; Acts 1:9☆

34 "You [R]will seek Me and not find *Me,* and where I am you cannot come." Hos. 5:6

35 Then the Jews said among themselves, "Where does He intend to go that we shall not find Him? Does He intend to go to [R]the Dispersion among the Greeks and teach the Greeks? James 1:1

36 "What is this thing that He said, 'You will seek Me and not find Me, and where I am you cannot come'?"

Christ Reveals the "Living Water"

37 [R]On the last day, that great *day* of the feast, Jesus stood and cried out, saying, [R]"If anyone thirsts, let him come to Me and drink. Lev. 23:36 • [Is. 55:1]

38 [R]"He who believes in Me, as the Scripture has said, [R]out of his heart will flow rivers of living water." Deut. 8:15 • Is. 12:3

39 But this He spoke concerning the Spirit, whom those believing* in Him would receive; for the Holy* Spirit was not yet *given,* because Jesus was not yet glorified.

Israel Is Divided over Christ

40 Therefore many* from the crowd, when they heard this saying, said, "Truly this is [R]the Prophet." Deut. 18:15, 18

41 Others said, "This is [R]the Christ." But some said, "Will the Christ come out of Galilee? John 4:42; 6:69

42 [R]"Has not the Scripture said that the Christ comes from the seed of David and from the town of Bethlehem, [R]where David was?" Mic. 5:2 • 1 Sam. 16:1, 4

43 So [R]there was a division among the people because of Him. John 7:12

44 Now [R]some of them wanted to take Him, but no one laid hands on Him. John 7:30

The Sanhedrin Is Confused over Christ

45 Then the officers came to the chief priests and Pharisees, who said to them, "Why have you not brought Him?"

46 The officers answered, [R]"No man ever spoke like this Man!" Luke 4:22

47 Then the Pharisees answered them, "Are you also deceived?

48 "Have any of the rulers or the Pharisees believed in Him?

49 "But this crowd that does not know the law is accursed."

50 Nicodemus (he who came to Jesus by night,* being one of them) said to them,

51 "Does our law judge a man before it hears him and knows what he is doing?"

52 They answered and said to him, "Are you also from Galilee? Search and look, for no prophet has arisen* out of Galilee."

53 And everyone went to his *own* house.*

CHAPTER 8

A Woman Is Caught in Adultery

BUT Jesus went to the Mount of Olives.

2 Now early* in the morning He came again into the temple, and all the people came to Him; and He sat down and [R]taught them. John 8:20; 18:20

3 Then the scribes and Pharisees brought to Him a woman caught in adultery. And when they had set her in the midst,

4 they said to Him, "Teacher, this woman was caught* in adultery, in the very act.

5 [R]"Now Moses, in the law, commanded* us that such should be stoned.* But what do You say?"* Lev. 20:10

6 This they said, testing Him, that they [R]might have *something* of which to accuse Him. But Jesus stooped down and wrote on the ground with *His* finger, as though He did not hear.* Matt. 22:15

7 So when they continued asking Him, He raised Himself up* and said to them, [R]"He who is without sin among you, let him throw a stone at her first." Deut. 17:7

8 And again He stooped down and wrote on the ground.

9 Then those who heard *it,* [R]being convicted by *their* conscience,* went out one by

7:29 NU, M omit *But* **7:33** NU, M omit *to them* **7:39** NU *who believed* • NU omits *Holy* **7:40** NU *some* **7:50** NU *before* **7:52** NU *is to rise* **7:53** NU brackets 7:53 through 8:11 as not in the original text. They are present in over 900 mss. of John. **8:2** M *very early* **8:4** M *we found this woman* **8:5** M *in our law Moses commanded* • NU, M *to stone such* • M adds *about her* **8:6** NU, M omit *as though He did not hear* **8:7** M *He looked up* **8:9** NU, M omit *being convicted by their conscience*

one, beginning with the oldest *even* to the last.
And Jesus was left alone, and the woman
standing in the midst. Rom. 2:22
10 When Jesus had raised Himself up and
saw no one but the woman, He said to her,*
"Woman, where are those accusers of yours?*
Has no one condemned you?"
11 She said, "No one, Lord." And Jesus said
to her, R"Neither do I condemn you; go and*
Rsin no more." [John 3:17] • [John 5:14]

"I Am the Light of the World"

12 Then Jesus spoke to them again, saying,
R"I am the light of the world. He who follows
Me shall not walk in darkness, but have the
light of life." John 1:4; 9:5; 12:35
13 The Pharisees therefore said to Him,
R"You bear witness of Yourself; Your witness is
not Ttrue." John 5:31 • *valid* as testimony
14 Jesus answered and said to them, "Even if
I bear witness of Myself, My witness is true,
for I know where I came from and where I am
going; but you do not know where I come
from and where I am going.
15 R"You judge according to the flesh; RI
judge no one. John 7:24 • [John 3:17; 12:47]
16 "And yet if I do judge, My judgment is
true; for RI am not alone, but I *am* with the Fa-
ther who sent Me. John 16:32
17 R"It is also written in your law that the tes-
timony of two men is true. Deut. 17:6
18 "I am One who bears witness of Myself,
and Rthe Father who sent Me bears witness of
Me." John 5:37
19 Then they said to Him, "Where is Your Fa-
ther?" Jesus answered, "You know neither Me
nor My Father. If you had known Me, you
would have known My Father also."
20 These words Jesus spoke in Rthe treas-
ury, as He taught in the temple; and Rno one
laid hands on Him, for His hour had not yet
come. Mark 12:41, 43 • John 2:4; 7:30
21 Then Jesus said to them again, "I am
going away, and you will seek Me, and Rwill
die in your sin. RWhere I go you cannot
come." John 8:24 • Mark 16:19; Acts 1:9☆
22 So the Jews said, "Will He kill Himself,
because He says, 'Where I go you cannot
come'?"
23 And He said to them, R"You are from be-
neath; I am from above. You are of this world;
I am not of this world. John 3:31
24 "Therefore I said to you that you will die
in your sins; for if you do not believe that I am
He, you will die in your sins."
25 Then they said to Him, "Who are You?"
And Jesus said to them, "Just what I have
been saying to you from the beginning.
26 "I have many things to say and to judge
concerning you, but RHe who sent Me is true;
and I speak to the world those things which I
heard from Him." John 7:28
27 They did not understand that He spoke to
them of the Father.
28 Then Jesus said to them, "When you Rlift
up the Son of Man, Rthen you will know that
I am *He,* and *that* I do nothing of Myself; but
as My Father taught Me, I speak these
things. John 3:14; 12:32; 19:18 • [Rom. 1:4]
29 "And RHe who sent Me is with Me. The Fa-
ther has not left Me alone, for I always do
those things that please Him." John 14:10
30 As He spoke these words, Rmany believed
in Him. John 7:31; 10:42; 11:45
31 Then Jesus said to those Jews who be-
lieved Him, "If you Rabide in My word, you are
My disciples indeed. [John 14:15, 23]
32 "And you shall know the truth, and the
truth shall make you free."
33 They answered Him, R"We are Abraham's
descendants, and have never been in bondage
to anyone. How *can* You say, 'You will be made
free'?" [Matt. 3:9]
34 Jesus answered them, "Most assuredly, I
say to you, Rwhoever commits sin is a slave of
sin. 2 Pet. 2:19
35 "And a slave does not abide in the house
forever, *but* a son abides forever.

8:10 NU omits *and saw no one but the woman;* M *He saw her and said,* • NU, M omit *of yours* **8:11** NU, M add *from now on*

8:31 God's Word Confirms—"To confirm" means "to fully establish a truth or fact." The Bible should be used to confirm the truth in our own hearts.

a. It confirms our salvation. Often Christians are troubled with doubts about their conversion experience. Did God really save them when they asked Him to do so? Are they still saved today? A number of verses may be used to confirm our salvation. One of the strongest is Jesus' own words in the Gospel of John: "Most assuredly, I say to you, he who hears My word and believes in Him who sent Me has everlasting life, and shall not come into judgment, but has passed from death into life" (Page 1086—John 5:24). Compare John 3:16; 6:27, 35, 37, 40; 10:27–29; Rom. 8:1.
b. It confirms the hand of God in all of life's bitter disappointments. Undoubtedly a most important verse of reassurance and comfort in the hour of great need is Rom. 8:28: "And we know that all things work together for good to those who love God, to those who are the called according to *His* purpose."
c. It confirms our forgiveness when we sin. Sometimes believers carry with them an unnecessary burden of guilt over past sins and failures. Even though these have been confessed, they have difficulty believing God has truly forgiven and cleansed them. But time and again the Bible assures us that all confessed sin is instantly and eternally forgiven (Page 561—Ps. 32:5; 103:12; Page 716—Is. 38:17).

Now turn to Page 649—Prov. 22:21: God's Word Equips.

36 [R]"Therefore if the Son makes you free,
you shall be free indeed. Gal. 5:1
37 "I know that you are Abraham's descen-
dants, but [R]you seek to kill Me, because My
word has no place in you. John 7:19
38 [R]"I speak what I have seen with My Fa-
ther, and you do what you have seen with*
your father." [John 3:32; 5:19, 30]
39 They answered and said to Him, [R]"Abra-
ham is our father." Jesus said to them, [R]"If you
were Abraham's children, you would do the
works of Abraham. Matt. 3:9 • [Rom. 2:28]
40 "But now you seek to kill Me, a Man who
has told you the truth which I heard from
God. Abraham did not do this.
41 "You do the deeds of your father." Then
they said to Him, "We were not born of forni-
cation; we have one Father—God."
42 Jesus said to them, [R]"If God were your Fa-
ther, you would love Me, for I proceeded forth
and came from God; nor have I come of My-
self, but He sent Me. 1 John 5:1
43 [R]"Why do you not understand My
speech? Because you are not able to listen to
My word. [John 7:17]
44 [R]"You are of *your* father the devil, and the
desires of your father you want to do. He was
a murderer from the beginning, and does not
stand in the truth, because there is no truth in
him. When he speaks a lie, he speaks from his
own *resources,* for he is a liar and the father
of it. Matt. 13:38
45 "But because I tell the truth, you do not
believe Me.
46 "Which of you convicts Me of sin? And if
I tell the truth, why do you not believe Me?
47 [R]"He who is of God hears God's words;
therefore you do not hear, because you are not
of God." 1 John 4:6
48 Then the Jews answered and said to Him,
"Do we not say rightly that You are a Samari-
tan and [R]have a demon?" John 7:20
49 Jesus answered, "I do not have a demon;
but I honor My Father, and [R]you dishonor
Me. John 5:41
50 "And [R]I do not seek My *own* glory; there
is One who seeks and judges. John 5:41
51 "Most assuredly, I say to you, if anyone
keeps My word he shall never see death."
52 Then the Jews said to Him, "Now we
know that You [R]have a demon! [R]Abraham is
dead, and the prophets; and You say, 'If any-
one keeps My word he shall never taste
death.' John 7:20; 10:20 • Zech. 1:5
53 "Are You greater than our father Abra-
ham, who is dead? And the prophets are dead.
Who do You make Yourself out to be?"
54 Jesus answered, [R]"If I honor Myself, My
honor is nothing. [R]It is My Father who hon-
ors Me, of whom you say that He is your*
God. John 5:31, 32 • Acts 3:13
55 "Yet [R]you have not known Him, but I
know Him. And if I say, 'I do not know Him,' I
shall be a liar like you; but I do know Him and
keep His word. John 7:28, 29
56 "Your father Abraham rejoiced to see My
day, and he saw *it* and was glad."
57 Then the Jews said to Him, "You are not
yet fifty years old, and have You seen Abra-
ham?"
58 Jesus said to them, "Most assuredly, I say
to you, before Abraham was, I AM."
59 Then [R]they took up stones to throw at
Him; but Jesus hid Himself and went out of
the temple,* going through the midst of them,
and so passed by. John 10:31; 11:8

CHAPTER 9

Christ Heals the Blind Man

NOW as *Jesus* passed by, He saw a man
who was blind from birth.
2 And His disciples asked Him, saying,
"Rabbi, [R]who sinned, this man or his parents,
that he was born blind?" John 9:34

8:38 NU *heard from* **8:54** NU, M *our* **8:59** NU omits the rest of v. 59.

8:44 Satan: Role in Fall of Humans—Jesus described Satan's role in the fall of humankind as that of murderer and liar. Satan murdered humankind with a lie. Jesus went on to imply that lying still kills and that liars reflect the character of Satan and reveal the abiding effects of the Fall on humanity.

In the Garden of Eden, Satan used the serpent as his tool of temptation. The serpent was a real creature, not a manifestation of the devil (Page 6—Gen. 3:1, 14, 15). First, the talking serpent approached Eve who had not directly received the commands from God, as had Adam. Second, he asked whether God had restricted human freedom in any way. Third, he accused God of misleading humankind about the results of violating His restrictions (v. 4). Finally, he asserted that disobeying God would lead to personal fulfillment, knowledge, and power (v. 5).

The serpent was cursed by God for its role in Satan's deception of the human race (Page 7—Gen. 3:14, 15). The literal serpent became a degraded animal that lives a lowly existence and generally inspires dread and uneasiness among humans. The great Serpent, Satan, who operated through the literal serpent also was cursed to be the enemy of humankind and would be mortally wounded by the Seed of the woman. This first messianic prophecy in the Bible foresaw the death of the Second Adam on the cross to pay the penalty for sin (Page 1152—Rom. 5:17; Page 1179—1 Cor. 15:45, 46), break the hold of Satan on humankind (Page 1059—Heb. 2:14, 15), and guarantee his doom in the lake of fire (Page 1105—Matt. 25:41; Page 1326—Rev. 20:10).

Now turn to Page 1185—2 Cor. 2:11: Satan: Strategies of Satan.

3 Jesus answered, "Neither this man nor his
parents sinned, [R]but that the works of God
should be revealed in him. John 11:4
4 "I* must work the works of Him who sent
Me while it is [R]day; *the* night is coming when
no one can work. John 11:9, 10; 12:35
5 "As long as I am in the world, [R]I am the
light of the world." [John 1:5, 9; 3:19; 8:12]
6 When He had said these things, [R]He spat
on the ground and made clay with the saliva;
and He anointed the eyes of the blind man
with the clay. Mark 7:33; 8:23
7 And He said to him, "Go, wash [R]in the
pool of Siloam" (which is translated, Sent).
So [R]he went and washed, and came back see-
ing. Neh. 3:15 • 2 Kin. 5:14
8 Therefore the neighbors and those who
previously had seen that he was blind* said,
"Is not this he who sat and begged?"
9 Some said, "This is he." Others *said,* "He
is like him."* He said, "I am *he.*"
10 Therefore they said to him, "How were
your eyes opened?"
11 He answered and said, [R]"A Man called
Jesus made clay and anointed my eyes and
said to me, 'Go to the pool of* Siloam and
wash.' So I went and washed, and I received
sight." John 9:6, 7
12 Then they said to him, "Where is He?" He
said, "I do not know."
13 They brought him who formerly was
blind to the Pharisees.
14 Now it was a Sabbath when Jesus made
the clay and opened his eyes.
15 Then the Pharisees also asked him again
how he had received his sight. He said to
them, "He put clay on my eyes, and I washed,
and I see."
16 Therefore some of the Pharisees said,
"This Man is not from God, because He does
not keep the Sabbath." Others said, "How can
a man who is a sinner do such signs?" And
there was a division among them.
17 They said to the blind man again, "What
do you say about Him because He opened
your eyes?" He said, "He is a prophet."
18 But the Jews did not believe concerning
him, that he had been blind and received his
sight, until they called the parents of him who
had received his sight.
19 And they asked them, saying, "Is this your
son, who you say was born blind? How then
does he now see?"
20 His parents answered them and said, "We
know that this is our son, and that he was
born blind;
21 "but by what means he now sees we do
not know, or who opened his eyes we do not
know. He is of age; ask him. He will speak for
himself."
22 His parents said these *things* because
[R]they feared the Jews, for the Jews had
agreed already that if anyone confessed *that*
He *was* Christ, he [R]would be put out of the
synagogue. Acts 5:13 • John 16:2
23 Therefore his parents said, "He is of age;
ask him."
24 So they again called the man who was
blind, and said to him, "Give God the glory!
We know that this Man is a sinner."
25 He answered and said, "Whether He is a
sinner *or not* I do not know. One thing I know:
that though I was blind, now I see."
26 Then they said to him again, "What did
He do to you? How did He open your
eyes?"
27 He answered them, "I told you already,
and you did not listen. Why do you want to
hear *it* again? Do you also want to become
His disciples?"
28 Then they reviled him and said, "You are
His disciple, but we are Moses' disciples.
29 "We know that God [R]spoke to [R]Moses; *as
for* this *fellow,* [R]we do not know where He is
from." Num. 12:6–8 • [John 5:45–47] • John 7:27, 28
30 The man answered and said to them,
[R]"Why, this is a marvelous thing, that you do
not know where He is from; yet He has
opened my eyes! John 3:10
31 "Now we know that [R]God does not hear
sinners; but if anyone is a worshiper of God
and does His will, He hears him. Zech. 7:13
32 "Since the world began it has been un-
heard of that anyone opened the eyes of one
who was born blind.
33 [R]"If this Man were not from God, He
could do nothing." John 3:2; 9:16
34 They answered and said to him, "You
were completely born in sins, and are you
teaching us?" And they cast him out.
35 Jesus heard that they had cast him out;
and when He had found him, He said to him,
"Do you believe in the Son of God?"*
36 He answered and said, "Who is He, Lord,
that I may believe in Him?"
37 And Jesus said to him, "You have both
seen Him and [R]it is He who is talking with
you." John 4:26
38 Then he said, "Lord, I believe!" And he
[R]worshiped Him. Matt. 8:2
39 And Jesus said, [R]"For judgment I have
come into this world, that those who do not
see may see, and that those who see may be
made blind." [John 3:17; 5:22, 27; 12:47]
40 Then *some* of the Pharisees who were
with Him heard these words, [R]and said to
Him, "Are we blind also?" [Rom. 2:19]
41 Jesus said to them, "If you were blind, you
would have no sin; but now you say, 'We see.'
Therefore your sin remains.

9:4 NU *We* **9:8** NU *a beggar* **9:9** NU *"No, but he is like him."* **9:11** NU omits *the pool of* **9:35** NU *Son of Man*

CHAPTER 10

"I Am the Good Shepherd"

"MOST assuredly, I say to you, he who
does not enter the sheepfold by the
door, but climbs up some other way, the same
is a thief and a robber.
2 "But he who enters by the door is the
shepherd of the sheep.
3 "To him the doorkeeper opens, and the
sheep hear his voice; and he calls his own
sheep by name and leads them out.
4 "And when he brings out his own sheep,
he goes before them; and the sheep follow
him, for they know his voice.
5 "Yet they will by no means follow a
stranger, but will flee from him, for they do
not know the voice of strangers."
6 Jesus used this illustration, but they did
not understand the things which He spoke to
them.
7 Then Jesus said to them again, "Most as-
suredly, I say to you, I am the door of the sheep.
8 "All who *ever* came before Me* are
thieves and robbers, but the sheep did not
hear them.
9 [R]"I am the door. If anyone enters by Me,
he will be saved, and will go in and out and
find pasture. [Eph. 2:18]
10 "The thief does not come except to steal,
and to kill, and to destroy. I have come that
they may have life, and that they may have *it*
more abundantly.
11 "I am the good shepherd. The good shep-
herd gives His life for the sheep.
12 "But a [T]hireling, *he who is* not the shep-
herd, one who does not own the sheep, sees
the wolf coming and [R]leaves the sheep and
flees; and the wolf catches the sheep and scat-
ters them. *hired man* • Zech. 11:16, 17
13 "The hireling flees because he is a
hireling and does not care about the sheep.
14 "I am the good shepherd; and I know My
sheep, and am known by My own.
15 [R]"As the Father knows Me, even so I know
the Father; [R]and I lay down My life for the
sheep. Matt. 11:27 • Matt. 27:50☆
16 "And [R]other sheep I have which are not of
this fold; them also I must bring, and they will
hear My voice; and there will be one flock *and*
one shepherd. Is. 42:6; 56:8★
17 "Therefore My Father [R]loves Me, [R]be-
cause I lay down My life that I may take it
again. John 5:20 • [Heb. 2:9]
18 "No one takes it from Me, but I lay it
down of Myself. I have power to lay it down,
and I have power to take it again. This com-
mand I have received from My Father."
19 Therefore there was a division again
among the Jews because of these sayings.
20 And many of them said, [R]"He has a
demon and is [T]mad. Why do you listen to
Him?" John 7:20 • *insane*
21 Others said, "These are not the words of
one who has a demon. [R]Can a demon open the
eyes of the blind?" [Ex. 4:11]

The Opposition at the Feast of Dedication in Jerusalem

22 Now it was the Feast of Dedication in Je-
rusalem, and it was winter.
23 And Jesus walked in the temple, [R]in Sol-
omon's porch. Acts 3:11; 5:12
24 Then the Jews surrounded Him and said
to Him, "How long do You keep us in doubt? If
You are the Christ, tell us plainly."

10:8 M omits *before Me*

10:10 The Earthly Life of the Son of God—Since the gospel narratives are mainly concerned with Jesus' earthly ministry, it is important that the main aspects of His teaching be recognized. The most important of these are: the kingdom of God (Page 981—Matt. 5—7; 24—25); His divine authority over humankind (Page 984—Matt. 7:28, 29; Page 1017—Mark 2:10); His own role as God and Messiah demonstrated by miracles and signs (Page 994—Matt. 16:15–20); the significance of His death and resurrection (Page 995—Matt. 16:21; Page 1075—Luke 24:26); the relationship His disciples and subsequent believers are to share with Him (Page 1098—John 13—16); and the urgency of His commission to believers to make disciples (Page 1011—Matt. 28:19, 20).

Of the many events of His earthly life the most significant, without a doubt, are His death and resurrection. On these two pivotal, historical incidents rests the validity of the entire Christian faith (Page 1178—1 Cor. 15:14). It is vital then to understand the nature of these two events. The death of Christ was first of all a humiliating physical death (Page 1104—John 19:18, 33). More than that, for a brief time it constituted a spiritual separation from God (Page 1009—Matt. 27:46). Within this moment there occurred the inexplicable mystery of the Father punishing the Son for the sins of the world (Page 1282—1 Pet. 3:18; Page 1187—2 Cor. 5:21). This event, though it was the greatest crime of human history, was in the plan of God (Page 1113—Acts 2:23), and thus became the basis of salvation for sinners (Page 731—Is. 53:5).

The power of the death of Christ would be nullified without His bodily resurrection. Though it does not justify us, the resurrection demonstrated that His death, by which believing sinners are justified, was valid (Page 1178—1 Cor. 15:12–20). While skeptics have denied the bodily resurrection of Christ, the historical evidence for it is overwhelming: the many separate accounts of post-Resurrection appearances, the empty tomb, and the transformed disciples. Every life that has been dramatically and wonderfully changed by believing in Christ since the first century is a testimony to its historical reality. Furthermore, it is the power of the Resurrection that marvelously empowers Christians today to live the Christian life (Page 1204—Eph. 1:19, 20; Page 1215—Phil. 3:10).

Now turn to page 1028—Mark 10:45: The Ministry of the Son of God.

25 Jesus answered them, "I told you, and you do not believe. The works that I do in My Father's name, they bear witness of Me.

26 "But you do not believe, because you are not of My sheep, as I said to you.*

27 [R]"My sheep hear My voice, and I know them, and they follow Me. John 10:4, 14

28 "And I give them eternal life, and they shall never perish; neither shall anyone snatch them out of My hand.

29 "My Father, who has given *them* to Me, is greater than all; and no one is able to snatch *them* out of My Father's hand.

30 "I and *My* Father are one."

31 Then [R]the Jews took up stones again to stone Him. John 8:59

32 Jesus answered them, "Many good works I have shown you from My Father. For which of those works do you stone Me?"

33 The Jews answered Him, saying, "For a good work we do not stone You, but for [R]blasphemy, and because You, being a Man, [R]make Yourself God." Matt. 9:3 • John 5:18

34 Jesus answered them, "Is it not written in your law, *'I said, "You are gods" '*?*

35 "If He called them gods, [R]to whom the word of God came (and the Scripture [R]cannot be broken), Matt. 5:17, 18 • 1 Pet. 1:25

36 "do you say of Him [R]whom the Father sanctified and [R]sent into the world, 'You are blaspheming,' [R]because I said, 'I am the Son of God'? John 6:27 • John 3:17 • John 5:17, 18

37 [R]"If I do not do the works of My Father, do not believe Me; John 10:25; 15:24

38 "but if I do, though you do not believe Me, [R]believe the works, that you may know and believe* [R]that the Father *is* in Me, and I in Him." John 5:36 • John 14:10, 11

39 Therefore they sought again to seize Him, but He escaped out of their hand.

40 And He went away again beyond the Jordan to the place [R]where John was baptizing at first, and there He stayed. John 1:28

41 Then many came to Him and said, "John performed no sign, but all the things that John spoke about this Man were true."

42 And many believed in Him there.

CHAPTER 11

Christ Raises Lazarus

NOW a certain *man* was sick, Lazarus of Bethany, the town of [R]Mary and her sister Martha. Luke 10:38, 39

2 It was *that* Mary who anointed the Lord with fragrant oil and wiped His feet with her hair, whose brother Lazarus was sick.

3 Therefore the sisters sent to Him, saying, "Lord, behold, he whom You love is sick."

4 When Jesus heard *that,* He said, "This sickness is not unto death, but for the glory of God, that the Son of God may be glorified through it."

5 Now Jesus loved Martha and her sister and Lazarus.

6 So, when He heard that he was sick, [R]He stayed two more days in the place where He was. John 10:40

7 Then after this He said to *the* disciples, "Let us go to Judea again."

8 *The* disciples said to Him, "Rabbi, lately the Jews sought to [R]stone You, and are You going there again?" John 8:59; 10:31

9 Jesus answered, "Are there not twelve hours in the day? [R]If anyone walks in the day, he does not stumble, because he sees the [R]light of this world. John 9:4; 12:35 • Is. 9:2

10 "But if one walks in the night, he stumbles, because the light is not in him."

11 These things He said, and after that He said to them, "Our friend Lazarus sleeps, but I go that I may wake him up."

12 Then His disciples said, "Lord, if he sleeps he will get well."

13 However, Jesus spoke of his death, but they thought that He was speaking about taking rest in sleep.

14 Then Jesus said to them plainly, "Lazarus is dead.

15 "And I am glad for your sakes that I was not there, that you may believe. Nevertheless let us go to him."

16 Then [R]Thomas, who is called the Twin, said to his fellow disciples, "Let us also go, that we may die with Him." John 14:5

17 So when Jesus came, He found that he had already been in the tomb four days.

18 Now Bethany was near Jerusalem, about two miles* away.

19 And many of the Jews had joined the women around Martha and Mary, to comfort them concerning their brother.

20 Then Martha, as soon as she heard that Jesus was coming, went and met Him, but Mary was sitting in the house.

21 Now Martha said to Jesus, "Lord, if You had been here, my brother would not have died.

22 "But even now I know that whatever You ask of God, God will give You."

23 Jesus said to her, "Your brother will rise again."

24 Martha said to Him, [R]"I know that he will rise again in the resurrection at the last day." [John 5:29]

25 Jesus said to her, "I am the resurrection and the life. He who believes in Me, though he may die, he shall live.

26 "And whoever lives and believes in Me shall never die. Do you believe this?"

27 She said to Him, "Yes, Lord, [R]I believe that You are the Christ, the Son of God, who is to come into the world." Matt. 16:16

10:26 NU omits *as I said to you* **10:34** Ps. 82:6
10:38 NU *understand* **11:18** Lit. *15 stadia*

28 And when she had said these things, she went her way and secretly called Mary her sister, saying, "The Teacher has come and is calling for you."

29 As soon as she heard *that,* she arose quickly and came to Him.

30 Now Jesus had not yet come into the town, but was* in the place where Martha met Him.

31 [R]Then the Jews who were with her in the house, and comforting her, when they saw that Mary rose up quickly and went out, followed her, saying, "She is going to the tomb to weep there."* John 11:19, 33

32 Then, when Mary came where Jesus was, and saw Him, she [R]fell down at His feet, saying to Him, "Lord, if You had been here, my brother would not have died." Rev. 1:17

33 Therefore, when Jesus saw her weeping, and the Jews who came with her weeping, He groaned in the spirit and was troubled.

34 And He said, "Where have you laid him?" They said to Him, "Lord, come and see."

35 [R]Jesus wept. Luke 19:41

36 Then the Jews said, "See how He loved him!"

37 And some of them said, "Could not this Man, who opened the eyes of the blind, also have kept this man from dying?"

38 Then Jesus, again groaning in Himself, came to the tomb. It was a cave, and a [R]stone lay against it. Matt. 27:60, 66

39 Jesus said, "Take away the stone." Martha, the sister of him who was dead, said to Him, "Lord, by this time there is a stench, for he has been *dead* four days."

40 Jesus said to her, "Did I not say to you that if you would believe you would [R]see the glory of God?" [John 11:4, 23]

41 Then they took away the stone *from the place* where the dead man was lying.* And Jesus lifted up *His* eyes and said, "Father, I thank You that You have heard Me.

42 "And I know that You always hear Me, but [R]because of the people who are standing by I said *this,* that they may believe that You sent Me." John 12:30; 17:21

43 Now when He had said these things, He cried with a loud voice, "Lazarus, come forth!"

44 And he who had died came out bound hand and foot with graveclothes, and his face was wrapped with a cloth. Jesus said to them, "Loose him, and let him go."

The Pharisees Plan to Kill Christ

45 Then many of the Jews who had come to Mary, [R]and had seen the things Jesus did, believed in Him. John 2:23; 10:42; 12:11, 18

46 But some of them went away to the Pharisees and [R]told them the things Jesus did. John 5:15

47 [R]Then the chief priests and the Pharisees gathered a council and said, [R]"What shall we do? For this Man works many signs. Ps. 2:2 • Acts 4:16

48 "If we let Him alone like this, everyone will believe in Him, and the Romans will come and take away both our place and nation."

49 And one of them, [R]Caiaphas, being high priest that year, said to them, "You know nothing at all, Luke 3:2

50 [R]"nor do you consider that it is expedient for us* that one man should die for the people, and not that the whole nation should perish." John 18:14

51 Now this he did not say on his own *authority;* but being high priest that year he prophesied that Jesus would die for the nation,

52 and not for that nation only, but also that He would gather together in one the children of God who were scattered abroad.

53 Then, from that day on, they plotted to [R]put Him to death. Matt. 26:4

54 [R]Therefore Jesus no longer walked openly among the Jews, but went from there into the country near the wilderness, to a city called [R]Ephraim, and there remained with His disciples. John 4:1, 3; 7:1 • 2 Chr. 13:19

55 [R]And the Passover of the Jews was near, and many went from the country up to Jerusalem before the Passover, to [R]purify themselves. John 2:13; 5:1; 6:4 • Num. 9:10, 13; 31:19, 20

56 [R]Then they sought Jesus, and spoke among themselves as they stood in the temple, "What do you think—that He will not come to the feast?" John 7:11

57 Now both the chief priests and the Pharisees had given a command, that if anyone knew where He was, he should report *it,* that they might [R]seize Him. Matt. 26:14–16

CHAPTER 12

Mary Anoints Christ
Matt. 26:6–12; Mark 14:3–9

THEN, six days before the Passover, Jesus came to Bethany, [R]where Lazarus was who had been dead,* whom He had raised from the dead. John 11:1, 43

2 [R]There they made Him a supper; and Martha served, but Lazarus was one of those who sat at the table with Him. Mark 14:3

3 Then Mary took a pound of very costly oil of spikenard, anointed the feet of Jesus, and wiped His feet with her hair. And the house was filled with the fragrance of the oil.

4 But one of His disciples, Judas Iscariot, Simon's *son,* who would betray Him, said,

5 "Why was this fragrant oil not sold for

11:30 NU adds *still* **11:31** NU *supposing that she was going to the tomb to weep there* **11:41** NU omits *from the place where the dead man was lying* **11:50** NU *you* **12:1** NU omits *who had been dead*

three hundred denarii* and given to the
poor?"
6 This he said, not that he cared for the
poor, but because he was a thief, and [R]had the
money box; and he used to take what was put
in it. John 13:29
7 But Jesus said, "Let her alone; she has
kept* this for the day of My burial.
8 "For the poor you have with you always,
but Me you do not have always."
9 Now a great many of the Jews knew that
He was there; and they came, not for Jesus'
sake only, but that they might also see
Lazarus, [R]whom He had raised from the
dead. John 11:43, 44
10 [R]But the chief priests plotted to put
Lazarus to death also, Luke 16:31
11 because on account of him many of the
Jews went away and believed in Jesus.

The Triumphal Entry
Matt. 21:1–9; Mark 11:1–10; Luke 19:29–38

12 The next day a great multitude that had
come to the feast, when they heard that Jesus
was coming to Jerusalem,
13 took branches of palm trees and went out
to meet Him, and cried out:

"Hosanna!
'Blessed is He who comes in the name of
*the LORD!'**
The King of Israel!"

14 Then Jesus, when He had found a young
donkey, sat on it; as it is written:

15 *"Fear not, daughter of Zion;*
Behold, your King is coming,
*Sitting on a donkey's colt."**

16 [R]His disciples did not understand these
things at first; but when Jesus was glorified,
then they remembered that these things were
written about Him and *that* they had done
these things to Him. Luke 18:34
17 Therefore the people, who were with Him
when He called Lazarus out of his tomb and
raised him from the dead, bore witness.
18 [R]For this reason the people also met Him,
because they heard that He had done this
sign. John 12:11
19 The Pharisees therefore said among
themselves, [R]"You see that you are accom-
plishing nothing. Look, the world has gone
after Him!" John 11:47, 48
20 Now there were certain Greeks among
those who came up to worship at the feast.
21 Then they came to Philip, who was from
Bethsaida of Galilee, and asked him, saying,
"Sir, we wish to see Jesus."
22 Philip came and told Andrew, and in turn
Andrew and Philip told Jesus.

The Messiah Teaches

23 But Jesus answered them, saying, [R]"The
hour has come [R]that the Son of Man should be
glorified. John 13:32 • Acts 3:13☆
24 "Most assuredly, I say to you, [R]unless a
grain of wheat falls into the ground and dies,
it remains alone; but if it dies, it produces
much [T]grain. 1 Cor. 15:36 • Lit. *fruit*
25 [R]"He who loves his life will lose it, and he
who hates his life in this world will keep it for
eternal life. Mark 8:35
26 "If anyone serves Me, let him [R]follow Me;
and [R]where I am, there My servant will be
also. If anyone serves Me, him *My* Father will
honor. [Matt. 16:24] • John 14:3; 17:24
27 "Now My soul is troubled, and what shall
I say? 'Father, save Me from this hour'? But for
this purpose I came to this hour.
28 "Father, glorify Your name." Then a voice
came from heaven, *saying,* "I have both glori-
fied *it* and will glorify *it* again."
29 Therefore the people who stood by and
heard *it* said that it had thundered. Others
said, "An angel has spoken to Him."
30 Jesus answered and said, [R]"This voice
did not come because of Me, but for your
sake. John 11:42
31 "Now is the judgment of this world; now
the ruler of this world will be cast out.
32 "And I, if I am lifted up from the earth,
will draw [R]all *peoples* to Myself." [Rom. 5:18]
33 [R]This He said, signifying by what death
He would die. John 18:32; 21:19
34 The people answered Him, [R]"We have
heard from the law that the Christ remains
forever; and how *can* You say, 'The Son of
Man must be lifted up'? Who is this Son of
Man?" Mic. 4:7
35 Then Jesus said to them, "A little while
longer [R]the light is with you. Walk while you
have the light, lest darkness overtake you; he
who walks in darkness does not know where
he is going. [John 1:9; 7:33; 8:12]
36 "While you have the light, believe in the
light, that you may become [R]sons of light."
These things Jesus spoke, and departed, and
was hidden from them. Luke 16:8
37 But although He had done so many
[R]signs before them, they did not believe in
Him, John 11:47
38 that the word of Isaiah the prophet might
be fulfilled, which he spoke:

"Lord, who has believed our report?
And to whom has the arm of the LORD
*been revealed?"**

39 Therefore they could not believe, because
Isaiah said again:

12:5 About one year's wages for a worker **12:7** NU *that she may keep* **12:13** Ps. 118:26★ **12:15** Zech. 9:9★ **12:38** Is. 53:1★

40 *"He has blinded their eyes and hardened*
their hearts,
[R]*Lest they should see with their eyes,*
Lest they should understand with their
hearts and turn, Matt. 13:14
*So that I should heal them."**

41 [R]These things Isaiah said when* he saw His glory and spoke of Him. Is. 6:1

42 Nevertheless even among the rulers many believed in Him, but because of the Pharisees they did not confess *Him,* lest they should be put out of the synagogue;

43 [R]for they loved the praise of men more than the praise of God. John 5:41, 44

44 Then Jesus cried out and said, [R]"He who believes in Me, believes not in Me [R]but in Him who sent Me. Mark 9:37 • [John 5:24]

45 "And [R]he who sees Me sees Him who sent Me. [John 14:9]

46 [R]"I have come *as* a light into the world, that whoever believes in Me should not abide in darkness. John 1:4, 5; 8:12; 12:35, 36

47 "And if anyone hears My words and does not believe,* [R]I do not judge him; for [R]I did not come to judge the world but to save the world. John 5:45 • John 3:17

48 "He who rejects Me, and does not receive My words, has that which judges him—[R]the word that I have spoken will judge him in the last day. Deut. 18:18, 19

49 "For [R]I have not spoken on My own *authority;* but the Father who sent Me gave Me a command, [R]what I should say and what I should speak. John 8:38 • Deut. 18:18

50 "And I know that His command is everlasting life. Therefore, whatever I speak, just as the Father has told Me, so I speak."

CHAPTER 13

Christ Washes the Disciples' Feet

NOW before the Feast of the Passover, when Jesus knew that His hour had come that He should depart from this world to the Father, having loved His own who were in the world, He loved them to the end.

2 And supper being ended,* the devil having already put it into the heart of Judas Iscariot, Simon's *son,* to betray Him,

3 Jesus, knowing that the Father had given all things into His hands, and that He had come from God and was going to God,

4 rose from supper and laid aside His garments, took a towel and girded Himself.

5 After that, He poured water into a basin and began to wash the disciples' feet, and to wipe *them* with the towel with which He was girded.

6 Then He came to Simon Peter. And *Peter* said to Him, [R]"Lord, are You washing my feet?" Matt. 3:14

7 Jesus answered and said to him, "What I am doing you do not understand now, [R]but you will know after this." John 13:19

8 Peter said to Him, "You shall never wash my feet!" Jesus answered him, "If I do not wash you, you have no part with Me."

9 Simon Peter said to Him, "Lord, not my feet only, but also *my* hands and *my* head!"

10 Jesus said to him, "He who is bathed needs only to wash *his* feet, but is completely clean; and [R]you are clean, but not all of you." [John 15:3]

11 For He knew who would betray Him; therefore He said, "You are not all clean."

12 So when He had washed their feet, taken His garments, and sat down again, He said to them, "Do you [T]know what I have done to you? *understand*

13 [R]"You call Me Teacher and Lord, and you say well, for *so* I am. Matt. 23:8, 10

14 [R]"If I then, *your* Lord and Teacher, have washed your feet, [R]you also ought to wash one another's feet. Luke 22:27 • [Rom. 12:10]

15 "For I have given you an example, that you should do as I have done to you.

16 "Most assuredly, I say to you, a servant is not greater than his master; nor is he who is sent greater than he who sent him.

17 [R]"If you know these things, blessed are you if you do them. [James 1:25]

18 "I do not speak concerning all of you. I know whom I have chosen; but that the [R]Scripture may be fulfilled, *'He who eats bread with Me* has lifted up his heel against Me.'** John 15:25; 17:12

19 [R]"Now I tell you before it comes, that when it does come to pass, you may believe that I am *He.* John 14:29; 16:4

20 [R]"Most assuredly, I say to you, he who receives whomever I send receives Me; and he who receives Me receives Him who sent Me." Matt. 10:40

Christ Announces Judas, the Betrayer
Matt. 26:21, 22; Mark 14:18, 19; Luke 22:21–23

21 When Jesus had said these things, [R]He was troubled in spirit, and testified and said, "Most assuredly, I say to you, [R]one of you will betray Me." John 12:27 • John 18:2☆

22 Then the disciples looked at one another, perplexed about whom He spoke.

23 Now there was leaning on Jesus' bosom one of His disciples, whom Jesus loved.

24 Simon Peter therefore motioned to him to ask who it was of whom He spoke.

25 Then, leaning back* on Jesus' breast, he said to Him, "Lord, who is it?"

26 Jesus answered, "It is he to whom I shall give a piece of bread when I have dipped *it.*"

12:40 Is. 6:10 **12:41** NU *because* **12:47** NU *keep them* **13:2** NU *And during supper* **13:18** NU *My bread* • Ps. 41:9★ **13:25** NU, M add *thus*

And having dipped the bread, He gave *it* to
Judas Iscariot, *the son* of Simon.
27 [R]Now after the piece of bread, Satan en-
tered him. Then Jesus said to him, "What you
do, do quickly." Luke 22:3
28 But no one at the table knew for what
reason He said this to him.
29 For some thought, because Judas had the
money box, that Jesus had said to him, "Buy
those things we need for the feast," or that he
should give something to the poor.
30 Having received the piece of bread, he
then went out immediately. And it was night.

Christ Announces His Departure

31 So, when he had gone out, Jesus said,
[R]"Now the Son of Man is glorified, and [R]God
is glorified in Him. John 12:23 • [1 Pet. 4:11]
32 "If God is glorified in Him, God will also
glorify Him in Himself, and [R]glorify Him im-
mediately. John 12:23
33 "Little children, I shall be with you a little
while longer. You will seek Me; and as I said to
the Jews, 'Where I am going, you cannot
come,' so now I say to you.
34 "A new commandment I give to you, that
you love one another; as I have loved you, that
you also love one another.
35 "By this all will know that you are My dis-
ciples, if you have love for one another."

Christ Foretells Peter's Denial
Matt. 26:34, 35; Mark 14:30, 31; Luke 22:33, 34

36 Simon Peter said to Him, "Lord, where
are You going?" Jesus answered him, "Where
I am going you cannot follow Me now, but
[R]you shall follow Me afterward." 2 Pet. 1:14
37 Peter said to Him, "Lord, why can I not
follow You now? I will [R]lay down my life for
Your sake." Mark 14:29–31
38 Jesus answered him, "Will you lay down
your life for My sake? Most assuredly, I say to
you, the rooster shall not [R]crow till you have
denied Me three times. John 18:25–27☆

CHAPTER 14

Christ Comforts His Disciples

"LET not your heart be troubled; you be-
lieve in God, believe also in Me.
2 "In My Father's house are many man-
sions;* if *it were* not so, I would have told you.
I go to prepare a place for you.*
3 "And if I go and prepare a place for you, I
will come again and receive you to Myself;
that where I am, *there* you may be also.
4 "And where I go you know, and the way
you know."

Christ Answers Thomas

5 [R]Thomas said to Him, "Lord, we do not
know where You are going, and how can we
know the way?" Matt. 10:3
6 Jesus said to him, "I am the way, the truth,
and the life. [R]No one comes to the Father ex-
cept through Me. 1 Tim. 2:5
7 [R]"If you had known Me, you would have
known My Father also; and from now on you
know Him and have seen Him." John 8:19

Christ Answers Philip

8 Philip said to Him, "Lord, show us the Fa-
ther, and it is sufficient for us."
9 Jesus said to him, "Have I been with you
so long, and yet you have not known Me,
Philip? [R]He who has seen Me has seen the Fa-
ther; so how can you say, 'Show us the Fa-
ther'? Col. 1:15
10 "Do you not believe that I am in the Fa-
ther, and the Father in Me? The words that I
speak to you [R]I do not speak on My own *au-
thority;* but the Father who dwells in Me does
the works. Deut. 18:18; John 5:19; 14:24★
11 "Believe Me that I *am* in the Father and
the Father in Me, [R]or else believe Me for the
sake of the works themselves. John 5:36
12 [R]"Most assuredly, I say to you, he who be-
lieves in Me, the works that I do he will do
also; and greater *works* than these he will do,
because I go to My Father. Luke 10:17
13 [R]"And whatever you ask in My name, that
I will do, that the Father may be [R]glorified in
the Son. Matt. 7:7 • John 13:31
14 "If you ask* anything in My name, I will
do *it.*
15 [R]"If you love Me, keep* My command-
ments. 1 John 5:3
16 "And I will pray the Father, and [R]He will
give you another Helper, that He may abide
with you forever— Acts 2:4, 33☆
17 "the Spirit of truth, whom the world can-
not receive, because it neither sees Him nor
knows Him; but you know Him, for He dwells
with you and will be in you.
18 [R]"I will not leave you orphans; [R]I will
come to you. [Matt. 28:20] • [John 14:3, 28]
19 "A little while longer and the world will
see Me no more, but [R]you will see Me. Be-
cause I live, you will live also. John 16:16, 22
20 "At that day you will know that I *am* in
My Father, and you in Me, and I in you.
21 "He who has My commandments and
keeps them, it is he who loves Me. And he who
loves Me will be loved by My Father, and I will
love him and manifest Myself to him."

Christ Answers Judas

22 [R]Judas (not Iscariot) said to Him, "Lord,
how is it that You will manifest Yourself to us,
and not to the world?" Luke 6:16

14:2 Lit. *dwellings* • NU *if it were not so, would I have told you that I go to prepare a place for you? or if it were not so, I would have told you; for I go to prepare a place for you.* **14:14** NU *ask Me* **14:15** NU *you will keep*

23 Jesus answered and said to him, "If anyone loves Me, he will keep My word; and My Father will love him, and We will come to him and make Our home with him.

24 "He who does not love Me does not keep My words; and the word which you hear is not Mine but the Father's who sent Me.

25 "These things I have spoken to you while being present with you.

26 "But the Helper, the Holy Spirit, whom the Father will send in My name, He will teach you all things, and bring to your remembrance all things that I said to you.

27 [R]"Peace I leave with you, My peace I give to you; not as the world gives do I give to you. Let not your heart be troubled, neither let it be afraid. Luke 1:79; [Phil. 4:7]★

28 "You have heard Me [R]say to you, 'I am going away and coming *back* to you.' If you loved Me, you would rejoice because I said,* [R]'I am going to the Father,' for My Father is greater than I. John 14:3, 18 • John 16:16

29 "And [R]now I have told you before it comes, that when it does come to pass, you may believe. John 13:19

30 "I will no longer talk much with you, [R]for the ruler of this world is coming, and he has [R]nothing in Me. [John 12:31] • [Heb. 4:15]

31 "But that the world may know that I love the Father, and [R]as the Father gave Me commandment, so I do. Arise, let us go from here. Is. 50:5; John 10:18★

CHAPTER 15

The Relationship of Believers to Christ

"I AM the true vine, and My Father is the vinedresser.

2 [R]"Every branch in Me that does not bear fruit He takes away;* and every *branch* that bears fruit He prunes, that it may bear [R]more fruit. Matt. 15:13 • [Matt. 13:12]

3 "You are already clean because of the word which I have spoken to you.

4 [R]"Abide in Me, and I in you. As the branch cannot bear fruit of itself, unless it abides in the vine, neither can you, unless you abide in Me. [Col. 1:23]

5 "I am the vine, you *are* the branches. He who abides in Me, and I in him, bears much fruit; for without Me you can do nothing.

6 "If anyone does not abide in Me, [R]he is cast out as a branch and is withered; and they gather them and throw *them* into the fire, and they are burned. Matt. 3:10

7 "If you abide in Me, and My words abide in you, you will* ask what you desire, and it shall be done for you.

8 "By this My Father is glorified, that you bear much fruit; so you will be My disciples.

9 "As the Father [R]loved Me, I also have loved you; abide in My love. John 5:20; 17:26

10 [R]"If you keep My commandments, you will abide in My love, just as I have kept My Father's commandments and abide in His love. John 14:15

11 "These things I have spoken to you, that My joy may remain in you, and [R]*that* your joy may be full. 1 John 1:4

The Relationship of Believers to Each Other

12 "This is My commandment, that you love one another as I have loved you.

13 "Greater love has no one than this, than to lay down one's life for his friends.

14 [R]"You are My friends if you do whatever I command you. [Matt. 12:50; 28:20]

15 "No longer do I call you servants, for a servant does not know what his master is doing; but I have called you friends, [R]for all things that I heard from My Father I have made known to you. Gen. 18:17

16 [R]"You did not choose Me, but I chose you and appointed you that you should go and bear fruit, and *that* your fruit should remain, that whatever you ask the Father in My name He may give you. John 6:70; 13:18

17 "These things I command you, that you love one another.

The Relationship of Believers to the World

18 [R]"If the world hates you, you know that it hated Me before *it hated* you. 1 John 3:13

19 "If you were of the world, the world would love its own. Yet because you are not of the world, but I chose you out of the world, therefore the world hates you.

20 "Remember the word that I said to you, [R]'A servant is not greater than his master.' If they persecuted Me, they will also persecute you. [R]If they kept My word, they will keep yours also. John 13:16 • Ezek. 3:7

21 "But [R]all these things they will do to you for My name's sake, because they do not know Him who sent Me. Matt. 10:22; 24:9

22 [R]"If I had not come and spoken to them, they would have no sin, but now they have no excuse for their sin. John 9:41; 15:24

23 [R]"He who hates Me hates My Father also. 1 John 2:23

24 "If I had not done among them the works which no one else did, they would have no sin; but now they have seen and also hated both Me and My Father.

25 "But *this happened* that the word might be fulfilled which is written in their law, *'They hated Me without a cause.'**

The Promise of the Holy Spirit

26 [R]"But when the Helper comes, whom I shall send to you from the Father, the Spirit of truth who proceeds from the Father, [R]He will testify of Me. Luke 24:49 • 1 John 5:6

14:28 NU omits *I said* **15:2** Or *lifts up* **15:7** NU omits *you will* **15:25** Ps. 69:4★

27 "And [R]you also will bear witness, be-
cause [R]you have been with Me from the be-
ginning. Luke 24:48 • Luke 1:2

CHAPTER 16

"THESE things I have spoken to you, that
you should not be made to stumble.
2 [R]"They will put you out of the syna-
gogues; yes, the time is coming [R]that whoever
kills you will think that he offers God ser-
vice. John 9:22 • Acts 8:1
3 "And [R]these things they will do to you*
because they have not known the Father nor
Me. John 8:19; 15:21
4 "But these things I have told you, that
when the* time comes, you may remember
that I told you of them. And these things I did
not say to you at the beginning, because I was
with you.
5 "But now I [R]go away to Him who sent Me,
and none of you asks Me, 'Where are You
going?' John 7:33; 13:33; 14:28; 17:11
6 "But because I have said these things to
you, sorrow has filled your heart.
7 "Nevertheless I tell you the truth. It is to
your advantage that I go away; for if I do not
go away, the Helper will not come to you; but
[R]if I depart, I will send Him to you. Acts 2:33☆
8 "And when He has come, [R]He will convict
the world of sin, and of righteousness, and of
judgment: Acts 1:8; 2:1–4, 37☆
9 [R]"of sin, because they do not believe in
Me; Acts 2:22
10 [R]"of righteousness, because I go to My Fa-
ther and you see Me no more; Acts 2:32
11 [R]"of judgment, because [R]the ruler of this
world is judged. Acts 26:18 • [Luke 10:18]
12 "I still have many things to say to you,
[R]but you cannot bear *them* now. Mark 4:33
13 "However, when He, the Spirit of truth,
has come, He will guide you into all truth; for
He will not speak on His own *authority*, but
whatever He hears He will speak; and [R]He
will tell you things to come. Acts 11:28; Rev. 1:19☆
14 "He will glorify Me, for He will take of
what is Mine and declare *it* to you.
15 [R]"All things that the Father has are Mine.
Therefore I said that He will take of Mine and
declare *it* to you.* Matt. 11:27

The Predictions of Christ's Death and Resurrection

16 "A [R]little while, and you will not see Me;
and again a little while, and you will see Me,
because I go to the Father." John 19:42; 20:19☆
17 **Then *some* of His disciples said among
themselves, "What is this that He says to us,** 'A
little while, and you will not see Me; and again
a little while, and you will see Me'; **and,** 'be-
cause I go to the Father'?"
18 **They said therefore, "What is this that He
says,** 'A little while'? **We do not [T]know what
He is saying."** understand
19 **Now Jesus knew that they desired to ask
Him, and He said to them,** "Are you inquiring
among yourselves about what I said, 'A little
while, and you will not see Me; and again a lit-
tle while, and you will see Me'?
20 "Most assuredly, I say to you that you will
weep and [R]lament, but the world will rejoice;
and you will be sorrowful, but your sorrow
will be turned into joy. John 20:20☆
21 [R]"A woman, when she is in labor, has
sorrow because her hour has come; but as
soon as she has given birth to the child, she
no longer remembers the anguish, for joy
that a human being has been born into the
world. Is. 13:8; 26:17; 42:14
22 "Therefore you now have sorrow; but I
will see you again and [R]your heart will re-
joice, and your joy no one will take from
you. John 20:20; Acts 2:46; 13:52; 1 Pet. 1:8☆
23 "And in that day you will ask Me nothing.
[R]Most assuredly, I say to you, whatever you ask
the Father in My name He will give you. Matt. 7:7
24 "Until now you have asked nothing in My
name. Ask, and you will receive, [R]that your
joy may be [R]full. John 17:13 • John 15:11
25 "These things I have spoken to you in fig-
urative language; but the time is coming when
I will no longer speak to you in figurative lan-
guage, but I will tell you [R]plainly about the Fa-
ther. John 7:13
26 "In that day you will ask in My name, and
I do not say to you that I shall pray the Father
for you;
27 [R]"for the Father Himself loves you, be-
cause you have loved Me, and have believed
that I came forth from God. [John 14:21, 23]
28 [R]"I came forth from the Father and have
come into the world. Again, I leave the world
and go to the Father." John 13:1, 3
29 **His disciples said to Him, "See, now You
are speaking plainly, and using no figure of
speech!**
30 **"Now we are sure that [R]You know all
things, and have no need that anyone should
question You. By this we believe that You came
forth from God."** John 21:17
31 **Jesus answered them,** "Do you now be-
lieve?
32 [R]"Indeed the hour is coming, yes, has
now come, that you will be scattered, [R]each
to his own, and will leave Me alone. And yet
I am not alone, because the Father is with
Me. Matt. 26:31, 56; Mark 14:50☆ • John 20:10
33 "These things I have spoken to you, that
in Me you may have peace. In the world you
will* have tribulation; but be of good cheer, I
have overcome the world."

16:3 NU, M omit *to you* **16:4** NU *their* **16:15** NU, M *He takes of Mine and will declare it to you.* **16:33** NU, M omit *will*

CHAPTER 17

Christ Prays for Himself

JESUS spoke these words, lifted up His eyes
to heaven, and said: "Father, [R]the hour has
come. Glorify Your Son, that Your Son also
may glorify You, John 12:23
2 [R]"as You have given Him authority over
all flesh, that He should* give eternal life to as
many as You have given Him. John 3:35
3 "And [R]this is eternal life, that they may
know You, the only true God, and Jesus Christ
whom You have sent. Jer. 9:23, 24
4 [R]"I have glorified You on the earth. I have
finished the work which You have given Me to
do. Is. 49:3; 50:5; John 13:31★
5 "And now, O Father, glorify Me together
with Yourself, with the glory [R]which I had with
You before the world was. Phil. 2:6

Christ Prays for His Disciples

6 "I have [T]manifested Your name to the men
whom You have given Me out of the world.
They were Yours, You gave them to Me, and
they have kept Your word. *revealed*
7 "Now they have known that all things
which You have given Me are from You.
8 "For [R]I have given to them the words
which You have given Me; and they have re-
ceived *them*, and have known surely that I
came forth from You; and they have believed
that You sent Me. Deut. 18:15, 18★
9 "I pray for them. [R]I do not pray for the
world but for those whom You have given Me,
for they are Yours. [1 John 5:19]
10 "And all Mine are Yours, and Yours are
Mine, and I am glorified in them.
11 [R]"Now I am no longer in the world, but
these are in the world, and I come to You. Holy
Father, [R]keep through Your name those whom
You have given Me,* that they may be one as
We *are*. John 13:1 • [1 Pet. 1:5]
12 "While I was with them in the world,* I
kept them in Your name. Those whom You
gave Me I have kept;* and none of them is lost
except the son of perdition, [R]that the Scripture
might be fulfilled. Ps. 41:9; 109:8
13 "But now I come to You, and these things
I speak in the world, that they may have My
joy fulfilled in themselves.
14 "I have given them Your word; and the
world has hated them because they are not of
the world, just as I am not of the world.
15 "I do not pray that You should take them
out of the world, but [R]that You should keep
them from the evil one. 1 John 5:18
16 "They are not of the world, just as I am
not of the world.
17 [R]"Sanctify them by Your truth. [R]Your word
is truth. [Eph. 5:26] • Ps. 119:9, 142, 151
18 [R]"As You sent Me into the world, I also
have sent them into the world. John 4:38
19 "And [R]for their sakes I sanctify Myself,
that they also may be sanctified by the
truth. [Heb. 10:10]

Christ Prays for All Believers

20 "I do not pray for these alone, but also for
those who will* believe in Me through their
word;
21 [R]"that they all may be one, as You, Father,
are in Me, and I in You; that they also may be
one in Us, that the world may believe that You
sent Me. [Gal. 3:28]
22 "And the [R]glory which You gave Me I have
given them, [R]that they may be one just as We
are one: 1 John 1:3 • [2 Cor. 3:18]
23 "I in them, and You in Me; that they may
be made perfect in one, and that the world
may know that You have sent Me, and have
loved them as You have loved Me.
24 [R]"Father, I desire that they also whom You
gave Me may be with Me where I am, that
they may behold My glory which You have
given Me; for You loved Me before the foun-
dation of the world. [1 Thess. 4:17]
25 "O righteous Father! The world has not
known You, but I have known You; and these
have known that You sent Me.
26 [R]"And I have declared to them Your
name, and will declare *it*, that the love [R]with
which You loved Me may be in them, and I in
them." John 17:6 • John 15:9

CHAPTER 18

The Arrest of Christ
Matt. 26:47–56; Mark 14:43–52; Luke 22:47–53

WHEN Jesus had spoken these words, He
went out with His disciples over the
Brook Kidron, where there was a garden,
which He and His disciples entered.
2 And Judas, who betrayed Him, also knew
the place; [R]for Jesus often met there with His
disciples. Luke 21:37; 22:39
3 Then Judas, having received a detach-
ment *of troops*, and officers from the chief
priests and Pharisees, came there with
lanterns, torches, and weapons.
4 Jesus therefore, knowing all things that
would come upon Him, went forward and said
to them, "Whom are you seeking?"
5 They answered Him, [R]"Jesus [T]of Naza-
reth." Jesus said to them, "I am *He*." And Ju-
das, who [R]betrayed Him, also stood with
them. Matt. 21:11 • Lit. *the Nazarene* • Ps. 41:9
6 Now when He said to them, "I am *He*,"
they drew back and fell to the ground.
7 Then He asked them again, "Whom are
you seeking?" And they said, "Jesus of Naza-
reth."

17:2 M *shall* **17:11** NU, M *keep them through Your name which You have given Me* **17:12** NU omits *in the world* • NU *in Your name which You gave Me. And I guarded them;* (or *it;*) **17:20** NU, M omit *will*

8 Jesus answered, "I have told you that I am *He*. Therefore, if you seek Me, let these go their way,"

9 that the saying might be fulfilled which He spoke, R"Of those whom You gave Me I have lost none." [John 6:39; 17:12]

10 RThen Simon Peter, having a sword, drew it and struck the high priest's servant, and cut off his right ear. The servant's name was Malchus. Matt. 26:51

11 So Jesus said to Peter, "Put your sword into the sheath. Shall I not drink the cup which My Father has given Me?"

First Jewish Trial Before Annas
Matt. 26:69, 70; Mark 14:66–68; Luke 22:55–57

12 Then the detachment *of troops* and the captain and the officers of the Jews arrested Jesus and bound Him.

13 And Rthey led Him away to Annas first, for he was the father-in-law of Caiaphas who was high priest that year. Matt. 26:57

14 RNow it was Caiaphas who advised the Jews that it was expedient that one man should die for the people. John 11:50

15 And Simon Peter followed Jesus, and so *did* another* disciple. Now that disciple was known to the high priest, and went with Jesus into the courtyard of the high priest.

16 But Peter stood at the door outside. Then the other disciple, who was known to the high priest, went out and spoke to her who kept the door, and brought Peter in.

17 Then the servant girl who kept the door said to Peter, "You are not also *one* of this Man's disciples, are you?" He said, "I am Rnot." Matt. 26:34

18 Now the servants and officers who had made a fire of coals stood there, for it was cold, and they warmed themselves. And Peter stood with them and warmed himself.

19 The high priest then asked Jesus about His disciples and His doctrine.

20 Jesus answered him, "I spoke openly to the world. I always taught in synagogues and in the temple, where the Jews always meet,* and in secret I have said nothing.

21 "Why do you ask Me? Ask Rthose who have heard Me what I said to them. Indeed they know what I said." Mark 12:37

22 And when He had said these things, one of the officers who stood by Rstruck Jesus with the palm of his hand, saying, "Do You answer the high priest like that?" Lam. 3:30★

23 Jesus answered him, "If I have spoken evil, bear witness of the evil; but if well, why do you strike Me?"

Second Jewish Trial Before Caiaphas
Matt. 26:57–68, 73–75; Mark 14:53–65, 70–72; Luke 22:59–65

24 RThen Annas sent Him bound to Caiaphas the high priest. Matt. 26:57

25 Now Simon Peter stood and warmed himself. Therefore they said to him, "You are not also *one* of His disciples, are you?" He denied *it* and said, "I am not!"

26 One of the servants of the high priest, a relative *of him* whose ear Peter cut off, said, "Did I not see you in the garden with Him?"

27 RPeter then denied again; and Rimmediately a rooster crowed. Matt. 26:34★ • John 13:38

First Roman Trial Before Pilate
Matt. 27:2, 11–14; Mark 15:1–5; Luke 23:1–5

28 RThen they led Jesus from Caiaphas to the Praetorium, and it was early morning. But they themselves did not go into the Praetorium, lest they should be defiled, but that they might eat the Passover. John 18:32★

29 RPilate then went out to them and said, "What accusation do you bring against this Man?" Matt. 27:11–14

30 They answered and said to him, "If He were not Tan evildoer, we would not have delivered Him up to you." *a criminal*

31 Then Pilate said to them, "You take Him and judge Him according to your law." Therefore the Jews said to him, "It is not lawful for us to put anyone to death,"

32 Rthat the saying of Jesus might be fulfilled which He spoke, signifying by what death He would die. Matt. 20:17–19; 26:2

33 RThen Pilate entered the Praetorium again, called Jesus, and said to Him, "Are You the King of the Jews?" Matt. 27:11

34 Jesus answered him, "Are you speaking for yourself about this, or did others tell you this concerning Me?"

35 Pilate answered, "Am I a Jew? Your own nation and the chief priests have delivered You to me. What have You done?"

36 RJesus answered, "My kingdom is not of this world. If My kingdom were of this world, My servants would fight, so that I should not be delivered to the Jews; but now My kingdom is not from here." 1 Tim. 6:13

37 Pilate therefore said to Him, "Are You a king then?" Jesus answered, "You say *rightly* that I am a king. For this cause I was born, and for this cause I have come into the world, Rthat I should bear Rwitness to the truth. Everyone who Ris of the truth hears My voice." [Matt. 5:17; 20:28] • Is. 55:4 • [John 14:6]

38 Pilate said to Him, "What is truth?" And when he had said this, he went out again to the Jews, and said to them, R"I find no fault in Him at all. John 19:4, 6

Second Roman Trial Before Pilate
Matt. 27:15–31; Mark 15:6–20; Luke 23:13–25

39 R"But you have a custom that I should release someone to you at the Passover. Do you

18:15 M *the other* **18:20** NU *where all the Jews meet*

therefore want me to release to you the King of the Jews?" Luke 23:17–25
40 [R]Then they all cried again, saying, "Not this Man, but Barabbas!" [R]Now Barabbas was a robber. Is. 53:3; Acts 3:14★ • Luke 23:19

CHAPTER 19

SO then [R]Pilate took Jesus and scourged *Him.* Is. 50:6; Matt. 20:19; 27:26★
2 And the soldiers twisted a crown of thorns and put *it* on His head, and they put on Him a purple robe.
3 Then they said,* "Hail, King of the Jews!" And they [R]struck Him with their hands. Is. 50:6
4 Pilate then went out again, and said to them, "Behold, I am bringing Him out to you, [R]that you may know that I find no fault in Him." John 18:33, 38
5 Then Jesus came out, wearing the crown of thorns and the purple robe. And *Pilate* said to them, "Behold the Man!"
6 [R]Therefore, when the chief priests and officers saw Him, they cried out, saying, "Crucify *Him,* crucify *Him!*" Pilate said to them, "You take Him and crucify *Him,* for I find no fault in Him." Acts 3:13
7 The Jews answered him, [R]"We have a law, and according to our* law [R]He ought to die, because [R]He made Himself the Son of God." Lev. 24:16 • Matt. 20:18★ • Matt. 26:63–66
8 Therefore, when Pilate heard that saying, he was the more afraid,
9 and went again into the Praetorium, and said to Jesus, "Where are You from?" [R]But Jesus gave him no answer. Ps. 38:13, 14; Is. 53:7★
10 Then Pilate said to Him, "Are You not speaking to me? Do You not know that I have [T]power to crucify You, and [T]power to release You?" *authority*
11 Jesus answered, "You could have no power at all against Me unless it had been given you from above. Therefore the one who delivered Me to you has the greater sin."
12 From then on Pilate sought to release Him, but the Jews cried out, saying, "If you let this Man go, you are not Caesar's friend. [R]Whoever makes himself a king speaks against Caesar." Luke 23:2
13 When Pilate therefore heard that saying, he brought Jesus out and sat down in the judgment seat in a place that is called *The* Pavement, but in Hebrew, Gabbatha.
14 Now it was the Preparation Day of the Passover, and about the sixth hour. And he said to the Jews, "Behold your King!"
15 [R]But they cried out, "Away with *Him,* away with *Him!* Crucify Him!" Pilate said to them, "Shall I crucify your King?" The chief priests answered, [R]"We have no king but Caesar!" Is. 53:3★ • [Gen. 49:10]
16 [R]Then he delivered Him to them to be crucified. So they took Jesus and led *Him* away.* Luke 23:24

The Crucifixion of Christ
Matt. 27:32–38, 48, 50; Mark 15:21–26, 36, 37; Luke 23:26–33, 38, 46

17 And He, bearing His cross, [R]went out to a place called *the Place* of a Skull, which is called in Hebrew, Golgotha, Num. 15:36
18 where they [R]crucified Him, and two others with Him, one on either side, and Jesus in the center. Ps. 22:16–18; Matt. 20:19; 26:2★
19 [R]Now Pilate wrote a title and put *it* on the cross. And the writing was: Matt. 27:37

JESUS OF NAZARETH,
THE KING OF THE JEWS.

20 Then many of the Jews read this title, for the place where Jesus was crucified was near the city; and it was written in Hebrew, Greek, *and* Latin.
21 Therefore the chief priests of the Jews said to Pilate, "Do not write, 'The King of the Jews,' but, 'He said, "I am the King of the Jews." ' "
22 Pilate answered, "What I have written, I have written."
23 [R]Then the soldiers, when they had crucified Jesus, took His garments and made four parts, to each soldier a part, and also the tunic. Now the tunic was without seam, woven from the top in one piece. Luke 23:34
24 They said therefore among themselves, "Let us not tear it, but cast lots for it, whose it shall be," that the Scripture might be fulfilled which says:

"They divided My garments among them,
*And for My clothing they cast lots."**

Therefore the soldiers did these things.
25 Now there stood by the cross of Jesus His mother, and His mother's sister, Mary the *wife* of Clopas, and Mary Magdalene.
26 When Jesus therefore saw His mother, and [R]the disciple whom He loved standing by, He said to His mother, [R]"Woman, behold your son!" John 13:23; 20:2; 21:7, 20, 24 • John 2:4
27 Then He said to the disciple, "Behold your mother!" And from that hour that disciple took her [R]to his own *home.* John 1:11
28 After this, Jesus, knowing* that all things were now accomplished, [R]that the Scripture might be fulfilled, said, "I thirst!" Ps. 22:15★
29 Now a vessel full of sour wine was sitting there; and [R]they filled a sponge with sour wine, put *it* on hyssop, and put *it* to His mouth. Ps. 69:21; Matt. 27:48, 50★
30 So when Jesus had received the sour

19:3 NU *And they came up to Him and said*
19:7 NU *the law* **19:16** NU omits *and led Him away*
19:24 Ps. 22:18★ **19:28** M *seeing*

wine, He said, [R]"It is finished!" And bowing
His head, He gave up His spirit. Zech. 11:10, 11★
31 Therefore, because it was the Preparation
Day, [R]that the bodies should not remain on
the cross on the Sabbath (for that Sabbath
was a high day), the Jews asked Pilate that
their legs might be broken, and *that* they
might be taken away. Deut. 21:23
32 Then the soldiers came and broke the
legs of the first and of the other who was cru-
cified with Him.
33 But when they came to Jesus and saw that
He was already dead, [R]they did not break His
legs. Ps. 34:20★
34 But one of the soldiers pierced His side
with a spear, and immediately [R]blood and
water came out. [1 John 5:6, 8]
35 And he who has seen has testified, and
his testimony is true; and he knows that he is
telling the truth, so that you may believe.
36 For these things were done that the Scrip-
ture should be fulfilled, "Not *one* of His bones
shall be broken."*
37 And again another Scripture says, *"They
shall look on Him whom they pierced."**

The Burial of Christ
Matt. 27:57–60; Mark 15:42–46; Luke 23:50–54

38 [R]After this, Joseph of Arimathea, being a
disciple of Jesus, but secretly, [R]for fear of the
Jews, asked Pilate that he might take away
the body of Jesus; and Pilate gave *him* per-
mission. So he came and took the body of Je-
sus. Is. 53:9; Luke 23:50–56★ • [John 7:13; 9:22]
39 And [R]Nicodemus, who at first came to
Jesus by night, also came, bringing a mix-
ture of [R]myrrh and aloes, about a hundred
pounds. John 3:1, 2; 7:50 • Matt. 2:11
40 Then they took the body of Jesus, and
bound it in strips of linen with the spices, as
the custom of the Jews is to bury.
41 Now in the place where He was crucified
there was a garden, and in the garden a new
tomb in which no one had yet been laid.
42 So [R]there they laid Jesus, because of the
Jews' Preparation *Day*, for the tomb was
nearby. Is. 53:9; Matt. 26:12; Mark 14:8★

CHAPTER 20

The Resurrection of Christ
Matt. 28:1–8; Mark 16:1–8; Luke 24:1–12

NOW on the first *day* of the week Mary
Magdalene went to the tomb early, while
it was still dark, and saw *that* the stone had
been taken away from the tomb.
2 Then she ran and came to Simon Peter,
and to the other disciple, whom Jesus loved,
and said to them, "They have taken away the
Lord out of the tomb, and we do not know
where they have laid Him."
3 Peter therefore went out, and the other
disciple, and were going to the tomb.
4 So they both ran together, and the other
disciple outran Peter and came to the tomb
first.
5 And he, stooping down and looking in,
saw [R]the linen cloths lying *there;* yet he did
not go in. John 19:40
6 Then Simon Peter came, following him,
and went into the tomb; and he saw the linen
cloths lying *there,*
7 and [R]the [T]handkerchief that had been
around His head, not lying with the linen
cloths, but folded together in a place by it-
self. John 11:44 • *face cloth*
8 Then the [R]other disciple, who came to the
tomb first, went in also; and he saw and be-
lieved. John 21:23, 24
9 For as yet they did not know the Scrip-
ture, that He must rise again from the dead.
10 Then the disciples went away again to
their own homes.

Christ Appears to Mary Magdalene

11 [R]But Mary stood outside by the tomb
weeping, and as she wept she stooped down
and looked into the tomb. Mark 16:5
12 And she saw two angels in white sitting,
one at the head and the other at the feet,
where the body of Jesus had lain.
13 Then they said to her, "Woman, why are
you weeping?" She said to them, "Because
they have taken away my Lord, and I do not
know where they have laid Him."
14 Now when she had said this, she turned
around and saw Jesus standing *there,* and did
not know that it was Jesus.
15 Jesus said to her, "Woman, why are you
weeping? Whom are you seeking?" She, sup-
posing Him to be the gardener, said to Him,
"Sir, if You have carried Him away, tell me
where You have laid Him, and I will take Him
away."
16 Jesus said to her, [R]"Mary!" She turned
and said to Him,* "Rabboni!" (which is to say,
Teacher). John 10:3
17 Jesus said to her, "Do not cling to Me, for
I have not yet ascended to My Father; but go
to My brethren and say to them, [R]'I am as-
cending to My Father and your Father, and *to*
My God and your God.'" Mark 16:19; Acts 1:9☆
18 Mary Magdalene came and told the disci-
ples that she had seen the Lord,* and *that* He
had spoken these things to her.

Christ Appears to the Disciples (Thomas Absent)—Mark 16:14; Luke 24:36–43

19 Then, the same day at evening, being the
first *day* of the week, when the doors were
shut where the disciples were assembled,* for

19:36 Ex. 12:46; Num. 9:12; Ps. 34:20★ **19:37** Zech. 12:10★ **20:16** NU adds *in Hebrew* **20:18** NU *disciples, "I have seen the Lord,"* **20:19** NU omits *assembled*

[R]fear of the Jews, [R]Jesus came and stood in the midst, and said to them, "Peace *be* with you." John 9:22; 19:38 • John 16:16★

20 When He had said this, He showed them *His* hands and His side. Then the disciples were glad when they saw the Lord.

21 So Jesus said to them again, "Peace to you! [R]As the Father has sent Me, I also send you." John 17:18, 19

22 [R]And when He had said this, He breathed on *them,* and said to them, "Receive the Holy Spirit. John 16:20–22★

23 [R]"If you forgive the sins of any, they are forgiven them; if you retain the *sins* of any, they are retained." Matt. 16:19; 18:18

24 Now Thomas, [R]called the Twin, one of the twelve, was not with them when Jesus came. John 11:16

25 The other disciples therefore said to him, "We have seen the Lord." So he said to them, "Unless I see in His hands the print of the nails, and put my finger into the print of the nails, and put my hand into His side, I will not believe."

Christ Appears to the Disciples (Thomas Present)—1 Cor. 15:5

26 And after eight days His disciples were again inside, and Thomas with them. Jesus came, the doors being shut, and stood in the midst, and said, "Peace to you!"

27 Then He said to Thomas, "Reach your finger here, and look at My hands; and reach your hand *here,* and put *it* into My side. Do not be unbelieving, but believing."

28 And Thomas answered and said to Him, "My Lord and my God!"

29 Jesus said to him, "Thomas,* because you have seen Me, you have believed. [R]Blessed *are* those who have not seen and *yet* have believed." 1 Pet. 1:8

The Purpose of John's Gospel

30 And [R]truly Jesus did many other signs in the presence of His disciples, which are not written in this book; John 21:25

31 [R]but these are written that [R]you may believe that Jesus [R]is the Christ, the Son of God, and that believing you may have life in His name. Luke 1:4 • 1 John 5:13 • Luke 2:11

CHAPTER 21

Christ Appears to the Seven Disciples

AFTER these things Jesus showed Himself again to the disciples at the Sea of Tiberias, and in this way He showed *Himself:*

2 Simon Peter, [R]Thomas called the Twin, [R]Nathanael of Cana in Galilee, the *sons* of Zebedee, and two others of His disciples were together. John 20:24 • John 1:45–51

3 Simon Peter said to them, "I am going fishing." They said to him, "We are going with you also." They went out and immediately* got into the boat, and that night they caught nothing.

4 But when the morning had now come, Jesus stood on the shore; yet the disciples [R]did not know that it was Jesus. John 20:14

5 Then [R]Jesus said to them, "Children, have you any food?" They answered Him, "No." Luke 24:41

6 And He said to them, [R]"Cast the net on the right side of the boat, and you will find *some.*" So they cast, and now they were not able to draw it in because of the multitude of fish. Luke 5:4, 6, 7

7 Therefore that disciple whom Jesus loved said to Peter, "It is the Lord!" Now when Simon Peter heard that it was the Lord, he put on *his* outer garment (for he had removed it), and plunged into the sea.

8 But the other disciples came in the little boat (for they were not far from land, but about two hundred cubits), dragging the net with fish.

9 Then, as soon as they had come to land, they saw a fire of coals there, and fish laid on it, and bread.

10 Jesus said to them, "Bring some of the fish which you have just caught."

11 Simon Peter went up and dragged the net to land, full of large fish, one hundred and fifty-three; and although there were so many, the net was not broken.

12 Jesus said to them, [R]"Come *and* eat breakfast." Yet none of the disciples dared ask Him, "Who are You?"—knowing that it was the Lord. Acts 10:41

13 Jesus then came and took the bread and gave it to them, and likewise the fish.

14 This *is* now [R]the third time Jesus showed Himself to His disciples after He was raised from the dead. John 20:19, 26

Christ Speaks to Peter

15 So when they had eaten breakfast, Jesus said to Simon Peter, "Simon, *son* of Jonah,* do you love Me more than these?" He said to Him, "Yes, Lord; You know that I love You." He said to him, "Feed My lambs."

16 He said to him again a second time, "Simon, *son* of Jonah,* do you love Me?" He said to Him, "Yes, Lord; You know that I [T]love You." [R]He said to him, "Tend My [R]sheep." *have affection for* • Heb. 13:20 • Ps. 79:13

17 He said to him the third time, "Simon, *son* of Jonah,* do you [T]love Me?" Peter was grieved because He said to him the third time, "Do you love Me?" And he said to Him, "Lord, You know all things; You know that I love You." Jesus said to him, "Feed My sheep. *have affection for*

20:29 NU, M omit *Thomas* **21:3** NU omits *immediately* **21:15** NU *John* **21:16** NU *John* **21:17** NU *John*

18 [R]"Most assuredly, I say to you, when you
were younger, you girded yourself and walked
where you wished; but when you are old, you
will stretch out your hands, and another will
gird you and carry *you* where you do not
wish." Acts 12:3, 4
19 **This He spoke, signifying by what death
he would glorify God. And when He had spo-
ken this, He said to him, "Follow Me."**
20 **Then Peter, turning around, saw the dis-
ciple [R]whom Jesus loved following, [R]who
also had leaned on His breast at the supper,
and said, "Lord, who is the one who betrays
You?"** John 13:23; 20:2 • John 13:25
21 **Peter, seeing him, said to Jesus, "But Lord,
what *about* this man?"**
22 **Jesus said to him, "If I [T]will that he re-
main [R]till I come, what *is that* to you? You fol-
low Me."** *desire* • [Rev. 2:25; 3:11; 22:7, 20]
23 **Then this saying went out among the
brethren that this disciple would not die. Yet
Jesus did not say to him that he would not die,
but, "If I will that he remain till I come, what
is that to you?"**

The Conclusion of John's Gospel

24 **This is the disciple who [R]testifies of these
things, and wrote these things; and we know
that his testimony is true.** John 19:35
25 **[R]And there are also many other things
that Jesus did, which if they were written one
by one, [R]I suppose that even the world itself
could not contain the books that would be
written. Amen.** John 20:30 • Amos 7:10

THE ACTS
OF THE APOSTLES

THE BOOK OF ACTS

Jesus' last recorded words have come to be known as the Great Commission: "You shall be witnesses to Me in Jerusalem, and in all Judea and Samaria, and to the end of the earth" (1:8). The Book of Acts, written by Luke, is the story of the men and women who took that commission seriously and began to spread the news of a risen Savior to the most remote corners of the known world.

Each section of the book (1—7; 8—12; 13—28) focuses on a particular audience, a key personality, and a significant phase in the expansion of the gospel message.

As the second volume in a two-part work by Luke, this book probably had no separate title. But all available Greek manuscripts designate it by the title *Praxeis*, "Acts," or by an expanded title like "The Acts of the Apostles." *Praxeis* was commonly used in Greek literature to summarize the accomplishments of outstanding men. While the apostles are mentioned collectively at several points, this book really records the acts of Peter (1—12) and of Paul (13—28).

THE AUTHOR OF ACTS

Acts 1:1 refers Theophilus to "The former account," that is, the Gospel of Luke. (See "The Author of Luke" for the internal and external support for Lucan authorship of Luke.) Luke's source for the "we" sections in this book (16:10–17; 20:5—21:18; 27:1—28:16) was his own memory if not some kind of diary. For the remainder of this book, Luke no doubt followed the same careful investigative procedures that he used in writing his gospel (Luke 1:1–4). As a close traveling companion of Paul, Luke had access to the principal eyewitness for chapters 13—28. It is also likely that he had opportunities to interview such key witnesses in Jerusalem as Peter and John for the information in chapters 1—12. Acts 15:23–29 and 23:26–30 indicate that Luke may have used written documents as well.

THE TIME OF ACTS

Suggested dates for the writing of Acts range from A.D. 62 to the middle of the second century. Twentieth-century archaeological discoveries have strikingly confirmed the trustworthiness and precision of Luke as a historian and show that his work should be dated in the first century. Luke's perplexingly abrupt ending with Paul awaiting trial in Rome has led many to believe that Acts was completed prior to Paul's trial (A.D. 62). If it was written after this crucial event, why didn't Luke mention the outcome? Luke may have had a reason, but the simplest explanation of his silence is that Paul had not yet stood before Caesar. Acts gives no hint of the persecution under Nero (A.D. 64), Paul's death (A.D. 68), or the destruction of Jerusalem (A.D. 70).

THE CHRIST OF ACTS

The resurrected Savior is the central theme of the sermons and defenses in Acts. The Old Testament Scriptures, the historical Resurrection, the apostolic testimony, and the convicting power of the Holy Spirit all bear witness that Jesus is both Lord and Christ (see Peter's sermons in 2:22–36 and 10:34–43). "To Him all the prophets witness that, through His name, whoever believes in Him will receive remission of sins" (10:43). "Nor is there salvation in any other, for there is no other name under heaven given among men by which we must be saved" (4:12).

KEYS TO ACTS

Key Word: The Growth of the Church—While there are four accounts of the life of Jesus, this is the only book that carries on the story from His ascension to the period of the New Testament epistles. Thus, Acts is the historical link between the Gospels and the Epistles. Because of Luke's strong emphasis on the ministry of the Holy Spirit, this book could be regarded as "the Acts of the Spirit of Christ working in and through the Apostles." As a missionary himself, Luke's interest in the progressive spread of the gospel is obviously reflected in this apostolic history. Luke was personally involved as a participant in this story, so it was not written from a detached point of view.

From a theological standpoint, Acts was written to trace the development of the body of Christ over the one-generation transition from a primarily Jewish to a predominantly Gentile membership. This apologetic work presents Christianity as distinct from Judaism but also as its fulfillment.

Key Verses: Acts 1:8 and 2:42–47—"But you shall receive power when the Holy Spirit has come upon you; and you shall be witnesses to Me in Jerusalem, and in all Judea and Samaria, and to the end of the earth" (1:8).

"And they continued steadfastly in the apostles' doctrine and fellowship, in the breaking of bread, and in prayers. Then fear came upon every soul, and many wonders and signs were done through the apostles. Now all who believed were together, and had all things in common, and sold their possessions and goods, and divided them among all, as anyone had need. So continuing daily with one accord in the temple, and breaking bread from house to house, they ate their food with gladness and simplicity of heart, praising God and having favor with all the people. And the Lord added to the church daily those who were being saved" (2:42–47).

Key Chapter: Acts 2—Chapter 2 records the earth-changing events of the Day of Pentecost when the Holy Spirit comes, fulfilling Christ's promise to wait until the Holy Spirit arrives to empower and direct the witness. The Spirit transforms a small group of fearful men into a thriving, worldwide church that is ever moving forward and fulfilling the Great Commission.

SURVEY OF ACTS

Luke begins the Book of Acts where he left off in his gospel. Acts records the initial fulfillment of the Great Commission of Matthew 28:19, 20 as it traces the beginning and growth of the New Testament church (this growth pattern can be seen in 1:15; 2:41, 47; 4:4; 5:14; 6:7; 9:31; 12:24; 13:49; 16:5; 19:20). Acts traces important events in the early history of Christianity from the ascension of Christ to the outpouring of the Holy Spirit to the rapid progress of the gospel, beginning in Jerusalem and spreading throughout the Roman Empire.

Acts is a pivotal book of transitions: from the Gospels to the Epistles (history), from Judaism to Christianity (religion), from law to grace (divine dealing), from Jews alone to Jews and Gentiles (people of God), and from kingdom to church (program of God).

The three movements in Acts follow its key verse (1:8): witness in Jerusalem (1:1—8:4); witness in Judea and Samaria (8:5—12:25); witness to the end of the earth (13—28).

Witness in Jerusalem (1:1—8:4): After appearing to His disciples for "forty days" (1:3), the Lord tells them to wait in Jerusalem for the fulfillment of His promise concerning the Holy Spirit. Ten days after His ascension, this promise is significantly fulfilled as the disciples are suddenly empowered and filled with the Holy Spirit. The disciples are transformed and filled with courage to proclaim the brand-new message of the resurrected Savior. Peter's powerful sermon, like all the sermons in Acts, is built upon the Resurrection, and 3,000 persons respond with saving faith. After dramatically healing a man who was lame from birth, Peter delivers a second crucial message to the people of Israel resulting in thousands of additional responses. The religious leaders arrest the apostles, and this gives Peter an opportunity to preach a special sermon to them.

The enthusiasm and joy of the infant church are marred by internal and external problems. Ananias and Sapphira receive the ultimate form of discipline because of their treachery, and the apostles are imprisoned and persecuted because of their witness. Seven men, including Stephen and Philip, are selected to assist the apostles. Stephen is brought before the Sanhedrin; in his defense, Stephen surveys the Scriptures to prove that the Man they condemned and killed was the Messiah Himself. The members of the Sanhedrin react to Stephen's words by dragging him out of the city and making him the first Christian martyr.

Witness in Judea and Samaria (8:5—12:25): Philip goes to the province of Samaria and successfully proclaims the new message to a people hated by the Jews. Peter and John confirm his work and exercise their apostolic authority by imparting the Holy Spirit to these

FOCUS	WITNESS IN JERUSALEM		WITNESS IN JUDEA AND SAMARIA	WITNESS TO THE REMOTEST PART OF THE EARTH	
REFERENCE	1:1———3:1———	——8:5———	———13:1———	———21:7———	——28:31
DIVISION	POWER OF THE CHURCH	PROGRESS OF THE CHURCH	EXPANSION OF THE CHURCH	PAUL'S THREE JOURNEYS	PAUL'S TRIALS
TOPIC	JEWS		SAMARITANS	GENTILES	
	PETER		PHILIP	PAUL	
LOCATION	JERUSALEM		JUDEA AND SAMARIA	UTTERMOST PART	
TIME	2 YEARS (A.D. 33–35)		13 YEARS (A.D. 35–48)	14 YEARS (A.D. 48–62)	

new members of the body of Christ. God sovereignly transforms Saul the persecutor into Paul the apostle to the Gentiles, but He uses Peter to introduce the gospel to the Gentiles. In a special vision Peter realizes that Christ has broken down the barrier between Jew and Gentile. After Cornelius and other Gentiles come to Christ through his preaching, Peter convinces the Jewish believers in Jerusalem that "the Gentiles had also received the word of God" (11:1). Even while experiencing more and more persecution, the church continues to increase, spreading throughout the Roman Empire.

Witness to the End of the Earth (13—28): Beginning with chapter 13, Luke switches the focus of Acts from Peter to Paul. Antioch in Syria gradually replaces Jerusalem as the headquarters of the church, and all three of Paul's missionary journeys originate from that city. The first journey (A.D. 48–49) concentrates on the Galatian cities of Pisidian Antioch, Iconium, Lystra, and Derbe. After this journey, a council is held among the apostles and elders of the church in Jerusalem to determine that the Gentile converts need not submit to the Law of Moses. The second missionary journey (A.D. 50–52) brings Paul once again to the Galatian churches, and then for the first time on to Macedonia and Greece. Paul spends much of his time in the cities of Philippi, Thessalonica, and Corinth, and later returns to Jerusalem and Antioch. In his third missionary journey (A.D. 53–57), Paul spends almost three years in the Asian city of Ephesus before visiting Macedonia and Greece for the second time. Although he is warned not to go to Jerusalem, Paul cannot be dissuaded.

It is not long before Paul is falsely accused of bringing Gentiles into the temple. Only the Roman commander's intervention prevents his being killed by the mob. Paul's defense before the people and before the Sanhedrin evokes violent reactions. When the commander learns of a conspiracy to assassinate Paul, he sends his prisoner to Felix, the governor in Caesarea. During his two-year imprisonment there (A.D. 57–59), Paul defends the Christian faith before Felix, Festus, and Agrippa. His appeal to Caesar requires a long voyage to Rome, where he is placed under house arrest until his trial.

OUTLINE OF ACTS

Part One: The Witness in Jerusalem (1:1—8:4)

I. The Power of the Church .... 1:1—2:47

A. Prologue to Acts 1:1, 2
B. Appearances of the Resurrected Christ .. 1:3–8
C. Ascension of Christ 1:9–11
D. Anticipation of the Spirit 1:12–14
E. Appointment of Matthias 1:15–26
F. Filling with the Holy Spirit 2:1–4
G. Speaking with Other Tongues 2:5–13
H. Peter Explains Pentecost 2:14–41
I. Practices of the Early Church 2:42–47

II. The Progress of the Church .... 3:1—8:4

A. Peter Heals the Lame Man 3:1–11
B. Peter's Second Sermon 3:12–26
C. Peter and John Are Put into Custody 4:1–4
D. Peter Preaches to the Sanhedrin 4:5–12
E. Sanhedrin Commands Peter Not to Preach 4:13–22
F. Apostles' Prayer for Boldness 4:23–31
G. Early Church Voluntarily Shares 4:32–37
H. Ananias and Sapphira Lie 5:1–11
I. Apostles' Mighty Miracles 5:12–16
J. Apostles' Persecution 5:17–42
   1. Apostles Are Miraculously Freed from Prison 5:17–28
   2. Apostles Preach to the Council 5:29–32
   3. Gamaliel's Advice 5:33–39
   4. Apostles Are Beaten 5:40–42
K. Deacons Are Appointed 6:1–8
L. Stephen Is Martyred .... 6:9—7:60
   1. Stephen Is Brought Before the Council 6:9–15
   2. Stephen Preaches to the Council 7:1–60
M. Saul Persecutes the Church 8:1–4

Part Two: The Witness in Judea and Samaria (8:5—12:25)

I. The Witness of Philip 8:5–40

A. Philip Witnesses to the Samaritans 8:5–25
B. Philip Witnesses to the Ethiopian Treasurer 8:26–40

II. The Conversion of Saul 9:1–31

A. Saul Is Converted and Blinded 9:1–9
B. Saul Is Filled with the Spirit 9:10–19
C. Saul Preaches at Damascus 9:20–22
D. Saul Witnesses in Jerusalem 9:23–31

III. The Witness of Peter .... 9:32—11:18

A. Peter Heals Aeneas at Lydda 9:32–35
B. Peter Raises Dorcas at Joppa 9:36–43
C. Peter Witnesses to Cornelius at Caesarea .... 10:1—11:18
   1. Cornelius Sends for Peter 10:1–8
   2. Peter Sees the Great Sheet 10:9–22
   3. Peter Preaches to the Gentiles 10:23–43
   4. Gentiles Are Converted and Speak in Tongues 10:44–48

Part Three: The Witness to the End of the Earth (13:1—28:31)

CHAPTER 1

Prologue to Acts

THE former account I made, O
[R]Theophilus, of all that Jesus began both
to do and teach, Luke 1:3
2 [R]until the day in which He was taken up,
after He through the Holy Spirit [R]had given
commandments to the apostles whom He had
chosen, Mark 16:19 • Matt. 28:19

Appearances of the Resurrected Christ Luke 24:44–49

3 [R]to whom He also presented Himself alive
after His suffering by many [T]infallible proofs,
being seen by them during forty days and
speaking of the things pertaining to the king-
dom of God. Mark 16:12, 14 • *unmistakable*
4 [R]And being assembled together with
them, He commanded them not to depart
from Jerusalem, but to wait for the Promise of
the Father, "which," *He said,* "you have [R]heard
from Me; Luke 24:49 • [John 14:16, 17, 26]
5 "for John truly baptized with water, [R]but
you shall be baptized with the Holy Spirit not
many days from now." [Joel 2:28]
6 Therefore, when they had come together,
they asked Him, saying, "Lord, will You at this
time restore the kingdom to Israel?"
7 And He said to them, [R]"It is not for you to
know times or seasons which the Father has
put in His own authority. 1 Thess. 5:1

8 [R]"But you shall receive power [R]when the
Holy Spirit has come upon you; and you shall
be witnesses to Me* in Jerusalem, and in all
Judea and Samaria, and to the end of the
earth." [Acts 2:1, 4] • Luke 24:49

Ascension of Christ Mark 16:19; Luke 24:50, 51

9 Now when He had spoken these things,
while they watched, He was taken up, and a
cloud received Him out of their sight.
10 And while they looked steadfastly toward
heaven as He went up, behold, two men stood
by them in white apparel,
11 who also said, "Men of Galilee, why do
you stand gazing up into heaven? This *same*
Jesus, who was taken up from you into
heaven, [R]will so come in like manner as you
saw Him go into heaven." Dan. 7:13

Anticipation of the Spirit—Luke 24:52

12 [R]Then they returned to Jerusalem from
the mount called Olivet, which is near Jerusa-
lem, a Sabbath day's journey. Luke 24:52
13 And when they had entered, they went
up [R]into the upper room where they were
staying: [R]Peter, James, John, and Andrew;
Philip and Thomas; Bartholomew and
Matthew; James *the son* of Alphaeus and
[R]Simon the Zealot; and Judas *the son* of
James. Acts 9:37, 39; 20:8 • Matt. 10:2–4 • Luke 6:15
14 [R]These all continued with one accord in
prayer and supplication,* with [R]the women
and Mary the mother of Jesus, and with [R]His
brothers. Acts 2:1, 46 • Luke 23:49, 55 • Matt. 13:55

Appointment of Matthias—Matt. 27:7, 8

15 And in those days Peter stood up in the
midst of the disciples* (altogether the number
[R]of names was about a hundred and twenty),
and said, Rev. 3:4
16 "Men *and* brethren, this Scripture had to
be fulfilled, [R]which the Holy Spirit spoke be-
fore by the mouth of David concerning Judas,
[R]who became a guide to those who arrested
Jesus; Ps. 41:9★ • Luke 22:47
17 "for [R]he was numbered with us and ob-
tained a part in this ministry." Matt. 10:4
18 [R](Now this man purchased a field with
[R]the wages of iniquity; and falling headlong,
he burst open in the middle and all his en-
trails gushed out. Matt. 27:3–10 • Mark 14:21
19 And it became known to all those
dwelling in Jerusalem; so that field is called in
their own language, Akel Dama, that is, Field
of Blood.)
20 "For it is written in the Book of Psalms:

1:8 NU *My witnesses* **1:14** NU omits *and supplication* **1:15** NU *brethren*

1:8 Empowered by God—One of the most common excuses for not becoming a Christian is the fear of failure to live the Christian life. Besides overlooking the fact that people cannot be saved on the basis of good works (Page 1250—Titus 3:5), this objection neglects the truth that God provides the power to live the Christian life. Before Christ was crucified He promised the coming of the Holy Spirit to help believers (Page 1101—John 16:13, 14). The subsequent events of the Book of Acts supply ample evidence of the fulfillment of this prophecy (Page 1115—Acts 4:7, 33; 6:8).

The power of the Holy Spirit was not designed solely for the first-century church. Rather, all Christians are indwelt by the Spirit and thus have His power available (Page 1170—1 Cor. 6:19). However, living the Christian life under the Spirit's power must not be thought of as simply allowing the Spirit to take control while the believer does nothing. Believers still must live the Christian life, though they do it through the Spirit's power. Rom. 8:13 says, "if by the Spirit you put to death the deeds of the body, you will live." It is you who are to put to death the sinful deeds of the body, but you are to do it through the Spirit's power.

Christians who struggle in their own strength to live the Christian life will fail. They must by faith appropriate *daily* the *power* of the Holy Spirit (Page 1154—Rom. 8:4, 5). Described practically, this means that believers trust the Spirit to empower them in specific instances such as sharing their faith with others, resisting temptation, being faithful, and so on. There is no *secret formula* that makes the Spirit's power available. It is simply a reliance on the Spirit to help.

Now turn to Page 1249—Titus 1:2: Promise of God.

'Let his dwelling place be [T]*desolate,*
*And let no one live in it';** deserted

and,

*'Let** *another take his office.'**

21 "Therefore, of these men who have ac-
companied us all the time that the Lord Jesus
went in and out among us,
22 "beginning from the baptism of John to
that day when [R]He was taken up from us, one
of these must [R]become a witness with us of
His resurrection." Acts 1:9 • Acts 1:8; 2:32
23 And they proposed two: Joseph called
[R]Barsabas, who was surnamed Justus, and
Matthias. Acts 15:22
24 And they prayed and said, "You, O Lord,
[R]who know the hearts of all, show which of
these two You have chosen 1 Sam.16:7
25 "to take part in this ministry and apostle-
ship from which Judas by transgression fell,
that he might go to his own place."
26 And they cast their lots, and the lot fell on
Matthias. And he was numbered with the
eleven apostles.

CHAPTER 2

Filling with the Holy Spirit

When [R]the Day of Pentecost had fully
come, [R]they were all with one accord* in
one place. Lev. 23:15 • Acts 1:14
2 And suddenly there came a sound from
heaven, as of a rushing mighty wind, and [R]it
filled the whole house where they were sit-
ting. Acts 4:31
3 Then there appeared to them divided
tongues, as of fire, and *one* sat upon each of
them.
4 And they were all filled with the Holy
Spirit and began to speak with other tongues,
as the Spirit gave them utterance.

Speaking with Other Tongues

5 And there were dwelling in Jerusalem
Jews, [R]devout men, from every nation under
heaven. Acts 8:2
6 And when this sound occurred, the [R]mul-
titude came together, and were confused, be-
cause everyone heard them speak in his own
language. Acts 4:32
7 Then they were all amazed and marveled,
saying to one another, "Look, are not all these
who speak [R]Galileans? Acts 1:11
8 "And how *is it that* we hear, each in our
own language in which we were born?
9 "Parthians and Medes and Elamites,
those dwelling in Mesopotamia, Judea and
[R]Cappadocia, Pontus and Asia, 1 Pet. 1:1
10 "Phrygia and Pamphylia, Egypt and the
parts of Libya adjoining Cyrene, visitors from
Rome, both Jews and proselytes,
11 "Cretans and [T]Arabs—we hear them
speaking in our own tongues the wonderful
works of God." Arabians
12 So they were all amazed and perplexed,
saying to one another, "Whatever could this
mean?"
13 Others mocking said, "They are full of
new wine."

Peter Explains Pentecost

14 But Peter, standing up with the eleven,
raised his voice and said to them, "Men of
Judea and all who dwell in Jerusalem, let this
be known to you, and heed my words.
15 "For these are not drunk, as you sup-
pose, [R]since it is *only* [T]the third hour of the
day. 1 Thess. 5:7 • 9 A.M.
16 "But this is what was spoken by the
prophet Joel:

17 *'And it shall come to pass in the last*
days, says God,
[R]*That I will pour out of My Spirit on all*
flesh; Acts 10:45
Your sons and [R]*your daughters shall*
prophesy, Acts 21:9
Your young men shall see visions,
Your old men shall dream dreams.
18 *And on My menservants and on My*
maidservants
I will pour out My Spirit in those days;
[R]*And they shall prophesy.* 1 Cor. 12:10
19 *I will show wonders in heaven above*
And signs in the earth beneath:
Blood and fire and vapor of smoke.
20 [R]*The sun shall be turned into darkness,*
And the moon into blood, Matt. 24:29
Before the coming of the great and
awesome day of the LORD.
21 *And it shall come to pass*
That [R]*whoever calls on the name of the*
LORD Rom. 10:13
*Shall be saved.'**

22 "Men of Israel, hear these words: Jesus of
Nazareth, [R]a Man attested by God to you [R]by
miracles, wonders, and signs which God did
through Him in your midst, as you yourselves
also know— Is. 50:5★ • John 3:2; 5:6
23 "Him, [R]being delivered by the determined
purpose and foreknowledge of God, you have
taken* by lawless hands, have crucified, and
put to death; Luke 22:22
24 "whom God raised up, having loosed the
pains of death, because it was not possible
that He should be held by it.
25 "For David says concerning Him:

1:20 Ps. 69:25 • Ps. 109:8★ • Gr. *episkopen,* position of overseer **2:1** NU *together* **2:21** Joel 2:28–32 **2:23** NU omits *have taken*

'*I foresaw the* LORD *always before my*
face,
For He is at my right hand, that I may
not be shaken.
26 *Therefore my heart rejoiced, and my*
tongue was glad;
Moreover my flesh also will rest in hope.
27 *For You will not leave my soul in Hades,*
Nor will You allow Your Holy One to
see [R]*corruption.* Acts 13:30–37
28 *You have made known to me the ways*
of life;
You will make me full of joy in Your
presence.'*

29 "Men *and* brethren, let *me* speak freely to
you [R]of the patriarch David, that he is both
dead and buried, and his tomb is with us to
this day. Acts 13:36
30 "Therefore, being a prophet, [R]and know-
ing that God had sworn with an oath to him
that of the fruit of his body, according to the
flesh, He would raise up the Christ to sit on
his throne,* Ps. 132:11
31 "he, foreseeing this, spoke concerning the
resurrection of the Christ, [R]that His soul was
not left in Hades, nor did His flesh see cor-
ruption. Ps. 16:10; Acts 13:35★
32 [R]"This Jesus God has raised up, of which
we are all witnesses. Ps. 68:18★
33 "Therefore [R]being exalted to [R]the right
hand of God, and [R]having received from the
Father the promise of the Holy Spirit, He
poured out this which you now see and
hear. [Acts 5:31] • [Heb. 10:12] • [John 14:26]
34 "For David did not ascend into the heav-
ens, but he says himself:

[R]'*The* LORD *said to my Lord,* Ps. 68:18★
"*Sit at My right hand,*
35 *Till I make Your enemies Your*
footstool." '*

36 "Therefore let all the house of Israel know
assuredly that God has made this Jesus,
whom you crucified, both Lord and Christ."
37 Now when they heard *this,* [R]they were cut
to the heart, and said to Peter and the rest of
the apostles, "Men *and* brethren, what shall
we do?" John 16:8★
38 Then Peter said to them, [R]"Repent, and
let every one of you be baptized in the name
of Jesus Christ for the [T]remission of sins;
and you shall receive the gift of the Holy
Spirit. Luke 24:47 • *forgiveness*
39 "For the promise is to you and to your
children, and to all who are afar off, as many
as the Lord our God will call."
40 And with many other words he testified
and exhorted them, saying, "Be saved from
this [T]perverse generation." *crooked*
41 Then those who gladly* received his word
were baptized; and that day about three thou-
sand souls were added *to them.*

Practices of the Early Church

42 And they continued steadfastly in the
apostles' doctrine and fellowship, in the
breaking of bread, and in prayers.
43 Then fear came upon every soul, and
[R]many wonders and signs were done through
the apostles. Acts 2:22
44 Now all who believed were together, and
[R]had all things in common, Acts 4:32, 34, 37
45 and [T]sold their possessions and goods,
and [R]divided[T] them among all, as anyone had
need. *would sell* • Is. 58:7 • *distributed*
46 [R]So continuing daily with one accord [R]in
the temple, and breaking bread from house to
house, they ate their food with gladness and
simplicity of heart, Acts 1:14 • Luke 24:53
47 praising God and having favor with all
the people. And the Lord added to the church*
daily those who were being saved.

CHAPTER 3

Peter Heals the Lame Man

NOW Peter and John went up together [R]to
the temple at the hour of prayer, [R]the
ninth *hour.* Acts 2:46 • Ps. 55:17
2 And [R]a certain man lame from his
mother's womb was carried, whom they laid
daily at the gate of the temple which is called
Beautiful, [R]to ask alms from those who en-
tered the temple; Acts 14:8 • John 9:8

2:28 Ps. 16:8–11★ **2:30** NU omits *according to the flesh, He would raise up the Christ* and completes the verse with *He would seat one on his throne.* **2:35** Ps. 110:1 **2:41** NU omits *gladly* **2:47** NU omits *to the church*

2:42–47 Benefits of Participation in the Local Church—The benefits of participation in a local church are immediately apparent. This passage records the first meeting of the first local church. From this passage seven benefits of participation in the local church are immediately apparent: instruction—"continued steadfastly in the apostles' doctrine"; fellowship—"and fellowship"; observance of the ordinances—"breaking of bread"; corporate prayer—"prayers"; effective outreach—"fear came upon every soul"; common cause—"had all things in common"; and mutual assistance—"divided them among all, as anyone had need." In addition to these, four other benefits of participation in the local church are clear: worship (Page 1135—Acts 20:7); discipline (Page 996—Matt. 18:15–17; Page 1192—2 Cor. 13:1–10); pastoral oversight (Page 1283—1 Pet. 5:1–3); and obedience to God's command (Page 1265—Heb. 10:25). Participation in the local church is not optional for the child of God. It is imperative and yields eternal benefits.

Now turn to Page 1011—Matt. 28:19: Sharing Our Faith: Why?

3 who, seeing Peter and John about to go into the temple, asked for alms.

4 And fixing his eyes on him, with John, Peter said, "Look at us."

5 So he gave them his attention, expecting to receive something from them.

6 Then Peter said, "Silver and gold I do not have, but what I do have I give you: [R]In the name of Jesus Christ of Nazareth, rise up and walk." Acts 4:10

7 And he took him by the right hand and lifted *him* up, and immediately his feet and ankle bones received strength.

8 So he, [R]leaping up, stood and walked and entered the temple with them—walking, leaping, and praising God. Is. 35:6

9 [R]And all the people saw him walking and praising God. Acts 4:16, 21

10 Then they knew that it was he who sat begging alms at the Beautiful Gate of the temple; and they were filled with wonder and amazement at what had happened to him.

11 Now as the lame man who was healed held on to Peter and John, all the people ran together to them in the porch which is called Solomon's, greatly amazed.

Peter's Second Sermon

12 So when Peter saw *it*, he responded to the people: "Men of Israel, why do you marvel at this? Or why look so intently at us, as though by our own power or godliness we had made this man walk?

13 [R]"The God of Abraham, Isaac, and Jacob, the God of our fathers, glorified His Servant Jesus, whom you delivered up and denied in the presence of Pilate, when he was determined to let *Him* go. John 5:30

14 "But you denied [R]the Holy One [R]and the Just, and asked for a murderer to be granted to you, Mark 1:24 • Acts 7:52

15 "and killed the [T]Prince of life, [R]whom God raised from the dead, [R]of which we are witnesses. Or *Originator* • Acts 2:24 • Acts 2:32

16 "And His name, through faith in His name, has made this man strong, whom you see and know. Yes, the faith which *comes* through Him has given him this perfect soundness in the presence of you all.

17 "Yet now, brethren, I know that you did *it* in ignorance, as *did* also your rulers.

18 "But those things which God foretold by the mouth of all His prophets, that the Christ would suffer, He has thus fulfilled.

19 [R]"Repent therefore and be converted, that your sins may be blotted out, so that times of refreshing may come from the presence of the Lord, [Acts 2:38; 26:20]

20 "and that He may send Jesus Christ, [R]who was preached to you before,* Mal. 3:1★

21 "whom heaven must receive until the times of [R]restoration of all things, which God has spoken by the mouth of all His holy prophets since the world began. Matt. 17:11

22 "For Moses truly said to the fathers, *'The* LORD *your God will raise up for you a Prophet like me from your brethren. Him you shall hear in all things, whatever He says to you.*

23 *'And it shall be that every soul who will not hear that Prophet shall be utterly destroyed from among the people.'**

24 "Yes, and all the prophets, from Samuel and those who follow, as many as have spoken, have also foretold* these days.

25 [R]"You are sons of the prophets, and of the covenant which God made with our fathers, saying to Abraham, [R]*'And in your seed all the families of the earth shall be blessed.'** [Rom. 9:4, 8] • Gen. 12:3; 18:18★

26 "To you [R]first, God, having raised up His Servant Jesus, sent Him to bless you, [R]in turning away every one *of you* from your iniquities." [Rom. 1:16; 2:9] • Matt. 1:21★

CHAPTER 4

Peter and John Are Put into Custody

NOW as they spoke to the people, the priests, the captain of the temple, and the Sadducees came upon them,

2 being greatly disturbed that they taught the people and preached in Jesus the resurrection from the dead.

3 And they laid hands on them, and put *them* in custody until the next day, for it was already evening.

4 However, many of those who heard the word believed; and the number of the men came to be about five thousand.

Peter Preaches to the Sanhedrin

5 And it came to pass, on the next day, that their rulers, elders, and scribes,

6 as well as [R]Annas the high priest, Caiaphas, John, and Alexander, and as many as were of the family of the high priest, were gathered together at Jerusalem. Luke 3:2

7 And when they had set them in the midst, they asked, "By what power or by what name have you done this?"

8 [R]Then Peter, filled with the Holy Spirit, said to them, "Rulers of the people and elders of Israel: Luke 12:11, 12

9 "If we this day are judged for a good deed *done* to a helpless man, by what means he has been made well,

10 "let it be known to you all, and to all the people of Israel, that by the name of Jesus Christ of Nazareth, whom you crucified, whom God raised from the dead, by Him this man stands here before you whole.

3:20 NU, M *Christ Jesus, who was ordained for you before* **3:23** Deut. 18:15, 18, 19★ **3:24** NU, M *proclaimed* **3:25** Gen. 22:18; 26:4; 28:14

11 "This is the *'stone which was rejected by you builders, which has become the chief cornerstone.'**
12 "Nor is there salvation in any other, for there is no other name under heaven given among men by which we must be saved."

Sanhedrin Commands Peter Not to Preach

13 Now when they saw the boldness of Peter
and John, [R]and perceived that they were un-
educated and untrained men, they marveled.
And they realized that they had been with Je-
sus. [1 Cor. 1:27]
14 And seeing the man who had been healed
[R]standing with them, they could say nothing
against it. Acts 3:11
15 But when they had commanded them to
go aside out of the council, they conferred
among themselves,
16 saying, [R]"What shall we do to these
men? For, indeed, that a [T]notable miracle has
been done through them *is* [R]evident to all
who dwell in Jerusalem, and we cannot deny
it. John 11:47 • *remarkable sign* • Acts 3:7–10
17 "But so that it spreads no further among
the people, let us severely threaten them, that
from now on they speak to no man in this
name."
18 [R]So they called them and commanded
them not to speak at all nor teach in the name
of Jesus. Acts 5:28, 40
19 But Peter and John answered and said to
them, [R]"Whether it is right in the sight of
God to listen to you more than to God, you
judge. Acts 5:29
20 [R]"For we cannot but speak the things
which we have seen and heard." Acts 1:8
21 So when they had further threatened
them, they let them go, finding no way of pun-
ishing them, [R]because of the people, since
they all [R]glorified God for [R]what had been
done. Acts 5:26 • Matt. 15:31 • Acts 3:7, 8
22 For the man was over forty years old on
whom this miracle of healing had been per-
formed.

Apostles' Prayer for Boldness

23 And being let go, they went to their own
companions and reported all that the chief
priests and elders had said to them.
24 So when they heard that, they raised their
voice to God with one accord and said: "Lord,
You *are* God, who made heaven and earth and
the sea, and all that is in them,
25 "who by the mouth of Your servant David*
have said:

'Why did the nations rage,
And the people plot vain things?
26 *The kings of the earth took their stand,*
And the rulers were gathered together
Against the L*ORD* *and against His*
*Christ.'**

27 "For truly against Your holy Servant Je-
sus, whom You anointed, both Herod and Pon-
tius Pilate, with the Gentiles and the people of
Israel, were gathered together
28 "to do whatever Your hand and Your pur-
pose determined before to be done.
29 "Now, Lord, look on their threats, and
grant to Your servants [R]that with all boldness
they may speak Your word, Acts 9:27
30 "by stretching out Your hand to heal, [R]and
that signs and wonders may be done
[R]through the name of [R]Your holy Servant Je-
sus." Acts 2:43; 5:12 • Acts 3:6, 16 • Acts 4:27
31 And when they had prayed, [R]the place
where they were assembled together was
shaken; and they were all filled with the Holy
Spirit, [R]and they spoke the word of God with
boldness. Acts 2:2, 4; 16:26 • Acts 4:29

Early Church Voluntarily Shares

32 Now the multitude of those who believed
[R]were of one heart and one soul; [R]neither did
anyone say that any of the things he pos-
sessed was his own, but they had all things in
common. Rom. 15:5, 6 • Acts 2:44
33 And with great power the apostles gave
witness to the resurrection of the Lord Jesus.
And great grace was upon them all.
34 Nor was there anyone among them who
lacked; for all who were possessors of lands
or houses sold them, and brought the pro-
ceeds of the things that were sold,
35 [R]and laid *them* at the apostles' feet;
[R]and they distributed to each as anyone had
need. Acts 4:37; 5:2 • Acts 2:45; 6:1
36 And Joses,* who was also named Bar-
nabas by the apostles (which is translated Son
of [T]Encouragement), a Levite of the country of
Cyprus, Or *Consolation*
37 having land, sold *it*, and brought the
money and laid *it* at the apostles' feet.

CHAPTER 5

Ananias and Sapphira Lie

BUT a certain man named Ananias, with
Sapphira his wife, sold a possession.
2 And he kept back *part* of the proceeds,
his wife also being aware *of it*, and brought a
certain part and laid *it* at the apostles' feet.
3 [R]But Peter said, "Ananias, why has [R]Satan
filled your heart to lie to the Holy Spirit and
keep back *part* of the price of the land for
yourself? Deut. 23:21 • Luke 22:3
4 "While it remained, was it not your own?
And after it was sold, was it not in your own
control? Why have you conceived this thing in
your heart? You have not lied to men but to
God."

4:11 Ps. 118:22 **4:25** NU *who through the Holy Spirit, by the mouth of our father, Your servant David,* **4:26** Ps. 2:1, 2★ **4:36** NU *Joseph*

5 Then Ananias, hearing these words, fell down and breathed his last. So great fear came upon all those who heard these things.

6 And the young men arose and wrapped him up, carried *him* out, and buried *him.*

7 Now it was about three hours later when his wife came in, not knowing what had happened.

8 And Peter answered her, "Tell me whether you sold the land for so much?" She said, "Yes, for so much."

9 Then Peter said to her, "How is it that you have agreed together [R]to test the Spirit of the Lord? Look, the feet of those who have buried your husband *are* at the door, and they will carry you out." Acts 5:3, 4

10 Then immediately she fell down at his feet and breathed her last. And the young men came in and found her dead, and carrying *her* out, buried *her* by her husband.

11 So great fear came upon all the church and upon all who heard these things.

Apostles' Mighty Miracles

12 And through the hands of the apostles many signs and wonders were done among the people. [R]And they were all with one accord in Solomon's Porch. Acts 3:11; 4:32

13 Yet none of the rest dared join them, but the people esteemed them highly.

14 And believers were increasingly added to the Lord, multitudes of both men and women,

15 so that they brought the sick out into the streets and laid *them* on beds and couches, that at least the shadow of Peter passing by might fall on some of them.

16 Also a multitude gathered from the surrounding cities to Jerusalem, bringing sick people and those who were tormented by unclean spirits, and they were all healed.

Apostles Are Miraculously Freed from Prison

17 [R]Then the high priest rose up, and all those who *were* with him (which is the sect of the Sadducees), and they were filled with [T]indignation, Acts 4:1, 2, 6 • *jealousy*

18 and laid their hands on the apostles and put them in the common prison.

19 But at night [R]an angel of the Lord opened the prison doors and brought them out, and said, Acts 12:7; 16:26

20 "Go, stand in the temple and speak to the people all the words of this life."

21 And when they heard *that,* they entered the temple early in the morning and taught. But the high priest and those with him came and called the council together, with all the elders of the children of Israel, and sent to the prison to have them brought.

22 But when the officers came and did not find them in the prison, they returned and reported,

23 saying, "Indeed we found the prison shut securely, and the guards standing outside* before the doors; but when we opened them, we found no one inside!"

24 Now when the high priest,* [R]the captain of the temple, and the chief priests heard these things, they wondered what the outcome would be. Acts 4:1; 5:26

25 So one came and told them, saying,* "Look, the men whom you put in prison are standing in the temple and teaching the people!"

26 Then the captain went with the officers and brought them without violence, [R]for they feared the people, lest they should be stoned. Matt. 21:26

27 And when they had brought them, they set *them* before the council. And the high priest asked them,

28 saying, [R]"Did we not strictly command you not to teach in this name? And look, you have filled Jerusalem with your doctrine, [R]and intend to bring this Man's [R]blood on us!" Acts 4:17, 18 • Acts 2:23, 36 • Matt. 23:35

Apostles Preach to the Council

29 But Peter and the *other* apostles answered and said: [R]"We ought to obey God rather than men. Acts 4:19

30 [R]"The God of our fathers raised up Jesus whom you murdered by [R]hanging on a tree. Acts 3:13, 15 • [1 Pet. 2:24]

31 "Him God has exalted to His right hand *to be* Prince and [R]Savior, to give repentance to Israel and forgiveness of sins. Matt. 1:21

32 "And we are His witnesses to these things, and *so* also *is* the Holy Spirit whom God has given to those who obey Him."

Gamaliel's Advice

33 When they heard *this,* they were [R]furious and plotted to kill them. Acts 2:37; 7:54

34 Then one in the council stood up, a Pharisee named [R]Gamaliel, a teacher of the law held in respect by all the people, and commanded them to put the apostles outside for a little while. Acts 22:3

35 And he said to them: "Men of Israel, [T]take heed to yourselves what you intend to do regarding these men. *be careful*

36 "For some time ago Theudas rose up, claiming to be somebody. A number of men, about four hundred, [T]joined him. He was slain, and all who obeyed him were scattered and came to nothing. *followed*

37 "After this man, Judas of Galilee rose up in the days of the census, and drew away many people after him. He also perished, and all who obeyed him were dispersed.

38 "And now I say to you, keep away from these men and let them alone; for if this plan or this work is of men, it will come to nothing;

5:23 NU, M omit *outside* **5:24** NU omits *the high priest* **5:25** NU, M omit *saying*

39 [R]"but if it is of God, you cannot overthrow
it—lest you even be found [R]to fight against
God." 1 Cor. 1:25 • Acts 7:51; 9:5

Apostles Are Beaten

40 And they agreed with him, and when they
had called for the apostles and beaten *them,*
they commanded that they should not speak
in the name of Jesus, and let them go.
41 So they departed from the presence of the
council, [R]rejoicing that they were counted wor-
thy to suffer shame for His* name. [1 Pet. 4:13–16]
42 And daily [R]in the temple, and in every
house, they did not cease teaching and
preaching Jesus *as* the Christ. Acts 2:46

CHAPTER 6

Deacons Are Appointed

NOW in those days, when *the number of*
the disciples was multiplying, there arose
a complaint against the Hebrews by the Hel-
lenists,* because their widows were neglected
in the daily distribution.
2 Then the twelve summoned the multitude
of the disciples and said, [R]"It is not desirable
that we should leave the word of God and
serve tables. Ex. 18:17
3 "Therefore, brethren, [R]seek out from
among you seven men of *good* reputation, full
of the Holy Spirit and wisdom, whom we may
appoint over this business; 1 Tim. 3:7
4 "but we will give ourselves continually to
prayer and to the ministry of the word."
5 And the saying pleased the whole multi-
tude. And they chose Stephen, [R]a man full of
faith and the Holy Spirit, and Philip, Proch-
orus, Nicanor, Timon, Parmenas, and Nicolas,
a proselyte from Antioch, Acts 6:3; 11:24
6 whom they set before the apostles; and
[R]when they had prayed, [R]they laid hands on
them. Acts 1:24 • [2 Tim. 1:6]
7 Then the word of God spread, and the
number of the disciples multiplied greatly in
Jerusalem, and a great many [R]of the priests
were obedient to the faith. John 12:42
8 And Stephen, full of faith* and power,
did great [R]wonders and signs among the peo-
ple. Acts 2:43; 5:12; 8:15; 14:3

Stephen Is Brought Before the Council

9 Then there arose some from what is
called the Synagogue of the Freedmen (Cyre-
nians, Alexandrians, and those from Cilicia
and Asia), disputing with Stephen.
10 And they were not able to resist the wis-
dom and the Spirit by which he spoke.
11 Then they secretly induced men to say,
"We have heard him speak blasphemous
words against Moses and God."
12 And they stirred up the people, the elders,
and the scribes; and they came upon *him,*
seized him, and brought *him* to the council.
13 They also set up false witnesses who said,
"This man does not cease to speak blasphe-
mous* words against this holy place and the
law;
14 [R]"for we have heard him say that this Je-
sus of Nazareth will destroy this place and
change the customs which Moses delivered to
us." Acts 10:38; 25:8
15 And all who sat in the council, looking
steadfastly at him, saw his face as the face of
an angel.

CHAPTER 7

Stephen Preaches to the Council

THEN the high priest said, "Are these
things so?"
2 And he said, "Brethren and fathers, listen:
The [R]God of glory appeared to our father
Abraham when he was in Mesopotamia, be-
fore he dwelt in [R]Haran, Ps. 29:3 • Gen. 11:31, 32
3 "and said to him, *'Get out of your country
and from your relatives, and come to a land
that I will show you.'**
4 "Then he came out of the land of the
Chaldeans and dwelt in Haran. And from
there, when his father was dead, He moved
him to this land in which you now dwell.
5 "And *God* gave him no inheritance in it,
not even *enough* to set his foot on. But even
when *Abraham* had no child, [R]He promised to
give it to him for a possession, and to his de-
scendants after him. Gen. 12:7; 13:15; 26:3
6 "But God spoke in this way: that his de-
scendants would dwell in a foreign land, and
that they would bring them into bondage and
oppress *them* four hundred years.
7 *'And the nation to whom they will be in
bondage I will* [R]*judge,'** said God, *'and after
that they shall come out and serve Me in this
place.'** Ex. 14:13–31
8 [R]"Then He gave him the covenant of cir-
cumcision; [R]and so *Abraham* begot Isaac and
circumcised him on the eighth day; and Isaac
begot Jacob, and Jacob *begot* the twelve pa-
triarchs. Gen. 17:9–14 • Gen. 21:1–5
9 [R]"And the patriarchs, becoming envious,
[R]sold Joseph into Egypt. [R]But God was with
him Gen. 37:4, 11, 28 • Gen. 37:28 • Gen. 39:2, 21, 23
10 "and delivered him out of all his trou-
bles, [R]and gave him favor and wisdom in the
presence of Pharaoh, king of Egypt; and he
made him governor over Egypt and all his
house. Gen. 41:38–44
11 "Now a famine and great [T]trouble came
over all the land of Egypt and Canaan, and
our fathers found no sustenance. *affliction*
12 "But when Jacob heard that there was
grain in Egypt, he sent out our fathers first.

5:41 NU *the name;* M *the name of Jesus*
6:1 Greek-speaking Jews **6:8** NU *grace* **6:13** NU
omits *blasphemous* **7:3** Gen. 12:1 **7:7** Gen. 15:14 •
Ex. 3:12

13 "And the second *time* Joseph was made
known to his brothers, and Joseph's family
became known to the Pharaoh.
14 [R]"Then Joseph sent and called his father
Jacob and [R]all his relatives to *him*, seventy-
five* people. Gen. 45:9, 27 • Deut. 10:22
15 [R]"So Jacob went down to Egypt; and he
died, he and our fathers. Gen. 46:1–7
16 "And they were carried back to Shechem
and laid in the tomb that Abraham bought for
a sum of money from the sons of Hamor, *the
father* of Shechem.
17 "But when the time of the promise drew
near which God had sworn to Abraham, the
people grew and multiplied in Egypt
18 "till another king [R]arose who did not
know Joseph. Ex. 1:8
19 "This man dealt treacherously with our
people, and oppressed our forefathers, [R]mak-
ing them expose their babies, so that they
might not live. Ex. 1:22
20 "At this time Moses was born, and was
well pleasing to God; and he was brought up
in his father's house for three months.
21 "But [R]when he was set out, [R]Pharaoh's
daughter took him away and brought him up
as her own son. Ex. 2:3, 4 • Ex. 2:5–10
22 "And Moses was learned in all the wis-
dom of the Egyptians, and was [R]mighty in
words and deeds. Luke 24:19
23 [R]"Now when he was forty years old, it
came into his heart to visit his brethren, the
children of Israel. Ex. 2:11, 12
24 "And seeing one of *them* suffer wrong, he
defended and avenged him who was op-
pressed, and struck down the Egyptian.
25 "For he supposed that his brethren would
have understood that God would deliver them
by his hand, but they did not understand.
26 "And the next day he appeared to two of
them as they were fighting, and *tried to* rec-
oncile them, saying, 'Men, you are brethren;
why do you wrong one another?'
27 "But he who did his neighbor wrong
pushed him away, saying, 'Who made you a
ruler and a judge over us?
28 *'Do you want to kill me as you did the
Egyptian yesterday?'**
29 [R]"Then, at this saying, Moses fled and be-
came a dweller in the land of Midian, where
he [R]had two sons. Heb. 11:27 • Ex. 18:3
30 [R]"And when forty years had passed, an
Angel of the Lord* appeared to him in a flame
of fire in a bush, in the wilderness of Mount
Sinai. Ex. 3:1–10
31 "When Moses saw *it*, he marveled at the
sight; and as he drew near to observe, the
voice of the Lord came to him,
32 *"saying, 'I am the God of your fathers—
the God of Abraham, the God of Isaac, and
the God of Jacob.'** And Moses trembled and
dared not look.
33 *'Then the LORD said to him, "Take your
sandals off your feet, for the place where you
stand is holy ground.*
34 *"I have surely* [R]*seen the oppression of My
people who are in Egypt; I have heard their
groaning and have come down to deliver
them. And now come, I will* [R]*send you to
Egypt."'** Ex. 2:24, 25 • Ps. 105:26
35 "This Moses whom they rejected, saying,
*'Who made you a ruler and a judge?'** is the
one God sent *to be* a ruler and a deliverer [R]by
the hand of the Angel who appeared to him in
the bush. Ex. 14:21
36 [R]"He brought them out, after he had
shown wonders and signs in the land of
Egypt, and in the Red Sea, and in the wilder-
ness forty years. Ex. 12:41; 33:1
37 "This is that Moses who said to the chil-
dren of Israel,* *'The LORD your God will raise
up for you a Prophet like me from your
brethren. Him you shall hear.'**
38 [R]"This is he who was in the congregation
in the wilderness with the Angel who spoke to
him on Mount Sinai, and *with* our fathers,
[R]the one who received the living oracles to
give to us, Ex. 19:3 • Deut. 5:27
39 "whom our fathers [R]would not obey, but
rejected. And in their hearts they turned back
to Egypt, Ps. 95:8–11

7:14 Or *seventy*, Ex. 1:5 **7:28** Ex. 2:14 **7:30** NU omits *of the Lord* **7:32** Ex. 3:6, 15 **7:34** Ex. 3:5, 7, 8, 10 **7:35** Ex. 2:14 **7:37** Deut. 18:15★ • NU, M omit *Him you shall hear*

7:38 The Meaning of the Church—In modern English the word "church" is used in five ways: (1) a building designated as a place of worship, that is, a church building; (2) all who profess faith in Christ regardless of particular theological beliefs; (3) a denomination; (4) a single organized Christian group, that is, a local church; and (5) the body of Christ, that is, the universal church. While all of these are legitimate uses for modern English, the word "church" is used in the NT in only the last two senses—a local church, or the body of Christ, the universal church. At its root, the word "church" means a "called-out group." It is used of the nation Israel (Page 1119—Acts 7:38), which was a group of people who were called out of the rest of the people of the world to have a special national relationship to God. It is used of a local church (Page 1226— 1 Thess. 1:1, church of the Thessalonians; Page 1313—Rev. 2:1, church of Ephesus, and so on), and of the universal church, the body of Christ (Page 1220—Col. 1:18). The universal church comprises all believers from the Day of Pentecost until the time God takes the church out of the world, and at which time His program for the church will be complete. The local church is a local, visible, temporal manifestation of the universal church. At one point in history the local and universal churches were identical (Page 1114—Acts 2:41). The universal church will not meet until "we all get to heaven" and once in session will never cease.

Now turn to Page 994—Matt. 16:18: The Origin of the Church.

40 "saying to Aaron, *'Make us gods to go before us; as for this Moses who brought us out of the land of Egypt, we do not know what has become of him.'**

41 [R]"And they made a calf in those days, offered sacrifices to the idol, and rejoiced in the works of their own hands. Deut. 9:16

42 "Then God turned and gave them up to worship [R]the host of heaven, as it is written in the book of the Prophets: 2 Kin. 21:3

'Did you offer Me slaughtered animals
and sacrifices during forty years in the
wilderness,
O house of Israel?
43 *You also took up the tabernacle of*
Moloch,
And the star of your god Remphan,
Images which you made to worship;
And [R]I will carry you away beyond
*Babylon.'** Jer. 25:9–12

44 "Our fathers had the tabernacle of witness in the wilderness, as He appointed, instructing Moses [R]to make it according to the pattern that he had seen, [Heb. 8:5]

45 [R]"which our fathers, having received it in turn, also brought with Joshua into the land possessed by the Gentiles, whom God drove out before the face of our fathers until the days of David, Josh. 3:14; 18:1; 23:9

46 [R]"who found favor before God and [R]asked to find a dwelling for the God of Jacob. 2 Sam. 7:1–13 • 1 Chr. 22:7

47 "But Solomon built Him a house.

48 "However, [R]the Most High does not dwell in temples made with hands, as the prophet says: 1 Kin. 8:27

49 *'Heaven is My throne,*
And earth is My footstool.
What house will you build for Me? says
the Lord,
Or what is the place of My rest?
50 *Has My hand not [R]made all these*
*things?'** Ps. 102:25

51 "*You* stiff-necked and uncircumcised in heart and ears! You always resist the Holy Spirit; as your fathers *did,* so *do* you.

52 [R]"Which of the prophets did your fathers not persecute? And they killed those who foretold the coming of [R]the Just One, of whom you now have become the betrayers and murderers, 2 Chr. 36:16 • Acts 3:14; 22:14

53 "who have received the law by the direction of angels and have not kept *it.*"

54 [R]When they heard these things they were [T]cut to the heart, and they gnashed at him with *their* teeth. Acts 5:33 • *furious*

55 But he, [R]being full of the Holy Spirit, gazed into heaven and saw the [R]glory of God, and Jesus standing at the right hand of God, Acts 6:5 • [Ex. 24:17]

56 and said, "Look! [R]I see the heavens opened and the [R]Son of Man standing at the right hand of God!" Matt. 3:16 • Dan. 7:13

57 Then they cried out with a loud voice, stopped their ears, and ran at him with one accord;

58 and they cast *him* out of the city and stoned *him.* And [R]the witnesses laid down their clothes at the feet of a young man named Saul. Acts 22:20

59 And they stoned Stephen as he was calling on *God* and saying, "Lord Jesus, [R]receive my spirit." Ps. 31:5

60 Then he knelt down and cried out with a loud voice, [R]"Lord, do not charge them with this sin." And when he had said this, he fell asleep. Matt. 5:44

CHAPTER 8

Saul Persecutes the Church

NOW Saul was consenting to his death. At that time a great persecution arose against the church which was at Jerusalem; and [R]they were all scattered throughout the regions of Judea and Samaria, except the apostles. Acts 8:4; 11:19

2 And devout men carried Stephen *to his burial,* and [R]made great lamentation over him. Gen. 23:2

3 As for Saul, [R]he made havoc of the church, entering every house, and dragging off men and women, committing *them* to prison. Phil. 3:6

4 Therefore those who were scattered went everywhere preaching the word.

Philip Witnesses to the Samaritans

5 Then Philip went down to the* city of Samaria and preached Christ to them.

6 And the multitudes with one accord heeded the things spoken by Philip, hearing and seeing the miracles which he did.

7 For [R]unclean spirits, crying with a loud voice, came out of many who were possessed; and many who were paralyzed and lame were healed. Mark 16:17

8 And there was great joy in that city.

9 But there was a certain man called Simon, who previously practiced sorcery in the city and astonished the people of Samaria, claiming that he was someone great,

10 to whom they all gave heed, from the least to the greatest, saying, "This man is the great power of God."

11 And they heeded him because he had astonished them with his [T]sorceries for a long time. *magic arts*

7:40 Ex. 32:1, 23 **7:43** Amos 5:25–27 **7:50** Is. 66:1, 2
8:5 Or *a*

12 But when they believed Philip as he preached the things concerning the kingdom of God and the name of Jesus Christ, both men and women were baptized.

13 Then Simon himself also believed; and when he was baptized he continued with Philip, and was amazed, seeing the miracles and signs which were done.

14 Now when the [R]apostles who were at Jerusalem heard that Samaria had received the word of God, they sent Peter and John to them, Acts 5:12, 29, 40

15 who, when they had come down, prayed for them [R]that they might receive the Holy Spirit. Acts 2:38; 19:2

16 For [R]as yet He had fallen upon none of them. They had only been baptized in the name of the Lord Jesus. Acts 19:2

17 Then [R]they laid hands on them, and they received the Holy Spirit. Acts 6:6; 19:6

18 And when Simon saw that through the laying on of the apostles' hands the Holy Spirit was given, he offered them money,

19 saying, "Give me this power also, that anyone on whom I lay hands may receive the Holy Spirit."

20 But Peter said to him, "Your money perish with you, because you thought that the gift of God could be purchased with money!

21 "You have neither part nor portion in this matter, for your [R]heart is not right in the sight of God. Jer. 17:9

22 "Repent therefore of this your wickedness, and pray God if perhaps the thought of your heart may be forgiven you.

23 "For I see that you are [R]poisoned by bitterness and bound by iniquity." Heb. 12:15

24 Then Simon answered and said, "Pray to the Lord for me, that none of the things which you have spoken may come upon me."

25 So when they had testified and preached the word of the Lord, they returned to Jerusalem, preaching the gospel in many villages of the Samaritans.

Philip Witnesses to the Ethiopian Treasurer

26 Now an angel of the Lord spoke to Philip, saying, "Arise and go toward the south along the road which goes down from Jerusalem to Gaza." This is desert.

27 So he arose and went. And behold, [R]a man of Ethiopia, a eunuch of great authority under Candace the queen of the Ethiopians, who had charge of all her treasury, and had come to Jerusalem to worship, Ps. 68:31

28 was returning. And sitting in his chariot, he was reading Isaiah the prophet.

29 Then the Spirit said to Philip, "Go near and overtake this chariot."

30 So Philip ran to him, and heard him reading the prophet Isaiah, and said, "Do you understand what you are reading?"

31 And he said, "How can I, unless someone guides me?" And he asked Philip to come up and sit with him.

32 The place in the Scripture which he read was this:

"He was led as a sheep to the slaughter;
And as a lamb before its shearer is
silent,
[R]*So He opened not His mouth.* John 19:9

33 *In His humiliation His* [R]*justice was taken*
away, Luke 23:1–25
And who will declare His generation?
*For His life is taken from the earth."**

34 So the eunuch answered Philip and said, "I ask you, of whom does the prophet say this, of himself or of some other man?"

35 Then Philip opened his mouth, [R]and beginning at this Scripture, preached Jesus to him. Luke 24:27

36 Now as they went down the road, they came to some water. And the eunuch said, "See, *here is* water. [R]What hinders me from being baptized?" Acts 10:47; 16:33

37 Then Philip said, [R]"If you believe with all your heart, you may." And he answered and said, [R]"I believe that Jesus Christ is the Son of God."* [Mark 16:16] • Matt. 16:16

38 So he commanded the chariot to stand still. And both Philip and the eunuch went down into the water, and he baptized him.

39 Now when they came up out of the water, the Spirit of the Lord caught Philip away, so that the eunuch saw him no more; and he went on his way rejoicing.

40 But Philip was found at Azotus. And passing through, he preached in all the cities till he came to [R]Caesarea. Acts 21:8

CHAPTER 9

Saul Is Converted and Blinded
Acts 22:4–11; 26:13–18

THEN [R]Saul, still breathing threats and murder against the disciples of the Lord, went to the high priest Acts 7:57; 8:1, 3

2 and asked [R]letters from him to the synagogues of Damascus, so that if he found any who were of the Way, whether men or women, he might bring them bound to Jerusalem. Acts 22:5

3 [R]As he journeyed he came near Damascus, and suddenly a light shone around him from heaven. 1 Cor. 15:8

4 Then he fell to the ground, and heard a voice saying to him, "Saul, Saul, [R]why are you persecuting Me?" [Matt. 25:40]

5 And he said, "Who are You, Lord?" Then the Lord said, "I am Jesus, whom you are

8:33 Is. 53:7, 8 **8:37** NU, M omit v. 37. It is found in Western texts, including the Latin tradition.

persecuting.* It *is* hard for you to kick against
the goads."
6 So he, trembling and astonished, said,
"Lord, what do You want me to do?" Then the
Lord *said* to him, "Arise and go into the city,
and you will be told what you must do."
7 And [R]the men who journeyed with him
stood speechless, hearing a voice but seeing
no one. [Acts 22:9; 26:13]
8 Then Saul arose from the ground, and
when his eyes were opened he saw no one.
But they led him by the hand and brought *him*
into Damascus.
9 And he was three days without sight, and
neither ate nor drank.

Saul Is Filled with the Spirit

10 Now there was a certain disciple at Da-
mascus [R]named Ananias; and to him the Lord
said in a vision, "Ananias." And he said, "Here
I am, Lord." Acts 22:12
11 So the Lord *said* to him, "Arise and go to
the street called Straight, and inquire at the
house of Judas for *one* called Saul of Tarsus,
for behold, he is praying.
12 "And in a vision he has seen a man named
Ananias coming in and putting *his* hand on
him, so that he might receive his sight."
13 Then Ananias answered, "Lord, I have
heard from many about this man, [R]how much
[T]harm he has done to Your saints in Jerusa-
lem. Acts 9:1 • *bad things*
14 "And here he has authority from the
chief priests to bind all [R]who call on Your
name." Acts 7:59; 9:2, 21
15 But the Lord said to him, "Go, for [R]he is a
chosen vessel of Mine to bear My name be-
fore [R]Gentiles, [R]kings, and the children of Is-
rael. Eph. 3:7, 8 • Rom. 1:5; 11:13 • Acts 25:22, 23
16 "For I will show him how many things he
must suffer for My name's sake."
17 And Ananias went his way and entered
the house; and laying his hands on him he
said, "Brother Saul, the Lord Jesus,* who ap-
peared to you on the road as you came, has
sent me that you may receive your sight and
be filled with the Holy Spirit."
18 Immediately there fell from his eyes
something like scales, and he received his
sight at once; and he arose and was baptized.
19 So when he had received food, he was
strengthened. [R]Then Saul spent some days
with the disciples at Damascus. Acts 26:20

Saul Preaches at Damascus

20 Immediately he preached the Christ* in
the synagogues, that He is the Son of God.
21 Then all who heard were amazed, and
said, [R]"Is this not he who destroyed those who
called on this name in Jerusalem, and has come
here for that purpose, so that he might bring
them bound to the chief priests?" Gal. 1:13, 23
22 But Saul increased all the more in
strength, [R]and confounded the Jews who
dwelt in Damascus, proving that this *Jesus* is
the Christ. Acts 18:28

Saul Witnesses in Jerusalem

23 Now after many days were past, [R]the
Jews plotted to kill him. 2 Cor. 11:26
24 [R]But their plot became known to Saul.
And they watched the gates day and night, to
kill him. 2 Cor. 11:32
25 Then the disciples took him by night and
[R]let *him* down through the wall in a large bas-
ket. Josh. 2:15
26 And [R]when Saul had come to Jerusalem,
he tried to join the disciples; but they were all
afraid of him, and did not believe that he was
a disciple. Acts 22:17–20; 26:20
27 [R]But Barnabas took him and brought *him*
to the apostles. And he declared to them how
he had seen the Lord on the road, and that
He had spoken to him, [R]and how he had
preached boldly at Damascus in the name of
Jesus. Acts 4:36; 13:2 • Acts 9:20, 22
28 So [R]he was with them at Jerusalem, com-
ing in and going out. Gal. 1:18
29 And he spoke boldly in the name of the
Lord Jesus and disputed against the Hel-
lenists, but they attempted to kill him.
30 When the brethren found out, they
brought him down to Caesarea and sent him
out to Tarsus.
31 [R]Then the churches* throughout all
Judea, Galilee, and Samaria had peace and
were edified. And walking in the fear of the
Lord and in the comfort of the Holy Spirit,
they were multiplied. Acts 5:11; 8:1; 16:5

Peter Heals Aeneas at Lydda

32 Now it came to pass, as Peter went
[R]through all *parts of the country,* that he
also came down to the saints who dwelt in
Lydda. Acts 8:14
33 There he found a certain man named Ae-
neas, who had been bedridden eight years
and was paralyzed.
34 And Peter said to him, "Aeneas, Jesus the
Christ heals you. Arise and make your bed."
Then he arose immediately.
35 So all who dwelt at Lydda and Sharon
saw him and turned to the Lord.

Peter Raises Dorcas at Joppa

36 At Joppa there was a certain disciple
named Tabitha, which is translated Dorcas.
This woman was full [R]of good works and
charitable deeds which she did. 1 Tim. 2:10
37 But it happened in those days that she be-
came sick and died. When they had washed
her, they laid *her* in an upper room.

9:5 NU, M omit the last sentence of v. 5 and begin v. 6 with *But arise and go* **9:17** M omits *Jesus* **9:20** NU *Jesus* **9:31** NU *church . . . was edified.*

38 And since Lydda was near Joppa, and the
disciples had heard that Peter was there, they
sent two men to him, imploring *him* not to
delay in coming to them.
39 Then Peter arose and went with them.
When he had come, they brought *him* to the
upper room. And all the widows stood by him
weeping, showing the tunics and garments
which Dorcas had made while she was with
them.
40 But Peter [R]put them all out, and [R]knelt
down and prayed. And turning to the body
he [R]said, "Tabitha, arise." And she opened
her eyes, and when she saw Peter she sat
up. Matt. 9:25 • Acts 7:60 • Mark 5:41, 42
41 Then he gave her *his* hand and lifted her
up; and when he had called the saints and
widows, he presented her alive.
42 And it became known throughout all
Joppa, and many believed on the Lord.
43 So it was that he stayed many days in
Joppa with [R]Simon, a tanner. Acts 10:6

CHAPTER 10

Cornelius Sends for Peter

THERE was a certain man in [R]Caesarea
called Cornelius, a centurion of what was
called the Italian Regiment, Acts 8:40; 23:23
2 [R]a devout *man* and one who [R]feared God
with all his household, who gave alms gener-
ously to the people, and prayed to God al-
ways. Acts 8:2; 9:22; 22:12 • [Acts 10:22, 35]
3 About the ninth hour of the day he saw
clearly in a vision an angel of God coming in
and saying to him, "Cornelius!"
4 And when he observed him, he was
afraid, and said, "What is it, lord?" So he said
to him, "Your prayers and your alms have
come up for a memorial before God.
5 "Now send men to Joppa, and send for Si-
mon whose surname is Peter.
6 "He is lodging with [R]Simon, a tanner,
whose house is by the sea.* [R]He will tell you
what you must do." Acts 9:43 • Acts 11:14
7 And when the angel who spoke to him
had departed, Cornelius called two of his
household servants and a devout soldier from
among those who waited on him continually.
8 So when he had explained all *these*
things to them, he sent them to Joppa.

Peter Sees the Great Sheet

9 The next day, as they went on their jour-
ney and drew near the city, [R]Peter went up
on the housetop to pray, about [T]the sixth
hour. Acts 10:9–32; 11:5–14 • Noon
10 Then he became very hungry and wanted
to eat; but while they made ready, he fell into
a trance
11 and saw heaven opened and an object
like a great sheet bound at the four corners,
descending to him and let down to the earth.
12 In it were all kinds of four-footed animals
of the earth, wild beasts, creeping things, and
birds of the air.
13 And a voice came to him, "Rise, Peter; kill
and eat."
14 But Peter said, "Not so, Lord! For I have
never eaten anything common or unclean."
15 And a voice *spoke* to him again the sec-
ond time, [R]"What God has cleansed you must
not call common." [Rom. 14:14]
16 This was done three times. And the object
was taken up into heaven again.
17 Now while Peter wondered within him-
self what this vision which he had seen
meant, behold, the men who had been sent
from Cornelius had made inquiry for Simon's
house, and stood before the gate.
18 And they called and asked whether Si-
mon, whose surname was Peter, was lodging
there.
19 While Peter thought about the vision, [R]the
Spirit said to him, "Behold, three men are
seeking you. Acts 11:12
20 [R]"Arise therefore, go down and go with
them, doubting nothing; for I have sent
them." Acts 15:7–9

10:6 NU, M omit the last sentence of v. 6.

10:14, 15 Reconciliation Between Enemies—The gospel of Jesus Christ not only reconciles humans to God but provides the basis for reconciliation between people who are natural enemies. In NT times the natural enemies who heard the gospel were Jews and Gentiles. Jews, whose faith rested on the OT, comprised all of the earliest converts to faith in Christ (Page 1114—Acts 2:41; 4:4; 11:19). The Jewish Christians did not want to consider Gentiles as Christians until they first became Jewish converts (Page 1129—Acts 15:1). One of the triumphs of the NT church was recognizing that all humans stand on level ground before the Cross of Christ—equally needy, equally redeemed by His death, equally worthwhile in His body (Page 1205—Eph. 2:11–18).

It is a scandal in the church of Jesus Christ when centuries later majority-race Christians exclude minority groups. That Native Americans, African-Americans, Asian-Americans, Hispanics, and other ethnic groups are despised and excluded from various Christian congregations is sin. One of the most powerful witnesses to the reality of the work of God in the modern world is interracial reconciliation (Page 1102—John 17:20–23). Hatred and suspicion cannot be solved by education and legislation. Only regeneration can change the fearful human heart (Page 1187—2 Cor. 5:16–20). Only the church has a compelling reason to reject natural racial hostility in favor of the supernatural love of Jesus Christ (Page 1205—Eph. 2:19–22).

Now turn to Page 1112—Acts 1:8: Empowered by God.

21 Then Peter went down to the men who
had been sent to him from Cornelius,* and
said, "Yes, I am he whom you seek. For what
reason have you come?"
22 And they said, "Cornelius *the* centurion, a
just man, one who fears God and [R]has a good
reputation among all the nation of the Jews,
was divinely instructed by a holy angel to
summon you to his house, and to hear words
from you." Acts 22:12

Peter Preaches to the Gentiles

23 Then he invited them in and lodged *them.*
On the next day Peter went away with them,
[R]and some brethren from Joppa accompanied
him. Acts 10:45; 11:12
24 And the following day they entered Caes-
area. Now Cornelius was waiting for them,
and had called together his relatives and close
friends.
25 As Peter was coming in, Cornelius met him
and fell down at his feet and worshiped *him.*
26 But Peter lifted him up, saying, [R]"Stand
up; I myself am also a man." Acts 14:14, 15
27 And as he talked with him, he went in and
found many who had come together.
28 Then he said to them, "You know how un-
lawful it is for a Jewish man to keep company
with or go to one of another nation. But God
has shown me that I should not call any man
common or unclean.
29 "Therefore I came without objection as
soon as I was sent for. I ask, then, for what
reason have you sent for me?"
30 So Cornelius said, "Four days ago I was
fasting until this hour; and at the ninth hour*
I prayed in my house, and behold, a man
stood before me in bright clothing,
31 "and said, 'Cornelius, [R]your prayer has
been heard, and your alms are remembered in
the sight of God. Dan. 10:12
32 'Send therefore to Joppa and call Simon
here, whose surname is Peter. He is lodging in
the house of Simon, a tanner, by the sea.*
When he comes, he will speak to you.'
33 "So I sent to you immediately, and you
have done well to come. Now therefore, we
are all present before God, to hear all the
things commanded you by God."
34 Then Peter opened *his* mouth and said:
[R]"In truth I perceive that God shows no par-
tiality. Deut. 10:17
35 "But [R]in every nation whoever fears Him
and works righteousness is [R]accepted by
Him. [Eph. 2:13] • Ps. 15:1, 2
36 "The word which *God* sent to the children
of Israel, [R]preaching peace through Jesus
Christ—He is Lord of all— Is. 57:19
37 "that word you know, which was pro-
claimed throughout all Judea, and [R]began
from Galilee after the baptism which John
preached: Luke 4:14
38 "how [R]God anointed Jesus of Nazareth
with the Holy Spirit and with power, who
[R]went about doing good and healing all who
were oppressed by the devil, [R]for God was
with Him. Luke 4:18 • Matt. 4:23 • John 3:2; 8:29
39 "And we are [R]witnesses of all things
which He did both in the land of the Jews and
in Jerusalem, whom they* [R]killed by hanging
on a tree. Acts 1:8 • Acts 2:23
40 "Him [R]God raised up on the third day, and
showed Him openly, Hos. 6:2; Matt. 12:39, 40★
41 [R]"not to all the people, but to witnesses
chosen before by God, *even* to us [R]who ate
and drank with Him after He arose from the
dead. [John 14:17, 19, 22; 15:27] • Luke 24:30, 41–43
42 "And [R]He commanded us to preach to the
people, and to testify [R]that it is He who was
ordained by God *to be* Judge of the living and
the dead. Matt. 28:19 • John 5:22, 27
43 [R]"To Him all the prophets witness that,
through His name, whoever believes in Him
will receive remission of sins." Zech. 13:1

Gentiles Are Converted and Speak in Tongues

44 While Peter was still speaking these
words, [R]the Holy Spirit fell upon all those who
heard the word. Acts 4:31
45 [R]And [T]those of the circumcision who be-
lieved were astonished, as many as came
with Peter, [R]because the gift of the Holy
Spirit had been poured out on the Gentiles
also. Acts 10:23 • The Jews • Acts 11:18
46 For they heard them speak with tongues
and magnify God. Then Peter answered,
47 "Can anyone forbid water, that these
should not be baptized who have received the
Holy Spirit [R]just as we *have?*" Acts 2:4
48 [R]And he commanded them to be baptized
in the name of the Lord. Then they asked him
to stay a few days. 1 Cor. 1:14–17

CHAPTER 11

Peter Defends His Ministry to the Gentiles

NOW the apostles and brethren who were
in Judea heard that the Gentiles had also
received the word of God.
2 And when Peter came up to Jerusalem,
[R]those of the circumcision contended with
him, Acts 10:45
3 saying, [R]"You went in to uncircumcised
men and ate with them!" Acts 10:28
4 But Peter explained *it* to them [R]in order
from the beginning, saying: Luke 1:3
5 "I was in the city of Joppa praying; and in
a trance I saw a vision, an object descending
like a great sheet, let down from heaven by
four corners; and it came to me.

10:21 NU, M omit *who had been sent to him from Cornelius* **10:30** NU *Four days ago to this hour, at the ninth hour* **10:32** NU omits the last sentence of v. 32. **10:39** NU, M add *also*

6 "When I observed it intently and considered, I saw four-footed animals of the earth, wild beasts, creeping things, and birds of the air.

7 "And I heard a voice saying to me, 'Rise, Peter; kill and eat.'

8 "But I said, 'Not so, Lord! For nothing common or unclean has at any time entered my mouth.'

9 "But the voice answered me again from heaven, 'What God has cleansed you must not call common.'

10 "Now this was done three times, and all were drawn up again into heaven.

11 "At that very moment, three men stood before the house where I was, having been sent to me from Caesarea.

12 "Then [R]the Spirit told me to go with them, doubting nothing. Moreover [R]these six brethren accompanied me, and we entered the man's house. [John 16:13] • Acts 10:23

13 [R]"And he told us how he had seen an angel standing in his house, who said to him, 'Send men to Joppa, and call for Simon whose surname is Peter, Acts 10:30

14 'who will tell you words by which you and all your household will be saved.'

15 "And as I began to speak, the Holy Spirit fell upon them, [R]as upon us at the beginning. Acts 2:1–4; 15:7–9

16 "Then I remembered the word of the Lord, how He said, [R]'John indeed baptized with water, but [R]you shall be baptized with the Holy Spirit.' John 1:26, 33 • Is. 44:3

17 [R]"If therefore God gave them the same gift as *He gave* us when we believed on the Lord Jesus Christ, [R]who was I that I could withstand God?" [Acts 15:8, 9] • Acts 10:47

18 When they heard these things they became silent; and they glorified God, saying, [R]"Then God has also granted to the Gentiles repentance to life." Rom. 10:12, 13; 15:9, 16

The Witness of the Antioch Church

19 [R]Now those who were scattered after the persecution that arose over Stephen traveled as far as Phoenicia, Cyprus, and Antioch, preaching the word to no one but the Jews only. Acts 8:1, 4

20 But some of them were men from Cyprus and Cyrene, who, when they had come to Antioch, spoke to [R]the Hellenists, preaching the Lord Jesus. Acts 6:1; 9:29

21 And [R]the hand of the Lord was with them, and a great number believed and [R]turned to the Lord. Luke 1:66 • Acts 9:35; 14:1

22 Then news of these things came to the ears of the church in Jerusalem, and they sent out Barnabas to go as far as Antioch.

23 When he came and had seen the grace of God, he was glad, and [R]encouraged them all that with purpose of heart they should continue with the Lord. Acts 13:43; 14:22

24 For he was a good man, [R]full of the Holy Spirit and of faith. [R]And a great many people were added to the Lord. Acts 6:5 • Acts 5:14

25 Then Barnabas departed for [R]Tarsus to seek Saul. Acts 9:11, 30

26 And when he had found him, he brought him to Antioch. So it was that for a whole year they assembled with the church and taught a great many people. And the disciples were first called Christians in Antioch.

27 And in these days [R]prophets came from Jerusalem to Antioch. 1 Cor. 12:28

28 Then one of them, named [R]Agabus, stood up and showed by the Spirit that there was going to be a great famine throughout all the world, which also happened in the days of Claudius Caesar. Acts 21:10

29 Then the disciples, each according to his ability, determined to send [R]relief to the brethren dwelling in Judea. 1 Cor. 16:1

30 This they also did, and sent it to the elders by the hands of Barnabas and Saul.

CHAPTER 12

Herod Kills James

NOW about that time Herod the king stretched out *his* hand to harass some from the church.

2 Then he killed James [R]the brother of John with the sword. Matt. 4:21; 20:23

Peter Is Miraculously Released from Prison

3 And because he saw that it pleased the Jews, he proceeded further to seize Peter also. Now it was *during* [R]the Days of Unleavened Bread. Ex. 12:15; 23:15

4 So when he had arrested him, he put *him* in prison, and delivered *him* to four squads of soldiers to keep him, intending to bring him before the people after Passover.

5 Peter was therefore kept in prison, but constant* prayer was offered to God for him by the church.

6 And when Herod was about to bring him out, that night Peter was sleeping, bound with two chains between two soldiers; and the guards before the door were [T]keeping the prison. *guarding*

7 Now behold, [R]an angel of the Lord stood by *him*, and a light shone in the prison; and he struck Peter on the side and raised him up, saying, "Arise quickly!" And his chains fell off *his* hands. Acts 5:19

8 Then the angel said to him, "Gird yourself and tie on your sandals"; and so he did. And he said to him, "Put on your garment and follow me."

9 So he went out and followed him, and [R]did not know that what was done by the

12:5 NU *constantly* or *earnestly*

angel was real, but thought [R]he was seeing a
vision. Ps. 126:1 • Acts 10:3, 17; 11:5
10 When they were past the first and the sec-
ond guard posts, they came to the iron gate
that leads to the city, [R]which opened to them
of its own accord; and they went out and went
down one street, and immediately the angel
departed from him. Acts 5:19
11 And when Peter had come to himself, he
said, "Now I know for certain that [R]the Lord
has sent His angel, and has delivered me from
the hand of Herod and *from* all the expecta-
tion of the Jewish people." [Ps. 34:7]
12 So, when he had considered *this,* he came
to the house of Mary, the mother of John
whose surname was Mark, where many were
gathered together praying.
13 And as Peter knocked at the door of the
gate, a girl named Rhoda came to answer.
14 When she recognized Peter's voice, be-
cause of *her* gladness she did not open the
gate, but ran in and announced that Peter
stood before the gate.
15 But they said to her, "You are beside your-
self!" Yet she kept insisting that it was so. So
they said, "It is his angel."
16 Now Peter continued knocking; and when
they opened *the door* and saw him, they were
astonished.
17 But [R]motioning to them with his hand to
keep silent, he declared to them how the Lord
had brought him out of the prison. And he
said, "Go, tell these things to James and to the
brethren." And he departed and went to an-
other place. Acts 13:16; 19:33; 21:40
18 Then, as soon as it was day, there was no
small [T]stir among the soldiers about what had
become of Peter. *disturbance*
19 But when Herod had searched for him
and not found him, he examined the guards
and commanded that *they* should be put to
death. And he went down from Judea to Caes-
area, and stayed *there.*

Herod Blasphemes and Dies

20 Now Herod had been very angry with
the people of [R]Tyre and Sidon; but they came
to him with one accord, and having made
Blastus the king's personal aide their friend,
they asked for peace, because [R]their country
was supplied with food by the king's *coun-
try.* Matt. 11:21 • Ezek. 27:17
21 So on a set day Herod, arrayed in royal
apparel, sat on his throne and gave an oration
to them.
22 And the people kept shouting, "The voice
of a god and not of a man!"
23 Then immediately an angel of the Lord
[R]struck him, because [R]he did not give glory
to God. And he was eaten by worms and
[T]died. 2 Sam. 24:16, 17 • Ps. 115:1 • *breathed his last*
24 But [R]the word of God grew and multi-
plied. Acts 6:7; 19:20
25 And Barnabas and Saul returned from*
Jerusalem when they had fulfilled *their* min-
istry, and they also took with them John
whose surname was Mark.

CHAPTER 13

Barnabas and Saul Are Sent from Antioch

NOW [R]in the church that was at Antioch
there were certain prophets and teach-
ers: [R]Barnabas, Simeon who was called
Niger, [R]Lucius of Cyrene, Manaen who had
been brought up with Herod the tetrarch, and
Saul. Acts 14:26 • Acts 11:22 • Rom. 16:21
2 As they ministered to the Lord and fasted,
the Holy Spirit said, [R]"Now separate to Me
Barnabas and Saul for the work to which I
have called them." Gal. 1:15; 2:9
3 Then, having fasted and prayed, and laid
hands on them, they sent *them* away.

Preaching in the Synagogues

4 So, being sent out by the Holy Spirit, they
went down to Seleucia, and from there they
sailed to [R]Cyprus. Acts 4:36
5 And when they arrived in Salamis, [R]they
preached the word of God in the synagogues
of the Jews. They also had [R]John as *their* as-
sistant. [Acts 13:46] • Acts 12:25; 15:37

Controversy with Bar-Jesus

6 Now when they had gone through the is-
land* to Paphos, they found [R]a certain sor-
cerer, a false prophet, a Jew whose name *was*
Bar-Jesus, Acts 8:9
7 who was with the proconsul, Sergius
Paulus, an intelligent man. This man called
for Barnabas and Saul and sought to hear the
word of God.
8 But Elymas the sorcerer (for so his name
is translated) withstood them, seeking to turn
the proconsul away from the faith.
9 Then Saul, who also *is called* Paul,
[R]filled with the Holy Spirit, looked intently
at him Acts 2:4; 4:8
10 and said, "O full of all deceit and all fraud,
[R]*you* son of the devil, *you* enemy of all right-
eousness, will you not cease perverting the
straight ways of the Lord? Matt. 13:38
11 "And now, indeed, the hand of the Lord *is*
upon you, and you shall be blind, not seeing
the sun for a time." And immediately a dark
mist fell on him, and he went around seeking
someone to lead him by the hand.
12 Then the proconsul believed, when he
saw what had been done, being astonished at
the teaching of the Lord.
13 Now when Paul and his party set sail
from Paphos, they came to Perga in Pam-
phylia; and [R]John, departing from them, re-
turned to Jerusalem. Acts 15:38

12:25 NU, M *to* **13:6** NU *the whole island*

Paul Preaches on First Sabbath

14 But when they departed from Perga, they came to Antioch in Pisidia, and [R]went into the synagogue on the Sabbath day and sat down. Acts 16:13

15 And [R]after the reading of the Law and the Prophets, the rulers of the synagogue sent to them, saying, "Men *and* brethren, if you have [R]any word of exhortation for the people, say on." Luke 4:16 • Heb. 13:22

16 Then Paul stood up, and motioning with *his* hand said, "Men of Israel, and [R]you who fear God, listen: Acts 10:35

17 "The God of this people Israel* [R]chose our fathers, and exalted the people [R]when they dwelt as strangers in the land of Egypt, and with an uplifted arm He [R]brought them out of it. Deut. 7:6–8 • Acts 7:17 • Ex. 14:8

18 "Now for a time of about forty years He put up with their ways in the wilderness.

19 "And when He had destroyed [R]seven nations in the land of Canaan, He distributed their land to them by allotment. Deut. 7:1

20 "After that [R]He gave *them* judges for about four hundred and fifty years, [R]until Samuel the prophet. Judg. 2:16 • 1 Sam. 3:20

21 "And afterward they asked for a king; so God gave them Saul the son of Kish, a man of the tribe of Benjamin, for forty years.

22 "And when He had removed him, He raised up for them David as king, to whom also He gave testimony and said, *'I have found David** the *son* of Jesse, *a man after My own heart,* who will do all My will.'*

23 [R]"From this man's seed, according [R]to *the* promise, God raised up for Israel [R]a Savior—Jesus—* Is. 11:1★ • Ps. 132:11 • [Matt. 1:21]

24 [R]"after John had first preached, before His coming, the baptism of repentance to all the people of Israel. [Luke 3:3]

25 "And as John was finishing his course, he said, [R]'Who do you think I am? I am not *He.* But behold, [R]there comes One after me, the sandals of whose feet I am not worthy to loose.' Mark 1:7 • John 1:20, 27

26 "Men *and* brethren, sons of the [T]family of Abraham, and [R]those among you who fear God, [R]to you the [T]word of this salvation has been sent. *stock* • Ps. 66:16 • Matt. 10:6 • *message*

27 "For those who dwell in Jerusalem, and their rulers, [R]because they did not know Him, nor even the voices of the Prophets which are read every Sabbath, have fulfilled *them* in condemning *Him.* Luke 23:34

28 [R]"And though they found no cause for death *in Him,* they asked Pilate that He should be put to death. Matt. 27:22, 23

29 "Now when they had fulfilled all that was written concerning Him, they took *Him* down from the tree and laid *Him* in a tomb.

30 "But God raised Him from the dead.

31 "He was seen for many days by those who came up with Him from Galilee to Jerusalem, who are His witnesses to the people.

32 "And we declare to you glad tidings—[R]that promise which was made to the fathers. [Gen. 3:15]

33 "God has fulfilled this for us their children, in that He has raised up Jesus. As it is also written in the second Psalm:

'You are My Son,
*Today I have begotten You.'**

34 "And that He raised Him from the dead, no more to return to [T]corruption, He has spoken thus: *the state of decay*

'I will give you the sure [T]mercies of
*David.'** *blessings*

35 "Therefore He also says in another *Psalm:*

'You will not allow Your Holy One to see
*corruption.'**

36 "For David, after he had served [T]his own generation by the will of God, [R]fell asleep, was buried with his fathers, and [T]saw corruption; *in his* • Acts 2:29 • *underwent decay*

37 "but He whom God raised up [T]saw no corruption. *underwent no decay*

38 "Therefore let it be known to you, brethren, that through this Man is preached to you the forgiveness of sins;

39 "and by Him everyone who believes is justified from all things from which you could not be justified by the law of Moses.

40 "Beware therefore, lest what has been spoken in the prophets come upon you:

41 *'Behold, you despisers,*
Marvel and perish!
For I work a work in your days,
A work which you will by no means
believe,
Though one were to declare it to
you.' "*

42 So when the Jews went out of the synagogue,* the Gentiles begged that these words might be preached to them the next Sabbath.

43 Now when the congregation had broken up, many of the Jews and devout proselytes followed Paul and Barnabas, who, speaking to them, [R]persuaded them to continue in [R]the grace of God. Acts 11:23 • Titus 2:11

13:17 M omits *Israel* **13:22** Ps. 89:20 • 1 Sam. 13:14 **13:23** M *for Israel salvation* **13:33** Ps. 2:7★ **13:34** Is. 55:3★ **13:35** Ps. 16:10★ **13:41** Hab. 1:5 **13:42** Or *And when they went out of the synagogue of the Jews;* NU *And when they went out, they begged*

Paul Preaches on Second Sabbath

44 On the next Sabbath almost the whole city came together to hear the word of God.

45 But when the Jews saw the multitudes, they were filled with envy; and contradicting and blaspheming, they [R]opposed the things spoken by Paul. 1 Pet. 4:4

46 Then Paul and Barnabas grew bold and said, [R]"It was necessary that the word of God should be spoken to you first; but [R]since you reject it, and judge yourselves unworthy of everlasting life, behold, [R]we turn to the Gentiles. Rom. 1:16 • Ex. 32:10 • Acts 18:6

47 "For so the Lord has commanded us:

[R]'*I have set you as a light to the Gentiles,*
That you should be for salvation to the
ends of the earth.' "* Is. 42:6

48 Now when the Gentiles heard this, they were glad and glorified the word of the Lord. [R]And as many as had been appointed to eternal life believed. [Acts 2:47]

49 And the word of the Lord was being spread throughout all the region.

50 But the Jews stirred up the devout and prominent women and the chief men of the city, [R]raised up persecution against Paul and Barnabas, and expelled them from their region. 2 Tim. 3:11

Ministry at Iconium

51 But they shook off the dust from their feet against them, and came to Iconium.

52 And the disciples [R]were filled with joy and with the Holy Spirit. John 16:22

CHAPTER 14

NOW it happened in Iconium that they went together to the synagogue of the Jews, and so spoke that a great multitude both of the Jews and of the Greeks believed.

2 But the unbelieving Jews stirred up the Gentiles and [T]poisoned their [T]minds against the brethren. *embittered* • Lit. *souls*

3 Therefore they stayed there a long time, speaking boldly in the Lord, [R]who was bearing witness to the word of His grace, granting signs and [R]wonders to be done by their hands. Heb. 2:4 • Acts 5:12

4 But the multitude of the city was [R]divided: part sided with the Jews, and part with the [R]apostles. Luke 12:51 • Acts 13:2, 3

5 And when a violent attempt was made by both the Gentiles and Jews, with their rulers, to abuse and stone them,

A Lame Man Is Healed

6 they became aware of it and [R]fled to Lystra and Derbe, cities of Lycaonia, and to the surrounding region. Matt. 10:23

7 And they were preaching the gospel there.

8 [R]And in Lystra a certain man without strength in his feet was sitting, a cripple from his mother's womb, who had never walked. Acts 3:2

9 *This* man heard Paul speaking. [T]Paul, observing him intently and seeing that he had faith to be healed, Lit. *Who*

10 said with a loud voice, [R]"Stand up straight on your feet!" And he leaped and walked. [Is. 35:6]

Paul and Barnabas Are Deified

11 Now when the people saw what Paul had done, they raised their voices, saying in the Lycaonian *language,* "The gods have come down to us in the likeness of men!"

12 And Barnabas they called [T]Zeus, and Paul, [T]Hermes, because he was the chief speaker. *Jupiter* • *Mercury*

13 Then the priest of Zeus, whose temple was in front of their city, brought oxen and garlands to the gates, [R]intending to sacrifice with the multitudes. Dan. 2:46

14 But when the apostles Barnabas and Paul heard this, they tore their clothes and ran in among the multitude, crying out

15 and saying, "Men, [R]why are you doing these things? [R]We also are men with the same nature as you, and preach to you that you should turn from [R]these useless things to the living God, who made the heaven, the earth, the sea, and all things that are in them, Acts 10:26 • James 5:17 • 1 Cor. 8:4

16 "who in bygone generations allowed all nations to walk in their own ways.

17 "Nevertheless He did not leave Himself without witness, in that He did good, gave us rain from heaven and fruitful seasons, filling our hearts with food and gladness."

18 And with these sayings they could scarcely restrain the multitudes from sacrificing to them.

Paul Is Stoned

19 Then Jews from Antioch and Iconium came there; and having persuaded the multitudes, they stoned Paul *and* dragged *him* out of the city, supposing him to be dead.

20 However, when the disciples gathered around him, he rose up and went into the city. And the next day he departed with Barnabas to Derbe.

Ministry on the Return Trip

21 And when they had preached the gospel to that city and made many disciples, they returned to Lystra, Iconium, and Antioch,

22 strengthening the souls of the disciples, [R]exhorting *them* to continue in the faith, and

13:47 Is. 49:6★

saying, "We must through many tribulations
enter the kingdom of God." Acts 11:23
23 So when they had [R]appointed elders in
every church, and prayed with fasting, they
commended them to the Lord in whom they
had believed. Titus 1:5
24 And after they had passed through Pi-
sidia, they came to Pamphylia.
25 Now when they had preached the word in
Perga, they went down to Attalia.

Report on the First Missionary Journey

26 From there they sailed to Antioch, where
they had been commended to the grace of
God for the work which they had completed.
27 Now when they had come and gathered
the church together, they reported all that
God had done with them, and that He had
opened the door of faith to the Gentiles.
28 So they stayed there a long time with the
disciples.

CHAPTER 15

Debate over Gentiles Keeping the Law

AND [R]certain *men* came down from Judea
and taught the brethren, "Unless you are
circumcised according to the custom of Mo-
ses, you cannot be saved." Gal. 2:12
2 Therefore, when Paul and Barnabas had
no small dissension and dispute with them,
they determined that [R]Paul and Barnabas and
certain others of them should go up to Jerusa-
lem, to the apostles and elders, about this
question. Gal. 2:1
3 So, [R]being sent on their way by the
church, they passed through Phoenicia and
Samaria, [R]describing the conversion of the
Gentiles; and they caused great joy to all the
brethren. Rom. 15:24 • Acts 14:27; 15:4, 12
4 And when they had come to Jerusalem,
they were received by the church and the
apostles and the elders; and they reported all
things that God had done with them.
5 But some of the sect of the Pharisees who
believed rose up, saying, "It is necessary to
circumcise them, and to command *them* to
keep the law of Moses."

Peter Preaches Salvation Through Grace

6 Now the apostles and elders came to-
gether to consider this matter.
7 And when there had been much dispute,
Peter rose up and said to them: [R]"Men and
brethren, you know that a good while ago
God chose among us, that by my mouth the
Gentiles should hear the word of the gospel
and believe. Acts 10:20
8 "So God, [R]who knows the heart, acknowl-
edged them by giving them the Holy Spirit,
just as *He did* to us, Acts 1:24
9 "and made no distinction between us and
them, purifying their hearts by faith.
10 "Now therefore, why do you test God [R]by
putting a yoke on the neck of the disciples
which neither our fathers nor we were able to
bear? Matt. 23:4
11 "But [R]we believe that through the grace of
the Lord Jesus Christ* we shall be saved in
the same manner as they." Rom. 3:4; 5:15

Paul and Barnabas Testify

12 Then all the multitude kept silent and lis-
tened to Barnabas and Paul declaring how
many miracles and wonders God had worked
through them among the Gentiles.

James Proves Gentiles Are Free from the Law

13 And after they had become silent, [R]James
answered, saying, "Men *and* brethren, listen
to me: Acts 12:17
14 [R]"Simon has declared how God at the first
visited the Gentiles to take out of them a peo-
ple for His name. Acts 15:7
15 "And with this the words of the prophets
agree, just as it is written:

16 '*After this I will return*
And will rebuild the tabernacle of David,
which has fallen down;
I will rebuild its ruins,
And I will set it up;
17 *So that the rest of mankind may seek*
the L*ORD*,
Even all the Gentiles who are called by
My name,
Says the L*ORD* *who does all these things.*'*

18 "Known to God from eternity are all His
works.*
19 "Therefore [R]I judge that we should not
trouble those from among the Gentiles who
are turning to God, Acts 15:28; 21:25
20 "but that we [R]write to them to abstain
from things polluted by idols, [R]*from* sexual
immorality,* [R]*from* things strangled, and *from*
blood. Acts 21:25 • [1 Cor. 6:9] • Lev. 3:17
21 "For Moses has had throughout many
generations those who preach him in every
city, [R]being read in the synagogues every Sab-
bath." Acts 13:15, 27

The Council Sends an Official Letter

22 Then it pleased the apostles and elders,
with the whole church, to send chosen men of
their own company to Antioch with Paul and
Barnabas, *namely*, Judas who was also named
[R]Barsabas,* and Silas, leading men among the
brethren. Acts 1:23
23 They wrote this *letter* by them:

15:11 NU, M omit *Christ* **15:17** Amos 9:11, 12
15:18 NU (combining with v. 17) *Says the Lord, who makes these things known from eternity (of old).*
15:20 Or *fornication* **15:22** NU, M *Barsabbas*

The apostles, the elders, and the brethren,
To the brethren who are of the Gentiles
in Antioch, Syria, and Cilicia:

Greetings.

24 Since we have heard that [R]some who
went out from us have troubled you with
words, unsettling your souls, saying,
"*You must* be circumcised and keep the
law"*—to whom we gave no *such*
commandment— Titus 1:10, 11
25 it seemed good to us, being assembled
with one [T]accord, to send chosen men to
you with our beloved Barnabas and
Paul, *purpose* or *mind*
26 men who have risked their lives for the
name of our Lord Jesus Christ.
27 We have therefore sent Judas and Silas,
who will also report the same things by
word of mouth.
28 For it seemed good to the Holy Spirit,
and to us, to lay upon you no greater
burden than these necessary things:
29 that you abstain from things offered to
idols, [R]from blood, from things strangled,
and from [R]sexual immorality.* If you
keep yourselves from these, you will do
well. Lev. 17:14 • Col. 3:5

Farewell.

Report to Antioch

30 So when they were sent off, they came to
Antioch; and when they had gathered the
multitude together, they delivered the letter.
31 When they had read it, they rejoiced over
its encouragement.
32 Now Judas and Silas, themselves being
[R]prophets also, exhorted and strengthened
the brethren with many words. Eph. 4:11
33 And after they had stayed *there* for a
time, they were sent back with greetings from
the brethren to the apostles.*
34 However, it seemed good to Silas to re-
main there.*
35 [R]Paul and Barnabas also remained in An-
tioch, teaching and preaching the word of the
Lord, with many others also. Acts 13:1

Contention over John Mark

36 Then after some days Paul said to Bar-
nabas, "Let us now go back and visit our
brethren in every city where we have
preached the word of the Lord, *and see* how
they are doing."
37 Now Barnabas [T]was determined to take
with them John called Mark. *resolved*
38 But Paul insisted that they should not
take with them [R]the one who had departed
from them in Pamphylia, and had not gone
with them to the work. Acts 13:13
39 Then the contention became so sharp that
they parted from one another. And so Barn-
abas took Mark and sailed to Cyprus;
40 but Paul chose Silas and departed, [R]being
[T]commended by the brethren to the grace of
God. Acts 11:23; 14:26 • *committed*
41 And he went through Syria and Cilicia,
[R]strengthening the churches. Acts 16:5

CHAPTER 16

Derbe and Lystra: Timothy Is Circumcised

THEN he came to [R]Derbe and Lystra. And
behold, a certain disciple was there,
[R]named Timothy, [R]*the* son of a certain Jewish
woman who believed, but his father *was*
Greek. Acts 14:6 • Rom. 16:21 • 2 Tim. 1:5; 3:15
2 He was well spoken of by the brethren
who were at Lystra and Iconium.
3 Paul wanted to have him go on with him.
And he took *him* and circumcised him be-
cause of the Jews who were in that region, for
they all knew that his father was Greek.
4 And as they went through the cities, they
delivered to them the [R]decrees to keep, [R]which
were determined by the apostles and elders at
Jerusalem. Acts 15:19–21 • Acts 15:28, 29
5 So the churches were strengthened in the
faith, and increased in number daily.

Troas: Macedonian Call

6 Now when they had gone through
Phrygia and the region of [R]Galatia, they were
forbidden by the Holy Spirit to preach the
word in Asia. Gal. 1:1, 2
7 After they had come to Mysia, they tried
to go into Bithynia, but the Spirit* did not per-
mit them.
8 So passing by Mysia, they [R]came down to
Troas. 2 Cor. 2:12
9 And a vision appeared to Paul in the
night. A [R]man of Macedonia stood and
pleaded with him, saying, "Come over to
Macedonia and help us." Acts 10:30
10 Now after he had seen the vision, imme-
diately we sought to go [R]to Macedonia, con-
cluding that the Lord had called us to preach
the gospel to them. 2 Cor. 2:13

Lydia Is Converted

11 Therefore, sailing from Troas, we ran a
straight course to Samothrace, and the next
day came to Neapolis,
12 and from there to [R]Philippi, which is the
[T]foremost city of that part of Macedonia, a
colony. And we were staying in that city for
some days. Phil. 1:1 • Lit. *first*
13 And on the Sabbath day we went out of

15:24 NU omits *saying, "You must be circumcised and keep the law"* **15:29** Or *fornication* **15:33** NU to *those who had sent them* **15:34** NU, M omit v. 34. **16:7** NU adds *of Jesus*

the city to the riverside, where prayer was customarily made; and we sat down and spoke to the women who met *there*.

14 Now a certain woman named Lydia heard *us*. She was a seller of purple from the city of [R]Thyatira, who worshiped God. [R]The Lord opened her heart to heed the things spoken by Paul. Rev. 1:11; 2:18, 24 • Luke 24:45

15 And when she and her household were baptized, she begged *us*, saying, "If you have judged me to be faithful to the Lord, come to my house and stay." So she persuaded us.

A Spirit of Divination Is Cast Out

16 Now it happened, as we went to prayer, that a certain slave girl possessed with a spirit of divination met us, who brought her masters much profit by fortune-telling.

17 This girl followed Paul and us, and cried out, saying, "These men are the servants of the Most High God, who proclaim to us the way of salvation."

18 And this she did for many days. But Paul, [R]greatly annoyed, turned and said to the spirit, "I command you in the name of Jesus Christ to come out of her." And he came out that very hour. Mark 1:25, 34

19 But [R]when her masters saw that their hope of profit was gone, they seized Paul and Silas and dragged *them* into the marketplace to the authorities. Acts 16:16; 19:25, 26

20 And they brought them to the magistrates, and said, "These men, being Jews, [R]exceedingly trouble our city; Acts 17:8

21 "and they teach customs which are not lawful for us, being Romans, to receive or observe."

22 Then the multitude rose up together against them; and the magistrates tore off their clothes [R]and commanded *them* to be beaten with rods. 1 Thess. 2:2

23 And when they had laid many stripes on them, they threw *them* into prison, commanding the jailer to keep them securely.

24 Having received such a charge, he put them into the inner prison and fastened their feet in the stocks.

Philippian Jailer Is Converted

25 But at midnight Paul and Silas were praying and singing hymns to God, and the prisoners were listening to them.

26 [R]Suddenly there was a great earthquake, so that the foundations of the prison were shaken; and immediately [R]all the doors were opened and everyone's chains were loosed. Acts 4:31 • Acts 5:19; 12:7, 10

27 And the keeper of the prison, awaking from sleep and seeing the prison doors open, supposing the prisoners had fled, drew his sword and was about to kill himself.

28 But Paul called with a loud voice, saying, "Do yourself no harm, for we are all here."

29 Then he called for a light, ran in, and fell down trembling before Paul and Silas.

30 And he brought them out and said, "Sirs, what must I do to be saved?"

31 So they said, [R]"Believe on the Lord Jesus Christ, and you will be saved, you and your household." [John 3:16, 36; 6:47]

32 Then they spoke the word of the Lord to him and to all who were in his house.

33 And he took them the same hour of the night and washed *their* stripes. And immediately he and all his family were baptized.

34 Now when he had brought them into his house, [R]he set food before them; and he rejoiced, having believed in God with all his household. Luke 5:29; 19:6

Paul Is Released from Prison

35 And when it was day, the magistrates sent the officers, saying, "Let those men go."

36 So the keeper of the prison reported these words to Paul, saying, "The magistrates have sent to let you go. Now therefore depart, and go in peace."

37 But Paul said to them, "They have beaten us openly, uncondemned Romans, *and* have thrown *us* into prison. And now do they put us out secretly? No indeed! Let them come themselves and get us out."

38 And the officers told these words to the

16:31 New Life: Received by Faith—The words spoken to the Philippian jailer are the best news human ears have ever heard, for they clearly tell how we receive God's gift of eternal life. When we receive God's gift of eternal life we are said to be "saved." The basic concept underlying "salvation" or "being saved" is deliverance. We are delivered from the penalty of sin (death, separation from God) and from the power of sin. Ultimately we will be delivered from the very presence of sin and will be delivered into the very presence of God. We receive new life by faith—believing that Jesus died for our sins, that His death was in our place, and that His payment for sin is fully acceptable in God's sight. Faith can be summarized in the acrostic:

F orsaking
A ll
I
T ake
H im

We are to forsake all (repent of our sins) and to take Him (by faith turn to God for our salvation) (Page 1136—Acts 20:21).

Now turn to Page 1086—John 5:24: Everlasting Life.

magistrates, and they were afraid when they heard that they were Romans.

39 Then they came and pleaded with them and brought *them* out, and [R]asked *them* to depart from the city. Matt. 8:34

40 So they went out of the prison [R]and entered *the house of* Lydia; and when they had seen the brethren, they encouraged them and departed. Acts 16:14

CHAPTER 17

Thessalonica: "Turned the World Upside Down"

1 NOW when they had passed through Amphipolis and Apollonia, they came to [R]Thessalonica, where there was a synagogue of the Jews. 1 Thess. 1:1

2 Then Paul, as his custom was, [R]went in to them, and for three Sabbaths reasoned with them from the Scriptures, Luke 4:16

3 explaining and demonstrating [R]that the Christ had to suffer and rise again from the dead, and *saying*, "This Jesus whom I preach to you is the Christ." Acts 18:5, 28

4 [R]And some of them were persuaded; and a great multitude of the devout Greeks, and not a few of the leading women, joined Paul and [R]Silas. Acts 28:24 • Acts 15:22, 27, 32, 40

5 But the Jews who were not persuaded, becoming [R]envious,* took some of the evil men from the marketplace, and gathering a mob, set all the city in an uproar and attacked the house of Jason, and sought to bring them out to the people. Acts 13:45

6 But when they did not find them, they dragged Jason and some brethren to the rulers of the city, crying out, [R]"These who have turned the world upside down have come here too. [Acts 16:20]

7 "Jason has harbored them, and these are all acting contrary to the decrees of Caesar, saying there is another king—Jesus."

8 And they troubled the crowd and the rulers of the city when they heard these things.

9 So when they had taken security from Jason and the rest, they let them go.

Berea: Many Receive the Word

10 Then [R]the brethren immediately sent Paul and Silas away by night to Berea. When they arrived, they went into the synagogue of the Jews. Acts 9:25; 17:14

11 These were more [T]fair-minded than those in Thessalonica, in that they received the word with all readiness, and [R]searched the Scriptures daily *to find out* whether these things were so. Lit. *noble* • John 5:39

12 Therefore many of them believed, and also not a few of the Greeks, prominent women as well as men.

13 But when the Jews from Thessalonica learned that the word of God was preached by Paul at Berea, they came there also and stirred up the crowds.

14 [R]Then immediately the brethren sent Paul away, to go to the sea; but both Silas and Timothy remained there. Matt. 10:23

15 So those who conducted Paul brought him to Athens; and [R]receiving a command for Silas and Timothy to come to him with all speed, they departed. Acts 18:5

Athens: Paul's Sermon on Mars' Hill

16 Now while Paul waited for them at Athens, [R]his spirit was provoked within him when he saw that the city was [T]given over to idols. 2 Pet. 2:8 • *full of idols*

17 Therefore he reasoned in the synagogue with the Jews and with the *Gentile* worshipers, and in the marketplace daily with those who happened to be there.

18 Then* certain Epicurean and Stoic philosophers encountered him. And some said, "What does this babbler want to say?" Others said, "He seems to be a proclaimer of foreign gods," because he preached to them [R]Jesus and the resurrection. 1 Cor. 15:12

19 And they took him and brought him to the Areopagus, saying, "May we know what this new doctrine *is* of which you speak?

20 "For you are bringing some strange things to our ears. Therefore we want to know what these things mean."

21 For all the Athenians and the foreigners who were there spent their time in nothing else but either to tell or to hear some new thing.

22 Then Paul stood in the midst of the Areopagus and said, "Men of Athens, I perceive that in all things you are very religious;

23 "for as I was passing through and considering the objects of your worship, I even found an altar with this inscription:

TO THE UNKNOWN GOD.

Therefore, the One whom you worship without knowing, Him I proclaim to you:

24 [R]"God, who made the world and everything in it, since He is [R]Lord of heaven and earth, [R]does not dwell in temples made with hands. Acts 14:15 • Matt. 11:25 • Acts 7:48–50

25 "Nor is He worshiped with men's hands, as though He needed anything, since He gives to all life, breath, and all things.

26 "And He has made from one blood* every nation of men to dwell on all the face of the earth, and has determined their preappointed times and [R]the boundaries of their dwellings, Deut. 32:8

27 [R]"so that they should seek the Lord, in the

17:5 NU omits *who were not persuaded;* M omits *becoming envious* **17:18** NU, M add *also* **17:26** NU omits *blood* hope that they might grope for Him and find Him, [R]though He is not far from each one of us; [Rom. 1:20] • Jer. 23:23, 24

28 "for in Him we live and move and have our being, as also some of your own poets have said, 'For we are also His offspring.'

29 "Therefore, since we are the offspring of God, we ought not to think that the Divine Nature is like gold or silver or stone, something shaped by art and man's devising.

30 "Truly, [R]these times of ignorance God overlooked, but now commands all men everywhere to repent, [Rom. 3:25]

31 "because He has appointed a day on which [R]He will judge the world in righteousness by the Man whom He has ordained. He has given assurance of this to all by [R]raising Him from the dead." Acts 10:42 • Acts 2:24

32 And when they heard of the resurrection of the dead, some mocked, while others said, "We will hear you again on this *matter*."

33 So Paul departed from among them.

34 However, some men joined him and believed, among them Dionysius the Areopagite, a woman named Damaris, and others with them.

CHAPTER 18

Paul Works with Aquila and Priscilla

AFTER these things Paul departed from Athens and went to Corinth.

2 And he found a certain Jew named [R]Aquila, born in Pontus, who had recently come from Italy with his wife Priscilla (because Claudius had commanded all the Jews to depart from Rome); and he came to them. 1 Cor. 16:19

3 So, because he was of the same trade, he stayed with them [R]and worked; for by occupation they were tentmakers. Acts 20:34

Jews Reject Paul

4 [R]And he reasoned in the synagogue every Sabbath, and persuaded both Jews and Greeks. Acts 17:2

5 [R]When Silas and Timothy had come from Macedonia, Paul was [R]compelled by the Spirit, and testified to the Jews *that* Jesus *is* the Christ. Acts 17:14, 15 • Acts 18:28

6 But when they opposed him and blasphemed, [R]he shook *his* garments and said to them, [R]"Your blood *be* upon your *own* heads; [R]I *am* clean. From now on I will go to the Gentiles." Neh. 5:13 • 2 Sam. 1:16 • [Ezek. 3:18, 19]

Crispus, the Gentile, Is Converted

7 And he departed from there and entered the house of a certain *man* named Justus,* *one* who worshiped God, whose house was next door to the synagogue.

8 Then Crispus, the ruler of the synagogue, believed on the Lord with all his household. And many of the Corinthians, hearing, believed and were baptized.

9 Now [R]the Lord spoke to Paul in the night by a vision, "Do not be afraid, but speak, and do not keep silent; Acts 23:11

10 [R]"for I am with you, and no one will attack you to hurt you; for I have many people in this city." Jer. 1:18, 19

11 And he continued *there* a year and six months, teaching the word of God among them.

Gallio Will Not Try Paul

12 When Gallio was proconsul of Achaia, the Jews with one accord rose up against Paul and brought him to the judgment seat,

13 saying, "This *fellow* persuades men to worship God contrary to the law."

14 And when Paul was about to open *his* mouth, Gallio said to the Jews, "If it were a matter of wrongdoing or wicked crimes, O Jews, there would be reason why I should bear with you.

15 "But if it is a [R]question of words and names and your own law, look *to it* yourselves; for I do not want to be a judge of such *matters*." Acts 23:29; 25:19

16 And he drove them from the judgment seat.

17 Then all the Greeks* took [R]Sosthenes, the ruler of the synagogue, and beat *him* before the judgment seat. But Gallio took no notice of these things. 1 Cor. 1:1

Return Trip to Antioch

18 So Paul still remained a good while. Then he took leave of the brethren and sailed for Syria, and Priscilla and Aquila *were* with him. He had *his* hair cut off at [R]Cenchrea, for he had taken a vow. Rom. 16:1

19 And he came to Ephesus, and left them there; but he himself entered the synagogue and reasoned with the Jews.

20 When they asked *him* to stay a longer time with them, he did not consent,

21 but took leave of them, saying, "I must by all means keep this coming feast in Jerusalem;* but I will return again to you, God willing." And he sailed from Ephesus.

22 And when he had landed at [R]Caesarea, and [T]gone up and greeted the church, he went down to Antioch. Acts 8:40 • To Jerusalem

Galatia and Phrygia: Strengthening the Disciples

23 After he had spent some time *there*, he departed and went over the region of [R]Galatia and Phrygia [T]in order, [R]strengthening all the disciples. Gal. 1:2 • *successively* • Acts 14:22

18:7 NU *Titius Justus* **18:17** NU *they all* **18:21** NU omits *I must* through *Jerusalem*

Apollos Teaches Effectively

24 Now a certain Jew named Apollos, born
at Alexandria, an eloquent man *and* mighty in
the Scriptures, came to Ephesus.
25 This man had been instructed in the way
of the Lord; and being [R]fervent in spirit, he
spoke and taught accurately the things of the
Lord, [R]though he knew only the baptism of
John. Rom. 12:11 • Acts 19:3
26 So he began to speak boldly in the syna-
gogue. When Aquila and Priscilla heard him,
they took him aside and explained to him the
way of God more accurately.
27 And when he desired to cross to Achaia,
the brethren wrote, exhorting the disciples to
receive him; and when he arrived, [R]he greatly
helped those who had believed through
grace; 1 Cor. 3:6
28 for he vigorously refuted the Jews pub-
licly, [R]showing from the Scriptures that Jesus
is the Christ. Acts 9:22; 17:3; 18:5

CHAPTER 19

Disciples of John Receive the Holy Spirit

AND it happened, while Apollos was at
Corinth, that Paul, having passed through
[R]the upper regions, came to Ephesus. And
finding some disciples Acts 18:23
2 he said to them, "Did you receive the Holy
Spirit when you believed?" So they said to
him, [R]"We have not so much as heard whether
there is a Holy Spirit." 1 Sam. 3:7
3 And he said to them, "Into what then were
you baptized?" So they said, [R]"Into John's
baptism." Acts 18:25
4 Then Paul said, [R]"John indeed baptized
with a baptism of repentance, saying to the
people that they should believe on Him who
would come after him, that is, on Christ Je-
sus." Matt. 3:11
5 When they heard *this*, they were baptized
in the name of the Lord Jesus.
6 And when Paul had laid hands on them,
the Holy Spirit came upon them, and they
spoke with tongues and prophesied.
7 Now the men were about twelve in all.

Paul Teaches in Tyrannus's School

8 [R]And he went into the synagogue and
spoke boldly for three months, reasoning and
persuading [R]concerning the things of the
kingdom of God. Acts 17:2; 18:4 • Acts 1:3
9 But [R]when some were hardened and did
not believe, but spoke evil [R]of the Way before
the multitude, he departed from them and
withdrew the disciples, reasoning daily in the
school of Tyrannus. 2 Tim. 1:15 • Acts 9:2
10 And this continued for two years, so that
all who dwelt in Asia heard the word of the
Lord Jesus, both Jews and Greeks.

Miracles Are Performed at Ephesus

11 Now [R]God worked unusual miracles by
the hands of Paul, Mark 16:20
12 [R]so that even handkerchiefs or aprons
were brought from his body to the sick, and
the diseases left them and the evil spirits went
out of them. Acts 5:15
13 Then some of the itinerant Jewish exor-
cists took it upon themselves to call the name
of the Lord Jesus over those who had evil
spirits, saying, "We* exorcise you by the Jesus
whom Paul preaches."
14 Also there were seven sons of Sceva, a
Jewish chief priest, who did so.
15 And the evil spirit answered and said, "Je-
sus I know, and Paul I know; but who are
you?"
16 Then the man in whom the evil spirit was
leaped on them, overpowered* them, and pre-
vailed against them,* so that they fled out of
that house naked and wounded.
17 This became known both to all Jews and
Greeks dwelling in Ephesus; and [R]fear fell on
them all, and the name of the Lord Jesus was
magnified. Luke 1:65; 7:16
18 And many who had believed came [R]con-
fessing and telling their deeds. Matt. 3:6
19 Also, many of those who had practiced
magic brought their books together and
burned *them* in the sight of all. And they
counted up the value of them, and *it* totaled
fifty thousand *pieces* of silver.
20 [R]So the word of the Lord grew mightily
and prevailed. Acts 6:7; 12:24

Timothy and Erastus Are Sent to Macedonia

21 [R]When these things were accomplished,
Paul purposed in the Spirit, when he had
passed through Macedonia and Achaia, to go
to Jerusalem, saying, "After I have been there,
I must also see Rome." Rom. 15:25
22 So he sent into Macedonia two of those
who ministered to him, Timothy and Erastus,
but he himself stayed in Asia for a time.

Demetrius Causes Uproar at Ephesus

23 And [R]about that time there arose a great
commotion about the Way. 2 Cor. 1:8
24 For a certain man named Demetrius, a
silversmith, who made silver shrines of Di-
ana,* brought [R]no small profit to the crafts-
men. Acts 16:16, 19
25 He called them together with the workers
of similar occupation, and said: "Men, you
know that we have our prosperity by this
trade.
26 "Moreover you see and hear that not only
at Ephesus, but throughout almost all Asia,
this Paul has persuaded and turned away

19:13 NU *I* **19:16** M *and they overpowered* • NU *both of them* **19:24** Gr. *Artemis*

many people, saying that they are not gods
which are made with hands.
27 "So not only is this trade of ours in danger of falling into disrepute, but also the temple of the great goddess Diana may be despised and her magnificence destroyed,* whom all Asia and the world worship."
28 Now when they heard *this,* they were full of wrath and cried out, saying, "Great *is* Diana of the Ephesians!"
29 So the whole city was filled with confusion, and rushed into the theater with one accord, having seized [R]Gaius and [R]Aristarchus, Macedonians, Paul's travel companions. Rom. 16:23 • Col. 4:10
30 And when Paul wanted to go in to the people, the disciples would not allow him.
31 Then some of the officials of Asia, who were his friends, sent to him pleading that he would not venture into the theater.
32 Some therefore cried one thing and some another, for the assembly was confused, and most of them did not know why they had come together.
33 And they drew Alexander out of the multitude, the Jews putting him forward. And [R]Alexander [R]motioned with his hand, and wanted to make his defense to the people. 2 Tim. 4:14 • Acts 12:17
34 But when they found out that he was a Jew, all with one voice cried out for about two hours, "Great *is* Diana of the Ephesians!"
35 And when the city clerk had quieted the crowd, he said: "Men of Ephesus, what man is there who does not know that the city of the Ephesians is temple guardian of the great goddess [T]Diana, and of the *image* which fell down from Zeus? Gr. *Artemis*
36 "Therefore, since these things cannot be denied, you ought to be quiet and do nothing rashly.
37 "For you have brought these men here who are neither robbers of temples nor blasphemers of your* goddess.
38 "Therefore, if Demetrius and his fellow craftsmen have a case against anyone, the courts are open and there are proconsuls. Let them bring charges against one another.
39 "But if you have any other inquiry to make, it shall be determined in the lawful assembly.
40 "For we are in danger of being called in question for today's uproar, there being no reason which we may give to account for this disorderly gathering."
41 And when he had said these things, he dismissed the assembly.

CHAPTER 20

Macedonia: Three Months of Ministry

AFTER the uproar had ceased, Paul called the disciples to *himself,* embraced *them,* and departed to go to Macedonia.
2 Now when he had gone over that region and encouraged them with many words, he came to [R]Greece Acts 17:15; 18:1
3 and stayed three months. And [R]when the Jews plotted against him as he was about to sail to Syria, he decided to return through Macedonia. 2 Cor. 11:26
4 And Sopater of Berea accompanied him to Asia—also [R]Aristarchus and Secundus of the Thessalonians, and [R]Gaius of Derbe, and [R]Timothy, and [R]Tychicus and Trophimus of Asia. Col. 4:10 • Acts 19:29 • Acts 16:1 • Eph. 6:21
5 These men, going ahead, waited for us at [R]Troas. 2 Tim. 4:13

Troas: Eutychus Falls from Loft

6 But we sailed away from Philippi after [R]the Days of Unleavened Bread, and in five days joined them [R]at Troas, where we stayed seven days. Ex. 12:14, 15 • 2 Tim. 4:13
7 Now on [R]the first *day* of the week, when the disciples came together [R]to break bread, Paul, ready to depart the next day, spoke to them and continued his message until midnight. 1 Cor. 16:2 • Acts 2:42, 46; 20:11
8 There were many lamps in the upper room where they* were gathered together.
9 And in a window sat a certain young man named Eutychus, who was sinking into a deep sleep. He was overcome by sleep; and as Paul continued speaking, he fell down from the third story and was taken up dead.
10 But Paul went down, [R]fell on him, and embracing *him* said, "Do not trouble yourselves, for his life is in him." 1 Kin. 17:21
11 Now when he had come up, had broken bread and eaten, and talked a long while, even till daybreak, he departed.
12 And they brought the young man in alive, and they were not a little comforted.

Miletus: Paul Bids Farewell to Ephesian Elders

13 Then we went ahead to the ship and sailed to Assos, there intending to take Paul on board; for so he had [T]given orders, intending himself to go on foot. *arranged it*
14 And when he met us at Assos, we took him on board and came to Mitylene.
15 We sailed from there, and the next *day* came opposite Chios. The following *day* we arrived at Samos and stayed at Trogyllium. The next *day* we came to Miletus.
16 For Paul had decided to sail past Ephesus, so that he would not have to spend time in Asia; for [R]he was hurrying [R]to be at Jerusalem, if possible, on [R]the Day of Pentecost. Acts 18:21; 19:21; 21:4 • Acts 24:17 • Acts 2:1
17 From Miletus he sent to Ephesus and called for the elders of the church.

19:27 NU *she be deposed from her magnificence*
19:37 NU *our* **20:8** NU, M *we*

18 And when they had come to him, he said
to them: "You know, [R]from the first day that I
came to Asia, in what manner I always lived
among you, Acts 18:19; 19:1, 10; 20:4, 16
19 "serving the Lord with all humility, with
many tears and trials which happened to me
[R]by the plotting of the Jews; Acts 20:3
20 "how I kept back nothing that was help-
ful, but proclaimed it to you, and taught you
publicly and from house to house,
21 "testifying to Jews, and also to Greeks,
[R]repentance toward God and faith toward our
Lord Jesus Christ. Mark 1:15
22 "And see, now [R]I go bound in the spirit to
Jerusalem, not knowing the things that will
happen to me there, Acts 19:21
23 "except that [R]the Holy Spirit testifies in
every city, saying that chains and tribulations
await me. Acts 21:4, 11
24 "But none of these things move me; nor
do I count my life dear to myself,* [R]so that
I may finish my race with joy, [R]and the
ministry [R]which I received from the Lord
Jesus, to testify to the gospel of the grace
of God. 2 Tim. 4:7 • Acts 1:17 • Gal. 1:1
25 "And indeed, now I know that you all,
among whom I have gone preaching the king-
dom of God, will see my face no more.
26 "Therefore I testify to you this day that I
am innocent of the blood of all *men.*
27 "For I have not shunned to declare to you
[R]the whole counsel of God. Luke 7:30
28 [R]"Therefore take heed to yourselves and
to all the flock, among which the Holy Spirit
[R]has made you overseers, to shepherd the
church of God* which He purchased with His
own blood. 1 Pet. 5:2 • 1 Cor. 12:28
29 "For I know this, that after my departure
[R]savage wolves will come in among you, not
sparing the flock. Matt. 7:15
30 "Also from among yourselves men will
rise up, speaking perverse things, to draw
away the disciples after themselves.
31 "Therefore watch, and remember that for
three years I did not cease to warn everyone
night and day with tears.
32 "So now, brethren, I commend you to God
and to the word of His grace, which is able to
build you up and give you an inheritance
among all those who are sanctified.
33 "I have coveted no one's silver or gold or
apparel.
34 "Yes,* you yourselves know [R]that these
hands have provided for my necessities, and
for those who were with me. Acts 18:3
35 "I have shown you in every way, [R]by la-
boring like this, that you must support the
weak. And remember the words of the Lord
Jesus, that He said, 'It is more blessed to give
than to receive.' " Rom. 15:1
36 And when he had said these things, he
knelt down and prayed with them all.
37 Then they all wept freely, and [R]fell on
Paul's neck and kissed him, Gen. 45:14
38 sorrowing most of all for the words which
he spoke, that they would see his face no
more. And they accompanied him to the ship.

CHAPTER 21

Tyre: Paul Is Warned About Jerusalem

NOW it came to pass, that when we had de-
parted from them and set sail, running a
straight course we came to Cos, the following
day to Rhodes, and from there to Patara.
2 And finding a ship sailing over to Phoe-
nicia, we went aboard and set sail.
3 When we had sighted Cyprus, we passed it
on the left, sailed to Syria, and landed at Tyre;
for there the ship was to unload her cargo.
4 And finding disciples,* we stayed there
seven days. They told Paul through the Spirit
not to go up to Jerusalem.
5 When we had come to the end of those
days, we departed and went on our way; and
they all accompanied us, with wives and chil-
dren, till *we were* out of the city. And we knelt
down on the shore and prayed.
6 When we had taken our leave of one an-
other, we boarded the ship, and they returned
[R]home. John 1:11

Caesarea: Agabus's Prediction

7 And when we had finished *our* voyage
from Tyre, we came to Ptolemais, greeted the
brethren, and stayed with them one day.
8 On the next *day* we who were Paul's com-
panions* departed and came to Caesarea, and
entered the house of Philip [R]the evangelist,
[R]who was *one* of the seven, and stayed with
him. Eph. 4:11 • Acts 6:5
9 Now this man had four virgin daughters
[R]who prophesied. Joel 2:28
10 And as we stayed many days, a certain
prophet named [R]Agabus came down from
Judea. Acts 11:28
11 When he had come to us, he took Paul's
belt, bound his *own* hands and feet, and said,
"Thus says the Holy Spirit, [R]'So shall the Jews
at Jerusalem bind the man who owns this
belt, and deliver *him* into the hands of the
Gentiles.' " Acts 20:23; 21:33
12 Now when we heard these things, both
we and those from that place pleaded with
him not to go up to Jerusalem.
13 Then Paul answered, [R]"What do you
mean by weeping and breaking my heart? For
I am ready not only to be bound, but also to
die at Jerusalem for the name of the Lord Je-
sus." Acts 20:24, 37

20:24 NU *But I do not count my life of any value or dear to myself* **20:28** M *of the Lord and God* **20:34** NU, M omit *Yes* **21:4** NU *the disciples* **21:8** NU omits *who were Paul's companions*

14 So when he would not be persuaded, we
ceased, saying, [R]"The will of the Lord be
done." Luke 11:2; 22:42
15 And after those days we [T]packed and
went up to Jerusalem. *made preparations*
16 Also some of the disciples from Caesarea
went with us and brought with them a certain
Mnason of Cyprus, an early disciple, with
whom we were to lodge.

Paul Conforms to Jewish Customs

17 [R]And when we had come to Jerusalem,
the brethren received us gladly. Acts 15:4
18 On the following *day* Paul went in with
us to [R]James, and all the elders were pres-
ent. Gal. 1:19; 2:9
19 When he had greeted them, he told in de-
tail those things which God had done among
the Gentiles through his ministry.
20 And when they heard *it*, they glorified the
Lord. And they said to him, "You see, brother,
how many myriads of Jews there are who
have believed, and they are all [R]zealous for
the law; Acts 15:1; 22:3
21 "but they have been informed about you
that you teach all the Jews who are among the
Gentiles to forsake Moses, saying that they
ought not to circumcise *their* children nor to
walk according to the customs.
22 "What then? The assembly must certainly
meet, for they will* hear that you have come.
23 "Therefore do what we tell you: We have
four men who have taken a vow.
24 "Take them and be purified with them,
and pay their expenses so that they may
[R]shave *their* heads, and that all may know
that those things of which they were in-
formed concerning you are nothing, but *that*
you yourself also walk orderly and keep the
law. Acts 18:18
25 "But concerning the Gentiles who believe,
[R]we have written *and* decided that they should
observe no such thing,* except that they should
keep themselves from *things* offered to idols,
from blood, from things strangled, and from
[T]sexual immorality." Acts 15:19, 20, 29 • *fornication*
26 Then Paul took the men, and the next
day, having been purified with them, [R]en-
tered the temple [R]to announce the [T]expira-
tion of the days of purification, at which time
an offering should be made for each one of
them. Acts 21:24; 24:18 • Num. 6:13 • *completion*

Paul's Arrest

27 Now when the seven days were almost
ended, [R]the Jews from Asia, seeing him in the
temple, stirred up the whole crowd and laid
hands on him, Acts 20:19; 24:18
28 crying out, "Men of Israel, help! This is the
man [R]who teaches all *men* everywhere against
the people, the law, and this place; and further-
more he also brought Greeks into the temple
and has defiled this holy place." Acts 6:13; 24:6
29 (For they had previously* seen [R]Troph-
imus the Ephesian with him in the city, whom
they supposed that Paul had brought into the
temple.) Acts 20:4
30 And [R]all the city was disturbed; and the
people ran together, seized Paul, and dragged
him out of the temple; and immediately the
doors were shut. Acts 16:19; 26:21
31 Now as they were seeking to kill him,
news came to the commander of the garrison
that all Jerusalem was in an uproar.
32 [R]He immediately took soldiers and centu-
rions, and ran down to them. And when they
saw the commander and the soldiers, they
stopped beating Paul. Acts 23:27; 24:7
33 Then the [R]commander came near and
took him, and [R]commanded *him* to be bound
with two chains; and he asked who he was
and what he had done. Acts 24:7 • Acts 20:23
34 And some among the multitude cried one
thing and some another. So when he could not
ascertain the truth because of the tumult, he
commanded him to be taken into the bar-
racks.
35 When he reached the stairs, he had to be
carried by the soldiers because of the violence
of the mob.
36 For the multitude of the people followed
after, crying out, "Away with him!"
37 Then as Paul was about to be led into the
barracks, he said to the commander, "May I
speak to you?" He replied, "Can you speak
Greek?
38 [R]"Are you not the Egyptian who some
time ago stirred up a rebellion and led the
four thousand assassins out into the wilder-
ness?" Acts 5:36
39 But Paul said, [R]"I am a Jew from Tarsus,
in Cilicia, a citizen of no [T]mean city; and I
implore you, permit me to speak to the peo-
ple." Acts 9:11; 22:3 • *insignificant*

Paul's Defense Before the Crowd
Acts 9:1–8, 17, 18; 26:13–18

40 So when he had given him permission,
Paul stood on the stairs and [R]motioned with
his hand to the people. And when there was a
great silence, he spoke to *them* in the [R]He-
brew language, saying, Acts 12:17 • Acts 22:2

CHAPTER 22

"BRETHREN[R] and fathers, hear my de-
fense before you now." Acts 7:2
2 And when they heard that he spoke to
them in the [R]Hebrew language, they kept all
the more silent. Then he said: Acts 21:40
3 "I am indeed a Jew, born in Tarsus of Cili-
cia, but brought up in this city at the feet of

21:22 NU *What then is to be done? They will certainly* **21:25** NU omits *that they should observe no such thing, except* **21:29** M omits *previously*

Gamaliel, taught according to the strictness of
our fathers' law, and was zealous toward God
as you all are today.
4 [R]"I persecuted this Way to the death, bind-
ing and delivering into prisons both men and
women, 1 Tim. 1:13
5 "as also the high priest bears me witness,
and [R]all the council of the elders, [R]from whom
I also received letters to the brethren, and
went to Damascus to bring in chains even
those who were there to Jerusalem to be pun-
ished. Acts 23:14; 24:1; 25:15 • Luke 22:66
6 "Now [R]it happened, as I journeyed and
came near Damascus at about noon, sud-
denly a great light from heaven shone around
me. Acts 9:3; 26:12, 13
7 "And I fell to the ground and heard a
voice saying to me, 'Saul, Saul, why are you
persecuting Me?'
8 "So I answered, 'Who are You, Lord?' And
He said to me, 'I am Jesus of Nazareth, whom
you are persecuting.'
9 "And those who were with me indeed saw
the light and were afraid,* but they did not
hear the voice of Him who spoke to me.
10 "So I said, 'What shall I do, Lord?' And
the Lord said to me, 'Arise and go into Damas-
cus, and there you will be told all things
which are appointed for you to do.'
11 "And since I could not see for the glory of
that light, being led by the hand of those who
were with me, I came into Damascus.
12 "Then a certain Ananias, a devout man
according to the law, having a good testimony
with all the Jews who dwelt *there*,
13 "came to me; and he stood and said to me,
'Brother Saul, receive your sight.' And at that
same hour I looked up at him.
14 "Then he said, [R]'The God of our fathers
[R]has chosen you that you should know His
will, and see the Just One, and hear the voice
of His mouth. Acts 3:13; 5:30 • Acts 9:15
15 'For you will be His witness to all men of
what you have seen and heard.
16 'And now why are you waiting? Arise and
be baptized, and wash away your sins, calling
on the name of the Lord.'
17 "Now [R]it happened, when I returned to Je-
rusalem and was praying in the temple, that I
was in a trance Acts 9:26; 26:20
18 "and [R]saw Him saying to me, [R]'Make
haste and get out of Jerusalem quickly, for
they will not receive your testimony concern-
ing Me.' Acts 22:14 • Matt. 10:14
19 "So I said, 'Lord, [R]they know that in every
synagogue I imprisoned and beat those who
believe on You. Acts 8:3; 22:4
20 'And when the blood of Your martyr
Stephen was shed, I also was standing by con-
senting to his death,* and guarding the
clothes of those who were killing him.'
21 "Then He said to me, 'Depart, for I will
send you far from here to the Gentiles.' "
22 And they listened to him until this word,
and *then* they raised their voices and said,
[R]"Away with such a *fellow* from the earth, for
[R]he is not fit to live!" Acts 21:36 • Acts 25:24
23 Then, as they cried out and tore off *their*
clothes and threw dust into the air,

Paul's Defense Before the Centurion

24 the commander ordered him to be
brought into the barracks, and said that he
should be examined under scourging, so that
he might know why they shouted so against
him.
25 And as they bound him with thongs, Paul
said to the centurion who stood by, [R]"Is it law-
ful for you to scourge a man who is a Roman,
and uncondemned?" Acts 16:37
26 When the centurion heard *that*, he went
and told the commander, saying, "Take care
what you do, for this man is a Roman."
27 Then the commander came and said to
him, "Tell me, are you a Roman?" He said,
"Yes."
28 The commander answered, "With a large
sum I obtained this citizenship." And Paul
said, "But I was born *a citizen*."
29 Then immediately those who were about
to examine him withdrew from him; and the
commander was also afraid after he found out
that he was a Roman, and because he had
bound him.

Paul's Defense Before the Sanhedrin

30 The next day, because he wanted to know
for certain why he was accused by the Jews,
he released him from *his* bonds, and com-
manded the chief priests and all their council
to appear, and brought Paul down and set him
before them.

CHAPTER 23

THEN Paul, looking earnestly at the coun-
cil, said, "Men *and* brethren, [R]I have lived
in all good conscience before God until this
day." 2 Tim. 1:3
2 And the high priest Ananias commanded
those who stood by him [R]to strike him on the
mouth. John 18:22
3 Then Paul said to him, "God will strike
you, *you* whitewashed wall! For you sit to
judge me according to the law, and [R]do you
command me to be struck contrary to the
law?" Deut. 25:1, 2
4 And those who stood by said, "Do you re-
vile God's high priest?"
5 Then Paul said, [R]"I did not know,
brethren, that he was the high priest; for it is
written, *'You shall not speak evil of a ruler of
your people.'* "* Lev. 5:17, 18

22:9 NU omits *and were afraid* **22:20** NU omits *to his death* **23:5** Ex. 22:28

6 But when Paul perceived that one part
were Sadducees and the other Pharisees, he
cried out in the council, "Men *and* brethren, [R]I
am a Pharisee, the son of a Pharisee; [R]concerning the hope and resurrection of the dead
I am being judged!" Phil. 3:5 • Acts 28:20
7 And when he had said this, a dissension
arose between the Pharisees and the Sadducees; and the assembly was divided.
8 [R]For Sadducees say that there is no resurrection—and no angel or spirit; but the Pharisees confess both. Matt. 22:23
9 Then there arose a loud outcry. And the
scribes of the Pharisees' party arose and
protested, saying, "We find no evil in this man;
but if a spirit or an angel has spoken to him,
let us not fight against God."*
10 Now when there arose a great dissension,
the commander, fearing lest Paul might be
pulled to pieces by them, commanded the soldiers to go down and take him by force from
among them, and bring *him* into the barracks.
11 But the following night the Lord stood by
him and said, "Be of good cheer, Paul; for as
you have testified for Me in Jerusalem, so you
must also bear witness at Rome."

Jews' Plan to Kill Paul

12 And when it was day, some of the Jews
banded together and bound themselves under
an oath, saying that they would neither eat
nor drink till they had killed Paul.
13 Now there were more than forty who had
formed this conspiracy.
14 They came to the chief priests and [R]elders, and said, "We have bound ourselves
under a great oath that we will eat nothing
until we have killed Paul. Acts 4:5, 23; 6:12
15 "Now you, therefore, together with the
council, suggest to the commander that he be
brought down to you tomorrow,* as though
you were going to make further inquiries concerning him; but we are ready to kill him before he comes near."
16 So when Paul's sister's son heard of their
ambush, he went and entered the barracks
and told Paul.
17 Then Paul called one of the centurions to
him and said, "Take this young man to the
commander, for he has something to tell him."
18 So he took him and brought *him* to the
commander and said, "Paul the prisoner called
me to *him* and asked *me* to bring this young
man to you. He has something to say to you."
19 Then the commander took him by the
hand, went aside, and asked privately, "What
is it that you have to tell me?"
20 And he said, [R]"The Jews have agreed to
ask that you bring Paul down to the council
tomorrow, as though they were going to inquire more fully about him. Acts 23:12
21 "But do not yield to them, for more than
forty of them lie in wait for him, men who
have bound themselves by an oath that they
will neither eat nor drink till they have killed
him; and now they are ready, waiting for the
promise from you."
22 So the commander let the young man depart, and commanded *him*, "Tell no one that
you have revealed these things to me."

Paul's Rescue

23 And he called for two centurions, saying,
"Prepare two hundred soldiers, seventy horsemen, and two hundred spearmen to go to Caesarea at the third hour of the night;
24 "and provide mounts to set Paul on, and
bring *him* safely to Felix the governor."
25 He wrote a letter in the following manner:

26 Claudius Lysias,

To the most excellent governor Felix:

Greetings.

27 This man was seized by the Jews and
was about to be killed by them. Coming
with the troops I rescued him, having
learned that he was a Roman.
28 [R]And when I wanted to know the reason
they accused him, I brought him before
their council. Acts 22:30
29 I found out that he was accused
concerning questions of their law, but
had nothing charged against him
deserving of death or chains.
30 And when it was told me that the Jews
lay in wait for the man,* I sent him
immediately to you, and also
commanded his accusers to state before
you the charges against him.

Farewell.

31 Then the soldiers, as they were commanded, took Paul and brought *him* by night
to Antipatris.
32 The next day they left the horsemen to go
on with him, and returned to the barracks.
33 When they came to [R]Caesarea and had
delivered the letter to the governor, they also
presented Paul to him. Acts 8:40

Paul Is Tried Before Felix

34 And when the governor had read *it*, he
asked what province he was from. And when
he understood that *he was* from Cilicia,
35 he said, "I will hear you when your accusers also have come." And he commanded him
to be kept in Herod's Praetorium.

23:9 NU *what if a spirit or an angel has spoken to him?* omitting the last clause **23:15** NU omits *tomorrow* **23:30** NU *there would be a plot against the man*

CHAPTER 24

NOW after five days Ananias the high priest came down with the elders and a certain orator *named* Tertullus. These gave evidence to the governor against Paul.

2 And when he was called upon, Tertullus began his accusation, saying: "Seeing that through you we enjoy great peace, and [T]prosperity is being brought to this nation by your foresight, Or *reforms are*

3 "we accept *it* always and in all places, most noble Felix, with all thankfulness.

4 "Nevertheless, not to be tedious to you any further, I beg you to hear, by your [T]courtesy, a few words from us. *graciousness*

5 [R]"For we have found this man a plague, a creator of dissension among all the Jews throughout the world, and a ringleader of the sect of the Nazarenes. 1 Pet. 2:12, 15

6 [R]"He even tried to profane the temple, and we seized him,* and wanted to judge him according to our law. Acts 21:28

7 [R]"But the commander Lysias came by and with great violence took *him* out of our hands, Acts 21:33; 23:10

8 [R]"commanding his accusers to come to you. By examining him yourself you may ascertain all these things of which we accuse him." Acts 23:30

9 And the Jews also assented,* maintaining that these things were so.

10 Then Paul, after the governor had nodded to him to speak, answered: "Inasmuch as I know that you have been for many years a judge of this nation, I do the more cheerfully answer for myself,

11 "because you may ascertain that it is no more than twelve days since I went up to Jerusalem [R]to worship. Acts 21:15, 18, 26, 27

12 [R]"And they neither found me in the temple disputing with anyone nor inciting the crowd, either in the synagogues or in the city. Acts 25:8; 28:17

13 "Nor can they prove the things of which they now accuse me.

14 "But this I confess to you, that according to [R]the Way which they call a sect, so I worship the [R]God of my fathers, believing all things which are written in the Law and in the Prophets. Acts 9:2; 24:22 • 2 Tim. 1:3

15 [R]"I have hope in God, which they themselves also accept, [R]that there will be a resurrection of *the* dead,* both of *the* just and *the* unjust. Acts 23:6; 26:6, 7; 28:20 • [Dan. 12:2]

16 [R]"This *being* so, I myself always strive to have a conscience without offense toward God and men. Acts 23:1

17 "Now after many years I came to bring alms and offerings to my nation,

18 "in the midst of which some Jews from Asia found me purified in the temple, neither with a mob nor with tumult.

19 [R]"They ought to have been here before you to object if they had anything against me. [Acts 23:30; 25:16]

20 "Or else let those who are *here* themselves say if they found any wrongdoing* in me while I stood before the council,

21 "unless *it is* for this one statement which I cried out, standing among them, 'Concerning the resurrection of the dead I am being judged by you this day.' "

22 But when Felix heard these things, having more accurate knowledge of *the* [R]Way, he adjourned the proceedings and said, "When Lysias the commander comes down, I will make a decision on your case." Acts 9:2

23 So he commanded the centurion to keep Paul and to let *him* have liberty, and [R]told him not to forbid any of his friends to provide for or visit him. Acts 23:16; 27:3; 28:16

24 And after some days, when Felix came with his wife Drusilla, who was Jewish, he sent for Paul and heard him concerning the [R]faith in Christ. [Rom. 10:9]

25 Now as he reasoned about righteousness, self-control, and the judgment to come, Felix was afraid and answered, "Go away for now; when I have a convenient time I will call for you."

26 Meanwhile he also hoped that [R]money would be given him by Paul, that he might release him.* Therefore he sent for him more often and conversed with him. Ex. 23:8

27 But after two years Porcius Festus succeeded Felix; and Felix, [R]wanting to do the Jews a favor, left Paul bound. Acts 12:3

CHAPTER 25

Paul Is Tried Before Festus

NOW when Festus had come to the province, after three days he went up from [R]Caesarea to Jerusalem. Acts 8:40

2 [R]Then the high priest* and the chief men of the Jews informed him against Paul; and they petitioned him, Acts 24:1; 25:15

3 asking a favor against him, that he would summon him to Jerusalem—[R]while *they* lay in ambush along the road to kill him. Acts 23:12, 15

4 But Festus answered that Paul should be kept at Caesarea, and that he himself was going *there* shortly.

5 "Therefore," he said, "let those who have authority among you go down with *me* and accuse this man, to see [R]if there is any fault in him." Acts 18:14; 25:18

6 And when he had remained among them

24:6 NU ends the sentence here and omits the rest of v. 6, all of v. 7, and the first clause of v. 8. **24:9** NU, M *joined the attack* **24:15** NU omits *of the dead* **24:20** NU, M *say what wrongdoing they found* **24:26** NU omits *that he might release him* **25:2** NU *chief priests*

more than ten days, he went down to Caesarea. And the next day, sitting on the judgment seat, he commanded Paul to be brought.

7 When he had come, the Jews who had come down from Jerusalem stood about and laid many serious complaints against Paul, which they could not prove,

8 while he answered for himself, [R]"Neither against the law of the Jews, nor against the temple, nor against Caesar have I offended in anything at all." Acts 6:13; 24:12; 28:17

9 But Festus, wanting to do the Jews a favor, answered Paul and said, "Are you willing to go up to Jerusalem and there be judged before me concerning these things?"

10 So Paul said, "I stand at Caesar's judgment seat, where I ought to be judged. To the Jews I have done no wrong, as you very well know.

11 [R]"For if I am an offender, or have committed anything deserving of death, I do not object to dying; but if there is nothing in these things of which these men accuse me, no one can deliver me to them. I appeal to Caesar." Acts 18:14; 23:29; 25:25; 26:31

12 Then Festus, when he had conferred with the council, answered, "You have appealed to Caesar? To Caesar you shall go!"

13 And after some days King Agrippa and Bernice came to Caesarea to greet Festus.

14 When they had been there many days, Festus laid Paul's case before the king, saying: [R]"There is a certain man left a prisoner by Felix, Acts 24:27

15 [R]"about whom the chief priests and the elders of the Jews informed *me*, when I was in Jerusalem, asking for a judgment against him. Acts 24:1; 25:2, 3

16 [R]"To them I answered, 'It is not the custom of the Romans to deliver any man to destruction* before the accused meets the accusers face to face, and has opportunity to answer for himself concerning the charge against him.' Acts 25:4, 5

17 "Therefore when they had come together, [R]without any delay, the next day I sat on the judgment seat and commanded the man to be brought in. Acts 25:6, 10

18 "When the accusers stood up, they brought no accusation against him of such things as I [T]supposed, *suspected*

19 [R]"but had some questions against him about their own religion and about a certain Jesus, who had died, whom Paul affirmed to be alive. Acts 18:14, 15; 23:29

20 "And because I was uncertain of such questions, I asked whether he was willing to go to Jerusalem and there be judged concerning these matters.

21 "But when Paul [R]appealed to be reserved for the decision of Augustus, I commanded him to be kept till I could send him to Caesar." Acts 25:11, 12

22 Then Agrippa said to Festus, "I also would like to hear the man myself." "Tomorrow," he said, "you shall hear him."

Paul Is Tried Before Agrippa

23 So the next day, when Agrippa and Bernice had come with great pomp, and had entered the auditorium with the commanders and the prominent men of the city, at Festus' command Paul was brought in.

24 And Festus said: "King Agrippa and all the men who are here present with us, you see this man about whom [R]the whole assembly of the Jews petitioned me, both at Jerusalem and here, crying out that he was [R]not fit to live any longer. Acts 25:2, 3, 7 • Acts 21:36

25 "But when I found that [R]he had committed nothing deserving of death, [R]and that he himself had appealed to Augustus, I decided to send him. Acts 23:9, 29; 26:31 • Acts 25:11, 12

26 "I have nothing certain to write to my lord concerning him. Therefore I have brought him out before you, and especially before you, King Agrippa, so that after the examination has taken place I may have something to write.

27 "For it seems to me unreasonable to send a prisoner and not to specify the charges against him."

CHAPTER 26

THEN Agrippa said to Paul, "You are permitted to speak for yourself." So Paul stretched out his hand and answered for himself:

2 "I think myself [R]happy, King Agrippa, because today I shall answer for myself before you concerning all the things of which I am accused by the Jews, [1 Pet. 3:14; 4:14]

3 "especially because you are expert in all customs and questions which have to do with the Jews. Therefore I beg you to hear me patiently.

4 "My manner of life from my youth, which was spent from the beginning among my own nation at Jerusalem, all the Jews know.

5 "They knew me from the first, if they were willing to testify, that according to [R]the strictest sect of our religion I lived a Pharisee. Phil. 3:5

6 [R]"And now I stand and am judged for the hope of [R]the promise made by God to our fathers. Acts 23:6 • Acts 13:32

7 "To this *promise* [R]our twelve tribes, earnestly serving *God* night and day, hope to attain. For this hope's sake, King Agrippa, I am accused by the Jews. James 1:1

8 "Why should it be thought incredible by you that God raises the dead?

9 [R]"Indeed, I myself thought I must do many things contrary to the name of [R]Jesus of Nazareth. 1 Tim. 1:12, 13 • Acts 2:22; 10:38

25:16 NU omits *to destruction,* although it is implied

10 [R]"This I also did in Jerusalem, and many
of the saints I shut up in prison, having re-
ceived authority from the chief priests; and
when they were put to death, I cast my vote
against *them*. Acts 8:1–3; 9:13
11 [R]"And I punished them often in every syn-
agogue and compelled *them* to blaspheme; and
being exceedingly enraged against them, I per-
secuted *them* even to foreign cities. Acts 22:19
12 [R]"While thus occupied, as I journeyed to
Damascus with authority and commission
from the chief priests, Acts 9:3–8; 22:6–11
13 "at midday, O king, along the road I saw a
light from heaven, brighter than the sun, shin-
ing around me and those who journeyed with
me.
14 "And when we all had fallen to the
ground, I heard a voice speaking to me and
saying in the Hebrew language, 'Saul, Saul,
why are you persecuting Me? *It is* hard for
you to kick against the goads.'
15 "So I said, 'Who are You, Lord?' And He
said, 'I am Jesus, whom you are persecuting.
16 'But rise and stand on your feet; for I have
appeared to you for this purpose, to make you
a minister and a witness both of the things
which you have seen and of the things which
I will yet reveal to you.
17 'I will [T]deliver you from the *Jewish* peo-
ple, as well as *from* the Gentiles, [R]to whom I
now* send you, *rescue* • Acts 22:21
18 [R]'to open their eyes, *in order* [R]to turn
them from darkness to light, and *from* the
power of Satan to God, [R]that they may re-
ceive forgiveness of sins and an inheritance
among those who are sanctified by faith in
Me.' Is. 35:5; 42:7, 16 • 1 Pet. 2:9 • Luke 1:77
19 "Therefore, King Agrippa, I was not
disobedient to the heavenly vision,
20 "but declared first to those in Damascus
and in Jerusalem, and throughout all the re-
gion of Judea, and *then* to the Gentiles, that
they should repent, turn to God, and do works
befitting repentance.
21 "For these reasons the Jews seized me in
the temple and tried to kill *me*.
22 "Therefore, having obtained help from
God, to this day I stand, witnessing both to
small and great, saying no other things than
those [R]which the prophets and [R]Moses said
would come— Rom. 3:21 • John 5:46
23 [R]"that the Christ would suffer, that He
would be the first to rise from the dead, and
[R]would proclaim light to the *Jewish* people
and to the Gentiles." Luke 24:26 • Luke 2:32
24 Now as he thus made his defense, Festus
said with a loud voice, "Paul, [R]you are beside
yourself! Much learning is driving you
mad!" [1 Cor. 1:23; 2:13, 14; 4:10]
25 But he said, "I am not [T]mad, most noble
Festus, but speak the words of truth and rea-
son. *out of my mind*
26 "For the king, before whom I also speak
freely, [R]knows these things; for I am con-
vinced that none of these things escapes his
attention, since this thing was not done in a
corner. Acts 26:3
27 "King Agrippa, do you believe the
prophets? I know that you do believe."
28 Then Agrippa said to Paul, "You almost
persuade me to become a Christian."
29 And Paul said, "I would to God that not
only you, but also all who hear me today,
might become both almost and altogether
such as I am, except for these chains."
30 When he had said these things, the king
stood up, as well as the governor and Bernice
and those who sat with them;
31 and when they had gone aside, they
talked among themselves, saying, [R]"This man
is doing nothing deserving of death or
chains." Acts 23:9, 29; 25:25
32 Then Agrippa said to Festus, "This man
might have been set [R]free [R]if he had not ap-
pealed to Caesar." Acts 28:18 • Acts 25:11

CHAPTER 27

Paul's Witness During the Shipwreck

AND when it was decided that we should
sail to Italy, they delivered Paul and some
other prisoners to *one* named Julius, a centu-
rion of the Augustan Regiment.
2 So, entering a ship of Adramyttium, we
put to sea, meaning to sail along the coasts of
Asia. [R]Aristarchus, a Macedonian of Thessa-
lonica, was with us. Acts 19:29
3 And the next *day* we landed at Sidon.
And Julius [R]treated Paul kindly and gave
him liberty to go to his friends and receive
care. Acts 24:23; 28:16
4 When we had put to sea from there, we
sailed under *the shelter of* Cyprus, because
the winds were contrary.
5 And when we had sailed over the sea
which is off Cilicia and Pamphylia, we came
to Myra, *a city* of Lycia.
6 There the centurion found [R]an Alexan-
drian ship sailing to Italy, and he put us on
board. Acts 28:11
7 When we had sailed slowly many days,
and arrived with difficulty off Cnidus, the
wind not permitting us to proceed, we sailed
under *the shelter of* Crete off Salmone.
8 Passing it with difficulty, we came to a
place called Fair Havens, near the city of
Lasea.
9 Now when much time had been spent,
and sailing was now dangerous [R]because
the Fast was already over, Paul advised
them, Lev. 16:29–31; 23:27–29
10 saying, "Men, I perceive that this voyage
will end with disaster and much loss, not only
of the cargo and ship, but also our lives."

26:17 NU, M omit *now*

11 Nevertheless the centurion was more per-
suaded by the helmsman and the owner of the
ship than by the things spoken by Paul.
12 And because the harbor was not suitable
to winter in, the majority advised to set sail
from there also, if by any means they could
reach Phoenix, a harbor of Crete opening to-
ward the southwest and northwest, *and* win-
ter *there.*
13 When the south wind blew softly, suppos-
ing that they had obtained *their* desire, put-
ting out to sea, they sailed close by Crete.
14 But not long after, a tempestuous head
wind arose, called Euroclydon.*
15 So when the ship was caught, and could
not head into the wind, we let *her* drive.
16 And running under *the shelter of* an is-
land called Clauda,* we secured the skiff with
difficulty.
17 When they had taken it on board, they
used cables to undergird the ship; and fearing
lest they should run aground on the Syrtis*
Sands, they struck sail and so were driven.
18 And because we were exceedingly tem-
pest-tossed, the next *day* they lightened the
ship.
19 On the third *day* we threw the ship's
tackle overboard with our own hands.
20 Now when neither sun nor stars appeared
for many days, and no small tempest beat on
us, all hope that we would be saved was fi-
nally given up.
21 But after long abstinence from food, then
Paul stood in the midst of them and said,
"Men, you should have listened to me, and not
have sailed from Crete and incurred this dis-
aster and loss.
22 "And now I urge you to take [T]heart, for
there will be no loss of life among you, but
only of the ship. *courage*
23 [R]"For there stood by me this night an
angel of the God to whom I belong and
[R]whom I serve, Acts 18:9; 23:11 • Dan. 6:16
24 "saying, 'Do not be afraid, Paul; you must
be brought before Caesar; and indeed God
has granted you all those who sail with you.'
25 "Therefore take heart, men, for I believe
God that it will be just as it was told me.
26 "However, [R]we must run aground on a
certain island." Acts 28:1
27 Now when the fourteenth night had come,
as we were driven up and down in the Adriatic
Sea, about midnight the sailors sensed that
they were drawing near some land.
28 And they took soundings and found *it* to
be twenty fathoms; and when they had gone a
little farther, they took soundings again and
found *it* to be fifteen fathoms.
29 Then, fearing lest we should run aground
on the rocks, they dropped four anchors from
the stern, and [T]prayed for day to come. Or *wished*
30 And as the sailors were seeking to escape
from the ship, when they had let down the
skiff into the sea, under pretense of putting
out anchors from the prow,
31 Paul said to the centurion and the sol-
diers, "Unless these men stay in the ship, you
cannot be saved."
32 Then the soldiers cut away the ropes of
the skiff and let it fall off.
33 And as day was about to dawn, Paul im-
plored *them* all to take food, saying, "Today is
the fourteenth day you have waited and con-
tinued without food, and eaten nothing.
34 "Therefore I urge you to take nourish-
ment, for this is for your survival, since not a
hair will fall from the head of any of you."
35 And when he had said these things, he
took bread and [R]gave thanks to God in the
presence of them all; and when he had broken
it he began to eat. [1 Tim. 4:3, 4]
36 Then they were all encouraged, and also
took food themselves.
37 And in all we were two hundred and sev-
enty-six [R]persons on the ship. Acts 2:41
38 So when they had eaten enough, they
lightened the ship and threw out the wheat
into the sea.
39 When it was day, they did not recognize
the land; but they observed a bay with a
beach, onto which they planned to run the
ship if possible.
40 And they [T]let go the anchors and left
them in the sea, meanwhile loosing the rud-
der ropes; and they hoisted the mainsail to the
wind and made for shore. *cast off*
41 But striking [T]a place where two seas met,
[R]they ran the ship aground; and the prow
stuck fast and remained immovable, but the
stern was being broken up by the violence of
the waves. A reef • 2 Cor. 11:25
42 And the soldiers' plan was to kill the pris-
oners, lest any of them should swim away and
escape.
43 But the centurion, wanting to save Paul,
kept them from *their* purpose, and com-
manded that those who could swim should
jump *overboard* first and get to land,
44 and the rest, some on boards and some on
parts of the ship. And so it was [R]that they all
escaped safely to land. Acts 27:22, 31

CHAPTER 28

Paul's Witness on Malta

NOW when they had escaped, they then
found out that [R]the island was called
Malta. Acts 27:26
2 And the [R]natives showed us unusual
kindness; for they kindled a fire and made us
all welcome, because of the rain that was
falling and because of the cold. Col. 3:11

27:14 A southeast wind that stirs up broad waves; NU *Euraquilon,* a northeaster **27:16** NU *Cauda*
27:17 M *Syrtes*

3 But when Paul had gathered a bundle of
sticks and laid *them* on the fire, a viper came
out because of the heat, and fastened on his
hand.
4 So when the natives saw the creature
hanging from his hand, they said to one an-
other, "No doubt this man is a murderer,
whom, though he has escaped the sea, yet jus-
tice does not allow to live."
5 But he shook off the creature into the fire
and [R]suffered no harm. Mark 16:18
6 However, they were expecting that he
would swell up or suddenly fall down dead.
But after they had looked for a long time and
saw no harm come to him, they changed their
minds and said that he was a god.
7 In that region there was an estate of the
leading citizen of the island, whose name was
Publius, who received us and entertained us
courteously for three days.
8 And it happened that the father of Publius
lay sick of a fever and dysentery. Paul went in
to him and prayed, and [R]he laid his hands on
him and healed him. Mark 5:23
9 So when this was done, the rest of those
on the island who had diseases also came and
were healed.
10 They also honored us in many [R]ways; and
when we departed, they provided such things
as were necessary. Matt. 15:6
11 After three months we sailed in [R]an
Alexandrian ship whose figurehead was the
Twin Brothers, which had wintered at the is-
land. Acts 27:6
12 And landing at Syracuse, we stayed three
days.
13 From there we circled round and reached
Rhegium. And after one day the south wind
blew; and the next day we came to Puteoli,
14 where we found [R]brethren, and were in-
vited to stay with them seven days. And so we
went toward Rome. Rom. 1:8
15 And from there, when the brethren heard
about us, they came to meet us as far as Appii
Forum and Three Inns. When Paul saw them,
he thanked God and took courage.

Paul's Witness in Rome

16 Now when we came to Rome, the centu-
rion delivered the prisoners to the captain of
the guard; but [R]Paul was permitted to dwell
by himself with the soldier who guarded
him. Acts 23:11; 24:25; 27:3
17 And it came to pass after three days that
Paul called the leaders of the Jews together.
So when they had come together, he said to
them: "Men *and* brethren, [R]though I have
done nothing against our people or the cus-
toms of our fathers, yet I was delivered as a
prisoner from Jerusalem into the hands of the
Romans, Acts 23:29; 24:12, 13; 26:31
18 "who, [R]when they had examined me,
wanted to let *me* go, because there was no
cause for putting me to death. Acts 22:24
19 "But when the Jews* spoke against *it*, [R]I
was compelled to appeal to Caesar, not that
I had anything of which to accuse my na-
tion. Acts 25:11, 21, 25
20 "For this reason therefore I have called
for you, to see *you* and speak with *you*, be-
cause [R]for the hope of Israel I am bound with
[R]this chain." Acts 26:6, 7 • Eph. 3:1; 4:1; 6:20
21 Then they said to him, "We neither re-
ceived letters from Judea concerning you, nor
have any of the brethren who came reported
or spoken any evil of you.
22 "But we desire to hear from you what you
think; for concerning this sect, we know that
it is spoken against everywhere."
23 So when they had appointed him a day,
many came to him at *his* lodging, to whom he
explained and solemnly testified of the king-
dom of God, persuading them concerning Je-
sus from both the Law of Moses and the
Prophets, from morning till evening.
24 And [R]some were persuaded by the
things which were spoken, and some disbe-
lieved. Acts 14:4; 19:9
25 So when they did not agree among them-
selves, they departed after Paul had said one
word: "The Holy Spirit spoke rightly through
Isaiah the prophet to our* fathers,
26 "saying,

[R]*'Go to this people and say:* Is. 6:9, 10★
"Hearing you will hear, and shall not
understand;
And seeing you will see, and not
perceive;
27 *For the hearts of this people have grown*
dull.
Their ears are hard of hearing,
And their eyes they have closed,
Lest they should see with their eyes and
hear with their ears,
Lest they should understand with their
hearts and turn,
*So that I should heal them."'**

28 "Therefore let it be known to you that the
salvation of God has been sent [R]to the Gen-
tiles, and they will hear it!" Is. 42:1; 49:6★
29 And when he had said these words, the
Jews departed and had a great dispute among
themselves.*
30 Then Paul dwelt two whole years in his
own rented house, and received all who came
to him,
31 [R]preaching the kingdom of God and
teaching the things which concern the Lord
Jesus Christ with all confidence, no one for-
bidding him. Eph. 6:19

28:19 The ruling authorities **28:25** NU *your*
28:27 Is. 6:9, 10 **28:29** NU omits v. 29.

THE EPISTLE OF PAUL THE APOSTLE TO THE

ROMANS

THE BOOK OF ROMANS

Romans, Paul's greatest work, is placed first among his thirteen epistles in the New Testament. While the four Gospels present the words and works of Jesus Christ, Romans explores the significance of His sacrificial death. Using a question-and-answer format, Paul records the most systematic presentation of doctrine in the Bible. Romans is more than a book of theology; it is also a book of practical exhortation. The good news of Jesus Christ is more than facts to be believed; it is also a life to be lived—a life of righteousness befitting the person "justified freely by [God's] grace through the redemption that is in Christ Jesus" (3:24).

Although some manuscripts omit "in Rome" in 1:7, 15, the title *Pros Romaious,* "To the Romans," has been associated with the epistle almost from the beginning.

THE AUTHOR OF ROMANS

All critical schools agree on the Pauline authorship (1:1) of this foundational book. The vocabulary, style, logic, and theological development are consistent with Paul's other epistles. Paul dictated this letter to a secretary named Tertius (16:22), who was allowed to add his own greeting.

The problem arises not with the authorship but with the disunity of the epistle. Some Latin (but no Greek) manuscripts omit 15:1—16:24, and the closing doxology (16:25–27) is placed at the end of chapter 14 in some manuscripts. These variations have led some scholars to conclude that the last two chapters were not originally part of the epistle or that Paul issued it in two editions. However, most scholars believe that chapter 15 fits in logically with the rest of the epistle. There is more debate over chapter 16, because Paul greets by name twenty-six persons in a church he has never visited. Some scholars contend that it was a separate letter, perhaps written to Ephesus, that was appended to this epistle. Such a letter would be surprising, to say the least (nothing but greetings), especially in the ancient world. It is simpler to understand the list of greetings as Paul's effort as a stranger to the Roman church to list his mutual friends. Paul met these people in the cities of his missionary journeys. Significantly, the only other Pauline epistle that lists individual greetings was addressed to the believers at Colosse, another church Paul had never visited. It may be that this portion was omitted from some copies of Romans because it did not seem relevant.

THE TIME OF ROMANS

Paul did not found the church at Rome, and the tradition that Peter was its founder is contrary to the evidence. It is possible that it began when some of the Jews and proselytes to Judaism who became followers of Christ on the Day of Pentecost (cf. Acts 2:10) returned to Rome, but it is more likely that Christians from churches established by Paul in Asia, Macedonia, and Greece settled in Rome and led others to Christ. According to this epistle, Gentiles were predominant in the church at Rome (1:13; 11:13, 28–31; 15:15, 16), but there were also Jewish believers (2:17—3:8; 3:21—4:1; 7:1–14; 14:1—15:12).

Rome was founded in 753 B.C., and by the time of Paul it was the greatest city in the world with over one million inhabitants (one inscription says over four million). It was full of magnificent buildings, but the majority of people were slaves: opulence and squalor coexisted in the Imperial City. The church in Rome was well known (1:8), and it had been established for several years by the time of this letter (see 14:14; 15:23). The believers there were probably numerous, and evidently they met in several places (16:1–16). The historian Tacitus referred to the Christians who were persecuted under Nero in A.D. 64 as "an immense multitude." The gospel filled the gap left by the practically defunct polytheism of Roman religion.

Paul wrote Romans in A.D. 57, near the end of his third missionary journey (Acts 18:23—21:14; cf. Rom. 15:19). It was evidently written during his three-month stay in Greece (Acts 20:3–6), more specifically, in Corinth. Paul was staying with Gaius of Corinth (16:23; cf. 1 Cor. 1:14); and he also mentioned "Erastus, the treasurer of the city" (16:23). A first-century inscription in Corinth mentions him: "Erastus, the commissioner of public works, laid this pavement at his own expense." Paul's collection from the churches of Macedonia and Achaia for the needy Christians in Jerusalem was complete (15:26), and he was ready to deliver it (15:25). Instead of sailing directly to Jerusalem, Paul avoided a plot by the Jews by first going north to Philippi. He evidently gave this letter to Phoebe from the church at Cenchrea, near Corinth, and she carried it to Rome (16:1, 2).

THE CHRIST OF ROMANS

Paul presents Jesus Christ as the Second Adam whose righteousness and substitutionary death have provided justification for all who place their faith in Him. He offers His righteousness as a gracious gift to sinful men, having borne God's condemnation and wrath for their sinfulness. His death and resurrection are the basis for the believer's redemption, justification, reconciliation, salvation, and glorification.

KEYS TO ROMANS

Key Word: The Righteousness of God—The theme of Romans is found in 1:16, 17: God offers the gift of His righteousness to everyone who comes to Christ by faith. Paul writes Romans to reveal God's sovereign plan of salvation (1—8), to show how Jews and Gentiles fit into that plan (9—11), and to exhort them to live righteous and harmonious lives (12—16). In his sweeping presentation of God's plan of salvation, Paul moves from condemnation to glorification and from positional truth to practical truth. Key words, such as *righteousness, faith, law, all,* and *sin* each appear at least sixty times in this epistle.

Key Verses: Romans 1:16, 17 and 3:21–25—"For I am not ashamed of the gospel of Christ, for it is the power of God to salvation for everyone who believes, for the Jew first and also for the Greek. For in it the righteousness of God is revealed from faith to faith; as it is written, 'The just shall live by faith' " (1:16, 17).

"But now the righteousness of God apart from the law is revealed, being witnessed by the Law and the Prophets, even the righteousness of God, through faith in Jesus Christ, to all and on all who believe. For there is no difference; for all have sinned and fall short of the glory of God, being justified freely by His grace through the redemption that is in Christ Jesus, whom God set forth *as* a propitiation by His blood, through faith, to demonstrate His righteousness, because in His forbearance God had passed over the sins that were previously committed" (3:21–25).

Key Chapters: Romans 6—8—Foundational to all teaching on the spiritual life is the central passage of Romans 6—8. The answers to the questions of how to be delivered from sin, how to live a balanced life under grace, and how to live the victorious Christian life through the power of the Holy Spirit are all contained here. Many consider this to be the principal passage on conforming to the image of Jesus Christ.

SURVEY OF ROMANS

The poet Samuel Taylor Coleridge regarded Romans as "the most profound book in existence," and the commentator Godet called it "the cathedral of the Christian faith." Because of its majestic declaration of the divine plan of salvation, Martin Luther wrote: "This epistle is the chief part of the New Testament and the very purest gospel. . . . It can never be read or pondered too much, and the more it is dealt with the more precious it becomes, and the better it tastes." The four Gospels present the words and works of the Lord Jesus, but Romans, "The Gospel According to Paul," delves more into the significance of His death and resurrection. The theology of Romans is balanced by practical exhortation, because Paul sees the believer's position as the basis for his practice. The theme of righteousness that runs through the book is reflected in the following outline: the revelation of the righteousness of God (1—8); the vindication of the righteousness of God (9—11); the application of the righteousness of God (12—16).

The Revelation of the Righteousness of God (1—8): The prologue (1:1–17) consists of a salutation (1:1–7), a statement of Paul's desire to minister in Rome (1:8–15), and the theme of the book (1:16, 17). This two-verse theme is the basic text of Romans because it combines the

FOCUS	REVELATION OF GOD'S RIGHTEOUSNESS			VINDICATION OF GOD'S RIGHTEOUSNESS			APPLICATION OF GOD'S RIGHTEOUSNESS	
REFERENCE	1:1	3:21	6:1	9:1	9:30	11:1	12:1	14:1—16:27
DIVISION	NEED FOR GOD'S RIGHTEOUSNESS	IMPUTATION OF GOD'S RIGHTEOUSNESS	DEMONSTRATION OF GOD'S RIGHTEOUSNESS	ISRAEL'S PAST: ELECTION	ISRAEL'S PRESENT: REJECTION	ISRAEL'S FUTURE: RESTORATION	CHRISTIAN DUTIES	CHRISTIAN LIBERTIES
TOPIC	SIN	SALVATION	SANCTIFICATION	SOVEREIGNTY			SERVICE	
	DOCTRINAL						BEHAVIORAL	
LOCATION	PROBABLY WRITTEN IN CORINTH							
TIME	C. A.D. 57							

three crucial concepts of salvation, righteousness, and faith.

In 1:18—3:20, Paul builds a solid case for the condemnation of all people under the holy God. The Gentiles are without excuse because they have suppressed the knowledge of God they received from nature and their conscience (1:18–32; their seven-step regression is traced in 1:21–31). The Jews are also under the condemnation of God, and Paul overcomes every objection they could raise to this conclusion (2:1—3:8). God judges according to truth (2:2–5), works (2:6–10), and impartiality (2:11–16), and both the moral and religious Jews fail to meet His standard. Paul concludes his discussion of the reasons for the guilt of the Jews by reminding them they do not obey the Law (2:17–29) nor believe the "oracles of God" (3:1–8). The divine verdict (3:9–20) is universal: "all have sinned and fall short of the glory of God" (3:23).

The section on justification (3:21—5:21) centers on and develops the theme of God's provision for man's need. The first eleven verses are the core of the book (3:21–31), revealing that in Christ, God is both Judge and Savior. Justification is by grace (the source of salvation; 3:21–24), by blood (the basis of salvation; 3:25, 26), and by faith (the condition of salvation; 3:27–31).

Chapter 4 illustrates the principle of justification by faith apart from works in the life of Abraham. Justification issues in reconciliation between God and man (5:1–11). It is brought about by the love of God which is causeless (5:6), measureless (5:7, 8), and ceaseless (5:9–11). In 5:12–21 Paul contrasts the two Adams and the opposite results of their two acts. The righteousness of the Second Adam is imputed to all who trust in Him, leading to reconciliation.

Chapter 6 describes the believer's relationship to sin: in his position he is dead to the principle of sin (6:1–14) and the practice of sin (6:15–23). The reality of identification with Christ is the basis for the sanctified Christian life. After describing the Christian's emancipation from the Law (7), Paul looks at the work of the Holy Spirit who indwells and empowers every believer (8:1–17). The next major topic after condemnation, justification, and sanctification is glorification (8:18–39). All Christians can anticipate a time when they will be perfectly conformed to Jesus Christ not only in their position (present) but also in their practice (the future resurrection).

The Vindication of the Righteousness of God (9—11): It appears that God has rejected His people, Israel, but it is really Israel who has rejected her Messiah. God's rejection of Israel is only partial (there is a spiritual remnant that has trusted in Christ) and temporary (they will be grafted back; 11:23–27). Paul appropriately quotes frequently from the Old Testament in this section, and he emphasizes that God will be faithful to His covenant promises and restore Israel.

The Application of the Righteousness of God (12—16): Paul recognizes that behavior must be built upon belief, and this is why the practical exhortations of this epistle appear after his teaching on the believer's position in Christ. The salvation described in the first eleven chapters should transform a Christian's life in relation to God (12:1, 2), society (12:3–21), higher powers (13:1–7); and one's neighbors (13:8–14). In chapters 14 and 15 the apostle discusses the whole concept of Christian liberty noting its principles (14) and its practice (15:1–13). A changed life is not a condition for salvation, but it should be the natural outcome of saving faith. The epistle closes with Paul's statement of his plans (15:14–33), a long series of personal greetings (16:1–16), and an admonition followed by a doxology (16:17–27).

OUTLINE OF ROMANS

Part One: The Revelation of the Righteousness of God (1:1—8:39)

I. Introduction **1:1–17**

II. Condemnation: The Need for God's Righteousness .... **1:18—3:20**

A. Guilt of the Gentile 1:18–32
1. Reason for Gentile Guilt 1:18–23
2. Results of Gentile Guilt 1:24–32

B. Guilt of the Jew .... 2:1—3:8
1. Jews Are Judged According to Truth 2:1–5
2. Jews Are Judged by Their Works 2:6–10
3. Jews Are Judged with Impartiality 2:11–16
4. Jews Do Not Obey the Law 2:17–29
5. Jews Do Not Believe the Oracles 3:1–8

C. Conclusion: All Are Guilty Before God 3:9–20

III. Justification: The Imputation of God's Righteousness .... **3:21—5:21**

A. Description of Righteousness 3:21–31

B. Illustration of Righteousness 4:1–25
1. Abraham's Righteousness Apart from Works 4:1–8
2. Abraham's Righteousness Apart from Circumcision 4:9–12
3. Abraham's Righteousness Apart from the Law 4:13–15
4. Abraham's Righteousness Was by Faith 4:16–25

C. Benefits of Righteousness 5:1–11
1. Peace with God 5:1, 2
2. Joy in Tribulation 5:3–8
3. Salvation from God's Wrath 5:9–11
D. Contrast of Righteousness and Condemnation 5:12–21

IV. Sanctification: The Demonstration of God's Righteousness ....6:1—8:39

A. Sanctification and Sin 6:1–23
1. Believer's Death to Sin in Principle 6:1–14
2. Believer's Death to Sin in Practice 6:15–23
B. Sanctification and the Law 7:1–25
1. Dead to the Law but Alive to God 7:1–6
2. Law Cannot Deliver from Sin 7:7–25
C. Sanctification and the Spirit 8:1–39
1. The Spirit Delivers from the Power of the Flesh 8:1–11
2. The Spirit Gives Sonship 8:12–17
3. The Spirit Assures of Future Glory 8:18–30
4. The Spirit Assures of Final Victory 8:31–39

Part Two: The Vindication of the Righteousness of God (9:1—11:36)

I. Israel's Past: The Election of God 9:1–29

A. Paul's Sorrow 9:1–5
B. God's Sovereignty 9:6–29

II. Israel's Present: The Rejection of God ....9:30—10:21

A. Israel Seeks Righteousness by Works 9:30–33
B. Israel Rejects Christ 10:1–15
C. Israel Rejects the Prophets 10:16–21

III. Israel's Future: The Restoration by God 11:1–36

A. Israel's Rejection Is Not Total 11:1–10
B. Israel's Rejection Is Not Final 11:11–32
1. Purpose of Israel's Rejection 11:11–24
2. Promise of Israel's Restoration 11:25–32
C. Israel's Restoration: The Occasion for Glorifying God 11:33–36

Part Three: The Application of the Righteousness of God (12:1—16:27)

I. Righteousness of God Demonstrated in Christian Duties ....12:1—13:14

A. Responsibilities Toward God 12:1, 2
B. Responsibilities Toward Society 12:3–21
C. Responsibilities Toward Higher Powers 13:1–7
D. Responsibilities Toward Neighbors 13:8–14

II. Righteousness of God Demonstrated in Christian Liberties ....14:1—15:13

A. Principles of Christian Liberty 14:1–23
B. Practices of Christian Liberty 15:1–13

III. Conclusion ....15:14—16:27

A. Paul's Purpose for Writing 15:14–21
B. Paul's Plans for Traveling 15:22–33
C. Paul's Praise and Greetings 16:1–27

CHAPTER 1

Introduction

PAUL, a bondservant of Jesus Christ,
[R]called *to be* an apostle, [R]separated to the
gospel of God 1 Tim. 1:11 • Acts 9:15; 13:2
2 [R]which He promised before through His
prophets in the Holy Scriptures, Acts 26:6
3 concerning His Son Jesus Christ our
Lord, who [T]was [R]born of the seed of David ac-
cording to the flesh, *came* • Gal. 4:4★
4 *and* [R]declared *to be* the Son of God with
power according to the Spirit of holiness, by
the resurrection from the dead. Ps. 2:7; 16:10, 11★
5 Through Him [R]we have received grace
and apostleship for obedience to the faith
among all nations for His name, Eph. 3:8
6 among whom you also are the called of
Jesus Christ;

7 To all who are in Rome, beloved of God,
[R]called *to be* saints: 1 Cor. 1:2, 24

[R]Grace to you and peace from God our Fa-
ther and the Lord Jesus Christ. 1 Cor. 1:3

8 First, [R]I thank my God through Jesus
Christ for you all, that your faith is spoken of
throughout the whole world. 1 Cor. 1:4
9 For [R]God is my witness, [R]whom I serve
with my spirit in the gospel of His Son, that
without ceasing I make mention of you al-
ways in my prayers, Rom. 9:1 • Acts 27:23
10 making request if, by some means, now at
last I may find a way in the will of God to
come to you.
11 For I long to see you, that [R]I may impart to
you some spiritual gift, so that you may be es-
tablished— Rom. 15:29
12 that is, that I may be encouraged together
with you by [R]the mutual faith both of you and
me. Titus 1:4
13 Now I do not want you to be unaware,
brethren, that I often planned to come to you
(but [R]was hindered until now), that I might

have some fruit among you also, just as
among the other Gentiles. [1 Thess. 2:18]
14 I am a debtor both to Greeks and to bar-
barians, both to wise and to unwise.
15 So, as much as is in me, *I am* ready to
preach the gospel to you who are in Rome also.
16 For [R]I am not ashamed of the gospel of
Christ,* for it is the power of God to salvation
for everyone who believes, for the Jew first
and also for the Greek. Ps. 40:9, 10
17 For [R]in it the righteousness of God is re-
vealed from faith to faith; as it is written, *"The
just shall live by faith."** Rom. 3:21

Reason for Gentile Guilt

18 [R]For the wrath of God is revealed from
heaven against all ungodliness and [R]unrigh-
teousness of men, who suppress the truth in
unrighteousness, [Acts 17:30] • 2 Thess. 2:10
19 because [R]what may be known of God is
manifest [T]in them, for [R]God has shown *it* to
them. [Acts 14:17; 17:24] • *among* • [John 1:9]
20 For since the creation of the world [R]His
invisible *attributes* are clearly seen, being un-
derstood by the things that are made, *even*
His eternal power and Godhead, so that they
are without excuse, Ps. 19:1–6
21 because, although they knew God, they
did not glorify *Him* as God, nor were thankful,
but [R]became futile in their thoughts, and their
foolish hearts were darkened. Jer. 2:5
22 [R]Professing to be wise, they became
fools, Jer. 10:14
23 and changed the glory of the incorrupt-
ible [R]God into an image made like corruptible
man—and birds and four-footed animals and
creeping things. Deut. 4:16–18

Results of Gentile Guilt

24 Therefore God also gave them up to
uncleanness, in the lusts of their hearts, to dis-
honor their bodies among themselves,
25 who exchanged [R]the truth of God [R]for the
lie, and worshiped and served the creature
rather than the Creator, who is blessed for-
ever. Amen. 1 Thess. 1:9 • Is. 44:20
26 For this reason God gave them up to
[R]vile passions. For even their [T]women ex-
changed the natural use for what is against
nature. Lev. 18:22 • Lit. *females*
27 Likewise also the [T]men, leaving the natu-
ral use of the [T]woman, burned in their lust
for one another, men with men committing
what is shameful, and receiving in them-
selves the penalty of their error which was
due. Lit. *males* • Lit. *female*
28 And even as they did not like to retain
God in *their* knowledge, God gave them over
to a debased mind, to do those things [R]which
are not fitting; Eph. 5:4
29 being filled with all unrighteousness,
sexual immorality,* wickedness, [T]covetous-
ness, [T]maliciousness; full of envy, murder,
strife, deceit, evil-mindedness; *they are* whis-
perers, *greed* • *malice*
30 backbiters, haters of God, violent, proud,
boasters, inventors of evil things, disobedient
to parents,
31 undiscerning, untrustworthy, unloving,
unforgiving,* unmerciful;
32 who, [R]knowing the righteous judgment
of God, that those who practice such things
[R]are deserving of death, not only do the same
but also [R]approve of those who practice
them. [Rom. 2:2] • [Rom. 6:21] • Hos. 7:3

CHAPTER 2

Jews Are Judged According to Truth

THEREFORE you are [R]inexcusable, O man,
whoever you are who judge, [R]for in what-
ever you judge another you condemn your-
self; for you who judge practice the same
things. [Rom. 1:20] • [Matt. 7:1–5]
2 But we know that the judgment of God is
according to truth against those who practice
such things.
3 And do you think this, O man, you who
judge those practicing such things, and doing
the same, that you will escape the judgment of
God?
4 Or do you despise the riches of His good-
ness, forbearance, and [R]longsuffering, [R]not
knowing that the goodness of God leads you
to repentance? Ex. 34:6 • Is. 30:18
5 But in accordance with your hardness
and your [T]impenitent heart [R]you are [T]treasur-
ing up for yourself wrath in the day of wrath
and revelation of the righteous judgment of
God, *unrepentant* • [Deut. 32:34] • *storing*

Jews Are Judged by Their Works

6 who *"will render to each one according to
his deeds"*:*
7 eternal life to those who by patient con-
tinuance in doing good seek for glory, honor,
and immortality;
8 but to those who are self-seeking and do
not obey the truth, but obey unrighteous-
ness—indignation and wrath,
9 tribulation and anguish, on every soul of
man who does evil, of the Jew [R]first and also
of the [T]Greek; 1 Pet. 4:17 • Gentile
10 [R]but glory, honor, and peace to everyone
who works what is good, to the Jew first and
also to the Greek. [1 Pet. 1:7]

Jews Are Judged with Impartiality

11 For there is no partiality with God.
12 For as many as have sinned without law
will also perish without law, and as many as
have sinned in the law will be judged by the law
13 (for [R]not the hearers of the law *are* just in

1:16 NU omits *of Christ* **1:17** Hab. 2:4 **1:29** NU omits *sexual immorality* **1:31** NU omits *unforgiving* **2:6** Ps. 62:12; Prov. 24:12

the sight of God, but the doers of the law will
be justified; [James 1:22, 25]
14 for when Gentiles, who do not have the
law, by nature do the things in the law, these,
although not having the law, are a law to
themselves,
15 who show the work of the law written in
their hearts, their conscience also bearing
witness, and between themselves *their*
thoughts accusing or else excusing *them*)
16 [R]in the day when God will judge the se-
crets of men [R]by Jesus Christ, according to my
gospel. [Matt. 25:31] • Acts 10:42; 17:31

Jews Do Not Obey the Law

17 Indeed* you are called a Jew, and rest on
the law, and make your boast in God,
18 and [R]know *His* will, and [R]approve the
things that are excellent, being instructed out
of the law, Deut. 4:8 • Phil. 1:10
19 and [R]are confident that you yourself are a
guide to the blind, a light to those who are in
darkness, Matt. 15:14
20 an instructor of the foolish, a teacher of
babes, [R]having the form of knowledge and
truth in the law. [2 Tim. 3:5]
21 You, therefore, who teach another, do you
not teach yourself? You who preach that a
man should not steal, do you steal?
22 You who say, "Do not commit adultery,"
do you commit adultery? You who abhor idols,
[R]do you rob temples? Mal. 3:8
23 You who [R]make your boast in the law,
do you dishonor God through breaking the
law? Rom. 2:17; 9:4
24 For [R]"*the name of God is blasphemed*
among the Gentiles because of you,"* as it is
written. Ezek. 16:27
25 [R]For circumcision is indeed profitable if
you keep the law; but if you are a breaker of
the law, your circumcision has become uncir-
cumcision. [Gal. 5:3]
26 Therefore, [R]if an uncircumcised man
keeps the righteous requirements of the law,
will not his uncircumcision be counted as cir-
cumcision? [Acts 10:34]
27 And will not the physically uncircum-
cised, if he fulfills the law, judge you who,
even with *your* written *code* and circumcision,
are a transgressor of the law?
28 For [R]he is not a Jew who *is one* outwardly,
nor *is* circumcision that which *is* outward in
the flesh; [Gal. 6:15]
29 but *he is* a Jew [R]who *is one* inwardly; and
circumcision *is that* of the heart, [R]in the
Spirit, not in the letter; whose praise *is* not
from men but from God. [1 Pet. 3:4] • Deut. 30:6

CHAPTER 3

Jews Do Not Believe the Oracles

WHAT advantage then has the Jew, or
what *is* the profit of circumcision?
2 Much in every way! Chiefly because to
them were committed the oracles of God.
3 For what if [R]some did not believe? [R]Will
their unbelief make the faithfulness of God
without effect? Heb. 4:2 • [2 Tim. 2:13]
4 Certainly not! Indeed, let God be true but
every man a liar. As it is written:

"That You may be justified in Your words,
And may overcome when You are
*judged."**

5 But if our unrighteousness demonstrates
the righteousness of God, what shall we say?
Is God unjust who inflicts wrath? [R](I speak as
a man.) Gal. 3:15
6 Certainly not! For then [R]how will God
judge the world? [Gen. 18:25]
7 For if the truth of God has increased
through my lie to His glory, why am I also still
judged as a sinner?
8 And *why* not *say,* [R]"Let us do evil that
good may come"?—as we are slanderously re-
ported and as some affirm that we say. Their
condemnation is just. Rom. 5:20

Conclusion: All Are Guilty Before God

9 What then? Are we better *than they*?
Not at all. For we have previously charged
both Jews and Greeks that [R]they are all
under sin. Gal. 3:22
10 As it is written:

"There is none righteous, no, not one;
11 *There is none who understands;*
There is none who seeks after God.
12 *They have all turned aside;*
They have together become unprofitable;
There is none who does good, no, not
*one."**
13 *"Their throat is an open* [T]*tomb;*
With their tongues they have practiced
*deceit";** grave
*"The poison of asps is under their lips";**
14 *"Whose mouth is full of cursing and*
*bitterness."**
15 *"Their feet are swift to shed blood;*
16 *Destruction and misery are in their*
ways;
17 *And the way of peace they have not*
*known."**
18 *"There is no fear of God before their*
*eyes."**

19 Now we know that whatever the law says,
it says to those who are under the law, that
every mouth may be stopped, and all the
world may become guilty before God.
20 Therefore [R]by the deeds of the law no

2:17 NU *But if* **2:24** Is. 52:5; Ezek. 36:22 **3:4** Ps. 51:4 **3:12** Ps. 14:1–3; 53:1–3; Eccl. 7:20 **3:13** Ps. 5:9 • Ps. 140:3 **3:14** Ps. 10:7 **3:17** Is. 59:7, 8 **3:18** Ps. 36:1

flesh will be justified in His sight, for by the law *is* the knowledge of sin. [Gal. 2:16]

Description of Righteousness

21 But now the righteousness of God apart from the law is revealed, being witnessed by the Law and the Prophets,

22 even the righteousness of God, through faith in Jesus Christ, to all and on all* who believe. For [R]there is no difference; [Col. 3:11]

23 for [R]all have sinned and fall short of the glory of God, Gal. 3:22

24 being justified [T]freely [R]by His grace [R]through the redemption that is in Christ Jesus, *without any cost* • [Eph. 2:8] • [Heb. 9:12, 15]

25 whom God set forth [R]*as* a propitiation by His blood, through faith, to demonstrate His righteousness, because in His forbearance God had passed over the sins that were previously committed, Lev. 16:15

26 to demonstrate at the present time His righteousness, that He might be just and the justifier of the one who has faith in Jesus.

27 [R]Where *is* boasting then? It is excluded. By what law? Of works? No, but by the law of faith. [1 Cor. 1:29]

28 Therefore we conclude [R]that a man is [T]justified by faith apart from the deeds of the law. Gal. 2:16 • *declared righteous*

29 Or *is He* the God of the Jews only? *Is He* not also the God of the Gentiles? Yes, of the Gentiles also,

30 since [R]*there is* one God who will justify the circumcised by faith and the uncircumcised through faith. [Gal. 3:8, 20]

31 Do we then make void the law through faith? Certainly not! On the contrary, we establish the law.

CHAPTER 4

Abraham's Righteousness Apart from Works

WHAT then shall we say that [R]Abraham our [R]father has found according to the flesh?* Is. 51:2 • James 2:21

2 For if Abraham was [R]justified by works, he has *something* to boast about, but not before God. Rom. 3:20, 27

3 For what does the Scripture say? *"Abraham believed God, and it was accounted to him for righteousness."**

4 Now to him who works, the wages are not counted as grace but as debt.

5 But to him who does not work but believes on Him who justifies the ungodly, his faith is accounted for righteousness,

6 just as David also describes the blessedness of the man to whom God imputes righteousness apart from works:

7 *"Blessed are those whose lawless deeds*
are forgiven,
And whose sins are covered;

8 *Blessed is the man to whom the* LORD
*shall not impute sin."**

Abraham's Righteousness Apart from Circumcision

9 *Does* this blessedness then *come* upon the circumcised *only,* or upon the uncircumcised also? For we say that faith was accounted to Abraham for righteousness.

10 How then was it accounted? While he was circumcised, or uncircumcised? Not while circumcised, but while uncircumcised.

11 And [R]he received the sign of circumcision, a seal of the righteousness of the faith which *he had while still* uncircumcised, that [R]he might be the father of all those who believe, though they are uncircumcised, that righteousness might be imputed to them also, Gen. 17:10 • Luke 19:9

12 and the father of circumcision to those who not only *are* of the circumcision, but who also walk in the steps of the faith which our father [R]Abraham *had while still* uncircumcised. Rom. 4:18–22

Abraham's Righteousness Apart from the Law

13 For the promise that he would be the [R]heir of the world *was* not to Abraham or to his seed through the law, but through the righteousness of faith. Gen. 17:4–6; 22:17

14 For [R]if those who are of the law *are* heirs, faith is made void and the promise made of no effect, Gal. 3:18

15 because [R]the law brings about wrath; for where there is no law *there is* no transgression. Rom. 3:20

Abraham's Righteousness Was by Faith

16 Therefore *it is* of faith that *it might be* [R]according to grace, [R]so that the promise might be sure to all the seed, not only to those who are of the law, but also to those who are of the faith of Abraham, [R]who is the father of us all [Rom. 3:24] • [Gal. 3:22] • Is. 51:2

17 (as it is written, *"I have made you a father of many nations"**) in the presence of Him whom he believed—God, who gives life to the dead and calls those [R]things which do not exist as though they did; Rom. 9:26

18 who, contrary to hope, in hope believed, so that he became the father of many nations, according to what was spoken, *"So shall your descendants be."**

19 And not being weak in faith, [R]he did not consider his own body, already dead (since he was about a hundred years old), and the deadness of Sarah's womb. Gen. 17:17

20 He did not waver at the promise of God

3:22 NU omits *and on all* **4:1** Or *Abraham our (fore-) father according to the flesh has found?* **4:3** Gen. 15:6 **4:8** Ps. 32:1, 2 **4:17** Gen. 17:5 **4:18** Gen. 15:5

through unbelief, but was strengthened in
faith, giving glory to God,
21 and being fully convinced that what He
had promised He was also able to perform.
22 And therefore "it was accounted to him
for righteousness."*
23 Now [R]it was not written for his sake alone
that it was imputed to him, Rom. 15:4
24 but also for us. It shall be imputed to us
who believe [R]in Him who raised up Jesus our
Lord from the dead, Acts 2:24
25 [R]who was delivered up because of our of-
fenses, and [R]was raised because of our justifi-
cation. Is. 53:4, 5 • [1 Cor. 15:17]

CHAPTER 5

Peace with God

THEREFORE, [R]having been justified by
faith, we have* [R]peace with God through
our Lord Jesus Christ, Is. 32:17 • [Eph. 2:14]
2 through whom also we have access by
faith into this grace in which we stand, and
[R]rejoice in hope of the glory of God. Heb. 3:6

Joy in Tribulation

3 And not only *that,* but [R]we also glory in
tribulations, [R]knowing that tribulation pro-
duces perseverance; Matt. 5:11, 12 • James 1:3
4 [R]and perseverance, [T]character; and char-
acter, hope. [James 1:12] • *approved character*
5 [R]Now hope does not disappoint, [R]because
the love of God has been poured out in our
hearts by the Holy Spirit who was given to
us. Phil. 1:20 • 2 Cor. 1:22
6 For when we were still without strength,
in due time Christ died for the ungodly.
7 For scarcely for a righteous man will one
die; yet perhaps for a good man someone
would even dare to die.
8 But [R]God demonstrates His own love to-
ward us, in that while we were still sinners,
Christ died for us. [John 3:16; 15:13]★

Salvation from God's Wrath

9 Much more then, having now been justi-
fied [R]by His blood, we shall be saved [R]from
wrath through Him. Eph. 2:13 • 1 Thess. 1:10
10 For [R]if when we were enemies we were
reconciled to God through the death of His
Son, much more, having been reconciled, we
shall be saved by His life. [Rom. 8:32]
11 And not only *that,* but we also [R]rejoice in
God through our Lord Jesus Christ, through
whom we have now received the reconcilia-
tion. [Gal. 4:9]

Contrast of Righteousness and Condemnation

12 Therefore, just as [R]through one man sin
entered the world, and [R]death through sin,
and thus death spread to all men, because all
sinned— [1 Cor. 15:21] • Gen. 2:17
13 (For until the law sin was in the world, but
[R]sin is not imputed when there is no law. 1 John 3:4
14 Nevertheless death reigned from Adam to
Moses, even over those who had not sinned
according to the likeness of the transgression
of Adam, [R]who is a type of Him who was to
come. [1 Cor. 15:21, 22]
15 But the free gift *is* not like the offense. For
if by the one man's offense many died, much
more the grace of God and the gift by the
grace of the one Man, Jesus Christ, abounded
[R]to many. [Is. 53:11]
16 And the gift *is* not like *that which came*
through the one who sinned. For the judg-
ment *which came* from one *offense resulted*
in condemnation, but the free gift *which*
came from many [T]offenses *resulted* in justifi-
cation. *trespasses*
17 For if by the one man's [T]offense death
reigned through the one, much more those
who receive abundance of grace and of the
gift of righteousness will reign in life through
the One, Jesus Christ.) *trespass*
18 Therefore, as through one man's offense
judgment came to all men, resulting in
condemnation, even so [R]through one Man's
righteous act *the free gift came* to all men, re-
sulting in justification of life. Is. 53:11, 12★
19 For as by one man's disobedience many
were made sinners, so also by one Man's obe-
dience many will be made righteous.
20 Moreover the law entered that the offense
might abound. But where sin abounded, grace
abounded much more,
21 so that as sin reigned in death, even so
grace might reign through righteousness to
eternal life through Jesus Christ our Lord.

CHAPTER 6

Believer's Death to Sin in Principle

WHAT shall we say then? Shall we con-
tinue in sin that grace may abound?
2 Certainly not! How shall we who [R]died to
sin live any longer in it? [Gal. 2:19]
3 Or do you not know that [R]as many of us
as were baptized into Christ Jesus were bap-
tized into His death? [Gal. 3:27]
4 Therefore we were [R]buried with Him
through baptism into death, that [R]just as
Christ was raised from the dead by the glory
of the Father, even so we also should walk in
newness of life. Col. 2:12 • 1 Cor. 6:14
5 For if we have been united together in the
likeness of His death, certainly we also shall
be *in the likeness* of *His* resurrection,
6 knowing this, that [R]our old man was cru-
cified with *Him,* that the body of sin might be
done away with, that we should no longer be
slaves of sin. Gal. 2:20; 5:24; 6:14

4:22 Gen. 15:6 **5:1** Another ancient reading *let us have peace*

7 For [R]he who has died has been [T]freed
from sin. 1 Pet. 4:1 • *cleared*
8 Now [R]if we died with Christ, we believe
that we shall also live with Him, 2 Tim. 2:11
9 knowing that [R]Christ, having been raised
from the dead, dies no more. Death no longer
has dominion over Him. Rev. 1:18
10 For *the death* that He died, [R]He died to sin
once for all; but *the life* that He lives, [R]He lives
to God. Heb. 9:27 • Luke 20:38
11 Likewise you also, [T]reckon yourselves to
be dead indeed to sin, but [R]alive to God in
Christ Jesus our Lord. *consider* • [Gal. 2:19]
12 [R]Therefore do not let sin reign in your
mortal body, that you should obey it in its
lusts. Ps. 19:13
13 And do not present your members *as* in-
struments of unrighteousness to sin, but pre-
sent yourselves to God as being alive from the
dead, and your members *as* instruments of
righteousness to God.
14 For [R]sin shall not have dominion over
you, for you are not under law but under
grace. [Gal. 5:18]

Believer's Death to Sin in Practice

15 What then? Shall we sin [R]because we are
not under law but under grace? Certainly
not! 1 Cor. 9:21
16 Do you not know that [R]to whom you pre-
sent yourselves slaves to obey, you are that
one's slaves whom you obey, whether of sin
leading to death, or of obedience *leading* to
righteousness? 2 Pet. 2:19
17 But God be thanked that *though* you were
slaves of sin, yet you obeyed from the heart
[R]that form of doctrine to which you were [T]de-
livered. 2 Tim. 1:13 • *entrusted*
18 And [R]having been set free from sin, you
became slaves of righteousness. John 8:32
19 I speak in human *terms* because of the
weakness of your flesh. For just as you pre-
sented your members *as* slaves of unclean-
ness, and of lawlessness *leading* to *more*
lawlessness, so now present your members *as*
slaves *of* righteousness for holiness.
20 For when you were slaves of sin, you were
free in regard to righteousness.
21 [R]What fruit did you have then in the
things of which you are now ashamed? For
the end of those things *is* death. Rom. 7:5
22 But now [R]having been set free from sin,
and having become slaves of God, you have
your fruit [T]to holiness, and the end, everlast-
ing life. Rom. 6:18; 8:2 • *unto sanctification*
23 For [R]the wages of sin *is* death, but [R]the
[T]gift of God *is* eternal life in Christ Jesus our
Lord. Gen. 2:17 • 1 Pet. 1:4 • *free gift*

CHAPTER 7

Dead to the Law but Alive to God

OR do you not know, brethren (for I speak
to those who know the law), that the law
[T]has dominion over a man as long as he
lives? *rules*
2 For the woman who has a husband is
bound by the law to *her* husband as long as he
lives. But if the husband dies, she is released
from the law of *her* husband.
3 So then if, while *her* husband lives, she
marries another man, she will be called an
adulteress; but if her husband dies, she is free
from that law, so that she is no adulteress,
though she has married another man.
4 Therefore, my brethren, you also have be-
come dead to the law through the body of
Christ, that you may be married to another—
to Him who was raised from the dead, that we
should bear fruit to God.
5 For when we were in the flesh, the sinful
passions which were aroused by the law
[R]were at work in our members [R]to bear fruit to
death. Rom. 6:13 • James 1:15
6 But now we have been delivered from the
law, having died to what we were held by, so that
we should serve [R]in the newness of the Spirit
and not *in* the oldness of the letter. Rom. 2:29

Law Cannot Deliver from Sin

7 What shall we say then? *Is* the law sin?
Certainly not! On the contrary, I would not
have known sin except through the law. For I
would not have known covetousness unless
the law had said, *"You shall not covet."**
8 But [R]sin, taking opportunity by the com-
mandment, produced in me all *manner of*
evil desire. For [R]apart from the law sin *was*
dead. Rom. 4:15 • 1 Cor. 15:56
9 I was alive once without the law, but

7:7 Ex. 20:17; Deut. 5:21

6:23 New Life: A Free Gift—You can work for sin but it is a cruel master. When it pays you off, its wage is death—separation from God forever. In stark contrast, God does not pay wages. He has a free gift to offer—eternal life. There is nothing that one can do to earn this gift. If one could earn it, it would not be a gift; it would be wages. Eternal life is just that—eternal—it never ceases. The basic concept underlying life is *union*. There are three kinds of life mentioned in the Bible: (1) physical life—union of the soul with the body; (2) spiritual life—union of the soul with God; and (3) eternal life—eternal union of the soul with God. Jesus said, "My sheep hear My voice . . . . And I give them eternal life; and they shall never perish" (Page 1095—John 10:27, 28). The gift of God is eternal life. We receive this gift when we believe in Jesus as our own personal Savior. Having eternal life, we will never perish.

Now turn to Page 1220—Col. 1:22: New Life: Based on Christ's Death.

when the commandment came, sin revived
and I died.
10 And the commandment, [R]which *was* to
bring life, I found to *bring* death. Lev. 18:5
11 For sin, taking occasion by the command-
ment, deceived me, and by it killed *me.*
12 Therefore the law *is* holy, and the com-
mandment holy and just and good.
13 Has then what is good become death to
me? Certainly not! But sin, that it might ap-
pear sin, was producing death in me through
what is good, so that sin through the com-
mandment might become exceedingly sinful.
14 For we know that the law is spiritual, but
I am carnal, sold under sin.
15 For what I am doing, I do not understand.
For what I will to do, that I do not practice; but
what I hate, that I do.
16 If, then, I do what I will not to do, I agree
with the law that *it is* good.
17 But now, *it is* no longer I who do it, but sin
that dwells in me.
18 For I know that [R]in me (that is, in my
flesh) nothing good dwells; for to will is pres-
ent with me, but *how* to perform what is good
I do not find. [Gen. 6:5; 8:21]
19 For the good that I will *to do,* I do not do;
but the evil I will not *to do,* that I practice.
20 Now if I do what I will not *to do,* it is no
longer I who do it, but sin that dwells in me.
21 I find then a law, that evil is present with
me, the one who wills to do good.
22 For I [R]delight in the law of God according
to [R]the inward man. Ps. 1:2 • [2 Cor. 4:16]
23 But [R]I see another law in my members,
warring against the law of my mind, and
bringing me into captivity to the law of sin
which is in my members. [Gal. 5:17]
24 O wretched man that I am! Who will de-
liver me from this body of death?
25 [R]I thank God—through Jesus Christ our
Lord! So then, with the mind I myself serve
the law of God, but with the flesh the law of
sin. 1 Cor. 15:57

CHAPTER 8

The Spirit Delivers from the Power of the Flesh

THERE is therefore now no condemnation
to those who are in Christ Jesus,* [R]who do
not walk according to the flesh, but according
to the Spirit. Gal. 5:16
2 For [R]the law of [R]the Spirit of life in Christ
Jesus has made me free from the law of sin
and death. Rom. 6:18, 22 • [1 Cor. 15:45]
3 For [R]what the law could not do in that it
was weak through the flesh, [R]God *did* by send-
ing His own Son in the likeness of sinful flesh,
on account of sin: He condemned sin in the
flesh, Acts 13:39 • [2 Cor. 5:21]
4 that the righteous requirement of the law
might be fulfilled in us who [R]do not walk ac-
cording to the flesh but according to the
Spirit. Gal. 5:16, 25
5 For [R]those who live according to the flesh
set their minds on the things of the flesh, but
those *who live* according to the Spirit, the
things of the Spirit. John 3:6
6 For to be carnally minded *is* death, but to
be spiritually minded *is* life and peace.
7 Because [R]the carnal mind *is* enmity
against God; for it is not subject to the law of
God, nor indeed can be. James 4:4
8 So then, those who are in the flesh cannot
please God.
9 But you are not in the flesh but in the
Spirit, if indeed the Spirit of God dwells in
you. Now if anyone does not have the Spirit of
Christ, he is not His.
10 And if Christ *is* in you, the body *is* dead
because of sin, but the Spirit *is* life because of
righteousness.
11 But if the Spirit of [R]Him who raised Jesus
from the dead dwells in you, [R]He who raised
Christ from the dead will also give life to your
mortal bodies through His Spirit who dwells
in you. Acts 2:24 • 1 Cor. 6:14

The Spirit Gives Sonship

12 [R]Therefore, brethren, we are debtors—
not to the flesh, to live according to the
flesh. [Rom. 6:7, 14]
13 For if you live according to the flesh you
will die; but if by the Spirit you put to death
the deeds of the body, you will live.
14 For [R]as many as are led by the Spirit of
God, these are sons of God. [Gal. 5:18]
15 For [R]you did not receive the spirit of
bondage again [R]to fear, but you received the
[R]Spirit of adoption by whom we cry out,
"Abba, Father." Heb. 2:15 • 2 Tim. 1:7 • [Is. 56:5]
16 The Spirit Himself bears witness with our
spirit that we are children of God,

8:1 NU omits the rest of v. 1.

8:15 God the Father of Believers—God is the Father of all who believe in Christ in a special sense not shared by unbelievers. God is called their Father, first of all, because they have a new standing before Him. While unbelievers are the offspring of God because He created them (Page 1133—Acts 17:28, 29), they do not have the standing of sons. Their standing is rather as condemned sinners before God the Judge (Page 1083—John 3:18; Page 1326—Rev. 20:11). When we believe in Christ as Savior, our estate is wonderfully changed from grim condemnation to privileged sonship. This new standing grants to all believers the legal right and spiritual privileges of divine sonship: "heirs of God and joint heirs with Christ" (Page 1155—Rom. 8:17).

17 and if children, then [R]heirs—heirs of God
and joint heirs with Christ, [R]if indeed we suf-
fer with *Him*, that we may also be glorified to-
gether. Acts 26:18 • Phil. 1:29

The Spirit Assures of Future Glory

18 For I consider that [R]the sufferings of
this present time are not worthy *to be com-
pared* with the glory which shall be revealed
in us. 2 Cor. 4:17
19 For [R]the earnest expectation of the cre-
ation eagerly waits for the revealing of the
sons of God. [2 Pet. 3:13]
20 For [R]the creation was subjected to futility,
not willingly, but because of Him who sub-
jected *it* in hope; Gen. 3:17–19
21 because the creation itself also will be
delivered from the bondage of [T]corruption
into the glorious [R]liberty of the children of
God. *decay* • [2 Cor. 3:17]
22 For we know that the whole creation
[R]groans and labors with birth pangs together
until now. Jer. 12:4, 11
23 Not only *that*, but we also who have the
firstfruits of the Spirit, even we ourselves
groan within ourselves, eagerly waiting for
the adoption, the redemption of our body.
24 For we were saved in this hope, but [R]hope
that is seen is not hope; for why does one still
hope for what he sees? Heb. 11:1
25 But if we hope for what we do not see, we
eagerly wait for *it* with perseverance.
26 Likewise the Spirit also helps in our
weaknesses. For we do not know what we
should pray for as we ought, but the Spirit
Himself makes intercession for us* with
groanings which cannot be uttered.
27 Now [R]He who searches the hearts knows
what the mind of the Spirit *is*, because He
makes intercession for the saints [R]according
to *the will of* God. 1 Chr. 28:9 • 1 John 5:14
28 And we know that all things work to-
gether for good to those who love God, to
those [R]who are the called according to *His*
purpose. 2 Tim. 1:9
29 For whom [R]He foreknew, He also predes-
tined *to be* conformed to the image of His
Son, [R]that He might be the firstborn among
many brethren. 2 Tim. 2:19 • Heb. 1:6
30 Moreover whom He predestined, these
He also [R]called; whom He called, these He
also [R]justified; and whom He justified, these
He also glorified. [1 Pet. 2:9; 3:9] • [Gal. 2:16]

The Spirit Assures of Final Victory

31 What then shall we say to these things? If
God *is* for us, who *can be* against us?
32 He who did not spare His own Son, but
delivered Him up for us all, how shall He not
with Him also freely give us all things?
33 Who shall bring a charge against God's
elect? [R]*It is* God who justifies. Is. 50:8, 9
34 [R]Who *is* he who condemns? *It is* Christ
who died, and furthermore is also risen, who
is even at the right hand of God, who also
makes intercession for us. John 3:18
35 Who shall separate us from the love of
Christ? *Shall* tribulation, or distress, or perse-
cution, or famine, or nakedness, or peril, or
sword?
36 As it is written:

> *"For Your sake we are killed all day long;*
> *We are accounted as sheep for the*
> *slaughter."**

37 Yet in all these things we are more than
conquerors through Him who loved us.
38 For I am persuaded that neither death nor
life, nor angels nor [R]principalities nor powers,
nor things present nor things to come, [Eph. 1:21]
39 nor height nor depth, nor any other cre-
ated thing, shall be able to separate us from
the love of God which is in Christ Jesus our
Lord.

CHAPTER 9

Paul's Sorrow

I [R]TELL the truth in Christ, I am not lying,
my conscience also bearing me witness in
the Holy Spirit, 2 Cor. 1:23
2 [R]that I have great sorrow and continual
grief in my heart. Rom. 10:1
3 For I could wish that I myself were ac-
cursed from Christ for my brethren, my coun-
trymen* according to the flesh,
4 who are Israelites, [R]to whom *pertain* the
adoption, [R]the glory, the covenants, [R]the giving

8:26 NU omits *for us* **8:36** Ps. 44:22 **9:3** Or *relatives*

God is the Father of believers also in the sense that He gives them new life (Page 1083—John 3:3). This relationship then is a family one involving many of the same realities that exist between an earthly father and child: birth of the child (Page 1083—John 3:3); partaking of the father's nature (Page 1287— 2 Pet. 1:4); the father's care for the child (Matt. 6:32, 33; 7:9–11); and the father's discipline of the child (Page 1267—Heb. 12:6–8). Furthermore, this new Father-child relationship carries with it new brothers and sisters (Page 1268—Heb. 13:1).

To obtain God as Father is not a result of one's own merit but a result of Christ's. The one who believes in Christ as Savior enters into the blessed Father-child relationship with God solely on the grounds of Christ's sonship (Page 1155—Rom. 8:17; Page 1259—Heb. 2:17). It is the grand privilege and calling of those who know God as Father to graciously invite unbelievers to meet God as Father and not as Judge.

Now turn to Page 691—Is. 9:6: The Person of the Son of God.

of the law, the service *of God*, and the prom-
ises; Ex. 4:22 • 1 Sam. 4:21 • Ps. 147:19
5 [R]of whom *are* the fathers and from
[R]whom, according to the flesh, Christ *came*,
[R]who is over all, *the* eternally blessed God.
Amen. Deut. 10:15 • [Luke 1:34, 35; 3:23] • Jer. 23:6

God's Sovereignty

6 [R]But it is not that the word of God has
taken no effect. For [R]they *are* not all Israel
who *are* of Israel, Num. 23:19 • [Gal. 6:16]
7 [R]nor *are they* all children because they
are the seed of Abraham; but, *"In Isaac your*
*seed shall be called."** [Gal. 4:23]
8 That is, those who *are* the children of the
flesh, these *are* not the children of God; but
[R]the children of the promise are counted as
the seed. Gal. 4:28
9 For this *is* the word of promise: *"At this*
*time I will come and Sarah shall have a son."**
10 And not only *this*, but when [R]Rebecca
also had conceived by one man, *even* by our
father Isaac Gen. 25:21
11 (for *the children* not yet being born, nor
having done any good or evil, that the purpose
of God according to election might stand, not
of works but of Him who calls),
12 it was said to her, *"The older shall serve*
*the younger."**
13 As it is written, *"Jacob I have loved, but*
*Esau I have hated."**
14 What shall we say then? *Is there* unrigh-
teousness with God? Certainly not!
15 For He says to Moses, *"I will have mercy*
on whomever I will have mercy, and I will
have compassion on whomever I will have
*compassion."**
16 So then *it is* not of him who wills, nor of
him who runs, but of God who shows mercy.
17 For the Scripture says to the Pharaoh,
"For this very purpose I have raised you up,
that I may show My power in you, and that
*My name may be declared in all the earth."**
18 Therefore He has mercy on whom He
wills, and whom He wills He hardens.
19 You will say to me then, "Why does He
still find fault? For [R]who has resisted His
will?" 2 Chr. 20:6
20 But indeed, O man, who are you to reply
against God? [R]Will the thing formed say to
him who formed *it*, "Why have you made me
like this?" Is. 29:16
21 Does not the potter have power over the
clay, from the same lump to make one vessel
for honor and another for dishonor?
22 *What* if God, wanting to show *His* wrath
and to make His power known, endured with
much longsuffering [R]the vessels of wrath pre-
pared for destruction, [1 Thess. 5:9]
23 and that He might make known [R]the
riches of His glory on the vessels of mercy,
which He had [R]prepared beforehand for
glory, [Col. 1:27] • [Rom. 8:28–30]
24 *even* us whom He called, not of the Jews
only, but also of the Gentiles?
25 As He says also in Hosea:

"I will call them My people, who were not
My people,
*And her beloved, who was not beloved."**
26*"And it shall come to pass in the place*
where it was said to them,
'You are not My people,'
There they shall be called sons of the
*living God."**

27 Isaiah also cries out concerning Israel:*

"Though the number of the children of
Israel be as the sand of the sea,
[R]*The remnant will be saved.* Rom. 11:5
28 *For He will finish the work and cut it*
short in righteousness,
[R]*Because the* LORD *will make a short*
*work upon the earth."** Is. 10:23; 28:22

29 And as Isaiah said before:

"Unless the LORD *of Sabaoth* had left us*
a seed,
[R]*We would have become like Sodom,*
And we would have been made like
*Gomorrah."** Is. 13:19

Israel Seeks Righteousness by Works

30 What shall we say then? [R]That Gentiles,
who did not pursue righteousness, have at-
tained to righteousness, [R]even the righteous-
ness of faith; Rom. 4:11 • Rom. 1:17; 3:21; 10:6
31 but Israel, [R]pursuing the law of righ-
teousness, [R]has not attained to the law of
righteousness.* [Rom. 10:2–4] • [Gal. 5:4]
32 Why? Because *they did* not *seek it* by faith,
but as it were, by the works of the law.* For [R]they
stumbled at that stumbling stone. [1 Cor. 1:23]
33 As it is written:

"Behold, I lay in Zion a stumbling stone
and rock of offense,
And [R]*whoever believes on Him will not*
*be put to shame."** Rom. 5:5; 10:11

CHAPTER 10

Israel Rejects Christ

BRETHREN, my heart's desire and prayer
to God for Israel* is that they may be
saved.

9:7 Gen. 21:12 **9:9** Gen. 18:10, 14 **9:12** Gen. 25:23 **9:13** Mal. 1:2, 3 **9:15** Ex. 33:19 **9:17** Ex. 9:16 **9:25** Hos. 2:23 **9:26** Hos. 1:10 **9:27** Is. 10:22, 23 **9:28** NU For the LORD will finish the work and cut it short upon the earth. **9:29** Lit., in Heb., *Hosts* • Is. 1:9 **9:31** NU omits *of righteousness* **9:32** NU *by works*, omitting *of the law* **9:33** Is. 8:14; 28:16★ **10:1** NU *them*

2 For I bear them witness [R]that they have a
zeal for God, but not according to knowl-
edge. Acts 21:20
3 For they being ignorant of [R]God's righ-
teousness, and seeking to establish their own
righteousness, have not submitted to the
righteousness of God. [Rom. 1:17]
4 For Christ *is* the end of the law for righ-
teousness to everyone who believes.
5 For Moses writes about the righteousness
which is of the law, *"The man who does those*
*things shall live by them."**
6 But the righteousness of faith speaks in
this way, *"Do not say in your heart, 'Who will*
*ascend into heaven?' "** (that is, to bring
Christ down *from above*)
7 or, *" 'Who will descend into the abyss?' "**
(that is, to bring Christ up from the dead).
8 But what does it say? *"The word is near*
*you, in your mouth and in your heart"** (that
is, the word of faith which we preach):
9 that [R]if you confess with your mouth the
Lord Jesus and believe in your heart that God
has raised Him from the dead, you will be
saved. Luke 12:8
10 For with the heart one believes unto righ-
teousness, and with the mouth confession is
made unto salvation.
11 For the Scripture says, *"Whoever believes*
*on Him will not be put to shame."**
12 For [R]there is no distinction between Jew
and Greek, for the same Lord over all is rich
to all who call upon Him. Rom. 3:22, 29
13 For *"whoever calls [R]on the name of the*
*LORD shall be saved."** Acts 9:14
14 How then shall they call on Him in whom
they have not believed? And how shall they
believe in Him of whom they have not heard?
And how shall they hear [R]without a
preacher? Titus 1:3
15 And how shall they preach unless they
are sent? As it is written:

"How beautiful are the feet of those who
*preach the gospel of peace,**
*Who bring glad tidings of good things!"**

Israel Rejects the Prophets

16 But they have not all obeyed the gospel.
For Isaiah says, *"LORD, who has believed our*
*report?"**
17 So then faith *comes* by hearing, and hear-
ing by the word of God.
18 But I say, have they not heard? Yes in-
deed:

"Their sound has gone out to all the
earth,
And their words to the ends of the
*world."**

19 But I say, did Israel not know? First Moses
says:

"I will provoke you to jealousy by those
who are not a nation,
I will move you to anger by a [R]foolish
*nation."** Titus 3:3

20 But Isaiah is very bold and says:

"I was found by those who did not seek Me;
I was made manifest to those who did
*not ask for Me."**

21 But to Israel he says:

"All day long I have stretched out My
hands
*To a disobedient and contrary people."**

CHAPTER 11

Israel's Rejection Is Not Total

I SAY then, [R]has God cast away His people?
[R]Certainly not! For I also am an Israelite, of
the seed of Abraham, *of* the tribe of Benja-
min. Jer. 46:28 • 1 Sam. 12:22
2 God has not cast away His people whom
[R]He foreknew. Or do you not know what the
Scripture says of Elijah, how he pleads with
God against Israel, saying, [Rom. 8:29]
3 *"LORD, they have killed Your prophets*
and torn down Your altars, and I alone am
*left, and they seek my life"?**
4 But what does the divine response say to
him? *"I have reserved for Myself seven thou-*
sand men who have not bowed the knee to
*Baal."**
5 [R]Even so then, at this present time there
is a remnant according to the election of
grace. Rom. 9:27
6 And [R]if by grace, then *it is* no longer of
works; otherwise grace is no longer grace.*
But if *it is* of works, it is no longer grace; oth-
erwise work is no longer work. Rom. 4:4
7 What then? [R]Israel has not obtained what
it seeks; but the elect have obtained it, and the
rest were blinded. Rom. 9:31
8 Just as it is written:

"God has given them a spirit of stupor,
Eyes that they should not see
And ears that they should not hear,
*To this very day."**

9 And David says:

"Let their table become a snare and a
trap,

10:5 Lev. 18:5 **10:6** Deut. 30:12 **10:7** Deut. 30:13 **10:8** Deut. 30:14 **10:11** Is. 28:16 **10:13** Joel 2:32 **10:15** NU omits *preach the gospel of peace, Who* • Is. 52:7; Nah. 1:15 **10:16** Is. 53:1★ **10:18** Ps. 19:4 **10:19** Deut. 32:21 **10:20** Is. 65:1 **10:21** Is. 65:2 **11:3** 1 Kin. 19:10, 14 **11:4** 1 Kin. 19:18 **11:6** NU omits the rest of v. 6. **11:8** Deut. 29:4; Is. 29:10

A stumbling block and a recompense to
them.
10 *Let their eyes be darkened, so that they*
do not see,
*And bow down their back always."**

Purpose of Israel's Rejection

11 I say then, have they stumbled that they
should fall? Certainly not! But [R]through their
fall, to provoke them to jealousy, salvation *has*
come to the Gentiles. Is. 42:6, 7
12 Now if their fall *is* riches for the world,
and their failure [R]riches for the Gentiles, how
much more their fullness! Hos. 1:10; 2:23★
13 For I speak to you Gentiles; inasmuch as
[R]I am an apostle to the Gentiles, I magnify my
ministry, Acts 9:15; 22:21
14 if by any means I may provoke to jealousy
those who are my flesh and [R]save some of
them. 1 Cor. 9:22
15 For if their being cast away *is* the recon-
ciling of the world, what *will* their acceptance
be but life from the dead?
16 For if [R]the firstfruit *is* holy, the lump *is*
also *holy;* and if the root *is* holy, so *are* the
branches. Lev. 23:10
17 And if [R]some of the branches were bro-
ken off, [R]and you, being a wild olive tree, were
grafted in among them, and with them be-
came a partaker of the root and [T]fatness of the
olive tree, Jer. 11:16 • [Eph. 2:12] • *richness*
18 do not boast against the branches. But if
you do boast, *remember that* you do not sup-
port the root, but the root supports you.
19 You will say then, "Branches were broken
off that I might be grafted in."
20 Well *said.* Because of [R]unbelief they were
broken off, and you stand by faith. Do not be
haughty, but fear. Heb. 3:19
21 For if God did not spare the natural
branches, He may not spare you either.
22 Therefore consider the goodness and
severity of God: on those who fell, severity;
but toward you, goodness,* [R]if you continue in
His goodness. Otherwise [R]you also will be cut
off. 1 Cor. 15:2 • [John 15:2]
23 And they also, [R]if they do not continue in
unbelief, will be grafted in, for God is able to
graft them in again. [2 Cor. 3:16]
24 For if you were cut out of the olive tree
which is wild by nature, and were grafted con-
trary to nature into a cultivated olive tree,
how much more will these, who *are* natural
branches, be grafted into their own olive tree?

Promise of Israel's Restoration

25 For I do not desire, brethren, that you
should be ignorant of this mystery, lest you
should be [R]wise in your own [T]opinion, that
[R]blindness in part has happened to Israel
[R]until the fullness of the Gentiles has come
in. Rom. 12:16 • *estimation* • 2 Cor. 3:14 • Luke 21:24
26 And so all Israel will be saved,* as it is
written:
"The Deliverer will come out of Zion,
And He will turn away ungodliness from
Jacob;
27 *For* [R]*this is My covenant with them,*
*When I take away their sins."** Is. 27:9
28 Concerning the gospel *they are* enemies
for your sake, but concerning the election
they are beloved for the sake of the fathers.
29 For the gifts and the calling of God *are*
[R]irrevocable. Num. 23:19
30 For as you [R]were once disobedient to God,
yet have now obtained mercy through their
disobedience, [Eph. 2:2]
31 even so these also have now been disobe-
dient, that through the mercy shown you they
also may obtain mercy.
32 For God has [T]committed them [R]all to
disobedience, that He might have mercy on
all. *shut them all up in* • [Gal. 3:22]

Israel's Restoration: The Occasion for Glorifying God

33 Oh, the depth of the riches both of the
wisdom and knowledge of God! How un-
searchable *are* His judgments and His ways
past finding out!
34 *"For who has known the mind of the*
LORD?
*Or who has become His counselor?"**
35 *"Or who has first given to Him*
*And it shall be repaid to him?"**
36 For [R]of Him and through Him and to Him
are all things, [R]to whom *be* glory forever.
Amen. Heb. 2:10 • Heb. 13:21

CHAPTER 12

Responsibilities Toward God

I [R]BESEECH[T] you therefore, brethren, by
the mercies of God, that you present
your bodies [R]a living sacrifice, holy, accept-
able to God, *which is* your [T]reasonable
service. 2 Cor. 10:1–4 • *urge* • Heb. 10:18, 20 • *rational*

11:10 Ps. 69:22, 23★ **11:22** NU adds *of God* **11:26** Or *delivered* **11:27** Is. 59:20, 21 **11:34** Is. 40:13; Jer. 23:18 **11:35** Job 41:11

12:1 Walking in the Spirit: Yielding—Confession of sin in itself is not enough to enable the believer to automatically walk in the Spirit. One must then become a yielded instrument for God's service. What is to be yielded is simply one's own self (Rom. 6:13; James 4:7). This involves both the body (Page 1158—Rom. 12:1; Page 1171—1 Cor. 6:20) and the mind (Page 1159—Rom. 12:2), since it is with the body that actions

2 And do not be conformed to this world,
but be transformed by the renewing of your
mind, that you may prove what *is* that good
and acceptable and perfect will of God.

Responsibilities Toward Society

3 For I say, through the grace given to me,
to everyone who is among you, not to think *of
himself* more highly than he ought to think,
but to think soberly, as God has dealt to each
one a measure of faith.
4 For [R]as we have many members in one
body, but all the members do not have the
same function, 1 Cor. 12:12–14
5 so [R]we, *being* many, are one body in
Christ, and individually members of one another. [1 Cor. 10:17]
6 Having then gifts differing according to
the grace that is [R]given to us, *let us use them:*
if prophecy, *let us* [R]*prophesy* in proportion to
our faith; [John 3:27] • Acts 11:27
7 or ministry, *let us use it* in *our* ministering; [R]he who teaches, in teaching; Eph. 4:11
8 [R]he who exhorts, in exhortation; [R]he who
gives, with liberality; [R]he who leads, with diligence; he who shows mercy, with cheerfulness. Acts 15:32 • [Matt. 6:1–3] • [Acts 20:28]
9 *Let* love *be* without hypocrisy. [R]Abhor
what is evil. Cling to what is good. Ps. 34:14
10 [R]*Be* kindly affectionate to one another
with brotherly love, [R]in honor giving preference to one another; Heb. 13:1 • Phil. 2:3
11 not lagging in diligence, fervent in spirit,
serving the Lord;
12 rejoicing in hope, patient in tribulation,
continuing steadfastly in prayer;
13 [R]distributing to the needs of the saints,
[R]given to hospitality. 1 Cor. 16:1 • 1 Tim. 3:2
14 [R]Bless those who persecute you; bless and
do not curse. [Matt. 5:44]
15 [R]Rejoice with those who rejoice, and
weep with those who weep. [1 Cor. 12:26]
16 Be of the same mind toward one another.
[R]Do not set your mind on high things, but associate with the humble. Do not be wise in
your own opinion. Jer. 45:5
17 Repay no one evil for evil. Have regard
for good things in the sight of all men.
18 If it is possible, as much as depends on
you, live peaceably with all men.
19 Beloved, [R]do not avenge yourselves, but
rather give place to wrath; for it is written,
*"Vengeance is Mine, I will repay,"** says the
Lord. Lev. 19:18
20 Therefore

"If your enemy is hungry, feed him;
If he is thirsty, give him a drink;
For in so doing you will heap coals of
*fire on his head."**

21 Do not be overcome by evil, but [R]overcome evil with good. [Rom. 12:1, 2]

CHAPTER 13

Responsibilities Toward Higher Powers

LET every soul be [R]subject to the governing
authorities. For there is no authority except from God, and the authorities that exist
are appointed by God. 1 Pet. 2:13
2 Therefore whoever resists the authority
resists the ordinance of God, and those who
resist will bring judgment on themselves.
3 For rulers are not a terror to good works,
but to evil. Do you want to be unafraid of the
authority? Do what is good, and you will have
praise from the same.
4 For he is God's minister to you for good.
But if you do evil, be afraid; for he does not
bear the sword in vain; for he is God's minister, an avenger to *execute* wrath on him who
practices evil.

12:19 Deut. 32:35 **12:20** Prov. 25:21, 22

---

conceived in the mind are carried out and with the mind that they are formulated. Stated another way, that which is conceived in the mind is carried out in the body; thus, one's whole being must be presented by a decisive act of the will to God for His service. Yielding must not be thought of simply as a willingness to do some specific thing. Rather, it consists of dedication by a person to do whatever God commands.

Yielding leads not only to dedication but also can result in separation: "do not be conformed to this world" (Page 1159—Rom. 12:2). Since the world is resolutely opposed to God, one cannot revel in its lusts and at the same time do the will of God (Page 1294—1 John 2:15–17). The concept of separation involves being "unfashionable" in spirit, thought, values, and actions according to the world's standards.

Finally, yielding includes transformation of the mind. This work is said to be accomplished through a lifetime of "renewing" the mind. The human mind has been darkened by sin (Page 1154—Rom. 8:7; Page 1220—Col. 1:21) and must be brought to the place where it thinks as God thinks (Page 1207—Eph. 4:23). This renewing is said to come especially through prayer to God in everything (Page 1215—Phil. 4:6, 7) and through constant meditation on the Word of God (Page 1610—Ps. 119:1). This transformation is a lifelong process that will not be completed until we are with Christ (Page 1213—Phil. 1:6; Page 1295—1 John 3:2). Along life's way, however, it brings a peace and delight that can only come from having embraced the mind of Christ.

Now turn to Page 1208—Eph. 5:18: Walking in the Spirit: Filling.

13:1–4 The Function of Human Government—The general function of human government, as instituted by God, may be said to be threefold: to protect, punish, and promote.

a. The Function of Protection: The moment Adam sinned it was obvious that civilizations would need some form of restraint and rule to protect citizens from themselves. An example of this function is seen in Acts

(continued on next page)

5 Therefore [R]*you* must be subject, not only because of wrath [R]but also for conscience' sake. Eccl. 8:2 • [1 Pet. 2:13, 19]

6 For because of this you also pay taxes, for they are God's ministers attending continually to this very thing.

7 [R]Render therefore to all their due: taxes to whom taxes *are due*, customs to whom customs, fear to whom fear, honor to whom honor. Matt. 22:21

Responsibilities Toward Neighbors

8 Owe no one anything except to love one another, for [R]he who loves another has fulfilled the law. [Gal. 5:13, 14]

9 For the commandments, *"You shall not commit adultery," "You shall not murder," "You shall not steal," "You shall not bear false witness,"** *"You shall not covet,"** and if *there is* any other commandment, are *all* summed up in this saying, namely, *"You shall love your neighbor as yourself."**

10 Love does no harm to a neighbor; therefore love *is* the fulfillment of the law.

11 And *do* this, knowing the time, that now *it is* high time [R]to awake out of sleep; for now our salvation *is* nearer than when we *first* believed. [1 Cor. 15:34]

12 The night is far spent, the day is at hand. [R]Therefore let us cast off the works of darkness, and [R]let us put on the armor of light. Eph. 5:11 • [Eph. 6:11, 13]

13 Let us walk properly, as in the day, not in revelry and drunkenness, not in lewdness and lust, not in strife and envy.

14 But [R]put on the Lord Jesus Christ, and [R]make no provision for the flesh, to *fulfill its* lusts. Gal. 3:27 • [Gal. 5:16]

CHAPTER 14

Principles of Christian Liberty

RECEIVE[R] one who is weak in the faith, *but* not to disputes over doubtful things. [1 Cor. 8:9; 9:22]

2 For one believes he may eat all things, but he who is weak eats *only* vegetables.

3 Let not him who eats despise him who does not eat, and [R]let not him who does not eat judge him who eats; for God has received him. [Col. 2:16]

4 [R]Who are you to judge another's servant? To his own master he stands or falls. Indeed, he will be made to stand, for God is able to make him stand. James 4:11, 12

5 One person esteems *one* day above another; another esteems every day *alike*. Let each be fully convinced in his own mind.

6 He who observes the day, observes *it* to the Lord;* and he who does not observe the day, to the Lord he does not observe *it*. He who eats, eats to the Lord, for he gives God thanks; and he who does not eat, to the Lord he does not eat, and gives God thanks.

7 For [R]none of us lives to himself, and no one dies to himself. [Gal. 2:20]

8 For if we live, we live to the Lord; and if we die, we die to the Lord. Therefore, whether we live or die, we are the Lord's.

9 For [R]to this end Christ died and rose* and lived again, that He might be Lord of both the dead and the living. 2 Cor. 5:15

10 But why do you judge your brother? Or why do you show contempt for your brother? For [R]we shall all stand before the judgment seat of Christ.* 2 Cor. 5:10

11 For it is written:

"As I live, says the LORD,
Every knee shall bow to Me,
*And every tongue shall confess to God."**

12 So then [R]each of us shall give account of himself to God. 1 Pet. 4:5

13 Therefore let us not judge one another [T]anymore, but rather resolve this, [R]not to put a stumbling block or a cause to fall in *our* brother's way. *any longer* • 1 Cor. 8:9

14 I know and am convinced by the Lord Jesus [R]that *there is* nothing unclean of itself; but to him who considers anything to be unclean, to him *it is* unclean. 1 Cor. 10:25

15 Yet if your brother is grieved because of *your* food, you are no longer walking in love. [R]Do not destroy with your food the one for whom Christ died. 1 Cor. 8:11

16 [R]Therefore do not let your good be spoken of as evil; [Rom. 12:17]

13:9 NU omits *"You shall not bear false witness."* • Ex. 20:13–15, 17; Deut. 5:17–19, 21 • Lev. 19:18
14:6 NU omits the rest of this sentence. **14:9** NU omits *and rose* **14:10** NU *of God* **14:11** Is. 45:23

(continued from previous page)

21:27–37 where Roman soldiers step in and save Paul from being murdered by his own enraged countrymen in Jerusalem.

b. The Function of Punishment: Both Paul and Peter bring this out. Paul writes that duly appointed human officials are to be regarded as God's servants to "bear the sword," that is, to impose punishment upon criminals (vv. 3, 4). Peter tells us that governors are "sent by him for the punishment of evildoers" (Page 1280—1 Pet. 2:13, 14).

c. The Function of Promotion: Human government is to promote the general welfare of the community where its laws are in effect. Paul commands us to pray for human leaders "that we may lead a quiet and peaceable life in all godliness and reverence" (Page 1237—1 Tim. 2:1, 2).

Now turn to Page 1280—1 Pet. 2:13: Our Responsibility to Human Government.

17 [R]for the kingdom of God is not eating and drinking, but righteousness and peace and joy in the Holy Spirit. 1 Cor. 8:8

18 For he who serves Christ in these things* [R]*is* acceptable to God and approved by men. 2 Cor. 8:21

19 [R]Therefore let us pursue the things *which make* for peace and the things by which one may edify another. Rom. 12:18

20 [R]Do not destroy the work of God for the sake of food. [R]All things indeed *are* pure, [R]but *it is* evil for the man who eats with offense. Rom. 14:15 • Acts 10:15 • 1 Cor. 8:9–12

21 *It is* good neither to eat meat nor drink wine nor *do anything* by which your brother stumbles or is offended or is made weak.*

22 Do you have faith?* Have *it* to yourself before God. Happy *is* he who does not condemn himself in what he approves.

23 But he who doubts is condemned if he eats, because *he does* not *eat* from faith; for whatever *is* not from faith is sin.*

CHAPTER 15

Practices of Christian Liberty

WE [R]then who are strong ought to bear with the [T]scruples of the weak, and not to please ourselves. [Gal. 6:1, 2] • *weaknesses*

2 [R]Let each of us please *his* neighbor for *his* good, leading to edification. 1 Cor. 9:22

3 For even Christ did not please Himself; but as it is written, *"The reproaches of those who reproached You fell on Me."**

4 For [R]whatever things were written before were written for our learning, that we through the patience and comfort of the Scriptures might have hope. 1 Cor. 10:11

5 Now may the God of patience and comfort grant you to be like-minded toward one another, according to Christ Jesus,

6 that you may [R]with one mind *and* one mouth glorify the God and Father of our Lord Jesus Christ. Acts 4:24

7 Therefore receive one another, just as Christ also received us,* to the glory of God.

8 Now I say that [R]Jesus Christ has become a [T]servant to the circumcision for the truth of God, [R]to confirm the promises *made* to the fathers, Matt. 15:24 • *minister* • 2 Cor. 1:20

9 and [R]that the Gentiles might glorify God for *His* mercy, as it is written: John 10:16

"For this reason I will confess to You
among the Gentiles,
*And sing to Your name."**

10 And again he says:

*"Rejoice, O Gentiles, with His people!"**

11 And again:

"Praise the LORD, all you Gentiles!
*Laud Him, all you peoples!"**

12 And again, Isaiah says:

"There shall be a root of Jesse;
And He who shall rise to reign over the
Gentiles,
*In Him the Gentiles shall hope."**

13 Now may the God of hope fill you with all [R]joy and peace in believing, that you may abound in hope by the power of the Holy Spirit. Rom. 12:12; 14:17

Paul's Purpose for Writing

14 Now [R]I myself am confident concerning you, my brethren, that you also are full of goodness, filled with all knowledge, able also to admonish one another.* 2 Pet. 1:12

15 Nevertheless, brethren, I have written more boldly to you on *some* points, as reminding you, [R]because of the grace given to me by God, Rom. 1:5; 12:3

16 that [R]I might be a minister of Jesus Christ to the Gentiles, ministering the gospel of God, that the [R]offering [T]of the Gentiles might be acceptable, sanctified by the Holy Spirit. Rom. 11:13 • [Is. 66:20] • Consisting of

17 Therefore I have reason to glory in Christ Jesus [R]in the things *which pertain* to God. Heb. 2:17; 5:1

18 For I will not dare to speak of any of those things which Christ has not accomplished through me, in word and deed, [R]to make the Gentiles obedient— Rom. 1:5

19 in mighty signs and wonders, by the power of the Spirit of God, so that from Jerusalem and round about to Illyricum I have fully preached the gospel of Christ.

20 And so I have made it my aim to preach the gospel, not where Christ was named, [R]lest I should build on another man's foundation, [2 Cor. 10:13, 15, 16]

21 but as it is written:

"To whom He was not announced, they
shall see;
And those who have not heard shall
*understand."**

Paul's Plan for Traveling

22 For this reason [R]I also have been much hindered from coming to you. Rom. 1:13

23 But now no longer having a place in these parts, and [R]having a great desire these many years to come to you, Acts 19:21; 23:11

14:18 NU *this* **14:21** NU omits *or is offended or is made weak* **14:22** NU *The faith which you have—have* **14:23** M puts Rom. 16:25–27 here. **15:3** Ps. 69:9★ **15:7** NU, M *you* **15:9** 2 Sam. 22:50; Ps. 18:49 **15:10** Deut. 32:43 **15:11** Ps. 117:1 **15:12** Is. 11:10★ **15:14** M *others* **15:21** Is. 52:15

24 whenever I journey to Spain, I shall
come to you.* For I hope to see you on my
journey, [R]and to be helped on my way there
by you, if first I may [R]enjoy your *company*
for a while. Acts 15:3 • Rom. 1:12
25 But now [R]I am going to Jerusalem to
[T]minister to the saints. Acts 19:21 • *serve*
26 For [R]it pleased those from Macedonia
and Achaia to make a certain contribution
for the poor among the saints who are in Je-
rusalem. 1 Cor. 16:1
27 It pleased them indeed, and they are
their debtors. For [R]if the Gentiles have been
partakers of their spiritual things, [R]their
duty is also to minister to them in material
things. Rom. 11:17 • 1 Cor. 9:11
28 Therefore, when I have performed this
and have sealed to them [R]this fruit, I shall go
by way of you to Spain. Phil. 4:17
29 [R]But I know that when I come to you, I
shall come in the fullness of the blessing of
the gospel* of Christ. [Rom. 1:11]
30 Now I beg you, brethren, through the
Lord Jesus Christ, and [R]through the love of
the Spirit, [R]that you strive together with me in
prayers to God for me, Phil. 2:1 • 2 Cor. 1:11
31 [R]that I may be delivered from those in
Judea who [T]do not believe, and that [R]my ser-
vice for Jerusalem may be acceptable to the
saints, 2 Tim. 3:11; 4:17 • *are disobedient* • 2 Cor. 8:4
32 [R]that I may come to you with joy [R]by the
will of God, and may [R]be refreshed together
with you. Rom. 1:10 • Acts 18:21 • 1 Cor. 16:18
33 Now [R]the God of peace *be* with you all.
Amen. 1 Cor. 14:33

CHAPTER 16

Paul's Praise and Greetings

I COMMEND to you Phoebe our sister, who
is a servant of the church in Cenchrea,
2 [R]that you may receive her in the Lord [R]in
a manner worthy of the saints, and assist her
in whatever business she has need of you; for
indeed she has been a helper of many and of
myself also. Phil. 2:29 • Phil. 1:27
3 Greet [R]Priscilla and Aquila, my fellow
workers in Christ Jesus, Acts 18:2, 18, 26
4 who risked their own necks for my life, to
whom not only I give thanks, but also all the
churches of the Gentiles.
5 Likewise *greet* the church that is in their
house. Greet my beloved Epaenetus, who is
the firstfruits of Achaia* to Christ.
6 Greet Mary, who labored much for us.
7 Greet Andronicus and Junia, my country-
men and my fellow prisoners, who are of note
among the [R]apostles, who also were in Christ
before me. Acts 1:13, 26
8 Greet Amplias, my beloved in the Lord.
9 Greet Urbanus, our fellow worker in
Christ, and Stachys, my beloved.
10 Greet Apelles, approved in Christ. Greet
those who are of the *household* of Aristobulus.
11 Greet Herodion, my countryman.* Greet
those who are of the *household* of Narcissus
who are in the Lord.
12 Greet Tryphena and Tryphosa, who have
labored in the Lord. Greet the beloved Persis,
who labored much in the Lord.
13 Greet Rufus, [R]chosen in the Lord, and his
mother and mine. 2 John 1
14 Greet Asyncritus, Phlegon, Hermas, Pat-
robas, Hermes, and the brethren who are with
them.
15 Greet Philologus and Julia, Nereus and
his sister, and Olympas, and all the saints who
are with them.
16 Greet one another with a holy kiss. The*
churches of Christ greet you.
17 Now I urge you, brethren, note those
[R]who cause divisions and offenses, contrary
to the doctrine which you learned, and [R]avoid
them. [Acts 15:1] • [1 Cor. 5:9]
18 For those who are such do not serve our
Lord Jesus* Christ, but their own belly, and
[R]by smooth words and flattering speech de-
ceive the hearts of the simple. Col. 2:4
19 For [R]your obedience has become known
to all. Therefore I am glad on your behalf; but
I want you to be wise in what is good, and
simple concerning evil. Rom. 1:8
20 And the God of peace will crush Satan
under your feet shortly. The grace of our Lord
Jesus Christ *be* with you. Amen.
21 [R]Timothy, my fellow worker, and [R]Lucius,
[R]Jason, and Sosipater, my countrymen, greet
you. Acts 16:1 • Acts 13:1 • Acts 17:5
22 I, Tertius, who wrote *this* epistle, greet
you in the Lord.
23 [R]Gaius, my host and *the host* of the
whole church, greets you. [R]Erastus, the trea-
surer of the city, greets you, and Quartus, a
brother. 1 Cor. 1:14 • Acts 19:22

15:24 NU omits *I shall come to you* and joins *Spain* with the next sentence. **15:29** NU omits *of the gospel* **16:5** NU *Asia* **16:11** Or *relative* **16:16** NU *All the churches* **16:18** NU, M omit *Jesus*

16:5 Definition of the Local Church—The local church is a geographically located, temporally limited, and visibly evident manifestation of the universal church, the body of Christ. In the early NT days the local church met in the Jewish synagogue and had a very simple organization (Page 1273—James 2:2). A little later the church met in the homes of believers (Rom. 16:5), and it was not uncommon to have a number of churches in an area (Page 1196—Gal. 1:2). The idea of meeting in a building constructed for that exclusive purpose is a post-NT idea. (For a more complete discussion of the church, read Acts 7:38 and THE CHRISTIAN'S GUIDE: The Meaning of the Church.)

Now turn to Page 1265—Heb. 10:25: The Reason for Participation in the Local Church.

24 [R]The grace of our Lord Jesus Christ *be*
with you all. Amen.* 1 Thess. 5:28
25 Now [R]to Him who is able to establish you
[R]according to my gospel and the preaching of
Jesus Christ, [R]according to the revelation of
the mystery kept secret since the world
began [Eph. 3:20] • Rom. 2:16 • Eph. 1:9
26 but now made manifest, and by the
prophetic Scriptures made known to all nations, according to the commandment of the
everlasting God, for obedience to the faith—
27 to [R]God, alone wise, *be* glory through Jesus Christ forever. Amen.* Jude 25

16:24 NU omits v. 24. **16:27** M puts Rom. 16:25–27 after Rom. 14:23.

Jewish Feasts

Feast of	*Month on Jewish Calendar*	*Day*	*Corresponding Month*	*References*
*Passover (Unleavened Bread)	Nisan	14–21	Mar.–Apr.	Ex. 12:43—13:10; Matt. 26:17–20
*Pentecost (Firstfruits or Weeks)	Sivan	6 (50 days after Passover)	May–June	Deut. 16:9–12; Acts 2:1
Trumpets, *Rosh Hashanah*	Tishri	1, 2	Sept.–Oct.	Num. 29:1–6
Day of Atonement, *Yom Kippur*	Tishri	10	Sept.–Oct.	Lev. 23:26–32; Heb. 9:7
*Tabernacles (Booths or Ingathering)	Tishri	15–22	Sept.–Oct.	Neh. 8:13–18; John 7:2
Dedication (Lights), *Hanukkah*	Chislev	25 (8 days)	Nov.–Dec.	John 10:22
Purim (Lots)	Adar	14, 15	Feb.–Mar.	Esth. 9:18–32

*The three major feasts for which all males of Israel were required to travel to the Temple in Jerusalem (Ex. 23:14–19).

THE FIRST EPISTLE OF PAUL THE APOSTLE TO THE

CORINTHIANS

THE BOOK OF 1 CORINTHIANS

Corinth, the most important city in Greece during Paul's day, was a bustling hub of worldwide commerce, degraded culture, and idolatrous religion. There Paul founded a church (Acts 18:1–17), and two of his letters are addressed "to the church of God which is at Corinth."

First Corinthians reveals the problems, pressures, and struggles of a church called out of a pagan society. Paul addresses a variety of problems in the lifestyle of the Corinthian church: factions, lawsuits, immorality, questionable practices, abuse of the Lord's Supper, and spiritual gifts. In addition to words of discipline, Paul shares words of counsel in answer to questions raised by the Corinthian believers.

The oldest recorded title of this epistle is *Pros Korinthious A,* in effect, the "First to the Corinthians." The *A* was no doubt a later addition to distinguish this book from 2 Corinthians.

THE AUTHOR OF 1 CORINTHIANS

Pauline authorship of 1 Corinthians is almost universally accepted. Instances of this widely held belief can be found as early as A.D. 95, when Clement of Rome wrote to the Corinthian church and cited this epistle in regard to their continuing problem of factions among themselves.

THE TIME OF 1 CORINTHIANS

Corinth was a key city in ancient Greece until it was destroyed by the Romans in 146 B.C. Julius Caesar rebuilt it as a Roman colony in 46 B.C.; and it grew and prospered, becoming the capital of the province of Achaia. Its official language was Latin, but the common language remained Greek. In Paul's day Corinth was the metropolis of the Peloponnesus, since it was strategically located on a narrow isthmus between the Aegean Sea and the Adriatic Sea that connects the Peloponnesus with northern Greece. Because of its two seaports it became a commercial center, and many small ships were rolled or dragged across the Corinthian isthmus to avoid the dangerous 200-mile voyage around southern Greece. Nero and others attempted to build a canal at the narrowest point, but this was not achieved until 1893. The city was filled with shrines and temples, but the most prominent was the Temple of Aphrodite on top of a 1,800-foot promontory called the Acrocorinthus. Worshipers of the "goddess of love" made free use of the 1,000 Hieroduli (consecrated prostitutes). This cosmopolitan center thrived on commerce, entertainment, vice, and corruption; pleasure-seekers came there to spend money on a holiday from morality. Corinth became so notorious for its evils that the term *Korinthiazomai* ("to act like a Corinthian") became a synonym for debauchery and prostitution.

In Paul's day the population of Corinth was approximately 700,000, about two-thirds of whom were slaves. The diverse population produced no philosophers, but Greek philosophy influenced any speculative thought that was there. In spite of these obstacles to the gospel, Paul was able to establish a church in Corinth on his second missionary journey (3:6, 10; 4:15; Acts 18:1–7). Persecution in Macedonia drove him south to Athens, and from there he proceeded to Corinth. He made tents with Aquila and Priscilla and reasoned with the Jews in the synagogue. Silas and Timothy joined him (they evidently brought a gift from Philippi; 2 Cor. 11:8, 9; Phil. 4:15), and Paul began to devote all his time to spreading the gospel. Paul wrote 1 and 2 Thessalonians, moved his ministry from the synagogue to the house of Titius Justus because of opposition, and converted Crispus, the leader of the synagogue. Paul taught the Word of God in Corinth for eighteen months in A.D. 51 and 52. After Paul's departure, Apollos came from Ephesus to minister in the Corinthian church (3:6; Acts 18:24–28).

When Paul was teaching and preaching in Ephesus during his third missionary journey, he was disturbed by reports from the household of Chloe concerning quarrels in the church at Corinth (1:11). The church sent a delegation of three men (16:17), who apparently brought a letter that requested Paul's judgment of certain issues (7:1). Paul wrote this epistle as his response to the problems and questions of the Corinthians (he had already written a previous letter; 5:9). It may be that the men who came from Corinth took this letter back with them. Paul was planning to leave Ephesus (16:5–8), indicating that 1 Corinthians was written in A.D. 56.

THE CHRIST OF 1 CORINTHIANS

This book proclaims the relevance of Christ Jesus to every area of the believer's life. He "became for us wisdom from God—and righteousness and sanctification and redemption—" (1:30), and these are the themes Paul addresses in this epistle.

KEYS TO 1 CORINTHIANS

Key Word: Correction of Carnal Living—The basic theme of this epistle is the application of Christian principles to carnality in the individual as well as in the church. The cross of Christ is a message that is designed to transform the lives of believers and make them different as people and as a corporate body from the surrounding world. However, the Corinthians are destroying their Christian testimony because of immorality and disunity. Paul writes this letter as his corrective response to the news of problems and disorders among the Corinthians. It is designed to refute improper attitudes and conduct and to promote a spirit of unity among the brethren in their relationships and worship. Paul's concern as their spiritual father (4:14, 15) is tempered with love, and he wants to avoid visiting them "with a rod" (4:21).

Key Verses: 1 Corinthians 6:19, 20 and 10:12, 13—"Or do you not know that your body is the temple of the Holy Spirit *who is* in you, whom you have from God, and you are not your own? For you were bought at a price; therefore glorify God in your body and in your spirit, which are God's" (6:19, 20).

"Therefore let him who thinks he stands take heed lest he fall. No temptation has overtaken you except such as is common to man; but God *is* faithful, who will not allow you to be tempted beyond what you are able, but with the temptation will also make the way of escape, that you may be able to bear *it*" (10:12, 13).

Key Chapter: 1 Corinthians 13—Read at weddings and often the text for sermons, 1 Corinthians 13 has won the hearts of people across the world as the best definition of "love" ever penned. Standing in stark contrast to the idea that love is an emotion, that one can fall into or fall out of love, this chapter clearly reveals that true love is primarily an action. This is why when "God so loved the world that He gave" (John 3:16).

SURVEY OF 1 CORINTHIANS

Through the missionary efforts of Paul and others, the church has been established in Corinth, but Paul finds it very difficult to keep Corinth out of the church. The pagan lifestyle of Corinth exerts a profound influence upon the Christians in that corrupt city—problems of every kind plague them. In this disciplinary letter, Paul is forced to exercise his apostolic authority as he deals firmly with problems of divisiveness, immorality, lawsuits, selfishness, abuses of the Lord's Supper and spiritual gifts, and denials of the Resurrection. This epistle is quite orderly in its approach as it sequentially addresses a group of problems that have come to Paul's attention. Paul also gives a series of perspectives on various questions and issues raised by the Corinthians in a letter. He uses the introductory words "Now concerning," or "Moreover," "Now" to delineate those topics (7:1, 25; 8:1; 11:2; 12:1; 15:1; 16:1). The three divisions of 1 Corinthians are: answer to Chloe's report of divisions (1—4); answer to report of fornication (5 and 6); and answer to letter of questions (7—16).

Answer to Chloe's Report of Divisions (1—4): Personality cults centering on Paul, Apollos, and Peter have led to divisions and false pride among the Corinthians (1). It is not their wisdom or cleverness that has brought them to Christ, because divine wisdom is contrary to human wisdom. The truth of the gospel is spiritually apprehended (2). Factions that exist among the saints at Corinth are indications of their spiritual immaturity (3). They should pride themselves in Christ, not in human leaders who are merely His servants (4).

FOCUS	ANSWER TO CHLOE'S REPORT OF DIVISIONS		ANSWER TO REPORT OF FORNICATION			ANSWER TO LETTER OF QUESTIONS				
REFERENCE	1:1——1:18——5:1——6:1——6:12——7:1——8:1——11:2——15:1——16:1——16:24									
DIVISION	REPORT OF DIVISIONS	REASON FOR DIVISIONS	INCEST	LITIGATION	IMMORALITY	MARRIAGE	OFFERINGS TO IDOLS	PUBLIC WORSHIP	RESURRECTION	COLLECTION FOR JERUSALEM
TOPIC	DIVISIONS IN THE CHURCH		DISORDER IN THE CHURCH			DIFFICULTIES IN THE CHURCH				
	CONCERN		CONDEMNATION			COUNSEL				
LOCATION	WRITTEN IN EPHESUS									
TIME	C. A.D. 56									

Answer to Report of Fornication (5 and 6): The next problem Paul addresses is that of incest between a member of the church and his stepmother (5). The Corinthians have exercised no church discipline in this matter, and Paul orders them to remove the offender from their fellowship until he repents. Another source of poor testimony is the legal action of believer against believer in civil courts (6:1–8). They must learn to arbitrate their differences within the Christian community. Paul concludes this section with a warning against immorality in general (6:9–20).

Answer to Letter of Questions (7—16): In these chapters the apostle Paul gives authoritative answers to thorny questions raised by the Corinthians. His first counsel concerns the issues of marriage, celibacy, divorce, and remarriage (7). The next three chapters are related to the problem of meat offered to idols (8:1—11:1). Paul illustrates from his own life the twin principles of Christian liberty and the law of love, and he concludes that believers must sometimes limit their liberty for the sake of weaker brothers (cf. Rom. 14). The apostle then turns to matters concerning public worship, including improper observance of the Lord's Supper and the selfish use of spiritual gifts (11:2—14:40). Gifts are to be exercised in love for the edification of the whole body. The Corinthians also have problems with the Resurrection, which Paul seeks to correct (15). His historical and theological defense of the Resurrection includes teaching on the nature of the resurrected body. The Corinthians probably have been struggling over this issue because the idea of a resurrected body is disdainful in Greek thought. The epistle closes with Paul's instruction for the collection he will make for the saints in Jerusalem (16:1–4), followed by miscellaneous exhortations and greetings (16:5–24).

OUTLINE OF 1 CORINTHIANS

Part One: In Answer to Chloe's Report of Divisions (1:1—4:21)

I. Introduction 1:1–9

A. Greetings of Grace 1:1–3
B. Prayer of Thanksgiving 1:4–9

II. Report of Divisions 1:10–17

III. Reasons for Divisions ......1:18—4:21

A. Misunderstanding of the Gospel Message ......1:18—3:4
1. The Gospel Is Not Earthly Wisdom ......1:18—2:5
2. The Gospel Is Heavenly Wisdom ...2:6—3:4
B. Misunderstanding of the Gospel Messenger ......3:5—4:5
1. Ministers Are Fellow Workers with God 3:5–17
2. Ministers Are Accountable to God ......3:18—4:5
C. Misunderstanding of Paul's Ministry 4:6–21

Part Two: In Answer to Reports of Fornication (5:1—6:20)

I. On Incest 5:1–13

A. Deliver the Fornicators for Discipline.....5:1–8
B. Separate Yourselves from Immoral Believers 5:9–13

II. Concerning Litigation Between Believers 6:1–11

III. Warning Against Sexual Immorality 6:12–20

Part Three: In Answer to the Letter of Questions (7:1—16:24)

I. Counsel Concerning Marriage 7:1–40

A. Principles for Married Life 7:1–9
B. Principles for the Married Believer.....7:10–16
C. Principle of Abiding in God's Call 7:17–24
D. Principles for the Unmarried 7:25–38
E. Principles for Remarriage 7:39, 40

II. Counsel Concerning Things Offered to Idols ......8:1—11:1

A. Principles of Liberty and the Weaker Brother 8:1–13
B. Illustration of Paul and His Liberty......9:1–27
1. Paul Lists His Rights as a Minister..9:1–14
2. Paul Limits His Rights for Ministry 9:15–27
C. Warning Against Forfeiting Liberty 10:1–13
D. Exhortation to Use Liberty to Glorify God ......10:14—11:1

III. Counsel Concerning Public Worship ......11:2—14:40

A. Principles of Public Prayer 11:2–16
B. Rebuke of Disorders at the Lord's Supper 11:17–34
C. Principles of Exercising Spiritual Gifts ......12:1—14:40
1. Test of the Spirit's Control 12:1–3
2. Diversity of the Gifts 12:4–11
3. Importance of All Gifts 12:12–31
4. Exercise Gifts with Love 13:1–13

CHAPTER 1

Greetings of Grace

PAUL, [R]called *to be* an apostle of Jesus
Christ [R]through the will of God, and Sos-
thenes *our* brother, Rom. 1:1 • 2 Cor. 1:1

2 To the church of God which is at Corinth,
to those who [R]are sanctified in Christ Jesus,
called *to be* saints, with all who in every place
call on the name of Jesus Christ our Lord,
both theirs and ours: [Acts 15:9]

3 [R]Grace to you and peace from God our Fa-
ther and the Lord Jesus Christ. Rom. 1:7

Prayer of Thanksgiving

4 [R]I thank my God always concerning you
for the grace of God which was given to you
by Christ Jesus, Rom. 1:8
5 that you were enriched in everything by
Him in all utterance and all knowledge,
6 even as [R]the testimony of Christ was con-
firmed [T]in you, 2 Tim. 1:8 • Or *among*
7 so that you come short in no gift, eagerly
[R]waiting for the revelation of our Lord Jesus
Christ, Phil. 3:20
8 [R]who will also confirm you to the end,
that you may be blameless in the day of our
Lord Jesus Christ. 1 Thess. 3:13; 5:23
9 [R]God *is* faithful, by whom you were called
into [R]the fellowship of His Son, Jesus Christ
our Lord. Is. 49:7 • [John 15:4]

Report of Divisions

10 Now I plead with you, brethren, by the
name of our Lord Jesus Christ, [R]that you all
speak the same thing, and *that* there be no di-
visions among you, but *that* you be perfectly
joined together in the same mind and in the
same judgment. 2 Cor. 13:11
11 For it has been declared to me concern-
ing you, my brethren, by those of Chloe's
household, that there are [T]contentions among
you. *quarrels*
12 Now I say this, that [R]each of you says, "I
am of Paul," or "I am of Apollos," or "I am of
Cephas," or "I am of Christ." 1 Cor. 3:4
13 [R]Is Christ divided? Was Paul crucified for
you? Or were you baptized in the name of
Paul? 2 Cor. 11:4
14 I thank God that I baptized [R]none of you
except Crispus and Gaius, John 4:2
15 lest anyone should say that I had baptized
in my own name.
16 Yes, I also baptized the household of
[R]Stephanas. Besides, I do not know whether I
baptized any other. 1 Cor. 16:15, 17
17 For Christ did not send me to baptize, but
to preach the gospel, [R]not with wisdom of
words, lest the cross of Christ should be made
of no effect. [1 Cor. 2:1, 4, 13]

The Gospel Is Not Earthly Wisdom

18 For the message of the cross is foolish-
ness to those who are perishing, but to us who
are being saved it is the power of God.
19 For it is written:

"I will destroy the wisdom of the wise,
And bring to nothing the understanding
*of the prudent."**

20 Where *is* the wise? Where *is* the scribe?
Where *is* the disputer of this age? Has not God
made foolish the wisdom of this world?
21 For since, in the wisdom of God, the world
through wisdom did not know God, it pleased
God through the foolishness of the message
preached to save those who believe.
22 For [R]Jews request a sign, and Greeks seek
after wisdom; Matt. 12:38
23 but we preach Christ crucified, [R]to the
Jews a stumbling block and to the Greeks*
[R]foolishness, Luke 2:34 • [1 Cor. 2:14]
24 but to those who are called, both Jews
and Greeks, Christ [R]the power of God and
[R]the wisdom of God. [Rom. 1:4] • Col. 2:3
25 Because the foolishness of God is wiser
than men, and the weakness of God is
stronger than men.
26 For [T]you see your calling, brethren,
[R]that not many wise according to the flesh,
not many mighty, not many [T]noble, *are*
called. *consider* • John 7:48 • *well-born*
27 But [R]God has chosen the foolish things
of the world to put to shame the wise, and

1:19 Is. 29:14 **1:23** NU *Gentiles*

God has chosen the weak things of the
world to put to shame the things which are
mighty; Matt. 11:25
28 and the base things of the world and the
things which are despised God has chosen,
and the things which are not, to bring to noth-
ing the things that are,
29 that no flesh should glory in His presence.
30 But of Him you are in Christ Jesus, who
became for us wisdom from God—and [R]righ-
teousness and sanctification and redemp-
tion— [2 Cor. 5:21]
31 that, as it is written, *"He who glories, let
him glory in the LORD."**

CHAPTER 2

AND I, brethren, when I came to you, did
not come with excellence of speech or of
wisdom declaring to you the testimony* of
God.
2 For I determined not to know anything
among you [R]except Jesus Christ and Him cru-
cified. Gal. 6:14
3 [R]I was with you [R]in weakness, in fear, and
in much trembling. Acts 18:1 • [2 Cor. 4:7]
4 And my speech and my preaching [R]*were*
not with persuasive words of human* wis-
dom, [R]but in demonstration of the Spirit and
of power, 2 Pet. 1:16 • Rom. 15:19
5 that your faith should not be in the wis-
dom of men but in the power of God.

The Gospel Is Heavenly Wisdom

6 However, we speak wisdom among those
who are mature, yet not the wisdom of this
age, nor of the rulers of this age, who are com-
ing to nothing.
7 But we speak the wisdom of God in a
mystery, the hidden *wisdom* which God or-
dained before the ages for our glory,
8 which none of the rulers of this age knew;
for [R]had they known, they would not have
crucified the Lord of glory. Luke 23:34
9 But as it is written:

"Eye has not seen, nor ear heard,
Nor have entered into the heart of man
The things which God has prepared for
*those who love Him."**

10 But God has revealed *them* to us through
His Spirit. For the Spirit searches all things,
yes, the deep things of God.
11 For what man knows the things of a man
except the [R]spirit of the man which is in him?
Even so no one knows the things of God ex-
cept the Spirit of God. [James 2:26]
12 Now we have received, not the spirit of
the world, but [R]the Spirit who is from God,
that we might know the things that have been
freely given to us by God. [Rom. 8:15]
13 These things we also speak, not in words
which man's wisdom teaches but which the
Holy* Spirit teaches, comparing spiritual
things with spiritual.
14 But the natural man does not receive the
things of the Spirit of God, for they are fool-
ishness to him; nor can he know *them,* be-
cause they are spiritually discerned.
15 But he who is spiritual judges all things,
yet he himself is *rightly* judged by no one.
16 For *"who has known the mind of the LORD
that he may instruct Him?"** [R]But we have the
mind of Christ. [John 15:15]

CHAPTER 3

AND I, brethren, could not speak to you as
to spiritual *people* but as to carnal, as to
[R]babes in Christ. Heb. 5:13
2 I fed you with milk and not with solid
food; for until now you were not able *to re-
ceive it,* and even now you are still not able;
3 for you are still carnal. For where *there
are* envy, strife, and divisions among you, are
you not carnal and [T]behaving like *mere*
men? Lit. *walking according to man*
4 For when one says, "I am of Paul," and an-
other, "I *am* of Apollos," are you not carnal?

Ministers Are Fellow Workers with God

5 Who then is Paul, and who *is* Apollos, but
[R]ministers through whom you believed, as the
Lord gave to each one? 2 Cor. 3:3, 6
6 [R]I planted, [R]Apollos watered, but God
gave the increase. Acts 18:4 • Acts 18:24–27
7 So then [R]neither he who plants is any-
thing, nor he who waters, but God who gives
the increase. [Gal. 6:3]
8 Now he who plants and he who waters
are one, and each one will receive his own re-
ward according to his own labor.
9 For we are God's fellow workers; you are
God's field, *you are* God's building.
10 [R]According to the grace of God which
was given to me, as a wise master builder I
have laid [R]the foundation, and another builds
on it. But let each one take heed how he builds
on it. Rom. 1:5 • 1 Cor. 4:15
11 For no other foundation can anyone lay
than [R]that which is laid, [R]which is Jesus
Christ. Is. 28:16 • Eph. 2:20
12 Now if anyone builds on this foundation
with gold, silver, precious stones, wood, hay,
straw,
13 each one's work will become clear; for
the Day [R]will declare it, because it will be re-
vealed by fire; and the fire will test each one's
work, of what sort it is. 1 Pet. 1:7
14 If anyone's work which he has built on *it*
endures, he will receive a reward.
15 If anyone's work is burned, he will suffer

1:31 Jer. 9:24 **2:1** NU *mystery* **2:4** NU omits *human*
2:9 Is. 64:4 **2:13** NU omits *Holy* **2:16** Is. 40:13

loss; but he himself will be saved, yet so as through fire.

16 [R]Do you not know that you are the temple of God and *that* the Spirit of God dwells in you? 2 Cor. 6:16

17 If anyone [T]defiles the temple of God, God will destroy him. For the temple of God is holy, which *temple* you are. *destroys*

Ministers Are Accountable to God

18 Let no one deceive himself. If anyone among you seems to be wise in this age, let him become a fool that he may become wise.

19 For the wisdom of this world is foolishness with God. For it is written, *"He catches the wise in their own craftiness"*;*

20 and again, *"The LORD knows the thoughts of the wise, that they are futile."**

21 Therefore let no one boast in men. For [R]all things are yours: [2 Cor. 4:5]

22 whether Paul or Apollos or Cephas, or the world or life or death, or things present or things to come—all are yours.

23 And [R]you *are* Christ's, and Christ *is* God's. 2 Cor. 10:7

CHAPTER 4

LET a man so consider us, as [R]servants of Christ [R]and stewards of the mysteries of God. Col. 1:25 • Titus 1:7

2 Moreover it is required in stewards that one be found faithful.

3 But with me it is a very small thing that I should be judged by you or by a human court.* In fact, I do not even judge myself.

4 For I know of nothing against myself, yet I am not justified by this; but He who judges me is the Lord.

5 Therefore judge nothing before the time, until the Lord comes, who will both bring to light the hidden things of darkness and reveal the counsels of the hearts. Then each one's praise will come from God.

Misunderstanding of Paul's Ministry

6 Now these things, brethren, I have figuratively transferred to myself and Apollos for your sakes, that you may learn in us not to think beyond what is written, that none of you may be [T]puffed up on behalf of one against the other. *arrogant*

7 For who makes you differ *from another?* And what do you have that you did not receive? Now if you did indeed receive *it*, why do you boast as if you had not received *it?*

8 You are already full! [R]You are already rich! You have reigned as kings without us—and indeed I could wish you did reign, that we also might reign with you! Rev. 3:17

9 For I think that God has displayed us, the apostles, last, as men condemned to death; for we have been made a spectacle to the world, both to angels and to men.

10 We *are* [R]fools for Christ's sake, but you *are* wise in Christ! [R]We *are* weak, but you *are* strong! You *are* distinguished, but we *are* dishonored! Acts 17:18; 26:24 • 2 Cor. 13:9

11 To the present hour we both hunger and thirst, and we are poorly clothed, and beaten, and homeless.

12 [R]And we labor, working with our own hands. [R]Being reviled, we bless; being persecuted, we endure; Acts 18:3; 20:34 • Matt. 5:44

13 being defamed, we entreat. [R]We have been made as the filth of the world, the offscouring of all things until now. Lam. 3:45

14 I do not write these things to shame you, but as my beloved children I warn *you.*

15 For though you might have ten thousand instructors in Christ, yet *you do* not *have* many fathers; for in Christ Jesus I have begotten you through the gospel.

16 Therefore I urge you, imitate me.

17 For this reason I have sent [R]Timothy to you, [R]who is my beloved and faithful son in the Lord, who will [R]remind you of my ways in Christ, as I teach everywhere in every church. Acts 19:22 • 1 Tim. 1:2, 18 • 1 Cor. 11:2

18 [R]Now some are [T]puffed up, as though I were not coming to you. 1 Cor. 5:2 • *arrogant*

19 But I will come to you shortly, if the Lord wills, and I will know, not the word of those who are puffed up, but the power.

20 For [R]the kingdom of God *is* not in word but in [R]power. 1 Thess. 1:5 • 1 Cor. 2:4

21 What do you want? [R]Shall I come to you with a rod, or in love and a spirit of gentleness? 2 Cor. 10:2

CHAPTER 5

Deliver the Fornicators for Discipline

IT is actually reported *that there is* sexual immorality among you, and such sexual immorality as is not even named* among the Gentiles—that a man has his father's [R]wife! Lev. 18:6–8

2 And you are puffed up, and have not rather mourned, that he who has done this deed might be taken away from among you.

3 [R]For I indeed, as absent in body but present in spirit, have already judged (as though I were present) him who has so done this deed. Col. 2:5

4 In the [R]name of our Lord Jesus Christ, when you are gathered together, along with my spirit, [R]with the power of our Lord Jesus Christ, [Matt. 18:20] • [John 20:23]

5 deliver such a one to Satan for the destruction of the flesh, that his spirit may be saved in the day of the Lord Jesus.*

3:19 Job 5:13 **3:20** Ps. 94:11 **4:3** Lit. *day* **5:1** NU omits *named* **5:5** NU omits *Jesus*

6 [R]Your glorying *is* not good. Do you not
know that [R]a little leaven leavens the whole
lump? 1 Cor. 3:21 • Gal. 5:9
7 Therefore purge out the old leaven, that
you may be a new lump, since you truly are
unleavened. For indeed [R]Christ, our Passover,
was sacrificed for us.* Is. 53:7
8 Therefore [R]let us keep the feast, not with
old leaven, nor with the leaven of malice and
wickedness, but with the unleavened *bread* of
sincerity and truth. Ex. 12:15

Separate Yourselves from Immoral Believers

9 I wrote to you in my epistle not to keep
company with sexually immoral people.
10 Yet *I* certainly *did* not *mean* with the sex-
ually immoral people of this world, or with
the covetous, or extortioners, or idolaters,
since then you would need to go [R]out of the
world. John 17:15
11 But now I have written to you not to
keep company [R]with anyone named a
brother, who is sexually immoral, or cov-
etous, or an idolater, or a reviler, or a drunk-
ard, or an extortioner—[R]not even to eat with
such a person. Matt. 18:17 • Gal. 2:12
12 For what *have* I *to do* with judging those
also who are outside? Do you not judge those
who are inside?
13 But those who are outside God judges.
Therefore *"put away from yourselves the evil
person."**

CHAPTER 6

Concerning Litigation Between Believers

DARE any of you, having a matter against
another, go to law before the unrigh-
teous, and not before the saints?
2 Do you not know that [R]the saints will
judge the world? And if the world will be
judged by you, are you unworthy to judge the
smallest matters? Ps. 49:14
3 Do you not know that we shall [R]judge an-
gels? How much more, things that pertain to
this life? 2 Pet. 2:4
4 If then you have [T]judgments concerning
things pertaining to this life, do you appoint
those who are least esteemed by the church to
judge? *courts*
5 I say this to your shame. Is it so, that there
is not a wise man among you, not even one,
who will be able to judge between his
brethren?
6 But brother goes to law against brother,
and that before unbelievers!
7 Now therefore, it is already an utter fail-
ure for you that you go to law against one an-
other. [R]Why do you not rather accept wrong?
Why do you not rather *let yourselves* be
cheated? [Prov. 20:22]
8 No, you yourselves do wrong and cheat,
and *you do* these things *to your* brethren!
9 Do you not know that the unrighteous
will not inherit the kingdom of God? Do not
be deceived. [R]Neither fornicators, nor idol-
aters, nor adulterers, nor homosexuals,* nor
[T]sodomites, Gal. 5:21 • *male homosexuals*
10 nor thieves, nor covetous, nor drunkards,
nor revilers, nor extortioners will inherit the
kingdom of God.

11 And such were some of you. But you were
washed, but you were sanctified, but you were
justified in the name of the Lord Jesus and by
the Spirit of our God.

Warning Against Sexual Immorality

12 [R]All things are lawful for me, but all
things are not [T]helpful. All things are lawful
for me, but I will not be brought under the
power of any. 1 Cor. 10:23 • *profitable*
13 [R]Foods for the stomach and the stomach
for foods, but God will destroy both it and
them. Now the body *is* not for [R]sexual im-

5:7 NU omits *for us* **5:13** Deut. 17:7; 19:19; 22:21, 24; 24:7 **6:9** *catamites,* those submitting to homosexuals

---

6:11 Changed Life—The first stanza of a famous Christian song begins: "What a wonderful change in my life has been wrought since Jesus came into my heart."

Without doubt the greatest proof of the new birth is changed life. Children of God now suddenly love the following:

a. They love Jesus. Before conversion sinners might hold Christ in high esteem, but after conversion they love the Savior (Page 1296—1 John 5:1, 2).
b. They love the Bible. We should love God's Word as the psalmist did in Psalm 119. He expresses his great love for God's Word no less than seventeen times! See verses 24, 40, 47, 48, 72, 97, 103, 111, 113, 127, 129, 140, 143, 159, 162, 165, 168.
c. They love other Christians. "We know that we have passed from death to life, because we love the brethren" (Page 1295—1 John 3:14).
d. They love their enemies. See Matthew 5:43–45.
e. They love the souls of all people. Like Paul, they too can cry out for the conversion of loved ones. "Brethren, my heart's desire and prayer to God for Israel is that they may be saved" (Page 1156—Rom. 10:1). See also Second Corinthians 5:14.
f. They love the pure life. John says if one loves the world, "the love of the Father is not in him" (Page 1294—1 John 2:15–17). See also First John 5:4.
g. They love to talk to God. "Speaking to one another in psalms and hymns and spiritual songs, singing and making melody in your heart to the Lord" (Page 1208—Eph. 5:19).

Now turn to Page 27—THE CHRISTIAN'S GUIDE: Growing in the New Life.

morality but [R]for the Lord, and the Lord for the body. Matt. 15:17 • Gal. 5:19 • 1 Thess. 4:3

14 And God both raised up the Lord and will also raise us up by His power.

15 Do you not know that [R]your bodies are members of Christ? Shall I then take the members of Christ and make *them* members of a harlot? Certainly not! Rom. 12:5

16 Or do you not know that he who is joined to a harlot is one body *with her?* For *"the two,"* He says, *"shall become one flesh."**

17 [R]But he who is joined to the Lord is one spirit *with Him.* [John 17:21–23]

18 [R]Flee sexual immorality. Every sin that a man does is outside the body, but he who commits sexual immorality sins [R]against his own body. Heb. 13:4 • Rom. 1:24

19 Or [R]do you not know that your body is the temple of the Holy Spirit *who is* in you, whom you have from God, [R]and you are not your own? 2 Cor. 6:16 • Rom. 14:7

20 For [R]you were bought at a price; therefore glorify God in your body* and in your spirit, which are God's. 2 Pet. 2:1

CHAPTER 7

Principles for Married Life

NOW concerning the things of which you wrote to me: [R]*It is* good for a man not to touch a woman. 1 Cor. 7:8, 26

2 Nevertheless, because of sexual immorality, let each man have his own wife, and let each woman have her own husband.

3 [R]Let the husband render to his wife the affection due her, and likewise also the wife to her husband. Ex. 21:10

4 The wife does not have authority over her own body, but the husband *does.* And likewise the husband does not have authority over his own body, but the wife *does.*

5 Do not deprive one another except with consent for a time, that you may give yourselves to fasting and prayer; and come together again so that Satan does not tempt you because of your lack of self-control.

6 But I say this as a concession, [R]not as a commandment. 2 Cor. 8:8

7 For [R]I wish that all men were even as I myself. But each one has his own gift from God, one in this manner and another in that. Acts 26:29

8 But I say to the unmarried and to the widows: [R]It is good for them if they remain even as I am; 1 Cor. 7:1, 26

9 but [R]if they cannot exercise self-control, let them marry. For it is better to marry than to burn *with passion.* 1 Tim. 5:14

Principles for the Married Believer

10 Now to the married I command, *yet* not I but the [R]Lord: [R]A wife is not to depart from *her* husband. Mark 10:6–10 • [Matt. 5:32]

11 But even if she does depart, let her remain unmarried or be reconciled to *her* husband. And a husband is not to divorce *his* wife.

12 But to the rest I, not the Lord, say: If any brother has a wife who does not believe, and she is willing to live with him, let him not divorce her.

13 And a woman who has a husband who does not believe, if he is willing to live with her, let her not divorce him.

14 For the unbelieving husband is sanctified by the wife, and the unbelieving wife is sanctified by the husband; otherwise [R]your children would be unclean, but now they are holy. Mal. 2:15

15 But if the unbeliever departs, let him depart; a brother or a sister is not under bondage in such *cases.* But God has called us [R]to peace. Rom. 12:18

16 For how do you know, O wife, whether you will [R]save *your* husband? Or how do you know, O husband, whether you will save *your* wife? 1 Pet. 3:1

6:16 Gen. 2:24 **6:20** NU ends v. 20 at *body.*

6:19 The Work of the Holy Spirit in Christian Living—As a loving and wise mother tenderly watches over her child, so the Holy Spirit cares for the children of God.

a. The Holy Spirit indwells Christians. The Bible teaches that all believers are indwelt by the Holy Spirit (1 Cor. 6:19). The purpose of this indwelling ministry is to control the newly created nature given at conversion (Page 1187—2 Cor. 5:17; Page 1206—Eph. 3:16).

b. The Holy Spirit fills believers. We are admonished to "be filled with the Spirit" (Page 1208—Eph. 5:18). The word "fill" means "to be controlled." The filling does not mean that the Christian gets more of the Holy Spirit, but rather, He gets more of us!

c. The Holy Spirit sanctifies the believer (Page 1161—Rom. 15:16; Page 1232—2 Thess. 2:13).

d. The Holy Spirit produces fruit in the life of the believer. This fruit is described by Paul: "But the fruit of the Spirit is love, joy, peace, longsuffering, kindness, goodness, faithfulness, gentleness, self-control" (Page 1200—Gal. 5:22, 23).

e. The Holy Spirit imparts gifts to Christians (Page 1159—Rom. 12:6–8; Page 1175—1 Cor. 12:1–11; Page 1207—Eph. 4:7–12). A spiritual gift is an ability imparted to every Christian (Page 1171—1 Cor. 7:7; Page 1283—1 Pet. 4:10). The purpose of these gifts is twofold, namely, to glorify God (Page 1315—Rev. 4:11) and to edify the body of Christ (Page 1207—Eph. 4:12, 13).

f. The Holy Spirit teaches believers. He will instruct us in all spiritual things as we read the Word of God (Page 1100—John 14:26) and abide in the Son of God (Page 1294—1 John 2:24–27).

Now turn to Page 5—Gen. 1:26: Unity of the Trinity.

Principle of Abiding in God's Call

17 But as God has distributed to each one, as the Lord has called each one, so let him walk. And so I ordain in all the churches.

18 Was anyone called while circumcised? Let him not become uncircumcised. Was anyone called while uncircumcised? [R]Let him not be circumcised. Acts 15:1

19 Circumcision is nothing and uncircumcision is nothing, but keeping the commandments of God *is what matters.*

20 Let each one remain in the same calling in which he was called.

21 Were you called *while* a slave? Do not be concerned about it; but if you can be made free, rather use *it.*

22 For he who is called in the Lord *while* a slave is the Lord's freedman. Likewise he who is called *while* free is Christ's slave.

23 [R]You were bought at a price; do not become slaves of men. 1 Pet. 1:18, 19

24 Brethren, let each one remain with God in that *state* in which he was called.

Principles for the Unmarried

25 Now concerning virgins: [R]I have no commandment from the Lord; yet I give judgment as one whom the Lord in His mercy *has made* trustworthy. 2 Cor. 8:8

26 I suppose therefore that this is good because of the present distress—that *it is* good for a man to remain as he is:

27 Are you bound to a wife? Do not seek to be loosed. Are you loosed from a wife? Do not seek a wife.

28 But even if you do marry, you have not sinned; and if a virgin marries, she has not sinned. Nevertheless such will have trouble in the flesh, but I would spare you.

29 But [R]this I say, brethren, the time *is* short, so that from now on even those who have wives should be as though they had none, 1 Pet. 4:7

30 those who weep as though they did not weep, those who rejoice as though they did not rejoice, those who buy as though they did not possess,

31 and those who use this world as not [R]misusing *it.* For [R]the form of this world is passing away. 1 Cor. 9:18 • [1 John 2:17]

32 But I want you to be without [T]care. He who is unmarried cares for the things of the Lord—how he may please the Lord. *concern*

33 But he who is married cares about the things of the world—how he may please *his* wife.

34 There is* a difference between a wife and a virgin. The unmarried woman cares about the things of the Lord, that she may be holy both in body and in spirit. But she who is married cares about the things of the world—how she may please *her* husband.

35 And this I say for your own profit, not that I may put a leash on you, but for what is proper, and that you may serve the Lord without distraction.

36 But if any man thinks he is behaving improperly toward his [T]virgin, if she is past the flower of youth, and thus it must be, let him do what he wishes. He does not sin; let them marry. Or *virgin daughter*

37 Nevertheless he who stands steadfast in his heart, having no necessity, but has power over his own will, and has so determined in his heart that he will keep his virgin,* does well.

38 [R]So then he who gives *her** in marriage does well, but he who does not give *her* in marriage does better. Heb. 13:4

Principles for Remarriage

39 [R]A wife is bound by law as long as her husband lives; but if her husband dies, she is at liberty to be married to whom she wishes, only in the Lord. Rom. 7:2

40 But she is happier if she remains as she is, [R]according to my judgment—and I think I also have the Spirit of God. 1 Cor. 7:6, 25

CHAPTER 8

Principles of Liberty and the Weaker Brother

NOW concerning things offered to idols: We know that we all have knowledge. Knowledge puffs up, but love edifies.

2 And [R]if anyone thinks that he knows anything, he knows nothing yet as he ought to know. [1 Cor. 13:8–12]

3 But if anyone loves God, this one is known by Him.

4 Therefore concerning the eating of things offered to idols, we know that [R]an idol *is* nothing in the world, [R]and that *there is* no other God but one. Is. 41:24 • Deut. 4:35, 39; 6:4

5 For even if there are [R]so-called gods, whether in heaven or on earth (as there are many gods and many lords), [John 10:34]

6 yet for us *there is* one God, the Father, of whom *are* all things, and we for Him; and one Lord Jesus Christ, through whom *are* all things, and through whom we *live.*

7 However, *there is* not in everyone that knowledge; for some, [R]with consciousness of the idol, until now eat *it* as a thing offered to an idol; and their conscience, being weak, is [R]defiled. [1 Cor. 10:28] • Rom. 14:14, 22

8 But [R]food does not commend us to God; for neither if we eat are we the better, nor if we do not eat are we the worse. [Rom. 14:17]

9 But [R]beware lest somehow this liberty of yours become [R]a stumbling block to those who are weak. Gal. 5:13 • Rom. 14:13, 21

7:34 M adds *also* **7:37** Or *virgin daughter* **7:38** NU *his own virgin*

10 For if anyone sees you who have knowl-
edge eating in an idol's temple, will not the
conscience of him who is weak be embold-
ened to eat those things offered to idols?
11 And [R]because of your knowledge shall
the weak brother perish, for whom Christ
died? Rom. 14:15, 20
12 But [R]when you thus sin against the
brethren, and wound their weak conscience,
you sin against Christ. Matt. 25:40
13 Therefore, [R]if food makes my brother
stumble, I will never again eat meat, lest I
make my brother stumble. Rom. 14:21

CHAPTER 9

Paul Lists His Rights as a Minister

AM [R]I not an apostle? Am I not free? Have
I not seen Jesus Christ our Lord? Are you
not my work in the Lord? Acts 9:15
2 If I am not an apostle to others, yet doubt-
less I am to you. For you are [R]the seal of my
apostleship in the Lord. 2 Cor. 12:12
3 My defense to those who examine me is
this:
4 Do we have no right to eat and drink?
5 Do we have no right to take along a be-
lieving wife, as *do* also the other apostles, the
brothers of the Lord, and Cephas?
6 Or *is it* only Barnabas and I [R]*who* have no
right to refrain from working? Acts 4:36
7 Who ever goes to war at his own ex-
pense? Who plants a vineyard and does not
eat of its fruit? Or who tends a flock and does
not drink of the milk of the flock?
8 Do I say these things as a *mere* man? Or
does not the law say the same also?
9 For it is written in the law of Moses, *"You
shall not muzzle an ox while it treads out the
grain."** Is it oxen God is concerned about?
10 Or does He say *it* altogether for our
sakes? For our sakes, no doubt, *this* is written,
that [R]he who plows should plow in hope, and
he who threshes in hope should be partaker
of his hope. 2 Tim. 2:6
11 [R]If we have sown spiritual things for you,
is it a great thing if we reap your material
things? Rom. 15:27
12 If others are partakers of *this* right over
you, *are* we not even more? Nevertheless we
have not used this right, but endure all things
lest we hinder the gospel of Christ.
13 Do you not know that those who minister
the holy things eat *of the things* of the temple,
and those who serve at the altar partake of
the offerings of the altar?
14 Even so [R]the Lord has commanded [R]that
those who preach the gospel should live from
the gospel. Matt. 10:10 • Rom. 10:15

Paul Limits His Rights for Ministry

15 But [R]I have used none of these things, nor
have I written these things that it should be
done so to me; for [R]it *would be* better for me
to die than that anyone should make my
boasting void. Acts 18:3; 20:33 • 2 Cor. 11:10
16 For if I preach the gospel, I have nothing
to boast of, for necessity is laid upon me; yes,
woe is me if I do not preach the gospel!
17 For if I do this willingly, [R]I have a reward;
but if against my will, I have been entrusted
with a stewardship. 1 Cor. 3:8, 14
18 What is my reward then? That when I
preach the gospel, I may present the gospel of
Christ* without charge, that I may not abuse
my authority in the gospel.
19 For though I am [R]free from all *men*, [R]I
have made myself a servant to all, that I might
win the more; 1 Cor. 9:1 • Gal. 5:13
20 and [R]to the Jews I became as a Jew, that I
might win Jews; to those *who are* under the
law, as under the law,* that I might win those
who are under the law; Acts 16:3
21 to those *who are* without law, as without
law (not being without law toward God,* but
under law toward Christ*), that I might win
those *who are* without law;
22 [R]to the weak I became as* weak, that I
might win the weak. [R]I have become all things
to all *men*, that I might by all means save
some. Rom. 14:1; 15:1 • 1 Cor. 10:33
23 Now this I do for the gospel's sake, that I
may be partaker of it with *you*.
24 Do you not know that those who run in a
race all run, but one receives the prize? Run in
such a way that you may obtain *it*.
25 And everyone who competes *for the prize*
is temperate in all things. Now they *do it* to
obtain a perishable crown, but we *for* [R]an
imperishable *crown*. James 1:12
26 Therefore I run thus: [R]not with uncer-
tainty. Thus I fight: not as *one who* beats the
air. 2 Tim. 2:5
27 [R]But I discipline my body and [R]bring *it*
into subjection, lest, when I have preached
to others, I myself should become [R]disquali-
fied. [Rom. 8:13] • [Rom. 6:18] • Jer. 6:30

CHAPTER 10

Warning Against Forfeiting Liberty

MOREOVER, brethren, I do not want you
to be unaware that all our fathers were
under [R]the cloud, all passed through [R]the
sea, Ex. 13:21, 22 • Ex. 14:21, 22, 29
2 all were baptized into Moses in the cloud
and in the sea,
3 all ate the same spiritual food,
4 and all drank the same spiritual drink.
For they drank of that spiritual Rock that fol-
lowed them, and that Rock was Christ.
5 But with most of them God was not well

9:9 Deut. 25:4 **9:18** NU omits *of Christ* **9:20** NU adds *though not being myself under the law* **9:21** NU *God's law* • NU *Christ's law* **9:22** NU omits *as*

pleased, for *their bodies* [R]were scattered in
the wilderness. Num. 14:29, 37; 26:65
6 Now these things became our examples,
to the intent that we should not lust after evil
things as they also lusted.
7 [R]And do not become idolaters as *were*
some of them. As it is written, *"The people*
sat down to eat and drink, and rose up to
*play."** 1 Cor. 5:11; 10:14
8 Nor let us commit sexual immorality, as
some of them did, and [R]in one day twenty-
three thousand fell; Ps. 106:29
9 nor let us [T]tempt Christ, as [R]some of them
also tempted, and [R]were destroyed by ser-
pents; *test* • Ex. 17:2, 7 • Num. 21:6–9
10 nor complain, as [R]some of them also com-
plained, and [R]were destroyed by [R]the de-
stroyer. Ex. 16:2 • Num. 14:37 • Ex. 12:23
11 Now all* these things happened to them
as examples, and [R]they were written for our
admonition, [R]upon whom the ends of the ages
have come. Rom. 15:4 • Phil. 4:5
12 Therefore [R]let him who thinks he stands
take heed lest he fall. Rom. 11:20
13 No temptation has overtaken you except
such as is common to man; but God *is* faithful,
who will not allow you to be tempted beyond
what you are able, but with the temptation
will also make the way of escape, that you
may be able to bear *it*.

Exhortation to Use Liberty to Glorify God

14 Therefore, my beloved, flee from idolatry.
15 I speak as to [R]wise men; judge for your-
selves what I say. 1 Cor. 8:1
16 The cup of blessing which we bless, is it
not the communion of the blood of Christ?
The bread which we break, is it not the com-
munion of the body of Christ?
17 For [R]we, *though* many, are one bread *and*
one body; for we all partake of that one
bread. 1 Cor. 12:12, 27
18 Observe [R]Israel [R]after the flesh: [R]Are not
those who eat of the sacrifices partakers of
the altar? Rom. 4:12 • Rom. 4:1 • Lev. 3:3; 7:6, 14
19 What am I saying then? [R]That an idol is
anything, or what is offered to idols is any-
thing? 1 Cor. 8:4
20 Rather, that the things which the Gentiles
[R]sacrifice they sacrifice to demons and not to
God, and I do not want you to have fellowship
with demons. Lev. 17:7
21 [R]You cannot drink the cup of the Lord
and [R]the cup of demons; you cannot partake
of the Lord's table and of the table of de-
mons. 2 Cor. 6:15, 16 • Deut. 32:38
22 Or do we [R]provoke the Lord to jealousy?
Are we stronger than He? Deut. 32:21
23 All things are lawful for me,* but not all
things are [R]helpful; all things are lawful for
me,* but not all things edify. 1 Cor. 6:12
24 Let no one seek his own, but each one
[R]the other's *well-being*. Phil. 2:4
25 [R]Eat whatever is sold in the meat mar-
ket, asking no questions for conscience'
sake; [1 Tim. 4:4]
26 for *"the earth is the LORD's, and all its full-*
*ness."**
27 If any of those who do not believe invites
you *to dinner*, and you desire to go, [R]eat what-
ever is set before you, asking no question for
conscience' sake. Luke 10:7, 8
28 But if anyone says to you, "This was of-
fered to idols," do not eat it [R]for the sake of the
one who told you, and for conscience' sake;*
for *"the earth is the LORD's, and all its full-*
*ness."** [1 Cor. 8:7, 10, 12]
29 "Conscience," I say, not your own, but that
of the other. For why is my liberty judged by
another *man's* conscience?
30 But if I partake with thanks, why am I evil
spoken of for *the food* [R]over which I give
thanks? Rom. 14:6
31 Therefore, whether you eat or drink, or
whatever you do, do all to the glory of God.
32 Give no offense, either to the Jews or to
the Greeks or to the church of God,
33 just as I also please all *men* in all *things*,
not seeking my own profit, but the *profit* of
many, that they may be saved.

CHAPTER 11

IMITATE me, just as I also *imitate* Christ.

Principles of Public Prayer

2 Now I praise you, brethren, that you re-
member me in all things and keep the tradi-
tions just as I delivered *them* to you.
3 But I want you to know that the head of
every man is Christ, the head of woman *is*
man, and the head of Christ *is* God.
4 Every man praying or prophesying, hav-
ing *his* head covered, dishonors his head.
5 But every woman who prays or prophe-
sies with *her* head uncovered dishonors her
head, for that is one and the same as if her
head were [R]shaved. Deut. 21:12
6 For if a woman is not covered, let her also be
shorn. But if it is [R]shameful for a woman to be
shorn or shaved, let her be covered. Num. 5:18
7 For a man indeed ought not to cover *his*
head, since he is the image and glory of God;
but woman is the glory of man.
8 For man is not from woman, but woman
[R]from man. Gen. 2:21–23
9 Nor was man created for the woman, but
woman [R]for the man. Gen. 2:18
10 For this reason the woman ought to have
a symbol of authority on *her* head, because of
the angels.

10:7 Ex. 32:6 **10:11** NU omits *all* **10:23** NU omits *for me* • NU omits *for me* **10:26** Ps. 24:1 **10:28** NU omits the rest of v. 28. • Ps. 24:1

11 Nevertheless, [R]neither *is* man independent of woman, nor woman independent of man, in the Lord. [Gal. 3:28]
12 For as woman *came* from man, even so man also *comes* through woman; but all things are from God.
13 Judge among yourselves. Is it proper for a woman to pray to God with her head uncovered?
14 Does not even nature itself teach you that if a man has long hair, it is a dishonor to him?
15 But if a woman has long hair, it is a glory to her; for *her* hair is given to her* for a covering.
16 But [R]if anyone seems to be contentious, we have no such custom, [R]nor *do* the churches of God. 1 Tim. 6:4 • 1 Cor. 7:17

Rebuke of Disorders at the Lord's Supper

17 Now in giving these instructions I do not praise *you,* since you come together not for the better but for the worse.
18 For first of all, when you come together as a church, I hear that there are divisions among you, and in part I believe it.
19 For there must also be factions among you, [R]that those who are approved may be recognized among you. [Deut. 13:3]
20 Therefore when you come together in one place, it is not to eat the Lord's Supper.
21 For in eating, each one takes his own supper ahead of *others;* and one is hungry and [R]another is drunk. Jude 12
22 What! Do you not have houses to eat and drink in? Or do you despise [R]the church of God and shame those who have nothing? What shall I say to you? Shall I praise you in this? I do not praise *you.* 1 Cor. 10:32
23 For [R]I received from the Lord that which I also delivered to you: [R]that the Lord Jesus on the *same* night in which He was betrayed took bread; 1 Cor. 15:3 • Matt. 26:26–28
24 and when He had given thanks, He broke *it* and said, "Take, eat;* this is My body which is broken* for you; do this in remembrance of Me."
25 In the same manner *He* also *took* the cup after supper, saying, "This cup is the new covenant in My blood. This do, as often as you drink *it,* in remembrance of Me."
26 For as often as you eat this bread and drink this cup, you proclaim the Lord's death [R]till He comes. John 14:3
27 Therefore whoever eats [R]this bread or drinks *this* cup of the Lord in an unworthy manner will be guilty of the body and blood* of the Lord. [John 6:51]
28 But [R]let a man examine himself, and so let him eat of the bread and drink of the cup. 2 Cor. 13:5
29 For he who eats and drinks in an unworthy manner* eats and drinks judgment to himself, not discerning the Lord's* body.
30 For this reason many *are* weak and sick among you, and many [T]sleep. Are dead
31 For [R]if we would judge ourselves, we would not be judged. [1 John 1:9]
32 But when we are judged, [R]we are chastened by the Lord, that we may not be condemned with the world. Ps. 94:12
33 Therefore, my brethren, when you come together to eat, wait for one another.
34 But if anyone is hungry, let him eat at home, lest you come together for judgment. And the rest I will set in order when I come.

CHAPTER 12

Test of the Spirit's Control

NOW concerning spiritual *gifts,* brethren, I do not want you to be ignorant:
2 You know [R]that* you were Gentiles, carried away to these [R]dumb idols, however you were led. Eph. 2:11 • Ps. 115:5
3 Therefore I make known to you that no one speaking by the Spirit of God calls Jesus accursed, and [R]no one can say that Jesus is Lord except by the Holy Spirit. Matt. 16:17

Diversity of the Gifts

4 [R]There are diversities of gifts, but [R]the same Spirit. Rom. 12:3–8 • Eph. 4:4
5 [R]There are differences of ministries, but the same Lord. Rom. 12:6
6 And there are diversities of activities, but it is the same God who works all in all.
7 But the manifestation of the Spirit is given to each one for the profit *of all:*
8 for to one is given the word of wisdom through the Spirit, to another the word of knowledge through the same Spirit,
9 [R]to another faith by the same Spirit, to another [R]gifts of healings by the same* Spirit, 2 Cor. 4:13 • Mark 3:15; 16:18

11:15 M omits *to her* **11:24** NU omits *Take, eat* • NU omits *broken* **11:27** NU, M *the blood* **11:29** NU omits *in an unworthy manner* • NU omits *Lord's* **12:2** NU, M add *when* **12:9** NU *one*

12:1–10 Using Spiritual Gifts—Spiritual gifts are discussed in detail in four New Testament passages: Romans 12:3–8; First Corinthians 12:1–10, 28–31; Ephesians 4:11, 12; and First Peter 4:10, 11. These lists are to be regarded as representative of spiritual gifts. Spiritual gifts are those gifts given by the Spirit of God for the accomplishment of God's purpose in the world and for the edification of the church, the body of Christ. Two things are important to remember concerning spiritual gifts: (1) every believer has been given spiritual gifts (Page 1159—Rom. 12:5, 6; 1 Cor. 12:7; Page 1175—1 Pet. 4:10); and (2) the gifts belong to God and are given for the believer to use for the glory of God (Page 1283—1 Pet. 4:11).

Now turn to Page 1199—Gal. 5:13: Serving.

10 [R]to another the working of miracles, to another [R]prophecy, to another [R]discerning of spirits, to another *different* kinds of tongues, to another the interpretation of tongues. Mark 16:17 • Rom. 12:6 • 1 John 4:1

11 But one and the same Spirit works all these things, [R]distributing to each one individually [R]as He wills. Rom. 12:6 • [John 3:8]

Importance of All Gifts

12 For [R]as the body is one and has many members, but all the members of that one body, being many, are one body, [R]so also *is* Christ. Rom. 12:4, 5 • [Gal. 3:16]

13 For [R]by one Spirit we were all baptized into one body—whether Jews or Greeks, whether slaves or free—and have all been made to drink into* one Spirit. [Rom. 6:5]

14 For in fact the body is not one member but many.

15 If the foot should say, "Because I am not a hand, I am not of the body," is it therefore not of the body?

16 And if the ear should say, "Because I am not an eye, I am not of the body," is it therefore not of the body?

17 If the whole body *were* an eye, where *would be* the hearing? If the whole *were* hearing, where *would be* the smelling?

18 But now [R]God has set the members, each one of them, in the body [R]just as He pleased. 1 Cor. 12:28 • Rom. 12:3

19 And if they *were* all one member, where *would* the body *be?*

20 But now indeed *there are* many members, yet one body.

21 And the eye cannot say to the hand, "I have no need of you"; nor again the head to the feet, "I have no need of you."

22 No, much rather, those members of the body which seem to be weaker are necessary.

23 And those *members* of the body which we think to be less honorable, on these we bestow greater honor; and our unpresentable *parts* have greater modesty,

24 but our presentable *parts* have no need. But God composed the body, having given greater honor to that *part* which lacks it,

25 that there should be no [T]schism in the body, but *that* the members should have the same care for one another. *division*

26 And if one member suffers, all the members suffer with *it;* or if one member is honored, all the members rejoice with *it.*

27 Now [R]you are the body of Christ, and [R]members individually. Rom. 12:5 • Eph. 5:30

28 And [R]God has appointed these in the church: first apostles, second prophets, third teachers, after that miracles, then gifts of healings, [R]helps, administrations, varieties of tongues. Eph. 4:11 • Num. 11:17

29 *Are* all apostles? *Are* all prophets? *Are* all teachers? *Are* all workers of miracles?

30 Do all have gifts of healings? Do all speak with tongues? Do all interpret?

31 But earnestly desire the best* gifts. And yet I show you a more excellent way.

CHAPTER 13

Exercise Gifts with Love

THOUGH I speak with the tongues of men and of angels, but have not love, I have become sounding brass or a clanging cymbal.

2 And though I have *the gift of* [R]prophecy, and understand all mysteries and all knowledge, and though I have all faith, so that I could remove mountains, but have not love, I am nothing. 1 Cor. 12:8–10, 28; 14:1

3 And [R]though I bestow all my goods to feed *the poor,* and though I give my body to be burned,* but have not love, it profits me nothing. Matt. 6:1, 2

4 [R]Love suffers long *and* is [R]kind; love does not envy; love does not parade itself, is not puffed up; Prov. 10:12; 17:9 • Eph. 4:32

5 does not behave rudely, does not seek its own, is not provoked, thinks no evil;

6 [R]does not rejoice in iniquity, but [R]rejoices in the truth; Rom. 1:32 • 2 John 4

7 bears all things, believes all things, hopes all things, endures all things.

8 Love never fails. But whether *there are* prophecies, they will fail; whether *there are* tongues, they will cease; whether *there is* knowledge, it will vanish away.

9 [R]For we know in part and we prophesy in part. 1 Cor. 8:2; 13:12

10 But when that which is [T]perfect has come, then that which is in part will be done away. *complete*

11 When I was a child, I spoke as a child, I understood as a child, I thought as a child; but when I became a man, I put away childish things.

12 For now we see in a mirror, dimly, but then face to face. Now I know in part, but then I shall know just as I also am known.

13 And now abide faith, hope, love, these three; but the greatest of these *is* love.

CHAPTER 14

Superiority of Prophecy

PURSUE love, and desire spiritual *gifts,* but especially that you may prophesy.

2 For he who [R]speaks in a tongue does not speak to men but to God, for no one understands *him;* however, in the spirit he speaks mysteries. Acts 2:4; 10:46

12:13 NU omits *into* **12:31** NU *greater* **13:3** NU *so I may boast*

3 But he who prophesies speaks edification and exhortation and comfort to men.

4 He who speaks in a tongue edifies himself, but he who prophesies edifies the church.

5 I wish you all spoke with tongues, but even more that you prophesied; for* he who prophesies *is* greater than he who speaks with tongues, unless indeed he interprets, that the church may receive edification.

6 But now, brethren, if I come to you speaking with tongues, what shall I profit you unless I speak to you either by [R]revelation, by knowledge, by prophesying, or by teaching? 1 Cor. 14:26

Gift of Tongues

7 Even things without life, whether flute or harp, when they make a sound, unless they make a distinction in the sounds, how will it be known what is piped or played?

8 For if the trumpet makes an uncertain sound, who will prepare for battle?

9 So likewise you, unless you utter by the tongue words easy to understand, how will it be known what is spoken? For you will be speaking into the air.

10 There are, it may be, so many kinds of languages in the world, and none of them *is* without [T]significance. *meaning*

11 Therefore, if I do not know the meaning of the language, I shall be a [T]foreigner to him who speaks, and he who speaks *will be* a foreigner to me. Lit. *barbarian*

12 Even so you, since you are [T]zealous for spiritual *gifts, let it be* for the edification of the church *that* you seek to excel. *eager*

13 Therefore let him who speaks in a tongue pray that he may interpret.

14 For if I pray in a tongue, my spirit prays, but my understanding is unfruitful.

15 What is *the conclusion* then? I will pray with the spirit, and I will also pray with the understanding. I will sing with the spirit, and I will also sing with the understanding.

16 Otherwise, if you bless with the spirit, how will he who occupies the place of the uninformed say "Amen" [R]at your giving of thanks, since he does not understand what you say? 1 Cor. 11:24

17 For you indeed give thanks well, but the other is not edified.

18 I thank my God I speak with tongues more than you all;

19 yet in the church I would rather speak five words with my understanding, that I may teach others also, than ten thousand words in a tongue.

20 Brethren, [R]do not be children in understanding; however, in malice be babes, but in understanding be mature. Ps. 131:2

21 [R]In the law it is written: John 10:34

> *"With men of other tongues and other lips*
> *I will speak to this people;*
> *And yet, for all that, they will not hear*
> *Me,"**

says the Lord.

22 Therefore tongues are for a [R]sign, not to those who believe but to unbelievers; but prophesying is not for unbelievers but for those who believe. Mark 16:17

23 Therefore if the whole church comes together in one place, and all speak with tongues, and there come in *those who are* uninformed or unbelievers, [R]will they not say that you are out of your mind? Acts 2:13

24 But if all prophesy, and an unbeliever or an uninformed person comes in, he is convinced by all, he is convicted by all.

25 And thus* the secrets of his heart are revealed; and so, falling down on *his* face, he will worship God and report [R]that God is truly among you. Is. 45:14

Exercising Gifts in Public Worship

26 How is it then, brethren? Whenever you come together, each of you has a psalm, [R]has a teaching, has a tongue, has a revelation, has an interpretation. Let all things be done for edification. 1 Cor. 12:8–10; 14:6

27 If anyone speaks in a tongue, *let there be* two or at the most three, *each* in turn, and let one interpret.

28 But if there is no interpreter, let him keep silent in church, and let him speak to himself and to God.

29 Let two or three prophets speak, and [R]let the others judge. 1 Cor. 12:10

30 But if *anything* is revealed to another who sits by, let the first keep silent.

31 For you can all prophesy one by one, that all may learn and all may be encouraged.

32 And [R]the spirits of the prophets are subject to the prophets. 1 John 4:1

33 For God is not *the author* of [T]confusion but of peace, [R]as in all the churches of the saints. *disorder* • 1 Cor. 11:16

34 [R]Let your* women keep silent in the churches, for they are not permitted to speak; but *they are* to be submissive, as the [R]law also says. 1 Tim. 2:11 • Gen. 3:16

35 And if they want to learn something, let them ask their own husbands at home; for it is shameful for women to speak in church.

36 Or did the word of God come *originally* from you? Or *was it* you only that it reached?

37 [R]If anyone thinks himself to be a prophet or spiritual, let him acknowledge that the things which I write to you are the commandments of the Lord. 2 Cor. 10:7

38 But if anyone is ignorant, let him be ignorant.*

39 Therefore, brethren, [R]desire earnestly to

14:5 NU *and* **14:21** Is. 28:11, 12 **14:25** NU omits *And thus* **14:34** NU omits *your* **14:38** NU *if anyone does not recognize this, he is not recognized.*

prophesy, and do not forbid to speak with tongues. 1 Cor. 12:31

40 [R]Let all things be done decently and in order. 1 Cor. 14:33

CHAPTER 15

Fact of Christ's Resurrection

MOREOVER, brethren, I declare to you the gospel [R]which I preached to you, which also you received and [R]in which you stand, [Gal. 1:11] • [Rom. 5:2; 11:20]

2 by which also you are saved, if you hold fast that word which I preached to you—unless you believed in vain.

3 For I delivered to you first of all that which I also received: that Christ died for our sins according to the Scriptures,

4 and that He was buried, and that He rose again the third day [R]according to the Scriptures, Ps. 16:10, 11; Is. 53:10; Luke 24:26★

5 [R]and that He was seen by [T]Cephas, then [R]by the twelve. Luke 24:34 • Peter • Matt. 28:17

6 After that He was seen by over five hundred brethren at once, of whom the greater part remain to the present, but some have [T]fallen asleep. Died

7 After that He was seen by James, then [R]by all the apostles. Acts 1:3, 4

8 [R]Then last of all He was seen by me also, as by one born out of due time. [Acts 9:3–8]

9 For I am the least of the apostles, who am not worthy to be called an apostle, because I persecuted the church of God.

10 But [R]by the grace of God I am what I am, and His grace toward me was not in vain; but I labored more abundantly than they all, [R]yet not I, but the grace of God *which was* with me. Eph. 3:7, 8 • Phil. 2:13

11 Therefore, whether *it was* I or they, so we preach and so you believed.

Importance of Christ's Resurrection

12 Now if Christ is preached that He has been raised from the dead, how do some among you say that there is no resurrection of the dead?

13 But if there is no resurrection of the dead, then Christ is not risen.

14 And if Christ is not risen, then our preaching *is* empty and your faith *is* also empty.

15 Yes, and we are found false witnesses of God, because we have testified of God that He raised up Christ, whom He did not raise up—if in fact the dead do not rise.

16 For if *the* dead do not rise, then Christ is not risen.

17 And if Christ is not risen, your faith *is* futile; [R]you are still in your sins! [Rom. 4:25]

18 Then also those who have [T]fallen [R]asleep in Christ have perished. Died • Job 14:12

19 If in this life only we have hope in Christ, we are of all men the most pitiable.

Order of the Resurrections

20 But now [R]Christ is risen from the dead, *and* has become [R]the firstfruits of those who have [T]fallen asleep. 1 Pet. 1:3 • Acts 26:23 • Died

21 For since by man *came* death, by Man also *came* the resurrection of the dead.

22 For as in Adam all die, even so in Christ all shall [R]be made alive. [John 5:28, 29]

23 But [R]each one in his own order: Christ the firstfruits, afterward those *who are* Christ's at His coming. [1 Thess. 4:15–17]

24 Then *comes* the end, when He delivers [R]the kingdom to God the Father, when He puts an end to all rule and all authority and power. [Dan. 2:44; 7:14, 27]☆

25 For He must reign [R]till He has put all enemies under His feet. Ps. 110:1; Acts 2:34, 35☆

26 [R]The last enemy *that* will be destroyed *is* death. [2 Tim. 1:10; Rev. 20:14]☆

27 For *"He has put all things under His feet."** But when He says "all things are put under Him," *it is* evident that He who put all things under Him is excepted.

28 [R]Now when all things are made subject to Him, then the Son Himself will also be subject

15:27 Ps. 8:6☆

15:3, 4 Sharing Our Faith: What?—Before discussing just what is to be shared concerning our faith, let us mention a few things we are not to do. We are not commanded to force Christian standards upon the unbelieving world (Page 1170—1 Cor. 5:12). We are not to confuse people by allowing them to believe that church membership, tithing, or any good works are somehow connected with becoming a Christian (Page 1205—Eph. 2:8–10).

Actually, we have but one thing to share with the unsaved, and that is the gospel of Christ. According to Paul it involves the death and resurrection of Christ (1 Cor. 15:1–4). A plan for sharing your faith might be as follows:

a. God's Word says all are sinners, condemned to hell (Page 731—Is. 53:6; Page 1150—Rom. 3:10, 11, 23; 5:8, 12; Page 1326—Rev. 20:15).
b. There is nothing lost persons can do on their own to save themselves (Page 741—Is. 64:6; Page 1205—Eph. 2:9).
c. Christ was born, crucified, and resurrected to save lost people from their sin (Page 1083—John 3:16; Page 1237—1 Tim. 1:15).
d. To be saved sinners must believe God's Word and invite Christ into their hearts by faith (Page 1086—John 5:24; Page 1131—Acts 16:31).

Now turn to Page 476—Ezra 7:10: Sharing Our Faith: How to Prepare.

to Him who put all things under Him, that God may be all in all. [Phil. 3:21]☆

Moral Implications of Christ's Resurrection

29 Otherwise, what will they do who are baptized for the dead, if the dead do not rise at all? Why then are they baptized for the dead?

30 And [R]why do we stand in [T]jeopardy every hour? 2 Cor. 11:26 • *danger*

31 I affirm, by the boasting in you which I have in Christ Jesus our Lord, I die daily.

32 If, in the manner of men, [R]I have fought with beasts at Ephesus, what advantage *is it* to me? If *the* dead do not rise, *"Let us eat and drink, for tomorrow we die!"** 2 Cor. 1:8

33 Do not be deceived: [R]"Evil company corrupts good habits." [1 Cor. 5:6]

34 Awake to righteousness, and do not sin; for some do not have the knowledge of God. I speak *this* to your shame.

Bodies of the Resurrected Dead

35 But someone will say, [R]"How are the dead raised up? And with what body do they come?" Ezek. 37:3

36 Foolish one, [R]what you sow is not made alive unless it dies. John 12:24

37 And what you sow, you do not sow that body that shall be, but mere grain—perhaps wheat or some other *grain.*

38 But God gives it a body as He pleases, and to each seed its own body.

39 All flesh *is* not the same flesh, but *there is* one *kind of* flesh* of men, another flesh of animals, another of fish, *and* another of birds.

40 *There are* also [T]celestial bodies and [T]terrestrial bodies; but the glory of the celestial *is* one, and the *glory* of the terrestrial *is* another. *heavenly • earthly*

41 *There is* one glory of the sun, another glory of the moon, and another glory of the stars; for *one* star differs from *another* star in glory.

42 [R]So also *is* the resurrection of the dead. *The body* is sown in corruption, it is raised in incorruption. [Dan. 12:3]

43 [R]It is sown in dishonor, it is raised in glory. It is sown in weakness, it is raised in power. [Phil. 3:21]

44 It is sown a natural body, it is raised a spiritual body. There is a natural body, and there is a spiritual body.

45 And so it is written, *"The first man Adam became a living being."** [R]The last Adam *became* a life-giving spirit. [Rom. 5:14]

46 However, the spiritual is not first, but the natural, and afterward the spiritual.

47 [R]The first man *was* of the earth, [R]*made* of dust; the second Man *is* the Lord* [R]from heaven. John 3:31 • Gen. 2:7; 3:19 • John 3:13

48 As *was* the [T]*man* of dust, so also *are* those *who are* [T]made of dust; [R]and as *is* the heavenly *Man,* so also *are* those *who are* heavenly. *earthy • earthy* • Phil. 3:20

49 And [R]as we have borne the image of the *man* of dust, [R]we shall also bear* the image of the heavenly *Man.* Gen. 5:3 • Rom. 8:29

50 Now this I say, brethren, that flesh and blood cannot inherit the kingdom of God; nor does corruption inherit incorruption.

Bodies of the Translated Living

51 Behold, I tell you a mystery: We shall not all sleep, but we shall all be changed—

52 in a moment, in the twinkling of an eye, at the last trumpet. For the trumpet will sound, and the dead will be raised incorruptible, and we shall be changed.

53 For this corruptible must put on incorruption, and [R]this mortal *must* put on immortality. 2 Cor. 5:4

54 So when this corruptible has put on incorruption, and this mortal has put on immortality, then shall be brought to pass the saying that is written: *"Death is swallowed up in victory."**

55 *"O Death, where is your sting?**
*O Hades, where is your victory?"**

56 The sting of death *is* sin, and [R]the strength of sin *is* the law. [Rom. 3:20; 4:15]

57 But thanks *be* to God, who gives us the victory through our Lord Jesus Christ.

58 [R]Therefore, my beloved brethren, be steadfast, immovable, always abounding in the work of the Lord, knowing that your labor is not in vain in the Lord. 2 Pet. 3:14

CHAPTER 16

Counsel Concerning the Collection for Jerusalem

NOW concerning the collection for the saints, as I have given orders to the churches of Galatia, so you must do also:

2 [R]On the first *day* of the week let each one of you lay something aside, storing up as he may prosper, that there be no collections when I come. Acts 20:7

3 And when I come, [R]whomever you approve by *your* letters I will send to bear your gift to Jerusalem. 2 Cor. 3:1; 8:18

4 [R]But if it is fitting that I go also, they will go with me. 2 Cor. 8:4, 19

Conclusion

5 Now I will come to you [R]when I pass through Macedonia (for I am passing through Macedonia). 2 Cor. 1:15, 16

15:32 Is. 22:13 **15:39** NU, M omit *of flies* **15:45** Gen. 2:7 **15:47** NU omits *the Lord* **15:49** M *let us also bear* **15:54** Is. 25:8 **15:55** Hos. 13:14 • NU *O Death, where is your victory? O Death, where is your sting?*

6 And it may be that I will remain, or even spend the winter with you, that you may send me on my journey, wherever I go.
7 For I do not wish to see you now on the way; but I hope to stay a while with you, [R]if the Lord permits. James 4:15
8 But I will tarry in Ephesus until [R]Pentecost. Lev. 23:15–22
9 For [R]a great and effective door has opened to me, and [R]*there are* many adversaries. Acts 14:27 • Acts 19:9
10 And [R]if Timothy comes, see that he may be with you without fear; for he does the work of the Lord, as I also *do*. Acts 19:22
11 [R]Therefore let no one despise him. But send him on his journey [R]in peace, that he may come to me; for I am waiting for him with the brethren. 1 Tim. 4:12 • Acts 15:33
12 Now concerning *our* brother [R]Apollos, I strongly urged him to come to you with the brethren, but he was quite unwilling to come at this time; however, he will come when he has a convenient time. 1 Cor. 1:12; 3:5
13 [R]Watch, [R]stand fast in the faith, be brave, be strong. Matt. 24:42 • Phil. 1:27; 4:1
14 Let all *that* you *do* be done with love.
15 I urge you, brethren—you know the household of Stephanas, that it is the firstfruits of Achaia, and *that* they have devoted themselves to the ministry of the saints—
16 that you also submit to such, and to everyone who works and labors with *us*.
17 I am glad about the coming of Stephanas, Fortunatus, and Achaicus, [R]for what was lacking on your part they supplied. 2 Cor. 11:9
18 [R]For they refreshed my spirit and yours. Therefore acknowledge such men. Col. 4:8
19 The churches of Asia greet you. Aquila and Priscilla greet you heartily in the Lord, with the church that is in their house.
20 All the brethren greet you. [R]Greet one another with a holy kiss. Rom. 16:16
21 [R]The salutation with my own hand—Paul's. Col. 4:18
22 If anyone [R]does not love the Lord Jesus Christ, [R]let him be accursed.* [R]O Lord, come!* Eph. 6:24 • Gal. 1:8, 9 • Jude 14, 15
23 [R]The grace of our Lord Jesus Christ *be* with you. Rom. 16:20
24 My love *be* with you all in Christ Jesus. Amen.

16:22 Gr. *anathema* • Aram. *Marana tha;* possibly *Maran atha, Our Lord has come*

THE SECOND EPISTLE OF PAUL THE APOSTLE TO THE

CORINTHIANS

THE BOOK OF 2 CORINTHIANS

Since Paul's first letter, the Corinthian church had been swayed by false teachers who stirred the people against Paul. They claimed he was fickle, proud, unimpressive in appearance and speech, dishonest, and unqualified as an apostle of Jesus Christ. Paul sent Titus to Corinth to deal with these difficulties, and upon his return, rejoiced to hear of the Corinthians' change of heart. Paul wrote this letter to express his thanksgiving for the repentant majority and to appeal to the rebellious minority to accept his authority. Throughout the book he defends his conduct, character, and calling as an apostle of Jesus Christ.

To distinguish this epistle from 1 Corinthians, it was given the title *Pros Korinthious B,* the "Second to the Corinthians." The *A* and *B* were probably later additions to *Pros Korinthious.*

THE AUTHOR OF 2 CORINTHIANS

External and internal evidence amply support the Pauline authorship of this letter. As with Romans, the problem of 2 Corinthians is with its lack of unity, not with its authorship. Many critics theorize that chapters 10—13 were not a part of this letter in its original form because their tone contrasts with that of chapters 1—9. It is held that the sudden change from a spirit of joy and comfort to a spirit of concern and self-defense points to a "seam" between two different letters. Many hypotheses have been advanced to explain the problem, but the most popular is that chapters 10—13 belong to a lost letter referred to in 2:4. Several problems arise with these attempts to dissect 2 Corinthians. Chapters 10—13 do not fit Paul's description of the "lost" letter of 2:4 because they are firm but not sorrowful and because they do not refer to the offender about whom that letter was written (2:5–11). Also, this earlier material would have been appended at the beginning of 2 Corinthians, not at the end. There is simply no external (manuscripts, church fathers, tradition) or internal basis for challenging the unity of this epistle. The difference in tone between 1—9 and 10—13 is easily explained by the change of focus from the repentant majority to the rebellious minority.

THE TIME OF 2 CORINTHIANS

Part of the background of 2 Corinthians can be found in "The Time of 1 Corinthians." Paul was in Ephesus when he wrote 1 Corinthians and expected Timothy to visit Corinth and return to him (1 Cor. 16:10–11). Timothy apparently brought Paul a report of the opposition that had developed against him in Corinth, and Paul made a brief and painful visit to the Corinthians (this visit is not mentioned in Acts, but it can be inferred from 2 Cor. 2:1; 12:14; 13:1, 2). Upon returning to Ephesus, Paul regretfully wrote his sorrowful letter to urge the church to discipline the leader of the opposition (2:1–11; 7:8). Titus carried this letter. Paul, anxious to learn the results, went to Troas and then to Macedonia to meet Titus on his return trip (2:12, 13; 7:5–16). Paul was greatly relieved by Titus's report that the majority of the Corinthians had repented of their rebelliousness against Paul's apostolic authority. However, a minority opposition still persisted, evidently led by a group of Judaizers (10—13). There in Macedonia Paul wrote 2 Corinthians and sent it with Titus and another brother (8:16–24). This took place late in A.D. 56, and the Macedonian city from which it was written may have been Philippi. Paul then made his third trip to Corinth (12:14; 13:1, 2; Acts 20:1–3) where he wrote his letter to the Romans.

There is an alternate view that the anguished letter of 2:4 and 7:8 is, in fact, 1 Corinthians and not a lost letter. This would require that the offender of 2 Corinthians 2:5–11 and 7:12 be identified with the offender of 1 Corinthians 5.

THE CHRIST OF 2 CORINTHIANS

Christ is presented as the believer's comfort (1:5), triumph (2:14), Lord (4:5), light (4:6), judge (5:10), reconciliation (5:19), substitute (5:21), gift (9:15), owner (10:7), and power (12:9).

KEYS TO 2 CORINTHIANS

Key Word: Paul's Defense of His Ministry—The major theme of 2 Corinthians is Paul's defense of his apostolic credentials and authority. This is especially evident in the portion directed to the still rebellious minority (10—13), but the theme of vindication is also clear in chapters 1—9. Certain false apostles had mounted an effective campaign against Paul in the church at Corinth, and Paul was forced to take a number of steps to overcome the opposition. This epistle expresses the apostle's joy over the triumph of the true gospel in Corinth (1—7), and it acknowledges the godly sorrow and repentance of the bulk of the believers. It also urges the Corinthians to fulfill their promise of making a liberal contribution for the poor among the Christians in Judea (8 and 9). This collection would not only assist the poor, but it would also demonstrate the concern of Gentile Christians in Macedonia and Achaia for Jewish Christians in Judea, thus displaying the unity of Jews and Gentiles in the body of Christ.

The opposition addressed in chapters 10—13 apparently consists of Jews (Palestinian or Hellenistic; 11:22) who claim to be apostles (11:5, 13; 12:11) but who preach a false gospel (11:4) and are enslaving in their leadership (11:20). Chapters 10—13 are intended to expose these "false apostles" (11:13) and defend Paul's God-given authority and ministry as an apostle of Jesus Christ.

Key Verses: 2 Corinthians 4:5, 6 and 5:17–19—"For we do not preach ourselves, but Christ Jesus the Lord, and ourselves your bondservants for Jesus' sake. For it is the God who commanded light to shine out of darkness, who has shone in our hearts to *give* the light of the knowledge of the glory of God in the face of Jesus Christ" (4:5, 6).

"Therefore, if anyone *is* in Christ, *he is* a new creation; old things have passed away; behold, all things have become new. Now all things *are* of God, who has reconciled us to Himself through Jesus Christ, and has given us the ministry of reconciliation, that is, that God was in Christ reconciling the world to Himself, not imputing their trespasses to them, and has committed to us the word of reconciliation" (5:17–19).

Key Chapters: 2 Corinthians 8 and 9—Chapters 8 and 9 are really one unit and comprise the most complete revelation of God's plan for giving found anywhere in the Scriptures. Contained therein are the principles for giving (8:1–6), the purposes for giving (8:7–15), the policies to be followed in giving (8:16—9:5), and the promises to be realized in giving (9:6–15).

SURVEY OF 2 CORINTHIANS

Second Corinthians describes the anatomy of an apostle. The Corinthian church has been swayed by false teachers who have stirred the people against Paul, especially in response to 1 Corinthians, Paul's disciplinary letter. Throughout this letter (2 Corinthians) Paul defends his apostolic conduct, character, and call. The three major sections are: Paul's explanation of his ministry (1—7); Paul's collection for the saints (8 and 9); and Paul's vindication of his apostleship (10—13).

Paul's Explanation of His Ministry (1—7): After his salutation and thanksgiving for God's comfort in his afflictions and perils (1:1–11), Paul explains why he has delayed his planned visit to Corinth. It is not a matter of vacillation: the apostle wants them to have enough time to repent (1:12—2:4). Paul graciously asks them to restore the repentant offender to fellowship (2:5–13). At this point, Paul embarks on an extended defense of his ministry in terms of his message, circumstances, motives, and conduct (2:14—6:10). He then admonishes the believers to separate themselves from defilement (6:11—7:1) and expresses his comfort at Titus's news of their change of heart (7:2–16).

Paul's Collection for the Saints (8 and 9): This is the longest discussion of the principles and practice of giving in the New Testament. The example of the Macedonians' liberal giving for the needy brethren in Jerusalem (8:1–6) is followed by an appeal to the Corinthians to keep their promise by doing the same (8:7—9:15). In this connection, Paul commends the messengers he has sent to Corinth to make arrangements for the large gift they have promised. Their generosity will be more than amply rewarded by God.

Paul's Vindication of His Apostleship (10—13): Paul concludes this epistle with a defense of his apostolic authority and credentials

FOCUS	EXPLANATION OF PAUL'S MINISTRY			COLLECTION FOR THE SAINTS		VINDICATION OF PAUL'S APOSTLESHIP		
REFERENCE	1:1——2:14	——6:11	——8:1	——8:7	——10:1	——11:1	——12:14–13:14	
DIVISION	HIS CHANGE OF PLANS	PHILOSOPHY OF MINISTRY	EXHORTATIONS TO THE CORINTHIANS	EXAMPLE OF THE MACEDONIANS	EXHORTATION TO THE CORINTHIANS	ANSWERS HIS ACCUSERS	DEFENDS HIS APOSTLESHIP	ANNOUNCES HIS UPCOMING VISIT
TOPIC	CHARACTER OF PAUL			COLLECTION FOR SAINTS		CREDENTIALS OF PAUL		
	EPHESUS TO MACEDONIA: CHANGE OF ITINERARY			MACEDONIA: PREPARATION FOR VISIT		TO CORINTH: IMMINENT VISIT		
LOCATION	WRITTEN IN MACEDONIA							
TIME	C. A.D. 56							

that is directed to the still rebellious minority in the Corinthian church. His meekness in their presence in no way diminishes his authority as an apostle (10). To demonstrate his apostolic credentials, Paul is forced to boast about his knowledge, integrity, accomplishments, sufferings, visions, and miracles (11:1—12:13). He reveals his plans to visit them for the third time and urges them to repent so that he will not have to use severity when he comes (12:14—13:10). The letter ends with exhortations, greetings, and a benediction (13:11–14).

OUTLINE OF 2 CORINTHIANS

Part One: Paul's Explanation of His Ministry (1:1—7:16)

Part Two: Paul's Collection for the Saints (8:1—9:15)

Part Three: Paul's Vindication of His Apostleship (10:1—13:14)

CHAPTER 1

Paul's Thanksgiving to God

PAUL, an apostle of Jesus Christ by the will of God, and Timothy *our* brother,

To the church of God which is at Corinth, [R]with all the saints who are in all Achaia: Col. 1:2

2 [R]Grace to you and peace from God our Father and the Lord Jesus Christ. Rom. 1:7

3 [R]Blessed *be* the God and Father of our Lord Jesus Christ, the Father of mercies and God of all comfort, 1 Pet. 1:3

4 who comforts us in all our tribulation, that we may be able to comfort those who are in any trouble, with the comfort with which we ourselves are comforted by God.

5 For as [R]the sufferings of Christ abound in us, so our [T]consolation also abounds through Christ. 2 Cor. 4:10 • *comfort*

6 Now if we are afflicted, [R]*it is* for your consolation and salvation, which is effective for enduring the same sufferings which we also suffer. Or if we are comforted, *it is* for your consolation and salvation. 2 Cor. 4:15

7 And our hope for you *is* steadfast, because we know that [R]as you are partakers of the sufferings, so also *you will partake* of the consolation. [Rom. 8:17]

Paul's Trouble in Asia

8 For we do not want you to be ignorant, brethren, of [R]our [T]trouble which came to us in Asia: that we were burdened beyond measure, above strength, so that we despaired even of life. Acts 19:23 • *tribulation*

9 Yes, we had the sentence of death in ourselves, that we should not trust in ourselves but in God who raises the dead,

10 [R]who delivered us from so great a death, and does* deliver us; in whom we trust that He will still deliver *us*, [2 Pet. 2:9]

11 you also [R]helping together in prayer for us, that thanks may be given by many persons on our* behalf [R]for the gift *granted* to us through many. Rom. 15:30 • 2 Cor. 4:15; 9:11

Paul's Original Plan

12 For our boasting is this: the testimony of our conscience that we conducted ourselves in the world in simplicity and [R]godly sincerity, [R]not with fleshly wisdom but by the grace of God, and more abundantly toward you. 2 Cor. 2:17 • [1 Cor. 2:4]

13 For we are not writing any other things to you than what you read or understand. Now I trust you will understand, even to the end

14 (as also you have understood us in part), that we are your boast as you also *are* ours, in the day of the Lord Jesus.

15 And in this confidence [R]I intended to come to you before, that you might have [R]a second benefit— 1 Cor. 4:19 • Rom. 1:11; 15:29

16 to pass by way of you to Macedonia, to come again from Macedonia to you, and be helped by you on my way to Judea.

17 Therefore, when I was planning this, did I do it lightly? Or the things I plan, do I plan [R]according to the flesh, that with me there should be Yes, Yes, and No, No? 2 Cor. 10:2

18 But *as* God *is* [R]faithful, our [T]word to you was not Yes and No. 1 John 5:20 • *message*

19 For [R]the Son of God, Jesus Christ, who was preached among you by us—by me, [R]Silvanus, and Timothy—was not Yes and No, but in Him was Yes. Mark 1:1 • 1 Pet. 5:12

20 [R]For all the promises of God in Him *are* Yes, and in Him Amen, to the glory of God through us. [Rom. 15:8, 9]

21 Now He who establishes us with you in Christ and has anointed us *is* God,

22 who also has sealed us and given us the Spirit in our hearts as a guarantee.

Paul's Change of Plans

23 Moreover [R]I call God as witness against my soul, [R]that to spare you I came no more to Corinth. Gal. 1:20 • 1 Cor. 4:21

24 Not [R]that we have dominion over your faith, but are fellow workers for your joy; for [R]by faith you stand. [1 Pet. 5:3] • Rom. 11:20

CHAPTER 2

BUT I determined this within myself, [R]that I would not come again to you in sorrow. 2 Cor. 1:23

2 For if I make you [R]sorrowful, then who is he who makes me glad but the one who is made sorrowful by me? 2 Cor. 7:8

3 And I wrote this very thing to you, lest, when I came, [R]I should have sorrow over those from whom I ought to have joy, [R]having confidence in you all that my joy is *the joy* of you all. 2 Cor. 12:21 • Gal. 5:10

4 For out of much [T]affliction and anguish of heart I wrote to you, with many tears, [R]not that you should be grieved, but that you might know the love which I have so abundantly for you. *tribulation* • [2 Cor. 2:9; 7:8, 12]

Paul's Appeal to Forgive

5 But [R]if anyone has caused grief, he has not grieved me, but all of you to some extent—not to be too severe. [1 Cor. 5:1]

6 This punishment which *was inflicted* by the majority *is* sufficient for such a man,

7 [R]so that, on the contrary, you *ought* rather to forgive and comfort *him*, lest perhaps such a one be swallowed up with too much sorrow. Gal. 6:1

1:10 NU *shall* **1:11** M *your behalf*

8 Therefore I urge you to reaffirm *your* love
to him.
9 For to this end I also wrote, that I might
put you to the test, whether you are [R]obedient
in all things. 2 Cor. 7:15; 10:6
10 Now whom you forgive anything, I also
forgive. For if indeed I have forgiven any-
thing, I have forgiven that one* for your sakes
in the presence of Christ,
11 lest Satan should take advantage of us;
for we are not ignorant of his devices.
12 Furthermore, [R]when I came to Troas to
preach Christ's gospel, and a door was
opened to me by the Lord, Acts 16:8
13 I had no rest in my spirit, because I did
not find Titus my brother; but taking my leave
of them, I departed for Macedonia.

Christ Causes Us to Triumph

14 Now thanks *be* to God who always leads
us in triumph in Christ, and through us [T]dif-
fuses the fragrance of His knowledge in every
place. *manifests*
15 For we are to God the fragrance of Christ
among those who are being saved and among
those who are perishing.
16 [R]To the one *we are* the aroma of death
leading to death, and to the other the aroma of
life *leading* to life. And [R]who *is* sufficient for
these things? Luke 2:34 • [1 Cor. 15:10]
17 For we are not, as so many,* [R]peddling[T]
the word of God; but as [R]of sincerity, but as
from God, we speak in the sight of God in
Christ. 2 Pet. 2:3 • *adulterating for gain* • 2 Cor. 1:12

CHAPTER 3

Changed Lives Prove Ministry

DO we begin again to commend ourselves?
Or do we need, as some *others,* [R]epistles
of commendation to you or *letters* of com-
mendation from you? Acts 18:27
2 You are our epistle written in our hearts,
known and read by all men;
3 clearly *you are* an epistle of Christ, [R]min-
istered by us, written not with ink but by the
Spirit of the living God, not [R]on tablets of
stone but on tablets of flesh, *that is,* of the
heart. 1 Cor. 3:5 • Ex. 24:12; 31:18
4 And we have such trust through Christ to-
ward God.
5 Not that we are sufficient of ourselves to
think of anything as *being* from ourselves, but
our sufficiency *is* from God,

New Covenant Is the Basis of Ministry

6 who also made us sufficient as [R]ministers
of [R]the new covenant, not of the letter but of
the Spirit;* for the letter kills, but the Spirit
gives life. 1 Cor. 3:5 • Jer. 31:31
7 But if [R]the ministry of death, [R]written
and engraved on stones, was glorious, [R]so
that the children of Israel could not look
steadily at the face of Moses because of the
glory of his countenance, which *glory* was
passing away, Rom. 7:10 • Ex. 34:1 • Ex. 34:29
8 how will [R]the ministry of the Spirit not be
more glorious? [Gal. 3:5]
9 For if the ministry of condemnation *had*
glory, the ministry [R]of righteousness exceeds
much more in glory. [Rom. 1:17; 3:21]
10 For even what was made glorious had no
glory in this respect, because of the glory that
excels.
11 For if what is passing away *was* glorious,
what remains *is* much more glorious.
12 Therefore, since we have such hope, [R]we
use great boldness of speech— Eph. 6:19
13 unlike Moses, [R]*who* put a veil over his
face so that the children of Israel could not
look steadily at [R]the end of what was passing
away. Ex. 34:33–35 • [Gal. 3:23]
14 [R]But their minds were blinded. For until
this day the same veil remains unlifted in the
reading of the Old Testament, because the *veil*
is taken away in Christ. Is. 29:10★

2:10 NU *For indeed, what I have forgiven, if I have forgiven anything, I did it for your sakes* **2:17** M *the rest* **3:6** Or *spirit*

2:11 Satan: Strategies of Satan—Some of the strategies of Satan are suggested by his many names:

a. The devil (Page 1274—James 4:7). He slanders God to people. He slanders people to God. He slanders people to one another and to themselves.
b. The wicked one (Page 1209—Eph. 6:16). He is out to harm people and create havoc in the natural, political, and social world.
c. The tempter (Page 1227—1 Thess. 3:5). He presents a false but appealing set of plausible reasons and advantages for sinning.
d. The god of this age (Page 1186—2 Cor. 4:4). He is the supernatural motivation for the secular and religious systems of thought that oppose biblical truth.
e. The ruler of this world (Page 1097—John 12:31). Satan has great influence over unrighteous political systems. Totalitarian power, injustice, oppression, and greed are among his trademarks.
f. The prince of the power of the air (Page 1205—Eph. 2:2). He directs the activity of his army of fallen angels who conspire to tempt, deceive, and corrupt in a seemingly endless variety of ways.

At a personal level, Satan appeals to men and women 1) by urging that there is a better way than God's way in the immediate situation, 2) by reminding how often they have failed in the past at this point, 3) by insinuating how pleasant sin will be, 4) by promoting the merits of hatred, bitterness, and revenge, 5) by advocating power over love, and 6) by urging them to destroy their enemies.

Now turn to Page 1006—Matt. 25:41: Satan: Destiny of Satan.

15 But even to this day, when Moses is read, a veil lies on their heart.

16 Nevertheless when one turns to the Lord, [R]the veil is taken away. Is. 25:7

17 Now the Lord is the Spirit; and where the Spirit of the Lord *is,* there *is* liberty.

18 But we all, with unveiled face, beholding [R]as in a mirror [R]the glory of the Lord, [R]are being transformed into the same image from glory to glory, just as by the Spirit of the Lord. 1 Cor. 13:12 • [2 Cor. 4:4, 6] • [Rom. 8:29, 30]

CHAPTER 4

Christ Is the Theme of Ministry

THEREFORE, since we have this ministry, [R]as we have received mercy, we [R]do not lose heart. 1 Cor. 7:25 • 2 Cor. 4:16

2 But we have renounced the hidden things of shame, not walking in craftiness nor handling the word of God deceitfully, but by manifestation of the truth [R]commending ourselves to every man's conscience in the sight of God. 2 Cor. 5:11

3 But even if our gospel is veiled, it is veiled to those who are perishing,

4 whose minds the god of this age has blinded, who do not believe, lest the light of the gospel of the glory of Christ, who is the image of God, should shine on them.

5 [R]For we do not preach ourselves, but Christ Jesus the Lord, and ourselves your bondservants for Jesus' sake. 1 Cor. 1:13

6 For it is the God [R]who commanded light to shine out of darkness, who has [R]shone in our hearts to *give* the light of the knowledge of the glory of God in the face of Jesus Christ. Gen. 1:3 • 2 Pet. 1:19

7 But we have this treasure in earthen vessels, [R]that the excellence of the power may be of God and not of us. 1 Cor. 2:5

Trials Abound in the Ministry

8 *We are* [R]hard-pressed on every side, yet not crushed; *we are* perplexed, but not in despair; 2 Cor. 1:8; 7:5

9 persecuted, but not forsaken; [R]struck down, but not destroyed— Ps. 37:24

10 always carrying about in the body the dying of the Lord Jesus, that the life of Jesus also may be manifested in our body.

11 For we who live are always delivered to death for Jesus' sake, that the life of Jesus also may be manifested in our mortal flesh.

12 So then death is working in us, but life in you.

13 And since we have [R]the same spirit of faith, according to what is written, *"I believed and therefore I spoke,"** we also believe and therefore speak, 2 Pet. 1:1

14 knowing that [R]He who raised up the Lord Jesus will also raise us up with Jesus, and will present *us* with you. [Rom. 8:11]

15 For [R]all things *are* for your sakes, that [R]grace, having spread through the many, may cause thanksgiving to abound to the glory of God. Col. 1:24 • 2 Cor. 1:11

Motivation of External Perspective

16 Therefore we [R]do not lose heart. Even though our outward man is perishing, yet the inward *man* is [R]being renewed day by day. 2 Cor. 4:1 • [Is. 40:29, 31]

17 For our light affliction, which is but for a moment, is working for us a far more exceeding *and* eternal weight of glory,

18 [R]while we do not look at the things which are seen, but at the things which are not seen. For the things which are seen *are* temporary, but the things which are not seen *are* eternal. [Heb. 11:1, 13]

CHAPTER 5

Motivation of the Future Presence of Christ

FOR we know that if [R]our earthly house, *this* tent, is destroyed, we have a building from God, a house [R]not made with hands, eternal in the heavens. Job 4:19 • Mark 14:58

2 For in this [R]we groan, earnestly desiring to be clothed with our [T]habitation which is from heaven, Rom. 8:23 • *dwelling*

3 if indeed, [R]having been clothed, we shall not be found naked. Rev. 3:18

4 For we who are in *this* tent groan, being burdened, not because we want to be unclothed, [R]but further clothed, that mortality may be swallowed up by life. 1 Cor. 15:53

5 Now He who has prepared us for this very thing *is* God, who also [R]has given us the Spirit as a guarantee. Rom. 8:23

6 So *we are* always confident, knowing that while we are at home in the body we are absent from the Lord.

7 For we walk by faith, not by sight.

8 We are confident, yes, [R]well pleased rather to be absent from the body and to be present with the Lord. Phil. 1:23

Motivation of Future Reward

9 Therefore we make it our aim, whether present or absent, to be well pleasing to Him.

10 [R]For we must all appear before the judgment seat of Christ, [R]that each one may receive the things *done* in the body, according to what he has done, whether good or bad. Rom. 2:16; 14:10, 12 • Eph. 6:8☆

Motivation of the Love of Christ

11 Knowing, therefore, [R]the terror of the Lord, we persuade men; but we are well known to God, and I also trust are well known in your consciences. [Heb. 10:31]

12 For [R]we do not commend ourselves again

4:13 Ps. 116:10

to you, but give you opportunity [R]to boast on
our behalf, that you may have *an answer* for
those who boast in appearance and not in
heart. 2 Cor. 3:1 • 2 Cor. 1:14
13 For if we are beside ourselves, *it is* for
God; or if we are of sound mind, *it is* for you.
14 For the love of Christ compels us, because
we judge thus: that [R]if One died for all, then
all died; [Rom. 5:15; 6:6]
15 and He died for all, that those who live
should live no longer for themselves, but for
Him who died for them and rose again.
16 Therefore, from now on, we regard no
one according to the flesh. Even though we
have known Christ according to the flesh, yet
now we know *Him thus* no longer.

Motivation of the Message of Reconciliation

17 Therefore, if anyone *is* in Christ, *he is* a
new creation; old things have passed away;
behold, all things have become new.

18 Now all things *are* of God, [R]who has rec-
onciled us to Himself through Jesus Christ,
and has given us the ministry of reconcilia-
tion, Rom. 5:10
19 that is, that [R]God was in Christ reconcil-
ing the world to Himself, not imputing their
trespasses to them, and has committed to us
the word of reconciliation. [Rom. 3:24]
20 Now then, we are [R]ambassadors for
Christ, as though God were pleading through
us: we implore *you* on Christ's behalf, be rec-
onciled to God. Eph. 6:20
21 For [R]He made Him who knew no sin *to be*
sin for us, that we might become the righ-
teousness of God in Him. Is. 53:6, 9★

CHAPTER 6

Giving No Offense in the Ministry

WE then, *as* [R]workers together *with Him*
also [R]plead with *you* not to receive the
grace of God in vain. 1 Cor. 3:9 • 2 Cor. 5:20
2 For He says:

"In an acceptable time I have heard you,
And in the day of salvation I have
*helped you."**

Behold, now *is* the accepted time; behold, now
is the day of salvation.
3 [R]We give no offense in anything, that our
ministry may not be blamed. Rom. 14:13
4 But in all *things* we commend ourselves
as ministers of God: in much patience, in
tribulations, in needs, in distresses,
5 [R]in stripes, in imprisonments, in tumults, in
labors, in sleeplessness, in fastings; 2 Cor. 11:23
6 by purity, by knowledge, by longsuffer-
ing, by kindness, by the Holy Spirit, by [T]sin-
cere love, Lit. *unhypocritical*
7 [R]by the word of truth, by the power of
God, by the armor of righteousness on the
right hand and on the left, 2 Cor. 7:14
8 by honor and dishonor, by evil report and
good report; as deceivers, and *yet* true;
9 as unknown, and [R]*yet* well known; as
dying, and behold we live; [R]as chastened, and
yet not killed; 2 Cor. 4:2; 5:11 • Ps. 118:18
10 as sorrowful, yet always rejoicing; as
poor, yet making many rich; as having noth-
ing, and *yet* possessing all things.

Paul's Appeal for Reconciliation

11 O Corinthians! We have spoken openly to
you, [R]our heart is wide open. 2 Cor. 7:3
12 You are not restricted by us, but you are
restricted by your *own* affections.
13 Now in return for the same [R](I speak as to
children), you also be open. 1 Cor. 4:14

Paul's Appeal for Separation from Unbelievers

14 Do not be unequally yoked together with
unbelievers. For what fellowship has righ-
teousness with lawlessness? And what com-
munion has light with darkness?
15 And what accord has Christ with Belial?
Or what part has a believer with an unbeliever?
16 And what agreement has the temple of
God with idols? For you* are the temple of the
living God. As God has said:

"I will dwell in them
And walk among them.

6:2 Is. 49:8★ **6:16** NU *we*

5:17 New Nature—The term "new nature" refers to the spiritual transformation that occurs within the individual when a person believes in Christ as Savior. The Christian becomes a "new man" (Page 1152—Rom. 6:6; Page 1205—Eph. 2:15; 4:22–24; Page 1221—Col. 3:9, 10). This concept of *newness* may be traced to an important choice between two Greek words, both meaning "new." One word means "new" in the sense of renovation (to repair), the other in the sense of fresh existence. The latter is used to describe the Christian. The Christian is not a renovated or refreshed version of the old; rather, the Christian is brand-new with a new family, a new set of values, new motivations, and new possessions.

The "old man" is still present in the new life and expresses himself in corrupting deeds such as lying (Page 1207—Eph. 4:22; Page 1221—Col. 3:9). The "new man," to be visible, must be *put on* as one would put on a new suit of clothes (Page 1221—Col. 3:10). In other words, the new nature must be cultivated or nurtured by spiritual decisiveness to grow in Christ. We must not revert to putting on the old suit of the former life; rather, we must continue to grow in this new life (Page 1208—Eph. 5:8).

The message of the new nature is a message of supreme hope: the Spirit of God can accomplish a life-changing transformation for all who will only believe in Christ.

Now turn to Page 738—Is. 61:10: Christ's Righteousness.

I will be their God,
*And they shall be My people."**
17 Therefore

"Come out from among them
And be separate, says the Lord.
Do not touch what is unclean,
*And I will receive you."**
18*"I will be a Father to you,*
And you shall be My [R]sons and
daughters, [Rom. 8:14]
*Says the LORD Almighty."**

CHAPTER 7

THEREFORE,[R] having these promises,
beloved, let us cleanse ourselves from all
filthiness of the flesh and spirit, perfecting ho-
liness in the fear of God. [1 John 3:3]

Paul's Meeting with Titus

2 Open *your hearts* to us. We have wronged
no one, we have corrupted no one, [R]we have
cheated no one. Acts 20:33
3 I do not say *this* to condemn; for [R]I have
said before that you are in our hearts, to die
together and to live together. 2 Cor. 6:11, 12
4 Great *is* my boldness of speech toward
you, great *is* my boasting on your behalf. [R]I
am filled with comfort. I am exceedingly joy-
ful in all our tribulation. Phil. 2:17
5 For indeed, [R]when we came to Macedo-
nia, our bodies had no rest, but we were trou-
bled on every side. [R]Outside *were* conflicts,
inside *were* fears. 2 Cor. 2:13 • Deut. 32:25
6 Nevertheless [R]God, who comforts the
downcast, comforted us by [R]the coming of Ti-
tus, 2 Cor. 1:3, 4 • 2 Cor. 2:13; 7:13
7 and not only by his coming, but also by
the [T]consolation with which he was comforted
in you, when he told us of your earnest desire,
your mourning, your zeal for me, so that I re-
joiced even more. comfort

Corinthians' Response to Paul's Letter

8 For even if I made you sorry with my let-
ter, I do not regret it; though I did regret it. For
I perceive that the same epistle made you
sorry, though only for a while.
9 Now I rejoice, not that you were made
sorry, but that your sorrow led to repentance.
For you were made sorry in a godly manner,
that you might suffer loss from us in noth-
ing.
10 For godly sorrow produces repentance
leading to salvation, not to be regretted; but
the sorrow of the world produces death.
11 For observe this very thing, that you sor-
rowed in a godly manner: What diligence it
produced in you, *what* [R]clearing *of your-*
selves, what indignation, *what* fear, *what* ve-
hement desire, *what* zeal, *what* vindication!
In all *things* you proved yourselves to be
[R]clear in this matter. Eph. 5:11 • 2 Cor. 2:5–11
12 Therefore, although I wrote to you, *I did*
not *do it* for the sake of him who had done the
wrong, nor for the sake of him who suffered
wrong, [R]but that our care for you in the sight
of God might appear to you. 2 Cor. 2:4
13 Therefore we have been comforted in
your comfort. And we rejoiced exceedingly
more for the joy of Titus, because his spirit
[R]has been refreshed by you all. Rom. 15:32
14 For if in anything I have boasted to him
about you, I am not ashamed. But as we spoke
all things to you in truth, even so our boasting
to Titus was found true.
15 And his affections are greater for you as
he remembers the obedience of you all, how
with fear and trembling you received him.
16 Therefore I rejoice that [R]I have confi-
dence in you in everything. 2 Thess. 3:4

CHAPTER 8

Example of the Macedonians

MOREOVER, brethren, we make known to
you the grace of God bestowed on the
churches of Macedonia:
2 that in a great trial of affliction the
abundance of their joy and [R]their deep
poverty abounded in the riches of their liber-
ality. Mark 12:44
3 For I bear witness that according to *their*
ability, yes, and beyond *their* ability, *they*
were freely willing,
4 imploring us with much urgency that we
would receive* the gift and the fellowship of
the ministering to the saints.
5 And not *only* as we had hoped, but they
first [R]gave themselves to the Lord, and *then* to
us by the will of God. [Rom. 12:1, 2]
6 So [R]we urged Titus, that as he had begun,
so he would also complete this grace in you as
well. 2 Cor. 8:17; 12:18

Example of Christ

7 But as [R]you abound in everything—in
faith, in speech, in knowledge, in all diligence,
and in your love for us—*see* that you abound
in this grace also. [1 Cor. 1:5; 12:13]
8 [R]I speak not by commandment, but I am
testing the sincerity of your love by the dili-
gence of others. 1 Cor. 7:6
9 For you know the grace of our Lord Jesus
Christ, that though He was rich, yet for your
sakes He became poor, that you through His
poverty might become rich.

6:16 Lev. 26:12; Jer. 32:38; Ezek. 37:27 **6:17** Is. 52:11; Ezek. 20:34, 41 **6:18** 2 Sam. 7:14 **8:4** NU, M omit *that we would receive,* thus changing text to *urgency for the favor and fellowship . . . .*

Purpose of Giving

10 And in this I give advice: It is to your advantage not only to be doing what you began and were desiring to do a year ago;
11 but now you also must complete the doing *of it;* that as *there was* a readiness to desire *it*, so *there* also *may be* a completion out of what *you* have.
12 For if there is first a willing mind, *it is* accepted according to what one has, *and* not according to what he does not have.
13 For *I do* not *mean* that others should be eased and you burdened;
14 but by an equality, *that* now at this time your abundance *may supply* their lack, that their abundance also may supply your lack—that there may be equality.
15 As it is written, *"He who gathered much had nothing left over, and he who gathered little had no lack."**

Policies in Giving

16 But thanks *be* to God who puts* the same earnest care for you into the heart of Titus.
17 For he not only accepted the exhortation, but being more diligent, he went to you of his own accord.
18 And we have sent with him [R]the brother whose praise *is* in the gospel throughout all the churches, 2 Cor. 12:18
19 and not only *that*, but who was also [R]chosen by the churches to travel with us with this gift, which is administered by us [R]to the glory of the Lord Himself and *to show* your ready mind, 1 Cor. 16:3, 4 • 2 Cor. 4:15
20 avoiding this: that anyone should blame us in this lavish gift which is administered by us—
21 [R]providing honorable things, not only in the sight of the Lord, but also in the sight of men. Rom. 12:17
22 And we have sent with them our brother whom we have often proved diligent in many things, but now much more diligent, because of the great confidence which *we have* in you.
23 If *anyone inquires* about [R]Titus, *he is* my partner and fellow worker concerning you. Or if our brethren *are inquired about, they are* [R]messengers of the churches, the glory of Christ. 2 Cor. 7:13, 14 • Phil. 2:25
24 Therefore show to them, and* before the churches, the proof of your love and of our [R]boasting on your behalf. 2 Cor. 7:4, 14

CHAPTER 9

Readiness in Giving

NOW concerning [R]the ministering to the saints, it is superfluous for me to write to you; Gal. 2:10
2 for I know your willingness, about which I boast of you to the Macedonians, that Achaia was ready a [R]year ago; and your zeal has stirred up the majority. 2 Cor. 8:10
3 Yet I have sent the brethren, lest our boasting of you should be in vain in this respect, that, as I said, you may be ready;
4 lest if *some* Macedonians come with me and find you unprepared, we (not to mention you!) should be ashamed of this confident boasting.*
5 Therefore I thought it necessary to [T]exhort the brethren to go to you ahead of time, and prepare your generous gift beforehand, which *you had* previously promised, that it may be ready as *a matter of* generosity and not as a grudging obligation. *encourage*

Principles in Giving

6 But this *I say:* He who sows sparingly will also reap sparingly, and he who sows bountifully will also reap bountifully.
7 *So let* each one *give* as he purposes in his heart, [R]not grudgingly or of necessity; for God loves a cheerful giver. Deut. 15:7

Promises from Giving

8 And God *is* able to make all grace abound toward you, that you, always having all sufficiency in all *things*, may have an abundance for every good work.

8:15 Ex. 16:18 **8:16** NU *has put* **8:24** NU, M omit *and* **9:4** NU *this confidence.*

9:6–8 Giving—There is no better indicator of growth in the new life than in the area of giving. This passage deals with the attitude one should have in giving—it should be cheerful. When giving is cheerful, it will also be generous. The important rule of thumb is not how much is given, but how much is left after the giving. God is not primarily occupied with the amount of the gift, but with the motive that lies behind it. All the money in the world belongs to God. My gift to Him does not make Him any richer; it makes me richer spiritually because of the realization that everything I have is His and that I am giving because I love Him and want to give.

The formula for giving is found in 1 Cor. 16:2 where three principles can be seen: (1) my giving is to be regular, "on the first *day* of the week"; (2) my giving is to be systematic, "let each one of you lay something aside"; and (3) my giving is to be proportionate, "as he may prosper."

Failure to give of the money that God has given is a serious matter. People who fail to honor God with their money actually rob God (Page 969—Mal. 3:8), not because it impoverishes God but because it denies the God-ordained means for the support of His work and His ministers. For the children of God who honor God with their money God promises abundant blessing (Page 969—Mal. 3:10; Page 1049—Luke 6:38) and the provision of his every need (Page 1216—Phil. 4:19). Giving, then, is a key to growth in the new life.

Now turn to Page 416—1 Chr. 16:29: The Meaning of Worship.

9 As it is written:

"He has dispersed abroad,
He has given to the poor;
*His righteousness endures forever."**

10 Now may* He who [R]supplies seed to the
sower, and bread for food, supply and multi-
ply the seed you have *sown* and increase the
fruits of your righteousness, Is. 55:10
11 while *you are* enriched in everything for
all liberality, [R]which causes thanksgiving
through us to God. 2 Cor. 1:11
12 For the administration of this service not
only [R]supplies the needs of the saints, but also
is abounding through many thanksgivings to
God, 2 Cor. 8:14
13 while, through the proof of this min-
istry, they [R]glorify God for the obedience of
your confession to the gospel of Christ, and
for *your* liberal [R]sharing with them and all
men, [Matt. 5:16] • [Heb. 13:16]
14 and by their prayer for you, who long for
you because of the exceeding [R]grace of God in
you. 2 Cor. 8:1
15 Thanks *be* to God [R]for His indescribable
gift! [James 1:17]

CHAPTER 10

The Charge of Cowardice Is Answered

NOW I, Paul, myself am pleading with
you by the meekness and gentleness of
Christ—who in presence *am* lowly among
you, but being absent am bold toward you.
2 But I beg *you* [R]that when I am present I may
not be bold with that confidence by which I in-
tend to be bold against some, who think of us as
if we walked according to the flesh. 1 Cor. 4:21

The Charge of Walking in the Flesh Is Answered

3 For though we walk in the flesh, we do not
war according to the flesh.
4 [R]For the weapons [R]of our warfare *are* not
carnal but mighty in God [R]for pulling down
strongholds, Eph. 6:13 • 1 Tim. 1:18 • Jer. 1:10
5 casting down arguments and every high
thing that exalts itself against the knowledge
of God, bringing every thought into captivity
to the obedience of Christ,
6 and being ready to punish all disobedi-
ence when your obedience is fulfilled.
7 Do you look at things according to the
outward appearance? If anyone is convinced
in himself that he is Christ's, let him again
consider this in himself, that just as he *is*
Christ's, even so we *are* Christ's.*
8 For even if I should boast somewhat more
about our authority, which the Lord gave us*
for edification and not for your destruction, I
shall not be ashamed—
9 lest I seem to terrify you by letters.

The Charge of Personal Weakness Is Answered

10 "For *his* letters," they say, "*are* weighty
and powerful, but *his* bodily presence *is* weak,
and *his* speech contemptible."
11 Let such a person consider this, that what
we are in word by letters when we are absent,
such *we will* also *be* in deed when we are
present.
12 [R]For we dare not class ourselves or com-
pare ourselves with those who commend
themselves. But they, measuring themselves
by themselves, and comparing themselves
among themselves, are not wise. 2 Cor. 5:12
13 [R]We, however, will not boast beyond
measure, but within the limits of the sphere
which God appointed us—a sphere which
especially includes you. 2 Cor. 10:15
14 For we are not overextending ourselves
(as though *our authority* did not extend to
you), [R]for it was to you that we came with the
gospel of Christ; 1 Cor. 3:5, 6
15 not boasting of things beyond measure,
that is, [R]in other men's labors, but having hope,
that as your faith is increased, we shall be
greatly enlarged by you in our sphere, Rom. 15:20
16 to preach the gospel in the *regions* be-
yond you, *and* not to boast in another man's
sphere of accomplishment.
17 But *"he who glories, let him glory in the*
*LORD."**
18 For not he who commends himself is ap-
proved, but whom the Lord commends.

CHAPTER 11

Paul's Declaration of His Apostleship

OH, that you would bear with me in a lit-
tle [R]folly—and indeed you do bear with
me. 2 Cor. 11:4, 16, 19
2 For I am jealous for you with godly jeal-
ousy. For [R]I have betrothed you to one hus-
band, that I may present *you* [R]*as* a chaste
virgin to Christ. Hos. 2:19 • Lev. 21:13
3 But I fear, lest somehow, as [R]the serpent
deceived Eve by his craftiness, so your minds
[R]may be corrupted from the simplicity* that is
in Christ. Gen. 3:4, 13 • Eph. 6:24
4 For if he who comes preaches another Je-
sus whom we have not preached, or *if* you re-
ceive a different spirit which you have not
received, or a [R]different gospel which you
have not accepted—you may well put up with
it! Gal. 1:6–8
5 For I consider that I am not at all inferior
to the most eminent apostles.
6 Even though [R]*I am* untrained in speech,
yet *I am* not [R]in knowledge. But [R]we have

9:9 Ps. 112:9 **9:10** NU *Now He who supplies . . . will supply . . . .* **10:7** NU *even as we are.* **10:8** NU omits *us* **10:17** Jer. 9:24 **11:3** NU adds *and purity*

been thoroughly manifested* among you in all things. [1 Cor. 1:17] • [Eph. 3:4] • [2 Cor. 12:12]

7 Did I commit sin in [T]humbling myself that you might be exalted, because I preached the gospel of God to you [R]free of charge? *putting myself down* • 1 Cor. 9:18

8 I robbed other churches, taking wages *from them* to minister to you.

9 And when I was present with you, and in need, [R]I was a burden to no one, for what I lacked [R]the brethren who came from Macedonia supplied. And in everything I kept myself from being burdensome to you, and so I will keep *myself.* Acts 20:33 • Phil. 4:10

10 [R]As the truth of Christ is in me, [R]no one shall stop me from this boasting in the regions of Achaia. Rom. 1:9; 9:1 • 1 Cor. 9:15

11 Why? [R]Because I do not love you? God knows! 2 Cor. 6:11; 12:15

12 But what I do, I will also continue to do, [R]that I may cut off the opportunity from those who desire an opportunity to be regarded just as we are in the things of which they boast. 1 Cor. 9:12

13 For such [R]*are* false apostles, [R]deceitful workers, transforming themselves into apostles of Christ. Phil. 1:15 • Phil. 3:2

14 And no wonder! For Satan himself transforms himself into an angel of light.

15 Therefore *it is* no great thing if his ministers also transform themselves into ministers of righteousness, [R]whose end will be according to their works. [Phil. 3:19]

Paul's Sufferings Support His Apostleship

16 I say again, let no one think me a fool. If otherwise, at least receive me as a fool, that I also may boast a little.

17 What I speak, [R]I speak not according to the Lord, but as it were, foolishly, in this confidence of boasting. 1 Cor. 7:6

18 Seeing that many boast according to the flesh, I also will boast.

19 For you put up with fools gladly, [R]since you *yourselves* are wise! 1 Cor. 4:10

20 For you put up with it [R]if one brings you into bondage, if one devours *you,* if one takes *from you,* if one exalts himself, if one strikes you on the face. [Gal. 2:4; 4:3, 9; 5:1]

21 To *our* shame I say that we were too weak for that! But in whatever anyone is bold—I speak foolishly—I am bold also.

22 Are they [R]Hebrews? So *am* I. Are they Israelites? So *am* I. Are they the seed of Abraham? So *am* I. Phil. 3:4–6

23 Are they ministers of Christ?—I speak as a fool—I *am* more: in labors more abundant, in stripes above measure, in prisons more frequently, in deaths often.

24 From the Jews five times I received [R]forty *stripes* minus one. Deut. 25:3

25 Three times I was [R]beaten with rods; [R]once I was stoned; three times I was shipwrecked; a night and a day I have been in the deep; Acts 16:22, 23; 21:32 • Acts 14:5, 19

26 *in* journeys often, *in* perils of waters, *in* perils of robbers, [R]*in* perils of *my own* countrymen, *in* perils of the Gentiles, *in* perils in the city, *in* perils in the wilderness, *in* perils in the sea, *in* perils among false brethren; Acts 9:23, 24; 13:45, 50; 17:5, 13

27 in weariness and toil, [R]in sleeplessness often, in hunger and thirst, in fastings often, in cold and nakedness— Acts 20:31

28 besides the other things, what comes upon me daily: [R]my deep concern for all the churches. Acts 20:18

29 [R]Who is weak, and I am not weak? Who is made to stumble, and I do not burn *with indignation?* [1 Cor. 8:9, 13; 9:22]

30 If I must boast, I will boast in the things which concern my infirmity.

31 [R]The God and Father of our Lord Jesus Christ, [R]who is blessed forever, knows that I am not lying. 1 Thess. 2:5 • Rom. 9:5

32 [R]In Damascus the governor, under Aretas the king, was guarding the city of the Damascenes with a garrison, desiring to arrest me; Acts 9:19–25

33 but I was let down in a basket through a window in the wall, and escaped from his hands.

CHAPTER 12

Vision of Paradise

IT is doubtless* not profitable for me to boast. I will come to visions and [R]revelations of the Lord: [Gal. 1:12; 2:2]

2 I know a man [R]in Christ who fourteen years ago—whether in the body I do not know, or whether out of the body I do not know, God knows—such a one [R]was caught up to the third heaven. Rom. 16:7 • Acts 22:17

3 And I know such a man—whether in the body or out of the body I do not know, God knows—

4 how he was caught up into [R]Paradise and heard inexpressible words, which it is not lawful for a man to utter. Luke 23:43

5 Of such a one I will boast; yet of myself I will not boast, except in my infirmities.

6 For though I might desire to boast, I will not be a fool; for I will speak the truth. But I refrain, lest anyone should think of me above what he sees me *to be* or hears from me.

Thorn in the Flesh

7 And lest I should be exalted above measure by the abundance of the revelations, a [R]thorn in the flesh was given to me, [R]a messenger of Satan to buffet me, lest I be exalted above measure. Ezek. 28:24 • Job 2:7

11:6 NU omits *been* **12:1** NU *necessary, though not profitable, to boast.*

8 [R]Concerning this thing I pleaded with the
Lord three times that it might depart from
me. Matt. 26:44
9 And He said to me, "My grace is sufficient
for you, for My strength is made perfect in
weakness." Therefore most gladly I will rather
boast in my infirmities, that the power of
Christ may rest upon me.
10 Therefore [R]I take pleasure in infirmities,
in reproaches, in needs, in persecutions, in
distresses, for Christ's sake. For when I am
weak, then I am strong. [Rom. 5:3; 8:35]

Paul's Signs Support His Apostleship

11 I have become [R]a fool in boasting;* you
have compelled me. For I ought to have been
commended by you; for [R]in nothing was I be-
hind the most eminent apostles, though I am
nothing. 2 Cor. 5:13; 11:1, 16; 12:6 • 2 Cor. 11:5
12 [R]Truly the signs of an apostle were ac-
complished among you with all persever-
ance, in signs and [R]wonders and mighty
[R]deeds. Rom. 15:18 • Acts 15:12 • Acts 14:8–10
13 For what is it in which you were inferior
to other churches, except that I myself was
not burdensome to you? Forgive me this
wrong!

Paul's Concern Not to Be a Financial Burden

14 Now *for* the third time I am ready to come
to you. And I will not be burdensome to you;
for I do not seek yours, but you. For the chil-
dren ought not to lay up for the parents, but
the parents for the children.
15 And I will very gladly spend and be spent
for your souls; though the more abundantly I
love you, the less I am loved.
16 But be that *as it may,* [R]I did not burden
you. Nevertheless, being crafty, I caught you
by cunning! 2 Cor. 11:9
17 Did I take advantage of you by any of
those whom I sent to you?
18 I urged Titus, and sent our [R]brother with
him. Did Titus take advantage of you? Did we
not walk in the same spirit? Did *we* not *walk*
in the same steps? 2 Cor. 8:18

Paul's Concern Not to Find Them Carnal

19 [R]Again, do you think* that we excuse our-
selves to you? We speak before God in Christ.
[R]But *we do* all things, beloved, for your edifi-
cation. 2 Cor. 5:12 • 1 Cor. 10:33
20 For I fear lest, when I come, I shall not
find you such as I wish, and *that* [R]I shall be
found by you such as you do not wish; lest
there be contentions, jealousies, outbursts of
wrath, selfish ambitions, backbitings, whis-
perings, conceits, tumults; 1 Cor. 4:21
21 lest, when I come again, my God [R]will
humble me among you, and I shall mourn
for many [R]who have sinned before and have
not repented of the uncleanness, [R]fornica-
tion, and lewdness which they have prac-
ticed. 2 Cor. 2:1, 4 • 2 Cor. 13:2 • 1 Cor. 5:1

CHAPTER 13

Paul's Warning to Examine Yourselves

THIS *will be* the third *time* I am coming to
you. *"By the mouth of two or three wit-*
*nesses every word shall be established."**
2 [R]I have told you before, and foretell as if I
were present the second time, and now being
absent I write* to those who have sinned be-
fore, and to all the rest, that if I come again I
will not spare— 2 Cor. 10:2
3 since you seek a proof of Christ [R]speak-
ing in me, who is not weak toward you, but
mighty [R]in you. Matt. 10:20 • [1 Cor. 9:2]
4 For though He was crucified in weakness,
yet He lives by the power of God. For we also
are weak in Him, but we shall live with Him
by the power of God toward you.
5 Examine yourselves *as to* whether you
are in the faith. Test yourselves. Do you not
know yourselves, that Jesus Christ is in
you?—unless indeed you are disqualified.
6 But I trust that you will know that we are
not disqualified.

12:11 NU omits *in boasting* **12:19** NU *You have been thinking for a long time . . . .* **13:1** Deut. 19:15 **13:2** NU omits *I write*

13:14 Persons of the Trinity—The one, indivisible divine essence has eternally existed in three Persons: The Father, Son, and Holy Spirit (Page 979—Matt. 3:16, 17; 28:19; Page 1175—1 Cor. 12:4–6; Page 1279—1 Pet. 1:2; 3:18). They are not a cosmic committee that meets eternally to rule over heaven and earth. The three Persons exist within one God; They comprise one divine Being—not as rooms in a house, but as notes in a chord.

While the "notes in a chord" analogy expresses the interrelatedness of the Persons of the Trinity, it fails to capture the fullness of each Person. If you examine one note of the chord, it is just the note, not the chord. But when you look at the Father, or the Son, or the Holy Spirit, each Person of the Trinity has the full divine nature. You are looking at God—not just a piece of Him (Page 1099—John 14:9; Page 1168—1 Cor. 2:10–16; Page 1258—Heb. 1:3).

Even the OT with its strict monotheism (Page 181—Deut. 6:4; Page 963—Zech. 14:9), hints at a plurality of Persons within the Godhead. There are glimpses of God deliberating with Himself as a plural Being (Page 4—Gen. 1:26; 11:7; Page 688—Is. 6:8). A reoccurring OT figure called the Angel of the Lord is also identified as God (Page 33—Gen. 31:11, 13; Page 57—Ex. 3:2–5). Even the "Holy, holy, holy *is* the LORD of hosts" from the mouth of the seraphim (Page 687—Is. 6:3) is consistent with three Persons in God's Being.

Now turn to Page 1204—Eph. 1:4, 7, 13: Interaction Within the Trinity.

7 Now I* pray to God that you do no evil,
not that we should appear approved, but that
you should do what is honorable, though [R]we
may seem disqualified. 2 Cor. 6:9
8 For we can do nothing against the truth,
but for the truth.
9 For we are glad [R]when we are weak and
you are strong. And this also we pray, that you
may be made complete. 1 Cor. 4:10
10 [R]Therefore I write these things being ab-
sent, lest being present I should use sharp-
ness, according to the [R]authority which the
Lord has given me for edification and not for
destruction. 1 Cor. 4:21 • 2 Cor. 10:8

Conclusion

11 Finally, brethren, farewell. Become com-
plete. [R]Be of good comfort, be of one mind,
live in peace; and the God of love [R]and peace
will be with you. Rom. 12:16, 18 • Rom. 15:33
12 Greet one another with a holy kiss.
13 All the saints greet you.

14 The grace of the Lord Jesus Christ, and
the love of God, and the communion of the
Holy Spirit *be* with you all. Amen.

13:7 NU *we*

THE EPISTLE OF PAUL THE APOSTLE TO THE

GALATIANS

THE BOOK OF GALATIANS

The Galatians, having launched their Christian experience by faith, seem content to leave their voyage of faith and chart a new course based on works—a course Paul finds disturbing. His letter to the Galatians is a vigorous attack against the gospel of works and a defense of the gospel of faith.

Paul begins by setting forth his credentials as an apostle with a message from God: blessing comes from God on the basis of faith, not law. The law declares men guilty and imprisons them; faith sets men free to enjoy liberty in Christ. But liberty is not license. Freedom in Christ means freedom to produce the fruits of righteousness through a Spirit-led lifestyle.

The book is called *Pros Galatas,* "To the Galatians," and it is the only letter of Paul that is specifically addressed to a number of churches ("To the churches of Galatia," 1:2). The name *Galatians* was given to this Celtic people because they originally lived in Gaul before their migration to Asia Minor.

THE AUTHOR OF GALATIANS

The Pauline authorship and the unity of this epistle are virtually unchallenged. The first verse clearly identifies the author as "Paul, an apostle." Also in 5:2, we read, "Indeed I, Paul, say to you." In fact, Paul actually wrote Galatians (6:11) instead of dictating it to a secretary, as was his usual practice.

THE TIME OF GALATIANS

The term *Galatia* was used in an ethnographic sense (that is, cultural and geographic origin) and in a political sense. The original ethnographic sense refers to the central part of Asia Minor where these Celtic tribes eventually settled after their conflicts with the Romans and Macedonians. Later, in 189 B.C. Galatia came under Roman domination, and in 25 B.C. Augustus declared it a Roman province. The political or provincial Galatia included territory to the south that was not originally considered part of Galatia (for example, the cities of Pisidian Antioch, Iconium, Lystra, and Derbe). There are two theories regarding the date and setting of Galatians.

The *North Galatian Theory* holds that Paul was speaking of Galatia in its earlier, more restricted sense. According to this theory, the churches of Galatia were north of the cities Paul visited on his first missionary journey. Paul visited the ethnographic Galatia (the smaller region to the North) for the first time on his second missionary journey, probably while he was on his way to Troas (Acts 16:6). On his third missionary journey, Paul revisited the Galatian churches he had established (Acts 18:23) and wrote this epistle either in Ephesus (A.D. 53–56) or in Macedonia (A.D. 56).

According to the *South Galatian Theory,* Paul was referring to Galatia in its wider political sense as a province of Rome. This means that the churches he had in mind in this epistle were in the cities he evangelized during his first missionary journey with Barnabas (Acts 13:13—14:23). This was just prior to the Jerusalem Council (Acts 15), so the Jerusalem visit in Galatians 2:1–10 must have been the Acts 11:27–30 famine-relief visit. Galatians was probably written in Syrian Antioch in A.D. 49 just before Paul went to the Council in Jerusalem.

Paul wrote this epistle in response to a report that the Galatian churches were suddenly taken over by the false teaching of certain Judaizers who professed Jesus yet sought to place Gentile converts under the requirements of the Mosaic Law (1:7; 4:17, 21; 5:2–12; 6:12, 13).

THE CHRIST OF GALATIANS

Christ has freed the believer from bondage to the law (legalism) and to sin (license) and has placed him in a position of liberty. The transforming Cross provides for the believer's deliverance from the curse of sin, law, and self (1:4; 2:20; 3:13; 4:5; 5:24; 6:14).

KEYS TO GALATIANS

Key Word: Freedom from the Law—This epistle shows that the believer is no longer under the law but is saved by faith alone. It has been said that Judaism was the cradle of Christianity, but also that it was very nearly its grave as well. God raised up Paul as the Moses of the Christian church to deliver them from this bondage. Galatians is the Christian's Declaration of Independence. The power of the Holy Spirit enables the Christian to enjoy freedom within the law of love.

Key Verses: Galatians 2:20, 21 and 5:1—"I have been crucified with Christ; it is no longer I who live, but Christ lives in me; and the *life* which I now live in the flesh I live by faith in the Son of God, who loved me and gave Himself for me. I do not set aside the grace of God; for if righteousness *comes* through the law, then Christ died in vain" (2:20, 21).

"Stand fast therefore in the liberty by which

Christ has made us free, and do not be entangled again with a yoke of bondage" (5:1).

Key Chapter: Galatians 5—The impact of the truth concerning freedom is staggering: freedom must not be used "as an opportunity for the flesh, but through love serve one another" (5:13). This chapter records the power, "Walk in the Spirit" (5:16), and the results, "the fruit of the Spirit" (5:22), of that freedom.

SURVEY OF GALATIANS

The Epistle to the Galatians has been called "the Magna Carta of Christian liberty." It is Paul's manifesto of justification by faith, and the resulting liberty. Paul directs this great charter of Christian freedom to a people who are willing to give up the priceless liberty they possess in Christ. The oppressive theology of certain Jewish legalizers has been causing the believers in Galatia to trade their freedom in Christ for bondage to the law. Paul writes this forceful epistle to do away with the false gospel of works and demonstrate the superiority of justification by faith. This carefully written polemic approaches the problem from three directions: the gospel of grace defended (1 and 2), the gospel of grace explained (3 and 4), and the gospel of grace applied (5 and 6).

The Gospel of Grace Defended (1 and 2): Paul affirms his divinely given apostleship and presents the gospel (1:1–5) because it has been distorted by false teachers among the Galatians (1:6–10). Paul launches into his biographical argument for the true gospel of justification by faith in showing that he received his message not from men but directly from God (1:11–24). When he submits his teaching of Christian liberty to the apostles in Jerusalem, they all acknowledge the validity and authority of his message (2:1–10). Paul also must correct Peter on the matter of freedom from the law (2:11–21).

The Gospel of Grace Explained (3 and 4): In this section Paul uses eight lines of reasoning to develop his theological defense of justification by faith: (1) The Galatians began by faith, and their growth in Christ must continue to be by faith (3:1–5). (2) Abraham was justified by faith, and the same principle applies today (3:6–9). (3) Christ has redeemed all who trust in Him from the curse of the law (3:10–14). (4) The promise made to Abraham was not nullified by the law (3:15–18). (5) The law was given to drive men to faith, not to save them (3:19–22). (6) Believers in Christ are adopted sons of God and are no longer bound by the law (3:23—4:7). (7) The Galatians must recognize their inconsistency and regain their original freedom in Christ (4:8–20). (8) Abraham's two sons allegorically reveal the superiority of the Abrahamic promise to the Mosaic Law (4:21–31).

The Gospel of Grace Applied (5 and 6): The Judaizers seek to place the Galatians under bondage to their perverted gospel of justification by law, but Paul warns them that law and grace are two contrary principles (5:1–12). So far, Paul has been contrasting the liberty of faith with the legalism of law, but at this point he warns the Galatians of the opposite extreme of license or antinomianism (5:13—6:10). The Christian is not only set free from bondage of law, but he is also free of the bondage of sin because of the power of the indwelling Spirit. Liberty is not an excuse to indulge in the deeds of the flesh; rather, it provides the privilege of bearing the fruit of the Spirit by walking in dependence upon Him. This letter closes with a contrast between the Judaizers—who are motivated by pride and a desire to avoid persecution—and Paul, who has suffered for the true gospel, but boasts only in Christ (6:11–18).

FOCUS	GOSPEL OF GRACE DEFENDED		GOSPEL OF GRACE EXPLAINED		GOSPEL OF GRACE APPLIED	
REFERENCE	1:1———	2:1———	3:1———	4:1———	5:1———	6:1———6:18
DIVISION	PAUL'S APOSTLESHIP	PAUL'S AUTHORITY	BONDAGE OF LAW	FREEEDOM OF GRACE	FRUIT OF THE SPIRIT	FRUITS OF THE SPIRIT
TOPIC	BIOGRAPHICAL EXPLANATION		DOCTRINAL EXPOSITION		PRACTICAL EXHORTATION	
	AUTHENTICATION OF LIBERTY		ARGUMENTATION FOR LIBERTY		APPLICATION OF LIBERTY	
LOCATION	SOUTH GALATIAN THEORY: SYRIAN ANTIOCH NORTH GALATIAN THEORY: EPHESUS OR MACEDONIA					
TIME	SOUTH GALATIAN THEORY: A.D. 49 NORTH GALATIAN THEORY: A.D. 53–56					

OUTLINE OF GALATIANS

I. The Gospel of Grace Defended ....1:1—2:21
- A. Introduction 1:1–9
  - 1. Salutation: The Ground of Grace 1:1–5
  - 2. Situation: The Departure from Grace............1:6–9
- B. Gospel of Grace Is Given by Divine Revelation 1:10–24
- C. Gospel of Grace Is Approved by Jerusalem Leadership 2:1–10
- D. Gospel of Grace Is Vindicated by Rebuking Peter..............2:11–21

II. The Gospel of Grace Explained ....3:1—4:31
- A. Holy Spirit Is Given by Faith, Not by Works..............3:1–5
- B. Abraham Was Justified by Faith, Not by Works..............3:6–9
- C. Justification Is by Faith, Not by the Law..............3:10—4:11
  - 1. Christ Redeems Us from the Curse of the Law..............3:10–14
  - 2. Abrahamic Covenant Is Not Voided by the Law 3:15–18
  - 3. Law Given to Drive Us to Faith.....3:19–22
  - 4. Believers Are Free from the Law..............3:23—4:11
- D. Galatians Receive Blessings by Faith, Not by the Law 4:12–20
- E. Law and Grace Cannot Coexist..........4:21–31

III. The Gospel of Grace Applied............5:1—6:18
- A. Position of Liberty: "Stand Fast" 5:1–12
- B. Practice of Liberty: Love One Another..............5:13–15
- C. Power for Liberty: Walk in the Spirit..............5:16–26
  - 1. Conflict Between the Spirit and the Flesh..............5:16–18
  - 2. "Works of the Flesh" 5:19–21
  - 3. "Fruit of the Spirit"..............5:22–26
- D. Performance in Liberty: Do Good to All Men..............6:1–10
  - 1. "Bear One Another's Burdens"..........6:1–5
  - 2. Do Not Be Weary While Doing Good 6:6–10
- E. Conclusion..............6:11–18
  - 1. Motives of the Circumcised 6:11–13
  - 2. Motives of the Apostle Paul..........6:14–18

CHAPTER 1

Salutation: The Ground of Grace

PAUL, an apostle (not from men nor
through man, but [R]through Jesus Christ
and God the Father [R]who raised Him from the
dead), Acts 9:6 • Acts 2:24
2 and all the brethren who are with me,

To the churches of Galatia:

3 Grace to you and peace from God the Fa-
ther and our Lord Jesus Christ,
4 who gave Himself for our sins, that He
might deliver us from this present evil age, ac-
cording to the will of our God and Father,
5 to whom *be* glory forever and ever. Amen.

Situation: The Departure from Grace

6 I marvel that you are turning away so
soon [R]from Him who called you in the grace
of Christ, to a different gospel, Gal. 1:15; 5:8
7 [R]which is not another; but there are some
[R]who trouble you and want to pervert the
gospel of Christ. 2 Cor. 11:4 • Gal. 5:10, 12
8 But even if [R]we, or an angel from
heaven, preach any other gospel to you than
what we have preached to you, let him be
[T]accursed. 1 Cor. 16:22 • Gr. *anathema*
9 As we have said before, so now I say
again, if anyone preaches any other gospel to
you [R]than what you have received, let him be
accursed. Deut. 4:2

Gospel of Grace Is Given by Divine Revelation

10 For [R]do I now [R]persuade men, or God?
Or [R]do I seek to please men? For if I still
pleased men, I would not be a bondservant of
Christ. 1 Thess. 2:4 • 1 Sam. 24:7 • 1 Thess. 2:4
11 [R]But I make known to you, brethren, that
the gospel which was preached by me is not
according to man. 1 Cor. 15:1
12 For [R]I neither received it from man, nor
was I taught *it*, but *it came* through the reve-
lation of Jesus Christ. 1 Cor. 15:1
13 For you have heard of my former con-
duct in Judaism, how [R]I persecuted the
church of God beyond measure and [R]*tried to*
destroy it. Acts 9:1 • Acts 8:3; 22:4, 5
14 And I advanced in Judaism beyond many
of my contemporaries in my own nation, be-
ing more exceedingly zealous [R]for the tradi-
tions of my fathers. Jer. 9:14
15 But when it pleased God, [R]who separated
me from my mother's womb and called *me*
through His grace, Is. 49:1, 5
16 to reveal His Son in me, that I might
preach Him among the Gentiles, I did not im-
mediately confer with flesh and blood,
17 nor did I go up to Jerusalem to those *who
were* apostles before me; but I went to Arabia,
and returned again to Damascus.
18 Then after three years [R]I went up to Jeru-
salem to see Peter,* and remained with him
fifteen days. Acts 9:26

1:18 NU *Cephas*

19 But [R]I saw none of the other apostles except James, the Lord's brother. 1 Cor. 9:5

20 (Now *concerning* the things which I write to you, indeed, before God, I do not lie.)

21 [R]Afterward I went into the regions of Syria and Cilicia. Acts 9:30

22 And I was unknown by face to the churches of Judea which *were* in Christ.

23 But they were hearing only, "He who formerly persecuted us now preaches the faith which he once *tried to* destroy."

24 And they glorified God in me.

CHAPTER 2

Gospel of Grace Is Approved by Jerusalem Leadership

THEN after fourteen years [R]I went up again to Jerusalem with Barnabas, and also took Titus with *me.* Acts 15:2

2 And I went up by revelation, and communicated to them that gospel which I preach among the Gentiles, but privately to those who were of reputation, lest by any means I might run, or had run, in vain.

3 Yet not even Titus who *was* with me, being a Greek, was compelled to be circumcised.

4 And *this occurred* because of [R]false brethren secretly brought in (who came in by stealth to spy out our [R]liberty which we have in Christ Jesus, that they might bring us into bondage), Acts 15:1, 24 • Gal. 3:25

5 to whom we did not yield submission even for an hour, that [R]the truth of the gospel might continue with you. [Gal. 1:6]

6 But from those who seemed to be something—whatever they were, it makes no difference to me; God shows personal favoritism to no man—for those who seemed *to be something* added nothing to me.

7 But on the contrary, when they saw that the gospel for the uncircumcised [R]had been committed to me, as *the gospel* for the circumcised *was* to Peter 1 Thess. 2:4

8 (for He who worked effectively in Peter for the apostleship to the [R]circumcised [R]also [R]worked effectively in me toward the Gentiles), 1 Pet. 1:1 • Acts 9:15 • [Gal. 3:5]

9 and when James, [T]Cephas, and John, who seemed to be [R]pillars, perceived the grace that had been given to me, they gave me and Barnabas the right hand of fellowship, that we *should go* to the Gentiles and they to the circumcised. Peter • Matt. 16:18

10 *They desired* only that we should remember the poor, [R]the very thing which I also was eager to do. Acts 11:30

Gospel of Grace Is Vindicated by Rebuking Peter

11 [R]Now when Peter* had come to Antioch, I [T]withstood him to his face, because he was to be blamed; Acts 15:35 • *opposed*

12 for before certain men came from James, [R]he would eat with the Gentiles; but when they came, he withdrew and separated himself, fearing [T]those who were of the circumcision. [Acts 10:28; 11:2, 3] • Jewish Christians

13 And the rest of the Jews also played the hypocrite with him, so that even Barnabas was carried away with their hypocrisy.

14 But when I saw that they were not straightforward about [R]the truth of the gospel, I said to Peter before *them* all, "If you, being a Jew, live in the manner of Gentiles and not as the Jews, why do you* compel Gentiles to live as Jews?* Gal. 1:6; 2:5

15 [R]"We *who are* Jews by nature, and not sinners of the Gentiles, [Acts 15:10]

16 [R]"knowing that a man is not justified by the works of the law but [R]by faith in Jesus Christ, even we have believed in Christ Jesus, that we might be justified by faith in Christ and not [R]by the works of the law; for by the works of the law no flesh shall be justified. Acts 13:38, 39 • Rom. 1:17 • Ps. 143:2

17 "But if, while we seek to be justified by Christ, we ourselves also are found [R]sinners, *is* Christ therefore a minister of sin? Certainly not! [1 John 3:8]

18 "For if I build again those things which I destroyed, I make myself a transgressor.

19 "For I [R]through the law died to the law that I might [R]live to God. Rom. 8:2 • [Rom. 6:11]

20 "I have been crucified with Christ; it is no longer I who live, but Christ lives in me; and the *life* which I now live in the flesh I live by faith in the Son of God, who loved me and [R]gave Himself for me. Is. 53:12★

21 "I do not set aside the grace of God; for [R]if righteousness *comes* through the law, then Christ died in vain." Heb. 7:11

CHAPTER 3

Holy Spirit Is Given by Faith, Not by Works

O FOOLISH Galatians! Who has bewitched you that you should not obey the truth,* before whose eyes Jesus Christ was clearly portrayed among you* as crucified?

2 This only I want to learn from you: Did you receive the Spirit by the works of the law, or by the hearing of faith?

3 Are you so foolish? [R]Having begun in the Spirit, are you now being made perfect by [R]the flesh? [Gal. 4:9] • Heb. 7:16

4 [R]Have you suffered so many things in vain—if indeed *it was* in vain? Heb. 10:35

5 Therefore He who supplies the Spirit to you and works miracles among you, *does He do it* by the works of the law, or by the hearing of faith?—

2:11 NU *Cephas* **2:14** NU *how can you* • Some interpreters stop the quotation here. **3:1** NU omits *that you should not obey the truth* • NU omits *among you*

Abraham Was Justified by Faith, Not by Works

6 just as Abraham *"believed God, and it was accounted to him for righteousness."**

7 Therefore know that *only* [R]those who are of faith are sons of Abraham. John 8:39

8 And the Scripture, foreseeing that God would justify the Gentiles by faith, preached the gospel to Abraham beforehand, *saying, "In you all the nations shall be blessed."**

9 So then those who *are* of faith are blessed with believing Abraham.

Christ Redeems Us from the Curse of the Law

10 For as many as are of the works of the law are under the curse; for it is written, *"Cursed is everyone who does not continue in all things which are written in the book of the law, to do them."**

11 But that no one is [T]justified by the law in the sight of God *is* evident, for *"the just shall live by faith."**
declared righteous

12 Yet the law is not of faith, but *"the man who does them shall live by them."**

13 [R]Christ has redeemed us from the curse of the law, having become a curse for us (for it is written, *"Cursed is everyone who hangs on a tree"**), [Rom. 8:3]

14 [R]that the blessing of Abraham might come upon the Gentiles in Christ Jesus, that we might receive the promise of the Spirit through faith. Is. 49:6; Rom. 4:9★

Abrahamic Covenant Is Not Voided by the Law

15 Brethren, I speak in the manner of men: Though *it is* only a man's covenant, yet *if it is* confirmed, no one annuls or adds to it.

16 Now [R]to Abraham and his Seed were the promises made. He does not say, "And to seeds," as of many, but as of one, *"And to your Seed,"** who is Christ. Gen. 12:3★

17 And this I say, *that* the law, [R]which was four hundred and thirty years later, cannot annul the covenant that was confirmed before by God in Christ,* that it should make the promise of no effect. Ex. 12:40

18 For if [R]the inheritance *is* of the law, [R]*it is* no longer of promise; but God gave *it* to Abraham by promise. [Rom. 8:17] • Rom. 4:14

Law Given to Drive Us to Faith

19 What purpose then *does* the law *serve?* It was added because of transgressions, till the Seed should come to whom the promise was made; *and it was* appointed through angels by the hand of a mediator.

20 Now a mediator does not *mediate* for one *only,* [R]but God is one. [Rom. 3:29]

21 *Is* the law then against the promises of God? Certainly not! For if there had been a law given which could have given life, truly righteousness would have been by the law.

22 But the Scripture has confined all under sin, that the promise by faith in Jesus Christ might be given to those who believe.

Believers Are Free from the Law

23 But before faith came, we were kept under guard by the law, kept for the faith which would afterward be revealed.

24 Therefore [R]the law was our tutor *to bring us* to Christ, [R]that we might be justified by faith. Rom. 10:4 • Acts 13:39

25 But after faith has come, we are no longer under a tutor.

26 For you [R]are all sons of God through faith in Christ Jesus. John 1:12

27 For [R]as many of you as were baptized into Christ have put on Christ. [Rom. 6:3]

28 [R]There is neither Jew nor Greek, [R]there is neither slave nor free, there is neither male nor female; for you are all one in Christ Jesus. Col. 3:11 • [1 Cor. 12:13]

29 And [R]if you *are* Christ's, then you are Abraham's [R]seed, and heirs according to the promise. Gen. 12:3; Heb. 11:18★ • Rom. 4:11

CHAPTER 4

NOW I say *that* the heir, as long as he is a child, does not differ at all from a slave, though he is master of all,

2 but is under guardians and stewards until the time appointed by the father.

3 Even so we, when we were children, [R]were in bondage under the elements of the world. Col. 2:8, 20

4 But when the fullness of the time had come, God sent forth His Son, [R]born* of a woman, born under the law, Is. 7:14★

5 [R]to redeem those who were under the law, [R]that we might receive the adoption as sons. [Matt. 20:28] • [John 1:12]

6 And because you are sons, God has sent forth the Spirit of His Son into your hearts, crying out, "Abba, Father!"

7 Therefore you are no longer a slave but a son, [R]and if a son, then an heir of* God through Christ. [Rom. 8:16, 17]

8 But then, indeed, [R]when you did not know God, [R]you served those which by nature are not gods. Eph. 2:12 • Rom. 1:25

9 But now [R]after you have known God, or rather are known by God, [R]how *is it that* you turn again to [R]the weak and beggarly elements, to which you desire again to be in bondage? [1 Cor. 8:3] • Col. 2:20 • Heb. 7:18

3:6 Gen. 15:6 **3:8** Gen 12:3; 18:18; 22:18; 26:4; 28:14 **3:10** Deut. 27:26 **3:11** Hab. 2:4 **3:12** Lev. 18:5 **3:13** Deut. 21:23 **3:16** Gen. 12:7; 13:15; 24:7 **3:17** NU omits *in Christ* **4:4** Or *made* **4:7** NU *through God* and omits *through Christ*

10 [R]You observe days and months and seasons and years. Rom. 14:5
11 I am afraid for you, [R]lest I have labored for you in vain. 1 Thess. 3:5

Galatians Receive Blessing by Faith, Not by the Law

12 Brethren, I urge you to become like me, for I *became* like you. [R]You have not injured me at all. 2 Cor. 2:5
13 You know that [R]because of physical infirmity I preached the gospel to you at the first. 1 Cor. 2:3
14 And my trial which was in my flesh you did not despise or reject, but you received me [R]as an [T]angel of God, [R]*even* as Christ Jesus. Mal. 2:7 • Or *messenger* • [Luke 10:16]
15 What* then was the blessing you *enjoyed?* For I bear you witness that, if possible, you would have plucked out your own eyes and given them to me.
16 Have I therefore become your enemy because I tell you the truth?
17 They [R]zealously court you, *but* for no good; yes, they want to exclude you, that you may be zealous for them. Rom. 10:2
18 But it is good to be zealous in a good thing always, and not only when I am present with you.
19 My little children, for whom I labor in birth again until Christ is formed in you,
20 I would like to be present with you now and to change my tone; for I have doubts about you.

Law and Grace Cannot Coexist

21 Tell me, you who desire to be under the law, do you not hear the law?
22 For it is written that Abraham had two sons: [R]the one by a bondwoman, [R]the other by a freewoman. Gen. 16:15 • Gen. 21:2
23 But he *who was* of the bondwoman was born according to the flesh, and he of the freewoman through promise,
24 which things are symbolic. For these are the* two covenants: the one from Mount [R]Sinai which gives birth to bondage, which is Hagar— Deut. 33:2
25 for this Hagar is Mount Sinai in Arabia, and corresponds to Jerusalem which now is, and is in bondage with her children—
26 but the [R]Jerusalem above is free, which is the mother of us all. [Is. 2:2]
27 For it is written:

"Rejoice, O barren,
You who do not bear!
Break forth and shout,
You who are not in labor!
For the desolate has many more children
*Than she who has a husband."**

28 Now [R]we, brethren, as Isaac *was,* are [R]children of promise. Gal. 3:29 • Acts 3:25
29 But, as he who was born according to the flesh then persecuted him *who was born* according to the Spirit, even so *it is* now.
30 Nevertheless what does the Scripture say? *"Cast out the bondwoman and her son, for the son of the bondwoman shall not be heir with the son of the freewoman."**
31 So then, brethren, we are not children of the bondwoman but of the free.

CHAPTER 5

Position of Liberty: "Stand Fast"

STAND[R] fast therefore in the liberty by which Christ has made us free,* and do not be entangled again with a [R]yoke of bondage. Phil. 4:1 • Acts 15:10
2 Indeed I, Paul, say to you that [R]if you become circumcised, Christ will profit you nothing. Acts 15:1
3 And I testify again to every man who becomes circumcised [R]that he is [T]a debtor to keep the whole law. [Rom. 2:25] • *obligated*
4 [R]You have become estranged from Christ, you who *attempt to* be justified by law; you have fallen from grace. [Rom. 9:31]
5 For we through the Spirit eagerly wait for the hope of righteousness by faith.
6 For [R]in Christ Jesus neither circumcision nor uncircumcision avails anything, but faith working through love. [Gal. 6:15]
7 You [R]ran well. Who hindered you from obeying the truth? 1 Cor. 9:24
8 This persuasion does not *come* from Him who calls you.
9 A little leaven leavens the whole lump.
10 I have confidence in you, in the Lord, that you will have no other mind; but he who troubles you shall bear his judgment, whoever he is.
11 And I, brethren, if I still preach circumcision, why do I still suffer persecution? Then the offense of the cross has ceased.
12 I could wish that those who trouble you would even cut themselves off!

Practice of Liberty: Love One Another

13 For you, brethren, have been called to liberty; only do not *use* liberty as an [R]opportunity for the flesh, but [R]through love serve one another. 1 Pet. 2:16 • 1 Cor. 9:19

4:15 NU *Where* **4:24** NU, M omit *the* **4:27** Is. 54:1 **4:30** Gen. 21:10 **5:1** NU *For freedom Christ has made us free; stand fast therefore,*

5:13 Serving—God intended that the Christian life should be dynamic, not static. We should sit under the teaching of the Word of God, understand and apply its meaning and implications, and serve God and

(continued on next page)

14 For [R]all the law is fulfilled in one word,
even in this: *"You shall love your neighbor as
yourself."** Matt. 7:12; 22:40
15 But if you bite and devour one another,
beware lest you be consumed by one another!

Conflict Between the Spirit and the Flesh

16 I say then: Walk in the Spirit, and you
shall not fulfill the lust of the flesh.
17 For the flesh lusts against the Spirit, and
the Spirit against the flesh; and these are con-
trary to one another, [R]so that you do not do
the things that you wish. Rom. 7:15
18 But [R]if you are led by the Spirit, you are
not under the law. [Rom. 6:14; 7:4; 8:14]

"Works of the Flesh"

19 Now [R]the works of the flesh are evident,
which are: adultery,* [T]fornication, unclean-
ness, lewdness, Eph. 5:3, 11 • *sexual immorality*
20 idolatry, sorcery, hatred, contentions, jeal-
ousies, outbursts of wrath, selfish ambitions,
dissensions, heresies,
21 envy, murders,* drunkenness, revelries,
and the like; of which I tell you beforehand,
just as I also told *you* in time past, that [R]those
who practice such things will not inherit the
kingdom of God. 1 Cor. 6:9, 10

"Fruit of the Spirit"

22 But [R]the fruit of the Spirit is [R]love, joy,
peace, longsuffering, kindness, goodness,
faithfulness, [John 15:2] • [Col. 3:12–15]
23 [T]gentleness, self-control. [R]Against such
there is no law. *meekness* • 1 Tim. 1:9
24 And those *who are* Christ's have crucified
the flesh with its passions and desires.
25 [R]If we live in the Spirit, let us also walk in
the Spirit. [Rom. 8:4, 5]
26 [R]Let us not become conceited, provoking
one another, envying one another. Phil. 2:3

CHAPTER 6

"Bear One Another's Burdens"

BRETHREN, if a man is overtaken in any
trespass, you who *are* spiritual restore
such a one in a spirit of gentleness, consider-
ing yourself lest you also be tempted.
2 [R]Bear one another's burdens, and so ful-
fill the law of Christ. Rom. 15:1
3 For [R]if anyone thinks himself to be some-
thing, when [R]he is nothing, he deceives him-
self. Rom. 12:3 • [2 Cor. 3:5]
4 But [R]let each one examine his own work,
and then he will have rejoicing in himself
alone, and not in another. 1 Cor. 11:28
5 For each one shall bear his own load.

Do Not Be Weary While Doing Good

6 Let him who is taught the word share in
all good things with him who teaches.
7 Do not be deceived, God is not mocked;
for [R]whatever a man sows, that he will also
reap. [Rom. 2:6]
8 For he who sows to his flesh will of the flesh
reap corruption, but he who sows to the Spirit
will of the Spirit reap [R]everlasting life. [Rom. 6:8]
9 And [R]let us not grow weary while doing
good, for in due season we shall reap [R]if we do
not lose heart. 1 Cor. 15:58 • [James 5:7, 8]
10 [R]Therefore, as we have opportunity, let us
do good to all, especially to those who are of
the household of faith. Prov. 3:27

Motives of the Circumcised

11 See with what large letters I have written
to you with my own hand!
12 As many as desire to make a good show-
ing in the flesh, these *would* compel you to be
circumcised, [R]only that they may not suffer
persecution for the cross of Christ. Gal. 5:11
13 For not even those who are circumcised
keep the law, but they desire to have you cir-
cumcised that they may boast in your flesh.

Motives of the Apostle Paul

14 But God forbid that I should boast except
in the [R]cross of our Lord Jesus Christ, by
whom* the world has been crucified to me,
and I to the world. [1 Cor. 1:18]
15 For [R]in Christ Jesus neither circumcision
nor uncircumcision avails anything, but a new
creation. 1 Cor. 7:19
16 And as many as walk according to this
rule, peace and mercy *be* upon them, and
upon the Israel of God.
17 From now on let no one trouble me, for I
bear in my body the marks of the Lord Jesus.
18 Brethren, the grace of our Lord Jesus
Christ *be* with your spirit. Amen.

5:14 Lev. 19:18 **5:19** NU omits *adultery* **5:21** NU omits *murders* **6:14** Or *by which* (the cross)

(continued from previous page)
our fellow believers. The Spirit of God has given us spiritual gifts, but those gifts are worthless unless they are put to use in the service of God and His church. Paul often uses the figure of the human body to show the dependence of the members of the body upon one another and the importance of each member serving the other (Page 1159—Rom. 12:4, 5; Page 1176—1 Cor. 12:12–31). While some members of the body have more prominent places of service than others, all are equally important. The worst thing that can happen to the human body is for one of its members to become nonfunctioning. Paralysis, sickness, deterioration, and sometimes death occur when a body member ceases to serve the other members of the body in the particular way that God intended. To maintain strength, health, and vitality, every member of the body must function and serve all the other members of the body. This is also true of the spiritual or new life. We will grow in the new life, become strong, and maintain good spiritual health as we use the talents and abilities that God has given us to meet the needs of the other members of the body.

Now turn to Page 1189—2 Cor. 9:6–8: Giving.

THE EPISTLE OF PAUL THE APOSTLE TO THE

EPHESIANS

THE BOOK OF EPHESIANS

Ephesians is addressed to a group of believers who are rich beyond measure in Jesus Christ, yet living as beggars, and only because they are ignorant of their wealth. Since they have yet to accept their wealth, they relegate themselves to living as spiritual paupers. Paul begins by describing in chapters 1—3 the contents of the Christian's heavenly "bank account": adoption, acceptance, redemption, forgiveness, wisdom, inheritance, the seal of the Holy Spirit, life, grace, citizenship—in short, every spiritual blessing. Drawing upon that huge spiritual endowment, the Christian has all the resources needed for living "to the praise of the glory of His grace" (1:6). Chapters 4—6 resemble an orthopedic clinic, where the Christian learns a spiritual walk rooted in his spiritual wealth. "For we are His workmanship, created in Christ Jesus [1—3] for good works, . . . that we should walk in them [4—6]" (2:10)

The traditional title of this epistle is *Pros Ephesious*, "To the Ephesians." Many ancient manuscripts, however, omit *en Epheso*, "in Ephesus," in 1:1. This has led a number of scholars to challenge the traditional view that this message was directed specifically to the Ephesians. The encyclical theory proposes that it was a circular letter sent by Paul to the churches of Asia. It is argued that Ephesians is really a Christian treatise designed for general use: it involves no controversy and deals with no specific problems in any particular church. This is also supported by the formal tone (no terms of endearment) and distant phraseology ("after I heard of your faith," 1:15; if they "have heard" of his message, 3:2). These things seem inconsistent with the relationship Paul must have had with the Ephesians after a ministry of almost three years among them. On the other hand, the absence of personal greetings is not a support for the encyclical theory because Paul would have done this to avoid favoritism. The only letters that greet specific people are Romans and Colossians, and they were addressed to churches Paul had not visited. Some scholars accept an ancient tradition that Ephesians is Paul's letter to the Laodiceans (Col. 4:16), but there is no way to be sure. If Ephesians began as a circular letter, it eventually became associated with Ephesus, the foremost of the Asian churches. Another plausible option is that this epistle was directly addressed to the Ephesians, but written in such a way as to make it helpful for all the churches in Asia.

THE AUTHOR OF EPHESIANS

All internal (1:1) and external evidence strongly supports the Pauline authorship of Ephesians. In recent years, however, critics have turned to internal grounds to challenge this unanimous ancient tradition. It has been argued that the vocabulary and style are different from other Pauline epistles, but this overlooks Paul's flexibility under different circumstances (cf. Rom. and 2 Cor.). The theology of Ephesians in some ways reflects a later development, but this must be attributed to Paul's own growth and meditation on the church as the body of Christ. Since the epistle clearly names the author in the opening verse, it is not necessary to theorize that Ephesians was written by one of Paul's pupils or admirers, such as Timothy, Luke, Tychicus, or Onesimus.

THE TIME OF EPHESIANS

At the end of his second missionary journey, Paul visited Ephesus where he left Priscilla and Aquila (Acts 18:18–21). This strategic city was the commercial center of Asia Minor, but heavy silting required a special canal to be maintained so that ships could reach the harbor. Ephesus was a religious center as well, famous especially for its magnificent temple of Diana (Roman name) or Artemis (Greek name), a structure considered to be one of the seven wonders of the ancient world (cf. Acts 19:35). The practice of magic and the local economy were clearly related to this temple. Paul remained in Ephesus for nearly three years on his third missionary journey (Acts 18:23—19:41); the Word of God was spread throughout the province of Asia. Paul's effective ministry began to hurt seriously the traffic in magic and images, leading to an uproar in the huge Ephesian theater. Paul then left for Macedonia, but afterward he met with the Ephesian elders while on his way to Jerusalem (Acts 20:17–38).

Paul wrote the "Prison Epistles" (Ephesians, Philippians, Colossians, and Philemon) during his first Roman imprisonment in A.D. 60–62. These epistles all refer to his imprisonment (Eph. 3:1; 4:1; 6:20; Phil. 1:7, 13, 14; Col. 4:3, 10, 18; Philem. 9, 10, 13, 23), and fit well against the background in Acts 28:16–31. This is especially true of Paul's references to the palace guard (governor's official residential guard, Phil. 1:13) and "Caesar's household" (Phil. 4:22). Some commentators believe that the imprisonment in one or more of these epistles refers to Paul's Caesarean imprisonment or to a hypothetical

Ephesian imprisonment, but the weight of evidence favors the traditional view that they were written in Rome. Ephesians, Colossians, and Philemon were evidently written about the same time (cf. Eph. 6:21, 22 with Col. 4:7–9) in A.D. 60–61. Philippians was written in A.D. 62, not long before Paul's release.

THE CHRIST OF EPHESIANS

Paul's important phrase "in Christ" (or its equivalent) appears about thirty-five times, more than in any other New Testament book. The believer is in Christ (1:1), in the heavenly places in Christ (1:3), chosen in Him (1:4), adopted through Christ (1:5), in the Beloved (1:6), redeemed in Him (1:7), given an inheritance in Him (1:11), given hope in Him (1:12), sealed in Him (1:13), made alive together with Christ (2:5), raised and seated with Him (2:6), created in Christ (2:10), brought near by His blood (2:13), growing in Christ (2:21), a partaker of the promise in Christ (3:6), and given access through faith in Him (3:12).

KEYS TO EPHESIANS

Key Word: Building the Body of Christ—Ephesians focuses on the believer's responsibility to walk in accordance with his heavenly calling in Christ Jesus (4:1). Ephesians was not written to correct specific errors in a local church, but to prevent problems in the church as a whole by encouraging the body of Christ to maturity in Him. It was also written to make believers more aware of their position in Christ because this is the basis for their practice on every level of life.

Key Verses: Ephesians 2:8–10 and 4:1–3—"For by grace you have been saved through faith, and that not of yourselves; *it is* the gift of God, not of works, lest anyone should boast. For we are His workmanship, created in Christ Jesus for good works, which God prepared beforehand that we should walk in them" (2:8–10).

"I, therefore, the prisoner of the Lord, beseech you to have a walk worthy of the calling with which you were called, with all lowliness and gentleness, with longsuffering, bearing with one another in love, endeavoring to keep the unity of the Spirit in the bond of peace" (4:1–3).

Key Chapter: Ephesians 6—Even though the Christian is blessed "with every spiritual blessing in the heavenly *places* in Christ" (1:3), spiritual warfare is still the daily experience of the Christian while in the world. Chapter 6 is the clearest advice for how to "be strong in the Lord and in the power of His might" (6:10).

SURVEY OF EPHESIANS

Paul wrote this epistle to make Christians more aware of their position in Christ and to motivate them to draw upon their spiritual source in daily living: "walk worthy of the calling with which you were called" (4:1; see 2:10). The first half of Ephesians lists the believer's heavenly possessions: adoption, redemption, inheritance, power, life, grace, citizenship, and the love of Christ. There are no imperatives in chapters 1—3, which focus only on divine gifts. But chapters 4—6 include thirty-five directives in the last half of Ephesians that speak of the believer's responsibility to conduct himself according to his individual calling. So Ephesians begins in heaven, but concludes in the home and in all other relationships of daily life. The two divisions are: the position of the Christian (1:1—3:21) and the practice of the Christian (4:1—6:20).

The Position of the Christian (1:1—3:21): After a two-verse prologue, in one long Greek sentence Paul extols the triune God for the riches of redemption (1:3–14). This hymn to God's grace praises the Father for choosing us (1:3–6), the Son for redeeming us (1:7–12), and

FOCUS	THE POSITION OF THE CHRISTIAN				THE PRACTICE OF THE CHRISTIAN			
REFERENCE	1:1——1:15——1:24——3:14——4:1——4:17——5:22——6:10——6:24							
DIVISION	PRAISE FOR REDEMPTION	PRAYER FOR REVELATION	POSITION OF THE CHRISTIAN	PRAYER FOR REALIZATION	UNITY IN THE CHURCH	HOLINESS IN LIFE	RESPONSIBILITIES AT HOME AND WORK	CONDUCT IN THE CONFLICT
TOPIC	BELIEF				BEHAVIOR			
	PRIVILEGES OF THE CHRISTIAN				RESPONSIBILITIES OF THE CHRISTIAN			
LOCATION	ROME							
TIME	A.D. 60–61							

the Spirit for sealing us (1:13, 14). The saving work of each divine Person is to the praise of the glory of His grace (1:6, 12, 14). Before continuing, Paul offers the first of two very significant prayers (1:15–23; cf. 3:14–21). Here he asks that the readers receive spiritual illumination so that they may come to perceive what is, in fact, true. Next, Paul describes the power of God's grace by contrasting their former condition with their present spiritual life in Christ, a salvation attained not by human works but by divine grace (2:1–10). This redemption includes Jews, yet also extends to those Gentiles who previously were "strangers from the covenants of promise" (2:12). In Christ, the two for the first time have become members of one body (2:11–22). The truth that Gentiles would become "fellow heirs, of the same body" (3:6) was formerly a mystery that has now been revealed (3:1–13). Paul's second prayer (3:14–21) expresses his desire that the readers be strengthened with the power of the Spirit and fully apprehend the love of Christ.

The Practice of the Christian (4:1–6:20): The pivotal verse of Ephesians is 4:1, because it draws a sharp line between the doctrinal and the practical divisions of this book. There is a cause-and-effect relationship between chapters 1—3 and 4—6 because the spiritual walk of a Christian must be rooted in his spiritual wealth. As Paul emphasized in Romans, behavior does not determine blessing; instead, blessing should determine behavior.

Because of the unity of all believers in the body of Christ, growth and maturity come from "the effective working by which every part does its share" (4:16). This involves the exercise of spiritual gifts in love. Paul exhorts the readers to "put off, concerning your former conduct, the old man" (4:22) and "put on the new man" (4:24) that will be manifested by a walk of integrity in the midst of all people. They are also to maintain a walk of holiness as children of light (5:1–21). Every relationship (wives, husbands, children, parents, slaves, and masters) must be transformed by their new life in Christ (5:22—6:9). Paul's colorful description of the spiritual warfare and the armor of God (6:10–20) is followed by a word about Tychicus and then a benediction (6:21–24).

OUTLINE OF EPHESIANS

Part One: The Position of the Christian (1:1—3:21)

I. Praise for Redemption....1:1–14

A. Salutation from Paul....1:1, 2
B. Chosen by the Father....1:3–6
C. Redeemed by the Son....1:7–12
D. Sealed by the Spirit....1:13, 14

II. Prayer for Revelation....1:15–23

III. Position of the Christian....2:1—3:13

A. The Christian's Position Individually....2:1–10
1. Old Condition: Dead to God....2:1–3
2. New Condition: Alive to God....2:4–10
B. The Christian's Position Corporately....2:11—3:13
1. Reconciliation of Jews and Gentiles....2:11–22
2. Revelation of the Mystery of the Church....3:1–13

IV. Prayer for Realization....3:14–21

Part Two: The Practice of the Christian (4:1—6:24)

I. Unity in the Church....4:1–16

A. Exhortation to Unity....4:1–3
B. Explanation of Unity....4:4–6
C. Means for Unity: The Gifts....4:7–11
D. Purpose of the Gifts....4:12–16

II. Holiness in Life....4:17—5:21

A. Put Off the Old Man....4:17–22
B. Put On the New Man....4:23–29
C. Grieve Not the Holy Spirit....4:30—5:12
D. Walk as Children of Light....5:13–17
E. Be Filled with the Spirit....5:18–21

III. Responsibilities in the Home and at Work....5:22—6:9

A. Wives: Submit to Your Husbands....5:22–24
B. Husbands: Love Your Wives....5:25–33
C. Children: Obey Your Parents....6:1–4
D. Service on the Job....6:5–9

IV. Conduct in the Conflict....6:10–24

A. Put On the Armor of God....6:10–17
B. Pray for Boldness....6:18–20
C. Conclusion....6:21–24

CHAPTER 1

Salutation from Paul

PAUL, an apostle of Jesus Christ by the will of God,

To the saints who are in Ephesus, and faithful in Christ Jesus:

2 Grace to you and peace from God our Father and the Lord Jesus Christ.

Chosen by the Father

3 [R]Blessed *be* the God and Father of our Lord Jesus Christ, who has blessed us with every spiritual blessing in the heavenly *places* in Christ, 2 Cor. 1:3

4 just as He chose us in Him before the foundation of the world, that we should be holy and without blame before Him in love,

5 [R]having predestined us to adoption as sons by Jesus Christ to Himself, according to the good pleasure of His will, [Rom. 8:29]

6 to the praise of the glory of His grace, [R]by which He made us accepted in [R]the Beloved. [Rom. 3:24] • Matt. 3:17

Redeemed by the Son

7 [R]In Him we have redemption through His blood, the forgiveness of sins, according to the riches of His grace [Heb. 9:12]

8 which He made to abound toward us in all wisdom and [T]prudence, *understanding*

9 having made known to us the mystery of His will, according to His good pleasure which He purposed in Himself,

10 that in the dispensation of the fullness of the times He might gather together in one all things in Christ, both* which are in heaven and which are on earth—in Him.

11 In Him also we have obtained an inheritance, being predestined according to [R]the purpose of Him who works all things according to the counsel of His will, Is. 46:10

12 that we who first trusted in Christ should be to the praise of His glory.

Sealed by the Spirit

13 In Him you also *trusted,* after you heard the word of truth, the gospel of your salvation; in whom also, having believed, you were sealed with the Holy Spirit of promise,

14 [R]who* is the guarantee of our inheritance [R]until the redemption of [R]the purchased possession, [R]to the praise of His glory. 2 Cor. 5:5 • Rom. 8:23 • [Acts 20:28] • 1 Pet. 2:9

Prayer for Revelation

15 Therefore I also, [R]after I heard of your faith in the Lord Jesus and your love for all the saints, Col. 1:4

16 do not cease to give thanks for you, making mention of you in my prayers:

17 that [R]the God of our Lord Jesus Christ, the Father of glory, [R]may give to you the spirit of wisdom and revelation in the knowledge of Him, John 20:17 • Col. 1:9

18 the eyes of your understanding* being enlightened; that you may know what is the hope of His calling, what are the riches of the glory of His inheritance in the saints,

19 and what *is* the exceeding greatness of His power toward us who believe, according to the working of His mighty power

20 which He worked in Christ when He raised Him from the dead and seated *Him* at His right hand in the heavenly *places,*

21 [R]far above all principality and power and might and dominion, and every name that is named, not only in this age but also in that which is to come. Phil. 2:9, 10

22 And [R]He put all *things* under His feet, and gave Him [R]*to be* head over all *things* to the church, Dan. 7:13, 14; Matt. 28:18☆ • Heb. 2:7

23 [R]which is His body, [R]the fullness of Him who fills all in all. Rom. 12:5 • Col. 2:9

1:10 NU, M omit *both* **1:14** NU *which* **1:18** NU, M *hearts*

1:4, 7, 13 Interaction Within the Trinity—The Bible glimpses interaction within the Trinity in creation (Page 4—Gen. 1:1, 2, 26) and the confusion of languages at Babel (11:7). In the NT emerges a clearer picture of the way the Father, Son, and Holy Spirit relate to one another in redeeming sinful humans.

The Father decrees the plans to be carried out on humanity's behalf (Eph. 1:4). The Son serves humankind to implement the Father's plans (Eph. 1:7). The Holy Spirit applies the work of the Son to the daily experience of believers in Christ (Eph. 1:13, 14).

A similar pattern appears at the baptism of Jesus (Page 979—Matt. 3:16, 17). The Father announced that Jesus was doing what pleased Him. Jesus identified with sinful Israel. The Holy Spirit descended as a sign for those who would believe.

In 1 Cor. 12:4–6 is a picture of the Persons of the Trinity interacting to direct the ministry of the church. The Holy Spirit personally gives the ministry gifts to each Christian. The Son establishes the pattern of ministry achieved by the gifted believers. The Father empowers what will be accomplished in a congregation as part of the church universal.

Now turn to Page 26—THE CHRISTIAN'S GUIDE: Understanding Other Spirit Beings.

1:22, 23 God's Work in the Church—Observation alone cannot reveal the awesome nature of the church, the body of Jesus Christ. It appears to be a human institution that serves religious purposes, but the Bible tells quite a different story.

CHAPTER 2

Old Condition: Dead to God

AND [R]you *He made alive,* who were dead
in trespasses and sins, Col. 2:13
2 in which you once walked according to
the course of this world, according to the
prince of the power of the air, the spirit who
now works in the sons of disobedience,
3 [R]among whom also we all once con-
ducted ourselves in the lusts of our flesh, ful-
filling the desires of the flesh and of the mind,
and [R]were by nature children of wrath, just as
the others. 1 Pet. 4:3 • [Ps. 51:5]

New Condition: Alive to God

4 But God, who is rich in mercy, because of
His great love with which He loved us,
5 [R]even when we were dead in trespasses,
made us alive together with Christ (by grace
you have been saved), Rom. 5:6, 8
6 and raised *us* up together, and made *us* sit
together [R]in the heavenly *places* in Christ Je-
sus, Eph. 1:20
7 that in the ages to come He might show
the exceeding riches of His grace in *His* kind-
ness toward us in Christ Jesus.
8 [R]For by grace you have been saved
[R]through faith, and that not of yourselves; *it is*
the gift of God, [2 Tim. 1:9] • Rom. 4:16
9 not of [R]works, lest anyone should
[R]boast. Rom. 4:4, 5; 11:6 • Rom. 3:27
10 For we are [R]His workmanship, created in
Christ Jesus for good works, which God pre-
pared beforehand that we should walk in
them. Is. 19:25

Reconciliation of Jews and Gentiles

11 Therefore remember that you, once Gen-
tiles in the flesh—who are called Uncircumci-
sion by what is called the Circumcision made
in the flesh by hands—
12 that at that time you were without Christ,
being aliens from the commonwealth of Israel
and strangers from the covenants of promise,
having no hope and without God in the world.
13 But now in Christ Jesus you who once
were far off have been brought near by the
blood of Christ.
14 [R]For He Himself is our peace, who has
made both one, and has broken down the
middle wall of separation, Is. 9:6★
15 having abolished in His flesh the en-
mity, *that is,* the law of commandments *con-
tained* in ordinances, so as to create in
Himself one [R]new man *from* the two, *thus*
making peace, Gal. 6:15
16 and that He might reconcile them both to
God in one body through the cross, thereby
putting to death the enmity.
17 And He came and preached peace to you
who were afar off and to those who were near.
18 For [R]through Him we both have access by
one Spirit to the Father. John 10:9
19 Now, therefore, you are no longer strang-
ers and foreigners, but fellow citizens with the
saints and members of the household of God,
20 having been built on the foundation of the
apostles and prophets, Jesus Christ Himself
being the chief corner*stone,*
21 [R]in whom the whole building, being fitted
together, grows into [R]a holy temple in the
Lord, Ps. 118:22★ • 1 Cor. 3:16, 17
22 [R]in whom you also are being built to-
gether for a [R]dwelling place of God in the
Spirit. 1 Pet. 2:5 • John 17:23

CHAPTER 3

Revelation of the Mystery of the Church

FOR this reason I, Paul, the prisoner of
Christ Jesus for you Gentiles—
2 if indeed you have heard of the [T]dispensa-
tion of the grace of God [R]which was given to
me for you, *stewardship* • Acts 9:15
3 [R]how that by revelation He made known
to me the mystery (as I have briefly written al-
ready, Acts 22:17, 21; 26:16
4 by which, when you read, you may under-
stand my knowledge in the mystery of Christ),
5 which in other ages was not made known
to the sons of men, as it has now been re-
vealed by the Spirit to His holy apostles and
prophets:
6 that the Gentiles should be fellow heirs,
of the same body, and partakers of His prom-
ise in Christ through the gospel,
7 of which I became a minister according to
the gift of the grace of God given to me by the
effective working of His power.
8 To me, [R]who am less than the least of all

First, the church is the congregation of all believers in Jesus Christ from all places and times (Page 1205—Eph. 2:19, 20; Page 1267—Heb. 12:23). It is all born-again men, women, and children called out of every tribe and nation (Page 1316—Rev. 5:9).

Second, the church is the bride of Christ, which will live and reign with Him throughout all eternity (Page 1209—Eph. 5:31, 32; Page 1325—Rev. 19:7).

Third, the church is entrusted with the mission of world evangelization during this age (Page 1011—Matt. 28:19, 20; Page 1112—Acts 1:8).

Fourth, the church exists in local congregations, which gather regularly for worship, instruction, fellowship, and outreach (Page 1114—Acts 2:42; 14:23; Page 1312—Rev. 1:4).

Fifth, the Holy Spirit gives the church leadership and spiritual abilities to bring its members to maturity in life and ministry (Page 1175—1 Cor. 12:4–11; Page 1207—Eph. 4:11–16).

Now turn to Page 1005—Matt. 25:31, 32: God's Work in the Future.

the saints, this grace was given, that I should preach among the Gentiles the unsearchable riches of Christ, [1 Cor. 15:9]

9 and to make all see what *is* the fellowship* of the mystery, which from the beginning of the ages has been hidden in God who created all things through Jesus Christ;*

10 [R]to the intent that now [R]the manifold wisdom of God might be made known by the church to the principalities and powers in the heavenly *places,* 1 Pet. 1:12 • [1 Tim. 3:16]

11 according to the eternal purpose which He accomplished in Christ Jesus our Lord,

12 in whom we have boldness and access with confidence through faith in Him.

13 [R]Therefore I ask that you do not lose heart at my tribulations for you, [R]which is your glory. Phil. 1:14 • 2 Cor. 1:6

Prayer for Realization

14 For this reason I bow my knees to the Father of our Lord Jesus Christ,*

15 from whom the whole family in heaven and earth is named,

16 that He would grant you, [R]according to the riches of His glory, [R]to be strengthened with might through His Spirit in [R]the inner man, [Phil. 4:19] • Col. 1:11 • Rom. 7:22

17 [R]that Christ may dwell in your hearts through faith; that you, [R]being rooted and grounded in love, John 14:23 • Col. 1:23

18 [R]may be able to comprehend with all the saints [R]what *is* the width and length and depth and height— Eph. 1:18 • Rom. 8:39

19 to know the love of Christ which passes knowledge; that you may be filled [R]with all the fullness of God. Eph. 1:23

20 Now [R]to Him who is able to do exceedingly abundantly [R]above all that we ask or think, [R]according to the power that works in us, Rom. 16:25 • 1 Cor. 2:9 • Col. 1:29

21 [R]to Him *be* glory in the church by Christ Jesus to all generations, forever and ever. Amen. Rom. 11:36

CHAPTER 4

Exhortation to Unity

I THEREFORE, the prisoner of the Lord, beseech you to [R]walk worthy of the calling with which you were called, 1 Thess. 2:12

2 with all lowliness and gentleness, with longsuffering, bearing with one another in love,

3 endeavoring to keep the unity of the Spirit [R]in the bond of peace. Col. 3:14

3:9 NU, M *stewardship* (dispensation) • NU omits *through Jesus Christ* **3:14** NU omits *of our Lord Jesus Christ*

3:21 The Purpose of the Church—The ultimate purpose of the church is to bring honor and glory to its head, Jesus Christ. It does this as it fulfills its two purposes related to God's program for the world.

The one purpose of the church, as it relates to the world, is evangelism. This program is spelled out in the Great Commission (Page 1011—Matt. 28:19, 20), which has never been rescinded. The program is to "make disciples of all the nations." The way this is to be done is twofold: by "baptizing them in the name of the Father and of the Son and of the Holy Spirit," and by "teaching them to observe all things that I have commanded you." Baptism is not an optional afterthought. It is a vital part of evangelism and making disciples. By baptism, one indicates that he has been identified with Christ in His death, burial, and resurrection (that is, he is a member of the universal church, the body of Christ) and wishes to be identified with the local church. A responsible parent not only brings a child into the world, but also provides what is necessary for the child's growth. So in the church, teaching must accompany evangelism so that the child of God can learn all that God expects of him and has provided for him.

Another purpose of the church, as it relates to the world, is edification. According to Eph. 4:12 the saints need to be edified (built up) for two goals: "for the equipping of the saints for the work of ministry." The believers who compose the church's membership need to be built up so that they may realize all that God has provided for Christian living and that they may come to spiritual maturity. They also need to be equipped to perform that work in the body of Christ that God wants them to perform. In a real sense each member of the church is to be a Christian worker so that the work that God wants to perform through the local church can be accomplished.

Now turn to Page 1238—1 Tim. 3:1–13: The Offices of the Church.

4:3 The Person of the Holy Spirit—One of the most serious errors in the minds of many people concerning the Holy Spirit is that He is simply a principle or an influence. On the contrary, the Holy Spirit is as much a Person (individual existence of a conscious being) as the Father and the Son.

a. The personality of the Holy Spirit. The Bible speaks of the mind (Page 1155—Rom. 8:27) and will (Page 1176—1 Cor. 12:11) of the Holy Spirit. He is often described as speaking directly to men in the Book of Acts. During Paul's second missionary journey the apostle was forbidden by the Spirit to visit a certain mission field (Page 1130—Acts 16:6, 7) and then was instructed to proceed toward another field of service (Page 1130—Acts 16:10). It was God's Spirit who spoke directly to Christian leaders in the Antioch church, commanding them to send Paul and Barnabas on their first missionary journey (Page 1126—Acts 13:2).

b. The deity of the Holy Spirit. He is not only a real Person, but He is also God. As is God the Father, He too is everywhere at once (Page 619—Ps. 139:7). As the Son is eternal, the Holy Spirit has also existed forever (Page 1263—Heb. 9:14). He is often referred to as God in the Bible. See Acts 5:3, 4. Finally, the Holy Spirit is equal with the Father and Son. This is seen during the baptism of Christ (Page 979—Matt. 3:16, 17) and is mentioned by Jesus Himself just prior to His ascension from the Mount of Olives (Page 1011—Matt. 28:19, 20).

Now turn to Page 1250—Titus 3:5: The Work of the Holy Spirit in Salvation.

Explanation of Unity

4 [R]*There is* one body and one Spirit, just as you were called in one hope of your calling; Rom. 12:5

5 one Lord, one faith, one baptism;

6 one God and Father of all, who *is* above all, and through all, and in you* all.

Means for Unity: The Gifts

7 But to each one of us grace was given according to the measure of Christ's gift.

8 Therefore He says:

"When He ascended on high,
He led captivity captive,
*And gave gifts to men."**

9 [R](Now this, "He ascended"—what does it mean but that He also first* descended into the lower parts of the earth? John 3:13

10 He who descended is also the One [R]who ascended far above all the heavens, [R]that He might fill all things.) Acts 1:9★ • [Eph. 1:23]

11 And He Himself gave some *to be* apostles, some prophets, some evangelists, and some pastors and teachers,

Purpose of the Gifts

12 for the equipping of the saints for the work of ministry, [R]for the edifying of [R]the body of Christ, 1 Cor. 14:26 • Col. 1:24

13 till we all come to the unity of the faith [R]and of the knowledge of the Son of God, to [R]a perfect man, to the measure of the stature of the fullness of Christ; Col. 2:2 • 1 Cor. 14:20

14 that we should no longer be [R]children, tossed to and fro and carried about with every wind of doctrine, by the trickery of men, in the cunning craftiness of [R]deceitful plotting, 1 Cor. 14:20 • Rom. 16:18

15 but, speaking the truth in love, may grow up in all things into Him who is the [R]head—Christ— Eph. 1:22

16 from whom the whole body, joined and knit together by what every joint supplies, according to the effective working by which every part does its share, causes growth of the body for the edifying of itself in love.

Put Off the Old Man

17 This I say, therefore, and testify in the Lord, that you should [R]no longer walk as the rest of* the Gentiles walk, in the futility of their mind, Eph. 2:2; 4:22

18 having their understanding darkened, being alienated from the life of God, because of the ignorance that is in them, because of the [R]blindness of their heart; Rom. 1:21

19 [R]who, being past feeling, have given themselves over to lewdness, to work all uncleanness with greediness. 1 Tim. 4:2

20 But you have not so learned Christ,

21 if indeed you have heard Him and have been taught by Him, as the truth is in Jesus:

22 that you put off, concerning your former conduct, the old man which grows corrupt according to the deceitful lusts,

Put On the New Man

23 and [R]be renewed in the spirit of your mind, [Rom. 12:2]

24 and that you [R]put on the new man which was created according to God, in true righteousness and holiness. [Rom. 6:4; 7:6]

25 Therefore, putting away lying, *"Let each one of you speak truth with his neighbor,"** for we are members of one another.

26 *"Be angry, and do not sin"*:* do not let the sun go down on your wrath,

27 nor give place to the devil.

28 Let him who stole steal no longer, but rather [R]let him labor, working with *his* hands what is good, that he may have something to give him who has need. Acts 20:35

29 [R]Let no corrupt word proceed out of your mouth, but [R]what is good for necessary edification, [R]that it may impart grace to the hearers. Col. 3:8 • 1 Thess. 5:11 • Col. 3:16

Grieve Not the Holy Spirit

30 And [R]do not grieve the Holy Spirit of God, by whom you were sealed for the day of redemption. Is. 7:13

31 [R]Let all bitterness, wrath, anger, clamor, and [R]evil speaking be put away from you, with all malice. Col. 3:8, 19 • James 4:11

32 And [R]be kind to one another, tenderhearted, [R]forgiving one another, even as God in Christ forgave you. 2 Cor. 6:10 • [Mark 11:25]

CHAPTER 5

THEREFORE[R] be imitators of God as dear [R]children. Luke 6:36 • 1 Pet. 1:14–16

2 And [R]walk in love, [R]as Christ also has loved us and given Himself for us, an offering and a sacrifice to God for a sweet-smelling aroma. 1 Thess. 4:9 • Gal. 1:4

3 But fornication and all uncleanness or covetousness, let it not even be named among you, as is fitting for saints;

4 [R]neither filthiness, nor foolish talking, nor coarse jesting, which are not fitting, but rather giving of thanks. Matt. 12:34, 35

5 For this you know,* that no fornicator, unclean person, nor covetous man, who is an idolater, has any [R]inheritance in the kingdom of Christ and God. 1 Cor. 6:9, 10

6 Let no one deceive you with empty words, for because of these things the wrath of God comes upon the sons of disobedience.

4:6 NU omits *you;* M *us* **4:8** Ps. 68:18☆ **4:9** NU omits *first* **4:17** NU omits *the rest of* **4:25** Zech. 8:16 **4:26** Ps. 4:4 **5:5** NU *For know this*

7 Therefore do not be [R]partakers with
them. 1 Tim. 5:22
8 For you were once darkness, but now *you*
are [R]light in the Lord. Walk as children of
light 1 Thess. 5:5
9 (for the fruit of the Spirit* *is* in all good-
ness, righteousness, and truth),
10 [R]finding out what is acceptable to the
Lord. [Rom. 12:1, 2]
11 And have [R]no fellowship with the unfruit-
ful works of darkness, but rather [T]expose
them. 2 Cor. 6:14 • *reprove*
12 [R]For it is shameful even to speak of
those things which are done by them in se-
cret. Rom. 1:24

Walk as Children of Light

13 But [R]all things that are exposed are made
manifest by the light, for whatever makes
manifest is light. [John 3:20, 21]
14 Therefore He says:

[R]"Awake, you who sleep, [Is. 26:19; 60:1]★
Arise from the dead,
And Christ will give you light."

15 [R]See then that you walk [T]circumspectly,
not as fools but as wise, Col. 4:5 • *carefully*
16 [R]redeeming the time, [R]because the days
are evil. Col. 4:5 • Eccl. 11:2
17 Therefore do not be unwise, but under-
stand what the will of the Lord *is*.

Be Filled with the Spirit

18 And [R]do not be drunk with wine, in
which is dissipation; but be filled with the
Spirit, Prov. 20:1; 23:31
19 speaking to one another in psalms and
hymns and spiritual songs, singing and mak-
ing melody in your heart to the Lord,
20 [R]giving thanks always for all things to
God the Father [R]in the name of our Lord Jesus
Christ, Ps. 34:1 • [1 Pet. 2:5]
21 [R]submitting to one another in the fear of
God.* [Phil. 2:3]

Wives: Submit to Your Husbands

22 Wives, [R]submit to your own husbands, as
to the Lord. Col. 3:18—4:1
23 For [R]the husband is head of the wife, as
also [R]Christ is head of the church; and He is
the Savior of the body. [1 Cor. 11:3] • Col. 1:18
24 Therefore, just as the church is subject to
Christ, so *let* the wives *be* to their own hus-
bands [R]in everything. Titus 2:4, 5

Husbands: Love Your Wives

25 [R]Husbands, love your wives, just as Christ
also loved the church and [R]gave Himself for
her, Col. 3:19 • Acts 20:28
26 that He might sanctify and cleanse her
with the washing of water by the word,
27 [R]that He might present her to Himself a
glorious church, [R]not having spot or wrinkle
or any such thing, but that she should be holy
and without blemish. Col. 1:22 • Song 4:7
28 So husbands ought to love their own
wives as their own bodies; he who loves his
wife loves himself.
29 For no one ever hated his own flesh, but
nourishes and cherishes it, just as the Lord
does the church.

5:9 NU *light* 5:21 NU *Christ*

5:18 Walking in the Spirit: Filling—To be filled with the Spirit is to be controlled by the Spirit and is therefore crucial to successfully living the Christian life. Unlike the indwelling of the Spirit, filling is a repeated experience. This is underscored by the use of the present tense ("be filled") as well as by biblical examples of Christians who were filled more than once (Page 1113—Acts 2:4; 4:31). Just as important, we must observe that filling is a command to be obeyed, not an option.

The next most important question is, How can someone be filled with the Spirit? The prerequisites are simply confession of sin and yielding to God. The former means to agree with God about the person's sin; the latter means primarily dedication of self to God. The believer who chooses to obey in these areas is filled with the Spirit and enabled to manifest Christ-like character. This obedience may be accompanied by prayer but is not necessarily so.

The certainty of being filled with the Spirit may be confirmed by the believer's faith and life. The believer must, of course, believe God's Word that meeting the conditions will result in the filling. The Spirit-filled person will exhibit the Christ-like character described in Gal. 5:22, 23 as the fruit of the Spirit. Included in that list are all the vibrant, attractive qualities desired by all Christians. How delightful it is that any Christian may possess them and be transformed by the filling of the Spirit.

Now turn to Page 28—THE CHRISTIAN'S GUIDE: Facing Problems in the New Life.

5:25–29 The Relationship of the Church to Christ—The wonderful relationship that exists between Christ and the church was initiated by Christ who loved the church and gave Himself for it. The intimacies of that relationship are described with seven figures:

a. "The shepherd and the sheep" emphasizes both the warm leadership and protection of Christ and the helplessness and dependency of believers (Page 1094—John 10:1–18).
b. "The vine and the branches" points out the necessity for Christians to depend on Christ's sustaining strength for growth (Page 1100—John 15:1–8).
c. "Christ as High Priest" and "the church as a kingdom of priests" stresses the joyful worship, fellowship, and service, which the church can render to God through Christ (Page 126—Heb. 5:1–10; 7:1; 8:6; Page 1280—1 Pet. 2:5–9; Page 1312—Rev. 1:6).
d. "The cornerstone and building stones" accents the foundational value of Christ to everything the church is and does, as well as Christ's value to the unity of believers. Love is to be the mortar which solidly

30 For [R]we are members of His body,* of His
flesh and of His bones. Gen. 2:23
31 *"For this reason a man shall leave his father and mother and be joined to his wife, and the two shall become one flesh."* *
32 This is a great mystery, but I speak concerning Christ and the church.
33 Nevertheless [R]let each one of you in particular so love his own wife as himself, and let the wife *see* that she [R]respects *her* husband. Col. 3:19 • 1 Pet. 3:1, 6

CHAPTER 6

Children: Obey Your Parents

CHILDREN, [R]obey your parents in the Lord, for this is right. Col. 3:20
2 *"Honor your father and mother,"* which is the first commandment with promise:
3 *"that it may be well with you and you may live long on the earth."**

4 And you, fathers, do not provoke your children to wrath, but bring them up in the training and admonition of the Lord.

Service on the Job

5 [R]Bondservants, be obedient to those who are your masters according to the flesh, [R]with fear and trembling, in sincerity of heart, as to Christ; [1 Tim. 6:1] • 2 Cor. 7:15
6 [R]not with eyeservice, as men-pleasers, but as bondservants of Christ, doing the will of God from the heart, Col. 3:22
7 with goodwill doing service, as to the Lord, and not to men,
8 [R]knowing that whatever good anyone does, he will receive the same from the Lord, whether *he is* a slave or free. Rom. 2:6
9 And you, masters, do the same things to them, giving up threatening, knowing that your own Master also* is in heaven, and [R]there is no partiality with Him. Rom. 2:11

Put On the Armor of God

10 Finally, my brethren, be strong in the Lord and in the power of His might.
11 [R]Put on the whole armor of God, that you may be able to stand against the [T]wiles of the devil. [2 Cor. 6:7] • *schemings*
12 For we do not wrestle against flesh and blood, but against principalities, against powers, against the rulers of the darkness of this age,* against spiritual *hosts* of wickedness in the heavenly *places.*
13 Therefore take up the whole armor of God, that you may be able to withstand in the evil day, and having done all, to stand.
14 Stand therefore, [R]having girded your waist with truth, [R]having put on the breastplate of righteousness, Is. 11:5 • Is. 59:17
15 [R]and having shod your feet with the preparation of the gospel of peace; Is. 52:7
16 above all, taking [R]the shield of faith with which you will be able to quench all the fiery darts of the wicked one. 1 John 5:4
17 And [R]take the helmet of salvation, and [R]the sword of the Spirit, which is the word of God; 1 Thess. 5:8 • [Heb. 4:12]

5:30 NU omits the rest of v. 30. **5:31** Gen. 2:24
6:3 Deut. 5:16 **6:9** NU *He who is both their Master and yours* **6:12** NU *rulers of this darkness,*

---

holds the living stones together (Page 1168—1 Cor. 3:9; 13:1–13; Page 1205—Eph. 2:19–22; Page 1280—1 Pet. 2:5).

e. "The head and many-membered body" is frequently used in Scripture to illustrate several tremendous truths: the church is a vibrant organism, not merely an organization; it draws its vitality and direction from Christ, the head; and each believer has a unique and necessary place in its growth (Page 1176—1 Cor. 12:12, 13, 27; Page 1207—Eph. 4:4).
f. "The last Adam and new creation" presents Christ as the initiator of a new creation of believers as Adam was of the old creation (Page 1178—1 Cor. 15:22, 45; Page 1187—2 Cor. 5:17).
g. "The bridegroom and bride" beautifully emphasizes the intimate fellowship and co-ownership existing between Christ and the church (Eph. 5:25–33; Page 1325—Rev. 19:7, 8; 21:9).

You have now completed The Christian's Guide to the New Life.

6:4 The Role of the Parents—While fathers are identified as the parents responsible for setting the pattern for child rearing, mothers usually do much more of the training and instructing of families' children. Mothers and fathers need to agree on their approach to child rearing and support one another in their efforts with their children. Both parents are to be obeyed and honored equally by their children (vv. 1, 2). Parental responsibility is set out in two ways: First, what they are *not* to do—"do not provoke your children to wrath." Parents are not to overdiscipline in a reign of terror that will result in bitterly hostile children (v. 4) or children who give up on life (Page 1222—Col. 3:21). Second, what parents *are* to do—"but bring them up in the training and admonition of the Lord." To "bring them up" involves three ideas:

a. Parenting is a continuous job. As long as a child is a dependent, parents are responsible for rearing them so they become the people God wants them to be.
b. Parenting is a loving job. To "bring up" means literally "to nourish tenderly." Children should be objects of tender, loving care.
c. Parenting is a twofold job involving 1) nurture (lit., "child training")—all that children need for physical, mental, and spiritual development—and 2) admonition (lit., "corrective" discipline) of the Lord.

Fathers and mothers are God's constituted home authority (Page 629—Prov. 1:8; 6:20–22) to nurture children along godly paths and to admonish them away from ungodly ones. Fathers and mothers who do not discipline their children are parents who are themselves undisciplined and disobedient to God's will.

Now turn to Page 648—Prov. 22:6: A Prescription for Rearing Children.

Pray for Boldness

18 [R]praying always with all prayer and sup-
plication in the Spirit, [R]being watchful to this
end with all perseverance and supplication
for all the saints— Luke 18:1 • [Matt. 26:41]
19 and for me, that utterance may be
given to me, that I may open my mouth
boldly to make known the mystery of the
gospel,
20 for which [R]I am an ambassador in chains;
that in it I may speak boldly, as I ought to
speak. 2 Cor. 5:20

Conclusion

21 But that you also may know my affairs
and how I am doing, Tychicus, a beloved
brother and faithful minister in the Lord, will
make all things known to you;
22 [R]whom I have sent to you for this very
purpose, that you may know our affairs, and
that he may comfort your hearts. Col. 4:8
23 Peace to the brethren, and love with faith,
from God the Father and the Lord Jesus Christ.
24 Grace *be* with all those who love our Lord
Jesus Christ in sincerity. Amen.

THE EPISTLE OF PAUL THE APOSTLE TO THE

PHILIPPIANS

THE BOOK OF PHILIPPIANS

Paul writes a thank-you note to the believers at Philippi for their help in his hour of need, and he uses the occasion to send along some instruction on Christian unity. His central thought is simple: Only in Christ are real unity and joy possible. With Christ as your model of humility and service, you can enjoy a oneness of purpose, attitude, goal, and labor—a truth Paul illustrates from his own life and one the Philippians desperately need to hear. Within their own ranks, fellow workers in the Philippian church are at odds, hindering the work in proclaiming new life in Christ. Because of this, Paul exhorts the church to "stand fast . . . be of the same mind . . . rejoice in the Lord always . . . but in everything by prayer and supplication, with thanksgiving, let your requests be made known . . . and the peace of God, which surpasses all understanding, will guard your hearts and minds through Christ Jesus" (4:1, 2, 4, 6, 7).

This epistle is called *Pros Philippesious,* "To the Philippians." The church at Philippi was the first church Paul founded in Macedonia.

THE AUTHOR OF PHILIPPIANS

The external and internal evidence for the Pauline authorship of Philippians is very strong, and there is scarcely any doubt that anyone but Paul wrote it.

THE TIME OF PHILIPPIANS

In 356 B.C. King Philip of Macedonia (the father of Alexander the Great) took this town and expanded it, renaming it Philippi. The Romans captured it in 168 B.C.; and in 42 B.C. the defeat of the forces of Brutus and Cassius by those of Anthony and Octavian (later Augustus) took place outside the city. Octavian turned Philippi into a Roman colony (cf. Acts 16:12) and a military outpost. The citizens of this colony were regarded as citizens of Rome and given a number of special privileges. Because Philippi was a military city and not a commercial center, there were not enough Jews for a synagogue when Paul came (Acts 16:13).

Paul's "Macedonian Call" in Troas during his second missionary journey led to his ministry in Philippi with the conversion of Lydia and others. Paul and Silas were beaten and imprisoned, but this resulted in the conversion of the Philippian jailer. The magistrates were placed in a dangerous position by beating Roman citizens without a trial (Acts 16:37–40), and that embarrassment may have prevented future reprisals against the new Christians in Philippi. Paul visited the Philippians again on his third missionary journey (Acts 20:1, 6). When they heard of his Roman imprisonment, the Philippian church sent Epaphroditus with financial help (4:18); they had helped Paul in this way on at least two other occasions (4:16). Epaphroditus almost died of an illness, yet remained with Paul long enough for the Philippians to receive word of his malady. Upon his recovery, Paul sent this letter back with him to Philippi (2:25–30).

Silas, Timothy, Luke, and Paul first came to Philippi in A.D. 51, eleven years before Paul wrote this letter. Philippians 1:13 and 4:22 suggest that it was written from Rome, although some commentators argue for Caesarea or Ephesus. Paul's life was at stake, and he was evidently awaiting the verdict of the Imperial Court (2:20–26).

THE CHRIST OF PHILIPPIANS

The great *kenosis* passage is one of several portraits of Christ in this epistle. In chapter 1, Paul sees Christ as his life ("For to me, to live *is* Christ," 1:21). In chapter 2 Christ is the model of true humility ("Let this mind be in you which was also in Christ Jesus," 2:5). Chapter 3 presents Him as the One "who will transform our lowly body that it may be conformed to His glorious body" (3:21). In chapter 4 He is the source of Paul's power over circumstances ("I can do all things through Christ who strengthens me," 4:13).

KEYS TO PHILIPPIANS

Key Word: To Live Is Christ—Central to Philippians is the concept of "For to me, to live *is* Christ, and to die *is* gain" (1:21). Every chapter resounds with the theme of the centrality of Jesus in the Christian's life. High points include the following: "Let this mind be in you which was also in Christ Jesus" (2:5); "I also count all things loss for the excellence of the knowledge of Christ Jesus" (3:8); and "I can do all things through Christ who strengthens me" (4:13).

Key Verses: Philippians 1:21 and 4:12—"For to me, to live *is* Christ, and to die *is* gain" (1:21).

"I know how to be abased, and I know how to abound. Everywhere and in all things I have learned both to be full and to be hungry, both to abound and to suffer need" (4:12).

Key Chapter: Philippians 2—The grandeur of the truth of the New Testament seldom exceeds the revelation of the humility of Jesus

Christ when He left heaven to become a servant of man. Christ is clearly the Christian's example; and Paul encourages, "Let this mind be in you which was also in Christ Jesus" (2:5).

SURVEY OF PHILIPPIANS

Philippians is the epistle of joy and encouragement in the midst of adverse circumstances. Paul freely expresses his fond affection for the Philippians, appreciates their consistent testimony and support, and lovingly urges them to center their actions and thoughts on the pursuit of the Person and power of Christ. Paul also seeks to correct the problems of disunity and rivalry (2:2–4) and to prevent the problems of legalism and antinomianism (3:1–19). Philippians focuses on: Paul's account of his present circumstances (1); Paul's appeal to have the mind of Christ (2); Paul's appeal to have the knowledge of Christ (3); Paul's appeal to have the peace of Christ (4).

Paul's Account of His Present Circumstances (1): Paul's usual salutation (1:1, 2) is followed by his thanksgiving, warm regard, and prayer on behalf of the Philippians (1:3–11). For years, they have participated in the apostle's ministry, and he prays for their continued growth in the real knowledge of Christ. Paul shares the circumstances of his imprisonment and rejoices in the spread of the gospel in spite of and because of his situation (1:12–26). As he considers the outcome of his approaching trial, he expresses his willingness to "depart and be with Christ" (1:23) or to continue in ministry. Paul encourages the Philippians to remain steadfast in the face of opposition and coming persecution (1:27–30).

Paul's Appeal to Have the Mind of Christ (2): Paul exhorts the Philippians to have a spirit of unity and mutual concern by embracing the attitude of humility (2:1–4), the greatest example of which is the incarnation and crucifixion of Christ (2:5–11). The *kenosis,* or "emptying," of Christ does not mean that He divested Himself of His deity, but that He withheld His preincarnate glory and voluntarily restricted His use of certain attributes (e.g., omnipresence and omniscience). Paul asks the Philippians to apply this attitude to their lives (2:12–18), and he gives two more examples of sacrifice—the ministries of Timothy and Epaphroditus (2:19–30).

Paul's Appeal to Have the Knowledge of Christ (3): It appears that Paul is about to close his letter ("Finally, my brethren," 3:1) when he launches into a warning about the continuing problem of legalism (3:1–9). Paul refutes this teaching with revealing autobiographical details about his previous attainments in Judaism. Compared to the goal of knowing Christ, those pursuits are as nothing. True righteousness is received through faith, not by mechanical obedience to any law. Paul yearns for the promised attainment of the resurrected body.

Paul's Appeal to Have the Peace of Christ (4): In a series of exhortations, Paul urges the Philippians to have peace with the brethren by living a lifestyle of unity, prayerful dependence, and holiness (4:13). In 4:4–9 Paul describes the secrets of having the peace of God as well as peace with God. He then rejoices over their gift, but explains that the power of Christ enables him to live above his circumstances (4:10–20). This joyous letter from prison closes with greetings and a benediction (4:21–23).

FOCUS	ACCOUNT OF CIRCUMSTANCES	THE MIND OF CHRIST	THE KNOWLEDGE OF CHRIST	THE PEACE OF CHRIST
REFERENCE	1:1—	2:1—	3:1—	4:1—4:23
DIVISION	PARTAKE OF CHRIST	PEOPLE OF CHRIST	PURSUIT OF CHRIST	POWER OF CHRIST
TOPIC	SUFFERING	SUBMISSION	SALVATION	SANCTIFICATION
	EXPERIENCE	EXAMPLES	EXHORTATION	
LOCATION	ROME			
TIME	c. A.D. 62			

OUTLINE OF PHILIPPIANS

Part One: The Supremacy of Christ in the Church (1:1—2:23)

I. Paul's Account of His Present Circumstance 1:1–30
- A. Paul's Prayer of Thanksgiving 1:1–11
- B. Paul's Afflictions Promote the Gospel 1:12–18
- C. Paul's Afflictions Exalt the Lord 1:19–26
- D. Paul's Exhortation to the Afflicted 1:27–30

II. Paul's Appeal to Have the Mind of Christ 2:1–30
- A. Paul's Exhortation to Humility 2:1–4
- B. Christ's Example of Humility 2:5–16
- C. Paul's Example of Humility 2:17, 18
- D. Timothy's Example of Humility 2:19–24
- E. Epaphroditus's Example of Humility .. 2:25–30

III. Paul's Appeal to Have the Knowledge of Christ 3:1–21
- A. Warning Against Confidence in the Flesh 3:1–9
- B. Exhortation to Know Christ 3:10–16
- C. Warning Against Living for the Flesh 3:17–21

IV. Paul's Appeal to Have the Peace of Christ 4:1–23
- A. Peace with the Brethren 4:1–3
- B. Peace with the Lord 4:4–9
- C. Peace in All Circumstances 4:10–19
- D. Conclusion 4:20–23

CHAPTER 1

Paul's Prayer of Thanksgiving

PAUL and Timothy, bondservants of Jesus
Christ,

To all the saints in Christ Jesus who are in
Philippi, with the bishops* and deacons:

2 Grace to you and peace from God our Fa-
ther and the Lord Jesus Christ.
3 [R]I thank my God upon every remem-
brance of you, 1 Cor. 1:4
4 always in [R]every prayer of mine making
request for you all with joy, Eph. 1:16
5 [R]for your fellowship in the gospel from
the first day until now, [Rom. 12:13]
6 being confident of this very thing, that He
who has begun a good work in you will com-
plete *it* until the day of Jesus Christ;
7 just as it is right for me to think this of
you all, because I have you in my heart, inas-
much as both in my chains and in the defense
and confirmation of the gospel, you all are
partakers with me of grace.
8 For God is my witness, how greatly I long
for you all with the affection of Jesus Christ.
9 And this I pray, that your love may
abound still more and more in knowledge and
all discernment,
10 that you may approve the things that are
excellent, that you may be sincere and with-
out offense till the day of Christ,
11 being filled with the fruits of righteous-
ness [R]which *are* by Jesus Christ, [R]to the glory
and praise of God. Col. 1:6 • John 15:8

Paul's Afflictions Promote the Gospel

12 But I want you to know, brethren, that the
things *which happened* to me have actually
turned out for the furtherance of the gospel,
13 so that it has become evident [R]to the
whole palace guard, and to all the rest, that
my chains are in Christ; Phil. 4:22
14 and most of the brethren in the Lord, hav-
ing become confident by my chains, are much
more bold to speak the word without fear.
15 Some indeed preach Christ even from
envy and strife, and some also from goodwill:
16 The former* preach Christ from selfish
ambition, not sincerely, supposing to add af-
fliction to my chains;
17 but the latter out of love, knowing that I
am appointed for the defense of the gospel.
18 What then? Only *that* in every way,
whether in pretense or in truth, Christ is
preached; and in this I rejoice, yes, and will
rejoice.

Paul's Afflictions Exalt the Lord

19 For I know that this will turn out for my
deliverance through your prayer and the sup-
ply of the Spirit of Jesus Christ,
20 according to my earnest expectation and
hope that in nothing I shall be ashamed, but
[R]with all boldness, as always, so now also
Christ will be magnified in my body, whether
by life [R]or by death. Eph. 6:19, 20 • [Rom. 14:8]
21 For to me, to live *is* Christ, and to die *is*
gain.
22 But if *I* live on in the flesh, this *will mean*
fruit from *my* labor; yet what I shall choose I
[T]cannot tell. *do not know*
23 For* I am hard-pressed between the two,
having a desire to depart and be with Christ,
which is [R]far better. [Ps. 16:11]
24 Nevertheless to remain in the flesh *is*
more needful for you.
25 And being confident of this, I know that I

1:1 Lit. *overseers* **1:16** NU reverses vv. 16 and 17.
1:23 NU, M *But*

shall remain and continue with you all for your progress and joy of faith,

26 that [R]your rejoicing for me may be more abundant in Jesus Christ by my coming to you again. 2 Cor. 1:14

Paul's Exhortation to the Afflicted

27 Only [R]let your conduct be worthy of the gospel of Christ, so that whether I come and see you or am absent, I may hear of your affairs, that you stand fast in one spirit, [R]with one mind [R]striving together for the faith of the gospel, Eph. 4:1 • Eph. 4:3 • Jude 3

28 and not in any way terrified by your adversaries, which is to them a proof of perdition, but to you of salvation,* and that from God.

29 For to you it has been granted on behalf of Christ, [R]not only to believe in Him, but also to suffer for His sake, Eph. 2:8

30 [R]having the same conflict which you saw in me and now hear *is* in me. Col. 1:29

CHAPTER 2

Paul's Exhortation to Humility

THEREFORE if *there is* any [T]consolation in Christ, if any comfort of love, if any fellowship of the Spirit, if any [R]affection and mercy, Or *encouragement* • Col. 3:12

2 [R]fulfill my joy [R]by being like-minded, having the same love, *being* of [R]one accord, of one mind. John 3:29 • Rom. 12:16 • Phil. 4:2

3 [R]*Let* nothing *be done* through selfish ambition or conceit, but [R]in lowliness of mind let each esteem others better than himself. Gal. 5:26 • Rom. 12:10

4 [R]Let each of you look out not only for his own interests, but also for the interests of [R]others. 1 Cor. 13:5 • Rom. 15:1, 2

Christ's Example of Humility

5 [R]Let this mind be in you which was also in Christ Jesus, [Matt. 11:29]

6 who, being in the form of God, did not consider it robbery to be equal with God,

7 [R]but made Himself of no reputation, taking the form [R]of a bondservant, *and* coming in the likeness of men. Ps. 22:6 • Is. 42:1

8 And being found in appearance as a man, He humbled Himself and [R]became [R]obedient to *the point of* death, even the death of the cross. Matt. 26:39 • Heb. 5:8

9 [R]Therefore God also [R]has highly exalted Him and given Him the name which is above every name, Heb. 2:9 • Acts 2:33★

10 that at the name of Jesus every knee should bow, of those in heaven, and of those on earth, and of those under the earth,

11 and [R]*that* every tongue should confess that Jesus Christ *is* Lord, to the glory of God the Father. John 13:13

12 Therefore, my beloved, [R]as you have always obeyed, not as in my presence only, but now much more in my absence, [R]work out your own salvation with [R]fear and trembling; Phil. 1:5, 6; 4:15 • John 6:27, 29 • Eph. 6:5

13 for it is God who works in you both to will and to do for *His* good pleasure.

14 Do all things [R]without [T]complaining and [R]disputing, 1 Pet. 4:9 • *grumbling* • Rom. 14:1

15 that you may become blameless and [T]harmless, children of God without fault in the midst of a crooked and perverse generation, among whom you shine as [R]lights in the world, *innocent* • Matt. 5:15, 16

16 holding fast the word of life, so that I may rejoice in the day of Christ that I have not run in vain or labored in vain.

Paul's Example of Humility

17 Yes, and if [R]I am being poured out *as a drink offering* on the sacrifice [R]and service of your faith, [R]I am glad and rejoice with you all. 2 Tim. 4:6 • Rom. 15:16 • 2 Cor. 7:4

18 For the same reason you also be glad and rejoice with me.

Timothy's Example of Humility

19 But I trust in the Lord Jesus to send Timothy to you shortly, that I also may be encouraged when I know your state.

20 For I have no one [R]like-minded, who will sincerely care for your state. 2 Tim. 3:10

21 For all seek their own, not the things which are of Christ Jesus.

22 But you know his proven character, [R]that as a son with *his* father he served with me in the gospel. 1 Cor. 4:17

23 Therefore I hope to send him at once, as soon as I see how it goes with me.

24 But I trust in the Lord that I myself shall also come shortly.

Epaphroditus's Example of Humility

25 Yet I considered it necessary to send to you [R]Epaphroditus, my brother, fellow worker, and [R]fellow soldier, [R]but your messenger and [R]the one who ministered to my need; Phil. 4:18 • Philem. 2 • 2 Cor. 8:23 • 2 Cor. 11:9

26 [R]since he was longing for you all, and was distressed because you had heard that he was sick. Phil. 1:8

27 For indeed he was sick almost unto death; but God had mercy on him, and not only on him but on me also, lest I should have sorrow upon sorrow.

28 Therefore I sent him the more eagerly, that when you see him again you may rejoice, and I may be less sorrowful.

29 Receive him therefore in the Lord with all gladness, and hold such men in esteem;

30 because for the work of Christ he came close to death, [T]not regarding his life, [R]to sup-

1:28 NU *of your salvation*

ply what was lacking in your service toward
me. *risking* • 1 Cor. 16:17

CHAPTER 3

Warning Against Confidence in the Flesh

FINALLY, my brethren, rejoice in the Lord.
For me to write the same things to you *is*
not tedious, but for you *it is* safe.
2 Beware of dogs, beware of [R]evil workers,
beware of the mutilation! Ps. 119:115
3 For we are the circumcision, who worship
God in the Spirit,* rejoice in Christ Jesus, and
have no confidence in the flesh,
4 though I also might have confidence in
the flesh. If anyone else thinks he may have
confidence in the flesh, I more so:
5 circumcised the eighth day, of the stock
of Israel, [R]*of* the tribe of Benjamin, [R]a Hebrew
of the Hebrews; concerning the law, [R]a Pharisee;
Rom. 11:1 • 2 Cor. 11:22 • Acts 23:6
6 concerning zeal, [R]persecuting the church;
concerning the righteousness which is in the
law, blameless. Acts 8:3; 22:4, 5
7 But [R]what things were gain to me, these I
have counted loss for Christ. Matt. 13:44
8 Yet indeed I also count all things loss [R]for
the excellence of the knowledge of Christ Jesus
my Lord, for whom I have suffered the
loss of all things, and count them as rubbish,
that I may gain Christ Jer. 9:23
9 and be found in Him, not having [R]my
own righteousness, which *is* from the law,
but [R]that which *is* through faith in Christ,
the righteousness which is from God by
faith; Rom. 10:3 • Rom. 1:17

Exhortation to Know Christ

10 that I may know Him and the power of
His resurrection, and the fellowship of His
sufferings, being conformed to His death,
11 if, by any means, I may [R]attain to the resurrection
from the dead. Acts 26:6–8
12 Not that I have already [R]attained, or am
already perfected; but I press on, that I may
lay hold of that for which Christ Jesus has
also laid hold of me. [1 Tim. 6:12, 19]
13 Brethren, I do not count myself to have
apprehended; but one thing *I do*, forgetting
those things which are behind and reaching
forward to those things which are ahead,
14 I press toward the goal for the prize of the
upward call of God in Christ Jesus.
15 Therefore let us, as many as are [R]mature,
[R]have this mind; and if in anything you
think otherwise, [R]God will reveal even this to
you. 1 Cor. 2:6 • Gal. 5:10 • Hos. 6:3
16 Nevertheless, to *the degree* that we have
already attained, [R]let us walk by the same
rule,* let us be of the same mind. Gal. 6:16

Warning Against Living for the Flesh

17 Brethren, [R]join in following my example,
and note those who so walk, as [R]you have us
for a pattern. [1 Cor. 4:16; 11:1] • Titus 2:7, 8
18 For many walk, of whom I have told you
often, and now tell you even weeping, *that
they are* the enemies of the cross of Christ:
19 [R]whose end *is* destruction, [R]whose god *is
their* belly, and [R]*whose* glory *is* in their
shame—[R]who set their mind on earthly
things. 2 Cor. 11:15 • 1 Tim. 6:5 • Hos. 4:7 • Rom. 8:5
20 For [R]our citizenship is in heaven, [R]from
which we also eagerly wait for the Savior, the
Lord Jesus Christ, Eph. 2:6, 19 • Acts 1:11
21 who will transform our lowly body that it
may be conformed to His glorious body, according
to the working by which He is able
even to subdue all things to Himself.

CHAPTER 4

Peace with the Brethren

THEREFORE, my beloved and [R]longed-for
brethren, [R]my joy and crown, so stand fast
in the Lord, beloved. Phil. 1:8 • 2 Cor. 1:14
2 I implore Euodia and I implore Syntyche
to be of the same mind in the Lord.
3 And* I urge you also, true companion,
help these women who [R]labored with me in
the gospel, with Clement also, and the rest of
my fellow workers, whose names *are* in [R]the
Book of Life. Rom. 16:3 • Luke 10:20

Peace with the Lord

4 [R]Rejoice in the Lord always. Again I will
say, rejoice! Rom. 12:12
5 Let your gentleness be known to all men.
[R]The Lord *is* at hand. [James 5:7–9]

6 [R]Be anxious for nothing, but in everything
by prayer and supplication, with
[R]thanksgiving, let your requests be made
known to God; Matt. 6:25 • [1 Thess. 5:17, 18]

3:3 NU, M *who worship in the Spirit of God* **3:16** NU omits *rule* and the rest of v. 16. **4:3** NU, M Yes

---

4:6 Thanksgiving—The importance and spiritual benefits of thanksgiving in our prayer life cannot be overemphasized. The Bible tells us God resists the proud, but gives grace to the humble (Page 1274—James 4:6). But the question is, How do you become humble? It is done by being thankful! A good rule is to be careful (worried) for nothing (Page 1215—Phil. 4:6), be prayerful in all things (Page 1228— 1 Thess. 5:18), and be thankful for anything. It was the sin of thanklessness that caused the ancient world to plunge into the terrible depths of sexual depravity (Page 1149—Rom. 1:21). In the OT a special group of priests was appointed to do nothing else but praise and thank the Lord (Page 459—2 Chr. 31:2).

(continued on next page)

7 and the peace of God, which surpasses all
understanding, will guard your hearts and
minds through Christ Jesus.
8 Finally, brethren, whatever things are
[R]true, whatever things *are* noble, whatever
things *are* [R]just, whatever things *are* pure,
whatever things *are* lovely, whatever things
are of good report, if *there is* any virtue and if
there is anything praiseworthy—meditate on
these things. Eph. 4:25 • Deut. 16:20
9 The things which you learned and re-
ceived and heard and saw in me, these do, and
the God of peace will be with you.

Peace in All Circumstances

10 But I rejoiced in the Lord greatly that now
at last [R]your care for me has flourished again;
though you surely did care, but you lacked op-
portunity. 2 Cor. 11:9
11 Not that I speak in regard to need, for I
have learned in whatever state I am, [R]to be
content: 1 Tim. 6:6, 8
12 [R]I know how to [T]be abased, and I know
how to [T]abound. Everywhere and in all
things I have learned both to be full and to
be hungry, both to abound and to suffer
need. 1 Cor. 4:11 • *live humbly* • *live in prosperity*
13 I can do all things [R]through Christ* who
strengthens me. John 15:5
14 Nevertheless you have done well that
[R]you shared in my distress. Phil. 1:7
15 Now you Philippians know also that in
the beginning of the gospel, when I departed
from Macedonia, [R]no church shared with me
concerning giving and receiving but you
only. 2 Cor. 11:8, 9
16 For even in Thessalonica you sent *aid*
once and again for my necessities.
17 Not that I seek the gift, but I seek the fruit
that abounds to your account.
18 Indeed I have all and abound. I am full,
having received from [R]Epaphroditus the
things *sent* from you, [R]a sweet-smelling
aroma, [R]an acceptable sacrifice, well pleasing
to God. Phil. 2:25 • Heb. 13:16 • 2 Cor. 9:12
19 And my God [R]shall supply all your need
according to His riches in glory by Christ Je-
sus. Ps. 23:1

Conclusion

20 [R]Now to our God and Father *be* glory for-
ever and ever. Amen. Rom. 16:27
21 Greet every saint in Christ Jesus. The
brethren who are with me greet you.
22 All the saints greet you, but especially
those who are of Caesar's household.
23 The grace of our Lord Jesus Christ be
with you all.* Amen.

4:13 NU *Him who* **4:23** NU *your spirit.*

(continued from previous page)

There are two main things we are to thank God for:

a. We are to thank Him for His work in Creation. David reminds us concerning this area of thanksgiving in Ps. 100. Later, John the apostle tells us we will thank God for His work in Creation throughout all eternity. Note the words of this song of praise: "You are worthy, O Lord, to receive glory and honor and power; for You created all things, and by Your will they exist and were created" (Page 1315—Rev. 4:11).
b. We are to thank Him for His work in redemption. John also informs us that our second song in heaven will feature thanksgiving for God's work in redemption: "And they sang a new song, saying: 'You are worthy to take the scroll, and to open its seals; for You were slain, and have redeemed us to God by Your blood' " (Page 1316—Rev. 5:9).

Now turn to Page 642—Prov. 16:3: Commitment.

THE EPISTLE OF PAUL THE APOSTLE TO THE

COLOSSIANS

THE BOOK OF COLOSSIANS

If Ephesians can be labeled the epistle portraying the "church of Christ," then Colossians must surely be the "Christ of the church." Ephesians focuses on the Body; Colossians focuses on the Head. Like Ephesians, the little Book of Colossians divides neatly in half with the first portion doctrinal (1 and 2) and the second practical (3 and 4). Paul's purpose is to show that Christ is preeminent—first and foremost in everything—and the Christian's life should reflect that priority. Because believers are rooted in Him, alive in Him, hidden in Him, and complete in Him, it is utterly inconsistent for them to live life without Him. Clothed in His love, with His peace ruling in their hearts, they are equipped to make Christ first in every area of life.

This epistle became known as *Pros Kolossaeis,* "To the Colossians," because of 1:2. Paul also wanted it to be read in the neighboring church at Laodicea (4:16).

THE AUTHOR OF COLOSSIANS

The external testimony to the Pauline authorship of Colossians is ancient and consistent, and the internal evidence also is very good. It not only claims to be written by Paul (1:1, 23; 4:18), but the personal details and close parallels with Ephesians and Philemon make the case even stronger. Nevertheless, the authenticity of this letter has been challenged on the internal grounds of vocabulary and thought. In its four chapters, Colossians uses fifty-five Greek words that do not appear in Paul's other epistles. However, Paul commanded a wide vocabulary; and the circumstances and subject of this epistle, especially the references to the Colossian heresy, account for these additional words. The high Christology of Colossians has been compared to John's later concept that Christ is the Logos (cf. 1:15–23 and John 1:1–18), with the conclusion that these concepts were too late for Paul's time. However, there is no reason to assume that Paul was unaware of Christ's work as Creator, especially in view of Philippians 2:5–11. It is also wrong to assume that the heresy refuted in Colossians 2 refers to the fully developed form of Gnosticism that did not appear until the second century. The parallels only indicate that Paul was dealing with an early form of Gnosticism.

THE TIME OF COLOSSIANS

Colosse was a minor city about one hundred miles east of Ephesus in the region of the seven Asian churches of Revelation 1—3. Located in the fertile Lycus Valley by a mountain pass on the road from Ephesus to the East, Colosse once was a populous center of commerce, famous for its glossy black wool. By the time of Paul, it had been eclipsed by its neighboring cities, Laodicea and Hierapolis (cf. 4:13), and was on the decline. Apart from this letter, Colosse exerted almost no influence on early church history. It is evident from 1:4–8 and 2:1 that Paul had never visited the church at Colosse, which was founded by Epaphras. On his third missionary journey, Paul devoted almost three years to an Asian ministry centered in Ephesus (cf. Acts 19:10; 20:31), and Epaphras probably came to Christ during this time. He carried the gospel to the cities in the Lycus Valley and years later came to visit Paul in his imprisonment (4:12, 13; Philem. 23).

Colossians, Philemon, and Ephesians were evidently written about the same time and under the same circumstances, judging by the overlapping themes and personal names (cf. Col. 4:9–17 and Philem. 2, 10, 23, 24). Although Caesarea and Ephesus have been suggested as the location of authorship, the bulk of the evidence indicates that Paul wrote all four Prison Epistles during his first Roman imprisonment (see "The Time of Ephesians" and "The Time of Philippians"). If so, Paul wrote it in A.D. 60 or 61 and sent it with Tychicus and the converted slave Onesimus to Colosse (4:7–9; see Eph. 6:21; Philem. 10–12).

Epaphras's visit and report about the conditions in Colosse prompted this letter. Although the Colossians had not yet succumbed (2:1–5), an encroaching heresy was threatening the predominantly Gentile (1:21, 27; 2:13) Colossian church. The nature of this heresy can only be deduced from Paul's incidental references to it in his refutation in 2:8–23. It was apparently a religious system that combined elements from Greek speculation (2:4, 8–10), Jewish legalism (2:11–17), and Oriental mysticism (2:18–23). It involved a low view of the body (2:20–23) and probably nature as a whole. Circumcision, dietary regulations, and ritual observances were included in this system, which utilized asceticism, worship of angels as intermediaries, and mystical experiences as an approach to the spiritual realm. Any attempt to fit Christ into such a system would undermine His Person and redemptive work.

THE CHRIST OF COLOSSIANS

This singularly Christological book is centered on the cosmic Christ—"the head of all principality and power" (2:10), the

Lord of creation (1:16, 17), and the Author of reconciliation (1:20–22; 2:13–15). He is the basis for the believer's hope (1:5, 23, 27), the source of the believer's power for a new life (1:11, 29), the believer's Redeemer and Reconciler (1:14, 20–22; 2:11–15), the embodiment of full deity (1:15, 19; 2:9), the Creator and Sustainer of all things (1:16, 17), the Head of the church (1:18), the resurrected God-Man (1:18; 3:1), and the all-sufficient Savior (1:28; 2:3, 10; 3:1–4).

KEYS TO COLOSSIANS

Key Word: The Preeminence of Christ—The resounding theme in Colossians is the preeminence and sufficiency of Christ in all things. The believer is complete in Him alone and lacks nothing because "in Him dwells all the fullness of the Godhead bodily" (2:9); He has "all the treasures of wisdom and knowledge" (2:3). There is no need for speculation, mystical visions, or ritualistic regulations as though faith in Christ were insufficient. Paul's predominant purpose, then, is to refute a threatening heresy that is devaluing Christ. This false teaching is countered by a positive presentation of His true attributes and accomplishments. A proper view of Christ is the antidote for heresy. Paul also writes this epistle to encourage the Colossians to "continue in the faith, grounded and steadfast" (1:23), so that they will grow and bear fruit in the knowledge of Christ (1:10). A firm adherence to the true gospel will give them stability and resistance to opposing influences.

Key Verses: Colossians 2:9, 10 and 3:1, 2—"For in Him dwells all the fullness of the Godhead bodily; and you are complete in Him, who is the head of all principality and power" (2:9, 10).

"If then you were raised with Christ, seek those things which are above, where Christ is, sitting at the right hand of God. Set your mind on things above, not on things on the earth" (3:1, 2).

Key Chapter: Colossians 3—Chapter 3 links the three themes of Colossians (see "Key Word") together showing their cause and effect relationships. Because the believer is risen with Christ (3:1–4), he is to put off the old man and put on the new (3:5–17), which will result in holiness in all relationships (3:18–25).

SURVEY OF COLOSSIANS

Colossians is perhaps the most Christ-centered book in the Bible. In it Paul stresses the preeminence of the Person of Christ and the completeness of the salvation He provides, in order to combat a growing heresy that is threatening the church at Colosse. This heresy seeks to devaluate Christ by elevating speculation, ritualism, mysticism, and asceticism. But Christ, the Lord of creation and Head of the Body, is completely sufficient for every spiritual and practical need of the believer. The last half of this epistle explores the application of these principles to daily life, because doctrinal truth (1 and 2) must bear fruit in practical conduct (3 and 4). The two major topics are: supremacy of Christ (1 and 2) and submission to Christ (3 and 4).

Supremacy of Christ (1 and 2): Paul's greeting (1:1, 2) is followed by an unusually extended thanksgiving (1:3–8) and prayer (1:9–14) on behalf of the believers at Colosse. Paul expresses his concern that the Colossians come to a deeper understanding of the Person and power of Christ. Even here Paul begins to develop his major theme of the preeminence of Christ, but the most potent statement of this theme is in 1:15–23. He is supreme both in creation (1:15–18) and in redemption (1:19–23), and this majestic passage builds a positive case for Christ as the most effective refutation of the heresy

FOCUS	SUPREMACY OF CHRIST			SUBMISSION TO CHRIST		
REFERENCE	1:1	1:15	2:4	3:1	3:5	4:7—4:18
DIVISION	INTRODUCTION	PREEMINENCE OF CHRIST	FREEDOM IN CHRIST	POSITION OF THE BELIEVER	PRACTICE OF THE BELIEVER	CONCLUSION
TOPIC	DOCTRINAL			PRACTICAL		
	WHAT CHRIST DID FOR US			WHAT CHRIST DOES THROUGH US		
LOCATION	ROME					
TIME	A.D. 60–61					

that will be exposed in chapter 2. Paul describes his own ministry of proclaiming the mystery of "Christ in you, the hope of glory" (1:27) to the Gentiles and assures his readers that although he has not personally met them, he strongly desires that they become deeply rooted in Christ alone, who is preeminent in the church (1:24—2:3). This is especially important in view of false teachers who would defraud them through enticing rationalisms (2:4–7), vain philosophy (2:8–10), legalistic rituals (2:11–17), improper mysticism (2:18, 19), and useless asceticism (2:20–23). In each case, Paul contrasts the error with the corresponding truth about Christ.

Submission to Christ (3 and 4): The believer's union with Christ in His death, resurrection, and exaltation is the foundation upon which his earthly life must be built (3:1–4). Because of his death with Christ, the Christian must regard himself as dead to the old sins and put them aside (3:5–11); because of his resurrection with Christ, the believer must regard himself as alive to Him in righteousness and put on the new qualities that are prompted by Christian love (3:12–17). Turning from the inward life (3:1–17) to the outward life (3:18—4:6), Paul outlines the transformation that faith in Christ should make in relationships inside and outside the home. This epistle concludes with a statement concerning its bearers (Tychicus and Onesimus), greetings and instructions, and a farewell note (4:7–18).

OUTLINE OF COLOSSIANS

Part One: The Supremacy of Christ in the Church (1:1—2:23)

I. Introduction 1:1–14

A. Paul's Greeting to the Colossians 1:1, 2
B. Paul's Thanksgiving for the Colossians ..1:3–8
C. Paul's Prayer for the Colossians 1:9–14

II. The Preeminence of Christ ....1:15—2:3

A. Christ Is Preeminent in Creation........1:15–18
B. Christ Is Preeminent in Redemption ..1:19–23
C. Christ Is Preeminent in the Church.1:24—2:3

III. The Freedom in Christ 2:4–23

A. Freedom from Enticing Words 2:4–7
B. Freedom from Vain Philosophy............2:8–10
C. Freedom from the Judgment of Men...2:11–17
D. Freedom from Improper Worship 2:18, 19
E. Freedom from the Doctrine of Men 2:20–23

Part Two: The Submission to Christ in the Church (3:1—4:18)

I. The Position of the Believer 3:1–4

II. The Practice of the Believer..............3:5—4:6

A. Put Off the Old Man...........................3:5–11
B. Put On the New Man 3:12–17
C. Personal Commands for Holiness.....3:18—4:6
1. Holiness in Family Life 3:18–21
2. Holiness in Work Life..................3:22—4:1
3. Holiness in Public Life 4:2–6

III. Conclusion 4:7–18

A. Commendation of Tychicus 4:7–9
B. Greetings from Paul's Friends 4:10–14
C. Introductions Regarding This Letter ..4:15–18

CHAPTER 1

Paul's Greeting to the Colossians

PAUL, an apostle of Jesus Christ by the will of God, and Timothy our brother,

2 To the saints [R]and faithful brethren in Christ *who are* in Colosse: 1 Cor. 4:17

Grace to you and peace from God our Father and the Lord Jesus Christ.*

Paul's Thanksgiving for the Colossians

3 [R]We give thanks to the God and Father of our Lord Jesus Christ, praying always for you, Phil. 1:3
4 since we heard of your faith in Christ Jesus and of your love for all the saints;
5 because of the hope which is laid up for you in heaven, of which you heard before in the word of the truth of the gospel,
6 which has come to you, as *it has* also in all the world, and is bringing forth fruit,* as *it is* also among you since the day you heard and knew the grace of God in truth;
7 as you also learned from [R]Epaphras, our dear fellow servant, who is a faithful minister of Christ on your behalf, Philem. 23
8 who also declared to us your [R]love in the Spirit. Rom. 15:30

Paul's Prayer for the Colossians

9 [R]For this reason we also, since the day we heard it, do not cease to pray for you, and to

1:2 NU omits *and the Lord Jesus Christ.* **1:6** NU, M add *and growing*

ask that you may be filled with the knowledge of His will in all wisdom and spiritual understanding; Eph. 1:15–17

10 [R]that you may walk worthy of the Lord, [R]fully pleasing *Him,* [R]being fruitful in every good work and increasing in the knowledge of God; Eph. 4:1 • 1 Thess. 4:1 • Heb. 13:21

11 [R]strengthened with all might, according to His glorious power, for all patience and longsuffering with joy; [Eph. 3:16; 6:10]

12 [R]giving thanks to the Father who has qualified us to be partakers of the inheritance of the saints in the light. [Eph. 5:20]

13 He has delivered us from [R]the power of darkness and conveyed *us* into the kingdom of the Son of His love, Eph. 6:12

14 [R]in whom we have redemption through His blood,* the forgiveness of sins. Eph. 1:7

Christ Is Preeminent in Creation

15 He is [R]the image of the invisible God, the firstborn over all creation. 2 Cor. 4:4

16 For by Him all things were created that are in heaven and that are on earth, visible and invisible, whether thrones or dominions or principalities or powers. All things were created through Him and for Him.

17 [R]And He is before all things, and in Him [R]all things consist. [John 17:5] • Heb. 1:3

18 And [R]He is the head of the body, the church, who is the beginning, [R]the firstborn from the dead, that in all things He may have the preeminence. Eph. 1:22 • Rev. 1:5

Christ Is Preeminent in Redemption

19 For it pleased *the Father that* [R]in Him all the fullness should dwell, John 1:16

20 and [R]by Him to reconcile all things to Himself, by Him, whether things on earth or things in heaven, having made peace through the blood of His cross. Eph. 2:14

21 And you, [R]who once were alienated and enemies in your mind [R]by wicked works, yet now He has reconciled [Eph. 2:1] • Titus 1:15

22 [R]in the body of His flesh through death, to present you holy, and blameless, and above reproach in His sight— 2 Cor. 5:18

23 if indeed you continue [R]in the faith, grounded and steadfast, and are [R]not moved away from the hope of the gospel which you heard, [R]which was preached to every creature under heaven, of which I, Paul, became a minister. Eph. 3:17 • [John 15:6] • Col. 1:6

Christ Is Preeminent in the Church

24 [R]I now rejoice in my sufferings for you, and fill up in my flesh what is lacking in the afflictions of Christ, for the sake of His body, which is the church, 2 Cor. 7:4

25 of which I became a minister according to [R]the [T]stewardship from God which was given to me for you, to fulfill the word of God, Gal. 2:7 • *dispensation* or *administration*

26 [R]the mystery which has been hidden from ages and from generations, but now has been revealed to His saints. [1 Cor. 2:7]

27 [R]To them God willed to make known what are the riches of the glory of this mystery among the Gentiles: which* is Christ in you, the hope of glory. 2 Cor. 2:14

28 Him we preach, [R]warning every man and teaching every man in all wisdom, [R]that we may present every man perfect in Christ Jesus. Acts 20:20 • Eph. 5:27

29 To this *end* I also labor, striving according to His working which works in me [R]mightily. Eph. 3:7

CHAPTER 2

FOR I want you to know what a great [R]conflict[T] I have for you and those in Laodicea, and *for* as many as have not seen my face in the flesh, Phil. 1:30 • *struggle*

2 that their hearts may be encouraged, being knit together in love, and *attaining* to all riches of the full assurance of understanding, to the knowledge of the mystery of God, both of the Father and* of Christ,

3 [R]in whom are hidden all the treasures of wisdom and knowledge. 1 Cor. 1:24, 30

Freedom from Enticing Words

4 Now this I say lest anyone should deceive you with persuasive words.

5 For [R]though I am absent in the flesh, yet I am with you in spirit, rejoicing to see [R]your *good* order and the steadfastness of your faith in Christ. 1 Thess. 2:17 • 1 Cor. 14:40

1:14 NU, M omit *through His blood* **1:27** M *who*
2:2 NU omits *both of the Father and*

1:22 New Life: Based on Christ's Death—Salvation is free, but it is not cheap. Salvation is a gift and costs me nothing, but it cost God everything—it cost Jesus His life. "The wages of sin is death" (separation from God). God's gift is "eternal life" (eternal union of the soul with God). This is possible because of the death of Jesus on Calvary's cross (Page 1153—Rom. 6:23). Jesus actually took sin's penalty for every man, woman, and child who ever has lived or ever will live. As He hung upon the cross, He cried, "Eli, Eli, lama sabachthani?" Being interpreted, He cried, "My God, My God, why have You forsaken Me?" (Page 1009—Matt. 27:46). Jesus was separated from God the Father so that you and I do not have to be. This is the heart of the Atonement. The marvel of it all is that He did this while we were His enemies: "But God demonstrates His own love toward us, in that while we were still sinners, Christ died for us" (Page 1152—Rom. 5:8).

Now turn to Page 1131—Acts 16:31: New Life: Received by Faith.

6 [R]As you therefore have received Christ Jesus the Lord, so walk in Him, 1 Thess. 4:1

7 rooted and built up in Him and established in the faith, as you have been taught, abounding in it* with thanksgiving.

Freedom from Vain Philosophy

8 Beware lest anyone cheat you through philosophy and empty deceit, according to [R]the tradition of men, according to the [R]basic principles of the world, and not according to Christ. Gal. 1:14 • Gal. 4:3, 9, 10

9 For [R]in Him dwells all the fullness of the Godhead [T]bodily; [John 1:14] • *in bodily form*

10 and you are complete in Him, who is the head of all principality and power.

Freedom from the Judgment of Men

11 In Him you were also circumcised with the circumcision made without hands, by putting off the body of the sins* of the flesh, by the circumcision of Christ,

12 [R]buried with Him in baptism, in which you also were raised with *Him* through [R]faith in the working of God, [R]who raised Him from the dead. Rom. 6:4 • Eph. 1:19, 20 • Acts 2:24

13 And you, being dead in your trespasses and the uncircumcision of your flesh, He has made alive together with Him, having forgiven you all trespasses,

14 having wiped out the handwriting of requirements that was against us, which was contrary to us. And He has taken it out of the way, having nailed it to the cross.

15 [R]Having disarmed principalities and powers, He made a public spectacle of them, triumphing over them in it. [Is. 53:12]

16 So let no one [R]judge you in food or in drink, or regarding a [T]festival or a new moon or sabbaths, Rom. 14:3 • *feast day*

17 which are a shadow of things to come, but the [T]substance is of Christ. Lit. *body*

Freedom from Improper Worship

18 Let no one cheat you of your reward, taking delight in *false* humility and worship of angels, intruding into those things which he has not* seen, vainly puffed up by his fleshly mind,

19 and not holding fast to [R]the Head, from whom all the body, nourished and knit together by joints and ligaments, grows with the increase *that is* from God. Eph. 4:15

Freedom from the Doctrine of Men

20 Therefore,* if you [R]died with Christ from the basic principles of the world, why, as *though* living in the world, do you subject yourselves to regulations— Rom. 6:2–5

21 [R]"Do not touch, do not taste, do not handle," 1 Tim. 4:3

22 which all concern things which perish with the using—[R]according to the commandments and doctrines of men? Titus 1:14

23 [R]These things indeed have an appearance of wisdom in self-imposed religion, *false* humility, and [T]neglect of the body, *but are* of no value against the indulgence of the flesh. 1 Tim. 4:8 • *severe treatment, asceticism*

CHAPTER 3

The Position of the Believer

IF then you were raised with Christ, seek those things which are above, where Christ is, sitting at the right hand of God.

2 Set your mind on things above, not on things on the [R]earth. [Matt. 6:19–21]

3 [R]For you died, [R]and your life is hidden with Christ in God. [Rom. 6:2] • [2 Cor. 5:7]

4 When Christ *who is* our life appears, then you also will appear with Him in glory.

Put Off the Old Man

5 [R]Therefore put to death your members which are on the earth: fornication, uncleanness, passion, evil desire, and covetousness, which is idolatry. [Rom. 8:13]

6 [R]Because of these things the wrath of God is coming upon [R]the sons of disobedience, Rom. 1:18 • [Eph. 2:2]

7 [R]in which you yourselves once walked when you lived in them. 1 Cor. 6:11

8 But now you yourselves are to put off all these: anger, wrath, malice, blasphemy, filthy language out of your mouth.

9 Do not lie to one another, since you have put off the old man with his deeds,

10 and have put on the new *man* who [R]is renewed in knowledge according to the image of Him who created him, Rom. 12:2

11 where there is neither [R]Greek nor Jew, circumcised nor uncircumcised, barbarian, Scythian, slave *nor* free, [R]but Christ *is* all and in all. Gal. 3:27, 28 • Eph. 1:23

Put On the New Man

12 Therefore, as *the* elect of God, holy and beloved, put on tender mercies, kindness, humility, meekness, longsuffering;

13 [R]bearing with one another, and forgiving one another, if anyone has a complaint against another; even as Christ forgave you, so you also *must do.* [Mark 11:25]

14 [R]But above all these things put on love, which is the bond of perfection. 1 Pet. 4:8

15 And let [R]the peace of God rule in your hearts, to which also you were called in one body; and be thankful. [John 14:27]

16 Let the word of Christ dwell in you richly in all wisdom, teaching and admonishing one another [R]in psalms and hymns and spiritual songs, singing with grace in your hearts to the Lord. Eph. 5:19

2:7 NU omits *in it* **2:11** NU omits *of the sins*
2:18 NU omits *not* **2:20** NU, M omit *Therefore*

17 And *whatever* you do in word or deed, *do*
all in the name of the Lord Jesus, giving
thanks to God the Father through Him.

Holiness in Family Life

18 [R]Wives, submit to your own husbands, as
is fitting in the Lord. 1 Pet. 3:1

19 [R]Husbands, love your wives and do not be
[R]bitter toward them. [Eph. 5:25] • Eph. 4:31

20 Children, obey your parents in all things,
for this is well pleasing to the Lord.
21 [R]Fathers, do not provoke your children,
lest they become discouraged. Eph. 6:4

Holiness in Work Life

22 [R]Bondservants, obey in all things your
masters according to the flesh, not with
eyeservice, as men-pleasers, but in sincerity
of heart, fearing God. Eph. 6:5
23 [R]And whatever you do, do it heartily, as to
the Lord and not to men, [Eccl. 9:10]
24 [R]knowing that from the Lord you will re-
ceive the reward of the inheritance; for* you
serve the Lord Christ. Eph. 6:8
25 But he who does wrong will be repaid
for what he has done, and [R]there is no par-
tiality. Rom. 2:11

CHAPTER 4

MASTERS,[R] give your bondservants what
is just and fair, knowing that you also
have a Master in heaven. Eph. 6:9

Holiness in Public Life

2 [R]Continue earnestly in prayer, being vigi-
lant in it with thanksgiving; Luke 18:1
3 [R]meanwhile praying also for us, that God
would [R]open to us a door for the word, to
speak the mystery of Christ, for which I am
also in chains, Eph. 6:19 • 1 Cor. 16:9
4 that I may make it manifest, as I ought to
speak.
5 [R]Walk in wisdom toward those *who are*
outside, redeeming the time. Eph. 5:15
6 *Let* your speech always *be* with grace,
seasoned with salt, that you may know how
you ought to answer each one.

Commendation of Tychicus

7 [R]Tychicus, a beloved brother, faithful min-
ister, and fellow servant in the Lord, will tell
you all the news about me. 2 Tim. 4:12
8 [R]I am sending him to you for this very
purpose, that he* may know your circum-
stances and comfort your hearts, Eph. 6:22
9 with [R]Onesimus, a faithful and beloved
brother, who is *one* of you. They will make
known to you all things which *are happening*
here. Philem. 10

Greetings from Paul's Friends

10 Aristarchus my fellow prisoner greets
you, with [R]Mark the cousin of Barnabas
(about whom you received instructions: if he
comes to you, welcome him), 2 Tim. 4:11
11 and Jesus who is called Justus. These *are*
my only fellow workers for the kingdom of
God who are of the circumcision; they have
proved to be a comfort to me.
12 [R]Epaphras, who is *one* of you, a bondser-
vant of Christ, greets you, always [R]laboring
fervently for you in prayers, that you may
stand perfect and complete* in all the will of
God. Philem. 23 • Rom. 15:30
13 For I bear him witness that he has a great
zeal* for you, and those who are in Laodicea,
and those in Hierapolis.
14 [R]Luke the beloved physician and [R]Demas
greet you. 2 Tim. 4:11 • 2 Tim. 4:10

3:24 NU omits *for* **4:8** NU *you may know our circumstances and he may* **4:12** NU *fully assured* **4:13** NU *concern*

3:19 The Role of the Husband—Paul tells the husband to love his wife (Page 1208—Eph. 5:25), while Peter tells the husband to dwell together with his wife (Page 1281—1 Pet. 3:7). The husband cannot live with his wife as Peter says unless he loves her in the way Paul means. The love that the husband is commanded to have for the wife is not primarily sexual or emotional (though both of those concepts are involved); it is a love that loves in spite of the response (or lack of it) in the one loved. It is the kind of love that God has for the world (Page 1083—John 3:16) and is the fruit of the Spirit (Page 1200—Gal. 5:22). A husband can only love his wife properly if he is a Christian and under the control of the Holy Spirit.

The two responsibilities the husband has in the family are to dwell with his wife according to knowledge and to render to his wife the honor that is due her because she is his wife. To "dwell together" with his wife means that the husband must take his wife into *every* aspect of his life. There are to be no areas of his life where there are signs that say, "Private, husband only—wife keep out."

The husband is to perform his two duties for a spiritual purpose: "that your prayers be not hindered." The man who is not taking his wife into every aspect of his life and rendering to her the honor that is due her because she is his wife cannot communicate with her in the way that God intended; hence, he cannot communicate with God either. To make sure that the channel of communication with God is open, the husband must make sure that the channel of communication with his wife is open. Only in this way can he truly love his wife as God intended and manifest his headship properly.

Now turn to Page 629—Prov. 1:8: The Role of Children.

Introductions Regarding This Letter

15 Greet the brethren who are in Laodicea,
and Nymphas and [R]the church that *is* in his*
house. Rom. 16:5
16 Now when [R]this epistle is read among
you, see that it is read also in the church of the
Laodiceans, and that you likewise read the
epistle from Laodicea. 1 Thess. 5:27
17 And say to [R]Archippus, "Take heed to the
ministry which you have received in the Lord,
that you may fulfill it." Philem. 2
18 [R]This salutation by my own hand—Paul.
[R]Remember my chains. Grace *be* with you.
Amen. 1 Cor. 16:21 • Heb. 13:3

4:15 NU *Nympha . . . her house.*

THE FIRST EPISTLE OF PAUL THE APOSTLE TO THE

THESSALONIANS

THE BOOK OF 1 THESSALONIANS

Paul has many pleasant memories of the days he spent with the infant Thessalonian church. Their faith, hope, love, and perseverance in the face of persecution are exemplary. Paul's labors as a spiritual parent to the fledgling church have been richly rewarded, and his affection is visible in every line of his letter.

Paul encourages them to excel in their newfound faith, to increase in their love for one another, and to rejoice, pray, and give thanks always. He closes his letter with instruction regarding the return of the Lord, whose advent signifies hope and comfort for believers both living and dead.

Because this is the first of Paul's two canonical letters to the church at Thessalonica, it received the title *Pros Thessalonikeis A,* the "First to the Thessalonians."

THE AUTHOR OF 1 THESSALONIANS

First Thessalonians went unchallenged as a Pauline epistle until the nineteenth century, when radical critics claimed that its dearth of doctrinal content made its authenticity suspect. But this is a weak objection on two counts: (1) the proportion of doctrinal teaching in Paul's epistles varies widely, and (2) 4:13—5:11 is a foundational passage for New Testament eschatology (future events). Paul had quickly grounded the Thessalonians in Christian doctrine, and the only problematic issue when this epistle was written concerned the matter of Christ's return. The external and internal evidence points clearly to Paul.

THE TIME OF 1 THESSALONIANS

In Paul's time, Thessalonica was the prominent seaport and the capital of the Roman province of Macedonia. This prosperous city was located on the Via Egnatia, the main road from Rome to the East, within sight of Mount Olympus, legendary home of the Greek pantheon. Cassander expanded and strengthened this site around 315 B.C. and renamed it after his wife, the half-sister of Alexander the Great. The Romans conquered Macedonia in 168 B.C. and organized it into a single province twenty-two years later with Thessalonica as the capital city. It became a "free city" under Augustus with its own authority to appoint a governing board of magistrates who were called "politarchs." The strategic location assured Thessalonica of commercial success, and it boasted a population of perhaps 200,000 in the first century. Thessalonica survives under the shortened name "Salonika."

Thessalonica had a sizable Jewish population, and the ethical monotheism of Judaism attracted many Gentiles who had become disenchanted with Greek paganism. These God-fearers quickly responded to Paul's reasoning in the synagogue when he ministered there on his second missionary journey (Acts 17:10). The Jews became jealous of Paul's success and organized a mob to oppose the Christian missionaries. Not finding Paul and Silas, they dragged Jason, Paul and Silas's host, before the politarchs and accused him of harboring traitors of Rome. The politarchs extracted a pledge guaranteeing the departure of Paul and Silas, who left that night for Berea. After a time, the Thessalonian Jews raised an uproar in Berea so that Paul departed for Athens, leaving orders for Silas and Timothy to join him there (Acts 17:11–16). Because of Luke's account in Acts, some scholars have reasoned that Paul was in Thessalonica for less than a month ("three Sabbaths," Acts 17:2), but other evidence suggests a longer stay: (1) Paul received two separate offerings from Philippi, 100 miles away, while he was in Thessalonica (Phil. 4:15, 16). (2) According to 1:9 and 2:14–16, most of the Thessalonian converts were Gentiles who came out of idolatry. This would imply an extensive ministry directed to the Gentiles after Paul's initial work with the Jews and Gentile God-fearers. (3) Paul worked "night and day" (2:9; 2 Thess. 3:7–9) during his time there. He may have begun to work immediately, but Paul supported himself by tent-making, which took many hours away from his ministry, requiring a longer stay to accomplish the extensive ministry of evangelism and teaching that took place in that city. After Silas and Timothy met Paul in Athens (3:1, 2), he sent Timothy to Thessalonica (Silas also went back to Macedonia, probably Philippi), and his assistants later rejoined him in Corinth (Acts 18:5; cf. 1 Thess. 1:1 where Silas is called Silvanus). There he wrote this epistle in A.D. 51 as his response to Timothy's good report.

THE CHRIST OF 1 THESSALONIANS

Christ is seen as the believer's hope of salvation both now and at His coming. When He returns, He will deliver (1:10; 5:4–11), reward (1:19), perfect (3:13), resurrect (4:13–18), and sanctify (5:23) all who trust Him.

KEYS TO 1 THESSALONIANS

Key Word: Holiness in Light of Christ's Return—Throughout this letter is an unmistakable emphasis upon steadfastness in the Lord (3:8) and a continuing growth in faith and love in view of the return of Christ (1:3–10; 2:12–20; 3:10–13; 4:1—5:28). The theme is not only the returning of Christ, but also the life of the believer in every practical relationship, each aspect of which can be transformed and illuminated by the glorious prospect of His eventual return.

Key Verses: 1 Thessalonians 3:12, 13 and 4:16–18—"And may the Lord make you increase and abound in love to one another and to all, just as we *do* to you, so that He may establish your hearts blameless in holiness before our God and Father at the coming of our Lord Jesus Christ with all His saints" (3:12, 13).

"For the Lord Himself will descend from heaven with a shout, with the voice of an archangel, and with the trumpet of God. And the dead in Christ will rise first. Then we who are alive *and* remain shall be caught up together with them in the clouds to meet the Lord in the air. And thus we shall always be with the Lord. Therefore comfort one another with these words" (4:16–18).

Key Chapter: 1 Thessalonians 4—Chapter 4 includes the central passage of the epistles on the coming of the Lord when the dead in Christ shall rise first, and those who remain are caught up together with them in the clouds.

SURVEY OF 1 THESSALONIANS

After Paul's forced separation from the Thessalonians, he grows increasingly concerned about the progress of their faith. His great relief upon hearing Timothy's positive report prompts him to write this warm epistle of commendation, exhortation, and consolation. They are commended for remaining steadfast under afflictions, exhorted to excel still more in their Christian walk, and consoled concerning their loved ones who have died in Christ. The theme of the coming of the Lord recurs throughout this epistle, and 4:13—5:11 is one of the fullest New Testament developments of this crucial truth. The two major sections of 1 Thessalonians are: Paul's personal reflections of the Thessalonians (1—3) and Paul's instructions for the Thessalonians (4 and 5).

Paul's Personal Reflections on the Thessalonians (1—3): Paul's typical salutation in the first verse combines the customary Greek ("grace") and Hebrew ("peace") greetings of his day and enriches them with Christian content. The opening chapter is a declaration of thanksgiving for the Thessalonians' metamorphosis from heathenism to Christian hope. Faith, love, and hope (1:3) properly characterize the new lives of these believers. In 2:1–16 Paul reviews his brief ministry in Thessalonica and defends his conduct and motives, apparently to answer enemies who are trying to impugn his character and message. He sends Timothy to minister to them and is greatly relieved when Timothy reports the stability of their faith and love (2:17—3:10). Paul therefore closes this historical section with a prayer that their faith may continue to deepen (3:11–13).

Paul's Instructions to the Thessalonians (4 and 5): The apostle deftly moves into a series of exhortations and instructions by encouraging the Thessalonians to continue progressing. He reminds them of his previous teaching on sexual and social matters (4:1–12), since these Gentile believers lack the moral upbringing in the Mosaic Law provided in the Jewish community. Now rooted in the Word of God (2:13), the readers must resist the constant pressures of a pagan society.

Paul has taught them about the return of

FOCUS	REFLECTIONS ON THE THESSALONIANS			INSTRUCTIONS TO THE THESSALONIANS			
REFERENCE	1:1	2:1	2:17	4:1	4:13	5:1	5:12—5:28
DIVISION	COMMENDATION FOR GROWTH	FOUNDING OF THE CHURCH	STRENGTHENING OF THE CHURCH	DIRECTION FOR GROWTH	THE DEAD IN CHRIST	THE DAY OF THE LORD	HOLY LIVING
TOPIC	PERSONAL EXPERIENCE			PRACTICAL EXHORTATION			
	LOOKING BACK			LOOKING FORWARD			
LOCATION	WRITTEN IN CORINTH						
TIME	C. A.D. 51						

Christ, and they have become distressed over the deaths of some among them. In 4:13–18 Paul comforts them with the assurance that all who die in Christ will be resurrected at His *parousia* ("presence," "coming," or "advent"). The apostle continues his discourse on eschatology by describing the coming day of the Lord (5:1–11). In anticipation of this day, believers are to "watch and be sober" as "sons of light" who are destined for salvation, not wrath. Paul requests the readers to deal with integrity toward one another and to continue growing spiritually (5:12–22). The epistle closes with a wish for their sanctification, three requests, and a benediction (5:23–28).

OUTLINE OF 1 THESSALONIANS

I. Paul's Personal Reflections on the Thessalonians .... 1:1—3:13

- A. Paul's Commendation for Their Growth 1:1–10
- B. Paul's Founding of the Church 2:1–16
- C. Timothy's Strengthening of the Church .... 2:17—3:13
  1. Satan Hinders Paul 2:17–20
  2. Paul Sends Timothy 3:1–5
  3. Timothy's Encouraging Report 3:6–10
  4. Paul's Desire to Visit Them 3:11–13

II. Paul's Instructions to the Thessalonians .... 4:1—5:28

- A. Directions for Growth 4:1–12
- B. Revelation Concerning the Dead in Christ 4:13–18
- C. Description of the Day of the Lord 5:1–11
- D. Instruction for Holy Living 5:12–22
- E. Conclusion 5:23–28

CHAPTER 1

Paul's Commendation for Their Growth

PAUL, [R]Silvanus, and Timothy, 1 Pet. 5:12

To the church of the Thessalonians in God the Father and the Lord Jesus Christ:

Grace to you and peace from God our Father and the Lord Jesus Christ.*

2 We give thanks to God always for you all, making mention of you in our prayers,
3 remembering without ceasing [R]your work of faith, [R]labor of love, and patience of hope in our Lord Jesus Christ in the sight of our God and Father, John 6:29 • Rom. 16:6
4 knowing, beloved brethren, [R]your election by God. Col. 3:12

5 For [R]our gospel did not come to you in word only, but also in power, [R]and in the Holy Spirit [R]and in much assurance, as you know what kind of men we were among you for your sake. Mark 16:20 • 2 Cor. 6:6 • Heb. 2:3

6 And you became followers of us and of the Lord, having received the word in much affliction, with joy of the Holy Spirit,
7 so that you became examples to all in Macedonia and Achaia who believe.
8 For from you the word of the Lord [R]has sounded forth, not only in Macedonia and Achaia, but also [R]in every place. Your faith toward God has gone out, so that we do not need to say anything. Rom. 10:18 • Rom. 1:8
9 For they themselves declare concerning us [R]what manner of entry we had to you, and how you turned to God from idols to serve the living and true God, 1 Thess. 2:1
10 and to wait for His Son from heaven,

1:1 NU omits *from God our Father and the Lord Jesus Christ*

1:5 Sharing Our Faith: How to Do It—Sharing our faith is a combination of spontaneous conversation about God and premeditated ideas about the gospel. The following is a set of practical steps to take in witnessing for Christ:

a. Regularly talk about God. Sprinkle your ordinary conversation with occasional references to God's activity in your life. It is much easier to share your faith when your friends know God is an integral part of your affairs.
b. Prepare your testimony. Learn to describe your pre-Christian life, your encounter with Christ, and subsequent changes in your life in fewer than 5 minutes. If you became a Christian as a child, focus on the impact Christ has had on your adult life.
c. Learn a brief summary of the gospel. If you have never learned a gospel presentation, ask your pastor to help you find one. Perhaps he will assist you to master it.

When you have opportunity to share Christ with someone, be sensitive to that person's spiritual readiness. Go as far as you can in the progression of mentioning the Lord, telling your story of faith, presenting the gospel, and appealing for a commitment of faith in Christ. Often you will sense that your friend has heard all he or she wants to. When you stop, be sure to mention that you want to talk more about the Lord another time. Keep the subject open.

Now turn to Page 1245—2 Tim. 4:2: Sharing Our Faith: When?

whom He raised from the dead, *even* Jesus
who delivers us from the wrath to come.

CHAPTER 2

Paul's Founding of the Church

FOR you yourselves know, brethren, that
our coming to you was not in vain.
2 But even* after we had suffered before
and were spitefully treated at [R]Philippi, as
you know, we were [R]bold in our God to
speak to you the gospel of God in much con-
flict. Acts 14:5; 16:19–24 • Acts 17:1–9
3 For our exhortation *did* not *come* from
error or uncleanness, nor *was it* in deceit.
4 But as [R]we have been approved by God
[R]to be entrusted with the gospel, even so we
speak, not as pleasing men, but God [R]who
tests our hearts. 1 Cor. 7:25 • Titus 1:3 • Prov. 17:3
5 For [R]neither at any time did we use flat-
tering words, as you know, nor a cloak for
covetousness—God *is* witness. 2 Cor. 2:17
6 Nor did we seek glory from men, either
from you or from others, when we might have
made demands as apostles of Christ.
7 But [R]we were gentle among you, just as
a nursing *mother* cherishes her own chil-
dren. 1 Cor. 2:3
8 So, affectionately longing for you, we
were well pleased to impart to you not only
the gospel of God, but also our own lives, be-
cause you had become dear to us.
9 For you remember, brethren, our labor
and toil; for laboring night and day, that we
might not be a burden to any of you, we
preached to you the gospel of God.
10 You *are* witnesses, and God *also*, how de-
voutly and justly and blamelessly we behaved
ourselves among you who believe;
11 as you know how we exhorted, and com-
forted, and charged* every one of you, as a fa-
ther *does* his own children,
12 [R]that you would walk worthy of God
[R]who calls you into His own kingdom and
glory. Eph. 4:1 • 1 Cor. 1:9
13 For this reason we also thank God
[R]without ceasing, because when you [R]re-
ceived the word of God which you heard
from us, you welcomed *it* [R]not *as* the word
of men, but as it is in truth, the word of God,
which also effectively works in you who be-
lieve. 1 Thess. 1:2, 3 • Mark 4:20 • [Gal. 4:14]
14 For you, brethren, became imitators of the
churches of God which are in Judea in Christ
Jesus. For you also suffered the same things
from your own countrymen, just as they *did*
from the Judeans,
15 [R]who killed both the Lord Jesus and their
own prophets, and have persecuted us; and
they do not please God [R]and are contrary to
all men, Acts 2:23 • Esth. 3:8
16 forbidding us to speak to the Gentiles that
they may be saved, so as always to fill up *the*
measure of their sins; but wrath has come
upon them to the uttermost.

Satan Hinders Paul

17 But we, brethren, having been taken away
from you for a short time [R]in presence, not in
heart, endeavored more eagerly to see your
face with great desire. 1 Cor. 5:3
18 Therefore we wanted to come to you—
even I, Paul, time and again—but [R]Satan hin-
dered us. Rom. 1:13; 15:22
19 For [R]what *is* our hope, or joy, or [R]crown
of rejoicing? *Is it* not even you in the [R]pres-
ence of our Lord Jesus Christ [R]at His com-
ing? 2 Cor. 1:14 • Prov. 16:31 • Jude 24 • 1 Cor. 15:23
20 For you are our glory and joy.

CHAPTER 3

Paul Sends Timothy

THEREFORE, when we could no longer en-
dure it, we thought it good to be left in
Athens alone,
2 and sent Timothy, our brother and minis-
ter of God, and our fellow laborer in the
gospel of Christ, to establish you and encour-
age you concerning your faith,
3 [R]that no one should be shaken by these
afflictions; for you yourselves know that [R]we
are appointed to this. Eph. 3:13 • Acts 9:16
4 For, in fact, we told you before when we
were with you that we would suffer tribula-
tion, just as it happened, and you know.
5 For this reason, when I could no longer
endure it, I sent to know your faith, [R]lest by
some means the tempter had tempted you,
and our labor might be in vain. 1 Cor. 7:5

Timothy's Encouraging Report

6 [R]But now that Timothy has come to us
from you, and brought us good news of your
faith and love, and that you always have good
remembrance of us, greatly desiring to see us,
as we also *to see* you— Acts 18:5
7 therefore, brethren, in all our affliction
and distress [R]we were comforted concerning
you by your faith. 2 Cor. 1:4
8 For now we live, if you [R]stand fast in the
Lord. Phil. 4:1
9 For what thanks can we render to God for
you, for all the joy with which we rejoice for
your sake before our God,
10 night and day praying exceedingly that
we may see your face [R]and perfect what is
lacking in your faith? 2 Cor. 13:9

Paul's Desire to Visit Them

11 Now may our God and Father Himself,
and our Lord Jesus Christ, [R]direct our way to
you. Mark 1:3
12 And may the Lord make you increase and

2:2 NU, M omit *even* **2:11** NU, M *implored*

[R]abound in love to one another and to all, just as we *do* to you, Phil. 1:9

13 so that He may establish [R]your hearts blameless in holiness before our God and Father at the coming of our Lord Jesus Christ with all His saints. 2 Thess. 2:17

CHAPTER 4

Directions for Growth

FINALLY then, brethren, we urge and exhort in the Lord Jesus [R]that you should abound more and more, [R]just as you received from us how you ought to walk and to please God; 1 Cor. 15:58 • Phil. 1:27

2 for you know what commandments we gave you through the Lord Jesus.

3 For this is [R]the will of God, [R]your sanctification: that you should abstain from sexual immorality; [Rom. 12:2] • Eph. 5:27

4 [R]that each of you should know how to possess his own vessel in sanctification and honor, Rom. 6:19

5 [R]not in passion of lust, [R]like the Gentiles who do not know God; Col. 3:5 • Eph. 4:17, 18

6 that no one should take advantage of and defraud his brother in this matter, because the Lord *is* the avenger of all such, as we also forewarned you and testified.

7 For God did not call us to uncleanness, [R]but in holiness. Lev. 11:44

8 [R]Therefore he who rejects *this* does not reject man, but God, [R]who has also given* us His Holy Spirit. Luke 10:16 • 1 Cor. 2:10

9 But concerning brotherly love you have no need that I should write to you, for [R]you yourselves are taught by God [R]to love one another; [Jer. 31:33, 34] • Matt. 22:39

10 and indeed you do so toward all the brethren who are in all Macedonia. But we urge you, brethren, [R]that you increase more and more; 1 Thess. 3:12

11 that you also aspire to lead a quiet life, [R]to mind your own business, and [R]to work with your own hands, as we commanded you, 2 Thess. 3:11 • Acts 20:35

12 [R]that you may walk properly toward those who are outside, and *that* you may lack nothing. Rom. 13:13

Revelation Concerning the Dead in Christ

13 But I do not want you to be ignorant, brethren, concerning those who have fallen [T]asleep, lest you sorrow [R]as others [R]who have no hope. Died • Lev. 19:28 • [Eph. 2:12]

14 For [R]if we believe that Jesus died and rose again, even so God will bring with Him those who sleep in Jesus.* 1 Cor. 15:13

15 For this we say to you by the word of the Lord, that we who are alive *and* remain until the coming of the Lord will by no means precede those who are asleep.

16 For the Lord Himself will descend from heaven with a shout, with the voice of an archangel, and with the trumpet of God. And the dead in Christ will rise first.

17 Then we who are alive *and* remain shall be caught up together with them in the clouds to meet the Lord in the air. And thus we shall always be with the Lord.

18 [R]Therefore comfort one another with these words. 1 Thess. 5:11

CHAPTER 5

Description of the Day of the Lord

BUT concerning [R]the times and the seasons, brethren, you have no need that I should write to you. Matt. 24:3

2 For you yourselves know perfectly that [R]the day of the Lord so comes as a thief in the night. [2 Pet. 3:10]

3 For when they say, "Peace and safety!" then [R]sudden destruction comes upon them, as labor pains upon a pregnant woman. And they shall not escape. Is. 13:6–9

4 [R]But you, brethren, are not in darkness, so that this Day should overtake you as a thief. 1 John 2:8

5 You are all sons of light and sons of the day. We are not of the night nor of darkness.

6 [R]Therefore let us not sleep, as others *do,* but let us watch and be sober. Matt. 25:5

7 For those who sleep, sleep at night, and those who get drunk are drunk at night.

8 But let us who are of the day be sober, putting on the breastplate of faith and love, and *as* a helmet the hope of salvation.

9 For [R]God did not appoint us to wrath, [R]but to obtain salvation through our Lord Jesus Christ, Rom. 9:22 • [2 Thess. 2:13]

10 who died for us, that whether we wake or sleep, we should live together with Him.

11 Therefore comfort each other and edify one another, just as you also are doing.

Instruction for Holy Living

12 And we urge you, brethren, to recognize those who labor among you, and are over you in the Lord and admonish you,

13 and to esteem them very highly in love for their work's sake. [R]Be at peace among yourselves. Mark 9:50

14 Now we exhort you, brethren, [R]warn those who are unruly, [R]comfort the fainthearted, uphold the weak, [R]be patient with all. 2 Thess. 3:6, 7, 11 • Heb. 12:12 • Gal. 5:22

15 [R]See that no one renders evil for evil to anyone, but always pursue what is good both for yourselves and for all. Lev. 19:18

16 [R]Rejoice always, [2 Cor. 6:10]

17 [R]pray without ceasing, Eph. 6:18

4:8 NU *who also gives* **4:14** Or *those who through Jesus sleep*

18 in everything give thanks; for this is the
will of God in Christ Jesus for you.
19 [R]Do not quench the Spirit. Eph. 4:30
20 Do not despise prophecies.
21 Test all things; hold fast what is good.
22 Abstain from every form of evil.

Conclusion

23 Now may [R]the God of peace Himself
[R]sanctify you completely; and may your
whole spirit, soul, and body [R]be preserved
blameless at the coming of our Lord Jesus
Christ. Phil. 4:9 • 1 Thess. 3:13 • 1 Cor. 1:8, 9

24 He who calls you *is* [R]faithful, who also
will [R]do *it*. [1 Cor. 10:13] • Phil. 1:6
25 Brethren, pray for us.
26 Greet all the brethren with a holy kiss.
27 I charge you by the Lord that this [T]epistle
be read to all the holy* brethren. *letter*
28 The grace of our Lord Jesus Christ *be*
with you. Amen.

5:27 NU omits *holy*

THE SECOND EPISTLE OF PAUL THE APOSTLE TO THE

THESSALONIANS

THE BOOK OF 2 THESSALONIANS

Since Paul's first letter, the seeds of false doctrine have been sown among the Thessalonians, causing them to waver in their faith. Paul removes these destructive seeds and again plants the seeds of truth. He begins by commending the believers on their faithfulness in the midst of persecution and encouraging them that present suffering will be repaid with future glory. Therefore, in the midst of persecution, expectation can be high.

Paul then deals with the central matter of his letter: a misunderstanding spawned by false teachers regarding the coming day of the Lord. Despite reports to the contrary, that day has not yet come, and Paul recounts the events that must first take place. Laboring for the gospel, rather than lazy resignation, is the proper response.

As the second letter in Paul's Thessalonian correspondence, this was entitled *Pros Thessalonikeis B,* the "Second to the Thessalonians."

THE AUTHOR OF 2 THESSALONIANS

The external attestation to the authenticity of 2 Thessalonians as a Pauline epistle is even stronger than that for 1 Thessalonians. Internally, the vocabulary, style, and doctrinal content support the claims in 1:1 and 3:17 that it was written by Paul.

THE TIME OF 2 THESSALONIANS

See "The Time of 1 Thessalonians" for the background to the Thessalonian correspondence. This letter was probably written a few months after 1 Thessalonians, while Paul was still in Corinth with Silas and Timothy (1:1; cf. Acts 18:5). The bearer of the first epistle may have brought Paul an update on the new developments, prompting him to write this letter. They were still undergoing persecution, and the false teaching about the day of the Lord led some of them to overreact by giving up their jobs. The problem of idleness recorded in 1 Thessalonians 4:11, 12 had become more serious (3:6–15). By this time, Paul was beginning to see the opposition he would face in his ministry in Corinth (3:2; see Acts 18:5–10).

THE CHRIST OF 2 THESSALONIANS

The return of Christ is mentioned more times (318) in the New Testament than any other doctrine, and this is certainly the major concept in chapters 1 and 2 of this epistle. The return of the Lord Jesus is a reassuring and joyful hope for believers, but His revelation from heaven holds awesome and terrifying implications for those who have not trusted in Him (1:6–10; 2:8–12).

KEYS TO 2 THESSALONIANS

Key Word: Understanding the Day of the Lord—The theme of this epistle is an understanding of the day of the Lord and the resulting lifestyle changes. The doctrinal error of chapter 2 has been causing the practical error that Paul seeks to overcome in chapter 3. Some of the believers have abandoned their work and have begun to live off others, apparently assuming that the end is at hand. Paul commands them to follow his example by supporting themselves and instructs the rest of the church to discipline them if they fail to do so.

Key Verses: 2 Thessalonians 2:2, 3 and 3:5, 6—"Not to be soon shaken in mind or troubled, either by spirit or by word or by letter, as if from us, as though the day of Christ had come. Let no one deceive you by any means; for *that Day will not come* unless the falling away comes first, and the man of sin is revealed, the son of perdition" (2:2, 3).

"Now may the Lord direct your hearts into the love of God and into the patience of Christ. But we command you, brethren, in the name of our Lord Jesus Christ, that you withdraw from every brother who walks disorderly and not according to the tradition which he received from us" (3:5, 6).

Key Chapter: 2 Thessalonians 2—The second chapter is written to correct the fallacious teaching that the day of the Lord has already come upon the Thessalonian church. This teaching, coupled with the afflictions they have been suffering, is causing a great disturbance among the believers who wonder when their "gathering together to Him" (2:1; 1 Thess. 4:13–18) will take place. Paul makes it clear that certain identifiable events will precede that day and that those events have not yet occurred.

SURVEY OF 2 THESSALONIANS

This epistle is the theological sequel to 1 Thessalonians, which developed the theme of the coming day of the Lord (1 Thess. 5:1–11). However, not long after the Thessalonians receive that letter, they fall prey to false teaching or outright deception, thinking the day of the Lord has already begun. Paul writes this brief letter to correct the error and also to encourage those believers whose faith is being tested by the difficulties presented by persecution. He also reproves those who have decided to cease working because they believe the coming of Christ is near. Second Thessalonians deals with Paul's encouragement in persecution (1); Paul's explanation of the day of the Lord (2); and Paul's exhortation to the church (3).

Paul's Encouragement in Persecution (1): After his two verse salutation, Paul gives thanks for the growing faith and love of the Thessalonians and assures them of their ultimate deliverance from those who are persecuting them (1:3–10). They are encouraged to patiently endure their afflictions, knowing that the Lord Jesus will judge their persecutors when He is "revealed from heaven with His mighty angels, in flaming fire" (1:7, 8). Before Paul moves to the next topic, he concludes this section with a prayer for the spiritual welfare of his readers (1:11, 12).

Paul's Explanation of the Day of the Lord (2): Because of the severity of their afflictions, the Thessalonians have become susceptible to false teaching (and possibly a fraudulent letter in the name of Paul), claiming that they are already in the day of the Lord (2:1, 2). This was particularly disturbing because Paul's previous letter had given them the comforting hope that they were not destined for the wrath of that day (1 Thess. 5:9). Paul therefore assures them that the day of the Lord is yet in the future and will not arrive unannounced (2:3–12). Paul then concludes with a word of encouragement and a benedictory prayer of comfort before moving to his next topic.

Paul's Exhortation to the Church (3:1–18): Paul requests the Thessalonian church to pray on his behalf and to wait patiently for the Lord (3:1–5). Having thus commended, corrected, and comforted his readers, the tactful apostle closes his letter with a sharp word of command to those who have been using the truth of Christ's return as an excuse for disorderly conduct (3:6–15; cf. 1 Thess. 4:11, 12). The doctrine of the Lord's return requires a balance between waiting and working. It is a perspective that should encourage holiness, not idleness. This final section, like the first two, closes on a benedictory note (3:16–18).

FOCUS	ENCOURAGEMENT IN PERSECUTION			EXPLANATION OF THE DAY OF THE LORD		EXHORTATION TO THE CHURCH	
REFERENCE	1:1—1:5—1:11—2:1—2:13—3:1—3:6—3:18						
DIVISION	THANKSGIVING FOR GROWTH	ENCOURAGEMENT IN PERSECUTION	PRAYER FOR BLESSING	EVENTS PRECEDING	COMFORT OF THE BELIEVER	WAIT PATIENTLY	WTHDRAW
TOPIC	DISCOURAGED BELIEVERS			DISTURBED BELIEVERS		DISOBEDIENT BELIEVERS	
	THAKSGIVING FOR THEIR LIFE			INSTRUCTION OF THEIR DOCTRINE		CORRECTION OF THEIR BEHAVIOR	
LOCATION	WRITTEN IN CORINTH						
TIME	C. A.D. 51						

OUTLINE OF 2 THESSALONIANS

I. Paul's Encouragement in Persecution 1:1–12

A. Thanksgiving for Their Growth..............1:1–4
B. Encouragement in Their Persecution....1:5–10
C. Prayer for God's Blessing....................1:11, 12

II. Paul's Explanation of the Day of the Lord...2:1–17

A. The Events Preceding the Day of the Lord..2:1–12
1. First a Falling Away 2:1–3
2. The Man of Sin Is Revealed 2:4, 5
3. The Restrainer Is Taken Out of the Way...2:6, 7
4. The Second Coming of Christ 2:8–12
B. The Comfort of the Believer on the Day of the Lord.......................................2:13–17

III. Paul's Exhortation to the Church........3:1–18

A. Wait Patiently for Christ.........................3:1–5
B. Withdraw from the Disorderly 3:6–15
C. Conclusion..3:16–18

CHAPTER 1

Thanksgiving for Their Growth

PAUL, Silvanus, and Timothy,

To the church of the Thessalonians in God
our Father and the Lord Jesus Christ:

2 Grace to you and peace from God our Fa-
ther and the Lord Jesus Christ.

3 We are bound to thank God always for
you, brethren, as it is fitting, because your
faith grows exceedingly, and the love of every
one of you all abounds toward each other,
4 so that we ourselves boast of you among
the churches of God for your patience and
faith in all your persecutions and tribulations
that you endure,

Encouragement in Their Persecution

5 *which is* [R]manifest[T] evidence of the righ-
teous judgment of God, that you may be
counted worthy of the kingdom of God, for
which you also suffer; Phil. 1:28 • *plain*
6 [R]since *it is* a righteous thing with God to
repay with [T]tribulation those who trouble
you, Rev. 6:10 • *affliction*
7 and to *give* you who are troubled rest
with us when the Lord Jesus is revealed from
heaven with His mighty angels,
8 in flaming fire taking vengeance on those
who do not know God, and on those who do
not obey the gospel of our Lord Jesus Christ.
9 These shall be punished with everlasting
destruction from the presence of the Lord and
from the glory of His power,
10 when He comes, in that Day, [R]to be glori-
fied in His saints and to be admired among all
those who believe,* because our testimony
among you was believed. Matt. 25:31

Prayer for God's Blessing

11 Therefore we also pray always for you
that our God would [R]count you worthy of
this calling, and fulfill all the good pleasure
of *His* goodness and [R]the work of faith with
power, Col. 1:12 • 1 Thess. 1:3
12 [R]that the name of our Lord Jesus Christ
may be glorified in you, and you in Him, ac-
cording to the grace of our God and the Lord
Jesus Christ. [Col. 3:17]

CHAPTER 2

The Events Preceding the Day of the Lord

NOW, brethren, concerning the coming of
our Lord Jesus Christ [R]and our gathering
together to Him, we ask you, Matt. 24:31
2 [R]not to be soon shaken in mind or trou-
bled, either by spirit or by word or by letter, as
if from us, as though the day of Christ* had
come. Matt. 24:4
3 Let no one deceive you by any means; for
that Day will not come [R]unless the falling
away comes first, and the man of sin* is re-
vealed, the son of perdition, 1 Tim. 4:1
4 who opposes and [R]exalts himself above
all that is called God or that is worshiped, so
that he sits as God* in the temple of God,
showing himself that he is God. Is. 14:13, 14
5 Do you not remember that when I was
still with you I told you these things?
6 And now you know what is restraining,
that he may be revealed in his own time.
7 For the mystery of lawlessness is already
at work; only He* who now restrains *will do
so* until He* is taken out of the way.
8 And then the lawless one will be revealed,
[R]whom the Lord will consume with the breath
of His mouth and destroy with the brightness
of His coming. Dan. 7:10
9 The coming of the *lawless one* is accord-
ing to the working of Satan, with all power,
[R]signs, and lying wonders, Deut. 13:1
10 and with all unrighteous deception
among [R]those who perish, because they did
not receive [R]the love of the truth, that they
might be saved. 2 Cor. 2:15 • 1 Cor. 16:22
11 And [R]for this reason God will send them
strong delusion, [R]that they should believe the
lie, Rom. 1:28 • 1 Tim. 4:1
12 that they all may be condemned who did
not believe the truth but [R]had pleasure in un-
righteousness. Rom. 1:32

The Comfort of the Believer on the Day of the Lord

13 But we are bound to give thanks to God
always for you, brethren beloved by the Lord,
because God from the beginning chose you
for salvation through sanctification by the
Spirit and belief in the truth,
14 to which He called you by our gospel, for
[R]the obtaining of the glory of our Lord Jesus
Christ. 1 Pet. 5:10
15 Therefore, brethren, stand fast and hold
the traditions which you were taught, whether
by word or our [T]epistle. *letter*
16 Now may our Lord Jesus Christ Himself,
and our God and Father, [R]who has loved us
and given *us* everlasting consolation and
[R]good hope by grace, [Rev. 1:5] • 1 Pet. 1:3
17 comfort your hearts [R]and establish you in
every good word and work. 1 Cor. 1:8

CHAPTER 3

Wait Patiently for Christ

FINALLY, brethren, [R]pray for us, that the
word of the Lord may run *swiftly* and be
glorified, just as *it is* with you, Eph. 6:19

1:10 NU, M *have believed* **2:2** NU *the Lord* **2:3** NU *lawlessness* **2:4** NU omits *as God* **2:7** Or *he* • Or *he*

2 and [R]that we may be delivered from
unreasonable and wicked men; [R]for not all
have faith. Rom. 15:31 • Acts 28:24
3 But the Lord is faithful, who will establish
you and guard *you* from the evil one.
4 And [R]we have confidence in the Lord con-
cerning you, both that you do and will do the
things we command you. 2 Cor. 7:16
5 Now may [R]the Lord direct your hearts
into the love of God and into the patience of
Christ. 1 Chr. 29:18

Withdraw from the Disorderly

6 But we command you, brethren, in the
name of our Lord Jesus Christ, that you with-
draw [R]from every brother who walks disor-
derly and not according to the tradition which
he* received from us. 1 Cor. 5:1
7 For you yourselves know how you ought
to follow us, for we were not disorderly
among you;
8 nor did we eat anyone's bread [T]free of
charge, but worked with [R]labor and toil night
and day, that we might not be a burden to any
of you, Lit. *for nothing* • 1 Thess. 2:9
9 not because we do not have [R]authority,
but to make ourselves an example of how you
should follow us. 1 Cor. 9:4, 6–14
10 For even when we were with you, we com-
manded you this: If anyone will not work, nei-
ther shall he eat.
11 For we hear that there are some who walk
among you in a disorderly manner, not work-
ing at all, but are busybodies.
12 Now those who are such we command
and [T]exhort through our Lord Jesus Christ
[R]that they work in quietness and eat their own
bread. *encourage* • Eph. 4:28
13 But *as for* you, brethren, [R]do not grow
weary *in* doing good. Gal. 6:9
14 And if anyone does not obey our word in
this [T]epistle, note that person and [R]do not
keep company with him, that he may be
ashamed. *letter* • Matt. 18:17
15 [R]Yet do not count *him* as an enemy, but
admonish *him* as a brother. Lev. 19:17

Conclusion

16 Now may [R]the Lord of peace Himself give
you peace always in every way. The Lord *be*
with you all. Rom. 15:33
17 [R]The salutation of Paul with my own
hand, which is a sign in every [T]epistle; so I
write. 1 Cor. 16:21 • *letter*
18 [R]The grace of our Lord Jesus Christ *be*
with you all. Amen. Rom. 16:20, 24

3:6 NU, M *they*

THE FIRST EPISTLE OF PAUL THE APOSTLE TO

TIMOTHY

THE BOOK OF 1 TIMOTHY

Paul, the aged and experienced apostle, writes to the young pastor Timothy who is facing a heavy burden of responsibility in the church at Ephesus. The task is challenging: false doctrine must be erased, public worship safeguarded, and mature leadership developed. In addition to the conduct of the church, Paul talks pointedly about the conduct of the minister. Timothy must be on his guard lest his youthfulness become a liability, rather than an asset, to the gospel. He must be careful to avoid false teachers and greedy motives, pursuing instead righteousness, godliness, faith, love, perseverance, and the gentleness that befits a man of God.

The Greek title for this letter is *Pros Timotheon A,* the "First to Timothy." The name "Timothy" means "Honoring God" or "Honored by God" and probably was given to him by his mother Eunice.

THE AUTHOR OF 1 TIMOTHY

Since the early nineteenth century, the Pastoral Epistles have been attacked more than any other Pauline epistles on the issue of authenticity. The similarity of these epistles requires that they be treated as a unit in terms of authorship because they stand or fall together.

The external evidence solidly supports the conservative position that Paul wrote the letters to Timothy and Titus. Postapostolic church fathers, such as Polycarp and Clement of Rome, allude to them as Paul's writing. In addition, these epistles are identified as Pauline by Irenaeus, Tertullian, Clement of Alexandria, and the Muratorian Canon. Only Romans and 1 Corinthians have better attestation among the Pauline Epistles.

Suggestions of an author other than Paul are supported wholly on the basis of internal evidence. Even though these letters claim to be written by Paul (1:1; 2 Tim. 1:1; Titus 1:1), critics assert that they are "pious forgeries" that appeared in the second century. There are several problems with this: (1) Pseudonymous writing was unacceptable to Paul (see 2 Thess. 2:2, 3:17) and to the early church, which was very sensitive to the problem of forgeries. (2) The adjective *pious* should deceive no one: a forgery was as deliberately deceptive then as it is now. (3) The many personal facts and names that appear in the Pastoral Epistles would have been avoided by a forger who would have taken refuge in vagueness. Nor would a forger have used expressions like those in 1:13, 15 if he had been an admirer of Paul. The doctrinal teaching and autobiographical details (cf. 1:12–17; 2:7; 2 Tim. 1:8–12; 4:9–22; Titus 1:5; 3:12, 13) fit very well with "Paul, the aged" (Philem. 9). (4) What purpose or advantage would these epistles serve as forgeries written years later? There are too many personal elements, and the doctrinal refutations do not refer to second-century Gnosticism. (5) The style and content of the postapostolic writings or apocryphal books differ greatly with these three letters.

THE TIME OF 1 TIMOTHY

Pauline authorship of the Pastoral Epistles requires Paul's release from his Roman imprisonment (Acts 28), the continuation of his missionary endeavors, and his imprisonment for a second time in Rome. Unfortunately, the order of events can only be reconstructed from hints, because there is no concurrent history paralleling Acts to chronicle the last years of the apostle. The following reconstruction, therefore, is only tentative:

As he anticipated in Philippians (1:19, 25, 26; 2:24), Paul was released from his first Roman imprisonment. It is possible that his Jewish accusers decided not to appear at his trial before Caesar. In fulfillment of his promise to the Philippians (Phil. 2:19–23), he sends Timothy to Philippi to relate the good news. Paul himself went to Ephesus (in spite of his earlier expectations in Acts 20:38) and to other Asian churches like Colosse (see Philem. 22). When Timothy rejoined him in Ephesus, Paul instructed his assistant to "remain in Ephesus" (1:3) while he journeyed to Macedonia. When he saw that he might be delayed in Macedonia, Paul wrote 1 Timothy, perhaps from Philippi (3:14, 15). After he saw Timothy in Ephesus, the apostle journeyed on to the island of Crete where, after a period of ministry, he left Titus to continue the work (Titus 1:5). In Corinth, Paul decided to write a letter to Titus because Zenas and Apollos were making a journey that would take them by way of Crete (Titus 3:13). He instructed Titus to join him in Nicopolis after the arrival of his replacement in Crete, Artemas or Tychicus (Titus 3:12).

If he went to Spain as he had planned (Rom. 15:24, 28), Paul probably departed with Titus for that western province after his winter in Nicopolis. Early church tradition holds that Paul did go to Spain. Before the end of the first century, Clement of Rome said that Paul "reached the limits of the West" (1 Clement 5:7). Since he was writing from Rome, he evidently had Spain in mind. Paul may have been in Spain from A.D. 64 to 66. He returned to Greece and Asia—to Corinth, Miletus, and Troas (2 Tim. 4:13, 20)—and may have been arrested in Troas where he left his valuable books and parchments (2 Tim. 4:13, 15).

Now that Christianity had become an illegal religion in the empire (the burning of Rome took place in A.D. 64), Paul's enemies were able to successfully accuse him. He was imprisoned in A.D. 67 and wrote 2 Timothy from his Roman cell after his first defense before the Imperial Court (2 Tim. 1:8, 17; 2:9; 4:16, 17). He was delivered from condemnation, but he held no hope of release and expected to be executed (2 Tim. 4:6–8, 18). He urged Timothy to come before that happened (2 Tim. 4:9, 21); and, according to tradition, the apostle was beheaded west of Rome on the Ostian Way.

Paul wrote 1 Timothy from Macedonia in A.D. 62 or 63 while Timothy was serving as his representative in Ephesus and perhaps in other churches in the province of Asia. Timothy was to appoint elders, combat false doctrine, and supervise church life as an apostolic representative.

THE CHRIST OF 1 TIMOTHY

Christ is the "one Mediator between God and men" (2:5), and "God was manifested in the flesh, justified in the Spirit, seen by angels, preached among the Gentiles, believed on in the world, received up in glory" (3:16). He is the source of spiritual strength, faith, and love (1:12, 14). He "came into the world to save sinners" (1:15) and "gave Himself a ransom for all" (2:6) as "*the* Savior of all men, especially of those who believe" (4:10).

KEYS TO 1 TIMOTHY

Key Word: Leadership Manual for Church Organization—The theme of this epistle is Timothy's organization and oversight of the Asian churches as a faithful minister of God. Paul writes this letter as a reference manual for leadership so that Timothy will have effective guidance for his work during Paul's absence in Macedonia (3:14, 15). Paul wants to encourage and exhort his younger assistant to become an example to others, exercise his spiritual gifts, and "fight the good fight of faith" (6:12; cf. 1:18; 4:12–16; 6:20). Timothy's personal and public life must be above reproach; and he must be ready to deal with matters of false teaching, organization, discipline, proclamation of the Scriptures, poverty and wealth, and the roles of various groups. Negatively, he is to refute error (1:7–11; 6:3–5); positively, he is to teach the truth (4:13–16; 6:2, 17, 18).

Key Verses: 1 Timothy 3:15, 16 and 6:11, 12—"But if I am delayed, *I write* so that you may know how you ought to conduct yourself in the house of God, which is the church of the living God, the pillar and ground of the truth. And without controversy great is the mystery of godliness: God was manifested in the flesh, justified in the Spirit, seen by angels, preached among the Gentiles, believed on in the world, received up in glory" (3:15, 16).

"But you, O man of God, flee these things and pursue righteousness, godliness, faith, love, patience, gentleness. Fight the good fight of faith, lay hold on eternal life, to which you were also called and have confessed the good confession in the presence of many witnesses" (6:11, 12).

Key Chapter: 1 Timothy 3—Listed in chapter 3 are the qualifications for the leaders of God's church, the elders and deacons. Notably absent are qualities of worldly success or position. Instead, Paul enumerates character qualities demonstrating that true leadership emanates from our walk with God rather than from achievements or vocational success.

SURVEY OF 1 TIMOTHY

Paul's last three recorded letters, written near the end of his full and fruitful life, were addressed to his authorized representatives Timothy and Titus. These were the only letters Paul wrote exclusively to individuals (Philemon was addressed primarily to its namesake, but also to others), and they were designed to exhort and encourage Timothy and Titus in their ministry of solidifying the churches in Ephesus and Crete. In the eighteenth century, these epistles came to be known as the Pastoral Epistles even though they do not use any terms such as shepherd, pastor, flock, or sheep. Still, this title is appropriate for 1 Timothy and Titus, since they focus on the oversight of church life. It is less appropriate in the case of 2 Timothy, which is a more personal than church-oriented letter. The Pastoral Epistles abound with principles for leadership and righteous living.

In his first letter to Timothy, Paul seeks to guide his younger and less experienced assistant in his weighty responsibility as the overseer of the work at Ephesus and other Asian cities. He writes, in effect, a challenge to Timothy to fulfill the task before him: combating false teaching with sound doctrine, developing qualified leadership, teaching God's Word, and encouraging Christian conduct. Because of the personal and conversational character of this letter, it is loosely structured around five clear charges that end each section (1:18–20; 3:14–16; 4:11–20; 5:21–25; 6:20, 21): Paul's charges concerning doctrine (1); Paul's charge concerning public worship (2 and 3); Paul's charge concerning false teachers (4); Paul's charge concerning church discipline (5); and Paul's charge concerning pastoral motives (6).

Paul's Charge Concerning Doctrine (1): After his greetings (1:1, 2), Paul warns Timothy about the growing problem of false doctrines, particularly as they relate to the misuse of the Mosaic Law (1:3–11). The aging apostle then recounts his radical conversion to Christ and subsequent calling to the ministry (1:12–17). Timothy, too, has received a divine calling, and Paul charges him to fulfill it without wavering in doctrine or conduct (1:18–20).

Paul's Charge Concerning Public Worship (2 and 3): Turning his attention to the church at large, Paul addresses the issues of church worship and leadership. Efficacious public prayer should be a part of worship, and Paul associates this with the role of men in the church (2:1–8). He then turns to the role of women (2:9–15), wherein he emphasizes the importance of the inner quality of godliness. In 3:1–7 Paul lists several qualifications for overseers or bishops. The word for "overseer" (*episkopos*) is used synonymously with the word for "elder" (*presbuteros*) in the New Testament, because both originally referred to the same office (see Acts 20:17, 28; Titus 1:5, 7). The qualifications for the office of deacon (*diakonos,* "servant") are listed in 3:8–13.

Paul's Charge Concerning False Teachers (4): Timothy obviously had difficulties with some of the older men (5:1) who had left the faith. Paul carefully advises on the issues of marriage, food, and exercise. The closing charge exhorts Timothy not to neglect the spiritual gift given to him.

Paul's Charge Concerning Church Discipline (5): One of the most difficult pastoral duties for the young minister is to lead in the exercise of church discipline. Commencing with the general advice of treating all members of the church as family (5:1, 2), Paul concentrates on the two special areas of widows and elders, focusing on Timothy's responsibility and providing practical instruction.

Paul's Charge Concerning Pastoral Duties (6): In addition, the insidious doctrine was being taught that godliness will eventually result in material blessing. Paul, in no uncertain terms, states "from such withdraw yourself" (6:5). The book closes with an extended charge (6:11–21), which is supplemented by an additional charge that Timothy is to give to the wealthy of this age (6:17–19).

FOCUS	DOCTRINE	PUBLIC WORSHIP	FALSE TEACHERS	CHURCH DISCIPLINE	PASTORAL MOTIVES
REFERENCE	1:1—	2:1—	4:1—	5:1—	6:1—6:21
DIVISION	PROBLEM OF FALSE DOCTRINE	PUBLIC WORSHIP AND LEADERSHIP	PRESERVE TRUE DOCTRINE	PRESCRIPTIONS FOR WIDOWS AND ELDERS	PASTORAL MOTIVATIONS
TOPIC	WARNING	WORSHIP	WISDOM	WIDOWS	WEALTH
	DANGERS OF FALSE DOCTRINE	DIRECTIONS FOR WORSHIP	DEFENSE AGAINST FALSE TEACHERS	DUTIES TOWARD OTHERS	DEALINGS WITH RICHES
LOCATION	WRITTEN IN MACEDONIA				
TIME	C. A.D. 62–63				

OUTLINE OF 1 TIMOTHY

I. Paul's Charge Concerning Doctrine.....1:1–20

A. Paul's Past Charge to Timothy 1:1–11
B. Christ's Past Charge to Paul..............1:12–17
C. First Charge: "Wage the Good Warfare"..............1:18–20

II. Paul's Charge Concerning Public Worship..............2:1—3:16

A. Prayer in Public Worship..............2:1–8
B. Women in Public Worship..............2:9–15
C. Qualifications of Bishops..............3:1–7
D. Qualifications of Deacons..............3:8–13
E. Second Charge: "Conduct Yourself in the House of God"..............3:14–16

III. Paul's Charge Concerning False Teachers..............4:1–16

A. Description of False Teachers..............4:1–5
B. Instruction for the True Teacher..............4:6–10
C. Third Charge: "Do Not Neglect the Gift"..............4:11–16

IV. Paul's Charge Concerning Church Discipline 5:1–25

A. How to Treat All People 5:1, 2
B. How to Treat Widows 5:3–16
C. How to Treat Elders 5:17–20
D. Fourth Charge: "Observe These Things Without Prejudice" 5:21–25

V. Paul's Charge Concerning Pastoral Motives..6:1–21

A. Exhortation to Servants...........................6:1, 2
B. Exhortation to Godliness with Contentment 6:3–16
C. Exhortation to the Rich.........................6:17–19
D. Fifth Charge: "Guard What Was Committed" 6:20, 21

CHAPTER 1

Paul's Past Charge to Timothy

PAUL, an apostle of Jesus Christ, by the
commandment of God our Savior and the
Lord Jesus Christ, our hope,

2 To Timothy, a true son in the faith:

[R]Grace, mercy, *and* peace from God our
Father and Jesus Christ our Lord. Gal. 1:3

3 As I urged you [R]when I went into Mace-
donia—remain in Ephesus that you may
[T]charge some [R]that they teach no other doc-
trine, Acts 20:1, 3 • *command* • Gal. 1:6, 7
4 nor give heed to fables and endless ge-
nealogies, which cause disputes rather than
godly edification which is in faith.
5 Now the purpose of the commandment is
love from a pure heart, *from* a good con-
science, and *from* sincere faith,
6 from which some, having strayed, have
turned aside to [R]idle talk, 1 Tim. 6:4, 20
7 desiring to be teachers of the law, under-
standing neither what they say nor the things
which they affirm.
8 But we know that the law *is* [R]good if one
uses it lawfully, Rom. 7:12, 16
9 knowing this: that the law is not made for
a righteous person, but for *the* lawless and in-
subordinate, for *the* ungodly and for sinners,
for *the* unholy and profane, for murderers of
fathers and murderers of mothers, for
manslayers,
10 for fornicators, for sodomites, for kidnap-
pers, for liars, for perjurers, and if there is any
other thing that is [T]contrary to sound doc-
trine, *opposed*
11 according to the glorious gospel of the
[R]blessed God which was [R]committed to my
trust. 1 Tim. 6:15 • 1 Cor. 9:17

Christ's Past Charge to Paul

12 And I thank Christ Jesus our Lord who
has enabled me, because He counted me faith-
ful, putting *me* into the ministry,
13 although [R]I was formerly a blasphemer, a
persecutor, and an [T]insolent man; but I ob-
tained mercy because [R]I did *it* ignorantly in
unbelief. Acts 8:3 • *violently arrogant* • John 4:21
14 [R]And the grace of our Lord was exceed-
ingly abundant, [R]with faith and love which
are in Christ Jesus. Rom. 5:20 • 2 Tim. 1:13
15 [R]This *is* a faithful saying and worthy of
all acceptance, that [R]Christ Jesus came into
the world to save sinners, of whom I am
chief. 2 Tim. 2:11 • Matt. 1:21; 9:13★
16 However, for this reason I obtained
mercy, that in me first Jesus Christ might
show all longsuffering, as a pattern to those
who are going to believe on Him for everlast-
ing life.
17 Now to the King eternal, immortal, invis-
ible, to God who alone is wise,* *be* honor and
glory forever and ever. Amen.

Final Charge: "Wage the Good Warfare"

18 This [T]charge I commit to you, son Timo-
thy, according to the prophecies previously
made concerning you, that by them you may
wage the good warfare, *command*
19 having faith and a good conscience,
which some having rejected, concerning the
faith have suffered shipwreck,
20 of whom are [R]Hymenaeus and Alexander,
whom I delivered to Satan that they may learn
not to blaspheme. 2 Tim. 2:17, 18

CHAPTER 2

Prayer in Public Worship

THEREFORE I exhort first of all that sup-
plications, prayers, intercessions, *and* giv-
ing of thanks be made for all men,
2 [R]for kings and all who are in authority,
that we may lead a quiet and peaceable life in
all godliness and reverence. Ezra 6:10
3 For this *is* [R]good and acceptable in the
sight [R]of God our Savior, Rom. 12:2 • 2 Tim. 1:9
4 who desires all men to be saved and to
come to the knowledge of the truth.
5 [R]For *there is* one God and [R]one Mediator
between God and men, *the* Man Christ Je-
sus, Gal. 3:20 • [Heb. 9:15]
6 [R]who gave Himself a ransom for all, to be
testified in due time, Mark 10:45
7 [R]for which I was appointed a preacher
and an apostle—I am speaking the truth in
Christ* *and* not lying—a teacher of the Gen-
tiles in faith and truth. Eph. 3:7, 8
8 I desire therefore that the men pray

1:17 NU *the only God,* **2:7** NU omits *in Christ*

[R]everywhere, [R]lifting up holy hands, without
wrath and doubting; Luke 23:34 • Ps. 134:2

Women in Public Worship

9 in like manner also, that the women
adorn themselves in modest apparel, with
propriety and moderation, not with braided
hair or gold or pearls or costly clothing,
10 but, which is proper for women profess-
ing godliness, with good works.
11 Let a woman learn in silence with all sub-
mission.
12 And [R]I do not permit a woman to teach or
to have authority over a man, but to be in si-
lence. 1 Cor. 14:34
13 For Adam was formed first, then Eve.
14 And Adam was not deceived, but the
woman being deceived, fell into transgres-
sion.
15 Nevertheless she will be saved in
childbearing if they continue in faith, love,
and holiness, with self-control.

CHAPTER 3

Qualifications of Bishops

THIS *is* a faithful saying: If a man desires
the position of a bishop,* he desires a
good work.
2 A bishop then must be blameless, the hus-
band of one wife, temperate, sober-minded, of
good behavior, hospitable, able to teach;
3 not [T]given to wine, not violent, not greedy
for money,* but gentle, not quarrelsome, not
[T]covetous; *addicted • loving money*
4 one who rules his own house well, having
his children in submission with all reverence
5 (for if a man does not know how to rule
his own house, how will he take care of the
church of God?);
6 not a [T]novice, lest being puffed up with
pride he fall into the *same* condemnation as
the devil. *new convert*
7 Moreover he must have a good testimony
among those who are outside, lest he fall into
reproach and the snare of the devil.

Qualifications of Deacons

8 Likewise deacons *must be* reverent, not
double-tongued, [R]not given to much wine, not
greedy for money, Ezek. 44:21
9 holding the [T]mystery of the faith with a
pure conscience. *hidden truth*
10 But let these also first be tested; then let
them serve as deacons, being *found* blame-
less.
11 Likewise, *their* wives *must be* reverent,
not [T]slanderers, temperate, faithful in all
things. *malicious gossips*
12 Let deacons be the husbands of one wife,
ruling *their* children and their own houses
well.
13 For those who have served well as dea-
cons [R]obtain for themselves a good standing
and great boldness in the faith which is in
Christ Jesus. Matt. 25:21

Second Charge:
"Conduct Yourself in the House of God"

14 These things I write to you, though I hope
to come to you shortly;
15 but if I am delayed, *I write* so that you
may know how you ought to conduct yourself
in the house of God, which is the church of
the living God, the pillar and [T]ground of the
truth. *foundation, mainstay*
16 And without controversy great is the
[T]mystery of godliness: *hidden truth*

God* was manifested in the flesh,
[R]Justified in the Spirit, [Matt. 3:16]
[R]Seen by angels, Matt. 28:2
Preached among the Gentiles,
[R]Believed on in the world, Col. 1:6, 23
[R]Received up in glory. Luke 24:51

3:1 Lit. *overseer* **3:3** NU omits *not greedy for money*
3:16 NU *Who*

3:1–13 The Offices of the Church—The NT uses four terms to describe the leadership of the church: (1) "elder" (Gr., *presbuteros*), which places emphasis upon the authority that the leadership has to teach or rule in the church; (2) "bishop" (Gr., *episkopos*—overseer), which emphasizes the fact that the leadership is charged with overseeing the local church and as such is responsible for the spiritual well-being of those in the church; (3) "pastor" (Gr., *poimen*—shepherd), which places emphasis upon the responsibility of the leadership of the church to shepherd the flock. No shepherd has ever given birth to his sheep. It is the responsibility of those in leadership to do for the sheep what they cannot do for themselves and to make sure that they are in good spiritual condition so that they can do what comes naturally, that is, beget other sheep; (4) "deacon" (Gr., *diakonos*—minister), which places emphasis upon the attitude that the leaders are to have in their leading. They are not to "lord it over" the flock, but are to realize that they are the ministers or servants of those whom the Lord has put under their care.

The function of the office of elder is twofold: (1) teaching and (2) ruling (Page 1239—1 Tim. 5:17). An elder is to be able to teach his people what the Word of God teaches and to give direction as to how that is to be accomplished in and through the local church.

The qualifications for the office of deacon are essentially the same as those for the elder except that the deacon need not be "able to teach." The deacons are to be spiritual and in tune with the elders and seek to assist them in implementing the goals that the elders feel the Spirit of God is leading them to pursue through the local church.

Now turn to Page 1208—Eph. 5:25–29: The Relationship of the Church to Christ.

CHAPTER 4

Description of False Teachers

NOW the Spirit [T]expressly says that in latter times some will depart from the faith, giving heed [R]to deceiving spirits and doctrines of demons, *explicitly* • Rev. 16:14
2 speaking lies in hypocrisy, having their own conscience seared with a hot iron,
3 forbidding to marry, *and commanding* to abstain from foods which God created to be received with thanksgiving by those who believe and know the truth.
4 For every creature of God *is* good, and nothing is to be refused if it is received with thanksgiving;
5 for it is [T]sanctified by the word of God and prayer. *set apart*

Instruction for the True Teacher

6 If you instruct the brethren in these things, you will be a good minister of Jesus Christ, [R]nourished in the words of faith and of the good doctrine which you have carefully followed. 2 Tim. 3:14
7 But reject profane and old wives' fables, and exercise yourself toward godliness.
8 For [R]bodily exercise profits a little, but godliness is profitable for all things, [R]having promise of the life that now is and of that which is to come. 1 Cor. 8:8 • Ps. 37:9
9 This *is* a faithful saying and worthy of all acceptance.
10 For to this *end* we both labor and suffer reproach,* because we trust in the living God, [R]who is *the* Savior of all men, especially of those who believe. Ps. 36:6

Third Charge: "Do Not Neglect the Gift"

11 These things command and teach.
12 Let no one despise your youth, but be an example to the believers in word, in conduct, in love, in spirit,* in faith, in purity.
13 Till I come, give attention to reading, to exhortation, to [T]doctrine. *teaching*
14 Do not neglect the gift that is in you, which was given to you by prophecy with the laying on of the hands of the eldership.
15 Meditate on these things; give yourself entirely to them, that your progress may be evident to all.
16 Take heed to yourself and to the doctrine. Continue in them, for in doing this you will save both yourself and those who hear you.

CHAPTER 5

How to Treat All People

DO not rebuke an older man, but exhort him as a father, younger men as brothers,
2 older women as mothers, younger women as sisters, with all purity.

How to Treat Widows

3 Honor widows who are really widows.
4 But if any widow has children or grandchildren, let them first learn to show piety at home and to repay their parents; for this is good and* acceptable before God.
5 Now she who is really a widow, and left alone, trusts in God and continues in supplications and prayers night and day.
6 But she who lives in [T]pleasure is dead while she lives. *indulgence*
7 And these things command, that they may be blameless.
8 But if anyone does not provide for his own, [R]and especially for those of his household, [R]he has denied the faith and is worse than an unbeliever. Is. 58:7 • 2 Tim. 3:5
9 Do not let a widow under sixty years old be taken into the number, *and not unless* she has been the wife of one man,
10 well reported for good works: if she has brought up children, if she has lodged strangers, if she has washed the saints' feet, if she has relieved the afflicted, if she has diligently followed every good work.
11 But refuse *the* younger widows; for when they have begun to grow wanton against Christ, they desire to marry,
12 having condemnation because they have cast off their first [T]faith. Or *solemn promise*
13 And besides they learn *to be* idle, wandering about from house to house, and not only idle but also gossips and busybodies, saying things which they ought not.
14 Therefore I desire that *the* younger *widows* marry, bear children, manage the house, give no opportunity to the adversary to speak reproachfully.
15 For some have already turned aside after Satan.
16 If any believing man or* woman has widows, let them [T]relieve them, and do not let the church be burdened, that it may relieve those who are really widows. *give aid to*

How to Treat Elders

17 Let the elders who rule well be counted worthy of double honor, especially those who labor in the word and doctrine.
18 For the Scripture says, *"You shall not muzzle an ox while it treads out the grain,"** and, "The laborer *is* worthy of his wages."*
19 Do not receive an accusation against an elder except from two or three witnesses.
20 Those who are sinning rebuke in the presence of all, that the rest also may fear.

4:10 NU *we labor and strive,* **4:12** NU omits *in spirit*
5:4 NU, M omit *good and* **5:16** NU omits *man or*
5:18 Deut. 25:4 • Luke 10:7

Fourth Charge: "Observe These Things Without Prejudice"

21 I charge *you* before God and the Lord Jesus Christ and the elect angels that you observe these things without [R]prejudice, doing nothing with partiality. Deut. 1:17

22 Do not lay hands on anyone hastily, nor [R]share in other people's sins; keep yourself pure. Eph. 5:6, 7

23 No longer drink only water, but use a little wine for your stomach's sake and your frequent [T]infirmities. *illnesses*

24 Some men's sins are [R]clearly evident, preceding *them* to judgment, but those of some *men* follow later. Gal. 5:19–21

25 Likewise, the good works *of some* are clearly evident, and those that are otherwise cannot be hidden.

CHAPTER 6

Exhortation to Servants

LET as many bondservants as are under the yoke count their own masters worthy of all honor, so that the name of God and *His* doctrine may not be blasphemed.

2 And those who have believing masters, let them not despise *them* because they are brethren, but rather serve *them* because those who are benefited are believers and beloved. Teach and exhort these things.

Exhortation to Godliness with Contentment

3 If anyone teaches otherwise and does not consent to wholesome words, *even* the words of our Lord Jesus Christ, and to the doctrine which accords with godliness,

4 he is proud, knowing nothing, but is obsessed with disputes and arguments over words, from which come envy, strife, reviling, evil suspicions,

5 useless wranglings* of men of corrupt minds and destitute of the truth, who suppose that godliness is a *means of* gain. From [R]such withdraw yourself.* 2 Tim. 3:5

6 Now godliness with [R]contentment is great gain. Heb. 13:5

7 For we brought nothing into *this* world, *and it is* certain* we can carry nothing out.

8 And having food and clothing, with these we shall be [R]content. Prov. 30:8, 9

9 But those who desire to be rich fall into temptation and a snare, and *into* many foolish and harmful lusts which drown men in destruction and perdition.

10 For the love of money is a root of all *kinds of* evil, for which some have strayed from the faith in their greediness, and pierced themselves through with many sorrows.

11 But you, O man of God, flee these things and pursue righteousness, godliness, faith, love, patience, gentleness.

12 Fight the good fight of faith, lay hold on eternal life, to which you were also called and have confessed the good confession in the presence of many witnesses.

13 I urge you in the sight of God who gives life to all things, and *before* Christ Jesus [R]who witnessed the good confession before Pontius Pilate, John 18:36, 37

14 that you keep *this* commandment without spot, blameless until our Lord Jesus Christ's appearing,

15 which He will manifest in His own time, *He who is* the blessed and only Potentate, the King of kings and Lord of lords,

16 who alone has immortality, dwelling in [R]unapproachable light, [R]whom no man has seen or can see, to whom *be* honor and everlasting power. Amen. Dan. 2:22 • John 6:46

Exhortation to the Rich

17 Command those who are rich in this present age not to be haughty, nor to trust in uncertain riches but in the living God, who gives us richly all things to enjoy.

18 *Let them* do good, that they be rich in good works, ready to give, willing to share,

19 [R]storing up for themselves a good foundation for the time to come, that they may lay hold on eternal life. [Matt. 6:20, 21; 19:21]

Fifth Charge: "Guard What Was Committed"

20 O Timothy! [R]Guard what was committed to your trust, avoiding the profane *and* idle babblings and contradictions of what is falsely called knowledge— [2 Tim. 1:12, 14]

21 by professing it some have strayed concerning the faith. Grace *be* with you. Amen.

6:5 NU, M *constant friction* • NU omits the rest of v. 5. **6:7** NU omits *and it is certain*

THE SECOND EPISTLE OF PAUL THE APOSTLE TO

TIMOTHY

THE BOOK OF 2 TIMOTHY

Prison is the last place from which to expect a letter of encouragement, but that is where Paul's second letter to Timothy originates. He begins by assuring Timothy of his continuing love and prayers, and he reminds him of his spiritual heritage and responsibilities. Only the one who perseveres, whether as a soldier, athlete, farmer, or minister of Jesus Christ, will reap the reward. Paul warns Timothy that his teaching will come under attack as men desert the truth for ear-"itching" words (4:3). But Timothy has Paul's example to guide him and God's Word to fortify him as he faces growing opposition and glowing opportunities in the last days.

Paul's last epistle received the title *Pros Timotheon B,* the "Second to Timothy." When Paul's epistles were collected together, the *B* was probably added to distinguish this letter from the first letter he wrote to Timothy.

THE AUTHOR OF 2 TIMOTHY

Since the Pastoral Epistles have to be treated as a unit on the matter of authorship, see "The Author of 1 Timothy" for comments on the origin of 2 Timothy.

Timothy's name is found more often in the salutations of the Pauline epistles than any other (2 Cor.; Phil.; Col.; 1 and 2 Thess.; 1 and 2 Tim.; Philem.). His father was a Greek (Acts 16:1), but his Jewish mother Eunice and grandmother Lois reared him in the knowledge of the Hebrew Scriptures (1:5; 3:15). Timothy evidently became a convert of Paul (1 Cor. 4:17; 1 Tim. 1:2; 2 Tim. 1:2) when the apostle was in Lystra on his first missionary journey (Acts 14:8–20). When he visited Lystra on his second missionary journey, Paul decided to take Timothy along with him and circumcised him because of the Jews (Acts 16:1–3). Timothy was ordained to the ministry (1 Tim. 4:14; 2 Tim. 1:6) and served as a devoted companion and assistant to Paul in Troas, Berea, Thessalonica, and Corinth (Acts 16—18; 1 Thess. 3:1, 2). During the third missionary journey, Timothy labored with Paul and ministered for him as his representative in Ephesus, Macedonia, and Corinth. He was with Paul during his first Roman imprisonment and evidently went to Philippi (2:19–23) after Paul's release. Paul left him in Ephesus to supervise the work there (1 Tim. 1:3) and years later summoned him to Rome (4:9, 21). According to Hebrews 13:23, Timothy was imprisoned and released, but the passage does not say where. Timothy was sickly (1 Tim. 5:23), timid (2 Tim. 1:7), and youthful (1 Tim. 4:12); but he was also a gifted teacher who was trustworthy and diligent.

THE TIME OF 2 TIMOTHY

For a tentative reconstruction of the events following Paul's first Roman imprisonment, see "The Time of 1 Timothy." The cruel and unbalanced Nero, emperor of Rome from A.D. 54 to 68, was responsible for the beginning of the Roman persecution of Christians. Half of Rome was destroyed in July A.D. 64 by a fire, and mounting suspicion that Nero was responsible for the conflagration caused him to use the unpopular Christians as his scapegoat. Christianity thus became a *religio illicito,* and persecution of those who professed Christ became severe. By the time of Paul's return from Spain to Asia in A.D. 66, his enemies were able to use the official Roman position against Christianity to their advantage. Fearing for their own lives, the Asian believers failed to support Paul after his arrest (1:15) and no one supported him at his first defense before the Imperial Court (4:16). Abandoned by almost everyone (4:10, 11), the apostle found himself in circumstances very different from those of his first Roman imprisonment (Acts 28:16–31). At that time he was merely under house arrest, people could freely visit him, and he had the hope of release. Now he was in a cold Roman cell (4:13), regarded "as an evildoer" (2:9), and without hope of acquittal in spite of the success of his initial defense (4:6–8, 17, 18). Under these conditions, Paul wrote this epistle in the fall of A.D. 67, hoping that Timothy would be able to visit him before the approaching winter (4:21). Timothy evidently was in Ephesus at the time of this letter (see 1:18, 4:19), and on his way to Rome he would go through Troas (4:13) and Macedonia. Priscilla and Aquila (4:19) probably returned from Rome (Rom. 16:3) to Ephesus after the burning of Rome and the beginning of the persecution. Tychicus may have been the bearer of this letter (4:12).

THE CHRIST OF 2 TIMOTHY

Christ Jesus appeared on earth, "abolished death and brought life and immortality to light through the gospel" (1:10). He rose from the dead (2:8) and provides salvation and "eternal glory" (2:10); for if believers "died with *Him,*" they will "also live with *Him*" (2:11). All who love His appearing will receive "the crown of righteousness" (4:8) and "reign with *Him*" (2:12).

KEYS TO 2 TIMOTHY

Key Word: Endurance in the Pastoral Ministry—In this letter, Paul commissions Timothy to faithfully endure and carry on the work that the condemned apostle must now relinquish. This set of instructions exhorts Timothy to use the Word of God constantly in order to overcome growing obstacles to the spread of the gospel. Timothy is in great need of encouragement because of the hardships he is facing, and Paul uses this letter to instruct him about handling persecution from the secular authorities and dissension and deception from within the church. As a spiritual father, Paul urges his young helper to overcome his natural timidity and boldly proclaim the gospel, even if it means that he will suffer for doing so.

Key Verses: 2 Timothy 2:3, 4 and 3:14–17—"You therefore must endure hardship as a good soldier of Jesus Christ. No one engaged in warfare entangles himself with the affairs of *this* life, that he may please him who enlisted him as a soldier" (2:3, 4).

"But you must continue in the things which you have learned and been assured of, knowing from whom you have learned *them,* and that from childhood you have known the Holy Scriptures, which are able to make you wise for salvation through faith which is in Christ Jesus. All Scripture *is* given by inspiration of God, and *is* profitable for doctrine, for reproof, for correction, for instruction in righteousness, that the man of God may be complete, thoroughly equipped for every good work" (3:14–17).

Key Chapter: 2 Timothy 2—The second chapter of 2 Timothy ought to be required daily reading for every pastor and full-time Christian worker. Paul lists the keys to an enduring successful ministry: (1) a reproducing ministry (1 and 2), an enduring ministry (3—13), a studying ministry (14—18), and a holy ministry (19—26).

SURVEY OF 2 TIMOTHY

Paul knows as he writes this final epistle that his days on earth are quickly drawing to a close. About to relinquish his heavy burdens, the godly apostle seeks to challenge and strengthen his somewhat timid but faithful associate, Timothy, in his difficult ministry in Ephesus. In spite of Paul's bleak circumstances, this is a letter of encouragement that urges Timothy on to steadfastness in the fulfillment of his divinely appointed task. Paul calls Timothy a "good soldier of Jesus Christ" (2:3), and it is clear from the sharp imperatives that this letter is really a combat manual for use in the spiritual warfare: "stir up" (1:6); "do not be ashamed" (1:8, 12, 13); "share with me in the sufferings" (1:8); "Hold fast . . . sound words" (1:13); "That good thing . . . keep" (1:14); "be strong" (2:1); "endure hardship" (2:3); "Be diligent to present yourself approved" (2:15); "Flee . . . pursue" (2:22); "avoid" (2:23); "You . . . must beware" (4:15). Central to everything in 2 Timothy is the sure foundation of the Word of God. Paul focuses on the need to persevere in present testing (1 and 2), and to endure in future testing (3 and 4).

Persevere in Present Testing (1 and 2): After his salutation to his "beloved son" (1:2), Paul expresses his thanksgiving for Timothy's "genuine faith" (1:5). He then encourages Timothy to stand firm in the power of the gospel and to overcome any fear in the face of opposition. At personal risk, Onesiphorus boldly sought out Paul in Rome, but most of the Asian Christians failed to stand behind Paul at the time of his arrest. Timothy must remain faithful and not fear possible persecution. Paul then exhorts his spiritual son to reproduce in the lives of others what he has received in Christ (four generations are mentioned in 2:2). He is responsible to work hard and discipline himself like a teacher, a soldier, a farmer, a workman, a vessel, and a ser-

FOCUS	PERSEVERE IN PRESENT TESTINGS			ENDURE IN FUTURE TESTINGS		
REFERENCE	1:1—	1:6—	2:1—	3:1—	4:1—	4:6—4:22
DIVISION	THANKSGIVING FOR TIMOTHY'S FAITH	REMINDER OF TIMOTHY'S RESPONSIBILITY	CHARACTERISTICS OF A FAITHFUL MINISTER	APPROACHING DAY OF APOSTASY	CHARGE TO PREACH THE WORD	APPROACHING DEATH OF PAUL
TOPIC	POWER OF THE GOSPEL		PERSEVERANCE OF THE GOSPEL	PROTECTOR OF THE GOSPEL	PROCLAMATION OF THE GOSPEL	
	REMINDER		REQUIREMENTS	RESISTANCE	REQUESTS	
LOCATION	ROMAN PRISON					
TIME	c. A.D. 67					

vant, following the example of Paul's perseverance (2:1–13). In his dealings with others, Timothy must not become entangled in false speculation, foolish quarrels, or youthful lusts, which would hamper his effectiveness. As he pursues "righteousness, faith, love, peace" (2:22), he must know how to overcome error graciously.

Endure in Future Testing (3 and 4): Paul anticipates a time of growing apostasy and wickedness when men and women will be increasingly susceptible to empty religiosity and false teaching (3:1–9). Arrogance and godlessness will breed further deception and persecution, but Timothy must not waver in using the Scripture to combat doctrinal error and moral evil (3:10–17). The Scriptures are inspired ("God-breathed") and with them Timothy is equipped to carry out the ministry to which he was called. Paul's final exhortation to Timothy (4:1–5) is a classic summary of the task of the man of God to proclaim the gospel in spite of opposing circumstances. This very personal letter closes with an update of Paul's situation in Rome along with certain requests (4:6–22). Paul longs to see Timothy before the end, and he also needs certain articles, especially "the parchments" (probably portions of the Old Testament Scriptures).

OUTLINE OF 2 TIMOTHY

I. Persevere in Present Testings..........1:1—2:26
- A. Thanksgiving for Timothy's Faith 1:1–5
- B. Reminder of Timothy's Responsibility...1:6–18
- C. Characteristics of a Faithful Minister...2:1–26
  1. Discipling Teacher..........2:1, 2
  2. Single-Minded Soldier..........2:3–5
  3. Enduring Farmer..........2:6–13
  4. Diligent Workman..........2:14–19
  5. Sanctified Vessel..........2:20–23
  6. Gentle Servant..........2:24–26

II. Endure in Future Testings..........3:1—4:22
- A. Approaching Day of Apostasy..........3:1–17
  1. Coming of Apostasy..........3:1–9
  2. Confronting Apostasy..........3:10–17
- B. Charge to Preach the Word..........4:1–5
- C. Approaching Death of Paul..........4:6–22
  1. Paul's Hope in Death..........4:6–8
  2. Paul's Situation in Prison..........4:9–18
  3. Paul's Closing Greetings..........4:19–22

CHAPTER 1

Thanksgiving for Timothy's Faith

PAUL, an apostle of Jesus Christ* by the will of God, according to the [R]promise of life which is in Christ Jesus, Titus 1:2

2 To Timothy, a [R]beloved son: 1 Tim. 1:2

Grace, mercy, *and* peace from God the Father and Christ Jesus our Lord.

3 I thank God, whom I serve with a pure conscience, as *my* [R]forefathers *did,* as without ceasing I remember you in my prayers night and day, Acts 24:14
4 greatly desiring to see you, being mindful of your tears, that I may be filled with joy,
5 when I call to remembrance the genuine faith that is in you, which dwelt first in your grandmother Lois and your mother Eunice, and I am persuaded is in you also.

Reminder of Timothy's Responsibility

6 Therefore I remind you [R]to stir up the gift of God which is in you through the laying on of my hands. 1 Tim. 4:14
7 For [R]God has not given us a spirit of fear, [R]but of power and of love and of a sound mind. Rom. 8:15 • [Acts 1:8]
8 Therefore do not be ashamed of the testimony of our Lord, nor of me His prisoner, but share with me in the sufferings for the gospel according to the power of God,
9 who has saved us and called *us* with a holy calling, [R]not according to our works, but [R]according to His own purpose and grace which was given to us in Christ Jesus before time began, [Rom. 3:20] • Rom. 8:28
10 but [R]has now been revealed by the appearing of our Savior Jesus Christ, *who* has abolished death and brought life and immortality to light through the gospel, Eph. 1:9
11 to which I was appointed a preacher, an apostle, and a teacher of the Gentiles.*
12 For this reason I also suffer these things; nevertheless I am not ashamed, for I know whom I have believed and am persuaded that He is able to keep what I have committed to Him until that Day.
13 [R]Hold fast the pattern of sound words which you have heard from me, in faith and love which are in Christ Jesus. Titus 1:9
14 That good thing which was committed to you, keep by the Holy Spirit who dwells in us.
15 This you know, that all those in Asia have turned away from me, among whom are Phygellus and Hermogenes.
16 The Lord grant mercy to the household of

1:1 NU, M *Christ Jesus* **1:11** NU omits *of the Gentiles*

Onesiphorus, for he often refreshed me, and was not ashamed of my chain;
17 but when he arrived in Rome, he sought me out very zealously and found *me.*
18 The Lord [R]grant to him that he may find mercy from the Lord in that Day—and you know very well how many ways he ministered *to me** at Ephesus. Mark 9:41

CHAPTER 2

Discipling Teacher

YOU therefore, [R]my son, be strong in the grace that is in Christ Jesus. 1 Tim. 1:2
2 And the things that you have heard from me among many witnesses, commit these to faithful men who will be able to teach others also.

Single-Minded Soldier

3 You therefore must endure* hardship as a good soldier of Jesus Christ.
4 [R]No one engaged in warfare entangles himself with the affairs of *this* life, that he may please him who enlisted him as a soldier. [2 Pet. 2:20]
5 And also [R]if anyone competes in athletics, he is not crowned unless he competes according to the rules. [1 Cor. 9:25]

Enduring Farmer

6 The hardworking farmer must be first to partake of the crops.
7 Consider what I say, and may* the Lord give you understanding in all things.
8 Remember that Jesus Christ, [R]of the seed of David, [R]was raised from the dead according to my gospel, Rom. 1:3, 4 • 1 Cor. 15:4
9 [R]for which I suffer trouble as an evildoer, *even* to the point of chains; but the word of God is not chained. Acts 9:16
10 Therefore [R]I endure all things for the sake of the [T]elect, [R]that they also may obtain the salvation which is in Christ Jesus with eternal glory. Eph. 3:13 • *chosen ones* • 2 Cor. 1:6
11 *This is* a faithful saying:

For [R]if we died with *Him,* Rom. 6:5, 8
We shall also live with *Him.*
12 [R]If we endure, [Rom. 5:17; 8:17]
We shall also reign with *Him.*
[R]If we deny *Him,* Matt. 10:33
He also will deny us.
13 If we are faithless,
He remains faithful;
He [R]cannot deny Himself. Num. 23:19

Diligent Workman

14 Remind *them* of these things, charging *them* before the Lord not to strive about words to no profit, to the ruin of the hearers.
15 Be diligent to present yourself approved to God, a worker who does not need to be ashamed, rightly dividing the word of truth.
16 But shun profane *and* idle babblings, for they will increase to more ungodliness.
17 And their message will spread like cancer. [R]Hymenaeus and Philetus are of this sort, 1 Tim. 1:20
18 who have strayed concerning the truth, saying that the resurrection is already past; and they overthrow the faith of some.
19 Nevertheless [R]the solid foundation of God stands, having this seal: "The Lord [R]knows those who are His," and, "Let everyone who names the name of Christ* depart from iniquity." [1 Cor. 3:11] • [Nah. 1:7]

Sanctified Vessel

20 But in a great house there are not only [R]vessels of gold and silver, but also of wood and clay, some for honor and some for dishonor. Rom. 9:21
21 Therefore if anyone cleanses himself from the latter, he will be a vessel for honor, sanctified and useful for the Master, [R]prepared for every good work. 2 Tim. 3:17
22 Flee also youthful lusts; but pursue righteousness, faith, love, peace with those who call on the Lord out of a pure heart.
23 But avoid foolish and ignorant disputes, knowing that they generate strife.

Gentle Servant

24 And [R]a servant of the Lord must not quarrel but be gentle to all, [R]able to teach, [R]patient, Titus 3:2 • Titus 1:9 • 1 Tim. 3:3
25 [R]in humility correcting those who are in opposition, [R]if God perhaps will grant them repentance, [R]so that they may know the truth, Gal. 6:1 • Acts 8:22 • 1 Tim. 2:4
26 and *that* they may come to their senses *and escape* the snare of the devil, having been taken captive by him to *do* his will.

CHAPTER 3

Coming of Apostasy

BUT know this, that [R]in the last days perilous times will come: 1 Tim. 4:1
2 For men will be lovers of themselves, lovers of money, boasters, proud, blasphemers, disobedient to parents, unthankful, unholy,
3 unloving, unforgiving, slanderers, without self-control, brutal, despisers of good,
4 traitors, headstrong, haughty, lovers of pleasure rather than lovers of God,
5 having a form of godliness but denying its power. And from such people turn away!
6 For [R]of this sort are those who creep into households and make captives of gullible women loaded down with sins, led away by various lusts, Matt. 23:14

1:18 *to me* from Vg., a few Gr. mss. **2:3** NU *You must share* **2:7** NU *the Lord will give you* **2:19** NU, M *the Lord*

7 always learning and never able [R]to come to the knowledge of the truth. 1 Tim. 2:4

8 [R]Now as Jannes and Jambres resisted Moses, so do these also resist the truth: men of corrupt minds, disapproved concerning the faith; Ex. 7:11, 12, 22; 8:7; 9:11

9 but they will progress no further, for their folly will be manifest to all, [R]as theirs also was. Ex. 7:11, 12; 8:18; 9:11

Confronting Apostasy

10 [R]But you have carefully followed my doctrine, manner of life, purpose, faith, longsuffering, love, perseverance, 1 Tim. 4:6

11 persecutions, afflictions, which happened to me at Antioch, at Iconium, at Lystra—what persecutions I endured. And out of *them* all the Lord delivered me.

12 Yes, and all who desire to live godly in Christ Jesus will suffer persecution.

13 [R]But evil men and impostors will grow worse and worse, deceiving and being deceived. 2 Thess. 2:11

14 But you must [R]continue in the things which you have learned and been assured of, knowing from whom you have learned *them,* 2 Tim. 1:13

15 and that from childhood you have known [R]the Holy Scriptures, which are able to make you wise for salvation through faith which is in Christ Jesus. John 5:39

16 [R]All Scripture *is* given by inspiration of God, [R]and *is* profitable for doctrine, for reproof, for correction, for instruction in righteousness, [2 Pet. 1:20] • Rom. 4:23; 15:4

17 that the man of God may be complete, thoroughly equipped for every good work.

CHAPTER 4

Charge to Preach the Word

I [R]CHARGE *you* therefore* before God and the Lord Jesus Christ, [R]who will judge the living and the dead at* His appearing and His kingdom: 1 Tim. 5:21 • Acts 10:42

2 Preach the word! Be ready in season *and* out of season. Convince, rebuke, exhort, with all longsuffering and teaching.

3 [R]For the time will come when they will not endure [R]sound doctrine, [R]but according to their own desires, *because* they have itching ears, they will heap up for themselves teachers; 2 Tim. 3:1 • 1 Tim. 1:10 • 2 Tim. 3:6

4 and they will turn *their* ears away from the truth, and be turned aside to fables.

5 But you be watchful in all things, [R]endure afflictions, do the work of an evangelist, fulfill your ministry. 2 Tim. 1:8

Paul's Hope in Death

6 For [R]I am already being poured out as a drink offering, and the time of [R]my departure is at hand. Phil. 2:17 • [Phil. 1:23]

7 I have fought the good fight, I have finished the race, I have kept the faith.

8 Finally, there is laid up for me [R]the crown of righteousness, which the Lord, the righteous Judge, will give to me on that Day, and not to me only but also to all who have loved His appearing. James 1:12

Paul's Situation in Prison

9 Be diligent to come to me quickly;

10 for [R]Demas has forsaken me, [R]having loved this present world, and has departed for Thessalonica—Crescens for Galatia, Titus for Dalmatia. Col. 4:14 • 1 John 2:15

11 Only Luke is with me. Get [R]Mark and bring him with you, for he is useful to me for ministry. Acts 12:12, 25; 15:37–39

12 And Tychicus I have sent to Ephesus.

13 Bring the cloak that I left with Carpus at Troas when you come—and the books, especially the parchments.

14 [R]Alexander the coppersmith did me much harm. May the Lord repay him according to his works. 1 Tim. 1:20

15 You also must beware of him, for he has greatly resisted our words.

16 At my first defense no one stood with me, but all forsook me. [R]May it not be charged against them. Acts 7:60

17 But the Lord stood with me and strengthened me, so that the message might be preached fully through me, and *that* all the

4:1 NU omits *therefore* • NU *and by* for *at*

4:2 Sharing Our Faith: When?—A famous evangelist once ended a revival meeting in Chicago by advising the unbelievers who were present that night to go home and seriously consider the claims of the gospel, and then return on the following night prepared to make a decision for Christ. But on that same night, October 8, 1871, the tragic Chicago fire broke out. Before it was finally extinguished, nearly four miles of buildings were consumed and 250 people had died. The evangelist then vowed never to end a service without giving an invitation to accept Christ immediately.

The question as to when we should share our faith is directly tied to when a sinner should accept Christ. The Bible is clear that God's accepted time is today. See Heb. 3:15; 4:7; 2 Cor. 6:2; Is. 55:6. The reason for this is very simple—sinners have no assurance whatsoever that they will live to see tomorrow. See Prov. 27:1; Luke 12:19; James 4:13–15.

Thus, we are to witness any time, all the time, in any place and in all places. The apostle Paul shows us how this should be done. He witnesses everywhere, in a prison at midnight (Page 1131—Acts 16:25–31), and even on a sinking ship during a dark and stormy day (Page 1143—Acts 27:20–25).

Now turn to Page 584—Ps. 73:1: Walking in the Spirit: Confession.

Gentiles might hear. Also I was delivered out of the mouth of the lion.
18 [R]And the Lord will deliver me from every evil work and preserve *me* for His heavenly kingdom. [R]To Him *be* glory forever and ever. Amen! Ps. 121:7 • Rom. 11:36

Paul's Closing Greetings

19 Greet [R]Prisca and Aquila, and the household of Onesiphorus. Acts 18:2

20 Erastus stayed in Corinth, but Trophimus I have left in Miletus sick.
21 Do your utmost to come before winter. Eubulus greets you, as well as Pudens, Linus, Claudia, and all the brethren.
22 The Lord Jesus Christ* be with your spirit. Grace be with you. Amen.

4:22 NU omits *Jesus Christ*

THE EPISTLE OF PAUL THE APOSTLE TO

TITUS

THE BOOK OF TITUS

Titus, a young pastor, faces the unenviable assignment of setting in order the church at Crete. Paul writes advising him to appoint elders, men of proven spiritual character in their homes and businesses, to oversee the work of the church. But elders are not the only individuals in the church who are required to excel spiritually. Men and women, young and old, each have their vital functions to fulfill in the church if they are to be living examples of the doctrine they profess. Throughout his letter to Titus, Paul stresses the necessary, practical working out of salvation in the daily lives of both the elders and the congregation. Good works are desirable and profitable for all believers.

This third Pastoral Epistle is simply titled *Pros Titon,* "To Titus." Ironically, this was also the name of the Roman general who destroyed Jerusalem in A.D. 70 and succeeded his father Vespasian as emperor.

THE AUTHOR OF TITUS

Since the Pastoral Epistles have to be treated as a unit on the matter of authorship, see "The Author of 1 Timothy" for the authorship of Titus.

Titus is not mentioned in Acts, but the thirteen references to him in the Pauline epistles make it clear that he was one of Paul's closest and most trusted companions. This convert of Paul ("a true son in *our* common faith," 1:4) was probably from Syrian Antioch, if he was one of the disciples of Acts 11:26. Paul brought this uncircumcised Greek believer to Jerusalem (Gal. 2:3) where he became a test case on the matter of Gentiles and liberty from the law. Years later when Paul set out from Antioch on his third missionary journey (Acts 18:22), Titus must have accompanied him because he was sent by the apostle to Corinth on three occasions during that time (2 Cor. 2:12, 13; 7:5–7, 13–15; 8:6, 16–24). He is not mentioned again until Paul leaves him in Crete to carry on the work (Titus 1:5). He was with Paul during his second Roman imprisonment but left to go to Dalmatia (2 Tim. 4:10), possibly on an evangelistic mission. Paul spoke of this reliable and gifted associate as his "brother" (2 Cor. 2:13), his "partner and fellow worker" (2 Cor. 8:23), and his "son" (1:4). He lauded Titus's character and conduct in 2 Corinthians 7:13–15 and 8:16, 17.

THE TIME OF TITUS

For a tentative reconstruction of the events following Paul's first Roman imprisonment, see "The Time of 1 Timothy."

The Mediterranean island of Crete is 156 miles long and up to 30 miles wide, and its first-century inhabitants were notorious for untruthfulness and immorality (1:12, 13). "To act the Cretan" became an idiom meaning "to play the liar." A number of Jews from Crete were present in Jerusalem at the time of Peter's sermon on the Day of Pentecost (Acts 2:11), and some of them may have believed in Christ and introduced the gospel to their countrymen. Certainly Paul would not have had opportunity to do evangelistic work during his brief sojourn in Crete while he was en route to Rome (Acts 27:7–13). The apostle spread the gospel in the cities of Crete after his release from Roman imprisonment and left Titus there to finish organizing the churches (1:5). Because of the problem of immorality among the Cretans, it was important for Titus to stress the need for righteousness in Christian living. False teachers, especially "those of the circumcision" (1:10), were also misleading and divisive. Paul wrote this letter about A.D. 63, perhaps from Corinth, taking advantage of the journey of Zenas and Apollos (3:13), whose destination would take them by way of Crete. Paul was planning to spend the winter in Nicopolis (western Greece), and he urged Titus in this letter to join him there upon his replacement by Artemas or Tychicus (3:12). Paul may have been planning to leave Nicopolis for Spain in the spring, and he wanted his useful companion Titus to accompany him.

THE CHRIST OF TITUS

The deity and redemptive work of Christ are beautifully stated in 2:13, 14: "Looking for the blessed hope and glorious appearing of our great God and Savior Jesus Christ, who gave Himself for us, that He might redeem us from every lawless deed and purify for Himself *His* own special people, zealous for good works."

KEYS TO TITUS

Key Word: Conduct Manual for Church Living—This brief letter focuses on Titus's role and responsibility in the organization and supervision of the churches in Crete. It is written to strengthen and exhort Titus to firmly exercise his authority as an apostolic representative to churches that need to be put in order, refuting false teachers and dissenters and replacing immoral behavior with good deeds. Paul uses this letter to remind Titus of some of the details related to his task, including the qualifications for elders and the behavior expected of various groups in the churches. Paul includes three doctrinal sections in this letter to stress that proper belief (orthodoxy) gives the basis for proper behavior (orthopraxy).

Key Verses: Titus 1:5 and 3:8—"For this reason I left you in Crete, that you should set in order the things that are lacking, and appoint elders in every city as I commanded you—"(1:5).

"This is a faithful saying, and these things I want you to affirm constantly, that those who have believed in God should be careful to maintain good works. These things are good and profitable to men" (3:8).

Key Chapter: Titus 2—Summarized in Titus 2 are the key commands to be obeyed which insure godly relationships within the church. Paul includes all categories of people instructing them to show "all good fidelity, that they may adorn the doctrine of God our Savior in all things" (2:10).

SURVEY OF TITUS

Titus, like 1 Timothy, was written by Paul after his release from Roman imprisonment and was also written to an associate who was given the task of organizing and supervising a large work as an apostolic representative. Paul left Titus on the island of Crete to "set in order the things that are lacking, and appoint elders in every city" (1:5). Not long after Paul's departure from Crete, he wrote this letter to encourage and assist Titus in his task. It stresses sound doctrine and warns against those who distort the truth, but it also is a conduct manual that emphasizes good deeds and the proper conduct of various groups within the churches. This epistle falls into two major sections: appoint elders (1); set things in order (2 and 3).

Appoint Elders (1): The salutation to Titus is actually a compact doctrinal statement, which lifts up "His word" as the source of the truth that reveals the way to eternal life (1:1–4). Paul reminds Titus of his responsibility to organize the churches of Crete by appointing elders (also called overseers; see 1:7) and rehearses the qualifications these spiritual leaders must meet (1:5–9). This is especially important in view of the disturbances that are being caused by false teachers who are upsetting a number of the believers with their Judaic myths and commandments (1:10–16). The natural tendency toward moral laxity among the Cretans coupled with that kind of deception is a dangerous force that must be overcome by godly leadership and sound doctrine.

Set Things in Order (2 and 3): Titus is given the charge to "speak the things which are proper for sound doctrine" (2:1), and Paul delineates Titus's role with regard to various groups in the church, including older men, older women, young women, young men, and servants (2:2–10). The knowledge of Christ must effect a transformation in each of these groups so that their testimony will "adorn the doctrine of God" (2:10). The second doctrinal statement of Titus (2:11–14) gives the basis for the appeals Paul has just made for righteous living. God in His grace redeems believers from being slaves of sin, assuring them the "blessed hope" of the coming of Christ that will eventually be realized. Paul urges Titus to authoritatively proclaim these truths (2:15).

In chapter 3 Paul moves from conduct in groups (2:1–10) to conduct in general (3:1–11). The behavior of believers as citizens must be different from the behavior of unbelievers because of their regeneration and renewal by the Holy Spirit. The third doctrinal statement in this book (3:4–7) emphasizes the kindness, love, and mercy of God who saves us "not by works of righteousness which we have done" (3:5). Nevertheless, the need for good deeds as a result of

FOCUS	APPOINT ELDERS		SET THINGS IN ORDER	
REFERENCE	1:1	1:10	2:1	3:1—3:15
DIVISION	ORDAIN QUALIFIED ELDERS	REBUKE FALSE TEACHERS	SPEAK SOUND DOCTRINE	MAINTAIN GOOD WORKS
TOPIC	PROTECTION OF SOUND DOCTRINE		PRACTICE OF SOUND DOCTRINE	
	ORGANIZATION	OFFENDERS	OPERATION	OBEDIENCE
LOCATION	PROBABLY WRITTEN IN CORINTH			
TIME	C. A.D. 63			

salvation is stressed six times in the three chapters of Titus (1:16; 2:7, 14; 3:1, 8, 14). Paul exhorts Titus to deal firmly with dissenters who would cause factions and controversies (3:9–11) and closes the letter with three instructions, a greeting, and a benediction (3:12–15).

OUTLINE OF TITUS

CHAPTER 1

Introduction

PAUL, a bondservant of God and an apostle
of Jesus Christ, according to the faith of
God's elect and the acknowledgment of the
truth which accords with godliness,

2 in hope of eternal life which God, who
cannot lie, promised before time began,

3 but has in due time manifested His word
through preaching, which was committed to
me according to the commandment of God
our Savior;

4 To [R]Titus, a true son in *our* common
faith: 2 Cor. 2:13; 8:23

Grace, mercy, *and* peace from God the Father and the Lord Jesus Christ* our Savior.

Ordain Qualified Elders

5 For this reason I left you in Crete, that you
should [R]set in order the things that are lacking, and appoint elders in every city as I commanded you— 1 Cor. 11:34

6 if a man is blameless, the husband of one
wife, having faithful children not accused of
dissipation or insubordination.

7 For a bishop* must be blameless, as a
steward of God, not self-willed, not quick-tempered, [R]not given to wine, not violent, not
greedy for money, Lev. 10:9

8 but hospitable, a lover of what is good,
sober-minded, just, holy, self-controlled,

9 holding fast the faithful word as he has
been taught, that he may be able, by sound
doctrine, both to exhort and convict those
who contradict.

Rebuke False Teachers

10 For there are many insubordinate, both
idle [R]talkers and deceivers, especially those of
the circumcision, James 1:26

11 whose mouths must be stopped, who subvert whole households, teaching things which
they ought not, [R]for the sake of dishonest
gain. 1 Tim. 6:5

12 [R]One of them, a prophet of their own,
said, "Cretans *are* always liars, evil beasts,
lazy gluttons." Acts 17:28

13 This testimony is true. [R]Therefore rebuke
them sharply, that they may be sound in the
faith, 2 Cor. 13:10

14 not giving heed to Jewish fables and
[R]commandments of men who turn from the
truth. Is. 29:13

15 [R]To the pure all things are pure, but to
those who are defiled and unbelieving nothing is pure; but even their mind and conscience are defiled. 1 Cor. 6:12

16 They profess to [R]know God, but [R]in
works they deny Him, being abominable,
disobedient, and disqualified for every good
work. Matt. 7:20–23; 25:12 • [2 Tim. 3:5, 7]

1:4 NU *and Christ Jesus* **1:7** Lit. *overseer*

1:2 Promise of God—Often the Christian will doubt his salvation simply because he doesn't feel saved, not understanding that the basis for that salvation is the promise of God and not emotional feelings. In fact, the entire Trinity is involved in this.

a. The promise and work of the Father in our salvation. He has promised graciously to accept in Christ all repenting sinners (Page 1204—Eph. 1:6; Page 1221—Col. 3:3). This means a Christian has the right to be in heaven someday, for he is in Christ. God guarantees to us that He will work out all things for our good (Page 1155—Rom. 8:28).

b. The promise and work of the Son. He has promised us eternal life (Page 1086—John 5:24) and abundant life (Page 1094—John 10:10). This covers not only our final destiny in heaven, but also our present Christian service here on earth. He is, in fact, right now praying for us and ministering to us at His Father's right hand (Page 1263—Heb. 8:1; 9:24).

c. The promise and work of the Holy Spirit. The Holy Spirit is said to indwell the believer (Page 1099—John 14:16). In addition, He places all believing sinners into the body of Christ, thus assuring us of union with God Himself (Page 1176—1 Cor. 12:13).

Now turn to Page 1296—1 John 3:24: Witness of the Spirit.

CHAPTER 2

Speak Sound Doctrine

BUT as for you, speak the things which are proper for sound doctrine:
2 that the older men be sober, reverent,
temperate, sound in faith, in love, in patience;
3 the older women likewise, that they be
reverent in behavior, not slanderers, not given
to much wine, teachers of good things—
4 that they admonish the young women to
love their husbands, to love their children,
5 to be discreet, chaste, homemakers, good,
obedient to their own husbands, that the word
of God may not be blasphemed.
6 Likewise, exhort the young men to be
sober-minded,
7 in all things showing yourself *to be* a pattern of good works; in doctrine *showing* integrity, reverence, incorruptibility,*
8 sound speech that cannot be condemned,
that one who is an opponent may be ashamed,
having nothing evil to say of you.*
9 *Exhort* [R]bondservants to be obedient to
their own masters, to be well pleasing in all
things, not answering back, 1 Tim. 6:1
10 not [T]pilfering, but showing all good fidelity, that they may adorn the doctrine of God
our Savior in all things. *thieving*
11 For [R]the grace of God that brings salvation has appeared to all men, [Rom. 5:15]
12 teaching us that, denying ungodliness
and worldly lusts, we should live soberly,
righteously, and godly in the present age,
13 [R]looking for the blessed [R]hope and glorious appearing of our great God and Savior Jesus Christ, 1 Cor. 1:7 • [Col. 3:4]
14 [R]who gave Himself for us, that He might
redeem us from every lawless deed and purify
for Himself *His* own special people, zealous
for good works. Is. 53:12; Gal. 1:4★
15 Speak these things, exhort, and rebuke
with all authority. Let no one despise you.

CHAPTER 3

Maintain Good Works

REMIND them [R]to be subject to rulers and authorities, to obey, [R]to be ready for every good work, 1 Pet. 2:13 • Col. 1:10
2 to speak evil of no one, to be peaceable,
gentle, showing all humility to all men.
3 For [R]we ourselves were also once foolish,
disobedient, deceived, serving various lusts
and pleasures, living in malice and envy, hateful and hating one another. 1 Cor. 6:11
4 But when the kindness and the love of
God our Savior toward man appeared,
5 not by works of righteousness which we
have done, but according to His mercy He
saved us, through the washing of regeneration
and renewing of the Holy Spirit,
6 whom He poured out on us abundantly
through Jesus Christ our Savior,
7 that having been justified by His grace
[R]we should become heirs according to the
hope of eternal life. [Rom. 8:17, 23, 24]
8 [R]This is a faithful saying, and these things
I want you to affirm constantly, that those
who have believed in God should be careful to
maintain good works. These things are good
and profitable to men. 1 Tim. 1:15
9 But avoid foolish disputes, genealogies,
contentions, and strivings about the law; for
they are unprofitable and useless.
10 [R]Reject a divisive man after the first and
second [T]admonition, Matt. 18:17 • *warning*
11 knowing that such a person is warped
and sinning, being self-condemned.

Conclusion

12 When I send Artemas to you, or Tychicus,
be diligent to come to me at Nicopolis, for I
have decided to spend the winter there.
13 Send Zenas the lawyer and [R]Apollos on
their journey with haste, that they may lack
nothing. Acts 18:24
14 And let our *people* also learn to maintain
good works, to *meet* urgent needs, that they
may not be unfruitful.
15 All who *are* with me greet you. Greet
those who love us in the faith. Grace *be* with
you all. Amen.

2:7 NU omits *incorruptibility* **2:8** NU, M *us*

3:5 The Work of the Holy Spirit in Salvation—There are three wonderful works performed by the Holy Spirit in preparing unsaved people to become Christians.

a. The work of the Holy Spirit in restraining. Satan would enjoy nothing more than to destroy people before they make their decision to accept Christ as Savior. But the Holy Spirit prevents this from occurring (Page 736—Is. 59:19).
b. The work of the Holy Spirit in convicting. Humankind's sin and righteousness are exposed by the Holy Spirit (Page 1101—John 16:8). There are two well-known examples of sinners being convicted by the Holy Spirit in the Book of Acts. Felix, a Roman governor, actually trembles under conviction as he hears Paul preach (Page 1140—Acts 24:25). The other case involves King Agrippa who responds to a gospel message by saying: " 'You almost persuade me to become a Christian'." (Page 1142—Acts 26:28).
c. The work of the Holy Spirit in regenerating. When repenting sinners accept Christ as Savior, they are given a new nature by the Holy Spirit. See 2 Cor. 5:17. Jesus carefully explained this ministry of the Holy Spirit to Nicodemus (Page 1083—John 3:3–7).

Now turn to Page 1171—1 Cor. 6:19: The Work of the Holy Spirit in Christian Living.

THE EPISTLE OF PAUL THE APOSTLE TO

PHILEMON

THE BOOK OF PHILEMON

Does Christian brotherly love really work, even in situations of extraordinary tension and difficulty? Will it work, for example, between a prominent slave owner and one of his runaway slaves? Paul has no doubt! He writes a "postcard" to Philemon, his beloved brother and fellow worker, on behalf of Onesimus—a deserter, thief, and formerly worthless slave, but now Philemon's brother in Christ. With much tact and tenderness, Paul asks Philemon to receive Onesimus back with the same gentleness with which he would receive Paul himself. Any debt Onesimus owes, Paul promises to make good. Knowing Philemon, Paul is confident that brotherly love and forgiveness will carry the day.

Since this letter is addressed to Philemon in verse 1, it becomes known as *Pros Philemona,* "To Philemon." Like 1 and 2 Timothy and Titus, it is addressed to an individual, but unlike the Pastoral Epistles, Philemon is also addressed to a family and a church (v. 2).

THE AUTHOR OF PHILEMON

The authenticity of Philemon was not called into question until the fourth century, when certain theologians concluded that its lack of doctrinal content made it unworthy of the apostle Paul. But men like Jerome and Chrysostom soon vindicated this epistle, and it was not challenged again until the nineteenth century. Some radical critics who denied the authenticity of Colossians also turned against the Pauline authorship of Philemon because of the close connection between the two epistles (e.g., the same people are associated with Paul in both letters: cf. Col. 4:9, 10, 12, 14 with Philem. 10, 23, 24). The general consensus of scholarship, however, recognized Philemon as Paul's work. There could have been no doctrinal motive for its forgery, and it is supported externally by consistent tradition and internally by no less than three references to Paul (vv. 1, 9, 19).

THE TIME OF PHILEMON

Reconstructing the background of this letter, it appears that a slave named Onesimus had robbed or in some other way wronged his master Philemon and had escaped. He had made his way from Colosse to Rome where he had found relative safety among the masses in the Imperial City. Somehow Onesimus had come into contact with Paul: it is possible that he had even sought out the apostle for help. (Onesimus no doubt had heard Philemon speak of Paul.) Paul had led him to Christ (v. 10); and although Onesimus had become a real asset to Paul, both knew that, as a Christian, Onesimus had a responsibility to return to Philemon. That day came when Paul wrote his epistle to the Colossians. Tychicus was the bearer of that letter. Paul decided to send Onesimus along with Tychicus to Colosse (Col. 4:7–9; Philem. 12), knowing that it would be safer, in view of slave-catchers, to send Onesimus with a companion.

Philemon is one of the four Prison Epistles (see Ephesians, Philippians, and especially "The Time of Colossians" for background). It was written in A.D. 60 or 61 and dispatched at the same time as Colossians during Paul's first Roman imprisonment (see vv. 1, 9, 10, 13, 23). Philemon 22 reflects Paul's confident hope of release: "prepare a guest room for me, for I trust that through your prayers I shall be granted to you."

Philemon was a resident of Colosse (Col. 4:9, 17; Philem. 1, 2) and a convert of Paul (v. 19), perhaps through an encounter with Paul in Ephesus during Paul's third missionary journey. Philemon's house was large enough to serve as the meeting place for the church there (v. 2). He was benevolent to other believers (vv. 5–7), and his son Archippus evidently held a position of leadership in the church (Col. 4:17; Philem. 2). Philemon may have had other slaves in addition to Onesimus, and he was not alone as a slaveholder among the Colossian believers (Col. 4:1). Thus this letter and his response would provide guidelines for other master-slave relationships.

According to Roman law, runaway slaves such as Onesimus could be severely punished or condemned to a violent death. It is doubtful that Onesimus would have returned to Philemon even with this letter if he had not become a believer in Christ.

THE CHRIST OF PHILEMON

The forgiveness that the believer finds in Christ is beautifully portrayed by analogy in Philemon. Although Onesimus is guilty of a great offense (vv. 11, 18), Paul is moved to intercede on his behalf (vv. 10–17). Paul lays aside his rights (v. 8) and becomes Onesimus's substitute by assuming his debt (vv. 18, 19). By Philemon's gracious act, Onesimus will be restored and placed in a new relationship (vv. 15, 16). In this analogy, we are as Onesimus. Paul's advocacy before Philemon is parallel to Christ's work of mediation before the Father. Onesimus was condemned by law but saved by grace.

KEYS TO PHILEMON

Key Word: Forgiveness from Slavery—Philemon develops the transition from bondage to brotherhood that is brought about by Christian love and forgiveness. Just as Philemon was shown mercy through the grace of Christ, so he must graciously forgive his repentant runaway who has returned as a brother in Christ. Paul writes this letter as his personal appeal that Philemon receive Onesimus even as he would receive Paul. This letter is also addressed to other Christians in Philemon's circle, because Paul wants it to have an impact on the Colossian church as a whole.

Key Verses: Philemon 16, 17—"No longer as a slave but more than a slave—a beloved brother, especially to me but how much more to you, both in the flesh and in the Lord. If then you count me as a partner, receive him as *you would* me" (vv. 16, 17).

SURVEY OF PHILEMON

This briefest of Paul's epistles (only 334 words in the Greek text) is a model of courtesy, discretion, and loving concern for the forgiveness of one who would otherwise face the sentence of death. This tactful and highly personal letter can be divided into three components: prayer of thanksgiving for Philemon (vv. 1–7); petition of Paul for Onesimus (vv. 8–16); promise of Paul to Philemon (vv. 17–25).

Prayer of Thanksgiving for Philemon (vv. 1–7): Writing this letter as a "prisoner of Christ Jesus," Paul addresses it personally to Philemon (a Christian leader in Colosse), to Apphia and Archippus (evidently Philemon's wife and son), as well as to the church that meets in Philemon's house. The main body of this compact letter begins with a prayer of thanksgiving for Philemon's faith and love.

Petition of Paul for Onesimus (vv. 8–16): Basing his appeal on Philemon's character, Paul refuses to command Philemon to pardon and receive Onesimus. Instead, Paul seeks to persuade his friend of his Christian responsibility to forgive even as he was forgiven by Christ. Paul urges Philemon not to punish Onesimus but to receive him "no longer as a slave" but as "a beloved brother" (v. 16).

Promise of Paul to Philemon (vv. 17–25): Paul places Onesimus's debt on his account, but then reminds Philemon of the greater spiritual debt Philemon himself owes as a convert to Christ (vv. 17–19).

Paul closes this effective epistle with a hopeful request (v. 22), greetings from his companions (vv. 23, 24), and a benediction (v. 25). The fact that it was preserved indicates Philemon's favorable response to Paul's pleas.

FOCUS	PRAYER OF THANKSGIVING	PETITION FOR ONESIMUS	PROMISE TO PHILEMON
REFERENCE	1———8	———17	———25
DIVISION	COMMENDATION OF PHILEMON'S LOVE	INTERCESSION FOR ONESIMUS	CONFIDENCE IN PHILEMON'S OBEDIENCE
TOPIC	PRAISE OF PHILEMON	PLEA OF PAUL	PLEDGE OF PAUL
	CHARACTER OF PHILEMON	CONVERSION OF ONESIMUS	CONFIDENCE OF PAUL
LOCATION	ROME		
TIME	c. A.D. 60–61		

OUTLINE OF PHILEMON

The Prayer of Thanksgiving for Philemon

PAUL, a [R]prisoner of Christ Jesus, and Tim-
othy *our* brother, Eph. 3:1
To Philemon our beloved *friend* and fel-
low laborer,
2 to the beloved* Apphia, [R]Archippus our
fellow soldier, and to the church in your
house: Col. 4:17

3 Grace to you and peace from God our Fa-
ther and the Lord Jesus Christ.

4 [R]I thank my God, making mention of you
always in my prayers, 2 Thess. 1:3
5 [R]hearing of your love and faith which you
have toward the Lord Jesus and toward all the
saints, Col. 1:4
6 that the sharing of your faith may be-
come effective [R]by the acknowledgment of
[R]every good thing which is in you* in Christ
Jesus. Phil. 1:9 • [1 Thess. 5:18]
7 For we have* great joy* and consolation
in your love, because the hearts of the saints
have been refreshed by you, brother.

The Petition of Paul for Onesimus

8 Therefore, though I might be very bold in
Christ to command you what is fitting,
9 *yet* for love's sake I rather appeal *to
you*—being such a one as Paul, the aged, and
now also a prisoner of Jesus Christ—
10 I appeal to you for my son Onesimus,
whom I have begotten *while* in my chains,
11 who once was unprofitable to you, but
now is profitable to you and to me.
12 I am sending him back.* You therefore re-
ceive him, that is, my own heart,
13 whom I wished to keep with me, that on
your behalf he might minister to me in my
chains for the gospel.
14 But without your consent I wanted to do
nothing, that your good deed might not be by
compulsion, as it were, but voluntary.
15 For perhaps he departed for a while for
this *purpose,* that you might receive him for-
ever,
16 no longer as a slave but more than a
slave—a beloved brother, especially to me but
how much more to you, both in the [R]flesh and
in the Lord. Col. 3:22

The Promise of Paul to Philemon

17 If then you count me as a partner, receive
him as *you would* me.
18 But if he has wronged you or owes any-
thing, put that on my account.
19 I, Paul, am writing with my own hand. I
will repay—not to mention to you that you
owe me even your own self besides.
20 Yes, brother, let me have joy from you in
the Lord; refresh my heart in the Lord.
21 [R]Having confidence in your obedience, I
write to you, knowing that you will do even
more than I say. 2 Cor. 7:16
22 But, meanwhile, also prepare a guest
room for me, for [R]I trust that through your
prayers I shall be granted to you. Phil. 1:25
23 [R]Epaphras, my fellow prisoner in Christ
Jesus, greets you, Col. 1:7; 4:12
24 *as do* [R]Mark, Aristarchus, Demas, Luke,
my fellow laborers. Acts 12:12, 25
25 [R]The grace of our Lord Jesus Christ *be*
with your spirit. Amen. 2 Tim. 4:22

2 NU *our sister Apphia* 6 NU, M *us* 7 NU *had* • M *thanksgiving* 12 NU *back to you in person, that is, my own heart,*

THE EPISTLE TO THE

HEBREWS

THE BOOK OF HEBREWS

Many Jewish believers, having stepped out of Judaism into Christianity, want to reverse their course in order to escape persecution by their countrymen. The writer of Hebrews exhorts them to "go on to perfection" (6:1). His appeal is based on the superiority of Christ over the Judaic system. Christ is better than the angels, for they worship Him. He is better than Moses, for He created him. He is better than the Aaronic priesthood, for His sacrifice was once for all time. He is better than the Law, for He mediates a better covenant. In short, there is more to be gained in Christ than to be lost in Judaism. Pressing on in Christ produces tested faith, self-discipline, and a visible love seen in good works.

Although the King James Version uses the title "The Epistle of Paul the Apostle to the Hebrews," there is no early manuscript evidence to support it. The oldest and most reliable title is simply *Pros Ebraious,* "To Hebrews."

THE AUTHOR OF HEBREWS

Like the ancestry of Melchizedek, the origin of Hebrews is unknown. Uncertainty plagues not only its authorship, but also where it was written, its date, and its readership. The question of authorship delayed its recognition in the West as part of the New Testament canon in spite of early support by Clement of Rome. Not until the fourth century was it generally accepted as authoritative in the Western church, when the testimonies of Jerome and Augustine settled the issue. In the Eastern church, there was no problem of canonical acceptance because it was regarded as one of the "fourteen" epistles of Paul. The issue of its canonicity was again raised during the Reformation, but the spiritual depth and quality of Hebrews bore witness to its inspiration, despite its anonymity.

Hebrews 13:18–24 tells us that this book was not anonymous to the original readers; they evidently knew the author. For some reason, however, early church tradition is divided over the identity of the author. Part of the church attributed it to Paul; others preferred Barnabas, Luke, or Clement; and some chose anonymity. Thus, external evidence will not help determine the author.

Internal evidence must be the final court of appeal, but here, too, the results are ambiguous. Some aspects of the language, style, and theology of Hebrews are very similar to Paul's epistles, and the author also refers to Timothy (13:23). However, significant differences have led the majority of biblical scholars to reject Pauline authorship of this book: (1) The Greek style of Hebrews is far more polished and refined than that found in any of Paul's recognized epistles. (2) In view of Paul's consistent claims to be an apostle and an eyewitness of Christ, it is very doubtful that he would have used the phraseology found in 2:3: "which at the first began to be spoken by the Lord, and was confirmed to us by those who heard *Him.*" (3) The lack of Paul's customary salutation, which includes his name, goes against the firm pattern found in all his other epistles. (4) While Paul used both the Hebrew text and the Septuagint to quote from the Old Testament, the writer of Hebrews apparently did not know Hebrew and quoted exclusively from the Septuagint. (5) Paul's common use of compound titles to refer to the Son of God is not followed in Hebrews, which usually refers to Him as "Christ," "Jesus," and "Lord." (6) Hebrews concentrates on Christ's present priestly ministry, but Paul's writings have very little to say about the present work of Christ. Thus, Hebrews appears not to have been written by Paul although the writer shows a Pauline influence. The authority of Hebrews in no way depends upon Pauline authorship, especially since it does not claim to have been written by Paul.

Tertullian referred to Barnabas as the author of Hebrews, but it is unlikely that this resident of Jerusalem (Acts 4:36, 37) would include himself as one of those who relied on others for eyewitness testimony about Jesus (2:3). Other suggestions include Luke, Clement of Rome, Apollos, Silvanus (Silas), Philip, and even Priscilla. Some of these are possibilities, but we must agree with the third-century theologian Origen who wrote: "Who it was that really wrote the Epistle, God only knows."

THE TIME OF HEBREWS

Because of the exclusive use of the Septuagint (Greek translation of the Hebrew Old Testament) and the elegant Greek style found in Hebrews, some recent scholars have argued that this book was written to a Gentile readership. However, the bulk of the evidence favors the traditional view that the original recipients of this letter were Jewish Christians. In addition to the ancient title "To Hebrews," there is also the frequent use of the Old Testament as an unquestioned authority, the assumed knowledge of the sacrificial ritual, and the many contrasts between Christianity and Judaism, which are designed to prevent the readers from lapsing into Judaism.

Many places have been suggested for the locality of the readers, but this letter's destination cannot be determined with any certainty. In the past, Jerusalem was most frequently suggested, but this view is hindered by four problems: (1) It is unlikely that a book addressed to Palestineans would quote exclusively from the Septuagint rather than the Hebrew Old Testament. (2) Palestinean believers were poor (Rom. 15:26), but these readers were able to assist other Christians financially (6:10). (3) Residents of Jerusalem would not be characterized by the description in 2:3 because some would have been eyewitnesses of the ministry of Christ. (4) "You have not yet resisted to bloodshed" (12:4) does not fit the situation in Jerusalem. The majority view today is that the recipients of Hebrews probably lived in Rome. The statement "Those from Italy greet you" in 13:24 seems to suggest that Italians away from Italy are sending their greetings home.

The recipients of this letter were believers (3:1) who had come to faith through the testimony of eyewitnesses of Christ (2:3). They were not novices (5:12), and they had successfully endured hardships because of their stand for the gospel (10:32–34). Unfortunately, they had become "dull of hearing" (5:11) and were in danger of drifting away (2:1; 3:12). This made them particularly susceptible to the renewed persecutions that were coming upon them (12:4–12), and the author found it necessary to check the downward spiral with "the word of exhortation" (13:22). While there is disagreement over the specific danger involved, the classic position that the readers were on the verge of lapsing into Judaism to avoid persecution directed at Christians seems to be supported by the whole tenor of the book. Hebrews' repeated emphasis on the superiority of Christianity over Judaism would have been pointless if the readers were about to return to Gnosticism or heathenism.

The place of writing is unknown, but a reasonable estimate of the date can be made. Hebrews was quoted in A.D. 95 by Clement of Rome, but its failure to mention the ending of the Old Testament sacrificial system with the destruction of Jerusalem in A.D. 70 indicates that it was written prior to that date. Timothy was still alive (13:23), persecution was mounting, and the old Jewish system was about to be removed (12:26, 27). All this suggests a date between A.D. 64 and 68.

THE CHRIST OF HEBREWS

Christ is our eternal High Priest according to the order of Melchizedek. He identified with man in His incarnation and offered no less a sacrifice than Himself on our behalf.

Hebrews presents Christ as the divine-human Prophet, Priest, and King. His deity (1:1–3, 8) and humanity (2:9, 14, 17, 18) are asserted with equal force, and over twenty titles are used to describe His attributes and accomplishments (e.g., Heir of all things, Apostle and High Priest, Mediator, Author and Perfecter of faith). He is superior to all who went before and offers the supreme sacrifice, priesthood, and covenant.

KEYS TO HEBREWS

Key Word: The Superiority of Christ—The basic theme of Hebrews is found in the word "better," describing the superiority of Christ in His Person and work (1:4; 6:9; 7:7, 19, 22; 8:6; 9:23; 10:34; 11:16, 35, 40; 12:24). The words *perfect* and *heavenly* are also prominent. He offers a better revelation, position, priesthood, covenant, sacrifice, and power. The writer develops this theme to prevent the readers from giving up the substance for the shadow

FOCUS	CHRIST'S PERSON			CHRIST'S WORK			THE WALK OF FAITH		
REFERENCE	1:1——	1:4——	3:1——	4:14——	8:1——	9:1——	10:19——	12:1——	13:1—13:25
DIVISION	CHRIST OVER PROPHETS	CHRIST OVER ANGELS	CHRIST OVER MOSES	PRIESTHOOD	COVENANT	SANCTUARY AND SACRIFICE	ASSURANCE OF FAITH	ENDURANCE OF FAITH	EXHORTATION TO LOVE
TOPIC	MAJESTY OF CHRIST			MINISTRY OF CHRIST			MINISTERS FOR CHRIST		
	DOCTRINE						DISCIPLINE		
LOCATION	PLACE OF WRITING UNKNOWN								
TIME	C. A.D. 64–68								

by abandoning Christianity and retreating into the old Judaic system. This epistle is also written to exhort them to become mature in Christ and to put away their spiritual dullness and degeneration. Thus, it places heavy stress on doctrine, concentrating on Christology and soteriology (the study of salvation).

Key Verses: Hebrews 4:14–16 and 12:1, 2—"Seeing then that we have a great High Priest who has passed through the heavens, Jesus the Son of God, let us hold fast *our* confession. For we do not have a High Priest who cannot sympathize with our weaknesses, but was in all *points* tempted as *we are, yet* without sin. Let us therefore come boldly to the throne of grace, that we may obtain mercy and find grace to help in time of need" (4:14–16).

"Therefore we also, since we are surrounded by so great a cloud of witnesses, let us lay aside every weight, and the sin which so easily ensnares *us,* and let us run with endurance the race that is set before us, looking unto Jesus, the author and finisher of *our* faith, who for the joy that was set before Him endured the cross, despising the shame, and has sat down at the right hand of the throne of God" (12:1, 2).

Key Chapter: Hebrews 11—The hall of fame of the Scriptures is located in Hebrews 11 and records those who willingly took God at His word even when there was nothing to cling to but His promise. Inherent to all those listed is the recognition that "without faith *it is* impossible to please *Him,* for he who comes to God must believe that He is, and *that* He is a rewarder of those who diligently seek Him" (Heb. 11:6).

SURVEY OF HEBREWS

Hebrews stands alone among the New Testament Epistles in its style and approach, and it is the only New Testament book whose authorship remains a real mystery. This profound work builds a case for the superiority of Christ through a cumulative argument in which Christ is presented as "better" in every respect. In His Person He is better than the angels, Moses, and Joshua; and in His performance He provides a better priesthood, covenant, sanctuary, and sacrifice. Evidently, the readers are in danger of reverting to Judaism because of the suffering they are beginning to experience for their faith in Christ. However, by doing so, they would be retreating from the substance back into the shadow. In addition to his positive presentation of the supremacy of Christ, the writer intersperses five solemn warnings about the peril of turning away from Christ (2:1–4; 3:7—4:13; 5:11—6:20; 10:19–39; 12:25–29). These parenthetical warnings include cautions against neglect (2:1–4) and refusal (12:25–29). After using the Old Testament to demonstrate the superiority of Christ's Person (1:1—4:13) and the superiority of Christ's work (4:14—10:18), the writer applies these truths in a practical way to show the superiority of the Christian's walk of faith (10:19—13:25).

The Superiority of Christ's Person (1:1—4:13): Instead of the usual salutation, this epistle immediately launches into its theme—the supremacy of Christ even over the Old Testament prophets (1:1–3). Christianity is built upon the highest form of divine disclosure: the personal revelation of God through His incarnate Son. Christ is therefore greater than the prophets, and He is also greater than the angels, the mediators of the Mosaic Law (1:4—2:18; see Acts 7:53; Heb. 2:2). This is seen in His name, His position, His worship by the angels, and His incarnation. The Son of God partook of flesh and blood and was "made like *His* brethren" in all things (2:17) in order to bring "many sons to glory" (2:10). Christ is also superior to Moses (3:1–6), for Moses was a servant in the house of God, but Christ is the Son over God's household. Because of these truths, the readers are exhorted to avoid the divine judgment that is visited upon unbelief (3:7—4:13). Their disbelief had prevented the generation of the Exodus from becoming the generation of the conquest, and the rest that Christ offers is so much greater than what was provided by Joshua. The readers are therefore urged to enter the eternal rest that is possessed by faith in Christ.

The Superiority of Christ's Work (4:14—10:18): The high priesthood of Christ is superior to the Aaronic priesthood (4:14—7:28). Because of His incarnation, Christ can "sympathize with our weaknesses," having been "in all *points* tempted as *we are, yet* without sin" (4:15). Christ was not a Levite, but He qualified for a higher priesthood according to the order of Melchizedek. The superiority of Melchizedek to Levi is seen in the fact that Levi, in effect, paid tithes through Abraham to Melchizedek (7:9–10). Abraham was blessed by Melchizedek, and "the lesser is blessed by the better" (7:7). The parenthetical warning in 5:11—6:20 exhorts the readers to "go on to perfection" by moving beyond the basics of salvation and repentance.

By divine oath (7:21), Christ has become a permanent and perfect High Priest and the "Mediator of a better covenant" (8:6). The new covenant has made the old covenant obsolete (8:6–13). Our Great High Priest similarly ministers in "the greater and more perfect tabernacle not made with hands, that is, not of this creation" (9:11). And unlike the former priests, He offers Himself as a sinless and voluntary sacrifice once and for all (9:1—10:18).

The Superiority of the Christian's Walk of Faith (10:19—13:25): The author applies what he has been saying about the superiority of Christ by warning his readers of the danger of discarding their faith in Christ (10:19–39). The faith that the readers must maintain is defined in 11:1–3 and illustrated in 11:4–40. The triumphs and accomplishments of faith in the lives of Old Testament believers should encourage the recipients of "something better" (11:40) in Christ to look "unto Jesus, the author and finisher of *our* faith" (12:2). Just as Jesus endured great hostility, those who believe in Him will sometimes have to endure divine discipline for the sake of holiness (12:1–29). The readers are warned not to turn away from Christ during such times, but to place their hope in Him. The character of their lives must be shaped by their dedication to Christ (13:1–19), and this will be manifested in their love of each other through their hospitality, concern, purity, contentment, and obedience. The author concludes this epistle with one of the finest benedictions in Scripture (13:20, 21) and some personal words (13:22–25).

OUTLINE OF HEBREWS

Part One: The Superiority of Christ's Person (1:1—4:13)

I. The Superiority of Christ over the Prophets 1:1–3

II. The Superiority of Christ over the Angels ....1:4—2:18

A. Christ Is Superior Because of His Deity 1:4–14
B. First Warning: Danger of Neglect 2:1–4
C. Christ Is Superior Because of His Humanity 2:5–18

III. The Superiority of Christ over Moses ....3:1—4:13

A. Christ Is Superior to Moses in His Work 3:1–4
B. Christ Is Superior to Moses in His Person 3:5, 6
C. Second Warning: Danger of Unbelief ....3:7—4:13
1. Danger of Hardening the Heart 3:7–19
2. Challenge to Enter His Rest 4:1–13

Part Two: The Superiority of Christ's Work (4:14—10:18)

I. The Superiority of Christ's Priesthood ....4:14—7:28

A. Christ Is Superior in His Position 4:14–16
B. Christ Is Superior in His Qualifications 5:1–10
1. Aaronic Priesthood 5:1–4
2. Melchizedekian Priesthood 5:5–10
C. Third Warning: Danger of Not Maturing ....5:11—6:20
1. Dullness of Hearing 5:11–14
2. Need for Maturity 6:1–8
3. Exhortation to Maturity 6:9–20
D. Christ Is Superior in His Priestly Order 7:1–28
1. Description of Melchizedek 7:1–3
2. Superiority of Melchizedek 7:4–10
3. Imperfection of Aaronic Priesthood 7:11–28

II. The Superiority of Christ's Covenant 8:1–13

A. A Better Covenant 8:1–6
B. A New Covenant 8:7–13

III. The Superiority of Christ's Sanctuary and Sacrifice ....9:1—10:18

A. Old Covenant's Sanctuary and Sacrifice 9:1–10
1. Old Covenant's Sanctuary 9:1–5
2. Old Covenant's Sacrifice 9:6–10
B. New Covenant's Sanctuary and Sacrifice ....9:11—10:18
1. New Covenant's Sanctuary 9:11
2. New Covenant's Sacrifice ....9:12—10:18

Part Three: The Superiority of the Christian's Walk of Faith (10:19—13:25)

I. Exhortation to Full Assurance of Faith ....10:19—11:40

A. Hold Fast the Confession of Faith 10:19–25
B. Fourth Warning: Danger of Drawing Back 10:26–39
C. Definition of Faith 11:1–3
D. Examples of Faith 11:4–40
1. Abel 11:4
2. Enoch 11:5, 6
3. Noah 11:7
4. Abraham and Sarah 11:8–19
5. Isaac 11:20
6. Jacob 11:21
7. Joseph 11:22
8. Moses' Parents 11:23
9. Moses 11:24–29
10. Joshua and Rahab 11:30, 31
11. Many Other Heroes of Faith 11:32–40

II. Endurance of Faith 12:1–29

A. Example of Christ's Endurance 12:1–4
B. Exhortation to Endure God's Chastening 12:5–24

CHAPTER 1

The Superiority of Christ over the Prophets

GOD, who at various times and [R]in various ways spoke in time past to the fathers by the prophets, Num. 12:6, 8

2 has in these last days spoken to us by *His* Son, whom He has appointed heir of all things, through whom also He made the [T]worlds; Or *ages*, Gr. *aiones*, aeons

3 [R]who being the brightness of *His* glory and the express [R]image of His person, and upholding all things by the word of His power, when He had by Himself* purged our* sins, [R]sat down at the right hand of the Majesty on high, John 1:14 • 2 Cor. 4:4 • Ps. 110:1★

Christ Is Superior Because of His Deity

4 having become so much better than the angels, as He has by inheritance obtained a more excellent name than they.

5 For to which of the angels did He ever say:

"You are My Son,
*Today I have begotten You"?**

And again:

"I will be to Him a Father,
*And He shall be to Me a Son"?**

6 But when He again brings [R]the firstborn into the world, He says: [Rom. 8:29]

*"Let all the angels of God worship Him."**

7 And of the angels He says:

"Who makes His angels spirits
*And His ministers a flame of fire."**

8 But to the Son *He says:*

"Your throne, O God, is forever and ever;
A scepter of righteousness is the scepter of Your kingdom.
9 *You have loved righteousness and hated lawlessness;*
Therefore God, Your God, [R]has anointed You Is. 61:1, 3★
*With the oil of gladness more than Your companions."**

10 And:

[R]*"You, LORD, in the beginning laid the foundation of the earth,* Ps. 102:25–27
And the heavens are the work of Your hands.
11 [R]*They will perish, but You remain;*
And [R]they will all grow old like a garment; [Is. 34:4] • Is. 50:9; 51:6
12 *Like a cloak You will fold them up,*
And they will be changed.
But You are the [R]same, Heb. 13:8
*And Your years will not fail."**

13 But to which of the angels has He ever said:

"Sit at My right hand,
*Till I make Your enemies Your footstool"?**

14 [R]Are they not all ministering spirits sent forth to minister for those who will [R]inherit salvation? Ps. 103:20 • Rom. 8:17

1:3 NU omits *by Himself* • NU omits *our* **1:5** Ps. 2:7 • 2 Sam. 7:14 **1:6** Deut. 32:43 (LXX, DSS); Ps. 97:7 **1:7** Ps. 104:4 **1:9** Ps. 45:6, 7★ **1:12** Ps. 102:25–27 **1:13** Ps. 110:1

1:14 Angels: Messengers and Servants—The ministry of good angels can be considered under six headings:

a. Angels attend and worship God. The basic activity of angels appears to be gathering around the throne of God and proclaiming His worthiness (Page 996—Matt. 18:10; Page 1316—Rev. 5:11).
b. Angels protect God's people. The Bible relates numerous instances of angels delivering heroes, such as Daniel and Peter, from threatening situations (Page 879—Dan. 6:22; Page 1117—Acts 5:19). However, all believers in Christ are objects of angelic concern (Page 1258—Heb. 1:14).
c. Angels guide God's people. Angels directed the women to see the empty tomb and told Jesus' disciples He was risen (Page 1010—Matt. 28:5–7). An angel guided Philip to the desert where he met the Ethiopian eunuch (Page 1121—Acts 8:26). An angel assured Paul that he would reach Rome safely (Page 1143—Acts 27:23, 24). They probably guide many Christians who do not realize where their help is coming from.
d. Angels bring judgment on the wicked. Angels participated in the destruction of Sodom and Gomorrah (Page 20—Gen. 19:12, 13). They struck down Herod when he received worship (Acts 12:23). They pour out bowls of judgment in Rev. (Page 1322—Rev. 16).

CHAPTER 2

First Warning: Danger of Neglect

THEREFORE we must give [T]the more ear-
nest heed to the things we have heard, lest
we drift away. *all the more careful attention*
2 For if the word spoken through angels
proved steadfast, and every transgression and
disobedience received a just reward,
3 [R]how shall we escape if we neglect so
great a salvation, which at the first began to
be spoken by the Lord, and was confirmed to
us by those who heard *Him,* Heb. 10:28
4 [R]God also bearing witness [R]both with
signs and wonders, with various miracles, and
gifts of the Holy Spirit, according to His own
will? Mark 16:20 • Acts 2:22, 43

Christ Is Superior Because of His Humanity

5 For He has not put the world to come, of
which we speak, in subjection to angels.
6 But one testified in a certain place, saying:

"What is man that You are mindful of him,
Or the son of man that You take care of
him?
7 *You have made him [T]a little lower than*
the angels; Or *for a little while*
You have crowned him with glory and
*honor,**
And set him over the works of Your
hands.
8 [R]*You have put all things in subjection*
*under his feet."** Matt. 28:18

For in that He put all in subjection under him,
He left nothing *that is* not put under him. But
now we do not yet see all things put under him.
9 But we see Jesus, [R]who was made a little
lower than the angels, for the suffering of
death [R]crowned with glory and honor, that
He, by the grace of God, might taste death for
everyone. Phil. 2:7–9 • Acts 2:33; 3:13
10 For it was fitting for Him, [R]for whom *are*
all things and by whom *are* all things, in
bringing many sons to glory, to make the cap-
tain of their salvation [R]perfect through suffer-
ings. Col. 1:16 • Heb. 5:8, 9; 7:28
11 For [R]both He who sanctifies and those
who are being sanctified [R]*are* all of one, for
which reason [R]He is not ashamed to call them
brethren, Heb. 10:10 • Acts 17:26 • Matt. 28:10
12 saying:

"I will declare Your name to My brethren;
In the midst of the assembly I will sing
*praise to You."**

13 And again:

*"I will put My trust in Him."**

And again:

"Here am I and the children whom God
*has given Me."**

14 Inasmuch then as the children have par-
taken of flesh and blood, He Himself likewise
shared in the same, that through death He
might destroy him who had the power of
death, that is, the devil,
15 and [R]release those who [R]through fear of
death were all their lifetime subject to bond-
age. Is. 42:7; 49:9; 61:1★ • [Luke 1:74]
16 For indeed He does not [T]give aid to an-
gels, but He does give aid to the seed of Abra-
ham. Or *take on* the nature of
17 Therefore, in all things He had [R]to be
made like *His* brethren, that He might be a
merciful and faithful High Priest in things
pertaining to God, to make propitiation for
the sins of the people. Phil. 2:7
18 [R]For in that He Himself has suffered,
being [T]tempted, He is able to aid those who
are tempted. [Heb. 4:15, 16] • *tested*

CHAPTER 3

Christ Is Superior to Moses in His Work

THEREFORE, holy brethren, partakers of
the heavenly calling, consider the Apostle
and [R]High Priest of our confession, Christ Je-
sus, Ps. 110:4★
2 who was faithful to Him who appointed
Him, as [R]Moses also *was faithful* in all His
house. Num. 12:7
3 For this One has been counted worthy of
more glory than Moses, inasmuch as [R]He who
built the house has more honor than the
house. Zech. 6:12, 13

2:7 NU, M omit the rest of v. 7. **2:8** Ps. 8:4–6
2:12 Ps. 22:22 **2:13** 2 Sam. 22:3; Is. 8:17 • Is. 8:18

e. Angels assisted Jesus on earth. Angels prepared Mary and Joseph for Jesus' birth (Page 978—Matt. 1:20; Page 1041—Luke 1:26–38). They announced Jesus' birth to the shepherds (Page 1043—Luke 2:8–15). They ministered to Jesus after His wilderness temptation (Page 1015—Mark 1:13). An angel strengthened Him in Gethsemane (Page 1072—Luke 22:43). Angels rolled away the rock from the tomb and ministered to the women (Page 1010—Matt. 28:2–7). Angels were present at Christ's ascension (Page 1112—Acts 1:11).

f. Angels will assist Christ at His return. An archangel will announce the return of Christ (Page 1228— 1 Thess. 4:16). Angels will gather all believers from the ends of the earth (Page 1004—Matt. 24:31). They will separate the true from the false (Page 991—Matt. 13:39, 49, 50). They will serve as an honor guard at the gates of the New Jerusalem (Page 1327—Rev. 21:12).

Now turn to Page 879—Dan. 6:22: Angels: Interaction with Humans.

4 For every house is built by someone, but
He who built all things *is* God.

Christ Is Superior to Moses in His Person

5 [R]And Moses indeed *was* faithful in all
His house as [R]a servant, [R]for a testimony of
those things which would be spoken *after-
ward,* Heb. 3:2 • Ex. 14:31 • Deut. 18:15, 18, 19
6 but Christ as [R]a Son over His own house,
[R]whose house we are if we hold fast the confi-
dence and the rejoicing of the hope firm to the
end.* Heb. 1:2 • [1 Cor. 3:16]

Danger of Hardening the Heart

7 Therefore, as the Holy Spirit says:

"Today, if you will hear His voice,
8 *Do not harden your hearts as in the
rebellion,*
In the day of trial in the wilderness,
9 *Where your fathers tested Me, tried Me,*
And saw My works forty years.
10 *Therefore I was angry with that
generation,*
*And said, 'They always go astray in
their* heart,
And they have not known My ways.'
11 *So I swore in My wrath,*
*'They shall not enter My rest.' "**

12 Beware, brethren, lest there be in any of
you an evil heart of unbelief in departing from
the living God;
13 but [T]exhort one another daily, while it is
called "*Today,*" lest any of you be hardened
through the deceitfulness of sin. encourage
14 For we have become partakers of Christ if
we hold the beginning of our confidence
steadfast to the end,
15 while it is said:

"Today, if you will hear His voice,
*Do not harden your hearts as in the
rebellion."**

16 [R]For who, having heard, rebelled? Indeed,
was it not all who came out of Egypt, *led* by
Moses? Num. 14:2, 11, 30
17 Now with whom was He angry forty
years? *Was it* not with those who sinned,
whose corpses fell in the wilderness?
18 And [R]to whom did He swear that they
would not enter His rest, but to those who did
not obey? Num. 14:30
19 So we see that they could not enter in be-
cause of [R]unbelief. 1 Cor. 10:11, 12

CHAPTER 4

Challenge to Enter His Rest

THEREFORE, since a promise remains of
entering His rest, let us fear lest any of
you seem to have come short of it.
2 For indeed the gospel was preached to us
as well as to them; but the word which they
heard did not profit them,* not being mixed
with faith in those who heard *it.*
3 For we who have believed do enter that
rest, as He has said:

"So I swore in My wrath,
*'They shall not enter My rest,' "**

although the works were finished from the
foundation of the world.
4 For He has spoken in a certain place of
the seventh *day* in this way: *"And God rested
on the seventh day from all His works";**
5 and again in this *place: "They shall not
enter My rest."**
6 Since therefore it remains that some *must*
enter it, and those to whom it was first
preached did not enter because of disobedi-
ence,
7 again He designates a certain day, saying
in David, *"Today,"* after such a long time, as it
has been said:

"Today, if you will hear His voice,
*Do not harden your hearts."**

8 For if Joshua had [R]given them rest, then
He would not afterward have spoken of an-
other day. Josh. 22:4
9 There remains therefore a rest for the
people of God.
10 For he who has entered His rest has him-
self also ceased from his works as God *did*
from His.
11 [R]Let us therefore be diligent to enter that
rest, lest anyone fall according to the same ex-
ample of disobedience. 2 Pet. 1:10
12 For the word of God *is* [R]living and power-
ful, and [R]sharper than any [R]two-edged sword,
piercing even to the division of soul and
spirit, and of joints and marrow, and is a dis-
cerner of the thoughts and intents of the
heart. Ps. 147:15 • Is. 49:2 • Eph. 6:17
13 [R]And there is no creature hidden from His
sight, but all things *are* [R]naked and open to
the eyes of Him to whom we *must give* ac-
count. Ps. 33:13–15; 90:8 • Job 26:6

Christ Is Superior in His Position

14 Seeing then that we have a great [R]High
Priest who has passed through the heavens,
Jesus the Son of God, [R]let us hold fast *our* con-
fession. Heb. 2:17; 7:26 • Heb. 10:23
15 For [R]we do not have a High Priest who
cannot sympathize with our weaknesses, but

3:6 NU omits *firm to the end* **3:11** Ps. 95:7–11
3:15 Ps. 95:7, 8 **4:2** NU, M *profit them, since they were not united by faith with those who heeded it*
4:3 Ps. 95:11 **4:4** Gen. 2:2 **4:5** Ps. 95:11 **4:7** Ps. 95:7, 8

[R]was in all *points* tempted as *we are,* [R]yet without sin. Is. 53:3–5 • Luke 22:28 • 2 Cor. 5:21

16 Let us therefore come boldly to the throne of grace, that we may obtain mercy and find grace to help in time of need.

CHAPTER 5

Aaronic Priesthood

FOR every high priest taken from among men [R]is appointed for men in things *pertaining* to God, that he may offer both gifts and sacrifices for sins. Heb. 2:17; 8:3

2 He can have compassion on those who are ignorant and going astray, since he himself is also subject to [R]weakness. Heb. 7:28

3 Because of this he is required as for the people, so also for [R]himself, to offer *sacrifices* for sins. Lev. 9:7; 16:6

4 And no man takes this honor to himself, but he who is called by God, just as [R]Aaron *was.* Ex. 28:1

Melchizedekian Priesthood

5 [R]So also Christ did not glorify Himself to become High Priest, *but it* was He who said to Him: John 8:54

"You are My Son,
*Today I have begotten You."**

6 As *He* also *says* in another *place:*

"You are a priest forever
According to the order of
*Melchizedek";**

7 who, in the days of His flesh, when He had offered up prayers and supplications, with vehement cries and tears to Him who was able to save Him from death, and was heard because of His godly fear,

8 though He was a Son, *yet* He learned obedience by the things which He suffered.

9 And [R]having been perfected, He became the author of eternal salvation to all who obey Him, Heb. 2:10

10 called by God as High Priest [R]*"according to the order of Melchizedek,"* Ps. 110:4★

Dullness of Hearing

11 of whom [R]we have much to say, and hard to explain, since you have become [R]dull of hearing. [John 16:12] • [Matt. 13:15]

12 For though by this time you ought to be teachers, you need *someone* to teach you again the first principles of the [T]oracles of God; and you have come to need [R]milk and not solid food. *sayings,* Scriptures • 1 Cor. 3:1–3

13 For everyone who partakes *only* of milk *is* unskilled in the word of righteousness, for he is [R]a babe. Eph. 4:14

14 But solid food belongs to those who are [T]of full age, *that is,* those who by reason of [T]use have their senses exercised [R]to discern both good and evil. *mature* • *practice* • Is. 7:15

CHAPTER 6

Need for Maturity

THEREFORE, [R]leaving the discussion of the elementary *principles* of Christ, let us go on to perfection, not laying again the foundation of repentance from [R]dead works and of faith toward God, Heb. 5:12 • [Heb. 9:14]

2 [R]of the doctrine of baptisms, of laying on of hands, of resurrection of the dead, and of eternal judgment. Acts 19:3–5

3 And this we will* do if God permits.

4 For *it is* impossible for those who were once enlightened, and have tasted [R]the heavenly gift, and [R]have become partakers of the Holy Spirit, [John 4:10] • [Gal. 3:2, 5]

5 and have tasted the good word of God and the powers of the age to come,

6 if they fall away,* to renew them again to repentance, [R]since they crucify again for themselves the Son of God, and put *Him* to an open shame. Heb. 10:29

7 For the earth which drinks in the rain that often comes upon it, and bears herbs useful for those by whom it is cultivated, [R]receives blessing from God; Ps. 65:10

8 [R]but if it bears thorns and briers, *it is* rejected and near to being cursed, whose end *is* to be burned. Is. 5:6

Exhortation to Maturity

9 But, beloved, we are confident of better things concerning you, yes, things that accompany salvation, though we speak in this manner.

10 For God *is* not unjust to forget your work and labor of* love which you have shown toward His name, *in that* you have ministered to the saints, and do minister.

11 And we desire that each one of you show the same diligence [R]to the full assurance of hope until the end, Col. 2:2

12 that you do not become [T]sluggish, but imitate those who through faith and patience [R]inherit the promises. *lazy* • Heb. 10:36

13 For when God made a promise to Abraham, because He could swear by no one greater, He swore by Himself,

14 saying, *"Surely blessing I will bless you, and multiplying I will multiply you."**

15 And so, after he had patiently endured, he obtained the [R]promise. Gen. 12:4; 21:5

16 For men indeed swear by the greater, and [R]an oath for confirmation *is* for them an end of all dispute. Ex. 22:11

5:5 Ps. 2:7★ **5:6** Ps. 110:4★ **6:3** M *let us do* **6:6** Or *and have fallen away* **6:10** NU omits *labor of* **6:14** Gen. 22:17

17 Thus God, determining to show more
abundantly to [R]the heirs of promise [R]the im-
mutability of His counsel, [T]confirmed *it* by an
oath, Heb. 11:9 • Rom. 11:29 • *guaranteed*
18 that by two immutable things, in which it
is impossible for God to lie, we might* have
strong consolation, who have fled for refuge
to lay hold of the hope set before *us*.
19 This *hope* we have as an anchor of the
soul, both sure and steadfast, and which en-
ters the *Presence* behind the veil,
20 [R]where the forerunner has entered for
us, *even* Jesus, [R]having become High Priest
forever according to the order of Melchize-
dek. [Heb. 4:14] • Heb. 3:1; 5:10, 11

CHAPTER 7

Description of Melchizedek

FOR this [R]Melchizedek, king of Salem,
priest of the Most High God, who met
Abraham returning from the slaughter of the
kings and blessed him, Gen. 14:18–20
2 to whom also Abraham gave a tenth part
of all, first being translated "king of righ-
teousness," and then also king of Salem,
meaning "king of peace,"
3 without father, without mother, without
genealogy, having neither beginning of days
nor end of life, but made like the Son of God,
remains a priest continually.

Superiority of Melchizedek

4 Now consider how great this man *was*, to
whom even the patriarch Abraham gave a
tenth of the [T]spoils. *plunder*
5 And indeed [R]those who are of the sons of
Levi, who receive the priesthood, have a com-
mandment to receive tithes from the people
according to the law, that is, from their
brethren, though they have come from the
loins of Abraham; Num. 18:21–26
6 but he whose genealogy is not derived
from them received tithes from Abraham and
blessed him who had the promises.
7 Now beyond all contradiction the lesser is
blessed by the better.
8 Here mortal men receive tithes, but there
he *receives them*, [R]of whom it is witnessed
that he lives. Heb. 5:6; 6:20
9 Even Levi, who receives tithes, paid tithes
through Abraham, so to speak,
10 for he was still in the loins of his father
when Melchizedek met him.

Imperfection of Aaronic Priesthood

11 Therefore, if perfection were through the
Levitical priesthood (for under it the people
received the law), what further need *was*
there that another priest should rise accord-
ing to the order of Melchizedek, and not be
called according to the order of Aaron?
12 For the priesthood being changed, of ne-
cessity there is also a change of the law.
13 For He of whom these things are spoken
belongs to another tribe, from which no man
has [T]officiated at the altar. *served*
14 For *it is* evident that [R]our Lord arose from
Judah, of which tribe Moses spoke nothing
concerning priesthood.* Is. 1:1★
15 And it is yet far more evident if, in the
likeness of Melchizedek, there arises another
priest
16 who has come, not according to the law of
a fleshly commandment, but according to the
power of an endless life.
17 For He testifies:*

"You are a priest forever
*According to the order of Melchizedek."**

18 For on the one hand there is an annulling
of the former commandment because of its
weakness and unprofitableness,
19 for [R]the law made nothing [T]perfect; on the
other hand, *there is the* bringing in of [R]a bet-
ter hope, through which [R]we draw near to
God. [Acts 13:39] • *complete* • Heb. 6:18, 19 • Rom. 5:2
20 And inasmuch as *He was* not *made priest*
without an oath
21 (for they have become priests without an
oath, but He with an oath by Him who said to
Him:

"The LORD has sworn
And will not relent,
*'You are a priest forever**
According to the order of
*Melchizedek' "),**

22 by so much more Jesus has become a
surety of a [R]better covenant. Heb. 8:6
23 Also there were many priests, because
they were prevented by death from continuing.
24 But He, because He continues forever, has
an unchangeable priesthood.
25 Therefore He is also [R]able to save to the
uttermost those who come to God through
Him, since He always lives [R]to make interces-
sion for them. Jude 24 • Rom. 8:34
26 For such a High Priest was fitting for us,
[R]*who is* holy, [T]harmless, undefiled, separate
from sinners, [R]and has become higher than
the heavens; Heb. 4:15 • *innocent* • Eph. 1:20
27 who does not need daily, as those high
priests, to offer up sacrifices, first for His
[R]own sins and then for the people's, for this
He did once for all when He offered up Him-
self. Lev. 9:7; 16:6
28 For the law appoints as high priests men
who have weakness, but the word of the oath,

6:18 M omits *might* **7:14** NU *priests* **7:17** NU *it is testified* • Ps. 110:4★ **7:21** NU ends the quotation after *forever*. • Ps. 110:4

which came after the law, *appoints* the Son who has been perfected forever.

CHAPTER 8

A Better Covenant

NOW *this is* the main point of the things we are saying: We have such a High Priest, who is seated at the right hand of the throne of the Majesty in the heavens,

2 a Minister of [R]the [T]sanctuary and of [R]the true tabernacle which the Lord erected, and not man. Heb. 9:8, 12 • Lit. *holies* • Heb. 9:11, 24

3 For [R]every high priest is appointed to offer both gifts and sacrifices. Therefore [R]*it is* necessary that this One also have something to offer. Heb. 5:1; 8:4 • [Eph. 5:2]

4 For if He were on earth, He would not be a priest, since there are priests who offer the gifts according to the law;

5 who serve [R]the copy and shadow of the heavenly things, as Moses was divinely instructed when he was about to make the tabernacle. For He said, *"See that you make all things according to the pattern shown you on the mountain."** Heb. 9:23, 24

6 But now [R]He has obtained a more excellent ministry, inasmuch as He is also Mediator of a better covenant, which was established on better promises. [2 Cor. 3:6–8]

A New Covenant

7 For if that [R]first *covenant* had been faultless, then no place would have been sought for a second. Ex. 3:8; 19:5

8 Because finding fault with them, He says: [R]*"Behold, the days are coming, says the* LORD*, when I will make a new covenant with the house of Israel and with the house of Judah—* Jer. 31:31–34★

9 *"not according to the covenant that I made with their fathers in the day when I took them by the hand to lead them out of the land of Egypt; because they did not continue in My covenant, and I disregarded them, says the* LORD.

10 *"For this is the covenant that I will make with the house of Israel after those days, says the* [R]LORD*: I will put My laws in their mind and write them on their hearts; and* [R]*I will be their God, and they shall be My people.* Jer. 31:33 • Zech. 8:8

11 [R]*"None of them shall teach his neighbor, and none his brother, saying, 'Know the* LORD*,' for all shall know Me, from the least of them to the greatest of them.* Is. 54:13

12 *"For I will be merciful to their unrighteousness, and their sins and their lawless deeds* I will remember no more."**

13 [R]In that He says, *"A new covenant,"* He has made the first obsolete. Now what is becoming obsolete and growing old is ready to vanish away. [2 Cor. 5:17]

CHAPTER 9

Old Covenant's Sanctuary

THEN indeed, even the first *covenant* had ordinances of divine service and [R]the earthly sanctuary. Ex. 25:8

2 For a tabernacle was prepared: the first *part,* in which *was* the lampstand, the table, and the showbread, which is called the [T]sanctuary; *holy place,* lit. *holies*

3 [R]and behind the second veil, the part of the tabernacle which is called the Holiest of All, Ex. 26:31–35; 40:3

4 which had the [R]golden censer and the ark of the covenant overlaid on all sides with gold, in which *were* the golden pot that had the manna, Aaron's rod that budded, and the tablets of the covenant; Lev. 16:12

5 and above it were the cherubim of glory overshadowing the mercy seat. Of these things we cannot now speak in detail.

Old Covenant's Sacrifice

6 Now when these things had been thus prepared, [R]the priests always went into the first part of the tabernacle, performing *the services.* Num. 18:2–6; 28:3

7 But into the second part the high priest *went* alone once a year, not without blood, which he offered for himself and *for* the people's sins *committed* in ignorance;

8 the Holy Spirit indicating this, that [R]the way into the Holiest of All was not yet made manifest while the first tabernacle was still standing. [John 14:6]

9 It *was* symbolic for the present time in which both gifts and sacrifices are offered which cannot make him who performed the service perfect in regard to the conscience—

10 *concerned* only with foods and drinks, various washings, and fleshly ordinances imposed until the time of reformation.

New Covenant's Sanctuary

11 But Christ came *as* High Priest of the good things to come,* with the greater and more perfect tabernacle not made with hands, that is, not of this creation.

New Covenant's Sacrifice

12 Not with the blood of goats and calves, but with His own blood He entered the Most Holy Place [R]once for all, [R]having obtained eternal redemption. Zech. 3:9 • [Dan. 9:24]★

13 For if [R]the blood of bulls and goats and [R]the ashes of a heifer, sprinkling the unclean, [T]sanctifies for the purifying of the flesh, Lev. 16:14, 15 • Num. 19:2 • *sets apart*

14 how much more shall the blood of Christ, who through the eternal Spirit [R]offered

8:5 Ex. 25:40 **8:12** NU omits *and their lawless deeds* • Jer. 31:31–34 **9:11** NU *that have come*

Himself without spot to God, [R]cleanse your conscience from [R]dead works to serve the living God? Is. 53:12★ • 1 John 1:7 • Heb. 6:1

15 And for this reason [R]He is the Mediator of the new covenant, by means of death, for the redemption of the transgressions under the first covenant, that [R]those who are called may receive the promise of the eternal inheritance. Rom. 3:25 • Heb. 3:1

16 For where there *is* a testament, there must also of necessity be the death of the testator.

17 For [R]a testament *is* in force after men are dead, since it has no power at all while the testator lives. Gal. 3:15

18 [R]Therefore not even the first *covenant* was dedicated without blood. Ex. 24:6

19 For when Moses had spoken every precept to all the people according to the law, he took the blood of calves and goats, with water, scarlet wool, and hyssop, and sprinkled both the book itself and all the people,

20 saying, *"This is the blood of the covenant which God has commanded you."**

21 Then likewise [R]he sprinkled with blood both the tabernacle and all the vessels of the ministry. Ex. 29:12, 36

22 And according to the law almost all things are purified with blood, and without shedding of blood there is no remission.

23 Therefore *it was* necessary that [R]the copies of the things in the heavens should be [T]purified with these, but the heavenly things themselves with better sacrifices than these. Heb. 8:5 • *cleansed*

24 For Christ has not entered the holy places made with hands, *which are* copies of the true, but into heaven itself, now to appear in the presence of God for us;

25 not that He should offer Himself often, as the high priest enters the Most Holy Place every year with blood of another—

26 He then would have had to suffer often since the foundation of the world; but now, once at the end of the ages, He has appeared to put away sin by the sacrifice of Himself.

27 And as it is appointed for men to die once, but after this the judgment,

28 so [R]Christ was offered once to bear the sins of many. To those who eagerly wait for Him He will appear a second time, apart from sin, for salvation. Is. 53:12; Rom. 6:10★

CHAPTER 10

FOR the law, having a shadow of the good things to come, *and* not the very image of the things, can never with these same sacrifices, which they offer continually year by year, make those who approach perfect.

2 For then would they not have ceased to be offered? For the worshipers, once [T]purified, would have had no more consciousness of sins. *cleansed*

3 But in those *sacrifices there is* a reminder of sins every year.

4 For *it is* not possible that the blood of bulls and goats could take away sins.

5 Therefore, when He came into the world, He said:

"Sacrifice and offering You did not desire,
But a body You have prepared for Me.
6 *In burnt offerings and sacrifices for sin*
You had no pleasure.
7 *Then I said, 'Behold, I have come—*
In the volume of the book it is written of
Me—
*To do Your will, O God.'"**

8 Previously saying, *"Sacrifice and offering, burnt offerings, and offerings for sin You did not desire, nor had pleasure in them"* (which are offered according to the law),

9 then He said, *"Behold, I have come to do Your will, O God."** He takes away the first that He may establish the second.

10 [R]By that will we have been sanctified [R]through the offering of the body of Jesus Christ once *for all.* John 17:19 • [Heb. 9:12]★

11 And every priest stands ministering daily and offering repeatedly the same sacrifices, which can never take away sins.

12 [R]But this Man, after He had offered one sacrifice for sins forever, sat down [R]at the right hand of God, Ps. 68:18; Col. 3:1★ • Ps. 110:1

13 from that time waiting [R]till His enemies are made His footstool. Ps. 110:1★

14 For by one offering He has perfected forever those who are being sanctified.

15 But the Holy Spirit also witnesses to us; for after He had said before,

16 *"This is the covenant that I will make with them after those days, says the* LORD: *I will put My laws into their hearts, and in their minds I will write them,"**

17 *then He adds, "Their sins and their lawless deeds I will remember no more."**

18 Now where there is remission of these, *there is* no longer an offering for sin.

Hold Fast the Confession of Faith

19 Therefore, brethren, having boldness to enter the Holiest by the blood of Jesus,

20 by a new and [R]living way which He consecrated for us, through the veil, that is, His flesh, John 14:6

21 and *having* a [R]High Priest over the house of God, Ps. 110:4★

22 let us [R]draw near with a true heart in full assurance of faith, having our hearts sprinkled from an evil conscience and our bodies washed with pure water. Heb. 7:19

23 Let us hold fast the confession of *our*

9:20 Ex. 24:8 **10:7** Ps. 40:6–8★ **10:9** NU, M omit *O God* **10:16** Jer. 31:33★ **10:17** Jer. 31:34★

hope without wavering, for [R]He who promised *is* faithful. 1 Cor. 1:9; 10:13

24 And let us consider one another in order to stir up love and good works,

25 not forsaking the assembling of ourselves together, as *is* the manner of some, but exhorting *one another,* and so much the more as you see the Day approaching.

Fourth Warning: Danger of Drawing Back

26 For if we sin willfully after we have received the knowledge of the truth, there no longer remains a sacrifice for sins,

27 but a certain fearful expectation of judgment, and [R]fiery indignation which will devour the adversaries. Zeph. 1:18

28 Anyone who has rejected Moses' law dies without mercy on the testimony of two or three [R]witnesses. Deut. 17:2–6; 19:15

29 [R]Of how much worse punishment, do you suppose, will he be thought worthy who has trampled the Son of God underfoot, counted the blood of the covenant by which he was sanctified a common thing, and insulted the Spirit of grace? [Heb. 2:3]

30 For we know Him who said, *"Vengeance is Mine, I will repay,"** says the Lord.* And again, *"The LORD will judge His people."**

31 [R]It is a fearful thing to fall into the hands of the living God. [Luke 12:5]

32 But [R]recall the former days in which, after you were illuminated, you endured a great struggle with sufferings: Gal. 3:4

33 partly while you were made [R]a spectacle both by reproaches and tribulations, and partly while you became companions of those who were so treated; 1 Cor. 4:9

34 for you had compassion on me* [R]in my chains, and [R]joyfully accepted the plundering of your goods, knowing that you have a better and an enduring possession for yourselves in heaven.* 2 Tim. 1:16 • Matt. 5:12

35 Therefore do not cast away your confidence, [R]which has great reward. Matt. 5:12

36 [R]For you have need of endurance, so that after you have done the will of God, you may receive the promise: Luke 21:19

37 *"For [R]yet a little while,* Luke 18:8
And He who is coming will come and*
will not [T]tarry. delay
38 *Now the* just shall live by faith;*
But if anyone draws back,
*My soul has no pleasure in him."**

39 But we are not of those [R]who draw back to perdition, but of those who [R]believe to the saving of the soul. 2 Pet. 2:20 • Acts 16:31

CHAPTER 11

Definition of Faith

NOW faith is the [T]substance of things hoped for, the [T]evidence [R]of things not seen. *realization* • Or *confidence* • Rom. 8:24

2 For by it the elders obtained a *good* testimony.

3 By faith we understand that [R]the worlds were framed by the word of God, so that the things which are seen were not made of things which are visible. Ps. 33:6

Abel

4 By faith [R]Abel offered to God a more excellent sacrifice than Cain, through which he obtained witness that he was righteous, God testifying of his gifts; and through it he being dead still [R]speaks. Gen. 4:3–5 • Heb. 12:24

Enoch

5 By faith Enoch was taken away so that he did not see death, *"and was not found, because God had taken him"*;* for before he was taken he had this testimony, that he pleased God.

6 But without faith *it is* impossible to please *Him,* for he who comes to God must believe that He is, and *that* He is a rewarder of those who diligently seek Him.

Noah

7 By faith [R]Noah, being divinely warned of things not yet seen, moved with godly fear, [R]prepared an ark for the saving of his household, by which he condemned the world and became heir of the righteousness which is according to faith. Gen. 6:13–22 • 1 Pet. 3:20

Abraham and Sarah

8 By faith Abraham obeyed when he was called to go out to the place which he would receive as an inheritance. And he went out, not knowing where he was going.

9 By faith he dwelt in the land of promise as *in* a foreign country, [R]dwelling in tents with

10:30 Deut. 32:35 • NU omits *says the Lord* • Deut. 32:36 **10:34** NU *the prisoners* instead of *me in my chains* • NU omits *in heaven* **10:37** Or *that which* **10:38** NU *My just one* • Hab. 2:3, 4☆ **11:5** Gen. 5:24

10:25 The Reason for Participation in the Local Church—The ultimate reason that we should participate in a local church is because it is specifically commanded by God. Even in NT days there were those who yielded to the temptation of absenting themselves from the worship services of the local church. The writer of Heb. points out that members of a local church have an obligation to one another. They are to provoke one another to good works and to exhort one another to live consistent lives worthy of God. This can best be done within the context of a local church; so believers are commanded not to forsake the assembling of themselves together.

Now turn to Page 1114—Acts 2:42–47: Benefits of Participation in the Local Church.

Isaac and Jacob, the heirs with him of the same promise; Gen. 12:8; 13:3, 18; 18:1, 9

10 for he waited for [R]the city which has foundations, [R]whose builder and maker *is* God. [Heb. 12:22; 13:14] • [Rev. 21:10]

11 By faith Sarah herself also received strength to conceive seed, and she bore a child* when she was past the age, because she judged Him faithful who had promised.

12 Therefore from one man, and him as good as dead, were born *as many* as the stars of the sky in multitude—innumerable as the sand which is by the seashore.

13 These all died in faith, not having received the [R]promises, but having seen them afar off were assured of them,* embraced *them* and confessed that they were strangers and pilgrims on the earth. Gen. 12:7

14 For those who say such things declare plainly that they seek a homeland.

15 And truly if they had called to mind that *country* from which they had come out, they would have had opportunity to return.

16 But now they desire a better, that is, a heavenly *country*. Therefore God is not ashamed [R]to be called their God, for He has prepared a city for them. Ex. 3:6, 15; 4:5

17 By faith Abraham, [R]when he was tested, offered up Isaac, and he who had received the promises offered up his only begotten *son,* James 2:21

18 [T]of whom it was said, *"In Isaac your seed shall be called,"** to

19 concluding that God *was* able to raise *him* up, even from the dead, from which he also received him in a figurative sense.

Isaac

20 By faith [R]Isaac blessed Jacob and Esau concerning things to come. Gen. 27:26–40

Jacob

21 By faith Jacob, when he was dying, blessed each of the sons of Joseph, and worshiped, *leaning* on the top of his staff.

Joseph

22 By faith [R]Joseph, when he was dying, made mention of the departure of the children of Israel, and gave instructions concerning his bones. Gen. 50:24, 25

Moses' Parents

23 By faith [R]Moses, when he was born, was hidden three months by his parents, because they saw *he was* a beautiful child; and they were not afraid of the king's [R]command. Ex. 2:1–3 • Ex. 1:16, 22

Moses

24 By faith [R]Moses, when he became of age, refused to be called the son of Pharaoh's daughter, Ex. 2:11–15

25 choosing rather to suffer affliction with the people of God than to enjoy the [T]passing pleasures of sin, *temporary*

26 esteeming the reproach of Christ greater riches than the treasures in* Egypt; for he looked to the [R]reward. Rom. 8:18

27 By faith [R]he forsook Egypt, not fearing the wrath of the king; for he endured as seeing Him who is invisible. Ex. 10:28

28 By faith [R]he kept the Passover and the sprinkling of blood, lest he who destroyed the firstborn should touch them. Ex. 12:21

29 By faith they passed through the Red Sea as by dry *land, whereas* the Egyptians, attempting *to do* so, were drowned.

Joshua and Rahab

30 By faith the walls of Jericho fell down after they were encircled for seven days.

31 By faith the harlot Rahab did not perish with those who did not believe, when she had received the spies with peace.

Many Other Heroes of Faith

32 And what more shall I say? For the time would fail me to tell of Gideon and Barak and Samson and Jephthah, also *of* David and [R]Samuel and the prophets: 1 Sam. 7:9–14

33 who through faith subdued kingdoms, worked righteousness, obtained promises, [R]stopped the mouths of lions, Dan. 6:22

34 quenched the violence of fire, escaped the edge of the sword, out of weakness were made strong, became valiant in battle, turned to flight the armies of the aliens.

35 [R]Women received their dead raised to life again. Others were [R]tortured, not accepting deliverance, that they might obtain a better resurrection. 1 Kin. 17:22 • Acts 22:25

36 Still others had trial of mockings and scourgings, yes, and [R]of chains and imprisonment. Gen. 39:20

37 [R]They were stoned, they were sawn in two, were tempted,* were slain with the sword. [R]They wandered about [R]in sheepskins and goatskins, being destitute, afflicted, tormented— 1 Kin. 21:13 • 2 Kin. 1:8 • Zech. 13:4

38 of whom the world was not worthy. They wandered in deserts and mountains, [R]*in* dens and caves of the earth. 1 Kin. 18:4, 13

39 And all these, [R]having obtained a good testimony through faith, did not receive the promise, Heb. 11:2, 13

40 God having provided something better for us, that they should not be [R]made perfect apart from us. Heb. 5:9

11:11 NU omits *she bore a child* **11:13** NU, M omit *were assured of them* **11:18** Gen. 21:12★ **11:26** NU, M *of* **11:37** NU omits *were tempted*

CHAPTER 12

Example of Christ's Endurance

THEREFORE we also, since we are surrounded by so great a cloud of witnesses, [R]let us lay aside every weight, and the sin which so easily ensnares *us*, and [R]let us run [R]with endurance the race that is set before us, Col. 3:8 • 1 Cor. 9:24 • Rom. 12:12
2 looking unto Jesus, the author and finisher of *our* faith, who for the joy that was set before Him [R]endured the cross, despising the shame, and has sat down at the right hand of the throne of God. Ps. 68:18; 69:7, 19★
3 [R]For consider Him who endured such hostility from sinners against Himself, [R]lest you become weary and discouraged in your souls. Matt. 10:24 • Gal. 6:9
4 [R]You have not yet resisted to bloodshed, striving against sin. [1 Cor. 10:13]

Exhortation to Endure God's Chastening

5 And you have forgotten the exhortation which speaks to you as to sons:

"My son, do not despise the [T]chastening
of the LORD, discipline
Nor be discouraged when you are
rebuked by Him;
6 *For [R]whom the LORD loves He chastens,*
And scourges every son whom He
*receives."** Rev. 3:19

7 [R]If* you endure chastening, God deals with you as with sons; for what son is there whom a father does not chasten? Deut. 8:5
8 But if you are without chastening, [R]of which all have become partakers, then you are illegitimate and not sons. 1 Pet. 5:9
9 Furthermore, we have had human fathers who corrected *us*, and we paid *them* respect. Shall we not much more readily be in subjection to [R]the Father of spirits and live? [Job 12:10]
10 For they indeed for a few days chastened *us* as seemed *best* to them, but He for *our* profit, [R]that *we* may be partakers of His holiness. Lev. 11:44
11 Now no [T]chastening seems to be joyful for the present, but painful; nevertheless, afterward it yields [R]the peaceable fruit of righteousness to those who have been trained by it. *discipline* • James 3:17, 18
12 Therefore [R]strengthen the hands which hang down, and the feeble knees, Is. 35:3
13 and make straight paths for your feet, so that what is lame may not be *dislocated*, but rather be healed.
14 [R]Pursue peace with all *people*, and holiness, [R]without which no one will see the Lord: Ps. 34:14 • Matt. 5:8
15 looking carefully lest anyone [R]fall short of the grace of God; lest any [R]root of bitterness springing up cause trouble, and by this many become defiled; Heb. 4:1 • Deut. 29:18
16 lest there *be* any fornicator or [T]profane person like Esau, [R]who for one morsel of food sold his birthright. *godless* • Gen. 25:33
17 For you know that afterward, when he wanted to inherit the blessing, he was rejected, for he found no place for repentance, though he sought it diligently with tears.
18 For you have not come to [R]the mountain that* may be touched and that burned with fire, and to blackness and darkness* and tempest, Deut. 4:11; 5:22
19 and the sound of a trumpet and the voice of words, so that those who heard *it* [R]begged that the word should not be spoken to them anymore. Ex. 20:18–26
20 (For they could not endure what was commanded: *"And if so much as a beast touches the mountain, it shall be stoned* or shot with an arrow."**
21 And so terrifying was the sight *that* Moses said, *"I am exceedingly afraid and trembling."**)
22 But you have come to Mount Zion and to the city of the living God, the heavenly Jerusalem, to an innumerable company of angels,
23 to the general assembly and church of the firstborn *who are* registered in heaven, to God [R]the Judge of all, to the spirits of just men made perfect, Ps. 50:6; 94:2
24 to Jesus the Mediator of the new covenant, and to the blood of sprinkling that speaks better things than *that of* Abel.

Fifth Warning: Danger of Refusing God

25 See that you do not refuse Him who speaks. For [R]if they did not escape who refused Him who spoke on earth, much more *shall we not escape* if we turn away from Him who *speaks* from heaven, Heb. 2:2, 3
26 whose voice then shook the earth; but now He has promised, saying, *"Yet once more I shake* not only the earth, but also heaven."**
27 Now this, *"Yet once more,"* indicates the removal of those things that are being shaken, as of things that are made, that the things which cannot be shaken may remain.
28 Therefore, since we are receiving [R]a kingdom which cannot be shaken, let us have grace, by which we may* serve God acceptably with reverence and godly fear. [Dan. 2:44]☆
29 For our God *is* a consuming fire.

12:6 Prov. 3:11, 12 **12:7** NU, M *It is for discipline that you endure; God . . .* **12:18** NU *to that which* • NU *gloom* **12:20** NU, M omit the rest of v. 20. • Ex. 19:12, 13 **12:21** Deut. 9:19 **12:26** NU *will shake* • Hag. 2:6 **12:28** M omits *may*

CHAPTER 13

Love in the Social Realm

LET [R]brotherly love continue. Rom. 12:10

2 [R]Do not forget to entertain strangers, for by so *doing* [R]some have unwittingly entertained angels. Matt. 25:35 • Gen. 18:1–22; 19:1

3 Remember the prisoners as if chained with them—those who are mistreated—since you yourselves are in the body also.

4 [R]Marriage *is* honorable among all, and the bed undefiled; [R]but fornicators and adulterers God will judge. Prov. 5:18, 19 • 1 Cor. 6:9

5 *Let your* conduct *be* without covetousness; *be* content with such things as you have. For He Himself has said, *"I will never leave you nor forsake you."**

6 So we may boldly say:

[R]*"The LORD is my helper;* Ps. 27:1
I will not fear.
*What can man do to me?"**

Love in the Religious Realm

7 Remember those who [T]rule over you, who have spoken the word of God to you, whose faith follow, considering the outcome of *their* conduct. *lead*

8 Jesus Christ *is* [R]the same yesterday, today, and forever. Heb. 1:12

9 Do not be carried about* with various and strange doctrines. For *it is* good that the heart be established by grace, not with foods which have not profited those who have been occupied with them.

10 We have an altar from which those who serve the tabernacle have no right to eat.

11 For the bodies of those animals, whose blood is brought into the sanctuary by the high priest for sin, are burned outside the camp.

12 Therefore Jesus also, that He might [T]sanctify the people with His own blood, suffered outside the gate. *set apart*

13 Therefore let us go forth to Him, outside the camp, bearing [R]His reproach. 1 Pet. 4:14

14 For here we have no continuing city, but we seek the one to come.

15 [R]Therefore by Him let us continually offer [R]the sacrifice of praise to God, that is, [R]the fruit of *our* lips, giving thanks to His name. Eph. 5:20 • Lev. 7:12 • Hos. 14:2

16 [R]But do not forget to do good and to share, for [R]with such sacrifices God is well pleased. Rom. 12:13 • Phil. 4:18

17 Obey those who [T]rule over you, and be submissive, for they watch out for your souls, as those who must give account. Let them do so with joy and not with grief, for that would be unprofitable for you. *lead*

Conclusion

18 [R]Pray for us; for we are confident that we have [R]a good conscience, in all things desiring to live honorably. Eph. 6:19 • Acts 23:1

19 But I especially urge *you* to do this, that I may be restored to you the sooner.

20 Now may the God of peace [R]who brought up our Lord Jesus from the dead, that great Shepherd of the sheep, through the blood of the everlasting covenant, Hos. 6:2★

21 make you complete in every good work to do His will, working in you* what is well pleasing in His sight, through Jesus Christ, to whom *be* glory forever and ever. Amen.

22 And I appeal to you, brethren, bear with the word of exhortation, for I have written to you in few words.

23 Know that *our* brother Timothy has been set free, with whom I shall see you if he comes shortly.

24 Greet all those who rule over you, and all the saints. Those from Italy greet you.

25 Grace *be* with you all. Amen.

13:5 Deut. 31:6, 8; Josh. 1:5 **13:6** Ps. 118:6 **13:9** NU, M *away* **13:21** NU, M *us*

13:15 The Expressions of Worship—Since worship encompasses thought, feeling, and deed, there are many expressions of it. Worship especially includes praise and thanksgiving, which may be expressed privately or publicly, either by grateful declarations (Heb. 13:15) or by joyful singing (Page 599—Ps. 100:2; Page 1208—Eph. 5:19; Page 1221—Col. 3:16). Portions of early Christian hymns of worship actually may be preserved in the NT (Page 1238—1 Tim. 3:16; Page 1244—2 Tim. 2:11–13).

One very important expression of worship for the church is remembering the death of Christ through the Lord's Supper (Page 1175—1 Cor. 11:26). The Lord's Supper was instituted by Christ Himself (Page 1007—Matt. 26:26–28) and judged by Paul not to be taken lightly (Page 1175—1 Cor. 11:28–32).

Since worship means giving something to God, the cheerful giving of money to God's work is certainly an act of worship (Page 1189—2 Cor. 9:7). The giving of one's time to the Lord's work may be considered worship as well. The use of one's spiritual gifts in ministry to the body of Christ constitutes an example of worship as service (Page 1175—1 Cor. 12), as does faithfully occupying a church office (Page 1207—Eph. 4:11; Page 1238—1 Tim. 3:1–13; Page 1249—Titus 1:5–9). Ministry in edifying saints and evangelizing sinners both likewise constitute services of worship.

The single most important act of worship for the Christian is the unqualified presentation of self to God as an obedient servant. This dedication involves the body and the mind (Page 1158—Rom. 12:1, 2): the body because it contains the tools by which the will of God is carried out; the mind because it coordinates the actions to be executed by the body. When these are gladly devoted to God, they become instruments by which He effects His will on the earth. Such faithful and joyous service makes one's entire life a performance of worship.

Now turn to Page 439—2 Chr. 7:3: The Reasons for Worship.

THE EPISTLE OF

JAMES

THE BOOK OF JAMES

Faith without works cannot be called faith. Faith without works is dead, and a dead faith is worse than no faith at all. Faith must work; it must produce; it must be visible. Verbal faith is not enough; mental faith is insufficient. Faith must be there, but it must be more. It must inspire action. Throughout his epistle to Jewish believers, James integrates true faith and everyday practical experience by stressing that true faith must manifest itself in works of faith.

Faith endures trials. Trials come and go, but a strong faith will face them head-on and develop endurance. Faith understands temptations. It will not allow us to consent to our lust and slide into sin. Faith obeys the Word. It will not merely hear and not do. Faith produces doers. Faith harbors no prejudice. For James, faith and favoritism cannot coexist. Faith displays itself in works. Faith is more than mere words; it is more than knowledge; it is demonstrated by obedience; and it overtly responds to the promises of God. Faith controls the tongue. This small but immensely powerful part of the body must be held in check. Faith can do it. Faith acts wisely. It gives us the ability to choose wisdom that is heavenly and to shun wisdom that is earthly. Faith produces separation from the world and submission to God. It provides us with the ability to resist the devil and humbly draw near to God. Finally, faith waits patiently for the coming of the Lord. Through trouble and trial it stifles complaining.

The name *Iakobos* (James) in 1:1 is the basis for the early title *Iakobou Epistole,* "Epistle of James." *Iakobos* is the Greek form of the Hebrew name "Jacob," a Jewish name common in the first century.

THE AUTHOR OF JAMES

Four men are named James in the New Testament: (1) James, the father of Judas (not Iscariot), is mentioned twice (Luke 6:16; Acts 1:13) as the father of one of the twelve disciples, but is otherwise completely unknown. (2) James, the son of Alphaeus (Matt. 10:3; Mark 3:18; Luke 6:15; Acts 1:13), elsewhere called James the Less (Mark 15:40), was one of the twelve disciples. Apart from being listed with the other disciples, this James is completely obscure, and it is doubtful that he is the authoritative figure behind the epistle. Some attempts have been made to identify this James with the Lord's brother (Gal. 1:19), but this view is difficult to reconcile with the gospel accounts. (3) James, the son of Zebedee and brother of John (Matt. 4:21; 10:2; 17:1; Mark 3:17; 10:35; 13:3; Luke 9:54; Acts 1:13), was one of Jesus' intimate disciples, but his martyrdom by A.D.44 (Acts 12:2) makes it very unlikely that he wrote this epistle. (4) James, the Lord's brother (Matt. 13:55; Mark 6:3; Gal. 1:19), was one of the "pillars" in the church in Jerusalem (Acts 12:17; 15:13–21; 21:18; Gal. 2:9, 12). Tradition points to this prominent figure as the author of the epistle, and this best fits the evidence of Scripture. There are several clear parallels between the language of the letter drafted under his leadership in Acts 15:23–29 and the epistle of James (e.g., the unusual word *chairein,* "greeting," is found only in Acts 15:23; 23:26; and James 1:1). The Jewish character of this epistle with its stress upon the law, along with the evident influence by the Sermon on the Mount (e.g., 4:11, 12; 5:12), complement what we know about James "the Just" from Scripture and early tradition.

It has been argued that the Greek of this epistle is too sophisticated for a Galilean such as James, but this assumes that he never had the opportunity or aptitude to develop proficiency in Koine ("common") Greek. As a prominent church leader, it would have been to his advantage to become fluent in the universal language of the Roman Empire.

For various reasons, some assert that James was a stepbrother of Jesus by a previous marriage of Joseph, or that the "brothers" of Jesus mentioned in Matthew 13:55 and Mark 6:3 were really His cousins. However, the most natural understanding of the gospel accounts is that James was the half-brother of Jesus, being the offspring of Joseph and Mary after the birth of Jesus (Matt. 1:24, 25). He apparently did not accept the claims of Jesus until the Lord appeared to him after His resurrection (1 Cor. 15:7). He and his brothers were among the believers who awaited the coming of the Holy Spirit on the Day of Pentecost (Acts 1:14). It was not long before he became an acknowledged leader of the Jerusalem church (Acts 12:17; Gal. 2:9, 12), and he was a central figure in the Jerusalem Council in Acts 15. Even after Paul's third missionary journey, James continued to observe the Mosaic Law as a testimony to other Jews (Acts 21:18–25). Early tradition stresses his Jewish piety and his role in bringing others to an understanding of Jesus as the Messiah. He suffered a violent martyr's death not long before the fall of Jerusalem.

The brevity and limited doctrinal emphasis of James kept it from wide circulation; and by the time it became known in the church as a whole, there was uncertainty about the identity of the James in 1:1. Growing recognition that it was written by the Lord's brother led to its acceptance as a canonical book.

THE TIME OF JAMES

James is addressed "to the twelve tribes which are scattered abroad" (1:1), and it is apparent from verses like 1:19 and 2:1, 7 that this greeting refers to Hebrew Christians outside of Palestine. Their place of meeting is called a "synagogue" in the Greek text of 2:2, and the whole epistle reflects Jewish thought and expressions (e.g., 2:19, 21; 4:11, 12; 5:4, 12). There are no references to slavery or idolatry, and this also fits an originally Jewish readership.

These Jewish believers were beset with problems that were testing their faith, and James was concerned that they were succumbing to impatience, bitterness, materialism, disunity, and spiritual apathy. As a resident of Jerusalem and a leader of the church, James no doubt had frequent contact with Jewish Christians from a number of Roman provinces. He therefore felt a responsibility to exhort and encourage them in their struggles of faith.

According to Josephus, James was martyred in A.D. 62 (Hegesippus, quoted in Eusebius, fixed the date of James's death at A.D. 66). Those who accept him as the author of this epistle have proposed a date of writing ranging from A.D. 45 to the end of his life. However, several factors indicate that this letter may have been the earliest writing of the New Testament (C. A.D. 46–49): (1) There is no mention of Gentile Christians or their relationship to Jewish Christians as would be expected in a later epistle. (2) Apart from references to the Person of Christ, there is practically no distinctive theology in James, suggesting an early date when Christianity was viewed in terms of Messianic Judaism. (3) The allusions to the teachings of Christ have such little verbal agreement with the synoptic Gospels that they probably preceded them. (4) James uses the word "synagogue" ("assembly," 2:2) in addition to "church" and indicates a very simple organization of elders and masters, that is, teachers (3:1; 5:14), which was patterned after the early synagogue. (5) James does not mention the issues involved in the Acts 15 Council in Jerusalem (A.D. 49).

THE CHRIST OF JAMES

In 1:1 and 2:1 James refers to the "Lord Jesus Christ," and in 5:7, 8 he anticipates "the coming of the Lord." Compared to other New Testament writers, James says little about Christ, and yet his speech is virtually saturated with allusions to the teaching of Christ. The Sermon on the Mount is especially prominent in James's thinking (there are about fifteen indirect references; e.g., James 1:2 and Matt. 5:10–12; James 1:4 and Matt. 5:48; James 2:13 and Matt. 6:14, 15; James 4:11 and Matt. 7:1, 2; James 5:2 and Matt. 6:19). This epistle portrays Christ in the context of early Messianic Judaism.

KEYS TO JAMES

Key Word: Faith That Works—Throughout his epistle, James develops the theme of the characteristics of true faith. He effectively uses these characteristics as a series of tests to help his readers evaluate the quality of their relationship to Christ. The purpose of this work is not doctrinal or apologetic but practical. James seeks to challenge these believers to examine the quality of their daily lives in terms of attitudes and actions. A genuine faith will produce real changes in a person's conduct and character, and the absence of change is a symptom of a dead faith.

FOCUS	TEST OF FAITH		CHARACTERISTICS OF FAITH	TRIUMPH OF FAITH		
REFERENCE	1:1—	1:13—	1:19—	5:7—	5:13—	5:19—5:20
DIVISION	PURPOSE OF TESTS	SOURCE OF TEMPTATION	OUTWARD DEMONSTRATION OF INNER FAITH	ENDURES WAITING	PRAYS FOR AFFLICTED	CONFRONTS SIN
TOPIC	DEVELOPMENT OF FAITH		WORKS OF FAITH	POWER OF FAITH		
	RESPONSE OF FAITH		REALITY OF FAITH	REASSURANCE OF FAITH		
LOCATION	PROBABLY JERUSALEM					
TIME	C. A.D. 46–49					

Key Verses: James 1:19–22 and 2:14–17— "So then, my beloved brethren, let every man be swift to hear, slow to speak, slow to wrath; for the wrath of man does not produce the righteousness of God. Therefore lay aside all filthiness and overflow of wickedness, and receive with meekness the implanted word, which is able to save your souls. But be doers of the word, and not hearers only, deceiving yourselves" (1:19–22).

"What *does it* profit, my brethren, if someone says he has faith but does not have works? Can faith save him? If a brother or sister is naked and destitute of daily food, and one of you says to them, 'Depart in peace, be warmed and filled,' but you do not give them the things which are needed for the body, what *does it* profit? Thus also faith by itself, if it does not have works, is dead" (2:14–17).

Key Chapter: James 1— One of the most difficult areas of the Christian life is that of testings and temptations. James reveals our correct response to both: to testings, count them all joy; to temptations, realize that God is not their source.

SURVEY OF JAMES

James is the Proverbs of the New Testament because it is written in the terse moralistic style of Wisdom Literature. It is evident that James was profoundly influenced by the Old Testament (especially by its Wisdom Literature) and by the Sermon on the Mount. But James's impassioned preaching against inequity and social injustice also earns him the title of the Amos of the New Testament. Because of the many subjects in this epistle, it is difficult to outline; suggestions have ranged from no connection between the various topics to a unified scheme. The outline used here is: the test of faith (1:1–18); the characteristics of faith (1:19—5:6); and the triumph of faith (5:7–20).

The Test of Faith (1:1–18): The first part of this epistle develops the qualities of genuine faith in regard to trials and temptations. After a one-verse salutation to geographically dispersed Hebrew Christians (1:1), James quickly introduces his first subject, outward tests of faith (1:2–12). These trials are designed to produce mature endurance and a sense of dependence upon God, to whom the believer turns for wisdom and enablement. Inward temptations (1:13–18) do not come from the One who bestows "every good gift" (1:17). These solicitations to evil must be checked at an early stage or they may result in disastrous consequences.

The Characteristics of Faith (1:19—5:6): A righteous response to testing requires that one be "swift to hear, slow to speak, slow to wrath" (1:19), and this broadly summarizes the remainder of the epistle. Quickness of hearing involves an obedient response to God's Word (1:19–27). True hearing means more than mere listening; the Word must be received and applied. After stating this principle (1:21, 22), James develops it with an illustration (1:23–25) and an application (1:26, 27). A genuine faith should produce a change in attitude from partiality to the rich to a love for the poor as well as the rich (2:1–13). True faith should also result in actions (2:14–26). In Romans 4, Paul used the example of Abraham to show that justification is by faith, not by works. But James says that Abraham was justified by works (2:21). In spite of the apparent contradiction, Romans 4 and James 2 are really two sides of the same coin. In context, Paul is writing about justification before God while James writes of the evidence of justification before men. A faith that produces no change is not saving faith.

Moving from works to words, James shows how a living faith controls the tongue ("slow to speak," 1:19). The tongue is small, but it has the power to accomplish great good or equally great evil. Only the power of God applied by an active faith can tame the tongue (3:1–12). Just as there are wicked and righteous uses of the tongue, so there are demonic and divine manifestations of wisdom (3:13–18). James contrasts seven characteristics of human wisdom with seven qualities of divine wisdom.

The strong pulls of worldliness (4:1–12) and wealth (4:13—5:6) create conflicts that are harmful to the growth of faith. The world system is at enmity with God; and the pursuit of its pleasures produces covetousness, envy, fighting, and arrogance (4:1–6). The believer's only alternative is submission to God out of a humble and repentant spirit. This will produce a transformed attitude toward others as well (4:7–12). This spirit of submission and humility should be applied to any attempts to accrue wealth (4:13–17), especially because wealth can lead to pride, injustice, and selfishness (5:1–6).

The Triumph of Faith (5:7–20): James encourages his readers to patiently endure the sufferings of the present life in view of the future prospect of the coming of the Lord (5:7–12). Believers may be oppressed by the rich or by other circumstances; but as the example of Job teaches, they can be sure that God has a gracious purpose in His dealings with them. James concludes his epistle with some practical words on prayer and restoration (5:13–20). The prayers of righteous men (e.g., elders in local churches) are efficacious for the healing and restoration of believers. When sin is not dealt with, it can contribute to illness and even death.

OUTLINE OF JAMES

I. The Test of Faith..1:1–18

- A. The Purpose of Tests 1:1–12
- B. The Source of Temptations 1:13–18

II. The Characteristics of Faith.............1:19—5:6

- A. Faith Obeys the Word...........................1:19–27
- B. Faith Removes Discrimination 2:1–13
- C. Faith Proves Itself by Works................2:14–26
- D. Faith Controls the Tongue 3:1–12
- E. Faith Produces Wisdom.........................3:13–18
- F. Faith Produces Humility...........................4:1–12
- G. Faith Produces Dependence on God 4:13—5:6

III. The Triumph of Faith.................................5:7–20

- A. Faith Endures Awaiting Christ's Return 5:7–12
- B. Faith Prays for the Afflicted 5:13–18
- C. Faith Confronts the Erring Brother..5:19, 20

CHAPTER 1

The Purpose of Tests

JAMES, [R]a bondservant of God and of the
Lord Jesus Christ, Acts 12:17

To the twelve tribes which are scattered
abroad:

Greetings.

2 My brethren, [R]count it all joy [R]when you
fall into various trials, Acts 5:41 • 1 Pet. 1:6
3 [R]knowing that the testing of your faith
produces patience. Rom. 5:3–5
4 But let patience have *its* perfect work,
that you may be [T]perfect and complete, lack-
ing nothing. *mature*
5 If any of you lacks wisdom, let him ask of
God, who gives to all liberally and without re-
proach, and it will be given to him.
6 But let him ask in faith, with no doubting,
for he who doubts is like a wave of the sea
driven and tossed by the wind.
7 For let not that man suppose that he will
receive anything from the Lord;
8 *he is* [R]a double-minded man, unstable in
all his ways. James 4:8
9 Let the lowly brother glory in his exalta-
tion,
10 but the rich in his humiliation, because as
a flower of the field he will pass away.
11 For no sooner has the sun risen with a
burning heat than it withers the grass; its
flower falls, and its beautiful appearance per-
ishes. So the rich man also will fade away in
his pursuits.
12 Blessed *is* the man who endures tempta-
tion; for when he has been approved, he will
receive the crown of life which the Lord has
promised to those who love Him.

The Source of Temptations

13 Let no one say when he is tempted, "I am
tempted by God"; for God cannot be tempted
by evil, nor does He Himself tempt anyone.
14 But each one is tempted when he is drawn
away by his own desires and enticed.
15 Then, [R]when desire has conceived, it
gives birth to sin; and sin, when it is full-
grown, brings forth death. Job 15:35
16 Do not be deceived, my beloved brethren.
17 Every good gift and every perfect gift is
from above, and comes down from the Father
of lights, [R]with whom there is no variation or
shadow of turning. Num. 23:19
18 [R]Of His own will He brought us forth by
the word of truth, that we might be a kind of
firstfruits of His creatures. John 1:13

Faith Obeys the Word

19 So then,* my beloved brethren, let every
man be swift to hear, slow to speak, [R]slow to
wrath; Prov. 14:17; 16:32
20 for the wrath of man does not produce the
righteousness of God.
21 Therefore [R]lay aside all filthiness and
overflow of wickedness, and receive with
meekness the implanted word, [R]which is able
to save your souls. Col. 3:8 • Acts 13:26
22 But [R]be doers of the word, and not hear-
ers only, deceiving yourselves. Matt. 7:21–28
23 For [R]if anyone is a hearer of the word and
not a doer, he is like a man observing his nat-
ural face in a mirror; Luke 6:47
24 for he observes himself, goes away, and
immediately forgets what kind of man he was.
25 But he who looks into the perfect law of
liberty and continues *in it*, and is not a forget-
ful hearer but a doer of the work, this one will
be blessed in what he does.
26 If anyone among you* thinks he is reli-
gious, and [R]does not bridle his tongue but de-
ceives his own heart, this one's religion *is*
useless. Ps. 34:13
27 Pure and undefiled religion before God
and the Father is this: [R]to visit orphans and
widows in their trouble, *and* to keep oneself
unspotted from the world. Is. 1:17

1:19 NU *Know this* or *This you know* **1:26** NU omits *among you*

CHAPTER 2

Faith Removes Discrimination

MY brethren, do not hold the faith of our Lord Jesus Christ, [R]*the Lord* of glory, with [R]partiality. 1 Cor. 2:8 • Lev. 19:15

2 For if there should come into your assembly a man with gold rings, in [T]fine apparel, and there should also come in a poor man in [T]filthy clothes, *bright* • *vile*

3 and you [T]pay attention to the one wearing the fine clothes and say to him, "You sit here in a good place," and say to the poor man, "You stand there," or, "Sit here at my footstool," Lit. *look upon*

4 have you not [T]shown partiality among yourselves, and become judges with evil thoughts? *differentiated*

5 Listen, my beloved brethren: Has God not chosen the poor of this world *to be* rich in faith and heirs of the kingdom [R]which He promised to those who love Him? Ex. 20:6

6 But [R]you have dishonored the poor man. Do not the rich oppress you [R]and drag you into the courts? 1 Cor. 11:22 • Acts 13:50

7 Do they not blaspheme that noble name by which you are [R]called? 1 Pet. 4:16

8 If you really fulfill *the* royal law according to the Scripture, *"You shall love your neighbor as yourself,"** you do well;

9 but if you [T]show partiality, you commit sin, and are convicted by the law as [R]transgressors. Lit. *receive the face* • Deut. 1:17

10 For whoever shall keep the whole law, and yet [R]stumble in one *point*, [R]he is guilty of all. Gal. 3:10 • Deut. 27:26

11 For He who said, *"Do not commit adultery,"** also said, *"Do not murder."** Now if you do not commit adultery, but you do murder, you have become a transgressor of the law.

12 So speak and so do as those who will be judged by [R]the law of liberty. James 1:25

13 For [R]judgment is without mercy to the one who has shown [R]no mercy. Mercy triumphs over judgment. Job 22:6 • Prov. 21:13

Faith Proves Itself by Works

14 [R]What *does it* profit, my brethren, if someone says he has faith but does not have works? Can faith save him? Matt. 21:28–32

15 [R]If a brother or sister is naked and destitute of daily food, Luke 3:11

16 and one of you says to them, "Depart in peace, be warmed and filled," but you do not give them the things which are needed for the body, what *does it* profit?

17 Thus also faith by itself, if it does not have works, is dead.

18 But someone will say, "You have faith, and I have works." [R]Show me your faith without your* works, and I will show you my faith by my* works. Heb. 6:10

19 You believe that there is one God. You do well. Even the demons believe—and tremble!

20 But do you want to know, O foolish man, that faith without works is dead?*

21 Was not Abraham our father justified by works [R]when he offered Isaac his son on the altar? Gen. 22:9, 10, 12, 16–18

22 Do you see [R]that faith was working together with his works, and by [R]works faith was made perfect? Heb. 11:17 • John 8:39

23 And the Scripture was fulfilled which says, *"Abraham believed God, and it was accounted to him for righteousness."** And he was called [R]the friend of God. 2 Chr. 20:7

24 You see then that a man is justified by works, and not by faith only.

25 Likewise, was not Rahab the harlot also justified by works when she received the messengers and sent *them* out another way?

26 For as the body without the spirit is dead, so faith without works is dead also.

CHAPTER 3

Faith Controls the Tongue

MY brethren, [R]let not many of you become teachers, knowing that we shall receive a stricter judgment. [Matt. 23:8]

2 For [R]we all stumble in many things. [R]If anyone does not stumble in word, [R]he *is* a perfect man, able also to bridle the whole body. 1 Kin. 8:46 • Ps. 34:13 • [Matt. 12:34–37]

3 Indeed,* [R]we put bits in horses' mouths that they may obey us, and we turn their whole body. Ps. 32:9

4 Look also at ships: although they are so large and are driven by fierce winds, they are turned by a very small rudder wherever the pilot desires.

5 Even so [R]the tongue is a little member and boasts great things. See how great a forest a little fire kindles! Prov. 12:18; 15:2

6 And [R]the tongue *is* a fire, a world of iniquity. The tongue is so set among our members that it [R]defiles the whole body, and sets on fire the course of nature; and it is set on fire by hell. Prov. 16:27 • [Matt. 12:36; 15:11, 18]

7 For every kind of beast and bird, of reptile and creature of the sea, is tamed and has been tamed by mankind.

8 But no man can tame the tongue. *It is* an unruly evil, full of deadly poison.

9 With it we bless our God and Father, and with it we curse men, who have been made [R]in the similitude of God. Gen. 1:26

10 Out of the same mouth proceed blessing and cursing. My brethren, these things ought not to be so.

2:8 Lev. 19:18 **2:11** Ex. 20:14; Deut. 5:18 • Ex. 20:13; Deut. 5:17 **2:18** NU omits *your* • NU omits *my* **2:20** NU *useless* **2:23** Gen. 15:6 **3:3** NU *Now if*

11 Does a spring send forth fresh *water* and
bitter from the same opening?
12 Can a fig tree, my brethren, bear olives, or
a grapevine bear figs? Thus no spring yields
both salt water and fresh.*

Faith Produces Wisdom

13 Who *is* wise and understanding among
you? Let him show by good conduct *that* his
works *are done* in the meekness of wisdom.
14 But if you have [R]bitter envy and self-
seeking in your hearts, [R]do not boast and lie
against the truth. Rom. 13:13 • Rom. 2:17
15 This wisdom does not descend from
above, but *is* earthly, sensual, demonic.
16 For where envy and self-seeking *exist*,
confusion and every evil thing *are* there.
17 But the wisdom that is from above is first
pure, then peaceable, gentle, willing to yield,
full of mercy and good fruits, without partial-
ity and without hypocrisy.
18 Now the fruit of righteousness is sown in
peace by those who make peace.

CHAPTER 4

Faith Produces Humility

WHERE do [T]wars and fights *come* from
among you? Do *they* not *come* from
your *desires for* pleasure [R]that war in your
members? *battles* • Rom. 7:23
2 You lust and do not have. You murder
and covet and cannot obtain. You fight and
[T]war. Yet* you do not have because you do
not ask. *battle*
3 [R]You ask and do not receive, [R]because
you ask amiss, that you may spend *it* on your
pleasures. Job 27:8, 9 • [Ps. 66:18]
4 Adulterers and* adulteresses! Do you not
know that [R]friendship with the world is en-
mity with God? [R]Whoever therefore wants to
be a friend of the world makes himself an
enemy of God. 1 John 2:15 • Gal. 1:4
5 Or do you think that the Scripture says in
vain, [R]"The Spirit who dwells in us yearns
jealously"? Gen. 6:5
6 But He gives more grace. Therefore He
says:

"God resists the proud,
*But gives grace to the humble."**

7 Therefore submit to God. [R]Resist the devil
and he will flee from you. [Eph. 4:27]
8 [R]Draw near to God and He will draw
near to you. [R]Cleanse *your* hands, *you* sin-
ners; and [R]purify *your* hearts, *you* double-
minded. 2 Chr. 15:2 • Is. 1:16 • 1 Pet. 1:22
9 [R]Lament and mourn and weep! Let your
laughter be turned to mourning and *your* joy
to gloom. Matt. 5:4
10 [R]Humble yourselves in the sight of the
Lord, and He will lift you up. Job 22:29

11 [R]Do not speak evil of one another,
brethren. He who speaks evil of a brother
[R]and judges his brother, speaks evil of the
law and judges the law. But if you judge the
law, you are not a doer of the law but a
judge. 1 Pet. 2:1–3 • [Matt. 7:1–5]
12 There is one Lawgiver,* [R]who is able to
save and to destroy. [R]Who* are you to judge
another?* [Matt. 10:28] • Rom. 14:4

Faith Produces Dependence on God

13 Come now, you who say, "Today or to-
morrow we will* go to such and such a city,
spend a year there, buy and sell, and make a
profit";
14 whereas you do not know what *will hap-
pen* tomorrow. For what *is* your life? [R]It is even
a vapor that appears for a little time and then
vanishes away. Job 7:7
15 Instead you *ought* to say, "If the Lord
wills, we shall live and do this or that."
16 But now you boast in your arrogance. [R]All
such boasting is evil. 1 Cor. 5:6
17 Therefore, to him who knows to do good
and does not do *it*, to him it is sin.

CHAPTER 5

COME now, *you* [R]rich, weep and howl for
your miseries that are coming upon
you! [Luke 6:24]
2 Your riches are corrupted, and [R]your gar-
ments are moth-eaten. Job 13:28
3 Your gold and silver are corroded, and
their corrosion will be a witness against you
and will eat your flesh like fire. You have
heaped up treasure in the last days.
4 Indeed [R]the wages of the laborers who
mowed your fields, which you kept back by
fraud, cry out; and [R]the cries of the reap-
ers have reached the ears of the Lord of
Sabaoth.* Lev. 19:13 • Deut. 24:15
5 You have lived on the earth in pleasure
and [T]luxury; you have fattened your hearts
as* in a day of slaughter. *indulgence*
6 You have condemned, you have murdered
the just; he does not resist you.

Faith Endures Awaiting Christ's Return

7 Therefore be patient, brethren, until the
coming of the Lord. See *how* the farmer waits
for the precious fruit of the earth, waiting pa-
tiently for it until it receives the early and lat-
ter rain.
8 You also be patient. Establish your
hearts, for the coming of the Lord [T]is at
hand. *has drawn near*
9 Do not [T]grumble against one another,

3:12 NU *Neither can a salty spring produce fresh water.* **4:2** NU, M omit *Yet* **4:4** NU omits *Adulterers and* **4:6** Prov. 3:34 **4:12** NU adds *and Judge* • NU, M *But who* • NU *a neighbor* **4:13** M *let us* **5:4** Lit., in Heb., *Hosts* **5:5** NU omits *as*

brethren, lest you be condemned.* Behold, the
Judge is standing at the door! Lit. *groan*
10 [R]My brethren, take the prophets, who
spoke in the name of the Lord, as an example
of suffering and patience. Matt. 5:12
11 Indeed [R]we count them blessed who en-
dure. You have heard of [R]the perseverance of
Job and seen the end *intended by* the Lord—
that the Lord is very compassionate and mer-
ciful. [Ps. 94:12] • Job 1:21, 22; 2:10
12 But above all, my brethren, [R]do not
swear, either by heaven or by earth or with
any other oath. But let your "Yes" be "Yes,"
and *your* "No," "No," lest you fall into judg-
ment.* Matt. 5:34–37

Faith Prays for the Afflicted

13 Is anyone among you suffering? Let him
[R]pray. Is anyone cheerful? [R]Let him sing
psalms. Ps. 50:14, 15 • Eph. 5:19
14 Is anyone among you sick? Let him call
for the elders of the church, and let them pray
over him, [R]anointing him with oil in the name
of the Lord. Mark 6:13; 16:18
15 And the prayer of faith will save the sick,
and the Lord will raise him up. And if he has
committed sins, he will be forgiven.
16 Confess *your* trespasses* to one another,
and pray for one another, that you may be
healed. [R]The effective, fervent prayer of a
righteous man avails much. Num. 11:2
17 Elijah was a man with a nature like ours,
and [R]he prayed earnestly that it would not
rain; and it did not rain on the land for three
years and six months. 1 Kin. 17:1; 18:1
18 And he prayed again, and the heaven
gave rain, and the earth produced its fruit.

Faith Confronts the Erring Brother

19 Brethren, if anyone among you wanders
from the truth, and someone [R]turns him
back, Gal. 6:1
20 let him know that he who turns a sinner
from the error of his way will save a soul*
from death and cover a multitude of sins.

5:9 NU, M *judged* **5:12** M *hypocrisy* **5:16** NU *Therefore confess your sins* **5:20** NU *his soul*

THE FIRST EPISTLE OF

PETER

THE BOOK OF 1 PETER

Persecution can cause either growth or bitterness in the Christian life. Response determines the result. In writing to Jewish believers struggling in the midst of persecution, Peter encourages them to conduct themselves courageously for the Person and program of Christ. Both their character and conduct must be above reproach. Having been born again to a living hope, they are to imitate the Holy One who has called them. The fruit of that character will be conduct rooted in submission: citizens to government, servants to masters, wives to husbands, husbands to wives, and Christians to one another. Only after submission is fully understood does Peter deal with the difficult area of suffering. The Christians are not to think it "strange concerning the fiery trial which is to try you, as though some strange thing happened to you" (4:12), but are to rejoice as partakers of the suffering of Christ. That response to life is truly the climax of one's submission to the good hand of God.

This epistle begins with the phrase *Petros apostolos Iesou Christou,* "Peter, an apostle of Jesus Christ." This is the basis of the early title *Petrou A,* the "First of Peter."

THE AUTHOR OF 1 PETER

The early church universally acknowledged the authenticity and authority of 1 Peter. The internal evidence supports this consistent external testimony in several ways. The apostle Peter's name is given in 1:1, and there are definite similarities between certain phrases in this letter and Peter's sermons as recorded in the Book of Acts (cf. 1 Pet. 1:20 and Acts 2:23; 1 Pet. 4:5 and Acts 10:42). Twice in Acts Peter used the Greek word *xylon,* "wood, tree," to speak of the cross, and this distinctive use is also found in 1 Peter (see Acts 5:30, 10:39; 1 Pet. 2:24). The epistle contains a number of allusions to events in the life of Christ that held special significance for Peter (e.g., 2:23; 3:18; 4:1; 5:1; cf. 5:5 and John 13:4).

Nevertheless, critics since the nineteenth century have challenged the authenticity of 1 Peter on several grounds. Some claim that 1:1, 2 and 4:12—5:14 were later additions that turned an anonymous address or a baptismal sermon into a Petrine epistle. Others argue that the sufferings experienced by readers of this letter must refer to the persecution of Christians that took place after the time of Peter in the reigns of the emperors Domitian (A.D. 81–96) and Trajan (A.D. 98–117). There is no basis for the first argument, and the second argument falsely assumes that Christians were not being reviled for their faith during the life of Peter. Another challenge asserts that the quality of the Greek of this epistle is too high for a Galilean like Peter. But Galileans were bilingual (Aramaic and Greek), and writers such as Matthew and James were skillful in their use of Greek. It is also likely that Peter used Silvanus as his scribe (5:12; Paul calls him Silvanus in 2 Cor. 1:19; 1 Thess. 1:1; 2 Thess. 1:1; Luke calls him Silas in Acts 15:40—18:5), and Silvanus may have smoothed out Peter's speech in the process.

THE TIME OF 1 PETER

This letter is addressed "to the strangers scattered," or more literally, "pilgrims of the Dispersion" (1:1). This, coupled with the injunction to keep their behavior "honorable among the Gentiles" (2:12), gives the initial appearance that the bulk of the readers are Hebrew Christians. A closer look, however, forms the opposite view that most of these believers were Gentiles. They were called "out of darkness" (2:9), and they "once *were* not a people but *are* now the people of God" (2:10). Their former "aimless conduct *received* by tradition from [their] fathers" was characterized by ignorance and futility (1:14, 18; cf. Eph. 4:17). Because they no longer engage in debauchery and idolatry, they are maligned by their countrymen (4:3, 4). These descriptions do not fit a predominantly Hebrew Christian readership. Though Peter was an apostle "to the circumcised" (Gal. 2:8), he also ministered to Gentiles (Acts 10:34–48; Gal. 2:12), and a letter like this would not be beyond the scope of his ministry.

This epistle was addressed to Christians throughout Asia Minor, indicating the spread of the gospel in regions not evangelized when Acts was written (Pontus, Cappadocia, Bithynia; 1:1). It is possible that Peter visited and ministered in some of these areas, but there is no evidence. He wrote this letter in response to the news of growing opposition to the believers in Asia Minor (1:6; 3:13–17; 4:12–19; 5:9, 10). Hostility and suspicion were mounting against Christians in the empire, and they were being reviled and abused for their lifestyles and subversive talk about another kingdom. Christianity had not yet received the official Roman ban, but the stage was being set for the persecution and martyrdom of the near future.

Peter's life was dramatically changed after the

Resurrection, and he occupied a central role in the early church and in the spread of the gospel to the Samaritans and Gentiles (Acts 2—10). After the Jerusalem Council in Acts 15, little is recorded of Peter's activities. He evidently traveled extensively with his wife (1 Cor. 9:5) and ministered in various Roman provinces. According to tradition, Peter was crucified upside down in Rome prior to Nero's death in A.D. 68.

This epistle was written from Babylon (5:13), but scholars are divided as to whether this refers literally to Babylon in Mesopotamia or symbolically to Rome. There is no tradition that Peter went to Babylon, and in his day it had few inhabitants. On the other hand, tradition consistently indicates that Peter spent the last years of his life in Rome. As a center of idolatry, the term "Babylon" was an appropriate figurative designation for Rome (cf. the later use of "Babylon" in Rev. 17; 18). Peter used other figurative expressions in this epistle, and it is not surprising that he would do the same with Rome. His mention of Mark (5:13) also fits this view because Mark was in Rome during Paul's first imprisonment (Col. 4:10). This epistle was probably written shortly before the outbreak of persecution under Nero in A.D. 64.

THE CHRIST OF 1 PETER

This epistle presents Christ as the believer's example and hope in time of suffering in a spiritually hostile world. He is the basis for the Christian's "living hope" and "inheritance" (1:3, 4), and the love relationship available with Him by faith is a source of inexpressible joy (1:8). His suffering and death provide redemption for all who trust in Him: "who Himself bore our sins in His own body on the tree, that we, having died to sins, might live for righteousness—by whose stripes you were healed" (2:24; cf. 1:18, 19; 3:18). Christ is the Chief Shepherd and Overseer of believers (2:25; 5:4); and when He appears, those who know Him will be glorified.

KEYS TO 1 PETER

Key Word: Suffering for the Cause of Christ—The basic theme of 1 Peter is the proper response to Christian suffering. Knowing that his readers will be facing more persecution than ever before, Peter writes this letter to give them a divine perspective on these trials so that they will be able to endure them without wavering in their faith. They should not be surprised at their ordeal because the One they follow also suffered and died (2:21; 3:18; 4;1, 12–14). Rather, they should count it a privilege to share the sufferings of Christ. Peter therefore exhorts them to be sure that their hardships are not being caused by their own wrongdoings, but for their Christian testimony. They are not the only believers who are suffering (5:9), and they must recognize that God brings these things into the lives of His children, not as a punishment but as a stimulus to "perfect" them in Christ (5:10). Peter wants to overcome the attitudes of bitterness and anxiety, replacing them with dependence on and confidence in God.

Another theme is stated in 5:12: "I have written to you briefly, exhorting and testifying that this is the true grace of God." In this epistle Peter frequently speaks of the believer's position in Christ and future hope, and he does so to remind his readers that they are merely sojourners on this planet: their true destiny is eternal glory "when His glory is revealed" (4:13). The grace of God in their salvation (1:1—2:10) shall give them an attitude of submission (2:11—3:12) in the context of suffering for the name of Christ (3:13—5:14).

Key Verses: 1 Peter 1:10–12 and 4:12, 13—"Of this salvation the prophets have inquired and searched carefully, who prophesied of the grace *that would come* to you, searching what, or what manner of time, the Spirit of Christ who was in

FOCUS	SALVATION OF THE BELIEVER		SUBMISSION OF THE BELIEVER	SUFFERING OF THE BELIEVER			
REFERENCE	1:1——1:13——	——2:13——		——3:13——	——3:18——	——4:7——	——5:1——5:14
DIVISION	SALVATION OF THE BELIEVER	SANCTIFICATION OF THE BELIEVER	GOVERNMENT BUSINESS, MARRIAGE, AND ALL OF LIFE	CONDUCT IN SUFFERING	CHRIST'S EXAMPLE OF SUFFERING	COMMANDS IN SUFFERING	MINISTER IN SUFFERING
TOPIC	BELIEF OF CHRISTIANS		BEHAVIOR OF CHRISTIANS	BUFFETING OF CHRISTIANS			
	HOLINESS		HARMONY	HUMILITY			
LOCATION	EITHER ROME OR BABYLON						
TIME	C. A.D. 63–64						

them was indicating when He testified beforehand the sufferings of Christ and the glories that would follow. To them it was revealed that, not to themselves, but to us they were ministering the things which now have been reported to you through those who have preached the gospel to you by the Holy Spirit sent from heaven—things which angels desire to look into" (1:10–12).

"Beloved, do not think it strange concerning the fiery trial which is to try you, as though some strange thing happened to you; but rejoice to the extent that you partake of Christ's sufferings, that when His glory is revealed, you may also be glad with exceeding joy" (4:12, 13).

Key Chapter: 1 Peter 4—Central in the New Testament revelation concerning how to handle persecution and suffering caused by one's Christian testimony is 1 Peter 4. Not only is Christ's suffering to be our model (4:1, 2), but also we are to rejoice in that we can share in His suffering (4:12–14).

SURVEY OF 1 PETER

Peter addresses this epistle to "pilgrims" in a world that is growing increasingly hostile to Christians. These believers are beginning to suffer because of their stand for Christ, and Peter uses this letter to give them counsel and comfort by stressing the reality of their living hope in the Lord. By standing firm in the grace of God (5:12) they will be able to endure their "fiery trial" (4:12), knowing that there is a divine purpose behind their pain. This letter logically proceeds through the themes of the salvation of the believer (1:1—2:12); the submission of the believer (2:13—3:12); and the suffering of the believer (3:13—5:14).

The Salvation of the Believer (1:1—2:12): Addressing his letter to believers in several Roman provinces, Peter briefly describes the saving work of the triune Godhead in his salutation (1:1, 2). He then extols God for the riches of this salvation by looking in three temporal directions (1:3–12). First, Peter anticipates the future realization of the Christian's manifold inheritance (1:3–5). Second, he looks at the present joy that this living hope produces in spite of various trials (1:6–9). Third, he reflects upon the prophets of the past who predicted the gospel of God's grace in Christ (1:10–12).

The proper response to this salvation is the pursuit of sanctification or holiness (1:13—2:10). This involves a purifying departure from conformity with the world to godliness in behavior and love. With this in mind, Peter exhorts his readers to "desire the pure milk of the word, that [they] may grow" (2:2) by applying "the word of God which lives and abides forever" (1:23) and acting as a holy priesthood of believers.

The Submission of the Believer (2:13—3:12): Peter turns to the believer's relationships in the world and appeals for an attitude of submission as the Christlike way to harmony and true freedom. Submission for the Lord's sake to those in governmental (2:13–17) and social (2:18–20) authority will foster a good testimony to outsiders. Before moving on to submission in marital relationships (3:1–7), Peter again picks up the theme of Christian suffering (mentioned in 1:6, 7 and 2:12, 18–20) and uses Christ as the supreme model: He suffered sinlessly, silently, and as a substitute for the salvation of others (2:21–25; cf. Is. 52:13—53:12). Peter summarizes his appeal for Christlike submission and humility in 3:8–12.

The Suffering of the Believer (3:13—5:14): Anticipating that growing opposition to Christianity will require a number of his readers to defend their faith and conduct, Peter encourages them to be ready to do so in an intelligent and gracious way (3:13–16). Three times he tells them that if they must suffer, it should be for righteousness' sake and not as a result of sinful behavior (3:17; see 2:20; 4:15, 16). The end of this chapter (3:18–22) is an extremely difficult passage to interpret, and several options have been offered. Verses 19 and 20 may mean that Christ, during the period between His death and resurrection, addressed demonic spirits or the spirits of those who were alive before the Flood. Another interpretation is that Christ preached through Noah to his pre-Flood contemporaries.

As believers in Christ, the readers are no longer to pursue the lusts of the flesh as they did formerly, but rather the will of God (4:1–6). In view of the hardships that they may suffer, Peter exhorts them to be strong in their mutual love and to exercise their spiritual gifts in the power of God so that they will be built up (4:7–11). They should not be surprised when they are slandered and reviled for their faith because God has a purpose in all things, and the time of judgment will come when His name and all who trust in Him will be vindicated (4:12–19). They must therefore "commit their souls *to Him* in doing good" (4:19).

In a special word to the elders of the churches in these Roman provinces, Peter urges them to be diligent but gentle shepherds over the flocks that have been divinely placed under their care (5:1–4). The readers as a whole are told to clothe themselves with humility toward one another and toward God who will exalt them at the proper time (5:5–7). They are to resist the Adversary in the sure knowledge that their calling to God's eternal glory in Christ will be realized (5:8–11). Peter ends his epistle by stating his theme ("the true grace of God") and conveying greetings and a benediction (5:12–14).

OUTLINE OF 1 PETER

CHAPTER 1

Salutation

PETER, an apostle of Jesus Christ,

To the pilgrims [R]of the Dispersion in
Pontus, Galatia, Cappadocia, Asia, and Bithy-
nia, James 1:1
2 elect [R]according to the foreknowledge of
God the Father, in sanctification of the Spirit,
for obedience and [R]sprinkling of the blood of
Jesus Christ: [Rom. 8:29] • Is. 52:15★

Grace to you and peace be multiplied.

Hope for the Future

3 [R]Blessed *be* the God and Father of our
Lord Jesus Christ, who [R]according to His
abundant mercy has begotten us again to a
living hope through the resurrection of Jesus
Christ from the dead, Eph. 1:3 • Gal. 6:16
4 to an inheritance [T]incorruptible and
undefiled and that does not fade away, [R]re-
served in heaven for you, *imperishable* • Col. 1:5

Trials for the Present

5 [R]who are kept by the power of God
through faith for salvation ready to be re-
vealed in the last time. John 10:28
6 [R]In this you greatly rejoice, though now
for a little while, if need be, you have been
grieved by various trials, Matt. 5:12
7 that [R]the genuineness of your faith, *being*
much more precious than gold that perishes,
though [R]it is tested by fire, may be found to
praise, honor, and glory at the revelation of
Jesus Christ, James 1:3 • Job 23:10
8 [R]whom having not seen* you love.
[R]Though now you do not see *Him,* yet believ-
ing, you rejoice with joy inexpressible and full
of glory, 1 John 4:20 • John 20:29
9 receiving the end of your faith—the sal-
vation of *your* souls.

Anticipation in the Past

10 Of this salvation the prophets have in-
quired and searched carefully, who prophe-
sied of the grace *that would come* to you,
11 searching what, or what manner of time,
[R]the Spirit of Christ who was in them was in-
dicating when He testified beforehand the
sufferings of Christ and the glories that would
follow. 2 Pet. 1:21
12 To them it was revealed that, not to
themselves, but to us* they were ministering
the things which now have been reported to
you through those who have preached the
gospel to you by the Holy Spirit sent from
heaven—things which [R]angels desire to look
into. Eph. 3:10

"Be Holy"

13 Therefore gird up the loins of your mind,
be sober, and rest *your* hope fully upon the
grace that is to be brought to you at the reve-
lation of Jesus Christ;

1:8 M *known* **1:12** NU, M *you*

14 as obedient children, not [R]conforming
yourselves to the former lusts, *as* in your ig-
norance; [Rom. 12:2]
15 [R]but as He who called you *is* holy, you
also be holy in all *your* conduct, [2 Cor. 7:1]
16 because it is written, *"Be holy, for I am*
*holy."**
17 And if you call on the Father, who [R]with-
out partiality judges according to each one's
work, conduct yourselves throughout the time
of your stay *here* in fear; Acts 10:34
18 knowing that you were not [R]redeemed
with [T]corruptible things, *like* silver or gold,
from your aimless conduct *received* by tradi-
tion from your fathers, Is. 52:3★ • *perishable*
19 but [R]with the precious blood of Christ,
[R]as of a lamb without blemish and without
spot. Acts 20:28 • Ex. 12:5; Is. 53:7★
20 [R]He indeed was foreordained before the
foundation of the world, but was manifest in
these last times for you Rom. 3:25
21 who through Him believe in God, [R]who
raised Him from the dead and [R]gave Him
glory, so that your faith and hope are in
God. Acts 2:24 • Acts 2:33

"Love One Another"

22 Since you [R]have purified your souls in
obeying the truth through the Spirit* in sin-
cere love of the brethren, love one another
fervently with a pure heart, Acts 15:9
23 [R]having been born again, not of [T]cor-
ruptible seed but incorruptible, [R]through the
word of God which lives and abides for-
ever,* John 1:13 • *perishable* • James 1:18
24 because

> *"All flesh is as grass,*
> *And all the glory of man* as the flower*
> *of the grass.*
> *The grass withers,*
> *And its flower falls away,*

25 *But the* [T]*word of the* LORD *endures*
*forever."** *spoken word*

[R]Now this is the word which by the gospel
was preached to you. [John 1:1]

CHAPTER 2

"Desire the Pure Milk of the Word"

THEREFORE, [R]laying aside all malice, all
deceit, hypocrisy, envy, and all evil speak-
ing, Heb. 12:1
2 [R]as newborn babes, desire the pure
[R]milk of the word, that you may grow
thereby,* [Matt. 18:3; 19:14] • 1 Cor. 3:2
3 if indeed you have [R]tasted that the Lord *is*
gracious. Heb. 6:5

"Offer Up Spiritual Sacrifices"

4 Coming to Him *as to* a living stone, [R]re-
jected indeed by men, but chosen by God *and*
precious, Ps. 118:22
5 you also, as living stones, are being built
up a spiritual house, a holy priesthood, to
offer up spiritual sacrifices acceptable to God
through Jesus Christ.
6 Therefore it is also contained in the Scrip-
ture,

> *"Behold, I lay in Zion*
> *A chief cornerstone, elect, precious,*
> *And he who believes on Him will by no*
> *means be put to shame."**

7 Therefore, to you who believe, *He is* pre-
cious; but to those who are disobedient,*

> *"The stone which the builders rejected*
> *Has become the chief cornerstone,"**

8 and

> *"A stone of stumbling*
> *And a rock of offense."**

They stumble, being disobedient to the word,
to which they also were appointed.
9 But you *are* a chosen generation, a royal
priesthood, a holy nation, His own special
people, that you may proclaim the praises of
Him who called you out of [R]darkness into His
marvelous light; [Acts 26:18]
10 who once *were* not a people but *are* now
the people of God, who had not obtained
mercy but now have obtained mercy.

"Abstain from Fleshly Lusts"

11 Beloved, I beg *you* as sojourners and pil-
grims, abstain from fleshly lusts [R]which war
against the soul, James 4:1
12 [R]having your conduct honorable among
the Gentiles, that when they speak against
you as evildoers, [R]they may, by *your* good
works which they observe, glorify God in the
day of visitation. Phil. 2:15 • Matt. 5:16; 9:8

Submission to the Government

13 Therefore submit yourselves to every or-
dinance of man for the Lord's sake, whether
to the king as supreme,

1:16 Lev. 11:44, 45; 19:2; 20:7 **1:22** NU omits *through the Spirit* **1:23** NU omits *forever* **1:24** NU *all its glory* **1:25** Is. 40:6–8 **2:2** NU adds *up to salvation* **2:6** Is. 28:16★ **2:7** NU *to those who disbelieve* • Ps. 118:22 **2:8** Is. 8:14★

2:13 Our Responsibility to Human Government—It is impossible for a believer to be a good Christian and a bad citizen at the same time. As children of God our responsibility to human government is threefold.

14 or to governors, as to those who are sent by him for the punishment of evildoers and *for the* praise of those who do good.
15 For this is the will of God, that by doing good you may put to silence the ignorance of foolish men—
16 as free, yet not using liberty as a cloak for vice, but as bondservants of God.
17 Honor all *people.* Love the brotherhood. Fear [R]God. Honor the king. Prov. 24:21

Submission in Business

18 [R]Servants, *be* submissive to *your* masters with all fear, not only to the good and gentle, but also to the harsh. Eph. 6:5–8
19 For this *is* [R]commendable, if because of conscience toward God one endures grief, suffering wrongfully. Matt. 5:10
20 For what credit *is it* if, when you are beaten for your faults, you take it patiently? But when you do good and suffer, if you take it patiently, this *is* commendable before God.
21 For to this you were called, because Christ also suffered for us,* leaving us* an example, that you should follow His steps:

22 "*Who committed no sin,*
Nor was deceit found in His mouth";*

23 [R]who, when He was reviled, did not revile in return; when He suffered, He did not threaten, but [R]committed *Himself* to Him who judges righteously; Is. 53:7★ • Luke 23:46
24 who Himself bore our sins in His own body on the tree, that we, having died to sins, might live for righteousness—[R]by whose stripes you were healed. Is. 53:5
25 For you were like sheep going astray, but have now returned [R]to the Shepherd and Overseer* of your souls. [Ezek. 34:23]; Zech. 13:7★

CHAPTER 3

Submission in Marriage

WIVES, likewise, *be* submissive to your own husbands, that even if some do not obey the word, they, without a word, may be won by the conduct of their wives,
2 [R]when they observe your chaste conduct *accompanied* by fear. 1 Pet. 2:12; 3:6
3 [R]Do not let your adornment be *merely* outward—arranging the hair, wearing gold, or putting on *fine* apparel— 1 Tim. 2:9
4 rather *let it be* [R]the hidden person of the heart, with the incorruptible *beauty* of a gentle and quiet spirit, which is very precious in the sight of God. Rom. 2:29
5 For in this manner, in former times, the holy women who trusted in God also adorned themselves, being submissive to their own husbands,
6 as Sarah obeyed Abraham, calling him lord, whose daughters you are if you do good and are not afraid with any terror.

7 [R]Husbands, likewise, dwell with *them* with understanding, giving honor to the wife,

2:21 NU *you* • NU, M *you* **2:22** Is. 53:9★ **2:25** Gr. *Episkopos*

a. We are to recognize and accept that the powers that be are ordained by God. "Let every soul be subject to the governing authorities. For there is no authority except from God, and the authorities that exist are appointed by God" (Page 1159—Rom. 13:1). This truth applies even to atheistic human governments unless, of course, the law is anti-scriptural. In that situation the believer must obey God rather than humans (Page 1116—Acts 4:18–20). In fact, when Paul wrote those words in Rom. 13:1, the evil emperor Nero was on the throne. See also Titus 3:1.
b. We are to pay our taxes to human government (see Page 996—Matt. 17:24–27; 22:21; Page 1160—Rom. 13:7).
c. We are to pray for the leaders in human government. "Therefore I exhort first of all that supplications, prayers, intercessions, *and* giving of thanks be made for all men, for kings and all who are in authority, that we may lead a quiet and peaceable life in all godliness and reverence. For this *is* good and acceptable in the sight of God our Savior" (Page 1237—1 Tim. 2:1–3).

Paul exhorts us to pray for those who are in authority that we may lead a quiet life. We are to pray that they hold their offices in godliness and honesty (Page 1237—1 Tim. 2:1–3).

Now turn to Page 910—Amos 3:2: Selection of Israel.

3:1–6 The Role of the Wife—This passage describes "subjection" to her husband as a fundamental responsibility of the married woman. (Other roles for women are covered in such passages as Page 657—Prov. 31:10–31 and Page 1250—Titus 2:3–5.) The wife is to submit to the authority of her husband, not to men in general. This does not mean the wife is by nature inferior to the husband. In marriage two people become one through the joining of their intellects, their emotions, and their wills. To keep their special union from fracturing and destroying itself, one member is charged to lead and one to submit.

The wife's submission to her husband is her "adorning," which makes her truly beautiful (3:3). This inner beauty is of great value in God's sight (3:4). The believing women of the OT who hoped to be the human channel for the Messiah to come into the world made themselves beautiful by being in subjection to their own husbands. This is supremely illustrated in the relationship between Sarah and Abraham. Wives are exhorted to do what Sarah did, to be in subjection to their husbands, letting the consequences rest with God, and thus become Sarah's daughters (3:6). For the wife who will do this God promises that, if her husband is either an unbeliever or out of fellowship with God, her subjection can be the very means God will use to bring her husband into a proper relationship with God (3:1, 2). The wife's subjection may lead to the husband's salvation.

Now turn to Page 1222—Col. 3:19: The Role of the Husband.

as to the weaker vessel, and as *being* heirs together of the grace of life, that your prayers may not be hindered. [Eph. 5:25]

8 Finally, all *of you be* of one mind, having compassion for one another; love as brothers, *be* tenderhearted, *be* courteous;*

Submission in All of Life

9 [R]not returning evil for evil or reviling for reviling, but on the contrary blessing, knowing that you were called to this, that you may inherit a blessing. [Prov. 17:13]

10 For

"He who would love life
And see good days,
Let him refrain his tongue from evil,
And his lips from speaking deceit.
11 *Let him* [R]*turn away from evil and do good;* Ps. 37:27
Let him seek peace and pursue it.
12 *For the eyes of the* LORD *are on the righteous,*
[R]*And His ears are open to their prayers;*
But the face of the LORD *is against those who do evil."** John 9:31

Conduct in Suffering

13 And who *is* he who will harm you if you become followers of what is good?

14 [R]But even if you should suffer for righteousness' sake, *you are* blessed. *"And do not be afraid of their threats, nor be troubled."** James 1:12

15 But [T]sanctify the Lord God* in your hearts, and always [R]*be* ready to *give* a defense to everyone who asks you a reason for the [R]hope that is in you, with meekness and fear; *set apart* • Ps. 119:46 • [Titus 3:7]

16 [R]having a good conscience, that when they defame you as evildoers, those who revile your good conduct in Christ may be ashamed. Heb. 13:18

17 For *it is* better, if it is the will of God, to suffer for doing good than for doing evil.

Christ's Example of Suffering

18 For Christ also suffered once for sins, the just for the unjust, that He might bring us* to God, being put to death in the flesh but made alive by the Spirit,

19 by whom also He went and preached to the spirits in prison,

20 who formerly were disobedient, when once the Divine longsuffering waited* in the days of Noah, while *the* ark was being prepared, in which a few, that is, eight souls, were saved through water.

21 [R]There is also an antitype which now saves us—baptism [R](not the removal of the filth of the flesh, but the answer of a good conscience toward God), through the resurrection of Jesus Christ, Eph. 5:26 • [Titus 3:5]

22 who has gone into heaven and [R]is at the right hand of God, [R]angels and authorities and powers having been made subject to Him. Ps. 110:1 • Rom. 8:38

CHAPTER 4

THEREFORE, since Christ suffered for us* in the flesh, arm yourselves also with the same mind, for he who has suffered in the flesh has ceased from sin,

2 that he no longer should live the rest of *his* time in the flesh for the lusts of men, [R]but for the will of God. John 1:13

3 For we *have spent* enough of our past lifetime* in doing the will of the Gentiles—when we walked in lewdness, lusts, drunkenness, revelries, drinking parties, and abominable idolatries.

4 In regard to these, they think it strange that you do not run with *them* in the same flood of dissipation, speaking evil of *you.*

5 They will give an account to Him who is ready to judge the living and the dead.

6 For this reason [R]the gospel was preached also to those who are dead, that they might be judged according to men in the flesh, but [R]live according to God in the spirit. 1 Pet. 1:12; 3:19 • [Rom. 8:9, 13]

3:8 NU *humble* **3:12** Ps. 34:12–16 **3:14** Is. 8:12 **3:15** NU *Christ as Lord* **3:18** NU, M *you* **3:20** NU, M *when the longsuffering of God waited patiently* **4:1** NU omits *for us* **4:3** NU *time*

3:17 Kinds of Suffering—There are three basic kinds of suffering, all of which can bring about much pain and discomfort to the believer.

a. Physical suffering. This, of course, occurs when a part of our body is injured or begins to malfunction, resulting in a disharmony between it and the rest of the body. Several factors can be involved in physical suffering. It can be caused by an accident or by carelessness (Page 309—2 Sam. 4:4). It can be due to birth deformities (Page 1092—John 9:1). It can result from internal disorders (Page 1053—Luke 8:43). Finally, physical suffering may actually be caused by Satan (Page 513—Job 2:7; Page 1061—Luke 13:16).
b. Mental suffering. In many ways this suffering is even more intense than physical suffering. Justified or unjustified concern over some matter can easily produce mental anguish. Paul himself experienced "fear, and much trembling" and "anguish of heart" (Page 1168—1 Cor. 2:3; Page 1184—2 Cor. 1:8; 2:4, 13; 7:5).
c. Spiritual suffering. Spiritual suffering can come from the world (Page 1294—1 John 2:15–17), the flesh (Page 1154—Rom. 7:18–24), or the devil. Often it is the latter. See Acts 13:8–11; 16:16–18; 1 Thess. 2:18.

Now turn to Page 513—Job 2:7: Purposes of Suffering.

Commands in Suffering

7 But [R]the end of all things is at hand;
therefore be serious and watchful in your
prayers. Rom. 13:11
8 And above all things have fervent love for
one another, for *"love will cover a multitude*
*of sins."**
9 [R]Be hospitable to one another [R]without
grumbling. Heb. 13:2 • 2 Cor. 9:7
10 [R]As each one has received a gift, minister
it to one another, as good stewards of the
manifold grace of God. Rom. 12:6–8
11 [R]If anyone speaks, *let him speak* as the
oracles of God. If anyone ministers, *let him*
do it as with the ability which God supplies,
that [R]in all things God may be glorified
through Jesus Christ, to whom belong the
glory and the [T]dominion forever and ever.
Amen. Eph. 4:29 • [1 Cor. 10:31] • *sovereignty*
12 Beloved, do not think it strange concern-
ing the fiery trial which is to try you, as
though some strange thing happened to you;
13 but rejoice [R]to the extent that you partake
of Christ's sufferings, that [R]when His glory is
revealed, you may also be glad with exceed-
ing joy. James 1:2 • 2 Tim. 2:12
14 If you are reproached for the name of
Christ, [R]blessed *are you,* for the Spirit of glory
and of God rests upon you.* On their part He
is blasphemed, [R]but on your part He is glori-
fied. Matt. 5:11 • Matt. 5:16
15 But let none of you suffer as a murderer,
a thief, an evildoer, or as a [T]busybody in other
people's matters. *meddler*
16 Yet if *anyone suffers* as a Christian, let
him not be ashamed, but let him glorify God
in this matter.*
17 For the time *has come* for judgment to
begin at the house of God; and if *it begins*
with us first, what will *be* the end of those
who do not obey the gospel of God?
18 Now

"If the righteous one is scarcely saved,
Where will the ungodly and the sinner
*appear?"**

19 Therefore let those who suffer according
to the will of God commit their souls *to Him*
in doing good, as to a faithful Creator.

CHAPTER 5

Elders, Shepherd the Flock

THE elders who are among you I exhort, I
who am a fellow elder and a witness of the
sufferings of Christ, and also a partaker of the
glory that will be revealed:
2 [R]Shepherd the flock of God which is
among you, serving as overseers, [R]not by
compulsion but willingly,* not for dishonest
gain but eagerly; Acts 20:28 • 1 Cor. 9:17
3 nor as [R]being [T]lords over [R]those en-
trusted to you, but [R]being examples to the
flock; Ezek. 34:4 • *masters* • Ps. 33:12 • Phil. 3:17
4 and when [R]the Chief Shepherd appears,
you will receive [R]the crown of glory that does
not fade away. Heb. 13:20 • 2 Tim. 4:8

Saints, Humble Yourselves

5 Likewise you younger people, submit
yourselves to *your* elders. Yes, [R]all of *you* be
submissive to one another, and be clothed
with humility, for Eph. 5:21

"God resists the proud,
*But gives grace to the humble."**

6 Therefore humble yourselves under the
mighty hand of God, that He may exalt you in
due time,
7 casting all your care upon Him, for He
cares for you.
8 Be sober, be vigilant; because* your ad-
versary the devil walks about like a roaring
lion, seeking whom he may devour.
9 Resist him, steadfast in the faith, knowing
that the same sufferings are experienced by
your brotherhood in the world.

Benediction

10 But may* the God of all grace, who called
us* to His eternal glory by Christ Jesus, after
you have suffered a while, perfect, establish,
strengthen, and settle *you.*
11 [R]To Him *be* the glory and the dominion
forever and ever. Amen. Rev. 1:6
12 By Silvanus, our faithful brother as I con-
sider him, I have written to you briefly, ex-
horting and testifying that this is the true
grace of God in which you stand.
13 She who is in Babylon, elect together
with *you,* greets you; and *so does* [R]Mark my
son. Acts 12:12, 25; 15:37, 39
14 Greet one another with a kiss of love.
Peace to you all who are in Christ Jesus.
Amen.

4:8 Prov. 10:12 **4:14** NU omits the rest of v. 14.
4:16 NU *name* **4:18** Prov. 11:31 **5:2** NU adds
according to God **5:5** Prov. 3:34 **5:8** NU, M omit
because **5:10** NU *But the God of all grace . . . will*
perfect, establish, strengthen, and settle you. • NU, M *you*

THE SECOND EPISTLE OF

PETER

THE BOOK OF 2 PETER

First Peter deals with problems from the outside; 2 Peter deals with problems from the inside. Peter writes to warn the believers about the false teachers who are peddling damaging doctrine. He begins by urging them to keep close watch on their personal lives. The Christian life demands diligence in pursuing moral excellence, knowledge, self-control, perseverance, godliness, brotherly kindness, and selfless love. By contrast, the false teachers are sensual, arrogant, greedy, and covetous. They scoff at the thought of future judgment and live their lives as if the present would be the pattern for the future. Peter reminds them that although God may be longsuffering in sending judgment, ultimately it will come. In view of that fact, believers should live lives of godliness, blamelessness, and steadfastness.

The statement of authorship in 1:1 is very clear: "Simon Peter, a bondservant and apostle of Jesus Christ." To distinguish this epistle from the first by Peter it was given the Greek title *Petrou B,* "Second of Peter."

THE AUTHOR OF 2 PETER

No other book in the New Testament poses as many problems of authenticity as does 2 Peter. Unlike 1 Peter, this letter has very weak external testimony, and its genuineness is hurt by internal difficulties as well. Because of these obstacles, many scholars reject the Petrine authorship of this epistle, but this does not mean that there is no case for the opposite position.

External Evidence: The external testimony for the Petrine authorship of 2 Peter is weaker than that for any other New Testament book, but by the fourth century it became generally recognized as an authentic work of the apostle Peter. There are no undisputed second-century quotations from 2 Peter, but in the third century it is quoted in the writings of several church fathers, notably Origen and Clement of Alexandria. Third-century writers were generally aware of 2 Peter and respected its contents, but it was still cataloged as a disputed book. The fourth century saw the official acknowledgment of the authority of 2 Peter in spite of some lingering doubts. For several reasons 2 Peter was not quickly accepted as a canonical book: (1) Slow circulation kept it from being widely known. (2) Its brevity and contents greatly limited the number of quotations from it in the writings of early church leaders. (3) The delay in recognition meant that 2 Peter had to compete with several later works that falsely claimed to be Petrine (e.g., the Apocalypse of Peter). (4) Stylistic differences between 1 and 2 Peter also raised doubts.

Internal Evidence: On the positive side, 2 Peter bears abundant testimony to its apostolic origin. It claims to be by "Simon Peter" (1:1), and 3:1 says "Beloved, I now write to you this second epistle." The writer refers to the Lord's prediction about the apostle's death in 1:14 (cf. John 21:18, 19) and says he was an eyewitness of the Transfiguration (1:16–18). As an apostle (1:1), he places himself on an equal level with Paul (3:15). There are also distinctive words that are found in 2 Peter and in Peter's sermons in Acts, as well as unusual words and phrases shared by 1 and 2 Peter.

On the negative side, a number of troublesome areas challenge the traditional position: (1) There are differences between the style and vocabulary of 1 and 2 Peter. The Greek of 2 Peter is rough and awkward compared to that of 1 Peter, and there are also differences in informality and in the use of the Old Testament. But these differences are often exaggerated, and they can be explained by Peter's use of Silvanus as his secretary for 1 Peter and his own hand for 2 Peter. (2) It is argued that 2 Peter used a passage from Jude to describe false teachers and that Jude was written after Peter's death. However, this is a debated issue, and it is possible that Jude quoted from Peter or that both used a common source (see "The Author of Jude"). (3) The reference to a collection of Paul's letters (3:15, 16) implies a late date for this epistle. But it is not necessary to conclude that all of Paul's letters were in mind here. Peter's contact with Paul and his associates no doubt made him familiar with several Pauline Epistles. (4) Some scholars claim that the false teaching mentioned in 2 Peter was a form of Gnosticism that emerged after Peter's day, but there is insufficient evidence to support this stand.

The alternative to Petrine authorship is a later forgery done in the name of Peter. Even the claim that 2 Peter was written by a disciple of Peter cannot overcome the problem of misrepresentation. In addition 2 Peter is clearly superior to any pseudonymous writings. In spite of the external and internal problems, the traditional position of Petrine authorship overcomes more difficulties than any other option.

THE TIME OF 2 PETER

Most scholars regard 3:1 ("Beloved, I now write to you this second epistle") as a reference to 1 Peter. If this is so, Peter had the same readers of Asia Minor in mind (see "The Time of 1 Peter"), although the more general salutation in 1:1 would also allow for a wider audience. Peter wrote this epistle in response to the spread of heretical teachings which were all the more insidious because they emerged from within the churches. These false teachers perverted the doctrine of justification and promoted a rebellious and immoral way of life.

This epistle was written just before the apostle's death (1:14), probably from Rome. His martyrdom took place between A.D. 64 and 66 (if Peter were alive in A.D. 67 when Paul wrote 2 Timothy during his second Roman imprisonment, it is likely that Paul would have mentioned him).

THE CHRIST OF 2 PETER

Apart from the first verse of his epistle, Peter employs the title "Lord" every time he names the Savior. The Lord Jesus Christ is the source of full knowledge and power for the attainment of spiritual maturity (1:2, 3, 8; 3:18). Peter recalls the glory of Jesus' transfiguration on the holy mountain and anticipates His *parousia,* "coming," when the whole world, not just three men on a mountain, will behold His glory.

KEYS TO 2 PETER

Key Word: Guard Against False Teachers—The basic theme that runs through 2 Peter is the contrast between the knowledge and practice of truth versus falsehood. This epistle is written to expose the dangerous and seductive work of false teachers, and to warn believers to be on their guard so that they will not be "led away with the error of the wicked" (3:17). It is also written to exhort the readers to "grow in the grace and knowledge of our Lord and Savior Jesus Christ" (3:18), because this growth into Christian maturity is the best defense against spiritual counterfeits. This letter serves to remind its readers of the foundational elements in the Christian life from which they must not waver (1:12, 13; 3:1, 2). This includes the certainty of the Lord's return in power and judgment.

Key Verses: 2 Peter 1:20, 21 and 3:9–11—"Knowing this first, that no prophecy of Scripture is of any private interpretation, for prophecy never came by the will of man, but holy men of God spoke *as they were* moved by the Holy Spirit" (1:20, 21).

"The Lord is not slack concerning *His* promise, as some count slackness, but is longsuffering toward us, not willing that any should perish but that all should come to repentance. But the day of the Lord will come as a thief in the night, in which the heavens will pass away with a great noise, and the elements will melt with fervent heat; both the earth and the works that are in it will be burned up. Therefore, since all these things will be dissolved, what manner *of persons* ought you to be in holy conduct and godliness" (3:9–11).

Key Chapter: 2 Peter 1—The Scripture clearest in defining the relationship between God and man on the issue of inspiration is contained in 1:19–21. Three distinct principles surface: (1) that the interpretation of Scriptures is not limited to a favored elect but is open for all who "rightly [divide] the word of truth" (2 Tim. 2:15); (2) that the divinely inspired prophet did not initiate the Scripture himself; and (3) that the Holy Spirit (not the emotion or circumstances of the moment) moved holy men.

SURVEY OF 2 PETER

Peter wrote his first epistle to encourage his readers to respond properly to external opposition. His second epistle focuses on

FOCUS	CULTIVATION OF CHRISTIAN CHARACTER		CONDEMNATION OF FALSE TEACHERS			CONFIDENCE IN CHRIST'S RETURN	
REFERENCE	1:1———1:15———2:1———2:4———2:10———3:1———3:8———3:18						
DIVISION	GROWTH IN CHRIST	GROUNDS OF BELIEF	DANGER	DESTRUCTION	DESCRIPTION	MOCKERY IN THE LAST DAYS	DAY OF THE LORD
TOPIC	TRUE PROPHECY		FALSE PROPHETS			PROPHECY: DAY OF THE LORD	
	HOLINESS		HERESY			HOPE	
LOCATION	PROBABLY ROME						
TIME	C. A.D. 64–66						

internal opposition caused by false teachers whose "destructive heresies" (2:1) can seduce believers into error and immorality. While 1 Peter speaks of the new birth through the living Word, 1 Peter stresses the need for growth in the grace and knowledge of Christ. The best antidote for error is a mature understanding of the truth. Second Peter divides into three parts: cultivation of Christian character (1); condemnation of false teachers (2); and confidence of Christ's return (3).

Cultivation of Christian Character (1): Peter's salutation (1:1, 2) is an introduction to the major theme of chapter 1, that is, the true knowledge of Jesus Christ. The readers are reminded of the "great and precious promises" that are theirs because of their calling to faith in Christ (1:3, 4). They have been called away from the corruption of the world to conformity with Christ, and Peter urges them to progress by forging a chain of eight Christian virtues from faith to love (1:5–7). If a believer does not transform profession into practice, he becomes spiritually useless, perverting the purpose for which he was called (1:8–11).

This letter was written not long before Peter's death (1:14) to remind believers of the riches of their position in Christ and their responsibility to hold fast to the truth (1:12–21). Peter knew that his departure from this earth was imminent, and he left this letter as a written legacy. As an eyewitness of the life of Christ (he illustrates this with a portrait of the Transfiguration in 1:16–18), Peter affirms the authority and reliability of the prophetic word. The clearest biblical description of the divine-human process of inspiration is found in 1:21: "but holy men of God spoke *as they were* moved by the Holy Spirit."

Condemnation of False Teachers (2): Peter's discussion of true prophecy leads him to an extended denunciation of false prophecy in the churches. These false teachers were especially dangerous because they arose within the church and undermined the confidence of believers (2:1–3). Peter's extended description of the characteristics of these false teachers (2:10–22) exposes the futility and corruption of their strategies. Their teachings and lifestyles reek of arrogance and selfishness, but their crafty words are capable of enticing immature believers.

Confidence of Christ's Return (3): Again Peter states that this letter is designed to stir up the minds of his readers "by way of reminder" (3:1; cf. 1:13). This very timely chapter is designed to remind them of the certain truth of the imminent *parousia* (this Greek word, used in 3:4, 12, refers to the second coming or advent of Christ) and to refute those mockers who will deny this doctrine in the last days. These scoffers will claim that God does not powerfully intervene in world affairs, but Peter calls attention to two past and one future divinely induced catastrophic events: the Creation, the Flood, and the dissolution of the present heavens and earth (3:1–7). It may appear that the promise of Christ's return will not be fulfilled, but this is untrue for two reasons: God's perspective on the passing of time is quite unlike that of men, and the apparent delay in the *parousia* is due to His patience in waiting for more individuals to come to a knowledge of Christ (3:8, 9). Nevertheless, the day of consummation will come, and all the matter of this universe will evidently be transformed into energy from which God will fashion a new cosmos (3:10–13).

In light of this coming day of the Lord, Peter exhorts his readers to live lives of holiness, steadfastness, and growth (3:14–18). He mentions the letters of "our beloved brother Paul" and significantly places them on a level with the Old Testament Scriptures (3:15, 16). After a final warning about the danger of false teachers, the epistle closes with an appeal to growth, and a doxology.

OUTLINE OF 2 PETER

I. Cultivation of Christian Character 1:1–21

- A. Salutation 1:1, 2
- B. Growth in Christ 1:3–14
- C. Grounds of Belief 1:15–21
  - 1. Experience of the Transfiguration 1:15–18
  - 2. Certainty of the Scriptures 1:19–21

II. Condemnation of False Teachers 2:1–22

- A. Danger of False Teachers 2:1–3
- B. Destruction of False Teachers 2:4–9
- C. Description of False Teachers 2:10–22

III. Confidence of Christ's Return 3:1–18

- A. Mockery in the Last Days 3:1–7
- B. Manifestation of the Day of the Lord 3:8–10
- C. Maturity in View of the Day of the Lord 3:11–18

CHAPTER 1

Salutation

SIMON Peter, a bondservant and [R]apostle of Jesus Christ, Gal. 2:8

To those who have obtained [R]like precious faith with us by the righteousness of our God and Savior Jesus Christ: Eph. 4:5

2 Grace and peace be multiplied to you in the knowledge of God and of Jesus our Lord,

Growth in Christ

3 as His [R]divine power has given to us all things that *pertain* to life and godliness, through the knowledge of Him [R]who called us by glory and virtue, 1 Pet. 1:5 • 1 Thess. 2:12

4 by which have been given to us exceedingly great and precious promises, that through these you may be partakers of the divine nature, having escaped the corruption *that is* in the world through lust.

5 But also for this very reason, [R]giving all diligence, add to your faith virtue, to virtue [R]knowledge, 2 Pet. 3:18 • 2 Pet. 1:2

6 to knowledge self-control, to self-control perseverance, to perseverance godliness,

7 to godliness brotherly kindness, and [R]to brotherly kindness love. Gal. 6:10

8 For if these things are yours and abound, *you will be* neither [T]barren [R]nor unfruitful in the knowledge of our Lord Jesus Christ. *useless* • [John 15:2]

9 For he who lacks these things is shortsighted, even to blindness, and has forgotten that he was cleansed from his old sins.

10 Therefore, brethren, be even more diligent [R]to make your call and election sure, for if you do these things you will never stumble; 1 John 3:19

11 for so an entrance will be supplied to you abundantly into the everlasting kingdom of our Lord and Savior Jesus Christ.

12 For this reason [R]I will not be negligent to remind you always of these things, [R]though you know and are established in the present truth. Phil. 3:1 • 1 Pet. 5:12

13 Yes, I think it is right, [R]as long as I am in this [T]tent, [R]to stir you up by reminding *you*, [2 Cor. 5:1, 4] • Body • 2 Pet. 3:1

14 [R]knowing that shortly I *must* put off my tent, just as [R]our Lord Jesus Christ showed me. [2 Tim. 4:6] • John 13:36; 21:18, 19

Experience of the Transfiguration
Matt. 17:5; Mark 9:7; Luke 9:35

15 Moreover I will be careful to ensure that you always have a reminder of these things after my [T]decease. Lit. *exodus, departure*

16 For we did not follow [R]cunningly devised fables when we made known to you the [R]power and [R]coming of our Lord Jesus Christ, but were eyewitnesses of His majesty. 1 Cor. 1:17 • [Eph. 1:19–22] • [1 Pet. 5:4]

17 For He received from God the Father honor and glory when such a voice came to Him from the Excellent Glory: "This is My beloved Son, in whom I am well pleased."

18 And we heard this voice which came from heaven when we were with Him on [R]the holy mountain. Matt. 17:1

Certainty of the Scriptures

19 And so we have the prophetic word confirmed,* which you do well to heed as a light that shines in a dark place, [R]until [R]the day dawns and the morning star rises in your hearts; Prov. 4:18 • Rev. 2:28; 22:16

20 knowing this first, that no prophecy of Scripture is of any private interpretation,*

21 for prophecy never came by the will of man, [R]but holy men of God* spoke *as they were* moved by the Holy Spirit. 2 Sam. 23:2

CHAPTER 2

Danger of False Teachers

BUT there were also false prophets among the people, even as there will be [R]false teachers among you, who will secretly bring in destructive heresies, even denying the Lord who bought them, *and* bring on themselves swift destruction. 1 Tim. 4:1, 2

2 And many will follow their destructive ways, because of whom the way of truth will be blasphemed.

3 By covetousness they will exploit you with deceptive words; for a long time their judgment has not been idle, and their destruction does* not slumber.

Destruction of False Teachers

4 For if God did not spare the angels who sinned, but cast *them* down to [T]hell and delivered *them* into chains of darkness, to be reserved for judgment; Lit. *Tartarus*

5 and did not spare the ancient world, but saved Noah, *one of* eight *people*, a preacher of righteousness, bringing in the flood on the world of the ungodly;

6 and turning the cities of Sodom and Gomorrah into ashes, condemned *them* to destruction, making *them* an example to those who afterward would live ungodly;

7 and [R]delivered righteous Lot, *who was* oppressed by the filthy conduct of the wicked Gen. 19:16, 29

8 (for that righteous man, dwelling among them, [R]tormented *his* righteous soul from day

1:19 Or *We also have the more sure prophetic word*
1:20 Or *origin* **1:21** NU *but men spoke from God*
2:3 M *will not*

to day by seeing and hearing *their* lawless deeds)— Ps. 119:139

9 *then* [R]the Lord knows how to deliver the godly out of temptations and to reserve the unjust under punishment for the day of judgment, Ps. 34:15–19

Description of False Teachers

10 and especially [R]those who walk according to the flesh in the lust of uncleanness and despise authority. [R]*They are* presumptuous, self-willed. They are not afraid to speak evil of dignitaries, Jude 4, 7, 8 • Jude 8

11 whereas angels, who are greater in power and might, do not bring a reviling accusation against them before the Lord.

12 But these, like natural brute beasts made to be caught and destroyed, speak evil of the things they do not understand, and will utterly perish in their own corruption,

13 *and* will receive the wages of unrighteousness, *as* those who count it pleasure to carouse in the daytime. *They are* spots and blemishes, carousing in their own deceptions while they feast with you,

14 having eyes full of adultery and that cannot cease from sin, enticing unstable souls. *They have* a heart trained in covetous practices, *and are* accursed children.

15 They have forsaken the right way and gone astray, following the way of [R]Balaam the *son* of Beor, who loved the wages of unrighteousness; Num. 22:5, 7

16 but he was rebuked for his iniquity: a dumb donkey speaking with a man's voice restrained the madness of the prophet.

17 These are wells without water, clouds* carried by a tempest, for whom is reserved the blackness of darkness forever.*

18 For when they speak great swelling *words* of emptiness, they allure through the lusts of the flesh, through lewdness, the ones who have actually escaped* from those who live in error.

19 While they promise them liberty, they themselves are slaves of [T]corruption; [R]for by whom a person is overcome, by him also he is brought into bondage. *depravity* • John 8:34

20 For if, after they [R]have escaped the pollutions of the world through the knowledge of the Lord and Savior Jesus Christ, they are [R]again entangled in them and overcome, the latter end is worse for them than the beginning. Matt. 12:45 • [Heb. 6:4–6]

21 For it would have been better for them not to have known the way of righteousness, than having known *it*, to turn from the holy commandment delivered to them.

22 But it has happened to them according to the true proverb: *"A dog returns to his own vomit,"** and, "a sow, having washed, to her wallowing in the mire."

CHAPTER 3

Mockery in the Last Days

BELOVED, I now write to you this second epistle (in *both of* which [R]I stir up your pure minds by way of reminder), 2 Pet. 1:13

2 that you may be mindful of the words which were spoken before by the holy prophets, and of the commandment of us,* the apostles of the Lord and Savior,

3 knowing this first: that scoffers will come in the last days, [R]walking according to their own lusts, 2 Pet. 2:10

4 and saying, "Where is the promise of His coming? For since the fathers fell asleep, all things continue as *they were* from the beginning of [R]creation." Gen. 6:1–7

5 For this they willfully forget: that [R]by the word of God the heavens were of old, and the earth [R]standing out of water and in the water, Gen. 1:6, 9 • Ps. 24:2; 136:6

6 by which the world *that* then existed perished, being flooded with water.

7 But [R]the heavens and the earth *which* are now preserved by the same word, are reserved for fire until the day of judgment and perdition of ungodly men. 2 Pet. 3:10, 12

Manifestation of the Day of the Lord

8 But, beloved, do not forget this one thing, that with the Lord one day *is* as a thousand years, and [R]a thousand years as one day. Ps. 90:4

9 [R]The Lord is not slack concerning *His* promise, as some count slackness, but [R]is longsuffering toward us,* [R]not willing that any should perish but that all should come to repentance. Hab. 2:3 • Is. 30:18 • Ezek. 33:11

10 But [R]the day of the Lord will come as a thief in the night, in which [R]the heavens will pass away with a great noise, and the elements will melt with fervent heat; both the earth and the works that are in it will be burned up.* Matt. 24:43☆ • Ps. 102:25, 26

Maturity in View of the Day of the Lord

11 Therefore, since all these things will be dissolved, what manner *of persons* ought you to be in holy conduct and godliness,

12 looking for and hastening the coming of the day of God, because of which the heavens will be dissolved, being on fire, and the elements will melt with fervent heat?

13 Nevertheless we, according to His promise, look for new heavens and a new earth in which righteousness dwells.

14 Therefore, beloved, looking forward to

2:17 NU *and mists* • NU omits *forever* **2:18** NU *are barely escaping* **2:22** Prov. 26:11 **3:2** NU, M *commandment of the apostles of your Lord and Savior or commandment of your apostles of the Lord and Savior* **3:9** NU *you* **3:10** NU *laid bare*, lit. *found*

these things, be diligent to be found by Him in
peace, without spot and blameless;
15 and consider *that* [R]the longsuffering of
our Lord *is* salvation—as also our beloved
brother Paul, according to the wisdom given
to him, has written to you, Rom. 2:4
16 as also in all his [R]epistles, speaking in
them of these things, in which are some
things hard to understand, which untaught
and unstable *people* twist to their own de-
struction, as *they do* also the [R]rest of the
Scriptures. 1 Cor. 15:24 • 2 Tim. 3:16
17 You therefore, beloved, [R]since you know
this beforehand, beware lest you also fall
from your own steadfastness, being led away
with the error of the wicked; Mark 13:23
18 but grow in the grace and knowledge
of our Lord and Savior Jesus Christ. To
Him *be* the glory both now and forever.
Amen.

THE FIRST EPISTLE OF

JOHN

THE BOOK OF 1 JOHN

God is light; God is love; and God is life. John is enjoying a delightful fellowship with that God of light, love, and life, and he desperately desires that his spiritual children enjoy the same fellowship.

God is light. Therefore, to engage in fellowship with Him we must walk in light and not in darkness. As we walk in the light, we will regularly confess our sins, allowing the blood of Christ continually to cleanse us. Christ will act as our defense attorney before the Father. Proof of our "walk in the light" will be keeping the commandments of God and replacing any hatred we have toward others with love. Two major roadblocks to hinder this walk will be falling in love with the world and falling for the alluring lies of false teachers.

God is love. Since we are His children, we must walk in love. In fact, John says that if we do not love, we do not know God. Additionally, our love needs to be practical. Love is more than just words; it is actions. Love is giving, not getting. Biblical love is unconditional in its nature. It is an "in spite of" love. Christ's love fulfilled those qualities and when that brand of love characterizes us, we will be free of self-condemnation and experience confidence before God.

God is life. Those who fellowship with Him must possess His quality of life. Spiritual life begins with spiritual birth. Spiritual birth occurs through faith in Jesus Christ. Faith in Jesus Christ infuses us with God's life—eternal life. Therefore, one who walks in fellowship with God will walk in light, love, and life.

Although the apostle John's name is not found in this book, it was given the title *Ioannou A*, "First of John."

THE AUTHOR OF 1 JOHN

The external evidence for the authorship of 1 John shows that from the beginning it was universally received without dispute as authoritative. It was used by Polycarp (who knew John in his youth) and Papias in the early second century, and later in that century Irenaeus (who knew Polycarp in his youth) specifically attributed it to the apostle John. All the Greek and Latin church fathers accepted this epistle as Johannine.

The internal evidence supports this universal tradition because the "we" (apostles), "you" (readers), and "they" (false teachers) phraseology places the writer in the sphere of the apostolic eyewitnesses (cf. 1:1–3; 4:14). John's name was well known to the readers, and it was unnecessary for him to mention it. The style and vocabulary of 1 John are so similar to those of the fourth Gospel that most scholars acknowledge these books to be by the same hand (see "The Author of John"). Both share many distinctively Johannine phrases, and the characteristics of limited vocabulary and frequent contrast of opposites are also common to them. Even so, some critics have assailed this conclusion on various grounds, but the theological and stylistic differences are not substantial enough to overcome the abundant similarities.

The traditional view is also rejected by those who hold that the fourth Gospel and these three epistles were written by John the "elder" or "presbyter," who is to be distinguished from John the apostle. But the only basis for this distinction is Eusebius's interpretation in his *Ecclesiastical History* (A.D. 323) of a statement by Papias. Eusebius understood the passage to refer to two distinct Johns, but the wording does not require this; the elder John and the apostle John may be one and the same. Even if they were different, there is no evidence for contradicting the consistent acknowledgment by the early church that this book was written by the apostle John.

THE TIME OF 1 JOHN

In Acts 8:14 John is associated with "the apostles who were at Jerusalem," and Paul calls him one of the "pillars" of the Jerusalem church in Galatians 2:9. Apart from Revelation 1, the New Testament is silent about his later years, but early Christian tradition uniformly tells us that he left Jerusalem (probably not long before its destruction in A.D. 70) and that he ministered in and around Ephesus. The seven churches in the Roman province of Asia, mentioned in Revelation 2 and 3, were evidently a part of this ministry. Although there is no address in 1 John, it is likely that the apostle directed this epistle to the Asian churches that were within the realm of his oversight.

The believers in these congregations were well established in Christian truth, and John wrote to them not as novices but as brethren grounded in apostolic doctrine (2:7, 18–27; 3:11). The apostle does not mention his own affairs, but his use of such terms of address as "beloved" and "my little children" gives this letter a personal touch that reveals his close relationship to the original recipients. First John was probably written in Ephesus after the Gospel of John, but the date cannot be fixed with certainty. No persecution is mentioned, suggesting a date prior to A.D. 95 when persecution broke out during the end of Domitian's reign (A.D. 81–96).

Advanced in years, John wrote this fatherly epistle out of loving concern for his "children," whose steadfastness in the truth was being threatened by the lure of worldliness and the guile of false teachers. The Gnostic heresy taught that matter is inherently evil, and a divine being therefore could not take on human flesh. This resulted in the distinction between the man Jesus and the spiritual Christ who came upon Jesus at His baptism but departed prior to His crucifixion. Another variation was Docetism (from *dokeo,* "to seem"), the doctrine that Christ only seemed to have a human body. The result in both cases was the same—a flat denial of the Incarnation.

The Gnostics also believed that their understanding of the hidden knowledge (*gnosis*) made them a kind of spiritual elite, who were above the normal distinctions of right and wrong. This led in most cases to deplorable conduct and complete disregard for Christian ethics.

THE CHRIST OF 1 JOHN

The present ministry of Christ is portrayed in 1:5—2:22. His blood continually cleanses the believer from all sin, and He is our righteous Advocate before the Father. This epistle places particular stress on the incarnation of God the Son and the identity of Jesus as the Christ (2:22; 4:2, 3), in refutation of Gnostic doctrine. Jesus Christ "came by water and blood" (5:6). He was the same indivisible Person from the beginning (His baptism) to the end (His crucifixion) of His public ministry.

KEYS TO 1 JOHN

Key Word: Fellowship with God— The major theme of 1 John is fellowship with God. John wants his readers to have assurance of the indwelling God through their abiding relationship with Him (2:28; 5:13). Belief in Christ should be manifested in the practice of righteousness and love for the brethren, which in turn produces joy and confidence before God. John writes this epistle to encourage this kind of fellowship and to emphasize the importance of holding fast to apostolic doctrine.

First John is also written to refute the destructive teachings of the Gnostics by stressing the reality of the Incarnation and the emptiness of profession without practice. These antichrists fail the three tests of righteous living, love for the brethren, and belief that Jesus is the Christ, the incarnate God-Man.

Key Verses: 1 John 1:3, 4 and 5:11–13— "That which we have seen and heard we declare to you, that you also may have fellowship with us; and truly our fellowship *is* with the Father and with His Son Jesus Christ. And these things we write to you that your joy may be full" (1:3, 4).

"And this is the testimony: that God has given us eternal life, and this life is in His Son. He who has the Son has life; he who does not have the Son of God does not have life. These things I have written to you who believe in the name of the Son of God, that you may know that you have eternal life, and that you may *continue to* believe in the name of the Son of God" (5:11–13).

Key Chapter: 1 John 1— The two central passages for continued fellowship with God are John 15 and 1 John 1. John 15 relates the positive side of fellowship, that is, abiding in Christ. First John 1 unfolds the other side, pointing out that when Christians do not abide in Christ, they must seek forgiveness before fellowship can be restored.

SURVEY OF 1 JOHN

John writes his first epistle at a time when apostolic doctrine is being challenged by a proliferation of false teachings. Like 2 Peter and Jude, 1 John has a negative and a positive thrust: it refutes erroneous doctrine and encourages its readership to walk in the knowledge of the truth. John lists the criteria and characteristics of fellowship with God and shows that those who abide in Christ can have confidence and assurance before Him. This simply written but profound work develops the meaning of fellowship in the basis of fellowship (1:1—2:27) and the behavior of fellowship (2:28— 5:21).

The Basis of Fellowship (1:1—2:27): John's prologue (1:1–4) recalls the beginning of apostolic contact with Christ. It relates his desire to transmit this apostolic witness to his readers so that they may share the same fellowship with Jesus Christ, the personification of life. This proclamation is followed by a description of the conditions of fellowship (1:5—2:14).

The readers' sins have been forgiven, and they enjoy fellowship with God. As a result, they know "Him *who is* from the beginning" and are strengthened to overcome the temptations of the Evil One (2:12–14). The cautions to fellowship are both practical (the lusts of the corrupt world system which opposes God, 2:15–17) and doctrinal (the teachings of those who differentiate between Jesus and the Christ, 2:18–23). In contrast to these antichrists, the readers have the knowledge of the truth and an anointing from the Holy One. Therefore, it would be foolish for them to turn away from the teachings of the apostles to the innovations of the antichrists. The antidote to these heretical teachings is abiding in the apostolic truths that they "heard from the beginning," which are authenticated by the anointing they have received (2:24–27).

The Behavior of Fellowship (2:28—5:21): The basic theme of 1 John is summarized in 2:28—assurance through abiding in Christ. The next verse introduces the motif of regeneration, and 2:29—3:10 argues that regeneration is manifested in the practice of righteousness. Because we are children of God through faith in Christ, we have a firm hope of being fully conformed to Him when He appears (3:1–3). Our present likeness to Christ places us in a position of incompatibility with sin, because sin is contrary to the Person and work of Christ (3:4–6). The concept in 3:6 does not contradict 1:8 because it is saying that the abider, insofar as he abides, does not sin. When the believer sins, he does not reflect the regenerate new man but Satan, the original sinner (3:7–10).

Regeneration is shown in righteousness (2:29—3:10), and righteousness is manifested in love (3:10–23). The apostle uses the example of Cain to illustrate what love is not: hatred is murdering in spirit, and it arises from the worldly sphere of death. John then uses the example of Christ to illustrate what love is: love is practiced in self-sacrifice, not mere profession. This practical expression of love results in assurance before God and answered prayers because the believer is walking in obedience to God's commands to believe in Christ and love one another.

In 3:24 John introduces two important motifs, which are developed in 4:1–16: the indwelling God, and the Spirit as a mark of this indwelling. The Spirit of God confesses the incarnate Christ and confirms apostolic doctrine (4:1–6). The mutual abiding of the believer in God and God in the believer is manifested in love for others, and this love produces a divine and human fellowship that testifies to and reflects the reality of the Incarnation (4:7–16). It also anticipates the perfect fellowship to come and creates a readiness to face the One from whom all love is derived (4:17–19).

John joins the concepts he has presented into a circular chain of six links that begins with love for the brethren (4:20—5:17): (1) Love for believers is the inseparable product of love for God (4:20—5:1). (2) Love for God arises out of obedience to His commandments (5:2, 3). (3) Obedience to God is the result of faith in His Son (5:4, 5). (4) This faith is in Jesus, who was the Christ not only at His baptism (the water), but also at His death (the blood; 5:6–8). (5) The divine witness to the Person of Christ is worthy of complete belief (5:9–13). (6) This belief produces confident access to God in prayer (5:14–17). Since intercessory prayer is a manifestation of love for others, the chain has come full circle.

The epilogue (5:18–21) summarizes the conclusions of the epistle in a series of three certainties: (1) Sin is a threat to fellowship, and it should be regarded as foreign to the believer's position in Christ (cf. Rom. 6). (2) The believer stands with God against the satanic world system. (3) The Incarnation produces true knowledge and communion with Christ. Since He is the true God and eternal life, the one who knows Him should avoid the lure of any substitute.

FOCUS	BASIS OF FELLOWSHIP		BEHAVIOR OF FELLOWSHIP	
REFERENCE	1:1———	2:15———	2:28———	5:4———5:21
DIVISION	CONDITIONS FOR FELLOWSHIP	CAUTIONS TO FELLOWSHIP	CHARACTERISTICS OF FELLOWSHIP	CONSEQUENCES OF FELLOWSHIP
TOPIC	MEANING OF FELLOWSHIP		MANIFESTATIONS OF FELLOWSHIP	
	ABIDING IN GOD'S LIGHT		ABIDING IN GOD'S LOVE	
LOCATION	WRITTEN IN EPHESUS			
TIME	C. A.D. 90			

OUTLINE OF 1 JOHN

Part One: The Basis of Fellowship (1:1—2:27)

I. Introduction 1:1–4

II. The Conditions for Fellowship .... 1:5—2:14

A. Walk in the Light 1:5–7
B. Confession of Sin .... 1:8—2:2
C. Obedience to His Commandments 2:3–6
D. Love for One Another 2:7–14

III. The Cautions to Fellowship 2:15–27

A. Love of the World 2:15–17
B. Spirit of the Antichrist 2:18–27

Part Two: The Behavior of Fellowship (2:28—5:21)

CHAPTER 1

Introduction

THAT [R]which was from the beginning, which we have heard, which we have seen with our eyes, which we have looked upon, and our hands have handled, concerning the Word of life— [John 1:1]

2 [R]the life was manifested, and we have seen, and bear witness, and declare to you that eternal life which was with the Father and was manifested to us— John 1:4

3 that which we have seen and heard we declare to you, that you also may have fellowship with us; and truly our fellowship *is* [R]with the Father and with His Son Jesus Christ. 1 Cor. 1:9

4 And these things we write to you [R]that your* joy may be full. John 15:11; 16:24

Walk in the Light

5 [R]This is the message which we have heard from Him and declare to you, that [R]God is light and in Him is no darkness at all. 1 John 3:11 • [1 Tim. 6:16]

6 [R]If we say that we have fellowship with Him, and walk in darkness, we lie and do not practice the truth. [1 John 2:9–11]

7 But if we [R]walk in the light as He is in the light, we have fellowship with one another, and the blood of Jesus Christ His Son cleanses us from all sin. Is. 2:5

Confession of Sin

8 If we say that we have no sin, we deceive ourselves, and the truth is not in us.

9 If we confess our sins, He is faithful and just to forgive us *our* sins and to cleanse us from all unrighteousness.

10 If we say that we have not sinned, we make Him a liar, and His word is not in us.

CHAPTER 2

MY little children, these things I write to you, so that you may not sin. And if anyone sins, we have an Advocate with the Father, Jesus Christ the righteous.

2 And [R]He Himself is the propitiation for our sins, and not for ours only but [R]also for the whole world. [Rom. 3:25] • John 1:29

Obedience to His Commandments

3 Now by this we know that we know Him, if we keep His commandments.

4 He who says, "I know Him," and does not keep His commandments, is a [R]liar, and the truth is not in him. Rom. 3:4

5 But [R]whoever keeps His word, truly the love of God is perfected in him. By this we know that we are in Him. John 14:21, 23

6 He who says he abides in Him ought himself also to walk just as He walked.

Love for One Another

7 Brethren,* I write no new commandment to you, but an old commandment which you have had [R]from the beginning. The old

1:4 NU, M *our* **2:7** NU *Beloved*

1:9 Confession—One of the most remarkable chapters in the OT is Ps. 51. This psalm contains the actual words of confession uttered by King David after his great sins of adultery and murder (Page 314—2 Sam. 11).

This prayer can serve as a pattern to Christians when guilty of sin today.

a. David begins his prayer by freely admitting his sin (Page 572—Ps. 51:3, 4). This honesty is vital in our confession. God will graciously forgive all our sins, but not on account of our excuses.
b. He then displays real sorrow over his sin (Page 573—Ps. 51:17). Paul writes (Page 1188—2 Cor. 7:10) that the main characteristic of true confession is godly sorrow.
c. He asks God's forgiveness (Page 572—Ps. 51:1, 7–9).
d. He believes that God has heard him and will restore him (Page 573—Ps. 51:12–15).

In the NT the most important single verse concerning confession is 1 John 1:9. In essence John tells us the means of forgiveness and cleansing is the blood of Christ, while the method of this forgiveness and cleansing is the confession of the Christian.

Like David, we must admit our sin, regret the actions of our sin, plead the blood of Christ, and believe that God has indeed done what He promised, namely, to cleanse us from sin and restore us to fellowship and service.

Now turn to Page 273—1 Sam. 1:17: Petition.

commandment is the word which you heard
from the beginning.* 1 John 4:21
8 Again, a new commandment I write to
you, which thing is true in Him and in you, be-
cause the darkness is passing away, and the
true light is already shining.
9 He who says he is in the light, and hates
his brother, is in darkness until now.
10 [R]He who loves his brother abides in the
light, and [R]there is no cause for stumbling in
him. [1 John 3:14] • 2 Pet. 1:10
11 But he who hates his brother is in dark-
ness and [R]walks in darkness, and does not
know where he is going, because the dark-
ness has blinded his eyes. John 12:35

12 I write to you, little children,
Because [R]your sins are forgiven you
for His name's sake. [1 Cor. 6:11]
13 I write to you, fathers,
Because you have known Him *who is*
[R]from the beginning. John 1:1
I write to you, young men,
Because you have overcome the
wicked one.
I write to you, little children,
Because you have known the Father.
14 I have written to you, fathers,
Because you have known Him *who is*
from the beginning.
I have written to you, young men,
Because [R]you are strong, and the word
of God abides in you,
And you have overcome the wicked
one. Eph. 6:10

Love of the World

15 [R]Do not love the world or the things in the
world. If anyone loves the world, the love of
the Father is not in him. [Rom. 12:2]

16 For all that *is* in the world—the lust of
the flesh, [R]the lust of the eyes, and the pride
of life—is not of the Father but is of the
world. [Eccl. 5:10, 11]

17 And [R]the world is passing away, and the
lust of it; but he who does the will of God
abides forever. 1 Cor. 7:31

Spirit of the Antichrist

18 [R]Little children, [R]it is the last hour; and
as you have heard that [R]the* Antichrist is
coming, even now many antichrists have
come, by which we know that it is the last
hour. John 21:5 • 1 Pet. 4:7 • 2 Thess. 2:3
19 [R]They went out from us, but they were not
of us; for if they had been of us, they would
have continued with us; but *they went out*
that they might be made manifest, that none
of them were of us. Deut. 13:13
20 But you have an anointing from the Holy
One, and you know all things.*
21 I have not written to you because you do
not know the truth, but because you know it,
and that no lie is of the truth.
22 [R]Who is a liar but he who denies that Je-
sus is the Christ? He is antichrist who denies
the Father and the Son. 2 John 7
23 [R]Whoever denies the Son does not have
the Father either; he who acknowledges the
Son has the Father also. John 15:23
24 Therefore let that abide in you [R]which
you heard from the beginning. If what you
heard from the beginning abides in you,
[R]you also will abide in the Son and in the Fa-
ther. 2 John 5, 6 • John 14:23
25 [R]And this is the promise that He has
promised us—eternal life. John 3:14–16; 6:40
26 These things I have written to you con-
cerning those who *try to* deceive you.
27 But the anointing which you have re-
ceived from Him abides in you, and you do
not need that anyone teach you; but as the
same anointing teaches you concerning all
things, and is true, and is not a lie, and just as
it has taught you, you will* abide in Him.

2:7 NU omits *from the beginning* **2:18** NU omits *the*
2:20 NU *you all know.* **2:27** NU *you abide*

2:15 Temptation by the World—The term "world" does not always refer to the universe as created by God. It often is used to describe the community of sinful humanity that possesses a spirit of rebellion against God (Page 1297—1 John 5:19). Because of its opposition to God, the world values those things that are contrary to God's will: "the lust of the flesh, and the lust of the eyes, and the pride of life" (1 John 2:16). Its temptations to the believer are thus twofold: lust for the sensual and pride in mastery of one's own life.

The attraction of the world is amplified by Satan who is head of its system. He is called the "ruler of this world" (Page 1097—John 12:31; 14:30; 16:11), and the whole world is said to be under his power (Page 1297—1 John 5:19, where "wickedness" can also be translated "wicked one").

Some of the tragic effects that love of the world will produce in the believer's life are:

a. A turning away from the Lord's work and other believers (Page 1245—2 Tim. 4:10);
b. Alienation from God (Page 1274—James 4:4);
c. Corrupting sins (Page 1287—2 Pet. 1:4; Page 1294—1 John 2:15–17);
d. Deception by false teachers (Page 1296—1 John 4:1; Page 1300—2 John 7).

The solution to the love of the world is to have a greater love for the Father (1 John 2:15). The Christian who seeks daily to please God in everything and who strives for spiritual growth through prayer, study of God's Word, and witnessing need not fall prey to the temptations of the world.

Now turn to Page 1033—Mark 14:38: Temptation by the Flesh.

Purity of Life

28 And now, little children, abide in Him,
that when* He appears, we may have [R]confi-
dence and not be ashamed before Him at His
coming. 1 John 3:21; 4:17; 5:14
29 [R]If you know that He is righteous, you
know that everyone who practices righ-
teousness is born of Him. Acts 22:14

CHAPTER 3

BEHOLD [R]what manner of love the Father
has bestowed on us, that [R]we should be
called children of God!* Therefore the world
does not know us,* because it did not know
Him. [1 John 4:10] • [John 1:12]
2 Beloved, [R]now we are children of God;
and it has not yet been revealed what we shall
be, but we know that when He is revealed, we
shall be like Him, for [R]we shall see Him as He
is. [Rom. 8:15, 16] • [Ps. 16:11]
3 And everyone who has this hope in Him
purifies himself, just as He is pure.

Practice of Righteousness

4 Whoever commits sin also commits law-
lessness, and [R]sin is lawlessness. Rom. 4:15
5 And you know [R]that He was manifested
[R]to take away our sins, and [R]in Him there is no
sin. 1 John 1:2; 3:8 • John 1:29 • [2 Cor. 5:21]
6 Whoever abides in Him does not sin.
Whoever sins has neither seen Him nor
known Him.
7 Little children, let no one deceive you. He
who practices righteousness is righteous, just
as He is righteous.
8 He who sins is of the devil, for the devil
has sinned from the beginning. For this pur-
pose the Son of God was manifested, that He
might destroy the works of the devil.
9 Whoever has been [R]born of God does
not sin, for [R]His seed remains in him; and he
cannot sin, because he has been born of
God. John 1:3; 3:3 • 1 Pet. 1:23
10 In this the children of God and the chil-
dren of the devil are manifest: Whoever does
not practice righteousness is not of God, nor
is he who does not love his brother.
11 For this is the message that you heard
from the beginning, [R]that we should love one
another, [John 13:34; 15:12]
12 not as [R]Cain *who* was of the wicked one
and murdered his brother. And why did he
murder him? Because his works were evil and
his brother's righteous. Gen. 4:4, 8

Love in Deed and Truth

13 Do not marvel, my brethren, if [R]the world
hates you. [John 15:18; 17:14]
14 We know that we have passed from death
to life, because we love the brethren. He who
does not love *his* brother* abides in death.
15 [R]Whoever hates his brother is a murderer,
and you know that no murderer has eternal
life abiding in him. Matt. 5:21
16 By this we know love, because He laid
down His life for us. And we also ought to lay
down *our* lives for the brethren.
17 But [R]whoever has this world's goods, and
sees his brother in need, and shuts up his
heart from him, how does the love of God
abide in him? Deut. 15:7
18 My little children, let us not love in word
or in tongue, but in deed and in truth.
19 And by this we know* [R]that we are of the
truth, and shall [T]assure our hearts before
Him. John 18:37 • *persuade, set at rest*
20 [R]For if our heart condemns us, God is
greater than our heart, and knows all
things. [1 Cor. 4:4, 5]
21 Beloved, if our heart does not condemn
us, we have confidence toward God.
22 And [R]whatever we ask we receive from

2:28 NU *if* **3:1** NU adds *And we are.* • M *you*
3:14 NU omits *his brother* **3:19** NU *we shall know*

3:2 Placed into God's Family—In a general sense all men and women are the offspring of God in that He is the Creator (Page 1133—Acts 17:28, 29). This relationship, however, is not sufficient to offset the penalty of sin, because all persons are sinners separated from God (Page 1151—Rom. 3:23). Therefore, for a sinful person to become a child of God, a miraculous transformation must take place. The Bible refers to this change as being "born again" (Page 1083—John 3:3). Individuals who place faith in Christ as Savior are born again into a new, spiritual, family relationship with God (Page 1198—Gal. 3:26). They gain God as Father (Page 1207—Eph. 4:6) and other Christians as brothers and sisters (Page 1259—Heb. 3:1). It is significant to note that the term "brotherly love," which Christians are commanded to have for each other (Page 1268—Heb. 13:1), is never used in the Greek language to refer to loving others as though they were your brothers. Rather, it is always used of loving those who actually are your brothers. So it is in the Christian faith: we actually are brothers and sisters with other Christians.

Not only are Christians the children of God by spiritual birth; they are adopted as well (Page 1204—Eph. 1:5). This figure implies a dramatic transformation of status from slave to son (Page 1198—Gal. 4:1–5). One is no longer in bondage to the master but becomes a free son possessing all the rights and privileges of sonship. One of these benefits is the right to call God *Abba,* an affectionate term meaning "Father" (Page 1154—Rom. 8:15). This marvelous relationship carries responsibilities with it, as well as privileges. All who have the hope of having their "sonship" perfected someday are presently purifying their own lives. Since they bear the family relationship to God, they must also exhibit the family character.

Now turn to Page 1123—Acts 10:14, 15: Reconciliation Between Enemies.

Him, because we keep His commandments
[R]and do those things that are pleasing in His
sight. Ps. 34:15 • John 8:29
23 And this is His commandment: that we
should believe on the name of His Son Jesus
Christ [R]and love one another, as He gave us*
commandment. Matt. 22:39

24 Now [R]he who keeps His commandments
abides in Him, and He in him. And by this we
know that He abides in us, by the Spirit whom
He has given us. John 14:23

CHAPTER 4

Testing the Spirits

BELOVED, do not believe every spirit, but
[R]test the spirits, whether they are of God;
because many false prophets have gone out
into the world. 1 Cor. 14:29
2 By this you know the Spirit of God: Every
spirit that confesses that Jesus Christ has
come in the flesh is of God,
3 and every spirit that does not confess
that* Jesus Christ has come in the flesh is not
of God. And this is the *spirit* of the Antichrist,
which you have heard was coming, and is now
already in the world.
4 You are of God, little children, and have
overcome them, because He who is in you is
greater than he who is in the world.
5 [R]They are of the world. Therefore they
speak *as* of the world, and [R]the world hears
them. John 3:31 • John 15:19; 17:14
6 We are of God. He who knows God hears
us; he who is not of God does not hear us. [R]By
this we know the spirit of truth and the spirit
of error. [1 Cor. 2:12–16]

Love as Christ Loved

7 Beloved, let us love one another, for love
is of God; and everyone who [R]loves is born of
God and knows God. 1 Thess. 4:9
8 He who does not love does not know God,
for God is love.
9 [R]In this the love of God was manifested
toward us, that God has sent His only begot-
ten [R]Son into the world, that we might live
through Him. Rom. 5:8 • John 3:16
10 In this is love, [R]not that we loved God, but
that He loved us and sent His Son *to be* the
propitiation for our sins. Titus 3:5
11 Beloved, [R]if God so loved us, we also
ought to love one another. Matt. 18:33
12 [R]No one has seen God at any time. If we
love one another, God abides in us, and His
love has been perfected in us. John 1:18
13 [R]By this we know that we abide in Him,
and He in us, because He has given us of His
Spirit. John 14:20
14 And [R]we have seen and testify that [R]the
Father has sent the Son *as* Savior of the
world. John 1:14 • John 3:17; 4:42
15 [R]Whoever confesses that Jesus is the
Son of God, God abides in him, and he in
God. [Rom. 10:9]
16 And we have known and believed the
love that God has for us. God is love, and [R]he
who abides in love abides in God, and God [R]in
him. [1 John 3:24] • [John 14:23]
17 Love has been perfected among us in this:
that [R]we may have boldness in the day of
judgment; because as He is, so are we in this
world. 1 John 2:28
18 There is no fear in love; but perfect love
casts out fear, because fear involves torment.
But he who fears has not been made perfect in
love.
19 We love Him* because He first loved us.
20 [R]If someone says, "I love God," and
hates his brother, he is a liar; for he who
does not love his brother whom he has seen,
how can* he love God [R]whom he has not
seen? [1 John 2:4] • 1 John 4:12
21 And [R]this commandment we have from
Him: that he who loves God *must* love his
brother also. [Matt. 5:43, 44; 22:39]

CHAPTER 5

WHOEVER believes that [R]Jesus is the
Christ is born of God, and everyone
who loves Him who begot also loves him who
is begotten of Him. 1 John 2:22; 4:2, 15
2 By this we know that we love the children
of God, when we love God and [R]keep His com-
mandments. John 15:10

3:23 M omits *us* **4:3** NU omits *that* and *Christ has come in the flesh* **4:19** NU omits *Him* **4:20** NU *he cannot*

3:24 Witness of the Spirit—While it is true that one need not always feel spiritual to have new life in Christ, nevertheless, feelings and emotions do play a role in our salvation. Both Paul (Page 1154—Rom. 8:16) and John (Page 1296—1 John 3:24) inform us we can experience that inner witness of the Holy Spirit to our spirit. What does this mean? It means we can enjoy the quiet confidence given by the Spirit that we have indeed passed from death unto life. It means we can now approach the mighty Creator of the vast universe and refer to Him as "Abba, Father" (Page 1154—Rom. 8:15). "Abba" is a very personal and intimate term for one's father. Prior to Pentecost only Christ had used the title for God (Page 1033—Mark 14:36). It is almost akin to our modern title "daddy," or "papa." It not only means we can approach the throne of grace with a holy boldness Page 1261—(Heb. 4:16), but we can also experience the blessing of knowing that the Father will hear and answer our prayers (Page 1295—1 John 3:22).

The apostle Paul experiences this witness during a crisis in his life while preaching in Corinth. See Acts 18:9, 10.

Now turn to Page 1170—1 Cor. 6:11: Changed Life.

3 [R]For this is the love of God, that we keep
His commandments. And His commandments
are not burdensome. John 14:15

Victory over the World

4 For [R]whatever is born of God overcomes
the world. And this is the victory that has
overcome the world—our* faith. John 16:33
5 Who is he who overcomes the world, but
[R]he who believes that Jesus is the Son of
God? 1 Cor. 15:57

Assurance of Salvation

6 This is He who came by water and
blood—Jesus Christ; not only by water, but by
water and blood. And it is the Spirit who
bears witness, because the Spirit is truth.
7 For there are three that bear witness in
heaven: the Father, the Word, and the Holy
Spirit; [R]and these three are one. John 10:30
8 And there are three that bear witness on
earth:* [R]the Spirit, the water, and the blood;
and these three agree as one. John 15:26
9 If we receive [R]the witness of men, the
witness of God is greater; [R]for this is the wit-
ness of God which* He has testified of His
Son. John 5:34, 37; 8:17, 18 • [Matt. 3:16, 17]
10 He who believes in the Son of God [R]has
the witness in himself; he who does not be-
lieve God [R]has made Him a liar, because he
has not believed the testimony that God has
given of His Son. [Rom. 8:16] • John 3:18, 33
11 And this is the testimony: that God has
given us eternal life, and this life is in His Son.
12 [R]He who has the Son has [T]life; he who
does not have the Son of God does not have
life. [John 3:15, 36; 6:47; 17:2, 3] • Or *the life*
13 These things I have written to you who
believe in the name of the Son of God, that
you may know that you have eternal life,* and
that you may *continue to* believe in the name
of the Son of God.

Guidance in Prayer

14 Now this is the confidence that we have in
Him, that [R]if we ask anything according to His
will, He hears us. [1 John 2:28; 3:21, 22]
15 And if we know that He hears us, what-
ever we ask, we know that we have the peti-
tions that we have asked of Him.
16 If anyone sees his brother sinning a sin
which does not *lead* to death, he will ask, and
[R]He will give him life for those who commit
sin not *leading* to death. There is sin *leading*
to death. I do not say that he should pray
about that. Job 42:8
17 [R]All unrighteousness is sin, and there is
sin not *leading* to death. 1 John 3:4

Freedom from Habitual Sin

18 We know that [R]whoever is born of God
does not sin; but he who has been born of God
[R]keeps himself,* and the wicked one does not
touch him. [1 Pet. 1:23] • James 1:27
19 We know that we are of God, and [R]the
whole world lies *under the sway of* the wicked
one. Gal. 1:4
20 And we know that the [R]Son of God has
come and [R]has given us an understanding,
[R]that we may know Him who is true; and
we are in Him who is true, in His Son Jesus
Christ. [R]This is the true God and eternal
life. 1 John 4:2 • Luke 24:45 • John 17:3 • Is. 9:6
21 Little children, keep yourselves from
idols. Amen.

5:4 M *your* **5:8** NU, M omit the words from *in heaven* (v. 7) through *on earth* (v. 8). Only 4 or 5 very late mss. contain these words in Greek. **5:9** NU *God, that* **5:13** NU omits the rest of v. 13. **5:18** NU *him*

THE SECOND EPISTLE OF

JOHN

THE BOOK OF 2 JOHN

"Let him who thinks he stands take heed lest he fall" (1 Cor. 10:12). These words of the apostle Paul could well stand as a subtitle for John's little epistle. The recipients, a chosen lady and her children, were obviously standing. They were walking in truth, remaining faithful to the commandments they had received from the Father. John is deeply pleased to be able to commend them. But he takes nothing for granted. Realizing that standing is just one step removed from falling, he hesitates not at all to issue a reminder: love one another. The apostle admits that this is not new revelation, but he views it sufficiently important to repeat. Loving one another, he stresses, is equivalent to walking according to God's commandments.

John indicates, however, that this love must be discerning. It is not a naive, unthinking, open to anything and anyone kind of love. Biblical love is a matter of choice; it is dangerous and foolish to float through life with undiscerning love. False teachers abound who do not acknowledge Christ as having come in the flesh. It is false charity to open the door to false teaching. We must have fellowship with God. We must have fellowship with Christians. But we must not have fellowship with false teachers.

The "Elder" of verse 1 has been traditionally identified with the apostle John, resulting in the Greek title *Ioannou B*, "Second of John."

THE AUTHOR OF 2 JOHN

Because of the similarity of the contents and circumstances of 2 and 3 John, the authorship of both will be considered here. These letters were not widely circulated at the beginning because of their brevity and their specific address to a small number of people. This limited circulation, combined with the fact that they have few distinctive ideas to add that are not found in 1 John, meant that they were seldom quoted in the patristic writings of the early church. Their place in the canon of New Testament books was disputed for a time, but it is significant that there was no question in the minds of those church fathers who lived closest to the time of John that these two epistles were written by the apostle. The second-century writers Irenaeus and Clement of Alexandria entertained no other view. Only as the details of their origin were forgotten did doubts arise, but the positive evidence in their favor eventually won for them the official recognition of the whole church.

It is obvious that the recipients of 2 and 3 John well knew the author's identity, although he did not use his name. Instead, he designated himself in the first verse of both letters as "the Elder." This is not an argument against the Johannine authorship of 2 and 3 John, since the context of these epistles reveals that his authority was far greater than that of an elder in a local church. The apostle Peter also referred to himself as an elder (1 Pet. 5:1), and John uses the distinguishing term "the elder."

The similarity of style, vocabulary, structure, and mood between 2 and 3 John makes it clear that these letters were written by the same author. In addition, both (especially 2 John) bear strong resemblances to 1 John and to the fourth Gospel. Thus, the external and internal evidence lends clear support to the traditional view that these epistles were written by the apostle John.

THE TIME OF 2 JOHN

The identification of the original readers of this epistle is difficult because of disagreement regarding the interpretation of "the elect lady and her children" (v. 1). Some scholars believe the address should be taken literally to refer to a specific woman and her children, while others prefer to take it as a figurative description of a local church.

The evidence is insufficient for a decisive conclusion, but in either case, the readers were well known to John and probably lived in the province of Asia, not far from Ephesus. If the figurative view is taken, "the children of your elect sister" (v. 13) refers to the members of a sister church.

In his first epistle, John wrote that a number of false teachers had split away from the church ("they went out from us, but they were not of us," 1 John 2:19). Some of these became traveling teachers who depended on the hospitality of individuals while they sought to infiltrate churches with their teachings.

Judging by the content and circumstances of 2 John, it was evidently contemporaneous with 1 John or was written slightly later. It was probably written about A.D. 90. All three of John's epistles may have been written in Ephesus (see "The Time of 1 John").

THE CHRIST OF 2 JOHN

John refutes the same error regarding the Person of Christ in this epistle as he did in his first epistle. Again he stresses that those "who do not confess Jesus Christ *as* coming in the flesh" (v. 7) are deceivers who must be avoided. One must abide "in the doctrine of Christ" (v. 9) to have a relationship with God. The doctrine of the Person and work of Jesus Christ affects every other area of theology.

KEYS TO 2 JOHN

Key Word: Avoid Fellowship with False Teachers—The basic theme of this brief letter is steadfastness in the practice and purity of the apostolic doctrine that the readers "have heard from the beginning" (v. 6). John writes it as a reminder to continue walking in obedience to God's commandment to love one another (practical exhortation, vv. 4–6). His primary purpose is to deliver a warning not to associate with or assist teachers who do not acknowledge the truth about Jesus Christ (doctrinal exhortation, vv. 7–11).

It has been suggested that 2 and 3 John were written as cover letters for 1 John to provide a personal word to a church (2 John) and to Gaius (3 John) that would supplement the longer epistle. However, there is no way to be sure.

Key Verses: 2 John 9, 10—"Whoever transgresses and does not abide in the doctrine of Christ does not have God. He who abides in the doctrine of Christ has both the Father and the Son. If anyone comes to you and does not bring this doctrine, do not receive him into your house nor greet him" (vv. 9, 10).

SURVEY OF 2 JOHN

This brief letter has much in common with 1 John, including a warning about the danger of false teachers who deny the incarnation of Jesus Christ. John encourages the readers to continue walking in love but exhorts them to be discerning in their expression of love. Second John breaks with two parts: abide in God's commandments (vv. 1–6) and abide not with false teachers (vv. 7–13).

Abide in God's Commandments (vv. 1–6): The salutation (vv. 1–3) centers on the concept of abiding in the truth (mentioned four times in these three verses). The recipients are loved for their adherence to the truth by "all those who have known the truth." The apostle commends his readers on their walk in truth in obedience to God's commandment (v. 4), and he reminds them that this commandment entails the practice of love for one another (vv. 5, 6). The divine command is given in verse 5 and the human response follows in verse 6.

Abide Not with False Teachers (vv. 7–13): Moving from the basic test of Christian behavior (love for the brethren) to the basic test of Christian belief (the Person of Christ), John admonishes the readers to beware of deceivers "who do not confess Jesus Christ *as* coming in the flesh" (vv. 7–9). In no uncertain terms, the apostle enjoins the readers to deny even the slightest assistance or encouragement to itinerant teachers who promote an erroneous view of Christ (and hence of salvation; vv. 10, 11).

This letter closes with John's explanation of its brevity: he anticipates a future visit during which he will be able to "speak face to face" with his readers (v. 12). The meaning of the greeting in verse 13 relates to the interpretation of verse 1.

FOCUS	ABIDE IN GOD'S COMMANDMENTS			ABIDE NOT WITH FALSE TEACHERS		
REFERENCE	1—4	—5	—7	—10	—11	—13
DIVISION	SALUTATION	WALK IN TRUTH	WALK IN LOVE	DOCTRINE OF FALSE TEACHERS	AVOID THE FALSE TEACHERS	BENEDICTION
TOPIC	WALK IN COMMANDMENTS			WATCH FOR COUNTERFEITS		
	PRACTICE THE TRUTH			PROTECT THE TRUTH		
LOCATION	WRITTEN IN EPHESUS					
TIME	C. A.D. 90					

OUTLINE OF 2 JOHN

I. Abide in God's Commandments 1–6

A. Salutation 1–3
B. Walk in Truth 4
C. Walk in Love 5, 6

II. Abide Not with False Teachers 7–13

A. Doctrine of the False Teachers 7–9
B. Avoid the False Teachers 10, 11
C. Benediction 12, 13

Salutation

THE Elder,

To the elect lady and her children, whom
I love in truth, and not only I, but also all those
who have known the truth,
2 because of the truth which abides in us
and will be with us forever:

3 [R]Grace, mercy, *and* peace will be with
you* from God the Father and from the Lord
Jesus Christ, the Son of the Father, in truth
and love. 1 Tim. 1:2

Walk in Truth

4 I rejoiced greatly that I have found *some*
of your children walking in truth, as we re-
ceived commandment from the Father.

Walk in Love

5 And now I plead with you, lady, not as
though I wrote a new commandment to you,
but that which we have had from the begin-
ning: that we love one another.
6 This is love, that we walk according to His
commandments. This is the commandment,
that [R]as you have heard from the beginning,
you should walk in it. 1 John 2:24

Doctrine of the False Teachers

7 For [R]many deceivers have gone out into
the world [R]who do not confess Jesus Christ *as*
coming in the flesh. This is a deceiver and an
antichrist. 1 John 2:19; 4:1 • 1 John 4:2
8 [R]Look to yourselves, that we* do not lose
those things we worked for, but *that* we* may
receive a full reward. Mark 13:9
9 Whoever transgresses* and does not
abide in the doctrine of Christ does not have
God. He who abides in the doctrine of Christ
has both the Father and the Son.

Avoid the False Teachers

10 If anyone comes to you and [R]does not
bring this doctrine, do not receive him into
your house nor greet him; Rom. 16:17
11 for he who greets him shares in his evil
deeds.

Benediction

12 [R]Having many things to write to you, I did
not wish *to do so* with paper and ink; but I
hope to come to you and speak face to face,
that our joy may be full. 3 John 13, 14
13 [R]The children of your elect sister greet
you. Amen. 1 Pet. 5:13

3 NU, M *us* **8** NU *you* • NU *you* **9** NU *goes ahead*

THE THIRD EPISTLE OF JOHN

THE BOOK OF 3 JOHN

In 1 John the apostle discusses fellowship with God; in 2 John he forbids fellowship with false teachers; and in 3 John he encourages fellowship with other Christians. Following his expression of love for Gaius, John assures him of his prayers for his health and voices his joy over Gaius's persistent walk in truth and for the manner in which he shows hospitality and support for missionaries who have come to his church. The phrase "send them forward on their journey" means to provide help for the missionaries' endeavors. Included in this help can be food, money, arrangements for companions, and means of travel. By supporting these men who are ministering for Christ, Gaius has become a fellow worker of the truth.

But not everyone in the church feels the same way. Diotrephes' heart is one hundred and eighty degrees removed from Gaius's heart. He is no longer living in love. Pride has taken precedence in his life. He has refused a letter John has written for the church, fearing that his authority might be superseded by that of the apostle. He also has accused John of evil words and refused to accept missionaries. He forbids others to do so and even expels them from the church if they disobey him. John uses this negative example as an opportunity to encourage Gaius to continue his hospitality. Demetrius has a good testimony and may even be one of those turned away by Diotrephes. He is widely known for his good character and his loyalty to the truth. Here he is well commended by John and stands as a positive example for Gaius.

The Greek titles of 1, 2, and 3 John are *Ioannou A, B,* and *G.* The *G* is *gamma,* the third letter of the Greek alphabet; *Ioannou G* means "Third of John."

THE AUTHOR OF 3 JOHN

The authorship of 2 and 3 John was considered together because the contents and circumstances of both books are similar (see "The Author of 2 John"). Although the external evidence for 2 and 3 John is limited (there is even less for 3 John than for 2 John), what little there is consistently points to the apostle John as author. The internal evidence is stronger, and it, too, supports the apostolic origin of both letters.

THE TIME OF 3 JOHN

The parallels between 2 and 3 John suggest that these epistles were written at about the same time (A.D. 90). Early Christian writers are unified in their testimony that the headquarters of John's later ministry was in Ephesus, the principal city of the Roman province of Asia (see "The Time of 1 John"). John evidently commissioned a number of traveling teachers to spread the gospel and to solidify the Asian churches, and these teachers were supported by believers who received them into their homes.

Third John, probably delivered by Demetrius, was occasioned by the report of some of these emissaries (called "brethren" in this letter), who returned to the apostle and informed him of the hospitality of Gaius and the hostility of Diotrephes. The arrogant Diotrephes seized the reins of an Asian church and vaunted himself as its preeminent authority. He maligned John's authority and rejected the teachers sent out by John, expelling those in his church who wanted to receive them.

"Gaius" was a common name in the Roman Empire, and three other men by that name are mentioned in the New Testament: (1) Gaius, one of Paul's traveling companions from Macedonia (Acts 19:29); (2) Gaius of Derbe (Acts 20:4); and (3) Gaius, Paul's host in Corinth, one of the few Corinthians Paul baptized (Rom. 16:23; 1 Cor. 1:14). The Gaius of 3 John evidently lived in Asia, and it is best to distinguish him from these other men.

In verse 9 John alludes to a previous letter that Diotrephes had spurned. This may have been 1 or 2 John, but it is more likely a letter that has been lost or perhaps was destroyed by Diotrephes.

THE CHRIST OF 3 JOHN

Unlike 1 and 2 John, 3 John makes no mention of the name of Jesus Christ. But verse 7 says "they went forth for His name's sake," an indirect reference to our Lord (cf. Acts 5:41, where the identical Greek construction is used to refer back to "the name of Jesus" in Acts 5:40). The concept of truth runs throughout this letter, and Christ is the source and incarnation of truth, as is obvious from John's other writings.

KEYS TO 3 JOHN

Key Word: Enjoy Fellowship with the Brethren—The basic theme of this letter is to enjoy and continue to have fellowship (hospitality) with fellow believers, especially full-time Christian workers. This is contrasted between the truth and servanthood of Gaius and the error and selfishness of Diotrephes. Moving through 3 John, five specific purposes can be discerned from its contents: (1) to commend Gaius for his adherence to the truth and his hospitality to the emissaries sent out by John (vv. 1–6); (2) to encourage Gaius to continue his support of these brethren (vv. 6–8); (3) to rebuke Diotrephes for his pride and misconduct (vv. 9–11); (4) to provide a recommendation for Demetrius (v. 12); and (5) to inform Gaius of John's intention to visit and straighten out the difficulties (vv. 10, 13, 14).

Key Verse: 3 John 11—"Beloved, do not imitate what is evil, but what is good. He who does good is of God, but he who does evil has not seen God" (v. 11).

SURVEY OF 3 JOHN

Third John is the shortest book in the Bible, but it is very personal and vivid. It offers a stark contrast between two men who respond in opposite ways to the itinerant teachers who have been sent out by the apostle. The faithful Gaius responds with generosity and hospitality, but the faithless Diotrephes responds with arrogance and opposition. Thus, John writes this letter to commend Gaius for walking in the truth (vv. 1–8) and to condemn Diotrephes for walking in error (vv. 9–14).

Commendation of Gaius (vv. 1–8): The "Elder" writes to one of his beloved "children" whose godly behavior has given the apostles great joy (vv. 1–4). The "brethren," upon returning to John, have informed him of Gaius's faithfulness, love, and generosity in their behalf. The apostle acknowledges these actions and urges Gaius to continue supporting traveling teachers and missionaries who go out "for His [Jesus'] name's sake" (vv. 5–8).

Condemnation of Diotrephes (vv. 9–14): The epistle suddenly shifts to a negative note as John describes a man whose actions are diametrically opposed to those of Gaius (vv. 9–11). Diotrephes boldly rejects John's apostolic authority and refuses to receive the itinerant teachers sent out by the apostle. Diotrephes evidently has been orthodox in his doctrine, but his evil actions indicate a blindness to God in his practice.

By contrast, John gives his full recommendation to Demetrius, another emissary and probably the bearer of this letter to Gaius (v. 12). John expresses his hope of a personal visit in the closing remarks (vv. 13, 14), as he does in 2 John.

FOCUS	COMMENDATION OF GAIUS			CONDEMNATION OF DIOTREPHES		
REFERENCE	1———2———5———			9———12———13———14		
DIVISION	SALUTATION	GODLINESS OF GAIUS	GENEROSITY OF GAIUS	PRIDE OF DIOTREPHES	PRAISE FOR DEMETRIUS	BENEDICTION
TOPIC	SERVANTHOOD			SELFISHNESS		
	DUTY OF HOSPITALITY			DANGER OF HAUGHTINESS		
LOCATION	WRITTEN IN EPHESUS					
TIME	C. A.D. 90					

OUTLINE OF 3 JOHN

Salutation

THE Elder,

To the beloved Gaius, [R]whom I love in truth: 2 John 1

Godliness of Gaius

2 Beloved, I pray that you may prosper in all things and be in health, just as your soul prospers.

3 For I [R]rejoiced greatly when brethren came and testified of the truth *that is* in you, just as you walk in the truth. 2 John 4

4 I have no greater joy than to hear that [R]my children walk in truth.* [1 Cor. 4:15]

Generosity of Gaius

5 Beloved, you do faithfully whatever you do for the brethren and* for strangers,

6 who have borne witness of your love before the church. *If* you send them forward on their journey in a manner worthy of God, you will do well,

7 because they went forth for His name's sake, taking nothing from the Gentiles.

8 We therefore ought to [R]receive* such, that we may become fellow workers for the truth. Matt. 10:40

Pride of Diotrephes

9 I wrote to the church, but Diotrephes, who loves to have the preeminence among them, does not receive us.

10 Therefore, if I come, I will call to mind his deeds which he does, prating against us with malicious words. And not content with that, he himself does not receive the brethren, and forbids those who wish to, putting *them* out of the church.

11 Beloved, do not imitate what is evil, but what is good. He who does good is of God, but* he who does evil has not seen God.

Praise for Demetrius

12 Demetrius [R]has a *good* testimony from all, and from the truth itself. And we also [T]bear witness, [R]and you know that our testimony is true. 1 Tim. 3:7 • *testify* • John 19:35

Benediction

13 I had many things to write, but I do not wish to write to you with pen and ink;

14 but I hope to see you shortly, and we shall speak face to face. Peace to you. Our friends greet you. Greet the friends by name.

4 NU *the truth* 5 NU adds *especially* 8 NU *support* 11 NU, M omit *but*

THE EPISTLE OF

JUDE

THE BOOK OF JUDE

Fight! Contend! Do battle! When apostasy arises, when false teachers emerge, when the truth of God is attacked, it is time to fight for the faith. Only believers who are spiritually "in shape" can answer the summons. At the beginning of his letter, Jude focuses on the believers' common salvation, but then feels compelled to challenge them to contend for the faith. The danger is real. False teachers have crept into the church, turning God's grace into unbounded license to do as they please. Jude reminds such men of God's past dealings with unbelieving Israel, disobedient angels, and wicked Sodom and Gomorrah. In the face of such danger, Christians should not be caught off guard. The challenge is great, but so is the God who is able to keep them from stumbling.

The Greek title *Iouda,* "Of Jude," comes from the name *Ioudas* which appears in verse 1. This name, which can be translated "Jude" or "Judas," was popular in the first century because of Judas Maccabaeus (died 160 B.C.), a leader of the Jewish resistance against Syria during the Maccabean revolt.

THE AUTHOR OF JUDE

In spite of its limited subject matter and size, Jude was accepted as authentic and quoted by early church fathers. There may be some older allusions, but undisputed references to this epistle appear in the last quarter of the second century. It was included in the Muratorian Canon (c. A.D. 170) and accepted as part of Scripture by early leaders, such as Tertullian and Origen. Nevertheless, doubts arose concerning the place of Jude in the canon because of its use of the Apocrypha. It was a disputed book in some parts of the church, but it eventually won universal recognition.

The author identifies himself as "a bondservant of Jesus Christ, and brother of James" (v. 1). This designation, combined with the reference in verse 17 to the apostles, makes it unlikely that this is the apostle Jude, called "Judas *the son* of James" in Luke 6:16 and in Acts 1:13. This leaves the traditional view that Jude was one of the Lord's brothers, called Judas in Matthew 13:55 and Mark 6:3 (see "The Author of James"). His older brother James (note his position on the two lists) was the famous leader of the Jerusalem church (Acts 15:13–21) and author of the epistle that bears his name. Like his brothers, Jude did not believe in Jesus before the Resurrection (John 7:1–9; Acts 1:14). The only other biblical allusion to him is in 1 Corinthians 9:5 where it is recorded that "the brothers of the Lord" took their wives along on their missionary journeys (the Judas of Acts 15:22, 32 may be another reference to him). Extrabiblical tradition adds nothing to our limited knowledge of Jude.

THE TIME OF JUDE

Jude's general address does not mark out any particular circle of readers, and there are no geographical restrictions. Nevertheless, he probably had in mind a specific region that was being troubled by false teachers. There is not enough information in the epistle to settle the question of whether his readers were predominately Jewish or Gentile Christians (there is probably a mixture of both). In any case, the progress of the faith in their region was threatened by a number of apostates who rejected Christ in practice and principle. These proud libertines were especially dangerous because of their deceptive flattery (v. 16) and infiltration of Christian meetings (v. 12). They perverted the grace of God (v. 4) and caused divisions in the church (v. 19).

Jude's description of these heretics is reminiscent of that found in 2 Peter and leads to the issue of the relationship between the two epistles (see "The Author of 2 Peter"). The strong similarity between 2 Peter 2:1—3:4 and Jude 4–18 can hardly be coincidental, but the equally obvious differences rule out the possibility that one is a mere copy of the other. It is also doubtful that both authors independently drew from an unknown third source, so the two remaining options are that Peter used Jude or Jude used Peter. Both views have their advocates, and a number of arguments have been raised in support of either side. But two arguments for the priority of 2 Peter are so strong that they tip the scales in favor of this position: (1) A comparison of the two books shows that 2 Peter anticipates the future rise of apostate teachers (2 Pet. 2:1, 2; 3:3) while Jude records the historical fulfillment of Peter's words (Jude 4, 11, 12, 17, 18); (2) Jude directly quotes 2 Peter 3:3 and acknowledges it as a quotation from the apostles (cf. 1 Tim. 4:1; 2 Tim. 3:1).

Because of the silence of the New Testament and tradition concerning Jude's later years, we cannot know where this epistle was written. Nor is there any way to be certain of its date. Assuming the priority of 2 Peter (A.D. 64–66), the probable range is A.D. 66–80. (Jude's silence concerning the destruction of Jerusalem does not prove that he wrote this letter before A.D. 70.)

THE CHRIST OF JUDE

In contrast to those who stand condemned by their licentiousness and denial of Christ (v. 4), the believer is "preserved in Jesus Christ" (v. 1). Jude tells his readers to "keep yourselves in the love of God, looking for the mercy of our Lord Jesus Christ unto eternal life" (v. 21). But at the same time, the Lord "is able to keep you from stumbling, and to present *you* faultless before the presence of His glory with exceeding joy" (v. 24).

KEYS TO JUDE

Key Word: Contend for the Faith—This epistle is intensely concerned with the threat of heretical teachers in the church and the believer's proper response to that threat. The contents reveal two major purposes: first, to condemn the practices of the ungodly libertines who were infesting the churches and corrupting believers; and second, to counsel the readers to stand firm, grow in their faith, and contend for the truth. Jude says little about the actual doctrines of these "raging waves of the sea," but they may have held to an antinomian version of Gnosticism (see "The Time of 1 John"). The readers are encouraged to reach out to those who have been misled by these men.

Key Verse: Jude 3—"Beloved, while I was very diligent to write to you concerning our common salvation, I found it necessary to write to you exhorting you to contend earnestly for the faith which was once for all delivered to the saints" (v. 3).

SURVEY OF JUDE

A surprisingly large number of the Pauline and non-Pauline epistles confront the problem of false teachers, and almost all of them allude to it. But Jude goes beyond all other New Testament epistles in its relentless and passionate denunciation of the apostate teachers who have "crept in unnoticed." With the exception of its salutation (vv. 1, 2) and doxology (vv. 24, 25), the entire epistle revolves around this alarming problem. Combining the theme of 2 Peter with the style of James, Jude is potent in spite of its brevity. This urgent letter has four major sections: purpose of Jude (vv. 1–4); description of false teachers (vv. 5–16); defense against false teachers (vv. 17–23); and doxology of Jude (vv. 24, 25).

Purpose of Jude (vv. 1–4): Jude addresses his letter to believers who are "called," "sanctified," and "preserved," and wishes for them the threefold blessing of mercy, peace, and love (vv. 1, 2). Grim news about the encroachment of false teachers in the churches has impelled Jude to put aside his commentary on salvation to write this timely word of rebuke and warning (vv. 3, 4). In view of apostates who turn "the grace of our God into lewdness" and deny Christ, it is crucial that believers "contend earnestly for the faith."

Description of False Teachers (vv. 5–16): Jude begins his extended exposæa of the apostate teachers by illustrating their ultimate doom with three examples of divine judgment from the Pentateuch (vv. 5–7).

Like unreasoning animals, these apostates are ruled by the things they revile, and they are destroyed by the things they practice (vv. 8–10). Even the archangel Michael is more careful in his dealings with superhuman powers than are these arrogant men. He compares these men to three spiritually rebellious men from Genesis (Cain) and Numbers (Balaam and Korah) who incurred the condemnation of God (v. 11). Verses 12 and 13 succinctly summarize their character with five highly descriptive metaphors taken from nature. After affirming the judgment of God upon such ungodly men with a quote from the noncanonical Book of Enoch (vv. 14, 15), Jude catalogs some of their practices (v. 16).

FOCUS	PURPOSE	DESCRIPTION OF FALSE TEACHERS			DEFENSE AGAINST FALSE TEACHERS	DOXOLOGY
REFERENCE	1—5	—8	—14	—17	—24	—25
DIVISION	INTRODUCTION	PAST JUDGMENT	PRESENT CHARACTERISTICS	FUTURE JUDGMENT	DUTY OF BELIEVERS	CONCLUSION
TOPIC	REASON TO CONTEND				HOW TO CONTEND	
	ANATOMY OF APOSTASY				ANTIDOTE FOR APOSTASY	
LOCATION	UNKNOWN					
TIME	C. A.D. 66–80					

Defense Against False Teachers (vv. 17–23): This letter has been exposing apostate teachers (vv. 8, 10, 12, 14, 16), but now Jude directly addresses his readers ("But you, beloved, remember" v. 17). He reminds them of the apostolic warning that such men would come (vv. 17–19) and encourages them to protect themselves against the onslaught of apostasy (vv. 20, 21). The readers must become mature in their own faith so that they will be able to rescue those who are enticed or already ensnared by error (vv. 22, 23).

Doxology of Jude (vv. 24, 25): Jude closes with one of the greatest doxologies in the Bible. It emphasizes the power of Christ to keep those who trust in Him from being overthrown by error.

OUTLINE OF JUDE

Purpose of Jude

JUDE, a bondservant of Jesus Christ, and
[R]brother of James, Acts 1:13

To those who are [R]called, sanctified* by
God the Father, and [R]preserved in Jesus
Christ: Rom. 1:7 • John 17:11, 12

2 Mercy, [R]peace, and love be multiplied to
you. 1 Pet. 1:2

3 Beloved, while I was very diligent to
write to you [R]concerning our common salvation, I found it necessary to write to you exhorting [R]you to contend earnestly for the faith which was once for all delivered to the saints. Titus 1:4 • Phil. 1:27

4 For certain men have crept in unnoticed,
who long ago were marked out for this condemnation, ungodly men, who turn the grace of our God into lewdness and deny the only Lord God* and our Lord Jesus Christ.

Past Judgment of False Teachers

5 But I want to remind you, though you
once knew this, that the Lord, having saved the people out of the land of Egypt, afterward destroyed those who did not believe.

6 And the angels who did not keep their
proper domain, but left their own abode, He has reserved in everlasting chains under darkness for the judgment of the great day;

7 as [R]Sodom and Gomorrah, and the cities
around them in a similar manner to these, having given themselves over to sexual immorality and gone after strange flesh, are set forth as an example, suffering the [T]vengeance of eternal fire. Gen. 19:24 • *punishment*

Present Characteristics of False Teachers

8 [R]Likewise also these dreamers defile the
flesh, reject authority, and [R]speak evil of dignitaries. 2 Pet. 2:10 • Ex. 22:28

9 Yet Michael the archangel, in [T]contending
with the devil, when he disputed about the body of Moses, dared not bring against him a reviling accusation, but said, [R]"The Lord rebuke you!" *arguing* • Zech. 3:2

10 [R]But these speak evil of whatever they do
not know; and whatever they know naturally, like brute beasts, in these things they corrupt themselves. 2 Pet. 2:12

11 Woe to them! For they have gone in the
way [R]of Cain, [R]have run greedily in the error of Balaam for profit, and perished in the rebellion of Korah. Gen. 4:3–8 • 2 Pet. 2:15

12 These are [T]spots in your love feasts, while
they feast with you without fear, serving *only* themselves. *They are* clouds without water, carried about* by the winds; late autumn trees without fruit, twice dead, pulled up by the roots; *stains,* or *hidden reefs*

13 [R]raging waves of the sea, [R]foaming up
their own shame; wandering stars [R]for whom is reserved the blackness of darkness forever. Is. 57:20 • [Phil. 3:19] • 2 Pet. 2:17

Future Judgment of False Teachers

14 [R]Now Enoch, the seventh from Adam,
prophesied about these men also, saying, "Behold, the Lord comes with ten thousands of His saints, Gen. 5:18; Dan. 7:10; Zech. 14:5☆

15 [R]"to execute judgment on all, to convict
all who are ungodly among them of all their ungodly deeds which they have committed in

1 NU *beloved* **4** NU omits *God* **12** NU, M *along*

an ungodly way, and of all the [R]harsh things
which ungodly sinners have spoken against
Him."
2 Pet. 2:6☆ • 1 Sam. 2:3
16 These are grumblers, complainers, walk-
ing according to their own lusts; and they
mouth great swelling *words*, [R]flattering peo-
ple to gain advantage.
Prov. 28:21

Defense Against False Teachers

17 [R]But you, beloved, remember the words
which were spoken before by the apostles of
our Lord Jesus Christ:
2 Pet. 3:2
18 how they told you that there would be
mockers in the last time who would walk ac-
cording to their own ungodly lusts.
19 These are sensual persons, who cause
divisions, not having the Spirit.
20 But you, beloved, [R]building yourselves up
on your most holy faith, [R]praying in the Holy
Spirit,
Col. 2:7 • [Rom. 8:26]
21 keep yourselves in the love of God, [R]look-
ing for the mercy of our Lord Jesus Christ
unto eternal life.
Titus 2:13
22 And on some have compassion, making a
distinction;*
23 but others save with fear, [R]pulling *them*
out of the fire,* hating even the garment de-
filed by the flesh.
Amos 4:11

Doxology of Jude

24 [R]Now to Him who is able to keep you*
from stumbling,
[Eph. 3:20]
And [R]to present *you* faultless
Col. 1:22
Before the presence of His glory with
exceeding joy,
25 To God our Savior,*
Who alone is wise,*
Be glory and majesty,
Dominion and power,*
Both now and forever.
Amen.

22 NU *who are doubting* (or *making distinctions*)
23 NU adds *and on some have mercy with fear* and omits *with fear* in first clause. 24 M *them* 25 NU *To the only God our Savior* • NU omits *Who . . . is wise* and adds *Through Jesus Christ our Lord,* • NU adds *Before all time,*

Measures of Length

Unit	*Length*	*Equivalents*	*Translations*
Day's journey	c. 20 miles		day's journey
Roman mile	4,854 feet	8 stadia	mile
Sabbath day's journey	3,637 feet	6 stadia	Sabbath day's journey
Stadion	606 feet	⅛ Roman mile	furlong
Rod	9 feet (10.5 feet in Ezekiel)	3 paces; 6 cubits	measuring reed, reed
Fathom	6 feet	4 cubits	fathom
Pace	3 feet	⅓ rod; 2 cubits	pace
Cubit	18 inches	½ pace; 2 spans	cubit
Span	9 inches	½ cubit; 3 handbreadths	span
Handbreadth	3 inches	⅓ span; 4 fingers	handbreadth
Finger	.75 inch	¼ handbreadth	finger

THE REVELATION
OF JESUS CHRIST

THE BOOK OF REVELATION

Just as Genesis is the book of beginnings, Revelation is the book of consummation. In it, the divine program of redemption is brought to fruition, and the holy name of God is vindicated before all creation. Although there are numerous prophecies in the Gospels and Epistles, Revelation is the only New Testament book that focuses primarily on prophetic events. Its title means "unveiling" or "disclosure." Thus, the book is an unveiling of the character and program of God. Penned by John during his exile on the island of Patmos, Revelation centers on visions and symbols of the resurrected Christ, who alone has authority to judge the earth, to remake it, and to rule it in righteousness.

The title of this book in the Greek text is *Apokalypsis Ioannou,* "Revelation of John." It is also known as the Apocalypse, a transliteration of the word *apokalypsis,* meaning "unveiling," "disclosure," or "revelation." Thus, the book is an unveiling of that which otherwise could not be known. A better title comes from the first verse: *Apokalypsis Iesou Christou,* "Revelation of Jesus Christ." This could be taken as a revelation that came from Christ or as a revelation that is about Christ—both are appropriate. Because of the unified contents of this book, it should not be called Revelations.

THE AUTHOR OF REVELATION

The style, symmetry, and plan of Revelation show that it was written by one author, four times named "John" (1:1, 4, 9; 22:8; see "The Author of John"). Because of its contents and its address to seven churches, Revelation quickly circulated and became widely known and accepted in the early church. It was frequently mentioned and quoted by second- and third-century Christian writers and was received as part of the canon of New Testament books. From the beginning, Revelation was considered an authentic work of the apostle John, the same John who wrote the gospel and three epistles. This was held to be true by Justin Martyr, the Shepherd of Hermas, Melito, Irenaeus, the Muratorian Canon, Tertullian, Clement of Alexandria, Origen, and others.

This view was seldom questioned until the middle of the third century when Dionysius presented several arguments against the apostolic authorship of Revelation. He observed a clear difference in style and thought between Revelation and the books that he accepted as Johannine, and he concluded that the Apocalypse must have been penned by a different John. Indeed, the internal evidence does pose some problems for the traditional view: (1) The Greek grammar of Revelation is not on par with the fourth Gospel or the Johannine Epistles. (2) There are also differences in vocabulary and expressions used. (3) The theological content of this book differs from John's other writings in emphasis and presentation. (4) John's other writings avoid the use of his name, but it is found four times in this book. While these difficulties exist, two things should be kept in mind: (1) There are a number of remarkable similarities between the Apocalypse and the other books traditionally associated with the apostle John (e.g., the distinctive use of terms, such as "word," "lamb," and "true," and the careful development of conflicting themes, such as light and darkness, love and hatred, good and evil). (2) Many of the differences can be explained by the unusual circumstances surrounding this book. The apocalyptic subject matter demands a different treatment, and John received the contents not by reflection but by a series of startling and ecstatic visions. It is also possible that John used a secretary who smoothed out the Greek style of his other writings, and that his exile on Patmos prevented the use of such a scribe when he wrote Revelation.

Thus, the internal evidence, while problematic, need not overrule the early and strong external testimony to the apostolic origin of this important book. The author was obviously well known to the recipients in the seven Asian churches, and this fits the unqualified use of the name "John" and the uniform tradition about his ministry in Asia. Alternate suggestions, such as John the Elder or a prophet named John, create more problems than they solve.

THE TIME OF REVELATION

John directed this prophetic word to seven selected churches in the Roman province of Asia (1:3, 4). The messages to these churches in chapters 2 and 3 begin with Ephesus, the most prominent, and continue in a clockwise direction until Laodicea is reached. It is likely that this book was initially carried along this circular route. While each of these messages had particular significance for these churches, they were also relevant for the church as a whole ("He who has an ear, let him hear what the Spirit says to the churches").

John's effective testimony for Christ led the Roman authorities to exile him to the small, desolate island of Patmos in the Aegean Sea (1:9). This island of volcanic rock was one of several places to which the Romans banished criminals and political offenders.

Revelation was written at a time when Roman hostility to Christianity was erupting into overt persecution (1:9; 2:10, 13). Some scholars believe that it should be given an early date during the persecution of Christians under Nero after the A.D. 64 burning of Rome. The Hebrew letters for Nero Caesar (*Neron Kesar*) add up to 666, the number of the Beast (13:18), and there was a legend that Nero would reappear in the East after his apparent death (cf. Rev. 13:3, 12, 14). This kind of evidence is weak, and a later date near the end of the reign of the emperor Domitian (A.D. 81–96) is preferable for several reasons: (1) This was the testimony of Irenaeus (disciple of Polycarp who was a disciple of John) and other early Christian writers. (2) John probably did not move from Jerusalem to Ephesus until about A.D. 67, shortly before the Roman destruction of Jerusalem in A.D. 70. The early dating would not give him enough time to have established an ongoing ministry in Asia by the time he wrote this book. (3) The churches of Asia appear to have been in existence for a number of years, long enough for some to reach a point of complacency and decline (cf. 2:4; 3:1, 15–18). (4) The deeds of Domitian are more relevant than those of Nero to the themes of the Apocalypse. Worship of deceased emperors had been practiced for years, but Domitian was the first emperor to demand worship while he was alive. This led to a greater clash between the state and the church, especially in Asia, where the worship of Caesar was widely practiced. The persecution under Domitian presaged the more severe persecutions to follow.

Thus, it is likely that John wrote this book in A.D. 95 or 96. The date of his release from Patmos is unknown, but he was probably allowed to return to Ephesus after the reign of Domitian. Passages such as 1:11; 22:7, 9, 10, 18, 19 suggest that the book was completed before John's release.

THE CHRIST OF REVELATION

Revelation has much to say about all three Persons of the Godhead, but it is especially clear in its presentation of the awesome resurrected Christ who has received all authority to judge the earth. He is called Jesus Christ (1:1), the faithful witness, the firstborn from the dead, the ruler over the kings of the earth (1:5), the First and the Last (1:17), He who lives (1:18), the Son of God (2:18), holy and true (3:7), the Amen, the Faithful and True Witness, the Beginning of the creation of God (3:14), the Lion of the tribe of Judah, the Root of David (5:5), a Lamb (5:6), Faithful and True (19:11), The Word of God (19:13), KING OF KINGS, AND LORD OF LORDS (19:16), Alpha and Omega (22:13), the Bright and Morning Star (22:16), and the Lord Jesus Christ (22:21).

This book is indeed "The Revelation of Jesus Christ" (1:1) since it comes from Him and centers on Him. It begins with a vision of His glory, wisdom, and power (1) and portrays His authority over the entire church (2; 3). He is the Lamb who was slain and declared worthy to open the book of judgment (5). His righteous wrath is poured out upon the whole earth (6—18), and He returns in power to judge His enemies and to reign as the Lord over all (19; 20). He will rule forever over the heavenly city in the presence of all who know Him (21; 22).

The Scriptures close with His great promise: " 'Behold, I am coming quickly!' " (22:7, 12). " 'Surely I am coming quickly.' Amen. Even so, come, Lord Jesus!" (22:20).

KEYS TO REVELATION

Key Word: The Revelation of the Coming of Christ—The purposes for which Revelation was written depend to some extent on how the book as a whole is interpreted. Because of its complex imagery and symbolism, Revelation is the most difficult biblical book to interpret, and there are four major alternatives: (1) The symbolic or idealist view maintains that Revelation is not a predictive prophecy, but a symbolic portrait of the cosmic conflict of spiritual principles. (2) The preterist view (the Latin word *praeter* means "past") maintains that it is a symbolic description of the Roman persecution of the church, emperor worship, and the divine judgment of Rome. (3) The historicist view approaches Revelation as an allegorical panorama of the history of the (Western) church from the first century to the Second Advent. (4) The futurist view acknowledges the obvious influence that the first-century conflict between Roman power and the church had upon the themes of this book. It also accepts the bulk of Revelation (4–22) as an inspired look into the time immediately preceding the Second Advent (the "Tribulation," usually seen as seven years; 6—18), and extending from the return of Christ to the creation of the new cosmos (19—22).

Advocates of all four interpretive approaches to Revelation agree that it was written to assure the recipients of the ultimate triumph of Christ over all who rise up against Him and His saints. The readers were facing dark times of persecution, and even worse times would follow. Therefore, they needed to be encouraged to persevere by standing firm in Christ in view of God's plan for the righteous and the wicked. This plan is especially clear in the stirring words of the epilogue (22:6–21). The book was also written to challenge complacent Christians to stop compromising with the world. According to futurists, Revelation serves the additional purpose of providing a perspective on end-time events that would have meaning and relevance to the spiritual lives of all succeeding generations of Christians.

Key Verses: Revelation 1:19 and 19:11–15—" 'Write the things which you have seen, and the things which are, and the things which will take place after this' " (1:19).

"Now I saw heaven opened, and behold, a white horse. And He who sat on him *was* called Faithful and True, and in righteousness He judges and makes war. His eyes *were* like a flame of fire, and on His head *were* many crowns. He had a name written that no one knew except Himself. He *was* clothed with a robe dipped in blood, and His name is called The Word of God. And the armies in heaven, clothed in fine linen, white and clean, followed Him on white horses. Now out of His mouth goes a sharp sword, that with it He should strike the nations. And He Himself will rule them with a rod of iron. He Himself treads the winepress of the fierceness and wrath of Almighty God" (19:11–15).

Key Chapters: Revelation 19—22—When the end of history is fully understood, its impact radically affects the present. In Revelation 19—22 the plans of God for the last days and for all of eternity are recorded in explicit terms. Careful study of and obedience to them will bring the blessings that are promised (1:3). Uppermost in the mind and deep in the heart should be guarded the words of Jesus, "Behold, I am coming quickly."

SURVEY OF REVELATION

Revelation is written in the form of apocalyptic literature (cf. Daniel and Zechariah) by a prophet (10:11; 22:9) and refers to itself as a prophetic book (1:3; 22:7, 10, 18, 19). The three major movements in this profound unveiling are captured in 1:19: "the things which you have seen" (1); "the things which are" (2 and 3); and "the things which must take place after this" (4—22).

"The Things Which You Have Seen" (1): Revelation contains a prologue (1:1–3) before the usual salutation (1:4–8). The Revelation was received by Christ from the Father and communicated by an angel to John. This is the only biblical book that specifically promises a blessing to those who read it (1:3), but it also promises a curse to those who add to or detract from it (22:18, 19). The salutation and closing benediction show that it was originally written as an epistle to seven Asian churches.

A rich theological portrait of the triune God (1:4–8) is followed by an overwhelming theophany (visible manifestation of God) in 1:9–20. The omnipotent and omniscient Christ who will subjugate all things under His authority is the central figure in this book.

"The Things Which Are" (2 and 3): The messages to the seven churches (2; 3) refer back to an aspect of John's vision of Christ and contain a command, a commendation and/or condemnation, a correction, and a challenge.

"The Things Which Must Take Place After This" (4—22): John is translated into heaven where he is given a vision of the divine majesty. In it, the Father ("*One* sat on the throne") and the Son (The Lion/Lamb) are worshiped by the twenty-four elders, the four living creatures, and the angelic host because of who they are and what they have done (creation and redemption; 4 and 5).

Three cycles of seven judgments in chapters 6—16 consist of seven seals, seven trumpets, and seven bowls. There is a prophetic insert be-

FOCUS	"THINGS WHICH YOU HAVE SEEN"	"THINGS WHICH ARE"	"THINGS WHICH WILL TAKE PLACE"				
REFERENCE	1:1—2:1—4:1—6:1—19:7—20:1—21:1—22:21						
DIVISION	THE LORD JESUS CHRIST	SEVEN CHURCHES	THE JUDGE	TRIBULATION	SECOND COMING	MILLENNIUM	ETERNAL STATE
TOPIC	VISION OF CHRIST		VISION OF CONSUMMATION				
	THEOPHANY	TALKS	TRIBULATIONS		TRUMPETS		TOGETHER
LOCATION	WRITTEN ON THE ISLAND OF PATMOS						
TIME	C. A.D. 95–96						

tween the sixth and seventh seal and trumpet judgments and an extended insert between the trumpet and bowl judgments. Because of the similarity of the seventh judgment in each series, it is possible that the three sets of judgments take place concurrently or with some overlap so that they all terminate with the return of Christ. An alternate approach views them as three consecutive series of judgments, so that the seventh seal is the seven trumpets and the seventh trumpet is the seven bowls.

The seven seals (6:1—8:5) include war, the famine and death that are associated with war, and persecution. The prophetic insert between the sixth and seventh seals (7) describes the protective sealing of 144,000 "children of Israel," 12,000 from every tribe. It also looks ahead to the multitudes from every part of the earth who come "out of the great tribulation." The catastrophic events in most of the trumpet judgments are called "woes" (8:2—11:19). The prophetic interlude between the sixth and seventh trumpets (10:1—11:14) adds more details about the nature of the tribulation period and mentions a fourth set of seven judgments (the "seven thunders"), which would have extended it if they had not been withdrawn. Two unnamed witnesses minister during three and one-half years of the Tribulation (forty-two months or 1,260 days). At the end of their ministry they are overcome by the Beast, but their resurrection and ascension confound their enemies.

Chapters 12—14 contain a number of miscellaneous prophecies that are inserted between the trumpet and bowl judgments to give further background on the time of tribulation. In chapter 12 a woman gives birth to a male child, who is caught up to God. The woman flees into the wilderness and is pursued by the Dragon, who is cast down to earth. Chapter 13 gives a graphic description of the beast and his False Prophet, both empowered by the Dragon. The first beast is given political, economic, and religious authority; and because of his power and the lying miracles performed by the second beast, he is worshiped as the ruler of the earth. Chapter 14 contains a series of visions including the 144,000 at the end of the Tribulation, the fate of those who follow the beast, and the outpouring of the wrath of God.

The seven bowl judgments of chapter 16 are prefaced by a heavenly vision of the power, holiness, and glory of God in chapter 15.

Chapters 17 and 18 anticipate the final downfall of Babylon, the great harlot sitting upon a scarlet-colored beast.

The marriage banquet of the Lamb is ready and the King of Kings, Lord of Lords leads the armies of heaven into battle against the beast and his False Prophet. They are cast into a lake of fire (19).

In chapter 20 the Dragon—Satan—is bound for a thousand years. He is cast into a bottomless pit. During this one thousand-year period Christ reigns over the earth with His resurrected saints, but by the end of this millennium, many have been born who refuse to submit their hearts to Christ. At the end of the thousand years, Satan is released and a final battle ensues. This is followed by the judgment at the Great White Throne.

A new universe is created, this time unspoiled by sin, death, pain, or sorrow. The New Jerusalem, described in 21:9—22:5, is shaped like a gigantic cube, 1,500 miles in length, width, and height (the Most Holy Place in the Old Testament tabernacle and the temple was also a perfect cube). Its multicolored stones will reflect the glory of God, and it will continually be filled with light. But the greatest thing of all is that believers will be in the presence of God and "they shall see His face."

Revelation concludes with an epilogue (22:6–21), which reassures the readers that Christ is coming quickly (22:7, 12, 20) and invites all who wish to "take the water of life freely" (22:17) to come to the Alpha and Omega, the Bright and Morning Star.

OUTLINE OF REVELATION

Part One: "The Things Which You Have Seen" (1:1–20)

I. Introduction **1:1–8**
II. Revelation of Christ **1:9–20**

Part Two: "The Things Which Are" (2:1—3:22)

I. Message to Ephesus **2:1–7**
II. Message to Smyrna **2:8–11**
III. Message to Pergamos **2:12–17**
IV. Message to Thyatira **2:18–29**
V. Message to Sardis **3:1–6**
VI. Message to Philadelphia **3:7–13**
VII. Message to Laodicea **3:14–22**

Part Three: "The Things Which Will Take Place After This" (4:1—22:21)

CHAPTER 1

Introduction

THE Revelation of Jesus Christ, [R]which
God gave Him to show His servants—
things which must shortly take place. And
[R]He sent and signified *it* by His angel to His
servant John, John 3:32 • Rev. 22:6
2 [R]who bore witness to the word of God,
and to the testimony of Jesus Christ, to all
things [R]that he saw. 1 Cor. 1:6 • 1 John 1:1
3 [R]Blessed *is* he who reads and those who
hear the words of this prophecy, and keep
those things which are written in it; for [R]the
time *is* near. Luke 11:28 • James 5:8

4 John, to the seven churches which are in
Asia:

Grace to you and peace from Him [R]who
is and [R]who was and who is to come, [R]and
from the seven Spirits who are before His
throne, Ex. 3:14 • John 1:1 • [Is. 11:2]
5 and from Jesus Christ, [R]the faithful wit-
ness, the firstborn from the dead, and [R]the
ruler over the kings of the earth. To Him who
loved us and washed* us from our sins in His
own blood, John 8:14 • Ps. 89:27★
6 and has made us kings* and priests to His
God and Father, to Him *be* glory and domin-
ion forever and ever. Amen.
7 Behold, He is coming with clouds, and
every eye will see Him, even they who pierced
Him. And all the tribes of the earth will mourn
because of Him. Even so, Amen.
8 [R]"I am the Alpha and the Omega, *the* Be-
ginning and *the* End,"* says the Lord,* [R]"who
is and who was and who is to come, the [R]Al-
mighty." Is. 41:4 • Rev. 4:8; 11:17 • Is. 9:6

Revelation of Christ

9 I, John, both* your brother and compan-
ion in the tribulation and kingdom and pa-
tience of Jesus Christ, was on the island that
is called Patmos for the word of God and for
the testimony of Jesus Christ.

1:5 NU *loves us and freed;* M *loves us and washed*
1:6 NU, M *a kingdom* 1:8 NU, M omit *the Beginning and the End* • NU, M add *God* 1:9 NU, M omit *both*

10 [R]I was in the Spirit on [R]the Lord's Day,
and I heard behind me [R]a loud voice, as of a
trumpet, Acts 10:10 • Acts 20:7 • Rev. 4:1
11 saying, "I am the Alpha and the Omega,
the First and the Last," and,* "What you see,
write in a book and send *it* to the seven
churches which are in Asia:* to Ephesus, to
Smyrna, to Pergamos, to Thyatira, to Sardis,
to Philadelphia, and to Laodicea."
12 Then I turned to see the voice that spoke
with me. And having turned [R]I saw seven
golden lampstands, Ex. 25:37
13 and in the midst of the seven lampstands
One like the Son of Man, clothed with a garment down to the feet and girded about the
chest with a golden band.
14 His head and [R]hair *were* white like wool,
as white as snow, and [R]His eyes like a flame of
fire; Dan. 7:9 • Dan. 10:6
15 [R]His feet *were* like fine brass, as if refined
in a furnace, and [R]His voice as the sound of
many waters; Ezek. 1:7 • Ezek. 1:24
16 He had in His right hand seven stars, [R]out
of His mouth went a sharp two-edged sword,
[R]and His countenance *was* like the sun shining in its strength. Is. 49:2★ • Matt. 17:2
17 And [R]when I saw Him, I fell at His feet as
dead. But [R]He laid His right hand on me, saying to me,* "Do not be afraid; I am the First
and the Last. Ezek. 1:28 • Dan. 8:18
18 "I *am* He who lives, and was dead, and behold, I am alive forevermore. Amen. And I
have the keys of Hades and of Death.
19 "Write* the things which you have seen,
and the things which are, and the things
which will take place after this.
20 "The mystery of the seven stars which
you saw in My right hand, and the seven
golden lampstands: The seven stars are [R]the
angels of the seven churches, and [R]the seven
lampstands which you saw* are the seven
churches. Rev. 2:1 • Zech. 4:2

CHAPTER 2

Message to Ephesus

"TO the [T]angel of the church of Ephesus
write, Or *messenger*
'These things says He who holds the
seven stars in His right hand, who walks in
the midst of the seven golden lampstands:
2 [R]"I know your works, your labor, your patience, and that you cannot bear those who
are evil. And [R]you have tested those who say
they are apostles and are not, and have found
them liars; Ps. 1:6 • 1 John 4:1
3 "and you have persevered and have patience, and have labored for My name's sake
and have [R]not become weary. Gal. 6:9
4 "Nevertheless I have *this* against you, that
you have left your first love.
5 "Remember therefore from where you
have fallen; repent and do the first works, [R]or
else I will come to you quickly and remove
your lampstand from its place—unless you repent. Matt. 21:41
6 "But this you have, that you hate the
deeds of the Nicolaitans, which I also hate.
7 [R]"He who has an ear, let him hear what
the Spirit says to the churches. To him who
overcomes I will give [R]to eat from [R]the tree of
life, which is in the midst of the Paradise of
God." ' Matt. 11:15 • [Rev. 22:2, 14] • [Gen. 2:9; 3:22]

Message to Smyrna

8 "And to the [T]angel of the church in
Smyrna write, Or *messenger*
'These things says the First and the Last,
who was dead, and came to life:
9 "I know your works, tribulation, and
poverty (but you are rich); and *I know* the
blasphemy of those who say they are Jews
and are not, but *are* a synagogue of Satan.
10 [R]"Do not fear any of those things which
you are about to suffer. Indeed, the devil is
about to throw *some* of you into prison, that
you may be tested, and you will have tribulation ten days. Be faithful until death, and I will
give you the crown of life. Matt. 10:22
11 [R]"He who has an ear, let him hear what
the Spirit says to the churches. He who overcomes shall not be hurt by [R]the second
death." ' Rev. 13:9 • [Rev. 20:6, 14; 21:8]

Message to Pergamos

12 "And to the [T]angel of the church in Pergamos write, Or *messenger*
'These things says [R]He who has the sharp
two-edged sword: Is. 49:2☆
13 "I know your works, and where you
dwell, where Satan's throne *is*. And you hold
fast to My name, and did not deny My faith
even in the days in which Antipas *was* My
faithful martyr, who was killed among you,
where Satan dwells.
14 "But I have a few things against you, because you have there those who hold the doctrine of [R]Balaam, who taught Balak to put a
stumbling block before the children of Israel,
to eat things sacrificed to idols, and to commit
sexual immorality. Num. 31:16
15 "Thus you also have those who hold the
doctrine of the Nicolaitans, which thing I
hate.*
16 "Repent, or else I will come to you quickly
and [R]will fight against them with the sword of
My mouth. 2 Thess. 2:8
17 "He who has an ear, let him hear what
the Spirit says to the churches. To him who
overcomes I will give some of the hidden
[R]manna to eat. And I will give him a white

1:11 NU, M omit *"I am* through third *and* • NU, M omit *which are in Asia* **1:17** NU, M omit *to me* **1:19** NU, M *Therefore, write* **1:20** NU, M omit *which you saw* **2:15** NU, M *likewise* for *which thing I hate*

stone, and on the stone [R]a new name written which no one knows except him who receives *it*." ' Ex. 16:33, 34 • Rev. 3:12

Message to Thyatira

18 "And to the [T]angel of the church in Thyatira write, Or *messenger*

'These things says the Son of God, [R]who has eyes like a flame of fire, and His feet like fine brass: Rev. 1:14, 15

19 "I know your works, love, service, faith,* and your patience; and *as* for your works, the last *are* more than the first.

20 "Nevertheless I have a few things against you, because you allow* that woman* [R]Jezebel, who calls herself a prophetess, to teach and seduce* My servants to commit sexual immorality and eat things sacrificed to idols. 1 Kin. 16:31; 21:25

21 "And I gave her time to repent of her sexual immorality, and she did not repent.*

22 "Indeed I will cast her into a sickbed, and those who commit adultery with her into great tribulation, unless they repent of their* deeds.

23 "I will kill her children with death, and all the churches shall know that I am He who [R]searches[T] the minds and hearts. And I will give to each one of you according to your works. Jer. 11:20; 17:10 • *examines*

24 "Now to you I say, and* to the rest in Thyatira, as many as do not have this doctrine, who have not known the [R]depths of Satan, as they say, [R]I will* put on you no other burden. 2 Tim. 3:1–9 • Acts 15:28

25 "But hold fast [R]what you have till I come. Rev. 3:11

26 "And he who overcomes, and keeps [R]My works until the end, [R]to him I will give power over the nations— [John 6:29] • [Matt. 19:28]

27 '*He shall rule them with a rod of iron;*
They shall be dashed to pieces like the potter's vessels'*—

as I also have received from My Father;

28 "and I will give him the morning star.

29 "He who has an ear, let him hear what the Spirit says to the churches." '

CHAPTER 3

Message to Sardis

"AND to the [T]angel of the church in Sardis write, Or *messenger*

'These things says He who [R]has the seven Spirits of God and the seven stars: "I know your works, that you have a name that you are alive, but you are dead. Rev. 1:4, 16

2 "Be watchful, and strengthen the things which remain, that are ready to die, for I have not found your works perfect before God.*

3 [R]"Remember therefore how you have received and heard; hold fast and repent. Therefore if you will not watch, I will come upon you as a thief, and you will not know what hour I will come upon you. 1 Tim. 6:20

4 "You* have [R]a few names even in Sardis who have not [R]defiled their garments; and they shall walk with Me [R]in white, for they are worthy. Acts 1:15 • [Jude 23] • Rev. 4:4; 6:11

5 "He who overcomes [R]shall be clothed in white garments, and I will not [R]blot out his name from the [R]Book of Life; but I will confess his name before My Father and before His angels. [Rev. 19:8] • Ex. 32:32 • Phil. 4:3

6 [R]"He who has an ear, let him hear what the Spirit says to the churches." ' Rev. 2:7

Message to Philadelphia

7 "And to the [T]angel of the church in Philadelphia write, Or *messenger*

'These things says [R]He who is holy, He who is true, *"He who has the key of David,* [R]*He who opens and no one shuts, and shuts and no one opens"*:* Acts 3:14 • [Matt. 16:19]

8 [R]"I know your works. See, I have set before you [R]an open door, and no one can shut it;* for you have a little strength, have kept My word, and have not denied My name. Rev. 3:1 • 1 Cor. 16:9

9 "Indeed I will make [R]*those* of the synagogue of Satan, who say they are Jews and are not, but lie—indeed I will make them come and worship before your feet, and to know that I have loved you. Rev. 2:9

10 "Because you have kept My command to persevere, [R]I also will keep you from the hour of trial which shall come upon [R]the whole world, to test those who dwell [R]on the earth. 2 Pet. 2:9 • Luke 2:1 • Is. 24:17

11 "Behold,* [R]I am coming quickly! [R]Hold fast what you have, that no one may take [R]your crown. Phil. 4:5 • Rev. 2:25 • [Rev. 2:10]

12 "He who overcomes, I will make him [R]a pillar in the temple of My God, and he shall go out no more. I will write on him the name of My God and the name of the city of My God, the New Jerusalem, which comes down out of heaven from My God. And *I will write on him* My new name. 1 Kin. 7:21

13 [R]"He who has an ear, let him hear what the Spirit says to the churches." ' Rev. 2:7

Message to Laodicea

14 "And to the [T]angel of the church of the Laodiceans* write, Or *messenger*

2:19 NU, M *faith, service* **2:20** NU, M *I have against you that you tolerate* • M *your wife Jezebel* • NU, M *and teaches and seduces* **2:21** NU, M *time to repent, and she does not want to repent of her sexual immorality.* **2:22** NU, M *her* **2:24** NU, M omit *and* • NU, M omit *will* **2:27** Ps. 2:9 **3:2** NU, M *My God* **3:4** NU, M *Nevertheless you have a few names in Sardis* **3:7** Is. 22:22 **3:8** NU, M *which no one can shut* **3:11** NU, M omit *Behold* **3:14** NU, M *in Laodicea*

[R]"These things says the Amen, [R]the Faith-
ful and True Witness, the Beginning of the cre-
ation of God: 2 Cor. 1:20 • Rev. 1:5; 3:7
15 [R]"I know your works, that you are neither
cold nor hot. I could wish you were cold or
hot. Rev. 3:1
16 "So then, because you are lukewarm, and
neither cold nor hot,* I will vomit you out of
My mouth.
17 "Because you say, 'I am rich, have become
wealthy, and have need of nothing'—and do
not know that you are wretched, miserable,
poor, blind, and naked—
18 "I counsel you [R]to buy from Me gold re-
fined in the fire, that you may be rich; and
[R]white garments, that you may be clothed,
that the shame of your nakedness may not be
revealed; and anoint your eyes with eye salve,
that you may see. Is. 55:1 • 2 Cor. 5:3
19 "As many as I love, I rebuke and chasten.
Therefore be zealous and repent.
20 "Behold, [R]I stand at the door and knock.
[R]If anyone hears My voice and opens the door,
I will come in to him and dine with him, and
he with Me. Song 5:2 • Luke 12:36, 37
21 "To him who overcomes I will grant to sit
with Me on My throne, as I also overcame and
sat down with My Father on His throne.
22 [R]"He who has an ear, let him hear what
the Spirit says to the churches." ' " Rev. 2:7

CHAPTER 4

The Throne of God

AFTER these things I looked, and behold, a
door *standing* [R]open in heaven. And the
first voice which I heard *was* like a trumpet
speaking with me, saying, "Come up here, and
I will show you things which must take place
after this." Ezek. 1:1
2 Immediately [R]I was in the Spirit; and be-
hold, [R]a throne set in heaven, and *One* sat on
the throne. Rev. 1:10 • Is. 6:1
3 And He who sat there was* like a jasper
and a sardius stone in appearance; and *there
was* a rainbow around the throne, in appear-
ance like an emerald.
4 Around the throne *were* twenty-four
thrones, and on the thrones I saw twenty-four
elders sitting, clothed in white robes; and they
had crowns* of gold on their heads.
5 And from the throne proceeded light-
nings, thunderings, and voices.* Seven lamps
of fire *were* burning before the throne, which
are the* seven Spirits of God.
6 Before the throne *there was** [R]a sea of
glass, like crystal. [R]And in the midst of the
throne, and around the throne, *were* four liv-
ing creatures full of eyes in front and in
back. Rev. 15:2 • Ezek. 1:5
7 [R]The first living creature *was* like a lion,
the second living creature like a calf, the
third living creature had a face like a man,
and the fourth living creature *was* like a fly-
ing eagle. Ezek. 1:10; 10:14
8 *The* four living creatures, each having
[R]six wings, were full of eyes around and
within. And they do not rest day or night, say-
ing: Is. 6:2

[R]"Holy, holy, holy,* Is. 6:3
[R]Lord God Almighty, Rev. 1:8
Who was and is and is to come!"

9 Whenever the living creatures give glory
and honor and thanks to Him who sits on the
throne, who lives forever and ever,
10 the twenty-four elders fall down before
Him who sits on the throne and worship Him
who lives forever and ever, and cast their
crowns before the throne, saying:

11 "You[R] are worthy, O Lord,* Rev. 1:6; 5:12
To receive glory and honor and power;
[R]For You created all things, Gen. 1:1
And by [R]Your will they exist* and were
created." Col. 1:16

CHAPTER 5

The Sealed Book

AND I saw in the right *hand* of Him who
sat on the throne [R]a scroll written in-
side and on the back, [R]sealed with seven
seals. Ezek. 2:9, 10 • Is. 29:11
2 Then I saw a strong angel proclaiming
with a loud voice, [R]"Who is worthy to open the
scroll and to loose its seals?" Rev. 4:11
3 And no one in heaven or on the earth or
under the earth was able to open the scroll, or
to look at it.
4 So I wept much, because no one was
found worthy to open and read* the scroll, or
to look at it.
5 But one of the elders said to me, "Do
not weep. Behold, [R]the Lion of the tribe of
[R]Judah, [R]the Root of David, has [R]prevailed
to open the scroll and to loose* its seven
seals." Gen. 49:9 • Heb. 7:14 • Is. 11:1, 10 • Rev. 3:21
6 And I looked, and behold,* in the midst
of the throne and of the four living crea-
tures, and in the midst of the elders, stood [R]a
Lamb as though it had been slain, having
seven horns and [R]seven eyes, which are [R]the
seven Spirits of God sent out into all the
earth. [John 1:29] • Zech. 3:9; 4:10 • Rev. 1:4; 3:1; 4:5
7 Then He came and took the scroll out of

3:16 NU, M *hot nor cold* **4:3** M omits *And He who sat there was*, making the following description in v. 3 modify the throne rather than God. **4:4** NU, M *robes, with crowns* **4:5** NU, M *voices, and thunderings.* • M omits *the* **4:6** NU, M add *something like* **4:8** M has *holy* nine times. **4:11** NU, M *our Lord and God* • NU, M *existed* **5:4** NU, M omit *and read* **5:5** NU, M omit *to loose* **5:6** NU, M *I saw in the midst . . . a Lamb standing*

the right hand [R]of Him who sat on the throne. Rev. 4:2

8 Now when He had taken the scroll, the four living creatures and the twenty-four elders fell down before the Lamb, each having a harp, and golden bowls full of incense, which are the prayers of the saints.

9 And they sang a new song, saying:

[R]"You are worthy to take the scroll,
And to open its seals; Rev. 4:11
For You were slain,
And [R]have redeemed us to God [R]by Your
blood John 1:29 • [Heb. 9:12]
Out of every tribe and tongue and
people and nation,
10 And have made us* [R]kings* and [R]priests
to our God; Ex. 19:6 • Is. 61:6
And we* shall reign on the earth."

11 Then I looked, and I heard the voice of many angels around the throne, the living creatures, and the elders; and the number of them was ten thousand times ten thousand, and thousands of thousands,

12 saying with a loud voice:

"Worthy is the Lamb who was slain
To receive power and riches and
wisdom,
And strength and honor and glory and
blessing!"

13 And [R]every creature which is in heaven and on the earth and under the earth and such as are in the sea, and all that are in them, I heard saying: Phil. 2:10

"Blessing and honor and glory and power
Be to Him who sits on the throne,
And to the Lamb, forever and ever!"*

14 Then the four living creatures said, "Amen!" And the twenty-four* elders fell down and worshiped Him who lives forever and ever.*

CHAPTER 6

First Seal

NOW [R]I saw when the Lamb opened one of the seals;* and I heard one of the four living creatures saying with a voice like thunder, "Come and see." [Rev. 5:5–7, 12]

2 And I looked, and behold, [R]a white horse. He who sat on it had a bow; and a crown was given to him, and he went out conquering and to conquer. Zech. 1:8; 6:3

Second Seal

3 When He opened the second seal, [R]I heard the second living creature saying, "Come and see."* Rev. 4:7

4 [R]Another horse, fiery red, went out. And it was granted to the one who sat on it to take peace from the earth, and that *people* should kill one another; and there was given to him a great sword. Zech. 1:8; 6:2

Third Seal

5 When He opened the third seal, [R]I heard the third living creature say, "Come and see." So I looked, and behold, [R]a black horse, and he who sat on it had a pair of [R]scales in his hand. Rev. 4:7 • Zech. 6:2, 6 • Matt. 24:7

6 And I heard a voice in the midst of the four living creatures saying, "A quart* of wheat for a denarius,* and three quarts of barley for a denarius; and [R]do not harm the oil and the wine." Rev. 7:3; 9:4

Fourth Seal

7 When He opened the fourth seal, [R]I heard the voice of the fourth living creature saying, "Come and see." Rev. 4:7

8 So I looked, and behold, a pale horse. And the name of him who sat on it was Death, and Hades followed with him. And power was given to them over a fourth of the earth, to kill with sword, with hunger, with death, and by the beasts of the earth.

Fifth Seal

9 When He opened the fifth seal, I saw under [R]the altar the souls of those who had been slain for the word of God and for the testimony which they held. Rev. 8:3

10 And they cried with a loud voice, saying, [R]"How long, O Lord, [R]holy and true, until You judge and avenge our blood on those who dwell on the earth?" Zech. 1:12 • Rev. 3:7

11 Then a [R]white robe was given to each of them; and it was said to them [R]that they should rest a little while longer, until both *the number of* their fellow servants and their brethren, who would be killed as they *were*, was completed. Rev. 3:4, 5; 7:9 • Heb. 11:40

Sixth Seal

12 I looked when He opened the sixth seal, and behold,* there was a great earthquake; and the sun became black as sackcloth of hair, and the moon* became like blood.

13 [R]And the stars of heaven fell to the earth, as a fig tree drops its late figs when it is shaken by a mighty wind. Rev. 8:10; 9:1

14 [R]Then the sky receded as a scroll when it is rolled up, and every mountain and island was moved out of its place. Is. 34:4

5:10 NU, M *them* • NU *a kingdom* • NU, M *they* **5:13** M adds *Amen* **5:14** NU, M omit *twenty-four* • NU, M omit *Him who lives forever and ever* **6:1** NU, M *seven seals* **6:3** NU, M omit *and see* **6:6** Gr. *choinix,* about 1 quart • About 1 day's wage for a worker **6:12** NU, M omit *behold* • NU, M *the whole moon*

15 And the [R]kings of the earth, the great
men, the rich men, the commanders,* the
mighty men, every slave and every free man,
hid themselves in the caves and in the rocks
of the mountains, Ps. 2:2–4
16 [R]and said to the mountains and rocks,
"Fall on us and hide us from the face of Him
who [R]sits on the throne and from the wrath of
the Lamb! Luke 23:29, 30 • Rev. 20:11
17 "For the great day of His wrath has come,
and who is able to stand?"

CHAPTER 7

144,000 Jews

AFTER these things I saw four angels
standing at the four corners of the earth,
[R]holding the four winds of the earth, [R]that the
wind should not blow on the earth, on the sea,
or on any tree. Dan. 7:2 • Rev. 7:3
2 Then I saw another angel ascending from
the east, having the seal of the living God.
And he cried with a loud voice to the four an-
gels to whom it was granted to harm the earth
and the sea,
3 saying, "Do not harm the earth, the sea, or
the trees till we have sealed the servants of
our God on their foreheads."
4 [R]And I heard the number of those who
were sealed. One hundred *and* forty-four
thousand [R]of all the tribes of the children of
Israel *were* sealed: Rev. 9:16 • Gen. 49:1–27

5 of the tribe of Judah
twelve thousand *were* sealed;*
of the tribe of Reuben
twelve thousand *were* sealed;
of the tribe of Gad
twelve thousand *were* sealed;
6 of the tribe of Asher
twelve thousand *were* sealed;
of the tribe of Naphtali
twelve thousand *were* sealed;
of the tribe of Manasseh
twelve thousand *were* sealed;
7 of the tribe of Simeon
twelve thousand *were* sealed;
of the tribe of Levi
twelve thousand *were* sealed;
of the tribe of Issachar
twelve thousand *were* sealed;
8 of the tribe of Zebulun
twelve thousand *were* sealed;
of the tribe of Joseph
twelve thousand *were* sealed;
of the tribe of Benjamin
twelve thousand *were* sealed.

Great Multitude of Gentiles

9 After these things I looked, and behold, a
great multitude which no one could number,
of all nations, tribes, peoples, and tongues,
standing before the throne and before the
Lamb, clothed with white robes, with palm
branches in their hands,
10 and crying out with a loud voice, saying,
[R]"Salvation *belongs* to our God who sits on
the throne, and to the Lamb!" Ps. 3:8
11 [R]All the angels stood around the throne
and the elders and the four living creatures,
and fell on their faces before the throne and
[R]worshiped God, Rev. 4:6 • Rev. 4:11; 5:9, 12, 14
12 [R]saying: Rev. 5:13, 14

"Amen! Blessing and glory and wisdom,
Thanksgiving and honor and power and
might,
Be to our God forever and ever.
Amen."

13 Then one of the elders answered, saying
to me, "Who are these arrayed in white robes,
and where did they come from?"
14 And I said to him, "Sir,* you know." So he
said to me, [R]"These are the ones who come out
of the great tribulation, and [R]washed their
robes and made them white in the blood of
the Lamb. Rev. 6:9 • [Heb. 9:14]
15 "Therefore they are before the throne of
God, and serve Him day and night in His tem-
ple. And He who sits on the throne will [R]dwell
among them. Is. 4:5, 6
16 [R]"They shall neither hunger anymore nor
thirst anymore; [R]the sun shall not strike them,
nor any heat; Is. 49:10 • Ps. 121:6
17 "for the Lamb who is in the midst of the
throne will shepherd them and lead them to
living fountains of waters.* And God will wipe
away every tear from their eyes."

CHAPTER 8

Seventh Seal

WHEN[R] He opened the seventh seal, there
was silence in heaven for about half an
hour. Rev. 6:1
2 [R]And I saw the seven angels who stand
before God, [R]and to them were given seven
trumpets. [Matt. 18:10] • 2 Chr. 29:25–28
3 Then another angel, having a golden
censer, came and stood at the altar. He was
given much incense, that he should offer *it*
with the prayers of all the saints upon the
golden altar which was before the throne.
4 And [R]the smoke of the incense, with the
prayers of the saints, ascended before God
from the angel's hand. Ps. 141:2
5 Then the angel took the censer, filled it
with fire from the altar, and threw *it* to the
earth. And [R]there were noises, thunderings,
lightnings, and an earthquake. Rev. 11:19

6:15 NU, M *the commanders, the rich men,* **7:5** NU, M *were sealed* is stated only in vv. 5a and 8c; the words are understood in the remainder of the passage. **7:14** NU, M *My lord* **7:17** NU, M *to fountains of the waters of life*

First Trumpet

6 So the seven angels who had the seven trumpets prepared themselves to sound.

7 The first angel sounded: [R]And hail and fire followed, mingled with blood, and they were thrown [R]to the earth.* And a third of the trees were burned up, and all green grass was burned up. Ezek. 38:22 • Rev. 16:2

Second Trumpet

8 Then the second angel sounded: [R]And *something* like a great mountain burning with fire was thrown into the sea, and a third of the sea became blood. Jer. 51:25

9 [R]And a third of the living creatures in the sea died, and a third of the ships were destroyed. Rev. 16:3

Third Trumpet

10 Then the third angel sounded: [R]And a great star fell from heaven, burning like a torch, [R]and it fell on a third of the rivers and on the springs of water. Is. 14:12 • Rev. 14:7

11 [R]The name of the star is Wormwood. [R]A third of the waters became wormwood, and many men died from the water, because it was made bitter. Ruth 1:20 • Ex. 15:23

Fourth Trumpet

12 Then the fourth angel sounded: And a third of the sun was struck, a third of the moon, and a third of the stars, so that a third of them were darkened. A third of the day did not shine, and likewise the night.

13 And I looked, [R]and I heard an angel* flying through the midst of heaven, saying with a loud voice, "Woe, woe, woe to the inhabitants of the earth, because of the remaining blasts of the trumpet of the three angels who are about to sound!" Rev. 14:6

CHAPTER 9

Fifth Trumpet

THEN the fifth angel sounded: [R]And I saw a star fallen from heaven to the earth. To him was given the key to [R]the [T]bottomless pit. Rev. 8:10 • Luke 8:31 • Lit. *shaft of the abyss*

2 And he opened the bottomless pit, and smoke arose out of the pit like the smoke of a great furnace. So the sun and the air were darkened because of the smoke of the pit.

3 Then out of the smoke locusts came upon the earth. And to them was given power, [R]as the scorpions of the earth have power. Judg. 7:12

4 They were commanded not to harm the grass of the earth, or any green thing, or any tree, but only those men who do not have the seal of God on their foreheads.

5 And [T]they were not given *authority* to kill them, but to torment them *for* five months. Their torment *was* like the torment of a scorpion when it strikes a man. The locusts

6 In those days [R]men will seek death and will not find it; they will desire to die, and death will flee from them. Jer. 8:3

7 The shape of the locusts was like horses prepared for battle. On their heads were crowns of something like gold, and their faces *were* like the faces of men.

8 They had hair like women's hair, and [R]their teeth were like lions' *teeth.* Joel 1:6

9 And they had breastplates like breastplates of iron, and the sound of their wings *was* [R]like the sound of chariots with many horses running into battle. Joel 2:5–7

10 They had tails like scorpions, and there were stings in their tails. Their power *was* to hurt men five months.

11 And they had as king over them [R]the angel of the bottomless pit, whose name in Hebrew *is* [T]Abaddon, but in Greek he has the name Apollyon. Eph. 2:2 • Lit. *Destruction*

12 One woe is past. Behold, still two more woes are coming after these things.

Sixth Trumpet

13 Then the sixth angel sounded: And I heard a voice from the four horns of the [R]golden altar which is before God, Rev. 8:3

14 saying to the sixth angel who had the trumpet, "Release the four angels who are bound at the great river Euphrates."

15 So the four angels, who had been prepared for the hour and day and month and year, were released to kill a [R]third of mankind. Rev. 8:7–9; 9:18

16 Now [R]the number of the army [R]of the horsemen *was* two hundred million; I heard the number of them. Dan. 7:10 • Ezek. 38:4

17 And thus I saw the horses in the vision: those who sat on them had breastplates of fiery red, hyacinth blue, and sulfur yellow; [R]and the heads of the horses *were* like the heads of lions; and out of their mouths came fire, smoke, and brimstone. Is. 5:28, 29

18 By these three *plagues* a third of mankind was killed—by the fire and the smoke and the brimstone which came out of their mouths.

19 For their power* is in their mouth and in their tails; [R]for their tails *are* like serpents, having heads; and with them they do harm. Is. 9:15

20 But the rest of mankind, who were not killed by these plagues, [R]did not repent of the works of their hands, that they should not worship demons, and idols of gold, silver, brass, stone, and wood, which can neither see nor hear nor walk. Deut. 31:29

21 And they did not repent of their murders [R]or their sorceries* or their sexual immorality or their thefts. Rev. 21:8; 22:15

8:7 NU, M add *and a third of the earth was burned up* **8:13** NU, M *eagle* **9:19** NU, M *the power of the horses* **9:21** NU, M *drugs*

CHAPTER 10

Little Book

I SAW still another mighty angel coming
down from heaven, clothed with a cloud.
[R]And a rainbow *was* on [R]his head, his face
was like the sun, and [R]his feet like pillars of
fire. Rev. 4:3 • Rev. 1:16 • Rev. 1:15
2 He had a little book open in his hand.
[R]And he set his right foot on the sea and *his*
left *foot* on the land, Matt. 28:18
3 and cried with a loud voice, as *when* a
lion roars. When he cried out, [R]seven thunders
uttered their voices. Ps. 29:3–9
4 Now when the seven thunders uttered
their voices,* I was about to write; but I heard
a voice from heaven saying to me,* "Seal up
the things which the seven thunders uttered,
and do not write them."
5 The angel whom I saw standing on the
sea and on the land [R]raised up his hand* to
heaven Dan. 12:7
6 and swore by Him who lives forever and
ever, who created heaven and the things that
are in it, the earth and the things that are in it,
and the sea and the things that are in it, that
there should be delay no longer,
7 but in the days of the sounding of the sev-
enth angel, when he is about to sound, the
mystery of God would be finished, as He de-
clared to His servants the prophets.
8 Then the voice which I heard from heaven
spoke to me again and said, "Go, take the lit-
tle book which is open in the hand of the
angel who stands on the sea and on the
earth."
9 So I went to the angel and said to him,
"Give me the little book." And he said to me,
[R]"Take and eat it; and it will make your stom-
ach bitter, but it will be as sweet as honey in
your mouth." Jer. 15:16
10 Then I took the little book out of the
angel's hand and ate it, [R]and it was as sweet
as honey in my mouth. But when I had eaten
it, my stomach became bitter. Ezek. 3:3
11 And he* said to me, "You must prophesy
again about many peoples, nations, tongues,
and kings."

CHAPTER 11

Two Witnesses

THEN I was given a reed like a measuring
rod. And the angel stood,* saying, [R]"Rise
and measure the temple of God, the altar, and
those who worship there. Num. 23:18
2 "But leave out [R]the court which is outside
the temple, and do not measure it, [R]for it has
been given to the Gentiles. And they will
[R]tread the holy city underfoot *for* forty-two
months. Ezek. 40:17, 20 • Ps. 79:1 • Dan. 8:10
3 "And I will give *power* to my two [R]wit-
nesses, [R]and they will prophesy [R]one thou-
sand two hundred and sixty days, clothed in
sackcloth." Rev. 20:4 • Rev. 19:10 • Rev. 12:6
4 These are the [R]two olive trees and the two
lampstands standing before the God* of the
earth. Zech. 4:2, 3, 11, 14
5 And if anyone wants to harm them, fire
proceeds from their mouth and devours their
enemies. And if anyone wants to harm them,
he must be killed in this manner.
6 These [R]have power to shut heaven, so that
no rain falls in the days of their prophecy; and
they have power over waters to turn them to
blood, and to strike the earth with all plagues,
as often as they desire. 1 Kin. 17:1
7 When they [R]finish their testimony, the
beast that ascends out of the bottomless pit
[R]will make war against them, overcome them,
and kill them. Luke 13:32 • Dan. 7:21
8 And their dead bodies *will lie* in the street
of [R]the great city which spiritually is called
Sodom and Egypt, [R]where also our* Lord was
crucified. Rev. 14:8 • Heb. 13:12
9 [R]Then *those* from the peoples, tribes,
tongues, and nations will see their dead
bodies three-and-a-half days, [R]and not
allow* their dead bodies to be put into
graves. Rev. 17:15 • Ps. 79:2, 3
10 [R]And those who dwell on the earth will
rejoice over them, make merry, [R]and send
gifts to one another, [R]because these two
prophets tormented those who dwell on the
earth. Rev. 12:12 • Esth. 9:19, 22 • Rev. 16:10
11 Now after the three-and-a-half days [R]the
breath of life from God entered them, and
they stood on their feet, and great fear fell on
those who saw them. Ezek. 37:5, 9, 10
12 And they* heard a loud voice from heaven
saying to them, "Come up here." [R]And they as-
cended to heaven in a cloud, and their ene-
mies saw them. Is. 14:13
13 In the same hour there was a great earth-
quake, [R]and a tenth of the city fell. In the
earthquake seven thousand people were
killed, and the rest were afraid and gave glory
to the God of heaven. Rev. 16:19
14 [R]The second woe is past. Behold, the third
woe is coming quickly. Rev. 8:13; 9:12

Seventh Trumpet

15 Then the seventh angel sounded: And
there were loud voices in heaven, saying, "The
kingdoms* of this world have become *the
kingdoms* of our Lord and of His Christ, and
He shall reign forever and ever!"
16 And [R]the twenty-four elders who sat be-
fore God on their thrones fell on their faces
and [R]worshiped God, Rev. 4:4 • Rev. 4:11; 7:11
17 saying:

10:4 NU, M *sounded,* • NU, M omit *to me* **10:5** NU, M *right hand* **10:11** NU, M *they* **11:1** NU, M omit *And the angel stood* **11:4** NU, M *Lord* **11:8** NU, M *their* **11:9** NU, M *nations see . . . and will not allow* **11:12** M *I* **11:15** NU, M *kingdom . . . has become*

"We give You thanks, O Lord God
Almighty, Rev. 20:4
The One [R]who is and who was and who
is to come,* Rev. 16:5
Because You have taken Your great
power [R]and reigned. Rev. 19:6
18 The nations were [R]angry, and Your
[T]wrath has come, Ps. 2:1 • *anger*
And the time of the [R]dead, that they
should be judged, Dan. 7:10
And that You should reward Your
servants the prophets and the saints,
And those who fear Your name, small
and great,
And should destroy those who destroy
the earth."

19 Then [R]the temple of God was opened in
heaven, and the ark of His covenant* was
seen in His temple. And [R]there were light-
nings, noises, thunderings, an earthquake,
and great hail. Rev. 4:1; 15:5, 8 • Rev. 8:5

CHAPTER 12

The Woman

NOW a great sign appeared in heaven: a
woman clothed with the sun, with the
moon under her feet, and on her head a gar-
land of twelve stars.
2 Then being with child, she cried out [R]in
labor and in pain to give birth. Is. 26:17
3 And another sign appeared in heaven: be-
hold, [R]a great, fiery red dragon having seven
heads and ten horns, and seven diadems on
his heads. Rev. 13:1; 17:3, 7, 9
4 [R]His tail drew a third of the stars of
heaven [R]and threw them to the earth. And the
dragon stood before the woman who was
ready to give birth, to devour her Child as
soon as it was born. Rev. 9:10, 19 • Dan. 8:10
5 She bore a male Child who was to rule all
nations with a rod of iron. And her Child was
caught up to God and His throne.
6 Then the woman fled into the wilderness,
where she has a place prepared by God, that
they should feed her there one thousand two
hundred and sixty days.

The War in Heaven

7 And war broke out in heaven: Michael
and his angels fought with the dragon; and
the dragon and his angels fought,
8 but they did not prevail, nor was a place
found for them* in heaven any longer.

9 So [R]the great dragon was cast out, [R]that
serpent of old, called the Devil and Satan,
[R]who deceives the whole world; he was cast to
the earth, and his angels were cast out with
him. John 12:31 • Gen. 3:1, 4 • Rev. 20:3

10 Then I heard a loud voice saying in
heaven, "Now salvation, and strength, and the
kingdom of our God, and the power of His
Christ have come, for the accuser of our
brethren, who accused them before our God
day and night, has been cast down.
11 "And [R]they overcame him by the blood of
the Lamb and by the word of their testimony,
[R]and they did not love their lives to the
death. Rom. 16:20 • Luke 14:26
12 "Therefore rejoice, O heavens, and you
who dwell in them! Woe to the inhabitants of
the earth and the sea! For the devil has come
down to you, having great wrath, because he
knows that he has a short time."

The War on Earth

13 Now when the dragon saw that he had
been cast to the earth, he persecuted the
woman who gave birth to the male *Child.*
14 [R]But the woman was given two wings of a
great eagle, that she might fly into the wilder-
ness to her place, where she is nourished for
a time and times and half a time, from the
presence of the serpent. Ex. 19:4
15 So the serpent [R]spewed water out of his
mouth like a flood after the woman, that he
might cause her to be carried away by the
flood. Is. 59:19
16 But the earth helped the woman, and the
earth opened its mouth and swallowed up the
flood which the dragon had spewed out of his
mouth.
17 And the dragon was enraged with the
woman, and he went to make war with the
rest of her offspring, who keep the command-
ments of God and have the testimony of Jesus
Christ.*

11:17 NU, M omit *and who is to come* **11:19** M *the covenant of the Lord* **12:8** M *him* **12:17** NU, M omit *Christ*

12:9 Demons: Fallen Angels—The Bible makes occasional references to the vast number of angels God created (Page 1007—Matt. 26:53; Page 1267—Heb. 12:22; Page 1316—Rev. 5:11). At some point in the indeterminate past, a chief angel Lucifer led perhaps a third of the angels in rebellion against God (Page 695—Is. 14:12; Page 1320—Rev. 12:3, 4, 9). These fallen angels who have been expelled from heaven to the realms of earth (Rev. 12:9) and the air (Page 1205—Eph. 2:2) are usually equated with the demons of the Gospels and Epistles. Some fallen angels engage in conflict with good angels (Page 884—Dan. 10:12, 13; Page 1306—Jude 9). Certain fallen angels are identified as guilty of especially terrible evil and as the objects of special present punishment (Page 1287—2 Pet. 2:4; Page 1306—Jude 6).

Now turn to Page 989—Matt. 12:24: Demons: Relation to Satan.

CHAPTER 13

The Beast Out of the Sea

THEN I* stood on the sand of the sea. And I saw [R]a beast rising up out of the sea, having seven heads and ten horns,* and on his horns ten crowns, and on his heads a blasphemous name. Dan. 7:2, 7

2 Now the beast which I saw was like a leopard, his feet were like *the feet of* a bear, and his mouth like the mouth of a lion. The [R]dragon gave him his power, his throne, and great authority. Rev. 12:3, 9; 13:4, 12

3 And *I saw* one of his heads [R]as if it had been mortally wounded, and his deadly wound was healed. And all the world marveled and followed the beast. Rev. 13:12, 14

4 So they worshiped the dragon who gave authority to the beast; and they worshiped the beast, saying, "Who *is* like the beast? Who is able to make war with him?"

5 And he was given [R]a mouth speaking great things and blasphemies, and he was given authority to continue* for [R]forty-two months. Dan. 7:8, 11, 20, 25; 11:36 • Rev. 11:2

6 Then he opened his mouth in blasphemy against God, to blaspheme His name, [R]His tabernacle, and those who dwell in heaven. [Col. 2:9]

7 It was granted to him [R]to make war with the saints and to overcome them. And [R]authority was given him over every tribe,* tongue, and nation. Dan. 7:21 • Rev. 11:18

8 All who dwell on the earth will worship him, [R]whose names have not been written in the Book of Life of the Lamb slain [R]from the foundation of the world. Ex. 32:32 • Rev. 17:8

9 If anyone has an ear, let him hear.

10 [R]He who leads into captivity shall go into captivity; he who kills with the sword must be killed with the sword. Here is the patience and the faith of the saints. Is. 33:1

The Beast Out of the Earth

11 Then I saw another beast [R]coming up out of the earth, and he had two horns like a lamb and spoke like a dragon. Rev. 11:7

12 And he exercises all the authority of the first beast in his presence, and causes the earth and those who dwell in it to worship the first beast, [R]whose deadly wound was healed. Rev. 13:3, 4

13 He performs great signs, [R]so that he even makes fire come down from heaven on the earth in the sight of men. 1 Kin. 18:38

14 [R]And he deceives those* who dwell on the earth by those signs which he was granted to do in the sight of the beast, telling those who dwell on the earth to make an image to the beast who was wounded by the sword [R]and lived. Rev. 12:9 • 2 Kin. 20:7

15 He was granted *power* to give breath to the image of the beast, that the image of the beast should both speak [R]and cause as many as would not worship the image of the beast to be killed. Rev. 16:2

16 He causes all, both small and great, rich and poor, free and slave, to receive a mark on their right hand or on their foreheads,

17 and that no one may buy or sell except one who has the mark or* the name of the beast, [R]or the number of his name. Rev. 15:2

18 [R]Here is wisdom. Let him who has [R]understanding calculate the number of the beast, for it is the number of a man: His number *is* 666. Rev. 17:9 • [1 Cor. 2:14]

CHAPTER 14

The 144,000

THEN I looked, and behold, a* [R]Lamb standing on Mount Zion, and with Him [R]one hundred *and* forty-four thousand, having* His Father's name [R]written on their foreheads. Rev. 5:6 • Rev. 7:4; 14:3 • Rev. 7:3

2 And I heard a voice from heaven, [R]like the voice of many waters, and like the voice of loud thunder. And I heard the sound of harpists playing their harps. Rev. 1:15; 19:6

3 They sang as it were a new song before the throne, before the four living creatures, and the elders; and no one could learn that song [R]except the hundred *and* forty-four thousand who were redeemed from the earth. Rev. 5:9

4 These are the ones who were not defiled with women, [R]for they are virgins. These are the ones [R]who follow the Lamb wherever He goes. These [R]were redeemed* from *among* men, *being* firstfruits to God and to the Lamb. [2 Cor. 11:2] • Rev. 3:4; 7:17 • Rev. 5:9

5 And [R]in their mouth was found no deceit,* for [R]they are without fault before the throne of God.* Ps. 32:2 • Eph. 5:27

The Three Angels' Announcements

6 Then I saw another angel [R]flying in the midst of heaven, [R]having the everlasting gospel to preach to those who dwell on the earth—[R]to every nation, tribe, tongue, and people— Rev. 8:13 • Eph. 3:9 • Rev. 13:7

7 saying with a loud voice, [R]"Fear God and give glory to Him, for the hour of His judgment has come; [R]and worship Him who made heaven and earth, the sea and springs of water." Rev. 11:18 • Neh. 9:6

8 And another angel followed, saying, "Babylon* is fallen, is fallen, that great city, because she has made all nations drink of the wine of the wrath of her fornication."

13:1 NU *he* • NU, M *ten horns and seven heads*
13:5 M *make war* **13:7** NU, M add *and people*
13:14 M *my own people* **13:17** NU, M omit *or*
14:1 NU, M *the* • NU, M add *His name and* **14:4** M adds *by Jesus* **14:5** NU, M *falsehood* • NU, M omit *before the throne of God.* **14:8** NU *Babylon the great is fallen, is fallen, which has made;* M *Babylon the great is fallen. She has made*

9 Then a third angel followed them, saying
with a loud voice, "If anyone worships the
beast and his image, and receives *his* mark on
his forehead or on his hand,
10 "he himself [R]shall also drink of the wine
of the wrath of God, which is poured out full
strength into the cup of His indignation. He
shall be tormented with fire and brimstone in
the presence of the holy angels and in the
presence of the Lamb. Ps. 75:8
11 "And [R]the smoke of their torment as-
cends forever and ever; and they have no rest
day or night, who worship the beast and his
image, and whoever receives the mark of his
name." Is. 34:8–10
12 Here is the patience of the saints; here *are*
those* who keep the commandments of God
and the faith of Jesus.
13 Then I heard a voice from heaven saying
to me,* "Write: 'Blessed *are* the dead who die
in the Lord from now on.' " "Yes," says the
Spirit, "that they may rest from their labors,
and their works follow them."

The Harvest Judgment

14 Then I looked, and behold, a white cloud,
and on the cloud sat *One* like the Son of Man,
having on His head a golden crown, and in
His hand a sharp sickle.
15 And another angel came out of the tem-
ple, crying with a loud voice to Him who sat
on the cloud, "Thrust in Your sickle and reap,
for the time has come for You* to reap, for the
harvest of the earth is ripe."
16 So He who sat on the cloud thrust in His
sickle on the earth, and the earth was reaped.
17 Then another angel came out of the tem-
ple which is in heaven, he also having a sharp
sickle.
18 And another angel came out from the
altar, who had power over fire, and he cried
with a loud cry to him who had the sharp
sickle, saying, "Thrust in your sharp sickle
and gather the clusters of the vine of the
earth, for her grapes are fully ripe."
19 So the angel thrust his sickle into the
earth and gathered the vine of the earth, and
threw *it* into [R]the great winepress of the wrath
of God. Rev. 19:15
20 And [R]the winepress was trampled outside
the city, and blood came out of the winepress,
up to the horses' bridles, for one thousand six
hundred furlongs. Is. 63:3

CHAPTER 15

Preparation for the Bowl Judgments

THEN [R]I saw another sign in heaven, great
and marvelous: [R]seven angels having the
seven last plagues, for in them the wrath of
God is complete. Rev. 12:1, 3 • Rev. 21:9
2 And I saw *something* like [R]a sea of glass
[R]mingled with fire, and those who have the
victory over the beast, over his image and
over his mark* *and* over the number of his
name, standing on the sea of glass, [R]having
harps of God. Rev. 4:6 • [Matt. 3:11] • Rev. 5:8
3 They sing [R]the song of Moses, the ser-
vant of God, and the song of the [R]Lamb, say-
ing: Ex. 15:1–21 • Rev. 15:3

[R]"Great and marvelous *are* Your works,
Lord God Almighty! Deut. 32:3, 4
[R]Just and true *are* Your ways,
O King of the saints!* Ps. 145:17
4 [R]Who shall not fear You, O Lord, and
glorify Your name? Ex. 15:14
For *You* alone *are* [R]holy. Lev. 11:44
For [R]all nations shall come and worship
before You, Is. 66:23
For Your judgments have been
manifested."

5 After these things I looked, and behold,*
[R]the temple of the tabernacle of the testimony
in heaven was opened. Num. 1:50
6 And out of the temple came the seven an-
gels having the seven plagues, [R]clothed in
pure bright linen, and having their chests
girded with golden bands. Ex. 28:6
7 [R]Then one of the four living creatures
gave to the seven angels seven golden bowls
full of the wrath of God [R]who lives forever
and ever. Rev. 4:6 • 1 Thess. 1:9
8 [R]The temple was filled with smoke [R]from
the glory of God and from His power, and no
one was able to enter the temple till the
seven plagues of the seven angels were com-
pleted. Ex. 19:18; 40:34 • 2 Thess. 1:9

CHAPTER 16

First Bowl

THEN I heard a loud voice from the temple
saying [R]to the seven angels, "Go and pour
out the bowls* [R]of the wrath of God on the
earth." Rev. 15:1 • Rev. 14:10
2 So the first went and poured out his bowl
[R]upon the earth, and a foul and [R]loathsome
sore came upon the men who had the mark of
the beast and those [R]who worshiped his
image. Rev. 8:7 • Ex. 9:9–11 • Rev. 13:14

Second Bowl

3 Then the second angel poured out his
bowl [R]on the sea, and [R]it became blood as of a
dead *man;* [R]and every living creature in the
sea died. Rev. 8:8; 11:6 • Ex. 7:17–21 • Rev. 8:9

14:12 NU, M omit *here are those* **14:13** NU, M omit *to me* **14:15** NU, M omit *for You* **15:2** NU, M omit *over his mark* **15:3** NU, M *nations* **15:5** NU, M omit *behold* **16:1** NU, M *seven bowls*

Third Bowl

4 Then the third angel poured out his bowl
on the rivers and springs of water, [R]and they
became blood. Ex. 7:17–20
5 And I heard the angel of the waters say-
ing:

[R]"You are righteous, O Lord,*
The One [R]who is and who was and who
is to be,* Rev. 15:3, 4 • Rev. 1:4, 8
Because You have judged these things.
6 For [R]they have shed the blood [R]of saints
and prophets, Matt. 23:34 • Rev. 11:18
[R]And You have given them blood to
drink. Is. 49:26
For* it is their just due."

7 And I heard another from* the altar say-
ing, "Even so, Lord God Almighty, true and
righteous *are* Your judgments."

Fourth Bowl

8 Then the fourth angel poured out his
bowl [R]on the sun, and power was given to him
to scorch men with fire. Rev. 8:12
9 And men were scorched with great heat,
and they blasphemed the name of God who
has power over these plagues; [R]and they did
not repent and give Him glory. Dan. 5:22

Fifth Bowl

10 Then the fifth angel poured out his bowl
on the throne of the beast, and his kingdom
became full of darkness; and they gnawed
their tongues because of the pain.
11 They blasphemed the God of heaven be-
cause of their pains and their sores, and did
not repent of their deeds.

Sixth Bowl

12 Then the sixth angel poured out his bowl
on the great river Euphrates, and its water
was dried up, so that the way of the kings
from the east might be prepared.
13 And I saw three unclean spirits like frogs
coming out of the mouth of the dragon, out of
the mouth of the beast, and out of the mouth
of the false prophet.
14 For they are spirits of demons, [R]perform-
ing signs, *which* go out to the kings of the
earth and* of [R]the whole world, to gather
them to [R]the battle of that great day of God
Almighty. 2 Thess. 2:9 • Luke 2:1 • Rev. 17:14
15 [R]"Behold, I am coming as a thief. Blessed
is he who watches, and keeps his gar-
ments, [R]lest he walk naked and they see his
shame." Matt. 24:43 • 2 Cor. 5:3
16 And they gathered them together to the
place called in Hebrew, Armageddon.*

Seventh Bowl

17 Then the seventh angel poured out his
bowl into the air, and a loud voice came out of
the temple of heaven, from the throne, saying,
[R]"It is done!" Rev. 10:6; 21:6
18 And [R]there were noises and thunderings
and lightnings; [R]and there was a great earth-
quake, such a mighty and great earthquake
[R]as had not occurred since men were on the
earth. Rev. 4:5 • Rev. 11:13 • Dan. 12:1
19 Now [R]the great city was divided into three
parts, and the cities of the nations fell. And
great Babylon was remembered before God,
[R]to give her the cup of the wine of the fierce-
ness of His wrath. Rev. 14:8 • Is. 51:17
20 Then [R]every island fled away, and the
mountains were not found. Rev. 6:14; 20:11
21 And great hail from heaven fell upon
men, *each hailstone* about the weight of a tal-
ent. Men blasphemed God because of the
plague of the hail, since that plague was ex-
ceedingly great.

CHAPTER 17

Great Harlot Is Described

THEN [R]one of the seven angels who had the
seven bowls came and talked with me,
saying to me,* "Come, I will show you the
judgment of [R]the great harlot who sits on
many waters, Rev. 1:1; 21:9 • Nah. 3:4
2 [R]"with whom the kings of the earth com-
mitted fornication, and [R]the inhabitants of the
earth were made drunk with the wine of her
fornication." Rev. 2:22; 18:3, 9 • Jer. 51:7
3 So he carried me away in the Spirit [R]into
the wilderness. And I saw a woman sitting [R]on
a scarlet beast *which was* full of [R]names of
blasphemy, having seven heads and ten
horns. Rev. 12:6, 14; 21:10 • Rev. 12:3 • Rev. 13:1
4 The woman was arrayed in purple and
scarlet, [R]and adorned with gold and precious
stones and pearls, having in her hand a
golden cup full of abominations and the filth-
iness of her fornication.* Dan. 11:38
5 And on her forehead a name *was* written:

MYSTERY,
BABYLON THE GREAT, THE
MOTHER OF HARLOTS AND OF THE
ABOMINATIONS OF THE EARTH.

6 I saw [R]the woman, drunk with the blood
of the saints and with the blood of the martyrs
of Jesus. And when I saw her, I marveled with
great amazement. Rev. 18:24

Great Harlot Is Destroyed

7 But the angel said to me, "Why did you
marvel? I will tell you the [T]mystery of the
woman and of the beast that carries her,

16:5 NU, M omit *O Lord* • NU, M *who was, the Holy One* **16:6** NU, M omit *For* **16:7** NU, M omit *another from* **16:14** NU, M omit *of the earth and* **16:16** Lit. *Mount Megiddo;* M *Megiddo* **17:1** NU, M omit *to me* **17:4** M *the filthiness of the fornication of the earth*

which has the seven heads and the ten horns. *hidden truth*

8 "The beast that you saw was, and is not, and [R]will ascend out of the bottomless pit and go to perdition. And those who dwell on the earth will marvel, whose names are not written in the Book of Life from the foundation of the world, when they see the beast that was, and is not, and yet is.* Rev. 11:7

9 [R]"Here *is* the mind which has wisdom: [R]The seven heads are seven mountains on which the woman sits. Rev. 13:18 • Rev. 13:1

10 "There are also seven kings. Five have fallen, one is, *and* the other has not yet come. And when he comes, he must [R]continue a short time. Rev. 13:5

11 "The [R]beast that was, and is not, is himself also the eighth, and is of the seven, and is going to perdition. Rev. 13:3, 12, 14; 17:8

12 [R]"The ten horns which you saw are ten kings who have received no kingdom as yet, but they receive authority for one hour as kings with the beast. Dan. 7:20

13 "These are of one mind, and they will give their power and authority to the beast.

14 [R]"These will make war with the Lamb, and the Lamb will [R]overcome them, for He is Lord of lords and King of kings; [R]and those *who are* with Him *are* called, chosen, and faithful." Rev. 16:14; 19:19 • Rev. 19:20 • Jer. 50:44

15 Then he said to me, [R]"The waters which you saw, where the harlot sits, are peoples, multitudes, nations, and tongues. Is. 8:7

16 "And the ten horns which you saw on* the beast, [R]these will hate the harlot, make her desolate [R]and naked, eat her flesh and burn her with fire. Jer. 50:41 • Ezek. 16:37, 39

17 [R]"For God has put it into their hearts to fulfill His purpose, to be of one mind, and to give their kingdom to the beast, until the words of God are fulfilled. 2 Thess. 2:11

18 "And the woman whom you saw [R]is that great city [R]which reigns over the kings of the earth." Rev. 11:8; 16:19 • Rev. 12:4

CHAPTER 18

Babylon the Great Is Destroyed

AFTER[R] these things I saw another angel coming down from heaven, having great authority, [R]and the earth was illuminated with his glory. Rev. 17:1, 7 • Ezek. 43:2

2 And he cried mightily* with a loud voice, saying, "Babylon the great is fallen, is fallen, and has become a dwelling place of demons, a prison for every foul spirit, and a cage for every unclean and hated bird!

3 "For all the nations [R]have drunk of the wine of the wrath of her fornication, the kings of the earth have committed fornication with her, [R]and the merchants of the earth have become rich through the abundance of her luxury." Rev. 14:8 • Is. 47:15

4 And I heard another voice from heaven saying, [R]"Come out of her, my people, lest you share in her sins, and lest you receive of her plagues. Is. 48:20

5 "For her sins have reached* to heaven, and God has remembered her iniquities.

6 [R]"Render to her just as she rendered to you,* and repay her double according to her works; [R]in the cup which she has mixed, mix double for her. Ps. 137:8 • Rev. 14:10

7 "In the measure that she glorified herself and lived luxuriously, in the same measure give her torment and sorrow; for she says in her heart, 'I sit *as* [R]queen, and am no widow, and will not see sorrow.' Is. 47:7, 8

8 "Therefore her plagues will come in one day—death and mourning and famine. And she will be utterly burned with fire, for strong *is* the Lord God who judges* her.

Earth Mourns Babylon's Destruction

9 "The kings of the earth who committed fornication and lived luxuriously with her [R]will weep and lament for her, when they see the smoke of her burning, Jer. 50:46

10 "standing at a distance for fear of her torment, saying, [R]'Alas, alas, that great city Babylon, that mighty city! For in one hour your judgment has come.' Is. 21:9

11 "And [R]the merchants of the earth will weep and mourn over her, for no one buys their merchandise anymore: Ezek. 27:27–34

12 [R]"merchandise of gold and silver, precious stones and pearls, fine linen and purple, silk and scarlet, every kind of citron wood, every kind of object of ivory, every kind of object of most precious wood, bronze, iron, and marble; Rev. 17:4

13 "and cinnamon and incense, fragrant oil and frankincense, wine and oil, fine flour and wheat, cattle and sheep, horses and chariots, and bodies and souls of men.

14 "The fruit that your soul longed for has gone from you, and all the things which are rich and splendid have gone from you,* and you shall find them no more at all.

15 "The merchants of these things, who became rich by her, will stand at a distance for fear of her torment, weeping and wailing,

16 "and saying, 'Alas, alas, [R]that great city [R]that was clothed in fine linen, purple, and scarlet, and adorned with gold and precious stones and pearls! Rev. 17:18 • Rev. 17:4

17 'For in one hour such great riches came to nothing.' Every shipmaster, all who travel by ship, sailors, and as many as trade on the sea, stood at a distance

17:8 NU, M *and shall be present* **17:16** NU, M *saw, and the beast* **18:2** NU, M omit *mightily* **18:5** NU, M *have been heaped up* **18:6** NU, M omit *to you* **18:8** NU, M *has judged* **18:14** NU, M *been lost to you*

18 [R]"and cried out when they saw the smoke of her burning, saying, [R]'What *is* like this great city?' Ezek. 27:30 • Rev. 13:4

19 [R]"They threw dust on their heads and cried out, weeping and wailing, and saying, 'Alas, alas, that great city, in which all who had ships on the sea became rich by her wealth! [R]For in one hour she [T]is made desolate.' Josh. 7:6 • Rev. 18:8 • *have been laid waste*

Heaven Rejoices Babylon's Destruction

20 [R]"Rejoice over her, O heaven, and *you* holy apostles* and prophets, for [R]God has avenged you on her!" Jer. 51:48 • Luke 11:49

21 Then a mighty angel took up a stone like a great millstone and threw *it* into the sea, saying, [R]"Thus with violence the great city Babylon shall be thrown down, and shall not be found anymore. Jer. 51:63, 64

22 [R]"The sound of harpists, musicians, flutists, and trumpeters shall not be heard in you anymore. No craftsman of any craft shall be found in you anymore, and the sound of a millstone shall not be heard in you anymore. Jer. 7:34; 16:9; 25:10

23 [R]"The light of a lamp shall not shine in you anymore, and the voice of bridegroom and bride shall not be heard in you anymore. For [R]your merchants were the great men of the earth, for by your sorcery all the nations were deceived. Jer. 25:10 • Is. 23:8

24 "And [R]in her was found the blood of prophets and saints, and of all who [R]were slain on the earth." Rev. 16:6; 17:6 • Jer. 51:49

CHAPTER 19

AFTER these things I heard* a loud voice of a great multitude in heaven, saying, "Alleluia! Salvation and glory and honor and power *belong* to the Lord* our God!

2 "For true and righteous *are* His judgments, because He has judged the great harlot who corrupted the earth with her fornication; and He [R]has avenged on her the blood of His servants *shed* by her." Deut. 32:43

3 Again they said, "Alleluia! [R]Her smoke rises up forever and ever!" Is. 34:10

4 And [R]the twenty-four elders and the four living creatures fell down and worshiped God who sat on the throne, saying, [R]"Amen! Alleluia!" Rev. 4:4, 6, 10 • 1 Chr. 16:36

5 Then a voice came from the throne, saying, [R]"Praise our God, all you His servants and those who fear Him, [R]both* small and great!" Ps. 134:1 • Rev. 11:18

6 [R]And I heard, as it were, the voice of a great multitude, as the sound of many waters and as the sound of mighty thunderings, saying, "Alleluia! For [R]the* Lord God Omnipotent reigns! Ezek. 1:24 • Rev. 11:15

Marriage Supper of the Lamb

7 "Let us be glad and rejoice and give Him glory, for the marriage of the Lamb has come, and His wife has made herself ready."

8 And to her it was granted to be arrayed in fine linen, clean and bright, for the fine linen is the righteous acts of the saints.

9 Then he said to me, "Write: [R]'Blessed *are* those who are called to the marriage supper of the Lamb!' " And he said to me, "These are the true sayings of God." Luke 14:15

10 And [R]I fell at his feet to worship him. But he said to me, [R]"See *that you do* not *do that!* I am your fellow servant, and of your brethren who have the testimony of Jesus. Worship God! For the testimony of Jesus is the spirit of prophecy." Rev. 22:8 • Acts 10:26

Second Coming of Christ

11 Now I saw heaven opened, and behold, a white horse. And He who sat on him *was* called Faithful and True, and [R]in righteousness He judges and makes war. Is. 11:4

12 [R]His eyes *were* like a flame of fire, and on His head *were* many crowns. [R]He had* a name written that no one knew except Himself. Rev. 1:14 • Rev. 2:17; 19:16

13 [R]He *was* clothed with a robe dipped in blood, and His name is called [R]The Word of God. Is. 63:2, 3 • [John 1:1, 14]

14 [R]And the armies in heaven, [R]clothed in fine linen, white and clean,* followed Him on white horses. Rev. 14:20 • Matt. 28:3

15 Now out of His mouth goes a sharp* sword, that with it He should strike the nations. And He Himself will rule them with a rod of iron. He Himself treads the winepress of the fierceness and wrath of Almighty God.

16 And [R]He has on *His* robe and on His thigh a name written: Rev. 2:17; 19:12

KING OF KINGS
AND LORD OF LORDS.

17 Then I saw an angel standing in the sun; and he cried with a loud voice, saying to all the birds that fly in the midst of heaven, [R]"Come and gather together for the supper of the great God,* Ezek. 39:17

18 "that you may eat the flesh of kings, the flesh of captains, the flesh of mighty men, the flesh of horses and of those who sit on them, and the flesh of all *people,* free* and slave, both small and great."

19 [R]And I saw the beast, the kings of the earth, and their armies, gathered together to

18:20 NU, M *saints and apostles* **19:1** NU, M add *something like* • NU, M omit *the Lord* **19:5** NU, M omit *both* **19:6** NU, M *our* **19:12** M adds *names written, and* **19:14** NU, M *pure white linen* **19:15** M adds *two-edged* **19:17** NU, M *the great supper of God* **19:18** NU, M *both free*

make war against Him who sat on the horse and against His army. Rev. 16:13–16

20 [R]Then the beast was captured, and with him the false prophet who worked signs in his presence, by which he deceived those who received the mark of the beast and those who worshiped his image. [R]These two were cast alive into the lake of fire burning with brimstone. Rev. 16:13 • Dan. 7:11

21 And the rest [R]were killed with the sword which proceeded from the mouth of Him who sat on the horse. And all the birds were filled with their flesh. Rev. 19:15

CHAPTER 20

Satan Is Bound 1,000 Years

THEN I saw an angel coming down from heaven, having the key to the bottomless pit and a great chain in his hand.

2 He laid hold of [R]the dragon, that serpent of old, who is *the* Devil and Satan, and bound him for a thousand years; 2 Pet. 2:4

3 and he cast him into the bottomless pit, and shut him up, and [R]set a seal on him, [R]so that he should deceive the nations no more till the thousand years were finished. But after these things he must be released for a little while. Dan. 6:17 • Rev. 12:9; 20:8, 10

Saints Reign 1,000 Years

4 And I saw thrones, and they sat on them, and judgment was committed to them. Then *I saw* the souls of those who had been beheaded for their witness to Jesus and for the word of God, who had not worshiped the beast or his image, and had not received *his* mark on their foreheads or on their hands. And they lived and reigned with Christ for a* thousand years.

5 But the rest of the dead did not live again until the thousand years were finished. This *is* the first resurrection.

6 Blessed and holy *is* he who has part in the first resurrection. Over such the second death has no power, but they shall be [R]priests of God and of Christ, and shall reign with Him a thousand years. Is. 61:6

Satan Is Released and Leads Rebellion

7 Now when the thousand years have expired, Satan will be released from his prison

8 and will go out [R]to deceive the nations which are in the four corners of the earth, [R]Gog and Magog, to gather them together to battle, whose number *is* as the sand of the sea. Rev. 12:9; 20:3, 10 • Ezek. 38:2; 39:1, 6

9 They went up on the breadth of the earth and surrounded the camp of the saints and the beloved city. And fire came down from God out of heaven and devoured them.

Satan Is Tormented Forever

10 The devil, who deceived them, was cast into the lake of fire and brimstone [R]where* the beast and the false prophet *are*. And they [R]will be tormented day and night forever and ever. Rev. 19:20; 20:14, 15 • Rev. 14:10

Great White Throne Judgment

11 Then I saw a great white throne and Him who sat on it, from whose face the earth and the heaven fled away. [R]And there was found no place for them. Dan. 2:35

12 And I saw the dead, small and great, standing before God,* and books were opened. And another book was opened, which is *the Book* of Life. And the dead were judged according to their works, by the things which were written in the books.

13 The sea gave up the dead who were in it, and Death and Hades delivered up the dead who were in them. And they were judged, each one according to his works.

14 Then Death and Hades were cast into the lake of fire. This is the second death.*

15 And anyone not found written in the Book of Life was cast into the lake of fire.

CHAPTER 21

New Heaven and Earth Are Created

NOW [R]I saw a new heaven and a new earth, [R]for the first heaven and the first earth had passed away. Also there was no more sea. [2 Pet. 3:13] • Rev. 20:11

New Jerusalem Descends

2 Then I, John,* saw [R]the holy city, New Jerusalem, coming down out of heaven from God, prepared [R]as a bride adorned for her husband. Is. 52:1 • 2 Cor. 11:2

3 And I heard a loud voice from heaven saying, "Behold, [R]the tabernacle of God *is* with men, and He will dwell with them, and they shall be His people. God Himself will be with them *and be* their God. Lev. 26:11

4 [R]"And God will wipe away every tear from their eyes; [R]there shall be no more death, [R]nor sorrow, nor crying. There shall be no more pain, for the former things have passed away." Is. 25:8 • 1 Cor. 15:26 • Is. 35:10

5 Then [R]He who sat on the throne said, [R]"Behold, I make all things new." And He said to me,* "Write, for these words are true and faithful." Rev. 4:2, 9; 20:11 • Is. 43:19

6 And He said to me, "It is done!* I am the Alpha and the Omega, the Beginning and the End. I will give of the fountain of the water of life freely to him who thirsts.

20:4 M *the* **20:10** NU, M add *also* **20:12** NU, M *the throne* **20:14** NU, M add *the lake of fire.* **21:2** NU, M omit *John* **21:5** NU, M omit *to me* **21:6** M omits *It is done*

7 "He who overcomes shall inherit all things,* and [R]I will be his God and he shall be My son. Zech. 8:8

8 "But the cowardly, unbelieving,* abominable, murderers, sexually immoral, sorcerers, idolaters, and all liars shall have their part in the lake which burns with fire and brimstone, which is the second death."

New Jerusalem Is Described

9 Then one of [R]the seven angels who had the seven bowls filled with the seven last plagues came to me* and talked with me, saying, "Come, I will show you [R]the bride, the Lamb's wife."* Rev. 15:1 • Rev. 19:7; 21:2

10 And he carried me away [R]in the Spirit to a great and high mountain, and showed me the great city, the holy* Jerusalem, descending out of heaven from God, Rev. 1:10

11 [R]having the glory of God. Her light *was* like a most precious stone, like a jasper stone, clear as crystal. Rev. 15:8; 21:23; 22:5

12 Also she had a great and high wall with [R]twelve gates, and twelve angels at the gates, and names written on them, which are *the names* of the twelve tribes of the children of Israel: Ezek. 48:31–34

13 [R]three gates on the east, three gates on the north, three gates on the south, and three gates on the west. Ezek. 48:31–34

14 Now the wall of the city had twelve foundations, and [R]on them were the names* of the twelve apostles of the Lamb. Eph. 2:20

15 And he who talked with me [R]had a gold reed to measure the city, its gates, and its wall. Ezek. 40:3

16 The city is laid out as a square; its length is as great as its breadth. And he measured the city with the reed: twelve thousand furlongs. Its length, breadth, and height are equal.

17 Then he measured its wall: one hundred *and* forty-four cubits, *according* to the measure of a man, that is, of an angel.

18 The construction of its wall was *of* jasper; and the city *was* pure gold, like clear glass.

19 [R]The foundations of the wall of the city *were* adorned with all kinds of precious stones: the first foundation *was* jasper, the second sapphire, the third chalcedony, the fourth emerald, Is. 54:11

20 the fifth sardonyx, the sixth sardius, the seventh chrysolite, the eighth beryl, the ninth topaz, the tenth chrysoprase, the eleventh jacinth, and the twelfth amethyst.

21 The twelve gates *were* twelve [R]pearls: each individual gate was of one pearl. [R]And the street of the city *was* pure gold, like transparent glass. Matt. 13:45, 46 • Rev. 22:2

22 But I saw no temple in it, for the Lord God Almighty and the Lamb are its temple.

23 The city had no need of the sun or of the moon to shine in it,* for the glory* of God illuminated it. The Lamb *is* its light.

24 [R]And the nations of those who are saved* shall walk in its light, and the kings of the earth bring their glory and honor into it.* Is. 60:3, 5; 66:12

25 [R]Its gates shall not be shut at all by day (there shall be no night there). Is. 60:11

26 [R]And they shall bring the glory and the honor of the nations into it.* Rev. 21:24

27 But there shall by no means enter it anything that defiles, or causes* an abomination or a lie, but only those who are written in the Lamb's [R]Book of Life. Phil. 4:3

CHAPTER 22

AND he showed me a pure* river of water of life, clear as crystal, proceeding from the throne of God and of the Lamb.

2 [R]In the middle of its street, and on either side of the river, *was* the tree of life, which bore twelve fruits, each *tree* yielding its fruit every month. The leaves of the tree *were* for the healing of the nations. Ezek. 47:12

3 And there shall be no more curse, but the throne of God and of the Lamb shall be in it, and His servants shall serve Him.

4 [R]They shall see His face, and His name *shall be* on their foreheads. [Matt. 5:8]

5 There shall be no night there: They need no lamp nor light of the sun, for [R]the Lord God gives them light. [R]And they shall reign forever and ever. Ps. 36:9 • Dan. 7:18, 27

Conclusion

6 Then he said to me, [R]"These words *are* faithful and true." And the Lord God of the holy* prophets [R]sent His angel to show His servants the things which must [R]shortly take place. Rev. 19:9 • Rev. 1:1 • Heb. 10:37

7 [R]"Behold, I am coming quickly! [R]Blessed *is* he who keeps the words of the prophecy of this book." [Rev. 3:11] • Rev. 1:3

8 Now I, John, saw and heard* these things. And when I heard and saw, [R]I fell down to worship before the feet of the angel who showed me these things. Rev. 19:10

9 Then he said to me, [R]"See *that you do* not *do that*. For* I am your fellow servant, and of your brethren the prophets, and of those who keep the words of this book. Worship God." Rev. 19:10

21:7 M *overcomes, I shall give him these things* **21:8** M adds *and sinners,* **21:9** NU, M omit *to me* • M *I will show you the woman, the Lamb's bride.* **21:10** NU, M omit *the great* and read *the holy city, Jerusalem* **21:14** NU, M *twelve names* **21:23** NU, M omit *in it* • M *the very glory* **21:24** NU, M omit *of those who are saved* • M *the glory and honor of the nations to Him* **21:26** M adds *that they may enter in.* **21:27** NU, M *anything profane, nor one who causes* **22:1** NU, M omit *pure* **22:6** NU, M *spirits of the prophets* **22:8** NU, M *am the one who heard and saw* **22:9** NU, M omit *For*

10 [R]And he said to me, "Do not seal the
words of the prophecy of this book, [R]for the
time is at hand. Dan. 8:26 • Rev. 1:3
11 "He who is unjust, let him be unjust still;
he who is filthy, let him be filthy still; he who
is righteous, let him be righteous* still; he who
is holy, let him be holy still."
12 "And behold, I am coming quickly, and
[R]My reward *is* with Me, to give to every one
according to his work. Is. 40:10; 62:11
13 [R]"I am the Alpha and the Omega, *the*
Beginning and *the* End, the First and the
Last."* Is. 41:4
14 [R]Blessed *are* those who do His command-
ments,* that they may have the right [R]to the
tree of life, and may enter through the gates
into the city. Dan. 12:12 • [Prov. 11:30]
15 But* [R]outside *are* [R]dogs and sorcerers
and sexually immoral and murderers and
idolaters, and whoever loves and practices a
lie. 1 Cor. 6:9 • Phil. 3:2
16 [R]"I, Jesus, have sent My angel to testify to
you these things in the churches. I am the
Root and the Offspring of David, [R]the Bright
and Morning Star." Rev. 1:1 • Num. 24:17
17 And the Spirit and the bride say, "Come!"
And let him who hears say, "Come!" And let
him who thirsts come. Whoever desires, let
him take the water of life freely.
18 For* I testify to everyone who hears the
words of the prophecy of this book: [R]If any-
one adds to these things, God will add* to
him the plagues that are written in this
book; Deut. 4:2; 12:32
19 and if anyone takes away from the words
of the book of this prophecy, [R]God shall take
away* his part from the Book* of Life, from
the holy city, and *from* the things which are
written in this book. Ex. 32:33
20 He who testifies to these things says,
"Surely I am coming quickly." Amen. Even so,
come, Lord Jesus!
21 The grace of our Lord Jesus Christ *be*
with you all.* Amen.

22:11 NU, M *do right* **22:13** NU, M *the First and the Last, the Beginning and the End.* **22:14** NU *wash their robes,* **22:15** NU, M omit *But* **22:18** NU, M omit *For* • M *may God add* **22:19** M *may God take away* • NU, M *tree of life* **22:21** NU *with all;* M *with all the saints*

Harmony of the Gospels

Date	Event	Location	Matthew	Mark	Luke	John	Related References
INTRODUCTIONS TO JESUS CHRIST							
	(1) Luke's Introduction				1:1–4		Acts 1:1
	(2) Pre-fleshly state of Christ					1:1–18	Heb. 1:1–14
	(3) Genealogy of Jesus Christ		1:1–17		3:23–38		Ruth 4:18–22 1 Chr. 1:1–4
BIRTH, INFANCY, AND ADOLESCENCE OF JESUS AND JOHN THE BAPTIST							
7 B.C.	(1) Announcement of Birth of John	Jerusalem (temple)			1:5–25		Num. 6:3
7 or 6 B.C.	(2) Announcement of Birth of Jesus to the Virgin	Nazareth			1:26–38		Is. 7:14
c. 5 B.C.	(3) Song of Elizabeth to Mary	Hill Country of Judea			1:39–45		
	(4) Mary's Song of Praise				1:46–56		Ps. 103:17
5 B.C.	(5) Birth, Infancy, and Purpose for Future of John the Baptist	Judea			1:57–80		Mal. 3:1
	(6) Announcement of Jesus' Birth to Joseph	Nazareth	1:18–25				Is. 9:6, 7
5–4 B.C.	(7) Birth of Jesus Christ	Bethlehem	1:24, 25		2:1–7		Is. 7:14
	(8) Proclamation by the Angels	Near Bethlehem			2:8–14		1 Tim. 3:16
	(9) The Visit of Homage by Shepherds	Bethlehem			2:15–20		
	(10) Jesus' Circumcision	Bethlehem			2:21		Lev. 12:3
4 B.C.	(11) First Temple Visit with Acknowledgments by Simeon and Anna	Jerusalem			2:22–38		Ex. 13:2 Lev. 12
	(12) Visit of the Wise Men	Jerusalem & Bethlehem	2:1–12				Num. 24:17
	(13) Flight into Egypt and Massacre of Innocents	Bethlehem, Jerusalem & Egypt	2:13–18				Jer. 31:15
	(14) From Egypt to Nazareth with Jesus		2:19–23		2:39		
Afterward	(15) Childhood of Jesus	Nazareth			2:40, 51		
A.D. 7–8	(16) Jesus, 12 Years Old, Visits the Temple	Jerusalem			2:41–50		Deut. 16:1–8
Afterward	(17) 18-Year Account of Jesus' Adolescence and Adulthood	Nazareth			2:51, 52		1 Sam. 2:26
TRUTHS ABOUT JOHN THE BAPTIST							
c. A.D. 28–30	(1) John's Ministry Begins	Judean Wilderness	3:1	1:1–4	3:1, 2	1:19–28	Mal. 3:1
	(2) Man and Message		3:2–12	1:2–8	3:3–14		Is. 40:3
	(3) His Picture of Jesus		3:11, 12	1:7, 8	3:15–18	1:26, 27	Acts 2:38
	(4) His Courage		14:4–12		3:19, 20		
BEGINNING OF JESUS' MINISTRY							
c. A.D. 30	(1) Jesus Baptized	Jordan River	3:13–17	1:9–11	3:21–23	1:29–34	Ps. 2:7
	(2) Jesus Tempted	Wilderness	4:1–11	1:12, 13	4:1–13		Ps. 91:11
	(3) Calls First Disciples	Beyond Jordan				1:35–51	
	(4) The First Miracle	Cana in Galilee				2:1–11	
	(5) First Stay in Capernaum	(Capernaum is "His" city)				2:12	
	(6) First Cleansing of the Temple	Jerusalem				2:13–22	Ps. 69:9
	(7) Received at Jerusalem	Judea				2:23–25	
	(8) Teaches Nicodemus about Second Birth	Judea				3:1–21	Num. 21:8, 9

Date	Event	Location	Matthew	Mark	Luke	John	Related References
A.D. 30	(9) Co-Ministry with John	Judea				3:22–30	
	(10) Leaves for Galilee	Judea	4:12	1:14	4:14	4:1–4	
	(11) Samaritan Woman at Jacob's Well	Samaria				4:5–42	Josh. 24:32
	(12) Returns to Galilee			1:15	4:15	4:43–45	

THE GALILEAN MINISTRY OF JESUS

Date	Event	Location	Matthew	Mark	Luke	John	Related References
A.D. 30–32							
A.D. 30	(1) Healing of the Nobleman's Son	Cana				4:46–54	
	(2) Rejected at Nazareth	Nazareth			4:16–30		Is. 61:1, 2
	(3) Moved to Capernaum	Capernaum	4:13–17				Is. 9:1, 2
	(4) Four Become Fishers of Men	Sea of Galilee	4:18–22	1:16–20	5:1–11		Ps. 33:9
	(5) Demoniac Healed on the Sabbath Day	Capernaum		1:21–28	4:31–37		
	(6) Peter's Mother-in-Law Cured, Plus Others	Capernaum	8:14–17	1:29–34	4:38–41		Is. 53:4
c. A.D. 30	(7) First Preaching Tour of Galilee	Galilee	4:23–25	1:35–39	4:42–44		
	(8) Leper Healed and Response Recorded	Galilee	8:1–4	1:40–45	5:12–16		Lev. 13:49
	(9) Paralytic Healed	Capernaum	9:1–8	2:1–12	5:17–26		Rom. 3:23
	(10) Matthew's Call and Reception Held	Capernaum	9:9–13	2:13–17	5:27–32		Hos. 6:6
	(11) Disciples Defended via a Parable	Capernaum	9:14–17	2:18–22	5:33–39		
A.D. 31	(12) Goes to Jerusalem for Second Passover; Heals Lame Man	Jerusalem				5:1–47	Ex. 20:10
	(13) Plucked Grain Precipitates Sabbath Controversy	En Route to Galilee	12:1–8	2:23–28	6:1–5		Deut. 5:14
	(14) Withered Hand Healed Causes Another Sabbath Controversy	Galilee	12:9–14	3:1–6	6:6–11		
	(15) Multitudes Healed	Sea of Galilee	12:15–21	3:7–12	6:17–19		
	(16) Twelve Apostles Selected After a Night of Prayer	Near Capernaum		3:13–19	6:12–16		
	(17) Sermon on the Mt.	Near Capernaum	5:1—7:29		6:20–49		
	(18) Centurion's Servant Healed	Capernaum	8:5–13		7:1–10		Is. 49:12, 13
	(19) Raises Widow's Son from Dead	Nain			7:11–17		Job 19:25
	(20) Jesus Allays John's Doubts	Galilee	11:2–19		7:18–35		Mal. 3:1
	(21) Woes Upon the Privileged		11:20–30				Gen. 19:24
	(22) A Sinful Woman Anoints Jesus	Simon's House, Capernaum			7:36–50		
	(23) Another Tour of Galilee	Galilee			8:1–3		
	(24) Jesus Accused of Blasphemy	Capernaum	12:22–37	3:20–30	11:14–23		
	(25) Jesus' Answer to a Demand for a Sign	Capernaum	12:38–45		11:24–26, 29–36		
	(26) Mother, Brothers Seek Audience	Capernaum	12:46–50	3:31–35	8:19–21		
	(27) Famous Parables of Sower, Seed, Tares, Mustard Seed, Leaven, Treasure, Pearl, Dragnet, Lamp Told	By Sea of Galilee	13:1–52	4:1–34	8:4–18		Joel 3:13
	(28) Sea Made Serene	Sea of Galilee	8:23–27	4:35–41	8:22–25		
	(29) Gadarene Demoniac Healed	E. Shore of Galilee	8:28–34	5:1–20	8:26–39		
	(30) Jairus's Daughter Raised and Woman with Hemorrhage Healed		9:18–26	5:21–43	8:40–56		

Date	Event	Location	Matthew	Mark	Luke	John	Related References
A.D. 31	(31) Two Blind Men's Sight Restored		9:27–31				
	(32) Mute Demoniac Healed		9:32–34				
	(33) Nazareth's Second Rejection of Christ	Nazareth	13:53–58	6:1–6			
	(34) Twelve Sent Out		9:35—11:1	6:7–13	9:1–6		1 Cor. 9:14
	(35) Fearful Herod Beheads John	Galilee	14:1–12	6:14–29	9:7–9		
Spring A.D. 32	(36) Return of 12, Jesus Withdraws, 5,000 Fed	Near Bethsaida	14:13–21	6:30–44	9:10–17	6:1–14	
	(37) Walks on the Water	Sea of Galilee	14:22–33	6:45–52		6:15–21	
	(38) Sick of Gennesaret Healed	Gennesaret	14:34–36	6:53–56			
	(39) Peak of Popularity Passes in Galilee	Capernaum				6:22–71 7:1	Is. 54:13
A.D. 32	(40) Traditions Attacked		15:1–20	7:1–23			Ex. 21:17
	(41) Aborted Retirement in Phoenicia: Syro-Phoenician Healed	Phoenicia	15:21–28	7:24–30			
	(42) Afflicted Healed	Decapolis	15:29–31	7:31–37			
	(43) 4,000 Fed	Decapolis	15:32–39	8:1–9			
	(44) Pharisees Increase Attack	Magdala	16:1–4	8:10–13			
	(45) Disciples' Carelessness Condemned; Blind Man Healed		16:5–12	8:14–26			Jer. 5:21
	(46) Peter Confesses Jesus Is the Christ	Near Caesarea Philippi	16:13–20	8:27–30	9:18–21		
	(47) Jesus Foretells His Death	Caesarea Philippi	16:21–26	8:31–38	9:22–25		
	(48) Kingdom Promised		16:27, 28	9:1	9:26, 27		Prov. 24:12
	(49) The Transfiguration	Mountain Unnamed	17:1–13	9:2–13	9:28–36		Is. 42:1
	(50) Epileptic Healed	Mt. of Transfiguration	17:14–21	9:14–29	9:37–42		
	(51) Again Tells of Death, Resurrection	Galilee	17:22, 23	9:30–32	9:43–45		
	(52) Taxes Paid	Capernaum	17:24–27				Ex. 30:11–15
	(53) Disciples Contend About Greatness; Jesus Defines; also Patience, Loyalty, Forgiveness	Capernaum	18:1–35	9:33–50	9:46–62		
	(54) Jesus Rejects Brothers' Advice	Galilee				7:2–9	
c. Sept. A.D. 32	(55) Galilee Departure and Samaritan Rejection		19:1		9:51–56	7:10	
	(56) Cost of Discipleship		8:18–22		9:57–62		

LAST JUDEAN AND PEREAN MINISTRY OF JESUS

Date	Event	Location	Matthew	Mark	Luke	John	Related References
A.D. 32–33 Oct. A.D. 32	(1) Feast of Tabernacles	Jerusalem				7:2, 10–52	
	(2) Forgiveness of Adulteress	Jerusalem				7:53—8:11	Lev. 20:10
A.D. 32	(3) Christ—the Light of the World	Jerusalem				8:12–20	
	(4) Pharisees Can't Meet the Prophecy Thus Try to Destroy the Prophet	Jerusalem—Temple				8:12–59	Is. 6:9
	(5) Man Born Blind Healed; Following Consequences	Jerusalem				9:1–41	
	(6) Parable of the Good Shepherd	Jerusalem				10:1–21	
	(7) The Service of the Seventy	Probably Judea			10:1–24		
	(8) Lawyer Hears the Story of the Good Samaritan	Judea (?)			10:25–37		
	(9) The Hospitality of Martha and Mary	Bethany			10:38–42		
	(10) Another Lesson on Prayer	Judea (?)			11:1–13		

Date	Event	Location	Matthew	Mark	Luke	John	Related References
A.D. 32	(11) Accused of Connection with Beelzebub				11:14–36		
	(12) Judgment Against Lawyers and Pharisees				11:37–54		Mic. 6:8
	(13) Jesus Deals with Hypocrisy, Covetousness, Worry, and Alertness				12:1–59		Mic. 7:6
	(14) Repent or Perish				13:1–5		
	(15) Barren Fig Tree				13:6–9		
	(16) Crippled Woman Healed on Sabbath				13:10–17		Deut. 5:12–15
	(17) Parables of Mustard Seed and Leaven	Probably Perea			13:18–21		
Winter A.D. 32	(18) Feast of Dedication	Jerusalem				10:22–39	Ps. 82:6
	(19) Withdrawal Beyond Jordan					10:40–42	
	(20) Begins Teaching Return to Jerusalem with Special Words About Herod	Perea			13:22–35		Ps. 6:8
	(21) Meal with a Pharisee Ruler Occasions Healing Man with Dropsy; Parables of Ox, Best Places, and Great Supper				14:1–24		
	(22) Demands of Discipleship	Perea			14:25–35		
	(23) Parables of Lost Sheep, Coin, Son				15:1–32		1 Pet. 2:25
	(24) Parables of Unjust Steward, Rich Man and Lazarus				16:1–31		
	(25) Lessons on Service, Faith, Influence				17:1–10		
	(26) Resurrection of Lazarus	Perea to Bethany				11:1–44	
	(27) Reaction to It: Withdrawal of Jesus					11:45–54	
A.D. 33	(28) Begins Last Journey to Jerusalem via Samaria & Galilee	Samaria, Galilee			17:11		
	(29) Heals Ten Lepers				17:12–19		Lev. 13:45, 46
	(30) Lessons on the Coming Kingdom				17:20–37		Gen. 6:1—7:24
	(31) Parables: Persistent Widow, Pharisee and Tax Collector				18:1–14		
	(32) Doctrine on Divorce		19:1–12	10:1–12			Deut. 24:1–4 Gen. 2:23–25
	(33) Jesus Blesses Children: Objections	Perea	19:13–15	10:13–16	18:15–17		Ps. 131:2
	(34) Rich Young Ruler	Perea	19:16–30	10:17–31	18:18–30		Ex. 20:1–17
	(35) Laborers of the 11th Hour		20:1–16				
	(36) Foretells Death and Resurrection	Near Jordan	20:17–19	10:32–34	18:31–34		Ps. 22
	(37) Ambition of James and John		20:20–28	10:35–45			
	(38) Blind Bartimaeus Healed	Jericho		10:46–52	18:35–43		
	(39) Interview with Zacchaeus	Jericho			19:1–10		
	(40) Parable: the Minas	Jericho			19:11–27		
	(41) Returns to Home of Mary and Martha	Bethany				11:55—12:1	
	(42) Plot to Kill Lazarus	Bethany				12:9–11	

JESUS' FINAL WEEK OF WORK AT JERUSALEM

Date	Event	Location	Matthew	Mark	Luke	John	Related References
Spring A.D. 33							
Sunday	(1) Triumphal Entry	Bethany, Jerusalem, Bethany	21:1–9	11:1–11	19:28–44	12:12–19	Zech. 9:9

Date	Event	Location	Matthew	Mark	Luke	John	Related References
Monday	(2) Fig Tree Cursed and Temple Cleansed	Bethany to Jerusalem	21:10–19	11:12–18	19:45–48		Jer. 7:11
	(3) The Attraction of Sacrifice	Jerusalem				12:20–50	Is. 6:10
Tuesday	(4) Withered Fig Tree Testifies	Bethany to Jerusalem	21:20–22	11:19–26			
	(5) Sanhedrin Challenges Jesus. Answered by Parables: Two Sons, Wicked Vinedressers and Marriage Feast	Jerusalem	21:23—22:14	11:27—12:12	20:1–19		Is. 5:1, 2
	(6) Tribute to Caesar	Jerusalem	22:15–22	12:13–17	20:20–26		
	(7) Sadducees Question the Resurrection	Jerusalem	22:23–33	12:18–27	20:27–40		Ex. 3:6
	(8) Pharisees Question Commandments	Jerusalem	22:34–40	12:28–34			
	(9) Jesus and David	Jerusalem	22:41–46	12:35–37	20:41–44		Ps. 110:1
	(10) Jesus' Last Sermon	Jerusalem	23:1–39	12:38–40	20:45–47		
	(11) Widow's Mite	Jerusalem		12:41–44	21:1–4		Lev. 27:30
	(12) Jesus Tells of the Future	Mt. of Olives	24:1–51	13:1–37	21:5–36		Dan. 12:1
	(13) Parables: Ten Virgins, Talents, The Day of Judgment	Mt. of Olives	25:1–46				Zech. 14:5
	(14) Jesus Tells Date of Crucifixion		26:1–5	14:1, 2	22:1, 2		
	(15) Anointing by Mary at Simon's Feast	Bethany	26:6–13	14:3–9		12:2–8	
	(16) Judas Contracts the Betrayal		26:14–16	14:10, 11	22:3–6		Zech. 11:12
Thursday	(17) Preparation for the Passover	Jerusalem	26:17–19	14:12–16	22:7–13		Ex. 12:14–28
Thursday P. M.	(18) Passover Eaten, Jealousy Rebuked	Jerusalem	26:20	14:17	22:14–16, 24–30		
	(19) Feet Washed	Upper Room				13:1–20	
	(20) Judas Revealed, Defects	Upper Room	26:21–25	14:18–21	22:21–23	13:21–30	Ps. 41:9
	(21) Jesus Warns About Further Desertion; Cries of Loyalty	Upper Room	26:31–35	14:27–31	22:31–38	13:31–38	Zech. 13:7
	(22) Institution of the Lord's Supper	Upper Room	26:26–29	14:22–25	22:17–20		1 Cor. 11:23–34
	(23) Last Speech to the Apostles and Intercessory Prayer	Jerusalem				14:1—17:26	Ps. 35:19
Thursday-Friday	(24) The Grief of Gethsemane	Mt. of Olives	26:30, 36–46	14:26, 32–42	22:39–46	18:1	Ps. 42:6
Friday	(25) Betrayal, Arrest, Desertion	Gethsemane	26:47–56	14:43–52	22:47–53	18:2–12	
	(26) First Examined by Annas	Jerusalem				18:12–14, 19–23	
	(27) Trial by Caiaphas and Council; Following Indignities	Jerusalem	26:57, 59–68	14:53, 55–65	22:54, 63–65	18:24	Lev. 24:16
	(28) Peter's Triple Denial	Jerusalem	26:58, 69–75	14:54, 66–72	22:54–62	18:15–18, 25–27	
	(29) Condemnation by the Council	Jerusalem	27:1	15:1	22:66–71		Ps. 110:1
	(30) Suicide of Judas	Jerusalem	27:3–10				Acts 1:18, 19
	(31) First Appearance Before Pilate	Jerusalem	27:2, 11–14	15:1–5	23:1–7	18:28–38	
	(32) Jesus Before Herod	Jerusalem			23:6–12		
	(33) Second Appearance Before Pilate	Jerusalem	27:15–26	15:6–15	23:13–25	18:39—19:16	Deut. 21:6–9
	(34) Mockery by Roman Soldiers	Jerusalem	27:27–30	15:16–19			
	(35) Led to Golgotha	Jerusalem	27:31–34	15:20–23	23:26–33	19:16, 17	Ps. 69:21
	(36) 6 Events of First 3 Hours on Cross	Calvary	27:35–44	15:24–32	23:33–43	19:18–27	Ps. 22:18
	(37) Last 3 Hours on Cross	Calvary	27:45–50	15:33–37	23:44–46	19:28–30	Ps. 22:1
	(38) Events Attending Jesus' Death		27:51–56	15:38–41	23:45, 47–49		
	(39) Burial of Jesus	Jerusalem	27:57–60	15:42–46	23:50–54	19:31–42	Ex. 12:46
Friday-Saturday	(40) Tomb Sealed	Jerusalem	27:61–66		23:55, 56		Ex. 20:8–11
	(41) Women Watch	Jerusalem		15:47			

Date	Event	Location	Matthew	Mark	Luke	John	Related References
	THE RESURRECTION THROUGH THE ASCENSION						
A.D. 33 Dawn of First Day (Sunday, "Lord's Day")	(1) Women Visit the Tomb	Near Jerusalem	28:1–8	16:1–8	24:1–11		
	(2) Peter and John See the Empty Tomb				24:12	20:1–10	
	(3) Jesus' Appearance to Mary Magdalene	Jerusalem		16:9–11		20:11–18	
	(4) Jesus' Appearance to the Other Women	Jerusalem	28:9, 10				
	(5) Guards' Report of the Resurrection		28:11–15				
Sunday Afternoon	(6) Jesus' Appearance to Two Disciples on Way to Emmaus			16:12, 13	24:13–35		1 Cor. 15:5
Late Sunday	(7) Jesus' Appearance to Ten Disciples Without Thomas	Jerusalem			24:36–43	20:19–25	
One Week Later	(8) Appearance to Disciples with Thomas	Jerusalem				20:26–31	
During 40 Days until Ascension	(9) Jesus' Appearance to Seven Disciples by Sea of Galilee	Galilee				21:1–25	
	(10) Appearance to 500	Mt. in Galilee					1 Cor. 15:6
	(11) Great Commission		28:16–20	16:14–18	24:44–49		
	(12) The Ascension	Mt. Olivet		16:19, 20	24:50–53		Acts 1:4–11

The Jewish Calendar

The Jews used two kinds of calendars:
Civil Calendar—official calendar of kings, childbirth, and contracts
Sacred Calendar—from which festivals were computed.

NAMES OF MONTHS	CORRESPONDS WITH	NO. OF DAYS	MONTH OF CIVIL YEAR	MONTH OF SACRED YEAR
TISHRI	Sept.–Oct.	30 days	1st	7th
HESHVAN	Oct.–Nov.	29 or 30	2nd	8th
CHISLEV	Nov.–Dec.	29 or 30	3rd	9th
TEBETH	Dec.–Jan.	29	4th	10th
SHEBAT	Jan.–Feb.	30	5th	11th
ADAR	Feb.–Mar.	29 or 30	6th	12th
NISAN	Mar.–Apr.	30	7th	1st
IYAR	Apr.–May	29	8th	2nd
SIVAN	May–June	30	9th	3rd
TAMMUZ	June–July	29	10th	4th
AB	July–Aug.	30	11th	5th
***ELUL**	Aug.–Sept.	29	12th	6th

The Jewish day was from sunset to sunset, in 8 equal parts:

FIRST WATCH ....SUNSET TO 9 P.M.
SECOND WATCH ....9 P.M. TO MIDNIGHT
THIRD WATCH..................MIDNIGHT TO 3 A.M.
FOURTH WATCH................3 A.M. TO SUNRISE

FIRST WATCH ....SUNRISE TO 9 A.M.
SECOND WATCH ....9 A.M. TO NOON
THIRD WATCH..................NOON TO 3 P.M.
FOURTH WATCH................3 P.M. TO SUNSET

*Hebrew months were alternately 30 and 29 days long. Their year, shorter than ours, had 354 days. Therefore, about every 3 years (7 times in 19 years) an extra 29-day-month, VEADAR, was added between ADAR and NISAN

TEACHINGS AND ILLUSTRATIONS OF CHRIST

Subject	*Reference*
Abiding in Christ	John 15:4–10
Ability	Matt. 25:14, 15
Ablution	Matt. 6:17, 18
Abode	John 14:23
Abraham	John 8:37, 56
Abstinence	Luke 21:34
Abundant life	John 10:10
Access to God	John 10:7, 9
Accountability	Luke 12:47, 48
Accusation, false	Matt. 5:11
Adultery	Matt. 5:27, 28
Adversity	Luke 24:46
Affliction	Matt. 24:7–12
Agreement	Matt. 18:19
Altar	Matt. 23:18, 19
Ambition	Luke 22:25–30
Angels	Matt. 13:39, 41
Anger	Matt. 5:22
Anxiety	Luke 12:22–31
Apostasy	Matt. 13:18–22
	Luke 8:13
Apostles	Luke 11:49
Appearance	Matt. 6:16
Appearance, outward	Matt. 23:27, 28
Authority	Matt. 21:24
	Luke 10:19
Avarice	Luke 12:16–21
Backsliding	Luke 9:62
Baptism	Matt. 28:19
	Acts 1:5
Beatitudes	Matt. 5:3–11
Beelzebub	Matt. 10:25
Begging	Luke 16:3
Beneficence	Matt. 5:42
Betrayal	Matt. 26:21
Bigotry	Luke 18:9–14
Birds	Matt. 8:20
Blasphemy	Matt. 12:31, 32
Blessings	Matt. 5:3–11
Blind guides	Matt. 15:14
Borrowing	Matt. 5:42
Bread of life	John 6:32–35
Brothers	Matt. 23:8
Builders	Matt. 7:24
	Luke 6:47–49
Burdens	Luke 11:46
Burial	Matt. 8:22
Caesar	Matt. 22:21
Call of God	Matt. 20:16
Called ones	Matt. 22:14
Capital and labor	Matt. 20:1–15
Capital punishment	Matt. 26:52
Care of God	Matt. 6:30, 33
Caution	Mark 4:24
Celibacy	Matt. 19:11, 12
Character	John 1:47
Charity	Luke 12:33
Cheating	Mark 10:19
Chosen	Matt. 22:14
Church	Matt. 18:17
Circumcision	John 7:22, 23
Cleansing	John 15:3
Coin	Matt. 22:19–21
Coldness	Matt. 24:12
Communication	Luke 24:17
Compassion	Matt. 15:32
	Luke 10:33
Compromise	Matt. 5:25, 26
Conceit	Luke 18:10–12
Conduct, Christian	Matt. 5:16
Confessing Christ	Matt. 10:32, 33
Confession of sin	Luke 18:13, 14
Confidence	Mark 10:24
Conflict	Matt. 10:34–36
Conscience	John 8:7–9
Contention	Matt. 18:15–17
Contentment	John 6:43
Conversion	Matt. 13:15
Convict	John 16:8
Corruption, moral	Luke 11:39
Courage	Matt. 9:22
Covenant	Mark 14:24
Coveting	Mark 7:21, 22
Cross-bearing	Matt. 10:38
Crucifixion	Luke 9:22
Cup of water	Matt. 10:42
Dancing	Luke 15:25–27
Daniel	Matt. 24:15
Darkness	Luke 11:35
David	Matt. 12:3
Day	John 11:9
Deaf	Matt. 13:13–15
Death	Luke 9:22
	John 8:51
Debts	Matt. 18:24
Deceivers	Matt. 24:4, 5
Decision	Matt. 6:24
Defilement	Matt. 15:11, 18, 19
Devil	Matt. 13:38, 39
Diligence	John 9:4
Disbelief	John 5:38
Discernment	Matt. 16:2, 3
Discipleship	Luke 14:33
Disputes	Mark 9:33, 34
Distress	Luke 21:23, 25
Divorce	Matt. 5:31, 32
Doctrine	Mark 7:7
Doubt	Matt. 21:21
Drunkard	Luke 7:34
Drunkenness	Luke 21:34
Dullness	Matt. 13:13
Duty	Luke 17:10
Dwelling places	John 14:2, 3
Earth	Matt. 5:18
Earthquakes	Mark 13:8
Economy	Matt. 15:37
	John 6:12
Elect	Matt. 24:24, 31
Election	Matt. 25:34
Elijah	Matt. 17:11, 12
Employer	Matt. 20:1–16
Encouragement	Matt. 9:2
Endowments	Matt. 25:14, 15
Endurance	Matt. 10:22
	Luke 21:19
Enemies	Matt. 5:43, 44
Eternal life	Matt. 19:29
Eternal sin	Mark 3:29
Etiquette	Luke 10:8
Evil	Matt. 15:19
Exaltation	Matt. 23:12
Example	John 13:15
Excuses	Luke 14:18–20
Extravagance	Luke 15:11–14
Fainting	Mark 8:2, 3
Faith	Matt. 6:25
	Mark 11:22
	Luke 7:50
Faithfulness	Matt. 25:21
Faithlessness	Matt. 25:24–30
False prophets	Matt. 24:11
False witness	Matt. 19:18
Farm	Matt. 22:2–6
Fasting	Matt. 6:16–18
Faultfinding	Matt. 7:3–5
Faults	Matt. 18:15
Fear of God	Matt. 10:28
Feast	Luke 14:8
Feet washing	John 13:12–15
Fellowship	Matt. 8:11
Flattery	Luke 6:26
Flesh	John 6:53
Flock	Matt. 26:31
Following Christ	Matt. 10:37, 38
Food	Matt. 6:11
	Matt. 6:25
	John 6:27
Fool	Matt. 5:22
Formalism	Matt. 23:23–28
Forsaking all	Luke 14:33
Foxes	Luke 9:58
Friends	Luke 11:5–8
Frugality	John 6:12
Fruitfulness	Matt. 13:23
Fruitlessness	Luke 13:6–9
Generosity	Matt. 25:34–40
Gentiles	Matt. 10:5–7

Subject	*Reference*
Gentleness	Matt. 5:5
Giving	Luke 6:38
Gladness	Luke 15:32
Glorifying God	Matt. 5:16
Gluttony	Luke 21:34
God	Matt. 19:17, 26
Godlessness	John 5:42, 44
Golden Rule	Matt. 7:12
Gospel	Luke 4:18
Grace	2 Cor. 12:9
Greatness	Matt. 5:19
Grumble	John 6:43
Guidance	John 16:13
Hairs numbered	Matt. 10:30
Hand of God	John 10:27–29
Happiness	Matt. 5:12
	John 13:16, 17
Harlots	Matt. 21:31
Harvest	Matt. 9:37, 38
Hatred	John 15:18, 19
Healing	Matt. 10:7, 8
	Mark 2:17
Heart	Matt. 13:19
Heaven	Luke 16:17
	John 3:13
Hell	Matt. 5:22
	Matt. 10:28
Helper	John 14:16
	John 15:26
Helpless	John 6:44
Hireling	John 10:11–13
Holy Spirit	John 14:26
Home	Mark 5:19
Honesty	Mark 10:19
	Luke 8:15
Honor of men	Matt. 6:2
Honor of parents	Matt. 15:3–6
Hospitality	Luke 14:12–14
Humility	Matt. 11:29
	John 13:14
Hunger, spiritual	Matt. 5:6
	Luke 6:21
Hypocrisy	Matt. 6:5
	Luke 6:42
Ignorance	Matt. 22:29
Immortality	Matt. 25:46
	John 11:25, 26
Impartiality of God	Matt. 5:45
Inconsistency	Matt. 7:3–5
	Luke 6:41, 42
Indecision	Luke 9:62
Indifference	Matt. 24:12
Industry	John 4:36
Infidelity	John 3:18
Influence	Matt. 5:13
Ingratitude	Luke 17:17, 18
Innocence	Matt. 10:16
Insincerity	Luke 16:15
Inspiration	Luke 12:12
Instability	Matt. 7:26, 27
Instruction	John 6:45
Insufficiency	Mark 10:21
Integrity	Luke 16:10
Intercession	John 17:9
Investment	Matt. 6:19, 20
Jealousy	Luke 15:25–30
John the Baptist	Luke 7:24–28
Jonah	Matt. 12:39–41
Joy	Matt. 25:21
	Luke 15:7, 10
Judge not	Matt. 7:1, 2
Judgment	Matt. 11:24
Judgment day	Matt. 25:31–46
Justice	John 5:30
Justification, self	Luke 16:15
Killing	Matt. 5:21, 22
Kindness	Luke 10:30–35
Kingdom	Luke 7:28
	John 18:36
Kiss	Luke 7:45
Knowledge	John 8:31, 32
Labor	Matt. 20:1–14
Laughter	Luke 6:21
Law	Luke 16:16
Lawsuit	Matt. 5:25, 40
Lawyers	Luke 11:46
Leaven	Matt. 16:6
	Luke 13:20, 21
Lending	Luke 6:34, 35
Lepers	Matt. 10:7, 8
Levite	Luke 10:30–32
Liars	John 8:44, 45
Liberality	Luke 6:30, 38
Liberty	Luke 4:18
Life	Matt. 6:25
	John 5:40
Light	Luke 11:33
	John 8:12
Living water	John 4:10
Log	Luke 6:41, 42
Loneliness	John 16:32
Lord's Supper	Matt. 26:26–29
Loss of soul	Matt. 16:25, 26
Lost opportunity	Matt. 25:7–12
Love	Matt. 22:37–40
Lukewarmness	Matt. 26:40, 41
Lunatic	Matt. 17:14, 15
Lust	Mark 4:18, 19
Magistrates	Luke 12:11, 58
Mammon	Matt. 6:24
Marriage	Matt. 19:4–6
	Mark 12:25
Martyrdom	John 16:1–3
Mary's choice	Luke 10:41, 42
Memorial	Matt. 26:13
Mercy	Matt. 5:7
	Luke 16:24
Minister	Luke 10:2
Miracles	Matt. 12:28
Money lender, creditor	Luke 7:41, 42
Moses	Matt. 19:8
Moses' Law	John 7:19
Mother	Matt. 10:37
Mourn	Matt. 5:4
Murder	Matt. 15:19
Mysteries of Heaven	Matt. 13:11
Narrow way	Matt. 7:13, 14
Neglect	Luke 12:47
Neighbor	Matt. 19:19
Neutrality	Matt. 12:30
New birth	John 3:3, 5–8
Noah	Luke 17:26, 27
Oath	Matt. 5:33–37
Obedience	Matt. 12:50
Offering	Matt. 5:25
Offerings	Luke 21:3, 4
Opportunity	Matt. 5:25
Parables	Mark 4:11, 12
Paradise	Luke 23:43
Pardoning	Luke 6:37
Parents	Matt. 10:21
Patriotism	Matt. 22:21
Peace	Mark 9:50
Peacemakers	Matt. 5:9
Penitence	Luke 18:13
Perception	John 8:43
Perfection	Matt. 5:48
Persecution	Matt. 24:9
Perseverance	Matt. 10:22
Pharisaism	Matt. 23:2–33
Pharisee and tax collector	Luke 18:10–14
Pharisees	Matt. 5:20
Philanthropy	Luke 11:41
Physician	Matt. 9:12
Piety	John 1:47
Pleasing God	John 8:29
Pleasures	Luke 8:14
Poison	Mark 16:17, 18
Poll tax	Matt. 22:19–21
Polygamy	Matt. 19:8, 9
Poor	Mark 14:7
Power	Matt. 6:13
Prayer	Matt. 6:9–13
	Matt. 7:7–11
Preaching	Mark 16:15, 16
Procrastination	Matt. 25:3
Profit and loss	Matt. 16:26
Prophets	Matt. 7:15
	Matt. 10:41
Proselyte	Luke 23:15
Protection	Luke 18:3
Providence	Matt. 6:25–33
Prudence	Matt. 10:16–20
Punishment	Matt. 21:41
Purity	Matt. 5:8
Ransom	Matt. 20:28
Reaping	John 4:35–38
Receiving Christ	Mark 9:37
Reconciliation	Matt. 5:23, 24
Regeneration	Matt. 19:28
Rejecting Christ	John 3:18

Subject	*Reference*
Rejoicing	Luke 10:20
Release	Luke 4:18
Religion	Matt. 25:34–36
	Mark 7:6–8
Repentance	Matt. 11:21
	Luke 13:28
Reproof	Matt. 11:21–23
Resignation	Matt. 26:39
Responsibility	Luke 12:47, 48
Rest	Matt. 11:28–30
	Matt. 26:45
Resurrection	John 6:40
Retaliation	Matt. 5:39–44
Retribution	Matt. 23:34, 35
Reward	Matt. 10:42
Riches	Mark 4:19
Righteousness	Matt. 5:6, 20
	John 16:10
Robbers	Luke 10:30
	John 10:1
Robbery	Matt. 23:25
Sabbath	Matt. 12:5–8
Sackcloth	Matt. 11:21
Sacrifice	Matt. 12:7
Sacrilege	Matt. 21:13
Sadducees	Matt. 16:6
Salt	Matt. 5:13
	Mark 9:50
Salvation	Luke 19:19
	John 4:22
Samaritan	Luke 10:30–35
Sanctification	John 17:17
Satan	Matt. 4:10
	Mark 4:15
Scripture	Matt. 21:42
	Luke 4:21
Secrecy	Luke 12:2, 3
Security	Luke 6:47, 48
Seduction	Mark 13:22
Seeking the kingdom	Matt. 6:19, 20
Self-condemnation	Matt. 23:29–32
	Luke 19:20–24
Self-control	Matt. 5:21
Self-deception	Luke 12:16–21
Self-denial	Matt. 16:24–26
Self-exaltation	Matt. 23:12
Self-examination	Matt. 7:3–5

Subject	*Reference*
Selfishness	Luke 6:32–35
Self-righteousness	Matt. 23:23–27
Self-sacrifice	Matt. 16:25
Serpents	Matt. 23:33
	John 3:14
Service	Luke 22:27
Sheep	Luke 15:4–7
Shepherd	John 10:1–18
Sickness	Matt. 10:8
Signs	Luke 11:16
	John 4:48
Silence	Matt. 17:9
Sin	Matt. 26:28
	John 8:34
Sincerity	Matt. 5:13–16
Skepticism	John 20:27, 29
Slaves	Matt. 18:23
	John 15:15
Sleep	Mark 4:26, 27
	Mark 13:35, 36
Slothfulness	Matt. 25:26–30
Son of Man	Luke 9:22
Sorrow	Matt. 19:22
	John 16:6
Soul	Matt. 10:28
	Luke 12:19, 20
Soul winners	Matt. 4:19
Sowing	Mark 4:14
Speech	John 8:43
Spirit	Matt. 26:41
	Mark 5:8
Statement	Matt. 5:37
Steadfastness	Matt. 10:22
Stealing	Matt. 19:18
Steward	Luke 12:42, 43
	Luke 16:1–8
Stewardship	Luke 19:13–27
Stomach	Matt. 15:17
Strife	Luke 22:24
Stubbornness	John 5:40
Stumbling block	Matt. 23:13
Submission	Matt. 26:39, 42
Suffering	Matt. 26:38
Supper, The Lord's	Luke 22:14–20
Swearing	Matt. 23:16–22
Talents	Matt. 18:24
Taxes	Matt. 22:19–21

Subject	*Reference*
Tax collectors	Matt. 5:46, 47
Teaching	Matt. 28:19, 20
	John 13:13–15
Temperance	Luke 21:34
Temptations	Matt. 4:1–11
	Luke 8:13
Thieves	Matt. 6:19
	John 10:1, 8
Timidness	Mark 4:40
Tithes	Luke 18:11, 12
Traditions	Mark 7:9, 13
Transgressions	Matt. 15:2
Treasures	Matt. 6:19–21
Tribulation	Matt. 24:9
	John 16:33
Truth	John 14:6
Unbelievers	Luke 12:46
Uncharitableness	John 7:24
Unchastity	Matt. 5:31, 32
Uncleanness	Matt. 23:27
Unity	John 17:20, 21
Unpardonable sin	Matt. 12:31, 32
Vengeance	Matt. 5:39, 40
Vine	John 15:1, 4, 5
Visions	Matt. 17:9
Walks of Life	John 8:12
	John 12:35
War	Matt. 24:26
Watchfulness	Matt. 24:42, 44
	Luke 12:37–40
Wedding	Luke 14:8–10
Widow	Mark 12:43, 44
Wine	Luke 5:37–39
Wisdom	Luke 21:15
Witness	John 8:14
Witness, false	Matt. 19:18
Witnessing	Acts 1:8
Wives	Luke 14:20, 26
Worker	Matt. 10:10
Worldliness	Luke 21:34
Worm	Mark 9:43–48
Worries of the world	Matt. 13:22
Worship	Matt. 4:10
Yoke	Matt. 11:28, 29
Zacchaeus	Luke 19:5
Zeal	John 2:17

PROPHECIES OF THE MESSIAH FULFILLED IN JESUS CHRIST

Presented Here in Their Order of Fulfillment

PROPHETIC SCRIPTURE	SUBJECT	FULFILLED
Gen. 3:15 "And I will put enmity between you and the woman, and between your seed and her Seed; He shall bruise your head, and you shall bruise his heel."	**seed of a woman**	***Gal. 4:4*** "But when the fullness of the time had come, God sent forth His Son, born of a woman, born under the law."
Gen. 12:3 "I will bless those who bless you, and I will curse him who curses you; and in you all the families of the earth shall be blessed."	**descendant of Abraham**	***Matt. 1:1*** "The book of the genealogy of Jesus Christ, the Son of David, the Son of Abraham."
Gen. 17:19 "Then God said, 'No, Sarah your wife shall bear you a son, and you shall call his name Isaac; I will establish My covenant with him for an everlasting covenant, *and* with his descendants after him.'"	**descendant of Isaac**	***Luke 3:34*** "*the son* of Jacob, *the son* of Isaac, *the son* of Abraham, *the son* of Terah, *the son* of Nahor."
Num. 24:17 "I see Him, but not now; I behold Him, but not near; a Star shall come out of Jacob; a Scepter shall rise out of Israel, and batter the brow of Moab, and destroy all the sons of tumult."	**descendant of Jacob**	***Matt. 1:2*** "Abraham begot Isaac, Isaac begot Jacob, and Jacob begot Judah and his brothers."
Gen. 49:10 "The scepter shall not depart from Judah, nor a lawgiver from between his feet, until Shiloh comes; and to Him *shall be* the obedience of the people."	**from the tribe of Judah**	***Luke 3:33*** "*the son* of Amminadab, *the son* of Ram, *the son* of Hezron, *the son* of Perez, *the son* of Judah."
Is. 9:7 "Of the increase of *His* government and peace *there will be* no end, upon the throne of David and over His kingdom, to order it and establish it with judgment and justice from that time forward, even forever. The zeal of the LORD of hosts will perform this."	**heir to the throne of David**	***Luke 1:32, 33*** "He will be great, and will be called the Son of the Highest; and the Lord God will give Him the throne of His father David. And He will reign over the house of Jacob forever, and of His kingdom there will be no end."
Ps. 45:6, 7; 102:25–27 "Your throne, O God, *is* forever and ever; a scepter of righteousness *is* the scepter of Your kingdom. You love righteousness, and hate wickedness; therefore God, Your God, has anointed You with the oil of gladness more than Your companions." "Of old You laid the foundation of the earth, and the heavens *are* the work of Your hands. They will perish, but You will endure; yes, all of them will grow old like a garment; like a cloak You will change them, and they will be changed. But You *are* the same, and Your years will have no end."	**anointed and eternal**	***Heb. 1:8–12*** "But to the Son *He says:* 'Your throne, O God, *is* forever and ever; a scepter of righteousness *is* the scepter of Your kingdom. You have loved righteousness and hated lawlessness; therefore God, Your God, has anointed You with the oil of gladness more than Your companions.' And: 'You, LORD, in the beginning laid the foundation of the earth, and the heavens are the work of Your hands. They will perish, but You remain; and they will all grow old like a garment; like a cloak You will fold them up, and they will be changed. But You are the same, and Your years will not fail.'"

PROPHETIC SCRIPTURE	SUBJECT	FULFILLED
Mic. 5:2 "But you, Bethlehem, Ephrathah, *though* you are little among the thousands of Judah, *yet* out of you shall come forth to Me the One to be Ruler in Israel, whose goings forth *are* from of old, from everlasting."	**born in Jerusalem**	***Luke 2:4, 5, 7*** "And Joseph also went up from Galilee, out of the city of Nazareth, into Judea, to the city of David, which is called Bethlehem, because he was of the house and lineage of David, to be registered with Mary, his betrothed wife, who was with child. . . . And she brought forth her firstborn Son, and wrapped Him in swaddling cloths, and laid Him in a manger, because there was no room for them in the inn."
Dan. 9:25 "Know therefore and understand, *that* from the going forth of the command to restore and build Jerusalem until Messiah the Prince, *there shall be* seven weeks, and sixty-two weeks; the street shall be built again, and the wall, even in troublesome times."	**time for His birth**	***Luke 2:1, 2*** "And it came to pass in those days *that* a decree went out from Caesar Augustus that all the world should be registered. This census first took place when Quirinius was governor of Syria."
Is. 7:14 "Therefore the Lord Himself will give you a sign: behold, the virgin shall conceive and bear a Son, and shall call His name Immanuel."	**to be born of a virgin**	***Luke 1:26, 27, 30, 31*** "Now in the sixth month the angel Gabriel was sent by God to a city of Galilee named Nazareth, to a virgin betrothed to a man whose name was Joseph, of the house of David. The virgin's name *was* Mary. . . . Then the angel said to her, 'Do not be afraid, Mary, for you have found favor with God. And behold, you will conceive in your womb, and bring forth a Son, and shall call His name JESUS.' "
Jer. 31:15 "Thus says the LORD: '*A voice was heard in Ramah, lamentation, and* bitter weeping, Rachel weeping for her children, refusing to be comforted for her children, because they *are* no more.' "	**slaughter of children**	***Matt. 2:16–18*** "Then Herod, when he saw that he was deceived by the wise men, was exceedingly angry; and he sent forth and put to death all the male children who were in Bethlehem and in all its districts, from two years old and under, according to the time which he had determined from the wise men. Then was fulfilled what was spoken by Jeremiah the prophet, saying: 'A voice was heard in Ramah, lamentation, weeping, and great mourning, Rachel weeping for her children, refusing to be comforted, because they are no more.' "
Hos. 11:1 "When Israel *was* a child, I loved him, and out of Egypt I called My son."	**flight to Egypt**	***Matt. 2:14, 15*** "When he arose, he took the young Child and His mother by night and departed for Egypt, and was there until the death of Herod, that it might be fulfilled which was spoken by the Lord through the prophet, saying, 'Out of Egypt I called My Son.' "
Is. 40:3–5 "The voice of one crying in the wilderness: 'Prepare the way of the LORD; make straight in the desert a highway for our God. Every valley shall be exalted, and every mountain and hill brought low; the crooked places shall be made straight, and the rough places smooth; the glory of the LORD shall be revealed, and all flesh shall see *it* together; for the mouth of the LORD has spoken.' "	**the way prepared**	***Luke 3:3–6*** "And he went into all the region around the Jordan, preaching a baptism of repentance for the remission of sins, as it is written in the book of the words of Isaiah the prophet, saying: 'The voice of one crying in the wilderness: "Prepare the way of the LORD; make His paths straight. Every valley shall be filled and every mountain and hill brought low; the crooked places shall be made straight and the rough ways smooth; and all flesh shall see the salvation of God." ' "

PROPHETIC SCRIPTURE	SUBJECT	FULFILLED
Mal. 3:1 "'Behold, I send My messenger, and he will prepare the way before Me. And the Lord, whom you seek, will suddenly come to His temple, even the Messenger of the covenant, in whom you delight. Behold, He is coming,' says the LORD of hosts."	**preceded by a forerunner**	***Luke 7:24, 27*** "When the messengers of John had departed, He began to speak to the multitudes concerning John: 'What did you go out into the wilderness to see? A reed shaken by the wind? . . . This is *he,* of whom it is written: "Behold, I send My messenger before Your face, who will prepare Your way before You." ' "
Mal. 4:5, 6 "Behold, I will send you Elijah the prophet before the coming of the great and dreadful day of the LORD. And he will turn the hearts of the fathers to the children, and the hearts of the children to their fathers, lest I come and strike the earth with a curse."	**preceded by Elijah**	***Matt. 11:13, 14*** "For all the prophets and the law prophesied until John. And if you are willing to receive *it,* he is Elijah who is to come."
Ps. 2:7 "I will declare the decree: the LORD has said to Me, 'You *are* My Son, today I have begotten You.' "	**declared the Son of God**	***Matt. 3:17*** "And suddenly a voice *came* from heaven, saying, 'This is My beloved Son, in whom I am well pleased.' "
Is. 9:1, 2 "Nevertheless the gloom *will* not *be* upon her who *is* distressed, as when at first He lightly esteemed the land of Zebulun and the land of Naphtali, and afterward more heavily oppressed *her, by* the way of the sea, beyond the Jordan, in Galilee of the Gentiles. The people who walked in darkness have seen a great light; those who dwelt in the land of the shadow of death, upon them a light has shined."	**Galilean ministry**	***Matt. 4:13–16*** "And leaving Nazareth, He came and dwelt in Capernaum, which is by the sea, in the regions of Zebulun and Naphtali, that it might be fulfilled which was spoken by Isaiah the prophet, saying: 'The land of Zebulun, and the land of Naphtali, *by* the way of the sea, beyond the Jordan, Galilee of the Gentiles: The people who sat in darkness have seen a great light, and upon those who sat in the region and shadow of death light has dawned.' "
Ps. 78:2–4 "I will open my mouth in a parable; I will utter dark sayings of old, which we have heard and known, and our fathers have told us. We will not hide *them* from their children, telling to the generation to come the praises of the LORD, and His strength and His wonderful works that He has done."	**speaks in parables**	***Matt. 13:34, 35*** "All these things Jesus spoke to the multitude in parables; and without a parable He did not speak to them, that it might be fulfilled which was spoken by the prophet, saying: 'I will open My mouth in parables; I will utter things which have been kept secret from the foundation of the world.' "
Deut. 18:15 "The LORD your God will raise up for you a Prophet like me from your midst, from your brethren. Him you shall hear."	**a prophet**	***Acts 3:20, 22*** "And that He may send Jesus Christ, who was preached to you before, . . . For Moses truly said to the fathers, 'The LORD your God will raise up for you a Prophet like me from your brethren. Him you shall hear in all things, whatever He says to you.' "
Is. 61:1, 2 "The Spirit of the Lord GOD *is* upon Me, because the LORD has anointed Me to preach good tidings to the poor; He has sent Me to heal the brokenhearted, to proclaim liberty to the captives, and the opening of the prison to *those who are* bound; to proclaim the acceptable year of the LORD, and the day of vengeance of our God; to comfort all who mourn."	**to bind up the brokenhearted**	***Luke 4:18, 19*** "The Spirit of the LORD *is* upon Me, because He has anointed Me to preach the gospel to *the* poor; He has sent Me to heal the brokenhearted, to proclaim liberty to *the* captives, and recovery of sight to *the* blind, to set at liberty those who are oppressed; to proclaim the acceptable year of the LORD."
Is. 53:3 "He is despised and rejected by men; a Man of sorrows and acquainted with grief. And we hid, as it were *our* faces from Him; He was despised, and we did not esteem Him."	**rejected by His own people, the Jews**	***John 1:11*** "He came to His own, and His own did not receive Him." ***Luke 23:18*** "And they all cried out at once, saying, 'Away with this *Man,* and release to us Barabbas.' "

PROPHETIC SCRIPTURE	SUBJECT	FULFILLED
Ps. 110:4 "The LORD has sworn and will not relent, 'You *are* a priest forever according to the order of Melchizedek.'"	**priest after order of Melchizedek**	***Heb. 5:5, 6*** "So also Christ did not glorify Himself to become High Priest, *but it* was He who said to Him: 'You are My Son, today I have begotten You.' As *He* also *says* in another *place:* 'You *are* a priest forever according to the order of Melchizedek.'"
Zech. 9:9 "Rejoice greatly, O daughter of Zion! Shout, O daughter of Jerusalem! Behold, your King is coming to you; He *is* just and having salvation, lowly and riding on a donkey, a colt, the foal of a donkey."	**triumphal entry**	***Mark 11:7, 9, 11*** "Then they brought the colt to Jesus and threw their clothes on it, and He sat on it. . . . Then those who went before and those who followed cried out, saying: 'Hosanna! Blessed *is* He who comes in the name of the LORD!' . . . And Jesus went into Jerusalem, and into the temple. So when He had looked around at all things, as the hour was already late, He went out to Bethany with the twelve."
Ps. 8:2 "Out of the mouth of babes and nursing infants You have ordained strength, because of Your enemies, that You may silence the enemy and the avenger."	**adored by infants**	***Matt. 21:15, 16*** "But when the chief priests and scribes saw the wonderful things that He did, and the children crying out in the temple and saying, 'Hosanna to the Son of David!' they were indignant and said to Him, 'Do you hear what these are saying?' And Jesus said to them, 'Yes. Have you never read, "Out of the mouth of babes and nursing infants You have perfected praise"?'"
Is. 53:1 "Who has believed our report? And to whom has the arm of the LORD been revealed?"	**not believed**	***John 12:37, 38*** "But although He had done so many signs before them, they did not believe in Him, that the word of Isaiah the prophet might be fulfilled, which he spoke: 'Lord, who has believed our report? And to whom has the arm of the LORD been revealed?'"
Ps. 41:9 "Even my own familiar friend in whom I trusted, who ate my bread, has lifted up *his* heel against me."	**betrayed by a close friend**	***Luke 22:47, 48*** "And while He was still speaking, behold, a multitude; and he who was called Judas, one of the twelve, went before them and drew near to Jesus to kiss Him. But Jesus said to him, 'Judas, are you betraying the Son of Man with a kiss?'"
Zech. 11:12 "Then I said to them, 'If it is agreeable to you, give *me* my wages; and if not, refrain.' So they weighed out for my wages thirty *pieces* of silver."	**betrayed for thirty pieces of silver**	***Matt. 26:14, 15*** "Then one of the twelve, called Judas Iscariot, went to the chief priests and said, 'What are you willing to give me if I deliver Him to you?' And they counted out to him thirty pieces of silver."
Ps. 35:11 "Fierce witnesses rise up; they ask me *things* that I do not know."	**accused by false witnesses**	***Mark 14:57, 58*** "Then some rose up and bore false witness against Him, saying, 'We heard Him say, "I will destroy this temple made with hands, and within three days I will build another made without hands."'"
Is. 53:7 "He was oppressed, and He was afflicted, yet He opened not His mouth; He was led as a lamb to the slaughter, and as a sheep before its shearers is silent, so He opened not His mouth."	**silent to accusations**	***Mark 15:4, 5*** "Then Pilate asked Him again, saying, 'Do You answer nothing? See how many things they testify against You!' But Jesus still answered nothing, so that Pilate marveled."

PROPHETIC SCRIPTURE	SUBJECT	FULFILLED
Is. 50:6 "I gave My back to those who struck *Me,* and My cheeks to those who plucked out the beard; I did not hide My face from shame and spitting."	**spat on and struck**	***Matt. 26:67*** "Then they spat in His face and beat Him; and others struck *Him* with the palms of their hands."
Ps. 35:19 "Let them not rejoice over me who are wrongfully my enemies; nor let them wink with the eye who hate me without a cause."	**hated without reason**	***John 15:24, 25*** "If I had not done among them the works which no one else did, they would have no sin; but now they have seen and also hated both Me and My Father. But *this happened* that the word might be fulfilled which is written in their law, 'They hated Me without a cause.'"
Is. 53:5 "But He *was* wounded for our transgressions, *He was* bruised for our iniquities; the chastisement for our peace *was* upon Him, and by His stripes we are healed."	**vicarious sacrifice**	***Rom. 5:6, 8*** "For when we were still without strength, in due time Christ died for the ungodly. . . . But God demonstrates His own love toward us, in that while we were still sinners, Christ died for us."
Is. 53:12 "Therefore I will divide Him a portion with the great, and He shall divide the spoil with the strong. Because He poured out His soul unto death, and He was numbered with the transgressors, and He bore the sin of many, and made intercession for the transgressors."	**crucified with malefactors**	***Mark 15:27, 28*** "With Him they also crucified two robbers, one on His right and the other on His left. So the Scripture was fulfilled which says, 'And He was numbered with the transgressors.'"
Zech. 12:10 "And I will pour on the house of David and on the inhabitants of Jerusalem the Spirit of grace and supplication; then they will look on Me whom they pierced. Yes, they will mourn for Him as one mourns for *his* only *son,* and grieve for Him as one grieves for a firstborn."	**pierced through hands and feet**	***John 20:27*** "Then He said to Thomas, 'Reach your finger here, and look at My hands; and reach your hand *here,* and put *it* into My side. Do not be unbelieving, but believing.'"
Ps. 22:7, 8 "All those who see Me ridicule Me; they shoot out the lip, they shake the head, *saying,* 'He trusted in the LORD, let Him rescue Him; let Him deliver Him, since He delights in Him!'"	**sneered and mocked**	***Luke 23:35*** "And the people stood looking on. But even the rulers with them sneered, saying, 'He saved others; let Him save Himself if He is the Christ, the chosen of God.'"
Ps. 69:9 "Because zeal for Your house has eaten me up, and the reproaches of those who reproach You have fallen on me."	**was reproached**	***Rom. 15:3*** "For even Christ did not please Himself; but as it is written, 'The reproaches of those who reproached You fell on Me.'"
Ps. 109:4 "In return for my love they are my accusers, but I give *myself to* prayer."	**prayer for His enemies**	***Luke 23:34*** "Then Jesus said, 'Father, forgive them, for they do not know what they do.' And they divided His garments and cast lots."
Ps. 22:17, 18 "I can count all My bones. They look *and* stare at Me. They divide My garments among them, and for My clothing they cast lots."	**soldiers gambled for His clothing**	***Matt. 27:35, 36*** "Then they crucified Him, and divided His garments, casting lots, that it might be fulfilled which was spoken by the prophet: 'They divided My garments among them, and for My clothing they cast lots.' Sitting down, they kept watch over Him there."
Ps. 22:1 "My God, My God, why have You forsaken Me? *Why are You so* far from helping Me, *and from* the words of My groaning?"	**forsaken by God**	***Matt. 27:46*** "And about the ninth hour Jesus cried out with a loud voice, saying, 'Eli, Eli, lama sabachthani?' that is, 'My God, My God, why have You forsaken Me?'"

PROPHETIC SCRIPTURE	SUBJECT	FULFILLED
Ps. 34:20 "He guards all his bones, not one of them is broken."	**no bones broken**	***John 19:32, 33, 36*** "Then the soliders came and broke the legs of the first and of the other who was crucified with Him. But when they came to Jesus and saw that He was already dead, they did not break His legs. . . . For these things were done that the Scripture should be fulfilled, 'Not *one* of His bones shall be broken.' "
Zech. 12:10 "And I will pour on the house of David and on the inhabitants of Jerusalem the Spirit of grace and supplication; then they will look on Me whom they have pierced. Yes, they will mourn for Him as one mourns for *his* only *son,* and grieve for Him as one grieves for a firstborn."	**His side pierced**	***John 19:34*** "But one of the soldiers pierced His side with a spear, and immediately blood and water came out."
Is. 53:9 "And they made His grave with the wicked—but with the rich at His death, because He had done no violence, nor *was any* deceit in His mouth."	**buried with the rich**	***Matt. 27:57–60*** "Now when evening had come, there came a rich man from Arimathea, named Joseph, who himself had also become a disciple of Jesus. This man went to Pilate and asked for the body of Jesus. Then Pilate commanded the body to be given to him. When Joseph had taken the body, he wrapped it in a clean linen cloth, and laid it in his new tomb which he had hewn out of the rock; and he rolled a large stone against the door of the tomb, and departed."
Ps. 16:10 "For You will not leave my soul in Sheol, nor will You allow Your Holy One to see corruption." ***Ps. 49:15*** "But God will redeem my soul from the power of the grave, for He shall receive me. Selah"	**to be resurrected**	***Mark 16:6, 7*** "But he said to them, 'Do not be alarmed. You seek Jesus of Nazareth, who was crucified. He is risen! He is not here. See the place where they laid Him. But go, tell His disciples—and Peter—that He is going before you into Galilee; there you will see Him, as He said to you.' "
Ps. 68:18 "You have ascended on high. You have led captivity captive; You have received gifts among men; even *from* the rebellious, that the LORD God might dwell *there.*"	**His ascension to God's right hand**	***Mark 16:19*** "So then, after the Lord had spoken to them, He was received up into heaven, and sat down at the right hand of God." ***1 Cor. 15:4*** "And that He was buried, and that He rose again the third day according to the Scriptures." ***Eph. 4:8*** "Therefore He says: 'When He ascended on high, He led captivity captive, and gave gifts to men.' "

THE PARABLES OF JESUS CHRIST

Parable	*Matthew*	*Mark*	*Luke*
1. Lamp Under a Basket	5:14–16	4:21, 22	8:16, 17 11:33–36
2. A Wise Man Builds on Rock and a Foolish Man Builds on Sand	7:24–27		6:47–49
3. Unshrunk (New) Cloth on an Old Garment	9:16	2:21	5:36
4. New Wine in Old Wineskins	9:17	2:22	5:37, 38
5. The Sower	13:3–23	4:2–20	8:4–15
6. The Tares (Weeds)	13:24–30		
7. The Mustard Seed	13:31, 32	4:30–32	13:18, 19
8. The Leaven	13:33		13:20, 21
9. The Hidden Treasure	13:44		
10. The Pearl of Great Price	13:45, 46		
11. The Dragnet	13:47–50		
12. The Lost Sheep	18:12–14		15:3–7
13. The Unforgiving Servant	18:23–35		
14. The Laborers in the Vineyard	20:1–16		
15. The Two Sons	21:28–32		
16. The Wicked Vinedressers	21:33–45	12:1–12	20:9–19
17. The Wedding Feast	22:2–14		
18. The Fig Tree	24:32–44	13:28–32	21:29–33
19. The Wise and Foolish Virgins	25:1–13		
20. The Talents	25:14–30		
21. The Growing Seed		4:26–29	
22. The Absent Householder		13:33–37	
23. The Creditor and Two Debtors			7:41–43
24. The Good Samaritan			10:30–37
25. A Friend in Need			11:5–13
26. The Rich Fool			12:16–21
27. The Faithful Servant and the Evil Servant			12:35–40
28. Faithful and Wise Steward			12:42–48
29. The Barren Fig Tree			13:6–9
30. The Great Supper			14:16–24
31. Building a Tower and a King Making War			14:25–35
32. The Lost Coin			15:8–10
33. The Prodigal Son			15:11–32
34. The Unjust Steward			16:1–13
35. The Rich Man and Lazarus			16:19–31
36. Unprofitable Servants			17:7–10
37. The Persistent Widow			18:1–8
38. The Pharisee and the Tax Collector			18:9–14
39. The Minas (Pounds)			19:11–27

THE MIRACLES OF JESUS CHRIST

Miracle	*Matthew*	*Mark*	*Luke*	*John*
1. Cleansing a Leper	8:2	1:40	5:12	
2. Healing a Centurion's Servant (of paralysis)	8:5		7:1	
3. Healing Peter's Mother-in-law	8:14	1:30	4:38	
4. Healing the Sick at Evening	8:16	1:32	4:40	
5. Stilling the Storm	8:23	4:35	8:22	
6. Demons Entering a Herd of Swine	8:28	5:1	8:26	
7. Healing a Paralytic	9:2	2:3	5:18	
8. Raising the Ruler's Daughter	9:18, 23	5:22, 35	8:40, 49	
9. Healing the Hemorrhaging Woman	9:20	5:25	8:43	
10. Healing Two Blind Men	9:27			
11. Curing a Demon-possessed, Mute Man	9:32			
12. Healing a Man's Withered Hand	12:9	3:1	6:6	
13. Curing a Demon-possessed, Blind and Mute Man	12:22		11:14	
14. Feeding the Five Thousand	14:13	6:30	9:10	6:1
15. Walking on the Sea	14:25	6:48		6:19
16. Healing the Gentile Woman's Daughter	15:21	7:24		
17. Feeding the Four Thousand	15:32	8:1		
18. Healing the Epileptic Boy	17:14	9:17	9:38	
19. Temple Tax in the Fish's Mouth	17:24			
20. Healing Two Blind Men	20:30	10:46	18:35	
21. Withering the Fig Tree	21:18	11:12		
22. Casting Out an Unclean Spirit		1:23	4:33	
23. Healing a Deaf and Dumb Man		7:31		
24. Healing a Blind Paralytic at Bethsaida		8:22		
25. Escape from the Hostile Multitude			4:30	
26. Draught of Fish			5:1	
27. Raising of a Widow's Son at Nain			7:11	
28. Healing the Infirm, Bowed Woman			13:11	
29. Healing the Man with Dropsy			14:1	
30. Cleansing the Ten Lepers			17:11	
31. Restoring a Servant's Ear			22:51	
32. Turning Water into Wine				2:1
33. Healing the Nobleman's Son (of fever)				4:46
34. Healing an Infirm Man at Bethesda				5:1
35. Healing the Man Born Blind				9:1
36. Raising of Lazarus				11:43
37. Second Draught of Fish				21:1

THE LAWS OF THE BIBLE

Page

2. Rape . . . . Deut. 22:25, 26 196
 Penalty . . . . Deut. 22:25–29 196
3. Prostitution . . . . Deut. 23:17 196
 Penalty . . . . Lev. 19:29; 21:9 117
4. Seduction . . . . Ex. 22:16, 17 76
 Penalty . . . . Deut. 22:28, 29 196
5. Incest . . . . Lev. 18:6–18 116
 . . . . Deut. 22:30 196
 Penalty . . . . Lev. 20:11–21 118
6. Sodomy . . . . Lev. 18:22, 23 116
 Deut. 23:17 196
 Penalty . . . . Ex. 22:19 76
 Lev. 20:13, 15, 16 118

C. *Crimes against persons*

1. Murder . . . . Ex. 20:13 74
 Penalty . . . . Gen. 9:6 12
 Ex. 21:12 75
2. Manslaughter . . . . Ex. 21:12–14 75
 Josh. 20:3–6 232
 Penalty . . . . Num. 35:11, 22–28 170
3. Assault . . . . Ex. 21:18–26 75
 Penalty . . . . Ex. 21:19–27 75
 Lev. 24:19, 20 122
4. Kidnapping . . . . Ex. 21:16 75
 Deut. 24:7 197
5. Slander . . . . Lev. 19:16 117

D. *Crimes against property*

1. Stealing . . . . Ex. 20:15; 74
 22:1–12 76
 Deut. 23:24, 25 197
2. Arson . . . . Ex. 22:6 76
3. Moving a landmark . . . . Deut. 19:14 193

V. LAWS PERTAINING TO DOMESTIC RELATIONS

A. *Marriage*

1. Ordained by God . . . . Gen. 1:27, 28; 4
 2:18, 24 6
2. Within the tribe . . . . Num. 36:6 171
3. Polygamy forbidden . . . . 1 Cor. 7:2 1171
 1 Tim. 3:2 1238
4. Marriage forbidden with:
 a. Stepmother . . . . Lev. 18:8; 20:11 116
 b. Aliens . . . . Ex. 34:13–17 88
 Deut. 7:1–3 182
 c. Sister . . . . Lev. 20:17 118
 d. Aunt . . . . Lev. 20:19 118
 e. Grandchild . . . . Lev. 18:10 116
 f. Daughter-in-law . . . . Lev. 18:15 116
5. Divorce . . . . Lev. 21:7; 22:13 119
 Is. 50:1 728
 1 Cor. 7:10, 11 1171
 a. Not to remarry woman divorced by another man . . . . Deut. 24:1–4 197
 b. For committing adultery . . . . Jer. 3:8 750
 Matt. 19:3–9 997
 Mark 10:2–12 1026
 Luke 16:8 1064

Page

B. *Parent and child*

1. Father has authority over child . . . . Num. 30:3–5 164
2. Father to arrange marriage . Gen. 24:2–4 24
3. Parents to educate . . . . . . Deut. 21:18–21 195
 Prov. 22:6 648
 Eph. 6:4 1209
4. Parents to discipline . . . . . Deut. 21:18–21 195
 Prov. 22:15 649
5. Children to honor parents . . . . Ex. 20:12; 21:15 75
6. Children to be regarded as gift of God . . . . Gen. 33:5; 48:9 35
 Josh. 24:3 236
7. Penalty for children who dishonor parents . . . . Lev. 20:9 118
 Deut. 21:18–21 195

VI. ESTATES—DESCENT AND DISTRIBUTION LAWS

A. *Inheritance*

1. Sons inherit father's estate . . . . Gen. 21:10–13 22
 1 Chr. 5:1 404
2. Double portion to first-born . . . . Deut. 21:15–17 195
3. Wife not heir, but descends with property to next of kin . . . . . Ruth 4:1–12 268
4. Daughters heirs when no sons . . . . Num. 27:8, 9 162
5. When no sons or daughters, inheritance to nearest relative . . . . Num. 27:9–11 162

B. *Real property—titles*

1. Real estate
 a. Land divided among tribes . . . . Num. 26:52–56 161
 Josh. 14:5 226
 b. Not transferable . . . . Num. 36:6–9 171
 c. Not permanently sold . . Lev. 25:23–28 123
 d. Value of land according to years after Jubilee . . . . Lev. 25:15, 16 123
 e. Release of land . . . . Lev. 25:8–34 123
 f. Mode of transfer
 (1) Deed made . . . . Jer. 32:9–14 782
 (2) Taking off sandal . . . . . Ruth 4:3–11 268
 (3) Deed delivered in presence of witnesses . . . . Jer. 32:10, 12 782
 (4) Deed recorded . . . . Jer. 32:14 782
2. Personal property
 (All property which is moveable, as against real property such as houses and lands)
 a. Sale recognized . . . . Lev. 25:14 123
 b. Pledges of:
 (1) Children given as . . . . . 2 Kin. 4:1–7 371
 (2) Upper and lower millstone prohibited . . . . Deut. 24:6 197
 (3) Not retained overnight . . . . Ex. 22:26, 27 76
 Deut. 24:13 197
 (4) Voluntary . . . . Deut. 24:10, 11 197

Page

1. Moses, first judge — Ex. 18:13–27 — 72
2. Priests judge in small matters — Ex. 18:22 — 72
3. King as judge — 1 Kin. 7:1–7 — 342

B. *Submission of cases*

1. Ordinary cases submitted to judges — Deut. 25:1, 2 — 197
2. Exceptional cases taken to Levitical priest for verdict — Deut. 17:8–11 — 191
3. Extreme cases submitted to the LORD for decision — Num. 5:11–31 — 137; Deut. 21:1–9 — 194
4. Judges must not pervert justice — Ex. 23:6–8 — 77
5. Bribery forbidden — Deut. 16:18–20 — 191

C. *Where courts were held*

1. At gate of city — Deut. 21:19 — 195
2. In Hall of Judgment — 1 Kin. 7:7 — 342

D. *Judgments*

1. Regarded as from God — Deut. 1:17 — 175
2. Righteous to be justified and wicked condemned — Deut. 25:1 — 197
3. Sentence to be executed — Deut. 25:2, 3 — 197

E. *Appeals*

1. To Moses — Ex. 18:26 — 73
2. To priests — Deut. 17:8–11 — 191
3. To the king — 1 Kin. 3:16–27 — 339

F. *Damages*

1. For disfiguring a person — Lev. 24:19, 20 — 122
2. For stealing — Ex. 22:4, 5 — 76
3. Kindling a fire which destroys property — Ex. 22:6 — 76
4. Breach of trust — Lev. 6:1–5 — 102
5. Killing an animal — Ex. 21:35, 36 — 76; Lev. 24:18, 21 — 122
6. Loss of animal falling into pit — Ex. 21:33, 34 — 75
7. Loss of borrowed property — Ex. 22:14 — 76

G. *Methods of punishment*

1. Infliction in kind — Gen. 9:6 — 12; Lev. 24:19, 20 — 122
2. Burning — Lev. 20:14 — 118
3. Mutilation — Deut. 25:11, 12 — 198
4. Hanging — Deut. 21:22, 23 — 195
5. Stoning — Lev. 24:16 — 122
6. Beating — Deut. 25:2, 3 — 197
7. Excommunication — Ezra 10:8 — 479
8. Imprisonment — Ezra 7:26 — 477
9. Compensation for damages — Ex. 21:19, 32, 36 — 75
10. Restitution for stolen or borrowed property — Ex. 22:12, 14, 15 — 76

Page

H. *Method of protection*

1. Cities of refuge appointed — Num. 35:6–15 — 170
2. Protection till trial could be held — Num. 35:12 — 170
3. Murderer unprotected — Num. 35:30, 31 — 170
4. Unintentional manslayer remained in city of refuge till death of high priest — Josh. 20:1–6 — 232

XI. TORT LAWS

A. *Assault* — Ex. 21:18, 19 — 75

B. *Compensation* — Ex. 21:18, 19, 32 — 75

C. *Damage by animals* — Ex. 21:32 — 75

D. *Damage by fire* — Ex. 22:6 — 76

E. *Injury to animals* — Ex. 21:33–36 — 75; Lev. 24:18, 21 — 122

F. *Loss of borrowed property* — Ex. 22:14, 15 — 76

G. *Personal injury* — Lev. 24:19, 20 — 122

H. *Rights of strangers* — Lev. 24:22 — 122

XII. LAWS OF SANITATION AND CLEANLINESS

A. *Cleansing of the woman after childbirth* — Lev. 12:1–8 — 109

B. *Test for leprosy* — Lev. 13:1–59 — 109

C. *Cleansing of the leper's house* — Lev. 14:33–57 — 112

D. *Cleansing of males with discharge* — Lev. 15:1–15 — 113

E. *Laws concerning the woman during menstruation* — Lev. 15:24–33 — 113

XIII. LAWS PERTAINING TO ANIMALS

A. *Beasts of burden* — Ex. 23:12 — 77; Deut. 25:4 — 198

B. *Beasts of the field* — Ex. 23:11 — 77

C. *Mother and young* — Lev. 22:28 — 120; Deut. 22:6, 7 — 195

D. *Enemy's animal* — Ex. 23:4, 5 — 76; Deut. 22:4 — 195

XIV. LAWS CONCERNING INTEREST AND LOANS

Interest on money was called usury in biblical times. (Now usury means excess interest.)

A. *Taking of interest forbidden among Jews* — Ex. 22:25 — 76; Deut. 23:19, 20 — 196

The money was borrowed for relief of distress.

B. *Allowed to be taken from foreigners* — Deut. 23:20 — 197

Money was borrowed by foreigner to develop trade.

C. *Property returned without interest* — Neh. 5:11–13 — 487

D. *Differing weights and measures forbidden* — Deut. 25:13–16 — 198

BETWEEN THE TESTAMENTS

The four hundred years between the prophecy of Malachi and the advent of Christ are frequently described as "silent," but they were in fact crowded with activity. Although no inspired prophet arose in Israel during those centuries, and the Old Testament was regarded as complete, events took place which gave to later Judaism its distinctive ideology and providentially prepared the way for the coming of Christ and the proclamation of His gospel.

The Persian Period

The Jews fared well under Persian rule. Cyrus had given them permission to return to Jerusalem and rebuild their temple and, although they met opposition from the inhabitants of Palestine, it was dedicated during the reign of Darius the Great. Ezra, the scribe, and Nehemiah, the layman, sought to strengthen the Palestinian Jewish community and encourage their loyalty to the Law of God. For about a century-and-a-half after Nehemiah's time, the Persian Empire exercised control over Judea, and the Jews were permitted to observe their religious ordinances without interference. Judea was ruled by high priests who were responsible to the Persian government, a fact which insured the Jews a large measure of autonomy. At the same time, however, it made a political office of the priesthood and sowed the seeds of future trouble. Contests for the office of high priest were marked by jealousy, intrigue, and even murder. **Johanan, son of Joiada** (Neh. 12:22), is reported to have slain his brother, Joshua, within the temple precincts.

Johanan was succeeded as high priest by his brother, **Jaddua,** whose brother Manasseh, according to Josephus, married the daughter of **Sanballat, governor of Samaria.** It was at this time that a Samaritan temple was built on Mount Gerizim which, rather than Zion, was regarded as sacred by the Samaritan community. The sanctuary on Mount Gerizim was destroyed by the Hasmonaean ruler John Hyrcanus (134–104 B.C.), but the mount itself continues to this day to be regarded as sacred by the Samaritans. The woman of Samaria wished to dispute with Jesus concerning the merits of the rival holy places, but the Saviour chose to emphasize the spiritual attitude of the worshiper rather than the place of worship (cf. John 4:20). The Sanballat of Josephus cannot have been the same individual as the man of the same name mentioned by Nehemiah (4:l). Josephus does, however, appear to reflect a valid tradition, for a temple seems to have been built on Mount Gerizim about this time. (In 1969 the Samaritans numbered fewer than 300.)

Persia's failure to conquer Greece encouraged subject peoples to seek their independence. Egypt was constantly attempting to throw off the Persian yoke, and Judea, geographically between the two powers, could not escape involvement. During the reign of **Artaxerxes III (Ochus),** many Jews were implicated in a revolt against Persia. When it failed, the Persians deported them to Babylonia and the southern shores of the Caspian Sea.

Jews had long been in Egypt. Following the murder of Gedaliah, the prophet Jeremiah was forced to join a group of refugees, who sought asylum at Tahpanhes in the eastern Delta (Jer. 43:4–13), and other Judeans doubtless found their way to Egypt to avoid capture by **Nebuchadnezzar.** Migration continued during the Persian Period, and by the fifth century before Christ a Jewish colony of mercenary soldiers was located at **Elephantine Island,** near modern Aswan, at the First Cataract of the Nile. Contrary to the Mosaic Law, these colonists built a temple for themselves, and they combined their devotion to the God of their fathers with pagan elements. **The Elephantine Jews** had correspondence with the Samaritans as well as the Judeans.

Alexander the Great

Persia never succeeded in subduing the Greeks, but an heir of Greek culture, **Alexander of Macedon**, eventually brought to an end the Persian Empire. Alexander was not simply a power-mad despot. A pupil of the philosopher Aristotle, he was thoroughly convinced that Greek culture was the one force that could unify the world. In 333 B.C. he passed from Macedonia into Asia Minor and defeated the Persian armies stationed there. Then he moved southward through Syria and Palestine to Egypt. Tyre and Gaza each offered stubborn resistance, but delays did not discourage Alexander, they simply strengthened his determination to win. There was no need for a campaign against the Jews, and legend makes Alexander a friend of the Jewish people. Jaddua, the high priest, is said to have come out to meet Alexander, telling him of Daniel's prophecy that the Greek army would be victorious (Dan. 8). Although historians do not take the story seriously, it does illustrate the friendly feelings between the Jews and the Macedonian conqueror. Alexander permitted the Jews to observe their laws, granted them exemption from tribute during sabbatical years, and, when he built **Alexandria** in Egypt (331 B.C.), he encouraged Jews to settle there and gave them privileges comparable to those of his Greek subjects.

Alexander was welcomed into Egypt as a deliverer from Persian oppression. His victorious armies retraced their steps through Palestine and Syria, then moved eastward. The cities of Babylon and Persia fell to Alexander, and he pressed on as far as the Punjab region of India. Although mighty in battle, it was **Hellenistic culture** rather than Macedonian rule that was Alexander's legacy to the Middle East. He determined to found a new city in each country of his empire, which would serve as a model for the reordering of the life of the country as a whole along Greek lines. Materially speaking, this meant the erection of fine public buildings, a gymnasium for games, an open-air theater, and whatever would approximate the life of a Greek city-state. Individuals were encouraged to take Greek names, adopt Greek dress and language—in short, to become Hellenized.

The material aspects of **Hellenism** must have seemed attractive for large segments of the population. Trade and commerce brought wealth to the new merchant class. Libraries and schools were welcomed by the scholar. Better housing and better food brought about a rise in the standard of living. Many in Israel, as elsewhere, were glad to accept this veneer of Greek culture. If idolatry had been the stumbling block to Israel in the preexilic period, Hellenism was the great postexilic temptation. A third-century B.C. writer observed, "In recent times, under the foreign rule of the Persians, and then of the Macedonians, by whom the Persian Empire was overthrown, intermingling with other races has led to many of the traditional Jewish ordinances losing their hold." Many Jews took Greek names, accepted a school of Greek philosophy, and tried to combine the wisdom of Greece with the faith of their fathers. Others resisted Hellenism and became more and more engrossed in the study of their Law.

At the age of thirty-three, Alexander died in Babylon. For a number of years the future of the Near East was uncertain, but the generals succeeded in dividing the Empire among themselves and the tide of Hellenism increased. While the Ptolemies of Egypt and the Seleucids of Syria fought among themselves for land and power, they were in complete agreement concerning their social and cultural mission. The historian W. W. Tarn says that Alexander "so changed the world [that] nothing after him could be as it was before."

The Ptolemies

Following the death of Alexander, Judea was first subject to Antigonus, one of his generals, but it quickly fell to another general, **Ptolemy I, surnamed Soter, "Deliverer,"** who seized Jerusalem on a Sabbath day in 320 B.C. Ptolemy, whose kingdom centered in Egypt, dealt kindly with the Jews. Many of them settled in Alexandria, which continued to be an important center of Jewish thought for many centuries. Under **Ptolemy II (Philadelphus)** the Alexandrian Jews translated their Old Testament into Greek. This translation was later known as the Septuagint from the legend of seventy (more correctly seventy-two, six from each of the twelve tribes) who were sent from Judea to produce the Greek translation of the Hebrew Scriptures.

The Jews in Palestine enjoyed a period of prosperity during Ptolemaic times. Tribute tax was paid to the government in Egypt, but local affairs were administered by high priests who had been responsible for governing their people since Persian times. The greatest figure among the Jews of the Ptolemaic period was **Simon the Just,** the high priest who is the subject of highest praise in the apocryphal book of Ecclesiasticus, which calls him, "Great among his brethren and the glory of his people." He is credited with rebuilding the walls of Jerusalem, which had been demolished by Ptolemy I, and is said to have repaired the temple and directed the excavation of a great reservoir to provide fresh water for Jerusalem in times of drought and siege. In addition to his reputation as high priest, Simon is also regarded as one of the great teachers of ancient Judaism. His favorite maxim was, "The world rests on three things, on the Law, on Divine Service, and on Charity" (*Pirke Aboth,* i. 2). The identity of Simon the Just poses a historical problem. A high priest known as Simon I lived during the middle of the third century, and Simon II lived about 200 B.C. One of these is doubtless the Simon the Just of Jewish tradition and legend.

During Ptolemaic times the priestly families of **Onias** and **Tobias** became bitter rivals. The house of Tobias was pro-Egyptian and represented the wealthy class of Jerusalem society. It may have been related to Tobiah the Ammonite (Neh. 2:10, 4:3, 7; 6:1-19), who gave so much trouble to Nehemiah. A papyrus from the time of Ptolemy II speaks of a Jew named Tobias, who was a cavalry commander in the Ptolemaic army stationed at Ammanitis, east of the Jordan. Archaeologists have discovered a mausoleum with the name "Tobiah" from the third century B.C. at Araq el-Emir in central Jordan. The Tobiahs are thought to have been tax collectors, occupying the same function as the New Testament tax gatherers.

Josephus states that Onias II refused to pay Ptolemy IV twenty talents of silver, which was evidently the tribute tax demanded of the high priests. By refusing payment, Onias seems to have renounced allegiance to Ptolemy. Joseph, a member of the house of Tobias, then succeeded in having himself appointed tax collector for the whole of Palestine. The tax collector had to go to Alexandria each year to bid for the renewal of the license to gather taxes. Joseph held this influential post for twenty years, under the Ptolemies and, after the victory of Antiochus III, under the Seleucids.

The Seleucids

The Syrian rulers are termed Seleucids because their kingdom, one of the successor states to Alexander's empire, was founded by **Seleucus I (Nicator).** Most of the early rulers bore the names of Seleucus or Antiochus, and they ruled from Antioch on the Orontes River. The energetic ruler Antiochus III, surnamed "the Great," waged a series of battles with Egypt until, in 199 B.C., he wrested Palestine from the Ptolemies after the Battle of Panion, near the sources of the Jordan River. This marked the beginning of a new era of Jewish history for, while the Ptolemies had been tolerant of Jewish institutions, the Seleucids determined to enforce Hellenism on the Jews.

The crisis came during the reign of **Antiochus IV, surnamed Epiphanes,** who found allies in the Hellenistic party in Judea. In the early days of the reign of Antiochus IV, Jerusalem was ruled by the high priest, Onias III, a descendant of Simon the Just and a strictly orthodox Jew. The Jews, who looked with favor on Greek culture, opposed Onias and espoused the cause of his brother, Jason. By promising large tribute to Antiochus, Jason succeeded in having himself appointed high priest. Although Antiochus looked upon the high priesthood as a political office which he had a right to fill as he pleased, pious Jews thought of the priesthood as divine in origin and considered its sale to the highest bidder a sin against God.

Jason encouraged the Hellenists who had sought his election. A gymnasium was built in Jerusalem, Greek names became commonplace, and Hebrew orthodoxy was considered obscurantist and obsolete. Yet, Jason argued with his close companion and fellow-Hellenist, **Menelaus,** of the tribe of Benjamin, who offered higher tribute to Antiochus than that paid by Jason, and had himself installed as high priest.

The orthodox Jews, who had been scandalized when Jason was named high priest, were more deeply disturbed when Menelaus, a Benjamite with no claim to priestly office, was installed. Jason raised an army to back his claim to the high priesthood, and Menelaus courted the favor of Antiochus. The Syrians, who were campaigning against Egypt, felt it essential to maintain effective control of Palestine. Antiochus staged a sneak attack on Jerusalem one Sabbath day (when the orthodox would not fight), and slaughtered a large number of the enemies of Menelaus. The city walls were destroyed, and a new fortress, the Akra, was built on the site of the citadel.

Antiochus was determined to remove all traces of orthodox Jewish faith. Israel's God was identified with Jupiter, and a bearded image of the pagan deity (perhaps in the likeness of Antiochus) was erected on the temple altar, where swine were offered in sacrifice. Jews were forbidden, under penalty of death, to practice circumcision, Sabbath observance, or the celebration of the Feasts of the Jewish calendar. Copies of the Scriptures were ordered destroyed. The laws were enforced with the utmost cruelty. An aged scribe named Eleazar was flogged to death because he would not eat swine's flesh.

By force of arms, Menelaus continued as high priest and the Hellenizing party gained a victory. Yet, the Hellenizers had gone too far, and their zeal to annihilate the old order proved their own undoing. The orthodox were willing to die for their faith, but not all were convinced that they should die passively.

The Maccabean Revolt

The oppressed Jews were not long in finding a champion. When the emissaries of Antiochus arrived at the village of Modin, about fifteen miles west of Jerusalem, they expected the aged priest, **Mattathias,** to set a good example to his people by coming forward to offer a pagan sacrifice. When Mattathias refused, a timid Jew came forward to perform the sacrifice. The enraged priest approached the altar and killed both the apostate Jew and the emissary of Antiochus. With his five sons, Mattathias destroyed the heathen altar and then fled to the hills to avoid reprisal. Others of orthodox persuasion joined the family of Mattathias in waging guerrilla warfare on the Syrians and the Hellenistic Jews who supported them. The orthodox would not fight on the Sabbath day, with the result that they were at a distinct military disadvantage. On one Sabbath, a group of the orthodox was surrounded and murdered, for they would not defend themselves. Following this episode, Mattathias suggested the principle that fighting in self-defense was permissible on the Sabbath day.

Soon after the beginning of the revolt, Mattathias died. He had urged his followers to choose as military leader his third son, **Judas (Hebrew Judah), known as "the Maccabee,"** a word usually interpreted to mean "the hammer." The choice was a good one, for more and more Jews rallied to the cause. The Maccabees, as the followers of Judas were called, were able to hold their own against a series of Syrian armies thrown against them. By a surprise night attack, Judas annihilated an army of Syrians and Hellenistically minded Jews at Emmaus, and then marched toward Jerusalem with the booty he had seized. The Maccabees entered the city and took everything except the Akra. They entered the temple and removed all the signs of paganism which had been installed there. The altar dedicated to Jupiter was removed and a new altar erected to Israel's God. The statue of Jupiter was ground to dust. Beginning with the twenty-fifth of Kislev (December), they celebrated an eight-day Feast of Dedication, known as Hanukkah, the Festival of Lights. In this way they marked the end of the three-year period during which the Temple had been desecrated.

Peace was short-lived. The Syrian general, **Lysias,** defeated the Maccabees in a battle near Jerusalem, and besieged the city. During the siege, however, Lysias learned of trouble at home and made an offer of peace to the Jews. The laws against the observance of Judaism would be repealed, and Syria would refrain from interference in the internal affairs of Judea. Menelaus was to be removed from office and the high priesthood given to a mild Hellenizer named **Alcimus.** Lysias promised that Judas and his followers would not be punished. However, the walls of Jerusalem would be destroyed.

A council comprising Maccabean army officers, respected scribes, and elders of the orthodox party was convened at Jerusalem to determine the action to be taken. Against the counsel of Judas, the peace terms were accepted. Alcimus became High Priest; Menelaus was executed, and Judas left the city with a few followers. The fears of Judas proved correct, for Alcimus seized and executed many of the orthodox party. Loyal Jews again turned to Judas and civil war was renewed. Judas, with an ill-equipped army of eight hundred men, met a large Syrian army and died in battle. Thus, the first phase of the Maccabean struggle was ended.

Jonathan, a brother of Judas, fled across the Jordan with several hundred Maccabean soldiers. They were ill-equipped to wage battle, but the next victories were in the field of diplomacy. Two pretenders to the Syrian throne each sought help from the Jews. They saw in Jonathan the man best able to raise and lead a Jewish army. By playing a delaying action, Jonathan was able to support the winning candidate and at the same time make treaties with Sparta and Rome. Before the war was over, Jonathan was High Priest, governor of Judea, and a member of the Syrian nobility. His brother, Simon, became governor of the Philistine coastal area. Jonathan was able to promote the internal prosperity of Judah, and when he died his brother, Simon, succeeded him as ruling High Priest.

Simon was advanced in years when he came to the throne. His major victory was in the field of diplomacy, for by recognizing **Demetrius** as rightful king of Syria he secured for the Jews immunity from taxation which amounted to an acknowledgment of independence. Simon was able also to starve out the Syrian garrison at the Akra and to occupy the cities of Joppa and Bethsura. In recognition of his wise rule, the leaders in Israel named Simon, "leader and High Priest for ever, until there shall arise a faithful prophet." Simon was the last of the sons of Mattathias, and this act legitimized a new dynasty which is termed Hasmonaean, presumably derived from an ancestor of the Maccabees named Asmonaeus or, in Hebrew, Hashmon. In 134 B.C., Simon and two of his sons were murdered by an ambitious son-in-law. A third son, **John Hyrcanus,** managed to escape and succeed his father as hereditary head of the Jewish state.

The Hasmonaeans

The Syrians recognized the government of John Hyrcanus on condition that he consider himself subject to Syria and promise help in Syrian military campaigns. Certain coastal cities annexed by Jonathan and Simon were also to be relinquished. The efficient rule of Hyrcanus, however, quickly effected the re-conquest of these cities and the addition of **Idumaea** (Old Testament Edom) to Judean territory. These conquests ensured the use of ancient trade routes by the merchant class, but they posed problems to the religiously oriented Jews. Hyrcanus compelled the Idumaeans to become circumcised and accept the Jewish faith, a practice which later Judaism disavows. Hyrcanus also campaigned in Samaria, where he destroyed the temple on Mount Gerizim. The success of Jewish arms might be applauded by the nationalistic element in Judea, but the religious fervor of the earlier Maccabees was no longer evident.

Before John Hyrcanus died in 104 B.C., the borders of the state had been extended on every side. The Maccabean struggle was long past and new rivalries developed. The older Hellenists were discredited, but their ideas were perpetuated in the party of the Sadducees. The orthodox of Maccabean times became the Pharisees of pre-Christian Judaism and the New Testament. Hyrcanus was devout and law-abiding, but his children had little sympathy with traditional Hebrew thought. They numbered themselves among the aristocrats, and they came to look with disdain on the rigidly orthodox Pharisees. Ironically, these heirs of the Maccabees became thoroughly Hellenized.

The death of John Hyrcanus precipitated a dynastic struggle among his children. His eldest son, who preferred his Greek name **Aristobulus** to his Hebrew name, Judah, emerged as victor and threw three of his brothers into prison—two of whom are thought to have starved to death. Another brother was murdered in the palace. In his short reign of but one year, Aristobulus pushed the borders of Judea north to Mount Lebanon and took the title of king. His life was cut short, however, by drink, disease, and the haunting fear of rebellion.

At the time of Aristobulus' death he had but one brother living, and he was in prison. Although his Hebrew name was Jonathan, history knows him by his Greek name **Alexander Jannaeus.** Under Jannaeus the policy of territorial expansion continued. The frontiers of Judea were extended along the Philistine coast toward the Egyptian frontier and in the Trans-jordan region. The Jewish state approximated the territory controlled by Israel in the days of David and Solomon. It included the whole of Palestine and adjacent areas from the borders of Egypt to Lake Huleh, north of the Sea of Galilee. Perea in Trans-jordan was subject to Jannaeus, as were the cities of the Coastal Plain except for Ascalon.

The territories incorporated into the Hasmonaean kingdom were, for the most part, quickly Judaised. The Idumaeans came to exercise an important place in Jewish life, and **Galilee** became an important center of Judaism. The Samaritans, however, continued to resist assimilation and cities such as Apollonia and Scythopolis (Old Testament Beth Shean), with only a small Jewish element in their population, kept their non-Jewish character.

Partisan strife marred the reign of Alexander Jannaeus, who showed open contempt for the Pharisees, precipitating civil war. The Pharisees accepted aid from the Syrians in their conflict with Jannaeus, and for a time Jewish independence was in the balance. When the Pharisees felt that they had gained their point, they withdrew their alliance with Syria and hoped for a Jewish state that would be both free of foreign control and tolerant of their viewpoint. Jannaeus sought out the leaders of the rebellion and crucified eight hundred Pharisees. Tradition says that Jannaeus repented on his deathbed, instructing his wife, **Salome Alexandra,** to dismiss his Sadducean advisors and reign with the help of the Pharisees. The tradition may have no historical basis, but Alexandra did turn to the Pharisees for support.

Salome Alexandra had been married successively to Aristobulus and to Alexander Jannaeus. The widow of two Hasmonaean rulers, she reigned in her own right for seven years. She was a woman of seventy when she came to the throne, dividing royal responsibilities between her two sons. **Hyrcanus,** the older son, became High Priest, and his brother, **Aristobulus,** received the military command. Her brother, **Simeon ben Shetah,** was a leader among the Pharisees and this fact may have disposed her to seek peace between the opposing factions of Judaism.

Under Alexandra, the Pharisees had their opportunity to make a constructive contribution to Jewish life. In many areas, particularly education, they were eminently successful. Under the presidency of Simeon ben Shetah, the Sanhedrin (the Jewish Council of State) decreed that every young man should be educated. A comprehensive system of elementary education was inaugurated so that the larger villages, towns, and cities of Judea would produce a literate, informed people. This education was centered in the Hebrew Scriptures.

The wounds of earlier strife were not healed during Alexandra's reign. Although the Pharisees were happy in their new-found recognition, the Sadducees were resentful of the fact that they had lost power. To compound the problem, the Pharisees sought to avenge the massacre of their leaders by Alexander Jannaeus. Sadducean blood was spilt and the makings of another civil war were in the air.

The Sadducees found in Aristobulus, the younger son of Jannaeus and Alexandra, the man they could support as Alexandra's successor. He was a soldier and appealed to the party that dreamed of imperial expansion and worldly power. Hyrcanus, the older brother and rightful heir, was acceptable to the Pharisees. With the death of Alexandra, the partisans of the two sons were ready for a showdown.

When his mother died, **Hyrcanus (II),** who had been serving as High Priest, succeeded to the throne, but his brother, **Aristobulus,** led an army of Sadducees against Jerusalem. Neither Hyrcanus nor the Pharisees were ready for war, and Hyrcanus surrendered his honors to Aristobulus (II), who became king and High Priest. Hyrcanus and Aristobulus thereupon vowed eternal friendship, and Aristobulus's eldest son,

Alexander, married Hyrcanus's only daughter, Alexandra. Peace between the brothers was short-lived. Hyrcanus had to flee and Antipater, governor of Idumaea, espoused his cause. With civil war threatening, Pompey appeared with his Roman Legions to ensure the peace of Judea and further the aims of Rome.

The Romans

When **Pompey** suspected Aristobulus of planning to rebel against Rome, he besieged Jerusalem. After three months, he breached the fortifications, entered the city, and reportedly murdered twelve thousand Jews. Pompey and his officers entered the Holy of Holies in the Temple, but he did not touch its costly furnishings and allowed Temple worship to continue. Jerusalem, however, was made tributary to the Romans, and the last vestige of Jewish independence was removed. Judea was incorporated into the Roman province of Syria and it lost the coastal cities, the district of Samaria, and the non-Jewish cities east of the Jordan. **Hyrcanus** was named Ethnarch of Judea, including Galilee, Idumaea, and Perea, and was confirmed again as High Priest. A yearly tribute was due Rome. Aristobulus and a number of other captives were taken to Rome to grace Pompey's triumph. During the voyage, Aristobulus's son Alexander escaped and attempted to organize a revolt against Hyrcanus. With the aid of the Romans, Hyrcanus was able to meet this challenge to his authority.

During the years of strife between **Aristobulus (II)** and **Hyrcanus (II),** the Idumaean governor **Antipater** (or **Antipas**) took a lively interest in the politics of Judea. Antipater was bitterly opposed to Aristobulus, partly through fear and partly because of his friendship with Hyrcanus. It appears that Hyrcanus relied much on Antipater, and that he was virtually the power behind the throne of Judea. The Jews resented the influence of Antipater almost as much as they smarted under Roman sovereignty. Although the Idumaeans had been incorporated into the Jewish state by John Hyrcanus, they had never been assimilated and ancient rivalries were not forgotten.

In the crisis which followed the murder of **Julius Caesar,** Antipater and his sons showed loyalty to the new regime of **Cassius** by zealously collecting tribute taxes. **Herod,** a son of Antipater, was given the title Procurator of Judea with the promise that he would one day be named king. When **Anthony** defeated Brutus and Cassius at Philippi, Asia again fell into the hands of a new regime. Herod, however, quickly changed loyalties and bribed his way into favor with Anthony.

The eastern part of the once mighty Persian Empire was occupied by a people known as **Parthians,** who had never been subdued by Rome. In 41 B.C. they attacked Jerusalem and made **Antigonus,** son of Aristobulus II, both king and High Priest. Herod, the son of Antipater, who had inherited the throne of Judea at the death of Hyrcanus, was forced to flee to Rome. There he won the favor of Anthony and was officially named "King of the Jews," although the title would have meaning only after the Parthians were driven out. Herod returned to Judea with Roman arms and triumphantly entered Jerusalem as king.

Herod's rule spanned the eventful years from 37 B.C. to 4 B.C. He is best known as the king who feared the birth of a rival "King of the Jews" and decreed the murder of infants in Bethlehem at the time of the birth of Jesus. While that act of Herod cannot be documented from secular records, his other atrocities are well known. He had ten wives in all, and the **Emperor Augustus** is reported to have commented of his family life, "I'd rather be Herod's hog than his son." The hog was an unclean animal and would not be butchered, but Herod's wives and children were violently removed when they interfered with his plans or were suspected of disloyalty.

Although detested by his Jewish subjects, Herod did seek to win their favor. He built and rebuilt cities throughout the land: Samaria became Sebaste in honor of Augustus; Straton's Tower became Caesarea, with a harbor protected by a moat and a wall with ten towers. Fortresses, baths, parks, market places, roads, and other luxuries of Hellenistic culture were part of his building program.

In the eighteenth year of his reign (20–19 B.C.), Herod began the work of rebuilding, on a grand scale, the Jewish Temple in Jerusalem. The main edifice was built by priests in a year and a half, but the work on the entire complex of courts and buildings was not completed until the procuratorship of **Albinus** (A.D. 62–64), less than a decade before it was totally destroyed by the armies of **Titus** (A.D. 70).

The Jewish Sects

The Pharisees, Sadducees, Herodians, and Zealots, who play so important a part in the gospel records, all have their origin during the two centuries before the birth of Christ. They represent different reactions to the continuing clash between Hellenism and Jewish religious life. While the Maccabean struggle had settled the political problem of the relationship between the Syrian Seleucids and Judea, it forced upon Judaism the necessity of determining its own relationship to the outside world.

The Pharisees

A party bearing the name of Pharisee is first mentioned during the reign of John Hyrcanus (134—104 B.C.), and it is evident that even then there was an antagonism between the "orthodox" Pharisee and the more open-minded Sadducee. The word **Pharisee** means "separated one," and the name probably meant, in the first instance, one who had separated himself from the corrupting influence of Hellenism in his zeal for the biblical Law. Josephus says that the Pharisees "appear more religious than others, and seem to interpret the laws more accurately."

Pharisees were punctilious in observing the laws regarding ceremonial purity. For this reason, they could not purchase items of food or drink from a "sinner" for fear of ceremonial defilement. Nor could a Pharisee eat in the house of a sinner, although he might entertain the sinner in his own home. Under such circumstances, the Pharisee would provide the sinner with clothes to wear, for the sinner's clothes might be ceremonially impure.

With a sincere desire to make the Law workable within the changing culture of the Greco-Roman world, the Pharisees developed systems of tradition which sought to apply the Law to a variety of circumstances. During the first century before Christ, two influential Pharisaic teachers gave their names to two schools of legal thought. **Hillel** was the more moderate of the two, ever considerate of the poor and willing to accept Roman rule as compatible with Jewish orthodoxy. **Shammai,** on the other hand, was more strict in his interpretation and bitterly opposed to Rome. His viewpoint ultimately found expression in the sect of **Zealots,** whose resistance to the Romans brought on the destruction of Jerusalem in A.D. 70. **The Talmud** preserves the record of three hundred sixteen controversies between the schools of Hillel and Shammai.

Tradition, in Pharisaic thought, began as a commentary on the Law, but it was ultimately raised to the level of Law itself. To justify this teaching, it was maintained that the "oral law" was given by God to Moses on Mount Sinai along with the "written law" or **Torah** (*Pirke Aboth,* 1.1). The ultimate in this development is reached when the **Mishna** states that oral law must be observed with greater stringency than the written law, because statutory law (that is, oral tradition) affects the life of the ordinary man more intimately than the more remote constitutional law (the written Torah) (*M. Sanhedrin,* 10.3).

In addition to the charge that Pharisaism involved little more than a concern for the minutia of the Law, the New Testament affirms that tradition had largely neglected the real intent of the Law (Matt. 15:3). As in many worthy movements, the early piety of those who had separated themselves from impurity at great cost was exchanged for an attitude of pride in the observance of legal precepts.

Men such as **Nicodemus, Joseph of Arimathea, Gamaliel,** and **Saul of Tarsus** represent some of the nobler souls from the Pharisaic tradition in the New Testament. To Saul, later Paul the apostle, the Pharisee represented the epitome of orthodoxy, "the strictest sect of our religion" (Acts 26:5). Pharisaism began well, and its perversion is a constant reminder that self-complacency and spiritual pride are temptations to which the pious are particularly susceptible.

The Sadducees

Although Pharisees and Sadducees are frequently denounced together in the New Testament, they had little in common except their antagonism to Jesus. The Sadducees were the party of the **Jerusalem aristocracy** and the **high priesthood.** They had made their peace with the political rulers and had attained positions of wealth and influence. Temple administration and ritual were their specific responsibilities. The Sadducees held themselves aloof from the masses and were unpopular with them.

The Pharisaic attempts at applying the Law to new situations were rejected by the Sadducees, who restricted their concept of authority to the Torah, or Mosaic Law. They did not believe in resurrection, spirits, or angels (cf. Mark 12:18; Luke 20:27; Acts 23:8). Their faith was largely a series of negations with the result that they left no positive religious or political system.

While the Pharisees welcomed proselytes (Matt. 23:15), the Sadducean party was closed. None but members of the high priestly and aristocratic families of Jerusalem could become members. With the destruction of the Temple in A.D. 70, the Sadducean party came to an end. Modern Judaism traces its roots to the Pharisees.

The Essenes

Essenes and Pharisees both trace their roots to the orthodox leaders of Maccabean times, who stood their ground against Hellenism. Pharisees maintained a strict orthodoxy within the framework of historical Judaism. They maintained their separation from defilement, but not from the Jewish community itself. Even though the Temple worship was conducted by Sadducees, the Pharisees esteemed it a basic part of their religious inheritance. While the Pharisee might hold himself aloof from "sinners," he lived among them and coveted their esteem.

A more extreme reaction against the influences which tended to corrupt Jewish life was taken by a sect which the ancient writers Philo, Josephus, and Pliny call the Essenes. They seem to have lived for the most part in **monastic communities** such as the one which maintained headquarters at Qumran, near the northwest corner of the Dead Sea.

In seeking to explain Judaism to the Greek speaking world, Josephus spoke of three "philosophies"—those of the Pharisees, Sadducees, and the Essenes. The term "Essene" seems to have had quite an elastic usage, including various groups of monastically minded Jews, who varied among themselves in certain of their practices. Pliny says that the Essenes avoided women and did not marry, but Josephus speaks of an order of marrying Essenes. The excavations at Qumran indicate that women were enrolled in the Qumran community.

Ancient writers speak favorably of the Essenes, who lived a life of rigor and simplicity. Members of the community studied Scripture and other religious books. Each Essene was required to perform manual labor in order to make the community self-supporting. Community of goods was practiced, and strict discipline was enforced by an overseer. Those groups which renounced marriage adopted boys at an early age in order to inculcate and perpetuate the ideals of Essenism. Slavery and war were repudiated.

The Essenes welcomed proselytes, but the novice was required to undergo a period of strict probation before he could become a full-fledged member. Numerically, the Essenes were never large. Philo says that there were four thousand of them, and Pliny speaks of a community north of En Gedi, corresponding to the Qumran area. That there were other settlements is clear, for we are told that all members of the sect were welcome in any of the Essene colonies.

Nothing certain is known of the early history of the sect for, like all reform movements, it traces its origins back to remote times. Philo states that Moses instituted the order, and Josephus says that they existed "ever since the ancient times of the fathers." It is certain that the Essene movement was at one time an extreme protest against the corruptions which were apparent in pre-Christian Judaism, and that ultimately many members withdrew from the Palestinian community life and sought spiritual purification in places such as the Qumran area.

Regarding themselves as the only true or pure **Israel,** the Essenes refused to cooperate with what they believed to be the corrupt religious observances at the Jerusalem Temple. The carefully regulated life at the Essene center seems to have served as a substitute for the Temple in the eyes of pious Essenes. The strictness of Essene discipline and the rigidity with which the Law was enforced are stressed by all who write about them. Josephus says that they were stricter than all Jews in abstaining from work on the Sabbath. A passage in **the Damascus Document** (which seems to be Essene in origin) says that it is unlawful to lift an animal from a pit on the Sabbath. Such a view was considered extreme, even by legalistic Pharisees (cf. Matt. 12:11).

The absence of Essenes from the main streams of Jewish life doubtless accounts for the fact that they are not mentioned in the New Testament or in the Jewish Talmud. Although the high morality of the Essenes is indeed commendable, the teaching and practice of Jesus was diametrically opposite to the legalism and asceticism of the Essene teaching. Although the Essenes considered that contact with a member of their own group of a lower order was ceremonially defiling, Jesus did not hesitate to eat and drink with "tax collectors and sinners" (Matt. 11:19; Luke 7:34). Although obedient to the Mosaic Law, Jesus had no sympathy with those who made of the Law a burden instead of a blessing. The Sabbath, according to Jesus, was made for man, and it is lawful to do good on the Sabbath Day (Matt. 12:1–12; Mark 2:23–28; Luke 6:6–11; 14:1–6).

Jesus denounced abuses in the Temple and prophesied its destruction, but He did not repudiate the Temple services. He came to Jerusalem for the great Jewish feasts, and after His resurrection, disciples still made their way to the Temple at the hour of prayer (cf. Acts 3). While asceticism and monasticism early gained a foothold in Christian thinking, Christianity in its earliest period was in no sense an ascetic movement. The ministry of Jesus was largely to the "common people," who were rejected by both Pharisee and Essene. Jesus was not ashamed to associate with the people of His generation, so the self-righteous called Him a drunkard, a friend of tax collectors and sinners (Matt. 11:19).

Other Sects

The New Testament mentions **Herodians** (Mark 3:6; Matt 22:16) and **Zealots** (Luke 6:15), groups of Jews at opposite ends of the political spectrum. The Herodians appear to have been Jews of influence and standing who were well disposed to the Herodian rule and, as a result, to the Romans who supported the Herods. The Zealots, on the other hand, were super patriots who determined to resist Rome at all costs. Their fanaticism brought on the war during which the army of Titus destroyed Jerusalem and its Temple (A.D. 70).

Chronology

Date B.C.	
612	**Nineveh** destroyed by Medes and Babylonians
587	**Jerusalem** destroyed by Nebuchadnezzar
559	**Cyrus** inherits kingdom of Anshan; beginning of Persian Empire
539	**Babylon** falls to Cyrus; end of Neo-Babylonian Empire
530–522	**Cambyses** succeeds Cyrus; conquest of Egypt
521–486	**Darius I** ruler of Persian Empire
515	**Second Temple** completed by Jews in Jerusalem
486–464	**Xerxes I** attempts the conquest of Greece; time of Esther
480	**Greek naval victory** at Salamis; Xerxes flees
464–423	**Artaxerxes I** rules Persia; age of Nehemiah
334–323	**Alexander of Macedon** conquers the East
311	**Seleucus** conquers Babylon; beginning of the Seleucid dynasty
223–187	**Antiochus (III) the Great,** Seleucid ruler of Syria
198	**Antiochus III** defeats Egypt, gains control of Palestine
175–163	**Antiochus (IV) Epiphanes** rules Syria; Judaism is proscribed
167	**Mattathias** and his sons rebel against Antiochus; beginning of Maccabean revolt
166–160	**Judas** is Maccabees' Leader
160–142	**Jonathan** is High Priest
142–135	**Simon** is High Priest; founds Hasmonaean dynasty
134–104	**John Hyrcanus** expands holdings of independent Jewish state
103	**Aristobulus's** Rule
102–76	**Alexander Jannaeus's Rule**
75–67	**Salome Alexandra** rules: Hyrcanus II High Priest
66–63	**Dynastic battle:** Aristobulus II and Hyrcanus II
63	**Pompey** invades Palestine; Roman rule begins
63–40	**Hyrcanus II** rules, subject to Rome. Antipater exercises increasing power
40–37	**Parthians** conquer Jerusalem; establish Aristohulus II as High Priest and king
37–4	**Herod the Great,** son of Antipater, rules as king; subject to Rome

THE APOCRYPHA

The term Apocrypha is used to designate a collection of ancient Jewish writings which were written between about 250 B.C. and the early Christian centuries. The apocryphal books have come to be regarded as inspired Scripture in the theology of the Roman Catholic Church, but the historic Protestant and Jewish viewpoint ascribes no real inspiration to them.

Why Protestants Reject the Apocrypha

While Protestants study the Apocrypha for the light it throws on the life and thought of pre-Christian Judaism, they reject it as inspired Scripture for the following reasons:

(1) The apocryphal books were not a part of the Old Testament of Jesus and the early Church. The threefold division of the Old Testament—the Law, the Prophets, and the Writings, still used in Hebrew Bibles and Jewish versions of the Old Testament—does not include the apocryphal books and never did. While the Apocrypha was known to Jesus and His disciples, they never quote from it as authoritative Scripture.

(2) Ancient Jewish writers who used the Greek Bible, notably **Philo** and **Josephus,** were acquainted with the Apocrypha but never quote it as Scripture. In fact, Josephus states that nothing had been added to Scripture "from Artaxerxes until our time." The apocryphal book of Second Esdras mentions twenty-four books, corresponding to the Hebrew Bible as it is known today, and seventy other writings which are esoteric in nature (2 Esdras 14:44–48). It is significant that this apocryphal book shows an acquaintance with the acknowledged Old Testament canon as known in the synagogue and in the Protestant churches.

(3) Church Fathers, who were familiar with the Hebrew canon, clearly distinguish between canonical and apocryphal writings. The writings of **Melito of Sardis, Cyril of Jerusalem,** and **St. Jerome** show a recognition of the difference between inspired Scripture and Apocrypha.

(4) The apocryphal books were never declared to be authoritative Scripture until the **Council of Trent** (A.D. 1546). At that time the following apocryphal books were declared canonical: Tobit, Judith, The Wisdom of Solomon, Ecclesiasticus, Baruch (including the Letter of Jeremiah), First and Second Maccabees, the additions to Esther, and the additions to Daniel (viz. Susanna, The Song of the Three Young Men, and Bel and the Dragon). Many Roman Catholic scholars distinguish between proto-canonical books (i.e., our Old Testament) and deuterocanonical books (i.e., the Apocrypha).

(5) Most readers feel that the apocryphal books represent a lower level of writing than that of the canonical Scriptures. They contain numerous historical and geographical inaccuracies and anachronisms and do not breathe the prophetic spirit so evident in canonical writings.

The **Westminster Confession** (1643) states that "the books commonly called Apocrypha, not being of divine inspiration, are not part of the Canon of Scripture, and therefore are of no authority in the Church of God, or to be any otherwise approved or made use of than other human writing." The Reformed Churches have not encouraged the use of the Apocrypha, and as a consequence it is seldom used in contemporary Protestantism. The Anglican Church in its Thirty-nine Articles takes a mediating position, holding that, "the Church doth read [the apocryphal books] for example of life and instruction of manners; but yet doth it not apply them to confess any doctrine."

In addition to the books commonly called Apocrypha, there is a wide variety of other ancient literature, both Jewish and Christian, to which the name **Pseudepigrapha** is often applied. Apocrypha, Pseudepigrapha, sectarian literature from the Qumran Caves, and a wide variety of other ancient writings provide helpful material for understanding the world of the New Testament and the early Church. While not on a par with inspired Scripture, such writings merit close examination.

The Books Commonly Termed Apocrypha Are:

First Esdras (Vulgate, 3 Esdras). The first book of Esdras relates a series of episodes from Old Testament history, beginning with the passover celebrated in Jerusalem by Josiah (*c.* 621 B.C.) and ending with the public reading of the law by Ezra (*c.* 444 B.C.). It reproduces the substance of Second Chronicles 33:1—36:23, the whole of Ezra, and Nehemiah 7:73—8:12. An addition to the biblical narrative appears in First Esdras 3:1—5:6, the **Tale of the Three Guardsmen.** Three young men who were acting as bodyguards to King Darius were keeping themselves awake by debating what was the strongest force in the world. One said wine, because of its peculiar power over men; another suggested the king, with unlimited power over his subjects; and the third (**Zerubbabel**) affirmed that woman, who gives birth to man, is strongest, but truth is victor over all things. The king, who was asked to decide the winner, favored Zerubbabel's answer and offered him any reward he might choose. Zerubbabel asked permission to return to Jerusalem to rebuild the Temple. The section ends with a description of the Jews departing from Babylon en route to Jerusalem. Most scholars suggest that First Esdras was composed in Egypt some time after 150 B.C.

Second Esdras (Vulgate, 4 Esdras). The core of Second Esdras (chapters 3—14) purports to describe seven **apocalyptic revelations** granted to Ezra in Babylon. They are concerned with the problem of Israel's suffering and attempt "to justify the ways of God to man." The author was evidently a Jew, who looked forward to the advent of Israel's Messiah and the period of blessedness which He would bring. The introduction (chapters 1 and 2) and the conclusion (chapters 15 and 16) contain additions written from a Christian viewpoint. The core was probably written in Aramaic toward the end of the first century A.D. About the middle of the second century, an introduction was added (in Greek), and a century later the concluding chapters were written. Oriental versions and many of the best Latin manuscripts contain only the core of the book.

Tobit. Tobit is a book of **religious fiction,** probably written in Aramaic during the second century B.C. It tells the story of a pious Jew of the tribe of Naphtali in Galilee who, with his wife Anna and their son Tobias, was taken to Nineveh by **Shalmaneser** (*c.* 721 B.C., 2 Kin. 18:9–12). In the land of exile they scrupulously obeyed the Jewish Law. When **Tobit** lost his eyesight, he sent his son to Rages in Media to obtain payment of a debt. An angel led him on to Ecbatana, where he fell in love with a beautiful widow whose seven husbands had successively been killed on their marriage day by an evil spirit. Tobias married the virgin-widow and escaped death by burning the inner part of a fish, the smoke of which put the evil spirit to flight. As an added blessing, the gall of the fish was used to cure the blindness of the aged Tobit.

Judith. The story of Judith was probably written in Hebrew by a Palestinian Jew during the years following the Maccabean revolt. It tells how Judith, a Jewish widow, delivered her people from the Assyrian commander, **Holofernes,** who was laying siege to Bethulia. Risking great personal danger, Judith made her way to the tent of Holofernes where she beguiled the Assyrian with her charms. Getting him into a drunken stupor, Judith took the sword of Holofernes, cut off his head, and brought it back to Bethulia as evidence that God had given His people victory over the Assyrians. Judith may be compared with biblical Jael, who killed the Caananite general Sisera (Judg. 4:17–22).

The Additions to the Book of Esther. During the second or the first century B.C., an Egyptian Jew translated the canonical Book of Esther into Greek, and at the same time interpolated a total of **107 verses** into six places where he felt that a religious note should be added. These pious insertions mention the name of God and prayer, neither of which appear in the canonical Esther. The apocryphal additions add ten verses to Esther 10, and six additional chapters, numbered 11 to 16. In the Greek Septuagint, however, the supplementary verses are distributed through the text so as to make one continuous narration.

The Wisdom of Solomon. An Alexandrian Jew, sometime between 150 and 50 B.C., composed an ethical treatise which he named The Wisdom of Solomon in order to gain for it a wider reading. He sought to protect the Jews in Egypt from falling into skepticism, materialism, and idolatry, and to teach his pagan readers the truth of Judaism and the folly of heathenism. The book begins with an exhortation to the rulers of the earth to seek wisdom and follow righteousness. Its theology is based on the Old Testament with modifications derived from Greek philosophical ideas current in Alexandria. Unlike the Old and New Testaments which honor the body, the Wisdom of Solomon (The New American Bible) regards it as something that "weighs down the soul," a mere "earthly tent" which "burdens the thoughtful mind" (9:15). The pre-existence (8:19,20) and immortality (3:1–5) of the soul are maintained, although the Hebrew-Christian doctrine of bodily resurrection is absent.

Ecclesiasticus, or the Wisdom of Jesus the Son of Sirach. Ecclesiasticus, an ethical treatise extolling the virtue of wisdom, was written in Hebrew between 200 and 175 B.C. by a pious scholar from Jerusalem, Jesus the son of Sirach. The author's grandson, an Alexandrian Jew, translated the work into Greek and added a prologue (*c.* 132 B.C.). It is the longest of the apocryphal books, and the only one with a known author. Like the canonical Proverbs, Ecclesiasticus deals with a wide variety of practical subjects—everything from diet to domestic relationships. The longest continuous section of the book (chapters 44 to 50) is the **Praise of Famous Men,** which briefly describes a long series of Hebrew worthies from **Enoch, Noah,** and **Abraham,** down to **Zerubbabel** and **Nehemiah,** and finally the **High Priest Simon,** a contemporary and friend of the author.

Baruch. The Book of Baruch, ostensibly written by Jeremiah's friend and secretary (Jer. 32:12; 36:4; 51:59), is a composite work which was not completed until the first century B.C. or later. Although the final recension was written in Greek, some sections may be traced to Hebrew originals. The book begins with a **prayer of penitence,** recognizing that the tragedies which befell Jerusalem are the just recompense for her sins (1:1—3:8). A second poetical section explains that **Israel's misfortunes** are due to her neglect of **Wisdom** (3:9—4:4). This Wisdom, whose praises are sung by a philosophically minded writer, is equated with God's law (4:1–3). The third section of the book, also poetic, is a message of **comfort and hope for distressed Israel.** The enemy will be destroyed and the children of Jerusalem will return in triumph! Baruch is the one book of the Apocrypha which breathes something of the fire of the Old Testament prophets, although it is lacking in originality.

The Letter of Jeremiah. Sometime about 300 B.C., or thereafter, an unknown author wrote **an impassioned sermon** based on **Jeremiah 11:10,** in which he showed the utter impotence of gods of wood, silver, and gold. This sermon, known as The Letter of Jeremiah, was originally written in Hebrew (or Aramaic), although it is extant only in Greek and translations derived from the Greek. Since many Greek and Syriac manuscripts, as well as the Latin version, attach the Letter of Jeremiah to the Book of Baruch, it appears as the sixth chapter of Baruch in most English translations of the Apocrypha. The Letter has no relation to Baruch, however, and some ancient codices place it after the biblical Book of Lamentations.

The Prayer of Azariah and the Song of the Three Young Men. (Additions to Daniel, inserted between 3:23 and 3:24.) Sometime during the second or first centuries B.C., the three "additions" to canonical Daniel, which exist as separate books of the Apocrypha, were written by unknown authors. The first of these, The Prayer of Azariah and the Song of the Three Young Men, was probably written in Hebrew by a pious Jew during the period when his people were suffering at the hand of **Antiochus Epiphanes,** or in the period of the **Maccabean revolt** which followed. During the ordeal of the fiery furnace, Azariah is represented as praising God, confessing his people's sins, and praying for national deliverance. The angel of the Lord then came into the furnace and drove out the fiery flame, so that the youths were unharmed. Then from the furnace they sang their praises to God in the Song, which is reminiscent of Psalm 148 in content and Psalm 136 in antiphonal form.

Susanna. It is uncertain whether the original of Susanna was written in Hebrew or Greek. Its unknown author lived sometime during the second or the first century B.C., but we are ignorant of other details concerning his life. Yet, the book itself is recognized as **one of the great short stories of world literature.** It tells how two immoral elders threatened to testify that they had found Susanna, the beautiful wife of an influential Babylonian Jew, in the arms of a lover, if she would not submit to them. When she repulsed them, they charged her with adultery through the testimony of two witnesses, and she was convicted and sentenced to death. A young man named Daniel, however, interrupted the proceedings and questioned the two witnesses separately. He asked each to identify the tree under which he had seen Susanna and her supposed lover. Betrayed by their own inconsistent answers, the guilty elders were put to death and Susanna was saved. In the Septuagint, the Story of Susanna precedes the canonical Book of Daniel; in the Vulgate it follows it.

Bel and the Dragon. The stories of Bel and the Dragon were probably written in Hebrew toward the middle of the first century B.C. and added to the Book of Daniel by its Greek translator. In the Septuagint it directly follows Daniel, while in the Vulgate it comes after Susanna. The story of Bel is one of the world's oldest detective stories. It tells how **Cyrus,** the Persian king, asked **Daniel** why he did not worship **Bel, the god of Babylon.** Cyrus told Daniel how much flour and oil and how many sheep the god Bel consumed each day. Then, Daniel persuaded Cyrus to deposit the usual provisions in the Temple and then to close and seal the Temple doors. In the meantime, Daniel scattered ashes over the Temple floor. When morning came the food was gone, and the floor was covered with footprints of the priests, their wives and children, who had used a secret entrance under the table to come by night into the Temple and consume the provisions. The king, convinced of the perfidy of Bel's priests, ordered them slain and their Temple destroyed. The Dragon is really a serpent which the king worshiped until Daniel killed it by feeding it lumps of pitch, fat, and hair. The Babylonians, furious at the destruction of their god, demanded that Daniel be put to death. The king reluctantly consented and Daniel was placed in a den of lions (cf. Dan. 6:1–28). The lions did not molest Daniel, who was miraculously fed by the prophet **Habakkuk,** who was caught up by an angel in Judea and taken to the lions' den in **Babylon.** On the seventh day the king took Daniel from the lions' den and cast his enemies into it, whereupon they were immediately devoured. The stories of Bel and the

Dragon were intended to ridicule idolatry and discredit heathen priestcraft.

The Prayer of Manasseh. The apocryphal Prayer of Manasseh was probably written sometime during the last two centuries B.C. by a Palestinian Jew. Scholars are uncertain whether it was composed in Hebrew, Aramaic, or Greek. The Prayer is ascribed to Manasseh, the king of Judah who, according to Second Chronicles 33, was taken to Babylon where he repented of the idolatry that had characterized the years of his reign. Mention is made of a prayer offered by Manasseh (2 Chr. 33:19), and a pious Jew appears to have attempted to write such a prayer as Manasseh would have uttered. The Prayer is typical of ancient Jewish liturgical forms. It opens with the ascription of **praise to the Lord,** whose majesty is seen in creation (1–4) and in His mercy toward sinners (5–8). This is followed by **personal confession** (9, 10) and **supplication for pardon** (11–13). The prayer concludes with a **petition for grace** (14) and a doxology (15).

First Maccabees. First Maccabees is a valuable historical record of the forty years beginning with the accession of **Antiochus Epiphanes** to the Syrian throne (175 B.C.) and ending with the death of **Simon the Maccabee** (135 B.C.). It was probably written by a Palestinian Jew, in Hebrew, about 100 B.C. The book gives us our best account of the Jewish resistance to Antiochus and the Maccabean wars which ultimately brought independence to the Jewish state. It relates the exploits of three of the sons of Mattathias, the priest who defied Antiochus and sparked the revolt: **Judas** (3:1—9:22), **Jonathan** (9:23—12:53), and **Simon** (13:1—16:24). The annual Jewish festival of Hanukkah, celebrated at the same season as Christmas, commemorates the rededication of the Temple as a result of the bravery of the Maccabees. The festival is mentioned in the New Testament as "the Feast of Dedication" (John 10:22).

Second Maccabees. Second Maccabees is primarily parallel to the first seven chapters of First Maccabees, covering the period from 175 to 160 B.C. It professes to be an abridgement of a five-volume history written by **Jason of Cyrene** (2:19–23), whose identity is a matter of conjecture. The author of Second Maccabees was evidently an Alexandrian Jew who wrote in Greek. He may have written as early as 120 B.C. or as late as the early first century A.D. Second Maccabees is less historical and more rhetorical than First Maccabees. It is written from the Pharisaic viewpoint and stresses the miraculous and the marvelous in contrast to the more prosaic and objective First Maccabees.

THE SCARLET THREAD OF REDEMPTION

Introduction

The Bible is a book of redemption. It is that or nothing at all. It is not merely a book of history, or of science, or of anthropology, or of cosmogony. It is a book of salvation and deliverance for lost humankind.

The idea in the word "redemption" is twofold: it refers to a deliverance; and it refers to the price paid for that deliverance, a ransom. We are redeemed from the penalty of sin, from the power of Satan and evil, by the price Jesus paid on the cross for us; and we are redeemed to a new freedom from sin, a new relationship to God, and a new life of love by the appropriation of that atonement for our sins.

The whole of the Bible, whether the Old Testament or the New Testament, looks to the mighty, redemptive atonement of Christ. His blood sacrifice is the ransom paid for our deliverance. He took our sinful nature upon Himself in order that He might satisfy the demands of the law. His sacrifice is accepted as the payment for the debt the sinner owes to God, and His death is accepted as the full payment for the individual's deliverance.

Our Lord's redemptive work for us is threefold: First, it is closely associated with forgiveness, since we receive forgiveness through the redemptive price of Christ's death. Second, it involves justification, since the deliverance establishes us in a restored position of favor before God. Third, it promises final deliverance from the power of sin at the coming of the Lord. This redemption is "The Scarlet Thread."

The Creation and the Fall

When God made the heavens and the earth, they must have been beautiful, perfect, and pure.

In the Garden of Eden, however, through a denial of the Word of God and through a deception of the woman, our first parents fell. Eve was deceived, but Adam chose to die by the side of the woman whom God had created and placed in his arms. When the Lord came to visit the man and his wife in the cool of the day, He could not find them. They were afraid and hid themselves from the Lord because they were naked and ashamed. To hide their guilt, they made for themselves aprons of fig leaves, but when God looked upon the covering, He said, "This will not do." Covering for sin (atonement for sin) cannot be woven by human hands. Therefore, somewhere in the Garden of Eden, the Lord took an innocent animal, and before the eyes of Eve and Adam, God slew that innocent animal as the ground drank up its blood. This is the beginning of "The Scarlet Thread of Redemption." Through the slaughter of an innocent victim, God took coats of skin and covered over the shame and the nakedness of the man and his wife. This is the first sacrifice, and it was offered by the hand of Almighty God. When Adam saw the gasping, spent life of that innocent creature, and when he saw the crimson stain which soiled the ground, it was his first experience of knowing what it meant to die because of sin. So the story of atonement and sacrifice begins and unfolds throughout the Word of God until finally in glory we shall see great throngs of the saints who have washed their robes and made them white in the blood of the Lamb. This is "The Scarlet Thread of Redemption."

From the Seventh Day in Eden to the Call of Abraham

In the Garden of Eden, as the Lord covered over the nakedness of the man and the woman, He turned to Satan and said, "And I will put enmity between you and the woman, and between your seed and her Seed; He shall bruise your head, and you shall bruise His heel" (Gen. 3:15). For centuries the rabbis studied that word of the Lord God to Satan. The Seed of the woman. Seed is masculine. The rabbis contemplated the promise of God that the "Seed" of the woman would bruise Satan's head. We now know that the promise is related to the long conflict and struggle between the hatred of Lucifer and the love of God in Christ Jesus. It speaks of Jesus at Calvary. Jesus suffered. His heel was bruised. But in that bruising, He defeated once and for all the power of that old serpent, the devil. He bruised his head.

As the man Adam and his wife, Eve, made their first home in earth cursed for their sakes, after a time there were born to them two sons. One was named Cain and the other Abel. In jealousy and insane fury, the older brother killed the younger brother. But the seed of God would be preserved. The Lord, therefore, gave to Eve another son, named Seth. Seth was a man of faith, as Cain was a man of the world. When the children of Seth, the godly remnant, intermarried with the children of Cain, the people of the world, the result was a fallen progeny that filled the earth with violence. Finally, God said it was enough. One hundred twenty years later, He would destroy the world by a flood. But a member of the line of Seth found grace in the sight of the Lord. His name was Noah. To preserve the righteous seed, God told Noah to build an ark; and into that ark of safety, salvation, and hope Noah brought his family. After the passing of the awesome judgment of the flood, the earth once again began its story of redemption through the life of this one man and his three sons.

It was not long, however, until the ravages of sin began to waste the select family of God. Instead of carrying out the great commission of the Lord for humankind to inhabit the whole earth, the people drew together into one plain and announced their purpose to build a tower around which they were to center their civilization and their collective, communal unity. When God looked down and saw their pride, He confused their speech and caused them to "babble." From this "Tower of Babel," therefore, the different parts of the human race, being unable to understand each other, scattered in different directions and so fathered the nations of the earth that grew up from those three great family lines of Noah.

From the Call of Abraham Through the Times of the Judges

We begin the story of Abraham in a dark era. The whole world had been plunged into abysmal idolatry, but God called out this man to leave his home, his place, his country, and his family to go into another country which he would afterward receive for an inheritance. In obedience, Abraham left the Mesopotamian valley and came as a pilgrim, a stranger, and a sojourner into the land of Canaan. There he dwelt, and there God gave him two sons. But the Lord God said to Abraham that Ishmael, the son of a slave woman, would not be the promised seed. When Abraham was a hundred years old and Sarah was ninety years old, God miraculously placed in the arms of the parents the child of promise, whom they named Isaac. Isaac was the father of two sons, Esau and Jacob. The Lord, refusing Esau, chose Jacob whom He renamed, after a deep conversion experience, the "prince of God" or "Israel."

Because of a severe famine in Canaan and because Jacob's son, Joseph, was in Egypt, the entire household of Jacob went down to live in the land of the Nile. Later, there arose a Pharaoh who "did not know" Joseph. The chosen family became slaves to this new ruler of Egypt, and their heavy groaning mounted up to the ears of the Lord God in heaven. The Lord, therefore, raised up the mighty prophet, Moses, to deliver his people from the bondage and slavery of the Egyptians. God worked this deliverance by a miracle called the Passover. For the Lord had said, "When I see the blood, I will pass over you and will spare you and your home." This way of salvation, through the blood, is once again "The Scarlet Thread of Redemption."

After the Lord God delivered the chosen family from Egypt, He brought them by the leadership of Moses through the parting of the Red Sea into the Sinaitic Peninsula to the base of Mount Horeb. There, for forty days and forty nights, Moses was with God, and there the Lord gave to Moses the pattern of the tabernacle, the ritual instructions of holy worship, and all of the other marvelous things in the Book of Leviticus that portray and prophesy the sacrifice of the Son of God.

After the death of Moses, Joshua went over Jordan and led the wars of conquest. In the first confrontation, at Jericho, an incident happened which gave rise to the title of this summary. The scouts sent out by Joshua to spy out Jericho were saved by the faith and kindness of Rahab. The men of Israel promised life and safety, both for her and her father's house, if she would bind a scarlet thread in her window. This she did, and, when Jericho fell into the hands of Joshua by the intervention of God, Rahab and her family were spared because of that scarlet line, "The Scarlet Thread of Redemption."

After the conquest of Canaan, under Joshua, we have the story of the Judges. The difference between a judge and a king was that a king gave to his son his throne by inheritance, but a judge was raised up in a crisis and endowed with special gifts from God for a period of time. The days of the Judges end with the birth of Samuel.

From the First of the Prophets to the Founding of the Kingdom

During the time of Samuel, the people began to cry for a king. It was the purpose of God in the beginning for the children of Israel to have a king (Deut. 17:14–20), but it hurt the heart of the Lord that the request should come in so vain and rebellious a way as they presented it to Samuel. But according to the word and instruction of God, Samuel anointed Saul to be king over Israel. In his beginning ministry, Saul was a mighty man and carried out the mandates of heaven, but he soon fell away from the instruction of Samuel and fell into gross disobedience to the will of God. The Word of the Lord, therefore, came to Samuel that he must anoint a man after God's own heart. That anointing was directed toward a lad from the shepherd field, a son of Jesse by the name of David.

David and the Kingdoms of Israel and Judah

The first part of David's life as king of Israel was magnificent. Then, in the very prime of his life, at the very height of his glory, he turned aside from the will of God and became self-indulgent and lustful like other Oriental kings. This brought to David an infinite tragedy, one by which the name of God was blasphemed. Nevertheless, God forgave the sin of David and chose him to be the father of that marvelous Son who would sit upon His throne as King forever. A type of that glorious Son of David was the *immediate* son of David, called Solomon. Solomon also began his reign gloriously and triumphantly, but like his father, Solomon also fell into tragic decline. Upon his death, the kingdom was divided.

Thereafter, the people of God were divided into two kingdoms: that of the north was called the kingdom of Israel, and that of the south was called the kingdom of Judah. The northern kingdom of Israel was taken away into captivity by the cruel and ruthless Assyrians in 722 B.C. The southern kingdom was carried away into Babylonian captivity in 587 B.C. In the days of the Babylonian captivity, Jeremiah prophesied in Jerusalem while Daniel, the prophet-statesman, and Ezekiel, the holy seer, comforted and strengthened the people of God in Mesopotamia.

Out of the Babylonian captivity came three great establishments by which God has blessed our world. First, the Jews were never idolatrous again. Second, the synagogue was born, and from the synagogue came the church. The services of the synagogue are the same type of services we have today. Third, from the captivity came the canon of the Holy Scriptures. Out of tears and suffering came our greatest blessing, "The Scarlet Thread of Redemption."

From the Prophets to the Christ to the Preaching of Paul

Out of the agonies of the days of the kingdoms of Israel and of Judah came the predictions by the prophets of a more glorious Savior and King, whom God would send to His people. When we read a passage like the twenty-second Psalm or the fifty-third chapter of Isaiah, we seem to be standing by the cross of the Son of God. More and more, the great spiritual leaders of Israel and of Judah began to depict the coming of a Redeemer who would save His people from their sins and bring to them the everlasting hope and righteousness of God. This messianic hope became stronger and more gloriously received as the centuries passed.

In 536 B.C. Cyrus the Persian gave the people the right to return from the Babylonian captivity to their homeland in Judah and to build their holy temple in Jerusalem. Thus, the remnant of the captivity returned under Zerubbabel, the political leader; under Joshua, the priestly leader; under Ezra, the scribe; and under Nehemiah, who had been the prime minister at the court of Shushan, the Persian capital. This holy remnant, thus seeking to restore the worship of the true God in Jerusalem and to recreate the political life of Judah, was encouraged by God's messengers, Haggai, Zechariah, and Malachi.

Of the three great restoration prophets, Zechariah is by far the greatest. Zechariah spoke much about Israel, about the end of time, and about the conversion of the people of the Lord. The last prophet is Malachi. He delivered his message from about 450 B.C. to about 425 B.C.

The four-hundred-year period between the Old Testament and the New Testament marks the rise of the Hellenistic empire. God used Alexander the Great to spread abroad throughout the civilized world one culture and one language, which made possible the later preaching of Christ to all men everywhere.

In that interbiblical period also arose the might of the Roman Empire. When Augustus Caesar was the Roman emperor, and when Rome had the entire world in her hand, the great prophecies of Isaiah, Micah, Nathan to David, Jacob to his son Judah, and the great promise of God Almighty to Eve in the Garden of Eden, came to pass. In the seed progeny of the woman and through the seed of Abraham, all the families of the earth were to be blessed—and our Savior was thus born into the world. "The Scarlet Thread of Redemption" has led us to the birth of Him who has come to redeem the human race from their fallen estate.

In His ministry Jesus early began to teach His disciples that He should suffer and die. When He was transfigured, there appeared Moses and Elijah talking to Him about His death, which He should accomplish in Jerusalem. When He was anointed by Mary of Bethany, He said it was for His burial. When the Greeks came to see Him from afar, He said, "And I, if I am lifted up from the earth, will draw all *peoples* to Myself" (John 12:32). At the Last Supper He said, "This is My body; eat in remembrance of Me." And again He said, "This is My blood; drink in remembrance of Me." Before He went to the cross, He gave Himself in Gethsemane in travail of soul for our redemption (Is. 53:11). And when He bowed His head and died, He said, "It is finished!" (John 19:30). When we preach the cross, when we preach the blood, when we preach the sacrificial death of Christ, we are preaching the meaning of His coming into the world. The sacrifice of Christ consummated the great redemptive plan and purpose of God on the earth. This is "The Scarlet Thread of Redemption."

After the resurrection of our Lord, after the

giving of the Great Commission to the apostles, and after the ascension of our Savior into heaven, the Lord poured out His Holy Spirit upon His church in Jerusalem on the day of Pentecost. Then the disciples of Jesus began to make known throughout the earth the Good News of our hope and salvation.

The epistles of Paul are divided into four distinct groups. The first group he wrote on his second missionary journey from Athens and Corinth. They are 1 and 2 Thessalonians. The second group of letters was born in his third missionary journey. While he was in Ephesus, he wrote 1 Corinthians. Somewhere between Ephesus and Corinth, he wrote 2 Corinthians in Macedonia. Then, either in Antioch or on his way to Antioch, he wrote Galatians and Romans. First and 2 Corinthians, Galatians, and Romans, therefore, center around the city of Ephesus. The third group of epistles Paul wrote from the prison in Rome, during his first Roman imprisonment. They are Ephesians, Philippians, Colossians, and Philemon. The fourth and last group of his epistles, written after his first Roman imprisonment were 1 Timothy, Titus, and 2 Timothy, called the pastoral epistles. In all of Paul's letters, there is the constant theme of redemptive love. It is a part of "The Scarlet Thread of Redemption."

The Apocalypse and the Consummation of the Age

We come now to the conclusion of the Bible.

On the Isle of Patmos, a rocky little point in the Mediterranean Sea, several miles southwest of Ephesus, John was exiled to die of exposure and starvation. But there the Lord appears to John in a glorious vision. The vision is called the Revelation, that is, "the unveiling." "The Apocalypse," the unveiling of Jesus Christ in His glory, in His majesty, and in His kingdom, is the reward that God gave to Jesus for saving us, Adam's fallen children, from our sins.

After the vision of the exalted and glorified Christ in chapter 1, and after the prophetic words in chapters 2 and 3, John is taken up through an open door into heaven. While John, the translated saint, is with the Savior in heaven, the judgments of Almighty God are poured out on the earth. They are depicted in the opening of the seven seals, the seven trumpets, and the seven bowls. In those dark days John sees a vision (Rev. 7), concerning the blood-washed redeemed souls in glory. Announcement is made to him through one of the elders that these are they who have come out of the great tribulation and have washed their robes and made them white in the blood of the Lamb. This is "The Scarlet Thread of Redemption" that began with the blood of covering in the Garden of Eden and finds its ultimate and final consummation in the blood-washed throng before the throne of God in glory.

After the seven seals and the judgments, the seven trumpets and the judgments, the seven bowls and the judgments, and the seven personages and the judgments, we come to the final great Judgment Day of Almighty God. The Antichrist, who professes to be the leader of the nations of the world, is seen gathering the armies of the entire earth together. They are converging from the north, from the east, from the south, from the west, and from the islands of the sea. They are converging for that great day of the Lord. That is the Battle of Armageddon, the last great war the world is going to fight. At Megiddo, the armies of the earth by the millions will converge to face that rendezvous with God. In the midst of this holocaust, Christ will intervene in human history. He comes with His saints. He will deliver His people, shut up in the holy city, and take Satan and bind him for a thousand years in the bottomless pit.

After the binding of Satan for a thousand years, which is called the Millennium, Satan is released and thereafter goes forth once again to lead rebellion against God. This is the final conflict which ends forever humankind's refusal to accept the will of God for their lives. At the end time, in the final resurrection of the wicked dead and the great white throne judgment, the books are opened, and those whose names are not found written in the Lamb's Book of Life are cast out and rewarded according to their deeds. Into the abyss of hell are flung Satan and his angels, along with those who choose Satan and his way of life, plus death and the grave—all are hurled into the fiery flames where the Beast and the False Prophet have already been for a thousand years.

After the purging of the earth of Satan and his minions, and after the judgment upon those who reject Christ and His grace, and after cleansing the earth of the heartache and tears of sickness, sin, death, and the grave, will come the renovation of earth and heaven. It is a new creation with a glorious new heaven and new earth. In it is the holy city, the heavenly Jerusalem, and in it is the dwelling place of God Himself. Tears, death, sorrow, pain, and crying are passed away. There are no graves on the hillsides of glory and no funeral wreaths on the doors of those mansions in the sky.

The book closes with the incomparable message of the hope, salvation, and redemption accomplished in the Person and work of the Lord Christ.

THE GREATEST ARCHAEOLOGICAL DISCOVERIES

and Their Effects on the Bible

I
Introduction

Definition and Importance of Biblical Archaeology

The last 150 years have witnessed the birth, growth, and phenomenal development of the science of biblical archaeology. This new science has performed many wonders in furnishing background material and in illustrating, illuminating, and in many cases authenticating the message and meaning of the Old and New Testament Scriptures.

Biblical archaeology may be defined as a study based on the excavation, decipherment, and critical evaluation of the records of the past as they affect the Bible. While the general field of archaeology is fascinating, much more so is the study of biblical archaeology, since it deals with the Holy Scriptures. This is the reason for the growing enthusiasm for biblical archaeology. The attraction lies in the supreme importance of the message and meaning of the Bible. The Scriptures, by virtue of their character as the inspired revelation of God to humankind and meeting humankind's deepest need, today as in the past, have naturally held a paramount place in the interest and affection of humankind. Biblical archaeology, illustrating the Bible in its historical background and contemporary life, attracts a measure of the interest that lies in the Bible itself. Accordingly, this science has a worthy ministry of expanding biblical horizons on the human plane.

No field of research has offered greater challenge and promise than that of biblical archaeology. Until the beginning of the 19th century very little was known of biblical times and biblical backgrounds, except what appeared on the pages of the Old Testament or what happened to be preserved in the writings of classical antiquity. This was considerable for the New Testament era but very little indeed for the Old Testament period. The reason for this is that Greek and Latin historians catalogued very little information before the 5th century B.C. As a result, the Old Testament period was very little known extrabiblically, and what was known was confined to what the Bible gave. This from the viewpoint of contemporary secular history was sparse. The result was that before the beginning of the science of modern archaeology there was practically nothing available to authenticate Old Testament history and literature. One can therefore imagine the fervor aroused among serious Bible students by illuminating discoveries in Bible lands, especially from c. 1800 to the present. In fact, modern archaeology may be said to have had its beginning in 1798, when the rich antiquities of the Nile Valley were opened up to scientific study by Napoleon's Egyptian Expedition.

II
Foundational Discoveries of the Nineteenth Century

Although the most notable discoveries affecting the Bible and particularly the Old Testament were not made until the 20th century, foundational discoveries were made in the 19th century and prepared the way for the modern era.

1. The Rosetta Stone—Key to Egypt's Splendid Past

This very important monument was discovered in 1798 at *Rosetta* (Rashid), near the westernmost mouth of the Nile River, by an officer in Napoleon's Expedition to Egypt. It was a slab of black basalt trilingually inscribed, which may be said to be the key that unlocked the door to knowledge of the language and literature of ancient Egypt and turned out to be the inscription that opened the modern era of scientific biblical archaeology.

The three languages in which this monument was found to be inscribed were the Greek of 200 B.C., two forms of Egyptian writing—the older, more complicated hieroglyphic script and the later simplified and more popular demotic writing, which was the common language of the people. The Greek could at once be read and provided the clue to the decipherment of the other two ancient Egyptian scripts. Sylvester de Sacy of France and J. D. Akerblad of Sweden succeeded in unraveling the demotic Egyptian by identifying the Greek personal names it contained, namely Ptolemy, Arsinoe, and Berenike.

Thomas Young of England then proceeded to identify the name of Ptolemy in the hieroglyphic portion, where groups of characters enclosed in oval frames, called cartouches, had already been surmised to be royal names. From this point on, the young Frenchman Jean François Champollion, 1790–1832, was able to decipher the hieroglyphics of the monument, show the true nature of this script, make a dictionary, formulate a grammar, and translate numerous Egyptian texts, from the year 1818 to 1832.

Champollion's achievement formally opened up the science of Egyptology. Scholars from henceforth were able to read Egyptian monumental inscriptions and reliefs. From that time forth the literary treasures of the Nile Valley have been opened to scholarly study. Today many universities maintain chairs in the language and culture of ancient Egypt. These studies have opened up vistas of history hitherto unknown so that, from the beginning of Egypt, c. 2800 B.C. to 63 B.C. when Rome took over, the entire history of the land of the Nile can fairly well be traced.

All of this has tremendous bearing on the background of the Bible. Egypt figures largely in the patriarchal narratives and the Book of Exodus and all through the Pentateuch. As a result, the background of the story of Joseph and of the sojourn of the children of Israel in Egypt, their deliverance under Moses, and much of their sojourn in the desert and later history in Canaan can now be set in the general framework of Egyptian history. It can be said that the whole context of Old Testament history, in its broad span from Abraham to Christ, is made immeasurably clearer because of the vast strides in our knowledge of Egypt. That great nation of antiquity interacted with the mighty Assyro-Babylonian empires on the Tigris-Euphrates and with the Hittite power on the Halys across the tiny bridge that was ancient Palestine.

2. The Behistun Inscription—Gateway to Assyrian-Babylonian Antiquity

This famous monument was the key to the languages of Assyria and Babylonia. It consists of a large relief panel containing numerous columns of inscription, which was boldly carved on the face of a mountain about 500 feet above the surrounding plain of Karmanshah on the old caravan route from Babylon to Ecbatana. Unlike the Rosetta Stone written in ancient Egyptian hieroglyphics, and later in popular demotic and in the Greek of the 3rd century B.C., the ***Behistun Inscription*** was written in the wedge-shaped characters of ancient Assyria-Babylonia. It contained about 1,200 lines of inscription. The three languages in which it was inscribed were all written in cuneiform characters, consisting of Old Persian, Elamite, and Akkadian. The third language, the Akkadian, was the wedge-shaped language of ancient Assyria and Babylonia, in which thousands upon thousands of clay tablets discovered in the Tigris-Euphrates region are inscribed.

Early excavations revealed a mass of material on which this curious wedge-shaped Babylonian-Akkadian writing appeared. But it was an unsolved riddle. Practically no progress was made until a young English officer in the Persian army, Henry C. Rawlinson, in 1835 and the following years made the dangerous climb to the Behistun Inscription and made copies and plaster of paris impressions of it. Rawlinson knew modern Persian and set to work to decipher the old Persian, the cuneiform part of the inscription. After a decade of labor, he finally succeeded in translating the five columns, nearly 400 lines of the old Persian portion of the Behistun Inscription, and sent it to Europe in 1845. The text translation and commentary on it were published in 1847 in the ***Journal of the Royal Asiatic Society***.

In conjunction with the literary part of the monument was a life-sized figure with numerous individuals bowing before it. This person turned out to be Darius the Great (522–486 B.C.), the Achemenid prince who saved the Persian Empire from a rebellion. The scene depicts the king, as Rawlinson's translation of the Persian portion of the inscription shows, receiving the submission of the rebels. The emperor is portrayed at the top of the relief accompanied by two attendants. His foot is placed upon the prostrate form of a leading rebel. The king's left hand holds a bow, while his right hand is lifted toward the winged disc symbolizing Ahura-Mazda, the spirit of good, whom Darius, an ardent follower of Zoroaster, worshiped. Behind the rebel stands a procession of rebel leaders, roped together by their necks. Beside and beneath the sculptured panel the numerous columns of the inscription appear, relating in three languages how Darius defended the throne and crushed the revolt.

Working on the supposition that the other inscriptions told the same story, scholars were soon enabled to read the second language, which was the Elamite or Susian. Then last, but most important, they could decipher the Akkadian or Assyro-Babylonian. This was a great discovery, for this wedge-shaped character of writing is recorded on numerous literary remains from the Tigris-Euphrates Valley. It opened up a vast new field of biblical background, so that today, as in the case of the Rosetta Stone opening up the science of Egyptology, the Behistun Inscription has

A gateway into Nebuchadnezzar's Palace in Babylon.
Matson Photo Service

given birth to the science of Assyriology. Moreover, both Egyptology and Assyriology offer great help in understanding biblical backgrounds and biblical history. No Bible dictionary, Bible handbook or commentary that is up to date can ignore the great findings of these sciences.

The task of deciphering cuneiform is increasing with every decade. Numerous cuneiform libraries have been discovered from antiquity. Two at Nineveh were unearthed. These contained thousands of clay tablets. ***The library of Ashurbanipal*** (669–625 B.C.) contained some 22,000 tablets. Among the tablets unearthed in this collection and sent to the British Museum were Assyrian copies of the Babylonian creation and flood stories. The identification and decipherment of these particular tablets by George Smith in 1872 produced great excitement in the archaeological world.

Not only in Babylonia but in many other places large bodies of cuneiform literature have been uncovered. For example, the famous ***Amarna Letters*** from Egypt were discovered in 1886 at Tell el-Amarna about 200 miles south of modern Cairo. These Amarna Tablets proved to be diplomatic correspondence of petty princes of Palestine in the 14th century B.C. with the Egyptian court at Amarna. The Amarna Letters give an inside glance into conditions in Palestine just before the conquest by Joshua and the Israelites. Many scholars actually think that they describe aspects of that invasion. One of the documents from the governor of Jerusalem (Urusalim) tells Amenophis IV that the "Habiru" (perhaps the Hebrews) were overrunning many Palestine cities and could not be held back.

Other important bodies of cuneiform literature bearing upon the Bible have been retrieved from Boghaz-Keui and Kanish in Asia Minor. Others come from Susa and Elam, others from the city of Mari on the middle Euphrates, others from Ras Shamra (ancient Ugarit), mentioned in the Amarna Letters and located in North Syria. Others stem from various sites within and without Babylonia. Of first-rate importance then is the Rosetta Stone from Egypt and the Behistun Inscription from Babylonia. These two monuments may be said to have laid the foundation for the key discoveries of the 20th century.

3. The Moabite Stone—A Sensational Literary Find

This important inscription, found in 1868, offers another example of the discoveries of the 19th century that prepared the way for the great finds of the 20th century. The inscription dates from c. 850 B.C. It was erected by Mesha, king of Moab, and is often styled the ***Mesha Stone.*** It tells of the wars of Mesha of Moab with Omri, king of Israel, and Omri's successors. It also tells

A replica of the Moabite Stone. *Matson Photo Service*

of Mesha's wars with the Edomites. The material recorded on the ***Moabite Stone*** parallels biblical history recorded in 2 Kings 1 and 3. Numerous places mentioned in the Old Testament occur on the stele (inscribed monument). Among them are Arnon (Num. 21:13; Deut. 2:24), Ataroth (Num. 32:34), Baal Meon or Beth Baal Meon (Josh. 13:17), Beth Bamoth or Bamoth Baal (Josh. 13:17), Beth Diblathaim (Jer. 48:22), Bezer (Josh. 20:8), Dibon (Num. 32:34), Jahaza (Josh. 13:18), Medeba (Josh. 13:9), and Nebo (Num. 32:38).

This inscribed monument or stele measures 3 feet 8½ inches in height, 2 feet 3½ inches in width, and 1 foot 1¾ inches in thickness. Its 34 lines constitute the longest single literary inscription yet recovered extrabiblically dealing with Palestine in the period 900–600 B.C. It records that Moab had been conquered by Omri and his son Ahab but was set free from the Israelite yoke by Mesha's god Chemosh. This deity is represented as commanding King Mesha to go to war against Israel, who, according to 2 Kings 3:27, offered up his eldest son as a burnt offering upon the wall to propitiate the god Chemosh and to secure his favor.

The Moabite Stone is written in the language of Moab, which was very similar to the Hebrew of the time of Omri and Ahab. This inscription, therefore, has great value in tracing the development of early Hebrew through the centuries. When it was discovered, the Mesha Stone was not only the longest and oldest Phoenician-Hebrew inscription then in existence, it was the only one. Now the ***Gezer Calendar*** is known and it dates from c. 925 B.C. It is a school boy's exercise written in perfect classical Hebrew. This small limestone tablet, found at ancient Gezer, gives an incidental sidelight on Palestinian agriculture as well as on ancient Hebrew writing. Such discoveries as the Gezer Calendar and the Mesha Stone not only give glimpses into the background of the Bible but form important links in the culture and history of the people outside the pale of Israel.

III
Great Discoveries of the Twentieth Century

Although such discoveries as the Rosetta Stone, the Behistun Inscription, the Mesha Stone, and the Siloam Inscription are important for their time and laid the foundations of scientific archaeology in the 19th century, it remained for the 20th century to produce the most thrilling and outstanding archaeological finds. During this period biblical archaeology came to be a refined and precise science, adding to the frontiers of biblical knowledge on the human plane and making tremendous contributions to the background, historical and cultural, of the written Word of God.

1. The Code of Hammurabi—Light on Mosaic Laws

A slab of black diorite, over 7 feet tall and some 6 feet around, was discovered in 1901. This record of the past contains engraved upon it almost 300 paragraphs of legal provision dealing with the commercial, social, domestic, and moral life of the Babylonians of King Hammurabi's time (1728–1676 B.C.). A copy of this code was found by Jacques de Morgan at Susa in Elam, where it had been carried off by the Elamites from Babylon. At the top of the stele the king is shown receiving the laws from the sun god Shamash, patron of law and justice. At some time when Babylon was weak, an Elamite conqueror carried away the monument to Susa. Its finding was one of the most startling legal discoveries in history.

The code is important in furnishing background material for comparison with other ancient bodies of law. It is also natural that it should offer comparative data for the study of the laws of the Pentateuch. The fact that the code is older by over three centuries than the laws of Moses has disposed of some untenable theories of the critics and given rise to others. For instance, the old critical view that detailed codes of law like those recorded in the Pentateuch are anachronistic for such an early period has been exploded by the discovery of Hammurabi's laws and much earlier codes in Mesopotamia.

A discovery of this sort illustrates how archaeology purges out radical critical views, which used to place the origin of many of the laws ascribed to Moses to much later times, such as the 9th, 8th, and 7th centuries B.C., or even later. These erroneous theories had to be drastically revised or entirely rejected. On the other hand, the discovery of the early extrabiblical legal material has led many to adopt an equally faulty view that Hebrew legislation is merely a selection and adaptation of Babylonian law. The only position that is valid as the two bodies of legal material are studied is that the Mosaic code is neither borrowed from, nor dependent upon, the Babylonian. It is divinely given, as it claims to be, and unique in those features that met Israel's peculiar need as an elect, theocratic nation.

The resemblances between the ***Mosaic laws*** and the ***Code of Hammurabi*** are clearly due to similarity of antecedents and general intellectual and cultural heritage. It is natural that in codes dealing with peoples in somewhat similar conditions, related racially and culturally, there should be some likeness in the incidents leading to litigation and likewise in the penalties imposed for infringement of common statutes. A striking difference, however, is obtained. These clearly demonstrate that there is no direct borrowing and that the Mosaic laws, although later by three centuries, are in no sense dependent upon the Babylonian.

The biblical law of divorce (Deut. 24:1), for instance, permits the man to put away his wife but does not extend the same right to the wife, as does the Babylonian code. Again the so-called ***Lex Talionis*** is a primitive Semitic law and would be expected to be reflected in various Semitic legal codes. Mosaic injunctions (Ex. 21:23–25; Deut. 19:21) state precisely the same principle of retaliation upon which a number of Hammurabi's laws are based, namely "life for life, eye for eye, tooth for tooth, hand for hand, foot for foot, burning for burning, wound for wound, stripe for stripe."

The Mosaic and Hammurabi codes are ***different in content.*** The Hebrew code contains many purely religious injunctions and ritual regulations. The Code of Hammurabi, on the other hand, is civil. However, the priestly laws of Leviticus contain many points of similarity with priestly ritual and practice in western Asia, whether in Canaan or Phoenicia or Mesopotamia. But this in no sense casts doubt on the fact that Israel's religious practices as recorded in the Pentateuch are divinely given and uniquely invested with significance to fit a nation divinely called to serve the one God. In some cases similar cultic practice among surrounding peoples was divinely given to Israel. But at the same time it was invested with a special significance for the worship of the Lord.

The two codes, of course, are ***different in their origin.*** The Babylonian laws are alleged to have been received by Hammurabi from the sun god Shamash. Moses received his laws directly from the Lord. Hammurabi, despite his reported reception from Shamash, takes credit for them in both the prologue and epilogue of the code. He, not Shamash, established order and

Elephantine Island seen from across the Nile. *Matson Photo Service*

equity throughout the land. Moses, in contrast, is only an instrument. The legislation is "Thus says the LORD."

The two codes govern a ***different type of society.*** Hammurabi's laws are fitted to the irrigation culture and highly commercialized urban society of Mesopotamia. The Mosaic injunctions, on the other hand, suit a simple, agricultural, pastoral people of a dry land like Palestine much less advanced in social and commercial development, but keenly conscious of their divine calling in all phases of their living.

The two codes ***differ in their morality.*** From the ethical and spiritual standpoint the Mosaic legislation, as would be expected, offers a considerable advance over the Babylonian code. Hammurabi's laws, for example, enumerate at least ten varieties of bodily mutilation prescribed for various offenses. If a doctor performs an operation that is unsuccessful, his hand is to be cut off. In the Mosaic legislation only one instance of mutilation occurs where a wife's hand is to be severed (Deut. 25:11, 12). Also in the Hebrew laws a greater value is set upon human life. A stricter regard for the honor of womanhood is seen, and more humane treatment of slaves is enjoined. In addition, the Babylonian code has nothing in it corresponding to that twofold golden thread running through the Mosaic legislation, namely, love to God and love to one's neighbor (Matt. 22:37–40).

The Israelite Torah and the Babylonian code may be contrasted as follows: In the Babylonian code there is no control of lust, no limitation of selfishness. The postulate of charity cannot be found. The religious motif is absent, which recognizes sin as the destruction of the people because it is in opposition to the fear of God. In the Hammurabi code every trace of religious thought is absent. Behind the Israelite laws stands the ruling will of a holy God. The laws are stamped throughout with a divine character.

2. The Elephantine Papyri—Light on the Ezra-Nehemiah Era

Discovered in 1903 on the island of Elephantine at the First Cataract of the Nile in Egypt, these important documents give an interesting glimpse of one of the outlying regions of the Persian Empire in the latter part of the 5th century B.C. ***The Elephantine Papyri*** come from a Jewish military colony which was settled at that place. Inscribed in Aramaic, the language of diplomacy and trade throughout western Asia in the Persian period, and which was gradually replacing Hebrew as the everyday tongue of the Jewish people, the contents are varied, ranging from the copy of the Behistun Inscription of Darius to such a document as a Jewish marriage contract. The letters tell us about the sacking of a Jewish temple at Elephantine in an anti-Jewish persecution about 411 B.C. The Jews at this far-off colony worshiped the Lord whom they referred to by the name of Yahu.

Other letters from Elephantine which have in

The city ruins at Ur. *Matson Photo Service*

The Ziggurat at Ur. *Matson Photo Service*

recent years become known and have been published by the Brooklyn Museum demonstrate that the temple was rebuilt after its destruction. They contain mention of Yahu as "the god who dwells in Yeb, the fortress." Compare Psalm 31:3. These new papyri demonstrate that Egypt was still under the authority of Persia in the first years of Artaxerxes II (404–359 B.C.).

The Elephantine Papyri therefore illuminate the general background of the period of Ezra-Nehemiah and the earlier Persian period. They shed important light on the life of the Jewish dispersion in a remote frontier place such as Elephantine in Egypt. They also are invaluable in giving the scholar a knowledge of the Aramaic language of that period, and many of the customs and names that appear in the Bible are illustrated by these important literary finds.

3. The Hittite Monuments from Boghaz-Keui—Mementos of an Imperial People

In 1906 Professor Hugo Winkler of Berlin began excavations at Boghaz-Keui, a site which lies 90 miles east of Ankara in the great bend of the Halys River in Asia Minor. It was discovered that this was an ancient Hittite capital. Numerous clay tablets were dug up written in texts containing six different languages. A large number of these were inscribed in the cuneiform characters of the Hittite language. Eventually deciphered through the labors of three men and particularly of the Czech scholar Friedrich Hrozny, this language proved to be the key to a great deal of background of interest to the biblical student.

Before the Boghaz-Keui tablets revealed the Hittites to be an ancient people, the biblical references to them used to be regarded in critical circles as historically worthless. In the five books of Moses, references to the Hittites as inhabiting the land of Canaan and as among those whom the Israelites drove out occur in several places (Ex. 33:2; Deut. 7:1; 20:17; Josh. 3:10; 24:11). In the various lists the order varies, and there is not an inkling that one reference might be the name of a powerful imperial people and the other a small local tribe. Less than a century ago the "Hittites" meant little more to the reader of the Bible than the "Hivite" or the "Perizzite" still does.

It was commonly known from the biblical record that when Abraham settled in Hebron he had Hittites as neighbors. It was everyday knowledge that one of David's eminent soldiers was Uriah, a Hittite. But who would have expected that "Hittites" were more prominent than "Gadites" or "Beerothites"?

Now it is known that two great periods of Hittite power are to be noted. The first goes back to c. 1800 B.C., and the second is dated from c. 1400–1200 B.C. In this latter period of Hittite supremacy the powerful rulers reigned at Boghaz-Keui. One of these was named Subbiluliuma. This great conqueror extended his empire to the confines of Syria-Palestine. The great Rameses II of Egypt, in the famous battle of Kadesh, collided with Hittite power. A Hittite treaty of peace with the Pharaoh in the 21st year of the latter's reign was confirmed by a royal marriage.

About 1200 B.C. the great Hittite Empire collapsed, and the Hittite city of Boghaz-Keui fell. However, important centers of Hittite power remained at Carchemish, Sengirli, Hamath, and other places in north Syria. As a result of the excavation and decipherment of various Hittite monuments, the whole context of the ancient biblical world has been illuminated.

Because of this increased background knowledge, such allusions as those to the "kings of the Hittites" (1 Kin. 10:29; 2 Chr. 1:17) are much better understood. Also Ezekiel's reference to unfaithful Jerusalem as having an Amorite for a father and a Hittite for a mother (Ezek. 16:45) are now comprehensible. The manner in which archaeology has brought to light the ancient Hittites furnishes a good example of the way this important science is expanding biblical horizons.

4. The City of Ur—Abraham's Home

An important metropolis of the ancient world, Ur was located on the Euphrates River in lower Mesopotamia, present-day Iraq. Several centuries before Abraham lived there as a boy and grew up there as a young man, this place was a very important city under the 2nd and 3rd dynasties of Ur, an important line of kings. But the glory of the city was suddenly destroyed in the period from c. 1960–1830 B.C. Foreigners stormed down from the surrounding hills and took the reigning king, Ibi-Sin, a captive and reduced the capital ***city of Ur*** to ruins. So complete was the eclipse of the city that it lay buried in oblivion for centuries until, like Nineveh, it was resurrected in modern times by the work of archaeologists.

So thoroughly was the ancient city blotted out that when it was referred to in Genesis 11:28–31 and 15:7 as Abraham's ancestral home and the place from which he started on his trek to Palestine, some scribe later had to append the descriptive phrase ***"of the Chaldeans"*** to the name of the city to give later readers some idea of where it had been located.

The long-lost and buried city was brought to the light of modern study by the work of numerous archaeologists, particularly by the work of Sir Leonard Woolley (1922–1934). Until the year 1854, the site of the ancient city was completely unknown. The Arabs used to call the location ***Al-muqayyer, "Mount of bitumen."*** It was a forbidding place in a climate of terrific heat and surrounded by intense desolation. In 1854, J. E. Taylor, an English archaeologist, assisted by others, made some preliminary excavations. Some cylinders turned up inscribed in cuneiform characters declaring that King Nabonidus of Babylon (556–539 B.C.) had restored the famous ziggurat of Ur-Nammu.

Later explorations were made by Campbell Thompson in 1918. H. R. Hall in 1918 continued other excavations, but it was left for the pivotal work of Sir Leonard Woolley, undertaken in 1922 as a joint expedition of the British Museum, the University of Pennsylvania, and the University Museum, to give a complete history and description of the city. The expedition completed twelve very successful archaeological campaigns, and by 1934 the long-lost and buried city of Ur, vanished from the pages of history, had become one of the best-known sites in all the ancient Near East.

Abraham's Native Town. Abraham lived in the city of Ur at the height of its splendor under the 3rd dynasty of kings. This is indicated if we follow the chronology of the Masoretic text of the Hebrew Bible. According to this system of reckoning, Abraham was born c. 2161 B.C. and entered Canaan c. 2086 B.C. Under this time arrangement, the patriarch left the city when it was near the acme of its prosperity. He entered Canaan precisely when Ur reached the pinnacle of its power, for the 3rd dynasty of kings (c. 2070–1969 B.C.) lifted the city to great prominence.

The first king was Ur-Nammu. This monarch had the title of "King of Sumer and Akkad." He built a splendid temple tower or ziggurat at this site. Today this is still preserved as the best monument of its type in all the flat alluvial territory of Lower Mesopotamia, the basin of Tigris-Euphrates rivers. It was this structure that Nabonidus, the last of the Babylonian kings, restored in the 6th century B.C.

In the famous ***monument of Ur-Nammu*** there is extant a contemporary record of the construction of the ziggurat at Ur. This stele is a slab of white limestone measuring 5 feet across and 10 feet in height. At the top of the monument the king is standing in an attitude of prayer. An account of the building of the monument is given, and scenes are inscribed denoting the actual construction. In the days of Ur-Nammu other buildings were built around the ziggurat, and the entire sacred area was dedicated to Nannar, the moon god (patron deity of the city) and his consort, whose name was Nin-Gal.

A king by the name of Dungi succeeded Ur-Nammu, whom Nabonidus declared completed the ziggurat. Dungi was a great ruler who built a magnificent mortuary temple and tomb for himself. His son Bur-Sin succeeded him. He was followed on the throne at Ur by Gimil-Sin and then by Ibi-Sin.

Ur and Abraham. When Abraham lived in the city before he left for Haran and Canaan, Ur was a center of religion and industry. The city was wholly given over to the worship of the moon god cult. The Babylonians were devotees of many deities. But at Ur the moon god Sin was supreme.

Sir Leonard Woolley's lengthy excavations in twelve highly rewarding campaigns have revealed the splendor and the size of the city and also have given details of the *temenos* or the religious section of the city. In other words, Abraham was surrounded on all sides by idolatry. This we have recorded in the Bible in Joshua 24:2. "Your fathers, *including* Terah, the father of Abraham and the father of Nahor, dwelt on the other side of the River in old times; and they served other gods."

The moon god Sin was given such epithets as "the exalted lord" and "the beautiful lord who shines in the heavens." The immense temple tower, built like a mountain with various stages, contained the holy chamber of Nannar on its uppermost level. Here in this lofty Babylonian temple mystic ritual in honor of the deity was conducted. In front of the immense ziggurat and on the lower level was an open court, a kind of holy market where the people brought their gifts and paid their taxes to the king, who was also their landlord. Accordingly, the city was a kind of theocracy centered in the moon deity.

The sacred area was called the *temenos.* In it were located other sacred buildings and shrines, including houses for the priests and priestesses of Nannar. To the west the river Euphrates flowed near the city walls, and there were canals running around and through the city. In Abraham's day instead of being a hot, forbidding, desertlike region, Ur was a flourishing and beautiful city because of irrigation and civilization. It was surrounded by fertile farms and a busy populace engaged in agriculture and in woolen and textile industries. All of this commerce was centered in religion.

The houses of Ur have been excavated and examined. It is conceivable that Abraham grew up as a lad in one of these residences. There is presumptive evidence that Terah's father worshiped the moon god and was a devotee of Nannar and Nin-Gal. In one of the dwellings, there is a small domestic chapel with altar niche and family burial vault. It is very likely that Terah worshiped at such an altar.

It is out of this polluted atmosphere of polytheism that God's sovereign grace called Abraham to begin a new line that was to be separated from idolatry and through which Messiah was to come, who would deliver the world from sin and idolatry.

The City Before the Time of Abraham. Ur existed as a brilliant city many hundreds of years before Abraham appeared on the scene. The lower regions of the Tigris-Euphrates basin with its flat land and very fertile soil have been the seat of many ancient empires—Sumer, Babylonia, Assyria, and Chaldea. The first of these civilizations was Sumer, one of the oldest civilized countries in the world. Wrapped in obscurity is the story of the beginnings of Sumer. At least by 3500 B.C. the Sumerians, that is the natives of the flat, alluvial lower courses of the Tigris-Euphrates plain, were advancing in civilization.

The Euphrates River. *Matson Photo Service*

In the next thousand years the ***Sumerian Empire*** diffused culture and civilization over most of western Asia. The extreme southern part of Sumer was called the land of Shinar. It was a flat, mud plain, immensely rich, formed by the sediment of the Tigris-Euphrates River. As these mighty streams flowed into the lower part of the Fertile Crescent, their current slackened, and they deposited huge amounts of a rich, sandy loam and formed a region which today is called Iraq, which is about as large as New Jersey.

With a network of canals running through this rich territory, this region blossomed like a rose. More than 150 years ago, travelers began to wonder about the strange mounds or hillocks of earth which dotted this flat region. What could they possibly be? Now and then antiquarian bits of carved marble or other remnants of bygone civilizations were exposed by the weather. Archaeologists began to dig beneath the truncated hillocks, and it was discovered that they were long-lost and buried cities.

One of these mounds proved to be the city of Ur of biblical fame. From these regions many tablets have been resurrected with cuneiform or wedge-shaped writing on them. These tablets were made of soft mud from the riverbank and carefully inscribed with a flat pen and set out in the sun to dry, or put in the fire to bake in a more firm form. And so, under these truncated mounds were not only buried artifacts and remnants of ancient civilizations but, what is most arresting, there are vast quantities of practically indestructible materials, all inscribed on clay tablets. These have been the basis of resurrecting the history and the civilization of Bible lands in Lower Mesopotamia in the land of Sumer.

The First Dynasty of Ur. In an ancient list of kings called the Sumerian King List in ***The Oxford Edition of Cuneiform Texts II,*** 1923, by F. Langdon, an interesting story is told of the early rulers of Sumer. Among the line of kings who reigned at Kish, Uruk (biblical Erech, Gen. 10:10), Awan, Adap, Mari, and Akshak are listed several dynasties who ruled at Ur. The first kings at Ur witnessed the culminating phase of the early dynastic period in Mesopotamia (c. 2800–2360 B.C.).

The King List goes on to say, "Uruk was smitten with weapons. Its kingship was carried to Ur. Mes-Anne-pada became king and ruled 80 years. A-Anne-pada, a son of Mes-Anne-pada, reigned . . . years. Meskiag-Nanna, a son of Mes-Anne-pada became king and reigned 36 years. Elulu reigned 25 years. Balulu reigned 36 years. Four kings reigned 177 years. Ur was smitten with weapons."

This line of kings was very powerful and lifted the city-state, since Ur was more than a city, to a high level of culture. This is demonstrated in the discoveries of the royal tombs by Sir Leonard Woolley, dating from c. 2500 B.C. These consisted of rooms and vaults built of brick and stone. Among one of the most interesting finds was the tomb of an important lady named ***Shubad of Ur.*** Her name is identified by an inscribed cylinder of lapis lazuli. Near her hand was a gold cup. Her lovely artistic headdress contained 9 yards of gold band.

Another exquisite find was the so-called ***"Standard of Ur."*** This was a wooden panel, 22 inches long by 9 inches wide, skillfully inlaid with mosaic work on both sides depicting scenes of war and peace. In the war panel the king is seen receiving captives. In another the phalanx of the royal army advances. Scenes of fighting with chariots and javelins are depicted. The panel of peace presents a royal family feast. Musicians entertain while servants wait in the banquet hall and bring in spoils captured from the enemy.

Certainly the archaeological resurrection of Abraham's ancient city of Ur has greatly illuminated the Bible references to the patriarch and given a much wider view of the historical horizons c. 2000 B.C. The early civilization of the Tigris-Euphrates Valley is becoming better known year after year. Bible dictionaries, encyclopedias, commentaries, and biblical works of every description are highly indebted to the restless and productive spade of the archaeologist. Certainly God has blessed, enabling scholars in our day to study these monuments and other remains of antiquity. The result is greater appreciation of the Bible on the human plane.

It must always be remembered that the Word of God is not only divine but human. It is God's Book for humankind. On the human side, God has so ordained that the horizons of biblical knowledge may be expanded and increased that we may on the spiritual plane better comprehend the Word of God. How unfortunate it is when the spiritual is divorced from the historical and archaeological, or vice versa, when the historical and archaeological are divorced from the spiritual. The two work hand in hand and help one another. Happy is the student of the Bible who will combine both of these disciplines in a better understanding of the Word of God.

5. The Religious Texts from Ras Shamra (Ugarit)—Canaanite Cults Exposed

One of the most important discoveries of the 20th century was the recovery of hundreds of clay tablets which have been housed in a library situated between two great temples, one dedicated to Baal and another dedicated to Dagon, in the city of ***Ugarit***—modern ***Ras Shamra*** in north Syria. These clay tablets date from the 15th to early 14th centuries B.C. They are inscribed in the earliest known alphabet written in wedge-shaped signs. Professor H. Bower of the University of Halle recognized this new writing as Semitic. Numbers of scholars such as E. Dhorme and Charles Virol-leaud began working on the decipherment of this new Semitic language.

The tablets turned out to be religious and cultic in nature and inscribed in a dialect that was closely akin to biblical Hebrew and Phoenician. Although Semitic in form, this new writing displayed evidences of Akkadian influence, since Mesopotamians wrote on clay tablets with wedge-shaped characters from left to right. First intimations of the archaeological importance of the ancient city of Ugarit, which was unknown until 1928, came in the spring of that year when a Syrian peasant plowing in his field a little north of present-day Minet el-Beida suddenly came across some antiquities. On April 2, 1929, work began at Minet el-Beida under the direction of Claude F. Schaffer. After a month's work he changed to the nearby tell of Ras Shamra. Only a few days' work demonstrated the importance of the new location. On May 20th the first tablets were uncovered. Schaffer continued excavations from 1929 to 1937. Between 1929 and 1933, the bulk of significant religious texts were recovered in the royal library in the area. Many of these were inscribed in an early Canaanite dialect, roughly contemporary with the Mosaic age.

The City of Ugarit. This flourishing second-millennium city, which had been known by scholars from Egyptian inscriptions from the ***Tell el-Amarna Letters*** and ***Hittite documents,*** was located on the north Syrian coast opposite the island of Cyprus, about 8 miles north of Latakia and 50 miles southwest of Antioch. It was situated on a bay and had a port which could be used by sea-going trade ships. It was a harbor town known in Greek times as Leukos Limen, the white harbor. It is now called ***Ras Shamra, "hill of fennel,"*** because fennel grows there.

The hill which comprises the ruin of the ancient city has the form of a trapezium with the long side about 670 yards north and south and the longer diagonal about 1,100 yards. The hill is about 22 yards high. The site was located on the important trade route along the coast from Egypt to Asia Minor, which was connected by a road with Aleppo, Mari on the Euphrates, and Babylon. The sea route from Ugarit to Alashiya—that is, Cyprus—was a short one.

Very early, Ugarit struck up a brisk trade with the Aegean Islands. It became an important harbor. One of the main exported articles was copper, which was used in the production of bronze. Copper was imported from Asia Minor and Cyprus. Bronze was produced in Ugarit. Being a Phoenician town, Ugarit, like its sister cities, delivered timber to Egypt. Not only cedars from the interior were exported but other kinds of wood as well. There were also purple dye factories; great heaps of murex shells indicate this. These shells, abundantly found along the east Mediterranean coast, produced a famous dye of antiquity.

Literary Importance of the Texts. After preliminary work by many scholars, Cyrus Gordon worked out a **Ugaritic Grammar** and later put out an edition of the texts called **Ugaritic Literature.** The decipherment of the texts showed the important parallels between Ugaritic and Hebrew literary style and vocabulary. By 1936 H. L. Ginsberg had made some far-reaching observations with regard to common structural elements. Ginsberg's study showed that Canaanite poetry, like Hebrew, was basically accentual, that is, consisted of numbers of feet, each of which was accented. A good example of the survival of Canaanite literary elements in Hebrew religious literature is the following tricolon (unit of three lines) from the ***Baal Epic of Ras Shamra:***

> **"Behold, thine enemies, O Baal;**
> **Behold, thine enemies shalt thou crush;**
> **Behold, thou shalt smite thy foes."**

In ***Psalm 92:9*** there is a striking parallel to this.

> **"For behold, Your enemies, O Lord,**
> **For behold, Your enemies shall perish;**
> **All the workers of iniquity shall be scattered."**

The following tricolon occurs frequently in the ***Aqhat Epic:***

> **"Do thou ask for life, O lad Aqhat;**
> **Do thou ask for life, I'll grant it thee,**
> **Eternal life, and I'll accord it thee."**

A similar literary device is found in the ***Song of Deborah*** (Judg. 5:30).

> **"For Sisera, plunder of dyed garments,**
> **Plunder of garments embroidered and dyed,**
> **Two pieces of dyed embroidery for the neck of the looter?"**

Background material such as this is an invaluable aid in the study of Hebrew poetry and the general literary qualities of style and vocabulary in Old Testament Hebrew. Since the Ugaritic language is very closely connected with biblical Hebrew, much light has been shed upon Hebrew lexicography. Any recent lexicon of Hebrew must take into consideration the vocabulary used at Ugarit. Future Hebrew dictionaries will include many words hitherto misunderstood or only partially known.

For example, the word *beth-heber* (Prov. 21:9; 25:24) hitherto rendered "house" has been shown from Ugaritic and Assyrian to mean specifically "a storehouse." These verses must then be rendered "*It is* better to dwell in a corner of the housetop, than with a brawling woman and in a storehouse." It is of interest to note that the Egyptian proverbs of Amenemope, which have many parallels to the biblical Book of Proverbs, employ a word for "storehouse" in exactly the same sense.

Religious Significance of the Ugaritic Inscriptions. By far the most important contribution of the religious texts from Ras Shamra (Ugarit) is in giving the Bible student background material for the study of Old Testament religions. The epics set forth very clearly the

Canaanite pantheon. We now know that this pantheon of the Canaanites was headed up by the god El, the supreme Canaanite deity. This is also a name by which God is known in the Old Testament (cf. Gen. 33:20). This name, "El," often occurs in Old Testament poetry (Ps. 18:31, 32; Job 8:3). It occurs frequently also in prose in compound names, for example, El Elyon, the God Most High (Gen. 14:18); El Shaddai, Almighty God (Gen. 17:1); El Hai, the living God (Josh. 3:10). This, however, does not mean any connection, of course, with Canaanite mythology. El is simply the common Semitic word for God. In Ugaritic, El was a bloody, lustful tyrant. The description of him, as well as of other Canaanite gods, fully substantiates the testimony of the Old Testament with regard to the degeneracy and polluting influence of Canaanite religion.

Baal was the son of El. He was the active king of the gods in the Canaanite pantheon and dominated the entire list of gods. He was the deity of the storm and the rain. Thunder was thought to be the reverberation of his voice in the heavens. At Ras Shamra a stele was discovered depicting Baal holding a stylized thunderbolt. Three of the Ugaritic poems concern Baal. Baalism, the worship of this god, was one of the most debilitating and destructive influences which threatened the Hebrews in Palestine and against which they had to be continually on guard.

As the giver of rain and all fertility, Baal figures very prominently in Canaanite mythology. He struggles with Mot, the god of death and the god of drought. In the fight Baal is slain. As a consequence, the seasonal drought occurs from June to late October. Then Anath, sister and lover of Baal, goes out in search of him, discovers his body, and slays his enemy, Mot. Baal is then brought back to life, thus ensuring the revival of vegetation for a seven-year period. The great Baal Epic of Ugarit finds in this representation a central theme.

The Phoenicians at Ugarit not only had gods who were polluted and immoral but also goddesses. Three of these who are prominent are Anath, Astarte, and Asherah. They are patronesses of war and sex. Their character, like that of El and Baal, bears out the pollution and damaging effects of Canaanite religion, since they portray war in its aspect of violence and murder and sex mainly in its lustful connotation of indulgence.

The new knowledge of Canaanite religion aids the Bible student correctly to evaluate the testimony of the Old Testament to the Canaanites. Higher criticism has impugned the morality of the Old Testament writers in such episodes as the divine command to exterminate these cults. Examples are the extermination of the people of Jericho, Saul's extermination of the Amalekites, and the driving out of the Canaanites in general. All of these examples appear in a different view when adjudged in the light of the vileness of Canaanite religion. In Genesis 15:16 the Lord declares, "the iniquity of the Amorites" was not yet "full" in Abraham's day. But archaeology shows Canaanite religious immorality was complete in Joshua's day, 400 years later, and had to be destroyed.

Now, as a result of the Ras Shamra literature, the nature of Canaanite religion comes before the scholar in its real light. No longer do we have to rely on the witness of early church fathers such as Eusebius, who quotes an earlier authority, or Philo of Byblos, who in turn goes back to a much earlier authority named Sanchuniathon. No longer must we doubt the veracity of this extrabiblical witness or doubt the authenticity of the Old Testament witness. Now, as a result of archaeology, an independent witness to the effete and degenerate nature of Canaanite cults is available. No longer can critics isolate the Old Testament and accuse it of a low morality in ordering the extermination of the Canaanites. The truth is, archaeology points out that the people had become so immoral, so honeycombed with the sins of violence and sexual immorality, that had Joshua and the children of Israel not appeared to take over the land, these people would have perished under the weight of their own iniquity.

"Like priest, like people" is an old adage. Never in all the annals of history was there such a mixture of violence and lust as was combined and made an intricate part of Canaanite cults. So the Scriptures stand as a warning, corroborated by archaeology, of the judgment of God falling upon apostate and sinful religionism. Archaeology helps us to see this in an entirely different light in regard to the Canaanites.

This is especially true when we consider the low moral tone of Canaanite goddesses and gods. El was a brutal and lustful tyrant who was guilty of incest and murder. Baal also was guilty of enormous crimes. How could people worship such deities and not themselves be polluted? No wonder the warning of God was issued again and again for separation from Baalism. No wonder the history of Baal contamination of Israel is a long story of woe and suffering, as God's people were trapped into complicity with Phoenician cults.

The era of Ahab and Jezebel, and the importation of Canaanite fertility cults and intermarriage with the Canaanites, show the devastating effect of such disobedience to the plain warning of God. Exterminating the Canaanites in the time of Joshua was not a question of destroying innocent people. It was a question of destroying or being destroyed, separating or being contaminated, being quarantined from the plague or having the plague destroy everyone.

Later Excavations at Ugarit. During World War II excavations at Ras Shamra were discontinued. They were resumed in 1948 and have been going on regularly. Work under the direction of C. F. Schaffer has been centered upon uncovering the great palace. The most important discoveries in connection with this structure were the royal archives. These archives, discovered in the palace, were of a historical nature in contrast to the mythological ritual texts of the early years, 1929–1937. The archives in the west wing of the building contained administrative documents to a large degree relating to the royal estates. Those in the east wing had documents relating to the capital city. Those in the central archive were mainly legal finds. Almost all documents were inscribed in the common language of these centuries, namely Akkadian. A few were written in Hurrian and Ugaritic. The names of twelve Ugaritic kings were found in the documents which date from the 18th to the 13th centuries B.C. The seals of the royal acts are remarkable as they all are identical in design at the top, without regard to the name of the reigning king. The motif is well known from Babylonian glyptic art and shows homage being paid to the deified king.

Numbers of fine objects have been recovered from the palace, especially pieces from the king's bedroom. Especially noteworthy was the large ivory foot panel of the royal bedstead, perhaps the largest single piece of ivory carving yet recovered in the Near East. Another remarkable piece found in the campaign of 1952–1953 is the ancient Ugaritic alphabet of thirty letters. This piece is now housed in the National Museum at Damascus.

6. The Nuzi Tablets and the Biblical Horites

From this city east of ancient Asshur and a short distance west of Arrapkha, which flourished in the middle centuries of the 2nd millennium B.C., have come several thousand cuneiform texts. These texts have proved of immense value, illustrating the rise of the Hurrians and patriarchal customs. The present site of Nuzi is Yoghlan-Tepe. It is a mound 150 miles north of Baghdad near the foothills of southern Khurdistan. Nuzi was excavated in 1925–1931 by the American School of Oriental Research in Baghdad and Harvard University. The name "Nuzi" was used during its occupation by the Hurrians.

Before the time of the Hurrian settlement the site of Nuzi was occupied by a different ethnic group, called the Subarians. In this older period, the city bore the name of Gasur, and its earliest occupation goes back to prehistoric times. But the vital interest in the town stems from its occupation by the Hurrians and the cuneiform texts, which have been excavated from it and from nearby Arrapkha, modern Kirkuk, some 9 miles to the east.

The Nuzi Tablets and the Hurrians. Modern archaeology has not only resurrected the ancient Hittites, who were for centuries practically unknown except for sporadic references on the pages of the Bible, but also the enigmatic Horites. In the books of the Pentateuch there are numbers of references to a perplexing people called Horites. These people were defeated by Chedorlaomer and the invading Mesopotamian army (Gen. 14:6). They were governed by chiefs (Gen. 36:20–30). They are said to have been destroyed by Esau's descendants (Deut. 2:12, 22).

This unknown people used to be thought of as a very local, restricted group of cave dwellers. The name "Horite" was thought to be derived from the Hebrew *hor*, "hole" or "cave." Other than this etymological description the Horites remained completely obscure, not appearing outside the Pentateuch or in extrabiblical literature. Within the last 35 years, however, archaeology has performed a miracle in resurrecting the ancient Hurrians, the biblical Horites. They are known not to be a local, restricted group but to be a prominent people who took a preeminent place on the stage of ancient history. It is now known that they not only existed but played a far-reaching role in ancient Near Eastern cultural history. As a result of the discovery of the Hurrians, the popular etymology which connects them with "cave dwellers" has had to be abandoned.

The Hurrians or Horites were non-Semitic peoples who, before the beginning of the 2nd millennium B.C., migrated into northeastern Mesopotamia. Their homeland was in the region south of the Caucasus. They appear first upon the horizon of history c. 2400 B.C. in the Zagros Mountains east of the Tigris River. In the period c. 2000–1400 B.C., the Hurrians were very common and widespread in Upper Mesopotamia.

The Nuzi Tablets and the Patriarchs. The main interest of the Nuzi Tablets lies in the illumination of patriarchal times and customs. In the patriarchal narratives, many local practices have been quite obscure to the modern reader. Numerous clay tablets from Nuzi and nearby Arrapkha have in many cases illuminated these customs, so that now we see them as they existed in the general historical background of the time. Although the Nuzi Tablets are to be dated in the 15th and 14th centuries B.C., sometime after the patriarchal period (c. 2000–1800 B.C.), nevertheless, they illustrate the times of the patriarchs. The reason is that when the patriarchs came out of Ur, they sojourned in Haran and mingled in west Hurrian society. But the same customs prevailed by extension among the west Hurrians as among the east Hurrians at Nuzi and Arrapkha. Hence, the results obtained at Nuzi are valid by extension for the west Hurrians, as well as for a period considerably later than the patriarchs.

In Genesis 15:2 Abraham laments his childless condition and the fact that his servant Eliezer was to be his heir. In the light of this situation, God assures the patriarch that he is to have a son of his own to inherit his property. The Nuzi Tablets explain this difficult matter. They tell how a trusted servant, an apparent outsider, could be heir. At ancient Nuzi, it was customary in Hurrian society for a couple who did not have a child to adopt a son to take care of his foster parents as long as they lived, take over when they died, and then in return for his filial duty to become their heir. But it is important to note that if a natural son was born, this agreement was nullified, at least in part, and the natural son became heir. Eliezer was plainly Abraham's adopted son. But the miraculous birth of Isaac, as the promised posterity, altered Eliezer's status as heir.

At Nuzi a marriage contract occasionally included the statement that a given slave girl is presented outright to a new bride, exactly as in the marriage of Leah (Gen. 29:24) and Rachel (29:29). Other marriage provisions specify that a wife of the upper classes who was childless was to furnish her husband with a slave girl as a concubine. In such a case, however, the wife was entitled to treat the concubine's offspring as her own. This last provision illuminates the difficult statement in Genesis 16:2 with its punning: "I shall obtain children by her," which means "I may be built up through her." It is interesting to note that the related law of Hammurabi, paragraph 144, offers no complete parallel. There the wife is a priestess and is not entitled to claim the children of the concubine for herself.

It is thus seen that in Nuzian law and society in which the patriarchs moved for a time, marriage was regarded primarily for bearing children and not mainly for companionship. In one way or another, it was considered necessary for the family to procreate. After Isaac's birth, Abraham's reluctance to comply with Sarah's demand that Hagar's child be driven out is illustrated by local practice at Nuzi. In the event the slave wife should have a son, that son must not be expelled. In Abraham's case, only a divine dispensation overruled human law and made the patriarch willing to comply.

Cases involving rights of the firstborn occurring in Genesis are also illustrated. In the Bible Esau sells his birthright to Jacob. In the Nuzi Tablets one brother sells a grove which he has inherited for three sheep. Evidently this in value is quite comparable to the savory food for which Esau sold his right.

In Hurrian society birthright was not so much the matter of being the firstborn as of paternal decree. Such decrees were binding above all others when handed down in the form of a deathbed declaration introduced by the following formula: "Behold now, I am old." This situation helps to illuminate Genesis 27, the chapter that tells of Jacob stealing the family blessing.

The obscure ***teraphim*** are also explained in Nuzian law. We know that the teraphim were small household deities. Possession of them implied headship of family. In the case of a married daughter, they assured her husband the right to her father's property. Laban had sons of his own when Jacob left for Canaan. They alone had the right to their father's gods. The theft of these important household idols by Rachel was a notorious offense (Gen. 31:19, 30, 35). She aimed at nothing less than to preserve for her husband the chief title to Laban's estate.

The texts from Arrapkha and Nuzi have at last supplied details for explaining these difficult customs. In special circumstances the property could pass to a daughter's husband, but only if the father had handed over his household gods to his son-in-law as a formal token that the arrangement had proper sanction.

Another custom illuminated is that found in Genesis 12:10–20; 20:2–6; 26:1–11, where the wife of a patriarch is introduced as his sister with no apparent worthy reason. The texts from Nuzi, however, show that among the Hurrians marriage bonds were most solemn, and the wife had legally, although not necessarily through ties of blood, the simultaneous status of sister, so that the term "sister" and "wife" could be interchangeable in an official use under certain circumstances. Thus, in resorting to the wife-sister relationship, both Abraham and Isaac were availing themselves of the strongest safeguards the law, as it existed then, could afford them.

Critical Value. Discoveries such as those at Nuzi and Arrapkha are forcing higher critics to abandon many radical and untenable theories. For example, not long ago it was customary for critics to view the patriarchal stories as retrojections from a much later period and not as authentic stories from the Mosaic age, namely the 15th century B.C. But now the question rises,

How could such authentic local color be retrojected from a later age? The Nuzi Letters have done a great service to students of early Bible history in not only attesting the influence of social customs in the patriarchal age and in the same portion of Mesopotamia from which the patriarchs come, but also have demonstrated these narratives are authentic to their time. Such discoveries add greatly to our historical background and enable us in our modern day to reveal them in their genuine local color and historical setting.

7. The Mari Letters—Light on the World of the Patriarchs

One of the most historically and archaeologically rewarding sites that has been discovered in Mesopotamia and Bible lands is the city of ***Mari,*** modern Tell el-Hariri on the Middle Euphrates, about 7 miles northwest of Abu-Kemal, a small town on the Syrian side of the Syro-Iraq frontier. The ancient city owed its importance to being a focal point on caravan routes crossing the Syrian desert and linking the city with Syria and the Mediterranean coast and with the civilizations of Assyria and Babylonia. This site was further identified by William Foxwell Albright in 1932.

Mari began to be excavated in 1933 by Andre Parrot under the auspices of the Musee du Louvre. The results were the digging up of an ancient imperial city of great importance and splendor. World War II interrupted excavations in 1939, after six highly successful campaigns had taken place. In 1951 this work was resumed. After four further campaigns it was broken off in 1956, as a result of the trouble over the Suez Canal.

Among the most important discoveries at Mari was the great ***temple of Ishtar,*** for the Babylonian goddess of propagation, and a temple tower or ziggurat. The temple itself had courts of the Sumerian type, columns, and a cella. The ziggurat or temple tower was similar to that at Ur and other Mesopotamian sites. Statuettes were uncovered to illustrate the popularity of the Ishtar fertility cult. One of the palace murals depicts the fact that the ruling monarch at Mari was believed to have received his staff and ring, the emblems of his authority, from Ishtar.

Another important discovery at Mari was the ***royal palace.*** A sprawling structure contemporary with the 1st dynasty of Babylon, it was built in the center of the mound and contained almost 300 rooms. The throne room furnished some rare specimens of well-preserved

The excavated ruins of the capital city of Babylon. *D. J. Wiseman*

wall paintings. This huge building with its beautifully colored mural paintings, its royal apartments, administrative offices, and scribal school is considered one of the best preserved palaces of the Middle East. The structure was built by later Amorites, who worshiped the deities Adad and Dagon. In the postwar campaign the excavation centered mainly around the older strata going back to buildings of the pre-Sargonic period from the time of the dynasty of Akkad.

The Royal Archives. The most interesting finds, however, were the so-called ***Mari Letters,*** some 20,000 clay tablets dug up and which have revolutionized knowledge of the ancient biblical world. These documents were written in the dialect of Old Babylonian. They date from the era of Hammurabi, c. 1700 B.C., the same monarch whose code was discovered in 1901 at Susa. These records constitute memoranda of the king and governors of the city-state of Mari, and belong to the time of the kings Yasmah-Adad, under whose reign the construction of the palace was begun, and Zimri-Lim, under whom it was completed. Some of the correspondence is that of King Yasmah-Adad with his father, the powerful empire builder King Shamshi-Adad I of Assyria, as well as with the representatives of the provinces of his realm. King Zimri-Lim's correspondence also figures in exchanges of diplomatic correspondence with King Hammurabi of Babylon, as well as with the king of Aleppo and other vassals. Two letters dispatched from Aleppo to Zimri-Lim deal with prophetic utterances delivered in the name of the god Adad of Aleppo. The subject and tenor of these remind one of biblical prophecies.

Biblical Value of the Mari Texts. These records are of great value to biblical students because they stem from the region which was the home of the Hebrew patriarchs for a number of years before going on to Canaan. However, Abraham's migration from Ur, according to preserved biblical chronology, apparently took place some 400 years before the era of Zimri-Lim and the fall of Mari. At this time of the 3rd dynasty of Ur, Mari was ruled by the governors of the kings of Ur. Eventually, however, a prince of Mari, Ishbi-Irra, who had brought the city-state of Isin under his dominion c. 2021 B.C., was instrumental in bringing about the downfall of the city of Ur.

Nahor, which figures prominently in the patriarchal narratives (Gen. 24:10), is mentioned quite often in the Mari Letters. One letter from Nahor is sent from a woman of that town to the king and runs as follows:

> **To my lord say, Thus Inib-Sharrim, thy maid servant. How long must I remain in Nahor? Peace is established and the road is unobstructed. Let my lord write and let me be brought that I may see the face of my lord from whom I am separated. Further, let my lord send me an answer to my tablet.**

The term "Habiru," very important since Abraham is the first individual in the Bible to be named a "Hebrew" (Gen. 14:13), is found frequently in the Mari Letters, as is also the case in the Nuzi Letters. In both instances the term apparently means "a wanderer," "one who crosses over," or "one who passes from one place to another." This explanation fits Abraham and the early patriarchs very well since they were nomadic travelers.

When Abraham left Ur in southern Mesopotamia to migrate to Canaan, he no doubt passed through the magnificent city of Mari. There can be little doubt that he and Terah with their families put up in one of the caravansaries there. Perhaps they spent days or weeks in the famous city and went sightseeing in the palace, traces of whose grandeur are still visible to the eye of the modern archaeologist.

The city of Mari was idolatrous and in it there was the widespread practice of divination. A diviner was an important official in all phases of daily life at Mari. People went to him for advice in ordinary difficulties of life. Commanders saw him for help in the movement of their troops.

The patriarchs were remarkably free from occult practices and contamination from paganism and divinatory phenomena in general. This fact is true despite the teraphim (household gods) of Rachel and despite the "foreign gods" which Jacob ordered put away and which he hid under a terebinth tree in Shechem (Gen. 35:2–4).

Interestingly, the Mari Letters refer to "sons of the right," that is, "sons of the south," since the directions were taken as one faced the east, and the south would be on one's right hand. These were a fierce tribe of wanderers and called Benjaminites, but they have no connection with the "Benjamites" of the Bible. The name "Benjamin," "son of the south," that is, "southerner," was a term suited to occur in various places, especially in Mari, where the parallel term "sons of the left," that is, "sons of the north," is found.

The Bible presents Benjamin as being of Palestinian birth after Jacob's return from Mesopotamia. He is set forth as never having been in Mesopotamia at all. Genesis 49:27 describes Benjamin as a ravenous wolf. This fits the description of the veteran tribe at Mari remarkably well. Any connection, however, is obviously dubious and purely imaginary.

Another interesting sidelight is the fact that

the word translated "chieftain," with reference to the plundering Benjaminites, is *dawidum,* meaning "leader." This sheds light on the etymology of the name of Israel's most renowned king, who evidently had a name meaning "the leader."

Historical Value of the Mari Letters. These documents establish that Shamshi-Adad I of Assyria, who ruled c. 1748–1716 B.C., and Hammurabi the Great of Babylon, were contemporaries. With these facts and other details furnished by the Mari documents, the date of Hammurabi can be fixed c. 1728–1676 B.C. This and other evidence have forced scholars to give up identifying Hammurabi of Babylon with Amraphel (Gen. 14:1). The high antiquity of Genesis 14 has been vindicated, but archaeology has not yet succeeded in furnishing the background of the four Mesopotamian kings who invaded the Trans-Jordanic country in the days of Abraham.

Hammurabi was a strong military leader and a great administrator. He was a member of the strong 1st dynasty of Babylon which reigned from 1830 to c. 1550 B.C. The power of this dynasty reached its height under Hammurabi's rule. He was the greatest of all Babylonian rulers. Hammurabi defeated Rim-Sin of Larsa and established himself over all the city-states of Lower Babylonia. His expanding military machine enabled him to destroy Mari. It was his code of laws, as we have seen, that was discovered at Susa in 1901. This famous codification has remained classic in illustrating and illuminating Israelite laws.

It was during the reign of Hammurabi that the Babylonian story of creation was composed. The poem glorified Marduk, the patron god of Babylon, whom Hammurabi established as the national god of Babylonia. In this period, the early Sumerian language became an antiquity and Semitic-Babylonian came into common usage.

The Mari Letters and the Amorites. About 2000 B.C. the Semitic-nomadic peoples, who lived along the desert fringes of the Fertile Crescent, invaded the centers of established civilization. Known as "Westerners," they are preserved in the Old Testament as "Amorites." Amorite states came into existence all over the Mesopotamian area. Nahor, Haran, Mari, Qatna, and Ugarit all appear as Amorite cities with Amorite kings. Babylon itself became the capital of an Amorite state under Hammurabi. This important historical fact is clearly reflected in the Mari Letters and in the peoples known as "Amorites" or "Westerners." In such a manner archaeology is slowly but surely outlining the historical framework of the patriarchal age. Such discoveries as the Mari Letters prove of incalculable assistance to the historian of the ancient biblical world.

8. The Lachish Ostraca—Jeremiah's Age Lives Again

In the excavations of Lachish, a southwestern Palestinian city, the most astonishing finds were some letters embedded in a layer of burnt charcoal and ashes. They were eighteen in number and were in Hebrew writing done in the ancient Phoenician script. Three more of these letters were discovered in later campaigns in 1938.

Almost all of the letters were written by one named Hoshiah, who was stationed at some military outpost, to Jaosh, who was evidently a high ranking officer in the garrison at Lachish. It was the era of the Babylonian overrunning of Palestine several years before the fall of Jerusalem in 587 B.C. The Babylonians had attacked and partly burned Lachish some ten years before in the reign of Jehoiakim. These particular letters were in the layer of ashes which represent the final destruction of the city. Accordingly, they are to be dated from 588 B.C., when Nebuchadnezzar was making the final siege of Jerusalem and also of Lachish and Azekah.

Identification of Lachish. This large mound, one of the largest occupied in Palestine, is located 30 miles southwest of Jerusalem, 20 miles inland from the Mediterranean, and 50 miles west of Hebron. It is mentioned in the Amarna Letters and in earlier Egyptian sources. Its strategic importance is attested by its being on the main route from central Palestine to Egypt. It overlooked the rich Shephelah (terrain which descended to the coastal lowland). The fortress city was an ideal barrier between the Philistine plains and the elevated Judean country. It was one of the principal fortified cities of Judah and one of the bastions taken by the Israelites in their conquest of Palestine (Josh. 10:31–35). The site of Umm-Lakis was first thought to be Lachish. Then the location was sought at Tell el-Hesy by Sir Flinders Petrie, a pioneer archaeologist. William Foxwell Albright finally identified it correctly with the large mound of Tell el-Duweir.

Nebuchadnezzar captured Lachish in 588–586 B.C. (Jer. 34:7). Marks of a huge conflagration on the road leading up to the gate and on the adjacent wall display that the attackers relied largely upon fire, for which felled olive trees not yet harvested supplied the fuel.

Excavations at Lachish. The Wellcome-Marston Archaeological Expedition in 1933 commenced work there, under the direction of J. L. Starkey. In 1938 Starkey was killed by Arab brigands, and the work was carried on by Lankester Harding and Charles H. Inge.

The Results of the Excavation. Besides evidences of earlier occupation, Lachish disclosed settlement by the Hyksos c. 1720–1550 B.C.

These people overran Egypt during this period. A typical Hyksos defense ditch or *fosse,* with a ramp of clay and lime that apparently provided an enclosure for their horses, was brought to light. In the fosse three Canaanite Egyptian temples built between 1450 and 1225 B.C. were excavated. A Persian temple of a much later period was also found. Cemeteries at Lachish yielded a great quantity of pottery, jewelry, scarabs, and skeletal evidence.

A well, 200 feet deep, was located within the city, the remains of a tremendous engineering excavation for water storage, which was not completed. A shaft about 85 feet terminates in a rectangle 80 x 70 feet cut to a depth of 80 feet. The aim was a water system which would have been much larger than that provided by Hezekiah for Jerusalem in the Siloam Tunnel and comparable to similar systems at Gezer and Megiddo.

A good quantity of inscribed material has been removed from the Lachish excavations. A bronze dagger from c. 1700 B.C. contains four pictographic signs, samples of the early script. A bowl and a ewer contain specimens of the same early writing as that found at Serabit el-Khadem. The name "Gedaliah" was found on a jar handle and may be the official whom Nebuchadnezzar set over the land after the fall of Jerusalem (cf. Jer. 40—42).

Contents of the Lachish Letters. But of all the epigraphic discoveries at Lachish, the most important are the Lachish Letters. These letters may be briefly described as follows: Letter 1 lists names, the majority of which are found in the Old Testament. Letters 2 and 5 consist largely of greetings. Letter 3, the longest, contains the most information. This concerns movements of Jewish troops and also makes an interesting note to an unnamed prophet and his word of warning. Letter 4 states that Hoshiah, though observing the signals of Lachish, cannot see those of Azekah. Azekah may well have fallen earlier, for this letter states, "We are watching for the signal station at Lachish according to all the signals you are giving, because we cannot see the signals of Azekah." Letter 6 contains the biblical expression, "to weaken the hands of the people." This recalls Jeremiah, who uses a similar expression (Jer. 38:4).

Historical Importance of the Letters. The Lachish Letters give us an independent view of conditions in Judah in the last days before the fall of Jerusalem. As the Neo-Babylonian army advanced, the doom of Jerusalem was sealed, in contrast to its deliverance under the Assyrian, Sennacherib, as Isaiah had predicted (2 Kin. 19:20, 32–36). Relentlessly, Nebuchadnezzar advanced on the city after a terrible eighteen-

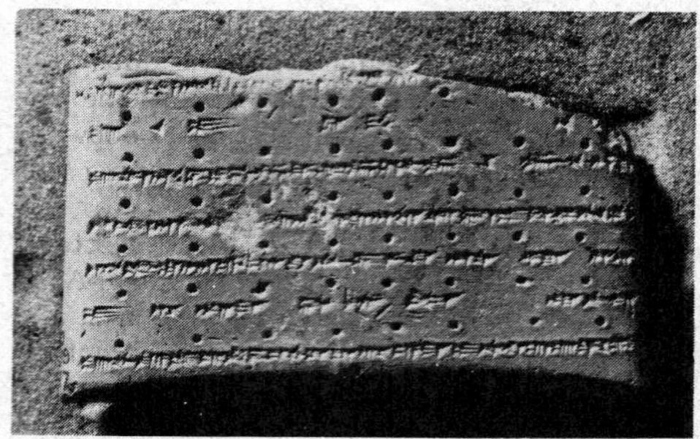

A clay tablet showing the colophon at the end of a typical Assyrian library tablet. Found at Nineveh. *British Museum*

month siege, 587 B.C. The walls of the city were broken down, the houses and the temple burned, and the people carried away to exile (2 Kin. 25:1–12).

Jeremiah conducted his difficult ministry in these agonizing times. His reference to Azekah and Lachish is most interesting. "When the king of Babylon's army fought against Jerusalem and all the cities of Judah that were left, against Lachish and Azekah; for *only* these fortified cities remained of the cities of Judah" (Jer. 34:7).

Tell Zakariya in the Shephelah region has been identified as Azekah. In 1898 it was excavated by Frederick K. Bliss of the Palestine Exploration Fund. It had a strong inner fortress buttressed with eight large towers.

The Lachish Letters concern the time just prior to the fall of the city and present the same conditions of turmoil and confusion that are revealed in the Book of Jeremiah. Numerous place names that occur in the Bible are found in the letters, as well as personal names. Hoshaiah appears in Jeremiah 42:1 and Nehemiah 12:32. God is referred to by the four-letter word *YHWH,* which are the consonants of the name "Jehovah" or "Yahweh." It is also interesting to note that many of the men's names have Yahweh endings. A prophet like Jeremiah is referred to in the letters. But this is most probably not Jeremiah himself.

So complete was the destruction by the Babylonians that it took many centuries for Judah to recover. The returned remnant was tiny and weak. The small Jewish state stamped its coins with the name "Yehud," that is, Judah, but not until after 300 B.C. do substantial archaeological remains appear, and then they are not abundant. Certainly the Babylonians did a thorough job of destroying Jewish power for many centuries.

The Paleographic Importance of the Letters. Being inscribed in biblical Hebrew, in which the Old Testament Scriptures were written, and with stylistic and vocabulary similarities to the Book of Jeremiah, these letters are of great paleographic importance. They help the scholar to trace the evolution of the Hebrew alphabet, noting the formation of the letters and their style. They also enable him to see how the Old Testament Scriptures, which were then written, appeared.

Surely research of this type, that makes it possible for the scholar to look back, to resurrect the past, and to see how the language of the Old Testament developed, is fascinating. Great strides are being made in this field of enquiry. It is the one truly bright spot in original biblical studies. This type of study is of immense value in expanding historical backgrounds and illuminating Holy Scripture on the human plane.

9. The Dead Sea Scrolls

The middle of the 20th century saw the greatest manuscript discovery of modern times. In 1947 a young Bedouin shepherd stumbled upon a cave south of Jericho, containing many leather scrolls of Hebrew and Aramaic writing and about 600 fragmentary inscriptions. Great excitement prevailed in the archaeological world. In 1952 new caves containing fragments of later scrolls in Hebrew, Greek, and Aramaic were found. These and other startling manuscript discoveries have been followed by news of additional manuscripts found in other caves in the Dead Sea area.

A. The Date of the Scrolls. After intensive study of the manuscripts from the Dead Sea area, scholars define three periods: 1. The Archaic Period c. 200–150 B.C. 2. The Hasmonean Period c. 150–30 B.C. 3. The Herodian Period c. 30 B.C. to A.D. 70. The great majority originated in the 2nd and 3rd periods, especially the last half of the 2nd period and last half of the 3rd period.

Although attacks have been made against the antiquity and authenticity of these manuscripts, two lines of evidence substantiate their antiquity. **The evidence of radiocarbon count.** This scientific method of dating places the linen in which the scrolls were wrapped in the general era of c. 175 B.C. to A.D. 225. **Paleographic evidence.** Scholars conversant in this science date these documents by the form of the letters and the way they are written in comparison with other eras of writing. They are able to demonstrate that they come in the intermediate period between the script of the 3rd century B.C. and of the middle of the 1st century A.D. W. F. Albright observes, "All competent students of writing conversant with the available material and with paleographic method date the scrolls in the 250 years before A.D. 70.

B. The Contents of the Scrolls. The Dead Sea cave manuscripts contain material partly biblical and partly intertestamental. The biblical includes two scrolls of Isaiah, one complete, and most of the first two chapters of Habakkuk,

The area near the Dead Sea where the Qumran scrolls were found. *Matson Photo Service*

and fragments of all Old Testament books except Esther. Large numbers of fragmentary manuscripts have been recovered from the Pentateuchal books and Isaiah. Fragments of Psalms, Jeremiah, and Daniel are numerous.

The scroll of ***Isaiah,*** in the initial finds from the site of Qumran, has remained the best known of the discoveries. It was the first major biblical manuscript of great antiquity to be recovered. It is earlier by a millennium than the oldest Hebrew text preserved in the Masoretic Hebrew Bible. This Masoretic Hebrew Bible is the basis of all recent translations and does not go back any earlier than A.D. 900.

This fact of the antiquity of the Hebrew text of Isaiah, dating as early as 150–125 B.C., constitutes these discoveries as the greatest of modern times. They are the oldest existing manuscripts of the Bible in any language.

In the original group of manuscripts of 1947 were a commentary on Habakkuk and so-called ***Manual of Discipline*** of a pre-Christian Jewish sect of Essenes. Of unusual interest were manuscripts later purchased by the Hebrew University of Jerusalem, containing a later Isaiah scroll more conformed to the traditional Hebrew, and a document of great interest called ***"The War Between the Children of Light and Darkness."*** This composition evidently issued from the Maccabean struggles against Greek paganism in 158–137 B.C.

In winter, 1949, the first manuscript-bearing cave was excavated by two well-known Palestinian archaeologists, Pierre de Vaux and Lankester Harding. Recovered were fragments of Genesis, Deuteronomy, and Judges with a fragment of Leviticus in Old Hebrew script. Nonbiblical finds included a fragment of the ***Book of Jubilees,*** a work related to the Enoch literature, and some unknown material.

C. Other Manuscript-Yielding Sites. In 1952 a cave was uncovered at Murabbaat in another part of the desert. This yielded manuscripts chiefly from the 2nd century A.D. in Hebrew, Greek, and Aramaic, including a few texts of Genesis, Exodus, Deuteronomy, and Isaiah. Several Hebrew letters were discovered from the period of Simon ben Keseba, that is, Bar Cocheba, who led the revolt in 132–135. A notable exception to the 2nd century A.D. date of this material is an archaic Hebrew papyrus piece, a palimpsest, a list of names and numbers, dated in the 6th century B.C.

In the same general area, other caves have been found, one group in Khirbet Mird, northeast of the monastery of Mar Saba. These contain Arabic papyri, Greek and Christo-Palestinian-Syrian documents, with fragments of biblical codices, all late Byzantine and early Arabic. Another group of manuscripts date from the period of the bulk of the Murabbaat material. Among them is a version of the minor prophets in Greek and a corpus of Nabatean papyri, both of great biblical and historical importance.

D. Excavations at Khirbet Qumran. Khirbet Qumran was excavated between 1951 and 1954. This Essene community, with the nearby caves, proved to be the richest manuscript-yielding center. Members of this Essenic community copied these manuscripts and preserved them by hiding them in the caves. The Essenes at Khirbet Qumran, 7 miles south of Jericho near the shores of the Dead Sea, were next to the Pharisees and Sadducees in importance in sectarian Judaism. This site has become one of the most publicized places in Palestine because of the phenomenal manuscript finds in the cave-dotted cliffs.

Excavations at Khirbet Qumran have fully authenticated this site as the center of Essenic Judaism. As the result of the recovery of coins, pottery, and architectural remains, the story of Qumran's occupation can now be told. Four periods in the later history of the site are traced.

Period 1 extends from its founding c. 110 B.C. under John Hyrcanus. Numerous coins of this ruler were dug up, as well as of other Hasmonean rulers including Antigonus, 40–37 B.C., the last ruler of this line, to the seventh year of Herod, 31 B.C. At this time an earthquake apparently leveled the site. Indications are that during Herod's reign the place was abandoned because of his antagonism.

Period 2 at Qumran dates from rebuilding and enlargement c. A.D. 1 and Roman destruction in June A.D. 68. During this era in the lifetime of Jesus, John the Baptist, and the early Christian apostles, Qumran flourished, influencing Judaism and the early Christian church. Coins have been found dating from the reign of Archelaus, 4 B.C. to A.D. 6, and from the time of the Roman procurators down to the second year of the first Jewish revolt in A.D. 66–70.

The Roman army, which took Jericho in June, A.D. 68, evidently likewise captured Qumran. One coin, marked with an X, belonged to the Tenth Legion. Iron arrowheads were found in a layer of burned ash in the excavation.

Qumran fell to Roman occupation. Some coins describe *Judaea Capta*. These date in the reign of Titus, A.D. 79–81, and mark **Period 3** as the Roman occupation after Jerusalem's destruction in A.D. 70. Evidence that Qumran structures were converted into army barracks indicates that a Roman garrison was stationed there from A.D. 68–c. A.D. 100. At this time the site apparently was abandoned.

Period 4. Qumran is distinguished by reoccupation of the site during the 2nd Jewish revolt, A.D. 132–135. Coins dating from this era indicate that here the Jews made their last stand to drive the Romans from their country. After that Qumran sank into obscurity.

Architectural Remains at Qumran. The main edifice at Qumran is 100 feet by 120 and formed the communal center and hub of the complex. At the northwest corner was a massive defense tower with thick walls enforced by stone embankments. Some coins from the time of the 2nd Jewish revolt (A.D. 132–135) attest its use as a fortress against Roman power.

Alongside the general meeting room is the largest hall of the main building. Here was located the scriptorium. Several inkwells of the Roman period, and even some dried ink, indicate that the manuscripts had been copied by the community's scribes.

Also in the complex were two cisterns (artificial reservoirs) carefully plastered. There were installations for ablutions and baptisms. Of the possibly 40 cisterns and reservoirs, the bulk of them must have been used for storage of water in the very hot, dry climate.

Of great interest is the cemetery, containing about 1,000 burial places. De Vaux excavated many of these tombs. They are noted for their lack of jewelry and any evidences of luxury.

E. Khirbet Qumran and the Essenes. Not only do the excavations at Khirbet Qumran demonstrate that it was the headquarters of Essenic Judaism but three authorities who were contemporary witnesses attest the same fact, namely, Josephus, Philo, and Pliny. Pliny, for example, locates the Essenes at precisely the spot where Qumran is situated, namely, "on the west side of the Dead Sea." He also designates the town of En-Gedi as situated "below the Essenes."

Josephus relates their unselfish character, industry, and communal life. He extols their love for common toil, says they dressed in white, and describes their three-year probationary period before admission to the sect, and other phases of discipline. He also mentions their various lustrations and says that they numbered about 4,000. He comments on their celibacy, piety, convictions concerning immortality, and their belief in rewards for righteousness.

Philo gives a similar description of this group in Judaism. The library at Qumran attests their delight in the Bible and literature. This is reflected in information given by Philo and Josephus. The Essenes carefully copied Holy Scripture and took pains to preserve it.

There are difficulties in equating the Essenes at Qumran with the sect described by Philo, Pliny, and Josephus. Nevertheless, the likenesses far outweigh the differences. The evidence would seem to equate Qumran with the Essenes of the 1st century A.D.

F. The Essenes at Qumran and John the Baptist. Concerning John, Luke wrote: "So the child grew and became strong in spirit, and was in the deserts till the day of his manifestation to Israel" (Luke 1:80). The home of John the Baptist's parents was in the hill country of Judea (Luke 1:39, 40, 65). Although nothing is known definitely, it is easy to believe that John the Baptist did in some way come in contact with the Essenes. There are many characteristics in his own life that parallel theirs.

Both John and the Qumranites feature Isaiah 40:3 with regard to preparing "the way of the LORD." But John must have early realized that there were some features of the Essenes that were not conducive to preparing the nation for the advent of the Messiah, and so if he ever had a connection with them, he must have broken with them, giving himself to an active ministry of preaching repentance and baptizing in the Jordan Valley.

John's message featured repentance (Matt. 3:2; Mark 1:4; Luke 3:3). Repentance was also a vital note in Qumran theology. They belonged to a "covenant of repentance" and they called themselves "the penitents of Israel." The baptism of repentance, which John administered, was also paralleled by the Essenes who practiced water baptism. John's baptism was an outer indication of inward spiritual renovation, enabling the recipients to recognize the Messiah when He came.

Baptism among the Qumranites, however, was purely ritual, and the recipients were enjoined to separate themselves rigidly from any who did not belong to their community. The severe indictment of the Jewish nation, which was characteristic of John, was also characteristic of the Essenes. They looked upon those not belonging to their sect as "sons of darkness" connected with Belial. They regarded themselves as true Israel, living in accordance with the law. For them alone the baptismal rite could have meaning.

John featured the baptism "with the Holy Spirit and fire" (Matt. 3:11), the baptism with fire being the judgment upon the unrepentant in an eschatological sense. Such judgment of fire is described in a Qumran hymn under the figure of a fiery river overflowing in wrath "on the outcasts" and in "the time of fury for all Belial."

The baptism of the Holy Spirit, on the other hand, is prophesied by John to be the portion of those who would repent and receive the coming Messiah (John 1:33). In Qumran literature not only does God "sprinkle upon him," the Messiah, the spirit of truth as purifying water to cleanse Him from all abominations of falsehood and from the spirit of impurity, but the Messiah sprinkles His people with His Holy Spirit, constituting them His anointed ones.

John the Baptist was intensely missionary and evangelistic in his message. The Qumranites were self-centered, strictly sectarian, and did not spread their convictions. They did adopt children to train in their ways.

John the Baptist was vouchsafed the honor of preparing the way for the Messiah and being His forerunner. The Qumran community did not recognize the Messiah when He came. Their asceticism led to a deadend. It never conducted them to Him who would take away the sin of the world (John 1:29).

G. The Essenes and Jesus the Messiah. Although the Qumran community had a messianic hope, it was strikingly different from that of the Old Testament. They could not comprehend the combination of King and Priest in *one* Person (Zech. 6:9–15). Neither could they comprehend in the union of the same Person the additional office of a Prophet, although they did feature in their writings the messianic prophecy of "a Prophet" (Deut. 18:18, 19).

Their great priest was Messiah of Aaron. Their great military leader, Messiah of Israel; their prophet comprehended in the rule of the community is set down alongside the "messiahs of Aaron and Israel," apparently as a separate messianic figure.

There are other similarities between the organization and teachings of the Qumran group and the teachings of Jesus and the formation of the Christian church. The passage in Matthew 18:15–17 has a striking parallel in Qumran literature.

It is easily seen that with this new material the background of the gospel stories is much more richly illustrated. The Last Supper, the Sermon on the Mount, and numerous other aspects of the earthly life and ministry of Jesus are fitted into a larger framework of historical background material, and to that extent are understood on the human side. However, it is transparently clear that the ministries of John the Baptist and Jesus remain unique. Qumran literature in no sense casts any shadow upon the unique Person and work of Jesus Christ. Christianity stands as authentically growing out of the Old Testament and not connected with later Gnosticism in a post-apostolic era that would jeopardize its historical genuineness.

H. The Dead Sea Scrolls and Literary Criticism of the New Testament. The Dead Sea material has had a stabilizing effect upon New Testament criticism. In the light of the new material, the New Testament appears as a Jewish book with a Christian theology with less Greek influence in its formation than Jewish, and there is reason to date the ***synoptic Gospels,*** beginning with ***Mark,*** between A.D. 60 and 65.

Jerusalem Temple inscription warning Gentiles against intrusion.
Matson Photo Service

Especially interesting is the dating of the ***Gospel of John.*** A radical criticism customarily dated this Gospel about A.D. 150 or later. Thus it was removed from apostolic tradition and treated more as an apocryphal book. Now it is well known that the fourth Gospel reflects the genuine Jewish background of John the Baptist and Jesus and not a later 2nd-century Gnostic milieu. This is clearly attested by the parallels to the conceptual imagery of John's Gospel in the Essenic literature from Qumran.

There is every evidence to believe in the authenticity of John's Gospel, and there is not the slightest reason critically to date the Gospel after A.D. 90. Indeed, it may be quite a bit earlier. Thus the Dead Sea discoveries and the excavations at Qumran not only give additional background material to the interbiblical and New Testament period but also help to stabilize higher criticism and purge out radical views that are now shown to be untenable.

The ***Book of Hebrews*** also is interesting. This is certainly to be definitely dated before the destruction of Jerusalem in A.D. 70. The treatise apparently was planned to offset the Essenic idea of "two anointed ones," one a prince and the other a priest. It was designed to present the Christian and Old Testament doctrine (cf. Zech. 6:9, 15; Ps. 110:1) that Messiah would be *both King and Priest in one Person.* Also the ***Book of the Revelation*** was doubtless penned toward the end of the 1st century, and, in the light of the Dead Sea Scrolls, may now possibly be dated earlier, that is, before A.D. 70. This conclusion is based on its Hebraic background, being illuminated by the evidence from the Dead Sea manuscripts.

10. Jerusalem

Probably no excavation ever carried out has been as important as that carried on by Israeli institutions at the western and southern walls of the temple mountain in Jerusalem. The actual steps and entrances of Herod's temple have been uncovered as have the tiny shops and narrow streets where the merchants must have hawked their wares. The giant stone blocks from the top of the wall, which were thrown down into the streets by Titus's troops in A.D. 70, were found where they fell. In a grave in another part of the city were found the remains of a Jew who had been crucified by the Romans, the first physical evidence of this form of execution ever found. So extensive were these finds that it will be a generation before they are all deciphered and integrated into the historical framework of the Roman Age.

11. Ebla

The modern Arabic name for this 140-acre mound in the Northwest corner of Syria is Tell Mardikh. Archaeologists of the University of Rome began digging this mound in 1964 and found an inscription in 1968 that identified this site as ancient Ebla. They uncovered portions of impressive ***buildings from the time of the biblical Patriarchs*** (1900–1700 B.C.); and beneath these were palaces and temples of the Early Bronze Age (2400–2250 B.C.). This was the discovery of an early but advanced civilization which was previously unknown.

In 1974, 1975, and 1976, three rooms of one palace yielded almost 7,000 well-preserved ***clay tablets*** and about 13,000 fragments of other tablets ***with cuneiform writing on them.*** This archive of ***ancient Sumerian and Canaanite literature*** is very important. The tablets contain economic, political, and legal records of Ebla. (Understanding the cultures of Israel's neighbors aids biblical interpretation.) They show that Ebla was a merchant empire. Its rulers controlled trade routes that reached into the Mesopotamian Valley, into the mountains of modern-day Turkey, and to the edge of the Nile Valley.

But more importantly, some tablets are ***dictionaries***—the earliest known—providing the meanings of words used in both the Sumerian and early Canaanite (Eblaite) languages. (Languages help archaeologists understand the cultures.) Many Canaanite words at Ugarit and ***Hebrew words in the Old Testament*** can be understood more accurately because they also occur on these early tablets.

Many ***place names*** occur in the Ebla records, including those familiar to readers of the Bible: Haran, Damascus, Hazor, Beth Shan, Shechem, Joppa, Eshkelon, Jerusalem, Dor—and some scholars believe also Sodom and Gomorrah. Since the Bible itself presents these as real places, the Ebla tablets help support its historical reliability.

About 10,000 names of people are found on the tablets. Among them are ***biblical names*** such as Adam, Eve, Noah, Jubal, Abram, Ishmael, Hagar, Keturah, Bilhah, Israel, Micah, Michael, Saul, David, Jehorum, and Jonah. Although these names do not refer to the biblical personages, they establish that the names in Scripture are authentic.

Sometimes, however, the tablets contain mythic and legendary stories which conflict with the Scriptures (e.g., different creation accounts). Such cases illumine the biblical authors' polemics against pagan worldviews.

The excavation project continues until the present and may be expected to cast more light on the Bible's meaning and reliability.

The thrilling story of biblical archaeology is not yet completed. Other great discoveries as a result of continuous research in Bible lands promise even greater contributions to biblical studies in future years. For example, the recovery of thirteen Coptic codices from Nag Hammadi in Upper Egypt, since 1945, have almost rivaled the Dead Sea Scrolls in actual biblical importance. These even include the apocryphal "Gospel of Thomas" and are of inestimable value, especially from a critical standpoint in dating New Testament literature.

What new and exciting discovery affecting the Bible may we not expect the archaeologist's spade to turn up next? The prospect should engender a love for the Scriptures and a desire to study them employing history, linguistics, and archaeology as the means under the Holy Spirit to a more accurate understanding of the Bible's message to humankind.

Acknowledgments: The publisher gratefully acknowledges the cooperation of these sources, whose photographs appear in this article:

British Museum (80–7–19, 277)
G. Eric Matson Collection, The Episcopal House
Professor D. J. Wiseman

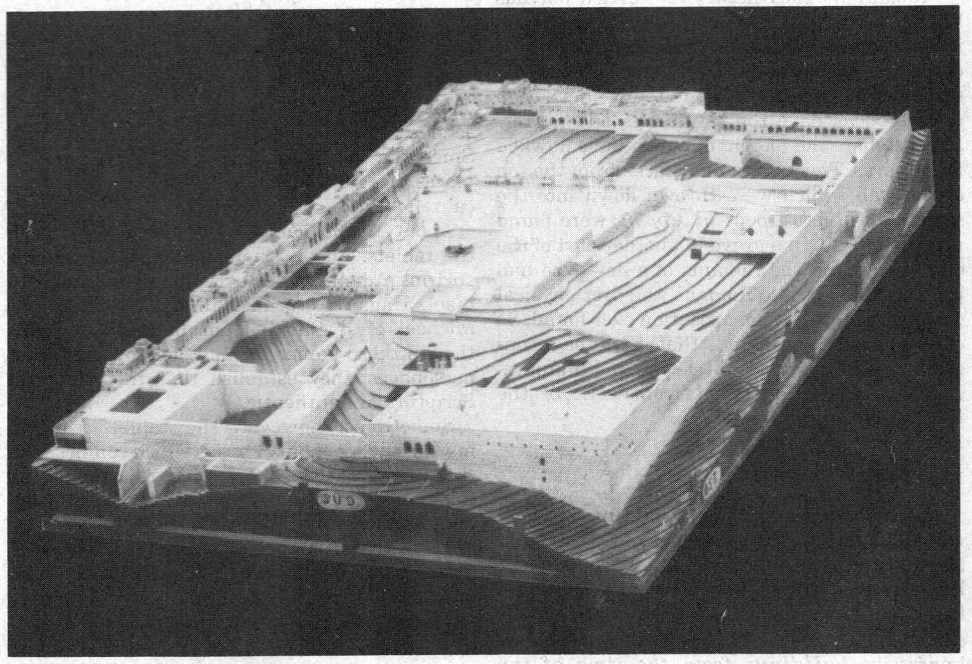

The Temple area in Jerusalem, showing the slope of the hill. *Matson Photo Service*

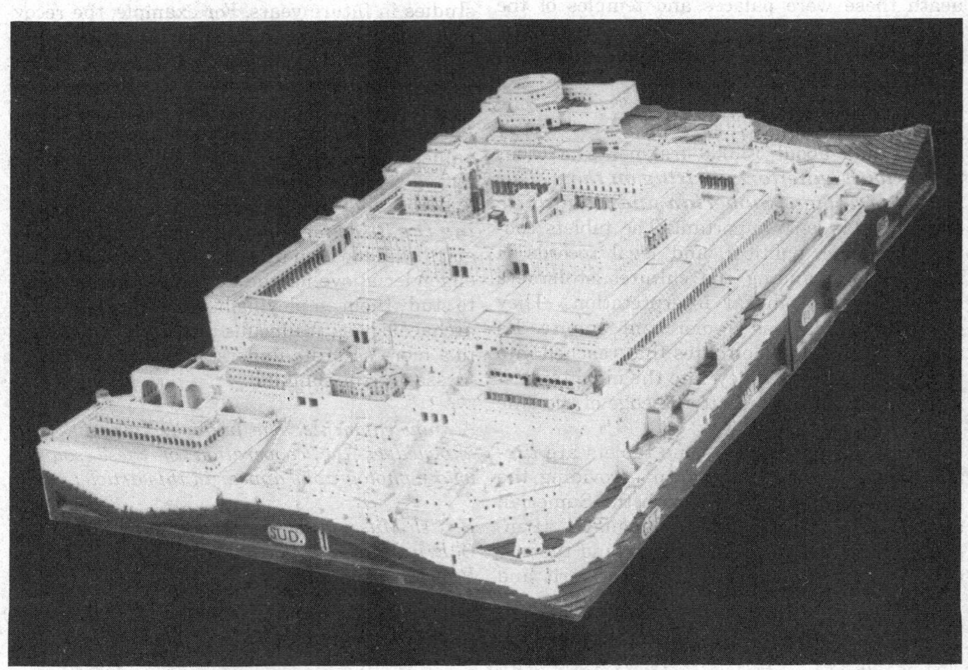

Model of the Temple of Solomon in Jerusalem. *Matson Photo Service*

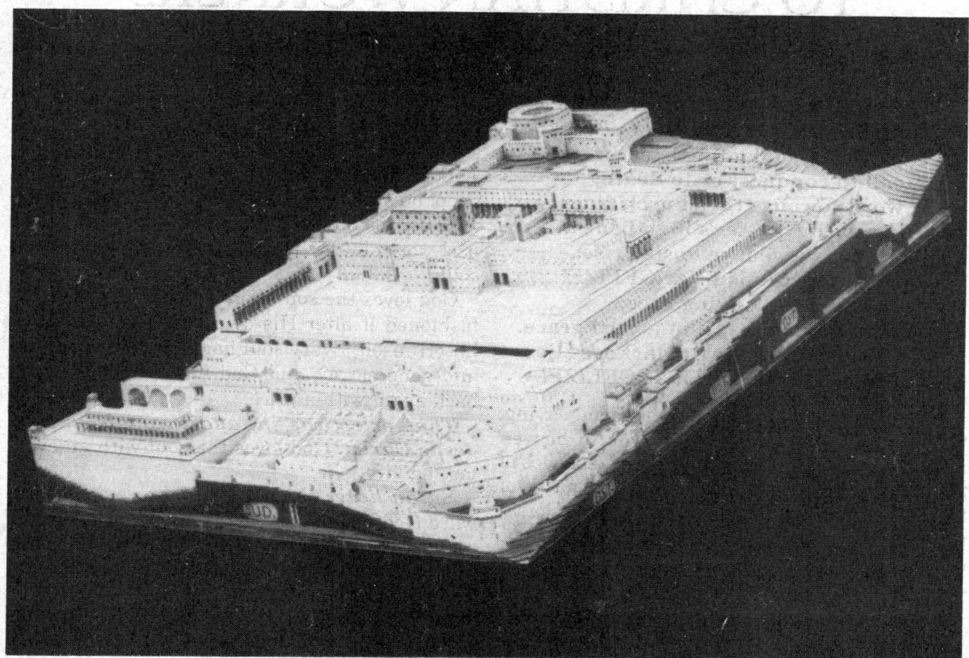

Model of the Temple of Zerubbabel in Jerusalem. *Matson Photo Service*

Model of the Temple of Herod in Jerusalem. *Matson Photo Service*

A GUIDE TO CHRISTIAN WORKERS

I. Commission

Give us a watchword for the hour,
A thrilling word, a word of power;
A battle cry, a flaming breath,
A call to conquest or to death;
A word to rouse the church from rest,
To heed the Master's high behest.
The call is given, ye hosts arise,
The watchword is EVANGELIZE!
To fallen men, a dying race,
Make known the gift of gospel grace.
The world that now in darkness lies,
O Church of Christ, EVANGELIZE!

"And Jesus came and spoke to them, saying, 'All authority has been given to Me in heaven and on earth. Go therefore and make disciples of all the nations, baptizing them in the name of the Father and of the Son and of the Holy Spirit, teaching them to observe all things that I have commanded you; and lo, I am with you always, *even* to the end of the age.' Amen" (Matt. 28:18–20).

"But you shall receive power when the Holy Spirit has come upon you; and you shall be witnesses to Me in Jerusalem, and in all Judea and Samaria, and to the end of the earth" (Acts 1:8).

"So you, son of man: I have made you a watchman for the house of Israel; therefore you shall hear a word from My mouth and warn them for Me. When I say to the wicked, 'O wicked *man,* you shall surely die!' and you do not speak to warn the wicked from his way, that wicked *man* shall die in his iniquity; but his blood I will require at your hand" (Ezek. 33:7, 8).

"You are the salt of the earth; but if the salt loses its flavor, how shall it be seasoned? It is then good for nothing but to be thrown out and trampled underfoot by men. You are the light of the world. A city that is set on a hill cannot be hidden. Nor do they light a lamp and put it under a basket, but on a lampstand, and it gives light to all *who are* in the house. Let your light so shine before men, that they may see your good works and glorify your Father in heaven" (Matt. 5:13–16).

II. Compassion

The story is told that Martinelli received $25,000 for singing only twice. Paul and Silas sang one night in a prison. Their song was not rendered with the skill or harmony of that of Martinelli, but its tenderness touched the heart of the keeper of the prison and echoed through the angel-crowded streets of heaven; and the listening King of kings rewarded those who sang with crowns of glory that will gleam in beauty throughout eternal ages.

An immortal soul is beyond all price. There is no trouble too great, no humiliation too deep, no suffering too severe, no love too strong, no labor too hard, no expense too large, but that it is worth it, if it is spent in the effort to win a soul.

God loves the soul more than all creation. He fashioned it after His own image, and made it like Himself. Every soul has departed from God and gone astray, and God has bought the soul back again with a price.

That price was in, and through, and by Jesus Christ. God loves the soul with an everlasting love.

Satan hates the soul. In Satan's enmity toward God he is using all his energy, using every snare, his utmost cunning, employing every means *with the single purpose of ruining the souls of humankind.*

When a million eternities have each lived their endless ages and have rolled by into the unthinkable past and time is no more, the soul will still be living, *a conscious personality* endowed with perpetual life reunited with the body.

God has said: "And he who wins souls is wise" (Prov. 11:30).

The Bible says: "Those who are wise shall shine like the brightness of the firmament, and those who turn many to righteousness like the stars forever and ever" (Dan. 12:3).

Compassion was the heartbeat of our Savior's ministry. "But when He saw the multitudes, He was moved with compassion for them, because they were weary and scattered, like sheep having no shepherd" (Matt. 9:36). "But You, O Lord, *are* a God full of compassion, and gracious, longsuffering and abundant in mercy and truth" (Ps. 86:15).

Heaven is geared for redemption. "I say to you that likewise there will be more joy in heaven over one sinner who repents than over ninety-nine just persons who need no repentance" (Luke 15:7).

No one who ever had a glimpse of hell would ever want a fellow human being to go there (see Luke 16:28).

"Those who sow in tears shall reap in joy. He who continually goes forth weeping, bearing seed for sowing, shall doubtless come again with rejoicing, bringing his sheaves *with him*" (Ps. 126:5, 6).

III. Concern

One of the first questions raised in recorded history was, "*Am* I my brother's keeper?" (Gen. 4:9). ***Do I have moral obligations toward others?*** "So I sought for a man among them who would make a wall, and stand in the gap before Me on behalf of the land, that I should not destroy it; but I found no one" (Ezek. 22:30).

"My sheep wandered through all the mountains, and on every high hill; yes, My flock was scattered over the whole face of the earth, and no one was seeking or searching *for them*" (Ezek. 34:6).

"*If* you extend your soul to the hungry and satisfy the afflicted soul, then your light shall dawn in the darkness, and your darkness shall *be* as the noonday" (Is. 58:10).

"I tell the truth in Christ, I am not lying, my conscience also bearing me witness in the Holy Spirit, that I have great sorrow and continual grief in my heart. For I could wish that I myself were accursed from Christ for my brethren, my countrymen according to the flesh" (Rom. 9:1–3). See also Psalm 106:23; Luke 19:41; Acts 20:31.

Intercession is the way that leads to the winning of souls. No church can prosper without it. No Christian can grow without it. The law of life demands reproduction—that kind should beget kind.

Jesus interceded for each of us. "Therefore I will divide Him a portion with the great, and He shall divide the spoil with the strong, because He poured out His soul unto death, and He was numbered with the transgressors, and He bore the sin of many, and made intercession for the transgressors" (Is. 53:12).

Christ left this command to us: "Therefore pray the Lord of the harvest to send out laborers into His harvest" (Matt. 9:38).

IV. Contact

It began with ***personal contact.***

"He first found his own brother Simon, and said to him, 'We have found the Messiah' (which is translated, the Christ)" (John 1:41).

With Christ came the emphasis of *seeking the lost.* "For the Son of Man has come to seek and to save that which was lost" (Luke 19:10).

The movement of Christianity in this world is scripturally based on personal contact. Anyone who really knows Jesus will want others to know Him.

The secret is in the words of Andrew, "We have *found.*" The search for satisfaction in an individual's soul is completed in a living knowledge of Jesus Christ. Personal evangelism is sharing this discovery.

"And he brought him to Jesus" (John 1:42).

How is this accomplished? Christ gives the answer. "Follow Me, and I will make you fishers of men" (Matt. 4:19). ***A love for Christ produces a love for humankind.***

We are to be workers "who [do] not need to be ashamed" (2 Tim. 2:15). Lives today are complicated by sin. They need more than slogans and formulas. They need personal help. A conscientious doctor must deal with each patient separately and so must a conscientious soulwinner.

These guidelines must be kept in mind:

1. I MUST LIVE IT. I can't say to others, "Do as I *say,* but don't do as I *do.*" They must see Christ in me (1 Cor. 4:9). My strongest testimony is my daily life.

2. I MUST LOVE PEOPLE. I cannot pretend. The other person knows my motive immediately. The power of evangelism is described in Revelation 22:17, "And the Spirit and the bride say, 'Come!' " When my *concern* for others is in keeping with the concern of the Holy Spirit toward humankind, there is a community of interest in the individual that results in *compulsion.*

3. I MUST MEET THE PUBLIC. Jesus was heaven's artist at this. He never met a stranger. Paul testified, "I have become all things to all *men,* that I might by all means save some" (1 Cor. 9:22).

Kindness will open doors (Eph. 4:32). It will bring an affirmative response.

4. I MUST LOOK FOR NEED. Jesus said, "Those who are well have no need of a physician, but those who are sick. I did not come to call *the* righteous, but sinners, to repentance" (Mark 2:17).

You will be surprised how many people are ready to talk. They simply need someone in whom they can have confidence. Zacchaeus was in trouble. Uninvited, he talked about his sin. *That is my point of contact—human need.*

5. I MUST COMMUNICATE. Keep away from technicalities. Refuse to become involved in debate. The Samaritan woman quibbled: "Our fathers worshiped on this mountain, and you *Jews* say that in Jerusalem is the place where one ought to worship" (John 4:20). It wasn't her *head* that was troubling her. It was her *heart.* She needed Christ before she needed a church; a Redeemer before she needed a ritual. "I know that Messiah is coming" (who is called Christ). "When He comes, He will tell us all things." Jesus said to her, "I who speak to you am *He*" (John 4:25, 26).

6. I MUST CONCENTRATE ON CHRIST. I can get so much "I" into my testimony that spiritual pride will offend the person to whom I am witnessing. The rule of the great Baptist still holds: "He must increase, but I *must* decrease"

(John 3:30). *My business is to present Jesus* (John 12:32). Christ is the attraction.

7. I MUST USE TACT. This suggests a sensitivity to the other person's feelings. It is a spirit of discernment. "If any of you lacks wisdom, let him ask of God, who gives to all liberally and without reproach, and it will be given to him" (James 1:5). Be natural. Be courteous. Be a good listener. Ask wise questions.

8. I MUST BRING A PERSON TO A DECISION. This can only be accomplished through the power and presence of the Holy Spirit (John 16:8).

The chance may never come again. *Opportunity is God-given.* Don't gamble with it. Press for a decision. "Yet you do not have because you do not ask" (James 4:2). Don't let people say of you at Judgment Day, "He (or she) never asked me to be a Christian!"

9. I MUST TEACH THEM TO LISTEN TO GOD'S VOICE. It is my business to *introduce* them to the Savior. So often the worker only introduces himself. "Now acquaint yourself with Him, and be at peace; thereby good will come to you" (Job 22:21). Let the person with whom you are dealing hear for the first time the voice of God speaking to him or her in reassurance and comfort, and you have built strength.

This is done by teaching the person two or three primary verses of Scripture. Tie the seeker to God's Word. Let your friend know before you leave that God has spoken these words to him or her. These words carry a guarantee.

Here is an *example:*

"Most assuredly, I say to you, he who hears My word and believes in Him who sent Me has everlasting life, and shall not come into judgment, but has passed from death into life" (John 5:24).

These are the words of the Son of God. They are spoken to *you.* They are spoken with finality and authority.

10. I MUST MAKE IT CRYSTAL CLEAR THAT THERE IS A DIFFERENCE BETWEEN KNOWING GOD AND KNOWING ABOUT GOD. Hearsay is not enough. *Birth is not something that is secondhand.* "And when he brings out his own sheep, he goes before them; and the sheep follow him, for they know his voice. Yet they will by no means follow a stranger, but will flee from him, for they do not know the voice of strangers" (John 10:4, 5).

I know God when I get down to business with Him. "Draw near to God and He will draw near to you" (James 4:8). God has expressed His willingness in a covenant, contract, or testament. It bears His signature in the death and resurrection of Jesus Christ. ***The moment I exercise faith toward this written word and become personally involved in agreement, that very moment the entire contract, or covenant, is in force toward me.***

If I do not associate the seeker with the Word of God, that person will miss his or her way. The devil will deceive the inquirer before breakfast. He will lie so cleverly that the inquirer will apologize to worldly associates before the day is over.

Remember! The authority is in the Word of God.

V. A Conversation

Dr. R. G. Lee calls this two-way conversation "convincing confutation." The following are answers to some excuses as Dr. Lee sets them forth.

1. Excuse: *"I want to get established in business first. After that I will be a Christian."*

Answer: No business should be allowed to cheat one out of heaven's blessings. Property should not kill the privilege of being a child of God. "For what will it profit a man if he gains the whole world, and loses his own soul?" (Mark 8:36). God called one man a fool to his face. "But God said to him, 'Fool! This night your soul will be required of you; then whose will those things be which you have provided?' " (Luke 12:20). He was the man who neglected his soul's welfare by building barns, enlarging crops, and feeding his soul on corn.

Further Scriptures that may be used: Matthew 6:33; Psalm 1:1, 2; Proverbs 29:25; Mark 10:29, 30.

2. Excuse: *"I am not a sinner."*

Answer: But God says *"There is none righteous, no, not one"* (Rom. 3:10). "But the Scripture has confined all under sin" (Gal. 3:22). If you are not a sinner, are you keeping God's commands? What about Matthew 22:37? "Jesus said to him, 'You shall love the LORD your God with all your heart, with all your soul, and with all your mind.' "

3. Excuse: *"I have no encouragement at home."*

Answer: Without families we came. Without our families we go. Guilt is personal. Then, too, if you have praying parents, a saintly wife or husband, and godly children, and you continue your selfish resistance to their accepted and your rejected Savior, your guilt is deeper.

4. Excuse: *"I am good enough as I am."*

Answer: God says you are bad enough—by nature. Humans in their natural state do wicked deeds, think evil thoughts, go to bad places, reject Jesus Christ—because their hearts are evil. No one is naturally good. If you are good, why not become acquainted with Jesus, who is supremely good?

5. Excuse: *"I am as good as others."*

Answer: Violin players do not take their tones from each other, but from the piano. Builders are constantly using the plumb line, the level, and the square. We need to live by standards—not comparisons. Nobody can claim health because he or she is better than another diabetic or stronger than another cancer victim. Measure yourself by Jesus if you want to know how good or bad you are. Do not be too sure you are better than many within the church. They have confessed Jesus before others—as Jesus asked. You have not. Moreover, you are forbidden to judge to justify yourself. You are not saved or lost by the deeds of others.

6. Excuse: *"I have no feeling."*

Answer: The world isn't run by feeling. Washington did not live at Valley Forge because he felt like it. Most people do most of their worthy acts contrary to feeling. The doctor does not deal with diseases because of feeling but because of necessity.

Scriptures that may be used: Revelation 3:20; John 3:36; Ephesians 1:13; 1 Peter 1:8.

7. Excuse: *"I am so weak."*

Answer: "You will keep *him* in perfect peace *whose* mind *is* stayed *on You,* because he trusts in You. Trust in the LORD forever, for in YAH, the LORD, *is* everlasting strength" (Is. 26:3, 4). Who will keep? The Almighty God. How? "In perfect peace." On what condition? "*Whose* mind *is* stayed" on God—not on self, nor circumstances, failures, successes, nor on others. Trust—not try or worry, but trust. In whom? God. How long? All the time. Why? For God is everlasting strength.

Further Scriptures that may be used: Jude 24; 1 Corinthians 10:13; Philippians 1:6; Isaiah 41:10, 13, 14; 2 Timothy 1:12.

8. Excuse: *"I am doing the best I can."*

Answer: How long have you been doing your best? Have you succeeded? How long will it take you to make yourself fit for heaven? Suppose you die now? The best you can do is to acknowledge you cannot do anything to save yourself—except believe.

9. Excuse: *"I am too big a sinner."*

Answer: Jesus came to save *all* sinners. "This *is* a faithful saying and worthy of all acceptance, that Christ Jesus came into the world to save sinners, of whom I am chief" (1 Tim. 1:15). Are your sins scarlet? " 'Come now, and let us reason together,' says the LORD, 'Though your sins are like scarlet, they shall be as white as snow; though they are red like crimson, they shall be as wool' " (Is. 1:18). Are you lost? "For the Son of Man has come to seek and to save that which was lost" (Luke 19:10). Are you without strength? "For when we were still without strength, in due time Christ died for the ungodly. For scarcely for a righteous man will one die; yet perhaps for a good man someone would even dare to die. But God demonstrates His own love toward us, in that while we were still sinners Christ died for us" (Rom. 5:6–8). "All that the Father gives Me will come to Me, and the one who comes to Me I will by no means cast out" (John 6:37).

Further Scriptures that may be used: Matthew 9:13; Hebrews 7:25; Luke 23:39–43.

10. Excuse: *"There are too many hypocrites."*

Answer: Hypocrites are lost. If you let hypocrites keep you from being saved, you will spend eternity in hell with them. Besides, you have to be smaller than what you hide behind. If you hide behind a hypocrite, you must be smaller than a hypocrite.

Further Scriptures that may be used: Zechariah 13:6; Acts 1:6; Hebrews 12:2; Acts 17:30, 31; Romans 2:1–6; 14:12; Matthew 7:1–5; 1 Samuel 16:7.

11. Excuse: *"A professing Christian wronged me."*

Answer: Granted. But is that any reason why you should wrong God and insult Christ, who loved you and gave Himself for you? "He who believes in the Son has everlasting life; and he who does not believe the Son shall not see life, but the wrath of God abides on him" (John 3:36).

12. Excuse: *"There is too much to give up."*

Answer: Better give up everything than lose the soul. Put Christ and your soul ahead of all else. Is it too much to give up paste pearls for glittering gems? Dirt for diamonds? Is it too much to give up rags for riches?

Further Scriptures that may be used: Psalm 16:11; 84:11; Proverbs 3:17; 13:15; Matthew 11:30; Isaiah 57:21; Romans 8:32; Mark 8:36, 37; Luke 18:29, 30.

13. Excuse: *"I cannot understand."*

Answer: Why let mystery cause you to refuse the Master? Do you understand the chemistry of digestion? Does your ignorance of it keep you from eating steak? Can you understand why the same sun and the same soil and the same rain get sweetness into the orange and sourness into the lemon and bitterness into the persimmon?

Lay aside your excuse of mystery and trust God as you trust the telephone to transmit your voice.

Further Scriptures that may be used: Romans 11:33; 1 Corinthians 1:8; 2:14.

14. Excuse: *"God is unjust."*

Answer: Who is God? Who are you? Injustice is sin. Do you mean to accuse God of sin? God is so just that He never demands two payments for one debt. Jesus paid your sin debt on the cross—

all of it. Therefore, when you accept Christ, you do not have that sin debt to pay.

15. Excuse: *"Folks would laugh."*

Answer: Better let them laugh than to have God laugh. "I also will laugh at your calamity; I will mock when your terror comes" (Prov. 1:26). Shun evil companions. "Do not enter the path of the wicked, and do not walk in the way of evil. . . . The way of the wicked *is* like darkness; they do not know what makes them stumble" (Prov. 4:14, 19). Do not be ashamed of Christ. "Therefore whoever confesses Me before men, him I will also confess before My Father who is in heaven. But whoever denies Me before men, him I will also deny before My Father who is in heaven" (Matt. 10:32, 33).

16. Excuse: *"Not now."*

Answer: Every time you say no, it is more difficult to say yes. The time and day is *now*. "For He says: 'In an acceptable time I have heard you, and in the day of salvation I have helped you' " (2 Cor. 6:2).

Seek the Lord while He may be found. Delay is decision for the wrong way. "Today—if you will," says the Lord. Tomorrow is the day when the idle one works, the thief becomes honest, the drunkard sober. Tomorrow is a period nowhere to be found except, perhaps, in the fool's calendar. God's call is not a call for tomorrow, but for *today*.

Dr. Lee says of the above, "In this manner do I deal with excuse-makers. With many excuse-makers I have had success. With some, I have not."

Further Scriptures that may be used: Proverbs 27:1; 29:1; Isaiah 55:6; Hebrews 2:3.

Some other common excuses and questions are:

17. Excuse: *"I think you are making too big a fuss about this."*

Answer: Why is Calvary such a big date in history? "But God demonstrates His own love toward us, in that while we were still sinners, Christ died for us" (Rom. 5:8).

Isn't your soul important? "For what profit is it to a man if he gains the whole world, and loses his own soul? Or what will a man give in exchange for his soul?" (Matt. 16:26).

Isn't life uncertain? "But God said to him, 'Fool! This night your soul will be required of you; then whose will those things be which you have provided?' " (Luke 12:20).

Death, judgment, and hell lie ahead (Gal. 6:7; Heb. 9:27).

The Son of God asks for your decision (Rev. 3:20).

18. Excuse: *"I will take my chances."*

Answer: God always has the last word. "So he said to him, 'Friend, how did you come in here without a wedding garment?' And he was speechless. Then the king said to the servants, 'Bind him hand and foot, take him away, and cast *him* into outer darkness; there will be weeping and gnashing of teeth' " (Matt. 22:12, 13).

Nebuchadnezzar gave this testimony, "That the Most High rules in the kingdom of men, gives it to whomever He will" (Dan. 4:17). "All the inhabitants of the earth *are* reputed as nothing; He does according to His will in the army of heaven and *among* the inhabitants of the earth. No one can restrain His hand or say to Him, 'What have you done?' " (Dan. 4:35).

God's Word has eternal force (Is. 55:11).

A judgment must be rendered on each life lived (John 5:27–29).

19. Excuse: *"My friends mean so much to me."*

Answer: Are they your friends or your enemies? "Adulterers and adulteresses! Do you not know that friendship with the world is enmity with God? Whoever therefore wants to be a friend of the world makes himself an enemy of God" (James 4:4).

Do your friends care for your soul? "But when he had spent all, there arose a severe famine in that land, and he began to be in want. Then he went and joined himself to a citizen of that country, and he sent him into his fields to feed swine. And he would gladly have filled his stomach with the pods that the swine ate, and no one gave him *anything*" (Luke 15:14–16).

You will gain a greater Friend and friends (John 15:15; Matt. 19:29).

Your example can lead your unsaved friends to Christ (John 1:45).

20. Excuse: *"I am going to have a good time in this world and let the next world take care of itself."*

Answer: Others have followed this course before. "Son, remember that in your lifetime you received your good things, and likewise Lazarus evil things; but now he is comforted and you are tormented" (Luke 16:25).

Your life can prove to be a *charade* (Luke 12:15).

Opportunity brings responsibility (Eccl. 11:9).

21. Excuse: *"Please do not talk to me about it."*

Answer: I am simply bringing God's message to you. "Therefore prepare yourself and arise, and speak to them all that I command you. Do not be dismayed before their faces, lest I dismay you before them" (Jer. 1:17). "And go, get to the captives, to the children of your people, and speak to them and tell them, 'Thus says the Lord GOD,' whether they hear, or whether they refuse" (Ezek. 3:11).

My business is to *witness* (2 Cor. 2:15, 16).

22. Excuse: *"I am my own boss."*

Answer: Wise men and women receive *counsel.* "There is a way *that seems* right to a man, but its end *is* the way of death" (Prov. 14:12).

The straight way is the best way (Matt. 7:13, 14).

The easiest thing in the world to get is *a wrong answer.*

23. Excuse: *"Frankly, I am skeptical about the whole matter."*

Answer: Are you honestly looking for *answers?* Will you accept evidence as it would be accepted before a court of law? Are you an *inquirer* or a *spiritual subversive* "who exchanged the truth of God for the lie, and worshiped and served the creature rather than the Creator" (Rom. 1:25). "And even as they did not like to retain God in *their* knowledge, God gave them over to a debased mind, to do those things which are not fitting" (Rom. 1:28).

Jesus Christ threw out this challenge: "He who is of God hears God's words; therefore you do not hear, because you are not of God" (John 8:47).

You can *doubt* to your own peril (2 Thess. 2:10, 12).

The way to find out whether or not a thing is true and worthy of one's acceptance is to put it to *a personal test* (Ps. 34:8).

24. Excuse: *"I want to be absolutely neutral about this matter."*

Answer: There are some things you can't be neutral about—food, drink, sleep, light, for instance. That is why Christ likened Himself to the *necessities* of life. "I am the bread of life" (John 6:48). "I am the light of the world. He who follows Me shall not walk in darkness, but have the light of life" (John 8:12).

Jesus said, "He who is not with Me is against Me, and he who does not gather with Me scatters abroad" (Matt. 12:30).

25. Excuse: *"I believe God is too good to damn anyone."*

Answer: That is not what the Bible says. "Therefore the ungodly shall not stand in the judgment, nor sinners in the congregation of the righteous. For the LORD knows the way of the righteous, but the way of the ungodly shall perish" (Ps. 1:5, 6).

God bases your salvation or damnation on your acceptance or rejection of Jesus Christ (John 12:48).

It is not God who is hard. It is you! "But in accordance with your hardness and your impenitent heart you are treasuring up for yourself wrath in the day of wrath and revelation of the righteous judgment of God" (Rom. 2:5).

Every agency of God seeks to lead you to repentance (2 Pet. 3:9).

26. Excuse: *"How can I reconcile the doctrine of hell with the Christian's God of salvation?"*

Answer: "Then He will also say to those on the left hand, 'Depart from Me, you cursed, into the everlasting fire prepared for the devil and his angels'" (Matt. 25:41).

"Judas by transgression fell, that he might go to his own place" (Acts 1:25).

"The Lord is not slack concerning *His* promise, as some count slackness, but is longsuffering toward us, not willing that any should perish but that all should come to repentance" (2 Pet. 3:9).

"'Do I have any pleasure at all that the wicked should die?' says the Lord GOD, '*and* not that he should turn from his ways and live?'" (Ezek. 18:23).

"And these will go away into everlasting punishment, but the righteous into eternal life" (Matt. 25:46).

"Son, remember that in your lifetime you received your good things, and likewise Lazarus evil things; but now he is comforted and you are tormented" (Luke 16:25).

"Serpents, brood of vipers! How can you escape the condemnation of hell?" (Matt. 23:33).

"And do not fear those who kill the body but cannot kill the soul. But rather fear Him who is able to destroy both soul and body in hell" (Matt. 10:28).

"Therefore Sheol has enlarged itself and opened its mouth beyond measure; their glory and their multitude and their pomp, and he who is jubilant, shall descend into it. People shall be brought down, each man shall be humbled, and the eyes of the lofty shall be humbled. But the LORD of hosts shall be exalted in judgment, and God who is holy shall be hallowed in righteousness" (Is. 5:14–16).

27. Excuse: *"I am religious."*

Answer: Religion is often something that is on the outside. "Many will say to Me in that day, 'Lord, Lord, have we not prophesied in Your name, cast out demons in Your name, and done many wonders in Your name?' And then I will declare to them, 'I never knew you; depart from Me, you who practice lawlessness!'" (Matt. 7:22, 23).

No one was more religious than Paul (Gal. 1:14; Phil. 3:6; 1 Tim. 1:13, 15).

Cornelius was a religious man who needed to be saved (Acts 11:14).

28. Excuse: *"I am trying to be a Christian."*

Answer: It is not *trying,* it is *trusting* that counts. A drowning man tries with all his might and perishes, but when he trusts in the saving power of another he is rescued. "Behold, God *is* my salvation, I will trust and not be afraid; 'For

YAH, the LORD, *is* my strength and song; He also has become my salvation' " (Is. 12:2).

Ishmael was Abraham's fleshly attempt to fulfill the promise of God (he tried). Isaac was God's provision (he trusted) (Rom. 4:3, 5).

No work that you can do for yourself can ever substitute in merit for the work that Jesus has done for you on the cross (Eph. 2:9).

"But we are all like an unclean *thing,* and all our righteousnesses *are* like filthy rags; we all fade as a leaf, and our iniquities, like the wind, have taken us away" (Is. 64:6). To try is to fail! "For whoever shall keep the whole law, and yet stumble in one *point,* he is guilty of all" (James 2:10).

29. Excuse: *"What is sin?"*

Answer: Sin is breaking God's law (1 John 3:10). All unrighteousness is sin, and there is no sin not *leading* to death (1 John 5:17).

Unbelief is sin (John 16:8, 9).

Questionable indulgences are sin (Rom. 14:23).

Missing the mark is sin (Rom. 3:23).

Undone duty is sin (James 4:17).

30. Excuse: *"My sins are small, so why worry?"*

Answer: Because any sin torments. " '*There is* no peace,' says the LORD, 'for the wicked' " (Is. 48:22).

Because any sin separates you from God (Is. 59:2).

Because any sin enslaves you (John 8:34).

Because any sin excludes from heaven (1 Cor. 6:9).

Because any sin ends in death (Rom. 6:23).

31. Excuse: *"I may be punished but not eternally."*

Answer: If God is eternal and heaven is eternal—hell will be eternal also. "Then He will also say to those on the left hand, 'Depart from Me, you cursed, into the everlasting fire prepared for the devil and his angels' " (Matt. 25:41).

There is "a resurrection of condemnation" (John 5:28, 29).

Don't forget there is the "second death" (Rev. 20:13–15).

32. Excuse: *"I am too old now to become a Christian."*

Answer: There is no age limit (2 Cor. 6:2).

God has foreseen your problem. "But from there you will seek the LORD your God, and you will find *Him* if you seek Him with all your heart and with all your soul. When you are in distress, and all these things come upon you in the latter days, when you turn to the LORD your God and obey His voice (for the LORD your God *is* a merciful God), He will not forsake you nor destroy you, nor forget the covenant of your fathers which He swore to them" (Deut. 4:29–31).

33. Excuse: *"I do not think I am old enough to make a decision."*

Answer: You have reached an age of accountability if you sense Christ's approach to your life. "Remember now your Creator in the days of your youth, before the difficult days come, and the years draw near when you say, 'I have no pleasure in them' " (Eccl. 12:1).

The time to make a decision is when your conscience is tender (2 Sam. 19:35).

The best time is *now* (Heb. 3:13).

34. Excuse: *"I intend to before I die."*

Answer: Can you determine the hour of your death? *Nothing is so uncertain as life* (Prov. 29:1; Job 34:20).

God warns against *presumption* (James 4:13–17).

There is no time like the present. "Seek the LORD while He may be found, call upon Him while He is near" (Is. 55:6).

35. Excuse: *"I am afraid I cannot hold out."*

Answer: Jesus not only saves but He keeps. He is the Good Shepherd (John 10:11, 14).

The same One who convicts you is concerned about you. "He who calls you *is* faithful, who also will do *it*" (1 Thess. 5:24).

Paul gives his experience. "And He said to me, 'My grace is sufficient for you, for My strength is made perfect in weakness.' Therefore most gladly I will rather boast in my infirmities, that the power of Christ may rest upon me" (2 Cor. 12:9).

God has made an investment in you, and He will work to protect that investment (Phil. 1:6).

To know Him is to have assurance. Commit your entire life to His care. Leave the future in your Master's hands (2 Tim. 1:12).

36. Excuse: *"I am afraid of persecution."*

Answer: It is a cowardly thing to deny Jesus Christ. "But the cowardly, unbelieving, abominable, murderers, sexually immoral, sorcerers, idolaters, and all liars shall have their part in the lake which burns with fire and brimstone, which is the second death" (Rev. 21:8).

"For whoever is ashamed of Me and My words in this adulterous and sinful generation, of him the Son of Man also will be ashamed when He comes in the glory of His Father with the holy angels" (Mark 8:38).

So little is asked for so much in return. "For I consider that the sufferings of this present time are not worthy *to be compared* with the glory which shall be revealed in us" (Rom. 8:18).

It is all or nothing. "If we endure, we shall also reign with *Him.* If we deny *Him,* He also will deny us" (2 Tim. 2:12).

You join a select company. It is a chance of a lifetime to do something worthwhile. "Blessed are you when men hate you, and when they exclude you, and revile *you,* and cast out your name as evil, for the Son of Man's sake. Rejoice in that day and leap for joy! For indeed your reward *is* great in heaven, for in like manner their fathers did to the prophets" (Luke 6:22, 23).

He does not ask you to do anything for Him that He did not do for you (Heb. 12:2).

37. Excuse: *"I think that Jesus Christ is only one of the great men in history."*

Answer: He claimed to be God. ". . . Who, being in the form of God, did not consider it robbery to be equal with God" (Phil. 2:6). He was put to death for this claim (Matt. 26:63–65). The Resurrection substantiated this claim: "Whom God raised up, having loosed the pains of death, because it was not possible that He should be held by it" (Acts 2:24).

The moral grandeur of His life surpasses anything on record. "Which of you convicts Me of sin? And if I tell the truth, why do you not believe Me?" (John 8:46).

No one has so influenced history (Luke 2:34).

There is the repeated testimony of personal experience. "Now we believe, not because of what you said, for we ourselves have heard *Him* and we know that this is indeed the Christ, the Savior of the world" (John 4:42).

There is the open challenge to prove His divinity for yourself. "If anyone wills to do His will, he shall know concerning the doctrine, whether it is from God or *whether* I speak on My own *authority*" (John 7:17).

38. Question: *"Why does God allow evil in this world?"*

Answer: Freedom of choice is the Creator's great gift to the human race. "I call heaven and earth as witnesses today against you, *that* I have set before you life and death, blessing and cursing; therefore choose life, that both you and your descendants may live" (Deut. 30:19).

Sin originated in human beings, not in God. God prevents sin's dominion (Rom. 6:14).

God has, at His own cost, provided a remedy. "I am the way, the truth, and the life. No one comes to the Father except through Me" (John 14:6).

39. Excuse: *"There is so much suffering."*

Answer: This is not the world as God planned it—the world that He said was "very good" (Gen. 1:31). It is the world in which humankind has spread their sin. "Even as I have seen, those who plow iniquity and sow trouble reap the same" (Job 4:8).

God has provided an alternative. "For the wages of sin *is* death, but the gift of God *is* eternal life in Christ Jesus our Lord" (Rom. 6:23).

It is not the world that God intends to establish (Is. 65:20).

40. Question: *"Does this have to be done publicly?"*

Answer: God makes the rules. He has undertaken our salvation completely; therefore He has the right to say how we are to receive it. "Therefore whoever confesses Me before men, him I will also confess before My Father who is in heaven. But whoever denies Me before men, him I will also deny before My Father who is in heaven" (Matt. 10:32, 33). "For with the heart one believes unto righteousness, and with the mouth confession is made unto salvation" (Rom. 10:10).

Like a true marriage—a miracle of trust happens in the heart first; then an open acknowledgment, through proper ordinances, is made to the public.

"For whoever is ashamed of Me and My words in this adulterous and sinful generation, of him the Son of Man also will be ashamed when He comes in the glory of His Father with the holy angels" (Mark 8:38).

"Also I say to you, whoever confesses Me before men, him the Son of Man also will confess before the angels of God. But he who denies Me before men will be denied before the angels of God" (Luke 12:8, 9).

"Nevertheless even among the rulers many believed in Him, but because of the Pharisees they did not confess *Him,* lest they should be put out of the synagogue; for they loved the praise of men more than the praise of God" (John 12:42, 43).

41. Question: *"What about baptism?"*

Answer: Baptism like Communion "shows the Lord's death." It is faith you show publicly when you are baptized.

"Or do you not know that as many of us as were baptized into Christ Jesus were baptized into His death? Therefore we were buried with Him through baptism into death, that just as Christ was raised from the dead by the glory of the Father, even so we also should walk in newness of life" (Rom. 6:3–5).

Baptism is our open profession before the world that we are now living a miracle, supernatural life of Christian grace by the quickening, regenerating power of God in us.

You should be baptized because like your Lord it fulfills ". . . all righteousness. . . ." It keeps setting forth the gospel of Jesus before this world. Baptism is one of the first tests of obedience.

42. Excuse: *"I cannot break with my sins."*

Answer: Salvation is a life-and-death choice. "I tell you, no; but unless you repent you will all likewise perish" (Luke 13:3).

You cannot live one way and die another way. "For he who sows to his flesh will of the flesh reap corruption, but he who sows to the Spirit will of the Spirit reap everlasting life" (Gal. 6:8; cf. Rev. 21:8).

You cannot do it in your own strength. "Therefore if the Son makes you free, you shall be free indeed" (John 8:36). "I can do all things through Christ who strengthens me" (Phil. 4:13).

Christ can reach you where you are (Heb. 7:25).

43. Excuse: *"I see no harm in worldly amusements."*

Answer: The approach to this question should always be *positive,* and not negative. Instead of asking, "What *harm* is there in it?" I should ask, "What *good* is there in it?"

"And *whatever* you do in word or deed, *do* all in the name of the Lord Jesus, giving thanks to God the Father through Him" (Col. 3:17).

"Therefore, whether you eat or drink, or whatever you do, do all to the glory of God" (1 Cor. 10:31).

"All things are lawful for me, but all things are not helpful. All things are lawful for me, but I will not be brought under the power of any" (1 Cor. 6:12).

As a Christian, I am responsible to use my body and my mind in trust for God's glory (1 Cor. 6:19, 20).

Sharp warnings appear in the New Testament: "If anyone defiles the temple of God, God will destroy him. For the temple of God is holy, which *temple* you are" (1 Cor. 3:17). "Come out from among them and be separate, says the Lord. Do not touch what is unclean, and I will receive you" (2 Cor. 6:17). "They profess to know God, but in works they deny Him, being abominable, disobedient, and disqualified for every good work" (Titus 1:16).

My aim should always be to give my utmost for His highest (2 Tim. 2:4).

44. Excuse: *"I am not respectable enough to be a Christian."*

Answer: It is your saving, active faith in Christ that counts, "And he arose and came to his father. But when he was still a great way off, his father saw him and had compassion, and ran and fell on his neck and kissed him. And the son said to him, 'Father, I have sinned against heaven and in your sight, and am no longer worthy to be called your son.' But the father said to his servants, 'Bring out the best robe and put *it* on him, and put a ring on his hand and sandals on *his* feet. And bring the fatted calf here and kill *it,* and let us eat and be merry; for this my son was dead and is alive again; he was lost and is found.' And they began to be merry" (Luke 15:20–24). See also Luke 18:10–14.

We can never make ourselves good enough. "But to him who does not work but believes on Him who justifies the ungodly, his faith is accounted for righteousness" (Rom. 4:5). See also Isaiah 41:13.

45. Excuse: *"I am afraid Jesus will not receive me."*

Answer: You have His word on it. "All that the Father gives Me will come to Me, and the one who comes to Me I will by no means cast out" (John 6:37).

God is no respecter of persons (Rom. 10:13; Luke 15:2). See also Revelation 22:17.

46. Excuse: *"I have tried before and failed."*

Answer: One failure need not mean final defeat. *Upon whom did you depend?* Did you make a complete surrender? Did you keep something back? Did you confess Christ publicly? Were you faithful in prayer? Did you seek guidance from the Word? "These were more fair-minded than those in Thessalonica, in that they received the word with all readiness, and searched the Scriptures daily *to find out* whether these things were so" (Acts 17:11). Did you go to work for Christ? (Luke 11:24–26). See also 1 Peter 2:2.

Make a full surrender. "I beseech you therefore, brethren, by the mercies of God, that you present your bodies a living sacrifice, holy, acceptable to God, *which is* your reasonable service" (Rom. 12:1).

Keep in touch! "Watch and pray, lest you enter into temptation. The spirit indeed *is* willing, but the flesh *is* weak" (Matt. 26:41).

Be present in church (Heb. 10:25).

47. Excuse: *"I think I have committed the unpardonable sin."*

Answer: You will *know* if you have committed this sin. The desire to be a Christian will be forever past. No spiritual impression will ever again come to your soul. *A hardening process will have taken place.*

"Therefore I say to you, every sin and blasphemy will be forgiven men, but the blasphemy *against* the Spirit will not be forgiven men. Anyone who speaks a word against the Son of Man, it will be forgiven him; but whoever speaks against the Holy Spirit, it will not be forgiven him, either in this age or in the *age* to come" (Matt. 12:31, 32).

In another passage we read: "but he who blasphemes against the Holy Spirit never has forgiveness, but is subject to eternal condemnation" (Mark 3:29).

The tragedy lies in *the eternally unforgiven soul.* Since the Holy Spirit is the agent in conviction and conversion, there can be no rebirth without the Holy Spirit. To sin against the Holy Spirit is to sin against your own soul. To blaspheme against the Holy Spirit is to shut yourself off forever from access to God.

"If anyone sees his brother sinning a sin *which does* not *lead* to death, he will ask, and He will give him life for those who commit sin not *leading* to death" (1 John 5:16).

You will *know* if you cross this line. Those who have committed this sin are completely given over to Satan and have not the slightest interest in spiritual matters. Paul describes it as being "past feeling" (Eph. 4:19).

On the other hand, Satan, *the deceiver*, will lie to you and tell you that you are unpardonable. God makes no exceptions in His offer of salvation.

"And by Him everyone who believes is justified from all things from which you could not be justified by the law of Moses" (Acts 13:39).

Murder is not unpardonable. David confessed his sin and was forgiven (Ps. 32:5).

Theft is not unpardonable. The penitent thief on the cross was pardoned (Luke 23:43).

Blasphemy is not unpardonable. Paul was a blasphemer, and he was pardoned (1 Tim. 1:13).

Adultery is not unpardonable. The woman of Samaria was saved (John 4:18).

One of the amazing records of forgiveness is found in 1 Corinthians 6:9–11.

The person who sincerely asks for pardon will never be refused. "Let the wicked forsake his way, and the unrighteous man his thoughts; let him return to the LORD, and He will have mercy on him; and to our God, for He will abundantly pardon" (Is. 55:7).

" 'Come now, and let us reason together,' says the LORD, 'though your sins are like scarlet, they shall be as white as snow; though they are red like crimson, they shall be as wool' " (Is. 1:18). See also Acts 10:43.

Paul was a great sinner, but he obtained salvation (1 Tim. 1:15, 16).

48. Question: *"Would not suicide be the best way out of my trouble?"*

Answer: There is only one solution for guilt consciousness—forgiveness and cleansing (Job 15:20; 1 John 1:9).

Self-murder only hastens judgment. "So then each of us shall give account of himself to God" (Rom. 14:12).

A correct relationship with Christ brings a new approach to living. "Therefore, if anyone *is* in Christ, *he is* a new creation; old things have passed away; behold, all things have become new" (2 Cor. 5:17).

Get the *sin-problem* settled first, and then the *trouble-problem* can be settled (Matt. 6:33).

49. Excuse: *"I am seeking but I cannot find Christ."*

Answer: Christ is not distant. His presence is noticeable, "so that they should seek the Lord, in the hope that they might grope for Him and find Him, though He is not far from each one of us; for in Him we live and move and have our being, as also some of your own poets have said, 'For we are also His offspring' " (Acts 17:27, 28).

Paul says that Christ makes Himself real to a person through the exercise of faith (Rom. 10:6–11).

Be sure you are looking in the right direction! "And you will seek Me and find *Me,* when you search for Me with all your heart" (Jer. 29:13).

50. Excuse: *"I am ashamed to come to Christ."*

Answer: "When Jesus heard *that,* He said to them, 'Those who are well have no need of a physician, but those who are sick. But go and learn what *this* means: "I desire mercy and not sacrifice." For I did not come to call the righteous, but sinners, to repentance' " (Matt. 9:12, 13).

Salvation is for the *lost.* "For when we were still without strength, in due time Christ died for the ungodly. For scarcely for a righteous man will one die; yet perhaps for a good man someone would even dare to die. But God demonstrates His own love toward us, in that while we were still sinners, Christ died for us" (Rom. 5:6–8).

51. Excuse: *"I would like to be a Christian, but I cannot forgive my enemies."*

Answer: Through God's help you can do what you cannot do otherwise. "With men this is impossible, but with God all things are possible" (Matt. 19:26).

I become a recipient of God's *grace.* "And God *is* able to make all grace abound toward you, that you, always having all sufficiency in all *things,* may have an abundance for every good work" (2 Cor. 9:8). See also 2 Corinthians 12:9.

Tell God only that *you are willing to be made willing* (Matt. 6:14, 15).

52. Excuse: *"I want to be saved, but I cannot believe."*

Answer: *Whom* does the Bible ask you to believe? "Believe on the Lord Jesus Christ, and you will be saved, you and your household" (Acts 16:31).

Do you believe that God has saved *others?* Do you believe that He wants to save *you?* Do you believe that He *can* save you? Will you trust Him to save you *now*?

You are saved through the Word, which is God's contract with you, and because God wants you to be saved (John 5:24). "But as many as received Him, to them He gave the right to become children of God, to those who believe in His name: who were born, not of blood, nor of the will of the flesh, nor of the will of man, but of God" (John 1:12, 13).

Use the faith that God gives you! "For by grace you have been saved through faith, and that not of yourselves; *it is* the gift of God" (Eph. 2:8). See also Romans 5:1.

53. Question: *"Does not the Bible have inconsistencies and contradictions in it?"*

Answer: Where are they? The Bible is *revelation.* " 'For My thoughts *are* not your thoughts, nor *are* your ways My ways,' says the LORD. 'For *as* the heavens are higher than the earth, so are My ways higher than your ways, and My thoughts than your thoughts" (Is. 55:8, 9).

The Bible is a *locked book* to a *locked heart.*

"Many shall be purified, made white, and refined, but the wicked shall do wickedly; and none of the wicked shall understand, but the wise shall understand" (Dan. 12:10). "But the natural man does not receive the things of the Spirit of God, for they are foolishness to him; nor can he know *them,* because they are spiritually discerned" (1 Cor. 2:14).

Certainly there are mysteries presented in God's Word! "As also in all his epistles, speaking in them of these things, in which are some things hard to understand, which untaught and unstable *people* twist to their own destruction, as *they do* also the rest of the Scriptures. You therefore, beloved, since you know *this* beforehand, beware lest you also fall from your own steadfastness, being led away with the error of the wicked; but grow in the grace and knowledge of our Lord and Savior Jesus Christ. To Him *be* the glory both now and forever. Amen" (2 Pet. 3:16–18).

Know Him and you will know His book!

54. Question: *"How can I know there is a God?"*

Answer: There are *three sources* of material. First, there is the Bible. Second, there is nature. Third, there is humankind. These point to the Creator. None are possible by happenstance. None could have been produced by accident.

"Because what may be known of God is manifest in them, for God has shown *it* to them" (Rom. 1:9).

"When I consider Your heavens, the work of Your fingers, the moon and the stars, which You have ordained" (Ps. 8:3).

"By the word of the LORD the heavens were made, and all the host of them by the breath of His mouth" (Ps. 33:6).

55. Question: *"Why do I need the blood?"*

Answer: "For the life of the flesh *is* in the blood, and I have given it to you upon the altar to make atonement for your souls; for it *is* the blood *that* makes atonement for the soul" (Lev. 17:11).

Jesus died for you and me (Matt. 26:28).

"And according to the law almost all things are purified with blood, and without shedding of blood there is no remission" (Heb. 9:22).

He tasted death for me. Thus He bore the supreme penalty of my sins (Rom. 5:9, 10).

It took the greatest price in the universe. "Knowing that you were not redeemed with corruptible things, *like* silver or gold, from your aimless conduct *received* by tradition from your fathers, but with the precious blood of Christ, as of a lamb without blemish and without spot" (1 Pet. 1:18, 19).

56. Question: *"Why should I accept the Bible as the final authority?"*

Answer: *The Bible has survived all unbelievers.* "For what if some did not believe? Will their unbelief make the faithfulness of God without effect? Certainly not! Indeed, let God be true but every man a liar" (Rom. 3:3, 4).

"All Scripture *is* given by inspiration of God, and *is* profitable for doctrine, for reproof, for correction, for instruction in righteousness" (2 Tim. 3:16).

God's character rests upon the authenticity and authority of the Bible (Mark 13:31).

57. Question: *"What must I do to be saved?"*

Answer: God, through Jesus Christ, His Son, has provided a way for you (Is. 53:5, 6). That sixth verse begins and ends with the same word, "all." It is a universal salvation for a universal need.

Your part is to "receive"; God's part is to give you "power to become." "But as many as received Him, to them He gave the right to become children of God, to those who believe in His name" (John 1:12).

Conversion and regeneration go together. When you have turned to God (conversion), He will turn over your life (regeneration). God's part is as essential as your part (John 3:7).

Saving faith reaches out and believes what God's Word says about you. "Most assuredly, I say to you, he who hears My word and believes in Him who sent Me has everlasting life, and shall not come into judgment, but has passed from death into life" (John 5:24).

Your salvation is in your acceptance of what Christ has done for you. Did He, or did He not, die for you? (Acts 16:31).

Outward form is useless until something has happened within your life. Salvation is like marriage. All the ceremony involved can't really marry a couple unless first of all something real toward each other has happened in each of their hearts. When that occurs, they want the whole world to know (Rom. 10:9–19).

God saves sinners only. Are you a sinner? Do you need two things—(1) FORGIVENESS and (2) CLEANSING?

What God has done for others, He will do for you. "For 'whoever calls on the name of the LORD shall be saved' " (Rom. 10:13).

Jesus foretold that excuses and alibis would be given. *Excuses* are never *reasons.*

"Then He said to him, 'A certain man gave a great supper and invited many, and sent his servant at supper time to say to those who were invited, "Come, for all things are now ready." But they all with one *accord* began to make excuses. The first said to him, "I have bought a piece of ground, and I must go and see it. I ask you to have me excused." And another said, "I have bought five yoke of oxen, and I am going to test them. I ask you to have me excused." Still another said, "I have married a wife, and therefore I cannot come." So that servant came and reported these things to his master. Then the master of the house, being angry, said to his servant, "Go out quickly into the streets and lanes of the city, and bring in here *the* poor, and *the* maimed and *the* lame and *the* blind." And the servant said, "Master, it is done as you commanded, and still there is room." Then the master said to the servant, "Go out into the highways and hedges, and compel *them* to come in, that my house may be filled. For I say to you that none of those men who were invited shall taste my supper" '" (Luke 14:16–24).

Let not conscience make you linger,
Nor of fitness fondly dream;
All the fitness he requireth
Is to feel your need of Him.
—Joseph Hart

VI. Conversion

Steps to the Christian Life:

1. REPENT. Turn around. Change your mind. "I tell you, no; but unless you repent you will all likewise perish" (Luke 13:3).

2. RECEIVE HIM. You need the Savior. Accept Him. "But as many as received Him, to them He gave the right to become children of God, to those who believe in His name" (John 1:12).

3. BE "BORN AGAIN." This is what God does for you. This is the New Birth—a miracle of spiritual life performed by the Holy Spirit. "Who were born, not of blood, nor of the will of the flesh, nor of the will of man, but of God" (John 1:13). See also John 11:25.

4. REJOICE PUBLICLY. Make your testimony for Christ, "that if you confess with your mouth the Lord Jesus and believe in your heart that God has raised Him from the dead, you will be saved. For with the heart one believes unto righteousness, and with the mouth confession is made unto salvation" (Rom. 10:9, 10). See also Matthew 10:32, 33.

5. REQUEST WATER BAPTISM. This is an outward testimony to an inward transaction. "He who believes and is baptized will be saved; but he who does not believe will be condemned" (Mark 16:16).

6. READ THE WORD. The Word is the source of your faith. "These things I have written to you who believe in the name of the Son of God, that you may know that you have eternal life, and that you may *continue to* believe in the name of the Son of God" (1 John 5:13). See also Romans 10:17; Psalm 119:105.

The Bible can never be the private and exclusive property of any one religion. God gave it to the world. Therefore, look for your eternal assurance from the Bible. *It is what God says that counts.*

7. REACH GOD IN PRAYER. Prayer is conversation with God. Life is sustained by union and communion (Eph. 6:18; James 4:2). "Now this is the confidence that we have in Him, that if we ask anything according to His will, He hears us. And if we know that He hears us, whatever we ask, we know that we have the petitions that we have asked of Him" (1 John 5:14, 15).

8. RELATE YOUR EXPERIENCE TO OTHERS. You maintain strength by exercise. "Nevertheless if you warn the wicked to turn from his way, and he does not turn from his way, he shall die in his iniquity; but you have delivered your soul. Therefore you, O son of man, say to the house of Israel: 'Thus you say, "If our transgressions and our sins *lie* upon us, and we pine away in them, how can we then live?"'" (Ezek. 33:9, 10).

9. RESIST THE DEVIL. Temptation is not sin. It is yielding to temptation that is sin. "That the genuineness of your faith, *being* much more precious than gold that perishes, though it is tested by fire, may be found to praise, honor, and glory at the revelation of Jesus Christ" (1 Pet. 1:7).

"For we do not have a High Priest who cannot sympathize with our weaknesses, but was in all *points* tempted as *we are, yet* without sin" (Heb. 4:15).

10. RESTITUTION. Your guilt is gone, and you can convert your influence for good. "Then Zacchaeus stood and said to the Lord, 'Look, Lord, I give half of my goods to the poor; and if I have taken anything from anyone by false accusation, I restore fourfold'" (Luke 19:8).

"This *being* so, I myself always strive to have a conscience without offense toward God and men" (Acts 24:16).

11. "RENDER .. TO GOD THE THINGS THAT ARE GOD'S." Start tithing your income immediately. "Will a man rob God? Yet you have robbed Me! But you say, 'In what way have we robbed You?' In tithes and offerings. . . . Bring all the tithes into the storehouse, that there may be food in My house, and try Me now in this," says the LORD of hosts, "if I will not open for you the windows of heaven and pour out for you *such* blessing that *there will* not *be room* enough *to receive it*" (Mal. 3:8, 10). See also 1 Corinthians 16:2.

12. REGULARLY ATTEND CHURCH AND SUNDAY SCHOOL. Associate yourself immediately with God's people. Become a church member (Heb. 10:25).

"So He came to Nazareth, where He had been brought up. And as His custom was, He went into the synagogue on the Sabbath day, and stood up to read" (Luke 4:16).

"As His divine power has given to us all things that *pertain* to life and godliness, through the knowledge of Him who called us by glory and virtue" (2 Pet. 1:3).

VII. Convincement

"In Him was life, and the life was the light of men" (John 1:4).

"But that you may know that the Son of Man has power on earth to forgive sins" (Luke 5:24).

It is too late in another world. Forgiveness of sins must be received on this side (1 John 3:2).

What is this assurance? How can I know for certain?

There are second chances in health, money, championships, and education; but when we pass from this life, we cannot return for a second chance. *Your religion must furnish your proof.* You have a right to demand it.

Calvary is ridiculous if your life can be changed and you do not know it. Something you may have and not know it, is something you can lose and never miss. ***The proof of your salvation is not by sensation. It is by Scripture.***

Certain evidences must be manifested in our lives immediately. These evidences are recorded in the Bible.

1. THERE IS AN INFALLIBLE INSIDE WITNESS. "He who believes in the Son of God has the witness in himself; he who does not believe God has made Him a liar, because he has not believed the testimony that God has given of His Son" (1 John 5:10). The preacher and the church may tell you that you are all right. But you *yourself* are the final judge in that matter.

Christ asked Peter about this. He asked, "Do you love Me more than these?" (John 21:15). There was no doubt in Peter's mind about his relationship to Jesus.

2. THERE IS A FAMILY RELATIONSHIP. "We know that we have passed from death to life, because we love the brethren" (1 John 3:14). ***You sense a different and vital relationship with God's children.*** You are at home with spiritual things. It is a tie stronger than any family background in this world (Gal. 6:10).

3. THERE IS A NEW IMAGE. "Therefore, if anyone *is* in Christ, *he is* a new creation; old things have passed away; behold, all things have become new" (2 Cor. 5:17). A New Testament Christian is not a patched-up job, a reformed sinner. There is a new will; there are new affections; there is a new purpose because there is a new nature.

The emptiest and unhappiest occupation in the world is trying to act like a Christian when you are not a Christian. You do not gradually stop stealing. You stop stealing. It is miracle, not magic.

4. THERE IS A RESPONSE OF VICTORY. "For whatever is born of God overcomes the world. And this is the victory that has overcome the world—our faith" (1 John 5:4). See also John 17:15, 16. ***The born-again man or woman is not motivated by this world-system.***

Fancy yourself on the farm. It is hot midsummer. Nearby is a big mud wallow. Here comes a pig. He grunts with contentment as he wades into the slime. You say, "Mr. Hog, why do you want to submerge in that filth? Why do you not seek a cleaner environment?" That pig has not the slightest interest in your ideas for his betterment. He loves the mud.

Now watch a sheep with long white wool. The moment a sheep notices mud it heads toward safer ground. The sheep has a different nature. So has a New Testament Christian.

These are Bible proofs. "These things I have written to you who believe in the name of the Son of God, that you may know that you have eternal life, and that you may *continue to* believe in the name of the Son of God" (1 John 5:13).

Paul testified on two continents (2 Tim. 3:11).

VIII. Camouflage

Today is a day of *substitutes.* Nylon has been substituted for silk. Oleomargarine has been substituted for butter. There also are many substitutes offered for salvation. Beware.

1. SERVICE IS NOT SALVATION. "Woe to you, scribes and Pharisees, hypocrites! For you travel land and sea to win one proselyte, and when he is won, you make him twice as much a son of hell as yourselves" (Matt. 23:15). How can you lead others to Christ when you do not know Christ yourself?

2. TURNING OVER A NEW LEAF IS NOT SALVATION. One does not get saved by *reforming,* saying, "I will clean up my life, and begin life anew."

"But we are all like an unclean *thing,* and all our righteousnesses *are* like filthy rags; we all fade as a leaf, and our iniquities, like the wind, have taken us away" (Is. 64:6). "How you turned to God from idols to serve the living and true God" (1 Thess. 1:9). *Notice the direction!* They did not turn from idols to God. The new birth is a divine miracle.

3. ASSERTING ONESELF IS NOT SALVATION. People "dead in trespasses and sins" (Eph. 2:1) cannot throw back their shoulders and assert their own ability for righteousness. ***The cross of Christ exposes human degradation.*** That is part of the "offense of the cross" (Gal. 5:11). It does not appeal to human pride. It unsparingly shows us that we cannot do anything for ourselves. We have no righteousness or decency to offer to God.

4. RIGHT THINKING IS NOT SALVATION. It is not cultivating and concentrating on a "divine spark" that is within you. "Behold, I was brought forth in iniquity, and in sin my mother conceived me" (Ps. 51:5). It is not keeping a picture of your mother, sweetheart, or your wife in your billfold, and looking at it frequently. ***It is not thinking high thoughts*** (Is. 55:8, 9). ***How can you think high thoughts with a base nature?***

5. DENYING THE EXISTENCE OF SIN IS NOT SALVATION. God does not deny sin. ***Calvary is God's recognition of sin.*** "And the LORD has laid on Him the iniquity of us all" (Is. 53:6). "But the Scripture has confined all under sin" (Gal. 3:22). One of the first steps toward salvation is to recognize your sin—not deny it.

6. TO DENY SELF IS NOT SALVATION. The heathen are masters at this. They practice all kinds of asceticism (1 Cor. 13:3). ***You are not saved by crucifying yourself.*** It is not proving to yourself that you can do hard things.

7. SACRIFICE IS NOT SALVATION. Dying for a great cause—the supreme sacrifice—is not salvation. ***Discipline does not cleanse a person from sin.*** If that were true, then everybody who entered a penitentiary would become a Christian. Paying for wrongdoing does not make one a Christian (1 Sam. 15:22).

There is no *side door* into heaven. Jesus said, "I am the door. If anyone enters by Me, he will be saved" (John 10:9).

"He who does not enter the sheepfold by the door, but climbs up some other way, the same is a thief and a robber" (John 10:1). You cannot steal your way into heaven.

IX. Christ

The Master has not asked us to do what He did not do constantly during His ministry upon earth. He says, "Follow Me, and I will make you fishers of men" (Matt. 4:19).

His record is one of personal contact from when He said to Andrew, "Come and see" to His assurance to the penitent thief, "Today you will be with Me in Paradise."

He is clear and concise about God's plan of salvation.

1. He came to meet a human need. "I have not come to call *the* righteous, but sinners . . ." (Luke 5:32). Salvation is for sinners only.

2. He came to be the sinner's substitute. "The good shepherd gives His life for the sheep" (John 10:11).

3. He came to do what none other can do. "I am the way, the truth, and the life. No one comes to the Father except through Me" (John 14:6).

4. He came to provide assurance to the trusting sinner. "Your sins are forgiven. . . . Go in peace" (Luke 7:48–50).

James remembers emphatically the passion that his brother manifested toward the lost. He reflects this when he says, "Let him know that he who turns a sinner from the error of his way will save a soul from death and cover a multitude of sins" (James 5:20).

X. Condensation

The story of salvation can be told in four words:

Sin
Calvary
Faith
Life

1. Salvation is needed. "For all have sinned and fall short of the glory of God" (Rom. 3:23).

2. Salvation is provided. "Who Himself bore our sins in His own body on the tree, that we, having died to sins, might live for righteousness—by whose stripes you were healed" (1 Pet. 2:24).

3. Salvation is offered. "For by grace you have been saved through faith, and that not of yourselves; *it is* the gift of God" (Eph. 2:8).

4. Salvation accepted. "He who has the Son has life; he who does not have the Son of God does not have life" (1 John 5:12).

There is a time, we know not when,
  A place, we know not where;
Which marks the destiny of men
  To glory or despair.

There is a line, by us unseen,
  Which crosses every path,
Which marks the boundary between
  God's mercy and his wrath.

To pass that limit is to die,
To die as if by stealth;
It does not dim the beaming eye,
Nor pale the glow of health.

The conscience may be still at ease,
The spirit light and gay;
And that which pleases still may please,
And care be thrust away.

But on that forehead God hath set
Indelibly a mark;
Unseen by man, for man as yet,
Is blind and in the dark.

He feels perchance that all is well
And every fear is calmed;
He lives, he dies, he walks in hell,
Not only doomed, but damned!

O, Where is that mysterious line
That may by men be crossed,
Beyond which God himself hath sworn,
That he who goes is lost?

An answer from the skies repeats,
"Ye who from God depart."
TODAY, O hear His voice,
TODAY repent and harden not your heart.

—Joseph Addison Alexander

PRAYERS OF THE BIBLE

Subject	Reference
Abijah's army—for victory	2 Chr. 13:14
Abraham—for a son	Gen. 15:1–6
Abraham—for Ishmael	Gen. 17:18–21
Abraham—for Sodom	Gen. 18:20–32
Abraham—for Abimelech	Gen. 20:17
Abraham's servant—for guidance	Gen. 24:12–52
Asa—for victory	2 Chr. 14:11
Cain—for mercy	Gen. 4:13–15
Centurion—for his servant	Matt. 8:5–13
Christians—for Peter	Acts 12:5–12
Christians—for kings in authority	1 Tim. 2:1, 2
Corinthians—for Paul	2 Cor. 1:9–11
Cornelius—for enlightenment	Acts 10:1–33
Criminal—for salvation	Luke 23:42, 43
Daniel—for the Jews	Dan. 9:3–19
Daniel—for knowledge	Dan. 2:17–23
David—for blessing	2 Sam. 7:18–29
David—for help	1 Sam. 23:10–13
David—for guidance	2 Sam. 2:1
David—for grace	Ps. 25:16
David—for justice	Ps. 9:17–20
Disciples—for boldness	Acts 4:24–31
Elijah—for drought and rain	James 5:17, 18
Elijah—for the raising to life of the widow's son	1 Kin. 17:20–23
Elijah—for triumph over Baal	1 Kin. 18:36–38
Elijah—for death	1 Kin. 19:4
Elisha—for blindness and sight	2 Kin. 6:17–23
Ezekiel—for undefilement	Ezek. 4:12–15
Ezra—for the sins of the people	Ezra 9:6–15
Gideon—for proof of his call	Judg. 6:36–40
Habakkuk—for deliverance	Hab. 3:1–19
Habakkuk—for justice	Hab. 1:1–4
Hagar—for consolation	Gen. 21:14–20
Hannah—for a son	1 Sam. 1:10–17
Hezekiah—for deliverance	2 Kin. 19:15–19
Hezekiah—for health	2 Kin. 20:1–11
Holy Spirit—for Christians	Rom. 8:26, 27
Isaac—for children	Gen. 25:21, 24–26
Israelites—for deliverance	Ex. 2:23–25 Ex. 3:7–10
Jabez—for prosperity	1 Chr. 4:10
Jacob—all night	Gen. 32:24–30
Jacob—for deliverance from Esau	Gen. 32:9–12
Jehoahaz—for victory	2 Kin. 13:1–5
Jehoshaphat—for protection	2 Chr. 20:5–12, 27
Jehoshaphat—for victory	2 Chr. 18:31
Jeremiah—for Judah	Jer. 42:1–6
Jeremiah—for mercy	Jer. 14:7–10
Jesus—Lord's Prayer	Matt. 6:9–13
Jesus—praise for revelation to babes	Matt. 11:25, 26
Jesus—at Lazarus's tomb	John 11:41, 42
Jesus—for the Father's glory	John 12:28
Jesus—for the church	John 17:1–26
Jesus—for deliverance	Matt. 26:39, 42, 44 Matt. 27:46
Jesus—for forgiveness for others	Luke 23:34
Jesus—in submission	Luke 23:46
Jews—for safe journey	Ezra 8:21, 23
Jonah—for deliverance from the fish	Jon. 2:1–10
Joshua—for help and mercy	Josh. 7:6–9
Leper—for healing	Matt. 8:2, 3
Manasseh—for deliverance	2 Chr. 33:12, 13
Manoah—for guidance	Judg. 13:8–15
Moses—for Pharaoh	Ex. 8:9–13
Moses—for water	Ex. 15:24, 25
Moses—for Israel	Ex. 32:31–35
Moses—for Miriam	Num. 12:11–14
Moses—that he might see the Promised Land	Deut. 3:23–25 Deut. 34:1–4
Moses—for a successor	Num. 27:15–17
Nehemiah—for the Jews	Neh. 1:4–11
Paul—for the healing of Publius's father	Acts 28:8
Paul—for the Ephesians	Eph. 3:14–21
Paul—for grace	2 Cor. 12:8, 9
People of Judah—for a covenant	2 Chr. 15:12–15
Peter—for the raising of Dorcas	Acts 9:40
Priests—for blessing	2 Chr. 30:27
Rebekah—for understanding	Gen. 25:22, 23
Reubenites—for victory	1 Chr. 5:18–20
Samson—for water	Judg. 15:18, 19
Samson—for strength	Judg. 16:29, 30
Samuel—for Israel	1 Sam. 7:5–12
Solomon—for wisdom	1 Kin. 3:6–14
Tax collector—for mercy	Luke 18:13
Zechariah—for a son	Luke 1:13

PRAYERS OF THE BIBLE

Subject	Reference
Abijah's army—for victory	2 Chr. 13:14
Abraham—for a son	Gen. 15:1–6
Abraham—for Ishmael	Gen. 17:18–21
Abraham—for Sodom	Gen. 18:20–32
Abraham—for Abimelech	Gen. 20:17
Abraham's servant—for guidance	Gen. 24:12–52
Asa—for victory	2 Chr. 14:11
Cain—for mercy	Gen. 4:13–15
Centurion—for his servant	Matt. 8:5–13
Christians—for Peter	Acts 12:5–12
Christians—for kings in authority	1 Tim. 2:1, 2
Corinthians—for Paul	2 Cor. 1:9–11
Cornelius—for enlightenment	Acts 10:1–33
Criminal—for salvation	Luke 23:42, 43
Daniel—for the Jews	Dan. 9:3–19
Daniel—for knowledge	Dan. 2:17–23
David—for blessing	2 Sam. 7:18–29
David—for help	1 Sam. 23:10–13
David—for guidance	2 Sam. 2:1
David—for grace	Ps. 25:16
David—for justice	Ps. 9:17–20
Disciples—for boldness	Acts 4:24–31
Elijah—for drought and rain	James 5:17, 18
Elijah—for the raising to life of the widow's son	1 Kin. 17:20–23
Elijah—for triumph over Baal	1 Kin. 18:36–38
Elijah—for death	1 Kin. 19:4
Elisha—for blindness and sight	2 Kin. 6:17–23
Ezekiel—for undefilement	Ezek. 4:12–15
Ezra—for the sins of the people	Ezra 9:5–15
Gideon—for proof of his call	Judg. 6:36–40
Habakkuk—for deliverance	Hab. 3:1–19
Habakkuk—for justice	Hab. 1:1–4
Hagar—for consolation	Gen. 21:14–20
Hannah—for a son	1 Sam. 1:10–17
Hezekiah—for deliverance	2 Kin. 19:15–19
Hezekiah—for health	2 Kin. 20:1–11
Holy Spirit—for Christians	Rom. 8:26, 27
Isaac—for children	Gen. 25:21, 24–26
Israelites—for deliverance	Ex. 2:23–25 Ex. 3:7–10
Jabez—for prosperity	1 Chr. 4:10
Jacob—all night	Gen. 32:24–30
Jacob—for deliverance from Esau	Gen. 32:9–12
Jehoahaz—for victory	2 Kin. 13:1–5
Jehoshaphat—for protection	2 Chr. 20:5–12, 27
Jehoshaphat—for victory	2 Chr. 18:31
Jeremiah—for Judah	Jer. 42:1–6
Jeremiah—for mercy	Jer. 14:7–10
Jesus—Lord's Prayer	Matt. 6:9–13
Jesus—praise for revelation to babes	Matt. 11:25, 26
Jesus—at Lazarus's tomb	John 11:41, 42
Jesus—for the Father's glory	John 12:28
Jesus—for the church	John 17:1–26
Jesus—for deliverance	Matt. 26:39, 42, 44 Matt. 27:46
Jesus—for forgiveness for others	Luke 23:34
Jesus—in submission	Luke 23:46
Jews—for safe journey	Ezra 8:21, 23
Jonah—for deliverance from the fish	Jon. 2:1–10
Joshua—for help and mercy	Josh. 7:6–9
Leper—for healing	Matt. 8:2, 3
Manasseh—for deliverance	2 Chr. 33:12, 13
Manoah—for guidance	Judg. 13:8–15
Moses—for Pharaoh	Ex. 8:9–13
Moses—for water	Ex. 15:24, 25
Moses—for Israel	Ex. 32:31–35
Moses—for Miriam	Num. 12:11–14
Moses—that he might see the Promised Land	Deut. 3:23–25 Deut. 34:1–4
Moses—for a successor	Num. 27:15–17
Nehemiah—for the Jews	Neh. 1:4–11
Paul—for the healing of Publius's father	Acts 28:8
Paul—for the Ephesians	Eph. 3:14–21
Paul—for grace	2 Cor. 12:8, 9
People of Judah—for a covenant	2 Chr. 15:12–15
Peter—for the raising of Dorcas	Acts 9:40
Priests—for blessing	2 Chr. 30:27
Rebekah—for understanding	Gen. 25:22, 23
Reubenites—for victory	1 Chr. 5:18–20
Samson—for water	Judg. 15:18, 19
Samson—for strength	Judg. 16:28–30
Samuel—for Israel	1 Sam. 7:5–12
Solomon—for wisdom	1 Kin. 3:6–9
Tax collector—for mercy	Luke 18:13
Zacharias—for a son	Luke 1:13

CONCORDANCE

New King James Version

A

ABASED
I know how to be *a* . . . . Phil 4:12

ABBA
And He said, "*A* . . . . Mark 14:36
whom we cry out, "*A* . . . . Rom 8:15

ABHOR
Therefore I *a* myself . . . . Job 42:6

ABHORRED
a His own inheritance . . . . Ps 106:40

ABIDE
the Most High Shall *a* . . . . Ps 91:1
Him, "If you *a* . . . . John 8:31
"If you *a* in Me . . . . John 15:7
a in My love . . . . John 15:9

ABIDES
He who *a* in Me . . . . John 15:5
will of God *a* forever . . . . 1 John 2:17

ABIDING
not have His word *a* . . . . John 5:38

ABILITY
to his own *a* . . . . Matt 25:15
a which God supplies . . . . 1 Pet 4:11

ABLE
shall give as he is *a* . . . . Deut 16:17
whom we serve is *a* . . . . Dan 3:17
God is *a* to raise up . . . . Matt 3:9
fear Him who is *a* . . . . Matt 10:28
you *a* to drink the . . . . Matt 20:22
that He is *a* . . . . 2 Tim 1:12
learning and never *a* . . . . 2 Tim 3:7
that God was *a* to . . . . Heb 11:19

ABOLISHED
having *a* in His flesh . . . . Eph 2:15
Christ, who has *a* . . . . 2 Tim 1:10

ABOMINABLE
deny Him, being *a* . . . . Titus 1:16
unbelieving, *a* . . . . Rev 21:8

ABOMINATION
Yes, seven are an *a* . . . . Prov 6:16
the scoffer is an *a* . . . . Prov 24:9
prayer is an *a* . . . . Prov 28:9
and place there the *a* . . . . Dan 11:31
the *a* of desolation . . . . Dan 12:11
the '*a* of desolation,' . . . . Matt 24:15

ABOMINATIONS
delights in their *a* . . . . Is 66:3
a golden cup full of *a* . . . . Rev 17:4

ABOUND
the offense might *a* . . . . Rom 5:20
sin that grace may *a* . . . . Rom 6:1
to make all grace *a* . . . . 2 Cor 9:8
and I know how to *a* . . . . Phil 4:12

ABOUNDED
But where sin *a* . . . . Rom 5:20

ABOUNDING
immovable, always *a* . . . . 1 Cor 15:58

ABOVE
that is in heaven *a* . . . . Ex 20:4
A it stood seraphim . . . . Is 6:2
"He who comes from *a* . . . . John 3:31
I am from *a* . . . . John 8:23
given you from *a* . . . . John 19:11
things which are *a* . . . . Col 3:1
perfect gift is from *a* . . . . James 1:17

ABSENT
in the body we are *a* . . . . 2 Cor 5:6

ABSTAIN
we write to them to *a* . . . . Acts 15:20
A from every form . . . . 1 Thess 5:22

ABUNDANCE
put in out of their *a* . . . . Mark 12:44
not consist in the *a* . . . . Luke 12:15

ABUNDANT
in labors more *a* . . . . 2 Cor 11:23

ABUNDANTLY
a satisfied with the . . . . Ps 36:8
may have it more *a* . . . . John 10:10
to do exceedingly *a* . . . . Eph 3:20

ACCEPT
offering, I will not *a* . . . . Jer 14:12
Should I *a* this from . . . . Mal 1:13

ACCEPTABLE
a time I have heard . . . . Is 49:8
proclaim the *a* year . . . . Is 61:2
proclaim the *a* year . . . . Luke 4:19
is that good and *a* . . . . Rom 12:2

ACCEPTABLY
we may serve God *a* . . . . Heb 12:28

ACCEPTED
Behold, now is the *a* . . . . 2 Cor 6:2
which He made us *a* . . . . Eph 1:6

ACCESS
whom also we have *a* . . . . Rom 5:2

ACCOMPLISHED
all things were now *a* . . . . John 19:28

ACCORD
continued with one *a* . . . . Acts 1:14

ACCOUNT
they will give *a* . . . . Matt 12:36
put that on my *a* . . . . Philem 18

ACCOUNTED
in the LORD, and He *a* . . . . Gen 15:6
his faith is *a* . . . . Rom 4:5
God, and it was *a* . . . . Gal 3:6
God, and it was *a* . . . . James 2:23

ACCURSED
not know the law is *a* . . . . John 7:49
of God calls Jesus *a* . . . . 1 Cor 12:3
to you, let him be *a* . . . . Gal 1:8

ACCUSATION
over His head the *a* . . . . Matt 27:37
they might find an *a* . . . . Luke 6:7

ACCUSE
they began to *a* Him . . . . Luke 23:2

ACCUSED
while He was being *a* . . . . Matt 27:12

ACCUSER
a of our brethren . . . . Rev 12:10

ACCUSING
their thoughts *a* . . . . Rom 2:15

ACKNOWLEDGE
a my transgressions . . . . Ps 51:3
In all your ways *a* . . . . Prov 3:6

ACKNOWLEDGES
a the Son has the . . . . 1 John 2:23

ACQUAINT
a yourself with Him . . . . Job 22:21

ACQUAINTED
A Man of sorrows and *a* .... Is 53:3
ACQUIT
at all *a* the wicked .... Nah 1:3
ACT
in the very *a* .... John 8:4
ACTIONS
by Him *a* are weighed .... 1 Sam 2:3
ACTS
of Your awesome *a* .... Ps 145:6
ADD
Do not *a* to His words .... Prov 30:6
ADDED
And the Lord *a* to the .... Acts 2:47
It was *a* because of .... Gal 3:19
ADMONISH
a him as a .... 2 Thess 3:15
ADMONITION
written for our *a* .... 1 Cor 10:11
in the training and *a* .... Eph 6:4
ADOPTION
the Spirit of *a* .... Rom 8:15
waiting for the *a* .... Rom 8:23
to whom pertain the *a* .... Rom 9:4
ADORN
also, that the women *a* .... 1 Tim 2:9
ADORNED
God also *a* themselves .... 1 Pet 3:5
prepared as a bride *a* .... Rev 21:2
ADRIFT
A among the dead .... Ps 88:5
ADULTERER
The eye of the *a* .... Job 24:15
ADULTERERS
nor idolaters, nor *a* .... 1 Cor 6:9
a God will judge .... Heb 13:4
ADULTEROUS
a generation .... Matt 12:39
ADULTERY
You shall not commit *a* .... Ex 20:14
already committed *a* .... Matt 5:28
is divorced commits *a* .... Matt 5:32
another commits *a* .... Mark 10:11
those who commit *a* .... Rev 2:22
ADVANTAGE
a that I go away .... John 16:7
Satan should take *a* .... 2 Cor 2:11
ADVERSARIES
and there are many *a* .... 1 Cor 16:9
terrified by your *a* .... Phil 1:28
ADVERSARY
"Agree with your *a* .... Matt 5:25
opportunity to the *a* .... 1 Tim 5:14
a the devil walks .... 1 Pet 5:8
ADVERSITY
I shall never be in *a* .... Ps 10:6
the day of *a* consider .... Eccl 7:14
ADVICE
in this I give my *a* .... 2 Cor 8:10
ADVOCATE
sins, we have an *A* .... 1 John 2:1
AFAR
and not a God *a* .... Jer 23:23
to you who were *a* .... Eph 2:17
having seen them *a* .... Heb 11:13
AFFAIRS
himself with the *a* .... 2 Tim 2:4
AFFECTION
to his wife the *a* .... 1 Cor 7:3
AFFECTIONATE
Be kindly *a* to one .... Rom 12:10
AFFIRM
you to *a* constantly .... Titus 3:8
AFFLICT
a Your heritage .... Ps 94:5
For He does not *a* .... Lam 3:33
AFFLICTED
To him who is *a* .... Job 6:14
hears the cry of the *a* .... Job 34:28
days of the *a* are evil .... Prov 15:15
Smitten by God, and *a* .... Is 53:4
"O you *a* one .... Is 54:11
being destitute, *a* .... Heb 11:37
AFFLICTING
A the just and taking .... Amos 5:12
AFFLICTION
is, the bread of *a* .... Deut 16:3
a take hold of me .... Job 30:16
and it is an evil *a* .... Eccl 6:2
For our light *a* .... 2 Cor 4:17
supposing to add *a* .... Phil 1:16
AFRAID
garden, and I was *a* .... Gen 3:10
saying, "Do not be *a* .... Gen 15:1
none will make you *a* .... Lev 26:6
ungodliness made me *a* .... Ps 18:4
Whenever I am *a* .... Ps 56:3
one will make them *a* .... Is 17:2
do not be *a* .... Matt 14:27
if you do evil, be *a* .... Rom 13:4
do good and are not *a* .... 1 Pet 3:6
AFTERWARD
a receive me to glory .... Ps 73:24
you shall follow Me *a* .... John 13:36
AGAIN
'You must be born *a* .... John 3:7
having been born *a* .... 1 Pet 1:23
AGAINST
come to 'set a man *a* .... Matt 10:35
or house divided *a* .... Matt 12:25
Me is *a* Me .... Matt 12:30
a the Spirit will not .... Matt 12:31
lifted up his heel *a* .... John 13:18
LORD and *a* His Christ .... Acts 4:26
to kick *a* the goads .... Acts 9:5
a the promises of God .... Gal 3:21
we do not wrestle *a* .... Eph 6:12
I have a few things *a* .... Rev 2:20
AGE
the grave at a full *a* .... Job 5:26
and in the *a* to come .... Mark 10:30
AGED
a one as Paul, the *a* .... Philem 9
AGES
ordained before the *a* .... 1 Cor 2:7
AGONY
And being in *a* .... Luke 22:44
AGREE
that if two of you *a* .... Matt 18:19
AGREED
unless they are *a* .... Amos 3:3
AGREEMENT
what *a* has the temple .... 2 Cor 6:16
AIR
the birds of the *a* .... Gen 1:26
of the *a* have nests .... Luke 9:58

of the power of the *a* ... Eph 2:2
the Lord in the *a* ... 1 Thess 4:17

ALIENATED
darkened, being *a* ... Eph 4:18
you, who once were *a* ... Col 1:21

ALIENS
A have devoured his ... Hos 7:9
Christ, being *a* ... Eph 2:12

ALIKE
esteems every day *a* ... Rom 14:5

ALIVE
I kill and I make *a* ... Deut 32:39
was dead and is *a* ... Luke 15:24
presented Himself *a* ... Acts 1:3
indeed to sin, but *a* ... Rom 6:11
all shall be made *a* ... 1 Cor 15:22
that we who are *a* ... 1 Thess 4:15
and behold, I am *a* ... Rev 1:18
These two were cast *a* ... Rev 19:20

ALLELUIA
Again they said, "*A* ... Rev 19:3

ALLOW
a Your Holy One ... Ps 16:10
a My faithfulness ... Ps 89:33
a Your Holy One ... Acts 2:27

ALLURE
of emptiness, they *a* ... 2 Pet 2:18

ALMOND
a tree blossoms ... Eccl 12:5

ALMOST
a persuade me to ... Acts 26:28

ALOES
of myrrh and *a* ... John 19:39

ALPHA
"I am the *A* and the ... Rev 1:8
"I am the *A* and the ... Rev 22:13

ALTAR
Then Noah built an *a* ... Gen 8:20
'An *a* of earth you ... Ex 20:24
it to you upon the *a* ... Lev 17:11
your gift to the *a* ... Matt 5:23
swears by the *a* ... Matt 23:18
I even found an *a* ... Acts 17:23
We have an *a* from ... Heb 13:10

ALTARS
Even Your *a*, O LORD ... Ps 84:3
and torn down Your *a* ... Rom 11:3

ALTERED
of His face was *a* ... Luke 9:29

ALWAYS
delight, Rejoicing *a* ... Prov 8:30
the poor with you *a* ... Matt 26:11
lo, I am with you *a* ... Matt 28:20
to them, that men *a* ... Luke 18:1
immovable, *a* ... 1 Cor 15:58
Rejoice in the Lord *a* ... Phil 4:4
thus we shall *a* ... 1 Thess 4:17
a be ready to give a ... 1 Pet 3:15

AM
to Moses, "I *A* WHO I ... Ex 3:14
First and I *a* the Last ... Is 44:6
in My name, I *a* ... Matt 18:20
a the bread of life ... John 6:35
a the light of the ... John 8:12
I *a* from above ... John 8:23
Abraham was, I *A* ... John 8:58
"I *a* the door ... John 10:9
a the good shepherd ... John 10:11
a the resurrection ... John 11:25
to him, "I *a* the way ... John 14:6
of God I *a* what I *a* ... 1 Cor 15:10

AMBASSADOR
for which I am an *a* ... Eph 6:20

AMBASSADORS
we are *a* for Christ ... 2 Cor 5:20

AMBITION
Christ from selfish *a* ... Phil 1:16

AMEN
are Yes, and in Him *A* ... 2 Cor 1:20
creatures said, "*A* ... Rev 5:14

ANCHOR
hope we have as an *a* ... Heb 6:19

ANCIENT
Do not remove the *a* ... Prov 23:10
"until the *A* of Days ... Dan 7:22

ANGEL
"Behold, I send an *A* ... Ex 23:20
Manoah said to the *A* ... Judg 13:17
the *A* of His Presence ... Is 63:9
things, behold, an *a* ... Matt 1:20
for an *a* of the Lord ... Matt 28:2
Then an *a* of the Lord ... Luke 1:11
And behold, an *a* ... Luke 2:9
a appeared to Him ... Luke 22:43
For an *a* went down at ... John 5:4
a has spoken to Him ... John 12:29
But at night an *a* ... Acts 5:19
A who appeared to him ... Acts 7:35
immediately an *a* ... Acts 12:23
himself into an *a* ... 2 Cor 11:14
even if we, or an *a* ... Gal 1:8
Then I saw a strong *a* ... Rev 5:2
Jesus, have sent My *a* ... Rev 22:16

ANGELS
If He charges His *a* ... Job 4:18
lower than the *a* ... Ps 8:5
He shall give His *a* ... Ps 91:11
He shall give His *a* ... Matt 4:6
not even the *a* ... Matt 24:36
and all the holy *a* ... Matt 25:31
twelve legions of *a* ... Matt 26:53
And she saw two *a* ... John 20:12
and worship of *a* ... Col 2:18
much better than the *a* ... Heb 1:4
entertained *a* ... Heb 13:2
things which *a* desire ... 1 Pet 1:12
did not spare the *a* ... 2 Pet 2:4
a who did not keep ... Jude 6

ANGER
For His *a* is but for a ... Ps 30:5
gracious, Slow to *a* ... Ps 103:8
Nor will He keep His *a* ... Ps 103:9
around at them with *a* ... Mark 3:5
bitterness, wrath, *a* ... Eph 4:31

ANGRY
Cain, "Why are you *a* ... Gen 4:6
"Let not the Lord be *a* ... Gen 18:30
the Son, lest He be *a* ... Ps 2:12
a man stirs up strife ... Prov 29:22
right for you to be *a* ... Jon 4:4
you that whoever is *a* ... Matt 5:22
"Be *a*, and do not ... Eph 4:26

ANGUISH
remembers the *a* ... John 16:21
tribulation and *a* ... Rom 2:9

ANIMAL
of every clean *a* ... Gen 7:2
set him on his own *a* ... Luke 10:34

ANIMALS
of *a* after their kind ... Gen 6:20
of four-footed *a* ... Acts 10:12

ANNUL
years later, cannot *a* ... Gal 3:17

ANNULS
is confirmed, no one *a* ... Gal 3:15

ANOINT
a my head with oil ... Ps 23:5
when you fast, *a* ... Matt 6:17
a My body for burial ... Mark 14:8
a your eyes with eye ... Rev 3:18

ANOINTED
"Surely the LORD's *a* ... 1 Sam 16:6
destroy the LORD's *a* ... 2 Sam 1:14
"Do not touch My *a* ... 1 Chr 16:22
Because He has *a* ... Luke 4:18
but this woman has *a* ... Luke 7:46
a the eyes of the ... John 9:6
that Mary who *a* ... John 11:2
Jesus, whom You *a* ... Acts 4:27
and has *a* us is God ... 2 Cor 1:21

ANOINTING
But you have an *a* ... 1 John 2:20

ANOTHER
that you love one *a* ... John 13:34

ANSWER
Call, and I will *a* ... Job 13:22
How shall I *a* Him ... Job 31:14
the day that I call, *a* ... Ps 102:2
In Your faithfulness *a* ... Ps 143:1
a turns away wrath ... Prov 15:1
a a fool according ... Prov 26:4
or what you should *a* ... Luke 12:11
you may have an *a* ... 2 Cor 5:12

ANT
Go to the *a* ... Prov 6:6

ANTICHRIST
heard that the *A* ... 1 John 2:18
a who denies the ... 1 John 2:22
is a deceiver and an *a* ... 2 John 7

ANTITYPE
a which now saves us ... 1 Pet 3:21

ANXIETIES
the multitude of my *a* ... Ps 94:19

ANXIETY
A in the heart of man ... Prov 12:25

ANXIOUS
Be *a* for nothing ... Phil 4:6

APART
justified by faith *a* ... Rom 3:28

APOSTLE
called to be an *a* ... Rom 1:1
consider the *A* ... Heb 3:1

APOSTLES
of the twelve *a* ... Matt 10:2
He also named *a* ... Luke 6:13
am the least of the *a* ... 1 Cor 15:9
none of the other *a* ... Gal 1:19
gave some to be *a* ... Eph 4:11

APOSTLESHIP
in this ministry and *a* ... Acts 1:25
are the seal of my *a* ... 1 Cor 9:2

APPAREL
gold rings, in fine *a* ... James 2:2
or putting on fine *a* ... 1 Pet 3:3

APPEAL
love's sake I rather *a* ... Philem 9

APPEAR
and let the dry land *a* ... Gen 1:9
also outwardly *a* ... Matt 23:28
God would *a* ... Luke 19:11
For we must all *a* ... 2 Cor 5:10

APPEARANCE
Do not look at his *a* ... 1 Sam 16:7
judge according to *a* ... John 7:24
those who boast in *a* ... 2 Cor 5:12
found in *a* as a man ... Phil 2:8

APPEARED
an angel of the Lord *a* ... Luke 1:11
who *a* in glory and ... Luke 9:31
brings salvation has *a* ... Titus 2:11
of the ages, He has *a* ... Heb 9:26

APPEARING
Lord Jesus Christ's *a* ... 1 Tim 6:14
and the dead at His *a* ... 2 Tim 4:1
who have loved His *a* ... 2 Tim 4:8

APPEARS
can stand when He *a* ... Mal 3:2
who is our life *a* ... Col 3:4
the Chief Shepherd *a* ... 1 Pet 5:4
that when He *a* ... 1 John 2:28

APPETITE
are a man given to *a* ... Prov 23:2

APPLE
And my law as the *a* ... Prov 7:2

APPLES
fitly spoken is like *a* ... Prov 25:11

APPLIED
a my heart to know ... Eccl 7:25

APPOINT
For God did not *a* ... 1 Thess 5:9

APPOINTED
And as it is *a* for men ... Heb 9:27

APPROACH
year, make those who *a* ... Heb 10:1

APPROACHING
as you see the Day *a* ... Heb 10:25

APPROVE
do the same but also *a* ... Rom 1:32

APPROVED
to God and *a* by men ... Rom 14:18
to present yourself *a* ... 2 Tim 2:15

ARBITRATOR
Me a judge or an *a* ... Luke 12:14

ARCHANGEL
the voice of an *a* ... 1 Thess 4:16

ARGUMENTS
casting down *a* and ... 2 Cor 10:5

ARISE
A, shine ... Is 60:1
But the LORD will *a* ... Is 60:2
you who sleep, *A* ... Eph 5:14

ARK
"Make yourself an *a* ... Gen 6:14
him, she took an *a* ... Ex 2:3
Bezalel made the *a* ... Ex 37:1
in heaven, and the *a* ... Rev 11:19

ARM
with an outstretched *a* ... Ex 6:6
Have you an *a* like God ... Job 40:9
strength with His *a* ... Luke 1:51
a yourselves also with ... 1 Pet 4:1

ARMED
a strong man, fully *a* ... Luke 11:21

ARMIES
And he sent out his *a* ... Matt 22:7
surrounded by *a* ... Luke 21:20
And the *a* in heaven ... Rev 19:14
the earth, and their *a* ... Rev 19:19

ARMOR
Put on the whole *a* .... Eph 6:11

ARMS
are the everlasting *a* .... Deut 33:27
took Him up in his *a* .... Luke 2:28

AROMA
the one we are the *a* .... 2 Cor 2:16
for a sweet-smelling *a* .... Eph 5:2

AROUSED
LORD was greatly *a* .... Num 11:10
Then Joseph, being *a* .... Matt 1:24

ARRAYED
his glory was not *a* .... Matt 6:29
"Who are these *a* .... Rev 7:13

ARROGANCE
Pride and *a* and the .... Prov 8:13

ARROW
a that flies by day .... Ps 91:5

ARROWS
a pierce me deeply .... Ps 38:2
Like *a* in the hand of .... Ps 127:4

ASCEND
Who may *a* into the .... Ps 24:3
If I *a* into heaven .... Ps 139:8
'I will *a* into heaven .... Is 14:13
see the Son of Man *a* .... John 6:62

ASCENDED
You have *a* on high .... Ps 68:18
"No one has *a* .... John 3:13
"When He *a* on high .... Eph 4:8

ASCENDING
the angels of God *a* .... John 1:51

ASCRIBE
A strength to God .... Ps 68:34

ASHAMED
Let me not be *a* .... Ps 25:2
And Israel shall be *a* .... Hos 10:6
For whoever is *a* .... Mark 8:38
am not *a* of the gospel .... Rom 1:16
Therefore God is not *a* .... Heb 11:16

ASHES
become like dust and *a* .... Job 30:19
in sackcloth and *a* .... Luke 10:13

ASIDE
lay something *a* .... 1 Cor 16:2
lay *a* all filthiness .... James 1:21
Therefore, laying *a* .... 1 Pet 2:1

ASK
when your children *a* .... Josh 4:6
"*A* a sign for yourself .... Is 7:11
whatever things you *a* .... Matt 21:22
a, and it will be .... Luke 11:9
that whatever You *a* .... John 11:22
a anything in My .... John 14:14
in that day you will *a* .... John 16:23
above all that we *a* .... Eph 3:20
wisdom, let him *a* .... James 1:5
But let him *a* in faith .... James 1:6
because you do not *a* .... James 4:2

ASKS
For everyone who *a* .... Matt 7:8
you who, if his son *a* .... Matt 7:9
Or if he *a* for a fish .... Luke 11:11

ASLEEP
But He was *a* .... Matt 8:24
some have fallen *a* .... 1 Cor 15:6
those who are *a* .... 1 Thess 4:15

ASSEMBLING
not forsaking the *a* .... Heb 10:25

ASSEMBLY
a I will praise You .... Ps 22:22
fast, Call a sacred *a* .... Joel 1:14
a I will sing praise .... Heb 2:12
to the general *a* .... Heb 12:23

ASSURANCE
riches of the full *a* .... Col 2:2
Spirit and in much *a* .... 1 Thess 1:5
to the full *a* of hope .... Heb 6:11

ASSURE
a our heats before .... 1 John 3:19

ASSURED
learned and been *a* .... 2 Tim 3:14

ASTONISHED
Just as many were *a* .... Is 52:14
who heard Him were *a* .... Luke 2:47

ASTRAY
one of them goes *a* .... Matt 18:12
like sheep going *a* .... 1 Pet 2:25

ATONEMENT
the blood that makes *a* .... Lev 17:11
for it is the Day of *A* .... Lev 23:28
there will be no *a* .... Is 22:14

ATTAIN
It is high, I cannot *a* .... Ps 139:6
worthy to *a* that age .... Luke 20:35
by any means, I may *a* .... Phil 3:11

ATTENTION
My son, give *a* to my .... Prov 4:20

ATTENTIVE
Let Your ears be *a* .... Ps 130:2

ATTESTED
a Man *a* by God to you .... Acts 2:22

AUSTERE
because you are an *a* .... Luke 19:21

AUTHOR
For God is not the *a* .... 1 Cor 14:33
unto Jesus, the *a* .... Heb 12:2

AUTHORITIES
a that exist are .... Rom 13:1

AUTHORITY
them as one having *a* .... Matt 7:29
"All *a* has been given .... Matt 28:18
a I will give You .... Luke 4:6
and has given Him *a* .... John 5:27
You have given Him *a* .... John 17:2
the flesh, reject *a* .... Jude 8

AUTUMN
a trees without fruit .... Jude 12

AVAILS
of a righteous man *a* .... James 5:16

AVENGE
Beloved, do not *a* .... Rom 12:19
a our blood on those .... Rev 6:10

AVENGER
the Lord is the *a* .... 1 Thess 4:6

AWAKE
be satisfied when I *a* .... Ps 17:15
it is high time to *a* .... Rom 13:11
A to righteousness .... 1 Cor 15:34

AWAY
the wind drives *a* .... Ps 1:4
Do not cast me *a* .... Ps 51:11
A time to cast *a* .... Eccl 3:5
fair one, And come *a* .... Song 2:10
minded to put her *a* .... Matt 1:19
and earth will pass *a* .... Matt 24:35
"I am going *a* .... John 8:21
they cried out, "*A* .... John 19:15

unless the falling *a* .... 2 Thess 2:3
in Asia have turned *a* .... 2 Tim 1:15
heard, lest we drift *a* .... Heb 2:1
if they fall *a* .... Heb 6:6
can never take *a* .... Heb 10:11
world is passing *a* .... 1 John 2:17
if anyone takes *a* .... Rev 22:19

AWESOME
a is this place .... Gen 28:17
God, the great and *a* .... Deut 7:21
By *a* deeds in .... Ps 65:5
O God, You are more *a* .... Ps 68:35
Your great and *a* name .... Ps 99:3

AWL
his ear with an *a* .... Ex 21:6

AX
If the *a* is dull .... Eccl 10:10
And even now the *a* .... Matt 3:10

B

BABBLER
"What does this *b* .... Acts 17:18

BABBLINGS
the profane and idle *b* .... 1 Tim 6:20

BABE
the *b* leaped in my .... Luke 1:44
You will find a *B* .... Luke 2:12
for he is a *b* .... Heb 5:13

BABES
Out of the mouth of *b* .... Ps 8:2
revealed them to *b* .... Matt 11:25
of the mouth of *b* .... Matt 21:16
as to carnal, as to *b* .... 1 Cor 3:1
as newborn *b* .... 1 Pet 2:2

BACK
for the fool's *b* .... Prov 26:3
I gave My *b* to those .... Is 50:6
plow, and looking *b* .... Luke 9:62
of those who draw *b* .... Heb 10:39
someone turns him *b* .... James 5:19

BACKBITERS
b, haters of God .... Rom 1:30

BACKBITING
b tongue an angry .... Prov 25:23

BACKSLIDER
The *b* in heart will be .... Prov 14:14

BACKSLIDINGS
And I will heal your *b* .... Jer 3:22

BACKWARD
ten degrees *b* .... 2 Kin 20:11

BAD
b tree bears *b* fruit .... Matt 7:17

BAG
"nor *b* for your .... Matt 10:10

BAKED
b unleavened cakes .... Ex 12:39

BAKER
the butler and the *b* .... Gen 40:1

BALANCES
Falsifying the *b* .... Amos 8:5

BALD
every head shall be *b* .... Jer 48:37

BALDHEAD
Go up, you *b* .... 2 Kin 2:23

BALM
no *b* in Gilead .... Jer 8:22

BANDAGED
and *b* his wounds .... Luke 10:34

BANKERS
my money with the *b* .... Matt 25:27

BANNERS
we will set up our *b* .... Ps 20:5
as an army with *b* .... Song 6:4

BANQUET
b that I have prepared .... Esth 5:4

BANQUETING
He brought me to the *b* .... Song 2:4

BAPTISM
coming to his *b* .... Matt 3:7
b that I am baptized .... Matt 20:22
"But I have a *b* .... Luke 12:50
said, "Into John's *b* .... Acts 19:3
Lord, one faith, one *b* .... Eph 4:5
buried with Him in *b* .... Col 2:12

BAPTISMS
of the doctrine of *b* .... Heb 6:2

BAPTIZE
"I indeed *b* you with .... Matt 3:11
Himself did not *b* .... John 4:2

BAPTIZED
b will be saved .... Mark 16:16
every one of you be *b* .... Acts 2:38
all his family were *b* .... Acts 16:33
Arise and be *b* .... Acts 22:16
were *b* into Christ .... Rom 6:3
I thank God that I *b* .... 1 Cor 1:14
Spirit we were all *b* .... 1 Cor 12:13

BAPTIZING
b them in the name of .... Matt 28:19

BARBARIAN
nor uncircumcised, *b* .... Col 3:11

BARLEY
here who has five *b* .... John 6:9

BARN
the wheat into my *b* .... Matt 13:30

BARNS
reap nor gather into *b* .... Matt 6:26
I will pull down my *b* .... Luke 12:18

BARREN
But Sarai was *b* .... Gen 11:30
"Sing, O *b* .... Is 54:1

BASE
and the *b* things of .... 1 Cor 1:28

BASIN
poured water into a *b* .... John 13:5

BASKET
and put it under a *b* .... Matt 5:15
I was let down in a *b* .... 2 Cor 11:33

BASKETS
they took up twelve *b* .... Matt 14:20

BATHED
to him, "He who is *b* .... John 13:10

BATS
To the moles and *b* .... Is 2:20

BATTLE
b is the LORD's .... 1 Sam 17:47
the *b* to the strong .... Eccl 9:11
became valiant in *b* .... Heb 11:34

BEAR
greater than I can *b* .... Gen 4:13
whom Sarah shall *b* .... Gen 17:21
not *b* false witness .... Ex 20:16
b their iniquities .... Is 53:11
child, and *b* a Son .... Matt 1:23
A good tree cannot *b* .... Matt 7:18
how long shall I *b* .... Matt 17:17

by, to *b* His cross .... Mark 15:21
whoever does not *b* .... Luke 14:27
are strong ought to *b* .... Rom 15:1
B one another's .... Gal 6:2
b the sins of many .... Heb 9:28

BEARD
the edges of your *b* .... Lev 19:27
Running down on the *b* .... Ps 133:2

BEARING
goes forth weeping, *B* .... Ps 126:6
And He, *b* His cross .... John 19:17
b His reproach .... Heb 13:13

BEARS
Every branch that *b* .... John 15:2

BEAST
You preserve man and *b* .... Ps 36:6
And I saw a *b* rising .... Rev 13:1
the mark of the *b* .... Rev 19:20

BEASTS
like brute *b* .... Jude 10

BEAT
b their swords into .... Is 2:4
spat in His face and *b* .... Matt 26:67

BEATEN
Three times I was *b* .... 2 Cor 11:25

BEAUTIFUL
B in elevation .... Ps 48:2
has made everything *b* .... Eccl 3:11
my love, you are as *b* .... Song 6:4
How *b* upon the .... Is 52:7
indeed appear *b* .... Matt 23:27

BEAUTIFY
b the place of My .... Is 60:13

BEAUTY
"The *b* of Israel is .... 2 Sam 1:19
To behold the *b* .... Ps 27:4
see the King in His *b* .... Is 33:17
no *b* that we should .... Is 53:2

BECAME
b a living being .... Gen 2:7
to the Jews I *b* .... 1 Cor 9:20

BED
I remember You on my *b* .... Ps 63:6
if I make my *b* in hell .... Ps 139:8
"Arise; take up your *b* .... Matt 9:6
be two men in one *b* .... Luke 17:34
and the *b* undefiled .... Heb 13:4

BEDS
sing aloud on their *b* .... Ps 149:5

BEFOREHAND
up, do not worry *b* .... Mark 43:11
told you all things *b* .... Mark 13:23
when He testified *b* .... 1 Pet 1:11

BEG
b you as sojourners .... 1 Pet 2:11

BEGAN
since the world *b* .... Luke 1:70

BEGGAR
there was a certain *b* .... Luke 16:20

BEGGARLY
weak and *b* elements .... Gal 4:9

BEGINNING
b God created the .... Gen 1:1
In the *b* was the Word .... John 1:1
a murderer from the *b* .... John 8:44
True Witness, the *B* .... Rev 3:14
and the Omega, the *B* .... Rev 21:6

BEGOTTEN
I have *b* You .... Ps 2:7
glory as of the only *b* .... John 1:14
loves him who is *b* .... 1 John 5:1

BEGUILING
b unstable souls .... 2 Pet 2:14

BEGUN
Having *b* in the Spirit .... Gal 3:3

BEHALF
you on Christ's *b* .... 2 Cor 5:20

BEHAVE
does not *b* rudely .... 1 Cor 13:5

BEHAVED
blamelessly we *b* .... 1 Thess 2:10

BEHAVIOR
of good *b*, hospitable .... 1 Tim 3:2

BEHEADED
and had John *b* .... Matt 14:10

BEHOLD
B, the virgin shall .... Is 7:14
Judah, "*B* your God .... Is 40:9
"'*B* the Lamb of God .... John 1:36
to them, "*B* the Man .... John 19:5
B what manner of .... 1 John 3:1

BEHOLDING
with unveiled face, *b* .... 2 Cor 3:18

BEING
move and have our *b* .... Acts 17:28
who, *b* in the form of .... Phil 2:6

BELIEVE
tears, "Lord, I *b* .... Mark 9:24
have no root, who *b* .... Luke 8:13
slow of heart to *b* .... Luke 24:25
to those who *b* .... John 1:12
this, that they may *b* .... John 11:42
that you may *b* .... John 20:31
the Lord Jesus and *b* .... Rom 10:9
Christ, not only to *b* .... Phil 1:29
comes to God must *b* .... Heb 11:6
b that there is one .... James 2:19
Even the demons *b* .... James 2:19

BELIEVED
And he *b* in the LORD .... Gen 15:6
Who has *b* our report .... Is 53:1
seen Me, you have *b* .... John 20:29
"Abraham *b* God .... Rom 4:3
whom I have *b* .... 2 Tim 1:12

BELIEVERS
example to the *b* .... 1 Tim 4:12

BELIEVES
The simple *b* every .... Prov 14:15
that whoever *b* in Him .... John 3:16
"He who *b* in the Son .... John 3:36
with the heart one *b* .... Rom 10:10

BELIEVING
you ask in prayer, *b* .... Matt 21:22

BELLY
On your *b* you shall go .... Gen 3:14
and Jonah was in the *b* .... Jon 1:17
whose god is their *b* .... Phil 3:19

BELOVED
so He gives His *b* .... Ps 127:2
My *b* is mine .... Song 2:16
"This is My *b* .... Matt 3:17
us accepted in the *B* .... Eph 1:6
Luke the *b* physician .... Col 4:14
"This is My *b* .... 2 Pet 1:17

BELT
with a leather *b* .... Matt 3:4

BEND
The wicked *b* their bow . . . . . Ps 11:2

BENEATH
"You are from *b* . . . . . John 8:23

BENEFACTORS
them are called '*b* . . . . . Luke 22:25

BENEFIT
have a second *b* . . . . . 2 Cor 1:15

BESEECH
b you therefore . . . . . Rom 12:1

BESIDE
He leads me *b* the . . . . . Ps 23:2
"Paul, you are *b* . . . . . Acts 26:24

BEST
desire the *b* . . . . . 1 Cor 12:31

BESTOWED
love the Father has *b* . . . . . 1 John 3:1

BETRAY
you, one of you will *b* . . . . . Matt 26:21

BETRAYED
Man is about to be *b* . . . . . Matt 17:22

BETRAYER
See, My *b* is at . . . . . Matt 26:46

BETRAYING
"Judas, are you *b* . . . . . Luke 22:48

BETRAYS
who is the one who *b* . . . . . John 21:20

BETROTH
"I will *b* you to Me . . . . . Hos 2:19

BETROTHED
to a virgin *b* to a man . . . . . Luke 1:27

BETTER
b than sacrifice . . . . . 1 Sam 15:22
It is *b* to trust in . . . . . Ps 118:8
For it is *b* to marry . . . . . 1 Cor 7:9
Christ, which is far *b* . . . . . Phil 1:23
b than the angels . . . . . Heb 1:4
b things concerning . . . . . Heb 6:9

BEWARE
"*B* of false prophets . . . . . Matt 7:15

BEWITCHED
b you that you should . . . . . Gal 3:1

BEYOND
advanced in Judaism *b* . . . . . Gal 1:14

BILLOWS
b have gone over me . . . . . Ps 42:7

BIND
and whatever you *b* . . . . . Matt 16:19
'*B* him hand and foot . . . . . Matt 22:13

BIRD
soul, "Flee as a *b* . . . . . Ps 11:1

BIRDS
b make their nests . . . . . Ps 104:17
"Look at the *b* . . . . . Matt 6:26
have holes and *b* . . . . . Matt 8:20

BIRTH
the day of one's *b* . . . . . Eccl 7:1
Now the *b* of Jesus . . . . . Matt 1:18
will rejoice at his *b* . . . . . Luke 1:14
conceived, it gives *b* . . . . . James 1:15

BIRTHDAY
was Pharaoh's *b* . . . . . Gen 40:20

BIRTHRIGHT
Esau despised his *b* . . . . . Gen 25:34

BISHOP
the position of a *b* . . . . . 1 Tim 3:1
b must be blameless . . . . . Titus 1:7

BIT
and they *b* the people . . . . . Num 21:6

BITE
A serpent may *b* . . . . . Eccl 10:11
But if you *b* and . . . . . Gal 5:15

BITTER
b herbs they . . . . . Ex 12:8
and do not be *b* . . . . . Col 3:19
But if you have *b* . . . . . James 3:14

BITTERLY
And Hezektah wept *b* . . . . . 2 Kin 20:3
went out and wept *b* . . . . . Matt 26:75

BITTERNESS
you are poisoned by *b* . . . . . Acts 8:23
b springing up cause . . . . . Heb 12:15

BLACK
one hair white or *b* . . . . . Matt 5:36
a *b* horse . . . . . Rev 6:5
and the sun became *b* . . . . . Rev 6:12

BLACKNESS
whom is reserved the *b* . . . . . Jude 13

BLACKSMITH
I have created the *b* . . . . . Is 54:16

BLADE
first the *b* . . . . . Mark 4:28

BLAME
be holy and without *b* . . . . . Eph 1:4

BLAMELESS
and that man was *b* . . . . . Job 1:1
body be preserved *b* . . . . . 1 Thess 5:23

BLAMELESSLY
b we behaved . . . . . 1 Thess 2:10

BLASPHEME
b Your name forever . . . . . Ps 74:10
compelled them to *b* . . . . . Acts 26:11
b that noble name . . . . . James 2:7

BLASPHEMED
who passed by *b* Him . . . . . Matt 27:39
great heat, and they *b* . . . . . Rev 16:9

BLASPHEMER
I was formerly a *b* . . . . . 1 Tim 1:13

BLASPHEMES
b the name of the . . . . . Lev 24:16
"This Man *b* . . . . . Matt 9:3

BLASPHEMIES
is this who speaks *b* . . . . . Luke 5:21

BLASPHEMY
but the *b* against . . . . . Matt 12:31
was full of names of *b* . . . . . Rev 17:3

BLEATING
"What then is this *b* . . . . . 1 Sam 15:14

BLEMISH
be holy and without *b* . . . . . Eph 5:27
as of a lamb without *b* . . . . . 1 Pet 1:19

BLEMISHED
to the Lord what is *b* . . . . . Mal 1:14

BLESS
b those who *b* you . . . . . Gen 12:3
You go unless You *b* . . . . . Gen 32:26
"The LORD *b* you and . . . . . Num 6:24
b the LORD at all . . . . . Ps 34:1
b You while I live . . . . . Ps 63:4
b His holy name . . . . . Ps 103:1
b those who curse . . . . . Luke 6:28
B those who . . . . . Rom 12:14
Being reviled, we *b* . . . . . 1 Cor 4:12

BLESSED
B is the man who walks ....Ps 1:1
B is the man to whom .... Ps 32:2
B is the nation whose .... Ps 33:12
B is he who comes .... Ps 118:26
rise up and call her *b* .... Prov 31:28
"*B* are the poor in .... Matt 5:3
B are those who mourn .... Matt 5:4
B are the meek .... Matt 5:5
B are those who hunger .... Matt 5:6
B are the merciful .... Matt 5:7
B are the pure in .... Matt 5:8
B are the peacemakers .... Matt 5:9
B are those who are .... Matt 5:10
B is He who comes .... Matt 21:9
'It is more *b* to give .... Acts 20:35
B be the God and .... Eph 1:3
"*B* are the dead who .... Rev 14:13

BLESSING
And you shall be a *b* .... Gen 12:2
before you today a *b* .... Deut 11:26
shall be showers of *b* .... Ezek 34:26
and you shall be a *b* .... Zech 8:13
that the *b* of Abraham .... Gal 3:14
with every spiritual *b* .... Eph 1:3

BLIND
To open *b* eyes .... Is 42:7
His watchmen are *b* .... Is 56:10
b leads the *b* .... Matt 15:14
to Him, "Are we *b* .... John 9:40
miserable, poor, *b* .... Rev 3:17

BLINDED
and the rest were *b* .... Rom 11:7

BLINDS
a bribe, for a bribe *b* .... Deut 16:19

BLOOD
of your brother's *b* .... Gen 4:10
b shall be shed .... Gen 9:6
b that makes : .... Lev 17:11
hands are full of *b* .... Is 1:15
And the moon into *b* .... Joel 2:31
For this is My *b* .... Matt 26:28
"His *b* be on us and .... Matt 27:25
covenant in My *b* .... Luke 22:20
were born, not of *b* .... John 1:13
b has eternal life .... John 6:54
with His own *b* .... Acts 20:28
propitiation by His *b* .... Rom 3:25
justified by His *b* .... Rom 5:9
through His *b* .... Eph 1:7
brought near by the *b* .... Eph 2:13
against flesh and *b* .... Eph 6:12
peace through the *b* .... Col 1:20
with the precious *b* .... 1 Pet 1:19
b of Jesus Christ His .... 1 John 1:7
our sins in His own *b* .... Rev 1:5
us to God by Your *b* .... Rev 5:9
them white in the *b* .... Rev 7:14
overcame him by the *b* .... Rev 12:11
a robe dipped in *b* .... Rev 19:13

BLOODSHED
me from the guilt of *b* .... Ps 51:14

BLOODTHIRSTY
The LORD abhors the *b* .... Ps 5:6

BLOSSOM
and *b* as the rose .... Is 35:1

BLOT
from my sins, and *b* .... Ps 51:9
and I will not *b* .... Rev 3:5

BLOTTED
your sins may be *b* .... Acts 3:19

BLOW
with a very severe *b* .... Jer 14:17

BLOWS
"The wind *b* where it .... John 3:8

BOAST
puts on his armor *b* .... 1 Kin 20:11
and make your *b* .... Rom 2:17
lest anyone should *b* .... Eph 2:9

BOASTERS
God, violent, proud, *b* .... Rom 1:30

BOASTING
Where is *b* then .... Rom 3:27

BODIES
b a living sacrifice .... Rom 12:1
not know that your *b* .... 1 Cor 6:15
wives as their own *b* .... Eph 5:28

BODILY
b form like a dove .... Luke 3:22
of the Godhead *b* .... Col 2:9

BODY
of the *b* is the eye .... Matt 6:22
those who kill the *b* .... Matt 10:28
this is My *b* .... Matt 26:26
of the temple of His *b* .... John 2:21
deliver me from this *b* .... Rom 7:24
redemption of our *b* .... Rom 8:23
members in one *b* .... Rom 12:4
But I discipline my *b* .... 1 Cor 9:27
b which is broken .... 1 Cor 11:24
baptized into one *b* .... 1 Cor 12:13
are the *b* of Christ .... 1 Cor 12:27
though I give my *b* .... 1 Cor 13:3
It is sown a natural *b* .... 1 Cor 15:44
in the *b* of His flesh .... Col 1:22
our sins in His own *b* .... 1 Pet 2:24

BOILS
Job with painful *b* .... Job 2:7

BOLDLY
therefore come *b* .... Heb 4:16

BOLDNESS
in whom we have *b* .... Eph 3:12
that we may have *b* .... 1 John 4:17

BOND
love, which is the *b* .... Col 3:14

BONDAGE
out of the house of *b* .... Ex 13:14
again with a yoke of *b* .... Gal 5:1

BONDS
"Let us break Their *b* .... Ps 2:3

BONDSERVANTS
B, be obedient to .... Eph 6:5
Masters, give your *b* .... Col 4:1

BONDWOMAN
the one by a *b* .... Gal 4:22

BONE
b clings to my skin .... Job 19:20

BONES
I can count all My *b* .... Ps 22:17
and my *b* waste away .... Ps 31:10
I kept silent, my *b* .... Ps 32:3
the wind, Or how the *b* .... Eccl 11:5
say to them, 'O dry *b* .... Ezek 37:4
of dead men's *b* .... Matt 23:27
b shall be broken .... John 19:36

BOOK
are written in the *b* .... Gal 3:10
in the Lamb's *B* .... Rev 21:27
the prophecy of this *b* .... Rev 22:18

BOOKS
b there is no end .... Eccl 12:12
not contain the *b* .... John 21:25
and *b* were opened .... Rev 20:12

BOOTH
of Zion is left as a *b* .... Is 1:8

BORDERS
and enlarge the *b* .... Matt 23:5

BORE
And to Sarah who *b* .... Is 51:2
b the sin of many .... Is 53:12
b our sicknesses .... Matt 8:17
Himself *b* our sins .... 1 Pet 2:24
b a male Child who was .... Rev 12:5

BORN
A time to be *b* .... Eccl 3:2
unto us a Child is *b* .... Is 9:6
b Jesus who is called .... Matt 1:16
unless one is *b* again .... John 3:3
"That which is *b* .... John 3:6
having been *b* again .... 1 Pet 1:23
who loves is *b* of God .... 1 John 4:7

BORROWER
b is servant to the .... Prov 22:7

BORROWS
The wicked *b* and does .... Ps 37:21

BOSOM
to Abraham's *b* .... Luke 16:22
Son, who is in the *b* .... John 1:18

BOTTOMLESS
ascend out of the *b* .... Rev 17:8
the key to the *b* .... Rev 20:1

BOUGHT
b the threshing floor .... 2 Sam 24:24
all that he had and *b* .... Matt 13:46
For you were *b* at a .... 1 Cor 6:20
denying the Lord who *b* .... 2 Pet 2:1

BOUND
on earth will be *b* .... Matt 16:19
And see, now I go *b* .... Acts 20:22
who has a husband is *b* .... Rom 7:2
Are you *b* to a wife .... 1 Cor 7:27
Devil and Satan, and *b* .... Rev 20:2

BOUNTIFULLY
and he who sows *b* .... 2 Cor 9:6

BOW
"You shall not *b* .... Ex 23:24
let us worship and *b* .... Ps 95:6
who sat on it had a *b* .... Rev 6:2

BOWED
stood all around and *b* .... Gen 37:7
And they *b* the knee .... Matt 27:29

BOWL
and poured out his *b* .... Rev 16:2

BOWLS
Go and pour out the *b* .... Rev 16:1

BOX
had the money *b* .... John 13:29

BOYS
Shall be full of *b* .... Zech 8:5

BRAIDED
not with *b* hair or .... 1 Tim 2:9

BRANCH
raise to David a *B* .... Jer 23:5
forth My Servant the *B* .... Zech 3:8
b that bears fruit He .... John 15:2

BRANCHES
vine, you are the *b* .... John 15:5

BRASS
become sounding *b* .... 1 Cor 13:1

BRAVE
in the faith, be *b* .... 1 Cor 16:13

BREAD
brought out *b* .... Gen 14:18
shall eat unleavened *b* .... Ex 23:15
not live by *b* alone .... Deut 8:3
b eaten in secret is .... Prov 9:17
B gained by deceit is .... Prov 20:17
Cast your *b* upon the .... Eccl 11:1
for what is not *b* .... Is 55:2
these stones become *b* .... Matt 4:3
not live by *b* alone .... Matt 4:4
this day our daily *b* .... Matt 6:11
eating, Jesus took *b* .... Matt 26:26
"I am the *b* of life .... John 6:48
betrayed took *b* .... 1 Cor 11:23

BREADTH
is as great as its *b* .... Rev 21:16

BREAK
covenant I will not *b* .... Ps 89:34
together to *b* bread .... Acts 20:7

BREAKING
in the *b* of bread .... Acts 2:42
b bread from house to .... Acts 2:46

BREAKS
Until the day *b* .... Song 2:17

BREAST
back on Jesus' *b* .... John 13:25

BREASTPLATE
righteousness as a *b* .... Is 59:17
having put on the *b* .... Eph 6:14

BREASTS
Your two *b* are like .... Song 4:5
b which nursed You .... Luke 11:27

BREATH
nostrils the *b* of life .... Gen 2:7
that there was no *b* .... 1 Kin 17:17
Man is like a *b* .... Ps 144:4
everything that has *b* .... Ps 150:6
"Surely I will cause *b* .... Ezek 37:5
gives to all life, *b* .... Acts 17:25
power to give *b* .... Rev 13:15

BREATHES
indeed he *b* his last .... Job 14:10

BRETHREN
and you are all *b* .... Matt 23:8
least of these My *b* .... Matt 25:40
among many *b* .... Rom 8:29
thus sin against the *b* .... 1 Cor 8:12
over five hundred *b* .... 1 Cor 15:6
perils among false *b* .... 2 Cor 11:26
sincere love of the *b* .... 1 Pet 1:22
we love the *b* .... 1 John 3:14
our lives for the *b* .... 1 John 3:16

BRIBE
you shall take no *b* .... Ex 23:8
b blinds the eyes .... Deut 16:19

BRIBES
hand is full of *b* .... Ps 26:10

BRICK
people straw to make *b* .... Ex 5:7

BRICKS
"Come, let us make *b* .... Gen 11:3

BRIDE
I will show you the *b* .... Rev 21:9
the Spirit and the *b* .... Rev 22:17

BRIDEGROOM
And as the *b* rejoices .... Is 62:5
mourn as long as the *b* .... Matt 9:15
went out to meet the *b* .... Matt 25:1
the friend of the *b* .... John 3:29

CHRIST
Jesus who is called *C* .... Matt 1:16
"You are the *C* .... Matt 16:16
a Savior, who is *C* .... Luke 2:11
It is *C* who died .... Rom 8:34
to be justified by *C* .... Gal 2:17
been crucified with *C* .... Gal 2:20
C is head of the .... Eph 5:23
to me, to live is *C* .... Phil 1:21
which is *C* in you .... Col 1:27
C who is our .... Col 3:4
Jesus *C* is the same .... Heb 13:8
C His Son cleanses us .... 1 John 1:7
that Jesus is the *C* .... 1 John 5:1

CHRISTIAN
anyone suffers as a *C* .... 1 Pet 4:16

CHRISTIANS
were first called *C* .... Acts 11:26

CHRISTS
"For false *c* and .... Matt 24:24

CHURCH
rock I will build My *c* .... Matt 16:18
c daily those who were .... Acts 2:47
Himself a glorious *c* .... Eph 5:27
as the Lord does the *c* .... Eph 5:29
body, which is the *c* .... Col 1:24
assembly and *c* .... Heb 12:23

CHURCHES
these things in the *c* .... Rev 22:16

CIRCLE
who sits above the *c* .... Is 40:22

CIRCUMCISE
is necessary to *c* them .... Acts 15:5

CIRCUMCISED
among you shall be *c* .... Gen 17:10
who will justify the *c* .... Rom 3:30
if you become *c* .... Gal 5:2

CIRCUMCISION
c is that of the heart .... Rom 2:29
C is nothing and .... 1 Cor 7:19
Christ Jesus neither *c* .... Gal 5:6

CIRCUMSPECTLY
then that you walk *c* .... Eph 5:15

CISTERN
from your own *c* .... Prov 5:15

CITIES
He overthrew those *c* .... Gen 19:25
three parts, and the *c* .... Rev 16:19

CITIZEN
But I was born a *c* .... Acts 22:28

CITIZENS
but fellow *c* with the .... Eph 2:19

CITIZENSHIP
For our *c* is in heaven .... Phil 3:20

CITY
shall make glad the *c* .... Ps 46:4
c has become a harlot .... Is 1:21
How lonely sits the *c* .... Lam 1:1
c that is set on a .... Matt 5:14
He has prepared a *c* .... Heb 11:16
have no continuing *c* .... Heb 13:14
John, saw the holy *c* .... Rev 21:2

CLAP
of the field shall *c* .... Is 55:12

CLAY
pit, out of the miry *c* .... Ps 40:2
We are the *c* .... Is 64:8
blind man with the *c* .... John 9:6
have power over the *c* .... Rom 9:21

CLEAN
He who has *c* hands and .... Ps 24:4
make yourselves *c* .... Is 1:16
c out His threshing .... Matt 3:12
You can make me *c* .... Matt 8:2
"You are not all *c* .... John 13:11
"You are already *c* .... John 15:3

CLEANSE
C me from secret .... Ps 19:12
And *c* me from my sin .... Ps 51:2
How can a young man *c* .... Ps 119:9
might sanctify and *c* .... Eph 5:26
us our sins and to *c* .... 1 John 1:9

CLEANSED
"Were there not ten *c* .... Luke 17:17

CLEANSES
Christ His Son *c* .... 1 John 1:7

CLEAR
of life, *c* as crystal .... Rev 22:1

CLIFF
secret places of the *c* .... Song 2:14

CLIMBS
c up some other way .... John 10:1

CLING
C to what is good .... Rom 12:9

CLINGS
And My tongue *c* .... Ps 22:15

CLOAK
let him have your *c* .... Matt 5:40
using liberty as a *c* .... 1 Pet 2:16

CLODS
The *c* of the valley .... Job 21:33

CLOSE
c friends abhor me .... Job 19:19

CLOSED
The deep *c* around me .... Jon 2:5

CLOTH
a piece of unshrunk *c* .... Matt 9:16

CLOTHE
He not much more *c* .... Matt 6:30

CLOTHED
of skin, and *c* them .... Gen 3:21
A man *c* in soft .... Matt 11:8
naked and you *c* .... Matt 25:36
legion, sitting and *c* .... Mark 5:15
desiring to be *c* .... 2 Cor 5:2
that you may be *c* .... Rev 3:18

CLOTHES
c became shining .... Mark 9:3
many spread their *c* .... Luke 19:36
a poor man in filthy *c* .... James 2:2

CLOTHING
c they cast lots .... Ps 22:18
do you worry about *c* .... Matt 6:28
to you in sheep's *c* .... Matt 7:15
c they cast lots .... John 19:24

CLOTHS
in swaddling *c* .... Luke 2:12

CLOUD
My rainbow in the *c* .... Gen 9:13
day in a pillar of *c* .... Ex 13:21
He led them with the *c* .... Ps 78:14
behold, a bright *c* .... Matt 17:5
of Man coming in a *c* .... Luke 21:27
c received Him out of .... Acts 1:9
by so great a *c* .... Heb 12:1

CLOUDS
Man coming on the *c* .... Matt 24:30
with them in the *c* .... 1 Thess 4:17

are *c* without water ... Jude 12
He is coming with *c* ... Rev 1:7

CLOUDY
them by day with a *c* ... Neh 9:12

CLOVEN
chew the cud or have *c* ... Deut 14:7

CLUSTER
beloved is to me a *c* ... Song 1:14

COAL
in his hand a live *c* ... Is 6:6

COALS
doing you will heap *c* ... Rom 12:20

COBRA
the lion and the *c* ... Ps 91:13

COBRA'S
shall play by the *c* ... Is 11:8

COFFIN
and he was put in a *c* ... Gen 50:26
touched the open *c* ... Luke 7:14

COIN
if she loses one *c* ... Luke 15:8

COLD
and harvest, *C* and ... Gen 8:22
of many will grow *c* ... Matt 24:12
that you are neither *c* ... Rev 3:15

COLLECTION
concerning the *c* ... 1 Cor 16:1

COLT
on a donkey, A *c* ... Zech 9:9
on a donkey, A *c* ... Matt 21:5

COME
He will *c* and save you ... Is 35:4
who have no money, *C* ... Is 55:1
Your kingdom *c* ... Matt 6:10
"*C* to Me ... Matt 11:28
I have *c* in My ... John 5:43
thirsts, let him *c* ... John 7:37
c as a light into the ... John 12:46
O Lord, *c* ... 1 Cor 16:22
the door, I will *c* ... Rev 3:20

COMELINESS
He has no form or *c* ... Is 53:2

COMES
Lord's death till He *c* ... 1 Cor 11:26

COMFORT
and Your staff, they *c* ... Ps 23:4
yes, *c* My people ... Is 40:1
c each other ... 1 Thess 5:11

COMFORTED
So Isaac was *c* after ... Gen 24:67
Refusing to be *c* ... Jer 31:15

COMFORTER
She had no *c* ... Lam 1:9

COMFORTS
I, even I, am He who *c* ... Is 51:12

COMING
see the Son of Man *c* ... Mark 13:26
mightier than I is *c* ... Luke 3:16
are Christ's at His *c* ... 1 Cor 15:23
Behold, I am *c* ... Rev 3:11
"Surely I am *c* ... Rev 22:20

COMMAND
c I have received ... John 10:18
and I know that His *c* ... John 12:50
If you do whatever I *c* ... John 15:14

COMMANDED
not endure what was *c* ... Heb 12:20

COMMANDMENT
c of the LORD is pure ... Ps 19:8
which is the great *c* ... Matt 22:36
"A new *c* I give to ... John 13:34
which is the first *c* ... Eph 6:2
And this is His *c* ... 1 John 3:23

COMMANDMENTS
covenant, the Ten *C* ... Ex 34:28
as doctrines the *c* ... Matt 15:9
c hang all the Law ... Matt 22:40
He who has My *c* ... John 14:21

COMMANDS
with authority He *c* ... Mark 1:27

COMMEND
But food does not *c* ... 1 Cor 8:8

COMMENDABLE
patiently, this is *c* ... 1 Pet 2:20

COMMENDED
c the unjust steward ... Luke 16:8

COMMENDS
but whom the Lord *c* ... 2 Cor 10:18

COMMIT
"You shall not *c* ... Ex 20:14
into Your hands I *c* ... Luke 23:46

COMMITS
sin also *c* lawlessness ... 1 John 3:4

COMMITTED
c Himself to Him who ... 1 Pet 2:23

COMMON
c people heard Him ... Mark 12:37
had all things in *c* ... Acts 2:44
concerning our *c* ... Jude 3

COMMOTION
there arose a great *c* ... Acts 19:23

COMMUNED
I *c* with my heart ... Eccl 1:16

COMMUNION
c of the Holy Spirit ... 2 Cor 13:14

COMPANION
a man my equal, My *c* ... Ps 55:13

COMPANIONS
while you became *c* ... Heb 10:33

COMPANY
Great was the *c* ... Ps 68:11
to an innumerable *c* ... Heb 12:22

COMPARE
c ourselves with ... 2 Cor 10:12

COMPARED
are not worthy to be *c* ... Rom 8:18

COMPASSION
are a God full of *c* ... Ps 86:15
He was moved with *c* ... Matt 9:36
whomever I will have *c* ... Rom 9:15
He can have *c* on those ... Heb 5:2

COMPASSIONATE
the Lord is very *c* ... James 5:11

COMPASSIONS
because His *c* fail not ... Lam 3:22

COMPEL
c them to come in ... Luke 14:23

COMPELS
the love of Christ *c* ... 2 Cor 5:14

COMPLAINED
some of them also *c* ... 1 Cor 10:10

COMPLAINERS
These are grumblers, *c* ... Jude 16

COMPLAINING
all things without *c* .... Phil 2:14
COMPLAINT
For the LORD has a *c* .... Mic 6:2
COMPLETE
work in you will *c* .... Phil 1:6
and you are *c* in Him .... Col 2:10
of God may be *c* .... 2 Tim 3:17
COMPLETELY
sanctify you *c* .... 1 Thess 5:23
COMPOSED
But God *c* the body .... 1 Cor 12:24
COMPREHEND
which we cannot *c* .... Job 37:5
the darkness did not *c* .... John 1:5
CONCEAL
of God to *c* a matter .... Prov 25:2
CONCEALED
Than love carefully *c* .... Prov 27:5
CONCEIT
selfish ambition or *c* .... Phil 2:3
CONCEITED
Let us not become *c* .... Gal 5:26
CONCEIVE
the virgin shall *c* .... Is 7:14
And behold, you will *c* .... Luke 1:31
CONCEIVED
in sin my mother *c* .... Ps 51:5
CONCERN
Neither do I *c* myself .... Ps 131:1
CONCERNED
Is it oxen God is *c* .... 1 Cor 9:9
CONCESSION
But I say this as a *c* .... 1 Cor 7:6
CONCLUSION
Let us hear the *c* .... Eccl 12:13
CONDEMN
world to *c* the world .... John 3:17
CONDEMNATION
can you escape the *c* .... Matt 23:33
“And this is the *c* .... John 3:19
Their *c* is just .... Rom 3:8
therefore now no *c* .... Rom 8:1
CONDEMNED
does not believe is *c* .... John 3:18
c sin in the flesh .... Rom 8:3
CONDEMNS
Who is he who *c* .... Rom 8:34
CONDUCT
from your aimless *c* .... 1 Pet 1:8
may be won by the *c* .... 1 Pet 3:1
CONFESS
c my transgressions .... Ps 32:5
that if you *c* with .... Rom 10:9
every tongue shall *c* .... Rom 14:11
If we *c* our sins .... 1 John 1:9
CONFESSED
c that He was Christ .... John 9:22
CONFESSES
c that Jesus is the .... 1 John 4:15
CONFESSION
with the mouth *c* .... Rom 10:10
High Priest of our *c* .... Heb 3:1
let us hold fast our *c* .... Heb 4:14
CONFIDENCE
c shall be Your .... Is 30:15
Jesus, and have no *c* .... Phil 3:3
CONFINED
the Scripture has *c* .... Gal 3:22
CONFIRM
who will also *c* .... 1 Cor 1:8
CONFIRMED
covenant that was *c* .... Gal 3:17
c it by an oath .... Heb 6:17
CONFIRMING
c the word through .... Mark 16:20
CONFLICT
to know what a great *c* .... Col 2:1
CONFLICTS
Outside were *c* .... 2 Cor 7:5
CONFORMED
predestined to be *c* .... Rom 8:29
And do not be *c* .... Rom 12:2
CONFUSE
c their language .... Gen 11:7
CONFUSED
the assembly was *c* .... Acts 19:32
CONGREGATION
Nor sinners in the *c* .... Ps 1:5
God stands in the *c* .... Ps 82:1
CONQUER
conquering and to *c* .... Rev 6:2
CONQUERORS
we are more than *c* .... Rom 8:37
CONSCIENCE
convicted by their *c* .... John 8:9
strive to have a *c* .... Acts 24:16
CONSECRATED
c this house which you .... 1 Kin 9:3
CONSENT
and does not *c* to .... 1 Tim 6:3
CONSENTED
He had not *c* to their .... Luke 23:51
CONSENTING
Now Saul was *c* to his .... Acts 8:1
CONSIDER
When I *c* Your heavens .... Ps 8:3
My people do not *c* .... Is 1:3
C the lilies of the .... Matt 6:28
“*C* the ravens .... Luke 12:24
c Him who endured .... Heb 12:3
CONSIST
in Him all things *c* .... Col 1:17
CONSOLATION
if there is any *c* .... Phil 2:1
us everlasting *c* .... 2 Thess 2:16
CONSOLE
c those who mourn .... Is 61:3
CONSTANT
c prayer was .... Acts 12:5
CONSUME
whom the Lord will *c* .... 2 Thess 2:8
CONSUMED
but the bush was not *c* .... Ex 3:2
mercies we are not *c* .... Lam 3:22
beware lest you be *c* .... Gal 5:15
CONSUMING
our God is a *c* fire .... Heb 12:29
CONTAIN
of heavens cannot *c* .... 2 Chr 2:6
c the books that .... John 21:25
CONTEMPT
and be treated with *c* .... Mark 9:12

COVENANT
I will establish My *c* .... Gen 6:18
the LORD made a *c* .... Gen 15:18
will show them His *c* .... Ps 25:14
sons will keep My *c* .... Ps 132:12
I will make a new *c* .... Jer 31:31
the Messenger of the *c* .... Mal 3:1
cup is the new *c* .... Luke 22:20
He says, "A new *c* .... Heb 8:13
Mediator of the new *c* .... Heb 12:24
of the everlasting *c* .... Heb 13:20

COVENANTS
the glory, the *c* .... Rom 9:4

COVER
He shall *c* you with .... Ps 91:4
c a multitude of sins .... James 5:20

COVERED
Whose sin is *c* .... Ps 32:1
c all their sin .... Ps 85:2
For there is nothing *c* .... Matt 10:26

COVERING
spread a cloud for a *c* .... Ps 105:39

COVERINGS
and made themselves *c* .... Gen 3:7

COVET
"You shall not *c* .... Ex 20:17

COVETED
c no one's silver .... Acts 20:33

COVETOUS
nor thieves, nor *c* .... 1 Cor 6:10

COVETOUSNESS
heed and beware of *c* .... Luke 12:15

COWARDLY
the *c*, unbelieving .... Rev 21:8

CRAFTILY
His people, to deal *c* .... Ps 105:25

CRAFTINESS
deceived Eve by his *c* .... 2 Cor 11:3
in the cunning *c* .... Eph 4:14

CRAFTSMAN
instructor of every *c* .... Gen 4:22

CRAFTY
the devices of the *c* .... Job 5:12
Nevertheless, being *c* .... 2 Cor 12:16

CREAM
were bathed with *c* .... Job 29:6

CREATE
peace and *c* calamity .... Is 45:7

CREATED
So God *c* man in His .... Gen 1:27
Has not one God *c* .... Mal 2:10
c in Christ Jesus .... Eph 2:10
new man which was *c* .... Eph 4:24

CREATION
know that the whole *c* .... Rom 8:22
Christ, he is a new *c* .... 2 Cor 5:17
anything, but a new *c* .... Gal 6:15

CREATOR
Remember now your *C* .... Eccl 12:1
God, the LORD, The *C* .... Is 40:28
rather than the *C* .... Rom 1:25

CREATURE
the gospel to every *c* .... Mark 16:15

CREATURES
firstfruits of His *c* .... James 1:18

CREDIT
For what *c* is it if .... 1 Pet 2:20

CREDITOR
There was a certain *c* .... Luke 7:41

CREEP
sort are those who *c* .... 2 Tim 3:6

CREEPING
c thing and beast of .... Gen 1:24

CREPT
For certain men have *c* .... Jude 4

CRIB
donkey its master's *c* .... Is 1:3

CRIED
the poor who *c* out .... Job 29:12
of the depths I have *c* .... Ps 130:1

CRIES
your brother's blood *c* .... Gen 4:10

CRIMES
land is filled with *c* .... Ezek 7:23

CRIMINALS
also two others, *c* .... Luke 23:32

CROOKED
c places shall be made .... Is 40:4
in the midst of a *c* .... Phil 2:15

CROSS
does not take his *c* .... Matt 10:38
to bear His *c* .... Matt 27:32
down from the *c* .... Matt 27:40
lest the *c* of Christ .... 1 Cor 1:17
boast except in the *c* .... Gal 6:14
the enemies of the *c* .... Phil 3:18
Him endured the *c* .... Heb 12:2
shall not follow a *c* .... Ex 23:2

CROWN
c the year with Your .... Ps 65:11
they had twisted a *c* .... Matt 27:29
obtain a perishable *c* .... 1 Cor 9:25
laid up for me the *c* .... 2 Tim 4:8
on his head a golden *c* .... Rev 14:14

CROWNED
angels, And You have *c* .... Ps 8:5
athletics, he is not *c* .... 2 Tim 2:5

CROWNS
His head were many *c* .... Rev 19:12

CRUCIFIED
"Let Him be *c* .... Matt 27:22
Calvary, there they *c* .... Luke 23:33
lawless hands, have *c* .... Acts 2:23
that our old man was *c* .... Rom 6:6
Jesus Christ and Him *c* .... 1 Cor 2:2
"I have been *c* .... Gal 2:20

CRUCIFY
out again, "*C* Him .... Mark 15:13

CRUEL
hate me with *c* hatred .... Ps 25:19

CRUELTY
the haunts of *c* .... Ps 74:20

CRUSH
of peace will *c* .... Rom 16:20

CRUSHED
every side, yet not *c* .... 2 Cor 4:8

CRUST
man is reduced to a *c* .... Prov 6:26

CRY
and their *c* came up to .... Ex 2:23
Does not wisdom *c* .... Prov 8:1
at midnight a *c* .... Matt 25:6
His own elect who *c* .... Luke 18:7

CRYING
nor sorrow, nor *c* .... Rev 21:4

CRYSTAL
a sea of glass, like *c* .... Rev 4:6
CUBIT
can add one *c* .... Matt 6:27
CUNNING
the serpent was more *c* .... Gen 3:1
c craftiness of deceitful .... Eph 4:14
CUP
My *c* runs over .... Ps 23:5
Then He took the *c* .... Matt 26:27
possible, let this *c* .... Matt 26:39
c is the new covenant .... Luke 22:20
cannot drink the *c* .... 1 Cor 10:21
c is the new .... 1 Cor 11:25
CURE
and to *c* diseases .... Luke 9:1
CURES
and perform *c* .... Luke 13:32
CURSE
c the ground for man's .... Gen 8:21
C God and die .... Job 2:9
"I will send a *c* .... Mal 2:2
law are under the *c* .... Gal 3:10
CURSED
c more than all cattle .... Gen 3:14
from Me, you *c* .... Matt 25:41
CURSES
I will curse him who *c* .... Gen 12:3
CURTAIN
the heavens like a *c* .... Ps 104:2
CUSTOM
according to the *c* .... Acts 15:1
CUT
evildoers shall be *c* .... Ps 37:9
the wicked will be *c* .... Prov 2:22
CYMBAL
or a clanging *c* .... 1 Cor 13:1

D

DAILY
Give us this day our *d* .... Matt 6:11
take up his cross *d* .... Luke 9:23
the Scriptures *d* .... Acts 17:11
DANCE
mourn, And a time to *d* .... Eccl 3:4
And you did not *d* .... Matt 11:17
DANCED
Then David *d* before .... 2 Sam 6:14
DANCING
saw the calf and the *d* .... Ex 32:19
he heard music and *d* .... Luke 15:25
DARE
someone would even *d* .... Rom 5:7
DARK
I tell you in the *d* .... Matt 10:27
shines in a *d* place .... 2 Pet 1:19
DARKENED
their understanding *d* .... Eph 4:18
DARKNESS
d He called Night .... Gen 1:5
Those who sat in *d* .... Ps 107:10
d Have seen a .... Is 9:2
And deep *d* the people .... Is 60:2
body will be full of *d* .... Matt 6:23
cast out into outer *d* .... Matt 8:12
d rather than light .... John 3:19
For you were once *d* .... Eph 5:8
called you out of *d* .... 1 Pet 2:9
d is reserved .... 2 Pet 2:17
and in Him is no *d* .... 1 John 1:5
d is passing away .... 1 John 2:8
DARTS
quench all the fiery *d* .... Eph 6:16
DASH
You shall *d* them to .... Ps 2:9
Lest you *d* your foot .... Matt 4:6
DASHED
infants shall be *d* .... Hos 13:16
DAUGHTER
"Rejoice greatly, O *d* .... Zech 9:9
"Fear not, *d* of Zion .... John 12:15
the son of Pharaoh's *d* .... Heb 11:24
DAUGHTERS
of God saw the *d* .... Gen 6:2
d shall prophesy .... Acts 2:17
DAY
God called the light *D* .... Gen 1:5
And *d* and night .... Gen 8:22
the Sabbath *d* .... Ex 20:8
For a *d* in Your courts .... Ps 84:10
d the LORD has .... Ps 118:24
not strike you by *d* .... Ps 121:6
For the *d* of the LORD .... Joel 2:11
who can endure the *d* .... Mal 3:2
d our daily bread .... Matt 6:11
sent Me while it is *d* .... John 9:4
person esteems one *d* .... Rom 14:5
D will declare it .... 1 Cor 3:13
again the third *d* .... 1 Cor 15:4
with the Lord one *d* .... 2 Pet 3:8
DAYS
d are swifter than a .... Job 7:6
of woman is of few *d* .... Job 14;1
The *d* of our lives are .... Ps 90:10
Before the difficult *d* .... Eccl 12:1
shortened those *d* .... Mark 13:20
raise it up in three *d* .... John 2:20
DAYSPRING
With which the *D* .... Luke 1:78
DEACONS
with the bishops and *d* .... Phil 1:1
d must be reverent .... 1 Tim 3:8
d be the husbands .... 1 Tim 3:12
DEAD
But the *d* know nothing .... Eccl 9:5
d bury their own *d* .... Matt 8:22
not the God of the *d* .... Matt 22:32
this my son was *d* .... Luke 15:24
d will hear the voice .... John 5:25
was raised from the *d* .... Rom 6:4
yourselves to be *d* .... Rom 6:11
be Lord of both the *d* .... Rom 14:9
resurrection of the *d* .... 1 Cor 15:12
And the *d* in Christ .... 1 Thess 4:16
without works is *d* .... James 2:26
And the *d* were judged .... Rev 20:12
DEADLY
drink anything *d* .... Mark 16:18
evil, full of *d* poison .... James 3:8
DEADNESS
the *d* of Sarah's womb .... Rom 4:19
DEAF
d shall be unstopped .... Is 35:5
are cleansed and the *d* .... Matt 11:5
DEAL
My Servant shall *d* .... Is 52:13
DEATH
d parts you and me .... Ruth 1:17
and the shadow of *d* .... Job 10:21
I sleep the sleep of *d* .... Ps 13:3

of the shadow of *d* ... Ps 23:4
house leads down to *d* ... Prov 2:18
who hate me love *d* ... Prov 8:36
swallow up *d* forever ... Is 25:8
no pleasure in the *d* ... Ezek 18:32
who shall not taste *d* ... Matt 16:28
but has passed from *d* ... John 5:24
Nevertheless *d* reigned ... Rom 5:14
D no longer has ... Rom 6:9
the wages of sin is *d* ... Rom 6:23
the Lord's *d* ... 1 Cor 11:26
since by man came *d* ... 1 Cor 15:21
D is swallowed up in ... 1 Cor 15:54
The sting of *d* is sin ... 1 Cor 15:56
is sin leading to *d* ... 1 John 5:16
Be faithful until *d* ... Rev 2:10
shall be no more *d* ... Rev 21:4
which is the second *d* ... Rev 21:8

DEBTOR
I am a *d* both to ... Rom 1:14
that he is a *d* to keep ... Gal 5:3

DEBTORS
as we forgive our *d* ... Matt 6:12
of his master's *d* ... Luke 16:5
brethren, we are *d* ... Rom. 8:12

DECEIT
Nor was any *d* in His ... Is 53:9
philosophy and empty *d* ... Col 2:8
no sin, nor was *d* ... 1 Pet 2:22
mouth was found no *d* ... Rev 14:5

DECEITFUL
deliver me from the *d* ... Ps 43:1
"The heart is *d* ... Jer 17:9
are false apostles, *d* ... 2 Cor 11:13

DECEITFULLY
an idol, Nor sworn *d* ... Ps 24:4
the word of God *d* ... 2 Cor 4:2

DECEITFULNESS
this world and the *d* ... Matt 13:22

DECEIVE
rise up and *d* many ... Matt 24:11
Let no one *d* you with ... Eph 5:6
we have no sin, we *d* ... 1 John 1:8

DECEIVED
"The serpent *d* ... Gen 3:13
the commandment, *d* ... Rom 7:11
deceiving and being *d* ... 2 Tim 3:13

DECEIVER
how that *d* said ... Matt 27:63
This is a *d* and an ... 2 John 7

DECEIVES
heed that no one *d* ... Matt 24:4

DECENTLY
all things be done *d* ... 1 Cor 14:40

DECEPTIVE
you with *d* words ... 2 Pet 2:3

DECISION
in the valley of *d* ... Joel 3:14

DECLARE
The heavens *d* the ... Ps 19:1
d Your name to My ... Ps 22:22
seen and heard we *d* ... 1 John 1:3

DECLARED
and *d* to be the Son of ... Rom 1:4

DECREE
"I will declare the *d* ... Ps 2:7
in those days that a *d* ... Luke 2:1

DEDICATION
it was the Feast of *D* ... John 10:22

DEED
you do in word or *d* ... Col 3:17

DEEDS
because their *d* ... John 3:19
"You do the *d* ... John 8:41
one according to his *d* ... Rom 2:6
you put to death the *d* ... Rom 8:13

DEEP
LORD God caused a *d* ... Gen 2:21
d uttered its voice ... Hab 3:10
"Launch out into the *d* ... Luke 5:4
I have been in the *d* ... 2 Cor 11:25

DEEPER
D than Sheol ... Job 11:8

DEEPLY
But He sighed *d* ... Mark 8:12

DEER
As the *d* pants for the ... Ps 42:1
shall leap like a *d* ... Is 35:6

DEFEATED
and Israel was *d* ... 1 Sam 4:10

DEFEND
D the fatherless ... Is 1:17

DEFENSE
For wisdom is a *d* ... Eccl 7:12
am appointed for the *d* ... Phil 1:17
be ready to give a *d* ... 1 Pet 3:15

DEFILE
also these dreamers *d* ... Jude 8

DEFILED
lest they should be *d* ... John 18:28
and conscience are *d* ... Titus 1:15

DEFILES
mouth, this *d* a man ... Matt 15:11
it anything that *d* ... Rev 21:27

DEFRAUD
d his brother in this ... 1 Thess 4:6

DEGREES
go forward ten *d* ... 2 Kin 20:9

DELICACIES
of the king's *d* ... Dan 1:5

DELICATE
a lovely and *d* woman ... Jer 6:2

DELIGHT
But his *d* is in the ... Ps 1:2
I *d* to do Your will ... Ps 40:8
And I was daily His *d* ... Prov 8:30
And let your soul *d* ... Is 55:2
call the Sabbath a *d* ... Is 58:13
For I *d* in the law of ... Rom 7:22

DELIGHTS
For the LORD *d* in you ... Is 62:4

DELIVER
Let Him *d* Him ... Ps 22:8
I will *d* him and honor ... Ps 91:15
into temptation, But *d* ... Matt 6:13
let Him *d* Him now if ... Matt 27:43
And the Lord will *d* ... 2 Tim 4:18
d the godly out of ... 2 Pet 2:9

DELIVERANCE
not accepting *d* ... Heb 11:35

DELIVERED
who was *d* up because ... Rom 4:25
was once for all *d* ... Jude 3

DELIVERER
D will come out of ... Rom 11:26

DELIVERS
even Jesus who *d* ... 1 Thess 1:10

DEVIL
to be tempted by the *d* .... Matt 4:1
prepared for the *d* .... Matt 25:41
of your father the *d* .... John 8:44
give place to the *d* .... Eph 4:27
the snare of the *d* .... 2 Tim 2:26
the works of the *d* .... 1 John 3:8

DEVIOUS
And who are *d* .... Prov 2:15

DEVISES
d wickedness on his .... Ps 36:4
But a generous man *d* .... Is 32:8

DEVOID
who is *d* of wisdom .... Prov 11:12

DEVOTED
Your servant, who is *d* .... Ps 119:38

DEVOUR
For you *d* widows' .... Matt 23:14
bite and *d* one another .... Gal 5:15
whom he may *d* .... 1 Pet 5:8
d her Child as .... Rev 12:4

DEVOURED
wild beast has *d* .... Gen 37:20
birds came and *d* them .... Matt 13:4
of heaven and *d* them .... Rev 20:9

DEVOUT
man was just and *d* .... Luke 2:25
d soldier from among .... Acts 10:7

DEW
God give you Of the *d* .... Gen 27:28

DIADEMS
ten horns, and seven *d* .... Rev 12:3

DIAMOND
d it is engraved .... Jer 17:1

DICTATES
according to the *d* .... Jer 23:17

DIE
it you shall surely *d* .... Gen 2:17
but a person shall *d* .... 2 Chr 25:4
I shall not *d* .... Ps 118:17
born, And a time to *d* .... Eccl 3:2
eat of it and not *d* .... John 6:50
to you that you will *d* .... John 8:24
though he may *d* .... John 11:25
one man should *d* .... John 11:50
the flesh you will *d* .... Rom 8:13
For as in Adam all *d* .... 1 Cor 15:22
and to *d* is gain .... Phil 1:21
for men to *d* once .... Heb 9:27
are the dead who *d* .... Rev 14:13

DIED
And all flesh *d* .... Gen 7:21
in due time Christ *d* .... Rom 5:6
Christ *d* for us .... Rom 5:8
Now if we *d* with .... Rom 6:8
and He *d* for all .... 2 Cor 5:15
for if we *d* with Him .... 2 Tim 2:11

DIES
alive unless it *d* .... 1 Cor 15:36

DIFFERS
for one star *d* from .... 1 Cor 15:41

DILIGENCE
d it produced in you .... 2 Cor 7:11

DILIGENT
d makes rich .... Prov 10:4

DILIGENTLY
d lest anyone fall .... Heb 12:15

DIM
His eyes were not *d* .... Deut 34:7

DIMLY
we see in a mirror, *d* .... 1 Cor 13:12

DINE
come in to him and *d* .... Rev 3:20

DINNER
invites you to *d* .... 1 Cor 10:27

DIP
d your piece of bread .... Ruth 2:14

DIPPED
clothed with a robe *d* .... Rev 19:13

DIRECT
Now may the Lord *d* .... 2 Thess 3:5

DIRT
cast up mire and *d* .... Is 57:20

DISARMED
d principalities .... Col 2:15

DISASTER
will end with *d* .... Acts 27:10

DISCERN
d the face of the sky .... Matt 16:3
senses exercised to *d* .... Heb 5:14

DISCERNED
they are spiritually *d* .... 1 Cor 2:14

DISCERNER
d of the thoughts .... Heb 4:12

DISCERNS
a wise man's heart *d* .... Eccl 8:5

DISCIPLE
he cannot be My *d* .... Luke 14:26
d whom Jesus loved .... John 21:7

DISCIPLES
word, you are My *d* .... John 8:31
but we are Moses' *d* .... John 9:28

DISCIPLINES
he who loves him *d* .... Prov 13:24

DISCORD
And one who sows *d* .... Prov 6:19

DISCOURAGED
lest they became *d* .... Col 3:21
become weary and *d* .... Heb 12:3

DISCRETION
D will preserve you .... Prov 2:11

DISFIGURE
d their faces that .... Matt 6:16

DISGUISES
And he *d* his face .... Job 24:15

DISHONOR
Father, and you *d* Me .... John 8:49
d their bodies among .... Rom 1:24
It is sown in *d* .... 1 Cor 15:43

DISHONORED
But you have *d* the .... James 2:6

DISHONORS
For son *d* father .... Mic 7:6

DISOBEDIENT
out My hands To a *d* .... Rom 10:21

DISORDERLY
for this *d* gathering .... Acts 19:40

DISPENSATION
d of the fullness of .... Eph 1:10

DISPERSION
the pilgrims of the *D* .... 1 Pet 1:1

DISPLEASE
LORD see it, and it *d* .... Prov 24:18

DISPLEASED
they were greatly *d* ... Matt 20:24
it, He was greatly *d* ... Mark 10:14

DISPUTE
there was also a *d* ... Luke 22:24

DISPUTER
Where is the *d* of this ... 1 Cor 1:20

DISPUTES
But avoid foolish *d* ... Titus 3:9

DISQUALIFIED
should become *d* ... 1 Cor 9:27

DISQUIETED
And why are you *d* ... Ps 42:5

DISSENSION
had no small *d* and ... Acts 15:2

DISSIPATION
not accused of *d* ... Titus 1:6

DISSOLVED
the heavens will be *d* ... 2 Pet 3:12

DISTINCTION
compassion, making a *d* ... Jude 22

DISTRESS
d them in His deep ... Ps 2:5
tribulation, or *d* ... Rom 8:35

DISTRESSED
and deeply *d* ... Mark 14:33

DISTRESSES
Bring me out of my *d* ... Ps 25:17

DISTRIBUTED
and they *d* to each as ... Acts 4:35

DISTRIBUTING
d to the needs of the ... Rom 12:13

DITCH
will fall into a *d* ... Matt 15:14

DIVERSITIES
There are *d* ... 1 Cor 12:4

DIVIDE
d the spoil with the ... Prov 16:19
"Take this and *d* ... Luke 22:17

DIVIDED
and the waters were *d* ... Ex 14:21
they were not *d* ... 2 Sam 1:23
"Every kingdom *d* ... Matt 12:25
Is Christ *d* ... 1 Cor 1:13

DIVIDES
at home *d* the spoil ... Ps 68:12

DIVIDING
rightly *d* the word of ... 2 Tim 2:15

DIVINATION
shall you practice *d* ... Lev 19:26
a spirit of *d* met us ... Acts 16:16

DIVINE
d service and the ... Heb 9:1

DIVISION
So there was a *d* ... John 7:43

DIVISIONS
those who cause *d* ... Rom 16:17
persons, who cause *d* ... Jude 19

DIVISIVE
Reject a *d* man after ... Titus 3:10

DIVORCE
her a certificate of *d* ... Deut 24:1
a certificate of *d* ... Mark 10:4

DO
men to *d* to you, *d* ... Matt 7:12
He sees the Father *d* ... John 5:19
without Me you can *d* ... John 15:5
"Sirs, what must I *d* ... Acts 16:30
d evil that good may ... Rom 3:8
or whatever you *d*, *d* ... 1 Cor 10:31

DOCTRINE
What new *d* is this ... Mark 1:27
"My *d* is not Mine ... John 7:16
with every wind of *d* ... Eph 4:14
is contrary to sound *d* ... 1 Tim 1:10
is profitable for *d* ... 2 Tim 3:16
not endure sound *d* ... 2 Tim 4:3

DOCTRINES
commandments and *d* ... Col 2:22
various and strange *d* ... Heb 13:9

DOERS
But be *d* of the word ... James 1:22

DOG
d is better than a ... Eccl 9:4
d returns to his own ... 2 Pet 2:22

DOGS
what is holy to the *d* ... Matt 7:6
d eat the crumbs ... Matt 15:27
But outside are *d* ... Rev 22:15

DOMINION
let them have *d* ... Gen 1:26
d is an everlasting ... Dan 4:34
sin shall not have *d* ... Rom 6:14
glory and majesty, *D* ... Jude 25

DONKEY
d its master's crib ... Is 1:3
and riding on a *d* ... Zech 9:9
colt, the foal of a *d* ... Matt 21:5
d speaking with a ... 2 Pet 2:16

DOOM
for the day of *d* ... Prov 16:4

DOOR
stone against the *d* ... Matt 27:60
to you, I am the *d* ... John 10:7
before you an open *d* ... Rev 3:8
I stand at the *d* ... Rev 3:20

DOORKEEPER
I would rather be a *d* ... Ps 84:10

DOORPOSTS
write them on the *d* ... Deut 6:9

DOORS
up, you everlasting *d* ... Ps 24:7

DOUBLE
from the LORD's hand *D* ... Is 40:2
worthy of *d* honor ... 1 Tim 5:17

DOUBLE-MINDED
he is a *d* man ... James 1:8

DOUBT
faith, why did you *d* ... Matt 14:31

DOUBTING
in faith, with no *d* ... James 1:6

DOUBTS
why do *d* arise in ... Luke 24:38
for I have *d* about you ... Gal 4:20

DOVE
d found no resting ... Gen 8:9
descending like a *d* ... Matt 3:16

DOVES
and harmless as *d* ... Matt 10:16

DOWNCAST
who comforts the *d* ... 2 Cor 7:6

DRAGNET
d that was cast ... Matt 13:47

E

cut off his right *e* .... John 18:10
not seen, nor *e* heard .... 1 Cor 2:9
"He who has an *e* .... Rev 2:7

EARLY
Very *e* in the morning .... Mark 16:2
arrived at the tomb *e* .... Luke 24:22

EARNESTLY
He prayed more *e* .... Luke 22:44
e that it would not .... James 5:17
you to contend *e* .... Jude 3

EARS
And hear with their *e* .... Is 6:10
"He who has *e* .... Matt 11:15
they have itching *e* .... 2 Tim 4:3

EARTH
to judge the *e* .... 1 Chr 16:33
foundations of the *e* .... Job 38:4
e is the LORD's .... Ps 24:1
You had formed the *e* .... Ps 90:2
there was ever an *e* .... Prov 8:23
e abides forever .... Eccl 1:4
for the meek of the *e* .... Is 11:4
e is My footstool .... Is 66:1
I will darken the *e* .... Amos 8:9
shall inherit the *e* .... Matt 5:5
heaven and *e* pass .... Matt 5:18
e as it is in heaven .... Matt 6:10
treasures on *e* .... Matt 6:19
then shook the *e* .... Heb 12:26
heaven and a new *e* .... Rev 21:1

EARTHLY
"If I have told you *e* .... John 3:12
that if our *e* house .... 2 Cor 5:1
their mind on *e* things .... Phil 3:19
from above, but is *e* .... James 3:15

EARTHQUAKE
after the wind an *e* .... 1 Kin 19:11
there was a great *e* .... Matt 28:2

EARTHQUAKES
And there will be *e* .... Mark 13:8

EASIER
"Which is *e*, to say .... Mark 2:9
"It is *e* for a camel .... Mark 10:25

EAST
goes toward the *e* .... Gen 2:14
wise men from the *E* .... Matt 2:1
many will come from *e* .... Matt 8:11
wilt come from the *e* .... Luke 13:29

EAT
you may freely *e* .... Gen 2:16
'You shall not *e* .... Gen 3:17
e this scroll .... Ezek 3:1
life, what you will *e* .... Matt 6:25
give us His flesh to *e* .... John 6:52
one believes he may *e* .... Rom 14:2
e meat nor drink wine .... Rom 14:21
I will never again *e* .... 1 Cor 8:13
neither shall he *e* .... 2 Thess 3:10

EATEN
Have you *e* from the .... Gen 3:11
he was *e* by worms .... Acts 12:23

EATS
receives sinners and *e* .... Luke 15:2
"Whoever *e* My flesh .... John 6:54
e this bread will live .... John 6:58
He who *e*, *e* to the .... Rom 14:6
unworthy manner *e* .... 1 Cor 11:29

EDIFICATION
has given me for *e* .... 2 Cor 13:10
rather than godly *e* .... 1 Tim 1:4

EDIFIES
puffs up, but love *e* .... 1 Cor 8:1

EDIFY
but not all things *e* .... 1 Cor 10:23

EDIFYING
of the body for the *e* .... Eph 4:16

ELDER
against an *e* except .... 1 Tim 5:19

ELDERS
the tradition of the *e* .... Matt 15:2
be rejected by the *e* .... Luke 9:22
they had appointed *e* .... Acts 14:23
e who rule well be .... 1 Tim 5:17
lacking, and appoint *e* .... Titus 1:5
e obtained a good .... Heb 11:2
e who are among you I .... 1 Pet 5:1
I saw twenty-four *e* .... Rev 4:4

ELDERSHIP
of the hands of the *e* .... 1 Tim 4:14

ELECT
gather together His *e* .... Matt 24:31
e have obtained it .... Rom 11:7
e according to the .... 1 Pet 1:2
A chief cornerstone, *e* .... 1 Pet 2:6

ELECTION
call and *e* sure .... 2 Pet 1:10

ELEMENTS
weak and beggarly *e* .... Gal 4:9
e will melt with .... 2 Pet 3:10

ELEVEN
numbered with the *e* .... Acts 1:26

ELOQUENT
an *e* man and mighty .... Acts 18:24

EMBALM
to *e* his father .... Gen 50:2

ENCOURAGED
is, that I may be *e* .... Rom 1:12
and all may be *e* .... 1 Cor 14:31

END
make me to know my *e* .... Ps 39:4
shall keep it to the *e* .... Ps 119:33
e is the way of death .... Prov 14:12
Declaring the *e* .... Is 46:10
what shall be the *e* .... Dan 12:8
the harvest is the *e* .... Matt 13:39
always, even to the *e* .... Matt 28:20
He loved them to the *e* .... John 13:1
For Christ is the *e* .... Rom 10:4
But the *e* of all .... 1 Pet 4:7
the latter *e* is worse .... 2 Pet 2:20
My works until the *e* .... Rev 2:26
Beginning and the *E* .... Rev 22:13

ENDLESS
and *e* genealogies .... 1 Tim 1:4
to the power of an *e* .... Heb 7:16

ENDURANCE
e the race that .... Heb 12:1

ENDURE
as the sun and moon *e* .... Ps 72:5
His name shall *e* .... Ps 72:17
persecuted, we *e* .... 1 Cor 4:12

ENDURED
he had patiently *e* .... Heb 6:15
e as seeing Him who .... Heb 11:27
consider Him who *e* .... Heb 12:3

ENDURES
And His truth *e* .... Ps 100:5
For His mercy *e* .... Ps 136:1
But he who *e* to the .... Matt 10:22
e only for a while .... Matt 13:21

for the food which *e* .... John 6:27
he has built on it *e* .... 1 Cor 3:14
hopes all things, *e* .... 1 Cor 13:7
word of the LORD *e* .... 1 Pet 1:25

ENDURING
the LORD is clean, *e* .... Ps 19:9

ENEMIES
the presence of my *e* .... Ps 23:5
e will lick the dust .... Ps 72:9
to you, love your *e* .... Matt 5:44
e will be those .... Matt 10:36
e we were reconciled .... Rom 5:10
till He has put all *e* .... 1 Cor 15:25
were alienated and *e* .... Col 1:21
His *e* are made His .... Heb 10:13

ENEMY
If your *e* is hungry .... Prov 25:21
rejoice over me, my *e* .... Mic 7:8
and hate your *e* .... Matt 5:43
last *e* that will be .... 1 Cor 15:26
become your *e* because .... Gal 4:16
count him as an *e* .... 2 Thess 3:15
makes himself an *e* .... James 4:4

ENJOY
richly all things to *e* .... 1 Tim 6:17
than to *e* the passing .... Heb 11:25

ENJOYMENT
So I commended *e* .... Eccl 8:15

ENLIGHTEN
E my eyes .... Ps 13:3

ENLIGHTENED
those who were once *e* .... Heb 6:4

ENMITY
And I will put *e* .... Gen 3:15
the carnal mind is *e* .... Rom 8:7
in His flesh the *e* .... Eph 2:15

ENRAPTURED
And always be *e* .... Prov 5:19

ENRICHED
while you are *e* .... 2 Cor 9:11

ENSNARED
The wicked is *e* .... Prov 12:13

ENSNARES
sin which so easily *e* .... Heb 12:1

ENTER
E into His gates .... Ps 100:4
you will by no means *e* .... Matt 5:20
"*E* by the narrow .... Matt 7:13
e the kingdom of God .... Matt 19:24
E into the joy of your .... Matt 25:21
and pray, lest you *e* .... Matt 26:41
"Strive to *e* through .... Luke 13:24
who have believed do *e* .... Heb 4:3
e the temple till the .... Rev 15:8

ENTERED
Then Satan *e* Judas .... Luke 22:3
through one man sin *e* .... Rom 5:12
ear heard, Nor have *e* .... 1 Cor 2:9
the forerunner has *e* .... Heb 6:20
e the Most Holy Place .... Heb 9:12

ENTERS
If anyone *e* by Me .... John 10:9

ENTHRONED
You are holy, *E* in .... Ps 22:3

ENTIRELY
give yourself *e* .... 1 Tim 4:15

ENTREAT
being defamed, we *e* .... 1 Cor 4:13

ENTREATED
e our God for this .... Ezra 8:23

ENVIOUS
patriarchs, becoming *e* .... Acts 7:9

ENVY
e slays a simple .... Job 5:2
e is rottenness .... Prov 14:30
not let your heart *e* .... Prov 23:17
full of *e* .... Rom 1:29
not in strife and *e* .... Rom 13:13
love does not *e* .... 1 Cor 13:4
e, murders .... Gal 5:21
living in malice and *e* .... Titus 3:3

EPISTLE
You are our *e* written .... 2 Cor 3:2

EPISTLES
as also in all his *e* .... 2 Pet 3:16

ERR
My people Israel to *e* .... Jer 23:13

ERROR
a sinner from the *e* .... James 5:20
led away with the *e* .... 2 Pet 3:17
run greedily in the *e* .... Jude 11

ERRORS
can understand his *e* .... Ps 19:12

ESCAPE
e all these things .... Luke 21:36
same, that you will *e* .... Rom 2:3
make the way of *e* .... 1 Cor 10:13
how shall we *e* if we .... Heb 2:3

ESCAPED
after they have *e* .... 2 Pet 2:20

ESTABLISH
seeking to *e* their own .... Rom 10:3
faithful, who will *e* .... 2 Thess 3:3
E your hearts .... James 5:8
a while, perfect, *e* .... 1 Pet 5:10

ESTABLISHED
Your throne is *e* .... Ps 93:2
built up In Him and *e* .... Col 2:7
covenant, which was *e* .... Heb 8:6

ESTEEM
and we did not *e* .... Is 53:3
e others better than .... Phil 2:3

ESTEEMED
For what is highly *e* .... Luke 16:15

ESTEEMS
One person *e* one day .... Rom 14:5

ETERNAL
e God is your refuge .... Deut 33:27
For man goes to his *e* .... Eccl 12:5
and inherit *e* life .... Matt 19:29
in the age to come. *e* .... Mark 10:30
not perish but have *e* .... John 3:15
you think you have *e* .... John 5:39
I give them *e* life .... John 10:28
"And this is *e* life .... John 17:3
the gift of God is *e* .... Rom 6:23
are not seen are *e* .... 2 Cor 4:18
lay hold on *e* life .... 1 Tim 6:12
e life which was .... 1 John 1:2

ETERNITY
Also He has put *e* .... Eccl 3:11
One who inhabits *e* .... Is 57:15

EUNUCH
of Ethiopia, a *e* .... Acts 8:27

EUNUCHS
made themselves *e* .... Matt 19:12

EVANGELIST
of Philip the *e* .... Acts 21:8
do the work of an *e* .... 2 Tim 4:5

EYES
e will be opened ... Gen 3:5
And my *e* shall behold ... Job 19:27
e are ever toward the ... Ps 25:15
The *e* of the LORD are ... Ps 34:15
I will lift up my *e* ... Ps 121:1
but the *e* of a fool ... Prov 17:24
be wise in his own *e* ... Prov 26:5
You have dove's *e* ... Song 1:15
e have seen the King ... Is 6:5
Who have *e* and see ... Jer 5:21
rims were full of *e* ... Ezek 1:18
You are of purer *e* ... Hab 1:13
blessed are your *e* ... Matt 13:16
"He put clay on my *e* ... John 9:15
e they have closed ... Acts 28:27
E that they should not ... Rom 11:8
have seen with our *e* ... 1 John 1:1
the lust of the *e* ... 1 John 2:16
as snow, and His *e* ... Rev 1:14
creatures full of *e* ... Rev 4:6
horns and seven *e* ... Rev 5:6

EYESERVICE
not with *e* ... Eph 6:6

EYEWITNESSES
the beginning were *e* ... Luke 1:2
e of His majesty ... 2 Pet 1:16

F

FABLES
nor give heed to *f* ... 1 Tim 1:4
cunningly devised *f* ... 2 Pet 1:16

FACE
"For I have seen God *f* ... Gen 32:30
f shone while he ... Ex 34:29
sins have hidden His *f* ... Is 59:2
f shone like the sun ... Matt 17:2
dimly, but then *f* ... 1 Cor 13:12
with unveiled *f* ... 2 Cor 3:18
withstood him to his *f* ... Gal 2:11
They shall see His *f* ... Rev 22:4

FADE
We all *f* as a leaf ... Is 64:6
rich man also will *f* ... James 1:11
and that does not *f* ... 1 Pet 1:4

FADES
withers, the flower *f* ... Is 40:7

FAIL
tittle of the law to *f* ... Luke 16:17
faith should not *f* ... Luke 22:32
they will *f* ... 1 Cor 13:8
Your years will not *f* ... Heb 1:12

FAILING
"men's hearts *f* ... Luke 21:26

FAILS
Love never *f* ... 1 Cor 13:8

FAINT
shall walk and not *f* ... Is 40:31

FAINTS
My soul *f* for Your ... Ps 119:81
And the whole heart *f* ... Is 1:5
the earth, Neither *f* ... Is 40:28

FAITH
shall live by his *f* ... Hab 2:4
you, O you of little *f* ... Matt 6:30
not found such great *f* ... Matt 8:10
that you have no *f* ... Mark 4:40
"Increase our *f* ... Luke 17:5
will He really find *f* ... Luke 18:8
are sanctified by *f* ... Acts 26:18
God is revealed from *f* ... Rom 1:17
f apart from the deeds ... Rom 3:28
his *f* is accounted for ... Rom 4:5
those who are of the *f* ... Rom 4:16
f which we preach ... Rom 10:8
f comes by hearing ... Rom 10:17
and you stand by *f* ... Rom 11:20
in proportion to our *f* ... Rom 12:6
Do you have *f* ... Rom 14:22
though I have all *f* ... 1 Cor 13:2
And now abide *f* ... 1 Cor 13:13
For we walk by *f* ... 2 Cor 5:7
the flesh I live by *f* ... Gal 2:20
f are sons of Abraham ... Gal 3:7
But after *f* has come ... Gal 3:25
of the household of *f* ... Gal 6:10
been saved through *f* ... Eph 2:8
one Lord, one *f* ... Eph 4:5
taking the shield of *f* ... Eph 6:16
your work of *f* ... 1 Thess 1:3
for not all have *f* ... 2 Thess 3:2
the mystery of the *f* ... 1 Tim 3:9
I have kept the *f* ... 2 Tim 4:7
in our common *f* ... Titus 1:4
not being mixed with *f* ... Heb 4:2
f is the substance ... Heb 11:1
without *f* it is ... Heb 11:6
says he has *f* ... James 2:14
Show me your *f* ... James 2:18
and not by *f* only ... James 2:24
f will save the sick ... James 5:15
add to your *f* virtue ... 2 Pet 1:5
the patience and the *f* ... Rev 13:10

FAITHFUL
God, He Is God, the *f* ... Deut 7:9
LORD preserves the *f* ... Ps 31:23
eyes shall be on the *f* ... Ps 101:6
But who can find a *f* ... Prov 20:6
the Holy One who is *f* ... Hos 11:12
"Who then is a *f* ... Matt 24:45
good and *f* servant ... Matt 25:23
"He who is *f* in what ... Luke 16:10
Judged me to be *f* ... Acts 16:15
God is *f* ... 1 Cor 1:9
is my beloved and *f* ... 1 Cor 4:17
But as God is *f* ... 2 Cor 1:18
f brethren in Christ ... Col 1:2
who calls you is *f* ... 1 Thess 5:24
This is a *f* saying and ... 1 Tim 1:15
f High Priest in ... Heb 2:17
He who promised is *f* ... Heb 10:23
He is *f* and just to ... 1 John 1:9
Be *f* until death ... Rev 2:10
words are true and *f* ... Rev 21:5

FAITHFULNESS
I have declared Your *f* ... Ps 40:10
Your *f* also surrounds ... Ps 89:8
f endures to all ... Ps 119:90
Great is Your *f* ... Lam 3:23
unbelief make the *f* ... Rom 3:3

FAITHLESS
"O *f* generation ... Mark 9:19
If we are *f* ... 2 Tim 2:13

FALL
a deep sleep to *f* ... Gen 2:21
Let them *f* by their ... Ps 5:10
righteous man may *f* ... Prov 24:16
But the wicked shall *f* ... Prov 24:16
the blind, both will *f* ... Matt 15:14
the stars will *f* ... Matt 24:29
"I saw Satan *f* ... Luke 10:18
take heed lest he *f* ... 1 Cor 10:12
if they *f* away ... Heb 6:6
lest anyone *f* short of ... Heb 12:15
and rocks, "*F* on us ... Rev 6:16

FALLEN
"Babylon is *f* ... Is 21:9
you have *f* from grace ... Gal 5:4
"Babylon is *f* ... Rev 14:8

FALLING
great drops of blood *f* ... Luke 22:44
f away comes first ... 2 Thess 2:3

FALSE
"You shall not bear *f* ... Ex 20:16
I hate every *f* way ... Ps 119:104
f witness shall perish ... Prov 21:28
"Beware of *f* prophets ... Matt 7:15
f christs and *f* ... Matt 24:24
and we are found *f* ... 1 Cor 15:15
of *f* brethren ... Gal 2:4
f prophets have gone ... 1 John 4:1
mouth of the *f* prophet ... Rev 16:13

FALSEHOOD
For their deceit is *f* ... Ps 119:118
Offspring of *f* ... Is 57:4

FALSELY
of evil against you *f* ... Matt 5:11
f called knowledge ... 1 Tim 6:20

FAMILIES
in you all the *f* ... Gen 12:3
the God of all the *f* ... Jer 31:1
in your seed all the *f* ... Acts 3:25

FAMILY
shall mourn, every *f* ... Zech 12:12
f were baptized ... Acts 16:33

FAMINES
And there will be *f* ... Matt 24:7

FAMISH
righteous soul to *f* ... Prov 10:3

FAMISHED
honorable men are *f* ... Is 5:13

FAR
Your judgments are *f* ... Ps 10:5
Be not *f* from Me ... Ps 22:11
The LORD is *f* from ... Prov 15:29
their heart is *f* from ... Matt 15:8
going to a *f* country ... Mark 13:34
though He is not *f* ... Acts 17:27
you who once were *f* ... Eph 2:13

FARMER
The hard-working *f* ... 2 Tim 2:6
See how the *f* waits ... James 5:7

FASHIONED
have made me and *f* ... Job 10:8

FASHIONS
He *f* their hearts ... Ps 33:15

FAST
f as you do this day ... Is 58:4
f that I have chosen ... Is 58:5
"Moreover, when you *f* ... Matt 6:16
disciples do not *f* ... Matt 9:14
I *f* twice a week ... Luke 18:12

FASTED
'When you *f* and ... Zech 7:5
And when He had *f* ... Matt 4:2

FASTING
by prayer and *f* ... Matt 17:21
give yourselves to *f* ... 1 Cor 7:5

FASTINGS
in sleeplessness, in *f* ... 2 Cor 6:5

FAT
and you will eat the *f* ... Gen 45:18
f is the LORD's ... Lev 3:16

FATHER
man shall leave his *f* ... Gen 2:24
and you shall be a *f* ... Gen 17:4
I was a *f* to the poor ... Job 29:16
A *f* of the fatherless ... Ps 68:5
f pities his children ... Ps 103:13
God, Everlasting *F* ... Is 9:6
You, O LORD, are our *F* ... Is 63:16
time cry to Me, 'My *F* ... Jer 3:4
For I am a *F* to Israel ... Jer 31:9
"A son honors his *f* ... Mal 1:6
Have we not all one *F* ... Mal 2:10
Our *F* in heaven ... Matt 6:9
"He who loves *f* ... Matt 10:37
know the *F* ... Matt 11:27
'He who curses *f* ... Matt 15:4
for One is your *F* ... Matt 23:9
"*F* will be divided ... Luke 12:53
F loves the Son ... John 3:35
F raises the dead ... John 5:21
F judges no one ... John 5:22
He has seen the *F* ... John 6:46
F who sent Me bears ... John 8:18
we have one *F* ... John 8:41
of your *f* the devil ... John 8:44
"I and My *F* are one ... John 10:30
'I am going to the *F* ... John 14:28
came forth from the *F* ... John 16:28
that he might be the *f* ... Rom 4:11
one God and *F* of all ... Eph 4:6
"I will be to Him a *F* ... Heb 1:5
down from the *F* ... James 1:17
if you call on the *F* ... 1 Pet 1:17
and testify that the *F* ... 1 John 4:14

FATHERLESS
the helper of the *f* ... Ps 10:14
He relieves the *f* ... Ps 146:9
do not defend the *f* ... Is 1:23
they may rob the *f* ... Is 10:2
You the *f* finds mercy ... Hos 14:3

FATHER'S
you in My *F* kingdom ... Matt 26:29
I must be about My *F* ... Luke 2:49
F house are many ... John 14:2
that a man has his *f* ... 1 Cor 5:1

FATHERS
the LORD God of our *f* ... Ezra 7:27
f trusted in You ... Ps 22:4
our ears, O God, our *f* ... Ps 44:1
f ate the manna ... John 6:31
of whom are the *f* ... Rom 9:5
unaware that all our *f* ... 1 Cor 10:1

FATNESS
of the root and *f* ... Rom 11:17

FAULT
I have found no *f* ... Luke 23:14
does He still find *f* ... Rom 9:19
of God without *f* ... Phil 2:15

FAULTLESS
covenant had been *f* ... Heb 8:7
to present you *f* ... Jude 24

FAULTS
"I remember my *f* ... Gen 41:9
me from secret *f* ... Ps 19:12

FAVOR
granted me life and *f* ... Job 10:12
His *f* is for life ... Ps 30:5
A good man obtains *f* ... Prov 12:2
and stature, and in *f* ... Luke 2:52
God and having *f* ... Acts 2:47

FAVORED
"Rejoice, highly *f* ... Luke 1:28

FAVORITISM
not show personal *f* . . . . . Luke 20:21
God shows personal *f* . . . . . Gal 2:6

FEAR
live, for I *f* God . . . . . Gen 42:18
to put the dread and *f* . . . . . Deut 2:25
said, "Does Job *f* . . . . . Job 1:9
Yes, you cast off *f* . . . . . Job 15:4
The *f* of the LORD is . . . . . Ps 19:9
of death, I will *f* . . . . . Ps 23:4
Whom shall I *f* . . . . . Ps 27:1
Oh, *f* the LORD . . . . . Ps 34:9
There is no *f* of God . . . . . Ps 36:1
The *f* of the LORD is . . . . . Ps 111:10
The *f* of man brings a . . . . . Prov 29:25
F God and keep His . . . . . Eccl 12:13
Let Him be your *f* . . . . . Is 8:13
"Be strong, do not *f* . . . . . Is 35:4
who would not *f* . . . . . Jer 10:7
f Him who is able . . . . . Matt 10:28
"Do not *f* . . . . . Luke 12:32
"Do you not even *f* . . . . . Luke 23:40
And walking in the *f* . . . . . Acts 9:31
given us a spirit of *f* . . . . . 2 Tim 1:7
those who through *f* . . . . . Heb 2:15
because of His godly *f* . . . . . Heb 5:7
F God . . . . . 1 Pet 2:17
love casts out *f* . . . . . 1 John 4:18

FEARED
He is also to be *f* . . . . . 1 Chr 16:25
f God more than . . . . . Neh 7:2
Yourself, are to be *f* . . . . . Ps 76:7
Then those who *f* . . . . . Mal 3:16

FEARFUL
It is a *f* thing to . . . . . Heb 10:31

FEARFULLY
f and wonderfully . . . . . Ps 139:14

FEARING
sincerity of heart, *f* . . . . . Col 3:22
forsook Egypt, not *f* . . . . . Heb 11:27

FEARS
upright man, one who *f* . . . . . Job 1:8
me from all my *f* . . . . . Ps 34:4
nation whoever *f* . . . . . Acts 10:35
f has not been made . . . . . 1 John 4:18

FEAST
and you shall keep a *f* . . . . . Num 29:12
hate, I despise your *f* . . . . . Amos 5:21
every year at the *F* . . . . . Luke 2:41
when you give a *f* . . . . . Luke 14:13
Now the Passover, a *f* . . . . . John 6:4
great day of the *f* . . . . . John 7:37

FEASTING
go to the house of *f* . . . . . Eccl 7:2

FEASTS
the best places at *f* . . . . . Luke 20:46
spots in your love *f* . . . . . Jude 12

FED
and *f* you with manna . . . . . Deut 8:3
f you with milk and . . . . . 1 Cor 3:2

FEEBLE
strengthened the *f* . . . . . Job 4:4
And there was none *f* . . . . . Ps 105:37
And my flesh is *f* . . . . . Ps 109:24
hang down, and the *f* . . . . . Heb 12:12

FEED
ravens to *f* you there . . . . . 1 Kin 17:4
and *f* your flocks . . . . . Is 61:5
to him, "*F* My lambs . . . . . John 21:15
your enemy hungers, *f* . . . . . Rom 12:20
goods to *f* the poor . . . . . 1 Cor 13:3

FEEDS
your heavenly Father *f* . . . . . Matt 6:26

FEET
all things under his *f* . . . . . Ps 8:6
He makes my *f* like the . . . . . Ps 18:33
You have set my *f* . . . . . Ps 31:8
For their *f* run to . . . . . Prov 1:16
Her *f* go down to death . . . . . Prov 5:5
mountains Are the *f* . . . . . Is 52:7
place of My *f* glorious . . . . . Is 60:13
in that day His *f* . . . . . Zech 14:4
two hands or two *f* . . . . . Matt 18:8
began to wash His *f* . . . . . Luke 7:38
wash the disciples' *f* . . . . . John 13:5
f are swift to shed . . . . . Rom 3:15
beautiful are the *f* . . . . . Rom 10:15
things under His *f* . . . . . 1 Cor 15:27
and having shod your *f* . . . . . Eph 6:15
fell at His *f* as dead . . . . . Rev 1:17

FELLOW
begins to beat his *f* . . . . . Matt 24:49
f citizens with the . . . . . Eph 2:19
Gentiles should be *f* . . . . . Eph 3:6
I am your *f* servant . . . . . Rev 19:10

FELLOWSHIP
doctrine and *f* . . . . . Acts 2:42
were called into the *f* . . . . . 1 Cor 1:9
f has righteousness . . . . . 2 Cor 6:14
the right hand of *f* . . . . . Gal 2:9
And have no *f* with the . . . . . Eph 5:11
of love, if any *f* . . . . . Phil 2:1
and the *f* of His . . . . . Phil 3:10
we say that we have *f* . . . . . 1 John 1:6
the light, we have *f* . . . . . 1 John 1:7

FERVENT
f prayer of a . . . . . James 5:16
will melt with *f* . . . . . 2 Pet 3:10

FERVENTLY
love one another *f* . . . . . 1 Pet 1:22

FEW
let your words be *f* . . . . . Eccl 5:2
and there are *f* . . . . . Matt 7:14
but the laborers are *f* . . . . . Matt 9:37
called, but *f* chosen . . . . . Matt 20:16
"Lord, are there *f* . . . . . Luke 13:23

FIDELITY
but showing all good *f* . . . . . Titus 2:10

FIELD
Let the *f* be joyful . . . . . Ps 96:12
"The *f* is the world . . . . . Matt 13:38
and buys that *f* . . . . . Matt 13:44
you are God's *f* . . . . . 1 Cor 3:9

FIERY
LORD sent *f* serpents . . . . . Num 21:6
shall make them as a *f* . . . . . Ps 21:9
burning *f* furnace . . . . . Dan 3:6
concerning the *f* . . . . . 1 Pet 4:12

FIG
f leaves together . . . . . Gen 3:7
"Look at the *f* . . . . . Luke 21:29
'I saw you under the *f* . . . . . John 1:50

FIGHT
"The LORD will *f* . . . . . Ex 14:14
Our God will *f* for us . . . . . Neh 4:20
My servants would *f* . . . . . John 18:36
to him, let us not *f* . . . . . Acts 23:9
F the good *f* . . . . . 1 Tim 6:12
have fought the good *f* . . . . . 2 Tim 4:7

FIGHTS
your God is He who *f* . . . . . Josh 23:10
because my lord *f* . . . . . 1 Sam 25:28
f come from among . . . . . James 4:1

F mock at sin .... Prov 14:9
We are *f* for Christ's .... 1 Cor 4:10

FOOT
will not allow your *f* .... Ps 121:3
f will not stumble .... Prov 3:23
From the sole of the *f* .... Is 1:6
f causes you to sin .... Matt 18:8
you dash your *f* .... Luke 4:11
If the *f* should say .... 1 Cor 12:15

FOOTSTOOL
Your enemies Your *f* .... Ps 110:1
Your enemies Your *f* .... Matt 22:44

FORBID
said, "Do not *f* .... Mark 9:39
"Can anyone *f* .... Acts 10:47
f that I should boast .... Gal 6:14

FORBIDDING
f to marry .... 1 Tim 4:3

FOREFATHERS
conscience, as my *f* .... 2 Tim 1:3

FOREHEADS
put a mark on the *f* .... Ezek 9:4
seal of God on their *f* .... Rev 9:4
his mark on their *f* .... Rev 20:4

FOREIGNER
"I am a *f* and a .... Gen 23:4
of me, since I am a *f* .... Ruth 2:10
to God except this *f* .... Luke 17:18

FOREIGNERS
f who were there .... Acts 17:21
longer strangers and *f* .... Eph 2:19

FOREKNEW
For whom He *f* .... Rom 8:29
His people whom He *f* .... Rom 11:2

FOREKNOWLEDGE
purpose and *f* of God .... Acts 2:23

FOREORDAINED
He indeed was *f* .... 1 Pet 1:20

FORESAW
'I *f* the LORD .... Acts 2:25

FORESEEING
f that God would .... Gal 3:8

FORESEES
A prudent man *f* .... Prov 22:3

FORETOLD
have also *f* these days .... Acts 3:24
killed those who *f* .... Acts 7:52

FOREVER
and eat, and live *f* .... Gen 3:22
to our children *f* .... Deut 29:29
LORD sits as King *f* .... Ps 29:10
Do not cast us off *f* .... Ps 44:23
throne, O God, is *f* .... Ps 45:6
"You are a priest *f* .... Ps 110:4
His mercy endures *f* .... Ps 136:1
of our God stands *f* .... Is 40:8
My salvation will be *f* .... Is 51:6
will not cast off *f* .... Lam 3:31
Like the stars *f* .... Dan 12:3
and the glory *f* .... Matt 6:13
the Christ remains *f* .... John 12:34
who is blessed *f* .... 2 Cor 11:31
to whom be glory *f* .... Gal 1:5
generation, *f* and ever .... Eph 3:21
and Father be glory *f* .... Phil 4:20
throne, O God, is *f* .... Heb 1:8
lives and abides *f* .... 1 Pet 1:23
of darkness *f* .... Jude 13
power, Both now and *f* .... Jude 25
And they shall reign *f* .... Rev 22:5

FOREVERMORE
Blessed be the LORD *f* .... Ps 89:52
this time forth and *f* .... Ps 113:2
behold, I am alive *f* .... Rev 1:18

FORGAVE
to repay, he freely *f* .... Luke 7:42
God in Christ *f* .... Eph 4:32
even as Christ *f* .... Col 3:13

FORGET
f the LORD who .... Deut 6:12
I will not *f* Your word .... Ps 119:16
If I *f* you .... Ps 137:5
My son, do not *f* .... Prov 3:1
f the LORD your Maker .... Is 51:13
f your work and labor .... Heb 6:10

FORGETFULNESS
in the land of *f* .... Ps 88:12

FORGETS
and immediately *f* .... James 1:24

FORGETTING
f those things which .... Phil 3:13

FORGIVE
f their sin and heal .... 2 Chr 7:14
good, and ready to *f* .... Ps 86:5
And *f* us our debts .... Matt 6:12
Father will also *f* .... Matt 6:14
his heart, does not *f* .... Matt 18:35
Who can *f* sins but God .... Mark 2:7
f the sins of any .... John 20:23
you ought rather to *f* .... 2 Cor 2:7
F me this wrong .... 2 Cor 12:13
f us our sins and to .... 1 John 1:9

FORGIVEN
sins be *f* them .... Mark 4:12
to whom little is *f* .... Luke 7:47
f you all trespasses .... Col 2:13
your sins are *f* .... 1 John 2:12

FORGIVENESS
But there is *f* with .... Ps 130:4
preached to you the *f* .... Acts 13:38
they may receive *f* .... Acts 26:18
His blood, the *f* .... Eph 1:7

FORGIVES
f all your iniquities .... Ps 103:3
is this who even *f* .... Luke 7:49

FORGIVING
tenderhearted, *f* .... Eph 4:32
and *f* one another .... Col 3:13

FORGOT
Joseph, but *f* .... Gen 40:23
They soon *f* His works .... Ps 106:13

FORGOTTEN
f the God who .... Deut 32:18
not one of them is *f* .... Luke 12:6
f the exhortation .... Heb 12:5
f that he was .... 2 Pet 1:9

FORM
earth was without *f* .... Gen 1:2
Who would *f* a god or .... Is 44:10
f the light and create .... Is 45:7
descended in bodily *f* .... Luke 3:22
time, nor seen His *f* .... John 5:37
For the *f* of this .... 1 Cor 7:31
Who, being in the *f* .... Phil 2:6
having a *f* of .... 2 Tim 3:5

FORMED
And the LORD God *f* .... Gen 2:7
f my inward parts .... Ps 139:13
say of him who *f* .... Is 29:16
"Before I *f* you in .... Jer 1:5

Will the thing *f* .... Rom 9:20
until Christ is *f* .... Gal 4:19

FORMER
f days better than .... Eccl 7:10
f rain to the earth .... Hos 6:3
f prophets preached .... Zech 1:4
your *f* conduct .... Eph 4:22
f things have passed .... Rev 21:4

FORMS
clay say to him who *f* .... Is 45:9
f the spirit of man .... Zech 12:1

FORNICATION
"We were not born of *f* .... John 8:41
of the wrath of her *f* .... Rev 14:8

FORNICATOR
you know, that no *f* .... Eph 5:5
lest there be any *f* .... Heb 12:16

FORNICATORS
but *f* and adulterers .... Heb 13:4

FORSAKE
But I did not *f* .... Ps 119:87
father, And do not *f* .... Prov 1:8
of you does not *f* .... Luke 14:33
never leave you nor *f* .... Heb 13:5

FORSAKEN
My God, why have You *f* .... Ps 22:1
seen the righteous *f* .... Ps 37:25
a mere moment I have *f* .... Is 54:7
God, why have You *f* .... Matt 27:46
persecuted, but not *f* .... 2 Cor 4:9
for Demas has *f* .... 2 Tim 4:10

FORSAKING
f the assembling .... Heb 10:25

FORSOOK
f God who made him .... Deut 32:15
all the disciples *f* .... Matt 26:56
with me, but all *f* .... 2 Tim 4:16

FORTRESS
is my rock, my *f* .... 2 Sam 22:2
my rock of refuge, a *f* .... Ps 31:2

FOUND
f a helper comparable .... Gen 2:20
a thousand I have *f* .... Eccl 7:28
LORD while He may be *f* .... Is 55:6
fruit on it and *f* none .... Luke 13:6
he was lost and is *f* .... Luke 15:24
f the Messiah" (which .... John 1:41
and be *f* in Him .... Phil 3:9

FOUNDATION
Of old You laid the *f* .... Ps 102:25
the earth without a *f* .... Luke 6:49
loved Me before the *f* .... John 17:24
I have laid the *f* .... 1 Cor 3:10
f can anyone lay than .... 1 Cor 3:11
us in Him before the *f* .... Eph 1:4
not laying again the *f* .... Heb 6:1
Lamb slain from the *f* .... Rev 13:8

FOUNDATIONS
when I laid the *f* .... Job 38:4
And the *f* of the wall .... Rev 21:19

FOUNTAIN
will become in him a *f* .... John 4:14

FOUNTAINS
on that day all the *f* .... Gen 7:11
lead them to living *f* .... Rev 7:17

FRAGRANCE
was filled with the *f* .... John 12:3
we are to God the *f* .... 2 Cor 2:15

FREE
'You will be made *f* .... John 8:33
And having been set *f* .... Rom 6:18
Jesus has made me *f* .... Rom 8:2
is neither slave nor *f* .... Gal 3:28
Christ has made us *f* .... Gal 5:1
he is a slave or *f* .... Eph 6:8

FREED
has died has been *f* .... Rom 6:7

FREEDMAN
slave is the Lord's *f* .... 1 Cor 7:22

FREELY
the garden you may *f* .... Gen 2:16
F you have received .... Matt 10:8
f give us all .... Rom 8:32
the water of life *f* .... Rev 22:17

FRIEND
of Abraham Your *f* .... 2 Chr 20:7
f who sticks closer .... Prov 18:24
a *f* of tax collectors .... Matt 11:19
of you shall have a *f* .... Luke 11:5
f Lazarus sleeps .... John 11:11
he was called the *f* .... James 2:23
wants to be a *f* .... James 4:4

FRIENDS
My *f* scorn me .... Job 16:20
the rich has many *f* .... Prov 14:20
one's life for his *f* .... John 15:13
I have called you *f* .... John 15:15
to forbid any of his *f* .... Acts 24:23

FROGS
your territory with *f* .... Ex 8:2
f coming out of the .... Rev 16:13

FRUIT
showed them the *f* .... Num 13:26
brings forth its *f* .... Ps 1:3
f is better than gold .... Prov 8:19
with good by the *f* .... Prov 12:14
like the first *f* .... Is 28:4
does not bear good *f* .... Matt 3:10
good tree bears good *f* .... Matt 7:17
not drink of this *f* .... Matt 26:29
and blessed is the *f* .... Luke 1:42
life, and bring no *f* .... Luke 8:14
and he came seeking *f* .... Luke 13:6
'And if it bears *f* .... Luke 13:9
branch that bears *f* .... John 15:2
that you bear much *f* .... John 15:8
should go and bear *f* .... John 15:16
God, you have your *f* .... Rom 6:22
that we should bear *f* .... Rom 7:4
But the *f* of the .... Gal 5:22
yields the peaceable *f* .... Heb 12:11
Now the *f* of .... James 3:18
autumn trees without *f* .... Jude 12
tree yielding its *f* .... Rev 22:2

FRUITFUL
them, saying, "Be *f* .... Gen 1:22
wife shall be like a *f* .... Ps 128:3
pleasing Him, being *f* .... Col 1:10

FRUITS
Therefore bear *f* .... Matt 3:8
know them by their *f* .... Matt 7:16
of mercy and good *f* .... James 3:17
which bore twelve *f* .... Rev 22:2

FULFILL
for us to *f* all .... Matt 3:15
f the law of Christ .... Gal 6:2
f my joy by being .... Phil 2:2
and *f* all the good .... 2 Thess 1:11
If you really *f* .... James 2:8

FULFILLED
the law till all is *f* ... Matt 5:18
of the Gentiles are *f* ... Luke 21:24
all things must be *f* ... Luke 24:44
of the law might be *f* ... Rom 8:4
loves another has *f* ... Rom 13:8
For all the law is *f* ... Gal 5:14

FULFILLMENT
love is the *f* of the ... Rom 13:10

FULL
and it was *f* of bones ... Ezek 37:1
whole body will be *f* ... Matt 6:22
your joy may be *f* ... John 15:11
You are already *f* ... 1 Cor 4:8
learned both to be *f* ... Phil 4:12

FULLNESS
f we have all received ... John 1:16
But when the *f* of the ... Gal 4:4
filled with all the *f* ... Eph 3:19
Him dwells all the *f* ... Col 2:9

FURNACE
you out of the iron *f* ... Deut 4:20
of a burning fiery *f* ... Dan 3:6
cast them into the *f* ... Matt 13:42
the smoke of a great *f* ... Rev 9:2

FURY
Thus will I spend My *f* ... Ezek 6:12
in anger and *f* On the ... Mic 5:15

G

GAIN
and to die is *g* ... Phil 1:21
rubbish, that I may *g* ... Phil 3:8
is a means of *g* ... 1 Tim 6:5
contentment is great *g* ... 1 Tim 6:6
for dishonest *g* ... 1 Pet 5:2

GAINED
g five more talents ... Matt 25:20

GAINS
g the whole world ... Matt 16:26

GALL
They also gave me *g* ... Ps 69:21
wine mingled with *g* ... Matt 27:34

GAP
and stand in the *g* ... Ezek 22:30

GARDEN
LORD God planted a *g* ... Gen 2:8
g enclosed Is my ... Song 4:12
Eden, the *g* of God ... Ezek 28:13
where there was a *g* ... John 18:1
g a new tomb in ... John 19:41

GARMENT
the hem of His *g* ... Matt 9:20
on a wedding *g* ... Matt 22:11
cloth on an old *g* ... Mark 2:21
all grow old like a *g* ... Heb 1:11
hating even the *g* ... Jude 23

GARMENTS
g did not wear out on ... Deut 8:4
They divide My *g* ... Ps 22:18
from Edom, With dyed *g* ... Is 63:1
"Take away the filthy *g* ... Zech 3:4
man clothed in soft *g* ... Matt 11:8
spread their *g* on the ... Matt 21:8
and divided His *g* ... Matt 27:35
by them in shining *g* ... Luke 24:4
g are moth-eaten ... James 5:2
be clothed in white *g* ... Rev 3:5

GATE
by the narrow *g* ... Matt 7:13
by the Sheep *G* a pool ... John 5:2
laid daily at the *g* ... Acts 3:2
suffered outside the *g* ... Heb 13:12

GATES
up your heads, O you *g* ... Ps 24:7
The LORD loves the *g* ... Ps 87:2
is known in the *g* ... Prov 31:23
Go through the *g* ... Is 62:10
and the *g* of Hades ... Matt 16:18
wall with twelve *g* ... Rev 21:12
g were twelve pearls ... Rev 21:21
g shall not be shut ... Rev 21:25

GATHER
And a time to *g* stones ... Eccl 3:5
g the lambs with His ... Is 40:11
g His wheat into the ... Matt 3:12
sow nor reap nor *g* ... Matt 6:26
Do men *g* grapes from ... Matt 7:16
g where I have not ... Matt 25:26
g together His ... Mark 13:27

GATHERED
g some of every kind ... Matt 13:47
the nations will be *g* ... Matt 25:32

GATHERING
g together of the ... Gen 1:10
g together to Him ... 2 Thess 2:1

GATHERS
The Lord GOD, who *g* ... Is 56:8
together, as a hen *g* ... Matt 23:37

GAVE
to be with me, she *g* ... Gen 3:12
g You this authority ... Matt 21:23
that He *g* His only ... John 3:16
Those whom You *g* ... John 17:12
but God *g* the increase ... 1 Cor 3:6
g Himself for our sins ... Gal 1:4
g Himself for me ... Gal 2:20
g Himself for it ... Eph 5:25

GENERATION
One *g* passes away ... Eccl 1:4
who will declare His *g* ... Is 53:8
and adulterous *g* ... Matt 12:39
this *g* will by no ... Matt 24:34
from this perverse *g* ... Acts 2:40
But you are a chosen *g* ... 1 Pet 2:9

GENERATIONS
be remembered in all *g* ... Ps 45:17
g will call me blessed ... Luke 1:48

GENEROUS
no longer be called *g* ... Is 32:5

GENTILES
G were separated ... Gen 10:5
As a light to the *G* ... Is 42:6
G shall come to your ... Is 60:3
all these things the *G* ... Matt 6:32
into the way of the *G* ... Matt 10:5
revelation to the *G* ... Luke 2:32
G are fulfilled ... Luke 21:24
My name before *G* ... Acts 9:15
poured out on the *G* ... Acts 10:45
a light to the *G* ... Acts 13:47
also the God of the *G* ... Rom 3:29
mystery among the *G* ... Col 1:27
a teacher of the *G* ... 1 Tim 2:7

GENTLE
from Me, for I am *g* ... Matt 11:29
we were *g* among ... 1 Thess 2:7
to be peaceable, *g* ... Titus 3:2
only to the good and *g* ... 1 Pet 2:18
ornament of a *g* ... 1 Pet 3:4

GENTLENESS
love and a spirit of *g* ... 1 Cor 4:21
g, self-control ... Gal 5:23

G be with all those ..... Eph 6:24
shaken, let us have *g* ..... Heb 12:28
But He gives more *g* ..... James 4:6
but grow in the *g* ..... 2 Pet 3:18

GRACIOUS
he said, "God be *g* ..... Gen 43:29
I will be *g* to whom I ..... Ex 33:19
at the *g* words which ..... Luke 4:22
that the Lord is *g* ..... 1 Pet 2:3

GRAFTED
In unbelief, will be *g* ..... Rom 11:23

GRAIN
it treads out the *g* ..... Deut 25:4
be revived like *g* ..... Hos 14:7
to pluck heads of *g* ..... Matt 12:1
unless a *g* of wheat ..... John 12:24

GRAPES
brought forth wild *g* ..... Is 5:2
have eaten sour *g* ..... Ezek 18:2
Do men gather *g* ..... Matt 7:16
g are fully ripe ..... Rev 14:18

GRASS
The *g* withers ..... Is 40:7
so clothes the *g* ..... Matt 6:30
"All Flesh is as *g* ..... 1 Pet 1:24

GRAVE
my soul up from the *g* ..... Ps 30:3
And they made His *g* ..... Is 53:9
the power of the *g* ..... Hos 13:14

GRAVES
g were opened ..... Matt 27:52
g which are not ..... Luke 11:44
g will hear His voice ..... John 5:28

GRAY
the man of *g* hairs ..... Deut 32:25

GREAT
and make your name *g* ..... Gen 12:2
For the LORD is *g* ..... 1 Chr 16:25
Who does *g* things ..... Job 5:9
g is the Holy One ..... Is 12:6
G is Your faithfulness ..... Lam 3:23
he shall be called *g* ..... Matt 5:19
one pearl of *g* price ..... Matt 13:46
desires to become *g* ..... Matt 20:26
g drops of blood ..... Luke 22:44
appearing of our *g* ..... Titus 2:13
g men, the rich men ..... Rev 6:15
Mystery, Babylon the *G* ..... Rev 17:5
the dead, small and *g* ..... Rev 20:12

GREATER
of heaven is *g* ..... Matt 11:11
place there is One *g* ..... Matt 12:6
g than Jonah is here ..... Matt 12:41
g than Solomon is ..... Matt 12:42
a servant is not *g* ..... John 13:16
"*G* love has no one ..... John 15:13
'A servant is not *g* ..... John 15:20
who prophesies is *g* ..... 1 Cor 14:5
God is *g* ..... 1 John 3:20
witness of God is *g* ..... 1 John 5:9

GREATEST
little child is the *g* ..... Matt 18:4
but the *g* of these is ..... 1 Cor 13:13

GREATNESS
is the exceeding *g* ..... Eph 1:19

GREED
part is full of *g* ..... Luke 11:39

GREEDINESS
all uncleanness with *g* ..... Eph 4:19

GREEDY
of everyone who is *g* ..... Prov 1:19
not violent, not *g* ..... 1 Tim 3:3

GREEK
written in Hebrew, *G* ..... John 19:20
and also for the *G* ..... Rom 1:16
is neither Jew not *G* ..... Gal 3:28

GREEN
lie down in *g* pastures ..... Ps 23:2

GRIEF
and acquainted with *g* ..... Is 53:3
joy and not with *g* ..... Heb 13:17

GRIEVE
g the Holy Spirit ..... Eph 4:30

GRIEVED
earth, and He was *g* ..... Gen 6:6
g His Holy Spirit ..... Is 63:10
with anger, being *g* ..... Mark 3:5

GROAN
even we ourselves *g* ..... Rom 8:23
who are in this tent *g* ..... 2 Cor 5:4

GROANING
I am weary with my *g* ..... Ps 6:6
Then Jesus, again *g* ..... John 11:38

GROANINGS
g which cannot ..... Rom 8:26

GROUND
"Cursed is the *g* ..... Gen 3:17
you stand is holy *g* ..... Ex 3:5
up your fallow *g* ..... Jer 4:3
others fell on good *g* ..... Matt 13:8
bought a piece of *g* ..... Luke 14:18
God, the pillar and *g* ..... 1 Tim 3:15

GROUNDED
being rooted and *g* ..... Eph 3:17

GROW
truth in love, may *g* ..... Eph 4:15
but *g* in the grace and ..... 2 Pet 3:18

GRUDGINGLY
in his heart, not *g* ..... 2 Cor 9:7

GUARANTEE
in our hearts as a *g* ..... 2 Cor 1:22
us the Spirit as a *g* ..... 2 Cor 5:5
who is the *g* of our ..... Eph 1:14

GUIDE
He will be our *g* ..... Ps 48:14
g our feet into the ..... Luke 1:79
has come, He will *g* ..... John 16:13

GUIDES
to you, blind *g* ..... Matt 23:16

GUILT
of your fathers' *g* ..... Matt 23:32

GUILTLESS
g who takes His name ..... Ex 20:7
have condemned the *g* ..... Matt 12:7

GUILTY
"We are truly *g* ..... Gen 42:21
world may become *g* ..... Rom 3:19
in one point, he is *g* ..... James 2:10

GULF
you there is a great *g* ..... Luke 16:26

H

HABITATION
Is God in His holy *h* ..... Ps 68:5
but He blesses the *h* ..... Prov 3:33
Jerusalem, a quiet *h* ..... Is 33:20

HAUGHTY
bring down *h* looks .... Ps 18:27
my heart is not *h* .... Ps 131:1
h spirit before a fall .... Prov 16:18

HEAD
He shall bruise your *h* .... Gen 3:15
and gave Him to be *h* .... Eph 1:22
For the husband is *h* .... Eph 5:23

HEAL
O LORD, *h* me .... Ps 6:2
h your backslidings .... Jer 3:22
torn, but He will *h* .... Hos 6:1
"*H* the sick .... Matt 10:8
So that I should *h* .... Matt 13:15
sent Me to *h* the .... Luke 4:18
Physician, *h* yourself .... Luke 4:23

HEALED
And return and be *h* .... Is 6:10
His stripes we are *h* .... Is 53:5
"When I would have *h* .... Hos 7:1
and He *h* them .... Matt 4:24
that you may be *h* .... James 5:16
his deadly wound was *h* .... Rev 13:3

HEALING
shall arise With *h* .... Mal 4:2
and *h* all kinds of .... Matt 4:23
tree were for the *h* .... Rev 22:2

HEALINGS
to another gifts of *h* .... 1 Cor 12:9

HEALS
h all your diseases .... Ps 103:3
Jesus the Christ *h* .... Acts 9:34

HEALTH
all things and be in *h* .... 3 John 2

HEAR
"*H*, O Israel .... Deut 6:4
Him you shall *h* .... Deut 18:15
H me when I call .... Ps 4:1
O You who *h* prayer .... Ps 65:2
ear, shall He not *h* .... Ps 94:9
h rather than to give .... Eccl 5:1
'Hearing you will *h* .... Matt 13:14
heed what you *h* .... Mark 4:24
that God does not *h* .... John 9:31
And how shall they *h* .... Rom 10:14
man be swift to *h* .... James 1:19
h what the Spirit says .... Rev 2:7

HEARD
h their cry because of .... Ex 3:7
that they will be *h* .... Matt 6:7
h the word believed .... Acts 4:4
not seen, nor ear *h* .... 1 Cor 2:9
things that you have *h* .... 2 Tim 2:2
the word which they *h* .... Heb 4:2
which we have *h* .... 1 John 1:1
Lord's Day, and I *h* .... Rev 1:10

HEARER
if anyone is a *h* .... James 1:23

HEARERS
for not the *h* of the .... Rom 2:13
the word, and not *h* .... James 1:22

HEARING
'Keep on *h* .... Is 6:9
h they do not .... Matt 13:13
h they may hear .... Mark 4:12
or by the *h* of faith .... Gal 3:2

HEARS
out and the LORD *h* .... Ps 34:17
of God *h* God's words .... John 8:47
"And if anyone *h* .... John 12:47
who is of the truth *h* .... John 18:37
He who knows God *h* .... 1 John 4:6
And let him who *h* .... Rev 22:17

HEART
h was only evil .... Gen 6:5
h rejoices in the LORD .... 1 Sam 2:1
gave him another *h* .... 1 Sam 10:9
LORD looks at the *h* .... 1 Sam 16:7
his wives turned his *h* .... 1 Kin 11:4
He pierces my *h* .... Job 16:13
My *h* also instructs me .... Ps 16:7
h is overflowing .... Ps 45:1
h shall depart from me .... Ps 101:4
look and a proud *h* .... Ps 101:5
with my whole *h* .... Ps 111:1
as he thinks in his *h* .... Prov 23:7
h reveals the man .... Prov 27:19
trusts in his own *h* .... Prov 28:26
The *h* of the wise is .... Eccl 7:4
And a wise man's *h* .... Eccl 8:5
h yearned for him .... Song 5:4
And the whole *h* .... Is 1:5
The yearning of Your *h* .... Is 63:15
h is deceitful above .... Jer 17:9
I will give them a *h* .... Jer 24:7
and take the stony *h* .... Ezek 11:19
yourselves a new *h* .... Ezek 18:31
are the pure in *h* .... Matt 5:8
is, there your *h* .... Matt 6:21
of the *h* proceed evil .... Matt 15:19
h will flow rivers .... John 7:38
"Let not your *h* .... John 14:1
Satan filled your *h* .... Acts 5:3
h that God has raised .... Rom 10:9
refresh my *h* in the .... Philem 20
and shuts up his *h* .... 1 John 3:17

HEARTILY
you do, do it *h* .... Col 3:23

HEARTS
God tests the *h* .... Ps 7:9
And he will turn The *h* .... Mal 4:6
h failing them from .... Luke 21:26
will guard your *h* .... Phil 4:7
of God rule in your *h* .... Col 3:15

HEATHEN
repetitions as the *h* .... Matt 6:7

HEAVEN
called the firmament *H* .... Gen 1:8
LORD looks down from *h* .... Ps 14:2
word is settled in *h* .... Ps 119:89
For God is in *h* .... Eccl 5:2
"*H* is My throne .... Is 66:1
for the kingdom of *h* .... Matt 3:2
your Father in *h* .... Matt 5:16
On earth as it is in *h* .... Matt 6:10
"*H* and earth will .... Matt 24:35
Him a sign from *h* .... Mark 8:11
have sinned against *h* .... Luke 15:18
you shall see *h* .... John 1:51
one has ascended to *h* .... John 3:13
the true bread from *h* .... John 6:32
a voice came from *h* .... John 12:28
sheet, let down from *h* .... Acts 11:5
laid up for you in *h* .... Col 1:5
there was silence in *h* .... Rev 8:1
Now I saw a new *h* .... Rev 21:1

HEAVENLY
your *h* Father will .... Matt 6:14
h host praising God .... Luke 2:13
if I tell you *h* things .... John 3:12
blessing in the *h* .... Eph 1:3
a better, that is, a *h* .... Heb 11:16
the living God, the *h* .... Heb 12:22

God, in His *h* mountain ... Ps 48:1
"*H, h, h* ... Is 6:3
child of the *H* Spirit ... Mark 1:18
baptize you with the *H* ... Mark 1:8
who speak, but the *H* ... Mark 13:11
H Spirit will come ... Luke 1:35
H Spirit descended ... Luke 3:22
Father give the *H* ... Luke 11:3
H Spirit will teach ... Luke 12:12
H Spirit was not ... John 7:39
H Spirit has come ... Acts 1:8
all filled with the *H* ... Acts 2:4
receive the *H* Spirit ... Acts 19:2
joy in the *H* ... Rom 14:17
H Spirit teaches ... 1 Cor 2:13
that we should be *h* ... Eph 1:4
were sealed with the *H* ... Eph 1:13
partakers of the *H* ... Heb 6:4
H Spirit sent from ... 1 Pet 1:12
it is written, "Be *h* ... 1 Pet 1:16
moved by the *H* Spirit ... 2 Pet 1:21
anointing from the *H* ... 1 John 2:20
says He who is *h* ... Rev 3:7
For You alone are *h* ... Rev 15:4
is *h*, let him be *h* ... Rev 22:11

HOME
sparrow has found a *h* ... Ps 84:3
to his eternal *h* ... Eccl 12:5
that while we are at *h* ... 2 Cor 5:6
to show piety at *h* ... 1 Tim 5:4

HOMEMAKERS
be discreet, chaste, *h* ... Titus 2:5

HONEY
and with *h* from the ... Ps 81:16
was locusts and wild *h* ... Matt 3:4

HONEYCOMB
than honey and the *h* ... Ps 19:10
fish and some *h* ... Luke 24:42

HONOR
"*H* your father and your ... Ex 20:12
will deliver him and *h* ... Ps 91:15
H and majesty are ... Ps 96:6
H the LORD with your ... Prov 3:9
before *h* is humility ... Prov 15:33
spirit will retain *h* ... Prov 29:23
Father, where is My *h* ... Mal 1:6
is not without *h* ... Matt 13:57
'*H* your father and ... Matt 15:4
h the Son Just as they ... John 5:23
"I do not receive *h* ... John 5:41
but I *h* My Father ... John 8:49
"If I *h* Myself ... John 8:54
him My Father will *h* ... John 12:26
to whom fear, *h* ... Rom 13:7
sanctification and *h* ... 1 Thess 4:4
alone is wise, be *h* ... 1 Tim 1:17
and clay, some for *h* ... 2 Tim 2:20
no man takes this *h* ... Heb 5:4
from God the Father *h* ... 2 Pet 1:17
give glory and *h* ... Rev 4:9

HONORABLE
His work is *h* and ... Ps 111:3
holy day of the LORD *h* ... Is 58:13
providing *h* things ... 2 Cor 8.21
Marriage is *h* among ... Heb 13:4
having your conduct *h* ... 1 Pet 2:12

HONORS
'This people *h* Me ... Mark 7:6
It is My Father who *h* ... John 8:54

HOPE
h He has uprooted ... Job 19:10
also will rest in *h* ... Ps 16:9
My *h* is in You ... Ps 39:7
For You are my *h* ... Ps 71:5
I *h* in Your word ... Ps 119:147
good that one should *h* ... Lam 3:26
to *h*, in *h* believed ... Rom 4:18
h does not disappoint ... Rom 5:5
were saved in this *h* ... Rom 8:24
now abide faith, *h* ... 1 Cor 13:13
life only we have *h* ... 1 Cor 15:19
may know what is the *h* ... Eph 1:18
were called in one *h* ... Eph 4:4
Christ in you, the *h* ... Col 1:27
Jesus Christ, our *h* ... 1 Tim 1:1
for the blessed *h* ... Titus 2:13
to lay hold of the *h* ... Heb 6:18
in of a better *h* ... Heb 7:19
who has this *h* in Him ... 1 John 3:3

HOPED
substance of things *h* ... Heb 11:1

HORSE
and behold, a white *h* ... Rev 6:2
and behold, a white *h* ... Rev 19:11

HOSANNA
H in the highest ... Matt 21:9

HOSPITABLE
Be *h* to one another ... 1 Pet 4:9

HOSTS
The LORD of *h* is with ... Ps 46:7
Praise Him, all His *h* ... Ps 148:2
against spiritual *h* ... Eph 6:12

HOUR
is coming at an *h* ... Matt 24:44
"But the *h* is coming ... John 4:23
save Me from this *h* ... John 12:27
keep you from the *h* ... Rev 3:10

HOUSE
as for me and my *h* ... Josh 24:15
Through wisdom a *h* ... Prov 24:3
better to go to the *h* ... Eccl 7:2
h was filled with ... Is 6:4
h divided against ... Matt 12:25
h shall be called a ... Matt 21:13
make My Father's *h* ... John 2:16
h are many mansions ... John 14:2
publicly and from *h* ... Acts 20:20
who rules his own *h* ... 1 Tim 3:4
the church in your *h* ... Philem 2
For every *h* is built ... Heb 3:4
His own *h*, whose *h* ... Heb 3:6

HOUSEHOLD
the ways of her *h* ... Prov 31:27
be those of his own *h* ... Matt 10:36
h were baptized ... Acts 16:15
saved, you and your *h* ... Acts 16:31
who are of Caesar's *h* ... Phil 4:22

HOUSEHOLDER
h who brings out of ... Matt 13:52

HOUSES
H and riches are an ... Prov 19:14
who has left *h* or ... Matt 19:29
you devour widows' *h* ... Matt 23:14

HOVERING
Spirit of God was *h* ... Gen 1:2

HUMBLE
man Moses was very *h* ... Num 12:3
the cry of the *h* ... Ps 9:12
h shall hear of it and ... Ps 34:2
contrite and *h* spirit ... Is 57:15
A meek and *h* people ... Zeph 3:12
associate with the *h* ... Rom 12:16
gives grace to the *h* ... James 4:6
H yourselves in the ... James 4:10
gives grace to the *h* ... 1 Pet 5:5
h yourselves under the ... 1 Pet 5:6

I

IMPUTED
might be *i* to them .... Rom 4:11
but sin is not *i* .... Rom 5:13

IMPUTES
i righteousness apart .... Rom 4:6

INCORRUPTIBLE
the glory of the *i* .... Rom 1:23
dead will be raised *i* .... 1 Cor 15:52
to an inheritance *i* .... 1 Pet 1:4

INCORRUPTION
corruption inherit *i* .... 1 Cor 15:50

INCREASE
Of the *i* of His .... Is 9:7
Lord "*I* our faith .... Luke 17:5
"He must *i* .... John 3:30
but God gave the *i* .... 1 Cor 3:6

INCREASES
who have no might He *i* .... Is 40:29

INCURABLE
Your sorrow is *i* .... Jer 30:15

INDIGNATION
i which will devour .... Heb 10:27
into the cup of His *i* .... Rev 14:10

INEXCUSABLE
Therefore you are *i* .... Rom 2:1

INEXPRESSIBLE
Paradise and heard *i* .... 2 Cor 12:4
you rejoice with joy *i* .... 1 Pet 1:8

INFALLIBLE
suffering by many *i* .... Acts 1:3

INFIRMITIES
"He Himself took our *i* .... Matt 8:17

INHERIT
love me to *i* wealth .... Prov 8:21
i the kingdom .... Matt 25:34
unrighteous will not *i* .... 1 Cor 6:9
who overcomes shall *i* .... Rev 21:7

INHERITANCE
"You shall have no *i* .... Num 18:20
is the place of His *i* .... Deut 32:9
the portion of my *i* .... Ps 16:5
i shall be forever .... Ps 37:18
He will choose our *i* .... Ps 47:4
will arise to your *i* .... Dan 12:13
God gave him no *i* .... Acts 7:5
and give you an *i* .... Acts 20:32
For if the *i* is of the .... Gal 3:18
we have obtained an *i* .... Eph 1:11
be partakers of the *i* .... Col 1:12
receive as an *i* .... Heb 11:8
i incorruptible .... 1 Pet 1:4

INIQUITIES
i have overtaken me .... Ps 40:12
forgives all your *i* .... Ps 103:3
LORD, should mark *i* .... Ps 130:3
was bruised for our *i* .... Is 53:5
He shall bear their *i* .... Is 53:11
i have separated you .... Is 59:2

INIQUITY
God, visiting the *i* of the .... Ex 20:5
was brought forth in *i* .... Ps 51:5
If I regard *i* in my .... Ps 66:18
i have dominion .... Ps 119:133
i will reap sorrow .... Prov 22:8
A people laden with *i* .... Is 1:4
i is taken away .... Is 6:7
has laid on Him the *i* .... Is 53:6
will remember their *i* .... Hos 9:9
to those who devise *i* .... Mic 2:1
like You, Pardoning *i* .... Mic 7:18

all you workers of *i* .... Luke 13:27
a fire, a world of *i* .... James 3:6

INJUSTICE
i have your fathers .... Jer 2:5

INN
room for them in the *i* .... Luke 2:7
brought him to an *i* .... Luke 10:34

INNOCENCE
washed my hands in *i* .... Ps 73:13

INNOCENT
because I was found *i* .... Dan 6:22
saying, "I am *i* .... Matt 27:24
this day that I am *i* .... Acts 20:26

INQUIRED
Therefore David *i* .... 1 Sam 23:2
the prophets have *i* .... 1 Pet 1:10

INQUIRY
shall make careful *i* .... Deut 19:18

INSANE
images, And they are *i* .... Jer 50:38

INSPIRATION
is given by *i* of God .... 2 Tim 3:16

INSTRUCT
I will *i* you and teach .... Ps 32:8
LORD that he may *i* .... 1 Cor 2:16

INSTRUCTED
This man had been *i* .... Acts 18:25
are excellent, being *i* .... Rom 2:18
Moses was divinely *i* .... Heb 8:5

INSTRUCTION
seeing you hate *i* .... Ps 50:17
Hear *i* and be wise .... Prov 8:33
Give *i* to a wise man .... Prov 9:9
for correction, for *i* .... 2 Tim 3:16

INSTRUCTS
My heart also *i* .... Ps 16:7

INSTRUMENTS
your members as *i* .... Rom 6:13

INSUBORDINATE
for the lawless and *i* .... 1 Tim 1:9

INSUBORDINATION
of dissipation or *i* .... Titus 1:6

INSULTED
will be mocked and *i* .... Luke 18:32
i the Spirit of grace .... Heb 10:29

INSULTS
nor be afraid of their *i* .... Is 51:7

INTEGRITY
in the *i* of my heart .... Gen 20:
in doctrine showing *i* .... Titus 2:

INTERCEDE
the LORD, who will *i* .... 1 Sam 2:25

INTERCESSION
of many, And made *i* .... Is 53:12
Spirit Himself makes *i* .... Rom 8:26
always lives to make *i* .... Heb 7:25

INTERCESSOR
that there was no *i* .... Is 59:16

INTEREST
collected it with *i* .... Luke 19:23

INTERPRET
Do all *i*? .... 1 Cor 12:30
pray that he may *i* .... 1 Cor 14:13

INTERPRETATION
to another the *i* .... 1 Cor 12:10
of any private *i* .... 2 Pet 1:20

dead, both of the *j* ... Acts 24:15
j shall live by faith ... Rom 1:17
that He might be *j* ... Rom 3:26
j men made perfect ... Heb 12:23
have murdered the *j* ... James 5:6
He is faithful and *j* ... 1 John 1:9

JUSTICE
j as the noonday ... Ps 37:6
And Your poor with *j* ... Ps 72:2
j the measuring line ... Is 28:17
the LORD is a God of *j* ... Is 30:18
He will bring forth *j* ... Is 42:1
J is turned back ... Is 59:14
I, the LORD, love *j* ... Is 61:8
truth, and His ways *j* ... Dan 4:37
'Execute true *j* ... Zech 7:9
"Where is the God of *j* ... Mal 2:17
And He will declare *j* ... Matt 12:18
His humiliation His *j* ... Acts 8:33

JUSTIFICATION
because of our *j* ... Rom 4:25
offenses resulted in *j* ... Rom 5:16

JUSTIFIED
Me that you may be *j* ... Job 40:8
words you will be *j* ... Matt 12:37
"But wisdom is *j* ... Luke 7:35
j rather than the ... Luke 18:14
who believes is *j* ... Acts 13:39
"That You may be *j* ... Rom 3:4
law no flesh will be *j* ... Rom 3:20
j freely by His grace ... Rom 3:24
having been *j* by ... Rom 5:1
these He also *j* ... Rom 8:30
that we might be *j* ... Gal 2:16
no flesh shall be *j* ... Gal 2:16
the harlot also *j* ... James 2:25

JUSTIFIES
He who *j* the wicked ... Prov 17:15
It is God who *j* ... Rom 8:33

JUSTIFY
wanting to *j* himself ... Luke 10:29
"You are those who *j* ... Luke 16:15
is one God who will *j* ... Rom 3:30

K

KEEP
k you wherever you ... Gen 28:15
day, to *k* it holy ... Ex 20:8
Let all the earth *k* ... Hab 2:20
k the commandments ... Matt 19:17
"If you love Me, *k* ... John 14:15
k through Your name ... John 17:11
orderly and *k* the law ... Acts 21:24
k the unity of the ... Eph 4:3
k His commandments ... 1 John 2:3

KEEPER
Am I my brother's *k* ... Gen 4:9
The LORD is your *k* ... Ps 121:5

KEEPS
k truth forever ... Ps 146:6
k the commandment ... Prov 19:16
none of you *k* the law ... John 7:19
born of God *k* ... 1 John 5:18
and *k* his garments ... Rev 16:15

KEPT
For I have *k* the ... 2 Sam 22:22
these things I have *k* ... Matt 19:20
love, just as I have *k* ... John 15:10
k back part of the ... Acts 5:2
I have *k* the faith ... 2 Tim 4:7
who are *k* by the power ... 1 Pet 1:5

KEY
taken away the *k* ... Luke 11:52
"He who has the *k* ... Rev 3:7

KEYS
I will give you the *k* ... Matt 16:19
And I have the *k* ... Rev 1:18

KILL
k the Passover ... Ex 12:21
I *k* and I make alive ... Deut 32:39
"Am I God, to *k* ... 2 Kin 5:7
A time to *k* ... Eccl 3:3
of them they will *k* ... Luke 11:49
afraid of those who *k* ... Luke 12:4
Why do you seek to *k* ... John 7:19
k and eat ... Acts 10:13

KILLED
Abel his brother and *k* ... Gen 4:8
for Your sake we are *k* ... Ps 44:22
and scribes, and be *k* ... Matt 16:21
Siloam fell and *k* them ... Luke 13:4
k the Prince of life ... Acts 3:15
Your sake we are *k* ... Rom 8:36
k both the Lord ... 1 Thess 2:15

KILLS
the one who *k* the ... Matt 23:37
for the letter *k* ... 2 Cor 3:6

KIND
animals after their *k* ... Gen 6:20
k can come out by ... Mark 9:29
suffers long and is *k* ... 1 Cor 13:4
And be *k* to one ... Eph 4:32

KINDLY
Julius treated Paul *k* ... Acts 27:3
k affectionate to one ... Rom 12:10

KINDNESS
For His merciful *k* ... Ps 117:2
k shall not depart ... Is 54:10
I remember you, The *k* ... Jer 2:2
by longsuffering, by *k* ... 2 Cor 6:6
longsuffering, *k* ... Gal 5:22
and to brotherly *k* ... 2 Pet 1:7

KING
"Yet I have set My *K* ... Ps 2:6
The LORD is *K* forever ... Ps 10:16
And the *K* of glory ... Ps 24:7
For God is my *K* ... Ps 74:12
when your *k* is a child ... Eccl 10:16
and the everlasting *K* ... Jer 10:10
the LORD shall be *K* ... Zech 14:9
who has been born *K* ... Matt 2:2
This Is Jesus The *K* ... Matt 27:37
"Behold your *K* ... John 19:14
Now to the *K* eternal ... 1 Tim 1:17
only Potentate, the *K* ... 1 Tim 6:15
this Melchizedek, *k* ... Heb 7:1
K of Kings and Lord ... Rev 19:16

KINGDOM
Yours is the *k* ... 1 Chr 29:11
k is the LORD's ... Ps 22:28
the scepter of Your *k* ... Ps 45:6
is an everlasting *k* ... Ps 145:13
k which shall never be ... Dan 2:44
High rules in the *k* ... Dan 4:17
"Repent, for the *k* ... Matt 3:2
for Yours is the *k* ... Matt 6:13
"But seek first the *k* ... Matt 6:33
the mysteries of the *k* ... Matt 13:11
are the sons of the *k* ... Matt 13:38
of such is the *k* ... Matt 19:14
back, is fit for the *k* ... Luke 9:62
against nation, and *k* ... Luke 21:10
he cannot see the *k* ... John 3:3
he cannot enter the *k* ... John 3:5

If My *k* were of this .... John 18:36
for the *k* of God is .... Rom 14:17
will not inherit the *k* .... Gal 5:21
the scepter of Your *k* .... Heb 1:8
we are receiving a *k* .... Heb 12:28

KINGDOMS
the *k* were moved .... Ps 46:6
showed Him all the *k* .... Matt 4:8
have become the *k* .... Rev 11:15

KINGS
The *k* of the earth set .... Ps 2:2
By me *k* reign .... Prov 8:15
governors and *k* .... Matt 10:18
k have desired to see .... Luke 10:24
You have reigned as *k* .... 1 Cor 4:8
and has made us *k* .... Rev 1:6
that the way of the *k* .... Rev 16:12

KISS
K the Son .... Ps 2:12
"You gave Me no *k* .... Luke 7:45
one another with a *k* .... 1 Pet 5:14

KISSED
they *k* one another .... 1 Sam 20:41
and *k* Him .... Matt 26:49
and she *k* His feet and .... Luke 7:38

KNEE
That to Me every *k* .... Is 45:23
have not bowed the *k* .... Rom 11:4
of Jesus every *k* .... Phil 2:10

KNEES
make firm the feeble *k* .... Is 35:3
this reason I bow my *k* .... Eph 3:14
and the feeble *k* .... Heb 12:12

KNEW
in the womb I *k* .... Jer 1:5
to them, 'I never *k* .... Matt 7:23
k what was in man .... John 2:25
He made Him who *k* .... 2 Cor 5:21

KNIT
be encouraged, being *k* .... Col 2:2

KNOCK
k, and it will be .... Matt 7:7
at the door and *k* .... Rev 3:20

KNOW
k good and evil .... Gen 3:22
k that I am the LORD .... Ex 6:7
k that my Redeemer .... Job 19:25
make me to *k* wisdom .... Ps 51:6
Who can *k* it .... Jer 17:9
saying, '*K* the LORD .... Jer 31:34
k what hour your .... Matt 24:42
an oath, "I do not *k* .... Matt 26:72
the world did not *k* .... John 1:10
We speak what We *k* .... John 3:11
k that You are .... John 6:69
My voice, and I *k* .... John 10:27
If you *k* these things .... John 13:17
k whom I have .... John 13:18
are sure that You *k* .... John 16:30
k that I love You .... John 21:15
k times or seasons .... Acts 1:7
and said, "Jesus I *k* .... Acts 19:15
wisdom did not *k* .... 1 Cor 1:21
nor can he *k* them .... 1 Cor 2:14
For we *k* in part and .... 1 Cor 13:9
k the love of Christ .... Eph 3:19
k whom I have .... 2 Tim 1:12
we *k* that we *k* Him .... 1 John 2:3
and you *k* all things .... 1 John 2:20
By this we *k* love .... 1 John 3:16
k that He abides .... 1 John 3:24
k that we are of God .... 1 John 5:19
"I *k* your works .... Rev 2:2

KNOWLEDGE
and the tree of the *k* .... Gen 2:9
unto night reveals *k* .... Ps 19:2
k is too wonderful .... Ps 139:6
people store up *k* .... Prov 10:14
k spares his words .... Prov 17:27
and he who increases *k* .... Eccl 1:18
k is that wisdom .... Eccl 7:12
k shall increase .... Dan 12:4
more accurate *k* .... Acts 24:22
having the form of *k* .... Rom 2:20
law is the *k* of sin .... Rom 3:20
whether there is *k* .... 1 Cor 13:8
Christ which passes *k* .... Eph 3:19
is falsely called *k* .... 1 Tim 6:20
in the grace and *k* .... 2 Pet 3:18

KNOWN
If you had *k* Me .... John 8:19
My sheep, and am *k* .... John 10:14
The world has not *k* .... John 17:25
peace they have not *k* .... Rom 3:17
"For who has *k* .... Rom 11:34
after you have *k* .... Gal 4:9
requests be made *k* .... Phil 4:6
k the Holy Scriptures .... 2 Tim 3:15

KNOWS
"For God *k* that in .... Gen 3:5
k what is in the .... Dan 2:22
k the things you have .... Matt 6:8
and hour no one *k* .... Matt 24:36
God *k* your hearts .... Luke 16:15
searches the hearts *k* .... Rom 8:27
k the things of God .... 1 Cor 2:11
k those who are His .... 2 Tim 2:19
to him who *k* to do .... James 4:17
and *k* all things .... 1 John 3:20

L

LABOR
Six days you shall *l* .... Ex 20:9
things are full of *l* .... Eccl 1:8
has man for all his *l* .... Eccl 2:22
He shall see the *l* .... Is 53:11
to Me, all you who *l* .... Matt 11:28
"Do not *l* for the .... John 6:27
knowing that your *l* .... 1 Cor 15:58
but rather let him *l* .... Eph 4:28
mean fruit from my *l* .... Phil 1:22
your work of faith, *l* .... 1 Thess; 1:3
forget your work and *l* .... Heb 6:10
your works, your *l* .... Rev 2:2

LABORED
l more abundantly .... 1 Cor 15:10
for you, lest I have *l* .... Gal 4:11

LABORERS
but the *l* are few .... Matt 9:37

LABORING
l night and day .... 1 Thess 2:9

LABORS
entered into their *l* .... John 4:38
creation groans and *l* .... Rom 8:22
l more abundant .... 2 Cor 11:23
may rest from their *l* .... Rev 14:13

LACK
What do I still *l* .... Matt 19:20
"One thing you *l* .... Mark 10:21

LADDER
and behold, a *l* .... Gen 28:12

LAID
the place where they *l* .... Mark 16:6
"Where have you *l* .... John 11:34

LAKE
cast alive into the *l* .... Rev 19:20

LAMB
but where is the *l* .... Gen 22:7
He was led as a *l* .... Is 53:7
The *L* of God who .... John 1:29
the elders, stood a *L* .... Rev 5:6
"Worthy is the *L* .... Rev 5:12
by the blood of the *L* .... Rev 12:11

LAME
l shall leap like a .... Is 35:6
blind see and the *l* .... Matt 11:5
And a certain man *l* .... Acts 3:2

LAMENTATION
was heard in Ramah, *l* .... Matt 2:18
and made great *l* .... Acts 8:2

LAMP
Your word is a *l* .... Ps 119:105
the *l* of the wicked .... Prov 13:9
his *l* will be put out .... Prov 20:20
"Nor do they light a *l* .... Matt 5:15
"The *l* of the body .... Matt 6:22
when he has lit a *l* .... Luke 8:16
l gives you light .... Luke 11:36
does not light a *l* .... Luke 15:8
burning and shining *l* .... John 5:35

LAMPS
he made its seven *l* .... Ex 37:23
and trimmed their *l* .... Matt 25:7

LAMPSTAND
branches of the *l* .... Ex 25:32
a basket, but on a *l* .... Matt 5:15
and remove your *l* .... Rev 2:5

LAND
l that I will show you .... Gen 12:1
l flowing with milk .... Ex 3:8
They will see the *l* .... Is 33:17
Bethlehem, in the *l* .... Matt 2:6

LANGUAGE
whole earth had one *l* .... Gen 11:1
speak in his own *l* .... Acts 2:6
blasphemy, filthy *l* .... Col 3:8

LANGUAGES
according to their *l* .... Gen 10:20

LAST
He shall stand at *l* .... Job 19:25
First and I am the *L* .... Is 44:6
l will be first .... Matt 20:16
the First and the *L* .... Rev 1:11

LATTER
l times some will .... 1 Tim 4:1

LAUGH
"Why did Sarah *l* .... Gen 18:13
Woe to you who *l* .... Luke 6:25

LAUGHS
The Lord *l* at him .... Ps 37:13

LAUGHTER
your *l* be turned to .... James 4:9

LAW
stones a copy of the *l* .... Josh 8:32
The *l* of the LORD is .... Ps 19:7
I delight in Your *l* .... Ps 119:70
Oh, how I love Your *l* .... Ps 119:97
And Your *l* is truth .... Ps 119:142
l will proceed from Me .... Is 51:4
in whose heart is My *l* .... Is 51:7
The *L* is no more .... Lam 2:9
The *l* of truth was in .... Mal 2:6
to destroy the *L* .... Matt 5:17
for this is the *L* .... Matt 7:12
hang all the *L* and the .... Matt 22:40
"The *l* and the .... Luke 16:1
l was given through .... John 1:1
"Does our *l* judge a .... John 7:5
l is the knowledge .... Rom 3:2
because the *l* brings .... Rom 4:1
when there is no *l* .... Rom 5:1
you are not under *l* .... Rom 6:1
For what the *l* could .... Rom 8:
l that I might live .... Gal 2:1
under guard by the *l* .... Gal 3:2
born under the *l* .... Gal 4:
l is fulfilled in one .... Gal 5:1
into the perfect *l* .... James 1:2
fulfill the royal *l* .... James 2:

LAWFUL
Is it *l* to pay taxes .... Matt 22:1
All things are *l* .... 1 Cor 6:1

LAWGIVER
There is one *L* .... James 4:1

LAWLESS
l one will be revealed .... 2 Thess 2:

LAWLESSNESS
Me, you who practice *l* .... Matt 7:2
l is already at work .... 2 Thess 2:

LAWYERS
"Woe to you also, *l* .... Luke 11:4

LAY
nowhere to *l* His head .... Matt 8:2
l hands may receive .... Acts 8:1

LAZINESS
l the building decays .... Eccl 10:1

LAZY
l man will be put to .... Prov 12:2
wicked and *l* servant .... Matt 25:2
liars, evil beasts, *l* .... Titus 1:1

LEAD
L me in Your truth and .... Ps 25:
And do not *l* us into .... Matt 6:1
"Can the blind *l* .... Luke 6:3

LEADS
He *l* me in the paths .... Ps 23:
And if the blind *l* .... Matt 15:1

LEAF
plucked olive *l* .... Gen 8:1

LEAN
all your heart, And *l* .... Prov 3:

LEAP
Then the lame shall *l* .... Is 35:

LEARN
L to do good .... Is 1:1
yoke upon you and *l* .... Matt 11:2

LEARNED
Me The tongue of the *l* .... Is 50:
have not so *l* Christ .... Eph 4:2
in all things I have *l* .... Phil 4:1

LEARNING
l is driving you mad .... Acts 26:2

LEAST
so, shall be called *l* .... Matt 5:1

LEAVE
a man shall *l* his .... Gen 2:2
For You will not *l* .... Ps 16:1
"I will never *l* .... Heb 13:

LEAVEN
of heaven is like *l* .... Matt 13:3
l leavens the whole .... Gal 5:

LEAVES
and they sewed fig *l* .... Gen 3:
The *l* of the tree .... Rev 22:

LED
l them forth by the ... Ps 107:7
For as many as are *l* ... Rom 8:14

LEFT
l hand know what your ... Matt 6:3

LEND
"And if you *l* ... Luke 6:34

LENDER
is servant to the *l* ... Prov 22:7

LENDS
ever merciful, and *l* ... Ps 37:26

LENGTH
is your life and the *l* ... Deut 30:20

LEOPARD
or the *l* its spots ... Jer 13:23

LEPERS
"And many *l* were in ... Luke 4:27

LET
"*L* there be light ... Gen 1:3

LETTER
for the *l* kills ... 2 Cor 3:6
or by word or by *l* ... 2 Thess 2:2

LETTERS
does this Man know *l* ... John 7:15

LEVIATHAN
"Can you draw out *L* ... Job 41:1

LEVITE
"Likewise a *L* ... Luke 10:32

LEWDNESS
wickedness, deceit, *l* ... Mark 7:22

LIAR
for he is a *l* and the ... John 8:44
but every man a *l* ... Rom 3:4
we make Him a *l* ... 1 John 1:10
his brother, he is a *l* ... 1 John 4:20

LIARS
"All men are *l* ... Ps 116:11
l shall have their ... Rev 21:8

LIBERALITY
he who gives, with *l* ... Rom 12:8

LIBERALLY
who gives to all *l* ... James 1:5

LIBERTY
year, and proclaim *l* ... Lev 25:10
'To proclaim *l* to the ... Luke 4:18
into the glorious *l* ... Rom 8:21
Lord is, there is *l* ... 2 Cor 3:17
therefore in the *l* ... Gal 5:1

LIE
Do not *l* to one ... Col 3:9
God, who cannot *l* ... Titus 1:2
an abomination or a *l* ... Rev 21:27

LIED
You have not *l* to men ... Acts 5:4

LIES
sin *l* at the door ... Gen 4:7
speaking *l* in ... 1 Tim 4:2

LIFE
the breath of *l* ... Gen 2:7
'For the *l* of the ... Lev 17:11
before you today *l* ... Deut 30:15
He will redeem their *l* ... Ps 72:14
word has given me *l* ... Ps 119:50
She is a tree of *l* ... Prov 3:18
finds me finds *l* ... Prov 8:35
L is more than ... Luke 12:23
l was the light ... John 1:4
so the Son gives *l* ... John 5:21
spirit, and they are *l* ... John 6:63
have the light of *l* ... John 8:12
and I lay down My *l* ... John 10:15
resurrection and the *l* ... John 11:25
you lay down your *l* ... John 13:38
l which I now live ... Gal 2:20
l is hidden with ... Col 3:3
For what is your *l* ... James 4:14
l was manifested ... 1 John 1:2
and the pride of *l* ... 1 John 2:16
has given us eternal *l* ... 1 John 5:11
the Lamb's Book of *L* ... Rev 21:27
right to the tree of *l* ... Rev 22:14
the water of *l* freely ... Rev 22:17
from the Book of *L* ... Rev 22:19

LIFT
I will *l* up my eyes to ... Ps 121:1
Lord, and He will *l* ... James 4:10

LIFTED
your heart is *l* ... Ezek 28:2
in Hades, he *l* up his ... Luke 16:23
the Son of Man be *l* ... John 3:14
"And I, if I am *l* ... John 12:32

LIGHT
"Let there be *l* ... Gen 1:3
The Lord is my *l* ... Ps 27:1
and a *l* to my path ... Ps 119:105
The *l* of the righteous ... Prov 13:9
The Lord gives *l* ... Prov 29:13
Truly the *l* is sweet ... Eccl 11:7
let us walk in the *l* ... Is 2:5
l shall break forth ... Is 58:8
"You are the *l* ... Matt 5:14
"Let your *l* so shine ... Matt 5:16
than the sons of *l* ... Luke 16:8
and the life was the *l* ... John 1:4
darkness rather than *l* ... John 3:19
saying, "I am the *l* ... John 8:12
God who commanded *l* ... 2 Cor 4:6
Walk as children of *l* ... Eph 5:8
You are all sons of *l* ... 1 Thess 5:5
into His marvelous *l* ... 1 Pet 2:9
to you, that God is *l* ... 1 John 1:5
l as He is in the ... 1 John 1:7
says he is in the *l* ... 1 John 2:9
The Lamb is its *l* ... Rev 21:23

LIGHTNING
"For as the *l* ... Matt 24:27
countenance was like *l* ... Matt 28:3

LIGHTNINGS
the throne proceeded *l* ... Rev 4:5

LIGHTS
"Let there be *l* ... Gen 1:14
whom you shine as *l* ... Phil 2:15

LIKENESS
according to Our *l* ... Gen 1:26
carved image—any *l* ... Ex 20:4
when I awake in Your *l* ... Ps 17:15
and coming in the *l* ... Phil 2:7

LILY
the *l* of the valleys ... Song 2:1

LIMIT
to the sea its *l* ... Prov 8:29

LINE
upon precept, *L* upon ... Is 28:10
I am setting a plumb *l* ... Amos 7:8

LINEN
wrapped Him in the *l* ... Mark 15:46

LINGER
salvation shall not *l* ... Is 46:13

LION
l shall eat straw ... Is 11:7

LIONS
the mouths of *l* ... Heb 11:33

LIPS
off all flattering *l* ... Ps 12:3
The *l* of the righteous ... Prov 10:21
But the *l* of ... Prov 20:15
am a man of unclean *l* ... Is 6:5
other *l* I will speak ... 1 Cor 14:21
from evil, And his *l* ... 1 Pet 3:10

LISTEN
you are not able to *l* ... John 8:43
you who fear God, *l* ... Acts 13:16

LISTENS
But whoever *l* to me ... Prov 1:33

LITTLE
Though you are *l* ... Mic 5:2
l ones only a cup ... Matt 10:42
"O you of *l* faith ... Matt 14:31
to whom *l* is forgiven ... Luke 7:47
faithful in a very *l* ... Luke 19:17

LIVE
eat, and *l* forever ... Gen 3:22
a man does, he shall *l* ... Lev 18:5
"Seek Me and *l* ... Amos 5:4
But the just shall *l* ... Hab 2:4
l by bread alone ... Matt 4:4
"for in Him we *l* ... Acts 17:28
l peaceably with all ... Rom 12:18
the life which I now *l* ... Gal 2:20
If we *l* in the Spirit ... Gal 5:25
to me, to *l* is Christ ... Phil 1:21

LIVED
died and rose and *l* ... Rom 14:9
And they *l* and reigned ... Rev 20:4

LIVES
but man *l* by every ... Deut 8:3
but Christ *l* in me ... Gal 2:20
to lay down our *l* ... 1 John 3:16
"I am He who *l* ... Rev 1:18

LIVING
and man became a *l* ... Gen 2:7
in the light of the *l* ... Ps 56:13
the dead, but of the *l* ... Matt 22:32
do you seek the *l* ... Luke 24;5
the word of God is *l* ... Heb 4:12
l creature was like a ... Rev 4:7

LOATHSOME
But a wicked man is *l* ... Prov 13:5

LOAVES
have here only five *l* ... Matt 14:17
you ate of the *l* ... John 6:26

LOCUST
What the chewing *l* ... Joel 1:4

LOCUSTS
and his food was *l* ... Matt 3:4

LOFTY
Wisdom is too *l* ... Prov 24:7

LONG
your days may be *l* ... Deut 5:16
Who *l* for death ... Job 3:21
I *l* for Your salvation ... Ps 119:174
go around in *l* robes ... Mark 12:38

LONGSUFFERING
is love, joy, peace, *l* ... Gal 5:22
and gentleness, with *l* ... Eph 4:2
for all patience and *l* ... Col 1:11
might show all *l* ... 1 Tim 1:16
once the Divine *l* ... 1 Pet 3:20
and consider that the *l* ... 2 Pet 3:15

LOOK
A proud *l* ... Prov 6:17
"*L* to Me ... Is 45:22
l on Me whom they ... Zech 12:10
say to you, '*L* here ... Luke 17:23
while we do not *l* ... 2 Cor 4:18

LOOKED
For He *l* down from ... Ps 102:19
He *l* for justice ... Is 5:7
the Lord turned and *l* ... Luke 22:61
for he *l* to the reward ... Heb 11:26

LOOKING
the plow, and *l* back ... Luke 9:62
l for the blessed hope ... Titus 2:13
l unto Jesus ... Heb 12:2
l carefully lest ... Heb 12:15
l for the mercy of ... Jude 21

LOOKS
The lofty *l* of man ... Is 2:11
to you that whoever *l* ... Matt 5:28

LOOSE
and whatever you *l* ... Matt 16:19
said to them, "*L* him ... John 11:44

LOOSED
the silver cord is *l* ... Eccl 12:6

LORD
L is my strength ... Ex 15:2
L our God, the *L* ... Deut 6:4
You alone are the *L* ... Neh 9:6
The *L* of hosts ... Ps 24:10
Gracious is the *L* ... Ps 116:5
L surrounds His people ... Ps 125:2
The *L* is righteous ... Ps 129:4
L is near to all who ... Ps 145:18
L is a God of justice ... Is 30:18
L Our Righteousness ... Jer 23:6
"The *L* is one ... Zech 14:9
shall not tempt the *L* ... Matt 4:7
shall worship the *L* ... Matt 4:10
Son of Man is also *L* ... Mark 2:28
who is Christ the *L* ... Luke 2:11
L is risen indeed ... Luke 24:34
Me Teacher and *L* ... John 13:13
He is *L* of all ... Acts 10:36
with your mouth the *L* ... Rom 10:9
say that Jesus is *L* ... 1 Cor 12:3
second Man is the *L* ... 1 Cor 15:47
the Spirit of the *L* ... 2 Cor 3:17
that Jesus Christ is *L* ... Phil 2:11
and deny the only *L* ... Jude 4
L God Omnipotent ... Rev 19:6

LORDS
for He is Lord of *l* ... Rev 17:14

LOSE
save his life will *l* ... Matt 16:25

LOSES
but if the salt *l* ... Matt 5:13
and *l* his own soul ... Matt 16:26

LOSS
count all things *l* ... Phil 3:8

LOST
save that which was *l* ... Matt 18:11
and none of them is *l* ... John 17:12
You gave Me I have *l* ... John 18:9

LOTS
garments, casting *l* ... Mark 15:24
And they cast their *l* ... Acts 1:26

LOUD
cried out with a *l* ... Matt 27:46
I heard behind me a *l* ... Rev 1:10

LOVE
l your neighbor as ... Lev 19:18
l the LORD your God ... Deut 6:5
Oh, *l* the LORD ... Ps 31:23
he has set his *l* ... Ps 91:14
Oh, how I *l* Your law ... Ps 119:97
l covers all sins ... Prov 10:12
A time to *l* ... Eccl 3:8
banner over me was *l* ... Song 2:4
l is as strong as ... Song 8:6
do justly, To *l* mercy ... Mic 6:8
to you, *l* your enemies ... Matt 5:44
which of them will *l* ... Luke 7:42
you do not have the *l* ... John 5:42
If you have *l* for one ... John 13:35
"If you *l* Me ... John 14:15
and My Father will *l* ... John 14:23
l one another as I ... John 15:12
l has no one than this ... John 15:13
because the *l* of God ... Rom 5:5
to *l* one another ... Rom 13:8
L suffers long and is ... 1 Cor 13:4
L never fails ... 1 Cor 13:8
greatest of these is *l* ... 1 Cor 13:13
For the *l* of Christ ... 2 Cor 5:14
of the Spirit is *l* ... Gal 5:22
Husbands, *l* your wives ... Eph 5:25
the commandment is *l* ... 1 Tim 1:5
For the *l* of money is ... 1 Tim 6:10
Let brotherly *l* ... Heb 13:1
having not seen you *l* ... 1 Pet 1:8
for "*l* will cover a ... 1 Pet 4:8
brotherly kindness *l* ... 2 Pet 1:7
By this we know *l* ... 1 John 3:16
Beloved, let us *l* ... 1 John 4:7
for God is *l* ... 1 John 4:8
There is no fear in *l* ... 1 John 4:18
l Him because He ... 1 John 4:19
loves God must *l* ... 1 John 4:21
For this is the *l* ... 1 John 5:3
have left your first *l* ... Rev 2:4

LOVED
L one and friend You ... Ps 88:18
Yet Jacob I have *l* ... Mal 1:2
forgiven, for she *l* ... Luke 7:47
so *l* the world that ... John 3:16
whom Jesus *l* ... John 13:23
"As the Father *l* ... John 15:9
l them as You have ... John 17:23
the Son of God, who *l* ... Gal 2:20
l the church and gave ... Eph 5:25
Beloved, if God so *l* ... 1 John 4:11
To Him who *l* us and ... Rev 1:5

LOVELY
he is altogether *l* ... Song 5:16
whatever things are *l* ... Phil 4:8

LOVES
"He who *l* father or ... Matt 10:37
l his life will lose ... John 12:25
l Me will be loved ... John 14:21
l a cheerful giver ... 2 Cor 9:7
If anyone *l* the world ... 1 John 2:15
l God must love his ... 1 John 4:21

LOVINGKINDNESS
To declare Your *l* ... Ps 92:2

LOWER
made him a little *l* ... Heb 2:7

LOWLINESS
with all *l* and ... Eph 4:2

LOWLY
for I am gentle and *l* ... Matt 11:29
in presence am *l* ... 2 Cor 10:1
l brother glory ... James 1:9

LUKEWARM
because you are *l* ... Rev 3:16

LUST
looks at a woman to *l* ... Matt 5:28
not fulfill the *l* ... Gal 5:16
You *l* and do not have ... James 4:2
the *l* of the flesh ... 1 John 2:16

LUSTS
to fulfill its *l* ... Rom 13:14
also youthful *l* ... 2 Tim 2:22
and worldly *l* ... Titus 2:12
to the former *l* ... 1 Pet 1:14
abstain from fleshly *l* ... 1 Pet 2:11
to their own ungodly *l* ... Jude 18

LUTE
Praise Him with the *l* ... Ps 150:3

LUXURY
in pleasure and *l* ... James 5:5
the abundance of her *l* ... Rev 18:3

LYING
I hate and abhor *l* ... Ps 119:163
righteous man hates *l* ... Prov 13:5
not trust in these *l* ... Jer 7:4
signs, and *l* wonders ... 2 Thess 2:9

M

MADE
m the stars also ... Gen 1:16
things My hand has *m* ... Is 66:2
All things were *m* ... John 1:3

MADNESS
m is in their hearts ... Eccl 9:3

MAGIC
m brought their books ... Acts 19:19

MAGNIFIED
let Your name be *m* ... 2 Sam 7:26
the Lord Jesus was *m* ... Acts 19:17
also Christ will be *m* ... Phil 1:20

MAGNIFIES
"My soul *m* the Lord ... Luke 1:46

MAGNIFY
m the LORD with me ... Ps 34:3

MAIDSERVANT
"Behold the *m* ... Luke 1:38

MAIDSERVANTS
m I will pour out My ... Acts 2:18

MAJESTY
right hand of the *M* ... Heb 1:3
eyewitnesses of His *m* ... 2 Pet 1:16
wise, Be glory and *m* ... Jude 25

MAKE
"Let Us *m* man in Our ... Gen 1:26
m you a great nation ... Gen 12:2
"You shall not *m* ... Ex 20:4
m Our home with ... John 14:23

MAKER
M is your husband ... Is 54:5
has forgotten his *M* ... Hos 8:14
builder and *m* is God ... Heb 11:10

MALICE
in *m* be babes ... 1 Cor 14:20
laying aside all *m* ... 1 Pet 2:1

MAN
"Let Us make *m* ... Gen 1:26
m that You are mindful ... Ps 8:4
of the Son of *M* ... Matt 24:27
"Behold the *M* ... John 19:5
by *m* came death ... 1 Cor 15:21
our outward *m* ... 2 Cor 4:16

the *m* of God may ... 2 Tim 3:17
is the number of a *m* ... Rev 13:18

MANGER
and laid Him in a *m* ... Luke 2:7

MANIFEST
m Myself to him ... John 14:21

MANIFESTATION
But the *m* of the ... 1 Cor 12:7

MANIFESTED
"I have *m* Your name ... John 17:6
God was *m* in the ... 1 Tim 3:16
the life was *m* ... 1 John 1:2

MANIFOLD
the *m* wisdom of God ... Eph 3:10

MANNA
of Israel ate *m* ... Ex 16:35
"Our fathers ate the *m* ... John 6:31

MANNER
Is this the *m* of man ... 2 Sam 7:19
in an unworthy *m* ... 1 Cor 11:27
what *m* of love ... 1 John 3:1

MANSIONS
house are many *m* ... John 14:2

MANTLE
Then he took the *m* ... 2 Kin 2:14

MARK
And the LORD set a *m* ... Gen 4:15
receives the *m* ... Rev 14:11

MARRED
So His visage was *m* ... Is 52:14

MARRIAGE
M is honorable among ... Heb 13:4

MARRIED
But he who is *m* ... 1 Cor 7:33

MARRY
they neither *m* nor ... Matt 22:30
forbidding to *m* ... 1 Tim 4:3

MARRYING
and drinking, *m* ... Matt 24:38

MARTYRS
the blood of the *m* ... Rev 17:6

MARVELED
Jesus heard it, He *m* ... Matt 8:10
so that Pilate *m* ... Mark 15:5

MARVELOUS
It is *m* in our eyes ... Ps 118:23
of darkness into His *m* ... 1 Pet 2:9

MASTER
a servant like his *m* ... Matt 10:25
greater than his *m* ... John 15:20
and useful for the *M* ... 2 Tim 2:21

MASTERS
can serve two *m* ... Luke 16:13
who have believing *m* ... 1 Tim 6:2

MATTERS
the weightier *m* ... Matt 23:23

MATURE
understanding be *m* ... 1 Cor 14:20
us, as many as are *m* ... Phil 3:15

MEANT
but God *m* it for good ... Gen 50:20

MEASURE
a perfect and just *m* ... Deut 25:15
give the Spirit by *m* ... John 3:34
to each one a *m* ... Rom 12:3

MEASURED
m the waters in the ... Is 40:12
you use, it will be *m* ... Matt 7:2

MEASURES
house differing *m* ... Deut 25:14

MEASURING
behold, a man with a *m* ... Zech 2:1
m themselves by ... 2 Cor 10:12

MEAT
will never again eat *m* ... 1 Cor 8:13

MEDIATOR
by the hand of a *m* ... Gal 3:19
is one God and one *M* ... 1 Tim 2:5
to Jesus the *M* of the ... Heb 12:24

MEDICINE
does good , like *m* ... Prov 17:22

MEDICINES
you will use many *m* ... Jer 46:11

MEDITATE
but you shall *m* ... Josh 1:8
M within your heart on ... Ps 4:4
I will *m* on Your ... Ps 119:15
m beforehand on ... Luke 21:14
m on these things ... Phil 4:8

MEDITATES
in His law he *m* ... Ps 1:2

MEDITATION
of my mouth and the *m* ... Ps 19:14
It is my *m* all the day ... Ps 119:97

MEDIUM
a woman who is a *m* ... Lev 20:27

MEDIUM'S
shall be like a *m* ... Is 29:4

MEDIUMS
"Seek those who are *m* ... Is 8:19

MEEK
with equity for the *m* ... Is 11:4
Blessed are the *m* ... Matt 5:5

MEEKNESS
are done in the *m* ... James 3:13

MEET
prepare to *m* your ... Amos 4:12
m the Lord in the ... 1 Thess 4:17

MELODY
singing and making *m* ... Eph 5:19

MELT
the elements will *m* ... 2 Pet 3:10

MEMBER
body is not one *m* ... 1 Cor 12:14

MEMBERS
you that one of your *m* ... Matt 5:29
do not present your *m* ... Rom 6:13
neighbor, for we are *m* ... Eph 4:25

MEMORIAL
and this is My *m* ... Ex 3:15
also be told as a *m* ... Matt 26:13

MEMORY
The *m* of the righteous ... Prov 10:7

MEN
m began to call on the ... Gen 4:26
make you fishers of *m* ... Matt 4:19
goodwill toward *m* ... Luke 2:14
heaven or from *m* ... Luke 20:
Likewise also the *m* ... Rom 1:2
the Lord, and not to *m* ... Eph 6:
between God and *m* ... 1 Tim 2:

MORNING
Evening and *m* and at .... Ps 55:17
Lucifer, son of the *m* .... Is 14:12
very early in the *m* .... Luke 24:1
the Bright and *M* Star .... Rev 22:16

MORTAL
sin reign in your *m* .... Rom 6:12
and this *m* must put .... 1 Cor 15:53

MORTALITY
m may be swallowed .... 2 Cor 5:4

MOTH
where *m* and rust .... Matt 6:19

MOTHER
because she was the *m* .... Gen 3:20
leave his father and *m* .... Matt 19:5
"Behold your *m* .... John 19:27
The *M* of Harlots .... Rev 17:5

MOUNT
come up to *M* Sinai .... Ex 19:23
They shall *m* up with .... Is 40:31

MOUNTAIN
to Horeb, the *m* .... Ex 3:1
let us go up to the *m* .... Is 2:3
became a great *m* .... Dan 2:35
are you, O great *m* .... Zech 4:7
you will say to this *m* .... Matt 17:20
Him on the holy *m* .... 2 Pet 1:18

MOUNTAINS
m were brought forth .... Ps 90:2
m shall depart And the .... Is 54:10
in Judea flee to the *m* .... Matt 24:16
that I could remove *m* .... 1 Cor 13:2

MOURN
A time to *m* .... Eccl 3:4
are those who *m* .... Matt 5:4
of the earth will *m* .... Rev 1:7

MOURNED
and have not rather *m* .... 1 Cor 5:2

MOURNING
shall be a great *m* .... Zech 12:11
be turned to *m* and .... James 4:9

MOUTH
"Who has made man's *m* .... Ex 4:11
Out of the *m* of babes .... Ps 8:2
knowledge, But the *m* .... Prov 10:14
The *m* of an immoral .... Prov 22:14
And a flattering *m* .... Prov 26:28
m speaking pompous .... Dan 7:8
m defiles a man .... Matt 15:11
m I will judge you .... Luke 19:22
I will give you a *m* .... Luke 21:15
m confession is made .... Rom 10:10
m great swelling words .... Jude 16
vomit you out of My *m* .... Rev 3:16

MOVED
she shall not be *m* .... Ps 46:5
spoke as they were *m* .... 2 Pet 1:21

MUCH
m study is .... Eccl 12:12
to whom *m* is given .... Luke 12:48

MULTIPLIED
of the disciples *m* .... Acts 6:7
of God grew and *m* .... Acts 12:24

MULTIPLY
"Be fruitful and *m* .... Gen 1:22
m the descendants .... Jer 33:22

MULTITUDE
stars of heaven in *m* .... Deut 1:10
In the *m* of words sin .... Prov 10:19
compassion on the *m* .... Matt 15:32
with the angel a *m* .... Luke 2:13

"love will cover a *m* .... 1 Pet 4:8
and behold, a great *m* .... Rev 7:9

MURDER
"You shall not *m* .... Ex 20:13
'You shall not *m* .... Matt 5:21
You *m* and covet and .... James 4:2

MURDERED
up Jesus whom you *m* .... Acts 5:30

MURDERER
He was a *m* from the .... John 8:44
his brother is a *m* .... 1 John 3:15

MURDERERS
and profane, for *m* .... 1 Tim 1:9
abominable, *m* .... Rev 21:8

MURDERS
evil thoughts, *m* .... Matt 15:19

MUSING
while I was *m* .... Ps 39:3

MUTILATION
beware of the *m* .... Phil 3:2

MUZZLE
"You shall not *m* .... 1 Tim 5:18

MYSTERIES
to you to know the *m* .... Matt 13:1
and understand all *m* .... 1 Cor 13:

MYSTERY
given to know the *m* .... Mark 4:1
wisdom of God in a *m* .... 1 Cor 2:
I tell you a *m* .... 1 Cor 15:5
made known to us the *m* .... Eph 1:
the *m* of godliness .... 1 Tim 3:1

N

NAILED
n it to the cross .... Col 2:1

NAKED
And they were both *n* .... Gen 2:2
knew that they were *n* .... Gen 3:
"*N* I came from my .... Job 1:2
'I was *n* and you .... Matt 25:3
but all things are *n* .... Heb 4:1
brother or sister is *n* .... James 2:1
poor, blind, and *n* .... Rev 3:1

NAKEDNESS
or famine, or *n* .... Rom 8:3
n may not be revealed .... Rev 3:1

NAME
Abram called on the *n* .... Gen 13
Israel shall be your *n* .... Gen 35:1
This is My *n* forever .... Ex 3:1
shall not take the *n* .... Ex 20
and awesome *n* .... Deut 28:5
excellent is Your *n* .... Ps 8
n will put their trust .... Ps 9:1
be His glorious *n* .... Ps 72:1
do not call on Your *n* .... Ps 79
to Your *n* give glory .... Ps 115
above all Your *n* .... Ps 138
A good *n* is to be .... Prov 22
what is His Son's *n* .... Prov 30
be called by a new *n* .... Is 62
Everlasting is Your *n* .... Is 63:
They will call on My *n* .... Zech 13
to you who fear My *n* .... Mal 4
Hallowed be Your *n* .... Matt 6
prophesied in Your *n* .... Matt 7:
n Gentiles will trust .... Matt 12:
together in My *n* .... Matt 18:
will come in My *n* .... Matt 24
who believe in His *n* .... John 1:
comes in his own *n* .... John 5:

and do not *o* the truth ... Rom 2:8
yourselves slaves to *o* ... Rom 6:16
o your parents in all ... Col 3:20
Bondservants, *o* in all ... Col 3:22
those who do not *o* ... 2 Thess 1:8
O those who rule ... Heb 13:17

OBEYED
of sin, yet you *o* ... Rom 6:17
they have not all *o* ... Rom 10:16
By faith Abraham *o* ... Heb 11:8

OBSERVATION
does not come with *o* ... Luke 17:20

OBSERVE
teaching them to *o* all ... Matt 28:20

OBTAIN
also may *o* mercy ... Rom 11:31
o salvation through ... 1 Thess 5:9

OBTAINED
o a part in this ... Acts 1:17
yet have now *o* mercy ... Rom 11:30
endured, he *o* the ... Heb 6:15

OBTAINS
o favor from the LORD ... Prov 8:35

OFFEND
lest we *o* them ... Matt 17:27
than that he should *o* ... Luke 17:2
them, "Does this *o* ... John 6:61

OFFENDED
they were *o* at Him ... Matt 13:57

OFFENSE
and a rock of *o* ... Is 8:14
You are an *o* to Me ... Matt 16:23
by the one man's *o* ... Rom 5:17
the *o* of the cross ... Gal 5:11
sincere and without *o* ... Phil 1:10
And a rock of *o* ... 1 Pet 2:8

OFFENSES
For *o* must come ... Matt 18:7
impossible that no *o* ... Luke 17:1

OFFER
come and *o* your gift ... Matt 5:24
let us continually *o* ... Heb 13:15

OFFERED
to eat those things *o* ... 1 Cor 8:10
so Christ was *o* ... Heb 9:28
o one sacrifice ... Heb 10:12

OFFERING
o You did not require ... Ps 40:6
You make His soul an *o* ... Is 53:10
Himself for us, an *o* ... Eph 5:2
o You did not ... Heb 10:5
o He has perfected ... Heb 10:14

OFFERINGS
and offered burnt *o* ... Gen 8:20
In burnt *o* ... Heb 10:6

OFFICE
sitting at the tax *o* ... Matt 9:9

OFFSPRING
wife and raise up *o* ... Matt 22:24
we are also His *o* ... Acts 17:28
am the Root and the *O* ... Rev 22:16

OFTEN
o I wanted to gather ... Luke 13:34
as *o* as you eat this ... 1 Cor 11:26

OIL
a bin, and a little *o* ... 1 Kin 17:12
very costly fragrant *o* ... Matt 26:7
anointing him with *o* ... James 5:14
and do not harm the *o* ... Rev 6:6

OLD
young, and now am *o* ... Ps 37:
was said to those of *o* ... Matt 5:
but when you are *o* ... John 21:
Your *o* men shall dream ... Acts 2:
o man was crucified ... Rom 6
o things have passed ... 2 Cor 5:
have put off the *o* man ... Col 3
that serpent of *o* ... Rev 20

OLDER
o shall serve the ... Gen 25:
not rebuke an *o* man ... 1 Tim 5

OLDEST
beginning with the *o* ... John 8

OLIVE
a freshly plucked *o* ... Gen 8:
o tree which is wild ... Rom 11:

OMNIPOTENT
For the Lord God *O* ... Rev 19

ONCE
died, He died to sin *o* ... Rom 6:
for men to die *o* ... Heb 9:
also suffered *o* ... 1 Pet 3:

ONE
"*O* thing you lack ... Mark 10:
o thing is needed ... Luke 10:
I and My Father are *o* ... John 10:
that they may be *o* ... John 17:
o accord in the temple ... Acts 2:
for you are all *o* ... Gal 3:
to create in Himself *o* ... Eph 2:
o Lord ... Eph 4
o faith ... Eph 4
o baptism ... Eph 4
o God and Father of ... Eph 4
For there is *o* God and ... 1 Tim 2
o Mediator between ... 1 Tim 2
a thousand years as *o* ... 2 Pet 3

OPENED
o not His mouth ... Is 53
o the Scriptures ... Luke 24:
o their understanding ... Luke 24:
Now I saw heaven *o* ... Rev 19:

OPENS
him the doorkeeper *o* ... John 10
and shuts and no one *o* ... Rev 3

OPINION
be wise in your own *o* ... Rom 11:

OPINIONS
falter between two *o* ... 1 Kin 18:

OPPORTUNITY
But sin, taking *o* ... Rom 7
as we have *o* ... Gal 6:
but you lacked *o* ... Phil 4:

OPPRESS
he loves to *o* ... Hos 12
o the widow or the ... Zech 7:
Do not the rich *o* ... James 2

OPPRESSED
for all who are *o* ... Ps 10
The tears of the *o* ... Eccl 4
He was *o* and He was ... Is 5
all who were *o* ... Acts 10:

OPPRESSES
o the poor reproaches ... Prov 14:

OPPRESSION
have surely seen the *o* ... Ex 3
their life from *o* ... Ps 72:
brought low through *o* ... Ps 107:
me from the *o* ... Ps 119:1
considered all the *o* ... Eccl 4

o destroys a wise ... Eccl 7:7
justice, but behold, *o* ... Is 5:7
surely seen the *o* ... Acts 7:34

ORACLES
received the living *o* ... Acts 7:38
were committed the *o* ... Rom 3:2
principles of the *o* ... Heb 5:12

ORDAINED
o you a prophet ... Jer 1:5
whom He has *o* ... Acts 17:31

ORDER
decently and in *o* ... 1 Cor 14:40

ORDERS
o his conduct aright I ... Ps 50:23

ORDINANCE
resists the *o* of God ... Rom 13:2

ORDINANCES
and fleshly *o* imposed ... Heb 9:10

ORPHANS
will not leave you *o* ... John 14:18
to visit *o* and widows ... James 1:27

OUGHT
These you *o* to have ... Matt 23:23
pray for as we *o* ... Rom 8:26
persons *o* you to be ... 2 Pet 3:11

OUTCAST
they called you an *o* ... Jer 30:17

OUTCASTS
will assemble the *o* ... Is 11:12

OUTRAN
the other disciple *o* ... John 20:4

OUTSIDE
and dish, that the *o* ... Matt 23:26
Pharisees make the *o* ... Luke 11:39
toward those who are *o* ... Col 4:5
to Him, *o* the camp ... Heb 13:13
But *o* are dogs and ... Rev 22:15

OUTSTRETCHED
and with an *o* arm ... Deut 26:8

OUTWARD
at the *o* appearance ... 1 Sam 16:7
adornment be merely *o* ... 1 Pet 3:3

OUTWARDLY
not a Jew who is one *o* ... Rom 2:28

OVERCAME
My throne, as I also *o* ... Rev 3:21
"And they *o* him by ... Rev 12:11

OVERCOME
good cheer, I have *o* ... John 16:33
and the Lamb will *o* ... Rev 17:14

OVERCOMES
of God *o* the world ... 1 John 5:4
o I will give to eat ... Rev 2:7
o shall not be hurt ... Rev 2:11
o shall inherit all ... Rev 21:7

OVERSEER
to the Shepherd and *O* ... 1 Pet 2:25

OVERSEERS
you, serving as *o* ... 1 Pet 5:2

OVERSHADOW
of the Highest will *o* ... Luke 1:35

OVERTHREW
As God *o* Sodom and ... Jer 50:40

OVERTHROW
o the faith of some ... 2 Tim 2:18

OVERTHROWN
and Nineveh shall be *o* ... Jon 3:4

OVERTHROWS
And *o* the mighty ... Job 12:19
o them in the night ... Job 34:25
o the words of the ... Prov 22:12

OVERWHELM
o the fatherless ... Job 6:27

OVERWHELMED
and my spirit was *o* ... Ps 77:3
my spirit is *o* within ... Ps 143:4

OVERWORK
Do not *o* to be rich ... Prov 23:4

OWE
O no one anything ... Rom 13:8

OWED
o him ten thousand ... Matt 18:24

OWN
He came to His *o* ... John 1:11
having loved His *o* ... John 13:1
would love its *o* ... John 15:19
you are not your *o* ... 1 Cor 6:19
But each one has his *o* ... 1 Cor 7:7
For all seek their *o* ... Phil 2:21
from our sins in His *o* ... Rev 1:5

OX
shall not muzzle an *o* ... Deut 25:4
o knows its owner ... Is 1:3
Sabbath loose his *o* ... Luke 13:15
shall not muzzle an *o* ... 1 Cor 9:9

P

PACIFIES
A gift in secret *p* ... Prov 21:14

PAIN
p you shall bring ... Gen 3:16
p as a woman in ... Is 13:8
Why is my *p* perpetual ... Jer 15:18
shall be no more *p* ... Rev 21:4

PAINED
My heart is severely *p* ... Ps 55:4
I am *p* in my very ... Jer 4:19

PAINFUL
for the present, but *p* ... Heb 12:11

PAINS
The *p* of death ... Ps 116:3
having loosed the *p* ... Acts 2:24

PAINT
your eyes with *p* ... Jer 4:30

PALACE
enter the King's *p* ... Ps 45:15
guards his own *p* ... Luke 11:21
evident to the whole *p* ... Phil 1:13

PALACES
Out of the ivory *p* ... Ps 45:8

PALE
behold, a *p* horse ... Rev 6:8

PALM
p branches in their ... Rev 7:9

PALMS
struck Him with the *p* ... Matt 26:67

PAMPERS
p his servant from ... Prov 29:21

PANGS
The *p* of death ... Ps 18:4
labors with birth *p* ... Rom 8:22

PARABLE
do You speak this *p* ... Luke 12:41

PARABLES
rest it is given in *p* ... Luke 8:10

PARADISE
will be with Me in *P* .... Luke 23:43
in the midst of the *P* .... Rev 2:7

PARDON
He will abundantly *p* .... Is 55:7
p all their iniquities .... Jer 33:8

PARDONING
is a God like You, *p* .... Mic 7:18

PARENTS
will rise up against *p* .... Matt 10:21
has left house or *p* .... Luke 18:29
disobedient to *p* .... Rom 1:30

PART
chosen that good *p* .... Luke 10:42
you, you have no *p* .... John 13:8
For we know in *p* .... 1 Cor 13:9
shall take away his *p* .... Rev 22:19

PARTAKE
for we all *p* of that .... 1 Cor 10:17

PARTAKER
in hope should be *p* .... 1 Cor 9:10
Christ, and also a *p* .... 1 Pet 5:1

PARTAKERS
Gentiles have been *p* .... Rom 15:27
know that as you are *p* .... 2 Cor 1:7
qualified us to be *p* .... Col 1:12

PARTIAL
You shall not be *p* .... Lev 19:15

PARTIALITY
that God shows no *p* .... Acts 10:34
doing nothing with *p* .... 1 Tim 5:21
good fruits, without *p* .... James 3:17

PASS
I will *p* over you .... Ex 12:13
When you *p* through the .... Is 43:2
and earth will *p* .... Matt 24:35

PASSED
forbearance God had *p* .... Rom 3:25
High Priest who has *p* .... Heb 4:14
know that we have *p* .... 1 John 3:14

PASSES
of Christ which *p* .... Eph 3:19

PASSION
uncleanness, *p* .... Col 3:5

PASSIONS
gave them up to vile *p* .... Rom 1:26

PASSOVER
It is the LORD's *P* .... Ex 12:11
I will keep the *P* .... Matt 26:18
indeed Christ, our *P* .... 1 Cor 5:7
By faith he kept the *P* .... Heb 11:28

PASTORS
and some *p* and .... Eph 4:11

PASTURE
the sheep of Your *p* .... Ps 74:1
in and out and find *p* .... John 10:9

PASTURES
to lie down in green *p* .... Ps 23:2

PATH
You will show me the *p* .... Ps 16:11

PATHS
He leads me in the *p* .... Ps 23:3
Make His *p* straight .... Matt 3:3
and make straight *p* .... Heb 12:13

PATIENCE
'Master, have *p* .... Matt 18:26
and bear fruit with *p* .... Luke 8:15
labor of love, and *p* .... 1 Thess 1:3
faith, love, *p* .... 1 Tim 6:11

your faith produces *p* .... James 1:3
p have its perfect .... James 1:4
in the kingdom and *p* .... Rev 1:9

PATIENT
rejoicing in hope, *p* .... Rom 12:12
the weak, be *p* .... 1 Thess 5:14

PATIENTLY
if you take it *p* .... 1 Pet 2:20

PATRIARCHS
begot the twelve *p* .... Acts 7:8

PATTERN
p which you were .... Ex 26:30
as you have us for a *p* .... Phil 3:17
p shown you on the .... Heb 8:5

PEACE
you, And give you *p* .... Num 6:2
both lie down in *p* .... Ps 4:
p have those who .... Ps 119:16
I am for *p* .... Ps 120:
war, And a time of *p* .... Eccl 3:
Father, Prince of *P* .... Is 9:
keep him in perfect *p* .... Is 26:
p they have not .... Is 59:
slightly, Saying, '*P* .... Jer 6:1
place I will give *p* .... Hag 2:
is worthy, let your *p* .... Matt 10:1
that I came to bring *p* .... Matt 10:3
And on earth *p* .... Luke 2:1
if a son of *p* is there .... Luke 10:
that make for your *p* .... Luke 19:4
leave with you, My *p* .... John 14:2
Me you may have *p* .... John 16:3
Grace to you and *p* .... Rom 1
by faith, we have *p* .... Rom 5
God has called us to *p* .... 1 Cor 7:1
p will be with you .... 2 Cor 13:1
Spirit is love, joy, *p* .... Gal 5:2
He Himself is our *p* .... Eph 2:1
and the *p* of God .... Phil 4
And let the *p* of God .... Col 3:1
faith, love, *p* .... 2 Tim 2:2
meaning "king of *p*," .... Heb 7

PEACEABLE
is first pure, then *p* .... James 3:1

PEACEABLY
on you, live *p* .... Rom 12:

PEACEFUL
in a *p* habitation .... Is 32:

PEACEMAKERS
Blessed are the *p* .... Matt 5

PEARL
had found one *p* .... Matt 13:

PEARLS
nor cast your *p* .... Matt 7
gates were twelve *p* .... Rev 21:

PENTECOST
P had fully come .... Acts 2

PEOPLE
will take you as My *p* .... Ex 6
p shall be my *p* .... Ruth 1:
p who know the joyful .... Ps 89:
We are His *p* and the .... Ps 10
"Blessed is Egypt My *p* .... Is 19:
to make ready a *p* .... Luke 1:
take out of them a *p* .... Acts 15:
who were not My *p* .... Rom 9:
they shall be My *p* .... 2 Cor 6:
LORD will judge His *p* .... Heb 10:
but are now the *p* .... 1 Pet 2:
tribe and tongue and *p* .... Rev
they shall be His *p* .... Rev 2

PERCEIVE
seeing, but do not *p* .... Is 6:9
may see and not *p* .... Mark 4:12

PERDITION
except the son of *p* .... John 17:12
revealed, the son of *p* .... 2 Thess 2:3
who draw back to *p* .... Heb 10:39

PERFECT
Noah was a just man, *p* .... Gen 6:9
Father in heaven is *p* .... Matt 5:48
they may be made *p* .... John 17:23
and *p* will of God .... Rom 12:2
when that which is *p* .... 1 Cor 13:10
present every man *p* .... Col 1:28
good gift and every *p* .... James 1:17
in word, he is a *p* .... James 3:2
p love casts out fear .... 1 John 4:18

PERFECTED
third day I shall be *p* .... Luke 13:32
or am already *p* .... Phil 3:12
Son who has been *p* .... Heb 7:28

PERFECTION
let us go on to *p* .... Heb 6:1

PERISH
so that we may not *p* .... Jon 1:6
little ones should *p* .... Matt 18:14
in Him should not *p* .... John 3:16
they shall never *p* .... John 10:28
among those who *p* .... 2 Thess 2:10
that any should *p* .... 2 Pet 3:9

PERISHABLE
do it to obtain a *p* .... 1 Cor 9:25

PERISHED
Truth has *p* and has .... Jer 7:28

PERISHING
We are *p* .... Matt 8:25

PERMIT
do not *p* a woman .... 1 Tim 2:12

PERMITS
we will do if God *p* .... Heb 6:3

PERMITTED
p no one to do them .... Ps 105:14
we are *p* .... 2 Cor 4:8

PERSECUTE
when they revile and *p* .... Matt 5:11

PERSECUTED
If they *p* Me .... John 15:20
p, but not forsaken .... 2 Cor 4:9

PERSECUTES
wicked in his pride *p* .... Ps 10:2

PERSECUTION
p arises because of .... Matt 13:21
At that time a great *p* .... Acts 8:1
do I still suffer *p* .... Gal 5:11

PERSECUTOR
a blasphemer, a *p* .... 1 Tim 1:13

PERSEVERANCE
tribulation produces *p* .... Rom 5:3

PERSEVERE
kept My command to *p* .... Rev 3:10

PERSISTENCE
p he will rise and .... Luke 11:8

PERSON
do not regard the *p* .... Matt 22:16
express image of His *p* .... Heb 1:3

PERSUADE
"You almost *p* me .... Acts 26:28

PERSUADED
neither will they be *p* .... Luke 16:31
p that He is able .... 2 Tim 1:12

PERSUASIVE
p words of human .... 1 Cor 2:4

PERVERSE
your way is *p* .... Num 22:32
p man sows strife .... Prov 16:28
from this *p* generation .... Acts 2:40

PERVERT
"You shall not *p* .... Deut 16:19
p the gospel of Christ .... Gal 1:7

PERVERTING
will you not cease *p* .... Acts 13:10

PERVERTS
p his ways will become .... Prov 10:9

PESTILENCE
from the perilous *p* .... Ps 91:3
Before Him went *p* .... Hab 3:5

PESTILENCES
will be famines, *p* .... Matt 24:7

PETITIONS
p that we have asked .... 1 John 5:15

PHARISEE
to pray, one a *P* .... Luke 18:10

PHILOSOPHERS
p encountered him .... Acts 17:18

PHILOSOPHY
cheat you through *p* .... Col 2:8

PHYSICIAN
have no need of a *p* .... Matt 9:12

PHYSICIANS
her livelihood on *p* .... Luke 8:43

PIECES
they took the thirty *p* .... Matt 27:9

PIERCE
a sword will *p* .... Luke 2:35

PIERCED
p My hands and My feet .... Ps 22:16
whom they have *p* .... Zech 12:10
of the soldiers *p* .... John 19:34
p themselves through .... 1 Tim 6:10
and they also who *p* .... Rev 1:7

PIERCING
p even to the division .... Heb 4:12

PILGRIMAGE
heart is set on *p* .... Ps 84:5
In the house of my *p* .... Ps 119:54

PILGRIMS
we are aliens and *p* .... 1 Chr 29:15
were strangers and *p* .... Heb 11:13

PILLAR
and she became a *p* .... Gen 19:26
and by night in a *p* .... Ex 13:21
the living God, the *p* .... 1 Tim 3:15

PILLARS
break their sacred *p* .... Ex 34:13
Blood and fire and *p* .... Joel 2:30
and his feet like *p* .... Rev 10:1

PIT
who go down to the *p* .... Ps 28:1
a harlot is a deep *p* .... Prov 23:27
my life in the *p* .... Lam 3:53
up my life from the *p* .... Jon 2:6
into the bottomless *p* .... Rev 20:3

PITIABLE
of all men the most *p* .... 1 Cor 15:19

PITS
The proud have dug *p* ... Ps 119:85

PITY
for someone to take *p* ... Ps 69:20
p He redeemed them ... Is 63:9
just as I had *p* ... Matt 18:33

PLACE
Come, see the *p* ... Matt 28:6
My word has no *p* ... John 8:37
I go to prepare a *p* ... John 14:2
might go to his own *p* ... Acts 1:25

PLACES
And the rough *p* ... Is 40:4
They love the best *p* ... Matt 23:6
in the heavenly *p* ... Eph 1:3

PLAGUE
bring yet one more *p* ... Ex 11:1

PLAGUES
p that are written ... Rev 22:18

PLANK
First remove the *p* ... Matt 7:5

PLANS
He makes the *p* of the ... Ps 33:10
that devises wicked *p* ... Prov 6:18

PLANT
A time to *p* ... Eccl 3:2
Him as a tender *p* ... Is 53:2
p of an alien vine ... Jer 2:21
p which My heavenly ... Matt 15:13

PLANTED
shall be like a tree *p* ... Ps 1:3
by the roots and be *p* ... Luke 17:6
I *p*, Apollos watered ... 1 Cor 3:6

PLANTS
neither he who *p* ... 1 Cor 3:7

PLATTER
head here on a *p* ... Matt 14:8

PLEASANT
food, that it was *p* ... Gen 3:6
how good and how *p* ... Ps 133:1

PLEASANTNESS
ways are ways of *p* ... Prov 3:17

PLEASE
in the flesh cannot *p* ... Rom 8:8
p his neighbor for his ... Rom 15:2
he may *p* the Lord ... 1 Cor 7:32
is impossible to *p* Him ... Heb 11:6

PLEASED
Then You shall be *p* ... Ps 51:19
in whom I am well *p* ... Matt 3:17
God was not well *p* ... 1 Cor 10:5
testimony, that he *p* ... Heb 11:5

PLEASES
Whatever the LORD *p* ... Ps 135:6

PLEASING
sacrifice, well *p* ... Phil 4:18
for this is well *p* ... Col 3:20
in you what is well *p* ... Heb 13:21

PLEASURE
Do good in Your good *p* ... Ps 51:18
p will be a poor man ... Prov 21:17
shall perform all My *p* ... Is 44:28
your Father's good *p* ... Luke 12:32
to the good *p* of His ... Eph 1:5
for sin You had no *p* ... Heb 10:6
My soul has no *p* ... Heb 10:38
p that war in your ... James 4:1

PLEASURES
Your right hand are *p* ... Ps 16:1
cares, riches, and *p* ... Luke 8:1
to enjoy the passing *p* ... Heb 11:2

PLOW
put his hand to the *p* ... Luke 9:6

PLOWED
You have *p* ... Hos 10:1

PLOWMAN
p shall overtake the ... Amos 9:1

PLUCK
p the heads of grain ... Mark 2:2

PLUCKED
cheeks to those who *p* ... Is 50
And His disciples *p* ... Luke 6
you would have *p* ... Gal 4:1

PLUNDER
p the Egyptians ... Ex 3:2
The *p* of the poor is ... Is 3:1
house and *p* his goods ... Matt 12:2

PLUNDERED
a people robbed and *p* ... Is 42:2
"And when you are *p* ... Jer 4:3

PLUNDERING
me Because of the *p* ... Is 22
accepted the *p* of your ... Heb 10:3

POETS
some of your own *p* ... Acts 17:2

POISON
"The *p* of asps is ... Rom 3:

POISONED
p by bitterness ... Acts 8:2

POLLUTIONS
have escaped the *p* ... 2 Pet 2:2

POMP
had come with great *p* ... Acts 25:2

POMPOUS
and a mouth speaking *p* ... Dan 7

PONDER
P the path of your ... Prov 4:2

PONDERED
p them in her heart ... Luke 2:

PONDERS
p all his paths ... Prov 5:2

POOR
p will never cease ... Deut 15:
So the *p* have hope ... Job 5:
I delivered the *p* ... Job 29:
p shall eat and be ... Ps 22:2
But I am *p* and needy ... Ps 40:
Let the *p* and needy ... Ps 74:2
He raises the *p* ... Ps 113
slack hand becomes *p* ... Prov 10
p man is hated even ... Prov 14:2
has mercy on the *p* ... Prov 14:2
who oppresses the *p* ... Prov 14:3
p reproaches his ... Prov 17
Do not rob the *p* ... Prov 22:2
that same *p* man ... Eccl 9:
The alien or the *p* ... Zech 7:
"Blessed are the *p* ... Matt 5
p have the gospel ... Matt 11
"For you have the *p* ... Matt 26:
sakes He became *p* ... 2 Cor 8
should remember the *p* ... Gal 2:
God not chosen the *p* ... James 2
wretched, miserable, *p* ... Rev 3:

PORTION
O LORD, You, are the *p* ... Ps 16
heart and my *p* forever ... Ps 73:

You are my *p* ... Ps 119:57
I will divide Him a *p* ... Is 53:12
rejoice in their *p* ... Is 61:7
The *P* of Jacob is not ... Jer 10:16
"The LORD is my *p* ... Lam 3:24
and appoint him his *p* ... Matt 24:51
to give them their *p* ... Luke 12:42
give me the *p* ... Luke 15:12

POSSESS
descendants shall *p* ... Gen 22:17
p the land which ... Josh 1:11
"By your patience *p* ... Luke 21:19
p his own vessel ... 1 Thess 4:4

POSSESSED
"The LORD *p* me at ... Prov 8:22

POSSESSING
and yet *p* all things ... 2 Cor 6:10

POSSESSION
as an everlasting *p* ... Gen 17:8
and an enduring *p* ... Heb 10:34

POSSESSIONS
and sold their *p* ... Acts 2:45

POSSIBLE
God all things are *p* ... Matt 19:26
p that the blood ... Heb 10:4

POUR
p My Spirit on your ... Is 44:3
P out Your fury ... Jer 10:25
That I will *p* out My ... Joel 2:28
"And I will *p* ... Zech 12:10
angels, "Go and *p* ... Rev 16:1

POURED
I am *p* out like water ... Ps 22:14
grace is *p* upon Your ... Ps 45:2
strong, Because He *p* ... Is 53:12
and My fury will be *p* ... Jer 7:20
broke the flask and *p* ... Mark 14:3
I am already being *p* ... 2 Tim 4:6
whom He *p* out on us ... Titus 3:6

POVERTY
leads only to *p* ... Prov 14:23
p put in all the ... Luke 21:4
and their deep *p* ... 2 Cor 8:2
p might become rich ... 2 Cor 8:9
tribulation, and *p* ... Rev 2:9

POWER
that I may show My *p* ... Ex 9:16
him who is without *p* ... Job 26:2
p who can understand ... Job 26:14
p belongs to God ... Ps 62:11
p Your enemies shall ... Ps 66:3
gives strength and *p* ... Ps 68:35
a king is, there is *p* ... Eccl 8:4
No one has *p* over the ... Eccl 8:8
Not by might nor by *p* ... Zech 4:6
the kingdom and the *p* ... Matt 6:13
the Son of Man has *p* ... Matt 9:6
Scriptures nor the *p* ... Matt 22:29
p went out from Him ... Luke 6:19
are endued with *p* ... Luke 24:49
I have *p* to lay it ... John 10:18
"You could have no *p* ... John 19:11
you shall receive *p* ... Acts 1:8
though by our own *p* ... Acts 3:12
man is the great *p* ... Acts 8:10
"Give me this *p* ... Acts 8:19
for it is the *p* ... Rom 1:16
saved it is the *p* ... 1 Cor 1:18
Greeks, Christ the *p* ... 1 Cor 1:24
that the *p* of Christ ... 2 Cor 12:9
greatness of His *p* ... Eph 1:19
the Lord and in the *p* ... Eph 6:10
to His glorious *p* ... Col 1:11
the glory of His *p* ... 2 Thess 1:9
of fear, but of *p* ... 2 Tim 1:7
by the word of His *p* ... Heb 1:3
p of death, that ... Heb 2:14
as His divine *p* ... 2 Pet 1:3
Dominion and *p* ... Jude 25
to him I will give *p* ... Rev 2:26
honor and glory and *p* ... Rev 5:13

POWERFUL
of the LORD is *p* ... Ps 29:4
of God is living and *p* ... Heb 4:12

POWERS
principalities and *p* ... Col 2:15
word of God and the *p* ... Heb 6:5

PRAISE
p shall be of You in ... Ps 22:25
the people shall *p* ... Ps 45:17
P is awaiting You ... Ps 65:1
Let all the peoples *p* ... Ps 67:3
p shall be continually ... Ps 71:6
And the heavens will *p* ... Ps 89:5
Seven times a day I *p* ... Ps 119:164
that has breath *p* ... Ps 150:6
Let another man *p* ... Prov 27:2
let her own works *p* ... Prov 31:31
And your gates *P* ... Is 60:18
He makes Jerusalem a *p* ... Is 62:7
For You are my *p* ... Jer 17:14
Me a name of joy, a *p* ... Jer 33:9
give you fame and *p* ... Zeph 3:20
You have perfected *p* ... Matt 21:16
men more than the *p* ... John 12:43
p is not from men but ... Rom 2:29
Then each one's *p* ... 1 Cor 4:5
should be to the *p* ... Eph 1:12
to the glory and *p* ... Phil 1:11
I will sing *p* to You ... Heb 2:12
the sacrifice of *p* ... Heb 13:15
and for the *p* of those ... 1 Pet 2:14
saying, "*P* our God ... Rev 19:5

PRAISED
daily He shall be *p* ... Ps 72:15
LORD's name is to be *p* ... Ps 113:3
and greatly to be *p* ... Ps 145:3
the Most High and *p* ... Dan 4:34

PRAISES
it is good to sing *p* ... Ps 147:1
and he *p* ... Prov 31:28

PRAISEWORTHY
If there is anything *p* ... Phil 4:8

PRAISING
They will still be *p* ... Ps 84:4
of the heavenly host *p* ... Luke 2:13
in the temple *p* ... Luke 24:53

PRAY
at noon I will *p* ... Ps 55:17
who hate you, and *p* ... Matt 5:44
"And when you *p* ... Matt 6:5
manner, therefore, *p* ... Matt 6:9
"Watch and *p* ... Matt 26:41
"Lord, teach us to *p* ... Luke 11:1
"And I will *p* ... John 14:16
I do not *p* for the ... John 17:9
"I do not *p* for ... John 17:20
p without ceasing ... 1 Thess 5:17
Brethren, *p* for us ... 1 Thess 5:25
Let him *p* ... James 5:13
to one another, and *p* ... James 5:16
say that he should *p* ... 1 John 5:16

PRAYED
p more earnestly ... Luke 22:44
p earnestly that it ... James 5:17

PRAYER
p made in this place .... 2 Chr 7:15
And my *p* is pure .... Job 16:17
A *p* to the God of my .... Ps 42:8
P also will be made .... Ps 72:15
He shall regard the *p* .... Ps 102:17
to the LORD, But the *p* .... Prov 15:8
go out except by *p* .... Matt 17:21
all night in *p* to God .... Luke 6:12
continually to *p* .... Acts 6:4
where *p* was .... Acts 16:13
steadfastly in *p* .... Rom 12:12
to fasting and *p* .... 1 Cor 7:5
always with all *p* .... Eph 6:18
but in everything by *p* .... Phil 4:6
the word of God and *p* .... 1 Tim 4:5
And the *p* of faith .... James 5:15

PRAYERS
though You make many *p* .... Is 1:15
pretense make long *p* .... Matt 23:14
fervently for you in *p* .... Col 4:12
p may not be hindered .... 1 Pet 3:7
which are the *p* .... Rev 5:8

PREACH
time Jesus began to *p* .... Matt 4:17
you hear in the ear, *p* .... Matt 10:27
P the gospel to the .... Luke 4:18
And how shall they *p* .... Rom 10:15
p Christ crucified .... 1 Cor 1:23
I or they, so we *p* .... 1 Cor 15:11
P the word .... 2 Tim 4:2

PREACHED
p that people .... Mark 6:12
out and *p* .... Mark 16:20
of sins should be *p* .... Luke 24:47
p Christ to them .... Acts 8:5
lest, when I have *p* .... 1 Cor 9:27
than what we have *p* .... Gal 1:8
the gospel was *p* .... Heb 4:2
also He went and *p* .... 1 Pet 3:19

PREACHER
they hear without a *p* .... Rom 10:14
I was appointed a *p* .... 1 Tim 2:7

PREACHES
the Jesus whom Paul *p* .... Acts 19:13
p another Jesus .... 2 Cor 11:4
p any other gospel .... Gal 1:9
p the faith which he .... Gal 1:23

PREACHING
p Jesus as the .... Acts 5:42
not risen, then our *p* .... 1 Cor 15:14

PRECEPTS
all His *p* are sure .... Ps 111:7
how I love Your *p* .... Ps 119:159

PRECIOUS
P in the sight of the .... Ps 116:15
She is more *p* than .... Prov 3:15
p things shall not .... Is 44:9
if you take out the *p* .... Jer 15:19
farmer waits for the *p* .... James 5:7
more *p* than gold .... 1 Pet 1:7
who believe, He is *p* .... 1 Pet 2:7
p in the sight of .... 1 Pet 3:4

PREDESTINED
foreknew, He also *p* .... Rom 8:29
having *p* us to .... Eph 1:5
inheritance, being *p* .... Eph 1:11

PREEMINENCE
He may have the *p* .... Col 1:18
loves to have the *p* .... 3 John 9

PREFERENCE
in honor giving *p* .... Rom 12:10

PREJUDICE
these things without *p* .... 1 Tim 5:2

PREMEDITATE
p what you will .... Mark 13:1

PREPARATION
Now it was the *P* .... John 19:1
your feet with the *p* .... Eph 6:1

PREPARE
p a table before me in .... Ps 23
P the way of the LORD .... Mark 1
p a place for you .... John 14

PREPARED
for whom it is *p* .... Matt 20:2
Which You have *p* .... Luke 2:3
mercy, which He had *p* .... Rom 9:2
things which God has *p* .... 1 Cor 2
Now He who has *p* .... 2 Cor 5
p beforehand that we .... Eph 2:1
God, for He has *p* .... Heb 11:1

PRESENCE
themselves from the *p* .... Gen 3
went out from the *p* .... Gen 4:1
P will go with you .... Ex 33:1
afraid in any man's *p* .... Deut 1:1
p is fullness of joy .... Ps 16:1
shall dwell in Your *p* .... Ps 140:1
not tremble at My *p* .... Jer 5:2
shall shake at My *p* .... Ezek 38:2
and drank in Your *p* .... Luke 13:2
full of joy in Your *p* .... Acts 2:2
but his bodily *p* .... 2 Cor 10:1
obeyed, not as in my *p* .... Phil 2:1

PRESENT
we are all *p* before .... Acts 10:3
evil is *p* with me .... Rom 7:2
p your bodies a living .... Rom 12
or death, or things *p* .... 1 Cor 3:2
absent in body but *p* .... 1 Cor 5
that He might *p* .... Eph 5:2
p you faultless .... Jude 2

PRESERVE
He shall *p* your soul .... Ps 121
The LORD shall *p* .... Ps 121
loses his life will *p* .... Luke 17:3
every evil work and *p* .... 2 Tim 4:1

PRESERVED
soul, and body be *p* .... 1 Thess 5:2

PRESERVES
For the LORD *p* the .... Ps 31:2
p the souls of His .... Ps 97:
who keeps his way *p* .... Prov 16:

PRETENSE
p make long prayers .... Matt 23:

PRICE
one pearl of great *p* .... Matt 13:
were bought at a *p* .... 1 Cor 6:

PRIDE
p serves as .... Ps 73
By *p* comes nothing .... Prov 13:
P goes before .... Prov 16:
her daughter had *p* .... Ezek 16:
was hardened in *p* .... Dan 5:
For the *p* of the .... Zech 11
evil eye, blasphemy, *p* .... Mark 7:
p he fall into the .... 1 Tim 3
eyes, and the *p* .... 1 John 2:

PRIEST
he was the *p* of God .... Gen 14:
p forever According .... Ps 110
So He shall be a *p* .... Zech 6:
and faithful High *P* .... Heb 2:
we have a great High *P* .... Heb 4:

PROPHETS
the Law or the *P* .... Matt 5:17
is the Law and the *P* .... Matt 7:12
or one of the *p* .... Matt 16:14
the tombs of the *p* .... Matt 23:29
indeed, I send you *p* .... Matt 23:34
one who kills the *p* .... Matt 23:37
Then many false *p* .... Matt 24:11
Moses and the *p* .... Luke 16:29
are sons of the *p* .... Acts 3:25
p did your fathers not .... Acts 7:52
"To Him all the *p* .... Acts 10:43
do you believe the *p* .... Acts 26:27
by the Law and the *P* .... Rom 3:21
have killed Your *p* .... Rom 11:3
to be apostles, some *p* .... Eph 4:11
this salvation the *p* .... 1 Pet 1:10
because many false *p* .... 1 John 4:1
found the blood of *p* .... Rev 18:24

PROPITIATION
set forth as a *p* .... Rom 3:25
to God, to make *p* .... Heb 2:17
He Himself is the *p* .... 1 John 2:2
His Son to be the *p* .... 1 John 4:10

PROPRIETY
modest apparel, with *p* .... 1 Tim 2:9

PROSPER
they *p* who love you .... Ps 122:6
of the LORD shall *p* .... Is 53:10
against you shall *p* .... Is 54:17
up as he may *p* .... 1 Cor 16:2
I pray that you may *p* .... 3 John 2

PROSPERED
since the LORD has *p* .... Gen 24:56

PROSPERING
His ways are always *p* .... Ps 10:5

PROSPERITY
p all your days .... Deut 23:6
p the destroyer .... Job 15:21
Now in my *p* I said .... Ps 30:6
has pleasure in the *p* .... Ps 35:27
When I saw the *p* .... Ps 73:3
I pray, send now *p* .... Ps 118:25
that we have our *p* .... Acts 19:25

PROSPEROUS
will make your way *p* .... Josh 1:8

PROSPERS
just as your soul *p* .... 3 John 2

PROUD
tongue that speaks *p* .... Ps 12:3
And fully repays the *p* .... Ps 31:23
does not respect the *p* .... Ps 40:4
a haughty look and a *p* .... Ps 101:5
p He knows from afar .... Ps 138:6
Everyone *p* .... Prov 16:5
by wine, He is a *p* .... Hab 2:5
He has scattered the *p* .... Luke 1:51
"God resists the *p* .... 1 Pet 5:5

PROVERB
of a drunkard Is a *p* .... Prov 26:9
one shall take up a *p* .... Mic 2:4
to the true *p* .... 2 Pet 2:22

PROVERBS
three thousand *p* .... 1 Kin 4:32
in order many *p* .... Eccl 12:9

PROVIDE
"My son, God will *p* .... Gen 22:8
"*P* neither gold nor .... Matt 10:9
if anyone does not *p* .... 1 Tim 5:8

PROVIDED
these hands have *p* .... Acts 20:34
p something better .... Heb 11:40

PROVISION
no *p* for the flesh .... Rom 13:14

PROVOKE
"Do they *p* Me to .... Jer 7:19
you, fathers, do not *p* .... Eph 6:4

PROVOKED
p the Most High .... Ps 78:56
his spirit was *p* .... Acts 17:16
seek its own, is not *p* .... 1 Cor 13:5

PRUDENCE
To give *p* to the .... Prov 1:4
wisdom, dwell with *p* .... Prov 8:12
us in all wisdom and *p* .... Eph 1:8

PRUDENT
p man covers shame .... Prov 12:1
A *p* man conceals .... Prov 12:2
The wisdom of the *p* .... Prov 14:8
p considers well .... Prov 14:1
heart will be called *p* .... Prov 16:2
p man foresees evil .... Prov 22:
Therefore the *p* .... Amos 5:1
from the wise and *p* .... Matt 11:2

PRUDENTLY
Servant shall deal *p* .... Is 52:1

PRUNES
that bears fruit He *p* .... John 15:

PSALM
each of you has a *p* .... 1 Cor 14:2

PSALMIST
And the sweet *p* .... 2 Sam 23:

PSALMS
to one another in *p* .... Eph 5:1
Let him sing *p* .... James 5:1

PUNISH
p the righteous is .... Prov 17:2
Shall I not *p* them for .... Jer 5:

PUNISHED
p them often in every .... Acts 26:1
These shall be *p* .... 2 Thess 1:

PUNISHES
will you say when He *p* .... Jer 13:2

PUNISHMENT
p is greater than I .... Gen 4:1
you do in the day of *p* .... Is 10:
p they shall perish .... Jer 10:1
not turn away its *p* .... Amos 1:
into everlasting *p* .... Matt 25:4
p which was inflicted .... 2 Cor 2
Of how much worse *p* .... Heb 10:2
sent by him for the *p* .... 1 Pet 2:1
the unjust under *p* .... 2 Pet 2:

PURE
a mercy seat of *p* gold .... Ex 25:1
'My doctrine is *p* .... Job 11
that he could be *p* .... Job 15:1
of the LORD are *p* .... Ps 12
ways of a man are *p* .... Prov 16
a generation that is *p* .... Prov 30:1
things indeed are *p* .... Rom 14:2
whatever things are *p* .... Phil 4
keep yourself *p* .... 1 Tim 5:2
p all things are *p* .... Titus 1:1
above is first *p* .... James 3:1
babes, desire the *p* .... 1 Pet 2
just as He is *p* .... 1 John 3

PURER
p eyes than to behold .... Hab 1:

PURGE
P me with hyssop .... Ps 51

PURGED
away, And your sin *p* ... Is 6:7
PURIFICATION
with the water of *p* ... Num 31:23
PURIFIED
all things are *p* ... Heb 9:22
Since you have *p* ... 1 Pet 1:22
PURIFIES
hope in Him *p* himself ... 1 John 3:3
PURIFY
and *p* your hearts ... James 4:8
PURIFYING
p their hearts by ... Acts 15:9
sanctifies for the *p* ... Heb 9:13
PURIM
called these days *P* ... Esth 9:26
PURITY
spirit, in faith, in *p* ... 1 Tim 4:12
PURPOSE
A time for every *p* ... Eccl 3:1
But for this *p* I came ... John 12:27
by the determined *p* ... Acts 2:23
to fulfill His *p* ... Rev 17:17
PURSUE
p righteousness ... Rom 9:30
P love ... 1 Cor 14:1
PURSUES
flee when no one *p* ... Prov 28:1

Q

QUAIL
and it brought *q* ... Num 11:31
QUARREL
He will not *q* nor cry ... Matt 12:19
the Lord must not *q* ... 2 Tim 2:24
QUARRELSOME
but gentle, not *q* ... 1 Tim 3:3
QUEEN
heart, 'I sit as *q* ... Rev 18:7
QUENCH
Many waters cannot *q* ... Song 8:7
flax He will not *q* ... Matt 12:20
q all the fiery ... Eph 6:16
Do not *q* the Spirit ... 1 Thess 5:19
QUENCHED
that shall never be *q* ... Mark 9:43
QUESTIONS
and asking them *q* ... Luke 2:46
QUICKLY
with your adversary *q* ... Matt 5:25
"Surely I am coming *q* ... Rev 22:20
QUIET
aspire to lead a *q* ... 1 Thess 4:11
a gentle and *q* spirit ... 1 Pet 3:4
QUIETNESS
a handful with *q* ... Eccl 4:6
In *q* and confidence ... Is 30:15
of righteousness, *q* ... Is 32:17
that they work in *q* ... 2 Thess 3:12

R

RABBI
be called by men, '*R* ... Matt 23:7
RACA
to his brother, '*R* ... Matt 5:22
RACE
man to run its *r* ... Ps 19:5
r is not to the swift ... Eccl 9:11
I have finished the *r* ... 2 Tim 4:7
with endurance the *r* ... Heb 12:1
RAGE
Why do the nations *r* ... Ps 2:1
'Why did the nations *r* ... Acts 4:25
RAIN
had not caused it to *r* ... Gen 2:5
And the *r* was on the ... Gen 7:12
I will *r* down on him ... Ezek 38:22
given you the former *r* ... Joel 2:23
the good, and sends *r* ... Matt 5:45
"and the *r* descended ... Matt 7:25
r that often comes ... Heb 6:7
that it would not *r* ... James 5:17
RAINBOW
"I set My *r* in the ... Gen 9:13
and there was a *r* ... Rev 4:3
RAINED
r fire and brimstone ... Luke 17:29
RAINS
r righteousness ... Hos 10:12
RAISE
third day He will *r* ... Hos 6:2
in three days I will *r* ... John 2:19
and I will *r* him up at ... John 6:40
and the Lord will *r* ... James 5:15
RAISED
be killed, and be *r* ... Matt 16:21
Just as Christ was *r* ... Rom 6:4
Spirit of Him who *r* ... Rom 8:11
"How are the dead *r* ... 1 Cor 15:35
the dead will be *r* ... 1 Cor 15:52
and *r* us up together ... Eph 2:6
RAISES
"For as the Father *r* ... John 5:21
but in God who *r* ... 2 Cor 1:9
RAN
You *r* well ... Gal 5:7
RANSOM
to give His life a *r* ... Mark 10:45
who gave Himself a *r* ... 1 Tim 2:6
RANSOMED
And the *r* of the LORD ... Is 35:10
redeemed Jacob, And *r* ... Jer 31:11
RASH
Do not be *r* with your ... Eccl 5:2
RASHLY
and do nothing *r* ... Acts 19:36
RAVENOUS
inwardly they are *r* ... Matt 7:15
RAVENS
"Consider the *r* ... Luke 12:24
REACHING
r forward to those ... Phil 3:13
READ
day, and stood up to *r* ... Luke 4:16
hearts, known and *r* ... 2 Cor 3:2
READER
the *r* understand ... Mark 13:14
READINESS
the word with all *r* ... Acts 17:11
READING
r the prophet Isaiah ... Acts 8:30
READS
Blessed is he who *r* ... Rev 1:3

READY
and those who were *r* ... Matt 25:10
"Lord, I am *r* ... Luke 22:33
Be *r* in season and out ... 2 Tim 4:2
and always be *r* ... 1 Pet 3:15

REAP
they neither sow nor *r* ... Matt 6:26
you knew that I *r* ... Matt 25:26

REAPED
You have *r* iniquity ... Hos 10:13

REAPERS
r are the angels ... Matt 13:39

REAPING
r what I did not ... Luke 19:22

REAPS
sows and another *r* ... John 4:37

REASON
"Come now, and let us *r* ... Is 1:18
who asks you a *r* ... 1 Pet 3:15

REASONED
for three Sabbaths *r* ... Acts 17:2

REBEL
if you refuse and *r* ... Is 1:20

REBELLING
more against Him By *r* ... Ps 78:17

REBELLION
hearts as in the *r* ... Heb 3:8

REBELLIOUS
day long to a *r* people ... Is 65:2

REBUILD
God, to *r* its ruins ... Ezra 9:9
r it as in the days of ... Amos 9:11

REBUKE
Turn at my *r* ... Prov 1:23
R a wise man ... Prov 9:8
r is better Than love ... Prov 27:5
R the oppressor ... Is 1:17
sins against you, *r* ... Luke 17:3
Do not *r* an older man ... 1 Tim 5:1
who are sinning *r* ... 1 Tim 5:20
"The Lord *r* you ... Jude 9
"As many as I love, I *r* ... Rev 3:19

REBUKED
r the winds and the ... Matt 8:26
r their unbelief ... Mark 16:14
but he was *r* for his ... 2 Pet 2:16

REBUKES
ear that hears the *r* ... Prov 15:31

RECEIVE
believing, you will *r* ... Matt 21:22
and His own did not *r* ... John 1:11
will come again and *r* ... John 14:3
the world cannot *r* ... John 14:17
Ask, and you will *r* ... John 16:24
"*R* the Holy Spirit ... John 20:22
"Lord Jesus, *r* ... Acts 7:59
r the Holy Spirit ... Acts 19:2
R one who is weak ... Rom 14:1
r the Spirit by the ... Gal 3:2
suppose that he will *r* ... James 1:7

RECEIVED
But as many as *r* ... John 1:12
for God has *r* him ... Rom 14:3
For I *r* from the Lord ... 1 Cor 11:23
r Christ ... Col 2:6
R up in glory ... 1 Tim 3:16

RECEIVES
r you *r* Me ... Matt 10:40
and whoever *r* Me ... Mark 9:37

RECONCILE
and that He might *r* ... Eph 2:16

RECONCILED
First be *r* to your ... Matt 5:24
we were *r* ... Rom 5:10
Christ's behalf, be *r* ... 2 Cor 5:20

RECONCILIATION
now received the *r* ... Rom 5:11
to us the word of *r* ... 2 Cor 5:19

RECONCILING
cast away is the *r* ... Rom 11:15
God was in Christ *r* ... 2 Cor 5:19

REDEEM
But God will *r* my soul ... Ps 49:15
r their life from ... Ps 72:14
was going to *r* Israel ... Luke 24:21
r those who were ... Gal 4:5
us, that He might *r* ... Titus 2:14

REDEEMED
Let the *r* of the LORD ... Ps 107:2
r shall walk there ... Is 35:9
sea a road For the *r* ... Is 51:10
And you shall be *r* ... Is 52:3
and *r* His people ... Luke 1:68
Christ has *r* us from ... Gal 3:13
that you were not *r* ... 1 Pet 1:18
were slain, And have *r* ... Rev 5:9

REDEEMER
For I know that my *R* ... Job 19:25
Our *R* from Everlasting ... Is 63:16

REDEEMING
r the time ... Eph 5:16

REDEMPTION
those who looked for *r* ... Luke 2:38
your *r* draws near ... Luke 21:28
grace through the *r* ... Rom 3:2
the adoption, the *r* ... Rom 8:2
sanctification and *r* ... 1 Cor 1:3
In Him we have *r* ... Eph 1:
for the day of *r* ... Eph 4:3
obtained eternal *r* ... Heb 9:1

REED
r He will not break ... Is 42:
r shaken by the wind ... Matt 11:

REFINED
us as silver is *r* ... Ps 66:1

REFINER
He will sit as a *r* ... Mal 3:

REFORMATION
until the time of *r* ... Heb 9:1

REFRESH
r my heart in the Lord ... Philem 2

REFRESHED
his spirit has been *r* ... 2 Cor 7:1
for he often *r* ... 2 Tim 1:1

REFRESHES
r the soul of his ... Prov 25:1

REFRESHING
r may come from the ... Acts 3:1

REFUGE
eternal God is your *r* ... Deut 33:2
God is our *r* and ... Ps 46
who have fled for *r* ... Heb 6:1

REGARD
r iniquity in my heart ... Ps 66:1
did not fear God nor *r* ... Luke 18

REGARDED
my hand and no one *r* ... Prov 1:2
r the lowly state ... Luke 1:4

RENEW
r a steadfast … Ps 51:10
on the LORD Shall *r* … Is 40:31

RENEWED
that your youth is *r* … Ps 103:5
inward man is being *r* … 2 Cor 4:16
and be *r* in the spirit … Eph 4:23

RENEWING
transformed by the *r* … Rom 12:2

RENOWN
were of old, men of *r* … Gen 6:4

REPAID
Shall evil be *r* … Jer 18:20

REPAY
again, I will *r* … Luke 10:35
they cannot *r* … Luke 14:14
R no one evil for evil … Rom 12:17
is Mine, I will *r* … Rom 12:19
r their parents … 1 Tim 5:4

REPAYS
the LORD, Who fully *r* … Is 66:6

REPENT
I abhor myself, And *r* … Job 42:6
"*R*, for the kingdom … Matt 3:2
you *r* you will all … Luke 13:3
said to them, "*R* … Acts 2:38
men everywhere to *r* … Acts 17:30
be zealous and *r* … Rev 3:19

REPENTANCE
you with water unto *r* … Matt 3:11
a baptism of *r* for the … Mark 1:4
persons who need no *r* … Luke 15:7
renew them again to *r* … Heb 6:6
found no place for *r* … Heb 12:17
all should come to *r* … 2 Pet 3:9

REPENTED
it, because they *r* … Matt 12:41

REPETITIONS
r as the heathen do … Matt 6:7

REPORT
Who has believed our *r* … Is 53:1
things are of good *r* … Phil 4:8

REPROACH
R has broken my heart … Ps 69:20
with dishonor comes *r* … Prov 18:3
not remember the *r* … Is 54:4
Because I bore the *r* … Jer 31:19
these things You *r* … Luke 11:45
lest he fall into *r* … 1 Tim 3:7
esteeming the *r* … Heb 11:26
and without *r* … James 1:5

REPROACHED
If you are *r* for the … 1 Pet 4:14

REPROACHES
is not an enemy who *r* … Ps 55:12
in infirmities, in *r* … 2 Cor 12:10

REPROOF
for doctrine, for *r* … 2 Tim 3:16

REPROOFS
R of instruction are … Prov 6:23

REPUTATION
seven men of good *r* … Acts 6:3
made Himself of no *r* … Phil 2:7

REQUEST
He gave them their *r* … Ps 106:15
For Jews *r* a sign … 1 Cor 1:22

REQUESTS
r be made known … Phil 4:6

REQUIRE
offering You did not *r* … Ps 40:6
what does the LORD *r* … Mic 6:8

REQUIRED
your soul will be *r* … Luke 12:20
him much will be *r* … Luke 12:48

REQUIREMENTS
keeps the righteous *r* … Rom 2:26
r that was against us … Col 2:14

RESERVED
"I have *r* for Myself … Rom 11:4
r in heaven for you … 1 Pet 1:4
habitation, He has *r* … Jude 6

RESIST
r an evil person … Matt 5:39
r the Holy Spirit … Acts 7:51
R the devil and he … James 4:7

RESISTED
For who has *r* His will … Rom 9:19
for he has greatly *r* … 2 Tim 4:15
You have not yet *r* … Heb 12:4

RESISTS
"God *r* the proud … James 4:6
for "God *r* the proud … 1 Pet 5:5

RESPECT
of the law held in *r* … Acts 5:34
and we paid them *r* … Heb 12:9

RESPECTED
And the LORD *r* Abel … Gen 4:4

REST
is the Sabbath of *r* … Ex 31:15
to build a house of *r* … 1 Chr 28:2
R in the LORD … Ps 37:7
fly away and be at *r* … Ps 55:6
"This is the *r* … Is 28:12
is the place of My *r* … Is 66:1
and I will give you *r* … Matt 11:28
shall not enter My *r* … Heb 3:11
remains therefore a *r* … Heb 4:9
that they should *r* … Rev 6:11
"that they may *r* … Rev 14:13
But the *r* of the dead … Rev 20:5

RESTED
He had done, and He *r* … Gen 2:2
"And God *r* on the … Heb 4:4

RESTORATION
until the times of *r* … Acts 3:21

RESTORE
R to me the joy … Ps 51:12
"So I will *r* to you … Joel 2:25
and will *r* all things … Matt 17:11
You at this time *r* … Acts 1:6
who are spiritual *r* … Gal 6:1

RESTORES
He *r* my soul … Ps 23:3

RESTRAINS
only He who now *r* … 2 Thess 2:7

RESTRAINT
They break all *r* … Hos 4:2

RESTS
r quietly in the heart … Prov 14:33

RESURRECTION
to her, "I am the *r* … John 11:25
them Jesus and the *r* … Acts 17:18
the likeness of His *r* … Rom 6:5
say that there is no *r* … 1 Cor 15:12
and the power of His *r* … Phil 3:10
obtain a better *r* … Heb 11:35
This is the first *r* … Rev 20:5

"There is none *r* .... Rom 3:10
r man will one die .... Rom 5:7
Jesus Christ the *r* .... 1 John 2:1

RIGHTEOUSLY
should live soberly, *r* .... Titus 2:12
to Him who judges *r* .... 1 Pet 2:23

RIGHTEOUSNESS
it to him for *r* .... Gen 15:6
I put on *r* .... Job 29:14
I call, O God of my *r* .... Ps 4:1
from the LORD, And *r* .... Ps 24:5
shall speak of Your *r* .... Ps 35:28
the good news of *r* .... Ps 40:9
heavens declare His *r* .... Ps 50:6
R and peace have .... Ps 85:10
R will go before Him .... Ps 85:13
r endures forever .... Ps 111:3
r delivers from death .... Prov 10:2
The *r* of the blameless .... Prov 11:5
the way of *r* is life .... Prov 12:28
R exalts a nation .... Prov 14:34
He who follows *r* .... Prov 21:21
R lodged in it .... Is 1:21
in the LORD I have *r* .... Is 45:24
r will be forever .... Is 51:8
I will declare your *r* .... Is 57:12
r as a breastplate .... Is 59:17
r goes forth as .... Is 62:1
The Lord Our *R* .... Jer 23:6
to David A Branch of *r* .... Jer 33:15
The *r* of the righteous .... Ezek 18:20
who turn many to *r* .... Dan 12:3
to fulfill all *r* .... Matt 3:15
exceeds the *r* of the .... Matt 5:20
to you in the way of *r* .... Matt 21:32
For in it the *r* .... Rom 1:17
even the *r* of God .... Rom 3:22
accounted to him for *r* .... Rom 4:22
r will reign in life .... Rom 5:17
might reign through *r* .... Rom 5:21
ignorant of God's *r* .... Rom 10:3
might become the *r* .... 2 Cor 5:21
the breastplate of *r* .... Eph 6:14
not having my own *r* .... Phil 3:9
r which we have .... Titus 3:5
not produce the *r* .... James 1:20
a preacher of *r* .... 2 Pet 2:5
a new earth in which *r* .... 2 Pet 3:13
who practices *r* .... 1 John 2:29
He who practices *r* .... 1 John 3:7

RIGHTLY
wise uses knowledge *r* .... Prov 15:2
r dividing the word .... 2 Tim 2:15

RISE
for He makes His sun *r* .... Matt 5:45
third day He will *r* .... Matt 20:19
third day He will *r* .... Luke 18:33
be the first to *r* .... Acts 26:23
in Christ will *r* .... 1 Thess 4:16

RISEN
there has not *r* .... Matt 11:11
disciples that He is *r* .... Matt 28:7
"The Lord is *r* .... Luke 24:34
then Christ is not *r* .... 1 Cor 15:13
if Christ is not *r* .... 1 Cor 15:17
But now Christ is *r* .... 1 Cor 15:20

RIVER
peace to her like a *r* .... Is 66:12
he showed me a pure *r* .... Rev 22:1

RIVERS
By the *r* of Babylon .... Ps 137:1
All the *r* run into the .... Eccl 1:7
his heart will flow *r* .... John 7:38

ROAR
The LORD also will *r* .... Joel 3:1

ROARING
and the waves *r* .... Luke 21:2
walks about like a *r* .... 1 Pet 5:

ROARS
"The LORD *r* from .... Amos 1:
as when a lion *r* .... Rev 10:

ROB
"Will a man *r* God .... Mal 3:

ROBBED
r other churches .... 2 Cor 11:

ROBBER
is a thief and a *r* .... John 10:
Barabbas was a *r* .... John 18:4

ROBBERS
also crucified two *r* .... Mark 15:2
Me are thieves and *r* .... John 10:

ROBBERY
did not consider it *r* .... Phil 2:

ROBE
'Bring out the best *r* .... Luke 15:2
on Him a purple *r* .... John 19:
Then a white *r* was .... Rev 6:1

ROBES
have stained all My *r* .... Is 63:
go around in long *r* .... Luke 20:4
clothed with white *r* .... Rev 7:

ROCK
you shall strike the *r* .... Ex 17:
and struck the *r* .... Num 20:1
For their *r* is not .... Deut 32:3
"The LORD is my *r* .... 2 Sam 22:
And who is a *r* .... 2 Sam 22:3
Blessed be my *R* .... 2 Sam 22:4
For You are my *r* .... Ps 31:
r that is higher than .... Ps 61:
been mindful of the *R* .... Is 17:1
shadow of a great *r* .... Is 32:
his house on the *r* .... Matt 7:2
r I will build My .... Matt 16:1
stumbling stone and *r* .... Rom 9:3
R that followed them .... 1 Cor 10:

ROD
Your *r* and Your staff .... Ps 23:
shall come forth a *R* .... Is 11:
rule them with a *r* .... Rev 2:2

ROOM
you a large upper *r* .... Mark 14:1
no *r* for them in the .... Luke 2:
into the upper *r* .... Acts 1:1

ROOT
day there shall be a *R* .... Is 11:1
because they had no *r* .... Matt 13:
of money is a *r* .... 1 Tim 6:1
lest any *r* of .... Heb 12:1
I am the *R* and the .... Rev 22:1

ROOTED
r and built up in Him .... Col 2:

ROSE
end Christ died and *r* .... Rom 14:
buried, and that He *r* .... 1 Cor 15:
Jesus died and *r* .... 1 Thess 4:1

RULE
And he shall *r* .... Gen 3:1
puts an end to all *r* .... 1 Cor 15:2
let the peace of God *r* .... Col 3:1
Let the elders who *r* .... 1 Tim 5:1
Remember those who *r* .... Heb 13:

RULER
to Me The One to be *r* ... Mic 5:2
by Beelzebub, the *r* ... Matt 12:24
the *r* of this world ... John 12:31
'Who made you a *r* ... Acts 7:27

RULERS
And the *r* take counsel ... Ps 2:2
"You know that the *r* ... Matt 20:25
which none of the *r* ... 1 Cor 2:8
powers, against the *r* ... Eph 6:12

RULES
That the Most High *r* ... Dan 4:17
that the Most High *r* ... Dan 4:32
r his own house well ... 1 Tim 3:4

RULING
r their children ... 1 Tim 3:12

RUMORS
hear of wars and *r* ... Matt 24:6

RUN
r and not be weary ... Is 40:31
us, and let us *r* ... Heb 12:1

S

SABAOTH
S had left us a ... Rom 9:29
ears of the Lord of *S* ... James 5:4

SABBATH
"Remember the *S* ... Ex 20:8
S was made for man ... Mark 2:27

SABBATHS
S you shall keep ... Ex 31:13

SACRIFICE
to the LORD than *s* ... Prov 21:3
For the LORD has a *s* ... Is 34:6
of My offerings they *s* ... Hos 8:13
LORD has prepared a *s* ... Zeph 1:7
desire mercy and not *s* ... Matt 9:13
an offering and a *s* ... Eph 5:2
put away sin by the *s* ... Heb 9:26
no longer remains a *s* ... Heb 10:26
offer the *s* of praise ... Heb 13:15

SACRIFICED
s their sons And their ... Ps 106:37

SACRIFICES
The *s* of God are a ... Ps 51:17
multitude of your *s* ... Is 1:11
priests, to offer up *s* ... Heb 7:27
s God is well pleased ... Heb 13:16

SAFE
he has received him *s* ... Luke 15:27

SAFELY
make them lie down *s* ... Hos 2:18

SAFETY
say, "Peace and *s* ... 1 Thess 5:3

SAINTS
s who are on the earth ... Ps 16:3
does not forsake His *s* ... Ps 37:28
Is the death of His *s* ... Ps 116:15
war against the *s* ... Dan 7:21
Jesus, called to be *s* ... 1 Cor 1:2
the least of all the *s* ... Eph 3:8
be glorified in His *s* ... 2 Thess 1:10
all delivered to the *s* ... Jude 3
shed the blood of *s* ... Rev 16:6

SALT
shall season with *s* ... Lev 2:13
"You are the *s* ... Matt 5:13
s loses its flavor ... Mark 9:50

SALVATION
still, and see the *s* ... Ex 14:13
S belongs to the LORD ... Ps 3:8
is my light and my *s* ... Ps 27:1
God is the God of *s* ... Ps 68:20
joy in the God of my *s* ... Hab 3:18
raised up a horn of *s* ... Luke 1:69
"Nor is there *s* ... Acts 4:12
the power of God to *s* ... Rom 1:16
now is the day of *s* ... 2 Cor 6:2
work out your own *s* ... Phil 2:12
chose you for *s* ... 2 Thess 2:13
neglect so great a *s* ... Heb 2:3

SAMARITAN
a drink from me, a *S* ... John 4:9

SANCTIFICATION
will of God, your *s* ... 1 Thess 4:3

SANCTIFIED
they also may be *s* ... John 17:19
but you were *s* ... 1 Cor 6:11
for it is *s* by the ... 1 Tim 4:5

SANCTIFIES
For both He who *s* ... Heb 2:11

SANCTIFY
s My great name ... Ezek 36:23
"*S* them by Your ... John 17:17
that He might *s* ... Eph 5:26

SANCTUARY
let them make Me a *s* ... Ex 25:8
and the earthly *s* ... Heb 9:1

SAND
descendants as the *s* ... Gen 32:12
innumerable as the *s* ... Heb 11:12

SAT
into heaven, and *S* ... Mark 16:19
And He who *s* there was ... Rev 4:3

SATAN
before the LORD, and *S* ... Job 1:6
"Away with you, *S* ... Matt 4:10
"Get behind Me, *S* ... Matt 16:23
"How can *S* cast out ... Mark 3:23
S has asked for you ... Luke 22:31
to the working of *S* ... 2 Thess 2:9
known the depths of *S* ... Rev 2:24
years have expired, *S* ... Rev 20:7

SATIATED
s the weary soul ... Jer 31:25

SATISFIED
I shall be *s* when I ... Ps 17:15
that are never *s* ... Prov 30:15
of His soul, and be *s* ... Is 53:11

SATISFIES
s the longing soul ... Ps 107:9

SATISFY
s us early with Your ... Ps 90:14
long life I will *s* ... Ps 91:16
for what does not *s* ... Is 55:2

SAVE
Oh, *s* me for Your ... Ps 6:4
s the children of the ... Ps 72:4
s the souls of the ... Ps 72:13
That it cannot *s* ... Is 59:1
s you And deliver you ... Jer 15:20
other, That he may *s* ... Hos 13:10
JESUS, for He will *s* ... Matt 1:21
s his life will ... Matt 16:25
s that which was ... Matt 18:11
let Him *s* Himself if ... Luke 23:35
but to *s* the world ... John 12:47
the world to *s* sinners ... 1 Tim 1:15

SHED
which is *s* for many ... Matt 26:28
SHEDDING
blood, and without *s* ... Heb 9:22
SHEEP
s will be scattered ... Zech 13:7
having a hundred *s* ... Luke 15:4
and I know My *s* ... John 10:14
"He was led as a *s* ... Acts 8:32
SHEEPFOLDS
lie down among the *s* ... Ps 68:13
SHEET
object like a great *s* ... Acts 10:11
SHELTER
the LORD will be a *s* ... Joel 3:16
SHELTERS
s him all the day long ... Deut 33:12
SHEOL
not leave my soul in *S* ... Ps 16:10
the belly of *S* I cried ... Jon 2:2
SHEPHERD
The LORD is my *S* ... Ps 23:1
His flock like a *s* ... Is 40:11
'I will strike the *S* ... Matt 26:31
"I am the good *s* ... John 10:11
the dead, that great *S* ... Heb 13:20
S the flock of God ... 1 Pet 5:2
when the Chief *S* ... 1 Pet 5:4
SHEPHERDS
"And I will give you *s* ... Jer 3:15
s have led them astray ... Jer 50:6
SHIELD
I am your *s* ... Gen 15:1
truth shall be your *s* ... Ps 91:4
all, taking the *s* ... Eph 6:16
SHINE
LORD make His face *s* ... Num 6:25
among whom you *s* ... Phil 2:15
SHINED
them a light has *s* ... Is 9:2
SHINES
heed as a light that *s* ... 2 Pet 1:19
SHINING
light is already *s* ... 1 John 2:8
SHIPS
down to the sea in *s* ... Ps 107:23
SHIPWRECK
faith have suffered *s* ... 1 Tim 1:19
SHOOT
They *s* out the lip ... Ps 22:7
SHORT
have sinned and fall *s* ... Rom 3:23
SHORTENED
those days were *s* ... Matt 24:22
SHOUT
heaven with a *s* ... 1 Thess 4:16
SHOW
a land that I will *s* ... Gen 12:1
s Him greater works ... John 5:20
SHOWBREAD
s which was not lawful ... Matt 12:4
SHOWERS
make it soft with *s* ... Ps 65:10
SHREWDLY
because he had dealt *s* ... Luke 16:8
SHRINES
who made silver *s* ... Acts 19:24

SHRIVELED
You have *s* me up ... Job 16:8
SHUFFLES
with his eyes, He *s* ... Prov 6:13
SHUNNED
feared God and *s* evil ... Job 1:1
SHUT
For you *s* up the ... Matt 23:13
SHUTS
s his eyes from seeing ... Is 33:15
who opens and no one *s* ... Rev 3:7
SICK
I was *s* and you ... Matt 25:36
faith will save the *s* ... James 5:15
SICKLE
"Thrust in Your *s* ... Rev 14:15
SICKNESS
will sustain him in *s* ... Prov 18:14
"This *s* is not unto ... John 11:4
SICKNESSES
And bore our *s* ... Matt 8:17
SIDE
The LORD is on my *s* ... Ps 118:6
SIFT
s the nations with the ... Is 30:28
SIGH
our years like a *s* ... Ps 90:9
SIGHING
For my *s* comes before ... Job 3:24
SIGHT
and see this great *s* ... Ex 3:3
by faith, not by *s* ... 2 Cor 5:7
SIGN
will give you a *s* ... Is 7:14
seeks after a *s* ... Matt 12:39
For Jews request a *s* ... 1 Cor 1:22
SIGNS
and let them be for *s* ... Gen 1:14
cannot discern the *s* ... Matt 16:3
did many other *s* ... John 20:30
SILENCE
That You may *s* ... Ps 8:2
seal, there was *s* ... Rev 8:1
SILENT
season, and am not *s* ... Ps 22:2
SILK
covered you with *s* ... Ezek 16:10
SILLY
They are *s* children ... Jer 4:22
SILVER
may buy the poor for *s* ... Amos 8:6
him thirty pieces of *s* ... Matt 26:15
SIMILITUDE
been made in the *s* ... James 3:9
SIMPLE
making wise the *s* ... Ps 19:7
SIMPLICITY
corrupted from the *s* ... 2 Cor 11:3
SIN
and be sure your *s* ... Num 32:23
Be angry, and do not *s* ... Ps 4:4
s is always before me ... Ps 51:3
soul an offering for *s* ... Is 53:10
And He bore the *s* ... Is 53:12
who takes away the *s* ... John 1:29
"He who is without *s* ... John 8:7
convict the world of *s* ... John 16:8
s entered the world ... Rom 5:12

s is not imputed .... Rom 5:13
s shall not have .... Rom 6:14
Shall we *s* because we .... Rom 6:15
Him who knew no *s* .... 2 Cor 5:21
man of *s* is revealed .... 2 Thess 2:3
we are, yet without *s* .... Heb 4:15
do it, to him it is *s* .... James 4:17
say that we have no *s* .... 1 John 1:8
and he cannot *s* .... 1 John 3:9

SINCERE
and from *s* faith .... 1 Tim 1:5

SINCERITY
simplicity and godly *s* .... 2 Cor 1:12

SINFUL
from me, for I am a *s* .... Luke 5:8
become exceedingly *s* .... Rom 7:13

SING
Let him *s* psalms .... James 5:13

SINGERS
The *s* went before .... Ps 68:25

SINGING
His presence with *s* .... Ps 100:2
and spiritual songs, *s* .... Eph 5:19

SINISTER
Who understands *s* .... Dan 8:23

SINK
I *s* in deep mire .... Ps 69:2
to *s* he cried out .... Matt 14:30

SINNED
You only, have I *s* .... Ps 51:4
"Father, I have *s* .... Luke 15:18
for all have *s* and .... Rom 3:23
that we have not *s* .... 1 John 1:10

SINNER
s who repents than .... Luke 15:7
the ungodly and the *s* .... 1 Pet 4:18

SINNERS
in the path of *s* .... Ps 1:1
the righteous, but *s* .... Matt 9:13
while we were still *s* .... Rom 5:8
many were made *s* .... Rom 5:19
the world to save *s* .... 1 Tim 1:15
such hostility from *s* .... Heb 12:3

SINS
from presumptuous *s* .... Ps 19:13
You, Our secret *s* .... Ps 90:8
The soul who *s* shall .... Ezek 18:4
if your brother *s* .... Matt 18:15
s according to the .... 1 Cor 15:3
the forgiveness of *s* .... Eph 1:7
If we confess our *s* .... 1 John 1:9
propitiation for our *s* .... 1 John 2:2

SISTER
is My brother and *s* .... Matt 12:50

SIT
but to *s* on My right .... Matt 20:23
"*S* at My right hand .... Heb 1:13
I will grant to *s* .... Rev 3:21

SITS
It is He who *s* above .... Is 40:22
so that he *s* as God .... 2 Thess 2:4

SITTING
where Christ is, *s* .... Col 3:1

SKILL
hand forget its *s* .... Ps 137:5

SKILLFULNESS
guided them by the *s* .... Ps 78:72

SKIN
God made tunics of *s* .... Gen 3:21
LORD and said, "*S* .... Job 2:4
Ethiopian change his *s* .... Jer 13:23

SKIP
He makes them also *s* .... Ps 29:6

SKIPPING
upon the mountains, *S* .... Song 2:8

SKULL
to say, Place of a *S* .... Matt 27:33

SKY
s receded as a scroll .... Rev 6:14

SLACK
The Lord is not *s* .... 2 Pet 3:9

SLAIN
is the Lamb who was *s* .... Rev 5:12

SLANDER
whoever spreads *s* .... Prov 10:18

SLANDERERS
be reverent, not *s* .... 1 Tim 3:11

SLANDEROUSLY
as we are *s* reported .... Rom 3:8

SLAUGHTER
led as a lamb to the *s* .... Is 53:7
as sheep for the *s* .... Rom 8:36

SLAVE
commits sin is a *s* .... John 8:34

SLAVES
should no longer be *s* .... Rom 6:6

SLAY
s the righteous .... Gen 18:25

SLEEP
God caused a deep *s* .... Gen 2:21
neither slumber nor *s* .... Ps 121:4
He gives His beloved *s* .... Ps 127:2
and many *s* .... 1 Cor 11:30
We shall not all *s* .... 1 Cor 15:51

SLEEPERS
gently the lips of *s* .... Song 7:9

SLEEPING
"Are you still *s* .... Matt 26:45

SLEEPLESSNESS
in labors, in *s* .... 2 Cor 6.5

SLEEPS
"Our friend Lazarus *s* .... John 11:11

SLEPT
I lay down and *s* .... Ps 3:5

SLIGHTED
is the one who is *s* .... Prov 12:9

SLING
he had, and his *s* .... 1 Sam 17:40

SLIP
Their foot shall *s* .... Deut 32:35

SLIPPERY
set them in *s* places .... Ps 73:18

SLOOPS
all the beautiful *s* .... Is 2:16

SLOW
hear, *s* to speak, *s* .... James 1:19

SLUGGARD
will you slumber, O *s* .... Prov 6:9

SLUMBERING
upon men, While *s* .... Job 33:15

SMALL
And I saw the dead, *s* .... Rev 20:12

SMELL
and he smelled the *s* ... Gen 27:27

SMELLS
s the battle from afar ... Job 39:25

SMITTEN
Him stricken, *S* ... Is 53:4

SMOKE
was filled with *s* ... Rev 15:8

SMOOTH
And the rough places *s* ... Is 40:4

SMOOTH-SKINNED
man, and I am a *s* ... Gen 27:11

SNAIL
s which melts away as ... Ps 58:8

SNARE
is a fowler's *s* ... Hos 9:8
it will come as a *s* ... Luke 21:35
and escape the *s* ... 2 Tim 2:26

SNARED
All of them are *s* ... Is 42:22

SNARES
who seek my life lay *s* ... Ps 38:12

SNATCH
neither shall anyone *s* ... John 10:28

SNATCHES
s away what was ... Matt 13:19

SNEER
And you *s* at it ... Mal 1:13

SNIFFED
They *s* at the wind ... Jer 14:6

SNORTING
s strikes terror ... Job 39:20

SNOW
shall be whiter than *s* ... Ps 51:7
shall be as white as *s* ... Is 1:18

SOAKED
Their land shall be *s* ... Is 34:7

SOAP
lye, and use much *s* ... Jer 2:22

SOBER
the older men be *s* ... Titus 2:2

SOBERLY
think, but to think *s* ... Rom 12:3

SODA
And like vinegar on *s* ... Prov 25:20

SODOMITES
nor homosexuals, nor *s* ... 1 Cor 6:9

SOJOURNER
no *s* had to lodge ... Job 31:32

SOJOURNERS
are strangers and *s* ... Lev 25:23

SOLD
s his birthright ... Gen 25:33
s all that he had ... Matt 13:46
but I am carnal, *s* ... Rom 7:14

SOLDIER
hardship as a good *s* ... 2 Tim 2:3

SOLDIERS
s twisted a crown ... John 19:2

SOLITARILY
heritage, Who dwell *s* ... Mic 7:14

SOLITARY
God sets the *s* in ... Ps 68:6

SOMEBODY
up, claiming to be *s* ... Acts 5:36

SOMETHING
thinks himself to be *s* ... Gal 6:3

SON
Me, 'You are My *S* ... Ps 2:7
is born, Unto us a *S* ... Is 9:6
fourth is like the *S* ... Dan 3:25
will bring forth a *S* ... Matt 1:21
"This is My beloved *S* ... Matt 3:17
Jesus, You *S* of God ... Matt 8:29
are the Christ, the *S* ... Matt 16:16
Whose *S* is He ... Matt 22:42
of the *S* of Man ... Matt 24:37
'I am the *S* of God ... Matt 27:43
of Jesus Christ, the *S* ... Mark 1:1
out, the only *s* ... Luke 7:12
The only begotten *S* ... John 1:18
that this is the *S* ... John 1:34
of the only begotten *S* ... John 3:18
S can do nothing ... John 5:19
s abides forever ... John 8:35
you believe in the *S* ... John 9:35
I said, 'I am the *S* ... John 10:36
behold your *s* ... John 19:26
Jesus Christ is the *S* ... Acts 8:37
by sending His own *S* ... Rom 8:3
not spare His own *S* ... Rom 8:32
live by faith in the *S* ... Gal 2:20
God sent forth His *S* ... Gal 4:4
the knowledge of the *S* ... Eph 4:13
"You are My *S* ... Heb 1:5
though He was a *S* ... Heb 5:8
but made like the *S* ... Heb 7:3
"This is My beloved *S* ... 2 Pet 1:17
denies the *S* ... 1 John 2:23
One like the *S* of Man ... Rev 1:13

SONG
Sing to Him a new *s* ... Ps 33:3
He has put a new *s* ... Ps 40:3
I will sing a new *s* ... Ps 144:9
they sang a new *s* ... Rev 5:9

SONGS
my Maker, Who gives *s* ... Job 35:10
and spiritual *s* ... Eph 5:19

SONS
s shall come from afar ... Is 60:4
He will purify the *s* ... Mal 3:3
you may become *s* ... John 12:36
who are of faith are *s* ... Gal 3:7
the adoption as *s* ... Gal 4:5
in bringing many *s* ... Heb 2:10
speaks to you as to *s* ... Heb 12:5

SOON
For it is *s* cut off ... Ps 90:10

SOOTHED
or bound up, Or *s* ... Is 1:6

SORCERER
But Elymas the *s* ... Acts 13:8

SORCERERS
outside are dogs and *s* ... Rev 22:15

SORCERESS
shall not permit a *s* ... Ex 22:18

SORCERY
idolatry, *s* ... Gal 5:20

SORES
and putrefying *s* ... Is 1:6

SORROW
multiply your *s* ... Gen 3:16
s is continually ... Ps 38:17
And He adds no *s* ... Prov 10:22
Your *s* is incurable ... Jer 30:15
them sleeping from *s* ... Luke 22:45
s will be turned ... John 16:20

s produces repentance ... 2 Cor 7:10
s as others who ... 1 Thess 4:13
no more death, nor *s* ... Rev 21:4

SORROWFUL
But I am poor and *s* ... Ps 69:29
he went away *s* ... Matt 19:22
soul is exceedingly *s* ... Matt 26:38
and I may be less *s* ... Phil 2:28

SORROWS
s shall be multiplied ... Ps 16:4
by men, A Man of *s* ... Is 53:3
are the beginning of *s* ... Matt 24:8

SORRY
s that He had made man ... Gen 6:6
For you were made *s* ... 2 Cor 7:9

SOUGHT
I *s* the LORD ... Ps 34:4
s what was lost ... Ezek 34:4

SOUL
with all your *s* ... Deut 6:5
"My *s* loathes my life ... Job 10:1
s draws near the Pit ... Job 33:22
will not leave my *s* ... Ps 16:10
converting the *s* ... Ps 19:7
He restores my *s* ... Ps 23:3
you cast down, O my *s* ... Ps 42:5
Let my *s* live ... Ps 119:175
No one cares for my *s* ... Ps 142:4
me wrongs his own *s* ... Prov 8:36
When You make His *s* ... Is 53:10
s delight itself ... Is 55:2
The *s* of the father As ... Ezek 18:4
able to destroy both *s* ... Matt 10:28
and loses his own *s* ... Matt 16:26
with all your *s* ... Matt 22:37
your whole spirit, *s* ... 1 Thess 5:23
to the saving of the *s* ... Heb 10:39
his way will save a *s* ... James 5:20
health, just as your *s* ... 3 John 2

SOULS
And will save the *s* ... Ps 72:13
And he who wins *s* ... Prov 11:30
unsettling your *s* ... Acts 15:24
is able to save your *s* ... James 1:21

SOUND
voice was like the *s* ... Ezek 43:2
do not *s* a trumpet ... Matt 6:2
s words which you ... 2 Tim 1:13

SOUNDNESS
him this perfect *s* ... Acts 3:16

SOUNDS
a distinction in the *s* ... 1 Cor 14:7

SOW
s trouble reap ... Job 4:8
Those who *s* in tears ... Ps 126:5
Blessed are you who *s* ... Is 32:20
"They *s* the wind ... Hos 8:7
s is not made alive ... 1 Cor 15:36

SOWER
"Behold. a *s* went ... Matt 13:3

SOWN
s spiritual things ... 1 Cor 9:11
of righteousness is *s* ... James 3:18

SOWS
s the good seed is the ... Matt 13:37
'One *s* and another ... John 4:37
for whatever a man *s* ... Gal 6:7

SPARE
He who did not *s* ... Rom 8:32
if God did not *s* ... 2 Pet 2:4

SPARES
s his rod hates his ... Prov 13:24

SPARK
the work of it as a *s* ... Is 1:31

SPARKLES
it is red, When it *s* ... Prov 23:31

SPARKS
to trouble, As the *s* ... Job 5:7

SPARROW
s has found a home ... Ps 84:3

SPARROWS
than many *s* ... Matt 10:31

SPAT
Then they *s* on Him ... Matt 27:30

SPEAK
only the word that I *s* ... Num 22:35
oh, that God would *s* ... Job 11:5
And a time to *s* ... Eccl 3:7
s anymore in His name ... Jer 20:9
or what you should *s* ... Matt 10:19
to you when all men *s* ... Luke 6:26
s what I have seen ... John 8:38
He hears He will *s* ... John 16:13
Spirit and began to *s* ... Acts 2:4

SPEAKING
envy, and all evil *s* ... 1 Pet 2:1

SPEAKS
to face, as a man *s* ... Ex 33:11
God has sent *s* ... John 3:34
When he *s* a lie ... John 8:44
he being dead still *s* ... Heb 11:4
of sprinkling that *s* ... Heb 12:24

SPEAR
His side with a *s* ... John 19:34

SPEARS
And their *s* into ... Is 2:4

SPECK
do you look at the *s* ... Matt 7:3

SPECTACLE
you were made a *s* ... Heb 10:33

SPEECH
one language and one *s* ... Gen 11:1
his *s* contemptible ... 2 Cor 10:10
s always be with grace ... Col 4:6

SPEECHLESS
your mouth for the *s* ... Prov 31:8

SPEED
they shall come with *s* ... Is 5:26

SPEEDILY
I call, answer me *s* ... Ps 102:2

SPEND
you *s* money for ... Is 55:2
amiss, that you may *s* ... James 4:3

SPENT
"But when he had *s* ... Luke 15:14

SPEW
nor hot, I will *s* ... Rev 3:16

SPIDER
s skillfully grasps ... Prov 30:28

SPIES
men who had been *s* ... Josh 6:23

SPIN
neither toil nor *s* ... Matt 6:28

SPINDLE
her hand holds the *s* ... Prov 31:19

SPIRIT
And the *S* of God was .... Gen 1:2
S shall not strive .... Gen 6:3
S that is upon you .... Num 11:17
portion of your *s* .... 2 Kin 2:9
Then a *s* passed .... Job 4:15
hand I commit my *s* .... Ps 31:5
The *s* of a man is the .... Prov 20:27
s will return to God .... Eccl 12:7
S has gathered them .... Is 34:16
I have put My *S* .... Is 42:1
"The *S* of the Lord .... Is 61:1
S entered me when He .... Ezek 2:2
and a new *s* .... Ezek 18:31
"I will put My *S* .... Ezek 36:27
walk in a false *s* .... Mic 2:11
and He saw the *S* .... Matt 3:16
I will put My *S* .... Matt 12:18
S descending upon .... Mark 1:10
s indeed is willing .... Mark 14:38
go before Him in the *s* .... Luke 1:17
manner of *s* you are of .... Luke 9:55
hands I commit My *s* .... Luke 23:46
they had seen a *s* .... Luke 24:37
"God is *S* .... John 4:24
I speak to you are *s* .... John 6:63
"the *S* of truth .... John 14:17
but if a *s* or an angel .... Acts 23:9
the flesh but in the *S* .... Rom 8:9
does not have the *S* .... Rom 8:9
s that we are children .... Rom 8:16
what the mind of the *S* .... Rom 8:27
to us through His *S* .... 1 Cor 2:10
gifts, but the same *S* .... 1 Cor 12:4
but the *S* gives life .... 2 Cor 3:6
Now the Lord is the *S* .... 2 Cor 3:17
Having begun in the *S* .... Gal 3:3
has sent forth the *S* .... Gal 4:6
with the Holy *S* .... Eph 1:13
the unity of the *S* .... Eph 4:3
stand fast in one *s* .... Phil 1:27
S expressly says that .... 1 Tim 4:1
S who dwells in us .... James 4:5
made alive by the *S* .... 1 Pet 3:18
do not believe every *s* .... 1 John 4:1
you know the *S* .... 1 John 4:2
has given us of His *S* .... 1 John 4:13
S who bears witness .... 1 John 5:6
not having the *S* .... Jude 19
I was in the *S* on the .... Rev 1:10
him hear what the *S* .... Rev 2:7
And the *S* and the .... Rev 22:17

SPIRITS
Who makes His angels *s* .... Ps 104:4
heed to deceiving *s* .... 1 Tim 4:1

SPIRITUAL
s judges all things .... 1 Cor 2:15
However, the *s* is not .... 1 Cor 15:46
s restore such a one .... Gal 6:1

SPIRITUALLY
s minded is life .... Rom 8:6

SPITEFULLY
for those who *s* .... Matt 5:44

SPITTING
face from shame and *s* .... Is 50:6

SPLENDOR
on the glorious *s* .... Ps 145:5

SPOIL
He shall divide the *s* .... Is 53:12

SPOILER
I have created the *s* .... Is 54:16

SPOKE
"No man ever *s* .... John 7:46
I was a child, I *s* .... 1 Cor 13:11
in various ways *s* .... Heb 1:1
s as they were moved .... 2 Pet 1:21

SPOKEN
I have not *s* in secret .... Is 45:19
why am I evil *s* .... 1 Cor 10:30

SPOKESMAN
"So he shall be your *s* .... Ex 4:16

SPONGE
them ran and took a *s* .... Matt 27:48

SPOT
church, not having *s* .... Eph 5:27
Himself without *s* .... Heb 9:14

SPOTS
These are *s* in your .... Jude 12

SPREAD
Then the word of God *s* .... Acts 6:7

SPREADS
s them out like a tent .... Is 40:22

SPRING
Truth shall *s* out of .... Ps 85:11
s send forth fresh .... James 3:11

SPRINGING
a fountain of water *s* .... John 4:14

SPRINGS
And the thirsty land *s* .... Is 35:7

SPRINKLE
"Then I will *s* .... Ezek 36:25

SPRINKLED
having our hearts *s* .... Heb 10:22

SPRINKLING
s that speaks .... Heb 12:24

SPROUT
and the seed should *s* .... Mark 4:27

SQUARES
voice in the open *s* .... Prov 1:20

STAFF
this Jordan with my *s* .... Gen 32:10
Your rod and Your *s* .... Ps 23:4
on the top of his *s* .... Heb 11:21

STAGGER
they will drink and *s* .... Jer 25:16

STAGGERS
As a drunken man *s* .... Is 19:14

STAKES
s will ever be removed .... Is 33:20

STALLS
be no herd in the *s* .... Hab 3:17

STAMMERERS
s will be ready .... Is 32:4

STAMMERING
s tongue that you .... Is 33:19

STAMPING
At the noise of the *s* .... Jer 47:3

STAND
one shall be able to *s* .... Deut 7:24
lives, And He shall *s* .... Job 19:25
ungodly shall not *s* .... Ps 1:5
not lack a man to *s* .... Jer 35:19
And who can *s* when He .... Mal 3:2
that kingdom cannot *s* .... Mark 3:24
he will be made to *s* .... Rom 14:4
Watch, *s* fast in the .... 1 Cor 16:13
for by faith you *s* .... 2 Cor 1:24
having done all, to *s* .... Eph 6:13
S therefore .... Eph 6:14

of God in which you *s* .... 1 Pet 5:12
"Behold, I *s* at the .... Rev 3:20

STANDARD
LORD will lift up a *s* .... Is 59:19

STANDING
they love to pray *s* .... Matt 6:5
and the Son of Man *s* .... Acts 7:56

STANDS
him who thinks he *s* .... 1 Cor 10:12

STAR
For we have seen His *s* .... Matt 2:2
Bright and Morning *S* .... Rev 22:16

STARS
He made the *s* also .... Gen 1:16
born as many as the *s* .... Heb 11:12

STATE
learned in whatever *s* .... Phil 4:11

STATURE
in wisdom and *s* .... Luke 2:52

STATUTE
shall be a perpetual *s* .... Lev 3:17

STATUTES
the *s* of the LORD are .... Ps 19:8
Teach me Your *s* .... Ps 119:12

STAY
S here and watch .... Matt 26:38

STEADFAST
brethren, be *s* .... 1 Cor 15:58
soul, both sure and *s* .... Heb 6:19
Resist him, *s* in the .... 1 Pet 5:9

STEADFASTLY
s set His face to go .... Luke 9:51
And they continued *s* .... Acts 2:42

STEADFASTNESS
good order and the *s* .... Col 2:5

STEADILY
could not look *s* .... 2 Cor 3:13

STEADY
and his hands were *s* .... Ex 17:12

STEAL
"You shall not *s* .... Ex 20:15
thieves break in and *s* .... Matt 6:19
night and *s* Him away .... Matt 27:64

STEM
forth a Rod from the *s* .... Is 11:1

STENCH
there will be a *s* .... Is 3:24
this time there is a *s* .... John 11:39

STEP
s has turned from the .... Job 31:7

STEPS
The *s* of a good man .... Ps 37:23
And established my *s* .... Ps 40:2
the LORD directs his *s* .... Prov 16:9
should follow His *s* .... 1 Pet 2:21

STEWARD
be blameless, as a *s* .... Titus 1:7

STEWARDS
of Christ and *s* .... 1 Cor 4:1

STEWARDSHIP
entrusted with a *s* .... 1 Cor 9:17

STICK
For Joseph, the *s* .... Ezek 37:16

STICKS
a man gathering *s* .... Num 15:32

STIFF
rebellion and your *s* .... Deut 31:27

STIFF-NECKED
"You *s* and .... Acts 7:51

STILL
When I awake, I am *s* .... Ps 139:18
sea, "Peace, be *s* .... Mark 4:39

STILLBORN
burial, I say that a *s* .... Eccl 6:3

STINGS
like a serpent, And *s* .... Prov 23:32

STIR
I remind you to *s* .... 2 Tim 1:6

STIRRED
So the LORD *s* up the .... Hag 1:14

STIRS
It *s* up the dead for .... Is 14:9

STOCKS
s that were in the .... Jer 20:2

STOIC
and *S* philosophers .... Acts 17:18

STOMACH
Foods for the *s* .... 1 Cor 6:13

STOMACH'S
little wine for your *s* .... 1 Tim 5:23

STONE
him, a pillar of *s* .... Gen 35:14
s shall be a witness .... Josh 24:27
s which the builders .... Ps 118:22
I lay in Zion a *s* .... Is 28:16
take the heart of *s* .... Ezek 36:26
will give him a *s* .... Matt 7.9
s will be broken .... Matt 21:44
s which the builders .... Luke 20:17
those works do you *s* .... John 10:32
Him as to a living *s* .... 1 Pet 2:4

STONED
s Stephen as he was .... Acts 7:59
They were *s* .... Heb 11:37

STONES
Abraham from these *s* .... Matt 3:9
command that these *s* .... Matt 4:3

STONY
fell on *s* ground .... Mark 4:5

STOOPED
And again He *s* down .... John 8:8

STOPPED
her flow of blood *s* .... Luke 8:44

STORE
exist are kept in *s* .... 2 Pet 3:7

STORK
s has her home in the .... Ps 104:17

STORM
He calms the *s* .... Ps 107:29
for a shelter from *s* .... Is 4:6

STRAIGHT
Make *s* in the desert A .... Is 40:3
and make *s* paths for .... Heb 12:13

STRAIGHTFORWARD
that they were not *s* .... Gal 2:14

STRAIN
"Blind guides, who *s* .... Matt 23:24

STRAITS
and desperate *s* .... Deut 28:53

STRANGE
s thing happened .... 1 Pet 4:12

STRANGER
and loves the *s* .... Deut 10:18
I was a *s* and you .... Matt 25:35

STRANGERS
know the voice of *s* ... John 10:5
you are no longer *s* ... Eph 2:19
STRANGLING
that my soul chooses *s* ... Job 7:15
STRAP
than I, whose sandal *s* ... Mark 1:7
STRAW
stones, wood, hay, *s* ... 1 Cor 3:12
STRAY
Who make my people *s* ... Mic 3:5
STRAYED
Yet I have not *s* ... Ps 119:110
some have *s* ... 1 Tim 6:10
STREAM
like a flowing *s* ... Is 66:12
STREAMS
He also brought *s* ... Ps 78:16
STREET
In the middle of its *s* ... Rev 22:2
STREETS
You taught in our *s* ... Luke 13:26
STRENGTH
s no man shall ... 1 Sam 2:9
The LORD is the *s* ... Ps 27:1
is our refuge and *s* ... Ps 46:1
They go from *s* to ... Ps 84:7
S and honor are her ... Prov 31:25
might He increases *s* ... Is 40:29
O LORD, my *s* and my ... Jer 16:19
were still without *s* ... Rom 5:6
s is made perfect ... 2 Cor 12:9
STRENGTHEN
And He shall *s* ... Ps 27:14
S the weak hands ... Is 35:3
s your brethren ... Luke 22:32
s the things ... Rev 3:2
STRENGTHENED
unbelief, but was *s* ... Rom 4:20
stood with me and *s* ... 2 Tim 4:17
STRENGTHENING
s the souls of the ... Acts 14:22
STRENGTHENS
through Christ who *s* ... Phil 4:13
STRETCH
are old, you will *s* ... John 21:18
STRETCHED
I have *s* out my hands ... Ps 88:9
"All day long I have *s* ... Rom 10:21
STRETCHES
For he *s* out his hand ... Job 15:25
STRICKEN
of My people He was *s* ... Is 53:8
STRIFE
man stirs up *s* ... Prov 15:18
even from envy and *s* ... Phil 1:15
which come envy, *s* ... 1 Tim 6:4
STRIKE
The sun shall not *s* ... Ps 121:6
"*S* the Shepherd ... Zech 13:7
'I will *s* the Shepherd ... Matt 26:31
STRINGED
of your *s* instruments ... Amos 5:23
STRIP
S yourselves ... Is 32:11
STRIPES
s we are healed ... Is 53:5
s you were healed ... 1 Pet 2:24

STRIVE
"My Spirit shall not *s* ... Gen 6:
"*S* to enter through ... Luke 13:2
the Lord not to *s* ... 2 Tim 2:1
STRIVING
for a man to stop *s* ... Prov 20:
STROKE
with a mighty *s* ... Jer 14:1
STRONG
The LORD *s* and mighty ... Ps 24:
S is Your hand ... Ps 89:1
"When a *s* man ... Luke 11:2
We then who are *s* ... Rom 15:
weak, then I am *s* ... 2 Cor 12:1
my brethren, be *s* ... Eph 6:1
were made *s* ... Heb 11:3
STRONGHOLD
of my salvation, my *s* ... Ps 18:
STRUCK
s the rock twice ... Num 20:1
the hand of God has *s* ... Job 19:2
Behold, He *s* the rock ... Ps 78:2
in My wrath I *s* ... Is 60:1
s the head from the ... Hab 3:1
took the reed and *s* ... Matt 27:3
STUBBLE
do wickedly will be *s* ... Mal 4:
STUBBORN
"If a man has a *s* ... Deut 21:1
STUBBORN-HEARTED
"Listen to Me, you *s* ... Is 46:1
STUBBORNNESS
do not look on the *s* ... Deut 9:2
STUDIED
having never *s* ... John 7:1
STUMBLE
have caused many to *s* ... Mal 2:
you will be made to *s* ... Matt 26:3
immediately they *s* ... Mark 4:1
who believe in Me to *s* ... Mark 9:4
For we all *s* in many ... James 3:
STUMBLED
s that they should ... Rom 11:1
STUMBLES
immediately he *s* ... Matt 13:2
STUMBLING
the deaf, nor put a *s* ... Lev 19:1
But a stone of *s* ... Is 8:1
Behold, I will lay *s* ... Jer 6:2
I lay in Zion a *s* ... Rom 9:3
this, not to put a *s* ... Rom 14:1
of yours become a *s* ... 1 Cor 8:
and "A stone of *s* ... 1 Pet 2:
to keep you from *s* ... Jude 2
STUPID
hates correction is *s* ... Prov 12:
SUBDUE
s all things to ... Phil 3:2
SUBJECT
for it is not *s* ... Rom 8:
Let every soul be *s* ... Rom 13:
all their lifetime *s* ... Heb 2:1
SUBJECTED
because of Him who *s* ... Rom 8:2
SUBJECTION
put all things in *s* ... Heb 2:
SUBMISSION
his children in *s* ... 1 Tim 3:

SUBMISSIVE
Yes, all of you be *s* ... 1 Pet 5:5
SUBMIT
Therefore *s* to God ... James 4:7
s yourselves to every ... 1 Pet 2:13
SUBSIDED
and the waters *s* ... Gen 8:1
SUBSTANCE
Bless his *s* ... Deut 33:11
SUCCESS
please give me *s* ... Gen 24:12
But wisdom brings *s* ... Eccl 10:10
SUCCESSFUL
Joseph, and he was a *s* ... Gen 39:2
SUDDENLY
s there was with the ... Luke 2:13
SUE
s you and take away ... Matt 5:40
SUFFER
for the Christ to *s* ... Luke 24:46
Christ, if indeed we *s* ... Rom 8:17
in Him, but also to *s* ... Phil 1:29
SUFFERED
s these things and to ... Luke 24:26
for whom I have *s* ... Phil 3:8
after you have *s* ... 1 Pet 5:10
SUFFERING
anyone among you *s* ... James 5:13
SUFFERINGS
I consider that the *s* ... Rom 8:18
perfect through *s* ... Heb 2:10
SUFFERS
Love *s* long and is ... 1 Cor 13:4
SUFFICIENCY
but our *s* is from God ... 2 Cor 3:5
SUFFICIENT
S for the day is its ... Matt 6:34
SUM
How great is the *s* ... Ps 139:17
SUMMER
and heat, Winter and *s* ... Gen 8:22
SUMPTUOUSLY
fine linen and fared *s* ... Luke 16:19
SUN
So the *s* stood still ... Josh 10:13
s shall not strike you ... Ps 121:6
s returned ten degrees ... Is 38:8
The *s* and moon grow ... Joel 2:10
s shall go down on the ... Mic 3:6
for He makes His *s* ... Matt 5:45
the *s* was darkened ... Luke 23:45
do not let the *s* ... Eph 4:26
s became black as ... Rev 6:12
had no need of the *s* ... Rev 21:23
SUPPER
to eat the Lord's *S* ... 1 Cor 11:20
took the cup after *s* ... 1 Cor 11:25
together for the *s* ... Rev 19:17
SUPPLICATION
by prayer and *s* ... Phil 4:6
SUPPLIES
by what every joint *s* ... Eph 4:16
SUPPLY
And my God shall *s* ... Phil 4:19
SUPPORT
this, that you must *s* ... Acts 20:35
SUPREME
to the king as *s* ... 1 Pet 2:13

SURE
s your sin will find ... Num 32:23
call and election *s* ... 2 Pet 1:10
SURETY
Be *s* for Your servant ... Ps 119:122
Jesus has become a *s* ... Heb 7:22
SURROUND
LORD, mercy shall *s* ... Ps 32:10
SURROUNDED
also, since we are *s* ... Heb 12:1
SURVIVOR
was no refugee or *s* ... Lam 2:22
SUSPICIONS
reviling, evil *s* ... 1 Tim 6:4
SUSTAIN
S me with cakes of ... Song 2:5
SWADDLING
Him in *s* cloths ... Luke 2:7
SWALLOW
a gnat and *s* a camel ... Matt 23:24
SWEAR
'You shall not *s* ... Matt 5:33
began to curse and *s* ... Matt 26:74
SWEARING
By *s* and lying ... Hos 4:2
SWEARS
but whoever *s* by the ... Matt 23:18
SWEAT
His *s* became like ... Luke 22:44
SWEET
s are Your words ... Ps 119:103
but it will be as *s* ... Rev 10:9
SWEETNESS
mouth like honey in *s* ... Ezek 3:3
SWELLING
they speak great *s* ... 2 Pet 2:18
SWIFT
let every man be *s* ... James 1:19
SWIM
night I make my bed *s* ... Ps 6:6
SWOON
As they *s* like the ... Lam 2:12
SWORD
s which turned every ... Gen 3:24
The *s* of the LORD is ... Is 34:6
'A *s* is sharpened ... Ezek 21:9
Bow and *s* of battle I ... Hos 2:18
to bring peace but a *s* ... Matt 10:34
for all who take the *s* ... Matt 26:52
the *s* of the Spirit ... Eph 6:17
than any two-edged *s* ... Heb 4:12
mouth goes a sharp *s* ... Rev 19:15
SWORDS
shall beat their *s* ... Is 2:4
SWORE
So I *s* in My wrath ... Heb 3:11
SWORN
"By Myself I have *s* ... Gen 22:16
"The LORD has *s* ... Heb 7:21
SYMBOLIC
which things are *s* ... Gal 4:24
SYMPATHIZE
Priest who cannot *s* ... Heb 4:15
SYMPATHY
My *s* is stirred ... Hos 11:8
SYNAGOGUE
but are a *s* of Satan ... Rev 2:9

T

TABERNACLE
t He shall hide me .... Ps 27:5
I will abide in Your *t* .... Ps 61:4
And will rebuild the *t* .... Acts 15:16
and more perfect *t* .... Heb 9:11

TABERNACLES
Feast of *T* was at hand .... John 7:2

TABLE
prepare a *t* before me .... Ps 23:5
dogs under the *t* .... Mark 7:28
of the Lord's *t* .... 1 Cor 10:21

TABLES
and overturned the *t* .... Matt 21:12

TABLET
is engraved On the *t* .... Jer 17:1

TAIL
t drew a third of the .... Rev 12:4

TAKE
t Your Holy Spirit .... Ps 51:11
"*T* My yoke upon .... Matt 11:29
and *t* up his cross .... Mark 8:34
My life that I may *t* .... John 10:17

TAKEN
He was *t* from prison .... Is 53:8
one will be *t* and the .... Matt 24:40
until He is *t* out of .... 2 Thess 2:7

TALEBEARER
t reveals secrets .... Prov 11:13

TALENT
went and hid your *t* .... Matt 25:25

TALK
shall *t* of them when .... Deut 6:7

TALKED
within us while He *t* .... Luke 24:32

TALKERS
both idle *t* and .... Titus 1:10

TAMBOURINE
The mirth of the *t* .... Is 24:8

TARES
the *t* also appeared .... Matt 13:26

TARGET
You set me as Your *t* .... Job 7:20

TARRY
come and will not *t* .... Heb 10:37

TASK
this burdensome *t* .... Eccl 1:13

TASTE
Oh, *t* and see that the .... Ps 34:8
might *t* death for .... Heb 2:9

TASTED
t the heavenly gift .... Heb 6:4

TAUGHT
as His counselor has *t* .... Is 40:13
from man, nor was I *t* .... Gal 1:12

TAUNT
and a byword, a *t* .... Jer 24:9

TAX
t collectors do the .... Matt 5:46

TAXES
t to whom *t* .... Rom 13:7

TEACH
"Can anyone *t* .... Job 21:22
T me Your paths .... Ps 25:4
t you the fear of the .... Ps 34:11
t transgressors Your .... Ps 51:1
So *t* us to number our .... Ps 90:1
t you again the first .... Heb 5:1

TEACHER
for One is your *T* .... Matt 23:
know that You are a *t* .... John 3:
named Gamaliel, a *t* .... Acts 5:3
a *t* of the Gentiles in .... 1 Tim 2:

TEACHERS
than all my *t* .... Ps 119:9
prophets, third *t* .... 1 Cor 12:2
and some pastors and *t* .... Eph 4:1
desiring to be *t* .... 1 Tim 1:
there will be false *t* .... 2 Pet 2:

TEACHES
the Holy Spirit *t* .... 1 Cor 2:1
the same anointing *t* .... 1 John 2:2

TEACHING
"*t* them to observe all .... Matt 28:2
t every man in all .... Col 1:2

TEAR
I, even I, will *t* .... Hos 5:1
will wipe away every *t* .... Rev 21:

TEARS
my couch with my *t* .... Ps 6:
mindful of your *t* .... 2 Tim 1:
it diligently with *t* .... Heb 12:1

TEETH
You have broken the *t* .... Ps 3:

TELL
"Who can *t* if God .... Jon 3:
t him his fault .... Matt 18:1
whatever they *t* .... Matt 23:
He comes, He will *t* .... John 4:2

TEMPERATE
prize is *t* in all .... 1 Cor 9:2
husband of one wife, *t* .... 1 Tim 3:

TEMPEST
And suddenly a great *t* .... Matt 8:2

TEMPLE
So Solomon built the *t* .... 1 Kin 6:1
LORD is in His holy *t* .... Ps 11:
One greater than the *t* .... Matt 12:
"Destroy this *t* .... John 2:1
your body is the *t* .... 1 Cor 6:1
grows into a holy *t* .... Eph 2:2
sits as God in the *t* .... 2 Thess 2:
and the Lamb are its *t* .... Rev 21:2

TEMPLES
t made with hands .... Acts 7:4

TEMPORARY
which are seen are *t* .... 2 Cor 4:1

TEMPT
t the LORD your God .... Matt 4:
does He Himself *t* .... James 1:1

TEMPTATION
do not lead us into *t* .... Matt 6:1
man who endures *t* .... James 1:1

TEMPTED
forty days, *t* by Satan .... Mark 1:1
lest you also be *t* .... Gal 6:
in all points *t* .... Heb 4:1

TEMPTER
Now when the *t* came .... Matt 4:

TENDER
your heart was *t* .... 2 Kin 22:1

TENDERHEARTED
to one another, *t* .... Eph 4:3

THROAT
t is an open tomb .... Rom 3:13

THRONE
Your *t*, O God, is .... Ps 45:6
Lord sitting on a *t* .... Is 6:1
"Heaven is My *t* .... Is 66:1
for it is God's *t* .... Matt 5:34
will give Him the *t* .... Luke 1:32
"Your *t*, O God, is .... Heb 1:8
come boldly to the *t* .... Heb 4:16
My Father on His *t* .... Rev 3:21
I saw a great white *t* .... Rev 20:11

THRONES
invisible, whether *t* .... Col 1:16

THRONG
house of God in the *t* .... Ps 55:14

THROW
t Yourself down .... Matt 4:6

THROWN
neck, and he were *t* .... Mark 9:42

THRUST
and rose up and *t* .... Luke 4:29

THUNDER
The voice of Your *t* .... Ps 77:18
the voice of loud *t* .... Rev 14:2

THUNDERED
"The LORD *t* from .... 2 Sam 22:14

THUNDERINGS
the sound of mighty *t* .... Rev 19:6

THUNDERS
The God of glory *t* .... Ps 29:3

TIDINGS
I bring you good *t* .... Luke 2:10

TILL
no man to *t* the ground .... Gen 2:5

TILLER
but Cain was a *t* .... Gen 4:2

TILLS
t his land will have .... Prov 28:19

TIME
pray to You In a *t* .... Ps 32:6
for the *t* is near .... Rev 1:3

TIMES
the signs of the *t* .... Matt 16:3
not for you to know *t* .... Acts 1:7
last days perilous *t* .... 2 Tim 3:1

TITHE
And he gave him a *t* .... Gen 14:20
For you pay *t* of mint .... Matt 23:23

TITHES
and to bring the *t* .... Neh 10:37
Bring all the *t* .... Mal 3:10

TITHING
the year of *t* .... Deut 26:12

TITLE
Now Pilate wrote a *t* .... John 19:19

TITTLE
away, one jot or one *t* .... Matt 5:18

TODAY
T I have begotten You .... Ps 2:7
t you will be with Me .... Luke 23:43
"*T*, if you will hear .... Heb 3:7
the same yesterday, *t* .... Heb 13:8

TOIL
t you shall eat of .... Gen 3:17

TOILED
"Master, we have *t* .... Luke 5:5

TOLD
Behold I have *t* .... Matt 28:7
so, I would have *t* .... John 14:2

TOLERABLE
you, it will be more *t* .... Matt 10:15

TOMB
in the garden a new *t* .... John 19:41

TOMBS
like whitewashed *t* .... Matt 23:27

TOMORROW
drink, for *t* we die .... Is 22:13
do not worry about *t* .... Matt 6:34
what will happen *t* .... James 4:14

TONGUE
remember you, Let my *t* .... Ps 137:6
forever, But a lying *t* .... Prov 12:19
t breaks a bone .... Prov 25:15
t should confess that .... Phil 2:11
does not bridle his *t* .... James 1:26
no man can tame the *t* .... James 3:8
every nation, tribe, *t* .... Rev 14:6

TONGUES
From the strife of *t* .... Ps 31:20
speak with new *t* .... Mark 16:17
divided *t*, as of fire .... Acts 2:3
I speak with the *t* .... 1 Cor 13:1

TOOTH
eye for an eye and a *t* .... Matt 5:38

TOPHET
the high places of *T* .... Jer 7:31

TORCH
and like a fiery *t* .... Zech 12:6

TORCHES
When he had set the *t* .... Judg 15:5
come with flaming *t* .... Nah 2:3

TORMENT
You come here to *t* .... Matt 8:29
t ascends forever .... Rev 14:11

TORMENTED
And they will be *t* .... Rev 20:10

TORMENTS
"And being in *t* .... Luke 16:23

TORN
of the temple was *t* .... Matt 27:51

TORTURED
Others were *t* .... Heb 11:35

TOSSED
t to and fro and .... Eph 4:14

TOTTER
drunkard, And shall *t* .... Is 24:20

TOUCH
"If only I may *t* .... Matt 9:21

TOUCHED
t my mouth with it .... Is 6:7

TOUCHES
He *t* the hills .... Ps 104:32

TOWER
t whose top is in the .... Gen 11:4
a watchman in the *t* .... Is 21:5

TRACKED
t our steps So that we .... Lam 4:18

TRADERS
are princes, Whose *t* .... Is 23:8

TRADITION
transgress the *t* .... Matt 15:2
according to the *t* .... Col 2:8

Savior in time of *t* .... Jer 14:8
there are some who *t* .... Gal 1:7

TROUBLED
worried and *t* .... Luke 10:41
shaken in mind or *t* .... 2 Thess 2:2

TROUBLES
Out of all their *t* .... Ps 25:22
will be famines and *t* .... Mark 13:8
him out of all his *t* .... Acts 7:10

TROUBLING
wicked cease from *t* .... Job 3:17

TRUE
He who sent Me is *t* .... John 7:28
Indeed, let God be *t* .... Rom 3:4
whatever things are *t* .... Phil 4:8
Him who is *t* .... 1 John 5:20
for these words are *t* .... Rev 21:5

TRUMPET
deed, do not sound a *t* .... Matt 6:2
t makes an uncertain .... 1 Cor 14:8
For the *t* will sound .... 1 Cor 15:52

TRUST
T in the LORD .... Ps 37:3
T in the LORD with all .... Prov 3:5
Do not *t* in a friend .... Mic 7:5
who *t* in riches .... Mark 10:24

TRUSTED
"He *t* in the LORD .... Ps 22:8
"He *t* in God .... Matt 27:43

TRUSTS
But he who *t* in the .... Ps 32:10

TRUTH
led me in the way of *t* .... Gen 24:48
Behold, You desire *t* .... Ps 51:6
t shall be your shield .... Ps 91:4
And Your law is *t* .... Ps 119:142
t is fallen in the .... Is 59:14
called the City of *T* .... Zech 8:3
you shall know the *t* .... John 8:32
"I am the way, the *t* .... John 14:6
He, the Spirit of *t* .... John 16:13
to Him. "What is *t* .... John 18:38
who suppress the *t* .... Rom 1:18
but, speaking the *t* .... Eph 4:15
your waist with *t* .... Eph 6:14
I am speaking the *t* .... 1 Tim 2:7
they may know the *t* .... 2 Tim 2:25
the knowledge of the *t* .... 2 Tim 3:7
that we are of the *t* .... 1 John 3:19
the Spirit is *t* .... 1 John 5:6

TRY
which is to *t* you .... 1 Pet 4:12

TUMULT
Your enemies make a *t* .... Ps 83:2

TUNIC
Also he made him a *t* .... Gen 37:3

TUNICS
the LORD God made *t* .... Gen 3:21

TURBAN
"Remove the *t* .... Ezek 21:26

TURN
you shall not *t* .... Deut 17:11
"Repent, *t* away from .... Ezek 14:6
on your right cheek, *t* .... Matt 5:39
t them from darkness .... Acts 26:18

TURNED
The wicked shall be *t* .... Ps 9:17
of Israel, They have *t* .... Is 1:4
and how you *t* .... 1 Thess 1:9

TURNING
marvel that you are *t* .... Gal 1:6
or shadow of *t* .... James 1:17

TURNS
A soft answer *t* .... Prov 15:1
that he who *t* .... James 5:20

TURTLEDOVE
t Is heard in our land .... Song 2:12

TUTOR
the law was our *t* .... Gal 3:24

TWIST
unstable people *t* to .... 2 Pet 3:16

TWO
T are better than one .... Eccl 4:9
t shall become one .... Matt 19:5
new man from the *t* .... Eph 2:15

TYPE
of Adam, who is a *t* .... Rom 5:14

U

UNAFRAID
Do you want to be *u* .... Rom 13:3

UNBELIEF
because of their *u* .... Matt 13:58
help my *u* .... Mark 9:24
did it ignorantly in *u* .... 1 Tim 1:13
enter in because of *u* .... Heb 3:19

UNBELIEVERS
yoked together with *u* .... 2 Cor 6:14

UNBELIEVING
Do not be *u* .... John 20:27
u nothing is pure .... Titus 1:15
"But the cowardly, *u* .... Rev 21:8

UNCIRCUMCISED
not the physically *u* .... Rom 2:27

UNCLEAN
I am a man of *u* lips .... Is 6:5
man common or *u* .... Acts 10:28
there is nothing *u* .... Rom 14:14
that no fornicator, *u* .... Eph 5:5

UNCLEANNESS
men's bones and all *u* .... Matt 23:27
flesh in the lust of *u* .... 2 Pet 2:10

UNCLOTHED
we want to be *u* .... 2 Cor 5:4

UNCOVERS
u deep things out of .... Job 12:22

UNDEFILED
incorruptible and *u* .... 1 Pet 1:4

UNDERMINE
And you *u* your friend .... Job 6:27

UNDERSTAND
if there are any who *u* .... Ps 14:2
hearing, but do not *u* .... Is 6:9
"Why do you not *u* .... John 8:43
lest they should *u* .... Acts 28:27
some things hard to *u* .... 2 Pet 3:16

UNDERSTANDING
His *u* is infinite .... Ps 147:5
lean not on your own *u* .... Prov 3:5
u will find good .... Prov 19:8
His *u* is unsearchable .... Is 40:28
also still without *u* .... Matt 15:16
also pray with the *u* .... 1 Cor 14:15
the Lord give you *u* .... 2 Tim 2:7
Who is wise and *u* .... James 3:13

UNDERSTANDS
There is none who *u* .... Rom 3:11

UNDERSTOOD
Then I *u* their end ... Ps 73:17
clearly seen, being *u* ... Rom 1:20

UNDESIRABLE
gather together, O *u* ... Zeph 2:1

UNDIGNIFIED
I will be even more *u* ... 2 Sam 6:22

UNDISCERNING
u, untrustworthy ... Rom 1:31

UNDONE
"Woe is me, for I am *u* ... Is 6:5

UNEDUCATED
that they were *u* ... Acts 4:13

UNFAITHFUL
way of the *u* is hard ... Prov 13:15

UNFAITHFULLY
back and acted *u* ... Ps 78:57

UNFORGIVING
unloving, *u* ... Rom 1:31

UNFORMED
substance, being yet *u* ... Ps 139:16

UNFRUITFUL
and it becomes *u* ... Mark 4:19

UNGODLINESS
heaven against all *u* ... Rom 1:18

UNGODLY
u shall not stand ... Ps 1:5
Christ died for the *u* ... Rom 5:6

UNHOLY
the holy and *u* ... Ezek 22:26

UNINFORMED
the place of the *u* ... 1 Cor 14:16

UNINTENTIONALLY
kills his neighbor *u* ... Deut 4:42

UNITE
U my heart to fear ... Ps 86:11

UNITY
to dwell together in *u* ... Ps 133:1
to keep the *u* of the ... Eph 4:3

UNJUST
commended the *u* ... Luke 16:8
of the just and the *u* ... Acts 24:15
For God is not *u* ... Heb 6:10

UNJUSTLY
long will you judge *u* ... Ps 82:2

UNKNOWN
To The *U* God ... Acts 17:23

UNLEAVENED
the Feast of *U* Bread ... Ex 12:17

UNLOVING
untrustworthy, *u* ... Rom 1:31

UNMERCIFUL
unforgiving, *u* ... Rom 1:31

UNPREPARED
with me and find you *u* ... 2 Cor 9:4

UNPRESENTABLE
u parts have greater ... 1 Cor 12:23

UNPROFITABLE
'We are *u* servants ... Luke 17:10
for that would be *u* ... Heb 13:17

UNPUNISHED
wicked will not go *u* ... Prov 11:21

UNQUENCHABLE
up the chaff with *u* ... Matt 3:12

UNRESTRAINED
that the people were *u* ... Ex 32:25

UNRIGHTEOUS
u man his thoughts ... Is 55:7
u will not inherit the ... 1 Cor 6:9

UNRIGHTEOUSNESS
all ungodliness and *u* ... Rom 1:18
cleanse us from all *u* ... 1 John 1:9
All *u* is sin ... 1 John 5:17

UNRULY
those who are *u* ... 1 Thess 5:14

UNSEARCHABLE
u are His judgments ... Rom 11:33

UNSKILLED
only of milk is *u* ... Heb 5:13

UNSPOTTED
to keep oneself *u* ... James 1:27

UNSTABLE
U as water ... Gen 49:4

UNSTOPPED
of the deaf shall be *u* ... Is 35:5

UNTAUGHT
which *u* and unstable ... 2 Pet 3:16

UNTRUSTWORTHY
undiscerning, *u* ... Rom 1:31

UNWASHED
eat bread with *u* hands ... Mark 7:5

UNWISE
Therefore do not be *u* ... Eph 5:17

UNWORTHY
u manner will be ... 1 Cor 11:27

UPHOLD
U me according to ... Ps 119:116

UPHOLDING
u all things by the ... Heb 1:3

UPHOLDS
LORD *u* all who fall ... Ps 145:14

UPPER
show you a large *u* ... Mark 14:15

UPRIGHT
u is His delight ... Prov 15:8

UPRIGHTNESS
princes for their *u* ... Prov 17:26

UPROOT
u the wheat with ... Matt 13:29

URIM
Thummim and Your *U* ... Deut 33:8

US
"God with *u* ... Matt 1:23
If God is for *u* ... Rom 8:31
of them were of *u* ... 1 John 2:19

USE
who spitefully *u* you ... Matt 5:44
u liberty as an ... Gal 5:13

USELESS
one's religion is *u* ... James 1:26

USES
if one *u* it lawfully ... 1 Tim 1:8

USING
u liberty as a ... 1 Pet 2:16

USURY
'Take no *u* or ... Lev 25:36

UTTER
u dark sayings of old ... Ps 78:2

UTTERANCE
the Spirit gave them *u* ... Acts 2:4

UTTERED
which cannot be *u* ... Rom 8:26

UTTERMOST
u those who come . . . Heb 7:25

UTTERS
Day unto day *u* speech . . . Ps 19:2

V

VAGABOND
v you shall be on the . . . Gen 4:12

VAIN
the people plot a *v* . . . Ps 2:1
you believed in *v* . . . 1 Cor 15:2

VALIANT
They are not *v* for the . . . Jer 9:3

VALIANTLY
God we will do *v* . . . Ps 60:12

VALLEY
v shall be exalted . . . Is 40:4

VALOR
a mighty man of *v* . . . 1 Sam 16:18

VALUE
of more *v* than they . . . Matt 6:26

VALUED
It cannot be *v* in the . . . Job 28:16

VANISH
knowledge, it will *v* . . . 1 Cor 13:8

VANISHED
and He *v* from their . . . Luke 24:31

VANITY
of vanities, all is *v* . . . Eccl 1:2

VAPOR
best state is but *v* . . . Ps 39:5
It is even a *v* that . . . James 4:14

VARIATION
whom there is no *v* . . . James 1:17

VEGETABLES
and let them give us *v* . . . Dan 1:12
is weak eats only *v* . . . Rom 14:2

VEHEMENT
of fire, A most *v* . . . Song 8:6

VEIL
v of the temple was . . . Matt 27:51
Presence behind the *v* . . . Heb 6:19

VENGEANCE
V is Mine . . . Deut 32:35

VENOM
It becomes cobra *v* . . . Job 20:14

VESSEL
like a potter's *v* . . . Ps 2:9
for he is a chosen *v* . . . Acts 9:15

VESSELS
treasure in earthen *v* . . . 2 Cor 4:7

VEXED
grieved, and I was *v* . . . Ps 73:21

VICE
as a cloak for *v* . . . 1 Pet 2:16

VICTIM
And plucked the *v* . . . Job 29:17

VICTORY
v that has overcome . . . 1 John 5:4

VIEW
"Go, *v* the land . . . Josh 2:1

VIGILANT
Be sober, be *v* . . . 1 Pet 5:8

VIGOR
nor his natural *v* . . . Deut 34:7

VILE
them up to *v* passions . . . Rom 1:26

VINDICATED
know that I shall be *v* . . . Job 13:18

VINDICATION
Let my *v* come from . . . Ps 17:2

VINE
"I am the true *v* . . . John 15:1

VINEDRESSER
and My Father is the *v* . . . John 15:1

VINEGAR
As *v* to the teeth and . . . Prov 10:26

VINES
foxes that spoil the *v* . . . Song 2:15

VINEYARD
Who plants a *v* and . . . 1 Cor 9:7

VIOLENCE
was filled with *v* . . . Gen 6:11
of heaven suffers *v* . . . Matt 11:12

VIOLENT
haters of God, *v* . . . Rom 1:30

VIPER
And stings like a *v* . . . Prov 23:32

VIPERS
to them, "Brood of *v* . . . Matt 3:7

VIRGIN
v shall conceive . . . Is 7:14
"Behold, the *v* shall . . . Matt 1:23

VIRGINS
v who took their lamps . . . Matt 25:1

VIRTUE
to your faith *v* . . . 2 Pet 1:5

VISAGE
v was marred more than . . . Is 52:14

VISIBLE
that are on earth, *v* . . . Col 1:16

VISION
in a trance I saw a *v* . . . Acts 11:5
to the heavenly *v* . . . Acts 26:19

VISIONS
young men shall see *v* . . . Joel 2:28

VISIT
v orphans and . . . James 1:27

VISITATION
God in the day of *v* . . . 1 Pet 2:12

VISITED
Israel, for He has *v* . . . Luke 1:68

VISITING
v the iniquity of the . . . Ex 20:5

VISITOR
am a foreigner and a *v* . . . Gen 23:4

VITALITY
v was turned into the . . . Ps 32:4

VOICE
fire a still small *v* . . . 1 Kin 19:12
if you will hear His *v* . . . Ps 95:7
"The *v* of one crying . . . Matt 3:3
And suddenly a *v* . . . Matt 3:17
for they know his *v* . . . John 10:4
the truth hears My *v* . . . John 18:37
If anyone hears My *v* . . . Rev 3:20

VOICES
And there were loud *v* . . . Rev 11:15

VOID
they are a nation *v* . . . Deut 32:28
heirs, faith is made *v* . . . Rom 4:14

WASTED
this fragrant oil *w* .... Mark 14:4
WASTELAND
w shall be glad .... Is 35:1
WASTING
that this man was *w* .... Luke 16:1
WATCH
is past, And like a *w* .... Ps 90:4
"*W* therefore .... Matt 24:42
WATCHED
he would have *w* .... Matt 24:43
WATCHES
Blessed is he who *w* .... Rev 16:15
WATCHFUL
But you be *w* in all .... 2 Tim 4:5
WATCHING
he comes, will find *w* .... Luke 12:37
WATCHMAN
I have made you a *w* .... Ezek 3:17
WATCHMEN
I have set *w* on your .... Is 62:6
WATER
Eden to *w* the garden .... Gen 2:10
I am poured out like *w* .... Ps 22:14
For I will pour *w* .... Is 44:3
given you living *w* .... John 4:10
rivers of living *w* .... John 7:38
can yield both salt *w* .... James 3:12
the Spirit, the *w* .... 1 John 5:8
are clouds without *w* .... Jude 12
let him take the *w* .... Rev 22:17
WATERED
I planted, Apollos *w* .... 1 Cor 3:6
WATERS
me beside the still *w* .... Ps 23:2
Though its *w* roar and .... Ps 46:3
your bread upon the *w* .... Eccl 11:1
thirsts, Come to the *w* .... Is 55:1
fountain of living *w* .... Jer 2:13
living fountains of *w* .... Rev 7:17
WAVE
Its fruit shall *w* .... Ps 72:16
WAVER
He did not *w* at the .... Rom 4:20
WAVERING
of our hope without *w* .... Heb 10:23
WAVES
sea, tossed by the *w* .... Matt 14:24
WAX
My heart is like *w* .... Ps 22:14
WAY
As for God, His *w* .... 2 Sam 22:31
the LORD knows the *w* .... Ps 1:6
Teach me Your *w* .... Ps 27:11
in the *w* everlasting .... Ps 139:24
w that seems right .... Prov 14:12
The *w* of the just is .... Is 26:7
wicked forsake his *w* .... Is 55:7
And pervert the *w* .... Amos 2:7
he will prepare the *w* .... Mal 3:1
and broad is the *w* .... Matt 7:13
will prepare Your *w* .... Matt 11:10
to him, "I am the *w* .... John 14:6
to him the *w* .... Acts 18:26
to have known the *w* .... 2 Pet 2:21
WAYS
For all His *w* are .... Deut 32:4
transgressors Your *w* .... Ps 51:13
w please the LORD .... Prov 16:7
"Stand in the *w* .... Jer 6:16

and owns all your *w* .... Dan 5:23
w are everlasting .... Hab 3:6
unstable in all his *w* .... James 1:8
and true are Your *w* .... Rev 15:3
WEAK
gives power to the *w* .... Is 40:29
knee will be as *w* .... Ezek 7:17
but the flesh is *w* .... Matt 26:41
Receive one who is *w* .... Rom 14:1
God has chosen the *w* .... 1 Cor 1:27
We are *w* .... 1 Cor 4:10
w I became as *w* .... 1 Cor 9:22
For when I am *w* .... 2 Cor 12:10
WEAKENED
w my strength in the .... Ps 102:23
WEAKENS
w the hands of the men .... Jer 38:4
WEAKER
the wife, as to the *w* .... 1 Pet 3:7
WEAKNESS
w were made strong .... Heb 11:34
WEAKNESSES
also helps in our *w* .... Rom 8:26
WEALTH
W gained by .... Prov 13:11
WEALTHY
rich, have become *w* .... Rev 3:17
WEANED
w child shall put his .... Is 11:8
WEAPON
w formed against you .... Is 54:17
WEAPONS
For the *w* of our .... 2 Cor 10:4
WEAR
'What shall we *w* .... Matt 6:31
WEARIED
You have *w* Me with .... Is 43:24
therefore, being *w* .... John 4:6
WEARINESS
say, 'Oh, what a *w* .... Mal 1:13
WEARISOME
and much study is *w* .... Eccl 12:12
WEARY
shall run and not be *w* .... Is 40:31
And let us not grow *w* .... Gal 6:9
do not grow *w* in .... 2 Thess 3:13
WEATHER
'It will be fair *w* .... Matt 16:2
WEDDING
day there was a *w* .... John 2:1
WEEK
the first day of the *w* .... Matt 28:1
WEEKS
w are determined .... Dan 9:24
WEEP
A time to *w* .... Eccl 3:4
You shall *w* no more .... Is 30:19
are you who *w* .... Luke 6:21
do not *w* .... Luke 23:28
w with those who *w* .... Rom 12:15
WEEPING
the noise of the *w* .... Ezra 3:13
They shall come with *w* .... Jer 31:9
There will be *w* .... Matt 8:12
by the tomb *w* .... John 20:11
WEIGH
O Most Upright, You *w* .... Is 26:7

WEIGHED
You have been *w* .... Dan 5:27
WEIGHS
eyes, But the LORD *w* .... Prov 16:2
WEIGHT
us lay aside every *w* .... Heb 12:1
WEIGHTIER
have neglected the *w* .... Matt 23:23
WELFARE
does not seek the *w* .... Jer 38:4
WELL
have done *w* .... Prov 31:29
wheel broken at the *w* .... Eccl 12:6
"Those who are *w* .... Matt 9:12
said to him, '*W* done .... Matt 25:21
WELLS
These are *w* without .... 2 Pet 2:17
WENT
They *w* out from us .... 1 John 2:19
WEPT
out and *w* bitterly .... Matt 26:75
saw the city and *w* .... Luke 19:41
Jesus *w* .... John 11:35
WET
his body was *w* with .... Dan 4:33
WHEAT
w falls into the .... John 12:24
WHEEL
in the middle of a *w* .... Ezek 1:16
WHEELS
noise of rattling *w* .... Nah 3:2
WHERE
not knowing *w* he was .... Heb 11:8
WHIP
A *w* for the horse .... Prov 26:3
WHIRLWIND
Job out of the *w* .... Job 38:1
has His way in the *w* .... Nah 1:3
WHISPER
my ear received a *w* .... Job 4:12
WHISPERER
w separates the best .... Prov 16:28
WHISPERERS
they are *w* .... Rom 1:29
WHISPERINGS
backbitings, *w* .... 2 Cor 12:20
WHITE
clothed in *w* garments .... Rev 3:5
behold, a *w* horse .... Rev 6:2
and made them *w* .... Rev 7:14
WHOLE
w body were an eye .... 1 Cor 12:17
WHOLESOME
not consent to *w* words .... 1 Tim 6:3
WHOLLY
w followed the LORD .... Deut 1:36
WICKED
w shall be silent .... 1 Sam 2:9
w shall be no more .... Ps 37:10
if there is any *w* .... Ps 139:24
w forsake his way .... Is 55:7
And desperately *w* .... Jer 17:9
the sway of the *w* .... 1 John 5:19
WICKEDLY
God will never do *w* .... Job 34:12
WICKEDNESS
LORD saw that the *w* .... Gen 6:5
in the tents of *w* .... Ps 84:10
man repented of his *w* .... Jer 8:6
is full of greed and *w* .... Luke 11:39
sexual immorality, *w* .... Rom 1:29
and overflow of *w* .... James 1:21
WIDE
open your hand *w* .... Deut 15:8
w is the gate and .... Matt 7:13
to you, our heart is *w* .... 2 Cor 6:11
WIDOW
the fatherless and *w* .... Ps 146:9
How like a *w* is she .... Lam 1:1
Then one poor *w* .... Mark 12:42
w has children or .... 1 Tim 5:4
WIDOW'S
And I caused the *w* .... Job 29:13
WIDOWS
w were neglected .... Acts 6:1
visit orphans and *w* .... James 1:27
WIFE
and be joined to his *w* .... Gen 2:24
w finds a good thing .... Prov 18:22
But a prudent *w* .... Prov 19:14
"Go, take yourself a *w* .... Hos 1:2
divorces his *w* .... Mark 10:11
'I have married a *w* .... Luke 14:20
"Remember Lot's *w* .... Luke 17:32
so love his own *w* .... Eph 5:33
the husband of one *w* .... Titus 1:6
bride, the Lamb's *w* .... Rev 21:9
WILD
olive tree which is *w* .... Rom 11:24
WILDERNESS
I will make the *w* .... Is 41:18
of one crying in the *w* .... Matt 3:3
the serpent in the *w* .... John 3:14
WILES
to stand against the *w* .... Eph 6:11
WILL
w be done On earth as .... Matt 6:10
but he who does the *w* .... Matt 7:21
not My *w* .... Luke 22:42
flesh, nor of the *w* .... John 1:13
not to do My own *w* .... John 6:38
w is present with me .... Rom 7:18
and perfect *w* of God .... Rom 12:2
works in you both to *w* .... Phil 2:13
according to His own *w* .... Heb 2:4
work to do His *w* .... Heb 13:21
WILLFULLY
For if we sin *w* .... Heb 10:26
For this they *w* .... 2 Pet 3:5
WILLING
If you are *w* and .... Is 1:19
The spirit indeed is *w* .... Matt 26:41
w that any should .... 2 Pet 3:9
WILLINGLY
by compulsion but *w* .... 1 Pet 5:2
WILLOWS
our harps Upon the *w* .... Ps 137:2
WILLS
to whom the Son *w* .... Matt 11:27
it is not of him who *w* .... Rom 9:16
say, "If the Lord *w* .... James 4:15
WIN
to all, that I might *w* .... 1 Cor 9:19
WIND
the chaff which the *w* .... Ps 1:4
reed shaken by the *w* .... Matt 11:7

“The *w* blows where ... John 3:8
of a rushing mighty *w* ... Acts 2:2

WINDOWS
not open for you the *w* ... Mal 3:10

WINDS
be, that even the *w* ... Matt 8:27

WINDSTORM
And a great *w* arose ... Mark 4:37

WINE
W is a mocker ... Prov 20:1
love is better than *w* ... Song 1:2
Yes, come, buy *w* ... Is 55:1
they gave Him sour *w* ... Matt 27:34
do not be drunk with *w* ... Eph 5:18
not given to much *w* ... Titus 2:3

WINEBIBBERS
Do not mix with *w* ... Prov 23:20

WINEPRESS
“I have trodden the *w* ... Is 63:3
into the great *w* ... Rev 14:19
Himself treads the *w* ... Rev 19:15

WINESKINS
new wine into old *w* ... Matt 9:17

WING
One *w* of the cherub ... 1 Kin 6:24

WINGS
the shadow of Your *w* ... Ps 36:7
With healing in His *w* ... Mal 4:2

WINNOW
You shall *w* them ... Is 41:16

WINS
w souls is wise ... Prov 11:30

WINTER
For lo, the *w* is past ... Song 2:11
flight may not be in *w* ... Matt 24:20

WIPE
w away every tear ... Rev 21:4

WISDOM
for this is your *w* ... Deut 4:6
man who finds *w* ... Prov 3:13
Get *w* ... Prov 4:5
is the beginning of *w* ... Prov 9:10
w is justified by her ... Matt 11:19
Jesus increased in *w* ... Luke 2:52
riches both of the *w* ... Rom 11:33
the gospel, not with *w* ... 1 Cor 1:17
w of this world ... 1 Cor 3:19
not with fleshly *w* ... 2 Cor 1:12
all the treasures of *w* ... Col 2:3
If any of you lacks *w* ... James 1:5
power and riches and *w* ... Rev 5:12

WISE
Do not be *w* in your ... Prov 3:7
who wins souls is *w* ... Prov 11:30
Therefore be *w* as ... Matt 10:16
five of them were *w* ... Matt 25:2
to God, alone *w* ... Rom 16:27
Where is the *w* ... 1 Cor 1:20
not as fools but as *w* ... Eph 5:15
able to make you *w* ... 2 Tim 3:15

WISELY
you do not inquire *w* ... Eccl 7:10

WISER
he was *w* than all men ... 1 Kin 4:31
of God is *w* than men ... 1 Cor 1:25

WISH
w it were already ... Luke 12:49

WISHED
Then he *w* death for ... Jon 4:8

WITCHCRAFT
is as the sin of *w* ... 1 Sam 15:2

WITHDRAW
From such *w* yourself ... 1 Tim 6:

WITHER
also shall not *w* ... Ps 1:

WITHERS
The grass *w* ... Is 40:
The grass *w* ... 1 Pet 1:2

WITHHELD
And your sins have *w* ... Jer 5:2

WITHHOLD
good thing will He *w* ... Ps 84:1

WITHOUT
pray *w* ceasing ... 1 Thess 5:1
w works is dead ... James 2:2

WITHSTAND
you may be able to *w* ... Eph 6:1

WITHSTOOD
I *w* him to his face ... Gal 2:1

WITNESS
all the world as a *w* ... Matt 24:1
This man came for a *w* ... John 1:
do not receive Our *w* ... John 3:1
Christ, the faithful *w* ... Rev 1:
beheaded for their *w* ... Rev 20:

WITNESSED
is revealed, being *w* ... Rom 3:2

WITNESSES
“You are My *w* ... Is 43:1
presence of many *w* ... 1 Tim 6:1
so great a cloud of *w* ... Heb 12:

WIVES
Husbands, love your *w* ... Eph 5:2
w must be reverent ... 1 Tim 3:1

WOLF
The *w* and the lamb ... Is 65:2

WOLVES
out as lambs among *w* ... Luke 10:
savage *w* ... Acts 20:2

WOMAN
She shall be called *W* ... Gen 2:2
whoever looks at a *w* ... Matt 5:2
Then the *w* of Samaria ... John 4:
“*W*, behold your ... John 19:2
natural use of the *w* ... Rom 1:2
His Son, born of a *w* ... Gal 4:
w being deceived ... 1 Tim 2:1
w clothed with the sun ... Rev 12:

WOMB
nations are in your *w* ... Gen 25:2
in the *w* I knew you ... Jer 1:
is the fruit of your *w* ... Luke 1:4

WOMEN
O fairest among *w* ... Song 1:
w will be grinding ... Matt 24:4
are you among *w* ... Luke 1:2
admonish the young *w* ... Titus 2:
times, the holy *w* ... 1 Pet 3:

WONDER
marvelous work and a *w* ... Is 29:1

WONDERFUL
Things too *w* for me ... Job 42:
name will be called *W* ... Is 9:

WONDERIFULLY
fearfully and *w* made ... Ps 139:1

WONDERS
“And I will show *w* ... Joel 2:3
signs, and lying *w* ... 2 Thess 2:

WONDROUS
w works declare that ... Ps 75:1

WONDROUSLY
God, Who has dealt *w* ... Joel 2:26

WOOD
precious stones, *w* ... 1 Cor 3:12

WOODCUTTERS
but let them be *w* ... Josh 9:21

WOOL
They shall be as *w* ... Is 1:18
hair were white like *w* ... Rev 1:14

WORD
w is very near you ... Deut 30:14
w I have hidden ... Ps 119:11
w is a lamp to my feet ... Ps 119:105
Every *w* of God is pure ... Prov 30:5
the *w* of our God ... Is 40:8
for every idle *w* ... Matt 12:36
The seed is the *w* ... Luke 8:11
beginning was the *W* ... John 1:1
W became flesh and ... John 1:14
Your *w* is truth ... John 17:17
Let the *w* of Christ ... Col 3:16
to you in *w* only ... 1 Thess 1:5
by the *w* of His power ... Heb 1:3
For the *w* of God is ... Heb 4:12
does not stumble in *w* ... James 3:2
through the *w* of God ... 1 Pet 1:23
let us not love in *w* ... 1 John 3:18
name is called The *W* ... Rev 19:13

WORDS
Let the *w* of my mouth ... Ps 19:14
The *w* of the wise are ... Eccl 12:11
pass away, but My *w* ... Matt 24:35
You have the *w* of ... John 6:68
not with wisdom of *w* ... 1 Cor 1:17
those who hear the *w* ... Rev 1:3

WORK
day God ended His *w* ... Gen 2:2
people had a mind to *w* ... Neh 4:6
the *w* of Your fingers ... Ps 8:3
Man goes out to his *w* ... Ps 104:23
w is honorable and ... Ps 111:3
will bring every *w* ... Eccl 12:14
For I will *w* a *w* ... Hab 1:5
could do no mighty *w* ... Mark 6:5
"This is the *w* of God ... John 6:29
"I must *w* the works ... John 9:4
w which You have ... John 17:4
know that all things *w* ... Rom 8:28
w is no longer *w* ... Rom 11:6
Do not destroy the *w* ... Rom 14:20
abounding in the *w* ... 1 Cor 15:58
If anyone will not *w* ... 2 Thess 3:10
but a doer of the *w* ... James 1:25

WORKED
which He *w* in Christ ... Eph 1:20

WORKER
w is worthy of his ... Matt 10:10
w who does not need ... 2 Tim 2:15

WORKERS
we are God's fellow *w* ... 1 Cor 3:9

WORKING
Father has been *w* ... John 5:17
through faith in the *w* ... Col 2:12

WORKMANSHIP
For we are His *w* ... Eph 2:10

WORKS
are Your wonderful *w* ... Ps 40:5
And let her own *w* ... Prov 31:31
'For I know their *w* ... Is 66:18
show Him greater *w* ... John 5:20
w that I do he will do ... John 14:12
might stand, not of *w* ... Rom 9:11
same God who *w* ... 1 Cor 12:6
not justified by the *w* ... Gal 2:16
Now the *w* of the flesh ... Gal 5:19
not of *w*, lest anyone ... Eph 2:9
for it is God who *w* ... Phil 2:13
but does not have *w* ... James 2:14
also justified by *w* ... James 2:25
"I know your *w* ... Rev 2:2
their *w* follow them ... Rev 14:13
according to their *w* ... Rev 20:12

WORLD
"The field is the *w* ... Matt 13:38
He was in the *w* ... John 1:10
God so loved the *w* ... John 3:16
His Son into the *w* ... John 3:17
w cannot hate you ... John 7:7
You are of this *w* ... John 8:23
overcome the *w* ... John 16:33
w may become guilty ... Rom 3:19
be conformed to this *w* ... Rom 12:2
loved this present *w* ... 2 Tim 4:10
Do not love the *w* ... 1 John 2:15
w is passing away ... 1 John 2:17

WORLDS
also He made the *w* ... Heb 1:2

WORM
But I am a *w* ... Ps 22:6
w does not die ... Mark 9:44

WORMS
he was eaten by *w* ... Acts 12:23

WORMWOOD
of the star is *W* ... Rev 8:11

WORRY
to you, do not *w* ... Matt 6:25

WORRYING
w can add one ... Matt 6:27

WORSE
w than their fathers ... Jer 7:26

WORSHIP
come to *w* Him ... Matt 2:2
w what you do not ... John 4:22
the angels of God *w* ... Heb 1:6

WORSHIPED
on their faces and *w* ... Rev 11:16

WORSHIPER
if anyone is a *w* ... John 9:31

WORTH
make my speech *w* ... Job 24:25

WORTHLESS
Indeed they are all *w* ... Is 41:29

WORTHLESSNESS
long will you love *w* ... Ps 4:2

WORTHY
present time are not *w* ... Rom 8:18
to walk *w* ... Eph 4:1
the world was not *w* ... Heb 11:38
"*W* is the Lamb who ... Rev 5:12

WOUND
And my *w* incurable ... Jer 15:18
and his deadly *w* ... Rev 13:3

WOUNDED
But He was *w* for our ... Is 53:5

WOUNDING
killed a man for *w* ... Gen 4:23

WOUNDS
Faithful are the *w* ... Prov 27:6

WRANGLINGS
useless *w* of men of . . . 1 Tim 6:5

WRATH
speak to them in His *w* . . . Ps 2:5
Surely the *w* of man . . . Ps 76:10
So I swore in My *w* . . . Ps 95:11
W is cruel and anger a . . . Prov 27:4
in My *w* I struck you . . . Is 60:10
w remember mercy . . . Hab 3:2
For the *w* of God is . . . Rom 1:18
up for yourself *w* . . . Rom 2:5
nature children of *w* . . . Eph 2:3
sun go down on your *w* . . . Eph 4:26
Let all bitterness, *w* . . . Eph 4:31
holy hands, without *w* . . . 1 Tim 2:8
So I swore in My *w* . . . Heb 3:11
not fearing the *w* . . . Heb 11:27
for the *w* of man . . . James 1:20
of the wine of the *w* . . . Rev 14:8
for in them the *w* . . . Rev 15:1
fierceness of His *w* . . . Rev 16:19

WRATHFUL
w man stirs up strife . . . Prov 15:18

WRESTLE
For we do not *w* . . . Eph 6:12

WRETCHED
w man that I am . . . Rom 7:24
know that you are *w* . . . Rev 3:17

WRETCHEDNESS
let me see my *w* . . . Num 11:15

WRINGING
w the nose produces . . . Prov 30:33

WRINKLE
not having spot or *w* . . . Eph 5:27

WRITE
w them on their hearts . . . Heb 8:10

WRITING
the *w* was the *w* . . . Ex 32:16

WRITINGS
do not believe his *w* . . . John 5:47

WRITTEN
tablets of stone, *w* . . . Ex 31:18
your names are *w* . . . Luke 10:20
"What I have *w* . . . John 19:22

WRONG
done nothing *w* . . . Luke 23:41
But he who does *w* . . . Col 3:25

WRONGED
We have *w* no one . . . 2 Cor 7:2

WRONGS
me *w* his own soul . . . Prov 8:36

WROTE
stooped down and *w* . . . John 8:6

WROUGHT
And skillfully *w* . . . Ps 139:15

Y

YEAR
the acceptable *y* . . . Is 61:2
of sins every *y* . . . Heb 10:3

YEARS
and for days and *y* . . . Gen 1:14
lives are seventy *y* . . . Ps 90:10
when He was twelve *y* . . . Luke 2:42
with Him a thousand *y* . . . Rev 20:6

YES
let your '*Y*' be '*Y*,' . . . Matt 5:37

YESTERDAY
For we were born *y* . . . Job 8:9

YOKE
"Take My *y* upon you . . . Matt 11:29

YOKED
Do not be unequally *y* . . . 2 Cor 6:14

YOUNG
I have been *y* . . . Ps 37:25
she may lay her *y* . . . Ps 84:3
I write to you, *y* . . . 1 John 2:13

YOUNGER
Likewise you *y* people . . . 1 Pet 5:5

YOURS
the battle is not *y* . . . 2 Chr 20:15
Y is the kingdom . . . Matt 6:13
all Mine are *Y* . . . John 17:10
for I do not seek *y* . . . 2 Cor 12:14

YOUTH
the sins of my *y* . . . Ps 25:7
and *y* are vanity . . . Eccl 11:10
I have kept from my *y* . . . Matt 19:20

YOUTHFUL
Flee also *y* lusts . . . 2 Tim 2:22

YOUTHS
y shall faint and be . . . Is 40:30

Z

ZEAL
The *z* of the LORD of . . . 2 Kin 19:31
"*Z* for Your house has . . . John 2:17
that they have a *z* . . . Rom 10:2

ZEALOUS
z for good works . . . Titus 2:14

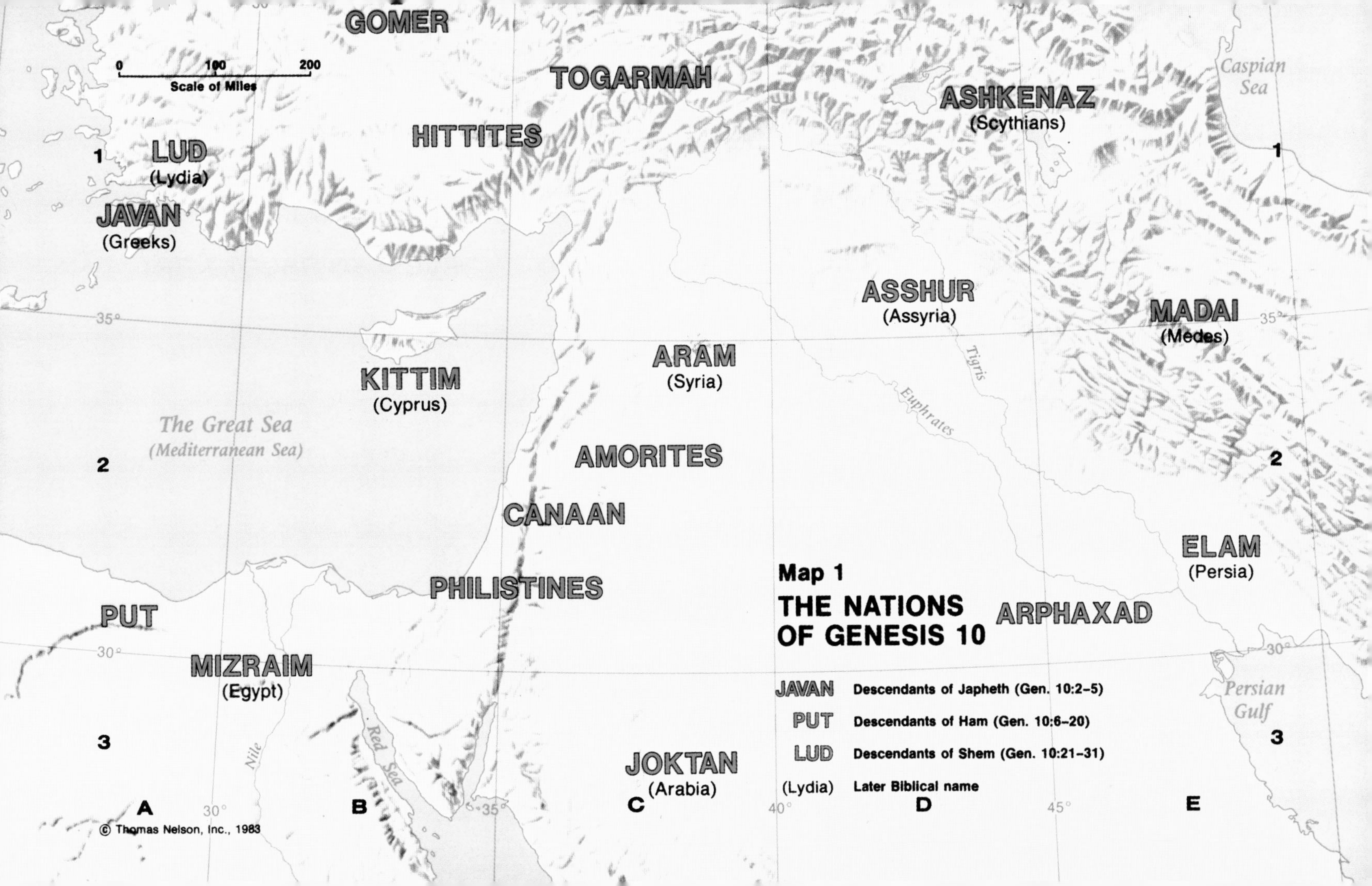
Map 1
THE NATIONS OF GENESIS 10
JAVAN Descendants of Japheth (Gen. 10:2–5)
PUT Descendants of Ham (Gen. 10:6–20)
LUD Descendants of Shem (Gen. 10:21–31)
(Lydia) Later Biblical name
GOMER
TOGARMAH
ASHKENAZ
(Scythians)
HITTITES
LUD
(Lydia)
JAVAN
(Greeks)
ASSHUR
(Assyria)
MADAI
(Medes)
ARAM
(Syria)
KITTIM
(Cyprus)
The Great Sea
(Mediterranean Sea)
AMORITES
CANAAN
ELAM
(Persia)
PHILISTINES
ARPHAXAD
PUT
MIZRAIM
(Egypt)
JOKTAN
(Arabia)
Caspian Sea
Persian Gulf
Red Sea
Nile
Tigris
Euphrates
0 100 200
Scale of Miles
35°
30°
40°
45°
A B C D E
1 2 3

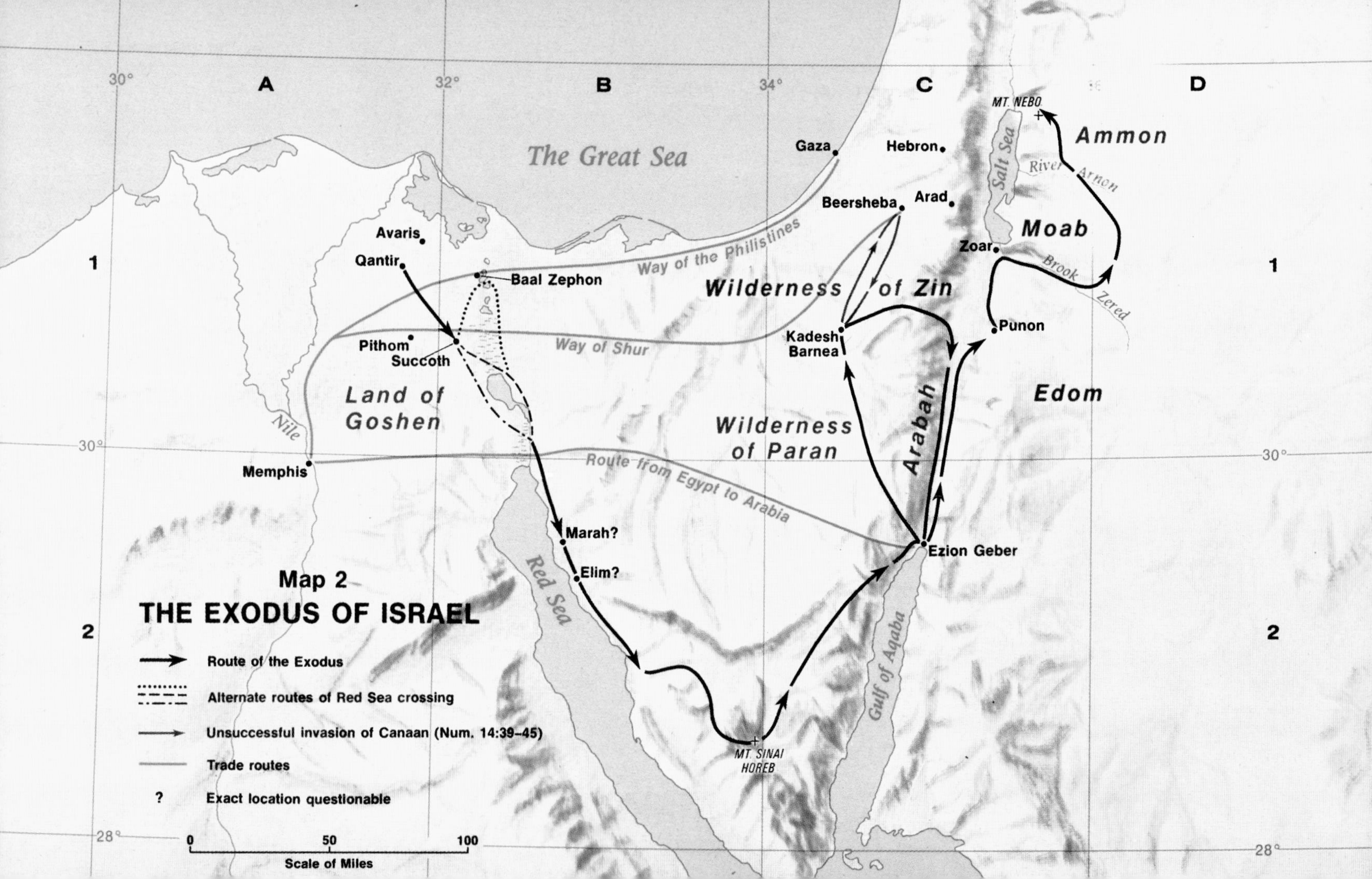
Map 2
THE EXODUS OF ISRAEL
Route of the Exodus
Alternate routes of Red Sea crossing
Unsuccessful invasion of Canaan (Num. 14:39–45)
Trade routes
? Exact location questionable
0 50 100
Scale of Miles
A
B
C
D
1
2
30°
32°
34°
28°
The Great Sea
Avaris
Qantir
Baal Zephon
Pithom
Succoth
Land of Goshen
Nile
Memphis
Way of the Philistines
Way of Shur
Route from Egypt to Arabia
Gaza
Hebron
Beersheba
Arad
Wilderness of Zin
Kadesh Barnea
Wilderness of Paran
Arabah
Marah?
Elim?
Red Sea
MT. SINAI HOREB
Gulf of Aqaba
Ezion Geber
Salt Sea
MT. NEBO
River Arnon
Ammon
Moab
Zoar
Brook Zered
Punon
Edom

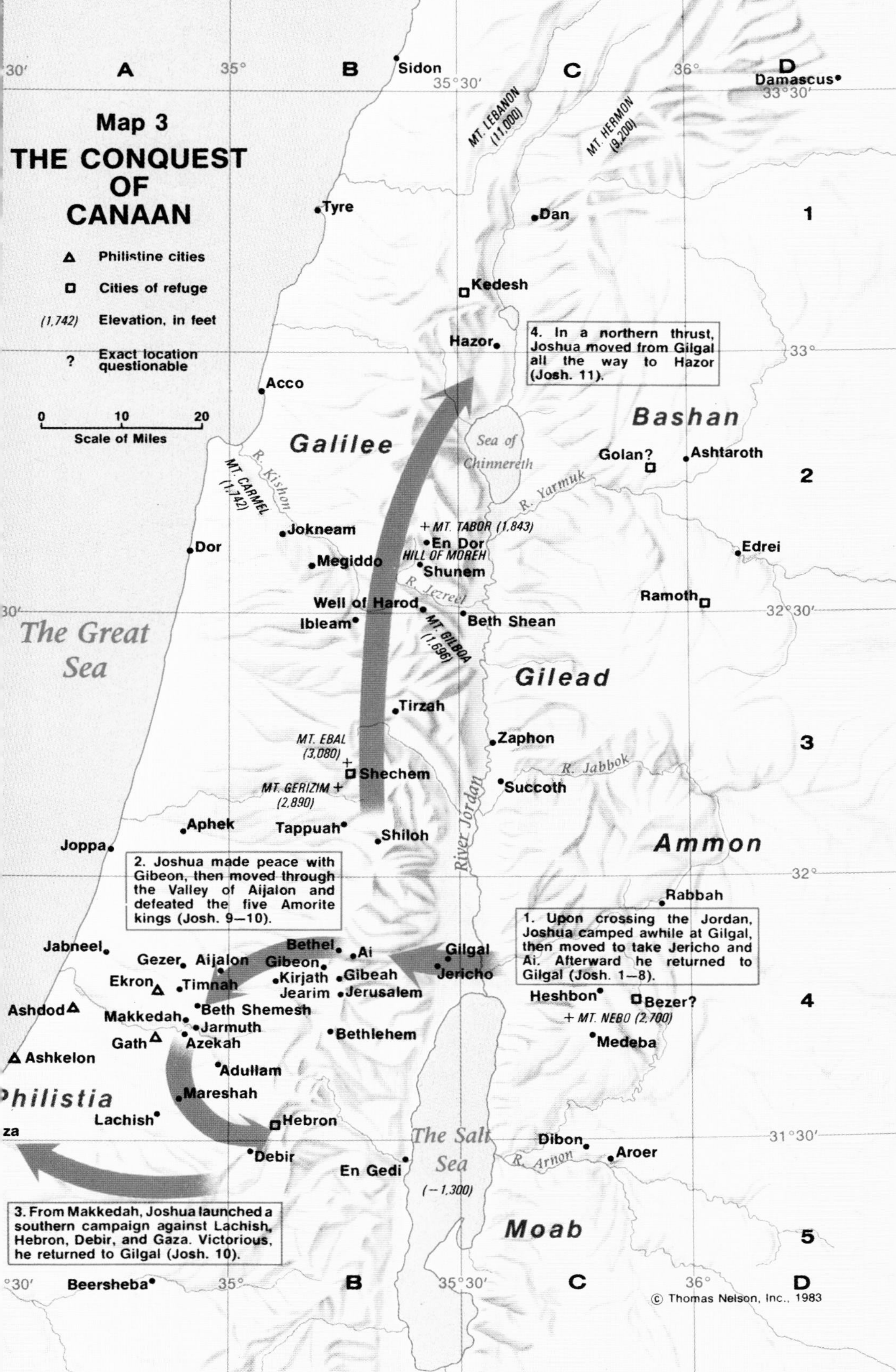

Map 3
THE CONQUEST OF CANAAN
Philistine cities
Cities of refuge
(1,742) Elevation, in feet
? Exact location questionable
0 10 20
Scale of Miles
A
B
C
D
35°
35°30′
36°
33°30′
33°
32°30′
32°
31°30′
1
2
3
4
5
Sidon
Damascus
MT. LEBANON (11,000)
MT. HERMON (9,200)
Tyre
Dan
Kedesh
Hazor
4. In a northern thrust, Joshua moved from Gilgal all the way to Hazor (Josh. 11).
Acco
Bashan
Galilee
Sea of Chinnereth
Golan?
Ashtaroth
MT. CARMEL (1,742)
R. Kishon
R. Yarmuk
MT. TABOR (1,843)
Jokneam
En Dor
HILL OF MOREH
Shunem
Dor
Megiddo
Edrei
R. Jezreel
Well of Harod
Ramoth
Ibleam
Beth Shean
MT. GILBOA (1,696)
The Great Sea
Gilead
Tirzah
Zaphon
MT. EBAL (3,080)
Shechem
R. Jabbok
MT. GERIZIM (2,890)
Succoth
River Jordan
Aphek
Tappuah
Shiloh
Joppa
Ammon
2. Joshua made peace with Gibeon, then moved through the Valley of Aijalon and defeated the five Amorite kings (Josh. 9—10).
Rabbah
1. Upon crossing the Jordan, Joshua camped awhile at Gilgal, then moved to take Jericho and Ai. Afterward he returned to Gilgal (Josh. 1—8).
Jabneel
Bethel
Ai
Gilgal
Gezer
Aijalon
Gibeon
Jericho
Ekron
Timnah
Kirjath Jearim
Gibeah
Jerusalem
Heshbon
Bezer?
Ashdod
Makkedah
Beth Shemesh
MT. NEBO (2,700)
Jarmuth
Gath
Azekah
Bethlehem
Medeba
Ashkelon
Adullam
Philistia
Mareshah
Lachish
Hebron
The Salt Sea
(−1,300)
Dibon
Aroer
R. Arnon
Debir
En Gedi
Moab
3. From Makkedah, Joshua launched a southern campaign against Lachish, Hebron, Debir, and Gaza. Victorious, he returned to Gilgal (Josh. 10).
Beersheba
© Thomas Nelson, Inc., 1983

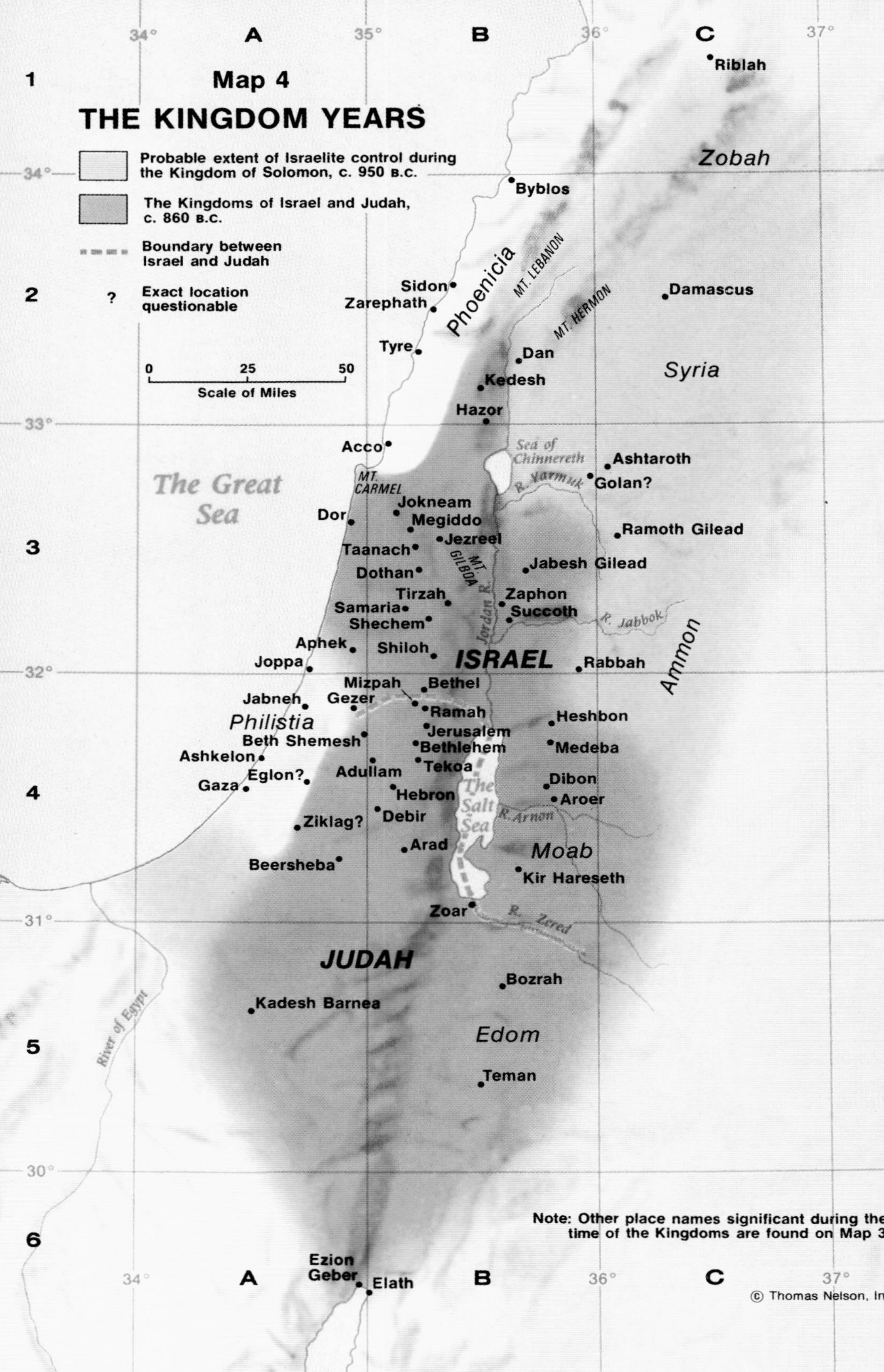
Map 4
THE KINGDOM YEARS
Probable extent of Israelite control during the Kingdom of Solomon, c. 950 B.C.
The Kingdoms of Israel and Judah, c. 860 B.C.
Boundary between Israel and Judah
? Exact location questionable
0 25 50
Scale of Miles
Note: Other place names significant during the time of the Kingdoms are found on Map 3.
A B C
1 2 3 4 5 6
34° 35° 36° 37°
33° 32° 31° 30°
The Great Sea
Riblah
Zobah
Byblos
Phoenicia
MT. LEBANON
MT. HERMON
Sidon
Zarephath
Tyre
Damascus
Dan
Syria
Kedesh
Hazor
Acco
Sea of Chinnereth
Ashtaroth
MT. CARMEL
R. Yarmuk
Golan?
Jokneam
Dor
Megiddo
Ramoth Gilead
Jezreel
Taanach
MT. GILBOA
Jabesh Gilead
Dothan
Tirzah
Zaphon
Samaria
Succoth
Shechem
R. Jabbok
Jordan R.
Aphek
Shiloh
Joppa
ISRAEL
Rabbah
Ammon
Mizpah
Bethel
Jabneh
Gezer
Ramah
Philistia
Heshbon
Jerusalem
Beth Shemesh
Bethlehem
Medeba
Ashkelon
Tekoa
Adullam
Dibon
Eglon?
Gaza
Hebron
Aroer
The Salt Sea
R. Arnon
Debir
Ziklag?
Arad
Moab
Beersheba
Kir Hareseth
Zoar
R. Zered
JUDAH
Bozrah
Kadesh Barnea
River of Egypt
Edom
Teman
Ezion Geber
Elath

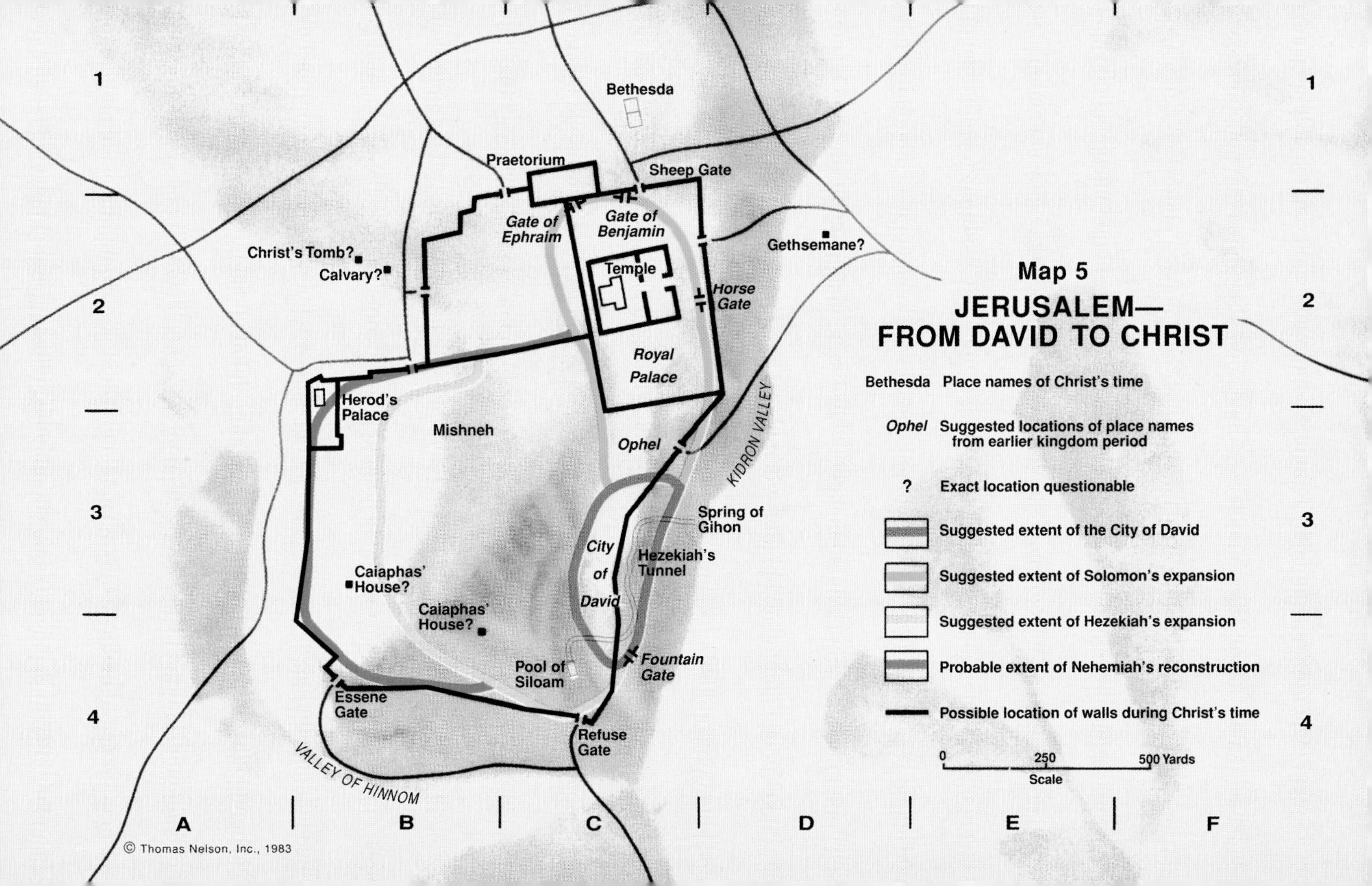

Map 5
JERUSALEM—
FROM DAVID TO CHRIST
Bethesda Place names of Christ's time
Ophel Suggested locations of place names from earlier kingdom period
? Exact location questionable
Suggested extent of the City of David
Suggested extent of Solomon's expansion
Suggested extent of Hezekiah's expansion
Probable extent of Nehemiah's reconstruction
Possible location of walls during Christ's time
0
250
500 Yards
Scale
Bethesda
Praetorium
Sheep Gate
Gate of Ephraim
Gate of Benjamin
Christ's Tomb?
Calvary?
Gethsemane?
Temple
Horse Gate
Royal Palace
Herod's Palace
Mishneh
Ophel
KIDRON VALLEY
Spring of Gihon
City of David
Hezekiah's Tunnel
Caiaphas' House?
Caiaphas' House?
Pool of Siloam
Fountain Gate
Essene Gate
Refuse Gate
VALLEY OF HINNOM
A
B
C
D
E
F
1
2
3
4

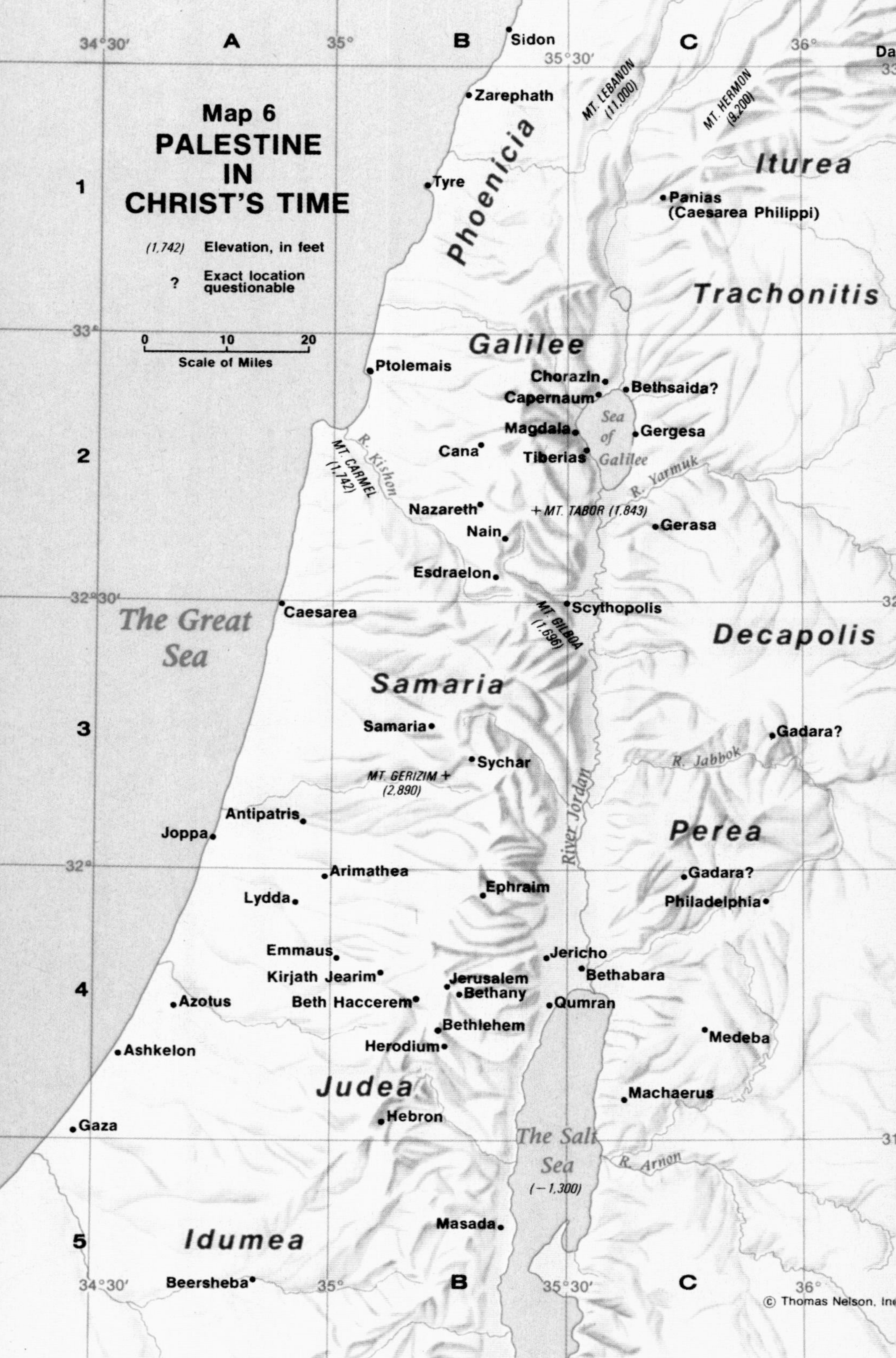

Map 6
PALESTINE IN CHRIST'S TIME
(1,742) Elevation, in feet
? Exact location questionable
0 10 20
Scale of Miles
A
B
C
34°30′
35°
35°30′
36°
1
2
3
4
5
33°
32°30′
32°
Sidon
Zarephath
MT. LEBANON (11,000)
MT. HERMON (9,200)
Phoenicia
Iturea
Tyre
Panias (Caesarea Philippi)
Trachonitis
Galilee
Ptolemais
Chorazin
Capernaum
Bethsaida?
Sea of Galilee
Magdala
Gergesa
Cana
Tiberias
MT. CARMEL (1,742)
R. Kishon
R. Yarmuk
Nazareth
+ MT. TABOR (1,843)
Gerasa
Nain
Esdraelon
Scythopolis
MT. GILBOA (1,696)
Caesarea
The Great Sea
Decapolis
Samaria
Samaria
Gadara?
Sychar
R. Jabbok
MT. GERIZIM + (2,890)
River Jordan
Antipatris
Joppa
Perea
Arimathea
Gadara?
Ephraim
Lydda
Philadelphia
Emmaus
Jericho
Kirjath Jearim
Bethabara
Jerusalem
Bethany
Azotus
Beth Haccerem
Qumran
Bethlehem
Medeba
Ashkelon
Herodium
Judea
Machaerus
Hebron
Gaza
The Salt Sea
(−1,300)
R. Arnon
Masada
Idumea
Beersheba
© Thomas Nelson, Inc

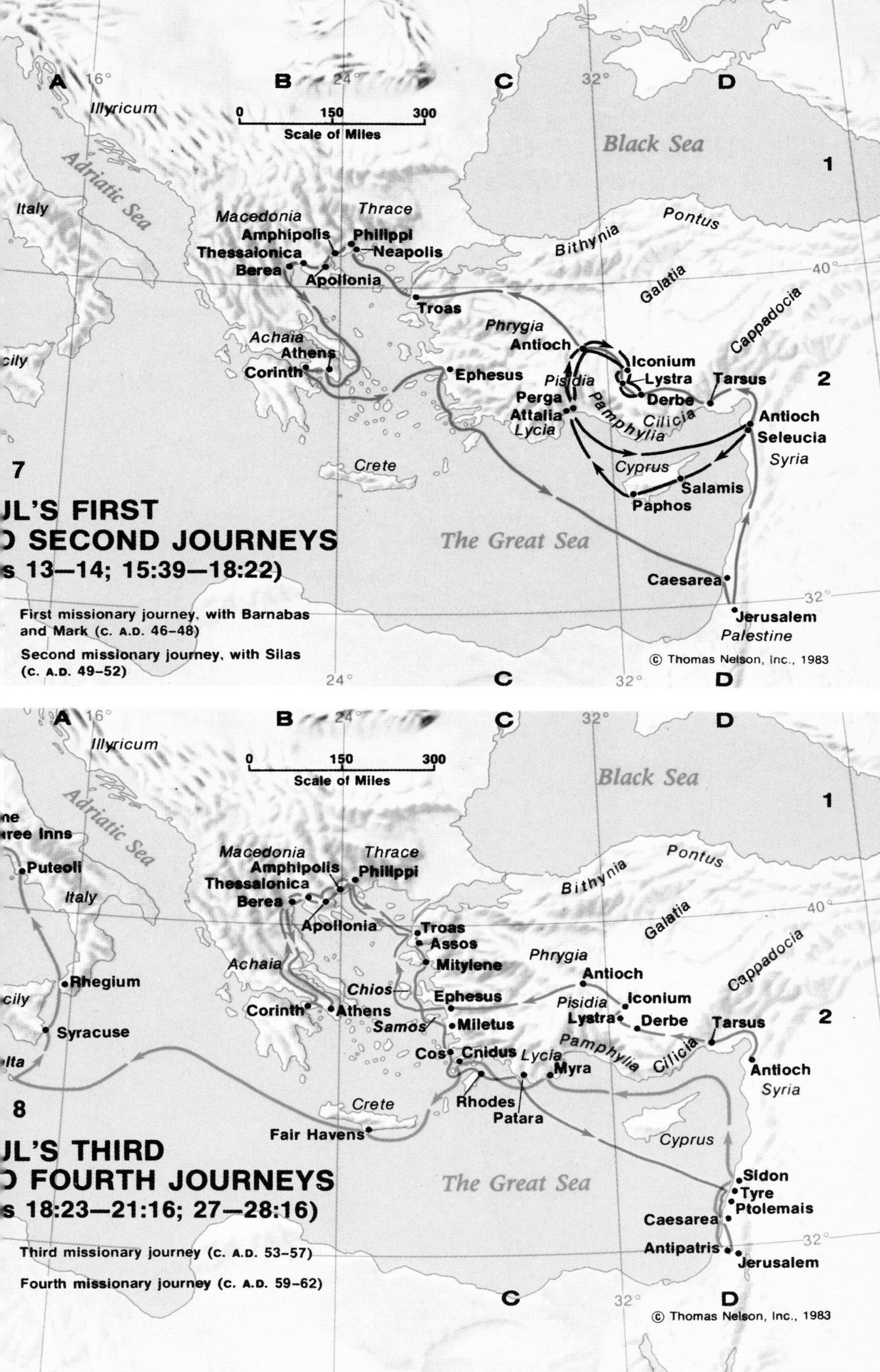

Illyricum
Scale of Miles
0
150
300
Black Sea
Adriatic Sea
Italy
Macedonia
Thrace
Amphipolis
Philippi
Thessalonica
Neapolis
Berea
Apollonia
Pontus
Bithynia
Galatia
Troas
Cappadocia
Phrygia
Antioch
Achaia
Athens
Iconium
Corinth
Ephesus
Lystra
Pisidia
Tarsus
Perga
Derbe
Attalia
Pamphylia
Antioch
Lycia
Cilicia
Seleucia
Syria
Cyprus
Crete
Salamis
Paphos
The Great Sea
Caesarea
Jerusalem
Palestine
7
JL'S FIRST
) SECOND JOURNEYS
s 13–14; 15:39–18:22)
First missionary journey, with Barnabas and Mark (c. A.D. 46–48)
Second missionary journey, with Silas (c. A.D. 49–52)
© Thomas Nelson, Inc., 1983
Illyricum
Scale of Miles
0
150
300
Black Sea
Adriatic Sea
ne
ree Inns
Puteoli
Italy
Macedonia
Thrace
Amphipolis
Philippi
Thessalonica
Berea
Apollonia
Pontus
Bithynia
Galatia
Troas
Assos
Mitylene
Achaia
Phrygia
Antioch
Cappadocia
Rhegium
Chios
Ephesus
Iconium
Pisidia
Corinth
Athens
Lystra
Derbe
Tarsus
Samos
Miletus
Syracuse
Cos
Cnidus
Lycia
Pamphylia
Cilicia
Myra
Antioch
Syria
Rhodes
Crete
Patara
8
Fair Havens
Cyprus
JL'S THIRD
) FOURTH JOURNEYS
s 18:23–21:16; 27–28:16)
The Great Sea
Sidon
Tyre
Ptolemais
Caesarea
Antipatris
Jerusalem
Third missionary journey (c. A.D. 53–57)
Fourth missionary journey (c. A.D. 59–62)
© Thomas Nelson, Inc., 1983

Map 9
THE HOLY LAND
IN MODERN TIMES
Area occupied by Israel
since June, 1967
0
25
50
Scale of Miles
A
B
C
D
1
2
3
4
5
6
34°
35°
36°
37°
33°
32°
31°
30°
LEBANON
SYRIA
JORDAN
ISRAEL
EGYPT
Tripoli
Beirut
Sidon
Tyre
Dan
Qiryat
Shemona
Damascus
BEKAA VALLEY
LEBANON MTS.
ANTI-LEBANON MTS.
U.N. Buffer Zone
1973 Line
Quneitra
1967 Cease-Fire Line
Golan
Heights
Nahariyya
Akko
Haifa
Safad
Sea of
Galilee
Tiberias
Nazareth
Afula
Dera
Ramtha
Mediterranean Sea
Beth Shean
Hadera
Netanya
Tulkarm
Nablus
Jarash
Herzliyya
Tel Aviv
Petah
Tiqwa
West
Bank
Jordan River
Yafo
Rishon le Zion
Lod
Ramla
Ramalah
Amman
Ashdod
Jericho
Jerusalem
Bethlehem
Madaba
Ashqelon
Qiryat
Gat
Gaza
Hebron
Dead
Sea
En Gedi
Dhiban
Beersheba
Al-Arish
Karak
Negev
Arabah
Sinai
Elat
Aqaba